# The Norton Anthology
# of American Literature

## SHORTER
## FOURTH EDITION

Nina Baym
UNIVERSITY OF ILLINOIS

Wayne Franklin
NORTHEASTERN UNIVERSITY

Ronald Gottesman
UNIVERSITY OF SOUTHERN CALIFORNIA

Laurence B. Holland
LATE OF THE JOHNS HOPKINS UNIVERSITY

David Kalstone
LATE OF RUTGERS, THE STATE UNIVERSITY OF NEW JERSEY

Arnold Krupat
SARAH LAWRENCE COLLEGE

Francis Murphy
SMITH COLLEGE

Hershel Parker
UNIVERSITY OF DELAWARE

William H. Pritchard
AMHERST COLLEGE

Patricia B. Wallace
VASSAR COLLEGE

# The Norton Anthology
# of American Literature

## SHORTER
## FOURTH EDITION

W • W • NORTON & COMPANY • *New York* • *London*

The text of this book is composed in Electra with the display set in Bernhard Modern.
Composition by Maple-Vail Composition. Manufacturing by R. R. Donnelley.
Book design by Antonina Krass.

Cover painting is *In the Patio #1* (1946) by Georgia O'Keeffe. Reproduced by courtesy of the
San Diego Museum of Art. Gift of Mr. and Mrs. Norton S. Walbridge. © 1995 The Georgia
O'Keeffe Foundation/Artists Rights Society (ARS), New York.

Since this page cannot legibly accommodate all the copyright notices, pages 2704–2712
constitute an extension of the copyright page.

The Norton anthology of American literature / [edited by] Nina Baym
. . . [et al.]. — 4th ed., shorter.
p.   cm.
Includes bibliographical references (p.   ) and index.
1. American literature.   2. United States—Literary collections.
I. Baym, Nina.
PS507.N65   1995
810.8—dc20                                                                94-42739
ISBN 0-393-96645-3

W. W. Norton & Company, Inc., 500 Fifth Avenue, New York, N.Y. 10110
W. W. Norton & Company Ltd., 10 Coptic Street, London WC1A 1PU

6 7 8 9 0

# Contents

## Early American Literature 1620–1820

## American Literature 1820–1865   385

## American Literature 1865–1914

## American Prose since 1945

# American Poetry since 1945 2423

# Preface to
# the Shorter Fourth Edition

This Shorter Fourth Edition of *The Norton Anthology of American Literature* distills in a single volume the full resources of the two parent volumes. It is designed to serve either a short course in American literature or one in which a teacher wishes to supplement a "core" anthology by a number of individual texts. The book retains the major innovations that have found favor with teachers and students in three earlier editions, but also introduces changes in response to useful suggestions by those who have used the anthology in the classroom. Like other Norton anthologies, it is the product of an ongoing collaboration between users and editors.

In response to significant changes in critical interest, the Shorter Fourth Edition introduces two major innovations. An entirely new section, Literature to 1620, gathers the writings of encounter—the journals and letters of the first European explorers. Texts such as Columbus's *Letter to Luis de Santangel* and Thomas Harriot's *Brief and True Report of the New Found Land of Virginia* bear witness to the natural wonders of the New World, a tradition that has remained strong in American writing ever since. At the same time, the literature of encounter tells of violence and devastation; *The Relation of Álvar Núñez Cabeza de Vaca* recounts the brutal treatment of the Native Americans by the "Christian slavers"; and the writings of the soldier-entrepreneur John Smith (moved to this section with other chroniclers of exploration) describe the harsh conditions of life in the early settlement of Jamestown.

Literature to 1620 also introduces the second major innovation in the Shorter Fourth Edition—the greatly increased attention to Native American oral and written traditions. The first of three new sections of oral materials, Stories of the Beginning of the World, includes creation stories from the Iroquois and the Pima. Headnotes here give special attention to the political, cultural, and linguistic complexities of transcription and translation.

Changes in critical and classroom interest have also led to innovations in every period of the anthology.

*Early American Literature 1620–1820.* Notable additions are five letters by Phillis Wheatley that reveal the strength of her opposition to slavery and deepen our understanding of her poetry. Countering the myth of the pastoral New World, a selection from Crèvecoeur's *Letter X, On Snakes; and on the Humming Bird*, shows a view of Nature as distinctly "red in tooth and claw."

*American Literature 1820–1865.* The additions to this great period enlarge instructors' options by expanding the kinds of texts offered. A chapter from William Apess's biographical work, *The Experiences of Five Christian Indians of the Pequot Tribe*, asserts that those who profess Christianity must also uphold racial equality. Six chapters from Harriet Jacobs's *Incidents in the Life of a Slave Girl* convey the drama of Linda Brent's bondage and escape, as well as Jacobs's skillful use of melodrama in the cause of abolition. New too is John Greenleaf Whittier's stirring abolitionist poem *Massachusetts to Virginia*. The period 1820–1865 also includes notable additions to two major authors. Freshly collated from manuscript is Walt Whitman's poem-sequence *Live Oak, with Moss*, celebrating sexual "adhesiveness" of man for man. These poems are here restored to Whitman's first and most personal ordering. The headnote to Emily Dickinson has been entirely rewritten and appropriately expanded; her poetry has been enriched with several new poems that reveal both her growing self-awareness as a poet and her sense of connection to other poets and writers—Shakespeare, the Brownings, the Brontës.

*American Literature 1865–1914.* Kate Chopin's evocative *At the 'Cadian Ball* now provides a companion piece for *The Storm*. Building on the Native American works earlier in the volume, two new sections of oral materials—Native American Oratory and Native American Chants and Songs—provide a rich introduction to several complex forms. While the selections from *The Night Chant* and the Chippewa and Ghost Dance songs may be read simply as poems in translation, to underscore their essential role as *performances* we accompany the texts with music notation and a period drawing illustrating the dance.

*American Literature between the Wars 1914–1945.* The outpouring between the wars of political poetry by women and African-American poets, eclipsed in the academy by High Modernism, is now significantly recovered with the inclusion of Muriel Rukeyser and Angelina Weld Grimké. The prominent imagist Amy Lowell is newly anthologized. Poems by Marianne Moore, Edna St. Vincent Millay, and Langston Hughes have been reselected to better show these poets' range and variety.

*American Prose since 1945.* A major figure in the Native American Renaissance, N. Scott Momaday is newly represented with selections chosen to show the "arc" of *The Way to Rainy Mountain*. Also newly included is Maxine Hong Kingston's *No Name Woman*, an autobiographical essay exploring family tragedy and its repercussions through the generations.

*American Poetry since 1945.* As the introduction to this section observes "What best characterizes the world of contemporary American poetry is its pluralism and the power of its best poets to absorb a variety of influences." This widely praised section has been updated with new poems by Gwendolyn Brooks, Adrienne Rich, and Rita Dove. Also added is a new poet: the vibrant and contemporary Li-Young Lee.

*Teaching with* The Norton Anthology of American Literature: *A Guide for Instructors,* by Marjorie Pryse, makes available to instructors teaching notes and suggested essay topics and exam questions for works in the anthology, as well as class plans for a variety of approaches to the survey course. Information for ordering the *Guide for Instructors* (in either print or disk versions) may be obtained from the publisher.

It will be clear from the foregoing that, in compiling the Shorter Fourth Edition, we have also held fast to two other important principles. First, teachers are offered more authors and more selections than they will have time to teach. Such copiousness is designed to allow flexibility within any course and variety from year to year. Second, on the principle of making the anthology self-sufficient—thereby minimizing the frustration of having to teach excerpts and eliminating the need for costly supplements—we include many long works in their entirety, all of them notable achievements in American literature. These range from Emerson's *Nature* to Clemens's *Huckleberry Finn* to O'Neill's *Long Day's Journey into Night*.

Readers already familiar with the anthology will have noticed that the present edition retains the larger trim size of its predecessor, which allows the volume, even in its middle section, to open out and stay flat. It retains, too, the page design and line-length that allow maximum ease of reading. The format is that of a book to be read for pleasure; the text is inviting to the eye, and the special paper makes it possible to keep each volume to a size and weight that allow it to be easily carried to a classroom.

Similarly, this edition continues to incorporate the editorial features that have established a standard in the classroom. The introductions, headnotes, and footnotes are concise but full and are designed to give the student the information needed, without preempting the interpretive function of the student or of the instructor. The Selected Bibliographies at the end of the volume provide guides to further readings and research and complete the self-sufficiency of the anthology, which permits each of its selections to be read, understood, and placed in historical context without dependence on reference books.

The editors have taken scrupulous care to represent the most accurate available version of each work. Indeed, several of the major texts—Franklin's *Autobiography* and some of the materials by Clemens—were edited from manuscript. Among the standard editions used in the Shorter Fourth Edition are those of Philip Barbour for John Smith, John Bierhorst for *The Night Chant*, Louis Martz for H. D., and Marc Simon for Hart Crane.

Our policy has been to reprint each text in the form that accords, as far as it is possible to determine, to the intention of its author. There is one exception: we have modernized most spellings and (very sparingly) the punctuation in the sections Literature to 1620 and Early American Literature 1620–1820, on the principle that nonfunctional features such as archaic spellings and typography pose unnecessary problems for beginning students. We have, however, since it is a new edition from the manuscript, left Franklin's *Autobiography* unchanged. For the convenience of the student, we have used square brackets to indicate titles supplied by the editors and have, whenever a portion of a text has been omitted, indicated that omission with three asterisks. To ensure the accuracy of all texts, the Shorter Fourth Edition has been proofread in its entirety against copy text.

The editors of this anthology were selected on the basis of their expertness in their individual areas. They combine respect for the best that has been thought and said about literature with alertness (as participants, as well as observers) to the altering interests of contemporary scholarship and criticism. Each editor was given ultimate responsibility for his or her period, but all collaborated in the final enterprise. New contributors to the Shorter Fourth Edition, Wayne Franklin edited Literature to 1620, and Arnold Krupat edited the Native American oral materials, as well as the Apess selection. In the

1820–1865 section, Ronald Gottesman prepared the texts and introductions for Lincoln, Stowe, and Douglass; and Nina Baym prepared the text and introduction for Harriet Jacobs.

In preparing these volumes, we have incurred obligations to hundreds of teachers throughout the country who have answered our questions; we take this opportunity to thank them warmly for their invaluable assistance. Those teachers who prepared detailed critiques or who offered special help in selecting or preparing texts are listed under Acknowledgments, on a separate page. The editors would like to express appreciation for their assistance to Kevin Affonso, Olivia Banner, Mark Canner, Daniel Chiasson, Joseph Coulombe, Sarah Hurley, Sharon Lee, Ted Loos, Thomas Osmond, Rilla Park, Heddy Richter, Danny Rose, Beth Shube, and Stellene Vollandes.

The publisher's editor, in turn, would like to express her special thanks to Marian Johnson, development editor of this Shorter Fourth Edition. She would also like to thank her coworkers Allen Clawson, Virginia Creeden, Anna Karvellas, Candace Levy, Polly Mancini, Mike McIver, Diane O'Connor, Hugh O'Neill, Nancy Palmquist, and Tara Parmiter. We also wish to acknowledge our debt to George P. Brockway, former president and chairman at Norton, who invented this anthology; to M. H. Abrams (Cornell), Norton's advisor on English texts, and to the late John G. Benedict and the late Barry K. Wade, anthology editors and mentors whose contribution is and will be ongoing. All have helped us to create an anthology that has been called "the standard of comparison for all American-literature survey texts."

# Acknowledgments

Among our many critics, advisors, and friends, the following were of especial help toward the preparation of the Shorter Fourth Edition either with advice or by providing critiques of particular periods of the anthology as a whole: M. H. Abrams (Cornell University); Donald Bahr (Arizona State University); Betty Louise Bell (University of Michigan); John Bierhorst; John Blassingame (Yale University); Joseph Boissé (University of California at Santa Barbara); William Dowling (Rutgers University); Michael Elliott (Columbia University); Everett Emerson; Larry Evers (University of Arizona); William Fenton; Robert Foulke (Skidmore College); George Hendrick (University of Illinois); Chris Lohman (Indiana University); Marianne Mithun (University of California at Santa Barbara); Mark Niemeyer (University of Reims); David Nordloh (Indiana University); Barry O'Connell (Amherst College); Robert Parker (University of Illinois); Donald Pizer (Tulane University); Joel Porte (Cornell University); Marjorie Pryse (State University of New York, College at Plattsburgh); Jarold Ramsey (University of Rochester); Mark W. Rocha (California State University at Northridge); Blair Rudes; A. LaVonne Brown Ruoff (University of Illinois at Chicago); Jack Stillinger (University of Illinois); Tom Wolfe (California State University at Northridge); Hertha D. Wong (University of California at Berkeley); Paul G. Zolbrod (Allegheny College).

We take pleasure in thanking, once again, those who advised us on the first three editions: Bruce Adams (Tuskegee University); Frederick Anderson (late General Editor of The Mark Twain Papers, University of California at Berkeley); Liahna Babener (Montana State University); John Bassett (Wayne State University); Peter J. Bellis (University of Miami); Alfred Bendixen (California State University); Ronald A. Bosco (State University of New York at Albany); Panthea Reid Broughton (Louisiana State University); Lawrence Buell (Harvard University); Sargent Bush, Jr. (University of Wisconsin); Edwin H. Cady (Duke University); D. Dean Cantrell (Berry College); Evan B. Carton (University of Texas); William Bedford Clark (Texas A & M University); Sarah Blacher Cohen (State University of New York at Albany); Thomas W. Cooley (The Ohio State University); James M. Cox (Dartmouth College); Donald H. Craver (Towson State University); Robert Creeley (State University of New York at Buffalo); Hugh J. Dawson (University of San Francisco); Sterling F. Delano (Villanova University); Joanne Feit Diehl (Bowdoin College); Doris I. Eder (University of New Haven); Thomas R. Edwards (Rutgers University); Allison Ensor (University of Tennessee); Jim Ewing (Mississippi College); Suzanne Ferguson (Case Western Reserve University); Judith Fetterley (State University of New York at Albany); Noel Riley Fitch (University of Southern California); Rosemary F. Franklin (University of Georgia); Vincent Freimarck (State University of New York at Binghamton); Lucy M. Friebert (University of Louisville); Albert Gelpi (Stanford University); Barbara Charlesworth Gelpi (Stanford University); Donna Gerstenberger (University of Washington); William M. Gibson (late of the University of Wisconsin);

Marshall Gilliland (University of Saskatchewan); Seymour Gross (University of Detroit); Harrison Hayford (Northwestern University); Carolyn Heilbrun (Columbia University); Anthony C. Hilfer (University of Texas at Austin); Faith Mackey Holland; C. Hugh Holman (late of University of North Carolina); Glen M. Johnson (The Catholic University of America); Myrl G. Jones (Radford University); Elaine H. Kim (University of California at Berkeley); Charles Klingler (Manchester College); Jerome F. Klinkowitz (University of Northern Iowa); Paul Lauter (Trinity College); J. A. Leo Lemay (University of Delaware); Perry Lentz (Kenyon College); Kenneth Lincoln (University of California at Los Angeles); Ilse Lind (New York University); Jay Martin (University of Southern California); Wendy Martin (Claremont Graduate School); Charlotte S. McClure (Georgia State University); Joseph R. McElrath, Jr. (Florida State University); Diane Middlebrook (Stanford University); Teresa McKenna (University of Southern California); Molly Francis Moore (University of Vermont); Adalaide K. Morris (University of Iowa); Thomas Moser (Stanford University); Frederick Newberry (Duquesne University); Robert O'Clair (late of Manhattanville College); Cheryl Z. Oreovicz (Purdue University); Nancy Packer (Stanford University); Raymund A. Paredes (University of California at Los Angeles); Thornton H. Parsons (Syracuse University); Alan Perlis (University of Alabama at Birmingham); Marjorie Perloff (Stanford University); William L. Phillips (University of Washington); Donald Pizer (Tulane University); Sidney Poger (University of Vermont); Carol H. Poston; William Powers (Michigan Technical University); Dorothy Redden (Douglass College); Jerome H. Rosenberg (Miami University of Ohio); M. L. Rosenthal (New York University); Nicholas Ruddick (University of Regina); Constantine Santas (Flagler College); Joan Schulz (State University of New York at Albany); George Sebouhian (State University of New York at Fredonia); Ann Semel; Judith L. Sensibar (Arizona State University); Daniel B. Shea (Washington University); Alan Shucard (University of Wisconsin at Parkside); Frank Shuffleton (University of Rochester); Merrill Skaggs (Drew University); Robert Spiegel (Central Connecticut State University); Catharine R. Stimpson (Rutgers University); Ely Stock (The College of Staten Island); J. Maurice Thomas (Wingate College); Eleanor M. Tilton (Barnard College); Darwin T. Turner (late of the University of Iowa); Linda C. Wagner-Martin (University of North Carolina); Laurence Wharton (University of Alabama); Sidney Howard White (University of Rhode Island); Kathleen Woodward (University of Wisconsin at Milwaukee).

# The Norton Anthology of American Literature

SHORTER
FOURTH EDITION

# Literature to 1620

In 1494 a man who had crossed the Atlantic in a large ship returned home to amaze those whom he had left behind with tales of a new world full of "marvels." None of those who listened to him had accomplished anything remotely like this. None had heard of this other world, let alone seen it, and none could begin to comprehend what its discovery might mean for their own familiar universe. As they listened with rapt attention, the voyager told of things undreamed of, plants and animals and most of all strange peoples whose uncanny customs, costumes, and beliefs astonished all who heard him.

The man in question might have been Christopher Columbus or any of the dozens of Europeans who accompanied him on his first voyage, but he was not. In fact, this teller of tales did join in that voyage, but he had not sailed from Palos, Spain, with the other men on August 6, 1492, and had not been with them when, at two in the morning of October 12, they sighted the Bahamian island they named San Salvador. Twice he crossed the Atlantic with Columbus, but in reverse: first to Spain from the Indies and then back again. We do not know his original name, but we know that he was a Taino Indian from the Bahamas, one of seven natives whom Columbus seized and took to Spain. There he was baptized and renamed Diego Colón, after the son of Columbus himself. (Colón was the Spanish version of the family's name.) Of the other natives, all of whom were similarly rechristened, one remained in Spain, where he died within a few years. Four others died of sickness on the passage back to America with Columbus and Colón. Colón and the sixth man escaped the same fate only "by a hair's breadth," as the fleet's physician, Diego Alvarez Chanca, wrote in his important letter on the second voyage. Returned to the Caribbean, the two served as translators for the much larger party of Spaniards, perhaps fifteen hundred strong, who arrived in seventeen ships early in November 1493. Colón himself already had seen service as an intermediary during the first voyage.

Of the two men, only Colón is reported by the historian Andrés Bernáldez, who knew Columbus and used the mariner's own lost account of the second voyage, to have regaled the other natives with tales of "the things which he had seen in Castile and the marvels of Spain, . . . the great cities and fortresses and churches, . . . the people and horses and animals, . . . the great nobility and wealth of the sovereigns and great lords, . . . the kinds of food, . . . the festivals and tournaments [and] bull-fighting." Perhaps the other man had died by this point in the second voyage. Perhaps Columbus singled out Colón for special mention because Colón had learned Castilian well enough to speak it and had shown himself to be an intelligent man and a good guide. He was to accompany Columbus on the whole of this voyage, which lasted three years.

The story of Colón catches in miniature the extraordinary changes that were to occur as natives of the Old World encountered natives of the New for the first time in recorded history. His story reminds us first that discovery was mutual rather than one sided. To be sure, far more Europeans voyaged to America than Americans to Europe, and they sent home thousands of reports and letters detailing what they saw and did in the New World. Because many of these European travelers came

1

to America to stay, however, the Indians soon had a colonial imitation of Europe developing before their eyes, complete with fortresses, churches, horses, new foods (on the second voyage, Columbus brought wheat, melons, onions, radishes, salad greens, grapevines, sugar cane, and various fruit trees) and much else that Colón in 1493 could have only found in Europe. Over time the natives of America could discover Europe encroaching on their villages and fields as the imported European landscape vied with their own. Europe was present in the textiles on the colonists' bodies, in the tools in their hands, for both of which the American Indians traded, and in the institutions of the church and state (slavery being the most obvious example) that had begun to reshape the identities and reorganize the lives of Native American peoples. In such concrete terms a new world was being created in the West Indies. It was not the new world Columbus himself was speaking of near the end of his life when he wrote in 1500 to the Spanish sovereigns Ferdinand and Isabella that he had "brought under [their] dominion . . . another world, whereby Spain, which was called poor, is now most rich." The new world that mattered was not just an expanse of space previously unknown to Europeans; it was a genuinely new set of social relationships that would evolve over the next centuries as Europe and the Americas continued to interact. With the European introduction of African slaves early in the sixteenth century, the terms of this new world became much more complex. The cultural and social relations of Americans took their origin in a great mixing of peoples from the whole Atlantic basin during the first century and a half after 1492.

Discovery began with wonder—that of Colón's listeners on his return in 1494 and that of Columbus as he descanted on the green beauty of the islands—evoking a mood that has remained strong in American writing ever since: he saw "trees of a thousand kinds" on San Salvador in November 1492, trees that seemed to "touch the sky . . . as green and as lovely as they are in Spain in May." But beyond that transcendent moment, discovery entailed a many-sided process of influence and exchange that ultimately produced the hybrid cultural universe of the Atlantic world, of which the English colonies were one small part. Much of this universe came through struggle rather than cooperation. Each people used its own traditions or elements recently borrowed from others to endure or conquer or outwit its opposite numbers, and violence often swallowed up the primal wonder glimpsed in the earliest documents. With gunpowder and steel, Europeans had the technological edge in warfare, and it would seem that—despite centuries of propaganda to the contrary—they took violence more seriously than the American Indians. The natives at first found the scale of European warfare appalling. In New England, the colonists' native allies against the Pequot tribe in 1637 complained that the English manner of fighting, as soldier John Underhill noted in his *Newes from America* (1638), "[was] too furious, and slay[ed] too many men." The natives were quick to adopt European weapons and tactics, however, applying them to their own disputes and to their disputes with the Europeans. The ferocity of what Europeans have called the "Indian wars" was the violent recoil in the face of violence from interlopers who threatened the very life of the native peoples.

Almost literally from 1492, the natives began to die in large numbers, if not from war then from enslavement, brutal mistreatment, despair, or disease. One of the more insidious forms of "exchange" involved the transfer to the American Indians of the microbes to which Europeans had become inured but to which the Indians had virtually no resistance. Nothing better displays the isolation of the continents and the drama of encounter that began in 1492 than the epidemic disasters that smallpox, measles, typhus, and other Old World maladies unleashed on the American natives. Whole populations plummeted as such diseases, combined with the other severe stresses placed on the natives, spread throughout the Caribbean and then on the mainland of Central and South America. The institutional disease of slavery further decimated the native peoples. It is widely agreed that the original population of the island of Hispaniola (estimated at anywhere from one hundred thousand to eight million in 1492) plunged once the Spanish took over the island, partly through disease and partly through the abuses of the *encomienda* system of virtual enslavement. In the face of this sudden decline in available native labor, Spain introduced African slavery into Hispaniola as early as 1501. By the middle of the sixteenth century the native population had been so completely displaced by African slaves that the Spanish historian Antonio de Herrera called the island "an effigy or an image of Ethiopia itself." Thus the destruction of one people was accompanied by the displacement and enslavement of another. By that point, the naive "wonder" of discovery was all but unrecoverable.

It would be inaccurate to picture the Indians, however, as merely victims, suffering decline. The natives made shrewd use of the European presence in America to forward their own aims, as Colón reminds us. In 1519 the disaffected natives in the Aztec empire clearly threw their lot in with Cortés because they saw in him a chance to settle the score with their overlord Montezuma, which they assuredly did. In New England, the Pequot War of 1637 saw a similar alignment on the English side of tribes such as the Narragansetts and the Mohegans, who had grievances with the fierce Pequots, interlopers in the region. Under ordinary circumstances, as among the Iroquois in the Northeast, European technology and the European market were seized on as a means of consolidating advantages gained before the arrival of the colonists. The Iroquois had begun to organize their famous League of the Five Nations before European settlement, but they solidified their earlier victories over other native peoples by forging canny alliances with the Dutch and then the English in New York. In the Southeast, remnant peoples banded together in the early eighteenth century to create the Catawba, a new political group that constructed what one recent historian has called a "new world" for itself. No longer known by a bewildering diversity of names, the former Nassaw and Suttirie and Charra and Succa peoples banded together with several others in an attempt to deal more effectively with the encroaching Euro-Americans of Charleston and the Low Country. This hardly was a case of diminishment or reduction. It suggests the important truth that Indians were not ahistorical before 1492, just as they were not monolithic culturally or politically then or afterward. Even as fewer and fewer of the original millions remained, they showed themselves resourceful in resisting, transforming, and exploiting the exotic cultures the Europeans were imposing on their original landscape.

## VOYAGES OF DISCOVERY

Columbus was still making voyages to America (1492–93; 1493–96; 1498; 1502–04) as other Europeans, following his example, found their way to the West Indies. Giovanni Caboto (known as John Cabot to the English for whom he sailed) and his fellow Italian Amerigo Vespucci both crossed the ocean before 1500, as did the Portuguese native Pedro Cabral. After that date the voyagers became too many to track. Unlike the Viking invasion of five hundred years before, which had established modest coastal settlements in North America that the natives soon wiped out, this second European wave quickly gathered momentum and extended itself far to the north and south of the Caribbean basin that Columbus explored. Cabot was near the mouth of the St. Lawrence in Canada the year before Vespucci found that of the Amazon, nearly five thousand miles away in South America. Soon the Europeans were leaving colonies everywhere. The first colonists lingered on the Caribbean island of Hispaniola following the departure of Columbus in 1493. Although that small settlement of La Navidad was soon destroyed in a clash with Taino natives under the cacique Caonabo of Maguana, the massive second voyage in 1493 came equipped to stay, and from that point on Spain and Europe generally maintained an aggressive presence in the West Indies. The constant battles along vague frontiers with Native Americans added fuel to the dissension and political in-fighting among the settlers themselves, whose riots and mutinies nearly ruined settlement after settlement. John Smith's experience during the first James-town voyage of 1607 provides probably the most famous example from Anglo-America. Arrested and nearly executed (probably for offending his "betters," something he had the habit of doing) en route to America in 1607, Smith was released in Virginia when the colony's sealed instructions were opened, revealing that this apparently modest soldier had been named to the prestigious governing council even before the ships had left England. Columbus himself became the focus of fierce competitions among greedy settlers and officials in Hispaniola by the time of his third voyage and, stripped of his property and powers by a royal official maddened by the uproar, went back to Spain in chains in 1500.

Europe continued to expand in the New World amid the disorder within settlement walls and the great violence outside. Columbus found the mainland of South America in 1498 and Central America in 1502, by which time John Cabot and the Portuguese Corte-Real brothers, Gaspar and Miguel, had been down the coast of North America from Labrador to the Chesapeake, and Cabral and Vespucci had covered the east coast of South America from the Orinoco River in present-day Venezuela to well south of the Río de la Plata on the border of present-day Uruguay and Argentina. Between 1515 and the 1520s, Spain, under the reign of Charles V, aggressively reached out over the Gulf of Mexico, toward the Yucatan peninsula and Mexico and Florida and the Isthmus of Panama, then sent expeditions into the heart of North America from the 1520s to the 1540s, covering a vast region stretching from Florida to the Gulf of California and north as far as Kansas and the Tennessee River. At the same time, other Spanish explorers and conquistadors spread out over South America, especially its west coast, where in imitation of Cortés' Conquest of Mexico a decade earlier Juan Pizarro overcame the Incan empire, recently beset with violent civil war. In that same period, the Portuguese established their first permanent settlements in Brazil, and the French explorer Jacques Cartier sailed into the Gulf of St. Lawrence, then up its chief river as far as the site of the future Montreal. Within fifty years of 1492, then, the east coasts of much of both continents had been explored, and many of their major regions had been traversed; the most spectacular of their peoples, the Aztecs and the Incas, had been conquered; and Europe had settled in for a long stay.

Spain under Ferdinand and Isabella and their grandson Charles V took the most aggressively expansive role in America. Other European nations, most conspicuously France and England, were more self-absorbed, awakening slowly to what was happening across the sea. Their first explorers enjoyed bad luck and inconsistent support. John and Sebastian Cabot had sailed for English merchants and the monarchs Henry VII and Henry VIII, but the first Cabot was lost on his voyage in 1498, and the second kept his interest in America alive only by entering the service of the Spanish Crown after 1512. A return to his adopted homeland of England and a royal pension from Edward VI came to him only in the 1540s, by which point he had committed himself to the search for an eastward route to China via the seas north of Russia. In France, Cartier enjoyed early support from Francis I, but his failure to find gold and other riches in the St. Lawrence valley and his dispute with the nobleman Roberval, whom the king appointed to command Cartier's third voyage in 1541, led to profound disenchantment in France. Fishermen from both nations continued to harvest the fabulous riches of the shoals off North America and summered on the shore, drying their catch. But not until the 1570s for England and the beginning of the next century for France, as a new generation of adventurers arose and a period of commercial expansion set in, did broad public support and governmental sanction combine to stir lasting curiosity and investment. A series of luckless North American voyages by the English under Martin Frobisher, Humphrey Gilbert, and then Walter Ralegh ended in the tragedy of the "Lost Colony" of Roanoke Island in the 1580s. For another twenty years few

English explorers made serious new efforts, although the press bubbled with publications regarding the New World, particularly the works of Richard Hakluyt the younger, whose great collections gathered the fugitive records of English, and indeed European, expansion overseas. Hakluyt's masterwork, *The Principall Navigations* (1598–1600), brought the literary productions of countless European mariners to the attention of a public newly stirred by what Shakespeare soon was to call this "brave new world" of Euro-America. Hakluyt notwithstanding, only in 1606 did a second Virginia colony set forth, and this one faltered grievously at the start with a shipwreck on Bermuda (which was to inspire Shakespeare's *The Tempest*), riots at Jamestown, near starvation, and violent encounters. By 1603 French interest had revived under the direction of a group of explorers and expansionists, Samuel de Champlain most significantly, who hoped for profit from the New World and, even more, a route through it to the fabled riches of Asia. Seasoned from his voyages to Spanish America, Champlain picked up where Cartier had left off sixty years earlier, founded permanent settlements in the St. Lawrence valley, and through his agents and followers pushed French exploration as far west as Lake Superior at a time when the English were still struggling in Virginia and New England settlement had just begun at Plymouth.

LITERARY CONSEQUENCES OF 1492

The period of European exploration in the New World produced a surprisingly large and intriguing body of literature. While many manuscripts were archived and out of reach until the nineteenth century, a number of texts found their way into print and were widely dispersed, thanks to the establishment of printing in the half century before 1492. Shortly after Columbus's return to Spain in early 1493, there appeared in print his letter to the court official Luis de Santangel, narrating the voyage and lushly describing the perpetual spring Columbus had found in the West Indies the previous autumn. From the appearance of that letter on, the printing press and the European expansion into America were reciprocal parts of a single engine. Without the ready dispersal of texts rich with imagery that stirred individual imagination and national ambition in regard to the West Indies, Europe's movement westward would have been blunted and perhaps thwarted. The sword of conquest found in the pen, and in the printing press, an indispensable ally.

The great mass of early American writings came from the hands of Europeans rather than the native peoples of the New World. Important exceptions happily exist. The natives had a lively oral culture that valued memory over mechanics as a means of preserving texts, although among some groups such as the Aztecs written traditions existed (in North America these records included shellwork belts and painted animal hides, tepees, and shields) and many more groups used visual records in subtle and sophisticated ways. Such cataclysms as the Conquest of Mexico produced not only the Spanish narratives of Cortés, Bernal Díaz del Castillo, and others but also native responses, many of which perished with those who knew them. Those that survived in original native characters or in transliterated form have inestimable ethnographic and literary value. For instance, anonymous native writers working in the Nahuatl language of the Aztecs in 1528—significantly, they used the Roman alphabet introduced by the Spanish—lamented the fall of their capital to Cortés in the following lines:

> Broken spears lie in the roads;
> we have torn our hair in our grief.
> The houses are roofless now, and their walls
> are red with blood.

No one reading these four lines will easily glorify the Conquest of Mexico or of the Americas more generally. The story of the transoceanic encounter, however, ceases to be a matter of easy contrasts once one reads widely in the texts on either side. Although Europeans committed atrocities in the New World, often they did so as a result of blundering and miscommunication rather than cool, deliberate policy. In fact, the split between policy and action goes to the heart of the infant Atlantic world of the sixteenth century and is mirrored in and influenced by the character of the writing that survives from the period. The great distance separating the hemispheres made the coordination of intention and performance extremely difficult. The authorities at home lacked the knowledge to form prudent or practical policy; as a result many texts written by explorers or colonists were intended as "briefs" meant to inform or influence policy decisions made at a distance. To cite a simple example, Columbus himself wrote a point-by-point description of his second voyage in 1495, addressed to Ferdinand and Isabella in a series of "items" to which the specific responses of the sovereigns were added by a court scribe. More complexly, Cortés sought to justify his patently illegal invasion of Mexico in 1519 by sending several long letters to Charles V defending his actions and promising lavish returns if his Conquest could proceed.

Most documents sent from America to the European powers reveal such generally political intentions. Europe responded by issuing directives aimed at controlling events across the sea. Even when good policies were articulated in Europe, however, applying them in the New World entailed further problems. By the time instructions arrived in Hispaniola or Mexico or Jamestown or Quebec, new events in the colony might have rendered them pointless. Distance made control both crucial and difficult. Whereas formal authority typically resided in Europe, power as an informal fact of life and experience and circumstance belonged to America, to those who could seize and use it or who acquired it by virtue of what they did rather than the official investitures they bore. Mutiny became so pervasive a fact or fear in America precisely because individuals and groups had, morally and geographically, great latitude in the thinly populated colonial enclaves. If writing served in this fluid, ambiguous universe as a means to influence official policy at home, it also emerged as a means of justifying actions (as with Cortés) that violated or ignored European directives.

Early American writing had, though, a third and more compelling purpose as a literature of witness. That we know so much about the European devastation of the West Indies comes from the fact that some Europeans responded powerfully to that devastation in writing. Although no one typifies this mood better than Bartolomé de las Casas, who assailed Spain's ruthless destruction of whole peoples in America, it is the rare European document that does not reveal the bloody truths of Europe's colonial dreams. Starting on the Columbian voyages themselves and flowering in the Spanish West Indies, especially in the 1540s and 1550s when debates about the mistreatment of the natives earnestly moved the clerics and government officials at home, the New World inspired an outpouring of written expression. Not all the literature of witness speaks to specific issues of policy, or particular public debates, but in many of the texts one senses a critical eye, a point of view not likely to be swayed by the slogans of empire or faith or even wealth. Writers such as Diaz del Castillo, the chronicler of Cortés, and England's John Smith came from the underclass of their native countries, where but for the opportunities represented by America they might well have spent their days in silence. As a result, their writing could be subversive, even mutinous, achieving its greatest depth when it captured a vision of America as more than a dependent province of the Old World, rather as a place where much that was genuinely new might be learned.

## NATIVE AMERICAN ORAL LITERATURE

When Columbus sailed from Europe in 1492, he left behind him a number of relatively centralized nation-states with largely agricultural economies. Europeans spoke some two or three dozen languages, most of them closely related; and they were generally Christian in religious belief and worldview, although many groups had had contact—and conflict—with adherents of Judaism and Islam. A written alphabet had been used by Europeans to preserve and communicate information for many centuries and Gutenberg's invention of moveable type in the mid-1400s had shown the way to a mechanical means of "writing"; by 1492, Europe was on its way to becoming a print culture.

By contrast, in 1492 in North America, native people spoke hundreds of languages, belonging to entirely different linguistic families (e.g., Athapascan, Uto-Aztecan, Chinookan, Siouan, and Algonquian) and structured their cultures in extraordinarily diverse economic and political forms. In the Great Basin of the West, small, loosely organized bands of Utes eked out a bare subsistence by hunting and gathering, while the sedentary Pueblo peoples of the Southwest and the Iroquoians of the Northeast had both highly developed agricultural economies and complex modes of political organization. In spite of some common features, religious and mythological beliefs were also diverse. Among North American peoples alone, eight different types of creation stories have been documented, with wide variations among them. All of these differ substantially from the creation stories of Judaism, Christianity, and Islam.

Also unlike European cultures, North American peoples did not use a written alphabet. Theirs were oral cultures, relying on the spoken word—whether chanted, sung, or presented in lengthy narratives—and the memory of those words to preserve important cultural information. The term *literature* comes from the Latin *littera*, "letter." Native American literatures were not, until long after the arrival of the Europeans, written "littera-tures." Indeed, as the phrase *oral literature* might appear to be a contradiction in terms, some have chosen to call the expressions of the oral tradition *orature*.

These expressions were, like the languages, political economies, and religious beliefs of Native American peoples, extremely various. Europeans in 1492 could name the tragedy, the comedy, the epic, the ode, and a variety of lyric forms as types of literature. In Native America there were probably (*probably*, because we have no actual records that predate 1492) such things as Kwakiutl winter ceremonies, Winnebago trickster tale cycles, Apache jokes, Hopi personal naming and grievance chants, Yaqui deer songs, Yuman dream songs, Piman shamanic chants, Iroquois condolence rituals, Navajo curing and blessing chants, and Chippewa songs of the Great Medicine Society, to name only some of the types of Native American verbal expression.

That there are many such types is unquestionable, but are these literary types? This question would not make sense to traditional native peoples, who do not have a category of language use corresponding to our category of literature. From a Western perspective, however, the types of native verbal expression could only be considered as literature after that late-eighteenth- and early-nineteenth-century revolution in European consciousness known as Romanticism. In that period the concept of literature shifted away from being defined by the *medium* of expression (all language preserved in *letters*) to the *kind* of expression (those texts that emphasized the imaginative and emotional possibilities of language). With this shift in the meaning of *literature*, many Native American verbal types could quite comfortably be considered literary.

We shall read these forms on the page, but it bears repeating that traditional Native American literatures originate as *oral* performances. They are offered to audiences as dramatic events in time, language for the ear, rather than objects in space for the eye. And in performance, a pause, a quickening of pace or a sudden retardation, a gesture, or a lowering of the voice affects meaning. Not surprisingly, scholars differ about the best way to transfer performance to the page. Some have opted for a stylized typography where type size and arrangement seek to convey something of the feeling of what an actual performance might have been like. Others, acknowledging that black marks on a white page cannot reproduce a living voice, have tried to translate the words as effectively as possible, leaving it to the reader to imagine these words in performance.

This matter of translating the words effectively is also controversial. When we know that the original performance used archaic and unfamiliar terms, should we use archaic and unfamiliar terms in the translation, even though they may appear stiff and old-fashioned on the page? What would the contemporary reader think of the following excerpt from J. N. B. Hewitt's rendition of the Iroquois creation story: "Through the crafty machinations of the Fire Dragon of the White Body, the consuming jealousy of the aged presiding chief was kindled against his young spouse." Should we instead opt for the nonstandard English, the Red English, or Reservation English as it has been called, of native collaborators in the translation process—even if it may strike some readers not as lively and colloquial but illiterate? Here are a few lines from a contemporary translation in Red English of a folktale from the Northwest: "He told the chief: 'Yes, I remember, I thought of it, I have a worker[,] a boy, and I asked him [to come] but no, he didn't want to leave his work and his eatings.' " Of course, if we translate these texts into standard, or "literary," English, we may have substantially misrepresented verbal expression that, in the original, would surely strike us as strange. Consider the following translation:

> You
> have been
> falling
> falling
> Have you
> fallen
> from the top
> of the salmon-
> berry bushes
> falling
> falling

This is attractive by contemporary standards, but for the sake of aesthetics, it gives up a good deal of fidelity to the original, which never appeared on the page.

While the question of how best to translate Native American verbal expression must remain open, reading the words of native oral literature conveys some sense of indigenous literary expression as it may have been before the coming of the Europeans.

---

# CHRISTOPHER COLUMBUS
## 1451–1506

Born into a family of wool workers near the once supreme Mediterranean port of Genoa, Christopher Columbus followed that rather sedentary trade for a time, but by his early adulthood he had left wool, Genoa, and land itself behind, venturing onto the broad Atlantic, north to England and perhaps beyond, and south along the African shore as far as the Gold Coast. During this time he began to develop a plan to find a new, commercially viable route to Asia by sailing west across the ocean. For eight years he sought support for such a journey. Then, in 1492,

the Spanish monarchs Ferdinand and Isabella, having just defeated the last of
Spain's Moorish rulers at Granada, finally agreed to back Columbus's "enterprise
of the Indies."

He made a quick passage across the sea, anxiously watching for signs of land,
until at two in the morning of October 12 the sailor Juan Rodríguez Bermejo saw
the outline of one of the Bahama Islands, and the three ships shortened sail and
waited for daylight. After sunrise, "some naked people" appeared on the beach as
Columbus and the others came ashore, carrying the royal standard and his own
ship's banners. On this island of Guanahaní and others, including Juana and
Española (Cuba and Hispaniola), he marveled at the natural scene ("my eyes never
weary of looking on this fine vegetation") and found the Taino Indians to be "of a
very acute intelligence," a people "so guileless and so generous" that although
naturally timid they approached the strangers and gave them anything they had.
Carried away on a flood of superlatives, Columbus even thought he heard European nightingales singing in the warm Caribbean autumn. Although the newness
of everything in this green paradise left him unable to identify few actual commodities, he kept a sharp eye out for anything he might take home, and by the time he
returned to Spain in early January 1493 he took many specimens with him—
including several of the Taino Indians. The flagship *Santa María* having been lost
in a wreck off Hispaniola on Christmas day, he left the forty-man crew of the
unlucky vessel as a colony there, confident that even if the peaceable Tainos should
turn against La Navidad ("the Nativity," named for the day of the shipwreck), the
well-armed Europeans could easily defend themselves. All seemed peaceful as the
two remaining vessels took their leave of Guacanagarí, the friendly Taino chieftain,
in the vicinity of La Navidad, on January 2, 1493.

When Columbus returned to Hispaniola on his second voyage in November
1493, at the head of a fleet of seventeen ships crammed with twelve to fifteen
hundred men, La Navidad was in ruins, and all the settlers were dead. Although
the greed of La Navidad's settlers for gold and women was revealed as the motive
for their annihilation by the Tainos, this bloody prelude to Spain's New World
empire accurately forecast much that was to follow. By the time Columbus left his
new Hispaniola settlement of Isabella in April 1494 to explore Cuba and Jamaica,
signs of disorder had appeared, and by the time he returned that August, wholesale
disorder was the norm. Columbus sought to restore some control, but he made
the strange mistake of punishing the Tainos who had resisted abuse by renegade
Spaniards, seizing them and enslaving them as rebels, and then subjugating the
island's whole population. With some irony, he was forced to leave for Spain again
in March 1496 to answer charges made against him by some of the Spanish rene-
gades.

Having cleared his name of the worst slanders in Spain, Columbus mounted a
third voyage in 1498, sailing south until he encountered the mainland of South
America near the Orinoco delta in modern Venezuela. Here, increasingly
absorbed in religious speculations and afflicted with arthritis and severe eye trouble,
Columbus took the vast outflow of fresh water as proof that he was near the site of
the Terrestrial Paradise, from which four great rivers were said to flow, and he
proclaimed that God had made him "the messenger" of "the new heaven and . . .
earth" of the Book of Revelation. Meanwhile, the new earth of Hispaniola fell ever
deeper into a hellish state marked by outright rebellion among the Spaniards and
uprisings among the Tainos. Columbus returned from the Orinoco to the new
Hispaniola capital of Santo Domingo at the end of August 1498 to find one of his
appointees, Chief Justice Francisco Roldán, in open rebellion against Columbus's
own brother, Bartolomew. Many of the ordinary Spaniards on the island sympathized with or openly supported Roldán, and he won some converts among the
Tainos as well by promising better treatment than they had so far received. The
promise was empty; when Columbus eventually reached a truce with Roldán and

his confederates, one of the rebels' key points, to which Columbus reluctantly assented, was that they be granted whole Taino communities to labor for them. Not even this sad agreement could end the disorder in the Spanish colony. When the newly appointed chief justice of the island, Francisco de Bobadilla, arrived from Spain in August 1500, he found seven Spanish rebels hanging from a gallows in Santo Domingo, and five more slated for execution the next day, for with the help of Roldán, Columbus was suppressing a rebellion led by an old lieutenant of Roldán. Bobadilla, charged by Ferdinand and Isabella to investigate (among other reported problems) the rumored abuse of ordinary Spanish colonists by the Italian Columbus, saw the corpses as proof that the rumors were correct. Overreacting, he seized the house and belongings of Columbus and by the end of a month seized Columbus himself, whom he sent back to Spain in chains.

Despite this turn of events, in Spain Columbus won the sympathy of the Crown and permission to undertake a fourth voyage in 1502, although he was to avoid visiting Hispaniola, which had been put under the rule of a royal governor, Nicolás de Ovando. After a passage of only twenty-one days across the Atlantic to the island of Martinique, this "High Voyage," as Columbus himself called it, turned disastrous. First came a hurricane off the south coast of Hispaniola and then, as he turned south following the long, thin shores of Central America, came the worst weather Columbus had ever encountered in his long experience at sea. In a place called Veragua (in modern Panama) he was led to expect great deposits of gold but instead found torrential rains. He took refuge in a shallow bay where his four ships, made leaky as sieves by worms, became landlocked for several months. One day as Columbus, sick with malaria, lay alone on one of the vessels, the stress and distress of this High Voyage overcame him. Climbing up the mast by a superhuman effort, he tried to shout to the men on shore for help, but the surf drowned out his voice. Still on the mast, he fell asleep and experienced a vision—or a delusion: "I heard a very compassionate voice, saying, 'O fool and slow to believe and serve thy God, the God of all!'" In this "trance" the voice assured Columbus that he had as much support from above as did David or Moses and that he should keep his faith.

At last he departed "on Easter night, with ships rotten, worm-eaten, all full of holes." By the end of June, the hulls in worse shape yet and more bad weather and contrary winds behind them, the ships arrived at Jamaica, unable to go farther. Columbus sent one of his company, Diego Mendez, in a Caribbean Indian canoe to Hispaniola for help. It was a desperate measure, but Mendez made it across the sea in five days.

Mendez carried with him a letter written in Jamaica in July 1503 by Columbus, a letter into which Columbus poured the accumulating despair of this final voyage and the life of frustration and sorrow it seemed to summarize. As he contemplated Hispaniola, now removed from his control, he thought of its "exhausted state," so different from what he had hoped for it. Rescued from Jamaica later that year, he never was rescued from the sadness that had overtaken him. And fate had reserved for him a last indignity: when he died in 1506, the hemisphere he had stumbled across in his search for Asia was about to be named for another Italian, Amerigo Vespucci, who had little to do with Europe's presence there.

Several documents regarding the four voyages survive from Columbus's hand. The supposed "Journal" of his first voyage is actually a summary prepared by the cleric and reformer Bartolomé de las Casas. A letter sent by Columbus to Luis de Santangel, a royal official and an early supporter of his venture, provides a more authentic account and served as the basis for the first printed description of America, issued in 1493 in Spain and widely translated and reprinted across Europe. A memorandum regarding the second voyage, intended by Columbus for the Spanish monarchs (whose responses to each point also survive), offers useful insights into the emerging ambiguities and problems of the colony on Hispaniola. For the third and fourth voyages, three letters from Columbus, two sent to the

Crown and one to a woman of the Spanish court, detail his deepening worldly and spiritual troubles.

## *From* Letter to Luis de Santangel Regarding the First Voyage [1]

[At sea, February 15, 1493]

Sir,

As I know that you will be pleased at the great victory with which Our Lord has crowned my voyage, I write this to you, from which you will learn how in thirty-three days, I passed from the Canary Islands to the Indies with the fleet which the most illustrious king and queen our sovereigns gave to me. And there I found very many islands filled with people innumerable, and of them all I have taken possession for their highnesses, by proclamation made and with the royal standard unfurled, and no opposition was offered to me. To the first island which I found I gave the name *San Salvador,* [2] in remembrance of the Divine Majesty, Who has marvelously bestowed all this; the Indians call it "Guanahani." To the second I gave the name *Isla de Santa María de Concepción;* to the third, *Fernandina;* to the fourth, *Isabella;* to the fifth, *Isla Juana,* and so to each one I gave a new name. [3]

When I reached Juana I followed its coast to the westward, and I found it to be so extensive that I thought that it must be the mainland, the province of Catayo. [4] And since there were neither towns nor villages on the seashore, but only small hamlets, with the people of which I could not have speech because they all fled immediately, I went forward on the same course, thinking that I should not fail to find great cities and towns. And at the end of many leagues, seeing that there was no change and that the coast was bearing me northwards, which I wished to avoid since winter was already beginning and I proposed to make from it to the south, and as moreover the wind was carrying me forward, I determined not to wait for a change in the weather and retraced my path as far as a certain harbor known to me. And from that point I sent two men inland to learn if there were a king or great cities. They traveled three days' journey and found an infinity of small hamlets and people without number, but nothing of importance. For this reason they returned.

I understood sufficiently from other Indians, whom I had already taken, that this land was nothing but an island. And therefore I followed its coast eastwards for one hundred and seven leagues to the point where it ended. And from that cape I saw another island distant eighteen leagues from the former, to the east, to which I at once gave the name "Española." [5] And I went there and followed its northern coast, as I had in the case of Juana, to the eastward for one hundred and eighty-eight great leagues in a straight line. This island and all the others are very fertile to a limitless degree, and this island is extremely so. In it there are many harbors on the coast of the sea, beyond

1. The text is from *Select Documents Illustrating the Four Voyages of Columbus,* translated and edited by Cecil Jane (1930–33). Luis de Santangel, a former merchant and a court official since 1478, had supported Columbus's proposal to the Spanish Crown and had helped secure financing for the first voyage.
2. The precise identity of the Bahamian island Co-

lumbus named San Salvador is not known today, although many theories have been put forward.
3. Of these four islands, only the identity of Juana (Cuba) is today certain.
4. I.e., China (or "Cathay").
5. I.e., Hispaniola, where the countries of Haiti and the Dominican Republic are located.

comparison with others which I know in Christendom, and many rivers, good and large, which is marvelous. Its lands are high, and there are in it very many sierras and very lofty mountains, beyond comparison with the island of Tenerife.[6] All are most beautiful, of a thousand shapes, and all are accessible and filled with trees of a thousand kinds and tall, and they seem to touch the sky. And I am told that they never lose their foliage, as I can understand, for I saw them as green and as lovely as they are in Spain in May, and some of them were flowering, some bearing fruit, and some in another stage, according to their nature. And the nightingale was singing and other birds of a thousand kinds in the month of November there where I went. There are six or eight kinds of palm, which are a wonder to behold on account of their beautiful variety, but so are the other trees and fruits and plants. In it are marvelous pine groves, and there are very large tracts of cultivatable lands, and there is honey,[7] and there are birds of many kinds and fruits in great diversity. In the interior are mines of metals, and the population is without number. Española is a marvel.

1493

## *From* Letter to Ferdinand and Isabella Regarding the Fourth Voyage [1]

[Jamaica, July 7, 1503]

✳   ✳   ✳

Of Española, Paria,[2] and the other lands, I never think without weeping. I believed that their example would have been to the profit of others; on the contrary, they are in an exhausted state; although they are not dead, the infirmity is incurable or very extensive; let him who brought them to this state come now with the remedy if he can or if he knows it; in destruction, everyone is an adept. It was always the custom to give thanks and promotion to him who imperiled his person. It is not just that he who has been so hostile to this undertaking should enjoy its fruits or that his children should. Those who left the Indies, flying from toils and speaking evil of the matter and of me, have returned with official employment.[3] So it has now been ordained in the case of Veragua.[4] It is an ill example and without profit for the business and for justice in the world.

The fear of this, with other sufficient reasons, which I saw clearly, led me to pray your highnesses before I went to discover these islands and Terra Firma, that you would leave them to me to govern in your royal name. It pleased you; it was a privilege and agreement, and under seal and oath, and you granted me the title of viceroy and admiral and governor general of all.

6. The largest of the Canary Islands.
7. The honeybee, presumably the source of the honey found on the island, is not native to the Western Hemisphere. Nor is the nightingale, mentioned above.
1. The text is from *Select Documents Illustrating the Four Voyages of Columbus*, translated and edited by Cecil Jane (1930–33). Written on Jamaica in 1503, this letter was hand carried from there to Hispaniola by Diego Mendez.

2. Paria was the mainland region of what is now Venezuela, near the island of Trinidad. Columbus, who had first landed in South America ("Terra Firma," as he terms it later) in 1498, argued that the terrestrial paradise lay nearby.
3. Although it appears that Columbus has specific personal enemies in mind, it is not clear whom he means.
4. I.e., Panama, where Columbus was shipwrecked earlier in this voyage.

And you fixed the boundary, a hundred leagues beyond the Azores and the Cape Verde Islands, by a line passing from pole to pole, and you gave me wide power over this and over all that I might further discover. The document states this very fully.

The other most important matter, which calls aloud for redress, remains inexplicable to this moment. Seven years I was at your royal court, where all to whom this undertaking was mentioned, unanimously declared it to be a delusion. Now all, down to the very tailors, seek permission to make discoveries. It can be believed that they go forth to plunder, and it is granted to them to do so, so that they greatly prejudice my honor and do very great damage to the enterprise. It is well to give to God that which is His due and to Caesar that which belongs to him. This is a just sentiment and based on justice.

The lands which here obey Your Highnesses are more extensive and richer than all other Christian lands. After I, by the divine will, had placed them under your royal and exalted lordship, and was on the point of securing a very great revenue, suddenly, while I was waiting for ships to come to your high presence with victory and with great news of gold, being very secure and joyful, I was made a prisoner and with my two brothers was thrown into a ship, laden with fetters, stripped to the skin, very ill-treated, and without being tried or condemned. Who will believe that a poor foreigner could in such a place rise against Your Highnesses, without cause, and without the support of some other prince, and being alone among your vassals and natural subjects, and having all my children at your royal court?

I came to serve at the age of twenty-eight years, and now I have not a hair on my body that is not gray, and my body is infirm, and whatever remained to me from those years of service has been spent and taken away from me and sold, and from my brothers, down to my very coat, without my being heard or seen, to my great dishonor. It must be believed that this was not done by your royal command. The restitution of my honor, the reparation of my losses, and the punishment of him who did this, will spread abroad the fame of your royal nobility. The same punishment is due to him who robbed me of the pearls, and to him who infringed my rights as admiral.[5] Very great will be your merit, fame without parallel will be yours, if you do this, and there will remain in Spain a glorious memory of Your Highnesses, as grateful and just princes.

The pure devotion which I have ever borne to the service of Your Highnesses, and the unmerited wrong that I have suffered, will not permit me to remain silent, although I would fain do so; I pray Your Highnesses to pardon me. I am so ruined as I have said; hitherto I have wept for others; now, Heaven have mercy upon me, and may the earth weep for me. Of worldly goods, I have not even a blanca[6] for an offering in spiritual things. Here in the Indies I have become careless of the prescribed forms of religion. Alone in my trouble, sick, in daily expectation of death, and encompassed about by a million savages, full of cruelty and our foes, and so separated from the holy Sacraments of Holy Church, my soul will be forgotten if it here leaves my body. Weep for me, whoever has charity, truth, and justice.

I did not sail upon this voyage to gain honor or wealth; this is certain, for

5. The reference is to Alonso de Ojeda (c. 1468–1516), who had taken pearls (part of what was reserved to Columbus under his agreement with the Spanish Crown) from Paria to Española.
6. A small Spanish coin.

already all hope of that was dead. I came to Your Highnesses with true devotion and with ready zeal, and I do not lie. I humbly pray Your Highnesses that if it please God to bring me forth from this place, that you will be pleased to permit me to go to Rome and to other places of pilgrimage. May the Holy Trinity preserve your life and high estate, and grant you increase of prosperity.

Done in the Indies in the island of Jamaica, on the seventh of July, in the year one thousand five hundred and three.

1505

---

# ÁLVAR NÚÑEZ CABEZA DE VACA
## c. 1490–1558

Among those who may have witnessed the disgrace of Columbus as he passed in chains through Cádiz in 1498 was a boy from the nearby village of Jerez de la Frontera. Álvar Núñez Cabeza de Vaca was the son of the village alderman, grandson of the conqueror of the Guanche people of Grand Canary Island, and a descendent on his mother's side from a hero of the wars against the Moors who was given the family name "Cabeza de Vaca" (or "cow's head") when he used a cow's skull to mark a strategic route through an unguarded mountain pass. Mindful of this family heritage, as a young man Cabeza de Vaca went off to the wars in Italy (he later was to say that the American Indians of Texas were as shrewd in battle "as if they had been reared in Italy in continual feuds") before coming home to serve as a steward to the duke of Medina Sidonia in campaigns against Spain's *communero* rebels and a French invasion force in the Spanish province of Navarre. His next exploit took him farther afield. In 1527, a few years after the Conquest of Mexico by Hernán Cortés set all Spain dreaming of golden realms in the New World, Cabeza de Vaca sailed on Pánfilo de Narváez's Florida expedition as *aquacil mayor* (provost marshal) and treasurer—an important royal appointee charged with ensuring that the Crown received its share of any riches gathered by Narváez.

The expedition endured many disasters. The first problem was Narváez himself, an impetuous, self-centered man and a bad leader. In 1520 Narváez had led an army from Cuba to the coast of Mexico with orders to arrest Cortés; instead Cortés convinced the army to switch sides, defeated Narváez, and jailed him for three years. Narvaéz, who lost an eye in the fray, finally had a chance to see the glories and the gold of Mexico's central valley shortly before Cortés released him in 1523, whereupon he returned to Spain to complain of Cortés and seek approval for a great conquest of his own. Once he had royal permission to sail for Florida in 1527, he led his six hundred men to Hispaniola, where a quarter of them deserted, and then to Cuba, where two of the six ships were lost in a hurricane. Ten months after leaving Spain the expedition landed in the vicinity of Sarasota Bay, on Florida's west coast. Against Cabeza de Vaca's advice, Narváez sent the ships farther along the shore in search of a rumored port where his army might rejoin them, but the ships were never seen again.

Now began a series of mistakes and follies on Narváez's part that resulted in the loss of all but four of his company. In a formal ceremony, Narváez took possession of Florida while the inhabitants of Sarasota Bay (probably Calusa Indians) made "many signs and threats [that] left little doubt that they were bidding us to go."

Soon the signs changed to arrows, and dwarfed by the great expanse of Florida, the expedition was reduced to eating its horses and trying to escape many groups of Florida natives, from the Timucuan of the Suwannee River area to the Apalachees of the Panhandle. Building clumsy "barges" out of any material at hand, the Spaniards retreated to the sea, hoping to go west to Panuco (modern Tampico, Mexico), which they took to be close, but which in fact was almost two thousand miles away. Narváez took the best oarsmen in his own barge and left the other barges behind him as they neared Mobile Bay; when he pulled away from the others he told them, with false magnanimity, that "it was no longer a time when one should command another"—that is, every man for himself! With that, Narváez and his crew disappeared, apparently lost at sea. It was a fitting last act for this commander of the ill-fated undertaking.

The other rafts passed the mouth of what must have been the Mississippi, and finally wrecked on Galveston Island, now Texas, in November 1528. Here began a further whittling away of the survivors and a time of extraordinary struggles for Cabeza de Vaca and the three men who survived with him: the Spaniards Andrés Dorantes and Alonso del Castillo Maldonado, and Dorantes's black slave, Estevánico, a native of the Moroccan town of Azemmor. The itinerary of Cabeza de Vaca's North American odyssey was long and involved. Alone or with drifting groups of other survivors, he spent his first two years on the Texas coast as a prisoner and slave of the Han and Capoque clans of the Karankawa Indians and then gradually progressed north and west, gaining status and power among the Caddos, Atakapas, Coahuiltecans, and other natives from his activities as a merchant and especially his skill as a healer. By 1535, he reached present-day New Mexico, where he encountered the Jumanos and Conchos, then headed southwest into Mexico as the leader of a vast crowd of Pimas and Opatas who, revering him, followed him from village to village.

The heady mood of the journey dissipated the following March, however, when he and the other survivors came across a party of Spaniards under the slave-hunter Diego de Alcaraz in western Mexico. Seeing the terror of his American Indian escorts at these Spaniards, Cabeza de Vaca felt genuine sympathy for the people of the region, who were being hunted down by what he acerbically called "Christian slavers." His closeness to the Pimas and Opatas and his obvious criticism of Alcaraz led to a falling-out with his countrymen, who arrested him, sent him south, and seized as slaves the six hundred natives in his company. From Mexico City, where he agitated against the cruel (and strictly illegal) activities of the likes of Alcaraz, Cabeza de Vaca went to Spain in 1537, intent on making similar representations to Emperor Charles V himself and hopeful that he would be allowed to lead an expedition back to the New World—one that would treat the Native Americans with justice and humanity.

In 1540 he secured appointment as governor of the South American region of Río de la Plata, but his attempt to enact an enlightened American Indian policy there met stiff resistance from those who benefited from more brutal ones; they removed him from office and sent him in chains back to Spain in 1545. After long delays in settling the dispute, in 1551 he was exiled to modern Algeria and forbidden to return to America.

During the three years he spent in Spain before his departure for Río de la Plata in 1540, Cabeza de Vaca completed his first narrative of the Narváez expedition. It was published in Spain in 1542; a corrected and expanded version that includes the story of his South American experience appeared in 1555. Addressed to Charles V, the 1542 account sought to justify his conclusions regarding Spanish policy and behavior in America as well as to argue for renewed explorations and settlement in the regions he had traversed (several later Spanish expeditions, including those of Coronado and De Soto, clearly drew on Cabeza de Vaca's arguments and knowledge). More important, however, *The Relation of Álvar Núñez Cabeza de Vaca* sought to recount (with remarkable understatement) his sufferings and many brushes with death and to explore his complex feelings regarding the Native Americans and his own countrymen's dealings with them.

# *From* The Relation of Álvar Núñez Cabeza de Vaca[1]

## [*Dedication*]

Sacred Caesarian Catholic Majesty:

Among all the princes who have reigned, I know of none who has enjoyed the universal esteem of Your Majesty[2] at this day, when strangers vie in approbation with those motivated by religion and loyalty.

Although everyone wants what advantage may be gained from ambition and action, we see everywhere great inequalities of fortune, brought about not by conduct but by accident, and not through anybody's fault but as the will of God. Thus the deeds of one far exceed his expectation, while another can show no higher proof of purpose than his fruitless effort, and even the effort may go unnoticed.

I can say for myself that I undertook the march abroad, on royal authorization, with a firm trust that my service would be as evident and distinguished as my ancestors', and that I would not need to speak to be counted among those Your Majesty honors for diligence and fidelity in affairs of state. But my counsel and constancy availed nothing toward those objectives we set out to gain, in your interests, for our sins. In fact, no other of the many armed expeditions into those parts has found itself in such dire straits as ours, or come to so futile and fatal a conclusion.

My only remaining duty is to transmit what I saw and heard in the nine years I wandered lost and miserable over many remote lands. I hope in some measure to convey to Your Majesty not merely a report of positions and distances, flora and fauna, but of the customs of the numerous, barbarous people I talked with and dwelt among, as well as any other matters I could hear of or observe. My hope of going out from among those nations was always small; nevertheless, I made a point of remembering all the particulars, so that should God our Lord eventually please to bring me where I am now, I might testify to my exertion in the royal behalf.

Since this narrative, in my opinion, is of no trivial value for those who go in your name to subdue those countries and bring them to a knowledge of the true faith and true Lord and bring them under the imperial dominion, I have written very exactly. Novel or, for some persons, difficult to believe though the things narrated may be, I assure you they can be accepted without hesitation as strictly factual. Better than to exaggerate, I have minimized all things; it is enough to say that the relation is offered Your Majesty for truth.

I beg that it may be received as homage, since it is the most one could bring who returned thence naked.

1. The text is based on *Adventures in the Unknown Interior of America*, edited and translated by Cyclone Covey (1961).

2. Emperor Charles V (1500–1558), grandson and successor of Ferdinand and Isabella.

\*   \*   \*

## [The Malhado Way of Life]

The people[3] we came to know there are tall and well-built. Their only weapons are bows and arrows, which they use with great dexterity. The men bore through one of their nipples, some both, and insert a joint of cane two and a half palms long by two fingers thick. They also bore their lower lip and wear a piece of cane in it half a finger in diameter.

Their women toil incessantly.

From October to the end of February every year, which is the season these Indians live on the island, they subsist on the roots I have mentioned,[4] which the women get from under water in November and December. Only in these two months, too, do they take fish in their cane weirs. When the fish is consumed, the roots furnish the one staple. At the end of February the islanders go into other parts to seek sustenance, for then the root is beginning to grow and is not edible.

These people love their offspring more than any in the world and treat them very mildly.

If a son dies, the whole village joins the parents and kindred in weeping. The parents set off the wails each day before dawn, again at noon, and at sunset, for one year. The funeral rites occur when the year of mourning is up. Following these rites, the survivors wash off the smoke stain of the ceremony in a symbolic purgation. All the dead are lamented this way except the aged, who merit no regrets. The dead are buried, except medicine-men, who are cremated. Everybody in the village dances and makes merry while the pyre of a medicine-man kindles, and until his bones become powder. A year later, when his rites are celebrated, the entire village again participating, this powder is presented in water for the relatives to drink.

Each man has an acknowledged wife, except the medicine-men, who may have two or three wives apiece. The several wives live together in perfect amity.

When a daughter marries, she must take everything her husband kills in hunting or catches in fishing to the house of her father, without daring to eat or to withhold any part of it, and the husband gets provided by female carrier from his father-in-law's house. Neither the bride's father nor mother may enter the son-in-law's house after the marriage, nor he theirs; and this holds for the children of the respective couples. If a man and his in-laws should chance to be walking so they would meet, they turn silently aside from each other and go a crossbow-shot out of their way, averting their glance to the ground. The woman, however, is free to fraternize with the parents and relatives of her husband. These marriage customs prevail for more than fifty leagues inland from the island.

At a house where a son or brother may die, no one goes out for food for three months, the neighbors and other relatives providing what is eaten. Because of this custom, which the Indians literally would not break to save their lives, great hunger reigned in most houses while we resided there, it

3. The Capoques and Hans of coastal Texas, near today's Galveston Island, which Cabeza de Vaca calls *Malhado*, or the Island of Doom.

4. I.e., "certain roots which taste like nuts, mostly grubbed from [under] the water with great labor."

being a time of repeated deaths. Those who sought food worked hard, but they could get little in that severe season. That is why Indians who kept me left the island by canoe for oyster bays on the main.

Three months out of every year they eat nothing but oysters and drink very bad water. Wood is scarce; mosquitoes, plentiful. The houses are made of mats; their floors consist of masses of oyster shells. The natives sleep on these shells—in animal skins, those who happen to own such.

Many a time I would have to go three days without eating, as would the natives. I thought it impossible that life could be so prolonged in such protracted hunger; though afterwards I found myself in yet greater want, as shall be seen.

The Indians who had Alonso del Castillo, Andrés Dorantes, and the others of their barge who remained alive, spoke a different dialect and claimed a different descent from these I lived among. They frequented the opposite shore of the main to eat oysters, staying till the first of April, then returning.

The distance to the main is two leagues at the widest part of the channel. The island itself, which supports the two tribes commodiously, is half a league wide by five long.

The inhabitants of all these parts go naked, except that the women cover some part of their persons with a wool that grows on trees,[5] and damsels dress in deerskin.

The people are generous to each other with what little they have. There is no chief. All belonging to the same lineage keep together. They speak two languages: Capoque and Han.

They have a strange custom when acquaintances meet or occasionally visit, of weeping for half an hour before they speak. This over, the one who is visited rises and gives his visitor all he has. The latter accepts it and, after a while, carries it away, often without a word. They have other strange customs, but I have told the principal and most remarkable of them.

In April [1529] we went to the seashore and ate blackberries all month, a time of [dance ceremonies] and *fiestas* among the Indians.

✳   ✳   ✳

## [Our Life among the Avavares and Arbadaos]

All the Indians of this region[6] are ignorant of time, either by the sun or moon; nor do they reckon by the month or year. They understand the seasons in terms of the ripening of fruits, the dying of fish, and the position of stars, in which dating they are adept.

The Avavares always treated us well. We lived as free agents, dug our own food, and lugged our loads of wood and water. The houses and our diet were like those of the nation we had just come from, but the Avavares suffer yet greater want, having no corn, acorns, or pecans. We always went naked like them and covered ourselves at night with deerskins.

Six of the eight months we dwelled with these people we endured acute hunger; for fish are not found where they are either. At the end of the eight

5. I.e., Spanish moss.
6. At this point in his story, having escaped from his captivity among the Capoques and Hans, Cabeza de

Vaca is among the Avavares and Arbadaos in inland Texas.

months, when the prickly pears were just beginning to ripen again [mid-June 1535], I traveled with the Negro[7]—unknown to our hosts—to others a day's journey farther on: the Maliacones.[8] When three days had passed, I sent Estevánico to fetch Castillo and Dorantes.

When they got there, the four of us set out with the Maliacones, who were going to find the small fruit of certain trees which they subsist on for ten or twelve days while the prickly pears are maturing. They joined another tribe, the Arbadaos, who astonished us by their weak, emaciated, swollen condition.

We told the Maliacones with whom we had come that we wanted to stop with these Arbadaos. The Maliacones despondently returned the way they came, leaving us alone in the brushland near the Arbadao houses. The observing Arbadaos talked among themselves and came up to us in a body. Four of them took each of us by the hand and led us to their dwellings.

Among them we underwent fiercer hunger than among the Avavares. We ate not more than two handfuls of prickly pears a day, and they were still so green and milky they burned our mouths. In our lack of water, eating brought great thirst. At nearly the end of our endurance we bought two dogs for some nets, with other things, and a skin I used for cover.

I have already said that we went naked through all this country; not being accustomed to going so, we shed our skins twice a year like snakes. The sun and air raised great, painful sores on our chests and shoulders, and our heavy loads caused the cords to cut our arms. The region is so broken and so overgrown that often, when we gathered wood, blood flowed from us in many places where the thorns and shrubs tore our flesh. At times, when my turn came to get wood and I had collected it at heavy cost in blood, I could neither drag nor bear it out. My only solace in these labors was to think of the sufferings of our Redeemer, Jesus Christ, and the blood He shed for me. How much worse must have been his torment from the thorns than mine here!

I bartered with these Indians in combs I made for them and in bows, arrows, and nets. We made mats, which are what their houses consist of and for which they feel a keen necessity. Although they know how to make them, they prefer to devote their full time to finding food; when they do not, they get too pinched with hunger.

Some days the Indians would set me to scraping and softening skins. These were my days of greatest prosperity in that place. I would scrape thoroughly enough to sustain myself two or three days on the scraps. When it happened that these or any people we had left behind gave us a piece of meat, we ate it raw. Had we put it to roast, the first native who came along would have filched it. Not only did we think it better not to risk this, we were in such a condition that roasted meat would have given us pain. We could digest it more easily raw.

Such was our life there, where we earned our meager subsistence by trade in items which were the work of our own hands.

## [Pushing On]

Eating the dogs seemed to give us strength enough to go forward; so commending ourselves to the guidance of God our Lord, we took leave of our

---

7. Estevánico, a Moorish slave from the west coast of Morocco.     8. Neighbors of the Avavares and Arbadaos.

hosts, who pointed out the way to others nearby who spoke their language.

Rain caught us. We traveled the day in the wet and got lost. At last, we made for an extensive scrub wood stretch, where we stopped and pulled prickly pear pads, which we cooked overnight in a hot oven we made. By morning they were ready.

After eating, we put ourselves again in the hands of God and set forth. We located the path we had lost and, after passing another scrub wood stretch, saw houses. Two women who were walking in the "forest" with some boys fled deep into it in fright to call their men, when they noticed us heading for the houses. The men arrived and hid behind trees to look at us. We called to them, and they came up very timidly. After some conversation, they told us their food was very scarce and that many houses of their people stood close by, to which they would conduct us.

At nightfall we came to a village of fifty dwellings. The residents looked at us in astonishment and fear. When they grew somewhat accustomed to our appearance, they felt our faces and bodies and then their own, comparing.

We stayed in that place overnight. In the morning the Indians brought us their sick, beseeching our blessing. They shared with us what they had to eat—prickly pear pads and the green fruit roasted. Because they did this with kindness and good will, gladly foregoing food to give us some, we tarried here several days.

Other Indians came from beyond in that interval and, when they were about to depart, we told our hosts we wanted to go with them. Our hosts felt quite uneasy at this and pressed us warmly to stay. In the midst of their weeping we left them.

### [Customs of That Region]

From the Island of Doom to this land, all the Indians we saw have the custom of not sleeping with their wives from the time they are discovered pregnant to two years after giving birth. Children are suckled until they are twelve, when they are old enough to find their own support. We asked why they thus prolonged the nursing period, and they said that the poverty of the land frequently meant—as we witnessed—going two or three days without eating, sometimes four; if children were not allowed to suckle in seasons of scarcity, those who did not famish would be weaklings.

Anyone who chances to fall sick on a foraging trip and cannot keep up with the rest is left to die, unless he be a son or brother; him they will help, even to carrying on their back.

It is common among them all to leave their wives when there is disagreement, and directly reconnect with whomever they please. This is the course of men who are childless. Those who have children never abandon their wives.

When Indian men get into an argument in their villages, they fist-fight until exhausted, then separate. Sometimes the women will go between and part them, but men never interfere. No matter what the disaffection, they do not resort to bows and arrows. After a fight, the disputants take their houses (and families) and go live apart from each other in the scrub wood until they have cooled off; then they return and from that moment are friends as if nothing had happened. No intermediary is needed to mend their friendship.

In case the quarrelers are single men, they repair to some neighboring people (instead of the scrub wood), who, even if enemies, welcome them warmly and give so largely of what they have that when the quarrelers' animosity subsides, they return to their home village rich.

*　*　*

## [The Long Swing-Around]

After the two days of indecision,[9] we concluded that our destiny lay toward the sunset and so took the trail north only as far as we had to in order to reach the westward one, and then swung down until eventually we came out at the South Sea. The seventeen *jornadas*[1] of hunger the Cow People warned us of, and which proved to be just as bad as they said, could not deter us.

During this desert ascent by the river, the Indians gave us many cowhides, but we passed up their *chacan*[2] in favor of about a handful of deep tallow a day, which we had long since learned to save for such times of famine.

After seventeen *jornadas* we forded the very wide, chest-deep, southern flowing river and traveled another seventeen.

One day as the sun went down out on the plains between massive mountains, we came upon people who for a third of the year eat nothing but powdered straw and, that being the season we passed through, we had to eat it ourselves until at last, at the end of the seventeen *jornadas*, we got to the people of permanent houses who had plenty of corn.[3]

They gave us a great quantity of corn, cornmeal, calabashes, beans, and cotton blankets, all of which we loaded onto the guides who had led us here, and they went back the happiest people on earth. We gave many thanks to God our Lord for bringing us to this land of abundance.

Some of the houses here are made of earth, the rest of cane mats. We marched more than a hundred leagues through continuously inhabited country of such domiciles, where corn and beans remained plentiful. The people gave us innumerable deerhide and cotton blankets, the latter better than those of New Spain, beads made of coral from the South Sea, fine turquoises from the north—in fact, everything they had, including a special gift to me of five emerald arrowheads such as they use in their singing and dancing. These looked quite valuable. I asked where they came from. They said from lofty mountains to the north, where there were towns of great population and great houses, and that the arrowheads had been purchased with feather bushes and parrot plumes.

Among this people, women are better treated than in any part of the Indies we had come through. They wear knee-length cotton shirts and, over them, half-sleeved skirts of scraped deerskin that reach to the ground and that are laced together in front with leather strips. The women soap this outer garment with a certain root which cleanses well and keeps the deerskin becoming. And they wear shoes.

All the people, sick and well, came to us in an attitude of urgency to be touched and blessed; only with great labor did we get through them all. Speak-

9. Tarrying in the Río Grande valley among the Cow People (so-called by the Spaniards because they hunted buffalo), Cabeza de Vaca's party was reluctant to leave the hospitality and easy living experienced there.
1. Roughly the distance covered in a day's journey, or between stops on a longer trip. The "seventeen *jorna-*

*das* of hunger" may refer to the infamous "Journey of Death," the ninety-mile stretch separating the Cow People from the Pueblo Indians of New Mexico.
2. Juniper berries, much used by Suma Indians.
3. These house-dwelling Opata Indians lived in the region of Sonora, in northwestern Mexico.

ing of labor, there were many times that women accompanying us gave birth to babies and, as soon as they were born, the mothers would bring them to us for our touch and blessing.

These Indians ever stayed with us until they safely delivered us to others. They were all convinced that we came from Heaven. (Anything that is new to them or beyond their comprehension is explained as coming from Heaven.) We Christians traveled all day without food, eating only at night—and then so little as to astonish our escort. We never felt tired, being so inured to hardship, which increased our enormous influence over them. To maintain this authority the better, we seldom talked with them directly, but made the Negro [Estevánico] our intermediary. He was constantly in conversation, finding out about routes, towns, and other matters we wished to know.

We passed from one strange tongue to another, but God our Lord always enabled each new people to understand us and we them. You would have thought, from the questions and answers in signs, that they spoke our language and we theirs. We did know six Indian languages, but could not always avail ourselves of them; there are a thousand dialectical differences.

Through all these nations, the people who were at war quickly made up so they could come meet us with everything they possessed. Thus we left all the land in peace. And we taught all the people by signs, which they understood, that in Heaven was a Man we called God, who had created the heavens and the earth; that all good came from Him and that we worshiped and obeyed Him and called him our Lord; and that if they would do the same, all would be well with them. They apprehended so readily that, if we had had enough command of their language to make ourselves perfectly understood, we would have left them all Christians.

We told them what we could and, from then on, at sunrise, they would raise their arms to the sky with a glad cry, then run their hands down the length of their bodies. They repeated this ritual at sunset.

They are a substantial people with a capacity for unlimited development.

## [The Town of Hearts]

In the town where the emeralds were presented us, the people gave Dorantes over 600 opened deer hearts, which they always kept in great supply for food. So we called this place the Town of Hearts. It is the gateway to many provinces on the South Sea, and whoever seeks them without entering here will surely be lost.

The timid, surly Indians of the coast, grow no corn; they eat powdered rushes, straw, and fish, which they catch from rafts, having no canoes. The women cover themselves somewhat, with grass and straw.

We think that near the coast, along the line of those permanent towns we came through, must be more than a thousand leagues of settled, productive land, where three crops a year of corn and beans are sown.

Deer in that belt are of three kinds, one of which are as big as yearling steers in Castile.

The houses are of the kind called *bahíos* in the West Indies.

These people get poison from a certain tree which is about the size of our apple trees. All they have to do is pick the fruit and wet the arrow with it or, if there be no fruit, break a twig and the milk will do as well. The tree is so deadly that, if deer or other animals drink where its bruised leaves have been steeped, they will burst.

We stayed in the Town of Hearts three days.

## [The Buckle and the Horseshoe Nail]

A few days farther on we came to another town where rain was falling so heavily that we could not cross the swollen river and had to wait fifteen days.

In this time Castillo happened to see an Indian wearing around his neck a little sword-belt buckle with a horseshoe nail stitched to it.

He took the amulet, and we asked the Indian what it was. He said it came from Heaven. But who had brought it? He and the Indians with him said that some bearded men like us had come to that river from Heaven, with horses, lances, and swords, and had lanced two natives.

Casually we inquired what had become of those men. They had gone to sea, said the Indians. They had put their lances into the water, got into the water themselves, and finally were seen moving on top of the water into the sunset.

We gave many thanks to God our Lord. Having almost despaired of finding Christians again, we could hardly restrain our excitement. Yet we anxiously suspected that these men were explorers who had merely made a flying visit on their voyage of discovery. But having at last some exact information to go on, we quickened our pace and, as we went, heard more and more of Christians. We told the natives we were going after those men to order them to stop killing, enslaving, and dispossessing the Indians; which made our friends very glad.

We hastened through a vast territory, which we found vacant, the inhabitants having fled to the mountains in fear of Christians. With heavy hearts we looked out over the lavishly watered, fertile, and beautiful land, now abandoned and burned and the people thin and weak, scattering or hiding in fright. Not having planted, they were reduced to eating roots and bark; and we shared their famine the whole way. Those who did receive us could provide hardly anything. They themselves looked as if they would willingly die. They brought us blankets they had concealed from the other Christians and told us how the latter had come through razing the towns and carrying off half the men and all the women and boys; those who had escaped were wandering about as fugitives. We found the survivors too alarmed to stay anywhere very long, unable or unwilling to till, preferring death to a repetition of their recent horror. While they seemed delighted with our company, we grew apprehensive that the Indians resisting farther on at the frontier would avenge themselves on us.

When we got there, however, they received us with the same awe and respect the others had—even more, which amazed us. Clearly, to bring all these people to Christianity and subjection to Your Imperial Majesty, they must be won by kindness, the only certain way.

They took us to a village on the crest of a range of mountains; it was a difficult ascent. The many people who had taken refuge there from the Christians received us well, giving us all they had: over 2,000 backloads of corn, which we distributed to the distressed, pathetic beings who had guided us to that place.

Next day, we despatched four heralds through the country, according to our custom, to call together all the rest of the Indians at a town three *jornadas* distant. We set out, ourselves, the day after that, with all who had congregated on the mountain top.

All along the way we could see the tracks of the Christians and traces of their camps. We met our messengers at noon. They had been unable to contact any Indians, who roved the woods out of sight, eluding the Christians. The night before, our heralds had spied on the Christians from behind trees and seen them marching many Indians in chains.

This intelligence terrified our escort, some of whom ran to spread the news that the Christians were coming, and many more would have followed if we had not managed to forbid them and to palliate their fright. We had with us Indians from a hundred leagues back whom we could not at this time discharge with the recompense due them.

For further reassurance to our escort, we held up where we were for the night. The following day we slept on the trail at the end of the *jornada*. The day after that, our heralds guided us to the place they had watched the Christians. We got there that afternoon and saw at once they had told the truth. We noted by the stakes the horses had been tied to that the men were mounted.

\* \* \*

### [The First Confrontation]

When we saw for certain that we were drawing near the Christians, we gave thanks to God our Lord for choosing to bring us out of such a melancholy and wretched captivity. The joy we felt can only be conjectured in terms of the time, the suffering, and the peril we had endured in that land.

The evening of the day we reached the recent campsite, I tried hard to get Castillo or Dorantes to hurry on three days, unencumbered, after the Christians who were now circling back into the area we had assured protection. They both reacted negatively, excusing themselves for weariness, though younger and more athletic than I; but they being unwilling, I took the Negro and eleven Indians next morning to track the Christians. We went ten leagues, past three villages where they had slept.

The day after that, I overtook four of them on their horses. They were dumbfounded at the sight of me, strangely undressed and in company with Indians. They just stood staring for a long time, not thinking to hail me or come closer to ask questions.

"Take me to your captain," I at last requested; and we went together half a league to a place where we found their captain, Diego de Alcaraz.

When we had talked awhile, he confessed to me that he was completely undone, having been unable to catch any Indians in a long time; he did not know which way to turn; his men were getting too hungry and exhausted. I told him of Castillo and Dorantes ten leagues away with an escorting multitude. He immediately dispatched three of his horsemen to them, along with fifty of his Indian allies. The Negro went, too, as a guide; I stayed behind.

I asked the Christians to furnish me a certificate of the year, month, and day I arrived here, and the manner of my coming; which they did.[4] From this river to the Christian town, Sant Miguel[5] within the government of the recently created province of New Galicia, is a distance of thirty leagues.

4. It was probably March 1536.
5. I.e., Culiacán, the northernmost Spanish settle- ment in Mexico at that time, located in Sinaloa near the mouth of the Gulf of California.

## [The Falling-Out with Our Countrymen]

After five days, Andrés Dorantes and Alonso del Castillo arrived with those who had gone for them; and they brought more than 600 natives of the vicinity whom the Indians who had been escorting us drew out of the woods and took to the mounted Christians, who thereupon dismissed their own escort.

When they arrived, Alcaraz begged us to order the villagers of this river out of the woods in the same way to get us food. It would be unnecessary to command them to bring food, if they came at all; for the Indians were always diligent to bring us all they could.

We sent our heralds to call them, and presently there came 600 Indians with all the corn they possessed. They brought it in clay-sealed earthen pots which had been buried. They also brought whatever else they had; but we wished only a meal, so gave the rest to the Christians to divide among themselves.

After this we had a hot argument with them, for they meant to make slaves of the Indians in our train. We got so angry that we went off forgetting the many Turkish-shaped bows, the many pouches, and the five emerald arrowheads, etc., which we thus lost. And to think we had given these Christians a supply of cowhides and other things that our retainers had carried a long distance!

It proved difficult to persuade our escorting Indians to go back to their homes, to feel apprehensive no longer, and to plant their corn. But they did not want to do anything until they had first delivered us into the hands of other Indians, as custom bound them. They feared they would die if they returned without fulfiling this obligation whereas, with us, they said they feared neither Christians nor lances.

This sentiment roused our countrymen's jealousy. Alcaraz bade his interpreter tell the Indians that we were members of his race who had been long lost; that his group were the lords of the land who must be obeyed and served, while we were inconsequential. The Indians paid no attention to this. Conferring among themselves, they replied that the Christians lied: We had come from the sunrise, they from the sunset; we healed the sick, they killed the sound; we came naked and barefoot, they clothed, horsed, and lanced; we coveted nothing but gave whatever we were given, while they robbed whomever they found and bestowed nothing on anyone.

                        ✻   ✻   ✻

To the last I could not convince the Indians that we were of the same people as the Christian slavers. Only with the greatest effort were we able to induce them to go back home. We ordered them to fear no more, reestablish their towns, and farm.

Already the countryside had grown rank from neglect. This is, no doubt, the most prolific land in all these Indies. It produces three crops a year; the trees bear a great variety of fruit; and beautiful rivers and brimming springs abound throughout. There are gold- and silver-bearing ores. The people are well disposed, serving such Christians as are their friends with great good will. They are comely, much more so than the Mexicans. This land, in short, lacks nothing to be regarded as blest.

When the Indians took their leave of us they said they would do as we commanded and rebuild their towns, if the Christians let them. And I solemnly swear that if they have not done so it is the fault of the Christians.

After we had dismissed the Indians in peace and thanked them for their toil in our behalf, the Christians subtly sent us on our way in the charge of an *alcalde* named Cebreros, attended by two horsemen.[6] They took us through forests and wastes so we would not communicate with the natives and would neither see nor learn of their crafty scheme afoot. Thus we often misjudge the motives of men; we thought we had effected the Indians' liberty, when the Christians were but poising to pounce.

*  *  *

ca. 1536–40                                                                                    1542

6. I.e., they were, in effect, under arrest.

---

## STORIES OF THE BEGINNING OF THE WORLD

Stories about the creation of the world tell people who they are by telling them where they come from. Native American creation stories, although never written down or gathered into a Bible, serve for native cultures in much the same way as the Book of Genesis serves for the Judeo-Christian world: they posit a general cultural outlook and offer perspectives on what life is and how to understand it. All native peoples have stories of the earliest times; anthologized here are two, one from the Iroquois of the Northeast and one from the Pima of the Southwest. These peoples encountered European explorers, missionaries, and colonists very early in the period of contact, and information and conjecture about the Iroquois and the Pima appear in European texts that go back almost four hundred years. But these early records offer only bare sketches of what native people said, sang, chanted, and narrated, and of course, North American Indians did not themselves write down their stories.

It was not until the mid to late nineteenth century that Euro-Americans developed the linguistic skills and cultural understanding necessary to translate and transcribe Native American creation stories in a manner that begins to do justice to them. It was also not until this time that native people collaborated extensively in recording the myths and legends of their people. In the Southwest, the army doctor Washington Matthews began to work on the Navajo Night Chant and Mountain Chant in the 1880s, while Frank Hamilton Cushing, employed by the Bureau of American Ethnology, had installed himself among the Zuni and begun to record their legends in 1879. J. W. Fewkes, after the turn of the century, and J. W. Lloyd, somewhat later, both worked with the Pima Indian known as Thin Leather to record stories of the earliest times. Among the Iroquois, David Cusick, a Tuscarora (the Tuscarora joined the Iroquois Confederacy early in the eighteenth century), had begun to document the legends of his people as early as 1825. He was followed by the distinguished Tuscarora anthropologist J. N. B. Hewitt shortly after the turn of the century.

For all the admirable labors of these Native American and Euro-American people, it is impossible to say with assurance whether one or another of the stories they recorded is more ancient or more authentic, more true to indigenous narrative practice before the arrival of Europeans. And while the stories do change with time and circumstance, because the oral tradition favors continuity, it seems reasonable to turn to later accounts for a window on what came before.

# THE IROQUOIS CREATION STORY

The people known as the Iroquois were made up of the Mohawk, Seneca, Oneida, Onondaga, and Cayuga nations. Joined in the early eighteenth century by the Tuscarora of North Carolina, the Five Nations became the Six Nations. The original Five Nations occupied lands that ranged from the area northeast of lakes Ontario and Erie around the St. Lawrence and Ottawa rivers, then south of the lakes, and eastward almost to the Hudson River. These inhabitants of the eastern woodlands spoke Algonquian languages, and it was an unidentified Algonquian word that early French explorers seized on to coin the term *Iroquois*. (Dutch and English settlers called all of these peoples Mohawk, Maqua, or Seneca.) The Iroquois, whose towns contained as many as two thousand people, called themselves People of the Longhouse (*Haudenosaunee* in Seneca, *Kanosoni* in Mohawk), in reference to their primary type of dwelling. Iroquois longhouses were some twenty feet wide and from forty to two hundred feet long, accommodating several families who shared cooking fires.

Warfare was an important element of Iroquois life. Late in the fifteenth century, in response to the terrible consequences of ongoing wars, a man named Hiawatha founded the League, or Confederacy, of the Five Nations. According to Iroquois legend, having lost all of his daughters in war, Hiawatha, in a rage of grief and despair, went by himself into the forest. There he encountered a supernatural being named Deganawidah, the Peacemaker, perhaps a reincarnation of the Good Twin of the Iroquois creation story. Deganawidah comforted Hiawatha and taught him Rituals of Condolence that were to be the core of a new creed, the Good News of Peace and Power. Thus the cultural ideal of peace was established. While war continued as a central reality of Iroquois life, there were now ritual means of comforting the bereaved—and an ongoing hope for more lasting peace.

Of special note is the importance of women in Iroquois life. Women owned the property and took responsibility for major decisions of social life (indeed, society is referred to as "she"), attending to agricultural duties in the clearings while the men hunted in the woods or warred against traditional enemies such as the fierce Huron to the north. The principal male figure in an Iroquois child's life was not the father but the mother's brother, and the image of mother-dominated families is established strongly in the creation legend. In the version printed here males are entirely absent at the beginning of the tale, appearing neither as husbands nor as fathers. Indeed, stories of fatherless boys who become heroes are common in Iroquois folk history.

The Iroquois creation myth exists in some twenty-five versions, the earliest of which was taken down by the Frenchman Gabriel Sagard in 1623 from the Huron, near neighbors and enemies of the Five Nations. Other early accounts derive from the Mohawk and the Seneca. There is, however, no actual transcription and translation of an Iroquois cosmogonic myth—a narrative of the establishment of the world—until that of David Cusick, a Tuscarora, in the nineteenth century.

Little is known about Cusick. He was born in Madison County, New York, before 1800, when his family moved to the lands granted the Tuscarora by the Seneca and Oneida in Niagara County, New York. Most likely, he attended a mission school where he learned to read and write English. He died in 1840. Cusick's Tuscarora version shares many elements with the creation stories of other members of the Iroquois League; indeed, it has surely been influenced by them. But it also omits much material that other versions include.

Other accounts begin with a man and a woman who live together in the sky world on opposite sides of a fire. Although these two do not sleep together, the woman finds herself pregnant and eventually gives birth to a daughter. The man falls ill and dies, and the daughter grieves intensely for him. When the young woman is grown, her father's spirit instructs her to make a difficult journey to a place where she will meet the man destined to become her husband. When at last she finds this man, he too is ill, but the young woman cures him. The two marry but do not sleep together; nonetheless, as had happened to her mother, she becomes pregnant. It is at this point that Cusick picks up the story of the woman who "would have the twin born." Other versions continue past the point where Cusick's terminates. Some tell, for example, of a toad that hoards water long enough for a flood to burst from its belly or armpit, an indigenous account of a flood uninfluenced by the Judeo-Christian account.

Cusick's English, as the phrase quoted above makes clear, is not standard. Aware of that, he noted in the preface to his work that he found himself "so small educated that it was impossible for me to compose the work without much difficulty." His style is a curious combination of an Indian-inflected English and what the Euro-American culture of the period would have defined as polite literary style. We have selected Cusick's version of the Iroquois creation story because it is early, because it is by a native person (Cusick was the first Native American to record on his own the founding myths of his own people), and because it is fairly accessible to the contemporary reader.

# The Iroquois Creation Story[1]

## A *Tale of the Foundation of the Great Island, Now North America;— the Two Infants Born, and the Creation of the Universe*

Among the ancients there were two worlds in existence. The lower world was in great darkness;—the possession of the great monster; but the upper world was inhabited by mankind; and there was a woman conceived[2] and would have the twin born. When her travail drew near, and her situation seemed to produce a great distress on her mind, and she was induced by some of her relations to lay herself on a mattrass which was prepared, so as to gain refreshments to her wearied body; but while she was asleep the very place sunk down towards the dark would.[3] The monsters[4] of the great water were alarmed at her appearance of descending to the lower world; in consequence all the species of the creatures were immediately collected into where it was expected she would fall. When the monsters were assembled, and they made consultation, one of them was appointed in haste to search the great deep, in order to procure some earth, if it could be obtained; accordingly the monster descends, which succeeds, and returns to the place. Another requisition was presented, who would be capable to secure the woman from the terrors of the great water, but none was able to comply except a large turtle came forward and made

1. From *Sketches of the Ancient History of the Six Nations* (1827).
2. The woman who conceives is, in most Iroquois accounts of the creation, the second generation of sky women to become pregnant without sexual activity. "Mankind": i.e., humans rather than "monsters"— undefined creatures of a time before the world as we know it was established—although these humans have

powers quite different from those humans usually possess.
3. Other versions have Sky Woman either being pushed out of the upper world or accidentally falling.
4. In other versions the monsters are a variety of familiar animals. Cusick's sense of them as monsters conveys the mysterious and dangerous state of affairs in the as-yet-unformed universe.

proposal to them to endure her lasting weight, which was accepted. The woman was yet descending from a great distance. The turtle executes upon the spot, and a small quantity of earth was varnished on the back part of the turtle. The woman alights on the seat prepared, and she receives a satisfaction.[5] While holding her, the turtle increased every moment and became a considerable island of earth, and apparently covered with small bushes. The woman remained in a state of unlimited darkness, and she was overtaken by her travail to which she was subject. While she was in the limits of distress one of the infants in her womb was moved by an evil opinion and he was determined to pass out under the side of the parent's arm, and the other infant in vain endeavoured to prevent his design.[6] The woman was in a painful condition during the time of their disputes, and the infants entered the dark world by compulsion, and their parent expired in a few moments. They had the power of sustenance without a nurse, and remained in the dark regions. After a time the turtle increased to a great Island and the infants were grown up, and one of them possessed with a gentle disposition, and named ENIGORIO, i.e. the good mind. The other youth possessed an insolence of character, and was named ENIGONHAHETGEA, i.e. the bad mind.[7] The good mind was not contented to remain in a dark situation, and he was anxious to create a great light in the dark world; but the bad mind was desirous that the world should remain in a natural state. The good mind determines to prosecute his designs, and therefore commences the work of creation. At first he took the parent's head, (the deceased) of which he created an orb, and established it in the centre of the firmament, and it became of a very superior nature to bestow light to the new world, (now the sun) and again he took the remnant of the body and formed another orb, which was inferior to the light (now moon). In the orb a cloud of legs appeared to prove it was the body of the good mind, (parent). The former was to give light to the day and the latter to the night; and he also created numerous spots of light, (now stars): these were to regulate the days, nights, seasons, years, etc. Whenever the light extended to the dark world the monsters were displeased and immediately concealed themselves in the deep places, lest they should be discovered by some human beings. The good mind continued the works of creation, and he formed numerous creeks and rivers on the Great Island, and then created numerous species of animals of the smallest and the greatest, to inhabit the forests, and fishes of all kinds to inhabit the waters. When he had made the universe he was in doubt respecting some being to possess the Great Island; and he formed two images of the dust of the ground in his own likeness, male and female, and by his breathing into their nostrils he gave them the living souls, and named them EA-GWE-HOWE, i.e., a real people;[8] and he gave the Great Island all the animals of game for their maintenance and he appointed thunder to water the earth by frequent

5. I.e., she lands safely, without harm.

6. Other versions of the story have Sky Woman give birth to a daughter, who again becomes supernaturally pregnant (perhaps by the spirit of the turtle), and it is *she* who conceives the twins. The twins argue even in the womb, the Evil Twin deciding not to be born in the normal way but to burst through his mother's side, which leads to her death. The theme of rival twins is widespread in the Americas.

7. More commonly, the Good Twin is called Tharonhiawagon (Sky-Grasper, Creator or Upholder of the Heavens), and the Evil Twin is named Tawiscaron (Evil-Minded, Flint, Ice, Patron of Winter, and other

disasters). Cusick's Enigorio is a rough translation of the Tuscarora word for "good minded" into Mohawk, while his Enigonhahetgea is an equally rough translation into Seneca, Onondaga, or Cayuga of the Tuscarora word for "bad minded." Cusick has probably changed the Tuscarora words best known to him into these other Iroquois languages, because they were considered to be more prestigious than Tuscarora, the Tuscaroras only recently having joined the Iroquois Confederacy.

8. Humans. *Ea-gwe-howe* is a Tuscarora term used by speakers of all the languages of the Six Nations and, today, simply means Indian, or Indians.

rains, agreeable of the nature of the system; after this the Island became fruitful and vegetation afforded the animals subsistance. The bad mind, while his brother was making the universe, went throughout the Island and made numerous high mountains and falls of water, and great steeps, and also creates various reptiles which would be injurious to mankind; but the good mind restored the Island to its former condition. The bad mind proceeded further in his motives and he made two images of clay in the form of mankind; but while he was giving them existence they became apes;[9] and when he had not the power to create mankind he was envious against his brother; and again he made two of clay. The good mind discovered his brothers contrivances, and aided in giving them living souls, (it is said these had the most knowledge of good and evil). The good mind now accomplishes the works of creation, notwithstanding the imaginations of the bad mind were continually evil; and he attempted to enclose all the animals of game in the earth, so as to deprive them from mankind; but the good mind released them from confinement, (the animals were dispersed, and traces of them were made on the rocks near the cave where it was closed). The good mind experiences that his brother was at variance with the works of creation, and feels not disposed to favor any of his proceedings, but gives admonitions of his future state. Afterwards the good mind requested his brother to accompany him, as he was proposed to inspect the game, etc., but when a short distance from their monina[1] [sic] residence, the bad mind became so unmanly that he could not conduct his brother any more.[2] The bad mind offered a challenge to his brother and resolved that who gains the victory should govern the universe; and appointed a day to meet the contest. The good mind was willing to submit to the offer, and he enters the reconciliation with his brother; which he falsely mentions that by whipping with flags would destroy his temporal life;[3] and he earnestly solicits his brother also to notice the instrument of death, which he manifestly relates by the use of deer horns, beating his body he would expire. On the day appointed the engagement commenced, which lasted for two days: after pulling up the trees and mountains as the track of a terrible whirlwind, at last the good mind gained the victory by using the horns, as mentioned the instrument of death, which he succeeded in deceiving his brother and he crushed him in the earth; and the last words uttered from the bad mind were, that he would have equal power over the souls of mankind after death; and he sinks down to eternal doom, and became the Evil Spirit.[4] After this tumult the good mind repaired to the battle ground, and then visited the people and retires from the earth.[5]

1827

---

9. Cusick may have seen an ape or a depiction of apes (there are no apes native to the New World) and decided to name them as the creatures made by the Evil Twin in contrast to the humans made by the Good Twin. John Buck and Chief John Gibson, in their later renditions of the Iroquois creation narrative also refer to apes at this point in the narrative.

1. Cusick perhaps means *nominal*, their named or designated residence.

2. I.e., the Evil Twin became so rude and obnoxious that the Good Twin could not lead ("conduct") his brother to the appointed place any longer.

3. The Good Twin tells his brother that he can be killed by being beaten with corn stalks, rushes, reeds, or cattails. Cusick calls this a deception; other accounts treat it as a confession of weakness. Below, the Evil Twin admits that he would die if beaten with the antlers of deer.

4. This may reflect an awareness of the Christian belief in the devil as the evil spirit, ruler over the lower depths.

5. Other versions go on to say that the Good Twin teaches the people how to grow corn and how to keep from harm by means of prayer and ritual.

# THE PIMA CREATION STORY

The Pima live along the Gila and Salt rivers in the desert of central Arizona and are close relations of the Tohono O'odham (formerly known as the Papago), who occupy lands in the mostly riverless desert to the south of them. Farming close to the rivers, the Pima grew corn and beans, gathered wild plants, and hunted small game. Late in the fifteenth century, they encountered the Spanish, who named them "Pima" sometime around 1600. Because of their remoteness from Spanish and Mexican centers of power, the Pima were not immediately subjected to strong European influence. In 1694 Spanish missionaries were sent out to convert them. Today, like many native people, most Pima are Christian, although their Christianity both includes and exists alongside traditional beliefs and practices.

The first Pima mythological narrative to be recorded dates from a 1694 journal account written by the Spaniard Juan Manje; Pedro Font, another Spaniard, also recorded a Pima story in 1775. These stories concern the ancestors of the Pima, the Hohokam (meaning, roughly, the "finished ones" or "those who are gone"). Of great importance to the Pima, the narratives offer an account of how the cultural practices of everyday Pima life came to be established. But these earliest stories do not tell of the creation of the world, of the origins of things, or the actions of the most distant ancestors. Such tales were not recorded until the turn of the twentieth century.

At the Pan-American Fair in Buffalo, New York, in July of 1901, J. W. Lloyd met a man named Edward H. Wood, a full-blood Pima, who told him that his greatest dream was to preserve the ancient legends and tales of his people. Wood's grand-uncle, Thin Leather, was a *see-nee-yaw-kum*, a recognized master who knew all the ancient stories. Thin Leather, as Wood told Lloyd, had no successor and feared that with his death the stories would be lost to his people and to the world. Wood persuaded Lloyd to go to the Southwest and work with him and his uncle to record the stories in English. In 1903 Lloyd traveled to Sacaton, Arizona, where he met Thin Leather and, with Wood acting as interpreter, recorded a number of his tales. Lloyd published the results of his work with Wood and Thin Leather privately in 1911, as *Aw-aw-tam, Indian Nights, Being the Myths and Legends of the Pimas of Arizona*. The title refers to the fact that these stories were traditionally told over a period of four nights.

Although the *Story of the Creation* was not narrated until the twentieth century, it is little influenced by the origin story in Genesis, which, however, Thin Leather probably knew. The important animals and vegetation, the chief protagonists, and their personalities and actions are all specific to Pima culture.

## The Story of the Creation[1]

In the beginning there was no earth, no water—nothing. There was only a Person, *Juh-wert-a-Mah-kai* (The Doctor of the Earth).[2]

He just floated, for there was no place for him to stand upon. There was no sun, no light, and he just floated about in the darkness, which was Darkness itself.

1. From *Aw-aw-tam, Indian Nights, Being the Myths and Legends of the Pimas of Arizona* (1911). The editor is indebted to Donald Bahr for his help with the annotation of the Pima selections.

2. This title is equivalent to respectfully calling Juh-wertamahkai a medicine person, or shaman, with great powers, although his powers seem, in a Western sense, to be godlike.

He wandered around in the nowhere till he thought he had wandered enough. Then he rubbed on his breast and rubbed out *moah-haht-tack,* that is perspiration, or greasy earth. This he rubbed out on the palm of his hand and held out. It tipped over three times, but the fourth time[3] it staid straight in the middle of the air and there it remains now as the world.

The first bush he created was the greasewood bush.[4]

And he made ants, little tiny ants, to live on that bush, on its gum which comes out of its stem.

But these little ants did not do any good, so he created white ants, and these worked and enlarged the earth; and they kept on increasing it, larger and larger, until at last it was big enough for himself to rest on.

Then he created a Person. He made him out of his eye, out of the shadow of his eyes, to assist him, to be like him, and to help him in creating trees and human beings and everything that was to be on the earth.

The name of this being was *Noo-ee* (the Buzzard).[5]

Nooee was given all power, but he did not do the work he was created for. He did not care to help Juhwertamahkai, but let him go by himself.

And so the Doctor of the Earth himself created the mountains and every-thing that has seed and is good to eat. For if he had created human beings first they would have had nothing to live on.

But after making Nooee and before making the mountains and seed for food, Juhwertamahkai made the sun.

In order to make the sun he first made water, and this he placed in a hollow vessel, like an earthen dish *(hwas-hah-ah)* to harden into something like ice. And this hardened ball he placed in the sky. First he placed it in the North, but it did not work; then he placed it in the West, but it did not work; then he placed it in the South, but it did not work; then he placed it in the East and there it worked as he wanted it to.

And the moon he made in the same way and tried in the same places, with the same results.

But when he made the stars he took the water in his mouth and spurted it up into the sky. But the first night his stars did not give light enough. So he took the Doctor-stone[6] (diamond), the *tone-dum-haw-teh,* and smashed it up, and took the pieces and threw them into the sky to mix with the water in the stars, and then there was light enough.

## Juhwertamahkai's *Song of Creation*

Juhwerta mahkai made the world—
Come and see it and make it useful!
He made it round—
Come and see it and make it useful!

---

3. This is the first of several actions that must be attempted four times before it is achieved [adapted from Lloyd's note]. Four is the pattern number of the Pima, as it is of a great many native peoples; it corresponds to the importance of three and seven as pattern numbers in Western cultures.
4. "The local touch in making the greasewood bush the first vegetation is very strong" [Lloyd's note]. Greasewood bushes are abundant in the Pima home-

lands.
5. He is a person and also a buzzard, which, in the earliest times, is not a contradiction or paradox to the Pima.
6. I.e., it is a particularly powerful stone. Lloyd's interpreter called it a diamond, but as diamonds are uncommon in North America, this is probably a quartz crystal.

And now Juhwertamahkai, rubbed again on his breast, and from the substance he obtained there made two little dolls, and these he laid on the earth. And they were human beings, man and woman.

And now for a time the people increased till they filled the earth. For the first parents were perfect, and there was no sickness and no death. But when the earth was full, then there was nothing to eat, so they killed and ate each other.

But Juhwertamahkai did not like the way his people acted, to kill and eat each other, and so he let the sky fall to kill them. But when the sky dropped he, himself, took a staff and broke a hole thru, thru which he and Nooee emerged and escaped, leaving behind them all the people dead.

And Juhwertamahkai, being now on the top of this fallen sky, again made a man and a woman, in the same way as before. But this man and woman became grey when old, and their children became grey still younger, and their children became grey younger still, and so on till the babies were gray in their cradles.

And Juhwertamahkai, who had made a new earth and sky, just as there had been before, did not like his people becoming grey in their cradles, so he let the sky fall on them again, and again made a hole and escaped, with Nooee, as before.

And Juhwertamahkai, on top of this second sky, again made a new heaven and a new earth, just as he had done before, and new people.

But these new people made a vice of smoking. Before human beings had never smoked till they were old, but now they smoked younger, and each generation still younger, till the infants wanted to smoke in their cradles.

And Juhwertamahkai did not like this, and let the sky fall again, and created everything new again in the same way, and this time he created the earth as it is now.

But at first the whole slope of the world was westward,[7] and tho there were peaks rising from this slope there were no true valleys, and all the water that fell ran away and there was no water for the people to drink. So Juhwertamahkai sent Nooee to fly around among the mountains, and over the earth, to cut valleys with his wings, so that the water could be caught and distributed and there might be enough for the people to drink.

Now the sun was male and the moon was female and they met once a month. And the moon became a mother and went to a mountain called *Tahs-my-et-tahn Toe-ahk* (sun striking mountain) and there was born her baby. But she had duties to attend to, to turn around and give light, so she made a place for the child by tramping down the weedy bushes and there left it. And the child, having no milk, was nourished on the earth.

And this child was the coyote,[8] and as he grew, he went out to walk and in his walk came to the house of Juhwertamahkai and Nooee, where they lived.

And when he came there Juhwertamahkai knew him and called him *Toe-hahvs*,[9] because he was laid on the weedy bushes of that name.

7. A specifically local element of the Pima story, as both the Gila and the Salt rivers, important to the Pima, flow westward [adapted from Lloyd's note].

8. It is appropriate that the night-prowling coyote is born of the moon, and there is a symmetry in having the buzzard serve as Juhwertamahkai's agent of the sky and the coyote as his agent of the earth [adapted from Lloyd's note].

9. Toehahvs, or Tohawes, means "brittlebush," a common plant in Pima country.

But now out of the North came another powerful personage, who has two names, *See-ur-huh* and *Ee-ee-toy*.[1]

Now Seeurhuh means older brother, and when this personage came to Juhwertamahkai, Nooee and Toehahvs he called them his younger brothers. But they claimed to have been here first, and to be older than he, and there was a dispute between them. But finally, because he insisted so strongly, and just to please him, they let him be called older brother.

1911

1. The name either means "drink it all up" or, according to present-day Pimas, just sounds like the word that means "drink it all up," i.e., it is not translatable. This character is "the most active and mysterious personality in Piman mythology. Out of the North, apparently self-existent, but little inferior in power to Juhwertamahkai, and claiming greater age, he appears, by pure 'bluff,' and persistent push and wheedling, to have induced the really more powerful, but goodnatured and rather lazy Juhwertakmahkai to give over most of the real work and government of the world to him" [Lloyd's note].

---

# THOMAS HARRIOT
## 1560–1621

An Oxford graduate who had entered Sir Walter Ralegh's employment in the early 1580s, Thomas Harriot probably trained Ralegh and the members of the first Roanoke expedition in navigational skills, and he may have accompanied the explorer Arthur Barlowe when the expedition left England in the spring of 1584. It is certain, in any case, that he went on the second voyage, in 1585, as a naturalist who was to collaborate with the painter John White. Having landed in America in April 1585, Harriot and White passed much of the time between then and July of the following year studying and collecting (the two spent that fall and winter, for instance, with an exploring party farther north, in the Chesapeake). In the process, Harriot must have compiled substantial notebooks. These do not survive, but we have a glimpse of them in his descriptive work, *A Brief and True Report of the New Found Land of Virginia* (1588). *A Brief and True Report* gives much information about the flora and fauna the two men found as well as about the American Indians from whom Harriot, having been taught their language (perhaps by Wanchese, a Roanoke Indian who returned with Barlowe to England in 1584), learned a great deal.

While Harriot and White were surveying the landscape, the infant colony— planted on Roanoke, an island off the coast of what is now the North Carolina mainland, at the suggestion of Granganimeo, brother of the Roanoke Indian chief Wingina—was struggling with political unrest. Ralegh's commander-in-chief, the hot-headed Sir Richard Grenville, exerted his authority by bullying the Native Americans and alienating and threatening his own people. When Grenville left for England in August 1585, one of his opponents, Governor Ralph Lane, expressed a relief many must have felt. But Lane himself dealt poorly with the Roanoke Indians and other nearby native groups, so that relations deteriorated, despite the fact that Wingina's people gave much aid to the colonists. Exasperated, the chief began to withhold crucial food supplies from the English, who were told by other Native Americans that he was plotting their annihilation. After nightfall on June 1, 1586, Lane led a preemptive attack on Dasemunkepeuc, Wingina's mainland village. Wounded while asleep, Wingina escaped but was chased down in the woods, killed, and beheaded.

Few of these increasingly serious events are mentioned by Harriot in his *Brief and True Report*. Harriot does glance at Lane's "fierce" dealings with Wingina's people, and he does give ample evidence that diseases imported by the English had already begun to decimate the Native Americans. Had Harriot's own purpose as a writer been less descriptive and propagandistic (apparently he wrote at Ralegh's direction as a new colony was being readied under John White's command), this history of England's first Virginia colony might have been more candid. Harriot's narrative does not acknowledge the disorderly end of the first colony, most of whose survivors were rescued from Roanoke Island by Sir Francis Drake during a severe storm in June 1586. When Grenville returned with reinforcements and supplies later that summer, he found the compound abandoned. Grenville left behind a handful of men (some of whom perished there, some of whom went off in a boat but were never seen again) when he departed on what was to prove a long, circuitous return to England via the Azores, Newfoundland, and then the Azores once again.

Harriot did not see his optimistic text through the press until 1588. By that point, a new group of colonists under his collaborator White's command had left England and sailed for Roanoke, and White had hastily returned to England for more supplies. The great naval encounter between England and the Spanish Armada in 1588 disrupted almost all English shipping, leaving White unable to return to America as quickly as he wished; he was forced to abandon his colonists, whose disappearance from Roanoke Island has never been adequately explained. Ironically, Harriot's propaganda came forth after the fate of the "Lost Colony" had been all but sealed.

# *From* A Brief and True Report of the New Found Land of Virginia

## From *Of the Nature and Manners of the People*[1]

[In] respect of troubling our inhabiting and planting [the natives] are not to be feared,[2] but * * * shall have cause both to fear and love us, that shall inhabit with them.

They are a people clothed with loose mantles made of deerskins, and aprons of the same round about their middles, all else naked, of such a difference of statures only as we in England,[3] having no edge tools or weapons of iron or steel to offend us with (neither know they how to make any). Those weapons that they have are only bows made of witch hazel, and arrows of reeds, [and] flat-edged truncheons[4] also of wood, about a yard long. Neither have they anything to defend themselves [with] but targets made of bark, and some armor made of sticks wickered[5] together with thread.

Their towns are but small, and near the seacoast but few, some containing but ten or twelve houses, some twenty. The greatest that we have seen has been out of thirty houses. If they be walled, it is only done with bark of trees made fast to stakes, or else with poles only fixed upright, and close, one by another.[6]

Their houses are made of small poles, made fast at the tops in round form,

1. The text is from Richard Hakluyt, *The Principall Navigations, Voyages, Traffiques & Discoveries of the English Nation*, vol. 8 (1904). "Manners": customs, practices.
2. I.e., they will not resist English settlement.
3. Varying in height much as the English do.
4. Heavy clubs.
5. Woven. "Targets": small shields.
6. I.e., with palisade fences.

after the manner as is used in many arbors[7] in our gardens in England. In most towns [they are] covered with bark, and in some with artificial mats made of long rushes,[8] from the tops of the houses down to the ground. The length of them is commonly double to the breadth. In some places they are but twelve and sixteen yards long, and in other some[9] we have seen [them] of four and twenty.

In some places of the country, one only[1] town belongs to the government of a Wiroans or chief Lord, in other some two or three, in some six, eight, and more. The greatest Wiroans that yet we had been dealing with, had but eighteen towns in his government, and [was] able to make[2] not above seven or eight hundred fighting men at the most. The language of every government is different from any other, and the further they are distant, the greater is the difference.

Their manner of wars amongst themselves is either by sudden surprising one another, most commonly about the dawning of the day, or moonlight, or else by ambushes, or some subtle devices. Set battles are very rare, except it falls out[3] where there are many trees, where either part may have some hope of defence, after the delivery of every arrow, in leaping behind some [tree] or other.

If there fall out any wars between us and them, what their fight[ing] is likely to be (we having advantages against them so many manner of ways, as by our discipline, our strange weapons and [other devices], especially ordinance great and small), it may easily be imagined. By the experience we have had in some places, the turning up of their heels against us in running away was their best defense.[4]

In respect of us, they are a poor people, and for want of skill and judgment in the knowledge and use of our things,[5] do esteem our trifles before things of greater value. Notwithstanding [this,] in their proper manner[6] (considering the want of such means as we have), they seem very ingenious, for although they have no such tools, nor any such crafts, sciences, and arts as we, yet in those things they do, they show excellence of wit. And by how much they upon due consideration shall find our manner of knowledges and crafts to exceed theirs in perfection, and speed for doing or execution, by so much the more is it probable that they should desire our friendship and love, and have the greater respect for pleasing and obeying us. Whereby may be hoped, if means of good government be used, that they may in short time be brought to civility, and the embracing of true religion.

Some religion they have already, which although it is far from the truth, yet being as it is, there is hope it may be easier and sooner reformed.

They believe that there are many gods, which they call Mantoac, but of different sorts and degrees, one only chief and great God, who has been from all eternity. Who (as they affirm) when he purposed to make the world, made first other gods of a principal order to be as means and instruments to be used

---

7. Small, open shelters.
8. Artfully made from reeds.
9. I.e., in other places.
1. Single, solitary.
2. Recruit, call on.
3. Happens.
4. Perhaps an obscure reference to Roanoke governor Ralph Lane's (1530–1603) surprise attack on Chief

Wingina. After he was attacked in his village, Wingina indeed ran away; he was tracked down, shot in the back, and then beheaded.
5. I.e., European weapons, tools, and so forth. "In respect of": by comparison with. "Want": lack.
6. I.e., within the limits of their own culture and technology.

in the creation and government to follow, and afterwards [made] the sun, moon, and stars as petty gods. * * * First (they say) were made waters, out of which by the gods was made all diversity of creatures that are visible or invisible.

For mankind they say a woman was made first, who by the working of one of the gods, conceived and brought forth children. And in such sort they say they had their beginning. But how many years or ages have passed since, they say they can make no relation,[7] having no letters or other such means as we to keep records of the particularities of times past, but only tradition from father to son.

They think that all the gods are of human shape, and therefore they represent them by images in the forms of men, which they call Kewasowok (one alone is called Kewas).[8] Them they place in houses appropriate, or temples, which they call Machicomuck, where they worship, pray, sing, and make many times [an] offering unto them. In some Machicomuck we have seen but one Kewas, in some two, and in other some three. The common sort think them to be also gods.[9]

They believe also [in] the immortality of the soul, that after this life as soon as the soul is departed from the body, according to the works it hath done, it is either carried to heaven the habitacle[1] of gods, there to enjoy perpetual bliss and happiness, or else to a great pit or hole, which they think to be in the furthest parts of their part of the world toward the sunset, there to burn continually—[that] place they call Popogusso.

For the confirmation of this opinion, they told me two stories, of two men that had been lately dead and revived again. The one [incident] happened but [a] few years before our coming into the country [to] a wicked man, who having [died and been] buried, the next day the earth of the grave being seen to move, [he] was taken up again. [He] made declaration where his soul had been, that is to say, very near entering into Popogusso, had not one of the gods saved him, and [given] him leave to return again, and teach his friends what they should do to avoid that terrible place of torment. The other [incident] happened in the same year we were there, but in a town that was sixty miles from us, and it was told [to] me for strange news, that one being dead, buried, and taken up again [like] the first, showed that although his body had lain dead in the grave, yet his soul was alive and had traveled far in a long broad way, on both sides whereof grew most delicate and pleasant trees, bearing more rare and excellent fruits than ever he had seen before, or was able to express. And at length [he] came to most brave and fair[2] houses, near which he met his father, [who] had been dead before, who gave him great charge to go back again, and show his friends what good they were to do to enjoy the pleasures of that place, which when he had done he should afterwards come again.

What subtlety soever [there may] be in the Wiroances and priests, this opin-

---

7. Narration.
8. In the 1590 edition of Harriot's text, which was published on the Continent and contained engravings taken from the watercolors of John White (c. 1545–93), one such idol is shown. The accompanying text explains, in part: "The people of this country have an Idol, which they call Kiwasa (it is carved of wood; in length, four foot), whose head is like the heads of the people of Florida. The face is of flesh color, the breast white, the rest is all black, the thighs are also spotted

with white. He hath a chain around his neck of white beads, between which are other round beads of copper which they esteem more than gold or silver."
9. This comment about the commoner's confusion of the image or icon with the god it represented would be of particular importance to a Protestant English audience, because there was a strong iconoclastic element in English religious thought.
1. Dwelling place.
2. Splendid, well-built.

ion works so much [effect] in many of the common and simple sort of people,
that it makes them have great respect to their Governors, and also great care
what they do, to avoid torment after death, and to enjoy bliss, although notwithstanding [this fact], there is punishment ordained for malefactors, [such]
as stealers, whoremongers, and other sorts of wicked doers, some punished
with death, some with forfeitures, some with beating, according to the greatness[3] of the facts.

And this is the sum of their religion, which I learned by having special
familiarity with some of their priests, wherein they were not so sure grounded,[4]
nor gave such credit to their traditions and stories, but through conversing
with us they were brought into great doubts of their own [faith], and no small
admiration of ours, [so that there was] earnest desire in many, to learn more
than we had means, for want of perfect utterance in their language, to express.

Most things they saw with us—[such] as mathematical instruments; sea
compasses; the virtue of the load-stone in drawing iron; a perspective glass[5]
whereby were shown many strange sights; burning glasses; wild fireworks; guns;
hooks; writing and reading; spring-clocks that seem to go of themselves; and
many other things that we had—were so strange unto them, and so far
exceeded their capacities to comprehend the reason and means how they
should be made and done, that they thought they were rather the works of
gods than of men, or at the [least] they had been given and taught [to] us [by]
the gods. Which made many of them to have such [an] opinion of us, that if
they knew not the truth of God and Religion already, it was rather to be had
from us whom God so specially loved, than from a people that were so simple,
as they found themselves to be in comparison [with] us. Whereupon greater
credit was given unto that [which] we spoke of, concerning such matters.

Many times and in every town where I came, according as I was able, I
made declaration of the contents of the Bible, [namely,] that therein was set
forth the true and only God, and his mighty works, that therein was contained
the true doctrine of salvation through Christ, with many particularities of Miracles and chief points of Religion, as I was able then to utter, and thought fit
for the time. And although I told them the book materially and of itself was
not of any such virtue, as I thought they did conceive, but only the doctrine
therein contained; yet would many be glad to touch it, to embrace it, to kiss
it, to hold it to their breasts and heads, and stroke over all their body with it,
to show their hungry desire of that knowledge which was spoken of.

The Wiroans with whom we dwelled, called Wingina, and many of his
people would be glad many times to be with us at our Prayers, and many times
would call upon us both in his own town [and] in others whither he sometimes
accompanied us, to pray and sing Psalms, hoping thereby to be partaker of the
same effects which we by that means also expected.

Twice this Wiroans was so grievously sick that he was like to die, and as he
lay languishing (doubting of any help [from] his own priests and thinking he
was in such danger for offending us and thereby our God), sent for some of us
to pray and be a means to our God, [so] that it would please Him either that
he might live, or after death dwell with Him in bliss, [and] so likewise were
the requests of many others in the like case.

---

3. I.e., seriousness.                              5. A device that produced distorted views of the world.
4. I.e., secure.                                   "Load-stone": magnet.

[At] a time also when their corn began to wither by reason of a drought which happened extraordinarily,[6] fearing that it had come to pass [because] in something they had displeased us, many would come to us and desire us to pray to our God of England, that he would preserve their corn, promising that when it was ripe we also should be partakers of the fruit.

There could at no time happen any strange sickness, losses, hurts, or any other cross[7] unto them, but that they would impute to us the cause or means thereof, for offending or not pleasing us. One other rare and strange accident, leaving others, will I mention before I end, which moved the whole country that either knew or heard of us, to [hold] us in wonderful admiration.[8]

There was no town where we had any subtle device practiced against us (we leaving it unpunished or not revenged because we sought by all means possible to win them by gentleness) but that within a few days after our departure from every such town, the people began to die very fast, and many in short space, in some towns about twenty, in some forty, and in one six score, which in truth was very many in respect of their numbers. This happened in no place that we could learn, but where we had been, where they used some practice against us, and after such time.[9] The disease also was so strange, that they neither knew what it was, nor how to cure it, [for] the like by report of the oldest men in the country never [had] happened before, time out of mind (a thing especially observed by us, as also by the natural inhabitants themselves). Insomuch that when some of the inhabitants which were our friends, and especially the Wiroans Wingina, had observed such effects in four or five towns [following] their wicked practices, they were persuaded that it was the work of God through our means, and that we by him might kill and slay whom we would without weapons, and not [have to] come near them. And thereupon when it had happened that they had understanding that any of their enemies had abused us in our journeys (hearing that we had wrought no revenge with our weapons, and fearing upon some cause the matter should so rest), [they] did come and entreat us that we would be a means to our God that they as others that had dealt ill with us might in like sort die, alleging how much it would be for our credit and profit (as also theirs) and hoping furthermore that we would do so much at their request [out] of the friendship we professed them.[1]

[We, however, argued that these requests] were ungodly, affirming that our God would not subject himself to any such prayers and requests of men; that indeed all things have been and were to be done according to his good pleasure as he had ordained; and that we, to show ourselves his true servants, ought rather to make petition for the contrary, [namely], that they with them[2] might live together with us, be made partakers of His truth, and serve Him in righteousness.

But, notwithstanding [our disavowals], * * * because the effect fell out so

6. I.e., the drought was extraordinarily severe.
7. Accident.
8. I.e., in awe. "Leaving": passing over.
9. I.e., it happened after the English had left.
1. Neither Harriot nor the Native Americans understood the accidental exchange of disease that was beginning to devastate the local population with European pathogens. That the ill effects were thought to be limited to villages in which some dispute had arisen between the two groups gave the American Indians the impression that the English were taking revenge. This pattern in the outbreaks has, however, a simpler explanation: the greater intimacy that may well have preceded and even produced the disagreements was one precondition for the spread of infection. Despite their confusion, Wingina's people seized on the usefulness of "English" sickness for their own political disputes with other Indian groups.
2. I.e., both Wingina's people and their enemies.

suddenly and shortly afterwards according to their desires,[3] they thought nevertheless [that] it came to pass by our means, and that we in using such speeches [with] them, did but dissemble the matter; and therefore [they] came unto us to give us thanks in their manner, [because] although we satisfied them not in promise,[4] yet in deeds and effect we had fulfilled their desires.

This marvelous accident[5] [produced] in all the country [such] strange opinions of us, that some people could not tell whether to think us gods or men, and the rather because that all the space of their sickness, there was no man of ours known to die, or [be] especially sick. They noted also that we had no women amongst us, [and] that we did [not] care for any of theirs.

Some therefore were of [the] opinion that we were not born of women, and therefore not mortal, but that we were men of an old generation many years past, then risen again to immortality.

Some would likewise seem to prophecy that there were more of our generation yet to come [to this land] to kill theirs and take their places, as some thought the purpose was, [judging] by that which was already done. Those that were immediately to come after us they imagined to be in the air, yet invisible and without bodies, and [imagined] that they by our entreaty and for the love of us, did make the people to die in [the way] they did, by shooting invisible bullets into them.

To confirm this opinion, their physicians (to excuse their ignorance in curing the disease)[6] would not be ashamed to * * * make the simple people believe that the strings of blood they sucked out of the sick bodies, were the strings wherewith the invisible bullets were tied and cast.[7] Some also thought that we shot them ourselves out of our pieces, from the place where we dwelled, and killed the people in any [such] town that had offended us, as we listed,[8] how far distant from us soever it was. And [others] said that it was the special work of God for our sakes, as we ourselves have cause in some sort to think no less. * * * Their opinions I have set down the more at large, that it may appear unto you that there is good hope they may be brought through discreet dealing and government[9] to the embracing of the truth, and consequently to honor, obey, fear, and love us.

And although some of our company towards the end of the year showed themselves too fierce in slaying some of the people in some towns, upon causes that on our part might easily enough have been borne * * * by carefulness of ourselves [there is] nothing at all to be feared.[1]

1588

3. I.e., the enemies for whose suffering they petitioned the English soon were visited with illness.
4. I.e., the English had not vowed to punish Wingina's enemies.
5. Occurrence, incident.
6. I.e., to find an excuse for their own failure to cure the illness.
7. Shot, thrown. The "strings" of blood may have been partly coagulated strands produced by the unknown illness.

8. Wished.
9. I.e., direction, control. "At large": at such length.
1. Here Harriot hints at the brutal behavior of Ralph Lane, who as governor of the infant colony reacted to rumors of a Roanoke Indian plot against the English by attacking the village of Dasemunkepeuc. By the time Harriot published his Relation in 1588, Wingina (one of "some of the people in some towns" whom Lane had killed) had been dead for two years.

# JOHN WHITE

## c. 1545–1593

According to the Elizabethan herbalist John Gerard, John White was "an excellent painter who carried very many people into Virginia . . . there to inhabite." White captured the sights of the Roanoke region and the Chesapeake with brush and pen in 1585 and 1586, collaborating with Thomas Harriot, who described the region in writing. In 1587 White was chosen governor of the tragic second colony sent to Roanoke. Although this man of modest background played a central role in the whole Ralegh enterprise, we know little of his life before 1585 or after 1590. His many excellent maps suggest that he was trained as a land surveyor, and his skills as an ethnographic artist may well have been honed during Sir Martin Frobisher's second voyage (1577) to Baffin Island, in the Canadian Arctic, located due west of Greenland. How many voyages White made to America is uncertain. The one he undertook in 1590 was described as his "fifth," so clearly he had been to the New World before the Roanoke voyage of 1585 and (like Harriot) may have been on one of the vessels that went there in 1584 as well.

White's last voyage, in 1590, was a desperate attempt to locate the survivors of the second Roanoke contingent, whom he last saw in 1587 before he sailed to England for fresh supplies. Unable to return quickly to America because of shipping disruptions caused by the great sea battle between England and the Spanish Armada, White at last arrived there in 1590, only to find that the settlers, including his daughter and her family, had vanished. At Roanoke, the capital "City of Ralegh" yielded only a clutter of broken objects and ruined houses, perhaps a testimony to Governor Ralph Lane's vicious attack in 1586 on Chief Wingina and his people. Further searching might have turned up clues, or perhaps even the colonists themselves, but White was not able to linger in Virginia. He had come as a passenger in a loosely allied group of privateers (private vessels licensed to disrupt enemy shipping) more interested in raiding Spanish ships in the Caribbean than in adding their own names to the death toll of Ralegh's Roanoke Colony. Though White found hints of the settlers' relocation to nearby Croatoan, the deaths of one of the privateer captains and several other men, together with fierce weather, forced him to abandon the search.

Anthologized here is White's account of what he found on the island in 1590, along with part of his record of the voyage home to England, prepared three years later for inclusion in the great collection of voyage narratives edited by Richard Hakluyt, *The Principall Navigations . . . of the English Nation* (1599–1600). In a letter to Hakluyt that accompanied his narrative, White summed up the course of his American career: "Thus may you plainly perceive the success [i.e., outcome] of my fifth and last voyage to Virginia, which was no less unfortunately ended than [adversely] begun, and [was] as luckless to many, as [it was] sinister to myself. But I would to God it had been as prosperous to all, as [it was troublesome] to the planters; and as joyfull to me, as discomfortable to them."

## *From* The Fifth Voyage of Mr. John White[1]

On the first of August the wind scanted, and from thence forward we had very foul weather with much rain, thundering, and great [water]spouts, which fell round about us nigh unto our ships.

1. The text is derived from Richard Hakluyt, *The Principall Navigations, Voyages, Traffiques, & Discoveries of the English Nation*, vol. 8 (1904).

The third we stood again in for the shore, and at midday we took the height[2] of the same. The height of that place we found to be 34° of latitude. Towards night we were within three leagues of the low sandy islands west of Wococon.[3] But the weather continued so exceedingly foul, that we could not come to an anchor nigh the coast, wherefore we stood off again to sea until Monday, the ninth of August.

On Monday the storm ceased, and we had very great likelihood of fair weather. Therefore, we stood in again for the shore, and came to an anchor at eleven fathoms in 35° of latitude, within a mile of the shore, where we went on land on the narrow sandy island, being one of the islands west of Wococon. In this island we took in some fresh water and caught great store of fish in the shallow water. Between the main[land] (as we supposed) and that island it was but a mile over, and three or four foot deep in most places.

On the twelfth in the morning we departed from thence and toward night we came to an anchor at the northeast end of the island of Croatoan, by reason of a breach which we perceived to lie out two or three leagues into the sea.[4] Here we rode all night.

The thirteenth in the morning, before we weighed our anchors, our boats were sent to sound[5] over this breach, our ships riding on the side thereof at five fathom, and a ship's length from us we found but four and a quarter, and then deepening and shallowing for the space of two miles; so that sometimes we found five fathom, and by and by seven, and within two casts with the lead nine, and then eight, next cast five, and then six, and then four, and then nine again, and deeper. [A mere] three fathoms was the last, two leagues off from the shore. This breach is in 35°30', and lies at the very northeast point of Croatoan, where [there is] a fret[6] out of the main sea into the inner waters, which part the islands and the mainland.

The fifteenth of August towards evening we came to an anchor at Hatorask, in 36°20', in five fathoms [of] water, three leagues from the shore. At our first coming to anchor on this shore we saw a great smoke rise on the isle [of] Roanoke, near the place where I left our colony in the year 1587, which smoke put us in good hope that some of the colony were there expecting my return out of England.

The sixteenth, [the] next morning, our two boats went ashore, and Captain Cocke and Captain Spicer and their company with me, with [the] intention to pass to the place at Roanoke where our countrymen were left. At our putting [off] from the ship, we commanded our master gunner to make ready two minions and a falcon,[7] well loaded, and to shoot them off with reasonable space between every shot, to the end that their reports might be heard to the place where we hoped to find some of our people. This was accordingly per-

---

2. They determined the latitude of this stretch of the coast by measuring the height of the sun above the horizon at noon, using a quadrant, or a cross-staff.
3. On the maps he drew of the Carolina coast, White identified Wococon as the southernmost of the four major islands of the Outer Banks, with Croatoan, Paquiwoc, and Hatorask ranging northward from it. Together, the four islands defined Pamlico Sound, within which (near Hatorask at the north end) lay Roanoke Island. The configuration of the barrier islands has changed much over the intervening centuries. Although the general features of the area remain roughly similar, White's "Hatorask" is not the same as

the modern Hatteras Island, "Croatoan" was roughly equivalent to the south end of modern Hatteras plus the north part of modern Ocracoke Island, and Wococon probably encompassed parts of modern Ocracoke and Portsmouth islands.
4. White means that they came to anchor for the night because, as they sailed by Croatoan on their way north, they could see dangerous shoals offshore. These would be the 16th-century predecessors of Diamond and Outer Shoals, located off modern Cape Hatteras.
5. I.e., check the depth of water over the shallows.
6. An opening or passage.
7. Kinds of light artillery.

formed, and our two boats put off unto the shore. In the admiral's boat[8] we sounded all the way and found from our ship until we came within a mile of the shore, nine, eight, and seven fathom; but before we were halfway between our ships and the shore we saw another great smoke to the southwest of Kenrick's Mounts.[9] We therefore thought [it] good to go to that second smoke first, but it was much farther from the harbor where we [had] landed [on Roanoke] than we supposed it to be, so that we were very sorely tired before we came to the smoke. But that which grieved us more was that when we came to the smoke we found no man nor [any] sign that any had been there lately, nor yet any fresh water in all this way to drink. Being thus wearied with this journey, we returned to the harbor where we [had] left our boats, [whose crews] in our absence had brought their casks ashore for fresh water, so we deferred our going to Roanoke until the next morning, and caused some of those sailors to dig in those sandy hills for fresh water, whereof we found sufficient [supply]. That night we returned aboard with our boats and our whole company in safety.

The next morning, being the seventeenth of August, our boats and company were prepared again to go up to Roanoke, but Captain Spicer had then sent his boat ashore for fresh water, by means whereof it was ten of the clock aforenoon before we put [off] from our ships, which were then come to an anchor within two miles of the shore. The admiral's boat was halfway toward the shore when Captain Spicer put off from his ship. The admiral's boat first passed the breach,[1] but not without some danger of sinking, for we had a sea break into our boat which filled us half full of water, but by the will of God and [the] careful steerage of Captain Cocke, we came safely ashore, saving only that our furniture, victuals, match,[2] and powder were much wet and spoiled. For at this time the wind blew at northeast and direct into the harbor, so great a gale that the sea broke extremely[3] on the bar and the tide went very forcibly at the entrance. By [the] time our admiral's boat was hauled ashore, and most of our things taken out to dry, Captain Spicer came to the entrance of the breach with his mast standing up, and was half passed over, but by the rash and indiscreet steerage of Ralph Skinner, his master's mate, a very dangerous sea broke into their boat and overset them quite. The men kept [to] the boat, some in it and some hanging on it, but the next sea set the boat on ground,[4] where it beat so that some of them were forced to let go their hold, hoping to wade ashore. But the sea still beat them down, so that they could neither stand nor swim, and the boat twice or thrice was turned the keel upward, whereon Captain Spicer and Skinner hung until they sunk, and were seen no more. But four that could swim a little kept themselves in deeper water and were saved by Captain Cocke's means, who so soon as he saw their oversetting, stripped himself, [as did] four others that could swim very well, and with all haste possible [they] rowed unto them, and saved [those] four.

8. I.e., the one from the largest ship, in this case the *Hopewell*.
9. High sand dunes on Cape Kenrick, then the outermost point of land on the Outer Banks, located between White's Hatorask and Paquiwoc. This cape disappeared toward the end of the following century. The boats of which White writes had headed roughly west (or perhaps northwest) to reach Roanoke and would have had to swing around to the south to seek out the place where this second fire had been lighted.

1. One of the channels separating the ends of the Outer Banks islands from each other. Because the water is typically shallow in such places, however, the word still carries the meaning it had in his earlier usage (see n. 4, p. 42).
2. Wick used in firing matchlock guns or cannons. "Steerage": steering. "Furniture": gear.
3. I.e., with extreme force.
4. I.e., forced it down against the sea bottom.

They were eleven in all, and seven of the chief were drowned, whose names were Edward Spicer, Ralph Skinner, Edward Kelley, Thomas Bevis, Hance the Surgeon, Edward Kelborne, [and] Robert Coleman. This mischance did so much discomfort the sailors, that they were all of one mind, [namely,] not to go any further to seek the planters. But in the end by the commandment and persuasion of me and Captain Cocke, they prepared the boats, and seeing the Captain and me so resolute, they seemed much more willing. Our boats and all things fitted again, we put off from Hatorask, being the number of nineteen persons in both boats, but before we could get to the place where our planters were left, it was so exceedingly dark that we overshot the place [by] a quarter of a mile. There we espied towards the north end of the island the light of a great fire through the woods, [toward] which we presently rowed. When we came right over against it, we let fall our grapnel[5] near the shore, and sounded with a trumpet a call, and afterwards many familiar English tunes of songs, and called to them friendly, but we had no answer. We therefore landed at daybreak, and coming to the fire, we found the grass and sundry rotten trees burning about the place. From hence we went through the woods to that part of the island directly over against Dasemunkepeuc,[6] and from thence we returned by the waterside, round about the north point of the island, until we came to the place where I left our colony in the year [1587]. In all this way we saw in the sand the print of the savages' feet, of two or three sorts, trodden [that] night, and as we entered up the sandy bank [we saw that], upon a tree in the very brow thereof,[7] were curiously carved these fair Roman letters,[8] C R O: which letters presently we knew to signify the place where I should find the planters seated, according to a secret token agreed upon between them and me at my last departure from them, which was that in any ways[9] they should not fail to write or carve on the trees or posts of the doors the name of the place where they should be seated, for at my coming away they were prepared to remove from Roanoke fifty miles into the main[land]. Therefore at my departure from them in Anno 1587, I willed them that if they should happen to be distressed in any of those places that then they should carve over the letters or name a cross ✚ in this form, but we found no such sign of distress. And having well considered of this, we passed toward the place where they were left in sundry houses, but we found the houses taken down, and the place very strongly enclosed with a high palisade of great [posts], with curtains and flankers,[1] very fort-like, and one of the chief trees or posts at the right side of the entrance had the bark taken off, and five feet from the ground in fair capital letters was graven CROATOAN, without any cross or sign of distress. This done, we entered into the palisade, where we found many bars of iron, two pigs of lead, four iron fowlers, iron saker-shot,[2] and such like heavy things, thrown here and there, almost overgrown with grass and weeds. From thence we went along by the waterside, towards the point of the creek to see if we could find any of their boats or [the] pinnace,[3] but we could perceive no sign of them, nor any of the last falcons and other small ordnance[4] which were left

5. Grappling hook, used as an anchor. "Over against it": directly opposite it.
6. Chief Wingina's principal village, located on the mainland across a narrow channel west of Roanoke Island.
7. I.e., at the very top ("brow") of the sandy bank.
8. I.e., in the style of inscriptions found on Roman buildings, consisting of simple large capitals.
9. I.e., by all means. "To Ken": sign.
1. Defensive walls on the front and sides.
2. Shot for a small cannon used in sieges and on shipboard. "Pigs": crude ingots.
3. A small sailing vessel.
4. Artillery. "Falcons": light artillery pieces.

with them, at my departure from them. At our return from the creek, some of our sailors, meeting us, told us that they had found where divers[5] chests had been hidden, and long [since] dug up again and broken up, and much of the goods in them spoiled and scattered about, but nothing left (of such things as the savages knew any use of) undefaced. Presently Captain Cocke and I went to the place, which was in the end of an old trench, made two years past by Captain Amadas,[6] where we found five chests that had been carefully hidden [by] the planters, and of the same chests three were my own, and about the place many of my things [lay] spoiled and broken, and my books torn from the covers, the frames of some of my pictures and maps rotten and spoiled with rain, and my armor almost eaten through with rust.[7] This could be [nothing] but the deed of the savages our enemies[8] at Dasemunkepeuc, who [must have] watched the departure of our men to Croatoan, and as soon as they were departed dug up every place where they suspected anything [was] buried. But although it much grieved me to see such spoil of my goods, yet on the other side I greatly joyed that I had safely found a certain token of their being safe at Croatoan, which is the place where Manteo[9] was born, and the savages of the island [were] our friends.

When we had seen in this place so much as we could, we returned to our boats and departed from the shore towards our ships with as much speed as we could, for the weather began to [be] overcast, and [it seemed] very likely that a foul and stormy night would ensure. Therefore, the same evening, with much danger and labor, we got ourselves aboard, by which time the wind and seas were so greatly risen that we doubted our cables and anchors would scarcely hold until morning. Wherefore the captain caused the boat to be manned with five lusty[1] men who could [all] swim well, and sent them to the little island on the righthand of the harbor, to bring aboard six of our men who had filled our casks with fresh water. The boat the same night returned aboard with our men, but all our casks, ready-filled, they left behind, impossible to be had aboard without danger of casting away both men and boats, for this night proved very stormy and foul.

The next morning it was agreed by the captain and myself, with the master and others, to weigh anchor and go for the place at Croatoan where our planters were, for that[2] then the wind was good for that place, and [we agreed] also to leave [those] casks with fresh water on shore [on] the island until our return. So then they brought the cable to the captain, but when the anchor was almost apeak[3] the cable broke, by means whereof we lost another anchor, wherewith we drove so fast [onto] the shore, that we were forced to let fall a third anchor, which came so fast home that the ship was almost aground by Kenrick's Mounts, so that we were forced to let slip [this] cable, end for end.[4] And if it had not chanced that we had fallen into a channel of deeper water, closer by the shore than we accounted of, we could never have gone clear of the point that lies to the southwards of Kenrick's Mounts. Being thus clear of some

5. Several.
6. Captain Philip Amadas (c. 1565–1586?), Arthur Barlowe's commander on the 1584 voyage, and "admiral of Virginia" in 1585–86.
7. The ruined objects suggest that considerable time had passed since the looting of the settlement.
8. Unlike Harriot, White acknowledges the antagonism between Wingina's people and the English.
9. One of the two natives who had been taken back to

England by Amadas and Barlowe in 1584, Manteo had come home with the 1585–86 expedition.
1. Strong.
2. Because.
3. Raised to the ship's railing.
4. Run out the cable rope so as to free the ship from the hold of the anchor, in this instance to gain maneuverability.

dangers, and gotten into deeper waters (but not without some loss: for we had but one cable and anchor left us of the four, and the weather grew to be fouler and fouler; our victuals [were] scarce, and our casks and fresh water lost), it was therefore determined that we should go for St. John[5] or some other island to the southward for fresh water. And it was further proposed that if we could anyway supply our wants of victuals and other necessaries either at Hispaniola, St. John, or Trinidad, that then we should continue in the [West] Indies all the winter following, with [the] hope to make two rich voyages of one,[6] and at our return to visit our countrymen [in] Virginia. The captain and the whole company in the admiral (with my earnest petitions) thereunto agreed, so that it rested only to know what the master of the *Moonlight*, our consort,[7] would do herein. But when we demanded [of] them if they would accompany us in that new determination, they alleged that their weak and leaky ship was not able to continue it; wherefore the same night we parted, leaving the *Moonlight* to go directly for England, and the admiral set [its] course for Trinidad, which course we kept two days.

On the twenty-eighth the wind changed, and it was set on foul weather every way. But this storm brought the wind west and northwest, and blew so forcibly that we were able to bear no sail, [except] our fore-course half mast high,[8] wherewith we ran upon the wind perforce, the due course for England, [so] that we were driven to change our first determination [of] Trinidad, and stood for the Islands of [the] Azores, where we purposed to take in fresh water, and also there hoped to meet with some English men of war about those islands, at whose hands we might obtain some supply of our wants. And thus continuing our course for the Azores, sometimes with calms, and sometimes with very scarce winds, on the fifteenth of September the wind came south-southeast and blew so exceedingly, that we were forced to lie atry[9] all that day. At this time by account we judged ourselves to be about twenty leagues to the west of Corvo and Flores,[1] but about night the storm ceased, and fair weather ensued.

*   *   *

1593                                                                    1600

5. San Juan, i.e., Puerto Rico.
6. The small fleet had already taken a Spanish ship as a prize before going to Roanoke, so a successful return to the West Indies would make "two rich voyages [out] of one."
7. Companion ship. "Rested": remained.
8. I.e., they shortened their foresail.
9. I.e., with the bow of the ship held to the weather by the counteraction of fore and aft sails.
1. Islands in the Azores.

---

# SAMUEL DE CHAMPLAIN

## c. 1570–1635

Born around 1570 in Brouage, an important seaport and center of the salt industry near La Rochelle on the Atlantic coast of France, Samuel de Champlain served more than any other Frenchman of his time to deepen his country's interest in America and to plant that interest solidly in American soil. Champlain served in the French army as a quartermaster during the 1590s (he fought in the battle in which the English explorer and French ally Sir Martin Frobisher was killed), but soon this merchant captain's son turned to the sea. In 1598 he sailed for Spain on a vessel commanded by an uncle, and the next year he crossed the Atlantic. He crossed it five more times in the next few years—in what capacity or for what purposes we do not know—traveled widely in the Spanish West Indies and Mexico, and then, after 1603, turned his attention toward what was to become France's main base of operations in the West, the northeastern part of North America.

The 1603 voyage to Canada, for which Champlain was recruited as "geographer royal" (perhaps at King Henri IV's urging), was under the command of François Pont-Gravé, who was sent out by a merchant holding the royal fur trade monopoly. Pont-Gravé followed Jacques Cartier's 1530 route up the St. Lawrence River as far as the future site of Montreal, where the expedition took on valuable furs before returning to the French port of Havre de Grace that fall. Early in 1604 Champlain published his official report, *Des Sauvages*, illustrated with his own maps, and in April returned to America along with Pont-Gravé under the command of the Sieur de Monts, the current holder of the royal monopoly and a Protestant merchant from Champlain's home region. Temporarily settled on an island in the St. Croix River between Maine and New Brunswick and then at Port-Royal in Nova Scotia, the Frenchmen spent much of their time exploring the coasts of what would become Maritime Canada and New England, reaching as far south as Cape Cod. Their first two winters in North America, especially that of 1604–05 on St. Croix Island, sorely tested their resolve, and although the third was milder, Champlain concluded, as he convinced the Sieur de Monts once back in France in 1607, that this northeastern coastal zone was not the ideal place for the permanent colony that they hoped to establish. Far better, argued Champlain, would be the valley of the St. Lawrence, first explored for France by Cartier seventy years earlier. On the next voyage, begun in 1608, Champlain returned up that river, on whose shores in that summer he founded Quebec City.

Although Champlain spent much of the rest of his life shuttling back and forth across the Atlantic, crossing it eighteen times between 1610 and 1633, he committed himself fully to the success of the new settlement of Quebec, and thereby ensured the survival of New France. Under his guidance, the French made bold claims to much of North America at a time when the English, with the exception of their small and frail coastal settlement in Virginia, had barely arrived. Champlain himself explored as far inland as Georgian Bay on Lake Huron. And Etienne Brulé, under the direction of Champlain, traveled as far as Lake Superior in the very year that the Pilgrims set out from England and, losing their route on the way to the Hudson River, settled at Plymouth, an area explored and mapped by Champlain fifteen years before.

As well as claiming new territory, Champlain did not neglect relations with the Native Americans. He established strong ties with the Montagnais Indians in the vicinity of his settlement, with the Algonkians farther upriver, and ultimately with the Hurons, who dwelled in what the French came to call Huronia, the large peninsula between lakes Erie and Huron. But in acquiring their friendship (such as it was: he long complained that no American Indian would lead him farther into the country), Champlain encountered and fought with a group of Mohawk, members of the Iroquois Confederacy, with whose expanding empire the French were to be long in conflict.

Like his English contemporary John Smith, Champlain assiduously recorded his experiences, leaving a large body of works that were mostly published in his own day, from *Des Sauvages* (1603) to *Les Voyages* (1613), *Voyages et Descouvertures* (1619), and the last and largest of his books, *Les Voyages de la Nouvelle France* (1632). Because he kept detailed journals of his explorations and of affairs in the French settlements where he lived, Champlain's narratives offer a great deal of information about colonial experience but also about Native American culture and life, particularly in the case of the Hurons, to whom a good part of *Voyages et*

*Descouvertures* is devoted. Champlain's accounts also offer a valuable perspective on the cultural and economic life of the Massachusetts and Cape Cod Indians before the coming of permanent European settlement (and disease). He describes an agricultural region, thickly settled, rather than the vacant "wilderness" (awaiting the impress of European order) that the English settlers in this region tended to find, especially as they later sought to justify their presence on the land. The different basis of French and English colonial economies, which were sustained by fur trading and agriculture, respectively, helps account for this difference of view. For the French the fur trade would flourish only if the American Indians themselves did, because the Indians with whom the French dealt hunted the fur-bearing animals and transported the pelts and trade goods over long distances. By contrast, the English, although also engaged in the fur trade, were more in competition with agricultural groups of Native Americans for the scarce farmland of New England and other regions to the south.

Part personal history, part propaganda, part communal record, Champlain's works were widely read and consulted during his lifetime. They accorded him a place in the history of New France that he has never lost.

## *From* The Voyages of Sieur de Champlain[1]

### From *Chapter VIII*

#### CONTINUATION OF THE EXPLORATION OF THE COAST OF THE ALMOUCHIQUOIS, AND WHAT OF NOTE WE THERE OBSERVED.

The next day we doubled cape St. Louis,[2] so named by the Sieur de Monts, a moderately low shore in latitude 42° 45'. That day we made two leagues along a sandy coast, and saw as we passed a number of wigwams and gardens. The wind coming ahead, we entered a little bay to await suitable weather for continuing our route. Two or three canoes approached us on their way back from fishing for cod and other fish, which are plentiful thereabouts. These they catch with hooks made of a piece of wood, to which they attach a bone shaped like a harpoon, which they fasten very securely for fear lest it come out. The whole thing has the form of a little crook. The line which is attached to it is made of tree-bark. They gave me one of them, which I took as a curiosity. In this the bone was attached with hemp, which in my opinion is like that of France. They informed me that they gathered this plant in their country without cultivating it, indicating its height as about four to five feet. The said canoe returned to shore to notify the people in the settlement, who made signal-smokes for us; and we perceived eighteen or twenty Indians who came down to the beach and began to dance. Our canoe went ashore to give them some trifles, with which they were much pleased. Some of them came out to beg us to enter their river. We raised anchor to do so, but were unable to get in because the tide was out and the water too shallow; and were obliged to anchor at the entrance. I went on shore, where I saw many more Indians, who received us very kindly. I went to explore the river, but saw only an arm of the sea which extends some little distance into the country, which is par-

1. The text is derived from *The Works of Samuel de Champlain*, edited by Henry P. Biggar, vol. 1 (1922). Champlain recorded these observations of the landscape and peoples of the Massachusetts coast from Gloucester to the southern shore of Cape Cod, during

two leisurely voyages in 1605 and 1606.
2. Champlain's party rounded Cape St. Louis (modern Brant Point), just north of what became Plymouth harbor, Massachusetts, on July 18, 1605. The Almouchiquois were inhabitants of this region.

tially cleared. Here it becomes only a brook, which cannot float boats except at high tide. The bay is about a league in circumference. On one side of the entrance is a kind of island covered with trees, especially pines, and it adjoins some sand-dunes which are fairly extensive: on the other side the land is rather high. Within the said bay are two islets, which cannot be seen unless one is inside, and round about them the sea recedes almost completely at low tide. This place is very conspicuous from the sea, inasmuch as the coast is very low except the cape at the entrance to this bay, which we named Cape St. Louis. harbor.[3] It is distant from the said cape two leagues, and from Island Cape ten. It lies in approximately the same latitude as cape St. Louis.

On the nineteenth of the month we set out from this place. Coasting toward the south we made four to five leagues, and passed close to a rock which lies on a level with the surface of the water. Continuing our route, we caught sight of some land which we took to be islands, but when nearer perceived that it was mainland, which continued to the north-north-west of us, and that it was the cape of a large bay more than eighteen to nineteen leagues in circumference.[4] We had run so far into this bay that we had to stand on the other tack to double the cape we had seen, which we named the White Cape, because there were sands and dunes which presented this appearance. The favorable wind was of great service here; for otherwise we should have been in danger of being driven upon the coast. This bay is very clear, provided one does not approach the shore nearer than a good league, there being no islands or rocks except the one I have mentioned, which is near a river that extends some distance inland and which we named Ste. Suzanne of the White Cape. From here to cape St. Louis the distance is ten leagues. The White Cape is a point of sand which bends southward some six leagues. This coast has fairly high sand-banks which are very conspicuous from the sea, where soundings are found of thirty, forty and fifty fathoms nearly fifteen or eighteen leagues from land, until one comes to ten fathoms in approaching the shore, which is very clear. There is a great extent of open country along the shore before one enters the woods, which are very delightful and pleasant to the eye. We cast anchor off shore and saw some Indians, toward whom four of our party advanced. Making their way along the sandy beach, they perceived as it were a bay with wigwams bordering it all around. When they were about a league and a half from us an Indian came toward them dancing all over (as they reported to us). He had come down from the high shore, but returned shortly after to give notice of our arrival to those in his settlement.

The next day, the twentieth of the month, we went to the place which our men had discovered, and found it to be a very dangerous port on account of the shoals and sand-banks, where we saw breakers on every side. It was almost low tide when we entered, and there were only four feet of water in the north passage; at high tide there are two fathoms. When we were inside, we saw that this place was rather large, being about three to four leagues in circumference, with all around it little houses about which each owner had as much land as was necessary for his support. A little river enters it which is very pretty; at low tide it has some three and a half feet of water. There are also two or three brooks bordered with meadows. The place would be very fine if only the harbor were good. I took an observation, and found the latitude 42°; and the

3. Plymouth harbor.          4. Cape Cod and Cape Cod Bay.

magnetic variation 18° 40'. There came to us from all sides, dancing, a number of Indians, both men and women. We named this place Malle-barre harbor.[5]

On the next day, the twenty-first of the month, the Sieur de Monts resolved to go and inspect their settlement, and nine or ten of us accompanied him with our arms; the remainder stayed behind to guard the pinnace. We went about a league along shore. Before reaching their wigwams we entered a field planted with Indian corn in the manner I have already described. The corn was in flower, and some five and a half feet in height. There was some less advanced, which they sow later. We saw an abundance of Brazilian beans, many edible squashes of various sizes, tobacco, and roots which they cultivate, the latter having the taste of artichoke. The woods are full of oaks, nut-trees, and very fine cypresses, which are of reddish color and have a very pleasant smell. There were also several fields not cultivated, for the reason that the Indians let them lie fallow. When they wish to plant them they set fire to the weeds and then dig up the field with their wooden spades. Their wigwams are round, and covered with heavy thatch made of reeds. In the middle of the roof is an opening, about a foot and a half wide, through which issues the smoke of their fire. We asked them if they had their permanent residence in this place, and whether there was much snow; but we could not find this out very well since we did not understand their language, although they attempted to explain by signs, taking up sand in their hand, then spreading it on the ground, and indicating that the snow was the same color as our collars and fell to the depth of a foot. Others indicated that it was less, giving us also to understand that the harbor never froze over; but we were unable to ascertain whether the snow lasted a long time. I consider, however, that this country is temperate and the winter not severe.[6] During the time we were there it blew a gale from the north-east which lasted four days, with the sky so overcast that the sun was hardly visible at all. It was very cold, so that we were obliged to put on our greatcoats which we had entirely laid aside. However, I believe this was exceptional, just as often happens in other localities out of season.

On the twenty-third of the said month of July, four or five sailors having gone ashore with some large kettles to fetch fresh water from among the sandhills at a distance from our pinnace, certain Indians, being desirous to possess some of these kettles,[7] watched for the time when our men went there, and snatched one by force out of the hands of a sailor who had filled his the first and who had no weapons. One of his companions, starting to run after the Indian, quickly returned, being unable to catch him, inasmuch as the latter was a swifter runner than himself. The other Indians, when they saw our sailors running toward our pinnace and shouting to us to discharge some musket-shots at the Indians who were in considerable numbers, took to flight. At that time there were a few Indians on board our pinnace who threw themselves into the sea, and we were able to seize only one of them. Those on shore who had taken to flight, seeing the others swimming, turned back straight to the

5. Modern Nauset Harbor, on the Atlantic side of Cape Cod.
6. Because this part of North America lay far south of the latitude of France and England, many early voyagers assumed it would have a mild climate. After visiting this landscape, however, William Bradford wrote, "They that know the winters of that country know them to be sharp and violent and subject to cruel and fierce storms, dangerous to travel to known places, much more to search an unknown coast."
7. Kettles made of iron and other metals were to be much sought after by Northeast Indian groups who traded their furs for European goods. "Pinnace": a small sailing vessel.

sailor from whom they had taken the kettle and shot several arrows at him from behind and brought him down. Perceiving his condition, they at once rushed upon him and despatched him with their knives. Meantime we made haste to go on shore, and fired muskets from our pinnace. Mine exploded in my hands and nearly killed me. The Indians, hearing this fusillade, again took to flight, and redoubled their speed when they saw that we had landed, being frightened on seeing us run after them. There was no likelihood of catching them; for they are as swift-footed as horses. The dead man[8] was brought in, and some hours later was buried. Meanwhile we kept our prisoner bound hand and foot on board our pinnace, fearing lest he should escape. The Sieur de Monts determined to let him go, feeling persuaded he was not to blame and knew nothing of what had occurred, as was the case also with those who were at the time on board and alongside our pinnace. A few hours later some Indians came toward us, making excuses by signs and outward show that it was not they who had done this evil deed but others farther off in the interior. We were unwilling to do them harm, although it was in our power to avenge ourselves.

* * *

## From *Chapter XIII*

### THE SIEUR DE POUTRINCOURT SETS OUT FROM PORT ROYAL TO MAKE DISCOVERIES. EVERYTHING WE SAW AND THAT HAPPENED AS FAR AS MALLEBARRE.

* * *

Continuing our route we went to Island Cape,[9] where we were delayed a little by bad weather and fog, and where we did not see much probability of spending the night, inasmuch as the place was not suitable for this purpose. Whilst we were in this predicament I remembered that when following this coast with the Sieur de Monts, I had noted on my map at a league's distance a place which appeared suitable for vessels, into which we had not entered because, at the time we were passing, the wind was favorable for holding on our course. This place lay behind us, on which account I said to the Sieur de Poutrincourt that we must stand in for a point which was then visible, where was situated the place in question which seemed to me suitable for passing the night. We proceeded to anchor at the entrance, and the next day went inside.[1]

The Sieur de Poutrincourt landed with eight or ten of our company. We saw some very fine grapes which were ripe, Brazilian peas, pumpkins, squashes, and some good roots with a flavor like that of chards, which the Indians cultivate. They presented us with a number of these in exchange for other little trifles which we gave them. They had already completed their harvest. We saw two hundred Indians in this place, which is pleasant enough; and here are many nut-trees, cypresses, sassafras, oaks, ashes, and beeches, which are very fine. The chief of this place, who is called Quiouhamenec, came to see us with another chief, a neighbor of his named Cohouepech, whom we entertained. Onemechin, chief of Saco,[2] also came to see us there, and we gave him a coat, which he did not keep long, but presented to another

8. A carpenter from the town of St. Malo.
9. Cape Ann, north of Boston. Champlain writes in this chapter of a voyage undertaken in the fall of 1606, under the Sieur de Poutrincourt, head of the French settlement of Port-Royal, Nova Scotia.
1. Gloucester Harbor, in the south shore of Cape Ann.
2. A river in Maine.

because, being uncomfortable in it, he could not adapt himself to it. At this place we also saw an Indian who wounded himself so badly in the foot, and lost so much blood, that he fainted. A number of other Indians gathered about him, and sang for some time before touching him. Afterward they made certain motions with their feet and hands, and shook his head; then while they breathed upon him, he came to. Our surgeon dressed his injuries, and afterward he was able to go off in good spirits.

The next day, as we were caulking our shallop,[3] the Sieur de Poutrincourt caught sight in the woods of a great many Indians, who with the intention of doing us some injury were on their way toward a little brook in the strait at the causeway leading to the mainland, where some of our men were washing their clothes. As I was walking along the causeway these Indians caught sight of me, and in order to put a good face upon the matter, since they saw clearly that I at the same time had discovered them, they began to shout and to dance; then they came toward me with their bows, arrows, quivers, and other arms. And inasmuch as there was a meadow between them and me, I made a sign to them to dance again, which they did in a circle, putting all their arms in the center. They had hardly begun when they espied in the woods the Sieur de Poutrincourt with eight musketeers, which astonished them. Nevertheless they did not fail to complete their dance, but when it was finished, they withdrew in all directions, being apprehensive lest some bad turn should be done to them. However, we said nothing to them, and showed them only evidences of good will. Then we returned to our shallop to launch it and to take our departure. They begged us to remain a day longer, saying that more than two thousand men would come to see us; but as we could not afford to lose time we were unwilling to delay any longer. I believe that their plan was to surprise us. Some of the land is cleared, and they were constantly clearing more, in the following fashion. They cut down the trees at a height of three feet from the ground; then they burn the branches upon the trunk, and sow their corn between the fallen timber; and in course of time they take out the roots. There are also fine meadows for supporting numbers of cattle. This port is very beautiful and a good one, with water enough for vessels, and shelter behind the islands. It lies in latitude 43°, and we have named it the Beautiful Port.

On the last day of September we departed from the Beautiful Port, and passed cape St. Louis; and we sailed all night to reach the White Cape. The next morning, an hour before daylight, we found ourselves in the White Bay to leeward of White Cape, in eight feet of water, at a distance of a league from the land. Here we cast anchor in order not to approach closer before daylight, and in order to see how we stood regarding the tide. Meanwhile we sent our shallop to make soundings, and they did not find more than eight feet of water, so that it was necessary to determine, while awaiting daylight, what we should do. The water fell to five feet, and our pinnace sometimes touched upon the sand, without, however, being injured or doing herself any damage; for the sea was calm; and we had not more than three feet of water under us, when the tide began to come in, which gave us great encouragement.

When day dawned we descried to leeward a very low sandy coast off which we lay. We sent the boat to make soundings in the direction of a tract of upland which is somewhat elevated, and where we judged there was much

---

3. A small vessel useful in coastal explorations.

water; and in fact we found there seven fathoms. We went there and cast anchor, and at once prepared the shallop with nine or ten men to go on shore and examine a place where we judged there was a good, safe harbor, in which we might find safety should the wind become stronger. Having explored it, we entered with two, three, and four fathoms of water. When we were inside, we found five and six. There were plenty of oysters, of very good quality, which we had not hitherto seen; and we named the port Oyster Harbor.[4] It is in latitude 42°. There came to us three canoes of Indians. That day the wind was favorable, and for this reason we weighed anchor to go to White Cape, distant from this place five leagues north a quarter north-east, and we doubled it.

The following day, the second of October, we arrived off Mallebarre, where we remained some time on account of the bad weather we experienced. During this time the Sieur de Poutrincourt, accompanied by twelve to fifteen men, paid a visit to the port in the shallop. There came to meet him some 150 Indians, singing and dancing, in accordance with their custom. After having viewed this place we returned to our vessel, and, the wind coming fair, made sail along the coast, steering south.

## Chapter XIV

### CONTINUATION OF THE ABOVE-MENTIONED DISCOVERIES; AND WHAT OF NOTE WAS OBSERVED DURING THESE.

When we were some six leagues from Mallebarre, we cast anchor near the shore because the wind was not favorable. Along this coast we observed smoke which the Indians were making; and this made us decide to go and visit them. For this purpose the shallop was got ready; but when we were near the shore, which is sandy, we were unable to land, as the swell was too great. The Indians, seeing this, launched a canoe; and eight or nine of them came out to us, singing and indicating by signs the joy it gave them to see us; and they showed us that lower down was a port where we could place our pinnace in safety.

Being unable to land, the shallop came back to the pinnace, and the Indians, who had been kindly treated, returned to the shore.

The next day, the wind being fair, we continued our course to the [south] five leagues, and we had no sooner gone this far than we found three and four fathoms of water at a distance of a league and a half from the shore. And going a little farther, the depth suddenly lessened to a fathom and a half and two fathoms, which made us apprehensive, since the sea was breaking everywhere, and we could perceive no passage along which we could return upon our course; for the wind was altogether against us.

So it came about that, being caught among the breakers and sand-banks, we had to run at haphazard where one judged there was water enough for our pinnace, which drew but at the most four feet. We kept on among these breakers until we found four feet and a half. Finally by God's favor we succeeded in passing over a sandy point which projects about three leagues into the sea to the south-south-east, making a very dangerous place. Doubling this cape, which we named Reef Cape,[5] and which is twelve or thirteen leagues from

4. Either Barnstable Harbor or Wellfleet Harbor, the major inlets on the inner shore of Cape Cod.
5. Some part of the group of dangerous shoals and reefs lying off Monomoy Point, Cape Cod's "elbow."

It was here, in 1620, that the *Mayflower* was forced to turn back from its intended route to the Hudson River, ultimately leaving William Bradford and the other Pilgrims at Plymouth.

Mallebarre, we anchored in two and a half fathoms of water, inasmuch as we found ourselves surrounded on all sides by breakers and shoals, save only in certain places where the sea was not breaking very much. We sent the shallop to seek out a channel in order that we might go to a place which we concluded was the one indicated to us by the Indians. We also believed there was a river there where we could lie in safety.

When our shallop reached the place, our men landed and inspected the locality, after which they came back with an Indian whom they brought with them. They informed us that at high tide we could enter, and it was resolved to do so. We at once weighed anchor and, under the guidance of the Indian, who acted as our pilot, proceeded to anchor in a roadstead[6] in front of the port, in six fathoms of water and good bottom; for we could not go inside because night had overtaken us.

The next day men were sent to place buoys upon the extremity of a sand-bank which lies at the harbor's mouth; then at high tide we entered the place with two fathoms of water. Once inside we gave praise to God for bringing us to a place of safety. Our rudder had broken and been mended with ropes, and we feared lest in the midst of these shallows and strong tides it should break again, which would have resulted in our destruction. Inside this harbor there is but one fathom of water, and at high tide two fathoms. Toward the east lies a bay which doubles to the north some three leagues, and therein is an island and two other little coves, which give beauty to the landscape. Here there is much cleared land and many little hills, whereon the Indians cultivate corn and other grains on which they live. Here are likewise very fine vines, plenty of nut-trees, oaks, cypresses, and a few pines. All the inhabitants of this place are much given to agriculture, and lay up a store of Indian corn for the winter, which they preserve in the following manner.

In the sand on the slope of the hills they dig holes some five to six feet deep more or less, and place their corn and other grains in large grass sacks, which they throw into the said holes, and cover them with sand to a depth of three or four feet above the surface of the ground. They take away this grain according to their needs, and it is preserved as well as it would be in our granaries.[7]

At this place we saw some five to six hundred Indians who were all naked except for their privy parts, which they cover with a little piece of deer or sealskin. The women are the same, and, like the men, cover their parts with skins or leaves. Both men and women wear their hair neatly combed and braided in various ways, after the fashion of the Indians at Saco, and are well-proportioned in body, with olive-colored skins. They adorn themselves with feathers, wampum beads, and other knick-knacks, which they arrange very neatly after the manner of embroidery. Their arms consist of bows, arrows, and clubs. They are not so much great hunters as good fishermen and tillers of the soil.

Regarding their polity, government, and religious belief, we were unable to form a judgment, and I believe that in this they do not differ from our Souri-quois[8] and Canadians, who worship neither moon nor sun nor any other thing, and pray no more than the beasts. They have indeed among them

---

6. An exposed anchoring place; the party evidently had rounded Monomoy Point and was about to enter modern Stage Harbor, which Champlain later names "Misfortune Harbor."

7. William Bradford notes that the Pilgrims dug up some of these caches during their exploration of Cape Cod fifteen years later.

8. The Micmac, who then inhabited Nova Scotia.

certain persons who, they say, have communication with the devil, and in these they have great faith. These persons tell them all that is to happen, in which for the most part they lie. Sometimes they succeed in hitting it right, and in telling them things similar to what actually happens. This is why they have faith in these persons, as if they were prophets, although they are naught but scamps who inveigle them, as the Egyptians and gypsies do the simple village folk. They have chiefs whom they obey in regard to matters of warfare but not in anything else. These chiefs work, and assume no higher rank than their companions. Each possesses only sufficient land for his own support.

Their lodges are separated from one another according to the extent of land that each is able to occupy. They are lofty, circular, and covered with matting made of grass or husks of Indian corn. Their only furniture consists of a bed or two raised one foot from the floor, and made of a number of saplings laid one against the other, whereon they place a reed-mat, in the Spanish manner (which is a kind of thick mattress two or three fingers in depth), and upon this they sleep. They have a great many fleas in summer, even in the fields. One day when we were out walking, we attracted such a number of them that we were obliged to change our clothes.

All the harbors, bays, and coasts from Saco onward are filled with every kind of fish like those we have near our settlements, and in such abundance that I can guarantee there was never a day or a night during which we did not see and hear more than a thousand porpoises passing alongside our pinnace and chasing the smaller fry. Here are likewise plenty of shellfish of several kinds, and especially oysters. Game birds are very plentiful.

This would prove a very good site for laying and constructing the foundations of a state, if the harbor were a little deeper and the entrance safer than it is.

Before leaving port our rudder was repaired, and we made bread from flour we had brought for our subsistence when our biscuit gave out. Meanwhile we sent the shallop with five or six men and an Indian to see whether they could find a passage more suitable for leaving than that by which we had entered.

When they had gone five or six leagues, and we were close inshore, the Indian took to flight. He gave those in the shallop to understand that he was afraid lest he should be carried off to other Indians farther south who are enemies of his tribe. Upon their return they reported that as far as they had gone, there were at least three fathoms of water, and that farther on there were neither shoals nor reefs.

We accordingly made haste to repair our pinnace and to provide bread for fifteen days. Meanwhile the Sieur de Poutrincourt, accompanied by ten or twelve musketeers, visited all the surrounding country, which is very fine, as I have already stated. Here and there we saw a good number of small lodges.

Some eight or nine days later, on the Sieur de Poutrincourt's going out walking as he had done before, we observed that the Indians were taking down their wigwams and were sending into the woods their wives, children and provisions, and other necessaries of life. This made us suspect some evil design, and that they wished to attack our people who were working on shore, where they remained every night to guard whatever could not be taken on board in the evening except with much labor. This proved to be quite true; for they had resolved among themselves that, when all their goods were in safety, they would surprise the men on shore as best they could, and would carry off everything these men had there. But if perchance they found them on their guard, they would come with signs of friendship, as they were accustomed to do, laying aside their bows and arrows.

Now in view of what the Sieur de Poutrincourt had seen, and of the mode of procedure he had been told they observed when they wished to do a bad turn, we passed among their wigwams where were a number of women, to whom we gave bracelets and rings, in order to keep them quiet and from becoming afraid of us, while to the majority of the prominent and older men we gave axes, knives, and other articles of which they stood in need. This pleased them much, repaying for all by dances, gambols, and speeches, which latter we did not in the least understand. We went about everywhere without their having the boldness to say anything to us. It amused us greatly to see them look so innocent as they made themselves appear.

We came back very quietly to our pinnace, accompanied by a few Indians. On the way we met with several small troops who were gradually collecting together, fully armed, and were much surprised to see us so far inland, little thinking that we had just made a tour of from four to five leagues through their country. When passing near us they trembled for fear lest we should harm them, which it was in our power to do; but we did nothing, although we were aware of their evil intentions. On reaching the spot where our men were at work, the Sieur de Poutrincourt asked if all things were in readiness to oppose the designs of these rascals.

He gave orders for every one on shore to be taken on board: which was done, except that the man who was making the bread remained behind to finish a baking, and two other men with him. They were told that the Indians had some evil design, and that they should make haste in order to come on board in the evening, as it was known that the Indians only put their plans into execution at night or at daybreak, which is the hour for making surprises in most of their schemes.

The evening having come, the Sieur de Poutrincourt ordered the shallop to be sent ashore to fetch the men who were left. This was done as soon as the tide would permit, and those on shore were told that they must embark for the reason already given them. This they refused to do despite the remonstrances made to them on the risks they were running and the disobedience they were showing to their chief. To these they paid no attention, except a servant of the Sieur de Poutrincourt, who came aboard; but two others disembarked from the boat and went off to the three on shore, who remained to eat some biscuits made at the same time as the bread. Since these were unwilling to do what they were told, the shallop returned alongside, but without informing the Sieur de Poutrincourt, who was asleep, and who believed they were all on board the vessel.

The next morning, the fifteenth of October, the Indians did not fail to come and see in what state were our men, whom they found asleep, except one who was before the fire. Seeing them in this condition, the Indians, to the number of four hundred, came quietly over a little hill, and shot such a salvo of arrows at them as to give them no chance of recovery before they were struck dead. Fleeing as fast as they could toward our pinnace, and crying out, "Help, help, they are killing us," some of them fell dead in the water, while the rest were all pierced with arrows, of whom one died a short time afterward.[9] These

9. Of the five Frenchmen ashore, the single one who escaped death, Jean Du Val, was executed in Quebec in 1608 for conspiring against Champlain. Marc Les- carbot (c. 1570–c. 1603), a lawyer and writer who accompanied this expedition, wrote that the mutinous shore party was led by a young braggart (probably of

Indians made a desperate row, with war-whoops which it was terrible to hear.

At this noise, and that of our men, the sentinel on our vessel cried out, "To arms; they are killing our men." Thereupon each quickly seized his weapons, and at the same time some fifteen or sixteen of us embarked in the shallop to go ashore. But being unable to land on account of a sand-bank which lay between us and the shore, we jumped into the water and waded from this bank to the mainland, a distance of a musket-shot. As soon as we reached it, the Indians, seeing us within bowshot, fled inland. To pursue them was useless, for they are wonderfully swift. All we could do was to carry off the dead bodies and bury them near a cross which had been set up the day before, and then to look about to see whether we could catch sight of any Indians; but in this we wasted our time. Realising this we returned. Three hours later they reappeared on the shore. We discharged several shots at them from our little brass cannon; and whenever they heard the report, they threw themselves flat on the ground to avoid the charge. In derision of us they pulled down the cross, and dug up the bodies, which displeased us greatly, and made us go after them a second time;[1] but they fled as they had done before. We again set up the cross, and reinterred the bodies, which they had scattered here and there among the heaths, where they had kindled a fire to burn them. We returned without having accomplished more than before, seeing clearly that there was hardly any chance of taking vengeance for this blow, and that we must postpone the matter until it should please God.

On the sixteenth of the month we set out from Misfortune harbor, so named by us on account of the misfortune which happened to us there. This place is in latitude 41° 20′, and distant some twelve or thirteen leagues from Malle-barre.

1613

---

noble background) who resented the fact that he had been denied alcohol on the ship. He was found dead on shore, Lescarbot wrote, "his face on the ground, having a little dog upon his back, both of them shot together, and pierced through with one and the selfsame arrow."

1. Lescarbot added that these Nauset Indians turned their backs to those on the ship and "cast sand with their two hands together betwixt their buttocks in derision, howling like wolves."

---

# JOHN SMITH
## 1580–1631

Under the patent granted to Sir Walter Ralegh by Queen Elizabeth I in 1584, the English undertook their first serious effort at colonization in Virginia. By 1590 this attempt, in the vicinity of Roanoke, had ended in disaster. When the English renewed their involvement in America in the 1600s, they replaced the older heroic model of exploration and colonization with a more corporate one. Under this new model, the single controlling figure of Ralegh's era was replaced by larger companies of investors (often merchants), who had more capital to support costly expansion overseas. In fact, King James I split the vaguely defined region of Virginia, which ran from Florida to Canada, into two more manageable parts, giving the direction of each to separate but related groups of investors who together composed the Virginia Company. The southern part (including the area now known as the state of Virginia) came under the care of the company's members from London, while the northern part (from which New England was to be developed) fell to members in the West Country towns of Bristol, Plymouth, and Exeter. Although the so-called First Charter was succeeded by new ones in 1609 and 1612, its broad base of formalized support set the standard for English colonial practice over the next hundred years. As a compromise between large-scale governmental action and isolated individual effort, the format of the colonial "company" proved both useful and enduring.

The push toward corporate structures did not mean that interesting individuals disappeared. Indeed, one of the most colorful of all the Englishmen ever involved in America, the legendary Captain John Smith, proved by his crucial role in the establishment and continuance of the new colony at Jamestown that success in such ventures still required individual initiative and commitment. Few people had more pertinent preparation to reteach the English this old lesson. When named by the London partners to the ruling council (that is, the local governing committee) for the Virginia colony sent out in late December 1606, John Smith brought rich experience to his charge. His early life was deceptively sedate: born into a farmer's family in Lincolnshire, he was apprenticed at fifteen to a shopkeeper near his home. But tales of exploration, piracy, and military adventure already had stirred his imagination. In 1593 he may have tried to join a punitive expedition Sir Francis Drake was thought to be readying against England's enemy Spain, although his father apparently intervened. Shortly after his father's death in 1596, the fiery sixteen-year-old managed to have his indenture to the shopkeeper canceled and went to the Netherlands as a volunteer soldier to fight for the Dutch in their long war of independence from Philip II.

Following his tour of duty in the Netherlands, he saw action in the Mediterranean on a privateer, winning a good share of the prize money when a Venetian galley was captured. Smith next joined the Austrian army in its continuing war (1593–1606) against the Turks, and while in the Austrian service, he fought valiantly in Hungary and was promoted to a captaincy. Eventually, after defeating and beheading a succession of three Turkish officers in single combat in Rumania (his coat of arms, awarded later, showed the three severed heads), Smith was wounded in battle, taken prisoner, and sold into slavery to a Turk. Smith was passed from place to place until, held prisoner on the Black Sea, he murdered his master and fled back to Rumania via Russia and Poland, returning to England in the winter of 1604–5.

Many of these details come to us only through Smith's own at times garbled narratives, most of them penned long after the events. But when the Jamestown backers encountered him as they readied their expedition, he must have had the air of someone deeply experienced in the skills that the quasi-military venture would require. Smith's military background (and temperament), however, also carried liabilities in that age when warfare was brutal and soldiers were far from professional: he sometimes used force unnecessarily, and his hard-to-control temper and stubborn self-reliance made him an often troublesome companion. Already on the voyage over, Smith ran afoul of those in charge, was placed under arrest while the fleet was near the Canary Islands in February 1607, and was threatened with execution in the West Indies the following month. By June 10, some weeks after the arrival in Virginia and the opening of the heretofore secret list of the council members (not revealed sooner so as to prevent difficulties on shipboard!), Smith had been given a reprieve and was sworn in to his seat on the council. From then until his final departure for England in October 1609, he was in the middle of the tumultuous colony's affairs. Smith survived the grim period of sickness in 1607 and missed the bleaker "starving time" that came shortly after his departure, but during his years there, he was always at the epicenter of the various political earthquakes that rocked early Virginia.

Placed in charge of its supplies in the fall of 1607, he was elected president of the council—in effect, the colony's governor—the following year, after a series of wide-ranging explorations that made him the most knowledgeable of the settlers regarding the new land. The explorations also led to his imprisonment at the hands of Powhatan, overlord of the Chesapeake Bay Indians, from whom he claimed (much later) that the king's young daughter Pocahontas rescued him. Whatever the role Pocahontas played, what Smith took to be his impending execution may have been nothing more than a harmless adoption ceremony inducting him into Powhatan's tribe. In this episode as in others, Smith's volatile and unpredictable relations with the Native Americans were characteristic. Also characteristic was the fact that as a writer Smith milked the story of his rescue by Pocahontas. Although he failed to have the lasting influence on Virginia's affairs that he sought, in recasting that story fifteen years after the fact he found the immortality that otherwise eluded him. How easily we forget that on his return to Jamestown from Powhatan's village he was charged with the loss of two soldiers and would have been hanged had a fleet with much-needed supplies not arrived from England. Or that when he left Virginia in 1609 (never to return), it was because he had been severely injured when his gunpowder bag mysteriously exploded in his lap while he napped on the deck of an exploring vessel.

Smith and his works form an important bridge between the first two permanent English colonies in North America. The first of his publications, A *True Relation of Such Occurrences and Accidents of Note as Hath Happened in Virginia* (1608), was a badly edited version of a letter he had sent back from the colony without intending that it be published. It was followed by a work to which many colonists including Smith contributed, A *Map of Virginia, with a Description of the Country* . . . [and] *The Proceedings of those Colonies* [sic] (1612). Some years later, Smith enlarged this book by adding more texts by other hands, expanding his own prose, and extending its geographical range and chronological coverage. More its editor than its author, Smith published the resulting *General History of Virginia, New England, and the Summer Isles* [i.e., Bermuda] in 1624. This book demonstrated the later reach of Smith's American ambitions beyond Virginia proper, for his knowledge of New England was based on a voyage he made there in 1614 and on his continuing involvement with the region—which in fact he, not the Puritans, named. During his life, Smith published more works on New England than on Virginia (A *Description of New England*, 1616; *New England's Trials*, 1620 and 1622; and *Advertisements for the Inexperienced Planters of New England, or Anywhere*, 1631). But for some unfortunate setbacks (bad weather several times forced him to abandon other voyages for New England), he might well have become more famous for this second aspect of his American career than for the first. An energetic promoter of the potential of this new region for English settlers, Smith offered the Pilgrims his services as guide for their voyage in 1620, but they chose instead to put Smith's helpful books in the hands of the more temperate Myles Standish. From that point on Smith's America was not the geographical realm about which he had entertained such bright hopes at the century's start but rather the verbal domain he continued to explore in his later writings. When he closed the Virginia part of his *General History* by writing "Thus far have I travelled in this Wilderness of Virginia," he was revealing how much like a country of his mind Virginia had become. Long gone from that still-struggling colony by then, he had internalized it so well that he helped to make it a permanent part of the English—and the Anglo-American—imagination.

# From The General History of Virginia, New England, and the Summer Isles[1]

## From The Third Book. From Chapter 2. What Happened till the First Supply

Being thus left to our fortunes, it fortuned that within ten days,[2] scarce ten amongst us could either go or well stand, such extreme weakness and sickness oppressed us. And thereat none need marvel if they consider the cause and reason which was this: While the ships stayed, our allowance was somewhat bettered by a daily proportion of biscuit which the sailors would pilfer to sell, give, or exchange with us for money, sassafras,[3] furs, or love. But when they departed, there remained neither tavern, beer-house, nor place of relief but the common kettle.[4] Had we been as free from all sins as [we were free from] gluttony and drunkenness we might have been canonized for saints, but our President would never have been admitted for engrossing to his private, oatmeal, sack, oil, aqua vitae, beef, eggs, or what not but the kettle;[5] that indeed he allowed equally to be distributed, and that was half a pint of wheat and as much barley boiled with water for a man a day, and this, having fried some twenty-six weeks in the ship's hold, contained as many worms as grains so that we might truly call it rather so much bran than corn; our drink was water,[6] our lodgings castles in the air.

With this lodging and diet, our extreme toil in bearing and planting palisades so strained and bruised us and our continual labor in the extremity of the heat had so weakened us, as were cause sufficient to have made us as miserable in our native country or any other place in the world.

From May to September, those that escaped lived upon sturgeon and sea crabs. Fifty in this time we buried; the rest seeing the President's[7] projects to escape these miseries in our pinnace by flight (who all this time had neither felt want nor sickness) so moved our dead spirits as we deposed him and established Ratcliffe in his place (Gosnold being dead), Kendall deposed. Smith newly recovered, Martin[8] and Ratcliffe were by his care preserved and relieved, and

---

1. The text used here is taken from *The Complete Works of Captain John Smith*, edited by Philip L. Barbour (1986). The Summer Isles are the Bermuda Islands. The *Third Book* is titled "The Proceedings and Accidents of the English Colony in Virginia," and is derived from Smith's Virginia book of 1612. The bulk of this chapter, which opens with an account of the sickness whose dire results were chronicled by George Percy in *Observations Gathered out of a Discourse of . . . Virginia* (1625), may have been written by John Smith himself, although at its publication in 1612 it was credited solely to Thomas Studley, chief storekeeper of the colony. In 1624, Smith added to Studley's signature at the end of this section of the text not only his own initials but also the names of Robert Fenton and Edward Harrington as part authors. According to George Percy, Thomas Studley died early in the first year, on August 28, 1607, four days after Harrington, so neither could have written much of what is in part attributed to them. Of Robert Fenton nothing is known.

2. By the end of June 1607, after Captain Christopher Newport (d. 1617) left to fetch new supplies from England. "Fortuned": happened.
3. The bark of the sassafras tree, sold for its supposed medicinal qualities, was a valuable commodity in London.
4. The communal resources.
5. I.e., President Edward Maria Wingfield (c. 1560–1613), a man of high connections in England, would not have been canonized as a saint because he diverted many supplies (everything except the contents of the common kettle) for his own use, including sack (wine) and aqua vitae (brandy).
6. It was more customary to drink wine or beer. "Corn": grain.
7. I.e., Wingfield.
8. Captain John Martin (c. 1567–1632?) was a colonist best known for his contentiousness. "Captain John Ratcliffe" was an alias of John Sicklemore (dates uncertain), master of one of the vessels on the voyage over and a member of the local council. The most enig-

the most of the soldiers recovered with the skillful diligence of Master Thomas Wotton our surgeon general.

But now was all our provision spent, the sturgeon gone, all helps abandoned, each hour expecting the fury of the savages, when God, the patron of all good endeavors, in that desperate extremity so changed the hearts of the savages that they brought such plenty of their fruits and provision as no man wanted.[9]

And now where some affirmed it was ill done of the Council to send forth men so badly provided, this incontradictable reason will show them plainly they are too ill advised to nourish such ill conceits: First, the fault of our going was our own; what could be thought fitting or necessary we had, but what we should find, or want, or where we should be, we were all ignorant and supposing to make our passage in two months, with victual to live and the advantage of the spring to work; we were at sea five months where we both spent our victual and lost the opportunity of the time and season to plant, by the unskillful presumption of our ignorant transporters that understood not at all what they undertook.

Such actions have ever since the world's beginning been subject to such accidents, and everything of worth is found full of difficulties, but nothing [is] so difficult as to establish a commonwealth so far remote from men and means and where men's minds are so untoward[1] as neither do well themselves nor suffer others. But to proceed.

The new President and Martin, being little beloved, of weak judgment in dangers, and less industry in peace, committed the managing of all things abroad[2] to Captain Smith, who, by his own example, good words, and fair promises, set some to mow, others to bind thatch, some to build houses, others to thatch them, himself always bearing the greatest task for his own share, so that in short time he provided most of them lodgings, neglecting any for himself.

This done, seeing the savages' superfluity begin to decrease, [Smith] (with some of his workmen) shipped himself in the shallop to search the country for trade. The want of[3] the language, knowledge to manage his boat without sails, the want of a sufficient power (knowing the multitude of the savages), apparel for his men, and other necessaries, were infinite impediments yet no discouragement.

Being but six or seven in company he went down the river to Kecoughtan[4] where at first they scorned him as a famished man and would in derision offer him a handful of corn, a piece of bread for their swords and muskets, and such like proportions also for their apparel. But seeing by trade and courtesy there was nothing to be had, he made bold to try such conclusions as necessity enforced; though contrary to his commission, [he] let fly[5] his muskets, ran his boat on shore; whereat they all fled into the woods.

So marching towards their houses, they might see great heaps of corn; much

matic figure in Jamestown, he was elected president of the council in September 1607, but later fell out with Smith. Captain Bartholomew Gosnold (c. 1572–1607), who had explored New England before the first Jamestown voyage, probably had been responsible for Smith's recruitment to the venture. Captain George Kendall (d. 1607) was executed for mutiny later in the year.

9. I.e., was in want.
1. Intractable.
2. I.e., outside the palisade.
3. Inability to speak. "Shallop": an open boat.
4. A village near the mouth of the James River whose inhabitants, the Kecoughtans, were members of the Powhatan Confederacy.
5. Fired.

ado he had to restrain his hungry soldiers from present taking of it, expecting as it happened that the savages would assault them, as not long after they did with a most hideous noise. Sixty or seventy of them, some black, some red, some white, some particolored, came in a square order,[6] singing and dancing out of the woods with their Okee (which was an idol made of skins, stuffed with moss, all painted and hung with chains and copper) borne before them, and in this manner, being well armed with clubs, targets, bows, and arrows, they charged the English that so kindly[7] received them with their muskets loaded with pistol shot that down fell their god, and divers lay sprawling on the ground; the rest fled again to the woods and ere long sent one of their Quiyoughkasoucks[8] to offer peace and redeem their Okee.

Smith told them if only six of them would come unarmed and load his boat, he would not only be their friend but restore them their Okee and give them beads, copper, and hatchets besides, which on both sides was to their contents[9] performed, and then they brought him venison, turkeys, wild fowl, bread, and what they had, singing and dancing in sign of friendship till they departed.

In his return he discovered the town and country of Warraskoyack.[1]

> Thus God unboundless by His power,
> Made them thus kind, would us devour.

Smith, perceiving (notwithstanding their late misery) not any regarded but from hand to mouth,[2] (the company being well recovered) caused the pinnace to be provided with things fitting to get provision for the year following, but in the interim he made three or four journeys and discovered the people of Chickahominy,[3] yet what he carefully provided the rest carelessly spent.

Wingfield and Kendall, living in disgrace * * * strengthened themselves with the sailors and other confederates to regain their former credit and authority, or at least such means aboard the pinnace (being fitted to sail as Smith had appointed for trade), to alter her course and to go for England.

Smith, unexpectedly returning, had the plot discovered to him, much trouble he had to prevent it, till with store of saker[4] and musket shot he forced them [to] stay or sink in the river: which action cost the life of Captain Kendall.

These brawls are so disgustful, as some will say they were better forgotten, yet all men of good judgment will conclude it were better their baseness should be manifest to the world, than the business bear the scorn and shame of their excused disorders.[5]

The President and Captain Archer[6] not long after intended also to have

---

6. Formation. "Particolored": i.e., painted for the battle.

7. In such a way. "Targets": small shields.

8. Smith elsewhere defines this term as referring to the "petty gods" of the Algonquian-speaking peoples, but here it may be used to mean priests. "Divers": several.

9. I.e., in mutual contentment.

1. A village on the south side of the James River near the mouth of the modern Pagan River, approximately opposite Smithfield.

2. I.e., none of the settlers, despite their recent sufferings, gave any thought to gathering a store of provision for the future.

3. The region along the Chickahominy River, which empties into the James River a short distance west of

Jamestown.

4. Shot for a small cannon used in sieges and on shipboard. "Discovered": revealed.

5. I.e., it is necessary to rehearse the troubles to lay the blame on the responsible individuals (Wingfield and Kendall), rather than let the whole "business" of the colony suffer ill repute.

6. Captain Gabriel Archer (c. 1575–1609?) had been an associate of Bartholomew Gosnold before the Jamestown voyage. Having gone back to England in 1608 as a confirmed opponent of Smith, he showed up in Virginia again the following year to head an anti-Smith faction but died during the starving time the next winter. Ratcliffe / Sicklemore was still president.

abandoned the country, which project also was curbed and suppressed by Smith.

The Spaniard never more greedily desired gold than he victual, nor his soldiers more to abandon the country than he to keep it. But [he found] plenty of corn in the river of Chickahominy, where hundreds of savages in divers places stood with baskets expecting his coming.

And now the winter approaching, the rivers became so covered with swans, geese, ducks, and cranes that we daily feasted with good bread, Virginia peas, pumpkins, and putchamins, fish, fowl, and divers sort of wild beasts as fast as we could eat them, so that none of our tuftaffety humorists[7] desired to go for England.

But our comedies never endured long without a tragedy, some idle exceptions[8] being muttered against Captain Smith for not discovering the head of Chickahominy river and [he being] taxed by the Council to be too slow in so worthy an attempt. The next voyage he proceeded so far that with much labor by cutting of trees asunder he made his passage, but when his barge could pass no farther, he left her in a broad bay out of danger of shot, commanding none should go ashore till his return; himself with two English and two savages went up higher in a canoe, but he was not long absent but his men went ashore, whose want of government gave both occasion and opportunity to the savages to surprise one George Cassen whom they slew and much failed not to have cut off the boat and all the rest.[9]

Smith little dreaming of that accident, being got to the marshes at the river's head twenty miles in the desert,[1] had his two men slain (as is supposed) sleeping by the canoe, while himself by fowling sought them victual, who finding he was beset with 200 savages, two of them he slew, still defending himself with the aid of a savage his guide, whom he bound to his arm with his garters and used him as a buckler,[2] yet he was shot in his thigh a little, and had many arrows that stuck in his clothes but no great hurt, till at last they took him prisoner.

When this news came to Jamestown, much was their sorrow for his loss, few expecting what ensued.

Six or seven weeks those barbarians kept him prisoner, many strange triumphs and conjurations they made of him, yet he so demeaned[3] himself amongst them, as he not only diverted them from surprising the fort, but procured his own liberty, and got himself and his company such estimation amongst them, that those savages admired him more than their own Quiyoughkasoucks.

The manner how they used and delivered him is as followeth:

The savages having drawn from George Cassen whither Captain Smith was gone, prosecuting that opportunity they followed him with 300 bowmen, conducted by the King of Pamunkey, who in divisions searching the turnings of the river found Robinson and Emry[4] by the fireside; those they shot full of arrows and slew. Then finding the Captain, as is said, that used the savage

---

7. Self-indulgent persons who might be given to wearing lace. "Putchamins": persimmons.
8. Objections.
9. I.e., only through fault of their own did they fail to wipe out Cassen's whole party. "Government": discipline.

1. Wilderness.
2. Shield. "Garters": laces used for tying clothing.
3. Behaved.
4. The two men mentioned above as having been killed while they slept. Thomas Emry was a carpenter. John Robinson was a "gentleman."

that was his guide as his shield (three of them being slain and divers others so galled[5]), all the rest would not come near him. Thinking thus to have returned to his boat, regarding them, as he marched, more than his way, [he] slipped up to the middle in an oozy creek and his savage with him, yet dared they not come to him till being near dead with cold he threw away his arms. Then according to their composition[6] they drew him forth and led him to the fire where his men were slain. Diligently they chafed his benumbed limbs.

He demanding for their captain, they showed him Opechancanough,[7] King of Pamunkey, to whom he gave a round ivory double compass dial. Much they marveled at the playing of the fly[8] and needle, which they could see so plainly and yet not touch it because of the glass that covered them. But when he demonstrated by that globe-like jewel the roundness of the earth and skies, the sphere of the sun, moon, and stars, and how the sun did chase the night round about the world continually, the greatness of the land and sea, the diversity of nations, variety of complexions, and how we were to them antipodes[9] and many other such like matters, they all stood as amazed with admiration.

Notwithstanding, within an hour after, they tied him to a tree, and as many as could stand about him prepared to shoot him, but the King holding up the compass in his hand, they all laid down their bows and arrows and in a triumphant manner led him to Orapaks[1] where he was after their manner kindly feasted and well used.

Their order in conducting him was thus: Drawing themselves all in file, the King in the midst had all their pieces and swords borne before him. Captain Smith was led after him by three great savages holding him fast by each arm, and on each side six went in file with their arrows nocked.[2] But arriving at the town (which was but only thirty or forty hunting houses made of mats, which they remove as they please, as we our tents), all the women and children staring to behold him, the soldiers first all in file performed the form of a bissom[3] so well as could be, and on each flank, officers as sergeants to see them keep their orders. A good time they continued this exercise and then cast themselves in a ring, dancing in such several postures and singing and yelling out such hellish notes and screeches; being strangely painted, every one [had] his quiver of arrows and at his back a club, on his arm a fox or an otter's skin or some such matter for his vambrace, their heads and shoulders painted red with oil and pocones mingled together, which scarlet-like color made an exceeding handsome show, his bow in his hand and the skin of a bird with her wings abroad,[4] dried, tied on his head, a piece of copper, a white shell, a long feather with a small rattle growing at the tails of their snakes tied to it, or some such like toy. All this while, Smith and the King stood in the midst, guarded as before is said, and after three dances they all departed. Smith they conducted to a long house where thirty or forty tall fellows did guard him, and ere long more bread and venison was brought him than would have served

---

5. Wounded.
6. Agreement for surrender.
7. Powhatan's younger half-brother and Smith's captor, Opechancanough (d. 1644) was to lead the Indian Confederacy's attack on the colonists in 1622 and as late as 1644 attempted one last time to expel them from the country.
8. Compass card.
9. On the opposite side of the globe.

1. A village located farther inland, later the residence of Powhatan.
2. Notched; i.e., with their arrows fitted on the bowstring ready to use.
3. From an Italian term denoting a snakelike formation.
4. Outspread. "Vambrace": forearm protection. "Pocones": a dye of vegetative origin.

twenty men. I think his stomach at that time was not very good; what he left they put in baskets and tied over his head. About midnight they set the meat again before him; all this time not one of them would eat a bit with him, till the next morning they brought him as much more, and then did they eat all the old and reserved the new as they had done the other, which made him think they would fat him to eat him. Yet in this desperate estate, to defend him from the cold, one Maocassater brought him his gown in requital[5] of some beads and toys Smith had given him at his first arrival in Virginia.

Two days after, a man would have slain him (but that the guard prevented it) for the death of his son, to whom they conducted him to recover the poor man then breathing his last. Smith told them that at Jamestown he had a water would do it, if they would let him fetch it, but they would not permit that, but made all the preparations they could to assault Jamestown, craving his advice, and for recompence he should have life, liberty, land, and women. In part of a table book[6] he wrote his mind to them at the fort, what was intended, how they should follow that direction to affright the messengers, and without fail send him such things as he wrote for. And an inventory with them. The difficulty and danger, he told the savages, of the mines, great guns, and other engines[7] exceedingly affrighted them, yet according to his request they went to Jamestown in as bitter weather as could be of frost and snow, and within three days returned with an answer.

But when they came to Jamestown, seeing men sally out as he had told them they would, they fled, yet in the night they came again to the same place where he had told them they should receive an answer and such things as he had promised them, which they found accordingly, and with which they returned with no small expedition to the wonder of them all that heard it, that he could either divine[8] or the paper could speak.

Then they led him to the Youghtanunds, the Mattapanients, the Piankatanks, the Nantaughtacunds, and Onawmanients[9] upon the rivers of Rappahannock and Potomac, over all those rivers and back again by divers other several nations[1] to the King's habitation at Pamunkey where they entertained him with most strange and fearful conjurations:[2]

> As if near led to hell
> Amongst the devils to dwell.

Not long after, early in a morning, a great fire was made in a long-house and a mat spread on the one side as on the other; on the one they caused him to sit, and all the guard went out of the house, and presently came skipping in a great grim fellow all painted over with coal[3] mingled with oil, and many snakes' and weasels' skins stuffed with moss, and all their tails tied together so as they met on the crown of his head in a tassel, and round about the tassel was as a coronet of feathers, the skins hanging round about his head, back, and shoulders and in a manner covered his face, with a hellish voice, and a rattle in his hand. With most strange gestures and passions be began his invo-

5. Payment.
6. A notebook.
7. Weaponry.
8. Perform magic. "Expedition": speed.
9. These groups were part of the confederacy that was under the rule of Powhatan.

1. Other Algonquian-speaking groups.
2. Incantations; but the following couplet Smith derived from a translation of Seneca published by Bishop Martin Fotherby in his *Atheomastix* (1622).
3. I.e., charcoal.

cation and environed[4] the fire with a circle of meal; which done, three more such like devils came rushing in with the like antic tricks, painted half black, half red, but all their eyes were painted white and some red strokes like mustaches along their cheeks. Round about him those fiends danced a pretty while, and then came in three more as ugly as the rest, with red eyes and white strokes over their black faces. At last they all sat down right against him, three of them on the one hand of the chief priest and three on the other. Then all with their rattles began a song; which ended, the chief priest laid down five wheat corns;[5] then straining his arms and hands with such violence that he sweat and his veins swelled, he began a short oration;[6] at the conclusion they all gave a short groan and then laid down three grains more. After that, began their song again, and then another oration, ever laying down so many corns as before till they had twice encircled the fire; that done, they took a bunch of little sticks prepared for that purpose, continuing still their devotion, and at the end of every song and oration they laid down a stick betwixt the divisions of corn. Till night, neither he nor they did either eat or drink, and then they feasted merrily with the best provisions they could make. Three days they used this ceremony; the meaning whereof, they told him, was to know if he intended them well or no. The circle of meal signified their country, the circles of corn the bounds of the sea, and the sticks his country. They imagined the world to be flat and round, like a trencher,[7] and they in the midst.

After this they brought him a bag of gunpowder, which they carefully preserved till the next spring, to plant as they did their corn, because they would be acquainted with the nature of that seed.

Opitchapam, the King's brother,[8] invited him to his house, where, with as many platters of bread, fowl, and wild beasts as did environ him, he bid him welcome, but not any of them would eat a bit with him but put up all the remainder in baskets.

At his return to Opechancanough's, all the King's women and their children flocked about him for their parts,[9] as a due by custom, to be merry with such fragments:

> But his waking mind in hideous dreams did
>     oft see wondrous shapes,
> Of bodies strange, and huge in growth, and
>     of stupendous makes.[1]

At last they brought him to Werowocomoco,[2] where was Powhatan, their Emperor. Here more than two hundred of those grim courtiers stood wondering at him, as [if] he had been a monster, till Powhatan and his train had put themselves in their greatest braveries.[3] Before a fire upon a seat like a bedstead, he sat covered with a great robe made of raccoon skins and all the tails hanging by. On either hand did sit a young wench of sixteen or eighteen years and along on each side [of] the house, two rows of men and behind them as many women, with all their heads and shoulders painted red, many of their heads bedecked with the white down of birds, but every one with something, and a great chain of white beads about their necks.

---

4. Encircled.
5. I.e., five kernels of Indian corn.
6. Prayer.
7. A flat wood dish.
8. Actually the chief's half-brother; he succeeded Powhatan in 1618.

9. Gifts.
1. From a translation of Lucretius by Fotherby.
2. Powhatan's village on the north shore of the York River, almost due north of Jamestown.
3. Finery; i.e., costumes.

At his entrance before the King, all the people gave a great shout. The Queen of Appomattoc[4] was appointed to bring him water to wash his hands, and another brought him a bunch of feathers, instead of a towel, to dry them; having feasted him after their best barbarous manner they could, a long consultation was held, but the conclusion was, two great stones were brought before Powhatan; then as many as could, laid hands on him, dragged him to them, and thereon laid his head and being ready with their clubs to beat out his brains, Pocahontas,[5] the King's dearest daughter, when no entreaty could prevail, got his head in her arms and laid her own upon his to save him from death, whereat the Emperor was contented he should live to make him hatchets, and her bells, beads, and copper, for they thought him as well of all occupations as themselves.[6] For the King himself will make his own robes, shoes, bows, arrows, pots; plant, hunt, or do anything so well as the rest.

> They say he bore a pleasant show,
> But sure his heart was sad.
> For who can pleasant be, and rest,
> That lives in fear and dread:
> And having life suspected, doth
> It still suspected lead.[7]

Two days after, Powhatan, having disguised himself in the most fearfulest manner he could, caused Captain Smith to be brought forth to a great house in the woods and there upon a mat by the fire to be left alone. Not long after, from behind a mat that divided the house, was made the most dolefulest noise he ever heard; then Powhatan more like a devil than a man, with some two hundred more as black as himself, came unto him and told him now they were friends, and presently he should go to Jamestown to send him two great guns and a grindstone for which he would give him the country of Capahowasic and forever esteem him as his son Nantaquoud.[8]

So to Jamestown with twelve guides Powhatan sent him. That night they quartered in the woods, he still expecting (as he had done all this long time of his imprisonment) every hour to be put to one death or other, for all their feasting. But almighty God (by His divine providence) had mollified the hearts of those stern barbarians with compassion. The next morning betimes they came to the fort, where Smith having used the savages with what kindness he could, he showed Rawhunt, Powhatan's trusty servant, two demi-culverins[9] and a millstone to carry [to] Powhatan; they found them somewhat too heavy, but when they did see him discharge them, being loaded with stones, among the boughs of a great tree loaded with icicles, the ice and branches came so tumbling down that the poor savages ran away half dead with fear. But at last we regained some conference with them and gave them such toys and sent to Powhatan, his women, and children such presents as gave them in general full content.

---

4. Opossunoquonuske was the weroansqua, or leader, of a small village (Appamatuck) near the future site of Petersburg, Virginia. In 1610, she was killed by the English in retaliation for the deaths of fourteen settlers.
5. Daughter of Powhatan (c. 1591–1617), she was mentioned in Smith's earlier versions of his captivity narrative, but first emerged as its heroine only in the *History*, which was published seven years after her death in England.
6. I.e., they thought him as variously skilled as themselves.
7. Derived from a translation of Euripides by Fotherby.
8. I.e., Powhatan would esteem him as highly as his own son Nantaquoud. Capahowasic was along the York River near where Smith was held prisoner.
9. Large cannons.

Now in Jamestown they were all in combustion, the strongest preparing once more to run away with the pinnace; which, with the hazard of his life, with saker falcon[1] and musket shot, Smith forced now the third time to stay or sink.

Some, no better than they should be, had plotted with the President the next day to have him put to death by the Levitical law,[2] for the lives of Robinson and Emry; pretending the fault was his that had led them to their ends; but he quickly took such order with such lawyers that he laid them by the heels till he sent some of them prisoners for England.

Now every once in four or five days, Pocahontas with her attendants brought him so much provision that saved many of their lives, that else for all this had starved with hunger.

> Thus from numb death our good God sent relief,
> The sweet assuager of all other grief.[3]

His relation of the plenty he had seen, especially at Werowocomoco, and of the state and bounty of Powhatan (which till that time was unknown), so revived their dead spirits (especially the love of Pocahontas)[4] as all men's fear was abandoned.

Thus you may see what difficulties still crossed any good endeavor; and the good success of the business being thus oft brought to the very period of destruction; yet you see by what strange means God hath still delivered it.

\*    \*    \*

## From *The Fourth Book*

### [SMITH'S FAREWELL TO VIRGINIA]

Thus far I have traveled in this Wilderness of Virginia, not being ignorant for all my pains this discourse will be wrested, tossed and turned as many ways as there is leaves;[5] that I have written too much of some, too little of others, and many such like objections. To such I must answer, in the Company's name I was requested to do it,[6] if any have concealed their approved experiences from my knowledge, they must excuse me: as for every fatherless or stolen relation,[7] or whole volumes of sophisticated rehearsals, I leave them to the charge of them that desire them. I thank God I never undertook anything yet [for which] any could tax me of carelessness or dishonesty, and what[8] is he to whom I am indebted or troublesome? Ah! were these my accusers but to change cases and places with me [for] but two years, or till they had done but so much as I, it may be they would judge more charitably of my imperfections.

---

1. Small falcon.
2. "And he that killeth any man shall surely be put to death" (Leviticus 24.17).
3. Apparently the first line is Smith's own, based on Fotherby, but the second is borrowed directly from Fotherby's translation from a quotation of Euripides found in Plutarch.
4. I.e., the evident affection of Pocahontas for Smith and the English was instrumental in reviving the colonists' spirits.
5. Pages.

6. Smith was not requested to write the whole *General History* by the Virginia Company, so it is not clear what his reference is here. Possibly the discourse to which he refers is the brief summary of recommendations for the "reformation" of Virginia that ends the *Fourth Book* and that he drew up at the request of the royal commissioners charged with effecting that reformation.
7. I.e., anonymous or "fugitive" narratives. "Approved": proven.
8. Who; i.e., he has been a burden to nobody.

But here I must leave all to the trial of time, both myself, Virginia's preparations, proceedings and good events, praying to that great God the protector of all goodness to send them as good success as the goodness of the action[9] and country deserveth, and my heart desireth.

1624

## *From* A Description of New England[1]

Who can desire more content, that hath small means; or but only his merit to advance his fortune, than to tread, and plant that ground he hath purchased by the hazard of his life? If he have but the taste of virtue, and magnanimity,[2] what to such a mind can be more pleasant, than planting and building a foundation for his posterity, got from the rude earth, by God's blessing and his own industry, without prejudice[3] to any? If he have any grain of faith or zeal in religion, what can he do less hurtful to any; or more agreeable to God, than to seek to convert those poor savages to know Christ, and humanity, whose labors with discretion will triple requite thy charge and pains? What so truly suits with honor and honesty, as the discovering things unknown? erecting townes, peopling countries, informing the ignorant, reforming things unjust, teaching virtue; and gain[ing] to our native mother country a kingdom to attend her; find[ing] employment for those that are idle, because they know not what to do: so far from wronging any, as to cause posterity to remember thee; and remembering thee, ever honor that remembrance with praise?

\*　\*　\*

Then, who would live at home idly (or think in himself any worth to live) only to eat, drink, and sleep, and so die? Or by consuming that carelessly, [which] his friends got worthily? Or by using that miserably, [which] maintained virtue honestly? Or, for being descended nobly, pine with the vain vaunt of great kindred, in penury?[4] Or (to maintain a silly show of bravery) toil out thy heart, soul, and time, basely, by shifts, tricks, cards, and dice? Or by relating news of others' actions, shark[5] here or there for a dinner, or supper; deceive thy friends, by fair promises, and dissimulation, in borrowing where thou never intendest to pay; offend the laws, surfeit with excess, burden thy country, abuse thyself, despair in want, and then cozen[6] thy kindred, yea even thine own brother, and wish thy parents' death (I will not say damnation) to have their estates? though thou seest what honors, and rewards, the world yet hath for them will seek them and worthily deserve them.

\*　\*　\*

Let this move you to embrace employment, for those whose educations, spirits, and judgments, want but your purses; not only to prevent such accustomed dangers, but also to gain more thereby than you have. And you fathers that are either so foolishly fond, or so miserably covetous, or so wilfully igno-

9. Venture. "Events": results.
1. The text is derived from *The Complete Works of Captain John Smith*, edited by Philip L. Barbour (1986).
2. Greatness of spirit.

3. Harm.
4. I.e., live in poverty while claiming great ancestors.
5. Sponge. "Bravery": fine appearances. "Shifts": expedients.
6. Deceive. "Excess": overindulge.

rant, or so negligently careless, as that you will rather maintain your children in idle wantonness, till they grow your masters; or become so basely unkind, as they wish nothing but your deaths; so that both sorts grow dissolute: and although you would wish them anywhere to escape the gallows, and ease your cares; though they spend you here one, two, or three hundred pound a year; you would grudge to give half so much in adventure with them, to obtain an estate, which in a small time but with a little assistance of your providence,[7] might be better than your own. But if an angel should tell you, that any place yet unknown can afford such fortunes; you would not believe him, no more than Columbus was believed there was any such land as is now the well-known abounding America; much less such large regions as are yet unknown, as well in America, as in Africa, and Asia, and Terra Incognita; where were courses for gentlemen (and them that would be so reputed) more suiting their qualities, than begging from their Prince's generous disposition, the labors of his subjects, and the very marrow of his maintenance.

I have not been so ill bred, but I have tasted of plenty and pleasure, as well as want and misery: nor doth necessity yet, or occasion of discontent, force me to these endeavors: nor am I ignorant what small thank I shall have for my pains; or that many would have the world imagine them to be of great judgment, that can but blemish these my designs, by their witty objections and detractions: yet (I hope) my reasons with my deeds, will so prevail with some, that I shall not want[8] employment in these affairs, to make the most blind see his own senselesness, and incredulity; hoping that gain will make them affect that, which religion, charity, and the common good cannot. It were but a poor device in me, to deceive myself; much more the king, and state, my friends, and country, with these inducements: which, seeing his Majesty hath given permission, I wish all sorts of worthy, honest, industrious spirits, would understand: and if they desire any further satisfaction, I will do my best to give it: Not to persuade them to go only;[9] but go with them: Not leave them there; but live with them there. I will not say, but by ill providing and undue managing, such courses may be taken, may make us miserable enough:[1] But if I may have the execution of what I have projected; if they want to eat, let them eat or never digest me.[2] If I perform what I say, I desire but that reward out of the gains may suit my pains, quality, and condition. And if I abuse you with my tongue, take my head for satisfaction. If any dislike at the year's end, defraying their charge,[3] by my consent they should freely return. I fear not want of company sufficient, were it but known what I know of those countries; and by the proof of that wealth I hope yearly to return, if God please to bless me from such accidents, as are beyond my power in reason to prevent: For, I am not so simple, to think, that ever any other motive than wealth, will ever erect there a Commonwealth; or draw company from their ease and humors at home, to stay in New England to effect my purposes. And lest any should think the toil might be insupportable, though these things may be had by labor, and diligence: I assure myself there are who delight extremely in vain pleasure, that take much more pains in England, to enjoy it, than I should do here to gain wealth sufficient: and yet I think they should not have half such sweet content:

---

7. Provision.
8. Lack.
9. Alone.
1. I.e., he won't promise that even with bad manage-

ment they'll succeed.
2. I.e., or never read Smith's works.
3. I.e., once they have paid the cost of their support for the year.

for, our pleasure here is still gains; in England, charges and loss. Here nature and liberty afford us that freely, which in England we want, or it costs us dearly. What pleasure can be more, than (being tired with any occasion ashore)[4] in planting vines, fruits, or herbs, in contriving their own grounds, to the pleasure of their own minds, their fields, gardens, orchards, buildings, ships, and other works, etc., to recreate themselves before their own doors, in their own boats upon the sea, where man, woman and child, with a small hook and line, by angling, may take diverse sorts of excellent fish, at their pleasures? And is it not pretty sport, to pull up two pence, six pence, and twelve pence, as fast as you can haul and veer[5] a line? He is a very bad fisher [who] cannot kill in one day with his hook and line, one, two, or three hundred cods: which dressed and dried, if they be sold there for ten shillings the hundred (though in England they will give more then twenty); may not both the servant, the master, and merchant, be well content with this gain? If a man work but three days in seven, he may get more than he can spend, unless he will be excessive. Now that carpenter, mason, gardener, tailor, smith, sailor, forgers,[6] or what other, may they not make this a pretty recreation though they fish but an hour in a day, to take more than they eat in a week: or if they will not eat it, because there is so much better choice; yet sell it, or change it, with the fishermen, or merchants, for anything they want. And what sport doth yield a more pleasing content, and less hurt or charge than angling with a hook, and crossing the sweet air from isle to isle, over the silent streams of a calm sea, wherein the most curious may find pleasure, profit, and content. Thus, though all men be not fishers: yet all men, whatsoever, may in other matters do as well. For necessity doth in these cases so rule a Commonwealth, and each in their several functions, as their labors in their qualities may be as profitable, because there is a necessary mutual use of all.

For Gentlemen, what exercise should more delight them, than ranging daily those unknown parts, using fowling and fishing, for hunting and hawking? and yet you shall see the wild hawks give you some pleasure, in seeing them stoop[7] (six or seven after one another) an hour or two together, at the schools of fish in the fair harbors, as those ashore at a fowl; and never trouble nor torment yourselves, with watching, mewing, feeding, and attending them: nor kill horse and man with running and crying, See you not a hawk?[8] For hunting also: the woods, lakes, and rivers, afford not only chase sufficient, for any that delights in that kind of toil, or pleasure; but such beasts to hunt, that besides the delicacy of their bodies for food, their skins are so rich, as may well recompence thy daily labor, with a captain's pay.

For laborers, if those that sow hemp, rape,[9] turnips, parsnips, carrots, cabbage, and such like; give twenty, thirty, forty, fifty shillings yearly for an acre of ground, and meat, drink, and wages to use it, and yet grow rich: when better, or at least as good ground, may be had and cost nothing but labor; it seems strange to me, any such should there grow poor.

My purpose is not to persuade children [to go] from their parents; men from their wives; nor servants from their masters: only, such as with free consent may be spared: But that each parish, or village, in city, or country, that will

4. Some casual occurrence.
5. I.e., fish.
6. I.e., ironworkers.
7. Swoop down.
8. Smith contrasts the delight of watching wild hawks

hunt their prey in America with the tedious care that keepers of trained hawks in England must give their birds—as when such birds fly away and must be hunted for all over the countryside.
9. I.e., the rape plant.

but apparel their fatherless children, of thirteen or fourteen years of age, or young married people, that have small wealth to live on; here by their labor may live exceedingly well: provided always that first there be a sufficient power to command them, houses to receive them, means to defend them, and meet provisions for them; for, any place may be overlain:[1] and it is most necessary to have a fortress (ere this grow to practice) and sufficient masters (as, carpenters, masons, fishers, fowlers, gardeners, husbandmen, sawyers, smiths, spinsters, tailors, weavers, and such like) to take ten, twelve, or twenty, or as there is occasion, for apprentices. The masters by this may quickly grow rich; these may learn their trades themselves, to do the like; to a general and an incredible benefit, for king, and country, master, and servant.

1616

## From New England's Trials[1]

Here I must entreate a little your favors to digress. They did not kill the English because they were Christians,[2] but for their weapons and commodities, that were rare novelties; but now they fear we may beat them out of their dens, which lions and tigers would not admit but by force. But must this be an argument for an Englishman,[3] or discourage any either in Virginia or New England? No: for I have tried them both. For Virginia, I kept that country with thirty-eight, and had not[4] to eat but what we had from the savages. When I had ten men able to go abroad, our commonwealth was very strong: with such a number I ranged that unknown country fourteen weeks; I had but eighteen to subdue them all, with which great army I stayed six weeks before their greatest king's habitations, till they had gathered together all the power they could; and yet the Dutchmen sent at a needless excessive charge did help Powhatan how to betray me.[5]

\*   \*   \*

For wronging a soldier but the value of a penny, I have caused Powhatan [to] send his own men to Jamestown to receive their punishment at my discretion. It is true in our greatest extremity they shot me, slew three of my men, and by the folly of them that fled took me prisoner; yet God made Pocahontas the king's daughter the means to deliver me: and thereby taught me to know their treacheries to preserve the rest. It was also my chance in single combat to take the king of Paspahegh[6] prisoner, and by keeping him, [I] forced his

1. Overcome.
1. The text is derived from *The Complete Works of Captain John Smith*, edited by Philip L. Barbour (1986). By "trials" Smith means tests or experiments, not sufferings.
2. Smith here is speaking of the massacre of settlers in Virginia in March 1622, news of which reached New England sometime in May of that year. In mustering support for settlement in New England, he obviously had to take into account the damping effect of events in Virginia.
3. I.e., such events are not strong enough to dissuade an Englishman. "Admit": allow.
4. Nothing. "With thirty-eight": i.e., he protected or secured Virginia by means of a very modest force.

5. Several "Dutch" (probably German) skilled workers had been shipped to Virginia in 1608. Sent to build a house for Powhatan, they hinted to him that they would take his side against the English, and soon were plotting against Smith and the colony. Arrested by the English and brought back to Jamestown for execution, they were saved when a new ship arrived from England, bringing fresh supplies and important new instructions for President Smith and Virginia's governing council.
6. Paspahegh was the Algonquian name for the region around Jamestown. Smith took its chief, Wowinchopunck, prisoner in 1609. An engraving in the 1st edition of the *General History* shows this episode.

subjects to work in chains, till I made all the country pay contribution, having little else whereon to live.

Twice in this time I was their president,[7] and none can say in all that time I had a man slain: but for keeping them in that fear I was much blamed both there and here: yet I left 500 behind me that through their confidence in six months came most to confusion, as you may read at large in the description of Virginia.[8] When I went first to those desperate designs, it cost me many a forgotten pound to hire men to go; and procrastination caused more [to] run away than went. But after the ice was broken, came many brave voluntaries: notwithstanding since I came from thence, the honorable Company have been humble suitors to his Majesty to get vagabonds and condemned men to go thither; nay so much scorned was the name of Virginia, some did choose to be hanged ere they would go thither, and were: yet for all the worst of spite, detraction and discouragement, and this lamentable massacre, there is more honest men now suitors to go, than ever hath been constrained knaves; and it is not unknown to most men of understanding, how happy many of those calumniators do think themselves, that they might be admitted, and yet pay for their passage to go now to Virginia: and had I but means to transport as many as would go, I might have choice of 10,000 that would gladly be in any of those new places, which were so basely condemned by ungrateful base minds.

To range this country of New England in like manner I had but eight, as is said, and amongst their brute[9] conditions I met many of their silly encounters, and without any hurt, God be thanked; when your West country men were many of them wounded and much tormented with the savages that assaulted their ship, as they did say themselves, in the first year I was there 1614, and though Master Hunt then master with me did most basely in stealing some savages from that coast to sell, when he was directed to have gone for Spain.[1] * * * I speak not this out of vainglory, as it may be some gleaners,[2] or some was never there may censure me, but to let all men be assured by those examples, what those savages are that thus strangely do murder and betray our countrymen. But to the purpose.

What is already written of the healthfulness of the air, the richness of the soil, the goodness of the woods, the abundance of fruits, fish, and fowl in their season, they still affirm that have been there now near two years, and at one draught[3] they have taken 1000 basses, and in one night twelve hogsheads of herring. They are building a strong fort, they hope shortly to finish, in the interim they are well provided: their number is about a hundred persons, all in health, and well near sixty acres of ground well planted with corn, besides their gardens well replenished with useful fruits; and if their adventurers would but furnish them with necessaries for fishing, their wants would quickly be

7. Smith was president of the Virginia council for only a single term; editors generally assume that he here means "twice during the time I was their president these things happened," although the passage may have been garbled.

8. I.e., Smith's first book, which contains a section so titled. "Confidence": i.e., overconfidence.

9. Tough.

1. Smith here refers to the tough going among earlier English voyagers to New England, especially Sir Ferdi-

nando Gorges (1568–1647), a backer of Smith, and Thomas Hunt (dates unknown), who had been with Smith on the latter's 1614 voyage to the region. Hunt had stirred up much trouble with the local American Indians by kidnapping more than twenty of them, including the Native American Tisquantum (called "Squanto" by the Pilgrims) to sell into slavery in Spain.

2. Those who pick through events in search of bits of scandal.

3. A single haul of the fish net.

supplied.[4] To supply them this sixteen of October is going the *Paragon* with sixty-seven persons, and all this is done by private men's purses. And to conclude in their own words, should they write of all plenties they have found, they think they should not be believed.

*   *   *

Thus you may see plainly the yearly success from New England (by Virginia)[5] which hath been so costly to this kingdom and so dear to me, which either to see perish or but bleed, pardon me though it passionate me beyond the bounds of modesty, to have been sufficiently able to foresee it, and had neither power nor means how to prevent it. By that acquaintance I have with them, I may call them my children, for they have been my wife, my hawks, my hounds, my cards, my dice, and in total my best content, as indifferent to my heart as my left hand to my right;[6] and notwithstanding all those miracles of disasters have crossed both them and me, yet were there not one Englishman remaining (as God be thanked there is some thousands) I would yet begin again with as small means as I did at the first; not for that I have any secret encouragement from any I protest, more than lamentable experiences: for all their discoveries I can yet hear of, are but pigs of my own sow;[7] nor more strange to me than to hear one tell me he hath gone from Billingsgate and discovered Greenwich, Gravesend, Tilbury, Queenborough, Leigh and Margate, which to those did never hear of them, though they dwell in England, might be made seem some rare secrets and great countries unknown, except the relations of Master Dirmer.[8]

*   *   *

What here I have written by relation, if it be not right, I humbly entreat your pardons, but I have not spared any diligence to learn the truth of them that have been actors or sharers in those voyages: in some particulars they might deceive me, but in the substances they could not, for few could tell me anything, except where they fished: but seeing all those [that] have lived there, do confirm more than I have written, I doubt not but all those testimonies with these new-begun examples of plantation, will move both city and country freely to adventure with me and my partners more than promises, seeing I have from his Majesty letters pattent, such honest, free and large conditions assured me from his commissioners, as I hope will satisfy any honest understanding.

1622

---

4. Here Smith speaks of the Plymouth settlers. "Adventurers": the investors who backed the Pilgrim venture.
5. I.e., by Virginia's example; Plymouth had barely been settled, but the longer experience of the English in Virginia (with all its faults) could be used to suggest the probable course of events in New England.
6. I.e., as equally dear to me as one hand or the other.
7. The offspring of Smith's deeds; i.e., the accomplishments of others would not have been possible had

he not gone before.
8. These are all well-known places in England. Smith's point is that once he had led the way into America, the English who followed him had accomplished nothing truly bold. The exception was Master Thomas Dermer (d. 1621), who had accompanied Smith to New England in 1614, had spent two years in Newfoundland (1616–18), and had returned to New England in 1619—in the process acquiring more knowledge about the region than Smith.

# Early American Literature 1620–1820

Long before Captain John Smith established Jamestown in 1607, the European imagination had been entranced by rumors of the New World's plenty. But it was probably Smith, rather than any other, who convinced English readers that there was an earthly paradise not far from their shores. In his *Description of New England* (1616) he wrote, "Here nature and liberty afford us that freely which in England we want [i.e., lack], or it costs us dearly." What greater satisfaction is there, he asked, than hauling in one's supper by dropping a hook and line into any plentiful river or stream; is it not "pretty sport" to "pull up two pence, six pence, and twelve pence" as fast as you can let out a line? One hundred twenty-five years later another Virginia planter, William Byrd, would add to the fabled accounts of the place in his *History of the Dividing Line*, and it is significant that Thomas Jefferson's one book, *Notes on the State of Virginia* (1785, 1787), was written in response to inquiries made by a French naturalist concerning the geography and resources of his state. In replying, however, Jefferson the scientist is quickly supplanted by Jefferson the artist: no country, he writes, has more sublime mountains, rivers, and waterfalls, all objects of such "stupendous" power that they are "worth crossing the Atlantic" to witness. European readers for three centuries were anxious to sort American fable from fact, but as American writers convinced them, the facts themselves were fabulous.

### THE PURITAN EXPERIMENT: PLYMOUTH PLANTATION

Although those Separatists from the Church of England whom we call Pilgrims were familiar with Smith's *Description* and followed his map of the Atlantic coast, they were not sympathetic to his proposal that he join their emigration to the New World; for Smith was primarily an adventurer, explorer, and trader, and while this group was not composed entirely of "reborn" Christians (only about twenty-seven of the one hundred persons aboard the *Mayflower* were Puritans), and even those were not indifferent to the material well-being of their venture, their leaders had more in mind than mercantile success. These pilgrims thought of themselves as soldiers in a war against Satan—the Arch-Enemy—who planned to ruin the kingdom of God on earth by sowing discord among those who professed to be Christians. This small band of believers saw no hope of reforming a national church and its Anglican hierarchy from within. In 1608, five years after the death of Queen Elizabeth and with an enemy of Puritanism, James Stuart, on the throne, they left England and settled in Holland, where, William Bradford tells us, they saw "fair and beautiful cities" and the "grisly face of poverty" confronting them. Isolated by their language, and unable to farm, they turned to mastering trades (Bradford himself became a weaver). Later, fearing that they would eventually lose their identity as a religious community living as strangers in a foreign land, they applied for a charter to settle in the Virginia Plantation—a vast tract of land that

75

included what is now New England. Sponsored by merchants who were anxious to receive repayment in goods from the New World, they sailed from Southampton, England, in September 1620. Sixty-six days later, taken by strong winds much farther north than they had anticipated, they dropped anchor at Cape Cod and established their colony at Plymouth.

In spite of the fact that their separatism does not make them representative of the large number of emigrants who came to these shores in the seventeenth century (Plymouth was eventually absorbed into the Massachusetts Bay Colony in 1691 when a new charter was negotiated), their story has become an integral part of our literature. Bradford's account of a chosen people, exiles in a "howling wilderness," who struggled against all adversity to bring into being the City of God on earth, is ingrained in our national consciousness. Both in the nineteenth century and in the twentieth, Americans have seen themselves as a "redeemer nation," without, of course, possessing Bradford's Christian ideals. What gives Bradford's book its great strength, in spite of his obvious prejudices, is his ability to keep the ideals of the Pilgrims before us as he describes the harsh reality of their struggle against not only the external forces of nature but the even more damaging corruption of worldliness within the community.

### THE PURITAN EXPERIMENT: THE MASSACHUSETTS BAY COLONY

Far more representative in attitude toward the Church of England were the Puritans who joined the Massachusetts Bay Colony under the leadership of John Winthrop. They were dissenting but nonseparating—although it might be argued that geographical distance from London and a charter that located the seat of their colony in Boston left them nonseparating in theory rather than practice. Whatever their difference with respect to the Church of England, however, the basic beliefs of both groups were identical: both held with Martin Luther that no pope or bishop had a right to impose any law on a Christian soul without consent and, following John Calvin, that God chose freely those He would save and those He would damn eternally.

Too much can be made of this doctrine of election; those who have not read the actual Puritan sermons often come away from secondary sources with the mistaken notion that Puritans talked about nothing but damnation. Puritans did indeed hold that God had chosen, before their birth, those whom He wished to save; but it does not follow that the Puritans considered most of us to be born damned. While Puritans argued that Adam broke the "Covenant of Works" (the promise God made to Adam that he was immortal and could live in Paradise forever as long as he obeyed God's commandments) when he disobeyed and ate of the tree of knowledge of good and evil, thereby bringing sin and death into the world, their central doctrine was the new "Covenant of Grace," a binding agreement Christ made with all men who believed in Him, and which He sealed with His Crucifixion, promising them eternal life. Puritans thus addressed themselves not to the hopelessly unregenerate but to the indifferent, and they addressed the heart more often than the mind, always distinguishing between "historical" or rational understanding and heartfelt "saving faith." There is more joy in Puritan life and thought than we often credit, and this joy is the direct result of meditation on the doctrine of Christ's redeeming power. Edward Taylor is not alone in making his rapturous litany of Christ's attributes: "He is altogether lovely in everything, lovely in His person, lovely in His natures, lovely in His properties, lovely in His offices, lovely in His titles, lovely in His practice, lovely in His purchases and lovely in His relations." All of Taylor's art is a meditation on the miraculous gift of the Incarnation, and, in this respect, his sensibility is typically Puritan. Anne Bradstreet, who is remarkably frank about confessing her religious doubts, told her children that it was "upon this rock Christ Jesus" that she built her faith.

Their lives, however, were hard. Anne Bradstreet's father told people in England to come over and join them if their lives were "endued with grace," but that others were "not fitted for this business"; that there was not a house where one had not died, and that if they survived the terrible winter they had to face the devastating infections that were the result of summer heat. Bradford's account of what he called "the starving time" is among the most moving in his history, and nothing in Smith's *Discovery* had hinted at how oppressive daily life might be. In her *Private Journal of a Journey from Boston to New York*, Sarah Kemble Knight provides a number of healthy antidotes to any sentimental notion we might have that life in the hinterland was invigorating. Puritan letters, diaries, histories, and poetry all attest to their faith in a larger plan, however, a "noble design" as Cotton Mather put it, which made daily life bearable.

In this Christocentric world it is not surprising that Puritans held to the strictest requirements regarding communion, or as they preferred to call it, the Lord's Supper. It was the most important of the two sacraments they recognized (baptism being the other), and they guarded it with a zeal that set them apart from all other dissenting churches. In the beginning, communion was taken only by church members—those who had stood before their minister and elders and given an account (or "relation") of their conversion—and was regarded as a sign of election. This insistence on challenging their members made these New England churches more rigorous than any others and confirmed the feeling that they were a special few. Thus, when John Winthrop addressed the immigrants to the Bay Colony aboard the flagship *Arbella* in 1630, he told them that the eyes of the world were on them and that they would be an example for all, a "city upon a hill."

### PURITAN HISTORIOGRAPHY

Puritans held the writing of history in high regard, for as heirs of Renaissance thought, they believed that lasting truths were to be gained by studying the lives of noble individuals. Cotton Mather urged students of the ministry to read not only early church historians but the classical historians Xenophon, Livy, Tacitus, and Plutarch as well. Puritans saw all of human time as a progression toward the fulfillment of God's design on earth. Therefore, pre-Christian history could be read as a preparation for Christ's entry into the world. They learned this lesson from medieval biblical scholars, who interpreted figures in the Old Testament as foreshadowings of Christ. This method of comparison, called typology, was an ingrained habit of Puritan thinking, and it made them compare themselves, as a chosen people, to the Israelites of old, who had been given the promise of a new land. Cotton Mather said that John Winthrop was the Puritan Moses whose education had prepared him to fulfill the "noble design of carrying a colony of chosen people into an American wilderness."

Puritans believed that God's hand was present in every human event and that He rewarded good and punished bad. History, therefore, revealed what God approved of or condemned, and if God looked favorably on a nation, His approval could be evidenced in its success. Puritans had enough confidence in God's design to believe that no facts were too small or insignificant to be included in that design; everything could emblemize something. In writing about Anne Bradstreet, Adrienne Rich observes that seventeenth-century Puritan life was perhaps "the most self-conscious ever lived"; that "faith underwent its hourly testing, the domestic mundanities were episodes in the drama; the piecemeal thoughts of a woman stirring a pot, clues to her 'justification' in Christ." John Winthrop in his diary records a struggle between a snake and a mouse and is surprised to see the seemingly weaker emerge the victor. His Boston friend, Mr. Wilson, however, saw the event as a battle between Satan and a "poor contemptible people, which God hath brought hither, which should overcome Satan here and disposses him of his kingdom." When a young sailor on board the *Mayflower* mocked those Puritans who were sick, Bradford found it fitting that the sailor should himself succumb to a "grievous disease." This sense of the universal significance of all things meant that drama was present in every believer's life and that individual lives could be as symbolic as the life of a nation. Mary Rowlandson, who had been captured by American Indians, saw her captivity as a lesson in the life of a representative soul who once wished to experience affliction and later experienced it only too well. Her captors were, to her, more than uncivilized savages; they were devils incarnate.

The greatest of all the Puritan historians was Cotton Mather, and in his *Magnalia Christi Americana* (1702) the myth of a chosen people took on its fullest resonance of meaning. By the time Mather undertook his history, the original Puritan community had vanished, leaving behind heirs to its lands and fortunes but not to its spirituality. Mather saw himself as one of the last defenders of the "old New England way," and all the churches as under attack from new forces of secularism. As a historian, Mather solved his problem by not focusing on the dissolution of the Puritan community but writing "saints' lives" instead, each of which (like those of Eliot, Bradford, and Winthrop) would serve as an example of the progress of the individual Christian soul and an allegory of the potential American hero. Under Mather's artistry, Winthrop's vision of a community of saints living in mutual concern and sympathy became an ideal rather than a historical reality. The words *New England* would symbolize the effort to realize the City of God on earth, and "whether New England may live anywhere else or no," he said, "it must live in our history."

### AN EXPANDING UNIVERSE

It should come as no surprise to learn that Mather was defensively retrospective in his ecclesiastical history of New England; for the enormous changes—economic, social, philosophical, and scientific—that occurred between Mather's birth in 1663 and the publication of the *Magnalia* in 1702 inevitably affected the influence and authority of Congregational churches. In 1686 Mather himself joined with Boston merchants in jailing their colonial governor, Sir Edmund Andros, and was successful in getting him sent back to England. It was a rare occasion when church and trade saw eye to eye; the Puritan clergy disliked Andros's Anglicanism as much as the merchants hated his taxes. It was an act celebrated annually in Boston until it was replaced by celebrations honoring American independence.

The increase in population alone would account for a greater diversity of opinion in the matter of churches. In 1670, for example, the population of the colonies numbered approximately 111,000. Thirty years later the colonies contained more than 250,000 persons; by 1760, if one included Georgia, they numbered 1,600,000, and the settled area had tripled. The demand for and price of colonial goods increased in England, and vast fortunes were to be made in New England with any business connected with shipbuilding: especially timber, tar, and pitch. Virginia planters became rich in tobacco, and rice and indigo from the Carolinas were in constant demand. New England Indians, on the other hand, estimated to number 25,000 in 1600, were reduced by one-third during the plague of 1616–18 and declined steadily thereafter; many communities disappeared entirely during this period of expansion.

New England towns were full of acrimonious debate between first settlers and newcomers. Town histories are full of accounts of splinter groups and the establishment of the "Second" church. In the beginning land was apportioned to settlers and allotted free, but by 1713 speculators in land were hard at work, buying as much as possible for as little as possible and selling high. The idea of a "community" of mutually helpful souls was fast disappearing. Life in the colonies was not easy, but the hardships and dangers the first settlers faced were mostly overcome, and compared with crowded cities like London, it was healthier, cheaper, and more hopeful. Those who could arrange their passage came in great numbers. Boston almost doubled in size from 1700 to 1720. It is also important to note that the great emigration to America that occurred in the first half of the eighteenth century was not primarily English. Dutch and Germans came in large numbers and so did French Protestants. Jewish merchants and craftsmen were well known in New York and Philadelphia.

By 1750 Philadelphia had become the unofficial capital of the colonies and was second only to London as a city of commerce. In 1681 the Quaker William Penn exchanged a large claim against the Crown for land in the New World. He was named proprietor (rather than governor, because he actually owned the territory) of Pennsylvania and immediately opened the land to settlement by people of all faiths. Penn had the genius to bestow the privilege of self-government on the people of Pennsylvania and in his "Frame of Government" told them that "Liberty without obedience is confusion, and obedience without liberty is slavery." These thousands of emigrants did not think of themselves as displaced British citizens; they thought of themselves as Americans. In 1702 no one would have dreamed of an independent union of colonies, but by 1752, fifty years later, it was a distinct possibility.

## THE ENLIGHTENMENT

Great challenges to seventeenth-century beliefs were posed by scientists and philosophers, and it has sometimes been suggested that the "modern" period dates from 1662 and the founding of the British scientific academy known, because of the patronage of King Charles II, as the Royal Society. The greatest scientists of the age like Sir Isaac Newton (1642–1727) and philosophers like John Locke (1632–1704) saw no conflict between their discoveries and traditionally held Christian truths. They saw nothing heretical in arguing that the universe was an orderly system and that by the application of reason humanity would comprehend its laws. But the inevitable result of their inquiries was to make the universe seem more rational and benevolent than it had been represented by Puritan doctrine. Because the world seemed more comprehensible, people paid less attention to revealed religion, and a number of seventeenth-century modes of thought—Bradford and Winthrop's penchant for the allegorical and emblematic, seeing every natural and human event as a message from God, for instance—seemed almost medieval and decidedly quaint. These new scientists and philosophers were called Deists; they deduced the existence of a supreme being from the construction of the universe itself rather than from the Bible. "A creation," as one distinguished historian has put it, "presupposes a creator." People were less interested in the metaphysical wit of introspective divines than in the progress of ordinary individuals as they made their way in the world. They assumed that humankind was naturally good and dwelt on neither the Fall nor the Incarnation. A harmonious universe proclaimed the beneficence of God, and Deists argued that humans should be as generous. They were not interested in theology but in humankind's own nature. American as well as English citizens knew Alexander Pope's famous couplet:

> Know then thyself, presume not God to scan,
> The proper study of mankind is man.

Locke said that "our business" here on earth "is not to know all things, but those which concern our conduct." In suggesting that we are not born with a set of innate ideas of good or evil and that the mind is rather like a blank wax tablet on which experiences are inscribed (a *tabula rasa*), Locke qualified traditional belief.

## THE GREAT AWAKENING

A conservative reaction against the worldview of the new science was bound to follow, and the first half of the eighteenth century witnessed a number of religious revivals in both England and America. They were sometimes desperate efforts to reassert the old values in the face of the new and, oddly enough, were themselves the direct product of the new cult of feeling, a philosophy that argued that our greatest pleasure was derived from the good we did for others and that our sympathetic emotions (our joy as well as our tears) should not be contained. Phillis Wheatley, whose poem on the death of the Methodist George Whitefield (1714–1770) made her famous, said that Whitefield prayed that "grace in every heart might dwell" and longed to see "America excell." Whitefield's revival meetings along the Atlantic seaboard were a great personal triumph, but they were no more famous than the "extraordinary circumstances" that occurred in Northampton, Massachusetts, under the leadership of Jonathan Edwards in the 1730s and that have come to be synonymous with the "Great Awakening."

Edwards also read his Locke, but he wished to liberate human beings from their senses, not define them by those senses. Edwards was fond of pointing out that the five senses are what we share with beasts, and that if our ultimate goal were merely a heightened sensibility, feverish sickness is the condition in which the senses are most acute. Edwards was interested in *supernatural* concerns, but he was himself influenced by Locke in arguing that true belief is something that we feel and do not merely comprehend intellectually. Edwards took the one doctrine most difficult for eighteenth-century minds to accept—election—and persuaded his congregation that God's sovereignty was not only the most reasonable doctrine but was the most "delightful" and appeared to him (using adjectives that suggest that the best analogy is to what can be apprehended sensually) "exceeding pleasant, bright, and sweet." In carefully reasoned, calmly argued prose, as harmonious and as ordered as anything the age produced, Edwards brought his great intellect to bear on doctrines that had been current the century before. Most people, when they think about the Puritans, remember Edwards's sermon Sinners in the Hands of an Angry God, forgetting that one hundred years had lapsed between that sermon and Winthrop's Model of Christian Charity. When Edwards tried to reassert "the old New England way" and demanded accounts of conversion before admission to church membership, he was accused of being a reactionary who thrived on hysteria, was removed from his pulpit, and was effectively silenced. He spent his last years as a missionary to the American Indians in Stockbridge, Massachusetts, a town forty miles to the west of Northampton, imitating the call of the Reverend David Brainard, a young man who, had he lived, would have married Edwards's daughter Jerusha. There he remained until invited to become president of the College of New Jersey. His death in Princeton was the direct result of his willingness to be vaccinated against smallpox and so to set an example for his frightened and superstitious students; it serves as a vivid reminder of how complicated in any one individual the response to the "new science" could become.

### THE AMERICAN CRISIS

On June 7, 1776, at the second Continental Congress, Richard Henry Lee of Virginia moved that "these united colonies are, and of a right ought to be, free and independent states." A committee was duly appointed to prepare a declaration of independence, and it was approved on July 4. Although these motions and their swiftness took some delegates by surprise—the purpose of the congress had, after all, not been to declare independence but to protest the usurpation of rights by king and Parliament and to effect a compromise with the homeland—others saw them as the inevitable consequence of the events of the decade preceding. The Stamp Act of 1764, taxing all newspapers, legal documents, and licenses, had infuriated Bostonians and resulted in the burning of the governor's palace; in Virginia, Patrick Henry had taken the occasion to speak impassionedly against taxation without representation. In 1770 a Boston mob had been fired on by British soldiers, and three years later the famous "Tea Party" occurred, an act that drew hard lines in the matter of acceptable limits of British rule. In adopting the dress of Native Americans, these protesters declared themselves antithetical to everything British. The news of the April confrontation with the British in Concord and Lexington, Massachusetts, was still on everyone's tongue in Philadelphia when the second Continental Congress convened in May of 1775.

Although the drama of these events cannot be underestimated, most historians agree that it was Thomas Paine's *Common Sense*, published in January 1776, that gave the needed push for revolution. In the course of two months it was read by almost every American. In arguing that separation from England was the only reasonable course and that "the Almighty" had planted these feelings in us "for good and wise purposes," Paine was appealing to basic tenets of the Enlightenment. His clarion call to those that "love mankind," those "that dare oppose not only the tyranny but the tyrant, stand forth!" did not go unheeded. Americans needed an apologist for the Revolution, and in December of 1776, when Washington's troops were at their most demoralized, it was, again, Paine's first *Crisis* paper—popularly called *The American Crisis*—that was read to all the regiments and was said to have inspired their future success.

Paine first came to America in 1774 with a note from Benjamin Franklin recommending him to publishers and editors. He was only one of a number of young writers who were able to take advantage of the times. This was, in fact, the great age of the newspaper and the moral essay; Franklin tells us that he modeled his own style on the clarity, good sense, and simplicity of the English essayists Joseph Addison and Richard Steele. The first newspaper in the colonies appeared in 1704, but by the time of the Revolution there were almost fifty papers and forty magazines. The great cry was for a "national literature" (meaning anti-British), and the political events of the 1770s were advantageous for a career. Philip Freneau made his first success as a writer as a satirist of the British, and after the publication of his *Poems Written Chiefly during the Late War* (1786) he turned to newspaper work, editing the *New York Daily Advertiser* and writing anti-Federalist party essays, making himself an enemy of Alexander Hamilton in the process. The most distinguished political writings of the period are, in fact, the essays Hamilton, John Jay, and James Madison wrote for New York newspapers in 1787 and 1788 and collectively known as *The Federalist Papers*. In attempting to get New Yorkers to support the new Constitution they provided an eloquent defense of the framework of the Republic. Joel Barlow also published anti-British satires in the *New Haven Gazette and Connecticut Magazine* and envisioned an American literature that would extol our government, our educational institutions, and the arts. He spent most of his life revising a long hymn to the Republic called *The Columbiad*. But Barlow never settled down to the life of the artist; he was too much the entrepreneur and world traveler for that. His best poems are not his philosophical epics but poems, like *The Hasty Pudding*, in praise of the simple life. Freneau's career was also marked by restlessness and indecision, although in his case financial necessity came between his life and his art. The first American writer able to live exclusively by his craft was Washington Irving.

The crisis in American life caused by the Revolution made artists self-conscious about American subjects. It would be another fifty years before writers discovered ways of being American without compromising their integrity. One of the ironies of our history is that the Revolution itself has rarely proved to be a usable subject for American literature and art.

THE PURSUIT OF HAPPINESS

When John Winthrop described his "model" for a Christian community, he envisioned a group of men and women working together for the common good, each one of whom knew his or her place in the social structure and accepted God's disposition of goods. At all times, he said, "some must be rich, some poor, some high and eminent in power and dignity," others low and "in subjection." Ideally, it was to be a community of love, all made equal by their fallen nature and their concern for the salvation of their souls, but it was to be a stable community, and Winthrop would not have imagined very much social change. One hundred forty years later John Adams, our second president, envisioned a model community, decreed by higher laws, when he said that the American colonies were a part of a "grand scheme and design in Providence for the illumination of the ignorant and the emancipation of the slavish part of mankind all over the earth." Adams witnessed social mobility of a kind and an extent, however, that no European before him would have dreamed possible. As historians have observed, European critics of America in the eighteenth and nineteenth centuries never understood that great social change was possible without social upheaval primarily because there was no feudal hierarchy to overthrow. When Crèvecoeur wanted to distinguish America from Europe, it was the medievalism of the latter that he wished to stress. The visitor to America, he said, "views not the hostile castle, and the haughty mansion, contrasted with the clay-built hut and miserable cabin, where cattle and men help to keep each other warm, and dwell in meanness, smoke and indigence."

Of course, not everyone was free, and for indentured servants and Native Americans, being "free" was relative. Some of our founding fathers, like Thomas Jefferson, were large slaveowners, and it was still not possible to vote without owning property. Women had hardly any rights at all: they could not vote and young women were educated at home, excluded by their studies from anything other than domestic employment. Nevertheless, the same forces that were undermining church authority in New England (in New York and Philadelphia no such hierarchy existed) were effecting social change. The two assumptions held to be true by most eighteenth-century Americans were, as Russel Nye once put it, "the perfectability of man, and the prospect of his future progress." Much of the imaginative energy of the second half of the eighteenth century was expanded in correcting institutional injustices: the tyranny of monarchy, the tolerance of slavery, the misuse of prisons. Few doubted that with the application of intelligence the human lot could be improved, and writers like Freneau, Franklin, and Crèvecoeur argued that, if it were not too late, the transplanted European might learn something about fellowship and manners from "the noble savages" rather than from rude white settlers, slaveowners, and backwoods pioneers.

In many ways it is Franklin who best represents the spirit of the Enlightenment in America: self-educated, social, assured, a man of the world, ambitious and public-spirited, speculative about the nature of the universe, but in matters of religion content to observe the actual conduct of humanity rather than to debate supernatural matters that are unprovable. When Ezra Stiles asked him about his religion, he said he believed in the "creator of the universe" but he doubted the "divinity of Jesus." He would never dogmatize about it, however, because he expected soon "an opportunity of knowing the truth with less trouble." Franklin always presents himself as a man depending on firsthand experience, too worldly wise to be caught off guard. His posture, however, belies one side of the eighteenth century that can be accounted for neither by the inheritance of Calvin nor by the empiricism of Locke: those idealistic assumptions that underlie the great public documents of the American Revolution, especially the Declaration of Independence. These are truths that, as the essayist and poet Joel Barlow once said, were "as perceptible when first presented to the mind as age or world of experience could make them." Given the representative nature of Franklin's character, it seems right that of the documents most closely associated with the formation of the American republic—the Declaration of Independence, the treaty of alliance with France, the Treaty of Paris, and the Constitution—only he should have signed all four.

The fact that Americans in the last quarter of the eighteenth century would hold that "certain truths are self-evident, that all men are created equal, that they are endowed by their Creator with certain unalienable Rights, that among these are Life, Liberty and the pursuit of Happiness" is the result, as both Leon Howard and Garry Wills have argued, of their reading the Scottish philosophers, particularly Francis Hutcheson and Lord Kames (Henry Home), who argued that all people in all places possess a sense common to all—a moral sense—that contradicted the notion of the mind as an empty vessel awaiting experience. This idealism paved the way for writers like Bryant, Emerson, Thoreau, and Whitman, but in the 1770s its presence is found chiefly in politics and ethics. The assurance of a universal sense of right and wrong made possible both the overthrow of tyrants and the restoration of order, and it allowed humankind to make new earthly covenants, not, as was the case with Bradford and Winthrop, for the glory of God, but, as Thomas Jefferson argued, for an individual's right to happiness on earth.

# WILLIAM BRADFORD
## 1590–1657

William Bradford epitomizes the spirit of determination and self-sacrifice that seems to us characteristic of our first "Pilgrims," a word Bradford himself used to describe the community of believers who sailed from Southampton, England, on the *Mayflower* and settled in Plymouth, Massachusetts, in 1620. For Bradford, as well as for the other members of this community, the decision to settle at Plymouth was the last step in a long march of exile from England, and the hardships they suffered in the new land were tempered with the knowledge that they were in a place they had chosen for themselves, where they were safe from persecution. Shortly after their arrival Bradford was elected governor. His duties involved more than that title might imply today: he was chief judge and jury, superintended agriculture and trade, and made allotments of land. It would be hard to imagine a historian better prepared to write the history of this colony.

Bradford's own life provides a model of the life of the community as a whole. He was born in Yorkshire, in the town of Austerfield, of parents who were modestly well off. Bradford's father died when he was an infant. His mother remarried in 1593, and he was brought up by his paternal grandparents and uncles. He did not receive a university education; instead, he was taught the arts of farming. When he was only twelve or thirteen, he heard the sermons of the Nonconformist minister Richard Clyfton, who preached in a neighboring parish; these sermons changed Bradford's life. For Clyfton was the religious guide of a small community of believers who met at the house of William Brewster in Scrooby, Nottinghamshire, and it was with this group, in 1606, that Bradford wished to be identified. Much against the opposition of uncles and grandparents, he left home and joined them. They were known as "Separatists," because unlike the majority of Puritans, they saw no hope of reforming the Church of England from within. They wished to follow Calvin's model and to set up "particular" churches, each one founded on a formal covenant, entered into by those who professed their faith and swore to the covenant. Their model was the Old Testament covenant God made with Adam and that Christ renewed. In their covenanted churches God offered himself as a contractual partner to each believer; it was a contract freely initiated but perpetually binding. They were not sympathetic to the idea of a national church. Separating was, however, by English law an act of treason, and many believers paid a high price for their dreams of purity. Sick of the hidden life that the Church of England forced on them, the Scrooby community took up residence in Holland. Bradford joined them in 1609 and there learned to be a weaver. When he came into his inheritance he went into business for himself.

Living in a foreign land was not easy, and eventually the Scrooby community petitioned for a grant of land in the New World. Their original grant was for land in the Virginia territory, but high seas prevented them from reaching those shores and they settled at Plymouth, Massachusetts, instead. In the second book of Bradford's history he describes the signing of the "Mayflower Compact," a civil covenant designed to allow the temporal state to serve the godly citizen. It was the first of a number of plantation covenants designed to protect the rights of citizens beyond the reach of established governments.

Bradford was a self-educated man, deeply committed to the Puritan cause. In his ecclesiastical history of New England, Cotton Mather describes him as "a person for study as well as action; and hence notwithstanding the difficulties which he passed in his youth, he attained unto a notable skill in languages. . . . but the Hebrew he most of all studied, because, he said, he would see with his own eyes the ancient oracles of God in their native beauty. . . . The crown of all his life was his holy, prayerful, watchful and fruitful walk with God, wherein he was exemplary." Bradford served as governor for all but five of the remaining years of his life.

The manuscript of Bradford's *History*, although known to early historians, disappeared from Boston after the revolution. The first book (through chapter IX) had been copied into the Plymouth church records and was thus preserved, but the second book was assumed lost. The manuscript was found in the residence of the bishop of London and published for the first time in 1856. In 1897 it was returned to this country by ecclesiastical decree and was deposited in the State House in Boston.

## *From* Of Plymouth Plantation[1]

### From Book I, Chapter I. [The Separatist Interpretation of the Reformation in England, 1550–1607]

\* \* \* When as by the travail and diligence of some godly and zealous preachers, and God's blessing on their labors, as in other places of the land, so in the North parts,[2] many became enlightened by the Word of God and had their ignorance and sins discovered[3] unto them, and began by His grace to reform their lives and make conscience of their ways; the work of God was no sooner manifest in them but presently they were both scoffed and scorned by the profane[4] multitude; and the ministers urged with the yoke of subscription,[5] or else must be silenced. And the poor people were so vexed with apparitors and pursuivants and the commissary courts,[6] as truly their affliction was not small. Which, notwithstanding, they bore sundry years with much patience, till they were occasioned by the continuance and increase of these troubles, and other means which the Lord raised up in those days, to see further into things by the light of the Word of God. How not only these base and beggarly ceremonies were unlawful, but also that the lordly and tyrannous power of the prelates ought not to be submitted unto; which thus, contrary to the freedom of the gospel, would load and burden men's consciences and by

---

1. The text is from *Of Plymouth Plantation*, edited by Samuel Eliot Morison (1953).
2. I.e., of England and Scotland.
3. Revealed.
4. Unholy.

5. I.e., to subscribe to the tenets of the Church of England. "Urged": threatened.
6. I.e., vexed with officers and summoners of the Church of England and the court of a bishop's jurisdiction.

their compulsive power make a profane mixture of persons and things in the worship of God. And that their offices and callings, courts and canons, etc. were unlawful and antichristian; being such as have no warrant in the Word of God, but the same that were used in popery and still retained. Of which a famous author thus writeth in his Dutch commentaries, at the coming of King James into England:

> The new king (saith he) found there established the reformed religion according to the reformed religion of King Edward VI, retaining or keeping still the spiritual state of the bishops, etc. after the old manner, much varying and differing from the reformed churches in Scotland, France and the Netherlands, Emden, Geneva, etc., whose reformation is cut, or shapen much nearer the first Christian churches, as it was used in the Apostles' times.[7]

So many, therefore, of these professors as saw the evil of these things in these parts, and whose hearts the Lord had touched with heavenly zeal for His truth, they shook off this yoke of antichristian bondage, and as the Lord's free people joined themselves (by a covenant[8] of the Lord) into a church estate, in the fellowship of the gospel, to walk in all His ways made known, or to be made known unto them, according to their best endeavors, whatsoever it should cost them, the Lord assisting them. And that it cost them something this ensuing history will declare.

These people became two distinct bodies or churches, and in regard of distance of place did congregate severally; for they were of sundry towns and villages, some in Nottinghamshire, some of Lincolnshire, and some of Yorkshire where they border nearest together. In one of these churches (besides others of note) was Mr. John Smith, a man of able gifts and a good preacher, who afterwards was chosen their pastor. But these afterwards falling into some errors in the Low Countries,[9] there (for the most part) buried themselves and their names.

But in this other church (which must be the subject of our discourse) besides other worthy men, was Mr. Richard Clyfton, a grave and reverend preacher, who by his pains and diligence had done much good, and under God had been a means of the conversion of many. And also that famous and worthy man Mr. John Robinson, who afterwards was their pastor for many years, till the Lord took him away by death. Also Mr. William Brewster[1] a reverend man, who afterwards was chosen an elder of the church and lived with them till old age.

But after these things they could not long continue in any peaceable condition, but were hunted and persecuted on every side, so as their former afflictions were but as flea-bitings in comparison of these which now came upon them. For some were taken and clapped up in prison, others had their houses beset and watched night and day, and hardly escaped their hands; and the

7. From Emanuel van Meteren's *General History of the Netherlands* (1608). King James (1566–1625) ascended the throne in 1603. Most Puritans preferred the model of the Calvinist system in Geneva or the Church of Scotland, which replaced a hierarchy of archbishops, bishops, and priests with a national assembly and a parish presbytery consisting of ministers and elders.
8. A solemn agreement between the members of a church to act together in harmony with the precepts of the Gospel.
9. Holland.
1. A church leader of the Pilgrims in both Leyden and Plymouth (1576–1644). John Smith was a Cambridge University graduate who seceded from the Church of England in 1605. Richard Clyfton and John Robinson were also Cambridge University graduates who were Separatists.

most were fain to flee and leave their houses and habitations, and the means of their livelihood.

Yet these and many other sharper things which afterward befell them, were no other than they looked for, and therefore were the better prepared to bear them by the assistance of God's grace and Spirit.

Yet seeing themselves thus molested, and that there was no hope of their continuance there, by a joint consent they resolved to go into the Low Countries, where they heard was freedom of religion for all men; as also how sundry from London and other parts of the land had been exiled and persecuted for the same cause, and were gone thither, and lived at Amsterdam and in other places of the land. So after they had continued together about a year, and kept their meetings every Sabbath in one place or other, exercising the worship of God amongst themselves, notwithstanding all the diligence and malice of their adversaries, they seeing they could no longer continue in that condition, they resolved to get over into Holland as they could. Which was in the year 1607 and 1608; of which more at large in the next chapter.

## Book I, Chapter IV. Showing the Reasons and Causes of Their Removal

After they had lived in this city about some eleven or twelve years (which is the more observable being the whole time of that famous truce between that state and the Spaniards)[2] and sundry of them were taken away by death and many others began to be well stricken in years (the grave mistress of Experience having taught them many things), those prudent governors with sundry of the sagest members began both deeply to apprehend their present dangers and wisely to foresee the future and think of timely remedy. In the agitation of their thoughts, and much discourse of things hereabout, at length they began to incline to this conclusion: of removal to some other place. Not out of any newfangledness or other such like giddy humor by which men are oftentimes transported to their great hurt and danger, but for sundry weighty and solid reasons, some of the chief of which I will here briefly touch.

And first, they saw and found by experience the hardness of the place and country to be such as few in comparison would come to them, and fewer that would bide it out and continue with them. For many that came to them, and many more that desired to be with them, could not endure that great labor and hard fare, with other inconveniences which they underwent and were contented with. But though they loved their persons, approved their cause and honored their sufferings, yet they left them as it were weeping, as Orpah did her mother-in-law Naomi, or as those Romans did Cato[3] in Utica who desired to be excused and borne with, though they could not all be Catos. For many, though they desired to enjoy the ordinances of God in their purity and the liberty of the gospel with them, yet (alas) they admitted of bondage with danger of conscience, rather than to endure these hardships. Yea, some preferred and chose the prisons in England rather than this liberty in Holland with these afflictions. But it was thought that if a better and easier place of living could

2. The struggle for independence by provinces of the Netherlands against Spain was interrupted by a twelve-year truce on March 30, 1609; that truce was now coming to a close. "This city": Leyden.
3. Roman statesman of unbending integrity, who committed suicide in 46 B.C. when Julius Caesar's cause triumphed. Orpah was the sister-in-law of Ruth: "And they lifted up their voice, and wept again: and Orpah kissed her mother-in-law; but Ruth clave unto her" (Ruth 1.14).

be had, it would draw many and take away these discouragements. Yea, their pastor would often say that many of those who both wrote and preached now against them, if they were in a place where they might have liberty and live comfortably, they would then practice as they did.

Secondly. They saw that though the people generally bore all these difficulties very cheerfully and with a resolute courage, being in the best and strength of their years; yet old age began to steal on many of them; and their great and continual labors, with other crosses and sorrows, hastened in before the time. So as it was not only probably thought, but apparently seen, that within a few years more they would be in danger to scatter, by necessities pressing them, or sink under their burdens, or both. And therefore according to the divine proverb, that a wise man seeth the plague when it cometh, and hideth himself, Proverbs xxii.3, so they like skillful and beaten soldiers were fearful either to be entrapped or surrounded by their enemies so as they should neither be able to fight nor fly. And therefore thought it better to dislodge betimes to some place of better advantage and less danger, if any such could be found.

Thirdly. As necessity was a taskmaster over them so they were forced to be such, not only to their servants but in a sort to their dearest children, the which as it did not a little wound the tender hearts of many a loving father and mother, so it produced likewise sundry sad and sorrowful effects. For many of their children that were of best dispositions and gracious inclinations, having learned to bear the yoke in their youth[4] and willing to bear part of their parents' burden, were oftentimes so oppressed with their heavy labors that though their minds were free and willing, yet their bodies bowed under the weight of the same, and became decrepit in their early youth, the vigor of nature being consumed in the very bud as it were. But that which was more lamentable, and of all sorrows most heavy to be borne, was that many of their children, by these occasions and the great licentiousness of youth in that country,[5] and the manifold temptations of the place, were drawn away by evil examples into extravagant and dangerous courses, getting the reins off their necks and departing from their parents. Some became soldiers, others took upon them far voyages by sea, and others some worse courses tending to dissoluteness and the danger of their souls, to the great grief of their parents and dishonor of God. So that they saw their posterity would be in danger to degenerate and be corrupted.

Lastly (and which was not least), a great hope and inward zeal they had of laying some good foundation, or at least to make some way thereunto, for the propagating and advancing the gospel of the kingdom of Christ in those remote parts of the world; yea, though they should be but even as stepping-stones unto others for the performing of so great a work.

These and some other like reasons moved them to undertake this resolution of their removal; the which they afterward prosecuted with so great difficulties, as by the sequel will appear.

The place they had thoughts on was some of those vast and unpeopled countries of America, which are fruitful and fit for habitation, being devoid of all civil inhabitants, where there are only savage and brutish men which range up and down, little otherwise than the wild beasts of the same. This proposi-

---

4. "It is good for a man that he bear the yoke in his youth" (Lamentations 3.27).
5. Morison notes that the Dutch did not keep the Sab-

bath Day in the strict sense that the English Puritans did.

tion being made public and coming to the scanning of all, it raised many variable opinions amongst men and caused many fears and doubts amongst themselves. Some, from their reasons and hopes conceived, labored to stir up and encourage the rest to undertake and prosecute the same; others again, out of their fears, objected against it and sought to divert from it; alleging many things, and those neither unreasonable nor unprobable; as that it was a great design and subject to many unconceivable perils and dangers; as, besides the casualties of the sea (which none can be freed from), the length of the voyage was such as the weak bodies of women and other persons worn out with age and travail (as many of them were) could never be able to endure. And yet if they should, the miseries of the land which they should be exposed unto, would be too hard to be borne and likely, some or all of them together, to consume and utterly to ruinate them. For there they should be liable to famine and nakedness and the want, in a manner, of all things. The change of air, diet and drinking of water would infect their bodies with sore sicknesses and grievous diseases. And also those which should escape or overcome these difficulties should yet be in continual danger of the savage people, who are cruel, barbarous and most treacherous, being most furious in their rage and merciless where they overcome; not being content only to kill and take away life, but delight to torment men in the most bloody manner that may be; flaying some alive with the shells of fishes, cutting off the members and joints of others by piecemeal and broiling on the coals, eat the collops[6] of their flesh in their sight whilst they live, with other cruelties horrible to be related.

And surely it could not be thought but the very hearing of these things could not but move the very bowels of men to grate within them and make the weak to quake and tremble. It was further objected that it would require greater sums of money to furnish such a voyage and to fit them with necessaries, than their consumed estates would amount to; and yet they must as well look to be seconded with supplies as presently to be transported. Also many precedents of ill success and lamentable miseries befallen others in the like designs were easy to be found, and not forgotten to be alleged; besides their own experience, in their former troubles and hardships in their removal into Holland, and how hard a thing it was for them to live in that strange place, though it was a neighbor country and a civil and rich commonwealth.

It was answered, that all great and honorable actions are accompanied with great difficulties and must be both enterprised and overcome with answerable courages. It was granted the dangers were great, but not desperate. The difficulties were many, but not invincible. For though there were many of them likely, yet they were not certain. It might be sundry of the things feared might never befall; others by provident care and the use of good means might in a great measure be prevented; and all of them, through the help of God, by fortitude and patience, might either be borne or overcome. True it was that such attempts were not to be made and undertaken without good ground and reason, not rashly or lightly as many have done for curiosity or hope of gain, etc. But their condition was not ordinary, their ends were good and honorable, their calling lawful and urgent; and therefore they might expect the blessing of God in their proceeding. Yea, though they should lose their lives in this action, yet might they have comfort in the same and their endeavors would be

---

6. Slices, portions.

honorable. They lived here but as men in exile and in a poor condition, and as great miseries might possibly befall them in this place; for the twelve years of truce were now out and there was nothing but beating of drums and preparing for war, the events whereof are always uncertain. The Spaniard might prove as cruel as the savages of America, and the famine and pestilence as sore here as there, and their liberty less to look out for remedy.

After many other particular things answered and alleged on both sides, it was fully concluded by the major part to put this design in execution and to prosecute it by the best means they could.

### From Book I, Chapter VII. Of Their Departure from Leyden, and Other Things Thereabout; with Their Arrival at Southampton, Where They All Met Together and Took in Their Provisions

#### [MR. ROBINSON'S LETTER]

At length, after much travel and these debates, all things were got ready and provided. A small ship[7] was bought and fitted in Holland, which was intended as to serve to help to transport them, so to stay in the country and attend upon fishing and such other affairs as might be for the good and benefit of the colony when they came there. Another was hired at London, of burthen about 9 score,[8] and all other things got in readiness. So being ready to depart, they had a day of solemn humiliation, their pastor taking his text from Ezra viii.21: "And there at the river, by Ahava, I proclaimed a fast, that we might humble ourselves before our God, and seek of him a right way for us, and for our children, and for all our substance." Upon which he spent a good part of the day very profitably and suitable to their present occasion; the rest of the time was spent in pouring out prayers to the Lord with great fervency, mixed with abundance of tears. And the time being come that they must depart, they were accompanied with most of their brethren out of the city, unto a town sundry miles off called Delftshaven, where the ship lay ready to receive them. So they left that goodly and pleasant city which had been their resting place near twelve years; but they knew they were pilgrims,[9] and looked not much on those things, but lift up their eyes to the heavens, their dearest country, and quieted their spirits.

When they came to the place they found the ship and all things ready, and such of their friends could not come with them followed after them, and sundry also came from Amsterdam to see them shipped and to take their leave of them. That night was spent with little sleep by the most, but with friendly entertainment and Christian discourse and other real expressions of true Christian love. The next day (the wind being fair) they went aboard and their friends with them, where truly doleful was the sight of that sad and mournful parting, to see what sighs and sobs and prayers did sound amongst them, what tears did gush from every eye, and pithy speeches pierced each heart; that sundry of the

---

7. "Of some 60 tun" [Bradford's note]. The Pilgrims left Amsterdam for Leyden because of disagreements "with the church that was there before them." They decided to leave Holland for reasons Bradford cites in the fourth chapter of book 1: economic hardship, the availability of inexpensive land for farming, the fear that their children were becoming Hollanders rather than English, and the advancement of the Gospel.

8. *The Mayflower*, a ship weighing 180 tons.

9. "Hebrews xi.31–16" [Bradford's note]. "These all died in faith, not having received the promises, but having seen them afar off, and were persuaded of them and embraced them, and confessed that they were strangers and pilgrims on the earth." It was this passage that caused the *Mayflower* company to be known as Pilgrims.

Dutch strangers that stood on the quay as spectators could not refrain from tears. Yet comfortable and sweet it was to see such lively and true expressions of dear and unfeigned love. But the tide, which stays for no man, calling them away that were thus loath to depart, their reverend pastor falling down on his knees (and they all with him) with watery cheeks commended them with most fervent prayers to the Lord and His blessing. And then with mutual embraces and many tears they took their leaves of one another, which proved to be the last leave to many of them.

*    *    *

At their parting Mr. Robinson writ a letter to the whole company; which though it hath already been printed;[1] yet I thought good here likewise to insert it. As also a brief letter writ at the same time to Mr. Carver,[2] in which the tender love and godly care of a true pastor appears.

My Dear Brother, I received enclosed in your last letter the note of information, which I shall carefully keep and make use of as there shall be occasion. I have a true feeling of your perplexity of mind and toil of body, but I hope that you who have always been able so plentifully to administer comfort unto others in their trials, are so well furnished for yourself, as that far greater difficulties than you have yet undergone (though I conceive them to have been great enough) cannot oppress you; though they press you, as the Apostle speaks.[3] The spirit of a man (sustained by the Spirit of God) will sustain his infirmity; I doubt not so will yours.[4] And the better much when you shall enjoy the presence and help of so many godly and wise brethren, for the bearing of the part of your burthen, who also will not admit into their hearts the least thought of suspicion of any the least negligence, at last presumption, to have been in you, whatsoever they think in others.

Now what shall I say or write unto you and your good wife my loving sister?[5] Even only this: I desire, and always shall unto you from the Lord, as unto my own soul. And assure yourself that my heart is with you, and that I will not forslow[6] my bodily coming at the first opportunity. I have written a large letter to the whole, and am sorry I shall not rather speak than write to them; and the more, considering the want of a preacher, which I shall also make some spur to my hastening after you. I do ever commend my best affection unto you, which if I thought you made any doubt of, I would express in more and the same more ample and full words.

And the Lord in whom you trust and whom you serve ever in this business and journey, guide you with His hand, protect you with His wing, and show you and us His salvation in the end, and bring us in the meanwhile together in this place desired, if such be His good will, for His Christ's sake. Amen.

Yours, etc.

July 27, 1620                                                      John Robinson

---

1. In *Mourt's Relation* (1622), an account of the first year of the plantation at Plymouth taken from the journals of Edward Winslow and William Bradford and brought to London for publication by Bradford's brother-in-law, George Mourt. Morison places the letters that follow in his appendix; we have restored them to their original position in the manuscript.
2. John Carver (d. 1621) was the first governor of the colony.
3. "For we would not, brethren, have you ignorant of our trouble which came to us in Asia, that we were pressed out of measure, above strength, insomuch that we despaired even of life" (2 Corinthians 1.8); "And when Silas and Timotheus were come from Macedonia, Paul was pressed in the spirit and testified to the Jews that Jesus was Christ" (Acts 18.5).
4. "Counsel is mine, and sound wisdom: I am understanding; I have strength" (Proverbs 8.14).
5. Mrs. Carver (d. 1621) was John Robinson's sister.
6. Delay.

This was the last letter that Mr. Carver lived to see from him. The other follows:

LOVING AND CHRISTIAN FRIENDS, I do heartily and in the Lord salute you all as being they with whom I am present in my best affection, and most earnest longings after you. Though I be constrained for a while to be bodily absent from you. I say constrained, God knowing how willingly and much rather than otherwise, I would have borne my part with you in this first brunt, were I not by strong necessity held back for the present. Make account of me in the meanwhile as of a man divided in myself with great pain, and as (natural bonds set aside) having my better part with you. And though I doubt not but in your godly wisdoms you both foresee and resolve upon that which concernth your present state and condition, both severally and jointly, yet have I thought it but my duty to add some further spur of provocation unto them who run already; if not because you need it, yet because I owe it in love and duty. And first, as we are daily to renew our repentance with our God, especially for our sins known, and generally for our unknown trespasses; so doth the Lord call us in a singular manner upon occasions of such difficulty and danger as lieth upon you, to a both more narrow search and careful reformation of your ways in His sight; lest He, calling to rememberance our sins forgotten by us or unrepented of, take advantage against us, and in judgment leave us for the same to be swallowed up in one danger or other. Whereas, on the contrary, sin being taken away by earnest repentance and the pardon thereof from the Lord, sealed up unto a man's conscience by His Spirit, great shall be his security and peace in all dangers, sweet his comforts in all distresses, with happy deliverance from all evil, whether in life or in death.

Now, next after this heavenly peace with God and our own consciences, we are carefully to provide for peace with all men what in us lieth, especially with our associates. And for that, watchfulness must be had that we neither at all in ourselves do give, no, nor easily take offense being given by others. Woe be unto the world for offenses, for though it be necessary (considering the malice of Satan and man's corruption) that offenses come, yet woe unto the man, or woman either, by whom the offense cometh, saith Christ, Matthew xviii.7. And if offenses in the unseasonable use of things, in themselves indifferent, be more to be feared than death itself (as the Apostle teacheth, I Corinthians ix.15) how much more in things simply evil, in which neither honor of God nor love of man is thought worthy to be regarded. Neither yet is it sufficient that we keep ourselves by the grace of God from giving offense, except withal we be armed against the taking of them when they be given by others. For how unperfect and lame is the work of grace in that person who wants charity to cover a multitude of offenses, as the Scriptures speak![7]

Neither are you to be exhorted to this grace only upon the common grounds of Christianity, which are, that persons ready to take offense either want[8] charity to cover offenses, or wisdom duly to weigh human frailty; or lastly, are gross, though close hypocrites as Christ our Lord teacheth (Matthew vii.1, 2, 3), as indeed in my own experience few or none have been found which sooner give offense than such as easily take it. Neither have they ever proved

---

7. "And above all things have fervent charity among    (1 Peter 4.8).
yourselves: for charity shall cover the multitude of sins"    8. Lack.

sound and profitable members in societies, which have nourished this touchy humor.

But besides these, there are divers motives provoking you above others to great care and conscience this way: As first, you are many of you strangers, as to the persons so to the infirmities one of another, and so stand in need of more watchfulness this way, lest when such things fall out in men and women as you suspected not, you be inordinately affected with them; which doth require at your hands much wisdom and charity for the covering and preventing of incident offenses that way. And, lastly, your intended course of civil community will minister continual occasion of offense, and will be as fuel for that fire, except you diligently quench it with brotherly forebearance. And if taking of offense causelessly or easily at men's doings be so carefully to be avoided, how much more heed is to be taken that we take not offense at God Himself, which yet we certainly do so for as we do murmur at His providence in our crosses, or bear impatiently such afflictions as wherewith He pleaseth to visit us. Store up, therefore, patience against that evil day, without which we take offense at the Lord Himself in His holy and just works.

A fourth thing there is carefully to be provided for, to wit, that with your common employments you join common affections truly bent upon the general good, avoiding as a deadly plague of your both common and special comfort all retiredness of mind for proper advantage, and all singularly affected any manner of way. Let every man repress in himself and the whole body in each person, as so many rebels against the common good, all private respects of men's selves, not sorting with the general coveniency. And as men are careful not to have a new house shaken with any violence before it be well settled and the parts firmly knit, so be you, I beseech you, brethren, much more careful that the house of God, which you are and are to be, be not shaken with unnecessary novelties or other oppositions at the first settling thereof.

Lastly, whereas you are become a body politic, using amongst yourselves civil government, and are not furnished with any persons of special eminency above the rest, to be chosen by you into office of government; let your wisdom and godliness appear, not only in choosing such persons as do entirely love and will promote the common good, but also in yielding unto them all due honor and obedience in their lawful administrations, not beholding in them the ordinariness of their persons, but God's ordinance for your good; not being like the foolish multitude who more honor the gay coat than either the virtuous mind of the man, or glorious ordinance of the Lord. But you know better things, and that the image of the Lord's power and authority which the magistrate beareth,[9] is honorable, in how mean persons soever. And this duty you both may the more willingly and ought the more conscionably to perform, because you are at least for the present to have only them for your ordinary governors, which yourselves shall make choice of for that work.

Sundry other things of importance I could put you in mind of, and of those before mentioned in more words, but I will not so far wrong your godly minds as to think you heedless of these things, there being also divers among you so well able to admonish both themselves and others of what concerneth them.

---

9. "For he is the minister of God to thee for good. But if thou do that which is evil, be afraid; for he beareth not the sword in vain: for he is the minister of God, a revenger to execute wrath upon him that doeth evil" (Romans 13.4). Morison notes that this passage "is sometimes said to have inspired the drafting of the Mayflower Compact."

These few things, therefore, and the same in few words, I do earnestly commend unto your care and conscience, joining therewith my daily incessant prayers unto the Lord, that He who hath made the heavens and the earth, the sea and all rivers of waters, and whose providence is over all His works, especially over all His dear children for good, would so guide and guard you in your ways, as inwardly by His Spirit, so outwardly by the hand of His power, as that both you and we also, for and with you, may have after matter of praising His name all the days of your and our lives. Fare you well in Him whom you trust, and in whom I rest.

An unfeigned wellwiller of your happy success in this hopeful voyage,

JOHN ROBINSON

This letter, though large, yet being so fruitful in itself and suitable to their occasion, I thought meet to insert in this place.

All things being now ready, and every business dispatched, the company was called together and this letter read amongst them, which had good acceptation with all, and after fruit with many. Then they ordered and distributed their company for either ship, as they conceived for the best; and chose a Governor and two or three assistants for each ship, to order the people by the way, and see to the disposing of their provisions and such like affairs. All which was not only with the liking of the masters of the ships but according to their desires. Which being done, they set sail from thence about the 5th of August. But what befell them further upon the coast of England will appear in the next chapter.

### Book I, Chapter IX. Of Their Voyage and How They Passed the Sea; and of Their Safe Arrival at Cape Cod

*September 6.* These troubles[1] being blown over, and now all being compact together in one ship, they put to sea again with a prosperous wind, which continued divers days together, which was some encouragement unto them; yet, according to the usual manner, many were afflicted with seasickness. And I may not omit here a special work of God's providence. There was a proud and very profane young man, one of the seamen, of a lusty,[2] able body, which made him the more haughty; he would always be condemning the poor people in their sickness and cursing them daily with grievous exercations; and did not let[3] to tell them that he hoped to help to cast half of them overboard before they came to their journey's end, and to make merry with what they had; and if he were by any gently reproved, he would curse and swear most bitterly. But it pleased God before they came half seas over, to smite this young man with a grievous disease, of which he died in a desperate manner, and so was himself the first that was thrown overboard. Thus his curses light on his own head, and it was an astonishment to all his fellows for they noted it to be the just hand of God upon him.

After they had enjoyed fair winds and weather for a season, they were encountered many times with cross winds and met with many fierce storms

---

1. Some of the Scrooby community originally sailed from Delftshaven about August 1, 1620, on board the *Speedwell,* but it proved unseaworthy and it was neces-  sary to transfer everything to the *Mayflower.*
2. Strong, energetic.
3. Hesitate.

with which the ship was shroudly[4] shaken, and her upper works made very leaky; and one of the main beams in the midships was bowed and cracked, which put them in some fear that the ship could not be able to perform the voyage. So some of the chief of the company, perceiving the mariners to fear the sufficiency of the ship as appeared by their mutterings, they entered into serious consultation with the master and other officers of the ship, to consider in time of the danger, and rather to return than to cast themselves into a desperate and inevitable peril. And truly there was great distraction and difference of opinion amongst the mariners themselves; fain would they do what could be done for their wages' sake (being now near half the seas over) and on the other hand they were loath to hazard their lives too desperately. But in examining of all opinions, the master and others affirmed they knew the ship to be strong and firm under water; and for the buckling of the main beam, there was a great iron screw the passengers brought out of Holland, which would raise the beam into his place; the which being done, the carpenter and master affirmed that with a post put under it, set firm in the lower deck and otherways bound, he would make it sufficient. And as for the decks and upper works, they would caulk them as well as they could, and though with the working of the ship they would not long keep staunch,[5] yet there would otherwise be no great danger, if they did not overpress her with sails. So they committed themselves to the will of God and resolved to proceed.

In sundry of these storms the winds were so fierce and the seas so high, as they could not bear a knot of sail, but were forced to hull[6] for divers days together. And in one of them, as they thus lay at hull in a mighty storm, a lusty young man called John Howland, coming upon some occasion above the gratings was, with a seele[7] of the ship, thrown into sea; but it pleased God that he caught hold of the topsail halyards which hung overboard and ran out at length. Yet he held his hold (though he was sundry fathoms under water) till he was hauled up by the same rope to the brim of the water, and then with a boat hook and other means got into the ship again and his life saved. And though he was something ill with it, yet he lived many years after and became a profitable member both in church and commonwealth. In all this voyage there died but one of the passengers, which was William Butten, a youth, servant to Samuel Fuller, when they drew near the coast.

But to omit other things (that I may be brief) after long beating at sea they fell with that land which is called Cape Cod; the which being made and certainly known to be it, they were not a little joyful. After some deliberation had amongst themselves and with the master of the ship, they tacked about and resolved to stand for the southward (the wind and weather being fair) to find some place about Hudson's River for their habitation. But after they had sailed that course about half the day, they fell amongst dangerous shoals and roaring breakers, and they were so far entangled therewith as they conceived themselves in great danger; and the wind shrinking upon them withal, they resolved to bear up again for the Cape and thought themselves happy to get out of those dangers before night overtook them, as by God's good providence they did. And the next day they got into the Cape Harbor[8] where they rid in safety.

---

4. Shrewdly, in its original sense of wickedly.
5. Watertight.
6. Drift with the wind under short sail.
7. Roll.

8. Cape Harbor is now Provincetown harbor; they arrived on November 11, 1620, the journey from England having taken sixty-five days.

A word or two by the way of this cape. It was thus first named by Captain Gosnold and his company, Anno 1602, and after by Captain Smith was called Cape James; but it retains the former name amongst seamen. Also, that point which first showed those dangerous shoals unto them they called Point Care, and Tucker's Terror; but the French and Dutch to this day call it Malabar[9] by reason of those perilous shoals and the losses they have suffered there.

Being thus arrived in a good harbor, and brought safe to land, they fell upon their knees and blessed the God of Heaven who had brought them over the vast and furious ocean, and delivered them from all the perils and miseries thereof, again to set their feet on the firm and stable earth, their proper element. And no marvel if they were thus joyful, seeing wise Seneca was so affected with sailing a few miles on the coast of his own Italy, as he affirmed, that he had rather remain twenty years on his way by land than pass by sea to any place in a short time, so tedious and dreadful was the same unto him.[1]

But here I cannot but stay and make a pause, and stand half amazed at this poor people's present condition; and so I think will the reader, too, when he well considers the same. Being thus passed the vast ocean, and a sea of troubles before in their preparation (as may be remembered by that which went before), they had now no friends to welcome them nor inns to entertain or refresh their weatherbeaten bodies; no houses or much less towns to repair to, to seek for succor. It is recorded in Scripture as a mercy to the Apostle and his shipwrecked company, that the barbarians showed them no small kindness in refreshing them,[2] but these savage barbarians, when they met with them (as after will appear) were readier to fill their sides full of arrows than otherwise. And for the season it was winter, and they that know the winters of that country know them to be sharp and violent, and subject to cruel and fierce storms, dangerous to travel to known places, much more to search an unknown coast. Besides, what could they see but a hideous and desolate wilderness, full of wild beasts and wild men—and what multitudes there might be of them they knew not. Neither could they, as it were, go up to the top of Pisgah[3] to view from this wilderness a more goodly country to feed their hopes; for which way soever they turned their eyes (saved upward to the heavens) they could have little solace or content in respect of any outward objects. For summer being done, all things stand upon them with a weatherbeaten face, and the whole country, full of woods and thickets, represented a wild and savage hue. If they looked behind them, there was the mighty ocean which they had passed and was now as a main bar and gulf to separate them from all the civil parts of the world. If it be said they had a ship to succor them, it is true; but what heard they daily from the master and company? But that with speed they should look out a place (with their shallop[4]) where they would be, at some near distance; for the season was such as he would not stir from thence till a safe harbor was discovered by them, where they would be, and he might go without danger; and that victuals consumed apace but he must and would keep sufficient for

---

9. The prefix *mal* means "bad"; the reference here is to the dangerous sandbars.

1. Bradford notes that this remark may be found in the *Moral Epistles to Lucilius*, line 5, of the Roman Stoic philosopher (4? B.C.–A.D. 65).

2. "And when they were escaped, then they knew that the island was called Melita. And the barbarous people showed us no little kindness: for they kindled a fire, and received us every one, because of the present rain, and because of the cold" (Acts 28.1–2).

3. Mountain from which Moses saw the Promised Land (Deuteronomy 34.1–4).

4. Small boat fitted with one or more masts.

themselves and their return. Yea, it was muttered by some that if they got not a place in time, they would turn them and their goods ashore and leave them. Let it also be considered what weak hopes of supply and succor they left behind them, that might bear up their minds in this sad condition and trials they were under; and they could not but be very small. It is true, indeed, the affections and love of their brethren at Leyden[5] was cordial and entire toward them, but they had little power to help them or themselves; and how the case stood between them and the merchants at their coming away hath already been declared.

What could now sustain them but the Spirit of God and His grace? May not and ought not the children of these fathers rightly say "Our fathers were Englishmen which came over this great ocean, and were ready to perish in this wilderness; but they cried unto the Lord, and He heard their voice and looked on their adversity,"[6] etc. "Let them therefore praise the Lord, because He is good: and His mercies endure forever." "Yea, let them which have been redeemed of the Lord, show how He hath delivered them from the hand of the oppressor. When they wandered in the desert wilderness out of the way, and found no city to dwell in, both hungry and thirsty, their soul was overwhelmed in them. Let them confess before the Lord His loving kindness and His wonderful works before the sons of men."[7]

## From *Book I, Chapter X. Showing How They Sought Out a Place of Habitation; and What Befell Them Thereabout*

Being thus arrived at Cape Cod the 11th of November, and necessity calling them to look out a place for habitation (as well as the master's and mariners' importunity); they having brought a large shallop with them out of England, stowed in quarters in the ship, they now got her out and set their carpenters to work to trim her up; but being much bruised and shattered in the ship with foul weather, they saw she would be long in mending. Whereupon a few of them tendered themselves to go by land and discover those nearest places, whilst the shallop was in mending; and the rather because as they went into that harbor there seemed to be an opening some two or three leagues off, which the master judged to be a river.[8] It was conceived there might be some danger in the attempt, yet seeing them resolute, they were permitted to go, being sixteen of them well armed under the conduct of Captain Standish,[9] having such instructions given them as was thought meet.

They set forth the 15th of November; and when they had marched about the space of a mile by the seaside, they espied five or six persons with a dog coming towards them, who were savages; but they fled from them and ran up into the woods, and the English followed them, partly to see if they could

5. In Holland. A substantial number of Separatists remained in the Netherlands.

6. "And the Egyptians evil entreated us, and afflicted us, and laid upon us hard bondage: And when we cried unto the Lord God of our fathers, the Lord heard our voice, and looked on our affliction, and our labor and our oppression: And the Lord brought us forth out of Egypt with a mighty hand" (Deuteronomy 26.6–8).

7. "O give thanks unto the Lord, for he is good: for his mercy endureth for ever. Let the redeemed of the Lord say so, whom he hath redeemed from the hand of the

enemy; And gathered them out of the lands, from the east, and from the west, from the north and from the south" (Psalm 107.1–5).

8. Morison observes that "Looking south from Provincetown Harbor where the Pilgrims were, the high land near Plymouth looks like an island on clear days, suggesting that there is a river or arm of the sea between it and Cape Cod."

9. Myles Standish (1584?–1656) was a professional soldier who had fought in the Netherlands; he was not a Pilgrim.

speak with them, and partly to discover if there might not be more of them lying in ambush. But the Indians seeing themselves thus followed, they again forsook the woods and ran away on the sands as hard[1] as they could, so as they could not come near them but followed them by the track of their feet sundry miles and saw that they had come the same way. So, night coming on, they made their rendezvous and set out their sentinels, and rested in quiet that night; and the next morning followed their track till they had headed a great creek and so left the sands, and turned another way into the woods. But they still followed them by guess, hoping to find their dwellings; but they soon lost both them and themselves, falling into such thickets as were ready to tear their clothes and armor in pieces; but were most distressed for want of drink. But at length they found water and refreshed themselves, being the first New England water they drunk of, and was now in great thirst as pleasant unto them as wine or beer had been in foretimes.

Afterwards they directed their course to come to the other shore, for they knew it was a neck of land they were to cross over, and so at length got to the seaside and marched to this supposed river, and by the way found a pond[2] of clear fresh water, and shortly after a good quantity of clear ground where the Indians had formerly set corn, and some of their graves. And proceeding further they saw new stubble where corn had been set the same year; also they found where lately a house had been, where some planks and a great kettle was remaining, and heaps of sand newly paddled with their hands. Which, they digging up, found in them divers fair Indian baskets filled with corn, and some in ears, fair and good, of divers colors, which seemed to them a very goodly sight (having never seen any such before). This was near the place of that supposed river they came to seek, unto which they went and found it to open itself into two arms with a high cliff of sand in the entrance[3] but more like to be creeks of salt water than any fresh, for aught they saw; and that there was good harborage for their shallop, leaving it further to be discovered by their shallop, when she was ready. So, their time limited them being expired, they returned to the ship lest they should be in fear of their safety; and took with them part of the corn and buried up the rest. And so, like the men from Eshcol, carried with them of the fruits of the land and showed their brethren;[4] of which, and their return, they were marvelously glad and their hearts encouraged.

After this, the shallop being got ready, they set out again for the better discovery of this place, and the master of the ship desired to go himself. So there went some thirty men but found it to be no harbor for ships but only for boats. There was also found two of their houses covered with mats, and sundry of their implements in them, but the people were run away and could not be seen.[5] Also there was found more of their corn and of their beans of various colors; the corn and beans they brought away, purposing to give them full satisfaction when they should meet with any of them as, about some six months afterward they did, to their good content.

And here is to be noted a special providence of God, and a great mercy to

---

1. Fast.
2. The pond from which Pond Village, Truro, Massachusetts, gets its name.
3. A salt creek known as Pamet River.
4. In the Numbers 13.23–26, Moses' scouts, after searching the wilderness for forty days, brought back clusters of grapes, which they found near the brook that they called "Eshcol."
5. Descendants of these Nauset Indians may still be found today at Mashpee on Cape Cod.

this poor people, that here they got seed to plant them corn the next year, or else they might have starved, for they had none nor any likelihood to get any till the season had been past, as the sequel did manifest. Neither is it likely they had had this, if the first voyage had not been made, for the ground was now all covered with snow and hard frozen; but the Lord is never wanting unto His in their greatest needs; let His holy name have all the praise.

The month of November being spent in these affairs, and much foul weather falling in, the 6th of December they sent out their shallop again with ten of their principal men and some seamen, upon further discovery, intending to circulate that deep bay of Cape Cod. The weather was very cold and it froze so hard as the spray of the sea lighting on their coats, they were as if they had been glazed. Yet that night betimes they got down into the bottom of the bay, and as they drew near the shore[6] they saw some ten or twelve Indians very busy about something. They landed about a league or two from them, and had much ado to put ashore anywhere—it lay so full of flats. Being landed, it grew late and they made themselves a barricado with logs and boughs as well as they could in the time, and set out their sentinel and betook them to rest, and saw the smoke of the fire the savages made that night. When morning was come they divided their company, some to coast along the shore in the boat, and the rest marched through the woods to see the land, if any fit place might be for their dwelling. They came also to the place where they saw the Indians the night before, and found they had been cutting up a great fish like a grampus,[7] being some two inches thick of fat like a hog, some pieces whereof they had left by the way. And the shallop found two more of these fishes dead on the sands, a thing usual after storms in that place, by reason of the great flats of sand that lie off.

So they ranged up and down all that day, but found no people, nor any place they liked. When the sun grew low, they hasted out of the woods to meet with their shallop, to whom they made signs to come to them into a creek[8] hard by, the which they did at high water; of which they were very glad, for they had not seen each other all that day since the morning. So they made them a barricado as usually they did every night, with logs, stakes and thick pine boughs, the height of a man, leaving it open to leeward, partly to shelter them from the cold and wind (making their fire in the middle and lying round about it) and partly to defend them from any sudden assaults of the savages, if they should surround them; so being very weary, they betook them to rest. But about midnight they heard a hideous and great cry, and their sentinel called "Arm! arm!" So they bestirred them and stood to their arms and shot off a couple of muskets, and then the noise ceased. They concluded it was a company of wolves or such like wild beasts, for one of the seamen told them he had often heard such a noise in Newfoundland.

So they rested till about five of the clock in the morning; for the tide, and their purpose to go from thence, made them be stirring betimes. So after prayer they prepared for breakfast, and it being day dawning it was thought best to be carrying things down to the boat. But some said it was not best to carry the arms down, others said they would be the readier, for they had lapped them up in their coats from the dew; but some three or four would not carry theirs

6. Somewhere near Eastham, Massachusetts.          8. The mouth of Herring River in Eastham.
7. Probably a blackfish (*Globicephala melæna*).

till they went themselves. Yet as it fell out, the water being not high enough, they laid them down on the bank side and came up to breakfast.

But presently, all on the sudden, they heard a great and strange cry, which they knew to be the same voices they heard in the night, though they varied their notes; and one of their company being abroad came running in and cried, "Men, Indians! Indians!" And withal, their arrows came flying amongst them. Their men ran with all speed to recover their arms, as by the good providence of God they did. In the meantime, of those that were there ready, two muskets were discharged at them, and two more stood ready in the entrance of their rendezvous but were commanded not to shoot till they could take full aim at them. And the other two charged again with all speed, for there were only four had arms there, and defended the barricado, which was first assaulted. The cry of the Indians was dreadful, especially when they saw the men run out of the rendezvous toward the shallop to recover their arms, the Indians wheeling about upon them. But some running out with coats of mail on, and cutlasses in their hands, they soon got their arms and let fly amongst them and quickly stopped their violence. Yet there was a lusty man, and no less valiant, stood behind a tree within half a musket shot, and let his arrows fly at them; he was seen [to] shoot three arrows, which were all avoided. He stood three shots of a musket, till one taking full aim at him and made the bark or splinters of the tree fly about his ears, after which he gave an extraordinary shriek and away they went, all of them. They[9] left some to keep the shallop and followed them about a quarter of a mile and shouted once or twice, and shot off two or three pieces, and so returned. This they did that they might conceive that they were not afraid of them or any way discouraged.

Thus it pleased God to vanquish their enemies and give them deliverance; and by His special providence so to dispose that not any one of them were either hurt or hit, though their arrows came close by them and on every side [of] them; and sundry of their coats, which hung up in the barricado, were shot through and through. Afterwards they gave God solemn thanks and praise for their deliverance, and gathered up a bundle of their arrows and sent them into England afterward by the master of the ship, and called that place the First Encounter.

From hence they departed and coasted all along but discerned no place likely for harbor; and therefore hasted to a place that their pilot (one Mr. Coppin who had been in the country before) did assure them was a good harbor, which he had been in, and they might fetch it before night; of which they were glad for it began to be foul weather.

After some hours' sailing it began to snow and rain, and about the middle of the afternoon the wind increased and the sea became very rough, and they broke their rudder, and it was as much as two men could do to steer her with a couple of oars. But their pilot bade them be of good cheer for he saw the harbor; but the storm increasing, and night drawing on, they bore what sail they could to get in, while they could see. But herewith they broke their mast in three pieces and their sail fell overboard in a very grown sea, so as they had like to have been cast away. Yet by God's mercy they recovered themselves, and having the flood[1] with them, struck into the harbor. But when it came to, the pilot was deceived in the place, and said the Lord be merciful unto them

9. I.e., the English.                    1. I.e., the flood tide.

for his eyes never saw that place before; and he and the master's mate would have run her ashore in a cove full of breakers before the wind. But a lusty seaman which steered bade those which rowed, if they were men, about with her or else they were all cast away; the which they did with speed. So he bid them be of good cheer and row lustily, for there was a fair sound before them, and he doubted not but they should find one place or other where they might ride in safety. And though it was very dark and rained sore, yet in the end they got under the lee of a small island and remained there all that night in safety. But they knew not this to be an island till morning, but were divided in their minds; some would keep the boat for fear they might be amongst the Indians, others were so wet and cold they could not endure but got ashore, and with much ado got fire (all things being so wet); and the rest were glad to come to them, for after midnight, the wind shifted to the northwest and it froze hard.

But though this had been a day and night of much trouble and danger unto them, yet God gave them a morning of comfort and refreshing (as usually He doth to His children) for the next day was a fair, sunshining day, and they found themselves to be on an island secure from the Indians, where they might dry their stuff, fix their pieces[2] and rest themselves; and gave God thanks for His mercies in their manifold deliverances. And this being the last day of the week, they prepared there to keep the Sabbath.

On Monday they sounded[3] the harbor and found it fit for shipping, and marched into the land and found divers cornfields and little running brooks, a place (as they supposed) fit for situation.[4] At least it was the best they could find, and the season and their present necessity made them glad to accept of it. So they returned to their ship again with this news to the rest of their people, which did much comfort their hearts.

On the 15th of December they weighed anchor to go to the place they had discovered, and came within two leagues of it, but were fain to bear up again; but the 16th day, the wind came fair, and they arrived safe in this harbor. And afterwards took better view of the place, and resolved where to pitch their dwelling; and the 25th day began to erect the first house for common use to receive them and their goods.

---

2. Armaments.
3. Measured the depth of.
4. Morison notes that this is "the only contemporary authority for the 'Landing of the Pilgrims at Plymouth Rock' on December 21, 1620" (or December 11 Old Style, since the Julian calendar differs from the present Gregorian calendar by ten days).

---

# JOHN WINTHROP
## 1588–1649

John Winthrop, the son of Adam Winthrop, a lawyer, and Anne Browne, the daughter of a tradesman, was born in Groton, England, on an estate that his father purchased from Henry VIII. It was a prosperous farm, and Winthrop had all the advantages that his father's social and economic position would allow. He went to Cambridge University for two years and married at the age of seventeen. It was probably at Cambridge University that Winthrop was exposed to Puritan ideas. Unlike Bradford and the Pilgrims, however, Winthrop was not a Separatist; that is, he wished to reform the national church from within, purging it of everything that harked back to Rome, especially the hierarchy of the clergy and all the traditional Catholic rituals. For a time Winthrop thought of becoming a clergyman himself, but instead he turned to the practice of law.

In the 1620s severe economic depression in England made Winthrop realize that he could not depend on the support of his father's estate. The ascension of Charles I to the throne—who was known to be sympathetic to Roman Catholicism and impatient with Puritan reformers—was also taken as an ominous sign for Puritans, and Winthrop was not alone in predicting that "God will bring some heavy affliction upon the land, and that speedily." Winthrop came to realize that he could not antagonize the king by expressing openly the Puritan cause without losing all that he possessed. The only recourse seemed to be to obtain the king's permission to emigrate. In March of 1629 a group of enterprising merchants, all sympathetic believers, were able to get a charter from the Council for New England for land in the New World. They called themselves "The Company of Massachusetts Bay in New England."

From four candidates, Winthrop was chosen governor in October 1629; for the next twenty years most of the responsibility for the colony rested in his hands. On April 8, 1630, an initial group of some seven hundred emigrants sailed from England. The ship carrying Winthrop was called the *Arbella*. Somewhere in the middle of the Atlantic Ocean Winthrop delivered his sermon *A Model of Christian Charity*. It set out clearly and eloquently the ideals of a harmonious Christian community and reminded all those on board that they would stand as an example to the world either of the triumph or else the failure of this Christian enterprise. When Cotton Mather wrote his history of New England some fifty years after Winthrop's death, he chose Winthrop as his model of the perfect earthly ruler. Although the actual history of the colony showed that Winthrop's ideal of a perfectly selfless community was impossible to realize in fact, Winthrop emerges from the story as a man of unquestioned integrity and deep humanity.

# A Model of Christian Charity[1]

## I

### A MODEL HEREOF

God Almighty in His most holy and wise providence, hath so disposed of the condition of mankind, as in all times some must be rich, some poor, some high and eminent in power and dignity; others mean and in subjection.

### THE REASON HEREOF

First, to hold conformity with the rest of His works, being delighted to show forth the glory of His wisdom in the variety and difference of the creatures; and the glory of His power, in ordering all these differences for the preservation and good of the whole; and the glory of His greatness, that as it is the glory of princes to have many officers, so this great King will have many stewards, counting Himself more honored in dispensing His gifts to man by man, than if He did it by His own immediate hands.

Secondly, that He might have the more occasion to manifest the work of His Spirit: first upon the wicked in moderating and restraining them, so that

---

1. The text is from Old South Leaflets, Old South Association, Old South Meetinghouse, Boston, Massachusetts, No. 207, edited by Samuel Eliot Morison. The original manuscript for Winthrop's sermon is lost, but a copy made during Winthrop's lifetime was published by the Massachusetts Historical Society in 1838.

the rich and mighty should not eat up the poor, nor the poor and despised rise up against their superiors and shake off their yoke; secondly in the regenerate, in exercising His graces, in them, as in the great ones, their love, mercy, gentleness, temperance, etc., in the poor and inferior sort, their faith, patience, obedience, etc.

Thirdly, that every man might have need of other, and from hence they might be all knit more nearly together in the bonds of brotherly affection. From hence it appears plainly that no man is made more honorable than another or more wealthy, etc., out of any particular and singular respect to himself, but for the glory of his Creator and the common good of the creature, man. Therefore God still reserves the property of these gifts to Himself as [in] Ezekiel: 16.17. He there calls wealth His gold and His silver.[2] [In] Proverbs: 3.9, he claims their service as His due: honor the Lord with thy riches, etc.[3] All men being thus (by divine providence) ranked into two sorts, rich and poor; under the first are comprehended all such as are able to live comfortably by their own means duly improved; and all others are poor according to the former distribution.

There are two rules whereby we are to walk one towards another: justice and mercy. These are always distinguished in their act and in their object, yet may they both concur in the same subject in each respect; as sometimes there may be an occasion of showing mercy to a rich man in some sudden danger of distress, and also doing of mere justice to a poor man in regard of some particular contract, etc.

There is likewise a double law by which we are regulated in our conversation one towards another in both the former respects: the law of nature and the law of grace, or the moral law or the law of the Gospel, to omit the rule of justice as not properly belonging to this purpose otherwise than it may fall into consideration in some particular cases. By the first of these laws man as he was enabled so withal [is] commanded to love his neighbor as himself.[4] Upon this ground stands all the precepts of the moral law, which concerns our dealings with men. To apply this to the works of mercy, this law requires two things: first, that every man afford his help to another in every want or distress; secondly, that he performed this out of the same affection which makes him careful of his own goods, according to that of our Savior. Matthew: "Whatsoever ye would that men should do to you."[5] This was practiced by Abraham and Lot in entertaining the Angels and the old man of Gibeah.[6]

The law of grace or the Gospel hath some difference from the former, as in these respects: First, the law of nature was given to man in the estate of innocency; this of the Gospel in the estate of regeneracy.[7] Secondly, the former

---

2. "Thou hast also taken that fair jewels of my gold and my silver, which I had given thee, and madest to thyself images of men, and didst commit whoredom with them."

3. "Honor the Lord with thy substance, and with the firstfruits of all thine increase: so shall thy barns be filled with plenty, and thy presses burst out with new wine" (Proverbs 3.9–10).

4. Matthew 5.43; 19.19.

5. "Therefore all things whatsoever ye would that men should do to you, do ye even so to them: for this is the law of the prophets" (Matthew 7.12).

6. Abraham entertains the angels in Genesis 18: "And the Lord appeared unto him in the plains of Mamre: and he sat in the tent door in the heat of the day; And

he lifted up his eyes and looked, and, lo, three men stood by him: and when he saw them, he ran to meet them" (Genesis 18.1–2). Lot was Abraham's nephew, and he escaped the destruction of the city of Sodom because he defended two angels who were his guests from a mob (Genesis 19.1–14). In Judges 19.16–21, an old citizen of Gibeah offered shelter to a traveling priest or Levite and defended him from enemies from a neighboring city.

7. Humanity lost its natural innocence when Adam and Eve fell; that state is called unregenerate. When Christ came to ransom humankind for Adam and Eve's sin, He offered salvation for those who believed in Him and became regenerate, or saved.

propounds one man to another, as the same flesh and image of God; this as a brother in Christ also, and in the communion of the same spirit and so teacheth us to put a difference between Christians and others. *Do good to all, especially to the household of faith:* Upon this ground the Israelites were to put a difference between the brethren of such as were strangers though not of Canaanites.[8] Thirdly, the law of nature could give no rules for dealing with enemies, for all are to be considered as friends in the state of innocency, but the Gospel commands love to an enemy. Proof. If thine Enemy hunger, feed him; Love your Enemies, do good to them that hate you. Matthew: 5.44.

This law of the Gospel propounds likewise a difference of seasons and occasions. There is a time when a Christian must sell all and give to the poor, as they did in the Apostles' times.[9] There is a time also when a Christian (though they give not all yet) must give beyond their ability, as they of Macedonia, Corinthians: 2.8.[1] Likewise community of perils calls for extraordinary liberality, and so doth community in some special service for the Church. Lastly, when there is no other means whereby our Christian brother may be relieved in his distress, we must help him beyond our ability, rather than tempt God in putting him upon help by miraculous or extraordinary means.

This duty of mercy is exercised in the kinds, *giving, lending* and *forgiving.—*

*Quest.* What rule shall a man observe in giving in respect of the measure?

*Ans.* If the time and occasion be ordinary, he is to give out of his abundance. Let him lay aside as God hath blessed him. If the time and occasion be extraordinary, he must be ruled by them; taking this withal, that then a man cannot likely do too much, especially if he may leave himself and his family under probable means of comfortable subsistence.

*Objection.* A man must lay up for posterity, the fathers lay up for posterity and children and he "is worse than an infidel" that "provideth not for his own."

*Ans.* For the first, it is plain that it being spoken by way of comparison, it must be meant of the ordinary and usual course of fathers and cannot extend to times and occasions extraordinary. For the other place, the Apostle speaks against such as walked inordinately, and it is without question, that he is worse than an infidel who through his own sloth and voluptuousness shall neglect to provide for his family.

*Objection.* "The wise man's eyes are in his head" saith Solomon, "and foreseeth the plague,"[2] therefore we must forecast and lay up against evil times when he or his may stand in need of all he can gather.

*Ans.* This very argument Solomon useth to persuade to liberality, Ecclesiastes: "Cast thy bread upon the waters," and "for thou knowest not what evil may come upon the land."[3] Luke: 16.9. "Make you friends of the riches of

8. One who lived in Canaan, the Land of Promise for the Israelites.

9. In Luke, Jesus tells a ruler who asks him what he must do to gain eternal life: "sell all that thou hast, and distribute unto the poor, and thou shalt have treasure in heaven: and come, follow me" (Luke 18.22).

1. "Moreover, brethren, we do you to wit of the grace of God bestowed on the churches of Macedonia; How that in a great trial of affliction, the abundance of their joy and their deep poverty abounded unto the riches of their liberality. For to their power, I bear record, yea, and beyond their power they were willing of themselves; Praying us with much entreaty that we would

receive the gift, and take upon us the fellowship of the ministering to the saints" (2 Corinthians 8.1–4).

2. Ecclesiastes 2.14. Solomon was the son of David and successor to David as king of all Israel.

3. "Cast thy bread upon the waters: for thou shalt find it after many days. Give a portion to seven, and also to eight; for thou knowest not what evil shall be upon the earth" (Ecclesiastes 11.1–2). Winthrop either makes his own translations from the Bible or uses the King James or Geneva versions; his quotations, therefore, differ occasionally from the King James version used in these notes.

iniquity."[4] You will ask how this shall be? very well. For first he that gives to
the poor, lends to the Lord and He will repay him even in this life an hundred
fold to him or his—The righteous is ever merciful and lendeth and his seed
enjoyeth the blessing; and besides we know what advantage it will be to us in
the day of account when many such witnesses shall stand forth for us to witness
the improvement of our talent.[5] And I would know of those who plead so
much for laying up for time to come, whether they hold that to be Gospel,
Matthew: 6.19: "Lay not up for yourselves treasures upon earth,"[6] etc. If they
acknowledge it, what extent will they allow it? if only to those primitive times,
let them consider the reason whereupon our Savior grounds it. The first is that
they are subject to the moth, the rust, the thief. Secondly, they will steal away
the heart; where the treasure is there will the heart be also. The reasons are of
like force at all times. Therefore the exhortation must be general and perpetual, with always in respect of the love and affection to riches and in regard of
the things themselves when any special service for the church or particular
distress of our brother do call for the use of them; otherwise it is not only lawful
but necessary to lay up as Joseph[7] did to have ready upon such occasions, as
the Lord (whose stewards we are of them) shall call for them from us. Christ
gives us an instance of the first, when he sent his disciples for the ass, and bids
them answer the owner thus, the Lord hath need of him.[8] So when the tabernacle was to be built he sends to His people to call for their silver and gold,
etc.; and yields them no other reason but that it was for His work. When
Elisha comes to the widow of Sareptah and finds her preparing to make ready
her pittance for herself and family, He bids her first provide for Him; he chal-
lengeth first God's part which she must first give before she must serve her
own family.[9] All these teach us that the Lord looks that when He is pleased to
call for His right in anything we have, our own interest we have must stand
aside till His turn be served. For the other, we need look no further than to
that of John: 1: "He who hath this world's goods and seeth his brother to need
and shuts up his compassion from him, how dwelleth the love of God in
him," which comes punctually to this conclusion: if thy brother be in want
and thou canst help him, thou needst not make doubt, what thou shouldst do,
if thou lovest God thou must help him.

    *Quest.* What rule must we observe in lending?

    *Ans.* Thou must observe whether thy brother hath present or probable, or
possible means of repaying thee, if there be none of these, thou must give him
according to his necessity, rather than lend him as he requires. If he hath
present means of repaying thee, thou art to look at him not as an act of mercy,
but by way of commerce, wherein thou art to walk by the rule of justice; but
if his means of repaying thee be only probable or possible, then is he an object
of thy mercy, thou must lend him, though there be danger of losing it, Deuteronomy: 15.7: "If any of thy brethren be poor," etc., "thou shalt lend him

---

4. The passage in Luke refers to the servant who, removed from his stewardship, resolves to be received in
the houses of his master's debtors and cuts their bills in
half. "And I say unto you, Make to yourselves friends
of the mammon of unrighteousness; that, when ye fail,
they may receive you into everlasting habitations"
(Luke 16.9).
5. Originally a measure of money.
6. "Lay not up for yourselves treasures upon earth,
where moth and rust doth corrupt, and where thieves

break through and steal: But lay up for yourselves treasures in heaven, where neither moth nor rust doth corrupt, and where thieves do not break through nor steal"
(Matthew 6.19–20).
7. Joseph, the son of Jacob and Rachel, stored up the
harvest in the seven good years before the famine (Genesis 41).
8. Matthew 21.5–7.
9. 1 Kings 17.8–24.

sufficient."[1] That men might not shift off this duty by the apparent hazard, He tells them that though the year of Jubilee[2] were at hand (when he must remit it, if he were not able to repay it before) yet he must lend him and that cheerfully: "It may not grieve thee to give him" saith He; and because some might object; "why so I should soon impoverish myself and my family," he adds "with all thy work,"[3] etc; for our Savior, Matthew: 5.42: "From him that would borrow of thee turn not away."

*Quest.* What rule must we observe in forgiving?

*Ans.* Whether thou didst lend by way of commerce or in mercy, if he have nothing to pay thee, [you] must forgive, (except in cause where thou hast a surety or a lawful pledge) Deuteronomy: 15.2. Every seventh year the creditor was to quit that which he lent to his brother if he were poor as appears—verse 8: "Save when there shall be no poor with thee." In all these and like cases, Christ was a general rule, Matthew: 7.22: "Whatsoever ye would that men should do to you, do ye the same to them also."

*Quest.* What rule must we observe and walk by in cause of community of peril?

*Ans.* The same as before, but with more enlargement towards others and less respect towards ourselves and our own right. Hence it was that in the primitive church they sold all, had all things in common, neither did any man say that which he possessed was his own. Likewise in their return out of the captivity, because the work was great for the restoring of the church and the danger of enemies was common to all, Nehemiah exhorts the Jews to liberality and readiness in remitting their debts to their brethren, and disposing liberally of his own to such as wanted, and stand not upon his own due, which he might have demanded of them.[4] Thus did some of our forefathers in times of persecution in England, and so did many of the faithful of other churches, whereof we keep an honorable remembrance of them; and it is to be observed that both in Scriptures and later stories of the churches that such as have been most bountiful to the poor saints, especially in these extraordinary times and occasions, God hath left them highly commended to posterity, as Zacheus, Cornelius, Dorcas, Bishop Hooper, the Cuttler of Brussells[5] and divers others. Observe again that the Scripture gives no caution to restrain any from being over liberal this way; but all men to the liberal and cheerful practice hereof by the sweetest promises; as to instance one for many, Isaiah: 58.6: "Is not this the fast I have chosen to loose the bonds of wickedness, to take off the heavy burdens, to let the oppressed go free and to break every yoke, to deal thy bread to the hungry and to bring the poor that wander into thy house, when thou seest the naked to cover them. And then shall thy light break forth as the morning, and thy health shall grow speedily, thy righteousness shall go before

---

1. "If there be among you a poor man of one of thy brethren within any of thy gates in thy land which the Lord thy God giveth thee, thou shalt not harden thine heart, nor shut thine hand from thy poor brother: But thou shalt open thine hand wide unto him, and shalt surely lend him sufficient for his need, in that which he wanteth" (Deuteronomy 15.7–8).

2. According to Mosaic law, every seventh year the lands would lie fallow, all work would cease, and all debts would be canceled. The Jubilee year concluded a cycle of seven sabbatical years.

3. "The seventh year, the year of release, is at hand; and thine eye be evil against thy poor brother, and thou

givest him nought; and he cry unto the Lord against thee, and it be sin unto thee. Thou shalt surely give him, and thine heart shall not be grieved when thou givest unto him: because that for this thing the Lord thy God shall bless thee in all thy works, and in all that thou puttest thine hand unto" (Deuteronomy 15.9–10).

4. Nehemiah was sent by King Artaxerxes to repair the walls of the city of Jerusalem; he saved the city as governor when he persuaded those lending money to charge no interest, and to think first of the common good (see Nehemiah 3).

5. Christian martyrs.

God, and the glory of the Lord shall embrace thee; then thou shalt call and the Lord shall answer thee" etc. [Verse] 10: "If thou pour out thy soul to the hungry, then shall thy light spring out in darkness, and the Lord shall guide thee continually, and satisfy thy soul in drought, and make fat thy bones; thou shalt be like a watered garden, and they shalt be of thee that shall build the old waste places" etc. On the contrary, most heavy curses are laid upon such as are straightened towards the Lord and His people, Judges: 5.[23]: "Curse ye Meroshe because ye came not to help the Lord," etc. Proverbs: [21.13]: "He who shutteth his ears from hearing the cry of the poor, he shall cry and shall not be heard." Matthew: 25: "Go ye cursed into everlasting fire" etc. "I was hungry and ye fed me not." 2 Corinthians: 9.6: "He that soweth sparingly shall reap sparingly."

Having already set forth the practice of mercy according to the rule of God's law, it will be useful to lay open the grounds of it also, being the other part of the commandment, and that is the affection from which this exercise of mercy must arise. The apostle[6] tells us that this love is the fulfilling of the law, not that it is enough to love our brother and so no further; but in regard of the excellency of his parts giving any motion to the other as the soul to the body and the power it hath to set all the faculties on work in the outward exercise of this duty. As when we bid one make the clock strike, he doth not lay hand on the hammer, which is the immediate instrument of the sound, but sets on work the first mover or main wheel, knowing that will certainly produce the sound which he intends. So the way to draw men to works of mercy, is not by force of argument from the goodness or necessity of the work; for though this course may enforce a rational mind to some present act of mercy, as is frequent in experience, yet it cannot work such a habit in a soul, as shall make it prompt upon all occasions to produce the same effect, but by framing these affections of love in the heart which will as natively bring forth the other, as any cause doth produce effect.

The definition which the Scripture gives us of love is this: "Love is the bond of perfection." First, it is a bond or ligament. Secondly it makes the work perfect. There is no body but consists of parts and that which knits these parts together gives the body its perfection, because it makes each part so contiguous to others as thereby they do mutually participate with each other, both in strength and infirmity, in pleasure and pain. To instance in the most perfect of all bodies: Christ and His church make one body. The several parts of this body, considered apart before they were united, were as disproportionate and as much disordering as so many contrary qualities or elements, but when Christ comes and by His spirit and love knits all these parts to Himself and each to other, it is become the most perfect and best proportioned body in the world. Ephesians: 4.16: "Christ, by whom all the body being knit together by every joint for the furniture thereof, according to the effectual power which is the measure of every perfection of parts," "a glorious body without spot or wrinkle," the ligaments hereof being Christ, or His love, for Christ is love (1 John: 4.8). So this definition is right: "Love is the bond of perfection."

From hence we may frame these conclusions. 1. First of all, true Christians are of one body in Christ, 1 Corinthians: 12.12, 27: "Ye are the body of Christ and members of their part." Secondly: The ligaments of this body which knit

---

6. St. Paul in his Epistle to the Romans 9.31.

together are love. Thirdly: No body can be perfect which wants its proper ligament. Fourthly. All the parts of this body being thus united are made so contiguous in a special relation as they must needs partake of each other's strength and infirmity; joy and sorrow, weal and woe. 1 Corinthians: 12.26: "If one member suffers, all suffer with it, if one be in honor, all rejoice with it." Fifthly. This sensibleness and sympathy of each other's conditions will necessarily infuse into each part a native desire and endeavor to strengthen, defend, preserve and comfort the other.

To insist a little on this conclusion being the product of all the former, the truth hereof will appear both by precept and pattern. 1 John: 3.10: "Ye ought to lay down your lives for the brethren." Galatians: 6.2: "bear ye one another's burthens and so fulfill the law of Christ." For patterns we have that first of our Savior who out of His good will in obedience to His father, becoming a part of this body, and being knit with it in the bond of love, found such a native sensibleness of our infirmities and sorrows as He willingly yielded Himself to death to ease the infirmities of the rest of His body, and so healed their sorrows. From the like sympathy of parts did the apostles and many thousands of the saints lay down their lives for Christ. Again, the like we may see in the members of this body among themselves. Romans: 9. Paul could have been contented to have been separated from Christ, that the Jews might not be cut off from the body. It is very observable what he professeth of his affectionate partaking with every member: "who is weak" saith he "and I am not weak? who is offended and I burn not;"[7] and again, 2 Corinthians: 7.13. "therefore we are comforted because ye were comforted." Of Epaphroditus[8] he speaketh, Philippians: 2.30. that he regarded not his own life to do him service. So Phoebe[9] and others are called the servants of the church. Now it is apparent that they served not for wages, or by constraint, but out of love. The like we shall find in the histories of the church in all ages, the sweet sympathy of affections which was in the members of this body one towards another, their cheerfulness in serving and suffering together, how liberal they were without repining, harborers without grudging and helpful without reproaching; and all from hence, because they had fervent love amongst them, which only make the practice of mercy constant and easy.

The next consideration is how this love comes to be wrought. Adam in his first estate[1] was a perfect model of mankind in all their generations, and in him this love was perfected in regard of the habit. But Adam rent himself from his creator, rent all his posterity also one from another; whence it comes that every man is born with this principle in him, to love and seek himself only, and thus a man continueth till Christ comes and takes possession of the soul and infuseth another principle, love to God and our brother. And this latter having continual supply from Christ, as the head and root by which he is united, gets the predomining in the soul, so by little and little expels the former. 1 John: 4.7. "love cometh of God and every one that loveth is borne of God," so that this love is the fruit of the new birth, and none can have it but the new creature. Now when this quality is thus formed in the souls of men,

---

7. 2 Corinthians 11.29.
8. St. Paul tells the Philippians that he will send to them as a spiritual guide "Epaphroditus, my brother and companion in labor, and fellow soldier, but your messenger, and he that ministered to my wants" (Phil-

ippians 2.25).
9. A Christian woman praised by St. Paul in Romans 16.1.
1. I.e., in his innocence.

it works like the spirit upon the dry bones. Ezekiel: 37: "bone came to bone." It gathers together the scattered bones, of perfect old man Adam, and knits them into one body again in Christ, whereby a man is become again a living soul.

The third consideration is concerning the exercise of this love which is twofold, inward or outward. The outward hath been handled in the former preface of this discourse. For unfolding the other we must take in our way that maxim of philosophy *simile simili gaudet*, or like will to like; for as it is things which are turned with disaffection to each other, the ground of it is from a dissimilitude arising from the contrary or different nature of the things themselves; for the ground of love is an apprehension of some resemblance in things loved to that which affects it. This is the cause why the Lord loves the creature, so far as it hath any of His image in it; He loves His elect because they are like Himself, He beholds them in His beloved son. So a mother loves her child, because she thoroughly conceives a resemblance of herself in it. Thus it is between the members of Christ. Each discerns, by the work of the spirit, his own image and resemblance in another, and therefore cannot but love him as he loves himself. Now when the soul, which is of a sociable nature, finds anything like to itself, it is like Adam when Eve was brought to him. She must have it one with herself. This is flesh of my flesh (saith the soul) and bone of my bone. She conceives a great delight in it, therefore she desires nearness and familiarity with it. She hath a great propensity to do it good and receives such content in it, as fearing the miscarriage of her beloved she bestows it in the inmost closet of her heart. She will not endure that it shall want any good which she can give it. If by occasion she be withdrawn from the company of it, she is still looking towards the place where she left her beloved. If she heard it groan, she is with it presently. If she find it sad and disconsolate, she sighs and moans with it. She hath no such joy as to see her beloved merry and thriving. If she see it wronged, she cannot bear it without passion. She sets no bounds to her affections, nor hath any thought of reward. She finds recompense enough in the exercise of her love towards it. We may see this acted to life in Jonathan and David.[2] Jonathan a valiant man endowed with the spirit of Christ, so soon as he discovers the same spirit in David had presently his heart knit to him by this lineament of love so that it is said he loved him as his own soul. He takes so great pleasure in him, that he strips himself to adorn his beloved. His father's kingdom was not so precious to him as his beloved David. David shall have it with all his heart, himself desires no more but that he may be near to him to rejoice in his good. He chooseth to converse with him in the wilderness even to the hazard of his own life, rather than with the great courtiers in his father's palace. When he sees danger towards him, he spares neither rare pains nor peril to direct it. When injury was offered his beloved David, he would not bear it, though from his own father; and when they must part for a season only, they thought their hearts would have broke for sorrow, had not their affections found vent by abundance of tears. Other instances might be brought to show the nature of this affection, as of Ruth and Naomi,[3] and many others; but this truth is cleared enough.

If any shall object that it is not possible that love should be bred or upheld without hope of requital, it is granted; but that is not our cause; for this love is

---

2. The story of David and Jonathan is told in 1 Samuel 19ff.
3. Naomi was the mother-in-law of Ruth, whom Ruth refused to leave when her husband died, telling her, "For whither thou goest, I will go; and where thou lodgest, I will lodge" (Ruth 1.16).

always under reward. It never gives, but it always receives with advantage; first, in regard that among the members of the same body, love and affection are reciprocal in a most equal and sweet kind of commerce. Secondly, in regard of the pleasure and content that the exercise of love carries with it, as we may see in the natural body. The mouth is at all the pains to receive and mince the food which serves for the nourishment of all the other parts of the body, yet it hath no cause to complain; for first the other parts send back by several passages a due proportion of the same nourishment, in a better form for the strengthening and comforting the mouth. Secondly, the labor of the mouth is accompanied with such pleasure and content as far exceeds the pains it takes. So is it in all the labor of love among Christians. The party loving, reaps love again, as was showed before, which the soul covets more than all the wealth in the world. Thirdly: Nothing yields more pleasure and content to the soul than when it finds that which it may love fervently, for to love and live beloved is the soul's paradise, both here and in heaven. In the state of wedlock there be many comforts to bear out the troubles of that condition; but let such as have tried the most, say if there be any sweetness in that condition comparable to the exercise of mutual love.

From former considerations arise these conclusions.

First: This love among Christians is a real thing, not imaginary.

Secondly: This love is as absolutely necessary to the being of the body of Christ, as the sinews and other ligaments of a natural body are to the being of that body.

Thirdly: This love is a divine, spiritual nature free, active, strong, courageous, permanent; undervaluing all things beneath its proper object; and of all the graces, this makes us nearer to resemble the virtues of our Heavenly Father.

Fourthly: It rests in the love and welfare of its beloved. For the full and certain knowledge of these truths concerning the nature, use, and excellency of this grace, that which the Holy Ghost hath left recorded, 1 Corinthians: 13, may give full satisfaction, which is needful for every true member of this lovely body of the Lord Jesus, to work upon their hearts by prayer, meditation, continual exercise at least of the special [influence] of His grace, till Christ be formed in them and they in Him, all in each other, knit together by this bond of love.

## II

It rests now to make some application of this discourse by the present design, which gave the occasion of writing of it. Herein are four things to be propounded: first the persons, secondly the work, thirdly the end, fourthly the means.

First, For the persons. We are a company professing ourselves fellow members of Christ, in which respect only though we were absent from each other many miles, and had our employments as far distant, yet we ought to account ourselves knit together by this bond of love, and live in the exercise of it, if we would have comfort of our being in Christ. This was notorious in the practice of the Christians in former times; as is testified of the Waldenses,[4] from the

4. The Waldenses took their name from Pater Valdes, an early French reformer of the church. They still survive as a religious community.

mouth of one of the adversaries *Æneas Sylvius*[5] "mutuo [ament] penè ante-
quam norunt," they used to love any of their own religion even before they
were acquainted with them.

Secondly, for the work we have in hand. It is by a mutual consent, through
a special overvaluing providence and a more than an ordinary approbation of
the Churches of Christ, to seek out a place of cohabitation and consortship
under a due form of government both civil and ecclesiastical. In such cases as
this, the care of the public must oversway all private respects, by which, not
only conscience, but mere civil policy, doth bind us. For it is a true rule that
particular estates cannot subsist in the ruin of the public.

Thirdly. The end is to improve our lives to do more service to the Lord; the
comfort and increase of the body of Christ whereof we are members; that
ourselves and posterity may be the better preserved from the common corruptions of this evil world, to serve the Lord and work out our salvation under the
power and purity of His holy ordinances.

Fourthly, for the means whereby this must be effected. They are twofold, a
conformity with the work and end we aim at. These we see are extraordinary,
therefore we must not content ourselves with usual ordinary means. Whatsoever we did or ought to have done when we lived in England, the same must
we do, and more also, where we go. That which the most in their churches
maintain as a truth in profession only, we must bring into familiar and constant practice, as in this duty of love. We must love brotherly without dissimulation; we must love one another with a pure heart fervently. We must bear
one another's burthens. We must not look only on our own things, but also
on the things of our brethren, neither must we think that the Lord will bear
with such failings at our hands as he doth from those among whom we have
lived; and that for three reasons.

First, In regard of the more near bond of marriage between Him and us,
where-in He hath taken us to be His after a most strict and peculiar manner,
which will make Him the more jealous of our love and obedience. So He tells
the people of Israel, you only have I known of all the families of the earth,
therefore will I punish you for your transgressions. Secondly, because the Lord
will be sanctified in them that come near Him. We know that there were
many that corrupted the service of the Lord, some setting up altars before His
own, others offering both strange fire and strange sacrifices also; yet there came
no fire from heaven or other sudden judgment upon them, as did upon Nadab
and Abihu,[6] who yet we may think did not sin presumptuously. Thirdly.
When God gives a special commission He looks to have it strictly observed in
every article. When He gave Saul a commission to destroy Amaleck, He
indented with him upon certain articles,[7] and because he failed in one of the
least, and that upon a fair pretense, it lost him the kingdom which should
have been his reward if he had observed his commission.

---

5. Aeneas Sylvius Piccolomini (1405–1464), Pope
Pius II, was a historian and scholar. *Solent amare* is a
closer approximation of the Latin than Morison's suggestion of *ament*.
6. "And Nadab and Abihu, the sons of Aaron, took
either of them his censer, and put fire therein, and put
incense thereon, and offered strange fire before the
Lord, which he commanded them not. And there went
out fire from the Lord, and devoured them, and they

died before the Lord" (Leviticus 10.1–2). Winthrop's
point is that the chosen people are often punished more
severly than unbelievers.
7. I.e., made an agreement with him on parts of a
contract or agreement. Saul was instructed to destroy
the Amalekites and all that they possessed, but he
spared their sheep and oxen, and in doing so disobeyed
the Lord's commandment and was rejected as king (1
Samuel 15.1–34).

Thus stands the cause between God and us. We are entered into covenant[8] with Him for this work. We have taken out a commission, the Lord hath given us leave to draw our own articles. We have professed to enterprise these actions, upon these and those ends, we have hereupon besought Him of favor and blessing. Now if the Lord shall please to hear us, and bring us in peace to the place we desire, then hath He ratified this covenant and sealed our commission, [and] will expect a strict performance of the articles contained in it; but if we shall neglect the observation of these articles which are the ends we have propounded, and, dissembling with our God, shall fall to embrace this present world and prosecute our carnal intentions, seeking great things for ourselves and our posterity, the Lord will surely break out in wrath against us; be revenged of such a perjured people and make us know the price of the breach of such a covenant.

Now the only way to avoid this shipwreck, and to provide for our posterity, is to follow the counsel of Micah,[9] to do justly, to love mercy, to walk humbly with our God. For this end, we must be knit together in this work as one man. We must entertain each other in brotherly affection, we must be willing to abridge ourselves of our superfluities, for the supply of other's necessities. We must uphold a familiar commerce together in all meekness, gentleness, patience and liberality. We must delight in each other, make other's conditions our own, rejoice together, mourn together, labor and suffer together, always having before our eyes our commission and community in the work, our community as members of the same body. So shall we keep the unity of the spirit in the bond of peace. The Lord will be our God, and delight to dwell among us as His own people, and will command a blessing upon us in all our ways, so that we shall see much more of His wisdom, power, goodness and truth, than formerly we have been acquainted with. We shall find that the God of Israel is among us, when ten of us shall be able to resist a thousand of our enemies; when He shall make us a praise and glory that men shall say of succeeding plantations, "the Lord make it like that of NEW ENGLAND." For we must consider that we shall be as a city upon a hill.[1] The eyes of all people are upon us, so that if we shall deal falsely with our God in this work we have undertaken, and so cause Him to withdraw His present help from us, we shall be made a story and a by-word through the world. We shall open the mouths of enemies to speak evil of the ways of God, and all professors for God's sake. We shall shame the faces of many of God's worthy servants, and cause their prayers to be turned into curses upon us till we be consumed out of the good land whither we are agoing.

And to shut up this discourse with that exhortation of Moses, that faithful servant of the Lord, in his last farewell to Israel, Deuteronomy 30.[2] Beloved, there is now set before us life and good, death and evil, in that we are com-

8. A legal contract; the Israelites entered into a covenant with God in which He promised to protect them if they kept His word and were faithful to Him.

9. The Book of Micah preserves the words of this 8th-century-B.C. prophet. Micah speaks continually of the judgment of God on His people and the necessity to hope for salvation: "I will bear the indignation of the Lord, because I have sinned against him, until he plead my cause, and execute judgment for me: he will bring me forth to the light, and I shall behold his righteousness" (Micah 7.9).

1. "Ye are the light of the world. A city that is set on a hill cannot be hid. Neither do men light a candle, and put it under a bushel, but on a candlestick; and it giveth light unto all that are in the house" (Matthew 5.14–15).

2. "And it shall come to pass, when all these things are come upon thee, the blessing and the curse, which I have set before thee, and thou shalt call them to mind among all the nations, whither the Lord thy God hath driven thee, And shalt return unto the Lord thy God, and shalt obey his voice according to all that I command thee this day, thou and thy children, with all thine heart, and with all thy soul; That then the Lord

manded this day to love the Lord our God, and to love one another, to walk in His ways and to keep His commandments and His ordinance and His laws, and the articles of our covenant with Him, that we may live and be multiplied, and that our Lord our God may bless us in the land whither we go to possess it. But if our hearts shall turn away, so that we will not obey, but shall be seduced, and worship other gods, our pleasures and profits, and serve them; it is propounded unto us this day, we shall surely perish out of the good land whither we pass over this vast sea to possess it.

> Therefore let us choose life,
> that we and our seed
> may live by obeying His
> voice and cleaving to Him,
> for He is our life and
> our prosperity.

1630                                                                        1838

## *From* The Journal of John Winthrop[1]

[June 8, 1630] The wind still W. and by S., fair weather, but close and cold. We stood N. N. W. with a stiff gale, and, about three in the afternoon, we had sight of land to the N. W. about ten leagues, which we supposed was the Isles of Monhegan, but it proved Mount Mansell.[2] Then we tacked and stood W. S. W. We had now fair sunshine weather, and so pleasant a sweet air as did much refresh us, and there came a smell off the shore like the smell of a garden.

There came a wild pigeon into our ship, and another small land bird.

[July 5, 1632] At Watertown there was (in view of divers witnesses) a great combat between a mouse and a snake; and, after a long fight, the mouse prevailed and killed the snake. The pastor of Boston, Mr. Wilson, a very sincere, holy man, hearing of it, gave this interpretation: That the snake was the devil; the mouse was a poor contemptible people, which God had brought hither, which should overcome Satan here, and dispossess him of his kingdom. Upon the same occasion, he told the governor,[3] that, before he was resolved to come into this country, he dreamed he was here, and that he saw a church arise out of the earth, which grew up and became a marvelous goodly church.

[December 27, 1633] The governor and assistants met at Boston, and took into consideration a treatise, which Mr. Williams[4] (then of Salem) had sent to them, and which he had formerly written to the governor and council of Plymouth, wherein, among other things, he disputes their right to the lands they possessed here, and concluded that, claiming by the king's grant, they could have no title, nor otherwise, except they compounded[5] with the natives. For

thy God will turn thy captivity, and have compassion upon thee, and will return and gather thee from all the nations, whither the Lord thy God hath scattered thee" (Deuteronomy 30.1–3).

1. The text used here is from *Winthrop's Journal: History of New England 1630–1649*, edited by James Kendall Hosmer (1908).

2. What Winthrop saw was Mount Desert, Maine,

named by the French explorer Champlain in 1604.

3. I.e., Winthrop himself.

4. Roger Williams (c.1603–1683), who had emigrated to New England in 1630 and refused a call to the First Church of Boston because he would not preach to "an unseparated people."

5. Arranged to purchase.

this, taking advice with some of the most judicious ministers, (who much condemned Mr. Williams's error and presumption,) they gave order, that he should be convented[6] at the next court, to be censured, etc. There were three passages chiefly whereat they were much offended: 1, for that he chargeth King James to have told a solemn public lie, because in his patent he blessed God that he was the first Christian prince that had discovered this land; 2, for that he chargeth him and others with blasphemy for calling Europe Christendom, or the Christian world; 3, for that he did personally apply to our present king, Charles, these three places in the Revelations,[7] viz., [blank].

Mr. Endicott being absent, the governor wrote to him and let him know what was done, and withal added divers arguments to confute the said errors, wishing him to deal with Mr. Williams to retract the same, etc. Whereto he returned a very modest and discreet answer. Mr. Williams also wrote to the governor,[8] and also to him and the rest of the council, very submissively, professing his intent to have been only to have written for the private satisfaction of the governor, etc., of Plymouth, without any purpose to have stirred any further in it, if the governor here had not required a copy of him; withal offering his book, or any part of it, to be burnt.

At the next court he appeared penitently, and gave satisfaction of his intention and loyalty. So it was left, and nothing done in it.

[January 20, 1634] Hall and the two others,[9] who went to Connecticut November 3, came now home, having lost themselves and endured much misery. They informed us that the small pox was gone as far as any Indian plantation was known to the west, and much people dead of it, by reason whereof they could have no trade.

At Naragansett, by the Indians' report, there died seven hundred; but, beyond Pascataquack, none to the eastward.

[January 24, 1634] The governor and council met again at Boston, to consider of Mr. Williams's letter, etc., when, with the advice of Mr. Cotton[1] and Mr. Wilson, and weighing his letter, and further considering of the aforesaid offensive passages in his book,[2] (which, being written in very obscure and implicative phrases, might well admit of doubtful interpretation,) they found the matters not to be so evil as at first they seemed. Whereupon they agreed, that, upon his retractation, etc., or taking an oath of allegiance to the king, etc., it should be passed over.

[January 11, 1636] The governor[3] and assistants met at Boston to consider about Mr. Williams, for that they were credibly informed, that, notwithstanding the injunction laid upon him (upon the liberty granted him to stay till the spring) not to go about to draw others to his opinions, he did use to entertain company in his house, and to preach to them, even of such points as he had been censured for; and it was agreed to send him into England by a ship then ready to depart. The reason was, because he had drawn above twenty persons to his opinion, and they were intended to erect a plantation about the Nara-

---

6. Summoned to appear.
7. I.e., the Book of Revelation. Winthrop never added the citations.
8. In 1633 Edward Winslow was governor.
9. Not further identified.
1. John Cotton (1584–1652) emigrated to Boston in 1633 and from that time until his death was a major figure in the hierarchy of the town. He was pastor of the First Church of Boston.
2. Winthrop is referring to a now-lost Williams manuscript or treatise, mentioned in the entry for December 27, 1633, rather than a published book.
3. John Hays (1594–1654). Winthrop was reelected governor in 1637.

gansett Bay,[4] from whence the infection would easily spread into these churches, (the people being, many of them, much taken with the apprehension of his godliness). Whereupon a warrant was sent to him to come presently to Boston, to be shipped,[5] etc. He returned answer, (and divers of Salem came with it,) that he could not come without hazard of his life, etc. Whereupon a pinnace[6] was sent with commission to Capt. Underhill, etc., to apprehend him, and carry him aboard the ship, (which then rode at Natascutt;) but, when they came at his house, they found he had been gone three days before; but whither they could not learn.

He had so far prevailed at Salem, as many there (especially of devout women) did embrace his opinions, and separated from the churches, for this cause, that some of their members, going into England, did hear the ministers there, and when they came home the churches here held [to be in] communion with them.

[October 21, 1636] One Mrs. Hutchinson,[7] a member of the church of Boston, a woman of a ready wit and bold spirit, brought over with her two dangerous errors: 1. That the person of the Holy Ghost dwells in a justified[8] person. 2. That no sanctification can help to evidence to us our justification.[9]—From these two grew many branches; as, 1. Our union with the Holy Ghost, so as a Christian remains dead to every spiritual action, and hath no gifts nor graces, other than such as are in hypocrites, nor any other sanctification but the Holy Ghost himself.

There joined with her in these opinions a brother of hers, one Mr. Wheelwright, a silenced[1] minister sometimes in England.

[October 25, 1636] The other ministers in the bay, hearing of these things, came to Boston at the time of a general court, and entered conference in private with them, to the end they might know the certainty of these things; that if need were, they might write to the church of Boston about them, to prevent (if it were possible) the dangers, which seemed hereby to hang over that and the rest of the churches. At this conference, Mr. Cotton was present, and gave satisfaction to them, so as he agreed with them all in the point of sanctification, and so did Mr. Wheelwright; so as they all did hold, that sanctification did help to evidence justification. The same he had delivered plainly in public, divers times; but, for the indwelling of the person of the Holy Ghost, he held that still, as some others of the ministers did, but not union with the person of the Holy Ghost, (as Mrs. Hutchinson and others did,) so as to amount to a personal union.

[November 1, 1637] There was great hope that the late general assembly would have had some good effect in pacifying the troubles and dissensions about matters of religion; but it fell out otherwise. For though Mr. Wheelwright and those of his party had been clearly confuted and confounded in the assembly, yet they persisted in their opinions, and were as busy in nourishing contentions (the principal of them) as before. * * *

4. Providence Plantation in Rhode Island received its patent in 1644.
5. I.e., returned to Boston by ship.
6. A small, light vessel, usually with two masts.
7. Anne Hutchinson (1591–1643), originally a follower of John Cotton, soon pursued an extreme position in which she argued that the elect were joined in personal union with God and superior to those lacking Inner Light. She also denied that good works were in any way a sign of God's favor, arguing that justification was by faith alone and had nothing to do with either piety or worldly success.
8. I.e., one elected or chosen for salvation by God.
9. I.e., that proper moral conduct is no sign of justification.
1. Mr. Wheelwright had probably refused to take an oath of loyalty to the Church of England.

The court also sent Mrs. Hutchinson, and charged her with divers matters, as her keeping two public lectures every week in her house, whereto sixty or eighty persons did usually resort, and for reproaching most of the ministers (viz., all except Mr. Cotton) for not preaching a covenant of free grace, and that they had not the seal of the spirit, nor were able ministers of the New Testament; which were clearly proved against her, though she sought to shift it off.[2] And, after many speeches to and fro, at last she was so full as she could not contain, but vented her revelations; amongst which this was one, that she had it revealed to her, that she should come into New England, and should here be persecuted, and that God would ruin us and our posterity, and the whole state, for the same. So the court proceeded and banished her; but, because it was winter, they committed her to a private house, where she was well provided, and her own friends and the elders permitted to go to her, but none else.

The court called also Capt. Underhill, and some five or six more of the principal, whose hands were to the said petition; and because they stood to justify it, they were disfranchised, and such as had public places were put from them.

The court also ordered, that the rest, who had subscribed the petition, (and would not acknowledge their fault, and which near twenty of them did,) and some others, who had been chief stirrers in these contentions, etc., should be disarmed. This troubled some of them very much, especially because they were to bring them in themselves; but at last, when they saw no remedy, they obeyed.[3]

All the proceedings of this court against these persons were set down at large, with the reasons and other observations, and were sent into England to be published there, to the end that all our godly friends might not be discouraged from coming to us, etc.

[March 1638] While Mrs. Hutchinson continued at Roxbury,[4] divers of the elders and others resorted to her, and finding her to persist in maintaining those gross errors beforementioned, and many others, to the number of thirty or thereabout, some of them wrote to the church at Boston, offering to make proof of the same before the church, etc., 15; whereupon she was called, (the magistrates being desired to give her license to come,) and the lecture was appointed to begin at ten. (The general court being then at Newtown, the governor[5] and the treasurer, being members of Boston, were permitted to come down, but the rest of the court continued at Newtown.) When she appeared, the errors were read to her. The first was, that the souls of men are mortal by generation,[6] but, after, made immortal by Christ's purchase. This she maintained a long time; but at length she was so clearly convinced by reason and scripture, and the whole church agreeing that sufficient had been delivered for her conviction, that she yielded she had been in an error. Then they proceeded to three other errors: 1. That there was no resurrection of these bodies, and that these bodies were not united to Christ, but every person united hath a new body, etc. These were also clearly confuted, but yet she held her own; so as the church (all but two of her sons) agreed she should be

---

2. I.e., to qualify her statements.
3. They were also forbidden to borrow to buy guns until "the court shall take further order therein."
4. Near Boston.

5. Winthrop himself.
6. I.e., from the beginning. Orthodox believers hold the soul immortal.

admonished, and because her sons would not agree to it, they were admonished also.

Mr. Cotton pronounced the sentence of admonition with great solemnity, and with much zeal and detestation of her errors and pride of spirit. The assembly continued till eight at night, and all did acknowledge the special presence of God's spirit therein; and she was appointed to appear again the next lecture day.

[March 22, 1638] Mrs. Hutchinson appeared again; (she had been licensed by the court, in regard she had given hope of her repentance, to be at Mr. Cotton's house, that both he and Mr. Davenport[7] might have the more opportunity to deal with her;) and the articles being again read to her, and her answer required, she delivered it in writing wherein she made a retractation of near all, but with such explanations and circumstances as gave no satisfaction to the church; so as she was required to speak further to them. Then she declared, that it was just with God to leave her to herself, as He had done, for her slighting His ordinances, both magistracy and ministry;[8] and confessed that what she had spoken against the magistrates at the court (by way of revelation) was rash and ungrounded; and desired the church to pray for her. This gave the church good hope of her repentance; but when she was examined about some particulars, as that she had denied inherent righteousness, etc., she affirmed that it was never her judgment; and though it was proved by many testimonies, that she had been of that judgment, and so had persisted, and maintained it by argument against divers, yet she impudently persisted in her affirmation, to the astonishment of all the assembly. So that, after much time and many arguments had been spent to bring her to see her sin, but all in vain, the church, with one consent, cast her out. Some moved to have her admonished[9] once more; but, it being for manifest evil in matter of conversation, it was agreed otherwise; and for that reason also the sentence was denounced[1] by the pastor, matter of manners belonging properly to his place.

After she was excommunicated,[2] her spirits, which seemed before to be somewhat dejected, revived again, and she gloried in her sufferings, saying, that it was the greatest happiness, next to Christ, that ever befell her. Indeed, it was a happy day to the churches of Christ here, and to many poor souls, who had been seduced by her, who, by what they heard and saw that day, were (through the grace of God) brought off quite from her errors, and settled again in the truth.

\* \* \*

After two or three days, the governor sent a warrant to Mrs. Hutchinson to depart this jurisdiction before the last of this month, according to the order of court, and for that end set her at liberty from her former constraint, so as she was not to go forth of her own house till her departure; and upon the 28th she went by water to her farm at the Mount, where she was to take water, with Mr. Wheelwright's wife and family, to go to Pascataquack; but she changed her mind, and went by land to Providence, and so to the island in the Narragansett Bay, which her husband and the rest of that sect had purchased of the Indians. \* \* \*

---

7. John Davenport (1597–1670), a Puritan minister.
8. Because her unorthodox beliefs threatened both civil and ecclesiastical law.
9. Warned.

1. Publicly condemned.
2. Excluded, banished; not to be confused with the rite of excommunication performed by the Roman Catholic Church.

[September 1638] . . . Mrs. Hutchinson, being removed to the Isle of Aquiday, in the Naragansett Bay, after her time was fulfilled, that she expected deliverance of a child, was delivered of a monstrous birth, which, being diversely related in the country, (and, in the open assembly at Boston, upon a lecture day, [was] declared by Mr. Cotton to be twenty-seven several lumps of man's seed, without any alteration or mixture of anything from the woman, and thereupon gathered that it might signify her error in denying inherent righteousness, but that all was Christ in us, and nothing of ours in our faith, love, etc.). Hereupon the governor wrote to Mr. Clarke, a physician and a preacher to those of the island, to know the certainty thereof.

\* \* \*

[July 3, 1645] \* \* \* Then was the deputy governor[3] desired by the court to go up and take his place again upon the bench, which he did accordingly, and the court being about to arise, he desired leave for a little speech, which was to this effect.

I suppose something may be expected from me, upon this charge that is befallen me, which moves me to speak now to you; yet I intend not to intermeddle in the proceedings of the court, or with any of the persons concerned therein. Only I bless God, that I see an issue of this troublesome business. I also acknowledge the justice of the court, and, for mine own part, I am well satisfied, I was publicly charged, and I am publicly and legally acquitted, which is all I did expect or desire. And though this be sufficient for my justification before men, yet not so before the God, who hath seen so much amiss in my dispensations (and even in this affair) as calls me to be humble. For to be publicly and criminally charged in this court, is matter of humiliation, (and I desire to make a right use of it,) notwithstanding I be thus acquitted. If her father had spit in her face, (saith the Lord concerning Miriam,) should she not have been ashamed seven days?[4] Shame had lien upon her, whatever the occasion had been. I am unwilling to stay you from your urgent affairs, yet give me leave (upon this special occasion) to speak a little more to this assembly. It may be of some good use, to inform and rectify the judgments of some of the people, and may prevent such distempers as have arisen amongst us. The great questions that have troubled the country, are about the authority of the magistrates and the liberty of the people. It is yourselves who have called us to this office, and being called by you, we have our authority from God, in way of an ordinance, such as hath the image of God eminently stamped upon it, the contempt and violation whereof hath been vindicated with examples of divine vengeance. I entreat you to consider, that when you choose magistrates, you take them from among yourselves, men subject to like passions as you are. Therefore when you see infirmities in us, you should reflect upon your own, and that would make you bear the more with us, and not be severe censurers of the failings of your magistrates, when you have continual experience of the like infirmities in yourselves and others. We account him a good servant, who breaks not his covenant. The covenant between you and us is the oath you have

3. Winthrop. The governor in 1645 was Thomas Dudley (1576–1654).
4. The sister of Moses and Aaron. "And the Lord said unto Moses, If her father had but spit in her face, should she not be ashamed seven days? let her be shut out from the camp seven days, and after that let her be received in again" (Numbers 12.14).

taken of us, which is to this purpose, that we shall govern you and judge your causes by the rules of God's laws and our own, according to our best skill. When you agree with a workman to build you a ship or house, etc., he undertakes as well for his skill as for his faithfulness, for it is his profession, and you pay him for both. But when you call one to be a magistrate, he doth not profess nor undertake to have sufficient skill for that office, nor can you furnish him with gifts, etc., therefore you must run the hazard of his skill and ability. But if he fail in faithfulness, which by his oath he is bound unto, that he must answer for. If it fall out that the case be clear to common apprehension, and the rule clear also, if he transgress here, the error is not in the skill, but in the evil of the will: it must be required of him. But if the case be doubtful, or the rule doubtful, to men of such understanding and parts as your magistrates are, if your magistrates should err here, yourselves must bear it.

For the other point concerning liberty, I observe a great mistake in the country about that. There is a twofold liberty, natural (I mean as our nature is now corrupt)[5] and civil or federal. The first is common to man with beasts and other creatures. By this, man, as he stands in relation to man simply, hath liberty to do what he lists; it is a liberty to evil as well as to good. This liberty is incompatible and inconsistent with authority, and cannot endure the least restraint of the most just authority. The exercise and maintaining of this liberty makes men grow more evil, and in time to be worse than brute beasts: *omnes sumus licentia deteriores.*[6] This is that great enemy of truth and peace, that wild beast, which all the ordinances of God are bent against, to restrain and subdue it. The other kind of liberty I call civil or federal, it may also be termed moral, in reference to the covenant between God and man, in the moral law, and the politic covenants and constitutions, amongst men themselves. This liberty is the proper end and object of authority, and cannot subsist without it; and it is a liberty to that only which is good, just, and honest. This liberty you are to stand for, with the hazard (not only of your goods, but) of your lives, if need be. Whatsoever crosseth this, is not authority, but a distemper thereof. This liberty is maintained and exercised in a way of subjection to authority; it is of the same kind of liberty wherewith Christ hath made us free. The woman's own choice makes such a man her husband; yet being so chosen, he is her lord, and she is to be subject to him, yet in a way of liberty, not of bondage; and a true wife accounts her subjection her honor and freedom, and would not think her condition safe and free, but in her subjection to her husband's authority. Such is the liberty of the church under the authority of Christ, her king and husband; his yoke is so easy and sweet to her as a bride's ornaments; and if through forwardness or wantonness, etc., she shake it off, at any time, she is at no rest in her spirit, until she take it up again; and whether her lord smiles upon her, and embraceth her in his arms, or whether he frowns, or rebukes, or smites her, she apprehends the sweetness of his love in all, and is refreshed, supported, and instructed by every such dispensation of his authority over her. On the other side, ye know who they are that complain of this yoke and say, let us break their bands, etc., we will not have this man to rule over us. Even so, brethren, it will be between you and your magistrates. If you stand for your natural corrupt

5. I.e., because we are fallen and subject to death.     6. We are all the worse for license (Latin).

liberties, and will do what is good in your own eyes, you will not endure the least weight of authority, but will murmur, and oppose, and be always striving to shake off that yoke; but if you will be satisfied to enjoy such civil and lawful liberties, such as Christ allows you, then will you quietly and cheerfully submit unto that authority which is set over you, in all the administrations of it, for your good. Wherein, if we fail at any time, we hope we shall be willing (by God's assistance) to hearken to good advice from any of you, or in any other way of God; so shall your liberties be preserved, in upholding the honor and power of authority amongst you.

The deputy governor having ended his speech, the court arose, and the magistrates and deputies retired to attend their other affairs. * * *

1630–49                                                           1826

---

# ANNE BRADSTREET

## c. 1612–1672

Anne Bradstreet's father, Thomas Dudley, was the manager of the country estate of the Puritan earl of Lincoln, and his daughter was very much the apple of his eye. He took great care to see that she received an education superior to that of most young women of the time. When she was only sixteen she married a young man, Simon Bradstreet, a recent graduate of Cambridge University, who was associated with her father in conducting the affairs of the earl of Lincoln's estate. He also shared her father's Puritan beliefs. A year after the marriage her husband was appointed to assist in the preparations of the Massachusetts Bay Company, and the following year the Bradstreets and the Dudleys sailed with Winthrop's fleet. Bradstreet tells us that when she first "came into this country" she "found a new world and new manners," at which her "heart rose" in resistance. "But after I was convinced it was the way of God, I submitted to it and joined the church at Boston."

We know very little of Bradstreet's daily life, except that it was a hard existence. The wilderness, Samuel Eliot Morison once observed, "made men stern and silent, children unruly, servants insolent." William Bradford's wife, Dorothy, staring at the barren dunes of Cape Cod is said to have preferred the surety of drowning to the unknown life ashore. Added to the hardship of daily living was the fact that Bradstreet was never very strong. She had rheumatic fever as a child and as a result suffered recurrent periods of severe fatigue; nevertheless, she risked death by childbirth eight times. Her husband was secretary to the company and later governor of the Bay Colony; he was always involved in the colony's diplomatic missions; and in 1661 he went to England to renegotiate the Bay Company charter with Charles II. All of Simon's tasks must have added to her responsibilities at home. And like any good Puritan she added to the care of daily life the examination of her conscience. She tells us in one of the "Meditations" written for her children that she was troubled many times about the truth of the Scriptures, that she never saw any convincing miracles, and that she always wondered if those of which read "were feigned." What proved to her finally that God exists was not her reading but the evidence of her own eyes. She is the first in a long line of American poets who took their consolation not from theology but from the "wondrous works," as she wrote, "that I see, the vast frame of the heaven and the earth, the order of all things, night and day, summer and winter, spring and autumn, the daily providing for this great household upon the earth, the preserving and directing of all to its proper end."

When Bradstreet was a young girl she had written poems to please her father, and he made much of their reading them together. After her marriage she continued writing. Quite unknown to her, her brother-in-law, John Woodbridge, pastor of the Andover church, brought with him to London a manuscript collection of her poetry and had it printed there in 1650. It was the first published volume of poems written by a resident in the New World and was widely read. Reverend Edward Taylor, also a poet, and living in the frontier community of Westfield, Massachusetts, had a copy of the second edition of Bradstreet's poems (1678) in his library. Although she herself probably took greatest pride in her long meditative poems on the ages of humankind and on the seasons, the poems that have attracted present-day readers are the more intimate ones, which reflect her concern for her family and home and the pleasures she took in everyday life rather than in the life to come.

The text used is the *Works of Anne Bradstreet*, edited by Jeannine Hensley (1967).

# The Prologue

### 1

To sing of wars, of captains, and of kings,
Of cities founded, commonwealths begun,
For my mean[1] pen are too superior things:
Or how they all, or each their dates have run
Let poets and historians set these forth,                    5
My obscure lines shall not so dim their worth.

### 2

But when my wond'ring eyes and envious heart
Great Bartas'[2] sugared lines do but read o'er,
Fool[3] I do grudge the Muses[4] did not part
'Twixt him and me that overfluent store;                    10
A Bartas can do what a Bartas will
But simple I according to my skill.

### 3

From schoolboy's tongue no rhet'ric we expect,
Nor yet a sweet consort[5] from broken strings,
Nor perfect beauty where's a main defect:                   15
My foolish, broken, blemished Muse so sings,
And this to mend, alas, no art is able,
'Cause nature made it so irreparable.

### 4

Nor can I, like that fluent sweet tongued Greek,
Who lisped at first, in future times speak plain.[6]         20
By art he gladly found what he did seek,
A full requital of his striving pain.
Art can do much, but this maxim's most sure:
A weak or wounded brain admits no cure.

---

1. Humble.
2. Guillaume du Bartas (1544–1590) was a French writer much admired by the Puritans. He was most famous as the author of *The Divine Weeks*, an epic poem translated by Joshua Sylvester and intended to recount the great moments in Christian history.

3. I.e., like a fool.
4. In Greek mythology, the nine goddesses of the arts and sciences.
5. Accord, harmony of sound.
6. The Greek orator Demosthenes (c. 383–322 B.C.) conquered a speech defect.

5

I am obnoxious to each carping tongue                    25
Who says my hand a needle better fits,
A poet's pen all scorn I should thus wrong,
For such despite they cast on female wits:
If what I do prove well, it won't advance,
They'll say it's stol'n, or else it was by chance.          30

6

But sure the antique Greeks were far more mild
Else of our sex, why feigned they those nine
And poesy made Calliope's[7] own child;
So 'mongst the rest they placed the arts divine:
But this weak knot they will full soon untie.              35
The Greeks did nought, but play the fools and lie.

7

Let Greeks be Greeks, and women what they are;
Men have precedency and still excel,
It is but vain unjustly to wage war;
Men can do best, and women know it well                    40
Preeminence in all and each is yours;
Yet grant some small acknowledgment of ours.

8

And oh ye high flown quills[8] that soar the skies,
And ever with your prey still catch your praise,
If e'er you deign these lowly lines your eyes              45
Give thyme or parsley wreath, I ask no bays;[9]
This mean and unrefined ore of mine
Will make your glist'ring gold but more to shine.

1650

## To Her Father with Some Verses

Most truly honored, and as truly dear,
If worth in me or ought[1] I do appear,
Who can of right better demand the same
Than may your worthy self from whom it came?
The principal[2] might yield a greater sum,                5
Yet handled ill, amounts but to this crumb;
My stock's so small I know not how to pay,
My bond[3] remains in force unto this day;
Yet for part payment take this simple mite,[4]
Where nothing's to be had, kings loose their right.        10
Such is my debt I may not say forgive,
But as I can, I'll pay it while I live;
Such is my bond, none can discharge but I,
Yet paying is not paid until I die.

1678

7. The muse of epic poetry.
8. Pens.
9. Garlands of laurel, used to crown the head of a poet.

1. Anything at all.
2. The capital that yields interest.
3. I.e., contract.
4. The smallest possible denomination.

# Contemplations

### 1

Some time now past in the autumnal tide,
When Phoebus[1] wanted but one hour to bed,
The trees all richly clad, yet void of pride,
Were gilded o'er by his rich golden head.
Their leaves and fruits seemed painted, but was true,                    5
Of green, of red, of yellow, mixed hue;
Rapt were my senses at this delectable view.

### 2

I wist not what to wish, yet sure thought I,
If so much excellence abide below,
How excellent is He that dwells on high,                    10
Whose power and beauty by His works we know?
Sure He is goodness, wisdom, glory, light,
That hath this under world so richly dight;[2]
More heaven than earth was here, no winter and no night.

### 3

Then on a stately oak I cast mine eye,                    15
Whose ruffling top the clouds seemed to aspire;
How long since thou wast in thine infancy?
Thy strength, and stature, more thy years admire,
Hath hundred winters past since thou wast born?
Or thousand since thou brakest thy shell of horn?                    20
If so, all these as nought, eternity doth scorn.

### 4

Then higher on the glistering Sun I gazed.
Whose beams was shaded by the leafy tree;
The more I looked, the more I grew amazed,
And softly said, "What glory's like to thee?"                    25
Soul of this world, this universe's eye,
No wonder some made thee a deity;
Had I not better known, alas, the same had I.

### 5

Thou as a bridegroom from thy chamber rushes,
And as a strong man, joys to run a race;[3]                    30
The morn doth usher thee with smiles and blushes;
The Earth reflects her glances in thy face.
Birds, insects, animals with vegative,
Thy heat from death and dullness doth revive,
And in the darksome womb of fruitful nature dive.                    35

### 6

Thy swift annual and diurnal course,
Thy daily straight and yearly oblique path,
Thy pleasing fervor and thy scorching force,
All mortals here the feeling knowledge hath.
Thy presence makes it day, thy absence night,                    40
Quaternal seasons causéd by thy might:
Hail creature, full of sweetness, beauty, and delight.

---

1. Apollo, the sun god.
2. Furnished, adorned.
3. The sun "is as a bridegroom coming out of his chamber, and rejoiceth as a strong man to run a race" (Psalm 19.5).

7

Art thou so full of glory that no eye
Hath strength thy shining rays once to behold?
And is thy splendid throne erect so high,                                    45
As to approach it, can no earthly mold?
How full of glory then must thy Creator be,
Who gave this bright light luster unto thee?
Admired, adored for ever, be that Majesty.

8

Silent alone, where none or saw, or heard,                                   50
In pathless paths I lead my wand'ring feet,
My humble eyes to lofty skies I reared
To sing some song, my mazéd[4] Muse thought meet.
My great Creator I would magnify,
That nature had thus decked liberally;                                       55
But Ah, and Ah, again, my imbecility!

9

I heard the merry grasshopper then sing.
The black-clad cricket bear a second part;
They kept one tune and played on the same string,
Seeming to glory in their little art.                                        60
Shall creatures abject thus their voices raise
And in their kind resound their Maker's praise
Whilst I, as mute, can warble forth no higher lays?

10

When present times look back to ages past,
And men in being fancy those are dead,                                       65
It makes things gone perpetually to last,
And calls back months and years that long since fled.
It makes a man more aged in conceit
Than was Methuselah,[5] or's grandsire great,
While of their persons and their acts his mind doth treat.                   70

11

Sometimes in Eden fair he seems to be,
Sees glorious Adam there made lord of all,
Fancies the apple, dangle on the tree,
That turned his sovereign to a naked thrall.[6]
Who like a miscreant's driven from that place,                              75
To get his bread with pain and sweat of face,
A penalty imposed on his backsliding race.

12

Here sits our grandame in retired place,
And in her lap her bloody Cain new-born;
The weeping imp oft looks her in the face,                                   80
Bewails his unknown hap[7] and fate forlorn;
His mother sighs to think of Paradise,
And how she lost her bliss to be more wise,
Believing him that was, and is, father of lies.[8]

4. Amazed.
5. Methuselah was thought to have lived 969 years
(Genesis 5.27). "Conceit": apprehension, the processes
of thought.
6. Slave.

7. Fortune, circumstances.
8. By believing in the "father of lies," Eve lost Paradise
(Genesis 3); her elder son, Cain, slew his brother, Abel
(Genesis 4.8).

13

Here Cain and Abel come to sacrifice,                                    85
Fruits of the earth and fatlings[9] each do bring.
On Abel's gift the fire descends from skies,
But no such sign on false Cain's offering;
With sullen hateful looks he goes his ways,
Hath thousand thoughts to end his brother's days,                       90
Upon whose blood his future good he hopes to raise.

14

There Abel keeps his sheep, no ill he thinks;
His brother comes, then acts his fratricide:
The virgin Earth of blood her first draught drinks,
But since that time she often hath been cloyed.                         95
The wretch with ghastly face and dreadful mind
Thinks each he sees will serve him in his kind,
Though none on earth but kindred near then could he find.

15

Who fancies not his looks now at the bar,
His face like death, his heart with horror fraught,                     100
Nor malefactor ever felt like war,
When deep despair with wish of life hath fought,
Branded with guilt and crushed with treble woes,
A vagabond to Land of Nod[1] he goes.
A city builds, that walls might him secure from foes.                   105

16

Who thinks not oft upon the father's ages,
Their long descent, how nephew's sons they saw,
The starry observations of those sages,
And how their precepts to their sons were law,
How Adam sighed to see his progeny,                                     110
Clothed all in his black sinful livery,
Who neither guilt nor yet the punishment could fly.

17

Our life compare we with their length of days
Who to the tenth of theirs doth now arrive?
And though thus short, we shorten many ways,                            115
Living so little while we are alive;
In eating, drinking, sleeping, vain delight
So unawares comes on perpetual night,
And puts all pleasures vain unto eternal flight.

18

When I behold the heavens as in their prime,                            120
And then the earth (though old) still clad in green,
The stones and trees, insensible of time,
Nor age nor wrinkle on their front are seen;
If winter come and greenness then do fade,
A spring returns, and they more youthful made;                          125
But man grows old, lies down, remains where once he's laid.

9. Animals for slaughter.
1. An unidentified region east of Eden where Cain dwelled after slaying Abel (Genesis 4.16).

19

By birth more noble than those creatures all,
Yet seems by nature and by custom cursed,
No sooner born, but grief and care makes fall
That state obliterate he had at first;                                  130
Nor youth, nor strength, nor wisdom spring again,
Nor habitations long their names retain,
But in oblivion to the final day remain.

20

Shall I then praise the heavens, the trees, the earth
Because their beauty and their strength last longer?                    135
Shall I wish there, or never to had birth,
Because they're bigger, and their bodies stronger?
Nay, they shall darken, perish, fade and die,
And when unmade, so ever shall they lie,
But man was made for endless immortality.                               140

21

Under the cooling shadow of a stately elm
Close sat I by a goodly river's side,
Where gliding streams the rocks did overwhelm,
A lonely place, with pleasures dignified.
I once that loved the shady woods so well,                              145
Now thought the rivers did the trees excel,
And if the sun would ever shine, there would I dwell.

22

While on the stealing stream I fixt mine eye,
Which to the longed-for ocean held its course,
I marked, nor crooks, nor rubs,[2] that there did lie                   150
Could hinder aught,[3] but still augment its force.
"O happy flood," quoth I, "that holds thy race
Till thou arrive at thy beloved place,
Nor is it rocks or shoals that can obstruct thy pace,

23

Nor is't enough, that thou alone mayst slide                            155
But hundred brooks in thy clear waves do meet,
So hand in hand along with thee they glide
To Thetis' house,[4] where all embrace and greet.
Thou emblem true of what I count the best,
O could I lead my rivulets to rest,                                     160
So may we press to that vast mansion, ever blest."

24

Ye fish, which in this liquid region 'bide,
That for each season have your habitation,
Now salt, now fresh where you think best to glide
To unknown coasts to give a visitation,                                 165
In lakes and ponds you leave your numerous fry;
So nature taught, and yet you know not why,
You wat'ry folk that know not your felicity.

2. Difficult ties.                          4. I.e., the sea; Thetis was Achilles' mother and a sea
3. Anything.                                nymph.

25

Look how the wantons frisk to taste the air,
Then to the colder bottom straight they dive;      170
Eftsoon to Neptune's[5] glassy hall repair
To see what trade they great ones there do drive,
Who forage o'er the spacious sea-green field,
And take the trembling prey before it yield,
Whose armor is their scales, their spreading fins their shield.    175

26

While musing thus with contemplation fed,
And thousand fancies buzzing in my brain,
The sweet-tongued Philomel[6] perched o'er my head
And chanted forth a most melodious strain
Which rapt me so with wonder and delight,      180
I judged my hearing better than my sight,
And wished me wings with her a while to take my flight.

27

"O merry Bird," said I, "that fears no snares,
That neither toils nor hoards up in thy barn,
Feels no sad thoughts nor cruciating[7] cares      185
To gain more good or shun what might thee harm.
Thy clothes ne'er wear, thy meat is everywhere,
Thy bed a bough, thy drink the water clear,
Reminds not what is past, nor what's to come dost fear."

28

"The dawning morn with songs thou dost prevent,[8]      190
Sets hundred notes unto thy feathered crew,
So each one tunes his pretty instrument,
And warbling out the old, begin anew,
And thus they pass their youth in summer season,
Then follow thee into a better region,      195
Where winter's never felt by that sweet airy legion."

29

Man at the best a creature frail and vain,
In knowledge ignorant, in strength but weak,
Subject to sorrows, losses, sickness, pain,
Each storm his state, his mind, his body break,      200
From some of these he never finds cessation,
But day or night, within, without, vexation,
Troubles from foes, from friends, from dearest, near'st relation.

30

And yet this sinful creature, frail and vain,
This lump of wretchedness, of sin and sorrow,      205
This weatherbeaten vessel wracked with pain,
Joys not in hope of an eternal morrow;
Nor all his losses, crosses, and vexation,
In weight, in frequency and long duration
Can make him deeply groan for that divine translation.[9]      210

5. Roman god of the ocean. "Eftsoon": soon afterward.
6. I.e., the nightingale. Philomela, the daughter of King Attica, was transformed into a nightingale after her brother-in-law raped her and tore out her tongue.
7. I.e., excruciating, painful.
8. Anticipate.
9. Transformation.

31

The mariner that on smooth waves doth glide
Sings merrily and steers his bark with ease,
As if he had command of wind and tide,
And now become great master of the seas:
But suddenly a storm spoils all the sport,                    215
And makes him long for a more quiet port,
Which 'gainst all adverse winds may serve for fort.

32

So he that saileth in this world of pleasure,
Feeding on sweets, that never bit of th' sour,
That's full of friends, of honor, and of treasure,           220
Fond fool, he takes this earth ev'n for heav'n's bower.
But sad affliction comes and makes him see
Here's neither honor, wealth, nor safety;
Only above is found all with security.

33

O Time the fatal wrack[1] of mortal things,                   225
That draws oblivion's curtains over kings;
Their sumptuous monuments, men know them not,
Their names without a record are forgot,
Their parts, their ports, their pomp's[2] all laid in th' dust
Nor wit nor gold, nor buildings scape times rust;             230
But he whose name is graved in the white stone[3]
Shall last and shine when all of these are gone.

1678

## The Flesh and the Spirit

In secret place where once I stood
Close by the banks of Lacrim[1] flood,
I heard two sisters reason on
Things that are past and things to come;
One Flesh was called, who had her eye                          5
On worldly wealth and vanity;
The other Spirit, who did rear
Her thoughts unto a higher sphere:
Sister, quoth Flesh, what liv'st thou on,
Nothing but meditation?                                        10
Doth contemplation feed thee so
Regardlessly to let earth go?
Can speculation satisfy
Notion[2] without reality?
Dost dream of things beyond the moon,                          15
And dost thou hope to dwell there soon?
Hast treasures there laid up in store

---

1. Destroyer.
2. Vanity. "Parts": features. "Ports": places of refuge.
3. "To him that overcometh will I give to eat of the hidden manna and will give him a white stone, and in

the stone a new name written, which no man knoweth saving he that receiveth it" (Revelation 2.17).
1. In Latin *lacrima* means "tear."
2. Thought.

That all in th' world thou count'st but poor?
Art fancy sick, or turned a sot[3]
To catch at shadows which are not?                              20
Come, come, I'll show unto thy sense,
Industry hath its recompense.
What canst desire, but thou may'st see
True substance in variety?
Dost honor like? Acquire the same,                             25
As some to their immortal fame,
And trophies[4] to thy name erect
Which wearing time shall ne'er deject.
For riches doth thou long full sore?
Behold enough of precious store.                               30
Earth hath more silver, pearls, and gold,
Than eyes can see or hands can hold.
Affect's thou pleasure? Take thy fill,
Earth hath enough of what you will.
Then let not go, what thou may'st find                         35
For things unknown, only in mind.

Spirit: Be still thou unregenerate[5] part,
Disturb no more my settled heart,
For I have vowed (and so will do)
Thee as a foe still to pursue.                                 40
And combat with thee will and must,
Until I see thee laid in th' dust.
Sisters we are, yea, twins we be,
Yet deadly feud 'twixt thee and me;
For from one father are we not,                                45
Thou by old Adam wast begot.
But my arise is from above,
Whence my dear Father I do love.
Thou speak'st me fair, but hat'st me sore,
Thy flatt'ring shows[6] I'll trust no more.                    50
How oft thy slave, hast thou me made,
When I believed what thou hast said,
And never had more cause of woe
Than when I did what thou bad'st do.
I'll stop mine ears at these thy charms,                       55
And count them for my deadly harms.
Thy sinful pleasures I do hate,
Thy riches are to me no bait,
Thine honors do, nor will I love;
For my ambition lies above.                                    60
My greatest honor it shall be
When I am victor over thee,
And triumph shall with laurel head,[7]
When thou my captive shalt be led,

3. Fool. "Art fancy sick": i.e., do you have hallucina-    6. Exhibitions, displays.
tions?                                                     7. In Roman times a crown of laurel was a sign of vic-
4. Monuments.                                              tory for poets, heroes, and athletes.
5. Unrepentant.

How I do live, thou need'st not scoff,                                65
For I have meat thou know'st not of;
The hidden manna[8] I do eat,
The word of life it is my meat.
My thoughts do yield me more content
Than can thy hours in pleasure spent.                                 70
Nor are they shadows which I catch,
Nor fancies vain at which I snatch,
But reach at things that are so high,
Beyond thy dull capacity:
Eternal substance I do see,                                           75
With which enrichéd I would be.
Mine eye doth pierce the heavens and see
What is invisible to thee.
My garments are not silk nor gold,
Nor such like trash which earth doth hold,                            80
But royal robes I shall have on,
More glorious than the glist'ring sun;
My crown not diamonds, pearls, and gold,
But such as angels' heads enfold.
The city[9] where I hope to dwell,                                    85
There's none on earth can parallel;
The stately walls both high and strong,
Are made of precious jasper stone;
The gates of pearl, both rich and clear,
And angels are for porters there;                                     90
The streets thereof transparent gold,
Such as no eye did e'er behold;
A crystal river there doth run,
Which doth proceed from the Lamb's throne.
Of life, there are the waters sure,                                   95
Which shall remain forever pure,
Nor sun, nor moon, they have no need,
For glory doth from God proceed.
No candle there, nor yet torchlight,
For there shall be no darksome night.                                 100
From sickness and infirmity
For evermore they shall be free;
Nor withering age shall e'er come there,
But beauty shall be bright and clear;
This city pure is not for thee,                                       105
For things unclean there shall not be.
If I of heaven may have my fill,
Take thou the world and all that will.

1678

---

8. The food sent by God to the Israelites in the wilderness (Exodus 16.15).
9. Lines 85 to 106 follow the description of the heavenly city of the New Jerusalem in Revelation 21
and 22.

## The Author to Her Book[1]

Thou ill-formed offspring of my feeble brain,
Who after birth didst by my side remain,
Till snatched from thence by friends, less wise than true,
Who thee abroad, exposed to public view,
Made thee in rags, halting to th' press to trudge,     5
Where errors were not lessened (all may judge).
At thy return my blushing was not small,
My rambling brat (in print) should mother call,
I cast thee by as one unfit for light,
Thy visage was so irksome in my sight;     10
Yet being mine own, at length affection would
Thy blemishes amend, if so I could:
I washed thy face, but more defects I saw,
And rubbing off a spot still made a flaw.
I stretched thy joints to make thee even feet,[2]     15
Yet still thou run'st more hobbling than is meet;
In better dress to trim thee was my mind,
But nought save homespun cloth i' th' house I find.
In this array 'mongst vulgars[3] may'st thou roam.
In critic's hands beware thou dost not come,     20
And take thy way where yet thou art not known;
If for thy father asked, say thou hadst none;
And for thy mother, she alas is poor,
Which caused her thus to send thee out of door.

1678

## Before the Birth of One of Her Children

All things within this fading world hath end,
Adversity doth still our joys attend;
No ties so strong, no friends so dear and sweet,
But with death's parting blow is sure to meet.
The sentence past is most irrevocable,     5
A common thing, yet oh, inevitable.
How soon, my Dear, death may my steps attend,
How soon't may be thy lot to lose thy friend,
We both are ignorant, yet love bids me
These farewell lines to recommend to thee,     10
That when that knot's untied that made us one,
I may seem thine, who in effect am none.
And if I see not half my days that's due,
What nature would, God grant to yours and you;
The many faults that well you know I have     15
Let be interred in my oblivious grave;
If any worth or virtue were in me,

1. *The Tenth Muse* was published in 1650 without Bradstreet's knowledge. She is thought to have written this poem in 1666 when a 2nd edition was contemplated.
2. I.e., metrical feet; to smooth out the lines.
3. The common people.

Let that live freshly in thy memory
And when thou feel'st no grief, as I no harms,
Yet love thy dead, who long lay in thine arms,                    20
And when thy loss shall be repaid with gains
Look to my little babes, my dear remains.
And if thou love thyself, or loved'st me,
These O protect from stepdame's[1] injury.
And if chance to thine eyes shall bring this verse,              25
With some sad sighs honor my absent hearse;
And kiss this paper for thy love's dear sake,
Who with salt tears this last farewell did take.

                                                        1678


## To My Dear and Loving Husband

If ever two were one, then surely we.
If ever man were loved by wife, then thee;
If ever wife was happy in a man,
Compare with me, ye women, if you can.
I prize thy love more than whole mines of gold                    5
Or all the riches that the East doth hold.
My love is such that rivers cannot quench,
Nor ought but love from thee, give recompense.
Thy love is such I can no way repay,
The heavens reward thee manifold, I pray.                        10
Then while we live, in love let's so persevere
That when we live no more, we may live ever.

                                                        1678


## A Letter to Her Husband,
## Absent upon Public Employment

My head, my heart, mine eyes, my life, nay, more,
My joy, my magazine[1] of earthly store,
If two be one, as surely thou and I,
How stayest thou there, whilst I at Ipswich[2] lie?
So many steps, head from the heart to sever,                      5
If but a neck, soon should we be together.
I, like the Earth this season, mourn in black,
My Sun is gone so far in's zodiac,
Whom whilst I 'joyed, nor storms, nor frost I felt,
His warmth such frigid colds did cause to melt.                  10
My chilled limbs now numbed lie forlorn;
Return, return, sweet Sol, from Capricorn;[3]
In this dead time, alas, what can I more

1. I.e., stepmother's.
1. Warehouse, storehouse.
2. Ipswich, Massachusetts, is north of Boston.

3. Capricorn, the tenth sign of the zodiac, represents
winter. "Sol": sun.

Than view those fruits which through thy heat I bore?
Which sweet contentment yield me for a space,                    15
True living pictures of their father's face.
O strange effect! now thou art southward gone,
I weary grow the tedious day so long;
But when thou northward to me shalt return,
I wish my Sun may never set, but burn                            20
Within the Cancer[4] of my glowing breast,
The welcome house of him my dearest guest.
Where ever, ever stay, and go not thence,
Till nature's sad decree shall call thee hence;
Flesh of thy flesh, bone of thy bone,                           25
I here, thou there, yet both but one.

1678

# In Memory of My Dear Grandchild Elizabeth Bradstreet, Who Deceased August, 1665, Being a Year and Half Old

1

Farewell dear babe, my heart's too much content,
Farewell sweet babe, the pleasure of mine eye,
Farewell fair flower that for a space was lent,
Then ta'en away unto eternity.
Blest babe, why should I once bewail thy fate,                  5
Or sigh thy days so soon were terminate,
Sith[1] thou art settled in an everlasting state.

2

By nature trees do rot when they are grown,
And plums and apples thoroughly ripe do fall,
And corn and grass are in their season mown,                    10
And time brings down what is both strong and tall.
But plants new set to be eradicate,
And buds new blown to have so short a date,
Is by His hand alone that guides nature and fate.

1678

# Here Follows Some Verses upon the Burning of Our House July 10th, 1666

### Copied Out of a Loose Paper

In silent night when rest I took
For sorrow near I did not look

---

4. Cancer, the fourth sign of the zodiac, represents     1. Since.
summer.

I wakened was with thund'ring noise
And piteous shrieks of dreadful voice.
That fearful sound of "Fire!" and "Fire!"    5
Let no man know is my desire.
I, starting up, the light did spy,
And to my God my heart did cry
To strengthen me in my distress
And not to leave me succorless.    10
Then, coming out, beheld a space
The flame consume my dwelling place.
And when I could no longer look,
I blest His name that gave and took,[1]
That laid my goods now in the dust.    15
Yea, so it was, and so 'twas just.
It was His own, it was not mine,
Far be it that I should repine;
He might of all justly bereft
But yet sufficient for us left.    20
When by the ruins oft I past
My sorrowing eyes aside did cast,
And here and there the places spy
Where oft I sat and long did lie:
Here stood that trunk, and there that chest,    25
There lay that store I counted best.
My pleasant things in ashes lie,
And them behold no more shall I.
Under thy roof no guest shall sit,
Nor at thy table eat a bit.    30
No pleasant tale shall e'er be told,
Nor things recounted done of old.
No candle e'er shall shine in thee,
Nor bridegroom's voice e'er heard shall be.
In silence ever shall thou lie,    35
Adieu, Adieu, all's vanity.
Then straight I 'gin my heart to chide,
And did thy wealth on earth abide?
Didst fix thy hope on mold'ring dust?
The arm of flesh didst make thy trust?    40
Raise up thy thoughts above the sky
That dunghill mists away may fly.
Thou hast an house on high erect,
Framed by that mighty Architect,
With glory richly furnished,    45
Stands permanent though this be fled.
It's purchaséd and paid for too
By Him who hath enough to do.
A price so vast as is unknown
Yet by His gift is made thine own;    50
There's wealth enough, I need no more,
Farewell, my pelf,[2] farewell my store.

1. "The Lord gave, and the Lord hath taken away;    2. Possessions, usually in the sense of being falsely
blessed be the name of the Lord" (Job 1.21).    gained.

The world no longer let me love,
My hope and treasure lies above.

1867

# From Meditations Divine and Moral[1]

### 1

There is no object that we see, no action that we do, no good that we enjoy, no evil that we feel or fear, but we may make some spiritual advantage of all; and he that makes such improvement is wise as well as pious.

### 5

It is reported of the peacock that, priding himself in his gay feathers, he ruffles them up, but spying his black feet, he soon lets fall his plumes; so he that glories in his gifts and adornings should look upon his corruptions, and that will damp his high thoughts.

### 13

The reason why Christians are so loath to exchange this world for a better is because they have more sense[2] than faith: they see what they enjoy; they do but hope for that which is to come.

### 38

Some children are hardly weaned; although the teat be rubbed with worm-wood or mustard,[3] they will either wipe it off, or else suck down sweet and bitter together. So is it with some Christians: let God embitter all the sweets of this life, that so they might feed upon more substantial food, yet they are so childishly sottish that they are still hugging and sucking these empty breasts that God is forced to hedge up their way with thorns or lay affliction on their loins that so they might shake hands with the world, before it bid them farewell.

### 40

The spring is a lively emblem of the Resurrection: after a long winter we see the leafless trees and dry stocks (at the approach of the sun) to resume their former vigor and beauty in a more ample manner than what they lost in the

1. These meditations are addressed to Bradstreet's son Simon. In the dedicatory letter, dated March 20, 1664, she writes: "Parents perpetuate their lives in their posterity and their manners; in their imitation children do naturally rather follow the failings than the virtues of their predecessors, but I am persuaded better things of you. You once desired me to leave something for you in writing that you might look upon, when you should see me no more; I could think of nothing more fit for you nor of more ease to myself than these short meditations following. Such as they are, I bequeath to you; small legacies are accepted by true friends, much more by dutiful children. I have avoided encroaching upon others' conceptions because I would leave you nothing but mine own, though in value they fall short of all in this kind; yet I presume they will be better prized by you for the author's sake. The Lord bless you with grace here and crown you with glory hereafter, that I may meet you with rejoicing at that great day of appearing, which is the continual prayer of your affectionate mother, A. B."

2. I.e., they are more concerned with physical sensation and the things of this world than with faith.

3. A common way of weaning children, making the mother's breast bitter.

autumn; so shall it be at that great day after a long vacation, when the Sun of Righteousness[4] shall appear; those dry bones shall arise in far more glory than that which they lost at their creation, and in this transcends the spring that their leaf shall never fail nor their sap decline.

## 48

There is nothing admits of more admiration than God's various dispensation of His gifts among the sons of men, betwixt whom He hath put so vast a disproportion that they scarcely seem made of the same lump or sprung out of the loins of one Adam, some set in the highest dignity that mortality is capable of, and some again so base that they are viler than the earth, some so wise and learned that they seem like angels among men, and some again so ignorant and sottish that they are more like beasts than men, some pious saints, some incarnate devils, some exceeding beautiful, and some extremely deformed, some so strong and healthful that their bones are full of marrow and their breasts of milk, and some again so weak and feeble that while they live they are accounted among the dead; and no other reason can be given of all this but so it pleased Him whose will is the perfect rule of righteousness.

## 51

The eyes and the ears are the inlets or doors of the soul, through which innumerable objects enter; yet is not that spacious room filled, neither doth it ever say it is enough, but like the daughters of the horseleach, cries, "Give, give";[5] and, which is most strange, the more it receives, the more empty it finds itself and sees an impossibility ever to be filled but by Him in whom all fullness dwells.

## 62

As a man is called the little world, so his heart may be called the little commonwealth; his more fixed and resolved thoughts are like to inhabitants, his slight and flitting thoughts are like passengers that travel to and fro continually; here is also the great court of justice erected, which is always kept by conscience, who is both accuser, excuser, witness, and judge, whom no bribes can pervert nor flattery cause to favor, but as he finds the evidence, so he absolves or condemns; yea, so absolute is this court of judicature that there is no appeal from it, no not to the court of heaven itself, for if our conscience condemn us, He also who is greater than our conscience will do it much more, but he that would have boldness to go to the throne of grace to be accepted there must be sure to carry a certificate from the court of conscience that he stands right there.

## 67

All the works and doings of God are wonderful, but none more awful than His great work of election and reprobation;[6] when we consider how many good

4. "But unto you that fear my name shall the Sun of righteousness arise with healing in his wings; and ye shall go forth, and grow up as calves of the stall" (Malachi 4.2). "Long vacation": i.e., the sleep of the dead, awaiting the Second Coming of Christ.
5. "The horseleach [veterinarian] hath two daughters, crying, Give, give. There are three things that are never satisfied, yea, four things say not, It is enough: The grave, and the barren womb; the earth that is not filled with water; and the fire that saith not, It is enough" (Proverbs 30.15–16).
6. God's decision upon those who are to be rejected and damned. "Election": God's choice of those who are to be eternally saved.

parents have had bad children, and again how many bad parents have had pious children, it should make us adore the sovereignty of God, who will not be tied to time nor place, nor yet to persons, but takes and chooses, when and where and whom He pleases; it should also teach the children of godly parents to walk with fear and trembling, lest they through unbelief fall short of a promise; it may also be a support to such as have or had wicked parents, that if they abide not in unbelief, God is able to gaff[7] them in. The upshot of all should make us with the apostle to admire the justice and mercy of God and say how unsearchable are His ways and His footsteps past finding out.[8]

71

All weak and diseased bodies have hourly mementos of their mortality, but the soundest of men, have likewise their nightly monitor by the emblem of death, which is their sleep (for so is death often called), and not only their death, but their grave is lively represented before their eyes by beholding their bed, the morning may mind them of the Resurrection, and the sun approaching of the appearing of the Sun of Righteousness, at Whose coming they shall all rise out of their beds, the long night shall fly away, and the day of eternity shall never end. Seeing these things must be, what manner of persons ought we to be, in all good conversation?

1664(?)                                                                      1867

## To My Dear Children

> This book by any yet unread,
> I leave for you when I am dead,
> That being gone, here you may find
> What was your living mother's mind.
> Make use of what I leave in love,                                    5
> And God shall bless you from above.
>                                               A. B.

*My dear children,*
  I, knowing by experience that the exhortations of parents take most effect when the speakers leave to speak,[1] and those especially sink deepest which are spoke latest, and being ignorant whether on my death bed I shall have opportunity to speak to any of you, much less to all, thought it the best, whilst I was able, to compose some short matters (for what else to call them I know not) and bequeath to you, that when I am no more with you, yet I may be daily in your remembrance (although that is the least in my aim in what I now do), but that you may gain some spiritual advantage by my experience. I have not studied in this you read to show my skill, but to declare the truth, not to set forth myself, but the glory of God. If I had minded the former, it had been perhaps better pleasing to you, but seeing the last is the best, let it be best pleasing to you.

---

7. Hook; to bring to shore a large fish by means of a long pole with a hook.
8. "O the depth of the riches both of the wisdom and knowledge of God! how unsearchable are his judg-ments, and his ways past finding out!" (Romans 11.33).
1. I.e., stop speaking.

The method I will observe shall be this: I will begin with God's dealing with me from my childhood to this day.

In my young years, about 6 or 7 as I take it, I began to make conscience of my ways, and what I knew was sinful, as lying, disobedience to parents, etc., I avoided it. If at any time I was overtaken with the like evils, it was as a great trouble, and I could not be at rest till by prayer I had confessed it unto God. I was also troubled at the neglect of private duties though too often tardy that way. I also found much comfort in reading the Scriptures, especially those places I thought most concerned my condition, and as I grew to have more understanding, so the more solace I took in them.

In a long fit of sickness which I had on my bed I often communed with my heart and made my supplication to the most High who set me free from that affliction.

But as I grew up to be about 14 or 15, I found my heart more carnal,[2] and sitting loose from God, vanity and the follies of youth take hold of me.

About 16, the Lord laid His hand sore upon me and smote me with the smallpox. When I was in my affliction, I besought the Lord and confessed my pride and vanity, and He was entreated of me and again restored me. But I rendered not to Him according to the benefit received.

After a short time I changed my condition and was married, and came into this country, where I found a new world and new manners, at which my heart rose. But after I was convinced it was the way of God, I submitted to it and joined to the church at Boston.

After some time I fell into a lingering sickness like a consumption together with a lameness, which correction I saw the Lord sent to humble and try me and do me good, and it was not altogether ineffectual.

It pleased God to keep me a long time without a child, which was a great grief to me and cost me many prayers and tears before I obtained one, and after him gave me many more of whom I now take the care, that as I have brought you into the world, and with great pains, weakness, cares, and fears brought you to this, I now travail[3] in birth again of you till Christ be formed in you.

Among all my experiences of God's gracious dealings with me, I have constantly observed this, that He hath never suffered me long to sit loose from Him, but by one affliction or other hath made me look home, and search what was amiss; so usually thus it hath been with me that I have no sooner felt my heart out of order, but I have expected correction for it, which most commonly hath been upon my own person in sickness, weakness, pains, sometimes on my soul, in doubts and fears of God's displeasure and my sincerity towards Him; sometimes He hath smote a child with a sickness, sometimes chastened by losses in estate,[4] and these times (through His great mercy) have been the times of my greatest getting and advantage; yea, I have found them the times when the Lord hath manifested the most love to me. Then have I gone to searching and have said with David, "Lord, search me and try me, see what ways of wickedness are in me, and lead me in the way everlasting,"[5] and seldom or never but I have found either some sin I lay under which God would have reformed, or some duty neglected which He would have performed, and

---

2. I.e., worldly.  
3. Toil, labor.  

4. Financial losses.  
5. Psalm 139.23–24.

by His help I have laid vows and bonds upon my soul to perform His righteous commands.

If at any time you are chastened of God, take it as thankfully and joyfully as in greatest mercies, for if ye be His, ye shall reap the greatest benefit by it. It hath been no small support to me in times of darkness when the Almighty hath hid His face from me that yet I have had abundance of sweetness and refreshment after affliction and more circumspection[6] in my walking after I have been afflicted. I have been with God like an untoward child, that no longer than the rod has been on my back (or at least in sight) but I have been apt to forget Him and myself, too. Before I was afflicted, I went astray, but now I keep Thy statutes.[7]

I have had great experience of God's hearing my prayers and returning comfortable answers to me, either in granting the thing I prayed for, or else in satisfying my mind without it, and I have been confident it hath been from Him, because I have found my heart through His goodness enlarged in thankfulness to Him.

I have often been perplexed that I have not found that constant joy in my pilgrimage and refreshing which I supposed most of the servants of God have, although He hath not left me altogether without the witness of His holy spirit, who hath oft given me His word and set to His seal that it shall be well with me. I have sometimes tasted of that hidden manna that the world knows not, and have set up my Ebenezer,[8] and have resolved with myself that against such a promise, such tastes of sweetness, the gates of hell shall never prevail; yet have I many times sinkings and droopings, and not enjoyed that felicity that sometimes I have done. But when I have been in darkness and seen no light, yet have I desired to stay myself upon the Lord, and when I have been in sickness and pain, I have thought if the Lord would but lift up the light of His countenance upon me, although He ground me to powder, it would be but light to me; yea, oft have I thought were I in hell itself and could there find the love of God toward me, it would be a heaven. And could I have been in heaven without the love of God, it would have been a hell to me, for in truth it is the absence and presence of God that makes heaven or hell.

Many times hath Satan troubled me concerning the verity of the Scriptures, many times by atheism how I could know whether there was a God; I never saw any miracles to confirm me, and those which I read of, how did I know but they were feigned? That there is a God my reason would soon tell me by the wondrous works that I see, the vast frame of the heaven and the earth, the order of all things, night and day, summer and winter, spring and autumn, the daily providing for this great household upon the earth, the preserving and directing of all to its proper end. The consideration of these things would with amazement certainly resolve me that there is an Eternal Being. But how should I know He is such a God as I worship in Trinity, and such a Savior as I rely upon? Though this hath thousands of times been suggested to me, yet God hath helped me over. I have argued thus with myself. That there is a God, I see. If ever this God hath revealed himself, it must be in His word, and this must be it or none. Have I not found that operation by it that no human invention can work upon the soul, hath not judgments befallen divers who

6. Prudence.
7. Psalm 119.8.
8. In 1 Samuel 7.12, a stone monument to commem-
orate a victory over the Philistines. "Manna": the "bread from heaven" (Exodus 16.4) that fed the Israelites in the wilderness.

have scorned and contemned it, hath it not been preserved through all ages maugre[9] all the heathen tyrants and all of the enemies who have opposed it? Is there any story but that which shows the beginnings of times, and how the world came to be as we see? Do we not know the prophecies in it fulfilled which could not have been so long foretold by any but God Himself?

When I have got over this block, then have I another put in my way, that admit this be the true God whom we worship, and that be His word, yet why may not the Popish religion be the right? They have the same God, the same Christ, the same word. They only interpret it one way, we another.

This hath sometimes stuck with me, and more it would, but the vain fooleries that are in their religion together with their lying miracles and cruel persecutions of the saints, which admit were they as they term them, yet not so to be dealt withal.

The consideration of these things and many the like would soon turn me to my own religion again.

But some new troubles I have had since the world has been filled with blasphemy and sectaries,[1] and some who have been accounted sincere Christians have been carried away with them, that sometimes I have said, "Is there faith upon the earth?" and I have not known what to think; but then I have remembered the words of Christ that so it must be, and if it were possible, the very elect should be deceived. "Behold," saith our Savior, "I have told you before." That hath stayed my heart, and I can now say, "Return, O my Soul, to thy rest, upon this rock Christ Jesus will I build my faith, and if I perish, I perish"; but I know all the Powers of Hell shall never prevail against it. I know whom I have trusted, and whom I have believed, and that He is able to keep that I have committed to His charge.

Now to the King, immortal, eternal and invisible, the only wise God, be honor, and glory for ever and ever, Amen.

This was written in much sickness and weakness, and is very weakly and imperfectly done, but if you can pick any benefit out of it, it is the mark which I aimed at.

1867

9. In spite of.                          1. Unbelievers, heretics.

---

# MARY ROWLANDSON
## c. 1636–1711

On June 20, 1675, Metacomet, who was called Philip by the colonists, led the first of a series of attacks on colonial settlements that lasted for more than a year. Before they were over, more than twelve hundred houses had been burned, about six hundred English colonials were dead, and three thousand American Indians killed. These attacks have become known as "King Philip's War." It was the direct result of the execution in Plymouth, Massachusetts, of three of Philip's Wampanoag tribesmen, but the indirect causes were many; not the least was the fact that the Native Americans were starving and desperate to retain their lands. In a sense, the war may be seen as a last-ditch effort by the Wampanoags and their allies against further expansion by the colonists. By the time the war was over, in August of 1676, with Philip slain and his wife and children sold into slavery in the West Indies, the independent power of the New England American Indians had ended.

Probably the most famous victim of these attacks is the author of A *Narrative of the Captivity and Restoration of Mrs. Mary Rowlandson*, the wife of the minister of the town of Lancaster. With the exception of the eleven weeks she spent as a captive among the Wampanoags, however, almost everything about Mrs. Rowlandson's life remains conjectural. She was probably born in England and brought to this country at an early age. Her father, John White, was a wealthy landholder in the Massachusetts Bay Colony who settled in Lancaster. About 1656 she married Joseph Rowlandson and for the next twenty years led a busy life of mother and minister's wife. The attack on Lancaster occurred on February 10, 1676, and she was not released until the second of May, having been ransomed for twenty pounds. The following year she went with her husband to Wethersfield, Connecticut; Mr. Rowlandson died there in 1678. The town voted to pay her an annuity "so long as she remains a widow among us." For lack of any further information, most biographical entries conclude here. Recently, David Greene has verified that Mary Rowlandson married Captain Samuel Talcott in Wethersfield on August 6, 1679, and that she died in that Connecticut Valley town on January 5, 1711, thirty-five years after her famous ordeal.

Shortly after her return to Lancaster, Mrs. Rowlandson began to make a record of her life in captivity. Her *Narrative* (published in 1682) is the only evidence we have of her skill as a writer. The account of her captivity became one of the most popular prose works of the seventeenth century, both in this country and in England. It combined high adventure, heroism, and exemplary piety and is the first and, in its narrative skill and delineation of character, the best of what have become popularly known as "Indian captivities." As transformed into fictional form by writers like James Fenimore Cooper (in *The Last of the Mohicans*) and William Faulkner (in *Sanctuary*), it is a genre that has proven to be an integral part of our American literary consciousness.

# A Narrative of the Captivity and Restoration of Mrs. Mary Rowlandson[1]

On the tenth of February 1675,[2] came the Indians with great numbers upon Lancaster:[3] their first coming was about sunrising; hearing the noise of some guns, we looked out; several houses were burning, and the smoke ascending to heaven. There were five persons taken in one house; the father, and the mother and a sucking child, they knocked on the head; the other two they took and carried away alive. There were two others, who being out of their garrison[4] upon some occasion were set upon; one was knocked on the head, the other escaped; another there was who running along was shot and wounded, and fell down; he begged of them his life, promising them money (as they told me) but

---

1. The text used is *Original Narratives of Early American History, Narratives of Indian Wars 1675–1699*, Vol. 14, edited by C. H. Lincoln (1952). The full title is *The sovereignty and goodness of GOD, together with the faithfulness of his promises displayed; being a narrative of the captivity and restoration of Mrs. Mary Rowlandson, commended by her, to all that desires to know the Lord's doings to, and dealings with her. Especially to her dear children and relations. The second Addition Corrected and amended. Written by her own hand for her private use, and now made public at the earnest*

desire of some friends, and for the benefit of the afflicted. Deut. 32.39. See now that I, even I am he, and there is no god with me; I kill and I make alive, I wound and I heal, neither is there any can deliver out of my hand.
2. A Thursday. Using the present Gregorian calendar, adopted in 1752, February 20, 1676.
3. Lancaster, Massachusetts, was a frontier town of approximately fifty families, about thirty miles west of Boston.
4. I.e., houses in the town where people gathered for defense.

they would not hearken to him but knocked him in head, and stripped him naked, and split open his bowels.[5] Another, seeing many of the Indians about his barn, ventured and went out, but was quickly shot down. There were three others belonging to the same garrison who were killed; the Indians getting up upon the roof of the barn, had advantage to shoot down upon them over their fortification. Thus these murderous wretches went on, burning, and destroying before them.

At length they came and beset our own house, and quickly it was the dolefulest day that ever mine eyes saw. The house stood upon the edge of a hill; some of the Indians got behind the hill, others into the barn, and others behind anything that could shelter them; from all which places they shot against the house, so that the bullets seemed to fly like hail; and quickly they wounded one man among us, then another, and then a third. About two hours (according to my observation, in that amazing time) they had been about the house before they prevailed to fire it (which they did with flax and hemp, which they brought out of the barn, and there being no defense about the house, only two flankers[6] at two opposite corners and one of them not finished); they fired it once and one ventured out and quenched it, but they quickly fired it again, and that took. Now is the dreadful hour come, that I have often heard of (in time of war, as it was the case of others), but now mine eyes see it. Some in our house were fighting for their lives, others wallowing in their blood, the house on fire over our heads, and the bloody heathen ready to knock us on the head, if we stirred out. Now might we hear mothers and children crying out for themselves, and one another, "Lord, what shall we do?" Then I took my children (and one of my sisters', hers) to go forth and leave the house: but as soon as we came to the door and appeared, the Indians shot so thick that the bullets rattled against the house, as if one had taken an handful of stones and threw them, so that we were fain to give back. We had six stout dogs belonging to our garrison, but none of them would stir, though another time, if any Indian had come to the door, they were ready to fly upon him and tear him down. The Lord hereby would make us the more acknowledge His hand, and to see that our help is always in Him. But out we must go, the fire increasing, and coming along behind us, roaring, and the Indians gaping before us with their guns, spears, and hatchets to devour us. No sooner were we out of the house, but my brother-in-law (being before wounded, in defending the house, in or near the throat) fell down dead, whereat the Indians scornfully shouted, and hallowed, and were presently upon him, stripping off his clothes, the bullets flying thick, one went through my side, and the same (as would seem) through the bowels and hand of my dear child in my arms. One of my elder sisters' children, named William, had then his leg broken, which the Indians perceiving, they knocked him on [his] head. Thus were we butchered by those merciless heathen, standing amazed, with the blood running down to our heels. My eldest sister being yet in the house, and seeing those woeful sights, the infidels hauling mothers one way, and children another, and some wallowing in their blood: and her elder son telling her that her son William was dead, and myself was wounded, she said, "And Lord, let me die with them," which was no sooner said, but she was struck with a bullet, and fell down dead over the threshold. I hope she is reaping the fruit of her

5. Belly.                                    6. Projecting fortifications.

good labors, being faithful to the service of God in her place. In her younger years she lay under much trouble upon spiritual accounts, till it pleased God to make that precious scripture take hold of her heart, "And he said unto me, my Grace is sufficient for thee" (2 Corinthians 12.9). More than twenty years after, I have heard her tell how sweet and comfortable that place was to her. But to return: the Indians laid hold of us, pulling me one way, and the children another, and said, "Come go along with us"; I told them they would kill me: they answered, if I were willing to go along with them, they would not hurt me.

Oh the doleful sight that now was to behold at this house! "Come, behold the works of the Lord, what desolations he has made in the earth."[7] Of thirty-seven persons who were in this one house, none escaped either present death, or a bitter captivity, save only one, who might say as he, "And I only am escaped alone to tell the News" (Job 1.15). There were twelve killed, some shot, some stabbed with their spears, some knocked down with their hatchets. When we are in prosperity, Oh the little that we think of such dreadful sights, and to see our dear friends, and relations lie bleeding out their heart-blood upon the ground. There was one who was chopped into the head with a hatchet, and stripped naked, and yet was crawling up and down. It is a solemn sight to see so many Christians lying in their blood, some here, and some there, like a company of sheep torn by wolves, all of them stripped naked by a company of hell-hounds, roaring, singing, ranting, and insulting, as if they would have torn our very hearts out; yet the Lord by His almighty power preserved a number of us from death, for there were twenty-four of us taken alive and carried captive.

I had often before this said that if the Indians should come, I should choose rather to be killed by them than taken alive, but when it came to the trial my mind changed; their glittering weapons so daunted my spirit, that I chose rather to go along with those (as I may say) ravenous beasts, than that moment to end my days; and that I may the better declare what happened to me during that grievous captivity, I shall particularly speak of the several removes[8] we had up and down the wilderness.

## The First Remove

Now away we must go with those barbarous creatures, with our bodies wounded and bleeding, and our hearts no less than our bodies. About a mile we went that night, up upon a hill within sight of the town, where they intended to lodge. There was hard by a vacant house (deserted by the English before, for fear of the Indians). I asked them whether I might not lodge in the house that night, to which they answered, "What, will you love English men still?" This was the dolefulest night that ever my eyes saw. Oh the roaring, and singing and dancing, and yelling of those black creatures in the night, which made the place a lively resemblance of hell. And as miserable was the waste that was there made of horses, cattle, sheep, swine, calves, lambs, roasting pigs, and fowl (which they had plundered in the town), some roasting, some lying and burning, and some boiling to feed our merciless enemies; who were joyful enough, though we were disconsolate. To add to the dolefulness of the

7. Psalm 46.8.    8. I.e., departures; movings from place to place.

former day, and the dismalness of the present night, my thoughts ran upon my losses and sad bereaved condition. All was gone, my husband gone (at least separated from me, he being in the Bay;[9] and to add to my grief, the Indians told me they would kill him as he came homeward), my children gone, my relations and friends gone, our house and home and all our comforts—within door and without—all was gone (except my life), and I knew not but the next moment that might go too. There remained nothing to me but one poor wounded babe, and it seemed at present worse than death that it was in such a pitiful condition, bespeaking compassion, and I had no refreshing for it, nor suitable things to revive it. Little do many think what is the savageness and brutishness of this barbarous enemy, Ay, even those that seem to profess more than others among them, when the English have fallen into their hands.

Those seven that were killed at Lancaster the summer before upon a Sabbath day, and the one that was afterward killed upon a weekday, were slain and mangled in a barbarous manner, by one-eyed John, and Marlborough's Praying Indians, which Capt. Mosely brought to Boston, as the Indians told me.[1]

## The Second Remove[2]

But now, the next morning, I must turn my back upon the town, and travel with them into the vast and desolate wilderness, I knew not whither. It is not my tongue, or pen, can express the sorrows of my heart, and bitterness of my spirit that I had at this departure: but God was with me in a wonderful manner, carrying me along, and bearing up my spirit, that it did not quite fail. One of the Indians carried my poor wounded babe upon a horse; it went moaning all along, "I shall die, I shall die." I went on foot after it, with sorrow that cannot be expressed. At length I took it off the horse, and carried it in my arms till my strength failed, and I fell down with it. Then they set me upon a horse with my wounded child in my lap, and there being no furniture upon the horse's back, as we were going down a steep hill we both fell over the horse's head, at which they, like inhumane creatures, laughed, and rejoiced to see it, though I thought we should there have ended our days, as overcome with so many difficulties. But the Lord renewed my strength still, and carried me along, that I might see more of His power; yea, so much that I could never have thought of, had I not experienced it.

After this it quickly began to snow, and when night came on, they stopped, and now down I must sit in the snow, by a little fire, and a few boughs behind me, with my sick child in my lap; and calling much for water, being now (through the wound) fallen into a violent fever. My own wound also growing so stiff that I could scarce sit down or rise up; yet so it must be, that I must sit all this cold winter night upon the cold snowy ground, with my sick child in my arms, looking that every hour would be the last of its life; and having no Christian friend near me, either to comfort or help me. Oh, I may see the wonderful power of God, that my Spirit did not utterly sink under my afflic-

9. I.e., Boston, or Massachusetts Bay.
1. On August 30, 1675, Captain Samuel Mosely, encouraged by a number of people who were skeptical of converted American Indians, brought to Boston by force fifteen Christianized American Indians who lived on their own lands in Marlborough, Massachusetts, and accused them of an attack on the town of Lancaster on August 22.
2. To Princeton, Massachusetts, near Mount Wachusett.

tion: still the Lord upheld me with His gracious and merciful spirit, and we were both alive to see the light of the next morning.

## The Third Remove[3]

The morning being come, they prepared to go on their way. One of the Indians got up upon a horse, and they set me up behind him, with my poor sick babe in my lap. A very wearisome and tedious day I had of it; what with my own wound, and my child's being so exceeding sick, and in a lamentable condition with her wound. It may be easily judged what a poor feeble condition we were in, there being not the least crumb of refreshing that came within either of our mouths from Wednesday night to Saturday night, except only a little cold water. This day in the afternoon, about an hour by sun, we came to the place where they intended, *viz.* an Indian town, called Wenimesset, northward of Quabaug. When we were come, Oh the number of pagans (now merciless enemies) that there came about me, that I may say as David, "I had fainted, unless I had believed, etc" (Psalm 27.13). The next day was the Sabbath. I then remembered how careless I had been of God's holy time; how many Sabbaths I had lost and misspent, and how evilly I had walked in God's sight; which lay so close unto my spirit, that it was easy for me to see how righteous it was with God to cut off the thread of my life and cast me out of His presence forever. Yet the Lord still showed mercy to me, and upheld me; and as He wounded me with one hand, so he healed me with the other. This day there came to me one Robert Pepper (a man belonging to Roxbury) who was taken in Captain Beers's fight, and had been now a considerable time with the Indians; and up with them almost as far as Albany, to see King Philip, as he told me, and was now very lately come into these parts.[4] Hearing, I say, that I was in this Indian town, he obtained leave to come and see me. He told me he himself was wounded in the leg at Captain Beer's fight; and was not able some time to go, but as they carried him, and as he took oaken leaves and laid to his wound, and through the blessing of God he was able to travel again. Then I took oaken leaves and laid to my side, and with the blessing of God it cured me also; yet before the cure was wrought, I may say, as it is in Psalm 38.5–6 "My wounds stink and are corrupt, I am troubled, I am bowed down greatly, I go mourning all the day long." I sat much alone with a poor wounded child in my lap, which moaned night and day, having nothing to revive the body, or cheer the spirits of her, but instead of that, sometimes one Indian would come and tell me one hour that "your master will knock your child in the head," and then a second, and then a third, "your master will quickly knock your child in the head."

This was the comfort I had from them, miserable comforters are ye all, as he[5] said. Thus nine days I sat upon my knees, with my babe in my lap, till my flesh was raw again; my child being even ready to depart this sorrowful world, they bade me carry it out to another wigwam (I suppose because they would not be troubled with such spectacles) whither I went with a very heavy heart, and down I sat with the picture of death in my lap. About two hours in the

3. February 12–27; they stopped at a Native American village on the Ware River near New Braintree.
4. Captain Beers had attempted to save the garrison of

Northfield, Massachusetts, on September 4, 1675.
5. I.e., as Job said. "I have heard many such things: miserable comforters are ye all" (Job 16.2).

night, my sweet babe like a lamb departed this life on Feb. 18, 1675. It being about six years, and five months old. It was nine days from the first wounding, in this miserable condition, without any refreshing of one nature or other, except a little cold water. I cannot but take notice how at another time I could not bear to be in the room where any dead person was, but now the case is changed; I must and could lie down by my dead babe, side by side all the night after. I have thought since of the wonderful goodness of God to me in preserving me in the use of my reason and senses in that distressed time, that I did not use wicked and violent means to end my own miserable life. In the morning, when they understood that my child was dead they sent for me home to my master's wigwam (by my master in this writing, must be understood Quinnapin, who was a Sagamore,[6] and married King Philip's wife's sister; not that he first took me, but I was sold to him by another Narragansett Indian, who took me when first I came out of the garrison). I went to take up my dead child in my arms to carry it with me, but they bid me let it alone; there was no resisting, but go I must and leave it. When I had been at my master's wigwam, I took the first opportunity I could get to go look after my dead child. When I came I asked them what they had done with it; then they told me it was upon the hill. Then they went and showed me where it was, where I saw the ground was newly digged, and there they told me they had buried it. There I left that child in the wilderness, and must commit it, and myself also in this wilderness condition, to Him who is above all. God having taken away this dear child, I went to see my daughter Mary, who was at this same Indian town, at a wigwam not very far off, though we had little liberty or opportunity to see one another. She was about ten years old, and taken from the door at first by a Praying Ind. and afterward sold for a gun. When I came in sight, she would fall aweeping; at which they were provoked, and would not let me come near her, but bade me be gone; which was a heart-cutting word to me. I had one child dead, another in the wilderness, I knew not where, the third they would not let me come near to: "Me (as he said) have ye bereaved of my Children, Joseph is not, and Simeon is not, and ye will take Benjamin also, all these things are against me."[7] I could not sit still in this condition, but kept walking from one place to another. And as I was going along, my heart was even overwhelmed with the thoughts of my condition, and that I should have children, and a nation which I knew not, ruled over them. Whereupon I earnestly entreated the Lord, that He would consider my low estate, and show me a token for good, and if it were His blessed will, some sign and hope of some relief. And indeed quickly the Lord answered, in some measure, my poor prayers; for as I was going up and down mourning and lamenting my condition, my son came to me, and asked me how I did. I had not seen him before, since the destruction of the town, and I knew not where he was, till I was informed by himself, that he was amongst a smaller parcel of Indians, whose place was about six miles off. With tears in his eyes, he asked me whether his sister Sarah was dead; and told me he had seen his sister Mary; and prayed me, that I would not be troubled in reference to himself. The occasion of his coming to see me at this time, was this: there was, as I said, about six miles from us, a small plantation of Indians, where it seems he had been during his captivity; and at

---

6. A subordinate chief among the Algonquin Indians. Quinnapin was the husband of Weetamoo, and Row-landson became her servant.

7. Jacob's lamentation in Genesis 42.36.

this time, there were some forces of the Ind. gathered out of our company, and some also from them (among whom was my son's master) to go to assault and burn Medfield.[8] In this time of the absence of his master, his dame brought him to see me. I took this to be some gracious answer to my earnest and unfeigned desire. The next day, *viz.* to this, the Indians returned from Medfield, all the company, for those that belonged to the other small company, came through the town that now we were at. But before they came to us, Oh! the outrageous roaring and hooping that there was. They began their din about a mile before they came to us. By their noise and hooping they signified how many they had destroyed (which was at that time twenty-three). Those that were with us at home were gathered together as soon as they heard the hooping, and every time that the other went over their number, these at home gave a shout, that the very earth rung again. And thus they continued till those that had been upon the expedition were come up to the Sagamore's wigwam; and then, Oh, the hideous insulting and triumphing that there was over some Englishmen's scalps that they had taken (as their manner is) and brought with them. I cannot but take notice of the wonderful mercy of God to me in those afflictions, in sending me a Bible. One of the Indians that came from Medfield fight, had brought some plunder, came to me, and asked me, if I would have a Bible, he had got one in his basket. I was glad of it, and asked him, whether he thought the Indians would let me read? He answered, yes. So I took the Bible, and in that melancholy time, it came into my mind to read first the 28th chapter of Deuteronomy,[9] which I did, and when I had read it, my dark heart wrought on this manner: that there was no mercy for me, that the blessings were gone, and the curses come in their room, and that I had lost my opportunity. But the Lord helped me still to go on reading till I came to Chap. 30, the seven first verses, where I found, there was mercy promised again, if we would return to Him by repentance;[1] and though we were scattered from one end of the earth to the other, yet the Lord would gather us together, and turn all those curses upon our enemies. I do not desire to live to forget this Scripture, and what comfort it was to me.

Now the Ind. began to talk of removing from this place, some one way, and some another. There were now besides myself nine English captives in this place (all of them children, except one woman). I got an opportunity to go and take my leave of them. They being to go one way, and I another, I asked them whether they were earnest with God for deliverance. They told me they did as they were able, and it was some comfort to me, that the Lord stirred up children to look to Him. The woman, *viz.* goodwife[2] Joslin, told me she should never see me again, and that she could find in her heart to run away. I wished her not to run away by any means, for we were near thirty miles from any English town, and she very big with child, and had but one week to reckon, and another child in her arms, two years old, and bad rivers there were to go over, and we were feeble, with our poor and coarse entertainment. I had my Bible with me, I pulled it out, and asked her whether she would read. We opened the Bible and lighted on Psalm 27, in which Psalm we

---

8. The attack on Medfield, Massachusetts, occurred on February 21.
9. This chapter of Deuteronomy is concerned with blessings for obedience to God and curses for disobedience.

1. "That then the Lord thy God will turn thy captivity, and have compassion upon thee, and will return and gather thee from all the nations." (Deuteronomy 30.3).
2. I.e., the mistress of a house.

especially took notice of that, *ver. ult.*, "Wait on the Lord, Be of good courage, and he shall strengthen thine Heart, wait I say on the Lord."[3]

## The Twelfth Remove[4]

It was upon a Sabbath-day-morning, that they prepared for their travel. This morning I asked my master whether he would sell me to my husband. He answered me "Nux,"[5] which did much rejoice my spirit. My mistress, before we went, was gone to the burial of a papoose, and returning, she found me sitting and reading in my Bible; she snatched it hastily out of my hand, and threw it out of doors. I ran out and catched it up, and put it into my pocket, and never let her see it afterward. Then they packed up their things to be gone, and gave me my load. I complained it was too heavy, whereupon she gave me a slap in the face, and bade me go; I lifted up my heart to God, hoping the redemption was not far off; and the rather because their insolency grew worse and worse.

But the thoughts of my going homeward (for so we bent our course) much cheered my spirit, and made my burden seem light, and almost nothing at all. But (to my amazement and great perplexity) the scale was soon turned; for when we had gone a little way, on a sudden my mistress gives out; she would go no further, but turn back again, and said I must go back again with her, and she called her *sannup*, and would have had him gone back also, but he would not, but said he would go on, and come to us again in three days. My spirit was, upon this, I confess, very impatient, and almost outrageous. I thought I could as well have died as went back; I cannot declare the trouble that I was in about it; but yet back again I must go. As soon as I had the opportunity, I took my Bible to read, and that quieting Scripture came to my hand, "Be still, and know that I am God" (Psalm 46.10). Which stilled my spirit for the present. But a sore time of trial, I concluded, I had to go through, my master being gone, who seemed to me the best friend that I had of an Indian, both in cold and hunger, and quickly so it proved. Down I sat, with my heart as full as it could hold, and yet so hungry that I could not sit neither; but going out to see what I could find, and walking among the trees, I found six acorns, and two chestnuts, which were some refreshment to me. Towards night I gathered some sticks for my own comfort, that I might not lie a-cold; but when we came to lie down they bade me to go out, and lie somewhere else, for they had company (they said) come in more than their own. I told them, I could not tell where to go, they bade me go look; I told them, if I went to another wigwam they would be angry, and send me home again. Then one of the company drew his sword, and told me he would run me through if I did not go presently. Then was I fain to stoop to this rude fellow, and to go out in the night, I knew not whither. Mine eyes have seen that fellow afterwards walking up and down Boston, under the appearance of a Friend Indian, and several others of the like cut. I went to one wigwam, and they told me they had no room. Then I went to another, and they said the same; at last an old Indian bade me to come to him, and his squaw gave me some ground nuts; she gave me also something to lay under my head, and a good fire we had;

3. Verse 14.
4. Sunday, April 9.
5. Yes.

and through the good providence of God, I had a comfortable lodging that night. In the morning, another Indian bade me come at night, and he would give me six ground nuts, which I did. We were at this place and time about two miles from [the] Connecticut river. We went in the morning to gather ground nuts, to the river, and went back again that night. I went with a good load at my back (for they when they went, though but a little way, would carry all their trumpery with them). I told them the skin was off my back, but I had no other comforting answer from them than this: that it would be no matter if my head were off too.

## The Twentieth Remove[6]

It was their usual manner to remove, when they had done any mischief, lest they should be found out; and so they did at this time. We went about three or four miles, and there they built a great wigwam, big enough to hold an hundred Indians, which they did in preparation to a great day of dancing. They would say now amongst themselves, that the governor would be so angry for his loss at Sudbury, that he would send no more about the captives, which made me grieve and tremble. My sister being not far from the place where we now were, and hearing that I was here, desired her master to let her come and see me, and he was willing to it, and would go with her; but she being ready before him, told him she would go before, and was come within a mile or two of the place. Then he overtook her, and began to rant as if he had been mad, and made her go back again in the rain; so that I never saw her till I saw her in Charlestown. But the Lord requited many of their ill doings, for this Indian her master, was hanged afterward at Boston. The Indians now began to come from all quarters, against their merry dancing day. Among some of them came one goodwife Kettle. I told her my heart was so heavy that it was ready to break. "So is mine too," said she, but yet said, "I hope we shall hear some good news shortly." I could hear how earnestly my sister desired to see me, and I as earnestly desired to see her; and yet neither of us could get an opportunity. My daughter was also now about a mile off, and I had not seen her in nine or ten weeks, as I had not seen my sister since our first taking. I earnestly desired them to let me go and see them: yea, I entreated, begged, and persuaded them, but to let me see my daughter; and yet so hard-hearted were they, that they would not suffer it. They made use of their tyrannical power whilst they had it; but through the Lord's wonderful mercy, their time was now but short.

On a Sabbath day, the sun being about an hour high in the afternoon, came Mr. John Hoar[7] (the council permitting him, and his own foreward spirit inclining him), together with the two forementioned Indians, Tom and Peter, with their third letter from the council. When they came near, I was abroad. Though I saw them not, they presently called me in, and bade me sit down and not stir. Then they catched up their guns, and away they ran, as if an enemy had been at hand, and the guns went off apace. I manifested some great trouble, and they asked me what was the matter? I told them I thought

---

6. April 28 to May 2, to an encampment at the southern end of Wachusett Lake, Princeton, Massachusetts.
7. John Hoar was from Concord, Massachusetts. He

had been delegated by Rowlandson's husband to represent him at the council for the Sagamore Indians, and to bargain for Rowlandson's redemption.

they had killed the Englishman (for they had in the meantime informed me that an Englishman was come). They said, no. They shot over his horse and under and before his horse, and they pushed him this way and that way, at their pleasure, showing what they could do. Then they let them come to their wigwams. I begged of them to let me see the Englishman, but they would not. But there was I fain to sit their pleasure. When they had talked their fill with him, they suffered me to go to him. We asked each other of our welfare, and how my husband did, and all my friends? He told me they were all well, and would be glad to see me. Amongst other things which my husband sent me, there came a pound of tobacco, which I sold for nine shillings in money; for many of the Indians for want of tobacco, smoked hemlock, and ground ivy. It was a great mistake in any, who thought I sent for tobacco; for through the favor of God, that desire was overcome. I now asked them whether I should go home with Mr. Hoar? They answered no, one and another of them, and it being night, we lay down with that answer. In the morning Mr. Hoar invited the Sagamores to dinner; but when we went to get it ready we found that they had stolen the greatest part of the provision Mr. Hoar had brought, out of his bags, in the night. And we may see the wonderful power of God, in that one passage, in that when there was such a great number of the Indians together, and so greedy of a little good food, and no English there but Mr. Hoar and myself, that there they did not knock us in the head, and take what we had, there being not only some provision, but also trading-cloth,[8] a part of the twenty pounds agreed upon. But instead of doing us any mischief, they seemed to be ashamed of the fact, and said, it were some matchit[9] Indian that did it. Oh, that we could believe that there is nothing too hard for God! God showed His power over the heathen in this, as He did over the hungry lions when Daniel was cast into the den.[1] Mr. Hoar called them betime to dinner, but they ate very little, they being so busy in dressing themselves, and getting ready for their dance, which was carried on by eight of them, four men and four squaws. My master and mistress being two. He was dressed in his holland[2] shirt, with great laces sewed at the tail of it; he had his silver buttons, his white stockings, his garters were hung round with shillings, and he had girdles of wampum[3] upon his head and shoulders. She had a kersey[4] coat, and covered with girdles of wampum from the loins upward. Her arms from her elbows to her hands were covered with bracelets; there were handfuls of necklaces about her neck, and several sorts of jewels in her ears. She had fine red stockings, and white shoes, her hair powdered and face painted red, that was always before black. And all the dancers were after the same manner. There were two others singing and knocking on a kettle for their music. They kept hopping up and down one after another, with a kettle of water in the midst, standing warm upon some embers, to drink of when they were dry. They held on till it was almost night, throwing out wampum to the standers by. At night I asked them again, if I should go home? They all as one said no, except[5] my husband would come for me. When we were lain down, my master went out of the wigwam, and by and by sent in an Indian called James the Printer,[6] who told

---

8. Cloth used for barter.
9. Bad.
1. The prophet Daniel was cast into a den of lions, but they did not harm him (see Daniel 6.1–29).
2. Linen.
3. Beads of polished shells used by some American In-

dians as currency.
4. Coarse cloth woven from long wool and usually ribbed.
5. Unless.
6. An American Indian who assisted the Rev. John Eliot in his printing of the Bible.

Mr. Hoar, that my master would let me go home tomorrow, if he would let him have one pint of liquors. Then Mr. Hoar called his own Indians, Tom and Peter, and bid them go and see whether he would promise it before them three; and if he would, he should have it; which he did, and he had it. Then Philip[7] smelling the business called me to him, and asked me what I would give him, to tell me some good news, and speak a good word for me. I told him I could not tell what to give him. I would [give him] anything I had, and asked him what he would have? He said two coats and twenty shillings in money, and half a bushel of seed corn, and some tobacco. I thanked him for his love; but I knew the good news as well as the crafty fox. My master after he had had his drink, quickly came ranting into the wigwam again, and called for Mr. Hoar, drinking to him, and saying, he was a good man, and then again he would say, "hang him rogue." Being almost drunk, he would drink to him, and yet presently say he should be hanged. Then he called for me. I trembled to hear him, yet I was fain to go to him, and he drank to me, showing no incivility. He was the first Indian I saw drunk all the while that I was amongst them. At last his squaw ran out, and he after her, round the wigwam, with his money jingling at his knees. But she escaped him. But having an old squaw he ran to her; and so through the Lord's mercy, we were no more troubled that night. Yet I had not a comfortable night's rest; for I think I can say, I did not sleep for three nights together. The night before the letter came from the council, I could not rest, I was so full of fears and troubles, God many times leaving us most in the dark, when deliverance is nearest. Yea, at this time I could not rest night nor day. The next night I was overjoyed, Mr. Hoar being come, and that with such good tidings. The third night I was even swallowed up with the thoughts of things, *viz.* that ever I should go home again; and that I must go, leaving my children behind me in the wilderness; so that sleep was now almost departed from mine eyes.

On Tuesday morning they called their general court (as they call it) to consult and determine, whether I should go home or no. And they all as one man did seemingly consent to it, that I should go home; except Philip, who would not come among them.

But before I go any further, I would take leave to mention a few remarkable passages of providence, which I took special notice of in my afflicted time.

1. Of the fair opportunity lost in the long march, a little after the fort fight, when our English army was so numerous, and in pursuit of the enemy, and so near as to take several and destroy them, and the enemy in such distress for food that our men might track them by their rooting in the earth for ground nuts, whilst they were flying for their lives. I say, that then our army should want provision, and be forced to leave their pursuit and return homeward; and the very next week the enemy came upon our town, like bears bereft of their whelps, or so many ravenous wolves, rending us and our lambs to death. But what shall I say? God seemed to leave his People to themselves, and order all things for His own holy ends. Shall there be evil in the City and the Lord hath not done it?[8] They are not grieved for the affliction of Joseph, therefore shall they go captive, with the first that go captive.[9] It is the Lord's doing, and it should be marvelous in our eyes.

---

7. An American Indian who aided Rowlandson earlier      8. Amos 3.6.
on the journey.      9. Amos 6.6–7.

2. I cannot but remember how the Indians derided the slowness, and dullness of the English army, in its setting out. For after the desolations at Lancaster and Medfield, as I went along with them, they asked me when I thought the English army would come after them? I told them I could not tell. "It may be they will come in May," said they. Thus did they scoff at us, as if the English would be a quarter of a year getting ready.

3. Which also I have hinted before, when the English army with new supplies were sent forth to pursue after the enemy, and they understanding it, fled before them till they came to Banquaug river, where they forthwith went over safely; that that river should be impassable to the English. I can but admire to see the wonderful providence of God in preserving the heathen for further affliction to our poor country. They could go in great numbers over, but the English must stop. God had an over-ruling hand in all those things.

4. It was thought, if their corn were cut down, they would starve and die with hunger, and all their corn that could be found, was destroyed, and they driven from that little they had in store, into the woods in the midst of winter; and yet how to admiration did the Lord preserve them for His holy ends, and the destruction of many still amongst the English! strangely did the Lord provide for them; that I did not see (all the time I was among them) one man, woman, or child, die with hunger.

Though many times they would eat that, that a hog or a dog would hardly touch; yet by that God strengthened them to be a scourge to His people.

The chief and commonest food was ground nuts. They eat also nuts and acorns, artichokes, lilly roots, ground beans, and several other weeds and roots, that I know not.

They would pick up old bones, and cut them to pieces at the joints, and if they were full of worms and maggots, they would scald them over the fire to make the vermine come out, and then boil them, and drink up the liquor, and then beat the great ends of them in a mortar, and so eat them. They would eat horse's guts, and ears, and all sorts of wild birds which they could catch; also bear, venison, beaver, tortoise, frogs, squirrels, dogs, skunks, rattlesnakes; yea, the very bark of trees; besides all sorts of creatures, and provision which they plundered from the English. I can but stand in admiration to see the wonderful power of God in providing for such a vast number of our enemies in the wilderness, where there was nothing to be seen, but from hand to mouth. Many times in a morning, the generality of them would eat up all they had, and yet have some further supply against they wanted. It is said, "Oh, that my People had hearkened to me, and Israel had walked in my ways, I should soon have subdued their Enemies, and turned my hand against their Adversaries" (Psalm 81.13–14). But now our perverse and evil carriages in the sight of the Lord, have so offended Him, that instead of turning His hand against them, the Lord feeds and nourishes them up to be a scourge to the whole land.

5. Another thing that I would observe is the strange providence of God, in turning things about when the Indians was at the highest, and the English at the lowest. I was with the enemy eleven weeks and five days, and not one week passed without the fury of the enemy, and some desolation by fire and sword upon one place or other. They mourned (with their black faces) for their own losses, yet triumphed and rejoiced in their inhumane, and many times devilish cruelty to the English. They would boast much of their victories; saying that

in two hours time they had destroyed such a captain and his company at such a place; and boast how many towns they had destroyed, and then scoff, and say they had done them a good turn to send them to Heaven so soon. Again, they would say this summer that they would knock all the rogues in the head, or drive them into the sea, or make them fly the country; thinking surely, Agag-like, "The bitterness of Death is past."[1] Now the heathen begins to think all is their own, and the poor Christians' hopes to fail (as to man) and now their eyes are more to God, and their hearts sigh heaven-ward; and to say in good earnest, "Help Lord, or we perish." When the Lord had brought His people to this, that they saw no help in anything but Himself; then He takes the quarrel into His own hand; and though they had made a pit, in their own imaginations, as deep as hell for the Christians that summer, yet the Lord hurled themselves into it. And the Lord had not so many ways before to preserve them, but now He hath as many to destroy them.

But to return again to my going home, where we may see a remarkable change of providence. At first they were all against it, except my husband would come for me, but afterwards they assented to it, and seemed much to rejoice in it; some asked me to send them some bread, others some tobacco, others shaking me by the hand, offering me a hood and scarfe to ride in; not one moving hand or tongue against it. Thus hath the Lord answered my poor desire, and the many earnest requests of others put up unto God for me. In my travels an Indian came to me and told me, if I were willing, he and his squaw would run away, and go home along with me. I told him no: I was not willing to run away, but desired to wait God's time, that I might go home quietly, and without fear. And now God hath granted me my desire. O the wonderful power of God that I have seen, and the experience that I have had. I have been in the midst of those roaring lions, and savage bears, that feared neither God, nor man, nor the devil, by night and day, alone and in company, sleeping all sorts together, and yet not one of them ever offered me the least abuse of unchastity to me, in word or action. Though some are ready to say I speak it for my own credit; but I speak it in the presence of God, and to His Glory. God's power is as great now, and as sufficient to save, as when He preserved Daniel in the lion's den; or the three children in the fiery furnace.[2] I may well say as his Psalm 107.12 "Oh give thanks unto the Lord for he is good, for his mercy endureth for ever." Let the redeemed of the Lord say so, whom He hath redeemed from the hand of the enemy, especially that I should come away in the midst of so many hundreds of enemies quietly and peaceably, and not a dog moving his tongue. So I took my leave of them, and in coming along my heart melted into tears, more than all the while I was with them, and I was almost swallowed up with the thoughts that ever I should go home again. About the sun going down, Mr. Hoar, and myself, and the two Indians came to Lancaster, and a solemn sight it was to me. There had I lived many comfortable years amongst my relations and neighbors, and now not one Christian to be seen, nor one house left standing. We went on to a farmhouse that was yet standing, where we lay all night, and a comfortable lodging we had, though nothing but straw to lie on. The Lord preserved us in safety that night, and raised us up again in the morning, and carried us along, that

1. 1 Samuel 15.32. Agag was the king of Amalek; he was defeated by Saul and thought himself spared, but was slain by Samuel (see 1 Samuel 15).

2. Shadrach, Meshach, and Abednego refused to worship false gods and were cast into a fiery furnace but saved from death by an angel (see Daniel 3.13–30).

before noon, we came to Concord. Now was I full of joy, and yet not without sorrow; joy to see such a lovely sight, so many Christians together, and some of them my neighbors. There I met with my brother, and my brother-in-law, who asked me, if I knew where his wife was? Poor heart! he had helped to bury her, and knew it not. She being shot down by the house was partly burnt, so that those who were at Boston at the desolation of the town, and came back afterward, and buried the dead, did not know her. Yet I was not without sorrow, to think how many were looking and longing, and my own children amongst the rest, to enjoy that deliverance that I had now received, and I did not know whether ever I should see them again. Being recruited[3] with food and raiment we went to Boston that day, where I met with my dear husband, but the thoughts of our dear children, one being dead, and the other we could not tell where, abated our comfort each to other. I was not before so much hemmed in with the merciless and cruel heathen, but now as much with pitiful, tender-hearted and compassionate Christians. In that poor, and distressed, and beggarly condition I was received in; I was kindly entertained in several houses. So much love I received from several (some of whom I knew, and others I knew not) that I am not capable to declare it. But the Lord knows them all by name. The Lord reward them sevenfold into their bosoms of His spirituals, for their temporals.[4] The twenty pounds, the price of my redemption, was raised by some Boston gentlemen, and Mrs. Usher, whose bounty and religious charity, I would not forget to make mention of. Then Mr. Thomas Shepard of Charlestown received us into his house, where we continued eleven weeks; and a father and mother they were to us. And many more tender-hearted friends we met with in that place. We were now in the midst of love, yet not without much and frequent heaviness of heart for our poor children, and other relations, who were still in affliction. The week following, after my coming in, the governor and council sent forth to the Indians again; and that not without success; for they brought in my sister, and goodwife Kettle. Their not knowing where our children were was a sore trial to us still, and yet we were not without secret hopes that we should see them again. That which was dead lay heavier upon my spirit, than those which were alive and amongst the heathen: thinking how it suffered with its wounds, and I was no way able to relieve it; and how it was buried by the heathen in the wilderness from among all Christians. We were hurried up and down in our thoughts, sometime we should hear a report that they were gone this way, and sometimes that; and that they were come in, in this place or that. We kept inquiring and listening to hear concerning them, but no certain news as yet. About this time the council had ordered a day of public thanksgiving. Though I thought I had still cause of mourning, and being unsettled in our minds, we thought we would ride toward the eastward, to see if we could hear anything concerning our children. And as we were riding along (God is the wise disposer of all things) between Ipswich and Rowley we met with Mr. William Hubbard, who told us that our son Joseph was come in to Major Waldron's, and another with him, which was my sister's son. I asked him how he knew it? He said the major himself told him so. So along we went till we came to Newbury; and their minister being absent, they desired my husband to preach the thanksgiving for them; but he was not willing to stay there that night, but would go over

3. Refreshed.                                                    4. Worldly goods and gifts.

to Salisbury, to hear further, and come again in the morning, which he did, and preached there that day. At night, when he had done, one came and told him that his daughter was come in at Providence. Here was mercy on both hands. Now hath God fulfilled that precious Scripture which was such a comfort to me in my distressed condition. When my heart was ready to sink into the earth (my children being gone, I could not tell whither) and my knees trembling under me, and I was walking through the valley of the shadow of death; then the Lord brought, and now has fulfilled that reviving word unto me: "Thus saith the Lord, Refrain thy voice from weeping, and thine eyes from tears, for thy Work shall be rewarded, saith the Lord, and they shall come again from the Land of the Enemy."[5] Now we were between them, the one on the east, and the other on the west. Our son being nearest, we went to him first, to Portsmouth, where we met with him, and with the Major also, who told us he had done what he could, but could not redeem him under seven pounds, which the good people thereabouts were pleased to pay. The Lord reward the major, and all the rest, though unknown to me, for their labor of Love. My sister's son was redeemed for four pounds, which the council gave order for the payment of. Having now received one of our children, we hastened toward the other. Going back through Newbury my husband preached there on the Sabbath day; for which they rewarded him many fold.

On Monday we came to Charlestown, where we heard that the governor of Rhode Island had sent over for our daughter, to take care of her, being now within his jurisdiction; which should not pass without our acknowledgments. But she being nearer Rehoboth than Rhode Island, Mr. Newman went over, and took care of her and brought her to his own house. And the goodness of God was admirable to us in our low estate, in that He raised up passionate[6] friends on every side to us, when we had nothing to recompense any for their love. The Indians were now gone that way, that it was apprehended dangerous to go to her. But the carts which carried provision to the English army, being guarded, brought her with them to Dorchester, where we received her safe. Blessed be the Lord for it, for great is His power, and He can do whatsoever seemeth Him good. Her coming in was after this manner: she was traveling one day with the Indians, with her basket at her back; the company of Indians were got before her, and gone out of sight, all except one squaw; she followed the squaw till night, and then both of them lay down, having nothing over them but the heavens and under them but the earth. Thus she traveled three days together, not knowing whither she was going; having nothing to eat or drink but water, and green hirtle-berries. At last they came into Providence, where she was kindly entertained by several of that town. The Indians often said that I should never have her under twenty pounds. But now the Lord hath brought her in upon free-cost, and given her to me the second time. The Lord make us a blessing indeed, each to others. Now have I seen that Scripture also fulfilled, "If any of thine be driven out to the outmost parts of heaven, from thence will the Lord thy God gather thee, and from thence will he fetch thee. And the Lord thy God will put all these curses upon thine enemies, and on them which hate thee, which persecuted thee" (Deuteronomy 30.4–7). Thus hath the Lord brought me and mine out of that horrible pit, and hath set us in the midst of tender-hearted and compassionate Christians. It is the desire of

5. Jeremiah 31.16.                        6. Compassionate.

my soul that we may walk worthy of the mercies received, and which we are receiving. Our family being now gathered together (those of us that were living), the South Church in Boston hired an house for us. Then we removed from Mr. Shephard's, those cordial friends, and went to Boston, where we continued about three-quarters of a year. Still the Lord went along with us, and provided graciously for us. I thought it somewhat strange to set up house-keeping with bare walls; but as Solomon says, "Money answers all things"[7] and that we had through the benevolence of Christian friends, some in this town, and some in that, and others; and some from England; that in a little time we might look, and see the house furnished with love. The Lord hath been exceeding good to us in our low estate, in that when we had neither house nor home, nor other necessaries, the Lord so moved the hearts of these and those towards us, that we wanted neither food, nor raiment for ourselves or ours: "There is a Friend which sticketh closer than a Brother" (Proverbs 18.24). And how many such friends have we found, and now living amongst? And truly such a friend have we found him to be unto us, in whose house we lived, *viz.* Mr. James Whitcomb, a friend unto us near hand, and afar off.

I can remember the time when I used to sleep quietly without workings in my thoughts, whole nights together, but now it is other ways with me. When all are fast about me, and no eye open, but His who ever waketh, my thoughts are upon things past, upon the awful dispensation of the Lord towards us, upon His wonderful power and might, in carrying of us through so many difficulties, in returning us in safety, and suffering none to hurt us. I remember in the night season, how the other day I was in the midst of thousands of enemies, and nothing but death before me. It is then hard work to persuade myself, that ever I should be satisfied with bread again. But now we are fed with the finest of the wheat, and, as I may say, with honey out of the rock.[8] Instead of the husk, we have the fatted calf.[9] The thoughts of these things in the particulars of them, and of the love and goodness of God towards us, make it true of me, what David said of himself, "I watered my Couch with my tears" (Psalm 6.6). Oh! the wonderful power of God that mine eyes have seen, affording matter enough for my thoughts to run in, that when others are sleeping mine eyes are weeping.

I have seen the extreme vanity of this world: One hour I have been in health, and wealthy, wanting nothing. But the next hour in sickness and wounds, and death, having nothing but sorrow and affliction.

Before I knew what affliction meant, I was ready sometimes to wish for it. When I lived in prosperity, having the comforts of the world about me, my relations by me, my heart cheerful, and taking little care for anything, and yet seeing many, whom I preferred before myself, under many trials and afflictions, in sickness, weakness, poverty, losses, crosses, and cares of the world, I should be sometimes jealous least I should have my portion in this life, and that Scripture would come to my mind, "For whom the Lord loveth he chasteneth, and scourgeth every Son whom he receiveth" (Hebrews 12.6). But now I see the Lord had His time to scourge and chasten me. The portion of some is to have their afflictions by drops, now one drop and then another; but

7. Ecclesiastes 10.19.
8. "He should have fed them also with the finest of the wheat: and with honey out of the rock should I have

satisfied thee" (Psalm 81.16).
9. "And bring hither the fatted calf, and kill it; and let us eat, and be merry" (Luke 15.23).

the dregs of the cup, the wine of astonishment, like a sweeping rain that leaveth no food, did the Lord prepare to be my portion. Affliction I wanted, and affliction I had, full measure (I thought), pressed down and running over. Yet I see, when God calls a person to anything, and through never so many difficulties, yet He is fully able to carry them through and make them see, and say they have been gainers thereby. And I hope I can say in some measure, as David did, "It is good for me that I have been afflicted."[1] The Lord hath showed me the vanity of these outward things. That they are the vanity of vanities, and vexation of spirit, that they are but a shadow, a blast, a bubble, and things of no continuance. That we must rely on God Himself, and our whole dependance must be upon Him. If trouble from smaller matters begin to arise in me, I have something at hand to check myself with, and say, why am I troubled? It was but the other day that if I had had the world, I would have given it for my freedom, or to have been a servant to a Christian. I have learned to look beyond present and smaller troubles, and to be quieted under them. As Moses said, "Stand still and see the salvation of the Lord" (Exodus 14.13).

Finis.

1682

1. Psalm 119.71.

---

# EDWARD TAYLOR

## c. 1642–1729

Given the importance of Edward Taylor's role in the town in which he lived for fifty-eight years, it is curious that we should know so little about his life. Taylor was probably born in Sketchly, Leicestershire County, England; his father was a "yeoman farmer"—that is, he was not a "gentleman" with large estates, but an independent landholder with title to his farm. Although his poetry contains no images that reflect his boyhood in Leicestershire, the dialect of that farming country is ever-present and gives his verse an air of provincial charm but also, it must be admitted, makes it difficult and complex for the modern reader. Taylor did not enter Harvard until he was twenty-nine years old and stayed only three years. It is assumed, therefore, that he had some university education in England, but it is not known where. We do know that he taught school and that he left his family and sailed to New England in 1668 because he would not sign an oath of loyalty to the Church of England. Rather than compromise his religious principles as a Puritan, he preferred exile in what he once called a "howling wilderness." It was at Harvard that he must have decided to leave teaching and prepare himself for the ministry.

In 1671 a delegation from the frontier town of Westfield, Massachusetts, asked Taylor to join them as their minister, and after a good deal of soul-searching he journeyed with them the hundred miles west to Westfield, where he remained the rest of his life. As by far the most educated member of that community, he served as minister, physician, and public servant. Taylor married twice and had fourteen children, many of whom died in infancy. A rigorous observer of all churchly functions, Taylor did not shy away from the religious controversies of the period. He was a strict observer of the "old" New England way, demanding a public account of conversion before admission to church membership and the right to partake of the sacrament of communion.

Taylor was a learned man as well as a pious one. Like most Harvard ministers, he knew Latin, Hebrew, and Greek. He had a passion for books and copied out in his own hand volumes that he borrowed from his college roommate, Samuel Sewall. He was known to Sewall and others as a good preacher, and on occasion he sent poems and letters to Boston friends, some parts of which were published during his lifetime. But Taylor's work as a poet was generally unknown until, in the 1930s, Thomas H. Johnson discovered that most of Taylor's poems had been deposited in the Yale University Library by Taylor's grandson, Ezra Stiles, a former president of Yale. It was one of the major literary discoveries of the twentieth century and revealed a body of work by a Puritan divine that was remarkable both in its quantity and quality.

Taylor's interest in poetry was lifelong, and he tried his hand at a variety of poetic genres: elegies on the death of public figures; lyrics in the manner of Elizabethan songs; a long poem, *God's Determinations*, in the tradition of the medieval debate; and an almost unreadable five-hundred-page *Metrical History of Christianity*, primarily a book of martyrs. But Taylor's best verse is to be found in a series called *Preparatory Meditations*. These poems, written for his own pleasure and never a part of any religious service, followed chiefly upon his preparation for a sermon to be delivered at monthly communion. They gave the poet an occasion to summarize the emotional and intellectual content of his sermon and to speak directly and fervently to God. Sometimes these poems are gnarled and difficult to follow, but they also reveal a unique voice, unmistakably Taylor's. They are written in an idiom that harks back to the verse Taylor must have known as a child in England—the Metaphysical lyrics of John Donne and George Herbert—and so delight in puns and paradoxes and a rich profusion of metaphors and images. Nothing previously discovered about Puritan literature had suggested that there was a writer in New England who had sustained such a long-term love affair with poetry.

## *From* Preparatory Meditations[1]

### Prologue

Lord, Can a Crumb of Dust the Earth outweigh,
    Outmatch all mountains, nay, the Crystal sky?
Embosom in't designs that shall Display
    And trace into the Boundless Deity?
Yea, hand a Pen whose moisture doth guide o'er       5
*Eternal Glory with a glorious glore.*[2]

*If it its Pen had of an Angel's Quill,*
    *And sharpened on a Precious Stone ground tight,*

1. The full title is *Preparatory Meditations before my Approach to the Lord's Supper. Chiefly upon the Doctrine preached upon the Day of Administration [of Communion]*. Taylor administered communion once a month to those members of his congregation who had made a declaration of their faith. He wrote these meditations in private; they are primarily the result of his contemplation of the biblical texts that served as the basis for the communion sermon. A total of 217 meditations survive, dating from 1682 to 1725. The text used here is from *Poems of Edward Taylor*, edited by Donald E. Stanford (1960).
2. Glory (Scottish).

And dipped in liquid Gold, and moved by Skill
   In Crystal leaves should golden Letters write,                    10
   It would but blot and blur, yea, jag, and jar
   Unless Thou mak'st the Pen, and Scrivener.

I am this Crumb of Dust which is designed
   To make my Pen unto Thy Praise alone,
And my dull Fancy³ I would gladly grind                              15
   Unto an Edge on Zion's⁴ Precious Stone.
And Write in Liquid Gold upon Thy Name
My Letters till Thy glory forth doth flame.

Let not th' attempts break down my Dust, I pray,
   Nor laugh Thou them to scorn but pardon give.                     20
Inspire this crumb of Dust till it display
   Thy Glory through't: and then Thy dust shall live.
Its failings then Thou'lt overlook, I trust,
   They being Slips slipped from Thy Crumb of Dust.

Thy Crumb of Dust breathes two words from its breast,               25
   That Thou wilt guide its pen to write aright
To Prove Thou art, and that Thou art the best
   And show Thy Properties to shine most bright.
And then Thy Works will shine as flowers on Stems
   Or as in Jewelry Shops, do gems.                                 30

c. 1682                                                           1939


## Meditation 8 (First Series)

*John 6.51. I am the Living Bread.*¹

I kenning through Astronomy Divine
   The World's bright Battlement,² wherein I spy
A Golden Path my Pencil cannot line,
   From that bright Throne unto my Threshold lie.
And while my puzzled thoughts about it pour,                         5
   I find the Bread of Life in't at my door.

When that this Bird of Paradise³ put in
   This Wicker Cage (my Corpse) to tweedle praise
Had pecked the Fruit forbade: and so did fling
   Away its Food; and lost its golden days;                         10

---

3. I.e., imagination.
4. The hill in Jerusalem on which Solomon built his
temple; the city of God on earth.
1. "The Jews then murmured at him, because he said,
I am the bread which came down from heaven. And
they said, Is not this Jesus, the son of Joseph, whose
father and mother we know? how is it then that he
saith, I came down from heaven? Jesus therefore answered . . . Verily, verily, I say unto you, He that believeth on me hath everlasting life. I am that bread of

life" (John 6.41–51). Christ offers a "New Covenant of
Faith" in place of the "Old Covenant of Works,"
which Adam broke when he disobeyed God's commandment.
2. I.e., discerning, by means of "divine astronomy,"
the towers of heaven. Taylor goes on to suggest that
there is an invisible golden path from this world to the
Gates of Heaven.
3. I.e., the soul, which is like a bird kept in the
body's cage.

It fell into Celestial Famine sore:
And never could attain a morsel more.

Alas! alas! Poor Bird, what wilt thou do?
The Ceatures' field no food for Souls e'er gave.
And if thou knock at Angels' doors they show          15
An Empty Barrel: they no soul bread have.
Alas! Poor Bird, the World's White Loaf is done.
And cannot yield thee here the smallest Crumb.

In this sad state, God's Tender Bowels[4] run
Out streams of Grace: and He to end all strife        20
The Purest Wheat in Heaven His dear-dear son
Grinds, and kneads up into this Bread of Life.
Which Bread of Life from Heaven down came and stands
Dished on Thy Table up by Angels' Hands.

Did God mold up this Bread in Heaven, and bake,       25
Which from His Table came, and to thine goeth?
Doth He bespeak thee thus, This Soul Bread take.
Come Eat thy fill of this thy God's White Loaf?
It's Food too fine for Angels, yet come, take
And Eat thy fill. It's Heaven's Sugar Cake.           30

What Grace is this knead in this Loaf? This thing
Souls are but petty things it to admire.
Ye Angels, help: This fill would to the brim
Heav'ns whelmed-down[5] Crystal meal Bowl, yea and higher.
This Bread of Life dropped in thy mouth, doth Cry:    35
Eat, Eat me, Soul, and thou shalt never die.

June 8, 1684                                          1939

## Meditation 16 (First Series)

*Luke 7.16. A Great Prophet is risen up.*[1]

Leaf Gold, Lord of Thy Golden wedge[2] o'erlaid
My Soul at first, Thy Grace in every part
Whose pert,[3] fierce Eye Thou such a Sight hadst made
Whose brightsome beams could break into Thy heart
Till Thy Cursed Foe had with my Fist mine Eye          5
Dashed out, and did my Soul Unglorify.

4. Here used in the sense of the interior of the body, the "seat of the tender and sympathetic emotions," the heart.
5. Turned over. The *Oxford English Dictionary* quotes a passage from Dryden that is relevant: "That the earth is like a trencher and the Heavens a dish whelmed over it."
1. Taylor refers to the passage in the New Testament in which Jesus raised from the dead the only son of a widow. When the dead man spoke, fear took hold of all the witnesses to this miracle and they said: "'That a great prophet is risen up among us; and, that God hath visited his people. And this rumor of him went forth throughout all Judea, and throughout all the region round about" (Luke 7.16–17).
2. In gilding it is customary to apply small squares of gold leaf to a surface; here the shape would seem to be triangular.
3. Sharp, quick to see.

I cannot see, nor Will Thy will aright.
Nor see to wail my Woe, my loss and hue
Nor all the Shine in all the Sun can light
    My Candle, nor its heat my Heart renew.                    10
    See, wail, and Will Thy Will, I must, or must
    From Heaven's sweet Shine to Hell's hot flame be thrust.

Grace then Concealed in God Himself, did roll
Even Snowball like into a Sunball Shine
And nestles all Its beams bunched in Thy soul              15
    My Lord, that sparkle in Prophetic Lines.
    Oh! Wonder more than Wonderful! this Will
    Lighten the Eye which Sight Divine did spill.

What art Thou, Lord, this Ball of Glory bright?
    A Bundle of Celestial Beams up bound                    20
In Grace's band fixed in Heaven's topmost height
    Pouring Thy golden beams thence, Circling round
    Which show Thy Glory, and Thy Glory's Way
    And Everywhere will make Celestial Day.

Lord, let Thy Golden Beams pierce through mine Eye          25
    And leave therein an Heavenly Light to glaze
My Soul with glorious Grace all o'er, whereby
    I may have Sight, and Grace in me may blaze.
    Lord ting⁴ my Candle at Thy Burning rays,
    To give a gracious Glory to Thy Praise                   30

Thou Lightning Eye, let some bright Beams of Thine
Stick in my Soul, to light and liven it:
Light, Life, and Glory, things that are Divine;
    I shall be graced withall for glory fit.
    My heart then stuffed with Grace, Light, Life, and Glee   35
    I'll sacrifice in Flames of Love to Thee.

March 6, 1686                                              1960


## Meditation 22 (First Series)

*Philippians 2.9. God hath highly exalted Him.*[1]

When Thy Bright Beams, my Lord, do strike mine Eye,
    Methinks I then could truly Chide outright

4. Perhaps to "ring" with light.
1. "Let this mind be in you, which was also in Christ Jesus: Who, being in the form of God, thought it not robbery to be equal with God: But made himself no reputation, and took upon him the form of a servant, and was made in the likeness of men: And being found in fashion as a man, he humbled himself, and became obedient unto death, even the death of the cross.

Wherefore God also hath highly exalted him, and given him a name which is above every name: That at the name of Jesus every knee should bow, of things in heaven, and things in earth, and things under the earth; And that every tongue should confess that Jesus Christ is Lord, to the glory of God the Father" (Philippians 2.5–11).

My Hide-bound Soul that stands so niggardly
    That scarce a thought gets glorified by't.
    My Quaintest[2] metaphors are ragged Stuff,                    5
    Making the Sun seem like a Mullipuff.[3]

It's my desire, Thou shouldst be glorified:
    But when Thy Glory shines before mine eye,
I pardon Crave, lest my desire be Pride,
    Or bed Thy Glory in a Cloudy Sky.                             10
    The Sun grows wan; and Angels palefaced shrink,
    Before Thy Shine, which I besmear with Ink.

But shall the Bird sing forth Thy Praise, and shall
    The little Bee present her thankful Hum?
But I who see Thy shining Glory fall                              15
    Before mine Eyes, stand Blockish, Dull, and Dumb?
    Whether I speak, or speechless stand, I spy,
    I fail Thy Glory: therefore pardon Cry.

But this I find; My Rhymes do better suit
    Mine own Dispraise than tune forth praise to Thee.            20
Yet being Chid, whether Consonant,[4] or Mute,
    I force my Tongue to tattle, as You see.
    That I Thy glorious Praise may Trumpet right,
    Be Thou my Song, and make, Lord, me Thy pipe.

This shining Sky will fly away apace,                             25
    When Thy bright Glory splits the same to make
Thy Majesty a Pass, whose Fairest Face
    Too foul a Path is for Thy Feet to take.
    What Glory then, shall tend Thee through the Sky
    Draining the Heaven much of Angels dry?                       30

What Light then flame will in Thy Judgment Seat,
    'Fore which all men and Angels shall appear?
How shall Thy Glorious Righteousness them treat,
    Rend'ring to each after his Works done here?
    Then Saints with Angels Thou wilt glorify:                    35
    And burn Lewd[5] Men, and Devils Gloriously.

One glimpse, my Lord, of Thy bright Judgment Day,
    And Glory piercing through, like fiery Darts,
All Devils, doth me make for Grace to pray,
    For filling Grace had I ten thousand Hearts.                  40
    I'd through ten Hells to see Thy Judgment Day
    Wouldst Thou but gild my Soul with Thy bright Ray.

June 12, 1687                                                    1960

---

2. Most skilled, wise.                    4. Talkative, making sounds.
3. Fuzz ball.                             5. Worthless, fallen.

# Meditation 42 (First Series)

*Revelation 3.21. I will give Him to sit with Me in my Throne.*[1]

Apples of gold, in silver pictures shrined[2]
   Enchant the appetite, make mouths to water.
And Loveliness in Lumps, tunn'd, and enrined[3]
   In Jasper[4] Cask, when tapped, doth briskly vapor:
   Bring forth a birth of Keys t'unlock Love's Chest,          5
   That Love, like Birds, may fly to't from its nest.

Such is my Lord, and more. But what strange thing
   Am I become? Sin rusts my Lock all o'er.
Though He ten thousand Keys all on a string
   Takes out, scarce one is found unlocks the Door.          10
   Which ope, my Love crinched[5] in a Corner lies
   Like some shrunk Crickling[6] and scarce can rise.

Lord, ope the Door: rub off my Rust, Remove
   My sin, and Oil my Lock. (Dust there doth shelf).
My Wards will trig[7] before Thy Key: my Love               15
   Then, as enlivened, leap will on Thyself.
   It needs must be, that giving hands receive
   Again Receivers Hearts furled in Love Wreath.

Unkey my Heart; unlock Thy Wardrobe: bring
   Out royal Robes: adorn my Soul, Lord: so,                20
My Love in rich attire shall on my King
   Attend, and honor on Him well bestow.
   In Glory He prepares for His a place
   Whom He doth all beglory here with Grace.

He takes them to the shining threshold clear                25
   Of His bright Palace, clothed in Grace's flame.
Then takes them in thereto, not only there
   To have a Prospect,[8] but possess the same.
   The Crown of Life, the throne of Glory's Place,
   The Father's House blanched o'er with orient Grace.      30

Canaan[9] in gold print enwalled with gems:
   A Kingdom rimmed with Glory round: in fine[1]
A glorious Crown paled[2] thick with all the stems
   Of Grace, and of all Properties Divine.
   How happy wilt Thou make me when these shall             35
   As a blest Heritage unto me fall?

1. "To him that overcometh will I grant to sit with me in my throne, even as I also overcame, and am set down with my Father in his throne. He that hath an ear, let him hear what the Spirit saith unto the churches" (Revelation 3.21–22).
2. Enshrined, enclosed.
3. Rendered, melted down. "Tunn'd": placed in a casket.
4. A precious stone, usually green in color.
5. Shrunken, gnarled up.
6. Properly "crinkling," a small, withered apple.
7. Open. "Wards": the protective ridges of a lock that prevent any but the proper key to open it.
8. View, range of vision.
9. The land promised by God to Abraham; the biblical name of Jerusalem (cf. Genesis 12.5–8).
1. In essence.
2. Striped.

Adorn me, Lord, with Holy Huswifry.[3]
All blanch my Robes with Clusters of Thy Graces:
Thus lead me to Thy threshold: give mine Eye
A Peephole there to see Bright Glory's Chases.[4]    40
Then take me in: I'll pay, when I possess
Thy Throne, to Thee the Rent in Happiness.

August 2, 1691                          1939

## Upon Wedlock, and Death of Children[1]

A Curious Knot[2] God made in Paradise,
    And drew it out enameled[3] neatly Fresh.
It was the True-Love Knot, more sweet than spice,
    And set with all the flowers of Grace's dress.
    It's Wedden's[4] Knot, that ne're can be untied:    5
    No Alexander's Sword[5] can it divide.

The slips[6] here planted, gay and glorious grow:
    Unless an Hellish breath do singe their Plumes.
Here Primrose, Cowslips, Roses, Lilies blow[7]
    With Violets and Pinks that void[8] perfumes:    10
    Whose beauteous leaves o'erlaid with Honey Dew,
    And Chanting birds Chirp out sweet Music true.

When in this Knot I planted was, my Stock[9]
    Soon knotted, and a manly flower out brake.[1]
And after it, my branch again did knot,    15
    Brought out another Flower, its sweet-breathed mate.
    One knot gave one tother[2] the tother's place.
    Whence Chuckling smiles fought in each other's face.

But Oh! a glorious hand from glory came
    Guarded with Angels, soon did crop this flower[3]    20
Which almost tore the root up of the same,
    At that unlooked for, Dolesome, darksome hour.
    In Prayer to Christ perfumed it did ascend,
    And Angels bright did it to heaven 'tend.

But pausing on't, this sweet perfumed my thought:    25
    Christ would in Glory have a Flower, Choice, Prime,
And having Choice, chose this my branch forth brought.

3. Cloth woven in the home, and the traditional task of the housewife.
4. The settings of precious stones.
1. The text used here is from *Poems of Edward Taylor*, edited by Donald E. Stanford (1960).
2. Flower bed.
3. Polished, shining.
4. I.e., wedding's.
5. Alexander the Great cut the Gordian knot devised by the king of Phyrgia when he learned that anyone who could undo it would rule Asia.
6. Cuttings.
7. Bloom.
8. Emit.
9. Stem.
1. Samuel Taylor was born on August 27, 1675, and lived to maturity.
2. To the other.
3. Elizabeth Taylor was born on December 27, 1676, and died on December 25, 1677.

Lord take't. I thank Thee, Thou tak'st ought of mine:
It is my pledge in glory, part of me
Is now in it, Lord, glorified with Thee.                              30

But praying o're my branch, my branch did sprout,
    And bore another manly flower, and gay,[4]
And after that another, sweet brake[5] out,
    The which the former hand soon got away.
    But Oh! the tortures, Vomit, screechings, groans,              35
    and six week's Fever would pierce hearts like stones.[6]

Grief o're doth flow: and nature fault would find
    Were not Thy Will, my Spell, Charm, Joy, and Gem:
That as I said, I say, take, Lord, they're Thine.
    I piecemeal pass to Glory bright in them.                       40
    In joy, may I sweet flowers for glory breed,
    Whether thou get'st them green, or lets them seed.

c. 1682                                                            1939


# Upon a Wasp Chilled with Cold[1]

The Bear that breathes the Northern blast[2]
Did numb, Torpedo-like,[3] a Wasp
Whose stiffened limbs encramped, lay bathing
In Sol's[4] warm breath and shine as saving,
Which with her hands she chafes and stands                          5
Rubbing her Legs, Shanks, Thighs, and hands.
Her petty toes, and fingers' ends
Nipped with this breath, she out extends
Unto the Sun, in great desire
To warm her digits at that fire.                                   10
Doth hold her Temples in this state
Where pulse doth beat, and head doth ache.
Doth turn, and stretch her body small,
Doth Comb her velvet Capital.[5]
As if her little brain pan were                                    15
A Volume of Choice precepts clear.
As if her satin jacket hot
Contained Apothecary's Shop
Of Nature's receipts,[6] that prevails
To remedy all her sad ails,                                        20
As if her velvet helmet high
Did turret[7] rationality.

4. James Taylor was born on October 12, 1678, and lived to maturity.
5. I.e., broke out.
6. Abigail Taylor was born on August 6, 1681, and died on August 22, 1682.
1. The text used here is from *Poems of Edward Taylor*, edited by Donald E. Stanford (1960).
2. The northern constellation the Big Dipper, also called Ursa Major, or the Great Bear.
3. The torpedo is a fish, like a stingray, and discharges a shock to one who touches it, causing numbness. Sir Thomas Browne writes: "Torpedoes deliver their opium at a distance and stupify beyond themselves" (1646).
4. The sun personified.
5. Head.
6. Remedies, prescriptions. "Apothecary's Shop": what we would now call a drugstore or pharmacy.
7. Contain, encompass.

She fans her wing up to the Wind
As if her Pettycoat were lined,
With reason's fleece, and hoists sails                    25
And humming flies in thankful gales
Unto her dun Curled[8] palace Hall
Her warm thanks offering for all.

Lord, clear my misted sight that I
May hence view Thy Divinity,                              30
Some sparks whereof Thou up dost hasp[9]
Within this little downy Wasp
In whose small Corporation[1] we
A school and a schoolmaster see,
Where we may learn, and easily find                      35
A nimble Spirit bravely mind
Her work in every limb: and lace
It up neat with a vital grace,
Acting each part though ne'er so small
Here of this Fustian[2] animal,                          40
Till I enravished Climb into
The Godhead on this Ladder do,
Where all my pipes inspired upraise
An Heavenly music furred[3] with praise.

1960

# Huswifery[1]

Make me, O Lord, Thy Spinning Wheel complete.
    Thy Holy Word my Distaff make for me.
Make mine Affections Thy Swift Flyers neat
    And make my Soul Thy holy Spool to be.
My conversation make to be Thy Reel                       5
And reel the yarn thereon spun of Thy Wheel.[2]

Make me Thy Loom then, knit therein this Twine:
    And make Thy Holy Spirit, Lord, wind quills:[3]
Then weave the Web Thyself. The yarn is fine.
    Thine Ordinances make my Fulling Mills.[4]           10
Then dye the same in Heavenly Colors Choice,
    All pinked with Varnished[5] Flowers of Paradise.

8. Dark curved.
9. Enclose, confine.
1. Body.
2. Coarse-clothed.
3. Trimmed or embellished, as with fur.
1. Housekeeping: used here to mean weaving. In Taylor's *Treatise Concerning the Lord's Supper* (see the following selection) he considers the significance of the sacrament of communion and takes as his text a passage from the New Testament: "And he saith unto him, Friend, how camest thou in hither not having a wedding garment? And he was speechless" (Matthew 22.12). Taylor argues that the wedding garment is the

proper sign of the regenerate Christian. The text used here is from *Poems of Edward Taylor*, edited by Donald E. Stanford (1960).
2. In the lines above Taylor refers to the working parts of a spinning wheel: the "distaff" holds the raw wool or flax; the "flyers" regulate the spinning; the "spool" twists the yarn; and the "reel" takes up the finished thread.
3. I.e., be like a spool or bobbin.
4. Where cloth is beaten and cleansed with fuller's earth, or soap.
5. Glossy, sparkling. "Pinked": adorned.

Then clothe therewith mine Understanding, Will,
　Affections, Judgment, Conscience, Memory,
My Words, and Actions, that their shine may fill　　　　15
My ways with glory and Thee glorify.
Then mine apparel shall display before Ye
That I am Clothed in Holy robes for glory.

1939

# SAMUEL SEWALL
## 1652–1730

Samuel Sewall's pursuit of the hand of the widow Katherine Winthrop has provided most readers of American literature with needed comic relief in the drama
of Puritan salvation. There is something very satisfying in looking over the shoulder
of the distinguished jurist subjecting his pride and reputation to the whims of courtship and adopting the role of a petitioner that, after a happy marriage of forty-two
years, he probably never thought he would have to assume again. But Sewall is a
more complicated figure than this small episode in his career would suggest. He
became a part of the public life of Massachusetts in his late twenties and rose to a
position of great authority. In the late 1870s, when the Massachusetts Historical
Society began to publish his diary, his private life intrigued colonial historians, but
before that Sewall was best known as the hanging judge of the Salem witch trials,
a man who presided over one of the saddest episodes in our history and was a
symbol of misguided authority and self-satisfied complacency.

　Sewall's self-confidence was derived, in part, from having had every material
advantage. Although his father had served briefly as a Puritan minister, his chief
interest was business, and when the vast land-holdings in New England held by
Samuel Sewall's grandfather, Henry Sewall, Sr., passed to him, he determined to
stay in Massachusetts rather than try to manage his estates while living abroad.
Sewall and his mother joined him in Boston on July 6, 1661. Samuel was only
nine.

　It was said of young Samuel that he was "born to be educated," and upon arrival
at the house in Newbury that his father had prepared for them, he was placed
under the care of the minister of the town and instructed in those subjects that
would make him eligible for admission to Harvard in the class of 1671. He loved
books and debated matters of theology with a passion. It seems fitting that Edward
Taylor became his "chum and bedfellow" their senior year. Both were a little old
before their time, very conservative in matters of church doctrine and apprehensive
about the secularization of the age. Sewall stayed on as a resident tutor and teaching fellow and after completing his master's degree (his thesis concerned the nature
of Original Sin) he was given an appointment as Keeper of the College Library.
He maintained close ties with Harvard and his classmates, eventually outliving
them all.

　Seven out of the eleven members of Sewall's class became ministers, and all of
Sewall's education was directed toward that end. He remained bookish and familiar
with new theological subtleties all his life, and because he traveled extensively in
Massachusetts regularly, few people were more informed than he about the activi-
ties of local churches. But it must have become clear to him in his last years at
Harvard that his true bent was in another direction; he refused a call to a pulpit in
Woodbridge, New Jersey. One reason must have been that the town of Boston was
attractive to him; for in spite of an introspective side, Sewall's temperament was

basically outgoing and social. His marriage in 1676 to Hannah Hull, the daughter of the affluent merchant John Hull, determined Sewall's career. He learned how to manage his father-in-law's interests and after John Hull's death in 1684 became a central figure in the great mercantile life of the town. He learned when to borrow and when to lend, filled his ships with goods Londoners were eager to buy (timber, molasses, pitch), and learned to anticipate public demand in New England for English goods (metalwares, fabrics, tiles), which his agent in London purchased for him and loaded in his ships for their return.

Sewall's ability to manage his fortune left him with the time to indulge his passion for civic duties. His diary, which he began in 1673 and continued for fifty-six years, reveals just how much the public and private life for Sewall were one. In 1679 he was elected a "constable" and represented the king in military affairs, and from then until 1729 he worked to become identified more as a public servant than as an importer. He represented Edward Taylor's town of Westfield in the General Court (or legislature) of Massachusetts, he moderated public meetings, he served as magistrate, he performed marriages and executed wills, and he became a judge of the Superior Court in 1692 and chief justice in 1717. He delighted in the ceremonies of his office and preferred the old forms to the new. His respect for tradition makes him seem at times inflexible and pompous, but for Sewall appearances mattered. He was not, however, ignorant of his own sins or the sins of the Commonwealth. On January 14, 1697, a fast day, Sewall placed in the hand of his minister, Samuel Willard, a statement acknowledging his wrong in the trials at Salem. He was the only witchcraft judge to do so. It was read aloud from the pulpit and posted for all to read. Three years later he published the first antislavery tract in America, *The Selling of Joseph*, and tells us that he received "frowns and hard words" for his pains. In matters of church discipline he was as strict as his friend Taylor, but in the matter of slavery he welcomed change. "Perfect servitude," he wrote, "can have no place by right . . . because our liberty in the natural account, is the very next thing to life itself, yea by many is preferred before it."

## *From* The Diary of Samuel Sewall[1]

*Mane.*[2] *March 21[, 1677.]* * * *
Remember, since I had thoughts of joining to the Church, I have been exceedingly tormented in my mind, sometimes lest the Third church [*the South*] should not be in God's way in breaking off from the old. (I resolved to speak with Mr. Torrey about that, but he passed home when I was called to business at the Warehouse. Another time I got Mr. Japheth Hobart to promise me a Meeting at our House after Lecture,—but she that is now his wife, being in town, prevented him.) Sometimes with my own unfitness and want of Grace: yet through importunity of friends, and hope that God might communicate himself to me in the ordinance, and because of my child (then hoped for) its being baptised, I offered myself, and was not refused. Besides what I had written, when I was speaking [*about admission to the church*] I resolved to confess what a great Sinner I had been, but going on in the method of the Paper, it came not to my mind. And now that Scruple of the Church vanished, and I began to be more afraid of myself. And on Saturday Goodman [Robert] Walker[3] came in, who used to be very familiar with me. But he said nothing

1. The first entry of Sewall's diary is dated December 3, 1673, and the last entry December 25, 1728. The text used here is from *The Diary of Samuel Sewall*, edited by M. Halsey Thomas (1973). To preserve the special flavor of Sewall's style, the text has been only slightly modernized. The dates, however, have been changed to conform to the modern calendar.
2. In the morning (Latin).
3. "Goodman" was the appropriate title for the head of a household. Robert Walker was one of the founders of the Old South Church in 1669.

of my coming into the Church, nor wished God to show me grace therein, at which I was almost overwhelmed, as thinking that he deemed me unfit for it. And I could hardly sit down to the Lord's Table. But I feared that if I went away I might be less fit next time, and thought that it would be strange for me who was just then joined to the Church, to withdraw, wherefore I stayed. But I never experienced more unbelief. I feared at least that I did not believe there was such an one as Jesus Xt.,[4] and yet was afraid that because I came to the ordinance without belief, that for the abuse of Xt. I should be stricken dead; yet I had some earnest desires that Xt. would, before the ordinance were done, though it were when he was just going away, give me some glimpse of himself; but I perceived none. Yet I seemed then to desire the coming of the next Sacrament day, that I might do better, and was stirred up hereby dreadfully to seek God who many times before had touched my heart by Mr. Thacher's praying and preaching more than now. The Lord pardon my former grieving of his Spirit, and circumcise my heart to love him with all my heart and soul.

*March 30, 1677.* I, together with Gilbert Cole, was admitted into Mr. Thacher's Church, making a Solemn covenant to take the L. Jehovah for our God, and to walk in Brotherly Love and watchfulness to Edification. Goodm. Cole first spake, then I, then the Relations of the Women were read: as we spake so were we admitted; then alltogether covenanted.[5] Prayed before, and after.

*Satterday, Jan^y 2^d[, 1686.]* Last night had a very unusual Dream; *viz.* That our Savior in the dayes of his Flesh when upon Earth, came to Boston and abode here sometime, and moreover that He Lodged in that time at Father Hull's; upon which in my Dream had two Reflections, One was how much more Boston had to say than Rome boasting of Peter's being there. The other a sense of great Respect that I ought to have shewed Father Hull since Christ chose when in town, to take up His Quarters at his House. Admired the goodness and Wisdom of Christ in coming hither and spending some part of His short Life here. The Chronological absurdity never came into my mind, as I remember. Jan^y 1, 1688, finished reading the Godly Learned ingenious Pareus[6] on the Revelation.

*April 11^th, 1692.* Went to Salem, where, in the Meeting-house, the persons accused of Witchcraft were examined; was a very great Assembly; 'twas awfull to see how the afflicted persons were agitated. Mr. Noyes pray'd at the beginning, and Mr. Higginson concluded. *[In the margin]*, Væ, Væ, Væ, Witchcraft.[7]

*July 30, 1692.* Mrs. Cary makes her escape out of Cambridge-Prison, who was Committed for Witchcraft.[8]

*Thorsday, Augt. 4, [1692.]* At Salem, Mr. Waterhouse brings the news of the desolation at Jamaica, June 7^th. 1700 persons kill'd, besides the Loss of Houses and Goods by the Earthquake.

*Augt. 19^th, 1692.* * * * This day *[in the margin, Dolefull Witchcraft]*

---

4. Christ.
5. Admitted to church membership. Statements of conversion for women were usually read from testimony recorded in conversations with the pastor.
6. David Pareus (1548–1622) was a theologian and biblical commentator and one of Sewall's favorite authors.
7. Woe, woe, woe, witchcraft (Latin). Governor William Phips (1651–1695) appointed Sewall one of seven

councillors of a court of Oyer and Terminer (i.e., to hear and determine) to judge those accused of witchcraft in Salem on May 24, 1692. The court met in Salem on June 2 and Bridget Bishop was hanged on June 10. On June 30 they met again and five more accused were executed on July 19. Unfortunately for us, Sewall kept his entries regarding the trials at Salem to a minimum.
8. Cary was given protection in New York.

George Burrough, John Willard, Jn° Procter, Martha Carrier and George Jacobs were executed at Salem, a very great number of Spectators being present. Mr. Cotton Mather was there, Mr. Sims, Hale, Noyes, Chiever, &c. All of them said they were innocent, Carrier and all. Mr. Mather says they all died by a Righteous Sentence. Mr. Burrough by his Speech, Prayer, protestation of his Innocence, did much move unthinking persons, which occasions their speaking hardly[9] concerning his being executed.

*Augt. 25*, [1692.] Fast at the old [*First*] Church, respecting the Witchcraft, Drought, &c.

*Monday, Sept. 19, 1692.* About noon, at Salem, Giles Corey was press'd to death[1] for standing Mute; much pains was used with him two days, one after another, by the Court and Capt. Gardner of Nantucket who had been of his acquaintance: but all in vain.

*Sept. 20,* [1692.] Now I hear from Salem that about 18 years agoe, he was suspected to have stamped and press'd a man to death, but was cleared. Twas not remembred till Anne Putnam was told of it by said Corey's Spectre the Sabbath-day night before Execution.[2]

*Sept. 20, 1692.* The Swan[3] brings in a rich French Prize of about 300 Tuns, laden with Claret, White Wine, Brandy, Salt, Linnen Paper, &c.

*Sept. 21,* [1692.] A petition is sent to Town in behalf of Dorcas Hoar, who now confesses: Accordingly an order is sent to the Sheriff to forbear her Execution, notwithstanding her being in the Warrant to die to morrow. This is the first condemned person who has confess'd.[4]

*Nov. 6*[, *1692.*] Joseph threw a knop of Brass and hit his Sister Betty on the forhead so as to make it bleed and swell; upon which, and for his playing at Prayer-time, and eating when Return Thanks, I whipd him pretty smartly. When I first went in (call'd by his Grandmother) he sought to shadow and hide himself from me behind the head of the Cradle: which gave me the sorrowfull remembrance of Adam's carriage.

*Jan^y 15,* [1697.] * * * Copy of the Bill I put up on the Fast day [January 14]; giving it to Mr. Willard as he pass'd by, and standing up at the reading of it, and bowing when finished; in the Afternoon.

Samuel Sewall, sensible of the reiterated strokes of God upon himself and family;[5] and being sensible, that as to the Guilt contracted, upon the opening of the late Commission of Oyer and Terminer at Salem (to which the order for this Day relates) he is, upon many accounts, more concerned than any that he knows of, Desires to take the Blame and Shame of it, Asking pardon of Men, And especially desiring prayers that God, who has an Unlimited Authority, would pardon that Sin and all other his Sins; personal and Relative: And according to his infinite Benignity, and Soveraignty, Not Visit the Sin of him, or of any other, upon himself or any of his, nor upon the Land: But that He would powerfully defend him against all Temptations to Sin, for the future; and vouchsafe him the Efficacious, Saving Conduct of his Word and Spirit.

*Fourth-day, June 19, 1700.* * * * Having been long and much dissatisfied

---

9. Vigorously.
1. Corey was eighty years old at the time. Heavy stones were placed on him until he died.
2. Putnam was only twelve when she made, along with her mother, accusations against "witches."
3. A ship.
4. Confession of witchcraft automatically set the accused free.

5. On May 22, 1696, Sewall buried a premature son born dead and on December 23 his daughter Sarah died. When his son Samuel read from Matthew 12.7 ("But if ye had known what this meaneth, I will have mercy, and not sacrifice, ye would not have condemned the guiltless.") it did "awfully bring to mind," Sewall noted, "the Salem tragedy."

with the Trade of fetching Negros from Guinea; at last I had a strong Inclina-
tion to Write something about it; but it wore off. At last reading Bayne,
Ephes.[6] about servants, who mentions Blackamoors; I began to be uneasy that
I had so long neglected doing any thing. When I was thus thinking, in came
Bro[r] Belknap to shew me a Petition he intended to present to the Gen[l] Court
for the freeing a Negro and his wife, who were unjustly held in Bondage. And
there is a Motion by a Boston Committee to get a Law that all Importers of
Negros shall pay 40[s] *per* head, to discourage the bringing of them. And Mr.
C. Mather resolves to publish a sheet to exhort Masters to labor their Conversion. Which makes me hope that I was call'd of God to Write this Apology[7]
for them; Let his Blessing accompany the same.

*Febr.* 6, [1718.] This morning wandering in my mind whether to live a
Single or a Married Life;[8] I had a sweet and very affectionat Meditation Concerning the Lord Jesus; Nothing was to be objected against his Person, Parentage, Relations, Estate, House, Home! Why did I not resolutely, presently
close with Him! And I cry'd mightily to God that He would help me so to
doe! * * *

*March,* 14, [1718.] Deacon Marion comes to me, sits with me a great while
in the evening; after a great deal of Discourse about his Courtship—He told
[me] the Olivers said they wish'd I would Court their Aunt.[9] I said little, but
said twas not five Moneths since I buried my dear Wife. Had said before 'twas
hard to know whether best to marry again or no; whom to marry. * * *

*Sept[r]* 5, [1720.] Mary Hirst goes to Board with Madam Oliver and her
Mother Loyd. Going to Son Sewall's I there meet with Madam Winthrop,
told her I was glad to meet her there, had not seen her a great while; gave her
Mr. Homes's Sermon.

*Sept.* 30, [1720.] Mr. Colman's Lecture: Daughter Sewall acquaints
Madam Winthrop that if she pleas'd to be within at 3. P.M. I would wait on
her. She answer'd she would be at home.

*Satterday,* October 1, [1720.] I dine at Mr. Stoddard's: from thence I went
to Madam Winthrop's just at 3. Spake to her, saying, my loving wife[1] died so
soon and suddenly, 'twas hardly convenient for me to think of Marrying again;
however I came to this Resolution, that I would not make my Court to any
person without first Consulting with her. * * *

*Octob[r]* 3, 2, [1720.] Waited on Madam Winthrop again; 'twas a little while
before she came in. Her daughter Noyes[2] being there alone with me, I said, I
hoped my Waiting on her Mother would not be disagreeable to her. She
answer'd she should not be against that that might be for her Comfort. I
Saluted her, and told her I perceiv'd I must shortly wish her a good Time; (her
mother had told me, she was with Child, and within a Moneth or two of her
Time). By and by in came Mr. Airs, Chaplain of the Castle,[3] and hang'd up
his Hat, which I was a little startled at, it seeming as if he was to lodge there.

---

6. Paul Baynes, *A Commentary upon the First Chapter of the Epistle of Saint Paul. Written to the Ephesians* (1618).
7. *The Selling of Joseph* was published on June 24,
1700.
8. Hannah Hull Sewall had died on October 19, 1717;
they had been married almost forty-two years. Sewall
married Abigail Tilley on October 29, 1719, and she
died suddenly in May of 1720. Sewall's courtship of
Madame Winthrop began seriously in the fall of 1720.

On March 29, 1722, Sewall married a widow, Mary
Gibbs, and she survived him.
9. Katherine Brattle Winthrop was the widow of Chief
Justice Wait Still Winthrop, Sewall's friend. Instead,
he married Tilley.
1. I.e., Abigail.
2. The wife of Dr. Oliver Noyes.
3. I.e., Castle Island in Boston Harbor. "Saluted":
kissed.

At last Madam Winthrop came in. After a considerable time, I went up to her and said, if it might not be inconvenient I desired to speak with her. She assented, and spake of going into another Room; but Mr. Airs and Mrs. Noyes presently rose up, and went out, leaving us there alone. Then I usher'd in Discourse from the names in the Fore-seat; at last I pray'd that Katharine [Mrs. Winthrop] might be the person assign'd for me. She instantly took it up in way of Denyal, as if she had catch'd at an Opportunity to do it, saying she could not do it before she was asked. Said that was her mind unless she should Change it, which she believed she should not; could not leave her Children. I express'd my Sorrow that she should do it so Speedily, pray'd her Consideration, and ask'd her when I should wait upon her agen. She setting no time, I mention'd that day Sennight.[4] Gave her Mr. Willard's Fountain[5] open'd with the little print and verses; saying I hop'd if we did well read that book, we should meet together hereafter, if we did not now. She took the Book, and put it in her Pocket. Took Leave.

[Oct.] 6th[, 1720.] A little after 6 P.M. I went to Madam Winthrop's. She was not within. I gave Sarah Chickering the Maid 2s, Juno, who brought in wood, 1s Afterward the Nurse came in, I gave her 18d, having no other small Bill. After awhile Dr. Noyes came in with his Mother; and quickly after his wife came in: They sat talking, I think, till eight aclock. I said I fear'd I might be some Interruption to their Business: Dr. Noyes reply'd pleasantly: He fear'd they might be an Interruption to me, and went away. Madam seem'd to harp upon the same string. Must take care of her Children; could not leave that House and Neighborhood where she had dwelt so long. I told her she might doe her children as much or more good by bestowing what she laid out in Hous-keeping, upon them. Said her Son would be of Age the 7th of August. I said it might be inconvenient for her to dwell with her Daughter-in-Law, who must be Mistress of the House. I gave her a piece of Mr. Belcher's Cake and Ginger-Bread wrapped up in a clean sheet of Paper; told her of her Father's kindness to me when Treasurer, and I Constable. My Daughter Judith was gon from me and I was more lonesom—might help to forward one another in our Journey to Canaan.[6] * * *

[Oct.] 12[, 1720.] At Madm Winthrop's Steps I took leave of Capt Hill, &c. Mrs. Anne Cotton came to door (twas before 8.) said Madam Winthrop was within, directed me into the little Room, where she was full of work[7] behind a Stand; Mrs. Cotton came in and stood. Madam Winthrop pointed to her to set me a Chair. Madam Winthrop's Countenance was much changed from what 'twas on Monday, look'd dark and lowering. At last, the work, (black stuff or Silk) was taken away, I got my Chair in place, had some Converse, but very Cold and indifferent to what 'twas before. Ask'd her to acquit me of Rudeness if I drew off her Glove. Enquiring the reason, I told her twas great odds between handling a dead Goat, and a living Lady. Got it off. I told her I had one Petition to ask of her, that was, that she would take off the Negative she laid on me the third of October; She readily answer'd she could not, and enlarg'd upon it; She told me of it so soon as she could; could not leave her house, children, neighbors, business. I told her she might do som Good to help and support me. * * * Sarah fill'd a Glass of Wine, she drank to me,

---

4. A week hence.
5. Samuel Willard, The Fountain Opened, or the Great Gospel Privilege of Having Christ Exhibited to

Sinful Men (1700).
6. I.e., to paradise.
7. I.e., her needlework.

I to her, She sent Juno home with me with a good Lantern, I gave her 6$^d$ and bid her thank her Mistress. In some of our Discourse, I told her I had rather go to the Stone-House[8] adjoining to her, than to come to her against her mind. Told her the reason why I came every other night was lest I should drink too deep draughts of Pleasure. She had talk'd of Canary,[9] her Kisses were to me better than the best Canary. * * *

Oct. 13, [1720.] I tell my Son and daughter Sewall, that the Weather was not so fair as I apprehended. * * *

Monday, [Oct.] 17, [1720.] Give Mr. Dan Willard, and Mr. Pelatiah Whittemore their Oaths to their Accounts; and Mr. John Briggs to his, as they are Attornys to Dr. Cotton Mather, Administrator to the estate of Nathan Howell deceased. In the Evening I visited Madam Winthrop, who Treated me Courteously, but not in Clean Linen as somtimes. She said, she did not know whether I would come again, or no. I ask'd her how she could so impute inconstancy to me. (I had not visited her since Wednesday night being unable to get over the Indisposition received by the Treatment received that night, and I *must* in it seem'd to sound like a made piece of Formality.) Gave her this day's Gazett. * * *

Midweek, [Oct.] 19, [1720.] Visited Madam Winthrop; Sarah told me she was at Mr. Walley's, would not come home till late. I gave her Hannah's 3 oranges with her Duty, not knowing whether I should find her or no. Was ready to go home: but said if I knew she was there, I would go thither. Sarah seemd to speak with pretty good Courage, She would be there. I went and found her there, with Mr. Walley and his wife in the little Room below. At 7 aclock I mentioned going home; at 8. I put on my Coat, and quickly waited on her home. She found occasion to speak loud to the servant, as if she had a mind to be known. Was Courteous to me; but took occasion to speak pretty earnestly about my keeping a Coach: I said 'twould cost £100. per annum: she said 'twould cost but £40. * * *

Oct. 20, [1720.] Mr. Colman preaches from Luke 15. 10. Joy among the Angels: made an Excellent Discourse.

At Council, Col. Townsend spake to me of my Hood: Should get a Wigg.[1] I said twas my chief[2] Ornament: I wore it for sake of the Day. Bro$^r$ Odlin, and Sam, Mary, and Jane Hirst dine with us. Promis'd to wait on the Gov$^r$ about 7. Madam Winthrop not being at Lecture, I went thither first; found her very Serene with her dâter Noyes, Mrs. Dering, and the widow Shipreev sitting at a little Table, she in her arm'd Chair. She drank to me, and I to Mrs. Noyes. After awhile pray'd the favor to speak with her. She took one of the Candles, and went into the best Room, clos'd the shutters, sat down upon the Couch. She told me Madam Usher had been there, and said the Coach must be set on Wheels, and not by Rusting. She spake something of my needing a Wigg. Ask'd me what her Sister said to me. I told her, She said, If her Sister were for it, She would not hinder it. But I told her, she did not say she would be glad to have me for her Brother. Said, I shall keep you in the Cold, and ask her if she would be within tomorrow night, for we had had but a running Feast. She said she could not tell whether she should, or no. I took Leave. As were

---

8. A prison.
9. A sweet wine from the Canary Isles.
1. I.e., in addition to Sewall's judicial hood, he should acquire a wig such as English judges wear to-

day, and to be distinguished from the periwig that Madame Winthrop wanted Sewall to wear to disguise his baldness. Sewall chose to wear a velvet cap instead.
2. Principal.

drinking at the Governor's, he said: In England the Ladies minded little more than that they might have Money, and Coaches to ride in. I said, And New-England brooks its Name.[3] At which Mr. Dudley smiled. Gov[r] said they were not quite so bad here.

*Friday, Oct. 21, [1720.]* My Son, the Minister, came to me p. m. by appointment and we pray one for another in the Old Chamber; more especially respecting my Courtship. About 6. aclock I go to Madam Winthrop's; Sarah told me her Mistress was gon out, but did not tell me whither she went. She presently order'd me a Fire; so I went in, having Dr. Sibb's Bowels[4] with me to read. I read the two first Sermons, still no body came in: at last about 9. aclock Mr. Jn° Eyre came in; I took the opportunity to say to him as I had done to Mrs. Noyes before, that I hoped my Visiting his Mother would not be disagreeable to him; He answered me with much Respect. When twas after 9. aclock He of himself said he would go and call her, she was but at one of his Brothers: A while after I heard Madam Winthrop's voice, enquiring somthing about John. After a good while and Clapping the Garden door twice or thrice, she came in. I mention'd somthing of the lateness; she banter'd me, and said I was later. She receiv'd me Courteously. I ask'd when our proceedings should be made publick: She said They were like to be no more publick than they were already. Offer'd me no Wine that I remember. I rose up at 11 aclock to come away, saying I would put on my Coat, She offer'd not to help me. I pray'd her that Juno might light me home, she open'd the Shutter, and said twas pretty light abroad; Juno was weary and gon to bed. So I came hôm by Star-light as well as I could. At my first coming in, I gave Sarah five Shillings. I writ Mr. Eyre his Name in his book with the date Octob[r] 21, 1720. It cost me 8[s]. Jehovah jireh![5] Madam told me she had visited M. Mico, Wendell, and W[m] Clark of the South [*Church*].

*Octob[r] 24, [1720.]* I went in the Hackny Coach through the Common, stop't at Madam Winthrop's (had told her I would take my departure from thence). Sarah came to the door with Katee in her Arms: but I did not think to take notice of the Child. Call'd her Mistress. I told her, being encourag'd by David Jeffries loving eyes, and sweet Words, I was come to enquire whether she could find in her heart to leave that House and Neighborhood, and go and dwell with me at the South-end; I think she said softly, Not yet. I told her It did not ly in my hands to keep a Coach. If I should, I should be in danger to be brought to keep company with her Neighbor Brooker, (he was a little before sent to prison for Debt). Told her I had an Antipathy against those who would pretend to give themselves; but nothing of their Estate. I would a proportion of my Estate with my self. And I suppos'd she would do so. As to a Perriwig, My best and greatest Friend, I could not possibly have a greater, began to find me with Hair before I was born, and had continued to do so ever since; and I could not find in my heart to go to another. She commended the book I gave her, Dr. Preston, the Church's Marriage; quoted him saying 'twas inconvenient keeping out of a Fashion commonly used. I said the Time and Tide did circumscribe my Visit. She gave me a Dram of Black-Cherry Brandy, and gave me a lump of the Sugar that was in it. She wish'd me a good Journy.

---

3. I.e., it is the same in New England.
4. Heart. Dr. Richard Sibbes was the author of *Bowels Opened; or a Discovery of the Neere and Deere Love, Union, and Communion between Christ and the*

*Church* (1641).
5. The Lord will provide (Hebrew), from Genesis 22.14.

I pray'd God to keep her, and came away. Had a very pleasant Journy to Salem.

*Midweek, Nov<sup>r</sup> 2, [1720.]* went again, and found Mrs. Alden there, who quickly went out. Gave her [Madam Winthrop] about ½ pound of Sugar Almonds, cost 3<sup>s</sup> per £. Carried them on Monday. She seem'd pleas'd with them, ask'd what they cost. Spake of giving her a Hundred pounds per annum if I dy'd before her. Ask'd her what sum she would give me, if she should dy first? Said I would give her time to Consider of it. She said she heard as if I had given all to my Children by Deeds of Gift. I told her 'twas a mistake, Point-Judith was mine &c. That in England, I own'd, my Father's desire was that it should go to my eldest Son; 'twas 20£ per annum; she thought 'twas forty. I think when I seem'd to excuse pressing this, she seem'd to think 'twas best to speak of it; a long winter was coming on. Gave me a Glass or two of Canary.

*Friday, Nov<sup>r</sup> 4<sup>th</sup>[, 1720.]* Went again about 7. aclock; found there Mr. John Walley and his wife: sat discoursing pleasantly. I shew'd them Isaac Moses's [*an Indian*] Writing. Madam W. serv'd Comfeits[6] to us. After awhile a Table was spread, and Supper was set. I urg'd Mr. Walley to Crave a Blessing; but he put it upon me. About 9. they went away. I ask'd Madam what fashioned Neck-lace I should present her with, She said, None at all. I ask'd her Where-about we left off last time; mention'd what I had offer'd to give her; Ask'd her what she would give me; She said she could not Change her Condition: She had said so from the beginning; could not be so far from her Children, the Lecture. Quoted the Apostle Paul affirming that a single Life was better than Married. I answer'd That was for the present Distress. Said she had not plea-sure in things of that nature as formerly: I said, you are the fitter to make me a Wife. If she held in that mind, I must go home and bewail my Rashness in making more haste than good Speed. However, considering the Supper, I desired her to be within next Monday night, if we liv'd so long. Assented. She charg'd me with saying, that she must put away Juno, if she came to me: I utterly deny'd it, it never came in my heart; yet she insisted upon it; saying it came in upon discourse about the Indian woman that obtained her Freedom this Court. About 10. I said I would not disturb the good orders of her House, and came away. She not seeming pleas'd with my Coming away. Spake to her about David Jeffries, had not seen him.

*Monday, Nov<sup>r</sup> 7<sup>th</sup>[, 1720.]* My son pray'd in the Old Chamber. Our time had been taken up by Son and Daughter Cooper's Visit; so that I only read the 130<sup>th</sup> and 143. Psalm. Twas on the Account of my Courtship. I went to Mad. Winthrop; found her rocking her little Katee in the Cradle. I excus'd my Com-ing so late (near Eight). She set me an arm'd Chair and Cusheon; and so the Cradle was between her arm'd Chair and mine. Gave her the remnant of my Almonds; She did not eat of them as before; but laid them away; I said I came to enquire whether she had alter'd her mind since Friday, or remained of the same mind still. She said, Thereabouts. I told her I loved her, and was so fond[7] as to think that she loved me: She said had a great respect for me. I told her, I had made her an offer, without asking any advice; she had so many to advise with, that twas a hindrance. The Fire was come to one short Brand besides the Block, which Brand was set up in end; at last it fell to pieces, and

---

6. Sweetmeats; fruits preserved in sugar.          7. Foolish.

no Recruit was made:[8] She gave me a Glass of Wine. I think I repeated again that I would go home and bewail my Rashness in making more haste than good Speed. I would endeavor to contain myself, and not go on to sollicit her to do that which she could not Consent to. Took leave of her. As came down the steps she bid me have a Care. Treated me Courteously. Told her she had enter'd the 4th year of her Widowhood. I had given her the News-Letter before: I did not bid her draw off her Glove as sometime I had done. Her Dress was not so clean as sometime it had been. Jehovah jireh!

*Midweek,* [*Nov.*] 9th[, *1720.*] Dine at Bro^r^ Stoddard's: were so kind as to enquire of me if they should invite M^m^ Winthrop; I answer'd No. * * *

*Nov^r^ 11,* [*1720.*] Went not to M^m^ Winthrop's. This is the 2^d^ Withdraw.[9]

*March, 29th,* [*1722.*] Samuel Sewall, and Mrs. Mary Gibbs were joined together in Marriage by the Rev^d^ Mr. William Cooper; Mr. Sewall pray'd once. Mr. Jn° Cotton was at Sandwich, sent for by Madam Cotton after her Husband's death.

1673–1729                                                        1878–82

8. Added logs would indicate that Sewall was expected     9. I.e., the second time he decided not to visit.
to stay longer.

---

# JONATHAN EDWARDS
## 1703–1758

Although it is certainly true that, as Perry Miller once put it, the true life of Jonathan Edwards is the life of a mind, the circumstances surrounding Edwards's career are not without their drama, and his rise to eminence and fall from power remain one of the most moving stories in American literature.

Edwards was born in East Windsor, Connecticut, a town not far from Hartford, the son of the Reverend Timothy Edwards and Esther Stoddard Edwards. There was little doubt from the beginning as to his career. Edwards's mother was the daughter of the Reverend Solomon Stoddard of Northampton, Massachusetts, one of the most influential and independent figures in the religious life of New England. Western Massachusetts clergymen were so anxious for his approval, that he was sometimes called the "Pope of the Connecticut Valley," and his gifted grandson, the only male child in a family of eleven children, was groomed to be his heir.

Edwards was a studious and dutiful child and from an early age showed remarkable gifts of observation and exposition. When he was eleven he wrote an essay on the flying spider, which is still very readable. Most of Edwards's early education he received at home. In 1716, when he was thirteen, Edwards was admitted to Yale College; he stayed on to read theology in New Haven for two years after his graduation in 1720. Like Benjamin Franklin, Edwards determined to perfect himself, and in one of his early notebooks he resolved "never to lose one moment of time, but to improve it in the most profitable way" he could. As a student he always rose at four in the morning, studied thirteen hours a day, and reserved part of each day for walking. It was a routine that Edwards varied little, even when, after spending two years in New York, he came to Northampton to assist his grandfather in his church. He married in 1727. In 1729 Solomon Stoddard died, and Edwards was named to succeed him. In the twenty-four years that Edwards lived in Northampton he managed to tend his duties as pastor of a growing congregation and deliver brilliant sermons, to write some of his most important books—concerned primarily with defining the nature of true religious experience—and watch his five children grow up. Until the mid-1740s his relations with the town seemed enviable.

In spite of the awesome—even imposing—quality of Edwards's mind, all of his work is of a piece and, in essence, readily graspable. What Edwards was trying to do was to restore to his congregation and to his readers that original sense of religious commitment that he felt had been lost since the first days of the Puritan exodus, and he wanted to do this by transforming his congregation from mere believers who understood the logic of Christian doctrine to converted Christians who were genuinely moved by the principles of their belief. Edwards says that he read the work of the English philosopher John Locke (1632–1704) with more pleasure "than the greedy miser finds when gathering up handfuls of silver and gold, from some newly discovered treasure." For Locke confirmed Edwards's conviction that we must do more than comprehend religious ideas; we must be *moved* by them, we must know them experientially: the difference, as he says, is like that between reading the word *fire* and actually being burned. Basic to this newly felt belief is the recognition that nothing that an individual can do warrants his or her salvation—that people are motivated entirely by self-love, and that it is only supernatural grace that alters their natural depravity. In his progress as a Christian, Edwards says that he experienced several steps toward conversion but that his true conversion came only when he had achieved a "full and constant sense of the absolute sovereignty of God, and a delight in that sovereignty." The word *delight* reminds us that Edwards is trying to inculcate and describe a religious feeling that approximates a physical sensation, recognizing always that supernatural feelings and natural ones are actually very different. In his patient and lucid prose Edwards became a master at the art of persuading his congregation that it could—and *must*—possess this intense awareness of humanity's precarious condition. The exaltation that his parishioners felt when they experienced delight in God's sovereignty was the characteristic fervid emotion of religious revivalism.

For fifteen years, beginning in 1734, this spirit of revivalism transformed complacent believers all along the eastern seaboard. This period of new religious fervor has been called the "Great Awakening," and in the early years Edwards could do no wrong. His meetinghouse was filled with newly converted believers, and the details of the spiritual life of Edwards and his congregation were the subject of inquiry by Christian believers everywhere. But in his attempt to restore the church to the position of authority it held in the years of his grandfather's reign, Edwards went too far. When he named backsliders from his pulpit—including the children and parents of the best families in town—and tried to return to the old order of communion, permitting the sacrament to be taken only by those who had publicly declared themselves to be saved, the people of the town turned against him. Residents of the Connecticut Valley everywhere were tired of religious controversy, and the hysterical behavior of a few fanatics turned many against the spirit of revivalism. On June 22, 1750, by a vote of two hundred to twenty, Edwards was dismissed from his church and effectively silenced. Although the congregation had difficulty naming a successor to Edwards, they preferred to have no sermons rather than let Edwards preach. For the next seven years he served as missionary to the Housatonnuck Indians in Stockbridge, Massachusetts, a town thirty-five miles to the west of Northampton. There he wrote his monumental treatises debating the doctrine of the freedom of the will and defining the nature of true virtue: "that consent, propensity and union of heart to Being in general, that is immediately exercised in a general good will." It was in Stockbridge that Edwards received, very reluctantly, a call to become president of the College of New Jersey (later called Princeton). Three months after his arrival in Princeton, Edwards died of smallpox, the result of the inoculation taken to prevent infection.

# Personal Narrative[1]

I had a variety of concerns and exercises[2] about my soul from my childhood, but had two more remarkable seasons of awakening[3] before I met with that change by which I was brought to those new dispositions and that new sense of things that I have since had. The first time was when I was a boy, some years before I went to college, at a time of remarkable awakening in my father's congregation. I was then very much affected[4] for many months and concerned about the things of religion and my soul's salvation and was abundant in duties. I used to pray five times a day in secret, and to spend much time in religious talk with other boys and used to meet with them to pray together. I experienced I know not what kind of delight in religion. My mind was much engaged in it, and had much self-righteous pleasure; and it was my delight to abound in religious duties. I, with some of my schoolmates, joined together and built a booth in a swamp, in a very secret and retired place, for a place of prayer. And besides, I had particular secret places of my own in the woods, where I used to retire by myself, and used to be from time to time much affected. My affections seemed to be lively and easily moved, and I seemed to be in my element, when engaged in religious duties. And I am ready to think, many are deceived with such affections and such a kind of delight, as I then had in religion, and mistake it for grace.

But in process of time, my convictions and affections wore off; and I entirely lost all those affections and delights, and left off secret prayer, at least as to any constant performance of it, and returned like a dog to his vomit, and went on in ways of sin.[5]

Indeed, I was at some times very uneasy, especially towards the latter part of the time of my being at college.[6] Till it pleased God, in my last year at college, at a time when I was in the midst of many uneasy thoughts about the state of my soul, to seize me with a pleurisy;[7] in which he brought me nigh to the grave, and shook me over the pit of hell.

But yet, it was not long after my recovery before I fell again into my old ways of sin. But God would not suffer me to go on with any quietness; but I had great and violent inward struggles: till after many conflicts with wicked inclinations and repeated resolutions and bonds that I laid myself under by a kind of vows to God, I was brought wholly to break off all former wicked ways and all ways of known outward sin, and to apply myself to seek my salvation and practice the duties of religion, but without that kind of affection and delight that I had formerly experienced. My concern now wrought more by inward struggles and conflicts and self-reflections. I made seeking my salvation the main business of my life. But yet it seems to me I sought after a miserable manner, which has made me sometimes since to question whether ever it issued in that which was saving,[8] being ready to doubt, whether such miserable

1. Because of Edwards's reference to an evening in January 1739, this essay must have been written after that date. Edwards's reasons for writing it are not known, and it was not published in his lifetime. After his death his friend Samuel Hopkins had access to his manuscripts and prepared *The Life and Character of the Late Rev. Mr. Jonathan Edwards*, which was published in 1765. In that volume the *Personal Narrative* appeared in section IV as a chapter titled "An account of his conversion, experiences, and religious exercises, given by himself."

2. Agitations.
3. I.e., spiritual awakenings, renewals.
4. Emotionally aroused, as opposed to merely understanding rationally the arguments for Christian faith.
5. "As a dog returneth to his vomit, so a fool returneth to his folly" (Proverbs 26.11).
6. Edwards was an undergraduate at Yale from 1716 to 1720 and a divinity student from 1720 to 1722.
7. A respiratory disorder.
8. I.e., truly redeeming, capable of making the penitent a "saint."

seeking was ever succeeded. But yet I was brought to seek salvation in a manner that I never was before. I felt a spirit to part with all things in the world for an interest in Christ. My concern continued and prevailed, with many exercising thoughts and inward struggles; but yet it never seemed to be proper to express my concern that I had, by the name of terror.

From my childhood up, my mind had been wont to be full of objections against the doctrine of God's sovereignty, in choosing whom He would to eternal life and rejecting whom He pleased, leaving them eternally to perish and be everlastingly tormented in hell. It used to appear like a horrible doctrine to me. But I remember the time very well when I seemed to be convinced, and fully satisfied, as to this sovereignty of God and His justice in thus eternally disposing of men according to His sovereign pleasure. But never could give an account how or by what means I was thus convinced; not in the least imagining, in the time of it nor a long time after, that there was any extraordinary influence of God's spirit in it; but only that now I saw further, and my reason apprehended the justice and reasonableness of it. However, my mind rested in it; and it put an end to all those cavils and objections, that had till then abode with me, all the proceeding part of my life. And there has been a wonderful alteration in my mind, with respect to the doctrine of God's sovereignty, from that day to this; so that I scarce ever have found so much as the rising of an objection against God's sovereignty, in the most absolute sense, in showing mercy to whom He will show mercy and hardening and eternally damning whom He will.[9] God's absolute sovereignty and justice, with respect to salvation and damnation, is what my mind seems to rest assured of, as much as of anything that I see with my eyes; at least it is so at times. But I have oftentimes since that first conviction had quite another kind of sense of God's sovereignty than I had then. I have often since not only had a conviction, but a delightful conviction. The doctrine of God's sovereignty has very often appeared an exceeding pleasant, bright and sweet doctrine to me; and absolute sovereignty is what I love to ascribe to God. But my first conviction was not with this.

The first that I remember that ever I found anything of that sort of inward, sweet delight in God and divine things, that I have lived much in since, was on reading those words, 1 Timothy 1.17, "Now unto the king eternal, immortal, invisible, the only wise God, be honor and glory for ever and ever, Amen." As I read the words, there came into my soul, and was as it were diffused through it, a sense of the glory of the Divine Being, a new sense, quite different from anything I ever experienced before. Never any words of scripture seemed to me as these words did. I thought with myself, how excellent a being that was, and how happy I should be if I might enjoy that God and be rapt[1] up to God in Heaven, and be as it were swallowed up in Him. I kept saying, and as it were singing over these words of scripture to myself; and went to prayer to pray to God that I might enjoy Him; and prayed in a manner quite different from what I used to do, with a new sort of affection. But it never came into my thought that there was anything spiritual or of a saving nature in this.

From about that time I began to have a new kind of apprehensions and ideas of Christ, and the work of redemption, and the glorious way of salvation by Him. I had an inward, sweet sense of these things, that at times came into my heart; and my soul was led away in pleasant views and contemplations of

---

9. "Therefore hath he mercy on whom he will have      9.18).
mercy, and whom he will be hardeneth" (Romans      1. Lifted.

them. And my mind was greatly engaged to spend my time in reading and meditating on Christ, and the beauty and excellency of His person, and the lovely way of salvation, by free grace in Him. I found no books so delightful to me as those that treated of these subjects. Those words Canticles 2.1, used to be abundantly with me: "I am the Rose of Sharon, the lily of the valleys." The words seemed to me, sweetly to represent the loveliness and beauty of Jesus Christ. And the whole book of Canticles[2] used to be pleasant to me; and I used to be much in reading it, about that time. And found, from time to time, an inward sweetness that used, as it were, to carry me away in my contemplations, in what I know not how to express otherwise, than by a calm, sweet abstraction of soul from all the concerns of this world, and a kind of vision, or fixed ideas and imaginations, of being alone in the mountains or some solitary wilderness, far from all mankind, sweetly conversing with Christ, and rapt and swallowed up in God. The sense I had of divine things would often of a sudden as it were, kindle up a sweet burning in my heart, an ardor of my soul, that I know not how to express.

Not long after I first began to experience these things, I gave an account to my father of some things that had passed in my mind. I was pretty much affected by the discourse we had together. And when the discourse was ended, I walked abroad alone, in a solitary place in my father's pasture, for contemplation. And as I was walking there, and looked up on the sky and clouds, there came into my mind a sweet sense of the glorious majesty and grace of God that I know not how to express. I seemed to see them both in a sweet conjunction, majesty and meekness joined together. It was a sweet and gentle, and holy majesty; and also a majestic meekness; an awful sweetness; a high, and great, and holy gentleness.

After this my sense of divine things gradually increased, and became more and more lively, and had more of that inward sweetness. The appearance of everything was altered: there seemed to be, as it were, a calm, sweet cast, or appearance of divine glory, in almost everything. God's excellency, His wisdom, His purity and love, seemed to appear in everything: in the sun, moon and stars; in the clouds, and blue sky; in the grass, flowers, trees; in the water, and all nature; which used greatly to fix my mind. I often used to sit and view the moon for a long time, and so in the daytime spent much time in viewing the clouds and sky to behold the sweet glory of God in these things, in the meantime, singing forth with a low voice my contemplations of the Creator and Redeemer. And scarce anything, among all the works of nature, was so sweet to me as thunder and lightning. Formerly, nothing had been so terrible to me. I used to be a person uncommonly terrified with thunder, and it used to strike me with terror when I saw a thunderstorm rising. But now, on the contrary, it rejoiced me. I felt God at the first appearance of a thunderstorm. And used to take the opportunity at such times to fix myself to view the clouds, and see the lightnings play, and hear the majestic and awful voice of God's thunder, which often times was exceeding entertaining, leading me to sweet contemplations of my great and glorious God. And while I viewed, used to spend my time, as it always seemed natural to me, to sing or chant forth my meditations, to speak my thoughts in soliloquies, and speak with a singing voice.

I felt then a great satisfaction as to my good estate.[3] But that did not content

---

2. I.e., Song of Solomon.                3. Condition of being.

me. I had vehement longings of soul after God and Christ, and after more holiness, wherewith my heart seemed to be full and ready to break: which often brought to my mind the words of the Psalmist, Psalm 119.28: "My soul breaketh for the longing it hath." I often felt a mourning and lamenting in my heart that I had not turned to God sooner, that I might have had more time to grow in grace. My mind was greatly fixed on divine things; I was almost perpetually in the contemplation of them. Spent most of my time in thinking of divine things, year after year. And used to spend abundance of my time in walking alone in the woods and solitary places for meditation, soliloquy and prayer, and converse with God. And it was always my manner, at such times, to sing forth my contemplations. And was almost constantly in ejaculatory prayer, wherever I was. Prayer seemed to be natural to me, as the breath by which the inward burnings of my heart had vent.

The delights which I now felt in things of religion were of an exceeding different kind from those forementioned, that I had when I was a boy. They were totally of another kind; and what I then had no more notion or idea of, than one born blind has of pleasant and beautiful colors. They were of a more inward, pure, soul-animating and refreshing nature. Those former delights never reached the heart, and did not arise from any sight of the divine excellency of the things of God or any taste of the soul-satisfying and life-giving good there is in them.

My sense of divine things seemed gradually to increase, till I went to preach at New York, which was about a year and a half after they began. While I was there, I felt them, very sensibly,[4] in a much higher degree, than I had done before. My longings after God and holiness, were much increased. Pure and humble, holy and heavenly Christianity appeared exceeding amiable to me. I felt in me a burning desire to be in everything a complete Christian, and conformed to the blessed image of Christ, and that I might live in all things, according to the pure, sweet and blessed rules of the gospel. I had an eager thirsting after progress in these things. My longings after it put me upon pursuing and pressing after them. It was my continual strife day and night, and constant inquiry, how I should be more holy, and live more holily, and more becoming a child of God, and disciple of Christ. I sought an increase of grace and holiness, and that I might live an holy life with vastly more earnestness than ever I sought grace, before I had it. I used to be continually examining myself, and studying and contriving for likely ways and means how I should live holily with far greater diligence and earnestness than ever I pursued anything in my life; but with too great a dependence on my own strength, which afterwards proved a great damage to me. My experience had not then taught me, as it has done since, my extreme feebleness and impotence, every manner of way, and the innumerable and bottomless depths of secret corruption and deceit that there was in my heart. However, I went on with my eager pursuit after more holiness, and sweet conformity to Christ.

The Heaven I desired was a heaven of holiness, to be with God, and to spend my eternity in divine love, and holy communion with Christ. My mind was very much taken up with contemplations on heaven, and the enjoyments of those there, and living there in perfect holiness, humility and love. And it used at that time to appear a great part of the happiness of heaven that there

---

4. Feelingly. Edwards was in New York from August 1722 to April 1723, assisting at a Presbyterian church.

the saints could express their love to Christ. It appeared to me a great clog and hindrance and burden to me that what I felt within I could not express to God and give vent to as I desired. The inward ardor of my soul seemed to be hindered and pent up, and could not freely flame out as it would. I used often to think how in heaven this sweet principle should freely and fully vent and express itself. Heaven appeared to me exceeding delightful as a world of love. It appeared to me that all happiness consisted in living in pure, humble, heavenly, divine love.

I remember the thoughts I used then to have of holiness. I remember I then said sometimes to myself, "I do certainly know that I love holiness such as the gospel prescribes." It appeared to me there was nothing in it but what was ravishingly lovely. It appeared to me to be the highest beauty and amiableness, above all other beauties, that it was a divine beauty, far purer than anything here upon earth; and that everything else, was like mire, filth and defilement in comparison of it.

Holiness, as I then wrote down some of my contemplations on it, appeared to me to be of a sweet, pleasant, charming, serene, calm nature. It seemed to me it brought an inexpressible purity, brightness, peacefulness and ravishment to the soul, and that it made the soul like a field or garden of God, with all manner of pleasant flowers; that is, all pleasant, delightful and undisturbed, enjoying a sweet calm, and the gently vivifying beams of the sun. The soul of a true Christian, as I then wrote my meditations, appeared like such a little white flower as we see in the spring of the year, low and humble on the ground, opening its bosom, to receive the pleasant beams of the sun's glory, rejoicing, as it were, in a calm rapture, diffusing around a sweet fragrancy, standing peacefully and lovingly in the midst of other flowers round about, all in like manner opening their bosoms, to drink in the light of the sun.

There was no part of creature holiness that I then, and at other times, had so great a sense of the loveliness of, as humility, brokenness of heart and poverty of spirit, and there was nothing that I had such a spirit to long for. My heart, as it were, panted after this to lie low before God, and in the dust; that I might be nothing, and that God might be all; that I might become as a little child.[5]

While I was there at New York, I sometimes was much affected with reflections on my past life, considering how late it was, before I began to be truly religious and how wickedly I had lived till then; and once so as to weep abundantly, and for a considerable time together.

On January 12, 1722–3 I made a solemn dedication of myself to God, and wrote it down; giving up myself, and all that I had to God; to be for the future in no respect my own; to act as one that had no right to himself, in any respect. And solemnly vowed to take God for my whole portion and felicity, looking on nothing else as any part of my happiness, nor acting as if it were: and His law for the constant rule of my obedience, engaging to fight with all my might against the world, the flesh and the devil, to the end of my life. But have reason to be infinitely humbled, when I consider, how much I have failed of answering my obligation.

I had then abundance of sweet religious conversation in the family where I

---

5. "Verily I say unto you, Whosoever shall not receive the kingdom of God as a little child, he shall not enter therein" (Mark 10.15).

lived, with Mr. John Smith, and his pious mother. My heart was knit in affection to those in whom were appearances of true piety, and I could bear the thoughts of no other companions but such as were holy, and the disciples of the blessed Jesus.

I had great longings for the advancement of Christ's kingdom in the world. My secret prayer used to be in great part taken up in praying for it. If I heard the least hint of anything that happened in any part of the world that appeared to me in some respect or other, to have a favorable aspect on the interest of Christ's kingdom, my soul eagerly catched at it; and it would much animate and refresh me. I used to be earnest to read public newsletters, mainly for that end, to see if I could not find some news favorable to the interest of religion in the world.

I very frequently used to retire into a solitary place, on the banks of Hudson's river, at some distance from the city, for contemplation on divine things and secret converse with God, and had many sweet hours there. Sometimes Mr. Smith and I walked there together to converse of the things of God, and our conversation used much to turn on the advancement of Christ's kingdom in the world, and the glorious things that God would accomplish for His church in the latter days.

I had then, and at other times, the greatest delight in the holy Scriptures, of any book whatsoever. Oftentimes in reading it, every word seemed to touch my heart. I felt an harmony between something in my heart, and those sweet and powerful words. I seemed often to see so much light exhibited by every sentence, and such a refreshing ravishing food communicated, that I could not get along in reading. Used oftentimes to dwell long on one sentence, to see the wonders contained in it; and yet almost every sentence seemed to be full of wonders.

I came away from New York in the month of April, 1723, and had a most bitter parting with Madam Smith and her son. My heart seemed to sink within me, at leaving the family and city, where I had enjoyed so many sweet and pleasant days. I went from New York to Weathersfield[6] by water. As I sailed away, I kept sight of the city as long as I could; and when I was out of sight of it, it would affect me much to look that way, with a kind of melancholy mixed with sweetness. However, that night after this sorrowful parting. I was greatly comforted in God at Westchester, where we went ashore to lodge, and had a pleasant time of it all the voyage to Saybrook.[7] It was sweet to me to think of meeting dear Christians in heaven, where we should never part more. At Saybrook we went ashore to lodge on Saturday, and there kept sabbath where I had a sweet and refreshing season, walking alone in the fields.

After I came home to Windsor, remained much in a like frame of my mind as I had been in at New York, but only sometimes felt my heart ready to sink with the thoughts of my friends at New York. And my refuge and support was in contemplations on the heavenly state, as I find in my diary of May 1, 1723. It was my comfort to think of that state where there is fulness of joy; where reigns heavenly, sweet, calm and delightful love, without alloy; where there are continually the dearest expressions of this love; where is the enjoyment of the persons loved without ever parting; where these persons that appear so

---

6. Wethersfield, Connecticut, is very near his father's home in Windsor.

7. Westchester and Saybrook are in New York and Connecticut, respectively.

lovely in this world will really be inexpressibly more lovely, and full of love to us. And how sweetly will the mutual lovers join together to sing the praises of God and the Lamb![8] How full will it fill us with joy to think that this enjoyment, these sweet exercises will never cease or come to an end, but will last to all eternity!

Continued much in the same frame in the general that I had been in at New York, till I went to New Haven to live there as tutor of the college, having some special seasons of uncommon sweetness; particularly once at Boston in a journey from Boston, walking out alone in the fields. After I went to New Haven, I sunk in religion, my mind being diverted from my eager and violent pursuits after holiness by some affairs that greatly perplexed and distracted my mind.

In September, 1725, was taken ill at New Haven, and endeavoring to go home to Windsor, was so ill at the North Village that I could go no further, where I lay sick for about a quarter of a year. And in this sickness, God was pleased to visit me again with the sweet influences of His spirit. My mind was greatly engaged there on divine, pleasant contemplations and longings of soul. I observed that those who watched with me would often be looking out for the morning, and seemed to wish for it. Which brought to my mind those words of the psalmist, which my soul with sweetness made its own language: "My soul waiteth for the Lord, more than they that watch for the morning, I say, more than they that watch for the morning."[9] And when the light of the morning came, and the beams of the sun came in at the windows, it refreshed my soul from one morning to another. It seemed to me to be some image of the sweet light of God's glory.

I remember, about that time, I used greatly to long for the conversion of some that I was concerned with. It seemed to me I could gladly honor them, and with delight be a servant to them, and lie at their feet, if they were but truly holy.

But sometime after this, I was again greatly diverted in my mind with some temporal concerns that exceedingly took up my thoughts, greatly to the wounding of my soul, and went on through various exercises, that it would be tedious to relate, that gave me much more experience of my own heart than ever I had before.

Since I came to this town, I have often had sweet complacency[1] in God, in views of His glorious perfections and the excellency of Jesus Christ. God has appeared to me a glorious and lovely Being, chiefly on the account of His holiness. The holiness of God has always appeared to me the most lovely of all His attributes. The doctrines of God's absolute sovereignty and free grace in showing mercy to whom He would show mercy, and man's absolute dependence on the operations of God's Holy Spirit, have very often appeared to me as sweet and glorious doctrines. These doctrines have been much my delight. God's sovereignty has ever appeared to me as great part of His glory. It has often been sweet to me to go to God and adore Him as a sovereign God, and ask sovereign mercy of Him.

I have loved the doctrines of the gospel; they have been to my soul like

---

8. In Revelation the symbol of Christ.
9. Psalm 130.6.
1. Contentment. "This town": Northampton, Massa-

chusetts, where, in 1726, Edwards came to help his grandfather in conducting the affairs of his parish.

green pastures. The gospel has seemed to me to be the richest treasure, the treasure that I have most desired and longed that it might dwell richly in me. The way of salvation by Christ has appeared in a general way glorious and excellent, and most pleasant and beautiful. It has often seemed to me that it would in a great measure spoil heaven to receive it in any other way. That text has often been affecting and delightful to me, Isaiah 32.2: "A man shall be an hiding place from the wind, and a covert from the tempest, etc."

It has often appeared sweet to me to be united to Christ; to have Him for my head, and to be a member of His body; and also to have Christ for my teacher and prophet. I very often think with sweetness and longings and pantings of soul, of being a little child, taking hold of Christ, to be led by Him through the wilderness of this world. That text, Matthew 18.3 at the beginning, has often been sweet to me, "Except ye be converted, and become as little children, etc." I love to think of coming to Christ, to receive salvation of Him, poor in spirit, and quite empty of self; humbly exalting Him alone; cut entirely off from my own root, and to grow into and out of Christ; to have God in Christ to be all in all; and to live by faith in the Son of God, a life of humble, unfeigned confidence in Him. That Scripture has often been sweet to me, Psalm 115.1: "Not unto us, O Lord, not unto us, but unto Thy name give glory, for Thy mercy, and for Thy truth's sake." And those words of Christ, Luke 10.21: "In that hour Jesus rejoiced in spirit, and said, I thank thee, O Father, Lord of heaven and earth, that Thou hast hid these things from the wise and prudent, and hast revealed them unto babes: Even so Father, for so it seemed good in Thy sight." That sovereignty of God that Christ rejoiced in seemed to me to be worthy to be rejoiced in, and that rejoicing of Christ seemed to me to show the excellency of Christ, and the spirit that He was of.

Sometimes only mentioning a single word causes my heart to burn within me, or only seeing the name of Christ or the name of some attribute of God. And God has appeared glorious to me on account of the Trinity. It has made me have exalting thoughts of God, that He subsists in three persons: Father, Son, and Holy Ghost.

The sweetest joys and delights I have experienced have not been those that have arisen from a hope of my own good estate,[2] but in a direct view of the glorious things of the Gospel. When I enjoy this sweetness it seems to carry me above the thoughts of my own safe estate. It seems at such times a loss that I cannot bear, to take off my eye from the glorious, pleasant object I behold without me, to turn my eye in upon myself, and my own good estate.

My heart has been much on the advancement of Christ's kingdom in the world. The histories of the past advancement of Christ's kingdom have been sweet to me. When I have read histories of past ages, the pleasantest thing in all my reading has been to read of the kingdom of Christ being promoted. And when I have expected in my reading to come to any such thing, I have lotted[3] upon it all the way as I read. And my mind has been much entertained and delighted with the Scripture promises and prophecies of the future glorious advancement of Christ's kingdom on earth.

I have sometimes had a sense of the excellent fullness of Christ, and His meetness and suitableness as a Savior; whereby He has appeared to me, far

---

2. Condition of being.                3. Rejoiced.

above all, the chief of ten thousands.[4] And His blood and atonement has appeared sweet, and His righteousness sweet; which is always accompanied with an ardency of spirit, and inward strugglings and breathings and groanings, that cannot be uttered, to be emptied of myself and swallowed up in Christ.

Once, as I rid out into the woods for my health, Anno[5] 1737, and having lit from my horse in a retired place, as my manner commonly has been, to walk for divine contemplation and prayer, I had a view, that for me was extraordinary, of the glory of the Son of God, as mediator between God and man, and His wonderful, great, full, pure and sweet grace and love, and meek and gentle condescension. This grace, that appeared to me so calm and sweet, appeared great above the heavens. The person of Christ appeared ineffably excellent, with an excellency great enough to swallow up all thought and conception, which continued, as near as I can judge, about an hour, which kept me, the bigger part of the time, in a flood of tears, and weeping aloud. I felt withal an ardency of soul to be, what I know not otherwise how to express, than to be emptied and annihilated; to lie in the dust, and to be full of Christ alone; to love Him with a holy and pure love; to trust in Him; to live upon Him; to serve and follow Him, and to be totally rapt up in the fullness of Christ; and to be perfectly sanctified and made pure with a divine and heavenly purity. I have several other times had views very much of the same nature and that have had the same effects.

I have many times had a sense of the glory of the third person in the Trinity in His office of Sanctifier; in His holy operations communicating divine light and life to the soul. God in the communications of His Holy Spirit has appeared as an infinite fountain of divine glory and sweetness, being full and sufficient to fill and satisfy the soul, pouring forth itself in sweet communications, like the sun in its glory, sweetly and pleasantly diffusing light and life.

I have sometimes had an affecting sense of the excellency of the word of God, as a word of life; as the light of life; a sweet, excellent, life-giving word, accompanied with a thirsting after that word, that it might dwell richly in my heart.

I have often, since I lived in this town, had very affecting views of my own sinfulness and vileness; very frequently so as to hold me in a kind of loud weeping, sometimes for a considerable time together, so that I have often been forced to shut myself up.[6] I have had a vastly greater sense of my wickedness, and the badness of my heart, since my conversion, than ever I had before. It has often appeared to me, that if God should mark iniquity against me, I should appear the very worst of all mankind, of all that have been since the beginning of the world of this time, and that I should have by far the lowest place in hell. When others that have come to talk with me about their soul concerns have expressed the sense they have had of their own wickedness by saying that it seemed to them that they were as bad as the devil himself, I thought their expressions seemed exceeding faint and feeble to represent my wickedness. I thought I should wonder that they should content themselves with such expressions as these, if I had any reason to imagine that their sin bore any proportion to mine. It seemed to me I should wonder at myself if I should express my wickedness in such feeble terms as they did.

---

4. "My beloved is white and ruddy, the chiefest among ten thousand" (Song of Solomon 5.10).

5. In the year (Latin).

6. I.e., retire to his study.

My wickedness, as I am in myself, has long appeared to me perfectly ineffable and infinitely swallowing up all thought and imagination, like an infinite deluge or infinite mountains over my head. I know not how to express better what my sins appear to me to be than by heaping infinite upon infinite, and multiplying infinite by infinite. I go about very often, for this many years, with these expressions in my mind and in my mouth, "Infinite upon infinite. Infinite upon infinite!" When I look into my heart and take a view of my wickedness, it looks like an abyss infinitely deeper than hell. And it appears to me that were it not for free grace, exalted and raised up to the infinite height of all the fullness and glory of the great Jehovah,[7] and the arm of His power and grace stretched forth, in all the majesty of His power and in all the glory of His sovereignty, I should appear sunk down in my sins infinitely below hell itself, far beyond sight of everything but the piercing eye of God's grace, that can pierce even down to such a depth and to the bottom of such an abyss.

And yet I be not in the least inclined to think that I have a greater conviction of sin than ordinary. It seems to me my conviction of sin is exceeding small and faint. It appears to me enough to amaze me that I have no more sense of my sin. I know certainly that I have very little sense of my sinfulness. That my sins appear to me so great don't seem to me to be because I have so much more conviction of sin than other Christians, but because I am so much worse and have so much more wickedness to be convinced of. When I have had these turns of weeping and crying for my sins, I thought I knew in the time of it that my repentance was nothing to my sin.

I have greatly longed of late for a broken heart and to lie low before God. And when I ask for humility of God, I can't bear the thoughts of being no more humble than other Christians. It seems to me that though their degrees of humility may be suitable for them, yet it would be a vile self-exaltation in me not to be the lowest in humility of all mankind. Others speak of their longing to be humbled to the dust. Though that may be a proper expression for them I always think for myself that I ought to be humbled down below hell. 'Tis an expression that it has long been natural for me to use in prayer to God. I ought to lie infinitely low before God.

It is affecting to me to think how ignorant I was, when I was a young Christian, of the bottomless, infinite depths of wickedness, pride, hypocrisy and deceit left in my heart.

I have vastly a greater sense of my universal, exceeding dependence on God's grace and strength and mere good pleasure, of late, than I used formerly to have, and have experienced more of an abhorrence of my own righteousness. The thought of any comfort or joy, arising in me, on any consideration or reflection on my own amiableness, or any of my performances or experiences, or any goodness of heart or life is nauseous and detestable to me. And yet I am greatly afflicted with a proud and self-righteous spirit, much more sensibly than I used to be formerly. I see that serpent rising and putting forth its head, continually, everywhere, all around me.

Though it seems to me that in some respects I was a far better Christian for two or three years after my first conversion than I am now, and lived in a more constant delight and pleasure, yet of late years I have had a more full and constant sense of the absolute sovereignty of God and a delight in that sover-

---

7. The name used for God in the Old Testament.

eignty, and have had more of a sense of the glory of Christ as a mediator as revealed in the Gospel. On one Saturday night in particular, had a particular discovery of the excellency of the Gospel of Christ, above all other doctrines, so that I could not but say to myself, "This is my chosen light, my chosen doctrine," and of Christ, "This is my chosen prophet." It appeared to me to be sweet beyond all expression to follow Christ and to be taught and enlightened and instructed by Him, to learn of Him, and live to Him.

Another Saturday night, January, 1738–9, had such a sense how sweet and blessed a thing it was to walk in the way of duty, to do that which was right and meet to be done and agreeable to the holy mind of God, that it caused me to break forth into a kind of a loud weeping, which held me some time, so that I was forced to shut myself up, and fasten the doors. I could not but as it were cry out, "How happy are they which do that which is right in the sight of God! They are blessed indeed, they are the happy ones!" I had at the same time, a very affecting sense how meet and suitable it was that God should govern the world, and order all things according to His own pleasure, and I rejoiced in it, that God reigned, and that His will was done.

c. 1740                                                                    1765

# A Divine and Supernatural Light[1]

IMMEDIATELY IMPARTED TO THE SOUL BY THE SPIRIT OF GOD, SHOWN
TO BE BOTH A SCRIPTURAL AND RATIONAL DOCTRINE

## Matthew 16.17

*And Jesus answered and said unto him, Blessed art thou, Simon Barjona;[2] for flesh and blood hath not revealed it unto thee, but my Father which is in heaven.*

Christ addresses these words to Peter upon occasion of his professing his faith in Him as the Son of God. Our Lord was inquiring of His disciples, whom men said that He was; not that He needed to be informed, but only to introduce and give occasion to what follows. They answer that some said He was John the Baptist, and some Elias, and others Jeremias, or one of the prophets.[3] When they had thus given an account whom others said that He was, Christ asks them, whom they said that He was? Simon Peter, whom we find always zealous and forward, was the first to answer: he readily replied to the question, Thou art Christ, the Son of the living God.

Upon this occasion, Christ says as He does to him and of him in the text: in which we may observe.

1. That Peter is pronounced blessed on this account.—Blessed art thou— "Thou art an happy man, that thou art not ignorant of this, that I am Christ, the Son of the living God. Thou art distinguishingly happy. Others are blinded, and have dark and deluded apprehensions, as you have now given an account, some thinking that I am Elias, and some that I am Jeremias, and

---

1. Edwards delivered this sermon in Northampton, Massachusetts, in 1733; it was published the following year at the request of his congregation. The text used is from *The Works of Jonathan Edwards*, vol. 6, edited

by Sereno E. Dwight (1829–30).
2. The apostle Peter (Simon, son of Jona).
3. Matthew 16.14. Elias is the name used in the New Testament for the prophet Elijah.

some one thing, and some another: but none of them thinking right, all of them are misled. Happy art thou, that art so distinguished as to know the truth in this matter."

2. The evidence of this his happiness declared, viz., That God, and He only, had revealed it to him. This is an evidence of his being blessed.

First. As it shows how peculiarly favored he was of God above others; q.d.,[4] "How highly favored art thou, that others, wise and great men, the scribes, Pharisees,[5] and rulers, and the nation in general, are left in darkness, to follow their own misguided apprehensions; and that thou shouldst be singled out, as it were, by name, that My heavenly Father should thus set His love on thee, Simon Bar-jona.—This argues thee blessed, that thou shouldst thus be the object of God's distinguishing love."

Secondly. It evidences his blessedness also, as it intimates that this knowledge is above any that flesh and blood can reveal. "This is such knowledge as only my Father which is in heaven can give. It is too high and excellent to be communicated by such means as other knowledge is. Thou art blessed, that thou knowest what God alone can teach thee."

The original of this knowledge is here declared, both negatively and positively. Positively, as God is here declared the author of it. Negatively, as it is declared, that flesh and blood had not revealed it. God is the author of all knowledge and understanding whatsoever. He is the author of all moral prudence, and of the skill that men have in their secular business. Thus it is said of all in Israel that were wise-hearted and skilled in embroidering, that God had filled them with the spirit of wisdom. Exodus 28.3.[6]

God is the author of such knowledge; yet so that flesh and blood reveals it. Mortal men are capable of imparting the knowledge of human arts and sciences, and skill in temporal affairs. God is the author of such knowledge by those means: flesh and blood is employed as the mediate or second cause of it; He conveys it by the power and influence of natural means. But this spiritual knowledge, spoken of in the text, is what God is the author of, and none else: He reveals it, and flesh and blood reveals it not. He imparts this knowledge immediately, not making use of any intermediate natural causes, as He does in other knowledge.

What had passed in the preceding discourse naturally occasioned Christ to observe this; because the disciples had been telling how others did not know Him, but were generally mistaken about him, divided and confounded in their opinions of Him: but Peter had declared his assured faith, that He was the Son of God. Now it was natural to observe how it was not flesh and blood that had revealed it to him, but God; for if this knowledge were dependent on natural causes or means, how came it to pass that they, a company of poor fishermen, illiterate men, and persons of low education, attained to the knowledge of the truth, while the Scribes and Pharisees, men of vastly higher advantages, and greater knowledge and sagacity, in other matters, remained in ignorance? This could be owing only to the gracious distinguishing influence and revelation of the Spirit of God. Hence, what I would make the subject of my present discourse from these words, is this:

---

4. I.e., *quasi dicat*: as if he should say (Latin).
5. A sect hostile to Jesus and known for their arrogance and pride (Matthew 9.9–13). "Scribes": interpreters of the Jewish law.

6. This passage from Exodus refers to God's command to the people of Israel to make proper garments for Aaron's priesthood.

## Doctrine

That there is such a thing as a spiritual and divine light, immediately imparted to the soul by God, of a different nature from any that is obtained by natural means. And on this subject I would,

I. Show what this divine light is.

II. How it is given immediately by God, and not obtained by natural means.

III. Show the truth of the doctrine.

And then conclude with a brief improvement.[7]

I. I would show what this spiritual and divine light is. And in order to it would show,

First, In a few things, what it is not. And here,

1. Those convictions that natural men may have of their sin and misery, is not this spiritual and divine light. Men, in a natural condition, may have convictions of the guilt that lies upon them, and of the anger of God, and their danger of divine vengeance. Such convictions are from the light of truth. That some sinners have a greater conviction of their guilt and misery than others is because some have more light, or more of an apprehension of truth than others. And this light and conviction may be from the Spirit of God; the Spirit convinces men of sin; but yet nature is much more concerned in it than in the communication of that spiritual and divine light that is spoken of in the doctrine; it is from the Spirit of God only as assisting natural principles, and not as infusing any new principles. Common grace differs from special in that it influences only by assisting of nature, and not by imparting grace, or bestowing anything above nature. The light that is obtained is wholly natural, or of no superior kind to what mere nature attains to, though more of that kind be obtained than would be obtained if men were left wholly to themselves; or, in other words, common grace only assists the faculties of the soul to do that more fully which they do by nature, as natural conscience or reason will by mere nature make a man sensible of guilt, and will accuse and condemn him when he has done amiss. Conscience is a principle natural to men; and the work that it doth naturally, or of itself, is to give an apprehension of right and wrong, and to suggest to the mind the relation that there is between right and wrong and a retribution. The Spirit of God, in those convictions which unregenerate men sometimes have, assists conscience to do this work in a further degree than it would do if they were left to themselves. He helps it against those things that tend to stupify it, and obstruct its exercise. But in the renewing and sanctifying work of the Holy Ghost, those things are wrought in the soul that are above nature, and of which there is nothing of the like kind in the soul by nature; and they are caused to exist in the soul habitually, and according to such a stated constitution or law, that lays such a foundation for exercises in a continued course, as is called a principle of nature. Not only are remaining principles assisted to do their work more freely and fully, but those principles are restored that were utterly destroyed by the fall; and the mind thenceforward habitually exerts those acts that the dominion of sin had made it as wholly destitute of as a dead body is of vital acts.

---

7. Literally, turning something to profit; here used in the sense of the lesson to be learned.

The Spirit of God acts in a very different manner in the one case, from what He doth in the other. He may, indeed, act upon the mind of a natural man, but He acts in the mind of a saint[8] as an indwelling vital principle. He acts upon the mind of an unregenerate[9] person as an extrinsic occasional agent; for, in acting upon them, He doth not unite himself to them: for, notwithstanding all His influences that they may possess, they are still sensual, having not the Spirit. Jude 19.[1] But He unites himself with the mind of a saint, takes him for His temple, actuates and influences him as a new supernatural principle of life and action. There is this difference, that the Spirit of God, in acting in the soul of a godly man, exerts and communicates Himself there in His own proper nature. Holiness is the proper nature of the Spirit of God. The Holy Spirit operates in the minds of the godly, by uniting Himself to them, and living in them, and exerting His own nature in the exercise of their faculties. The Spirit of God may act upon a creature, and yet not in acting communicate Himself. The Spirit of God may act upon inanimate creatures, as, the Spirit moved upon the face of the waters,[2] in the beginning of the creation; so the Spirit of God may act upon the minds of men many ways, and communicate Himself no more than when He acts upon an inanimate creature. For instance, He may excite thoughts in them, may assist their natural reason and understanding, or may assist other natural principles, and this without any union with the soul, but may act, as it were, upon an external object. But as He acts in His holy influences and spiritual operations, He acts in a way of peculiar communication of Himself; so that the subject is thence denominated spiritual.

2. This spiritual and divine light does not consist in any impression made upon the imagination. It is no impression upon the mind, as though one saw anything with the bodily eyes. It is no imagination or idea of an outward light or glory, or any beauty of form or countenance, or a visible luster or brightness of any object. The imagination may be strongly impressed with such things; but this is not spiritual light. Indeed when the mind has a lively discovery of spiritual things, and is greatly affected with the power of divine light, it may, and probably very commonly doth, much affect the imagination; so that impressions of an outward beauty or brightness may accompany those spiritual discoveries. But spiritual light is not that impression upon the imagination, but an exceedingly different thing. Natural men may have lively impressions on their imaginations; and we cannot determine but that the devil, who transforms himself into an angel of light, may cause imaginations of an outward beauty, or visible glory, and of sounds and speeches, and other such things; but these are things of a vastly inferior nature to spiritual light.

3. This spiritual light is not the suggesting of any new truths or propositions not contained in the word of God. This suggesting of new truths or doctrines to the mind, independent of any antecedent revelations of those propositions, either in word or writing, is inspiration; such as the prophets and apostles had, and such as some enthusiasts[3] pretend to. But this spiritual light that I am speaking of, is quite a different thing from inspiration. It reveals no new doc-

8. Here, a living Christian who has passed from mere understanding of Christ's doctrine to heartfelt commitment; such people were often called "visible saints."
9. One who is not yet saved.
1. "These be they who separate themselves, sensual, having not the Spirit."
2. Genesis 1.2.
3. People who erroneously claim to be inspired by the spirit of God.

trine, it suggests no new proposition to the mind, it teaches no new thing of God, or Christ, or another world, not taught in the Bible, but only gives a due apprehension of those things that are taught in the word of God.

4. It is not every affecting view that men have of religious things that is this spiritual and divine light. Men by mere principles of nature are capable of being affected with things that have a special relation to religion as well as other things. A person by mere nature, for instance, may be liable to be affected with the story of Jesus Christ, and the sufferings he underwent, as well as by any other tragical story. He may be the more affected with it from the interest he conceives mankind to have in it. Yea, he may be affected with it without believing it; as well as a man may be affected with what he reads in a romance, or sees acted in a stage play. He may be affected with a lively and eloquent description of many pleasant things that attend the state of the blessed in heaven, as well as his imagination be entertained by a romantic[4] description of the pleasantness of fairyland, or the like. And a common belief of the truth of such things, from education or otherwise, may help forward their affection. We read in Scripture of many that were greatly affected with things of a religious nature, who yet are there represented as wholly graceless, and many of them very ill[5] men. A person therefore may have affecting views of the things of religion, and yet be very destitute of spiritual light. Flesh and blood may be the author of this; one man may give another an affecting view of divine things with but common assistance; but God alone can give a spiritual discovery of them.—But I proceed to show.

Secondly, Positively what this spiritual and divine light is.

And it may be thus described: A true sense of the divine excellency of the things revealed in the word of God, and a conviction of the truth and reality of them thence arising. This spiritual light primarily consists in the former of these, viz., a real sense and apprehension of the divine excellency of things revealed in the word of God. A spiritual and saving conviction of the truth and reality of these things, arises from such a sight of their divine excellency and glory; so that this conviction of their truth is an effect and natural consequence of this sight of their divine glory. There is therefore in this spiritual light,

1. A true sense of the divine and superlative excellency of the things of religion; a real sense of the excellency of God and Jesus Christ, and of the work of redemption, and the ways and works of God revealed in the gospel. There is a divine and superlative glory in these things; an excellency that is of a vastly higher kind, and more sublime nature than in other things; a glory greatly distinguishing them from all that is earthly and temporal. He that is spiritually enlightened truly apprehends and sees it, or has a sense of it. He does not merely rationally believe that God is glorious, but he has a sense of the gloriousness of God in his heart. There is not only a rational belief that God is holy, and that holiness is a good thing, but there is a sense of the loveliness of God's holiness. There is not only a speculatively judging that God is gracious, but a sense how amiable God is on account of the beauty of this divine attribute.

There is a twofold knowledge of good of which God has made the mind of man capable. The first, that which is merely notional; as when a person only speculatively judges that anything is, which by the agreement of mankind, is

---

4. Fanciful, imaginary.                5. I.e., evil.

called good or excellent, viz., that which is most to general advantage, and between which and a reward there is a suitableness,—and the like. And the other is, that which consists in the sense of the heart; as when the heart is sensible[6] of pleasure and delight in the presence of the idea of it. In the former is exercised merely the speculative faculty, or the understanding, in distinction from the will or disposition of the soul. In the latter, the will, or inclination, or heart, are mainly concerned.

Thus there is a difference between having an opinion, that God is holy and gracious, and having a sense of the loveliness and beauty of that holiness and grace. There is a difference between having a rational judgment that honey is sweet, and having a sense of its sweetness. A man may have the former, that knows not how honey tastes; but a man cannot have the latter unless he has an idea of the taste of honey in his mind. So there is a difference between believing that a person is beautiful, and having a sense of his beauty. The former may be obtained by hearsay, but the latter only by seeing the countenance. When the heart is sensible of the beauty and amiableness of a thing, it necessarily feels pleasure in the apprehension. It is implied in a person's being heartily sensible of the loveliness of a thing, that the idea of it is pleasant to his soul; which is a far different thing from having a rational opinion that it is excellent.

2. There arises from this sense of the divine excellency of things contained in the word of God, a conviction of the truth and reality of them; and that, either indirectly or directly.

First, Indirectly, and that two ways:

1. As the prejudices of the heart, against the truth of divine things, are hereby removed; so that the mind becomes susceptive of the due force of rational arguments for their truth. The mind of man is naturally full of prejudices against divine truth. It is full of enmity against the doctrines of the gospel; which is a disadvantage to those arguments that prove their truth, and causes them to lose their force upon the mind. But when a person has discovered to him the divine excellency of Christian doctrines, this destroys the enmity, removes those prejudices, sanctifies the reason, and causes it to lie open to the force of arguments for their truth.

Hence was the different effect that Christ's miracles had to convince the disciples, from what they had to convince the Scribes and Pharisees. Not that they had a stronger reason, or had their reason more improved; but their reason was sanctified, and those blinding prejudices, that the Scribes and Pharisees were under, were removed by the sense they had of the excellency of Christ, and his doctrine.

It not only removes the hindrances of reason, but positively helps reason. It makes even the speculative notions more lively. It engages the attention of the mind, with more fixedness and intenseness to that kind of objects; which causes it to have a clearer view of them, and enables it more clearly to see their mutual relations, and occasions it to take more notice of them. The ideas themselves that otherwise are dim and obscure are by this means impressed with the greater strength, and have a light cast upon them, so that the mind can better judge of them. As he that beholds objects on the face of the earth, when the light of the sun is cast upon them, is under greater advantage to

6. Aware.

discern them in their true forms and natural relations, than he that sees them in a dim twilight.

The mind, being sensible of the excellency of divine objects, dwells upon them with delight; and the powers of the soul are more awakened and enlivened to employ themselves in the contemplation of them, and exert themselves more fully and much more to the purpose. The beauty of the objects draws on the faculties, and draws forth their exercises; so that reason itself is under far greater advantages for its proper and free exercises, and to attain its proper end, free of darkness and delusion.—But,

Secondly, A true sense of the divine excellency of the things of God's word doth more directly and immediately convince us of their truth; and that because the excellency of these things is so superlative. There is a beauty in them so divine and godlike, that it greatly and evidently distinguishes them from things merely human, or that of which men are the inventors and authors; a glory so high and great, that when clearly seen, commands assent to their divine reality. When there is an actual and lively discovery of this beauty and excellency, it will not allow of any such thought as that it is the fruit of men's invention. This is a kind of intuitive and immediate evidence. They believe the doctrines of God's word to be divine, because they see a divine, and transcendent, and most evidently distinguishing glory in them; such a glory as, if clearly seen, does not leave room to doubt of their being of God, and not of men.

Such a conviction of the truths of religion as this, arising from a sense of their divine excellency, is included in saving faith. And this original of it is that by which it is most essentially distinguished from that common assent, of which unregenerate men are capable.

II. I proceed now to the second thing proposed, viz., to show how this light is immediately given by God, and not obtained by natural means. And here,

1. It is not intended that the natural faculties are not used in it. They are the subject of this light: and in such a manner, that they are not merely passive, but active in it. God, in letting in this light into the soul, deals with man according to his nature, and makes use of his rational faculties. But yet this light is not the less immediately from God for that; the faculties are made use of as the subject, and not as the cause. As the use we make of our eyes in beholding various objects, when the sun arises, is not the cause of the light that discovers those objects to us.

2. It is not intended that outward means have no concern in this affair. It is not in this affair, as in inspiration, where new truths are suggested; for, by this light is given only a due apprehension of the same truths that are revealed in the word of God, and therefore it is not given without the word. The gospel is employed in this affair. This light is the "light of the glorious gospel of Christ" (2 Corinthians 4.3–4).[7] The gospel is as a glass, by which this light is conveyed to us (1 Corinthians 13.12): "Now we see through a glass."[8]—But,

3. When it is said that this light is given immediately by God, and not obtained by natural means, hereby is intended that it is given by God without

7. "But if our gospel be hid, it is hid to them that are lost: In whom the god of this world hath blinded the minds of them which believe not, lest the light of the glorious gospel of Christ, who is the image of God, should shine unto them."
8. "For now we see through a glass, darkly; but then face to face."

making use of any means that operate by their own power or natural force. God makes use of means; but it is not as mediate causes to produce this effect. There are not truly any second causes of it; but it is produced by God immediately. The word of God is no proper cause of this effect, but is made use of only to convey to the mind the subject matter of this saving instruction: And this indeed it doth convey to us by natural force or influence. It conveys to our minds these doctrines; it is the cause of a notion of them in our heads, but not of the sense of their divine excellency in our hearts. Indeed a person cannot have spiritual light without the word. But that does not argue, that the word properly causes that light. The mind cannot see the excellency of any doctrine, unless that doctrine be first in the mind; but seeing the excellency of the doctrine may be immediately from the Spirit of God; though the conveying of the doctrine, or proposition, itself, may be by the word. So that the notions which are the subject matter of this light are conveyed to the mind by the word of God; but that due sense of the heart, wherein this light formally consists, is immediately by the Spirit of God. As, for instance, the notion that there is a Christ, and that Christ is holy and gracious, is conveyed to the mind by the word of God: But the sense of the excellency of Christ, by reason of that holiness and grace, is nevertheless, immediately the work of the Holy Spirit.— I come now,

III. To show the truth of the doctrine; that is, to show that there is such a thing as that spiritual light that has been described, thus immediately let into the mind by God. And here I would show, briefly, that this doctrine is both scriptural and rational.

First, It is scriptural. My text is not only full to the purpose, but it is a doctrine with which the Scripture abounds. We are there abundantly taught, that the saints differ from the ungodly in this; that they have the knowledge of God, and a sight of God, and of Jesus Christ. I shall mention but few texts out of many: 1 John 3.6: "Whosoever sinneth, hath not seen him, nor known him." 3 John 11: "He that doeth good, is of God: but he that doeth evil, hath not seen God." John 14.19: "The world seeth me no more; but ye see me." John 17.3: "And this is eternal life, that they might know thee, the only true God, and Jesus Christ whom thou hast sent." This knowledge, or sight of God and Christ, cannot be a mere speculative knowledge, because it is spoken of as that wherein they differ from the ungodly. And by these scriptures, it must not only be a different knowledge in degree and circumstances, and different in its effects, but it must be entirely different in nature and kind.

And this light and knowledge is always spoken of as immediately given of God; Matthew 11.25–27: "At that time, Jesus answered and said, I thank thee, O Father, Lord of heaven and earth, because thou hast hid these things from the wise and prudent, and hast revealed them unto babes. Even so, Father, for so it seemed good in thy sight. All things are delivered unto me of my Father: and no man knoweth the Father, save the Son, and he to whomsoever the Son will reveal him." Here this effect is ascribed exclusively to the arbitrary operation and gift of God bestowing this knowledge on whom He will, and distinguishing those with it who have the least natural advantage or means for knowledge, even babes, when it is denied to the wise and prudent. And imparting this knowledge is here appropriated to the Son of God, as His sole prerogative. And again, 2 Corinthians 4.6: "For God, who commanded the light to shine out of darkness, hath shined in our hearts, to give the light of the knowledge of the glory of God, in the face of Jesus Christ." This plainly shows, that there is a discovery of the divine superlative glory and excellency of God and Christ, peculiar to the saints: and, also, that it is as immediately from God, as light from the sun, and that it is the immediate effect of His power and will. For it is compared to God's creating the light by his powerful word in the beginning of the creation; and is said to be by the Spirit of the Lord, in the 18th verse of the preceding chapter. God is spoken of as giving the knowledge of Christ in conversion, as of what before was hidden and unseen; Galatians 1.15–16: "But when it pleased God, who separated me from my mother's womb, and called me by his grace, to reveal his son in me." The scripture also speaks plainly of such a knowledge of the word of God, as has been described as the immediate gift of God; Psalm 119.18: "Open thou mine eyes, that I may behold wondrous things out of thy law." What could the Psalmist mean, when he begged of God to open his eyes? Was he ever blind? Might he not have resort to the law, and see every word and sentence in it when he pleased? And what could he mean by those wondrous things? Were they the wonderful stories of the creation, and deluge, and Israel's passing through the Red Sea,[9] and the like? Were not his eyes open to read these strange things when he would? Doubtless, by wondrous things in God's law, he had respect to those distinguishing and wonderful excellencies, and marvelous manifestations of the divine perfections and glory contained in the commands and doctrines of the word, and those works and counsels of God that were there revealed. So the scripture speaks of a knowledge of God's dispensation, and covenant of mercy,[1] and way of grace towards His people, as peculiar to the saints, and given only by God; Psalm 25.14: "The secret of the Lord is with them that fear him; and he will show them his covenant."

And that a true and saving belief of the truth of religion is that which arises from such a discovery is, also, what the scripture teaches. As John 6.40: "And this is the will of him that sent me, that every one who seeth the Son, and believeth on him, may have everlasting life"; where it is plain that a true faith is what arises from a spiritual sight of Christ. And John 17.6–8: "I have manifested thy name unto the men which thou gavest me out of the world. Now, they have known, that all things whatsoever thou hast given me, are of thee. For I have given unto them the words which thou gavest me, and they have received them, and have known surely, that I came out from thee, and they have believed that thou didst send me"; where Christ's manifesting God's name to the disciples, or giving them the knowledge of God, was that whereby they knew that Christ's doctrine was of God, and that Christ Himself proceeded from Him, and was sent by Him. Again, John 12.44–46: "Jesus cried, and said, He that believeth on me, believeth not on me but on him that sent me. And he that seeth me, seeth him that sent me. I am come a light into the world, that whosoever believeth on me, should not abide in darkness." Their believing in Christ, and spiritually seeing Him, are parallel.

Christ condemns the Jews, that they did not know that He was the Messiah, and that His doctrine was true, from an inward distinguishing taste and relish of what was divine, in Luke 12.56–57. He having there blamed the Jews, that,

---

9. The waters of the Red Sea divided for the Israelites in their exodus from Egypt (Exodus 14.21).
1. The agreement between Christ and those who be-lieve in him that they would be saved; also known as the Covenant of Faith, as distinct from the Covenant of Works, which Adam broke.

though they could discern the face of the sky and of the earth, and signs of the weather, that yet they could not discern those times—or, as it is expressed in Matthew, the signs of those times—adds, "yea, and why even of your own-selves, judge ye not what is right?" i.e., without extrinsic signs. Why have ye not that sense of true excellency, whereby ye may distinguish that which is holy and divine? Why have ye not that savor of the things of God, by which you may see the distinguishing glory, and evident divinity of me and my doctrine?

The apostle Peter mentions it as what gave him and his companions good and well-grounded assurance of the truth of the gospel, that they had seen the divine glory of Christ. 2 Peter 1.16: "For we have not followed cunningly devised fables, when we made known unto you the power and coming of our Lord Jesus Christ, but were eye-witnesses of his majesty." The apostle has respect to that visible glory of Christ which they saw in His transfiguration. That glory was so divine, having such an ineffable appearance and semblance of divine holiness, majesty, and grace, that it evidently denoted Him to be a divine person. But if a sight of Christ's outward glory might give a rational assurance of His divinity, why may not an apprehension of His spiritual glory do so too? Doubtless Christ's spiritual glory is in itself as distinguishing, and as plainly shows His divinity, as His outward glory—nay, a great deal more, for His spiritual glory is that wherein His divinity consists; and the outward glory of His transfiguration showed Him to be divine, only as it was a remarkable image or representation of that spiritual glory. Doubtless, therefore, he that has had a clear sight of the spiritual glory of Christ, may say, "I have not followed cunningly devised fables, but have been an eyewitness of His majesty, upon as good grounds as the apostle, when he had respect to the outward glory of Christ that he had seen." But this brings me to what was proposed next, viz., to show that,

Secondly, This doctrine is rational.[2]

1. It is rational to suppose, that there is really such an excellency in divine things—so transcendent and exceedingly different from what is in other things—that if it were seen, would most evidently distinguish them. We cannot rationally doubt but that things divine, which appertain to the supreme Being, are vastly different from things that are human; that there is a high, glorious, and godlike excellency in them that does most remarkably difference them from the things that are of men, insomuch that if the difference were but seen, it would have a convincing, satisfying influence upon anyone that they are divine. What reason can be offered against it unless we would argue that God is not remarkably distinguished in glory from men.

If Christ should now appear to any one as he did on the mount at His transfiguration,[3] or if He should appear to the world in His heavenly glory, as He will do at the Day of Judgment,[4] without doubt, His glory and majesty would be such as would satisfy everyone that He was a divine person, and that His religion was true; and it would be a most reasonable, and well grounded conviction too. And why may there not be that stamp of divinity or divine glory on the word of God, on the scheme and doctrine of the gospel, that may be in like manner distinguishing and as rationally convincing, provided it be

---

2. Capable of being grasped by the mind, understandable.
3. In Matthew 17.1–8, Christ appeared to Peter, James, and John shining "as the sun" and his garments "white as the light."
4. See Revelation 4.

but seen? It is rational to suppose, that when God speaks to the world, there should be something in His word vastly different from men's word. Supposing that God never had spoken to the world, but we had notice that He was about to reveal Himself from heaven and speak to us immediately Himself, or that He should give us a book of His own inditing;[5] after what manner should we expect that He would speak? Would it not be rational to suppose, that His speech would be exceeding different from men's speech, that there should be such an excellency and sublimity in His word, such a stamp of wisdom, holiness, majesty, and other divine perfections, that the word of men, yea of the wisest of men, should appear mean and base in comparison of it? Doubtless it would be thought rational to expect this, and unreasonable to think otherwise. When a wise man speaks in the exercise of His wisdom, there is something in everything He says, that is very distinguishable from the talk of a little child. So, without doubt, and much more is the speech of God, to be distinguished from that of the wisest of men; agreeable to Jeremiah 23.28–29. God, having there been reproving the false prophets that prophesied in his name, and pretended that what they spake was His word, when indeed it was their own word, says, "The prophet that hath a dream, let him tell a dream; and he that hath my word let him speak my word faithfully: what is the chaff to the wheat? saith the Lord. Is not my word like as a fire? saith the Lord: and like a hammer that breaketh the rock in pieces?"

2. If there be such a distinguishing excellency in divine things, it is rational to suppose that there may be such a thing as seeing it. What should hinder but that it may be seen? It is no argument that there is no such distinguishing excellency, or that it cannot be seen, because some do not see it, though they may be discerning men in temporal matters. It is not rational to suppose, if there be any such excellency in divine things, that wicked men should see it. It is rational to suppose that those whose minds are full of spiritual pollution, and under the power of filthy lusts, should have any relish or sense of divine beauty or excellency; or that their minds should be susceptive of that light that is in its own nature so pure and heavenly? It need not seem at all strange that sin should so blind the mind, seeing that men's particular natural tempers and dispositions will so much blind them in secular matters; as when men's natural temper is melancholy, jealous, fearful, proud, or the like.

3. It is rational to suppose that this knowledge should be given immediately by God, and not be obtained by natural means. Upon what account should it seem unreasonable that there should be any immediate communication between God and the creature? It is strange, that men should make any matter of difficulty of it. Why should not He that made all things still have something immediately to do with the things that He has made? Where lies the great difficulty, if we own the being of a God, and that He created all things out of nothing, of allowing some immediate influence of God on the creation still? And if it be reasonable to suppose it with respect to any part of the creation, it is especially so with respect to reasonable, intelligent creatures; who are next to God in the gradation of the different orders of beings, and whose business is most immediately with God; and reason teaches that man was made to serve and glorify his Creator. And if it be rational to suppose that God immediately communicates Himself to man in any affair, it is in this. It is rational to

5. Composition.

suppose that God would reserve that knowledge and wisdom, which is of such a divine and excellent nature, to be bestowed immediately by Himself, and that it should not be left in the power of second causes. Spiritual wisdom and grace is the highest and most excellent gift that ever God bestows on any creature; in this, the highest excellency and perfection of a rational creature consists. It is also immensely the most important of all divine gifts: it is that wherein man's happiness consists, and on which his everlasting welfare depends. How rational is it to suppose that God, however He has left lower gifts to second causes, and in some sort in their power, yet should reserve this most excellent, divine, and important of all divine communications in His own hands to be bestowed immediately by Himself, as a thing too great for second causes to be concerned in. It is rational to suppose that this blessing should be immediately from God, for there is no gift or benefit that is in itself so nearly related to the divine nature. Nothing which the creature receives is so much a participation of the Deity; it is a kind of emanation of God's beauty, and is related to God as the light is to the sun. It is, therefore, congruous and fit, that when it is given of God, it should be immediately from Himself, and by Himself, according to His own sovereign will.

It is rational to suppose, that it should be beyond man's power to obtain this light by the mere strength of natural reason; for it is not a thing that belongs to reason to see the beauty and loveliness of spiritual things; it is not a speculative thing, but depends on the sense of the heart. Reason, indeed, is necessary, in order to it, as it is by reason only that we are become the subjects of the means of it; which means, I have already shown to be necessary in order to it, though they have no proper causal influence in the affair. It is by reason that we become possessed of a notion of those doctrines that are the subject matter of this divine light or knowledge; and reason may many ways be indirectly and remotely an advantage to it. Reason has also to do in the acts that are immediately consequent on this discovery: for, seeing the truth of religion from hence, is by reason, though it be but by one step, and the inference be immediate. So reason has to do in that accepting of and trusting in Christ that is consequent on it. But if we take reason strictly—not for the faculty of mental perception in general, but for ratiocination, or a power of inferring by arguments— the perceiving of spiritual beauty and excellency no more belongs to reason than it belongs to the sense of feeling to perceive colors, or to the power of seeing to perceive the sweetness of food. It is out of reason's province to perceive the beauty or loveliness of anything; such a perception does not belong to that faculty. Reason's work is to perceive truth and not excellency. It is not ratiocination that gives men the perception of the beauty and amiableness of a countenance, though it may be many ways indirectly an advantage to it; yet it is no more reason that immediately perceives it than it is reason that perceives the sweetness of honey; it depends on the sense of the heart. Reason may determine that a countenance is beautiful to others, it may determine that honey is sweet to others, but it will never give me a perception of its sweetness.

I will conclude with a very brief improvement of what has been said.

First, this doctrine may lead us to reflect on the goodness of God, that has so ordered it, that a saving evidence of the truth of the Gospel is such as is attainable by persons of mean capacities and advantages, as well as those that are of the greatest parts and learning. If the evidence of the Gospel depended only on history and such reasonings as learned men only are capable of, it would be above the reach of far the greatest part of mankind. But persons with an ordinary degree of knowledge are capable, without a long and subtle train of reasoning, to see the divine excellency of the things of religion; they are capable of being taught by the Spirit of God, as well as learned men. The evidence that is this way obtained is vastly better and more satisfying than all that can be obtained by the arguings of those that are most learned and greatest masters of reason. And babes are as capable of knowing these things as the wise and prudent; and they are often hid from these when they are revealed to those. 1 Corinthians 1.26–27: "For ye see your calling, brethren, how that not many wise men, after the flesh, not many mighty, not many noble, are called. But God hath chosen the foolish things of the world."

Secondly, This doctrine may well put us upon examining ourselves, whether we have ever had this divine light let into our souls. If there be such a thing, doubtless it is of great importance whether we have thus been taught by the Spirit of God; whether the light of the glorious gospel of Christ, who is the image of God, hath shined unto us, giving us the light of the knowledge of the glory of God in the face of Jesus Christ; whether we have seen the Son, and believed on Him, or have that faith of gospel doctrines which arises from a spiritual sight of Christ.

Thirdly, All may hence be exhorted earnestly to seek this spiritual light. To influence and move to it, the following things may be considered.

1. This is the most excellent and divine wisdom that any creature is capable of. It is more excellent than any human learning; it is far more excellent than all the knowledge of the greatest philosophers or statesmen. Yea, the least glimpse of the glory of God in the face of Christ doth more exalt and ennoble the soul than all the knowledge of those that have the greatest speculative understanding in divinity without grace. This knowledge has the most noble object that can be, viz., the divine glory and excellency of God and Christ. The knowledge of these objects is that wherein consists the most excellent knowledge of the angels, yea, of God Himself.

2. This knowledge is that which is above all others sweet and joyful. Men have a great deal of pleasure in human knowledge, in studies of natural things; but this is nothing to that joy which arises from this divine light shining into the soul. This light gives a view of those things that are immensely the most exquisitely beautiful and capable of delighting the eye of the understanding. The spiritual light is the dawning of the light of glory in the heart. There is nothing so powerful as this to support persons in affliction, and to give the mind peace and brightness in this stormy and dark world.

3. This light is such as effectually influences the inclination and changes the nature of the soul. It assimilates our nature to the divine nature, and changes the soul into an image of the same glory that is beheld. 2 Corinthians 3.18: "But we all with open face, beholding as in a glass the glory of the Lord, are changed into the same image, from glory to glory, even as by the Spirit of the Lord." This knowledge will wean[6] from the world, and raise the inclination to heavenly things. It will turn the heart to God as the fountain of good, and to choose Him for the only portion. This light, and this only, will bring the soul to a saving close with Christ. It conforms the heart to the gospel, mortifies its enmity and opposition against the scheme of salvation therein

---

6. Draw us away from.

revealed; it causes the heart to embrace the joyful tidings, and entirely to adhere to, and acquiesce in, the revelation of Christ as our Savior; it causes the whole soul to accord and symphonize with it, admitting it with entire credit and respect, cleaving to it with full inclination and affection; and it effectually disposes the soul to give up itself entirely to Christ.

4. This light, and this only, has its fruit in an universal holiness of life. No merely notional or speculative understanding of the doctrines of religion will ever bring to this. But this light, as it reaches the bottom of the heart, and changes the nature, so it will effectually dispose to an universal obedience. It shows God as worthy to be obeyed and served. It draws forth the heart in a sincere love to God, which is the only principle of a true, gracious, and universal obedience, and it convinces of the reality of those glorious rewards that God has promised to them that obey Him.

1733                                                                    1734

## Sinners in the Hands of an Angry God[1]

### Deuteronomy 32.35

Their foot shall slide in due time.[2]

In this verse is threatened the vengeance of God on the wicked unbelieving Israelites, who were God's visible people, and who lived under the means of grace,[3] but who, notwithstanding all God's wonderful works towards them, remained (as in verse 28)[4] void of counsel, having no understanding in them. Under all the cultivations of heaven, they brought forth bitter and poisonous fruit, as in the two verses next preceding the text.[5] The expression I have chosen for my text, "Their foot shall slide in due time," seems to imply the following things, relating to the punishment and destruction to which these wicked Israelites were exposed.

1. That they were always exposed to destruction; as one that stands or walks in slippery places is always exposed to fall. This is implied in the manner of their destruction coming upon them, being represented by their foot sliding. The same is expressed, Psalm 73.18: "Surely thou didst set them in slippery places; thou castedst them down into destruction."

2. It implies that they were always exposed to sudden unexpected destruc-

---

1. Edwards delivered this sermon in Enfield, Connecticut, a town about thirty miles south of Northampton, on Sunday, July 8, 1741. In Benjamin Trumbull's *A Complete History of Connecticut* (1797, 1818) we are told that Edwards read his sermon in a level voice with his sermon book in his left hand, and in spite of his calm, "there was such a breathing of distress, and weeping, that the preacher was obliged to speak to the people and desire silence, that he might be heard." The text is from *The Works of Jonathan Edwards*, vol. 7, edited by Sereno E. Dwight (1829–30).
2. "To me belongeth vengeance, and recompense; their foot shall slide in due time: for the day of their calamity is at hand, and the things that shall come upon them make haste."

3. I.e., the Ten Commandments. For Protestants following the Westminster Confession (1646), the "means of grace" consist of "preaching of the word and the administration of the sacraments of baptism and the Lord's Supper."
4. "They are a nation void of counsel, neither is there any understanding in them" (Deuteronomy 32.28).
5. "For their vine is of the vine of Sodom, and the fields of Gomorrah: their grapes are grapes of gall, their clusters are bitter: Their wine is the poison of dragons, and the cruel venom of asps" (Deuteronomy 32.32–33). Sodom and Gomorrah were wicked cities destroyed by a rain of fire and sulfur from heaven (Genesis 19.24).

tion. As he that walks in slippery places is every moment liable to fall, he cannot foresee one moment whether he shall stand or fall the next; and when he does fall, he falls at once without warning: which is also expressed in Psalm 73.18–19: "Surely thou didst set them in slippery places; thou castedst them down into destruction: How are they brought into desolation as in a moment!"

3. Another thing implied is, that they are liable to fall of themselves, without being thrown down by the hand of another; as he that stands or walks on slippery ground needs nothing but his own weight to throw him down.

4. That the reason why they are not fallen already, and do not fall now, is only that God's appointed time is not come. For it is said that when that due time, or appointed times comes, their foot shall slide. Then they shall be left to fall, as they are inclined by their own weight. God will not hold them up in these slippery places any longer, but will let them go; and then, at that very instant, they shall fall into destruction; as he that stands on such slippery declining ground, on the edge of a pit, he cannot stand alone, when he is let go he immediately falls and is lost.

The observation from the words that I would now insist upon is this. "There is nothing that keeps wicked men at any one moment out of hell, but the mere pleasure of God." By the mere pleasure of God, I mean His sovereign pleasure, His arbitrary will, restrained by no obligation, hindered by no manner of difficulty, any more than if nothing else but God's mere will had in the least degree, or in any respect whatsoever, any hand in the preservation of wicked men one moment. The truth of this observation may appear by the following considerations.

1. There is no want of power in God to cast wicked men into hell at any moment. Men's hands cannot be strong when God rises up. The strongest have no power to resist Him, not can any deliver[6] out of His hands. He is not only able to cast wicked men into hell, but He can most easily do it. Sometimes an earthly prince meets with a great deal of difficulty to subdue a rebel, who has found means to fortify himself, and has made himself strong by the numbers of his followers. But it is not so with God. There is no fortress that is any defense from the power of God. Though hand join in hand, and vast multitudes of God's enemies combine and associate themselves, they are easily broken in pieces. They are as great heaps of light chaff before the whirlwind; or large quantities of dry stubble before devouring flames. We find it easy to tread on and crush a worm that we see crawling on the earth; so it is easy for us to cut or singe a slender thread that any thing hangs by: thus easy is it for God, when he pleases, to cast His enemies down to hell. What are we, that we should think to stand before Him, at whose rebuke the earth trembles, and before whom the rocks are thrown down?

2. They deserve to be cast into hell; so that divine justice never stands in the way, it makes no objection against God's using His power at any moment to destroy them. Yea, on the contrary, justice calls aloud for an infinite punishment of their sins. Divine justice says of the tree that brings forth such grapes of Sodom, "Cut it down, why cumbereth it the ground? Luke 13.7. The sword of divine justice is every moment brandished over their heads, and it is nothing but the hand of arbitrary mercy, and God's will, that holds it back.

3. They are already under a sentence of condemnation to hell. They do not

---

6. I.e., rescue others.

only justly deserve to be cast down thither, but the sentence of the law of God, that eternal and immutable rule of righteousness that God has fixed between Him and mankind, is gone out against them, and stands against them; so that they are bound over already to hell. John 3.18: "He that believeth not is condemned already." So that every unconverted man properly belongs to hell; that is his place; from thence he is, John 8.23: "Ye are from beneath." And thither he is bound; it is the place that justice, and God's word, and the sentence of his unchangeable law assign to him.

4. They are now the objects of that very same anger and wrath of God that is expressed in the torments of hell. And the reason why they do not go down to hell at each moment is not because God, in whose power they are, is not then very angry with them as He is with many miserable creatures now tormented in hell, who there feel and bear the fierceness of His wrath. Yea, God is a great deal more angry with great numbers that are now on earth: yea, doubtless, with many that are now in this congregation, who it may be are at ease, than He is with many of those who are now in the flames of hell.

So that it is not because God is unmindful of their wickedness, and does not resent it, that He does not let loose His hand and cut them off. God is not altogether such an one as themselves, though they may imagine Him to be so. The wrath of God burns against them, their damnation does not slumber; the pit is prepared, the fire is made ready, the furnace is now hot, ready to receive them; the flames do now rage and glow. The glittering sword is whet,[7] and held over them, and the pit hath opened its mouth under them.

5. The devil stands ready to fall upon them, and seize them as his own, at what moment God shall permit him. They belong to him; he has their souls in his possession, and under his dominion. The Scripture represents them as his goods, Luke 11.12.[8] The devils watch them; they are ever by them at their right hand; they stand waiting for them, like greedy hungry lions that see their prey, and expect to have it, but are for the present kept back. If God should withdraw His hand, by which they are restrained, they would in one moment fly upon their poor souls. The old serpent is gaping for them; hell opens its mouth wide to receive them; and if God should permit it, they would be hastily swallowed up and lost.

6. There are in the souls of wicked men those hellish principles reigning that would presently kindle and flame out into hell fire, if it were not for God's restraints. There is laid in the very nature of carnal men a foundation for the torments of hell. There are those corrupt principles, in reigning power in them, and in full possession of them, that are seeds of hell fire. These principles are active and powerful, exceeding violent in their nature, and if it were not for the restraining hand of God upon them, they would soon break out, they would flame out after the same manner as the same corruptions, the same enmity does in the hearts of damned souls, and would beget the same torments as they do in them. The souls of the wicked are in Scripture compared to the troubled sea, Isaiah 57.20.[9] For the present, God restrains their wickedness by His mighty power, as He does the raging waves of the troubled sea, saying, "Hitherto shalt thou come, but no further;"[1] but if God should withdraw that restraining power, it would soon carry all before it. Sin is the ruin and misery

7. Sharpened.
8. "Or if he shall ask an egg, will he offer him a scorpion?"

9. "But the wicked are like the troubled sea, when it cannot rest, whose waters cast up mire and dirt."
1. Job 38.11.

of the soul; it is destructive in its nature; and if God should leave it without restraint, there would need nothing else to make the soul perfectly miserable. The corruption of the heart of man is immoderate and boundless in its fury; and while wicked men live here, it is like fire pent up by God's restraints, whereas if it were let loose, it would set on fire the course of nature; and as the heart is now a sink of sin, so if sin was not restrained, it would immediately turn the soul into a fiery oven, or a furnace of fire and brimstone.

7. It is no security to wicked men for one moment that there are no visible means of death at hand. It is no security to a natural man that he is now in health and that he does not see which way he should now immediately go out of the world by any accident, and that there is no visible danger in any respect in his circumstances. The manifold and continual experience of the world in all ages, shows this is no evidence that a man is not on the very brink of eternity, and that the next step will not be into another world. The unseen, unthought-of ways and means of persons going suddenly out of the world are innumerable and inconceivable. Unconverted men walk over the pit of hell on a rotten covering, and there are innumerable places in this covering so weak that they will not bear their weight, and these places are not seen. The arrows of death fly unseen at noonday;[2] the sharpest sight cannot discern them. God has so many different unsearchable ways of taking wicked men out of the world and sending them to hell, that there is nothing to make it appear that God had need to be at the expense of a miracle, or go out of the ordinary course of His providence, to destroy any wicked man at any moment. All the means that there are of sinners going out of the world are so in God's hands, and so universally and absolutely subject to His power and determination, that it does not depend at all the less on the mere will of God whether sinners shall at any moment go to hell than if means were never made use of or at all concerned in the case.

8. Natural men's prudence and care to preserve their own lives, or the care of others to preserve them, do not secure them a moment. To this, divine providence and universal experience do also bear testimony. There is this clear evidence that men's own wisdom is no security to them from death; that if it were otherwise we should see some difference between the wise and politic men of the world, and others, with regard to their liableness to early and unexpected death: but how is it in fact? Ecclesiastes 2.16: "How dieth the wise man? even as the fool."

9. All wicked men's pains and contrivance which they use to escape hell, while they continue to reject Christ, and so remain wicked men, do not secure them from hell one moment. Almost every natural[3] man that hears of hell, flatters himself that he shall escape it; he depends upon himself for his own security; he flatters himself in what he has done, in what he is now doing, or what he intends to do. Every one lays out matters in his own mind how he shall avoid damnation, and flatters himself that he contrives well for himself, and that his schemes will not fail. They hear indeed that there are but few saved, and that the greater part of men that have died heretofore are gone to hell; but each one imagines that he lays out matters better for his own escape than others have done. He does not intend to come to that place of torment;

---

2. "Thou shalt not be afraid for the terror by night; nor    3. I.e., unregenerate, unsaved.
for the arrow that flieth by day" (Psalm 91.5).

he says within himself that he intends to take effectual care, and to order matters so for himself as not to fail.

But the foolish children of men miserably delude themselves in their own schemes, and in confidence in their own strength and wisdom; they trust to nothing but a shadow. The greater part of those who heretofore have lived under the same means of grace, and are now dead, are undoubtedly gone to hell; and it was not because they were not as wise as those who are now alive: it was not because they did not lay out matters as well for themselves to secure their own escape. If we could speak with them, and inquire of them, one by one, whether they expected when alive, and when they used to hear about hell, ever to be the subjects of that misery, we doubtless, should hear one and another reply, "No, I never intended to come here: I had laid out matters otherwise in my mind; I thought I should contrive well for myself: I thought my scheme good. I intended to take effectual care; but it came upon me unexpected; I did not look for it at that time, and in that manner; it came as a thief: Death outwitted me: God's wrath was too quick for me. Oh, my cursed foolishness! I was flattering myself, and pleasing myself with vain dreams of what I would do hereafter; and when I was saying, peace and safety, then suddenly destruction came upon me."

10. God has laid Himself under no obligation by any promise to keep any natural man out of hell one moment. God certainly has made no promises either of eternal life or of any deliverance or preservation from eternal death but what are contained in the covenant of grace,[4] the promises that are given in Christ, in whom all the promises are yea and amen. But surely they have no interest in the promises of the covenant of grace who are not the children of the covenant, who do not believe in any of the promises, and have no interest in the Mediator of the covenant.[5]

So that, whatever some have imagined and pretended[6] about promises made to natural men's earnest seeking and knocking, it is plain and manifest that whatever pains a natural man takes in religion, whatever prayers he makes, till he believes in Christ, God is under no manner of obligation to keep him a moment from eternal destruction.

So that, thus it is that natural men are held in the hand of God, over the pit of hell; they have deserved the fiery pit, and are already sentenced to it; and God is dreadfully provoked. His anger is as great towards them as to those that are actually suffering the executions of the fierceness of His wrath in hell, and they have done nothing in the least to appease or abate that anger, neither is God in the least bound by any promise to hold them up one moment; the devil is waiting for them, hell is gaping for them, the flames gather and flash about them, and would fain lay hold on them, and swallow them up; the fire pent up in their own hearts is struggling to break out: and they have no interest in any Mediator, there are no means within reach that can be any security to them. In short, they have no refuge, nothing to take hold of; all that preserves them every moment is the mere arbitrary will, and uncovenanted, unobliged forbearance of an incensed God.

---

4. The original covenant God made with Adam is called the Covenant of Works; the second covenant Christ made with fallen humanity—declaring that if they believed in Him they would be saved—is called the Covenant of Grace.
5. I.e., Christ, who took upon Himself the sins of the world and suffered for them.
6. Claimed.

## Application

The use of this awful[7] subject may be for awakening unconverted persons in this congregation. This that you have heard is the case of every one of you that are out of Christ. That world of misery, that lake of burning brimstone, is extended abroad under you. There is the dreadful pit of the glowing flames of the wrath of God; there is hell's wide gaping mouth open; and you have nothing to stand upon, nor any thing to take hold of; there is nothing between you and hell but the air; it is only the power and mere pleasure of God that holds you up.

You probably are not sensible[8] of this; you find you are kept out of hell, but do not see the hand of God in it; but look at other things, as the good state of your bodily constitution, your care of your own life, and the means you use for your own preservation. But indeed these things are nothing; if God should withdraw His hand, they would avail no more to keep you from falling, than the thin air to hold up a person that is suspended in it.

Your wickedness makes you as it were heavy as lead, and to tend downwards with great weight and pressure towards hell; and if God should let you go, you would immediately sink and swiftly descend and plunge into the bottomless gulf, and your healthy constitution, and your own care and prudence, and best contrivance, and all your righteousness, would have no more influence to uphold you and keep you out of hell, than a spider's web would have to stop a fallen rock. Were it not for the sovereign pleasure of God, the earth would not bear you one moment; for you are a burden to it; the creation groans with you; the creature is made subject to the bondage of your corruption, not willingly; the sun does not willingly shine upon you to give you light to serve sin and Satan; the earth does not willingly yield her increase to satisfy your lusts; nor is it willingly a stage for your wickedness to be acted upon; the air does not willingly serve you for breath to maintain the flame of life in your vitals, while you spend your life in the service of God's enemies. God's creatures are good, and were made for men to serve God with, and do not willingly subserve to any other purpose, and groan when they are abused to purposes so directly contrary to their nature and end. And the world would spew you out, were it not for the sovereign hand of Him who hath subjected it in hope. There are black clouds of God's wrath now hanging directly over your heads, full of the dreadful storm, and big with thunder; and were it not for the restraining hand of God, it would immediately burst forth upon you. The sovereign pleasure of God, for the present, stays His rough wind; otherwise it would come with fury, and your destruction would come like a whirlwind, and you would be like the chaff of the summer threshing floor.

The wrath of God is like great waters that are dammed for the present; they increase more and more, and rise higher and higher, till an outlet is given; and the longer the stream is stopped, the more rapid and mighty is its course when once it is let loose. It is true that judgment against your evil works has not been executed hitherto; the floods of God's vengeance have been withheld; but your guilt in the meantime is constantly increasing, and you are every day treasuring up more wrath; the waters are constantly rising, and waxing more and more mighty; and there is nothing but the mere pleasure of God that holds

---

7. Awesome.                                8. Aware.

the waters back, that are unwilling to be stopped, and press hard to go forward. If God should only withdraw His hand from the floodgate, it would immediately fly open, and the fiery floods of the fierceness and wrath of God, would rush forth with inconceivable fury, and would come upon you with omnipotent power; and if your strength were ten thousand times greater than it is, yea, ten thousand times greater than the strength of the stoutest, sturdiest devil in hell, it would be nothing to withstand or endure it.

The bow of God's wrath is bent, and the arrow made ready on the string, and justice bends the arrow at your heart, and strains the bow, and it is nothing but the mere pleasure of God, and that of an angry God, without any promise or obligation at all, that keeps the arrow one moment from being made drunk with your blood. Thus all you that never passed under a great change of heart, by the mighty power of the Spirit of God upon your souls, all you that were never born again, and made new creatures, and raised from being dead in sin, to a state of new, and before altogether unexperienced light and life, are in the hands of an angry God. However you may have reformed your life in many things, and may have had religious affections,[9] and may keep up a form of religion in your families and closets,[1] and in the house of God, it is nothing but His mere pleasure that keeps you from being this moment swallowed up in everlasting destruction. However unconvinced you may now be of the truth of what you hear, by and by you will be fully convinced of it. Those that are gone from being in the like circumstances with you see that it was so with them; for destruction came suddenly upon most of them; when they expected nothing of it and while they were saying, peace and safety: now they see that those things on which they depended for peace and safety, were nothing but thin air and empty shadows.

The God that holds you over the pit of hell, much as one holds a spider or some loathsome insect over the fire, abhors you, and is dreadfully provoked: His wrath towards you burns like fire; He looks upon you as worthy of nothing else but to be cast into the fire; He is of purer eyes than to bear to have you in His sight; you are ten thousand times more abominable in His eyes than the most hateful venomous serpent is in ours. You have offended Him infinitely more than ever a stubborn rebel did his prince; and yet it is nothing but His hand that holds you from falling into the fire every moment. It is to be ascribed to nothing else, that you did not go to hell the last night; that you was suffered to awake again in this world, after you closed your eyes to sleep. And there is no other reason to be given, why you have not dropped into hell since you arose in the morning, but that God's hand has held you up. There is no other reason to be given why you have not gone to hell, since you have sat here in the house of God, provoking His pure eyes by your sinful wicked manner of attending His solemn worship. Yea, there is nothing else that is to be given as a reason why you do not this very moment drop down into hell.

O sinner! Consider the fearful danger you are in: it is a great furnace of wrath, a wide and bottomless pit, full of the fire of wrath, that you are held over in the hand of that God, whose wrath is provoked and incensed as much against you, as against many of the damned in hell. You hang by a slender thread, with the flames of divine wrath flashing about it, and ready every moment to singe it, and burn it asunder; and you have no interest in any Mediator, and nothing to lay hold of to save yourself, nothing to keep off the

---

9. Feelings.                    1. Studies; rooms for meditation.

flames of wrath, nothing of your own, nothing that you ever have done, nothing that you can do, to induce God to spare you one moment. And consider here more particularly.

1. Whose wrath it is: it is the wrath of the infinite God. If it were only the wrath of man, though it were of the most potent prince, it would be comparatively little to be regarded. The wrath of kings is very much dreaded, especially of absolute monarchs, who have the possessions and lives of their subjects wholly in their power, to be disposed of at their mere will. Proverbs 20.2: "The fear of a king is as the roaring of a lion: Whoso provoketh him to anger, sinneth against his own soul." The subject that very much enrages an arbitrary prince is liable to suffer the most extreme torments that human art can invent, or human power can inflict. But the greatest earthly potentates in their greatest majesty, and strength, and when clothed in their greatest terrors, are but feeble, despicable worms of the dust, in comparison of the great and almighty Creator and King of heaven and earth. It is but little that they can do, when most enraged, and when they have exerted the utmost of their fury. All the kings of the earth, before God, are as grasshoppers; they are nothing, and less than nothing: both their love and their hatred is to be despised. The wrath of the great King of kings, is as much more terrible than theirs, as His majesty is greater. Luke 12.4–5: "And I say unto you, my friends, Be not afraid of them that kill the body, and after that, have no more that they can do. But I will forewarn you whom you shall fear: fear him, which after he hath killed, hath power to cast into hell: yea, I say unto you, Fear him."

2. It is the fierceness of His wrath that you are exposed to. We often read of the fury of God; as in Isaiah 59.18: "According to their deeds, accordingly he will repay fury to his adversaries." So Isaiah 66.15: "For behold, the Lord will come with fire, and with his chariots like a whirlwind, to render his anger with fury, and his rebuke with flames of fire." And in many other places. So, Revelation 19.15: we read of "the wine press of the fierceness and wrath of Almighty God."[2] The words are exceeding terrible. If it had only been said, "the wrath of God," the words would have implied that which is infinitely dreadful: but it is "the fierceness and wrath of God." The fury of God! the fierceness of Jehovah![3] Oh, how dreadful must that be! Who can utter or conceive what such expressions carry in them! But it is also "the fierceness and wrath of Almighty God." As though there would be a very great manifestation of His almighty power in what the fierceness of His wrath should inflict, as though omnipotence should be as it were enraged, and exerted, as men are wont to exert their strength in the fierceness of their wrath. Oh! then, what will be the consequence! What will become of the poor worms that shall suffer it! Whose hands can be strong? And whose heart can endure? To what a dreadful, inexpressible, inconceivable depth of misery must the poor creature be sunk who shall be the subject of this!

Consider this, you that are here present that yet remain in an unregenerate state. That God will execute the fierceness of His anger implies that He will inflict wrath without any pity. When God beholds the ineffable extremity of your case, and sees your torment to be so vastly disproportioned to your strength, and sees how your poor soul is crushed, and sinks down, as it were, into an infinite gloom; He will have no compassion upon you, He will not forbear the executions of His wrath, or in the least lighten His hand; there

2. "He treadeth the winepress of the fierceness and wrath of Almighty God."

3. The name used for God in the Old Testament.

shall be no moderation or mercy, nor will God then at all stay His rough wind; He will have no regard to your welfare, nor be at all careful lest you should suffer too much in any other sense, than only that you shall not suffer beyond what strict justice requires. Nothing shall be withheld because it is so hard for you to bear. Ezekiel 8.18: "Therefore will I also deal in fury: mine eye shall not spare, neither will I have pity; and though they cry in mine ears with a loud voice, yet I will not hear them." Now God stands ready to pity you; this is a day of mercy; you may cry now with some encouragement of obtaining mercy. But when once the day of mercy is past, your most lamentable and dolorous cries and shrieks will be in vain; you will be wholly lost and thrown away of God as to any regard to your welfare. God will have no other use to put you to, but to suffer misery; you shall be continued in being to no other end; for you will be a vessel of wrath fitted to destruction; and there will be no other use of this vessel, but to be filled full of wrath. God will be so far from pitying you when you cry to Him, that it is said He will only "laugh and mock." Proverbs 1.25–26, etc.[4]

How awful are those words, Isaiah 63.3, which are the words of the great God: "I will tread them in mine anger, and will trample them in my fury, and their blood shall be sprinkled upon my garments, and I will stain all my raiment." It is perhaps impossible to conceive of words that carry in them greater manifestations of these three things, viz., contempt, and hatred, and fierceness of indignation. If you cry to God to pity you, He will be so far from pitying you in your doleful case, or showing you the least regard or favor, that instead of that, He will ony tread you under foot. And though He will know that you cannot bear the weight of omnipotence treading upon you, yet He will not regard that, but He will crush you under His feet without mercy; He will crush out your blood, and make it fly and it shall be sprinkled on His garments, so as to stain all His raiment. He will not only hate you, but He will have you in the utmost contempt: no place shall be thought fit for you, but under His feet to be trodden down as the mire of the streets.

3. The misery you are exposed to is that which God will inflict to that end, that He might show what that wrath of Jehovah is. God hath had it on His heart to show to angels and men both how excellent His love is, and also how terrible His wrath is. Sometimes earthly kings have a mind to show how terrible their wrath is, by the extreme punishments they would execute on those that would provoke them. Nebuchadnezzar, that mighty and haughty monarch of the Chaldean empire, was willing to show his wrath when enraged with Shadrach, Meshech, and Abednego; and accordingly gave orders that the burning fiery furnace should be heated seven times hotter than it was before; doubtless, it was raised to the utmost degree of fierceness that human art could raise it.[5] But the great God is also willing to show His wrath, and magnify His awful majesty and mighty power in the extreme sufferings of His enemies. Romans 9.22: "What if God, willing to show his wrath, and to make his power known, endure with much long-suffering the vessels of wrath fitted to destruction?" And seeing this is His design, and what He has determined, even to show how terrible the restrained wrath, the fury and fierceness of Jehovah is, He will do it to effect. There will be something accomplished and brought to pass that will be dreadful with a witness. When the great and angry God

---

4. "But ye have set at nought all my counsel, and would none of my reproof: I also will laugh at your   calamity; I will mock you when your fear cometh."
5. See Daniel 3.1–30.

hath risen up and executed His awful vengeance on the poor sinner, and the wretch is actually suffering the infinite weight and power of His indignation, then will God call upon the whole universe to behold that awful majesty and mighty power that is to be seen in it. Isaiah 33.12–14: "And the people shall be as the burnings of lime, as thorns cut up shall they be burnt in the fire. Hear ye that are far off, what I have done; and ye that are near, acknowledge my might. The sinners in Zion are afraid; fearfulness hath surprised the hypocrites," etc.

Thus it will be with you that are in an unconverted state, if you continue in it; the infinite might, and majesty, and terribleness of the omnipotent God shall be magnified upon you, in the ineffable strength of your torments. You shall be tormented in the presence of the holy angels, and in the presence of the Lamb; and when you shall be in this state of suffering, the glorious inhabitants of heaven shall go forth and look on the awful spectacle, that they may see what the wrath and fierceness of the Almighty is; and when they have seen it, they will fall down and adore that great power and majesty. Isaiah 66.23–24: "And it shall come to pass, that from one new moon to another, and from one sabbath to another, shall all flesh come to worship before me, saith the Lord. And they shall go forth and look upon the carcasses of the men that have transgressed against me; for their worm shall not die, neither shall their fire be quenched, and they shall be an abhorring unto all flesh."

4. It is everlasting wrath. It would be dreadful to suffer this fierceness and wrath of Almighty God one moment; but you must suffer it to all eternity. There will be no end to this exquisite horrible misery. When you look forward, you shall see a long forever, a boundless duration before you, which will swallow up your thoughts, and amaze your soul; and you will absolutely despair of ever having any deliverance, any end, any mitigation, any rest at all. You will know certainly that you must wear out long ages, millions of millions of ages, in wrestling and conflicting with this almighty merciless vengeance; and then when you have so done, when so many ages have actually been spent by you in this manner, you will know that all is but a point to what remains. So that your punishment will indeed be infinite. Oh, who can express what the state of a soul in such circumstances is! All that we can possibly say about it gives but a very feeble, faint representation of it; it is inexpressible and inconceivable: For "who knows the power of God's anger?"[6]

How dreadful is the state of those that are daily and hourly in the danger of this great wrath and infinite misery! But this is the dismal case of every soul in this congregation that has not been born again, however moral and strict, sober and religious, they may otherwise be. Oh that you would consider it, whether you be young or old! There is reason to think that there are many in this congregation now hearing this discourse that will actually be the subjects of this very misery to all eternity. We know not who they are, or in what seats they sit, or what thoughts they now have. It may be they are now at ease, and hear all these things without much disturbance, and are now flattering themselves that they are not the persons, promising themselves that they shall escape. If they knew that there was one person, and but one, in the whole congregation, that was to be the subject of this misery, what an awful thing would it be to think of! If we knew who it was, what an awful sight would it be to see such a person! How might all the rest of the congregation lift up a

6. "Who knoweth the power of thine anger? even according to thy fear, so is thy wrath" (Psalm 90.11).

lamentable and bitter cry over him! But, alas! instead of one, how many is it likely will remember this discourse in hell? And it would be a wonder, if some that are now present should not be in hell in a very short time, even before this year is out. And it would be no wonder if some persons, that now sit here, in some seats of this meetinghouse, in health, quiet and secure, should be there before tomorrow morning. Those of you that finally continue in a natural condition, that shall keep out of hell longest will be there in a little time! your damnation does not slumber; it will come swiftly, and, in all probability, very suddenly upon many of you. You have reason to wonder that you are not already in hell. It is doubtless the case of some whom you have seen and known, that never deserved hell more than you, and that heretofore appeared as likely to have been now alive as you. Their case is past all hope; they are crying in extreme misery and perfect despair; but here you are in the land of the living and in the house of God, and have an opportunity to obtain salvation. What would not those poor damned hopeless souls give for one day's opportunity such as you now enjoy!

And now you have an extraordinary opportunity, a day wherein Christ has thrown the door of mercy wide open, and stands in calling and crying with a loud voice to poor sinners; a day wherein many are flocking to Him, and pressing into the kingdom of God. Many are daily coming from the east, west, north and south; many that were very lately in the same miserable condition that you are in are now in a happy state, with their hearts filled with love to Him who has loved them, and washed them from their sins in His own blood, and rejoicing in hope of the glory of God. How awful is it to be left behind at such a day! To see so many others feasting, while you are pining and perishing! To see so many rejoicing and singing for joy of heart, while you have cause to mourn for sorrow of heart, and howl for vexation of spirit! How can you rest one moment in such a condition? Are not your souls as precious as the souls of the people at Suffield,[7] where they are flocking from day to day to Christ?

Are there not many here who have lived long in the world, and are not to this day born again? and so are aliens from the commonwealth of Israel,[8] and have done nothing ever since they have lived, but treasure up wrath against the day of wrath? Oh, sirs, your case, in an especial manner, is extremely dangerous. Your guilt and hardness of heart is extremely great. Do you not see how generally persons of your years are passed over and left, in the present remarkable and wonderful dispensation of God's mercy? You had need to consider yourselves, and awake thoroughly out of sleep. You cannot bear the fierceness and wrath of the infinite God. And you, young men, and young women, will you neglect this precious season which you now enjoy, when so many others of your age are renouncing all youthful vanities, and flocking to Christ? You especially have now an extraordinary opportunity; but if you neglect it, it will soon be with you as with those persons who spent all the precious days of youth in sin, and are now come to such a dreadful pass in blindness and hardness. And you, children, who are unconverted, do not you know that you are going down to hell, to bear the dreadful wrath of that God, who is now angry with you every day and every night? Will you be content to be the children of the devil, when so many other children in the land are converted, and are become the holy and happy children of the King of kings?

7. "A town in the neighborhood" [Edwards's note].
8. I.e., not among the chosen people and, therefore, saved.

And let every one that is yet of Christ, and hanging over the pit of hell, whether they be old men and women, or middle-aged, or young people, or little children, now hearken to the loud calls of God's word and providence. This acceptable year of the Lord, a day of such great favors to some, will doubtless be a day of as remarkable vengeance to others. Men's hearts harden, and their guilt increases apace at such a day as this, if they neglect their souls; and never was there so great danger of such person being given up to hardness of heart and blindness of mind. God seems now to be hastily gathering in His elect in all parts of the land; and probably the greater part of adult persons that ever shall be saved, will be brought in now in a little time, and that it will be as it was on the great outpouring of the Spirit upon the Jews in the apostles' days;[9] the election will obtain, and the rest will be blinded. If this should be the case with you, you will eternally curse this day, and will curse the day that ever you was born, to see such a season of the pouring out of God's Spirit, and will wish that you had died and gone to hell before you had seen it. Now undoubtedly it is, as it was in the days of John the Baptist, the ax is in an extraordinary manner laid at the root of the trees,[1] that every tree which brings not forth good fruit, may be hewn down and cast into the fire.

Therefore, let everyone that is out of Christ, now awake and fly from the wrath to come. The wrath of Almighty God is now undoubtedly hanging over a great part of this congregation: Let everyone fly out of Sodom: "Haste and escape for your lives, look not behind you, escape to the mountain, lest you be consumed."[2]

1741

9. In Acts 2 the apostle Peter admonishes a crowd to repent and be converted, saying, "Save yourselves from this untoward generation. Then they that gladly received his word were baptized: and the same day there were added unto them about three thousand souls" (Acts 2.40–41).

1. "And now also the ax is laid unto the root of the trees: therefore every tree which bringeth not forth good fruit is hewn down, and cast into the fire" (Matthew 3.10).
2. Genesis 19.17.

# BENJAMIN FRANKLIN
## 1706–1790

Benjamin Franklin was born on Milk Street in Boston, the tenth son in a family of fifteen children. His father, Josiah, was a tallow chandler and soap boiler who came to Boston in 1682 from Ecton in Northamptonshire, England, and was proud of his Protestant ancestors. He married Abiah Folger, whose father was a teacher to the Native Americans. Josiah talked of offering his son Benjamin as his "tithe" to the church and enrolled him in Boston Grammar School as a preparation for the study of the ministry, but his plans were too ambitious and Benjamin was forced to leave school and work for his father. He hated his father's occupation and threatened to run away to sea. A compromise was made, and when Benjamin was twelve he was apprenticed to his brother, a printer. He must have been a natural student of the printing trade; he loved books and reading, he learned quickly, and he liked to write. His brother unwittingly published Benjamin's first essay when he printed an editorial left on his desk signed "Silence Dogood." When his brother was imprisoned in 1722 for offending Massachusetts officials, Franklin carried on publication of the paper by himself.

In 1723 Franklin broke with his brother and ran away to Philadelphia. It was a serious act for an apprentice, and his brother was justly indignant and angry. But the break was inevitable; for Franklin was proud and independent by nature and too clever for his brother by far. At seventeen, with little money in his pocket but already an expert printer, he proceeded to make his way in the world, subject to the usual "errata," as he liked to call his mistakes, but confident that he could profit from lessons learned and not repeat them. His most serious error was in trusting a foolish man who wanted to be important to everyone. As a result of Governor Keith's "favors," Benjamin found himself alone and without employment in London in 1724. He returned to the colonies two years later.

Franklin had an uncanny instinct for success. He taught himself French, Spanish, Italian, and Latin yet was shrewd enough to know that people did not like to do business with merchants who were smarter than they. He dressed plainly and sometimes carried his own paper in a wheelbarrow through Philadelphia streets to assure future customers that he was hardworking and not above doing things for himself. By the time he was twenty-four he was the sole owner of a successful printing shop and editor and publisher of the *Pennsylvania Gazette*. He offered his *Poor Richard's Almanac* for sale in 1733 and made it an American institution, filling it with maxims for achieving wealth and preaching hard work and thrift. In 1730 he married Deborah Read, the daughter of his first landlady, and they had two children. Franklin had two illegitimate children, and Deborah took Franklin's son William into the household. He was later to become governor of New Jersey and a Loyalist during the Revolution; Franklin addressed the first part of his *Autobiography* to him. Before he retired from business at the age of forty-two, Franklin had founded a library, invented a stove, established a fire company, subscribed to an academy that was to become the University of Pennsylvania, and served as secretary to the American Philosophical Society. It was his intention when he retired to devote himself to public affairs and his lifelong passion for the natural sciences, especially the phenomena of sound, vapors, earthquakes, and electricity.

Franklin's observations on electricity were published in London in 1751 and, despite his disclaimers in the *Autobiography*, brought him the applause of British scientists. Science was Franklin's great passion, the only thing, the American historian Charles Beard once said, about which Franklin was not ironic. His inquiring mind was challenged most by the mechanics of the ordinary phenomena of the world, and he was convinced that the mind's rational powers would enable him to solve riddles that had puzzled humankind for centuries. Franklin believed that people were naturally innocent, that all the mysteries that charmed the religious mind could be explained to our advantage and that education, properly undertaken, would transform our lives and set us free from the tyrannies of church and monarchy. Franklin had no illusions about the errata of humankind, but his metaphor suggests that we can change and alter our past in a way that the word *sins* does not.

Franklin's remaining years, however, were not spent in a laboratory, but at the diplomatic table in London, Paris, and Philadelphia, where his gift for irony served him well. For he was a born diplomat, detached, adaptable, witty, urbane, charming, and clever and of the slightly more than forty years left to him after his retirement, more than half were spent abroad. In 1757 he went to England to represent the colonies and stayed for five years, returning in 1763. It was in England in 1768 that Franklin first noted his growing sense of alienation and the impossibility of compromise with the homeland. Parliament can make *all* laws for the colonies or *none*, he said, and "I think the arguments for the latter more numerous and weighty, than those for the former." When he returned to Philadelphia in May 1775, he was chosen as a representative to the Second Continental Congress, and he served on the committee to draft the Declaration of Independence. In October 1776, he was appointed minister to France, where he successfully negotiated a treaty of allegiance and became something of a cult hero. In 1781 he was a member of the American delegation to the Paris peace conference, and he signed the Treaty of Paris, which brought the Revolutionary War to an end. Franklin protested his too-long stay in Europe and returned to Philadelphia in 1785, serving as a delegate to the Constitutional Convention. When he died in 1790, he was one of the most beloved Americans. Twenty thousand people attended his funeral.

This hero of the eighteenth century, however, has not universally charmed our own. For a number of readers, Franklin has been identified as a garrulous but insensitive man of the world, too adaptable for a man of integrity and too willing to please. D. H. Lawrence is only one of a number of Franklin's critics who have charged him with insensitivity and indifference to the darker recesses of the soul. There is no question but that Franklin, like Emerson, has been reduced by his admirers—the hero of those who seek only the way to wealth. But such single-mindedness does not do justice to Franklin's complexity. A reading of his letters will serve as a proper antidote; for the voice we find there is fully alert to the best and worst in all of humankind.

All the Franklin texts used here—with the exception of *The Autobiography*—are from *The Writings of Benjamin Franklin*, edited by Albert Henry Smyth (1907).

# The Way to Wealth[1]

### Preface to Poor Richard Improved

Courteous Reader,

I have heard that nothing gives an author so great pleasure, as to find his works respectfully quoted by other learned authors. This pleasure I have seldom enjoyed; for though I have been, if I may say it without vanity, an eminent author of almanacs annually now a full quarter of a century, my brother authors in the same way, for what reason I know not, have ever been very sparing in their applauses, and no other author has taken the least notice of me, so that did not my writings produce me some solid pudding, the great deficiency of praise would have quite discouraged me.

I concluded at length, that the people were the best judges of my merit; for they buy my works; and besides, in my rambles, where I am not personally known, I have frequently heard one or other of my adages repeated with "as Poor Richard says" at the end on 't; this gave me some satisfaction, as it showed not only that my instructions were regarded, but discovered likewise some respect for my authority; and I own, that to encourage the practice of remembering and repeating those wise sentences, I have sometimes quoted myself with great gravity.

Judge, then, how much I must have been gratified by an incident I am going to relate to you. I stopped my horse lately where a great number of people were collected at a vendue[2] of merchant goods. The hour of sale not being come, they were conversing on the badness of the times and one of the company called to a plain clean old man, with white locks, "Pray, Father

---

1. Franklin composed this essay for the twenty-fifth anniversary issue of his *Almanac*, the first issue of which, under the fictitious editorship of "Richard Saunders," appeared in 1733. For this essay Franklin brought together the best of his maxims in the guise of a speech by Father Abraham. It is frequently reprinted as *The Way to Wealth*, but is also known by earlier titles: *Poor Richard Improved* and *Father Abraham's Speech*.
2. Auction or sale.

Abraham, what think you of the times? Won't these heavy taxes quite ruin the country? How shall we be ever able to pay them? What would you advise us to?" Father Abraham stood up, and replied, "If you'd have my advice, I'll give it you in short, for a *word to the wise is enough, and many words won't fill a bushel*, as Poor Richard says." They joined in desiring him to speak his mind, and gathering round him, he proceeded as follows:

"Friends," says he, "and neighbors, the taxes are indeed very heavy, and if those laid on by the government were the only ones we had to pay, we might more easily discharge them; but we have many others, and much more griev-ous to some of us. We are taxed twice as much by our idleness, three times as much by our pride, and four times as much by our folly; and from these taxes the commissioners cannot ease or deliver us by allowing an abatement. However, let us hearken to good advice, and something may be done for us; *God helps them that help themselves*, as Poor Richard says, in his Almanac of 1733.

"It would be thought a hard government that should tax its people one-tenth part of their time, to be employed in its service. But idleness taxes many of us much more, if we reckon all that is spent in absolute sloth, or doing of noth-ing, with that which is spent in idle employments, or amusements, that amount to nothing. Sloth, by bringing on diseases, absolutely shortens life. *Sloth, like rust, consumes faster than labor wears; while the used key is always bright*, as Poor Richard says. *But dost thou love life, then do not squander time, for that's the stuff life is made of*, as Poor Richard says. How much more than is necessary do we spend in sleep, forgetting that *the sleeping fox catches no poultry* and that *there will be sleeping enough in the grave*, as Poor Rich-ard says.

"*If time be of all things the most precious, wasting time must be*, as Poor Richard says, *the greatest prodigality*; since, as he elsewhere tells us, *lost time is never found again; and what we call time enough, always proves little enough*: let us then up and be doing, and doing to the purpose; so by diligence shall we do more with less perplexity. *Sloth makes all things difficult, but industry all easy*, as Poor Richard says; *and he that riseth late must trot all day, and shall scarce overtake his business at night*; while *laziness travels so slowly, that poverty soon overtakes him*, as we read in Poor Richard, who adds, *drive thy business, let not that drive thee*, and *early to bed, and early to rise, makes a man healthy, wealthy, and wise*.

"So what signifies wishing and hoping for better times. We may make these times better, if we bestir ourselves. *Industry need not wish*, as Poor Richard says, *and he that lives upon hope will die fasting. There are no gains without pains; then help hands, for I have no lands*, or if I have, they are smartly taxed. And, as Poor Richard likewise observes, *he that hath a trade hath an estate; and he that hath a calling, hath an office of profit and honor*; but then the trade must be worked at, and the calling well followed, or neither the estate nor the office will enable us to pay our taxes. If we are industrious, we shall never starve; for, as Poor Richard says, *at the workingman's house hunger looks in, but dares not enter*. Nor will the bailiff or the constable enter, for *industry pays debts, while despair increaseth them*, says Poor Richard. What though you have found no treasure, nor has any rich relation left you a legacy, *diligence is the mother of good luck*, as Poor Richard says, and *God gives all things to industry. Then plow deep, while sluggards sleep, and you shall have corn to sell and to keep*, says Poor Dick. Work while it is called today, for you know not how much you may be hindered tomorrow, which makes Poor Richard says, *one today is worth two tomorrows*, and farther, *have you somewhat to do tomorrow, do it today*. If you were a servant, would you not be ashamed that a good master should catch you idle? Are you then your own master, *be ashamed to catch yourself idle*, as Poor Dick says. When there is so much to be done for yourself, your family, your country, and your gracious king, be up by peep of day; *let not the sun look down and say, inglorious here he lies*. Handle your tools without mittens; remember that *the cat in gloves catches no mice*, as Poor Richard says. 'Tis true there is much to be done, and perhaps you are weak-handed, but stick to it steadily; and you will see great effects, for *constant dropping wears away stones*, and *by diligence and patience the mouse ate in two the cable*; and *little strokes fell great oaks*, as Poor Richard says in his Almanac, the year I cannot just now remember.

"Methinks I hear some of you say, 'must a man afford himself no leisure?' I will tell thee, my friend, what Poor Richard says, *employ thy time well, if thou meanest to gain leisure; and, since thou art not sure of a minute, throw not away an hour*. Leisure is time for doing something useful; this leisure the diligent man will obtain, but the lazy man never; so that, as Poor Richard says *a life of leisure and a life of laziness are two things*. Do you imagine that sloth will afford you more comfort than labor? No, for as Poor Richard says, *trouble springs from idleness, and grievous toil from needless ease. Many without labor, would live by their wits only, but they break for want of stock*. Whereas industry gives comfort, and plenty, and respect: *fly pleasures, and they'll follow you. The diligent spinner has a large shift;*[3] *and now I have a sheep and a cow, everybody bids me good morrow*; all of which is well said by Poor Richard.

"But with our industry, we must likewise be steady, settled, and careful, and oversee our own affairs with our own eyes, and not trust too much to others; for, as Poor Richard says

> *I never saw an oft-removed tree,*
> *Nor yet an oft-removed family,*
> *That throve so well as those that settled be.*

And again, *three removes*[4] *is as bad as a fire*; and again, *keep thy shop, and thy shop will keep thee*; and again, *if you would have your business done, go; if not, send*. And again,

> *He that by the plow would thrive,*
> *Himself must either hold or drive.*

And again, *the eye of a master will do more work than both his hands*; and again, *want of care does us more damage than want of knowledge*; and again, *not to oversee workmen is to leave them your purse open*. Trusting too much to others' care is the ruin of many; for, as the Almanac says, *in the affairs of this world, men are saved, not by faith, but by the want of it*; but a man's own care is profitable; for, saith Poor Dick, *learning is to the studious, and riches to the careful*, as well as *power to the bold*, and *heaven to the virtuous*, and farther, *if you would have a faithful servant, and one that you like, serve yourself*. And again, he adviseth to circumspection and care, even in the smallest matters, because sometimes *a little neglect may breed great mischief*; adding, *for want of a nail the shoe was lost; for want of a shoe the horse was lost; and for want*

---

3. Wardrobe.                    4. Moves.

*of a horse the rider was lost, being overtaken and slain by the enemy; all for want of care about a horseshoe nail.*

"So much for industry, my friends, and attention to one's own business; but to these we must add frugality, if we would make our industry more certainly successful. A man may, if he knows not how to save as he gets, keep his nose all his life to the grindstone, and die not worth a groat[5] at last. *A fat kitchen makes a lean will,* as Poor Richard says; and

> *Many estates are spent in the getting,*
> *Since women for tea forsook spinning and knitting,*
> *And men for punch forsook hewing and splitting.*

*If you would be wealthy,* says he, in another Almanac, *think of saving as well as of getting: the Indies have not made Spain rich, because her outgoes are greater than her incomes.*

"Away then with your expensive follies, and you will not then have so much cause to complain of hard times, heavy taxes, and chargeable families; for, as Poor Dick says,

> *Women and wine, game and deceit,*
> *Make the wealth small and the wants great.*

And farther, *what maintains one vice would bring up two children.* You may think perhaps, that a little tea, or a little punch now and then, diet a little more costly, clothes a little finer, and a little entertainment now and then, can be no great matter; but remember what Poor Richard says, *many a little makes a mickle;*[6] and farther, *Beware of little expenses; a small leak will sink a great ship;* and again, *who dainties love shall beggars prove;* and moreover, *fools make feasts, and wise men eat them.*

"Here you are all got together at this vendue of fineries and knicknacks. You call them goods; but if you do not take care, they will prove evils to some of you. You expect they will be sold cheap, and perhaps they may for less than they cost; but if you have no occasion for them, they must be dear to you. Remember what Poor Richard says; *buy what thou hast no need of, and ere long thou shalt sell thy necessaries.* And again, *at a great pennyworth pause a while:* he means, that perhaps the cheapness is apparent only, and not real; or the bargain, by straightening thee in thy business, may do thee more harm than good. For in another place he says, *many have been ruined by buying good pennyworths.* Again, Poor Richard says, *'tis foolish to lay out money in a purchase of repentance;* and yet this folly is practiced every day at vendues, for want of minding the Almanac. *Wise men,* as Poor Dick says, *learn by others' harms, fools scarcely by their own;* but *felix quem faciunt aliena pericula cautum.*[7] Many a one, for the sake of finery on the back, have gone with a hungry belly, and half-starved their families. *Silks and satins, scarlet and velvets,* as Poor Richard says, *put out the kitchen fire.*

"These are not the necessaries of life; they can scarcely be called the conveniences; and yet only because they look pretty, how many want to have them! The artificial wants of mankind thus become more numerous than the natural; and, as Poor Dick says, *for one poor person, there are an hundred indigent.* By these, and other extravagancies, the genteel are reduced to poverty, and forced to borrow of those whom they formerly despised, but who through industry

5. A silver coin worth about four pence.                    7. A Latin version of the proverb just quoted.
6. Lot.

and frugality have maintained their standing; in which case it appears plainly, that *a plowman on his legs is higher than a gentleman on his knees*, as Poor Richard says. Perhaps they have had a small estate left them, which they knew not the getting of; they think, " 'Tis day, and will never be night"; that a little to be spent out of so much is not worth minding; *a child and a fool*, as Poor Richard says, *imagine twenty shillings and twenty years can never be spent* but, *always taking out of the meal-tub, and never putting in, soon comes to the bottom*; as Poor Dick says, *when the well's dry, they know the worth of water*. But this they might have known before, if they had taken his advice; *if you would know the value of money, go and try to borrow some; for, he that goes a-borrowing goes a-sorrowing*; and indeed so does he that lends to such people, when he goes to get it in again. Poor Dick farther advises, and says,

> Fond pride of dress is sure a very curse;
> E'er fancy you consult, consult your purse.

And again, *pride is as loud a beggar as want, and a great deal more saucy*. When you have bought one fine thing, you must buy ten more, that your appearance may be all of a piece; but Poor Dick says, *'tis easier to suppress the first desire, than to satisfy all that follow it*. And 'tis as truly folly for the poor to ape the rich, as for the frog to swell, in order to equal the ox.

> Great estates may venture more,
> But little boats should keep near shore.

'Tis, however, a folly soon punished; for *pride that dines on vanity sups on contempt*, as Poor Richard says. And in another place, *pride breakfasted with plenty, dined with poverty, and supped with infamy*. And after all, of what use is this pride of appearance, for which so much is risked so much is suffered? It cannot promote health, or ease pain; it makes no increase of merit in the person, it creates envy, it hastens misfortune.

> What is a butterfly? At best
> He's but a caterpillar dressed.
> The gaudy fop's his picture just,

as Poor Richard says.

"But what madness must it be to run in debt for these superfluities! We are offered, by the terms of this vendue, *six months' credit*; and that perhaps has induced some of us to attend it, because we cannot spare the ready money, and hope now to be fine without it. But, ah, think what you do when you run in debt; you give to another power over your liberty. If you cannot pay at the time, you will be ashamed to see your creditor; you will be in fear when you speak to him; you will make poor pitiful sneaking excuses, and by degrees come to lose your veracity, and sink into base downright lying; for, as Poor Richard says, *the second vice is lying, the first is running in debt*. And again, to the same purpose, *lying rides upon debt's back*. Whereas a free-born Englishman ought not to be ashamed or afraid to see or speak to any man living. But poverty often deprives a man of all spirit and virtue: *'tis hard for an empty bag to stand upright*, as Poor Richard truly says.

"What would you think of that prince, or that government, who should issue an edict forbidding you to dress like a gentleman or a gentlewoman, on pain of imprisonment or servitude? Would you not say, that you were free, have a right to dress as you please, and that such an edict would be a breach of your privileges, and such a government tyrannical? And yet you are about to put yourself under that tyranny, when you run in debt for such dress! Your creditor has authority, at his pleasure to deprive you of your liberty, by confining you in gaol[8] for life, or to sell you for a servant, if you should not be able to pay him! When you have got your bargain, you may, perhaps, think little of payment; but *creditors*, Poor Richard tells us, *have better memories than debtors*; and in another place says, *creditors are a superstitious sect, great observers of set days and times*. The day comes round before you are aware, and the demand is made before you are prepared to satisfy it, or if you bear your debt in mind, the term which at first seemed so long will, as it lessens, appear extremely short. Time will seem to have added wings to his heels as well as shoulders. *Those have a short Lent*, saith Poor Richard, *who owe money to be paid at Easter*. Then since, as he says, *The borrower is a slave to the lender, and the debtor to the creditor*, disdain the chain, preserve your freedom; and maintain your independency: be industrious and free; be frugal and free. At present, perhaps, you may think yourself in thriving circumstances, and that you can bear a little extravagance without injury; but,

> *For age and want, save while you may;*
> *No morning sun lasts a whole day,*

as Poor Richard says. Gain may be temporary and uncertain, but ever while you live, expense is constant and certain; and *'tis easier to build two chimneys than to keep one in fuel*, as Poor Richard says. So, *rather go to bed supperless than rise in debt*.

> *Get what you can, and what you get hold;*
> *'Tis the stone that will turn all your lead into gold,*

as Poor Richard says. And when you have got the philosopher's stone,[9] sure you will no longer complain of bad times, or the difficulty of paying taxes.

"This doctrine, my friends, is reason and wisdom; but after all, do not depend too much upon your own industry, and frugality, and prudence, though excellent things, for they may all be blasted without the blessing of heaven; and therefore, ask that blessing humbly, and be not uncharitable to those that at present seem to want it, but comfort and help them. Remember, Job[1] suffered, and was afterwards prosperous.

"And now to conclude, *experience keeps a dear[2] school, but fools will learn in no other, and scarce in that*; for it is true, *we may give advice, but we cannot give conduct*, as Poor Richard says: however, remember this, *they that won't be counseled, can't be helped*, as Poor Richard says: and farther, that, *if you will not hear reason, she'll surely rap your knuckles.*"

Thus the old gentleman ended his harangue. The people heard it, and approved the doctrine, and immediately practiced the contrary, just as if it had been a common sermon; for the vendue opened, and they began to buy extravagantly, notwithstanding his cautions and their own fear of taxes. I found the good man had thoroughly studied my almanacs, and digested all I had dropped on these topics during the course of five and twenty years. The frequent mention he made of me must have tired any one else, but my vanity

---

8. Jail.
9. A substance thought to transform base metals into gold, much sought after by alchemists.

1. The Old Testament patriarch whose faith was tested by suffering.
2. Expensive.

was wonderfully delighted with it, though I was conscious that not a tenth part of the wisdom was my own, which he ascribed to me, but rather the gleanings I had made of the sense of all ages and nations. However, I resolved to be the better for the echo of it; and though I had at first determined to buy stuff for a new coat, I went away resolved to wear my old one a little longer. Reader, if thou wilt do the same, thy profit will be as great as mine. I am, as ever, thine to serve thee,

Richard Saunders<br>July 7, 1757

1757                                                                              1758

# Remarks Concerning the Savages of North America

Savages we call them, because their manners differ from ours, which we think the perfection of civility; they think the same of theirs.

Perhaps, if we could examine the manners of different nations with impartiality, we should find no people so rude, as to be without any rules of politeness; nor any so polite, as not to have some remains of rudeness.

The Indian men, when young, are hunters and warriors; when old, counselors; for all their government is by counsel of the sages; there is no force, there are no prisons, no officers to compel obedience, or inflict punishment. Hence they generally study oratory, the best speaker having the most influence. The Indian women till the ground, dress the food, nurse and bring up the children, and preserve and hand down to posterity the memory of public transactions. These employments of men and women are accounted natural and honorable. Having few artificial wants, they have abundance of leisure for improvement by conversation. Our laborious manner of life, compared with theirs, they esteem slavish and base; and the learning, on which we value ourselves, they regard as frivolous and useless. An instance of this occurred at the Treaty of Lancaster, in Pennsylvania, anno 1744, between the government of Virginia and the Six Nations.[1] After the principal business was settled, the commissioners from Virginia acquainted the Indians by a speech, that there was at Williamsburg a college, with a fund for educating Indian youth; and that, if the Six Nations would send down half a dozen of their young lads to that college, the government would take care that they should be well provided for, and instructed in all the learning of the white people. It is one of the Indian rules of politeness not to answer a public proposition the same day that it is made; they think it would be treating it as a light matter, and that they show it respect by taking time to consider it, as of a matter important. They therefore deferred their answer till the day following; when their speaker began, by expressing their deep sense of the kindness of the Virginia government, in making them that offer; "for we know," says he, "that you highly esteem the kind of learning taught in those Colleges, and that the maintenance of our young men, while with you, would be very expensive to you. We are convinced, therefore, that you mean to do us good by your proposal; and we thank you heartily. But you, who are wise, must know that different nations have different conceptions of

---

1. A confederation of Iroquois tribes: Seneca, Cayuga, Oneida, Onondaga, Mohawk, and Tuscarora.

things; and you will therefore not take it amiss, if our ideas of this kind of education happen not to be the same with yours. We have had some experience of it; several of our young people were formerly brought up at the colleges of the northern provinces; they were instructed in all your sciences; but, when they came back to us, they were bad runners, ignorant of every means of living in the woods, unable to bear either cold or hunger, knew neither how to build a cabin, take a deer, or kill an enemy, spoke our language imperfectly, were therefore neither fit for hunters, warriors, nor counselors; they were totally good for nothing. We are however not the less obliged by your kind offer, though we decline accepting it; and, to show our grateful sense of it, if the gentlemen of Virginia will send us a dozen of their sons, we will take great care of their education, instruct them in all we know, and make *men* of them."

Having frequent occasions to hold public councils, they have acquired great order and decency in conducting them. The old men sit in the foremost ranks, that warriors in the next, and the women and children in the hindmost. The business of the women is to take exact notice of what passes, imprint it in their memories (for they have no writing), and communicate it to their children. They are the records of the council, and they preserve traditions of the stipulations in treaties 100 years back; which, when we compare with our writings, we always find exact. He that would speak, rises. The rest observe a profound silence. When he has finished and sits down, they leave him 5 or 6 minutes to recollect, that, if he has omitted anything he intended to say, or has anything to add, he may rise again and deliver it. To interrupt another, even in common conversation, is reckoned highly indecent. How different this from the conduct of a polite British House of Commons, where scarce a day passes without some confusion, that makes the speaker hoarse in calling to *order*; and how different from the mode of conversation in many polite companies of Europe, where, if you do not deliver your sentence with great rapidity, you are cut off in the middle of it by the impatient loquacity of those you converse with, and never suffered to finish it!

The politeness of these savages in conversation is indeed carried to excess, since it does not permit them to contradict or deny the truth of what is asserted in their presence. By this means they indeed avoid disputes; but then it becomes difficult to know their minds, or what impression you make upon them. The missionaries who have attempted to convert them to Christianity, all complain of this as one of the great difficulties of their mission. The Indians hear with patience the truths of the Gospel explained to them, and give their usual tokens of assent and approbation; you would think they were convinced. No such matter. It is mere civility.

A Swedish minister, having assembled the chiefs of the Susquehanah Indians, made a sermon to them, acquainting them with the principal historical facts on which our religion is founded; such as the fall of our first parents by eating an apple, the coming of Christ to repair the mischief, His miracles and suffering, etc. When he had finished, an Indian orator stood up to thank him. "What you have told us," he says, "is all very good. It is indeed bad to eat apples. It is better to make them all into cider. We are much obliged by your kindness in coming so far, to tell us these things which you have heard from your mothers. In return, I will tell you some of those we have heard from ours. In the beginning, our fathers had only the flesh of animals to subsist on; and if their hunting was unsuccessful, they were starving. Two of our young hunters, having killed a deer, made a fire in the woods to broil some part of it.

When they were about to satisfy their hunger, they beheld a beautiful young woman descend from the clouds, and seat herself on that hill, which you see yonder among the blue mountains. They said to each other, it is a spirit that has smelled our broiling vension, and wishes to eat of it; let us offer some to her. They presented her with the tongue; she was pleased with the taste of it, and said, 'Your kindness shall be rewarded; come to this place after thirteen moons, and you shall find something that will be of great benefit in nourishing you and your children to the latest generations.' They did so, and, to their surprise, found plants they had never seen before; but which, from that ancient time, have been constantly cultivated among us, to our great advantage. Where her right hand had touched the ground, they found maize; where her left hand had touched it, they found kidney-beans; and where her backside had sat on it, they found tobacco." The good missionary, disgusted with this idle tale, said, "What I delivered to you were sacred truths; but what you tell me is mere fable, fiction, and falsehood." The Indian, offended, replied, "My brother, it seems your friends have not done you justice in your education; they have not well instructed you in the rules of common civility. You saw that we, who understand and practice those rules, believed all your stories; why do you refuse to believe ours?"

When any of them come into our towns, our people are apt to crowd round them, gaze upon them, and incommode them, where they desire to be private; this they esteem great rudeness, and the effect of the want of instruction in the rules of civility and good manners. "We have," say they, "as much curiosity as you, and when you come into our towns, we wish for opportunities of looking at you, but for this purpose we hide ourselves behind bushes, where you are to pass, and never intrude ourselves into your company."

Their manner of entering one another's village has likewise its rules. It is reckoned uncivil in traveling strangers to enter a village abruptly, without giving notice of their approach. Therefore, as soon as they arrive within hearing, they stop and hollow,[2] remaining there till invited to enter. Two old men usually come out to them, and lead them in. There is in every village a vacant dwelling, called *the stranger's house*. Here they are placed, while the old men go round from hut to hut, acquainting the inhabitants, that strangers are arrived, who are probably hungry and weary; and every one sends them what he can spare of victuals, and skins to repose on. When the strangers are refreshed, pipes and tobacco are brought; and then, but not before, conversation begins, with inquiries who they are, whither bound, what news, etc.; and it usually ends with offers of service, if the strangers have occasion of guides, or any necessaries for continuing their journey; and nothing is exacted for the entertainment.

The same hospitality, esteemed among them as a principal virtue, is practiced by private persons; of which Conrad Weiser, our interpreter, gave me the following instances. He had been naturalized among the Six Nations, and spoke well the Mohawk language. In going through the Indian country, to carry a message from our Governor to the Council at Onondaga, he called at the habitation of Canassatego, an old acquaintance, who embraced him, spread furs for him to sit on, placed before him some boiled beans and venison, and mixed some rum and water for his drink. When he was well refreshed, and had lit his pipe, Canassatego began to converse with him; asked

2. Cry out; announce themselves.

how he had fared the many years since they had seen each other; whence he then came; what occasioned the journey, etc. Conrad answered all his questions; and when the discourse began to flag, the Indian, to continue it, said, "Conrad, you have lived long among the white people, and know something of their customs; I have been sometimes at Albany, and have observed, that once in seven days they shut up their shops, and assemble all in the great house; tell me what it is for? What do they do there?" "They meet there," says Conrad, "to hear and learn *good things.*" "I do not doubt," says the Indian, "that they tell you so; they have told me the same; but I doubt the truth of what they say, and I will tell you my reasons. I went lately to Albany to sell my skins and buy blankets, knives, powder, rum, etc. You know I used generally to deal with Hans Hanson; but I was a little inclined this time to try some other merchant. However, I called first upon Hans, and asked him what he would give for beaver. He said he could not give any more than four shillings a pound; 'but,' says he, 'I cannot talk on business now; this is the day when we meet together to learn *good things,* and I am going to the meeting.' So I thought to myself, 'Since we cannot do any business today, I may as well go to the meeting too,' and I went with him. There stood up a man in black, and began to talk to the people very angrily. I did not understand what he said; but, perceiving that he looked much at me and at Hanson, I imagined he was angry at seeing me there; so I went out, sat down near the house, struck fire, and lit my pipe, waiting till the meeting should break up. I thought too, that the man had mentioned something of beaver, and I suspected it might be the subject of their meeting. So, when they came out, I accosted my merchant. 'Well, Hans,' says I, 'I hope you have agreed to give more than four shillings a pound.' 'No,' says he, 'I cannot give so much; I cannot give more than three shillings and sixpence.' I then spoke to several other dealers, but they all sung the same song,—three and sixpence,—three and sixpence. This made it clear to me, that my suspicion was right; and, that whatever they pretended of meeting to learn *good things,* the real purpose was to consult how to cheat Indians in the price of beaver. Consider but a little, Conrad, and you must be of my opinion. If they met so often to learn *good things,* they would certainly have learned some before this time. But they are still ignorant. You know our practice. If a white man, in traveling through our country, enters one of our cabins, we all treat him as I treat you; we dry him if he is wet, we warm him if he is cold, we give him meat and drink, that he may allay his thirst and hunger; and we spread soft furs for him to rest and sleep on; we demand nothing in return. But, if I go into a white man's house at Albany, and ask for victuals and drink, they say, 'Where is your money?' and if I have none, they say, 'Get out, you Indian dog.' You see they have not yet learned those little *good things,* that we need no meetings to be instructed in, because our mothers taught them to us when we were children; and therefore it is impossible their meetings should be, as they say, for any such purpose, or have any such effect; they are only to contrive *the cheating of Indians in the price of beaver.*"[3]

1784

3. "It is remarkable that in all ages and countries hospitality has been allowed as the virtue of those whom the civilized were pleased to call barbarians. The Greeks celebrated the Scythians for it. The Saracens possessed it eminently, and it is to this day the reigning virtue of the wild Arabs. St. Paul, too, in the relation of his voyage and shipwreck on the island of Melité says the barbarous people showed us no little kindness; for they kindled a fire, and received us every one, because of the present rain, and because of the cold" [Franklin's note]. St. Paul's account of his visit to Melita may be found in Acts 28. The Scythians were nomadic tribes of southeastern Europe known for their plundering.

# Letters

## To Peter Collinson[1]

[WHIRLWINDS]

Philadelphia, Aug. 25, 1755.

Dear Sir,—

As you have my former papers on Whirlwinds, etc., I now send you an account of one which I had lately an opportunity of seeing and examining myself.

Being in *Maryland*, riding with Colonel *Tasker*, and some other gentlemen to his country-seat, where I and my son were entertained by that amiable and worthy man with great hospitality and kindness, we saw in the vale below us, a small whirlwind beginning in the road, and showing itself by the dust it raised and contained. It appeared in the form of a sugar-loaf,[2] spinning on its point, moving up the hill towards us, and enlarging as it came forward. When it passed by us, its smaller part near the ground, appeared no bigger than a common barrel, but widening upwards, it seemed, at 40 or 50 feet high, to be 20 or 30 feet in diameter. The rest of the company stood looking after it, but my curiosity being stronger, I followed it, riding close by its side, and observed its licking up, in its progress, all the dust that was under its smaller part. As it is a common opinion that a shot, fired through a water-spout,[3] will break it, I tried to break this little whirlwind, by striking my whip frequently through it, but without any effect. Soon after, it quitted the road and took into the woods, growing every moment larger and stronger, raising, instead of dust, the old dry leaves with which the ground was thick covered, and making a great noise with them and the branches of the trees, bending some tall trees round in a circle swiftly and very surprisingly, though the progressive motion of the whirl was not so swift but that a man on foot might have kept pace with it; but the circular motion was amazingly rapid. By the leaves it was now filled with, I could plainly perceive that the current of air they were driven by, moved upwards in a spiral line; and when I saw the trunks and bodies of large trees enveloped in the passing whirl, which continued entire after it had left them I no longer wondered that my whip had no effect on it in its smaller state. I accompanied it about three quarters of a mile, till some limbs of dead trees, broken off by the whirl, flying about and falling near me, made me more apprehensive of danger; and then I stopped, looking at the top of it as it went on, which was visible, by means of the leaves contained in it, for a very great height above the trees. Many of the leaves, as they got loose from the upper and widest part, were scattered in the wind; but so great was their height in the air, that they appeared no bigger than flies. My son, who was by this time come up with me, followed the whirlwind till it left the woods, and crossed an old tobacco-field, where, finding neither dust nor leaves to take up, it gradually became invisible below as it went away over that field. The course of the general wind then blowing was along with us as we traveled, and the progressive motion of the whirlwind was in a direction nearly opposite, though it did not keep a straight line, nor was its progressive motion uniform, it making

---

1. English scientist and friend of Franklin's (d. 1768). He had Franklin's *Experiments and Observations on Electricity* printed in 1751; it was Franklin's first pub-

lished pamphlet.
2. A cone shape.
3. Geyser.

little sallies on either hand as it went, proceeding sometimes faster and sometimes slower, and seeming sometimes for a few seconds almost stationary, then starting forward pretty fast again. When we rejoined the company, they were admiring the vast height of the leaves now brought by the common wind, over our heads. These leaves accompanied us as we traveled, some falling now and then round about us, and some not reaching the ground till we had gone near three miles from the place where we first saw the whirlwind begin. Upon my asking Colonel *Tasker* if such whirlwinds were common in *Maryland*, he answered pleasantly, "No, not at all common; but we got this on purpose to treat Mr. Franklin." And a very high treat it was, to

Dear Sir,<br>
Your affectionate friend and humble servant,<br>
B. F[RANKLIN.]

1755                                                                    1769


*To Ezra Stiles*[4]

[MY RELIGION]

Philadelphia, March 9, 1790
Reverend and Dear Sir,
    I received your kind letter of January 28, and am glad you have at length received the portrait of Governor Yale[5] from his family, and deposited it in the college library. He was a great and good man, and had the merit of doing infinite service to your country by his munificence to that institution. The honor you propose doing me by placing mine in the same room with his is much too great for my deserts; but you always had a partiality for me, and to that it must be ascribed. I am however too much obliged to Yale College, the first learned society that took notice of me[6] and adorned me with its honors, to refuse a request that comes from it through so esteemed a friend. But I do not think any one of the portraits you mention, as in my possession, worthy of the place and company you propose to place it in. You have an excellent artist lately arrived. If he will undertake to make one for you, I shall cheerfully pay the expense; but he must not delay setting about it, or I may slip through his fingers, for I am now in my eighty-fifty year, and very infirm.[7]
    I send with this a very learned work, as it seems to me, on the ancient Samaritan coins, lately printed in Spain, and at least curious for the beauty of the impression. Please to accept it for your college library. I have subscribed for the Encyclopædia[8] now printing here, with the intention of presenting it to the college. I shall probably depart before the work is finished, but shall leave directions for its continuance to the end. With this you will receive some of the first numbers.

4. Ezra Stiles (1727–95) was the grandson of the poet Edward Taylor and president of Yale College. He wrote to Franklin on January 28, 1780, asking Franklin to provide him with some information about his "religious sentiments" and his opinion "concerning Jesus of Nazareth." Stiles hoped Franklin would not think his inquiry an "impertinence" because he revered Franklin with an affection "bordering on adoration."
5. Elihu Yale (1649–1721) was an official in the East India Company, and governor of Fort Saint George.

Yale College was named for him after the receipt from London of books and goods in 1714 and 1718.
6. Franklin was awarded an honorary master's degree from Yale in 1753.
7. Franklin died on April 17, 1790.
8. The 3rd edition of the *Encyclopaedia Britannica*, printed in the United States for the first time. It was customary in undertaking expensive publishing ventures to get customers to subscribe for future volumes and ensure the success of the undertaking.

You desire to know something of my religion. It is the first time I have been questioned upon it. But I cannot take your curiosity amiss, and shall endeavor in a few words to gratify it. Here is my creed. I believe in one God, Creator of the Universe. That He governs it by His providence. That He ought to be worshiped. That the most acceptable service we render to Him is doing good to His other children. That the soul of man is immortal, and will be treated with justice in another life respecting its conduct in this. These I take to be the fundamental principles of all sound religion, and I regard them as you do in whatever sect I meet with them.

As to Jesus of Nazareth, my opinion of whom you particularly desire, I think the system of morals and his religion, as he left them to us, the best the world ever saw or is likely to see; but I apprehend it has received various corrupting changes, and I have with most of the present dissenters in England, some doubts as to his divinity; though it is question I do not dogmatize upon, having never studied it, and think it needless to busy myself with it now, when I expect soon an opportunity of knowing the truth with less trouble. I see no harm, however, in its being believed, if that belief has the good consequence, as probably it has, of making his doctrines more respected and better observed; especially as I do not perceive, that the Supreme takes it amiss, by distinguishing the unbelievers in His government of the world with any peculiar marks of His displeasure.

I shall only add, respecting myself, that, having experienced the goodness of that Being in conducting me prosperously through a long life, I have no doubt of its continuance in the next, though without the smallest conceit of meriting such goodness. My sentiments on this head you will see in the copy of an old letter enclosed, which I wrote in answer to one from a zealous religionist, whom I had relieved in a paralytic case by electricity, and who, being afraid I should grow proud upon it, sent me his serious though rather impertinent caution. I send you also the copy of another letter,[9] which will show something of my disposition relating to religion. With great and sincere esteem and affection, I am, your obliged old friend and most obedient humble servant,

B. FRANKLIN.

1790                                                                          1907

P.S. Had not your college some present of books from the King of France? Please to let me know, if you had an expectation given you of more, and the nature of that expectation? I have a reason for the inquiry.

I confide, that you will not expose me to criticism and censure by publishing any part of this communication to you. I have ever let others enjoy their religious sentiments, without reflecting on them for those that appeared to me unsupportable and even absurd. All sects here, and we have a great variety, have experienced my good will in assisting them with subscriptions for building their new places of worship; and, as I have never opposed any of their doctrines, I hope to go out of the world in peace with them all.

1790                                                                          1840

---

9. It has been suggested that this letter was addressed to Thomas Paine.

The Autobiography        Franklin turned to the manuscript of *The Autobiogra-*
*phy* on four different occasions over a period of nineteen years. The first part,
addressed to his son William Franklin (c.

1731–1813), who was governor of New
Jersey when Franklin was writing this section, was composed while Franklin was
visiting the country home of Bishop Jonathan Shipley at Twyford, a village about
fifty miles from London. It was begun on July 30 and concluded on or about
August 13, 1771. Franklin did not work on the manuscript again until he was
living in France and was minister of the newly formed United States, about thirteen years later. The last two sections were written in August 1788 and the winter
of 1789–90, when Franklin stopped because of illness. Before he died he carried
his life up to the year 1758. The account ends, therefore, before Franklin's great
triumphs as a diplomat and public servant.

The first part of *The Autobiography* was published in 1791 by Jacques Buisson
in a French translation; William Temple Franklin, Franklin's grandson, published
an edition of *The Autobiography* in 1818, but he did not possess the last section
that his grandfather wrote because he unwittingly exchanged it for the French
translator's Part One. It was not until 1868 that John Bigelow published *The Autobiography* as we know it, with all four sections complete.

The text for the two parts of *The Autobiography* here reprinted is the first to have
been taken directly from the manuscript itself (all other editors have merely corrected earlier printed texts). Established by J. A. Leo Lemay and Paul Zall for their
Norton Critical Edition of *The Autobiography*, the text is here reprinted with their
kind permission. It has been only slightly modernized. All manuscript abbreviations and symbols have been expanded. The editors note that they have omitted
short dashes, which Franklin often wrote after sentences, and punctuation marks
that "have been clearly superseded by revisions or additions." Careless slips have
been corrected silently but may be found in their section on emendations in their
complete text. Professors Lemay and Zall have been generous in letting us see their
footnotes and biographical sketches. Every student of Franklin's *Autobiography*
must also acknowledge the helpful edition of Leonard W. Labaree et al. (1964).

# The Autobiography

## [*Part One*]

Twyford, at the Bishop of St. Asaph's 1771.

Dear Son,

I have ever had a Pleasure in obtaining any little Anecdotes of my Ancestors.
You may remember the Enquiries I made among the Remains[1] of my Relations when you were with me in England; and the Journey I took for that
purpose. Now imagining it may be equally agreeable to you to know the Circumstances of *my* Life, many of which you are yet unacquainted with; and
expecting a Week's uninterrupted Leisure in my present Country Retirement,
I sit down to write them for you. To which I have besides some other Inducements. Having emerg'd from the Poverty and Obscurity in which I was born
and bred, to a State of Affluence and some Degree of Reputation in the World,
and having gone so far thro' Life with a considerable Share of Felicity, the
conducting Means I made use of, which, with the Blessing of God, so well

---

1. I.e., the remaining representatives of a family. Franklin and his son toured England in 1758 and visited ancestral homes at Ecton and Banbury, Northhamptonshire, England.

succeeded, my Posterity may like to know, as they may find some of them suitable to their own Situations, and therefore fit to be imitated. That Felicity, when I reflected on it, has induc'd me sometimes to say, that were it offer'd to my Choice, I should have no Objection to a Repetition of the same Life from its Beginning, only asking the Advantage Authors have in a second Edition to correct some Faults of the first. So would I if I might, besides correcting the Faults, change some sinister Accidents and Events of it for others more favorable, but tho' this were denied, I should still accept the Offer. However, since such a Repetition is not to be expected, the Thing most like living one's Life over again, seems to be a *Recollection* of that Life; and to make that Recollection as durable as possible, the putting it down in Writing. Hereby, too, I shall indulge the Inclination so natural in old Men, to be talking of themselves and their own past Actions, and I shall indulge it, without being troublesome to others who thro' respect to Age might think themselves oblig'd to give me a Hearing, since this may be read or not as any one pleases. And lastly, (I may as well confess it, since my Denial of it will be believ'd by no body) perhaps I shall a good deal gratify my own *Vanity*. Indeed I scarce ever heard or saw the introductory Words, *Without Vanity I may say*, etc. but some vain thing immediately follow'd. Most People dislike Vanity in others whatever Share they have of it themselves, but I give it fair Quarter wherever I meet with it, being persuaded that it is often productive of Good to the Possessor and to others that are within his Sphere of Action: And therefore in many Cases it would not be quite absurd if a Man were to thank God for his Vanity among the other Comforts of Life.

And now I speak of thanking God, I desire with all Humility to acknowledge, that I owe the mention'd Happiness of my past Life to his kind Providence, which led me to the Means I us'd and gave them Success. My Belief of This, induces me to *hope*, tho' I must not *presume*, that the same Goodness will still be exercis'd towards me in continuing that Happiness, or in enabling me to bear a fatal Reverso,[2] which I may experience as others have done, the Complexion of my future Fortune being known to him only: and in whose Power it is to bless to us even our Afflictions.

The Notes one of my Uncles (who had the same kind of Curiosity in collecting Family Anecdotes) once put into my Hands, furnish'd me with several Particulars, relating to our Ancestors. From those Notes I learned that the Family had liv'd in the same Village, Ecton in Northamptonshire, for 300 Years, and how much longer he knew not, (perhaps from the Time when the Name *Franklin* that before was the Name of an Order of People,[3] was assum'd by them for a Surname, when others took Surnames all over the Kingdom)[4] on a Freehold of about 30 Acres, aided by the Smith's Business which had continued in the Family till his Time, the eldest Son being always bred to that Business. A Custom which he and my Father both followed as to their eldest Sons. When I search'd the Register at Ecton, I found an Account of their Births, Marriages and Burials, from the Year 1555 only, there being no Register kept in that Parish at any time preceding. By that Register I perceiv'd that I was the youngest Son of the youngest Son for 5 Generations back. My Grandfather Thomas, who was born in 1598, lived at Ecton till he grew too old to

2. I.e., a backhanded stroke, a word used in dueling with rapiers.
3. A "franklin" was a freeholder—an individual who

owned land but was not of noble birth.
4. "Here a note" [Franklin intended to insert a note here, but did not].

follow Business longer, when he went to live with his Son John, a Dyer at Banbury in Oxfordshire, with whom my Father serv'd an Apprenticeship. There my Grandfather died and lies buried. We saw his Gravestone in 1758. His eldest Son Thomas liv'd in the House at Ecton, and left it with the Land to his only Child, a Daughter, who with her Husband, one Fisher of Wellingborough, sold it to Mr. Isted, now Lord of the Manor there.

My Grandfather had 4 Sons that grew up, viz., Thomas, John, Benjamin and Josiah. I will give you what Account I can of them at this distance from my Papers, and if those are not lost in my Absence, you will among them find many more Particulars. Thomas was bred a Smith under his Father, but being ingenious, and encourag'd in Learning (as all his Brothers likewise were,) by an Esquire[5] Palmer then the principal Gentleman in that Parish, he qualified himself for the Business of Scrivener,[6] became a considerable Man in the County Affairs, was a chief Mover of all public Spirited Undertakings for the County or Town of Northampton and his own Village, of which many Instances were told us at Ecton, and he was much taken Notice of and patroniz'd by the then Lord Halifax. He died in 1702, Jan. 6, old Stile,[7] just 4 Years to a Day before I was born. The Account we receiv'd of his Life and Character from some old People at Ecton, I remember struck you as something extraordinary from its Similarity to what you knew of mine. Had he died on the same Day, you said one might have suppos'd a Transmigration.[8]

John was bred a Dyer, I believe of Woollens. Benjamin was bred a Silk Dyer, serving an Apprenticeship at London. He was an ingenious Man. I remember him well, for when I was a Boy he came over to my Father in Boston, and lived in the House with us some Years. He lived to a great Age. His Grandson Samuel Franklin now lives in Boston. He left behind him two Quarto[9] Volumes, Manuscript of his own Poetry, consisting of little occasional Pieces address'd to his Friends and Relations, of which the following sent to me, is a Specimen.[1] He had form'd a Shorthand of his own, which he taught me, but never practicing it I have now forgot it. I was nam'd after this Uncle, there being a particular Affection between him and my Father. He was very pious, a great Attender of Sermons of the best Preachers, which he took down in his Shorthand and had with him many Volumes of them. He was also much of a Politician, too much perhaps for his Station. There fell lately into my Hands in London a Collection he had made of all the principal Pamphlets relating to Public Affairs from 1641 to 1717. Many of the Volumes are wanting, as appears by the Numbering, but there still remains 8 Volumes Folio, and 24 in Quarto and Octavo. A Dealer in old Books met with them, and knowing me by my sometimes buying of him, he brought them to me. It seems my Uncle must have left them here when he went to America, which was above 50 Years since. There are many of his Notes in the Margins.

This obscure Family of ours was early in the Reformation, and continu'd

5. An honorific originally extended to a young man of gentle birth, but extended as a courtesy to any gentleman.

6. A professional copier of documents.

7. Until September 1752 England used the Julian calendar, in which the New Year began on March 25. Because the Julian calendar did not have leap years, the English skipped eleven days (September 3 to September 13, 1752) when adopting the Gregorian calendar. Franklin's birthday is either January 6, 1705–6

"old Stile" or January 17, 1706, New Style.

8. The passage of the soul to another's body upon death.

9. The terms folio, quarto, and octavo designate book sizes from large to small. A single sheet folded once makes a folio, or four sides for printing; a quarto is obtained if the sheet is folded again; an octavo is the sheet folded once more.

1. "Here insert it" [Franklin's note, but the example was not included].

Protestants thro' the Reign of Queen Mary,[2] when they were sometimes in Danger of Trouble on Account of their Zeal against Popery. They had got an English Bible,[3] and to conceal and secure it, it was fastened open with Tapes under and within the Frame of a Joint Stool.[4] When my Great Great Grandfather read in it to his Family, he turn'd up the Joint Stool upon his Knees, turning over the Leaves then under the Tapes. One of the Children stood at the Door to give Notice if he saw the Apparitor[5] coming, who was an Officer of the Spiritual Court. In that Case the Stool was turn'd down again upon its feet, when the Bible remain'd conceal'd under it as before. This Anecdote I had from my Uncle Benjamin. The Family continu'd all of the Church of England till about the End of Charles the Second's Reign,[6] when some of the Ministers that had been outed for Nonconformity, holding Conventicles[7] in Northamptonshire, Benjamin and Josiah adher'd to them, and so continu'd all their Lives. The rest of the Family remain'd with the Episcopal Church.

Josiah, my Father, married young, and carried his Wife with three Children unto New England, about 1682.[8] The Conventicles having been forbidden by Law, and frequently disturbed, induced some considerable Men of his Acquaintance to remove to that Country, and he was prevail'd with to accompany them thither, where they expected to enjoy their Mode of Religion with Freedom. By the same Wife he had 4 Children more born there, and by a second Wife ten more, in all 17, of which I remember 13 sitting at one time at his Table, who all grew up to be Men and Women, and married. I was the youngest Son and the youngest Child but two, and was born in Boston, New England.

My Mother the second Wife was Abiah Folger, a Daughter of Peter Folger, one of the first Settlers of New England, of whom honorable mention is made by Cotton Mather, in his Church History of that Country, (entitled Magnalia Christi Americana) as a *godly learned Englishman*, if I remember the Words rightly.[9] I have heard that he wrote sundry small occasional Pieces, but only one of them was printed which I saw now many Years since. It was written in 1675, in the homespun Verse of that Time and People, and address'd to those then concern'd in the Government there. It was in favor of Liberty of Conscience, and in behalf of the Baptists, Quakers, and other Sectaries,[1] that had been under Persecution; ascribing the Indian Wars and other Distresses that had befallen the Country to that Persecution, as so many Judgments of God, to punish so heinous an Offence; and exhorting a Repeal of those uncharitable Laws. The whole appear'd to me as written with a good deal of Decent Plainness and manly Freedom. The six last concluding Lines I remember, tho' I have forgotten the two first of the Stanza, but the Purport of them was that his Censures proceeded from *Goodwill*, and therefore he would be known as the Author,

---

2. From 1553 to 1558, Mary, the older sister of Elizabeth I, tried to restore Roman Catholicism as the national church.
3. A Bible known as the "Geneva" version, translated by Reformed English Protestants living in Switzerland; this version, used by the Puritans, was outlawed by the Church of England.
4. A small four-legged stool.
5. An officer of an ecclesiastical court, in this case a court established to eliminate heresy.
6. Charles II (1630–1685) reigned from 1660 to 1685.

7. Secret and illegal meetings of Nonconformists, outlawed in 1664. Nonconformists refused to adopt the rituals and acknowledge the hierarchy of the Church of England.
8. More correctly, October 1683.
9. Cotton Mather's ecclesiastical history *The Wonderful Work of Christ in America*, which was published in London in 1702; the quotation is properly "an Able Godly Englishman."
1. Believers or followers of a particular religious teaching.

because to be a Libeler, (says he)
I hate it with my Heart.
From Sherburne Town[2] where now I dwell,
    My Name I do put here,
Without Offence, your real Friend,
    It is Peter Folgier.

My elder Brothers were all put Apprentices to different Trades. I was put to
the Grammar School at Eight Years of Age, my Father intending to devote
me as the Tithe[3] of his Sons to the Service of the Church. My early Readiness
in learning to read (which must have been very early, as I do not remember
when I could not read) and the Opinion of all his Friends that I should certainly make a good Scholar, encourag'd him in this Purpose of his. My Uncle
Benjamin too approv'd of it, and propos'd to give me all his Shorthand Volumes of Sermons, I suppose as a Stock to set up with, if I would learn his
Character.[4] I continu'd however at the Grammar School not quite one Year,
tho' in that time I had risen gradually from the Middle of the Class of that
Year to be the Head of it, and farther was remov'd into the next Class above
it, in order to go with that into the third at the End of the Year. But my Father
in the meantime, from a View of the Expense of a College Education which,
having so large a Family, he could not well afford, and the mean Living many
so educated were afterwards able to obtain, Reasons that he gave to his Friends
in my Hearing, altered his first Intention, took me from the Grammar School,
and sent me to a School for Writing and Arithmetic kept by a then famous
Man, Mr. George Brownell, very successful in his Profession generally, and
that by mild encouraging Methods. Under him I acquired fair Writing pretty
soon, but I fail'd in the Arithmetic, and made no Progress in it.

At Ten Years old, I was taken home to assist my Father in his Business,
which was that of a Tallow Chandler and Soap-Boiler.[5] A Business he was not
bred to, but had assumed on his Arrival in New England and on finding his
Dying Trade would not maintain his Family, being in little Request. Accordingly I was employed in cutting Wick for the Candles, filling the Dipping
Mold, and the Molds for cast Candles, attending the Shop, going of Errands,
etc. I dislik'd the Trade and had a strong Inclination for the Sea; but my Father
declar'd against it; however, living near the Water, I was much in and about
it, learned early to swim well, and to manage Boats, and when in a Boat or
Canoe with other Boys I was commonly allow'd to govern,[6] especially in any
case of Difficulty; and upon other Occasions I was generally a Leader among
the Boys, and sometimes led them into Scrapes, of which I will mention one
Instance, as it shows an early projecting public Spirit, tho' not then justly
conducted. There was a Salt Marsh that bounded part of the Mill Pond, on
the Edge of which at Highwater, we us'd to stand to fish for Minnows. By
much Trampling, we had made it a mere Quagmire. My Proposal was to build
a Wharf there fit for us to stand upon, and I show'd my Comrades a large
Heap of Stones which were intended for a new House near the Marsh, and
which would very well suit our Purpose. Accordingly in the Evening when the
Workmen were gone, I assembled a Number of my Playfellows, and working
with them diligently like so many Emmets,[7] sometimes two or three to a

2. "In the Island of Nantucket" [Franklin's note].
3. I.e., as if he were the tenth part of his income, traditionally given to the church.
4. Here, his system of shorthand.

5. Maker of candles and soap.
6. Steer.
7. Ants.

Stone, we brought them all away and built our little Wharf. The next Morning the Workmen were surpris'd at Missing the Stones; which were found in our Wharf; Enquiry was made after the Removers; we were discovered and complain'd of; several of us were corrected by our Fathers; and tho' I pleaded the Usefulness of the Work, mine convinc'd me that nothing was useful which was not honest.

I think you may like to know something of his Person and Character. He had an excellent Constitution of Body, was of middle Stature, but well set and very strong. He was ingenious, could draw prettily, was skill'd a little in Music and had a clear pleasing Voice, so that when he play'd Psalm Tunes on his Violin and sung withal as he some times did in an Evening after the Business of the Day was over, it was extremely agreeable to hear. He had a mechanical Genius too, and on occasion was very handy in the Use of other Tradesmen's Tools. But his great Excellence lay in a sound Understanding, and solid Judgment in prudential Matters, both in private and public Affairs. In the latter indeed he was never employed, the numerous Family he had to educate and the Straitness of his Circumstances, keeping him close to his Trade, but I remember well his being frequently visited by leading People, who consulted him for his Opinion on Affairs of the Town or of the Church he belong'd to and show'd a good deal of Respect for his Judgment and Advice. He was also much consulted by private Persons about their Affairs when any Difficulty occur'd, and frequently chosen an Arbitrator between contending Parties. At his Table he lik'd to have as often as he could, some sensible Friend or Neighbor, to converse with, and always took care to start some ingenious or useful Topic for Discourse, which might tend to improve the Minds of his Children. By this means he turn'd our Attention to what was good, just, and prudent in the Conduct of Life; and little or no Notice was ever taken of what related to the Victuals on the Table, whether it was well or ill drest, in or out of season, of good or bad flavor, preferable or inferior to this or that other thing of the kind; so that I was brought up in such a perfect Inattention to those Matters as to be quite Indifferent what kind of Food was set before me; and so unobservant of it, that to this Day, if I am ask'd I can scarce tell, a few Hours after Dinner, what I din'd upon. This has been a Convenience to me in traveling, where my Companions have been sometimes very unhappy for want of a suitable Gratification of their more delicate because better instructed Tastes and Appetites.

My Mother had likewise an excellent Constitution. She suckled all her 10 Children. I never knew either my Father or Mother to have any Sickness but that of which they died, he at 89 and she at 85 Years of age. They lie buried together at Boston, where I some Years since plac'd a Marble stone over their Grave with this Inscription:

Josiah Franklin
And Abiah his Wife
Lie here interred.
They lived lovingly together in Wedlock
Fifty-five Years.
Without an Estate or any gainful Employment,[8]
By constant Labor and Industry,
With God's Blessing,

8. Privileged employment.

They maintained a large Family
Comfortably;
And brought up thirteen Children,
And seven Grandchildren
Reputably.
From this Instance, Reader,
Be encouraged to Diligence in thy Calling,
And distrust not Providence.
He was a pious and prudent Man,
She a discreet and virtuous Woman.
Their youngest Son,
In filial Regard to their Memory,
Places this Stone.
J.F. born 1655—Died 1744. Ætat[9] 89
A.F. born 1667—died 1752——85.

By my rambling Digressions I perceive myself to be grown old. I us'd to write more methodically. But one does not dress for private Company as for a public Ball. 'Tis perhaps only Negligence.

To return. I continu'd thus employ'd in my Father's Business for two Years, that is till I was 12 Years old; and my Brother John[1] who was bred to that Business having left my Father, married and set up for himself at Rhode Island, there was all Appearance that I was destin'd to supply his Place and be a Tallow Chandler. But my Dislike to the Trade continuing, my Father was under Apprehensions that if he did not find one for me more agreeable, I should break away and get to Sea, as his Son Josiah had done to his great Vexation. He therefore sometimes took me to walk with him, and see Joiners, Bricklayers, Turners, Braziers,[2] etc. at their Work, that he might observe my Inclination, and endeavor to fix it on some Trade or other on Land. It has ever since been a Pleasure to me to see good Workmen handle their Tools; and it has been useful to me, having learned so much by it, as to be able to do little Jobs myself in my House, when a Workman could not readily be got; and to construct little Machines for my Experiments while the Intention of making the Experiment was fresh and warm in my Mind. My Father at last fix'd upon the Cutler's Trade, and my Uncle Benjamin's Son Samuel who was bred to that Business in London being about that time establish'd in Boston, I was sent to be with him some time on liking. But his Expectations of a Fee with me displeasing my Father, I was taken home again.

From a Child I was fond of Reading, and all the little Money that came into my Hands was ever laid out in Books. Pleas'd with the Pilgrim's Progress, my first Collection was of John Bunyan's[3] Works, in separate little Voumes. I afterwards sold them to enable me to buy R. Burton's[4] Historical Collections; they were small Chapmen's Books[5] and cheap, 40 or 50 in all. My Father's little Library consisted chiefly of Books in polemic Divinity, most of which I

9. Aged.
1. John Franklin (1690–1756), Franklin's favorite brother; he was to become postmaster of Boston.
2. Woodworkers, bricklayers, latheworkers, brassworkers.
3. John Bunyan (1628–1688) published *Pilgrim's Progress* in 1678; his works were enormously popular and available in cheap one-shilling editions. The book

is an allegory in which the hero, Christian, flees the City of Destruction and makes his way to the Celestial City with the help of Mr. Worldly-Wiseman, Faithful, Hopeful, etc.
4. "Burton" was a pseudonym for Nathaniel Crouch (1632?–1725?), a popularizer of British history.
5. Peddlers' books, hence inexpensive.

read, and have since often regretted, that at a time when I had such a Thirst for Knowledge, more proper Books had not fallen in my Way, since it was now resolv'd I should not be a Clergyman. Plutarch's Lives[6] there was, in which I read abundently, and I still think that time spent to great Advantage. There was also a Book of Defoe's called an Essay on Projects[7] and another of Dr. Mather's call'd Essays to do Good,[8] which perhaps gave me a Turn of Thinking that had an Influence on some of the principal future Events of my Life.

This Bookish Inclination at length determin'd my Father to make me a Printer, tho' he had already one Son, (James) of that Profession. In 1717 my Brother James return'd from England with a Press and Letters[9] to set up his Business in Boston. I lik'd it much better than that of my Father, but still had a Hankering for the Sea. To prevent the apprehended Effect of such an Inclination, my Father was impatient to have me bound[1] to my Brother. I stood out some time, but at last was persuaded and signed the Indentures,[2] when I was yet but 12 Years old. I was to serve as an Apprentice till I was 21 Years of Age, only I was to be allow'd Journeyman's Wages[3] during the last Year. In a little time I made great Proficiency in the Business, and became a useful Hand to my Brother. I now had Access to better Books. An Acquaintance with the Apprentices of Booksellers enabled me sometimes to borrow a small one, which I was careful to return soon and clean. Often I sat up in my Room reading the greatest Part of the Night, when the Book was borrow'd in the Evening and to be return'd early in the Morning lest it should be miss'd or wanted. And after some time an ingenious Tradesman[4] who had a pretty[5] Collection of Books, and who frequented our Printing-House, took Notice of me, invited me to his Library, and very kindly lent me such Books as I chose to read. I now took a Fancy to Poetry, and made some little Pieces. My Brother, thinking it might turn to account encourag'd me, and put me on composing two occasional Ballads. One was called the *Light House Tragedy*, and contain'd an Account of the drowning of Capt. Worthilake with his Two Daughters; the other was a Sailor Song on the Taking of *Teach* or Blackbeard the Pirate.[6] They were wretched Stuff, in the Grubstreet Ballad Style,[7] and when they were printed he sent me about the Town to sell them. The first sold wonderfully, the Event being recent, having made a great Noise. This flatter'd my Vanity. But my Father discourag'd me, by ridiculing my Performances, and telling me Verse-makers were generally Beggars; so I escap'd being a Poet, most probably a very bad one. But as Prose Writing has been of great Use to me in the Course of my Life, and was a principal Means of my Advancement, I shall tell you how in such a Situation I acquir'd what little Ability I have in that Way.

6. Plutarch (A.D. 46?–120?), Greek biographer who wrote *Parallel Lives* of noted Greek and Roman figures.
7. Daniel Defoe's (1659?–1731) *Essay on Projects* (1697) offered suggestions for economic improvement (see also n. 2, p. 239).
8. Cotton Mather published *Bonifacius: An Essay upon the Good* in 1710.
9. Type.
1. Apprenticed.
2. A contract binding him to work for his brother for nine years. James Franklin (1697–1735) had learned the printer's trade in England.

3. I.e., be paid for each day's work, having served his apprenticeship.
4. "Mr. Matthew Adams" [Franklin's note].
5. Exceptionally fine.
6. The full texts of these ballads cannot be found; George Worthylake, lighthouse keeper on Beacon Island, Boston Harbor, and his wife and daughter were drowned on November 3, 1718; the pirate Blackbeard, Edward Teach, was killed off the Carolina coast on November 22, 1718.
7. Grub Street in London was inhabited by poor literary hacks who capitalized on poems of topical interest.

There was another Bookish Lad in the Town, John Collins by Name, with whom I was intimately acquainted. We sometimes disputed, and very fond we were of Argument, and very desirous of confuting one another. Which disputatious Turn, by the way, is apt to become a very bad Habit, making People often extremely disagreeable in Company, by the Contradiction that is necessary to bring it into Practice, and thence, besides souring and spoiling the Conversation, is productive of Disgusts and perhaps Enmities where you may have occasion for Friendship. I had caught it by reading my Father's Books of Dispute about Religion. Persons of good Sense, I have since observ'd, seldom fall into it, except Lawyers, University Men, and Men of all Sorts that have been bred at Edinburgh.[8] A Question was once some how or other started between Collins and me, of the Propriety of educating the Female Sex in Learning, and their Abilities for Study. He was of Opinion that it was improper; and that they were naturally unequal to it. I took the contrary Side, perhaps a little for Dispute sake. He was naturally more eloquent, had a ready Plenty of Words, and sometimes as I thought bore me down more by his Fluency than by the Strength of his Reasons. As we parted without settling the Point, and were not to see one another again for some time, I sat down to put my Arguments in Writing, which I copied fair and sent to him. He answer'd and I replied. Three or four Letters of a Side had pass'd, when my Father happen'd to find my Papers, and read them. Without entering into the Discussion, he took occasion to talk to me about the Manner of my Writing, observ'd that tho' I had the Advantage of my Antagonist in correct Spelling and pointing[9] (which I ow'd to the Printing-House) I fell far short in elegance of Expression, in Method and in Perspicuity, of which he convinc'd me by several Instances. I saw the Justice of his Remarks, and thence grew more attentive to the *Manner* in Writing, and determin'd to endeavor at Improvement.

About this time I met with an odd Volume of the Spectator.[1] I had never before seen any of them. I bought it, read it over and over, and was much delighted with it. I thought the Writing excellent, and wish'd if possible to imitate it. With that View, I took some of the Papers, and making short Hints of the Sentiment in each Sentence, laid them by a few Days, and then without looking at the Book, tried to complete the Papers again, by expressing each hinted Sentiment at length and as fully as it had been express'd before, in any suitable Words that should come to hand.

Then I compar'd my Spectator with the Original, discover'd some of my Faults and corrected them. But I found I wanted a Stock of Words or a Readiness in recollecting and using them, which I thought I should have acquir'd before that time, if I had gone on making Verses, since the continual Occasion for Words of the same Import but of different Length, to suit the Measure,[2] or of different Sound for the Rhyme, would have laid me under a constant Necessity of searching for Variety, and also have tended to fix that Variety in my Mind, and make me Master of it. Therefore I took some of the Tales and turn'd them into Verse: And after a time, when I had pretty well forgotten the Prose, turn'd them back again. I also sometimes jumbled my Collections of

8. Scottish Presbyterians were noted for their argumentative nature.
9. Punctuation. Spelling and punctuation were not standardized at this time.
1. An English periodical published daily from March 1, 1711, to December 6, 1712, and revived in 1714. It contained esays by Joseph Addison (1672–1719) and Richard Steele (1672–1729). It addressed itself primarily to matters of literature and morality. Its aim was to "enliven morality with wit" and "temper wit with morality."
2. Meter.

Hints into Confusion, and after some Weeks, endeavor'd to reduce them into the best Order, before I began to form the full Sentences, and complete the Paper. This was to teach me Method in the Arrangement of Thoughts. By comparing my Work afterwards with the original, I discover'd many faults and amended them; but I sometimes had the Pleasure of Fancying that in certain Particulars of small Import, I had been lucky enough to improve the Method or the Language and this encourag'd me to think I might possibly in time come to be a tolerable English Writer, of which I was extremely ambitious.

My Time for these Exercises and for Reading, was at Night after Work, or before Work began in the Morning; or on Sundays, when I contrived to be in the Printing-House alone, evading as much as I could the common Attendance on public Worship, which my Father used to exact of me when I was under his Care: And which indeed I still thought a Duty; tho' I could not, as it seemed to me, afford the Time to practice it.

When about 16 Years of Age, I happen'd to meet with a Book written by one Tryon,[3] recommending a Vegetable Diet. I determined to go into it. My Brother being yet unmarried, did not keep House, but boarded himself and his Apprentices in another Family. My refusing to eat Flesh occasioned an Inconveniency, and I was frequently chid for my singularity. I made myself acquainted with Tryon's Manner of preparing some of his Dishes, such as Boiling Potatoes or Rice, making Hasty Pudding,[4] and a few others, and then propos'd to my Brother, that if he would give me Weekly half the Money he paid for my Board, I would board myself. He instantly agreed to it, and I presently found that I could save half what he paid me. This was an additional Fund for buying Books: But I had another Advantage in it. My Brother and the rest going from the Printing-House to their Meals, I remain'd there alone, and dispatching presently my light Repast, (which often was no more than a Biscuit or a Slice of Bread, a Handful of Raisins or a Tart from the Pastry Cook's, and a Glass of Water) had the rest of the Time till their Return, for Study, in which I made the greater Progress from that greater Clearness of Head and quicker Apprehension which usually attend Temperance in Eating and Drinking. And now it was that being on some Occasion made asham'd of my Ignorance in Figures, which I had twice fail'd in learning when at School, I took Cocker's Book of Arithmetic,[5] and went thro' the whole by myself with great Ease. I also read Seller's and Sturmy's Books of Navigation,[6] and became acquainted with the little Geometry they contain, but never proceeded far in that Science. And I read about this Time Locke on Human Understanding and the Art of Thinking by Messrs. du Port Royal.[7]

While I was intent on improving my Language, I met with an English Grammar (I think it was Greenwood's[8]) at the End of which there were two little Sketches of the Arts of Rhetoric and Logic, the latter finishing with a Specimen of a Dispute in the Socratic Method.[9] And soon after I procur'd

3. Thomas Tryon, whose Way to Health, Wealth, and Happiness appeared in 1682; a digest titled Wisdom's Dictates appeared in 1691.
4. I.e., cornmeal or oatmeal mush.
5. Edward Cocker's Arithmetic, published in 1677, was reprinted twenty times by 1700.
6. John Seller published An Epitome of the Art of Navigation in 1681. Samuel Sturmy published The Mariner's Magazine: Or Sturmy's Mathematical and Practical Arts in 1699.

7. John Locke (1632–1704) published An Essay Concerning Human Understanding in 1690. Antoine Arnauld (1612–94) and Pierre Nicole (1625?–95), of Port Royal, published the English edition of Logic: Or the Art of Thinking in 1687. It was originally published in Latin in 1662.
8. James Greenwood, An Essay towards a Practical English Grammar (1711).
9. I.e., in the form of a debate.

Xenophon's Memorable Things of Socrates,[1] wherein there are many Instances of the same Method. I was charm'd with it, adopted it, dropped my abrupt Contradiction and positive Argumentation, and put on the humble Enquirer and Doubter. And being then, from reading Shaftesbury and Collins,[2] became a real Doubter in many Points of our Religious Doctrine, I found this Method safest for myself and very embarrassing to those against whom I used it, therefore I took a Delight in it, practic'd it continually and grew very artful and expert in drawing People even of superior Knowledge into Concessions the Consequences of which they did not foresee, entangling them in Difficulties out of which they could not extricate themselves, and so obtaining Victories that neither myself nor my Cause always deserved. I continu'd this Method some few Years, but gradually left it, retaining only the Habit of expressing myself in Terms of modest Diffidence, never using when I advance any thing that may possibly be disputed, the Words, *Certainly, undoubtedly*, or any others that give the Air of Positiveness to an Opinion; but rather say, *I conceive*, or *I apprehend* a Thing to be so or so, *It appears to me*, or *I should think it so or so for such and such Reasons*, or *I imagine* it to be so, or *it is so if I am not mistaken*. This Habit I believe has been of great Advantage to me, when I have had occasion to inculcate my Opinions and persuade Men into Measures that I have been from time to time engag'd in promoting. And as the chief Ends of Conversation are to *inform*, or to be *informed*, to *please* or to *persuade*, I wish well-meaning sensible Men would not lessen their Power of doing Good by a Positive assuming Manner that seldom fails to disgust, tends to create Opposition, and to defeat every one of those Purposes for which Speech was given us, to wit, giving or receiving Information, or Pleasure: For If you would *inform*, a positive dogmatical Manner in advancing your Sentiments, may provoke Contradiction and prevent a candid Attention. If you wish Information and Improvement from the Knowledge of others and yet at the same time express yourself as firmly fix'd in your present Opinions, modest sensible Men, who do not love Disputation, will probably leave you undisturb'd in the Possession of your Error; and by such a Manner you can seldom hope to recommend yourself in *pleasing* your Hearers, or to persuade those whose Concurrence you desire. Pope says, judiciously.

> Men should be taught as if you taught them not,
> And things unknown propos'd as things forgot,

farther recommending it to us,

> To speak tho' sure, with seeming Diffidence.[3]

And he might have coupled with this Line that which he has coupled with another, I think less properly,

> For want of Modesty is want of Sense.

If you ask why *less properly*, I must repeat the Lines;

---

1. Xenophon's (434?–355 B.C.) *The Memorable Things of Socrates* was translated by Edward Bysshe in 1712.
2. Anthony Ashley Cooper, third earl of Shaftesbury (1671–1713), was a religious skeptic. Anthony Collins (1676–1729) argued that the world could satisfactorily be explained in terms of itself. Perhaps Franklin read Shaftesbury's *Characteristics of Men, Manners, Opin-* ions, *Times* (1711) and Collins's A *Discourse of Free Thinking* (1713).
3. From Alexander Pope's An *Essay on Criticism* (1711), lines 574–75 and 567, respectively. Franklin is quoting from memory. The first line should read, "Men must be taught as if you taught them not," and the third, "And speak, tho' sure, with seeming diffidence."

"Immodest Words admit of *no* Defence;
*For* Want of Modesty is Want of Sense."[4]

Now is not *Want of Sense*, (where a Man is so unfortunate as to want it) some Apology for his *Want of Modesty?* and would not the Lines stand more justly thus?

Immodest Words admit *but this* Defence,
That Want of Modesty is Want of Sense.

This however I should submit to better Judgments.

My Brother had in 1720 or 21, begun to print a Newspaper. It was the second[5] that appear'd in America, and was called *The New England Courant.* The only one before it, was *The Boston News Letter.* I remember his being dissuaded by some of his Friends from the Undertaking, as not likely to succeed, one Newspaper being in their Judgment enough for America. At this time 1771 there are not less than five and twenty. He went on however with the Undertaking, and after having work'd in composing the Types and printing off the Sheets I was employ'd to carry the Papers thro' the Streets to the Customers. He had some ingenious Men among his Friends who amus'd themselves by writing little Pieces for this Paper, which gain'd it Credit, and made it more in Demand; and these Gentlemen often visited us. Hearing their Conversations, and their Accounts of the Approbation their Papers were receiv'd with, I was excited to try my Hand among them. But being still a Boy, and suspecting that my Brother would object to printing any Thing of mine in his Paper if he knew it to be mine, I contriv'd to disguise my Hand, and writing an anonymous Paper I put it in at Night under the Door of the Printing-House. It was found in the Morning and communicated to his Writing Friends when they call'd in as Usual. They read it, commented on it in my Hearing, and I had the exquisite Pleasure, of finding it met with their Approbation, and that in their different Guesses at the Author none were named but Men of some Character among us for Learning and Ingenuity. I suppose now that I was rather lucky in my Judges: And that perhaps they were not really so very good ones as I then esteem'd them. Encourag'd however by this, I wrote and convey'd in the same Way to the Press several more Papers,[6] which were equally approv'd, and I kept my Secret till my small Fund of Sense for such Performances was pretty well exhausted, and then I discovered[7] it; when I began to be considered a little more by my Brother's Acquaintance, and in a manner that did not quite please him, as he thought, probably with reason, that it tended to make me too vain. And perhaps this might be one Occasion of the Differences that we began to have about this Time. Tho' a Brother, he considered himself as my Master, and me as his Apprentice; and accordingly expected the same Services from me as he would from another; while I thought he demean'd me too much in some he requir'd of me, who from a Brother expected more Indulgence, Our Disputes were often brought before our Father, and I fancy I was either generally in the right, or else a better Pleader, because the Judgment was generally in my favor. But my Brother was passion-

4. Franklin is mistaken here: the lines are from Wentworth Dillon, fourth earl of Roscommon (1633?–1685), from his *Essay on Translated Verse* (1684), lines 113–14. The second line should read, "For want of decency is want of sense." "Want": lack.

5. Actually the fifth; James Franklin's paper appeared on August 7, 1721.
6. *The Silence Dogood Letters* (April 12–October 8, 1722) were the earliest essay series in America.
7. Revealed.

ate and had often beaten me, which I took extremely amiss; and thinking my Apprenticeship very tedious, I was continually wishing for some Opportunity of shortening it, which at length offered in a manner unexpected.[8]

One of the Pieces in our Newspaper, on some political Point which I have now forgotten, gave Offence to the Assembly. He was taken up, censur'd and imprison'd[9] for a Month by the Speaker's Warrant, I suppose because he would not discover his Author. I too was taken up and examin'd before the Council; but tho' I did not give them any Satisfaction, they contented themselves with admonishing me, and dismiss'd me; considering me perhaps as an Apprentice who was bound to keep his Master's Secrets. During my Brother's Confinement, which I resented a good deal, notwithstanding our private Differences, I had the Management of the Paper, and I made bold to give our Rulers some Rubs[1] in it, which my Brother took very kindly, while others began to consider me in an unfavorable Light, as a young Genius that had a Turn for Libeling and Satire.[2] My Brother's Discharge was accompanied with an Order of the House, (a very odd one) *that James Franklin should no longer print the Paper called the New England Courant.* There was a Consultation held in our Printing-House among his Friends what he should do in this Case. Some propos'd to evade the Order by changing the Name of the Paper; but my Brother seeing Inconveniences in that, it was finally concluded on as a better Way, to let it be printed for the future under the Name of *Benjamin Franklin.* And to avoid the Censure of the Assembly that might fall on him, as still printing it by his Apprentice, the Contrivance was, that my old Indenture should be return'd to me with a full Discharge on the Back of it, to be shown on Occasion; but to secure to him the Benefit of my Service I was to sign new Indentures for the Remainder of the Term, which were to be kept private. A very flimsy Scheme it was, but however it was immediately executed, and the Paper went on accordingly under my Name for several Months.[3] At length a fresh Difference arising between my Brother and me, I took upon me to assert my Freedom, presuming that he would not venture to produce the new Indentures. It was not fair in me to take this Advantage, and this I therefore reckon one of the first Errata[4] of my Life: But the Unfairness of it weigh'd little with me, when under the Impressions of Resentment, for the Blows his Passion too often urg'd him to bestow upon me. Tho' he was otherwise not an ill-natur'd Man: Perhaps I was too saucy and provoking.

When he found I would leave him, he took care to prevent my getting Employment in any other Printing-House of the Town, by going round and speaking to every Master, who accordingly refus'd to give me Work. I then thought of going to New York as the nearest Place where there was a Printer: and I was the rather inclin'd to leave Boston, when I reflected that I had already made myself a little obnoxious to the governing Party; and from the arbitrary Proceedings of the Assembly in my Brother's Case it was likely I might if I stay'd soon bring myself into Scrapes; and farther that my indiscreet

8. "I fancy his harsh and tyrannical Treatment of me, might be a means of impressing me with that Aversion to arbitrary Power that has stuck to me thro' my whole Life" [Franklin's note].
9. On June 11, 1722, the *Courant* hinted that there was collusion between local authorities and pirates raiding off Boston Harbor. James Franklin was jailed from June 12 to July 7. "Assembly": Massachusetts

legislative body; the lower house, with representatives elected by towns of the Massachusetts general court.
1. Insults, annoyances.
2. Satirizing.
3. The paper continued under Franklin's name until 1726, nearly three years after he left Boston.
4. Printer's term for errors (Latin).

Disputations about Religion began to make me pointed at with Horror by good People, as an Infidel or Atheist; I determin'd on the Point: but my Father now siding with my Brother, I was sensible that if I attempted to go openly, Means would be used to prevent me. My Friend Collins therefore undertook to manage a little for me. He agreed with the Captain of a New York Sloop for my Passage, under the Notion of my being a young Acquaintance of his that had got a naughty Girl with Child, whose Friends would compel me to marry her, and therefore I could not appear or come away publicly. So I sold some of my Books to raise a little Money, was taken on board privately, and as we had a fair Wind, in three Days I found myself in New York near 300 Miles from home, a Boy of but 17, without the least Recommendation to or Knowledge of any Person in the Place, and with very little Money in my Pocket.

My Inclinations for the Sea, were by this time worn out, or I might now have gratified them. But having a Trade, and supposing myself a pretty good Workman, I offer'd my Service to the Printer of the Place, old Mr. William Bradford.[5] He could give me no Employment, having little to do, and Help enough already: But, says he, my Son at Philadelphia has lately lost his principal Hand, Aquila Rose, by Death. If you go thither I believe he may employ you. Philadelphia was 100 Miles farther. I set out, however, in a Boat for Amboy;[6] leaving my Chest and Things to follow me round by Sea. In crossing the Bay we met with a Squall that tore our rotten Sails to pieces, prevented our getting into the Kill,[7] and drove us upon Long Island. In our Way a drunken Dutchman, who was a Passenger too, fell overboard; when he was sinking I reach'd thro' the Water to his shock Pate[8] and drew him up so that we got him in again. His Ducking sober'd him a little, and he went to sleep, taking first out of his Pocket a Book which he desir'd I would dry for him. It prov'd to be my old favorite Author Bunyan's Pilgrim's Progress[9] in Dutch, finely printed on good Paper with copper Cuts,[1] a Dress better than I had ever seen it wear in its own Language. I have since found that it has been translated into most of the Languages of Europe, and suppose it has been more generally read than any other Book except perhaps the Bible. Honest John was the first that I know of who mix'd Narration and Dialogue, a Method of Writing very engaging to the Reader, who in the most interesting Parts finds himself as it were brought into the Company, and present at the Discourse. Defoe in his Crusoe, his Moll Flanders, Religious Courtship, Family Instructor, and other Pieces, has imitated it with Success.[2] And Richardson has done the same in his Pamela,[3] etc.

When we drew near the Island we found it was at a Place where there could be no Landing, there being a great Surf on the stony Beach. So we dropped Anchor and swung round towards the Shore. Some People came down to the Water Edge and hallow'd to us, as we did to them. But the Wind was so high and the Surf so loud, that we could not hear so as to understand each other.

---

5. William Bradford (1663–1752), one of the first American printers and father of Andrew Bradford (1686–1742), Franklin's future competitor in Philadelphia.
6. Perth Amboy, New Jersey.
7. The narrow channel with separates Staten Island, New York, from New Jersey.
8. Shaggy head of hair.
9. See n. 3, p. 232.

1. Engravings.
2. Daniel Defoe (1659?–1731) published Robinson Crusoe in 1719, Moll Flanders in 1722, Religious Courtship in 1772, and The Family Instructor in 1715–18.
3. Samuel Richardson (1689–1761) published his novel Pamela: Or Virtue Rewarded in 1740. Franklin reprinted Richardson's first novel in 1744 and in doing so published the first novel in America.

There were Canoes on the Shore, and we made Signs and hallow'd that they
should fetch us, but they either did not understand us, or thought it impracticable. So they went away, and Night coming on, we had no Remedy but to
wait till the Wind should abate, and in the mean time the Boatman and I
concluded to sleep if we could, and so crowded into the Scuttle[4] with the
Dutchman who was still wet, and the Spray beating over the Head of our Boat,
leak'd thro' to us, so that we were soon almost as wet as he. In this Manner we
lay all Night with very little Rest. But the Wind abating the next Day, we
made a Shift to reach Amboy before Night, having been 30 hours on the
Water without Victuals, or any Drink but a Bottle of filthy Rum: The Water
we sail'd on being salt.

In the Evening I found myself very feverish, and went ill to Bed. But having
read somewhere that cold Water drank plentifully was good for a Fever, I
follow'd the Prescription, sweat plentifully most of the Night, my Fever left
me, and in the Morning crossing the Ferry, proceeded on my Journey, on
foot, having 50 Miles to Burlington,[5] where I was told I should find Boats that
would carry me the rest of the Way to Philadelphia.

It rain'd very hard all the Day, I was thoroughly soak'd, and by Noon a good
deal tir'd, so I stopped at a poor Inn, where I stayed all Night, beginning now
to wish I had never left home. I cut so miserable a Figure too, that I found by
the Questions ask'd me I was suspected to be some runaway Servant, and in
danger of being taken up on that Suspicion. However I proceeded the next
Day, and got in the Evening to an Inn within 8 or 10 Miles of Burlington,
kept by one Dr. Browne.[6]

He entered into Conversation with me while I took some Refreshment, and
finding I had read a little, became very sociable and friendly. Our Acquaintance continu'd as long as he liv'd. He had been, I imagine, an itinerant
Doctor, for there was no Town in England, or Country in Europe, of which
he could not give a very particular Account. He had some Letters,[7] and was
ingenious, but much of an Unbeliever, and wickedly undertook some Years
after to travesty the Bible in doggerel Verse as Cotton had done Virgil.[8] By this
means he set many of the Facts in a very ridiculous Light, and might have
hurt weak minds if his Work had been publish'd: but it never was. At his
House I lay that Night, and the next Morning reach'd Burlington.—But had
the Mortification to find that the regular Boats were gone a little before my
coming, and no other expected to go till Tuesday, this being Saturday. Wherefore I return'd to an old Woman in the Town of whom I had bought Ginger-
bread to eat on the Water, and ask'd her Advice; she invited me to lodge at her
House till a Passage by Water should offer; and being tired with my foot Traveling, I accepted the Invitation. She understanding I was a Printer, would have
had me stay at that Town and follow my Business, being ignorant of the Stock
necessary to begin with. She was very hospitable, gave me a Dinner of Ox
Cheek with great Goodwill, accepting only of a Pot of Ale in return. And I
thought myself fix'd till Tuesday should come. However walking in the Eve-

4. A hole or opening in a ship's deck provided with a
movable cover or lid.
5. Then the capital of West Jersey, about eighteen
miles north of Philadelphia.
6. Dr. John Browne (c. 1667–1737), innkeeper in
Burlington, and a noted religious skeptic as well as

physician.
7. I.e., education.
8. Charles Cotton (1630–87), who parodied the first
and fourth books of the *Aeneid* in his *Scarronides*
(1664). The opening lines are: "I sing the Man (read
it who list), / A Trojan true as ever pissed."

ning by the Side of the River a Boat came by, which I found was going towards Philadelphia with several People in her. They took me in, and as there was no Wind, we row'd all the Way; and about Midnight not having yet seen the City, some of the Company were confident we must have pass'd it, and would row no farther, the others knew not where we were, so we put towards the Shore, got into a Creek, landed near an old Fence with the Rails of which we made a Fire, the Night being cold, in October, and there we remain'd till Daylight. Then one of the Company knew the Place to be Cooper's Creek a little above Philadelphia, which we saw as soon as we got out of the Creek, and arriv'd there about 8 or 9 aClock, on the Sunday morning, and landed at the Market Street Wharf.[9]

I have been the more particular in this Description of my Journey, and shall be so of my first Entry into that City, that you may in your Mind compare such unlikely Beginning with the Figure I have since made there. I was in my working Dress, my best Clothes being to come round by Sea. I was dirty from my Journey; my Pockets were stuff'd out with Shirts and Stockings; I knew no Soul, nor where to look for Lodging. I was fatigu'd with Traveling, Rowing and Want of Rest. I was very hungry, and my whole Stock of Cash consisted of a Dutch Dollar and about a Shilling in Copper. The latter I gave the People of the Boat for my Passage, who at first refus'd it on Account of my Rowing; but I insisted on their taking it, a Man being sometimes more generous when he has but a little Money than when he has plenty, perhaps thro' Fear of being thought to have but little. Then I walk'd up the Street, gazing about, till near the Market House I met a Boy with Bread. I had made many a Meal on Bread, and inquiring where he got it, I went immediately to the Baker's he directed me to in Second Street; and ask'd for Biscuit, intending such as we had in Boston, but they it seems were not made in Philadelphia, then I ask'd for a three-penny Loaf, and was told they had none such: so not considering or knowing the Difference of Money and the greater Cheapness nor the Names of his Bread, I bad him give me three pennyworth of any sort. He gave me accordingly three great Puffy Rolls. I was surpris'd at the Quantity, but took it, and having no Room in my Pockets, walk'd off, with a Roll under each Arm, and eating the other. Thus I went up Market Street as far as Fourth Street, passing by the Door of Mr. Read, my future Wife's Father, when she standing at the Door saw me, and thought I made as I certainly did a most awkward ridiculous Appearance. Then I turn'd and went down Chestnut Street and part of Walnut Street, eating my Roll all the Way, and coming round found myself again at Market Street Wharf, near the Boat I came in, to which I went for a Drought of the River Water, and being fill'd with one of my Rolls, gave the other two to a Woman and her Child that came down the River in the Boat with us and were waiting to go farther. Thus refresh'd I walk'd again up the Street, which by this time had many clean dress'd People in it who were all walking the same Way; I join'd them, and thereby was led into the great Meeting House of the Quakers near the Market. I sat down among them, and after looking round a while and hearing nothing said, being very drowsy thro' Labor and want of Rest the preceding Night, I fell fast asleep, and continu'd so till the Meeting broke up, when one was kind enough to rouse me. This was therefore the first House I was in or slept in, in Philadelphia.

9. October 6, 1723.

Walking again down towards the River, and looking in the Faces of People, I met a young Quaker Man whose Countenance I lik'd, and accosting him requested he would tell me where a Stranger could get Lodging. We were then near the Sign of the Three Mariners. Here, says he, is one Place that entertains Strangers, but it is not a reputable House; if thee wilt walk with me, I'll show thee a better. He brought me to the Crooked Billet in Water Street. Here I got a Dinner. And while I was eating it, several sly Questions were ask'd me, as it seem'd to be suspected from my youth and Appearance, that I might be some Runaway. After Dinner my Sleepiness return'd: and being shown to a Bed, I lay down without undressing, and slept till Six in the Evening; was call'd to Supper; went to Bed again very early and slept soundly till the next Morning. Then I made myself as tidy as I could, and went to Andrew Bradford the Printer's. I found in the Shop the old Man his Father, whom I had seen at New York, and who traveling on horse back had got to Philadelphia before me. He introduc'd me to his Son, who receiv'd me civilly, gave me a Breakfast, but told me he did not at present want a Hand, being lately supplied with one. But there was another Printer in town lately set up, one Keimer,[1] who perhaps might employ me; if not, I should be welcome to lodge at his House, and he would give me a little Work to do now and then till fuller Business should offer.

The old Gentleman said, he would go with me to the new Printer: And when we found him, Neighbor, says Bradford, I have brought to see you a young Man of your Business, perhaps you may want such a One. He ask'd me a few Questions, put a Composing Stick[2] in my Hand to see how I work'd, and then said he would employ me soon, tho' he had just then nothing for me to do. And taking old Bradford whom he had never seen before, to be one of the Townspeople that had a Goodwill for him, enter'd into a Conversation on his present Undertaking and Prospects; while Bradford not discovering that he was the other Printer's Father; on Keimer's Saying he expected soon to get the greatest Part of the Business into his own Hands, drew him on by artful Questions and starting little Doubts, to explain all his Views, what Interest he relied on, and in what manner he intended to proceed. I who stood by and heard all, saw immediately that one of them was a crafty old Sophister,[3] and the other a mere Novice. Bradford left me with Keimer, who was greatly surpris'd when I told him who the old Man was.

Keimer's Printing-House I found, consisted of an old shatter'd Press and one small worn-out Font of English,[4] which he was then using himself, composing in it an Elegy on Aquila Rose[5] before-mentioned, an ingenious young Man of excellent Character much respected in the Town, Clerk of the Assembly,[6] and a pretty Poet. Keimer made Verses, too, but very indifferently. He could not be said to write them, for his Manner was to compose them in the Types directly out of his Head; so there being no Copy, but one Pair of Cases,[7] and the Elegy likely to require all the Letter, no one could help him. I endeavor'd to put his Press (which he had not yet us'd, and of which he understood noth-

1. Samuel Keimer (c. 1688–1742) was a printer in London before coming to Philadelphia.
2. An instrument of adjustable width in which type is set before being put on a galley.
3. Trickster, rationalizer.
4. An oversized type, not practicable for books and newspapers.

5. Journeyman printer (c. 1695–1723) for Andrew Bradford; his son Joseph apprenticed with Franklin.
6. One who has charge of the records, documents, and correspondence of any organized body; here, the Pennsylvania legislative council.
7. Two shallow trays that contain uppercase and lowercase type.

ing) into Order fit to be work'd with; and promising to come and print off his Elegy as soon as he should have got it ready, I return'd to Bradford's who gave me a little Job to do for the present, and there I lodged and dieted.[8] A few Days after Keimer sent for me to print off the Elegy. And now he had got another Pair of Cases, and a Pamphlet to reprint, on which he set me to work.

These two Printers I found poorly qualified for their Business. Bradford had not been bred to it, and was very illiterate; and Keimer tho' something of a Scholar, was a mere Compositor, knowing nothing of Presswork. He had been one of the French Prophets[9] and could act their enthusiastic Agitations. At this time he did not profess any particular Religion, but something of all on occasion; was very ignorant of the World, and had, as I afterwards found, a good deal of the Knave in his Composition. He did not like my Lodging at Bradford's while I work'd with him. He had a House indeed, but without Furniture, so he could not lodge me: But he got me a Lodging at Mr. Read's before-mentioned, who was the Owner of his House. And my Chest and Clothes being come by this time, I made rather a more respectable Appearance in the Eyes of Miss Read, than I had done when she first happen'd to see me eating my Roll in the Street.

I began now to have some Acquaintance among the young People of the Town, that were Lovers of Reading with whom I spent my Evenings very pleasantly and gaining Money by my Industry and Frugality, I lived very agreeably, forgetting Boston as much as I could, and not desiring that any there should know where I resided except my Friend Collins who was in my Secret, and kept it when I wrote to him. At length an Incident happened that sent me back again much sooner than I had intended.

I had a Brother-in-law, Robert Homes,[1] Master of a Sloop that traded between Boston and Delaware. He being at New Castle 40 Miles below Philadelphia, heard there of me, and wrote me a Letter, mentioning the Concern of my Friends in Boston at my abrupt Departure, assuring me of their Goodwill to me, and that everything would be accommodated to my Mind if I would return, to which he exhorted me very earnestly. I wrote an Answer to his Letter, thank'd him for his Advice, but stated my Reasons for quitting Boston fully, and in such a Light as to convince him I was not so wrong as he had apprehended. Sir William Keith[2] Governor of the Province, was then at New Castle, and Captain Homes happening to be in Company with him when my Letter came to hand, spoke to him of me, and show'd him the Letter. The Governor read it, and seem'd surpris'd when he was told my Age. He said I appear'd a young Man of promising Parts, and therefore should be encouraged: The Printers at Philadelphia were wretched ones, and if I would set up there, he made no doubt I should succeed; for his Part, he would procure me the public Business, and do me every other Service in his Power. This my Brother-in-Law afterwards told me in Boston. But I knew as yet nothing of it; when one Day Keimer and I being at Work together near the Window, we saw the Governor and another Gentleman (which prov'd to be Colonel French, of New Castle) finely dress'd, come directly across the Street to our House, and heard them at the Door.

8. Boarded.
9. An English sect that preached doomsday and cultivated emotional fits.
1. Husband of Franklin's sister Mary, and a ship's captain (d. before 1743).
2. Keith (1680–1749) was governor of Pennsylvania from 1717 to 1726; he fled to England in 1728 to escape debtor's prison.

Keimer ran down immediately, thinking it a Visit to him. But the Governor enquir'd for me, came up, and with a Condescension and Politeness I had been quite unus'd to, made me many Compliments, desired to be acquainted with me, blam'd me kindly for not having made myself known to him when I first came to the Place, and would have me away with him to the Tavern where he was going with Colonel French to taste as he said some excellent Madeira. I was not a little surpris'd, and Keimer star'd like a Pig poison'd. I went however with the Governor and Colonel French, to a Tavern the Corner of Third Street, and over the Madeira he propos'd my Setting up my Business, laid before me the Probabilities of Success, and both he and Colonel French assur'd me I should have their Interest and Influence in procuring the Public-Business of both Governments. On my doubting whether my Father would assist me in it, Sir William said he would give me a Letter to him, in which he would state the Advantages, and he did not doubt of prevailing with him. So it was concluded I should return to Boston in the first Vessel with the Governor's Letter recommending me to my Father.

In the meantime the Intention was to be kept secret, and I went on working with Keimer as usual, the Governor sending for me now and then to dine with him, a very great Honor I thought it, and conversing with me in the most affable, familiar, and friendly manner imaginable. About the End of April 1724, a little Vessel offer'd for Boston. I took Leave of Keimer as going to see my Friends. The Governor gave me an ample Letter, saying many flattering things of me to my Father, and strongly recommending the Project of my setting up at Philadelphia, as a Thing that must make my Fortune. We struck on a Shoal in going down the Bay and sprung a Leak, we had a blustring time at Sea, and were oblig'd to pump almost continually, at which I took my Turn. We arriv'd safe however at Boston in about a Fortnight. I had been absent Seven Months and my Friends had heard nothing of me, for my Brother Homes was not yet return'd; and had not written about me. My unexpected Appearance surpris'd the Family; all were however very glad to see me and made me Welcome, except my Brother.

I went to see him at his Printing-House: I was better dress'd than ever while in his Service, having a genteel new Suit from Head to foot, a Watch, and my Pockets lin'd with near Five Pounds Sterling in Silver. He receiv'd me not very frankly, look'd me all over, and turn'd to his Work again. The Journeymen were inquisitive where I had been, what sort of a Country it was, and how I lik'd it? I prais'd it much, and the happy Life I led in it; expressing strongly my Intention of returning to it; and one of them asking what kind of Money we had there, I produc'd a handful of Silver and spread it before them, which was a kind of Raree-Show[3] they had not been us'd to, Paper being the Money of Boston. Then I took an Opportunity of letting them see my Watch: and lastly, (my Brother still grum and sullen) I gave them a Piece of Eight to drink[4] and took my Leave. This Visit of mine offended him extremely. For when my Mother some time after spoke to him of a Reconciliation, and of her Wishes to see us on good Terms together, and that we might live for the future as Brothers, he said, I had insulted him in such a Manner before his People that he could never forget or forgive it. In this however he was mistaken.

---

3. A sidewalk peep show; silver coins were rare in the colonies.

4. A Spanish dollar with which they could buy drinks.

My Father receiv'd the Governor's Letter with some apparent Surprise; but said little of it to me for some Days; when Captain Homes returning, he show'd it to him, ask'd if he knew Keith, and what kind of a Man he was: Adding his Opinion that he must be of small Discretion, to think of setting a Boy up in Business who wanted yet 3 Years of being at Man's Estate. Homes said what he could in favor of the Project; but my Father was clear in the Impropriety of it; and at last gave a flat Denial to it. Then he wrote a civil Letter to Sir William thanking him for the Patronage he had so kindly offered me, but declining to assist me as yet in Setting up, I being in his Opinion too young to be trusted with the Management of a Business so important; and for which the Preparation must be so expensive.

My Friend and Companion Collins, who was a Clerk at the Post-Office, pleas'd with the Account I gave him of my new Country, determin'd to go thither also: And while I waited for my Father's Determination,[5] he set out before me by Land to Rhode Island, leaving his Books which were a pretty Collection of Mathematics and Natural Philosophy,[6] to come with mine and me to New York where he propos'd to wait for me. My Father, tho' he did not approve Sir William's Proposition, was yet pleas'd that I had been able to obtain so advantageous a Character from a Person of such Note where I had resided, and that I had been so industrious and careful as to equip myself so handsomely in so short a time: therefore seeing no Prospect of an Accommodation between my Brother and me, he gave his Consent to my Returning again to Philadelphia, advis'd me to behave respectfully to the People there, endeavor to obtain the general Esteem, and avoid lampooning and libeling to which he thought I had too much Inclination; telling me, that by steady Industry and a prudent Parsimony, I might save enough by the time I was One and Twenty to set me up, and that if I came near the Matter he would help me out with the Rest. This was all I could obtain, except some small Gifts as Tokens of his and my Mother's Love, when I embark'd again for New York, now with their Approbation and their Blessing.

The Sloop putting in at Newport, Rhode Island, I visited my Brother John, who had been married and settled there some Years. He received me very affectionately, for he always lov'd me. A Friend of his, one Vernon, having some Money due to him in Pennsylvania, about 35 Pounds Currency, desired I would receive it for him, and keep it till I had his Directions what to remit it in. Accordingly he gave me an Order. This afterwards occasion'd me a good deal of Uneasiness. At Newport we took in a Number of Passengers for New York: Among which were two young Women, Companions, and a grave, sensible Matron-like Quaker-Woman with her Attendants. I had shown an obliging Readiness to do her some little Services which impress'd her I suppose with a degree of Goodwill towards me. Therefore when she saw a daily growing Familiarity between me and the two Young Women, which they appear'd to encourage, she took me aside and said, Young Man, I am concern'd for thee, as thou has no Friend with thee, and seems not to know much of the World, or of the Snares Youth is expos'd to; depend upon it those are very bad Women, I can see it in all their Actions, and if thee art not upon thy Guard, they will draw thee into some Danger: they are Strangers to thee, and I advise thee in a friendly Concern for thy Welfare, to have no Acquaintance with

5. Decision.                    6. I.e., natural science.

them. As I seem'd at first not to think so ill of them as she did, she mention'd some Things she had observ'd and heard that had escap'd my Notice; but now convinc'd me she was right. I thank'd her for her kind Advice, and promis'd to follow it. When we arriv'd at New York, they told me where they liv'd, and invited me to come and see them: but I avoided it. And it was well I did: For the next Day, the Captain miss'd a Silver Spoon and some other Things that had been taken out of his Cabin, and knowing that these were a Couple of Strumpets, he got a Warrant to search their Lodgings, found the stolen Goods, and had the Thieves punish'd. So tho' we had escap'd a sunken Rock which we scrap'd upon in the Passage, I thought this Escape of rather more Importance to me.

At New York I found my Friend Collins, who had arriv'd there some Time before me. We had been intimate from[7] Children, and had read the same Books together. But he had the Advantage of more time for Reading, and Studying and a wonderful Genius for Mathematical Learning in which he far outstripped me. While I liv'd in Boston most of my Hours of Leisure for Conversation were spent with him, and he continu'd a sober as well as an industrious Lad; was much respected for his Learning by several of the Clergy and other Gentlemen, and seem'd to promise making a good Figure in Life: but during my Absence he had acquir'd a Habit of Sotting[8] with Brandy; and I found by his own Account and what I heard from others, that he had been drunk every day since his Arrival at New York, and behav'd very oddly. He had gam'd too and lost his Money, so that I was oblig'd to discharge[9] his Lodgings, and defray his Expences to and at Philadelphia: Which prov'd extremely inconvenient to me. The then Governor of New York, Burnet,[1] Son of Bishop Burnet, hearing form the Captain that a young Man, one of his Passengers, had a great many Books, desired he would bring me to see him. I waited upon him accordingly, and should have taken Collins with me but that he was not sober. The Governor treated me with great Civility, show'd me his Library, which was a very large one, and we had a good deal of Conversation about Books and Authors. This was the second Governor who had done me the Honor to take Notice of me, which to a poor Boy like me was very pleasing.

We proceeded to Philadelphia. I received on the Way Vernon's Money, without which we could hardly have finish'd our Journey. Collins wish'd to be employ'd in some Counting House; but whether they discover'd his Dramming by his Breath, or by his Behavior, tho' he had some Recommendations, he met with no Success in any Application, and continu'd Lodging and Boarding at the same House with me and at my Expense. Knowing I had that Money of Vernon's he was continually borrowing of me, still promising Repayment as soon as he should be in Business. At length he had got so much of it, that I was distress'd to think what I should do, in case of being call'd on to remit it. His Drinking continu'd, about which we sometimes quarrel'd, for when a little intoxicated he was very fractious. Once in a Boat on the Delaware with some other young Men, he refused to row in his Turn: I will be row'd home, says he. We will not row you, says I. You must, says he, or stay all Night on the Water, just as you please. The others said, Let us row; What signifies it? But my Mind being soured with his other Conduct, I continu'd to refuse. So he swore he would make me row, or throw me overboard; and coming along

---

7. I.e., since.
8. Getting stupefied on.
9. To release him from debt by paying his bills.

1. William Burnet (1688–1729), governor of New York and New Jersey from 1720 to 1728, and governor of Massachusetts from 1728 to 1729.

stepping on the Thwarts[2] towards me, when he came up and struck at me, I clapped my Hand under his Crotch, and rising, pitch'd him headforemost into the River. I knew he was a good Swimmer, and so was under little Concern about him; but before he could get round to lay hold of the Boat, we had with a few Strokes pull'd her out of his Reach. And ever when he drew near the Boat, we ask'd if he would row, striking a few Strokes to slide her away from him. He was ready to die with Vexation, and obstinately would not promise to row; however seeing him at last beginning to tire, we lifted him in; and brought him home dripping wet in the Evening. We hardly exchang'd a civil Word afterwards; and a West India Captain who had a Commission to procure a Tutor for the Sons of a Gentleman at Barbados,[3] happening to meet with him, agreed to carry him thither. He left me then, promising to remit me the first Money he should receive in order to discharge the Debt. But I never heard of him after.

The Breaking into this Money of Vernon's was one of the first great Errata of my Life. And this Affair show'd that my Father was not much out in his Judgment when he suppos'd me too Young to manage Business of Importance. But Sir William, on reading his Letter, said he was too prudent. There was great Difference in Persons, and Discretion did not always accompany Years, nor was Youth always without it. And since he will not set you up, says he, I will do it myself. Give me an Inventory of the Things necessary to be had from England, and I will send for them. You shall repay me when you are able; I am resolv'd to have a good Printer here, and I am sure you must succeed. This was spoken with such an Appearance of Cordiality, that I had not the least doubt of his meaning what he said. I had hitherto kept the Proposition of my Setting up a Secret in Philadelphia, and I still kept it. Had it been known that I depended on the Governor, probably some Friend that knew him better would have advis'd me not to rely on him, as I afterwards heard it as his known Character to be liberal of Promises which he never meant to keep. Yet unsolicited as he was by me, how could I think his generous Offers insincere? I believ'd him one of the best Men in the World.

I presented him an Inventory of a little Printing-House, amounting by my Computation to about 100 Pounds Sterling. He lik'd it, but ask'd me if my being on the Spot in England to choose the Types and see that everything was good of the kind, might not be of some Advantage. Then, says he, when there, you may make Acquaintances and establish Correspondences in the Bookselling, and Stationery Way. I agreed that this might be advantageous. Then says he, get yourself ready to go with Annis;[4] which was the annual Ship, and the only one at that Time usually passing between London and Philadelphia. But it would be some Months before Annis sail'd, so I continu'd working with Keimer, fretting about the Money Collins had got from me, and in daily Apprehensions of being call'd upon by Vernon, which however did not happen for some Years after.

I believe I have omitted mentioning that in my first Voyage from Boston, being becalm'd off Block Island,[5] our People set about catching Cod and haul'd up a great many. Hitherto I had stuck to my Resolution of not eating animal Food; and on this Occasion, I consider'd with my Master Tryon, the taking every Fish as a kind of unprovok'd Murder, since none of them had or

---

2. The seat on which an oarsman sits.
3. Island in the British West Indies.
4. Thomas Annis, captain of the *London Hope*, the

packet boat on which Franklin sailed to London in 1724.
5. Off the coast of Rhode Island.

ever could do us any Injury that might justify the Slaughter. All this seem'd very reasonable. But I had formerly been a great Lover of Fish, and when this came hot out of the Frying Pan, it smelt admirably well. I balanc'd some time between Principle and Inclination: till I recollected, that when the Fish were opened, I saw smaller Fish taken out of their Stomachs: Then, thought I, if you eat one another, I don't see why we mayn't eat you. So I din'd upon Cod very heartily and continu'd to eat with other People, returning only now and then occasionally to a vegetable Diet. So convenient a thing it is to be a *reasonable Creature*, since it enables one to find or make a Reason for everything one has a mind to do.

Keimer and I liv'd on a pretty good familiar Footing and agreed tolerably well: for he suspected nothing of my Setting up. He retain'd a great deal of his old Enthusiasms, and lov'd an Argumentation. We therefore had many Disputations. I us'd to work him so with my Socratic Method, and had trapann'd[6] him so often by Questions apparently so distant from any Point we had in hand, and yet by degrees led to the Point, and brought him into Difficulties and Contradictions, that at last he grew ridiculously cautious, and would hardly answer me the most common Question, without asking first, *What do you intend to infer from that?* However it gave him so high an Opinion of my Abilities in the Confuting Way, that he seriously propos'd my being his Colleague in a Project he had of setting up a new Sect. He was to preach the Doctrines, and I was to confound all Opponents. When he came to explain with me upon the Doctrines, I found several Conundrums[7] which I objected to, unless I might have my Way a little too, and introduce some of mine. Keimer wore his Beard at full Length, because somewhere in the Mosaic Law it is said, *thou shalt not mar the Corners of thy Beard.*[8] He likewise kept the seventh-day Sabbath; and these two Points were Essentials with him. I dislik'd both, but agreed to admit them upon Condition of his adopting the Doctrine of using no animal Food. I doubt, says he, my Constitution will not bear that. I assur'd him it would, and that he would be the better for it. He was usually a great Glutton, and I promis'd myself some Diversion in half-starving him. He agreed to try the Practice if I would keep him Company. I did so and we held it for three Months. We had our Victuals dress'd and brought to us regularly by a Woman in the Neighborhood, who had from me a List of 40 Dishes to be prepar'd for us at different times, in all which there was neither Fish Flesh nor Fowl, and the Whim suited me the better at this time from the Cheapness of it, not costing us about 18 Pence Sterling each, per Week. I have since kept several Lents most strictly, leaving the common Diet for that, and that for the common, abruptly, without the least Inconvenience: So that I think there is little in the Advice of making those Changes by easy Gradations. I went on pleasantly, but Poor Keimer suffer'd grievously, tir'd of the Project, long'd for the Flesh Pots of Egypt,[9] and order'd a roast Pig. He invited me and two Women Friends to dine with him, but it being brought too soon upon table, he could not resist the Temptation, and ate it all up before we came.

I had made some Courtship during this time to Miss Read. I had a great

---

6. Trapped.
7. Puzzles, difficult questions.
8. "Ye shall not round the corners of your heads, neither shalt thou mar the corners of thy beard" (Leviticus 19.27). Keimer probably also wore his hair long.
9. "And the whole congregation of the children of Israel murmured against Moses and Aaron in the wilderness: And the children of Israel said unto them, Would to God we had died by the hand of the Lord in the land of Egypt, when we sat by the flesh pots, and when we did eat bread to the full" (Exodus 16.2–3).

Respect and Affection for her, and had some Reason to believe she had the same for me: but as I was about to take a long Voyage, and we were both very young, only a little above 18, it was thought most prudent by her Mother to prevent our going too far at present, as a Marriage if it was to take place would be more convenient after my Return, when I should be as I expected set up in my Business. Perhaps too she thought my Expectations not so well founded as I imagined them to be.

My chief Acquaintances at this time were, Charles Osborne, Joseph Watson, and James Ralph;[1] All Lovers of Reading. The two first were Clerks to an eminent Scrivener or Conveyancer in the Town, Charles Brockden;[2] the other was Clerk to a Merchant. Watson was a pious sensible young Man, of great integrity. The others rather more lax in their Principles of Religion, particularly Ralph, who as well as Collins had been unsettled by me, for which they both made me suffer. Osborne was sensible, candid, frank, sincere, and affectionate to his Friends; but in literary Matters too fond of Criticizing. Ralph, was ingenious, genteel in his Manners, and extremely eloquent; I think I never knew a prettier Talker. Both of them great Admirers of Poetry, and began to try their Hands in little Pieces. Many pleasant Walks we four had together, on Sundays into the Woods near Skuylkill,[3] where we read to one another and conferr'd on what we read. Ralph was inclin'd to pursue the Study of Poetry, not doubting but he might become eminent in it and make his Fortune by it, alledging that the best Poets must when they first began to write, make as many Faults as he did. Osborne dissuaded him, assur'd him he had no Genius for Poetry, and advis'd him to think of nothing beyond the Business he was bred to; that in the mercantile way tho' he had no Stock, he might by his Diligence and Punctuality recommend himself to Employment as a Factor,[4] and in time acquire wherewith to trade on his own Account. I approv'd the amusing oneself with Poetry now and then, so far as to improve one's Language, but no farther. On this it was propos'd that we should each of us at our next Meeting produce a Piece of our own Composing, in order to improve by our mutual Observations, Criticisms and Corrections. As Language and Expression was what we had in View, we excluded all Considerations of Invention,[5] by agreeing that the Task should be a Version of the 18th Psalm, which describes the Descent of a Deity.[6] When the Time of our Meeting drew nigh, Ralph call'd on me first, and let me know his Piece was ready. I told him I had been busy, and having little Inclination had done nothing. He then show'd me his Piece for my Opinion; and I much approv'd it, as it appear'd to me to have great Merit. Now, says he, Osborne never will allow the least Merit in any thing of mine, but makes 1000 Criticisms out of mere Envy. He is not so jealous of you. I wish therefore you would take this Piece, and produce it as yours. I will pretend not to have had time, and so produce nothing. We shall then see what he will say to it. It was agreed, and I immediately transcrib'd it that it might appear in my own hand. We met.

Watson's Performance was read: there were some Beauties in it: but many Defects. Osborne's was read: It was much better. Ralph did it Justice, remark'd some Faults, but applauded the Beauties. He himself had nothing to produce.

1. Charles Osborne's dates are unknown. Joseph Watson died about 1728. James Ralph (c. 1695–1762) became well known as a political journalist.
2. Brockden (1683–1769) came to Philadelphia in 1706. "Conveyancer": one who draws up leases and deeds.

3. Schuylkill River, at Philadelphia.
4. Business agent.
5. I.e., originality.
6. "He bowed the heavens also, and came down: and darkness was under his feet" (Psalm 18.9).

I was backward, seem'd desirous of being excus'd, had not had sufficient Time to correct; etc., but no Excuse could be admitted, produce I must. It was read and repeated; Watson and Osborne gave up the Contest; and join'd in applauding it immoderately. Ralph only made some Criticisms and propos'd some Amendments, but I defended my Text. Osborne was against Ralph, and told him he was no better a Critic than Poet; so he dropped the Argument. As they two went home together, Osborne express'd himself still more strongly in favor of what he thought my Production, having restrain'd himself before as he said, lest I should think it Flattery. But who would have imagin'd, says he, that Franklin had been capable of such a Performance; such Painting, such Force! such Fire! He has even improv'd the Original! In his common Conversation, he seems to have no Choice of Words; he hesitates and blunders; and yet, good God, how he writes!

When we next met, Ralph discover'd the Trick we had played him, and Osborne was a little laughed at. This Transaction fix'd Ralph in his Resolution of becoming a Poet. I did all I could to dissuade him from it, but he continu'd scribbling Verses, till Pope[7] cur'd him. He became however a pretty good Prose Writer. More of him hereafter. But as I may not have occasion again to mention the other two, I shall just remark here, that Watson died in my Arms a few Years after, much lamented, being the best of our Set. Osborne went to the West Indies, where he became an eminent Lawyer and made Money, but died young. He and I had made a serious Agreement, that the one who happen'd first to die, should if possible make a friendly Visit to the other, and acquaint him how he found things in that separate State. But he never fulfill'd his Promise.

The Governor, seeming to like my Company, had me frequently to his House; and his Setting me up was always mention'd as a fix'd thing. I was to take with me Letters recommendatory to a Number of his Friends, besides the Letter of Credit to furnish me with the necessary Money for purchasing the Press and Types, Paper, etc. For these Letters I was appointed to call at different times, when they were to be ready, but a future time was still[8] named. Thus we went on till the ship whose Departure too had been several times postponed was on the Point of sailing. Then when I call'd to take my Leave and receive the Letters, his Secretary, Dr. Bard,[9] came out to me and said the Governor was extremely busy, in writing, but would be down at New Castle[1] before the Ship, and there the Letters would be delivered to me.

Ralph, tho' married and having one Child, had determined to accompany me in this Voyage. It was thought he intended to establish a Correspondence, and obtain Goods to sell on Commission. But I found afterwards, that thro' some Discontent with his Wife's Relations, he purposed to leave her on their Hands, and never return again. Having taken leave of my Friends, and interchang'd some Promises with Miss Read, I left Philadelphia in the Ship, which anchor'd at New Castle. The Governor was there. But when I went to his Lodging, the Secretary came to me from him with the civilest Message in the World, that he could not then see me being engag'd in Business of the utmost Importance, but should send the Letters to me on board, wish'd me

---

7. In the 2nd edition of the *Dunciad* (1728), a poem that attacks ignorance of all kinds, Alexander Pope responded to Ralph's slur against him in *Sawney:* "Silence, ye Wolves; while Ralph to Cynthia howls. / And makes Night hideous—Answer him ye Owls" (book 3, lines 159–60). In the 1742 edition Pope included an-

other dig at Ralph: "And see: The very Gazeteers give o'er, / Ev'n Ralph repents" (book 1, lines 215–16).
8. Always.
9. Patrick Bard, or Baird, resided in Philadelphia as port physician after 1720.
1. Delaware.

heartily a good Voyage and a speedy Return, etc. I return'd on board, a little puzzled, but still not doubting.

Mr. Andrew Hamilton,[2] a famous Lawyer of Philadelphia, had taken Passage in the same Ship for himself and Son: and with Mr. Denham[3] a Quaker Merchant, and Messrs. Onion and Russel Masters of an Iron Work in Maryland, had engag'd the Great Cabin; so that Ralph and I were forc'd to take up with a Berth in the Steerage: And none on board knowing us, were considered as ordinary Persons. But Mr. Hamilton and his Son (it was James, since Governor) return'd from New Castle to Philadelphia the Father being recall'd by a great Fee to plead for a seized Ship. And just before we sail'd Colonel French coming on board, and showing me great Respect, I was more taken Notice of, and with my Friend Ralph invited by the other Gentlemen to come into the Cabin, there being now Room. Accordingly we remov'd thither.

Understanding that Colonel French had brought on board the Governor's Dispatches, I ask'd the Captain for those Letters that were to be under my Care. He said all were put into the Bag together; and he could not then come at them; but before we landed in England, I should have an Opportunity of picking them out. So I was satisfied for the present, and we proceeded on our Voyage. We had a sociable Company in the Cabin, and lived uncommonly well, having the Addition of all Mr. Hamilton's Stores, who had laid in plentifully. In this Passage Mr. Denham contracted a Friendship for me that continued during his Life. The Voyage was otherwise not a pleasant one, as we had a great deal of bad Weather.

When we came into the Channel, the Captain kept his Word with me, and gave me an Opportunity of examining the Bag for the Governor's Letters. I found none upon which my Name was put, as under my Care; I pick'd out 6 or 7 that by the Handwriting I thought might be the promis'd Letters, especially as one of them was directed to Basket[4] the King's Printer, and another to some Stationer. We arriv'd in London the 24th of December, 1724. I waited upon the Stationer who came first in my Way, delivering the Letter as from Governor Keith. I don't know such a Person, says he: but opening the Letter, O, this is from Riddlesden;[5] I have lately found him to be a complete Rascal, and I will have nothing to do with him, nor receive any Letters from him. So putting the Letter into my Hand, he turn'd on his Heel and left me to serve some Customer. I was surprised to find these were not the Governor's Letters. And after recollecting and comparing Circumstances, I began to doubt his Sincerity. I found my Friend Denham, and opened the whole Affair to him. He let me into Keith's Character, told me there was not the least Probability that he had written any Letters for me, that no one who knew him had the smallest Dependence on him, and he laughed at the Notion of the Governor's giving me a Letter of Credit, having as he said no Credit to give. On my expressing some Concern about what I should do: He advis'd me to endeavor getting some Employment in the Way of my Business. Among the Printers here, says he, you will improve yourself; and when you return to America, you will set up to greater Advantage.

We both of us happen'd to know, as well as the Stationer, that Riddlesden

2. Andrew Hamilton (c. 1678–1741), American-born lawyer; his successful defense of John Peter Zenger against a charge of libel established freedom of the press in the colonies and earned for Hamilton the so-briquet "the Philadelphia Lawyer." His son James Hamilton (c. 1710–1783) was governor of Pennsylva-

nia four times between 1748 and 1773.
3. Thomas Denham (d. 1728), merchant and benefactor, left Bristol, England, in 1715.
4. John Baskett (d. 1742).
5. William Riddlesden (d. before 1733), well known in Maryland as a man of "infamy."

the Attorney, was a very Knave. He had half ruin'd Miss Read's Father by drawing him in to be bound[6] for him. By his Letter it appear'd, there was a secret Scheme on foot to the Prejudice of Hamilton, (Suppos'd to be then coming over with us,) and that Keith was concern'd in it with Riddlesden. Denham, who was a Friend of Hamilton's, thought he ought to be acquainted with it. So when he arriv'd in England, which was soon after, partly from Resentment and Ill-Will to Keith and Riddlesden, and partly from Goodwill to him: I waited on him, and gave him the Letter. He thank'd me cordially, the Information being of Importance to him. And from that time he became my Friend, greatly to my Advantage afterwards on many Occasions.

But what shall we think of a Governor's playing such pitiful Tricks, and imposing so grossly on a poor ignorant Boy! It was a Habit he had acquired. He wish'd to please everybody; and having little to give, he gave Expectations. He was otherwise an ingenious sensible Man, a pretty good Writer, and a good Governor for the People, tho' not for his Constituents the Proprietaries,[7] whose Instructions he sometimes disregarded. Several of our best Laws were of his Planning, and pass'd during his Administration.

Ralph and I were inseparable Companions. We took Lodgings together in Little Britain[8] at 3 shillings 6 pence per Week, as much as we could then afford. He found some Relations, but they were poor and unable to assist him. He now let me know his Intentions of remaining in London, and that he never meant to return to Philadelphia. He had brought no Money with him, the whole he could muster having been expended in paying his Passage. I had 15 Pistoles.[9] So he borrowed occasionally of me, to subsist while he was looking out for Business. He first endeavor'd to get into the Playhouse, believing himself qualified for an Actor; but Wilkes,[1] to whom he applied, advis'd him candidly not to think of that Employment, as it was impossible he should succeed in it. Then he propos'd to Roberts, a Publisher in Paternoster Row,[2] to write for him a Weekly Paper like the Spectator, on certain Conditions, which Roberts did not approve. Then he endeavor'd to get Employment as a Hackney Writer[3] to copy for the Stationers and Lawyers about the Temple[4] but could find no Vacancy.

I immediately got into Work at Palmer's, then a famous Printing-House in Bartholomew Close;[5] and here I continu'd near a Year. I was pretty diligent; but spent with Ralph a good deal of my Earnings in going to Plays and other Places of Amusement. We had together consum'd all my Pistoles, and now just rubb'd[6] on from hand to mouth. He seem'd quite to forget his Wife and Child, and I by degrees my Engagements with Miss Read, to whom I never wrote more than one Letter, and that was to let her know I was not likely soon to return. This was another of the great Errata of my Life, which I should wish to correct if I were to live it over again. In fact, by our Expenses, I was constantly kept unable to pay my Passage.

6. I.e., as a cosigner of a document and legally bound to be responsible for his debts.
7. Members of the Penn family were the Proprietors of Pennsylvania and the legal owners of the state. "Constituents": those who appointed him their representative; in this case, the Penn family, which retained control of Pennsylvania until the Revolution.
8. A street in London near St. Paul's Cathedral.
9. A Spanish gold coin worth approximately eighteen shillings.

1. Robert Wilks (1665?–1732), an Irish actor, dominated London theater life from 1709 to 1730.
2. The center of the London printing business.
3. A copyist.
4. The Inner and Middle Temples were two of four buildings in London that were centers for the legal profession.
5. Just off Little Britain, and a square known for its printers and typesetters.
6. Proceeded with difficulty.

At Palmer's I was employ'd in Composing for the second Edition of Wollaston's Religion of Nature.[7] Some of his Reasonings not appearing to me well-founded, I wrote a little metaphysical Piece, in which I made Remarks on them. It was entitled, A *Dissertation on Liberty and Necessity, Pleasure and Pain*.[8] I inscrib'd it to my Friend Ralph. I printed a small Number. I occasion'd my being more consider'd by Mr. Palmer, as a young Man of some Ingenuity, tho' he seriously expostulated with me upon the Principles of my Pamplet which to him appear'd abominable. My printing this Pamphlet was another Erratum.

While I lodg'd in Little Britain I made an Acquaintance with one Wilcox a Bookseller, whose Shop was at the next Door. He had an immense Collection of second-hand Books. Circulating Libraries were not then in Use; but we agreed that on certain reasonable Terms which I have now forgotten, I might take, read and return any of his Books. This I esteem'd a great Advantage, and I made as much Use of it as I could.

My Pamphlet by some means falling into the Hands of one Lyons,[9] a Surgeon, Author of a Book entitled *The Infallibility of Human Judgment*, it occasioned an Acquaintance between us; he took great Notice of me, call'd on me often, to converse on these Subjects, carried me to the Horns a pale Ale-House in [blank] Lane, Cheapside, and introduc'd me to Dr. Mandeville,[1] Author of the Fable of the Bees who had a Club there, of which he was the Soul, being a most facetious entertaining Companion. Lyons too introduc'd me to Dr. Pemberton, at Batson's Coffee House,[2] who promis'd to give me an Opportunity some time or other of seeing Sir Isaac Newton,[3] of which I was extremely desirous; but this never happened.

I had brought over a few Curiosities among which the principal was a Purse made of the Asbestos, which purifies by Fire. Sir Hans Sloane[4] heard of it, came to see me, and invited me to his House in Bloomsbury Square; where he show'd me all his Curiosities, and persuaded me to let him add that to the Number, for which he paid me handsomely.

In our House there lodg'd a young Woman, a Millener, who I think had a shop in the Cloisters.[5] She had been genteelly bred, was sensible and lively, and of most pleasing Conversation. Ralph read Plays to her in the Evenings, they grew intimate, she took another Lodging, and he follow'd her. They liv'd together some time, but he being still out of Business, and her Income not sufficient to maintain them with her Child, he took a Resolution of going from London, to try for a Country School, which he thought himself well qualified to undertake, as he wrote an excellent Hand, and was a Master of Arithmetic and Accounts. This however he deem'd a Business below him, and confident of future better Fortune when he should be unwilling to have it

7. William Wollaston's *Religion of Nature* was first published in 1725. Franklin set the type for the 4th edition, which appeared in April 1726.
8. Franklin's pamphlet, of which only four copies are known to survive. By denying the existence of virtue and vice Franklin laid himself open to accusations of atheism.
9. William Lyons, a surgeon and author of *The Infallibility, Dignity, and Excellence of Human Judgment* (1719).
1. Bernard Mandeville (c. 1670–1733), a Dutch physician and man of letters residing in London. His *Fable of the Bees* was published in 1714.

2. Batson's in Cornhill was a favorite meeting place of physicians. Henry Pemberton (1694–1771) was a friend of Isaac Newton's and a member of the Royal Society.
3. Isaac Newton (1642–1727), best known for explaining the theories of gravity, light, and color, president of the Royal Society 1703–27.
4. Physician and naturalist (1660–1753), was the successor to Newton as president of the Royal Society; his library and museum served as the basis for the present collection at the British Museum.
5. Probably near St. Bartholomew's Church, London.

known that he once was so meanly employ'd, he chang'd his Name, and did me the Honor to assume mine. For I soon after had a Letter from him, acquainting me, that he was settled in a small Village in Berkshire, I think it was, where he taught reading and writing to 10 or a dozen Boys at 6 pence each per Week, recommending Mrs. T. to my Care, and desiring me to write to him directing for Mr. Franklin Schoolmaster at such a Place. He continu'd to write frequently, sending me large Specimens of an Epic Poem, which he was then composing, and desiring my Remarks and Corrections. These I gave him from time to time, but endeavor'd rather to discourage his Proceeding. One of Young's Satires was then just publish'd.[6] I copied and sent him a great Part of it, which set in a strong Light the Folly of pursuing the Muses with any Hope of Advancement by them. All was in vain. Sheets of the Poem continu'd to come by every Post. In the mean time Mrs. T. having on his Account lost her Friends and Business, was often in Distresses, and us'd to send for me, and borrow what I could spare to help her out of them. I grew fond of her Company, and being at this time under no Religious Restraints, and presuming on my Importance to her, I attempted Familiarities, (another Erratum) which she repuls'd with a proper Resentment, and acquainted him with my Behavior. This made a Breach between us, and when he return'd again to London, he let me know he thought I had cancel'd all the Obligations he had been under to me. So I found I was never to expect his Repaying me what I lent to him or advanc'd for him. This was however not then of much Consequence, as he was totally unable. And in the Loss of his Friendship I found myself reliev'd from a Burden. I now began to think of getting a little Money beforehand; and expecting better Work, I left Palmer's to work at Watts's[7] near Lincoln's Inn Fields, a still greater Printing-House. Here I continu'd all the rest of my Stay in London.

At my first Admission into this Printing-House, I took to working at Press, imagining I felt a Want of the Bodily Exercise I had been us'd to in America, where Presswork is mix'd with Composing. I drank only Water; the other Workmen, near 50 in Number, were great Guzzlers of Beer. On occasion I carried up and down Stairs a large Form of Types[8] in each hand, when others carried but one in both Hands. They wonder'd to see from this and several Instances that the Water-American as they call'd me was *stronger* than themselves who drunk *strong*[9] Beer. We had an Alehouse Boy who attended always in the House to supply the Workmen. My Companion at the Press drank every day a Pint before Breakfast, a Pint at Breakfast with his Bread and Cheese; a Pint between Breakfast and Dinner; a Pint at Dinner; a Pint in the Afternoon about Six o'clock, and another when he had done his Day's Work. I thought it a detestable Custom. But it was necessary, he suppos'd, to drink *strong* Beer that he might be *strong* to labor. I endeavor'd to convince him that the Bodily Strength afforded by Beer could only be in proportion to the Grain or Flour of the Barley dissolved in the Water of which it was made; that there was more Flour in a Penny-worth of Bread, and therefore if he would eat that with a Pint of Water, it would give him more Strength than a Quart of Beer. He drank on however, and had 4 or 5 Shillings to pay out of his Wages every

6. Edward Young (1683–1765) published the first four parts of *Love of Fame, the Universal Passion* in 1725.

7. John Watts (c. 1678–1763).
8. Type set and locked in metal frames.
9. Intoxicating.

Saturday Night for that muddling Liquor; an Expense I was free from. And thus these poor Devils keep themselves always under.[1]

Watts after some Weeks desiring to have me in the Composing-Room, I left the Pressmen. A new *Bienvenu*[2] or Sum for Drink, being 5 Shillings, was demanded of me by the Compositors.[3] I thought it an Imposition, as I had paid below. The Master thought so too, and forbad my Paying it. I stood out two or three Weeks, was accordingly considered as an Excommunicate, and had so many little Pieces of private Mischief done me, by mixing my Sorts,[4] transposing my Pages, breaking my Matter,[5] etc., etc. if I were ever so little out of the Room, and all ascrib'd to the Chapel[6] Ghost, which they said ever haunted those not regularly admitted, that notwithstanding the Master's Protection, I found myself oblig'd to comply and pay the Money; convinc'd of the Folly of being on ill Terms with those one is to live with continually. I was now on a fair Footing with them, and soon acquir'd considerable Influence. I propos'd some reasonable Alterations in their Chapel Laws, and carried them against all Opposition. From my Example a great Part of them, left their muddling Breakfast of Beer and Bread and Cheese, finding they could with me be supplied from a neighboring House with a large Porringer of hot Water-gruel, sprinkled with Pepper, crumb'd with Bread, and a Bit of Butter in it, for the Price of a Pint of Beer, viz., three halfpence. This was a more comfortable as well as cheaper Breakfast, and kept their Heads clearer. Those who continu'd sotting with Beer all day, were often, by not paying, out of Credit at the Alehouse, and us'd to make Interest with me to get Beer, *their Light*, as they phras'd it, *being out*. I watch'd the Pay table on Saturday Night, and collected what I stood engag'd for them, having to pay some times near Thirty Shillings a Week on their Accounts. This and my being esteem'd a pretty good Riggite,[7] that is a jocular verbal Satirist, supported my Consequence in the Society. My constant Attendance, (I never making a St. Monday),[8] recommended me to the Master; and my uncommon Quickness at Composing, occasion'd my being put upon all Work of Dispatch, which was generally better paid. So I went on now very agreeably.

My Lodging in Little Britain being too remote, I found another in Duke Street opposite to the Romish Chapel.[9] It was two pair of Stairs backwards at an Italian Warehouse. A Widow Lady kept the House; she had a Daughter and a Maid Servant, and a Journeyman who attended the Warehouse, but lodg'd abroad. After sending to enquire my Character at the House where I last lodg'd, she agreed to take me in at the same Rate, 3 Shillings 6 Pence per Week, cheaper as she said from the Protection she expected in having a Man lodge in the House. She was a Widow, an elderly Woman, had been bred a Protestant, being a Clergyman's Daughter, but was converted to the Catholic Religion by her Husband, whose Memory she much revered, had lived much among People of Distinction, and knew a 1000 Anecdotes of them as far back as the Times of Charles the second. She was lame in her Knees with the Gout, and therefore seldom stirr'd out of her Room, so sometimes wanted Company; and hers was so highly amusing to me that I was sure to spend an Evening

1. I.e., in poverty.
2. Welcome (French, literal trans.).
3. Typesetters.
4. Type, letters.
5. Type set up for printing.
6. "A Printing House is always called a Chappel by the Workmen" [Franklin's note]. The workers set their own customs, practices, and fines.
7. One who makes fun of others.
8. Taking Monday off as if it were a religious holiday.
9. The Roman Catholic Chapel of St. Anselm and St. Cecilia.

with her whenever she desired it. Our Supper was only half an Anchovy each, on a very little Strip of Bread and Butter, and half a Pint of Ale between us. But the Entertainment was in her Conversation. My always keeping good Hours, and giving little Trouble in the Family, made her unwilling to part with me; so that when I talk'd of a Lodging I had heard of, nearer my Business, for 2 Shillings a Week, which, intent as I now was on saving Money, made some Difference; she bid me not think of it, for she would abate me two Shillings a Week for the future, so I remain'd with her at 1 Shilling 6 Pence as long as I stayed in London.

In a Garret of her House there lived a Maiden Lady of 70 in the most retired Manner, of whom my Landlady gave me this Account, that she was a Roman Catholic, had been sent abroad when young and lodg'd in a Nunnery with an Intent of becoming a Nun: but the Country not agreeing with her, she return'd to England, where there being no Nunnery, she had vow'd to lead the Life of a Nun as near as might be done in those Circumstances: Accordingly She had given all her Estate to charitable Uses, reserving only Twelve Pounds a year to live on, and out of this Sum she still gave a great deal in Charity, living herself on Watergruel only, and using no Fire but to boil it. She had lived many Years in that Garret, being permitted to remain there gratis by successive catholic Tenants of the House below, as they deem'd it a Blessing to have her there. A Priest visited her, to confess her every Day. I have ask'd her, says my Landlady, how she, as she liv'd, could possibly find so much Employment for a Confessor? O, says she, it is impossible to avoid *vain Thoughts*. I was permitted once to visit her: She was cheerful and polite, and convers'd pleasantly. The Room was clean, but had no other Furniture than a Mattress, a Table with a Crucifix and Book, a Stool, which she gave me to sit on, and a Picture over the Chimney of *St. Veronica*,[1] displaying her Handkerchief with the miraculous Figure of Christ's bleeding Face on it, which she explain'd to me with great Seriousness. She look'd pale, but was never sick, and I give it as another Instance on how small an Income Life and Health may be supported.

At Watts's Printing-House I contracted an Acquaintance with an ingenious young Man, one Wygate, who having wealthy Relations, had been better educated than most Printers, was a tolerable Latinist, spoke French, and lov'd Reading. I taught him, and a Friend of his, to swim at twice going into the River, and they soon became good Swimmers. They introduc'd me to some Gentlemen from the Country who went to Chelsea by Water to see the College and Don Saltero's Curiosities.[2] In our Return, at the Request of the Company, whose Curiosity Wygate had excited, I stripped and leaped into the River, and swam from near Chelsea to Blackfriars,[3] performing on the Way many Feats of Activity both upon and under Water, that surpris'd and pleas'd those to whom they were Novelties. I had from a Child been ever delighted with this Exercise, had studied and practic'd all Thevenot's[4] Motions and Positions, added some of my own, aiming at the graceful and easy, as well as the Useful. All these I took this Occasion of exhibiting to the Company, and was much flatter'd by their Admiration. And Wygate, who was desirous of becom-

1. According to tradition, as Christ bore the cross, St. Veronica wiped his face with a cloth that miraculously retained the image of his face.
2. James Salter was a former barber of Sir Hans Sloane; he kept supposed curios, like Job's tears and pieces of the True Cross, on view. He was dubbed

Don Saltero by the *Tatler*. "College": i.e., Chelsea Hospital, erected on the site of the former Chelsea College.
3. I.e., more than three miles.
4. Melchisédeck de Thevenot, *The Art of Swimming* (1699).

ing a Master, grew more and more attach'd to me on that account, as well as from the Similarity of our Studies. He at length propos'd to me traveling all over Europe together, supporting ourselves every where by working at our Business. I was once inclin'd to it. But mentioning it to my good Friend Mr. Denham, with whom I often spent an Hour when I had Leisure, he dissuaded me from it; advising me to think only of returning to Pennsylvania, which he was now about to do.

I must record one Trait of this good Man's Character. He had formerly been in Business at Bristol, but fail'd in Debt to a Number of People, compounded[5] and went to America. There, by a close Application to Business as a Merchant, he acquir'd a plentiful Fortune in a few Years. Returning to England in the Ship with me, He invited his old Creditors to an Entertainment, at which he thank'd them for the easy Composition[6] they had favor'd him with, and when they expected nothing but the Treat, every Man at the first Remove[7] found under his Plate an Order on a Banker for the full Amount of the unpaid Remainder with Interest.

He now told me he was about to return to Philadelphia, and should carry over a great Quantity of Goods in order to open a Store there: He propos'd to take me over as his Clerk, to keep his Books (in which he would instruct me), copy his Letters, and attend the Store. He added, that as soon as I should be acquainted with mercantile Business he would promote me by sending me with a Cargo of Flour and Bread, etc., to the West Indies, and procure me Commissions from others; which would be profitable, and if I manag'd well, would establish me handsomely. The Thing pleas'd me, for I was grown tired of London, remember'd with Pleasure the happy Months I had spent in Pennsylvania, and wish'd again to see it. Therefore I immediately agreed, on the Terms of Fifty Pounds a Year, Pennsylvania Money; less indeed than my then Gettings as a Compositor, but affording a better Prospect.

I now took Leave of Printing, as I thought for ever, and was daily employ'd in my new Business; going about with Mr. Denham among the Tradesmen, to purchase various Articles, and see them pack'd up, doing Errands, calling upon Workmen to dispatch, etc., and when all was on board, I had a few Days' Leisure. On one of these Days I was to my Surprise sent for by a great Man I knew only by Name, a Sir William Wyndham and I waited upon him. He had heard by some means or other of my Swimming from Chelsey to Blackfriars, and of my teaching Wygate and another young Man to swim in a few Hours. He had two Sons about to set out on their Travels; he wish'd to have them first taught Swimming; and propos'd to gratify me handsomely if I would teach them. They were not yet come to Town and my Stay was uncertain, so I could not undertake it. But from this Incident I thought it likely, that if I were to remain in England and open a Swimming School, I might get a good deal of Money. And it struck me so strongly, that had the Overture been sooner made me, probably I should not so soon have returned to America. After Many Years, you and I had something of more Importance to do with one of these Sons of Sir William Wyndham,[8] become Earl of Egremont, which I shall mention in its Place.[9]

5. Settled part payment on his debts.
6. Conditions for accepting a declaration of bankruptcy.
7. I.e., the first time the plates were cleared.

8. Chancellor of the exchequer and Tory leader in Parliament (1687–1740).
9. Franklin does not mention Charles Wyndham (1710–1763) again.

Thus I spent about 18 Months in London. Most Part of the Time, I work'd hard at my Business, and spent but little upon myself except in seeing Plays, and in Books. My Friend Ralph had kept me poor. He owed me about 27 Pounds; which I was now never likely to receive; a great Sum out of my small Earnings. I lov'd him notwithstanding, for he had many amiable Qualities. Tho' I had by no means improv'd my Fortune, I had pick'd up some very ingenious Acquaintance whose Conversation was of great Advantage to me, and I had read considerably.

We sail'd from Gravesend on the 23d of July 1726. For The Incidents of the Voyage, I refer you to my Journal, where you will find them all minutely related. Perhaps the most important Part of that Journal is the *Plan*[1] to be found in it which I formed at Sea for regulating my future Conduct in Life. It is the more remarkable, as being form'd when I was so young, and yet being pretty faithfully adhered to quite thro' to old Age. We landed in Philadelphia the 11th of October, where I found sundry Alterations. Keith was no longer Governor, being superseded by Major Gordon:[2] I met him walking the Streets as a common Citizen. He seem'd a little asham'd at seeing me, but pass'd without saying anything. I should have been as much asham'd at seeing Miss Read, had not her Friends despairing with Reason of my Return, after the Receipt of my Letter, persuaded her to marry another, one Rogers, a Potter, which was done in my Absence. With him however she was never happy, and soon parted from him, refusing to cohabit with him, or bear his Name. It being now said that he had another Wife. He was a worthless Fellow tho' an excellent Workman which was the Temptation to her Friends. He got into Debt, and ran away in 1727 or 28, went to the West Indies, and died there. Keimer had got a better House, a Shop well supplied with Stationery, plenty of new Types, a number of Hands tho' none good, and seem'd to have a great deal of Business.

Mr. Denham took a Store in Water Street, where we open'd our Goods. I attended the Business diligently, studied Accounts, and grew in a little Time expert at selling. We lodg'd and boarded together, he counsel'd me as a Father, having a sincere Regard for me: I respected and lov'd him: and we might have gone on together very happily: But in the Beginning of February 1726/7 when I had just pass'd my 21st Year, we both were taken ill. My Distemper was a Pleurisy,[3] which very nearly carried me off: I suffered a good deal, gave up the Point[4] in my own mind, and was rather disappointed when I found myself recovering; regretting in some degree that I must now sometime or other have all that disagreeable Work to do over again. I forget what his Distemper was. It held him a long time, and at length carried him off. He left me a small Legacy in a nuncupative Will,[5] as a Token of his Kindness for me, and he left me once more to the wide World. For the Store was taken into the Care of his Executors, and my Employment under him ended: My Brother-in-law Homes, being now at Philadelphia, advis'd my Return to my Business. And Keimer tempted me with an Offer of large Wages by the Year to come and take the Management of his Printing-House that he might better attend his Stationer's Shop. I had heard a bad Character of him in London, from his

1. Only the "Outline" and "Preamble" of Franklin's *Plan* survive.
2. Patrick Gordon (1644–1736), governor of Pennsylvania from 1726 to 1736.
3. A disease of the lungs.
4. End; i.e., resigned himself to death.
5. An oral will.

Wife and her Friends, and was not fond of having any more to do with him. I tried for farther Employment as a Merchant's Clerk; but not readily meeting with any, I clos'd again with Keimer.

I found in *his* House these Hands; Hugh Meredith[6] a Welsh-Pennsylvanian, 30 Years of Age, bred to Country Work: honest, sensible, had a great deal of solid Observation, was something of a Reader, but given to drink: Stephen Potts,[7] a young Country Man of full Age, bred to the Same, of uncommon natural Parts[8] and great Wit and Humor, but a little idle. These he had agreed with at extreme low Wages, per Week, to be rais'd a Shilling every 3 Months, as they would deserve by improving in their Business, and the Expectation of these high Wages to come on hereafter was what he had drawn them in with. Meredith was to work at Press, Potts at Bookbinding, which he by Agreement, was to teach them, tho' he knew neither one nor t'other. John ——— a wild Irishman brought up to no Business, whose Service for 4 Years Keimer had purchas'd[9] from the Captain of a Ship. He too was to be made a Pressman. George Webb,[1] an Oxford Scholar, whose Time for 4 Years he had likewise bought, intending him for a Compositor: of whom more presently. And David Harry,[2] a Country Boy, whom he had taken Apprentice. I soon perceiv'd that the Intention of engaging me at Wages so much higher than he had been us'd to give, was to have these raw cheap Hands form'd thro' me, and as soon as I had instructed them, then, they being all articled to him, he should be able to do without me. I went on however, very cheerfully; put his Printing-House in Order, which had been in great Confusion, and brought his Hands by degrees to mind their Business and to do it better.

It was an odd Thing to find an Oxford Scholar in the Situation of a bought Servant. He was not more than 18 Years of Age, and gave me this Account of himself; that he was born in Gloucester, educated at a Grammar School there, had been distinguish'd among the Scholars for some apparent Superiority in performing his Part when they exhibited Plays; belong'd to the Witty Club there, and had written some Pieces in Prose and Verse which were printed in the Gloucester Newspapers. Thence he was sent to Oxford; there he continu'd about a Year, but not well-satisfied, wishing of all things to see London and become a Player. At length receiving his Quarterly Allowance of 15 Guineas, instead of discharging his Debts, he walk'd out of Town, hid his Gown in a Furz Bush,[3] and footed it to London, where having no Friend to advise him, he fell into bad Company, soon spent his Guineas, found no means of being introduc'd among the Players, grew necessitous, pawn'd his Clothes and wanted Bread. Walking the Street very hungry, and not knowing what to do with himself, a Crimp's Bill[4] was put into his Hand, offering immediate Entertainment and Encouragement to such as would bind themselves to serve in America. He went directly, sign'd the Indentures, was put into the Ship and came over; never writing a Line to acquaint his Friends what was become of him. He was lively, witty, good-natur'd and a pleasant Companion, but idle, thoughtless and imprudent to the last Degree.

6. Hugh Meredith (c. 1696–1749), later a business partner of Franklin's.
7. Later a bookseller and innkeeper (d. 1758).
8. I.e., handsome.
9. I.e., Keimer had paid for his passage in exchange for his service.
1. Later a member of Franklin's Junto Club and

printer (1708–1736?).
2. A Welsh Quaker (1708–1760) and later first printer in the Barbados.
3. An evergreen shrub; gorse. "Gown": academic robe worn regularly by Oxford students.
4. An advertisement for free passage to the colonies for those who would work as indentured servants.

John the Irishman soon ran away. With the rest I began to live very agreeably; for they all respected me, the more as they found Keimer incapable of instructing them, and that from me they learned something daily. We never work'd on a Saturday, that being Keimer's Sabbath. So I had two Days for Reading. My Acquaintance with ingenious People in the Town increased. Keimer himself treated me with great Civility and apparent Regard; and nothing now made me uneasy but my Debt to Vernon, which I was yet unable to pay, being hitherto but a poor Economist. He however kindly made no Demand of it.

Our Printing-House often wanted Sorts,[5] and there was no Letter Founder in America. I had seen Types cast at James's[6] in London, but without much Attention to the Manner: However I now contriv'd a Mold, made use of the Letters we had as Puncheons, struck the Matrices[7] in Lead, and thus supplied in a pretty tolerable way all Deficiencies. I also engrav'd several Things on occasion. I made the Ink, I was Warehouse-man and everything, in short quite a Factotum.[8]

But however serviceable I might be, I found that my Services became every Day of less Importance, as the other Hands improv'd in the Business. And when Keimer paid my second Quarter's Wages, he let me know that he felt them too heavy, and thought I should make an Abatement. He grew by degrees less civil, put on more of the Master, frequently found Fault, was captious and seem'd ready for an Out-breaking. I went on nevertheless with a good deal of Patience, thinking that his encumber'd Circumstances were partly the Cause. At length a Trifle snapped our Connection. For a great Noise happening near the Courthouse, I put my Head out of the Window to see what was the Matter. Keimer being in the Street look'd up and saw me, call'd out to me in a loud Voice and angry Tone to mind my Business, adding some reproachful Words, that nettled me the more for their Publicity, all the Neighbors who were looking out on the same Occasion being Witnesses how I was treated. He came up immediately into the Printing-House, continu'd the Quarrel, high Words pass'd on both Sides, he gave me the Quarter's Warning we had stipulated, expressing a Wish that he had not been oblig'd to so long a Warning: I told him his Wish was unnecessary for I would leave him that Instant; and so taking my Hat walk'd out of Doors; desiring Meredith whom I saw below to take care of some Things I left, and bring them to my Lodging.

Meredith came accordingly in the Evening, when we talk'd my Affair over. He had conceiv'd a great Regard for me, and was very unwilling that I should leave the House while he remain'd in it. He dissuaded me from returning to my native Country[9] which I began to think of. He reminded me that Keimer was in debt for all he possess'd, that his Creditors began to be uneasy, that he kept his Shop miserably, sold often without Profit for ready Money, and often trusted without keeping Account. That he must therefore fail; which would make a Vacancy I might profit of. I objected my Want of Money. He then let me know, that his Father had a high Opinion of me, and from some Discourse that had pass'd between them, he was sure would advance Money to set us up, if I would enter into Partnership with him. My Time, says he, will be out with

5. Letters of type.
6. Thomas James's foundry in London.
7. Molds for casting types. "Puncheons": stamping

tools.
8. Jack-of-all-trades.
9. I.e., Boston.

Keimer in the Spring. By that time we may have our Press and Types in from London: I am sensible I am no Workman. If you like it, Your Skill in the Business shall be set against the Stock I furnish; and we will share the Profits equally.—The Proposal was agreeable, and I consented. His Father was in Town, and approv'd of it, the more as he saw I had great Influence with his Son, had prevail'd on him to abstain long from Dramdrinking,[1] and he hop'd might break him of that wretched Habit entirely, when we came to be so closely connected. I gave an Inventory to the Father, who carried it to a Merchant; the Things were sent for; the Secret was to be kept till they should arrive, and in the mean time I was to get Work if I could at the other Printing-House. But I found no Vacancy there, and so remain'd idle a few Days, when Keimer, on a Prospect of being employ'd to print some Paper-money, in New Jersey, which would require Cuts and various Types that I only could supply, and apprehending Bradford might engage me and get the Job from him, sent me a very civil Message, that old Friends should not part for a few Words, the Effect of sudden Passion, and wishing me to return. Meredith persuaded me to comply, as it would give more Opportunity for his Improvement under my daily Instructions. So I return'd, and we went on more smoothly than for some time before. The New Jersey Job was obtain'd. I contriv'd a Copper-Plate Press for it, the first that had been seen in the Country. I cut several Ornaments and Checks for the Bills. We went together to Burlington,[2] where I executed the Whole to Satisfaction, and he received so large a Sum for the Work, as to be enabled thereby to keep his Head much longer above Water.

At Burlington I made an Acquaintance with many principal People of the Province. Several of them had been appointed by the Assembly a Committee to attend the Press, and take Care that no more Bills were printed than the Law directed. They were therefore by Turns constantly with us, and generally he who attended brought with him a Friend or two for Company. My Mind having been much more improv'd by Reading than Keimer's, I suppose it was for that Reason my Conversation seem'd to be more valu'd. They had me to their Houses, introduc'd me to their Friends and show'd me much Civility, while he, tho' the Master, was a little neglected. In truth he was an odd Fish, ignorant of common Life, fond of rudely opposing receiv'd Opinions, slovenly to extreme dirtiness, enthusiastic[3] in some Points of Religion, and a little Knavish withal. We continu'd there near 3 Months, and by that time I could reckon among my acquired Friends, Judge Allen, Samuel Bustill, the Secretary of the Province, Isaac Pearson, Joseph Cooper and several of the Smiths, Members of Assembly, and Isaac Decow the Surveyor General. The latter was a shrewd sagacious old Man, who told me that he began for himself when young by wheeling Clay for the Brickmakers, learned to write after he was of Age, carried the Chain for Surveyors, who taught him Surveying, and he had now by his Industry acquir'd a good Estate; and says he, I foresee, that you will soon work this Man out of his Business and make a Fortune in it at Philadelphia. He had not then the least Intimation of my Intention to set up there or anywhere. These Friends were afterwards of great Use to me, as I occasionally was to some of them. They all continued their Regard for me as long as they lived.

---

1. Frequently drinking small measures of alcohol.      3. Highly emotional.
2. New Jersey.

Before I enter upon my public Appearance in Business, it may be well to let you know the then State of my Mind, with regard to my Principles and Morals, that you may see how far those influenc'd the future Events of my Life. My Parents had early given me religious Impressions, and brought me through my Childhood piously in the Dissenting Way.[4] But I was scarce 15 when, after doubting by turns of several Points as I found them disputed in the different Books I read, I began to doubt of Revelation itself. Some Books against Deism fell into my Hands; they were said to be the Substance of Sermons preached at Boyle's Lectures.[5] It happened that they wrought an Effect on me quite contrary to what was intended by them: For the Arguments of the Deists which were quoted to be refuted, appeared to me much Stronger than the Refutations. In short I soon became a thorough Deist. My Arguments perverted some others, particularly Collins and Ralph: but each of them having afterwards wrong'd me greatly without the least Compunction, and recollecting Keith's Conduct towards me, (who was another Freethinker) and my own towards Vernon and Miss Read which at Times gave me great Trouble, I began to suspect that this Doctrine tho' it might be true, was not very useful. My London pamphlet, which had for its Motto those Lines of Dryden

> ——Whatever is, is right
> Tho' purblind Man Sees but a Part of
> The Chain, the nearest Link,
> His Eyes not carrying to the equal Beam,
> That poizes all, above.[6]

And from the Attributes of God, his infinite Wisdom, Goodness and Power concluded that nothing could possibly be wrong in the World, and that Vice and Virtue were empty Distinctions, no such Things existing: appear'd now not so clever a Performance as I once thought it; and I doubted whether some Error had not insinuated itself unperceiv'd into my Argument, so as to infect all that follow'd, as is common in metaphysical Reasonings. I grew convinc'd that *Truth*, *Sincerity* and *Integrity* in Dealings between Man and Man, were of the utmost Importance to the Felicity of Life, and I form'd written Resolutions, (which still remain in my Journal Book) to practice them ever while I lived. Revelation had indeed no weight with me as such; but I entertain'd an Opinion, that tho' certain Actions might not be bad *because* they were forbidden by it, or good *because* it commanded them; yet probably those Actions might be forbidden *because* they were bad for us, or commanded *because* they were beneficial to us, in their own Natures, all the Circumstances of things considered. And this Persuasion, with the kind hand of Providence, or some guardian Angel, or accidental favorable Circumstances and Situations, or all together, preserved me (thro' this dangerous Time of Youth and the hazardous Situations I was sometimes in among Strangers, remote from the Eye and Advice of my Father) without any *willful* gross Immorality or Injustice that might have been expected from my Want of Religion. I say *willful*, because

---

4. I.e., in the Congregational or Presbyterian way, as opposed to the Church of England.
5. Robert Boyle (1627–1691), English physicist and chemist, endowed annual lectures for preaching eight sermons a year against "infidels." Deism accepts a supreme being as the author of finite existence, but denies Christian doctrines of revelation and supernatu-

ralism.
6. The first line is not from John Dryden (1631–1700) but from Alexander Pope's *Essay on Man* (1733), Epistle I, line 294; however, Dryden's line is close: "Whatever is, is in its Causes just." The rest of the poem is recalled accurately from Dryden's *Oedipus* (3.1.244–48).

the Instances I have mentioned, had something of *Necessity* in them, from my Youth, Inexperience, and the Knavery of others. I had therefore a tolerable Character to begin the World with, I valued it properly, and determin'd to preserve it.

We had not been long return'd to Philadelphia, before the New Types arriv'd from London. We settled with Keimer, and left him by his Consent before he heard of it. We found a House to hire near the Market, and took it. To lessen the Rent, (which was then but 24 Pounds a Year tho' I have since known it let for 70) we took in Thomas Godfrey a Glazier,[7] and his Family, who were to pay a considerable Part of it to us, and we to board with them. We had scarce opened our Letters and put our Press in Order, before George House, an Acquaintance of mine, brought a Countryman to us; whom he had met in the Street enquiring for a Printer. All our Cash was now expended in the Variety of Particulars we had been obliged to procure, and this Country-man's Five Shillings, being our First Fruits and coming so seasonably, gave me more Pleasure than any Crown[8] I have since earn'd; and from the Grati-tude I felt towards House, has made me often more ready than perhaps I should otherwise have been to assist young Beginners.

There are Croakers in every Country always boding its Ruin. Such a one then lived in Philadelphia, a Person of Note, an elderly Man, with a wise Look and very grave Manner of Speaking. His Name was Samuel Mickle. This Gentleman, a Stranger to me, stopped one Day at my Door, and ask'd me if I was the young Man who had lately opened a new Printing-House: Being answer'd in the Affirmative; He said he was sorry for me; because it was an expensive Undertaking, and the Expense would be lost, for Philadelphia was a sinking[9] Place, the People already half Bankrupts or near being so; all Appearances of the contrary such as new Buildings and the Rise of Rents, being to his certain Knowledge fallacious, for they were in fact among the Things that would soon ruin us. And he gave me such a Detail of Misfortunes now existing or that were soon to exist, that he left me half-melancholy. Had I known him before I engag'd in this Business, probably I never should have done it. This Man continu'd to live in this decaying Place, and to declaim in the same Strain, refusing for many Years to buy a House there, because all was going to Destruction, and at last I had the Pleasure of seeing him give five times as much for one as he might have bought it for when he first began his Croaking.

I should have mention'd before, that in the Autumn of the preceding Year, I had form'd most of my ingenious Acquaintance into a Club, for mutual Improvement, which we call'd the Junto.[1] We met on Friday Evenings. The Rules I drew up, requir'd that every Member in his Turn should produce one or more Queries on any Point of Morals, Politics or Natural Philosophy, to be discuss'd by the Company, and once in three Months produce and read an Essay of his own Writing on any Subject he pleased. Our Debates were to be under the Direction of a President, and to be conducted in the sincere Spirit of Enquiry after Truth, without fondness for Dispute, or Desire of Victory; and to prevent Warmth, all expressions of Positiveness in Opinion, or of direct Contradiction, were after some time made contraband and prohibited under

---

7. A man who sets glass for windowpanes.
8. A coin worth five shillings.
9. Economically declining.

1. I.e., a small, select group (the name is taken from the Spanish word *junta*, or fraternity).

small pecuniary Penalties. The first Members were, Joseph Breintnall,[2] a Copier of Deeds for the Scriveners; a good-natur'd friendly middle-ag'd Man, a great Lover of Poetry, reading all he could meet with, and writing some that was tolerable; very ingenious in many little Nicknackeries, and of sensible Conversation. Thomas Godfrey,[3] a self-taught Mathematician, great in his Way, and afterwards Inventor of what is now call'd Hadley's Quadrant.[4] But he knew little out of his way, and was not a pleasing Companion, as like most Great Mathematicians I have met with, he expected unusual Precision in everything said, or was forever denying or distinguishing upon Trifles, to the Disturbance of all Conversation. He soon left us. Nicholas Scull,[5] a Surveyor, afterwards Surveyor-General, Who lov'd Books, and sometimes made a few Verses. William Parsons,[6] bred a Shoemaker, but loving Reading, had acquir'd a considerable Share of Mathematics, which he first studied with a View to Astrology that he afterwards laughed at. He also became Surveyor General. William Maugridge,[7] a Joiner, and a most exquisite Mechanic, and a solid sensible Man. Hugh Meredith, Stephen Potts, and George Webb, I have Characteris'd before. Robert Grace,[8] a young Gentleman of some Fortune, generous, lively and witty, a Lover of Punning and of his Friends. And William Coleman,[9] then a Merchant's Clerk, about my Age, who had the coolest clearest Head, the best Heart, and the exactest Morals, of almost any Man I ever met with. He became afterwards a Merchant of great Note, and one of our Provincial Judges: Our Friendship continued without Interruption to his Death, upwards of 40 Years. And the Club continu'd almost as long and was the best School of Philosophy, Morals and Politics that then existed in the Province; for our Queries which were read the Week preceding their Discussion, put us on reading with Attention upon the several Subjects, that we might speak more to the purpose: and here too we acquired better Habits of Conversation, everything being studied in our Rules which might prevent our disgusting each other. From hence the long Continuance of the Club, which I shall have frequent Occasion to speak farther of hereafter; But my giving this Account of it here, is to show something of the Interest I had, everyone of these exerting themselves in recommending Business to us.

Breintnall particularly procur'd us from the Quakers, the Printing 40 Sheets of their History, the rest being to be done by Keimer: and upon this we work'd exceeding hard, for the Price was low. It was a Folio, Pro Patria Size, in Pica with Long Primer Notes.[1] I compos'd of it a Sheet a Day, and Meredith work'd it off at Press. It was often 11 at Night and sometimes later, before I had finish'd my Distribution[2] for the next day's Work: For the little Jobs sent in by our other Friends now and then put us back. But so determin'd I was to continue doing a Sheet a Day of the Folio, that one Night when having impos'd my Forms,[3] I thought my Day's Work over, one of them by accident was broken and two Pages reduc'd to Pie,[4] I immediately distributed and compos'd

---

2. Brientnal (d. 1746) shared Franklin's interest in science.
3. Godfrey (1704–1749).
4. An instrument for measuring altitudes in navigation and astronomy.
5. Nicholas Scull II (1687–1761).
6. Became surveyor general in 1741 and librarian of the Library Company (1701–1757).
7. A ship's carpenter (d. 1766).
8. Franklin's landlord for thirty-seven years (1709–

1766).
9. Coleman (1704–1769).
1. A book of large size, with the main text in twelve-point type and the notes in ten-point type.
2. I.e., of type, returning letters to their cases so that they may be used again.
3. Locked the type into its form and readied it for printing.
4. A confused pile.

it over again before I went to bed. And this Industry visible to our Neighbors began to give us Character and Credit; particularly I was told, that mention being made of the new Printing Office at the Merchants' Every-night-Club, the general Opinion was that it must fail, there being already two Printers in the Place, Keimer and Bradford; but Doctor Baird (whom you and I saw many Years after at his native Place, St. Andrews in Scotland) gave a contrary Opinion; for the Industry of that Franklin, says he, is superior to anything I ever saw of the kind: I see him still at work when I go home from Club; and he is at Work again before his Neighbors are out of bed. This struck the rest, and we soon after had Offers from one of them to supply us with Stationery. But as yet we did not choose to engage in Shop Business.

I mention this Industry the more particularly and the more freely, tho' it seems to be talking in my own Praise, that those of my Posterity who shall read it, may know the Use of that Virtue, when they see its Effects in my Favor throughout this Relation.

George Webb, who had found a Friend that lent him wherewith to purchase his Time of Keimer, now came to offer himself as a Journeyman to us. We could not then employ him, but I foolishly let him know, as a Secret, that I soon intended to begin a Newspaper, and might then have Work for him. My Hopes of Success as I told him were founded on this, that the then only Newspaper,[5] printed by Bradford was a paltry thing, wretchedly manag'd, no way entertaining; and yet was profitable to him. I therefore thought a good Paper could scarcely fail of good Encouragement. I requested Webb not to mention it, but he told it to Keimer, who immediately, to be beforehand with me, published Proposals for Printing one himself, on which Webb was to be employ'd. I resented this, and to counteract them, as I could not yet begin our Paper, I wrote several Pieces of Entertainment for Bradford's Paper, under the Title of the Busy Body which Breintnall continu'd some Months.[6] By this means the Attention of the Public was fix'd on that Paper, and Keimer's Proposals which we burlesqu'd and ridicul'd, were disregarded. He began his Paper however, and after carrying it on three Quarters of a Year, with at most only 90 Subscribers, he offer'd it to me for a Trifle, and I having been ready some time to go on with it, took it in hand directly, and it prov'd in a few Years extremely profitable to me.[7]

I perceive that I am apt to speak in the singular Number, though our Partnership still continu'd. The Reason may be, that in fact the whole Management of the Business lay upon me. Meredith was no Compositor, a poor Pressman, and seldom sober. My Friends lamented my Connection with him, but I was to make the best of it.

Our first Papers made a quite different Appearance from any before in the Province, a better Type and better printed: but some spirited Remarks of my Writing on the Dispute then going on between Governor Burnet[8] and the Massachusetts Assembly, struck the principal People, occasion'd the Paper and the Manager of it to be much talk'd of, and in a few Weeks brought them all to be our Subscribers. Their Example was follow'd by many, and our Number went on growing continually. This was one of the first good Effects of my

5. The *American Weekly Mercury*.
6. From February 4, 1728, to September 25, 1729.
7. Franklin took over Keimer's The *Universal Instructor in All Arts and Sciences: and Pennsylvania Gazette*

in October 1729 and shortened the name to the *Pennsylvania Gazette*.
8. See n. 1, p. 246.

having learned a little to scribble. Another was, that the leading Men, seeing a Newspaper now in the hands of one who could also handle a Pen, thought it convenient to oblige and encourage me. Bradford still printed the Votes and Laws and other Public Business. He had printed an Address of the House[9] to the Governor in a coarse blundering manner; We reprinted it elegantly and correctly, and sent one to every Member. They were sensible of the Difference, it strengthen'd the Hands of our Friends in the House, and they voted us their Printers for the Year ensuing.

Among my Friends in the House I must not forget Mr. Hamilton[1] before-mentioned, who was then returned from England and had a Seat in it. He interested himself[2] for me strongly in that Instance, as he did in many others afterwards, continuing his Patronage till his Death. Mr. Vernon about this time put me in mind of the Debt I ow'd him: but did not press me. I wrote him an ingenuous Letter of Acknowledgments, crav'd his Forbearance a little longer which he allow'd me, and as soon as I was able I paid the Principal with Interest and many Thanks. So that Erratum was in some degree corrected.

But now another Difficulty came upon me, which I had never the least Reason to expect. Mr. Meredith's Father, who was to have paid for our Printing-House according to the Expectations given me, was able to advance only one Hundred Pounds, Currency, which had been paid, and a Hundred more was due to the Merchant; who grew impatient and su'd us all. We gave Bail, but saw that if the Money could not be rais'd in time, the Suit must come to a Judgment and Execution, and our hopeful Prospects must with us be ruined, as the Press and Letters must be sold for Payment, perhaps at half-Price. In this Distress two true Friends whose Kindness I have never forgotten nor ever shall forget while I can remember anything, came to me separately unknown to each other, and without any Application from me, offering each of them to advance me all the Money that should be necessary to enable me to take the whole Business upon myself if that should be practicable, but they did not like my continuing the Partnership with Meredith, who as they said was often seen drunk in the Streets, and playing at low Games in Alehouses, much to our Discredit. These two Friends were *William Coleman* and *Robert Grace*.

I told them I could not propose a Separation while any Prospect remain'd of the Merediths fulfilling their Part of our Agreement. Because I thought myself under great Obligations to them for what they had done and would do if they could. But if they finally fail'd in their Performance, and our Partnership must be dissolv'd, I should then think myself at Liberty to accept the Assistance of my Friends. Thus the matter rested for some time. When I said to my Partner, perhaps your Father is dissatisfied at the Part you have undertaken in this Affair of ours, and is unwilling to advance for you and me what he would for you alone: If that is the Case, tell me, and I will resign the whole to you and go about my Business. No—says he, my Father has really been disappointed and is really unable; and I am unwilling to distress him farther. I see this is a Business I am not fit for. I was bred a Farmer, and it was a Folly in me to come to Town and put myself at 30 Years of Age an Apprentice to learn a new Trade. Many of our Welsh People are going to settle in North Carolina where Land is cheap: I am inclin'd to go with them, and follow my

9. I.e., the Pennsylvania Assembly.
1. Andrew Hamilton (see n. 2, p. 251).
2. "I got his Son once £500" [Franklin's note]. Frank-

lin was able to get the legislature to pay Governor James Hamilton his salary when they were at odds with him.

old Employment. You may find Friends to assist you. If you will take the Debts of the Company upon you, return to my Father the hundred Pound he has advanc'd, pay my little personal Debts, and give me Thirty Pounds and a new Saddle, I will relinquish the Partnership and leave the whole in your Hands. I agreed to this Proposal. It was drawn up in Writing, sign'd and seal'd immediately. I gave him what he demanded and he went soon after to Carolina; from whence he sent me next Year two long Letters, containing the best Account that had been given of that Country, the Climate, Soil, Husbandry, etc., for in those Matters he was very judicious. I printed them in the Papers,[3] and they gave great Satisfaction to the Public.

As soon as he was gone, I recurr'd to my two Friends; and because I would not give an unkind Preference to either, I took half what each had offered and I wanted, of one, and half of the other; paid off the Company Debts, and went on with the Business in my own Name, advertising that the Partnership was dissolved. I think this was in or about the Year 1729.[4]

About this Time there was a Cry among the People for more Paper-Money, only 15,000 Pounds being extant in the Province and that soon to be sunk.[5] The wealthy Inhabitants oppos'd any Addition, being against all Paper Currency, from an Apprehension that it would depreciate as it had done in New England to the Prejudice of all Creditors. We had discuss'd this Point in our Junto, where I was on the Side of an Addition, being persuaded that the first small Sum struck in 1723 had done much good, by increasing the Trade, Employment, and Number of Inhabitants in the Province, since I now saw all the old Houses inhabited, and many new ones building, where as I remember'd well, that when I first walk'd about the Streets of Philadelphia, eating my Roll, I saw most of the Houses in Walnut Street between Second and Front Streets with Bills[6] on their Doors, to be let; and many likewise in Chestnut Street, and other Streets; which made me then think the Inhabitants of the City were one after another deserting it. Our Debates possess'd me so fully of the Subject, that I wrote and printed an anonymous Pamphlet on it, entitled, *The Nature and Necessity of a Paper Currency.*[7] It was well receiv'd by the common People in general; but the Rich Men dislik'd it; for it increas'd and strengthen'd the Clamor for more Money; and they happening to have no Writers among them that were able to answer it, their Opposition slacken'd, and the Point was carried by a Majority in the House. My Friends there, who conceiv'd I had been of some Service, thought fit to reward me, by employing me in printing the Money,[8] a very profitable Job, and a great Help to me. This was another Advantage gain'd by my being able to write. The Utility of this Currency became by Time and Experience so evident, as never afterwards to be much disputed, so that it grew soon to 55,000 Pounds, and in 1739 to 80,000 Pounds, since which it arose during War to upwards of 350,000 Pounds—Trade, Building and Inhabitants all the while increasing. Tho' I now think there are Limits beyond which the Quantity may be hurtful.

I soon after obtain'd, thro' my Friend Hamilton, the Printing of the New

---

3. In the *Pennsylvania Gazette*, May 6, and 13, 1732.
4. More accurately, July 14, 1730.
5. Destroyed. In 1723 paper money had become so scarce that the Assembly issued new money secured by real estate mortgages; when the mortgages were paid off, the bills were "sunk." But by 1729 the value of the currency was so low that the money was recalled before

the mortgages were paid.
6. Signs.
7. *A Modest Inquiry into the Nature and Necessity of a Paper Currency* (April 3, 1729).
8. Franklin received the contract to print money in 1731.

Castle[9] Paper Money, another profitable Job, as I then thought it; small Things appearing great to those in small Circumstances. And these to me were really great Advantages, as they were great Encouragements. He procured me also the Printing of the Laws and Votes of that Government which continu'd in my Hands as long as I follow'd the Business.

I now open'd a little Stationer's Shop.[1] I had in it Blanks of all Sorts the correctest that ever appear'd among us, being assisted in that by my Friend Breintnall; I had also Paper, Parchment, Chapmen's Books,[2] etc. One Whitmarsh[3] a Compositor I had known in London, an excellent Workman now came to me and work'd with me constantly and diligently, and I took an Apprentice the Son of Aquila Rose. I began now gradually to pay off the Debt I was under for the Printing-House. In order to secure my Credit and Character as a Tradesman, I took care not only to be in *Reality* Industrious and frugal, but to avoid all *Appearances* of the contrary. I dressed plainly; I was seen at no Places of idle Diversion; I never went out a-fishing or shooting; a Book, indeed, sometimes debauch'd me from my Work; but that was seldom, snug, and gave no Scandal: and to show that I was not above my Business, I sometimes brought home the Paper I purchas'd at the Stores, thro' the Streets on a Wheelbarrow. Thus being esteem'd an industrious thriving young Man, and paying duly for what I bought, the Merchants who imported Stationery solicited my Custom, others propos'd supplying me with Books, and I went on swimmingly. In the mean time Keimer's Credit and Business declining daily, he was at last forc'd to sell his Printing-House to satisfy his Creditors. He went to Barbados, and there lived some Years, in very poor Circumstances.

His Apprentice David Harry, whom I had instructed while I work'd with him, set up in his Place at Philadelphia, having bought his Materials. I was at first apprehensive of a powerful Rival in Harry, as his Friends were very able, and had a good deal of Interest. I therefore propos'd a Partnership to him; which he, fortunately for me, rejected with Scorn. He was very proud, dress'd like a Gentleman, liv'd expensively, took much Diversion and Pleasure abroad, ran in debt, and neglected his Business, upon which all Business left him; and finding nothing to do, he follow'd Keimer to Barbados; taking the Printing-House with him. There this Apprentice employ'd his former Master as a Journeyman. They quarrel'd often. Harry went continually behind-hand, and at length was forc'd to sell his Types, and return to his Country Work in Pennsylvania. The Person that bought them employ'd Keimer to use them, but in a few years he died. There remain'd now no Competitor with me at Philadelphia, but the old one, Bradford, who was rich and easy, did a little Printing now and then by straggling Hands, but was not very anxious about the Business. However, as he kept the Post Office, it was imagined he had better Opportunities of obtaining News, his Paper was thought a better Distributer of Advertisements than mine, and therefore had many more, which was a profitable thing to him and a Disadvantage to me. For tho' I did indeed receive and send Papers by the Post, yet the public Opinion was otherwise; for what I did send was by Bribing the Riders[4] who took them privately: Bradford

---

9. New Castle, Delaware. Delaware had a separate legislature but the same proprietary governor as Pennsylvania.
1. In July 1730.
2. Inexpensive paper pamphlets.

3. Thomas Whitmarsh (d. 1733); the following year Whitmarsh went to South Carolina.
4. I.e., the postal riders or carriers. Franklin did this to have his papers delivered on the same day as Bradford's.

being unkind enough to forbid it: which occasion'd some Resentment on my Part; and I thought so meanly of him for it, that when I afterwards came into his Situation,[5] I took care never to imitate it.

I had hitherto continu'd to board with Godfrey who lived in Part of my House with his Wife and Children, and had one Side of the Shop for his Glazier's Business, tho' he work'd little, being always absorb'd in his Mathematics. Mrs. Godfrey projected a Match for me with a Relation's Daughter, took Opportunities of bringing us often together, till a serious Courtship on my Part ensu'd, the Girl being in herself very deserving. The old Folks encourag'd me by continual Invitations to Supper, and by leaving us together, till at length it was time to explain. Mrs. Godfrey manag'd our little Treaty. I let her know that I expected as much Money with their Daughter as would pay off my Remaining Debt for the Printing-House, which I believe was not then above a Hundred Pounds.[6] She brought me Word they had no such Sum to spare. I said they might mortgage their House in the Loan Office. The Answer to this after some Days was, that they did not approve the Match; that on Enquiry of Bradford they had been inform'd the Printing Business was not a profitable one, the Types would soon be worn out and more wanted, that S. Keimer and D. Harry had fail'd one after the other, and I should probably soon follow them; and therefore I was forbidden the House, and the Daughter shut up.

Whether this was a real Change of Sentiment, or only Artifice, on a Supposition of our being too far engag'd in Affection to retract, and therefore that we should steal a Marriage, which would leave them at Liberty to give or withhold what they pleas'd, I know not: But I suspected the latter, resented it, and went no more. Mrs. Godfrey brought me afterwards some more favorable Accounts of their Disposition, and would have drawn me on again: But I declared absolutely my Resolution to have nothing more to do with that Family. This was resented by the Godfreys, we differ'd, and they removed, leaving me the whole House, and I resolved to take no more Inmates. But this Affair having turn'd my Thoughts to Marriage, I look'd round me, and made Overtures of Acquaintance in other Places; but soon found that the Business of a Printer being generally thought a poor one, I was not to expect Money with a Wife unless with such a one, as I should not otherwise think agreeable. In the mean time, that hard-to-be-govern'd Passion of Youth, had hurried me frequently into Intrigues with low Women that fell in my Way, which were attended with some Expense and great Inconvenience, besides a continual Risk to my Health by a Distemper[7] which of all Things I dreaded, tho' by great good Luck I escaped.

A friendly Correspondence as Neighbors and old Acquaintances, had continued between me and Mrs. Read's Family who all had a Regard for me from the time of my first Lodging in their House. I was often invited there and consulted in their Affairs, wherein I sometimes was of Service. I pitied poor Miss Read's unfortunate Situation, who was generally dejected, seldom cheerful, and avoided Company. I consider'd my Giddiness and Inconstancy when in London as in a great degree the Cause of her Unhappiness; tho' the Mother

---

5. Franklin assumed Bradford's office as postmaster of Philadelphia in October 1737.
6. Franklin's expectations were not unusual: marriages

were often arranged on agreeable financial considerations.
7. I.e., syphilis.

was good enough to think the Fault more her own than mine, as she had prevented our Marrying before I went thither, and persuaded the other Match in my Absence. Our mutual Affection was revived, but there were now great Objections to our Union. That Match was indeed look'd upon as invalid, a preceding Wife being said to be living in England; but this could not easily be prov'd, because of the Distance, etc. And tho' there was a Report of his Death, it was not certain. Then, tho' it should be true, he had left many Debts which his Successor might be call'd upon to pay. We ventured however, over all these Difficulties, and I took her to Wife Sept. 1, 1730.[8] None of the Inconveniencies happened that we had apprehended, she prov'd a good and faithful Helpmate, assisted me much by attending the Shop, we throve together, and have ever mutually endeavor'd to make each other happy. Thus I corrected that great Erratum as well as I could.

About this Time our Club meeting, not at a Tavern, but in a little Room of Mr. Grace's set apart for that Purpose; a Proposition was made by me, that since our Books were often referr'd to in our Disquisitions upon the Queries, it might be convenient to us to have them all together where we met, that upon Occasion they might be consulted; and by thus clubbing our Books to a common Library, we should, while we lik'd to keep them together, have each of us the Advantage of using the Books of all the other Members, which would be nearly as beneficial as if each owned the whole. It was lik'd and agreed to, and we fill'd one End of the Room with such Books as we could best spare. The Number was not so great as we expected; and tho' they had been of great Use, yet some Inconveniencies occurring for want of due Care of them, the Collection after about a Year was separated, and each took his Books home again.

And now I set on foot my first Project of a public Nature, that for a Subscription Library. I drew up the Proposals, got them put into Form by our great Scrivener Brockden, and by the help of my Friends in the Junto, procur'd Fifty Subscribers of 40 Shillings each to begin with and 10 Shillings a Year for 50 Years, the Term our Company was to continue. We afterwards obtain'd a Charter, the Company being increas'd to 100. This was the Mother of all the North American Subscription Libraries now so numerous. It is become a great thing itself, and continually increasing. These Libraries have improv'd the general Conversation of the Americans, made the common Tradesmen and Farmers as intelligent as most Gentlemen from other Countries, and perhaps have contributed in some degree to the Stand so generally made throughout the Colonies in Defense of their Privileges.

Memo.

Thus far was written with the Intention express'd in the Beginning and therefore contains several little family Anecdotes of no Importance to others. What follows was written many Years after in compliance with the Advice contain'd in these Letters, and accordingly intended for the Public. The Affairs of the Revolution occasion'd the Interruption.

---

8. Because there was no proof that John Rogers, Deborah Read's first husband, was dead, she and Franklin entered into a common-law marriage without civil ceremony.

## [*Part Two*][9]

### LETTER FROM MR. ABEL JAMES,[1] WITH NOTES ON MY LIFE, (RECEIVED IN PARIS)

My dear and honored Friend.

I have often been desirous of writing to thee, but could not be reconciled to the Thought that the Letter might fall into the Hands of the British,[2] lest some Printer or busy Body should publish some Part of the Contents and give our Friends Pain and myself Censure.

Some Time since there fell into my Hands to my great Joy about 23 Sheets in thy own handwriting containing an Account of the Parentage and Life of thyself, directed to thy Son ending in the Year 1730 with which there were Notes[3] likewise in thy writing, a Copy of which I enclose in Hopes it may be a means if thou continuedst it up to a later period, that the first and latter part may be put together; and if it is not yet continued, I hope thou wilt not delay it. Life is uncertain as the Preacher tells us, and what will the World say if kind, humane and benevolent Ben Franklin should leave his Friends and the World deprived of so pleasing and profitable a Work, a Work which would be useful and entertaining not only to a few, but to millions.

The Influence Writings under that Class have on the Minds of Youth is very great, and has no where appeared so plain as in our public Friends' Journals. It almost insensibly leads the Youth into the Resolution of endeavoring to become as good and as eminent as the Journalist. Should thine for Instance when published, and I think it could not fail of it, lead the Youth to equal the Industry and Temperance of thy early Youth, what a Blessing with that Class would such a Work be. I know of no Character living nor many of them put together, who has so much in his Power as Thyself to promote a greater Spirit of Industry and early Attention to Business, Frugality and Temperance with the American Youth. Not that I think the Work would have no other Merit and Use in the World, far from it, but the first is of such vast Importance, that I know nothing that can equal it.

The foregoing letter and the minutes accompanying it being shown to a friend, I received from him the following:

### LETTER FROM MR. BENJAMIN VAUGHAN[4]

MY DEAREST SIR,            *Paris, January 31, 1783.*

When I had read over your sheets of minutes of the principal incidents of your life, recovered for you by your Quaker acquaintance; I told you I would send you a letter expressing my reasons why I thought it would be

9. Franklin wrote the second part of his autobiography at the Hôtel de Valentenois in Passy, a Paris suburb. He had been sent to Paris as American representative to the peace treaty, ending the war with Britain, September 3, 1783. Franklin remained in Paris until July 1785, when Thomas Jefferson replaced him as minister.
1. A Quaker merchant in Philadelphia (c. 1726–1790).

2. James's letter was written in 1782, when Britain was still at war with the colonies.
3. Franklin's outline for his *Autobiography*, written in 1771. Reprinted in the Yale University edition, 1964.
4. The wealthy son (1751–1835) of a Jamaican merchant and Maine mother; private secretary to Lord Shelburne, and personal emissary to Franklin during the Paris peace talks (1782–85).

useful to complete and publish it as he desired. Various concerns have
for some time past prevented this letter being written, and I do not know
whether it was worth any expectation: happening to be at leisure however
at present, I shall by writing at least interest and instruct myself; but as the
terms I am inclined to use may tend to offend a person of your manners, I
shall only tell you how I would address any other person, who was as
good and as great as yourself, but less diffident. I would say to him, Sir, I
*solicit* the history of your life from the following motives.

Your history is so remarkable, that if you do not give it, somebody else
will certainly give it; and perhaps so as nearly to do as much harm, as
your own management of the thing might do good.

It will moreover present a table of the internal circumstances of your
country, which will very much tend to invite to it settlers of virtuous and
manly minds. And considering the eagerness with which such information is sought by them, and the extent of your reputation, I do not know
of a more efficacious advertisement than your Biography would give.

All that has happened to you is also connected with the detail of the
manners and situation of *a rising* people; and in this respect I do not think
that the writings of Caesar and Tacitus[5] can be more interesting to a true
judge of human nature and society.

But these, Sir, are small reasons in my opinion, compared with the
chance which your life will give for the forming of future great men; and
in conjunction with your *Art of Virtue*,[6] (which you design to publish) of
improving the features of private character, and consequently of aiding
all happiness both public and domestic.

The two works I allude to, Sir, will in particular give a noble rule and
example of *self-education*. School and other education constantly proceed
upon false principles, and show a clumsy apparatus pointed at a false
mark; but your apparatus is simple, and the mark a true one; and while
parents and young persons are left destitute of other just means of estimating and becoming prepared for a reasonable course in life, your discovery
that the thing is in many a man's private power, will be invaluable!

Influence upon the private character late in life, is not only an influence late in life, but a weak influence. It is in *youth* that we plant our
chief habits and prejudices; it is in youth that we take our party[7] as to
profession, pursuits, and matrimony. In youth therefore the turn is given;
in youth the education even of the next generation is given; in youth the
private and public character is determined: and the term of life extending
from youth to age, life ought to begin well from youth; and more especially *before* we take our party as to our principal objects.

But your Biography will not merely teach self-education, but the education of *a wise man;* and the wisest man will receive lights and improve
his progress, by seeing detailed the conduct of another wise man. And
why are weaker men to be deprived of such helps, when we see our race
has been blundering on in the dark, almost without a guide in this particular, from the farthest trace of time. Show then, Sir, how much is to be

5.  Gaius Julius Caesar (100–44 B.C.) and Publius Cornelius Tacitus (late 1st and early 2nd centuries A.D.).
6.  Vaughan is referring to Franklin's intention to write
"a little work for the benefit of youth" to be called *The*

*Art of Virtue.* Part Two of the *Autobiography* is, in
part, an answer to Vaughan's reminder.
7.  Make our decision.

done, *both to sons and fathers*; and invite all wise men to become like yourself; and other men to become wise.

When we see how cruel statesmen and warriors can be to the humble race, and how absurd distinguished men can be to their acquaintance, it will be instructive to observe the instances multiply of pacific acquiescing manners; and to find how compatible it is to be great and *domestic*; enviable and yet *good-humored*.

The little private incidents which you will also have to relate, will have considerable use, as we want above all things, *rules of prudence in ordinary affairs*; and it will be curious to see how you have acted in these. It will be so far a sort of key to life, and explain many things that all men ought to have once explained to them, to give them a chance of becoming wise by foresight.

The nearest thing to having experience of one's own, is to have other people's affairs brought before us in a shape that is interesting; this is sure to happen from your pen. Your affairs and management will have an air of simplicity or importance that will not fail to strike; and I am convinced you have conducted them with as much originality as if you had been conducting discussions in politics or philosophy; and what more worthy of experiments and system, (its importance and its errors considered) than human life!

Some men have been virtuous blindly, others have speculated fantastically, and others have been shrewd to bad purposes; but you, Sir, I am sure, will give under your hand, nothing but what is at the same moment, wise, practical, and good.

Your account of yourself (for I suppose the parallel I am drawing for Dr. Franklin, will hold not only in point of character but of private history), will show that you are ashamed of no origin; a thing the more important, as you prove how little necessary all origin is to happiness, virtue, or greatness.

As no end likewise happens without a means, so we shall find, Sir, that even you yourself framed a plan by which you became considerable; but at the same time we may see that though the event is flattering, the means are as simple as wisdom could make them; that is, depending upon nature, virtue, thought, and habit.

Another thing demonstrated will be the propriety of every man's waiting for his time for appearing upon the stage of the world. Our sensations being very much fixed to the moment, we are apt to forget that more moments are to follow the first, and consequently that man should arrange his conduct so as to suit the *whole* of a life. Your attribution appears to have been applied to your *life*, and the passing moments of it have been enlivened with content and enjoyment, instead of being tormented with foolish impatience or regrets. Such a conduct is easy for those who make virtue and themselves their standard, and who try to keep themselves in countenance by examples of other truly great men, of whom patience is so often the characteristic.

Your Quaker correspondent, Sir (for here again I will suppose the subject of my letter resembling Dr. Franklin,) praised your frugality, diligence, and temperance, which he considered as a pattern for all youth: but it is singular that he should have forgotten your modesty, and your disinterestedness, without which you never could have waited for your advancement, or found your situation in the mean time comfortable; which is a strong lesson to show the poverty of glory, and the importance of regulating our minds.

If this correspondent had known the nature of your reputation as well as I do, he would have said; your former writings and measures would secure attention to your Biography, and Art of Virtue; and your Biography and Art of Virtue, in return, would secure attention to them. This is an advantage attendant upon a various character, and which brings all that belongs to it into greater play; and it is the more useful, as perhaps more persons are at a loss for the *means* of improving their minds and characters, than they are for the time or the inclination to do it.

But there is one concluding reflection, Sir, that will show the use of your life as a mere piece of biography. This style of writing seems a little gone out of vogue, and yet it is a very useful one; and your specimen of it may be particularly serviceable, as it will make a subject of comparison with the lives of various public cut-throats and intriguers, and with absurd monastic self-tormentors, or vain literary triflers. If it encourages more writings of the same kind with your own, and induces more men to spend lives fit to be written; it will be worth all Plutarch's Lives put together.

But being tired of figuring to myself a character of which every feature suits only one man in the world, without giving him the praise of it; I shall end my letter, my dear Dr. Franklin, with a personal application to your proper self.

I am earnestly desirous then, my dear Sir, that you should let the world into the traits of your genuine character, as civil broils may otherwise tend to disguise or traduce it. Considering your great age, the caution of your character, and your peculiar style of thinking, it is not likely that any one besides yourself can be sufficiently master of the facts of your life, or the intentions of your mind.

Besides all this, the immense revolution of the present period, will necessarily turn our attention towards the author of it; and when virtuous principles have been pretended in it, it will be highly important to show that such have really influenced; and, as your own character will be the principal one to receive a scrutiny, it is proper (even for its effects upon your vast and rising country, as well as upon England and upon Europe), that it should stand respectable and eternal. For the furtherance of human happiness, I have always maintained that it is necessary to prove that man is not even at present a vicious and detestable animal; and still more to prove that good management may greatly amend him; and it is for much the same reason, that I am anxious to see the opinion established, that there are fair characters existing among the individuals of the race; for the moment that all men, without exception, shall be conceived abandoned, good people will cease efforts deemed to be hopeless, and perhaps think of taking their share in the scramble of life, or at least of making it comfortable principally for themselves.

Take then, my dear Sir, this work most speedily into hand: show yourself good as you are good, temperate as you are temperate; and above all things, prove yourself as one who from your infancy have loved justice, liberty, and concord, in a way that has made it natural and consistent for you to have acted, as we have seen you act in the last seventeen years of your life. Let Englishmen be made not only to respect, but even to love you. When they think well of individuals in your native country, they will go nearer to thinking well of your country; and when your countrymen see themselves well thought of by Englishmen, they will go nearer to thinking well of England. Extend your views even further; do not stop at those who speak the English tongue, but after having settled so many points in nature and politics, think of bettering the whole race of men.

As I have not read any part of the life in question, but know only the character that lived it, I write somewhat at hazard. I am sure however, that the life, and the treatise I allude to (on the Art of Virtue), will necessarily fullfil the chief of my expectations; and still more so if you take up the measure of suiting these performances to the several views above stated. Should they even prove unsuccessful in all that a sanguine admirer of yours hopes from them, you will at least have framed pieces to interest the human mind; and whoever gives a feeling of pleasure that is innocent to man, has added so much to the fair side of a life otherwise too much darkened by anxiety, and too much injured by pain.

In the hope therefore that you will listen to the prayer addressed to you in this letter, I beg to subscribe myself, my dearest Sir, etc., etc.

Signed    BENJ. VAUGHAN.

### CONTINUATION OF THE ACCOUNT OF MY LIFE.
### BEGUN AT PASSY, 1784.

It is some time since I receiv'd the above Letters, but I have been too busy till now to think of complying with the Request they contain. It might too be much better done if I were at home among my Papers, which would aid my Memory, and help to ascertain Dates. But my Return being uncertain, and having just now a little Leisure, I will endeavor to recollect and write what I can; if I live to get home, it may there be corrected and improv'd.

Not having any Copy here of what is already written, I know not whether an Account is given of the means I used to establish the Philadelphia public Library, which from a small Beginning is now become so considerable, though I remember to have come down to near the Time of that Transaction, 1730. I will therefore begin here, with an Account of it, which may be struck out if found to have been already given.

At the time I establish'd myself in Pennsylvania, there was not a good Bookseller's Shop in any of the Colonies to the Southward of Boston. In New York and Philadelphia the Printers were indeed Stationers, they sold only Paper, etc., Almanacs, Ballads, and a few common School Books. Those who lov'd Reading were oblig'd to send for their Books from England. The Members of the Junto had each a few. We had left the Alehouse where we first met, and hired a Room to hold our Club in. I propos'd that we should all of us bring our Books to that Room, where they would not only be ready to consult in our Conferences, but become a common Benefit, each of us being at Liberty to borrow such as he wish'd to read at home. This was accordingly done, and for some time contented us. Finding the Advantage of this little Collection, I propos'd to render the Benefit from Books more common by commencing a Public Subscription Library. I drew a Sketch of the Plan and Rules that would be necessary, and got a skillful Conveyancer Mr. Charles Brockden[8] to put the whole in Form of Articles of Agreement to be subscribed, by which each Subscriber engag'd to pay a certain Sum down for the first Purchase of Books and an annual Contribution for increasing them. So few were the Readers at that time in Philadelphia, and the Majority of us so poor, that I was not able with great Industry to find more than Fifty Persons, mostly young Tradesmen, willing to pay down for this purpose Forty shillings each, and Ten Shillings per Annum. On this little Fund we began. The Books were imported. The Library was open one Day in the Week for lending them to the Subscribers, on their Promissory Notes to pay Double the Value if not duly returned. The Institution soon manifested its Utility, was imitated by other Towns and in other Provinces, the Libraries were augmented by Donations, Reading became fashionable, and our People having no public Amusements to divert their Attention from Study became better acquainted with Books, and in a few Years were observ'd by Strangers to be better instructed and more intelligent than People of the same Rank generally are in other Countries.

When we were about to sign the above-mentioned Articles, which were to be binding on us, our Heirs, etc., for fifty Years, Mr. Brockden, the Scrivener, said to us, "You are young Men, but it is scarce probable that any of you will live to see the Expiration of the Term fix'd in this Instrument." A Number of us, however, are yet living: But the Instrument was after a few Years rendered null by a Charter that incorporated and gave Perpetuity to the Company.

The Objections, and Reluctances I met with in Soliciting the Subscriptions, made me soon feel the Impropriety of presenting oneself as the Proposer of any useful Project that might be suppos'd to raise one's Reputation in the smallest degree above that of one's Neighbors, when one has need of their Assistance to accomplish that Project. I therefore put myself as much as I could out of sight, and stated it as a Scheme of *a Number of Friends*, who had requested me to go about and propose it to such as they thought Lovers of Reading. In this way my Affair went on more smoothly, and I ever after practic'd it on such Occasions; and from my frequent Successes, can heartily recommend it. The present little Sacrifice of your Vanity will afterwards be amply repaid. If it remains a while uncertain to whom the Merit belongs, someone more vain than yourself will be encourag'd to claim it, and then even Envy will be dispos'd to do you Justice, by plucking those assum'd Feathers, and restoring them to their right Owner.

This Library afforded me the Means of Improvement by constant Study, for which I set apart an Hour or two each Day; and thus repair'd in some Degree the Loss of the Learned Education my Father once intended for me. Reading was the only Amusement I allow'd myself. I spent no time in Taverns, Games, or Frolics of any kind. And my Industry in my Business continu'd as indefatigable as it was necessary. I was in debt for my Printing-House, I had a young Family[9] coming on to be educated, and I had to contend with for Business two Printers who were establish'd in the Place before me. My Circumstances however grew daily easier: my original Habits of Frugality continuing. And My Father having among his Instructions to me when a Boy, frequently repeated a Proverb of Solomon, "*Seest thou a Man diligent in his Calling, he shall stand*

---

8. Philadelphia's leading drafter of legal documents (1683–1769). "Conveyancer": an attorney who specializes in the transfer of real estate and property.

9. Franklin had three children: William, born c. 1731; Francis, born in 1732; Sarah, born in 1743.

*before Kings, he shall not stand before mean Men.*"[1] I from thence consider'd Industry as a Means of obtaining Wealth and Distinction, which encourag'd me: tho' I did not think that I should ever literally stand before Kings, which however has since happened; for I have stood before five,[2] and even had the honor of sitting down with one, the King of Denmark, to Dinner.

We have an English Proverb that says,

> He that would thrive
> Must ask his Wife,[3]

it was lucky for me that I had one as much dispos'd to Industry and Frugality as myself. She assisted me cheerfully in my Business, folding and stitching Pamphlets, tending Shop, purchasing old Linen Rags for the Paper-makers, etc., etc. We kept no idle Servants, our Table was plain and simple, our Furniture of the cheapest. For instance my Breakfast was a long time Bread and Milk, (no Tea,) and I ate it out of a two penny earthen Porringer[4] with a Pewter Spoon. But mark how Luxury will enter Families, and make a Progress, in Spite of Principle. Being Call'd one Morning to Breakfast, I found it in a China[5] Bowl with a Spoon of Silver. They had been bought for me without my Knowledge by my Wife, and had cost her the enormous Sum of three and twenty Shillings, for which she had no other Excuse or Apology to make, but that she thought *her* Husband deserv'd a Silver Spoon and China Bowl as well as any of his Neighbors. This was the first Appearance of Plate[6] and China in our House, which afterwards in a Course of Years as our Wealth increas'd, augmented gradually to several Hundred Pounds in Value.

I had been religiously educated as a Presbyterian, and tho' some of the Dogmas of that Persuasion, such as the Eternal Decrees of God, Election, Reprobation,[7] etc., appear'd to me unintelligible, others doubtful, and I early absented myself from the Public Assemblies of the Sect, Sunday being my Studying-Day, I never was without some religious Principles; I never doubted, for instance, the Existence of the Deity, that he made the World, and govern'd it by his Providence; that the most acceptable Service of God was the doing Good to Man; that our Souls are immortal; and that all Crime will be punished and Virtue rewarded either here or hereafter; these I esteem'd the Essentials of every Religion, and being to be found in all the Religions we had in our Country I respected them all, tho' with different degrees of Respect as I found them more or less mix'd with other Articles which without any Tendency to inspire, promote or confirm Morality, serv'd principally to divide us and make us unfriendly to one another. This Respect to all, with an Opinion that the worst had some good Effects, induc'd me to avoid all Discourse that might tend to lessen the good Opinion another might have of his own Religion; and as our Province increas'd in People and new Places of worship were continually wanted, and generally erected by voluntary Contribution, my Mite[8] for such purpose, whatever might be the Sect, was never refused.

Tho' I seldom attended any Public Worship, I had still an Opinion of its Propriety, and of its Utility when rightly conducted, and I regularly paid my

1. Proverbs 22.29.
2. Louis XV and Louis XVI of France, George II and George III of England, and Christian VI of Denmark.
3. More commonly: "He that will thrive must ask leave of his wife."
4. Bowl.
5. I.e., porcelain.
6. Silver.
7. Punishment. "Election": God's choosing who is to be saved and who is to be damned.
8. Small contribution.

BENJAMIN FRANKLIN

annual Subscription for the Support of the only Presbyterian Minister or Meeting we had in Philadelphia. He us'd to visit me sometimes as a Friend, and admonish me to attend his Administrations, and I was now and then prevail'd on to do so, once for five Sundays successively. Had he been, *in my Opinion*, a good Preacher perhaps I might have continued, notwithstanding the occasion I had for the Sunday's Leisure in my Course of Study: But his Discourses were chiefly either polemic Arguments, or Explications of the peculiar Doctrines of our Sect, and were all to me very dry, uninteresting and unedifying, since not a single moral Principle was inculcated or enforc'd, their Aim seeming to be rather to make us Presbyterians than good Citizens. At length he took for his Text that Verse of the 4th Chapter of Philippians, *Finally, Brethren, Whatsoever Things are true, honest, just, pure, lovely, or of good report, if there be any virtue, or any praise, think on these Things;*[9] and I imagin'd in a Sermon on such a Text, we could not miss of having some Morality: But he confin'd himself to five Points only as meant by the Apostle, viz., 1. Keeping holy the Sabbath Day. 2. Being diligent in Reading the Holy Scriptures. 3. Attending duly the Public Worship. 4. Partaking of the Sacrament. 5. Paying a due Respect to God's Ministers.—These might be all good Things, but as they were not the kind of good Things that I expected from that Text, I despaired of ever meeting with them from any other, was disgusted, and attended his Preaching no more. I had some Years before compos'd a little Liturgy or Form of Prayer for my own private Use, viz., in 1728, entitled, *Articles of Belief and Acts of Religion.*[1] I return'd to the Use of this, and went no more to the public Assemblies. My Conduct might be blameable, but I leave it without attempting farther to excuse it, my present purpose being to relate Facts, and not to make Apologies for them.

It was about this time that I conceiv'd the bold and arduous Project of arriving at moral Perfection. I wish'd to live without committing any Fault at anytime; I would conquer all that either Natural Inclination, Custom, or Company might lead me into. As I knew, or thought I knew, what was right and wrong, I did not see why I might not *always* do the one and avoid the other. But I soon found I had undertaken a Task of more Difficulty than I had imagined: While my Care was employ'd in guarding against one Fault, I was often surpris'd by another. Habit took the Advantage of Inattention. Inclination was sometimes too strong for Reason. I concluded at length, that the mere speculative Conviction that it was our Interest to be completely virtuous, was not sufficient to prevent our Slipping, and that the contrary Habits must be broken and good Ones acquired and established, before we can have any Dependence on a steady uniform Rectitude of Conduct. For this purpose I therefore contriv'd the following Method.

In the various Enumerations of the moral Virtues I had met with in my Reading, I found the Catalog more or less numerous, as different Writers included more or fewer Ideas under the same Name. Temperance, for Example, was by some confin'd to Eating and Drinking, while by others it was extended to mean the moderating every other Pleasure, Appetite, Inclination or Passion, bodily or mental, even to our Avarice and Ambition. I propos'd to myself, for the sake of Clearness, to use rather more Names with fewer Ideas

9. A paraphrase of Philippians 4.8.
1. Only the first part of Franklin's *Articles of Belief and Acts of Religion* survives. It can be found in *The Papers*

*of Benjamin Franklin,* vol. 1, edited by Leonard W. Labaree et al. (1964).

annex'd to each, than a few Names with more Ideas; and I included after Thirteen Names of Virtues all that at that time occurr'd to me as necessary or desirable, and annex'd to each a short Precept, which fully express'd the Extent I gave to its Meaning.

These Names of Virtues with their Precepts were

### 1. TEMPERANCE.

Eat not to Dullness. Drink not to Elevation.

### 2. SILENCE.

Speak not but what may benefit others or yourself. Avoiding trifling Conversation.

### 3. ORDER.

Let all your Things have their Places. Let each Part of your Business have its Time.

### 4. RESOLUTION.

Resolve to perform what you ought. Perform without fail what you resolve.

### 5. FRUGALITY.

Make no Expense but to do good to others or yourself: i.e., Waste nothing.

### 6. INDUSTRY.

Lose no Time. Be always employ'd in something useful. Cut off all unnecessary Actions.

### 7. SINCERITY.

Use no hurtful Deceit. Think innocently and justly; and, if you speak; speak accordingly.

### 8. JUSTICE.

Wrong none, by doing Injuries or omitting the Benefits that are your Duty.

### 9. MODERATION.

Avoid Extremes. Forbear resenting Injuries so much as you think they deserve.

### 10. CLEANLINESS.

Tolerate no Uncleanness in Body, Clothes or Habitation.

### 11. TRANQUILITY.

Be not disturbed at Trifles, or Accidents common or unavoidable.

### 12. CHASTITY.

Rarely use Venery but for Health or Offspring; Never to Dullness, Weakness, or the Injury of your own or another's Peace or Reputation.

### 13. HUMILITY.

Imitate Jesus and Socrates.

My intention being to acquire the *Habitude*[2] of all these Virtues, I judg'd it would be well not to distract my Attention by attempting the whole at once, but to fix it on one of them at a time, and when I should be Master of that, then to proceed to another, and so on till I should have gone thro' the thirteen. And as the previous Acquisition of some might facilitate the Acquisition of

---

2. I.e., making these virtues an integral part of his nature.

*Form of the Pages*

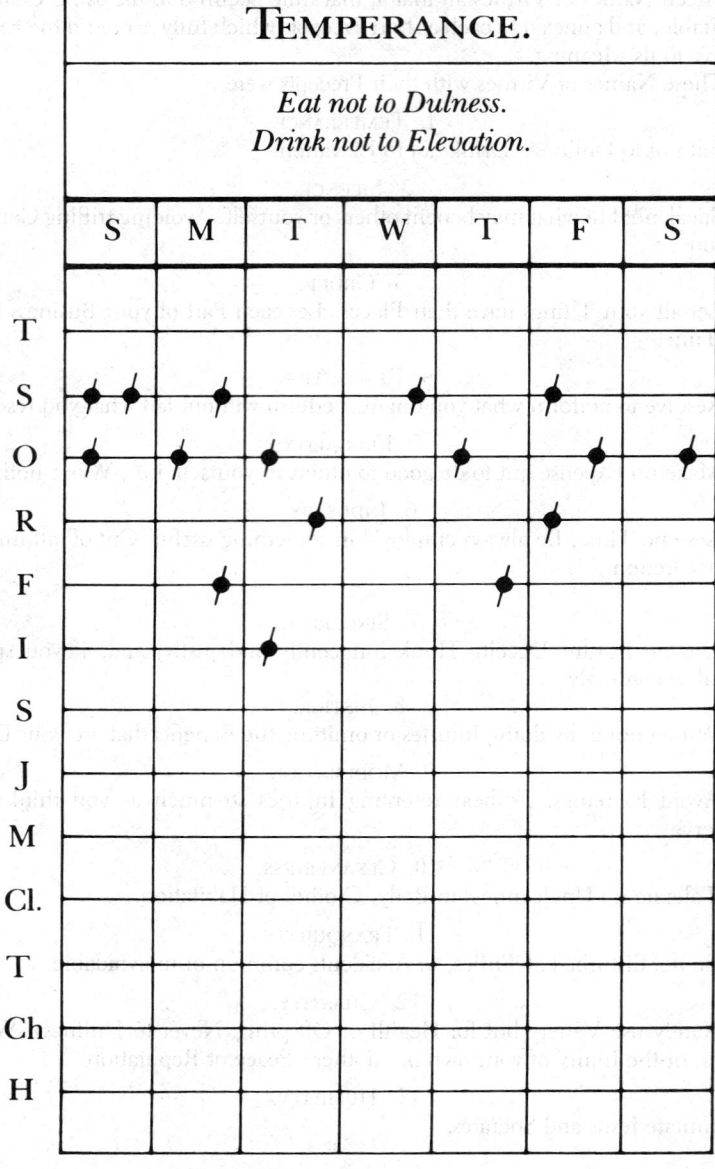

certain others, I arrang'd them with that View as they stand above. *Temperance* first, as it tends to procure that Coolness and Clearness of Head, which is so necessary where constant Vigilance was to be kept up, and Guard maintained, against the unremitting Attraction of ancient Habits, and the Force of perpetual Temptations. This being acquir'd and establish'd, *Silence* would be more easy, and my Desire being to gain Knowledge at the same time that I improv'd in Virtue, and considering that in Conversation it was obtain'd rather by the Use of the Ears than of the Tongue, and therefore wishing to break a Habit I was getting into of Prattling, Punning and Joking, which only made me acceptable to trifling Company, I gave *Silence* the second Place. This, and the next, *Order*, I expected would allow me more Time for attending to my Project and my studies; RESOLUTION once become habitual, would keep me firm in my Endeavors to obtain all the subsequent Virtues; *Frugality* and *Industry*, by freeing me from my remaining Debt, and producing Affluence and Independence would make more easy the Practice of *Sincerity* and *Justice*, etc., etc. Conceiving then that agreeable to the Advice of Pythagoras[3] in his Golden Verses, daily Examination would be necessary, I contriv'd the following Method for conducting that Examination.

I made a little Book in which I allotted a Page for each of the Virtues. I rul'd each Page with red Ink so as to have seven Columns, one for each Day of the Week, marking each Column with a Letter for the Day. I cross'd these Columns with thirteen red Lines, marking the Beginning of each Line with the first Letter of one of the Virtues, on which Line and in its proper Column I might mark by a little black Spot every Fault I found upon Examination, to have been committed respecting that Virtue upon that Day.

I determined to give a Week's strict Attention to each of the Virtues successively. Thus in the first Week my great Guard was to avoid every the least Offence against Temperance, leaving the other Virtues to their ordinary Chance, only marking every Evening the Faults of the Day. Thus if in the first Week I could keep my first Line marked T clear of Spots, I suppos'd the Habit of that Virtue so much strengthen'd and its opposite weaken'd, that I might venture extending my Attention to include the next, and for the following Week keep both Lines clear of Spots. Proceeding thus to the last, I could go thro' a Course complete in Thirteen Weeks, and four Courses in a Year. And like him who having a Garden to weed, does not attempt to eradicate all the bad Herbs at once, which would exceed his Reach and his Strength, but works on one of the Beds at a time, and having accomplish'd the first proceeds to a second; so I should have, (I hoped) the encouraging Pleasure of seeing on my Pages the Progress I made in Virtue, by clearing successively my Lines of their Spots, till in the End by a Number of Courses, I should be happy in viewing a clean Book after a thirteen Weeks' daily Examination.

This my little Book had for its Motto these Lines from *Addison's Cato*,[4]

> *Here will I hold: If there is a Pow'r above us,*
> *(And that there is, all Nature cries aloud*
> *Thro' all her Works) he must delight in Virtue,*
> *And that which he delights in must be happy.*

---

3. Pythagoras (6th century B.C.) was a Greek philosopher and mathematician. Franklin added a note here: "Insert those Lines that direct it in a Note," and wished to include verses translated: "Let sleep not close your eyes till you have thrice examined the transactions of the day: where have I strayed, what have I done, what good have I omitted?"

4. Joseph Addison, *Cato, a Tragedy* (1713; 5.1.15–18). Franklin also used these lines as an epigraph for his *Articles of Belief and Acts of Religion*.

| | | |
|---|---|---|
| The Morning Question, What Good shall I do this Day? | 5<br>6<br>7 | Rise, wash, and address *Powerful Goodness;* contrive Day's Business and take the Resolution of the Day; prosecute the present Study: and breakfast.— |
| | 8<br>9<br>10<br>11 | Work. |
| | 12<br>1 | Read, or overlook my Accounts, and dine. |
| | 2<br>3<br>4<br>5 | Work. |
| | 6<br>7<br>8<br>9 | Put Things in their Places, Supper, Musick, or Diversion, or Conversation, Examination of the Day. |
| Evening Question, What Good have I done to day? | 10<br>11<br>12<br>1<br>2<br>3<br>4 | Sleep.— |

Another from *Cicero*.[5]

> *O Vitæ Philosophia Dux! O Virtutum indagatrix, expultrixque vitiorum! Unus dies bene, et ex preceptis tuis actus, peccanti immortalitati est anteponendus.*

Another from the Proverbs of Solomon speaking of Wisdom or Virtue;

> Length of Days is in her right hand, and in her Left Hand Riches and Honors; Her Ways are Ways of Pleasantness, and all her Paths are Peace.
>                                                                    III, 16, 17

And conceiving God to be the Fountain of Wisdom, I thought it right and necessary to solicit his Assistance for obtaining it; to this End I form'd the following little Prayer, which was prefix'd to my Tables of Examination, for daily Use.

> *O Powerful Goodness! bountiful Father! merciful Guide! Increase in me that Wisdom which discovers my truest Interests; Strengthen my Resolutions to perform what that Wisdom dictates. Accept my kind Offices to thy other Children, as the only Return in my Power for thy continual Favors to me.*

I us'd also sometimes a little Prayer which I took from *Thomson's*[6] Poems, viz.,

> *Father of Light and Life, thou Good supreme,*
> *O teach me what is good, teach me thy self!*
> *Save me from Folly, Vanity and Vice,*
> *From every low Pursuit, and fill my Soul*
> *With Knowledge, conscious Peace, and Virtue pure,*
> *Sacred, substantial, neverfading Bliss!*

The Precept of *Order* requiring that *every Part of my Business should have its allotted Time*, one Page in my little Book contain'd the following Scheme of Employment for the Twenty-four Hours of a natural Day.

I enter'd upon the Execution of this Plan for Self-examination, and continu'd it with occasional Intermissions for some time. I was surpris'd to find myself so much fuller of Faults than I had imagined, but I had the Satisfaction of seeing them diminish. To avoid the Trouble of renewing now and then my little Book, which by scraping out the Marks on the Paper of old Faults to make room for new Ones in a new Course, became full of Holes: I transferr'd my Tables and Precepts to the Ivory Leaves of a Memorandum Book, on which the Lines were drawn with red Ink that made a durable Stain, and on those Lines I mark'd my Faults with a black Lead Pencil, which Marks I could easily wipe out with a wet Sponge. After a while I went thro' one Course only in a Year, and afterwards only one in several Years; till at length I omitted them entirely, being employ'd in Voyages and Business abroad with a Multiplicity of Affairs, that interfered. But I always carried my little Book with me.

My Scheme of ORDER, gave me the most Trouble, and I found, that tho' it

---

5. Marcus Tullius Cicero (106–43 B.C.), Roman philosopher and orator. The quotation is from *Tusculan Disputations* (5.2.5), but several lines are omitted after *vitiorum:* Oh, philosophy, guide of life: Oh, searcher out of virtues and expeller of vices! . . . One day lived well and according to thy precepts is to be preferred to an eternity of sin (Latin).
6. James Thomson (1700–1748), *The Seasons*, "Winter" (1726), lines 218–23.

might be practicable where a Man's Business was such as to leave him the
Disposition of his Time, that of a Journeyman Printer for instance, it was not
possible to be exactly observ'd by a Master, who must mix with the World,
and often receive People of Business at their own Hours. Order too, with
regard to Places for Things, Papers, etc., I found extremely difficult to acquire.
I had not been early accustomed to it, and having an exceeding good Memory,
I was not so sensible of the Inconvenience attending Want of Method. This
Article therefore cost me so much painful Attention and my Faults in it vex'd
me so much, and I made so little Progress in Amendment, and had such
frequent Relapses, that I was almost ready to give up the Attempt, and content
myself with a faulty Character in that respect. Like the Man who in buying an
Ax of a Smith my Neighbor, desired to have the whole of its Surface as bright
as the Edge; the Smith consented to grind it bright for him if he would turn
the Wheel. He turn'd while the Smith press'd the broad Face of the Ax hard
and heavily on the Stone, which made the Turning of it very fatiguing. The
Man came every now and then from the Wheel to see how the Work went on;
and at length would take his Ax as it was without farther Grinding. No, says
the Smith, Turn on, turn on; we shall have it bright by and by; as yet 'tis only
speckled. Yes, says the Man; but—I *think I like a speckled* Ax *best.*—And I
believe this may have been the Case with many who having for want of some
such Means as I employ'd found the Difficulty of obtaining good, and breaking
bad Habits, in other Points of Vice and Virtue, have given up the Struggle,
and concluded that *a speckled* Ax *was best.* For something that pretended to
be Reason was every now and then suggesting to me, that such extreme Nicety
as I exacted of myself might be a kind of Foppery in Morals, which if it were
known would make me ridiculous; that a perfect Character might be attended
with the Inconvenience of being envied and hated; and that a benevolent Man
should allow a few Faults in himself, to keep his Friends in Countenance.

    In Truth I found myself incorrigible with respect to *Order;* and now I am
grown old, and my Memory bad, I feel very sensibly the want of it. But on the
whole, tho' I never arrived at the Perfection I had been so ambitious of
obtaining, but fell far short of it, yet I was by the Endeavor made a better and
a happier Man than I otherwise should have been, if I had not attempted it;
As those who aim at perfect Writing by imitating the engraved Copies,[7] tho'
they never reach the wish'd for Excellence of those Copies, their Hand is
mended by the Endeavor, and is tolerable while it continues fair and legible.

    And it may be well my Posterity should be informed, that to this little Arti-
fice, with the Blessing of God, their Ancestor ow'd the constant Felicity of his
Life down to his 79th Year in which this is written. What Reverses may attend
the Remainder is in the Hand of Providence: But if they arrive, the Reflection
on past Happiness enjoy'd ought to help his Bearing them with more Resignation. To *Temperance* he ascribes his long-continu'd Health, and what is still
left to him of a good Constitution. To *Industry* and *Frugality* the early Easi-
ness of his Circumstances, and Acquisition of his Fortune, with all that
Knowledge which enabled him to be an useful Citizen, and obtain'd for him
some Degree of Reputation among the Learned. To *Sincerity* and *Justice* the
Confidence of his Country, and the honorable Employs it conferr'd upon him.
And to the joint Influence of the whole Mass of the Virtues, even in their
imperfect State he was able to acquire them, all that Evenness of Temper, and

---

7. I.e., the models in the printed book.

that Cheerfulness in Conversation which makes his Company still sought for, and agreeable even to his younger Acquaintance. I hope therefore that some of my Descendants may follow the Example and reap the Benefit.

It will be remark'd[8] that, tho' my Scheme was not wholly without Religion there was in it no Mark of any of the distinguishing Tenets of any particular Sect. I had purposely avoided them; for being fully persuaded of the Utility and Excellency of my Method, and that it might be serviceable to People in all Religions, and intending some time or other to publish it, I would not have anything in it that should prejudice anyone of any Sect against it. I purposed writing a little Comment on each Virtue, in which I would have shown the Advantages of possessing it, and the Mischiefs attending its opposite Vice; and I should have called my Book the ART of Virtue, because it would have shown the Means and Manner of obtaining Virtue; which would have distinguish'd it from the mere Exhortation to be good, that does not instruct and indicate the Means; but is like the Apostle's Man of verbal Charity, who only, without showing to the Naked and the Hungry how or where they might get Clothes or Victuals, exhorted them to be fed and clothed. James II, 15, 16.[9]

But it so happened that my Intention of writing and publishing this Comment was never fulfilled. I did indeed, from time to time put down short Hints of the Sentiments, Reasonings, etc., to be made use of in it; some of which I have still by me: But the necessary close Attention to private Business in the earlier part of Life, and public Business since, have occasioned my postponing it. For it being connected in my Mind with a great and extensive Project that required the whole Man to execute, and which an unforeseen Succession of Employs prevented my attending to, it has hitherto remain'd unfinish'd.

In this Piece it was my Design to explain and enforce this Doctrine, that vicious Actions are not hurtful because they are forbidden, but forbidden because they are hurtful, the Nature of Man alone consider'd: That it was therefore every one's Interest to be virtuous, who wish'd to be happy even in this World. And I should from this Circumstance (there being always in the World a Number of rich Merchants, Nobility, States and Princes, who have need of honest Instruments for the Management of their Affairs, and such being so rare) have endeavored to convince young Persons, that no Qualities were so likely to make a poor Man's Fortune as those of Probity and Integrity.

My List of Virtues contain'd at first but twelve: But a Quaker Friend having kindly inform'd me that I was generally thought proud; that my Pride show'd itself frequently in Conversation; that I was not content with being in the right when discussing any Point, but was overbearing and rather insolent; of which he convinc'd me by mentioning several Instances; I determined endeavoring to cure myself if I could of this Vice or Folly among the rest, and I added Humility to my List, giving an extensive Meaning to the Word. I cannot boast of much Success in acquiring the Reality of this Virtue; but I had a good deal with regard to the Appearance of it. I made it a Rule to forbear all direct Contradiction to the Sentiments of others, and all positive Assertion of my own. I even forbid myself, agreeable to the old Laws of our Junto, the Use of every Word or Expression in the Language that imported[1] a fix'd Opinion; such as certainly, undoubtedly, etc., and I adopted instead of them, I conceive,

---

8. Observed.
9. "If a brother or sister be naked, and destitute of daily food, And one of you say unto them, Depart in peace, be ye warmed and filled: notwithstanding ye give them not those things which are needful to the body; what doth it profit?"
1. Suggested.

I *apprehend*, or I *imagine* a thing to be so or so, or it so appears to me at present. When another asserted something that I thought an Error, I denied myself the Pleasure of contradicting him abruptly, and of showing immediately some Absurdity in his Proposition; and in answering I began by observing that in certain Cases or Circumstances his Opinion would be right, but that in the present case there *appear'd* or *seem'd* to me some Difference, etc., I soon found the Advantage of this Change in my Manners. The Conversations I engag'd in went on more pleasantly. The modest way in which I propos'd my Opinions, procur'd them a readier Reception and less Contradiction; I had less Mortification when I was found to be in the wrong, and I more easily prevail'd with others to give up their Mistakes and join with me when I happen'd to be in the right. And this Mode, which I at first put on, with some violence to natural Inclination, became at length so easy and so habitual to me, that perhaps for these Fifty Years past no one has ever heard a dogmatical Expression escape me. And to this Habit (after my Character of Integrity) I think it principally owing, that I had early so much Weight with my Fellow Citizens, when I proposed new Institutions, or Alterations in the old; and so much Influence in public Councils when I became a Member. For I was but a bad Speaker, never eloquent, subject to much Hesitation in my choice of Words, hardly correct in Language, and yet I generally carried my Points.

In reality there is perhaps no one of our natural Passions so hard to subdue as *Pride*. Disguise it, struggle with it, beat it down, stifle it, mortify it as much as one pleases, it is still alive, and will every now and then peep out and show itself. You will see it perhaps often in this History. For even if I could conceive that I had completely overcome it, I should probably be proud of my Humility.

Thus far written at Passy, 1784.

---

# ELIZABETH ASHBRIDGE

## 1713–1755

The spiritual autobiography is as old as Christianity, but in the seventeenth and eighteenth centuries Christians turned the history of their conversions into an art form of its own. In the Reverend Edward Taylor's congregation in Westfield, Massachusetts, for example, men were accustomed to describing the drama of their spiritual lives before church members to be admitted into full fellowship in the Lord's Supper. Such public accounts led to no great unveiling of the hidden private life: Taylor told the congregation that it was his sister's retelling of the story of the Creation and of Jesus's life, particularly the Christmas story, that filled him with a new devotion. Women did not customarily make public accounts of their conversions: these moments were reserved for private meetings in the minister's study.

Anyone familiar with these Congregational "relations" and their rather predictable progressions, therefore, will be struck with the decidedly more frank and novelistic account given of her life in Christ by Elizabeth Ashbridge of Mount Holly, New Jersey, who came to these shores at the age of nineteen, "a stranger in a strange land." Ashbridge found her spiritual home in America, but she soon learned that Americans were not as tolerant of religious beliefs as they sometimes claimed and were easily threatened by any religion that asserted the truth of the heart over traditional forms of masculine authority.

We know almost nothing whatsoever about Ashbridge other than what she tells us in *Some Account*. She was born in 1713 in Middlewich, Cheshire County, England, and came from a conventional home. Her father was a ship's surgeon and had little to do with her growing up. After her teenage transgression he involved himself not at all in her life, and it was her mother who cared for her. She was not an easy child to raise, for in spite of talk of her love of dancing and her innocence, she clearly had a strong will and was easily pleased with herself, judgmental, and disobedient. When she was little more than fourteen she ran away with a man who died five months later. Unwanted by her father at home, she left England for Ireland, first going to Dublin, where her Quaker relatives annoyed her, and then to the west of Ireland, where country manners were more to her liking. When she met a woman going to America she joined her and indentured herself to her without knowing her at all. Kidnapped for a time, she turned around and sailed on the very ship whose captain held her prisoner. She seems to have escaped from a life of near white slavery only to find herself attached to an aggressive bully whose one redeeming grace was that he allowed her to purchase her freedom from a four-year indenture after serving three years. At twenty-two she married again, this time to a man named Sullivan (his name is not mentioned in her *Account*). He loved her for her dancing. She neither loved him nor valued him at all.

All this, of course, sounds more like the trappings of an eighteenth-century popular novel than a description of a religious conversion, but it is precisely this accumulated detail that makes Ashbridge's life so intriguing. Had she written her *Account* after becoming a successful Quaker preacher and not shortly after her third, and happy, marriage (to Aaron Ashbridge in New Jersey in 1746), we might not have been given quite so many particulars. But in concentrating on the early part of her life, Ashbridge provides us with an unfamiliar glimpse of an America, one that we are inclined to repress: its cruelty to women, its intolerance, its injustice and prejudices, its terrible city and country poverty, and its indifference to all those who lacked money and, consequently, power. Surely one reason she petitioned her community in New Jersey to permit her to return to England and Ireland in 1753 to preach was that she wanted to complete the circle of her life: to prove that the child who stood in awe of religion, who loved the poor and hated hypocrisy, and who wished that she were a boy so that she might take Holy Orders, was no longer a stranger but a saint. Ashbridge was ill almost from the moment of her arrival and died in Ireland on May 16, 1755.

# Some Account of the Fore-Part of the Life of Elizabeth Ashbridge[1]

My life being attended with many uncommon occurrences, some of which I brought upon myself, which I believe were for my good, I have therefore thought proper to make some remarks on the dealings of Divine Goodness with me, having often had cause with David, to say, "It is good for me that I have been afflicted";[2] and I most earnestly desire that whosoever reads the following lines may take warning and shun the evils that through the deceitfulness of Satan I have been drawn into.

1. The text is that of the 1st edition, published in Nantwich, England, in 1774. Some of the spelling and punctuation has been altered for easier reading.

2. Psalm 119.71.

I was born in Middlewich, in Cheshire,[3] in the year 1713, of honest parents. My father's name was Thomas Sampson, he was a surgeon; my mother's name was Mary. My father was a man that bore a good character, but not so strictly religious as my mother, who was a pattern of virtue to me. I was the only child of my father, but my mother had a son and a daughter by a former husband. Soon after my birth my father took to the sea, and followed his profession on board a ship many long voyages, till I was twelve years old, about which time he settled at home; so that my education lay mostly on my mother, in which she discharged her duty by endeavoring to instill into me the principles of virtue during my tender age, for which I have since had cause to be thankful to the Lord, that He blessed me with such a parent, tho' her good advice and counsel have been as cast upon the water, etc.[4] In short, she was a good example to all about her, and beloved by most that knew her, tho' not of the same religious persuasion I am now of. But oh! alas, when the time came that she might reasonably have expected the benefit of her labor, and have had comfort from me, I left her, of which I shall mention in its proper place.

In my very infancy I had an awful[5] regard for religion and a great love for religious people, particularly the ministers, and sometimes grieved at my not being a boy and therefore could not be one, as I thought they were good men, and beloved of God. I also had a great love for the poor, remembering I had read they were blessed of the Lord; this I took to mean such as were poor in this world, and often went to their poor cottages to see them, and if I had any money or other things, I used to give them some, remembering that saying, that they that give to the poor lend to the Lord, and I had when very young an earnest desire to be beloved of Him. I used also to make remarks on those called gentlemen, and when I heard them swear it would grieve me much; for my mother had informed me that if I used any naughty words, God would not love me. As I grew up I took notice that there were several different religious societies, wherefore I often went alone and wept, desiring that I might be directed to the right. Thus my young years were attended with such like tender desires, tho' I was sometimes guilty of those things incident to children, but then I always found something in me that made me sorry for what I did amiss. Till I arrived at the age of fourteen years, I was as innocent as most children, about which time my sorrows began, and have continued most part of my life, through my giving way to a foolish passion, in setting my affections on a young man, who became a suitor to me, without my parent's consent, till I suffered myself (I may say with sorrow of heart) to be carried off in the night, and to be married before my parents found me; altho' as soon as they missed me all possible search was made after me, but all in vain, till too late to recover me.

This precipitate act plunged me into a vast scene of sorrow, for I was soon smote with remorse for thus leaving my parents, who had a right to have disposed of me, or at least their approbation ought to have been consulted in the affair, for I was soon chastised for my disobedience. Divine Providence let me see my error, and in five months I was stripped of the darling of my soul, and left a young and disconsolate widow.

I had then no home to fly to. My father was so displeased that he would do nothing for me, but my dear mother had some compassion towards me, and

3. A former county in the west of England.
4. "Cast thy bread upon the waters: for thou shalt find

it after many days" (Ecclesiastes 11.1).
5. I.e., awe-inspired, reverential.

kept me amongst the neighbors for some time, till by her advice I went to Dublin,[6] to a relation of hers, in hopes that absence would help to regain my father's affection. But he continued inflexible and would not send for me, and I dared not to return without his permission.——This relation with whom I lived was one of the people called Quakers. His conduct was so different from the manner of my education, which was in the way of the Church of England, that it made my situation disagreeable; for tho', as I said, I had a religious education, yet I was allowed to sing and dance, which my cousins were against, and I having a great vivacity in my natural disposition could not bear to give way to the gloomy scene of sorrow, and conviction gave it the wrong effect, and made me more wild and airy[7] than before, for which I was often reproved. But I then thought, as a great many do now, that it was the effect of singularity[8] and therefore would not be subject to it.

I having at that time a distant relation in the west of Ireland, I left Dublin, and went there, where I was entertained, and what rendered me disagreeable in the former place was quite pleasing to the latter. Between these two relations I spent 3 years and 2 months. While I was in Ireland I contracted an intimacy with a widow and her daughter, who were Papists, with whom I used to discourse about religion, they in defense of their faith, and I of mine; and altho' I was then very wild, it made me very thoughtful. The old woman would tell me of such mighty miracles done by their priests that I began to be disturbed in my mind, and thought that if those things were so, they must be the Apostle's successors.[9] The old woman perceiving it one day, said in rapture, that if I, under God, can be instrumental to convert you to the holy Catholic faith, all the sins that ever I committed will be forgiven me. In a while it got so far that the priests came to converse with me, and I being young and my judgment weak was ready to believe what they said. And tho' wild as I was, it cost me many a tear with desires that I might be rightly directed. For some time I frequented their place of worship, but none of my relations knew I had any intention of going with them. At length I concluded never to be led darkly into their belief, and thought to myself—if their articles of faith are good, they will not be against my knowing them. Therefore the next time I had an opportunity with the priest, I told him I had some thoughts of becoming one of his flock, but I did not like to join with them till I knew all I was to agree to, and therefore desired to see their principles. He answered I must first confess my sins to him, and gave me till next day to consider of them. I was not much against that, having done nothing that any person could hurt me, and if, thought I, what the man says be true, it will be for my good. So when he came again, I told him all I could remember, which I thought bad enough; but he thought me, as he said, the most innocent creature that ever made confession to him. When he had done he took a book out of his pocket, and read all which I was to swear to, if I joined with them.

Tho' I was but young, I made my remarks as he went on, but I do not think it worth my writing, nor the reader's hearing. It was a great deal of ridiculous stuff. But what made me sick of my new intention was (I believe I should have swallowed the rest), I was to swear "I believed the Pretender to be the true heir to the crown of England, and that he was King James' son, and also, that

6. In Ireland.
7. Vivacious.
8. I.e., that the Quakers were peculiar and not to be

taken seriously.
9. I.e., the true successors of Peter, who founded the (Catholic) church.

whosoever died out of the pale[1] of the church were damned." As to the first, I did not believe it essential to salvation, whether I believed it or not, and to take an oath to any such thing would be very unsafe; and the second I saw struck directly against charity, which the Apostles preferred before all other Graces. And besides, I had a religious mother who was out of that opinion.[2] I therefore thought it would be wicked in me to believe she was damned. I therefore concluded to consider about it, but before I saw him again a sudden turn took hold of me, which put a final end to it.

My father still keeping me at so great a distance, I thought myself quite shut out of his affections, and therefore concluded, since my absence was most agreeable he should have it, and getting acquaintance with a gentlewoman lately come from Pennsylvania, who was going back again, where I had an uncle, my mother's brother, I soon agreed with her for my passage, and being ignorant in the nature of an indenture[3] consented to be bound. As soon as this was over, she invited me to go and see the vessel we was to sail in, [to] which I readily consented, not knowing what would follow. When I came on board I found a young woman, who I afterwards understood was of a good family and had been deluded away by this creature. I was extremely glad to think I should have such an agreeable companion, but while we were in discourse, our kidnapper left us, and went ashore, and when I wanted to go was not permitted. I was kept there near three weeks, in which time the young woman's friends found her and fetched her away, by which means my friends found me, and went to the water bailiff, who brought me on shore, and our gentlewoman was obliged to conceal herself, or she would have been laid fast.[4] My friends kept me close for two weeks, but at last I found means to get away, for my thoughts being full of going to America, I was determined to proceed with my intention, and one day meeting with the captain, I inquired of him when they sailed, and entered on board the same ship that I was on board before, and I have since thought there was [a] Providential hand in it.

There was sixty Irish servants on board, and several English passengers, but none of the English, excepting myself, understood a word of the Irish language. As for me, I had been at no small pains to learn it, by which I had acquired so much as to discover anything they discoursed upon in Irish, which was of service to us all. There was on board the aforesaid gentlewoman and her husband's brother. While we were on the coast of Ireland, for the wind kept us there some time, I overheard the servants contriving how they should get their liberty when they came to America. To accomplish which they concluded to rise and kill the ship's crew, and all the English passengers on board, and the above mentioned young man was to navigate the ship. I took a private opportunity of informing the captain with their wicked intentions, and he let the English know of it. The next day they bore for the shore, and at a small distance from the Cove of Cork they lowered sail and cast anchor, under pretense of the wind not being fair to stand[5] their course, then hoisted out their boat and invited the passengers to go on shore to divert themselves. And among the rest this young man that was to be this rabble's captain went, by which our

---

1. I.e., protection. The "Pretender" was James Francis Edward Stuart (1688–1766), son of James II and a Roman Catholic, who claimed he was the true heir to the English throne.
2. I.e., was a member of the Church of England and thus damned.

3. A contract in which she would be bound as a servant for a specific time.
4. Arrested. "Water bailiff": officer of the court supervising matters concerning shipping.
5. Maintain.

end was answered. And as soon as he was on shore the rest left him and came on board, and our captain immediately ordered to weigh anchor and hoist sail. At this there was a great outcry for the young man on shore, but the captain told them the wind was fresh up, and he would not stay, [even] if it was for his own son. So their treachery was betrayed in good time, and in a manner they did not mistrust; for it was thought most advisable to keep it private least any of them should do me a mischief. But at length they found out that I understood Irish by my smiling at a story that they were telling in that language, and from that time they devised many ways to do me hurt, for which several of them were put in irons.

In nine weeks from the time I left Dublin we arrived at New York, viz., on the 15 of the 7th month, 1732.[6] Now those to whom I had been instrumental to preserve life proved treacherous to me.—I was a stranger in a strange land.[7]

The captain got an indenture and demanded of me to sign it, at the same time threatening me if I refused it. I told him I could find means to satisfy him for my passage without being bound, but he told me I might take my choice: either to sign that or have the other in force which I signed in Ireland. By this time I had learned the character of the before-mentioned woman, by which she appeared to be a vile person, and I feared if ever I was in her power she would use me ill on her brother's account. I therefore in a fright signed the latter, and tho' there was no magistrate present it proved sufficient to make me a servant for four years. In two weeks time I was sold, and were it possible to convey in characters[8] a scene of the sufferings of my servitude, it would affect the most stony heart with pity for a young creature who had been so tenderly brought up. For tho' my father had no great estate yet he lived well, and I had been used to little but the school, tho' it had been better for me now if I had been brought up to greater hardships.

For a while I was pretty well used, but in a little time the scale turned, which was occasioned by a difference between my master and me, wherein I was innocent; but from that time he set himself against me, and was so inhuman that he would not suffer me to have clothes to be decent in, making me to go barefoot in the snowy weather, and to be employed in the meanest drudgery, wherein I suffered the utmost hardships that my body was able to bear, and which the rest of my troubles had like to have been my ruin to all eternity, had not Almighty God interposed. My master would seem to be a religious man, often taking the Sacrament, so called, and used to pray every night in his family, except when his prayer book was lost, for he never prayed without it as I remember, but the difference was of such a kind, that I was sick of his religion. For tho' I had but little myself, I had an idea what sort of people they should be who professed[9] much. But at length the enemy[1] by his insinuations made me believe there was no such a thing as religion, and that the convictions I had felt in my youth were nothing more than the prejudice of education, which convictions were at times so strong that I have gone and fallen on the ground, crying for mercy. But now I began to be hardened and for some months don't remember I felt any such thing, so that I was ready to conclude

---

6. September was the seventh month under the old calendar. The new calendar with January as the first month began March 25, 1752. "Viz.": namely (Latin).
7. "And she bare him a son, and he called his name Gershom: for he said, I have been a stranger in a strange land" (Exodus 2.22).
8. Writing.
9. Believed.
1. Satan.

there was no God, and that all was priestcraft, I having a different opinion of those sort of men than what I had in my youth. And what corroborated with my atheistical opinion was this: my master's house used to be a place of great resort for the clergy, which gave me an opportunity of making my remarks on them;[2] for sometimes those that came out of the country used to lodge there, and their evening diversions often was playing at cards and singing, and in a few moments after, praying and singing psalms to Almighty God. But I thought, if there be a God, He must be a Pure Being and will not hear the prayers of polluted lips; for He hath in an abundant manner shown mercy to me as will be shown in the sequel, which did not suffer me to doubt in this manner any longer. For when my feet were near the bottomless pit, He plucked me back.

I had to one woman and no other discovered[3] the occasion of this difference, and the nature of it, which two years before had happened betwixt my master and me, and by that means he heard of it, and tho' he knew it to be true, he sent for the town whipper to correct me for it, and upon his appearing, I was called in and ordered to strip, without asking whether I deserved it or not, at which my heart was ready to burst, for I could as freely have given up my life, as suffer such ignominy. And I then said, "If there be a God, be graciously pleased to look down on one of the most unhappy creatures, and plead my cause, for Thou knowest what I have said is the truth, and had it not been from a principle more noble than he was capable of, I would have told it before his wife." Then fixing my eyes on the barbarous man, in a flood of tears, I said to him, "Sir, if you have no pity on me, yet for my father's sake spare me from this shame" (for before this he had heard of my father several ways), "and if you think I deserve such punishment do it yourself." He then took a turn about the room and bid the whipper go about his business, so I came off without a blow, which I thought something remarkable.

I now began to think my credit was gone, for they said several things of me, which (I bless God) were not true; and here I suffered so much cruelty that I knew not how to bear it, and the enemy immediately came in and put me in a way how to get rid of it all, by tempting me to end my miserable life, which I joined with, and for that purpose went into the garret in order to hang myself, at which time I was convinced there was a God, for as my feet entered the place, horror seized me to that[4] degree that I trembled much, and while I stood in amazement, it seemed as tho' I heard a voice say, "There is a hell beyond the grave," at which I was greatly astonished and convinced of an Almighty Power, to whom I prayed, saying "God be merciful and enable me to bear whatsoever Thou of Thy Providence shall bring or suffer to come upon me for my disobedience." I then went downstairs but let none know what I had been about.

Soon after this I had a dream, and tho' some may ridicule dreams, yet this seems very significant to me, therefore I shall mention it.——I thought somebody knocked at the door, which when I had opened there stood a grave[5] woman, holding in her right hand an oil lamp burning, who with a solid countenance fixed her eyes on me, and said, "I am sent to tell thee, that if thou wilt return to the Lord thy God, He will have mercy on thee, and thy

---

2. I.e., observing them.                    4. I.e., such.
3. Revealed.                                5. Somber.

lamp shall not be put out in obscure darkness"; upon which the light flamed from the lamp in a very radiant manner and the vision left me. But oh! alas, I did not give up to join with the heavenly vision, as I think I may call it; for, after all this, I was near being caught in another snare, which if I had, would probably have been my ruin, from which I was also preferred.[6]

I was accounted a fine singer and dancer, in which I took great delight, and once falling in company with some of the stage players, then at New York, they took a great fancy to me, as they said, and persuaded me to become an actress amongst them, and they would find means to get me from my servitude, and that I should live like a lady. The proposal took with me, and I used much pains to qualify myself for the stage, by reading plays, even when I should have slept, but after all this I found a stop in my mind, when I came to consider what my father would think when he heard of it, who had not only forgiven my disobedience in marriage, but had sent for me home, tho' my proud heart would not suffer me to return in so mean a condition I was then in, but rather chose bondage.

When I had served three years I bought the remainder of my time, and got a genteel maintenance by my needle, but alas! I was not sufficiently punished by my former servitude but got into another, and that for life; for a few months after this, I married a young man, who fell in love with me for my dancing— a poor motive for a man to choose a wife, or a woman to choose a husband.[7]

As to my part I fell in love for nothing I saw in him, and it seems unaccountable, that I, who had refused several offers, both in this country and in Ireland, should at last marry a man I had no value for.

In a week after we were married, my husband, who was a school-master, removed from New York, and took me along with him to New England, and settled at a place called Westerley, in Rhode Island government. With respect to religion, he was much like myself, without any; for when he was in drink he would use the worst of oaths. I don't mention this to expose my husband, but to show the effect it had upon me, for I now saw myself ruined, as I thought, being joined to a man I had no love for, and who was a pattern of no good to me. I therefore began to think we were like two joining hands and going to destruction, which made me conclude that if I was not forsaken of God, to alter my course of life. But to love the Divine Being, and not to love my husband, I saw was an inconfidency, and seemed impossible; therefore I requested, with tears, that my affections might increase towards my husband, and I can say in truth that my love was sincere to him. I now resolved to do my duty towards God, and expecting that I must come to the knowledge of it by reading the Scriptures, I read them with a strong resolution of following their directions, but the more I read the more uneasy I grew, especially about baptism, for altho' I had reason to believe I was sprinkled[8] in my infancy, because at the age of fourteen I passed under the bishop's hands for confirmation, as it is called, yet I could not find any precedent for that practice, and upon reading where it is said, "he that believes and is baptized, etc.,"[9] I observed that belief went before baptism, which I was not capable of when I

---

6. Esteemed enough to be saved.
7. Ashbridge's second husband, like her first, is never named. She married her third husband, Aaron Ashbridge, in Burlington County, New Jersey, in 1746.
8. Baptized with holy water by the priest in infancy, as distinguished from total immersion after the age of

reason.
9. "He that believeth and is baptized shall be saved; but he that believeth not shall be damned" (Mark 16.16). "Confirmation" is the ceremony admitting young adults to full church membership.

was sprinkled, at which I grew very uneasy, and living in a neighborhood that were mostly Seventh Day Baptists, I conversed with them, and at length thinking it to be really my duty, I was baptized by one of their teachers, but did not join strictly with them, tho' I began to think the seventh-day[1] the true sabbath, and for some time kept it as such. My husband did not yet oppose me, for he saw I grew more affectionate to him, but I did not yet leave off singing and dancing so much, but I could divert him whenever he desired it.

Soon after this my husband and I concluded to go for England, and for that purpose went to Boston, where we found a ship bound for Liverpool, and agreed for our passage, expecting to sail in two weeks. But my time was not yet come, for there came one called a gentleman, who hired the ship to carry him and his attendants to Philadelphia, and to take no other passengers. There being no other ship near sailing, we for that time gave it over.

We stayed several weeks at Boston, and I remained still dissatisfied as to religion, tho' I had reformed my conduct so as to be accounted by those that knew me a sober woman. But that was not sufficient; for even then I expected to find the sweets of such a change, and though several thought me religious, I dared not to think myself so, and what to do to be so, I seemed still an utter stranger to. I used to converse with people of all societies, as opportunity offered, and, like many others, had got a deal of head knowledge, and several societies thought me of their opinion, but I joined strictly with none, resolving never to leave searching till I found the TRUTH. This was in the 22d year of my age.

While we were at Boston, I went one day to the Quakers' meeting, not expecting to find what I wanted, but from a motive of curiosity. At this meeting there was a woman spoke, at which I was a little surprised, for I had never heard one before. I looked on her with pity for her ignorance, and in contempt of her practice said to myself, "I am sure you're a fool, for if ever I should turn Quaker, which will never be, I could not be a preacher." In these and such like thoughts I sat while she was speaking. After she had done, there stood up a man, which I could better bear; he spoke well, as I thought, from good Joshua's resolutions, viz., "As for me and my house we will serve the Lord."[2] After a time of silence he went to prayer, which was attended with something so awful and affecting that I was reduced to tears, yet a stranger to the cause.

Soon after this we left Boston, for my husband was given to ramble, which was very disagreeable to me, but I must submit. We went to Rhode Island, where he hired a place to keep a school. This place was mostly inhabited with Presbyterians, where I soon got acquainted with some of the most religious amongst them; for tho' I was poor, I was favored with respect amongst people of the best credit, and had frequent discourses with them, but the more I was acquainted with their principles, the worse I liked them, so that I remained dissatisfied, and the old enemy of my happiness,[3] knowing I was resolved to abandon him, assaulted me afresh, and laid a bait with which I had like to have been caught. For one day having been abroad, at my return home, I found the people, at whose house we had taken a room, had left some flax in an apartment through which I went to my own, at sight of which I was tempted to steal some to make some thread, and I went and took a small bunch in my

---

1. Saturday.
2. "And if it seem evil unto you to serve the Lord, choose you this day whom ye will serve; whether the gods which your father served that were on the other side of the flood, or the gods of the Amorites in whose land ye dwell: but as for me and my house, we will serve the Lord" (Joshua 24.15).
3. I.e., Satan.

hand, at which I was smote with remorse, and immediately laid it down, saying, "Lord help me from such a vile act as this." But the twisting serpent did not leave me yet, his assaults were so strong and prevalent that I took it into my room; when I came there horror seized me, and bursting into tears, I cried, "O God of mercy, enable me to resist this temptation," which He of His mercy did, and gave me power to say, "I will regard thy convictions." So I carried it back, and returning to my room, I was so filled with thanksgiving to God, and wrapped into such a frame as I have not words to express, neither can any guess but those who have resisted temptation, and tasted of the same sweet peace by experience.

Soon after this my husband hired[4] a place further up the island, where we were nearer a Church of England, to which place I used to go, for tho' I disliked some of their ways, yet I approved of them the best.

At this time a new exercise fell upon me,[5] and of such a sort as I had never heard of before, and while I was under it I thought myself alone.——It was in the 2d month of the year.[6] I was sitting by a fire in company with several persons, amongst whom my husband was one; there arose a thunder gust and with the noise that struck my ear, a voice attending, even as the sound of a mighty trumpet piercing through me with these words: "Oh, eternity! eternity! the endless term of long eternity!" at which I was exceedingly surprised and sat speechless as in a trance, and in a moment saw myself in such a state as made me despair of ever being happy. I seemed to behold a roll,[7] wrote in black characters, at sight of which I heard a voice say, "These are thy sins"; and immediately followed another saying: "The Blood of Christ is not sufficient to wash them away, and this is shown thee that thou mayst confess thy damnation is just, and not in order that they should be forgiven thee."

All this while I sat speechless, but at last I got up trembling, and threw myself upon a bed. The company thought my indisposition proceeded only from the fright of the thunder, but oh! alas, it was of another kind, and from that time for several months I was in the utmost despair, for if I at any time did endeavor to hope or lay hold of a gracious promise, the old accuser[8] would come in telling me it was now too late, that I had withstood the day of mercy, and that I should add to my sins by praying for pardon and provoke the Divine Vengeance to make a monument of wrath of me.

I now was like one already in torment. My sleep departed from me, I ate little, became extremely melancholy, and took no delight in anything. Had this world been mine and the glory of it, I would gladly have given it for a glimpse of hope. My husband was shocked to see me so changed. I that once could divert him with a song, in which he took great delight, nay after I grew religious as to the outward form, and till I could do it no longer. But now my singing was turned into mourning, and my dancing into lamentations; for my nights and days were one continual scene of sorrow. I let none know my desperate condition. My husband used all means to divert my melancholy state, but all in vain; the wound was too deep to be healed with anything short of the true Balm of Gilead.[9] I durst not go much alone for fear of evil spirits, but if I would, my husband would not suffer[1] it, and if I took the Bible he would take it from me, saying, "How you are altered; you used to be agreeable company, but now I have no comfort of you." I endeavored to bear all with patience, expecting soon to bear more than man could inflict upon me.

At length I went to a priest to see if he could relieve me, but he was a stranger to my condition, and advised me to take the Sacrament, and to use some innocent diversions,[2] and sent me a book of prayers which he said was for my condition. But all was in vain. As to the Sacrament, I thought myself in a state very unfit to receive it worthily, and I then could not use my prayers, for I thought that if ever my prayers should be acceptable, I should be enabled to pray without a book, and diversions were burdensome, for as I said, my husband used all means tending that way to no purpose. Yet he with some others once persuaded me to the raising of a building, where much people were got, in hopes of diverting my grief. But instead of relief, it added to my sorrow; for to this place came an officer to summon a jury to inquire concerning the body of a man that had hanged himself, which as soon as I understood, it seemed to be attended with a voice, saying, "Thou shalt be the next monument of wrath, for thou art not worthy to die a natural death."

For two months after this I was daily tempted to destroy myself, and sometimes the temptation was so strong I could scarce resist, through fear of which, when I went alone I used to throw off my apron and garters, and if I had a knife, to cast it from me, crying, "Lord keep me from taking away that life Thou gave me, and which Thou wouldst have made happy, if I had joined with the offers of Thy grace, and had regarded the convictions I've had from my youth—the fault is my own, Thou, O Lord, [art] clear." And yet so great was my agony that I desired death, that I might know the worst of my torments; all this while I was so hardened that I could not shed a tear. But God in His own good time delivered my soul out of this thralldom.

For one night as I lay in my bed, my husband by me asleep, bemoaning my miserable condition, I had strength to cry, "O my God, had Thou no mercy left? Look down I beseech Thee for Christ's sake, who has promised that all manner of sin and blasphemy shall be forgiven. Therefore Lord, if Thou wilt graciously please to extend this promise to me, an unworthy creature, trembling before Thee, there is nothing Thou shalt command, but I will obey." In an instant my heart tendered and dissolved into a flood of tears, abhorring my past offenses, and admiring the mercies of God; for I was made to hope in Christ my redeemer, and enabled to look upon Him with an eye of faith, and saw fulfilled what I believed when the priest lent me his book, that if ever my prayers would be acceptable to God, I should be enabled to pray without form,[3] and so used it no more. Nevertheless I thought to join with some religious society, but met with none that I liked in everything. Yet the Church of England seemed nearest, upon which I joined with them and received the Sacrament, so called, and can say in truth that I did it with reverence and fear.

Being thus released from deep distress, I seemed like another creature, and went often alone without fear and tears flowed abundantly from my eyes; and once as I was abhorring myself, in great humility of mind, I heard a gracious voice say, "I will not forsake thee, only obey what I shall make known unto

---

2. Amusements. "The Sacrament": Holy Communion.    3. Without reading a prayer book.

thee." I then entered into covenant,[4] saying, "My soul doth magnify Thee the God of mercy; if Thou will vouchsafe Thy Grace, the rest of my days shall be devoted to Thee, and if it be Thy will that I beg my bread, I will be content and submit to Thy Providence."

I now began to think of my relations in Pennsylvania, whom I had not yet seen, and having a great desire to see them, I got leave of my husband to go, and also a certificate from the priest, in order that if I made any stay, I might be received as a member wherever I came. Then setting out, my husband bore me company to the Blazing Star Ferry, saw me safe over, and then returned. In the way near a place called Maidenhead, I fell from my horse and was disabled from traveling for some time, and abode at the house of an honest Dutchman, who with his wife was very kind to me—and tho' they had much trouble in going to the doctor and waiting upon me, for I was several days unable to help myself—yet would have nothing for it, which I thought very kind, and charged me[5] if ever I came that way again to call and lodge there.— I mention this because I shall have occasion to remark this place again.

I arrived next at Trent town Ferry,[6] where I met with no small mortification upon hearing that my relations were Quakers, and what was worst of all, my aunt was a preacher. I was sorry to hear of it, for I was exceedingly prejudiced against those people, and have often wondered with what face they could call themselves Christians; and I began to repent my coming, sometimes having a mind to return back without seeing them. At last I concluded to go see them, since I was so far on my journey, tho' I expected little comfort from my visit. But see how God brings unforeseen things to pass, for by my going there I was brought to the knowledge of the TRUTH.

I went from Trent town Ferry to Philadelphia by water, and thence to my uncle's on horseback, where I met with a very kind reception; for tho' my own uncle was dead and my aunt married again, yet both she and her husband received me in a very kind manner. I had not been there 3 hours before I met with a shock, and my opinion began to alter with respect to these people; for seeing a book lie on the table, and being much given to reading, I took it up, which my aunt observing, said, "Cousin, that is a Quaker's book, Samuel Crisp's *Two Letters*,"[7] and I suppose she thought I should not like it, at perceiving that I was not one. I made her no answer, but thought to myself, "What can these people write about, for I have heard that they deny the Scripture, and have no other bible but George Foxe's *Journal*,[8] and that they deny all the holy Ordinances;" for I resolved to read a little, and had not read two pages before my very heart burned within me, and tears came into my eyes, which I was afraid would be seen. I therefore walked with the book into the garden, and the piece being small, read it through before I went in, and sometimes uttering these involuntary expressions: "My God, if ever I come to the true knowledge of the truth, must I be of this man's opinion, who has fought Thee as I have done, and join with these people that I preferred the Papists to, but a [few] hours ago. Oh! Thou the God of my salvation and of my life, who hast in an abundant manner manifested Thy long-suffering and tender mercy

---

4. Formal agreement.
5. Made me promise.
6. Trenton, New Jersey.
7. Samuel Crisp (n.d.) was an English schoolmaster and the author of *A Libeller Exposed: being a Vindica-*

*tion of the People Called Quaker* (1704).
8. George Fox (1624–1691), an Englishman and founder of the Society of Friends, popularly called Quakers. His *Journal* appeared in 1694, revised by a committee headed by William Penn.

in redeeming me as from the lowest hell, a monument of Thy grace. Lord my soul beseeches Thee to direct me in the right way, and keep me from error; and then according to my covenant, I'll think nothing too near to part with for Thy name's sake, if these things be so. Oh! happy people thus beloved of God."

After I came a little to myself I washed my face, least any in the house should perceive I had been weeping. At night I got very little sleep, for the old enemy began to suggest that I was one of those that wavered and was not steadfast in the faith, advancing several texts of Scripture against me and them that mention in the latter days there shall be those that will deceive the very elect, and these people were them, and that I was in danger of being deluded. Here the subtle serpent transformed himself so hiddenly that I verily thought this to be a timely caution from a good angel, so resolved to beware of these deceivers, and for some weeks did not touch any of their books.

The next day being the first of the week, I wanted to have gone to church, which was distant about four miles, but being a stranger and having nobody to go with me, was forced to give it up, and as most of the family was going to meeting, I went with them. But with this conclusion: not to like them. And so it was; for as they sat in silence, I looked over the meeting, thinking within myself, how like fools these people sit, how much better were it to stay at home and read the Bible, or some good book, than to come here and go to sleep; for I being very sleepy thought they were no better than me. Indeed, at length I fell asleep and had like to have fallen down, but this was the last time I ever fell asleep in a meeting, tho' often assaulted with it.

I now began to be lifted up with spiritual pride, and thought myself better than they, but through mercy this did not last long, for in a little time I was brought low, and saw that they were the people to whom I must join. It may seem strange that I, who had lived so long with one of this society in Dublin, should yet be so great a stranger to them. In answer, let it be considered, that during the time I was there, I never read one of their books or went to one meeting, and besides, I had heard such ridiculous stories of them as made me think they were the worst of any society of people. But God that knew the sincerity of my heart, looked with pity on my weakness, and soon let me see my error; for in a few weeks there was an afternoon's meeting held at my uncle's to which came that servant of the Lord, William Hammons,[9] who was then made instrumental in convincing me of the TRUTH more perfectly, and helping me over some great doubts, tho' I believe no one did ever sit in greater opposition than I did when he first stood up. But I was soon brought down, for he preached the Gospel with such power that I was forced to give up and confess it was the TRUTH.

As soon as meeting was ended, I endeavored to get alone, for I was not fit to be seen, being so broken; yet afterwards the restless adversary assaulted me again in the manner following. The morning before this meeting I had been disputing with my uncle about Baptism,[1] which was the subject this good man dwelt upon and which he handled so clearly as to answer all my scruples beyond objection. Yet the crooked serpent farther alleged that the sermon I had heard did not proceed from Divine Revelation, but that my uncle and

9. Evidently a Quaker of some renown.
1. In the 1774 edition, "Baptism" was misprinted as *Babylon*.

aunt had acquainted the Friend[2] of me, which being strongly suggested, I fell to accusing them of it, and of which they both cleared themselves, saying they had not seen him since my coming to these parts until he came to the meeting.

I then concluded he was a messenger sent from God to me, and with fervent cries desired I might be directed right. And now I laid aside all prejudice and set my heart to receive TRUTH, and the Lord in His own good time revealed to my soul not only the beauty there is in it, and that those should shine who continued faithful to it, but also the emptiness of all shadows, which in their way were glorious, but now the Son of Glory was come to put an end to them all and establish everlasting righteousness in the room thereof, which is a work in the soul. He likewise let me see that all I had gone through was to prepare me for this day, and that the time was near that He would require me to go forth and declare to others what the God of mercy had done for my soul; at which I was surprised and desired I might be excused, for fear I should bring dishonor to the TRUTH, and cause His holy Name to be evil spoken of.

All this while I did not let anybody know the condition I was in, nor did appear like a Friend,[3] and feared a discovery. I now began to think of returning to my husband, but found a restraint to stay where I was. I then hired a place to keep a school, and hearing of a place for him wrote desiring him to come to me, but let him know nothing how it was with me.

I loved to go to meetings, but did not like to be seen to go on week days, and therefore to shun it used to go from my school through the woods to them. But notwithstanding all my care, the neighbors that were not Friends soon began to revile, calling me Quaker, saying they supposed I intended to be a fool and turn preacher. I then received the same censure that I, a little above a year before, had passed on[4] one of the handmaids of the Lord at Boston, and so weak was I, alas, I could not bear the reproach, and in order to change their opinions got in to greater excess in apparel than I had freedom to wear for some time before I became acquainted with Friends. In this condition I continued till my husband came, and then began the trial of my faith. Before he reached me he heard I was turned Quaker, at which he stamped, saying, I had rather have heard she had been dead, well as I love her, for if so all my comfort is gone; he then came to me, and had not seen me for four months; I got up and met him, saying, "My dear, I am glad to see thee," at which he fell in a great passion, and said, "The devil THEE thee, don't THEE me." I used all the mild means I could to pacify him, and at length got him fit to go and speak to my relations, but he was alarmed, and as soon as he got alone he said, "So I see your Quaker relations have made you one." I told him they had not, which was true, nor had I ever told them how it was with me. But he would have it that I was one, and therefore should not stay amongst them, and having found a place to his mind,[5] hired it, and came directly back to fetch me, and in one afternoon walked near thirty miles to keep me from meeting, the next day being the first-day,[6] and on the morrow took me to the aforesaid place, hired lodgings at a Church-man's house, who was one of the wardens,[7] and a bitter enemy to Friends, and would tell me a great deal of ridiculous stuff. But my judgment was too clearly convinced to believe. I still did not appear like a

2. I.e., Hammons.
3. I.e., did not dress in Quaker clothes.
4. I.e., the criticism that I . . . had made of.
5. Suitable to him.

6. Sunday. Quakers preferred not to use the traditional names for the days of the week because they are derived from the names of pagan gods.
7. Lay officer in the Anglican, or Episcopal, church.

Friend, but they all believed I was one. When my husband and him used to be making their diversions and revilings, I used to sit in silence, but now and then an involuntary sigh would break from me, at which he would say to my husband, "There, did not I tell you your wife was a Quaker, and she will be a preacher soon," upon which my husband once in a great rage came up to me, and shaking his hand over me said, "You had better be hanged on that day." I then, Peter like,[8] in a panic denied my being a Quaker, at which great horror seized upon me, and continued for near three months, so that I again feared that by denying the Lord who bought me the heavens were shut against me; for great darkness surrounded me, and I was again plunged in despair.

I used to walk much alone in the woods, where no eye saw, or ear heard me, and there lamented my miserable condition, and have often gone from morning till night without breaking my fast, with which I was brought so low that my life was a burden to me. The devil seemed to vaunt[9] [that although] the sins [of] my youth were forgiven, yet now he was sure of me, for that I had committed the unpardonable sin, and hell would inevitably be my portion, and my torments would be greater than if I had hanged myself at the first.

In this doleful condition I had now to bewail my misery, and even in the night, when I could not sleep, under the painful distress of my mind. And if my husband perceived me weeping he used to revile me for it. At last, when he and his friends thought themselves too weak to overset me, tho' I feared it was already done, he went to the priest at Chester to advise what to do with me. This man knew I was a member of the Church, for I had shown him my certificate. His advice was to take me out of Pennsylvania, and find some place where there was no Quakers, and there my opinion would wear off. To this my husband agreed, saying he did not care where he went, if he could but restore me to that liveliness of temper I was naturally of, and to that Church of which I was a member. I, on my part, had no spirit to oppose their proposals, neither much cared where I was; for I seemed to have nothing to hope for, but daily expected to be made a spectacle of Divine Wrath, and I was possessed it would be by thunder.

The time of removal came and I was not suffered[1] to bid my relations farewell. My husband was poor and kept no horse, so I must travel on foot. We came to Wilmington, 15 miles thence to Philadelphia, by water; here he took me to a tavern, where I soon became a spectacle and discourse of the company. My husband told them his wife was turned Quaker, and that he designed, if possible, to find out some place where there was none. Oh, thought I, I was once in condition of deserving that name, but now it was over with me. Oh, that I might, from a true hope, once more have an opportunity to confess to the TRUTH, tho' sure of all manner of cruelties yet I would not regard it. These were my concerns while he was entertaining the company with my story, in which he told them that I had been a good dancer, but now he could neither get me to dance nor sing; upon which one of the company starts up, saying, "I'll go fetch my fiddle and we'll have a dance," at which my husband was pleased. The fiddle came, the sight of which put me in a sad condition, for fear, if I refused, my husband would be in a great passion. However I took up this resolution not to comply whatever might be the conse-

---

8. Peter denied Christ three times in Mark 14.66–72.          1. Allowed.
9. Brag.

quence. He came to me and took me by the hand, saying, "Come my dear, shake off that gloom, let's have a civil dance, you would now and then, when you were a good Church-woman and that is better than a stiff Quaker." I, trembling, desired to be excused. But he insisted on it, and knowing his temper to be exceeding choleric, I durst not say much, but would not consent. He then pulled me round the room till tears affected my eyes, at sight of which the musician stopped, and said, "I'll play no more, let your wife alone," of which I was glad. There was also a man in [this] company who came from Freehold, in West Jersey,[2] who said, "I see your wife is a Quaker, but if you'll take my advice, you need not go so far (for my husband designed to go to Staten Island), come and live amongst us and we'll soon cure her from her Quakerism, and we want both a school-master and mistress." To which he agreed, and a happy turn it was for me as will be seen by and by, and the wonderful turn of Providence, who had not yet abandoned me, but raised a glimmering hope and afforded the answer of peace in refusing to dance, for which I was more rejoiced than if I were made a mistress of much riches, and in floods of tears, said, "Lord, I dread to ask, and yet without Thy gracious pardon I am miserable, I therefore fall down before Thy throne, imploring mercy at Thy hand. O Lord, once more I beseech Thee try my obedience, and then whatsoever Thou commands, I will obey, and not fear to confess Thee before men." Thus was my soul engaged before God in sincerity, and He of His tender mercy heard my cries, and in me has shewn that He delights not in the death of a sinner, for He again set my soul at liberty and I could praise Him.

I now again longed for an opportunity to confess to His TRUTH, which He showed me should come, tho' in what manner I did not see, but believed the words I had heard, which in a little time were fulfilled to me. My husband, as aforesaid, agreed to go to Freehold, and in our way thither came to Maiden-head, where I went to see the kind Dutchman, aforementioned, who made us welcome, and invited us to stay a few days. While we were there, there was held a great meeting of the Presbyterians, not only of worship, but business also; for one of their preachers being charged with drunkenness was this day to have his trial before a great number of priests, and we went to it, of which I was afterwards glad; for here I perceived great divisions amongst the people about who should be their shepherd, and for which I greatly pitied their condition. I now saw beyond the men-made ministers,[3] and what they preached for, and which all those at this meeting might have done, had not the prejudice of education, which is very prevalent, blinded their eyes. Some insisted to have the old offender restored; some to have a young man they had upon trial[4] some weeks; a third party was for sending for one from New England. At length one stood up, and, addressing himself to the chief speaker, said, "Sir, when we have been at the expense, which will be no small matter, of fetching this gentleman from New England, perhaps he won't stay with us." [Answered.] "Don't you know how to make him?" [Replied.] "No, Sir." "I'll tell you then," said he, to which I gave good attention: "Give him a good salary, and I'll engage he'll stay." O, thought I, these mercenary creatures, they are actuated by one and the same thing, ever the love of money, and not the regard of

---

2. Now the western part of the state of New Jersey, where many Quakers lived.

3. I.e., ministers without a divine calling.

4. I.e., on probation as a replacement for the accused.

souls. This, [so-]called reverend gentleman, whom these poor people almost adored, to my knowledge had left his flock on Long Island and moved to Philadelphia, where he could get more money. I myself had heard some of them on the Island say that they had almost impoverished themselves to keep him, but not being able to equal Philadelphia's invitation, he left them without a shepherd. This man therefore, knowing their ministry proceeded from one cause, might be purchased with the same thing.—Surely these and such like are the shepherds that regard the fleece more than the flock, and in whose mouth are lies, saying the Lord hath sent them, and that they were Christ's ambassadors, whose command to those He sent was "Freely ye have received, freely give."[5] I durst not say anything to my husband of the remarks I had made, but laid them up in my heart, and they did help to strengthen me in my resolutions.

Hence we set forward for Freehold, and coming through Stony Brook, my husband turning towards me said tauntingly, "There's one of Satan's Synagogues, don't you want to be in it? I hope I shall see you carried off [by] this new religion." I made no answer but went on. In a little time we came to a large run of water, over which was no bridge, and we being strangers knew no way to get over. But through we was obliged to go. My husband carried our clothes, which we had in bundles, and I pulled off my shoes and waded through in my stockings, which served somewhat to prevent the chill of the water from [freezing] me, it being very cold and a fall of snow, in the 12th month.[6] My heart was concerned in prayer that the Lord would sanctify all my afflictions to me, and give me patience to bear whatsoever should be suffered to come upon me.

We walked most part of a mile before we came to a house, which proved to be a sort of a tavern. My husband called for some spirituous liquors, but I got some cider mulled, which when I had drank of t, the cold being struck to my heart, made me extremely sick, insomuch, that when we were a little past the house I expected I should have fainted, and not being able to stand, fell down under a fence. Which my husband observing, tauntingly said, "What's the matter now? What are you drunk? Where's your religion now?" He knew better, and at that time I believe he pitied me, yet was suffered grievously to afflict me. In a little time I grew better, and going on came to another tavern at which place we lodged. The next day I was indifferent well, and as we proceeded on our journey a young man with an empty cart overtook us, and I desired my husband to ask the young man to let us ride, which he did and it was readily granted. I now thought myself well off, and took it as a great favor, for my proud heart was humbled, and I did not regard the looks of it, tho' the time had been that I would not have been seen in a cart. This cart belonged to a man at Shrewsbury and was to go through the place that we were going to, so we rode on. We soon had the care of the team to ourselves, from a failure in the driver, to the place where I was intended to have been made a prey on. But see how unforeseen things are brought to pass by a Providential hand. It is said and answered, Shall we do evil that good may come? God forbid.[7] Yet hence good came to me. Here my husband would fain have me stay, while he went to see the team safe at home, but I told him no, since he

5. "Heal the sick, cleanse the lepers, raise the dead, cast out devils: freely ye have received, freely give" (Matthew 10.8).

6. February.
7. "Shall we continue in sin, that grace may abound? God forbid" (Romans 6.1–2).

had led me through the country like a vagabond, I would not stay behind him; so we went on, and lodged that night at the man's house who owned the cart. Next day on our return to Freehold, we met a man riding full speed, who stopped, and said to my husband, "Sir, are you a school-master?" and was answered yes. "I came to tell you," replied the stranger, "of two new school houses, and each want a master and are two miles apart." How this stranger came to hear of us, who came but the night before, I never knew, but I was glad he was not one called a Quaker, lest my husband should have thought it had been a plot. I said to my husband: "My dear, look on me with pity. If thou hast any affections left for me, which I hope thou hast, for I am not conscious of having done anything to alienate them here; here is," continued I, "an opportunity to settle us both, and I am willing to do all in my power towards an honest livelihood."

My expressions took place, and after a little pause he consented to the young man's directions and made towards the place, and in our way we came to the house of a worthy Friend, whose wife was a preacher, tho' we did not know it. I was surprised to see the people so kind to us who were strangers. We had not been long in the house before we were invited to lodge there that night, it being the last of the week. I said nothing, but waited to hear my master speak. He soon consented, saying, "My wife has had a tedious travel, and I pity her," at which kind expressions I was greatly affected, for they were now very seldom used to me.

The Friends' kindness could not have proceeded from my appearing in the garb of a Quaker, for I had not yet altered my dress; but the woman of the house, after we had concluded to stay, fixed her eyes on me and said, I believe thou hast met with a deal of troubles, to which I made but little answer. My husband observing they were of that sort of people he had so much endeavored to shun would give us no opportunity for any discourse that night, but the next morning I let the Friend know a little how it was with me. Meeting time came, to which I longed to go, but durst not ask my husband leave, for fear of disturbing him, till we were settled, and then thought I, "If ever I am favored to be in this place, come life or death, I'll fight through, for my salvation is at stake." The Friends, getting ready for meeting, asked my husband if he would go, saying they knew who were to be his employers, and if they were at meeting, they would speak to them. He then consented to go. Then said the woman, "Friend, and wilt thou let thy wife go?" to which he denied, making several objections, all which she answered so prudently, that he could not be angry and at last he consented. With joy I went, for I had not been at one for near 4 months, and an heavenly meeting it was to me. I now renewed my covenant, and saw the word of the Lord made good, that I should have another opportunity to confess to His name, for which, "My soul did magnify the Lord, and my spirit did rejoice in the God of my salvation,"[8] who had brought strange things to pass. May I ever be preserved in humility, never forgetting His tender mercies to me.

Here according to my desire we settled, my husband got one school and I the other. We took a room at a Friend's house, a mile from each school, and 8 miles from the meeting-house. Before the next first-day we were got to our

---

8. "And Mary said, My soul doth magnify the Lord, and my spirit hath rejoiced in God my Savior" (Luke 1.46–47).

new settlement, and now I concluded to let my husband see that I was determined to join with Friends. When the first-day came I directed myself to him in this manner: "My dear, art thou willing to let me go to meeting?" at which he fell into a rage, saying, "No, you shan't." I then drew up a resolution and told him that as a dutiful wife ought, so was I ready to obey all his commands, but where they imposed on my conscience I no longer durst, for I had already done it too long, and had wronged myself by it, and tho' he was near and I loved him as a wife ought, yet God was nearer than all the world to me, and had made me sensible this was the way I ought to go, which I assured him was no small cross to my own will. Yet I had given up my heart, and hoped he that had called for it would enable me the residue of my life to keep it steadily devoted to him whatever I suffered, adding I hoped not to make him any worse a wife for it. But all I could say was in vain. I had now put my hand to the plow and resolved not to look back, so went without leave, but expected to be immediately followed and forced back. He did not follow me as I expected, so I went to a neighbor's and got a girl to show me the way; and then went on rejoicing and praising God in my heart who had thus far given me power, and another opportunity to confess to the TRUTH.

Thus for some time I had to go 8 miles on foot to meeting, which I never thought hard. My husband now bought a horse, but would not let me ride him, neither when my shoes were wore out would he let me have a new pair, thinking by that means to keep me from meetings. But this did not hinder me, for I have taken strings and tied round to keep them on. He now finding no hard usage could alter my resolution, neither threatening to beat me, nor denying it, for he several times struck me with sore blows, which I endeavored to bear with patience, believing the time would come when he would see I was in the right, which accordingly [he] did. He once came up to me and took out his penknife, saying, "If you offer to go to meeting to-morrow, with this knife I'll cripple you, for you shall not be a Quaker." I made him no answer but when morning came I set out as usual, and he was not suffered to hurt me.

In despair of recovering me himself, he now fled to the priest for help, and told him that I had been a very religious woman in the way of the Church of England, was a member of it, and had a good certificate from Long Island, but now was bewitched and turned Quaker, which almost broke his heart. He therefore desired, as he was one who had the care of souls, he would come and pay me a visit, and use his best endeavors to reclaim me, and he hoped by the blessing of God it would be done.

The priest consented to come, and the time was fixed, which was to be that day two weeks, for he said he could not come sooner. My husband came home extremely pleased, and told me of it, at which I smiled and said I hope to be enabled to give a reason for the hope that is in me, at the same time believing the priest would never trouble me nor he never did. Before this appointed time came it was required of me in a more public manner to confess to the world what I was, and to give up in prayer at the meeting. The fight of which and the power that attended it made me tremble, and I could not hold myself still. I now again desired death and could have freely given up my natural life as ransom. And what made it harder to me, I was not taken under the care of Friends; and what kept me from requesting it was for fear I should be overcome, and bring a scandal on the Society. I begged to be excused till I was joined, and then I would give up freely, to which I received this answer, as tho' I had heard a distinct voice, "I am a covenant-keeping God, and the words that I spoke to thee when I found thee in distress, even that I would never leave thee, nor forsake thee, if thou wouldst be obedient to what I should make known to thee, which I will assuredly make good; but if thou refuse, my Spirit shall not always strive. Fear not, I will make way for thee through all thy difficulties, which shall be many, for My name's sake, but be faithful, and I will give thee a crown of life." I then being sure it was God that spoke, said, "Thy will, O God, be done, I am in Thy hand, do with me according to Thy word." And I gave up, but after it was over the enemy came in like a flood, telling me I had done what I ought not, and should now bring dishonor to this people. But this shock did not last long.

This day, as usual, I had gone on foot. My husband, as he afterwards told me, lying on the bed, these words ran through him, "Lord where shall I fly to shun thee," at which he arose, and seeing it rain, got the horse and came to fetch me, and coming just as the meeting broke up, I got on horseback as quick as possible, least he should hear what had happened. Nevertheless he had heard, and as soon as we were got into the woods he began, saying, "What do you mean thus to make my life unhappy? could you not be a Quaker without turning fool after this manner?" I answered in tears, saying, "My dear, look on me with pity, if thou hast any; can'st thou think that I in the bloom of my days would bear all that thou knowest of, and a great deal which thou knowest not of, if I did not believe it to be my duty?" This took hold of him, and he taking my hand said, "Well, I'll even give you up, for I see it don't avail to strive. If it be of God, I cannot overthrow it, and if it be of yourself it will soon fall," and I saw the tears stand in his eyes, at which my heart was overcome with joy, and I would not have changed conditions with a queen. I already began to reap the fruit of my obedience, but my trials did not end here. The time being up that the priest was to come, but no priest appeared, my husband went to fetch him, but he would not come, saying he was busy and could not, which so displeased my husband that he'd never go near him more, and for some time went to no place of worship.

Now the Unwearied Adversary found out another scheme, and with it assaulted me so strong, that I thought all I had gone through was but little to this. It came upon me in such an unexpected manner, I hearing a woman relate a book she had read, in which it was asserted that Christ was not the Son of God. As soon as she had spoke the words, if a man had spoke I could not more distinctly have heard these words, "No more He is, it's all a fancy, and the contrivance of man," and an horror of great darkness fell upon me which continued for three weeks. The exercise[9] I was in I am not able to express, neither durst I let any one know how it was with me. I again sought desolate places, where I might make my moan, and have lain whole nights and don't know that my eyes have been shut to sleep. I again thought myself alone, but would never let go my faith in Him, after saying in my heart, I'll believe till I die, and keep a hope that He who delivered me out of the paw of the bear and from the jaws of the devouring lion would in His own good time deliver me out of this temptation also, which He of His mercy did, and let me see this was for my good in order to prepare me for further service, which He had for me to do, and that it was necessary that His ministers should be dipped

9. As above, spiritual struggle or trial.

into all states,[1] that thereby they might be abler to speak to all, for which my soul was thankful to Him, the God of mercies, who had at several times redeemed me out of great distress. And I found the truth of His words that all things should work for good to those that loved and feared Him, which I did with my whole heart, and I hope ever shall while I have a being.

This happened soon after my first appearance, and Friends had not been to talk with me, nor did they know what to do till I had appeared again, which was not for some time, when at the monthly meeting, four Friends came to pay me a visit, which I was glad of, and gave them such satisfaction that they left me well satisfied. I then joined with Friends, my husband went to no place of worship. One day he said, "I'd go to meeting, only I'm afraid I shall hear your clack, which I cannot bear." I used no persuasions, yet when meeting-time came he got the horse, and took me behind him and went to meeting. But for several months, if he saw me offer to rise,[2] he would go out, till one time I got up before he was aware, and then, as he afterward said, was ashamed to do it, and from that time never did nor hindered me from going to meeting, and tho' he, poor man, could not take up the Cross, yet his judgment was convinced, and sometimes in a flood of tears would say, "My dear, I've seen the beauty there is in the TRUTH, and that thou art in the right, and I pray God preserve thee in it, but as for me the Cross is too heavy, I cannot bear it." I told him I hoped He that had given me strength would also favor him. "Oh!" said he, "I can't bear the reproach thou dost to be called turn-coat, and become a laughing stock to the world. But I'll no longer hinder thee from it;" which I looked on as a great favor that my way was thus far made easy, and a little hope remained that my prayers would be heard on his account.

In this place he had got linked in with some that he was afraid would make game of him, which indeed they already did, asking him when he designed to commence preacher, for that they saw he intended to turn Quaker, and seemed to love his wife better since she did than before. We were now got to a little house by ourselves, which tho' mean, and little to put in it, our bed being no better than chaff,[3] yet I was truly content, and did not envy the rich their riches. The only desires I now had was my own persuasion, and to be blessed with the reformation of my husband. These men used to come to our house and there provoke my husband to sit up and drink sometimes till near day, while I have been sorrowing in a stable. As I once sat in this condition I heard my husband say to his company, "I cannot bear any longer to afflict my poor wife in this manner, for whatever you may think of her, I do believe she is a good woman," upon which he came to me, and said, "Come in, my dear, God has given thee a deal of patience, I'll put an end to this practice." And so he did, for this was the last time they sat up at nights. My husband now thought if he was in any place where it was not known that he had been so bitter against Friends he could do better than here, but I was much against his moving, fearing it would turn out to his hurt, having been for some months much altered for the better, establishing me in the TRUTH, and therefore would not have him be afflicted about that, and according to the measure of Grace received did what I could both by example and advice for his good, and my advice was for him to fight through it here, fearing he would grow weaker, and

1. I.e., spiritual or mental states.                    3. Straw. "Mean": inferior.
2. I.e., to stand up and speak at a Quaker meeting.

the enemy gain advantage over him, if he thus fled. But all I could say did not prevail against his moving, and hearing of a place at Burdon Town [Bordentown], [he] went there. But that did not suit. He then moved to Mount Holy [New Jersey], and there we settled. He got a good school and so did I, and here we might have done very well. We got our house pretty well furnished for poor folks. I now began to think I wanted but one thing to complete my happiness, viz., the reformation of my husband, to which also I had too much reason to doubt, for it fell out according to my fears, and he grew worse here, and took to drinking, so that it seemed as tho' my life was to be a continual scene of sorrow, and most earnestly I prayed to Almighty God, to endue me with patience to bear my afflictions, and submit to His providence, which I can say in truth I did without murmuring, or ever uttering an unsavory expression, to the best of my knowledge, except once when my husband coming home a little in drink, in which frame he was very fractious, and finding me at work by a candle, came to me, put it out, and fetching me a box on the ear said, "You don't earn your light," which unkind usage—for he had not struck me of two years before—went hard with me, and I uttered these [sic] rash expressions, "Thou art a vile man," and was a little angry, but soon recovered and was sorry for it. He struck me again, which I received without so much as a word in return, and [he] went on in a distracted manner, uttering several rash expressions that bespoke despair, as that he now believed he was predestined to damnation, and he did not care how soon God would strike him dead and the like. I durst say but little, but at length I broke out in these words, "Lord look down on my afflictions, and deliver me by some means or other." I was answered I should soon be, and so I was, but in such a manner as I verily believed it would have killed me.

In a little time he went to Burlington, where he got in drink, and enlisted for a common soldier to go to Cuba, anno dom. 1740. I had drank many bitter cups, but this seemed to exceed them all; for indeed my very senses seemed shaken. I now a thousand times blamed myself for making such an undevised[4] request, fearing I had displeased God by it, and tho' He had granted it, it was in displeasure and suffered to be in this manner to punish me. But I can say I never desired his death more than my own, nay not so much. I have since had cause to believe his mind was benefited by the undertaking, which hope makes up for all I have suffered from him, being informed that he did in the army what he could not do at home, viz., suffer for the testimony of TRUTH. When they came to an engagement he refused to fight, for which he was whipped, and brought before the general, who asked him why he enlisted, if he would not fight. "I did it," said he, "in a drunken frolic, when the devil had the better of me, but my judgment is convinced, that I ought not, neither will I, whatever I suffer. I have but one life and you may take that if you please, but I'll never take up arms." They used him with much cruelty to make him yield, but could not, by means whereof he was so disabled that the general sent him to the hospital at Chelsea, near London, where in nine months he died, and I hope made a good end, for which I prayed both night and day, till I heard of his death.

Thus I thought it my duty to say what I could in his favor, as I have been obliged to say so much of his hard usage to me, all which I hope did me good,

4. I.e., thoughtless.

and altho' he was so bad yet had several good properties, and I never thought him the worst of men. He was one I loved, and had he let religion have its perfect work, I should have thought myself happy in the lowest state of life, and I have cause to bless God who enabled me in the station of a wife to do my duty, and now a widow, to submit to His will, always believing every thing He doth to be right. May He in all stations of life so preserve me by the arm of Divine Power, that I may never forget His tender mercies to me, the remembrance whereof doth often bow down my soul in humility before His throne, saying, "Lord, what was I, that Thou should'st have revealed to my soul the knowledge of the TRUTH, and done so much for me, who deserved Thy displeasure rather. But in me Thou hast shown Thy long-suffering and tender mercy. May Thou, O God, be glorified, and I abased, for it is Thy own works that praise Thee, and, of a truth, to the humble soul makest everything sweet."[5]

1774

5. In an "Appendix" to the 1774 edition Aaron Ashbridge informed the reader that Elizabeth's second husband left her in debt for the sum of eighty pounds and that she repaid it with great difficulty. In 1753 she left New Jersey for Ireland, called to service abroad. She died in Ireland "the sixteenth day of the fifth month [July], 1755."

# J. HECTOR ST. JOHN DE CRÈVECOEUR
## 1735–1813

Crèvecoeur was a man with a mysterious past, and a number of details of his life have puzzled his biographers. He was born Michel-Guillaume Jean de Crèvecoeur in Caen, Normandy, in 1735. When he was nineteen, he left home and sailed to England, where he took up residence with distant relatives. He planned to marry, but his fiancée died before the ceremony took place, and in 1755 he went to Canada; he enlisted in the Canadian militia, served the government as a surveyor and cartographer, and was wounded in the defense of Quebec. His military career came to an end in 1759, at which time he traveled to New York and changed his name to J. Hector St. John, later expanding his surname to J. Hector St. John de Crèvecoeur. For the next ten years Crèvecoeur traveled extensively in the colonies as a surveyor and trader with American Indians. In 1769 he bought land in Orange County, New York, and, newly married, settled into the life of an American farmer.

Given the history of Crèvecoeur's restlessness, it is hard to know whether or not he would have been happy forever at Pine Hill, but the advent of the American Revolution and his Tory sympathies were enough to determine his return to France. He claimed that he wished to reestablish ownership of family lands, and it is ironic, given his political sympathies, that he was arrested and imprisoned as a rebel spy when he tried to sail from the port of New York. Not until 1780 did Crèvecoeur succeed in reaching London. He remained in France until 1783, when he returned as French consul to New York, Connecticut, and New Jersey, only to learn that his farm had been burned in an Indian attack, his wife was dead, and his children were housed with strangers.

Crèvecoeur was a great success as a diplomat—he was made an honorary citizen of a number of American cities, and the town of St. Johnsbury, Vermont, was named in his honor—but he did not remain long in America. He returned to

France in 1785 and after 1790 remained there permanently, first living in Paris and retiring, after 1793, to Normandy. The first year that Crèvecoeur spent at Pine Hill he began to write a series of essays about America based on his travels and experience as a farmer. He brought them to London in 1780 and, suppressing those essays most unsympathetic to the American cause, sold them to the bookseller Thomas Davies. *Letters from an American Farmer* appeared in 1782 and was an immediate success. Crèvecoeur found himself a popular hero when the expanded French edition (dated 1784) appeared. Its publication followed close enough on the American Revolution to satisfy an almost insatiable demand for things American and confirmed, for most readers, a vision of a new land, rich and promising, where industry prevailed over class and fashion. George Washington said the book was "too flattering" to be true, but more careful readers of these twelve letters will take note of a more ambiguous attitude throughout: Crèvecoeur's hymn to the land does not make him blind to the ignorant frontier settlers or the calculating slaveholder. His final letter, "Distresses of a Frontiersman," affirms the possibility of a harmonious relationship with nature, but he writes from an American Indian village and with no successful historical models in mind.

# From Letters from an American Farmer[1]

## From *Letter III. What Is an American*

I wish I could be acquainted with the feelings and thoughts which must agitate the heart and present themselves to the mind of an enlightened Englishman, when he first lands on this continent. He must greatly rejoice that he lived at a time to see this fair country discovered and settled; he must necessarily feel a share of national pride, when he views the chain of settlements which embellishes these extended shores. When he says to himself, this is the work of my countrymen, who, when convulsed by factions,[2] afflicted by a variety of miseries and wants, restless and impatient, took refuge here. They brought along with them their national genius,[3] to which they principally owe what liberty they enjoy, and what substance they possess. Here he sees the industry of his native country displayed in a new manner, and traces in their works the embryos of all the arts, sciences, and ingenuity which flourish in Europe. Here he beholds fair cities, substantial villages, extensive fields, an immense country filled with decent houses, good roads, orchards, meadows, and bridges, where an hundred years ago all was wild, woody, and uncultivated! What a train of pleasing ideas this fair spectacle must suggest; it is a prospect which must inspire a good citizen with the most heartfelt pleasure. The difficulty consists in the manner of viewing so extensive a scene. He is arrived on a new continent; a modern society offers itself to his contemplation, different from what he had hitherto seen. It is not composed, as in Europe, of great lords who possess everything, and of a herd of people who have nothing. Here are no aristocratical families, no courts, no kings, no bishops, no ecclesiastical dominion, no invisible power giving to a few a very visible one; no great manufacturers employing thousands, no great refinements of luxury. The rich and the poor are not so far removed from each other as they are in Europe.

---

1. From *Letters from an American Farmer*, edited by
Albert Boni and Charles Boni (1925).

2. Disputes.
3. Spirit; distinctive national character.

Some few towns excepted, we are all tillers of the earth, from Nova Scotia to West Florida. We are a people of cultivators, scattered over an immense territory, communicating with each other by means of good roads and navigable rivers, united by the silken bands of mild government, all respecting the laws, without dreading their power, because they are equitable. We are all animated with the spirit of an industry which is unfettered and unrestrained, because each person works for himself. If he travels through our rural districts he views not the hostile castle, and the haughty mansion, contrasted with the clay-built hut and miserable cabin, where cattle and men help to keep each other warm, and dwell in meanness, smoke, and indigence. A pleasing uniformity of decent competence appears throughout our habitations. The meanest of our log-houses is a dry and comfortable habitation. Lawyer or merchant are the fairest titles our towns afford; that of a farmer is the only appellation of the rural inhabitants of our country. It must take some time ere he can reconcile himself to our dictionary, which is but short in words of dignity, and names of honor. There, on a Sunday, he sees a congregation of respectable farmers and their wives, all clad in neat homespun, well mounted, or riding in their own humble wagons. There is not among them an esquire, saving the unlettered magistrate. There he sees a parson as simple as his flock, a farmer who does not riot[4] on the labor of others. We have no princes, for whom we toil, starve, and bleed; we are the most perfect society now existing in the world. Here man is free as he ought to be; nor is this pleasing equality so transitory as many others are. Many ages will not see the shores of our great lakes replenished with inland nations, nor the unknown bounds of North America entirely peopled. Who can tell how far it extends? Who can tell the millions of men whom it will feed and contain? for no European foot has as yet traveled half the extent of this mighty continent!

The next wish of this traveler will be to know whence came all these people? They are a mixture of English, Scotch, Irish, French, Dutch, Germans and Swedes. From this promiscuous breed, that race now called Americans have arisen. The eastern provinces[5] must indeed be excepted, as being the unmixed descendants of Englishmen. I have heard many wish that they had been more intermixed also: for my part, I am no wisher, and think it much better as it has happened. They exhibit a most conspicuous figure in this great and variegated picture; they too enter for a great share in the pleasing perspective displayed in these thirteen provinces. I know it is fashionable to reflect on them, but respect them for what they have done; for the accuracy and wisdom with which they have settled their territory; for the decency of their manners; for their early love of letters; their ancient college,[6] the first in this hemisphere; for their industry, which to me who am but a farmer is the criterion of everything. There never was a people, situated as they are, who with so ungrateful a soil have done more in so short a time. Do you think that the monarchical ingredients which are more prevalent in other governments have purged them from all foul stains? Their histories assert the contrary.

In this great American asylum, the poor of Europe have by some means met together, and in consequence of various causes; to what purpose should they ask one another what countrymen they are? Alas, two thirds of them had

---

4. I.e., indulge himself.                        6. Harvard College was founded in 1636.
5. New England.

no country. Can a wretch who wanders about, who works and starves, whose life is a continual scene of sore affliction or pinching penury, can that man call England or any other kingdom his country? A country that had no bread for him, whose fields procured him no harvest, who met with nothing but the frowns of the rich, the severity of the laws, with jails and punishments; who owned not a single foot of the extensive surface of this planet? No! Urged by a variety of motives, here they came. Everything has tended to regenerate them; new laws, a new mode of living, a new social system; here they are become men: in Europe they were as so many useless plants, wanting vegetative mold and refreshing showers; they withered, and were mowed down by want, hunger, and war; but now by the power of transplantation, like all other plants they have taken root and flourished! Formerly they were not numbered in any civil lists[7] of their country, except in those of the poor; here they rank as citizens. By what invisible power has this surprising metamorphosis been performed? By that of the laws and that of their industry. The laws, the indulgent laws, protect them as they arrive, stamping on them the symbol of adoption; they receive ample rewards for their labors; these accumulated rewards procure them lands; those lands confer on them the title of freemen, and to that title every benefit is affixed which men can possibly require. This is the great operation daily performed by our laws. From whence proceed these laws? From our government. Whence the government? It is derived from the original genius and strong desire of the people ratified and confirmed by the crown. This is the great chain which links us all, this is the picture which every province exhibits, Nova Scotia excepted. There the crown has done all;[8] either there were no people who had genius, or it was not much attended to: the consequence is that the province is very thinly inhabited indeed; the power of the crown in conjunction with the mosquitoes has prevented men from settling there. Yet some parts of it flourished once, and it contained a mild, harmless set of people. But for the fault of a few leaders, the whole were banished. The greatest political error the crown ever committed in America was to cut off men from a country which wanted nothing but men!

What attachment can a poor European emigrant have for a country where he had nothing? The knowledge of the language, the love of a few kindred as poor as himself, were the only cords that tied him: his country is now that which gives him land, bread, protection, and consequence: *Ubi panis ibi patria*[9] is the motto of all emigrants. What then is the American, this new man? He is either a European, or the descendant of a European, hence that strange mixture of blood, which you will find in no other country. I could point out to you a family whose grandfather was an Englishman, whose wife was Dutch, whose son married a French woman, and whose present four sons have now four wives of different nations. He is an American, who, leaving behind him all his ancient prejudices and manners, receives new ones from the new mode of life he has embraced, the new government he obeys, and the new rank he holds. He becomes an American by being received in the broad lap of our great *Alma Mater.*[1] Here individuals of all nations are melted into a new race of men, whose labors and posterity will one day cause great changes

---

7. Recognized employees of the civil government: ambassadors, judges, secretaries, etc.
8. In 1755 the French Acadians were banished from Nova Scotia by the British, who took it in 1710.

9. Where there is bread, there is one's fatherland (Latin).
1. Dear mother (Latin, literal trans.).

in the world. Americans are the western pilgrims, who are carrying along with them that great mass of arts, sciences, vigor, and industry which began long since in the east; they will finish the great circle. The Americans were once scattered all over Europe; here they are incorporated into one of the finest systems of population which has ever appeared, and which will hereafter become distinct by the power of the different climates they inhabit. The American ought therefore to love this country much better than that wherein either he or his forefathers were born. Here the rewards of his industry follow with equal steps the progress of his labor; his labor is founded on the basis of nature, *self-interest*; can it want a stronger allurement? Wives and children, who before in vain demanded of him a morsel of bread, now, fat and frolicsome, gladly help their father to clear those fields whence exuberant crops are to arise to feed and to clothe them all; without any part being claimed, either by a despotic prince, a rich abbot, or a mighty lord. Here religion demands but little of him; a small voluntary salary to the minister, and gratitude to God; can he refuse these? The American is a new man, who acts upon new principles; he must therefore entertain new ideas, and form new opinions. From involuntary idleness, servile dependence, penury, and useless labor, he has passed to toils of a very different nature, rewarded by ample subsistence.— This is an American.

British America is divided into many provinces, forming a large association, scattered along a coast 1,500 miles extent and about 200 wide. This society I would fain examine, at least such as it appears in the middle provinces; if it does not afford that variety of tinges and gradations which may be observed in Europe, we have colors peculiar to ourselves. For instance, it is natural to conceive that those who live near the sea must be very different from those who live in the woods; the intermediate space will afford a separate and distinct class.

Men are like plants; the goodness and flavor of the fruit proceeds from the peculiar soil and exposition in which they grow. We are nothing but what we derive from the air we breathe, the climate we inhabit, the government we obey, the system of religion we profess, and the nature of our employment. Here you will find but few crimes; these have acquired as yet no root among us. I wish I was able to trace all my ideas; if my ignorance prevents me from describing them properly, I hope I shall be able to delineate a few of the outlines, which are all I propose.

Those who live near the sea feed more on fish than on flesh, and often encounter that boisterous element. This renders them more bold and enterprising; this leads them to neglect the confined occupations of the land. They see and converse with a variety of people, their intercourse with mankind becomes extensive. The sea inspires them with a love of traffic, a desire of transporting produce from one place to another; and leads them to a variety of resources which supply the place of labor. Those who inhabit the middle settlements, by far the most numerous, must be very different; the simple cultivation of the earth purifies them, but the indulgences of the government, the soft remonstrances of religion, the rank of independent freeholders, must necessarily inspire them with sentiments, very little known in Europe among people of the same class. What do I say? Europe has no such class of men; the early knowledge they acquire, the early bargains they make, give them a great degree of sagacity. As freemen they will be litigious; pride and obstinancy are often the cause of lawsuits; the nature of our laws and governments may be another. As citizens it is easy to imagine that they will carefully read the newspapers, enter into every political disquisition, freely blame or censure governors and others. As farmers they will be careful and anxious to get as much as they can, because what they get is their own. As northern men they will love the cheerful cup. As Christians, religion curbs them not in their opinions; the general indulgence leaves everyone to think for themselves in spiritual matters; the laws inspect our actions, our thoughts are left to God. Industry, good living, selfishness, litigiousness, country politics, the pride of freemen, religious indifference are their characteristics. If you recede still farther from the sea, you will come into more modern settlements; they exhibit the same strong lineaments, in a ruder appearance. Religion seems to have still less influence, and their manners are less improved.

Now we arrive near the great woods, near the last inhabited districts;[2] there men seem to be placed still farther beyond the reach of government, which in some measure leaves them to themselves. How can it pervade every corner; as they were driven there by misfortunes, necessity of beginnings, desire of acquiring large tracts of land, idleness, frequent want of economy,[3] ancient debts; the reunion of such people does not afford a very pleasing spectacle. When discord, want of unity and friendship; when either drunkenness or idleness prevail in such remote districts; contention, inactivity, and wretchedness must ensue. There are not the same remedies to these evils as in a long-established community. The few magistrates they have are in general little better than the rest; they are often in a perfect state of war; that of man against man, sometimes decided by blows, sometimes by means of the law; that of man against every wild inhabitant of these venerable woods, of which they are come to dispossess them. There men appear to be no better than carnivorous animals of a superior rank, living on the flesh of wild animals when they can catch them, and when they are not able, they subsist on grain. He who would wish to see America in its proper light, and have a true idea of its feeble beginnings and barbarous rudiments, must visit our extended line of frontiers where the last settlers dwell, and where he may see the first labors of settlement, the mode of clearing the earth, in all their different appearances; where men are wholly left dependent on their native tempers and on the spur of uncertain industry, which often fails when not sanctified by the efficacy of a few moral rules. There, remote from the power of example and check of shame, many families exhibit the most hideous parts of our society. They are a kind of forlorn hope, preceding by ten or twelve years the most respectable army of veterans which come after them. In that space, prosperity will polish some, vice and the law will drive off the rest, who uniting again with others like themselves will recede still farther; making room for more industrious people, who will finish their improvements, convert the loghouse into a convenient habitation, and rejoicing that the first heavy labors are finished, will change in a few years that hitherto barbarous country into a fine fertile, well-regulated district. Such is our progress, such is the march of the Europeans toward the interior parts of this continent. In all societies these are offcasts; this impure part serves as our precursors or pioneers; my father himself was one of

---

2. I.e., the frontier; the land west of the original colonies and east of the Mississippi.

3. I.e., they were improvident and spent beyond their means.

that class,[4] but he came upon honest principles, and was therefore one of the few who held fast; by good conduct and temperance, he transmitted to me his fair inheritance, when not above one in fourteen of his contemporaries had the same good fortune.

Forty years ago his smiling country was thus inhabited; it is now purged, a general decency of manners prevails throughout, and such has been the fate of our best countries.

Exclusive of those general characteristics, each province has its own, founded on the government, climate, mode of husbandry, customs, and peculiarity of circumstances. Europeans submit insensibly to these great powers, and become, in the course of a few generations, not only Americans in general, but either Pennsylvanians, Virginians, or provincials under some other name. Whoever traverses the continent must easily observe those strong differences, which will grow more evident in time. The inhabitants of Canada, Massachusetts, the middle provinces, the southern ones will be as different as their climates; their only points of unit will be those of religion and language.

As I have endeavored to show you how Europeans become Americans, it may not be disagreeable to show you likewise how the various Christian sects introduced wear out, and how religious indifference becomes prevalent. When any considerable number of a particular sect happen to dwell contiguous to each other, they immediately erect a temple, and there worship the Divinity agreeably to their own peculiar ideas. Nobody disturbs them. If any new sect springs up in Europe it may happen that many of its professors[5] will come and settle in America. As they bring their zeal with them, they are at liberty to make proselytes if they can, and to build a meeting and to follow the dictates of their consciences; for neither the government nor any other power interferes. If they are peaceable subjects, and are industrious, what is it to their neighbors how and in what manner they think fit to address their prayers to the Supreme Being? But if the sectaries are not settled close together, if they are mixed with other denominations, their zeal will cool for want of fuel, and will be extinguished in a little time. Then the Americans become as to religion what they are as to country, allied to all. In them the name of Englishman, Frenchman, and European is lost, and in like manner, the strict modes of Christianity as practiced in Europe are lost also. This effect will extend itself still farther hereafter, and though this may appear to you as a strange idea, yet it is a very true one. I shall be able perhaps hereafter to explain myself better; in the meanwhile, let the following example serve as my first justification.

Let us suppose you and I to be traveling; we observe that in this house, to the right, lives a Catholic, who prays to God as he has been taught, and believes in transubstantiation;[6] he works and raises wheat, he has a large family of children, all hale and robust; his belief, his prayers offend nobody. About one mile farther on the same road, his next neighbor may be a good honest plodding German Lutheran, who addresses himself to the same God, the God of all, agreeably to the modes he has been educated in, and believes in consubstantiation;[7] by so doing he scandalizes nobody; he also works in his fields,

4. His father never came to America.
5. Believers.
6. The doctrine followed by Roman Catholics that the substance of the bread and wine used in the sacrament of communion are changed at the consecration to the substance of the body and blood of Christ.

7. As distinguished from transubstantiation; the doctrine that affirms that Christ's body is not present in or under the elements of bread and wine, but that the bread and wine are signs of Christ's presence through faith.

embellishes the earth, clears swamps, etc. What has the world to do with his Lutheran principles? He persecutes nobody, and nobody persecutes him, he visits his neighbors, and his neighbors visit him. Next to him lives a seceder,[8] the most enthusiastic of all sectaries;[9] his zeal is hot and fiery, but separated as he is from others of the same complexion, he has no congregation of his own to resort to, where he might cabal and mingle religious pride with worldly obstinacy. He likewise raises good crops, his house is handsomely painted, his orchard is one of the fairest in the neighborhood. How does it concern the welfare of the country, or of the province at large, what this man's religious sentiments are, or really whether he has any at all? He is a good farmer, he is a sober, peaceable, good citizen: William Penn[1] himself would not wish for more. This is the visible character, the invisible one is only guessed at, and is nobody's business. Next again lives a Low Dutchman, who implicitly believes the rules laid down by the synod of Dort.[2] He conceives no other idea of a clergyman than that of a hired man; if he does his work well he will pay him the stipulated sum; if not he will dismiss him, and do without his sermons, and let his church be shut up for years. But notwithstanding this coarse idea, you will find his house and farm to be the neatest in all the country; and you will judge by his wagon and fat horses that he thinks more of the affairs of this world than of those of the next. He is sober and laborious, therefore he is all he ought to be as to the affairs of this life; as for those of the next, he must trust to the great Creator. Each of these people instruct their children as well as they can, but these instructions are feeble compared to those which are given to the youth of the poorest class in Europe. Their children will therefore grow up less zealous and more indifferent in matters of religion than their parents. The foolish vanity, or rather the fury of making proselytes, is unknown here; they have no time, the seasons call for all their attention, and thus in a few years, this mixed neighborhood will exhibit a strange religious medley, that will be neither pure Catholicism nor pure Calvinism. A very perceptible indifference, even in the first generation, will become apparent; and it may happen that the daughter of the Catholic will marry the son of the seceder, and settle by themselves at a distance from their parents. What religious education will they give their children? A very imperfect one. If there happens to be in the neighborhood any place of worship, we will suppose a Quaker's meeting; rather than not show their fine clothes, they will go to it, and some of them may perhaps attach themselves to that society. Others will remain in a perfect state of indifference; the children of these zealous parents will not be able to tell what their religious principles are, and their grandchildren still less. The neighborhood of a place of worship generally leads them to it, and the action of going thither is the strongest evidence they can give of their attachment to any sect. The Quakers are the only people who retain a fondness for their own mode of worship; for be they ever so far separated from each other, they hold a sort of communion with the society, and seldom depart from its rules, at least in this country. Thus all sects are mixed as well as all nations; thus religious indifference is imperceptibly disseminated from one end

8. A Presbyterian who has separated from the established Church of Scotland.
9. One who dissents or withdraws from an established church.
1. William Penn (1644–1718), English Quaker and founder of Pennsylvania.
2. The Synod of Dort met in Holland in 1618 and attempted to settle disputes between Protestant reformed churches. "Low Dutchman": someone from Holland, not Belgium.

of the continent to the other; which is at present one of the strongest characteristics of the Americans. Where this will reach no one can tell, perhaps it may leave a vacuum fit to receive other systems. Persecution, religious pride, the love of contradiction are the food of what the world commonly calls religion. These motives have ceased here; zeal in Europe is confined; here it evaporates in the great distance it has to travel; there it is a grain of power inclosed, here it burns away in the open air, and consumes without effect.

But to return to our back settlers. I must tell you that there is something in the proximity of the woods which is very singular. It is with men as it is with the plants and animals that grow and live in the forests; they are entirely different from those that live in the plains. I will candidly tell you all my thoughts but you are not to expect that I shall advance any reasons. By living in or near the woods, their actions are regulated by the wildness of the neighborhood. The deer often come to eat their grain, the wolves to destroy their sheep, the bears to kill their hogs, the foxes to catch their poultry. This surrounding hostility immediately puts the gun into their hands; they watch these animals, they kill some; and thus by defending their property, they soon become professed hunters; this is the progress; once hunters, farewell to the plow. The chase renders them ferocious, gloomy, and unsociable; a hunter wants no neighbor, he rather hates them, because he dreads the competition. In a little time their success in the woods makes them neglect their tillage. They trust to the natural fecundity of the earth, and therefore do little; carelessness in fencing often exposes what little they sow to destruction; they are not at home to watch; in order therefore to make up the deficiency, they go oftener to the woods. That new mode of life brings along with it a new set of manners, which I cannot easily describe. These new manners, being grafted on the old stock, produce a strange sort of lawless profligacy, the impressions of which are indelible. The manners of the Indian natives are respectable, compared with this European medley. Their wives and children live in sloth and inactivity; and having no proper pursuits, you may judge what education the latter receive. Their tender minds have nothing else to contemplate but the example of their parents; like them they grow up a mongrel breed, half civilized, half savage, except nature stamps on them some constitutional propensities. That rich, that voluptuous sentiment is gone that struck them so forcibly; the possession of their freeholds[3] no longer conveys to their minds the same pleasure and pride. To all these reasons you must add their lonely situation, and you cannot imagine what an effect on manners the great distances they live from each other has! Consider one of the last settlements in its first view: of what is it composed? Europeans who have not that sufficient share of knowledge they ought to have, in order to prosper; people who have suddenly passed from oppression, dread of government, and fear of laws into the unlimited freedom of the woods. This sudden change must have a very great effect on most men, and on that class particularly. Eating of wild meat, whatever you may think, tends to alter their temper: though all the proof I can adduce is that I have seen it: and having no place of worship to resort to, what little society this might afford is denied them. The Sunday meetings, exclusive of religious benefits, were the only social bonds that might have inspired them with some degree of emulation in neatness. Is it then surprising to see men thus situated, immersed in

3. Land held outright for a specified period of time.

great and heavy labors, degenerate a little? It is rather a wonder the effect is not more diffusive. The Moravians[4] and the Quakers are the only instances in exception to what I have advanced. The first never settle singly, it is a colony of the society which emigrates; they carry with them their forms, worship, rules, and decency: the others never begin so hard, they are always able to buy improvements, in which there is a great advantage, for by that time the country is recovered from its first barbarity. Thus our bad people are those who are half cultivators and half hunters; and the worst of them are those who have degenerated altogether into the hunting state. As old plowmen and new men of the woods, as Europeans and new-made Indians, they contract the vices of both; they adopt the moroseness and ferocity of a native, without his mildness, or even his industry at home. If manners are not refined, at least they are rendered simple and inoffensive by tilling the earth; all our wants are supplied by it, our time is divided between labor and rest, and leaves none of the commission of great misdeeds. As hunters it is divided between the toil of the chase, the idleness of repose, or the indulgence of inebriation. Hunting is but a licentious idle life, and if it does not always pervert good dispositions; yet, when it is united with bad luck, it leads to want: want stimulates that propensity to rapacity and injustice, too natural to needy men, which is the fatal gradation. After this explanation of the effects which follow by living in the woods, shall we yet vainly flatter ourselves with the hope of converting the Indians? We should rather begin with converting our back-settlers; and now if I dare mention the name of religion, its sweet accents would be lost in the immensity of these woods. Men thus placed are not fit either to receive or remember its mild instructions; they want[5] temples and ministers, but as soon as men cease to remain at home, and begin to lead an erratic life, let them be either tawny or white, they cease to be its disciples.

* * *

Europe contains hardly any other distinctions but lords and tenants; this fair country alone is settled by freeholders, the possessors of the soil they cultivate, members of the government they obey, and the framers of their own laws, by means of their representatives. This is a thought which you have taught me to cherish; our difference from Europe, far from diminishing, rather adds to our usefulness and consequence as men and subjects. Had our forefathers remained there, they would only have crowded it, and perhaps prolonged those convulsions which had shook it so long. Every industrious European who transports himself here may be compared to a sprout growing at the foot of a great tree; it enjoys and draws but a little portion of sap; wrench it from the parent roots, transplant it, and it will become a tree bearing fruit also. Colonists are therefore entitled to the consideration due to the most useful subjects; a hundred families barely existing in some parts or Scotland will here in six years cause an annual exportation of 10,000 bushels of wheat; 100 bushels being but a common quantity for an industrious family to sell, if they cultivated good land. It is here then that the idle may be employed, the useless become useful, and the poor become rich; but by riches I do not mean gold

4. The Moravians were followers of Jacob Hutter, who was executed in 1536; they were Christian family communities who gave up private property and were noted for their industry and thrift. They suffered a number of persecutions in the 17th century and emigrated to other lands.
5. Lack.

and silver, we have but little of those metals; I mean a better sort of wealth, cleared lands, cattle, good houses, good clothes, and an increase of people to enjoy them.

There is no wonder that this country has so many charms, and presents to Europeans so many temptations to remain in it. A traveler in Europe becomes a stranger as soon as he quits his own kingdom; but it is otherwise here. We know, properly speaking, no strangers; this is every person's country; the variety of our soils, situations, climates, governments, and produce hath something which must please everybody. No sooner does a European arrive, no matter of what condition, than his eyes are opened upon the fair prospect; he hears his language spoken, he retraces many of his own country manners, he perpetually hears the names of families and towns with which he is acquainted; he sees happiness and prosperity in all places disseminated; he meets with hospitality, kindness, and plenty everywhere; he beholds hardly any poor; he seldom hears of punishments and executions; and he wonders at the elegance of our towns, those miracles of industry and freedom. He cannot admire enough our rural districts, our convenient roads, good taverns, and our many accommodations; he involuntarily loves a country where everything is so lovely.

*    *    *

After a foreigner from any part of Europe is arrived, and become a citizen, let him devoutly listen to the voice of our great parent, which says to him, "Welcome to my shores, distressed European; bless the hour in which thou didst see my verdant fields, my fair navigable rivers, and my green mountains!—If thou wilt work, I have bread for thee; if thou wilt be honest, sober, and industrious, I have greater rewards to confer on thee—ease and independence. I will give thee fields to feed and clothe thee; a comfortable fireside to sit by, and tell thy children by what means thou hast prospered; and a decent bed to repose on. I shall endow thee beside with the immunities of a freeman. If thou wilt carefully educate thy children, teach them gratitude to God, and reverence to that government, the philanthropic government, which has collected here so many men and made them happy. I will also provide for thy progeny; and to every good man this ought to be the most holy, the most powerful, the most earnest wish he can possibly form, as well as the most consolatory prospect when he dies. Go thou and work and till; thou shalt prosper, provided thou be just, grateful, and industrious."

### From *Letter IX. Description of Charles-Town; Thoughts on Slavery; on Physical Evil; A Melancholy Scene*

Charles-Town is, in the north, what Lima is in the south; both are capitals of the richest provinces of their respective hemispheres: you may therefore conjecture, that both cities must exhibit the appearances necessarily resulting from riches. Peru abounding in gold, Lima is filled with inhabitants who enjoy all those gradations of pleasure, refinement, and luxury, which proceed from wealth. Carolina produces commodities, more valuable perhaps than gold, because they are gained by greater industry; it exhibits also on our northern stage, a display of riches and luxury, inferior indeed to the former, but far superior to what are to be seen in our northern towns. Its situation is admirable, being built at the confluence of two large rivers, which receive in their course a great number of inferior streams; all navigable in the spring, for flatboats. Here the produce of this extensive territory concenters; here therefore is the seat of the most valuable exportation; their wharfs, their docks, their magazines,[6] are extremely convenient to facilitate this great commercial business. The inhabitants are the gayest in America; it is called the center of our beau monde, and it [is] always filled with the richest planters of the province, who resort hither in a quest of health and pleasure. Here are always to be seen a great number of valetudinarians from the West Indies, seeking for the renovation of health, exhausted by the debilitating nature of their sun, air, and modes of living. Many of these West Indians have I seen, at thirty, loaded with the infirmities of old age; for nothing is more common in those countries of wealth, than for persons to lose the abilities of enjoying the comforts of life, at a time when we northern men just begin to taste the fruits of our labor and prudence. The round of pleasure, and the expenses of those citizens' tables, are much superior to what you would imagine: indeed the growth of this town and province has been astonishingly rapid. It is [a] pity that the narrowness of the neck on which it stands prevents it from increasing; and which is the reason why houses are so dear. The heat of the climate, which is sometimes very great in the interior parts of the country, is always temperate in Charles-Town; though sometimes when they have no sea breezes the sun is too powerful. The climate renders excesses of all kinds very dangerous, particularly those of the table; and yet, insensible or fearless of danger, they live on, and enjoy a short and a merry life: the rays of their sun seem to urge them irresistably to dissipation and pleasure: on the contrary, the women, from being abstemious, reach to a longer period of life, and seldom die without having had several husbands. An European at his first arrival must be greatly surprised when he sees the elegance of their houses, their sumptuous furniture, as well as the magnificence of their tables. Can he imagine himself in a country, the establishment of which is so recent?

The three principal classes of inhabitants are, lawyers, planters, and merchants; this is the province which has afforded to the first the richest spoils, for nothing can exceed their wealth, their power, and their influence. They have reached the *ne plus ultra*[7] of worldly felicity; no plantation is secured, no title is good, no will is valid, but what they dictate, regulate, and approve. The whole mass of provincial property is become tributary to this society; which, far above priests and bishops, disdain to be satisfied with the poor Mosaical portion of the tenth.[8] I appeal to the many inhabitants, who, while contending perhaps for their right to a few hundred acres, have lost by the mazes of the law their whole patrimony. These men are more properly law givers than interpreters of the law; and have united here, as well as in most other provinces, the skill and dexterity of the scribe with the power and ambition of the prince: who can tell where this may lead in a future day? The nature of our laws, and the spirit of freedom, which often tends to make us litigious, must necessarily throw the greatest part of the property of the colonies into the hands of these gentlemen. In another century, the law will possess in the north, what now the church possesses in Peru and Mexico.

While all is joy, festivity, and happiness in Charles-Town, would you imag-

6. Warehouses.
7. No more beyond (Latin, literal trans.); the point of highest achievement.

8. The law set forth in the first five books of the Old Testament that one-tenth of one's worldly goods should be offered to God.

ine that scenes of misery overspread in the country? Their ears by habit are become deaf, their hearts are hardened; they neither see, hear, nor feel for the woes of their poor slaves, from whose painful labors all their wealth proceeds. Here the horrors of slavery, the hardship of incessant toils, are unseen; and no one thinks with compassion of those showers of sweat and of tears which from the bodies of Africans, daily drop, and moisten the ground they till. The cracks of the whip urging these miserable beings to excessive labor, are far too distant from the gay capital to be heard. The chosen race eat, drink, and live happy, while the unfortunate one grubs up the ground, raises indigo, or husks the rice; exposed to a sun full as scorching as their native one; without the support of good food, without the cordials of any cheering liquor. This great contrast has often afforded me subjects of the most afflicting meditation. On the one side, behold a people enjoying all that life affords most bewitching and pleasurable, without labor, without fatigue, hardly subjected to the trouble of wishing. With gold, dug from Peruvian mountains, they order vessels to the coasts of Guinea; by virtue of that gold, wars, murders, and devastations are committed in some harmless, peaceable African neighborhood, where dwelt innocent people, who even knew not but that all men were black. The daughter torn from her weeping mother, the child from the wretched parents, the wife from the loving husband; whose families swept away and brought through storms and tempests to this rich metropolis! There, arranged like horses at a fair, they are branded like cattle, and then driven to toil, to starve, and to languish for a few years on the different plantations of these citizens. And for whom must they work? For persons they know not, and who have no other power over them than that of violence; no other right than what this accursed metal has given them! Strange order of things! Oh, Nature, where are thou?—Are not these blacks thy children as well as we? On the other side, nothing is to be seen but the most diffusive misery and wretchedness, unrelieved even in thought or wish! Day after day they drudge on without any prospect of ever reaping for themselves; they are obliged to devote their lives, their limbs, their will, and every vital exertion to swell the wealth of masters; who look not upon them with half the kindness and affection with which they consider their dogs and horses. Kindness and affection are not the portion of those who till the earth, who carry the burdens, who convert the logs into useful boards. This reward, simple and natural as one would conceive it, would border on humanity; and planters must have none of it!

* * *

A clergyman settled a few years ago at George-Town, and feeling as I do now, warmly recommended to the planters, from the pulpit, a relaxation of severity; he introduced the benignity of Christianity, and pathetically made use of the admirable precepts of that system to melt the hearts of his congregation into a greater degree of compassion toward their slaves than had been hitherto customary; "Sir (said one of his hearers) we pay you a genteel salary to read to us the prayers of the liturgy, and to explain to us such parts of the Gospel as the rule of the church directs; but we do not want you to teach us what we are to do with our blacks." The clergyman found it prudent to withhold any farther admonition. Whence this astonishing right, or rather this barbarous custom, for most certainly we have no kind of right beyond that of force? We are told, it is true, that slavery cannot be so repugnant to human nature as we at first imagine, because it has been practiced in all ages, and in all nations: the Lacedemonians[9] themselves, those great assertors of liberty, conquered the Helotes with the design of making them their slaves; the Romans, whom we consider as our masters in civil and military policy, lived in the exercise of the most horrid oppression; they conquered to plunder and to enslave. What a hideous aspect the face of the earth must then have exhibited! Provinces, towns, districts, often depopulated; their inhabitants driven to Rome, the greatest market in the world, and there sold by thousands! The Roman dominions were tilled by the hands of unfortunate people, who had once been, like their victors free, rich, and possessed of every benefit society can confer; until they became subject to the cruel right of war, and to lawless force. Is there then no superintending power who conducts the moral operations of the world, as well as the physical? The same sublime hand which guides the planets round the sun with so much exactness, which preserves the arrangement of the whole with such exalted wisdom and paternal care, and prevents the vast system from falling into confusion; doth it abandon mankind to all the errors, the follies, and the miseries, which their most frantic rage, and their most dangerous vices and passions can produce?

*   *   *

Everywhere one part of the human species are taught the art of shedding the blood of the other; of setting fire to their dwellings; of leveling the works of their industry: half of the existence of nations regularly employed in destroying other nations. What little political felicity is to be met with here and there, has cost oceans of blood to purchase; as if good was never to be the portion of unhappy man. Republics, kingdoms, monarchies, founded either on fraud or successful violence, increase by pursuing the steps of the same policy, until they are destroyed in their turn, either by the influence of their own crimes, or by more successful but equally criminal enemies.

If from this general review of human nature, we descend to the examination of what is called civilized society; there the combination of every natural and artificial want, makes us pay very dear for what little share of political felicity we enjoy. It is a strange heterogeneous assemblage of vices and virtues, and of a variety of other principles, forever at war, forever jarring, forever producing some dangerous, some distressing extreme. Where do you conceive then that nature intended we should be happy? Would you prefer the state of men in the woods, to that of men in a more improved situation? Evil preponderates in both; in the first they often eat each other for want of food, and in the other they often starve each other for want of room. For my part, I think the vices and miseries to be found in the latter, exceed those of the former; in which real evil is more scarce, more supportable, and less enormous. Yet we wish to see the earth peopled; to accomplish the happiness of kingdoms, which is said to consist in numbers. Gracious God! to what end is the introduction of so many beings into a mode of existence in which they must grope amidst as many errors, commit as many crimes, and meet with as many diseases, wants, and sufferings!

The following scene will I hope account for these melancholy reflections, and apologize for the gloomy thoughts with which I have filled this letter: my

9. Another name for Spartans, who enslaved the people of Helos, a town in Laconia.

mind is, and always has been, oppressed since I became a witness to it. I was not long since invited to dine with a planter who lived three miles from ——, where he then resided. In order to avoid the heat of the sun, I resolved to go on foot, sheltered in a small path, leading through a pleasant wood. I was leisurely traveling along, attentively examining some peculiar plants which I had collected, when all at once I felt the air strongly agitated; though the day was perfectly calm and sultry. I immediately cast my eyes toward the cleared ground, from which I was but at a small distance, in order to see whether it was not occasioned by a sudden shower; when at that instant a sound resembling a deep rough voice, uttered, as I thought, a few inarticulate monosyllables. Alarmed and surprised, I precipitately looked all round, when I perceived at about six rods distance something resembling a cage, suspended to the limbs of a tree; all the branches of which appeared covered with large birds of prey, fluttering about, and anxiously endeavoring to perch on the cage. Actuated by an involuntary motion of my hands, more than by any design of my mind, I fired at them; they all flew to a short distance, with a most hideous noise: when, horrid to think and painful to repeat, I perceived a Negro, suspended in the cage, and left there to expire! I shudder when I recollect that the birds had already picked out his eyes, his cheek bones were bare; his arms had been attacked in several places, and his body seemed covered with a multitude of wounds. From the edges of the hollow sockets and from the lacerations with which he was disfigured, the blood slowly dropped, and tinged the ground beneath. No sooner were the birds flown, than swarms of insects covered the whole body of this unfortunate wretch, eager to feed on his mangled flesh and to drink his blood. I found myself suddenly arrested by the power of affright and terror; my nerves were convulsed; I trembled, I stood motionless, involuntarily contemplating the fate of this Negro, in all its dismal latitude. The living specter, though deprived of his eyes, could still distinctly hear, and in his uncouth dialect begged me to give him some water to allay his thirst. Humanity herself would have recoiled back with horror; she would have balanced whether to lessen such reliefless distress, or mercifully with one blow to end this dreadful scene of agonizing torture! Had I had a ball in my gun, I certainly should have dispatched him; but finding myself unable to perform so kind an office, I sought, though trembling, to relieve him as well as I could. A shell ready fixed to a pole, which had been used by some Negroes, presented itself to me; filled it with water, and with trembling hands I guided it to the quivering lips of the wretched sufferer. Urged by the irresistible power of thirst, he endeavored to meet it, as he instinctively guessed its approach by the noise it made in passing through the bars of the cage. "Tankè, you whitè man, tankè you, putè somè poison and givè me." "How long have you been hanging there?" I asked him. "Two days, and me no die; the birds, the birds; aaah me!" Oppressed with the reflections which this shocking spectacle afforded me, I mustered strength enough to walk away, and soon reached the house at which I intended to dine. There I heard that the reason for this slave being thus punished was on account of his having killed the overseer of the plantation. They told me that the laws of self-preservation rendered such executions necessary; and supported the doctrine of slavery with the arguments generally made use of to justify the practice; with the repetition of which I shall not trouble you at present.

Adieu.

From *Letter X. On Snakes; and on the Humming Bird*

\* \* \*

As I was one day sitting solitary and pensive in my primitive arbor, my attention was engaged by a strange sort of rustling noise at some paces distant. I looked all around without distinguishing anything, until I climbed one of my great hemp stalks; when to my astonishment, I beheld two snakes of considerable length, the one pursuing the other with great celerity through a hemp stubble field. The aggressor was of the black kind, six feet long; the fugitive was a water snake, nearly of equal dimensions. They soon met, and in the fury of their first encounter, they appeared in an instant firmly twisted together; and whilst their united tails beat the ground, they mutually tried with open jaws to lacerate each other. What a fell[1] aspect did they present! their heads were compressed to a very small size, their eyes flashed fire; and after this conflict had lasted about five minutes, the second found means to disengage itself from the first, and hurried toward the ditch. Its antagonist instantly assumed a new posture, and half creeping and half erect, with a majestic mein, overtook and attacked the other again, which placed itself in the same attitude, and prepared to resist. The scene was uncommon and beautiful; for thus opposed they fought with their jaws, biting each other with the utmost rage; but notwithstanding this appearance of mutual courage and fury, the water snake still seemed desirous of retreating toward the ditch, its natural element. This was no sooner perceived by the keen-eyed black one, than twisting its tail twice round a stalk of hemp, and seizing its adversary by the throat, not by means of its jaws, but by twisting its own neck twice round that of the water snake, pulled it back from the ditch. To prevent a defeat the latter took hold likewise of a stalk on the bank, and by the acquisition of that point of resistance became a match for its fierce antagonist. Strange was this to behold; two great snakes strongly adhering to the ground mutually fastened together by means of the writhings which lashed them to each other, and stretched at their full length, they pulled but pulled in vain, and in the moments of greatest exertions that part of their bodies which was entwined, seemed extremely small, while the rest appeared inflated, and now and then convulsed with strong undulations, rapidly following each other. Their eyes seemed on fire, and ready to start out of their heads; at one time the conflict seemed decided; the water-snake bent itself into two great folds, and by that operation rendered the other more than commonly outstretched; the next minute the new struggles of the black one gained an unexpected superiority, it acquired two great folds likewise, which necessarily extended the body of its adversary in proportion as it had contracted its own. These efforts were alternate; victory seemed doubtful, inclining sometimes to the one side and sometimes to the other; until at last the stalk to which the black snake fastened, suddenly gave way, and in consequence of this accident they both plunged into the ditch. The water did not extinguish their vindictive rage; for by their agitations I could trace, though not distinguish their mutual attacks. They soon reappeared on the surface twisted together, as in their first onset; but the black snake seemed to retain its wonted superiority, for its head was exactly fixed above that of the other, which it incessantly pressed down under the water, until it was stifled,

1. Evil.

and sunk. The victor no sooner perceived its enemy incapable of farther resistance, than abandoning it to the current, it returned on shore and disappeared.

c. 1769–80                                                                          1782

# THOMAS PAINE
## 1737–1809

The author of two of the most popular books in eighteenth-century America, and the most persuasive rhetorician of the cause for independence that our country has ever known, Thomas Paine was born in England in 1737, the son of a Quaker father and an Anglican mother, and did not come to America until he was thirty-seven years old. Paine's early years prepared him to be a supporter of the Revolution. The discrepancy between his high intelligence and the limitations imposed on him by poverty and caste made him long for a new social order. He once said that a sermon he heard at the age of eight impressed him with the cruelty inherent in Christianity and made him a rebel forever. When he arrived in Philadelphia with letters of introduction from Benjamin Franklin, recommending him as an "ingenious, worthy young man," he had already had a remarkably full life. Until he was thirteen he went to grammar school and then was apprenticed in his father's corset shop; at nineteen he ran away from home to go to sea. From 1757 to 1774 he was a corset maker, a tobacconist and grocer, a schoolteacher, and an exciseman (a government employee who taxed goods). His efforts to organize the excisemen and make Parliament raise their salary was unprecedented. He lost his job when he admitted he had stamped as examined goods that had not been opened. His first wife died less than a year after his marriage, and he was separated from his second wife after three years. Scandals about his private life and questions about his integrity while employed as an exciseman provided his critics with ammunition for the rest of his life. Franklin was right, however, in recognizing Paine's genius; for, like Franklin himself, he was a remarkable man, self-taught and curious about everything, from the philosophy of law to natural science.

In Philadelphia he seemed to find himself as a journalist, and he made his way quickly in that city, first as a spokesman against slavery and then as the anonymous author of *Common Sense*, the first pamphlet published in this country to urge immediate independence from Britain. Paine was obviously the right man in the right place at the right time. Relations with England were at their lowest ebb: Boston was under seige, and the Second Continental Congress had convened in Philadelphia. *Common Sense* sold almost half a million copies, and its authorship (followed by the charge of traitor) could not be kept a secret for long. Paine enlisted in the Revolutionary Army and served as an aide-de-camp in battles in New York, New Jersey, and Pennsylvania. He followed his triumph of *Common Sense* with the first of sixteen pamphlets titled *Crisis*. The first *Crisis* paper ("These are the times that try men's souls") was read to Washington's troops at Trenton and did much to shore up the spirits of the Revolutionary soldiers.

Paine received a number of political appointments as rewards for his services as a writer for the American cause, but he misused his privileges and lost the most lucrative offices. He was too indiscreet and hot tempered for public employment. In 1787 he returned to England, determined to get financial assistance to construct an iron bridge for which he had devised plans. It came to nothing. But in England he wrote his second most successful work, his *Rights of Man* (1791–92), an impassioned plea against hereditary monarchy, the traditional institution Paine never tired of arguing against. Paine was charged with treason and fled to France, where he was made a citizen and lionized as a spokesman for revolution. The horrors of the French Revolution, however, brought home to Paine the fact that the mere overthrow of monarchy did not usher in light and order. When he protested the execution of Louis XVI, he was accused of sympathy with the Crown and imprisoned. He was saved from trial by the American ambassador, James Monroe, who offered him an American citizenship and safe passage back to New York.

Paine spent the last years of his life in New York City and in New Rochelle, New York. They were unhappy, impoverished years, and his reputation suffered enormously as a result of *The Age of Reason* (1794). Paine's attempt to define his beliefs was viewed as an attack on Christianity and, by extension, on conventional society. He was ridiculed and despised. Even George Washington, who had supported Paine's early writing, thought English criticism of him was "not a bad thing." Paine had clearly outlived his time. He was buried on his farm at New Rochelle after his request for a Quaker grave site was refused. Ten years later an enthusiastic admirer exhumed his bones with the intention of having him reburied in England. The admirer's plans came to nothing, and the whereabouts of Paine's grave is, at present, unknown.

Paine's great gift as a stylist was "plainness." He said he needed no "ceremonious expressions." "It is my design," he wrote, "to make those who can scarcely read understand," to put his arguments in a language "as plain as the alphabet," and to shape everything "to fit the powers of thinking and the turn of language to the subject, so as to bring out a clear conclusion that shall hit the point in question and nothing else."

## From Common Sense[1]

### Introduction

Perhaps the sentiments contained in the following pages are not yet sufficiently fashionable to procure them general favor; a long habit of not thinking a thing wrong gives it a superficial appearance of being right, and raises at first a formidable outcry in defence of custom. But the tumult soon subsides. Time makes more converts than reason.

As a long and violent abuse of power is generally the means of calling the right of it in question (and in matters too which might never have been thought of, had not the sufferers been aggravated into the inquiry), and as the King of England hath undertaken in his own right, to support the Parliament in what he calls theirs, and as the good people of this country are grievously oppressed by the combination, they have an undoubted privilege to inquire into the pretensions of both, and equally to reject the usurpation of either.

In the following sheets, the author hath studiously avoided everything which is personal among ourselves. Compliments as well as censure to individuals make no part thereof. The wise and the worthy need not the triumph of a pamphlet; and those whose sentiments are injudicious or unfriendly will cease of themselves, unless too much pains is bestowed upon their conversions.

The cause of America is in a great measure the cause of all mankind. Many

1. The full title is *Common Sense: Addressed to the Inhabitants of America, on the following Interesting Subjects: viz.:* I. *Of the Origin and Design of Government; with Concise Remarks on the English Constitution.* II. *Of Monarchy and Hereditary Succes-* sion. III. *Thoughts on the Present State of American Affairs.* IV. *Of the Present Ability of America; with* some *Miscellaneous Reflections.* The text used here is from *The Writings of Thomas Paine*, vol. 1, edited by M. D. Conway (1894–96).

circumstances have, and will, arise which are not local, but universal, and through which the principles of all lovers of mankind are affected, and in the event of which their affections are interested. The laying a country desolate with fire and sword, declaring war against the natural rights of all mankind, and extirpating the defenders thereof from the face of the earth, is the concern of every man to whom nature hath given the power of feeling; of which class, regardless of party censure, is

The Author

## From III. Thoughts on the Present State of American Affairs

In the following pages I offer nothing more than simple facts, plain arguments, and common sense: and have no other preliminaries to settle with the reader, than that he will divest himself of prejudice and prepossession, and suffer his reason and his feelings to determine for themselves: that he will put on, or rather that he will not put off, the true character of a man, and generously enlarge his views beyond the present day.

Volumes have been written on the subject of the struggle between England and America. Men of all ranks have embarked in the controversy, from different motives, and with various designs; but all have been ineffectual, and the period of debate is closed. Arms as the last resource decide the contest; the appeal was the choice of the King, and the continent has accepted the challenge.

It hath been reported of the late Mr. Pelham[2] (who though an able minister was not without his faults) that on his being attacked in the House of Commons on the score that his measures were only of a temporary kind, replied, "they will last my time." Should a thought so fatal and unmanly possess the colonies in the present contest, the name of ancestors will be remembered by future generations with detestation.

The sun never shined on a cause of greater worth. 'Tis not the affair of a city, a county, a province, or a kingdom; but of a continent—of at least one eighth part of the habitable globe. 'Tis not the concern of a day, a year, or an age; posterity are virtually involved in the contest, and will be more or less affected even to the end of time, by the proceedings now. Now is the seed time of continental union, faith and honor. The least fracture now will be like a name engraved with the point of a pin on the tender rind of a young oak; the wound would enlarge with the tree, and posterity read it in full grown characters.

By referring the matter from argument to arms, a new era for politics is struck—a new method of thinking hath arisen. All plans, proposals, etc., prior to the nineteenth of April, i.e., to the commencement of hostilities,[3] are like the almanacs of the last year; which though proper then, are superceded and useless now. Whatever was advanced by the advocates on either side of the question then, terminated in one and the same point, viz., a union with Great Britain; the only difference between the parties was the method of effecting it; the one proposing force, the other friendship; but it hath so far happened that the first hath failed, and the second hath withdrawn her influence.

2. Henry Pelham (c. 1695–1754), prime minister of Britain (1743–54).
3. The "Minutemen" of Lexington, Massachusetts, defended their ammunition stores against the British on April 19, 1775, and engaged in the first armed conflict of the American Revolution.

As much hath been said of the advantages of reconciliation, which, like an agreeable dream, hath passed away and left us as we were, it is but right that we should examine the contrary side of the argument, and inquire into some of the many material injuries which these colonies sustain, and always will sustain, by being connected with and dependent on Great Britain. To examine that connection and dependence, on the principles of nature and common sense, to see what we have to trust to, if separated, and what we are to expect, if dependent.

I have heard it asserted by some, that as America has flourished under her former connection with Great Britain, the same connection is necessary towards her future happiness, and will always have the same effect. Nothing can be more fallacious than this kind of argument. We may as well assert that because a child has thrived upon milk, that it is never to have meat, or that the first twenty years of our lives is to become a precedent for the next twenty. But even this is admitting more than is true; for I answer roundly, that America would have flourished as much, and probably much more, had no European power taken any notice of her. The commerce by which she hath enriched herself are the necessaries of life, and will always have a market while eating is the custom of Europe.

But she has protected us, say some. That she hath engrossed[4] us is true, and defended the continent at our expense as well as her own, is admitted; and she would have defended Turkey from the same motive, viz., for the sake of trade and dominion.

Alas! we have been long led away by ancient prejudices and made large sacrifices to superstition. We have boasted the protection of Great Britain without considering that her motive was interest not attachment; and that she did not protect us from our enemies on our account; but from her enemies on her own account, from those who had no quarrel with us on any other account, and who will always be our enemies on the same account. Let Britain waive her pretensions to the continent, or the continent throw off the dependence, and we should be at peace with France and Spain, were they at war with Britain. The miseries of Hanover's last war[5] ought to warn us against connections.

It hath lately been asserted in Parliament, that the colonies have no relation to each other but through the parent country, i.e., that Pennsylvania and the Jerseys,[6] and so on for the rest, are sister colonies by the way of England; this is certainly a very roundabout way of proving relationship, but it is the nearest and only true way of proving enmity (or enemyship, if I may so call it). France and Spain never were, nor perhaps ever will be, our enemies as Americans, but as our being the subjects of Great Britain.

But Britain is the parent country, say some. Then the more shame upon her conduct. Even brutes do not devour their young, nor savages make war upon their families; wherefore, the assertion, if true, turns to her reproach; but it happens not to be true, or only partly so, and the phrase parent or mother country hath been jesuitically[7] adopted by the King and his parasites, with a

---

4. Dominated.
5. King George III of Great Britain was a descendant of the Prussian House of Hanover; Paine is referring to the Seven Years' War (1756–63), which originally involved Prussia and Austria and grew to involve all the major European powers. American losses in the French and Indian War were heavy, even though the war was settled in Britain's favor.
6. The colony was divided into East and West Jersey.
7. I.e., cunningly.

low papistical design of gaining an unfair bias on the credulous weakness of our minds. Europe, and not England, is the parent country of America. This new world hath been the asylum for the persecuted lovers of civil and religious liberty from every part of Europe. Hither have they fled, not from the tender embraces of the mother, but from the cruelty of the monster; and it is so far true of England, that the same tyranny which drove the first emigrants from home, pursues their descendants still.

In this extensive quarter of the globe, we forget the narrow limits of three hundred and sixty miles (the extent of England) and carry our friendship on a larger scale; we claim brotherhood with every European Christian, and triumph in the generosity of the sentiment.

It is pleasant to observe by what regular gradations we surmount the force of local prejudices, as we enlarge our acquaintance with the world. A man born in any town in England divided into parishes, will naturally associate most with his fellow parishioners (because their interests in many cases will be common) and distinguish him by the name of neighbor; if he meet him but a few miles from home, he drops the narrow idea of a street, and salutes him by the name of townsman; if he travel out of the county and meet him in any other, he forgets the minor divisions of street and town, and calls him countryman, i.e., countyman: but if in their foreign excursions they should associate in France, or any other part of Europe, their local remembrance would be enlarged into that of Englishmen. And by a just parity of reasoning, all Europeans meeting in America, or any other quarter of the globe, are countrymen; for England, Holland, Germany, or Sweden, when compared with the whole, stand in the same places on the larger scale, which the divisions of street, town, and county do on the smaller ones; distinctions too limited for continental minds. Not one third of the inhabitants, even of this province,[8] are of English descent. Wherefore, I reprobate the phrase of parent or mother country applied to England only, as being false, selfish, narrow and ungenerous.

But, admitting that we were all of English descent, what does it amount to? Nothing. Britain, being now an open enemy, extinguishes every other name and title: and to say that reconciliation is our duty is truly farcical. The first King of England of the present line (William the Conqueror) was a Frenchman, and half the peers of England are descendants from the same country; wherefore, by the same method of reasoning, England ought to be governed by France.

Much hath been said of the united strength of Britain and the colonies, that in conjunction they might bid defiance to the world: but this is mere presumption; the fate of war is uncertain, neither do the expressions mean anything; for this continent would never suffer itself to be drained of inhabitants to support the British arms in either Asia, Africa, or Europe.

Besides, what have we to do with setting the world at defiance? Our plan is commerce, and that, well attended to, will secure us the peace and friendship of all Europe; because it is the interest of all Europe to have America a free port. Her trade will always be a protection, and her barrenness of gold and silver secure her from invaders.

I challenge the warmest advocate for reconciliation to show a single advantage that this continent can reap by being connected with Great Britain. I

8. I.e., Pennsylvania.

repeat the challenge; not a single advantage is derived. Our corn will fetch its price in any market in Europe, and our imported goods must be paid for buy them where we will.

But the injuries and disadvantages which we sustain by that connection, are without number; and our duty to mankind at large, as well as to ourselves, instruct us to renounce the alliance: because, any submission to, or dependence on, Great Britain tends directly to involve this continent in European wars and quarrels, and set us at variance with nations who would otherwise seek our friendship, and against whom we have neither anger nor complaint. As Europe is our market for trade, we ought to form no partial connection with any part of it. It is the true interest of America to steer clear of European contentions, which she never can do, while, by her dependence on Britain, she is made the makeweight in the scale of British politics.

Europe is too thickly planted with kingdoms to be long at peace, and whenever a war breaks out between England and any foreign power, the trade of America goes to ruin, because of her connection with Britain. The next war may not turn out like the last,[9] and should it not, the advocates for reconciliation now will be wishing for separation then, because neutrality in that case would be a safer convoy than a man of war. Everything that is right or reasonable pleads for separation. The blood of the slain, the weeping voice of nature cries, " 'Tis time to part." Even the distance at which the Almighty hath placed England and America is a strong and natural proof that the authority of the one over the other was never the design of Heaven. The time likewise at which the continent was discovered adds weight to the argument, and the manner in which it was peopled increases the force of it. The Reformation was preceded by the discovery of America: as if the Almighty graciously meant to open a sanctuary to the persecuted in future years, when home should afford neither friendship nor safety.

The authority of Great Britain over this continent is a form of government which sooner or later must have an end: and a serious mind can draw no true pleasure by looking forward, under the painful and positive conviction that what he calls "the present constitution" is merely temporary. As parents, we can have no joy, knowing that this government is not sufficiently lasting to insure anything which we may bequeath to posterity: and by a plain method of argument, as we are running the next generation into debt, we ought to do the work of it, otherwise we use them meanly and pitifully. In order to discover the line of our duty rightly, we should take our children in our hand, and fix our station a few years farther into life; that eminence will present a prospect which a few present fears and prejudices conceal from our sight.

Though I would carefully avoid giving unnecessary offense, yet I am inclined to believe that all those who espouse the doctrine of reconciliation may be included within the following descriptions.

Interested men who are not to be trusted, weak men who cannot see, prejudiced men who will not see, and a certain set of moderate men who think better of the European world than it deserves; and this last class, by an ill-judged deliberation, will be the cause of more calamities to this continent than all the other three.

---

9. The Seven Years' War concluded with the Treaty of Paris (1763), and Britain gained all the French territory in North America.

It is the good fortune of many to live distant from the scene of present sorrow; the evil is not sufficiently brought to their doors to make them feel the precariousness with which all American property is possessed. But let our imaginations transport us a few moments to Boston;[1] that seat of wretchedness will teach us wisdom, and instruct us forever to renounce a power in whom we can have no trust. The inhabitants of that unfortunate city, who but a few months ago were in ease and affluence, have now no other alternative than to stay and starve, or turn out to beg. Endangered by the fire of their friends if they continue within the city, and plundered by the soldiery if they leave it, in their present situation they are prisoners without the hope of redemption, and in a general attack for their relief they would be exposed to the fury of both armies.

Men of passive tempers look somewhat lightly over the offenses of Great Britain, and, still hoping for the best, are apt to call out, "Come, come, we shall be friends again for all this." But examine the passions and feelings of mankind: bring the doctrine of reconciliation to the touchstone of nature, and then tell me whether you can hereafter love, honor, and faithfully serve the power that hath carried fire and sword into your land? If you cannot do all these, then are you only deceiving yourselves, and by your delay bringing ruin upon posterity. Your future connection with Britain, whom you can neither love nor honor, will be forced and unnatural, and, being formed only on the plan of present convenience, will in a little time fall into a relapse more wretched than the first. But if you say, you can still pass the violations over, then I ask, hath your house been burnt? Hath your property been destroyed before your face? Are your wife and children destitute of a bed to lie on, or bread to live on? Have you lost a parent or a child by their hands, and yourself the ruined and wretched survivor? If you have not, then are you not a judge of those who have. But if you have, and can still shake hands with the murderers, then are you unworthy the name of husband, father, friend, or lover, and whatever may be your rank or title in life, you have the heart of a coward, and the spirit of a sycophant.

This is not inflaming or exaggerating matters, but trying them by those feelings and affections which nature justifies, and without which we should be incapable of discharging the social duties of life, or enjoying the felicities of it. I mean not to exhibit horror for the purpose of provoking revenge, but to awaken us from fatal and unmanly slumbers, that we may pursue determinately some fixed object. 'Tis not in the power of Britain or of Europe to conquer America, if she doth not conquer herself by delay and timidity. The present winter is worth an age if rightly employed, but if lost or neglected the whole continent will partake of the misfortune; and there is no punishment which that man doth not deserve, be he who, or what, or where he will, that may be the means of sacrificing a season so precious and useful.

'Tis repugnant to reason, to the universal order of things, to all examples from former ages, to suppose that this continent can long remain subject to any external power. The most sanguine in Britain doth not think so. The utmost stretch of human wisdom cannot, at this time, compass a plan, short of separation, which can promise the continent even a year's security. Reconciliation is now a fallacious dream. Nature hath deserted the connection, and

---

1. Boston was under British military occupation and blockaded for six months.

art cannot supply her place. For, as Milton wisely expresses, "never can true reconcilement grow where wounds of deadly hate have pierced so deep."[2]

\* \* \*

A government of our own is our natural right: and when a man seriously reflects on the precariousness of human affairs, he will become convinced that it is infinitely wiser and safer to form a constitution of our own in a cool deliberate manner, while we have it in our power, than to trust such an interesting event to time and chance. If we omit it now, some Massanello[3] may hereafter arise, who, laying hold of popular disquietudes, may collect together the desperate and the discontented, and by assuming to themselves the powers of government, finally sweep away the liberties of the continent like a deluge. Should the government of America return again into the hands of Britain, the tottering situation of things will be a temptation for some desperate adventurer to try his fortune; and in such a case, what relief can Britain give? Ere she could hear the news, the fatal business might be done; and ourselves suffering like the wretched Britons under the oppression of the conqueror. Ye that oppose independence now, ye know not what ye do: ye are opening a door to eternal tyranny by keeping vacant the seat of government. There are thousands and tens of thousands, who would think it glorious to expel from the continent that barbarous and hellish power, which hath stirred up the Indians and the Negroes to destroy us; the cruelty hath a double guilt: it is dealing brutally by us, and treacherously by them.

To talk of friendship with those in whom our reason forbids us to have faith, and our affections wounded through a thousand pores instruct us to detest, is madness and folly. Every day wears out the little remains of kindred between us and them; and can there be any reason to hope, that as the relationship expires, the affection will increase, or that we shall agree better when we have ten times more and greater concerns to quarrel over than ever?

Ye that tell us of harmony and reconciliation, can ye restore to us the time that is past? Can ye give to prostitution its former innocence? Neither can ye reconcile Britain and America. The last cord now is broken, the people of England are presenting addresses against us. There are injuries which nature cannot forgive; she would cease to be nature if she did. As well can the lover forgive the ravisher of his mistress, as the continent forgive the murders of Britain. The Almighty hath implanted in us these unextinguishable feelings for good and wise purposes. They are the guardians of His image in our hearts. They distinguish us from the herd of common animals. The social compact would dissolve, and justice be extirpated from the earth, or have only a casual existence were we callous to the touches of affection. The robber and the murderer would often escape unpunished, did not the injuries which our tempers sustain provoke us into justice.

O! ye that love mankind! Ye that dare oppose not only the tyranny but the tyrant, stand forth! Every spot of the old world is overrun with oppression. Freedom hath been hunted round the globe. Asia and Africa have long expelled her. Europe regards her like a stranger, and England hath given her

---

2. *Paradise Lost* 4.98–99.
3. "Thomas Anello, otherwise Massanello, a fisherman of Naples, who after spiriting up his countrymen in the public market place, against the oppression of

the Spaniards, to whom the place was then subject, prompted them to revolt, and in the space of a day became King" [Paine's note].

warning to depart. O! receive the fugitive, and prepare in time an asylum for mankind.

1776

# The Crisis,[1] No. 1

These are the times that try men's souls. The summer soldier and the sunshine patriot will, in this crisis, shrink from the service of their country; but he that stands it now, deserves the love and thanks of man and woman. Tyranny, like hell, is not easily conquered; yet we have this consolation with us, that the harder the conflict, the more glorious the triumph. What we obtain too cheap, we esteem too lightly: it is dearness only that gives everything its value. Heaven knows how to put a proper price upon its goods; and it would be strange indeed if so celestial an article as freedom should not be highly rated. Britain, with an army to enforce her tyranny, has declared that she has a right (not only to tax) but "to bind us in all cases whatsoever," and if being bound in that manner is not slavery, then is there not such a thing as slavery upon earth. Even the expression is impious; for so unlimited a power can belong only to God.

Whether the independence of the continent was declared too soon, or delayed too long, I will not now enter into as an argument; my own simple opinion is, that had it been eight months earlier, it would have been much better. We did not make a proper use of last winter, neither could we, while we were in a dependent state. However, the fault, if it were one, was all our own;[2] we have none to blame but ourselves. But no great deal is lost yet. All that Howe[3] has been doing for this month past is rather a ravage than a conquest, which the spirit of the Jerseys,[4] a year ago, would have quickly repulsed, and which time and a little resolution will soon recover.

I have as little superstition in me as any man living, but my secret opinion has ever been, and still is, that God Almighty will not give up a people to military destruction, or leave them unsupportedly to perish, who have so earnestly and so repeatedly sought to avoid the calamities of war, by every decent method which wisdom could invent. Neither have I so much of the infidel in me as to suppose that He has relinquished the government of the world, and given us up to the care of devils; and as I do not, I cannot see on what grounds the King of Britain can look up to heaven for help against us: a common murderer, a highwayman, or a housebreaker has as good a pretense as he.

'Tis surprising to see how rapidly a panic will sometimes run through a country. All nations and ages have been subject to them: Britain has trembled

---

1. The first of sixteen pamphlets that appeared under this title. Paine sometimes referred to this particular essay as The American Crisis. There were three pamphlet editions in one week: one undated, one dated December 19, and the one reprinted here, dated December 23. The text used here is from The Writings of Thomas Paine, vol. 1, edited by M. D. Conway (1894–96).
2. "The present winter is worth an age, if rightly employed; but, if lost or neglected, the whole continent

will partake of the evil; and there is no punishment that man does not deserve, be he who, or what, or where he will, that may be the means of sacrificing a season so precious and useful" [Paine's note, taken from Common Sense]. Paine wanted an immediate declaration of independence, uniting the colonies and enlisting the aid of France and Spain.
3. Lord William Howe (1729–1814) was commander of the British Army in America from 1775 to 1778.
4. The colony was divided into East and West Jersey.

like an ague[5] at the report of a French fleet of flat-bottomed boats; and in the fourteenth[6] century the whole English army, after ravaging the kingdom of France, was driven back like men petrified with fear; and this brave exploit was performed by a few broken forces collected and headed by a woman, Joan of Arc. Would that heaven might inspire some Jersey maid to spirit up her countrymen, and save her fair fellow sufferers from ravage and ravishment! Yet panics, in some cases, have their uses; they produce as much good as hurt. Their duration is always short; the mind soon grows through them, and acquires a firmer habit than before. But their peculiar advantage is that they are the touchstones of sincerity and hypocrisy, and bring things and men to light, which might otherwise have lain forever undiscovered. In fact, they have the same effect on secret traitors, which an imaginary apparition would have upon a private murderer. They sift out the hidden thoughts of man, and hold them up in public to the world. Many a disguised tory[7] has lately shown his head, that shall penitentially solemnize with curses the day on which Howe arrived upon the Delaware.

As I was with the troops at Fort Lee, and marched with them to the edge of Pennsylvania, I am well acquainted with many circumstances, which those who live at a distance know but little or nothing of. Our situation there was exceedingly cramped, the place being a narrow neck of land between the North River[8] and the Hackensack. Our force was inconsiderable, being not one fourth so great as Howe could bring against us. We had no army at hand to have relieved the garrison, had we shut ourselves up and stood on our defense. Our ammunition, light artillery, and the best part of our stores had been removed on the apprehension that Howe would endeavor to penetrate the Jerseys, in which case Fort Lee could be of no use to us; for it must occur to every thinking man, whether in the army or not, that these kind of field forts are only for temporary purposes, and last in use no longer than the enemy directs his force against the particular object, which such forts are raised to defend. Such was our situation and condition at Fort Lee on the morning of the 20th of November, when an officer arrived with information that the enemy with 200 boats had landed about seven miles above: Major General Green,[9] who commanded the garrison, immediately ordered them under arms, and sent express to General Washington at the town of Hackensack, distant, by the way of the ferry, six miles. Our first object was to secure the bridge over the Hackensack, which laid up the river between the enemy and us, about six miles from us, and three from them. General Washington arrived in about three quarters of an hour, and marched at the head of the troops towards the bridge, which place I expected we should have a brush for; however, they did not choose to dispute it with us, and the greatest part of our troops went over the bridge, the rest over the ferry, except some which passed at a mill on a small creek, between the bridge and the ferry, and made their way through some marshy grounds up to the town of Hackensack, and there passed the river. We brought off as much baggage as the wagons could contain, the rest was lost. The simple object was to bring off the garrison, and march them on till they could be strengthened by the Jersey or Pennsylvania militia,

---

5. I.e., like one who is chilled.
6. Properly, the 15th century. Joan of Arc led the French to victory over the English in 1429.
7. I.e., supporter of the king.

8. I.e., the Hudson River.
9. Paine was aide-de-camp to Major General Nathanael Greene (1742–1786).

so as to be enabled to make a stand. We staid four days at Newark, collected our outposts with some of the Jersey militia, and marched out twice to meet the enemy, on being informed that they were advancing, though our numbers were greatly inferior to theirs. Howe, in my little opinion, committed a great error in generalship in not throwing a body of forces off from Staten Island through Amboy, by which means he might have seized all our stores at Brunswick, and intercepted our march into Pennsylvania; but if we believe the power of hell to be limited, we must likewise believe that their agents are under some providential control.[1]

I shall not now attempt to give all the particulars of our retreat to the Delaware; suffice it for the present to say, that both officers and men, though greatly harassed and fatigued, frequently without rest, covering, or provision, the inevitable consequences of a long retreat, bore it with a manly and martial spirit. All their wishes centered in one, which was that the country would turn out and help them to drive the enemy back. Voltaire has remarked that King William never appeared to full advantage but in difficulties and in action;[2] the same remark may be made on General Washington, for the character fits him. There is a natural firmness in some minds which cannot be unlocked by trifles, but which, when unlocked, discovers a cabinet[3] of fortitude; and I reckon it among those kind of public blessings, which we do not immediately see, that God hath blessed him with uninterrupted health, and given him a mind that can even flourish upon care.

I shall conclude this paper with some miscellaneous remarks on the state of our affairs; and shall begin with asking the following question: Why is it that the enemy have left the New England provinces, and made these middle ones the seat of war? The answer is easy: New England is not infested with tories, and we are. I have been tender in raising the cry against these men, and used numberless arguments to show them their danger, but it will not do to sacrifice a world either to their folly or their baseness. The period is now arrived, in which either they or we must change our sentiments, or one or both must fall. And what is a tory? Good God! what is he? I should not be afraid to go with a hundred whigs[4] against a thousand tories, were they to attempt to get into arms. Every tory is a coward; for servile, slavish, self-interested fear is the foundation of toryism; and a man under such influence, though he may be cruel, never can be brave.

But, before the line of irrecoverable separation be drawn between us, let us reason the matter together: Your conduct is an invitation to the enemy, yet not one in a thousand of you has heart enough to join him. Howe is as much deceived by you as the American cause is injured by you. He expects you will all take up arms, and flock to his standard, with muskets on your shoulders. Your opinions are of no use to him, unless you support him personally, for 'tis soldiers, and not tories, that he wants.

I once felt all that kind of anger, which a man ought to feel, against the mean principles that are held by the tories: a noted one, who kept a tavern at Amboy,[5] was standing at his door, with as pretty a child in his hand, about

---

1. The American losses were larger than Paine implies. General Howe took three thousand prisoners and a large store of military supplies when he captured Fort Lee. Paine wrote *The Crisis, No. 1* while serving with Washington's army as it retreated through New Jersey.
2. Voltaire (1694–1778) made this remark about King William III of England (1650–1702) in his *History of Louis the Fourteenth* (1751).
3. Storehouse.
4. Supporters of the Revolution.
5. Paine was stationed at Perth Amboy, New Jersey, while in the Continental Army.

eight or nine years old, as I ever saw, and after speaking his mind as freely as he thought was prudent, finished with this unfatherly expression, "Well! give me peace in my day." Not a man lives on the continent but fully believes that a separation must some time or other finally take place, and a generous parent should have said, "If there must be trouble, let it be in my day, that my child may have peace"; and this single reflection, well applied, is sufficient to awaken every man to duty. Not a place upon earth might be so happy as America. Her situation is remote from all the wrangling world, and she has nothing to do but to trade with them. A man can distinguish himself between temper and principle, and I am as confident, as I am that God governs the world, that America will never be happy till she gets clear of foreign dominion. Wars, without ceasing, will break out till that period arrives, and the continent must in the end be conqueror; for though the flame of liberty may sometimes cease to shine, the coal can never expire.

America did not, nor does not, want force; but she wanted a proper application of that force. Wisdom is not the purchase of a day, and it is no wonder that we should err at the first setting off. From an excess of tenderness, we were unwilling to raise an army, and trusted our cause to the temporary defense of a well-meaning militia. A summer's experience has now taught us better; yet with those troops, while they were collected, we were able to set bounds to the progress of the enemy, and thank God! they are again assembling. I always considered militia as the best troops in the world for a sudden exertion, but they will not do for a long campaign. Howe, it is probable, will make an attempt on this city;[6] should he fail on this side of the Delaware, he is ruined: if he succeeds, our cause is not ruined. He stakes all on his side against a part on ours; admitting he succeeds, the consequence will be that armies from both ends of the continent will march to assist their suffering friends in the middle states; for he cannot go everywhere, it is impossible. I consider Howe as the greatest enemy the tories have; he is bringing a war into their country, which, had it not been for him and partly for themselves, they had been clear of. Should he now be expelled, I wish with all the devotion of a Christian, that the names of whig and tory may never more be mentioned; but should the tories give him encouragement to come, or assistance if he come, I as sincerely wish that our next year's arms may expel them from the continent, and the congress appropriate their possessions to the relief of those who have suffered in well-doing. A single successful battle next year will settle the whole. America could carry on a two years' war by the confiscation of the property of disaffected persons, and be made happy by their expulsion. Say not that this is revenge; call it rather the soft resentment of a suffering people, who, having no object in view but the good of all, have staked their own all upon a seemingly doubtful event. Yet it is folly to argue against determined hardness; eloquence may strike the ear, and the language of sorrow draw forth the tear of compassion, but nothing can reach the heart that is steeled with prejudice.

Quitting this class of men, I turn with the warm ardor of a friend to those who have nobly stood, and are yet determined to stand the matter out: I call not upon a few, but upon all: not on this state or that state, but on every state: up and help us; lay your shoulders to the wheel; better have too much force than too little, when so great an object is at stake. Let it be told to the future

6. I.e., Philadelphia.

world that in the depth of winter, when nothing but hope and virtue could survive, that the city and the country, alarmed at one common danger, came forth to meet and to repulse it. Say not that thousands are gone, turn out your tens of thousands;[7] throw not the burden of the day upon Providence, but "show your faith by your works"[8] that God may bless you. It matters not where you live, or what rank of life you hold, the evil or the blessing will reach you all. The far and the near, the home counties and the back,[9] the rich and poor will suffer or rejoice alike. The heart that feels not now is dead: the blood of his children will curse his cowardice who shrinks back at a time when a little might have saved the whole, and made them happy. I love the man that can smile in trouble, that can gather strength from distress, and grow brave by reflection. 'Tis the business of little minds to shrink; but he whose heart is firm, and whose conscience approves his conduct, will pursue his principles unto death. My own line of reasoning is to myself as straight and clear as a ray of light. Not all the treasures of the world, so far as I believe, could have induced me to support an offensive war, for I think it murder; but if a thief breaks into my house, burns and destroys my property, and kills or threatens to kill me, or those that are in it, and to "bind me in all cases whatsoever"[1] to his absolute will, am I to suffer it? What signifies it to me, whether he who does it is a king or a common man; my countryman or not my countryman; whether it be done by an individual villain, or an army of them? If we reason to the root of things we shall find no difference; neither can any just cause be assigned why we should punish in the one case and pardon in the other. Let them call me rebel, and welcome, I feel no concern from it; but I should suffer the misery of devils were I to make a whore of my soul by swearing allegiance to one whose character is that of a sottish, stupid, stubborn, worthless, brutish man. I conceive likewise a horrid idea in receiving mercy from a being, who at the last day shall be shrieking to the rocks and mountains to cover him, and fleeing with terror from the orphan, the widow, and the slain of America.

There are cases which cannot be overdone by language, and this is one. There are persons, too, who see not the full extent of the evil which threatens them; they solace themselves with hopes that the enemy, if he succeed, will be merciful. It is the madness of folly to expect mercy from those who have refused to do justice; and even mercy, where conquest is the object, is only a trick of war; the cunning of the fox is as murderous as the violence of the wolf, and we ought to guard equally against both. Howe's first object is, partly by threats and partly by promises, to terrify or seduce the people to deliver up their arms and receive mercy. The ministry recommended the same plan to Gage,[2] and this is what the tories call making their peace, "a peace which passeth all understanding"[3] indeed! A peace which would be the immediate forerunner of a worse ruin than any we have yet thought of. Ye men of Pennsylvania, do reason upon these things! Were the back counties to give up their arms, they would fall an easy prey to the Indians, who are all armed: this

---

7. "Saul hath slain his thousands, and David his ten thousands" (1 Samuel 18.7).
8. "Shew me thy faith without thy works, and I will shew thee my faith by my works" (James 2.18).
9. I.e., the backwoods.
1. From the Declaratory Act of Parliament, February 24, 1766, establishing British authority over the Amer-

ican colonies.
2. General Thomas Gage, who commanded the British armies in America from 1763 to 1775, before Howe.
3. "And the peace of God, which passeth all understanding, shall keep your hearts and minds through Christ Jesus" (Philippians 4.7).

perhaps is what some tories would not be sorry for. Were the home counties to deliver up their arms, they would be exposed to the resentment of the back counties, who would then have it in their power to chastise their defection at pleasure. And were any one state to give up its arms, that state must be garrisoned by all Howe's army of Britons and Hessians[4] to preserve it from the anger of the rest. Mutual fear is the principal link in the chain of mutual love, and woe be to that state that breaks the compact. Howe is mercifully inviting you to barbarous destruction, and men must be either rogues or fools that will not see it. I dwell not upon the vapors of imagination: I bring reason to your ears, and, in language as plain as A, B, C, hold up truth to your eyes.

I thank God that I fear not. I see no real cause for fear. I know our situation well, and can see the way out of it. While our army was collected, Howe dared not risk a battle; and it is no credit to him that he decamped from the White Plains,[5] and waited a mean opportunity to ravage the defenseless Jerseys; but it is great credit to us, that, with a handful of men, we sustained an orderly retreat for near an hundred miles, brought off our ammunition, all our field pieces, the greatest part of our stores, and had four rivers to pass. None can say that our retreat was precipitate, for we were near three weeks in performing it, that the country[6] might have time to come in. Twice we marched back to meet the enemy, and remained out till dark. The sign of fear was not seen in our camp, and had not some of the cowardly and disaffected inhabitants spread false alarms through the country, the Jerseys had never been ravaged. Once more we are again collected and collecting; our new army at both ends of the continent is recruiting fast, and we shall be able to open the next campaign with sixty thousand men, well armed and clothed. This is our situation, and who will may know it. By perseverance and fortitude we have the prospect of a glorious issue; by cowardice and submission, the sad choice of a variety of evils—a ravaged country—a depopulated city—habitations without safety, and slavery without hope—our homes turned into barracks and bawdyhouses for Hessians, and a future race to provide for, whose fathers we shall doubt of. Look on this picture and weep over it! and if there yet remains one thoughtless wretch who believes it not, let him suffer it unlamented.

Common Sense

1776

4. German mercenaries.
5. At White Plains, New York, on October 28, 1776, General Howe successfully overcame Washington's

troops, but failed to take full advantage of his victory.
6. I.e., the local volunteers.

---

# THOMAS JEFFERSON
## 1743–1826

President of the United States, first secretary of state, and minister to France, governor of Virginia, and congressman, Thomas Jefferson once said that he wished to be remembered for only three things: drafting the Declaration of Independence, writing and supporting the Virginia Statute for Religious Freedom (1786), and founding the University of Virginia. Jefferson might well have included a number of other accomplishments in this list: he was a remarkable architect and designed the Virginia state capital, his residence Monticello, and the original buildings for the University of Virginia; he farmed thousands of acres and built one of the most beautiful plantations in America; he had a library of some ten thousand volumes, which served as the basis for the Library of Congress, and a collection of paintings and sculpture that made him America's greatest patron of the arts; and was known the world over for his spirit of scientific inquiry and as the creator of a number of remarkable inventions. The three acts for which he wished to be remembered, however, have this in common: they all testify to Jefferson's lifelong passion to liberate the human mind from tyranny, whether imposed by the state, the church, or our own ignorance.

Jefferson was born at Shadwell, in what is now Albermarle County, Virginia. His mother, Jane Randolph, came from one of the most distinguished families in Virginia. Peter Jefferson, his father, was a county official and surveyor. He made the first accurate map of Virginia, something of which Jefferson was always proud. When his father died Thomas was only fourteen. Peter Jefferson left his son 2,750 acres of land, and Jefferson added to this acreage until he died; at one time he owned almost ten thousand acres. Jefferson tells us in his *Autobiography* that his father's education had been "quite neglected" but that he was always "eager after information" and determined to improve himself. In 1760, when Jefferson entered William and Mary College in Williamsburg, Virginia, he had mastered Latin and Greek, played the violin respectably, and was a skilled horseman. He was tall and a bit awkward looking, but a good companion. Williamsburg was the capital of Virginia as well as a college town, and Jefferson was fortunate enough to make the acquaintance of three men who strongly influenced his life: Governor Francis Fauquier, a fellow of the Royal Society; George Wythe, one of the best teachers of law in the country; and Dr. William Small, an emigrant from Scotland who taught mathematics and philosophy and who introduced Jefferson, as Garry Wills has put it, "to the invigorating realm of the Scottish Enlightenment," especially the work of Francis Hutcheson, author of An *Inquiry into the Original of Our Ideas of Beauty and Virtue* (1725), and Lord Kames (Henry Home), author of *Essays on the Principles of Morality and Natural Religion* (1751). Jefferson flourished in Williamsburg, and it is hard to imagine a city in America where his natural interests and talents could have been more sympathetically encouraged.

Jefferson stayed on in Williamsburg to read law after graduation and was admitted to the bar. In 1769 he was elected to the Virginia House of Burgesses and began a distinguished career in the legislature. In 1774 he wrote an influential and daring pamphlet called A *Summary View of the Rights of British America*, denying all parliamentary authority over America and arguing that ties to the British monarchy were voluntary and not irrevocable. Jefferson's reputation as a writer preceded him to Philadelphia, where he was a delegate to the Second Continental Congress, and on June 11, 1776, he was elected to join Benjamin Franklin, John Adams, Roger Sherman, and Robert Livingston in drafting a declaration of independence. Although committee members made suggestions, the draft was very much Jefferson's own. As Garry Wills has recently shown, Jefferson was unhappy with the changes made by Congress to his draft, and rightly so; for congressional changes went contrary to some of his basic arguments. Jefferson wished to place the British *people* on record as the ultimate cause of the Revolution, because they tolerated a corrupt parliament and king; and he wished to include a strong statement against slavery. Congress tolerated neither passage. Jefferson was justified, however, in asking that he be remembered as the author of the Declaration. It was, as Dumas Malone, Jefferson's biographer, once put it, a "dangerous but glorious opportunity." Whether as the result of these frustrations or merely Jefferson's wish to be nearer his family, he left the Congress in September 1776, and entered the Virginia House of Delegates. In 1779 he was elected governor, and although reelected the following year, Jefferson's term of office came to an ignominious end when he resigned. After the British captured Richmond in 1781, Jefferson and the legislature moved to Charlottesville, and he and the legislators barely escaped imprisonment when the pursuing British army descended on them at Monticello. Jefferson's resignation and the lack of preparations for the defense of the city were held against him, and it was some time before he regained the confidence of Virginians.

From 1781 to 1784 Jefferson withdrew from public life and remained at Monticello, completing his only book, Notes on the State of Virginia. In 1784 he was appointed minister to France and served with Benjamin Franklin on the commission that signed the Treaty of Paris, ending the Revolutionary War. He returned to Monticello in 1789, and in 1790 Washington appointed him the first secretary of state under the newly adopted Constitution. After three years he announced his plans for retirement once again and withdrew to Monticello, where he rotated his crops and built a grist mill. But Jefferson's political blood was too thick for retirement, and in 1796 he ran for the office of president, losing to John Adams and taking the office of vice president instead. In 1800 he was elected president, the first to be inaugurated in Washington. He named Benjamin Latrobe surveyor of public buildings, and he worked with Latrobe in planning a great city.

When Jefferson returned to Monticello in 1809, he knew that this time his public life was over. For the final seventeen years of his life he kept a watchful eye on everything that grew in Monticello. But Jefferson was never far from the world. He rose every morning to attack his voluminous correspondence. The Library of Congress holds more than fifty-five thousand Jefferson manuscripts and letters, and the most recent edition of his writings will run to sixty volumes. Jefferson left no treatise on political philosophy and, in a sense, was no political thinker. He was always more interested in the practical consequences of ideas. He remained an agrarian aristocrat all his life, and it is to the liberty of mind and the values of the land that he always returned. As Dumas Malone puts it: he was a "homely aristocrat in manner of life and personal tastes; he distrusted all rulers and feared the rise of an industrial proletariat, but more than any of his eminent contemporaries, he trusted the common man, if measurably enlightened and kept in rural virtue." Jefferson died a few hours before John Adams on the Fourth of July, 1826.

# From The Autobiography of Thomas Jefferson[1]

## From The Declaration of Independence

*       *       *

It appearing in the course of these debates, that the colonies of New York, New Jersey, Pennsylvania, Delaware, Maryland, and South Carolina were not yet matured for falling from the parent stem, but that they were fast advancing to that state, it was thought most prudent to wait a while for them, and to postpone the final decision to July 1st; but, that this might occasion as little delay as possible, a committee was appointed to prepare a Declaration of Independence. The committee were John Adams, Dr. Franklin, Roger Sherman,

1. On June 7, 1776, Richard Henry Lee of Virginia proposed to the Second Continental Congress, meeting in Philadelphia, that "these united Colonies are, and of a right ought to be, free and independent states." On June 11, a committee of five—John Adams of Massachusetts, Benjamin Franklin of Pennsylvania, Roger Sherman of Connecticut, Robert Livingston of New York, and Thomas Jefferson of Virginia—was instructed to draft a declaration of independence. The draft presented to Congress on June 28 was primarily the work of Jefferson. Lee's resolution was passed on July 2, and the Declaration was adopted on July 4 with the changes noted by Jefferson in this text, taken from his Autobiography. Jefferson observes that "As the sentiments of men are known not only by what they receive, but what they reject also, I will state the form of the declaration as originally reported. The parts struck out by Congress shall be distinguished by a black line drawn under them; and those inserted by them shall be placed in the margin or in a concurrent column." On August 2 a copy in parchment was signed by all the delegates but three, and they signed later. The text used here is from The Writings of Thomas Jefferson, edited by A. A. Lipscomb and A. E. Bergh (1903).

Robert R. Livingston, and myself. Committees were also appointed, at the same time, to prepare a plan of confederation for the colonies, and to state the terms proper to be proposed for foreign alliance. The committee for drawing the Declaration of Independence, desired me to do it. It was accordingly done, and being approved by them, I reported it to the House on Friday, the 28th of June, when it was read, and ordered to lie on the table. On Monday, the 1st of July, the House resolved itself into a committee of the whole, and resumed the consideration of the original motion made by the delegates of Virginia, which, being again debated through the day, was carried in the affirmative by the votes of New Hampshire, Connecticut, Massachusetts, Rhode Island, New Jersey, Maryland, Virginia, North Carolina and Georgia. South Carolina and Pennsylvania voted against it. Delaware had but two members present, and they were divided. The delegates from New York declared they were for it themselves, and were assured their constituents were for it; but that their instructions having been drawn near a twelve-month before, when reconciliation was still the general object, they were enjoined by them to do nothing which should impede that object. They, therefore, thought themselves not justifiable in voting on either side, and asked leave to withdraw from the question: which was given them. The committee rose and reported their resolution to the House. Mr. Edward Rutledge, of South Carolina, then requested the determination might be put off to the next day, as he believed his colleagues, though they disapproved of the resolution, would then join in it for the sake of unanimity. The ultimate question, whether the House would agree to the resolution of the committee, was accordingly postponed to the next day, when it was again moved, and South Carolina concurred in voting for it. In the meantime, a third member had come post[2] from the Delaware counties, and turned the vote of that colony in favor of the resolution. Members of a different sentiment attending that morning from Pennsylvania also, her vote was changed, so that the whole twelve colonies who were authorized to vote at all, gave their voices for it; and, within a few days, the convention of New York approved of it, and thus supplied the void occasioned by the withdrawing of her delegates from the vote.

Congress proceeded the same day to consider the Declaration of Independence, which had been reported and lain on the table the Friday preceding, and on Monday referred to a committee of the whole. The pusillanimous idea that we had friends in England worth keeping terms with, still haunted the minds of many. For this reason, those passages which conveyed censures on the people of England were struck out, lest they should give them offense. The clause too, reprobating the enslaving the inhabitants of Africa, was struck out in complaisance to South Carolina and Georgia, who had never attempted to restrain the importation of slaves, and who, on the contrary, still wished to continue it. Our northern brethren also, I believe, felt a little tender under those censures; for though their people had very few slaves themselves, yet they had been pretty considerable carriers of them to others. The debates, having taken up the greater parts of the 2d, 3d, and 4th days of July, were, on the evening of the last, closed; the Declaration was reported by the committee, agreed to by the House, and signed by every member present, except Mr. Dickinson.[3] As the sentiments of men are known not only by what they

---

2. Speedily, posthaste.                3. John Dickinson of Pennsylvania, who opposed it.

receive, but what they reject also, I will state the form of the Declaration as originally reported. The parts struck out by Congress shall be distinguished by a black line drawn under them, and those inserted by them shall be placed in the margin, or in a concurrent column.

A DECLARATION BY THE REPRESENTATIVES OF THE UNITED STATES OF AMERICA, IN GENERAL CONGRESS ASSEMBLED.

When, in the course of human events, it becomes necessary for one people to dissolve the political bands which have connected them with another, and to assume among the powers of the earth the separate and equal station to which the laws of nature and of nature's God entitle them, a decent respect to the opinions of mankind requires that they should declare the causes which impel them to the separation.

We hold these truths to be self evident: that all men are created equal;[4] that they are endowed by their Creator with inherent and   certain inalienable rights; that among these are life, liberty, and the pursuit of happiness;[5] that to secure these rights, governments are instituted among men, deriving their just powers from the consent of the governed; that whenever any form of government becomes destructive of these ends, it is the right of the people to alter or to abolish it, and to institute new government, laying its foundation on such principles, and organizing its powers in such form, as to them shall seem most likely to effect their safety and happiness. Prudence, indeed, will dictate that governments long established should not be changed for light and transient causes; and accordingly all experience hath shown that mankind are more disposed to suffer while evils are sufferable, than to right themselves by abolishing the forms to which they are accustomed. But when a long train of abuses and usurpations, begun at a distinguished[6] period and pursuing invariably the same object, evinces a design to reduce them under absolute despotism, it is their right, it is their duty to throw off such government, and to provide new guards for their future security. Such has been the patient sufferance of these colonies; and such is now the necessity which constrains them to expunge their former systems of government. The   alter history of the present king of Great Britain[7] is a history of unremit-   repeated ting injuries and usurpations, among which appears no solitary   all having fact to contradict the uniform tenor of the rest, but all have in direct object the establishment of an absolute tyranny over these

4. Garry Wills, in his study of the Declaration (*Inventing America*, 1978), tells us that Jefferson means *equal* in possessing a moral sense: "The moral sense is not only man's *highest* faculty, but the one that is *equal* to all men."
5. In his *Second Treatise on Government* (1689) John Locke defined man's natural rights to "life, liberty, and property." Jefferson's substitution of "pursuit of happiness" has puzzled a number of critics. Wills suggests that Jefferson was less influenced by Locke than the Scottish philosophers, particularly Francis Hutcheson and his *Inquiry into the Original of Our Ideas of Beauty*

*and Virtue* (1725). Wills tells us that "the pursuit of happiness is a phenomenon both obvious and paradoxical. It supplies us with the ground of human right and the goal of human virtue. It is the basic drive of the self, and the only means given for transcending the self. . . . Men in the eighteenth century felt they could become conscious of their freedom by discovering how they were bound: When they found what they *must* pursue, they knew they had a *right* to pursue it."
6. I.e., discernible.
7. King George III (1738–1820).

states. To prove this, let facts be submitted to a candid world <u>for the truth of which we pledge a faith yet unsullied by falsehood.</u>

He has refused his assent to laws the most wholesome and necessary for the public good.

He has forbidden his governors to pass laws of immediate and pressing importance, unless suspended in their operation till his assent should be obtained; and, when so suspended, he has utterly neglected to attend to them.

He has refused to pass other laws for the accommodation of large districts of people, unless those people would relinquish the right of representation in the legislature, a right inestimable to them, and formidable to tyrants only.

He has called together legislative bodies at places unusual, uncomfortable, and distant from the depository of their public records, for the sole purpose of fatiguing them into compliance with his measures.

He has dissolved representative houses repeatedly <u>and continually</u> for opposing with manly firmness his invasions on the rights of the people.

He has refused for a long time after such dissolutions to cause others to be elected, whereby the legislative powers, incapable of annihilation, have returned to the people at large for their exercise, the state remaining, in the meantime, exposed to all the dangers of invasion from without and convulsions within.

He has endeavored to prevent the population of these states; for that purpose obstructing the laws for naturalization of foreigners, refusing to pass others to encourage their migrations hither, and raising the conditions of new appropriations of lands.

He has <u>suffered</u> the administration of justice <u>totally to cease in</u> <u>some of these states</u> refusing his assent to laws for establishing judiciary powers. [margin: obstructed by]

He has made <u>our</u> judges dependent on his will alone for the tenure of their offices, and the amount and payment of their salaries.

He has erected a multitude of new offices, <u>by a self-assumed power</u> and sent hither swarms of new officers to harass our people and eat out their substance.

He has kept among us in times of peace standing armies <u>and ships of war</u> without the consent of our legislatures.

He has affected to render the military independent of, and superior to, the civil power.

<u>He has combined with others[8] to subject us to a jurisdiction foreign to our constitutions and unacknowledged by our laws, giving his assent to their acts of pretended legislation for quartering large bodies of armed troops among us; for protecting them by a mock trial from punishment for any murders which they should commit on the inhabitants of these states; for cutting off our trade with all parts of the world; for imposing taxes on us without our</u>

8. I.e., the British Parliament.

consent; for depriving us [    ] of the benefits of trial by jury; for in many cases transporting us beyond seas to be tried for pretended offenses; for abolishing the free system of English laws in a neighboring province,[9] establishing therein an arbitrary government, and enlarging its boundaries, so as to render it at once an example and fit instrument for introducing the same absolute rule into these states; for colonies; taking away our charters, abolishing our most valuable laws, and altering fundamentally the forms of our governments; for suspending our own legislatures, and declaring themselves invested with power to legislate for us in all cases whatsoever.

He has abdicated government here withdrawing his governors, by declaring us out of his and declaring us out of his allegiance and protection. protection,

He has plundered our seas, ravaged our coasts, burnt our and waging war against towns, and destroyed the lives of our people. us.

He is at this time transporting large armies of foreign mercenaries[1] to complete the works of death, desolation and tyranny already begun with circumstances of cruelty and perfidy [    ] scarcely unworthy the head of a civilized nation. paralleled

He has constrained our fellow citizens taken captive on the high in the most barbarous seas, to bear arms against their country, to become the executioners of their friends and brethren, or to fall themselves by their ages, and totally hands.

He has [    ] endeavored to bring on the inhabitants of our frontiers, the merciless Indian savages, whose known rule of warfare excited domestic insurrection is an undistinguished destruction of all ages, sexes and conditions among us, and has of existence.

He has incited treasonable insurrections of our fellow citizens, with the allurements of forfeiture and confiscation of our property.

He has waged cruel war against human nature itself, violating its most sacred rights of life and liberty in the persons of a distant people who never offended him, captivating and carrying them into slavery in another hemisphere, or to incur miserable death in their transportation thither. This piratical warfare, the opprobrium of INFIDEL powers, is the warfare of the CHRISTIAN king of Great Britain. Determined to keep open a market where MEN should be bought and sold, he has prostituted his negative for suppressing every legislative attempt to prohibit or to restrain this execrable commerce. And that this assemblage of horrors might want no fact of distinguished die, he is now exciting those very people to rise in arms among us, and to purchase that liberty of which he has deprived them, by murdering the people on whom he also obtruded them: thus paying off former crimes committed against the LIBERTIES of one people, with crimes which he urges them to commit against the LIVES of another.

In every stage of these oppressions we have petitioned for redress

---

9. The Quebec Act of 1774 recognized the Roman Catholic religion in Quebec and extended the borders of the province to the Ohio River; it restored French civil law and thus angered the New England colonies.

It was often referred to as one of the "intolerable acts." 1. German soldiers hired by the king for colonial service.

in the most humble terms: our repeated petitions have been answered only by repeated injuries.

A prince whose character is thus marked by every act which may define a tyrant is unfit to be the ruler of a [ ] people who *free* mean to be free. Future ages will scarcely believe that the hardiness of one man adventured, within the short compass of twelve years only, to lay a foundation so broad and so undisguised for tyranny over a people fostered and fixed in principles of freedom.

Nor have we been wanting in attentions to our British brethren. We have warned them from time to time of attempts by their legislature to extend a jurisdiction over these our states. We have *an unwarrantable us* reminded them of the circumstances of our emigration and settlement here, no one of which could warrant so strange a pretension: that these were effected at the expense of our own blood and treasure, unassisted by the wealth or the strength of Great Britain: that in constituting indeed our several forms of government, we had adopted one common king, thereby laying a foundation for perpetual league and amity with them: but that submission to their parliament was no part of our constitution, nor ever in idea, if history may be credited: and, we [ ] appealed to their native jus- *have and we have conjured them by would inevitably* tice and magnanimity as well as to the ties of our common kindred to disavow these usurpations which were likely to interrupt our connection and correspondence. They too have been deaf to the voice of justice and of consanguinity, and when occasions have been given them, by the regular course of their laws, of removing from their councils the disturbers of our harmony, they have, by their free election, reestablished them in power. At this very time too, they are permitting their chief magistrate to send over not only soldiers of our common blood, but Scotch and foreign mercenaries to invade and destroy us. These facts have given the last stab to agonizing affection, and manly spirit bids us to renounce forever these unfeeling brethren. We must endeavor to forget our former love for them, and hold them as we hold the rest of mankind, enemies in war, in peace friends. We might have been a free and a great people together; but a communication of grandeur and of freedom, it seems, is below their dignity. Be it so, since *We must therefore* they will have it. The road to happiness and to glory is open to us, too. We will tread it apart from them, and acquiesce in the *and hold them as we hold the rest of mankind, enemies in war, in peace friends.* necessity which denounces[2] our eternal separation [ ]!

We therefore the representatives of the United States of America in General Congress assembled, do in the name, and by the authority of the good people of these states reject and renounce all allegiance and subjec-

We, therefore, the representatives of the United States of America in General Congress assembled, appealing to the supreme judge of the world for the rectitude of our intentions, do in the name, and by the

2. Proclaims.

tion to the kings of Great Britain and all others who may hereafter claim by, through or under them; we utterly dissolve all political connection which may heretofore have subsisted between us and the people or parliament of Great Britain: and finally we do assert and declare these colonies to be free and independent states, and that as free and independent states, they have full power to levy war, conclude peace, contract alliances, establish commerce, and to do all other acts and things which independent states may of right do.

And for the support of this declaration, we mutually pledge to each other our lives, our fortunes, and our sacred honor.

authority of the good people of these colonies, solemnly publish and declare, that these united colonies are, and of right ought to be free and independent states; that they are absolved from all allegiance to the British crown, and that all political connection between them and the state of Great Britain is, and ought to be, totally dissolved; and that as free and independent states, they have full power to levy war, conclude peace, contract alliances, establish commerce, and to do all other acts and things which independent states may of right do.

And for the support of this declaration, with a firm reliance on the protection of divine providence, we mutually pledge to each other our lives, our fortunes, and our sacred honor.

The Declaration thus signed on the 4th, on paper, was engrossed on parchment, and signed again on the 2d of August.

1821                                                  1829

# From Notes on the State of Virginia[1]

## From Query VI. Productions Mineral, Vegetable, and Animal

\*   \*   \*

The opinion advanced by the Count de Buffon[2] is 1. That the animals common both to the old and new world are smaller in the latter. 2. That those peculiar to the new are on a smaller scale. 3. That those which have been domesticated in both have degenerated in America. and 4. That on the whole it exhibits fewer species. And the reason he thinks is that the heats of America are less; that more waters are spread over its surface by nature, and fewer of these drained off by the hand of man. In other words, that *heat* is friendly, and *moisture* adverse to the production and development of large quadrupeds.

1. In 1781, the year Jefferson retired as governor of Virginia, he received a request from the Marquis de Barbé-Marbois, secretary of the French legation at Philadelphia, to answer twenty-three questions concerning the geographical boundaries, the ecology, and the social history of Virginia. Jefferson took the occasion to make some observations on slavery, manufacturing, and government. He wanted especially to counter the notion, prevalent among European naturalists, that species in North America had degenerated and were inferior to Old World types. Jefferson's replies were published privately in 1784–85. The threat of an unauthorized French translation prompted Jefferson to publish an authorized edition in London in 1787. The text used here is from the Norton edition, edited by William Peden (1954).

2. Georges Louis Leclerc de Buffon (1707–1788), French naturalist and keeper of the Royal Gardens. Buffon suggested that North American species were degenerate in his *Natural History* (1749–88).

I will not meet this hypothesis on its first doubtful ground, whether the climate of America be comparatively more humid? Because we are not furnished with observations sufficient to decide this question. And though, till it be decided, we are as free to deny, as others are to affirm, the fact, yet for a moment let it be supposed. The hypothesis, after this supposition, proceeds to another; that *moisture* is unfriendly to animal growth. The truth of this is inscrutable to us by reasonings a priori.[3] Nature has hidden from us her modus agendi.[4] Our only appeal on such questions is to experience; and I think that experience is against the supposition. It is by the assistance of *heat* and *moisture* that vegetables are elaborated from the elements of earth, air, water, and fire. We accordingly see the more humid climates produce the greater quantity of vegetables. Vegetables are mediately or immediately the food of every animal: and in proportion to the quantity of food, we see animals not only multiplied in their numbers, but improved in their bulk, as far as the laws of their nature will admit. Of this opinion is the Count de Buffon himself in another part of his work: "in general it seems that somewhat cold countries are better suited to our oxen than hot countries, and they are the heavier and bigger in proportion as the climate is damper and more abounding in pasture lands. The oxen of Denmark, of Podolie,[5] of the Ukraine, and of Tartary which is inhabited by the Calmouques,[6] are the largest of all." Here then a race of animals, and one of the largest too, has been increased in its dimensions by *cold* and *moisture*, in direct opposition to the hypothesis, which supposes that these two circumstances diminish animal bulk, and that it is their contraries *heat* and *dryness* which enlarge it. But when we appeal to experience, we are not to rest satisfied with a single fact. Let us therefore try our question on more general ground. Let us take our portions of the earth, Europe and America for instance, sufficiently extensive to give operation to general causes; let us consider the circumstances peculiar to each, and observe their effect on animal nature. America, running through the torrid as well as temperate zone, has more *heat*, collectively taken, than Europe. But Europe, according to our hypothesis, is the *dryest*. They are equally adapted then to animal productions; each being endowed with one of those causes which befriend animal growth, and with one which opposes it. If it be thought unequal to compare Europe with America, which is so much larger, I answer, not more so than to compare America with the whole world. Besides, the purpose of the comparison is to try an hypothesis, which makes the size of animals depend on the *heat* and *moisture* of climate. If therefore we take a region, so extensive as to comprehend a sensible distinction of climate, and so extensive too as that local accidents, or the intercourse of animals on its borders, may not materially affect the size of those in its interior parts, we shall comply with those conditions which the hypothesis may reasonably demand. The objection would be the weaker in the present case, because any intercourse of animals which may take place on the confines of Europe and Asia, is to the advantage of the former, Asia producing certainly larger animals than Europe. * * *

Hitherto I have considered this hypothesis as applied to brute animals only, and not in its extension to the man of America, whether aboriginal or transplanted. It is the opinion of Mons. de Buffon that the former furnishes no

---

3. Assumptions; previously held ideas (Latin).
4. The mode by which a thing acts or operates (Latin).
5. A village in northeast India.

6. More commonly spelled "Kalmucks," a nomadic Mongol tribe.

exception to it: "Although the savage of the new world is about the same height as man in our world, this does not suffice for him to constitute an exception to the general fact that all living nature has become smaller on that continent. The savage is feeble, and has small organs of generation; he has neither hair nor beard, and no ardor whatever for his female; although swifter than the European because he is better accustomed to running, he is, on the other hand, less strong in body; he is also less sensitive, and yet more timid and cowardly; he has no vivacity, no activity of mind; the activity of his body is less an exercise, a voluntary motion, than a necessary action caused by want; relieve him of hunger and thirst, and you deprive him of the active principle of all his movements; he will rest stupidly upon his legs or lying down entire days. There is no need for seeking further the cause of the isolated mode of life of these savages and their repugnance for society: the most precious spark of the fire of nature has been refused to them; they lack ardor for their females, and consequently have no love for their fellow men: not knowing this strongest and most tender of all affections, their other feelings are also cold and languid; they love their parents and children but little; the most intimate of all ties, the family connection, binds them therefore but loosely together; between family and family there is no tie at all; hence they have no communion, no commonwealth, no state of society. Physical love constitutes their only morality; their heart is icy, their society cold, and their rule harsh. They look upon their wives only as servants for all work, or as beasts of burden, which they load without consideration with the burden of their hunting, and which they compel without mercy, without gratitude, to perform tasks which are often beyond their strength. They have only few children, and they take little care of them. Everywhere the original defect appears: they are indifferent because they have little sexual capacity, and this indifference to the other sex is the fundamental defect which weakens their nature, prevents its development, and—destroying the very germs of life—uproots society at the same time. Man is here no exception to the general rule. Nature, by refusing him the power of love, has treated him worse and lowered him deeper than any animal." An afflicting picture indeed, which, for the honor of human nature, I am glad to believe has no original. Of the Indian of South America I know nothing; for I would not honor with the appelation of knowledge, what I derive from the fables published of them. These I believe to be just as true as the fables of Aesop.[7] This belief is founded on what I have seen of man, white, red, and black, and what has been written of him by authors, enlightened themselves, and writing amidst an enlightened people. The Indian of North America being more within our reach, I can speak of him somewhat from my own knowledge, but more from the information of others better acquainted with him, and on whose truth and judgment I can rely. From these sources I am able to say, in contradiction to this representation, that he is neither more defective in ardor, nor more impotent with his female, than the white reduced to the same diet and exercise: that he is brave, when an enterprise depends on bravery; education with him making the point of honor consist in the destruction of an enemy by stratagem, and in the preservation of his own person free from injury; or perhaps this is nature; while it is education which teaches us to honor force more than finesse; that he will defend himself against an host of

7. A Greek slave (c. 620–560 B.C.), reported to be the author of fables.

enemies, always choosing to be killed, rather than to surrender, though it be to the whites, who he knows will treat him well: that in other situations also he meets death with more deliberation, and endures tortures with a firmness unknown almost to religious enthusiasm with us: that he is affectionate to his children, careful of them, and indulgent in the extreme: that his affections comprehend his other connections, weakening, as with us, from circle to circle, as they recede from the center: that his friendships are strong and faithful to the uttermost extremity: that his sensibility is keen, even the warriors weeping most bitterly on the loss of their children, though in general they endeavor to appear superior to human events: that his vivacity and activity of mind is equal to ours in the same situation; hence his eagerness for hunting, and for games of chance. The women are submitted to unjust drudgery. This I believe is the case with every barbarous people. With such, force is law. The stronger sex therefore imposes on the weaker. It is civilization alone which replaces women in the enjoyment of their natural equality. That first teaches us to subdue the selfish passions, and to respect those rights in others which we value in ourselves. Were we in equal barbarism, our females would be equal drudges. The man with them is less strong than with us, but their woman stronger than ours; and both for the same obvious reason; because our man and their woman is habituated to labor, and formed by it. With both races the sex which is indulged with ease is least athletic. An Indian man is small in the hand and wrist for the same reason for which a sailor is large and strong in the arms and shoulders, and a porter in the legs and thighs.—They raise fewer children than we do. The causes of this are to be found, not in a difference of nature, but of circumstance. The women are frequently attending the men in their parties of war and of hunting, childbearing becomes extremely inconvenient to them. It is said, therefore, that they have learnt the practice of procuring abortion by the use of some vegetable; and that it even extends to prevent conception for a considerable time after. During these parties they are exposed to numerous hazards, to excessive exertions, to the greatest extremities of hunger. Even at their homes the nation depends for food, through a certain part of every year, on the gleanings of the forest: that is, they experience a famine once in every year. With all animals, if the female be badly fed, or not fed at all, her young perish: and if both male and female be reduced to like want, generation becomes less active, less productive. To the obstacles then of want and hazard, which nature has opposed to the multiplication of wild animals, for the purpose of restraining their numbers within certain bounds, those of labor and of voluntary abortion are added with the Indian. No wonder then if they multiply less than we do. Where food is regularly supplied, a single farm will show more of cattle, than a whole country of forests can of buffaloes. The same Indian women, when married to white traders, who feed them and their children plentifully and regularly, who exempt them from excessive drudgery, who keep them stationary and unexposed to accident, produce and raise as many children as the white women. Instances are known, under these circumstances, of their rearing a dozen children. An inhuman practice once prevailed in this country of making slaves of the Indians. (This practice commenced with the Spaniards with the first discovery of America). It is a fact well known with us, that the Indian women so enslaved produced and raised as numerous families as either the whites or blacks among whom they lived.—It has been said, that Indians have less hair than the whites, except on the head.

But this is a fact of which fair proof can scarcely be had. With them it is disgraceful to be hairy on the body. They say it likens them to hogs. They therefore pluck the hair as fast as it appears. But the traders who marry their women, and prevail on them to discontinue this practice, say, that nature is the same with them as with the whites. Nor, if the fact be true, is the consequence necessary which has been drawn from it. Negroes have notoriously less hair than the whites; yet they are more ardent. But if cold and moisture be the agents of nature for diminishing the races of animals, how comes she all at once to suspend their operation as to the physical man of the new world, whom the Count acknowledges to be "about the same size as the man of our hemisphere," and to let loose their influence on his moral faculties? How has this "combination of the elements and other physical causes, so contrary to the enlargement of animal nature in this new world, these obstacles to the development and formation of great germs," been arrested and suspended, so as to permit the human body to acquire its just dimensions, and by what inconceivable process has their action been directed on his mind alone? To judge of the truth of this, to form a just estimate of their genius and mental powers, more facts are wanting, and great allowance to be made for those circumstances of their situation which call for a display of particular talents only. This done, we shall probably find that they are formed in mind as well as in body, on the same module with the "Homo sapiens Europæus."[8] The principles of their society forbidding all compulsion, they are to be led to duty and to enterprise by personal influence and persuasion. Hence eloquence in council, bravery and address in war, become the foundations of all consequence with them. To these acquirements all their faculties are directed. Of their bravery and address in war we have multiplied proofs, because we have been the subjects on which they were exercised. Of their eminence in oratory we have fewer examples, because it is displayed chiefly in their own councils. Some, however, we have of very superior luster. I may challenge the whole orations of Demosthenes and Cicero,[9] and of any more eminent orator, if Europe has furnished more eminent, to produce a single passage, superior to the speech of Logan, a Mingo chief, to Lord Dunmore,[1] when governor of this state. And, as a testimony of their talents in this line, I beg leave to introduce it, first stating the incidents necessary for understanding it. In the spring of the year 1774, a robbery was committed by some Indians on certain land-adventurers on the river Ohio. The whites in that quarter, according to their custom, undertook to punish this outrage in a summary way. Captain Michael Cresap,[2] and a certain Daniel Great-house, leading on these parties, surprised, at different times, traveling and hunting parties of the Indians, having their women and children with them, and murdered many. Among these were unfortunately the family of Logan, a chief celebrated in peace and war, and long distinguished as the friend of the whites. This unworthy return provoked his vengeance. He accordingly signalized himself in the war which ensued. In the autumn of the same year a decisive battle was fought at the mouth of the Great Kanhaway, between the collected forces of the Shawanese, Mingoes, and Delawares, and a detachment of the Virginia militia. The Indians were

8. European man (Latin).
9. Demosthenes (385?–322 B.C.) was an Athenian orator. Cicero (106–43 B.C.) was a Roman orator and statesman.

1. John Murray, earl of Dunmore (1732–1809), was the colonial governor of Virginia from 1771 to 1775. "Mingo": an Iroquois tribe.
2. A Maryland soldier and frontiersman (1742–1775).

defeated, and sued for peace. Logan however disdained to be seen among the suppliants. But, lest the sincerity of a treaty should be distrusted, from which so distinguished a chief absented himself, he sent by a messenger the following speech to be delivered to Lord Dunmore.

"I appeal to any white man to say, if ever he entered Logan's cabin hungry, and he gave him not meat; if ever he came cold and naked, and he clothed him not. During the course of the last long and bloody war, Logan remained idle in his cabin, an advocate for peace. Such was my love for the whites, that my countrymen pointed as they passed, and said, 'Logan is the friend of white men.' I had even thought to have lived with you, but for the injuries of one man. Col. Cresap, the last spring, in cold blood, and unprovoked, murdered all the relations of Logan, not sparing even my women and children. There runs not a drop of my blood in the veins of any living creature. This called on me for revenge. I have sought it: I have killed many: I have fully glutted my vengeance. For my country, I rejoice at the beams of peace. But do not harbor a thought that mine is the joy of fear. Logan never felt fear. He will not turn on his heel to save his life. Who is there to mourn for Logan?—Not one."

Before we condemn the Indians of this continent as wanting genius,[3] we must consider that letters have not yet been introduced among them. Were we to compare them in their present state with the Europeans North of the Alps, when the Roman arms and arts first crossed those mountains, the comparison would be unequal, because, at that time, those parts of Europe were swarming with numbers; because numbers produce emulation, and multiply the chances of improvement, and one improvement begets another. Yet I may safely ask, How many good poets, how many able mathematicians, how many great inventors in arts or sciences had Europe North of the Alps then produced? And it was sixteen centuries after this before a Newton[4] could be formed. I do not mean to deny, that there are varieties in the race of man, distinguished by their powers both of body and mind. I believe there are, as I see to be the case in the races of other animals. I only mean to suggest a doubt, whether the bulk and faculties of animals depend on the side of the Atlantic on which their food happens to grow, or which furnishes the elements of which they are compounded? Whether nature has enlisted herself as a Cis[5] or transatlantic partisan? I am induced to suspect, there has been more eloquence than sound reasoning displayed in support of this theory; that it is one of those cases where the judgment has been seduced by a glowing pen: and whilst I render every tribute of honor and esteem to the celebrated zoologist, who has added, and is still adding, so many precious things to the treasures of science, I must doubt whether in this instance he has not cherished error also, by lending her for a moment his vivid imagination and bewitching language. * * *

---

3. Lacking intelligence.
4. Sir Isaac Newton (1642–1727), English philosopher and mathematician, most frequently identified with his theory of gravitation.
5. On this side.

# Letter to John Adams[1]

## [The Natural Aristocrat]

Monticello, October 28, 1813

Dear Sir,—According to the reservation between us, of taking up one of the subjects of our correspondence at a time, I turn to your letters of August the 16th and September the 2d. * * * I agree with you that there is a natural aristocracy among men. The grounds of this are virtue and talents. Formerly, bodily powers gave place among the aristoi.[2] But since the invention of gunpowder has armed the weak as well as the strong with missile death, bodily strength, like beauty, good humor, politeness and other accomplishments, has become but an auxiliary ground of distinction. There is also an artificial aristocracy, founded on wealth and birth, without either virtue or talents; for with these it would belong to the first class. The natural aristocracy I consider as the most precious gift of nature for the instruction, the trusts, and government of society. And indeed, it would have been inconsistent in creation to have formed man for the social state, and not to have provided virtue and wisdom enough to manage the concerns of the society. May we not even say that that form of government is the best which provides the most effectually for a pure selection of these natural aristoi into the offices of government? The artificial aristocracy is a mischievous ingredient in government, and provision should be made to prevent its ascendency. On the question, what is the best provision, you and I differ; but we differ as rational friends, using the free exercise of our own reason, and mutually indulging its errors. You think it best to put the pseudo-aristoi into a separate chamber of legislation, where they may be hindered from doing mischief by their co-ordinate branches, and where, also, they may be a protection to wealth against the agrarian and plundering enterprises of the majority of the people. I think that to give them power in order to prevent them from doing mischief is arming them for it, and increasing instead of remedying the evil. For if the co-ordinate branches can arrest their action, so may they that of the co-ordinates. Mischief may be done negatively as well as positively. Of this, a cabal in the Senate of the United States has furnished many proofs. Nor do I believe them necessary to protect the wealthy; because enough of these will find their way into every branch of the legislation, to protect themselves. From fifteen to twenty legislatures of our own, in action for thirty years past, have proved that no fears of an equalization of property are to be apprehended from them. I think the best remedy is exactly that provided by all our constitutions, to leave to the citizens the free election and separation of the aristoi from the pseudo-aristoi, of the wheat from the chaff. In general they will elect the really good and wise. In some instances, wealth may corrupt, and birth blind them; but not in sufficient degree to endanger the society.

1. Thomas Jefferson and John Adams (1735–1826) became estranged when Adams was elected second president in 1796. Adams's Federalist positions were opposed by Jefferson, who succeeded him as president in 1801. In 1812 they began to correspond and were able to debate their differences. The text used here is from *The Writings of Thomas Jefferson*, vol. 13, edited by A. A. Lipscomb and A. E. Bergh (1903).
2. The best (Greek). On July 9, 1813, Adams wrote to Jefferson that he recalled a maxim from the work of the Greek elegiac poet Theognis (6th century B.C.) that said that " 'nobility in men is worth as much as it is in horses, asses, or rams; but the meanest [i.e., poorest] blooded puppy in the world, if he gets a little money is as good a man as the best of them.' Yet birth and wealth together have prevailed over virtue and talents in all ages. The many will acknowledge no other *aristoi*."

It is probable that our difference of opinion may, in some measure, be produced by a difference of character in those among whom we live. From what I have seen of Massachusetts and Connecticut myself, and still more from what I have heard, and the character given of the former by yourself,[3] who know them so much better, there seems to be in those two states a traditionary reverence for certain families, which has rendered the offices of the government nearly hereditary in those families. I presume that from an early period of your history, members of those families happening to possess virtue and talents, have honestly exercised them for the good of the people, and by their services have endeared their names to them. In coupling Connecticut with you, I mean it politically only, not morally. For having made the Bible the common law of their land, they seem to have modeled their morality on the story of Jacob and Laban.[4] But although this hereditary succession to office with you, may, in some degree, be founded in real family merit, yet in a much higher degree, it has proceeded from your strict alliance of Church and State. These families are canonized in the eyes of the people on common principles, "you tickle me, and I will tickle you." In Virginia we have nothing of this. Our clergy, before the Revolution, having been secured against rivalship by fixed salaries, did not give themselves the trouble of acquiring influence over the people. Of wealth, there were great accumulations in particular families, handed down from generation to generation, under the English law of entails.[5] But the only object of ambition for the wealthy was a seat in the King's Council.[6] All their court then was paid to the crown and its creatures; and they philippized[7] in all collisions between the King and the people. Hence they were unpopular; and that unpopularity continues attached to their names. A Randolph, a Carter, or a Burwell[8] must have great personal superiority over a common competitor to be elected by the people even at this day. At the first session of our legislature after the Declaration of Independence, we passed a law abolishing entails. And this was followed by one abolishing the privilege of primogeniture, and dividing the lands of intestates[9] equally among all their children, or other representatives. These laws, drawn by myself, laid the axe to the foot of pseudo-aristocracy. And had another which I prepared been adopted by the legislature, our work would have been complete. It was a bill for the more general diffusion of learning. This proposed to divide every county into wards of five or six miles square, like your townships; to establish in each ward a free school for reading, writing and common arithmetic; to provide for the annual selection of the best subjects from these schools, who might receive, at the public expense, a higher degree of education at a district school; and from these district schools to select a certain number of the most promising subjects, to be completed at an university, where all the useful sciences should be taught. Worth and genius would thus have been sought out from every condition of life, and completely prepared by education for defeating the competition of wealth and birth for public trusts. My proposition

3. "Vol, 1, page 111" [Jefferson's note]. A reference to Adams's *Defense of the Constitutions of Government of the United States of America*, 3 vols. (1797). This work was first published in 1787.
4. I.e., a dynastic family, founded on the marital relations between the daughters of Jacob and Laban (Genesis 24–31).
5. An estate that cannot be willed but must pass from a proscribed list of successors.

6. The Privy Council, a select group of advisers, appointed by the king.
7. Argued against liberty for the people; spoke corrupted by their desire to please the king.
8. John Randolph, Landon Carter, and Lewis Burwell were all Virginia aristocrats.
9. Those who died without wills. "Primogeniture": a law that gives estates to the eldest son.

had, for a further object, to impart to these wards those portions of self-government for which they are best qualified, by confiding to them the care of their
poor, their roads, police, elections, the nomination of jurors, administration
of justice in small cases, elementary exercises of militia; in short, to have made
them little republics, with a warden at the head of each, for all those concerns
which, being under their eye, they would better manage than the larger republics of the county or state. A general call of ward meetings by their wardens on
the same day through the state, would at any time produce the genuine sense
of the people on any required point, and would enable the state to act in mass,
as your people have so often done, and with so much effect by their town
meetings. The law for religious freedom,[1] which made a part of this system,
having put down the aristocracy of the clergy, and restored to the citizen the
freedom of the mind, and those of entails and descents nurturing an equality
of condition among them, this on education would have raised the mass of
the people to the high ground of moral respectability necessary to their own
safety, and to orderly government; and would have completed the great object
of qualifying them to select the veritable aristoi, for the trusts of government,
to the exclusion of the pseudalists; and the same Theognis who has furnished
the epigraphs of your two letters, assures us that "Ονδεμιαν πω, Κυρν',
αγαθοι πολιν ωλεσαν ανδρε."[2] Although this law has not yet been acted on
but in a small and inefficient degree, it is still considered as before the legislature, with other bills of the revised code, not yet taken up, and I have great
hope that some patriotic spirit will, at a favorable moment, call it up, and
make it the keystone of the arch of our government.

With respect to aristocracy, we should further consider, that before the
establishment of the American states, nothing was known to history but the
man of the old world, crowded within limits either small or overcharged, and
steeped in the vices which that situation generates. A government adapted to
such men would be one thing; but a very different one, that for the man of
these states. Here every one may have land to labor for himself, if he chooses;
or, preferring the exercise of any other industry, may exact for it such compensation as not only to afford a comfortable subsistence, but wherewith to provide
for a cessation from labor in old age. Every one, by his property, or by his
satisfactory situation, is interested in the support of law and order. And such
men may safely and advantageously reserve to themselves a wholesome control
over their public affairs, and a degree of freedom, which, in the hands of the
canaille[3] of the cities of Europe, would be instantly perverted to the demolition
and destruction of everything public and private. The history of the last twenty-
five years of France,[4] and of the last forty years in America, nay of its last two
hundred years, proves the truth of both parts of this observation.

But even in Europe a change has sensibly taken place in the mind of man.
Science had liberated the ideas of those who read and reflect, and the American example had kindled feelings of right in the people. An insurrection has
consequently begun, of science, talents, and courage, against rank and birth,
which have fallen into contempt. It has failed in its first effort, because the
mobs of the cities, the instrument used for its accomplishment, debased by
ignorance, poverty, and vice, could not be restrained to rational action. But

1. Passed in 1786.                          3. Mob.
2. Curnis, good men have never harmed any city   4. I.e., since the French Revolution (1789).
(Greek).

the world will recover from the panic of this first catastrophe. Science is progressive, and talents and enterprise on the alert. Resort may be had to the people of the country, a more governable power from their principles and subordination; and rank, and birth, and tinsel-aristocracy will finally shrink into insignificance, even there. This, however, we have no right to meddle with. It suffices for us, if the moral and physical condition of our own citizens qualifies them to select the able and good for the direction of their government, with a recurrence of elections at such short periods as will enable them to displace an unfaithful servant, before the mischief he meditates may be irremediable.

I have thus stated my opinion on a point on which we differ, not with a view to controversy, for we are both too old to change opinions which are the result of a long life of inquiry and reflection; but on the suggestions of a former letter of yours, that we ought not to die before we have explained ourselves to each other. We acted in perfect harmony, through a long and perilous contest for our liberty and independence. A constitution has been acquired, which, though neither of us thinks perfect, yet both consider as competent to render our fellow citizens the happiest and the securest on whom the sun has ever shone. If we do not think exactly alike as to its imperfections, it matters little to our country, which, after devoting to it long lives of disinterested labor, we have delivered over to our successors in life, who will be able to take care of it and of themselves.

Of the pamphlet on aristocracy which has been sent to you, or who may be its author, I have heard nothing but through your letter. If the person you suspect, it may be known from the quaint, mystical, and hyperbolical ideas, involved in affected, newfangled and pedantic terms which stamp his writings. Whatever it be, I hope your quiet is not to be affected at this day by the rudeness or intemperance of scribblers; but that you may continue in tranquility to live and to rejoice in the prosperity of our country, until it shall be your own wish to take your seat among the aristoi who have gone before you. Ever and affectionately yours.

---

# OLAUDAH EQUIANO

## c. 1745–1797

*The Interesting Narrative of the Life of Olaudah Equiano, or Gustavus Vassa, the African* was published in London in 1789 and found an enthusiastic American audience when it was reprinted in New York in 1791. In the next five years it went through eight more editions and it was reprinted again in the nineteenth century. No black voice before Frederick Douglass in his *Narrative* of 1845 spoke so movingly to American readers about inhumanity. In a literature replete with self-made figures who voyage from innocence to experience—some fictive, some not—Equiano's story stands, in view of the actual horrors he suffered, in a class quite by itself. He defined himself, of course, as neither African-American (his first owner in the New World was a Virginian) nor Anglo-African (with London as his adopted home). He was "the African," even at the end of his life, a man set apart from everyone else by his color and his bondage, shaped as much by what he left behind as what he saw before him.

Equiano was born about 1745 in what is now Nigeria, in an unlocated Ibo village called Essaka; he was sold to British slavers in 1756 and transported first to the Barbadoes in the West Indies and then to a plantation in Virginia. He was with his second owner, Lt. Michael Henry Pascal, all during the Seven Years' War between England and France and was present at the siege of Fort Louisburg on Cape Breton Island in Nova Scotia. Eventually, he was sold to a Quaker merchant from Philadelphia, Robert King, who carried on much of his business in the West Indies. King often traded in "live cargo," or slaves, and Equiano saw much that made him grateful for his Quaker master's treatment of him, without having, for a moment, any illusions about what the loss of freedom entailed. He saw the ugliest side of American life in both the North and the South. Even in Philadelphia, a city built on the premise of "brotherly love," Equiano observed that the freed black was treated with profound contempt, "plundered" and "universally insulted," with no possibility of redress. King, however, did make it possible for Equiano to purchase his freedom in 1766. Once having gained his freedom by saving forty pounds—earned by his own instincts for enterprise, carrying on his own business while managing King's—he never set foot on American soil again.

It was Equiano's intention to settle in London for the rest of his life. He made his living there as a free servant, a musician (he played the French horn), and a barber. But Equiano's skill as a seaman, and his always remarkable curiosity, made him restless for new adventures, and before he died he had traveled as far as Turkey; had heard opera in Rome; and had seen Jamaica, Honduras, and Nicaragua. In 1783 Equiano brought the case of the infamous ship *Zong* to the British public: the owners had thrown overboard 132 shackled slaves and later made insurance claims against their loss. He lectured widely on the abolition of slavery and approved a project to resettle poor blacks in Sierra Leone, Africa. He was, in fact, given an official post in this undertaking, but lost it after he made accusations of misdeeds against some officials. Although he always spoke about his desire to return to the place of his birth, Africa always lay beyond his reach. In a letter written to his hosts in Birmingham, England, after lecturing there, he wrote:

> These acts of kindness and hospitality have filled me with a longing desire to see these worthy friends on my own estate in Africa, where the richest produce of it should be devoted to their entertainment. There they should partake of the luxuriant pineapples, and the well-flavored virgin palm-wine, and to heighten the bliss I would burn a certain tree, that would afford us light as clear and brilliant as the virtue of my guests.

In 1792 Equiano married Susanna Cullen, and their marriage was duly noticed in the London *Gentleman's Magazine*. He died on March 31, 1797, and his only child, a daughter, died shortly after him.

# *From* The Interesting Narrative of the Life of Olaudah Equiano, or Gustavas Vassa, the African, Written by Himself[1]

## Chapter II

I hope the reader will not think I have trespassed on his patience in introducing myself to him, with some account of the manners and customs of my

---

1. The text used here is taken from the 1st edition, published in two volumes for the author in London in 1789. The original paragraphing has been altered to facilitate reading.

country. They had been implanted in me with great care, and made an impression on my mind, which time could not erase, and which all the adversity and variety of fortune I have since experienced, served only to rivet and record; for, whether the love of one's country be real or imaginary, or a lesson of reason, or an instinct of nature, I still look back with pleasure on the first scenes of my life, though that pleasure has been for the most part mingled with sorrow.

I have already acquainted the reader with the time and place of my birth. My father, besides many slaves, had a numerous family, of which seven lived to grow up, including myself and a sister, who was the only daughter. As I was the youngest of the sons, I became, of course, the greatest favorite with my mother, and was always with her; and she used to take particular pains to form my mind. I was trained up from my earliest years in the art of war: my daily exercise was shooting and throwing javelins; and my mother adorned me with emblems, after the manner of our greatest warriors. In this way I grew up till I was turned the age of eleven, when an end was put to my happiness in the following manner:—generally when the grown people in the neighborhood were gone far in the fields to labor, the children assembled together in some of the neighboring premises to play; and commonly some of us used to get up a tree to look out for any assailant, or kidnapper, that might come upon us— for they sometimes took those opportunities of our parents' absence, to attack and carry off as many as they could seize. One day as I was watching at the top of a tree in our yard, I saw one of those people come into the yard of our next neighbor but one to kidnap, there being many stout[2] young people in it. Immediately on this I gave the alarm of the rogue, and he was surrounded by the stoutest of them, who entangled him with cords, so that he could not escape till some of the grown people came and secured him. But, alas! ere long it was my fate to be thus attacked, and to be carried off, when none of the grown people were nigh. One day, when all our people were gone out to their works as usual, and only I and my dear sister were left to mind the house, two men and a woman got over our walls, and in a moment seized us both, and, without giving us time to cry out, or make resistance, they stopped our mouths, and ran off with us into the nearest wood. Here they tied our hands, and continued to carry us as far as they could, till night came on, when we reached a small house, where the robbers halted for refreshment, and spent the night. We were then unbound, but were unable to take any food; and, being quite overpowered by fatigue and grief, our only relief was some sleep, which allayed our misfortune for a short time. The next morning we left the house, and continued traveling all the day. For a long time we had kept the woods, but at last we came into a road which I believed I knew. I had now some hopes of being delivered; for we had advanced but a little way before I discovered some people at a distance, on which I began to cry out for their assistance; but my cries had no other effect than to make them tie me faster and stop my mouth, and then they put me into a large sack. They also stopped my sister's mouth, and tied her hands; and in this manner we proceeded till we were out of sight of these people. When we went to rest the following night, they offered us some victuals, but we refused it; and the only comfort we had was in being in one another's arms all that night, and bathing each

2. Strong.

other with our tears. But alas! we were soon deprived of even the small comfort of weeping together. The next day proved a day of greater sorrow than I had yet experienced; for my sister and I were then separated, while we lay clasped in each other's arms. It was in vain that we besought them not to part us; she was torn from me, and immediately carried away, while I was left in a state of distraction not to be described. I cried and grieved continually; and for several days did not eat any thing but what they forced into my mouth. At length, after many days traveling, during which I had often changed masters, I got into the hands of a chieftain, in a very pleasant country. This man had two wives and some children, and they all used me extremely well, and did all they could to comfort me; particularly the first wife, who was something like my mother. Although I was a great many days' journey from my father's house, yet these people spoke exactly the same language with us. This first master of mine, as I may call him, was a smith,[3] and my principal employment was working his bellows, which were the same kind as I had seen in my vicinity. They were in some respects not unlike the stoves here in gentlemen's kitchens, and were covered over with leather; and in the middle of that leather a stick was fixed, and a person stood up, and worked it in the same manner as is done to pump water out of a cask with a hand pump. I believe it was gold he worked, for it was of a lovely bright yellow color, and was worn by the women on their wrists and ankles. I was there I suppose about a month, and they at last used to trust me some little distance from the house. This liberty I used in embracing every opportunity to inquire the way to my own home; and I also sometimes, for the same purpose, went with the maidens, in the cool of the evenings, to bring pitchers of water from the springs for the use of the house. I had also remarked where the sun rose in the morning, and set in the evening, as I had traveled along; and I had observed that my father's house was towards the rising of the sun. I therefore determined to seize the first opportunity of making my escape, and to shape my course for that quarter; for I was quite oppressed and weighed down by grief after my mother and friends; and my love of liberty, ever great, was strengthened by the mortifying circumstance of not daring to eat with the free-born children, although I was mostly their companion. While I was projecting my escape one day, an unlucky event happened, which quite disconcerted my plan, and put an end to my hopes. I used to be sometimes employed in assisting an elderly slave to cook and take care of the poultry; and one morning, while I was feeding some chickens, I happened to toss a small pebble at one of them, which hit it on the middle, and directly killed it. The old slave, having soon after missed the chicken, inquired after it; and on my relating the accident (for I told her the truth, for my mother would never suffer me to tell a lie), she flew into a violent passion, and threatened that I should suffer for it; and, my master being out, she immediately went and told her mistress what I had done. This alarmed me very much, and I expected an instant flogging, which to me was uncommonly dreadful, for I had seldom been beaten at home. I therefore resolved to fly; and accordingly I ran into a thicket that was hard by, and hid myself in the bushes. Soon afterwards my mistress and the slave returned, and, not seeing me, they searched all the house, but not finding me, and I not making answer when they called to me, they thought I had run away, and the whole neighbor-

3. A metalworker; here, a goldsmith.

hood was raised in the pursuit of me. In that part of the country, as in ours, the houses and villages were skirted with woods, or shrubberies, and the bushes were so thick that a man could readily conceal himself in them, so as to elude the strictest search. The neighbors continued the whole day looking for me, and several times many of them came within a few yards of the place where I lay hid. I expected every moment, when I heard a rustling among the trees, to be found out, and punished by my master; but they never discovered me, though they were often so near that I even heard their conjectures as they were looking about for me; and I now learned from them that any attempts to return home would be hopeless. Most of them supposed I had fled towards home; but the distance was so great, and the way so intricate, that they thought I could never reach it, and that I should be lost in the woods. When I heard this I was seized with a violent panic, and abandoned myself to despair. Night, too, began to approach, and aggravated all my fears. I had before entertained hopes of getting home, and had determined when it should be dark to make the attempt; but I was now convinced it was fruitless, and began to consider that, if possibly I could escape all other animals, I could not those of the human kind; and that, not knowing the way, I must perish in the woods. Thus was I like the hunted deer—

> —"Every leaf and every whisp'ring breath,
> Convey'd a foe, and every foe a death."

I heard frequent rustlings among the leaves, and being pretty sure they were snakes, I expected every instant to be stung by them. This increased my anguish, and the horror of my situation became now quite insupportable. I at length quitted the thicket, very faint and hungry, for I had not eaten or drank any thing all the day, and crept to my master's kitchen, from whence I set out at first, which was an open shed, and laid myself down in the ashes with an anxious wish for death, to relieve me from all my pains. I was scarcely awake in the morning, when the old woman slave, who was the first up, came to light the fire, and saw me in the fire place. She was very much surprised to see me, and could scarcely believe her own eyes. She now promised to intercede for me, and went for her master, who soon after came, and, having slightly reprimanded me, ordered me to be taken care of, and not ill treated.

Soon after this, my master's only daughter, and child by his first wife, sickened and died, which affected him so much that for some time he was almost frantic, and really would have killed himself, had he not been watched and prevented. However, in short time afterwards he recovered, and I was again sold. I was now carried to the left of the sun's rising, through many dreary wastes and dismal woods, amidst the hideous roarings of wild beasts. The people I was sold to used to carry me very often, when I was tired, either on their shoulders or on their backs. I saw many convenient well built sheds along the road, at proper distances, to accommodate the merchants and travelers, who lay in those buildings along with their wives, who often accompany them; and they always go well armed.

From the time I left my own nation, I always found somebody that understood me till I came to the sea coast. The languages of different nations did not totally differ, nor were they so copious as those of the Europeans, particularly the English. They were therefore, easily learned; and, while I was journeying thus through Africa, I acquired two or three different tongues. In this manner I had been traveling for a considerable time, when, one evening, to my great surprise, whom should I see brought to the house where I was but my dear sister! As soon as she saw me, she gave a loud shriek, and ran into my arms—I was quite overpowered: neither of us could speak; but, for a considerable time, clung to each other in mutual embraces, unable to do any thing but weep. Our meeting affected all who saw us; and, indeed, I must acknowledge, in honor of those sable destroyers of human rights, that I never met with any ill treatment, or saw any offered to their slaves, except tying them, when necessary, to keep them from running away. When these people knew we were brother and sister, they indulged us to be together; and the man, to whom I supposed we belonged, lay with us, he in the middle, while she and I held one another by the hands across his breast all night; and thus for a while we forgot our misfortunes, in the joy of being together; but even this small comfort was soon to have an end; for scarcely had the fatal morning appeared when she was again torn from me forever! I was now more miserable, if possible, than before. The small relief which her presence gave me from pain was gone, and the wretchedness of my situation was redoubled by my anxiety after her fate, and my apprehensions lest her sufferings should be greater than mine, when I could not be with her to alleviate them. Yes, thou dear partner of all my childish sports! thou sharer of my joys and sorrows! happy should I have ever esteemed myself to encounter every misery for you and to procure your freedom by the sacrifice of my own.—Though you were early forced from my arms, your image has been always riveted in my heart, from which neither time nor fortune have been able to remove it; so that, while the thoughts of your sufferings have damped my prosperity, they have mingled with adversity and increased its bitterness. To that Heaven which protects the weak from the strong, I commit the care of your innocence and virtues, if they have not already received their full reward, and if your youth and delicacy have not long since fallen victims to the violence of the African trader, the pestilential stench of a Guinea ship, the seasoning in the European colonies, or the lash and lust of a brutal and unrelenting overseer.

I did not long remain after my sister. I was again sold, and carried through a number of places, till after traveling a considerable time, I came to a town called Tinmah, in the most beautiful country I had yet seen in Africa. It was extremely rich, and there were many rivulets which flowed through it, and supplied a large pond in the center of the town, where the people washed. Here I first saw and tasted cocoa nuts, which I thought superior to any nuts I had ever tasted before; and the trees which were loaded, were also interspersed among the houses, which had commodious shades adjoining, and were in the same manner as ours, the insides being neatly plastered and whitewashed. Here I also saw and tasted for the first time, sugar cane. Their money consisted of little white shells, the size of the finger nail. I was sold here for one hundred and seventy-two of them, by a merchant who lived and brought me there. I had been about two or three days at his house, when a wealthy widow, a neighbor of his, came there one evening, and brought with her an only son, a young gentleman about my own age and size. Here they saw me; and, having taken a fancy to me, I was bought of the merchant, and went home with them. Her house and premises were situated close to one of those rivulets I have mentioned, and were the finest I ever saw in Africa: they were very extensive, and she had a number of slaves to attend her. The next day I was washed and perfumed, and when mealtime came, I was led into the presence of my mistress, and ate and drank before her with her son. This filled me with astonishment; and I could scarce help expressing my surprise that the young gentleman should suffer[4] me, who was bound, to eat with him who was free; and not only so, but that he would not at any time either eat or drink till I had taken first, because I was the eldest, which was agreeable to our custom. Indeed, every thing here, and all their treatment of me, made me forget that I was a slave. The language of these people resembled ours so nearly, that we understood each other perfectly. They had also the very same customs as we. There were likewise slaves daily to attend us, while my young master and I, with other boys, sported with our darts and bows and arrows, as I had been used to do at home. In this resemblance to my former happy state, I passed about two months; and I now began to think I was to be adopted into the family, and was beginning to be reconciled to my situation, and to forget by degrees my misfortunes, when all at once the delusion vanished; for, without the least previous knowledge, one morning early, while my dear master and companion was still asleep, I was awakened out of my reverie to fresh sorrow, and hurried away even amongst the uncircumcised.

Thus, at the very moment I dreamed of the greatest happiness, I found myself most miserable; and it seemed as if fortune wished to give me this taste of joy only to render the reverse more poignant.—The change I now experienced, was as painful as it was sudden and unexpected. It was a change indeed, from a state of bliss to a scene which is inexpressible by me, as it discovered to me an element I had never before beheld, and till then had no idea of, and wherein such instances of hardship and cruelty continually occurred, as I can never reflect on but with horror.

All the nations and people I had hitherto passed through, resembled our own in their manners, customs, and language: but I came at length to a country, the inhabitants of which differed from us in all those particulars. I was very much struck with this difference, especially when I came among a people who did not circumcise, and ate without washing their hands. They cooked also in iron pots, and had European cutlasses and cross bows, which were unknown to us, and fought with their fists among themselves. Their women were not so modest as ours, for they ate, and drank, and slept with their men. But above all, I was amazed to see no sacrifices or offerings among them. In some of those places the people ornamented themselves with scars, and likewise filed their teeth very sharp. They wanted sometimes to ornament me in the same manner, but I would not suffer them; hoping that I might some time be among a people who did not thus disfigure themselves, as I thought they did. At last I came to the banks of a large river which was covered with canoes, in which the people appeared to live with their household utensils, and provisions of all kinds. I was beyond measure astonished at this, as I had never before seen any water larger than a pond or a rivulet: and my surprise was mingled with no small fear when I was put into one of these canoes, and we began to paddle and move along the river. We continued going on thus till night, and when we came to land, and made fires on the banks, each family by themselves; some dragged their canoes on shore, others stayed and cooked in theirs, and laid in them all night. Those on the land had mats, of which they made

4. Allow.

tents, some in the shape of little houses; in these we slept; and after the morning meal, we embarked again and proceeded as before. I was often very much astonished to see some of the women, as well as the men, jump into the water, dive to the bottom, come up again, and swim about.—Thus I continued to travel, sometimes by land, sometimes by water, through different countries and various nations, till, at the end of six or seven months after I had been kidnapped, I arrived at the sea coast. It would be tedious and uninteresting to relate all the incidents which befell me during this journey, and which I have not yet forgotten; of the various hands I passed through, and the manners and customs of all the different people among whom I lived—I shall therefore only observe, that in all the places where I was, the soil was exceedingly rich; the pumpkins, eadas,[5] plaintains, yams, etc., etc., were in great abundance, and of incredible size. There were also vast quantities of different gums, though not used for any purpose, and every where a great deal of tobacco. The cotton even grew quite wild, and there was plenty of red-wood. I saw no mechanics[6] whatever in all the way, except such as I have mentioned. The chief employment in all these countries was agriculture, and both the males and females, as with us, were brought up to it, and trained in the arts of war.

The first object which saluted my eyes when I arrived on the coast, was the sea, and a slave ship, which was then riding at anchor, and waiting for its cargo. These filled me with astonishment, which was soon converted into terror, when I was carried on board. I was immediately handled, and tossed up to see if I were sound, by some of the crew; and I was now persuaded that I had gotten into a world of bad spirits, and that they were going to kill me. Their complexions, too, differing so much from ours, their long hair, and the language they spoke (which was very different from any I had ever heard), united to confirm me in this belief. Indeed, such were the horrors of my views and fears at the moment, that, if ten thousand worlds had been my own, I would have freely parted with them all to have exchanged my condition with that of the meanest slave in my own country. When I looked round the ship too, and saw a large furnace of copper boiling, and a multitude of black people of every description chained together, every one of their countenances expressing dejection and sorrow, I no longer doubted of my fate; and, quite overpowered with horror and anguish, I fell motionless on the deck and fainted. When I recovered a little, I found some black people about me, who I believed were some of those who had brought me on board, and had been receiving their pay; they talked to me in order to cheer me, but all in vain. I asked them if we were not to be eaten by those white men with horrible looks, red faces, and long hair. They told me I was not: and one of the crew brought me a small portion of spirituous liquor in a wine glass, but, being afraid of him, I would not take it out of his hand. One of the blacks, therefore, took it from him and gave it to me, and I took a little down my palate, which, instead of reviving me, as they thought it would, threw me into the greatest consternation at the strange feeling it produced, having never tasted any such liquor before. Soon after this, the blacks who brought me on board went off, and left me abandoned to despair.

I now saw myself deprived of all chance of returning to my native country,

---

5. More commonly spelled "eddoes": edible roots    6. Artisans, manual workers.
found in the tropics.

or even the least glimpse of hope of gaining the shore, which I now considered as friendly; and I even wished for my former slavery in preference to my present situation, which was filled with horrors of every kind, still heightened by my ignorance of what I was to undergo. I was not long suffered to indulge my grief; I was soon put down under the decks, and there I received such a salutation in my nostrils as I had never experienced in my life: so that, with the loathsomeness of the stench, and crying together, I became so sick and low that I was not able to eat, nor had I the least desire to taste any thing. I now wished for the last friend, death, to relieve me; but soon, to my grief, two of the white men offered me eatables; and, on my refusing to eat, one of them held me fast by the hands, and laid me across, I think the windlass, and tied my feet, while the other flogged me severely. I had never experienced any thing of this kind before, and although not being used to the water, I naturally feared that element the first time I saw it, yet, nevertheless, could I have got over the nettings, I would have jumped over the side, but I could not; and besides, the crew used to watch us very closely who were not chained down to the decks, lest we should leap into the water; and I have seen some of these poor African prisoners most severely cut, for attempting to do so, and hourly whipped for not eating. This indeed was often the case with myself. In a little time after, amongst the poor chained men, I found some of my own nation, which in a small degree gave ease to my mind. I inquired of these what was to be done with us? They gave me to understand we were to be carried to these white people's country to work for them. I then was a little revived, and thought, if it were no worse than working, my situation was not so desperate; but still I feared I should be put to death, the white people looked and acted, as I thought, in so savage a manner; for I had never seen among any people such instances of brutal cruelty; and this not only shown towards us blacks, but also to some of the whites themselves. One white man in particular I saw, when we were permitted to be on deck, flogged so unmercifully with a large rope near the foremast, that he died in consequence of it; and they tossed him over the side as they would have done a brute. This made me fear these people the more; and I expected nothing less than to be treated in the same manner. I could not help expressing my fears and apprehensions to some of my countrymen; I asked them if these people had no country, but lived in this hollow place (the ship)? They told me they did not, but came from a distant one. "Then," said I, "how comes it in all our country we never heard of them?" They told me because they lived so very far off. I then asked where were their women? had they any like themselves? I was told they had. "And why," said I, "do we not see them?" They answered, because they were left behind. I asked how the vessel could go? they told me they could not tell; but that there was cloth put upon the masts by the help of the ropes I saw, and then the vessel went on; and the white men had some spell or magic they put in the water when they liked, in order to stop the vessel. I was exceedingly amazed at this account, and really thought they were spirits. I therefore wished much to be from amongst them, for I expected they would sacrifice me; but my wishes were vain—for we were so quartered that it was impossible for any of us to make our escape.

While we stayed on the coast I was mostly on deck; and one day, to my great astonishment, I saw one of these vessels coming in with the sails up. As soon as the whites saw it, they gave a great shout, at which we were amazed;

and the more so, as the vessel appeared larger by approaching nearer. At last, she came to an anchor in my sight, and when the anchor was let go, I and my countrymen who saw it, were lost in astonishment to observe the vessel stop— and were now convinced it was done by magic. Soon after this the other ship got her boats out, and they came on board of us, and the people of both ships seemed very glad to see each other.—Several of the strangers also shook hands with us black people, and made motions with their hands, signifying I suppose, we were to go to their country, but we did not understand them.

At last, when the ship we were in had got in all her cargo, they made ready with many fearful noises, and we were all put under deck, so that we could not see how they managed the vessel. But this disappointment was the least of my sorrow. The stench of the hold while we were on the coast was so intolera- bly loathsome, that it was dangerous to remain there for any time, and some of us had been permitted to stay on the deck for the fresh air; but now that the whole ship's cargo were confined together, it became absolutely pestilential. The closeness of the place, and the heat of the climate, added to the number in the ship, which was so crowded that each had scarcely room to turn himself, almost suffocated us. This produced copious perspirations, so that the air soon became unfit for respiration, from a variety of loathsome smells, and brought on a sickness among the slaves, of which many died—thus falling victims to the improvident avarice, as I may call it, of their purchasers. This wretched situation was again aggravated by the galling of the chains, now become insup- portable, and the filth of the necessary tubs, into which the children often fell, and were almost suffocated. The shrieks of the women, and the groans of the dying, rendered the whole a scene of horror almost inconceivable. Happily perhaps, for myself, I was soon reduced so low here that it was thought neces- sary to keep me almost always on deck; and from my extreme youth I was not put in fetters. In this situation I expected every hour to share the fate of my companions, some of whom were almost daily brought upon deck at the point of death, which I began to hope would soon put an end to my miseries. Often did I think many of the inhabitants of the deep much more happy than myself. I envied them the freedom they enjoyed, and as often wished I could change my condition for theirs. Every circumstance I met with, served only to render my state more painful, and heightened my apprehensions, and my opinion of the cruelty of the whites.

One day they had taken a number of fishes; and when they had killed and satisfied themselves with as many as they thought fit, to our astonishment who were on deck, rather than give any of them to us to eat, as we expected, they tossed the remaining fish into the sea again, although we begged and prayed for some as well as we could, but in vain; and some of my countrymen, being pressed by hunger, took an opportunity, when they thought no one saw them, of trying to get a little privately; but they were discovered, and the attempt procured them some very severe floggings. One day, when we had a smooth sea and moderate wind, two of my wearied countrymen who were chained together (I was near them at the time), preferring death to such a life of misery, somehow made through the nettings and jumped into the sea: immediately, another quite dejected fellow, who, on account of his illness, was suffered to be out of irons, also followed their example; and I believe many more would very soon have done the same, if they had not been prevented by the ship's crew, who were instantly alarmed. Those of us that were the most active, were in a moment put down under the deck, and there was such a noise and confusion amongst the people of the ship as I never heard before, to stop her, and get the boat out to go after the slaves. However, two of the wretches were drowned, but they got the other, and afterwards flogged him unmercifully, for thus attempting to prefer death to slavery. In this manner we continued to undergo more hardships than I can now relate, hardships which are inseparable from this accursed trade. Many a time we were near suffocation from the want of fresh air, which we were often without for whole days together. This, and the stench of the necessary tubs, carried off many.

During our passage, I first saw flying fishes, which surprised me very much; they used frequently to fly across the ship, and many of them fell on the deck. I also now first saw the use of the quadrant; I had often with astonishment seen the mariners make observations with it, and I could not think what it meant. They at last took notice of my surprise; and one of them, willing to increase it, as well as to gratify my curiosity, made me one day look through it. The clouds appeared to me to be land, which disappeared as they passed along. This heightened my wonder; and I was now more persuaded than ever, that I was in another world, and that every thing about me was magic. At last, we came in sight of the island of Barbadoes,[7] at which the whites on board gave a great shout, and made many signs of joy to us. We did not know what to think of this; but as the vessel drew nearer, we plainly saw the harbor, and other ships of different kinds and sizes, and we soon anchored amongst them, off Bridgetown. Many merchants and planters now came on board, though it was in the evening. They put us in separate parcels,[8] and examined us attentively. They also made us jump, and pointed to the land, signifying we were to go there. We thought by this, we should be eaten by these ugly men, as they appeared to us; and, when soon after we were all put down under the deck again, there was much dread and trembling among us, and nothing but bitter cries to be heard all the night from these apprehensions, insomuch, that at last the white people got some old slaves from the land to pacify us. They told us we were not to be eaten, but to work, and were soon to go on land, where we should see many of our country people. This report eased us much. And sure enough, soon after we were landed, there came to us Africans of all languages.

We were conducted immediately to the merchant's yard, where we were all pent up together, like so many sheep in a fold, without regard to sex or age. As every object was new to me, every thing I saw filled me with surprise. What struck me first, was, that the houses were built with bricks and stories,[9] and in every other respect different from those I had seen in Africa; but I was still more astonished on seeing people on horseback. I did not know what this could mean; and, indeed, I thought these people were full of nothing but magical arts. While I was in this astonishment, one of my fellow prisoners spoke to a countryman of his, about the horses, who said they were the same kind they had in their country. I understood them, though they were from a distant part of Africa; and I thought it odd I had not seen any horses there; but afterwards, when I came to converse with different Africans, I found they had many horses amongst them, and much larger than those I then saw.

We were not many days in the merchant's custody, before we were sold after their usual manner, which is this:—On a signal given (as the beat of a

7. In the West Indies.                          9. I.e., the buildings were two storied.
8. Groups.

drum), the buyers rush at once into the yard where the slaves are confined, and make choice of that parcel they like best. The noise and clamor with which this is attended, and the eagerness visible in the countenances of the buyers, serve not a little to increase the apprehension of terrified Africans, who may well be supposed to consider them as the ministers of that destruction to which they think themselves devoted. In this manner, without scruple, are relations and friends separated, most of them never to see each other again. I remember, in the vessel in which I was brought over, in the men's apartment, there were several brothers, who, in the sale, were sold in different lots; and it was very moving on this occasion, to see and hear their cries at parting. O, ye nominal Christians![1] might not an African ask you—Learned you this from your God, who says unto you, Do unto all men as you would men should do unto you? Is it not enough that we are torn from our country and friends, to toil for your luxury and lust of gain? Must every tender feeling be likewise sacrificed to your avarice? Are the dearest friends and relations, now rendered more dear by their separation from their kindred, still to be parted from each other, and thus prevented from cheering the gloom of slavery, with the small comfort of being together, and mingling their sufferings and sorrows? Why are parents to lose their children, brothers their sisters, or husbands their wives? Surely, this is a new refinement in cruelty, which, while it has no advantage to atone for it, thus aggravates distress, and adds fresh horrors even to the wretchedness of slavery.

1789

1. Christians in name only.

---

# PHILIP FRENEAU
## 1752–1832

Philip Freneau had all the advantages that wealth and social position could bestow, and the Freneau household in Manhattan was frequently visited by well-known writers and painters. Philip received a good education at the hands of tutors and at fifteen entered the sophomore class at the College of New Jersey (now Princeton University). There he became fast friends with his roommate, James Madison, a future president, and a classmate, Hugh Henry Brackenridge, who was to become a successful novelist. In their senior year Freneau and Brackenridge composed an ode on *The Rising Glory of America*, and Brackenridge read the poem at commencement. It establishes early in Freneau's career his recurrent vision of a glorious future in which America would fulfill the collective hope of humankind:

> Paradise anew
> Shall flourish, by no second Adam lost,
> No dangerous tree with deadly fruit shall grow,
> No tempting serpent to allure the soul
> From native innocence. . . . The lion and the lamb
> In mutual friendship linked, shall browse the shrub,
> And timorous deer with softened tigers stray
> O'er mead, or lofty hill, or grassy plain . . .

For a short time Freneau taught school and hoped to make a career as a writer, but it was an impractical wish. When he was offered a position as secretary on a plantation in the West Indies in 1776, he sailed to Santa Cruz and remained there almost three years. It was in that country, where "Sweet orange groves in lonely valleys rise," that Freneau wrote some of his most sensuous lyrics, but as he tells us in *To Sir Toby*, he could not talk of "blossoms" and an "endless spring" forever in a land that abounded in poverty and misery and where the owners grew wealthy on a slave economy. In 1778 he returned home and enlisted as a seaman on a blockade runner; two years later he was captured at sea and imprisoned on the British ship *Scorpion*, anchored in New York harbor. He was treated brutally, and when he was exchanged from the hospital ship *Hunter* his family feared for his life.

Freneau was to spend ten more years of his life at sea, first as a master of a merchant ship in 1784, and again in 1803, but immediately after he regained his health, he moved to Philadelphia to work in the post office, and it was in that city that he gained his reputation as a satirist, journalist, and poet. As editor of the *Freeman's Journal*, Freneau wrote impassioned verse in support of the American Revolution and turned all his rhetorical gifts against anyone who was thought to be in sympathy with the British monarchy. It was during this period in his life that he became identified as the "Poet of the American Revolution." In 1791, after he returned from duties at sea, Jefferson, as secretary of state, offered him a position as translator in his department, understanding that Freneau would have plenty of free time to devote to his newspaper, the *National Gazette*. Like Thomas Paine, Freneau was a strong supporter of the French Revolution, and he had a sharp eye for anyone not sympathetic to the democratic cause. He had a special grudge against Alexander Hamilton, secretary of the treasury, as chief spokesman for the Federalists. President Washington thought it was ironic that "that rascal Freneau" should be employed by his administration when he attacked it so outspokenly.

The *National Gazette* ceased publication in 1793, and after Jefferson resigned his office, Freneau left Philadelphia for good, alternating between ship's captain and newspaper editor in New York and New Jersey. He spent his last years on his New Jersey farm, unable to make it self-supporting and with no hope of further employment. Year after year he sold off the land he inherited from his father and was finally reduced to applying for a pension as a veteran of the American Revolution. He died impoverished and unknown, lost in a blizzard.

Freneau's biographer, Lewis Leary, subtitled his book A *Study in Literary Failure* and began that work by observing that "Philip Freneau failed in almost everything he attempted." Freneau's most sympathetic readers have always believed that he was born in a time not ripe for poetry and that his genuine lyric gifts were always in conflict with his political pamphleteering. Had he been born fifty years later, perhaps he could have joined Cooper and Irving in a life devoted exclusively to letters. There is no doubt that he did much to pave the way for these later writers. Freneau is not "the father of American poetry" (as his readers, anxious for an advocate for a national literary consciousness, liked to call him), but his obsession with the beautiful, transient things of nature and the conflict in his art between the sensuous and the didactic are central to the concerns of American poetry.

Texts used are *The Poems of Philip Freneau*, edited by F. L. Pattee (1902); *The Poems of Freneau*, edited by H. H. Clark (1929); and *The Last Poems of Philip Freneau*, edited by Lewis Leary (1945).

# On the Emigration to America and Peopling the Western Country

To western woods, and lonely plains,
Palemon[1] from the crowd departs,

---

1. Conventionally, any young man setting out on a journey. Palamon appears in Chaucer's *Knight's Tale*, an adaptation of Boccaccio's *Teseide*.

Where Nature's wildest genius reigns,
To tame the soil, and plant the arts—
What wonders there shall freedom show,                    5
What mighty states successive grow!

From Europe's proud, despotic shores
Hither the stranger takes his way,
And in our new found world explores
A happier soil, a milder sway,                           10
Where no proud despot holds him down,
No slaves insult him with a crown.

What charming scenes attract the eye,
On wild Ohio's savage stream!
There Nature reigns, whose works outvie                  15
The boldest pattern art can frame;
There ages past have rolled away,
And forests bloomed but to decay.

From these fair plains, these rural seats,
So long concealed, so lately known,                      20
The unsocial Indian far retreats,
To make some other clime his own,
Where other streams, less pleasing flow,
And darker forests round him grow.

Great sire[2] of floods! whose varied wave               25
Through climes and countries takes its way,
To whom creating Nature gave
Ten thousand streams to swell thy sway!
No longer shall *they* useless prove,
Nor idly through the forests rove;                       30

Nor longer shall your princely flood
From distant lakes be swelled in vain,
Nor longer through a darksome wood
Advance, unnoticed, to the main,[3]
Far other ends, the heavens decree—                      35
And commerce plans new freights for thee.

While virtue warms the generous breast,
There heaven-born freedom shall reside,
Nor shall the voice of war molest,
Nor Europe's all-aspiring pride—                         40
There Reason shall new laws devise,
And order from confusion rise.

Forsaking kings and regal state,
With all their pomp and fancied bliss,
The traveler owns,[4] convinced though late,            45
No realm so free, so blessed as this—

2. "Mississippi" [Freneau's note].          4. Admits.
3. Ocean.

The east is half to slaves consigned,
Where kings and priests enchain the mind.

O come the time, and haste the day,
When man shall man no longer crush,                50
When Reason shall enforce her sway,
Nor these fair regions raise our blush,
Where still the *African* complains,
And mourns his yet unbroken chains.

Far brighter scenes a future age,                 55
The muse predicts, these states will hail,
Whose genius may the world engage,
Whose deeds may over death prevail,
And happier systems bring to view,
Than all the eastern sages knew.                  60

1785

## The Wild Honey Suckle

Fair flower, that dost so comely grow,
Hid in this silent, dull retreat,
Untouched thy honeyed blossoms blow,[1]
Unseen thy little branches greet:
   No roving foot shall crush thee here,     5
   No busy hand provoke a tear.

By Nature's self in white arrayed,
She bade thee shun the vulgar[2] eye,
And planted here the guardian shade,
And sent soft waters murmuring by;                10
   Thus quietly thy summer goes,
   Thy days declining to repose.

Smit with those charms, that must decay,
I grieve to see your future doom;
They died—nor were those flowers more gay,        15
The flowers that did in Eden bloom;
   Unpitying frosts, and Autumn's power
   Shall leave no vestige of this flower.

From morning suns and evening dews
At first thy little being came:                   20
If nothing once, you nothing lose,
For when you die you are the same;
   The space between, is but an hour,
   The frail duration of a flower.

1786

---

1. Bloom.                    2. Common; unfeeling.

# On Mr. Paine's Rights of Man[1]

Thus briefly sketched the sacred rights of man,
How inconsistent with the royal plan!
Which for itself exclusive honor craves,
Where some are masters born, and millions slaves.
With what contempt must every eye look down　　　5
On that base, childish bauble called a *crown*,
The gilded bait, that lures the crowd, to come,
Bow down their necks, and meet a slavish doom;
The source of half the miseries men endure,
The quack[2] that kills them, while it seems to cure,　　　10
　Roused by the reason of his manly page,
Once more shall Paine a listening world engage:
From Reason's source, a bold reform he brings,
In raising up *mankind*, he pulls down *kings*,
Who, source of discord, patrons of all wrong,　　　15
On blood and murder have been fed too long:
Hid from the world, and tutored to be base,
The curse, the scourge, the ruin of our race,
Their's was the task, a dull designing few,
To shackle beings that they scarcely knew,　　　20
Who made this globe the residence of slaves,
And built their thrones on systems formed by knaves
—Advance, bright years, to work their final fall,
And haste the period that shall crush them all.
　Who, that has read and scanned the historic page　　　25
But glows, at every line, with kindling rage,
To see by them the rights of men aspersed,
Freedom restrained, and Nature's law reversed,
Men, ranked with beasts, by monarchs willed away,
And bound young fools, or madmen to obey:　　　30
Now driven to wars, and now oppressed at home,
Compelled in crowds o'er distant seas to roam,
From India's climes the plundered prize to bring
To glad the strumpet, or to glut the king.
　Columbia, hail! immortal be thy reign:　　　35
Without a king, we till the smiling plain;
Without a king, we trace the unbounded sea,
And traffic round the globe, through each degree;
Each foreign clime our honored flag reveres,
Which asks no monarch, to support the stars:　　　40
Without a *king*, the laws maintain their sway,
While honor bids each generous heart obey.
Be ours the task the ambitious to restrain,
And this great lesson teach—that kings are vain;
That warring realms to certain ruin haste,　　　45
That kings subsist by war, and wars are waste:

---

1. The original title was *To a Republican with Mr. Paine's Rights of Man*. Paine read Edmund Burke's *Reflections on the French Revolution* (1790), a defense of monarchy and an attack on revolution, when he was living in England. In his *Rights of Man* (1791–92) Paine argued for the overthrow of monarchy and the right of the people to govern themselves.
2. False physician.

So shall our nation, formed on Virtue's plan,
Remain the guardian of the Rights of Man,
A vast republic, famed through every clime,
Without a king, to see the end of time.                    50

                                                          1795

## On the Religion of Nature

The power, that gives with liberal hand
   The blessings man enjoys, while here,
And scatters through a smiling land
   Abundant products of the year;
     That power of nature, ever blessed,                    5
     Bestowed religion with the rest.

Born with ourselves, her early sway
   Inclines the tender mind to take
The path of right, fair virtue's way
   Its own felicity to make.                    10
     This universally extends
     And leads to no mysterious ends.

Religion, such as nature taught,
   With all divine perfection suits;
Had all mankind this system sought                    15
   Sophists[1] would cease their vain disputes,
     And from this source would nations know
     All that can make their heaven below.

This deals not curses on mankind,
   Or dooms them to perpetual grief,                    20
If from its aid no joys they find,
   It damns them not for unbelief;
     Upon a more exalted plan
     Creatress nature dealt with man—

Joy to the day, when all agree                    25
   On such grand systems to proceed,
From fraud, design, and error free,
   And which to truth and goodness lead:
     Then persecution will retreat
     And man's religion be complete.                    30

                                                          1795

1. Teachers of philosophy.

# PHILLIS WHEATLEY

## c. 1753–1784

Phillis Wheatley was either nineteen or twenty years old when her *Poems on Various Subjects, Religious and Moral* was published in London in 1773. At the time of their publication she was the object of considerable public attention because, in addition to being a child prodigy, Wheatley was a black slave, born in Africa (probably in present-day Senegal or Gambia), and brought to Boston in 1761. She had been purchased by a wealthy tailor, John Wheatley, for his wife, Susannah, probably as a companion, and named for the vessel that carried her to our shores. Wheatley was fortunate in her surroundings, for Susannah Wheatley was sympathetic toward this very frail and remarkably intelligent child. In an age in which few white women were given an education, Wheatley was taught to read and write, and in a short time began to read Latin writers. She came to know the Bible well, and three English poets—Milton, Pope, and Gray—touched her deeply and exerted a strong influence on her verse. The Wheatleys moved in a circle of enlightened Boston Christians and Phillis, as James Levernier has recently shown, was introduced early on to a community that challenged the role of slavery as incompatible with Christian life. Wheatley's poem on the death of the Reverend George Whitefield, the great egalatarian English evangelist who frequently toured New England, made her famous. In June 1773, she arrived in London with her manuscript in the company of the Wheatleys' son Nathaniel. She came to England partly for reasons of health and partly to seek support for her first book. Benjamin Franklin and the lord mayor of London were among those who paid their respects. Her literary gifts, intelligence, and piety were a striking example to her English and American admirers of the triumph of the human spirit over the circumstances of birth. Her poems appeared early in September and the governor of Massachusetts, along with John Wheatley and John Hancock, were among the eighteen prominent citizens testifying that "under the Disadvantage of serving as a Slave in a Family in this Town," Wheatley "had been examined and thought qualified to write them."

Wheatley did not remain long enough in London to witness their publication; for she was called back to Boston with the news that Susannah Wheatley was dying. Early in the fall of 1773 she was manumitted. Susannah Wheatley died in 1774 and John Wheatley, four years later. In that same year, 1778, she married John Peters, a freedman, about whom almost nothing is known other than that the Wheatleys did not like him, that he petitioned for a license to sell liquor in 1784, and that he may have been in debtor's prison when Wheatley died, having endured poverty and the loss of two children in her last years. On her deathbed her third child lay ill beside her and succumbed shortly after Wheatley herself. They were buried together in an unmarked grave. Five years earlier, and only one year after her marriage, a proposal appeared for a second volume of poetry to include thirteen letters and thirty-three poems. The volume was never published and most of the poems and letters have yet to be found.

Wheatley's poetry was rediscovered in the 1830s by the New England abolitionists, but it is no exaggeration to say that she has never been better understood than at the present. Her recent critics have not only corrected a number of biographical errors but, more important, have provided a context in which her work can be best read and her life understood. This reconsideration shows Wheatley to be a bold and canny spokesperson for her faith and her politics; she early on joined the cause of American independence and the abolition of slavery, anticipating her friend the Reverend Samuel Hopkins's complaint that when American Negroes first heard the "sons of liberty" cry for freedom they were shocked by indifference to their own "abject slavery and utter wretchedness." It doesn't take a philosopher, Wheatley told Samson Occom, a Presbyterian minister and Mohegan tribesman, to see that the exercise of slavery cannot be reconciled with a "principle" that God has implanted in every human breast, "Love of Freedom." She was mistaken in thinking that the conservative earl of Dartmouth (William Legge) might be sympathetic to the American cause but correct in reminding him that there could be no justice anywhere if people in authority were deaf to the history of human sorrow:

> Should you, my lord, while you peruse my song,
> Wonder from whence my love of *Freedom* sprung,
> Whence flow these wishes for the common good,
> By feeling hearts best understood,
> I, young in life, by seeming cruel fate
> Was snatched from *Afric's* fancied happy seat:
> What pangs excruciating must molest,
> What sorrows labor in my parent's breast?
> Steeled was that soul and by no misery moved
> That from a father seized his babe beloved:
> Such, such my case. And can I then but pray
> Others may never feel tyrannic sway?

With the publication of Wheatley's *Poems*, Henry Louis Gates, Jr., has argued, "Wheatley launched two traditions at once—the black American literary tradition *and* the black woman's literary tradition. It is extraordinary that not just one but both of these traditions were founded simultaneously by a black woman—certainly an event unique in the history of literature—it is also ironic that this important fact of common, coterminous literary origin seems to have escaped most scholars."

The text used here for both the letters and the poems is from *The Poems of Phillis Wheatley*, edited by Julian D. Mason, Jr. (1966, rev. 1989). Wheatley's letters retain her original spelling.

## On Being Brought from Africa to America

> 'Twas mercy brought me from my pagan land,
> Taught my benighted soul to understand
> That there's a God, that there's a Savior too:
> Once I redemption neither sought nor knew.
> Some view our sable[1] race with scornful eye.          5
> "Their color is a diabolic dye."
> Remember, Christians, Negroes, black as Cain,[2]
> May be refined, and join the angelic train.

                                                                1773

## To the University of Cambridge, in New England[1]

> While an intrinsic ardor prompts to write,
> The muses promise to assist my pen;

---

1. Black.
2. Cain slew his brother Abel and was "marked" by God for doing so. This mark has sometimes been taken

to be the origin of dark-skinned peoples (Genesis 4.1–15).
1. Harvard.

'Twas not long since I left my native shore
The land of errors,[2] and Egyptian gloom:[3]
Father of mercy, 'twas Thy gracious hand                          5
Brought me in safety from those dark abodes.

Students, to you 'tis given to scan the heights
Above, to traverse the ethereal space,
And mark the systems of revolving worlds.
Still more, ye sons of science[4] ye receive                     10
The blissful news by messengers from Heav'n,
How Jesus' blood for your redemption flows.
See Him with hands outstretched upon the cross;
Immense compassion in His bosom glows;
He hears revilers, nor resents their scorn:                      15
What matchless mercy in the Son of God!
When the whole human race by sin had fall'n,
He deigned to die that they might rise again,
And share with Him in the sublimest skies,
Life without death, and glory without end.                       20

Improve your privileges while they stay,
Ye pupils, and each hour redeem, that bears
Or good or bad report of you to Heav'n.
Let sin, that baneful evil to the soul,
By you be shunned, nor once remit your guard;                    25
Suppress the deadly serpent in its egg.
Ye blooming plants of human race divine,
An Ethiop[5] tells you 'tis your greatest foe;
Its transient sweetness turns to endless pain,
And in immense perdition sinks the soul.                         30

1767                                                           1773

# On the Death of the
# Rev. Mr. George Whitefield, 1770[1]

Hail, happy saint, on thine immortal throne,
Possessed of glory, life, and bliss unknown;
We hear no more the music of thy tongue,
Thy wonted[2] auditories cease to throng.
Thy sermons in unequaled accents flowed,                         5
And every bosom with devotion glowed;
Thou didst in strains of eloquence refined
Inflame the heart, and captivate the mind.

2. I.e., theological errors, because Africa was unconverted.
3. "And Moses stretched forth his hand toward
heaven; and there was a thick darkness in all the land
of Egypt three days" (Exodus 10.22).
4. Knowledge.
5. Ethiopian. In Wheatley's time "Ethiopian" was a
conventional name for the black peoples of Africa.

1. George Whitefield (1714–1770), an English follower of John Wesley, was the best-known revivalist in
the 18th century. He made several visits to America
and died in Newburyport, Massachusetts. This was
Wheatley's first published poem, and it made her
famous.
2. Accustomed.

Unhappy we the setting sun deplore,
So glorious once, but ah! it shines no more.          10

Behold the prophet in his towering flight!
He leaves the earth for heav'n's unmeasured height,}
And worlds unknown receive him from our sight.
There Whitefield wings with rapid course his way,
And sails to Zion[3] through vast seas of day.          15
Thy prayers, great saint, and thine incessant cries
Have pierced the bosom of thy native skies.
Thou moon hast seen, and all the stars of light,
How he has wrestled with his God by night.
He prayed that grace in every heart might dwell,          20
He longed to see America excel;
He charged[4] its youth that every grace divine
Should with full luster in their conduct shine;
That Savior, which his soul did first receive,
The greatest gift that ev'n a God can give,          25
He freely offered to the numerous throng,
That on his lips with listening pleasure hung.

"Take Him, ye wretched, for your only good,
Take Him ye starving sinners, for your food;
Ye thirsty, come to this life-giving stream,          30
Ye preachers, take Him for your joyful theme;
Take Him my dear Americans," he said,
"Be your complaints on His kind bosom laid:
Take Him, ye Africans, He longs for you,
Impartial Savior is His title due:          35
Washed in the fountain of redeeming blood,
You shall be sons, and kings, and priests to God."

Great *Countess*,[5] we Americans revere
Thy name, and mingle in thy grief sincere;
New England deeply feels, the orphans mourn,          40
Their more than father will no more return.

But, though arrested by the hand of death,
Whitefield no more exerts his laboring breath,
Yet let us view him in the eternal skies,
Let every heart to this bright vision rise;          45
While the tomb safe retains its sacred trust,
Till life divine re-animates his dust.

1770                                        1770, 1773

---

3. Here, the heavenly city of God.
4. Exhorted.
5. Selina Shirley Hastings (1707–1791), countess of

Huntington, was a strong supporter of George
Whitefield and active in Methodist church affairs.
Wheatley visited her in England in 1773.

# Thoughts on the Works of Providence

Arise, my soul, on wings enraptured, rise
To praise the monarch of the earth and skies,
Whose goodness and beneficence appear
As round its center moves the rolling year,
Or when the morning glows with rosy charms, 5
Or the sun slumbers in the ocean's arms:
Of light divine by a rich portion lent
To guide my soul, and favor my intent.
Celestial muse, my arduous flight sustain,
And raise my mind to a seraphic[1] strain! 10

Adored forever be the God unseen,
Which round the sun revolves this vast machine,
Though to His eye its mass a point appears:
Adored the God that whirls surrounding spheres,
Which first ordained that mighty Sol[2] should reign 15
The peerless monarch of the ethereal train:
Of miles twice forty millions is his height,
And yet his radiance dazzles mortal sight
So far beneath—from him the extended earth
Vigor derives, and every flowery birth: 20
Vast through her orb she moves with easy grace
Around her Phœbus[3] in unbounded space;
True to her course the impetuous storm derides,
Triumphant o'er the winds, and surging tides.

Almighty, in these wond'rous works of Thine, 25
What Power, what Wisdom, and what Goodness shine!
And are Thy wonders, Lord, by men explored,
And yet creating glory unadored!

Creation smiles in various beauty gay,
While day to night, and night succeeds to day: 30
That wisdom, which attends Jehovah's ways,
Shines most conspicuous in the solar rays:
Without them, destitute of heat and light,
This world would be the reign of endless night:
In their excess how would our race complain, 35
Abhorring life! how hate its lengthened chain!
From air adust[4] what numerous ills would rise?
What dire contagion taint the burning skies?
What pestilential vapors, fraught with death,
Would rise, and overspread the lands beneath? 40

Hail, smiling morn, that from the orient main[5]
Ascending dost adorn the heavenly plain!
So rich, so various are thy beauteous dyes,

---

1. Angelic.
2. The sun.
3. Apollo, the Greek sun god.

4. Dried up.
5. Ocean. "Orient": eastern.

That spread through all the circuit of the skies,
That, full of thee, my soul in rapture soars,                    45
And thy great God, the cause of all adores.

O'er beings infinite His love extends,
His wisdom rules them, and His power defends.
When tasks diurnal[6] tire the human frame,
The spirits faint, and dim the vital flame,                      50
Then too that ever active bounty shines,
Which not infinity of space confines.
The sable veil, that night in silence draws,
Th)TConceals effects, but shows the almighty cause;
Night seals in sleep the wide creation fair,                     55
And all is peaceful but the brow of care.
Again, gay Phœbus, as the day before,
Wakes every eye, but what shall wake no more;
Again the face of nature is renewed,
Which still appears harmonious, fair, and good.                  60
May grateful strains salute the smiling morn,
Before its beams the eastern hills adorn!

Shall day to day, and night to night conspire
To show the goodness of the Almighty Sire?
This mental voice shall man regardless hear,                     65
And never, never raise the filial prayer?
Today, O hearken, nor your folly mourn
For time misspent, that never will return.

But see the sons of vegetation rise,
And spread their leafy banners to the skies.                     70
All-wise Almighty providence we trace
In trees, and plants, and all the flowery race;
As clear as in the nobler frame of man,
All lovely copies of the Maker's plan.
The power the same that forms a ray of light,                    75
That called creation from eternal night.
"Let there be light," He said: from His profound[7]
Old Chaos heard, and trembled at the sound:
Swift as the word, inspired by power divine,
Behold the light around its maker shine,                         80
The first fair product of the omnific God,
And now through all His works diffused abroad.

As reason's powers by day our God disclose,
So we may trace Him in the night's repose:
Say what is sleep? and dreams how passing strange!               85
When action ceases, and ideas range
Licentious and unbounded o'er the plains,
Where Fancy's[8] queen in giddy triumph reigns.
Hear in soft strains the dreaming lover sigh
To a kind fair, or rave in jealousy;                             90

6. Daily.                              Let there be light: and there was light" (Genesis 1.3).
7. A place in the depths of the ocean. "And God said,   8. The imagination in its image-making aspect.

On pleasure now, and now on vengeance bent,
The laboring passions struggle for a vent.
What power, O man! thy reason then restores,
So long suspended in nocturnal hours?
What secret hand returns the mental train,                    95
And gives improved thine active powers again?
From thee, O man, what gratitude should rise!
And, when from balmy sleep thou op'st thine eyes,⎫
Let thy first thoughts be praises to the skies.  ⎭
How merciful our God who thus imparts                         100
O'erflowing tides of joy to human hearts,
When wants and woes might be our righteous lot,
Our God forgetting, by our God forgot!

Among the mental powers a question rose,
"What most the image of the Eternal shows?"                   105
When thus to Reason (so let Fancy rove)
Her great companion spoke, immortal Love.

"Say, mighty power, how long shall strife prevail,
And with its murmurs load the whispering gale?
Refer the cause to Recollection's shrine,                     110
Who loud proclaims my origin divine,
The cause whence heaven and earth began to be,
And is not man immortalized by me?
Reason let this most causeless strife subside."
Thus Love pronounced, and Reason thus replied.               115

"Thy birth, celestial queen! 'tis mine to own,
In thee resplendent is the Godhead shown;
Thy words persuade, my soul enraptured feels
Resistless beauty which thy smile reveals."
Ardent she spoke, and, kindling at her charms,               120
She clasped the blooming goddess in her arms.

Infinite Love wher'er we turn our eyes
Appears: this every creature's wants supplies;
This most is heard in Nature's constant voice,
This makes the morn, and this is the eve rejoice;            125
This bids the fostering rains and dews descend
To nourish all, to serve one general end,
The good of man: yet man ungrateful pays
But little homage, and but little praise.
To Him, whose works arrayed with mercy shine,                130
What songs should rise, how constant, how divine!

                                                          1773

# To S.M.,[1] a Young African Painter, on Seeing His Works

To show the laboring bosom's deep intent,
And thought in living characters to paint,

1. Scipio Moorhead, a servant to the Rev. John Moorhead of Boston.

When first thy pencil did those beauties give,
And breathing figures learnt from thee to live,
How did those prospects give my soul delight,                    5
A new creation rushing on my sight?
Still, wond'rous youth! each noble path pursue,
On deathless glories fix thine ardent view:
Still may the painter's and the poet's fire
To aid thy pencil, and thy verse conspire!                      10
And may the charms of each seraphic² theme
Conduct thy footsteps to immortal fame!
High to the blissful wonders of the skies
Elate thy soul, and raise thy wishful eyes.
Thrice happy, when exalted to survey                            15
That splendid city, crowned with endless day,
Whose twice six gates³ on radiant hinges ring:
Celestial Salem⁴ blooms in endless spring.

Calm and serene thy moments glide along,
And may the muse inspire each future song!                      20
Still, with the sweets of contemplation blest,
May peace with balmy wings your soul invest!
But when these shades of time are chased away,
And darkness ends in everlasting day,
On what seraphic pinions shall we move,                         25
And view the landscape in the realms above?
There shall thy tongue in heavenly murmurs flow,
And there my muse with heavenly transport glow:
No more to tell of Damon's⁵ tender sighs,
Or rising radiance of Aurora's⁶ eyes,                           30
For nobler themes demand a nobler strain,
And purer language on the ethereal plain.
Cease, gentle muse! the solemn gloom of night
Now seals the fair creation from my sight.

                                                               1773


# To His Excellency General Washington[1]

Sir. I have taken the freedom to address your Excellency in the enclosed
poem, and entreat your acceptance, though I am not insensible of its inaccura-
cies. Your being appointed by the Grand Continental Congress to be Generalissimo of the armies of North America, together with the fame of your virtues,
excite sensations not easy to suppress. Your generosity, therefore, I presume,
will pardon the attempt. Wishing your Excellency all possible success in the
great cause you are so generously engaged in. I am,

Your Excellency's most obedient humble servant,
Phillis Wheatley

2. Angelic.
3. Heaven, like the city of Jerusalem, is thought to
have had twelve gates (as many gates as tribes of Israel).
4. Heavenly Jerusalem.
5. In classical mythology Damon pledged his life for
his friend Pythias.

6. The Roman goddess of the dawn.
1. This poem was first published in the *Pennsylvania
Magazine* when Thomas Paine was editor. Washington invited Wheatley to meet him in Cambridge, Massachusetts, in February 1776, after reading it.

Providence, Oct. 26, 1775.
His Excellency Gen. Washington.

> Celestial choir! enthroned in realms of light,
>   Columbia's[2] scenes of glorious toils I write.
> While freedom's cause her anxious breast alarms,
> She flashes dreadful in refulgent arms.
> See mother earth her offspring's fate bemoan,            5
> And nations gaze at scenes before unknown!
> See the bright beams of heaven's revolving light
> Involved in sorrows and the veil of night!
>   The goddess comes, she moves divinely fair,
> Olive and laurel[3] binds her golden hair:              10
> Wherever shines this native of the skies,
> Unnumbered charms and recent graces rise.
>   Muse! bow propitious while my pen relates
> How pour her armies through a thousand gates,
> As when Eolus[4] heaven's fair face deforms,            15
> Enwrapped in tempest and a night of storms;
> Astonished ocean feels the wild uproar,
> The refluent surges beat the sounding shore;
> Or thick as leaves in Autumn's golden reign,
> Such, and so many, moves the warrior's train.           20
> In bright array they seek the work of war,
> Where high unfurled the ensign[5] waves in air.
> Shall I to Washington their praise recite?
> Enough thou know'st them in the fields of fight.
> Thee, first in place and honors—we demand              25
> The grace and glory of thy martial band.
> Famed for thy valor, for thy virtues more,
> Heart every tongue thy guardian aid implore!
>   One century scarce performed its destined round,
> When Gallic[6] powers Columbia's fury found;           30
> And so may you, whoever dares disgrace
> The land of freedom's heaven-defended race!
> Fixed are the eyes of nations on the scales,
> For in their hopes Columbia's arm prevails.
> Anon Britannia droops the pensive head,               35
> While round increase the rising hills of dead.
> Ah! cruel blindness to Columbia's state!
> Lament thy thirst of boundless power too late.
>   Proceed, great chief, with virtue on thy side,
> Thy every action let the goddess guide.               40
> A crown, a mansion, and a throne that shine,
> With gold unfading, WASHINGTON! be thine.

1775–76                                              1776, 1834

---

2. This reference to America as "the land Columbus found" is believed to be the first in print.
3. Emblems of victory.
4. Keeper of the winds.

5. Flag or banner.
6. The French and Indian War (1754–63) comprised four wars between France and England, which actually ended the French colonial empire in North America.

PHILLIS WHEATLEY

# Letters

## To John Thornton,[1] London

[THE BIBLE MY CHIEF STUDY]

[Boston, April 21, 1772]

Hon'd, Sir

I rec'd your instructive fav[2] of Feb. 29, for which, return you ten thousand thanks, I did not flatter myself with the tho'ts of your honouring me with an Answer to my letter, I thank you for recommending the Bible to be my chief Study, I find and Acknowledge it the best of Books, it contains an endless treasure of wisdom, and knowledge. O that my eyes were more open'd to see the real worth, and true excellence of the word of truty, my flinty heart Soften'd with the grateful dews of divine grace and the Stubborn will, and affections, bent on God alone their proper object, and the vitiated palate may be corrected to relish heav'nly things. It has pleas'd God to lay me on a bed of Sickness, and I knew not but my deathbed, but he has been graciously pleas'd to restore me in a great measure. I beg your prayers, that I may be made thankful for his paternal corrections, and that I may make a proper use of them to the glory of his grace. I am Still very weak & the Physicians, seem to think there is danger of a consumpsion. And O that when my flesh and my heart fail me God would be my strength and portion for ever. that I might put my whole trust and Confidence in him, who has promis'd never to forsake those who Seek him with the whole heart. You could not, I am sure have express greater tenderness and affection for me, than by being a welwisher to my Soul, the friends of Souls bear Some resemblance to the father of Spirits and are made partakers of his divine Nature.

I am affraid I have entruded on your patient, but if I had not tho't it ungrateful to omit writing in answer to your favour Should not have troubl'd you, but I can't expect you to answer this,

I am Sir with greatest respect,
your very hum. sert.
Phillis Wheatley

## To Arbour Tanner,[3] Newport, Rhode Island

[A SENSE OF THE BEAUTIES AND EXCELLENCE OF THE CRUCIFIED SAVIOUR]

[Boston, May 19, 1772]

Dear Sister

I rec'd your favour of February 6th for which I give you my sincere thanks, I greatly rejoice with you in that realizing view,[4] and I hope experience, of the Saving change which you So emphatically describe. Happy were it for us if we could arrive to that evangelical Repentance, and the true holiness of heart which you mention. Inexpressibly happy Should we be could we have a due

---

1. A London merchant (1720–1790), who was a devout Anglican and lived outside London at Clapham, where a small group of Christians were committed to helping the poor and abolishing slavery. He was a friend of John and Susannah Wheatley and sent them money to be used for work among the American Indians.

2. Favor, i.e., letter.
3. There are more extant Wheatley letters to Arbour (sometimes spelled "Obour") Tanner, a black servant in the family of James Tanner, than to any other person.
4. I.e., to a new realization of Christianity.

Sense of the Beauties and excellence of the Crucified Saviour. In his Crucifixion may be seen marvellous displays of Grace and Love, Sufficient to draw
and invite us to the rich and endless treasures of his mercy, let us rejoice in
and adore the wonders of God's infinite Love in bringing us from a land Sem-
blant of darkness itself, and where the divine light of revelation (being
obscur'd) is as darkness. Here, the knowledge of the true God and eternal life
are made manifest; But there, profound ignorance overshadows the Land,
Your observation is true, namely, that there was nothing in us to recommend
us to God. Many of our fellow creatures are pass'd by, when the bowels[5] of
divine love expanded towards us. May this goodness & long Suffering of God
lead us to unfeign'd repentance

It gives me very great pleasure to hear of so many of my Nation, Seeking
with eagerness the way to true felicity, O may we all meet at length in that
happy mansion. I hope the correspondence between us will continue, (my
being much indispos'd this winter past was the reason of my not answering
yours before now) which correspondence I hope may have the happy effect of
improving our mutual friendship. Till we meet in the regions of consummate
blessedness, let us endeavor by the assistance of divine grace, to live the life,
and we Shall die the death of the Righteous. May this be our happy case and
of those who are travelling to the region of Felicity is the earnest request of
your affectionate

Friend & hum. Sert.   Phillis Wheatley

### To John Thornton, London

[THE GIFT OF GOD IS ETERNAL LIFE]

[Boston, December 1, 1773]

Hon'd Sir

It is with great satisfaction, I acquaint you with my experience of the goodness of God in safely conducting my passage over the mighty waters, and
returning me in safety to my American Friends.[6] I presume you will Join with
them and m[e] in praise to God for so distinguishing a favour, it was amazing
Mercy, altogether unmerited by me: and if possible it is augmented by the
consideration of the bitter r[e]verse, which is the deserved wages of my evil
doings. The Apostle Paul, tells us that the wages of Sin is death.[7] I don't
imagine he excepted any sin whatsoever being equally hateful in its nature in
the sight of God, who is essential Purity.

Should we not sink hon'd Sir, under this Sentence of Death, pronounced
on every Sin, from the comparatively least to the greatest, were not this blessed
Co[n]trast annexed to it, "But the Gift of God is eternal Life,["] through Jesus
Christ our Lord? It is his Gift. O let us be thankful for it! What a load is taken
from the Sinner's Shoulder when he thinks that Jesus has done that work for
him which he could never have done, and Suffer'd, that punishment of his
imputed Rebellions, for which a long Eternity of Torments could not have
made sufficient expiation. O that I could meditate continually on this work of
wonde[r] in Deity itself. This, which Kings & Prophets have desir'd to see, &
have not See[n]. This, which Angels are continually exploring, et are not

---

5. The seat of compassion.
6. Wheatley accompanied John Wheatley to London
in the spring of 1773 and returned to Boston hurriedly
when they received news of Susannah Wheatley's ill-

ness. They arrived in Boston on September 13.
7. "The wages of sin is death; but the gift of God is
eternal life" (Romans 6.23).

equal to the search,—Millions of Ages shall roll away, and they may try in vain to find out to perfection, the sublime mysteries of Christ's Incarnation. Nor will this desir[e] to look into the deep things of God, cease, in the Breasts of glorified Saints & Angels. It's duration will be coeval with Eternity. This Eternity how dreadf[ul,] how delightful! Delightful to those who have an interest in the Crucifi[ed] Saviour, who has dignified our Nature, by seating it at the Right Hand of the divine Majesty.—They alone who are thus interested have Cause to rejoi[ce] even on the brink of that Bottomless Profound: and I doubt not (without the [lea]st Adulation) that you are one of that happy number. O pray that I may be one also, who Shall Join with you in Songs of praise at the Throne of him, who is no respecter of Persons: being equally the great Maker of all:—Therefor disdain not to be called the Father of Humble Africans and Indians; though despisd on earth on account of our colour, we have this Consolation, if he enables us to deserve it. "That God dwells in the humble & contrite heart." O that I were more & more possess'd of this inestimable blessing; to be directed by the immediate influence of the divine Spirit in my daily walk & Conversation.

Do you, my hon'd Sir, who have abundant Reason to be thankful for the great Share you possess of it, be always mindful in your Closet, of those who want it—of me in particular.— When I first arrivd at home my mistress was so bad as not to be expected to live above two or three days, but through the goodness of God She is still alive, but remains in a very weak & languishing Condition, She begs a continued interest in your most earnest prayers, that she may be surly prepar'd for that great Change which [She] is likely Soon to undergo; She intreats you, as her Son is Still in England, that you would take all opportun[i]ties to advise & counsel him; She says she is going to leave him & desires you'd be a Spiritual Fath[er] to hi[m]. She will take it very kind. *She thanks you heartily for the kind notice you took of me while in England.* Pleas[e] to give my best Respects to Mrs. & miss Thornton, and masters Henry and Robert who held with me a long conversation on many subjects which Mrs. Drinkwater[8] knows very well, hope she is in better Health than when I left her. Please to remember me to your whole family & I than[k] them for their kindness to me. begging Still an interest in your best hours
I am Hon'd Sir

most respectfully your Humble Servt.

Phillis Wheatley

I have written to Mrs. Wilberforce[9] Sometime since Please to give my duty to her; Since writing the above the Rev'd Mr. Moorhead[1] has made his Exit from this world, in whom we lament the loss of the Zealous Pious & true christian

## To Rev. Samson Occom,[2] New London, Connecticut

[THE NATURAL RIGHTS OF NEGROES]

[February 11, 1774]

"Rev'd and honor'd Sir,

I have this Day received your obliging kind Epistle, and am greatly satisfied with your Reasons respecting the Negroes, and think highly reasonable what

---

8. A mutual friend.
9. Thornton's sister.
1. The Rev. John Moorhead (d. 1773) came to Boston from Scotland in 1730 and was the pastor of a Scotch Presbyterian church near the Wheatley home.

Wheatley wrote an elegy on his death and dedicated it to his daughter Mary.
2. A Mohegan Indian (1723–1792) born and living in New London; he was in England from 1766 to 1767. Mason notes that Occom, an ordained Presbyterian

you offer in Vindication of their natural Rights: Those that invade them cannot be insensible that the divine Light is chasing away the thick Darkness[3]
which broods over the Land of Africa; and the Chaos which has reign'd so
long, is converting into beautiful Order, and [r]eveals more and more clearly,
the glorious Dispensation of civil and religious Liberty, which are so insepara-
bly united, that there is little or no Enjoyment of one without the other: Otherwise, perhaps, the Israelites had been less solicitous for their Freedom from
Egyptian slavery; I do not say they would have been contented without it, by
no means, for in every human Breast, God has implanted a Principle, which
we call Love of Freedom; it is impatient of Oppression, and pants for Deliverance; and by the Leave of our modern Egyptians I will assert, that the same
Principle lives in us. God grant Deliverance in his own Way and Time, and
get him honour upon all those whose Avarice impels them to countenance
and help forward the Calamities of their fellow Creatures. This I desire not for
their Hurt, but to convince them of the strange Absurdity of their Conduct
whose Words and Actions are so diametrically opposite. How well the Cry for
Liberty, and the reverse Disposition for the exercise of oppressive Power over
others agree,—I humbly think it does not require the Penetration of a philosopher to determine."—

## To John Thornton, London

### [THE DEATH OF MRS. WHEATLEY]

[Boston, March 29, 1774]

Much honoured Sir,
   I should not so soon have troubled you with the 2d. Letter, but the mournful *Occasion* will sufficiently Apologize. It is the death of Mrs. Wheatley. She
has been labouring under a languishing illness for many months past and has
at length took he flight from hence to those blissful regions, which need not
the light of any, but the Sun of Righteousness. O could you have been present,
to See how She long'd to drop the tabernacle of Clay, and to be freed from the
cumbrous Shackles of a mortal Body, which had so many Times retarded her
desires when Soaring upward. She has often told me how your Letters hav[e]
quicken'd her in her spiritual Course: when She has been in darkness of mind
they have rais'd and enliven'd her insomuch, that She went on, with chearful-
n[ess] and alacrity in the path of her duty. She did truely, *run with patience
the race that was Set before her*,[4] and hath, at length obtained the celestial
Goal. She is now Sure, that the afflictions of this present time, were not worthy to be compared to the Glory, which is now, revealed in her, Seeing they
have wrought out for her, *a far more exceeding and eternal weight of Glory*:[5]
This, Sure, is Sufficient encouragement under the bitterest Sufferings, which
we can endure.—About half an hour before her Death, She Spoke with a
more audible voice, than She had for 3 months before. She calld. her friends
& relations around her, and charg'd them not to leave their great work undone
till *that* hour, but to fear God, and keep his Commandments. being ask'd if

---

minister and friend of the Wheatleys, suggested to
Wheatley that she go to Africa as a missionary, but she
rejected the idea.
3. "And Moses stretched forth his hand toward
heaven; and there was a thick darkness in all the land
of Egypt three days" (Exodus 10.22).
4. "Wherefore seeing we also are compassed about

with so great a cloud of witnesses, let us lay aside every
weight, and the sin which doth so easily beset us, and
let us run with patience the race that is set before us"
(Hebrews 12.1).
5. "For our light affliction, which is but for a moment,
worketh for us a far more exceeding and eternal weight
of glory" (2 Corinthians 4.17).

her faith faild her She answer'd, No. Then Spr[ead] out her arms crying come! come quickly! come, come! O pray for an eas[y] and quick Passage! She eagerly longed to depart to be with Christ. She retaind her Senses till the very last moment when "fare well, fare well." with a very low voice, were the last words She utter'd. I sat the whole time by her bed Side, and Saw with Grief and Wonder, the Effects of Sin on the human race. Had not Christ taken away the envenom'd Sting, where had been our hopes? what might we not have fear'd, what might we not have expectd from the dreadful King of Terrors? But *this* is matter of endless praise, to the King eternal immortal, invisible, that, *it is finished.* I hope her Son will be interested in Your Closet duties,[6] & that the prayers which she was continually putting up, & wch. are recorded before God, in the Book of his remembrance for her Son & for me may be answer'd, I can Scarcely think that an Object of so many prayers, will fail of the Blessings implor'd for him ever Since he was born. I intreat the same Interest in your best thoughts for my Self, that her prayers, in my behalf, may be favour'd with an Answer of *Peace.* We received and forwarded your Letter to the rev'd Mr. Occom, but first, took the freedom to peruse it, and am exceeding glad, that you have order'd him to draw immediately for £25. for I really think he is in absolute necessity for that and as much more, he is so loth to run in debt for fear he Shall not be able to repay, that he has not the Least Shelter for his Creatures to defend them from the inclemencies of the weather, and he has lost some already for want of it, His hay is quite as defenceless, thus the former are in a fair way of being lost, and the latter to be wasted; It were to be wished that his *dwelling house* was like the Ark, with appartments, to contain the beasts and their provision; He said Mrs. Wheatley and the rev'd Mr. Moorhead were his best friends in Boston, But alass! they are gone. I trust gone to recieve the rewards promis'd to those, who Offer a Cup of cold water in the name & for the sake of Jesus—They have both been very instrum[ental in meetin]g the wants of that child of God, Mr. Occom— but I fear your pa[tience has been] exhausted, it remains only that we thank you for your kind Letter to my mistress it came above a fortnight after her Death.—Hoping for an interest in your prayers for these [and then] Sanctification of this bereaving Providence, I am hon'd Sir with dutiful respect ever your obliged

and devoted Humble Servant   Phillis Wheatley

---

6. I.e., his meditations and prayers.

# American Literature
# 1820–1865

THE INFLUENCE OF WASHINGTON IRVING

In a painting popular during the late nineteenth century, Christian Schussele reverentially depicted *Washington Irving and His Literary Friends at Sunnyside.* Working in 1863, four years after Irving's death, Schussele portrayed an astonishing number of elegantly clad notables in Irving's snug study in his Gothic cottage-castle on the Hudson River, north of New York City. Among them were several writers in this anthology: Irving himself, Nathaniel Hawthorne, Henry Wadsworth Longfellow, Ralph Waldo Emerson, William Cullen Bryant, and James Fenimore Cooper. Intermingled with these men were poets and novelists now seldom read: William Gilmore Simms, Fitz-Greene Halleck, Nathaniel Parker Willis, James Kirke Paulding, John Pendleton Kennedy, and Henry T. Tuckerman, along with the historians William H. Prescott and George Bancroft. The Schussele painting was a pious hoax, for these guests never assembled together at one time, at Sunnyside or anywhere else, and while a few of those depicted were indeed among Irving's friends, he barely knew some of them and never met others at all. But in several ways the scene is profoundly true to American literary history.

As Schussele's painting suggests, Irving, beloved by ordinary readers and by most of his fellow writers, was the central figure in the American literary world between 1809 (the year of his parody *History of New York*) and the Civil War, especially after he demonstrated in *The Sketch Book* (1819–20) that memorable fiction—*Rip Van Winkle* and *The Legend of Sleepy Hollow*—could be set in the United States; he also proved, by the book's international success, that an American writer could win a British and Continental audience. Irving's legion of imitators included several of the men in the painting, and among his fellow writers Irving's reputation was enhanced by his generosity, as in his gallantly relinquishing the subject of the conquest of Mexico to Prescott or in urging the publisher George P. Putnam to bring out an American edition of the first book by the unknown Herman Melville. Although James Fenimore Cooper's fame as a fiction writer rivaled Irving's in the 1820s and 1830s, his influence never approached the breadth of Irving's. Nor did the influence of Ralph Waldo Emerson, despite his profoundly provocative effects on such writers as Margaret Fuller, Henry David Thoreau, Walt Whitman, Herman Melville, and Emily Dickinson—effects that make modern literary historians see him as the seminal writer of the century.

Mentioning the names of Fuller, Thoreau, Melville, and Dickinson suggests still another way the Schussele painting is exemplary. Because the painter set out to depict representative literary men (not literary women) as much as to depict genuine intimates of Irving, it is striking that he omitted writers who now seem among the most important of the century: Edgar Allan Poe, Thoreau, Whitman, Melville, John Greenleaf Whittier (who was frowned on as a militant abolitionist until 1866, when *Snow-Bound* made him seem a safe poet to admire), and Dickinson (in the 1860s an all but unpublished recluse). The painter would probably have considered Augustus Baldwin Longstreet, George Washington Harris, and other southern or backwoods humorists to be subliterary, despite the fact that Irving had influenced such writing and had delighted in reading it.

### THE SMALL WORLD OF AMERICAN WRITERS

Perhaps most important, paintings like the one by Schussele (and the similar wishful fad of depicting famous literary people in cozy association through the then-new technique of composite photography) capture the fact that in the nineteenth century the American literary world was very small indeed, so small that most of the writers in this period knew each other, often intimately, or else knew much about each other. They lived, if not in each other's pockets, at least in each other's houses, or boardinghouses: Lemuel Shaw, from 1830 to 1860 chief justice of the Massachusetts Supreme Court, and Herman Melville's father-in-law after 1847, for a time stayed in a Boston boardinghouse run by Ralph Waldo Emerson's widowed mother; the Longfellows summered in the 1840s at the Pittsfield boardinghouse run by Melville's cousin, a house where Melville had stayed in his early teens; in Pittsfield and Lenox, Hawthorne and Melville paid each other overnight visits, in Concord the Hawthornes rented the Old Manse, the Emerson ancestral home, and later bought a house there from the educator Bronson Alcott and made it famous as the Wayside; in Concord the Emersons welcomed many guests, including Margaret Fuller, and when the master was away Thoreau sometimes stayed in the house to help Mrs. Emerson with the children and the property. The popular Manhattan hostess Anne Lynch assigned the young travel-writer Bayard Taylor to write a valentine for a slightly older travel-writer, Herman Melville, in 1848, and three years later, apparently with matchmaking in mind, brought together Taylor's intimate friend R. H. Stoddard and Elizabeth Barstow, a distant relative of Hawthorne. In 1853 Hawthorne received at Wayside young Mr. Stoddard, by then husband of Elizabeth Barstow, and pulled wires to get him a job in the New York Custom House, Hawthorne having the year before written the campaign biography for his old friend, the candidate for president, Franklin Pierce. (When Melville finally got his own appointment to the Custom House in 1866, Stoddard was on desk duty to welcome him; Stoddard kept Melville from being fired once, but Melville outlasted him many years in that nest of corruption.) On a visit to Washington after the Civil War had broken out, the still reclusive, and ailing, Hawthorne seriously considered making the hazardous trip to Wheeling to meet the extraordinary new contributor to the *Atlantic Monthly*, Rebecca Harding; later he welcomed her at Wayside. At Litchfield, Connecticut, the young Georgian Longstreet greatly admired one of the minister Lyman Beecher's daughters (not Harriet, then a small child).

Many of the writers of this period came together casually for dining and drinking, the hospitality at the editor Evert A. Duyckinck's house in New York being famous, open to southerners like Simms as well as New Yorkers like Melville and Bostonians like the elder Richard Henry Dana. In the late 1850s a Bohemian group of newspaper and theater people and writers drank together at Pfaff's saloon on Broadway above Bleecker Street; for a time Whitman was a fixture there. Of the clubs formed by writers, artists, and other notables (usually male), the four most memorable are the Bread and Cheese Club, which Cooper organized in 1824 in the back room of his publisher's Manhattan bookstore; the Transcendental Club, started in Boston in 1836 and lasting four years; the Saturday Club, a more convivial Boston group formed in 1856; and the Authors Club, founded in New York in 1882. Members of the Bread and Cheese Club included the poet William Cullen Bryant, Samuel F. B. Morse (the painter who later invented the telegraph), the poet Fitz-Greene Halleck, and Thomas Cole (the English-born painter of the American landscape). Emerson was the leading spirit of the Transcendental Club, but other members included Bronson Alcott, later Margaret Fuller, and George

Ripley (the organizer of the Transcendental commune at Brook Farm, near Roxbury). Among the members of the Saturday Club were Emerson, James Russell
Lowell, Henry Wadsworth Longfellow, Oliver Wendell Holmes, and the historians John Lothrop Motley and William H. Prescott; Nathaniel Hawthorne attended
some meetings. Brander Matthews cofounded the Authors Club, from the first a
beloved resource for the literary establishment, which included dominant magazine editors of the time such as Richard Watson Gilder and critics and poets such
as R. H. Stoddard and Edmund Clarence Stedman (an intimate of Samuel L.
Clemens and William Dean Howells who also befriended Melville in his last years
and whose son Arthur became Melville's literary executor); Matthews recalled that
once or twice "the shy and elusive Herman Melville dropped in for an hour or
two."

### THE SMALL COUNTRY

Such intimacy was inevitable in a country that had only a few literary and publishing centers, all of them along the Atlantic seaboard. Despite the acquisition of the
Louisiana Territory from France in 1803 and the vast Southwest from Mexico in
1848, most of the writers we still read lived all their lives in the original thirteen
states, except for trips abroad, and their practical experience was of a compact
country: in 1840 the "northwestern" states were those covered by the Northwest
Ordinance of 1787 (Ohio, Indiana, Illinois, and Michigan; Wisconsin was still a
territory), while the "southwestern" humor writers such as George Washington
Harris, Thomas Bangs Thorpe, and Johnson Jones Hooper wrote in the region
bounded by Georgia, Louisiana, and Tennessee.

Improvements in transportation were shrinking the country even while territorial
gains were enlarging it. When Irving went from Manhattan to Albany in 1800,
steamboats had not yet been invented, although William Longstreet, the father of
the writer, had been planning one for a decade; the Hudson voyage was slow and
dangerous, and in 1803 the wagons of Irving's Canada-bound party barely made it
through the bogs beyond Utica. The Erie Canal, completed in 1825, changed
things: in the 1830s and 1840s Hawthorne, Melville, and Fuller took the canal
boats in safety, suffering only from crowded and stuffy sleeping conditions. When
Irving went buffalo hunting in Indian territory (now Oklahoma) in 1832 he left the
steamboat at St. Louis and went on horseback, camping out at night except when
his party reached one of the line of missions built to accommodate whites who were
Christianizing the Plains Indians. By the 1840s railroads had replaced stagecoaches
between many eastern towns, although to get to New Orleans in 1848 Whitman
had to change from railroad to stagecoach to steamboat. Despite frequent train
wrecks, steamboat explosions, and Atlantic shipwrecks, by the 1850s travel had
ceased to be the hazardous adventure it had been. But the few American writers
who saw much of the country were still provincials in their practical attitude toward
their literary careers, for their publishers and purchasers were concentrated mainly
in or near New York, Philadelphia, and Boston.

And the New York, Philadelphia, and Boston of this period were themselves
tiny in comparison to their modern size. The site of Brook Farm, now long since
a victim of urban sprawl, was chosen because it was nine miles remote from Boston
and two miles away from the nearest farm. The population of New York City at
the start of the 1840s was only a third of a million and was concentrated in lower
Manhattan: Union Square was the edge of town. Horace Greeley, the editor of the
*New York Tribune*, escaped the bustle of the city by living on a ten-acre farm up
the East River on Turtle Bay, where the East Fifties are now; there he and his wife
provided a bucolic retreat for Margaret Fuller when she was his literary critic and
metropolitan reporter. In 1853 the Crystal Palace, an exposition of arts, crafts, and
sciences, created in imitation of the great Crystal Palace at the London World's
Fair of 1851, failed—largely because it was too far out of town, up west of the new

Croton Water Reservoir that had recently brought running water to the city. The reservoir was on the spot where the New York Public Library now stands, at Forty-second Street and Fifth Avenue, and the Crystal Palace was on the site of the modern Bryant Park, named for the nature poet.

### THE ECONOMICS OF AMERICAN LETTERS

Geography and modes of transportation bore directly on publishing procedures in the United States of this period. For a long time writers who wanted to publish a book carried the manuscript to a local printer and paid job rates to have it printed and bound. Longfellow worked in this fashion with a firm in Brunswick, Maine, when he printed his translation of *Elements of French Grammar* and other text-books during his first years as a teacher. Fiction was also sometimes sent to a local printer, as when Longstreet had his own firm in Augusta print *Georgia Scenes* or when Johnson Jones Hooper paid a firm in Tuscaloosa, Alabama, to print *A Ride with Old Kit Kuncker* before having it brought out the next year by a regular Philadelphia publisher. However, the true publishing centers were major seaports that could receive the latest British books by the fastest ships and, hastily reprinting them, distribute them inland by river traffic as well as in coastal cities. After 1820 the leading publishing towns were New York and Philadelphia, with the Erie Canal soon giving New York an advantage in the Ohio trade. Boston remained only a provincial publishing center until after 1850, when publishers realized the value of the new railroad connections to the West. Despite the aggressive merchandising techniques of a few firms, the creation of a national book-buying market for literature, especially American literature, was long delayed.

The problem was that the economic interests of American publisher-booksellers were antithetical to the interests of American writers. A national copyright law became effective in the United States in 1790, but it was 1891 before American writers had international protection and foreign writers received protection in the United States. Until the end of the century, American printers routinely pirated English writers, paying nothing to Sir Walter Scott or Charles Dickens for their novels, which were rushed into print and sold very cheaply in New York, Philadelphia, and other cities. American readers benefited from the situation, for they could buy the best British—and Continental—writings cheaply, but American writers suffered, because if they were to receive royalties, their books had to be priced above the prices charged for works of the most famous British writers. American publishers were willing to carry a few native novelists and poets as prestige items for a while, but they were businesspeople, not philanthropists.

To compound the problem, Irving's apparent conquest of the British publishing system, by which he received large sums for *The Sketch Book* and succeeding volumes, proved delusory. Cooper and others followed in Irving's track and were paid by magnanimous British publishers under a system whereby works first printed in Great Britain were presumed to hold a British copyright. But this practice was ruled illegal by a British judge in 1849, and the British market dried up for American writers.

Throughout this period, making a serious American contribution to the literature of the world was no guarantee at all of monetary rewards. Except possibly for a few authors of sentimental best-sellers, including what Hawthorne jealously called "that damned mob of scribbling women," the United States was not a country in which one could make a living by writing. It was not even a place where the best authors could always publish what they wrote. The only writers who could consistently find a publisher were Irving and Cooper, who kept their appeal on the basis of early success (though more copies had to be sold to make the same profit) and the magazine or newspaper editors who could fill some of their own columns when they wanted. These editors included (for various periods of time) Poe, Longstreet, Harris, Thorpe, Hooper, Lowell, and four other notable examples: Fuller, who for several years reported for the *New York Tribune* at home and from Europe; Whitman, who for much of the 1840s and 1850s was free to editorialize in one Brooklyn or Manhattan newspaper or another; Whittier, who for more than two decades before the Civil War was corresponding editor of the *Washington National Era*; and most conspicuous, Bryant, long-time owner of the *New York Evening Post*. Whitman was his own publisher for most editions of *Leaves of Grass* and filled mail orders himself, as Thoreau also did when an occasional request came for one of the seven hundred copies of his first book, which the publisher had turned back to him. At crucial moments in his career Melville was balked from writing what he wanted to write, as when he sacrificed his literary aspirations after the failure of *Mardi* and wrote *Redburn* and *White-Jacket*, which he regarded as mere drudgery; and at other times he was "prevented from publishing" works he had written, including at least one that was subsequently destroyed. Ironically, the writer freest to pursue literary greatness in this period was probably Emily Dickinson, whose "letter to the world" remained unmailed during her lifetime.

## THE QUEST FOR AN AMERICAN LITERARY DESTINY

In the first half of the nineteenth century, lobbying for the existence of an American literature in magazines seemed to take up more space than the literature itself. Especially after the War of 1812 confirmed American independence, theorists called for a great literature that would match the emerging political greatness of the nation. Huckstering critics soon developed specific notions as to the subjects that would-be writers should choose: preferably the distant colonial past (the nearest we could hope to come to the medieval settings that were serving Sir Walter Scott so well), or possibly American Indian legends, or still less desirable (because too near the mundane present), subjects from the recent Revolutionary past. Such exhortations were the stock-in-trade of commencement speakers and literary critics in the 1820s and 1830s. But in *The Poet* (1842) Emerson boldly called for a poet who would write of the United States as it was, not as it might have been:

> We have yet had no genius in America, with tyrannous eye, which knew the value of our incomparable materials, and saw, in the barbarism and materialism of the times, another carnival of the same gods whose picture he so much admires in Homer; then in the middle age; then in Calvinism. Banks and tariffs, the newspaper and caucus, methodism and unitarianism, are flat and dull to dull people, but rest on the same foundations of wonder as the town of Troy, and the temple of Delphos, and are as swiftly passing away. Our logrolling, our stumps and their politics, our fisheries, our Negroes, and Indians, our boasts, and our repudiations, the wrath of rogues, and the pusillanimity of honest men, the northern trade, the southern planting, the western clearing, Oregon, and Texas, are yet unsung. Yet America is a poem in our eyes; its ample geography dazzles the imagination, and it will not wait long for metres.

Later Whitman was to say that he had remained simmering, simmering, until Emerson brought him to a boil.

During the 1840s Evert A. Duyckinck and other New York literary men and women (primarily through the columns of the *Democratic Review* and the *Literary World*) mustered a squad of promoters of the great literature that was to come. The propagandists perfected the rhetorical strategy of linking literary destiny to geography and political destiny: the "great nation of futurity" must have a literature to match Niagara Falls and the Rocky Mountains. Herman Melville for several years was associated with Duyckinck's magazines, and he half-champions and half-spoofs the chauvinistic rhetoric in the essay on Hawthorne that he wrote for the *Literary World* in 1850. An American, he proclaimed, was "bound to carry republican progressiveness into Literature, as well as into Life," even to the point of believing that sooner or later American writers would rival Shakespeare, whom a generation of Bardolators regarded as unapproachable. This was literary manifest destiny with a vengeance, warranted only because as he wrote the essay Melville had already written his way well into what he later titled *Moby-Dick.*

None of the American writers of the period was chauvinistic enough to think that a great American literature could be written without reference to past English and European literature. As Cooper protested in *Notions of the Americans* (1828), writers in the United States possessed the same literary heritage that writers in Great Britain did. Shakespeare, Spenser, Milton, Bunyan, Addison, Pope, Fielding, Johnson, and Burns, along with many others (especially some now neglected writers of the eighteenth century) were the possession of all educated Americans born in the late eighteenth century or early in the nineteenth. Americans were not long behind the British in responding to the Romantics Wordsworth and Coleridge, then to Byron, Moore, and Scott. By the 1830s Carlyle was a force in the lives of several American writers through his translations of recent German philosophical works and his own jeremiads against contemporary British values. Americans had access to the latest British and continental discussions of art, religion, politics, and science, for British magazines, especially the quarterly reviews, were imported promptly and widely reprinted. Nineteenth-century American writing reveals its full meanings only in the light of European influences and parallel developments.

THE NEW AMERICANNESS OF AMERICAN LITERATURE

Despite the cultural cross-connections with Europe, the best literature that emerged in the United States was distinctively new, and a few perceptive critics very early began trying to define its special quality. This analysis from the review of *The Whale* (the English title of *Moby-Dick*) in the London *Leader* had currency in America as well, for the popular *Harper's New Monthly Magazine* quoted it approvingly:

> Want [lack] of originality has long been the just and standing reproach to American literature; the best of its writers were but second-hand Englishmen. Of late some have given evidence of originality, not *absolute* originality, but such genuine outcomings of the American intellect as can be safely called national. Edgar Poe, Nathaniel Hawthorne, Herman Melville are assuredly no British offshoots; nor is Emerson—the *German* American that he is! The observer of this commencement of an American literature, properly so called, will notice as significant that these writers have a wild and mystic love of the supersensual, peculiarly their own. To move a horror skilfully, with something of the earnest faith in the Unseen, and with weird imagery to shape these Phantasms so vividly that the most incredulous mind is hushed, absorbed—to do this no European pen has apparently any longer the power— to do this American literature is without a rival. What *romance* writer can be named with Hawthorne? Who knows the terrors of the seas like Herman Melville?"

Plainly, this was meant as praise, but to employ "weird imagery" to "move a horror skilfully" was hardly the ambition of any American writer of the period besides Poe; for their part Hawthorne and Melville were not concerned with the supernatural except as stage devices for heightening their psychological analyses.

But literary historians have not improved much on the reviewer in the *Leader* in deciding what was American about American literature. American writers were not achieving originality in form: Irving's sentences were accepted as models of English prose style precisely because they were themselves modeled on the sentences of Addison and Goldsmith, long the prime exemplars of decorous English prose. Melville's sentences often looked like those of whatever powerful master of the English language he had most recently been reading—Shakespeare, Milton, Burton, Taylor, Sterne, De Quincey, or Carlyle. Nor was the content of the best American writing of this period original in anything like an "absolute" sense. Modern scholars have shown that in his most "American" stories, *Rip Van Winkle* and *The Legend of Sleepy Hollow*, Irving drew on, and even closely translated, parts of German tales. In *Moby-Dick* Melville's metaphysics are recognizably of the generation of Goethe, Byron, and Carlyle. Thoreau's recurrent ideas came mainly from Emerson (at least Emerson himself insisted they did), but Emerson had picked them up from dozens of ancient and modern philosophers.

Yet, as everyone in the country sensed by the 1850s, there was some elusive quality about its new literature that was *American*. Irving's German-influenced stories were profoundly moving to Americans, who knew more than most Britons what it was to feel the trauma of rapid change, especially to experience repeated physical uprootings, and Americans found in the ne'er-do-well Rip a model for making a success of failure. In Cooper's novels was a sense of the immensity of physical nature and the power of human beings to destroy nature that most European writers could experience only vicariously. In Melville's *Moby-Dick* was a sense (long suppressed in European consciousness) of the grandeur of the physical universe and of the place of human beings in that universe. In *Leaves of Grass* Whitman undertook another elemental task—to become the national poet of a new people on a new continent. What proved most enduringly "American" about Emerson was his wide streak of Yankee individualism best displayed in *Self-Reliance*, which became an inspiration to thousands of Americans who were determined to hitch their wagons, as Emerson said, to a star. Even Thoreau's *Walden*, which many contemporaries took merely as an American counterpart of the English naturalist Gilbert White's *Natural History and Antiquities of Selbourne*, was in fact consciously an American counterscripture, a Franklinesque retort to Poor Richard, a how-to book on getting a living by working at what you love. At a time when grandiloquence in political rhetoric was often taken for eloquence, Abraham Lincoln mastered both the majestic cadences of the King James Version of the Bible and the extravagant toughness of backwoods tall talk. Dickinson's poems in their minute intensity were as ambitious as Whitman's, magnificent attempts to define her experience at whatever cost in wrenched syntax and rhyme. At best, beyond question, American writers were accomplishing things yet unattempted in the English language.

THE AESTHETICS OF A NATIONAL LITERATURE

The great writers of the period for the most part defined their aesthetic problems by themselves, though Emerson's *The Poet* aided some of the others. The primary difficulty of how to keep from being secondhand English writers had not been squarely faced by the theorists of nationality in literature, who most often seemed to think that adoption of an American setting or, more vaguely, the infusion of an American "spirit" guaranteed Americanness. Insofar as the issues had been addressed by Americans before the 1840s, it was primarily by painters and sculptors, the most prominent of whom had received their training abroad but then had found it impossible to reconcile their European notions of noble subject and style with Americanness. The Hudson River school of painters, led by Thomas Cole, found a pantheistic majesty in American landscapes not anticipated by the history-filled landscapes of European painting. Some of Cole's own work was marred by a tendency to allegorize as inveterate as Hawthorne's own, but others of the Hudson River school, including Frederic Edwin Church, faced in North—and South—America a New World, a landscape with primeval power both to awe and to destroy. Artistic tributes could be as clichéd as Whitman's catalogs (everyone from Church to T. B. Thorpe painted inevitable Niagaras), but Church's rediscovered

*Icebergs* (1861) is only a decade away from *Moby-Dick*, a work by a spirit that was in truth kindred. Other Americans, notably Martin Johnson Heade, born the same year as Melville, found compelling mystery not only in the exotica of South America but also in the salt hay marshes and low coasts of New England. The genre painters who formed so conspicuous a part of the artistic establishment— Melville's and Whitman's acquaintance William Sidney Mount, for instance— were pleasantly but unchallengingly continuing the familiar Dutch tradition— familiar from paintings brought across the Atlantic by Dutch settlers as well as those more recently brought over. Of the major writers of the period Whitman, from his friendships with the members of the Brooklyn Art Union in the early 1850s, was exposed to controversies in art in time to have them affect his poetry— his own aesthetic statements reflect Horatio Greenough's championship of the nude and his disparagement of mere embellishment. Most of the writers, despite the theorizing about painting and sculpting and the actual painting and sculpting available for them to see, were pretty much on their own when they were solving their crucial aesthetic problems—such as Hawthorne's attempts to strike a balance between the allegorical and the realistic, Emerson's difficulty in achieving unity from the mutually repellent particles of his thought, Thoreau's attempts to unite the Transcendentalist and the naturalist in himself, Whitman's struggle to domesticate the epic catalog without falling into self-parody, Melville's attempt to create a tragedy in a democracy, and Dickinson's attempt to walk the hairline between mere coyness and psychological precision.

### THE WRITERS AND THEIR AMERICA

When the great American writers of the mid-nineteenth century took stock of their country, they sometimes caught the contagion of an ebullient, expansionist mood that struck many observers as the dominant one of the time, and even Thoreau, the most relentless critic of the values of his society, insisted that to some extent he counted himself among "those who find their encouragement and inspiration in precisely the present condition of things, and cherish it with the fondness and enthusiasm of lovers." But often they felt a profound alienation. Emerson was a preacher who had renounced his pulpit, and the other great writers—also preachers without pulpits—devoted much of their artistic effort to analyzing conditions of life in America and to exhorting their fellow citizens to live more wisely.

### CONFORMITY, MATERIALISM, AND THE ECONOMY

The eccentricity of Americans, especially in rural areas and smaller towns, was notorious among visitors from abroad and was recorded in some of its aspects by writers as diverse as Longstreet, Harris, Melville, and Stowe. In Stowe's novels of the late 1850s and early 1860s there is a gallery of portraits of such mentally angular or gnarled characters. In Amherst, Emily Dickinson out-Thoreaued Thoreau in her resolute privacy, idiosyncrasies, and individuality. But she could be understood in relation to real and fictional characters. The night her correspondent Thomas Wentworth Higginson met her in 1870 he strove to convey her character in a letter to his wife without staying up too late; "if you had read Mrs. Stoddard's novels you could understand a house where each member runs his or her own selves." Despite such powerful individualists, it seemed to some of the writers that Americans, even while deluding themselves that they were the most self-reliant populace in the world, were systematically selling out their individuality. Emerson sounded the alarm: "Society everywhere is in conspiracy against the manhood of every one of its members. Society is a joint-stock company in which the members agree for the better securing of his bread to each shareholder, to surrender the liberty and culture of the eater. The virtue in most request is conformity." In *The Celestial Railroad* Hawthorne satirically described the condition at the Vanity Fair of modern America, where there was a "species of machine for the wholesale manufacture of individual morality." He went on: "This excellent result is effected by societies for all manner of virtuous purposes; with which a man has merely to connect himself, throwing, as it were, his quota of virtue into the common stock; and the president and directors will take care that the aggregate amount be well applied." Thoreau repeatedly satirized America as a nation of joiners that tried to force every newcomer "to belong to their desperate odd-fellow society": to Thoreau, members of the Odd Fellows and other social organizations were simply not odd *enough*, not individual enough.

But none of the writers found anything comical in the wholesale loss of Yankee individualism as both men and women deserted worn-out farms for factories, where many began to feel what Emerson called "the disproportion between their faculties and the work offered them." Far too often, the search for a better life had degenerated into a desire to possess factory-made objects. "Things are in the saddle," Emerson said sweepingly, "and ride mankind." In elaboration of that accusation, Thoreau wrote *Walden* as a treatise on expanding the spiritual life by simplifying material wants. Informing Thoreau's outrage at the materialism of his time was the bitter knowledge that even the most impoverished were being led to waste their money (and, therefore, their lives) on trumpery. In a vocabulary echoing Benjamin Franklin, he condemned the emerging consumer economy that was devoted, even in the infancy of advertising, to the creation of "artificial wants" for things that were unneeded or outright pernicious. And to counter the loss of an archetypal Yankee virtue, he made himself into a jack-of-all-trades and strong master of one, the art of writing. In strangely different ways the four to speak out most profoundly about the emerging American economic system were Melville, Stowe, Whitman, and Harding.

### SEX AND SEXUAL ROLES

At a time when sex was banished from the magazines and from almost all books except medical treatises, Whitman alone called for a healthy sense of the relation between body and soul and created a forum for discussing sexual joy and anguish. The other male writers made no challenge to conventional sexual roles; when Emerson, for instance, said that society "is in conspiracy against the manhood of every one of its members," he meant "*manhood*," not "manhood and womanhood." Only Whitman among the male authors regularly employed what we would call nonsexist language, and only Whitman rejected the opinion that woman's proper "sphere" was a limited, subservient, supportive one. While the attitudes of most male—and female—writers of the time reflected and embodied the prevailing sexism, Whitman rejected the "empty dish, gallantry" as a degraded attitude: "This tepid wash, this diluted deferential love, as in songs, fictions, and so forth, is enough to make a man vomit." Instead, he insisted on equality: "Women in These States approach the day of that organic equality with me, without which, I see, men cannot have organic equality among themselves." Of the other writers only Margaret Fuller thought so deeply about sexual roles. Ironically, as the mother of a tardily acknowledged child (and perhaps not the wife of its Italian father), Fuller was an incalculable threat to the little Boston literary society in the months before her death by shipwreck prevented her arrival home. Of the women writers of the time, Dickinson, who never married, was the most bitterly ironic observer of the sacrifices marriage often required of a woman, as in her depiction of the bride who "rose to His Requirement—dropt / The Playthings of Her Life / To take the honorable Work / Of Woman, and of Wife," and Elizabeth Stoddard, overshadowed by her husband, wrote controlled, ironic analyses of the restricted roles women were allowed to assume. But women had no monopoly on sexual anguish. Melville, who as a young man had known the pagan Eden of the South Seas, found that the claims of his intellect and imagination, his pursuit of a literary career, could not be met while also meeting the claims of his wife and children. And Whitman, the only writer of the period to advance a "Programme" for honest depiction of sex in literature, privately recorded the torments he endured from his homoerotic longings.

### NATURE

In "a new country," Thoreau said, "fuel is an encumbrance," and his generation acted as if trees existed to be burned (and mountains to be graded and wild animals to be slaughtered). But while Thoreau faced the possibility that like villains we might grub our forests all up, "poaching on our own national domains," he had no deep anxiety that primeval nature like the Maine woods would be destroyed. Melville was likewise sure that the whale would not perish: "hunted from the savannas and glades of the middle seas, the whale-bone whales can at last resort to their Polar citadels, and diving under the ultimate glassy barriers and walls there, come up among icy fields and floes; and in a charmed circle of everlasting December, bid defiance to all pursuit from man." Of the major writers of the period, Emerson, Thoreau, and Whitman felt an intensity of communion with nature that warrants their being called nature-mystics, and Dickinson, bounded by town lots and fields near her house in Amherst, found a profoundly un-Christian, "Druidic difference" that enhanced nature for her with a sense of harmony between it and human beings. The writers diverged in their wider views of the universe, Melville describing in *Moby-Dick* the maddening of a cabin boy abandoned in the immensity of ocean, and Thoreau, by contrast, insisting that he was not lonely at Walden. "Why should I feel lonely? is not our planet in the Milky Way?" But whatever their sense of the place of human beings in the cosmos, they all found nature a force in their lives in ways out of keeping with the times, when the Romantic sense of nature as restorer and healer of humankind seemed to persist, as Thoreau pointed out, in the absurd form of uneasy rest-day strollers anxious to pass their allotted time in the woods and return to town.

### ORTHODOX RELIGION AND TRANSCENDENTALISM

All the major writers found themselves at odds with the dominant religion of their time, a nominal Protestant Christianity that exerted practical control over what could be printed in books and magazines. This church, Emerson said, acted "as if God were dead." Whitman was more bitter still: "The churches are one vast lie; the people do not believe them, and they do not believe themselves." The writers all came of Protestant backgrounds in which Calvinism was more or less watered down (less in the cases of Melville and Dickinson), but they tended to apply absolute standards toward what passed for Christianity. In *The Celestial Railroad* Hawthorne memorably satirized the American urge to be progressive and liberal in theology as well as in politics, and Melville extended the satire throughout an entire book, *The Confidence-Man*.

Awareness of the fact of religious ecstasy was not at issue. Emerson, for instance, showed in *The Over-Soul* a clinical sense of the varieties of religious experience, the "varying forms of that shudder of awe and delight with which the individual soul always mingles with the universal soul." Similarly, Thoreau acknowledged the validity of the "second birth and peculiar religious experience" available to the "solitary hired man on a farm in the outskirts of Concord" but felt that any religious denomination in America would pervert that mystical experience into something available only under its auspices and something to be brought into line with its particular doctrines. Like Thoreau, Whitman saw all religious ecstasy as equally valid and came forth in *Song of Myself* outbidding "the old cautious hucksters" like Jehovah, Kronos, Zeus, and Hercules, gods who held too low an estimate of the value of men and women. Among these writers Melville was alone in his anguish at the realization that Christianity was impracticable. Melville also felt the brutal power of the Calvinistic Jehovah with special keenness: human beings were "god-bullied" even as the hull of the *Pequod* was in *Moby-Dick*, and the best way people had of demonstrating their own divinity lay in defying the omnipotent tyrant. To Dickinson also God was a bully—a "Mastiff," whom subservience might, or might not, appease. In a series of novels Harriet Beecher Stowe best described the way rigid Calvinism could cripple young minds.

Transcendentalism in the late 1830s and early 1840s was treated in newspapers and magazines as something between a national laughingstock and a clear menace to organized religion. The running journalistic joke, which Hawthorne echoed in *The Celestial Railroad*, was that no one could define the term, other than that it was highfalutin, foreign, and obscurely dangerous. The conservative Christian view is well represented by a passage that appeared in Stowe's newspaper serialization of *Uncle Tom's Cabin* (1851) but was omitted from the book version, a sarcastic indictment of the reader who might find it hard to believe that Tom could be stirred by a passage in the Bible: "I mention this, of course, philosophic friend, as a psychological phenomenon. Very likely it would do no such a thing for you, because you are an enlightened man, and have out-grown the old myths of past centuries. But then you have Emerson's Essays and Carlyle's Miscellanies, and other productions of the latter day, suited to your advanced development." Such early observers understood well enough that Transcendentalism was more pantheistic than Christian. The "defiant Pantheism" infusing Thoreau's shorter pieces helped keep them out of the magazines, and James Russell Lowell for the *Atlantic Monthly* publication of a section of *The Maine Woods* censored a sentence in which Thoreau declared that a pine tree was as immortal as he was and perchance would "go to as high a heaven."

Melville also was at least once kept from publication by the religious scruples of the magazines, and often he was harshly condemned for what he had managed to publish. For years he bore the wrath of reviewers such as the one who denounced him for writing *Moby-Dick* and the Harpers for publishing it: "The Judgment day will hold him liable for not turning his talents to better account, when, too, both authors and publishers of injurious books will be cojointly answerable for the influence of those books upon the wide circle of immortal minds on which they have written their mark. The book-maker and the book-publisher had better do their work with a view to the trial it must undergo at the bar of God." The ultimate result was that Melville was silenced. This was extreme, but Emerson, Thoreau, and Whitman all suffered in comparable ways for transgressing the code of the Doctors of Divinity (Thoreau said he wished it were not the D.D.'s but the chickadee-dees who acted as censors). Lowell himself indiscriminately censored Thoreau, Whitman, and Stoddard.

### IMMIGRATION AND XENOPHOBIA

However threatened conservative Protestants felt by Transcendentalism and by religious speculations like Melville's, they felt far more threatened by Catholicism when refugees from the Napoleonic Wars were followed by refugees from oppressed and famine-struck Ireland. In Boston, Lyman Beecher, father of Harriet Beecher Stowe, thundered out antipapist sermons, then professed dismay when in 1834 a mob in Charlestown, across the Charles River from Boston, burned the Ursuline Convent School where daughters of many wealthy families were educated. Through the 1830s and 1840s and long afterward, the country was saturated with lurid books and pamphlets purporting to reveal the truth about sexual practices in nunneries and monasteries (accounts of how priests and nuns disposed of their babies were specially prized) and about the pope's schemes to take over the Mississippi Valley (Samuel F. B. Morse and others warned that Jesuits were prowling the Ohio Valley, in disguise). An extreme of xenophobia was reached in the summer of 1844, when rioters in Philadelphia (the city, everyone pointed out, of brotherly love) burned Catholic churches and a seminary. Melville was replying to the current hostility when he followed a description of the pestilent conditions of steerage passengers in emigrant ships with this plea: "Let us waive that agitated national topic, as to whether such multitudes of foreign poor should be landed on our American shores; let us waive it, with the one only thought, that if they can get here, they have God's right to come; though they bring all Ireland and her miseries with them. For the whole world is the patrimony of the whole world; there is no telling who does not own a stone in the Great Wall of China."

For all his humanitarian eloquence, Melville, like the other writers, realized that the new immigrants were changing the country from the cozy, homogeneous land it had been, or had seemed to be. By the end of the Civil War many native Americans shared Stowe's profound nostalgia for the days before the railroads, before the influx of Catholics, before the even more alien influx of immigrants from Southern and Eastern Europe, few of whom spoke English and many of whom were not Christian at all. The view of many in the literary establishment was reflected by Thomas Bailey Aldrich in *The Stillwater Tragedy* (1880): what you do with the widow and children of the unionizing Italian (once he has conveniently and agonizingly died) is ship them back to Italy.

POLITICS AND WARS

The major writers of the period lived with the anguishing paradox that the most idealistic nation in the world was implicated in continuing national sins: the near-genocide of the American Indians (whole tribes in colonial times had already become, in Melville's phrase for the Massachusetts Pequots, as extinct as the ancient Medes), the enslavement of blacks, and (partly a by-product of slavery) the staged "Executive's War" against Mexico, started by President Polk before being declared by Congress. Emerson was an exception, but most writers were silent about the successive removal of eastern Indian tribes to less desirable lands west of the Mississippi River, as legislated by the Indian Removal Act of 1830. American destiny plainly required a little practical callousness, most whites felt, in a secular version of the colonial notion that God had willed the extirpation of the American Indian. The imperialistic Mexican War was so gaudily exotic—and so distant— that only a small minority of American writers voiced more than perfunctory opposition; an exception was Thoreau, who spent a night in the Concord jail in symbolic protest against being taxed to support the war.

It was black slavery, what Melville called "man's foulest crime," which most stirred the consciences of the white writers, and in describing his own enslavement, the fugitive Frederick Douglass developed a notable capacity to stir readers as well as audiences in the lecture halls. When the Fugitive Slave Law was enforced in Boston in 1851 (by Melville's father-in-law, Chief Justice Shaw), Thoreau worked his outrage into his journals; then after another famous case in 1854 he combined the experiences into his most scathing speech, *Slavery in Massachusetts*, for delivery at a Fourth of July countercelebration at which a copy of the Constitution was burned because slavery was written into it. In that speech Thoreau summed up the disillusionment that many of his generation shared. He had felt a vast but indefinite loss after the 1854 case, he said: "I did not know at first what ailed me. At last it occurred to me that what I had lost was a country." (Successive generations of American writers would experience the same trauma: Howells, Twain, and others when the United States turned from savior to conqueror in the Philippines after the Spanish-American War; Robert Lowell and many others after it became clear that the involvement of the United States in Vietnam was not purely a gesture of compassion toward a grateful, beleaguered nation.) More obliquely than Thoreau, Melville explored black slavery in *Benito Cereno* as an index to the emerging national character. At his bitterest, he felt in the mid-1850s that "free Ameriky" was "intrepid, unprincipled, reckless, predatory, with boundless ambition, civilized in externals but a savage at heart."

John Brown's raid on Harpers Ferry in 1859, immediately repudiated by the new Republican party, drew from the now tubercular Thoreau a passionate defense. During the Civil War itself, Lincoln found the genius to suit diverse occasions with right language and length of utterance, but the major writers fell silent. When the war began on April 12, 1861, with the firing of Confederate guns on Fort Sumter, in Charleston harbor, Irving, Cooper, Poe, and Fuller were dead (the younger two earlier than the older two), and before Robert E. Lee's surrender to Ulysses S. Grant at Appomattox, Virginia, on April 9, 1865, Thoreau had been dead three years and Hawthorne one. Some writers in this anthology had in their ways, directly and indirectly, helped to bring the war on: Lincoln was not wholly jesting if in fact he called Stowe "the little woman who had started the big war"; Whittier had by 1861 devoted decades of his life to the struggle against slavery, arousing furious resistance to him both in the North and in the South; and Douglass's oratory had revealed to many white Northerners a sense of the evils of slavery and the humanness of those of another race (or of mixed races). Firebrand Yankees such as Thoreau and firebrand Southerners such as G. W. Harris had roused the passions of at least some members of their own communities and regions. When the war came, most Northern writers were slow to have a sense of its reality. As Rebecca Harding saw during her visit to Concord in 1862, fresh from a portion of a slave state that had chosen to stay with the Union, Emerson had no notion what suffering was involved. Hawthorne, who received her with enthusiasm, had faced the start of the war as a Southern sympathizer in a village that had welcomed John Brown, then had seen Washington in wartime, and retained, as he always did, a practical politician's sense of things. It was for many Northerners an oddly informal war. A man did not have to go when he was drafted: Dickinson's brother Austin was drafted in 1864 but paid five hundred dollars for a substitute to be hired. Dickinson, who at first felt the war as "an oblique place," worried about the wounding of the "preceptor" she had not yet seen, Thomas Wentworth Higginson, earlier a co-conspirator with John Brown, then in 1862 the commander of the first black regiment, the First South Carolina Volunteers. When his son Charley ran away to join the Union Army, Longfellow had Senator Charles Sumner forward boxes to the boy and was baffled if they did not arrive promptly; he fussed about Charley's not having his rubber overcoat, and sent him a servant and two horses. Melville went down to camp to see a soldier cousin and, borrowing a flannel shirt, went along on a scouting party. Henry James's brother Wilkinson, injured at Charleston when Colonel Robert Gould Shaw's black regiment was half-slaughtered in July 1863, was saved by the civilian father of his closest friend, who did not find the son he was hunting for among the wounded, but found Wilky and delivered him on a stretcher to the James home in Newport. Whitman went to seek his wounded brother, passing piles of amputated limbs on his way to the field hospital, and stayed, nursing the wounded in Washington hospitals, in the single most courageous sacrifice any of these writers made to the war. All the Northern writers felt the reality before the war was over. James Russell Lowell was not a greatly exceptional case in losing three nephews.

Simply because the South was almost exclusively the battlefield, Southerners lived more immediately with the horrors of wounding and death than did most Northerners, and because the South became effectively blockaded from medical supplies and other necessities, Southern civilians suffered directly in deprivation of food, disruption of livelihoods, forced evacuations, and destroyed property as well as deaths of friends and family members. Harris and Longstreet were made refugees; Simms's magnificent library at Woodlands was burned by stragglers from Sherman's army, with the loss (among other riches) of many letters from Poe and many letters from Evert Duyckinck (which must have contained mentions of Poe, Melville, and other writers, especially New Yorkers and Southerners).

None of the writers in this anthology fought in the war, though Thorpe held federal office in occupied New Orleans. A younger Connecticut writer, John William DeForest, recruited a company of volunteers at New Haven and served through the war as their captain. His *The First Time under Fire*, published in the September 1864 *Harper's*, deserves to be better known and may find a place in some future edition of this anthology; surely in the opening of the nineteenth-century canon his *Miss Ravenel's Conversion from Secession to Loyalty* will be taught in survey courses as a supplemental text. Samuel L. Clemens after a brief fling at patrolling in Missouri (an episode he later winsomely if speciously recorded in *The Private History of a Campaign that Failed*) saw the war out safely in the west; William Dean Howells sat it out in Venice; and Henry James, seeing both younger brothers off to the war, the opening of which coincided with his suffering what he called an "obscure" injury, spent the war years in Newport and Cambridge. No writer really escaped it, and for most of them, as for most citizens, it was a chasm in personal and national history. In *Clarel* (1876) Melville called the winter of 1860–61 a "sad arch between contrasted eras"; his modern critics have forgivably misapplied the words to the years 1861–65.

DeForest's masterpiece aside, the war did not soon evoke great fiction, but Melville's uneven *Battle-Pieces* (1866) included some remarkable meditative poems as well as the technically interesting *Donelson*, in which he conveyed vividly the anxiety of civilians awaiting news during a prolonged and dubious battle and eagerly reading aloud the latest bulletins posted outside the telegraph office. (His contemporaries such as Richard Henry Stoddard liked best the brisk derivative poems such as *Sheridan's Ride*.) Whitman's *Drum-Taps* (1865) also is uneven but contains several great poems. After a few copies had been dispersed, Whitman held back the edition for a "Sequel" mainly consisting of newly written poems on Lincoln, among them *When Lilacs Last in the Dooryard Bloom'd*, the greatest literary work to come out of the war and one of the world's great elegies. Both volumes summed up the national experience. Both writers looked ahead as well as backward, Whitman calling "reconciliation" the "word over all," and Melville urging in a prose "Supplement" that the victorious North "be Christians toward our fellow-whites, as well as philanthropists toward the blacks, our fellow-men." Later in *Specimen Days* Whitman made a memorable attempt to do the impossible—to put the real war realistically into a book.

Both Whitman and Melville, especially in their later years, saw American politics cease to be concerned with great national struggles over momentous issues; rather, politics meant corruption, on a petty or a grand scale. Melville lived out the Gilded Age as an employee at the notoriously corrupt Custom House in New York City. In *Clarel*, foreseeing a descent from the present "civic barbarism" to "the Dark Ages of Democracy," he portrayed his American pilgrims to the Holy Land as recognizing sadly that the time might come to honor the God of Limitations in what had been the Land of Opportunity, a time when Americans might cry: "To Terminus build fanes! / Columbus ended earth's romance: / No New World to mankind remains!"

### THE HEROISM OF AMERICAN WRITERS

Against a society that often lost sight of principles, whether aesthetic, social, or political, Emerson offered the challenge that the other great writers took up: "Let us affront and reprimand the smooth mediocrity and squalid contentment of the times, and hurl in the face of custom, and trade, and office, the fact which is the upshot of all history, that there is a great responsible Thinker and Actor moving wherever moves a man: that a true man belongs to no other time or place, but is the centre of things." In the same spirit Melville looked bravely at the risks that lay beyond the imitation of Irving:

> But the graceful writer, who perhaps of all Americans has received the most plaudits from his own country for his productions,—that very popular and

amiable writer, however good, and self-reliant in many things, perhaps owes his chief reputation to the self-acknowledged imitation of a foreign model, and to the studied avoidance of all topics but smooth ones. But it is better to fail in originality, than to succeed in imitation. He who has never failed somewhere, that man can not be great. Failure is the true test of greatness.

In the same spirit Whitman commanded his readers: "Re-examine all you have been told at school or church or in any book, dismiss whatever insults your own soul, and your very flesh shall be a great poem and have the richest fluency not only in its words but in the silent lines of its lips and face and between the lashes of your eyes and in every motion and joint of your body." As Emerson had warned them they must, the great writers of this time relinquished "display and immediate fame" to wrestle, in Melville's phrase, "with the angel—Art," making their writings into classics from which later generations, and sometimes even their own, would date eras in their lives. As the selections in this volume demonstrate, all of Emerson's great fellow writers fervently shared his conviction that "nothing is of any value in books, excepting the transcendental and extraordinary."

---

# WASHINGTON IRVING
## 1783–1859

Washington Irving, the first American to achieve an international literary reputation, was born in New York City on April 3, 1783, the last of eleven children of a Scottish-born father and English-born mother. Well into his thirties his brothers routinely tried to make plans for him, and his own devotion to his family was a dominant emotion throughout his life. He read widely in English literature at home, modeling his early prose on the graceful *Spectator* papers by Joseph Addison, but delighted by many other writers, including Shakespeare, Oliver Goldsmith, and Laurence Sterne. His brothers enjoyed writing poems and essays as pleasant, companionable recreation, and at nineteen Irving wrote a series of satirical essays on the theater and New York society for his brother Peter's newspaper, the *Morning Courier*.

When Irving showed signs of tuberculosis in 1804, his brothers sent him abroad for a two-year tour of Europe, where in his notebooks he steadily became an acute observer and felicitous recorder of what he witnessed. On his return, he began studying law with Judge Josiah Hoffman, but more important for his career, he and his brother William (along with William's brother-in-law, James Kirke Paulding) started an anonymous satirical magazine, *Salmagundi* (the name of a spicy hash), which ran through 1807 with sketches and poems on politics and drama as well as familiar essays on a great range of topics. Then in 1808 Irving began work on A *History of New York*, at first conceiving it as a parody of Samuel Latham Mitchell's pompously titled *The Picture of New-York; or The Traveller's Guide through the Commercial Metropolis of the United States*, then taking on a variety of satiric targets, including President Jefferson, whom he portrayed as an early Dutch governor of New Amsterdam, William the Testy. Exuberant, broadly comic, the *History* spoofed historians' pedantries but was itself the result of many months of antiquarian reading in local libraries, where his researches gave Irving refuge from grief over the sudden death of Judge Hoffman's daughter Matilda, to whom he had become engaged. Then the *History* was launched by a charming publicity campaign. First a newspaper noted the disappearance of a "small elderly gentleman, dressed in an old black coat and cocked hat, by the name of KNICK-ERBOCKER," adding that there were "some reasons for believing he is not entirely in his right mind." After further "news" items the old man's fictitious landlord announced that he had found in Knickerbocker's room a *"very curious kind of a written book"* which he intended to dispose of to pay the bill that was owed him, and the book at last appeared, ascribed to Diedrich Knickerbocker. With its publication Irving became an American celebrity. Reprinted in England, the *History* reached Sir Walter Scott, who declared that it made his sides hurt from laughter. Like all but the rarest of topical satires, however, it has become increasingly inaccessible to later generations of readers, who can hardly comprehend Irving's strategies and targets without precisely the sort of antiquarian footnotes he found delight in mocking.

During the War of 1812 Irving was editor of the *Analectic Magazine*, which he filled mainly with essays from British periodicals but where he printed his own timely series of patriotic biographical sketches of American naval heroes. Toward the end of the war he was made a colonel in the New York State Militia. Then in May 1815, a major break occurred in his life: he left for Europe and stayed away for seventeen years. At first he worked in Liverpool with his brother Peter, an importer of English hardware. In 1818 Peter went bankrupt, shortly after their mother died in New York; profoundly grieved and shamed, Irving once again took refuge in writing. During his work on *The Sketch Book* he met Scott, who buoyed him by admiration for the *History* and helpfully directed Irving's attention to the wealth of unused literary material in German folktales; there, as scholars have shown, Irving found the source for *Rip Van Winkle*, some passages of which are close paraphrases of the original. In 1819 Irving began sending *The Sketch Book* to the United States for publication in installments. When the full version was printed in England the next year, it made Irving famous and brought him the friendship of many of the leading British writers of the time. His new pseudonym, Geoffrey Crayon, became universally recognized, and over the next years selections from *The Sketch Book* entered the classroom as models of English prose just as selections from Addison had long been used. As Irving knew, part of his British success derived from general astonishment that a man born in the United States could write in such an English way about English scenes: Addison lay behind the sketches of English country life, just as Oliver Goldsmith's essays on the Boar's-head Tavern in Eastcheap and on Westminster Abbey lay behind Irving's on the same topics. But in among the graceful, tame tributes to English scenes and characters were two vigorous tales set in rural New York, *Rip Van Winkle* and *The Legend of Sleepy Hollow*. Everyone who read them knew instantly that they were among the literary treasures of the language, and it very soon became hard to remember that they had not always been among the English classics.

Irving's next book, *Bracebridge Hall* (1822), a worshipful tribute to old-fashioned English country life, was, as the author realized, a feeble follow-up, and *Tales of a Traveller* (1824) was widely taken as a sign that he had written himself out. At a loss to sustain his career, Irving gambled on accepting an invitation from an acquaintance, the American minister to Spain: he was to come to Spain as an attaché of the legation (a device for giving him entrée into manuscript collections) and translate Martín Fernández de Navarrete's new compilation of accounts of the voyages of Columbus, including Columbus's own lost journals as copied by an earlier historian. Helped by the American consul in Madrid, Obadiah Rich, who owned a magnificent collection of books and manuscripts on Spanish and Latin American history, Irving worked intensely and in 1828 published *The Life and Voyages of Christopher Columbus*, not a translation of Navarrete (though the Spaniard's volume supplied most of the facts) but a biography of Irving's own, shaped by his skill at evocative re-creation of history. Out of these Spanish years came also *The Conquest of Granada* (1829), *Voyages and Discoveries of the Companions of Columbus* (1831), and *The Alhambra* (1832), which became known as "the Spanish *Sketch Book*."

In 1829 Irving was appointed secretary to the American legation in London,

where he became a competent, hardworking diplomat, aided by his access to the
highest levels of British society. No longer the latest rage, Irving by now was a
solidly established author. On his return to the United States in 1832 his reputation
was in need of redemption from a different charge—that of becoming too Europeanized. As if in an effort to make amends, Irving turned to three studies of the
American West: A *Tour on the Prairies* (1835), based on his horseback journey into
what is now Oklahoma; *Astoria* (1836), an account of John Jacob Astor's fur-trad-
ing colony in Oregon, written in Astor's own library and based on published
accounts as well as research in Astor's archives (in which task Irving was assisted by
his nephew Peter); and *The Adventures of Captain Bonneville, U.S.A.* (1837), an
account of a Frenchman's explorations in the Rockies and the Far West.

In the late 1830s Irving bought and began refurbishing a house near Tarrytown,
along the Hudson north of New York City, just where he had dreamed of settling
down in *The Legend of Sleepy Hollow*. At Sunnyside he made a home for several
members of his family, including as many as five nieces at a time, but he wrote
little. From this somewhat purposeless stage of his life he was rescued by appointment as minister to Spain in 1842; he served four years in Madrid with great
success. After his return he arranged with G. P. Putnam to publish a collected
edition of his writings and took the occasion to revise some of them. Using essays
he had written years before, he also prepared for the edition a derivative biography
of Oliver Goldsmith (1849), after which critics more than ever compared him to
the Irish prince of hack writers. Irving's main work after 1851 was his long-contem-
plated life of George Washington. He worked in libraries, read old newspapers,
studied government records, and visited battlefields, but once again he drew very
heavily on published biographies, especially the recent one by Jared Sparks. He
forced himself, in the most heroic effort of his career, to complete the successive
five volumes, the first of which was published in 1855. Just after finishing the last
he collapsed, and died a few months later, on November 28, 1859.

Decades before his death, Irving had achieved the status of a classic writer; in
his own country he had no rival as a stylist. As schoolboys, Hawthorne and Longfellow were inspired by the success of *The Sketch Book*, and their prose, as well as
that of a horde of now-unread writers, owed much to Irving. Although Melville,
in his essay on Hawthorne's *Mosses from an Old Manse*, declared his preference
for creative geniuses over adept imitators like Irving, he could not escape Irving's
influence, which emerges both in his short stories and in a late poem, *Rip Van
Winkle's Lilacs*, which showed he saw Rip as an archetypal artist figure. (Melville's
debt was even more tangible, for early in 1846 Irving had passed the word to
Putnam that *Typee* was worth reprinting in New York, but then Irving had been
generous to younger writers all his life, as in his supervision of the London publication of Bryant's poems in 1832.) The southwestern humorists of the 1840s, whom
Irving read and enjoyed, were much more robust than Irving in his mature years,
yet they learned from him that realistic details of rural life in America could be
worked memorably into fiction. From the beginning, Americans identified with
Rip as a counterhero, an anti-Franklinian who made a success of failure, and
successive generations have responded profoundly to Irving's pervasive theme of
mutability, especially as localized in his portrayal of the bewildering and destructive rapidity of change in American life.

# Rip Van Winkle[1]

[The following Tale was found among the papers of the late Diedrich Knickerbocker, an old gentleman of New-York, who was very curious in the Dutch

1. *Rip Van Winkle* was the last of the sketches printed in the May 1819 first installment of *The Sketch Book*, the
source of the present text.

history of the province, and the manners of the descendants from its primitive settlers. His historical researches, however, did not lay so much among books, as among men; for the former are lamentably scanty on his favourite topics; whereas he found the old burghers, and still more, their wives, rich in that legendary lore, so invaluable to true history. Whenever, therefore, he happened upon a genuine Dutch family, snugly shut up in its low-roofed farm house, under a spreading sycamore, he looked upon it as a little clasped volume of black-letter,[2] and studied it with the zeal of a bookworm.

The result of all these researches was a history of the province, during the reign of the Dutch governors, which he published some years since. There have been various opinions as to the literary character of his work, and, to tell the truth, it is not a whit better than it should be. Its chief merit is its scrupulous accuracy, which, indeed, was a little questioned, on its first appearance, but has since been completely established;[3] and it is now admitted into all historical collections, as a book of unquestionable authority.

The old gentleman died shortly after the publication of his work, and now, that he is dead and gone, it cannot do much harm to his memory, to say, that his time might have been much better employed in weightier labours. He, however, was apt to ride his hobby his own way; and though it did now and then kick up the dust a little in the eyes of his neighbours, and grieve the spirit of some friends, for whom he felt the truest deference and affection; yet his errors and follies are remembered "more in sorrow than in anger,"[4] and it begins to be suspected, that he never intended to injure or offend. But however his memory may be appreciated by critics, it is still held dear among many folk, whose good opinion is well worth having; particularly certain biscuit bakers, who have gone so far as to imprint his likeness on their new year cakes, and have thus given him a chance for immortality, almost equal to being stamped on a Waterloo medal, or a Queen Anne's farthing.[5]]

### Rip Van Winkle
#### A Posthumous Writing of Diedrich Knickerbocker

> By Woden, God of Saxons,
> From whence comes Wensday, that is Wodensday,
> Truth is a thing that ever I will keep
> Unto thylke day in which I creep into
> My sepulchre—
>
> —Cartwright[6]

Whoever has made a voyage up the Hudson, must remember the Kaatskill mountains. They are a dismembered branch of the great Appalachian family, and are seen away to the west of the river, swelling up to a noble height, and

2. Typeface in early printed books, resembling medieval script; such books, because of their value, were often equipped with clasps so they could be shut tightly and even locked.
3. Irving knew that most of his first readers would remember with delight the wildly inaccurate Knickerbocker *History*. He is also echoing Cervantes' humorous assurance of accuracy at the outset of *Don Quixote*.
4. Shakespeare's *Hamlet* 1.1.231–32. To this quotation Irving appended the following footnote: "Vide [see] the excellent discourse of G. C. Verplanck, Esq. before the New-York Historical Society." If Irving's

friend Gulian C. Verplanck ever made such an address, it was in fun.
5. Irving's irony cuts in different directions: Waterloo medals were minted liberally after the defeat of Napoleon in 1815, whereas farthings (tiny coins) from the reign of Queen Anne of England (1702–14) were commonly, though wrongly, considered rare, one story saying only three were minted.
6. In this quotation from *The Ordinary*, 3.1.1050–54, a play by the English writer William Cartwright (1611–1643), the speaker is a pedant named Moth. "Woden": Norse god of war.

lording it over the surrounding country. Every change of season, every change of weather, indeed, every hour of the day, produces some change in the magical hues and shapes of these mountains, and they are regarded by all the good wives, far and near, as perfect barometers. When the weather is fair and settled, they are clothed in blue and purple, and print their bold outlines on the clear evening sky; but some times, when the rest of the landscape is cloudless, they will gather a hood of gray vapours about their summits, which, in the last rays of the setting sun, will glow and light up like a crown of glory.

At the foot of these fairy mountains, the voyager may have descried the light smoke curling up from a village, whose shingle roofs gleam among the trees, just where the blue tints of the upland melt away into the fresh green of the nearer landscape. It is a little village of great antiquity, having been founded by some of the Dutch colonists, in the early times of the province, just about the beginning of the government of the good Peter Stuyvesant,[7] (may he rest in peace!) and there were some of the houses of the original settlers standing within a few years, with lattice windows, gable fronts surmounted with weathercocks, and built of small yellow bricks brought from Holland.

In that same village, and in one of these very houses, (which, to tell the precise truth, was sadly time worn and weather beaten,) there lived many years since, while the country was yet a province of Great Britain, a simple good natured fellow, of the name of Rip Van Winkle. He was a descendant of the Van Winkles who figured so gallantly in the chivalrous days of Peter Stuyvesant, and accompanied him to the siege of Fort Christina. He inherited, however, but little of the martial character of his ancestors. I have observed that he was a simple good natured man; he was moreover a kind neighbour, and an obedient, henpecked husband. Indeed, to the latter circumstance might be owing that meekness of spirit which gained him such universal popularity; for those men are most apt to be obsequious and conciliating abroad, who are under the discipline of shrews at home. Their tempers, doubtless, are rendered pliant and malleable in the fiery furnace of domestic tribulation, and a curtain lecture[8] is worth all the sermons in the world for teaching the virtues of patience and long suffering. A termagant wife may, therefore, in some respects, be considered a tolerable blessing; and if so, Rip Van Winkle was thrice blessed.

Certain it is, that he was a great favourite among all the good wives of the village, who, as usual with the amiable sex, took his part in all family squabbles, and never failed, whenever they talked those matters over in their evening gossippings, to lay all the blame on Dame Van Winkle. The children of the village, too, would shout with joy whenever he approached. He assisted at their sports, made their playthings, taught them to fly kites and shoot marbles, and told them long stories of ghosts, witches, and Indians. Whenever he went dodging about the village, he was surrounded by a troop of them, hanging on his skirts, clambering on his back, and playing a thousand tricks on him with impunity; and not a dog would bark at him throughout the neighbourhood.

The great error in Rip's composition was an insuperable aversion to all kinds of profitable labour. It could not be for the want of assiduity or perseverance; for he would sit on a wet rock, with a rod as long and heavy as a Tartar's lance,

---

7. Peter Stuyvesant (1592–1672), last governor of the Dutch province of New Netherlands, in 1655 (as mentioned below) defeated Swedish colonists at Fort Chris- tina, near what is now Wilmington, Delaware.
8. Tirade delivered by a wife after the curtains around the four-poster bed have been drawn for the night.

and fish all day without a murmur, even though he should not be encouraged by a single nibble. He would carry a fowling piece on his shoulder, for hours together, trudging through woods and swamps, and up hill and down dale, to shoot a few squirrels or wild pigeons. He would never even refuse to assist a neighbour in the roughest toil, and was a foremost man at all country frolicks for husking Indian corn, or building stone fences; the women of the village, too, used to employ him to run their errands, and to do such little odd jobs as their less obliging husbands would not do for them;—in a word, Rip was ready to attend to any body's business but his own; but as to doing family duty, and keeping his farm in order, it was impossible.

In fact, he declared it was no use to work on his farm; it was the most pestilent little piece of ground in the whole country; every thing about it went wrong, and would go wrong, in spite of him. His fences were continually falling to pieces; his cow would either go astray, or get among the cabbages; weeds were sure to grow quicker in his fields than any where else; the rain always made a point of setting in just as he had some out-door work to do. So that though his patrimonial estate had dwindled away under his management, acre by acre, until there was little more left than a mere patch of Indian corn and potatoes, yet it was the worst conditioned farm in the neighbourhood.

His children, too, were as ragged and wild as if they belonged to nobody. His son Rip, an urchin begotten in his own likeness, promised to inherit the habits, with the old clothes of his father. He was generally seen trooping like a colt at his mother's heels, equipped in a pair of his father's cast-off galligas-kins,[9] which he had much ado to hold up with one hand, as a fine lady does her train in bad weather.

Rip Van Winkle, however, was one of those happy mortals, of foolish, well-oiled dispositions, who take the world easy, eat white bread or brown, which ever can be got with least thought or trouble, and would rather starve on a penny than work for a pound. If left to himself, he would have whistled life away, in perfect contentment; but his wife kept continually dinning in his ears about his idleness, his carelessness, and the ruin he was bringing on his family. Morning, noon, and night, her tongue was incessantly going, and every thing he said or did was sure to produce a torrent of household eloquence. Rip had but one way of replying to all lectures of the kind, and that, by frequent use, had grown into a habit. He shrugged his shoulders, shook his head, cast up his eyes, but said nothing. This, however, always provoked a fresh volley from his wife, so that he was fain to draw off his forces, and take to the outside of the house—the only side which, in truth, belongs to a henpecked husband.

Rip's sole domestic adherent was his dog Wolf, who was as much henpecked as his master; for Dame Van Winkle regarded them as companions in idleness, and even looked upon Wolf with an evil eye, as the cause of his master's so often going astray. True it is, in all points of spirit befitting an honourable dog, he was as courageous an animal as ever scoured the woods—but what courage can withstand the ever-during and all-besetting terrors of a woman's tongue? The moment Wolf entered the house, his crest fell, his tail drooped to the ground, or curled between his legs, he sneaked about with a gallows air, casting many a sidelong glance at Dame Van Winkle, and at the least flourish of a broomstick or ladle, would fly to the door with yelping precipitation.

9. Loose, wide breeches.

Times grew worse and worse with Rip Van Winkle as years of matrimony rolled on; a tart temper never mellows with age, and a sharp tongue is the only edge tool that grows keener by constant use. For a long while he used to console himself, when driven from home, by frequenting a kind of perpetual club of the sages, philosophers, and other idle personages of the village, that held its sessions on a bench before a small inn, designated by a rubicund portrait of his majesty George the Third. Here they used to sit in the shade, of a long lazy summer's day, talk listlessly over village gossip, or tell endless sleepy stories about nothing. But it would have been worth any statesman's money to have heard the profound discussions that sometimes took place, when by chance an old newspaper fell into their hands, from some passing traveller. How solemnly they would listen to the contents, as drawled out by Derrick Van Bummel, the schoolmaster, a dapper learned little man, who was not to be daunted by the most gigantic word in the dictionary; and how sagely they would deliberate upon public events some months after they had taken place.

The opinions of this junto[1] were completely controlled by Nicholas Vedder, a patriarch of the village, and landlord of the inn, at the door of which he took his seat from morning till night, just moving sufficiently to avoid the sun, and keep in the shade of a large tree; so that the neighbours could tell the hour by his movements as accurately as by a sun dial. It is true, he was rarely heard to speak, but smoked his pipe incessantly. His adherents, however, (for every great man has his adherents,) perfectly understood him, and knew how to gather his opinions. When any thing that was read or related displeased him, he was observed to smoke his pipe vehemently, and send forth short, frequent, and angry puffs; but when pleased, he would inhale the smoke slowly and tranquilly, and emit it in light and placid clouds, and sometimes taking the pipe from his mouth, and letting the fragrant vapour curl about his nose, would gravely nod his head in token of perfect approbation.

From even this strong hold the unlucky Rip was at length routed by his termagant wife, who would suddenly break in upon the tranquillity of the assemblage, call the members all to nought, nor was that august personage, Nicholas Vedder himself, sacred from the daring tongue of this terrible virago, who charged him outright with encouraging her husband in habits of idleness.

Poor Rip was at last reduced almost to despair; and his only alternative to escape from the labour of the farm and the clamour of his wife, was to take gun in hand, and stroll away into the woods. Here he would sometimes seat himself at the foot of a tree, and share the contents of his wallet[2] with Wolf, with whom he sympathised as a fellow sufferer in persecution. "Poor Wolf," he would say, "thy mistress leads thee a dogs' life of it; but never mind, my lad, while I live thou shalt never want a friend to stand by thee!" Wolf would wag his tail, look wistfully in his master's face, and if dogs can feel pity, I verily believe he reciprocated the sentiment with all his heart.

In a long ramble of the kind on a fine autumnal day, Rip had unconsciously scrambled to one of the highest parts of the Kaatskill mountains. He was after his favourite sport of squirrel shooting, and the still solitudes had echoed and re-echoed with the reports of his gun. Panting and fatigued, he threw himself, late in the afternoon, on a green knoll, covered with mountain herbage, that

---

1. Ruling committee (Spanish).          2. Knapsack.

crowned the brow of a precipice. From an opening between the trees, he could overlook all the lower country for many a mile of rich woodland. He saw at a distance the lordly Hudson, far, far below him, moving on its silent but majestic course, the reflection of a purple cloud, or the sail of a lagging bark, here and there sleeping on its glassy bosom, and at last losing itself in the blue highlands.

On the other side he looked down into a deep mountain glen, wild, lonely, and shagged, the bottom filled with fragments from the impending cliffs, and scarcely lighted by the reflected rays of the setting sun. For some time Rip lay musing on this scene, evening was gradually advancing, the mountains began to throw their long blue shadows over the valleys, he saw that it would be dark long before he could reach the village, and he heaved a heavy sigh when he thought of encountering the terrors of Dame Van Winkle.

As he was about to descend, he heard a voice from a distance, hallooing, "Rip Van Winkle! Rip Van Winkle!" He looked around, but could see nothing but a crow winging its solitary flight across the mountain. He thought his fancy must have deceived him, and turned again to descend, when he heard the same cry ring through the still evening air; "Rip Van Winkle! Rip Van Winkle!"—at the same time Wolf bristled up his back, and giving a low growl, skulked to his master's side, looking fearfully down into the glen. Rip now felt a vague apprehension stealing over him; he looked anxiously in the same direction, and perceived a strange figure slowly toiling up the rocks, and bending under the weight of something he carried on his back. He was surprised to see any human being in this lonely and unfrequented place, but supposing it to be some one of the neighbourhood in need of his assistance, he hastened down to yield it.

On nearer approach, he was still more surprised at the singularity of the stranger's appearance. He was a short square built old fellow, with thick bushy hair, and a grizzled beard. His dress was of the antique Dutch fashion—a cloth jerkin[3] strapped round the waist—several pair of breeches, the outer one of ample volume, decorated with rows of buttons down the sides, and bunches at the knees. He bore on his shoulder a stout keg, that seemed full of liquor, and made signs for Rip to approach and assist him with the load. Though rather shy and distrustful of this new acquaintance, Rip complied with his usual alacrity, and mutually relieving each other, they clambered up a narrow gully, apparently the dry bed of a mountain torrent. As they ascended, Rip every now and then heard long rolling peals, like distant thunder, that seemed to issue out of a deep ravine, or rather cleft between lofty rocks, toward which their rugged path conducted. He paused for an instant, but supposing it to be the muttering of one of those transient thunder showers which often take place in mountain heights, he proceeded. Passing through the ravine, they came to a hollow, like a small amphitheatre, surrounded by perpendicular precipices, over the brinks of which impending trees shot their branches, so that you only caught glimpses of the azure sky, and the bright evening cloud. During the whole time, Rip and his companion had laboured on in silence; for though the former marvelled greatly what could be the object of carrying a keg of liquor up this wild mountain, yet there was something strange and incomprehensible about the unknown, that inspired awe, and checked familiarity.

3. Jacket fitted tightly at the waist.

On entering the amphitheatre, new objects of wonder presented themselves. On a level spot in the centre was a company of odd-looking personages playing at nine-pins. They were dressed in a quaint, outlandish fashion: some wore short doublets,[4] others jerkins, with long knives in their belts, and most had enormous breeches, of similar style with that of the guide's. Their visages, too, were peculiar: one had a large head, broad face, and small piggish eyes; the face of another seemed to consist entirely of nose, and was surmounted by a white sugarloaf hat, set off with a little red cockstail. They all had beards, of various shapes and colours. There was one who seemed to be the commander. He was a stout old gentleman, with a weather-beaten countenance; he wore a laced doublet, broad belt and hanger,[5] high crowned hat and feather, red stockings, and high heeled shoes, with roses in them. The whole group reminded Rip of the figures in an old Flemish painting, in the parlour of Dominie[6] Van Schaick, the village parson, and which had been brought over from Holland at the time of the settlement.

What seemed particularly odd to Rip, was, that though these folks were evidently amusing themselves, yet they maintained the gravest faces, the most mysterious silence, and were, withal, the most melancholy party of pleasure he had ever witnessed. Nothing interrupted the stillness of the scene, but the noise of the balls, which, whenever they were rolled, echoed along the mountains like rumbling peals of thunder.

As Rip and his companion approached them, they suddenly desisted from their play, and stared at him with such fixed statue-like gaze, and such strange, uncouth, lack lustre countenances, that his heart turned within him, and his knees smote together. His companion now emptied the contents of the keg into large flagons, and made signs to him to wait upon the company. He obeyed with fear and trembling; they quaffed the liquor in profound silence, and then returned to their game.

By degrees, Rip's awe and apprehension subsided. He even ventured, when no eye was fixed upon him, to taste the beverage, which he found had much of the flavour of excellent Hollands.[7] He was naturally a thirsty soul, and was soon tempted to repeat the draught. One taste provoked another, and he re-iterated his visits to the flagon so often, that at length his senses were overpowered, his eyes swam in his head, his head gradually declined, and he fell into a deep sleep.

On awaking, he found himself on the green knoll from whence he had first seen the old man of the glen. He rubbed his eyes—it was a bright sunny morning. The birds were hopping and twittering among the bushes, and the eagle was wheeling aloft, and breasting the pure mountain breeze. "Surely," thought Rip, "I have not slept here all night." He recalled the occurrences before he fell asleep. The strange man with the keg of liquor—the mountain ravine—the wild retreat among the rocks—the wo-begone party at nine-pins— the flagon—"Oh! that flagon! that wicked flagon!" thought Rip—"what excuse shall I make to Dame Van Winkle?"

He looked round for his gun, but in place of the clean well-oiled fowling-piece, he found an old firelock lying by him, the barrel encrusted with rust, the lock falling off, and the stock worm-eaten. He now suspected that the grave

---

4. Male garment covering from neck to upper thighs,        6. Minister.
where it hooked to hose.                                   7. Kind of gin.
5. Short, curved sword.

roysters of the mountain had put a trick upon him, and having dosed him with liquor, had robbed him of his gun. Wolf, too, had disappeared, but he might have strayed away after a squirrel or partridge. He whistled after him, shouted his name, but all in vain; the echoes repeated his whistle and shout, but no dog was to be seen.

He determined to revisit the scene of the last evening's gambol, and if he met with any of the party, to demand his dog and gun. As he arose to walk he found himself stiff in the joints, and wanting in his usual activity. "These mountain beds do not agree with me," thought Rip, "and if this frolick should lay me up with a fit of the rheumatism, I shall have a blessed time with Dame Van Winkle." With some difficulty he got down into the glen: he found the gully up which he and his companion had ascended the preceding evening, but to his astonishment a mountain stream was now foaming down it, leaping from rock to rock, and filling the glen with babbling murmurs. He, however, made shift to scramble up its sides, working his toilsome way through thickets of birch, sassafras, and witch hazle, and sometimes tripped up or entangled by the wild grape vines that twisted their coils and tendrils from tree to tree, and spread a kind of network in his path.

At length he reached to where the ravine had opened through the cliffs, to the amphitheatre; but no traces of such opening remained. The rocks presented a high impenetrable wall, over which the torrent came tumbling in a sheet of feathery foam, and fell into a broad deep basin, black from the shadows of the surrounding forest. Here, then, poor Rip was brought to a stand. He again called and whistled after his dog; he was only answered by the cawing of a flock of idle crows, sporting high in air about a dry tree that overhung a sunny precipice; and who, secure in their elevation, seemed to look down and scoff at the poor man's perplexities. What was to be done? the morning was passing away, and Rip felt famished for his breakfast. He grieved to give up his dog and gun; he dreaded to meet his wife; but it would not do to starve among the mountains. He shook his head, shouldered the rusty firelock, and, with a heart full of trouble and anxiety, turned his steps homeward.

As he approached the village, he met a number of people, but none that he knew, which somewhat surprised him, for he had thought himself acquainted with every one in the country round. Their dress, too, was of a different fashion from that to which he was accustomed. They all stared at him with equal marks of surprise, and whenever they cast eyes upon him, invariably stroked their chins. The constant recurrence of this gesture, induced Rip, involuntarily, to do the same, when, to his astonishment, he found his beard had grown a foot long!

He had now entered the skirts of the village. A troop of strange children ran at his heels, hooting after him, and pointing at his gray beard. The dogs, too, not one of which he recognized for his old acquaintances, barked at him as he passed. The very village seemed altered: it was larger and more populous. There were rows of houses which he had never seen before, and those which had been his familiar haunts had disappeared. Strange names were over the doors—strange faces at the windows—every thing was strange. His mind now began to misgive him, that both he and the world around him were bewitched. Surely this was his native village, which he had left but the day before. There stood the Kaatskill mountains—there ran the silver Hudson at a distance— there was every hill and dale precisely as it had always been—Rip was sorely

perplexed—"That flagon last night," thought he, "has addled my poor head
sadly!"

It was with some difficulty he found the way to his own house, which he
approached with silent awe, expecting every moment to hear the shrill voice
of Dame Van Winkle. He found the house gone to decay—the roof fallen in,
the windows shattered, and the doors off the hinges. A half starved dog, that
looked like Wolf, was skulking about it. Rip called him by name, but the cur
snarled, showed his teeth, and passed on. This was an unkind cut indeed—
"My very dog," sighed poor Rip, "has forgotten me!"

He entered the house, which, to tell the truth, Dame Van Winkle had
always kept in neat order. It was empty, forlorn, and apparently abandoned.
This desolateness overcame all his connubial fears—he called loudly for his
wife and children—the lonely chambers rung for a moment with his voice,
and then all again was silence.

He now hurried forth, and hastened to his old resort, the little village inn—
but it too was gone. A large ricketty wooden building stood in its place, with
great gaping windows, some of them broken, and mended with old hats and
petticoats, and over the door was painted, "The Union Hotel, by Jonathan
Doolittle." Instead of the great tree that used to shelter the quiet little Dutch
inn of yore, there now was reared a tall naked pole, with something on top
that looked like a red night cap,[8] and from it was fluttering a flag, on which
was a singular assemblage of stars and stripes—all this was strange and incomprehensible. He recognised on the sign, however, the ruby face of King
George, under which he had smoked so many a peaceful pipe, but even this
was singularly metamorphosed. The red coat was changed for one of blue and
buff,[9] a sword was stuck in the hand instead of a sceptre, the head was decorated with a cocked hat, and underneath was painted in large characters,
GENERAL WASHINGTON.

There was, as usual, a crowd of folk about the door, but none that Rip
recollected. The very character of the people seemed changed. There was a
busy, bustling, disputatious tone about it, instead of the accustomed phlegm
and drowsy tranquillity. He looked in vain for the sage Nicholas Vedder, with
his broad face, double chin, and fair long pipe, uttering clouds of tobacco
smoke instead of idle speeches; or Van Bummel, the schoolmaster, doling
forth the contents of an ancient newspaper. In place of these, a lean bilious
looking fellow, with his pockets full of handbills, was haranguing vehemently
about rights of citizens—election—members of congress—liberty—Bunker's
hill—heroes of seventy-six—and other words, that were a perfect Babylonish
jargon[1] to the bewildered Van Winkle.

The appearance of Rip, with his long grizzled beard, his rusty fowling piece,
his uncouth dress, and the army of women and children that had gathered at
his heels, soon attracted the attention of the tavern politicians. They crowded
around him, eyeing him from head to foot, with great curiosity. The orator
bustled up to him, and drawing him partly aside, inquired "which side he
voted?" Rip stared in vacant stupidity. Another short but busy little fellow

8. Limp, close-fitting cap adopted during the French
Revolution as a symbol of liberty; the pole is a "liberty
pole"—i.e., a tall flagstaff topped by a liberty cap.
9. Colors of the Revolutionary uniform. Irving's joke
is that the new proprietor, being a Yankee, is so parsi-

monious that he will only touch up the sign, not replace it with a true portrait of Washington.
1. Cf. Genesis 11.1–9, Babel being confused with
Babylon.

pulled him by the arm, and raising on tiptoe, inquired in his ear, "whether he was Federal or Democrat."[2] Rip was equally at a loss to comprehend the question; when a knowing, self-important old gentleman, in a sharp cocked hat, made his way through the crowd, putting them to the right and left with his elbows as he passed, and planting himself before Van Winkle, with one arm akimbo, the other resting on his cane, his keen eyes and sharp hat penetrating, as it were, into his very soul, demanded, in an austere tone, "what brought him to the election with a gun on his shoulder, and a mob at his heels, and whether he meant to breed a riot in the village?" "Alas! gentlemen," cried Rip, somewhat dismayed, "I am a poor quiet man, a native of the place, and a loyal subject of the King, God bless him!"

Here a general shout burst from the bystanders—"A tory! a tory! a spy! a refugee! hustle him! away with him!" It was with great difficulty that the self-important man in the cocked hat restored order; and having assumed a tenfold austerity of brow, demanded again of the unknown culprit, what he came there for, and whom he was seeking. The poor man humbly assured them that he meant no harm; but merely came there in search of some of his neighbours, who used to keep about the tavern.

"Well—who are they?—name them."

Rip bethought himself a moment, and inquired, "where's Nicholas Vedder?"

There was a silence for a little while, when an old man replied, in a thin piping voice, "Nicholas Vedder? why he is dead and gone these eighteen years! There was a wooden tombstone in the church yard that used to tell all about him, but that's rotted and gone too."

"Where's Brom Dutcher?"

"Oh he went off to the army in the beginning of the war; some say he was killed at the battle of Stoney-Point—others say he was drowned in a squall, at the foot of Antony's Nose.[3] I don't know—he never came back again."

"Where's Van Bummel, the schoolmaster?"

"He went off to the wars too, was a great militia general, and is now in Congress."

Rip's heart died away, at hearing of these sad changes in his home and friends, and finding himself thus alone in the world. Every answer puzzled him, too, by treating of such enormous lapses of time, and of matters which he could not understand: war—congress—Stoney-Point;—he had no courage to ask after any more friends, but cried out in despair, "does nobody here know Rip Van Winkle?"

"Oh, Rip Van Winkle!" exclaimed two or three, "Oh, to be sure! that's Rip Van Winkle yonder, leaning against the tree."

Rip looked, and beheld a precise counterpart of himself, as he went up the mountain: apparently as lazy, and certainly as ragged. The poor fellow was now completely confounded. He doubted his own identity, and whether he was himself or another man. In the midst of his bewilderment, the man in the cocked hat demanded who he was, and what was his name?

"God knows," exclaimed he, at his wit's end; "I'm not myself—I'm some-

2. Political parties that developed in the Washington administrations, Alexander Hamilton leading the Federalists and Thomas Jefferson, the Democrats.
3. A mountain near West Point. "Stoney Point": on the west bank of the Hudson south of West Point, captured by General Anthony Wayne (1745–1796) during the Revolution.

body else—that's me yonder—no—that's somebody else, got into my shoes—
I was myself last night, but I fell asleep on the mountain, and they've changed
my gun, and every thing's changed, and I'm changed, and I can't tell what's
my name, or who I am!"

The bystanders began now to look at each other, nod, wink significantly,
and tap their fingers against their foreheads. There was a whisper, also, about
securing the gun, and keeping the old fellow from doing mischief. At the very
suggestion of which, the self-important man in the cocked hat retired with
some precipitation. At this critical moment a fresh likely woman pressed
through the throng to get a peep at the graybearded man. She had a chubby
child in her arms, which, frightened at his looks, began to cry. "Hush, Rip,"
cried she, "hush, you little fool, the old man wont hurt you." The name of
the child, the air of the mother, the tone of her voice, all awakened a train of
recollections in his mind.

"What is your name, my good woman?" asked he.

"Judith Gardenier."

"And your father's name?"

"Ah, poor man, his name was Rip Van Winkle; it's twenty years since he
went away from home with his gun, and never has been heard of since—his
dog came home without him; but whether he shot himself, or was carried
away by the Indians, nobody can tell. I was then but a little girl."

Rip had but one question more to ask; but he put it with a faltering voice:
"Where's your mother?"

Oh, she too had died but a short time since; she broke a blood vessel in a fit
of passion at a New-England pedlar.

There was a drop of comfort, at least, in this intelligence. The honest man
could contain himself no longer.—He caught his daughter and her child in
his arms.—"I am your father!" cried he—"Young Rip Van Winkle once—old
Rip Van Winkle now!—Does nobody know poor Rip Van Winkle!"

All stood amazed, until an old woman, tottering out from among the crowd,
put her hand to her brow, and peering under it in his face for a moment,
exclaimed, "Sure enough! it is Rip Van Winkle—it is himself. Welcome
home again, old neighbour—Why, where have you been these twenty long
years?"

Rip's story was soon told, for the whole twenty years had been to him but as
one night. The neighbours stared when they heard it; some were seen to wink
at each other, and put their tongues in their cheeks; and the self-important
man in the cocked hat, who, when the alarm was over, had returned to the
field, screwed down the corners of his mouth, and shook his head—upon
which there was a general shaking of the head throughout the assemblage.

It was determined, however, to take the opinion of old Peter Vanderdonk,
who was seen slowly advancing up the road. He was a descendant of the historian of that name,[4] who wrote one of the earliest accounts of the province.
Peter was the most ancient inhabitant of the village, and well versed in all the
wonderful events and traditions of the neighbourhood. He recollected Rip at
once, and corroborated his story in the most satisfactory manner. He assured
the company that it was a fact, handed down from his ancestor the historian,
that the Kaatskill mountains had always been haunted by strange beings. That

---

4. Adriaen Van der Donck (1620–1655?) wrote a history of New Netherlands (1655).

it was affirmed that the great Hendrick Hudson, the first discoverer of the river and country, kept a kind of vigil there every twenty years, with his crew of the Half-moon, being permitted in this way to revisit the scenes of his enterprize, and keep a guardian eye upon the river, and the great city[5] called by his name. That his father had once seen them in their old Dutch dresses playing at nine pins in a hollow of the mountain; and that he himself had heard, one summer afternoon, the sound of their balls, like long peals of thunder.

To make a long story short, the company broke up, and returned to the more important concerns of the election. Rip's daughter took him home to live with her; she had a snug, well-furnished house, and a stout cheery farmer for a husband, whom Rip recollected for one of the urchins that used to climb upon his back. As to Rip's son and heir, who was the ditto of himself, seen leaning against the tree, he was employed to work on the farm; but evinced an hereditary disposition to attend to any thing else but his business.

Rip now resumed his old walks and habits; he soon found many of his former cronies, though all rather the worse for the wear and tear of time; and preferred making friends among the rising generation, with whom he soon grew into great favour.

Having nothing to do at home, and being arrived at that happy age when a man can do nothing with impunity, he took his place once more on the bench, at the inn door, and was reverenced as one of the patriarchs of the village, and a chronicle of the old times "before the war." It was some time before he could get into the regular track of gossip, or could be made to comprehend the strange events that had taken place during his torpor. How that there had been a revolutionary war—that the country had thrown off the yoke of old England—and that, instead of being a subject of his Majesty George the Third, he was now a free citizen of the United States. Rip, in fact, was no politician; the changes of states and empires made but little impression on him. But there was one species of despotism under which he had long groaned, and that was—petticoat government. Happily, that was at an end; he had got his neck out of the yoke of matrimony, and could go in and out whenever he pleased, without dreading the tyranny of Dame Van Winkle. Whenever her name was mentioned, however, he shook his head, shrugged his shoulders, and cast up his eyes; which might pass either for an expression of resignation to his fate, or joy at his deliverance.

He used to tell his story to every stranger that arrived at Mr. Doolittle's hotel. He was observed, at first, to vary on some points every time he told it, which was, doubtless, owing to his having so recently awaked. It at last settled down precisely to the tale I have related, and not a man, woman, or child in the neighbourhood, but knew it by heart. Some always pretended to doubt the reality of it, and insisted that Rip had been out of his head, and that this was one point on which he always remained flighty. The old Dutch inhabitants, however, almost universally gave it full credit. Even to this day they never hear a thunder storm of a summer afternoon, about the Kaatskill, but they say Hendrick Hudson and his crew are at their game of nine pins; and it is a common wish of all henpecked husbands in the neighbourhood, when life hangs heavy on their hands, that they might have a quieting draught out of Rip Van Winkle's flagon.

5. Henry Hudson (d. 1611), English navigator in the service of the Dutch. "Great city" is ironic, for the town named for him on the east bank of the Hudson River was flourishing but not a metropolis.

NOTE

The foregoing tale, one would suspect, had been suggested to Mr. Knicker-bocker by a little German superstition about Charles V.[6] and the Kypphauser mountain; the subjoined note, however, which he had appended to the tale, shows that it is an absolute fact, narrated with his usual fidelity:

"The story of Rip Van Winkle may seem incredible to many, but neverthe-less I give it my full belief, for I know the vicinity of our old Dutch settlements to have been very subject to marvellous events and appearances. Indeed, I have heard many stranger stories than this, in the villages along the Hudson; all of which were too well authenticated to admit of a doubt. I have even talked with Rip Van Winkle myself, who, when last I saw him, was a very venerable old man, and so perfectly rational and consistent on every other point, that I think no conscientious person could refuse to take this into the bargain; nay, I have seen a certificate on the subject taken before a country justice, and signed with a cross, in the justice's own hand writing. The story, therefore, is beyond the possibility of doubt.                                D.K."

1819

6. Later Irving changed "Charles V." (Holy Roman emperor 1519–1556) to "The Emperor Frederick der Rothbart" (i.e., Frederick Barbarossa; Holy Roman emperor 1152–1190). ("Rothbart" and "Barbarossa" both mean "redbeard.") In either form, the allusion is a red herring, a disarming way of suggesting indebtedness to a German source while concealing the most specific source, the story of Peter Klaus in the folktales of J. C. C. N. Otmar.

---

# JAMES FENIMORE COOPER
## 1789–1851

James Fenimore Cooper, the first successful American novelist, was born on September 15, 1789, in Burlington, New Jersey, but taken in infancy to Cooperstown, on Otsego Lake in central New York, where his wealthy father owned great tracts of land. A few years before, the region had been wilderness, but during Cooper's boyhood there were few of the early backwoods settlers left, and fewer American Indians; in his novels the information about Indian tribes came from older people and from books. In 1801 his father sent him to study in Albany in preparation for Yale, where he spent two years in his midteens before being expelled for pranks, thereby acquiring a lifelong distaste for New Englanders. He became a sailor in 1806, then two years later a midshipman in the navy. At twenty he inherited a fortune from his father and married Susan De Lancey, whose family had lost pos-sessions by siding with the British in the Revolution but still owned lands in West-chester County. For several years Cooper and his wife wavered between Scarsdale and Otsego as a permanent home. Wherever they settled, Cooper seemed certain to live as a landed gentleman. His first book, *Precaution* (1820), a novel dealing with English high society, was the result of his casual bet with his wife that he could write a better book than the one he had been reading to her. Following that insignificant start, he wrote *The Spy* (1821), the first important historical romance of the Revolution, and on its success he moved to New York City to take up his new career. From the first his faults (such as syntactical awkwardness, arbitrary plotting, and heavy-handed attempts at humor) were obvious enough, but so were his genuine achievements in opening up new American scenes and themes for fiction. Founding the Bread and Cheese Club, he became the center of a circle that included notable painters of the Hudson River school as well as writers (William Cullen Bryant among them) and professionals. In 1823 he published *The Pioneers*, the first of what eventually consisted of five books about Natty Bumppo, known collectively as the *Leather-Stocking Tales*; the second, *The Last of the Mohicans*, followed in 1826. Cooper has other claims to fame—the virtual creation of the sea novel (starting with *The Pilot*, 1824), authorship of the first serious American novels of manners and the first American sociopolitical novels—but with Natty Bumppo, the aged hunter, he had created one of the most popular characters in world literature.

In 1826, at the height of his fame, Cooper sailed for Europe. In Paris, where he became intimate with the aged Lafayette, he wrote *The Prairie* (1827) and *Notions of the Americans* (1828), a defense of the United States against the attacks of European travelers. Smarting under the half-complimentary, half-patronizing epithet of "The American Scott," he wrote three historical novels set in medieval Europe as a realistic corrective to Sir Walter Scott's glorifications of the past. On his return to the United States in 1833 Cooper was so stung by a review of one of these novels that he renounced novel writing in the angry *Letter to His Countrymen* (1834). Then at Cooperstown he gave notice that a point of land on Otsego Lake where the townspeople had been picnicking was private property and not to be used without permission. Newspapers began attacking him as a would-be aristocrat poisoned by his residence abroad, and for years Cooper embroiled himself in lawsuits designed not to gain damages for the journalistic libels but to tame the irresponsible press. Legally in the right, Cooper sacrificed his peace of mind to establish the principle that reviewers must work within the bounds of truth when they deal with the author rather than the book. Even as he was becoming the great national scold of his time, Cooper managed to write book after book—social and political satires growing out of his experiences with the press, a reactionary primer, *The American Democrat* (1838), and despite his avowal in 1834, a series of sociopolitical novels and two more *Leather-Stocking Tales: The Pathfinder* (1840), and *The Deerslayer* (1841). His monumental *History of the Navy of the United States of America* (1839) became the focus of new quarrels and a new lawsuit.

When Cooper died on September 14, 1851, a day before his sixty-second birthday, he was a byword for litigiousness and social pretentiousness. A lifelong defender of American democracy as he knew it in his youth against European aristocracy and then against what American democracy had become, he was out of step with his countrypeople. Yet throughout the century and into the next his *Leather-Stocking Tales* had an incalculable vogue in the United States and abroad. In his own time and shortly afterward major European writers as diverse as Honoré de Balzac and Leo Tolstoy were profoundly moved by *The Pioneers* and the subsequent Natty Bumppo novels, but gradually the *Leather-Stocking Tales* became something only schoolchildren read. Not until the 1920s did scholars begin to see Cooper's value as the country's first great social critic. It now seems clear that no revolution in taste will lead to widespread admiration of Cooper as a literary artist, but he will always be a major source for the student of ideas in America. Some of his opinions now seem hopelessly reactionary, as when he defends American slavery as legal and, after all, mild ("physical suffering cannot properly be enumerated among its evils") or when he deplores the dangers of universal manhood suffrage and argues for restricting voting on certain issues to property owners, who have the greater stake in society. What most appeals to modern readers are his profoundly ambivalent dramatizations of such enduring American conflicts as natural right versus legal right, order versus change, primeval wilderness versus civilization. And new readers will always encounter the *Leather-Stocking Tales* with a sense of something long known and loved, for if Cooper is no longer read even by children, everyone has read books—and seen films—that are directly and indirectly influenced by his grand conception of Natty Bumppo.

# *From* The Pioneers

## [*The Slaughter of the Pigeons*][1]

"Men, boys, and girls.
Desert th' unpeopled village; and wild crowds
Spread o'er the plain, by the sweet frenzy driven."[2]
—Somerville

From this time to the close of April, the weather continued to be a succession of great and rapid changes. One day, the soft airs of spring would seem to be stealing along the valley, and, in unison with an invigorating sun, attempting, covertly, to rouse the dormant powers of the vegetable world; while on the next, the surly blasts from the north would sweep across the lake, and erase every impression left by their gentle adversaries. The snow, however, finally disappeared, and the green wheat fields were seen in every direction, spotted with the dark and charred stumps that had, the preceding season, supported some of the proudest trees of the forest.[3] Ploughs were in motion, wherever those useful implements could be used, and the smokes of the sugar-camps[4] were no longer seen issuing from the summits of the woods of maple. The lake had lost all the characteristic beauty of a field of ice, but still a dark and gloomy covering concealed its waters, for the absence of currents left them yet hid under a porous crust, which, saturated with the fluid, barely retained enough of its strength to preserve the contiguity of its parts. Large flocks of wild geese were seen passing over the country, which would hover, for a time, around the hidden sheet of water, apparently searching for an opening, where they might obtain a resting-place; and then, on finding themselves excluded by the chill covering, would soar away to the north, filling the air with their discordant screams, as if venting their complaints at the tardy operations of nature.

For a week, the dark covering of the Otsego was left to the undisturbed possession of two eagles, who alighted on the centre of its field, and sat proudly eyeing the extent of their undisputed territory. During the presence of these monarchs of the air, the flocks of migrating birds avoided crossing the plain of ice, by turning into the hills, and apparently seeking the protection of the forests, while the white and bald heads of the tenants of the lake were turned upward, with a look of majestic contempt, as if penetrating to the very heavens, with the acuteness of their vision. But the time had come, when even these kings of birds were to be dispossessed. An opening had been gradually increasing, at the lower extremity of the lake, and around the dark spot where

1. *The Pioneers, or The Sources of the Susquehanna; A Descriptive Tale* (1823) is the first of five Cooper novels in which Natty Bumppo is the major character. The text is that of the 1st edition, chap. 3 (chap. 22 in later one-volume editions). *The Pioneers* begins in December 1793 at the settlement of Templeton (modeled on Cooperstown) at Otsego Lake in central New York, some fifty miles west of Albany. The episode reprinted here occurs in the spring of 1794. Natty Bumppo is in his early seventies, six feet tall (then a great height), gray-eyed, with lank, sandy hair, sunburned, robust, but thin almost to emaciation. One yellow tooth survives in his enormous mouth, and he gives forth a remarkable kind of inward laugh. He wears a foxskin hat and is clad in deerskin—coat, moccasins, and even the leggings, which fasten over the knees of his buckskin breeches and give him the nickname of Leather-stocking. For his old and unusually long rifle he carries gunpowder in an enormous ox horn slung over his shoulder by a strap of deerskin. This was the unprepossessing figure who captured the imagination of the United States and Europe.

2. From *The Chace*, 2.197–99, by the English poet William Somerville (1675–1742). The last word should be *seized*, not "driven."

3. The practice was to chop timber down in the spring, let it dry through the summer, then burn the cleared area so that only blackened logs and stumps remained. Nothing was salvaged except some ashes used as the basis for potash.

4. Where sugar was made from maple sap.

the current of the river had prevented the formation of ice, during even the coldest weather; and the fresh southerly winds, that now breathed freely up the valley, obtained an impression on the waters. Mimic waves begun to curl over the margin of the frozen field, which exhibited an outline of crystallizations, that slowly receded towards the north. At each step the power of the winds and the waves increased, until, after a struggle of a few hours, the turbulent little billows succeeded in setting the whole field in an undulating motion, when it was driven beyond the reach of the eye, with a rapidity, that was as magical as the change produced in the scene by this expulsion of the lingering remnant of winter. Just as the last sheet of agitated ice was disappearing in the distance, the eagles rose over the border of crystals, and soared with a wide sweep far above the clouds, while the waves tossed their little caps of snow into the air, as if rioting in their release from a thraldom of five months duration.

The following morning Elizabeth[5] was awakened by the exhilarating sounds of the martins, who were quarrelling and chattering around the little boxes which were suspended above her windows, and the cries of Richard,[6] who was calling, in tones as animating as the signs of the season itself—

"Awake! awake! my lady fair! the gulls are hovering over the lake already, and the heavens are alive with the pigeons. You may look an hour before you can find a hole, through which, to get a peep at the sun. Awake! awake! lazy ones! Benjamin[7] is overhauling the ammunition, and we only wait for our breakfasts, and away for the mountains and pigeon-shooting."

There was no resisting this animated appeal, and in a few minutes Miss Temple and her friend[8] descended to the parlour. The doors of the hall were thrown open, and the mild, balmy air of a clear spring morning was ventilating the apartment, where the vigilance of the ex-steward had been so long maintaining an artificial heat, with such unremitted diligence. All of the gentlemen, we do not include Monsieur Le Quoi,[9] were impatiently waiting their morning's repast, each being equipt in the garb of a sportsman. Mr. Jones made many visits to the southern door, and would cry—

"See, cousin Bess! see, 'duke![1] the pigeon-roosts of the south have broken up! They are growing more thick every instant. Here is a flock that the eye cannot see the end of. There is food enough in it to keep the army of Xerxes[2] for a month, and feathers enough to make beds for the whole county. Xerxes, Mr. Edwards,[3] was a Grecian king, who—no, he was a Turk, or a Persian, who wanted to conquer Greece, just the same as these rascals will overrun our wheat-fields, when they come back in the fall.—Away! away! Bess; I long to pepper them from the mountain."

In this wish both Marmaduke and young Edwards seemed equally to participate, for really the sight was most exhilarating to a sportsman; and the ladies soon dismissed the party, after a hasty breakfast.

---

5. Elizabeth Temple, daughter of Judge Marmaduke Temple, the founder of Templeton and its chief landowner; at the outset of the story she returns from four years at school.
6. Richard (Dickon) Jones, the sheriff, a cousin of Judge Temple; he superintends "all the minor concerns of Temple's business."
7. Benjamin Penguillan (called Ben Pump), a Cornishman and former sailor, majordomo, or steward under Jones. In the next paragraph Pump is called "the ex-steward" because he had been the steward to the

captain in his seagoing years. One of his charges at the Templeton house is to keep the stove in the parlor hot in winter.
8. Louisa Grant, daughter of the Episcopal minister.
9. Once a West Indian planter, now a refugee because of the French Revolution.
1. Short for "Marmaduke," the judge.
2. Xerxes the Great (519?–465 B.C.) was king of Persia (486–65 B.C.).
3. Oliver Edwards, a mysterious young stranger.

If the heavens were alive with pigeons, the whole village seemed equally in motion, with men, women, and children. Every species of fire-arms, from the French ducking-gun, with its barrel of near six feet in length, to the common horseman's pistol, was to be seen in the hands of the men and boys; while bows and arrows, some made of the simple stick of a walnut sapling, and others in a rude imitation of the ancient cross-bows, were carried by many of the latter.

The houses, and the signs of life apparent in the village, drove the alarmed birds from the direct line of their flight, towards the mountains, along the sides and near the bases of which they were glancing in dense masses, that were equally wonderful by the rapidity of their motion, as by their incredible numbers.

We have already said, that across the inclined plane which fell from the steep ascent of the mountain to the banks of the Susquehanna, ran the highway, on either side of which a clearing of many acres had been made, at a very early day. Over those clearings, and up the eastern mountain, and along the dangerous path that was cut into its side, the different individuals posted themselves, as suited their inclinations; and in a few moments the attack commenced.

Amongst the sportsmen was to be seen the tall, gaunt form of Leather-stocking,[4] who was walking over the field, with his rifle hanging on his arm, his dogs following close at his heels, now scenting the dead or wounded birds, that were beginning to tumble from the flocks, and then crouching under the legs of their master, as if they participated in his feelings, at this wasteful and unsportsmanlike execution.

The reports of the fire-arms became rapid, whole volleys rising from the plain, as flocks of more than ordinary numbers darted over the opening, covering the field with darkness, like an interposing cloud; and then the light smoke of a single piece would issue from among the leafless bushes on the mountain, as death was hurled on the retreat of the affrighted birds, who would rise from a volley, for many feet into the air, in a vain effort to escape the attacks of man. Arrows, and missiles of every kind, were seen in the midst of the flocks; and so numerous were the birds, and so low did they take their flight, that even long poles, in the hands of those on the sides of the mountain, were used to strike them to the earth.

During all this time, Mr. Jones, who disdained the humble and ordinary means of destruction used by his companions, was busily occupied, aided by Benjamin, in making arrangements for an assault of a more than ordinarily fatal character. Among the relics of the old military excursions, that occasionally are discovered throughout the different districts of the western part of New-York, there had been found in Templeton, at its settlement, a small swivel,[5] which would carry a ball of a pound weight. It was thought to have been deserted by a war-party of the whites, in one of their inroads into the Indian settlements, when, perhaps, their convenience or their necessities induced them to leave such an encumbrance to the rapidity of their march, behind them in the woods. This miniature cannon had been released from the rust, and mounted on little wheels, in a state for actual service. For several years, it

4. I.e., Natty Bumppo.
5. Small cannon capable of being swung higher or lower.

was the sole organ for extraordinary rejoicings that was used in those mountains. On the mornings of the Fourth of July, it would be heard, with its echoes ringing among the hills, and telling forth its sounds, for thirteen times, with all the dignity of a two-and-thirty pounder; and even Captain Hollister,[6] who was the highest authority in that part of the country on all such occasions, affirmed that, considering its dimensions, it was no despicable gun for a salute. It was somewhat the worse for the service it had performed, it is true, there being but a trifling difference in size between the touch-hole and the muzzle.[7] Still, the grand conceptions of Richard had suggested the importance of such an instrument, in hurling death at his nimble enemies. The swivel was dragged by a horse into a part of the open space, that the sheriff thought most eligible for planting a battery of the kind, and Mr. Pump proceeded to load it. Several handfuls of duck-shot were placed on top of the powder, and the Major-domo soon announced that his piece was ready for service.

The sight of such an implement collected all the idle spectators to the spot, who, being mostly boys, filled the air with their cries of exultation and delight. The gun was pointed on high, and Richard, holding a coal of fire in a pair of tongs, patiently took his seat on a stump, awaiting the appearance of a flock that was worthy of his notice.

So prodigious was the number of the birds, that the scattering fire of the guns, with the hurling of missiles, and the cries of the boys, had no other effect than to break off small flocks from the immense masses that continued to dart along the valley, as if the whole creation of the feathered tribe were pouring through that one pass. None pretended to collect the game, which lay scattered over the fields in such profusion, as to cover the very ground with the fluttering victims.

Leather-stocking was a silent, but uneasy spectator of all these proceedings, but was able to keep his sentiments to himself until he saw the introduction of the swivel into the sports.

"This comes of settling a country" he said—"here have I known the pigeons to fly for forty long years, and, till you made your clearings, there was nobody to scare or to hurt them. I loved to see them come into the woods, for they were company to a body; hurting nothing; being, as it was, as harmless as a garter-snake. But now it gives me sore thoughts when I hear the frighty things whizzing through the air, for I know it's only a motion to bring out all the brats in the village at them. Well! the Lord won't see the waste of his creaters for nothing, and right will be done to the pigeons, as well as others, by-and-by.—There's Mr. Oliver, as bad as the rest of them, firing into the flocks as if he was shooting down nothing but the Mingo[8] warriors."

Among the sportsmen was Billy Kirby,[9] who, armed with an old musket, was loading, and, without even looking into the air, was firing, and shouting as his victims fell even on his own person. He heard the speech of Natty, and took upon himself to reply—

"What's that, old Leather-stocking!" he cried; "grumbling at the loss of a few pigeons! If you had to sow your wheat twice, and three times, as I have done, you wouldn't be so massyfully[1] feeling'd to'ards the divils.—Hurrah,

---

6. The landlord of the major village inn, The Bold Dragoon; his rank comes from his having been an early commander of local militia.
7. Ordinarily the muzzle (or mouth) would be considerably larger than the touchhole, the vent by which fire is communicated to the powder.

8. In the *Leather-Stocking* novels set in New York, the Mingos (Iroquois) are made out to be the "bad Indians," whereas the Delawares are the "good Indians."
9. A woodchopper.
1. Mercifully.

boys! scatter the feathers. This is better than shooting at a turkey's head[2] and neck, old fellow."

"It's better for you, maybe, Billy Kirby," returned the indignant old hunter, "and all them as don't know how to put a ball down a rifle-barrel, or how to bring it up ag'in with a true aim; but it's wicked to be shooting into flocks in this wastey manner; and none do it, who know how to knock over a single bird. If a body has a craving for pigeon's flesh, why! it's made the same as all other creaters, for man's eating, but not to kill twenty and eat one. When I want such a thing, I go into the woods till I find one to my liking, and then I shoot him off the branches without touching a feather of another, though there might be a hundred on the same tree. But you couldn't do such a thing, Billy Kirby—you couldn't do it if you tried."

"What's that you say, you old, dried cornstalk! you sapless stub!" cried the wood-chopper. "You've grown mighty boasting, sin[3] you killed the turkey; but if you're for a single shot, here goes at that bird which comes on by himself."

The fire from the distant part of the field had driven a single pigeon below the flock to which it had belonged, and, frightened with the constant reports of the muskets, it was approaching the spot where the disputants stood, darting first from one side, and then to the other, cutting the air with the swiftness of lightning, and making a noise with its wings, not unlike the rushing of a bullet. Unfortunately for the wood-chopper, notwithstanding his vaunt, he did not see his bird until it was too late for him to fire as it approached, and he pulled his trigger at the unlucky moment when it was darting immediately over his head. The bird continued its course with incredible velocity.

Natty had dropped his piece from his arm, when the challenge was made, and, waiting a moment, until the terrified victim had got in a line with his eyes, and had dropped near the bank of the lake, he raised his rifle with uncommon rapidity, and fired. It might have been chance, or it might have been skill, that produced the result; it was probably a union of both; but the pigeon whirled over in the air, and fell into the lake, with a broken wing. At the sound of his rifle, both his dogs started from his feet, and in a few minutes the "slut"[4] brought out the bird, still alive.

The wonderful exploit of Leather-stocking was noised through the field with great rapidity, and the sportsmen gathered in to learn the truth of the report.

"What," said young Edwards, "have you really killed a pigeon on the wing, Natty, with a single ball?"

"Haven't I killed loons before now, lad, that dive at the flash?" returned the hunter. "It's much better to kill only such as you want, without wasting your powder and lead, than to be firing into God's creaters in such a wicked manner. But I come out for a bird, and you know the reason why I like small game, Mr. Oliver, and now I have got one I will go home, for I don't like to see these wasty ways that you are all practysing, as if the least thing was not made for use, and not to destroy."

"Thou sayest well, Leather-stocking," cried Marmaduke, "and I begin to think it time to put an end to this work of destruction."

"Put an ind, Judge, to your clearings. An't the woods his work as well as the pigeons? Use, but don't waste. Wasn't the woods made for the beasts and birds to harbour in? and when man wanted their flesh, their skins, or their feathers,

---

2. In an earlier chapter Natty Bumppo had beaten Kirby in a turkey-shooting contest.

3. Since.

4. Bitch, female dog.

there's the place to seek them. But I'll go to the hut with my own game, for I wouldn't touch one of the harmless things that kiver the ground here, looking up with their eyes at me, as if they only wanted tongues to say their thoughts."

With this sentiment in his mouth, Leather-stocking threw his rifle over his arm, and, followed by his dogs, stepped across the clearing with great caution, taking care not to tread on one, of the hundreds of the wounded birds that lay in his path. He soon entered the bushes on the margin of the lake, and was hid from view.

Whatever might be the impression the morality of Natty made on the Judge, it was utterly lost on Richard. He availed himself of the gathering of the sportsmen, to lay a plan for one "fell swoop"[5] of destruction. The musket-men were drawn up in battle array, in a line extending on each side of his artillery, with orders to await the signal of firing from himself.

"Stand by, my lads," said Benjamin, who acted as an aid-de-camp on this momentous occasion, "stand by, my hearties, and when Squire Dickens heaves out the signal for to begin the firing, d'ye see, you may open upon them in a broadside. Take care and fire low, boys, and you'll be sure to hull the flock."

"Fire low!" shouted Kirby—"hear the old fool! If we fire low, we may hit the stumps, but not ruffle a pigeon."

"How should you know, you lubber?"[6] cried Benjamin, with a very unbecoming heat, for an officer on the eve of battle—"how should you know, you grampus? Havn't I sailed aboard of the Boadishy[7] for five years? and wasn't it a standing order to fire low, and to hull your enemy? Keep silence at your guns, boys, and mind the order that is passed."

The loud laughs of the musketmen were silenced by the authoritative voice of Richard, who called to them for attention and obedience to his signals.

Some millions of pigeons were supposed to have already passed, that morning, over the valley of Templeton; but nothing like the flock that was now approaching had been seen before. It extended from mountain to mountain in one solid blue mass, and the eye looked in vain over the southern hills to find its termination. The front of this living column was distinctly marked by a line, but very slightly indented, so regular and even was the flight. Even Marmaduke forgot the morality of Leather-stocking as it approached, and, in common with the rest, brought his musket to his shoulder.

"Fire!" cried the Sheriff, clapping his coal to the priming of the cannon. As half of Benjamin's charge escaped through the touch-hole, the whole volley of the musketry preceded the report of the swivel. On receiving this united discharge of small-arms, the front of the flock darted upward, while, at the same instant, myriads of those in their rear rushed with amazing rapidity into their places, so that when the column of white smoke gushed from the mouth of the little cannon, an accumulated mass of objects was gliding over its point of direction. The roar of the gun echoed along the mountains, and died away to the north, like distant thunder, while the whole flock of alarmed birds seemed, for a moment, thrown into one disorderly and agitated mass. The air was filled with their irregular flights, layer rising over layer, far above the tops

5. Shakespeare's *Macbeth* 4.3.219, in Macduff's lament for his dead wife and children.
6. Landlubber, clumsy fellow.
7. The *Boadicea*, a ship named for the British queen who led a rebellion against the Roman rulers in A.D. 62. "Grampus": variety of small whale, used here as a term of contempt.

of the highest pines, none daring to advance beyond the dangerous pass; when, suddenly, some of the leaders of the feathered tribe shot across the valley, taking their flight directly over the village, and the hundreds of thousands in their rear followed their example, deserting the eastern side of the plain to their persecutors and the fallen.

"Victory!" shouted Richard, "victory! we have driven the enemy from the field."

"Not so, Dickon," said Marmaduke; "the field is covered with them; and, like the Leather-stocking, I see nothing but eyes, in every direction, as the innocent sufferers turn their heads in terror, to examine my movements. Full one half of those that have fallen are yet alive: and I think it is time to end the sport; if sport it be."

"Sport!" cried the Sheriff; "it is princely sport. There are some thousands of the blue-coated boys on the ground, so that every old woman in the village may have a pot-pie for the asking."

"Well, we have happily frightened the birds from this pass," said Marmaduke, "and our carnage must of necessity end, for the present.—Boys, I will give thee sixpence a hundred for the pigeons' heads only; so go to work, and bring them into the village, when I will pay thee."

This expedient produced the desired effect, for every urchin on the ground went industriously to work to wring the necks of the wounded birds. Judge Temple retired towards his dwelling with that kind of feeling, that many a man has experienced before him, who discovers, after the excitement of the moment has passed, that he has purchased pleasure at the price of misery to others. Horses were loaded with the dead; and, after this first burst of sporting, the shooting of pigeons became a business, for the remainder of the season, more in proportion to the wants of the people.[8] Richard, however, boasted for many a year, of his shot with the "cricket;"[9] and Benjamin gravely asserted, that he thought that they killed nearly as many pigeons on that day, as there were Frenchmen destroyed on the memorable occasion of Rodney's victory.[1]

1823

8. The pigeons described in this chapter—the passenger pigeons—are extinct, the last known specimen dying in 1914 at the Cincinnati Zoological Garden.
9. I.e., the little cannon.
1. The British admiral George Brydges, Baron Rodney (1719–1792), defeated the French off Dominica, in the West Indies, in April 1782. Penguillan's nickname comes from his tall tale about manning the pumps to keep the ship from sinking after Rodney's victory.

---

# WILLIAM CULLEN BRYANT
## 1794–1878

William Cullen Bryant was born in the backwoods of Massachusetts, at Cummington, but his father was a physician who loved the classics, and Cullen, as the boy was called, was trained early in Greek and Latin. For religion he was taught a harsh Calvinism that held that the Fall of Adam and Eve had brought about the Fall of Nature as well. But Bryant's first published poem was political, not about nature and religion: when he wrote an anti-Jefferson lampoon, *The Embargo*, his Federalist father printed it as a pamphlet (1808). Bryant entered Williams College in 1810 but dropped out after a few months with the expectation of entering Yale. His father could not afford that expense, and instead Bryant read for the law, being admitted to practice in 1815. Meanwhile, in 1813 or 1814, Bryant wrote the first, shorter version of *Thanatopsis*, the poem by which he is best remembered. Since his early teens Bryant had been reading the melancholy and sometimes scarifying meditations of the British "graveyard poets" of the previous decades, especially Robert Blair (*The Grave*), Thomas Gray (*Elegy Written in a Country Churchyard*), Bishop Beilby Porteus (*Death*), and various poems by Henry Kirke White. Such poems by their luxurious sonorousness tempered the Calvinism instilled in the boy, but they often poeticized religious doctrine, as in Blair's account of the resurrection at the Judgment Day: "The time draws on / When not a single spot of burial-earth, / Whether on land, or on the spacious sea, / But must give back its long-committed dust / Inviolate" (*The Grave*). In 1810 or soon afterward Bryant read *Lyrical Ballads* and responded strongly to Wordsworth's near-pantheistic view of nature. *Thanatopsis* as published in the *North American Review* in 1817 is nondoctrinally meditative. The fuller version of 1821 concludes with a fervent injunction to trust in something or someone who remains unspecified: Bryant's Calvinistic earnestness was outliving his commitment to particular doctrines. (Symptomatically, a reference to the Fall of Nature in the first version of *The Prairies*, 1834, was later removed.) *Thanatopsis* won Bryant immediate acknowledgment in 1817, but a full-time career as a poet was economically impossible. In 1820, the year his father died, Bryant was appointed as justice of the peace in Berkshire County. Early in 1821 he married Frances Fairchild in Great Barrington, Massachusetts, and later that year published the very slim volume *Poems*.

Stirred by the conflict between his literary ambition and his need to support his family, Bryant in 1825 chanced a move to New York City as an editor of the *New-York Review and Atheneum Magazine*. He was welcomed as a literary celebrity and quickly fitted into metropolitan life, becoming an early member of James Fenimore Cooper's Bread and Cheese Club. His magazine failed, as almost all periodicals did at that time, but Bryant stayed on in New York as editorial assistant on the *Evening Post* (1826), then soon became part owner and editor-in-chief. Bryant was not immune to the pettier temptations of the then-brawling occupation of journalism, but over the decades he made the *Evening Post* one of the most respected newspapers in the country, mainly through editorials in which he argued out his position on many momentous issues. A deeply committed Jacksonian Democrat, despite his youthful Federalism, Bryant rarely let party loyalty interfere with principle. He led the antislavery Free-Soil movement within the Democratic party as long as this seemed a feasible way of achieving his ends, then helped to form the Republican party. In 1860 he was an influential advocate of Abraham Lincoln.

As he prospered with his newspaper, Bryant became a great traveler, at home and abroad, and through his letters to the *Evening Post* he helped to shape a sense of the world for his countrypeople. *Letters of a Traveller* appeared in 1850; *Letters of a Traveller, Second Series*, in 1859; and *Letters from the East* (that is, the Mideast) in 1869. His community service took many forms, most tangibly in his campaign for the creation of Central Park. His private life was happy. In 1844 he moved his family to a fine old farmhouse on the Sound in then-rural Long Island, and for many years he relieved his strenuous urban activity with peaceful respites at his estate, Cedarmere. Left a widower in 1866, Bryant continued to work at the *Evening Post*. Blessed with patriarchal fame and great wealth as well as astonishing health, which owed much to a daily set of vigorous exercises, Bryant in his seventies undertook the remarkably ambitious task of translating Homer. His version of the *Iliad* was published in 1870, and that of the *Odyssey* two years later. Together with the 1876 printing of his *Poems* (a new accumulation of many old and a few new verses), these translations crowned his career.

Bryant died of the consequences of a fall suffered after he gave a speech at the unveiling of a statue of the Italian patriot Joseph Mazzini in Central Park. In New York City flags were lowered to half mast, and he was mourned throughout the country as a great poet and editor.

Bryant had, in fact, written very little poetry; his translations from Homer are many times as long as his own verses. And his poems, early and late, are for the most part limited to a few subjects treated in ways that soon become predictable. His collected poetry consists of accurately rhymed or sonorously unrhymed blank verse on landscapes, flora, meteorological phenomena, historical personages and events, friends, Indian legends, and a few other topics. Yet the country's response showed plainly that he was providing what it needed at a time of national self-consciousness about the scarcity of talented poets—a loftiness of diction that at best seemed securely Miltonic, a way of making American landscapes and subjects as worthy of celebration as Old World scenes and topics, and a moral stance that blended ecumenical vagueness with didactic earnestness. Bryant's fame as a poet was accurately analyzed by his early biographer, W. A. Bradley: "He appeared much more remarkable to his early contemporaries than he ever can to us, because of the contrast which he presented with what had gone before. And later, after a period in which he suffered somewhat of an eclipse through the rise of new schools and new poets to contest with him the palm of supremacy, his great age, the traditions of an earlier day which he represented, his personality which so perfectly embodied the prophetic and seer-like aspect of the poetic ideal, and finally local pride in the possession of a poet whom New York could produce to oppose the claims of its rival, Boston, to literary supremacy,—all these tended to create a regard for Bryant that was rather personal than literary." On the strength of a few— mainly very early—poems and a notable public life, Bryant passed into what seemed, to his own time, literary immortality. Only as historians describe his part in the great political issues of his time is he passing into a perhaps truer immortality as a man who may not have been a great American poet but who led a great American life.

# Thanatopsis[1]

To him who in the love of Nature holds
Communion with her visible forms, she speaks
A various language; for his gayer hours
She has a voice of gladness, and a smile
And eloquence of beauty, and she glides                                5
Into his darker musings, with a mild
And gentle sympathy, that steals away
Their sharpness, ere he is aware. When thoughts
Of the last bitter hour come like a blight
Over thy spirit, and sad images                                       10
Of the stern agony, and shroud, and pall,
And breathless darkness, and the narrow house,
Make thee to shudder, and grow sick at heart;—
Go forth under the open sky, and list
To Nature's teachings, while from all around—                         15
Earth and her waters, and the depths of air,—
Comes a still voice—Yet a few days, and thee

---

1. The text is that of the first full printing, in Bryant's *Poems* (1821). The title ("Meditation on death") was supplied by an editor for the central section of the poem (lines 17–73) when that section was printed in the *North American Review* (September 1817).

The all-beholding sun shall see no more
In all his course; nor yet in the cold ground,
Where thy pale form was laid, with many tears,                    20
Nor in the embrace of ocean shall exist
Thy image. Earth, that nourished thee, shall claim
Thy growth, to be resolv'd to earth again;
And, lost each human trace, surrend'ring up
Thine individual being, shalt thou go                            25
To mix forever with the elements,
To be a brother to th' insensible rock
And to the sluggish clod, which the rude swain
Turns with his share,[2] and treads upon. The oak
Shall send his roots abroad, and pierce thy mould.               30
Yet not to thy eternal resting place
Shalt thou retire alone—nor couldst thou wish
Couch more magnificent. Thou shalt lie down
With patriarchs of the infant world—with kings
The powerful of the earth—the wise, the good,                   35
Fair forms, and hoary seers of ages past,
All in one mighty sepulchre.—The hills
Rock-ribb'd and ancient as the sun,—the vales
Stretching in pensive quietness between;
The venerable woods—rivers that move                            40
In majesty, and the complaining brooks
That make the meadows green; and pour'd round all,
Old ocean's grey and melancholy waste,—
Are but the solemn decorations all
Of the great tomb of man. The golden sun,                       45
The planets, all the infinite host of heaven,
Are shining on the sad abodes of death,
Through the still lapse of ages. All that tread
The globe are but a handful to the tribes
That slumber in its bosom.—Take the wings                       50
Of morning—and the Barcan desert[3] pierce,
Or lose thyself in the continuous woods
Where rolls the Oregan,[4] and hears no sound,
Save his own dashings—yet—the dead are there,
And millions in those solitudes, since first                    55
The flight of years began, have laid them down
In their last sleep—the dead reign there alone.—
So shalt thou rest—and what if thou shalt fall
Unnoticed by the living—and no friend
Take note of thy departure? All that breathe                    60
Will share thy destiny. The gay will laugh
When thou art gone, the solemn brood of care
Plod on, and each one as before will chase
His favourite phantom; yet all these shall leave
Their mirth and their employments, and shall come,              65
And make their bed with thee. As the long train
Of ages glide away, the sons of men,

2. Plowshare. "Swain": farmer.
3. In Barca (northeast Libya).
4. An early variant spelling of Oregon; now the Columbia River. (For his distant examples Bryant ranges
across the Atlantic and then westward across the North
American continent.)

The youth in life's green spring, and he who goes
In the full strength of years, matron, and maid,
The bow'd with age, the infant in the smiles          70
And beauty of its innocent age cut off,—
Shall one by one be gathered to thy side,
By those, who in their turn shall follow them.
So live, that when thy summons comes to join
The innumerable caravan, that moves          75
To the pale realms of shade, where each shall take
His chamber in the silent halls of death,
Thou go not, like the quarry-slave at night,
Scourged to his dungeon, but sustain'd and sooth'd
By an unfaltering trust, approach thy grave,          80
Like one who wraps the drapery of his couch
About him, and lies down to pleasant dreams.

c. 1814                                        1821


# To a Waterfowl[1]

Whither, 'midst falling dew,
While glow the heavens with the last steps of day,
Far, through their rosy depths, dost thou pursue
          Thy solitary way?

Vainly the fowler's eye          5
Might mark thy distant flight to do thee wrong,
As, darkly painted on the crimson sky,
          Thy figure floats along.

Seek'st thou the plashy[2] brink
Of weedy lake, or marge of river wide,          10
Or where the rocking billows rise and sink
          On the chafed ocean side?

There is a Power whose care
Teaches thy way along that pathless coast,—
The desert and illimitable air,—          15
          Lone wandering, but not lost.

All day thy wings have fann'd
At that far height, the cold thin atmosphere:
Yet stoop not, weary, to the welcome land,
          Though the dark night is near.          20

And soon that toil shall end,
Soon shalt thou find a summer home, and rest,
And scream among thy fellows; reeds shall bend
          Soon o'er thy sheltered nest.

1. The text is that of the printing in *Poems* (1821); the
poem was drafted in Bridgewater, Massachusetts, during July 1815.          2. Marshy; a plash is a pool.

Thou'rt gone, the abyss of heaven                                    25
Hath swallowed up thy form; yet, on my heart
Deeply hath sunk the lesson thou hast given,
      And shall not soon depart.

He, who, from zone to zone,
Guides through the boundless sky thy certain flight,      30
In the long way that I must tread alone,
      Will lead my steps aright.

1815                                                                      1821

# The Prairies[1]

These are the Gardens of the Desert, these
The unshorn fields, boundless and beautiful,
And fresh as the young earth, ere man had sinned—
The Prairies. I behold them for the first,
And my heart swells, while the dilated sight              5
Takes in the encircling vastness. Lo! they stretch
In airy undulations, far away,
As if the ocean, in his gentlest swell,
Stood still, with all his rounded billows fixed,
And motionless for ever.—Motionless?—                    10
No—they are all unchained again. The clouds
Sweep over with their shadows, and beneath
The surface rolls and fluctuates to the eye;
Dark hollows seem to glide along and chase
The sunny ridges. Breezes of the South!                  15
Who toss the golden and the flame-like flowers,
And pass the prairie-hawk that, poised on high,
Flaps his broad wings, yet moves not—ye have played
Among the palms of Mexico and vines
Of Texas, and have crisped the limpid brooks             20
That from the fountains of Sonora[2] glide
Into the calm Pacific—have ye fanned
A nobler or a lovelier scene than this?
Man hath no part in all this glorious work:
The hand that built the firmament hath heaved            25
And smoothed these verdant swells, and sown their slopes
With herbage, planted them with island groves,
And hedged them round with forests. Fitting floor
For this magnificent temple of the sky—
With flowers whose glory and whose multitude             30
Rival the constellations! The great heavens
Seem to stoop down upon the scene in love,—

---

1. From the first printing in *Poems* (1834). Bryant wrote the poem over a year after visiting his brothers in Illinois during 1832. Later he removed the reference to the Fall of Adam and Eve by substituting this as the third line: "For which the speech of England has no name—" (alluding to the fact that the word *prairies* was adopted from French explorers and trappers).
2. River in northwest Mexico.

A nearer vault, and of a tenderer blue,
Than that which bends above the eastern hills.
As o'er the verdant waste I guide my steed,                    35
Among the high rank grass that sweeps his sides,
The hollow beating of his footstep seems
A sacrilegious sound. I think of those
Upon whose rest he tramples. Are they here—
The dead of other days!—and did the dust                      40
Of these fair solitudes once stir with life
And burn with passion? Let the mighty mounds[3]
That overlook the rivers, or that rise
In the dim forest crowded with old oaks,
Answer. A race, that long has passed away,                    45
Built them;—a disciplined and populous race
Heaped, with long toil, the earth, while yet the Greek
Was hewing the Pentelicus[4] to forms
Of symmetry, and rearing on its rock
The glittering Parthenon. These ample fields                  50
Nourished their harvests, here their herds were fed,
When haply by their stalls the bison lowed,
And bowed his maned shoulder to the yoke.
All day this desert murmured with their toils,
Till twilight blushed and lovers walked, and wooed            55
In a forgotten language, and old tunes,
From instruments of unremembered form,
Gave the soft winds a voice. The red man came—
The roaming hunter tribes, warlike and fierce,
And the mound-builders vanished from the earth.               60
The solitude of centuries untold
Has settled where they dwelt. The prairie wolf
Hunts in their meadows, and his fresh dug den
Yawns by my path. The gopher mines the ground
Where stood their swarming cities. All is gone—               65
All—save the piles of earth that hold their bones—
The platforms where they worshipped unknown gods—
The barriers which they builded from the soil
To keep the foe at bay—till o'er the walls
The wild beleaguerers broke, and, one by one,                 70
The strong holds of the plain were forced, and heaped
With corpses. The brown vultures of the wood
Flocked to those vast uncovered sepulchres,
And sat, unscared and silent, at their feast.
Haply some solitary fugitive,                                 75
Lurking in marsh and forest, till the sense
Of desolation and of fear became
Bitterer than death, yielded himself to die.
Man's better nature triumphed. Kindly words
Welcomed and soothed him; the rude conquerors                 80

3. The burial mounds common in Illinois; Bryant follows a contemporary theory that they were built by a
culture older than the American Indians.
4. Greek mountain from which a fine white marble

was quarried, including that used in building the Parthenon, the temple of Athena on the Acropolis in
Athens.

Seated the captive with their chiefs. He chose
A bride among their maidens. And at length
Seemed to forget,—yet ne'er forgot,—the wife
Of his first love, and her sweet little ones
Butchered, amid their shrieks, with all his race.                    85
    Thus change the forms of being. Thus arise
Races of living things, glorious in strength,
And perish, as the quickening breath of God
Fills them, or is withdrawn. The red man too—
Has left the blooming wilds he ranged so long,                       90
And, nearer to the Rocky Mountains, sought
A wider hunting ground. The beaver builds
No longer by these streams, but far away,
On waters whose blue surface ne'er gave back
The white man's face—among Missouri's springs,                      95
And pools whose issues swell the Oregan,[5]
He rears his little Venice.[6] In these plains
The bison feeds no more. Twice twenty leagues
Beyond remotest smoke of hunter's camp,
Roams the majestic brute, in herds that shake                       100
The earth with thundering steps—yet here I meet
His ancient footprints stamped beside the pool.
    Still this great solitude is quick with life.
Myriads of insects, gaudy as the flowers
They flutter over, gentle quadrupeds,                               105
And birds, that scarce have learned the fear of man
Are here, and sliding reptiles of the ground,
Startlingly beautiful. The graceful deer
Bounds to the wood at my approach. The bee,
A more adventurous colonist than man,                              110
With whom he came across the eastern deep,
Fills the savannas with his murmurings,
And hides his sweets, as in the golden age,
Within the hollow oak. I listen long
To his domestic hum, and think I hear                              115
The sound of that advancing multitude
Which soon shall fill these deserts. From the ground
Comes up the laugh of children, the soft voice
Of maidens, and the sweet and solemn hymn
Of Sabbath worshippers. The low of herds                           120
Blends with the rustling of the heavy grain
Over the dark-brown furrows. All at once
A fresher wind sweeps by, and breaks my dream,
And I am in the wilderness alone.

1833                                                              1834

---

5. The Columbia River.                    6. I.e., builds a city in the water.

# WILLIAM APESS
## 1798–1839

Little is known of William Apess's life other than what he tells us in A *Son of the Forest* (1829), the first extensive autobiography published by a Native American. His grandfather, says Apess, was a white man who married the granddaughter of the Wampanoag leader King Philip, or Metacom, the loser, in 1678, of "King Philip's War." Philip increasingly occupied Apess's thoughts during his lifetime, serving as the subject of his last published work. Apess's father was of mixed blood, but he joined the Pequot tribe and married a full-blood Indian woman. Born in Colrain, Massachusetts, Apess drops from public record after 1838. Only recently have obituaries in the New York *Sun* and the New York *Observer* been found recording his death, from alcoholism, in New York, in the spring of 1839.

In A *Son of the Forest*, Apess details the pains of his early life: at three he was taken into the home of his poor, alcoholic maternal grandparents; he was severely beaten and, at four or five, sold as an indentured laborer. His first master allowed him to attend school for six years, which constituted his entire formal education; he also introduced Apess to Christianity. Apess served as a soldier in the abortive American attack on Montreal in the War of 1812 and converted to evangelical Methodism after leaving the army. At the conclusion of A *Son of the Forest*, Apess writes that he achieved an "exhorter's" license from his church, enabling him to earn a living as an itinerant preacher; only later would he realize his goal of ordination as a Methodist minister.

A fervent Christian, Apess early understood Christianity as incompatible with any form of race prejudice, sounding a note that presages Christian abolitionists later in the nineteenth century. In 1833, Apess went to preach at Mashpee, the only remaining Indian town in Massachusetts. There he became involved in the Mashpees' struggle to preserve their resources and rights, which were threatened by the overseers imposed on them by the Commonwealth of Massachusetts. The Mashpee eventually drew up petitions, probably composed by Apess, requiring that no whites cut wood or hay on Mashpee lands without the Indians' consent for "we, as a tribe, will rule ourselves, and have the right to do so; for all men are born free and equal, says the Constitution of the Country." Such unprecedented assertiveness on the part of the Indians alarmed the governor of Massachusetts, who announced his readiness to put down the unrest with troops. Apess's version of the controversy appears in his *Indian Nullification of the Unconstitutional Laws of Massachusetts Relative to the Marshpee* [sic] *Tribe; or, The Pretended Riot Explained* (1835). A year before the book appeared, its case was won when the state legislature granted the Mashpee the same rights of self-governance that other Massachusetts townships possessed.

Apess's career as a preacher and an author comes to a close with his *Eulogy on King Philip*, delivered in 1836 at the Odeon in Boston, one of the city's largest public lecture halls, and published that same year. In the *Eulogy* Apess meditated on his distant relation, naming Philip the foremost man that America had thus far produced. He reminds his audience, descendants of the Pilgrims, of the crimes of their ancestors, although "you and I have to rejoice that we have not to answer for our fathers' crimes; neither shall we do right to charge them one to another." Nonetheless, he notes, "in vain have I looked for the Christian to take me by the hand and bid me welcome to his cabin, as my fathers did them [the Christians], before we were born." Apess concludes that a "different course must be pursued. . . . And while you ask yourselves, 'What do they, the Indians, want?' you have only to look at the unjust laws made for them and say, 'They want what I want' ": justice and Christian fellowship.

Our selection comes from *The Experiences of Five Christian Indians of the Pequot Tribe*, published in 1833, the year Apess came to Mashpee. The first of these "experiences" is Apess's own, an account of his life and conversion that repeats some of the material in *A Son of the Forest* but intensifies considerably the condemnation of Euro-American treatment of native peoples. Apess concludes this book with the text anthologized here, *An Indian's Looking Glass for the White Man*, a searing indictment of race prejudice against people of color generally and Native Americans particularly. The forceful beginning of *Indian's Looking Glass* is marked by the hortatory style of the practiced preacher as well as by a remembered sense of the power of the spoken word in native cultures. Although his punctuation and syntax do not conform to the conventions of standard written English, Apess writes in a style that powerfully imitates oral performance. His provocative, ironic voice calls to mind that of the later moralist and orator for justice, Henry David Thoreau.

# An Indian's Looking-Glass for the White Man[1]

Having a desire to place a few things before my fellow creatures who are traveling with me to the grave, and to that God who is the maker and preserver both of the white man and the Indian, whose abilities are the same and who are to be judged by one God, who will show no favor to outward appearances but will judge righteousness. Now I ask if degradation has not been heaped long enough upon the Indians? And if so, can there not be a compromise? Is it right to hold and promote prejudices? If not, why not put them all away? I mean here, among those who are civilized. It may be that many are ignorant of the situation of many of my brethren within the limits of New England. Let me for a few moments turn your attention to the reservations in the different states of New England, and, with but few exceptions, we shall find them as follows: the most mean, abject, miserable race of beings in the world—a complete place of prodigality and prostitution.

Let a gentleman and lady of integrity and respectability visit these places, and they would be surprised; as they wandered from one hut to the other they would view, with the females who are left alone, children half-starved and some almost as naked as they came into the world. And it is a fact that I have seen them as much so—while the females are left without protection, and are seduced by white men, and are finally left to be common prostitutes for them and to be destroyed by that burning, fiery curse, that has swept millions, both of red and white men, into the grave with sorrow and disgrace—rum. One reason why they are left so is because their most sensible and active men are absent at sea. Another reason is because they are made to believe they are minors and have not the abilities given them from God to take care of themselves, without it is to see to a few little articles, such as baskets and brooms. Their land is in common stock, and they have nothing to make them enterprising.

---

1. The text is from *The Experiences of Five Christian Indians of the Pequot Tribe* (1833) reprinted in *On Our Own Ground: The Complete Writings of William Apess, a Pequot*, edited by Barry O'Connell (1992).

Another reason is because those men who are Agents,[2] many of them are unfaithful and care not whether the Indians live or die; they are much imposed upon by their neighbors, who have no principle. They would think it no crime to go upon Indian lands and cut and carry off their most valuable timber, or anything else they chose; and I doubt not but they think it clear gain. Another reason is because they have no education to take care of themselves; if they had, I would risk them to take care of their own property.

Now I will ask if the Indians are not called the most ingenious people among us. And are they not said to be men of talents? And I would ask: Could there be a more efficient way to distress and murder them by inches than the way they have taken? And there is no people in the world but who may be destroyed in the same way. Now, if these people are what they are held up in our view to be, I would take the liberty to ask why they are not brought forward and pains taken to educate them, to give them all a common education, and those of the brightest and first-rate talents put forward and held up to office. Perhaps some unholy, unprincipled men would cry out, "The skin was not good enough"; but stop, friends—I am not talking about the skin but about principles. I would ask if there cannot be as good feelings and principles under a red skin as there can be under a white. And let me ask: Is it not on the account of a bad principle that we who are red children have had to suffer so much as we have? And let me ask: Did not this bad principle proceed from the whites or their forefathers? And I would ask: Is it worthwhile to nourish it any longer? If not, then let us have a change, although some men no doubt will spout their corrupt principles against it, that are in the halls of legislation and elsewhere. But I presume this kind of talk will seem surprising and horrible. I do not see why it should so long as they (the whites) say that they think as much of us as they do of themselves.

This I have heard repeatedly, from the most respectable gentlemen and ladies—and having heard so much precept, I should now wish to see the example. And I would ask who has a better right to look for these things than the naturalist[3] himself—the candid man would say none.

I know that many say that they are willing, perhaps the majority of the people, that we should enjoy our rights and privileges as they do. If so, I would ask, Why are not we protected in our persons and property throughout the Union? Is it not because there reigns in the breast of many who are leaders a most unrighteous, unbecoming, and impure black principle, and as corrupt and unholy as it can be—while these very same unfeeling, self-esteemed characters pretend to take the skin as a pretext to keep us from our unalienable and lawful rights? I would ask you if you would like to be disfranchised from all your rights, merely because your skin is white, and for no other crime. I'll venture to say, these very characters who hold the skin to be such a barrier in the way would be the first to cry out, "Injustice! awful injustice!"

But, reader, I acknowledge that this is a confused world, and I am not seeking for office, but merely placing before you the black inconsistency that you place before me—which is ten times blacker than any skin that you will find in the universe. And now let me exhort you to do away that principle, as it appears ten times worse in the sight of God and candid men than skins of color—more disgraceful than all the skins that Jehovah ever made. If black or red skins or any other skin of color is disgraceful to God, it appears that he has disgraced himself a great deal—for he has made fifteen colored people to one white and placed them here upon this earth.

Now let me ask you, white man, if it is a disgrace for to eat, drink, and sleep with the image of God, or sit, or walk and talk with them. Or have you the folly to think that the white man, being one in fifteen or sixteen, are the only beloved images of God? Assemble all nations together in your imagination, and then let the whites be seated among them, and then let us look for the whites, and I doubt not it would be hard finding them; for to the rest of the nations, they are still but a handful. Now suppose these skins were put together, and each skin had its national crimes written upon it—which skin do you think would have the greatest? I will ask one question more. Can you charge the Indians with robbing a nation almost of their whole continent, and murdering their women and children, and then depriving the remainder of their lawful rights, that nature and God require them to have? And to cap the climax, rob another nation to till their grounds and welter out their days under the lash with hunger and fatigue under the scorching rays of a burning sun?[4] I should look at all the skins, and I know that when I cast my eye upon that white skin, and if I saw those crimes written upon it, I should enter my protest against it immediately and cleave to that which is more honorable. And I can tell you that I am satisfied with the manner of my creation, fully—whether others are or not.

But we will strive to penetrate more fully into the conduct of those who profess to have pure principles and who tell us to follow Jesus Christ and imitate him and have his Spirit. Let us see if they come anywhere near him and his ancient disciples. The first thing we are to look at are his precepts, of which we will mention a few. "Thou shalt love the Lord thy God with all thy heart, with all thy soul, with all thy mind, and with all thy strength. The second is like unto it. Thou shalt love thy neighbor as thyself. On these two precepts hang all the law and the prophets" (Matthew 22.37, 38, 39, 40). "By this shall all men know that they are my disciples, if ye have love one to another" (John 13.35). Our Lord left this special command with his followers, that they should love one another.

Again, John in his Epistles says, "He who loveth God loveth his brother also" (1 John 4.21). "Let us not love in word but in deed" (1 John 3.18). "Let your love be without dissimulation. See that ye love one another with a pure heart fervently" (1 Peter 1.22). "If any man say, I love God, and hateth his brother, he is a liar" (1 John 4.20). "Whosoever hateth his brother is a murderer, and no murderer hath eternal life abiding in him" (1 John 3.15). The first thing that takes our attention is the saying of Jesus, "Thou shalt love," etc. The first question I would ask my brethren in the ministry, as well as that of the membership: What is love, or its effects? Now, if they who teach are not essentially affected with pure love, the love of God, how can they teach as they ought? Again, the holy teachers of old said, "Now if any man have not the spirit of Christ, he is none of his" (Romans 8.9). Now, my brethren in the ministry, let me ask you a few sincere questions. Did you ever hear or read of Christ teaching his disciples that they ought to despise one because his skin

---

4. The reference is to the "nation" of Africa, many of whose people were brought to the United States as slaves.

was different from theirs? Jesus Christ being a Jew, and those of his Apostles certainly were not whites—and did not he who completed the plan of salvation complete it for the whites as well as for the Jews, and others? And were not the whites the most degraded people on the earth at that time? And none were more so, for they sacrificed their children to dumb idols![5] And did not St. Paul labor more abundantly for building up a Christian nation among you than any of the Apostles? And you know as well as I that you are not indebted to a principle beneath a white skin for your religious services but to a colored one.

What then is the matter now? Is not religion the same now under a colored skin as it ever was? If so, I would ask, why is not a man of color respected? You may say, as many say, we have white men enough. But was this the spirit of Christ and his Apostles? If it had been, there would not have been one white preacher in the world—for Jesus Christ never would have imparted his grace or word to them, for he could forever have withheld it from them. But we find that Jesus Christ and his Apostles never looked at the outward appearances. Jesus in particular looked at the hearts, and his Apostles through him, being discerners of the spirit, looked at their fruit without any regard to the skin, color, or nation; as St. Paul himself speaks, "Where there is neither Greek nor Jew, circumcision nor uncircumcision, Barbarian nor Scythian, bond nor free—but Christ is all, and in all" (Colossians 3.11). If you can find a spirit like Jesus Christ and his Apostles prevailing now in any of the white congregations, I should like to know it. I ask: Is it not the case that everybody that is not white is treated with contempt and counted as barbarians? And I ask if the word of God justifies the white man in so doing. When the prophets prophesied, of whom did they speak? When they spoke of heathens, was it not the whites and others who were counted Gentiles? And I ask if all nations with the exception of the Jews were not counted heathens. And according to the writings of some, it could not mean the Indians, for they are counted Jews. And now I would ask: Why is all this distinction made among these Christian societies? I would ask: What is all this ado about missionary societies, if it be not to Christianize those who are not Christians? And what is it for? To degrade them worse, to bring them into society where they must welter out their days in disgrace merely because their skin is of a different complexion. What folly it is to try to make the state of human society worse than it is. How astonished some may be at this—but let me ask: Is it not so? Let me refer you to the churches only. And, my brethren, is there any agreement? Do brethren and sisters love one another? Do they not rather hate one another? Outward forms and ceremonies, the lusts of the flesh, the lusts of the eye, and pride of life is of more value to many professors[6] than the love of God shed abroad in their hearts, or an attachment to his altar, to his ordinances, or to his children. But you may ask: Who are the children of God? Perhaps you may say, none but white. If so, the word of the Lord is not true.

I will refer you to St. Peter's precepts (Acts 10): "God is no respecter of persons," etc. Now if this is the case, my white brother, what better are you than God? And if no better, why do you, who profess his Gospel and to have his spirit, act so contrary to it? Let me ask why the men of a different skin are so despised. Why are not they educated and placed in your pulpits? I ask if his

---

5. The ancient Hebrews considered various Mideastern peoples idolators whose practices presumably in-

cluded child sacrifice.
6. I.e., those who profess the Christian faith.

services well performed are not as good as if a white man performed them. I ask if a marriage or a funeral ceremony or the ordinance of the Lord's house would not be as acceptable in the sight of God as though he was white. And if so, why is it not to you? I ask again: Why is it not as acceptable to have men to exercise their office in one place as well as in another? Perhaps you will say that if we admit you to all of these privileges you will want more. I expect that I can guess what that is—Why, say you, there would be intermarriages. How that would be I am not able to say—and if it should be, it would be nothing strange or new to me; for I can assure you that I know a great many that have intermarried, both of the whites and the Indians—and many are their sons and daughters and people, too, of the first respectability. And I could point to some in the famous city of Boston and elsewhere. You may look now at the disgraceful act in the statute law passed by the legislature of Massachusetts, and behold the fifty-pound fine levied upon any clergyman or justice of the peace that dare to encourage the laws of God and nature by a legitimate union in holy wedlock between the Indians and whites. I would ask how this looks to your lawmakers. I would ask if this corresponds with your sayings—that you think as much of the Indians as you do of the whites. I do not wonder that you blush, many of you, while you read; for many have broken the ill-fated laws made by man to hedge up the laws of God and nature. I would ask if they who have made the law have not broken it—but there is no other state in New England that has this law but Massachusetts; and I think, as many of you do not, that you have done yourselves no credit.

But as I am not looking for a wife, having one of the finest cast, as you no doubt would understand while you read her experience and travail of soul in the way to heaven, you will see that it is not my object. And if I had none, I should not want anyone to take my right from me and choose a wife for me; for I think that I or any of my brethren have a right to choose a wife for themselves as well as the whites—and as the whites have taken the liberty to choose my brethren, the Indians, hundreds and thousands of them, as partners in life, I believe the Indians have a much right to choose their partners among the whites if they wish. I would ask you if you can see anything inconsistent in your conduct and talk about the Indians. And if you do, I hope you will try to become more consistent. Now, if the Lord Jesus Christ, who is counted by all to be a Jew—and it is well known that the Jews are a colored people,[7] especially those living in the East, where Christ was born—and if he should appear among us, would he not be shut out of doors by many, very quickly? And by those too who profess religion?

By what you read, you may learn how deep your principles are. I should say they were skin-deep. I should not wonder if some of the most selfish and ignorant would spout a charge of their principles now and then at me. But I would ask: How are you to love your neighbors as yourself? Is it to cheat them? Is it to wrong them in anything? Now, to cheat them out of any of their rights is robbery. And I ask: Can you deny that you are not robbing the Indians daily, and many others? But at last you may think I am what is called a hard and uncharitable man. But not so. I believe there are many who would not hesitate to advocate our cause; and those too who are men of fame and respectability—as well as ladies of honor and virtue. There is a Webster, an Everett, and a

---

7. Referring to the belief that Moses and the biblical Hebrews, including Jesus, were people of color.

Wirt,[8] and many others who are distinguished characters—besides a host of my fellow citizens, who advocate our cause daily. And how I congratulate such noble spirits—how they are to be prized and valued; for they are well calculated to promote the happiness of mankind. They well know that man was made for society, and not for hissing-stocks[9] and outcasts. And when such a principle as this lies within the hearts of men, how much it is like its God— and how it honors its Maker—and how it imitates the feelings of the Good Samaritan, that had his wounds bound up, who had been among thieves and robbers.

Do not get tired, ye noble-hearted—only think how many poor Indians want their wounds done up daily; the Lord will reward you, and pray you stop not till this tree of distinction shall be leveled to the earth, and the mantle of prejudice torn from every American heart—then shall peace pervade the Union.[1]

8. William Wirt (1772–1834), lawyer, politician, orator, and writer; he served as attorney general under President James Monroe and was nominated by the Whig party for president. Daniel Webster (1782–1852), orator, legislator, statesman, and interpreter of the Constitution; he served as congressman from New Hampshire, senator from Massachusetts, and secretary of state under President William Henry Harrison. Edward Everett (1794–1865), the first Eliot Professor of Greek at Harvard and the editor of the prestigious *North American Review*; he served in Congress and as governor of Massachusetts.
9. Those who are laughed at or hissed at (cf. laughing-stocks).
1. "In the 1837 edition, *Experience of Five Christian Indians*, Apess removed this entire essay and substituted the following (entitled 'An Indian's Thought') in its place and thus ended the book: 'He would ask the white Christian thus: How can you let your light shine among Indians unless you do it by example? Proof of the Savior's light. Not by precept only, that he loved the world, but by example. Such as doing all manner

of cures, by working miracles, to the astonishment of all the world; and to test his love for them, he laid down his life for them, even while they were enemies. Now, if we have his spirit, as we profess to have, we shall most certainly want the indigent of all classes made comfortable. And who that understands the history of the world, does not know that ignorance is the cause of the major part of the vices that exist in the world. Now, does not the white man know that it is his duty to educate the Indians, to help them build houses of worship, and such like, in order to raise them up and make them comfortable as yourselves? And do you not know it was the intent of Christ's dying to make you and them equal with himself in holiness and peace? Now, this is just the way you ought to feel toward all the race of mankind. And you can never make ignorant people know that you love them, unless you do something for them. And be it known to all men, that your light can never shine unless you do it by works of righteousness. Judge ye, what that is.—William Apess' " [O'Connell's note]

---

# RALPH WALDO EMERSON

## 1803–1882

Ralph Waldo Emerson was a man who had no personal excesses such as doomed Poe, no mysterious decade such as lent glamor to Hawthorne, no exotic adventures such as Melville founded his career on, no dramatic struggles for artistic recognition such as Whitman waged, no local notoriety as a crank and extremist such as Thoreau acquired. He led a respectable, conventional life as a family man and decent, solid citizen. Yet in both literature and philosophy this man of conventional life became the American writer with whom every other significant writer of his time had to come to terms. At one extreme, Melville reacted so hostilely to the optimistic side of Emerson's thought that he satirized him in *The Confidence-Man* as a great American philosophical con man. At the other extreme, without Emerson's inspiration the writings of Thoreau are all but unthinkable and Whitman's great poetry might never have been written. Emerson's persisting influence on twentieth-century American writers is evident in astonishing permutations, on writers as diverse as Theodore Dreiser, Robert Frost, Wallace Stevens, his name-sake Ralph Waldo Ellison, and A. R. Ammons.

Emerson was born in Boston on May 25, 1803, son of a Unitarian minister and the second of five surviving boys. He was eight years old when the death of his father left the family to the meager charity of the church. Determined to send four sons to Harvard (another son, mentally retarded, was cared for by rural relatives), Emerson's mother kept a succession of boardinghouses. Emerson grew up in the city, protected from the lower-class "rough boys" in his early years and sent at nine to the Boston Public Latin School. So poorly clothed that two brothers had to make do at times with one coat, the boys were encouraged by a brilliant eccentric aunt, Mary Moody Emerson, to regard deprivation as ecstatic self-denial. Emerson showed no remarkable literary promise either in his early prose exercises or in his adolescent satires in imitation of Alexander Pope. His Harvard years, 1817–21, were frugal, industrious, and undistinguished. After graduation he served, he said, as "a hopeless Schoolmaster," unable to impose his authority on his pupils. Escaping into the study of theology in 1825, he began preaching in October 1826, and early in 1829 was ordained as junior pastor of Boston's Second Church, where Increase Mather and Cotton Mather had preached a century and more before.

Biographers have pointed out that Emerson's dedication to the ministry at the age of twenty-one was to a life of public service through eloquence, not to a life of preserving and disseminating religious dogma. In any case, Boston was no longer a Puritan stronghold. Boston Unitarianism, led in the 1820s by William Ellery Channing, still accepted the Bible as the revelation of God's intentions for humankind, but no longer held that human beings were innately depraved or that Jesus was more than the highest type of mortal individual. Emerson's skepticism toward Christianity was strengthened by his exposure to the German "higher criticism," which heretically interpreted biblical miracles in the light of comparable stories in other cultures. Emerson was gradually developing a faith greater in individual moral sentiment than in revealed religion. Around 1830–31 his reading of Samuel Taylor Coleridge's Aids to Reflection provided him with a basic terminology in his postulation of an intuitive "Reason," which is superior to the mere "Understanding," or ordinary rationality operating on the materials of sense experience. Undogmatic about Christianity as he became, Emerson nevertheless seems to have undergone an intense religious experience around these same years, 1830 or 1831, something comparable with the sweet inward burning that the Calvinist Jonathan Edwards had delighted in describing. Emerson's knowledge of this emotion is clear from his later essay The Over-Soul, but he felt no impulse to account for it according to the tenets of a particular church.

In the year of his ordination, Emerson married a young woman from New Hampshire, Ellen Tucker. She died sixteen months later of tuberculosis, the disease that had already infected Emerson and others in his family. Early in 1832 Emerson notified his church that he had become so skeptical of the validity of the Lord's Supper that he could no longer administer it. A few months later he resigned, keeping the sober goodwill of many in his flock, and embarked on a leisurely European tour, which constituted a postgraduate education in art and natural science. In the custom of that time, he called on well-known writers, meeting Walter Savage Landor in Italy, listening to Coleridge converse with such cogent volubility that he seemed to be reading aloud, and hearing William Wordsworth recite his poetry. Most important for his intellectual growth and for his reputation was his visit to Thomas Carlyle at Craigenputtock in Scotland, beginning a lifelong alliance in which each helped to publish and create an audience for the other.

In 1834 Emerson drifted into a quiet retreat at Concord, Massachusetts, where generations of his ancestors had been ministers. That year he received the first installment of his wife's legacy. Soon he was assured of more than a thousand dollars annually, enough so that he did not need to hold a steady job again. He continued to preach occasionally and began lecturing at New England lyceums, the public halls that brought a variety of speakers and performers both to the cities and to smaller towns. In 1835, after a prudent courtship, he married Lydia Jackson of Plymouth, having explained to her his work and the conditions under which he must pursue it. One condition was that he must live in rural Concord rather than move into the bustle of Plymouth. His assessment of his accomplishments was focused on his being a "poet," even when writing prose: "I am a poet, of a low class without doubt yet a poet. That is my nature & vocation. My singing be sure is very 'husky,' & is for the most part in prose. Still am I a poet in the sense of a perceiver & dear lover of the harmonies that are in the soul & in matter, & specially of the correspondences between these & those. A sunset, a forest, a snow storm, a certain river-view, are more to me than many friends & do ordinarily divide my day with books. Wherever I go therefore I guard & study my rambling propensities with a care that is ridiculous to people, but to me is the care of my high calling."

At this time, before *Nature* was published and before his essays were written, Emerson may well have hoped to gain his literary fame by his verse, and in fact the poems he had written thus far were not so husky or unmelodious as he implied. His main problem as a poet was not the huskiness he complained of but the more serious failure first to arrive at, then to apply, his great insight: that in true poetry the thought creates its own meter, the content creates its own form. Emerson's first little book, *Nature* (1836), did not establish him as an important American writer (for one thing, it was anonymous, and not every reviewer was in on what became an open secret around Boston), but it did confirm his future as a prose writer, however poetic that prose might be. One reviewer noticed the influence of Wordsworth and Coleridge in the tendency to "look on Nature with the spiritual eye," so that one creates Nature in perceiving it. Another found that the author had adopted "the Berkeleyan system" of philosophy, which denies "the outward and real existence" of Nature, and noticed also that the new school of philosophy called Transcendentalism was "a revival of the Old Platonic school" in rejecting a scientific attitude toward Nature. Yet another reviewer stressed the influence of Wordsworth's *Immortality* ode and of Coleridge's *Dejection: An Ode* in the author's concept of Nature. Another hailed the book as revealing a mind cognate with Thomas Carlyle's, "however inferior in energies and influences," and defined the philosophy of the book as "an Idealistic Pantheism" like that of Carlyle's *Sartor Resartus* (1834). A Swedenborgian writer in London took *Nature* as self-evidently the work of an American Swedenborgian, especially in "the beautiful and heart-cheering doctrine of correspondences" between moods of Nature and moods of human beings. As all these reviewers understood, *Nature* was not a Christian book but one influenced by a range of idealistic philosophies, ancient and very modern, Transcendentalism being merely the latest name for an old way of thinking. Although the favorable reception of the book in England encouraged some American journalists, hitherto skeptical, to take Emerson more seriously as a force in modern thought, Emerson's immediate reward was having the book become the unofficial manifesto for "the Symposium" or the Transcendental Club, which held its first meeting only a few days after *Nature* was published.

The Transcendental Club had influences, on Emerson and on the intellectual life of the country, out of proportion to its small membership and its short life of four years. It was composed mainly of ministers who were repelled by John Locke's views that the mind is a passive receiver of sense impressions and enthusiastic about Coleridge's alternative view of the mind as creative in perception. Among the members were the educator Bronson Alcott, the abolitionist and Unitarian minister Theodore Parker, and the Unitarian minister Orestes A. Brownson (later a major force in American Catholicism). Such friends were welcome, for during the early 1830s deaths broke up the close-knit band of Emerson brothers. Emerson himself had gone south to recover from tuberculosis in 1826–27; weakened by the same disease, Edward Emerson became mentally deranged in 1827 and died in 1834; and the youngest brother, Charles, died in 1836. There was compensation for Emerson in the circle of admirers who began forming about him at the time of his second marriage and the publication of *Nature*. Alcott, Margaret Fuller, and others sought him out, some paying him frequent and prolonged visits or even settling in Concord to be near him.

*Nature* reached a smaller audience than did many of his lectures, which were often reported by newspapers in substantial part; his formal Harvard addresses to the Phi Beta Kappa Society in 1837 on the American scholar and to the Divinity School graduates in 1838 on the state of Christianity were both printed as pamphlets, according to the custom of the time. The second of these speeches occasioned a brief, virulent series of attacks in the press for its heresies, giving Emerson a notoriety that barred him from speaking at Harvard for three decades. His unsigned contributions to the Transcendentalists' magazine *The Dial* did not enhance his reputation; indeed, he sometimes was attacked in newspapers as the author of Alcott's *Orphic Sayings*, which jocular contemporaries took as the ultimate of transcendental gibberish. Only with the publication of *Essays* (1841) did Emerson's lasting reputation begin. Far more than *Nature*, this book was directed to a popular audience. The essays had been tried out, in whole or large part, in his lectures, so that their final form was shaped by the responses of many audiences.

By the early 1840s, Emerson's life had settled into its enduring routine. He gave intermittent lectures in Boston and made lecture tours in the Northeast and, later, in the Middle Atlantic states to supplement the income from his legacy. Early in 1842 his first son, Waldo, died at the age of five, the last of the untimely deaths in Emerson's immediate family; after that Emerson devoted himself more and more to the personal problems of his circle of family and friends. His editing of *The Dial* from 1842 till 1844, for instance, was undertaken mainly to support his friends, especially Margaret Fuller. He worked steadily at a succession of essays, usually derived from his extensive journals by way of one or more intervening lectures. *Essays* (1841) was followed by *Essays: Second Series* (1844). The second collection demonstrated even more thoroughly than the first that Emerson's intellect had sharpened in the years since *Nature*. In *The Poet* especially his grappling with aesthetic problems was more incisive; he spoke from practical experience as well as theoretical speculation in defining the present state of literature in America, and he brilliantly foretold the nature of the great national poets to come. In *Experience* and other essays he resolutely and realistically faced the conflict between idealism and ordinary life. The deferential minister and the once-tentative lecturer had become a confident American prophet. Emerson slowly gained recognition for his poems, which he collected at the end of 1846. A second trip to Europe (1847–48) capped his secure middle age. He became something of a country squire, buying up many pieces of property in and around Concord. Always aware that there was a certain coldness in his disposition, he deliberately set out to make himself into a more sociable man, taking part in Boston club life (and smoking cigars to mask his diffidence). As his reputation expanded, he widened his lecture tours into the Midwest. His newer books, among them *Representative Men* (1849) and *Conduct of Life* (1860), were less forceful than his earlier ones, though they sold better because of the enlarged market and his established fame. After long resisting attempts by reformers to gain his support for various social issues, Emerson became a fervent advocate in the 1850s for abolitionism, though his efforts were too late and too local to make him a national leader. The rest of Emerson's writing, like the rest of his life, was a slow anticlimax to the intellectual ferment of the years between the mid-1830s and the mid-1840s, though it was only during these later decades that his earlier work first won general recognition. Emerson's memory began to fail more than ten years before his death, and he declined into a benign senility during which the English-speaking world, and even many who read him in translation, continued to honor the intellectual liberator that he had been in his middle life.

Although Emerson's contemporary reputation rested on his essays, he had all along been writing another masterpiece, his journals, which were not published in full until the 1960s and 1970s under the title *Journals and Miscellaneous Notebooks*. It will take time before readers fully grasp the importance of these writings as the historical record of a response to people and events, the most thorough documentation we possess of the growth of a nineteenth-century American writer, and the remarkable account of a spiritual life.

A critic said that Emerson wanted to get his whole philosophy into each essay; more than that, he got as much of it as he could into everything he wrote. Emerson's point of view may shift from one pole of a subject to the other even within a single work, for his mind moved like that of a dramatist who embodies felt or imagined moods in various characters, but the subject remains Emersonian. In this there is challenge for the new reader to find pattern in diversity. And for those who have already cherished Emerson through the various stages of life there is the warmth of familiarity, however unsettling this mild-mannered man always remains to any receptive reader.

Nature    Since its anonymous publication (1836), a little book paid for by the author himself, *Nature* has been recognized as a major document in American Romanticism and Transcendentalism. Merton M. Sealts, Jr., and Alfred R. Ferguson in their *Emerson's "Nature"—Origin, Growth, Meaning* point out "how wide the divergence has been over how to read such a work—whether as doctrine or mysticism, philosophy or poetry." In an earlier Norton anthology, *Eight American Writers* (1963), one of the most conscientious Emersonians, the late Stephen E. Whicher, took the book as "an audacious attempt to rescue nature from the natural scientists and to sketch instead a human or poetical science"; he took Emerson's question "To what end is nature?" as asking how nature can help "to restore our confidence and release our powers, the fact of historical religion once did." Underlying many passages in *Nature* is the defensiveness of a man who has chosen to be a thinker rather than taking what his contemporaries would have seen as an active role in affairs, a defensiveness, in the sexist terminology which he regularly employed, against the charge of "effeminancy." For modern readers there is inescapable pain at Emerson's confidence that wild nature is inexhaustible and invulnerable and at the undreamed-of consequences of the belief that nature is created for human benefit.

We have drawn on the Sealts-Ferguson list of emendations for the corrections of a few obvious typographical errors and have followed Sealts and Ferguson in two corrections Emerson made in presentation copies at the beginning of Chapter 4, but we have left several oddities of punctuation, spelling, and rough-and-ready subject-verb agreements. The text is thus the one Emerson offered to his circle of American and British friends in the fall of 1836 as his first bid for a national and international reputation.

The Sealts-Ferguson volume is indispensable to serious study of *Nature* for, among other virtues, its printing of source passages in the Harvard University Press edition of *The Journals and Miscellaneous Notebooks of Ralph Waldo Emerson* (abbreviated here *JMN*). We have given the journal and lecture citations only when they reveal Emerson's literary borrowings (which are as often as not second-hand—a quotation from a Greek philosopher in a work by Samuel Taylor Coleridge, for example).

# Nature

*"Nature is but an image or imitation of wisdom, the last thing of the soul;
nature being a thing which doth only do, but not know."*

—*Plotinus*[1]

## Introduction

Our age is retrospective. It builds the sepulchres of the fathers. It writes
biographies, histories, and criticism. The foregoing generations beheld God
and nature face to face; we, through their eyes. Why should not we also enjoy
an original relation to the universe? Why should not we have a poetry and
philosophy of insight and not of tradition, and a religion by revelation to us,
and not the history of theirs? Embosomed for a season in nature, whose floods
of life stream around and through us, and invite us by the powers they supply,
to action proportioned to nature, why should we grope among the dry bones
of the past,[2] or put the living generation into masquerade out of its faded
wardrobe? The sun shines to-day also. There is more wool and flax in the
fields. There are new lands, new men, new thoughts. Let us demand our own
works and laws and worship.

Undoubtedly we have no questions to ask which are unanswerable. We
must trust the perfection of the creation so far, as to believe that whatever
curiosity the order of things has awakened in our minds, the order of things
can satisfy. Every man's condition is a solution in hieroglyphic to those inquiries he would put. He acts it as life, before he apprehends it as truth. In like
manner, nature is already, in its forms and tendencies, describing its own
design. Let us interrogate the great apparition, that shines so peacefully around
us. Let us inquire, to what end is nature?

All science has one aim, namely, to find a theory of nature. We have theories of races and of functions, but scarcely yet a remote approximation to an
idea of creation. We are now so far from the road to truth, that religious
teachers dispute and hate each other, and speculative men are esteemed
unsound and frivolous. But to a sound judgment, the most abstract truth is
the most practical. Whenever a true theory appears, it will be its own evidence.
Its test is, that it will explain all phenomena. Now many are thought not only
unexplained but inexplicable; as language, sleep, dreams, beasts, sex.

Philosophically considered, the universe is composed of Nature and the
Soul. Strictly speaking, therefore, all that is separate from us, all which Philosophy distinguishes as the NOT ME,[3] that is, both nature and art, all other men
and my own body, must be ranked under this name, NATURE. In enumerating
the values of nature and casting up their sum, I shall use the word in both
senses;—in its common and in its philosophical import. In inquiries so general
as our present one, the inaccuracy is not material; no confusion of thought
will occur. *Nature*, in the common sense, refers to essences unchanged by
man; space, the air, the river, the leaf. *Art* is applied to the mixture of his will
with the same things, as in a house, a canal, a statue, a picture. But his

---

1. Emerson found the motto from the Roman philosopher Plotinus (205?–270?) in his copy of Ralph Cud-
worth's *The True Intellectual System of the Universe*
(1820).
2. An echo of Ezekiel 37.1–14, esp. 37.4, where God
tells Ezekiel to "Prophesy upon these bones, and say
unto them, O ye dry bones, hear the word of the

Lord." Emerson had left the ministry but was still writing as a prophet.
3. Emerson takes "not me" from Thomas Carlyle's
*Sartor Resartus* (1833–34), where it appears as a translation of the recent German philosophical term for everything but the self.

operations taken together are so insignificant, a little chipping, baking, patching, and washing, that in an impression so grand as that of the world on the human mind, they do not vary the result.

## Chapter I. *Nature*

To go into solitude, a man needs to retire as much from his chamber as from society. I am not solitary whilst I read and write, though nobody is with me. But if a man would be alone, let him look at the stars. The rays that come from those heavenly worlds, will separate between him and vulgar things. One might think the atmosphere was made transparent with this design, to give man, in the heavenly bodies, the perpetual presence of the sublime. Seen in the streets of cities, how great they are! If the stars should appear one night in a thousand years, how would men believe and adore; and preserve for many generations the remembrance of the city of God which had been shown! But every night come out these preachers of beauty, and light the universe with their admonishing smile.

The stars awaken a certain reverence, because though always present, they are always inaccessible; but all natural objects make a kindred impression, when the mind is open to their influence. Nature never wears a mean appearance. Neither does the wisest man extort all her secret, and lose his curiosity by finding out all her perfection. Nature never became a toy to a wise spirit. The flowers, the animals, the mountains, reflected all the wisdom of his best hour, as much as they had delighted the simplicity of his childhood.

When we speak of nature in this manner, we have a distinct but most poetical sense in the mind. We mean the integrity of impression made by manifold natural objects. It is this which distinguishes the stick of timber of the woodcutter, from the tree of the poet. The charming landscape which I saw this morning, is indubitably made up of some twenty or thirty farms. Miller owns this field, Locke that, and Manning the woodland beyond. But none of them owns the landscape. There is a property in the horizon which no man has but he whose eye can integrate all the parts, that is, the poet. This is the best part of these men's farms, yet to this their land-deeds give them no title.[4]

To speak truly, few adult persons can see nature. Most persons do not see the sun. At least they have a very superficial seeing. The sun illuminates only the eye of the man, but shines into the eye and the heart of the child. The lover of nature is he whose inward and outward senses are still truly adjusted to each other; who has retained the spirit of infancy even into the era of manhood.[5] His intercourse with heaven and earth, becomes part of his daily food. In the presence of nature, a wild delight runs through the man, in spite of real sorrows. Nature says,—he is my creature, and maugre[6] all his impertinent griefs, he shall be glad with me. Not the sun or the summer alone, but every hour and season yields its tribute of delight; for every hour and change corresponds to and authorizes a different state of the mind, from breathless noon to grimmest midnight. Nature is a setting that fits equally well a comic or a mourning piece. In good health, the air is a cordial of incredible virtue. Crossing a bare common, in snow puddles, at twilight, under a clouded sky, without

4. Cf., *Where I Lived, and What I Lived For* (p. 830) in Thoreau's *Walden*.
5. An echo of Samuel Taylor Coleridge's *Biographia Literaria*, chap. 4, in which Coleridge defines the character and privilege of genius as the ability to carry the feelings of childhood into the powers of adulthood.
6. Despite.

having in my thoughts any occurrence of special good fortune, I have enjoyed a perfect exhilaration. Almost I fear to think how glad I am. In the woods too, a man casts off his years, as the snake his slough, and at what period soever of life, is always a child. In the woods, is perpetual youth. Within these plantations of God, a decorum and sanctity reign, a perennial festival is dressed, and the guest sees not how he should tire of them in a thousand years. In the woods, we return to reason and faith. There I feel that nothing can befal me in life,—no disgrace, no calamity, (leaving me my eyes,) which nature cannot repair. Standing on the bare ground,—my head bathed by the blithe air, and uplifted into infinite space,—all mean egotism vanishes. I become a transparent eye-ball.[7] I am nothing. I see all. The currents of the Universal Being circulate through me; I am part or particle of God. The name of the nearest friend sounds then foreign and accidental. To be brothers, to be acquaintances,—master or servant, is then a trifle and a disturbance. I am the lover of uncontained and immortal beauty. In the wilderness, I find something more dear and connate[8] than in streets or villages. In the tranquil landscape, and especially in the distant line of the horizon, man beholds somewhat as beautiful as his own nature.

The greatest delight which the fields and woods minister, is the suggestion of an occult relation between man and the vegetable. I am not alone and unacknowledged. They nod to me and I to them. The waving of the boughs in the storm, is new to me and old. It takes me by surprise, and yet is not unknown. Its effect is like that of a higher thought or a better emotion coming over me, when I deemed I was thinking justly or doing right.

Yet it is certain that the power to produce this delight, does not reside in nature, but in man, or in a harmony of both. It is necessary to use these pleasures with great temperance. For, nature is not always tricked in holiday attire, but the same scene which yesterday breathed perfume and glittered as for the frolic of the nymphs, is overspread with melancholy today. Nature always wears the colors of the spirit.[9] To a man laboring under calamity, the heat of his own fire hath sadness in it. Then, there is a kind of contempt of the landscape felt by him who has just lost by death a dear friend. The sky is less grand as it shuts down over less worth in the population.

## Chapter II.  Commodity[1]

Whoever considers the final cause[2] of the world, will discern a multitude of uses that enter as parts into that result. They all admit of being thrown into one of the following classes; Commodity; Beauty; Language; and Discipline.

Under the general name of Commodity, I rank all those advantages which our senses owe to nature. This, of course, is a benefit which is temporary and mediate, not ultimate, like its service to the soul. Yet although low, it is perfect in its kind, and is the only use of nature which all men apprehend. The misery of man appears like childish petulance, when we explore the steady and prodigal provision that has been made for his support and delight on this

7. The most famous phrase in the essay, endlessly ridiculed and explicated. As Sealts says in *The Composition of Nature*, Emerson is not "merely repeating what he had already said about the implications of the preceding sentence on the bare common." When the speaker leaves the village for the woods, "the level of discourse is significantly shifted along with the setting,

and the ensuing episode takes place on what Emerson would later call another 'platform' of experience."
8. Related.
9. See Emerson's maturer broodings on subjectivity in *Experience* (p. 523).
1. Usefulness.
2. In the sense of "purpose."

green ball which floats him through the heavens. What angels invented these splendid ornaments, these rich conveniences, this ocean of air above, this ocean of water beneath, this firmament of earth between? this zodiac of lights, this tent of dropping clouds, this striped coat of climates, this fourfold year? Beasts, fire, water, stones, and corn serve him. The field is at once his floor, his work-yard, his play-ground, his garden, and his bed.

> "More servants wait on man
> Than he'll take notice of."[3]——

Nature, in its ministry to man, is not only the material, but is also the process and the result. All the parts incessantly work into each other's hands for the profit of man. The wind sows the seed; the sun evaporates the sea; the wind blows the vapor to the field; the ice, on the other side of the planet, condenses rain on this; the rain feeds the plant; the plant feeds the animal; and thus the endless circulations of the divine charity nourish man.

The useful arts are but reproductions or new combinations by the wit of man, of the same natural benefactors. He no longer waits for favoring gales, but by means of steam, he realizes the fable of Æolus's bag,[4] and carries the two and thirty winds in the boiler of his boat. To diminish friction, he paves the road with iron bars, and, mounting a coach with a ship-load of men, animals, and merchandise behind him, he darts through the country, from town to town, like an eagle or a swallow through the air. By the aggregate of these aids, how is the face of the world changed, from the era of Noah to that of Napoleon! The private poor man hath cities, ships, canals, bridges, built for him. He goes to the post-office, and the human race run on his errands; to the book-shop, and the human race read and write of all that happens, for him; to the court-house, and nations repair his wrongs. He sets his house upon the road, and the human race go forth every morning, and shovel out the snow, and cut a path for him.

But there is no need of specifying particulars in this class of uses. The catalogue is endless, and the examples so obvious, that I shall leave them to the reader's reflection, with the general remark, that this mercenary benefit is one which has respect to a farther good. A man is fed, not that he may be fed, but that he may work.

## Chapter III. Beauty

A nobler want of man is served by nature, namely, the love of Beauty.

The ancient Greeks called the world κοσμο,[5] beauty. Such is the constitution of all things, or such the plastic[6] power of the human eye, that the primary forms, as the sky, the mountain, the tree, the animal, give us a delight in and for themselves; a pleasure arising from outline, color, motion, and grouping. This seems partly owing to the eye itself. The eye is the best of artists. By the mutual action of its structure and of the laws of light, perspective is produced, which integrates every mass of objects, of what character soever, into a well colored and shaded globe, so that where the particular objects are mean and

---

3. From *Man*, by the English poet George Herbert (1593–1633), quoted at length in chap. 8, "Prospects."
4. In the *Odyssey* 10, Aeolus, the god of winds, gives Odysseus a bag containing favorable winds, but they create a storm when his unwary sailors let them all out

at once; here, Emerson refers only to the harnessing of the powers of nature by human beings. "Realizes": brings into real existence.
5. Cosmos, or order.
6. Creative.

unaffecting, the landscape which they compose, is round and symmetrical. And as the eye is the best composer, so light is the first of painters. There is no object so foul that intense light will not make beautiful. And the stimulus it affords to the sense, and a sort of infinitude which it hath, like space and time, make all matter gay. Even the corpse hath its own beauty. But beside this general grace diffused over nature, almost all the individual forms are agreeable to the eye, as is proved by our endless imitations[7] of some of them, as the acorn, the grape, the pine-cone, the wheat-ear, the egg, the wings and forms of most birds, the lion's claw, the serpent, the butterfly, sea-shells, flames, clouds, buds, leaves, and the forms of many trees, as the palm.

For better consideration, we may distribute the aspects of Beauty in a three-fold manner.

1. First, the simple perception of natural forms is a delight. The influence of the forms and actions in nature, is so needful to man, that, in its lowest functions, it seems to lie on the confines of commodity and beauty. To the body and mind which have been cramped by noxious work or company, nature is medicinal and restores their tone. The tradesman, the attorney comes out of the din and craft[8] of the street, and sees the sky and the woods, and is a man again. In their eternal calm, he finds himself. The health of the eye seems to demand a horizon. We are never tired, so long as we can see far enough.

But in other hours, Nature satisfies the soul purely by its loveliness, and without any mixture of corporeal benefit. I have seen the spectacle of morning from the hill-top over against my house, from day-break to sun-rise, with emotions which an angel might share. The long slender bars of cloud float like fishes in the sea of crimson light. From the earth, as a shore, I look out into that silent sea. I seem to partake its rapid transformations: the active enchantment reaches my dust, and I dilate and conspire with[9] the morning wind. How does Nature deify us with a few and cheap elements! Give me health and a day, and I will make the pomp of emperors ridiculous. The dawn is my Assyria; the sun-set and moon-rise my Paphos, and unimaginable realms of faerie, broad noon shall be my England of the senses and the understanding; the night shall be my Germany of mystic philosophy and dreams.[1]

Not less excellent, except for our less susceptibility in the afternoon, was the charm, last evening, of a January sunset. The western clouds divided and subdivided themselves into pink flakes modulated with tints of unspeakable softness; and the air had so much life and sweetness, that it was a pain to come within doors. What was it that nature would say? Was there no meaning in the live repose of the valley behind the mill, and which Homer or Shakspeare could not re-form for me in words? The leafless trees become spires of flame in the sunset, with the blue east for their background, and the stars of the dead calices of flowers, and every withered stem and stubble rimed[2] with frost, contribute something to the mute music.

The inhabitants of cities suppose that the country landscape is pleasant only half the year. I please myself with observing the graces of the winter scenery,

---

7. As in architectural and furniture design and decoration.
8. Craftiness, materialism.
9. Breathe with.
1. "Assyria": the ancient Near Eastern empire. "Paphos": the ancient city in Cyprus (site of worship of

Aphrodite). In the next part of the passage Emerson is contrasting the Scottish Common Sense philosophy with German post-Kantian idealism.
2. Coated. "Calices": i.e., calyxes; the outer whorls of leaves or sepals at the bases of flowers.

and believe that we are as much touched by it as by the genial[3] influences of summer. To the attentive eye, each moment of the year has its own beauty, and in the same field, it beholds, every hour, a picture which was never seen before, and which shall never be seen again. The heavens change every moment, and reflect their glory or gloom on the plains beneath. The state of the crop in the surrounding farms alters the expression of the earth from week to week. The succession of native plants in the pastures and roadsides, which make the silent clock by which time tells the summer hours, will make even the divisions of the day sensible to a keen observer. The tribes of birds and insects, like the plants punctual to their time, follow each other, and the year has room for all. By water-courses, the variety is greater. In July, the blue pontederia or pickerel-weed blooms in large beds in the shallow parts of our pleasant river,[4] and swarms with yellow butterflies in continual motion. Art cannot rival this pomp of purple and gold. Indeed the river is a perpetual gala, and boasts each month a new ornament.

But this beauty of Nature which is seen and felt as beauty, is the least part. The shows of day, the dewy morning, the rainbow, mountains, orchards in blossom, stars, moonlight, shadows in still water, and the like, if too eagerly hunted, become shows merely, and mock us with their unreality. Go out of the house to see the moon, and 't is mere tinsel; it will not please as when its light shines upon your necessary journey. The beauty that shimmers in the yellow afternoons of October, who ever could clutch it? Go forth to find it, and it is gone: 't is only a mirage as you look from the windows of the diligence.

2. The presence of a higher, namely, of the spiritual element is essential to its perfection. The high and divine beauty which can be loved without effeminacy, is that which is found in combination with the human will, and never separate. Beauty is the mark God sets upon virtue. Every natural action is graceful. Every heroic act is also decent,[5] and causes the place and the bystanders to shine. We are taught by great actions that the universe is the property of every individual in it. Every rational creature has all nature for his dowry and estate. It is his, if he will. He may divest himself of it; he may creep into a corner, and abdicate his kingdom, as most men do, but he is entitled to the world by his constitution. In proportion to the energy of his thought and will, he takes up the world into himself. "All those things for which men plough, build, or sail, obey virtue;" said an ancient historian.[6] "The winds and waves," said Gibbon,[7] "are always on the side of the ablest navigators." So are the sun and moon and all the stars of heaven. When a noble act is done,—perchance in a scene of great natural beauty; when Leonidas and his three hundred martyrs consume one day in dying, and the sun and moon come each and look at them once in the steep defile of Thermopylæ; when Arnold Winkelried,[8] in the high Alps, under the shadow of the avalanche, gathers in his side a sheaf of Austrian spears to break the line for his comrades; are not these heroes entitled to add the beauty of the scene to the beauty of the deed? When the bark of Columbus nears the shore of America;—before it, the

---

3. Generative, creative.
4. The Concord River.
5. Beautiful.
6. Sallust (1st century B.C.), Roman historian, in *The Conspiracy of Cataline*, chap. 2.
7. Edward Gibbon (1737–1794), English historian, from *The Decline and Fall of the Roman Empire*, chap.

68 (*JMN* 5.108).
8. Arnold von Winkelried, a Swiss hero, was killed (1386) in a battle against the Austrians at Sempach. Leonidas, king of Sparta, was killed (c. 480 B.C.) defending the pass at Thermopylae against the Persian army led by Xerxes.

beach lined with savages, fleeing out of all their huts of cane; the sea behind; and the purple mountains of the Indian Archipelago around, can we separate the man from the living picture? Does not the New World clothe his form with her palm-groves and savannahs as fit drapery? Ever does natural beauty steal in like air, and envelope great actions. When Sir Harry Vane[9] was dragged up the Tower-hill, sitting on a sled, to suffer death, as the champion of the English laws, one of the multitude cried out to him, "You never sate on so glorious a seat." Charles II., to intimidate the citizens of London, caused the patriot Lord Russel[1] to be drawn in an open coach, through the principal streets of the city, on his way to the scaffold. "But," to use the simple narrative of his biographer, "the multitude imagined they saw liberty and virtue sitting by his side." In private places, among sordid objects, an act of truth or heroism seems at once to draw to itself the sky as its temple, the sun as its candle. Nature stretcheth out her arms to embrace man, only let his thoughts be of equal greatness. Willingly does she follow his steps with the rose and the violet, and bend her lines of grandeur and grace to the decoration of her darling child. Only let his thoughts be of equal scope, and the frame will suit the picture. A virtuous man, is in unison with her works, and makes the central figure of the visible sphere. Homer, Pindar, Socrates, Phocion,[2] associate themselves fitly in our memory with the whole geography and climate of Greece. The visible heavens and earth sympathize with Jesus. And in common life, whosoever has seen a person of powerful character and happy genius, will have remarked how easily he took all things along with him,—the persons, the opinions, and the day, and nature became ancillary to a man.

3. There is still another aspect under which the beauty of the world may be viewed, namely, as it becomes an object of the intellect. Beside the relation of things to virtue, they have a relation to thought. The intellect searches out the absolute order of things as they stand in the mind of God, and without the colors of affection.[3] The intellectual and the active powers seem to succeed each other in man, and the exclusive activity of the one, generates the exclusive activity of the other. There is something unfriendly in each to the other, but they are like the alternate periods of feeding and working in animals; each prepares and certainly will be followed by the other. Therefore does beauty, which, in relation to actions, as we have seen comes unsought, and comes because it is unsought, remain for the apprehension and pursuit of the intellect; and then again, in its turn, of the active power. Nothing divine dies. All good is eternally reproductive. The beauty of nature reforms itself in the mind, and not for barren contemplation, but for new creation.

All men are in some degree impressed by the face of the world. Some men even to delight. This love of beauty is Taste. Others have the same love in such excess, that, not content with admiring, they seek to embody it in new forms. The creation of beauty is Art.

The production of a work of art throws a light upon the mystery of humanity. A work of art is an abstract or epitome of the world. It is the result or expression of nature, in miniature. For although the works of nature are innu-

9. A Puritan, once colonial governor of Massachusetts; he was executed for treason in 1662.
1. William, Lord Russel (b. 1639) was executed for treason in 1683 after perjurous testimony. *JMN* (5.76) cites Emerson's source as Alexander Chalmer's *General Biographical Dictionary*.
2. Athenian statesman and general of the 4th century

B.C., of whom Emerson knew from Plutarch's *Lives*. Homer was the legendary Greek author of *The Iliad* and *The Odyssey*. Pindar was a Greek lyric poet of the 5th and 6th centuries B.C. Socrates was a Greek philosopher of the 5th century B.C.
3. Modifying emotions.

merable and all different, the result or the expression of them all is similar and single. Nature is a sea of forms radically alike and even unique.[4] A leaf, a sunbeam, a landscape, the ocean, make an analogous impression on the mind. What is common to them all,—that perfectness and harmony, is beauty. Therefore the standard of beauty, is the entire circuit of natural forms,—the totality of nature; which the Italians expressed by defining beauty "il piu nell' uno."[5] Nothing is quite beautiful alone: nothing but is beautiful in the whole. A single object is only so far beautiful as it suggests this universal grace. The poet, the painter, the sculptor, the musician, the architect seek each to concentrate this radiance of the world on one point, and each in his several work to satisfy the love of beauty which stimulates him to produce. Thus is Art, a nature passed through the alembic[6] of man. Thus in art, does nature work through the will of a man filled with the beauty of her first works.

The world thus exists to the soul to satisfy the desire of beauty. Extend this element to the uttermost, and I call it an ultimate end. No reason can be asked or given why the soul seeks beauty. Beauty, in its largest and profoundest sense, is one expression for the universe. God is the all-fair. Truth, and goodness, and beauty, are but different faces of the same All. But beauty in nature is not ultimate. It is the herald of inward and eternal beauty, and is not alone a solid and satisfactory good. It must therefore stand as a part and not as yet the last or highest expression of the final cause of Nature.

## Chapter IV. Language

A third use which Nature subserves to man is that of Language. Nature is the vehicle of thought, and in a simple, double, and threefold degree.

1. Words are signs of natural facts.
2. Particular natural facts are symbols of particular spiritual facts.
3. Nature is the symbol of spirit.

1. Words are signs of natural facts. The use of natural history is to give us aid in supernatural history. The use of the outer creation is to give us language for the beings and changes of the inward creation. Every word which is used to express a moral or intellectual fact, if traced to its root, is found to be borrowed from some material appearance. *Right* originally means *straight; wrong* means *twisted. Spirit* primarily means *wind; transgression*, the crossing of a *line; supercilious*, the *raising of the eye-brow*. We say the *heart* to express emotion, the *head* to denote thought; and *thought* and *emotion* are, in their turn, words borrowed from sensible things, and now appropriated to spiritual nature. Most of the process by which this transformation is made, is hidden from us in the remote time when language was framed; but the same tendency may be daily observed in children. Children and savages use only nouns or names of things, which they continually convert into verbs, and apply to analogous mental acts.

2. But this origin of all words that convey a spiritual import,—so conspicuous a fact in the history of language,—is our least debt to nature. It is not words only that are emblematic; it is things which are emblematic. Every natural fact is a symbol of some spiritual fact.[7] Every appearance in nature

---

4. Similar to the point of being identical.
5. The many in one (a borrowing from Coleridge).
6. A distilling apparatus.
7. This passage owes much to the Swedish theologian

and mystic Emanuel Swedenborg (1688–1772), whose doctrine of correspondence between the inner and outer worlds underlies much of Emerson's thought.

corresponds to some state of the mind, and that state of the mind can only be described by presenting that natural appearance as its picture. An enraged man is a lion, a cunning man is a fox, a firm man is a rock, a learned man is a torch. A lamb is innocence; a snake is subtle spite; flowers express to us the delicate affections. Light and darkness are our familiar expression for knowledge and ignorance; and heat for love. Visible distance behind and before us, is respectively our image of memory and hope.

Who looks upon a river in a meditative hour, and is not reminded of the flux of all things? Throw a stone into the stream, and the circles that propagate themselves are the beautiful type of all influence. Man is conscious of a universal soul within or behind his individual life, wherein, as in a firmament, the natures of Justice, Truth, Love, Freedom, arise and shine. This universal soul, he calls Reason: it is not mine or thine or his, but we are its; we are its property and men.[8] And the blue sky in which the private earth is buried, the sky with its eternal calm, and full of everlasting orbs, is the type of Reason. That which, intellectually considered, we call Reason, considered in relation to nature, we call Spirit. Spirit is the Creator. Spirit hath life in itself. And man in all ages and countries, embodies it in his language, as the FATHER.

It is easily seen that there is nothing lucky or capricious in these analogies, but that they are constant, and pervade nature. These are not the dreams of a few poets, here and there, but man is an analogist, and studies relations in all objects. He is placed in the centre of beings, and a ray of relation passes from every other being to him. And neither can man be understood without these objects, nor these objects without man. All the facts in natural history taken by themselves, have no value, but are barren like a single sex. But marry it to human history, and it is full of life. Whole Floras, all Linnæus' and Buffon's[9] volume, are but dry catalogues of facts; but the most trivial of these facts, the habit of a plant, the organs, or work, or noise of an insect, applied to the illustration of a fact in intellectual philosophy, or, in any way associated to human nature, affects us in the most lively and agreeable manner. The seed of a plant,—to what affecting analogies in the nature of man, is that little fruit made use of, in all discourse, up to the voice of Paul, who calls the human corpse a seed,—"It is sown a natural body; it is raised a spiritual body."[1] The motion of the earth round its axis, and round the sun, makes the day, and the year. These are certain amounts of brute light and heat. But is there no intent of an analogy between man's life and the seasons? And do the seasons gain no grandeur or pathos from that analogy? The instincts of the ant are very unimportant considered as the ant's; but the moment a ray of relation is seen to extend from it to man, and the little drudge is seen to be a monitor, a little body with a mighty heart, then all its habits, even that said to be recently observed, that it never sleeps, become sublime.

Because of this radical[2] correspondence between visible things and human thoughts, savages, who have only what is necessary, converse in figures. As we go back in history, language becomes more picturesque, until its infancy, when it is all poetry; or, all spiritual facts are represented by natural symbols.[3]

8. As he regularly does, Emerson uses *reason* to mean something like what we think of as the intuitive powers of the mind and *understanding* to mean the rational powers.
9. French naturalist (1707–1788). "Linnaeus": Carl von Linné (1707–1778), Swedish botanist.

1. 1 Corinthians 15.44.
2. Fundamental (literally "from the root").
3. The superseded theory of language was a Romantic commonplace, familiar to Emerson from Percy Bysshe Shelley's A *Defense of Poetry* (1821): "In the infancy of society every author is necessarily a poet."

The same symbols are found to make the original elements of all languages. It has moreover been observed, that the idioms of all languages approach each other in passages of the greatest eloquence and power. And as this is the first language, so is it the last. This immediate dependence of language upon nature, this conversion of an outward phenomenon into a type of somewhat in human life, never loses its power to affect us. It is this which gives that piquancy to the conversation of a strong-natured farmer or back-woodsman, which all men relish.

Thus is nature an interpreter, by whose means man converses with his fellow men. A man's power to connect his thought with its proper symbol, and so utter it, depends on the simplicity of his character, that is, upon his love of truth and his desire to communicate it without loss. The corruption of man is followed by the corruption of language. When simplicity of character and the sovereignty of ideas is broken up by the prevalence of secondary desires, the desire of riches, the desire of pleasure, the desire of power, the desire of praise,—and duplicity and falsehood take place of simplicity and truth, the power over nature as an interpreter of the will, is in a degree lost; new imagery ceases to be created, and old words are perverted to stand for things which are not; a paper currency is employed when there is no bullion in the vaults. In due time, the fraud is manifest, and words lose all power to stimulate the understanding or the affections. Hundreds of writers may be found in every long-civilized nation, who for a short time believe, and make others believe, that they see and utter truths, who do not of themselves clothe one thought in its natural garment, but who feed unconsciously upon the language created by the primary writers of the country, those, namely, who hold primarily on nature.

But wise men pierce this rotten diction and fasten words again to visible things; so that picturesque language is at once a commanding certificate that he who employs it, is a man in alliance with truth and God. The moment our discourse rises above the ground line of familiar facts, and is inflamed with passion or exalted by thought, it clothes itself in images. A man conversing in earnest, if he watch his intellectual processes, will find that always a material image, more or less luminous, arises in his mind, contemporaneous with every thought, which furnishes the vestment of the thought. Hence, good writing and brilliant discourse are perpetual allegories. This imagery is spontaneous. It is the blending of experience with the present action of the mind. It is proper creation. It is the working of the Original Cause through the instruments he has already made.

These facts may suggest the advantage which the country-life possesses for a powerful mind, over the artificial and curtailed life of cities. We know more from nature than we can at will communicate. Its light flows into the mind evermore, and we forget its presence. The poet, the orator, bred in the woods, whose scenes have been nourished by their fair and appeasing changes, year after year, without design and without heed,—shall not lose their lesson altogether, in the roar of cities or the broil of politics. Long hereafter, amidst agitation and terror in national councils,—in the hour of revolution,—these solemn images shall reappear in their morning lustre, as fit symbols and words of the thoughts which the passing events shall awaken. At the call of a noble sentiment, again the woods wave, the pines murmur, the river rolls and shines, and the cattle low upon the mountains, as he saw and heard them in

his infancy. And with these forms, the spells of persuasion, the keys of power
are put into his hands.

3. We are thus assisted by natural objects in the expression of particular
meanings. But how great a language to convey such pepper-corn informations!
Did it need such noble races of creatures, this profusion of forms, this host of
orbs in heaven, to furnish man with the dictionary and grammar of his municipal speech? Whilst we use this grand cipher to expedite the affairs of our pot
and kettle, we feel that we have not yet put it to its use, neither are able. We
are like travellers using the cinders of a volcano to roast their eggs. Whilst we
see that it always stands ready to clothe what we would say, we cannot avoid
the question, whether the characters are not significant of themselves. Have
mountains, and waves, and skies, no significance but what we consciously
give them, when we employ them as emblems of our thoughts? The world is
emblematic. Parts of speech are metaphors because the whole of nature is a
metaphor of the human mind. The laws of moral nature answer to those of
matter as face to face in a glass. "The visible world and the relation of its parts,
is the dial plate of the invisible."[4] The axioms of physics translate the laws of
ethics.[5] Thus, "the whole is greater than its part;" "reaction is equal to action;"
"the smallest weight may be made to lift the greatest, the difference of weight
being compensated by time;" and many the like propositions, which have an
ethical as well as physical sense. These propositions have a much more extensive and universal sense when applied to human life, than when confined to
technical use.

In like manner, the memorable words of history, and the proverbs of
nations, consist usually of a natural fact, selected as a picture or parable of a
moral truth. Thus; A rolling stone gathers no moss; A bird in the hand is worth
two in the bush; A cripple in the right way, will beat a racer in the wrong;
Make hay whilst the sun shines; 'T is hard to carry a full cup even; Vinegar is
the son of wine; The last ounce broke the camel's back; Long-lived trees make
roots first;—and the like.[6] In their primary sense these are trivial facts, but we
repeat them for the value of their analogical import. What is true of proverbs,
is true of all fables, parables, and allegories.

This relation between the mind and matter is not fancied by some poet, but
stands in the will of God, and so is free to be known by all men. It appears to
men, or it does not appear. When in fortunate hours we ponder this miracle,
the wise man doubts, if, at all other times, he is not blind and deaf;

> ——"Can these things be,
> And overcome us like a summer's cloud,
> Without our special wonder?"[7]

for the universe becomes transparent, and the light of higher laws than its
own, shines through it. It is the standing problem which has exercised the
wonder and the study of every fine genius since the world began; from the era
of the Egyptians and the Brahmins, to that of Pythagoras, of Plato, of Bacon,

4. Emerson copied the Swedenborg quotation from
the New Jerusalem Magazine (July 1832), 437 (JMN
4.33).
5. Adapted from Mme. De Stael's Germany (1813):
"Not a mathematical axiom but is a moral rule"
(JMN 3.255).
6. A list of proverbs in JMN (6.138–41) includes sev-

eral of these, the one about the cripple in the race being attributed to Francis Bacon's The Advancement of
Learning, II, and the one about the full cup being attributed to Robert Leighton's Select Works.
7. Macbeth, 3.4.110–12 (Emerson misquotes "these"
for "such").

of Leibnitz, of Swedenborg.[8] There sits the Sphinx at the road-side, and from age to age, as each prophet comes by, he tries his fortune at reading her riddle.[9] There seems to be a necessity in spirit to manifest itself in material forms; and day and night, river and storm, beast and bird, acid and alkali, preëxist in necessary Ideas in the mind of God, and are what they are by virtue of preceding affections,[1] in the world of spirit. A Fact is the end or last issue of spirit. The visible creation is the terminus or the circumference of the invisible world. "Material objects," said a French philosopher, "are necessarily kinds of *scoriæ* of the substantial thoughts of the Creator, which must always preserve an exact relation to their first origin; in other words, visible nature must have a spiritual and moral side."[2]

This doctrine is abstruse, and though the images of "garment," "scoriæ," "mirror," &c., may stimulate the fancy, we must summon the aid of subtler and more vital expositors to make it plain. "Every scripture is to be interpreted by the same spirit which gave it forth,"—is the fundamental law of criticism.[3] A life in harmony with nature, the love of truth and of virtue, will purge the eyes to understand her text. By degrees we may come to know the primitive sense of the permanent objects of nature, so that the world shall be to us an open book, and every form significant of its hidden life and final cause.

A new interest surprises us, whilst, under the view now suggested, we contemplate the fearful extent and multitude of objects; since "every object rightly seen, unlocks a new faculty of the soul."[4] That which was unconscious truth, becomes, when interpreted and defined in an object, a part of the domain of knowledge,—a new amount to the magazine[5] of power.

## Chapter V. Discipline[6]

In view of this significance of nature, we arrive at once at a new fact, that nature is a discipline. This use of the world includes the preceding uses, as parts of itself.

Space, time, society, labor, climate, food, locomotion, the animals, the mechanical forces, give us sincerest lessons, day by day, whose meaning is unlimited. They educate both the Understanding and the Reason. Every property of matter is a school for the understanding,—its solidity or resistance, its inertia, its extension, its figure, its divisibility. The understanding adds, divides, combines, measures, and finds everlasting nutriment and room for its activity in this worthy scene. Meantime, Reason transfers all these lessons into its own world of thought, by perceiving the analogy that marries Matter and Mind.

1. Nature is a discipline of the understanding in intellectual truths. Our

8. For Emerson, representatives of "every fine genius since the world began" (*Early Lectures*, 1.224).
9. In Greek mythology, the winged monster with a lion's body and the head and breasts of a woman perched on a rock near Thebes and challenged every passerby with a riddle; if they answered incorrectly, she killed them. When Oedipus answered it correctly, she killed herself.
1. Modifying emotions.
2. Guillaume Oegger, *The True Messiah* (1829), which Emerson had seen in a manuscript translation, perhaps by Elizabeth Peabody. "Scoriæ": i.e., scoria; slag or refuse left after metal has been smelted from

ore.
3. From the English Quaker, George Fox (1624–91) (*JMN* 4.31).
4. From Coleridge's *Aids to Reflection* (1829), 150–51 (*JMN* 5.189).
5. Storehouse.
6. Whicher quotes the American literature anthologists Bradley, Beatty, and Long for their caution about the term *discipline*: "A trained ecclesiastic, Emerson utilizes the dualism of this word, signifying at once a controlled obedience to the absolute, and, secondly, the ecclesiastical discipline of practical rules affecting conduct."

dealing with sensible objects is a constant exercise in the necessary lessons of difference, of likeness, of order, of being and seeming, of progressive arrangement;[7] of ascent from particular to general; of combination to one end of manifold forces. Proportioned to the importance of the organ to be formed, is the extreme care with which its tuition is provided,—a care pretermitted[8] in no single case. What tedious training, day after day, year after year, never ending, to form the common sense; what continual reproduction of annoyances, inconveniences, dilemmas; what rejoicing over us of little men; what disputing of prices, what reckonings of interest,—and all to form the Hand of the mind;—to instruct us that "good thoughts are no better than good dreams, unless they be executed!"[9]

The same good office is performed by Property and its filial systems of debt and credit. Debt, grinding debt, whose iron face the widow, the orphan, and the sons of genius fear and hate;—debt, which consumes so much time, which so cripples and disheartens a great spirit with cares that seem so base, is a preceptor whose lessons cannot be foregone, and is needed most by those who suffer from it most. Moreover, property, which has been well compared to snow,—"if it fall level to-day, it will be blown into drifts tomorrow,"—is merely the surface action of internal machinery, like the index on the face of a clock. Whilst now it is the gymnastics of the understanding, it is hiving in the foresight of the spirit, experience in profounder laws.

The whole character and fortune of the individual is affected by the least inequalities in the culture of the understanding; for example, in the perception of differences. Therefore is Space, and therefore Time, that man may know that things are not huddled and lumped, but sundered and individual. A bell and a plough have each their use, and neither can do the office of the other. Water is good to drink, coal to burn, wool to wear; but wool cannot be drunk, nor water spun, nor coal eaten. The wise man shows his wisdom in separation, in gradation, and his scale of creatures and of merits, is as wide as nature. The foolish have no range in their scale, but suppose every man is as every other man. What is not good they call the worst, and what is not hateful, they call the best.

In like manner, what good heed, nature forms in us! She pardons no mistakes. Her yea is yea, and her nay, nay.

The first steps in Agriculture, Astronomy, Zoölogy, (those first steps which the farmer, the hunter, and the sailor take,) teach that nature's dice are always loaded; that in her heaps and rubbish are concealed sure and useful results.

How calmly and genially the mind apprehends one after another the laws of physics! What noble emotions dilate the mortal as he enters into the counsels of the creation, and feels by knowledge the privilege to BE! His insight refines him. The beauty of nature shines in his own breast. Man is greater that he can see this, and the universe less, because Time and Space relations vanish as laws are known.

Here again we are impressed and even daunted by the immense Universe to be explored. 'What we know, is a point to what we do not know.'[1] Open any

7. A borrowing from Coleridge's *The Friend* (1818). Emerson made a note on "what Coleridge defines Method, viz. progressive arrangement" (*JMN* 3.299).
8. Neglected. "Tuition": guardianship.
9. Adapted from Francis Bacon's essay *Of Great Place*

(*JMN* 5.136).
1. A saying ascribed both to Sir Isaac Newton (1642–1727), English mathematician and philosopher, and to Bishop Joseph Butler (1692–1752), the moralist.

recent journal of science, and weigh the problems suggested concerning Light, Heat, Electricity, Magnetism, Physiology, Geology, and judge whether the interest of natural science is likely to be soon exhausted.

Passing by many particulars of the discipline of nature we must not omit to specify two.

The exercise of the Will or the lesson of power is taught in every event. From the child's successive possession of his several senses up to the hour when he saith, "thy will be done!"[2] he is learning the secret, that he can reduce under his will, not only particular events, but great classes, nay the whole series of events, and so conform all facts to his character. Nature is thoroughly mediate. It is made to serve. It receives the dominion of man as meekly as the ass on which the Saviour rode.[3] It offers all its kingdoms to man as the raw material which he may mould into what is useful. Man is never weary of working it up. He forges the subtile and delicate air into wise and melodious words, and gives them wing as angels of persuasion and command. More and more, with every thought, does his kingdom stretch over things, until the world becomes, at last, only a realized will,—the double of the man.

2. Sensible objects conform to the premonitions of Reason and reflect the conscience. All things are moral; and in their boundless changes have an unceasing reference to spiritual nature. Therefore is nature glorious with form, color, and motion, that every globe in the remotest heaven; every chemical change from the rudest crystal up to the laws of life; every change of vegetation from the first principle of growth in the eye of a leaf, to the tropical forest and antediluvian[4] coal-mine; every animal function from the sponge up to Hercules,[5] shall hint or thunder to man the laws of right and wrong, and echo the Ten Commandments. Therefore is nature always the ally of Religion: lends all her pomp and riches to the religious sentiment. Prophet and priest, David, Isaiah, Jesus, have drawn deeply from this source.

This ethical character so penetrates the bone and marrow of nature, as to seem the end for which it was made. Whatever private purpose is answered by any member or part, this is its public and universal function, and is never omitted. Nothing in nature is exhausted in its first use. When a thing has served an end to the uttermost, it is wholly new for an ulterior service. In God, every end is converted into a new means. Thus the use of Commodity, regarded by itself, is mean and squalid. But it is to the mind an education in the great doctrine of Use, namely, that a thing is good only so far as it serves; that a conspiring of parts and efforts to the production of an end, is essential to any being. The first and gross manifestation of this truth, is our inevitable and hated training in values and wants, in corn and meat.

It has already been illustrated, in treating of the significance of material things, that every natural process is but a version of a moral sentence. The moral law lies at the centre of nature and radiates to the circumference. It is the pith and marrow of every substance, every relation, and every process. All things with which we deal, preach to us. What is a farm but a mute gospel? The chaff and the wheat, weeds and plants, blight, rain, insects, sun,—it is a sacred emblem from the first furrow of spring to the last stack which the snow of winter overtakes in the fields. But the sailor, the shepherd, the miner, the

2. Matthew 6.10 and 26.42.
3. Matthew 21.5.
4. Before the Flood, which destroyed all living crea-

tures not in Noah's ark (Genesis 6–9).
5. In Greek mythology the hero renowned for feats of strength.

merchant, in their several resorts, have each an experience precisely parallel and leading to the same conclusions. Because all organizations are radically alike. Nor can it be doubted that this moral sentiment which thus scents the air, and grows in the grain, and impregnates the waters of the world, is caught by man and sinks into his soul. The moral influence of nature upon every individual is that amount of truth which it illustrates to him. Who can estimate this? Who can guess how much firmness the sea-beaten rock has taught the fisherman? how much tranquillity has been reflected to man from the azure sky, over whose unspotted deeps the winds forevermore drive flocks of stormy clouds, and leave no wrinkle or stain? how much industry and providence and affection we have caught from the pantomime of brutes? What a searching preacher of self-command is the varying phenomenon of Health!

Herein is especially apprehended the Unity of Nature,—the Unity in Variety,—which meets us everywhere. All the endless variety of things make a unique, an identical impression. Xenophanes[6] complained in his old age, that, look where he would, all things hastened back to Unity. He was weary of seeing the same entity in the tedious variety of forms. The fable of Proteus has a cordial[7] truth. Every particular in nature, a leaf, a drop, a crystal, a moment of time is related to the whole, and partakes of the perfection of the whole. Each particle is a microcosm, and faithfully renders the likeness of the world.

Not only resemblances exist in things whose analogy is obvious, as when we detect the type of the human hand in the flipper of the fossil saurus, but also in objects wherein there is great superficial unlikeness. Thus architecture is called 'frozen music,' by De Stael and Goethe.[8] 'A Gothic church,' said Coleridge,[9] 'is a petrified religion.' Michael Angelo maintained, that, to an architect, a knowledge of anatomy is essential.[1] In Haydn's[2] oratorios, the notes present to the imagination not only motions, as, of the snake, the stag, and the elephant, but colors also; as the green grass. The granite is differenced in its laws only by the more or less of heat, from the river that wears it away. The river, as it flows, resembles the air that flows over it; the air resembles the light which traverses it with more subtile currents; the light resembles the heat which rides with it through Space. Each creature is only a modification of the other; the likeness in them is more than the difference, and their radical law is one and the same. Hence it is, that a rule of one art, or a law of one organization, holds true throughout nature. So intimate is this Unity, that, it is easily seen, it lies under the undermost garment of nature, and betrays its source in universal Spirit. For, it pervades Thought also. Every universal truth which we express in words, implies or supposes every other truth. *Omne verum vero consonat.*[3] It is like a great circle on a sphere, comprising all possible circles; which, however, may be drawn, and comprise it, in like manner. Every such truth is the absolute Ens[4] seen from one side. But it has innumerable sides.

6. Greek philosopher of 5th and 6th centuries B.C. who taught the unity of all existence (*JMN* 3.369 and 5.136).
7. Vital, heartwarming. "Proteus": sea god who could change his shape so as to evade any captor.
8. Johann Wolfgang von Goethe (1749–1832), in his *Conversations with Eckermann* (*JMN* 4.337). Mme. de Stael (1766–1817), in *Corinne*, book 4, chap. 3 (*JMN* 4.40).
9. In his *Lecture on the General Character of the*

*Gothic Mind in the Middle Ages* (1836) (*JMN* 5.36).
1. From the sketch of Michelangelo in *Lives of Eminent Persons* (1833), p. 57 (*JMN* 5.367–68).
2. Franz Joseph Haydn (1732–1809), Austrian composer (*JMN* 5.137).
3. Every truth agrees with every other truth (Latin). "We say every truth supposes or implies every other truth" (*JMN* 4.376).
4. Abstract being.

The same central Unity is still more conspicuous in actions. Words are finite organs of the infinite mind. They cannot cover the dimensions of what is in truth. They break, chop, and impoverish it. An action is the perfection and publication of thought. A right action seems to fill the eye, and to be related to all nature. "The wise man, in doing one thing, does all; or, in the one thing he does rightly, he sees the likeness of all which is done rightly."[5]

Words and actions are not the attributes of mute and brute nature. They introduce us to that singular form which predominates over all other forms. This is the human. All other organizations appear to be degradations of the human form. When this organization appears among so many that surround it, the spirit prefers it to all others. It says, 'From such as this, have I drawn joy and knowledge. In such as this, have I found and beheld myself. I will speak to it. It can speak again. It can yield me thought already formed and alive.' In fact, the eye,—the mind,—is always accompanied by these forms, male and female; and these are incomparably the richest informations[6] of the power and order that lie at the heart of things. Unfortunately, every one of them bears the marks as of some injury; is marred and superficially defective. Nevertheless, far different from the deaf and dumb nature around them, these all rest like fountain-pipes on the unfathomed sea of thought and virtue whereto they alone, of all organizations, are the entrances.

It were a pleasant inquiry to follow into detail their ministry to our education, but where would it stop? We are associated in adolescent and adult life with some friends, who, like skies and waters, are coextensive with our idea; who, answering each to a certain affection of the soul, satisfy our desire on that side; whom we lack power to put at such focal distance from us, that we can mend or even analyze them. We cannot chuse but love them. When much intercourse with a friend has supplied us with a standard of excellence, and has increased our respect for the resources of God who thus sends a real person to outgo our ideal; when he has, moreover, become an object of thought, and, whilst his character retains all its unconscious effect, is converted in the mind into solid and sweet wisdom,—it is a sign to us that his office is closing, and he is commonly withdrawn from our sight in a short time.

## Chapter VI. Idealism

Thus is the unspeakable but intelligible and practicable meaning of the world conveyed to man, the immortal pupil, in every object of sense. To this one end of Discipline, all parts of nature conspire.

A noble doubt perpetually suggests itself, whether this end be not the Final Cause of the Universe; and whether nature outwardly exists. It is a sufficient account of that Appearance we call the World, that God will teach a human mind, and so makes it the receiver of a certain number of congruent sensations, which we call sun and moon, man and woman, house and trade. In my utter impotence to test the authenticity of the report of my senses, to know whether the impressions they make on me correspond with outlying objects, what difference does it make, whether Orion is up there in heaven, or some god paints the image in the firmament of the soul? The relations of parts and the end of the whole remaining the same, what is the difference, whether land

---

5. Paraphrase of Goethe's *Wilhelm Meister* from Carlyle's translation (*JMN* 4.75).

6. Products of the inward, form-giving capacity.

and sea interact, and worlds revolve and intermingle without number or end,—deep yawning under deep,[7] and galaxy balancing galaxy, throughout absolute space, or, whether, without relations of time and space, the same appearances are inscribed in the constant faith of man. Whether nature enjoy a substantial existence without, or is only in the apocalypse[8] of the mind, it is alike useful and alike venerable to me. Be it what it may, it is ideal to me, so long as I cannot try the accuracy of my senses.

The frivolous make themselves merry with the Ideal theory,[9] as if its consequences were burlesque; as if it affected the stability of nature. It surely does not. God never jests with us, and will not compromise the end of nature, by permitting any inconsequence in its procession. Any distrust of the permanence of laws, would paralyze the faculties of man. Their permanence is sacredly respected, and his faith therein is perfect. The wheels and springs of man are all set to the hypothesis of the permanence of nature. We are not built like a ship to be tossed, but like a house to stand. It is a natural consequence of this structure, that, so long as the active powers predominate over the reflective, we resist with indignation any hint that nature is more short-lived or mutable than spirit. The broker, the wheelwright, the carpenter, the tollman, are much displeased at the intimation.

But whilst we acquiesce entirely in the permanence of natural laws, the question of the absolute existence of nature, still remains open. It is the uniform effect of culture on the human mind, not to shake our faith in the stability of particular phenomena, as of heat, water, azote;[1] but to lead us to regard nature as a phenomenon, not a substance; to attribute necessary existence to spirit; to esteem nature as an accident and an effect.

To the senses and the unrenewed understanding, belongs a sort of instinctive belief in the absolute existence of nature. In their view, man and nature are indissolubly joined. Things are ultimates, and they never look beyond their sphere. The presence of Reason mars this faith. The first effort of thought tends to relax this despotism of the senses, which binds us to nature as if we were a part of it, and shows us nature aloof, and, as it were, afloat. Until this higher agency intervened, the animal eye sees, with wonderful accuracy, sharp outlines and colored surfaces. When the eye of Reason opens, to outline and surface are at once added, grace and expression. These proceed from imagination and affection, and abate somewhat of the angular distinctness of objects. If the Reason be stimulated to more earnest vision, outlines and surfaces become transparent, and are no longer seen; causes and spirits are seen through them. The best, the happiest moments of life, are these delicious awakenings of the higher powers, and the reverential withdrawing of nature before its God.

Let us proceed to indicate the effects of culture. 1. Our first institution[2] in the Ideal philosophy is a hint from nature herself.

Nature is made to conspire with spirit to emancipate us. Certain mechanical changes, a small alteration in our local position apprizes us of a dualism. We are strangely affected by seeing the shore from a moving ship, from a balloon, or through the tints of an unusual sky. The least change in our point of view,

---

7. From Psalm 42.7: "Deep calleth unto deep at the noise of thy waterspouts: all thy waves and thy billows are gone over me."
8. Revelation.
9. Emerson uses Bishop George Berkeley (1685–1753) as representative of the notion that we can only know

ideas in the mind and cannot know material things in themselves.
1. Nitrogen.
2. Instruction. "Effects of culture": in the sense of the effects of awakening thought.

gives the whole world a pictorial air. A man who seldom rides, needs only to get into a coach and traverse his own town, to turn the street into a puppet-show. The men, the women,—talking, running, bartering, fighting,—the earnest mechanic, the lounger, the beggar, the boys, the dogs, are unrealized[3] at once, or, at least, wholly detached from all relation to the observer, and seen as apparent, not substantial beings. What new thoughts are suggested by seeing a face of country quite familiar, in the rapid movement of the rail-road car! Nay, the most wonted objects, (make a very slight change in the point of vision,) please us most. In a camera obscura,[4] the butcher's cart, and the figure of one of our own family amuse us. So a portrait of a well-known face gratifies us. Turn the eyes upside down, by looking at the landscape through your legs, and how agreeable is the picture, though you have seen it any time these twenty years!

In these cases, by mechanical means, is suggested the difference between the observer and the spectacle,—between man and nature. Hence arises a pleasure mixed with awe; I may say, a low degree of the sublime is felt from the fact, probably, that man is hereby apprized, that, whilst the world is a spectacle, something in himself is stable.

2. In a higher manner, the poet communicates the same pleasure. By a few strokes he delineates, as on air, the sun, the mountain, the camp, the city, the hero, the maiden, not different from what we know them, but only lifted from the ground and float before the eye. He unfixes the land and the sea, makes them revolve around the axis of his primary thought, and disposes them anew. Possessed himself by a heroic passion, he uses matter as symbols of it. The sensual man conforms thoughts to things; the poet conforms things to his thoughts.[5] The one esteems nature as rooted and fast; the other, as fluid, and impresses his being thereon. To him, the refractory world is ductile and flexible; he invests dusts and stones with humanity and makes them the words of the Reason. The imagination may be defined to be, the use which the Reason makes of the material world. Shakspeare possesses the power of subordinating nature for the purposes of expression, beyond all poets. His imperial muse tosses the creation like a bauble from hand to hand, to embody any capricious shade of thought that is uppermost in his mind. The remotest spaces of nature are visited, and the farthest sundered things are brought together, by a subtile spiritual connexion. We are made aware that magnitude of material things is merely relative, and all objects shrink and expand to serve the passion of the poet. Thus, in his sonnets, the lays of birds, the scents and dyes of flowers, he finds to be the *shadow* of his beloved; time, which keeps her from him, is his *chest*; the suspicion she has awakened, is her *ornament*;[6]

---

3. Made unsubstantial. "Mechanic": manual laborer.
4. Dark chamber or box with a lens or opening through which an image is projected in natural colors onto an opposite surface.
5. From Bacon's *The Advancement of Learning* (2.4.2), but more directly from William Hazlitt's adaptation (*JMN* 6.227).
6. Emerson summarizes Shakespeare's *Sonnet 98*:

From you have I been absent in the spring,
When proud-pied April, dress'd in all his trim,
Hath put a spirit of youth in every thing,
That heavy Saturn laugh'd and leap'd with him.
Yet nor the lays of birds, nor the sweet smell

Of different flowers in odour and in hue,
Could make me any summer's story tell,
Or from their proud lap pluck them where they grew;
Nor did I wonder at the lily's white,
Nor praise the deep vermilion in the rose:
They were but sweet, but figures of delight.
Drawn after you, you pattern of all
  those.
Yet seemed it winter still, and you away,
As with your shadow I with these did play.

Then Emerson refers to *Sonnet 65* ("Shall Time's best jewel from Time's chest lie hid?")

> The ornament of beauty is Suspect,
> A crow which flies in heaven's sweetest air.[7]

His passion is not the fruit of chance; it swells, as he speaks, to a city, or a state.

> No, it was builded far from accident;
> It suffers not in smiling pomp, nor falls
> Under the brow of thralling discontent;
> It fears not policy, that heretic,
> That works on leases of short numbered hours,
> But all alone stands hugely politic.[8]

In the strength of his constancy, the Pyramids[9] seem to him recent and transitory. And the freshness of youth and love dazzles him with its resemblance to morning.

> Take those lips away
> Which so sweetly were forsworn;
> And those eyes,—the break of day,
> Lights that do mislead the morn.[1]

The wild beauty of this hyperbole, I may say, in passing, it would not be easy to match in literature.

This transfiguration which all material objects undergo through the passion of the poet,—this power which he exerts, at any moment, to magnify the small, to micrify the great,—might be illustrated by a thousand examples from his Plays. I have before me the Tempest, and will cite only these few lines.

> PROSPERO. The strong based promontory
> Have I made shake, and by the spurs plucked up
> The pine and cedar.[2]

Prospero calls for music to sooth the frantic Alonzo, and his companions;

> A solemn air, and the best comforter
> To an unsettled fancy, cure thy brains
> Now useless, boiled within thy skull.

Again;

> The charm dissolves space
> And, as the morning steals upon the night,
> Melting the darkness, so their rising senses
> Begin to chase the ignorant fumes that mantle
> Their clearer reason.

> Their understanding
> Begins to swell: and the approaching tide
> Will shortly fill the reasonable shores
> That now lie foul and muddy.

7. Shakespeare's Sonnet 70.
8. Shakespeare's Sonnet 124.
9. Shakespeare's Sonnet 123: "No, Time, thou shalt not boast that I do change: / Thy pyramids built up with newer might / To me are nothing novel, nothing strange: / They are but dressings of a former sight."

1. From Shakespeare's Measure for Measure (5.1.1–4).
2. The Tempest 5.1.46–48 (the 1836 text says "Ariel" instead of Prospero, a careless slip not preserved here): later quotations are from 5.1.58–60, 64–68, and 79–82.

The perception of real affinities between events, (that is to say, of *ideal* affinities, for those only are real,) enables the poet thus to make free with the most imposing forms and phenomena of the world, and to assert the predominance of the soul.

3. Whilst thus the poet delights us by animating[3] nature like a creator, with his own thoughts, he differs from the philosopher only herein, that the one proposes Beauty as his main end; the other Truth. But, the philosopher, not less than the poet, postpones the apparent order and relations of things to the empire of thought. "The problem of philosophy," according to Plato, "is, for all that exists conditionally, to find a ground unconditioned and absolute."[4] It proceeds on the faith that a law determines all phenomena, which being known, the phenomena can be predicted. That law, when in the mind, is an idea. Its beauty is infinite. The true philosopher and the true poet are one, and a beauty, which is truth, and a truth, which is beauty, is the aim of both. Is not the charm of one of Plato's or Aristotle's definitions, strictly like that of the Antigone of Sophocles?[5] It is, in both cases, that a spiritual life has been imparted to nature; that the solid seeming block of matter has been pervaded and dissolved by a thought; that this feeble human being has penetrated the vast masses of nature with an informing soul, and recognised itself in their harmony, that is, seized their law. In physics, when this is attained, the memory disburthens itself of its cumbrous catalogues of particulars, and carries centuries of observation in a single formula.

Thus even in physics, the material is ever degraded before the spiritual. The astronomer, the geometer, rely on their irrefragable analysis, and disdain the results of observation. The sublime remark of Euler[6] on his law of arches, "This will be found contrary to all experience, yet it is true;" had already transferred nature into the mind, and left matter like an outcast corpse.

4. Intellectual science has been observed to beget invariably a doubt of the existence of matter. Turgot[7] said, "He that has never doubted the existence of matter, may be assured he has no aptitude for metaphysical inquiries." It fastens the attention upon immortal necessary uncreated natures, that is, upon Ideas; and in their beautiful and majestic presence, we feel that our outward being is a dream and a shade. Whilst we wait in this Olympus of gods, we think of nature as an appendix to the soul. We ascend into their region, and know that these are the thoughts of the Supreme Being. "These are they who were set up from everlasting, from the beginning, or ever the earth was. When he prepared the heavens, they were there; when he established the clouds above, when he strengthened the fountains of the deep. Then they were by him, as one brought up with him. Of them took he counsel."[8]

Their influence is proportionate. As objects of science, they are accessible to few men. Yet all men are capable of being raised by piety or by passion, into their region. And no man touches these divine natures, without becoming, in some degree, himself divine. Like a new soul, they renew the body. We become physically nimble and lightsome; we tread on air; life is no longer

3. Giving life to.
4. Emerson draws this quotation from Coleridge's *The Friend* (1818) (*JMN* 6.202).
5. Greek dramatist of the 5th century B.C., wrote the tragedy *Antigone* in which the title character chooses death rather than violate her sacred duty to perform funeral rites for her slain brother.
6. Leonhard Euler (1707–1783), Swiss mathematician and physicist; Emerson took the quotation from Coleridge's *Aids to Reflection* (1829) (*JMN* 4.327, 332).
7. Anne Robert Jacques Turgot (1727–1781), French economist and author of a book on proofs of the existence of God (*JMN* 2.212–13).
8. Cf. Proverbs 8.23–30.

irksome, and we think it will never be so. No man fears age or misfortune or death, in their serene company, for he is transported out of the district of change. Whilst we behold unveiled the nature of Justice and Truth, we learn the difference between the absolute and the conditional or relative. We apprehend the absolute. As it were, for the first time, *we exist.* We become immortal, for we learn that time and space are relations of matter; that, with a perception of truth, or a virtuous will, they have no affinity.[9]

5. Finally, religion and ethics, which may be fitly called,—the practice of ideas, or the introduction of ideas into life,—have an analogous effect with all lower culture, in degrading nature and suggesting its dependence on spirit. Ethics and religion differ herein; that the one is the system of human duties commencing from man; the other, from God. Religion includes the personality of God; Ethics does not. They are one to our present design. They both put nature under foot. The first and last lesson of religion is, "The things that are seen, are temporal; the things that are unseen are eternal."[1] It puts an affront upon nature. It does that for the unschooled, which philosophy does for Berkeley and Viasa.[2] The uniform language that may be heard in the churches of the most ignorant sects, is,—'Contemn the unsubstantial shows of the world; they are vanities, dreams, shadows, unrealities; seek the realities of religion.' The devotee flouts nature. Some theosophists[3] have arrived at a certain hostility and indignation towards matter, as the Manichean and Plotinus. They distrusted in themselves any looking back to these flesh-pots of Egypt. Plotinus was ashamed of his body.[4] In short, they might all better say of matter, what Michael Angelo said of external beauty, "it is the frail and weary weed, in which God dresses the soul, which he has called into time."[5]

It appears that motion, poetry, physical and intellectual science, and religion, all tend to affect our convictions of the reality of the external world. But I own there is something ungrateful in expanding too curiously the particulars of the general proposition, that all culture tends to imbue us with idealism. I have no hostility to nature, but a child's love to it. I expand and live in the warm day like corn and melons. Let us speak her fair. I do not wish to fling stones at my beautiful mother, nor soil my gentle nest. I only wish to indicate the true position of nature in regard to man, wherein to establish man, all right education tends; as the ground which to attain is the object of human life, that is, of man's connexion with nature. Culture inverts the vulgar views of nature, and brings the mind to call that apparent, which it uses to call real, and that real, which it uses to call visionary. Children, it is true, believe in the external world. The belief that it appears only, is an afterthought, but with culture, this faith will as surely arise on the mind as did the first.

The advantage of the ideal theory over the popular faith, is this, that it presents the world in precisely that view which is most desirable to the mind.

---

9. An echo of Socrates' speech in the *Symposium.*
1. 2 Corinthians 4.18.
2. Reputed author of the Vedas, the ancient sacred literature of Hinduism (*JMN* 5.123). George Berkeley (1685–1753), Irish idealist philosopher.
3. In the broad sense of those who attempt to establish direct contact with divine principle through contemplation and revelation.
4. Plotinus, Greek neoplatonical philosopher of the 3rd century, was not so much "ashamed of his body" as of the fact that his soul had to be contained in a body

(*JMN* 3.251). (Neoplatonism is a mystical religious system, combining features of Platonic and other Greek philosophies with features of Judaism and Christianity.) The Israelites yearned for the fleshpots of Egypt while in the wilderness (Exodus 16.3). "Manichean": from Mani or Manes, 3rd-century Persian, who founded a religion based on the dualism of good and evil.
5. Michelangelo's *Sonnet 51* (Emerson's *Early Lectures,* 1.229).

It is, in fact, the view which Reason, both speculative and practical, that is, philosophy and virtue, take. For, seen in the light of thought, the world always is phenomenal;[6] and virtue subordinates it to the mind. Idealism sees the world in God. It beholds the whole circle of persons and things, of actions and events, of country and religion, not as painfully accumulated, atom after atom, act after act, in an aged creeping Past, but as one vast picture, which God paints on the instant eternity, for the contemplation of the soul. Therefore the soul holds itself off from a too trivial and microscopic study of the universal tablet. It respects the end too much, to immerse itself in the means. It sees something more important in Christianity, than the scandals of ecclesiastical history or the niceties of criticism; and, very incurious concerning persons or miracles, and not at all disturbed by chasms of historical evidence, it accepts from God the phenomenon, as it finds it, as the pure and awful form of religion in the world. It is not hot and passionate at the appearance of what it calls its own good or bad fortune, at the union or opposition of other persons. No man is its enemy. It accepts whatsoever befalls, as part of its lesson. It is a watcher more than a doer, and it is a doer, only that it may the better watch.

## Chapter VII. Spirit

It is essential to a true theory of nature and of man, that it should contain somewhat progressive. Uses that are exhausted or that may be, and facts that end in the statement, cannot be all that is true of this brave lodging wherein man is harbored, and wherein all his faculties find appropriate and endless exercise. And all the uses of nature admit of being summed in one, which yields the activity of man an infinite scope. Through all its kingdoms, to the suburbs and outskirts of things, it is faithful to the cause whence it had its origin. It always speaks of Spirit. It suggests the absolute. It is a perpetual effect. It is a great shadow pointing always to the sun behind us.

The aspect of nature is devout. Like the figure of Jesus, she stands with bended head, and hands folded upon the breast. The happiest man is he who learns from nature the lesson of worship.

Of that ineffable essence which we call Spirit, he that thinks most, will say least. We can foresee God in the coarse and, as it were, distant phenomena of matter; but when we try to define and describe himself, both language and thought desert us, and we are as helpless as fools and savages. That essence refuses to be recorded in propositions, but when man has worshipped him intellectually, the noblest ministry of nature is to stand as the apparition[7] of God. It is the great organ through which the universal spirit speaks to the individual, and strives to lead back the individual to it.

When we consider Spirit, we see that the views already presented do not include the whole circumference of man. We must add some related thoughts. Three problems are put by nature to the mind; What is matter? Whence is it? and Whereto? The first of these questions only, the ideal theory answers. Idealism saith: matter is a phenomenon, not a substance. Idealism acquaints us with the total disparity between the evidence of our own being, and the evidence of the world's being. The one is perfect, the other, incapable of any assurance; the mind is a part of the nature of things; the world is a divine

---

6. Only an appearance.　　　　　7. Visible state.

dream, from which we may presently awake to the glories and certainties of day. Idealism is a hypothesis to account for nature by other principles than those of carpentry and chemistry. Yet, if it only deny the existence of matter, it does not satisfy the demands of the spirit. It leaves God out of me. It leaves me in the splendid labyrinth of my perceptions, to wander without end. Then the heart resists it, because it baulks the affections in denying substantive being to men and women. Nature is so pervaded with human life, that there is something of humanity in all, and in every particular. But this theory makes nature foreign to me, and does not account for that consanguinity which we acknowledge to it.

Let it stand then, in the present state of our knowledge, merely as a useful introductory hypothesis, serving to apprize us of the eternal distinction between the soul and the world.

But when, following the invisible steps of thought, we come to inquire, Whence is matter? and Whereto? many truths arise to us out of the recesses of consciousness. We learn that the highest is present to the soul of man, that the dread universal essence, which is not wisdom, or love, or beauty, or power, but all in one, and each entirely, is that for which all things exist, and that by which they are; that spirit creates; that behind nature, throughout nature, spirit is present; that spirit is one and not compound; that spirit does not act upon us from without, that is, in space and time, but spiritually, or through ourselves. Therefore, that spirit, that is, the Supreme Being, does not build up nature around us, but puts it forth through us, as the life of the tree puts forth new branches and leaves through the pores of the old. As a plant upon the earth, so a man rests upon the bosom of God: he is nourished by unfailing fountains, and draws, at his need, inexhaustible power. Who can set bounds to the possibilities of man? Once inspire the infinite, by being admitted to behold the absolute natures of justice and truth, and we learn that man has access to the entire mind of the Creator, is himself the creator in the finite. This view, which admonishes me where the sources of wisdom and power lie, and points to virtue as to

> "The golden key
> When opes the palace of eternity,"[8]

carries upon its face the highest certificate of truth, because it animates me to create my own world through the purification of my soul.

The world proceeds from the same spirit as the body of man. It is a remoter and inferior incarnation of God, a projection of God in the unconscious. But it differs from the body in one important respect. It is not, like that, now subjected to the human will. Its serene order is inviolable by us. It is therefore, to us, the present expositor of the divine mind. It is a fixed point whereby we may measure our departure. As we degenerate, the contrast between us and our house is more evident. We are as much strangers in nature, as we are aliens from God. We do not understand the notes of the birds. The fox and the deer run away from us; the bear and tiger rend us. We do not know the uses of more than a few plants, as corn and the apple, the potato and the vine. Is not the landscape, every glimpse of which hath a grandeur, a face of him? Yet this may show us what discord is between man and nature, for you cannot

8. John Milton's *Comus*, 13–14.

freely admire a noble landscape, if laborers are digging in the field hard by. The poet finds something ridiculous in his delight, until he is out of the sight of men.

## Chapter VIII. Prospects

In inquiries respecting the laws of the world and the frame of things, the highest reason is always the truest. That which seems faintly possible—it is so refined, is often faint and dim because it is deepest seated in the mind among the eternal verities. Empirical science is apt to cloud the sight, and, by the very knowledge of functions and processes, to bereave the student of the manly contemplation of the whole. The savant[9] becomes unpoetic. But the best read naturalist who lends an entire and devout attention to truth, will see that there remains much to learn of his relation to the world, and that it is not to be learned by any addition or subtraction or other comparison of known quantities, but is arrived at by untaught sallies of the spirit, by a continual self-recovery, and by entire humility. He will perceive that there are far more excellent qualities in the student than preciseness and infallibility; that a guess is often more fruitful than an indisputable affirmation, and that a dream may let us deeper into the secret of nature than a hundred concerted experiments.

For, the problems to be solved are precisely those which the physiologist and the naturalist omit to state. It is not so pertinent to man to know all the individuals of the animal kingdom, as it is to know whence and whereto is this tyrannizing unity in his constitution, which evermore separates and classifies things, endeavouring to reduce the most diverse to one form. When I behold a rich landscape, it is less to my purpose to recite correctly the order and superposition of the strata, than to know why all thought of multitude is lost in a tranquil sense of unity. I cannot greatly honor minuteness in details, so long as there is no hint to explain the relation between things and thoughts; no ray upon the *metaphysics* of conchology, of botany, of the arts, to show the relation of the forms of flowers, shells, animals, architecture, to the mind, and build science upon ideas. In a cabinet[1] of natural history, we become sensible of a certain occult recognition and sympathy in regard to the most bizarre forms of beast, fish, and insect. The American who has been confined, in his own country, to the sight of buildings designed after foreign models, is surprised on entering York Minister or St. Peter's at Rome, by the feeling that these structures are imitations also,—faint copies of an invisible archetype. Nor has science sufficient humanity, so long as the naturalist overlooks that wonderful congruity which subsists between man and the world; of which he is lord, not because he is the most subtile inhabitant, but because he is its head and heart, and finds something of himself in every great and small thing, in every mountain stratum, in every new law of color, fact of astronomy, or atmospheric influence which observation or analysis lay open. A perception of this mystery inspires the muse of George Herbert, the beautiful psalmist of the seventeenth century. The following lines are part of his little poem on Man[2]

"Man is all symmetry,
  Full of proportions, one limb to another,

---

9. Learned person.
1. Display case, or room containing many display
 cases.
2. Herbert's *Man* (stanzas 1–4 and 6).

And to all the world besides.
Each part may call the farthest, brother;
For head with foot hath private amity,
And both with moons and tides.

"Nothing hath got so far
But man hath caught and kept it as his prey;
His eyes dismount the highest star;
He is in little all the sphere.
Herbs gladly cure our flesh, because that they
Find their acquaintance there.

"For us, the winds do blow.
The earth doth rest, heaven move, and fountains flow;
Nothing we see, but means our good,
As our delight, or as our treasure;
The whole is either our cupboard of food,
Or cabinet of pleasure.

"The stars have us to bed;
Night draws the curtain; which the sun withdraws.
Music and light attend our head.
All things unto our flesh are kind,
In their descent and being; to our mind,
In their ascent and cause.

"More servants wait on man
Than he'll take notice of. In every path,
He treads down that which doth befriend him
When sickness makes him pale and wan.
Oh mighty love! Man is one world, and hath
Another to attend him."

The perception of this class of truths makes the eternal attraction which draws men to science, but the end is lost sight of in attention to the means. In view of this half-sight of science, we accept the sentence of Plato, that, "poetry comes nearer to vital truth than history."[3] Every surmise and vatication[4] of the mind is entitled to a certain respect, and we learn to prefer imperfect theories, and sentences, which contain glimpses of truth, to digested systems which have no one valuable suggestion. A wise writer will feel that the ends of study and composition are best answered by announcing undiscovered regions of thought, and so communicating, through hope, new activity to the torpid spirit.

I shall therefore conclude this essay with some traditions of man and nature, which a certain poet[5] sang to me; and which, as they have always been in the world, and perhaps reappear to every bard, may be both history and prophecy.

3. In copying two quotations from the *Edinburgh Review* Emerson blurred the attributions; here he quotes not from Plato but from section 9 of Aristotle's *Poetics* (*JMN* 4.261 and 173).
4. Foretelling, prophesying.
5. The poet is Emerson himself, in the same sort of

private joke that he later uses in *The Poet*, but before writing this passage he had been seeing his neighbor, the arch-Transcendentalist and idealist Bronson Alcott, who was full of his own "Orphic Sayings," so the device is a little joke with Alcott, one of the first readers and admirers of *Nature*.

The foundations of man are not in matter, but in spirit. But the element of spirit is eternity. To it, therefore, the longest series of events, the oldest chronologies are young and recent. In the cycle of the universal man, from whom the known individuals proceed, centuries are points, and all history is but the epoch of one degradation.

'We distrust and deny inwardly our sympathy with nature. We own and disown our relation to it, by turns. We are, like Nebuchadnezzar, dethroned, bereft of reason, and eating grass like an ox.[6] But who can set limits to the remedial force of spirit?

'A man is a god in ruins. When men are innocent, life shall be longer, and shall pass into the immortal, as gently as we awake from dreams. Now, the world would be insane and rabid, if these disorganizations should last for hundreds of years. It is kept in check by death and infancy. Infancy is the perpetual Messiah, which comes into the arms of fallen men, and pleads with them to return to paradise.

'Man is the dwarf of himself. Once he was permeated and dissolved by spirit. He filled nature with his overflowing currents. Out from him sprang the sun and moon; from man, the sun; from woman, the moon. The laws of his mind, the periods of his actions externized themselves into day and night, into the year and the seasons. But, having made for himself this huge shell, his waters retired; he no longer fills the veins and veinlets; he is shrunk to a drop. He sees, that the structure still fits him, but fits him colossally. Say, rather, once it fitted him, now it corresponds to him from far and on high. He adores timidly his own work. Now is man the follower of the sun, and woman the follower of the moon. Yet sometimes he starts in his slumber, and wonders at himself and his house, and muses strangely at the resemblance betwixt him and it. He perceives that if his law is still paramount, if still he have elemental power, "if his word is sterling yet in nature," it is not conscious power, it is not inferior but superior to his will. It is Instinct.' Thus my Orphic poet sang.

At present, man applies to nature but half his force. He works on the world with his understanding alone. He lives in it, and masters it by a penny-wisdom; and he that works most in it, is but a half-man and whilst his arms are strong and his digestion good, his mind is imbruted and he is a selfish savage. His relation to nature, his power over it, is through the understanding; as by manure; the economic use of fire, wind, water, and the mariner's needle; steam, coal, chemical agriculture; the repairs of the human body by the dentist and the surgeon. This is such a resumption of power, as if a banished king should buy his territories inch by inch, instead of vaulting at once into his throne. Meantime, in the thick darkness, there are not wanting gleams of a better light,—occasional examples of the action of man upon nature with his entire force,—with reason as well as understanding. Such examples are; the traditions of miracles in the earliest antiquity of all nations; the history of Jesus Christ; the achievements of a principle, as in religious and political revolutions, and in the abolition of the Slave-trade; the miracles of enthusiasm,[7] as those reported of Swedenborg, Hohenlohe, and the Shakers;[8] many obscure and yet contested facts, now arranged under the name of Animal Magnetism;[9] prayer; eloquence, self-healing; and the wisdom of children. These are exam-

---

6. See Daniel 4.31–33.
7. Those in a supernatural ecstasy or possession.
8. An offshoot of the Quakers; the group believed in

miraculous cures. Leopold Franz Emmerich, prince of Hohnlohe (1794–1849), reputed miracle healer.
9. Hypnotism.

ples of Reason's momentary grasp of the sceptre, the exertions of a power which exists not in time or space, but an instantaneous in-streaming causing power. The difference between the actual and the ideal force of man is happily figured by the schoolmen,[1] in saying, that the knowledge of man is an evening knowledge, *vespertina cognitio*, but that of God is a morning knowledge, *matutina cognitio.*

The problem of restoring to the world original and eternal beauty, is solved by the redemption of the soul. The ruin or the blank, that we see when we look at nature, is in our own eye. The axis of vision is not coincident with the axis of things, and so they appear not transparent but opake. The reason why the world lacks unity, and lies broken and in heaps, is, because man is disunited with himself. He cannot be a naturalist, until he satisfies all the demands of the spirit. Love is as much its demand, as perception. Indeed, neither can be perfect without the other. In the uttermost meaning of the words, thought is devout, and devotion is thought. Deep calls unto deep.[2] But in actual life, the marriage is not celebrated. There are innocent men who worship God after the tradition of their fathers, but their sense of duty has not yet extended to the use of all their faculties. And there are patient naturalists, but they freeze their subject under the wintry light of the understanding. Is not prayer also a study of truth,—a sally of the soul into the unfound infinite? No man ever prayed heartily, without learning something. But when a faithful thinker, resolute to detach every object from personal relations, and see it in the light of thought, shall, at the same time, kindle science with the fire of the holiest affections, then will God go forth anew into the creation.

It will not need, when the mind is prepared for study, to search for objects. The invariable mark of wisdom is to see the miraculous in the common. What is a day? What is a year? What is summer? What is woman? What is a child? What is sleep? To our blindness, these things seem unaffecting. We make fables to hide the baldness of the fact and conform it, as we say, to the higher law of the mind. But when the fact is seen under the light of an idea, the gaudy fable fades and shrivels. We behold the real higher law. To the wise, therefore, a fact is true poetry, and the most beautiful of fables. These wonders are brought to our own door. You also are a man. Man and woman, and their social life, poverty, labor, sleep, fear, fortune, are known to you. Learn that none of these things is superficial, but that each phenomenon hath its roots in the faculties and affections of the mind. Whilst the abstract question occupies your intellect, nature brings it in the concrete to be solved by your hands. It were a wise inquiry for the closet,[3] to compare, point by point, especially at remarkable crises in life, our daily history, with the rise and progress of ideas in the mind.

So shall we come to look at the world with new eyes. It shall answer the endless inquiry of the intellect,—What is truth? and of the affections,—What is good? by yielding itself passive to the educated Will. Then shall come to pass what my poet said; 'Nature is not fixed but fluid. Spirit alters, moulds, makes it. The immobility or bruteness of nature, is the absence of spirit; to pure spirit, it is fluid, it is volatile, it is obedient. Every spirit builds itself a house; and beyond its house, a world; and beyond its world, a heaven. Know

1. Medieval scholastic philosophers (see *JMN* 6.179).          3. The scholar's private workroom.
2. Psalm 42.7.

then, that the world exists for you. For you is the phenomenon perfect. What we are, that only can we see. All that Adam had, all that Cæsar could, you have and can do. Adam called his house, heaven and earth; Cæsar called his house, Rome; you perhaps call yours, a cobler's trade; a hundred acres of ploughed land; or a scholar's garret. Yet line for line and point for point, your dominion is as great as theirs, though without fine names. Build, therefore your own world. As fast as you can conform your life to the pure idea in your mind, that will unfold its great proportions. A correspondent revolution in things will attend the influx of the spirit. So fast will disagreeable appearances, swine, spiders, snakes, pests, mad-houses, prisons, enemies, vanish; they are temporary and shall be no more seen. The sordor and filths of nature, the sun shall dry up, and the wind exhale. As when the summer comes from the south, the snow-banks melt, and the face of the earth becomes green before it, so shall the advancing spirit create its ornaments along its path, and carry with it the beauty it visits, and the song which enchants it; it shall draw beautiful faces, and warm hearts, and wise discourse, and heroic acts, around its way, until evil is no more seen. The kingdom of man over nature, which cometh not with observation,[4]—a dominion such as now is beyond his dream of God,—he shall enter without more wonder than the blind man feels who is gradually restored to perfect sight.'

1836

# The American Scholar[1]

Mr. President, and Gentlemen,

I greet you on the re-commencement of our literary year. Our anniversary is one of hope, and, perhaps, not enough of labor. We do not meet for games of strength or skill, for the recitation of histories, tragedies and odes, like the ancient Greeks; for parliaments of love and poesy, like the Troubadours;[2] nor for the advancement of science, like our cotemporaries in the British and European capitals. Thus far, our holiday has been simply a friendly sign of the survival of the love of letters amongst a people too busy to give to letters any more. As such, it is precious as the sign of an indestructible instinct. Perhaps the time is already come, when it ought to be, and will be something else; when the sluggard intellect of this continent will look from under its iron lids and fill the postponed expectation of the world with something better than the exertions of mechanical skill. Our day of dependence, our long apprentice-ship to the learning of other lands, draws to a close. The millions that around us are rushing into life, cannot always be fed on the sere remains of foreign harvests. Events, actions arise, that must be sung, that will sing themselves. Who can doubt that poetry will revive and lead in a new age, as the star in the constellation Harp which now flames in our zenith, astronomers announce, shall one day be the pole-star for a thousand years.

---

4. Luke 17.20

1. The text printed here is that of the first publication (1837) as a pamphlet titled *An Oration, Delivered before the Phi Beta Kappa Society at Cambridge, August 31, 1837.* By altering the title to *The American Scholar* when he republished it in *Essays* (1841), Emerson ex-

panded the application to all American college students and all others who dedicate themselves to thought.

2. Courtly poets of southern France, especially Provence, in the 12th and 13th centuries.

In the light of this hope, I accept the topic which not only usage, but the nature of our association, seem to prescribe to this day,—the AMERICAN SCHOLAR. Year by year, we come up hither to read one more chapter of his biography. Let us inquire what new lights, new events and more days have thrown on his character, his duties and his hopes.

It is one of those fables, which out of an unknown antiquity, convey an unlooked for wisdom, that the gods, in the beginning, divided Man into men, that he might be more helpful to himself;[3] just as the hand was divided into fingers, the better to answer its end.

The old fable covers a doctrine ever new and sublime; that there is One Man,—present to all particular men only partially, or through one faculty; and that you must take the whole society to find the whole man. Man is not a farmer, or a professor, or an engineer, but he is all. Man is priest, and scholar, and statesman, and producer, and soldier. In the *divided* or social state, these functions are parcelled out to individuals, each of whom aims to do his stint of the joint work, whilst each other performs his. The fable implies that the individual to possess himself, must sometimes return from his own labor to embrace all the other laborers. But unfortunately, this original unit, this fountain of power, has been so distributed to multitudes, has been so minutely subdivided and peddled out, that it is spilled into drops, and cannot be gathered. The state of society is one in which the members have suffered amputation from the trunk, and strut about so many walking monsters,—a good finger, a neck, a stomach, an elbow, but never a man.

Man is thus metamorphosed into a thing, into many things. The planter, who is Man sent out into the field to gather food, is seldom cheered by any idea of the true dignity of his ministry. He sees his bushel and his cart, and nothing beyond, and sinks into the farmer, instead of Man on the farm. The tradesman scarcely ever gives an ideal worth to his work, but is ridden by the routine of his craft, and the soul is subject to dollars. The priest becomes a form; the attorney, a statute-book; the mechanic, a machine; the sailor, a rope of a ship.

In this distribution of functions, the scholar is the delegated intellect. In the right state, he is, *Man Thinking.* In the degenerate state, when the victim of society, he tends to become a mere thinker, or, still worse, the parrot of other men's thinking.

In this view of him, as Man Thinking, the whole theory of his office[4] is contained. Him nature solicits, with all her placid, all her monitory pictures. Him the past instructs. Him the future invites. Is not, indeed, every man a student, and do not all things exist for the student's behoof? And, finally, is not the true scholar the only true master? But, as the old oracle said, "All things have two handles. Beware of the wrong one." In life, too often, the scholar errs with mankind and forfeits his privilege. Let us see him in his school, and consider him in reference to the main influences he receives.

I. The first in time and the first in importance of the influences upon the mind is that of nature. Every day, the sun; and, after sunset, night and her stars. Ever the winds blow; ever the grass grows. Every day, men and women, conversing, beholding and beholden. The scholar must needs stand wistful

---

3. One such fable Emerson knew from Plato's *Sym-*     4. Function.
*posium.*

and admiring before this great spectacle. He must settle its value in his mind. What is nature to him? There is never a beginning, there is never an end to the inexplicable continuity of this web of God, but always circular power returning into itself. Therein it resembles his own spirit, whose beginning, whose ending he never can find—so entire, so boundless. Far, too, as her splendors shine, system on system shooting like rays, upward, downward, without centre, without circumference,—in the mass and in the particle nature hastens to render account of herself to the mind. Classification begins. To the young mind, every thing is individual, stands by itself. By and by, it finds how to join two things, and see in them one nature; then three, then three thousand; and so, tyrannized over by its own unifying instinct, it goes on tying things together, diminishing anomalies, discovering roots running under ground, whereby contrary and remote things cohere, and flower out from one stem. It presently learns, that, since the dawn of history, there has been a constant accumulation and classifying of facts. But what is classification but the perceiving that these objects are not chaotic, and are not foreign, but have a law which is also a law of the human mind? The astronomer discovers that geometry, a pure abstraction of the human mind, is the measure of planetary motion. The chemist finds proportions and intelligible method throughout matter: and science is nothing but the finding of analogy, identity in the most remote parts. The ambitious soul sits down before each refractory fact; one after another, reduces all strange constitutions, all new powers, to their class and their law, and goes on forever to animate the last fibre of organization, the outskirts of nature, by insight.

Thus to him, to this school-boy under the bending dome of day, is suggested, that he and it proceed from one root; one is leaf and one is flower; relation, sympathy, stirring in every vein. And what is that Root? Is not that the soul of his soul?—A thought too bold—a dream too wild. Yet when this spiritual light shall have revealed the law of more earthly natures,—when he has learned to worship the soul, and to see that the natural philosophy that now is, is only the first gropings of its gigantic hand, he shall look forward to an ever expanding knowledge as to a becoming creator. He shall see that nature is the opposite of the soul, answering to it part for part. One is seal, and one is print. Its beauty is the beauty of his own mind. Its laws are the laws of his own mind. Nature then becomes to him the measure of his attainments. So much of nature as he is ignorant of, so much of his own mind does he not yet possess. And, in fine, the ancient precept, "Know thyself," and the modern precept, "Study nature," become at last one maxim.

II. The next great influence[5] into the spirit of the scholar, is, the mind of the Past,—in whatever form, whether of literature, of art, of institutions, that mind is inscribed. Books are the best type of the influence of the past, and perhaps we shall get at the truth—learn the amount of this influence more conveniently—by considering their value alone.

The theory of books is noble. The scholar of the first age received into him the world around; brooded thereon; gave it the new arrangement of his own mind, and uttered it again. It came into him—life; it went out from him— truth. It came to him—short-lived actions; it went out from him—immortal thoughts. It came to him—business; it went from him—poetry. It was—dead

5. Inflowing.

fact; now, it is quick[6] thought. It can stand, and it can go. It now endures, it now flies, it now inspires.[7] Precisely in proportion to the depth of mind from which it issued, so high does it soar, so long does it sing.

Or, I might say, it depends on how far the process had gone, of transmuting life into truth. In proportion to the completeness of the distillation, so will the purity and imperishableness of the product be. But none is quite perfect. As no air-pump can by any means make a perfect vacuum, so neither can any artist entirely exclude the conventional, the local, the perishable from his book, or write a book of pure thought that shall be as efficient, in all respects, to a remote posterity, as to cotemporaries, or rather to the second age. Each age, it is found, must write its own books; or rather, each generation for the next succeeding. The books of an older period will not fit this.

Yet hence arises a grave mischief. The sacredness which attaches to the act of creation,—the act of thought,—is instantly transferred to the record. The poet chanting, was felt to be a divine man. Henceforth the chant is divine also. The writer was a just and wise spirit. Henceforward it is settled, the book is perfect; as love of the hero corrupts into worship of his statue. Instantly, the book becomes noxious. The guide is a tyrant. We sought a brother, and lo, a governor. The sluggish and perverted mind of the multitude, always slow to open to the incursions of Reason, having once so opened, having once received this book, stands upon it, and makes an outcry, if it is disparaged. Colleges are built on it. Books are written on it by thinkers, not by Man Thinking; by men of talent, that is, who start wrong, who set out from accepted dogmas, not from their own sight of principles. Meek young men grow up in libraries, believing it their duty to accept the views which Cicero, which Locke, which Bacon have given, forgetful that Cicero, Locke and Bacon were only young men in libraries when they wrote these books.[8]

Hence, instead of Man Thinking, we have the bookworm. Hence, the book-learned class, who value books, as such; not as related to nature and the human constitution, but as making a sort of Third Estate[9] with the world and the soul. Hence, the restorers of readings, the emendators, the bibliomaniacs of all degrees.

This is bad; this is worse than it seems. Books are the best of things, well used; abused, among the worst. What is the right use? What is the one end which all means go to effect? They are for nothing but to inspire. I had better never see a book than to be warped by its attraction clean out of my own orbit, and made a satellite instead of a system. The one thing in the world of value, is, the active soul,—the soul, free, sovereign, active. This every man is entitled to; this every man contains within him, although in almost all men, obstructed, and as yet unborn. The soul active sees absolute truth; and utters truth, or creates. In this action, it is genius; not the privilege of here and there a favorite, but the sound estate of every man. In its essence, it is progressive. The book, the college, the school of art, the institution of any kind, stop with

---

6. Living. "Business": busyness, activity.
7. Breathes in. "Go": walk.
8. These examples are not especially apt, since none of the three wrote books at an unusually precocious age. As a young man Marcus Tullius Cicero (106–143 B.C., Roman statesman, was best known for his oratory. John Locke (1632–1704), English philosopher and political thinker, wrote *Essay Concerning Human*

*Understanding* (1690) before he was forty. Sir Francis Bacon (1561–1626), English statesman and philosopher, wrote his *Essays*.
9. On the analogy of the three-part division of estates of the realm, in which the third estate is the common people; the first estate is the nobility and the second, the clergy.

some past utterance of genius. This is good, say they,—let us hold by this. They pin me down. They look backward and not forward. But genius always looks forward. The eyes of man are set in his forehead, not in his hindhead. Man hopes. Genius creates. To create,—to create,—is the proof of a divine presence. Whatever talents may be, if the man create not, the pure efflux[1] of the Deity is not his:—cinders and smoke, there may be, but not yet flame. There are creative manners, there are creative actions, and creative words; manners, actions, words, that is, indicative of no custom or authority, but springing spontaneous from the mind's own sense of good and fair.

On the other part, instead of being its own seer, let it receive always from another mind its truth, though it were in torrents of light, without periods of solitude, inquest and self-recovery, and a fatal disservice is done. Genius is always sufficiently the enemy of genius by over-influence. The literature of every nation bear me witness. The English dramatic poets have Shakspearized now for two hundred years.

Undoubtedly, there is a right way of reading,—so it be sternly subordinated. Man Thinking must not be subdued by his instruments. Books are for the scholar's idle times. When he can read God directly, the hour is too precious to be wasted in other mens' transcripts of their readings. But when the intervals of darkness come, as come they must,—when the soul seeth not, when the sun is hid, and the stars withdraw their shining,—we repair to the lamps which were kindled by their ray to guide our steps to the East again, where the dawn is. We hear that we may speak. The Arabian proverb says, "A fig tree looking on a fig tree, becometh fruitful."

It is remarkable, the character of the pleasure we derive from the best books. They impress us ever with the conviction that one nature wrote and the same reads. We read the verses of one of the great English poets, of Chaucer, of Marvell, of Dryden, with the most modern joy,—with a pleasure, I mean, which is in great part caused by the abstraction of all *time* from their verses. There is some awe mixed with the joy of our surprise, when this poet, who lived in some past world, two or three hundred years ago, says that which lies close to my own soul, that which I also had well nigh thought and said. But for the evidence thence afforded to the philosophical doctrine of the identity of all minds, we should suppose some pre-established harmony, some foresight of souls that were to be, and some preparation of stores for their future wants, like the fact observed in insects, who lay up food before death for the young grub they shall never see.

I would not be hurried by any love of system, by any exaggeration of instincts, to underrate the Book. We all know, that as the human body can be nourished on any food, though it were boiled grass and the broth of shoes, so the human mind can be fed by any knowledge. And great and heroic men have existed, who had almost no other information than by the printed page. I only would say, that it needs a strong head to bear that diet. One must be an inventor to read well. As the proverb says, "He that would bring home the wealth of the Indies, must carry out the wealth of the Indies." There is then creative reading, as well as creative writing. When the mind is braced by labor and invention, the page of whatever book we read becomes luminous with manifold allusion. Every sentence is doubly significant, and the sense of our

1. Flowing forth.

author is as broad as the world. We then see, what is always true, that as the seer's hour of vision is short and rare among heavy days and months, so is its record, perchance, the least part of his volume. The discerning will read in his Plato or Shakspeare, only that least part,—only the authentic utterances of the oracle,—and all the rest he rejects, were it never so many times Plato's and Shakspeare's.

Of course, there is a portion of reading quite indispensable to a wise man. History and exact science he must learn by laborious reading. Colleges, in like manner, have their indispensable office,—to teach elements. But they can only highly serve us, when they aim not to drill, but to create; when they gather from far every ray of various genius to their hospitable halls, and, by the concentrated fires, set the hearts of their youth on flame. Thought and knowledge are natures in which apparatus and pretension avail nothing. Gowns, and pecuniary foundations, though of towns of gold, can never countervail the least sentence or syllable of wit. Forget this, and our American colleges will recede in their public importance whilst they grow richer every year.

III. There goes in the world a notion that the scholar should be a recluse, a valetudinarian,—as unfit for any handiwork or public labor, as a penknife for an axe. The so called "practical men" sneer at speculative men, as if, because they speculate or *see*, they could do nothing. I have heard it said that the clergy,—who are always more universally than any other class, the scholars of their day,—are addressed as women: that the rough, spontaneous conversation of men they do not hear, but only a mincing and diluted speech. They are often virtually disfranchised; and, indeed, there are advocates for their celibacy. As far as this is true of the studious classes, it is not just and wise. Action is with the scholar subordinate, but it is essential. Without it, he is not yet man. Without it, thought can never ripen into truth. Whilst the world hangs before the eye as a cloud of beauty, we can not even see its beauty. Inaction is cowardice, but there can be no scholar without the heroic mind. The preamble of thought, the transition through which it passes from the unconscious to the conscious, is action. Only so much do I know, as I have lived. Instantly, we know whose words are loaded with life, and whose not.

The world,—this shadow of the soul, or *other me*, lies wide around. Its attractions are the keys which unlock my thoughts and make me acquainted with myself. I launch eagerly into this resounding tumult. I grasp the hands of those next me, and take my place in the ring to suffer and to work, taught by an instinct that so shall the dumb abyss be vocal with speech. I pierce its order; I dissipate its fear; I dispose of it within the circuit of my expanding life. So much only of life as I know by experience, so much of the wilderness have I vanquished and planted, or so far have I extended my being, my dominion. I do not see how any man can afford, for the sake of his nerves and his nap, to spare any action in which he can partake. It is pearls and rubies to his discourse. Drudgery, calamity, exasperation, want, are instructers in eloquence and wisdom. The true scholar grudges every opportunity of action past by, as a loss of power.

It is the raw material out of which the intellect moulds her splendid products. A strange process too, this, by which experience is converted into thought, as a mulberry leaf is converted into satin. The manufacture goes forward at all hours.

The actions and events of our childhood and youth are now matters of calmest observation. They lie like fair pictures in the air. Not so with our recent actions,—with the business which we now have in hand. On this we are quite unable to speculate. Our affections as yet circulate through it. We no more feel or know it, than we feel the feet, or the hand, or the brain of our body. The new deed is yet a part of life,—remains for a time immersed in our unconscious life. In some contemplative hour, it detaches itself from the life like a ripe fruit, to become a thought of the mind. Instantly, it is raised, transfigured; the corruptible has put on incorruption.[2] Always now it is an object of beauty, however base its origin and neighborhood. Observe, too, the impossibility of antedating this act. In its grub state, it cannot fly, it cannot shine,—it is a dull grub. But suddenly, without observation, the selfsame thing unfurls beautiful wings, and is an angel of wisdom. So is there no fact, no event, in our private history, which shall not, sooner or later, lose its adhesive inert form, and astonish us by soaring from our body into the empyrean.[3] Cradle and infancy, school and playground, the fear of boys, and dogs, and ferules,[4] the love of little maids and berries, and many another fact that once filled the whole sky, are gone already; friend and relative, profession and party, town and country, nation and world, must also soar and sing.

Of course, he who has put forth his total strength in fit actions, has the richest return of wisdom. I will not shut myself out of this globe of action and transplant an oak into a flower pot, there to hunger and pine; nor trust the revenue of some single faculty, and exhaust one vein of thought, much like those Savoyards,[5] who, getting their livelihood by carving shepherds, shepherdesses, and smoking Dutchmen, for all Europe, went out one day to the mountain to find stock, and discovered that they had whittled up the last of their pine trees. Authors we have in numbers, who have written out their vein, and who, moved by a commendable prudence, sail for Greece or Palestine, follow the trapper into the prairie, or ramble round Algiers to replenish their merchantable stock.[6]

If it were only for a vocabulary the scholar would be covetous of action. Life is our dictionary. Years are well spent in country labors; in town—in the insight into trades and manufactures; in frank intercourse with many men and women; in science; in art; to the one end of mastering in all their facts a language, by which to illustrate and embody our perceptions. I learn immediately from any speaker how much he has already lived, through the poverty or the splendor of his speech. Life lies behind us as the quarry from whence we get tiles and copestones for the masonry of to-day. This is the way to learn grammar. Colleges and books only copy the language which the field and the workyard made.

But the final value of action, like that of books, and better than books, is, that it is a resource. That great principle of Undulation in nature, that shows itself in the inspiring and expiring of the breath; in desire and satiety; in the ebb and flow of the sea, in day and night, in heat and cold, and as yet more

2. "For this corruptible must put on incorruption, and this mortal must put on immortality" (I Corinthians 15.53).
3. The highest reaches of heaven.
4. Rods used for punishing children.
5. Savoy is in the western Alps, where France, Italy, and Switzerland converge.

6. Emerson's contemporaries would have understood a reference to writers now unread, such as Nathaniel Parker Willis, as well as to two still-famous writers, James Fenimore Cooper, author of *The Prairie* (1827), and Washington Irving, author of *A Tour on the Prairies* (1835).

deeply ingrained in every atom and every fluid, is known to us under the name of Polarity,—these "fits of easy transmission and reflection," as Newton[7] called them, are the law of nature because they are the law of spirit.

The mind now thinks; now acts; and each fit reproduces the other. When the artist has exhausted his materials, when the fancy no longer paints, when thoughts are no longer apprehended, and books are a weariness,—he has always the resource to *live*. Character is higher than intellect. Thinking is the function. Living is the functionary. The stream retreats to its source. A great soul will be strong to live, a well as strong to think. Does he lack organ or medium to impart his truths? He can still fall back on this elemental force of living them. This is a total act. Thinking is a partial act. Let the grandeur of justice shine in his affairs. Let the beauty of affection cheer his lowly roof. Those "far from fame" who dwell and act with him, will feel the force of his constitution in the doings and passages of the day better than it can be measured by any public and designed display. Time shall teach him that the scholar loses no hour which the man lives. Herein he unfolds the sacred germ of his instinct screened from influence. What is lost in seemliness is gained in strength. Not out of those on whom systems of education have exhausted their culture, comes the helpful giant to destroy the old or to build the new, but out of unhandselled[8] savage nature, out of terrible Druids and Berserkirs, come at last Alfred[9] and Shakspear.

I hear therefore with joy whatever is beginning to be said of the dignity and necessity of labor to every citizen. There is virtue yet in the hoe and the spade, for learned as well as for unlearned hands. And labor is every where welcome; always we are invited to work; only be this limitation observed, that a man shall not for the sake of wider activity sacrifice any opinion to the popular judgments and modes of action.

I have now spoken of the education of the scholar by nature, by books, and by action. It remains to say somewhat of his duties.

They are such as become Man Thinking. They may all be comprised in self-trust. The office of the scholar is to cheer, to raise, and to guide men by showing them facts amidst appearances. He plies the slow, unhonored, and unpaid task of observation. Flamsteed and Herschel, in their glazed[1] observatory, may catalogue the stars with the praise of all men, and the results being splendid and useful, honor is sure. But he, in his private observatory, cataloguing obscure and nebulous stars of the human mind, which as yet no man has thought of as such,—watching days and months, sometimes, for a few facts; correcting still his old records;—must relinquish display and immediate fame. In the long period of his preparation, he must betray often an ignorance and shiftlessness in popular arts, incurring the disdain of the able who shoulder him aside. Long he must stammer in his speech; often forego the living for the dead. Worse yet, he must accept—how often! poverty and solitude. For the ease and pleasure of treading the old road, accepting the fashions, the education, the religion of society, he takes the cross of making his own, and, of

---

7. From the *Optics* (1704) of Sir Isaac Newton (1642–1727), English scientist and mathematician.
8. A handsel is a gift to express good wishes at the outset of some enterprise; apparently Emerson uses the word to mean something like unauspicious.
9. The enlightened 9th-century king of the West Saxons. "Terrible Druids and Berserkirs": uncivilized Celts

and Anglo-Saxons.
1. Glass-roofed. John Flamsteed (1646–1719), English astronomer, first royal astronomer at Greenwich Observatory. Sir William Herschel (1738–1822), German-born English astronomer, founder of sideral astronomy.

course, the self accusation, the faint heart, the frequent uncertainty and loss of time which are the nettles and tangling vines in the way of the self-relying and self-directed; and the state of virtual hostility in which he seems to stand to society, and especially to educated society. For all this loss and scorn, what offset? He is to find consolation in exercising the highest functions of human nature. He is one who raises himself from private considerations, and breathes and lives on public and illustrious thoughts. He is the world's eye. He is the world's heart. He is to resist the vulgar prosperity that retrogrades ever to barbarism, by preserving and communicating heroic sentiments, noble biographies, melodious verse, and the conclusions of history. Whatsoever oracles the human heart in all emergencies, in all solemn hours has uttered as its commentary on the world of actions,—these he shall receive and impart. And whatsoever new verdict Reason from her inviolable seat pronounces on the passing men and events of to-day,—this he shall hear and promulgate.

These being his functions, it becomes him to feel all confidence in himself, and to defer never to the popular cry. He and he only knows the world. The world of any moment is the merest appearance. Some great decorum, some fetish of a government, some ephemeral trade, or war, or man, is cried up by half mankind and cried down by the other half, as if all depended on this particular up or down. The odds are that the whole question is not worth the poorest thought which the scholar has lost in listening to the controversy. Let him not quit his belief that a popgun is a popgun, though the ancient and honorable of the earth affirm it to be the crack of doom. In silence, in steadiness, in severe abstraction, let him hold by himself; add observation to observation; patient of neglect, patient of reproach, and bide his own time,—happy enough if he can satisfy himself alone that this day he has seen something truly. Success treads on every right step. For the instinct is sure that prompts him to tell his brother what he thinks. He then learns that in going down into the secrets of his own mind, he has descended into the secrets of all minds. He learns that he who has mastered any law in his private thoughts, is master to that extent of all men whose language he speaks, and of all into whose language his own can be translated. The poet in utter solitude remembering his spontaneous thoughts and recording them, is found to have recorded that which men in "cities vast" find true for them also. The orator distrusts at first the fitness of his frank confessions,—his want of knowledge of the persons he addresses,—until he finds that he is the complement of his hearers;—that they drink his words because he fulfils for them their own nature; the deeper he dives into his privatest secretest presentiment,—to his wonder he finds, this is the most acceptable, most public, and universally true. The people delight in it; the better part of every man feels, This is my music: this is myself.

In self-trust, all the virtues are comprehended. Free should the scholar be,—free and brave. Free even to the definition of freedom, "without any hindrance that does not arise out of his own constitution." Brave; for fear is a thing which a scholar by his very function puts behind him. Fear always springs from ignorance. It is a shame to him if his tranquillity, amid dangerous times, arise from the presumption that like children and women, his is a protected class; or if he seek a temporary peace by the diversion of his thoughts from politics or vexed questions, hiding his head like an ostrich in the flowering bushes, peeping into microscopes, and turning rhymes, as a boy whistles to keep his courage up. So is the danger a danger still: so is the fear worse.

Manlike let him turn and face it. Let him look into its eye and search its nature, inspect its origin—see the whelping of this lion,—which lies no great way back; he will then find in himself a perfect comprehension of its nature and extent; he will have made his hands meet on the other side, and can henceforth defy it, and pass on superior. The world is his who can see through its pretension. What deafness, what stone-blind custom, what overgrown error you behold, is there only by sufferance,—by your sufferance. See it to be a lie, and you have already dealt it its mortal blow.

Yes, we are the cowed,—we the trustless. It is a mischievous notion that we are come late into nature; that the world was finished a long time ago. As the world was plastic and fluid in the hands of God, so it is ever to so much of his attributes as we bring to it. To ignorance and sin, it is flint. They adapt themselves to it as they may; but in proportion as a man has anything in him divine, the firmament flows before him, and takes his signet[2] and form. Not he is great who can alter matter, but he who can alter my state of mind. They are the kings of the world who give the color of their present thought to all nature and all art, and persuade men by the cheerful serenity of their carrying the matter, that this thing which they do, is the apple which the ages have desired to pluck, now at last ripe, and inviting nations to the harvest. The great man makes the great thing. Wherever Macdonald sits, there is the head of the table.[3] Linnæus makes botany the most alluring of studies and wins it from the farmer and the herb-woman. Davy, chemistry: and Cuvier,[4] fossils. The day is always his, who works in it with serenity and great aims. The unstable estimates of men crowd to him whose mind is filled with a truth, as the heaped waves of the Atlantic follow the moon.

For this self-trust, the reason is deeper than can be fathomed,—darker than can be enlightened. I might not carry with me the feeling of my audience in stating my own belief. But I have already shown the ground of my hope, in adverting to the doctrine that man is one. I believe man has been wronged: he has wronged himself. He has almost lost the light that can lead him back to his prerogatives. Men are become of no account. Men in history, men in the world of to-day are bugs, are spawn, and are called "the mass" and "the herd." In a century, in a millenium, one or two men; that is to say—one or two approximations to the right state of every man. All the rest behold in the hero or the poet their own green and crude being—ripened; yes, and are content to be less, so *that* may attain to its full stature. What a testimony—full of grandeur, full of pity, is borne to the demands of his own nature, by the poor clansman, the poor partisan, who rejoices in the glory of his chief. The poor and the low find some amends to their immense moral capacity, for their acquiescence in a political and social inferiority. They are content to be brushed like flies from the path of a great person, so that justice shall be done by him to that common nature which it is the dearest desire of all to see enlarged and glorified. They sun themselves in the great man's light, and feel it to be their own element. They cast the dignity of man from their downtrod selves upon the shoulders of a hero, and will perish to add one drop of blood to make that great heart beat, those giant sinews combat and conquer. He lives for us, and we live in him.

2. Seal.
3. An old proverb says, "Where Macgregor sits, there is the head of the table"; Emerson substitutes another typical name for a Scottish chief.

4. Georges Cuvier (1769–1832), French pioneer in comparative anatomy and paleontology. Carl von Linné ("Linnaeus") (1707–1778), Swedish botanist. Sir Humphry Davy (1778–1829), English chemist.

Men such as they are, very naturally seek money or power; and power because it is as good as money,—the "spoils," so called, "of office." And why not? for they aspire to the highest, and this, in their sleep-walking, they dream is highest. Wake them, and they shall quit the false good and leap to the true, and leave government to clerks and desks. This revolution is to be wrought by the gradual domestication of the idea of Culture. The main enterprise of the world for splendor, for extent, is the upbuilding of a man. Here are the materials strown along the ground. The private life of one man shall be a more illustrious monarchy,—more formidable to its enemy, more sweet and serene in its influence to its friend, than any kingdom in history. For a man, rightly viewed, comprehendeth the particular natures of all men. Each philosopher, each bard, each actor, has only done for me, as by a delegate, what one day I can do for myself. The books which once we valued more than the apple of the eye, we have quite exhausted. What is that but saying that we have come up with the point of view which the universal mind took through the eyes of that one scribe; we have been that man, and have passed on. First, one; then another; we drain all cisterns, and waxing greater by all these supplies, we crave a better and more abundant food. The man has never lived that can feed us ever. The human mind cannot be enshrined in a person who shall set a barrier on any one side to this unbounded, unboundable empire. It is one central fire which flaming now out of the lips of Etna, lightens the capes of Sicily; and now out of the throat of Vesuvius, illuminates the towers and vineyards of Naples.[5] It is one light which beams out of a thousand stars. It is one soul which animates all men.

But I have dwelt perhaps tediously upon this abstraction of the Scholar. I ought not to delay longer to add what I have to say, of nearer reference to the time and to this country.

Historically, there is thought to be a difference in the ideas which predominate over successive epochs, and there are data for marking the genius of the Classic, of the Romantic, and now of the Reflective or Philosophical age.[6] With the views I have intimated of the oneness or the identity of the mind through all individuals, I do not much dwell on these differences. In fact, I believe each individual passes through all three. The boy is a Greek; the youth, romantic; the adult, reflective. I deny not, however, that a revolution in the leading idea may be distinctly enough traced.

Our age is bewailed as the age of Introversion. Must that needs be evil? We, it seems, are critical. We are embarrassed with second thoughts. We cannot enjoy any thing for hankering to know whereof the pleasure consists. We are lined with eyes. We see with our feet. The time is infected with Hamlet's unhappiness,—

"Sicklied o'er with the pale cast of thought."[7]

Is it so bad then? Sight is the last thing to be pitied. Would we be blind? Do we fear lest we should outsee nature and God, and drink truth dry? I look upon the discontent of the literary class as a mere announcement of the fact that they find themselves not in the state of mind of their fathers, and regret the coming state as untried; as a boy dreads the water before he has learned that

---

5. Active volcanoes in eastern Sicily and western Italy.
6. Emerson proceeds to refute the self-excusing notion that his age was merely a time for criticism, not for genuinely creative achievements.
7. Shakespeare's *Hamlet* (3.1.85–87).

he can swim. If there is any period one would desire to be born in,—is it not the age of Revolution; when the old and the new stand side by side, and admit of being compared; when the energies of all men are searched by fear and by hope; when the historic glories of the old, can be compensated by the rich possibilities of the new era? This time, like all times, is a very good one, if we but know what to do with it.

I read with joy some of the auspicious signs of the coming days as they glimmer already through poetry and art, through philosophy and science, through church and state.

One of these signs is the fact that the same movement which effected the elevation of what was called the lowest class in the state, assumed in literature a very marked and as benign an aspect. Instead of the sublime and beautiful, the near, the low, the common, was explored and poetised. That which had been negligently trodden under foot by those who were harnessing and provisioning themselves for long journies into far countries, is suddenly found to be richer than all foreign parts. The literature of the poor, the feelings of the child, the philosophy of the street, the meaning of household life, are the topics of the time. It is a great stride. It is a sign—is it not? of new vigor, when the extremities are made active, when currents of warm life run into the hands and the feet. I ask not for the great, the remote, the romantic; what is doing in Italy or Arabia; what is Greek art, or Provencal Minstrelsy; I embrace the common, I explore and sit at the feet of the familiar, the low. Give me insight into to-day, and you may have the antique and future worlds. What would we really know the meaning of? The meal in the firkin; the milk in the pan; the ballad in the street; the news of the boat; the glance of the eye; the form and the gait of the body;—show me the ultimate reason of these matters;—show me the sublime presence of the highest spiritual cause lurking, as always it does lurk, in these suburbs and extremities of nature; let me see every trifle bristling with the polarity that ranges it instantly on an eternal law; and the shop, the plough, and the ledger, referred to the like cause by which light undulates and poets sing;—and the world lies no longer a dull miscellany and lumber room,[8] but has form and order; there is no trifle; there is no puzzle; but one design unites and animates the farthest pinnacle and the lowest trench.

This idea has inspired the genius of Goldsmith, Burns, Cowper, and in a newer time, of Goethe, Wordsworth, and Carlyle. This idea they have differently followed and with various success. In contrast with their writing, the style of Pope, of Johnson, of Gibbon, looks cold and pedantic.[9] This writing is blood-warm. Man is surprised to find that things near are not less beautiful and wondrous than things remote. The near explains the far. The drop is a small ocean. A man is related to all nature. This perception of the worth of the vulgar, is fruitful in discoveries. Goethe, in this very thing the most modern of the moderns, has shown us, as none ever did, the genius of the ancients.

There is one man of genius who has done much for this philosophy of life, whose literary value has never yet been rightly estimated;—I mean Emanuel Swedenborg.[1] The most imaginative of men, yet writing with the precision of

---

8. Junk room.
9. Himself nurtured on such "cold and pedantic" writers as Alexander Pope, Samuel Johnson, and Edward Gibbon, in this passage Emerson conventionally contrasts them with the so-called pre-Romantics like Oliver Goldsmith, Robert Burns, and William Cowper and Romantics like Goethe, Wordsworth, and Carlyle,

supposedly marked by greater attention to aspects of ordinary life.
1. No important critic after Emerson has taken up this advocacy of literary greatness in Swedenborg (1688–1772), Swedish scientist and theologian. He was a passion of Emerson's because of his intellectual and spiritual affinities not his intrinsic literary merit.

a mathematician, he endeavored to engraft a purely philosophical Ethics on the popular Christianity of his time. Such an attempt, of course, must have difficulty which no genius could surmount. But he saw and showed the connexion between nature and the affections of the soul. He pierced the emblematic or spiritual character of the visible, audible, tangible world. Especially did his shade-loving muse hover over and interpret the lower parts of nature; he showed the mysterious bond that allies moral evil to the foul material forms, and has given in epical parables a theory of insanity, of beasts, of unclean and fearful things.

Another sign of our times, also marked by an analogous political movement is, the new importance given to the single person. Every thing that tends to insulate the individual,—to surround him with barriers of natural respect, so that each man shall feel the world is his, and man shall treat with man as a sovereign state with a sovereign state;—tends to true union as well as greatness. "I learned," said the melancholy Pestalozzi,[2] "that no man in God's wide earth is either willing or able to help any other man." Help must come from the bosom alone. The scholar is that man who must take up into himself all the ability of the time, all the contributions of the past, all the hopes of the future. He must be an university of knowledges. If there be one lesson more than another which should pierce his ear, it is, The world is nothing, the man is all; in yourself is the law of all nature, and you know not yet how a globule of sap ascends; in yourself slumbers the whole of Reason; it is for you to know all, it is for you to dare all. Mr. President and Gentlemen, this confidence in the unsearched might of man, belongs by all motives, by all prophecy, by all preparation, to the American Scholar. We have listened too long to the courtly muses of Europe. The spirit of the American freeman is already suspected to be timid, imitative, tame. Public and private avarice make the air we breathe thick and fat. The scholar is decent, indolent, complaisant.[3] See already the tragic consequence. The mind of this country taught to aim at low objects, eats upon itself. There is no work for any but the decorous and the complaisant. Young men of the fairest promise, who begin life upon our shores, inflated by the mountain winds, shined upon by all the stars of God, find the earth below not in unison with these,—but are hindered from action by the disgust which the principles on which business is managed inspire, and turn drudges, or die of disgust,—some of them suicides. What is the remedy? They did not yet see, and thousands of young men as hopeful now crowding to the barriers for the career, do not yet see, that if the single man plant himself indomitably on his instincts, and there abide, the huge world will come round to him. Patience—patience;—with the shades of all the good and great for company; and for solace, the perspective of your own infinite life; and for work, the study and the communication of principles, the making those instincts prevalent, the conversion of the world. Is it not the chief disgrace in the world, not to be an unit;—not to be reckoned one character;—not to yield that peculiar fruit which each man was created to bear, but to be reckoned in the gross, in the hundred, or the thousand, of the party, the section, to which we belong; and our opinion predicted geographically, as the north, or the south. Not so, brothers and friends,—please God, ours shall not be so. We

---

2. Johann Heinrich Pestalozzi (1746–1827), Swiss educator and benefactor of poor children, whose ideas on education influenced Emerson's friends Bronson Al- cott and Elizabeth Peabody.
3. Too ready to please others.

will walk on our own feet; we will work with our own hands; we will speak our own minds. Then shall man be no longer a name for pity, for doubt, and for sensual indulgence. The dread of man and the love of man shall be a wall of defence and a wreath of love around all. A nation of men will for the first time exist, because each believes himself inspired by the Divine Soul which also inspires all men.

1837

## The Divinity School Address[1]

In this refulgent summer it has been a luxury to draw the breath of life. The grass grows, the buds burst, the meadow is spotted with fire and gold in the tint of flowers. The air is full of birds, and sweet with the breath of the pine, the balm-of-Gilead,[2] and the new hay. Night brings no gloom to the heart with its welcome shade. Through the transparent darkness pour the stars their almost spiritual rays. Man under them seems a young child, and his huge globe a toy. The cool night bathes the world as with a river, and prepares his eyes again for the crimson dawn. The mystery of nature was never displayed more happily. The corn and the wine have been freely dealt to all creatures, and the never-broken silence with which the old bounty goes forward, has not yielded yet one word of explanation. One is constrained to respect the perfection of this world, in which our senses converse. How wide; how rich; what invitation from every property it gives to every faculty of man! In its fruitful soils; in its navigable sea; in its mountains of metal and stone; in its forests of all woods; in its animals; in its chemical ingredients; in the powers and path of light, heat, attraction, and life, is it well worth the pith and heart of great men to subdue and enjoy it. The planters, the mechanics, the inventors, the astronomers, the builders of cities, and the captains, history delights to honor.

But the moment the mind opens, and reveals the laws which traverse the universe, and make things what they are, then shrinks the great world at once into a mere illustration and fable of this mind. What am I? and What is? asks the human spirit with a curiosity new-kindled, but never to be quenched. Behold these outrunning laws, which our imperfect apprehension can see tend this way and that, but not come full circle. Behold these infinite relations, so like, so unlike; many, yet one. I would study, I would know, I would admire forever. These works of thought have been the entertainments of the human spirit in all ages.

A more secret, sweet, and overpowering beauty appears to man when his heart and mind open to the sentiment of virtue. Then instantly he is instructed in what is above him. He learns that his being is without bound; that, to the

1. An Address Delivered before the Senior Class in Divinity College, Cambridge, Sunday Evening 15 July, 1838 was published as a pamphlet in Boston soon after it was given. That original text is followed here, though with the title used in Essays (1841). Outraged attacks appeared in newspapers and pamphlets, and Emerson cautioned himself in his journal to remain "steady." (Perry Miller, in The Transcendentalists [1950], reprints some of the documents in this brief furor, including the most notorious attack on Emerson, Andrews Norton's The Latest Form of Infidelity.) Emerson retracted nothing privately or publicly and was not invited back to Harvard for three decades, after the university had become more secular and Emerson's own international reputation had muted the charges against him.

2. An aromatic evergreen tree, named for the curative resin associated with Gilead in Jeremiah 8.22: "Is there no balm in Gilead; is there no physician there?"

good, to the perfect, he is born, low as he now lies in evil and weakness. That which he venerates is still his own, though he has not realized it yet. *He ought.* He knows the sense of that grand word, though his analysis fails entirely to render account of it. When in innocency, or when by intellectual perception, he attains to say,—'I love the Right; Truth is beautiful within and without, forevermore. Virtue, I am thine: save me: use me: thee will I serve, day and night, in great, in small, that I may be not virtuous, but virtue;'—then is the end of the creation answered, and God is well pleased.

The sentiment of virtue is a reverence and delight in the presence of certain divine laws. It perceives that this homely game of life we play, covers, under what seem foolish details, principles that astonish. The child amidst his baubles, is learning the action of light, motion, gravity, muscular force; and in the game of human life, love, fear, justice, appetite, man, and God, interact. These laws refuse to be adequately stated. They will not by us or for us be written out on paper, or spoken by the tongue. They elude, evade our persevering thought, and yet we read them hourly in each other's faces, in each other's actions, in our own remorse. The moral traits which are all globed into every virtuous act and thought,—in speech, we must sever, and describe or suggest by painful enumeration of many particulars. Yet, as this sentiment is the essence of all religion, let me guide your eyes to the precise objects of the sentiment, by an enumeration of some of those classes of facts in which this element is conspicuous.

The intuition of the moral sentiment is an insight of the perfection of the laws of the soul. These laws execute themselves. They are out of time, out of space, and not subject to circumstance. Thus; in the soul of man there is a justice whose retributions are instant and entire. He who does a good deed, is instantly ennobled himself. He who does a mean deed, is by the action itself contracted. He who puts off impurity, thereby puts on purity. If a man is at heart just, then in so far is he God; the safety of God, the immortality of God, the majesty of God do enter into that man with justice. If a man dissemble, deceive, he deceives himself, and goes out of acquaintance with his own being. A man in the view of absolute goodness, adores, with total humility. Every step so downward, is a step upward. The man who renounces himself, comes to himself by so doing.

See how this rapid intrinsic energy worketh everywhere, righting wrongs, correcting appearances, and bringing up facts to a harmony with thoughts. Its operation in life, though slow to the senses, is, at last, as sure as in the soul. By it, a man is made the Providence to himself, dispensing good to his goodness, and evil to his sin. Character is always known. Thefts never enrich; alms never impoverish; murder will speak out of stone walls. The least admixture of a lie,—for example, the smallest mixture of vanity, the least attempt to make a good impression, a favorable appearance,—will instantly vitiate the effect. But speak the truth, and all nature and all spirits help you with unexpected furtherance. Speak the truth, and all things alive or brute are vouchers, and the very roots of the grass underground there, do seem to stir and move to bear you witness. See again the perfection of the Law as it applies itself to the affections, and becomes the law of society. As we are, so we associate. The good, by affinity, seek the good; the vile, by affinity, the vile. Thus of their own volition, souls proceed into heaven, into hell.

These facts have always suggested to man the sublime creed, that the world is not the product of manifold power, but of one will, of one mind; and that one mind is everywhere, in each ray of the star, in each wavelet of the pool, active; and whatever opposes that will, is everywhere baulked and baffled, because things are made so, and not otherwise. Good is positive. Evil is merely privative,[3] not absolute. It is like cold, which is the privation of heat. All evil is so much death or nonentity. Benevolence is absolute and real. So much benevolence as a man hath, so much life hath he. For all things proceed out of this same spirit, which is differently named love, justice, temperance, in its different applications, just as the ocean receives different names on the several shores which it washes. All things proceed out of the same spirit, and all things conspire with it. Whilst a man seeks good ends, he is strong by the whole strength of nature. In so far as he roves from these ends, he bereaves himself of power, of auxiliaries; his being shrinks out of all remote channels, he becomes less and less, a mote, a point, until absolute badness is absolute death.

The perception of this law of laws always awakens in the mind a sentiment which we call the religious sentiment, and which makes our highest happiness. Wonderful is its power to charm and to command. It is a mountain air. It is the embalmer of the world. It is myrrh and storax, and chlorine and rosemary.[4] It makes the sky and the hills sublime, and the silent song of the stars is it. By it, is the universe made safe and habitable, not by science or power. Thought may work cold and intransitive in things, and find no end or unity. But the dawn of the sentiment of virtue on the heart, gives and is the assurance that Law is sovereign over all natures; and the worlds, time, space, eternity, do seem to break out into joy.

This sentiment is divine and deifying. It is the beatitude of man. It makes him illimitable. Through it, the soul first knows itself. It corrects the capital mistake of the infant man, who seeks to be great by following the great, and hopes to derive advantages *from another*,—by showing the fountain of all good to be in himself, and that he, equally with every man, is a door into the deeps of Reason. When he says, "I ought;" when love warms him; when he chooses, warned from on high, the good and great deed; then, deep melodies wander through his soul from Supreme Wisdom. Then he can worship, and be enlarged by his worship; for he can never go behind this sentiment. In the sublimest flights of the soul, rectitude is never surmounted, love is never outgrown.

This sentiment lies at the foundation of society, and successively creates all forms of worship. The principle of veneration never dies out. Man fallen into superstition, into sensuality, is never wholly without the visions of the moral sentiment. In like manner, all the expressions of this sentiment are sacred and permanent in proportion to their purity. The expressions of this sentiment affect us deeper, greatlier, than all other compositions. The sentences of the oldest time, which ejaculate this piety, are still fresh and fragrant. This thought dwelled always deepest in the minds of men in the devout and contemplative East; not alone in Palestine, where it reached its purest expression, but in Egypt, in Persia, in India, in China. Europe has always owed to oriental

3. I.e., not an active power, but the absence of a power.
4. An aromatic evergeen shrub of Southern Europe and Asia Minor, used in cookery and perfumery. "Myrrh": one of the gifts the wise men brought to Je-

sus, a perfume made from aromatic resins. "Storax": an aromatic resin. "Chlorine": in this sense, a greenish yellow gas used for purification.

genius, its divine impulses. What these holy bards said, all sane men found agreeable and true. And the unique impression of Jesus upon mankind, whose name is not so much written as ploughed into the history of this world, is proof of the subtle virtue of this infusion.

Meantime, whilst the doors of the temple stand open, night and day, before every man, and the oracles of this truth cease never, it is guarded by one stern condition; this, namely; It is an intuition. It cannot be received at second hand. Truly speaking, it is not instruction, but provocation, that I can receive from another soul. What he announces, I must find true in me, or wholly reject; and on his word, or as his second, be he who he may, I can accept nothing. On the contrary, the absence of this primary faith is the presence of degradation. As is the flood so is the ebb. Let this faith depart, and the very words it spake, and the things it made, become false and hurtful. Then falls the church, the state, art, letters, life. The doctrine of the divine nature being forgotten, a sickness infects and dwarfs the constitution. Once man was all; now he is an appendage, a nuisance. And because the indwelling Supreme Spirit cannot wholly be got rid of, the doctrine of it suffers this perversion, that the divine nature is attributed to one or two persons, and denied to all the rest, and denied with fury. The doctrine of inspiration is lost; the base doctrine of the majority of voices, usurps the place of the doctrine of the soul. Miracles, prophecy, poetry, the ideal life, the holy life, exist as ancient history merely; they are not in the belief, nor in the aspiration of society; but, when suggested, seem ridiculous. Life is comic or pitiful, as soon as the high ends of being fade out of sight, and man becomes near-sighted, and can only attend to what addresses the senses.

These general views, which, whilst they are general, none will contest, find abundant illustration in the history of religion, and especially in the history of the Christian church. In that, all of us have had our birth and nurture. The truth contained in that, you, my young friends, are now setting forth to teach. As the Cultus, or established worship of the civilized world, it has great historical interest for us. Of its blessed words, which have been the consolation of humanity, you need not that I should speak. I shall endeavor to discharge my duty to you, on this occasion, by pointing out two errors in its administration, which daily appear more gross from the point of view we have just now taken.

Jesus Christ belonged to the true race of prophets. He saw with open eye the mystery of the soul. Drawn by its severe harmony, ravished with its beauty, he lived in it, and had his being there. Alone in all history, he estimated the greatness of man. One man was true to what is in you and me. He saw that God incarnates himself in man, and evermore goes forth anew to take possession of his world. He said, in this jubilee of sublime emotion, 'I am divine. Through me, God acts; through me, speaks. Would you see God, see me; or, see thee, when thou also thinkest as I now think.' But what a distortion did his doctrine and memory suffer in the same, in the next, and the following ages! There is no doctrine of the Reason which will bear to be taught by the Understanding.[5] The understanding caught this high chant from the poet's lips, and said, in the next age, 'This was Jehovah come down out of heaven. I will kill you, if you say he was a man.' The idioms of his language, and the figures of

---

5. Emerson reverses the common meaning of *reason*, using it in the sense of intuitive, suprarational knowledge, while by *understanding* he means knowledge arrived at through a logical reasoning process.

his rhetoric, have usurped the place of his truth; and churches are not built on his principles, but on his tropes. Christianity became a Mythus,[6] as the poetic teaching of Greece and of Egypt, before. He spoke of miracles; for he felt that man's life was a miracle, and all that man doth, and he knew that this daily miracle shines, as the man is diviner. But the very word Miracle, as pronounced by Christian churches, gives a false impression; it is Monster. It is not one with the blowing clover and the falling rain.

He felt respect for Moses and the prophets; but no unfit tenderness at postponing their initial revelations, to the hour and the man that now is; to the eternal revelation in the heart. Thus was he a true man. Having seen that the law in us is commanding, he would not suffer it to be commanded. Boldly, with hand, and heart, and life, he declared it was God. Thus was he a true man. Thus is he, as I think, the only soul in history who has appreciated the worth of a man.

1. In thus contemplating Jesus, we become very sensible of the first defect of historical Christianity. Historical Christianity has fallen into the error that corrupts all attempts to communicate religion. As it appears to us, and as it has appeared for ages, it is not the doctrine of the soul, but an exaggeration of the personal, the positive, the ritual. It has dwelt, it dwells, with noxious exaggeration about the *person* of Jesus. The soul knows no persons. It invites every man to expand to the full circle of the universe, and will have no preferences but those of spontaneous love. But by this eastern monarchy of a Christianity, which indolence and fear have built, the friend of man is made the injurer of man. The manner in which his name is surrounded with expressions, which were once sallies of admiration and love, but are now petrified into official titles, kills all generous sympathy and liking. All who hear me, feel, that the language that describes Christ to Europe and America, is not the style of friendship and enthusiasm to a good and noble heart, but is appropriated and formal,—paints a demigod, as the Orientals or the Greeks would describe Osiris or Apollo.[7] Accept the injurious impositions of our early catechetical instruction, and even honesty and self-denial were but splendid sins, if they did not wear the Christian name. One would rather be

'A pagan suckled in a creed outworn,'[8]

than to be defrauded of his manly right in coming into nature, and finding not names and places, not land and professions, but even virtue and truth foreclosed and monopolized. You shall not be a man even. You shall not own the world; you shall not dare, and live after the infinite Law that is in you, and in company with the infinite Beauty which heaven and earth reflect to you in all lovely forms; but you must subordinate your nature to Christ's nature; you must accept our interpretations; and take his portrait as the vulgar draw it.

That is always best which gives me to myself. The sublime is excited in me by the great stoical doctrine, Obey thyself. That which shows God in me, fortifies me. That which shows God out of me, makes me a wart and a wen. There is no longer a necessary reason for my being. Already the long shadows of untimely oblivion creep over me, and I shall decease forever.

The divine bards are the friends of my virtue, of my intellect, of my

---

6. A cult deliberately fostered.
7. Emerson associates Egypt (where Osiris was a fertility god) with the Orient and associates Greece (where

Apollo was the god of the sun) with European culture.
8. From Wordsworth's sonnet *The World Is Too Much with Us.*

strength. They admonish me, that the gleams which flash across my mind, are not mine, but God's; that they had the like, and were not disobedient to the heavenly vision.[9] So I love them. Noble provocations go out from them, inviting me also to emancipate myself; to resist evil; to subdue the world; and to Be. And thus by his holy thoughts, Jesus serves us, and thus only. To aim to convert a man by miracles, is a profanation of the soul. A true conversion, a true Christ, is now, as always, to be made, by the reception of beautiful sentiments. It is true that a great and rich soul, like his, falling among the simple, does so preponderate, that, as his did, it names the world. The world seems to them to exist for him, and they have not yet drunk so deeply of his sense, as to see that only by coming again to themselves, or to God in themselves, can they grow forevermore. It is a low benefit to give me something; it is a high benefit to enable me to do somewhat of myself. The time is coming when all men will see, that the gift of God to the soul is not a vaunting, overpowering, excluding sanctity, but a sweet, natural goodness, a goodness like thine and mine, and that so invites thine and mine to be and to grow.

The injustice of the vulgar tone of preaching is not less flagrant to Jesus, than it is to the souls which it profanes. The preachers do not see that they make his gospel not glad, and shear him of the locks of beauty and the attributes of heaven. When I see a majestic Epaminondas,[1] or Washington; when I see among my contemporaries, a true orator, an upright judge, a dear friend; when I vibrate to the melody and fancy of a poem; I see beauty that is to be desired. And so lovely, and with yet more entire consent of my human being, sounds in my ear the severe music of the bards that have sung of the true God in all ages. Now do not degrade the life and dialogues of Christ out of the circle of this charm, by insulation and peculiarity. Let them lie as they befel, alive and warm, part of human life, and of the landscape, and of the cheerful day.

2. The second defect of the traditionary and limited way of using the mind of Christ is a consequence of the first; this, namely; that the Moral Nature, that Law of laws, whose revelations introduce greatness,—yea, God himself, into the open soul, is not explored as the fountain of the established teaching in society. Men have come to speak of the revelation as somewhat long ago given and done, as if God were dead. The injury to faith throttles the preacher; and the goodliest of institutions becomes an uncertain and inarticulate voice.

It is very certain that it is the effect of conversation with the beauty of the soul, to beget a desire and need to impart to others the same knowledge and love. If utterance is denied, the thought lies like a burden on the man. Always the seer is a sayer. Somehow his dream is told. Somehow he publishes it with solemn joy. Sometimes with pencil on canvas; sometimes with chisel on stone; sometimes in towers and aisles of granite, his soul's worship is builded; sometimes in anthems of indefinite music; but clearest and most permanent, in words.

The man enamored of this excellency, becomes its priest or poet. The office is coeval with the world. But observe the condition, the spiritual limitation of the office. The spirit only can teach. Not any profane man, not any sensual, not any liar, not any slave can teach, but only he can give, who has; he only

<hr>

9. "I was not disobedient unto the heavenly vision"
(Acts 26.19).

1. Theban general (418?–362 B.C) whose military innovations helped end Sparta's dominance in Greece.

can create, who is. The man on whom the soul descends, through whom the soul speaks, alone can teach. Courage, piety, love, wisdom, can teach; and every man can open his door to these angels, and they shall bring him the gift of tongues. But the man who aims to speak as books enable, as synods use, as the fashion guides, and as interest commands, babbles. Let him hush.

To this holy office, you propose to devote yourselves. I wish you may feel your call in throbs of desire and hope. The office is the first in the world. It is of that reality, that it cannot suffer the deduction of any falsehood. And it is my duty to say to you, that the need was never greater of new revelation than now. From the views I have already expressed, you will infer the sad conviction, which I share, I believe, with numbers, of the universal decay and now almost death of faith in society. The soul is not preached. The Church seems to totter to its fall, almost all life extinct. On this occasion, any complaisance, would be criminal, which told you, whose hope and commission it is to preach the faith of Christ, that the faith of Christ is preached.

It is time that this ill-suppressed murmur of all thoughtful men against the famine of our churches; this moaning of the heart because it is bereaved of the consolation, the hope, the grandeur, that come alone out of the culture of the moral nature; should be heard through the sleep of indolence, and over the din of routine. This great and perpetual office of the preacher is not discharged. Preaching is the expression of the moral sentiment in application to the duties of life. In how many churches, by how many prophets, tell me, is man made sensible that he is an infinite Soul; that the earth and heavens are passing into his mind; that he is drinking forever the soul of God? Where now sounds the persuasion, that by its very melody imparadises my heart, and so affirms its own origin in heaven? Where shall I hear words such as in elder ages drew men to leave all and follow,—father and mother, house and land, wife and child?[2] Where shall I hear these august laws of moral being so pronounced, as to fill my ear, and I feel ennobled by the offer of my uttermost action and passion? The test of the true faith, certainly, should be its power to charm and command the soul, as the laws of nature control the activity of the hands,—so commanding that we find pleasure and honor in obeying. The faith should blend with the light of rising and of setting suns, with the flying cloud, the singing bird, and the breath of flowers. But now the priest's Sabbath has lost the splendor of nature; it is unlovely; we are glad when it is done; we can make, we do make, even sitting in our pews, a far better, holier, sweeter, for ourselves.

Whenever the pulpit is usurped by a formalist, then is the worshipper defrauded and disconsolate. We shrink as soon as the prayers begin, which do not uplift, but smite and offend us. We are fain to wrap our cloaks about us, and secure, as best we can, a solitude that hears not. I once heard a preacher who sorely tempted me to say, I would go to church no more. Men go, thought I, where they are wont to go, else had no soul entered the temple in the afternoon. A snowstorm was falling around us. The snowstorm was real; the preacher merely spectral; and the eye felt the sad contrast in looking at him, and then out of the window behind him, into the beautiful meteor of

2. See Matthew 19.28–29: "And Jesus said unto them, Verily I say unto you, That ye which have followed me, in the regeneration when the Son of man shall sit in the throne of his glory, ye also shall sit upon twelve thrones, judging the twelve tribes of Israel. And every one that hath forsaken houses, or brethren, or sisters, or father, or mother, or wife, or children, or lands, for my name's sake, shall receive an hundredfold, and shall inherit everlasting life."

the snow. He had lived in vain. He had no one word intimating that he had laughed or wept, was married or in love, had been commended, or cheated, or chagrined. If he had ever lived and acted, we were none the wiser for it. The capital secret of his profession, namely, to convert life into truth, he had not learned. Not one fact in all his experience, had he yet imported into his doctrine. This man had ploughed, and planted, and talked, and bought, and sold; he had read books; he had eaten and drunken; his head aches; his heart throbs; he smiles and suffers; yet was there not a surmise, a hint, in all the discourse, that he had ever lived at all. Not a line did he draw out of real history. The true preacher can always be known by this, that he deals out to the people his life,—life passed through the fire of thought. But of the bad preacher, it could not be told from his sermon, what age of the world he fell in; whether he had a father or a child; whether he was a freeholder or a pauper; whether he was a citizen or a countryman; or any other fact of his biography.

It seemed strange that the people should come to church. It seemed as if their houses were very unentertaining, that they should prefer this thoughtless clamor. It shows that there is a commanding attraction in the moral sentiment, that can lend a faint tint of light to dulness and ignorance, coming in its name and place. The good hearer is sure he has been touched sometimes; is sure there is somewhat to be reached, and some word that can reach it. When he listens to these vain words, he comforts himself by their relation to his remembrance of better hours, and so they clatter and echo unchallenged.

I am not ignorant that when we preach unworthily, it is not always quite in vain. There is a good ear, in some men, that draws supplies to virtue out of very indifferent nutriment. There is poetic truth concealed in all the common-places of prayer and of sermons, and though foolishly spoken, they may be wisely heard; for, each is some select expression that broke out in a moment of piety from some stricken or jubilant soul, and its excellency made it remembered. The prayers and even the dogmas of our church, are like the zodiac of Denderah,[3] and the astronomical monuments of the Hindoos, wholly insulated from anything now extant in the life and business of the people. They mark the height to which the waters once rose. But this docility is a check upon the mischief from the good and devout. In a large portion of the community, the religious service gives rise to quite other thoughts and emotions. We need not chide the negligent servant. We are struck with pity, rather, at the swift retribution of his sloth. Alas for the unhappy man that is called to stand in the pulpit, and *not* give bread of life. Everything that befals, accuses him. Would he ask contributions for the missions, foreign or domestic? Instantly his face is suffused with shame, to propose to his parish, that they should send money a hundred or a thousand miles, to furnish such poor fare as they have at home, and would do well to go the hundred or the thousand miles, to escape. Would he urge people to a godly way of living;—and can he ask a fellow creature to come to Sabbath meetings, when he and they all know what is the poor uttermost they can hope for therein? Will he invite them privately to the Lord's Supper? He dares not. If no heart warm this rite, the hollow, dry, creaking formality is too plain, than that he can face a man of wit and energy, and put the invitation without terror. In the street, what has he to say to the

---

3. At Dandarah, a village in Upper Egypt, the ceiling of a ruined ancient temple is sculpted with astronomical scenes.

bold village blasphemer? The village blasphemer sees fear in the face, form, and gait of the minister.

Let me not taint the sincerity of this plea by any oversight of the claims of good men. I know and honor the purity and strict conscience of numbers of the clergy. What life the public worship retains, it owes to the scattered company of pious men, who minister here and there in the churches, and who, sometimes accepting with too great tenderness the tenet of the elders, have not accepted from others, but from their own heart, the genuine impulses of virtue, and so still command our love and awe, to the sanctity of character. Moreover, the exceptions are not so much to be found in a few eminent preachers, as in the better hours, the truer inspirations of all,—nay, in the sincere moments of every man. But with whatever exception, it is still true, that tradition characterizes the preaching of this country; that it comes out of the memory, and not out of the soul; that it aims at what is usual, and not at what is necessary and eternal; that thus, historical Christianity destroys the power of preaching, by withdrawing it from the exploration of the moral nature of man, where the sublime is, where are the resources of astonishment and power. What a cruel injustice it is to that Law, the joy of the whole earth, which alone can make thought dear and rich; that Law whose fatal sureness the astronomical orbits poorly emulate, that it is travestied and depreciated, that it is behooted and behowled, and not a trait, not a word of it articulated. The pulpit in losing sight of this Law, loses all its inspiration, and gropes after it knows not what. And for want of this culture, the soul of the community is sick and faithless. It wants nothing so much as a stern, high, stoical, Christian discipline, to make it know itself and the divinity that speaks through it. Now man is ashamed of himself; he skulks and sneaks through the world, to be tolerated, to be pitied, and scarcely in a thousand years does any man dare to be wise and good, and so draw after him the tears and blessings of his kind.

Certainly there have been periods when, from the inactivity of the intellect on certain truths, a greater faith was possible in names and persons. The Puritans in England and America, found in the Christ of the Catholic Church, and in the dogmas inherited from Rome, scope for their austere piety, and their longings for civil freedom. But their creed is passing away, and none arises in its room. I think no man can go with his thoughts about him, into one of our churches, without feeling that what hold the public worship had on men, is gone or going. It has lost its grasp on the affection of the good, and the fear of the bad. In the country,—neighborhoods, half parishes are *signing off*,—to use the local term. It is already beginning to indicate character and religion to withdraw from the religious meetings. I have heard a devout person, who prized the Sabbath, say in bitterness of heart, "On Sundays, it seems wicked to go to church." And the motive, that holds the best there, is now only a hope and a waiting. What was once a mere circumstance, that the best and the worst men in the parish, the poor and the rich, the learned and the ignorant, young and old, should meet one day as fellows in one house, in sign of an equal right in the soul,—has come to be a paramount motive for going thither.

My friends, in these two errors, I think, I find the causes of that calamity of a decaying church and a wasting unbelief, which are casting malignant influences around us, and making the hearts of good men sad. And what greater calamity can fall upon a nation, than the loss of worship? Then all things go to decay. Genius leaves the temple, to haunt the senate, or the market. Literature becomes frivolous. Science is cold. The eye of youth is not lighted by the hope of other worlds, and age is without honor. Society lives to trifles, and when men die, we do not mention them.

And now, my brothers, you will ask, What in these desponding days can be done by us? The remedy is already declared in the ground of our complaint of the Church. We have contrasted the Church with the Soul. In the soul, then, let the redemption be sought. In one soul, in your soul, there are resources for the world. Wherever a man comes, there comes revolution. The old is for slaves. When a man comes, all books are legible, all things transparent, all religions are forms. He is religious. Man is the wonderworker. He is seen amid miracles. All men bless and curse. He saith yea and nay, only. The stationariness of religion; the assumption that the age of inspiration is past, that the Bible is closed; the fear of degrading the character of Jesus by representing him as a man; indicate with sufficient clearness the falsehood of our theology. It is the office of a true teacher to show us that God is, not was; that He speaketh, not spake. The true Christianity,—a faith like Christ's in the infinitude of man,—is lost. None believeth in the soul of man, but only in some man or person old and departed. Ah me! no man goeth alone. All men go in flocks to this saint or that poet, avoiding the God who seeth in secret. They cannot see in secret; they love to be blind in public. They think society wiser than their soul, and know not that one soul, and their soul, is wiser than the whole world. See how nations and races flit by on the sea of time, and leave no ripple to tell where they floated or sunk, and one good soul shall make the name of Moses, or of Zeno, or of Zoroaster,[4] reverend forever. None assayeth the stern ambition to be the Self of the nation, and of nature, but each would be an easy secondary to some Christian scheme, or sectarian connexion, or some eminent man. Once leave your own knowledge of God, your own sentiment, and take secondary knowledge, as St. Paul's, or George Fox's, or Swedenborg's,[5] and you get wide from God with every year this secondary form lasts, and if, as now, for centuries,—the chasm yawns to that breadth, that men can scarcely be convinced there is in them anything divine.

Let me admonish you, first of all, to go alone; to refuse the good models, even those most sacred in the imagination of men, and dare to love God without mediator or veil. Friends enough you shall find who will hold up to your emulation Wesleys and Oberlins,[6] Saints and Prophets. Thank God for these good men, but say, 'I also am a man.' Imitation cannot go above its model. The imitator dooms himself to hopeless mediocrity. The inventor did it, because it was natural to him, and so in him it has a charm. In the imitator, something else is natural, and he bereaves himself of his own beauty, to come short of another man's.

Yourself a newborn bard of the Holy Ghost,—cast behind you all confor-

---

4. Iranian religious reformer (6 century B.C.), founder of religion still practiced by the Parsees. Moses, Hebrew lawgiver who led the exodus from Egypt. Zeno (342?–270? B.C.), Greek philosopher and founder of Stoicism.
5. Emanuel Swedenborg (1688–1772), Swedish scientist and theologian. St. Paul, the apostle to the Gentiles, hero of the Book of Acts, and author of other books of the New Testament. George Fox (1624–

1691), English founder of the Society of Friends (Quakers).
6. Jean Frédéric Oberlin (1740–1826), Alsatian Lutheran clergyman and philanthropist, innovator in children's education; the town and college in Ohio are named in his honor. John Wesley (1703–1791) and his brother Charles (1707–1788) founded the Methodist movement in the Church of England.

mity, and acquaint men at first hand with Deity. Be to them a man. Look to it first and only, that you are such; that fashion, custom, authority, pleasure, and money are nothing to you,—are not bandages over your eyes, that you cannot see,—but live with the privilege of the immeasurable mind. Not too anxious to visit periodically all families and each family in your parish connexion,—when you meet one of these men or women, be to them a divine man; be to them thought and virtue; let their timid aspirations find in you a friend; let their trampled instincts be genially tempted out in your atmosphere; let their doubts know that you have doubted, and their wonder feel that you have wondered. By trusting your own soul, you shall gain a greater confidence in other men. For all our penny-wisdom, for all our soul-destroying slavery to habit, it is not to be doubted, that all men have sublime thoughts; that all men do value the few real hours of life; they love to be heard; they love to be caught up into the vision of principles. We mark with light in the memory the few interviews, we have had in the dreary years of routine and of sin, with souls that made our souls wiser; that spoke what we thought; that told us what we knew; that gave us leave to be what we inly were. Discharge to men the priestly office, and, present or absent, you shall be followed with their love as by an angel.

And, to this end, let us not aim at common degrees of merit. Can we not leave, to such as love it, the virtue that glitters for the commendation of society, and ourselves pierce the deep solitudes of absolute ability and worth? We easily come up to the standard of goodness in society. Society's praise can be cheaply secured, and almost all men are content with those easy merits; but the instant effect of conversing with God, will be, to put them away. There are sublime merits; persons who are not actors, not speakers, but influences; persons too great for fame, for display; who disdain eloquence; to whom all we call art and artist, seems too nearly allied to show and by-ends, to the exaggeration of the finite and selfish, and loss of the universal. The orators, the poets, the commanders encroach on us only as fair women do, by our allowance and homage. Slight them by preoccupation of mind, slight them, as you can well afford to do, by high and universal aims, and they instantly feel that you have right, and that it is in lower places that they must shine. They also feel your right; for they with you are open to the influx of the all-knowing Spirit, which annihilates before its broad noon the little shades and gradations of intelligence in the compositions we call wiser and wisest.

In such high communion, let us study the grand strokes of rectitude: a bold benevolence, an independence of friends, so that not the unjust wishes of those who love us, shall impair our freedom, but we shall resist for truth's sake the freest flow of kindness, and appeal to sympathies far in advance; and,— what is the highest form in which we know this beautiful element,—a certain solidity of merit, that has nothing to do with opinion, and which is so essentially and manifestly virtue, that it is taken for granted, that the right, the brave, the generous step will be taken by it, and nobody thinks of commending it. You would compliment a coxcomb doing a good act, but you would not praise an angel. The silence that accepts merit as the most natural thing in the world, is the highest applause. Such souls, when they appear, are the Imperial Guard of Virtue, the perpetual reserve, the dictators of fortune. One needs not praise their courage,—they are the heart and soul of nature. O my friends, there are resources in us on which we have not drawn. There are men who rise refreshed on hearing a threat; men to whom a crisis which intimidates and paralyzes the majority—demanding not the faculties of prudence and thrift, but comprehension, immovableness, the readiness of sacrifice,—comes graceful and beloved as a bride. Napoleon said of Massena,[7] that he was not himself until the battle began to go against him; then, when the dead began to fall in ranks around him, awoke his powers of combination, and he put on terror and victory as a robe. So it is in rugged crises, in unweariable endurance, and in aims which put sympathy out of question, that the angel is shown. But these are heights that we can scarce remember and look up to, without contrition and shame. Let us thank God that such things exist.

And now let us do what we can to rekindle the smouldering, nigh quenched fire on the altar. The evils of that church that now is, are manifest. The question returns. What shall we do? I confess, all attempts to project and establish a Cultus with new rites and forms, seem to me vain. Faith makes us, and not we it, and faith makes its own forms. All attempts to contrive a system, are as cold as the new worship introduced by the French to the goddess of Reason,[8]—today, pasteboard and fillagree, and ending to-morrow in madness and murder. Rather let the breath of new life be breathed by you through the forms already existing. For, if once you are alive, you shall find they shall become plastic[9] and new. The remedy to their deformity is, first, soul, and second, soul, and evermore, soul. A whole popedom[1] of forms, one pulsation of virtue can uplift and vivify. Two inestimable advantages Christianity has given us; first; the Sabbath, the jubilee of the whole world; whose light dawns welcome alike into the closet of the philosopher, into the garret of toil, and into prison cells, and everywhere suggests, even to the vile, a thought of the dignity of spiritual being. Let is stand forevermore, a temple, which new love, new faith, new sight shall restore to more than its first splendor to mankind. And secondly, the institution of preaching;—the speech of man to men,—essentially the most flexible of all organs, of all forms. What hinders that now, everywhere, in pulpits, in lecture-rooms, in houses, in fields, wherever the invitation of men or your own occasions lead you, you speak the very truth, as your life and conscience teach it, and cheer the waiting, fainting hearts of men with new hope and new revelation.

I look for the hour when that supreme Beauty, which ravished the souls of those Eastern men, and chiefly of those Hebrews, and through their lips spoke oracles to all time, shall speak in the West also. The Hebrew and Greek Scriptures contain immortal sentences, that have been bread of life to millions. But they have no epical integrity; are fragmentary; are not shown in their order to the intellect. I look for the new Teacher, that shall follow so far those shining laws, that he shall see them come full circle; shall see their rounding complete grace; shall see the world to be the mirror of the soul; shall see the identity of the law of gravitation with purity of heart; and shall show that the Ought, that Duty, is one thing with Science, with Beauty, and with Joy.

1838, 1841

---

7. André Masséna (1758–1817), marshal of the empire under Napoleon; the anecdote is taken from Barry Edward O'Meara's *Napoleon in Exile* (1823).
8. A reference to the French "worship of Reason"

promulgated in 1793 during the Reign of Terror.
9. Receptive to influences, capable of receiving new shapes.
1. I.e., rigid hierarchy.

# Self-Reliance[1]

*Ne te quæsiveris extra.*[2]

*"Man is his own star, and the soul that can*
*Render an honest and a perfect man,*
*Command all light, all influence, all fate,*
*Nothing to him falls early or too late.*
*Our acts our angels are, or good or ill,*
*Our fatal shadows that walk by us still."*
—Epilogue to Beaumont and Fletcher's *Honest Man's Fortune*[3]

*Cast the bantling*[4] *on the rocks,*
*Suckle him with the she-wolf's teat:*
*Wintered with the hawk and fox,*
*Power and speed be hands and feet.*

I read the other day some verses written by an eminent painter which were original and not conventional. Always the soul hears an admonition in such lines, let the subject be what it may. The sentiment they instil is of more value than any thought they may contain. To believe your own thought, to believe that what is true for you in your private heart, is true for all men,—that is genius. Speak your latent conviction and it shall be the universal sense; for always the inmost becomes the outmost,—and our first thought is rendered back to us by the trumpets of the Last Judgment. Familiar as the voice of the mind is to each, the highest merit we ascribe to Moses, Plato, and Milton, is that they set at naught books and traditions, and spoke not what men wrote but what they thought. A man should learn to detect and watch that gleam of light which flashes across his mind from within, more than the lustre of the firmament of bards and sages. Yet he dismisses without notice his thought, because it is his. In every work of genius we recognize our own rejected thoughts: they come back to us with a certain alienated majesty. Great works of art have no more affecting lesson for us than this. They teach us to abide by our spontaneous impression with good humored inflexibility then most when the whole cry of voices is on the other side. Else, to-morrow a stranger will say with masterly good sense precisely what we have thought and felt all the time, and we shall be forced to take with shame our own opinion from another.

There is a time in every man's education when he arrives at the conviction that envy is ignorance; that imitation is suicide; that he must take himself for better, for worse, as his portion; that though the wide universe is full of good, no kernel of nourishing corn can come to him but through his toil bestowed on that plot of ground which is given to him to till. The power which resides in him is new in nature, and none but he knows what that is which he can do, nor does he know until he has tried. Not for nothing one face, one character, one fact makes much impression on him, and another none. It is not without preëstablished harmony, this sculpture in the memory. The eye was placed where one ray should fall, that it might testify of that particular ray.

---

1. *Self-Reliance*, first published in *Essays* (1841), the source of the present text, is even more than most of Emerson's essays a collection of thoughts from his journals, often by way of various lectures over a period of years. The earliest of the journal entries reused in this essay is from 1832, the year Emerson renounced his pulpit, and numerous other reused journal entries and lecture reworkings are from the years 1838–40, when *The Divinity School Address* provided a major test of his own self-trust.
2. Persius, *Satire* 1.7: "Do not search outside yourself" (Latin), i.e., meaning do not imitate.
3. 1613.
4. Baby. The stanza is Emerson's.

Bravely let him speak the utmost syllable of his confession. We but half express ourselves, and are ashamed of that divine idea which each of us represents. It may be safely trusted as proportionate and of good issues, so it be faithfully imparted, but God will not have his work made manifest by cowards. It needs a divine man to exhibit any thing divine. A man is relieved and gay when he has put his heart into his work and done his best; but what he has said or done otherwise, shall give him no peace. It is a deliverance which does not deliver. In the attempt his genius deserts him; no muse befriends; no invention, no hope.

Trust thyself: every heart vibrates to that iron string. Accept the place the divine Providence has found for you; the society of your contemporaries, the connexion of events. Great men have always done so and confided themselves childlike to the genius of their age, betraying their perception that the Eternal was stirring at their heart, working through their hands, predominating in all their being. And we are now men, and must accept in the highest mind the same transcendent destiny; and not pinched in a corner, not cowards fleeing before a revolution, but redeemers and benefactors, pious aspirants to be noble clay plastic under the Almighty effort, let us advance and advance on Chaos and the Dark.

What pretty oracles nature yields us on this text in the face and behavior of children, babes and even brutes. That divided and rebel mind, that distrust of a sentiment because our arithmetic has computed the strength and means opposed to our purpose, these have not. Their mind being whole, their eye is as yet unconquered, and when we look in their faces, we are disconcerted. Infancy conforms to nobody: all conform to it, so that one babe commonly makes four or five out of the adults who prattle and play to it. So God has armed youth and puberty and manhood no less with its own piquancy and charm, and made it enviable and gracious and its claims not to be put by, if it will stand by itself. Do not think the youth has no force because he cannot speak to you and me. Hark! in the next room, who spoke so clear and emphatic? Good Heaven! it is he! it is that very lump of bashfulness and phlegm which for weeks has done nothing but eat when you were by, that now rolls out these words like bell-strokes. It seems he knows how to speak to his contemporaries. Bashful or bold, then, he will know how to make us seniors very unnecessary.

The nonchalance of boys who are sure of a dinner, and would disdain as much as a lord to do or say aught to conciliate one, is the healthy attitude of human nature. How is a boy the master of society; independent, irresponsible, looking out from his corner on such people and facts as pass by, he tries and sentences them on their merits, in the swift summary way of boys, as good, bad, interesting, silly, eloquent, troublesome. He cumbers himself never about consequences, about interests: he gives an independent, genuine verdict. You must court him: he does not court you. But the man is, as it were, clapped into jail by his consciousness. As soon as he has once acted or spoken with eclat, he is a committed person, watched by the sympathy or the hatred of hundreds whose affections must now enter into his account. There is no Lethe[5] for this. Ah, that he could pass again into his neutral, godlike independence! Who can thus lose all pledge, and having observed, observe again from

5. Oblivion-producing water from the river of the underworld in Greek mythology.

the same unaffected, unbiased, unbribable, unaffrighted innocence, must always be formidable, must always engage the poet's and the man's regards. Of such an immortal youth the force would be felt. He would utter opinions on all passing affairs, which being seen to be not private but necessary, would sink like darts into the ear of men, and put them in fear.

These are the voices which we hear in solitude, but they grow faint and inaudible as we enter into the world. Society everywhere is in conspiracy against the manhood of every one of its members. Society is a joint-stock company[6] in which the members agree for the better securing of his bread to each shareholder, to surrender the liberty and culture of the eater. The virtue in most request is conformity. Self-reliance is its aversion. It loves not realities and creators, but names and customs.

Whoso would be a man must be a nonconformist. He who would gather immortal palms must not be hindered by the name of goodness, but must explore if it be goodness. Nothing is at last sacred but the integrity of our own mind. Absolve you to yourself, and you shall have the suffrage of the world. I remember an answer which when quite young I was prompted to make to a valued adviser who was wont to importune me with the dear old doctrines of the church. On my saying, What have I to do with the sacredness of traditions, if I live wholly from within? my friend suggested—"But these impulses may be from below, not from above." I replied, 'They do not seem to me to be such; but if I am the devil's child, I will live then from the devil.' No law can be sacred to me but that of my nature. Good and bad are but names very readily transferable to that or this; the only right is what is after my constitution, the only wrong what is against it. A man is to carry himself in the presence of all opposition as if every thing were titular and ephemeral but he. I am ashamed to think how easily we capitulate to badges and names, to large societies and dead institutions. Every decent and well-spoken individual affects and sways me more than is right. I ought to go upright and vital, and speak the rude truth in all ways. If malice and vanity wear the coat of philanthropy, shall that pass? If an angry bigot assumes this bountiful cause of Abolition, and comes to me with his last news from Barbadoes,[7] why should I not say to him, 'Go love thy infant; love thy wood-chopper: be good-natured and modest: have that grace; and never varnish your hard, uncharitable ambition with this incredible tenderness for black folk a thousand miles off. Thy love afar is spite at home.' Rough and graceless would be such greeting, but truth is handsomer than the affectation of love. Your goodness must have some edge to it—else it is none. The doctrine of hatred must be preached as the counteraction of the doctrine of love when that pules and whines. I shun father and mother and wife and brother, when my genius calls me.[8] I would write on the lintels of the door-post, Whim.[9] I hope it is somewhat better than whim at last, but we cannot spend the day in explanation. Expect me not to show cause why I seek or why I exclude company. Then, again, do not tell me, as a good man did

6. Business for which the capital is held by its joint owners in transferable shares.
7. Island in the eastern Caribbean where slavery was officially abolished in 1834 and all slaves freed by 1838.
8. For shunning family to obey a divine command see Matthew 10.34–37.
9. See Exodus 12 for God's instructions to Moses on

marking with blood the "two side posts" and the "upper door post" (or lintel) of houses so that God would spare those within when he passed through to "smite all the firstborn in the land of Egypt, both man and beast." Emerson equates importunate distractions from other people with a death threat to his intellectual and spiritual life.

to-day, of my obligation to put all poor men in good situations. Are they *my* poor? I tell thee, thou foolish philanthropist, that I grudge the dollar, the dime, the cent I give to such men as do not belong to me and to whom I do not belong. There is a class of persons to whom by all spiritual affinity I am bought and sold; for them I will go to prison, if need be; but your miscellaneous popular charities; the education at college of fools; the building of meeting-houses to the vain end to which many now stand; alms to sots; and the thousandfold Relief Societies;—though I confess with shame I sometimes succumb and give the dollar, it is a wicked dollar which by-and-by I shall have the manhood to withhold.

Virtues are in the popular estimate rather the exception than the rule. There is the man *and* his virtues. Men do what is called a good action, as some piece of courage or charity, much as they would pay a fine in expiation of daily non-appearance on parade. Their works are done as an apology or extenuation of their living in the world,—as invalids and the insane pay a high board. Their virtues are penances. I do not wish to expiate, but to live. My life is not an apology, but a life. It is for itself and not for a spectacle. I much prefer that it should be of a lower strain, so it be genuine and equal, than that it should be glittering and unsteady. I wish it to be sound and sweet, and not to need diet and bleeding.[1] My life should be unique; it should be an alms, a battle, a conquest, a medicine. I ask primary evidence that you are a man, and refuse this appeal from the man to his actions. I know that for myself it makes no difference whether I do or forbear those actions which are reckoned excellent. I cannot consent to pay for a privilege where I have intrinsic right. Few and mean as my gifts may be, I actually am, and do not need for my own assurance or the assurance of my fellows any secondary testimony.

What I must do, is all that concerns me, not what the people think. This rule, equally arduous in actual and in intellectual life, may serve for the whole distinction between greatness and meanness. It is the harder, because you will always find those who think they know what is your duty better than you know it. It is easy in the world to live after the world's opinion; it is easy in solitude to live after our own; but the great man is he who in the midst of the crowd keeps with perfect sweetness the independence of solitude.

The objection to conforming to usages that have become dead to you, is, that it scatters your force. It loses your time and blurs the impression of your character. If you maintain a dead church, contribute to a dead Bible-Society, vote with a great party either for the Government or against it, spread your table like base housekeepers,—under all these screens, I have difficulty to detect the precise man you are. And, of course, so much force is withdrawn from your proper life. But do your thing, and I shall know you. Do your work, and you shall reinforce yourself. A man must consider what a blindman's-buff is this game of conformity. If I know your sect, I anticipate your argument. I hear a preacher announce for his text and topic the expediency of one of the institutions of his church. Do I not know beforehand that not possibly can he say a new and spontaneous word? Do I not know that with all this ostentation of examining the grounds of the institution, he will do no such thing? Do I not know that he is pledged to himself not to look but at one side; the permitted side, not as a man, but as a parish minister? He is a retained attorney, and

1. The old medical treatment of bloodletting.

these airs of the bench are the emptiest affectation. Well, most men have bound their eyes with one or another handkerchief, and attached themselves to some one of these communities of opinion. This conformity makes them not false in a few particulars, authors of a few lies, but false in all particulars. Their every truth is not quite true. Their two is not the real two, their four not the real four: so that every word they say chagrins us, and we know not where to begin to set them right. Meantime nature is not slow to equip us in the prison-uniform of the party to which we adhere. We come to wear one cut of face and figure, and acquire by degrees the gentlest asinine expression. There is a mortifying experience in particular which does not fail to wreak itself also in the general history; I mean, "the foolish face of praise,"[2] the forced smile which we put on in company where we do not feel at ease in answer to conversation which does not interest us. The muscles, not spontaneously moved, but moved by a low usurping wilfulness, grow tight about the outline of the face and make the most disagreeable sensation, a sensation of rebuke and warning which no brave young man will suffer twice.

For non-conformity the world whips you with its displeasure. And therefore a man must know how to estimate a sour face. The bystanders look askance on him in the public street or in the friend's parlor. If this aversation had its origin in contempt and resistance like his own, he might well go home with a sad countenance; but the sour faces of the multitude, like their sweet faces, have no deep cause,—disguise no god, but are put on and off as the wind blows, and a newspaper directs. Yet is the discontent of the multitude more formidable than that of the senate and the college. It is easy enough for a firm man who knows the world to brook the rage of the cultivated classes. Their rage is decorous and prudent, for they are timid as being very vulnerable themselves. But when to their feminine rage the indignation of the people is added, when the ignorant and the poor are aroused, when the unintelligent brute force that lies at the bottom of society is made to growl and mow, it needs the habit of magnanimity and religion to treat it godlike as a trifle of no concernment.

The other terror that scares us from self-trust is our consistency; a reverence for our past act or word, because the eyes of others have no other data for computing our orbit than our past acts, and we are loath to disappoint them.

But why should you keep your head over your shoulder? Why drag about this monstrous corpse of your memory, lest you contradict somewhat you have stated in this or that public place? Suppose you should contradict yourself; what then? It seems to be a rule of wisdom never to rely on your memory alone, scarcely even in acts of pure memory, but bring the past for judgment into the thousand-eyed present, and live ever in a new day. Trust your emotion. In your metaphysics you have denied personality to the Deity: yet when the devout motions of the soul come, yield to them heart and life, though they should clothe God with shape and color. Leave your theory as Joseph his coat in the hand of the harlot, and flee.[3]

A foolish consistency is the hobgoblin of little minds, adored by little statesmen and philosophers and divines. With consistency a great soul has simply nothing to do. He may as well concern himself with his shadow on the wall.

2. Alexander Pope, *Epistle to Dr. Arbuthnot*, line 212.
3. The story of Joseph and Potiphar's wife is in Genesis 39.

Out upon your guarded lips! Sew them up with packthread, do. Else, if you would be a man, speak what you think to-day in words as hard as cannon balls, and to-morrow speak what to-morrow thinks in hard words again, though it contradict every thing you said to-day. Ah, then, exclaim the aged ladies, you shall be sure to be misunderstood. Misunderstood! It is a right fool's word. Is it so bad then to be misunderstood? Pythagoras was misunderstood, and Socrates, and Jesus, and Luther, and Copernicus, and Galileo, and Newton, and every pure and wise spirit that ever took flesh. To be great is to be misunderstood.

I suppose no man can violate his nature. All the sallies of his will are rounded in by the law of his being as the inequalities of Andes and Himmaleh[4] are insignificant in the curve of the sphere. Nor does it matter how you gauge and try him. A character is like an acrostic or Alexandrian stanza;[5]—read it forward, backward, or across, it still spells the same thing. In this pleasing contrite wood-life which God allows me, let me record day by day my honest thought without prospect or retrospect, and, I cannot doubt, it will be found symmetrical, though I mean it not, and see it not. My book should smell of pines and resound with the hum of insects. The swallow over my window should interweave that thread or straw he carries in his bill into my web also. We pass for what we are. Character teaches above our wills. Men imagine that they communicate their virtue or vice only by overt actions and do not see that virtue or vice emit a breath every moment.

Fear never but you shall be consistent in whatever variety of actions, so they be each honest and natural in their hour. For of one will, the actions will be harmonious, however unlike they seem. These varieties are lost sight of when seen at a little distance, at a little height of thought. One tendency unites them all. The voyage of the best ship is a zigzag line of a hundred tacks. This is only microscopic criticism. See the line from a sufficient distance, and it straightens itself to the average tendency. Your genuine action will explain itself and will explain your other genuine actions. Your conformity explains nothing. Act singly, and what you have already done singly, will justify you now. Greatness always appeals to the future. If I can be great enough now to do right and scorn eyes, I must have done so much right before, as to defend me now. Be it how it will, do right now. Always scorn appearances, and you always may. The force of character is cumulative. All the foregone days of virtue work their health into this. What makes the majesty of the heroes of the senate and the field, which so fills the imagination? The consciousness of a train of great days and victories behind. There they all stand and shed an united light on the advancing actor. He is attended as by a visible escort of angels to every man's eye. That is it which throws thunder into Chatham's voice, and dignity into Washington's port, and America into Adams's[6] eye. Honor is venerable to us because it is no ephemeris. It is always ancient virtue. We worship it to-day, because it is not of to-day. We love it and pay it homage, because it is not a

---

4. Mountain ranges in South America and Asia, the latter (now spelled Himalayas) separates India from China.
5. A palindrome, reading the same backward as forward.
6. Adams may be Samuel Adams (1722–1803), leader of Revolutionary movement in Massachusetts or, more likely, his younger relative John Quincy Adams (1767–

1848), sixth president of the United States and, afterward, long-time member of the House of Representatives, known as "Old Man Eloquence." William Pitt, first earl of Chatham (1708–1778), English statesman and great orator. George Washington (1732–1799), first president of the United States. "Port": carriage or physical bearing.

trap for our love and homage, but is self-dependent, self-derived, and therefore
of an old immaculate pedigree, even if shown in a young person.

I hope in these days we have heard the last of conformity and consistency.
Let the words be gazetted and ridiculous henceforward.[7] Instead of the gong
for dinner, let us hear a whistle from the Spartan fife.[8] Let us bow and apologize never more. A great man is coming to eat at my house. I do not wish to
please him: I wish that he should wish to please me. I will stand here for
humanity, and though I would make it kind, I would made it true. Let us
affront and reprimand the smooth mediocrity and squalid contentment of the
times, and hurl in the face of custom, and trade, and office, the fact which is
the upshot of all history, that there is a great responsible Thinker and Actor
moving wherever moves a man; that a true man belongs to no other time or
place, but is the centre of things. Where he is, there is nature. He measures
you, and all men, and all events. You are constrained to accept his standard.
Ordinarily every body in society reminds us of somewhat else or of some other
person. Character, reality, reminds you of nothing else. It takes place of the
whole creation. The man must be so much that he must make all circumstances indifferent,—put all means into the shade. This all great men are and
do. Every true man is a cause, a country, and an age; requires infinite spaces
and numbers and time fully to accomplish his thought;—and posterity seem
to follow his steps as a procession. A man Cæsar is born, and for ages after, we
have a Roman Empire. Christ is born, and millions of minds so grow and
cleave to his genius, that he is confounded with virtue and the possible of man.
An institution is the lengthened shadow of one man; as, the Reformation, of
Luther; Quakerism, of Fox; Methodism, of Wesley; Abolition, of Clarkson.[9]
Scipio,[1] Milton called "the height of Rome;" and all history resolves itself very
easily into the biography of a few stout and earnest persons.

Let a man then know his worth, and keep things under his feet. Let him
not peep or steal, or skulk up and down with the air of a charity-boy, a bastard,
or an interloper, in the world which exists for him. But the man in the street
finding no worth in himself which corresponds to the force which built a tower
or sculptured a marble god, feels poor when he looks on these. To him a
palace, a statue, or a costly book have an alien and forbidding air, much like
a gay equipage, and seem to say like that, 'Who are you, sir?' Yet they all are
his, suitors for his notice, petitioners to his faculties that they will come out
and take possession. The picture waits for my verdict: it is not to command
me, but I am to settle its claims to praise. That popular fable of the sot who
was picked up dead drunk in the street, carried to the duke's house, washed
and dressed and laid in the duke's bed, and, on his waking, treated with all
obsequious ceremony like the duke, and assured that he had been insane,[2]—
owes its popularity to the fact, that it symbolizes so well the state of man, who
is in the world a sort of sot, but now and then wakes up, exercises his reason,
and finds himself a true prince.

Our reading is mendicant and sycophantic. In history, our imagination
makes fools of us, plays us false. Kingdom and lordship, power and estate are
a gaudier vocabulary than private John and Edward in a small house and

---

7. Labeled in public as not to be used henceforth.
8. Emerson is associating the gong with lax ease and
the Spartan fife with disciplined alertness.
9. These founders are Martin Luther (1483–1546),
George Fox (1624–1691), John Wesley (1703–1791),

and Thomas Clarkeson (1760–1846).
1. Scipio Africanus (237–183 B.C.), the conqueror of
Carthage.
2. The best-known version of the fable is in the "Induction" to Shakespeare's *The Taming of the Shrew*.

common day's work: but the things of life are the same to both: the sum total
of both is the same. Why all this deference to Alfred, and Scanderbeg, and
Gustavus?[3] Suppose they were virtuous: did they wear out virtue? As great a
stake depends on your private act to-day, as followed their public and
renowned steps. When private men shall act with vast views, the lustre will be
transferred from the actions of kings to those of gentlemen.

The world has indeed been instructed by its kings, who have so magnetized
the eyes of nations. It has been taught by this colossal symbol the mutual
reverence that is due from man to man. The joyful loyalty with which men
have every where suffered the king, the noble, or the great proprietor to walk
among them by a law of his own, make his own scale of men and things, and
reverse theirs, pay for benefits not with money but with honor, and represent
the Law in his person, was the hieroglyphic by which they obscurely signified
their consciousness of their own right and comeliness, the right of every man.

The magnetism which all original action exerts is explained when we
inquire the reason of self-trust. Who is the Trustee? What is the aboriginal
Self on which a universal reliance may be grounded? What is the nature and
power of that science-baffling star, without parallax,[4] without calculable elements, which shoots a ray of beauty even into trivial and impure actions, if
the least mark of independence appear? The inquiry leads us to that source, at
once the essence of genius, the essence of virtue, and the essence of life, which
we call Spontaneity or Instinct. We denote this primary wisdom as Intuition,
whilst all later teachings are tuitions. In that deep force, the last fact behind
which analysis cannot go, all things find their common origin. For the sense
of being which in calm hours rises, we know not how, in the soul, is not
diverse from things, from space, from light, from time, from man, but one
with them, and proceedeth obviously from the same source whence their life
and being also proceedeth. We first share the life by which things exist, and
afterwards see them as appearances in nature, and forget that we have shared
their cause. Here is the fountain of action and the fountain of thought. Here
are the lungs of that inspiration which giveth man wisdom, of that inspiration
of man which cannot be denied without impiety and atheism. We lie in the
lap of immense intelligence, which makes us organs of its activity and receivers
of its truth. When we discern justice, when we discern truth, we do nothing
of ourselves, but allow a passage to its beams. If we ask whence this comes, if
we seek to pry into the soul that causes,—all metaphysics, all philosophy is at
fault. Its presence or its absence is all we can affirm. Every man discerns
between the voluntary acts of his mind, and his involuntary perceptions. And
to his involuntary perceptions, he knows a perfect respect is due. He may err
in the expression of them, but he knows that these things are so, like day and
night, not to be disputed. All my wilful actions and acquisitions are but roving;—the most trivial reverie, the faintest native emotion are domestic and
divine. Thoughtless people contradict as readily the statement of perceptions as
of opinions, or rather much more readily; for, they do not distinguish between
perception and notion. They fancy that I choose to see this or that thing. But
perception is not whimsical, but fatal. If I see a trait, my children will see it
after me, and in course of time, all mankind,—although it may chance that

---

3. National heroes: Alfred (849–899), of England;
Scanderbeg (1404?–1468), of Albania; and Gustavis
(1594–1632), of Sweden.
4. An apparent change in the direction of an object

caused by a change in the position from which it is
observed. Apparently Emerson means without an ob-
servational position.

no one has seen it before me. For my perception of it is as much a fact as the sun.

The relations of the soul to the divine spirit are so pure that it is profane to seek to interpose helps. It must be that when God speaketh, he should communicate not one thing, but all things; should fill the world with his voice; should scatter forth light, nature, time, souls from the centre of the present thought; and new date and new create the whole. Whenever a mind is simple, and receives a divine wisdom, then old things pass away,—means, teachers, texts, temples fall; it lives now and absorbs past and future into the present hour. All things are made sacred by relation to it,—one thing as much as another. All things are dissolved to their centre by their cause, and in the universal miracle petty and particular miracles disappear. This is and must be. If, therefore, a man claims to know and speak of God, and carries you backward to the phraseology of some old mouldered nation in another country, in another world, believe him not. Is the acorn better than the oak which is its fulness and completion? Is the parent better than the child into whom he has cast his ripened being? Whence then this worship of the past? The centuries are conspirators against the sanity and majesty of the soul. Time and space are but physiological colors which the eye maketh, but the soul is light; where it is, is day; where it was, is night; and history is an impertinence and an injury, if it be anything more than a cheerful apologue or parable of my being and becoming.

Man is timid and apologetic. He is not longer upright. He dares not say 'I think,' 'I am,' but quotes some saint or sage. He is ashamed before the blade of grass or the blowing rose. These roses under my window make no reference to former roses or to better ones; they are for what they are; they exist with God to-day. There is no time to them. There is simply the rose; it is perfect in every moment of its existence. Before a leaf-bud has burst, its whole life acts; in the full-blown flower, there is no more; in the leafless root, there is no less. Its nature is satisfied, and it satisfies nature, in all moments alike. There is no time to it. But man postpones or remembers; he does not live in the present, but with reverted eye laments the past, or, heedless of the riches that surround him, stands on tiptoe to foresee the future. He cannot be happy and strong until he too lives with nature in the present, above time.

This should be plain enough. Yet see what strong intellects dare not yet hear God himself, unless he speak the phraseology of I know not what David, or Jeremiah, or Paul.[5] We shall not always set so great a price on a few texts, on a few lines. We are like children who repeat by rote the sentences of grandames and tutors, and, as they grow older, of the men of talents and character they chance to see,—painfully recollecting the exact words they spoke; afterwards, when they come into the point of view which those had who uttered these sayings, they understand them, and are willing to let the words go; for, at any time, they can use words as good, when occasion comes. So was it with us, so will it be, if we proceed. If we live truly, we shall see truly. It is as easy for the strong man to be strong, as it is for the weak to be weak. When we have new perception, we shall gladly disburthen the memory of its hoarded treasures as old rubbish. When a man lives with God, his voice shall be as sweet as the murmur of the brook and the rustle of the corn.

And now at last the highest truth on this subject remains unsaid; probably,

5. Biblical authors of the Book of Psalms, the Book of Jeremiah, and various New Testament Epistles, respectively.

cannot be said; for all that we say is the far off remembering of the intuition. That thought, by what I can now nearest approach to say it, is this. When good is near you, when you have life in yourself,—it is not by any known or appointed way; you shall not discern the foot-prints of any other; you shall not see the face of man; you shall not hear any name;—the way, the thought, the good shall be wholly strange and new. It shall exclude all other being. You take the way from man not to man. All persons that ever existed are its fugitive ministers. There shall be no fear in it. Fear and hope are alike beneath it. It asks nothing. There is somewhat low even in hope. We are then in vision. There is nothing that can be called gratitude nor properly joy. The soul is raised over passion. It seeth identity and eternal causation. It is a perceiving that Truth and Right are. Hence it becomes a Tranquillity out of the knowing that all things go well. Vast spaces of nature; the Atlantic Ocean, the South Sea; vast intervals of time, years, centuries, are of no account. This which I think and feel, underlay that former state of life and circumstances, as it does underlie my present, and will always all circumstance, and what is called life, and what is called death.

Life only avails, not the having lived. Power ceases in the instant of repose; it resides in the moment of transition from a past to a new state; in the shooting of the gulf; in the darting to an aim. This one fact the world hates, that the soul *becomes*; for, that forever degrades the past; turns all riches to poverty; all reputation to a shame; confounds the saint with the rogue; shoves Jesus and Judas equally aside. Why then do we prate of self-reliance? Inasmuch as the soul is present, there will be power not confident but agent. To talk of reliance, is a poor external way of speaking. Speak rather of that which relies, because it works and is. Who has more soul than I, masters me, though he should not raise his finger. Round him I must revolve by the gravitation of spirits; who has less, I rule with like facility. We fancy it rhetoric when we speak of eminent virtue. We do not yet see that virtue is Height, and that a man or a company of men plastic and permeable to principles, by the law of nature must overpower and ride all cities, nations, kings, rich men, poets, who are not.

This is the ultimate fact which we so quickly reach on this as on every topic, the resolution of all into the ever blessed ONE. Virtue is the governor, the creator, the reality. All things real are so by so much of virtue as they contain. Hardship, husbandry, hunting, whaling, war, eloquence, personal weight, are somewhat, and engage my respect as examples of the soul's presence and impure action. I see the same law working in the nature for conservation and growth. The poise of a planet, the bended tree recovering itself from the strong wind, the vital resources of every vegetable and animal, are also demonstrations of the self-sufficing, and therefore self-relying soul. All history from its highest to its trivial passages is the various record of this power.

Thus all concentrates; let us not rove; let us sit at home with the cause. Let us stun and astonish the intruding rabble of men and books and institutions by a simple declaration of the divine fact. Bid them take the shoes from off their feet,[6] for God is here within. Let our simplicity judge them, and our docility to our own law demonstrate the poverty of nature and fortune beside our native riches.

But now we are a mob. Man does not stand in awe of man, nor is the soul

6. Exodus 3.5.

admonished to stay at home, to put itself in communication with the internal ocean, but it goes abroad to beg a cup of water of the urns of men. We must go alone. Isolation must precede true society. I like the silent church before the service begins, better than any preaching. How far off, how cool, how chaste the persons look, begirt each one with a precinct or sanctuary. So let us always sit. Why should we assume the faults of our friend, or wife, or father, or child, because they sit around our hearth, or are said to have the same blood? All men have my blood, and I have all men's. Not for that will I adopt their petulance or folly, even to the extent of being ashamed of it. But your isolation must not be mechanical, but spiritual, that is, must be elevation. At times the whole world seems to be in conspiracy to importune you with emphatic trifles. Friend, client, child, sickness, fear, want, charity, all knock at once at thy closet door and say, 'Come out unto us.'—Do not spill thy soul; do not all descend; keep thy state; stay at home in thine own heaven; come not for a moment into their facts, into their hubbub of conflicting appearances, but let in the light of thy law on their confusion. The power men possess to annoy me, I give them by a weak curiosity. No man can come near me but through my act. "What we love that we have, but by desire we bereave ourselves of the love."

If we cannot at once rise to the sanctities of obedience and faith, let us at least resist our temptations, let us enter into the state of war, and wake Thor and Woden,[7] courage and constancy in our Saxon breasts. This is to be done in our smooth times by speaking the truth. Check this lying hospitality and lying affection. Live no longer to the expectation of these deceived and deceiving people with whom we converse. Say to them, O father, O mother, O wife, O brother, O friend, I have lived with you after appearances hitherto. Henceforward I am the truth's. Be it known unto you that henceforward I obey no law less than the external law. I will have no covenants but proximities. I shall endeavor to nourish my parents, to support my family, to be the chaste husband of one wife,—but these relations I must fill after a new and unprecedented way. I appeal from your customs. I must be myself. I cannot break myself any longer for you, or you. If you can love me for what I am, we shall be the happier. If you cannot, I will still seek to deserve that you should. I must be myself. I will not hide my tastes or aversions. I will so trust that what is deep is holy, that I will do strongly before the sun and moon whatever inly rejoices me, and the heart appoints. If you are noble, I will love you; if you are not, I will not hurt you and myself by hypocritical attentions. If you are true, but not in the same truth with me, cleave to your companions; I will seek my own. I do this not selfishly, but humbly and truly. It is alike your interest and mine and all men's, however long we have dwelt in lies, to live in truth. Does this sound harsh to-day? You will soon love what is dictated by your nature as well as mine, and if we follow the truth, it will bring us out safe at last.—But so you may give these friends pain. Yes, but I cannot sell my liberty and my power, to save their sensibility. Besides, all persons have their moments of reason when they look out into the region of absolute truth; then will they justify me and do the same thing.

The populace think that your rejection of popular standards is a rejection of

---

7. Norse gods, here taken as ancestral gods of the Anglo-Saxon as well, associated respectively with courage and endurance. Emerson took seriously the idea of racial traits.

all standard, and mere antinomianism;[8] and the bold sensualist will use the name of philosophy to gild his crimes. But the law of consciousness abides. There are two confessionals, in one or the other of which we must be shriven. You may fulfil your round of duties by clearing yourself in the *direct*, or, in the *reflex* way. Consider whether you have satisfied your relations to father, mother, cousin, neighbor, town, cat, and dog; whether any of these can upbraid you. But I may also neglect this reflex standard, and absolve me to myself. I have my own stern claims and perfect circle. It denies the name of duty to many offices that are called duties. But if I can discharge its debts, it enables me to dispense with the popular code. If any one imagines that this law is lax, let him keep its commandment one day.

And truly it demands something godlike in him who has cast off the common motives of humanity, and has ventured to trust himself for a task-master. High be his heart, faithful his will, clear his sight, that he may in good earnest be doctrine, society, law to himself, that a simple purpose may be to him as strong as iron necessity is to others.

If any man consider the present aspects of what is called by distinction *society*, he will see the need of these ethics. The sinew and heart of man seem to be drawn out, and we are become timorous desponding whimperers. We are afraid of truth, afraid of fortune, afraid of death, and afraid of each other. Our age yields no great and perfect persons. We want men and women who shall renovate life and our social state, but we see that most natures are insolvent; cannot satisfy their own wants, have an ambition out of all proportion to their practical force, and so do lean and beg day and night continually. Our housekeeping is mendicant, our arts, our occupations, our marriages, our religion we have not chosen, but society has chosen for us. We are parlor soldiers. The rugged battle of fate, where strength is born, we shun.

If our young men miscarry in their first enterprizes, they lose all heart. If the young merchant fails, men say he is *ruined*. If the finest genius studies at one of our colleges, and is not installed in an office within one year afterwards in the cities or suburbs of Boston or New York, it seems to his friends and to himself that he is right in being disheartened and in complaining the rest of his life. A sturdy lad from New Hampshire or Vermont, who in turn tries all the professions, who *teams it, farms it, peddles*, keeps a school, preaches, edits a newspaper, goes to Congress, buys a township, and so forth, in successive years, and always, like a cat, falls on his feet, is worth a hundred of these city dolls.[9] He walks abreast with his days, and feels no shame in not 'studying a profession,' for he does not postpone his life, but lives already. He has not one chance, but a hundred chances. Let a stoic arise who shall reveal the resources of man, and tell men they are not leaning willows, but can and must detach themselves; that with the exercise of self-trust, new powers shall appear; that a man is the word made flesh, born to shed healing to the nations, that he should be ashamed of our compassion, and that the moment he acts from himself, tossing the laws, the books, idolatries, and customs out of the window,—we pity him no more but thank and revere him,—and that teacher shall restore the life of man to splendor, and make his name dear to all History.

It is easy to see that a greater self-reliance,—a new respect for the divinity

8. Rejection of moral and religious laws.
9. Emerson's journal entry for May 27, 1839, shows

that this passage was originally modeled on the young Thoreau.

in man,—must work a revolution in all the offices and relations of men; in their religion; in their education; in their pursuits; their modes of living; their association; in their property; in their speculative views.

1. In what prayers do men allow themselves! That which they call a holy office, is not so much as brave and manly. Prayer looks abroad and asks for some foreign addition to come through some foreign virtue, and loses itself in endless mazes of natural and supernatural, and mediatorial and miraculous. Prayer that craves a particular commodity—any thing less than all good, is vicious. Prayer is the contemplation of the facts of life from the highest point of view. It is the soliloquy of a beholding and jubilant soul. It is the spirit of God pronouncing his works good. But prayer as a means to effect a private end, is theft and meanness. It supposes dualism and not unity in nature and consciousness. As soon as the man is at one with God, he will not beg. He will then see prayer in all action. The prayer of the farmer kneeling in his field to weed it, the prayer of the rower kneeling with the stroke of his oar, are true prayers heard throughout nature, though for cheap ends. Caratach, in Fletcher's Bonduca, when admonished to inquire the mind of the god Audate, replies,

> "His hidden meaning lies in our endeavors,
> Our valors are our best gods."[1]

Another sort of false prayers are our regrets. Discontent is the want of self-reliance; it is infirmity of will. Regret calamities, if you can thereby help the sufferer; if not, attend your own work, and already the evil begins to be repaired. Our sympathy is just as base. We come to them who weep foolishly, and sit down and cry for company, instead of imparting to them truth and health in rough electric shocks, putting them once more in communication with the soul. The secret of fortune is joy in our hands. Welcome evermore to gods and men is the self-helping man. For him all doors are flung wide. Him all tongues greet, all honors crown, all eyes follow with desire. Our love goes out to him and embraces him, because he did not need it. We solicitously and apologetically caress and celebrate him, because he held on his way and scorned our disapprobation. The gods love him because men hated him. "To the persevering mortal," said Zoroaster,[2] "the blessed Immortals are swift."

As men's prayers are a disease of the will, so are their creeds a disease of the intellect. They say with those foolish Israelites, 'Let not God speak to us, lest we die. Speak thou, speak any man with us, and we will obey.'[3] Everywhere I am bereaved of meeting God in my brother, because he has shut his own temple doors, and recites fables merely of his brother's, or his brother's brother's God. Every new mind is a new classification. If it prove a mind of uncommon activity and power, a Locke, a Lavoisier, a Hutton, a Bentham, a Spurzheim,[4] it imposes its classification on other men, and lo! a new system. In proportion always to the depth of the thought, and so to the number of the

---

1. Lines 1294–95, slightly misquoted.
2. Religious prophet of ancient Persia.
3. See the fearful words of the Hebrews after God has given Moses the Ten Commandments, Exodus 20.19: "And they said unto Moses, Speak thou with us, and we will hear: but let not God speak with us, lest we die."
4. These innovators are John Locke (1632–1704), En-glish philosopher; Antoine Lavoisier (1726–1797), French chemist; James Hutton (1726–1797), Scottish geologist; Jeremy Bentham (1748–1832), English philosopher; and Johann Kaspar Spurzheim (1776–1832), German physician whose work led to the pseudoscience of phrenology, reading character by the bumps on the skull.

objects it touches and brings within reach of the pupil, is his complacency. But chiefly is this apparent in creeds and churches, which are also classifications of some powerful mind acting on the great elemental thought of Duty, and man's relation to the Highest. Such is Calvinism, Quakerism, Swedenborgianism.[5] The pupil takes the same delight in subordinating every thing to the new terminology that a girl does who has just learned botany, in seeing a new earth and new seasons thereby. It will happen for a time, that the pupil will feel a real debt to the teacher,—will find his intellectual power has grown by the study of his writings. This will continue until he has exhausted his master's mind. But in all unbalanced minds, the classification is idolized, passes for the end, and not for a speedily exhaustible means, so that the walls of the system blend to their eye in the remote horizon with the walls of the universe; the luminaries of heaven seem to them hung on the arch their master built. They cannot imagine how you aliens have any right to see,—how you can see; 'It must be somehow that you stole the light from us.' They do not yet perceive, that, light unsystematic, indomitable, will break into any cabin, even into theirs. Let them chirp awhile and call it their own. If they are honest and do well, presently their neat new pinfold will be too strait and low, will crack, will lean, will rot and vanish, and the immortal light, all young and joyful, million-orbed, million-colored, will beam over the universe as on the first morning.

2. It is for want of self-culture that the idol of Travelling, the idol of Italy, of England, of Egypt, remains for all educated Americans. They who made England, Italy, or Greece venerable in the imagination, did so not by rambling round creation as a moth round a lamp, but by sticking fast where they were, like an axis of the earth. In manly hours, we feel that duty is our place, and that the merrymen of circumstance should follow as they may. The soul is no traveller: the wise man stays at home with the soul, and when his necessities, his duties, on any occasion call him from his house, or into foreign lands, he is at home still, and is not gadding abroad from himself, and shall make men sensible by the expression of his countenance, that he goes the missionary of wisdom and virtue, and visits cities and men like a sovereign, and not like an interloper or a valet.

I have no churlish objection to the circumnavigation of the globe, for the purposes of art, of study, and benevolence, so that the man is first domesticated, or does not go abroad with the hope of finding somewhat greater than he knows. He who travels to be amused, or to get somewhat which he does not carry, travels away from himself, and grows old even in youth among old things. In Thebes, in Palmyra, his will and mind have become old and dilapidated as they. He carries ruins to ruins.

Travelling is a fool's paradise. We owe to our first journeys the discovery that place is nothing. At home I dream that at Naples, at Rome, I can be intoxicated with beauty, and lose my sadness. I pack my trunk, embrace my friends, embark on the sea, and at last wake up in Naples, and there beside me is the stern Fact, the sad self, unrelenting, identical, that I fled from. I seek the Vatican, and the palaces. I affect to be intoxicated with sights and suggestions, but I am not intoxicated. My giant goes with me wherever I go.

3. But the rage of travelling is itself only a symptom of a deeper unsoundness

---

5. Three widely varying religious movements founded by or based on the teachings of, respectively, John Calvin (1509–1564), French theologian; George Fox (1624–1691), English clergyman; and Emanuel Swedenborg (1688–1772), Swedish scientist and theologian.

affecting the whole intellectual action. The intellect is vagabond, and the universal system of education fosters restlessness. Our minds travel when our bodies are forced to stay at home. We imitate; and what is imitation but the travelling of the mind? Our houses are built with foreign taste; our shelves are garnished with foreign ornaments; our opinions, our tastes, our whole minds lean, and follow the Past and the Distant, as the eyes of a maid follow her mistress. The soul created the arts wherever they have flourished. It was in his own mind that the artist sought his model. It was an application of his own thought to the thing to be done and the conditions to be observed. And why need we copy the Doric or the Gothic model?[6] Beauty, convenience, grandeur of thought, and quaint expression are as near to us as to any, and if the American artist will study with hope and love the precise thing to be done by him, considering the climate, the soil, the length of the day, the wants of the people, the habit and form of the government, he will create a house in which all these will find themselves fitted, and taste and sentiment will be satisfied also.

Insist on yourself; never imitate. Your own gift you can present every moment with the cumulative force of a whole life's cultivation; but of the adopted talent of another, you have only an extemporaneous, half possession. That which each can do best, none but his Maker can teach him. No man yet knows what it is, nor can, till that person has exhibited it. Where is the master who could have taught Shakspeare? Where is the master who could have instructed Franklin, or Washington, or Bacon, or Newton. Every great man is an unique. The Scipionism[7] of Scipio is precisely that part he could not borrow. If any body will tell me whom the great man imitates in the original crisis when he performs a great act, I will tell him who else than himself can teach him. Shakspeare will never be made by the study of Shakspeare. Do that which is assigned thee, and thou canst not hope too much or dare too much. There is at this moment, there is for me an utterance bare and grand as that of the colossal chisel of Phidias,[8] or trowel of the Egyptians, or the pen of Moses, or Dante, but different from all these. Now possibly will the soul all rich, all eloquent, with thousand-cloven tongue, deign to repeat itself; but if I can hear what these patriarchs say, surely I can reply to them in the same pitch of voice: for the ear and the tongue are two organs of one nature. Dwell up there in the simple and noble regions of thy life, obey thy heart, and thou shalt reproduce the Foreworld again.

4. As our Religion, our Education, our Art look abroad, so does our spirit of society. All men plume themselves on the improvement of society, and no man improves.

Society never advances. It recedes as fast on one side as it gains on the other. Its progress is only apparent, like the workers of a treadmill. It undergoes continual changes: it is barbarous, it is civilized, it is christianized, it is rich, it is scientific; but this change is not amelioration. For every thing that is given, something is taken. Society acquires new arts and loses old instincts. What a contrast between the well-clad, reading, writing, thinking American, with a watch, a pencil, and a bill of exchange in his pocket, and the naked New Zealander, whose property is a club, a spear, a mat, and an undivided

---

6. I.e., Greek or medieval architecture.          8. Greek sculptor of 5th century B.C.
7. I.e., the essence of the man.

twentieth of a shed to sleep under. But compare the health of the two men, and you shall see that his aboriginal strength the white man has lost. If the traveller tell us truly, strike the savage with a broad axe, and in a day or two the flesh shall unite and heal as if you struck the blow into soft pitch, and the same blow shall send the white to his grave.

The civilized man has built a coach, but has lost the use of his feet. He is supported on crutches, but loses so much support of muscle. He has got a fine Geneva watch, but he has lost the skill to tell the hour by the sun. A Greenwich nautical almanac he has, and so being sure of the information when he wants it, the man in the street does not know a star in the sky. The solstice he does not observe; the equinox he knows as little; and the whole bright calendar of the year is without a dial in his mind. His notebooks impair his memory; his libraries overload his wit; the insurance office increases the number of accidents; and it may be a question whether machinery does not encumber; whether we have not lost by refinement some energy, by a christianity entrenched in establishments and forms, some vigor of wild virtue. For every stoic was a stoic;[9] but in Christendom where is the Christian?

There is no more deviation in the moral standard than in the standard of height or bulk. No greater men are now than ever were. A singular equality may be observed between the great men of the first and of the last ages; nor can all the science, art, religion and philosophy of the nineteenth century avail to educate greater men than Plutarch's heroes,[1] three or four and twenty centuries ago. Not in time is the race progressive. Phocion, Socrates, Anaxagoras, Diogenes,[2] are great men, but they leave no class. He who is really of their class will not be called by their name, but be wholly his own man, and, in his turn the founder of a sect. The arts and inventions of each period are only its costume, and do not invigorate men. The harm of the improved machinery may compensate its good. Hudson and Behring[3] accomplished so much in their fishing-boats, as to astonish Parry and Franklin,[4] whose equipment exhausted the resources of science and art. Galileo, with an opera-glass, discovered a more splendid series of facts than any one since. Columbus found the New world in an undecked boat. It is curious to see the periodical disuse and perishing of means and machinery which were introduced with loud laudation, a few years or centuries before. The great genius returns to essential man. We reckoned the improvements of the art of war among the triumphs of science, and yet Napoleon conquered Europe by the Bivouac, which consisted of falling back on naked valor, and disencumbering it of all aids. The Emperor held it impossible to make a perfect army, says Las Cases,[5] "without abolishing our arms, magazines, commissaries, and carriages, until in imitation of the Roman custom, the soldier should receive his supply of corn, grind it in his hand-mill, and bake his bread himself."

Society is a wave. The wave moves onward, but the water of which it is

---

9. Emerson refers particularly to the Stoics, members of the Greek school of philosophy founded by Zeno about 308 B.C. It taught the ideal of a calm, passionless existence in which any occurrence is accepted as inevitable.

1. The lives of famous Greeks and Romans written by Plutarch (46?–120?), Greek biographer.

2. Four Greek philosophers: Phocion (402?–317 B.C.), Socrates (470?–399 B.C.), Anaxagoras (500?–428 B.C.), and Diogenes (412?–323 B.C.).

3. Vitus Jonassen Bering (1680–1741), Danish navigator who explored the northern Pacific Ocean. Henry Hudson (d. 1611) English navigator (sometimes in service of the Dutch).

4. Sir William Edward Perry (1790–1855) and Sir John Franklin (1786–1847), English explorers of the Arctic.

5. Comte Emmanuel de Las Cases (1766–1842), author of a book recording his conversations with the exiled Napoleon at St. Helena.

composed, does not. The same particle does not rise from the valley to the ridge. Its unity is only phenomenal. The persons who make up a nation to-day, next year die, and their experience with them.

And so the reliance on Property, including the reliance on governments which protect it, is the want of self-reliance. Men have looked away from themselves and at things so long, that they have come to esteem what they call the soul's progress, namely, the religious, learned, and civil institutions, as guards of property, and they deprecate assaults on these, because they feel them to be assaults on property. They measure their esteem of each other, by what each has, and not by what each is. But a cultivated man becomes ashamed of his property, ashamed of what he has, out of new respect for his being. Especially, he hates what he has, if he see that it is accidental,—came to him by inheritance, or gift, or crime; then he feels that it is not having; it does not belong to him, has no root in him, and merely lies there, because no revolution or no robber takes it away. But that which a man is, does always by necessity acquire, and what the man acquires is permanent and living property, which does not wait the beck of rulers, or mobs, or revolutions, or fire, or storm, or bankruptcies, but perpetually renews itself wherever the man is put. "Thy lot or portion of life," said the Caliph Ali,[6] "is seeking after thee; therefore be at rest from seeking after it." Our dependence on these foreign goods leads us to our slavish respect for numbers. The political parties meet in numerous conventions; the greater the concourse, and with each new uproar of announcement, The delegation from Essex![7] The Democrats from New Hampshire! The Whigs of Maine! the young patriot feels himself stronger than before by a new thousand of eyes and arms. In like manner the reformers summon conventions, and vote and resolve in multitude. But not so, O friends! will the God deign to enter and inhabit you, but by a method precisely the reverse. It is only as a man puts off from himself all external support, and stands alone, that I see him to be strong and to prevail. He is weaker by every recruit to his banner. Is not a man better than a town? Ask nothing of men, and in the endless mutation, thou only firm column must presently appear the upholder of all that surrounds thee. He who knows that power is in the soul, that he is weak only because he has looked for good out of him and elsewhere, and so perceiving, throws himself unhesitatingly on his thought, instantly rights himself, stands in the erect position, commands his limbs, works miracles; just as a man who stands on his feet is stronger than a man who stands on his head.

So use all that is called Fortune. Most men gamble with her, and gain all, and lose all, as her wheel rolls. But do thou leave as unlawful these winnings, and deal with Cause and Effect, the chancellors of God. In the Will work and acquire, and thou hast chained the wheel of Chance, and shalt always drag her after thee. A political victory, a rise of rents, the recovery of your sick, or the return of your absent friend, or some other quite external event, raises your spirits, and you think good days are preparing for you. Do not believe it. It can never be so. Nothing can bring you peace but yourself. Nothing can bring you peace but the triumph of principles.

1841

6. Fourth Moslem caliph of Mecca (602?–661).        7. County in Massachusetts.

# The Poet[1]

*A moody child and wildly wise*
*Pursued the game with joyful eyes,*
*Which chose, like meteors, their way,*
*And rived the dark with private ray:*
*They overleapt the horizon's edge,*
*Searched with Apollo's privilege;*
*Through man, and woman, and sea, and star,*
*Saw the dance of nature forward far;*
*Through worlds, and races, and terms, and times,*
*Saw musical order, and pairing rhymes.*

*Olympian bards who sung*
*Divine ideas below,*
*Which always find us young,*
*And always keep us so.*

Those who are esteemed umpires of taste, are often persons who have acquired some knowledge of admired pictures or sculptures, and have an inclination for whatever is elegant; but if you inquire whether they are beautiful souls, and whether their own acts are like fair pictures, you learn that they are selfish and sensual. Their cultivation is local, as if you should rub a log of dry wood in one spot to produce fire, all the rest remaining cold. Their knowledge of the fine arts is some study of rules and particulars, or some limited judgment of color or form, which is exercised for amusement or for show. It is a proof of the shallowness of the doctrine of beauty, as it lies in the minds of our amateurs, that men seem to have lost the perception of the instant dependence of form upon soul. There is no doctrine of forms in our philosophy. We were put into our bodies, as fire is put into a pan, to be carried about; but there is no accurate adjustment between the spirit and the organ, much less is the latter the germination of the former. So in regard to other forms, the intellectual men do not believe in any essential dependence of the material world on thought and volition. Theologians think it a pretty air-castle to talk of the spiritual meaning of a ship or a cloud, of a city or a contract, but they prefer to come again to the solid ground of historical evidence; and even the poets are contented with a civil and conformed manner of living, and to write poems from the fancy, at a safe distance from their own experience. But the highest minds of the world have never ceased to explore the double meaning, or, shall I say, the quadruple, or the centuple, or much more manifold meaning, of every sensuous fact: Orpheus, Empedocles, Heraclitus, Plato, Plutarch, Dante, Swedenborg,[2] and the masters of sculpture, picture, and poetry. For we are not pans and barrows, nor even porters of the fire and torchbearers, but children of the fire, made of it, and only the same divinity transmuted, and at two or three removes, when we know least about it. And this hidden truth, that the foundations whence all this river of Time, and its creatures, floweth, are intrinsically ideal and beautiful, draws us to the consideration of the nature

1. First published in *Essays, Second Series* (1844), the source of the present text, *The Poet* contains the fullest elaboration of Emerson's aesthetic ideas and his most incisive comments on contemporary poetry and criticism. The first prefatory poem is from one of Emerson's own uncompleted poems, and the second is from his *Ode to Beauty*.

2. Emanuel Swedenborg (1688–1772), Swedish scientist and mystic. Orpheus, a legendary Greek poet. Empedocles (5th century B.C.), Heraclitus (6th century B.C.), and Plato (4th century B.C.) were Greek philosophers. Plutarch (1st century), Greek biographer. Dante (1265–1321), Italian poet.

and functions of the Poet, or the man of Beauty, to the means and materials he uses, and to the general aspect of the art in the present time. The breadth of the problem is great, for the poet is representative. He stands among partial men for the complete man, and apprises us not of his wealth, but of the commonwealth. The young man reveres men of genius, because, to speak truly, they are more himself than he is. They receive of the soul as he also receives, but they more. Nature enhances her beauty, to the eye of loving men, from their belief that the poet is beholding her shows at the same time. He is isolated among his contemporaries, by truth and by his art, but with this consolation in his pursuits, that they will draw all men sooner or later. For all men live by truth, and stand in need of expression. In love, in art, in avarice, in politics, in labor, in games, we study to utter our painful secret. The man is only half himself, the other half is his expression.

Notwithstanding this necessity to be published, adequate expression is rare. I know not how it is that we need an interpreter; but the great majority of men seem to be minors, who have not yet come into possession of their own, or mutes, who cannot report the conversation they have had with nature. There is no man who does not anticipate a supersensual utility in the sun, and stars, earth, and water. These stand and wait to render him a peculiar service. But there is some obstruction, or some excess of phlegm in our constitution, which does not suffer them to yield the due effect. Too feeble fall the impressions of nature on us to make us artists. Every touch should thrill. Every man should be so much an artist, that he could report in conversation what had befallen him. Yet, in our experience, the rays or appulses have sufficient force to arrive at the senses, but not enough to reach the quick, and compel the reproduction of themselves in speech. The poet is the person in whom these powers are in balance, the man without impediment, who sees and handles that which others dream of, traverses the whole scale of experience, and its representative of man, in virtue of being the largest power to receive and to impart.

For the Universe has three children, born at one time, which reappear, under different names, in every system of thought, whether they be called cause, operation, and effect; or, more poetically, Jove, Pluto, Neptune; or, theologically, the Father, the Spirit, and the Son; but which we will call here, the Knower, the Doer, and the Sayer. These stand respectively for the love of truth, for the love of good, and for the love of beauty. These three are equal. Each is that which he is essentially, so that he cannot be surmounted or analyzed, and each of these three has the power of the others latent in him, and his own patent.

The poet is the sayer, the namer, and represents beauty. He is a sovereign, and stands on the centre. For the world is not painted or adorned, but is from the beginning beautiful; and God has not made some beautiful things, but Beauty is the creator of the universe. Therefore the poet is not any permissive potentate, but is emperor in his own right. Criticism is infested with a cant of materialism, which assumes that manual skill and activity is the first merit of all men, and disparages such as say and do not, overlooking the fact that some men, namely, poets, are natural sayers, sent into the world to the end of expression, and confounds them with those whose province is action, but who quit it to imitate the sayers. But Homer's words are as costly and admirable to Homer, as Agamemnon's victories are to Agamemnon.[3] The poet does not

---

3. Emerson is comparing the author (Homer) with his character (Agamemnon, in *The Iliad*).

wait for the hero or the sage, but, as they act and think primarily, so he writes primarily what will and must be spoken, reckoning the others, though primaries also, yet, in respect to him, secondaries and servants; as sitters or models in the studio of a painter, or as assistants who bring building materials to an architect.

For poetry was all written before time was, and whenever we are so finely organized that we can penetrate into that region where the air is music, we hear those primal warblings, and attempt to write them down, but we lose ever and anon a word, or a verse, and substitute something of our own, and thus miswrite the poem. The men of more delicate ear write down these cadences more faithfully, and these transcripts, though imperfect, become the songs of the nations. For nature is as truly beautiful as it is good, or as it is reasonable, and must as much appear, as it must be done, or be known. Words and deeds are quite indifferent modes of the divine energy. Words are also actions, and actions are a kind of words.

The sign and credentials of the poet are, that he announces that which no man foretold. He is the true and only doctor;[4] he knows and tells; he is the only teller of news, for he was present and privy to the appearance which he describes. He is a beholder of ideas, and an utterer of the necessary and causal. For we do not speak now of men of poetical talents, or of industry and skill in metre, but of the true poet. I took part in a conversation the other day, concerning a recent writer of lyrics, a man of subtle mind, whose head appeared to be a music-box of delicate tunes and rhythms, and whose skill, and command of language, we could not sufficiently praise. But when the question arose, whether he was not only a lyrist, but a poet, we were obliged to confess that he is plainly a contemporary, not an eternal man. He does not stand out of our low limitations, like a Chimborazo under the line,[5] running up from the torrid base through all the climates of the globe, with belts of the herbage of every latitude on its high and mottled sides; but this genius is the landscape-garden of a modern house, adorned with fountains and statues, with well-bred men and women standing and sitting in the walks and terraces. We hear, through all the varied music, the ground-tone of conventional life. Our poets are men of talents who sing, and not the children of music. The argument is secondary, the finish of the versus is primary.

For it is not metres, but a metre-making argument, that makes a poem,—a thought so passionate and alive, that, like the spirit of a plant or an animal, it has an architecture of its own, and adorns nature with a new thing. The thought and the form are equal in the order of time, but in the order of genesis the thought is prior to the form. The poet has a new thought: he has a whole new experience to unfold; he will tell us how it was with him, and all men will be the richer in his fortune. For, the experience of each new age requires a new confession, and the world seems always waiting for its poet. I remember, when I was young, how much I was moved one morning by tidings that genius had appeared in a youth who sat near me at table. He had left his work, and gone rambling none knew whither, and had written hundreds of lines, but could not tell whether that which was in him was therein told: he could tell nothing but that all was changed,—man, beast, heaven, earth, and sea. How gladly we listened! how credulous! Society seemed to be compromised. We sat in the aurora of a sunrise which was to put out all the stars. Boston seemed to

---

4. Teacher.     5. Equator. "Chimborazo": a mountain in Ecuador.

be at twice the distance it had the night before, or was much farther than that.
Rome,—what was Rome! Plutarch and Shakspeare were in the yellow leaf,
and Homor no more should be heard of. It is much to know that poetry has
been written this very day, under this very roof, by your side. What! that
wonderful spirit has not expired! these stony moments are still sparkling and
animated! I had fancied that the oracles were all silent, and nature had spent
her fires, and behold! all night, from every pore, these fine auroras have been
streaming. Every one has some interest in the advent of the poet, and no one
knows how much it may concern him. We know that the secret of the world
is profound, but who or what shall be our interpreter, we know not. A mountain ramble, a new style of face, a new person, may put the key into our hands.
Of course, the value of genius to us is in the veracity of its report. Talent may
frolic and juggle; genius realizes and adds. Mankind, in good earnest, have
availed so far in understanding themselves and their work, that the foremost
watchman on the peak announces his news. It is the truest word ever spoken,
and the phrase will be the fittest, most musical, and the unerring voice of the
world for that time.

All that we call sacred history attests that the birth of a poet is the principal
event in chronology. Man, never so often deceived, still watches for the arrival
of a brother who can hold him steady to a truth, until he has made it his own.
With what joy I begin to read a poem, which I confide in as an inspiration!
And now my chains are to be broken; I shall mount above these clouds and
opaque airs in which I live,—opaque, though they seem transparent,—and
from the heaven of truth I shall see and comprehend my relations. That will
reconcile me to life, and renovate nature, to see trifles animated by a tendency,
and to know what I am doing. Life will no more be a noise; now I shall see
men and women, and know the signs by which they may be discerned from
fools and satans. This day shall be better than my birth-day: then I became an
animal: now I am invited into the science of the real. Such is the hope, but
the fruition is postponed. Oftener it falls, that this winged man, who will carry
me into the heaven, whirls me into the clouds, then leaps and frisks about
with me from cloud to cloud, still affirming that he is bound heavenward; and
I, being myself a novice, am slow in perceiving that he does not know the way
into the heavens, and is merely bent that I should admire his skill to rise, like
a fowl or a flying fish, a little way from the ground or the water; but the all-
piercing, all-feeding, and ocular[6] air of heaven, that man shall never inhabit.
I tumble down again soon into my old nooks, and lead the life of exaggerations
as before, and have lost my faith in the possibility of any guide who can lead
me thither where I would be.

But leaving these victims of vanity, let us, with new hope, observe how
nature, by worthier impulses, has ensured the poet's fidelity to his office of
announcement and affirming, namely, by the beauty of things, which
becomes a new, and higher beauty, when expressed. Nature offers all her
creatures to him as a picture-language. Being used as a type, a second wonderful value appears in the object, far better than its old value, as the carpenter's
stretched cord, if you hold your ear close enough, is musical in the breeze.
"Things more excellent than every image," says Jamblichus,[7] "are expressed

6. Visible.
7. Neoplatonic philosopher of the 4th century A.D.
(Neoplatonism is a mystical religious system, combin-

ing features of Platonic and other Greek philosophies
with features of Judaism and Christianity.)

through images." Things admit of being used as symbols, because nature is a symbol, in the whole, and in every part. Every line we can draw in the sand, has expression; and there is no body without its spirit or genius. All form is an effect of character; all condition, of the quality of the life; all harmony, of health; (and, for this reason, a perception of beauty should be sympathetic, or proper only to the good.) The beautiful rests on the foundations of the necessary. The soul makes the body, as the wise Spenser teaches:—

> "So every spirit, as it is most pure,
> And hath in it the more of heavenly light,
> So it the fairer body doth procure
> To habit in, and it more fairly dight,
> With cheerful grace and amiable sight.
> For, of the soul, the body form doth take,
> For soul is form, and doth the body make."[8]

Here we find ourselves, suddenly, not in a critical speculation, but in a holy place, and should go very warily and reverently. We stand before the secret of the world, there where Being passes into Appearance, and Unity into Variety.

The Universe is the externisation of the soul. Wherever the life is, that bursts into appearance around it. Our science is sensual, and therefore superficial. The earth, and the heavenly bodies, physics, and chemistry, we sensually treat, as if they were self-existent; but these are the retinue of that Being we have. "The mighty heaven," said Proclus,[9] "exhibits, in its transfigurations, clear images of the splendor of intellectual perceptions; being moved in conjunction with the unapparent periods of intellectual natures." Therefore, science always goes abreast with the just elevation of the man, keeping step with religion and metaphysics; or, the state of science is an index of our self-knowledge. Since everything in nature answers to a moral power, if any phenomenon remains brute and dark, it is that the corresponding faculty in the observer is not yet active.

No wonder, then, if these waters be so deep, that we hover over them with a religious regard. The beauty of the fable proves the importance of the sense; to the poet, and to all others; or, if you please, every man is so far a poet as to be susceptible of these enchantments of nature: for all men have the thoughts whereof the universe is the celebration. I find that the fascination resides in the symbol. Who loves nature? Who does not? Is it only poets, and men of leisure and cultivation, who live with her? No; but also hunters, farmers, grooms, and butchers, though they express their affection in their choice of life, and not in their choice of words. The writer wonders what the coachman or the hunter values in riding, in horses, and dogs. It is not superficial qualities. When you talk with him, he holds these at as slight a rate as you. His worship is sympathetic; he has no definitions, but he is commanded in nature, by the living power which he feels to be there present. No imitation, or playing of these things, would content him; he loves the earnest of the northwind, of rain, of stone, and wood, and iron. A beauty not explicable, is dearer than a beauty which we can see to the end of. It is nature the symbol, nature certifying the supernatural, body overflowed by life, which he worships, with coarse, but sincere rites.

---

8. *An Hymn in Honour of Beauty* (1596), by the English poet Edmund Spenser (1552–1599).     9. Greek neoplatonic philosopher (411–485).

The inwardness, and mystery, of this attachment, drives men of every class to the use of emblems. The schools of poets, and philosophers, are not more intoxicated with their symbols, than the populace with theirs. In our political parties, compute the power of badges and emblems. See the great ball which they roll from Baltimore to Bunker hill! In the political processions, Lowell goes in a loom, and Lynn in a shoe, and Salem in a ship.[1] Witness the ciderbarrel, the log-cabin, the hickory-stick, the palmetto, and all the cognizances of party. See the power of national emblems. Some stars, lilies, leopards, a crescent, a lion, an eagle, or other figure, which came into credit God knows how, on an old rag of bunting, blowing in the wind, on a fort, at the ends of the earth, shall make the blood tingle under the rudest, or the most conventional exterior. The people fancy they hate poetry, and they are all poets and mystics!

Beyond this universality of the symbolic language, we are apprised of the divineness of this superior use of things, whereby the world is a temple, whose walls are covered with emblems, pictures, and commandments of the Deity, in this, that there is no fact in nature which does not carry the whole sense of nature; and the distinctions which we make in events, and in affairs, of low and high, honest and base, disappear when nature is used as a symbol. Thought makes every thing fit for use. The vocabulary of an omniscient man would embrace words and images excluded from polite conversation. What would be base, or even obscene, to the obscene, becomes illustrious, spoken in a new connexion of thought. The piety of the Hebrew prophets purges their grossness. The circumcision is an example of the power of poetry to raise the low and offensive. Small and mean things serve as well as great symbols. The meaner the type by which a law is expressed, the more pungent it is, and the more lasting in the memories of men: just as we choose the smallest box, or case, in which any needful utensil can be carried. Bare lists of words are found suggestive, to an imaginative and excited mind; as it is related of Lord Chatham,[2] that he was accustomed to read in Bailey's Dictionary, when he was preparing to speak in Parliament. The poorest experience is rich enough for all the purposes of expressing thought. Why covet a knowledge of new facts? Day and night, house and garden, a few books, a few actions, serve us as well as would all trades and all spectacles. We are far from having exhausted the significance of the few symbols we use. We can come to use them yet with a terrible simplicity. It does not need that a poem should be long. Every word was once a poem. Every new relation is a new word. Also, we use defects and deformaties to a sacred purpose, so expressing our sense that the evils of the world are such only to the evil eye. In the old mythology, mythologists observe, defects are ascribed to divine natures, as lameness to Vulcan, blindness to Cupid, and the like, to signify exuberances.

For, as it is dislocation and detachment from the life of God, that makes things ugly, the poet, who re-attaches things to nature and the Whole,—re-attaching even artificial things, and violations of nature, to nature, by a deeper insight,—disposes very easily of the most disagreeable facts. Readers of poetry see the factory-village, and the railway, and fancy that the poetry of the land-

1. Towns are symbolized by major products. "The great ball": a recent political stunt.
2. Nathan (or Nathaniel) Bailey (d. 1742) published *An Universal Etymological English Dictionary* (1721), which ran through many editions. "Lord Chatham": William Pitt (1708–1778), English statesman, famous for his oratory.

scape is broken up by these; for these works of art are not yet consecrated in their reading; but the poet sees them fall within the great Order not less than the bee-hive, or the spider's geometrical web. Nature adopts them very fast into her vital circles, and the gliding train of cars she loves like her own. Besides, in a centred mind, it signifies nothing how many mechanical inventions you exhibit. Though you add millions, and never so surprising, the fact of mechanics has not gained a grain's weight. The spiritual fact remains unalterable, by many or by few particulars; as no mountain is of any appreciable height to break the curve of the sphere. A shrewd country-boy goes to the city for the first time, and the complacent citizen is not satisfied with his little wonder. It is not that he does not see all the fine houses, and know that he never saw such before, but he disposes of them as easily as the poet finds place for the railway. The chief value of the new fact, is to enhance the great and constant fact of Life, which can dwarf any and every circumstance, and to which the belt of wampum, and the commerce of America, are alike.

The world being thus put under the mind for verb and noun, the poet is he who can articulate it. For, though life is great, and fascinates, and absorbs,— and though all men are intelligent of the symbols through which it is named,—yet they cannot originally use them. We are symbols, and inhabit symbols; workmen, work, and tools, words and things, birth and death, all are emblems; but we sympathize with the symbols, and, being infatuated with the economical uses of things, we do not know that they are thoughts. The poet, by an ulterior intellectual perception, gives them a power which makes their old use forgotten, and puts eyes, and a tongue, into every dumb and inanimate object. He perceives the independence of the thought on the symbol, the stability of the thought, the accidency and fugacity of the symbol. As the eyes of Lyncæus[3] were said to see through the earth, so the poet turns the world to glass, and shows us all things in their right series and procession. For, through that better perception, he stands one step nearer to things, and sees the flowing or metamorphosis; perceives that thought is multiform; that within the form of every creature is a force impelling it to ascend into a higher form; and, following with his eyes the life, uses the forms which express that life, and so his speech flows with the flowing of nature. All the facts of the animal economy, sex, nutriment, gestation, birth, growth, are symbols of the passage of the world into the soul of man, to suffer there a change, and reappear a new and higher fact. He uses forms according to the life, and not according to the form. This is true science. The poet alone knows astronomy, chemistry, vegetation, and animation, for he does not stop at these facts, but employs them as signs. He knows why the plain, or meadow of space, was strown with these flowers we call suns, and moons, and stars; why the great deep is adorned with animals, with men, and gods; for, in every word he speaks he rides on them as the horses of thought.

By virtue of this science the poet is the Namer, or Language-maker, naming things sometimes after their appearance, sometimes after their essence, and giving to every one its own name and not another's, thereby rejoicing the intellect, which delights in detachment or boundary. The poets made all the words, and therefore language is the archives of history, and, if we must say

3. In Greek mythology, the keenest-sighted crewman on the *Argo*, in which Jason sailed in search of the Golden Fleece.

it, a sort of tomb of the muses. For, though the origin of most of our words is forgotten, each word was at first a stroke of genius, and obtained currency, because for the moment it symbolized the world to the first speaker and to the hearer. The etymologist finds the deadest word to have been once a brilliant picture. Language is fossil poetry. As the limestone of the continent consists of infinite masses of the shells of animalcules, so language is made up of images, or tropes, which now, in their secondary use, have long ceased to remind us of their poetic origin. But the poet names the thing because he sees it, or comes one step nearer to it than any other. This expression, or naming, is not art, but a second nature, grown out of the first, as a leaf out of a tree. What we call nature, is a certain self-regulated motion, or change; and nature does all things by her own hands, and does not leave another to baptise her, but baptises herself; and this through the metamorphosis again. I remember that a certain poet[4] described it to me thus:

> Genius is the activity which repairs the decays of things, whether wholly or partly of a material and finite kind. Nature, through all her kingdoms, insures herself. Nobody cares for planting the poor fungus: so she shakes down from the gills of one agaric countless spores, any one of which, being preserved, transmits new billions of spores to-morrow or next day. The new agaric of this hour has a chance which the old one had not. This atom of seed is thrown into a new place, not subject to the accidents which destroyed its parent two rods off. She makes a man; and having brought him to ripe age, she will no longer run the risk of losing this wonder at a blow, but she detaches from him a new self, that the kind may be safe from accidents to which the individual is exposed. So when the soul of the poet has come to ripeness of thought, she detaches and sends away from it its poems or songs,—a fearless, sleepless, deathless progeny, which is not exposed to the accidents of the weary kingdom of time: a fearless, vivacious offspring, clad with wings (such was the virtue of the soul out of which they came), which carry them fast and far, and infix them irrecoverably into the hearts of men. These wings are the beauty of the poet's soul. The songs, thus flying immortal from their mortal parent, are pursued by clamorous flights of censures, which swarm in far greater numbers, and threaten to devour them; but these last are not winged. At the end of a very short leap they fall plump down, and rot, having received from the souls out of which they came no beautiful wings. But the melodies of the poet ascend, and leap, and pierce into the deeps of infinite time.

So far the bard taught me, using his freer speech. But nature has a higher end, in the production of new individuals, than security, namely, *ascension*, or, the passage of the soul into higher forms. I knew, in my younger days, the sculptor who made the statue of the youth which stands in the public garden. He was, as I remember, unable to tell directly, what made him happy, or unhappy, but by wonderful indirections he could tell. He rose one day, according to his habit, before the dawn, and saw the morning break, grand as the eternity out of which it came, and, for many days after, he strove to express this tranquillity, and, lo! his chisel had fashioned out of marble the form of a

---

4. A private joke: the poet is Emerson himself.

beautiful youth, Phosphorus,[5] whose aspect is such, that, it is said, all persons who look on it become silent. The poet also resigns himself to his mood, and that thought which agitated him is expressed, but *alter idem,*[6] in a manner totally new. The expression is organic, or, the new type which things themselves take when liberated. As, in the sun, objects paint their images on the retina of the eye, so they, sharing the aspiration of the whole universe, tend to paint a far more delicate copy of their essence in his mind. Like the metamorphosis of things into higher organic forms, is their change into melodies. Over everything stands its dæmon, or soul, and, as the form of the thing is reflected by the eye, so the soul of the thing is reflected by a melody. The sea, the mountain-ridge, Niagara, and every flower-bed, pre-exist, or super-exist, in pre-cantations, which sail like odors in the air, and when any man goes by with an ear sufficiently fine, he overhears them, and endeavors to write down the notes, without diluting or depraving them. And herein is the legitimation of criticism, in the mind's faith, that the poems are a corrupt version of some text in nature, with which they ought to be made to tally. A rhyme in one of our sonnets should not be less pleasing than the iterated nodes of a seashell, or the resembling difference of a group of flowers. The pairing of the birds is an idyl, not tedious as our idyls are; a tempest is a rough ode, without falsehood or rant: a summer, with its harvest sown, reaped, and stored, is an epic song, subordinating how many admirably executed parts. Why should not the symmetry and truth that modulate these, glide into our spirits, and we participate the invention of nature?

This insight, which expresses itself by what is called Imagination, is a very high sort of seeing, which does not come by study, but by the intellect being where and what it sees, by sharing the path, or circuit of things through forms, and so making them translucid to others. The path of things is silent. Will they suffer a speaker to go with them? A spy they will not suffer; a lover, a poet, is the transcendency of their own nature,—him they will suffer. The condition of true naming, on the poet's part, is his resigning himself to the divine *aura*[7] which breathes through forms, and accompanying that.

It is a secret which every intellectual man quickly learns, that, beyond the energy of his possessed and conscious intellect, he is capable of a new energy (as of an intellect doubled on itself), by abandonment to the nature of things; that, beside his privacy of power as an individual man, there is a great public power, on which he can draw, by unlocking, at all risks, his human doors, and suffering the ethereal tides to roll and circulate through him: then he is caught up into the life of the Universe, his speech is thunder, his thought is law, and his words are universally intelligible as the plants and animals. The poet knows that he speaks adequately, then, only when he speaks somewhat wildly, or, "with the flower of the mind;" not with the intellect, used as an organ, but with the intellect released from all service, and suffered to take its direction from its celestial life; or, as the ancients were wont to express themselves, not with intellect alone, but with the intellect inebriated by nectar. As the traveller who has lost his way, throws his reins on his horse's neck, and trusts to the instinct of the animal to find his road, so must we do with the divine animal who carries us through this world. For if in any manner we can

---

5. The Greek god associated with the morning star.   7. Distinctive quality.
6. The same, yet different (Latin).

stimulate this instinct, new passages are opened for us into nature, the mind flows into and through things hardest and highest, and the metamorphosis is possible.

This is the reason why bards love wine, mead, narcotics, coffee, tea, opium, the fumes of sandal-wood and tobacco, or whatever other species of animal exhilaration. All men avail themselves of such means as they can, to add this extraordinary power to their normal powers; and to this end they prize conversation, music, pictures, sculpture, dancing, theatres, travelling, war, mobs, fires, gaming, politics, or love, or science, or animal intoxication, which are several coarser or finer *quasi*-mechanical substitutes for the true nectar, which is the ravishment of the intellect by coming nearer to the fact. These are auxiliaries to the centrifugal tendency of a man, to his passage out into free space, and they help him to escape the custody of that body in which he is pent up, and of that jail-yard of individual relations in which he is enclosed. Hence a great number of such as were professionally expressors of Beauty, as painters, poets, musicians, and actors, have been more than others wont to lead a life of pleasure and indulgence; all but the few who received the true nectar; and, as it was a spurious mode of attaining freedom, as it was an emancipation not into the heavens, but into the freedom of baser places, they were punished for that advantage they won, by a dissipation and deterioration. But never can any advantage be taken of nature by a trick. The spirit of the world, the great calm presence of the creator, comes not forth to the sorceries of opium or of wine. The sublime vision comes to the pure and simple soul in a clean and chaste body. That is not an inspiration which we owe to narcotics, but some counterfeit excitement and fury. Milton says, that the lyric poet may drink wine and live generously, but the epic poet, he who shall sing of the gods, and their descent unto men, must drink water out of a wooden bowl.[8] For poetry is not 'Devil's wine,' but God's wine. It is with this as it is with toys. We fill the hands and nurseries of our children with all manner of dolls, drums, and horses, withdrawing their eyes from the plain face and sufficing objects of nature, the sun, and moon, the animals, the water, and stones, which should be their toys. So the poet's habit of living should be set on a key so low and plain, that the common influences should delight him. His cheerfulness should be the gift of the sunlight; the air should suffice for his inspiration, and he should be tipsy with water. That spirit which suffices quiet hearts, which seems to come forth to such from every dry knoll of sere grass, from every pine-stump, and half-imbedded stone, on which the dull March sun shines, comes forth to the poor and hungry, and such as are of simple taste. If thou fill thy brain with Boston and New York, with fashion and covetousness, and wilt stimulate thy jaded senses with wine and French coffee, thou shalt find no radiance of wisdom in the lonely waste of the pine-woods.

If the imagination intoxicates the poet, it is not inactive in other men. The metamorphosis excites in the beholder an emotion of joy. The use of symbols has a certain power of emancipation and exhilaration for all men. We seem to be touched by a wand, which makes us dance and run about happily, like children. We are like persons who come out of a cave or cellar into the open air. This is the effect on us of tropes,[9] fables, oracles, and all poetic forms.

---

8. In Milton's *Sixth Latin Elegy*.          9. Figures of speech.

Poets are thus liberating gods. Men have really got a new sense, and found within their world, another world, or nest of worlds; for, the metamorphosis once seen, we divine that it does not stop. I will not now consider how much this makes the charm of algebra and the mathematics, which also have their tropes, but it is felt in every definition; as, when Aristotle defines *space* to be an immovable vessel, in which things are contained;—or, when Plato defines a *line* to be a flowing point; or, *figure* to be a bound of solid; and many the like. What a joyful sense of freedom we have, when Vitruvius announces the old opinion of artists, that no architect can build any house well, who does not know something of anatomy. When Socrates, in Charmides, tells us that the soul is cured of its maladies by certain incantations, and that these incantations are beautiful reasons, from which temperance is generated in souls; when Plato calls the world an animal; and Timæus affirms that the plants also are animals; or affirms a man to be a heavenly tree, growing with his root, which is his head, upward; and, as George Chapman, following him, writes,—

> "So in our tree of man, whose nervie root
> Springs in his top;"

when Orpheus speaks of hoariness as "that white flower which marks extreme old age;" when Proclus calls the universe the statue of the intellect; when Chaucer, in his praise of 'Gentilesse,' compares good blood in mean condition to fire, which, though carried to the darkest house betwixt this and the mount of Caucasus, will yet hold its natural office, and burn as bright as if twenty thousand men did it behold; when John saw, in the apocalypse, the ruin of the world through evil, and the stars fall from heaven, as the figtree casteth her untimely fruit; when Æsop reports the whole catalogue of common daily relations through the masquerade of birds and beasts;—we take the cheerful hint of the immortality of our essence, and its versatile habit and escapes, as when the gypsies say, "it is in vain to hang them, they cannot die."[1]

The poets are thus liberating gods. The ancient British bards had for the title of their order, "Those who are free throughout the world." They are free, and they make free. An imaginative book renders us much more service at first, by stimulating us through its tropes, than afterward, when we arrive at the precise sense of the author. I think nothing is of any value in books, excepting the transcendental and extraordinary. If a man is inflamed and carried away by his thought, to that degree that he forgets the authors and the public, and heeds only this one dream, which holds him like an insanity, let me read his paper, and you may have all the arguments and histories and criticism. All the value which attaches to Pythagoras, Paracelsus, Cornelius Agrippa, Cardan, Kepler, Swedenborg, Schelling, Oken,[2] or any other who introduces questionable facts into his cosmogony, as angels, devils, magic, astrology, palmistry, mesmerism,[3] and so on, is the certificate we have of departure from

1. Emerson's freewheeling allusiveness embodies the liberation he is celebrating: *Charmides* and *Timaeus* are two of Plato's Dialogues. The Chapman quotation is from his dedication to his translation of Homer. Chaucer's praise of "gentilesse" is in *The Wife of Bath's Tale*. John's vision is in Revelation 6.13. The Greek Aesop in the 6th century B.C. wrote beast fables, which commented on human foibles. The saying attributed to gypsies is unlocated.
2. Lorenz Oken (1779–1851), German naturalist. Py-

thagoras (6th century B.C.), Greek mathematician and mystic philosopher. Paracelsus (1493–1541), German alchemist. Agrippa (1486–1535), German physician. Girolamo Cardano (1501–1576), Italian mathematician. Johann Kepler (1571–1630), German astronomer. Swedenborg, see n. 2, p. 1074. Friedrich Wilhelm Joseph von Schelling (1775–1854), German philosopher.
3. Hypnotism.

routine, and that here is a new witness. That also is the best success in conversation, the magic of liberty, which puts the world, like a ball, in our hands. How cheap even the liberty then seems; how mean to study, when an emotion communicates to the intellect the power to sap and upheave nature; how great the perspective! nations, times, systems, enter and disappear, like threads in tapestry of large figure and many colors; dream delivers us to dream, and, while the drunkenness lasts, we will sell our bed, our philosophy, our religion, in our opulence.

There is good reason why we should prize this liberation. The fate of the poor shepherd, who, blinded and lost in the snowstorm, perishes in a drift within a few feet of his cottage door, is an emblem of the state of man. On the brink of the waters of life and truth, we are miserably dying. The inaccessibleness of every thought but that we are in, is wonderful. What if you come near to it,—you are as remote, when you are nearest, as when you are farthest. Every thought is also a prison; every heaven is also a prison. Therefore we love the poet, the inventor, who in any form, whether in an ode, or in an action, or in looks and behavior, has yielded us a new thought. He unlocks our chains, and admits us to a new scene.

This emancipation is dear to all men, and the power to impart it, as it must come from greater depth and scope of thought, is a measure of intellect. Therefore all books of the imagination endure, all which ascend to that truth, that the writer sees nature beneath him, and uses it as his exponent.[4] Every verse or sentence, possessing this virtue, will take care of its own immortality. The religions of the world are the ejaculations[5] of a few imaginative men.

But the quality of the imagination is to flow, and not to freeze. The poet did not stop at the color, or the form, but read their meaning; neither may he rest in this meaning, but he makes the same objects exponents of his new thought. Here is the difference betwixt the poet and the mystic, that the last nails a symbol to one sense, which was a true sense for a moment, but soon becomes old and false. For all symbols are fluxional; all language is vehicular and transitive, and is good, as ferries and horses are, for conveyance, not as farms and houses are, for homestead. Mysticism consists in the mistake of an accidental and individual symbol for an universal one. The morning-redness happens to be the favorite meteor to the eyes of Jacob Behmen,[6] and comes to stand to him for truth and faith; and he believes should stand for the same realities to every reader. But the first reader prefers as naturally the symbol of a mother and child, or a gardener and his bulb, or a jeweller polishing a gem. Either of these, or of a myriad more, are equally good to the person to whom they are significant. Only they must be held lightly, and be very willingly translated into the equivalent terms which others use. And the mystic must be steadily told,—All that you say is just as true without the tedious use of that symbol as with it. Let us have a little algebra, instead of this trite rhetoric,— universal signs, instead of these village symbols,—and we shall both be gainers. The history of hierarchies seems to show, that all religious error consisted in making the symbol too stark and solid, and, at last, nothing but an excess of the organ of language.

Swedenborg, of all men in the recent ages, stands eminently for the transla-

---

4. Means of expounding his beliefs.
5. Throwings forth.

6. German mystic (1575–1624).

tor of nature into thought. I do not know the man in history to whom things stood so uniformly for words. Before him the metamorphosis continually plays. Everything on which his eye rests, obeys the impulses of moral nature. The figs become grapes whilst he eats them. When some of his angels affirmed a truth, the laurel twig which they held blossomed in their hands. The noise which, at a distance, appeared like gnashing and thumping, on coming nearer was found to be the voice of disputants. The men, in one of his visions, seen in heavenly light, appeared like dragons, and seemed in darkness: but, to each other, they appeared as men, and, when the light from heaven shone into their cabin, they complained of the darkness, and were compelled to shut the window that they might see.

There was this perception in him, which makes the poet or seer, an object of awe and terror, namely, that the same man, or society of men, may wear one aspect to themselves and their companions, and a different aspect to higher intelligences. Certain priests, whom he describes as conversing very learnedly together, appeared to the children, who were at some distance, like dead horses: and many the like misappearances. And instantly the mind inquires, whether these fishes under the bridge, yonder oxen in the pasture, those dogs in the yard, are immutably fishes, oxen, and dogs, or only so appear to me, and perchance to themselves appear upright men; and whether I appear as a man to all eyes. The Bramins and Pythagoras propounded the same question, and if any poet has witnessed the transformation, he doubtless found it in harmony with various experiences. We have all seen changes as considerable in wheat and caterpillars. He is the poet, and shall draw us with love and terror, who sees, through the flowing vest, the firm nature, and can declare it.

I look in vain for the poet whom I describe. We do not, with sufficient plainness, or sufficient profoundness, address ourselves to life, nor dare we chaunt our own times and social circumstance. If we filled the day with bravery, we should not shrink from celebrating it. Time and nature yield us many gifts, but not yet the timely man, the new religion, the reconciler, whom all things await. Dante's praise is, that he dared to write his autobiography in colossal cipher, or into universality. We have yet had no genius in America, with tyrannous eye, which knew the value of our incomparable materials, and saw, in the barbarism and materialism of the times, another carnival of the same gods whose picture he so much admires in Homer; then in the middle age; then in Calvinism. Banks and tariffs, the newspaper and caucus, methodism and unitarianism, are flat and dull to dull people, but rest on the same foundations of wonder as the town of Troy, and the temple of Delphos,[7] and are as swiftly passing away. Our logrolling, our stumps and their politics,[8] our fisheries, our Negroes, and Indians, our boasts, and our repudiations, the wrath of rogues, and the pusillanimity of honest men, the northern trade, the southern planting, the western clearing, Oregon, and Texas, are yet unsung. Yet America is a poem in our eyes; its ample geography dazzles the imagination, and it will not wait long for metres. If I have not found that excellent combination of gifts in my countrymen which I seek, neither could I aid

---

7. The home of the Delphic oracle, or prophetess, in Greece. Troy is the site of the Trojan War in Asia Minor.
8. "Boasts" is the common correction for the 1st edition's "boats." "Logrolling" seems to be used in the metaphorical sense of exchanging political favors.

"Stumps" refers to the practice political orators had of addressing audiences from any makeshift platform, even a tree stump. Emerson is contrasting the optimism of the states as they sold bonds here and abroad with their seemingly blithe repudiation of states' debts when grandiose projects fell through.

myself to fix the idea of the poet by reading now and then in Chalmers's collection of five centuries of English poets.[9] These are wits, more than poets, though there have been poets among them. But when we adhere to the ideal of the poet, we have our difficulties even with Milton and Homer. Milton is too literary, and Homer too literal and historical.

But I am not wise enough for a national criticism, and must use the old largeness a little longer, to discharge my errand from the muse to the poet concerning his art.

Art is the path of the creator to his work. The paths, or methods, are ideal and eternal, though few men ever see them, not the artist himself for years, or for a lifetime, unless he comes into the conditions. The painter, the sculptor, the composer, the epic rhapsodist, the orator, all partake one desire, namely, to express themselves symmetrically and abundantly, not dwarfishly and fragmentarily. They found or put themselves in certain conditions, as, the painter and sculptor before some impressive human figures; the orator, into the assembly of the people; and the others, in such scenes as each has found exciting to his intellect; and each presently feels the new desire. He hears a voice, he sees a beckoning. Then he is apprised, with wonder, what herds of dæmons hem him in. He can no more rest; he says, with the old painter, "By God, it is in me, and must go forth of me." He pursues a beauty, half seen, which flies before him. The poet pours out verses in every solitude. Most of the things he says are conventional, no doubt; but by and by he says something which is original and beautiful. That charms him. He would say nothing else but such things. In our way of talking, we say, "That is yours, this is mine;' but the poet knows well that it is not his; that it is as strange and beautiful to him as to you; he would fain hear the like eloquence at length. Once having tasted this immortal ichor,[1] he cannot have enough of it, and, as an admirable creative power exists in these intellections, it is of the last importance that these things get spoken. What a little of all we know is said! What drops of all the sea of our science are bailed up! and by what accident it is that these are exposed, when so many secrets sleep in nature! Hence the necessity of speech and song; hence these throbs and heart-beatings in the orator, at the door of the assembly, to the end, namely, that thought may be ejaculated as Logos, or Word.

Doubt not, O Poet, but persist. Say, 'It is in me, and shall out.' Stand there, baulked and dumb, stuttering and stammering, hissed and hooted, stand and strive, until, at last, rage draw out of thee that *dream*-power which every night shows thee is thine own; a power transcending all limit and privacy, and by virtue of which a man is the conductor of the whole river of electricity. Nothing walks, or creeps, or grows, or exists, which must not in turn arise and walk before him as exponent of his meaning. Comes he to that power, his genius is no longer exhaustible. All the creatures, by pairs and by tribes, pour into his mind as into a Noah's ark, to come forth again to people a new world. This is like the stock of air for our respiration, or for the combustion of our fireplace, not a measure of gallons, but the entire atmosphere if wanted. And therefore the rich poets, as Homer, Chaucer, Shakspeare, and Raphael, have obviously no limits to their works, except the limits of their lifetime, and resemble a mirror carried through the street, ready to render an image of every created thing.

---

9. A commonly used set compiled by Alexander Chalmers (1759–1834), Scottish journalist and biographer.

1. In Greek myth, blood of the gods, but Emerson may mean nectar, the drink of the gods.

O poet! a new nobility is conferred in groves and pastures, and not in castles, or by the sword-blade, any longer. The conditions are hard, but equal. Thou shalt leave the world, and know the muse only. Thou shalt not know any longer the times, customs, graces, politics, or opinions of men, but shalt take all from the muse. For the time of towns is tolled from the world by funereal chimes, but in nature the universal hours are counted by succeeding tribes of animals and plants, and by growth of joy on joy. God wills also that thou abdicate a manifold and duplex life, and that thou be content that others speak for thee. Others shall be thy gentlemen, and shall represent all courtesy and worldly life for thee; others shall do the great and resounding actions also. Thou shalt lie close hid with nature, and canst not be afforded to the Capitol or the Exchange.[2] The world is full of renunciations and apprenticeships, and this is thine: thou must pass for a fool and a churl for a long season. This is the screen and sheath in which Pan[3] has protected his well-beloved flower, and thou shalt be known only to thine own, and they shall console thee with tenderest love. And thou shalt not be able to rehearse the names of thy friends in thy verse, for an old shame before the holy ideal. And this is the reward: that the ideal shall be real to thee; and the impressions of the actual world shall fall like summer rain, copious, but not troublesome, to thy invulnerable essence. Thou shalt have the whole land for thy park and manor, the sea for thy bath and navigation, without tax and without envy; the woods and the rivers thou shalt own; and thou shalt possess that wherein others are only tenants and boarders. Thou true land-lord! sea-lord! air-lord! Wherever snow falls, or water flows, or birds fly, wherever day and night meet in twilight, wherever the blue heaven is hung by clouds, or sown with stars, wherever are forms with transparent boundaries, wherever are outlets into celestial space, wherever is danger, and awe, and love, there is Beauty, plenteous as rain, shed for thee, and though thou shouldest walk the world over, thou shalt not be able to find a condition inopportune or ignoble.

1844

# Experience[1]

*The lords of life, the lords of life,—*
*I saw them pass,*
*In their own guise,*
*Like and unlike,*
*Portly and grim,*
*Use and Surprise,*
*Surface and Dream,*
*Succession swift, and spectral Wrong,*
*Temperament without a tongue,*
*And the inventor of the game*
*Omnipresent without name;—*
*Some to see, some to be guessed,*

2. Stock exchange.
3. In Greek myth, the god of woods and fields, represented with goat's legs, horns, and ears.
1. First published in *Essays, Second Series* (1844), *Experience* emerged in 1843 and 1844 during Emerson's broodings following the death of his young son Waldo in January 1842, rather than being derived from a lecture, as most of his essays were. David W. Hill has shown that some of the more optimistic passages derive from journal entries made after Waldo's death, while some of the darker passages were first drafted before 1842, so no simple autobiographical reading is tenable. Still, it is the intensity of concentration following Waldo's death and the new and ruthless determination to tell the truth as he saw it that give the essay a strong claim to being Emerson's masterpiece. The epigraph is by Emerson.

*They marched from east to west:*
*Little man, least of all,*
*Among the legs of his guardians tall,*
*Walked about with puzzled look:—*
*Him by the hand dear nature took;*
*Dearest nature, strong and kind,*
*Whispered, 'Darling, never mind!*
*Tomorrow they will wear another face,*
*The founder thou! these are thy race!"*

Where do we find ourselves? In a series of which we do not know the extremes, and believe that it has none. We wake and find ourselves on a stair; there are stairs below us, which we seem to have ascended; there are stairs above us, many a one, which go upward and out of sight. But the Genius[2] which, according to the old belief, stands at the door by which we enter, and gives us the lethe[3] to drink, that we may tell no tales, mixed the cup too strongly, and we cannot shake off the lethargy now at noonday. Sleep lingers all our lifetime about our eyes; as night hovers all day in the boughs of the fir-tree. All things swim and glitter. Our life is not so much threatened as our perception. Ghostlike we glide through nature, and should not know our place again. Did our birth fall in some fit of indigence and frugality in nature, that she was so sparing of her fire and so liberal of her earth, that it appears to us that we lack the affirmative principle, and though we have health and reason, yet we have no superfluity of spirit for new creation? We have enough to live and bring the year about, but not an ounce to impart or to invest. Ah that our Genius were a little more of a genius! We are like millers on the lower levels of a stream, when the factories above them have exhausted the water. We too fancy that the upper people must have raised their dams.

If any of us knew what we were doing, or where we are going, then when we think we best know! We do not know today whether we are busy or idle. In times when we thought ourselves indolent, we have afterwards discovered, that much was accomplished, and much was begun in us. All our days are so unprofitable while they pass, that 'tis wonderful where or when we ever got anything of this which we call wisdom, poetry, virtue. We never got it on any dated calendar day. Some heavenly days must have been intercalated somewhere, like those that Hermes won with dice of the Moon, that Osiris[4] might be born. It is said, all martyrdoms looked mean when they were suffered. Every ship is a romantic object, except that we sail in. Embark, and the romance quits our vessel, and hangs on every other sail in the horizon. Our life looks trivial, and we shun to record it. Men seem to have learned of the horizon the art of perpetual retreating and reference. 'Yonder uplands are rich pasturage, and my neighbor has fertile meadow, but my field,' says the querulous farmer, 'only holds the world together.' I quote another man's saying; unluckily, that other withdraws himself in the same way, and quotes me. 'Tis the trick of nature thus to degrade today; a good deal of buzz, and somewhere a result slipped magically in. Every roof is agreeable to the eye, until it is lifted; then we find tragedy and moaning women, and hard-eyed husbands, and deluges of lethe, and the men ask, 'What's the news?' as if the old were so bad.

2. Governing or guardian spirit.
3. Water from the river of forgetfulness in the underworld of Greek myth.
4. Chief Egyptian god. The following story is told in Plutarch's *Morals:* the sun god forbade his wife, Rhea, to give birth on any day of the year, but Hermes won five new days from the moon, during which Osiris could be born.

How many individuals can we count in society? how many actions? how many opinions? So much of our time is preparation, so much is routine, and so much retrospect, that the pith of each man's genius contracts itself to a very few hours. The history of literature—take the net result of Tiraboschi, Warton, or Schlegel,[5]—is a sum of very few ideas, and of very few original tales,—all the rest being variation of these. So in this great society wide lying around us, a critical analysis would find very few spontaneous actions. It is almost all custom and gross sense. There are even few opinions, and these seem organic in the speakers, and do not disturb the universal necessity.

What opium is instilled into all disaster! It shows formidable as we approach it, but there is at last no rough rasping friction, but the most slippery sliding surfaces. We fall soft on a thought. Ate Dea[6] is gentle,

> "Over men's heads walking aloft,
> With tender feet treading so soft."[7]

People grieve and bemoan themselves, but it is not half so bad with them as they say. There are moods in which we court suffering, in the hope that here, at least, we shall find reality, sharp peaks and edges of truth. But it turns out to be scene-painting and counterfeit. The only thing grief has taught me, is to know how shallow it is. That, like all the rest, plays about the surface, and never introduces me into the reality, for contact with which, we would even pay the costly price of sons and lovers. Was it Boscovich[8] who found out that bodies never come in contact? Well, souls never touch their objects. An innavigable sea washes with silent waves between us and the things we aim at and converse with. Grief too will make us idealists. In the death of my son, now more than two years ago, I seem to have lost a beautiful estate,—no more. I cannot get it nearer to me. If tomorrow I should be informed of the bankruptcy of my principal debtors, the loss of my property would be a great inconvenience to me, perhaps, for many years; but it would leave me as it found me,—neither better nor worse. So is it with this calamity: it does not touch me: some thing which I fancied was a part of me, which could not be torn away without tearing me, nor enlarged without enriching me, falls off from me, and leaves no scar. It was caducous.[9] I grieve that grief can teach me nothing, nor carry me one step into real nature. The Indian who was laid under a curse, that the wind should not blow on him, nor water flow to him, nor fire burn him, is a type of us all. The dearest events are summer-rain, and we the Para coats[1] that shed every drop. Nothing is left us now but death. We look to that with a grim satisfaction, saying, there at least is reality that will not dodge us.

I take this evanescence and lubricity of all objects, which lets them slip through our fingers then when we clutch hardest, to be the most unhandsome part of our condition. Nature does not like to be observed, and likes that we should be her fools and playmates. We may have the sphere for our cricket-ball, but not a berry for our philosophy. Direct strokes she never gave us power

5. Either Friedrich von Schlegel (1772–1829) or his brother August Wilhelm von Schlegel (1767–1845), historians of European literature. Girolamo Tiraboschi (1731–1794), historian of Italian literature. Thomas Warton (1728–1790), historian of British literature.
6. The goddess of mischief or fatal recklessness.
7. The Iliad, book 19.
8. Ruggiero Giuseppe Boscovich (1711–1787), Italian physicist who advanced a molecular theory of matter.
9. Not long lasting.
1. Rubber overcoats.

to make; all our blows glance, all our hits are accidents. Our relations to each other are oblique and casual.

Dream delivers us to dream, and there is no end to illusion. Life is a train of moods like a string of beads, and, as we pass through them, they prove to be many-colored lenses which paint the world their own hue, and each shows only what lies in its focus. From the mountain you see the mountain. We animate what we can, and we see only what we animate. Nature and books belong to the eyes that see them. It depends on the mood of the man, whether he shall see the sunset or the fine poem. There are always sunsets, and there is always genius; but only a few hours so serene that we can relish nature or criticism. The more or less depends on structure or temperament. Temperament is the iron wire on which the beads are strung. Of what use is fortune or talent to a cold and defective nature? Who cares what sensibility or discrimination a man has at some time shown, if he falls asleep in his chair? or if he laugh and giggle? or if he apologize? or is affected with egotism? or thinks of his dollar? or cannot go by food? or has gotten a child in his boyhood? Of what use is genius, if the organ is too convex or too concave, and cannot find a focal distance within the actual horizon of human life? Of what use, if the brain is too cold or too hot, and the man does not care enough for results, to stimulate him to experiment, and hold him up in it? or if the web is too finely woven, too irritable by pleasure and pain, so that life stagnates from too much reception, without due outlet? Of what use to make heroic vows of amendment, if the same old law-breaker is to keep them? What cheer can the religious sentiment yield, when that is suspected to be secretly dependent on the seasons of the year, and the state of the blood? I knew a witty physician who found theology in the biliary duct, and used to affirm that if there was disease in the liver, the man became a Calvinist, and if that organ was sound, he became a Unitarian.[2] Very mortifying is the reluctant experience that some unfriendly excess or imbecility neutralizes the promise of genius. We see young men who owe us a new world, so readily and lavishly they promise, but they never acquit the debt; they die young and dodge the account: or if they live, they lose themselves in the crowd.

Temperament also enters fully into the system of illusions, and shuts us in a prison of glass which we cannot see. There is an optical illusion about every person we meet. In truth, they are all creatures of given temperament, which will appear in a given character, whose boundaries they will never pass: but we look at them, they seem alive, and we presume there is impulse in them. In the moment it seems impulse; in the year, in the lifetime, it turns out to be a certain uniform tune which the revolving barrel of the music-box must play. Men resist the conclusion in the morning, but adopt it as the evening wears on, that temper prevails over everything of time, place, and condition, and is inconsumable in the flames of religion. Some modifications the moral sentiment avails to impose, but the individual texture holds its dominion, if not to bias the moral judgments, yet to fix the measure of activity and of enjoyment.

I thus express the law as it is read from the platform of ordinary life, but must not leave it without noticing the capital exception. For temperament is

2. I.e., the Calvinistic sense of Original Sin is seen as an intellectual manifestation of a bodily disease; the Unitarian view of humanity has none of the Calvinistic preoccupation with eternal damnation for all but the select few, the elect.

a power which no man willingly hears any one praise but himself. On the platform of physics, we cannot resist the contracting influences of so-called science. Temperament puts all divinity to rout. I know the mental proclivity of physicians. I hear the chuckle of the phrenologists.[3] Theoretic kidnappers and slave-drivers, they esteem each man the victim of another, who winds him round his finger by knowing the law of his being, and by such cheap signboards as the color of his beard, or the slope of his occiput, reads the inventory of his fortunes and character. The grossest ignorance does not disgust like this impudent knowingness. The physicians say, they are not materialists; but they are:—Spirit is matter reduced to an extreme thinness: O so thin!— But the definition of *spiritual* should be, *that which is its own evidence.* What notions do they attach to love! what to religion! One would not willingly pronounce these words in their hearing, and give them the occasion to profane them. I saw a gracious gentleman who adapts his conversation to the form of the head of the man he talks with! I had fancied that the value of life lay in its inscrutable possibilities; in the fact that I never know, in addressing myself to a new individual, what may befall me. I carry the keys of my castle in my hand, ready to throw them at the feet of my lord, whenever and in what disguise soever he shall appear. I know he is in the neighborhood hidden among vagabonds. Shall I preclude my future, by taking a high seat, and kindly adapting my conversation to the shape of heads? When I come to that, the doctors shall buy me for a cent.——'But, sir, medical history; the report to the Institute; the proven facts!'—I distrust the facts and the inferences. Temperament is the veto or limitation-power in the constitution, very justly applied to restrain an opposite excess in the constitution, but absurdly offered as a bar to original equity. When virtue is in presence, all subordinate powers sleep. On its own level, or in view of nature, temperament is final. I see not, if one be once caught in this trap of so-called sciences, any escape for the man from the links of the chain of physical necessity. Given such an embryo, such a history must follow. On this platform, one lives in a sty of sensualism, and would soon come to suicide. But it is impossible that the creative power should exclude itself. Into every intelligence there is a door which is never closed, through which the creator passes. The intellect, seeker of absolute truth, or the heart, lover of absolute good, intervenes for our succor, and at one whisper of these high powers, we awake from ineffectual struggles with this nightmare. We hurl it into its own hell, and cannot again contract ourselves to so base a state.

The secret of the illusoriness is in the necessity of a succession of moods or objects. Gladly we would anchor, but the anchorage is quicksand. This onward trick of nature is too strong for us: *Pero si muove.*[4] When, at night, I look at the moon and stars, I seem stationary, and they to hurry. Our love of the real draws us to permanence, but health of body consists in circulation, and sanity of mind in variety or facility of association. We need change of objects. Dedication to one thought is quickly odious. We house with the insane, and must humor them; then conversation dies out. Once I took such

3. Pseudoscientists who claimed to read character by bumps on the skull.
4. It moves, all the same (Italian); Galileo's muttered protest after the Inquisition (tribunal of the Roman Catholic church charged with suppressing heresy) had forced him to retract the idea that the earth revolves around the sun.

delight in Montaigne, that I thought I should not need any other book; before that, in Shakspeare; then in Plutarch; then in Plotinus; at one time in Bacon; afterwards in Goethe; even in Bettine;[5] but now I turn the pages of either of them languidly, whilst I still cherish their genius. So with pictures; each will bear an emphasis of attention once, which it cannot retain, though we fain would continue to be pleased in that manner. How strongly I have felt of pictures, that when you have seen one well, you must take your leave of it; you shall never see it again. I have had good lessons from pictures, which I have since seen without emotion or remark. A deduction must be made from the opinion, which even the wise express of a new book or occurrence. Their opinion gives me tidings of their mood, and some vague guess at the new fact, but is nowise to be trusted as the lasting relation between that intellect and that thing. The child asks, 'Mamma, why don't I like the story as well as when you told it me yesterday?' Alas, child, it is even so with the oldest cherubim of knowledge. But will it answer thy question to say, Because thou wert born to a whole, and this story is a particular? The reason of the pain this discovery causes us (and we make it late in respect to works of art and intellect), is the plaint of tragedy which murmurs from it in regard to persons, to friendship and love.

That immobility and absence of elasticity which we find in the arts, we find with more pain in the artist. There is no power of expansion in men. Our friends early appear to us as representatives of certain ideas, which they never pass or exceed. They stand on the brink of the ocean of thought and power, but they never take the single step that would bring them there. A man is like a bit of Labrador spar,[6] which has no lustre as you turn it in your hand, until you come to a particular angle; then it shows deep and beautiful colors. There is no adaptation or universal applicability in men, but each has his special talent, and the mastery of successful men consists in adroitly keeping them-selves where and when that turn shall be oftenest to be practised. We do what we must, and call it by the best names we can, and would fain have the praise of having intended the result which ensues. I cannot recall any form of man who is not superfluous sometimes. But is not this pitiful? Life is not worth the taking, to do tricks in.

Of course, it needs the whole society, to give the symmetry we seek. The parti-colored wheel must revolve very fast to appear white. Something is learned too by conversing with so much folly and defect. In fine, whoever loses, we are always of the gaining party. Divinity is behind our failures and follies also. The plays of children are nonsense, but very educative nonsense. So it is with the largest and solemnest things, with commerce, government, church, marriage, and so with the history of every man's bread, and the ways by which he is to come by it. Like a bird which alights nowhere, but hops perpetually from bough to bough, is the Power which abides in no man and in no woman, but for a moment speaks from this one, and for another moment from that one.

5. Elizabeth ("Bettine") von Arnim (1785–1859), whose purported correspondence with Goethe was published in 1835. Michel de Montaigne (1533–1592), French essayist. Plutarch (46?–120?), Greek biographer of famous Greeks and Romans. Plotinus (205?–270?), Egyptian-born Roman neoplatonist philosopher. (Neoplatonism is a mystic religious system, combining features of Platonic and other Greek philosophies with features of Judaism and Christianity.) Sir Francis Bacon (1561–1626), English essayist, philosopher, and statesman. Johann Wolfgang von Goethe (1749–1832), German poet and dramatist.
6. Labradorite, crystalline rock.

But what help from these fineries or pedantries? What help from thought? Life is not dialectics. We, I think, in these times, have had lessons enough of the futility of criticism. Our young people have thought and written much on labor and reform, and for all that they have written, neither the world nor themselves have got on a step. Intellectual tasting of life will not supersede muscular activity. If a man should consider the nicety of the passage of a piece of bread down his throat, he would starve. At Education-Farm,[7] the noblest theory of life sat on the noblest figures of young men and maidens, quite powerless and melancholy. It would not rake or pitch a ton of hay; it would not rub down a horse; and the men and maidens it left pale and hungry. A political orator wittily compared our party promises to western roads, which opened stately enough, with planted trees on either side, to tempt the traveller, but soon became narrow and narrower, and ended in a squirrel-track, and ran up a tree. So does culture with us; it ends in head-ache. Unspeakably sad and barren does life look to those, who a few months ago were dazzled with the splendor of the promise of the times. "There is now no longer any right course of action, nor any self-devotion left among the Iranis."[8] Objections and criticism we have had our fill of. There are objections to every course of life and action, and the practical wisdom infers an indifferency, from the omnipresence of objection. The whole frame of things preaches indifferency. Do not craze yourself with thinking, but go about your business anywhere. Life is not intellectual or critical, but sturdy. Its chief good is for well-mixed people who can enjoy what they find, without question. Nature hates peeping and our mothers speak her very sense when they say, "Children, eat your victuals, and say no more of it." To fill the hour,—that is happiness; to fill the hour, and leave no crevice for a repentance or an approval. We live amid surfaces, and the true art of life is to skate well on them. Under the oldest mouldiest conventions, a man of native force prospers just as well as in the newest world, and that by skill of handling and treatment. He can take hold anywhere. Life itself is a mixture of power and form, and will not bear the least excess of either. To finish the moment, to find the journey's end in every step of the road, to live the greatest number of good hours, is wisdom. It is not the part of men, but of fanatics, or of mathematicians, if you will, to say, that, the shortness of life considered, it is not worth caring whether for so short a duration we were sprawling in want, or sitting high. Since our office is with moments, let us husband them. Five minutes of today are worth as much to me, as five minutes in the next millennium. Let us be poised, and wise, and our own, today. Let us treat the men and women well: treat them as if they were real: perhaps they are. Men live in their fancy, like drunkards whose hands are too soft and tremulous for successful labor. It is a tempest of fancies, and the only ballast I know, is a respect to the present hour. Without any shadow of doubt amidst this vertigo of shows and politics, I settle myself ever the firmer in the creed, that we should not postpone and refer and wish, but do broad justice where we are, by whomsoever we deal with, accepting our actual companions and circumstances, however humble or odious, as the mystic officials to whom the universe has delegated its whole pleasure for us. If these are mean and malignant, their contentment, which is the last victory of justice, is a more

7. Brook Farm, the Transcendentalist commune at West Roxbury, Massachusetts.
8. From the Persian *Desatir*, ancient scriptures cred-ited to Zoroaster (6th century B.C.), founder of the Parsee religion.

satisfying echo to the heart, than the voice of poets and the casual sympathy of admirable persons. I think that however a thoughtful man may suffer from the defects and absurdities of his company, he cannot without affectation deny to any set of men and women, a sensibility to extraordinary merit. The coarse and frivolous have an instinct of superiority, if they have not a sympathy, and honor it in their blind capricious way with sincere homage.

The fine young people despise life, but in me, and in such as with me are free from dyspepsia, and to whom a day is a sound and solid good, it is a great excess of politeness to look scornful and to cry for company. I am grown by sympathy a little eager and sentimental, but leave me alone, and I should relish every hour and what it brought me, the potluck of the day, as heartily as the oldest gossip in the bar-room. I am thankful for small mercies. I compared notes with one of my friends who expects everything of the universe, and is disappointed when anything is less than the best, and I found that I begin at the other extreme, expecting nothing, and am always full of thanks for moderate goods. I accept the clangor and jangle of contrary tendencies. I find my account in sots and bores also. They give a reality to the circumjacent picture, which such a vanishing meteorous appearance can ill spare. In the morning I awake, and find the old world, wife, babes, and mother, Concord and Boston, the dear old spiritual world, and even the dear old devil not far off. If we will take the good we find, asking no questions, we shall have heaping measures. The great gifts are not got by analysis. Everything good is on the highway. The middle region of our being is the temperate zone. We may climb into the thin and cold realm of pure geometry and lifeless science, or sink into that of sensation. Between these extremes is the equator of life, of thought, of spirit, of poetry,—a narrow belt. Moreover, in popular experience, everything good is on the highway. A collector peeps into all the picture-shops of Europe, for a landscape of Poussin, a crayon-sketch of Salvator; but the Transfiguration, the Last Judgment, the Communion of St. Jerome, and what are as transcendent as these, are on the walls of the Vatican, the Uffizii, or the Louvre, where every footman may see them;[9] to say nothing of nature's pictures in every street, of sunsets and sunrises every day, and the sculpture of the human body never absent. A collector recently bought at public auction, in London, for one hundred and fifty-seven guineas,[1] an autograph of Shakspeare: but for nothing a school-boy can read Hamlet, and can detect secrets of highest concernment yet unpublished therein. I think I will never read any but the commonest books,—the Bible, Homer, Dante, Shakspeare, and Milton. Then we are impatient of so public a life and planet, and run hither and thither for nooks and secrets. The imagination delights in the woodcraft of Indians, trappers, and bee-hunters. We fancy that we are strangers, and not so intimately domesticated in the planet as the wild man, and the wild beast and bird. But the exclusion reaches them also; reaches the climbing, flying, gliding, feathered and four-footed man. Fox and woodchuck, hawk and snipe, and bittern, when nearly seen, have no more root in the deep world than man, and are just such superficial tenants of the globe. Then the new molecular

9. I.e., the collector hunts for minor paintings in out-of-the-way shops while the great paintings are in museums where anyone may see them. Nicolas Poussin (1594–1665), French painter. Salvator Rosa (1615–1673), Italian painter of wild landscapes. The Trans- / figuration is that by Raphael, in Rome. The Last Judgment is Michelangelo's, in Florence. The Communion of St. Jerome is that by Il Domenichino in Paris. / 1. British gold coin worth one shilling more than a pound.

philosophy shows astronomical interspaces betwixt atom and atom, shows that the world is all outside: it has no inside. The mid-world is best. Nature, as we know her, is no saint. The lights of the church, the ascetics, Gentoos and Grahamites,[2] she does not distinguish by any favor. She comes eating and drinking and sinning. Her darlings, the great, the strong, the beautiful, are not children of our law, do not come out of the Sunday School, nor weigh their food, nor punctually keep the commandments. If we will be strong with her strength, we must not harbor such disconsolate consciences, borrowed too from the consciences of other nations. We must set up the strong present tense against all the rumors of wrath, past or to come. So many things are unsettled which it is of the first importance to settle,—and, pending their settlement, we will do as we do. Whilst the debate goes forward on the equity of commerce, and will not be closed for a century or two, New and Old England may keep shop. Law of copyright and international copyright[3] is to be discussed, and, in the interim, we will sell our books for the most we can. Expediency of literature, reason of literature, lawfulness of writing down a thought, is questioned; much is to say on both sides, and, while the fight waxes hot, thou, dearest scholar, stick to thy foolish task, add a line every hour, and between whiles add a line. Right to hold land, right of property, is disputed, and the conventions convene, and before the vote is taken, dig away in your garden, and spend your earnings as a waif or godsend to all serene and beautiful purposes. Life itself is a bubble and a skepticism, and a sleep within a sleep. Grant it, and as much more as they will—but thou, God's darling! heed thy private dream: thou wilt not be missed in the scorning and skepticism: there are enough of them: stay there in thy closet, and toil, until the rest are agreed what to do about it. Thy sickness, they say, and thy puny habit, require that thou do this or avoid that, but know that thy life is a flitting state, a tent for a night, and do thou, sick or well, finish that stint. Thou art sick, but shalt not be worse, and the universe, which holds thee dear, shall be the better.

Human life is made up of the two elements, power and form, and the proportion must be invariably kept, if we would have it sweet and sound. Each of these elements in excess makes a mischief as hurtful as its defect. Everything runs to excess: every good quality is noxious, if unmixed, and, to carry the danger to the edge of ruin, nature causes each man's peculiarity to super-abound. Here, among the farms, we adduce the scholars as examples of this treachery. They are nature's victims of expression. You who see the artist, the orator, the poet, too near, and find their life no more excellent than that of mechanics or farmers, and themselves victims of partiality, very hollow and haggard, and pronounce them failures,—not heroes, but quacks,—conclude very reasonably, that these arts are not for man, but are disease. Yet nature will not bear you out. Irresistible nature made men such, and makes legions more of such, every day. You love the boy reading in a book, gazing at a drawing, or a cast: yet what are these millions who read and behold, but incipient writers and sculptors? Add a little more of that quality which now reads and sees, and they will seize the pen and chisel. And if one remembers how innocently he began to be an artist, he perceives that nature joined with his

2. Contemporary food-faddists; from Sylvester Graham (1794–1851), vegetarian whose efforts at food reform are memorialized in the graham cracker. "Gentoos": Hindu sectarians.
3. Not passed by the American Congress until 1891.

enemy. A man is a golden impossibility. The line he must walk is a hair's breadth. The wise through excess of wisdom is made a fool.

How easily, if fate would suffer it, we might keep forever these beautiful limits, and adjust ourselves, once for all, to the perfect calculation of the kingdom of known cause and effect. In the street and in the newspapers, life appears so plain a business, that manly resolution and adherence to the multi-plication-table through all weathers, will insure success. But ah! presently comes a day, or is it only a half-hour, with its angel-whispering,—which dis-comfits the conclusions of nations and of years! Tomorrow again, everything looks real and angular, the habitual standards are reinstated, common sense is as rare as genius,—is the basis of genius, and experience is hands and feet to every enterprise;—and yet, he who should do his business on this understand-ing, would be quickly bankrupt. Power keeps quite another road than the turnpikes of choice and will, namely, the subterranean and invisible tunnels and channels of life. It is ridiculous that we are diplomatists, and doctors, and considerate people: there are no dupes like these. Life is a series of surprises, and would not be worth taking or keeping, if it were not. God delights to isolate us every day, and hide from us the past and the future. We would look about us, but with grand politeness he draws down before us an impenetrable screen of purest sky, and another behind us of purest sky. 'You will not remember,' he seems to say, 'and you will not expect.' All good conversation, manners, and action, come from a spontaneity which forgets usages, and makes the moment great. Nature hates calculators; her methods are saltatory and impulsive. Man lives by pulses; our organic movements are such; and the chemical and ethereal agents are undulatory and alternate; and the mind goes antagonizing on, and never prospers but by fits. We thrive by casualties. Our chief experiences have been casual. The most attractive class of people are those who are powerful obliquely, and not by the direct stroke: men of genius, but not yet accredited: one gets the cheer of their light, without paying too great a tax. Theirs is the beauty of the bird, or the morning light, and not of art. In the thought of genius there is always a surprise; and the moral sentiment is well called "the newness," for it is never other; as new to the oldest intelli-gence as to the young child.—"the kingdom that cometh without observa-tion."[4] In like manner, for practical success, there must not be too much design. A man will not be observed in doing that which he can do best. There is a certain magic about his properest action, which stupefies your powers of observation, so that though it is done before you, you wist not of it. The art of life has a pudency, and will not be exposed. Every man is an impossibility, until he is born; every thing impossible, until we see a success. The ardors of piety agree at last with the coldest skepticism,—that nothing is of us or our works,—that all is of God. Nature will not spare us the smallest leaf of laurel. All writing comes by the grace of God, and all doing and having. I would gladly be moral, and keep due metes and bounds, which I dearly love, and allow the most to the will of man, but I have set my heart on honesty in this chapter, and I can see nothing at last, in success or failure, than more or less of vital force supplied from the Eternal. The results of life are uncalculated and uncalculable. The years teach much which the days never know. The persons who compose our company, converse, and come and go, and design

4. Luke 17.20.

and execute many things, and somewhat comes of it all, but an unlooked for result. The individual is always mistaken. He designed many things, and drew in other persons as coadjutors, quarrelled with some or all, blundered much, and something is done; all are a little advanced, but the individual is always mistaken. It turns out somewhat new, and very unlike what he promised himself.

The ancients, stuck with this irreducibleness of the elements of human life to calculation, exalted Chance into a divinity, but that is to stay too long at the spark,—which glitters truly at one point,—but the universe is warm with the latency of the same fire. The miracle of life which will not be expounded, but will remain a miracle, introduces a new element. In the growth of the embryo, Sir Everard Home,[5] I think, noticed that the evolution was not from one central point, but co-active from three or more points. Life has no memory. That which proceeds in succession might be remembered, but that which is co-existent, or ejaculated from a deeper cause, as yet far from being conscious, knows not its own tendency. So it is with us, now skeptical, or without unity, because immersed in forms and effects all seeming to be of equal yet hostile value, and now religious, whilst in the reception of spiritual law. Bear with these distractions, with this coetaneous growth of the parts: they will one day be *members*, and obey one will. On that one will, on that secret cause, they nail our attention and hope. Life is hereby melted into an expectation or a religion. Underneath the inharmonious and trivial particulars, is a musical perfection, the Ideal journeying always with us, the heaven without rent or seam. Do but observe the mode of our illumination. When I converse with a profound mind, or if at any time being alone I have good thoughts, I do not at once arrive at satisfactions, as when, being thirsty, I drink water, or go to the fire, being cold: no! but I am at first apprised of my vicinity to a new and excellent region of life. By persisting to read or to think, this region gives further sign of itself, as it were in flashes of light, in sudden discoveries of its profound beauty and repose, as if the clouds that covered it parted at intervals, and showed the approaching traveller the inland mountains, with the tranquil eternal meadows spread at their base, whereon flocks graze, and shepherds pipe and dance. But every insight from this realm of thought is felt as initial, and promises a sequel. I do not make it; I arrive there, and behold what was there already. I make! O no! I clap my hands in infantine joy and amazement, before the first opening to me of this august magnificence, old with the love and homage of innumerable ages, young with the life of life, the sunbright Mecca of the desert. And what a future it opens! I feel a new heart beating with the love of the new beauty. I am ready to die out of nature, and be born again into this new yet unapproachable America I have found in the West.

> "Since neither now nor yesterday began
> These thoughts, which have been ever, nor yet can
> A man be found who their first entrance knew."[6]

If I have described life as a flux of moods, I must now add, that there is that in us which changes not, and which ranks all sensations and states of mind. The consciousness in each man is a sliding scale, which identifies him now with the First Cause, and now with the flesh of his body; life above life, in

5. Scottish surgeon (1756–1832).
6. A free translation of the conclusion of one of the

heroine's speeches in Sophocles' *Antigone* (lines 456–57).

infinite degrees. The sentiment from which it sprung determines the dignity of any deed, and the question ever is, not, what you have done or forborne, but, at whose command you have done or forborne it.

Fortune, Minerva,[7] Muse, Holy Ghost,—these are quaint names, too narrow to cover this unbounded substance. The baffled intellect must still kneel before this cause, which refuses to be named—ineffable cause, which every fine genius has essayed to represent by some emphatic symbol, as, Thales by water, Anaximenes by air, Anaxagoras by (Νοῦς) thought, Zoroaster[8] by fire, Jesus and the moderns by love: and the metaphor of each has become a national religion. The Chinese Mencius[9] has not been the least successful in his generalization. "I fully understand language," he said, "and nourish well my vast-flowing vigor."—"I beg to ask what you call vast-flowing vigor?"—said his companion. "The explanation," replied Mencius, "is difficult. This vigor is supremely great, and in the highest degree unbending. Nourish it correctly, and do it no injury, and it will fill up the vacancy between heaven and earth. This vigor accords with and assists justice and reason, and leaves no hunger."—In our more correct writing, we give to this generalization the name of Being, and thereby confess that we have arrived as far as we can go. Suffice it for the joy of the universe, that we have not arrived at a wall, but at interminable oceans. Our life seems not present, so much as prospective; not for the affairs on which it is wasted, but as a hint of this vast-flowing vigor. Most of life seems to be mere advertisement of faculty: information is given us not to sell ourselves cheap; that we are very great. So, in particulars, our greatness is always in a tendency or direction, not in an action. It is for us to believe in the rule, not in the exception. The noble are thus known from the ignoble. So in accepting the leading of the sentiments, it is not what we believe concerning the immortality of the soul, or the like, but *the universal impulse to believe*, that is the material circumstance, and is the principal fact in the history of the globe. Shall we describe this cause as that which works directly? The spirit is not helpless or needful of mediate organs. It has plentiful powers and direct effects. I am explained without explaining, I am felt without acting, and where I am not. Therefore all just persons are satisfied with their own praise. They refuse to explain themselves, and are content that new actions should do them that office. They believe that we communicate without speech, and above speech, and that no right action of ours is quite unaffecting to our friends, at whatever distance; for the influence of action is not to be measured by miles. Why should I fret myself, because a circumstance has occurred, which hinders my presence where I was expected? If I am not at the meeting, my presence where I am, should be as useful to the commonwealth of friendship and wisdom, as would be my presence in that place. I exert the same quality of power in all places. Thus journeys the mighty Ideal before us; it never was known to fall into the rear. No man ever came to an experience which was satiating, but his good is tidings of a better. Onward and onward! In liberated moments, we know that a new picture of life and duty is already possible; the elements already exist in many minds around you, of a doctrine of life which shall transcend any written record we have. The new statement

---

7. Roman goddess of wisdom.
8. The 6th-century Persian founder of the fire worship of the Parsees. Thales (7th century B.C.), Anaximenes (6th century B.C.), and Anaxagoras (5th century B.C.),

Greek philosophers.
9. Meng-tsu (3rd century B.C.), compiler of doctrines of Confucianism.

will comprise the skepticisms, as well as the faiths of society, and out of unbeliefs a creed shall be formed. For, skepticisms are not gratuitous or lawless, but are limitations of the affirmative statement, and the new philosophy must take them in, and make affirmations outside of them, just as much as it must include the oldest beliefs.

It is very unhappy, but too late to be helped, the discovery we have made, that we exist. That discovery is called the Fall of Man. Ever afterwards, we suspect our instruments. We have learned that we do not see directly, but mediately, and that we have no means of correcting these colored and distorting lenses which we are, or of computing the amount of their errors. Perhaps these subject-lenses have a creative power; perhaps there are no objects. Once we lived in what we saw; now, the rapaciousness of this new power, which threatens to absorb all things, engages us. Nature, art, persons, letters, religions,—objects, successively tumble in, and God is but one of its ideas. Nature and literature are subjective phenomena; every evil and every good thing is a shadow which we cast. The street is full of humiliations to the proud. As the fop contrived to dress his bailiffs in his livery, and make them wait on his guests at table, so the chagrins[1] which the bad heart gives off as bubbles, at once take form as ladies and gentlemen in the street, shopmen or barkeepers in hotels, and threaten or insult whatever is threatenable and insultable in us. 'Tis the same with our idolatries. People forget that it is the eye which makes the horizon, and the rounding mind's eye which makes this or that man a type or representative of humanity with the name of hero or saint. Jesus the "providential man," is a good man on whom many people are agreed that these optical laws shall take effect. By love on one part, and by forbearance to press objection on the other part, it is for a time settled, that we will look at him in the centre of the horizon, and ascribe to him the properties that will attach to any man so seen. But the longest love or aversion has a speedy term. The great and crescive[2] self, rooted in absolute nature, supplants all relative existence, and ruins the kingdom of mortal friendship and love. Marriage (in what is called the spiritual world) is impossible, because of the inequality between every subject and every object. The subject is the receiver of Godhead, and at every comparison must feel his being enhanced by that cryptic might. Though not in energy, yet by presence, this magazine[3] of substance cannot be otherwise than felt: nor can any force of intellect attribute to the object the proper deity which sleeps or wakes forever in every subject. Never can love make consciousness and ascription equal in force. There will be the same gulf between every me and thee, as between the original and the picture. The universe is the bride of the soul. All private sympathy is partial. Two human beings are like globes, which can touch only in a point, and, whilst they remain in contact, all other points of each of the spheres are inert; their turn must also come, and the longer a particular union lasts, the more energy of appetency[4] the parts not in union acquire.

Life will be imaged, but cannot be divided nor doubled. Any invasion of its unity would be chaos. The soul is not twin-born, but the only begotten, and though revealing itself as child in time, child in appearance, is of a fatal and universal power, admitting no co-life. Every day, every act betrays the ill-

---

1. Ill-humored feelings.
2. Increasing.

3. Stored supply.
4. Strong impulse toward union.

concealed deity. We believe in ourselves, as we do not believe in others. We permit all things to ourselves, and that which we call sin in others, is experiment for us. It is an instance of our faith in ourselves, that men never speak of crime as lightly as they think: or, every man thinks a latitude safe for himself, which is nowise to be indulged to another. The act looks very differently on the inside, and on the outside; in its quality, and in its consequences. Murder in the murderer is no such ruinous thought as poets and romancers will have it; it does not unsettle him, or fright him from his ordinary notice of trifles: it is an act quite easy to be contemplated, but in its sequel, it turns out to be a horrible jangle and confounding of all relations. Especially the crimes that spring from love, seem right and fair from the actor's point of view, but, when acted, are found destructive of society. No man at last believes that he can be lost, nor that the crime in him is as black as in the felon. Because the intellect qualifies in our own case the moral judgments. For there is no crime to the intellect. That is antinomian or hypernomian,[5] and judges law as well as fact. "It is worse than a crime, it is a blunder," said Napoleon, speaking the language of the intellect. To it, the world is a problem in mathematics or the science of quantity, and it leaves out praise and blame, and all weak emotions. All stealing is comparative. If you come to absolutes, pray who does not steal? Saints are sad, because they behold sin, (even when they speculate,) from the point of view of the conscience, and not of the intellect; a confusion of thought. Sin seen from the thought, is a diminution or *less:* seen from the conscience or will, it is pravity or *bad.* The intellect names it shade, absence of light, and no essence. The conscience must feel it as essence, essential evil. This it is not: it has an objective existence, but no subjective.

Thus inevitably does the universe wear our color, and every object fall successively into the subject itself. The subject exists, the subject enlarges; all things sooner or later fall into place. As I am, so I see; use what language we will, we can never say anything but what we are; Hermes, Cadmus, Columbus, Newton, Buonaparte, are the mind's ministers.[6] Instead of feeling a poverty when we encounter a great man, let us treat the new comer like a travelling geologist, who passes through our estate, and shows us good slate, or limestone, or anthracite, in our brush pasture. The partial action of each strong mind in one direction, is a telescope for the objects on which it is pointed. But every other part of knowledge is to be pushed to the same extravagance, ere the soul attains her due sphericity. Do you see that kitten chasing so prettily her own tail? If you could look with her eyes, you might see her surrounded with hundreds of figures performing complex dramas, with tragic and comic issues, long conversations, many characters, many ups and downs of fate,—and meantime it is only puss and her tail. How long before our masquerade will end its noise of tamborines, laughter, and shouting, and we shall find it was a solitary performance?—A subject and an object,—it takes so much to make the galvanic circuit complete, but magnitude adds nothing. What imports it whether it is Kepler and the sphere; Columbus and America; a reader and his book; or puss with her tail?

5. Against or beyond the control of law.
6. I.e., great gods or men of legend and history are servants of the human mind because our subjectivity uses them to light up areas of our own being. Hermes is the Greek god of invention. Cadmus is the mythical inventor of the alphabet and creator of the Thebans by sowing dragon's teeth. Columbus sailed to America. Newton discovered the law of gravity. Napoleon Bonaparte in Emerson's childhood was the conquerer of much of Europe.

It is true that all the muses and love and religion hate these developments, and will find a way to punish the chemist, who publishes in the parlor the secrets of the laboratory. And we cannot say too little of our constitutional necessity of seeing things under private aspects, or saturated with our humors. And yet is the God the native of these bleak rocks. That need makes in morals the capital virtue of self-trust. We must hold hard to this poverty, however scandalous, and by more vigorous self-recoveries, after the sallies of action, possess our axis more firmly. The life of truth is cold, and so far mournful; but it is not the slave of tears, contritions, and perturbations. It does not attempt another's work, nor adopt another's facts. It is a main lesson of wisdom to know your own from another's. I have learned that I cannot dispose of other people's facts; but I possess such a key to my own, as persuades me against all their denials, that they also have a key to theirs. A sympathetic person is placed in the dilemma of a swimmer among drowning men, who all catch at him, and if he give so much as a leg or a finger, they will drown him. They wish to be saved from the mischiefs of their vices, but not from their vices. Charity would be wasted on this poor waiting on the symptoms. A wise and hardy physician will say, *Come out of that*, as the first condition of advice.

In this our talking America, we are ruined by our good nature and listening on all sides. This compliance takes away the power of being greatly useful. A man should not be able to look other than directly and forthright. A preoccupied attention is the only answer to the importunate frivolity of other people: an attention, and to an aim which makes their wants frivolous. This is a divine answer, and leaves no appeal, and no hard thoughts. In Flaxman's drawing of the Eumenides of Æschylus, Orestes supplicates Apollo, whilst the Furies sleep on the threshold.[7] The face of the god expresses a shade of regret and compassion, but calm with the conviction of the irreconcilableness of the two spheres. He is born into other politics, into the eternal and beautiful. The man at his feet asks for his interest in turmoils of the earth, into which his nature cannot enter. And the Eumenides there lying express pictorially this disparity. The god is surcharged with his divine destiny.

Illusion, Temperament, Succession, Surface, Surprise, Reality, Subjectiveness,—these are threads on the loom of time, these are the lords of life. I dare not assume to give their order, but I name them as I find them in my way. I know better than to claim any completeness for my picture. I am a fragment, and this is a fragment of me. I can very confidently announce one or another law, which throws itself into relief and form, but I am too young yet by some ages to compile a code. I gossip for my hour concerning the eternal politics. I have seen many fair pictures not in vain. A wonderful time I have lived in. I am not the novice I was fourteen, nor yet seven years ago. Let who will ask, where is the fruit? I find a private fruit sufficient. This is a fruit,—that I should not ask for a rash effect from meditations, counsels, and the hiving of truths. I should feel it pitiful to demand a result on this town and county, an overt effect on the instant month and year. The effect is deep and secular[8] as the cause. It works on periods in which mortal lifetime is lost. All

---

7. John Flaxman (1755–1826), English illustrator. In the clearer modern usage, the title of Aeschylus's play *The Eumenides* would be italicized; in the scene depicted by Flaxman, the Furies, or Eumenides, who have pursued Orestes since his murder of his adulterous mother, are temporarily lulled by the power of Apollo, who sanctioned the murder.
8. Lasting from century to century.

I know is reception; I am and I have: but I do not get, and when I have fancied I had gotten anything, I found I did not. I worship with wonder the great Fortune. My reception has been so large, that I am not annoyed by receiving this or that superabundantly. I say to the Genius, if he will pardon the proverb, *In for a mill, in for a million.* When I receive a new gift, I do not macerate my body to make the account square, for, if I should die, I could not make the account square. The benefit overran the merit the first day, and has over-ran the merit ever since. The merit itself, so-called, I reckon part of the receiving.

Also, that hankering after an overt or practical effect seems to me an apostasy. In good earnest, I am willing to spare this most unnecessary deal of doing. Life wears to me a visionary face. Hardest, roughest action is visionary also. It is but a choice between soft and turbulent dreams. People disparage knowing and the intellectual life, and urge doing. I am very content with knowing, if only I could know. That is an august entertainment, and would suffice me a great while. To know a little, would be worth the expense of this world. I hear always the law of Adrastia,[9] "that every soul which had acquired any truth, should be safe from harm until another period."

I know that the world I converse with in the city and in the farms, is not the world I *think.* I observe that difference, and shall observe it. One day, I shall know the value and law of this discrepance. But I have not found that much was gained by manipular attempts to realize the world of thought. Many eager persons successively make an experiment in this way, and make themselves ridiculous. They acquire democratic manners, they foam at the mouth, they hate and deny. Worse, I observe, that, in the history of mankind, there is never a solitary example of success,—taking their own tests of success. I say this polemically, or in reply to the inquiry, why not realize your world? But far be from me the despair which prejudges the law by a paltry empiricism,— since there never was a right endeavor, but it succeeded. Patience and patience, we shall win at the last. We must be very suspicious of the deceptions of the element of time. It takes a good deal of time to eat or to sleep, or to earn a hundred dollars, and a very little time to entertain a hope and an insight which becomes the light of our life. We dress our garden, eat our dinners, discuss the household with our wives, and these things make no impression, are forgotten next week; but in the solitude to which every man is always returning, he has a sanity and revelations, which in his passage into new worlds he will carry with him. Never mind the ridicule, never mind the defeat: up again, old heart!—it seems to say,—there is victory yet for all justice; and the true romance which the world exists to realize, will be the transformation of genius into practical power.

1844


## Each and All

Little thinks, in the field, yon red-cloaked clown,[1]
Of thee from the hill-top looking down;

9. Another name for Nemesis or Destiny. The quota-        1. Peasant.
tion is from the *Phaedrus* by Plato.

The heifer that lows in the upland farm,
Far-heard, lows not thine ear to charm;
The sexton, tolling his bell at noon,                    5
Deems not that great Napoleon
Stops his horse, and lists with delight,
Whilst his files sweep round yon Alpine height;
Nor knowest thou what argument
Thy life to thy neighbor's creed has lent.               10
All are needed by each one;
Nothing is fair or good alone.
I thought the sparrow's note from heaven,
Singing at dawn on the alder bough;
I brought him home, in his nest, at even;               15
He sings the song, but it cheers not now,
For I did not bring home the river and sky;—
He sang to my ear,—they sang to my eye.
The delicate shells lay on the shore;
The bubbles of the latest wave                         20
Fresh pearls to their enamel gave;
And the bellowing of the savage sea
Greeted their safe escape to me.
I wiped away the weeds and foam,
I fetched my sea-born treasures home;                  25
But the poor, unsightly, noisome things
Had left their beauty on the shore,
With the sun, and the sand, and the wild uproar.
The lover watched his graceful maid,
As 'mid the virgin train she strayed,                  30
Nor knew her beauty's best attire
Was woven still by the snow-white choir.
At last she came to his hermitage,
Like the bird from the woodlands to the cage;—
The gay enchantment was undone,                        35
A gentle wife, but fairy none.
Then I said, 'I covet truth;
Beauty is unripe childhood's cheat;
I leave it behind with the games of youth.'—
As I spoke, beneath my feet                            40
The ground-pine curled its pretty wreath,
Running over the club-moss burrs;
I inhaled the violet's breath;
Around me stood the oaks and firs;
Pine-cones and acorns lay on the ground,               45
Over me soared the eternal sky,
Full of light and of deity;
Again I saw, again I heard,
The rolling river, the morning bird;—
Beauty through my senses stole;                        50
I yielded myself to the perfect whole.

1847

# The Rhodora

## On Being Asked, Whence Is the Flower?

In May, when sea-winds pierced our solitudes,
I found the fresh Rhodora in the woods,
Spreading its leafless blooms in a damp nook,
To please the desert and the sluggish brook.
The purple petals, fallen in the pool,                            5
Made the black water with their beauty gay;
Here might the red-bird come his plumes to cool,
And court the flower that cheapens his array.
Rhodora! if the sages ask thee why
This charm is wasted on the earth and sky,              10
Tell them, dear, that if eyes were made for seeing,
Then Beauty is its own excuse for being:
Why thou wert there, O rival of the rose!
I never thought to ask, I never knew;
But, in my simple ignorance, suppose                        15
The self-same Power that brought me there brought you.

1847

# Ode, Inscribed to W. H. Channing[1]

Though loath to grieve
The evil time's sole patriot,
I cannot leave
My honied thought
For the priest's cant,                                                5
Or statesman's rant.

If I refuse
My study for their politique,
Which at the best is trick,
The angry Muse                                                       10
Puts confusion in my brain.

But who is he that prates
Of the culture of mankind,
Of better arts and life?
Go, blindworm, go,                                                 15
Behold the famous States
Harrying Mexico
With rifle and with knife!

Or who, with accent bolder,
Dare praise the freedom-loving mountaineer?        20

1. A young clergyman, nephew of the famous Unitarian minister William Ellery Channing; as the poem makes clear, he had urged Emerson to take an overt political role in resisting the war waged by the United States against Mexico.

I found by thee, O rushing Contoocook!
And in thy valleys, Agiochook![2]
The jackals of the negro-holder.

The God who made New Hampshire
Taunted the lofty land                                25
With little men;—
Small bat and wren
House in the oak:—
If earth-fire cleave
The upheaved land, and bury the folk,                 30
The southern crocodile would grieve.

Virtue palters; Right is hence;
Freedom praised, but hid;
Funeral eloquence
Rattles the coffin-lid.                                35

What boots thy zeal,
O glowing friend,
That would indignant rend
The northland from the south?
Wherefore? to what good end?                           40
Boston Bay and Bunker Hill[3]
Would serve things still;—
Things are of the snake.

The horseman serves the horse,
The neatherd serves the neat,[4]                       45
The merchant serves the purse,
The eater serves his meat;
'Tis the day of the chattel,
Web to weave, and corn to grind;
Things are in the saddle,                              50
And ride mankind.

There are two laws discrete,
Not reconciled,—
Law for man, and law for thing;
The last builds town and fleet,                        55
But it runs wild,
And doth the man unking.

'Tis fit the forest fall,
The steep be graded,
The mountain tunnelled,                                60

2. New Hampshire had gone Democratic, which meant in effect proslavery, reason enough for Emerson to taunt the debased inhabitants of that state with the majesty of their rivers like Contoocook and mountains like Agiochook.
3. Emerson does not spare his own state from accusa-

tion of materialism, whatever its heroic past memorialized in the Bunker Hill Monument. One manifestation of that materialism was a commercial alliance between the South, which grew cotton, and the North, which shipped and manufactured it.
4. The cowherd serves the cow.

The sand shaded,
The orchard planted,
The glebe[5] tilled,
The prairie granted,
The steamer built.                                              65

Let man serve law for man;
Live for friendship, live for love,
For truth's and harmony's behoof;
The state may follow how it can,
As Olympus follows Jove.[6]                                     70

   Yet do not I invite[7]
The wrinkled shopman to my sounding woods,
Nor bid the unwilling senator
Ask votes of thrushes in the solitudes.
Every one to his chosen work;—                                  75
Foolish hands may mix and mar;
Wise and sure the issues are.
Round they roll till dark is light,
Sex to sex, and even to odd;—
The over-god                                                    80
Who marries Right to Might,
Who peoples, unpeoples,—
He who exterminates
Races by stronger races,
Black by white faces,—                                          85
Knows to bring honey
Out of the lion;[8]
Grafts gentlest scion
On pirate and Turk.

The Cossack eats Poland,[9]                                     90
Like stolen fruit,
Her last noble is ruined,
Her last poet mute:
Straight, into double band
The victors divide;                                             95
Half for freedom strike and stand;—
The astonished Muse finds thousands at her side.

1847

---

5. Soil.
6. As minor gods follow the supreme god.
7. Later texts read "implore."
8. A reference to the riddle (Judges 14) that Samson
propounded after finding the carcass of a lion in which
bees had made honey: "Out of the eater came forth
meat, and out of the strong came forth sweetness."
9. Poland had been partitioned three times in the late
18th century, with Russia (the Cossack) getting the
lion's share.

# FROM JOURNALS AND LETTERS[1]

## [Sadness after Thirty]

August 1, 1835 [Concord]

After thirty a man wakes up sad every morning excepting perhaps five or six until the day of his death.

## [Protest; Writing; America]

June 18, 1838 [Concord]

C[aroline]. S[turgis].[2] protests. That is a good deal. In these times you shall find a small number of persons of whom only that can be affirmed that they protest. Yet is it as divine to say no, as to say yes. You say they go too much alone. Yea, but they shun society to the end of finding society. They repudiate the false out of love of the true. Extravagance is a good token. In an Extravagance, there is hope; in Routine, none.

\* \* \*

The art of writing consists in putting two things together that are unlike and that belong together like a horse & cart. Then have we somewhat far more goodly & efficient than either.

\* \* \*

Ah my country! In thee is the reasonable hope of mankind not fulfilled. It should be that when all feudal straps & bandages were taken off an unfolding of the Titans[3] had followed & they had laughed & leaped young giants along the continent & ran up the mountains of the West with the errand of Genius & of love. But the utmost thou hast yet produced, is a puny love of beauty in Allston, in Greenough; in Bryant; in Everett; in Channing; in Irving; an imitative love of grace.[4] A vase of fair outline but empty, which whoso seeth may fill with what wit & character is in him but which does not like the charged cloud overflow with terrible beauty & emit lightnings on all beholders. Ah me! the cause is one; the diffidence of Ages in the Soul has crept over thee too, America. No man here believeth in the soul of man but only in some name

1. Emerson's journals and notebooks have been newly edited by several scholars, led by the late William H. Gilman and published meticulously by Harvard University Press as The Journals and Miscellaneous Notebooks of Ralph Waldo Emerson. Because the Harvard edition does not print "clear text" but shows Emerson's revisions, some of the quotations here have been simplified to show only the final readings. The six-volume edition of The Letters of Ralph Waldo Emerson excludes most letters previously published in one collection or another, so the letters printed here are drawn from various sources indicated in the footnotes. Passages from the journals and letters are printed chronologically, but because Emerson sometimes failed to date journal entries the date given may be merely the first one that occurs before the entry. Annotations are light, because the selections are meant to be suggestive of the diverse contents of the journals and letters, not comprehensive.
2. From Boston, who had been visiting the Emersons; later she was a contributor to the Dial under Emer-

son's editorship.
3. The gigantic pre-Olympian gods of Greek mythology; in revolt against their father, Uranus, they stormed heaven.
4. I.e., instead of an American artistic flourishing comparable to the revolt of the Titans there occurred only a puny stirring. Here Emerson catalogs the best the country had yet produced in the arts. The South Carolina painter Washington Allston (1779–1843) had an enormously inflated reputation in his adopted Boston. Horatio Greenough (1805–1852) was both a sculptor and an aesthetician who made important comments on architecture. William Cullen Bryant (1794–1878) was revered as our best serious poet. Edward Everett (1794–1865) was a clergyman famous for his oratory. William Ellery Channing (1780–1842) was the leading Unitarian clergyman of Boston and a major influence on Emerson during Emerson's young manhood. Washington Irving (1783–1859) had no rival as the best-loved American fiction writer, despite the popularity of James Fenimore Cooper.

or person old & departed. Ah me! No man goeth alone[,] all men go in flocks
to this saint or that poet avoiding the God who seeth in secret. They cannot
see in secret. They love to be blind in public. They think society wiser than
their soul, & know not that one soul, & their soul is wiser than the whole
world. See how nations & races flit by on the sea of time & leave no ripple to
tell where they floated or sunk, & one good soul shall make the name of Moses
or of Zeno or Zoroaster[5] reverend forever. None assayeth the austere ambition
to be the Man, the Self of the nation & of nature, but each would be an easy
Secondary to some English Literature or Christian Scheme or American government.

### [Aftermath of the Divinity School Address]

August 31, 1838 [Concord]

Yesterday at φ B.K.[6] anniversary. Steady, steady. I am convinced that if a
man will be a true scholar, he shall have perfect freedom. The young people
& the mature hint at odium, & aversion of faces to be presently encountered
in society. I say no: I fear it not. No scholar need fear it. For if it be true that
he is merely an observer, a dispassionate reporter, no partisan, a singer merely
for the love of music, his is a position of perfect immunity: to him no disgusts
can attach; he is invulnerable. The vulgar[7] think he would found a sect &
would be installed & made much of. He knows better & much prefers his
melons & his woods. Society has no bribe for me, neither in politics, nor
church, nor college, nor city. My resources are far from exhausted. If they
will not hear me lecture, I shall have leisure for my book which wants me.
Beside[,] it is an universal maxim worthy of all acceptation that a man may
have that allowance which he takes. Take the place & attitude to which you
see your unquestionable right, & all men acquiesce. Who are these murmur-
ers, these haters, these revilers? Men of no knowledge, & therefore no stability.
The scholar on the contrary is sure of his point, is fast-rooted, & can securely
predict the hour when all this roaring multitude shall roar for him.

Analyze the chiding opposition & it is made up of such timidities, uncertainties, & no opinions, that it is not worth dispersing.

## To Thomas Carlyle

### [Delayed Reactions to the Divinity School Address]

[Concord, October 17, 1838]

* * * In a letter within a twelvemonth I have urged you to pay us a visit in
America, & in Concord. I have believed that you would come, one day, & do
believe it. But if, on your part, you have been generous & affectionate enough
to your friends here—or curious enough concerning our society to wish to

---

5. Zoroaster (6th century B.C.), a Persian prophet,
founded Zoroastrianism, a major tenet of which is that
forces of light and darkness are engaged in a universal
struggle. Moses was the lawgiver who led the Israelities
out of Egypt toward Israel, as described in Exodus.
Zeno (342?–270? B.C.), a Greek philosopher, was the
founder of Stoicism.
6. Phi Beta Kappa. Emerson had delivered his oration

The American Scholar at the previous celebration, but
on the 1838 anniversary he was merely in the audience. The warnings of ostracism that he heard on
August 30, 1838, had to do with the growing hostility
toward the address he had made on July 15, 1838, to
the senior class of the Divinity School.
7. The masses; ordinary, insensitive people.

come, I think you must postpone, for the present, the satisfaction of your friendship & your curiosity. At this moment, I would not have you here, on any account. The publication of my "Address to the Divinity College," (copies of which I sent you) has been the occasion of an outcry in all our leading local newspapers against my "infidelity," "pantheism," & "atheism." The writers warn all & sundry against me, & against whatever is supposed to be related to my connexion of opinion, &c; against Transcendentalism, Goethe & Carlyle. I am heartily sorry to see this last aspect of the storm in our washbowl.[8] For, as Carlyle is nowise guilty, & has unpopularities of his own, I do not wish to embroil him in my parish-differences. You were getting to be a great favorite with us all here, and are daily a greater, with the American public, but just now, *in Boston*, where I am known as your editor, I fear you lose by the association. Now it is indispensable to your right influence here, that you should never come before our people as one of a clique, but as a detached, that is, universally associated man; so I am happy, as I could not have thought, that you have not yet yielded yourself to my entreaties. Let us wait a little until this foolish clam[or] be overblown. My position is fortunately such as to put me quite out of the reach of any real inconvenience from the panic strikers or the panic struck; &, indeed, so far as this uneasiness is a necessary result of mere inaction of mind, it seems very clear to me that, if I live, my neighbors must look for a great many more shocks, & perhaps harder to bear. * * *

## From Journals

### [Challenging Thoreau to Write His Opinions into Good Poetry]

November 10, 1838 [Concord]

My brave Henry Thoreau walked with me to Walden this P.M. and complained of the proprietors who compelled him to whom as much as to any the whole world belonged, to walk in a strip of road & crowded him out of all the rest of God's earth. He must not get over the fence: but to the building of that fence he was no party. Suppose, he said, some great proprietor, before he was born, had bought up the whole globe. So had he been hustled out of nature. Not having been privy to any of these arrangements he does not feel called on to consent to them & so cuts fishpoles in the woods without asking who has a better title to the wood than he. I defended of course the good Institution as a scheme not good but the best that could be hit on for making the woods & waters & fields available to Wit & Worth, & for restraining the bold bad man. At all events, I begged him, having this maggot of Freedom & Humanity in his brain, to write it out into good poetry & so clear himself of it. He replied, that he feared that that was not the best way; that in doing justice to the thought, the man did not always do justice to himself: the poem ought to sing itself: if the man took too much pains with the expression he was not any longer the Idea himself. I acceded & confessed that this was the tragedy of Art that the Artist was at the expense of the Man; & hence, in the first age, as they tell, the Sons of God printed no epics, carved no stone, painted no picture,

8. The intense, though sporadic and local, hostility resulting from his address to the Harvard Divinity School (see n. 6, p. 544).

built no railroad; for the sculpture, the poetry, the music, & architecture, were in the Man. And truly Bolts & Bars do not seem to me the most exalted or exalting of our institutions. And what other spirit reigns in our intellectual works? We have literary property. The very recording of a thought betrays a distrust that there is any more or much more as good for us. If we felt that the Universe was ours[,] that we dwelled in eternity & advance into all wisdom we should be less covetous of these sparks & cinders. Why should we covetously build a St Peter's, if we had the seeing Eye which beheld all the radiance of beauty & majesty in the matted grass & the overarching boughs? Why should a man spend years upon the carving an Apollo who looked Apollos into the landscape with every glance he threw?

## To William Emerson[9]

### [What to Expect from Thoreau]

Concord, 6 May, 1843

Dear William,

I received yesterday your letter with its enclosure $47.06 which comes in good time. Yet our Concord rapacity is greater than one would look for in a quiet town, & we spend faster than the utmost generosity of cities can keep up with. I have advanced Henry Thoreau $10.00 more, since I wrote before, & this sum having been expanded in outfit, I paid him last night $7.00 for travelling expenses, so that I charge you with 17.—And now goes our brave youth into the new house, the new connexion, the new City. I am sure no truer & no purer person lives in wide New York; and he is a bold & a profound thinker though he may easily chance to pester you with some accidental crotchets and perhaps a village exaggeration of the value of facts. Yet I confide, if you should content each other, in Willie's soon coming to value him for his real power to serve & instruct him. I shall eagerly look, though not yet for some time, for tidings how you speed in this new relation. * * *

Affectionately your brother
Waldo

## To Walter Whitman

### [The Wonderful Gift of Leaves of Grass]

July 21, 1855, Concord

* * * I am not blind to the worth of the wonderful gift of "Leaves of Grass." I find it the most extraordinary piece of wit and wisdom that America has yet contributed. I am very happy in reading it, as great power makes us happy. It meets the demand I am always making of what seemed the sterile & stingy nature, as if too much handiwork or too much lymph[1] in the temperament, were making our western wits fat & mean. I give you joy of your free & brave thought. I have great joy in it. I find incomparable things said incomparably

---

9. Emerson's brother, the father of the "Willie" mentioned in the letter whom Thoreau was to tutor.

1. Here, a sluggish or phlegmatic substance.

well, as they must be. I find the courage of treatment, which so delights me, and which large perception only can inspire. I greet you at the beginning of a great career, which yet must have had a long foreground somewhere, for such a start. I rubbed my eyes a little to see if this sunbeam were no illusion; but the solid sense of the book is a sober certainty. It has the best of merits, namely, of fortifying & encouraging.

I did not know until I, last night, saw the book advertised in a newspaper, that I could trust the name as real & available for a post-office. I wish to see my benefactor, & have felt much like striking my tasks, & visiting New York to pay you my respects. * * *

---

# NATHANIEL HAWTHORNE
## 1804–1864

Nathaniel Hawthorne was born on Independence Day, 1804, in Salem, Massachusetts, a descendant of Puritan immigrants; one ancestor had been a judge in the Salem witchcraft trials. The family, like the seaport town, was on the decline. When his sea-captain father died in Dutch Guiana in 1808, his mother's brothers took responsibility for his education. In his early teens he lived three years as free as "a bird of the air" at Sebago Lake, in Maine (then still a part of Massachusetts), acquiring a love of tramping, which he always kept. By his mid-teens he was reading eighteenth-century novelists like Henry Fielding, Tobias Smollett, and Horace Walpole as well as contemporary writers like William Godwin and Sir Walter Scott and forming an ambition to be a writer himself. At Bowdoin College shyness caused him to try to evade the obligatory public declamations, but in social clubs he formed smoking, card-playing, and drinking friendships; two fellow members of the Democratic literary society, Horatio Bridge and Franklin Pierce, later president, became lifelong friends; Longfellow, another classmate, belonged to the rival Federalist society. Hawthorne kept outdoors a good deal as the bucolic college but managed, as he later said, to read "desultorily right and left." At the graduation ceremonies in 1825, Longfellow spoke optimistically on the possibility that "Our Native Writers" could achieve lasting fame. Hawthorne went home to Salem and became a writer, but he was agonizingly slow in winning acclaim.

Hawthorne's years between 1825 and 1837 have fascinated his biographers and critics. Hawthorne himself took pains to propagate the notion that he had lived as a hermit who left his upstairs room only for nighttime walks and hardly communicated even with his mother and sisters. Twentieth-century scholars have shown that although in fact Hawthorne was intensely committed to his writing and was steeping himself in colonial history more than the political issues of his time, he socialized in Salem, had several more or less serious flirtations, kept in touch with Pierce and Bridge, among others, and spent most of the summers knocking about all over New England (an uncle owned stage lines). He even got as far as Detroit one year. Often called his apprenticeship, these dozen years in fact encompassed as well his period of finest creativity. The first surviving piece of his true apprenticework is the historical novel *Fanshawe*, which Hawthorne paid to have published in 1828 and then quickly suppressed.

Over the next several years Hawthorne tried unsuccessfully to find a publisher for collections of the tales he was writing. In chagrin he burned *Seven Tales of My Native Land* (including one or two stories of witchcraft) although at least one of the seven, *Alice Doane's Appeal*, survives in an altered form. By 1829 he was negotiating—again fruitlessly—for the publication of a volume called *Provincial Tales*, which included *The Gentle Boy* as well, apparently, as *Roger Malvin's Burial* and *My Kinsman, Major Molineux*. In tales like these he had found his special—though highly unsatisfactory—outlets for publication: magazines and the literary annuals that were issued each fall as genteel Christmas gifts. For his tales Hawthorne got a few dollars each and no fame at all, since publication in the annuals was anonymous. He continued to strive to interest a bookseller in his tales, offering what could have been a remarkable volume called *The Story Teller*, in which the title character wandered about New England telling his stories in dramatic settings and circumstances. One story, *Mr. Higginbotham's Catastrophe*, reached print in its narrative frame, but the editor of the *New-England Magazine* scrapped the frame for *Young Goodman Brown* and others that are now known as isolated items instead of interrelated elements in a larger whole. The biographer Randall Stewart plausibly suggests that "*The Story Teller* would have united in one work Hawthorne's imaginative and reportorial faculties as none of his published writings quite do." In 1836 Hawthorne turned to literary hackwork, making an encyclopedia for the Boston publisher Samuel G. Goodrich, whose annual, *The Token*, had become the regular market for his tales. In the same year Bridge secretly persuaded Goodrich to publish a collection of Hawthorne's tales by promising to repay any losses. *Twice-Told Tales* appeared in March 1837, with Hawthorne's name on the title page; the title was a self-deprecating allusion to Shakespeare's *King John* 3.4: "Life is as tedious as a twice-told tale / Vexing the dull eare of a drowsie man." The book was reviewed in England as well as the United States, and opened up what Hawthorne called "an intercourse with the world." A notebook entry written sometime in 1836 was only a little premature: "In this dismal and sordid chamber FAME was won."

Throughout the early stories, both those collected in *Twice-Told Tales* and those he left for later gleaning, Hawthorne mused obsessively over a small range of psychological themes: the consequences of pride, selfishness, and secret guilt; the conflict between lighthearted and somber attitudes toward life; the difficulty of preventing isolation from leading to coldness of heart; the impingement of the past (especially the Puritan past) on the present; the futility of comprehensive social reforms; and the impossibility of eradicating sin from the human heart. Above all, his theme was curiosity about the recesses of other men's and women's beings. About this theme he was always ambivalent, for he knew that his success as a writer depended on his keen psychological analysis of people he met, while he could never forget that invasion of the sanctity of another's personality may harden the heart even as it enriches the mind. He knew that there was "something of the hawk-eye" about him and that the line was vague between prurient curiosity and legitimate artistic study of character. At his best, he was a master of psychological insight, and some of his power of psychological burrowing remained with him throughout his career, even in the romances that were left unfinished at his death.

The year 1837 was the start of Hawthorne's public literary career; it also marked the end of his single-minded dedication to his work. In the fall of 1838 Elizabeth Peabody, a Salemite who was to become a major force in American educational reform, sought out the new local celebrity. When Hawthorne met her sister Sophia, twenty-nine and an invalid, his life abruptly changed course. Within a few months he and Sophia were engaged. To save money for marriage, Hawthorne worked as salt and coal measurer in the Boston Custom House during 1839 and 1840, then the next year invested in the utopian community Brook Farm, more as a business venture than as a philosophical gesture; the only return, however, was the locale he later used for *The Blithedale Romance* (1852). During his engagement, Hawthorne's main literary productions were letters to Sophia—full of ironical self-deprecation, satirical reportage, and romantic effusions. In December 1841, he wrote Evert A. Duyckinck and Cornelius Mathews, New York magazine editors, that his early stories had grown out of quietude and seclusion, the lack of which would probably prevent him from writing any more. Marriage, not literature, became Hawthorne's new career long before the actual ceremony in July 1842. As he rather severely put it, "when a man has taken upon himself to beget children, he has no longer any right to a life of his own."

The first three years of marriage, spent at the Old Manse in Concord, the home of Emerson's ancestors, seemed idyllic to the Hawthornes, but a hoped-for novel never materialized. By now comfortably familiar with accounts of the Puritan and Revolutionary past, he wrote a child's history of colonial and revolutionary New England, *Grandfather's Chair* (1841), and four years later produced a rewriting of Bridge's *Journal of an African Cruiser*. *Mosses from an Old Manse* (1846) consisted mainly of new tales, but among the early ones first collected in it were *Roger Malvin's Burial* and *Young Goodman Brown*. His literary earnings were not rising, but his reputation was, partly through his own shrewd creation of a public persona. Knowing that certain readers who delight in realism would be disturbed by the shadowiness of some of his stories, he anticipated the worst that could be said, declaring in the whimsical survey of his career in the headnote to *Rappaccini's Daughter* that "M. de l'Aubépine" (French for "Hawthorne") had "an inveterate love of allegory, which is apt to invest his plots and characters with the aspect of scenery and people in the clouds, and to steal away the human warmth out of his conceptions." Any hostility, of course, was disarmed by such self-criticism, and in the introductory essay for *Mosses from an Old Manse* Hawthorne pursued his strategy of evoking for himself an equivalent of the Miltonic fit audience though few, yet enlarging that audience without letting his readers feel they were part of a mob. Hawthorne insisted winningly both on his ultimate reserve—his refusal to "serve up" his own heart delicately fried—and on his eagerness to communicate with his chosen audience. Even after he attained a large readership, he knew the value of trading on his own early obscurity so as to make a reader feel like a special discoverer of a rarity yet unshared by the many. In the 1851 edition of *Twice-Told Tales*, Hawthorne observed that the author, "on the internal evidence of his sketches, came to be regarded as a mild, shy, gentle, melancholic, exceedingly sensitive, and not very forcible man, hiding his blushes under an assumed name, the quaintness of which was supposed, somehow or other, to symbolize his personal and literary traits." While summarizing the image critics had conceived of him, he helped fix that image for a century and more as *the* Hawthorne.

Through long service to the local Democrats, Hawthorne was named Surveyor of the Port of Salem in 1846. The office was something of a sinecure, but his forenoons—always his most productive hours—had to be spent at the Custom House, and he wrote little. Hawthorne was thrown out of office by the new Whig administration in June 1849, amid a furious controversy in the newspapers. He then spent a summer of "great diversity and severity" of emotion climaxed by his mother's death. In September he was at work on *The Scarlet Letter*, which he planned as a long tale to make up half a volume called *Old Time Legends; together with Sketches, Experimental and Ideal*. Besides the long introduction, *The Custom House*, which was Hawthorne's means of revenging himself on the Salem Whigs who had ousted him, he planned to include some still-uncollected tales. James Fields, the young associate of the publisher William D. Ticknor, persuaded him that a long piece of fiction would sell better than another collection of stories, and Hawthorne obligingly omitted the stories. (Fields was the source of a false story that he also persuaded Hawthorne to expand *The Scarlet Letter* from a story to a novel.) Although it was frequently denounced as licentious or morbid, *The Scarlet Letter* (1850) was nevertheless a literary sensation in the United States and Great Britain, and Hawthorne was proclaimed as the finest American romancer. There had already been many novels set in Puritan New England, and many more followed, but *The Scarlet Letter* remains the single classic of the group, appealing to tastes of changing generations in different ways; perhaps the most powerful appeal has not changed at all: the remarkable way Hawthorne manages to evoke emotional sympathy for the heroine even when he is condemning her actions.

During a year and a half in the Berkshires of western Massachusetts, where Melville became his "not-too-distant neighbor," Hawthorne wrote *The House of the Seven Gables* (1851), assembled *The Snow Image*, mainly from very early pieces, and wrote for children *A Wonder-Book* (1852). Escaping from the rigors of the Berkshire winters, he wrote *The Blithedale Romance* (1852) in West Newton; then in the first home he had owned, the Wayside at Concord, he put together a political biography of his friend Franklin Pierce for the campaign of 1852 and worked up *The Tanglewood Tales* (1853), prettified stories from mythology. This productivity was broken when President Pierce appointed him American consul at Liverpool. The consulship came as a blessing despite the disruption of his new life at Concord, for his literary income was not enough to support his family, which now included a son and two daughters.

At Liverpool (1853–57) Hawthorne was an uncommonly industrious consul; he had always been more comfortable among businesspeople and politicians than among literary people. Tireless in sightseeing among ancient inns, castles, and other public buildings, he also set himself a rigorous course of gallery going and elaborately recorded his observations in his notebooks. Exposed to great museums for the first time, Hawthorne surprised himself with his affinity for the seventeenth-century Dutch masters of genre painting, deciding that those painters "accomplish all they aim at,—a praise, methinks, which can be given to no other men since the world began." He forced himself—fortified with liquor—to make the required public speeches, and late in his consulship let himself be lionized during an extended trip to London. A stay in Italy—starting in the miserably cold first months of 1858—ate deeply into the more than $30,000 he had earned at Liverpool, and malaria nearly killed his daughter Una. Except during her illness, he kept up his minutely detailed tourist's account as well as a record of the family's contacts with the English and American colony of painters, sculptors, and writers. Many pages of the notebooks went nearly verbatim into a book that he began in Florence in 1858 and finished late in 1859, after his return to England. This romance, suggested by the statue of a faun attributed to the classical Greek sculptor Praxiteles, was published in London (1860) as *Transformation* and in the United States under Hawthorne's preferred title, *The Marble Faun*.

The Hawthornes came home in June 1860, during the general acclaim of the new romance, and set about fitting up the Wayside; this project was a considerable drain on Hawthorne's savings, which were already depleted by prolonged residence abroad after resigning his consulship and by generous, though unwise, loans to friends. His literary stature made even his abolitionist neighbors respectful toward him, but Hawthorne was keenly aware that his sympathy for the South ran counter to the mood of neighbors such as Emerson and Thoreau. For the *Atlantic Monthly* Fields solicited a series of sketches that Hawthorne adapted from his English notebooks. Fields paid well, but he was pressing Hawthorne into overwork. Despite short excursions designed to restore his vigor, Hawthorne's physical and psychic energies waned steadily. Humiliated by his weakness, he intermittently forced himself to work on his literary projects, especially the English sketches, which he published as *Our Old Home* (1863), loyally dedicating it to Pierce, who because of his Southern sympathies was now anathema to many Northerners. Hawthorne began four romances, overlapping attempts to grapple with two major themes: an American claimant to an ancestral English estate and the search for an elixir of life. He finished none of them before his death in May 1864, while traveling in New Hampshire with Pierce. He was buried in the Sleepy Hollow Cemetery at Concord. Alcott, Emerson, Fields, Holmes, Longfellow, and Lowell were among his pallbearers.

# My Kinsman, Major Molineux[1]

After the kings of Great Britain had assumed the right of appointing the colonial governors,[2] the measures of the latter seldom met with the ready and general approbation, which had been paid to those of their predecessors, under the original charters. The people looked with most jealous scrutiny to the exercise of power, which did not emanate from themselves, and they usually rewarded the rulers with slender gratitude, for the compliances, by which, in softening their instructions from beyond the sea, they had incurred the reprehension of those who gave them. The annals of Massachusetts Bay will inform us, that of six governors, in the space of about forty years from the surrender of the old charter, under James II., two were imprisoned by a popular insurrection; a third, as Hutchinson[3] inclines to believe, was driven from the province by the whizzing of a musket ball; a fourth, in the opinion of the same historian, was hastened to his grave by continual bickerings with the house of representatives; and the remaining two, as well as their successors, till the Revolution, were favored with few and brief intervals of peaceful sway. The inferior members of the court party,[4] in times of high political excitement, led scarcely a more desirable life. These remarks may serve as preface to the following adventures, which chanced upon a summer night, not far from a hundred years ago. The reader, in order to avoid a long and dry detail of colonial affairs, is requested to dispense with an account of the train of circumstances, that had caused much temporary inflammation of the popular mind.

It was near nine o'clock of a moonlight evening, when a boat crossed the ferry with a single passenger, who had obtained his conveyance, at that unusual hour, by the promise of an extra fare. While he stood on the landing-place, searching in either pocket for the means of fulfilling his agreement, the ferryman lifted a lantern, by the aid of which, and the newly risen moon, he took a very accurate survey of the stranger's figure. He was a youth of barely eighteen years, evidently country-bred, and now, as it should seem, upon his first visit to town. He was clad in a coarse grey coat, well worn, but in excellent repair; his under garments were durably constructed of leather, and sat tight to a pair of serviceable and well-shaped limbs; his stockings of blue yarn, were the incontrovertible handiwork of a mother or a sister; and on his head was a three-cornered hat, which in its better days had perhaps sheltered the graver brow of the lad's father. Under his left arm was a heavy cudgel, formed of an oak sapling, and retaining a part of the hardened root; and his equipment was completed by a wallet,[5] not so abundantly stocked as to incommode the vigorous shoulders on which it hung. Brown, curly hair, well-shaped features, and bright, cheerful eyes, were nature's gifts, and worth all that art could have done for his adornment.

The youth, one of whose names was Robin, finally drew from his pocket the half of a little province-bill[6] of five shillings, which, in the depreciation of

1. The text here is that of the first printing in *The Token* for 1832, where the story is identified as being "By the Author of 'Sights from a Steeple.' "
2. I.e., after 1684, when the British government annulled the Massachusetts charter.
3. Thomas Hutchinson (1711–1780), the last royal governor. The particular annals, or year-by-year histories, that Hawthorne has in mind are *The History of the Colony and Province of Massachusetts-Bay* (1764, 1767) by Hutchinson. James II (1633–1701) reigned briefly (1685–88) before being exiled to France in the Glorious Revolution.
4. The pro-Crown party.
5. Knapsack.
6. Local paper money.

that sort of currency, did but satisfy the ferryman's demand, with the surplus of a sexangular piece of parchment valued at three pence. He then walked forward into the town, with as light a step, as if his day's journey had not already exceeded thirty miles, and with as eager an eye, as if he were entering London city, instead of the little metropolis of a New England colony. Before Robin had proceeded far, however, it occurred to him, that he knew not whither to direct his steps; so he paused, and looked up and down the narrow street, scrutinizing the small and mean wooden buildings, that were scattered on either side.

'This low hovel cannot be my kinsman's dwelling,' thought he, 'nor yonder old house, where the moonlight enters at the broken casement; and truly I see none hereabouts that might be worthy of him. It would have been wise to inquire my way of the ferryman, and doubtless he would have gone with me, and earned a shilling from the Major for his pains. But the next man I meet will do as well.'

He resumed his walk, and was glad to perceive that the street now became wider, and the houses more respectable in their appearance. He soon discerned a figure moving on moderately in advance, and hastened his steps to overtake it. As Robin drew nigh, he saw that the passenger was a man in years, with a full periwig of grey hair, a wide-skirted coat of dark cloth, and silk stockings rolled about his knees. He carried a long and polished cane, which he struck down perpendicularly before him, at every step; and at regular intervals he uttered two successive hems, of a peculiarly solemn and sepulchral intonation. Having made these observations, Robin laid hold of the skirt of the old man's coat, just when the light from the open door and windows of a barber's shop, fell upon both their figures.

'Good evening to you, honored Sir,' said he, making a low bow, and still retaining his hold of the skirt. 'I pray you to tell me whereabouts is the dwelling of my kinsman, Major Molineux?'

The youth's question was uttered very loudly; and one of the barbers, whose razor was descending on a well-soaped chin, and another who was dressing a Ramillies wig,[7] left their occupations, and came to the door. The citizen, in the meantime, turned a long favored countenance upon Robin, and answered him in a tone of excessive anger and annoyance. His two sepulchral hems, however, broke into the very centre of his rebuke, with most singular effect, like a thought of the cold grave obtruding among wrathful passions.

'Let go my garment, fellow! I tell you. I know not the man you speak of. What! I have authority, I have—hem, hem—authority; and if this be the respect you show your betters, your feet shall be brought acquainted with the stocks,[8] by daylight, tomorrow morning!'

Robin released the old man's skirt, and hastened away, pursued by an ill-mannered roar of laughter from the barber's shop. He was at first considerably surprised by the result of his question, but, being a shrewd youth, soon thought himself able to account for the mystery.

'This is some country representative,' was his conclusion, 'who has never seen the inside of my kinsman's door, and lacks the breeding to answer a stranger civilly. The man is old, or verily—I might be tempted to turn back

7. Elaborately plaited wig named for Ramillies, Belgium.
8. Instrument of punishment having a heavy wooden frame with holes for confining the ankles and sometimes the wrists as well.

and smite him on the nose. Ah, Robin, Robin! even the barber's boys laugh at you, for choosing such a guide! You will be wiser in time, friend Robin.'

He now became entangled in a succession of crooked and narrow streets, which crossed each other, and meandered at no great distance from the waterside. The smell of tar was obvious to his nostrils, the masts of vessels pierced the moonlight above the tops of the buildings, and the numerous signs, which Robin paused to read, informed him that he was near the centre of business. But the streets were empty, the shops were closed, and lights were visible only in the second stories of a few dwelling-houses. At length, on the corner of a narrow lane, through which he was passing, he beheld the broad countenance of a British hero swinging before the door of an inn, whence proceeded the voices of many guests. The casement of one of the lower windows was thrown back, and a very thin curtain permitted Robin to distinguish a party at supper, round a well-furnished table. The fragrance of good cheer steamed forth into the outer air, and the youth could not fail to recollect, that the last remnant of his travelling stock of provision had yielded to his morning appetite, and that noon had found, and left him, dinnerless.

'Oh, that a parchment three-penny might give me a right to sit down at yonder table,' said Robin, with a sigh. 'But the Major will make me welcome to the best of his victuals; so I will even step boldly in, and inquire my way to his dwelling.'

He entered the tavern, and was guided by the murmur of voices, and fumes of tobacco, to the public room. It was a long and low apartment, with oaken walls, grown dark in the continual smoke, and a floor, which was thickly sanded, but of no immaculate purity. A number of persons, the larger part of whom appeared to be mariners, or in some way connected with the sea, occupied the wooden benches, or leather-bottomed chairs, conversing on various matters, and occasionally lending their attention to some topic of general interest. Three or four little groups were draining as many bowls of punch, which the great West India trade had long since made a familiar drink in the colony. Others, who had the aspect of men who lived by regular and laborious handicraft, preferred the insulated bliss of an unshared potation, and became more taciturn under its influence. Nearly all, in short, evinced a predilection for the Good Creature in some of its various shapes, for this is a vice, to which, as the Fast-day[9] sermons of a hundred years ago will testify, we have a long hereditary claim. The only guests to whom Robin's sympathies inclined him, were two or three sheepish countrymen, who were using the inn somewhat after the fashion of a Turkish Caravansary;[1] they had gotten themselves into the darkest corner of the room, and, heedless of the Nicotian[2] atmosphere, were supping on the bread of their own ovens, and the bacon cured in their own chimney-smoke. But though Robin felt a sort of brotherhood with these strangers, his eyes were attracted from them, to a person who stood near the door, holding whispered conversation with a group of ill-dressed associates. His features were separately striking almost to grotesqueness, and the whole face left a deep impression in the memory. The forehead bulged out into a double prominence, with a vale between; the nose came boldly forth in an irregular curve,

9. Days set apart for public penitence. "Good Creature": rum; Hawthorne is playing on the warning against food fanatics in 1 Timothy 4.4: "For every creature of God is good, and nothing to be refused, if it be received with thanksgiving."

1 An inn built around a court for accommodating caravans.
2. Heavy with tobacco fumes (from Jean Nicot, who introduced tobacco into France when he was French ambassador at Lisbon).

and its bridge was of more than a finger's breadth; the eyebrows were deep and shaggy, and the eyes glowed beneath them like fire in a cave.

While Robin deliberated of whom to inquire respecting his kinsman's dwelling, he was accosted by the innkeeper, a little man in a stained white apron, who had come to pay his professional welcome to the stranger. Being in the second generation from a French protestant, he seemed to have inherited the courtesy of his parent nation; but no variety of circumstance was ever known to change his voice from the one shrill note in which he now addressed Robin.

'From the country, I presume, Sir?' said he, with a profound bow. 'Beg to congratulate you on your arrival, and trust you intend a long stay with us. Fine town here, Sir, beautiful buildings, and much that may interest a stranger. May I hope for the honor of your commands in respect to supper?'

'The man sees a family likeness! the rogue has guessed that I am related to the Major!' thought Robin, who had hitherto experienced little superfluous civility.

All eyes were now turned on the country lad, standing at the door, in his worn three-cornered hat, grey coat, leather breeches, and blue yarn stockings, leaning on an oaken cudgel, and bearing a wallet on his back. Robin replied to the courteous innkeeper, with such an assumption of consequence, as befitted the Major's relative.

'My honest friend,' he said, 'I shall make it a point to patronise your house on some occasion, when—' here he could not help lowering his voice—'I may have more than a parchment three-pence in my pocket. My present business,' continued he, speaking with lofty confidence, 'is merely to inquire the way to the dwelling of my kinsman, Major Molineux.'

There was a sudden and general movement in the room, which Robin interpreted as expressing the eagerness of each individual to become his guide. But the innkeeper turned his eyes to a written paper on the wall, which he read, or seemed to read, with occasional recurrences to the young man's figure.

'What have we here?' said he, breaking his speech into little dry fragments, "Left the house of the subscriber, bounden servant,[3] Hezekiah Mudge—had on when he went away, grey coat, leather breeches, master's third best hat. One pound currency reward to whoever shall lodge him in any jail in the province." 'Better trudge, boy, better trudge.'

Robin had begun to draw his hand towards the lighter end of the oak cudgel, but a strange hostility in every countenance, induced him to relinquish his purpose of breaking the courteous innkeeper's head. As he turned to leave the room, he encountered a sneering glance from the bold-featured personage whom he had before noticed; and no sooner was he beyond the door, than he heard a general laugh, in which the innkeeper's voice might be distinguished, like the dropping of small stones in a kettle.

'Now is it not strange,' thought Robin, with his usual shrewdness, 'is it not strange, that the confession of an empty pocket, should outweigh the name of my kinsman, Major Molineux? Oh, if I had one of these grinning rascals in the woods, where I and my oak sapling grew up together, I would teach him that my arm is heavy, though my purse be light!'

On turning the corner of the narrow lane, Robin found himself in a spa-

---

3. A person bound by contract to servitude for seven years (or another set period), usually in repayment for transportation to the colonies.

cious street, with an unbroken line of lofty houses on each side, and a steepled building at the upper end, whence the ringing of a bell announced the hour of nine. The light of the moon, and the lamps from numerous shop windows, discovered people promenading on the pavement, and amongst them, Robin hoped to recognise his hitherto inscrutable relative. The result of his former inquiries made him unwilling to hazard another, in a scene of such publicity, and he determined to walk slowly and silently up the street, thrusting his face close to that of every elderly gentleman, in search of the Major's lineaments. In his progress, Robin encountered many gay and gallant figures. Embroidered garments, of showy colors, enormous periwigs, gold-laced hats, and silver hilted swords, glided past him and dazzled his optics. Travelled youths, imitators of the European fine gentlemen of the period, trod jauntily along, half-dancing to the fashionable tunes which they hummed, and making poor Robin ashamed of his quiet and natural gait. At length, after many pauses to examine the gorgeous display of goods in the shop windows, and after suffering some rebukes for the impertinence of his scrutiny into people's faces, the Major's kinsman found himself near the steepled building, still unsuccessful in his search. As yet, however, he had seen only one side of the thronged street; so Robin crossed, and continued the same sort of inquisition down the opposite pavement, with stronger hopes than the philosopher seeking an honest man,[4] but with no better fortune. He had arrived about midway towards the lower end, from which his course began, when he overheard the approach of some one, who struck down a cane on the flag-stones at every step, uttering, at regular intervals, two sepulchral hems.

'Mercy on us!' quoth Robin, recognising the sound.

Turning a corner, which chanced to be close at his right hand, he hastened to pursue his researches, in some other part of the town. His patience was now wearing low, and he seemed to feel more fatigue from his rambles since he crossed the ferry, than from his journey of several days on the other side. Hunger also pleaded loudly within him, and Robin began to balance the propriety of demanding, violently and with lifted cudgel, the necessary guidance from the first solitary passenger, whom he should meet. While a resolution to this effect was gaining strength, he entered a street of mean appearance, on either side of which, a row of ill-built houses was straggling towards the harbor. The moonlight fell upon no passenger along the whole extent, but in the third domicile which Robin passed, there was a half-opened door, and his keen glance detected a woman's garment within.

'My luck may be better here,' said he to himself.

Accordingly, he approached the door, and beheld it shut closer as he did so; yet an open space remained, sufficing for the fair occupant to observe the stranger, without a corresponding display on her part. All that Robin could discern was a strip of scarlet petticoat, and the occasional sparkle of an eye, as if the moonbeams were trembling on some bright thing.

'Pretty mistress,'—for I may call her so with a good conscience, thought the shrewd youth, since I know nothing to the contrary—'my sweet pretty mistress, will you be kind enough to tell me whereabouts I must seek the dwelling of my kinsman, Major Molineux?'

Robin's voice was plaintive and winning, and the female, seeing nothing to

<hr>

4. Diogenes, the Greek philosopher (412?–323 b.c.), carried a lantern about in daytime in his search for an honest man.

be shunned in the handsome country youth, thrust open the door, and came forth into the moonlight. She was a dainty little figure, with a white neck, round arms, and a slender waist, at the extremity of which her scarlet petticoat jutted out over a hoop, as if she were standing in a balloon. Moreover, her face was oval and pretty, her hair dark beneath the little cap, and her bright eyes possessed a sly freedom, which triumphed over those of Robin.

'Major Molineux dwells here,' said this fair woman.

Now her voice was the sweetest Robin had heard that night, the airy counterpart of a stream of melted silver; yet he could not help doubting whether that sweet voice spoke gospel truth. He looked up and down the mean street, and then surveyed the house before which they stood. It was a small, dark edifice of two stories, the second of which projected over the lower floor; and the front apartment had the aspect of a shop for petty commodities.

'Now truly I am in luck,' replied Robin, cunningly, 'and so indeed is my kinsman, the Major, in having so pretty a housekeeper. But I prithee trouble him to step to the door; I will deliver him a message from his friends in the country, and then go back to my lodgings at the inn.'

'Nay, the Major has been a-bed this hour or more, said the lady of the scarlet petticoat; 'and it would be to little purpose to disturb him to night, seeing his evening draught was of the strongest. But he is a kind-hearted man, and it would be as much as my life's worth, to let a kinsman of his turn away from the door. You are the good old gentleman's very picture, and I could swear that was his rainy-weather hat. Also, he has garments very much resembling those leather—But come in, I pray, for I bid you hearty welcome in his name.'

So saying, the fair and hospitable dame took our hero by the hand; and though the touch was light, and the force was gentleness, and though Robin read in her eyes what he did not hear in her words, yet the slender waisted woman, in the scarlet petticoat, proved stronger than the athletic country youth. She had drawn his half-willing footsteps nearly to the threshold, when the opening of a door in the neighborhood, startled the Major's housekeeper, and, leaving the Major's kinsman, she vanished speedily into her own domicile. A heavy yawn preceded the appearance of a man, who, like the Moonshine of Pyramus and Thisbe, carried a lantern,[5] needlessly aiding his sister luminary in the heavens. As he walked sleepily up the street, he turned his broad, dull face on Robin, and displayed a long staff, spiked at the end.

'Home, vagabond, home!' said the watchman, in accents that seemed to fall asleep as soon as they were uttered. 'Home, or we'll set you in the stocks by peep of day!'

'This is the second hint of the kind,' thought Robin. 'I wish they would end my difficulties, by setting me there to-night.'

Nevertheless, the youth felt an instinctive antipathy towards the guardian of midnight order, which at first prevented him from asking his usual question. But just when the man was about to vanish behind the corner, Robin resolved not to lose the opportunity, and shouted lustily after him—

'I say, friend! will you guide me to the house of my kinsman, Major Molineux?'

The watchman made no reply, but turned the corner and was gone; yet

5. In Shakespeare's *Midsummer Night's Dream* 5.1, the craftsmen's play within a play.

Robin seemed to hear the sound of drowsy laughter stealing along the solitary street. At that moment, also, a pleasant titter saluted him from the open window above his head; he looked up, and caught the sparkle of a saucy eye; a round arm beckoned to him, and next he heard light footsteps descending the staircase within. But Robin, being of the household of a New England clergyman, was a good youth, as well as a shrewd one; so he resisted temptation, and fled away.

He now roamed desperately, and at random, through the town, almost ready to believe that a spell was on him, like that, by which a wizard of his country, had once kept three pursuers wandering, a whole winter night, within twenty paces of the cottage which they sought. The streets lay before him, strange and desolate, and the lights were extinguished in almost every house. Twice, however, little parties of men, among whom Robin distinguished individuals in outlandish attire, came hurrying along, but though on both occasions they paused to address him, such intercourse did not at all enlighten his perplexity. They did but utter a few words in some language of which Robin knew nothing, and perceiving his inability to answer, bestowed a curse upon him in plain English, and hastened away. Finally, the lad determined to knock at the door of every mansion that might appear worthy to be occupied by his kinsman, trusting that perseverance would overcome the fatality which had hitherto thwarted him. Firm in this resolve, he was passing beneath the walls of a church, which formed the corner of two streets, when, as he turned into the shade of its steeple, he encountered a bulky stranger, muffled in a cloak. The man was proceeding with the speed of earnest business, but Robin planted himself full before him, holding the oak cudgel with both hands across his body, as a bar to further passage.

'Halt, honest man, and answer me a question,' said he, very resolutely, 'Tell me, this instant, whereabouts is the dwelling of my kinsman, Major Molineux?'

'Keep your tongue between your teeth, fool, and let me pass,' said a deep, gruff voice, which Robin partly remembered. 'Let me pass, I say, or I'll strike you to the earth!'

'No, no, neighbor!' cried Robin, flourishing his cudgel, and then thrusting its larger end close to the man's muffled face. 'No, no, I'm not the fool you take me for, nor do you pass, till I have an answer to my question. Whereabouts is the dwelling of my kinsman, Major Molineux?'

The stranger, instead of attempting to force his passage, stept back into the moonlight, unmuffled his own face and stared full into that of Robin.

'Watch here an hour, and Major Molineux will pass by,' said he.

Robin gazed with dismay and astonishment, on the unprecedented physiognomy of the speaker. The forehead with its double prominence, the broad-hooked nose, the shaggy eyebrows, and fiery eyes, were those which he had noticed at the inn, but the man's complexion had undergone a singular, or more properly, a two-fold change. One side of the face blazed of an intense red, while the other was black as midnight, the division line being in the broad bridge of the nose; and a mouth, which seemed to extend from ear to ear, was black or red, in contrast to the color of the cheek. The effect was as if two individual devils, a fiend of fire and a fiend of darkness, had united themselves to form this infernal visage. The stranger grinned in Robin's face, muffled his party-colored features, and was out of sight in a moment.

'Strange things we travellers see!' ejaculated Robin.

He seated himself, however, upon the steps of the church-door, resolving to wait the appointed time for his kinsman's appearance. A few moments were consumed in philosophical speculations, upon the species of the *genus homo*, who had just left him, but having settled this point shrewdly, rationally, and satisfactorily, he was compelled to look elsewhere for amusement. And first he threw his eyes along the street; it was of more respectable appearance than most of those into which he had wandered, and the moon, 'creating, like the imaginative power, a beautiful strangeness in familiar objects,' gave something of romance to a scene, that might not have possessed it in the light of day. The irregular, and often quaint architecture of the houses, some of whose roofs were broken into numerous little peaks; while others ascended, steep and narrow, into a single point; and others again were square; the pure milk-white of some of their complexions, the aged darkness of others, and the thousand sparklings, reflected from bright substances in the plastered walls of many; these matters engaged Robin's attention for awhile, and then began to grow wearisome. Next he endeavored to define the forms of distant objects, starting away with almost ghostly indistinctness, just as his eye appeared to grasp them; and finally he took a minute survey of an edifice, which stood on the opposite side of the street, directly in front of the church-door, where he was stationed. It was a large square mansion, distinguished from its neighbors by a balcony, which rested on tall pillars, and by an elaborate gothic window, communicating therewith.

'Perhaps this is the very house I have been seeking,' thought Robin.

Then he strove to speed away the time, by listening to a murmur, which swept continually along the street, yet was scarcely audible, except to an unaccustomed ear like his; it was a low, dull, dreamy sound, compounded of many noises, each of which was at too great a distance to be separately heard. Robin marvelled at this snore of a sleeping town, and marvelled more, whenever its continuity was broken, by now and then a distant shout, apparently loud where it originated. But altogether it was a sleep-inspiring sound, and to shake off its drowsy influence, Robin arose, and climbed a window-frame, that he might view the interior of the church. There the moonbeams came trembling in, and fell down upon the deserted pews, and extended along the quiet aisles. A fainter, yet more awful radiance, was hovering round the pulpit, and one solitary ray had dared to rest upon the opened page of the great bible. Had Nature, in that deep hour, become a worshipper in the house, which man had builded? Or was that heavenly light the visible sanctity of this place, visible because no earthly and impure feet were within the walls? The scene made Robin's heart shiver with a sensation of loneliness, stronger than he had ever felt in the remotest depths of his native woods; so he turned away, and sat down again before the door. There were graves around the church, and now an uneasy thought obtruded into Robin's breast. What if the object of his search, which had been so often and so strangely thwarted, were all the time mouldering in his shroud? What if his kinsman should glide through yonder gate, and nod and smile to him in passing dimly by?

'Oh, that any breathing thing were here with me!' said Robin.

Recalling his thoughts from this uncomfortable track, he sent them over forest, hill, and stream, and attempted to imagine how that evening of ambiguity and weariness, had been spent by his father's household. He pictured them assembled at the door, beneath the tree, the great old tree, which had been spared for its huge twisted trunk, and venerable shade, when a thousand leafy brethren fell. There, at the going down of the summer sun, it was his father's custom to perform domestic worship, that the neighbors might come and join with him like brothers of the family, and that the wayfaring man might pause to drink at that fountain, and keep his heart pure by freshening the memory of home. Robin distinguished the seat of every individual of the little audience; he saw the good man in the midst, holding the scriptures in the golden light that shone from the western clouds; he beheld him close the book, and all rise up to pray. He heard the old thanksgivings for daily mercies, the old supplications for their continuance, to which he had so often listened in weariness, but which were now among his dear remembrances. He perceived the slight inequality of his father's voice when he came to speak of the Absent One; he noted how his mother turned her face to the broad and knotted trunk, how his elder brother scorned, because the beard was rough upon his upper lip, to permit his features to be moved; how his younger sister drew down a low hanging branch before her eyes; and how the little one of all, whose sports had hitherto broken the decorum of the scene, understood the prayer for her playmate, and burst into clamorous grief. Then he saw them go in at the door; and when Robin would have entered also, the latch tinkled into its place, and he was excluded from his home.

'Am I here, or there?' cried Robin, starting; for all at once, when his thoughts had become visible and audible in a dream, the long, wide, solitary street shone out before him.

He aroused himself, and endeavored to fix his attention steadily upon the large edifice which he had surveyed before. But still his mind kept vibrating between fancy and reality; by turns, the pillars of the balcony lengthened into the tall, bare stems of pines, dwindled down to human figures, settled again in their true shape and size, and then commenced a new succession of changes. For a single moment, when he deemed himself awake, he could have sworn that a visage, one which he seemed to remember, yet could not absolutely name as his kinsman's, was looking towards him from the Gothic window. A deeper sleep wrestled with, and nearly overcame him, but fled at the sound of footsteps along the opposite pavement. Robin rubbed his eyes, discerned a man passing at the foot of the balcony, and addressed him in a loud, peevish, and lamentable cry.

'Halloo, friend! must I wait here all night for my kinsman, Major Molineux?'

The sleeping echoes awoke, and answered the voice; and the passenger, barely able to discern a figure sitting in the oblique shade of the steeple, traversed the street to obtain a nearer view. He was himself a gentleman in his prime, of open, intelligent, cheerful and altogether prepossessing countenance. Perceiving a country youth, apparently homeless and without friends, he accosted him in a tone of real kindness, which had become strange to Robin's ears.

'Well, my good lad, why are you sitting here?' inquired he. 'Can I be of service to you in any way?'

'I am afraid not, Sir,' replied Robin, despondingly; 'yet I shall take it kindly, if you'll answer me a single question. I've been searching half the night for one Major Molineux; now, Sir, is there really such a person in these parts, or am I dreaming?'

'Major Molineux! The name is not altogether strange to me,' said the gentleman smiling. 'Have you any objection to telling me the nature of your business with him?'

Then Robin briefly related that his father was a clergyman, settled on a small salary, at a long distance back in the country, and that he and Major Molineux were brothers' children. The Major, having inherited riches, and acquired civil and military rank, had visited his cousin in great pomp a year or two before; had manifested much interest in Robin and an elder brother, and, being childless himself, had thrown out hints respecting the future establishment of one of them in life. The elder brother was destined to succeed to the farm, which his father cultivated, in the interval of sacred duties; it was therefore determined that Robin should profit by his kinsman's generous intentions, especially as he had seemed to be rather the favorite, and was thought to possess other necessary endowments.

'For I have the name of being a shrewd youth,' observed Robin, in this part of his story.

'I doubt not you deserve it,' replied his new friend, good naturedly; 'but pray proceed.'

'Well, Sir, being nearly eighteen years old, and well grown, as you see,' continued Robin, raising himself to his full height, 'I thought it high time to begin the world. So my mother and sister put me in handsome trim, and my father gave me half the remnant of his last year's salary, and five days ago I started for this place, to pay the Major a visit. But would you believe it, Sir? I crossed the ferry a little after dusk, and have yet found nobody that would show me the way to his dwelling; only an hour or two since, I was told to wait here, and Major Molineux would pass by.'

'Can you describe the man who told you this?' inquired the gentleman.

'Oh, he was a very ill-favored fellow, Sir,' replied Robin, 'with two great bumps on his forehead, a hook nose, fiery eyes, and, what struck me as the strangest, his face was of two different colors. Do you happen to know such a man, Sir?'

'Not intimately,' answered the stranger, 'but I chanced to meet him a little time previous to your stopping me. I believe you may trust his word, and that the Major will very shortly pass through this street. In the mean time, as I have a singular curiosity to witness your meeting, I will sit down here upon the steps, and bear you company.'

He seated himself accordingly, and soon engaged his companion in animated discourse. It was but of brief continuance, however, for a noise of shouting, which had long been remotely audible, drew so much nearer, that Robin inquired its cause.

'What may be the meaning of this uproar?' asked he. 'Truly, if your town be always as noisy, I shall find little sleep, while I am an inhabitant.'

'Why, indeed, friend Robin, there do appear to be three or four riotous fellows abroad to-night,' replied the gentleman. 'You must not expect all the stillness of your native woods, here in our streets. But the watch will shortly be at the heels of these lads, and—'

'Aye, and set them in the stocks by peep of day,' interrupted Robin, recollecting his own encounter with the drowsy lantern-bearer. 'But, dear Sir, if I may trust my ears, an army of watchmen would never make head against such a multitude of rioters. There were at least a thousand voices went to make up that one shout.'

'May not one man have several voices, Robin, as well as two complexions?' said his friend.

'Perhaps a man may; but heaven forbid that a woman should!' responded the shrewd youth, thinking of the seductive tones of the Major's housekeeper.

The sounds of a trumpet in some neighboring street, now became so evident and continual, that Robin's curiosity was strongly excited. In addition to the shouts, he heard frequent bursts from many instruments of discord, and a wild and confused laughter filled up the intervals. Robin rose from the steps, and looked wistfully towards a point, whither several people seemed to be hastening.

'Surely some prodigious merrymaking is going on,' exclaimed he. 'I have laughed very little since I left home, Sir, and should be sorry to lose an opportunity. Shall we just step round the corner by that darkish house, and take our share of the fun?'

'Sit down again, sit down, good Robin,' replied the gentleman, laying his hand on the skirt of the grey coat. 'You forget that we must wait here for your kinsman; and there is reason to believe that he will pass by, in the course of a very few moments.'

The near approach of the uproar had now disturbed the neighborhood; windows flew open on all sides; and many heads, in the attire of the pillow, and confused by sleep suddenly broken, were protruded to the gaze of whoever had leisure to observe them. Eager voices hailed each other from house to house, all demanding the explanation, which not a soul could give. Half-dressed men hurried towards the unknown commotion, stumbling as they went over the stone steps, that thrust themselves into the narrow foot-walk. The shouts, the laughter, and the tuneless bray, the antipodes of music, came onward with increasing din, till scattered individuals, and then denser bodies, began to appear round a corner, at a distance of a hundred yards.

'Will you recognise your kinsman, Robin, if he passes in this crowd?' inquired the gentleman.

'Indeed, I can't warrant it, Sir; but I'll take my stand here, and keep a bright look out,' answered Robin, descending to the outer edge of the pavement.

A mighty stream of people now emptied into the street, and came rolling slowly towards the church. A single horseman wheeled the corner in the midst of them, and close behind him came a band of fearful wind-instruments, sending forth a fresher discord, now that no intervening buildings kept it from the ear. Then a redder light disturbed the moonbeams, and a dense multitude of torches shone along the street, concealing by their glare whatever object they illuminated. The single horseman, clad in a military dress, and bearing a drawn sword, rode onward as the leader, and, by his fierce and variegated countenance, appeared like war personified; the red of one cheek was an emblem of fire and sword; the blackness of the other betokened the mourning which attends them. In his train, were wild figures in the Indian dress, and many fantastic shapes without a model, giving the whole march a visionary air, as if a dream had broken forth from some feverish brain, and were sweeping visibly through the midnight streets. A mass of people, inactive, except as applauding spectators, hemmed the procession in, and several women ran along the sidewalks, piercing the confusion of heavier sounds, with their shrill voices of mirth or terror.

'The double-faced fellow has his eye upon me,' muttered Robin, with an indefinite but uncomfortable idea, that he was himself to bear a part in the pageantry.

The leader turned himself in the saddle, and fixed his glance full upon the country youth, as the steed went slowly by. When Robin had freed his eyes from those fiery ones, the musicians were passing before him, and the torches were close at hand; but the unsteady brightness of the latter formed a veil which he could not penetrate. The rattling of wheels over the stones sometimes found its way to his ear, and confused traces of a human form appeared at intervals, and then melted into the vivid light. A moment more, and the leader thundered a command to halt; the trumpets vomited a horrid breath, and held their peace; the shouts and laughter of the people died away, and there remained only an universal hum, nearly allied to silence. Right before Robin's eyes was an uncovered cart. There the torches blazed the brightest, there the moon shone out like day, and there, in tar-and-feathery dignity, sate his kinsman, Major Molineux!

He was an elderly man, of large and majestic person, and strong, square features, betokening a steady soul; but steady as it was, his enemies had found the means to shake it. His face was pale as death, and far more ghastly; the broad forehead was contracted in his agony, so that the eyebrows formed one dark grey line; his eyes were red and wild, and the foam hung white upon his quivering lip. His whole frame was agitated by a quick, and continual tremor, which his pride strove to quell, even in those circumstances of overwhelming humiliation. But perhaps the bitterest pang of all was when his eyes met those of Robin; for he evidently knew him on the instant, as the youth stood witnessing the foul disgrace of a head that had grown grey in honor. They stared at each other in silence, and Robin's knees shook, and his hair bristled, with a mixture of pity and terror. Soon, however, a bewildering excitement began to seize upon his mind; the preceding adventures of the night, the unexpected appearance of the crowd, the torches, the confused din, and the hush that followed, the spectre of his kinsman reviled by that great multitude, all this, and more than all, a perception of tremendous ridicule in the whole scene, affected him with a sort of mental inebriety. At that moment a voice of sluggish merriment saluted Robin's ears; he turned instinctively, and just behind the corner of the church stood the lantern-bearer, rubbing his eyes, and drowsily enjoying the lad's amazement. Then he heard a peal of laughter like the ringing of silvery bells; a woman twitched his arm, a saucy eye met his, and he saw the lady of the scarlet petticoat. A sharp, dry cachinnation appealed to his memory, and, standing on tiptoe in the crowd, with his white apron over his head, he beheld the courteous little innkeeper. And lastly, there sailed over the heads of the multitude a great, broad laugh, broken in the midst by two deep sepulchral hems; thus—

'Haw, haw, haw—hem, hem—haw, haw, haw, haw!'

The sound proceeded from the balcony of the opposite edifice, and thither Robin turned his eyes. In front of the Gothic window stood the old citizen, wrapped in a wide gown, his grey periwig exchanged for a nightcap, which was thrust back from his forehead, and his silk stockings hanging down about his legs. He supported himself on his polished cane in a fit of convulsive merriment, which manifested itself on his solemn old features, like a funny inscription on a tomb-stone. Then Robin seemed to hear the voices of the barbers; of the guests of the inn; and of all who had made sport of him that night. The contagion was spreading among the multitude, when, all at once, it seized upon Robin, and he sent forth a shout of laughter that echoed through the street; every man shook his sides, every man emptied his lungs, but Robin's shout was the loudest there. The cloud-spirits peeped from their silvery islands, as the congregated mirth went roaring up the sky! The Man in the Moon heard the far bellow; 'Oho,' quoth he, 'the old Earth is frolicsome to-night!'

When there was a momentary calm in that tempestuous sea of sound, the leader gave the sign, and the procession resumed its march. On they went, like fiends that throng in mockery round some dead potentate, mighty no more, but majestic still in his agony. On they went, in counterfeited pomp, in senseless uproar, in frenzied merriment, trampling all on an old man's heart. On swept the tumult, and left a silent street behind.

· · · · ·

'Well, Robin, are you dreaming?' inquired the gentleman, laying his hand on the youth's shoulder.

Robin started, and withdrew his arm from the stone post, to which he had instinctively clung, while the living stream rolled by him. His cheek was somewhat pale, and his eye not quite so lively as in the earlier part of the evening.

'Will you be kind enough to show me the way to the Ferry?' said he, after a moment's pause.

'You have then adopted a new subject of inquiry?' observed his companion, with a smile.

'Why, yes, Sir,' replied Robin, rather dryly. 'Thanks to you, and to my other friends, I have at last met my kinsman, and he will scarce desire to see my face again. I begin to grow weary of a town life, Sir. Will you show me the way to the Ferry?'

'No, my good friend Robin, not to-night, at least,' said the gentleman. 'Some few days hence, if you continue to wish it, I will speed you on your journey. Or, if you prefer to remain with us, perhaps, as you are a shrewd youth, you may rise in the world, without the help of your kinsman, Major Molineux.'

1832, 1837

## Roger Malvin's Burial[1]

One of the few incidents of Indian warfare, naturally susceptible of the moonlight of romance, was that expedition, undertaken, for the defence of the frontiers, in the year 1725, which resulted in the well-remembered 'Lovell's Fight.'[2] Imagination, by casting certain circumstances judiciously into the shade, may see much to admire in the heroism of a little band, who gave battle to twice their number in the heart of the enemy's country. The open bravery displayed by both parties was in accordance with civilized ideas of valor, and chivalry itself might not blush to record the deeds of one or two individuals. The battle, though so fatal to those who fought, was not unfortunate in its consequences to the country; for it broke the strength of a tribe, and

---

1. The text is that of the first printing, in *The Token* for 1832.  2. An incident in the Penobscot War in Maine (then part of Massachusetts) during 1725.

conduced to the peace which subsisted during several ensuing years. History and tradition are unusually minute in their memorials of this affair; and the captain of a scouting party of frontier-men has acquired as actual a military renown, as many a victorious leader of thousands. Some of the incidents contained in the following pages will be recognised, notwithstanding the substitution of fictitious names, by such as have heard, from old men's lips, the fate of the few combatants who were in a condition to retreat, after 'Lovell's Fight.'

• • • • •

The early sunbeams hovered cheerfully upon the tree-tops, beneath which two weary and wounded men had stretched their limbs the night before. Their bed of withered oak leaves was strewn upon the small level space, at the foot of a rock, situated near the summit of one of the gentle swells, by which the face of the country is there diversified. The mass of granite, rearing its smooth, flat surface, fifteen or twenty feet above their heads, was not unlike a gigantic grave-stone, upon which the veins seemed to form an inscription in forgotten characters. On a tract of several acres around this rock, oaks and other hardwood trees had supplied the place of the pines, which were the usual growth of the land; and a young and vigorous sapling stood close beside the travellers.

The severe wound of the elder man had probably deprived him of sleep; for, so soon as the first ray of sunshine rested on the top of the highest tree, he reared himself painfully from his recumbent posture, and sat erect. The deep lines of his countenance, and the scattered grey of his hair, marked him as past the middle age; but his muscular frame would, but for the effects of his wound, have been as capable of sustaining fatigue, as in the early vigor of life. Languor and exhaustion now sat upon his haggard features, and the despairing glance which he sent forward through the depths of the forest, proved his own conviction that his pilgrimage was at an end. He next turned his eyes to the companion, who reclined by his side. The youth, for he had scarcely attained the years of manhood, lay, with his head upon his arm, in the embrace of an unquiet sleep, which a thrill of pain from his wounds seemed each moment on the point of breaking. His right hand grasped a musket, and, to judge from the violent action of his features, his slumbers were bringing back a vision of the conflict, of which he was one of the few survivors. A shout,—deep and loud to his dreaming fancy,—found its way in an imperfect murmur to his lips, and, starting even at the slight sound of his own voice, he suddenly awoke. The first act of reviving recollection, was to make anxious inquiries respecting the condition of his wounded fellow traveller. The latter shook his head.

'Reuben, my boy,' said he, 'this rock, beneath which we sit, will serve for an old hunter's grave-stone. There is many and many a long mile of howling wilderness before us yet; nor would it avail me anything, if the smoke of my own chimney were but on the other side of that swell of land. The Indian bullet was deadlier than I thought.'

'You are weary with our three days' travel,' replied the youth, 'and a little longer rest will recruit you. Sit you here, while I search the woods for the herbs and roots, that must be our sustenance; and having eaten, you shall lean on me, and we will turn our faces homeward. I doubt not, that, with my help, you can attain to some one of the frontier garrisons.'

'There is not two days' life in me, Reuben,' said the other, calmly, 'and I will no longer burthen you with my useless body, when you can scarcely support your own. Your wounds are deep, and your strength is failing fast; yet, if you hasten onward alone, you may be preserved. For me there is no hope; and I will await death here.'

'If it must be so, I will remain and watch by you,' said Reuben, resolutely.

'No, my son, no,' rejoined his companion. 'Let the wish of a dying man have weight with you; give me one grasp of your hand, and get you hence. Think you that my last moments will be eased by the thought, that I leave you to die a more lingering death? I have loved you like a father, Reuben, and, at a time like this, I should have something of a father's authority. I charge you to be gone, that I may die in peace.'

'And because you have been a father to me, should I therefore leave you to perish, and to lie unburied in the wilderness?' exclaimed the youth. 'No; if your end be in truth approaching, I will watch by you, and receive your parting words. I will dig a grave here by the rock, in which, if my weakness overcome me, we will rest together; or, if Heaven gives me strength, I will seek my way home.'

'In the cities, and wherever men dwell,' replied the other, 'they bury their dead in the earth; they hide them from the sight of the living; but here, where no step may pass, perhaps for a hundred years, wherefore should I not rest beneath the open sky, covered only by the oak-leaves, when the autumn winds shall strew them? And for a monument, here is this grey rock, on which my dying hand shall carve the name of Roger Malvin: and the traveller in days to come will know, that here sleeps a hunter and a warrior. Tarry not, then, for a folly like this, but hasten away, if not for your own sake, for hers who will else be desolate.'

Malvin spoke the last few words in a faultering voice, and their effect upon his companion was strongly visible. They reminded him that there were other, and less questionable duties, than that of sharing the fate of a man whom his death could not benefit. Nor can it be affirmed that no selfish feeling strove to enter Reuben's heart, though the consciousness made him more earnestly resist his companion's entreaties.

'How terrible, to wait the slow approach of death, in this solitude!' exclaimed he. 'A brave man does not shrink in the battle, and, when friends stand round the bed, even women may die composedly; but here'—

'I shall not shrink, even here, Reuben Bourne;' interrupted Malvin, 'I am a man of no weak heart; and, if I were, there is a surer support than that of earthly friends. You are young, and life is dear to you. Your last moments will need comfort far more than mine; and when you have laid me in the earth, and are alone, and night is settling on the forest, you will feel all the bitterness of the death that may now be escaped. But I will urge no selfish motive to your generous nature. Leave me for my sake; that, having said a prayer for your safety, I may have space to settle my account, undisturbed by worldly sorrows.'

'And your daughter! How shall I dare to meet her eye?' exclaimed Reuben. 'She will ask the fate of her father, whose life I vowed to defend with my own. Must I tell her, that he travelled three days' march with me from the field of battle, and that then I left him to perish in the wilderness? Were it not better to lie down and die by your side, than to return safe, and say this to Dorcas?'

'Tell my daughter,' said Roger Malvin, 'that, though yourself sore wounded, and weak, and weary, you led my tottering footsteps many a mile, and left me only at my earnest entreaty, because I would not have your blood upon my soul. Tell her, that through pain and danger you were faithful, and that, if your life-blood could have saved me, it would have flowed to its last drop. And tell her, that you will be something dearer than a father, and that my blessing is with you both, and that my dying eyes can see a long and pleasant path, in which you will journey together.'

As Malvin spoke, he almost raised himself from the ground, and the energy of his concluding words seemed to fill the wild and lonely forest with a vision of happiness. But when he sank exhausted upon his bed of oak-leaves, the light, which had kindled in Reuben's eye, was quenched. He felt as if it were both sin and folly to think of happiness at such a moment. His companion watched his changing countenance, and sought, with generous art, to wile him to his own good.

'Perhaps I deceive myself in regard to the time I have to live,' he resumed. 'It may be, that, with speedy assistance, I might recover my wound. The foremost fugitives must, ere this, have carried tidings of our fatal battle to the frontiers, and parties will be out to succour those in like condition with ourselves. Should you meet one of these, and guide them hither, who can tell but that I may sit by my own fireside again?'

A mournful smile strayed across the features of the dying man, as he insinuated that unfounded hope; which, however, was not without its effect on Reuben. No merely selfish motive, nor even the desolate condition of Dorcas, could have induced him to desert his companion, at such a moment. But his wishes seized upon the thought, that Malvin's life might be preserved, and his sanguine nature heightened, almost to certainty, the remote possibility of procuring human aid.

'Surely there is reason, weighty reason, to hope that friends are not far distant,' he said, half aloud. 'There fled one coward, unwounded, in the beginning of the fight, and most probably he made good speed. Every true man on the frontier would shoulder his musket, at the news; and though no party may range so far into the woods as this, I shall perhaps encounter them in one day's march. Counsel me faithfully,' he added, turning to Malvin, in distrust of his own motives. 'Were your situation mine, would you desert me while life remained?'

'It is now twenty years,' replied Roger Malvin, sighing, however, as he secretly acknowledged the wide dissimilarity between the two cases,—'it is now twenty years, since I escaped, with one dear friend, from Indian captivity, near Montreal. We journeyed many days through the woods, till at length, overcome with hunger and weariness, my friend lay down, and besought me to leave him; for he knew, that, if I remained, we both must perish. And, with but little hope of obtaining succour, I heaped a pillow of dry leaves beneath his head, and hastened on.'

'And did you return in time to save him?' asked Reuben, hanging on Malvin's words, as if they were to be prophetic of his own success.

'I did,' answered the other, 'I came upon the camp of a hunting party, before sunset of the same day. I guided them to the spot where my comrade was expecting death; and he is now a hale and hearty man, upon his own farm, far within the frontiers, while I lie wounded here, in the depths of the wilderness.'

This example, powerful in effecting Reuben's decision, was aided, unconsciously to himself, by the hidden strength of many another motive. Roger Malvin perceived that the victory was nearly won.

'Now go, my son, and Heaven prosper you!' he said. 'Turn not back with our friends, when you meet them, lest your wounds and weariness overcome you; but send hitherward two or three, that may be spared, to search for me. And believe me, Reuben, my heart will be lighter with every step you take towards home.' Yet there was perhaps a change, both in his countenance and voice, as he spoke thus; for, after all, it was a ghastly fate, to be left expiring in the wilderness.

Reuben Bourne, but half convinced that he was acting rightly, at length raised himself from the ground, and prepared for his departure. And first, though contrary to Malvin's wishes, he collected a stock of roots and herbs, which had been their only food during the last two days. This useless supply he placed within reach of the dying man, for whom, also, he swept together a fresh bed of dry oak-leaves. Then, climbing to the summit of the rock, which on one side was rough and broken, he bent the oak-sapling downwards, and bound his handkerchief to the topmost branch. This precaution was not unnecessary, to direct any who might come in search of Malvin; for every part of the rock, except its broad, smooth front, was concealed, at a little distance, by the dense undergrowth of the forest. The handkerchief had been the bandage of a wound upon Reuben's arm; and, as he bound it to the tree, he vowed, by the blood that stained it, that he would return, either to save his companion's life, or to lay his body in the grave. He then descended, and stood, with downcast eyes, to receive Roger Malvin's parting words.

The experience of the latter suggested much and minute advice, respecting the youth's journey through the trackless forest. Upon this subject he spoke with calm earnestness, as if he were sending Reuben to the battle or the chase, while he himself remained secure at home; and not as if the human countenance, that was about to leave him, were the last he would ever behold. But his firmness was shaken, before he concluded.

'Carry my blessing to Dorcas, and say that my last prayer shall be for her and you. Bid her have no hard thoughts because you left me here'—Reuben's heart smote him—'for that your life would not have weighed with you, if its sacrifice could have done me good. She will marry you, after she has mourned a little while for her father; and Heaven grant you long and happy days! and may your children's children stand round your death-bed! And, Reuben,' added he, as the weakness of mortality made its way at last, 'return, when your wounds are healed and your weariness refreshed, return to this wild rock, and lay my bones in the grave, and say a prayer over them.'

An almost superstitious regard, arising perhaps from the customs of the Indians, whose war was with the dead, as well as the living, was paid by the frontier inhabitants to the rites of sepulture; and there are many instances of the sacrifice of life, in the attempt to bury those who had fallen by the 'sword of the wilderness.' Reuben, therefore, felt the full importance of the promise, which he most solemnly made, to return, and perform Roger Malvin's obsequies. It was remarkable, that the latter, speaking his whole heart in his parting words, no longer endeavored to persuade the youth, that even the speediest succour might avail to the preservation of his life. Reuben was internally convinced, that he should see Malvin's living face no more. His generous nature would fain have delayed him, at whatever risk, till the dying scene were past; but the desire of existence, and the hope of happiness had strengthened in his heart, and he was unable to resist them.

'It is enough,' said Roger Malvin, having listened to Reuben's promise. 'Go, and God speed you!'

The youth pressed his hand in silence, turned, and was departing. His slow and faultering steps, however, had borne him but a little way, before Malvin's voice recalled him.

'Reuben, Reuben,' said he, faintly; and Reuben turned and knelt down by the dying man.

'Raise me and let me lean against the rock,' was his last request. 'My face will be turned towards home, and I shall see you a moment longer, as you pass among the trees.'

Reuben, having made the desired alteration in his companion's posture, again began his solitary pilgrimage. He walked more hastily at first, than was consistent with his strength; for a sort of guilty feeling, which sometimes torments men in their most justifiable acts, caused him to seek concealment from Malvin's eyes. But, after he had trodden far upon the rustling forest-leaves, he crept back, impelled by a wild and painful curiosity, and, sheltered by the earthy roots of an uptorn tree, gazed earnestly at the desolate man. The morning sun was unclouded, and the trees and shrubs imbibed the sweet air of the month of May; yet there seemed a gloom on Nature's face, as if she sympathized with mortal pain and sorrow. Roger Malvin's hands were uplifted in a fervent prayer, some of the words which stole through the stillness of the woods, and entered Reuben's heart, torturing it with an unutterable pang. They were the broken accents of a petition for his own happiness and that of Dorcas; and, as the youth listened, conscience, or something in its similitude, pleaded strongly with him to return, and lie down again by the rock. He felt how hard was the doom of the kind and generous being whom he had deserted in his extremity. Death would come, like the slow approach of a corpse, stealing gradually towards him through the forest, and showing its ghastly and motionless features from behind a nearer, and yet a nearer tree. But such must have been Reuben's own fate, had he tarried another sunset; and who shall impute blame to him, if he shrank from so useless a sacrifice? As he gave a parting look, a breeze waved the little banner upon the sapling-oak, and reminded Reuben of his vow.

•  •  •  •  •  •

Many circumstances contributed to retard the wounded traveller, in his way to the frontiers. On the second day, the clouds, gathering densely over the sky, precluded the possibility of regulating his course by the position of the sun; and he knew not but that every effort of his almost exhausted strength, was removing him farther from the home he sought. His scanty sustenance was supplied by the berries, and other spontaneous products of the forest. Herds of deer, it is true, sometimes bounded past him, and partridges frequently whirred up before his footsteps; but his ammunition had been expended in the fight, and he had no means of slaying them. His wounds, irritated by the constant exertion in which lay the only hope of life; wore away his strength, and at intervals confused his reason. But, even in the wanderings of intellect, Reuben's young heart clung strongly to existence, and it was only through absolute incapacity of motion, that he at last sank down beneath a tree, compelled there to await death. In this situation he was discovered by a party, who, upon the first intelligence of the fight, had been despatched to the relief of the survivors. They conveyed him to the nearest settlement, which chanced to be that of his own residence.

Dorcas, in the simplicity of the olden time, watched by the bed-side of her wounded lover, and administered all those comforts, that are in the sole gift of woman's heart and hand. During several days, Reuben's recollection strayed drowsily among the perils and hardships through which he had passed, and he was incapable of returning definite answers to the inquiries, with which many were eager to harass him. No authentic particulars of the battle had yet been circulated; nor could mothers, wives, and children tell, whether their loved ones were detained by captivity, or by the stronger chain of death. Dorcas nourished her apprehensions in silence, till one afternoon, when Reuben awoke from an unquiet sleep, and seemed to recognise her, more perfectly than at any previous time. She saw that his intellect had become composed, and she could no longer restrain her filial anxiety.

'My father, Reuben?' she began; but the change in her lover's countenance made her pause.

The youth shrank, as if with a bitter pain, and the blood gushed vividly into his wan and hollow cheeks. His first impulse was to cover his face; but, apparently with a desperate effort, he half raised himself, and spoke vehemently, defending himself against an imaginary accusation.

'Your father was sore wounded in the battle, Dorcas; and he bade me not burthen myself with him, but only to lead him to the lakeside, that he might quench his thirst and die. But I would not desert the old man in his extremity, and, though bleeding myself, I supported him; I gave him half my strength, and led him away with me. For three days we journeyed on together, and your father was sustained beyond my hopes; but, awaking at sunrise on the fourth day, I found him faint and exhausted,—he was unable to proceed,—his life had ebbed away fast,—and'—

'He died!' exclaimed Dorcas, faintly.

Reuben felt it impossible to acknowledge, that his selfish love of life had hurried him away, before her father's fate was decided. He spoke not; he only bowed his head; and, between shame and exhaustion, sank back and hid his face in the pillow. Dorcas wept, when her fears were thus confirmed; but the shock, as it had been long anticipated, was on that account the less violent.

'You dug a grave for my poor father, in the wilderness, Reuben?' was the question by which her filial piety manifested itself.

'My hands were weak, but I did what I could,' replied the youth in a smothered tone. 'There stands a noble tomb-stone above his head, and I would to Heaven I slept as soundly as he!'

Dorcas, perceiving the wildness of his latter words, inquired no farther at that time; but her heart found ease in the thought, that Roger Malvin had not lacked such funeral rites as it was possible to bestow. The tale of Reuben's courage and fidelity lost nothing, when she communicated it to her friends; and the poor youth, tottering from his sick chamber to breathe the sunny air, experienced from every tongue the miserable and humiliating torture of unmerited praise. All acknowledged that he might worthily demand the hand of the fair maiden, to whose father he had been 'faithful unto death;' and, as my tale is not of love, it shall suffice to say, that, in the space of two years,

Reuben became the husband of Dorcas Malvin. During the marriage ceremony, the bride was covered with blushes, but the bridegroom's face was pale.

There was now in the breast of Reuben Bourne an incommunicable
thought; something which he was to conceal most heedfully from her whom
he most loved and trusted. He regretted, deeply and bitterly, the moral cowardice that had restrained his words, when he was about to disclose the truth
to Dorcas; but pride, the fear of losing her affection, the dread of universal
scorn, forbade him to rectify this falsehood. He felt, that, for leaving Roger
Malvin, he deserved no censure. His presence, the gratuitous sacrifice of his
own life, would have added only another, and a needless agony to the last
moments of the dying man. But concealment had imparted to a justifiable act,
much of the secret effect of guilt; and Reuben, while reason told him that he
had done right, experienced in no small degree, the mental horrors, which
punish the perpetrator of undiscovered crime. By a certain association of ideas,
he at times almost imagined himself a murderer. For years, also, a thought
would occasionally recur, which, though he perceived all its folly and extravagance, he had not power to banish from his mind; it was a haunting and
torturing fancy, that his father-in-law was yet sitting at the foot of the rock, on
the withered forest-leaves, alive, and awaiting his pledged assistance. These
mental deceptions, however, came and went, nor did he ever mistake them
for realities; but in the calmest and clearest moods of his mind, he was conscious that he had a deep vow unredeemed, and that an unburied corpse was
calling to him, out of the wilderness. Yet, such was the consequence of his
prevarication, that he could not obey the call. It was now too late to require
the assistance of Roger Malvin's friends, in performing his long-deferred sepulture; and superstitious fears, of which none were more susceptible than the
people of the outward settlements, forbade Reuben to go alone. Neither did
he know where, in the pathless and illimitable forest, to seek that smooth and
lettered rock, at the base of which the body lay; his remembrance of every
portion of his travel thence was indistinct, and the latter part had left no
impression upon his mind. There was, however, a continual impulse, a voice
audible only to himself, commanding him to go forth and redeem his vow;
and he had a strange impression, that, were he to make the trial, he would be
led straight to Malvin's bones. But, year after year, that summons, unheard
but felt, was disobeyed. His one secret thought, became like a chain, binding
down his spirit, and, like a serpent, gnawing into his heart; and he was transformed into a sad and downcast, yet irritable man.

In the course of a few years after their marriage, changes began to be visible
in the external prosperity of Reuben and Dorcas. The only riches of the former
had been his stout heart and strong arm; but the latter, her father's sole heiress,
had made her husband master of a farm, under older cultivation, larger, and
better stocked than most of the frontier establishments. Reuben Bourne, however, was a neglectful husbandman; and while the lands of the other settlers
became annually more fruitful, his deteriorated in the same proportion. The
discouragements to agriculture were greatly lessened by the cessation of Indian
war, during which men held the plough in one hand, and the musket in the
other; and were fortunate if the products of their dangerous labor were not
destroyed, either in the field or in the barn, by the savage enemy. But Reuben
did not profit by the altered condition of the country; nor can it be denied,
that his intervals of industrious attention to his affairs were but scantily

rewarded with success. The irritability, by which he had recently become distinguished, was another cause of his declining prosperity, as it occasioned frequent quarrels, in his unavoidable intercourse with the neighboring settlers. The results of these were innumerable law-suits; for the people of New England, in the earliest stages and wildest circumstances of the country, adopted, whenever attainable, the legal mode of deciding their differences. To be brief, the world did not go well with Reuben Bourne, and, though not till many years after his marriage, he was finally a ruined man, with but one remaining expedient against the evil fate that had pursued him. He was to throw sunlight into some deep recess of the forest, and seek subsistence from the virgin bosom of the wilderness.

The only child of Reuben and Dorcas was a son, now arrived at the age of fifteen years, beautiful in youth, and giving promise of a glorious manhood. He was peculiarly qualified for, and already began to excel in, the wild accomplishments of frontier life. His foot was fleet, his aim true, his apprehension quick, his heart glad and high; and all, who anticipated the return of Indian war, spoke of Cyrus Bourne as a future leader in the land. The boy was loved by his father, with a deep and silent strength, as if whatever was good and happy in his own nature had been transferred to his child, carrying his affections with it. Even Dorcas, though loving and beloved, was far less dear to him; for Reuben's secret thoughts and insulated emotions had gradually made him a selfish man; and he could no longer love deeply, except where he saw, or imagined, some reflection or likeness of his own mind. In Cyrus he recognised what he had himself been in other days; and at intervals he seemed to partake of the boy's spirit, and to be revived with a fresh and happy life. Reuben was accompanied by his son in the expedition, for the purpose of selecting a tract of land, and felling and burning the timber, which necessarily preceded the removal of the household gods.[3] Two months of autumn were thus occupied; after which Reuben Bourne and his young hunter returned, to spend their last winter in the settlements.

•  •  •  •  •

It was early in the month of May, that the little family snapped asunder whatever tendrils of affection had clung to inanimate objects, and bade farewell to the few, who, in the blight of fortune, called themselves their friends. The sadness of the parting moment had, to each of the pilgrims, its peculiar alleviations. Reuben, a moody man, and misanthropic because unhappy, strode onward, with his usual stern brow and downcast eye, feeling few regrets, and disdaining to acknowledge any. Dorcas, while she wept abundantly over the broken ties by which her simple and affectionate nature had bound itself to everything, felt that the inhabitants of her inmost heart moved on with her, and that all else would be supplied wherever she might go. And the boy dashed one tear-drop from his eye, and thought of the adventurous pleasures of the untrodden forest. Oh! who, in the enthusiasm of a day-dream, has not wished that he were a wanderer in a world of summer wilderness, with one fair and gentle being hanging lightly on his arm? In youth, his free and exulting step would know no barrier but the rolling ocean or the snow-topt mountains; calmer manhood would choose a home, where Nature had strewn a double

---

3. I.e., prized possessions, because of the value placed on personal idols in many cultures. In Genesis 31.19 Rachel, without telling her husband, Jacob, steals her father's household gods.

wealth, in the vale of some transparent stream; and when hoary age, after long, long years of that pure life, stole on and found him there, it would find him the father of a race, the patriarch of a people, the founder of a mighty nation yet to be. When death, like the sweet sleep which we welcome after a day of happiness, came over him, his far descendants would mourn over the venerated dust. Enveloped by tradition in mysterious attributes, the men of future generations would call him godlike; and remote posterity would see him standing, dimly glorious, far up the valley of a hundred centuries!

The tangled and gloomy forest, through which the personages of my tale were wandering, differed widely from the dreamer's Land of Fantasië; yet there was something in their way of life that Nature asserted as her own; and the gnawing cares, which went with them from the world, were all that now obstructed their happiness. One stout and shaggy steed, the bearer of all their wealth, did not shrink from the added weight of Dorcas; although her hardy breeding sustained her, during the larger part of each day's journey, by her husband's side. Reuben and his son, their muskets on their shoulders, and their axes slung behind them, kept an unwearied pace, each watching with a hunter's eye for the game that supplied their food. When hunger bade, they halted and prepared their meal on the bank of some unpolluted forest-brook, which, as they knelt down with thirsty lips to drink, murmured a sweet unwillingness, like a maiden, at love's first kiss. They slept beneath a hut of branches, and awoke at peep of light, refreshed for the toils of another day. Dorcas and the boy went on joyously, and even Reuben's spirit shone at intervals with an outward gladness; but inwardly there was a cold, cold sorrow, which he compared to the snow-drifts, lying deep in the glens and hollows of the rivulets, while the leaves were brightly green above.

Cyrus Bourne was sufficiently skilled in the travel of the woods, to observe, that his father did not adhere to the course they had pursued, in their expedition of the preceding autumn. They were now keeping farther to the north, striking out more directly from the settlements, and into a region, of which savage beasts and savage men were as yet the sole possessors. They boy sometimes hinted his opinions upon the subject, and Reuben listened attentively, and once or twice altered the direction of their march in accordance with his son's counsel. But having so done, he seemed ill at ease. His quick and wandering glances were sent forward, apparently in search of enemies lurking behind the tree-trunks; and seeing nothing there, he would cast his eyes backward, as if in fear of some pursuer. Cyrus, perceiving that his father gradually resumed the old direction, forbore to interfere; nor, though something began to weigh upon his heart, did his adventurous nature permit him to regret the increased length and the mystery of their way.

On the afternoon of the fifth day, they halted and made their simple encampment, nearly an hour before sunset. The face of the country, for the last few miles, had been diversified by swells of land, resembling huge waves of a petrified sea; and in one of the corresponding hollows, a wild and romantic spot, had the family reared their hut, and kindled their fire. There is something chilling, and yet heart-warming, in the thought of three, united by strong bands of love, and insulated from all that breathe beside. The dark and gloomy pines looked down upon them, and, as the wind swept through their tops, a pitying sound was heard in the forest; or did those old trees groan, in fear that men were come to lay the axe to their roots at last? Reuben and his son, while Dorcas made ready their meal, proposed to wander out in search of game, of which that day's march had afforded no supply. The boy, promising not to quit the vicinity of the encampment, bounded off with a step as light and elastic as that of the deer he hoped to slay; while his father, feeling a transient happiness as he gazed after him, was about to pursue an opposite direction. Dorcas, in the meanwhile, had seated herself near their fire of fallen branches, upon the moss-grown and mouldering trunk of a tree, uprooted years before. Her employment, diversified by an occasional glance at the pot, now beginning to simmer over the blaze, was the perusal of the current year's Massachusetts Almanac, which, with the exception of an old black-letter[4] Bible, comprised all the literary wealth of the family. None pay a greater regard to arbitrary divisions of time, than those who are excluded from society; and Dorcas mentioned, as if the information were of importance, that it was now the twelfth of May. Her husband started.

'The twelfth of May! I should remember it well,' muttered he, while many thoughts occasioned a momentary confusion in his mind. 'Where am I? Whither am I wandering? Where did I leave him?'

Dorcas, too well accustomed to her husband's wayward moods to note any peculiarity of demeanor, now laid aside the Almanac, and addressed him in that mournful tone, which the tender-hearted appropriate to griefs long cold and dead.

'It was near this time of the month, eighteen years ago, that my poor father left this world for a better. He had a kind arm to hold his head, and a kind voice to cheer him, Reuben, in his last moments; and the thought of the faithful care you took of him, has comforted me, many a time since. Oh! death would have been awful to a solitary man, in a wild place like this!'

'Pray Heaven, Dorcas,' said Reuben, in a broken voice, 'pray Heaven, that neither of us three die solitary, and lie unburied, in this howling wilderness!' And he hastened away, leaving her to watch the fire, beneath the gloomy pines.

Reuben Bourne's rapid pace gradually slackened, as the pang, unintentionally inflicted by the words of Dorcas, became less acute. Many strange reflections, however, thronged upon him; and, straying onward, rather like a sleepwalker than a hunter, it was attributable to no care of his own, that his devious course kept him in the vicinity of the encampment. His steps were imperceptibly led almost in a circle, nor did he observe that he was on the verge of a tract of land heavily timbered, but not with pine-trees. The place of the latter was here supplied by oaks, and other of the harder woods; and around their roots clustered a dense and bushy undergrowth, leaving, however, barren spaces between the trees, thick-strewn with withered leaves. Whenever the rustling of the branches, or the creaking of the trunks made a sound, as if the forest were waking from slumber, Reuben instinctively raised the musket that rested on his arm, and cast a quick, sharp glance on every side; but, convinced by a partial observation that no animal was near, he would again give himself up to his thoughts. He was musing on the strange influence, that had led him away from his premeditated course, and so far into the depths of the wilderness. Unable to penetrate to the secret place of his soul, where his motives lay hidden, he believed that a supernatural voice had called him onward, and that

4. Printed in early type resembling the shapes of letters used by medieval and early Renaissance scribes.

a supernatural power had obstructed his retreat. He trusted that it was Heaven's intent to afford him an opportunity of expiating his sin; he hoped that he might find the bones, so long unburied; and that, having laid the earth over them, peace would throw its sunlight into the sepulchre of his heart. From these thoughts he was aroused by a rustling in the forest, at some distance from the spot to which he had wandered. Perceiving the motion of some object behind a thick veil of undergrowth, he fired, with the instinct of a hunter, and the aim of a practised marksman. A low moan, which told his success, and by which even animals can express their dying agony, was unheeded by Reuben Bourne. What were the recollections now breaking upon him?

The thicket, into which Reuben had fired, was near the summit of a swell of land, and was clustered around the base of a rock, which, in the shape and smoothness of one of its surfaces, was not unlike a gigantic gravestone. As if reflected in a mirror, its likeness was in Reuben's memory. He even recognised the veins which seemed to form an inscription in forgotten characters; everything remained the same, except that a thick covert of bushes shrouded the lower part of the rock, and would have hidden Roger Malvin, had he still been sitting there. Yet, in the next moment, Reuben's eye was caught by another change, that time had effected, since he last stood, where he was now standing again, behind the earthy roots of the uptorn tree. The sapling, to which he had bound the blood-stained symbol of his vow, had increased and strengthened into an oak, far indeed from its maturity, but with no mean spread of shadowy branches. There was one singularity, observable in this tree, which made Reuben tremble. The middle and lower branches were in luxuriant life, and an excess of vegetation had fringed the trunk, almost to the ground; but a blight had apparently stricken the upper part of the oak, and the very topmost bough was withered, sapless, and utterly dead. Reuben remembered how the little banner had fluttered on that topmost bough, when it was green and lovely, eighteen years before. Whose guilt had blasted it?

·  ·  ·  ·  ·

Dorcas, after the departure of the two hunters, continued her preparations for their evening repast. Her sylvan table was the moss-covered trunk of a large fallen tree, on the broadest part of which she had spread a snow-white cloth, and arranged what were left of the bright pewter vessels, that had been her pride in the settlements. It had a strange aspect—that one little spot of homely comfort, in the desolate heart of Nature. The sunshine yet lingered upon the higher branches of the trees that grew on rising ground; but the shades of evening had deepened into the hollow, where the encampment was made; and the fire-light began to redden as it gleamed up the tall trunks of the pines, or hovered on the dense and obscure mass of foliage, that circled round the spot. The heart of Dorcas was not sad; for she felt that it was better to journey in the wilderness, with two whom she loved, than to be a lonely woman in a crowd that cared not for her. As she busied herself in arranging seats of mouldering wood, covered with leaves, for Reuben and her son, her voice danced through the gloomy forest, in the measure of a song that she had learned in youth. The rude melody, the production of a bard who won no name, was descriptive of a winter evening in a frontier-cottage, when, secured from savage inroad by the high-piled snow-drifts, the family rejoiced by their own fire-side. The whole song possessed that nameless charm, peculiar to unborrowed thought; but four continually-recurring lines shone out from the rest, like the blaze of the hearth whose joys they celebrated. Into them, working magic with a few simple words, the poet had instilled the very essence of domestic love and household happiness, and they were poetry and picture joined in one. As Dorcas sang, the walls of her forsaken home seemed to encircle her; she no longer saw the gloomy pines, nor heard the wind, which still, as she began each verse, sent a heavy breath through the branches, and died away in a hollow moan, from the burthen of the song. She was aroused by the report of a gun, in the vicinity of the encampment; and either the sudden sound, or her loneliness by the glowing fire, caused her to tremble violently. The next moment, she laughed in the pride of a mother's heart.

'My beautiful young hunter! my boy has slain a deer!' she exclaimed, recollecting that, in the direction whence the shot proceeded, Cyrus had gone to the chase.

She waited a reasonable time, to hear her son's light step bounding over the rustling leaves, to tell of his success. But he did not immediately appear, and she sent her cheerful voice among the trees, in search of him.

'Cyrus! Cyrus!'

His coming was still delayed, and she determined, as the report of the gun had apparently been very near, to seek for him in person. Her assistance, also, might be necessary in bringing home the venison, which she flattered herself he had obtained. She therefore set forward, directing her steps by the long-past sound, and singing as she went, in order that the boy might be aware of her approach, and run to meet her. From behind the trunk of every tree, and from every hiding place in the thick foliage of the undergrowth, she hoped to discover the countenance of her son, laughing with the sportive mischief that is born of affection. The sun was now beneath the horizon, and the light that came down among the trees was sufficiently dim to create many illusions in her expecting fancy. Several times she seemed indistinctly to see his face gazing out from among the leaves; and once she imagined that he stood beckoning to her, at the base of a craggy rock. Keeping her eyes on this object, however, it proved to be no more than the trunk of an oak, fringed to the very ground with little branches, one of which, thrust out farther than the rest, was shaken by the breeze. Making her way round the foot of the rock, she suddenly found herself close to her husband, who had approached in another direction. Leaning upon the butt of his gun, the muzzle of which rested upon the withered leaves, he was apparently absorbed in the contemplation of some object at his feet.

'How is this, Reuben? Have you slain the deer, and fallen asleep over him?' exclaimed Dorcas, laughing cheerfully, on her first slight observation of his posture and appearance.

He stirred not, neither did he turn his eyes towards her; and a cold, shuddering fear, indefinite in its source and object, began to creep into her blood. She now perceived that her husband's face was ghastly pale, and his features were rigid, as if incapable of assuming any other expression than the strong despair which had hardened upon them. He gave not the slightest evidence that he was aware of her approach.

'For the love of Heaven, Reuben, speak to me!' cried Dorcas, and the strange sound of her own voice affrighted her even more than the dead silence.

Her husband started, stared into her face; drew her to the front of the rock, and pointed with his finger.

Oh! there lay the boy, asleep, but dreamless, upon the fallen forest-leaves!

His cheek rested upon his arm, his curled locks were thrown back from his brow, his limbs were slightly relaxed. Had a sudden weariness overcome the youthful hunter? Would his mother's voice arouse him? She knew that it was death.

'This broad rock is the grave-stone of your near kindred, Dorcas,' said her husband. 'Your tears will fall at once over your father and your son.'

She heard him not. With one wild shriek, that seemed to force its way from the suffer's inmost soul, she sank insensible by the side of her dead boy. At that moment, the withered topmost bough of the oak loosened itself, in the stilly air, and fell in soft, light fragments upon the rock, upon the leaves, upon Reuben, upon his wife and child, and upon Roger Malvin's bones. Then Reuben's heart was stricken, and the tears gushed out like water from a rock. The vow that the wounded youth had made, the blighted man had come to redeem. His sin was expiated, the curse was gone from him; and, in the hour, when he had shed blood dearer to him than his own, a prayer, the first for years, went up to Heaven from the lips of Reuben Bourne.

1832                                                                    1846

# Young Goodman Brown[1]

Young goodman Brown came forth, at sunset, into the street of Salem village, but put his head back, after crossing the threshold, to exchange a parting kiss with his young wife. And Faith, as the wife was aptly named, thrust her own pretty head into the street, letting the wind play with the pink ribbons of her cap, while she called to goodman Brown.

'Dearest heart,' whispered she, softly and rather sadly, when her lips were close to his ear, 'pr'y thee, put off your journey until sunrise, and sleep in your own bed to-night. A lone woman is troubled with such dreams and such thoughts, that she's afeard of herself, sometimes. Pray, tarry with me this night, dear husband, of all nights in the year!'

'My love and my Faith,' replied young goodman Brown, 'of all nights in the year, this one night must I tarry away from thee. My journey, as thou callest it, forth and back again, must needs be done 'twixt now and sunrise. What, my sweet, pretty wife, dost thou doubt me already, and we but three months married!'

'Then, God bless you!' and Faith, with the pink ribbons, 'and may you find all well, when you come back.'

'Amen!' cried goodman Brown. 'Say thy prayers, dear Faith, and go to bed at dusk, and no harm will come to thee.'

So they parted; and the young man pursued his way, until, being about to turn the corner by the meeting-house, he looked back, and saw the head of Faith still peeping after him, with a melancholy air, in spite of her pink ribbons.

1. The text followed here is that of the first publication, in the *New-England Magazine* (April 1835); the story was ascribed to "the author of 'The Gray Champion,'" which had appeared in the same magazine three months earlier. "Goodman": Hawthorne puns on the title used to address a man of humble birth and the moral implications of "good man"; what with "Brown" as a surname, the hero is equivalent to Young Mister Anybody.

'Poor little Faith!' thought he, for his heart smote him. 'What a wretch am I, to leave her on such an errand! She talks of dreams, too. Methought, as she spoke, there was trouble in her face, as if a dream had warned her what work is to be done to-night. But, no, no! 't would kill her to think it. Well; she's a blessed angel on earth; and after this one night, I'll cling to her skirts and follow her to Heaven.'

With this excellent resolve for the future, goodman Brown felt himself justified in making more haste on his present evil purpose. He had taken a dreary road, darkened by all the gloomiest trees of the forest, which barely stood aside to let the narrow path creep through, and closed immediately behind. It was all as lonely as could be; and there is this peculiarity in such a solitude, that the traveler knows not who may be concealed by the innumerable trunks and the thick boughs overhead; so that, with lonely footsteps, he may yet be passing through an unseen multitude.

'There may be a devilish Indian behind every tree,' said goodman Brown, to himself; and he glanced fearfully behind him, as he added, 'What if·the devil himself should be at my very elbow!'

His head being turned back, he passed a crook of the road, and looking forward again, beheld the figure of a man, in grave and decent attire, seated at the foot of an old tree. He arose, at goodman Brown's approach, and walked onward, side by side with him.

'You are late, goodman Brown,' said he. 'The clock of the Old South was striking as I came through Boston; and that is full fifteen minutes agone.'[2]

'Faith kept me back awhile,' replied the young man, with a tremor in his voice, caused by the sudden appearance of his companion, though not wholly unexpected.

It was now deep dusk in the forest, and deepest in that part of it where these two were journeying. As nearly as could be discerned, the second traveler was about fifty years old, apparently in the same rank of life as goodman Brown, and bearing a considerable resemblance to him, though perhaps more in expression than features. Still, they might have been taken for father and son. And yet, though the elder person was as simply clad as the younger, and as simple in manner too, he had an indescribable air of one who knew the world, and would not have felt abashed at the governor's dinner-table, or in king William's[3] court, were it possible that his affairs should call him thither. But the only thing about him, that could be fixed upon as remarkable, was his staff, which bore the likeness of a great black snake, so curiously wrought, that it might almost be seen to twist and wriggle itself, like a living serpent. This, of course, must have been an ocular deception, assisted by the uncertain light.

'Come, goodman Brown!' cried his fellow-traveler, 'this is a dull pace for the beginning of a journey. Take my staff, if you are so soon weary.'

'Friend,' said the other, exchanging his slow pace for a full stop, 'having kept covenant by meeting thee here, it is my purpose now to return whence I came. I have scruples, touching the matter thou wot'st of.'

'Sayest thou so?' replied he of the serpent, smiling apart. 'Let us walk on, nevertheless, reasoning as we go, and if I convince thee not, thou shalt turn back. We are but a little way in the forest, yet.'

2. This speed could only be supernatural.
3. William of Orange, first cousin and husband of   Queen Mary II, with whom he jointly ruled England, 1689–1702.

'Too far, too far!' exclaimed the goodman, unconsciously resuming his walk. 'My father never went into the woods on such an errand, nor his father before him. We have been a race of honest men and good Christians, since the days of the martyrs.[4] And shall I be the first of the name of Brown, that ever took this path, and kept'—

'Such company, thou wouldst say,' observed the elder person, interpreting his pause. 'Good, goodman Brown! I have been as well acquainted with your family as with ever a one among the Puritans; and that's no trifle to say. I helped your grandfather, the constable, when he lashed the Quaker woman so smartly through the streets of Salem. And it was I that brought your father a pitch-pine knot, kindled at my own hearth, to set fire to an Indian village, in king Philip's[5] war. They were my good friends, both; and many a pleasant walk have we had along this path, and returned merrily after midnight. I would fain be friends with you, for their sake.'

'If it be as thou sayest,' replied goodman Brown, 'I marvel they never spoke of these matters. Or, verily, I marvel not, seeing that the least rumor of the sort would have driven them from New-England. We are a people of prayer, and good works, to boot, and abide no such wickedness.'

'Wickedness or not,' said the traveler with the twisted staff, 'I have a very general acquaintance here in New-England. The deacons of many a church have drunk the communion wine with me; the selectmen, of divers towns, make me their chairman; and a majority of the Great and General Court[6] are firm supporters of my interest. The governor and I, too—but these are state-secrets.'

'Can this be so!' cried goodman Brown, with a stare of amazement at his undisturbed companion. 'Howbeit, I have nothing to do with the governor and council; they have their own ways, and are no rule for a simple husband-man,[7] like me. But, were I to go on with thee, how should I meet the eye of that good old man, our minister, at Salem village? Oh, his voice would make me tremble, both Sabbath-day and lecture-day!'[8]

Thus far, the elder traveler had listened with due gravity, but now burst into a fit of irrepressible mirth, shaking himself so violently, that his snake-like staff actually seemed to wriggle in sympathy.

'Ha! ha! ha!' shouted he, again and again; then composing himself, 'Well, go on, goodman Brown, go on; but, pr'y thee, don't kill me with laughing!'

'Well, then, to end the matter at once,' said goodman Brown, considerably nettled, 'there is my wife, Faith. It would break her dear little heart; and I'd rather break my own!'

'Nay, if that be the case,' answered the other, 'e'en go thy ways, goodman Brown. I would not, for twenty old women like the one hobbling before us, that Faith should come to any harm.'

As he spoke, he pointed his staff at a female figure on the path, in whom goodman Brown recognized a very pious and exemplary dame, who had taught him his catechism, in youth, and was still his moral and spiritual adviser, jointly with the minister and deacon Gookin.

4. I.e., during the reign of the Catholic Mary Tudor of England (1553–58), called "Bloody Mary" for her persecution of Protestants. Common reading in New England was John Foxe's Acts and Monuments (1563), soon known as the Book of Martyrs; it concluded with horrifically detailed accounts of martyrdoms under

Mary.
5. Leader of the Wampanoag Indians who waged war (1675–76) against the New England colonists.
6. The legislature.
7. Usually, farmer; here, man of ordinary status.
8. Midweek sermon day, Wednesday or Thursday.

'A marvel, truly, that goody Cloyse[9] should be so far in the wilderness, at night-fall!' said he. 'But, with your leave, friend, I shall take a cut through the woods, until we have left this Christian woman behind. Being a stranger to you, she might ask whom I was consorting with, and whither I was going.'

'Be it so,' said his fellow-traveler. 'Betake you to the woods, and let me keep the path.'

Accordingly, the young man turned aside, but took care to watch his companion, who advanced softly along the road, until he had come within a staff's length of the old dame. She, meanwhile, was making the best of her way, with singular speed for so aged a woman, and mumbling some indistinct words, a prayer, doubtless, as she went. The traveler put forth his staff, and touched her withered neck with what seemed the serpent's tail.

'The devil!' screamed the pious old lady.

'Then goody Cloyse knows her old friend?' observed the traveler, confronting her, and leaning on his writhing stick.

'Ah, forsooth, and is it your worship, indeed?' cried the good dame. 'Yea, truly is it, and in the very image of my old gossip, goodman Brown, the grandfather of the silly fellow that now is. But, would your worship believe it? my broomstick hath strangely disappeared, stolen, as I suspect, by that unhanged witch, goody Cory, and that, too, when I was all anointed with the juice of smallage and cinque-foil and wolf's-bane'[1]—

'Mingled with fine wheat and the fat of a new-born babe,' said the shape of old goodman Brown.

'Ah, your worship knows the receipt,' cried the old lady, cackling aloud. 'So, as I was saying, being all ready for the meeting, and no horse to ride on, I made up my mind to foot it; for they tell me, there is a nice young man to be taken into communion to-night. But now your good worship will lend me your arm, and we shall be there in a twinkling.'

'That can hardly be,' answered her friend. 'I may not spare you my arm, goody Cloyse, but here is my staff, if you will.'

So saying, he threw it down at her feet, where, perhaps, it assumed life, being one of the rods which its owner had formerly lent to the Egyptian Magi.[2] Of this fact, however, goodman Brown could not take cognizance. He had cast up his eyes in astonishment, and looking down again, beheld neither goody Cloyse nor the serpentine staff, but his fellow-traveler alone, who waited for him as calmly as if nothing had happened.

'That old woman taught me my catechism!' said the young man; and there was a world of meaning in this simple comment.

They continued to walk onward, while the elder traveler exhorted his companion to make good speed and persevere in the path, discoursing so aptly, that his arguments seemed rather to spring up in the bosom of his auditor, than to be suggested by himself. As they went, he plucked a branch of maple, to serve for a walking-stick, and began to strip it of the twigs and little boughs, which were wet with evening dew. The moment his fingers touched them, they became strangely withered and dried up, as with a week's sunshine. Thus

9. Hawthorne uses historical names of people involved in the Salem witchcraft trials. "Goody": i.e., "goodwife"; the polite title for a married woman of humble rank.
1. Plants associated with witchcraft. "Smallage": wild celery or parsley. "Cinque-foil": a five-lobed plant of

the rose family (from the Latin for "five fingers"). "Wolf's-bane": hooded, poisonous plant known as monkshood (bane means "poison").
2. See Exodus 7.11 for the magicians of Egypt who duplicated Aaron's feat of casting down his rod before Pharaoh and making it turn into a serpent.

the pair proceeded, at a good free pace, until suddenly, in a gloomy hollow of the road, goodman Brown sat himself down on the stump of a tree, and refused to go any farther.

'Friend,' said he, stubbornly, 'my mind is made up. Not another step will I budge on this errand. What if a wretched old woman do choose to go to the devil, when I thought she was going to Heaven! Is that any reason why I should quit my dear Faith, and go after her?'

'You will think better of this, by-and-by,' said his acquaintance, composedly. 'Sit here and rest yourself awhile; and when you feel like moving again, there is my staff to help you along.'

Without more words, he threw his companion the maple stick, and was as speedily out of sight, as if he had vanished into the deepening gloom. The young man sat a few moments, by the roadside, applauding himself greatly, and thinking with how clear a conscience he should meet the minister, in his morning-walk, nor shrink from the eye of good old deacon Gookin. And what calm sleep would be his, that very night, which was to have been spent so wickedly, but purely and sweetly now, in the arms of Faith! Amidst these pleasant and praiseworthy meditations, goodman Brown heard the tramp of horses along the road, and deemed it advisable to conceal himself within the verge of the forest, conscious of the guilty purpose that had brought him thither, though now so happily turned from it.

On came the hoof-tramps and the voices of the riders, two grave old voices, conversing soberly as they drew near. These mingled sounds appeared to pass along the road, within a few yards of the young man's hiding-place; but owing, doubtless, to the depth of the gloom, at that particular spot, neither the travelers nor their steeds were visible. Though their figures brushed the small boughs by the way-side, it could not be seen that they intercepted, even for a moment, the faint gleam from the strip of bright sky, athwart which they must have passed. Goodman Brown alternately crouched and stood on tip-toe, pulling aside the branches, and thrusting forth his head as far as he durst, without discerning so much as a shadow. It vexed him the more, because he could have sworn, were such a thing possible, that he recognized the voices of the minister and deacon Gookin, jogging along quietly, as they were wont to do, when bound to some ordination or ecclesiastical council. While yet within hearing, one of the riders stopped to pluck a switch.

'Of the two, reverend Sir,' said the voice like the deacon's, 'I had rather miss an ordination-dinner than to-night's meeting. They tell me that some of our community are to be here from Falmouth and beyond, and others from Connecticut and Rhode-Island; besides several of the Indian powows,[3] who, after their fashion, know almost as much deviltry as the best of us. Moreover, there is a goodly young woman to be taken into communion.'

'Mighty well, deacon Gookin!' replied the solemn old tones of the minister. 'Spur up, or we shall be late. Nothing can be done, you know, until I get on the ground.'

The hoofs clattered again, and the voices, talking so strangely in the empty air, passed on through the forest, where no church had ever been gathered, nor solitary Christian prayed. Whither, then, could these holy men be journeying, so deep into the heathen wilderness? Young goodman Brown caught

---

3. Medicine men. Usually spelled "pow-wow" and later used to refer to any conference or gathering. Falmouth is a town on Cape Cod, about seventy miles from Salem.

hold of a tree, for support, being ready to sink down on the ground, faint and overburthened with the heavy sickness of his heart. He looked up to the sky, doubting whether there really was a Heaven above him. Yet, there was the blue arch, and the stars brightening in it.

'With Heaven above, and Faith below, I will yet stand firm against the devil!' cried goodman Brown.

While he still gazed upward, into the deep arch of the firmament, and had lifted his hands to pray, a cloud, though no wind was stirring, hurried across the zenith, and hid the brightening stars. The blue sky was still visible, except directly overhead, where this black mass of cloud was sweeping swiftly northward. Aloft in the air, as if from the depths of the cloud, came a confused and doubtful sound of voices. Once, the listener fancied that he could distinguish the accents of town's-people of his own, men and women, both pious and ungodly, many of whom he had met at the communion-table, and had seen others rioting at the tavern. The next moment, so indistinct were the sounds, he doubted whether he had heard aught but the murmur of the old forest, whispering without a wind. Then came a stronger swell of those familiar tones, heard daily in the sunshine, at Salem village, but never, until now, from a cloud of night. There was one voice, of a young woman, uttering lamentations, yet with an uncertain sorrow, and entreating for some favor, which, perhaps, it would grieve her to obtain. And all the unseen multitude, both saints and sinners, seemed to encourage her onward.

'Faith!' shouted goodman Brown, in a voice of agony and desperation; and the echoes of the forest mocked him, crying—'Faith! Faith!' as if bewildered wretches were seeking her, all through the wilderness.

The cry of grief, rage, and terror, was yet piercing the night, when the unhappy husband held his breath for a response. There was a scream, drowned immediately in a louder murmur of voices, fading into far-off laughter, as the dark cloud swept away, leaving the clear and silent sky above goodman Brown. But something fluttered lightly down through the air, and caught on the branch of a tree. The young man seized it, and beheld a pink ribbon.

'My Faith is gone!' cried he, after one stupefied moment. 'There is no good on earth; and sin is but a name. Come, devil! for to thee is this world given.'

And maddened with despair, so that he laughed loud and long, did goodman Brown grasp his staff and set forth again, at such a rate, that he seemed to fly along the forest-path, rather than to walk or run. The road grew wilder and drearier, and more faintly traced, and vanished at length, leaving him in the heart of the dark wilderness, still rushing onward, with the instinct that guides mortal man to evil. The whole forest was peopled with frightful sounds; the creaking of the trees, the howling of wild beasts, and the yell of Indians; while, sometimes, the wind tolled like a distant church-bell, and sometimes gave a broad roar around the traveler, as if all Nature were laughing him to scorn. But he was himself the chief horror of the scene, and shrank not from its other horrors.

'Ha! ha! ha!' roared goodman Brown, when the wind laughed at him. 'Let us hear which will laugh loudest! Think not to frighten me with your deviltry! Come witch, come wizard, come Indian powow, come devil himself! and here comes goodman Brown. You may as well fear him as he fear you!'

In truth, all through the haunted forest, there could be nothing more frightful than the figure of goodman Brown. On he flew, among the black pines, brandishing his staff with frenzied gestures, now giving vent to an inspiration of horrid blasphemy, and now shouting forth such laughter, as set all the echoes of the forest laughing like demons around him. The fiend in his own shape is less hideous, than when he rages in the breast of man. Thus sped the demoniac on his course, until, quivering among the trees, he saw a red light before him, as when the felled trunks and branches of a clearing have been set on fire, and throw up their lurid blaze against the sky, at the hour of midnight. He paused, in a lull of the tempest that had driven him onward, and heard the swell of what seemed a hymn, rolling solemnly from a distance, with the weight of many voices. He knew the tune; it was a familiar one in the choir of the village meeting-house. The verse died heavily away, and was lengthened by a chorus, not of human voices, but of all the sounds of the benighted wilderness, pealing in awful harmony together. Goodman Brown cried out; and his cry was lost to his own ear, by its unison with the cry of the desert.

In the interval of silence, he stole forward, until the light glared full upon his eyes. At one extremity of an open space, hemmed in by the dark wall of the forest, arose a rock, bearing some rude, natural resemblance either to an altar or a pulpit, and surrounded by four blazing pines, their tops a flame, their stems untouched, like candles at an evening meeting. The mass of foliage, that had overgrown the summit of the rock, was all on fire, blazing high into the night, and fitfully illuminating the whole field. Each pendent twig and leafy festoon was in a blaze. As the red light arose and fell, a numerous congregation alternately shone forth, then disappeared in shadow, and again grew, as it were, out of the darkness, peopling the heart of the solitary woods at once.

'A grave and dark-clad company!' quoth goodman Brown.

In truth, they were such. Among them, quivering to-and-fro, between gloom and splendor, appeared faces that would be seen, next day, at the council-board of the province, and others which, Sabbath after Sabbath, looked devoutly heavenward, and benignantly over the crowded pews, from the holiest pulpits in the land. Some affirm, that the lady of the governor was there. At least, there were high dames well known to her, and wives of honored husbands, and widows, a great multitude, and ancient maidens, all of excellent repute, and fair young girls, who trembled, lest their mothers should espy them. Either the sudden gleams of light, flashing over the obscure field, bedazzled goodman Brown, or he recognized a score of the church-members of Salem village, famous for their especial sanctity. Good old deacon Gookin had arrived, and waited at the skirts of that venerable saint, his revered pastor. But, irreverently consorting with these grave, reputable, and pious people, these elders of the church, these chaste dames and dewy virgins, there were men of dissolute lives and women of spotted fame, wretches given over to all mean and filthy vice, and suspected even of horrid crimes. It was strange to see, that the good shrank not from the wicked, nor were the sinners abashed by the saints. Scattered, also, among their pale-faced enemies, were the Indian priests, or powows, who had often scared their native forest with more hideous incantations than any known to English witchcraft.

'But, where is Faith?' thought goodman Brown; and, as hope came into his heart, he trembled.

Another verse of the hymn arose, a slow and solemn strain, such as the pious love, but joined to words which expressed all that our nature can conceive of sin, and darkly hinted at far more. Unfathomable to mere mortals is the lore of fiends. Verse after verse was sung, and still the chorus of the desert swelled between, like the deepest tone of a mighty organ. And, with the final peal of that dreadful anthem, there came a sound, as if the roaring wind, the rushing streams, the howling beasts, and every other voice of the unconverted wilderness, were mingling and according with the voice of guilty man, in homage to the prince of all. The four blazing pines threw up a loftier flame, and obscurely discovered shapes and visages of horror on the smoke-wreaths, above the impious assembly. At the same moment, the fire on the rock shot redly forth, and formed a glowing arch above its base, where now appeared a figure. With reverence be it spoken, the apparition bore no slight similitude, both in garb and manner, to some grave divine of the New-England churches.

'Bring forth the converts!' cried a voice, that echoed through the field and rolled into the forest.

At the word, goodman Brown stept forth from the shadow of the trees, and approached the congregation, with whom he felt a loathful brotherhood, by the sympathy of all that was wicked in his heart. He could have well nigh sworn, that the shape of his own dead father beckoned him to advance, looking downward from a smoke-wreath, while a woman, with dim features of despair, threw out her hand to warn him back. Was it his mother? But he had no power to retreat one step, nor to resist, even in thought, when the minister and good old deacon Gookin, seized his arms, and led him to the blazing rock. Thither came also the slender form of a veiled female, led between Goody Cloyse, that pious teacher of the catechism, and Martha Carrier, who had received the devil's promise to be queen of hell. A rampant hag was she! And there stood the proselytes, beneath the canopy of fire.

'Welcome, my children,' said the dark figure, 'to the communion of your race![4] Ye have found, thus young, your nature and your destiny. My children, look behind you!"

They turned; and flashing forth, as it were, in a sheet of flame, the fiend-worshippers were seen; the smile of welcome gleamed darkly on every visage.

'There,' resumed the sable form, 'are all whom ye have reverenced from youth. Ye deemed them holier than yourselves, and shrank from your own sin, contrasting it with their lives of righteousness, and prayerful aspirations heavenward. Yet, here are they all, in my worshipping assembly! This night it shall be granted you to know their secret deeds; how hoary-bearded elders of the church have whispered wanton words to the young maids of their households; how many a woman, eager for widow's weeds, has given her husband a drink at bed-time, and let him sleep his last sleep in her bosom; how beardless youths have made haste to inherit their fathers' wealth; and how fair damsels—blush not, sweet ones!—have dug little graves in the garden, and bidden me, the sole guest, to an infant's funeral. By the sympathy of your human hearts for sin, ye shall scent out all the places—whether in church, bed-chamber, street, field, or forest—where crime has been committed, and shall exult to behold the whole earth one stain of guilt, one mighty blood-spot. Far more than this! It shall be your's to penetrate, in every bosom, the deep mystery of sin, the fountain of all wicked arts, and which, inexhaustibly supplies more evil impulses than human power—than my power, at its utmost!—can make manifest in deeds. And now, my children, look upon each other.'

4. The New-England Magazine erroneously printed "grave," corrected to "race" in Mosses from an Old Manse (1846).

They did so; and, by the blaze of the hell-kindled torches, the wretched man beheld his Faith, and the wife her husband, trembling before that unhallowed altar.

'Lo! there ye stand, my children,' said the figure, in a deep and solemn tone, almost sad, with its despairing awfulness, as if his once angelic nature could yet mourn for our miserable race. 'Depending upon one another's hearts, ye had still hoped, that virtue were not all a dream. Now are ye undeceived! Evil is the nature of mankind. Evil must be your only happiness. Welcome, again, my children, to the communion of your race!'

'Welcome!' repeated the fiend-worshippers, in one cry of despair and triumph.

And there they stood, the only pair, as it seemed, who were yet hesitating on the verge of wickedness, in this dark world. A basin was hollowed, naturally, in the rock. Did it contain water, reddened by the lurid light? or was it blood? or, perchance, a liquid flame? Herein did the Shape of Evil dip his hand, and prepare to lay the mark of baptism upon their foreheads, that they might be partakers of the mystery of sin, more conscious of the secret guilt of others, both in deed and thought, than they could now be of their own. The husband cast one look at his pale wife, and Faith at him. What polluted wretches would the next glance shew them to each other, shuddering alike at what they disclosed and what they saw!

'Faith! Faith!' cried the husband. 'Look up to Heaven, and resist the Wicked One!'

Whether Faith obeyed, he knew not. Hardly had he spoken, when he found himself amid calm night and solitude, listening to a roar of the wind, which died heavily away through the forest. He staggered against the rock and felt it chill and damp, while a hanging twig, that had been all on fire, besprinkled his cheek with the coldest dew.

The next morning, young goodman Brown came slowly into the street of Salem village, staring around him like a bewildered man. The good old minister was taking a walk along the graveyard, to get an appetite for breakfast and meditate his sermon, and bestowed a blessing, as he passed, on goodman Brown. He shrank from the venerable saint, as if to avoid an anathema. Old deacon Gookin was at domestic worship, and the holy words of his prayer were heard through the open window. 'What God doth the wizard pray to?' quoth goodman Brown. Goody Cloyse, that excellent old Christian, stood in the early sunshine, at her own lattice, catechising a little girl, who had brought her a pint of morning's milk. Goodman Brown snatched away the child, as from the grasp of the fiend himself. Turning the corner by the meeting-house, he spied the head of Faith, with the pink ribbons, gazing anxiously forth, and bursting into such joy at sight of him, that she skipt along the street, and almost kissed her husband before the whole village. But, goodman Brown looked sternly and sadly into her face, and passed on without a greeting.

Had goodman Brown fallen asleep in the forest, and only dreamed a wild dream of a witch-meeting?

Be it so, if you will. But, alas! it was a dream of evil omen for young goodman Brown. A stern, a sad, a darkly meditative, a distrustful, if not a desperate man, did he become, from the night of that fearful dream. On the Sabbath-day, when the congregation were singing a holy psalm, he could not listen, because an anthem of sin rushed loudly upon his ear, and drowned all the blessed strain. When the minister spoke from the pulpit, with power and fervid eloquence, and, with his hand on the open bible, of the sacred truths of our religion, and of saint-like lives and triumphant deaths, and of future bliss or misery unutterable, then did goodman Brown turn pale, dreading, lest the roof should thunder down upon the gray blasphemer and his hearers. Often, awakening suddenly at midnight, he shrank from the bosom of Faith, and at morning or eventide, when the family knelt down at prayer, he scowled, and muttered to himself, and gazed sternly at his wife, and turned away. And when he had lived long, and was borne to his grave, a hoary corpse, followed by Faith, an aged woman, and children and grand-children, a goodly procession, besides neighbors, not a few, they carved no hopeful verse upon his tomb-stone; for his dying hour was gloom.

1835

# The May-Pole of Merry Mount[1]

*There is an admirable foundation for a philosophic romance, in the curious history of the early settlement of Mount Wallaston, or Merry Mount. In the slight sketch here attempted, the facts, recorded on the grave pages of our New England annalists, have wrought themselves, almost spontaneously, into a sort of allegory. The masques, mummeries, and festive customs, described in the text, are in accordance with the manners of the age. Authority, on these points may be found in Strutt's Book of English Sports and Pastimes.[2]*

Bright were the days at Merry Mount, when the May-Pole was the banner-staff of that gay colony! They who reared it, should their banner be triumphant, were to pour sun-shine over New England's rugged hills, and scatter flower-seeds throughout the soil. Jollity and gloom were contending for an empire. Midsummer eve[3] had come, bringing deep verdure to the forest, and roses in her lap, of a more vivid hue than the tender buds of Spring. But May, or her mirthful spirit, dwelt all the year round at Merry Mount, sporting with the Summer months, and revelling with Autumn, and basking in the glow of Winter's fireside. Through a world of toil and care, she flitted with a dreamlike smile, and came hither to find a home among the lightsome hearts of Merry Mount.

Never had the May-Pole been so gaily decked as at sunset on mid-summer eve. This venerated emblem was a pine tree, which had preserved the slender grace of youth, while it equalled the loftiest height of the old wood monarchs. From its top streamed a silken banner, colored like the rainbow. Down nearly to the ground, the pole was dressed with birchen boughs, and others of the liveliest green, and some with silvery leaves, fastened by ribbons that fluttered in fantastic knots of twenty different colors, but no sad ones. Garden flowers, and blossoms of the wilderness, laughed gladly forth amid the verdure, so fresh

1. The text is that of the first printing in *The Token* (1836), where the story is ascribed to "the Author of 'The Gentle Boy.'" "May-pole": in English tradition the tall pole placed in a prominent site in a village where on May 1 flower-bedecked young people could dance around it after a night of gathering new vegetation and blossoms in the woods. Puritans condemned the custom as a sexual orgy.

2. Joseph Strutt, *The Sports and Pastimes of the People of England* (1801). Hawthorne also knew Nathaniel Morton's *New England Memorial* (1669), which drew on William Bradford's manuscript history *Of Plymouth Plantation*.

3. June 20, the day before the longest day of the year.

and dewy, that they must have grown by magic on that happy pine tree. Where this green and flowery splendor terminated, the shaft of the May-Pole was stained with the seven brilliant hues of the banner at its top. On the lowest green bough hung an abundant wreath of roses, some that had been gathered in the sunniest spots of the forest, and others, of still richer blush, which the colonists had reared from English seed. Oh, people of the Golden Age, the chief of your husbandry, was to raise flowers!

But what was the wild throng that stood hand in hand about the May-Pole? It could not be, that the Fauns and Nymphs, when driven from their classic groves and homes of ancient fable, had sought refuge, as all the persecuted did, in the fresh woods of the West. These were Gothic monsters, though perhaps of Grecian ancestry. On the shoulders of a comely youth, uprose the head and branching antlers of a stag; a second, human in all other points, had the grim visage of a wolf; a third, still with the trunk and limbs of a mortal man, showed the beard and horns of a venerable he-goat. There was the likeness of a bear erect, brute in all but his hind legs, which were adorned with pink silk stockings. And here again, almost as wondrous, stood a real bear of the dark forest, lending each of his fore paws to the grasp of a human hand, and as ready for the dance as any in that circle. This inferior nature rose halfway, to meet his companions as they stooped. Other faces wore the similitude of man or woman, but distorted or extravagant, with red noses pendulous before their mouths, which seemed of awful depth, and stretched from ear to ear in an eternal fit of laughter. Here might be seen the Salvage Man,[4] well known in heraldry, hairy as a baboon, and girdled with green leaves. By his side, a nobler figure, but still a counterfeit, appeared an Indian hunter, with feathery crest and wampum belt. Many of this strange company wore foolscaps, and had little bells appended to their garments, tinkling with a silvery sound, responsive to the inaudible music of their gleesome spirits. Some youths and maidens were of soberer garb, yet well maintained their places in the irregular throng, by the expression of wild revelry upon their features. Such were the colonists of Merry Mount, as they stood in the broad smile of sunset, round their venerated May-Pole.

Had a wanderer, bewildered in the melancholy forest, heard their mirth, and stolen a half-affrighted glance, he might have fancied them the crew of Comus,[5] some already transformed to brutes, some midway between man and beast, and the others rioting in the flow of tipsey jollity that foreran the change. But a band of Puritans, who watched the scene, invisible themselves, compared the masques to those devils and ruined souls, with whom their superstition peopled the black wilderness.

Within the ring of monsters, appeared the two airiest forms, that had ever trodden on any more solid footing than a purple and golden cloud. One was a youth, in glistening apparel, with a scarf of the rainbow pattern crosswise on his breast. His right hand held a gilded staff, the ensign[6] of high dignity among the revellous, and his left grasped the slender fingers of a fair maiden, not less gaily decorated than himself. Bright roses glowed in contrast with the dark and glossy curls of each, and were scattered round their feet, or had sprung up spontaneously there. Behind this lightsome couple, so close to the May-Pole

---

4. Person clad in foliage to represent a savage, as in medieval and Renaissance pageantry.
5. The god of revelry, here associated with Milton's

*Comus* (1634).
6. Sign, token.

that its boughs shaded his jovial face, stood the figure of an English priest, canonically dressed, yet decked with flowers, in Heathen fashion, and wearing a chaplet of the native vine leaves. By the riot of his rolling eye, and the pagan decorations of his holy garb, he seemed the wildest monster there, and the very Comus of the crew.

'Votaries of the May-Pole,' cried the flower-decked priest, 'merrily, all day long, have the woods echoed to your mirth. But be this your merriest hour, my hearts! Lo, here stand the Lord and Lady of the May, whom I, a clerk[7] of Oxford, and high priest of Merry Mount, am presently to join in holy matrimony. Up with your nimble spirits, ye morrice-dancers, green-men, and glee-maidens,[8] bears and wolves, and horned gentlemen! Come; a chorus now, rich with the old mirth of Merry England, and the wilder glee of this fresh forest; and then a dance, to show the youthful pair what life is made of, and how airily they should go through it! All ye that love the May-Pole, lend your voices to the nuptial song of the Lord and Lady of the May!'

This wedlock was more serious than most affairs of Merry Mount, where jest and delusion, trick and fantasy, kept up a continual carnival. The Lord and Lady of the May, though their titles must be laid down at sunset, were really and truly to be partners for the dance of life, beginning the measure that same bright eve. The wreath of roses, that hung from the lowest green bough of the May-Pole, had been twined for them, and would be thrown over both their heads, in symbol of their flowery union. When the priest had spoken, therefore, a riotous uproar burst from the rout of monstrous figures.

'Begin you the stave,[9] reverend Sir,' cried they all; 'and never did the woods ring to such a merry peal, as we of the May-Pole shall send up!'

Immediately a prelude of pipe, cittern,[1] and viol, touched with practised minstrelsy, began to play from a neighboring thicket, in such a mirthful cadence, that the boughs of the May-Pole quivered to the sound. But the May Lord, he of the gilded staff, chancing to look into his Lady's eyes, was wonderstruck at the almost pensive glance that met his own.

'Edith, sweet Lady of the May,' whispered he, reproachfully, 'is your wreath of roses a garland to hang above our graves, that you look so sad? Oh, Edith, this is our golden time! Tarnish it not by any pensive shadow of the mind; for it may be, that nothing of futurity will be brighter than the mere remembrance of what is now passing.'

'That was the very thought that saddened me! How came it in your mind too?' said Edith, in a still lower tone than he; for it was high treason to be sad at Merry Mount. 'Therefore do I sigh amid this festive music. And besides, dear Edgar, I struggle as with a dream, and fancy that these shapes of our jovial friends are visionary, and their mirth unreal, and that we are no true Lord and Lady of the May. What is the mystery in my heart?'

Just then, as if a spell had loosened them, down came a little shower of withering rose leaves from the May-Pole. Alas, for the young lovers! No sooner had their hearts glowed with real passion, than they were sensible of something vague and unsubstantial in their former pleasures, and felt a dreary presentiment of inevitable change. From the moment that they truly loved, they had

7. In Anglican usage, lay minister who assists the parish clergyman.
8. Participants in an English folk dance, which was originally "Moorish dance." "Green-men": men be-

decked in greenery. "Glee-maidens": girl singers.
9. Stanza.
1. Guitar with pear-shaped body.

subjected themselves to earth's doom of care, and sorrow, and troubled joy, and had no more a home at Merry Mount. That was Edith's mystery. Now leave we the priest to marry them, and the masquers to sport round the May-Pole, till the last sunbeam be withdrawn from its summit, and the shadows of the forest mingle gloomily in the dance. Meanwhile, we may discover who these gay people were.

Two hundred years ago, and more, the old world and its inhabitants became mutually weary of each other. Men voyaged by thousands to the West; some to barter glass beads, and such like jewels, for the furs of the Indian hunter; some to conquer virgin empires; and one stern band to pray. But none of these motives had much weight with the colonists of Merry Mount. Their leaders were men who had sported so long with life, that when Thought and Wisdom came, even these unwelcome guests were led astray, by the crowd of vanities which they should have put to flight. Erring Thought and perverted Wisdom were made to put on masques, and play the fool. The men of whom we speak, after losing the heart's fresh gaiety, imagined a wild philosophy of pleasure, and came hither to act out their latest day-dream. They gathered followers from all that giddy tribe, whose whole life is like the festal days of soberer men. In their train were minstrels, not unknown in London streets; wandering players, whose theatres had been the halls of noblemen; mummeries, rope-dancers, and mountebanks,[2] who would long be missed at wakes, church-ales, and fairs; in a word, mirth-makers of every sort, such as abounded in that age, but now began to be discountenanced by the rapid growth of Puritanism. Light had their footsteps been on land, and as lightly they came across the sea. Many had been maddened by their previous troubles into a gay despair; others were as madly gay in the flush of youth, like the May Lord and his Lady; but whatever might be the quality of their mirth, old and young were gay at Merry Mount. The young deemed themselves happy. The elder spirits, if they knew that mirth was but the counterfeit of happiness, yet followed the false shadow wilfully, because at least her garments glittered brightest. Sworn triflers of a life-time, they would not venture among the sober truths of life, not even to be truly blest.

All the hereditary pastimes of Old England were transplanted hither. The King of Christmas was duly crowned, and the Lord of Misrule[3] bore potent sway. On the eve of Saint John,[4] they felled whole acres of the forest to make bonfires, and danced by the blaze all night, crowned with garlands, and throwing flowers into the flame. At harvest time, though their crop was of the smallest, they made an image with the sheaves of Indian corn, and wreathed it with autumnal garlands, and bore it home triumphantly. But what chiefly characterized the colonists of Merry Mount, was their veneration for the May-Pole. It has made their true history a poet's tale. Spring decked the hallowed emblem with young blossoms and fresh green boughs; Summer brought roses of the deepest blush, and the perfected foliage of the forest; Autumn enriched it with that red and yellow gorgeousness, which converts each wildwood leaf into a painted flower; and Winter silvered it with sleet, and hung it round with icicles, till it flashed in the cold sunshine, itself a frozen sunbeam. Thus each alternate season did homage to the May-Pole, and paid it a tribute of its own

---

2. Showmen who "climb on a bench" to hawk medicines or (as here) to tell stories or do tricks. "Mummeries": masked actors. "Rope-dancers": tightrope walkers.

3. Master of the traditional Christmas revelry.
4. Midsummer eve.

richest splendor. Its votaries danced round it, once, at least, in every month; sometimes they called it their religion, or their altar; but always, it was the banner-staff of Merry Mount.

Unfortunately, there were men in the new world, of a sterner faith than these May-Pole worshippers. Not far from Merry Mount was a settlement of Puritans, most dismal wretches, who said their prayers before daylight, and then wrought in the forest or the cornfield, till evening made it prayer time again. Their weapons were always at hand, to shoot down the straggling savage. When they met in conclave, it was never to keep up the old English mirth, but to hear sermons three hours long, or to proclaim bounties on the heads of wolves and the scalps of Indians. Their festivals were fast-days, and their chief pastime the singing of psalms. Woe to the youth or maiden, who did but dream of a dance! The selectman nodded to the constable; and there sat the light-heeled reprobate in the stocks; or if he danced, it was round the whipping-post, which might be termed the Puritan May-Pole.

A party of these grim Puritans, toiling through the difficult woods, each with a horse-load of iron armor to burthen his footsteps, would sometimes draw near the sunny precincts of Merry Mount. There were the silken colonists, sporting round their May-Pole; perhaps teaching a bear to dance, or striving to communicate their mirth to the grave Indian; or masquerading in the skins of deer and wolves, which they had hunted for that especial purpose. Often, the whole colony were playing at blindman's bluff, magistrates and all with their eyes bandaged, except a single scape-goat, whom the blinded sinners pursued by the tinkling of the bells at his garments. Once, it is said, they were seen following a flower-decked corpse, with merriment and festive music, to his grave. But did the dead man laugh? In their quietest times, they sang ballads and told tales, for the edification of their pious visiters; or perplexed them with juggling tricks; or grinned at them through horse-collars; and when sport itself grew wearisome, they made game of their own stupidity, and began a yawning match. At the very least of these enormities, the men of iron shook their heads and frowned so darkly, that the revellers looked up, imagining that a momentary cloud had overcast the sunshine, which was to be perpetual there. On the other hand, the Puritans affirmed, that, when a psalm was pealing from their place of worship, the echo, which the forest sent them back, seemed often like the chorus of a jolly catch, closing with a roar of laughter. Who but the fiend, and his fond slaves, the crew of Merry Mount, had thus disturbed them! In due time, a feud arose, stern and bitter on one side, and as serious on the other as any thing could be, among such light spirits as had sworn allegiance to the May-Pole. The future complexion of New England was involved in this important quarrel. Should the grisly saints establish their jurisdiction over the gay sinners, then would their spirits darken all the clime, and make it a land of clouded visages, of hard toil, of sermon and psalm, forever. But should the banner-staff of Merry Mount be fortunate, sunshine would break upon the hills, and flowers would beautify the forest, and late posterity do homage to the May-Pole!

After these authentic passages from history, we return to the nuptials of the Lord and Lady of the May. Alas! we have delayed too long, and must darken our tale too suddenly. As we glanced again at the May-Pole, a solitary sunbeam is fading from the summit, and leaves only a faint golden tinge, blended with the hues of the rain bow banner. Even that dim light is now withdrawn, relinquishing the whole domain of Merry Mount to the evening gloom, which has rushed so instantaneously from the black surrounding woods. But some of these black shadows have rushed forth in human shape.

Yes: with the setting sun, the last day of mirth had passed from Merry Mount. The ring of gay masquers was disordered and broken; the stag lowered his antlers in dismay; the wolf grew weaker than a lamb; the bells of the morrice dancers tinkled with tremulous affright. The Puritans had played a characteristic part in the May-Pole mummeries. Their darksome figures were intermixed with the wild shapes of their foes, and made the scene a picture of the moment, when waking thoughts start up amid the scattered fantasies of a dream. The leader of the hostile party stood in the centre of the circle, while the rout of monsters cowered around him, like evil spirits in the presence of a dread magician. No fantastic foolery could look him in the face. So stern was the energy of his aspect, that the whole man, visage, frame, and soul, seemed wrought of iron, gifted with life and thought, yet all of one substance with his head-piece and breast-plate. It was the Puritan of Puritans; it was Endicott[5] himself!

'Stand off, priest of Baal!' said he, with a grim frown, and laying no reverent hand upon the surplice. 'I know thee, Claxton![6] Thou art the man, who couldst not abide the rule even of thine own corrupted church,[7] and hast come hither to preach iniquity, and to give example of it in thy life. But now shall it be seen that the Lord hath sanctified this wilderness for his peculiar people. Woe unto them that would defile it! And first for this flower-decked abomination, the altar of thy worship!'

And with his keen sword, Endicott assaulted the hallowed May-Pole. Nor long did it resist his arm. It groaned with a dismal sound; it showered leaves and rose-buds upon the remorseless enthusiast; and finally, with all its green boughs, and ribbons, and flowers, symbolic of departed pleasures, down fell the banner-staff of Merry Mount. As it sank, tradition says, the evening sky grew darker, and the woods threw forth a more sombre shadow.

'There,' cried Endicott, looking triumphantly on his work, 'there lies the only May-Pole in New-England! The thought is strong within me, that, by its fall, is shadowed forth the fate of light and idle mirth-makers, amongst us and our posterity. Amen, saith John Endicott!'

'Amen!' echoed his followers.

But the votaries of the May-Pole gave one groan for their idol. At the sound, the Puritan leader glanced at the crew of Comus, each a figure of broad mirth, yet, at this moment, strangely expressive of sorrow and dismay.

'Valiant captain,' quoth Peter Palfrey, the Ancient[8] of the band, 'what order shall be taken with the prisoners?'

'I thought not to repent me of cutting down a May-Pole,' replied Endicott, 'yet now I could find in my heart to plant it again, and give each of these bestial pagans one other dance round their idol. It would have served rarely for a whipping-post!'

'But there are pine trees enow,' suggested the lieutenant.

---

5. John Endicott (1589?–1665), several times governor of the Massachusetts colony.
6. "Did Governor Endicott speak less positively, we should suspect a mistake here. The Reverend Mr. Claxton, though an eccentric, is not known to have been an immoral man. We rather doubt his identity with the priest of Merry Mount" [Hawthorne's note]. For the slaying of the prophets of the fertility god Baal, see 1 Kings 18.
7. I.e., the Anglican church.
8. Lieutenant.

'True, good Ancient,' said the leader. 'Wherefore, bind the heathen crew, and bestow on them a small matter of stripes apiece, as earnest of our future justice. Set some of the rogues in the stocks to rest themselves, so soon as Providence shall bring us to one of our own well-ordered settlements, where such accommodations may be found. Further penalties, such as branding and cropping of ears, shall be thought of hereafter.'

'How many stripes for the priest?' inquired Ancient Palfrey.

'None as yet,' answered Endicott, bending his iron frown upon the culprit. 'It must be for the Great and General Court[9] to determine, whether stripes and long imprisonment, and other grievous penalty, may atone for his transgressions. Let him look to himself! For such as violate our civil order, it may be permitted us to show mercy. But woe to the wretch that troubleth our religion!'

'And this dancing bear,' resumed the officer. 'Must he share the stripes of his fellows?'

'Shoot him through the head!' said the energetic Puritan. 'I suspect witchcraft in the beast.'

'Here be a couple of shining ones,' continued Peter Palfrey, pointing his weapon at the Lord and Lady of the May. 'They seem to be of high station among these mis-doers. Methinks their dignity will not be fitted with less than a double share of stripes.'

Endicott rested on his sword, and closely surveyed the dress and aspect of the hapless pair. There they stood, pale, downcast, and apprehensive. Yet there was an air of mutual support, and of pure affection, seeking aid and giving it, that showed them to be man and wife, with the sanction of a priest upon their love. The youth, in the peril of the moment, had dropped his gilded staff, and thrown his arm about the Lady of the May, who leaned against his breast, too lightly to burthen him, but with weight enough to express that their destinies were linked together, for good or evil. They looked first at each other, and then into the grim captain's face. There they stood, in the first hour of wedlock, while the idle pleasures, of which their companions were the emblems, had given place to the sternest cares of life, personified by the dark Puritans. But never had their youthful beauty seemed so pure and high, as when its glow was chastened by adversity.

'Youth,' said Endicott, 'ye stand in an evil case, thou and thy maiden wife. Make ready presently; for I am minded that ye shall both have a token to remember your wedding-day!'

'Stern man,' exclaimed the May Lord, 'How can I move thee? Were the means at hand, I would resist to the death. Being powerless, I entreat! Do with me as thou wilt; but let Edith go untouched!'

'Not so,' replied the immitigable zealot. 'We are not wont to show an idle courtesy to that sex, which requireth the stricter discipline. What sayest thou, maid? Shall thy silken bridegroom suffer thy share of the penalty, besides his own?'

'Be it death,' said Edith, 'and lay it all on me!'

Truly, as Endicott had said, the poor lovers stood in a woeful case. Their foes were triumphant, their friends captive and abased, their home desolate, the benighted wilderness around them, and a rigorous destiny, in the shape of

9. Massachusetts legislature.

the Puritan leader, their only guide. Yet the deepening twilight could not altogether conceal, that the iron man was softened; he smiled, at the fair spectacle of early love; he almost sighed, for the inevitable blight of early hopes.

'The troubles of life have come hastily on this young couple,' observed Endicott. 'We will see how they comport themselves under their present trials, ere we burthen them with greater. If, among the spoil, there be any garments of a more decent fashion, let them be put upon this May Lord and his Lady, instead of their glistening vanities. Look to it, some of you.'

'And shall not the youth's hair be cut?' asked Peter Palfrey, looking with abhorrence at the love-lock and long glossy curls of the young man.

'Crop it forthwith, and that in the true pumpkin shell fashion,'[1] answered the captain. 'Then bring them along with us, but more gently than their fellows. There be qualities in the youth, which may make him valiant to fight, and sober to toil, and pious to pray; and in the maiden, that may fit her to become a mother in our Israel,[2] bringing up babes in better nurture than her own hath been. Nor think ye, young ones, that they are the happiest, even in our lifetime of a moment, who misspend it in dancing round a May-Pole!'

And Endicott, the severest Puritan of all who laid the rock-foundation of New England, lifted the wreath of roses from the ruin of the May-Pole, and threw it, with his own gauntleted hand, over the heads of the Lord and Lady of the May. It was a deed of prophecy. As the moral gloom of the world overpowers all systematic gaiety, even so was their home of wild mirth made desolate amid the sad forest. They returned to it no more. But, as their flowery garland was wreathed of the brightest roses that had grown there, so, in the tie that united them, were intertwined all the purest and best of their early joys. They went heavenward, supporting each other along the difficult path which it was their lot to tread, and never wasted one regretful thought on the vanities of Merry Mount.

1835

# Wakefield[1]

In some old magazine or newspaper, I recollect a story, told as truth, of a man—let us call him Wakefield—who absented himself for a long time, from his wife. The fact, thus abstractedly stated, is not very uncommon, nor—without a proper distinction of circumstances—to be condemned either as naughty or nonsensical. Howbeit, this, though far from the most aggravated, is perhaps the strangest instance, on record, of marital delinquency; and, moreover, as remarkable a freak as may be found in the whole list of human oddities. The wedded couple lived in London. The man, under pretence of going a journey, took lodgings in the next street to his own house, and there, unheard of by his wife or friends, and without the shadow of a reason for such self-banishment, dwelt upwards of twenty years. During that period, he beheld his home every day, and frequently the forlorn Mrs. Wakefield. And after so great a gap in his matrimonial felicity—when his death was reckoned certain,

---

1. Roundhead style, close-cropped in Puritan fashion.
2. Endicott makes the standard 17th-century Puritan identification of the New England settlers with the

Jews, another persecuted, God-chosen minority.
1. The text is from the first publication, in the *New-England Magazine* (May 1835).

his estate settled, his name dismissed from memory, and his wife, long, long ago, resigned to her autumnal widowhood—he entered the door one evening, quietly, as from a day's absence, and became a loving spouse until death. This outline is all that I remember. But the incident, though of the purest originality, unexampled, and probably never to be repeated, is one, I think, which appeals to the general sympathies of mankind. We know, each for himself, that none of us would perpetrate such a folly, yet feel as if some other might. To my own contemplations, at least, it has often recurred, always exciting wonder, but with a sense that the story must be true, and a conception of its hero's character. Whenever any subject so forcibly affects the mind, time is well spent in thinking of it. If the reader choose, let him do his own meditation; or if he prefer to ramble with me through the twenty years of Wakefield's vagary, I bid him welcome; trusting that there will be a pervading spirit and a moral, even should we fail to find them, done up neatly, and condensed into the final sentence. Thought has always its efficacy, and every striking incident its moral.

What sort of a man was Wakefield? We are free to shape out our own idea, and call it by his name. He was now in the meridian of life; his matrimonial affections, never violent, were sobered into a calm, habitual sentiment; of all husbands, he was likely to be the most constant, because a certain sluggishness would keep his heart at rest, wherever it might be placed. He was intellectual, but not actively so; his mind occupied itself in long and lazy musings, that tended to no purpose, or had not vigor to attain it; his thoughts were seldom so energetic as to seize hold of words. Imagination, in the proper meaning of the term, made no part of Wakefield's gifts. With a cold, but not depraved nor wandering heart, and a mind never feverish with riotous thoughts, nor perplexed with originality, who could have anticipated, that our friend would entitle himself to a foremost place among the doers of eccentric deeds? Had his acquaintances been asked, who was the man in London, the surest to perform nothing to-day which should be remembered on the morrow, they would have thought of Wakefield. Only the wife of his bosom might have hesitated. She, without having analyzed his character, was partly aware of a quiet selfishness, that had rusted into his inactive mind—of a peculiar sort of vanity, the most uneasy attribute about him—of a disposition to craft, which had seldom produced more positive effects than the keeping of petty secrets, hardly worth revealing—and, lastly, of what she called a little strangeness, sometimes, in the good man. This latter quality is indefinable, and perhaps non-existent.

Let us now imagine Wakefield bidding adieu to his wife. It is the dusk of an October evening. His equipment is a drab great-coat, a hat covered with an oil-cloth, top-boots, an umbrella in one hand and a small portmanteau in the other. He has informed Mrs. Wakefield that he is to take the night-coach into the country. She would fain inquire the length of his journey, its object, and the probable time of his return; but, indulgent to his harmless love of mystery, interrogates him only by a look. He tells her not to expect him positively by the return coach, nor to look alarmed should he tarry three or four days; but, at all events, to look for him at supper on Friday evening. Wakefield himself, be it considered, has no suspicion of what is before him. He holds out his hand; she gives her own, and meets his parting kiss, in the matter-of-course way of a ten years' matrimony; and forth goes the middle-aged Mr. Wakefield, almost resolved to perplex his good lady by a whole week's absence. After the door has closed behind him, she perceives it thrust partly open, and a vision of her husband's face, through the aperture, smiling on her, and gone in a moment. For the time, this little incident is dismissed without a thought. But, long afterwards, when she has been more years a widow than a wife, that smile recurs, and flickers across all her reminiscences of Wakefield's visage. In her many musings, she surrounds the original smile with a multitude of fantasies, which make it strange and awful; as, for instance, if she imagines him in a coffin, that parting look is frozen on his pale features; or, if she dreams of him in Heaven, still his blessed spirit wears a quiet and crafty smile. Yet, for its sake, when all others have given him up for dead, she sometimes doubts whether she is a widow.

But, our business is with the husband. We must hurry after him, along the street, ere he lose his individuality, and melt into the great mass of London life. It would be vain searching for him there. Let us follow close at his heels, therefore, until, after several superfluous turns and doublings, we find him comfortably established by the fireside of a small apartment, previously bespoken. He is in the next street to his own, and at his journey's end. He can scarcely trust his good fortune, in having got thither unperceived—recollecting that, at one time, he was delayed by the throng, in the very focus of a lighted lantern; and, again, there were foot-steps, that seemed to tread behind his own, distinct from the multitudinous tramp around him; and, anon, he heard a voice shouting afar, and fancied that it called his name. Doubtless, a dozen busy-bodies had been watching him, and told his wife the whole affair. Poor Wakefield! Little knowest thou thine own insignificance in this great world! No mortal eye but mine has traced thee. Go quietly to thy bed, foolish man; and, on the morrow, if thou wilt be wise, get thee home to good Mrs. Wakefield, and tell her the truth. Remove not thyself, even for a little week, from thy place in her chaste bosom. Were she, for a single moment, to deem thee dead, or lost, or lastingly divided from her, thou wouldst be woefully conscious of a change in thy true wife, forever after. It is perilous to make a chasm in human affections; not that they gape so long and wide—but so quickly close again!

Almost repenting of his frolic, or whatever it may be termed, Wakefield lies down betimes, and starting from his first nap, spreads forth his arms into the wide and solitary waste of the unaccustomed bed. 'No'—thinks he, gathering the bed-clothes about him—'I will not sleep alone another night.'

In the morning, he rises earlier than usual, and sets himself to consider what he really means to do. Such are his loose and rambling modes of thought, that he has taken this very singular step, with the consciousness of a purpose, indeed, but without being able to define it sufficiently for his own contemplation. The vagueness of the project, and the convulsive effort with which he plunges into the execution of it, are equally characteristic of a feeble-minded man. Wakefield sifts his ideas, however, as minutely as he may, and finds himself curious to know the progress of matters at home—how his exemplary wife will endure her widowhood, of a week; and, briefly, how the little sphere of creatures and circumstances, in which he was a central object, will be affected by his removal. A morbid vanity, therefore, lies nearest the bottom of the affair. But, how is he to attain his ends? Not, certainly, by keeping close in this comfortable lodging, where, though he slept and awoke in the next street to his home, he is as effectually abroad, as if the stage-coach had been whirling him away all night. Yet, should he reappear, the whole project is knocked in the head. His poor brains being hopelessly puzzled with this dilemma, he at length ventures out, partly resolving to cross the head of the street, and send one hasty glance towards his forsaken domicile. Habit—for he is a man of habits—takes him by the hand, and guides him, wholly unaware, to his own door, where, just at the critical moment, he is aroused by the scraping of his foot upon the step. Wakefield! whither are you going?

At that instant, his fate was turning on the pivot. Little dreaming of the doom to which his first backward step devotes him, he hurries away, breathless with agitation hitherto unfelt, and hardly dares turn his head, at the distant corner. Can it be, that nobody caught sight of him? Will not the whole household—the decent Mrs. Wakefield, the smart maid-servant, and the dirty little foot-boy—raise a hue-and-cry, through London streets, in pursuit of their fugitive lord and master? Wonderful escape! He gathers courage to pause and look homeward, but is perplexed with a sense of change about the familiar edifice, such as affects us all, when, after a separation of months or years, we again see some hill or lake, or work of art, with which we were friends, of old. In ordinary cases, this indescribable impression is caused by the comparison and contrast between our imperfect reminiscences and the reality. In Wakefield, the magic of a single night has wrought a similar transformation, because, in that brief period, a great moral change has been effected. But this is a secret from himself. Before leaving the spot, he catches a far and momentary glimpse of his wife, passing athwart the front window, with her face turned towards the head of the street. The crafty nincompoop takes to his heels, scared with the idea, that, among a thousand such atoms of mortality, her eye must have detected him. Right glad is his heart, though his brain be somewhat dizzy, when he finds himself by the coal-fire of his lodgings.

So much for the commencement of this long whim-wham. After the critical conception, and the stirring up of the man's sluggish temperament to put it in practice, the whole matter evolves itself in a natural train. We may suppose him, as the result of deep deliberation, buying a new wig, of reddish hair, and selecting sundry garments, in a fashion unlike his customary suit of brown, from a Jew's old-clothes bag. It is accomplished. Wakefield is another man. The new system being now established, a retrograde movement to the old would be almost as difficult as the step that placed him in his unparalleled position. Furthermore, he is rendered obstinate by a sulkiness, occasionally incident to his temper, and brought on, at present, by the inadequate sensation which he conceived to have been produced in the bosom of Mrs. Wakefield. He will not go back until she be frightened half to death. Well; twice or thrice has she passed before his sight, each time with a heavier step, a paler cheek, and more anxious brow; and, in the third week of his non-appearance, he detects a portent of evil entering the house, in the guise of an apothecary. Next day, the knocker is muffled. Towards night-fall, comes the chariot of a physician, and deposits its big-wigged and solemn burthen at Wakefield's door, whence, after a quarter of an hour's visit, he emerges, perchance the herald of a funeral. Dear woman! Will she die? By this time, Wakefield is excited to something like energy of feeling, but still lingers away from his wife's bedside, pleading with his conscience, that she must not be disturbed at such a juncture. If aught else restrains him, he does not know it. In the course of a few weeks, she gradually recovers; the crisis is over; her heart is sad, perhaps, but quiet; and, let him return soon or late, it will never be feverish for him again. Such ideas glimmer through the mist of Wakefield's mind, and render him indistinctly conscious that an almost impassible gulf divides his hired apartment from his former home. 'It is but in the next street!' he sometimes says. Fool! it is in another world. Hitherto, he has put off his return from one particular day to another; henceforward, he leaves the precise time undetermined. Not to-morrow—probably next week—pretty soon. Poor man! The dead have nearly as much chance of re-visiting their earthly homes, as the self-banished Wakefield.

Would that I had a folio to write, instead of a brief article in the New-England! Then might I exemplify how an influence, beyond our control, lays its strong hand on every deed which we do, and weaves its consequences into an iron tissue of necessity. Wakefield is spell-bound. We must leave him, for ten years or so, to haunt around his house, without once crossing the threshold, and to be faithful to his wife, with all the affection of which his heart is capable, while he is slowly fading out of hers. Long since, it must be remarked, he has lost the perception of singularity in his conduct.

Now for a scene! Amid the throng of a London street, we distinguish a man, now waxing elderly, with few characteristics to attract careless observers, yet bearing, in his whole aspect, the hand-writing of no common fate, for such as have the skill to read it. He is meagre; his low and narrow forehead is deeply wrinkled; his eyes, small and lustreless, sometimes wander apprehensively about him, but oftener seem to look inward. He bends his head, and moves with an indescribable obliquity of gait, as if unwilling to display his full front to the world. Watch him, long enough to see what we have described, and you will allow, that circumstances—which often produce remarkable men from nature's ordinary handiwork—have produced one such here. Next, leaving him to sidle along the foot-walk, cast your eyes in the opposite direction, where a portly female, considerably in the wane of life, with a prayer-book in her hand, is proceeding to yonder church. She has the placid mien of settled widowhood. Her regrets have either died away, or have become so essential to her heart, that they would be poorly exchanged for joy. Just as the lean man and well conditioned woman are passing, a slight obstruction occurs, and brings these two figures directly in contact. Their hands touch; the pressure of the crowd forces her bosom against his shoulder; they stand, face to face, staring into each other's eyes. After a ten years' separation, thus Wakefield meets his wife!

The throng eddies away, and carries them asunder. The sober widow, resuming her former pace, proceeds to church, but pauses in the portal, and throws a perplexed glance along the street. She passes in, however, opening her prayer-book as she goes. And the man? With so wild a face, that busy and selfish London stands to gaze after him, he hurries to his lodgings, bolts the door, and throws himself upon the bed. The latent feelings of years break out; his feeble mind acquires a brief energy from their strength; all the miserable strangeness of his life is revealed to him at a glance; and he cries out, passionately—'Wakefield! Wakefield! You are mad!'

Perhaps he was so. The singularity of his situation must have so moulded him to itself, that, considered in regard to his fellow-creatures and the business of life, he could not be said to possess his right mind. He had contrived, or rather he had happened, to dissever himself from the world—to vanish—to give up his place and privileges with living men, without being admitted among the dead. The life of a hermit is nowise parallel to his. He was in the bustle of the city, as of old; but the crowd swept by, and saw him not; he was, we may figuratively say, always beside his wife, and at his hearth, yet must never feel the warmth of the one, nor the affection of the other. It was Wakefield's unprecedented fate, to retain his original share of human sympathies, and to be still involved in human interests, while he had lost his reciprocal influence on them. It would be a most curious speculation, to trace out the effect of such circumstances on his heart and intellect, separately, and in unison. Yet, changed as he was, he would seldom be conscious of it, but deem himself the same man as ever; glimpses of the truth, indeed, would come, but only for the moment; and still he would keep saying—'I shall soon go back!'— nor reflect, that he had been saying so for twenty years.

I conceive, also, that these twenty years would appear, in the retrospect, scarcely longer than the week to which Wakefield had at first limited his absence. He would look on the affair as no more than an interlude in the main business of his life. When, after a little while more, he should deem it time to re-enter his parlor, his wife would clap her hands for joy, on beholding the middle-aged Mr. Wakefield. Alas, what a mistake! Would Time but await the close of our favorite follies, we should be young men, all of us, and till Doom's Day.

One evening, in the twentieth year since he vanished, Wakefield is taking his customary walk towards the dwelling which he still calls his own. It is a gusty night of autumn, with frequent showers, that patter down upon the pavement, and are gone, before a man can put up his umbrella. Pausing near the house, Wakefield discerns, through the parlor-windows of the second floor, the red glow, and the glimmer and fitful flash, of a comfortable fire. On the ceiling, appears a grotesque shadow of good Mrs. Wakefield. The cap, the nose and chin, and the broad waist, form an admirable caricature, which dances, moreover, with the up-flickering and down-sinking blaze, almost too merrily for the shade of an elderly widow. At this instant, a shower chances to fall, and is driven, by the unmannerly gust, full into Wakefield's face and bosom. He is quite penetrated with its autumnal chill. Shall he stand, wet and shivering here, when his own hearth has a good fire to warm him, and his own wife will run to fetch the gray coat and small-clothes, which, doubtless, she has kept carefully in the closet of their bed-chamber? No! Wakefield is no such fool. He ascends the steps—heavily!—for twenty years have stiffened his legs, since he came down—but he knows it not. Stay, Wakefield! Would you go to the sole home that is left you? Then step into your grave! The door opens. As he passes in, we have a parting glimpse of his visage, and recognize the crafty smile, which was the precursor of the little joke, that he has ever since been playing off at his wife's expense. How unmercifully has he quizzed the poor woman! Well; a good night's rest to Wakefield!

This happy event—supposing it to be such—could only have occurred at an unpremeditated moment. We will not follow our friend across the threshold. He has left us much food for thought, a portion of which shall lend its wisdom to a moral, and be shaped into a figure. Amid the seeming confusion of our mysterious world, individuals are so nicely adjusted to a system, and systems to one another, and to a whole, that, by stepping aside for a moment, a man exposes himself to a fearful risk of losing his place forever. Like Wakefield, he may become, as it were, the Outcast of the Universe.

1835

# The Minister's Black Veil

## A Parable[1]

### BY THE AUTHOR OF 'SIGHTS FROM A STEEPLE'

The sexton stood in the porch of Milford meeting-house, pulling lustily at the bell-rope. The old people of the village came stooping along the street. Children, with bright faces, tript merrily beside their parents, or mimicked a graver gait, in the conscious dignity of their sunday clothes. Spruce bachelors looked sidelong at the pretty maidens, and fancied that the sabbath sunshine made them prettier than on week-days. When the throng had mostly streamed into the porch, the sexton began to toll the bell, keeping his eye on the Reverend Mr. Hooper's door. The first glimpse of the clergyman's figure was the signal for the bell to cease its summons.

'But what has good Parson Hooper got upon his face?' cried the sexton in astonishment.

All within hearing immediately turned about, and beheld the semblance of Mr. Hooper, pacing slowly his meditative way towards the meeting-house. With one accord they started, expressing more wonder than if some strange minister were coming to dust the cushions of Mr. Hooper's pulpit.

'Are you sure it is our parson?' inquired Goodman Gray of the sexton.

'Of a certainty it is good Mr. Hooper,' replied the sexton. 'He was to have exchanged pulpits with Parson Shute of Westbury; but Parson Shute sent to excuse himself yesterday, being to preach a funeral sermon.'

The cause of so much amazement may appear sufficiently slight. Mr. Hooper, a gentlemanly person of about thirty, though still a bachelor, was dressed with due clerical neatness, as if a careful wife had starched his band, and brushed the weekly dust from his Sunday's garb. There was but one thing remarkable in his appearance. Swathed about his forehead, and hanging down over his face, so low as to be shaken by his breath, Mr. Hooper had on a black veil. On a nearer view, it seemed to consist of two folds of crape, which entirely concealed his features, except the mouth and chin, but probably did not intercept his sight, farther than to give a darkened aspect to all living and inanimate things. With this gloomy shade before him, good Mr. Hooper walked onward, at a slow and quiet pace, stooping somewhat and looking on the ground, as is customary with abstracted men, yet nodding kindly to those of his parishioners who still waited on the meeting-house steps. But so wonder-struck were they, that his greeting hardly met with a return.

'I can't really feel as if good Mr. Hooper's face was behind that piece of crape,' said the sexton.

'I don't like it,' muttered an old woman, as she hobbled into the meeting-

---

1. The text is that of the first printing in *The Token* (1836). "Another clergyman in New-England, Mr. Joseph Moody, of York, Maine, who died about eighty years since, made himself remarkable by the same eccentricity that is here related of the Reverend Mr. Hooper. In his case, however, the symbol had a different import. In early life he had accidentally killed a beloved friend; and from that day till the hour of his own death, he hid his face from men" [Hawthorne's note].

house. 'He has changed himself into something awful, only by hiding his face.'

'Our parson has gone mad!' cried Goodman Gray, following him across the threshhold.

A rumor of some unaccountable phenomenon had preceded Mr. Hooper into the meeting-house, and set all the congregation astir. Few could refrain from twisting their heads towards the door; many stood upright, and turned directly about; while several little boys clambered upon the seats, and came down again with a terrible racket. There was a general bustle, a rustling of the women's gowns and shuffling of the men's feet, greatly at variance with that hushed repose which should attend the entrance of the minister. But Mr. Hooper appeared not to notice the perturbation of his people. He entered with an almost noiseless step, bent his head mildly to the pews on each side, and bowed as he passed his oldest parishioner, a white-haired great-grandsire, who occupied an arm-chair in the centre of the aisle. It was strange to observe, how slowly this venerable man became conscious of something singular in the appearance of his pastor. He seemed not fully to partake of the prevailing wonder, till Mr. Hooper had ascended the stairs, and showed himself in the pulpit, face to face with his congregation, except for the black veil. That mysterious emblem was never once withdrawn. It shook with his measured breath as he gave out the psalm; it threw its obscurity between him and the holy page, as he read the Scriptures; and while he prayed, the veil lay heavily on his uplifted countenance. Did he seek to hide it from the dread Being whom he was addressing?

Such was the effect of this simple piece of crape, that more than one woman of delicate nerves was forced to leave the meeting-house. Yet perhaps the pale-faced congregation was almost as fearful a sight to the minister, as his black veil to them.

Mr. Hooper had the reputation of a good preacher, but not an energetic one: he strove to win his people heavenward, by mild persuasive influences, rather than to drive them thither, by the thunders of the Word. The sermon which he now delivered, was marked by the same characteristics of style and manner, as the general series of his pulpit oratory. But there was something, either in the sentiment of the discourse itself, or in the imagination of the auditors, which made it greatly the most powerful effort that they had ever heard from their pastor's lips. It was tinged, rather more darkly than usual, with the gentle gloom of Mr. Hooper's temperament. The subject had reference to secret sin, and those sad mysteries which we hide from our nearest and dearest, and would fain conceal from our own consciousness, even forgetting that the Omniscient can detect them. A subtle power was breathed into his words. Each member of the congregation, the most innocent girl, and the man of hardened breast, felt as if the preacher had crept upon them, behind his awful veil, and discovered their hoarded iniquity of deed or thought. Many spread their clasped hands on their bosoms. There was nothing terrible in what Mr. Hooper said; at least, no violence; and yet, with every tremor of his melancholy voice, the hearers quaked. An unsought pathos came hand in hand with awe. So sensible were the audience of some unwonted attribute in their minister, that they longed for a breath of wind to blow aside the veil, almost believing that a stranger's visage would be discovered, though the form, gesture, and voice were those of Mr. Hooper.

At the close of the services, the people hurried out with indecorous confusion, eager to communicate their pent-up amazement, and conscious of lighter spirits, the moment they lost sight of the black veil. Some gathered in little circles, huddled closely together, with their mouths all whispering in the centre; some went homeward alone, wrapt in silent meditation; some talked loudly, and profaned the Sabbath-day with ostentatious laughter. A few shook their sagacious heads, intimating that they could penetrate the mystery; while one or two affirmed that there was no mystery at all, but only that Mr. Hooper's eyes were so weakened by the midnight lamp, as to require a shade. After a brief interval, forth came good Mr. Hooper also, in the rear of his flock. Turning his veiled face from one group to another, he paid due reverence to the hoary heads, saluted the middle-aged with kind dignity, as their friend and spiritual guide, greeted the young with mingled authority and love, and laid his hands on the little children's heads to bless them. Such was always his custom on the Sabbath-day. Strange and bewildered looks repaid him for his courtesy. None, as on former occasions, aspired to the honor of walking by their pastor's side. Old Squire Saunders, doubtless by an accidental lapse of memory, neglected to invite Mr. Hooper to his table, where the good clergyman had been wont to bless the food, almost every Sunday since his settlement. He returned, therefore, to the parsonage, and, at the moment of closing the door, was observed to look back upon the people, all of whom had their eyes fixed upon the minister. A sad smile gleamed faintly from beneath the black veil, and flickered about his mouth, glimmering as he disappeared.

'How strange,' said a lady, 'that a simple black veil, such as any woman might wear on her bonnet, should become such a terrible thing on Mr. Hooper's face!'

'Something must surely be amiss with Mr. Hooper's intellects,' observed her husband, the physician of the village. 'But the strangest part of the affair is the effect of this vagary, even on a sober-minded man like myself. The black veil, though it covers only our pastor's face, throws its influence over his whole person, and makes him ghost-like from head to foot. Do you not feel it so?'

'Truly do I,' replied the lady; 'and I would not be alone with him for the world. I wonder he is not afraid to be alone with himself!'

'Men sometimes are so,' said her husband.

The afternoon service was attended with similar circumstances. At its conclusion, the bell tolled for the funeral of a young lady. The relatives and friends were assembled in the house, and the more distant acquaintances stood about the door, speaking of the good qualities of the deceased, when their talk was interrupted by the appearance of Mr. Hooper, still covered with his black veil. It was now an appropriate emblem. The clergyman stepped into the room where the corpse was laid, and bent over the coffin, to take a last farewell of his deceased parishioner. As he stooped, the veil hung straight down from his forehead, so that, if her eye-lids had not been closed for ever, the dead maiden might have seen his face. Could Mr. Hooper be fearful of her glance, that he so hastily caught back the black veil? A person, who watched the interview between the dead and living, scrupled not to affirm, that, at the instant when the clergyman's features were disclosed, the corpse had slightly shuddered, rustling the shroud and muslin cap, though the countenance retained the composure of death. A superstitious old woman was the only witness of this prodigy. From the coffin, Mr. Hooper passed into the chambers of the mourners, and thence to the head of the staircase, to make the funeral prayer. It was a tender and heart-dissolving prayer, full of sorrow, yet so imbued with celestial hopes, that the music of a heavenly harp, swept by the fingers of the dead, seemed faintly to be heard among the saddest accents of the minister. The people trembled, though they but darkly understood him, when he prayed that they, and himself, and all of mortal race, might be ready, as he trusted this young maiden had been, for the dreadful hour that should snatch the veil from their faces. The bearers went heavily forth, and the mourners followed, saddening all the street, with the dead before them, and Mr. Hooper in his black veil behind.

'Why do you look back?' said one in the procession to his partner.

'I had a fancy,' replied she, 'that the minister and the maiden's spirit were walking hand in hand.'

'And so had I, at the same moment,' said the other.

That night, the handsomest couple in Milford village were to be joined in wedlock. Though reckoned a melancholy man, Mr. Hooper had a placid cheerfulness for such occasions, which often excited a sympathetic smile, where livelier merriment would have been thrown away. There was no quality of his disposition which made him more beloved than this. The company at the wedding awaited his arrival with impatience, trusting that the strange awe, which had gathered over him throughout the day, would now be dispelled. But such was not the result. When Mr. Hooper came, the first thing that their eyes rested on was the same horrible black veil, which had added deeper gloom to the funeral, and could portend nothing but evil to the wedding. Such was its immediate effect on the guests, that a cloud seemed to have rolled duskily from beneath the black crape, and dimmed the light of the candles. The bridal pair stood up before the minister. But the bride's cold fingers quivered in the tremulous hand of the bridegroom, and her death-like paleness caused a whisper, that the maiden who had been buried a few hours before, was come from her grave to be married. If ever another wedding were so dismal, it was that famous one, where they tolled the wedding-knell.[2] After performing the ceremony, Mr. Hooper raised a glass of wine to his lips, wishing happiness to the new-married couple, in a strain of mild pleasantry that ought to have brightened the features of the guests, like a cheerful gleam from the hearth. At that instant, catching a glimpse of his figure in the looking-glass, the black veil involved his own spirit in the horror with which it overwhelmed all others. His frame shuddered—his lips grew white—he spilt the untasted wine upon the carpet—and rushed forth into the darkness. For the Earth, too, had on her Black Veil.

The next day, the whole village of Milford talked of little else than Parson Hooper's black veil. That, and the mystery concealed behind it, supplied a topic for discussion between acquaintances meeting in the street, and good women gossiping at their open windows. It was the first item of news that the tavern-keeper told to his guests. The children babbled of it on their way to school. One imitative little imp covered his face with an old black handkerchief, thereby so affrighting his playmates, that the panic seized himself, and he well nigh lost his wits by his own waggery.

It was remarkable, that, of all the busy-bodies and impertinent people in the parish, not one ventured to put the plain question to Mr. Hooper, wherefore

2. A reference to Hawthorne's own *The Wedding Knell*, which appeared in *The Token* for 1836 along with this story.

he did this thing. Hitherto, whenever there appeared the slightest call for such interference, he had never lacked advisers, nor shown himself averse to be guided by their judgment. If he erred at all, it was by so painful a degree of self-distrust, that even the mildest censure would lead him to consider an indifferent action as a crime. Yet, though so well acquainted with this amiable weakness, no individual among his parishioners chose to make the black veil a subject of friendly remonstrance. There was a feeling of dread, neither plainly confessed nor carefully concealed, which caused each to shift the responsibility upon another, till at length it was found expedient to send a deputation of the church, in order to deal with Mr. Hooper about the mystery, before it should grow into a scandal. Never did an embassy so ill discharge its duties. The minister received them with friendly courtesy, but became silent, after they were seated, leaving to his visitors the whole burthen[3] of introducing their important business. The topic, it might be supposed, was obvious enough. There was the black veil, swathed round Mr. Hooper's forehead, and conceal-ing every feature above his placid mouth, on which, at times, they could perceive the glimmering of a melancholy smile. But that piece of crape, to their imagination, seemed to hang down before his heart, the symbol of a fearful secret between him and them. Were the veil but cast aside, they might speak freely of it, but not till then. Thus they sat a considerable time, speech-less, confused, and shrinking uneasily from Mr. Hooper's eye, which they felt to be fixed upon them with an invisible glance. Finally, the deputies returned abashed to their constituents, pronouncing the matter too weighty to be han-dled, except by a council of the churches, if, indeed, it might not require a general synod.

But there was one person in the village, unappalled by the awe with which the black veil had impressed all beside herself. When the deputies returned without an explanation, or even venturing to demand one, she, with the calm energy of her character, determined to chase away the strange cloud that appeared to be settling round Mr. Hooper, every moment more darkly than before. As his plighted wife, it should be her privilege to know what the black veil concealed. At the minister's first visit, therefore, she entered upon the subject, with a direct simplicity, which made the task easier both for him and her. After he had seated himself, she fixed her eyes steadfastly upon the veil, but could discern nothing of the dreadful gloom that had so overawed the multitude: it was but a double fold of crape, hanging down from his forehead to his mouth, and slightly stirring with his breath.

'No,' said she aloud, and smiling, 'there is nothing terrible in this piece of crape, except that it hides a face which I am always glad to look upon. Come, good sir, let the sun shine from behind the cloud. First lay aside your black veil: then tell me why you put it on.'

Mr. Hooper's smile glimmered faintly.

'There is an hour to come,' said he, 'when all of us shall cast aside our veils. Take it not amiss, beloved friend, if I wear this piece of crape till then.'

'Your words are a mystery too,' returned the young lady. 'Take away the veil from them, at least.'

'Elizabeth, I will,' said he, 'so far as my vow may suffer me. Know, then, this veil is a type[4] and a symbol, and I am bound to wear it ever, both in light

3. Burden.
4. Symbol (the phrase "a type and a symbol" is redundant).

and darkness, in solitude and before the gaze of multitudes, and as with strangers, so with my familiar friends. No mortal eye will see it withdrawn. This dismal shade must separate me from the world: even you, Elizabeth, can never come behind it!'

'What grievous affliction hath befallen you,' she earnestly inquired, 'that you should thus darken your eyes for ever?'

'If it be a sign of mourning,' replied Mr. Hooper, 'I, perhaps, like most other mortals, have sorrows dark enough to be typified by a black veil.'

'But what if the world will not believe that it is the type of an innocent sorrow?' urged Elizabeth. 'Beloved and respected as you are, there may be whispers, that you hide your face under the consciousness of secret sin. For the sake of your holy office, do away this scandal!'

The color rose into her cheeks, as she intimated the nature of the rumors that were already abroad in the village. But Mr. Hooper's mildness did not forsake him. He even smiled again—that same sad smile, which always appeared like a faint glimmering of light, proceeding from the obscurity beneath the veil.

'If I hide my face for sorrow, there is cause enough,' he merely replied; 'and if I cover it for secret sin, what mortal might not do the same?'

And with this gentle, but unconquerable obstinacy, did he resist all her entreaties. At length Elizabeth sat silent. For a few moments she appeared lost in thought, considering, probably, what new methods might be tried, to withdraw her lover from so dark a fantasy, which, if it had no other meaning, was perhaps a symptom of mental disease. Though of a firmer character than his own, the tears rolled down her cheeks. But, in an instant, as it were, a new feeling took the place of sorrow: her eyes were fixed insensibly on the black veil, when, like a sudden twilight in the air, its terrors fell around her. She arose, and stood trembling before him.

'And do you feel it then at last?' said he mournfully.

She made no reply, but covered her eyes with her hand, and turned to leave the room. He rushed forward and caught her arm.

'Have patience with me, Elizabeth!' cried he passionately. 'Do not desert me, though this veil must be between us here on earth. Be mine, and hereafter there shall be no veil over my face, no darkness between our souls! It is but a mortal veil—it is not for eternity! Oh, you know not how lonely I am and how frightened to be alone behind my black veil. Do not leave me in this miserable obscurity for ever!'

'Lift the veil but once, and look me in the face,' said she.

'Never! It cannot be!' replied Mr. Hooper.

'Then, farewell!' said Elizabeth.

She withrew her arm from his grasp, and slowly departed, pausing at the door, to give one long, shuddering gaze, that seemed almost to penetrate the mystery of the black veil. But, even amid his grief, Mr. Hooper smiled to think that only a material emblem had separated him from happiness, though the horrors which it shadowed forth, must be drawn darkly between the fondest of lovers.

From that time no attempts were made to remove Mr. Hooper's black veil, or, by a direct appeal, to discover the secret which it was supposed to hide. By persons who claimed a superiority to popular prejudice, it was reckoned merely an eccentric whim, such as often mingles with the sober actions of men otherwise rational, and tinges them all with its own semblance of insanity. But with the multitude, good Mr. Hooper was irreparably a bugbear.[5] He could not walk the street with any peace of mind, so conscious was he that the gentle and timid would turn aside to avoid him, and that others would make it a point of hardihood to throw themselves in his way. The impertinence of the latter class compelled him to give up his customary walk, at sunset, to the burial ground; for when he leaned pensively over the gate, there would always be faces behind the grave-stones, peeping at his black veil. A fable went the rounds, that the stare of the dead people drove him thence. It grieved him, to the very depth of his kind heart, to observe how the children fled from his approach, breaking up their merriest sports, while his melancholy figure was yet afar off. Their instinctive dread caused him to feel, more strongly than aught else, that a preternatural horror was interwoven with the threads of the black crape. In truth, his own antipathy to the veil was known to be so great, that he never willingly passed before a mirror, nor stooped to drink at a still fountain, lest, in its peaceful bosom, he should be affrighted by himself. This was what gave plausibility to the whispers, that Mr. Hooper's conscience tortured him for some great crime, too horrible to be entirely concealed, or otherwise than so obscurely intimated. Thus, from beneath the black veil, there rolled a cloud into the sunshine, an ambiguity of sin or sorrow, which enveloped the poor minister, so that love or sympathy could never reach him. It was said, that ghost and fiend consorted with him there. With self-shudderings and outward terrors, he walked continually in its shadow, groping darkly within his own soul, or gazing through a medium that saddened the whole world. Even the lawless wind, it was believed, respected his dreadful secret, and never blew aside the veil. But still good Mr. Hooper sadly smiled, at the pale visages of the worldly throng as he passed by.

Among all its bad influences, the black veil had the one desirable effect, of making its wearer a very efficient clergyman. By the aid of his mysterious emblem—for there was no other apparent cause—he became a man of awful power, over souls that were in agony for sin. His converts always regarded him with a dread peculiar to themselves, affirming, though but figuratively, that, before he brought them to celestial light, they had been with him behind the black veil. Its gloom, indeed, enabled him to sympathize with all dark affections. Dying sinners cried aloud for Mr. Hooper, and would not yield their breath till he appeared; though ever, as he stooped to whisper consolation, they shuddered at the veiled face so near their own. Such were the terrors of the black veil, even when death had bared his visage! Strangers came long distances to attend service at his church, with the mere idle purpose of gazing at his figure, because it was forbidden them to behold his face. But many were made to quake ere they departed! Once, during Governor Belcher's administration, Mr. Hooper was appointed to preach the election sermon.[6] Covered with his black veil, he stood before the chief magistrate, the council, and the representatives, and wrought so deep an impression, that the legislative measures of that year, were characterized by all the gloom and piety of our earliest ancestral sway.

In this manner Mr. Hooper spent a long life, irreproachable in outward act,

---

5. Object of dread.
6. A sermon was preached at the installing of each new governor (in this case, at one of Belcher's installations

for a new term). Jonathan Belcher (1682–1757) was governor of Massachusetts and New Hampshire (1730–41).

yet shrouded in dismal suspicions; kind and loving, though unloved, and dimly feared; a man apart from men, shunned in their health and joy, but ever summoned to their aid in mortal anguish. As years wore on, shedding their snows above his sable veil, he acquired a name throughout the New-England churches, and they called him Father Hooper. Nearly all his parishioners, who were of mature age when he was settled, had been borne away by many a funeral: he had one congregation in the church, and a more crowded one in the church-yard; and having wrought so late into the evening, and done his work so well, it was now good Father Hooper's turn to rest.

Several persons were visible by the shaded candlelight, in the death-chamber of the old clergyman. Natural connections he had none. But there was the decorously grave, though unmoved physician, seeking only to mitigate the last pangs of the patient whom he could not save. There were the deacons, and other eminently pious members of his church. There, also, was the Reverend Mr. Clark, of Westbury, a young and zealous divine, who had ridden in haste to pray by the bed-side of the expiring minister. There was the nurse, no hired handmaiden of death, but one whose calm affection had endured thus long, in secresy, in solitude, amid the chill of age, and would not perish, even at the dying hour. Who, but Elizabeth! And there lay the hoary head of good Father Hooper upon the death-pillow, with the black veil still swathed about his brow and reaching down over his face, so that each more difficult gasp of his faint breath caused it to stir. All through life that piece of crape had hung between him and the world: it had separated him from cheerful brotherhood and woman's love, and kept him in that saddest of all prisons, his own heart; and still it lay upon his face, as if to deepen the gloom of his darksome chamber, and shade him from the sunshine of eternity.

For some time previous, his mind had been confused, wavering doubtfully between the past and the present, and hovering forward, as it were, at intervals, into the indistinctness of the world to come. There had been feverish turns, which tossed him from side to side, and wore away what little strength he had. But in his most convulsive struggles, and in the wildest vagaries of his intellect, when no other thought retained its sober influence, he still showed an awful solicitude lest the black veil should slip aside. Even if his bewildered soul could have forgotten, there was a faithful woman at his pillow, who, with averted eyes, would have covered that aged face, which she had last beheld in the comeliness of manhood. At length the death-stricken old man lay quietly in the torpor of mental and bodily exhaustion, with an imperceptible pulse, and breath that grew fainter and fainter, except when a long, deep, and irregular inspiration seemed to prelude the flight of his spirit.

The minister of Westbury approached the bedside.

'Venerable Father Hooper,' said he, 'the moment of your release is at hand. Are you ready for the lifting of the veil, that shuts in time from eternity?'

Father Hooper at first replied merely by a feeble motion of his head; then, apprehensive, perhaps, that his meaning might be doubtful, he exerted himself to speak.

'Yea,' said he, in faint accents, 'my soul hath a patient weariness until that veil be lifted.'

'And is it fitting,' resumed the Reverend Mr. Clark, 'that a man so given to prayer, of such a blameless example, holy in deed and thought, so far as mortal judgment may pronounce; is it fitting that a father in the church should leave a shadow on his memory, that may seem to blacken a life so pure? I pray you, my venerable brother, let not this thing be! Suffer us to be gladdened by your triumphant aspect, as you go to your reward. Before the veil of eternity be lifted, let me cast aside this black veil from your face!'

And thus speaking, the reverend Mr. Clark bent forward to reveal the mystery of so many years. But, exerting a sudden energy, that made all the beholders stand aghast, Father Hooper snatched both his hands from beneath the bed-clothes, and pressed them strongly on the black veil, resolute to struggle, if the minister of Westbury would contend with a dying man.

'Never!' cried the veiled clergyman. 'On earth, never!'

'Dark old man!' exclaimed the affrighted minister, 'with what horrible crime upon your soul are you now passing to the judgment?'

Father Hooper's breath heaved; it rattled in his throat; but, with a mighty effort, grasping forward with his hands, he caught hold of life, and held it back till he should speak. He even raised himself in bed; and there he sat, shivering with the arms of death around him, while the black veil hung down, awful, at that last moment, in the gathered terrors of a life-time. And yet the faint, sad smile, so often there, now seemed to glimmer from its obscurity, and linger on Father Hooper's lips.

'Why do you tremble at me alone?' cried he, turning his veiled face round the circle of pale spectators. 'Tremble also at each other! Have men avoided me, and women shown no pity, and children screamed and fled, only for my black veil? What, but the mystery which it obscurely typifies, has made this piece of crape so awful? When the friend shows his inmost heart to his friend; the lover to his best-beloved; when man does not vainly shrink from the eye of his Creator, loathsomely treasuring up the secret of his sin; then deem me a monster, for the symbol beneath which I have lived, and die! I look around me, and lo! on every visage a black veil!'

While his auditors shrank from one another, in mutual affright, Father Hooper fell back upon his pillow, a veiled corpse, with a faint smile lingering on the lips. Still veiled, they laid him in his coffin, and a veiled corpse they bore him to the grave. The grass of many years has sprung up and withered on that grave, the burial-stone is moss-grown, and good Mr. Hooper's face is dust; but awful is still the thought, that it mouldered beneath the black veil!

1836

# Rappaccini's Daughter[1]

## Writings of Aubépine

We do not remember to have seen any translated specimens of the productions of M. de l'Aubépine;[2] a fact the less to be wondered at, as his very name is unknown to many of his own countrymen, as well as to the student of foreign literature. As a writer, he seems to occupy an unfortunate position between the Transcendentalists (who, under one name or another, have their share in all the current literature of the world), and the great body of pen-and-

---

1. The text is from the first publication in *The Demo-cratic Review* (December 1844).

2. French for "Hawthorne." What follows is a facetious account of Hawthorne's own career.

ink men who address the intellect and sympathies of the multitude. If not too refined, at all events too remote, too shadowy and unsubstantial in his modes of development, to suit the taste of the latter class, and yet too popular to satisfy the spiritual or metaphysical requisitions of the former, he must necessarily find himself without an audience; except here and there an individual, or possibly an isolated clique. His writings, to do them justice, are not altogether destitute of fancy and originality; they might have won him greater reputation but for an inveterate love of allegory, which is apt to invest his plots and characters with the aspect of scenery and people in the clouds, and to steal away the human warmth out of his conceptions. His fictions are sometimes historical, sometimes of the present day, and sometimes, so far as can be discovered, have little or no reference either to time or space. In any case, he generally contents himself with a very slight embroidery of outward manners,—the faintest possible counterfeit of real life,—and endeavors to create an interest by some less obvious peculiarity of the subject. Occasionally, a breath of nature, a rain-drop of pathos and tenderness, or a gleam of humor, will find its way into the midst of his fantastic imagery, and make us feel as if, after all, we were yet within the limits of our native earth. We will only add to this very cursory notice, that M. de l'Aubépine's productions, if the reader chance to take them in precisely the proper point of view, may amuse a leisure hour as well as those of a brighter man; if otherwise, they can hardly fail to look excessively like nonsense.

Our author is voluminous; he continues to write and publish with as much praiseworthy and indefatigable prolixity, as if his efforts were crowned with the brilliant success that so justly attends those of Eugene Sue.[3] His first appearance was by a collection of stories, in a long series of volumes, entitled "*Contes deux fois racontées.*"[4] The titles of some of his more recent works (we quote from memory) are as follows:—"*Le Voyage Céleste à Chemin de Fer*," 3 tom. 1838. "*Le nouveau père Adam et la nouvelle mère Eve*," 2 tom. 1839. "*Roderic; ou le Serpent à l'estomac*," 2 tom. 1840. "*Le Culte du Feu*," a folio volume of ponderous research into the religion and ritual of the old Persian Ghebers, published in 1841. "*La Soirée du Château en Espagne*," 1 tom. 8vo. 1842; and "*L'Artiste du Beau; ou le Papillon Mécanique*," 5 tom. 4to. 1843.[5] Our somewhat wearisome persual of this startling catalogue of volumes has left behind it a certain personal affection and sympathy, though by no means admiration, for M. de l'Aubépine; and we would fain do the little in our power towards introducing him favorably to the American public. The ensuing tale is a translation of his "*Béatrice; ou La Belle Empoisonneuse*," recently published in "*La Revue Anti-Aristocratique.*" This journal, edited by the Comte de Bearhaven,[6] has, for some years past, led the defence of liberal principles and popular rights, with a faithfulness and ability worthy of all praise.

3. French novelist (1804–1857), author of *The Wandering Jew* and other popular works.
4. *Twice-Told Tales* (French), Hawthorne's first volume (1837), except for the anonymous and suppressed *Fanshawe*.
5. In these mock bibliographical citations "tom." (French abbreviation for *tome*, "volume") and "8vo" (octavo) and "4vo" (quarto) are jokes: Hawthorne's tales took up only a few magazine pages each. All but one

of these French titles refer to stories by Hawthorne. In order, the titles are *The Celestial Railroad, The New Adam and Eve, Egotism: or, the Boston-Serpent, Fire-Worship, Evening in a Castle in Spain* (imaginary), and *The Artist of the Beautiful.*
6. Hawthorne's friend, John O'Sullivan, editor of *The Democratic Review* (here, "*La Revue Anti-Aristocratique*").

## Rappaccini's Daughter

A young man, named Giovanni Guasconti, came, very long ago, from the more southern region of Italy, to pursue his studies at the University of Padua. Giovanni, who had but a scanty supply of gold ducats in his pocket, took lodgings in a high and gloomy chamber of an old edifice, which looked not unworthy to have been the palace of a Paduan noble, and which, in fact, exhibited over its entrance the armorial bearings of a family long since extinct. The young stranger, who was not unstudied in the great poem of his country, recollected that one of the ancestors of this family, and perhaps an occupant of this very mansion, had been pictured by Dante as a partaker of the immortal agonies of his Inferno. These reminiscences and associations, together with the tendency to heart-break natural to a young man for the first time out of his native sphere, caused Giovanni to sigh heavily, as he looked around the desolate and ill-furnished apartment.

"Holy Virgin, signor," cried old dame Lisabetta, who, won by the youth's remarkable beauty of person, was kindly endeavoring to give the chamber a habitable air, "what a sigh was that to come out of a young man's heart! Do you find this old mansion gloomy? For the love of heaven, then, put your head out of the window, and you will see as bright sunshine as you have left in Naples."

Guasconti mechanically did as the old woman advised, but could not quite agree with her that the Lombard sunshine was as cheerful as that of southern Italy. Such as it was, however, it fell upon a garden beneath the window, and expended its fostering influences on a variety of plants, which seemed to have been cultivated with exceeding care.

"Does this garden belong to the house?" asked Giovanni.

"Heaven forbid, signor!—unless it were fruitful of better pot-herbs than any that grow there now," answered old Lisabetta. "No: that garden is cultivated by the own hands of Signor Giacomo Rappaccini, the famous Doctor, who, I warrant him, has been heard of as far as Naples. It is said he distils these plants into medicines that are as potent as a charm. Oftentimes you may see the signor Doctor at work, and perchance the signora his daughter, too, gathering the strange flowers that grow in the garden."

The old woman had now done what she could for the aspect of the chamber, and, commending the young man to the protection of the saints, took her departure.

Giovanni still found no better occupation than to look down into the garden beneath his window. From its appearance, he judged it to be one of those botanic gardens, which were of earlier date in Padua than elsewhere in Italy, or in the world. Or, not improbably, it might once have been the pleasure-place of an opulent family; for there was the ruin of a marble fountain in the centre, sculptured with rare art, but so wofully shattered that it was impossible to trace the original design from the chaos of remaining fragments. The water, however, continued to gush and sparkle into the sunbeams as cheerfully as ever. A little gurgling sound ascended to the young man's window, and made him feel as if the fountain were an immortal spirit, that sung its song unceasingly, and without heeding the vicissitudes around it; while one century embodied it in marble, and another scattered the garniture on the soil. All about the pool into which the water subsided, grew various plants, that seemed to require a plentiful supply of moisture for the nourishment of gigantic leaves, and, in some instances, flowers gorgeously magnificent. There was one shrub in particular, set in a marble vase in the midst of the pool, that bore a profusion of purple blossoms, each of which had the lustre and richness of a gem; and the whole together made a show so resplendent that it seemed enough to illuminate the garden, even had there been no sunshine. Every portion of the soil was peopled with plants and herbs, which, if less beautiful, still bore tokens of assiduous care; as if all had their individual virtues, known to the scientific mind that fostered them. Some were placed in urns, rich with old carving, and others in common garden-pots; some crept serpent-like along the ground, or climbed on high, using whatever means of ascent was offered them. One plant had wreathed itself round a statue of Vertumnus,[7] which was thus quite veiled and shrouded in a drapery of hanging foliage, so happily arranged that it might have served a sculptor for a study.

While Giovanni stood at the window, he heard a rustling behind a screen of leaves, and became aware that a person was at work in the garden. His figure soon emerged into view, and showed itself to be that of no common laborer, but a tall, emaciated, sallow, and sickly-looking man, dressed in a scholar's garb of black. He was beyond the middle term of life, with grey hair, a thin grey beard, and a face singularly marked with intellect and cultivation, but which could never, even in his more youthful days, have expressed much warmth of heart.

Nothing could exceed the intentness with which this scientific gardener examined every shrub which grew in his path; it seemed as if he was looking into their inmost nature, making observations in regard to their creative essence, and discovering why one leaf grew in this shape, and another in that, and wherefore such and such flowers differed among themselves in hue and perfume. Nevertheless, in spite of the deep intelligence on his part, there was no approach to intimacy between himself and these vegetable existences. On the contrary, he avoided their actual touch, or the direct inhaling of their odors, with a caution that impressed Giovanni most disagreeably; for the man's demeanor was that of one walking among malignant influences, such as savage beasts, or deadly snakes, or evil spirits, which, should he allow them one moment of license, would wreak upon him some terrible fatality. It was strangely frightful to the young man's imagination, to see this air of insecurity in a person cultivating a garden, that most simple and innocent of human toils, and which had been alike the joy and labor of the unfallen parents of the race. Was this garden, then, the Eden of the present world?—and this man, with such a perception of harm in what his own hands caused to grow, was he the Adam?

The distrustful gardener, while plucking away the dead leaves or pruning the too luxuriant growth of the shrubs, defended his hands with a pair of thick gloves. Nor were these his only armor. When, in his walk through the garden, he came to the magnificent plant that hung its purple gems beside the marble fountain, he placed a kind of mask over his mouth and nostrils, as if all this beauty did but conceal a deadlier malice. But finding his task still too dangerous, he drew back, removed the mask, and called loudly, but in the infirm voice of a person affected with inward disease:

7. The god of the seasons (and vegetation produced by the changing seasons).

"Beatrice!—Beatrice!"

"Here am I, my father! What would you?" cried a rich and youthful voice from the window of the opposite house; a voice as rich as a tropical sunset, and which made Giovanni, though he knew not why, think of deep hues of purple or crimson, and of perfumes heavily delectable.—"Are you in the garden?"

"Yes, Beatrice," answered the gardener, "and I need your help."

Soon there emerged from under a sculptured portal the figure of a young girl, arrayed with as much richness of taste as the most splendid of the flowers, beautiful as the day, and with a bloom so deep and vivid that one shade more would have been too much. She looked redundant with life, health, and energy; all of which attributes were bound down and compressed, as it were, and girdled tensely, in their luxuriance, by her virgin zone.[8] Yet Giovanni's fancy must have grown morbid, while he looked down into the garden; for the impression which the fair stranger made upon him was as if here were another flower, the human sister of those vegetable ones, as beautiful as they—more beautiful than the richest of them—but still to be touched only with a glove, nor to be approached without a mask. As Beatrice came down the garden-path, it was observable that she handled and inhaled the odor of several of the plants, which her father had most sedulously avoided.

"Here, Beatrice," said the latter,—"see how many needful offices require to be done to our chief treasure. Yet, shattered as I am, my life might pay the penalty of approaching it so closely as circumstances demand. Henceforth, I fear, this plant must be consigned to your sole charge."

"And gladly will I undertake it," cried again the rich tones of the young lady, as she bent towards the magnificent plant, and opened her arms as if to embrace it. "Yes, my sister, my splendor, it shall be Beatrice's task to nurse and serve thee; and thou shalt reward her with thy kisses and perfumed breath, which to her is as the breath of life!"

Then, with all the tenderness in her manner that was so strikingly expressed in her words, she busied herself with such attentions as the plant seemed to require; and Giovanni, at his lofty window, rubbed his eyes, and almost doubted whether it were a girl tending her favorite flower, or one sister performing the duties of affection to another. The scene soon terminated. Whether Doctor Rappaccini had finished his labors in the garden, or that his watchful eye had caught the stranger's face, he now took his daughter's arm and retired. Night was already closing in; oppressive exhalations seemed to proceed from the plants, and steal upward past the open window; and Giovanni, closing the lattice, went to his couch, and dreamed of a rich flower and beautiful girl. Flower and maiden were different and yet the same, and fraught with some strange peril in either shape.

But there is an influence in the light of morning that tends to rectify whatever errors of fancy, or even of judgment, we may have incurred during the sun's decline, or among the shadows of the night, or in the less wholesome glow of moonshine. Giovanni's first movement on starting from sleep, was to throw open the window, and gaze down into the garden which his dreams had made so fertile of mysteries. He was surprised, and a little ashamed, to find how real and matter-of-fact an affair it proved to be, in the first rays of the sun,

8. Wide girdlelike belt customarily worn by unmarried girls.

which gilded the dew-drops that hung upon leaf and blossom, and, while giving a brighter beauty to each rare flower, brought everything within the limits of ordinary experience. The young man rejoiced, that, in the heart of the barren city, he had the privilege of overlooking this spot of lovely and luxuriant vegetation. It would serve, he said to himself, as a symbolic language, to keep him in communion with nature. Neither the sickly and thought-worn Doctor Giacomo Rappaccini, it is true, nor his brilliant daughter were now visible; so that Giovanni could not determine how much of the singularity which he attributed to both, was due to their own qualities, and how much to his wonder-working fancy. But he was inclined to take a most rational view of the whole matter.

In the course of the day, he paid his respects to Signor Pietro Baglioni, professor of medicine in the University, a physician of eminent repute, to whom Giovanni had brought a letter of introduction. The professor was an elderly personage, apparently of genial nature, and habits that might almost be called jovial; he kept the young man to dinner, and made himself very agreeable by the freedom and liveliness of his conversation, especially when warmed by a flask or two of Tuscan wine. Giovanni, conceiving that men of science, inhabitants of the same city, must needs be on familiar terms with one another, took an opportunity to mention the name of Dr. Rappaccini. But the professor did not respond with so much cordiality as he had anticipated.

"Ill would it become a teacher of the divine art of medicine," said Professor Pietro Baglioni, in answer to a question of Giovanni, "to withhold due and well-considered praise of a physician so eminently skilled as Rappaccini. But, on the other hand, I should answer it but scantily to my conscience, were I to permit a worthy youth like yourself, Signor Giovanni, the son of an ancient friend, to imbibe erroneous ideas respecting a man who might hereafter chance to hold your life and death in his hands. The truth is, our worshipful Doctor Rappaccini has as much science as any member of the faculty—with perhaps one single exception—in Padua, or all Italy. But there are certain grave objections to his professional character."

"And what are they?" asked the young man.

"Has my friend Giovanni any disease of body or heart, that he is so inquisitive about physicians?" said the Professor, with a smile. "But as for Rappaccini, it is said of him—and I, who know the man well, can answer for its truth—that he cares infinitely more for science than for mankind. His patients are interesting to him only as subjects for some new experiment. He would sacrifice human life, his own among the rest, or whatever else was dearest to him, for the sake of adding so much as a grain of mustard-seed to the great heap of his accumulated knowledge."

"Methinks he is an awful[9] man, indeed," remarked Guasconti, mentally recalling the cold and purely intellectual aspect of Rappaccini. "And yet, worshipful Professor, is it not a noble spirit? Are there many men capable of so spiritual a love of science?"

"God forbid," answered the Professor, somewhat testily—"at least, unless they take sounder views of the healing art than those adopted by Rappaccini. It is his theory, that all medicinal virtues are comprised within those substances which we term vegetable poisons. These he cultivates with his own hands, and

---

9. The word carries some of the sense of "awe-striking."

is said even to have produced new varieties of poison, more horribly deleterious than Nature, without the assistance of this learned person, would ever have plagued the world with. That the signor Doctor does less mischief than might be expected, with such dangerous substances, is undeniable. Now and then, it must be owned, he has effected—or seemed to effect—a marvellous cure. But, to tell you my private mind, Signor Giovanni, he should receive little credit for such instances of success—they being probably the work of chance—but should be held strictly accountable for his failures, which may justly be considered his own work."

The youth might have taken Baglioni's opinions with many grains of allowance, had he known that there was a professional warfare of long continuance between him and Doctor Rappaccini, in which the latter was generally thought to have gained the advantage. If the reader be inclined to judge for himself, we refer him to certain black-letter tracts on both sides, preserved in the medical department of the University of Padua.

"I know not, most learned Professor," returned Giovanni, after musing on what had been said of Rappaccini's exclusive zeal for science—"I know not how dearly this physician may love his art; but surely there is one object more dear to him. He has a daughter."

"Aha!" cries the Professor with a laugh. "So now our friend Giovanni's secret is out. You have heard of this daughter, whom all the young men in Padua are wild about, though not half a dozen have ever had the good hap to see her face. I know little of the Signora Beatrice, save that Rappaccini is said to have instructed her deeply in his science, and that, young and beautiful as fame reports her, she is already qualified to fill a professor's chair. Perchance her father destines her for mine! Other absurd rumors there be, not worth talking about, or listening to. So now, Signor Giovanni, drink off your glass of Lacryma."[1]

Guasconti returned to his lodgings somewhat heated with the wine he had quaffed, and which caused his brain to swim with strange fantasies in reference to Doctor Rappaccini and the beautiful Beatrice. On his way, happening to pass by a florist's, he bought a fresh bouquet of flowers.

Ascending to his chamber, he seated himself near the window, but within the shadow thrown by the depth of the wall, so that he could look down into the garden with little risk of being discovered. All beneath his eye was a solitude. The strange plants were basking in the sunshine, and now and then nodding gently to one another, as if in acknowledgment of sympathy and kindred. In the midst, by the shattered fountain, grew the magnificent shrub, with its purple gems clustering all over it; they glowed in the air, and gleamed back again out of the depths of the pool, which thus seemed to overflow with colored radiance from the rich reflection that was steeped in it. At first, as we have said, the garden was a solitude. Soon, however,—as Giovanni had half-hoped, half-feared, would be the case,—a figure appeared beneath the antique sculptured portal, and came down between the rows of plants, inhaling their various perfumes, as if she were one of those beings of old classic fable, that lived upon sweet odors. On again beholding Beatrice, the young man was even startled to perceive how much her beauty exceeded his recollection of it; so brilliant, so vivid in its character, that she glowed amid the sunlight, and,

1. A still Italian wine grown near Vesuvius.

as Giovanni whispered to himself, positively illuminated the more shadowy intervals of the garden path. Her face being now more revealed than on the former occasion, he was struck by its expression of simplicity and sweetness; qualities that had not entered into his idea of her character, and which made him ask anew, what manner of mortal she might be. Nor did he fail again to observe, or imagine, an analogy between the beautiful girl and the gorgeous shrub that hung its gem-like flowers over the fountain; a resemblance which Beatrice seemed to have indulged a fantastic humor in heightening, both by the arrangement of her dress and the selection of its hues.

Approaching the shrub, she threw open her arms, as with a passionate ardor, and drew its branches into an intimate embrace; so intimate, that her features were hidden in its leafy bosom, and her glistening ringlets all intermingled with the flowers.

"Give me thy breath, my sister," exclaimed Beatrice; "for I am faint with common air! And give me this flower of thine, which I separate with gentlest fingers from the stem, and place it close beside my heart."

With these words, the beautiful daughter of Rappaccini plucked one of the richest blossoms of the shrub, and was about to fasten it in her bosom. But now, unless Giovanni's draughts of wine had bewildered his senses, a singular incident occurred. A small orange-colored reptile of the lizard or chameleon species, chanced to be creeping along the path, just at the feet of Beatrice. It appeared to Giovanni—but, at the distance from which he gazed, he could scarcely have seen anything so minute—it appeared to him, however, that a drop or two of moisture from the broken stem of the flower descended upon the lizard's head. For an instant, the reptile contorted itself violently, and then lay motionless in the sunshine. Beatrice observed this remarkable phenomenon, and crossed herself, sadly, but without surprise; nor did she therefore hesitate to arrange the fatal flower in her bosom. There it blushed, and almost glimmered with the dazzling effect of a precious stone, adding to her dress and aspect the one appropriate charm, which nothing else in the world could have supplied. But Giovanni, out of the shadow of his window bent forward and shrank back, and murmured and trembled.

"Am I awake? Have I my senses?" said he to himself. "What is this being?—beautiful, shall I call her?—or inexpressibly terrible?"

Beatrice now strayed carelessly through the garden, approaching closer beneath Giovanni's window, so that he was compelled to thrust his head quite out of its concealment in order to gratify the intense and painful curiosity which she excited. At this moment, there came a beautiful insect over the garden wall; it had perhaps wandered through the city and found no flowers nor verdure among those antique haunts of men, until the heavy perfumes of Doctor Rappaccini's shrubs had lured it from afar. Without alighting on the flowers, this winged brightness seemed to be attracted by Beatrice, and lingered in the air and fluttered about her head. Now here it could not be but that Giovanni Guasconti's eyes deceived him. Be that as it might, he fancied that while Beatrice was gazing at the insect with childish delight, it grew faint and fell at her feet!—its bright wings shivered! it was dead!—from no cause that he could discern, unless it were the atmosphere of her breath. Again Beatrice crossed herself and sighed heavily, as she bent over the dead insect.

An impulsive movement of Giovanni drew her eyes to the window. There she beheld the beautiful head of the young man—rather a Grecian than an

Italian head, with fair, regular features, and a glistening of gold among his ringlets—gazing down upon her like a being that hovered in mid-air. Scarcely knowing what he did, Giovanni threw down the bouquet which he had hitherto held in his hand.

"Signora," said he, "there are pure and healthful flowers. Wear them for the sake of Giovanni Guasconti!"

"Thanks, Signor," replied Beatrice, with her rich voice, that came forth as it were like a gush of music; and with a mirthful expression half childish and half woman-like. "I accept your gift, and would fain recompense it with this precious purple flower; but if I toss it into the air, it will not reach you. So Signor Guasconti must even content himself with my thanks."

She lifted the bouquet from the ground, and then as if inwardly ashamed at having stepped aside from her maidenly reserve to respond to a stranger's greeting, passed swiftly homeward through the garden. But, few as the moments were, it seemed to Giovanni when she was on the point of vanishing beneath the sculptured portal, that his beautiful bouquet was already beginning to wither in her grasp. It was an idle thought; there could be no possibility of distinguishing a faded flower from a fresh one at so great a distance.

For many days after the incident, the young man avoided the window that looked into Doctor Rappaccini's garden, as if something ugly and monstrous would have blasted his eye-sight, had he been betrayed into a glance. He felt conscious of having put himself, to a certain extent, within the influence of an unintelligible power, by the communication which he had opened with Beatrice. The wisest course would have been, if his heart were in any real danger, to quit his lodgings and Padua itself, at once; the next wiser, to have accustomed himself, as far as possible, to the familiar and day-light view of Beatrice; thus bringing her rigidly and systematically within the limits of ordinary experience. Least of all, while avoiding her sight, should Giovanni have remained so near this extraordinary being, that the proximity and possibility even of intercourse, should give a kind of substance and reality to the wild vagaries which his imagination ran riot continually in producing. Guasconti had not a deep heart—or at all events, its depths were not sounded now—but he had a quick fancy, and an ardent southern temperament, which rose every instant to a higher fever-pitch. Whether or no Beatrice possessed those terrible attributes—that fatal breath—the affinity with those so beautiful and deadly flowers—which were indicated by what Giovanni had witnessed, she had at least instilled a fierce and subtle poison into his sytem. It was not love, although her rich beauty was a madness to him; nor horror, even while he fancied her spirit to be imbued with the same baneful essence that seemed to pervade her physical frame; but a wild offspring of both love and horror that had each parent in it, and burned like one and shivered like the other. Giovanni knew not what to dread; still less did he know what to hope; *hope* and *dread* kept a continual warfare in his breast, alternately vanquishing one another and starting up afresh to renew the contest. Blessed are all simple emotions, be they dark or bright! It is the lurid intermixture of the two that produces the illuminating blaze of the infernal regions.

Sometimes he endeavored to assuage the fever of his spirit by a rapid walk through the streets of Padua, or beyond its gates; his footsteps kept time with the throbbings of his brain, so that the walk was apt to accelerate itself to a race. One day, he found himself arrested; his arm was seized by a portly personage who had turned back on recognizing the young man, and expended much breath in overtaking him.

"Signor Giovanni!—stay, my young friend!" cried he. "Have you forgotten me? That might well be the case, if I were as much altered as yourself."

It was Baglioni, whom Giovanni had avoided, ever since their first meeting, from a doubt that the professor's sagacity would look too deeply into his secrets. Endeavoring to recover himself, he stared forth wildly from his inner world into the outer one, and spoke like a man in a dream:

"Yes; I am Giovanni Guasconti. You are Professor Pietro Baglioni. Now let me pass!"

"Not yet—not yet, Signor Giovanni Guasconti," said the Professor, smiling, but at the same time scrutinizing the youth with an earnest glance.—"What; did I grow up side by side with your father, and shall his son pass me like a stranger, in these old streets of Padua? Stand still, Signor Giovanni; for we must have a word or two, before we part."

"Speedily, then, most worshipful Professor, speedily!" said Giovanni, with feverish impatience. "Does not your worship see that I am in haste?"

Now, while he was speaking, there came a man in black along the street, stooping and moving feebly, like a person in inferior health. His face was all overspread with a most sickly and sallow hue, but yet so pervaded with an expression of piercing and active intellect, that an observer might easily have overlooked the merely physical attributes, and have seen only this wonderful energy. As he passed, this person exchanged a cold and distant salutation with Baglioni, but fixed his eyes upon Giovanni with an intentness that seemed to bring out whatever was within him worthy of notice. Nevertheless, there was a peculiar quietness in the look, as if taking merely a speculative, not a human interest, in the young man.

"It is Doctor Rappaccini!" whispered the Professor, when the stranger had passed.—"Has he ever seen your face before?"

"Not that I know," answered Giovanni, starting at the name.

"He *has* seen you!—he must have seen you!" said Baglioni, hastily. "For some purpose or other, this man of science is making a study of you. I know that look of his! It is the same that coldly illuminates his face, as he bends over a bird, a mouse, or a butterfly, which, in pursuance of some experiment, he has killed by the perfume of a flower;—a look as deep as nature itself, but without nature's warmth of love. Signor Giovanni, I will stake my life upon it, you are the subject of one of Rappaccini's experiments!"

"Will you make a fool of me?" cried Giovanni, passionately. "*That*, Signor Professor, were an untoward experiment."

"Patience, patience!" replied the imperturbable Professor.—"I tell thee, my poor Giovanni, that Rappaccini has a scientific interest in thee. Thou hast fallen into fearful hands! And the Signora Beatrice? What part does she act in this mystery?"

But Guasconti, finding Baglioni's pertinacity intolerable, here broke away, and was gone before the Professor could again seize his arm. He looked after the young man intently, and shook his head.

"This must not be," said Baglioni to himself. "The youth is the son of my old friend, and should not come to any harm from which the arcana of medical science can preserve him. Besides, it is too insufferable an impertinence in Rappaccini, thus to snatch the bud out of my own hands, as I may say, and make use of him for his infernal experiments. This daughter of his! It shall be looked to. Perchance, most learned Rappaccini, I may foil you where you little dream of it!"

Meanwhile, Giovanni had pursued a circuitous route, and at length found himself at the door of his lodgings. As he crossed the threshold, he was met by old Lisabetta, who smirked and smiled, and was evidently desirous to attract his attention; vainly, however, as the ebullition of his feelings had momentarily subsided into a cold and dull vacuity. He turned his eyes full upon the withered face that was puckering itself into a smile, but seemed to behold it not. The old dame, therefore, laid her grasp upon his cloak.

"Signor!—Signor!" whispered she, still with a smile over the whole breadth of her visage, so that it looked not unlike a grotesque carving in wood, darkened by centuries—"Listen, Signor! There is a private entrance into the garden!"

"What do you say?" exclaimed Giovanni, turning quickly about, as if an inanimate thing should start into feverish life.—"A private entrance into Doctor Rappaccini's garden!"

"Hush! hush!—not so loud!" whispered Lisabetta, putting her hand over his mouth. "Yes; into the worshipful Doctor's garden, where you may see all his fine shrubbery. Many a young man in Padua would give gold to be admitted among those flowers."

Giovanni put a piece of gold into her hand.

"Show me the way," said he.

A surmise, probably excited by his conversation with Baglioni, crossed his mind, that this interposition of old Lisabetta might perchance be connected with the intrigue, whatever were its nature, in which the Professor seemed to suppose that Doctor Rappaccini was involving him. But such a suspicion, though it disturbed Giovanni, was inadequate to restrain him. The instant he was aware of the possibility of approaching Beatrice, it seemed an absolute necessity of his existence to do so. It mattered not whether she were angel or demon; he was irrevocably within her sphere, and must obey the law that whirled him onward, in ever lessening circles, towards a result which he did not attempt to foreshadow. And yet, strange to say, there came across him a sudden doubt, whether this intense interest on his part were not delusory— whether it were really of so deep and positive a nature as to justify him in now thrusting himself into an incalculable position—whether it were not merely the fantasy of a young man's brain, only slightly, or not at all, connected with his heart!

He paused—hesitated—turned half about—but again went on. His withered guide led him along several obscure passages, and finally undid a door, through which, as it was opened, there came the sight and sound of rustling leaves, with the broken sunshine glimmering among them. Giovanni stepped forth, and forcing himself through the entanglement of a shrub that wreathed its tendrils over the hidden entrance, he stood beneath his own window, in the open area of Doctor Rappaccini's garden.

How often is it the case, that, when impossibilities have come to pass, and dreams have condensed their misty substance into tangible realities, we find ourselves calm, and even coldly self-possessed, amid circumstances which it would have been a delirium of joy or agony to anticipate! Fate delights to thwart us thus. Passion will choose his own time to rush upon the scene, and lingers sluggishly behind, when an appropriate adjustment of events would seem to summon his appearance. So was it now with Giovanni. Day after day, his pulses had throbbed with feverish blood, at the improbable idea of an interview with Beatrice, and of standing with her, face to face, in this very garden, basking in the oriental sunshine of her beauty, and snatching from her full gaze the mystery which he deemed the riddle of his own existence. But now there was a singular and untimely equanimity within his breast. He threw a glance around the garden to discover if Beatrice or her father were present, and perceiving that he was alone, began a critical observation of the plants.

The aspect of one and all of them dissatisfied him; their gorgeousness seemed fierce, passionate, and even unnatural. There was hardly an individual shrub which a wanderer, straying by himself through a forest, would not have been startled to find growing wild, as if an unearthly face had glared at him out of the thicket. Several, also, would have shocked a delicate instinct by an appearance of artificialness, indicating that there had been such commixture, and, as it were, adultery of various vegetable species, that the production was no longer of God's making, but the monstrous offspring of man's depraved fancy, glowing with only an evil mockery of beauty. They were probably the result of experiment, which, in one or two cases, had succeeded in mingling plants individually lovely into a compound possessing the questionable and ominous character that distinguished the whole growth of the garden. In fine, Giovanni recognized but two or three plants in the collection, and those of a kind that he well knew to be poisonous. While busy with these contemplations, he heard the rustling of a silken garment, and turning, beheld Beatrice emerging from beneath the sculptured portal.

Giovanni had not considered with himself what should be his deportment; whether he should apologize for his intrusion into the garden, or assume that he was there with the privity, at least, if not the desire of Doctor Rappaccini or his daughter. But Beatrice's manner placed him at his ease, though leaving him still in doubt by what agency he had gained admittance. She came lightly along the path, and met him near the broken fountain. There was surprise in her face, but brightened by a simple and kind expression of pleasure.

"You are a connoisseur in flowers, Signor," said Beatrice with a smile, alluding to the bouquet which he had flung her from the window. "It is no marvel, therefore, if the sight of my father's rare collection has tempted you to take a nearer view. If he were here, he could tell you many strange and interesting facts as to the nature and habits of these shrubs, for he has spent a lifetime in such studies, and this garden is his world."

"And yourself, lady"—observed Giovanni—"if fame says true—you, likewise, are deeply skilled in the virtues indicated by these rich blossoms, and these spicy perfumes. Would you deign to be my instructress, I should prove an apter scholar than under Signor Rappaccini himself."

"Are there such idle rumors?" asked Beatrice, with the music of a pleasant laugh. "Do people say that I am skilled in my father's science of plants? What a jest is there! No; though I have grown up among these flowers, I know no more of them than their hues and perfume; and sometimes, methinks I would fain rid myself of even that small knowledge. There are many flowers here, and those not the least brilliant, that shock and offend me, when they meet my eye. But, pray, Signor, do not believe these stories about my science. Believe nothing of me save what you see with your own eyes."

"And must I believe all that I have seen with my own eyes?" asked Giovanni pointedly, while the recollection of former scenes made him shrink. "No, Signora, you demand too little of me. Bid me believe nothing, save what comes from your own lips."

It would appear that Beatrice understood him. There came a deep flush to her cheek; but she looked full into Giovanni's eyes, and responded to his gaze of uneasy suspicion with a queen-like haughtiness.

"I do so bid you, Signor!" she replied. "Forget whatever you may have fancied in regard to me. If true to the outward senses, still it may be false in its essence. But the words of Beatrice Rappaccini's lips are true from the heart outward. Those you may believe!"

A fervor glowed in her whole aspect, and beamed upon Giovanni's consciousness like the light of truth itself. But while she spoke, there was a fragrance in the atmosphere around her, rich and delightful, though evanescent, yet which the young man, from an indefinable reluctance, scarcely dared to draw into his lungs. It might be the odor of the flowers. Could it be Beatrice's breath, which thus embalmed her words with a strange richness, as if by steeping them in her heart? A faintness passed like a shadow over Giovanni, and flitted away; he seemed to gaze through the beautiful girl's eyes into her transparent soul, and felt no more doubt or fear.

The tinge of passion that had colored Beatrice's manner vanished; she became gay, and appeared to derive a pure delight from her communion with the youth, not unlike what the maiden of a lonely island might have felt, conversing with a voyager from the civilized world. Evidently her experience of life had been confined within the limits of that garden. She talked now about matters as simple as the day-light or summer-clouds, and now asked questions in reference to the city, or Giovanni's distant home, his friends, his mother, and his sisters; questions indicating such seclusion, and such lack of familiarity with modes and forms, that Giovanni responded as if to an infant. Her spirit gushed out before him like a fresh rill, that was just catching its first glimpse of the sunlight, and wondering at the reflections of earth and sky which were flung into its bosom. There came thoughts, too, from a deep source, and fantasies of a gem-like brilliancy, as if diamonds and rubies sparkled upward among the bubbles of the fountain. Ever and anon, there gleamed across the young man's mind a sense of wonder, that he should be walking side by side with the being who had so wrought upon his imagination—whom he had idealized in such hues of terror—in whom he had positively witnessed such manifestations of dreadful attributes—that he should be conversing with Beatrice like a brother, and should find her so human and so maiden-like. But such reflections were only momentary; the effect of her character was too real, not to make itself familiar at once.

In this free intercourse, they had strayed through the garden, and now, after many turns among its avenues, were come to the shattered fountain, beside which grew the magnificent shrub with its treasury of glowing blossoms. A fragrance was diffused from it, which Giovanni recognized as identical with that which he had attributed to Beatrice's breath, but incomparably more powerful. As her eyes fell upon it, Giovanni beheld her press her hand to her bosom, as if her heart were throbbing suddenly and painfully.

"For the first time in my life," murmured she, addressing the shrub, "I had forgotten thee!"

"I remember, Signora," said Giovanni, "that you once promised to reward me with one of these living gems for the bouquet, which I had the happy boldness to fling to your feet. Permit me now to pluck it as a memorial of this interview."

He made a step towards the shrub, with extended hand. But Beatrice darted forward, uttering a shriek that went through his heart like a dagger. She caught his hand, and drew it back with the whole force of her slender figure. Giovanni felt her touch thrilling through his fibres.

"Touch it not!" exclaimed she, in a voice of agony. "Not for thy life! It is fatal!"

Then, hiding her face, she fled from him, and vanished beneath the sculptured portal. As Giovanni followed her with his eyes, he beheld the emaciated figure and pale intelligence of Doctor Rappaccini, who had been watching the scene, he knew not how long, within the shadow of the entrance.

No sooner was Guasconti alone in his chamber, than the image of Beatrice came back to his passionate musings, invested with all the witchery that had been gathering around it ever since his first glimpse of her, and now likewise imbued with a tender warmth of girlish womanhood. She was human: her nature was endowed with all gentle and feminine qualities; she was worthiest to be worshipped; she was capable, surely, on her part, of the height and heroism of love. Those tokens, which he had hitherto considered as proofs of a frightful peculiarity in her physical and moral system, were now either forgotten, or, by the subtle sophistry of passion, transmuted into a golden crown of enchantment, rendering Beatrice the more admirable, by so much as she was the more unique. Whatever had looked ugly, was now beautiful; or, if incapable of such a change, it stole away and hid itself among those shapeless half-ideas, which throng the dim region beyond the day-light of our perfect consciousness. Thus did Giovanni spend the night, nor fell asleep, until the dawn had begun to awake the slumbering flowers in Doctor Rappaccini's garden, whither his dreams doubtless led him. Up rose the sun in his due season, and flinging his beams upon the young man's eyelids, awoke him to a sense of pain. When thoroughly aroused, he became sensible of a burning and tingling agony in his hand—in his right hand—the very hand which Beatrice had grasped in her own, when he was on the point of plucking one of the gem-like flowers. On the back of that hand there was now a purple print, like that of four small fingers, and the likeness of a slender thumb upon his wrist.

Oh, how stubbornly does love—or even that cunning semblance of love which flourishes in the imagination, but strikes no depth of root into the heart—how stubbornly does it hold its faith, until the moment come, when it is doomed to vanish into thin mist! Giovanni wrapt a handkerchief about his hand, and wondered what evil thing had stung him, and soon forgot his pain in a reverie of Beatrice.

After the first interview, a second was in the inevitable course of what we call fate. A third; a fourth; and a meeting with Beatrice in the garden was no longer an incident in Giovanni's daily life, but the whole space in which he might be said to live; for the anticipation and memory of that ecstatic hour made up the remainder. Nor was it otherwise with the daughter of Rappaccini. She watched for the youth's appearance, and flew to his side with confidence as unreserved as if they had been playmates from early infancy—as if they were such playmates still. If, by any unwonted chance, he failed to come at the appointed moment, she stood beneath the window, and sent up the rich sweetness of her tones to float around him in his chamber, and echo and reverberate throughout his heart—"Giovanni! Giovanni! Why tarriest thou? Come down!"—And down he hastened into that Eden of poisonous flowers.

But, with all this intimate familiarity, there was still a reserve in Beatrice's demeanor, so rigidly and invariably sustained, that the idea of infringing it scarcely occurred to his imagination. By all appreciable signs, they loved; they had looked love, with eyes that conveyed the holy secret from the depths of one soul into the depths of the other, as if it were too sacred to be whispered by the way; they had even spoken love, in those gushes of passion when their spirits darted forth in articulated breath, like tongues of long-hidden flame; and yet there had been no seal of lips, no clasp of hands, nor any slightest caress, such as love claims and hallows. He had never touched one of the gleaming ringlets of her hair; her garment—so marked was the physical barrier between them—had never been waved against him by a breeze. On the few occasions when Giovanni had seemed tempted to overstep the limit, Beatrice grew so sad, so stern, and withal wore such a look of desolate separation, shuddering at itself, that not a spoken word was requisite to repel him. At such times, he was startled at the horrible suspicions that rose, monster-like, out of the caverns of his heart, and stared him in the face; his love grew thin and faint as the morning-mist; his doubts alone had substance. But when Beatrice's face brightened again, after the momentary shadow, she was transformed at once from the mysterious, questionable being, whom he had watched with so much awe and horror; she was now the beautiful and unsophisticated girl, whom he felt that his spirit knew with a certainty beyond all other knowledge.

A considerable time had now passed since Giovanni's last meeting with Baglioni. One morning, however, he was disagreeably surprised by a visit from the Professor, whom he had scarcely thought of for whole weeks, and would willingly have forgotten still longer. Given up, as he had long been, to a pervading excitement, he could tolerate no companions, except upon condition of their perfect sympathy with his present state of feeling. Such sympathy was not to be expected from Professor Baglioni.

The visitor chatted carelessly, for a few moments, about the gossip of the city and the University, and then took up another topic.

"I have been reading an old classic author lately," said he, "and met with a story[2] that strangely interested me. Possibly you may remember it. It is of an Indian prince, who sent a beautiful woman as a present to Alexander the Great. She was as lovely as the dawn, and gorgeous as the sunset; but what especially distinguished her was a certain rich perfume in her breath—richer than a garden of Persian roses. Alexander, as was natural to a youthful conqueror, fell in love at first sight with this magnificent stranger. But a certain sage physician, happening to be present, discovered a terrible secret in regard to her."

"And what was that?" asked Giovanni, turning his eyes downward to avoid those of the Professor.

"That this lovely woman," continued Baglioni, with emphasis, "had been nourished with poisons from her birth upward, until her whole nature was so imbued with them, that she herself had become the deadliest poison in exis-

---

2. In Sir Thomas Browne's *Vulgar Errors* (1646) or elsewhere.

tence. Poison was her element of life. With that rich perfume of her breath, she blasted the very air. Her love would have been poison!—her embrace death! Is not this a marvellous tale?"

"A childish fable," answered Giovanni, nervously starting from his chair. "I marvel how your worship finds time to read such nonsense, among your graver studies."

"By the by," said the Professor, looking uneasily about him, "what singular fragrance is this in your apartment? Is it the perfume of your gloves? It is faint, but delicious, and yet, after all, by no means agreeable. Were I to breathe it long, methinks it would make me ill. It is like the breath of a flower—but I see no flowers in the chamber."

"Nor are there any," replied Giovanni, who had turned pale as the Professor spoke; "nor, I think, is there any fragrance, except in your worship's imagination. Odors, being a sort of element combined of the sensual and the spiritual, are apt to deceive us in this manner. The recollection of a perfume—the bare idea of it—may easily be mistaken for a present reality."

"Aye; but my sober imagination does not often play such tricks," said Baglioni; "and were I to fancy any kind of odor, it would be that of some vile apothecary drug, wherewith my fingers are likely enough to be imbued. Our worshipful friend Rappaccini, as I have heard, tinctures his medicaments with odors richer than those of Araby. Doubtless, likewise, the fair and learned Signora Beatrice would minister to her patients with draughts as sweet as a maiden's breath. But wo to him that sips them!"

Giovanni's face evinced many contending emotions. The tone in which the Professor alluded to the pure and lovely daughter of Rappaccini was a torture to his soul; and yet, the intimation of a view of her character, opposite to his own, gave instantaneous distinctness to a thousand dim suspicions, which now grinned at him like so many demons. But he strove hard to quell them, and to respond to Baglioni with a true lover's perfect faith.

"Signor Professor," said he, "you were my father's friend—perchance, too, it is your purpose to act a friendly part towards his son. I would fain feel nothing towards you, save respect and deference. But I pray you to observe, Signor, that there is one subject on which we must not speak. You know not the Signora Beatrice. You cannot, therefore, estimate the wrong—the blasphemy, I may even say—that is offered to her character by a light or injurious word."

"Giovanni!—my poor Giovanni!" answered the Professor, with a calm expression of pity, "I know this wretched girl far better than yourself. You shall hear the truth in respect to the poisoner Rappaccini, and his poisonous daughter. Yes; poisonous as she is beautiful! Listen; for even should you do violence to my grey hairs, it shall not silence me. That old fable of the Indian woman has become a truth, by the deep and deadly science of Rappaccini, and in the person of the lovely Beatrice!"

Giovanni groaned and hid his face.

"Her father," continued Baglioni, "was not restrained by natural affection from offering up his child, in this horrible manner, as the victim of his insane zeal for science. For—let us do him justice—he is as true a man of science as ever distilled his own heart in an alembic. What, then, will be your fate? Beyond a doubt, you are selected as the material of some new experiment. Perhaps the result is to be death—perhaps a fate more awful still! Rappaccini, with what he calls the interest of science before his eyes, will hesitate at nothing."

"It is a dream!" muttered Giovanni to himself, "surely it is a dream!"

"But," resumed the professor, "be of good cheer, son of my friend! It is not yet too late for the rescue. Possibly, we may even succeed in bringing back this miserable child within the limits of ordinary nature, from which her father's madness has estranged her. Behold this little silver vase! It was wrought by the hands of the renowned Benvenuto Cellini,[3] and is well worthy to be a love-gift to the fairest dame in Italy. But its contents are invaluable. One little sip of this antidote would have rendered the most virulent poisons of the Borgias[4] innocuous. Doubt not that it will be as efficacious against those of Rappaccini. Bestow the vase, and the precious liquid within it, on your Beatrice, and hopefully await the result."

Baglioni laid a small, exquisitely wrought silver phial on the table, and withdrew, leaving what he had said to produce its effect upon the young man's mind.

"We will thwart Rappaccini yet!" thought he, chuckling to himself, as he descended the stairs. "But, let us confess the truth of him, he is a wonderful man!—a wonderful man indeed! A vile empiric, however, in his practice, and therefore not to be tolerated by those who respect the good old rules of the medical profession!"

Throughout Giovanni's whole acquaintance with Beatrice, he had occasionally, as we have said, been haunted by dark surmises as to her character. Yet, so thoroughly had she made herself felt by him as a simple, natural, most affectionate and guileless creature, that the image now held up by Professor Baglioni, looked as strange and incredible, as if it were not in accordance with his own original conception. True, there were ugly recollections connected with his first glimpses of the beautiful girl; he could not quite forget the bouquet that withered in her grasp, and the insect that perished amid the sunny air, by no ostensible agency, save the fragrance of her breath. These incidents, however, dissolving in the pure light of her character, had no longer the efficacy of facts, but were acknowledged as mistaken fantasies, by whatever testimony of the senses they might appear to be substantiated. There is something truer and more real, than what we can see with the eyes, and touch with the finger. On such better evidence, had Giovanni founded his confidence in Beatrice, though rather by the necessary force of her high attributes, than by any deep and generous faith, on his part. But, now, his spirit was incapable of sustaining itself at the height to which the early enthusiasm of passion had exalted it; he fell down, grovelling among earthly doubts, and defiled therewith the pure whiteness of Beatrice's image. Not that he gave her up; he did but distrust. He resolved to institute some decisive test that should satisfy him, once for all, whether there were those dreadful peculiarities in her physical nature, which could not be supposed to exist without some corresponding monstrosity of soul. His eyes, gazing down afar, might have deceived him as to the lizard, the insect, and the flowers. But if he could witness, at the distance of a few paces, the sudden blight of one fresh and healthful flower in Beatrice's hand, there would be room for no further question. With this idea, he hastened to the florist's, and purchased a bouquet that was still gemmed with the morning dew-drops.

3. Italian goldsmith and sculptor (1500–1571).
4. Renaissance Italian family influential in church and government and notorious for cruelty and licentiousness.

It was now the customary hour of his daily interview with Beatrice. Before descending into the garden, Giovanni failed not to look at his figure in the mirror; a vanity to be expected in a beautiful young man, yet, as displaying itself at that troubled and feverish moment, the token of a certain shallowness of feeling and insincerity of character. He did gaze, however, and said to himself, that his features had never before possessed so rich a grace, nor his eyes such vivacity, nor his cheeks so warm a hue of superabundant life.

"At least," thought he, "her poison has not yet insinuated itself into my system. I am no flower to perish in her grasp!"

With that thought, he turned his eyes on the bouquet, which he had never once laid aside from his hand. A thrill of indefinable horror shot through his frame, on perceiving that those dewy flowers were already beginning to droop; they wore the aspect of things that had been fresh and lovely, yesterday. Giovanni grew white as marble, and stood motionless before the mirror, staring at his own reflection there, as at the likeness of something frightful. He remembered Baglioni's remark about the fragrance that seemed to pervade the chamber. It must have been the poison in his breath! Then he shuddered— shuddered at himself! Recovering from his stupor, he began to watch, with curious eye, a spider that was busily at work, hanging its web from the antique cornice of the apartment, crossing and re-crossing the artful system of interwoven lines, as vigorous and active a spider as ever dangled from an old ceiling. Giovanni bent towards the insect, and emitted a deep, long breath. The spider suddenly ceased its toil; the web vibrated with a tremor originating in the body of the small artizan. Again Giovanni sent forth a breath, deeper, longer, and imbued with a venomous feeling out of his heart; he knew not whether he were wicked or only desperate. The spider made a convulsive gripe with his limbs, and hung dead across the window.

"Accursed! Accursed!" muttered Giovanni, addressing himself. "Hast thou grown so poisonous, that this deadly insect perishes by the breath?"

At that moment, a rich, sweet voice came floating up from the garden:—

"Giovanni! Giovanni! It is past the hour! Why tarriest thou! Come down!"

"Yes," muttered Giovanni again. "She is the only being whom my breath may not slay! Would that it might!"

He rushed down, and in an instant, was standing before the bright and loving eyes of Beatrice. A moment ago, his wrath and despair had been so fierce that he could have desired nothing so much as to wither her by a glance. But, with her actual presence, there came influences which had too real an existence to be at once shaken off; recollections of the delicate and benign power of her feminine nature, which had so often enveloped him in a religious calm; recollections of many a holy and passionate outgush of her heart, when the pure fountain had been unsealed from its depths, and made visible in its transparency to his mental eye; recollections which, had Giovanni known how to estimate them, would have assured him that all this ugly mystery was but an earthly illusion, and that, whatever mist of evil might seem to have gathered over her, the real Beatrice was a heavenly angel. Incapable as he was of such high faith, still her presence had not utterly lost its magic. Giovanni's rage was quelled into an aspect of sullen insensibility. Beatrice, with a quick spiritual sense, immediately felt that there was a gulf of blackness between them, which neither he nor she could pass. They walked on together, sad and silent, and came thus to the marble fountain, and to its pool of water on the ground, in the midst of which grew the shrub that bore gem-like blossoms. Giovanni was affrighted at the eager enjoyment—the appetite, as it were—with which he found himself inhaling the fragrance of the flowers.

"Beatrice," asked he abruptly, "whence came this shrub?"

"My father created it," answered she, with simplicity.

"Created it! created it!" repeated Giovanni. "What mean you, Beatrice?"

"He is a man fearfully acquainted with the secrets of nature," replied Beatrice; "and, at the hour when I first drew breath, this plant sprang from the soil, the offspring of his science, of his intellect, while I was but his earthly child. "Approach it not!" continued she, observing with terror that Giovanni was drawing nearer to the shrub. "It has qualities that you little dream of. But I, dearest Giovanni,—I grew up and blossomed with the plant, and was nourished with its breath. It was my sister, and I loved it with a human affection: for—alas! hast thou not suspected it? there was an awful doom."

Here Giovanni frowned so darkly upon her that Beatrice paused and trembled. But her faith in his tenderness re-assured her, and made her blush that she had doubted for an instant.

"There was an awful doom," she continued,—"the effect of my father's fatal love of science—which estranged me from all society of any kind. Until Heaven sent thee, dearest Giovanni, Oh! how lonely was thy poor Beatrice!"

"Was it a hard doom?" asked Giovanni, fixing his eyes upon her.

"Only of late have I known how hard it was," answered she tenderly. "Oh, yes; but my heart was torpid, and therefore quiet."

Giovanni's rage broke forth from his sullen gloom like a lightning-flash out of a dark cloud.

"Accursed one!" cried he, with venomous scorn and anger. "And finding thy solitude wearisome, thou hast severed me, likewise, from all the warmth of life, and enticed me into thy region of unspeakable horror!"

"Giovanni!" exclaimed Beatrice, turning her large bright eyes upon his face. The force of his words had not found its way into her mind; she was merely wonder-struck.

"Yes, poisonous thing!" repeated Giovanni, beside himself with passion. "Thou has done it! Thou has blasted me! Thou hast filled my veins with poison! Thou hast made me as hateful, as ugly, as loathsome and deadly a creature as thyself,—a world's wonder of hideous monstrosity! Now—if our breath be happily as fatal to ourselves as to all others—let us join our lips in one kiss of unutterable hatred, and so die!"

"What has befallen me?" murmured Beatrice, with a low moan out of her heart. "Holy Virgin pity me, a poor heart-broken child!"

"Thou! Dost thou pray?" cried Giovanni, still with the same fiendish scorn. "Thy very prayers, as they come from thy lips, taint the atmosphere with death. Yes, yes; let us pray! Let us to church, and dip our fingers in the holy water at the portal! They that come after us will perish as by a pestilence. Let us sign crosses in the air! It will be scattering curses abroad in the likeness of holy symbols!"

"Giovanni," said Beatrice calmly, for her grief was beyond passion, "why dost thou join thyself with me thus in those terrible words? I, it is true, am the horrible thing thou namest me. But thou!—what hast thou to do, save with one other shudder at my hideous misery, to go forth out of the garden and mingle with thy race, and forget that there ever crawled on earth such a monster as poor Beatrice?"

"Dost thou pretend ignorance?" asked Giovanni, scowling upon her. "Behold! This power have I gained from the pure daughter of Rappaccini!"

There was a swarm of summer-insects flitting through the air, in search of the food promised by the flower-odors of the fatal garden. They circled round Giovanni's head, and were evidently attracted towards him by the same influence which had drawn them, for an instant, within the sphere of several of the shrubs. He sent forth a breath among them, and smiled bitterly at Beatrice, as at least a score of the insects fell dead upon the ground.

"I see it! I see it!" shrieked Beatrice. "It is my father's fatal science! No, no, Giovanni; it was not I! Never, never! I dreamed only to love thee, and be with thee a little time, and so to let thee pass away, leaving but thine image in mine heart. For, Giovanni—believe it—though my body be nourished with poison, my spirit is God's creature, and craves love as its daily food. But my father!— he has united us in this fearful sympathy. Yes; spurn me!—tread upon me!— kill me! Oh, what is death, after such words as thine? But it was not I! Not for a world of bliss would I have done it!"

Giovanni's passion had exhausted itself in its outburst from his lips. There now came across a sense, mournful, and not without tenderness, of the intimate and peculiar relationship between Beatrice and himself. They stood, as it were, in an utter solitude, which would be made none the less solitary by the densest throng of human life. Ought not, then, the desert of humanity around them to press this insulated pair close together? If they should be cruel to one another, who was there to be kind to them? Besides, thought Giovanni, might there not still be a hope of his returning within the limits of ordinary nature, and leading Beatrice—the redeemed Beatrice—by the hand? Oh, weak, and selfish, and unworthy spirit, that could dream of an earthly union and earthly happiness as possible, after such deep love had been so bitterly wronged as was Beatrice's love by Giovanni's blighting words! No, no; there could be no such hope. She must pass heavily, with that broken heart, across the borders—she must bathe her hurts in some fount of Paradise, and forget her grief in the light of immortality—and *there* be well!

But Giovanni did not know it.

"Dear Beatrice," said he, approaching her, while she shrank away, as always at his approach, but now with a different impulse—"dearest Beatrice, our fate is not yet so desperate. Behold! There is a medicine, potent, as a wise physician has assured me, and almost divine in its efficacy. It is composed of ingredients the most opposite to those by which thy awful father has brought this calamity upon thee and me. It is distilled of blessed herbs. Shall we not quaff it together, and thus be purified from evil?"

"Give it me!" said Beatrice, extending her hand to receive the little silver phial which Giovanni took from his bosom. She added, with a peculiar emphasis; "I will drink—but do thou await the result."

She put Baglioni's antidote to her lips; and, at the same moment, the figure of Rappaccini emerged from the portal, and came slowly towards the marble fountain. As he drew near, the pale man of science seemed to gaze with a triumphant expression at the beautiful youth and maiden, as might an artist who should spend his life in achieving a picture or a group of statuary, and finally be satisfied with his success. He paused—his bent form grew erect with conscious power, he spread out his hand over them, in the attitude of a father imploring a blessing upon his children. But those were the same hands that had thrown poison into the stream of their lives! Giovanni trembled. Beatrice shuddered nervously, and pressed her hand upon her heart.

"My daughter," said Rappaccini, "thou art no longer lonely in the world! Pluck one of those precious gems from thy sister shrub, and bid thy bridegroom wear it in his bosom. It will not harm him now! My science, and the sympathy between thee and him, have so wrought within his system, that he now stands apart from common men, as thou dost, daughter of my pride and triumph, from ordinary women. Pass on, then, through the world, most dear to one another, and dreadful to all besides!"

"My father," said Beatrice, feebly—and still, as she spoke, she kept her hand upon her heart—"wherefore didst thou inflict this miserable doom upon thy child?"

"Miserable!" exclaimed Rappaccini. "What mean you, foolish girl? Dost thou deem it misery to be endowed with marvellous gifts, against which no power nor strength could avail an enemy? Misery, to be able to quell the mightiest with a breath? Misery, to be as terrible as thou art beautiful? Wouldst thou, then, have preferred the condition of a weak woman, exposed to all evil, and capable of none?"

"I would fain have been loved, not feared," murmured Beatrice, sinking down upon the ground.—"But now it matters not; I am going, father, where the evil, which thou hast striven to mingle with my being, will pass away like a dream—like the fragrance of these poisonous flowers, which will no longer taint my breath among the flowers of Eden. Farewell, Giovanni! Thy words of hatred are like lead within my heart—but they, too, will fall away as I ascend. Oh, was there not, from the first, more poison in thy nature than in mine?"

To Beatrice—so radically had her earthly part been wrought upon by Rappaccini's skill—as poison had been life, so the powerful antidote was death. And thus the poor victim of man's ingenuity and of thwarted nature, and of the fatality that attends all such efforts of perverted wisdom, perished there, at the feet of her father and Giovanni. Just at that moment, Professor Pietro Baglioni looked forth from the window, and called loudly, in a tone of triumph mixed with horror, to the thunder-stricken man of science:

"Rappaccini! Rappaccini! And is *this* the upshot of your experiment?"

1844

# Preface to *The House of the Seven Gables*[1]

When a writer calls his work a Romance, it need hardly be observed that he wishes to claim a certain latitude, both as to its fashion and material, which he would not have felt himself entitled to assume, had he professed to be writing a Novel. The latter form of composition is presumed to aim at a very minute fidelity, not merely to the possible, but to the probable and ordinary course of man's experience. The former—while, as a work of art, it must rigidly subject itself to laws, and while it sins unpardonably so far as it may swerve aside from the truth of the human heart—has fairly a right to present that truth under circumstances, to a great extent, of the writer's own choosing

---

1. The text is from *The House of the Seven Gables: A Romance* (1851).

or creation. If he think fit, also, he may so manage his atmospherical medium as to bring out or mellow the lights, and deepen and enrich the shadows, of the picture. He will be wise, no doubt, to make a very moderate use of the privileges here stated, and, especially, to mingle the Marvellous rather as a slight, delicate, and evanescent flavor, than as any portion of the actual substance of the dish offered to the public. He can hardly be said, however, to commit a literary crime, even if he disregard this caution.

In the present work, the author has proposed to himself—but with what success, fortunately, it is not for him to judge—to keep undeviatingly within his immunities. The point of view in which this tale comes under the Romantic definition lies in the attempt to connect a by-gone time with the very present that is flitting away from us. It is a legend, prolonging itself, from an epoch now gray in the distance, down into our own broad daylight, and bringing along with it some of its legendary mist, which the reader, according to his pleasure, may either disregard, or allow it to float almost imperceptibly about the characters and events, for the sake of a picturesque effect. The narrative, it may be, is woven of so humble a texture as to require this advantage, and, at the same time, to render it the more difficult of attainment.

Many writers lay very great stress upon some definite moral purpose, at which they profess to aim their works. Not to be deficient in this particular, the author has provided himself with a moral;—the truth, namely, that the wrong-doing of one generation lives into the successive ones, and, divesting itself of every temporary advantage, becomes a pure and uncontrollable mischief;—and he would feel it a singular gratification, if this romance might effectually convince mankind—or, indeed, any one man—of the folly of tumbling down an avalanche of ill-gotten gold, or real estate, on the heads of an unfortunate posterity, thereby to maim and crush them, until the accumulated mass shall be scattered abroad in its original atoms. In good faith, however, he is not sufficiently imaginative to flatter himself with the slightest hope of this kind. When romances do really teach anything, or produce any effective operation, it is usually through a far more subtile process than the ostensible one. The author has considered it hardly worth his while, therefore, relentlessly to impale the story with its moral, as with an iron rod,—or, rather as by sticking a pin through a butterfly,—thus at once depriving it of life, and causing it to stiffen in an ungainly and unnatural attitude. A high truth, indeed, fairly, finely, and skilfully wrought out, brightening at every step, and crowning the final development of a work of fiction, may add an artistic glory, but is never any truer, and seldom any more evident, at the last page than at the first.

The reader may perhaps choose to assign an actual locality to the imaginary events of this narrative. If permitted by the historical connection,—which, though slight, was essential to his plan,—the author would very willingly have avoided anything of this nature. Not to speak of other objections, it exposes the romance to an inflexible and exceedingly dangerous species of criticism, by bringing his fancy-pictures almost into positive contact with the realities of the moment. It has been no part of his object, however, to describe local manners, nor in any way to meddle with the characteristics of a community for whom he cherishes a proper respect and a natural regard. He trusts not to be considered as unpardonably offending, by laying out a street that infringes upon nobody's private rights, and appropriating a lot of land which had no visible owner, and building a house, of materials long in use for constructing castles in the air. The personages of the tale—though they give themselves out to be of ancient stability and considerable prominence—are really of the author's own making, or, at all events, of his own mixing; their virtues can shed no lustre, nor their defects redound, in the remotest degree, to the discredit of the venerable town[2] of which they profess to be inhabitants. He would be glad, therefore, if—especially in the quarter to which he alludes—the book may be read strictly as a Romance, having a great deal more to do with the clouds overhead than with any portion of the actual soil of the County of Essex.

LENOX, *January 27, 1851*.

2. Salem, Massachusetts.

---

# HENRY WADSWORTH LONGFELLOW
## 1807–1882

Henry Wadsworth Longfellow was born in Portland, Maine (then still a part of Massachusetts), on February 27, 1807, and died on March 24, 1882, in Cambridge, Massachusetts, the most beloved American poet of his time. His father sent him to Bowdoin, thinking that he would become a lawyer. Instead, Longfellow became so proficient a student of languages that Bowdoin created for him a professorship of modern languages, then one of only a handful in the country. With support from his father, Longfellow studied languages in Europe for three years before taking up his work at Bowdoin in 1829. In Spain, Washington Irving was hospitable, and Longfellow's prose romance *Outre-Mer* (1833–35) was in loving imitation of *The Sketch-Book*. Having concentrated on the Romance languages during his first European stay, Longfellow returned to perfect himself in Germanic languages, a condition for his becoming a professor at Harvard late in 1836. He took teaching seriously, although in the early years he spent most of his time instilling the rudiments of foreign languages (for which he wrote and published his own textbooks) without being able to teach the literatures. Later, at Harvard, he taught an extraordinary range of European literatures of many periods and thereby became an incalculable force in American cultural life. It would be hard, also, to overestimate the importance of his anthology *The Poets and Poetry of Europe* (1845) in bringing home to the ordinary reader the rich variety of European literatures. His own poetry became a means of teaching readers of his day something of the possible range of poetic subject matter and techniques, ancient, medieval, and modern. Irving had been notably successful in domesticating European subject matter while employing a British prose style; now Longfellow domesticated European meters, as in his adaptation of classical Greek meters to tell the story of Evangeline Bellefontaine, set in the recent North American past or in using Finnish folk meter in his celebration of American Indian legends in *Hiawatha*. Longfellow became a great teacher of the masses. If his worst fault is that he made poetry seem so easy to write that anyone could do it, his greatest virtue is that he made poetry seem worth reading and worth writing.

Longfellow married in 1831, during his professorship at Bowdoin, but in 1835, during his second European trip, his wife died after miscarrying. Longfellow stayed on, fulfilling his commitment to Harvard, and before he returned home he had met Fanny Appleton, the Boston heiress who was to become his second wife. She was slow to return his affection, and he embarrassed her by the transparent account of their meeting in the prose romance *Hyperion* (1839), but after their marriage in 1843 their life was idyllic. Longfellow's father-in-law bought the couple, as a wedding gift, Craigie House in Cambridge, a mansion George Washington had used as headquarters and where Longfellow himself had been renting rooms. Their life was elegant. Emerson, who lived amply enough in Concord, was intimidated: "If Socrates were here, we could go and talk with him; but Longfellow we cannot go and talk with; there is a palace, and servants, and a row of bottles of different colored wines, and wine glasses, and fine coats." But the sumptuousness proved supportive and encouraging to Longfellow's poetry and to his work at Harvard until he resigned in 1854. Popular as he was, Longfellow could not make a living from his poetry. In 1855 and 1856, for instance, the phenomenal sales of *Hiawatha* brought his total earnings from poetry to around $3,700 and $7,400, but in the 1840s and 1850s his average annual income from poetry hardly exceeded his Harvard salary of $1,500 ($1,800 after 1845). In 1861 Fanny Longfellow was fatally burned as she was sealing up locks of her daughters' hair. In his grief Longfellow turned to translating the entire *Divine Comedy* of Dante, making the labor the occasion for regular meetings with friends such as James Russell Lowell and the young William Dean Howells, who had lived in Venice. Longfellow's last decades were uneventful, except for one final visit to Europe in 1868–69, during which Queen Victoria gave him a private audience. His seventy-fifth birthday was celebrated nationally. Of his death his brother and official biographer wrote: "The long, busy, blameless life was ended. The loneliness of separation was over. He was dead. But the world was better and happier for his having lived."

# A Psalm of Life[1]

'Life that shall send
A challenge to its end,
And when it comes, say, 'Welcome, friend.'[2]

## What the Heart of the Young Man Said to the Psalmist

I

Tell me not, in mournful numbers,[3]
    Life is but an empty dream!
For the soul is dead that slumbers,
    And things are not what they seem.

II

Life is real—life is earnest—                                    5
    And the grave is not its goal:
Dust thou art, to dust returnest,
    Was not spoken of the soul.

III

Not enjoyment, and not sorrow,
    Is our destin'd end or way;                                  10
But to *act*, that each to-morrow
    Find us farther than to-day.

---

1. The text is that of the first publication, in the *Knickerbocker or New-York Monthly Magazine* (September 1838). The poem was collected in *Voices of the Night* (1839).
2. Slightly misquoted from *Wishes to His Supposed*

*Mistress* by the English poet Richard Crashaw (c. 1613–1649). Longfellow included the Crashaw poem in a volume he edited, *The Waif: A Collection of Poems* (1845).
3. Meters, rhythms.

IV

Art is long, and time is fleeting,[4]
    And our hearts, though stout and brave,
Still, like muffled drums, are beating                          15
    Funeral marches to the grave.

V

In the world's broad field of battle,
    In the bivouac of Life,
Be not like dumb, driven cattle!
    Be a hero in the strife!                                    20

VI

Trust no Future, howe'er pleasant!
    Let the dead Past bury its dead!
Act—act in the glorious Present!
    Heart within, and God o'er head!

VII

Lives of great men all remind us                               25
    We can make *our* lives sublime,
And, departing, leave behind us
    Footsteps on the sands of time.

VIII

Footsteps, that, perhaps another,
    Sailing o'er life's solemn main,                            30
A forlorn and shipwreck'd brother,
    Seeing, shall take heart again.

IX

Let us then be up and doing,
    With a heart for any fate;
Still achieving, still pursuing,                                35
    Learn to labor and to wait.

1838, 1839

# My Lost Youth[1]

Often I think of the beautiful town
    That is seated by the sea;
Often in thought go up and down
The pleasant streets of that dear old town,
    And my youth comes back to me.                               5
    And a verse of a Lapland song
    Is haunting my memory still:
"A boy's will is the wind's will,
And the thoughts of youth are long, long thoughts."

---

4. A paraphrase of Seneca's complaint, *"Vita brevis est, ars longa"* (*De Brevitate vitae* 1.1). The meaning of *ars* or *art* is clearer in Chaucer's *The Parliament of Fowls*, line 1: "The lyf so short, the craft so long to lerne."
1. Longfellow wrote this poem about his hometown of Portland, Maine, in March 1855, at Cambridge, deriving the refrain from lines in John Scheffer's *The History*

of Lapland (1674): "A Youth's desire is the desire of the wind, / All his essaies / Are long delaies, / No issue can they find." ("Essaies," or essays, means attempts and "issue" means outlet.) The text is that of the first printing in *Putnam's Monthly Magazine*, vol. 6 (August 1855). It was reprinted in *The Courtship of Miles Standish and Other Poems* (1858).

I can see the shadowy lines of its trees,                    10
    And catch, in sudden gleams,
The sheen of the far-surrounding seas,
And islands that were the Hesperides[2]
    Of all my boyish dreams.
        And the burden of that old song,                     15
            It murmurs and whispers still:
        "A boy's will is the wind's will,
And the thoughts of youth are long, long thoughts."

I remember the black wharves and the slips,
    And the sea-tides tossing free;                          20
And Spanish sailors with bearded lips,
And the beauty and mystery of the ships,
    And the magic of the sea.
        And the voice of that wayward song
            Is singing and saying still:                     25
        "A boy's will is the wind's will,
And the thoughts of youth are long, long thoughts."

I remember the bulwarks by the shore,
    And the fort upon the hill;
The sun-rise gun, with its hollow roar,                      30
The drum-beat repeated o'er and o'er,
    And the bugle wild and shrill.
        And the music of that old song
            Throbs in my memory still:
        "A boy's will is the wind's will,                    35
And the thoughts of youth are long, long thoughts."

I remember the sea-fight far away,
    How it thundered o'er the tide![3]
And the dead captains, as they lay
In their graves, o'erlooking the tranquil bay,               40
    Where they in battle died.
        And the sound of that mournful song
            Goes through me with a thrill:
        "A boy's will is the wind's will,
And the thoughts of youth are long, long thoughts."         45

I can see the breezy dome of groves,
    The shadows of Deering's Woods;
And the friendships old and the early loves
Come back with a Sabbath sound, as of doves
    In quiet neighborhoods.                                  50
        And the verse of that sweet old song,
            It flutters and murmurs still:
        "A boy's will is the wind's will,
And the thoughts of youth are long, long thoughts."

2. In Greek mythology, fabled islands where the golden apples grew.
3. The American *Enterprise* and the British *Boxer* fought near Portland in 1813. Both captains were killed and carried ashore for burial.

I remember the gleams and glooms that dart                          55
  Across the schoolboy's brain;
The song and the silence in the heart,
That in part are prophecies, and in part
  Are longings wild and vain.
    And the voice of that fitful song                               60
    Sings on, and is never still:
    "A boy's will is the wind's will,
And the thoughts of youth are long, long thoughts."

There are things of which I may not speak;
  There are dreams that cannot die;                                 65
There are thoughts that make the strong heart weak,
And bring a pallor into the cheek,
  And a mist before the eye.
    And the words of that fatal song
    Come over me like a chill:                                      70
    "A boy's will is the wind's will,
And the thoughts of youth are long, long thoughts."

Strange to me now are the forms I meet
  When I visit the dear old town;
But the native air is pure and sweet,                               75
And the trees that o'ershadow each well-known street,
  As they balance up and down,
    Are singing the beautiful song,
    Are sighing and whispering still:
    "A boy's will is the wind's will,                               80
And the thoughts of youth are long, long thoughts."

And Deering's Woods are fresh and fair,
  And with joy that is almost pain
My heart goes back to wander there,
And among the dreams of the days that were,                        85
  I find my lost youth again.
    And the strange and beautiful song,
    The groves are repeating it still:
    "A boy's will is the wind's will,
And the thoughts of youth are long, long thoughts."                90

1855                                                               1855

---

# JOHN GREENLEAF WHITTIER
## 1807–1892

John Greenleaf Whittier was born on December 17, 1807, on a farm near Haverhill, Massachusetts, of a Quaker family. No longer persecuted in New England,
Quakers were still a people apart, and Whittier grew up with a sense of being
different from most of his neighbors. Labor on the debt-ridden farm overstrained
his health in adolescence, and thereafter throughout his long life he suffered from

intermittent physical collapses. At fourteen, having had only meager education in a household suspicious of non-Quaker literature, he found in the Scottish poet Robert Burns a model for imitation, one using a regional dialect, dealing with homely subjects, and displaying a strong social conscience. His first poem was published in 1826 in a local newspaper run by another young man, William Lloyd Garrison, whose dedication to the antislavery movement was to affect Whittier's life profoundly. In 1827 Garrison helped persuade Whittier's father that the young poet deserved more education, and Whittier supported himself through two terms at Haverhill Academy. During this time and later Whittier was near serious courtships, but like many of his relatives, he never married; among the obstacles were his Quakerism, his poverty, and his commitment to abolitionism. In 1836, six years after his father's death, Whittier and his mother and sisters moved from the farm to the house in nearby Amesbury, Massachusetts, which he owned until his death.

In his twenties Whittier became editor of various newspapers, some of regional importance. He was elected for a term to the Massachusetts legislature (1835) and became a behind-the-scenes force in the Whig party and, later, in the antislavery Liberty party, which he helped to found in 1839. The turning point in his career came in 1833 with the publication of his abolitionist manifesto *Justice and Expediency*, in which Whittier concluded that there was only one practicable and just scheme of emancipation: "Immediate abolition of slavery; an immediate acknowledgment of the great truth, that man cannot hold property in man; an immediate surrender of baneful prejudice to Christian love; an immediate practical obedience to the command of Jesus Christ: 'Whatsoever ye would that men should do unto you, do ye even so to them.' " Over the next three decades Whittier paid for his principles in many ways, some subtle, some as overt as being mobbed and stoned in 1835. The climactic danger came in 1838 when Whittier, in disguise, joined a mob to save some of his papers as his office was ransacked and burned. As early as 1833, Whittier began publishing abolitionist poems, which eventually numbered nearly one hundred. The strongest of them, like *Massachusetts to Virginia*, conveyed both a poetic and a moral complexity inspired, perhaps, by Whittier's own sense of conflict as a Quaker between the goal of "immediate abolition" and the violence it would inevitably impose on individuals and on the nation.

From the 1830s through the 1850s Whittier was a working editor associated with abolitionist papers, becoming the sort of man he was to describe in *The Tent on the Beach* (1867): A "dreamer born, / Who, with a mission to fulfil, / Had left the Muses' haunts to turn / The crank of an opinion-mill, / Making his rustic reed of song / A weapon in the war with wrong." Yet he continued to write about his own region, one legacy from his family being a rich oral history. His first book, *Legends of New England* (1831), had included stories in both prose and poetry. His first book of poetry was *Lays of My Home* (1843), and the prose *Supernaturalism of New England* followed in 1847. *Leaves from Margaret Smith's Journal* (1849) is a fictional re-creation of colonial life in the form of the diary of a young woman. Through his fictional and historical prose and through his poetry Whittier was setting a very early example of faithful treatment of American village and rural life that later local colorists and regionalists were to follow: the elderly Whittier's paternal interest in the career of Sarah Orne Jewett epitomizes this influence. But from the beginning a crucial problem for Whittier had been how to be true to the occasional beauty of rural life without portraying it in the sentimental manner that prevailed at the time. Whittier succeeded best in some late poems, especially *Snow-Bound* (1866) and the Prelude to *Among the Hills* (1868). Whittier's reputation began undergoing a change in the late 1850s, when abolitionism had ceased to be almost as much abhorred in the North as in the South; partly the new favor he received was a result of the founding in 1857 of the *Atlantic Monthly*, which was always hospitable to his poems, humorous folk legends as well as militant odes. *Snow-Bound* brought Whittier extraordinary acclaim and immediate financial

security; although one of the themes of the poem was his sense of his own
approaching death, Whittier ironically lived another quarter century, during which
he was revered as a great American poet. He died on September 7, 1892.

## Massachusetts to Virginia[1]

The blast from Freedom's Northern hills, upon its Southern way,
Bears greeting to Virginia, from Massachusetts Bay:—
No word of haughty challenging, nor battle-bugle's peal,
Nor steady tread of marching files, nor clang of horsemen's steel.

No trains of deep-mouthed cannon along our high-ways go—   5
Around our silent arsenals untrodden lies the snow;
And to the land breeze of our ports, upon their errands far,
A thousand sails of Commerce swell, but none are spread for War.

We hear thy threats, Virginia! thy stormy words and high,
Swell harshly on the Southern winds which melt along our sky;  10
Yet, not one brown, hard hand foregoes its honest labor here—
No hewer of our mountain oaks suspends his axe in fear.

Wild are the waves which lash the reefs along St. George's bank—
Cold on the shore of Labrador[2] the fog lies white and dank;
Through storm, and wave, and blinding mist, stout are the hearts
 which man   15
The fishing smacks of Marblehead, the sea-boats of Cape Ann.[3]

The cold North light and wintry sun glare on their icy forms,
Bent grimly o'er their straining lines or wrestling with the storms;
Free as the winds they drive before, rough as the waves they roam,
They laugh to scorn the slaver's threat against their rocky home. 20

What means the Old Dominion?[4] Hath she forgot the day
When o'er her conquered vallies swept the Briton's steel array?
How side by side, with sons of hers, the Massachusetts men
Encountered Tarleton's charge of fire, and stout Cornwallis,[5] then?

Forgets she how the Bay State,[6] in answer to the call   25
Of her old House of Burgesses, spoke out from Faneuil Hall[7]?

1. First collected in *Voices of Freedom* (1846), the text
of which is used here. Fugitive Slave Laws required
northern states to return escaped slaves to the South.
Following is a note Whittier later appended to the
poem: "Written on reading an account of the proceedings of the citizens of Norfolk, Va., in reference to
George Latimer, the alleged fugitive slave, who was
seized in Boston without warrant at the request of
James B. Grey, of Norfolk, claiming to be his master.
The case caused great excitement North and South,
and led to the presentation of a petition to Congress,
signed by more than fifty thousand citizens of Massachusetts, calling for such laws and proposed amendments to the Constitution as should relieve the Commonwealth from all further participation in the crime
of oppression. George Latimer himself was finally
given his free papers for the sum of four hundred
dollars."
2. Large peninsula divided between the Canadian
provinces of Newfoundland and Quebec. "St. George's
bank": off the southwestern coast of Newfoundland.
3. On the northern coast of Massachusetts. "Smacks":
sailing vessels. "Marblehead": Massachusetts town
northeast of Boston and on the Atlantic Ocean.
4. Virginia.
5. Commanders of British troops in Virginia during
the American Revolution.
6. Massachusetts.
7. Boston meeting hall. "House of Burgesses": lower
house of Virginia's colonial legislature.

When, echoing back her Henry's[8] cry, came pulsing on each breath
Of Northern winds, the thrilling sounds of 'LIBERTY OR DEATH!'

What asks the Old Dominion? If now her sons have proved
False to their fathers' memory—false to the faith they loved;⁣ 30
If she can scoff at Freedom, and its Great Charter[9] spurn,
Must we of Massachusetts from Truth and Duty turn?

We hunt your bondmen[1], flying from Slavery's hateful hell—
Our voices, at your bidding, take up the bloodhound's yell—
We gather, at your summons, above our fathers' graves,⁣ 35
From Freedom's holy altar horns[2] to tear your wretched slaves!

Thank God! not set so vilely can Massachusetts bow;
The spirit of her early time is with her even now;
Dream not because her pilgrim blood moves slow, and calm, and cool,
She thus can stoop her chainless neck, a sister's slave and tool!⁣ 40

All that a *sister* State should do, all that a *free* State may,
Heart, hand and purse we proffer, as in our early day:
But that one dark loathsome burden ye must stagger with alone,
And reap the bitter harvest which ye yourselves have sown!

Hold, while ye may, your struggling slaves, and burden God's free air⁣ 45
With woman's shriek beneath the lash, and manhood's wild despair;
Cling closer to the 'cleaving curse';[3] that writes upon your plains
The blasting of Almighty wrath against a land of chains

Still shame your gallant ancestry, the cavaliers of old,
By watching round the shambles[4] where human flesh is sold—⁣ 50
Gloat o'er the new born child, and count his market value, when
The maddened mother's cry of woe shall pierce the slaver's den!

Lower than plummet[5] soundeth, sink the Virginian name
Plant, if ye will, your fathers' graves with rankest weeds of shame;
Be, if ye will, the scandal of God's fair universe—⁣ 55
We wash our hands forever, of your sin, and shame, and curse.

A voice from lips whereon the coal from Freedom's shrine hath been,[6]
Thrilled, as but yesterday, the hearts of Berkshire's[7] mountain men:
The echoes of that solemn voice are sadly lingering still
In all our sunny valleys, on every wind-swept hill.⁣ 60

And when the prowling man-thief[8] came hunting for his prey
Beneath the very shadow of Bunker's shaft of grey,[9]

8. Patrick Henry (1736–1799), Virginia statesman.
9. Declaration of Independence.
1. Slaves.
2. In 1 Kings 1.50–53 and 2.28, the fugitives Adonijah and Joab gained asylum by grasping horns protruding from the altars of the Israelites.
3. Deuteronomy 13.12–17.
4. Slaughterhouse or meat market, where slave markets were often established.

5. Lead weight attached to a line and used to measure, or sound, the depth of water.
6. Isaiah 6.6–7.
7. County in western Massachusetts, with a mountain range of the same name.
8. Slave hunter.
9. Monument of Bunker Hill, site of the early Revolutionary War battle.

How, through the free lips of the son, the father's warning spoke;
How, from its bonds of trade and sect, the Pilgrim city[1] broke!

A hundred thousand right arms were lifted up on high,—       65
A hundred thousand voices sent back their loud reply;
Through the thronged towns of Essex[2] the startling summons rang,
And up from bench and loom and wheel her young mechanics sprang!

The voice of free, broad Middlesex—of thousands as of one—
The shaft of Bunker calling to that of Lexington—[3]      70
From Norfolk's ancient villages; from Plymouth's rocky bound
To where Nantucket[4] feels the arms of ocean close her round;—

From rich and rural Worcester, where through the calm repose
Of cultured vales and fringing woods the gentle Nashua[5] flows,
To where Wachusett's[6] wintry blasts the mountain larches stir,   75
Swelled up to heaven the thrilling cry of 'God save Latimer!'

And sandy Barnstable rose up, wet with the salt sea spray—
And Bristol sent her answering shout down Narragansett Bay![7]
Along the broad Connecticut[8] old Hampden felt the thrill,
And the cheer of Hampshire's woodmen swept down from Holyoke Hill.  80

The voice of Massachusetts! Of her free sons and daughters—
Deep calling unto deep aloud—the sound of many waters![9]
Against the burden of that voice what tyrant power shall stand?
*No fetters in the Bay State? No slave upon her land!*

Look to it well, Virginians! In calmness we have borne,     85
In answer to our faith and trust, your insult and your scorn;
You've spurned our kindest counsels—you've hunted for our lives—
And shaken round our hearths and homes your manacles and gyves![1]

We wage no war—we lift no arm—we fling no torch within
The fire-damps[2] of the quaking mine beneath your soil of sin;  90
We leave ye with your bondmen—to wrestle while ye can,
With the strong upward tendencies and God-like soul of man!

But for us and for our children, the vow which we have given
For Freedom and humanity, is registered in Heaven;
*No slave-hunt in our borders—no pirate on our strand!*     95
*No fetters in the Bay State—no slave upon our Land!*

                            1842

1. Boston.
2. Whittier's home county. Middlesex, Norfolk, Plymouth, Worcester, Barnstable, Bristol, Hampden, and Hampshire, mentioned below, are all Massachusetts counties.
3. Town in eastern Massachusetts where the first battle of the American Revolution was fought; the site is marked by a monument.
4. Island off the Massachusetts coast.

5. River in New Hampshire and Massachusetts.
6. Mountain in central Massachusetts.
7. A finger of this bay in southeastern Rhode Island extends into Massachusetts.
8. The Connecticut River flows through Massachusetts.
9. Psalms 42.7 and Ezekiel 43.2.
1. Shackles.
2. Combustible mine gas.

# Ichabod![1]

So fallen! so lost! the light withdrawn
    Which once he wore!
The glory from his gray hairs gone
    Forevermore!

Revile him not—the Tempter hath            5
    A snare for all;
And pitying tears, not scorn and wrath,
    Befit his fall!

Oh! dumb be passion's stormy rage,
    When he who might               10
Have lighted up and led his age,
    Falls back in night.

Scorn! would the angels laugh, to mark
    A bright soul driven,
Fiend-goaded, down the endless dark,        15
    From hope and heaven!

Let not the land, once proud of him,
    Insult him now,
Nor brand with deeper shame his dim,
    Dishonored brow.               20

But let its humbled sons, instead,
    From sea to lake,
A long lament, as for the dead,
    In sadness make.

Of all we loved and honored, nought       25
    Save power remains—
A fallen angel's pride of thought,
    Still strong in chains.

All else is gone; from those great eyes
    The soul has fled:             30
When faith is lost, when honor dies,
    The man is dead!

Then, pay the reverence of old days
    To his dead fame;
Walk backward, with averted gaze,         35
    And hide the shame![2]

1850

1. *Ichabod!* is an attack on the statesman Daniel Webster, whose championing of the Fugitive Slave Bill (the part of the Compromise of 1850 which provided that Northern states must return runaway slaves caught within their borders) made him anathema to the abolitionists. The title is from 1 Samuel 4.21: "And she named the child Ichabod, saying, The glory is departed from Israel." The text is that of the first printing in *Songs of Labor, and Other Poems* (1850).
2. By this allusion to Genesis 9.20–25 Whittier equates Webster's shame to that of Noah after the Flood, who in drunkenness sprawled naked in his cave.

## Prelude to *Among the Hills*[1]

Along the roadside, like the flowers of gold
That tawny Incas[2] for their gardens wrought,
Heavy with sunshine droops the golden-rod,
And the red pennons of the cardinal-flowers
Hang motionless upon their upright staves.                        5
The sky is hot and hazy, and the wind,
Wing-weary with its long flight from the south,
Unfelt; yet, closely scanned, yon maple leaf
With faintest motion, as one stirs in dreams,
Confesses it. The locust by the wall                             10
Stabs the noon-silence with his sharp alarm.
A single hay-cart down the dusty road
Creaks slowly, with its driver fast asleep
On the load's top. Against the neighboring hill,
Huddled along the stone wall's shady side,                       15
The sheep show white, as if a snow-drift still
Defied the dog-star.[3] Through the open door
A drowsy smell of flowers—gay heliotrope,
And white sweet-clover, and shy mignonette—
Comes faintly in, and silent chorus lends                        20
To the pervading symphony of peace.

No time is this for hands long overworn
To task their strength; and (unto Him be praise
Who giveth quietness!) the stress and strain
Of years that did the work of centuries                          25
Have ceased, and we can draw our breath once more
Freely and full. So, as yon harvesters
Make glad their nooning underneath the elms
With tale and riddle and old snatch of song,
I lay aside grave themes, and idly turn                          30
The leaves of Memory's sketch-book, dreaming o'er
Old summer pictures of the quiet hills,
And human life, as quiet, at their feet.

And yet not idly all. A farmer's son,
Proud of field-lore and harvest craft, and feeling              35
All their fine possibilities, how rich
And restful even poverty and toil
Become when beauty, harmony, and love
Sit at their humble hearth as angels sat
At evening in the patriarch's tent, when man                    40
Makes labor noble, and his farmer's frock
The symbol of a Christian chivalry
Tender and just and generous to her
Who clothes with grace all duty; still, I know

1. From the first printing, in *Among the Hills, and
Other Poems* (1869).
2. An allusion to the belief that gold was so plentiful
among the Inca Indians of Peru that they fashioned
golden ornamental flowers for their gardens.
3. Sirius, star visible near the sun at dawn during the
torrid "dog days" of August.

Too well the picture has another side,— 45
How wearily the grind of toil goes on
Where love is wanting, how the eye and ear
And heart are starved amidst the plenitude
Of nature, and how hard and colorless
Is life without an atmosphere. I look 50
Across the lapse of half a century,
And call to mind old homesteads, where no flower
Told that the spring had come, but evil weeds,
Nightshade and rough-leaved burdock in the place
Of the sweet doorway greeting of the rose 55
And honeysuckle, where the house walls seemed
Blistering in sun, without a tree or vine
To cast the tremulous shadow of its leaves
Across the curtainless windows from whose panes
Fluttered the signal rags of shiftlessness; 60
Within, the cluttered kitchen-floor, unwashed
(Broom-clean I think they called it); the best room
Stifling with cellar damp, shut from the air
In hot midsummer, bookless, pictureless
Save the inevitable sampler hung 65
Over the fireplace, or a mourning-piece,[4]
A green-haired woman, peony-cheeked, beneath
Impossible willows; the wide-throated hearth
Bristling with faded pine-boughs half concealing
The piled-up rubbish at the chimney's back; 70
And, in sad keeping with all things about them,
Shrill, querulous women, sour and sullen men,
Untidy, loveless, old before their time,
With scarce a human interest save their own
Monotonous round of small economies,[5] 75
Or the poor scandal of the neighborhood;
Blind to the beauty everywhere revealed,
Treading the May-flowers with regardless feet;
For them the song-sparrow and the bobolink
Sang not, nor winds made music in the leaves; 80
For them in vain October's holocaust
Burned, gold and crimson, over all the hills,
The sacramental mystery of the woods.
Church-goers, fearful of the unseen Powers,
But grumbling over pulpit-tax and pew-rent,[6] 85
Saving, as shrewd economists, their souls
And winter pork with the least possible outlay
Of salt and sanctity; in daily life
Showing as little actual comprehension
Of Christian charity and love and duty, 90
As if the Sermon on the Mount[7] had been
Outdated like a last year's almanac:

---

4. A piece of art in memory of a departed relative.
5. Management of domestic affairs, particularly those involving the budget.
6. Fees to support the minister and pay for the use of a pew.
7. Matthew 5–7, Jesus' fullest statement of the absolute behavior he expects of his followers in contrast to the conventional ways of this world.

Rich in broad woodlands and in half-tilled fields,
And yet so pinched and bare and comfortless,
The veriest straggler limping on his rounds,                        95
The sun and air his sole inheritance,
Laughed at a poverty that paid its taxes,
And hugged his rags in self-complacency!

Not such should be the homesteads of a land
Where whoso wisely wills and acts may dwell                        100
As king and lawgiver, in broad-acred state,
With beauty, art, taste, culture, books, to make
His hour of leisure richer than a life
Of fourscore to the barons of old time,
Our yeoman[8] should be equal to his home                          105
Set in the fair, green valleys, purple walled,
A man to match his mountains, not to creep
Dwarfed and abased below them. I would fain
In this light way (of which I needs must own
With the knife-grinder of whom Canning sings,                      110
"Story, God bless you! I have none to tell you!")[9]
Invite the eye to see and heart to feel
The beauty and the joy within their reach,—
Home, and home loves, and the beatitudes
Of nature free to all. Haply in years                              115
That wait to take the places of our own,
Heard where some breezy balcony looks down
On happy homes, or where the lake in the moon
Sleeps dreaming of the mountains, fair as Ruth,
In the old Hebrew pastoral, at the feet                            120
Of Boaz,[1] even this simple lay of mine
May seem the burden of a prophecy,
Finding its late fulfilment in a change
Slow as the oak's growth, lifting manhood up
Through broader culture, finer manners, love,                      125
And reverence, to the level of the hills.

O Golden Age, whose light is of the dawn,
And not of sunset, forward, not behind,
Flood the new heavens and earth, and with thee bring
All the old virtues, whatsoever things                             130
Are pure and honest and of good repute,
But add thereto whatever bard has sung
Or seer has told of when in trance and dream
They saw the Happy Isles of prophecy!
Let Justice hold her scale, and Truth divide                       135
Between the right and wrong; but give the heart

8. Farmer.
9. During the 1790s, as a way of turning English public opinion against the French Revolution, the statesman George Canning (1770–1827) wrote for The Anti-
Jacobin, a paper, as its title says, opposed to the most
radical French faction. Canning's The Friend of Humanity and the Knife-Grinder, extremely popular in
Whittier's time, is a satire of misplaced humanitarian-
ism and bleeding-heart liberalism. The line Whittier
quotes is the drink-loving knife-grinder's brusque retort
to the torrential address of the would-be philanthropist.
1. See Ruth 3 for the story of how the young widow,
an ancestor of David, reminded Boaz of his family obligation to marry her.

The freedom of its fair inheritance;
Let the poor prisoner, cramped and starved so long,
At Nature's table feast his ear and eye
With joy and wonder; let all harmonies                    140
Of sound, form, color, motion, wait upon
The princely guest, whether in soft attire
Of leisure clad, or the coarse frock of toil.
And, lending life to the dead form of faith,
Give human nature reverence for the sake                    145
Of One who bore it, making it divine
With the ineffable tenderness of God;
Let common need, the brotherhood of prayer,
The heirship of an unknown destiny,
The unsolved mystery round about us, make                    150
A man more precious than the gold of Ophir.[2]
Sacred, inviolate, unto whom all things
Should minister, as outward types and signs
Of the eternal beauty which fulfils
The one great purpose of creation, Love,                    155
The sole necessity of Earth and Heaven!

1869

2. Source of treasures of gold brought to King Solomon (1 Kings 10.1).

---

# EDGAR ALLAN POE
## 1809–1849

The life of Edgar Allan Poe is the most melodramatic of any of the major American writers of his generation. Determining the facts has proved difficult, as lurid legend became entwined with fact even before he died. Some legends were spread by Poe himself. Given to claiming that he was born in 1811 or 1813 and had written certain poems far earlier than he had, Poe also exaggerated the length of his attendance at the University of Virginia and, in imitation of Lord Byron, fabricated a "quixotic expedition to join the Greeks, then struggling for liberty." Two days after Poe's death his supposed friend Rufus Griswold, a prominent anthologizer of American literature, began a campaign of character assassination in which he ultimately rewrote Poe's correspondence so as to alienate many of his friends who could only assume that Poe had treacherously maligned them behind their backs. Griswold's forgeries went unexposed for many years, poisoning every biographer's image of Poe, and legend still feeds on half-truth in much writing on him.

Yet biographers now possess a great deal of factual evidence about most periods of Poe's life. His mother, Elizabeth Arnold, had been an actress, prominent among the wandering seaport players in a profession that was then considered disreputable. She was a teenage widow when she married David Poe, Jr., in 1806. Poe, also an actor, worked up to choice supporting roles before liquor destroyed his career. Edgar, the Poes' second child, was born in Boston on January 19, 1809; a year later David Poe deserted the family. In December 1811, Elizabeth Poe died at twenty-four while acting in Richmond, Virginia, and her husband disappeared completely, probably dying soon afterward at the age of twenty-seven.

The disruptions of Poe's first two years were followed by apparent security, for John Allan, a young Richmond merchant, took him in as the children were parceled out. As "Master Allan," Poe accompanied the family to England in 1815, where he attended good schools. On their return in 1820 the boy continued in school, but under his own last name. During Poe's adolescence, uncertainty about his future and shameful certainty about his past affected his feelings—and those of his prosperous playmates. Around 1824, Allan's attitude toward the boy changed; one rumor suggests that Edgar took the side of his foster mother in a quarrel. Poe spent most of 1826 at the new University of Virginia, doing well in his studies, although he was already drinking. Under the pretext that Allan had not provided him an adequate allowance, he gambled, and lost some two thousand dollars— "debts of honor," which a gentleman must repay. Allan had just inherited a fortune of several hundred thousand dollars (with purchasing power of several million today), but he refused to pay Poe's debts. After a quarrel with Allan in March 1827, Poe looked up his father's relatives in Baltimore and then went on to his birthplace, where he paid for the printing of *Tamerlane and Other Poems*, "By a Bostonian." Before its publication, "Edgar A. Perry" had joined the army. Poe was partially reconciled with Allan in March 1829, just after Mrs. Allan died. Released from the army with the rank of sergeant major, Poe sought Allan's influence to gain him an appointment to West Point, although he was past the age limit for admission.

While he was waiting for the appointment, Poe shortened *Tamerlane*, revised other poems, and added new ones to make up a second volume, *Al Aaraaf, Tamerlane, and Minor Poems*, published at Baltimore in December 1829. He entered West Point in June 1830, but felt he could not fit into life at the academy without supplemental income, and Allan was interested in his own life, not Poe's. Just after Poe went to West Point a woman in Richmond bore Allan twin sons. In October 1830 Allan married again and within a month his new wife was pregnant. Losing any remaining hope that if he dutifully pursued a military career he might become Allan's heir, Poe got himself expelled by missing classes and roll calls. Supportive friends among the cadets made up a subscription for his *Poems*, published in May 1831. In this third volume Poe revised some earlier poems and for the first time included versions of both *To Helen* (the famous "Helen, thy beauty is to me," not a later, inferior poem of the same title) and *Israfel*.

Poe's mature career—from his twenty-first year to his death in his fortieth year— was spent in four literary centers: Baltimore, Richmond, Philadelphia, and New York. The Baltimore years—mid-1831 to late 1835—were marked by great industry and comparative sobriety. Poe lived in sordid poverty among his once-prosperous relatives, including his poetaster brother who died in 1831; his grandmother Poe, whose death in 1835 cut off a Revolutionary widow's pension of $240 per annum on which the household relied; his aunt Maria Poe Clemm; and her daughter Virginia, whom Poe secretly married in 1835, when she was thirteen. Poe's first story, *Metzengerstein* (later subtitled *In Imitation of the German*), was published in the Philadelphia *Saturday Courier*, anonymously, in January 1832, and other stories appeared in the same paper through the year. By early 1833 Poe was projecting a volume of eleven stories, *Tales of the Folio Club*, never published under that title. In May 1833 he sent the *New-England Magazine* one of a set of *Eleven Tales of the Arabesque*—apparently the same eleven; a postscript added to the manuscript said simply, "I am poor." With his *Tales of the Folio Club*, Poe impressed all three judges of a contest in the Baltimore *Saturday Visiter*. One judge, the novelist John P. Kennedy, became a loyal mentor, offering timely money and advice.

Poe returned to Richmond in 1835, twenty-six years old, as assistant editor of T. L. White's new *Southern Literary Messenger*, at a salary of $540 a year, subsistence wages even in the 1830s. Allan was dead, survived by three small legitimate sons, and Poe had no contact with the widow. From the start, White deplored what he called Poe's tendency to "sip the juice" and gave him editorial duties without commensurate recognition or authority, even though the circulation of the magazine rose swiftly under Poe's guidance. The *Messenger* published stories by Poe, but it was through his critical pieces that he gained a national reputation as a reviewer in the virulently sarcastic British manner—a literary hatchetman.

Fired from the *Messenger* early in 1837, Poe took his aunt and his wife (whom he had publicly remarried in May 1836) to New York City, where for two years he lived hand to mouth on the fringes of the publishing world, selling a few stories and reviews. He had written a short novel, *The Narrative of Arthur Gordon Pym*, in Richmond, where White ran two installments in the *Messenger* early in 1837. *Harper's* finally brought it out in July 1838, but it earned him no money, because it purported only to be edited by Poe, and not much reputation either. In 1838 Poe moved to Philadelphia, where for weeks the family survived on bread and molasses. But he continued writing, and *Ligeia* appeared in the Baltimore *American Museum* in September 1838, where other stories and poems followed. Resorting to literary hackwork just as Hawthorne was doing, Poe put his name on *The Conchologist's First Book* (1839). In May 1839 he got his first steady job in over two years, as coeditor of *Burton's Gentleman's Magazine*. There he published book reviews and stories, among them *The Fall of the House of Usher* and *William Wilson*. Late in 1839, a Philadelphia firm published *Tales of the Grotesque and Arabesque*, but it sold badly. Poe was now at the height of his powers as a writer of tales, though his personal life continued unstable, as did his career as an editor. William Burton fired him for drinking in May 1840 but recommended him to George Graham, who carried on Burton's magazine as *Graham's*. Throughout 1841, Poe was with *Graham's* as coeditor, courting subscribers by articles on cryptography and on character as revealed in handwriting. In January 1842, Virginia Poe, not yet twenty, burst a blood vessel in her throat (she lived only five more years). Leaving *Graham's* in some unhappiness, Poe revived a project for his own magazine, now to be called *The Stylus*. In 1843 he worked at times for the Philadelphia weekly *Saturday Museum*. On a trip to Washington seeking a patronage job (and subscriptions to *The Stylus*) he reportedly was so drunk when he called on President Tyler that he wore his cloak inside out.

In April 1844 Poe moved his family to New York City, where he wrote for newspapers and worked as subeditor on the *Sunday Times*. Poe's most successful year was 1845. The February issue of *Graham's* contained James Russell Lowell's complimentary article on Poe, and *The Raven* appeared in the February *American Review* after advance publication in the New York *Evening Mirror*. Capitalizing on the sensation the poem created, Poe lectured on "Poets of America" and became a principal reviewer for the new weekly, the *Broadway Journal*. *The Raven* won him entrée into the literary life of New York. One new literary acquaintance, Evert A. Duyckinck, soon to be Melville's friend also, selected a dozen of Poe's stories for a collection brought out by Wiley & Putnam in June and arranged for the same firm to publish *The Raven and Other Poems* in November. Having acquired critical clout despite a growing number of enemies, Poe had great hopes for the *Broadway Journal*, of which he became sole owner; but it failed early in 1846. Meanwhile Poe was marring his new opportunities by drinking.

With fame the tempo of Poe's life spun into a blur of literary feuds, flirtations with literary ladies, and drinking bouts that ended in quarrels. Virginia's death in January 1847 slowed the tempo: during much of that year Poe was seriously ill himself—perhaps with a brain lesion—and drinking steadily. He worked away at *Eureka*, a prose statement of a theory of the universe, and soon after Virginia's death he wrote *Ulalume*. The year 1848 was frenetic, culminating in a brief engagement to Helen Power Whitman of Providence; his letters to her are effusively hysterical. He flirted with Mrs. Nancy Richmond of Lowell, Massachusetts, in equally desperate letters, and may—as he wrote her—have tried to commit suicide by taking laudanum. He managed to write a little still, the story *Hop-Frog* and the poem *Annabel Lee*. While headed south in June 1849, he drank on the train and got off in Philadelphia to seek asylum, he said, from two men who were trying to kill him. In Richmond he spent two improbably happy months, being received into society by his childhood friends and becoming engaged to the sweetheart of his teens, the now-widowed Elmira Royster Shelton. He gave lectures and readings, and joined the Sons of Temperance. On the way to accept a hundred dollars for editing the poems of a Philadelphia woman, he stopped off in Baltimore, broke his temperance pledge, and was found senseless near a polling place on an Election Day (October 3). Taken to a hospital, he died on October 7, 1849, "of congestion of the brain."

If Poe had disappeared from the American literary scene after publishing his third volume of poems in 1831, a literary historian grubbing among privately printed nineteenth-century collections of poetry would have classified him (once his authorship of the anonymous *Tamerlane* had been established) as an odd American imitator of major British Romantics like Lord Byron and Percy Bysshe Shelley as well as then-popular ones like Thomas Moore. In both form and content Poe's early poetry is typically Romantic, although of an unusually limited range. Well before his twenty-first birthday he had earned the right to call himself a poet, but by British standards he was not an important one.

It was the handful of poems that Poe wrote a decade and a half later that made him famous as a poet. *The Raven* brought him international celebrity, and poems like *Ulalume* and *The Bells* soon enhanced that fame among Poe's constantly enlarging posthumous audience. These poems became standard declamation pieces in schools and remained so well into the present century. In subject matter they progress little beyond the Romantic gothicism of Poe's early years, but in technique they are remarkable. Innumerable young people have learned to love poetry from them and have continued to love poetry even after they stopped loving only Poe. There could be worse fates for a man who started out as a belated, second-rate imitator of first- and second-rate British Romantics.

But the bulk of Poe's collected writings consists of his criticism, and his most abiding ambition was to become a powerful critic. Just as he had modeled his poems and first tales on British examples (or British imitations of the German), he took his critical concepts from treatises on aesthetics by late-eighteenth-century Scottish Common Sense philosophers (later modified by his borrowings from A. W. Schlegel and Coleridge) and took his stance as a reviewer from the slashing critics of the British quarterlies. Poe's employers were often uneasy about their reviewer, both because his virulence brought reproaches (though it was good for business) and because they suspected that for all his stress on aesthetic principles, Poe's reviews were apt to be unjust to writers he was jealous of and laudatory toward others he wished to curry favor with. But Poe's basic critical principles were consistent enough, however he deviated from them in his reviewing. He thought poetry should appeal only to the sense of beauty, not truth; informational poetry, poetry of ideas, or any sort of didactic poetry was illegitimate. Holding that the true poetic emotion was a vague sensory state, he set himself against realistic details in poetry, although the prose tale, with truth as one object, could profit from the discreet use of specifics. Both poems and tales should be short enough to be read in one sitting; otherwise the unity of effect would be dissipated. In Poe's view, good writers calculate their effects precisely. At a time when even famous poets such as Longfellow rarely wrote a poem of sustained coherence, Poe's reaction, with the stress on forethought, seems understandable. But his criticism is often dogmatic and self-serving, weakened partly because it was applied to some of the most wretched writing a reviewer ever had to discuss, for Poe never had the luxury of reviewing only worthwhile volumes.

Poe's first tales have proved hard to classify—are they burlesques of popular kinds of fiction or serious attempts at contributing to or somehow altering those genres? Poe's own comments tend to becloud his intentions rather than to clarify them. In 1836 his benefactor John P. Kennedy wrote him: "Some of your *bizarreries* have been mistaken for satire—and admired too in that character. *They* deserved it, but *you* did not, for you did not intend them so. I like your grotesque—it is of the very best stamp; and I am sure you will do wonders for yourself in the comic—I mean the seriotragicomic." Poe's reply is tantalizing: "You are nearly, but not altogether right in relation to the satire of some of my Tales. Most of them were *intended* for half banter, half satire—although I might not have fully acknowledged this to be their aim even to myself." The problem of determining the nature of a given work—imitation? satire? spoof? hoax?—is crucial in Poe criticism.

At the core of Poe's defenses of his stories is the hardheadedness of a professional writer who wanted to crack the popular market. Such stories, he claimed, were the products of superior minds disciplining themselves to the task at hand, not the indulgences of Romantic genius. Poe worked hard at structuring his tales of aristocratic madmen, self-tormented murderers, neurasthenic necrophiliacs, and other deviant types so as to produce the greatest possible horrific effects on the reader. In the detective story, which Poe created when he was thirty-two, with all its major conventions complete, the structuring was equally contrived, although the effect desired was one of awe at the brilliance of his preternatural logician-hero. Seriously as he took the writing of his tales, Poe never claimed that prose writing was for him, as he said poetry was, a "passion," not merely a "purpose."

Other American writers, from Poe's time to ours, have often been uneasy about him. The "jingle man," Ralph Waldo Emerson is supposed to have called him, and Henry James thought that enthusiasm for Poe was "the mark of a decidedly primitive stage of reflection," while T. S. Eliot said Poe's intellect was that of "a highly gifted young person before puberty." Yet no other American writer, except possibly Mark Twain, has been so thoroughly absorbed by later writers—writers as diverse as E. A. Robinson, Frank Norris, Theodore Dreiser, and William Faulkner, as well as the great Russian-American player of complex Poesque games, Vladimir Nabokov. Some American literary critics and historians have always been hard pressed to understand why foreign writers like Charles Baudelaire and Stéphane Mallarmé could idolize Poe and translate his works lovingly, why the French Symbolist poets could draw on him for their aesthetic ideas, how August Strindberg could fantasize that because he was born in 1849 Poe's spirit had passed to him, how the influence of someone so childish could seem profound when it came back to English indirectly, through foreigners Poe had influenced. Some American critics have often felt reproached when British writers such as Dante Gabriel Rosetti, Algernon Swinburne, Robert Louis Stevenson, Arthur Conan Doyle, and George Bernard Shaw expressed delight in Poe or indebtedness to him. More than a century and a quarter after his death, American critics are still taking sides about Poe, hailing him as a pioneering aesthetician, psychological investigator, and literary technician, or else reviling him as an absurd fraud, a subliterary vulgarian. But whatever his influence on artists of the past and present, and whatever his status with literary critics and historians, Poe's reputation with the reading public— through the whole range of literacy—is more assured than that of any other major American writer of his century, again with the possible exception of Mark Twain. For the professional writer that Poe struggled to be, that is probably a fate even better than being precisely understood and logically classified.

## Sonnet—To Science[1]

SCIENCE! meet daughter of old Time thou art
Who alterest all things with thy peering eyes!
Why prey'st thou thus upon the poet's heart,
Vulture! whose wings are dull realities!
How should he love thee—or how deem thee wise     5
Who woulds't not leave him, in his wandering,
To seek for treasure in the jewell'd skies
Albeit, he soar with an undaunted wing?
Hast thou not dragg'd Diana from her car,
And driv'n the Hamadryad from the wood     10
To seek a shelter in some happier star?
The gentle Naiad[2] from her fountain-flood?
The elfin from the green grass? and from me
The summer dream beneath the shrubbery?

1829, 1845

## To Helen[1]

Helen, thy beauty is to me
   Like those Nicéan barks[2] of yore,
That gently, o'er a perfumed sea,
   The weary, way-worn wanderer bore
To his own native shore.     5

On desperate seas long wont to roam,
   Thy hyacinth hair, thy classic face,
Thy Naiad[3] airs have brought me home
   To the glory that was Greece,
And the grandeur that was Rome.     10

Lo! in yon brilliant window-niche
   How statue-like I see thee stand,
The agate lamp within thy hand!
   Ah, Psyche,[4] from the regions which
Are Holy-Land!     15

1831, 1845

1. The text is from *The Raven and Other Poems* (1845). Both in 1829 and 1831 the sonnet, untitled, was printed as a proem to *Al Aaraaf*; in 1845 the poem retained its place but carried the title first used in an 1843 reprinting. *Sonnet—To Science* is built on the Romantic commonplace that the scientific spirit destroys beauty, a notion well exemplified by Wordsworth's *The Tables Turned* ("Sweet is the lore which Nature brings; / Our medling intellect / Misshapes the beauteous forms of things:— / We murder to dissect") and by Keats's *Lamia* ("Philosophy will clip an angel's wings").
2. Nymph living in brooks or fountains. "Diana": Roman goddess of the moon (imaged as a chariot or car

that she drives through the sky). "Hamadryad": wood nymph in Greek and Roman mythology, often thought of as living within a tree and perishing with it.
1. The text is that of 1845, with two errors of indentation corrected. The poem was first published in 1831 where, among other differences, lines 9 and 10 read: "To the beauty of fair Greece, / And the grandeur of old Rome."
2. Variously annotated by Poe scholars, the Nicéan boats are more important for their musicality and vaguely classical suggestiveness than for their vaguely Mediterranean reference.
3. Nymphlike, fairylike.
4. Goddess of the soul.

# Israfel[1]

In Heaven a spirit doth dwell
  "Whose heart-strings are a lute;"
None sing so wildly well
As the angel Israfel,
And the giddy stars (so legends tell)           5
Ceasing their hymns, attend the spell
  Of his voice, all mute.

Tottering above
  In her highest noon,
  The enamoured moon           10
Blushes with love,
  While, to listen, the red levin
  (With the rapid Pleiads,[2] even,
  Which were seven,)
  Pauses in Heaven.           15

And they say (the starry choir
  And the other listening things)
That Israfeli's fire
Is owing to that lyre
  By which he sits and sings—           20
The trembling living wire
  Of those unusual strings.

But the skies that angel trod,
  Where deep thoughts are a duty—
Where Love's a grown-up God—           25
  Where the Houri[3] glances are
Imbued with all the beauty
  Which we worship in a star.

Therefore, thou art not wrong,
  Israfeli, who despisest           30
An unimpassioned song;
  To thee the laurels belong,
  Best bard, because the wisest!
Merrily live, and long!

The ecstasies above           35
  With thy burning measures suit—
Thy grief, thy joy, thy hate, thy love,

1. "And the angel Israfel, whose heartstrings are a lute, and who has the sweetest voice of all God's creatures.—Koran" [Poe's note]. A version of this poem appeared in the 1831 volume; the present text is from 1845. In 1831 the footnote to the title read (correctly): "And the angel Israfel, who has the sweetest voice of all God's creatures.—Koran." Poe later expanded the quotation. Parallels among English Romantic poems include Coleridge's *Kubla Khan*, where glimpses of heavenly song also inspire but ultimately frustrate the speaker.
2. In Greek mythology the seven daughters of Atlas became stars, making up a constellation.
3. Beautiful virgin waiting in paradise for the devout Mohammedan.

With the fervour of thy lute—
Well may the stars be mute!

Yes, Heaven is thine; but this                                    40
Is a world of sweets and sours;
Our flowers are merely—flowers,
And the shadow of thy perfect bliss
Is the sunshine of ours.

If I could dwell                                                 45
Where Israfel
Hath dwelt, and he where I,
He might not sing so wildly well
A mortal melody,
While a bolder note than this might swell                        50
From my lyre within the sky.

                                                     1831, 1845


# The Raven[1]

## By———Quarles

*[The following lines from a correspondent—besides the deep quaint strain of
the sentiment, and the curious introduction of some ludicrous touches amidst
the serious and impressive, as was doubtless intended by the author—appear to
us one of the most felicitous specimens of unique rhyming which has for some
time met our eye. The resources of English rhythm for varieties of melody, measure, and sound, producing corresponding diversities of effect, have been thoroughly studied, much more perceived, by very few poets in the language. While
the classic tongues, especially the Greek, possess, by power of accent, several
advantages for versification over our own, chiefly through greater abundance of
spondaic feet,[2] we have other and very great advantages of sound by the modern
usage of rhyme. Alliteration is nearly the only effect of that kind which the
ancients had in common with us. It will be seen that much of the melody of
"The Raven" arises from alliteration, and the studious use of similar sounds in
unusual places. In regard to its measure, it may be noted that if all the verses
were like the second, they might properly be placed merely in short lines, producing a not uncommon form; but the presence in all the others of one line—mostly
the second in the verse—which flows continuously, with only an aspirate pause
in the middle, like that before the short line in the Sapphic Adonic,[3] while the
fifth has at the middle pause no similarity of sound with any part besides, gives
the versification an entirely different effect. We could wish the capacities of our
noble language, in prosody, were better understood.—ED. AM. REV.]*

Once upon a midnight dreary, while I pondered, weak and weary,
Over many a quaint and curious volume of forgotten lore,
While I nodded, nearly napping, suddenly there came a tapping,

1. This printing of Poe's most famous poem is taken
from the *American Review: A Whig Journal of Politics,
Literature, Art and Science* 1 (February 1845), where
it was first set in type; the New York *Evening Mirror*
printed the poem, on January 29, 1845, from the pages
of the *American Review*. The prefatory paragraph,
signed as if it were by the editor of the *American Review*, is retained here because Poe most likely had a
hand in it, if he did not write it all. Many minor variations appear in later texts.
2. A spondee is a metrical foot consisting of two
stressed syllables.
3. A Greek lyric form. In prosody an adonic is a dactyl
(a foot with one long syllable and two short ones) followed by a spondee.

As of some one gently rapping, rapping at my chamber door.
" 'Tis some visiter," I muttered, "tapping at my chamber door—        5
                    Only this, and nothing more."

Ah, distinctly I remember it was in the bleak December,
And each separate dying ember wrought its ghost upon the floor.
Eagerly I wished the morrow;—vainly I had tried to borrow
From my books surcease of sorrow—sorrow for the lost Lenore—        10
For the rare and radiant maiden whom the angels name Lenore—
                    Nameless here for evermore.

And the silken sad uncertain rustling of each purple curtain
Thrilled me—filled me with fantastic terrors never felt before;
So that now, to still the beating of my heart, I stood repeating        15
" 'Tis some visiter entreating entrance at my chamber door—
Some late visiter entreating entrance at my chamber door;—
                    This it is, and nothing more."

Presently my soul grew stronger; hesitating then no longer,
"Sir," said I, "or Madam, truly your forgiveness I implore;        20
But the fact is I was napping, and so gently you came rapping,
And so faintly you came tapping, tapping at my chamber door,
That I scarce was sure I heard you"—here I opened wide the door;—
                    Darkness there, and nothing more.

Deep into that darkness peering, long I stood there wondering, fearing,        25
Doubting, dreaming dreams no mortal ever dared to dream before;
But the silence was unbroken, and the darkness gave no token,
And the only word there spoken was the whispered word, "Lenore!"
This I whispered, and an echo murmured back the word, "Lenore!"
                    Merely this, and nothing more.  30

Then into the chamber turning, all my soul within me burning,
Soon I heard again a tapping somewhat louder than before.
"Surely," said I, "surely that is something at my window lattice;
Let me see, then, what thereat is, and this mystery explore—
Let my heart be still a moment and this mystery explore;—        35
                    'Tis the wind, and nothing more!"

Open here I flung the shutter, when, with many a flirt and flutter,
In there stepped a stately raven of the saintly days of yore;
Not the least obeisance made he; not an instant stopped or stayed he;
But, with mien of lord or lady, perched above my chamber door—        40
Perched upon a bust of Pallas[4] just above my chamber door—
                    Perched, and sat, and nothing more.

Then this ebony bird beguiling my sad fancy into smiling,
By the grave and stern decorum of the countenance it wore,
"Though thy crest be shorn and shaven, thou," I said, "art sure no craven,  45

4. Athena, the Greek goddess of wisdom and the arts.

Ghastly grim and ancient raven wandering from the Nightly shore—
Tell me what thy lordly name is on the Night's Plutonian[5] shore!"
Quoth the raven, "Nevermore."

Much I marvelled this ungainly fowl to hear discourse so plainly,
Though its answer little meaning—little relevancy bore;                    50
For we cannot help agreeing that no sublunary[6] being
Ever yet was blessed with seeing bird above his chamber door—
Bird or beast upon the sculptured bust above his chamber door,
With such name as "Nevermore."

But the raven, sitting lonely on the placid bust, spoke only                    55
That one word, as if his soul in that one word he did outpour.
Nothing farther then he uttered—not a feather then he fluttered—
Till I scarcely more than muttered, "Other friends have flown before—
On the morrow *he* will leave me, as my hopes have flown before."
Quoth the raven, "Nevermore."   60

Wondering at the stillness broken by reply so aptly spoken,
"Doubtless," said I, "what it utters is its only stock and store,
Caught from some unhappy master whom unmerciful Disaster
Followed fast and followed faster—so, when Hope he would adjure,
Stern Despair returned, instead of the sweet Hope he dared adjure—                    65
That sad answer, "Nevermore!"[7]

But the raven still beguiling all my sad soul into smiling,
Straight I wheeled a cushioned seat in front of bird, and bust, and door;
Then upon the velvet sinking, I betook myself to linking
Fancy unto fancy, thinking what this ominous bird of yore—                    70
What this grim, ungainly, ghastly, gaunt, and ominous bird of yore
Meant in croaking "Nevermore."

This I sat engaged in guessing, but no syllable expressing
To the fowl whose fiery eyes now burned into my bosom's core;
This and more I sat divining, with my head at ease reclining                    75
On the cushion's velvet lining that the lamplight gloated o'er,
But whose velvet violet lining with the lamplight gloating o'er,
*She* shall press, ah, nevermore!

Then, methought, the air grew denser, perfumed from an unseen censer
Swung by angels whose faint foot-falls tinkled on the tufted floor.                    80
"Wretch," I cried, "thy God hath lent thee—by these angels he hath sent thee
Respite—respite and Nepenthe[8] from thy memories of Lenore!
Let me quaff this kind Nepenthe and forget this lost Lenore!"
Quoth the raven, "Nevermore."

"Prophet!" said I, "thing of evil!—prophet still, if bird or devil!—                    85
Whether Tempter sent, or whether tempest tossed thee here ashore,

---

5. Black, as in the underworld of Greek mythology.
6. Earthly, beneath the moon.
7. This stanza concluded in the 1845 volume with these lines: "Followed fast and followed faster till his songs one burden bore— / Till the dirges of his Hope that melancholy burden bore of 'Never—nevermore.'"
8. Drug that induces oblivion.

Desolate, yet all undaunted, on this desert land enchanted—
On this home by Horror haunted—tell me truly, I implore—
Is there—*is* there balm in Gilead?[9]—tell me—tell me, I implore!"
                              Quoth the raven, "Nevermore."  90

"Prophet!" said I, "thing of evil!—prophet still, if bird or devil!
By that Heaven that bends above us—by that God we both adore—
Tell this soul with sorrow laden if, within the distant Aidenn,[1]
It shall clasp a sainted maiden whom the angels name Lenore—
Clasp a rare and radiant maiden whom the angels name Lenore."   95
                              Quoth the raven, "Nevermore."

"Be that word our sign of parting, bird or fiend!" I shrieked, upstarting—
"Get thee back into the tempest and the Night's Plutonian shore!
Leave no black plume as a token of that lie thy soul hath spoken!
Leave my loneliness unbroken—quit the bust above my door!   100
Take thy beak from out my heart, and take thy form from off my door!"
                              Quoth the raven, "Nevermore."

And the raven, never flitting, still is sitting, still is sitting
On the pallid bust of Pallas just above my chamber door;
And his eyes have all the seeming of a demon that is dreaming,   105
And the lamp-light o'er him streaming throws his shadow on the floor;
And my soul from out that shadow that lies floating on the floor
                              Shall be lifted—nevermore!

                                                    1845

## To —— —— ——.[1] Ulalume: A Ballad

 The skies they were ashen and sober;
  The leaves they were crispéd and sere—
  The leaves they were withering and sere;
 It was night in the lonesome October
  Of my most immemorial year;    5
 It was hard by the dim lake of Auber,
  In the misty mid region of Weir[2]—
 It was down by the dank tarn[3] of Auber.
 In the ghoul-haunted woodland of Weir.

 Here once, through an alley Titanic,[4]    10
  Of cypress, I roamed with my Soul—
  Of cypress, with Psyche, my Soul.
 These were days when my heart was volcanic

9. An echo of the ironic words in Jeremiah 8.22: "Is there no balm in Gilead; is there no physician there?" Gilead is a mountainous area east of the Jordan River between the Sea of Galilee and the Dead Sea; evergreens growing there were an ample source of medicinal resins.
1. One of Poe's vaguely evocative place names, designed to suggest Eden.
1. This is the longer version of the poem; Poe sometimes dropped the tenth stanza. The source is the *American Review* 6 (December 1847), 599–600, the first printing.
2. "Auber" and "Weir" are surnames Poe probably knew; as place names they are chosen for their rhyme value and connotative suggestions ("Weir," for instance, suggesting "weird").
3. A small mountain lake.
4. The alley—the pathway—is titanic because the cypress trees on either side are enormous, on a scale to match that of the pre-Olympian Greek gods.

As the scoriac rivers[5] that roll—
As the lavas that restlessly roll      15
Their sulphurous currents down Yaanek
In the ultimate climes of the pole—
That groan as they roll down Mount Yaanek
In the realms of the boreal pole.[6]

Our talk had been serious and sober,      20
But our thoughts they were palsied and sere—
Our memories were treacherous and sere—
For we knew not the month was October,
And we marked not the night of the year—
(Ah, night of all nights in the year!)      25
We noted not the dim lake of Auber—
(Though once we had journeyed down here)—
We remembered not the dank tarn of Auber,
Nor the ghoul-haunted woodland of Weir.

And now, as the night was senescent      30
And star-dials pointed to morn—
As the star-dials hinted of morn—
At the end of our path a liquescent
And nebulous lustre was born,
Out of which a miraculous crescent      35
Arose with a duplicate horn—
Astarte's[7] bediamonded crescent
Distinct with its duplicate horn.

And I said—"She is warmer than Dian:[8]
She rolls through an ether of sighs—      40
She revels in a region of sighs:
She has seen that the tears are not dry on
These cheeks, where the worm never dies,
And has come past the stars of the Lion[9]
To point us the path to the skies—      45
To the Lethean[1] peace of the skies—
Come up, in despite of the Lion,
To shine on us with her bright eyes—
Come up through the lair of the Lion
With Love in her luminous eyes."      50

But Psyche,[2] uplifting her finger,
Said—"Sadly this star I mistrust—
Her pallor I strangely mistrust:—
Oh, hasten!—oh, let us not linger!
Oh, fly!—let us fly!—for we must."      55
In terror she spoke, letting sink her
Wings till they trailed in the dust—
In agony sobbed, letting sink her

5. Rivers of lava.
6. North pole.
7. Phoenician fertility goddess, here described as a moon goddess; the horns are the ends of a new moon.
8. The chaste Roman goddess of the moon.

9. The constellation Leo.
1. Absolute peace, as if bathed in the oblivion-giving waters of Lethe.
2. The soul, imaged as a butterfly.

Plumes till they trailed in the dust—
Till they sorrowfully trailed in the dust.     60

I replied—"This is nothing but dreaming:
Let us on by this tremulous light!
Let us bathe in this crystalline light!
Its Sybillic[3] splendor is beaming
    With Hope and in Beauty to-night:—     65
See!—it flickers up the sky through the night!
Ah, we safely may trust to its gleaming,
    And be sure it will lead us aright—
We safely may trust to a gleaming
    That cannot but guide us aright,     70
Since it flickers up to Heaven through the night."

Thus I pacified Psyche and kissed her,
    And tempted her out of her gloom—
    And conquered her scruples and gloom:
And we passed to the end of the vista,     75
    And were stopped by the door of a tomb—
    By the door of a legended tomb;
And I said—"What is written, sweet sister,
    On the door of this legended tomb?"
She replied—"Ulalume—Ulalume—     80
'Tis the vault of thy lost Ulalume!"

Then my heart it grew ashen and sober
    As the leaves that were crispéd and sere—
    As the leaves that were withering and sere,
And I cried—"It was surely October     85
    On *this* very night of last year
That I journeyed—I journeyed down here—
    That I brought a dread burden down here—
On this night of all nights in the year,
    Oh, what demon has tempted me here?     90
Well I know, now, this dim lake of Auber—
    This misty mid region of Weir—
Well I know, now, this dank tarn of Auber,
    In the ghoul-haunted woodland of Weir."

Said *we*, then—the two, then—"Ah, can it     95
    Have been that the woodlandish ghouls—
    The pitiful, the merciful ghouls—
To bar up our way and to ban it
    From the secret that lies in these wolds—
    From the thing that lies hidden in these wolds—     100
Had drawn up the spectre of a planet
    From the limbo of lunary souls—
This sinfully scintillant[4] planet
    From the Hell of the planetary souls?"

1847

---

3. Mysterious prophetic—now spelled "sibyllic."      4. Sparkling, shining.

# Annabel Lee[1]

It was many and many a year ago,
    In a kingdom by the sea
That a maiden there lived whom you may know.
    By the name of ANNABEL LEE;
And this maiden she lived with no other thought         5
    Than to love and be loved by me.

*I* was a child and *she* was a child,
    In this kingdom by the sea;
But we loved with a love that was more than love—
    I and my ANNABEL LEE—            10
With a love that the wingèd seraphs of heaven
    Coveted her and me.

And this was the reason that, long ago,
    In this kingdom by the sea,
A wind blew out of a cloud, chilling          15
    My beautiful ANNABEL LEE;
So that her highborn kinsmen came
    And bore her away from me,
To shut her up in a sepulchre
    In this kingdom by the sea.          20

The angels, not half so happy in heaven,
    Went envying her and me—
Yes!—that was the reason (as all men know,
    In this kingdom by the sea)
That the wind came out of the cloud by night,      25
    Chilling and killing my ANNABEL LEE.

But our love it was stronger by far than the love
    Of those who were older than we—
    Of many far wiser than we—
And neither the angels in heaven above,        30
    Nor the demons down under the sea,
Can ever dissever my soul from the soul
    Of the beautiful ANNABEL LEE:

For the moon never beams, without bringing me dreams
    Of the beautiful ANNABEL LEE;        35
And the stars never rise, but I feel the bright eyes
    Of the beautiful ANNABEL LEE:
And so, all the night tide, I lie down by the side
Of my darling—my darling—my life and my bride,
    In her sepulchre there by the sea—      40
    In her tomb by the sounding sea.

1849

---

1. The text is that of the first printing, in Rufus Griswold's article in the New York *Tribune* (October 9, 1849), signed "Ludwig."

# Ligeia[1]

*And the will therein lieth, which dieth not. Who knoweth the mysteries of
the will, with its vigour? For God is but a great will pervading all things by
nature of its intentness. Man doth not yield himself to the angels, nor unto
death utterly, save only through the weakness of his feeble will.*

—Joseph Glanvill[2]

I cannot, for my soul, remember how, when, or even precisely where I first
became acquainted with the lady Ligeia. Long years have since elapsed, and
my memory is feeble through much suffering: or, perhaps, I cannot *now* bring
these points to mind, because, in truth, the character of my beloved, her rare
learning, her singular yet placid cast of beauty, and the thrilling and enthralling eloquence of her low, musical language, made their way into my heart by
paces, so steadily and stealthily progressive, that they have been unnoticed and
unknown. Yet I know that I met her most frequently in some large, old,
decaying city near the Rhine. Of her family—I have surely heard her speak—
that they are of a remotely ancient date cannot be doubted. Ligeia! Buried in
studies of a nature, more than all else, adapted to deaden impressions of the
outward world, it is by that sweet word alone—by Ligeia, that I bring before
mine eyes in fancy the image of her who is no more. And now, while I write,
a recollection flashes upon me that I have *never known* the paternal name of
her who was my friend and my betrothed, and who became the partner of my
studies, and eventually the wife of my bosom. Was it a playful charge on the
part of my Ligeia? or was it a test of my strength of affection that I should
institute no inquiries upon this point? or was it rather a caprice of my own—a
wildly romantic offering on the shrine of the most passionate devotion? I but
indistinctly recall the fact itself—what wonder that I have utterly forgotten the
circumstances which originated or attended it? And indeed, if ever that spirit
which is entitled *Romance*—if ever she, the wan, and the misty-winged *Ashto-
phet*[3] of idolatrous Egypt, presided, as they tell, over marriages illomened,
then most surely she presided over mine.

There is one dear topic, however, on which my memory faileth me not. It
is the person of Ligeia. In stature she was tall, somewhat slender, and in her
latter days even emaciated. I would in vain attempt to pourtray the majesty,
the quiet ease of her demeanour, or the incomprehensible lightness and elasticity of her footfall. She came and departed like a shadow. I was never made
aware of her entrance into my closed study save by the dear music of her low
sweet voice, as she placed her delicate hand upon my shoulder. In beauty of
face no maiden ever equalled her. It was the radiance of an opium dream—
an airy and spirit-lifting vision more wildly divine than the phantasies which
hovered about the slumbering souls of the daughters of Delos.[4] Yet her features were not of that regular mould which we have been falsely taught to
worship in the classical labors of the Heathen. "There is no exquisite[5] beauty,"

---

1. *Ligeia* was first published in the *American Museum* 1
(September 1838), the source of the present text. Poe
later revised the tale slightly and added to it the poem
*The Conqueror Worm*.
2. Like others of Poe's epigraphs (often added after first
publication), this one is fabricated to fit the desired effect. Joseph Glanvill (1636–1680) was one of the Cambridge Platonists, 17th-century English religious philosophers who tried to reconcile Christianity and

Renaissance science.
3. Variant of Ashtoreth, Phoenician goddess of fertility.
4. Probably the maidens attending Artemis, goddess of
wild nature and the hunt; she was born on Delos,
among the Cyclades in the Aegean Sea.
5. In his essay *Of Beauty* Francis Bacon, Baron Veru-
lam (1561–1626), wrote "excellent," not "exquisite."

saith Verülam, Lord Bacon, speaking truly of all the forms and *genera* of beauty, "without some *strangeness* in the proportions." Yet, although I saw that the features of Ligeia were not of classic regularity, although I perceived that her loveliness was indeed "exquisite," and felt that there was much of "strangeness" pervading it, yet I have tried in vain to detect the irregularity, and to trace home my own perception of "the strange." I examined the contour of the lofty and pale forehead—it was faultless—how cold indeed that word when applied to a majesty so divine! The skin rivaling the purest ivory, the commanding breadth and repose, the gentle prominence of the regions above the temples, and then the raven-black, the glossy, the luxuriant and naturally-curling tresses, setting forth the full force of the Homeric epithet, "hyacin-thine;" I looked at the delicate outlines of the nose—and nowhere but in the graceful medallions of the Hebrews had I beheld a similar perfection. There was the same luxurious smoothness of surface, the same scarcely perceptible tendency to the aquiline, the same harmoniously curved nostril speaking the free spirit. I regarded the sweet mouth. Here was indeed the triumph of all things heavenly—the magnificent turn of the short upper lip—the soft, volup-tuous repose of the under—the dimples which sported, and the colour which spoke—the teeth glancing back, with a brilliancy almost startling, every ray of the holy light which fell upon them in her serene, and placid, yet most exultingly radiant of all smiles. I scrutinized the formation of the chin—and here, too, I found the gentleness of breadth, the softness and the majesty, the fulness and the spirituality, of the Greek, the contour which the God Apollo revealed but in a dream to Cleomenes, the son of the Athenian.[6] And then I peered into the large eyes of Ligeia.

For eyes we have no models in the remotely antique. It might have been, too, that in these eyes of my beloved lay the secret to which Lord Verülam alludes. They were, I must believe, far larger than the ordinary eyes of our race. They were even far fuller than the fullest of the Gazelle eyes of the tribe of the valley of Nourjahad.[7] Yet it was only at intervals—in moments of intense excitement—that this peculiarity became more than slightly noticeable in Ligeia. And at such moments was her beauty—in my heated fancy thus it appeared perhaps—the beauty of beings either above or apart from the earth—the beauty of the fabulous Houri[8] of the Turk. The colour of the orbs was the most brilliant of black, and far over them hung jetty lashes of great length. The brows, slightly irregular in outline, had the same hue. The "strangeness," however, which I have found in the eyes of my Ligeia was of a nature distinct from the formation, or the colour, or the brilliancy of the feature, and must, after all, be referred to the *expression*. Ah, word of no meaning! behind whose vast latitude of mere sound we intrench our ignorance of so much of the spiritual. The expression of the eyes of Ligeia! How, for long hours have I pondered upon it! How have I, through the whole of a mid-summer night, struggled to fathom it! What was it—that something more profound than the well of Democritus[9]—which lay far within the pupils of my beloved? What *was* it? I was possessed with a passion to discover. Those eyes! those large,

---

6. Classical Greek sculptor whose name (possibly forged) is signed to the Venus de' Medici. The god Apollo was the patron of artists.
7. Frances Sheridan (1724–1766) wrote *The History of Nourjahad*, an Oriental romance.
8. Beautiful virgin waiting in paradise for the devout Mohammedan.
9. The Greek "laughing philosopher" (5th century B.C.); Greece; one of his proverbs is "Truth lies at the bottom of a well."

those shining, those divine orbs! they became to me twin stars of Leda,[1] and I to them devoutest of astrologers. Not for a moment was the unfathomable meaning of their glance, by day or by night, absent from my soul.

There is no point, among the many incomprehensible anomalies of the science of mind, more thrillingly exciting than the fact—never, I believe noticed in the schools—that in our endeavours to recall to memory something long forgotten we often find ourselves *upon the very verge* of remembrance without being able, in the end, to remember. And thus, how frequently, in my intense scrutiny of Ligeia's eyes, have I felt approaching the full knowledge of the secret of their expression—felt it approaching—yet not quite be mine— and so at length utterly depart. And (strange, oh strangest mystery of all!) I found, in the commonest objects of the universe, a circle of analogies to that expression. I mean to say that, subsequently to the period when Ligeia's beauty passed into my spirit, there dwelling as in a shrine, I derived from many existences in the material world, a sentiment, such as I felt always aroused within me by her large and luminous orbs. Yet not the more could I define that sentiment, or analyze, or even steadily view it. I recognized it, let me repeat, sometimes in the commonest objects of the universe. It has flashed upon me in the survey of a rapidly-growing vine—in the contemplation of a moth, a butterfly, a chrysalis, a stream of running water. I have felt it in the ocean, in the falling of a meteor. I have felt it in the glances of unusually aged people. And there are one or two stars in heaven—(one especially, a star of the sixth magnitude, double and changeable, to be found near the large star in Lyra)[2] in a telescopic scrutiny of which I have been made aware of the feeling. I have been filled with it by certain sounds from stringed instruments, and not unfrequently by passages from books. Among innumerable other instances, I well remember something in a volume of Joseph Glanvill, which, perhaps merely from its quaintness—who shall say? never failed to inspire me with the sentiment.—"And the will therein lieth, which dieth not. Who knoweth the mysteries of the will, with its vigor? For God is but a great will pervading all things by nature of its intentness. Man doth not yield him to the angels, nor unto death utterly, but only through the weakness of his feeble will."

Length of years, and subsequent reflection, have enabled me to trace, indeed, some remote connexion between this passage in the old English moralist and a portion of the character of Ligeia. An *intensity* in thought, action, or speech was possibly, in her, a result, or at least an index, of that gigantic volition which, during our long intercourse, failed to give other and more immediate evidence of its existence. Of all women whom I have ever known, she, the outwardly calm, the ever placid Ligeia, was the most violently a prey to the tumultuous vultures of stern passion. And of such passion I could form no estimate, save by the miraculous expansion of those eyes which at once so delighted and appalled me, by the almost magical melody, modulation, distinctness and placidity of her very low voice, and by the fierce energy, (rendered doubly effective by contrast with her manner of utterance) of the words which she uttered.

I have spoken of the learning of Ligeia: it was immense—such as I have

1. Queen of Sparta whom Zeus, in the form of a swan, raped, thereby begetting Helen of Troy and (according to some versions) the twin sons Castor and Pollux, whom their father transformed into the constellation Gemini.
2. The lesser star is Epsilon Lyrae, the large one Vega or Alpha Lyrae.

never known in woman. In all the classical tongues was she deeply proficient, and as far as my own acquaintance extended in regard to the modern dialects of Europe, I have never known her at fault. Indeed upon any theme of the most admired, because simply the most abstruse, of the boasted erudition of the academy, have I *ever* found Ligeia at fault? How singularly, how thrillingly, this one point in the nature of my wife has forced itself, at this late period, only, upon my attention! I said her knowledge was such as I had never known in woman. Where breathes the man who, like her, has traversed, and successfully, *all* the wide areas of moral, natural, and mathematical science? I saw not then what I now clearly perceive, that the acquisitions of Ligeia were gigantic, were astounding—yet I was sufficiently aware of her infinite supremacy to resign myself, with a childlike confidence, to her guidance through the chaotic world of metaphysical investigation at which I was most busily occupied during the earlier years of our marriage. With how vast a triumph—with how vivid a delight—with how much of all that is ethereal in hope—did I *feel*, as she bent over me, in studies but little sought for—but less known that delicious vista by slow but very perceptible degrees expanding before me, down whose long, gorgeous, and all untrodden path I might at length pass onward to the goal of a wisdom too divinely precious not to be forbidden!

How poignant, then, must have been the grief with which, after some years, I beheld my well-grounded expectations take wings to themselves and flee away! Without Ligeia I was but as a child groping benighted. Her presence, her readings alone, rendered vividly luminous the many mysteries of the transcendentalism in which we were immersed. Letters, lambent and golden, grew duller than Saturnian[3] lead wanting the radiant lustre of her eyes. And now those eyes shone less and less frequently upon the pages over which I poured. Ligeia grew ill. The wild eye blazed with a too—too glorious effulgence; the pale fingers became of the transparent waxen hue of the grave—and the blue veins upon the lofty forehead swelled and sunk impetuously with the tides of the most gentle emotion. I saw that she must die—and I struggled desperately in spirit with the grim Azrael.[4] And the struggles of the passionate Ligeia were, to my astonishment, even more energetic than my own. There had been much in her stern nature to impress me with the belief that, to her, death would have come without its terrors—but not so. Words are impotent to convey any just idea of the fierceness of resistance with which Ligeia wrestled with the dark shadow. I groaned in anguish at the pitiable spectacle. I would have soothed—I would have reasoned; but in the intensity of her wild desire for life—for life—*but* for life, solace and reason were alike the uttermost of folly. Yet not for an instant, amid the most convulsive writhings of her fierce spirit, was shaken the external placidity of her demeanor. Her voice grew more gentle—grew more low—yet I would not wish to dwell upon the wild meaning of the quietly-uttered words. My brain reeled as I hearkened, entranced, to a melody more than mortal—to assumptions and aspirations which mortality had never before known.

That Ligeia loved me, I should not have doubted; and I might have been easily aware that, in a bosom such as hers, love would have reigned no ordinary passion. But in death only, was I fully impressed with the intensity of her

3. Sluggish; in alchemy *saturnus* is the name for lead.
4. The Angel of Death (in Judaism and Mohammedanism).

affection. For long hours, detaining my hand, would she pour out before me the overflowings of a heart whose more than passionate devotion amounted to idolatry. How had I deserved to be so blessed by such confessions.—How had I deserved to be so cursed with the removal of my beloved in the hour of her making them? But upon this subject I cannot bear to dilate. Let me say only, that in Ligeia's more than womanly abandonment to a love, alas, all unmerited, all unworthily bestowed; I at length recognised the principle of her longing, with so wildly earnest a desire for the life which was now fleeing so rapidly away. It is this wild longing—it is this eager intensity of desire for life—*but* for life—that I have no power to pourtray—no utterance capable to express. Methinks I again behold the terrific struggles of her lofty, her nearly idealized nature, with the might and the terror, and the majesty of the great Shadow. But she perished. The giant *will* succumbed to a power more stern. And I thought, as I gazed upon the corpse, of the wild passage in Joseph Glanvill. "The will therein lieth, which dieth not. Who knoweth the mysteries of the will, with its vigor? For God is but a great will pervading all things by nature of its intentness. Man doth not yield him to the angels, *nor unto death utterly,* save only through the weakness of his feeble will."

She died—and I, crushed into the very dust with sorrow, could no longer endure the lonely desolation of my dwelling in the dim and decaying city by the Rhine. I had no lack of what the world terms wealth—Ligeia had brought me far more, very far more, than falls ordinarily to the lot of mortals. After a few months, therefore, of weary and aimless wandering, I purchased, and put in some repair, an abbey, which I shall not name, in one of the wildest and least frequented portions of fair England. The gloomy and dreary grandeur of the building, the almost savage aspect of the domain, the many melancholy and time-honored memories connected with both, had much in unison with the feelings of utter abandonment which had driven me into that remote and musical region of the country. Yet, although the external abbey, with its verdant decay hanging about it suffered but little alteration, I gave way with a child-like perversity, and perchance with a faint hope of alleviating my sorrows, to a display of more than regal magnificence within. For such follies even in childhood I had imbibed a taste, and now they came back to me as if in the dotage of grief. Alas, I now feel how much even of incipient madness might have been discovered in the gorgeous and fantastic draperies, in the solemn carvings of Egypt, in the wild cornices and furniture of Arabesque, in the bedlam patterns of the carpets of tufted gold! I had become a bounden slave in the trammels of opium, and my labors and my orders had taken a colouring from my dreams. But these absurdities I must not pause to detail. Let me speak only of that one chamber, ever accursed, whither, in a moment of mental alienation, I led from the altar as my bride—as the successor of the unforgotten Ligeia—the fair-haired and blue-eyed lady Rowena Trevanion, of Tremaine.

There is not any individual portion of the architecture and decoration of that bridal chamber which is not now visibly before me. Where were the souls of the haughty family of the bride, when, through thirst of gold, they permitted to pass the threshold of an apartment *so* bedecked, a maiden and a daughter so beloved? I have said that I minutely remember the details of the chamber— yet I am sadly forgetful on topics of deep moment—and here there was no system, no keeping, in the fantastic display, to take hold upon the memory.

The room lay in a high turret of the castellated abbey, was pentagonal in shape, and of capacious size. Occupying the whole southern face of the pentagon was the sole window—an immense sheet of unbroken glass from Venice— a single pane, and tinted of a leaden hue, so that the rays of either the sun or moon, passing through it, fell with a ghastly lustre upon the objects within. Over the upper portion of this huge window extended the open trellice-work of an aged vine which clambered up the massy walls of the turret. The ceiling, of gloomy-looking oak, was excessively lofty, vaulted, and elaborately fretted with the wildest and most grotesque specimens of a semi-Gothic, semi-druidical device. From out the most central recess of this melancholy vaulting, depended, by a single chain of gold, with long links, a huge censer of the same metal, Arabesque in pattern, and with many perforations so contrived that there writhed in and out of them, as if endued with a serpent vitality, a continual succession of parti-coloured fires. Some few ottomans and golden candelabras of Eastern figure were in various stations about—and there was the couch, too, the bridal couch, of an Indian model, and low, and sculptured of solid ebony, with a canopy above. In each of the angles of the chamber, stood on end a gigantic sarcophagus of black granite, from the tombs of the kings over against Luxor,[5] with their aged lids full of immemorial sculpture. But in the draping of the apartment lay, alas! the chief phantasy of all. The lofty walls— gigantic in height—even unproportionally so, were hung from summit to foot, in vast folds with a heavy and massy looking tapestry—tapestry of a material which was found alike as a carpet on the floor, as a covering for the ottomans, and the ebony bed, as a canopy for the bed, and as the gorgeous volutes[6] of the curtains which partially shaded the window. This material was the richest cloth of gold. It was spotted all over, at irregular intervals, with Arabesque figures, of about a foot in diameter, and wrought upon the cloth in patterns of the most jetty black. But these figures partook of the true character of the Arabesque only when regarded from a single point of view. By a contrivance now common, and indeed traceable to a very remote period of antiquity, they were made changeable in aspect. To one entering the room they bore the appearance of ideal monstrosities; but, upon a farther advance, this appearance suddenly departed; and, step by step, as the visitor moved his station in the chamber, he saw himself surrounded by an endless succession of the ghastly forms which belong to the superstition of the Northman, or arise in the guilty slumbers of the monk. The phantasmagoric effect was vastly heightened by the artificial introduction of a strong continual current of wind behind the draperies—giving a hidious and uneasy vitality to the whole.

In halls such as these—in a bridal chamber such as this, I passed, with the lady of Tremaine, the unhallowed hours of the first month of our marriage— passed them with but little disquietude. That my wife dreaded the fierce moodiness of my temper—that she shunned me, and loved me but little, I could not help perceiving—but it gave me rather pleasure than otherwise. I loathed her with a hatred belonging more to demon than to man. My memory flew back, (oh, with what intensity of regret!) to Ligeia, the beloved, the beautiful, the entombed. I revelled in recollections of her purity, of her wisdom, of her lofty, her ethereal nature, of her passionate, her idolatrous love. Now, then, did my spirit fully and freely burn with more than all the fires of her own. In

5. In middle Egypt, near Thebes; site of famous ruins,　　6. Scroll-like ornaments.
including the temple of Amun.

the excitement of my opium dreams (for I was habitually fettered in the iron shackles of the drug)[7] I would call aloud upon her name, during the silence of the night, or among the sheltered recesses of the glens by day, as if, by the wild eagerness, the solemn passion, the consuming intensity of my longing for the departed Ligeia, I could restore the departed Ligeia to the pathways she had abandoned upon earth.

About the commencement of the second month of the marriage, the lady Rowena was attacked with sudden illness from which her recovery was slow. The fever which consumed her, rendered her nights uneasy, and, in her perturbed state of half-slumber, she spoke of sounds, and of motions, in and about the chamber of the turret which had no origin save in the distemper of her fancy, or, perhaps, in the phantasmagoric influences of the chamber itself. She became at length convalescent—finally well. Yet but a brief period elapsed, ere a second more violent disorder again threw her upon a bed of suffering—and from this attack her frame, at all times feeble, never altogether recovered. Her illnesses were, after this period, of alarming character, and of more alarming recurrence, defying alike the knowledge and the great exertions of her medical men. With the increase of the chronic disease which had thus, apparently, taken too sure hold upon her constitution to be eradicated by human means, I could not fail to observe a similar increase in the nervous irritability of her temperament, and in her excitability by trivial causes of fear. Indeed reason seemed fast tottering from her throne. She spoke again, and now more frequently and pertinaciously, of the sounds, of the slight sounds, and of the unusual motions among the tapestries, to which she had formerly alluded. It was one night near the closing in of September, when she pressed this distressing subject with more than usual emphasis upon my attention. She had just awakened from a perturbed slumber, and I had been watching, with feelings half of anxiety, half of a vague terror, the workings of her emaciated countenance. I sat by the side of her ebony bed, upon one of the ottomans of India. She partly arose, and spoke, in an earnest low whisper, of sounds which she *then* heard, but which I could not hear, of motions which she *then* saw, but which I could not perceive. The wind was rushing hurriedly behind the tapestries, and I wished to show her (what, let me confess it, I could not *all* believe) that those faint, almost articulate, breathings, and the very gentle variations of the figures upon the wall, were but the natural effects of that customary rushing of the wind. But a deadly pallor overspreading her face, had proved to me that my exertions to re-assure her would be fruitless. She appeared to be fainting, and no attendants were within call. I remembered where was deposited a decanter of some light wine which had been ordered by her physicians, and hastened across the chamber to procure it. But, as I stepped beneath the light of the censer, two circumstances of a startling nature attracted my attention. I had felt that some palpable object had passed lightly by my person; and I saw that there lay a faint, indefinite shadow upon the golden carpet in the very middle of the rich lustre, thrown from the censer. But I was wild with the excitement of an immoderate dose of opium, and heeded these things but little, nor spoke of them to Rowena. Finding the wine, I re-crossed the chamber, and poured out a goblet-ful, which I held to the lips of the fainting lady. But she had now partially recovered, and took, herself,

7. The *American Museum* has no punctuation after "dreams" or "drug" in this sentence; parentheses are added to the present text.

the vessel, while I sank upon the ottoman near me, with my eyes rivetted upon her person. It was then that I became distinctly aware of a gentle foot-fall upon the carpet, and near the couch; and, in a second thereafter, as Rowena was in the act of raising the wine to her lips, I saw, or may have dreamed that I saw, fall within the goblet, as if from some invisible spring in the atmosphere of the room, three or four large drops of a brilliant and ruby colored fluid. If this I saw—not so Rowena. She swallowed the wine unhesitatingly, and I forbore to speak to her of a circumstance which must, after all, I considered, have been but the suggestion of a vivid imagination, rendered morbidly active by the terror of the lady, by the opium, and by the hour.

Yet I cannot conceal it from myself, after this period, a rapid change for the worse took place in the disorder of my wife, so that, on the third subsequent night, the hands of her menials prepared her for the tomb, and on the fourth, I sat alone, with her shrouded body, in that fantastical chamber which had received her as my bride. Wild visions, opium engendered, flitted, shadow-like, before me. I gazed with unquiet eye upon the sarcophagi in the angles of the room, upon the varying figures of the drapery, and upon the writhing of the parti-colored fires in the censer overhead. My eyes then fell, as I called to mind the circumstances of a former night, to the spot beneath the glare of the censer where I had beheld the faint traces of the shadow. It was there, however, no longer, and, breathing with greater freedom, I turned my glances to the pallid and rigid figure upon the bed. Then rushed upon me a thousand memories of Ligeia—and then came back upon my heart, with the turbulent violence of a flood, the whole of that unutterable woe with which I had regarded *her* thus enshrouded. The night waned; and still, with a bosom full of bitter thoughts of the one only and supremely beloved, I remained with mine eyes rivetted upon the body of Rowena.

It might have been midnight, or perhaps earlier, or later, for I had taken no note of time, when a sob, low, gentle, but very distinct, startled me from my revery. I *felt* that it came from the bed of ebony—the bed of death. I listened in an agony of superstitious terror—but there was no repetition of the sound; I strained my vision to detect any motion in the corpse, but there was not the slightest perceptible. Yet I could not have been deceived. I had heard the noise, however faint, and my whole soul was awakened within me, as I reso-lutely and perseveringly kept my attention rivetted upon the body. Many minutes elapsed before any circumstance occurred tending to throw light upon the mystery. At length it became evident that a slight, a very faint, and barely noticeable tinge of colour had flushed up within the cheeks, and along the sunken small veins of the eyelids. Through a species of unutterable horror and awe, for which the language of mortality has no sufficiently energetic expres-sion, I felt my brain reel, my heart cease to beat, my limbs grow rigid where I sat. Yet a sense of duty finally operated to restore my self-possession. I could no longer doubt that we had been precipitate in our preparations for inter-ment—that Rowena still lived. It was necessary that some immediate exertion be made; yet the turret was altogether apart from the portion of the Abbey tenanted by the servants—there were none within call, and I had no means of summoning them to my aid without leaving the room for many minutes— and this I could not venture to do. I therefore struggled alone in my endeavors to call back the spirit still hovering. In a short period it became evident how-ever, that a relapse had taken place; the color utterly disappeared from both eyelid and cheek, leaving a wanness even more than that of marble; the lips became doubly shrivelled and pinched up in the ghastly expression of death; a coldness surpassing that of ice, overspread rapidly the surface of the body, and all the usual rigorous stiffness immediately supervened. I fell back with a shudder upon the ottoman from which I had been so startlingly aroused, and again gave myself up to passionate waking visions of Ligeia.

An hour thus elapsed when, (could it be possible?) I was a second time aware of some vague sound issuing from the region of the bed. I listened—in extremity of horror. The sound came again—it was a sigh. Rushing to the corpse, I saw—distinctly saw—a tremor upon the lips. In a minute after they slightly relaxed, disclosing a bright line of the pearly teeth. Amazement now struggled in my bosom with the profound awe which had hitherto reigned therein alone. I felt that my vision grew dim, that my brain wandered, and it was only by a convulsive effort that I at length succeeded in nerving myself to the task which duty thus, once more, had pointed out. There was now a partial glow upon the forehead, upon the cheek and throat—a perceptible warmth pervaded the whole frame—there was even a slight pulsation at the heart. The lady lived; and with redoubled ardour I betook myself to the task of restoration. I chafed, and bathed the temples, and the hands, and used every exertion which experience, and no little medical reading, could suggest. But in vain. Suddenly, the colour fled, the pulsation ceased, the lips resumed the expression of the dead, and, in an instant afterwards, the whole body took upon itself the icy chillness, the livid hue, the intense rigidity, the sunken outline, and each and all of the loathsome peculiarities of that which has been, for many days, a tenant of the tomb.

And again I sunk into visions of Ligeia—and again (what marvel that I shudder while I write?) *again* there reached my ears a low sob from the region of the ebony bed. But why shall I minutely detail the unspeakable horrors of that night? Why shall I pause to relate how, time after time, until near the period of the grey dawn, this hideous drama of revivification was repeated, and how each terrific relapse was only into a sterner and apparently more irredeemable death? Let me hurry to a conclusion.

The greater part of the fearful night had worn away, and the corpse of Rowena once again stirred—and now more vigorously than hitherto, although arousing from a dissolution more appalling in its utter hopelessness than any. I had long ceased to struggle or to move, and remained sitting rigidly upon the ottoman, a helpless prey to a whirl of violent emotions, of which extreme awe was perhaps the least terrible, the least consuming. The corpse, I repeat, stirred, and now more vigorously than before. The hues of life flushed up with unwonted energy into the countenance—the limbs relaxed—and, save that the eyelids were yet pressed heavily together, and that the bandages and draperies of the grave still imparted their charnel character to the figure, I might have dreamed that Rowena had indeed shaken off, utterly, the fetters of Death. But if this idea was not, even then, altogether adopted, I could, at least, doubt no longer, when, arising from the bed, tottering, with feeble steps, with closed eyes, and with the air of one bewildered in a dream, the lady of Tremaine stood bodily and palpably before me.

I trembled not—I stirred not—for a crowd of unutterable fancies connected with the air, the demeanour of the figure, rushing hurriedly through my brain, sent the purple blood ebbing in torrents from the temples to the heart. I stirred not—but gazed upon her who was before me. There was a mad disorder in my thoughts—a tumult unappeasable. Could it, indeed, be the *living* Rowena who confronted me? Why, *why* should I doubt it? The bandage lay heavily about the mouth—but then it was the mouth of the breathing lady of Tremaine. And the cheeks—there were the roses as in her noon of health—yes, these were indeed the fair cheeks of the living lady of Tremaine. And the chin, with its dimples, as in health, was it not hers?—but—but *had she then grown taller since her malady?* What inexpressible madness seized me with that thought? One bound, and I had reached her feet! Shrinking from my touch, she let fall from her head, unloosened, the ghastly cerements which had confined it, and there streamed forth, into the rushing atmosphere of the chamber, huge masses of long and dishevelled hair. *It was blacker than the raven wings of the midnight!* And now the eyes opened of the figure which stood before me. "Here then at least," I shrieked aloud, "can I never—can I never be mistaken—these are the full, and the black, and the wild eyes of the lady— of the lady Ligeia!"

1838

# The Fall of the House of Usher[1]

During the whole of a dull, dark, and soundless day in the autumn of the year, when the clouds hung oppressively low in the heavens, I had been passing alone, on horseback, through a singularly dreary tract of country; and at length found myself, as the shades of the evening drew on, within view of the melancholy House of Usher. I know not how it was—but, with the first glimpse of the building, a sense of insufferable gloom pervaded my spirit. I say insufferable; for the feeling was unrelieved by any of that half-pleasurable, because poetic, sentiment, with which the mind usually receives even the sternest natural images of the desolate or terrible. I looked upon the scene before me—upon the mere house, and the simple landscape features of the domain—upon the bleak walls—upon the vacant eye-like windows—upon a few rank sedges—and upon a few white trunks of decayed trees—with an utter depression of soul which I can compare to no earthly sensation more properly than to the after-dream of the reveller upon opium—the bitter lapse into common life—the hideous dropping off of the veil. There was an iciness, a sinking, a sickening of the heart—an unredeemed dreariness of thought which no goading of the imagination could torture into aught of the sublime. What was it— I paused to think—what was it that so unnerved me in the contemplation of the House of Usher? It was a mystery all insoluble; nor could I grapple with the shadowy fancies that crowded upon me as I pondered. I was forced to fall back upon the unsatisfactory conclusion, that while, beyond doubt, there *are* combinations of very simple natural objects which have the power of thus affecting us, still the reason, and the analysis, of this power, lie among considerations beyond our depth. It was possible, I reflected, that a mere different arrangement of the particulars of the scene, of the details of this picture, would be sufficient to modify, or perhaps to annihilate its capacity for sorrowful

---

1. The text is that of the first publication in *Burton's Gentleman's Magazine, and American Monthly Review* 5 (September 1839).

impression; and, acting upon this idea, I reined my horse to the precipitous brink of a black and lurid tarn[2] that lay in unruffled lustre by the dwelling, and gazed down—but with a shudder even more thrilling than before—upon the re-modelled and inverted images of the gray sedge, and the ghastly tree-stems, and the vacant and eye-like windows.

Nevertheless, in this mansion of gloom I now proposed to myself a sojourn of some weeks. Its proprietor, Roderick Usher, had been one of my boon companions in boyhood; but many years had elapsed since our last meeting. A letter, however, had lately reached me in a distant part of the country—a letter from him—which, in its wildly importunate nature, had admitted of no other than a personal reply. The MS. gave evidence of nervous agitation. The writer spoke of acute bodily illness—of a pitiable mental idiosyncrasy which oppressed him—and of an earnest desire to see me, as his best, and indeed, his only personal friend, with a view of attempting, by the cheerfulness of my society, some alleviation of his malady. It was the manner in which all this, and much more, was said—it was the apparent *heart* that went with his request—which allowed me no room for hesitation—and I accordingly obeyed, what I still considered a very singular summons, forthwith.

Although, as boys, we had been even intimate associates, yet I really knew little of my friend. His reserve had been always excessive and habitual. I was aware, however, that his very ancient family had been noted, time out of mind, for a peculiar sensibility of temperament, displaying itself, through long ages, in many works of exalted art, and manifested, of late, in repeated deeds of munificent yet unobtrusive charity, as well as in a passionate devotion to the intricacies, perhaps even more than to the orthodox and easily recogniz-able beauties, of musical science. I had learned, too, the very remarkable fact, that the stem of the Usher race, all time-honored as it was, had put forth, at no period, any enduring branch; in other words, that the entire family lay in the direct line of descent, and had always, with very trifling and very temporary variation, so lain. It was this deficiency, I considered, while running over in thought the perfect keeping of the character of the premises with the accredited character of the people, and while speculating upon the possible influence which the one, in the long lapse of centuries, might have exercised upon the other—it was this deficiency, perhaps, of collateral issue, and the consequent undeviating transmission, from sire to son, of the patrimony with the name, which had, at length, so identified the two as to merge the original title of the estate in the quaint and equivocal appellation of the "House of Usher"—an appellation which seemed to include, in the minds of the peasantry who used it, both the family and the family mansion.

I have said that the sole effect of my somewhat childish experiment, of looking down within the tarn, had been to deepen the first singular impression. There can be no doubt that the consciousness of the rapid increase of my superstition—for why should I not so term it?—served mainly to accelerate the increase itself. Such, I have long known, is the paradoxical law of all senti-ments having terror as a basis. And it might have been for this reason only, that, when I again uplifted my eyes to the house itself, from its image in the pool, there grew in my mind a strange fancy—a fancy so ridiculous, indeed, that I but mention it to show the vivid force of the sensations which oppressed

2. A small lake, normally in the mountains.

me. I had so worked upon my imagination as really to believe that around about the whole mansion and domain there hung an atmosphere peculiar to themselves and their immediate vicinity—an atmosphere which had no affinity with the air of heaven, but which had reeked up from the decayed trees, and the gray walls, and the silent tarn, in the form of an inelastic vapor or gas—dull, sluggish, faintly discernible, and leaden-hued. Shaking off from my spirit what *must* have been a dream, I scanned more narrowly the real aspect of the building. Its principal feature seemed to be that of an excessive antiquity. The discoloration of ages had been great. Minute fungi overspread the whole exterior, hanging in a fine tangled web-work from the eaves. Yet all this was apart from any extraordinary dilapidation. No portion of the masonry had fallen; and there appeared to be a wild inconsistency between its still perfect adaptation of parts, and the utterly porous, and evidently decayed condition of the individual stones. In this there was much that reminded me of the specious totality of old wood-work which has rotted for long years in some neglected vault, with no disturbance from the breath of the external air. Beyond this indication of extensive decay, however, the fabric gave little token of instability. Perhaps the eye of a scrutinizing observer might have discovered a barely perceptible fissure, which, extending from the roof of the building in front, made its way down the wall in a zigzag direction, until it became lost in the sullen waters of the tarn.

Noticing these things, I rode over a short causeway to the house. A servant in waiting took my horse, and I entered the Gothic archway of the hall. A valet, of stealthy step, thence conducted me, in silence, through many dark and intricate passages in my progress to the studio of his master. Much that I encountered on the way contributed, I know not how, to heighten the vague sentiments of which I have already spoken. While the objects around me—while the carvings of the ceilings, the sombre tapestries of the walls, the ebon blackness of the floors, and the phantasmagoric armorial trophies which rattled as I strode, were but matters to which, or to such as which, I had been accustomed from my infancy—while I hesitated not to acknowledge how familiar was all this—I still wondered to find how unfamiliar were the fancies which ordinary images were stirring up. On one of the staircases, I met the physician of the family. His countenance, I thought, wore a mingled expression of low cunning and perplexity. He accosted me with trepidation and passed on. The valet now threw open a door and ushered me into the presence of his master.

The room in which I found myself was very large and excessively lofty. The windows were long, narrow, and pointed, and at so vast a distance from the black oaken floor as to be altogether inaccessible from within. Feeble gleams of encrimsoned light made their way through the trelliced panes, and served to render sufficiently distinct the more prominent objects around; the eye, however, struggled in vain to reach the remoter angles of the chamber, or the recesses of the vaulted and fretted ceiling. Dark draperies hung upon the walls. The general furniture was profuse, comfortless, antique, and tattered. Many books and musical instruments lay scattered about, but failed to give any vitality to the scene. I felt that I breathed an atmosphere of sorrow. An air of stern, deep, and irredeemable gloom hung over and pervaded all.

Upon my entrance, Usher arose from a sofa upon which he had been lying at full length, and greeted me with a vivacious warmth which had much in it, I at first thought of an overdone cordiality—of the constrained effort of the ennuyé[3] man of the world. A glance, however, at his countenance convinced me of his perfect sincerity. We sat down; and for some moments, while he spoke not, I gazed upon him with a feeling half of pity, half of awe. Surely, man had never before so terribly altered, in so brief a period, as had Roderick Usher! It was with difficulty that I could bring myself to admit the identity of the wan being before me with the companion of my early boyhood. Yet the character of his face had been at all times remarkable. A cadaverousness of complexion; an eye large, liquid, and luminous beyond comparison; lips somewhat thin and very pallid, but of a surpassingly beautiful curve; a nose of a delicate Hebrew model, but with a breadth of nostril unusual in similar formations; a finely moulded chin, speaking, in its want of prominence, of a want of moral energy; hair of a more than web-like softness and tenuity; these features, with an inordinate expansion above the regions of the temple, made up altogether a countenance not easily to be forgotten. And now in the mere exaggeration of the prevailing character of these features, and of the expression they were wont to convey, lay so much of change that I doubted to whom I spoke. The now ghastly pallor of the skin, and the now miraculous lustre of the eye, above all things startled and even awed me. The silken hair, too, had been suffered to grow all unheeded, and as, in its wild gossamer texture, it floated rather than fell about the face, I could not, even with effort, connect its arabesque expression with any idea of simple humanity.

In the manner of my friend I was at once struck with an incoherence—an inconsistency; and I soon found this to arise from a series of feeble and futile struggles to overcome an habitual trepidancy, an excessive nervous agitation. For something of this nature I had indeed been prepared, no less by his letter, than by reminiscences of certain boyish traits, and by conclusions deduced from his peculiar physical conformation and temperament. His action was alternately vivacious and sullen. His voice varied rapidly from a tremulous indecision (when the animal spirits seemed utterly in abeyance) to that species of energetic concision—that abrupt, weighty, unhurried, and hollow-sounding enunciation—that leaden, self-balanced and perfectly modulated guttural utterance, which may be observed in the moments of the intensest excitement of the lost drunkard, or the irreclaimable eater of opium.

It was thus that he spoke of the object of my visit, of his earnest desire to see me, and of the solace he expected me to afford him. He entered, at some length, into what he conceived to be the nature of his malady. It was, he said, a constitutional and a family evil, and one for which he despaired to find a remedy—a mere nervous affection, he immediately added, which would undoubtedly soon pass off. It displayed itself in a host of unnatural sensations. Some of these, as he detailed them, interested and bewildered me—although, perhaps, the terms, and the general manner of the narration had their weight. He suffered much from a morbid acuteness of the senses; the most insipid food was alone endurable; he could wear only garments of certain texture; the odors of all flowers were oppressive; his eyes were tortured by even a faint light; and there were but peculiar sounds, and these from stringed instruments, which did not inspire him with horror.

To an anomalous species of terror I found him a bounden slave. "I shall perish," said he, "I *must* perish in this deplorable folly. Thus, thus, and not

3. Bored (from French).

otherwise, shall I be lost. I dread the events of the future, not in themselves, but in their results. I shudder at the thought of any, even the most trivial, incident, which may operate upon this intolerable agitation of soul. I have, indeed, no abhorrence of danger, except in its absolute effect—in terror. In this unnerved—in this pitiable condition—I feel that I must inevitably abandon life and reason together in my struggles with some fatal demon of fear."

I learned, moreover, at intervals, and through broken and equivocal hints, another singular feature of his mental condition. He was enchained by certain superstitious impressions in regard to the dwelling which he tenanted, and from which, for many years, he had never ventured forth—in regard to an influence whose supposititious force was conveyed in terms too shadowy here to be restated—an influence which some peculiarities in the mere form and substance of his family mansion, had, by dint of long sufferance, he said, obtained over his spirit—an effect which the *physique* of the gray walls and turrets, and of the dim tarn into which they all looked down, had, at length, brought about upon the *morale* of his existence.

He admitted, however, although with hesitation, that much of the peculiar gloom which thus afflicted him could be traced to a more natural and far more palpable origin—to the severe and long-continued illness—indeed to the evidently approaching dissolution—of a tenderly beloved sister; his sole companion for long years—his last and only relative on earth. "Her decease," he said, with a bitterness which I can never forget, "would leave him (him the hopeless and the frail) the last of the ancient race of the Ushers." As he spoke, the lady Madeline (for so was she called) passed slowly through a remote portion of the apartment, and, without having noticed my presence, disappeared. I regarded her with an utter astonishment not unmingled with dread. Her figure, her air, her features—all, in their very minutest development were those—were identically (I can use no other sufficient term) were identically those of the Roderick Usher who sat beside me. A feeling of stupor oppressed me, as my eyes followed her retreating steps. As a door, at length, closed upon her exit, my glance sought instinctively and eagerly the countenance of the brother—but he had buried his face in his hands, and I could only perceive that a far more than ordinary wanness had overspread the emaciated fingers through which trickled many passionate tears.

The disease of the lady Madeline had long baffled the skill of her physicians. A settled apathy, a gradual wasting away of the person, and frequent although transient affections of a partially cataleptical character, were the unusual diagnosis. Hitherto she had steadily borne up against the pressure of her malady, and had not betaken herself finally to bed; but, on the closing in of the evening of my arrival at the house, she succumbed, as her brother told me at night with inexpressible agitation, to the prostrating power of the destroyer—and I learned that the glimpse I had obtained of her person would thus probably be the last I should obtain—that the lady, at least while living, would be seen by me no more.

For several days ensuing, her name was unmentioned by either Usher or myself; and, during this period, I was busied in earnest endeavors to alleviate the melancholy of my friend. We painted and read together—or I listened, as if in a dream, to the wild improvisations of his speaking guitar. And thus, as a closer and still closer intimacy admitted me more unreservedly into the recesses of his spirit, the more bitterly did I perceive the futility of all attempt at cheering a mind from which darkness, as if an inherent positive quality, poured forth upon all objects of the moral and physical universe, in one unceasing radiation of gloom.

I shall ever bear about me, as Moslemin their shrouds at Mecca; a memory of the many solemn hours I thus spent alone with the master of the House of Usher. Yet I should fail in any attempt to convey an idea of the exact character of the studies, or of the occupations, in which he involved me, or led me the way. An excited and highly distempered ideality threw a sulphurous lustre over all. His long improvised dirges will ring for ever in my ears. Among other things, I bear painfully in mind a certain singular perversion and amplification of the wild air of the last waltz of Von Weber.[4] From the paintings over which his elaborate fancy brooded, and which grew, touch by touch, into vaguenesses at which I shuddered the more thrillingly, because I shuddered knowing not why, from these paintings (vivid as their images now are before me) I would in vain endeavor to educe more than a small portion which should lie within the compass of merely written words. By the utter simplicity, by the nakedness, of his designs, he arrested and over-awed attention. If ever mortal painted an idea, that mortal was Roderick Usher. For me at least—in the circumstances then surrounding me—there arose out of the pure abstractions which the hypochondriac contrived to throw upon his canvas, an intensity of intolerable awe, no shadow of which felt I ever yet in the contemplation of the certainly glowing yet too concrete reveries of Fuseli.[5]

One of the phantasmagoric conceptions of my friend, partaking not so rigidly of the spirit of abstraction, may be shadowed forth, although feebly, in words. A small picture presented the interior of an immensely long and rectangular vault or tunnel, with low walls, smooth, white, and without interruption or device. Certain accessory points of the design served well to convey the idea that this excavation lay at an exceeding depth below the surface of the earth. No outlet was observed in any portion of its vast extent, and no torch, or other artificial source of light was discernible—yet a flood of intense rays rolled throughout, and bathed the whole in a ghastly and inappropriate splendor.

I have just spoken of that morbid condition of the auditory nerve which rendered all music intolerable to the sufferer, with the exception of certain effects of stringed instruments. It was, perhaps, the narrow limits to which he thus confined himself upon the guitar, which gave birth, in great measure, to the fantastic character of his performances. But the fervid *facility* of his impromptus could not be so accounted for. They must have been, and were, in the notes, as well as in the words of his wild fantasias, (for he not unfrequently accompanied himself with rhymed verbal improvisations,) the result of that intense mental collectedness and concentration to which I have previously alluded as observable only in particular moments of the highest artificial excitement. The words of one of these rhapsodies I have easily borne away in memory. I was, perhaps, the more forcibly impressed with it, as he gave it, because, in the under or mystic current of its meaning, I fancied that I perceived, and for the first time, a full consciousness on the part of Usher, of the tottering of his lofty reason upon her throne. The verses, which were entitled "The Haunted Palace," ran very nearly, if not accurately, thus:[6]

4. Karl Maria von Weber (1786–1826) established Romanticism in German opera; *The Last Waltz of Von Weber* was composed by Karl Gottlieb Reissiger (1798–1859).

5. Henry Fuseli (1741–1825), Swiss painter who made his reputation in London; noted for his interest in the supernatural.

6. In the original printing this note appeared at the end of the story: "The ballad of 'The Haunted Palace,' introduced in this tale, was published separately, some months ago, in the Baltimore 'Museum.'"

### I

In the greenest of our valleys,
   By good angels tenanted,
Once a fair and stately palace—
   Snow-white palace—reared its head.
In the monarch Thought's dominion—
   It stood there!
Never seraph spread a pinion
   Over fabric half so fair.

### II

Banners yellow, glorious, golden,
   On its roof did float and flow;
(This—all this—was in the olden
   Time long ago)
And every gentle air that dallied,
   In that sweet day,
Along the ramparts plumed and pallid,
   A winged odor went away.

### III

Wanderers in that happy valley
   Through two luminous windows saw
Spirits moving musically
   To a lute's well-tunéd law,
Round about a throne, where sitting
   (Porphyrogene!)[7]
In state his glory well befitting,
   The sovereign of the realm was seen.

### IV

And all with pearl and ruby glowing
   Was the fair palace door,
Through which came flowing, flowing, flowing,
   And sparkling evermore,
A troop of Echoes whose sole duty
   Was but to sing,
In voices of surpassing beauty,
   The wit and wisdom of their king.

### V

But evil things, in robes of sorrow,
   Assailed the monarch's high estate;
(Ah, let us mourn, for never morrow
   Shall dawn upon him, desolate!)
And, round about his home, the glory
   That blushed and bloomed
Is but a dim-remembered story
   Of the old time entombed.

### VI

And travellers now within that valley,
   Through the red-litten windows, see
Vast forms that move fantastically
   To a discordant melody;

7. Born to the purple, of royal birth.

> While, like a rapid ghastly river,
> Through the pale door,
> A hideous throng rush out forever,
> And laugh—but smile no more.

I well remember that suggestions arising from this ballad led us into a train of thought wherein there became manifest an opinion of Usher's which I mention not so much on account of its novelty, (for other men have thought thus,) as on account of the pertinacity with which he maintained it. This opinion, in its general form, was that of the sentience of all vegetable things. But, in his disordered fancy, the idea had assumed a more daring character, and trespassed, under certain conditions, upon the kingdom of inorganization. I lack words to express the full extent, or the earnest *abandon* of his persuasion. The belief, however, was connected (as I have previously hinted) with the gray stones of the home of his forefathers. The condition of the sentience had been here, he imagined, fulfilled in the method of collocation of these stones—in the order of their arrangement, as well as in that of the many fungi which overspread them, and of the decayed trees which stood around—above all, in the long undisturbed endurance of this arrangement, and in its reduplication in the still waters of the tarn. Its evidence—the evidence of the sentience—was to be seen, he said, (and I here started as he spoke,) in *the gradual yet certain condensation of an atmosphere of their own about the waters and the walls.* The result was discoverable, he added, in that silent, yet importunate and terrible influence which for centuries had moulded the destinies of his family, and which made *him* what I now saw him—what he was. Such opinions need no comment, and I will make none.

Our books—the books which, for years, had formed no small portion of the mental existence of the invalid—were, as might be supposed, in strict keeping with this character of phantasm. We pored together over such works as the Ververt et Chartreuse of Gresset; the Belphegor of Machiavelli; the Selenography of Brewster; the Heaven and Hell of Swedenborg; the Subterranean Voyage of Nicholas Klimm de Holberg; the Chiromancy of Robert Flud, of Jean d'Indaginé, and of De la Chambre; the Journey into the Blue Distance of Tieck; and the City of the Sun of Campanella. One favorite volume was a small octavo edition of the Directorium Inquisitorium, by the Dominican Eymeric de Gironne; and there were passages in Pomponius Mela, about the old African Satyrs and Œgipans, over which Usher would sit dreaming for hours. His chief delight, however, was found in the earnest and repeated perusal of an exceedingly rare and curious book in quarto Gothic—the manual of a forgotten church—the *Vigilae Mortuorum secundum Chorum Ecclesiae Maguntinae.*[8]

8. The titles are real, although the way they sound in the narrator's inventory is at least as important as their precise contents. Jean Baptiste Gresset (1709–1777) wrote the anticlerical *Vairvert* and *Ma Chartreuse*. In *Belphegor*, by Niccolò Machiavelli (1469–1527), a demon comes to earth to prove that women damn men to hell. Sir David Brewster (1781–1868), Scotish physicist who studied optics and polarized light. Emanuel Swedenborg (1688–1772), Swedish scientist and mystic, presents a fantastically precise anatomy of living conditions in heaven and hell, seeing the two places as mutually attractive opposites. Ludwig Holberg (1684–1754), Danish dramatist and historian, deals with a voyage to the land of death and back. Robert Flud (1574–1637), English physician and noted Rosicrucian (the Rosicrucians then being a new organization of esoteric philosophy and theology that purported to be based on ancient lore from the Middle East), and two Frenchmen, Jean D'Indaginé (fl. early 16th century) and Maria Cireau de la Chambre (1594–1669), all wrote on chiromancy (palm reading). The German Ludwig Tieck (1773–1853) wrote *Das Alte Buch; oder Reise ins Blaue hinein*, which deals with a journey to another world. *The City of the Sun* by the Italian Tommaso Campanella (1568–1639) is a famous utopian work. Nicholas Eymeric de Gerone, who was inquisi-

I could not help thinking of the wild ritual of this work, and of its probable influence upon the hypochondriac, when, one evening, having informed me abruptly that the lady Madeline was no more, he stated his intention of preserving her corpse for a fortnight, previously to its final interment, in one of the numerous vaults within the main walls of the building. The worldly reason, however, assigned for this singular proceeding, was one which I did not feel at liberty to dispute. The brother had been led to his resolution (so he told me) by considerations of the unusual character of the malady of the deceased, of certain obtrusive and eager inquiries on the part of her medical men, and of the remote and exposed situation of the burial ground of the family. I will not deny that when I called to mind the sinister countenance of the person whom I met upon the staircase, on the day of my arrival at the house, I had no desire to oppose what I regarded as at best but a harmless, and not by any means an unnatural precaution.[9]

At the request of Usher, I personally aided him in the arrangements for the temporary entombment. The body having been encoffined, we two alone bore it to its rest. The vault in which we placed it (and which had been so long unopened that our torches, half smothered in its oppressive atmosphere, gave us little opportunity for investigation) was small, damp, and utterly without means of admission for light; lying, at great depth, immediately beneath that portion of the building in which was my own sleeping apartment. It had been used, apparently, in remote feudal times, for the worst purposes of a donjon-keep, and, in later days, as a place of deposit for powder, or other highly combustible substance, as a portion of its floor, and the whole interior of a long archway through which we reached it, were carefully sheathed with copper. The door, of massive iron, had been, also, similarly protected. Its immense weight caused an unusually sharp grating sound, as it moved upon its hinges.

Having deposited our mournful burden upon tressels within this region of horror, we partially turned aside the yet unscrewed lid of the coffin, and looked upon the face of the tenant. The exact similitude between the brother and sister even here again startled and confounded me. Usher, divining, perhaps, my thoughts, murmured out some few words from which I learned that the deceased and himself had been twins, and that sympathies of a scarcely intelligible nature had always existed between them. Our glances, however, rested not long upon the dead—for we could not regard her unawed. The disease which had thus entombed the lady in the maturity of youth, had left, as usual in all maladies of a strictly cataleptical character, the mockery of a faint blush upon the bosom and the face, and that suspiciously lingering smile upon the lip which is so terrible in death. We replaced and screwed down the lid, and, having secured the door of iron, made our way, with toil, into the scarcely less gloomy apartments of the upper portion of the house.

And now, some days of bitter grief having elapsed, an observable change came over the features of the mental disorder of my friend. His ordinary manner had vanished. His ordinary occupations were neglected or forgotten. He

---

tor-general for Castile in 1356, recorded procedures for torturing heretics. Pomponius Mela (1st century) was a Roman whose widely used book on geography (printed in Italy in 1471) described strange beasts ("oegipans" are African goat-men). A book called *The Vigils of the Dead, According to the Church-Choir of Mayence* was printed in Basel around 1500.

9. The shortage of corpses for dissection had led to the new profession of "resurrection men," who dug up fresh corpses and sold them to medical students and surgeons.

roamed from chamber to chamber with hurried, unequal, and objectless step. The pallor of his countenance had assumed, if possible, a more ghastly hue— but the luminousness of his eye had utterly gone out. The once occasional huskiness of his tone was heard no more; and a tremulous quaver, as if of extreme terror, habitually characterized his utterance.—There were times, indeed, when I thought his unceasingly agitated mind was laboring with an oppressive secret, to divulge which he struggled for the necessary courage. At times, again, I was obliged to resolve all into the mere inexplicable vagaries of madness, as I beheld him gazing upon vacancy for long hours, in an attitude of the profoundest attention, as if listening to some imaginary sound. It was no wonder that his condition terrified—that it infected me. I felt creeping upon me, by slow yet certain degrees, the wild influences of his own fantastic yet impressive superstitions.

It was, most especially, upon retiring to bed late in the night of the seventh or eighth day after the entombment of the lady Madeline, that I experienced the full power of such feelings. Sleep came not near my couch—while the hours waned and waned away. I struggled to reason off the nervousness which had dominion over me. I endeavored to believe that much, if not all of what I felt, was due to the phantasmagoric influence of the gloomy furniture of the room—of the dark and tattered draperies, which, tortured into motion by the breath of a rising tempest, swayed fitfully to and fro upon the walls, and rustled uneasily about the decorations of the bed. But my efforts were fruitless. An irrepressible tremor gradually pervaded my frame; and, at length, there sat upon my very heart an incubus[1] of utterly causeless alarm. Shaking this off with a gasp and a struggle, I uplifted myself upon the pillows, and, peering earnestly within the intense darkness of the chamber, harkened—I know not why, except that an instinctive spirit prompted me—to certain low and indefinite sounds which came, through the pauses of the storm, at long inter- vals, I knew not whence. Overpowered by an intense sentiment of horror, unaccountable yet unendurable, I threw on my clothes with haste, for I felt that I should sleep no more during the night, and endeavored to arouse myself from the pitiable condition into which I had fallen, by pacing rapidly to and fro through the apartment.

I had taken but few turns in this manner, when a light step on an adjoining staircase arrested my attention. I presently recognized it as that of Usher. In an instant afterwards he rapped, with a gentle touch, at my door, and entered, bearing a lamp. His countenance was, as usual, cadaverously wan—but there was a species of mad hilarity in his eyes—an evidently restrained hysteria in his whole demeanor. His air appalled me—but any thing was preferable to the solitude which I had so long endured, and I even welcomed his presence as a relief.

"And you have not seen it?" he said abruptly, after having stared about him for some moments in silence—"you have not then seen it?—but, stay! you shall." Thus speaking, and having carefully shaded his lamp, he hurried to one of the gigantic casements, and threw it freely open to the storm.

The impetuous fury of the entering gust nearly lifted us from our feet. It was, indeed, a tempestuous yet sternly beautiful night, and one wildly singular in its terror and its beauty. A whirlwind had apparently collected its force in

---

1. An evil spirit supposed to lie upon people in their sleep.

our vicinity; for there were frequent and violent alterations in the direction of the wind; and the exceeding density of the clouds (which hung so low as to press upon the turrets of the house) did not prevent our perceiving the life-like velocity with which they flew careering from all points against each other, without passing away into the distance. I say that even their exceeding density did not prevent our perceiving this—yet we had no glimpse of the moon or stars—nor was there any flashing forth of the lightning. But the under surfaces of the huge masses of agitated vapor, as well as all terrestrial objects immediately around us, were glowing in the unnatural light of a faintly luminous and distinctly visible gaseous exhalation which hung about and enshrouded the mansion.

"You must not—you shall not behold this!" said I, shudderingly, to Usher, as I led him, with a gentle violence, from the window to a seat. "These appearances, which bewilder you, are merely electrical phenomena not uncommon—or it may be that they have their ghastly origin in the rank miasma of the tarn. Let us close this casement—the air is chilling and dangerous to your frame. Here is one of your favorite romances. I will read, and you shall listen—and so we will pass away this terrible night together."

The antique volume which I had taken up was the "Mad Trist" of Sir Launcelot Canning[2]—but I had called it a favorite of Usher's more in sad jest than in earnest; for, in truth, there is little in its uncouth and unimaginative prolixity which could have had interest for the lofty and spiritual ideality of my friend. It was, however, the only book immediately at hand; and I indulged a vague hope that the excitement which now agitated the hypochondriac might find relief (for the history of mental disorder is full of similar anomalies) even in the extremeness of the folly which I should read. Could I have judged, indeed, by the wild, overstrained air of vivacity with which he harkened, or apparently harkened, to the words of the tale, I might have well congratulated myself upon the success of my design.

I had arrived at that well-known portion of the story where Ethelred, the hero of the Trist, having sought in vain for peaceable admission into the dwelling of the hermit, proceeds to make good an entrance by force. Here, it will be remembered, the words of the narrative run thus—

"And Ethelred, who was by nature of a doughty heart, and who was now mighty withal, on account of the powerfulness of the wine which he had drunken, waited no longer to hold parley with the hermit, who, in sooth, was of an obstinate and maliceful turn, but, feeling the rain upon his shoulders, and fearing the rising of the tempest, uplifted his mace outright, and, with blows, made quickly room in the plankings of the door for his gauntleted hand, and now pulling therewith sturdily, he so cracked, and ripped, and tore all asunder, that the noise of the dry and hollow-sounding wood alarummed and reverberated throughout the forest."

At the termination of this sentence I started, and, for a moment, paused; for it appeared to me (although I at once concluded that my excited fancy had deceived me)—it appeared to me that, from some very remote portion of the mansion or of its vicinity, there came, indistinctly, to my ears, what might have been, in its exact similarity of character, the echo (but a stifled and dull one certainly) of the very cracking and ripping sound which Sir Launcelot had

---

2. Not a real book. "Trist" here means simply meeting, or prearranged or fated encounter, not the lovers' meeting implied in the modern use of "tryst."

so particularly described. It was, beyond doubt, the coincidence alone which had arrested my attention; for, amid the rattling of the sashes of the casements, and the ordinary commingled noises of the still increasing storm, the sound, in itself, had nothing, surely, which should have interested or disturbed me. I continued the story.

"But the good champion Ethelred, now entering within the door, was sore enraged and amazed to perceive no signal of the maliceful hermit; but, in the stead thereof, a dragon of scaly and prodigious demeanor, and of a fiery tongue, which sate in guard before a palace of gold, with a floor of silver; and upon the wall there hung a shield of shining brass with this legend enwritten—

Who entereth herein, a conqueror hath bin,
Who slayeth the dragon, the shield he shall win.

And Ethelred uplifted his mace, and struck upon the head of the dragon, which fell before him, and gave up his pesty breath, with a shriek so horrid and harsh, and withal so piercing, that Ethelred had fain to close his ears with his hands against the dreadful noise of it, the like whereof was never before heard."

Here again I paused abruptly, and now with a feeling of wild amazement— for there could be no doubt whatever that, in this instance, I did actually hear (although from what direction it proceeded I found it impossible to say) a low and apparently distant, but harsh, protracted, and most unusual screaming or grating sound—the exact counterpart of what my fancy had already conjured up as the sound of the dragon's unnatural shriek as described by the romancer.

Oppressed, as I certainly was, upon the occurrence of this second and most extraordinary coincidence, by a thousand conflicting sensations, in which wonder and extreme terror were predominant, I still retained sufficient presence of mind to avoid exciting, by any observation, the sensitive nervousness of my companion. I was by no means certain that he had noticed the sounds in question; although, assuredly, a strange alteraton had, during the last few minutes, taken place in his demeanor. From a position fronting my own, he had gradually brought round his chair, so as to sit with his face to the door of the chamber, and thus I could but partially perceive his features, although I saw that his lips trembled as if he were murmuring inaudibly. His head had dropped upon his breast—yet I knew that he was not asleep, from the wide and rigid opening of the eye, as I caught a glance of it in profile. The motion of his body, too, was at variance with his idea—for he rocked from side to side with a gentle yet constant and uniform sway. Having rapidly taken notice of all this, I resumed the narrative of Sir Launcelot, which thus proceeded:—

"And now, the champion, having escaped from the terrible fury of the dragon, bethinking himself of the brazen shield, and of the breaking up of the enchantment which was upon it, removed the carcass from out of the way before him, and approached valorously over the silver pavement of the castle to where the shield was upon the wall; which in sooth tarried not for his full coming, but fell down at his feet upon the silver floor, with a mighty great and terrible ringing sound."

No sooner had these syllables passed my lips, than—as if a shield of brass had indeed, at the moment, fallen heavily upon a floor of silver—I became aware of a distinct, hollow, metallic, and clangorous, yet apparently muffled reverberation. Completely unnerved, I started convulsively to my feet, but the measured rocking movement of Usher was undisturbed. I rushed to the chair in which he sat. His eyes were bent fixedly before him, and throughout his whole countenance there reigned a more than stony rigidity. But, as I laid my hand upon his shoulder, there came a strong shudder over his frame; a sickly smile quivered about his lips; and I saw that he spoke in a low, hurried, and gibbering murmur, as if unconscious of my presence. Bending closely over his person, I at length drank in the hideous import of his words.

"Not hear it?—yes, I hear it, and *have* heard it. Long—long—long—many minutes, many hours, many days, have I heard it—yet I dared not—oh, pity me, miserable wretch that I am!—I dared not—I *dared* not speak! *We have put her living in the tomb!* Said I not that my senses were acute?—I *now* tell you that I heard her first feeble movements in the hollow coffin. I heard them—many, many days ago—yet I dared not—*I dared not speak!* And now—to-night—Ethelred—ha! ha!—the breaking of the hermit's door, and the death-cry of the dragon, and the clangor of the shield—say, rather, the rending of the coffin, and the grating of the iron hinges, and her struggles within the coppered archway of the vault! Oh wither shall I fly? Will she not be here anon? Is she not hurrying to upbraid me for my haste? Have I not heard her footsteps on the stair? Do I not distinguish that heavy and horrible beating of her heart? Madman!"—here he sprung violently to his feet, and shrieked out his syllables, as if in the effort he were giving up his soul—"Madman! *I tell you that she now stands without the door!*"

As if in the superhuman energy of his utterance there had been found the potency of a spell—the huge antique pannels to which the speaker pointed, threw slowly back, upon the instant, their ponderous and ebony jaws. It was the work of the rushing gust—but then without those doors there *did* stand the lofty and enshrouded figure of the lady Madeline of Usher. There was blood upon her white robes, and the evidence of some bitter struggle upon every portion of her emaciated frame. For a moment she remained trembling and reeling to and fro upon the threshold—then, with a low moaning cry, fell heavily inward upon the person of her brother, and in her horrible and now final death-agonies, bore him to the floor a corpse, and a victim to the terrors he had dreaded.

From that chamber, and from that mansion, I fled aghast. The storm was still abroad in all its wrath as I found myself crossing the old causeway. Suddenly there shot along the path a wild light, and I turned to see whence a gleam so unusual could have issued—for the vast house and its shadows were alone behind me. The radiance was that of the full, setting, and blood-red moon, which now shone vividly through that once barely-discernible fissure, of which I have before spoken, as extending from the roof of the building, in a zig-zag direction, to the base. While I gazed, this fissure rapidly widened—there came a fierce breath of the whirlwind—the entire orb of the satellite burst at once upon my sight—my brain reeled as I saw the mighty walls rushing asunder—there was a long tumultuous shouting sound like the voice of a thousand waters—and the deep and dank tarn at my feet closed sullenly and silently over the fragments of the *"House of Usher."*

1839

# William Wilson. A Tale[1]

*What say of it? what say of conscience grim,*
*That spectre in my path?*
—*Chamberlaine's Pharronida*[2]

Let me call myself, for the present, William Wilson. The fair page now lying before me need not be sullied with my real appellation. This has been already too much an object for the scorn, for the horror, for the detestation of my race. To the uttermost regions of the globe have not the indignant winds bruited its unparalleled infamy? oh, outcast of all outcasts most abandoned! To the earth art thou not for ever dead? to its honours, to its flowers, to its golden aspirations? and a cloud, dense, dismal, and limitless, does it not hang eternally between thy hopes and heaven?

I would not, if I could, here or to-day, embody a record of my later years of unspeakable misery, and unpardonable crime. This epoch—these later years—took unto themselves a sudden elevation in turpitude, whose origin alone it is my present purpose to assign. Men usually grow base by degrees. From me, in an instant, all virtue dropped bodily as a mantle. I shrouded my nakedness in triple guilt. From comparatively trivial wickedness I passed, with the stride of a giant, into more than the enormities of an Elah-Gabalus.[3] What chance, what one event brought this evil thing to pass, bear with me while I relate. Death approaches; and the shadow which foreruns him has thrown a softening influence over my spirit. I long, in passing through the dim valley, for the sympathy—I had nearly said for the pity— of my fellow-men. I would fain have them believe that I have been, in some measure, the slave of circumstances beyond human control. I would wish them to seek out for me, in the details I am about to give, some little oasis of *fatality* amid a wilderness of error. I would have them allow—what they cannot refrain from allowing— that, although temptation may have erewhile existed as great, man was never *thus*, at least, tempted before—certainly, never *thus* fell. And therefore has he never thus suffered. Have I not indeed been living in a dream? And am I not now dying a victim to the horror and the mystery of the wildest of all sublunary visions?

I am come of a race whose imaginative and easily excitable temperament has at all times rendered them remarkable; and, in my earliest infancy, I gave evidence of having fully inherited the family character. As I advanced in years it was more strongly developed; becoming, for many reasons, a cause of serious disquietude to my friends, and of positive injury to myself. I grew self-willed, addicted to the wildest caprices, and a prey to the most ungovernable passions. Weak-minded, and beset with constitutional infirmities akin to my own, my parents could do but little to check the evil propensities which distinguished me. Some feeble and ill-directed efforts resulted in complete failure on their

1. This tale is reprinted from its first appearance in the Philadelphia annual *The Gift*, dated 1840 but published in September 1839. Into it Poe worked some memories of the school he attended at Stoke-Newington (Bransby was the name of his own principal there). January 19 is Poe's own birthday as well as William Wilson's, and in different printings of the story Wilson's birth year appears as 1809, 1811, and 1813, the latter two dates being those Poe also used in autobiographical accounts to make him even more precocious than he was.
2. The epigraph is not in this 1659 poem by William Chamberlayne.
3. Elagabalus (b. 204), boy emperor of Rome (218–222), murdered by his imperial guards. Among the "enormities" were the imposition of the worship of Baal, the Semitic fertility god, and the favor displayed toward handsome homosexual boys.

part, and of course, in total triumph on mine. Thenceforward my voice was a household law; and at an age when few children have abandoned their leading-strings, I was left to the guidance of my own will, and became, in all but name, the master of my own actions.

My earliest recollections of a school-life are connected with a large, rambling, cottage-built, and somewhat decayed building in a misty-looking village of England, where were a vast number of gigantic and gnarled trees, and where all the houses were excessively ancient and inordinately tall. In truth, it was a dream-like and spirit-soothing place, that venerable old town. At this moment, in fancy, I feel the refreshing chilliness of its deeply-shadowed avenues, inhale the fragrance of its thousand shrubberies, and thrill anew with undefinable delight, at the deep, hollow note of the church-bell, breaking each hour, with sullen and sudden roar, upon the stillness of the dusky atmosphere in which the old, fretted, Gothic steeple lay imbedded and asleep.

It gives me, perhaps, as much of pleasure as I can now in any manner experience, to dwell upon minute recollections of the school and its concerns. Steeped in misery as I am—misery, alas! only too real—I shall be pardoned for seeking relief, however slight and temporary, in the weakness of a few rambling details. These, moreover, utterly trivial, and even ridiculous in themselves, assume, to my fancy, adventitious importance as connected with a period and a locality, when and where I recognise the first ambiguous monitions of the destiny which afterwards so fully overshadowed me. Let me then remember.

The house, I have said, was old, irregular, and cottage-built. The grounds were extensive, and an enormously high and solid brick wall, topped with a bed of mortar and broken glass, encompassed the whole. This prison-like rampart formed the limit of our domain; beyond it we saw but thrice a week—once every Saturday afternoon, when, attended by two ushers,[4] we were permitted to take brief walks in a body through some of the neighbouring fields—and twice during Sunday, when we were paraded in the same formal manner to the morning and evening service in the one church of the village. Of this church the principal of our school was pastor. With how deep a spirit of wonder and perplexity was I wont to regard him from our remote pew in the gallery, as, with step solemn and slow he ascended the pulpit! This reverend man, with countenance so demurely benign, with robes so glossy and so clerically flowing, with wig so minutely powdered, so rigid and so vast—could this be he who of late, with sour visage, and in snuffy habiliments, administered, ferule in hand, the Draconian[5] laws of the academy? Oh, gigantic paradox too utterly monstrous for solution!

At an angle of the ponderous wall frowned a more ponderous gate. It was riveted and studded with iron bolts, and surmounted with jagged iron spikes. What impressions of deep awe it inspired! It was never opened save for the three periodical egressions and ingressions already mentioned; then, in every creak of its mighty hinges we found a plenitude of mystery, a world of matter for solemn remark, or for far more solemn meditation.

The extensive enclosure was irregular in form, having many capacious recesses. Of these, three or four of the largest constituted the play-ground. It was level, and covered with fine hard gravel. I well remember it had no trees, nor benches, nor any thing similar within it. Of course it was in the rear of

4. Assistant schoolmasters.
5. Merciless, from Draco, Athenian lawgiver, whose    code (621? B.C.) set death as the penalty for numerous    crimes.

the house. In front lay a small parterre, planted with box and other shrubs; but through this sacred division we passed only upon rare occasions indeed, such as a first advent or final departure from school, or perhaps, when a parent or friend having called for us, we joyfully took our way home for the Christmas or Mid-summer holydays.

But the house—how quaint an old building was this!—to me how veritably a palace of enchantment! There was really no end to its windings, to its incomprehensible sub-divisions. It was impossible, at any given time, to say with certainty upon which of its two stories one happened to be. From each room to every other there were sure to be found three or four steps either in ascent or descent. Then the lateral branches were innumerable—inconceivable, and so returning in upon themselves, that our most exact ideas in regard to the whole mansion were not very far different from those with which we pondered upon infinity. During the five years of my residence here I was never able to ascertain with precision, in what remote locality lay the little sleeping apartment assigned to myself and some eighteen or twenty other scholars.

The school-room was the largest in the house—I could not help thinking, in the world. It was very long, narrow, and dismally low, with pointed Gothic windows and a ceiling of oak. In a remote and terror-inspiring angle was a square enclosure of eight or ten feet, comprising the sanctum, "during hours," of our principal, the Reverend Dr. Bransby. It was a solid structure, with massy door, sooner than open which in the absence of "the Dominie,"[6] we would all have willingly perished by the *peine forte et dure.*[7] In other angles were two other similar boxes, far less reverenced, indeed, but still greatly matters of awe. One of these was the pulpit of "the classical" usher, one of the "English and mathematical." Interspersed about the room, crossing and recrossing in endless irregularity, were innumerable benches and desks, black, ancient, and time-worn, piled desperately with much-bethumbed books, and so beseamed with initial letters, names at full length, meaningless gashes, grotesque figures, and other multiplied efforts of the knife, as to have utterly lost what little of original form might have been their portion in days long departed. A huge bucket with water stood at one extremity of the room, and a clock of stupendous dimensions at the other.

Encompassed by the massy walls of this venerable academy I passed, yet not in tedium or disgust, the years of the third lustrum[8] of my life. The teeming brain of childhood requires no external world of incident to occupy or amuse it, and the apparently dismal monotony of a school, was replete with more intense excitement than my riper youth has derived from luxury, or my full manhood from crime. Yet I must believe that my first mental developement had in it much of the uncommon, even much of the *outré.*[9] Upon mankind at large the events of very early existence rarely leave in mature age any definite impression. All is gray shadow—a weak and irregular remembrance—an indistinct regathering of feeble pleasures and phantasmagoric pains. With me this is not so. In childhood I must have felt with the energy of a man what I now find stamped upon memory in lines as vivid, as deep, and as durable as the exergues of the Carthaginian medals.[1]

Yet in fact—in the fact of the world's view—how little was there to remem-

6. Minister or schoolteacher (Bransby was both).
7. Pressing to death, as with large flat rocks (French).
8. Five-year period.
9. Extreme, exaggerated (French).
1. Perhaps Poe has in mind no particular medal of

Carthage (the ancient sea power on the Mediterranean near modern Tunis, defeated by Rome in the 2nd century B.C.). "Exergues": the spaces beneath the central design on the reverse of coins.

ber! The morning's awakening, the nightly summons to bed; the connings,[2] the recitations; the periodical half-holidays and perambulations; the play-ground, with its broils, its pastimes, its intrigues—these, by a mental sorcery long forgotten, were made to involve a wilderness of sensation, a world of rich incident, an universe of varied emotion, of excitement the most passionate and spirit-stirring. *"Oh, le bon temps, que ce siecle de fer!"*[3]

In truth, the ardency, the enthusiasm, and the imperiousness of my disposition soon rendered me a marked character among my schoolmates, and by slow but natural gradations, gave me an ascendency over all not greatly older than myself—over all with one single exception. This exception was found in the person of a scholar, who although no relation, bore the same Christian and surname as myself—a circumstance, in truth, little remarkable, for, not-withstanding a noble descent, mine was one of those every-day appellations which seem, by prescriptive right, to have been, time out of mind, the com-mon property of the mob. In this narrative I have therefore designated myself as William Wilson—a fictitious title not very dissimilar to the real. My name-sake alone, of those who in school phraseology constituted "our set," presumed to compete with me in the studies of the class, in the sports and broils of the play-ground—to refuse implicit belief in my assertions, and submission to my will—indeed to interfere with my arbitrary dictation in any respect whatsoever. If there be on earth a supreme and unqualified despotism, it is the despotism of a master mind in boyhood over the less energetic spirits of his companions.

Wilson's rebellion was to me a source of the greatest embarrassment—the more so as, in spite of the bravado with which in public I made a point of treating him and his pretensions, I secretly felt that I feared him, and could not help thinking the equality which he maintained so easily with myself a proof of his true superiority, since not to be overcome cost me a perpetual struggle. Yet this superiority—even this equality—was in truth acknowledged by no one but myself; our companions, by some unaccountable blindness, seemed not even to suspect it. Indeed, his competition, his resistance, and especially his impertinent and dogged interference with my purposes, were not more pointed than private. He appeared to be utterly destitute alike of the ambition which urged, and of the passionate energy of mind which enabled me to excel. In his rivalry he might have been supposed actuated solely by a whimsical desire to thwart, astonish, or mortify myself; although there were times when I could not help observing, with a feeling made up of wonder, abasement, and pique, that he mingled with his injuries, his insults, or his contradictions, a certain most inappropriate, and assuredly most unwelcome *affectionateness* of manner. I could only conceive this singular behaviour to arise from a consummate self-conceit assuming the vulgar airs of patronage and protection.

Perhaps it was this latter trait in Wilson's conduct, conjoined with our iden-tity of name, and the mere accident of our having entered the school upon the same day, which set afloat the notion that we were brothers, among the senior classes in the academy. These do not usually inquire with much strictness into the affairs of their juniors. I have before said, or should have said, that Wilson was not, in the most remote degree, connected with my family. But assuredly if we *had* been brothers we must have been twins, for, since leaving Dr. Bran-

---

2. Memorizings.
3. From Voltaire's *Le Mondain* (1736): "Oh, this age

of iron is a good time" (French). Iron implies dull utili-tarianism in contrast to the fabled heroic age of gold.

sby's, I casually learned that my namesake—a somewhat remarkable coincidence—was born on the nineteenth of January, 1811—and this is precisely
the day of my own nativity.

It may seem strange that in spite of the continual anxiety occasioned me by
the rivalry of Wilson, and his intolerable spirit of contradiction, I could not
bring myself to hate him altogether. We had, to be sure, nearly every day a
quarrel, in which, yielding me publicly the palm of victory, he, in some manner, contrived to make me feel that it was he who had deserved it; yet a sense
of pride upon my part, and a veritable dignity upon his own, kept us always
upon what are called "speaking terms," while there were many points of strong
congeniality in our tempers, operating to awake in me a sentiment which our
position alone, perhaps, prevented from ripening into friendship. It is difficult,
indeed, to define, or even to describe, my real feelings towards him. They
were formed of a heterogeneous mixture—some petulant animosity, which
was not yet hatred, some esteem, more respect, much fear, with a world of
uneasy curiosity. To the moralist fully acquainted with the minute springs of
human action, it will be unnecessary to say, in addition, that Wilson and
myself were the most inseparable of companions.

It was no doubt the anomalous state of affairs existing between us which
turned all my attacks upon him, and they were many, either open or covert,
into the channel of banter or practical joke (giving pain while assuming the
aspect of mere fun) rather than into that of a more serious and determined
hostility. But my endeavours on this head were by no means uniformly successful, even when my plans were the most wittily concocted; for my namesake
had much about him, in character, of that unassuming and quiet austerity
which, while enjoying the poignancy of its own jokes, has no heel of Achilles[4]
in itself, and absolutely refuses to be laughed at. I could find, indeed, but one
vulnerable point, and that, lying in a personal peculiarity arising, perhaps,
from constitutional disease, would have been spared by any antagonist less at
his wit's end than myself—my rival had a weakness in the faucial or guttural
organs which precluded him from raising his voice at any time *above a very
low whisper.* Of this defect I did not fail to take what poor advantage lay in
my power.

Wilson's retaliations in kind were many, and there was one form of his
practical wit that disturbed me beyond measure. How his sagacity first discovered at all that so petty a thing would vex me is a question I never could
solve—but, having discovered, he habitually practised the annoyance. I had
always felt aversion to my uncourtly patronymic, and its very common, if not
plebeian, praenomen. The words were venom in my ears; and when, upon
the day of my arrival, a second William Wilson came also to the academy, I
felt angry with him for bearing the name, and doubly disgusted with the name
because a stranger bore it who would be the cause of its twofold repetition,
who would be constantly in my presence, and whose concerns, in the ordinary
routine of the school business, must, inevitably, on account of the detestable
coincidence, be often confounded with my own.

The feeling of vexation thus engendered, grew stronger with every circumstance tending to show resemblance, moral or physical, between my rival and

4. I.e., no vulnerable spot. The mother of Achilles, the hero of Homer's *Iliad*, tried to make her son im- mortal by dipping him into the river Styx. But no water touched the heel she held him by, and in that heel he received his death wound.

myself. I had not then discovered the remarkable fact that we were of the same age; but I saw that we were of the same height, and I perceived that we were not altogether unlike in general contour of person and outline of feature. I was galled, too, by the rumour touching a relationship which had grown current in the upper forms. In a word, nothing could more seriously disturb me, (although I scrupulously concealed such disturbance,) than any allusion to a similarity of mind, person, or condition existing between us. But, in truth, I had no reason to believe that (with the exception of the matter of relationship, and in the case of Wilson himself,) this similarity had ever been made a subject of comment, or even observed at all by our schoolfellows. That *he* observed it in all its bearings, and as fixedly as I, was apparent, but that he could discover in such circumstances so fruitful a field of annoyance for myself can only be attributed, as I said before, to his more than ordinary penetration.

His cue, which was to perfect an imitation of myself, lay both in words and in actions; and most admirably did he play his part. My dress it was an easy matter to copy; my gait and general manner were, without difficulty, appropriated; in spite of his constitutional defect, even my voice did not escape him. My louder tones were, of course, unattempted, but then the key, it was identical; *and his singular whisper, it grew the very echo of my own.*

How greatly this most exquisite portraiture harassed me, (for it could not justly be termed a caricature,) I will not now venture to describe. I had but one consolation—in the fact that the imitation, apparently, was noticed by myself alone, and that I had to endure only the knowing and strangely sarcastic smiles of my namesake himself. Satisfied with having produced in my bosom the intended effect, he seemed to chuckle in secret over the sting he had inflicted, and was characteristically disregardful of the public applause which the success of his witty endeavours might have so easily elicited. That the school, indeed, did not feel his design, perceive its accomplishment, and participate in his sneer, was, for many anxious months, a riddle I could not resolve. Perhaps the *gradation* of his copy rendered it not so readily perceptible, or, more possibly, I owed my security to the masterly air of the copyist, who, disdaining the letter, which in a painting is all the obtuse can see, gave but the full spirit of his original for my individual contemplation and chagrin.

I have already more than once spoken of the disgusting air of patronage which he assumed towards me, and of his frequent officious interference with my will. This interference often took the ungracious character of advice; advice not openly given, but hinted or insinuated. I received it with a repugnance which gained strength as I grew in years. Yet, at this distant day, let me do him the simple justice to acknowledge that I can recall no occasion when the suggestions of my rival were on the side of those errors or follies so usual to his immature age, and seeming inexperience; that his moral sense, at least, if not his general talents and worldly wisdom, was far keener than my own; and that I might, to-day, have been a better, and thus a happier man, had I more seldom rejected the counsels embodied in those meaning whispers which I then but too cordially hated, and too bitterly derided.

As it was, I at length grew restive in the extreme, under his distasteful supervision, and daily resented more and more openly what I considered his intolerable arrogance. I have said that, in the first years of our connexion as schoolmates, my feelings in regard to him might have been easily ripened into friendship; but, in the latter months of my residence at the academy, although the intrusion of his ordinary manner had, beyond doubt, in some measure, abated, my sentiments, in nearly similar proportion, partook very much of positive hatred. Upon one occasion he saw this, I think, and afterwards avoided, or made a show of avoiding me.

It was about the same period, if I remember aright, that, in an altercation of violence with him, in which he was more than usually thrown off his guard, and spoke and acted with an openness of demeanour rather foreign to his nature, I discovered, or fancied I discovered, in his accent, his air, and general appearance, a something which first startled, and then deeply interested me, by bringing to mind dim visions of my earliest infancy; wild, confused, and thronging memories of a time when memory herself was yet unborn. I cannot better describe the sensation which oppressed me than by saying that I could with difficulty shake off the belief that myself and the being who stood before me had been acquainted at some epoch very long ago; some point of the past even infinitely remote. The delusion, however, faded rapidly as it came; and I mention it at all but to define the day of the last conversation I there held with my singular namesake.

The huge old house, with its countless subdivisions, had several enormously large chambers communicating with each other, where slept the greater number of the students. There were, however, as must necessarily happen in a building so awkwardly planned, many little nooks or recesses, the odds and ends of the structure; and these the economic ingenuity of Dr. Bransby had also fitted up as dormitories—although, being the merest closets, they were capable of accommodating only a single individual. One of these small apartments was occupied by Wilson.

It was upon a gloomy and tempestuous night of an early autumn, about the close of my fifth year at the school, and immediately after the altercation just mentioned, that, finding every one wrapped in sleep, I arose from bed, and, lamp in hand, stole through a wilderness of narrow passages from my own bed-room to that of my rival. I had been long plotting one of those ill-natured pieces of practical wit at his expense in which I had hitherto been so uniformly unsuccessful. It was my intention, now, to put my scheme in operation, and I resolved to make him feel the whole extent of the malice with which I was imbued. Having reached his closet, I noiselessly entered, leaving the lamp with a shade over it, on the outside. I advanced a step, and listened to the sound of his tranquil breathing. Assured of his being asleep, I returned, took the light, and with it again approached the bed. Close curtains were around it, which, in the prosecution of my plan, I slowly and quietly withdrew, when the bright rays fell vividly upon the sleeper, and my eyes, at the same moment upon his countenance. I looked, and a numbness, an iciness of feeling instantly pervaded my frame. My breast heaved, my knees tottered, my whole spirit became possessed with an objectless yet intolerable horror. Gasping for breath, I lowered the lamp in still nearer proximity to the face. Were these— *these* the lineaments of William Wilson? I saw, indeed, that they were his, but I shook as with a fit of the ague in fancying they were not. What *was* there about them to confound me in this manner? I gazed—while my brain reeled with a multitude of incoherent thoughts. Not thus he appeared—assuredly not *thus*—in the vivacity of his waking hours. The same name; the same contour of person; the same day of arrival at the academy! And then his dogged and meaningless imitation of my gait, my voice, my habits, and my manner! Was it, in truth, within the bounds of human possibility that *what I now witnessed* was the result of the habitual practice of this sarcastic imitation? Awe-stricken, and with a creeping shudder, I extinguished the lamp, passed silently from the chamber, and left, at once, the halls of that old academy, never to enter them again.

After a lapse of some months, spent at home in mere idleness, I found myself a student at Eton. The brief interval had been sufficient to enfeeble my remembrance of the events at Dr. Bransby's, or at least, to effect a material change in the nature of the feelings with which I remembered them. The truth—the tragedy—of the drama was no more. I could now find room to doubt the evidence of my senses; and seldom called up the subject at all but with wonder at the extent of human credulity, and a smile at the vivid force of the imagination which I hereditarily possessed. Neither was this species of scepticism likely to be diminished by the character of the life I led at Eton. The vortex of thoughtless folly into which I there so immediately and so recklessly plunged, washed away all but the froth of my past hours—engulfed, at once, every solid or serious impression, and left to memory only the veriest levities of a former existence.

I do not wish, however, to trace the course of my miserable profligacy here—a profligacy which set at defiance the laws, while it eluded the vigilance of the institution. Three years of folly, passed without profit, had but given me rooted habits of vice, and added, in a somewhat unusual degree, to my bodily stature, when, after a week of soulless dissipation, I invited a small party of the most dissolute students to a secret carousal in my chamber. We met at a late hour of the night, for our debaucheries were to be faithfully protracted until morning. The wine flowed freely, and there were not wanting other, perhaps more dangerous, seductions; so that the gray dawn had already faintly appeared in the east, while our delirious extravagance was at its height. Madly flushed with cards and intoxication, I was in the act of insisting upon a toast of more than intolerable profanity, when my attention was suddenly diverted by the violent, although partial unclosing of the door of the apartment, and by the eager voice from without of a servant. He said that some person, apparently in great haste, demanded to speak with me in the hall.

Wildly excited with the potent *Vin de Barac*, the unexpected interruption rather delighted than surprised me. I staggered forward at once, and a few steps brought me to the vestibule of the building. In this low and small room there hung no lamp; and now no light at all was admitted, save that of the exceedingly feeble dawn which made its way through a semicircular window. As I put my foot over the threshold I became aware of the figure of a youth about my own height, and (what then peculiarly struck my mad fancy) habited in a white cassimere morning frock, cut in the novel fashion of the one I myself wore at the moment. This the faint light enabled me to perceive—but the features of his face I could not distinguish. Immediately upon my entering he strode hurriedly up to me, and, seizing me by the arm with a gesture of petulant impatience, whispered the words "William Wilson!" in my ear. I grew perfectly sober in an instant.

There was that in the manner of the stranger, and in the tremulous shake of his uplifted finger, as he held it between my eyes and the light, which filled me with unqualified amazement—but it was not this which had so violently moved me. It was the pregnancy of solemn admonition in the singular, low, hissing utterance; and, above all, it was the character, the tone, *the key*, of those few, simple, and familiar, yet whispered, syllables, which came with a thousand thronging memories of by-gone days, and struck upon my soul with the shock of a galvanic battery. Ere I could recover the use of my senses he was gone.

Although this event failed not of a vivid effect upon my disordered imagination, yet was it evanescent as vivid. For some weeks, indeed, I busied myself in earnest inquiry, or was wrapped in a cloud of morbid speculation. I did not pretend to disguise from my perception the identity of the singular individual who thus perseveringly interfered with my affairs, and harassed me with his insinuated counsel. But who and what was this Wilson?—and whence came he?—and what were his purposes? Upon neither of these points could I be satisfied—merely ascertaining, in regard to him, that a sudden accident in his family had caused his removal from Dr. Bransby's Academy on the afternoon of the day in which I myself had eloped. But in a brief period I ceased to think upon the subject; my attention being all absorbed in a contemplated departure for Oxford. Thither I soon went; the uncalculating vanity of my parents furnished me with an outfit, and annual establishment, which would enable me to indulge at will in the luxury already so dear to my heart—to vie in profuseness of expenditure with the haughtiest heirs of the wealthiest earldoms in Great Britain.

Excited by such appliances to vice, my constitutional temperament broke forth with redoubled ardour, and I spurned even the common restraints of decency in the mad infatuation of my revels. But it were absurd to pause in the detail of my extravagance. Let it suffice, that among spendthrifts I out-heroded Herod,[5] and that, giving name to a multitude of novel follies, I added no brief appendix to the long catalogue of vices then usual in the most dissolute university of Europe.

It could hardly be credited, however, that I had, even here, so utterly fallen from the gentlemanly estate as to seek acquaintance with the vilest arts of the gambler by profession, and, having become an adept in his despicable science, to practise it habitually as a means of increasing my already enormous income at the expense of the weak-minded among my fellow-collegians. Such, nevertheless, was the fact. And the very enormity of this offence against all manly and honourable sentiment proved, beyond doubt, the main, if not the sole reason of the impunity with which it was committed. Who, indeed, among my most abandoned associates, would not rather have disputed the clearest evidence of his senses, than have suspected of such courses the gay, the frank, the generous William Wilson—the noblest and most liberal commoner at Oxford—him whose follies (said his parasites) were but the follies of youth and unbridled fancy—whose errors but inimitable whim—whose darkest vice but a careless and dashing extravagance.

I had been now two years successfully busied in this way, when there came to the university a young *parvenu* nobleman, Glendinning—rich, said report, as Herodes Atticus[6]—his riches, too, as easily acquired. I soon found him of weak intellect, and, of course, marked him as a fitting subject for my skill. I

---

5. I.e., exceeded excesses, from Hamlet's advice to the players in Shakespeare's *Hamlet* 3.2. In medieval mystery plays a favorite luridly acted villain was Herod (73–4 B.C.), the cruel king of Judea (see Matthew 2).

6. Athenian rhetorician (2nd century), proverbial for his extreme wealth. *"Parvenu"*: upstart, newly rich (French).

frequently engaged him in play, and contrived, with a gambler's usual art, to let him win considerable sums, the more effectually to entangle him in my snares. At length, my schemes being ripe, I met him (with the full intention that this meeting should be final and decisive) at the chambers of a fellow-commoner, (Mr. Preston,) equally intimate with both, but who, to do him justice, entertained not even a remote suspicion of my design. To give to this a better colouring, I had contrived to have assembled a party of some eight or ten, and was solicitously careful that the introduction of cards should appear accidental, and originate in the proposal of my contemplated dupe himself. To be brief upon a vile topic, none of the low finesse was omitted, so customary upon similar occasions that it is a just matter for wonder how any are still found so besotted as to fall its victim.

We had protracted our sitting far into the night, and I had at length effected the manœuvre of getting Glendinning as my sole antagonist. The game, too, was my favourite écarté. The rest of the company, interested in the extent of our play, had abandoned their own cards, and were standing around us as spectators. The *parvenu*, who had been induced by my artifices in the early part of the evening to drink deeply, now shuffled, dealt, or played with a wild nervousness of manner for which his intoxication, I thought, might partially, but could not altogether, account. In a very short period he had become my debtor to a large amount of money, when, having taken a long draught of port, he did precisely what I had been cooly anticipating, proposed to double our already extravagant stakes. With a well feigned show of reluctance, and not until after my repeated refusal had seduced him into some angry words which gave a colour of *pique* to my compliance, did I finally comply. The result, of course, did but prove how entirely the prey was in my toils—in less than a single hour he had quadrupled his debt. For some time his countenance had been losing the florid tinge lent it by the wine—but now, to my astonishment, I perceived that it had grown to a pallor truly fearful. I say to my astonishment. Glendinning had been represented to my eager inquiries as immeasurably wealthy; and the sums which he had as yet lost, although in themselves vast, could not, I supposed, very seriously annoy, much less so violently affect him. That he was overcome by the wine just swallowed, was the idea which most readily presented itself; and, rather with a view to the preservation of my own character in the eyes of my associates, than from any less interested motive, I was about to insist, peremptorily, upon a discontinuance of the play, when some expressions at my elbow from among the company, and an ejaculation evincing utter despair on the part of Glendinning, gave me to understand that I had effected his total ruin under circumstances which, rendering him an object for the pity of all, should have protected him from the ill offices of a fiend.

What now might have been my conduct it is difficult to say. The pitiable condition of my dupe had thrown an air of embarrassed gloom over all, and, for some moments, a profound and unbroken silence was maintained, during which I could not help feeling my cheeks tingle with the many burning glances of scorn or reproach cast upon me by the less abandoned of the party. I will even own that an intolerable weight of anxiety was for a brief instant lifted from my bosom by the sudden and extraordinary interruption which ensued. The wide, heavy folding doors of the apartment were all at once thrown open, to their full extent, with a vigorous and rushing impetuosity that extinguished, as if by magic, every candle in the room. Their light, in dying, enabled us just to perceive that a stranger had entered of about my own height, and closely muffled in a cloak. The darkness, however, was now total; and we could only feel that he was standing in our midst. Before any one of us could recover from the extreme astonishment into which this rudeness had thrown all, we heard the voice of the intruder.

"Gentlemen"—he said, in a low, distinct, and never-to-be-forgotten *whisper* which thrilled to the very marrow of my bones—"Gentlemen, I make no apology for this behaviour, because in thus behaving I am but fulfilling a duty. You are, beyond doubt, uninformed of the true character of the person who has to-night won at écarté a large sum of money from Lord Glendinning. I will therefore put you upon an expeditious and decisive plan of obtaining this very necessary information. Please to examine, at your leisure, the inner linings of the cuff of his left sleeve, and the several little packages which may be found in the somewhat capacious pockets of his embroidered morning wrapper."

While he spoke, so profound was the stillness that one might have heard a pin dropping upon the floor. In ceasing, he at once departed, and as abruptly as he had entered. Can I—shall I describe my sensations?—must I say that I felt all the horrors of the damned? Most assuredly I had but little time given for reflection. Many hands roughly seized me upon the spot, and lights were immediately reprocured. A search ensued. In the lining of my sleeve were found all of the court-cards essential in écarté, and, in the pockets of my wrapper, a number of packs, fac-similes of those used at our sittings, with the single exception that mine were of the species called, technically, *arrondé*; the honours[7] being slightly convex at the ends, the lower cards slightly convex at the sides. In this disposition, the dupe who cuts, as customary, at the breadth of the pack, will invariably find that he cuts his antagonist an honour; while the gambler, cutting at the length, will, as certainly, cut nothing for his victim which may count in the records of the game.

Any outrageous burst of indignation upon this shameful discovery would have affected me less than the silent contempt, or the sarcastic composure with which it was received.

"Mr. Wilson," said our host, stooping to remove from beneath his feet an exceedingly luxurious cloak of rare furs, "Mr. Wilson, this is your property." (The weather was cold; and, upon quitting my own room, I had thrown a cloak over my dressing wrapper, putting it off upon reaching the scene of play.) "I presume it is supererogatory to seek here (eyeing the folds of the garment with a bitter smile,) for any farther evidence of your skill. Indeed we have had enough. You will see the necessity, I hope, of quitting Oxford—at all events, of quitting, instantly, my chambers."

Abased, humbled to the dust as I then was, it is probable that I should have resented this galling language by immediate personal violence, had not my whole attention been immediately arrested, by a fact of the most startling character. The cloak which I had worn was of a rare description of fur; how rare, how extravagantly costly, I shall not venture to say. Its fashion, too, was of my own fantastic invention; for I was fastidious, to a degree of absurd coxcombry, in matters of this frivolous nature. When, therefore, Mr. Preston reached me

7. Face cards.

that which he had picked up upon the floor, and near the folding doors of the apartment, it was with an astonishment nearly bordering upon terror, that I perceived my own already hanging on my arm, (where I had no doubt unwittingly placed it,) and that the one presented me was but its exact counterpart in every, in even the minutest possible particular. The singular being who had so disastrously exposed me, had been muffled, I remembered, in a cloak; and none had been worn at all by any of the members of our party with the exception of myself. Retaining some presence of mind, I took the one offered me by Preston, placed it, unnoticed, over my own, left the apartment with a resolute scowl of defiance, and, next morning ere dawn of day, commenced a hurried journey from Oxford to the continent, in a perfect agony of horror and of shame.

I fled in vain. My evil destiny pursued me as if in exultation, and proved, indeed, that the exercise of its mysterious dominion had as yet only begun. Scarcely had I set foot in Paris ere I had fresh evidence of the detestable interest taken by this Wilson in my concerns. Years flew, while I experienced no relief. Villain!—at Rome, with how untimely, yet with how spectral an officiousness, stepped he in between me and my ambition! At Vienna, too, at Berlin, and at Moscow! Where, in truth, had I not bitter cause to curse him within my heart? From his inscrutable tyranny did I at length flee, panic-stricken, as from a pestilence; and to the very ends of the earth I fled in vain.

And again, and again, in secret communion with my own spirit, would I demand the questions "Who is he?—whence came he?—and what are his objects?" But no answer was there found. And now I scrutinized, with a minute scrutiny, the forms, and the methods, and the leading traits of his impertinent supervision. But even here there was very little upon which to base a conjecture. It was noticeable, indeed, that, in no one of the multiplied instances in which he had of late crossed my path, had he so crossed it except to frustrate those schemes, or to disturb those actions, which, fully carried out, might have resulted in bitter mischief. Poor justification this, in truth, for an authority so imperiously assumed! Poor indemnity for natural rights of self-agency so pertinaciously, so insultingly denied!

I had also been forced to notice that my tormentor, for a very long period of time, (while scrupulously and with miraculous dexterity maintaining his whim of an identity of apparel with myself,) had so contrived it, in the execution of his varied interference with my will, that I saw not, at any moment, the features of his face. Be Wilson what he might, this, at least, was but the veriest of affection, or of folly. Could he, for an instant, have supposed that, in my admonisher at Eton, in the destroyer of my honour at Oxford, in him who thwarted my ambition at Rome, my revenge in Paris, my passionate love at Naples, or what he falsely termed my avarice in Egypt, that in this, my arch-enemy and evil genius, I could fail to recognize the William Wilson of my schoolboy days, the namesake, the companion, the rival, the hated and dreaded rival at Dr. Bransby's? Impossible!—But let me hasten to the last eventful scene of the drama.

Thus far I had succumbed supinely to this imperious domination. The sentiments of deep awe with which I habitually regarded the elevated character, the majestic wisdom, the apparent omnipresence and omnipotence of Wilson, added to a feeling of even terror, with which certain other traits in his nature and assumptions inspired me, had operated, hitherto, to impress me with an idea of my own utter weakness and helplessness, and to suggest an implicit, although bitterly reluctant submission to his arbitrary will. But, of late days, I had given myself up entirely to wine; and its maddening influency upon my hereditary temper rendered me more and more impatient of control. I began to murmur, to hesitate, to resist. And was it only fancy which induced me to believe that, with the increase of my own firmness, that of my tormentor underwent a proportional diminution? Be this as it may, I now began to feel the inspirations of a burning hope, and at length nurtured in my secret thoughts a stern and desperate resolution that I would submit no longer to be enslaved.

It was at Rome, during the carnival of 18—, that I attended a masquerade in the palazzo of the Neapolitan Duke Di Broglio. I had indulged more freely than usual in the excesses of the wine-table; and now the suffocating atmosphere of the crowded rooms irritated me beyond endurance. The difficulty, too, of forcing my way through the mazes of the company contributed not a little to the ruffling of my temper; for I was anxiously seeking, let me not say with what unworthy motive, the young, the gay, the beautiful wife of the aged and doting Di Broglio. With a too unscrupulous confidence she had previously communicated to me the secret of the costume in which she would be habited, and now, having caught a glimpse of her person, I was hurrying to make my way into her presence. At this moment I felt a light hand laid upon my shoulder, and that ever-remembered, low, damnable whisper within my ear.

In a perfect whirlwind of wrath, I turned at once upon him who had thus interrupted me, and seized him violently by the collar. He was attired, as I expected, like myself; wearing a large Spanish cloak, and a mask of black silk which entirely covered his features.

"Scoundrel!" I said, in a voice husky with rage, while every syllable I uttered seemed as new fuel to my fury, "scoundrel! impostor! accursed villain! you shall not—you *shall not* dog me unto death! Follow me, or I stab you where I stand," and I broke my way from the room into a small antechamber adjoining, dragging him unresistingly with me as I went.

Upon entering, I thrust him furiously from me. He staggered against the wall, while I closed the door with an oath, and commanded him to draw. He hesitated but for an instant, then, with a slight sigh, drew in silence, and put himself upon his defence.

The contest was brief indeed. I was frantic with every species of wild excitement, and felt within my single arm the energy and the power of a multitude. In a few seconds I forced him by sheer strength against the wainscoting, and thus, getting him at mercy, plunged my sword, with brute ferocity, repeatedly through and through his bosom.

At this instant some person tried the latch of the door. I hastened to prevent an intrusion, and then immediately returned to my dying antagonist. But what human language can adequately portray *that* astonishment, *that* horror which possessed me at the spectacle then presented to view. The brief moment in which I averted my eyes had been sufficient to produce, apparently, a material change in the arrangements at the upper or farther end of the room. A large mirror, it appeared to me, now stood where none had been perceptible before; and, as I stepped up to it in extremity of terror, mine own image, but with features all pale and dabbled in blood, advanced, with a feeble and tottering gait, to meet me.

Thus it appeared, I say, but was not. It was my antagonist—it was Wilson, who then stood before me in the agonies of his dissolution. Not a line in all the marked and singular lineaments of that face which was not, even identically, mine own! His mask and cloak lay, where he had thrown them, upon the floor.

It was Wilson, but he spoke no longer in a whisper, and I could have fancied that I myself was speaking while he said—

"*You have conquered, and I yield. Yet, henceforward art thou also dead— dead to the world and its hopes. In me didst thou exist—and, in my death, see by this image, which is thine, how utterly thou hast murdered thyself.*"

1839

# The Purloined Letter[1]

At Paris, just after dark one gusty evening in the autumn of 18—, I was enjoying the twofold luxury of meditation and a meerschaum, in company with my friend C. Auguste Dupin, in his little back library, or book-closet, *au troisiême,*[2] *No. 33, Rue Dunôt, Faubourg St. Germain.* For one hour at least we had maintained a profound silence; while each, to any casual observer, might have seemed intently and exclusively occupied with the curling eddies of smoke that oppressed the atmosphere of the chamber. For myself, however, I was mentally discussing certain topics which had formed matter for conversation between us at an earlier period of the evening; I mean the affair of the Rue Morgue, and the mystery attending the murder of Marie Roget. I looked upon it, therefore, as something of coincidence, when the door of our apartment was thrown open and admitted our old acquaintance, Monsieur G——, the Prefect of the Parisian police.

We gave him a hearty welcome; for there was nearly half as much of the entertaining as of the contemptible about the man, and we had not seen him for several years. We had been sitting in the dark, and Dupin now arose for the purpose of lighting a lamp, but sat down again, without doing so, upon G.'s saying that he had called to consult us, or rather to ask the opinion of my friend, about some official business which had occasioned a great deal of trouble.

"If it is any point requiring reflection," observed Dupin, as he forebore to enkindle the wick, "we shall examine it to better purpose in the dark."

"That is another of your odd notions," said the Prefect, who had a fashion of calling every thing "odd" that was beyond his comprehension, and thus lived amid an absolute legion of "oddities."

---

1. The text is that of the first publication in *The Gift,* a Philadelphia annual dated 1845 but for sale late in 1844. Historians of detective fiction usually cite Poe's three stories about C. Auguste Dupin as the first of the genre. This is the third Dupin story, the others being *The Murders in the Rue Morgue* (1841) and *The Mystery of Marie Rôget* (1842). Here the criminal is known from the beginning and the solution comes from Dupin's analytical powers. In *The Murders in the Rue Morgue,* however, Poe is at some pains to stress that Dupin's powers are not of mere "calculation," rather "the analyst throws himself into the spirit of his opponent, identifies himself therewith, and not unfre-

quently sees thus, at a glance, the sole methods (sometimes indeed absurdly simple ones) by which he may seduce into error or hurry into miscalculation."

2. Actually the fourth floor (because the French do not count the first, the *rez-de-chaussée*). In *The Murders in the Rue Morgue* the narrator describes his and Dupin's quarters, "a time-eaten and grotesque mansion, long deserted through superstitions," "tottering to its fall in a retired and desolate portion of the Faubourg St. Germain," but meanwhile furnished "in a style which suited the rather fantastic gloom" of their common temperament.

"Very true," said Dupin, as he supplied his visiter with a pipe, and rolled towards him a very comfortable chair.

"And what is the difficulty now?" I asked. "Nothing more in the assassination way, I hope?"

"Oh no; nothing of that nature. The fact is, the business is *very* simple indeed, and I make no doubt that we can manage it sufficiently well ourselves; but then I thought Dupin would like to hear the details of it, because it is so excessively *odd*."

"Simple and odd," said Dupin.

"Why, yes; and not exactly that, either. The fact is, we have all been a good deal puzzled because the affair *is* so simple, and yet baffles us altogether."

"Perhaps it is the very simplicity of the thing which puts you at fault," said my friend.

"What nonsense you *do* talk!" replied the Prefect, laughing heartily.

"Perhaps the mystery is a little *too* plain," said Dupin.

"Oh, good heavens! who ever heard of such an idea?"

"A little *too* self-evident."

"Ha! ha! ha!—ha! ha! ha!—ho! ho! ho!" roared out our visiter, profoundly amused, "oh, Dupin, you will be the death of me yet!"

"And what, after all, *is* the matter on hand?" I asked.

"Why, I will tell you," replied the Prefect, as he gave a long, steady, and contemplative puff, and settled himself in his chair. "I will tell you in a few words; but, before I begin, let me caution you that this is an affair demanding the greatest secrecy, and that I should most probably lose the position I now hold, were it known that I confided it to any one."

"Proceed," said I.

"Or not," said Dupin.

"Well, then; I have received personal information, from a very high quarter, that a certain document of the last importance, has been purloined from the royal apartments. The individual who purloined it is known; this beyond a doubt; he was seen to take it. It is known, also, that it still remains in his possession."

"How is this known?" asked Dupin.

"It is clearly inferred," replied the Prefect, "from the nature of the document, and from the non-appearance of certain results which would at once arise from its passing *out* of the robber's possession;—that is to say, from his employing it as he must design in the end to employ it."

"Be a little more explicit," I said.

"Well, I may venture so far as to say that the paper gives its holder a certain power in a certain quarter where such power is immensely valuable." The Prefect was fond of the cant of diplomacy.

"Still I do not quite understand," said Dupin.

"No? Well; the disclosure of the document to a third person, who shall be nameless, would bring in question the honour of a personage of most exalted station; and this fact gives the holder of the document an ascendancy over the illustrious personage whose honour and peace are so jeopardized."

"But this ascendancy," I interposed, "would depend upon the robber's knowledge of the loser's knowledge of the robber. Who would dare—"

"The thief," said G, "is the—Minister D——, who dares all things, those unbecoming as well as those becoming a man. The method of the theft was not less ingenious than bold. The document in question—a letter, to be frank—had been received by the personage robbed while alone in the royal *boudoir*. During its perusal she was suddenly interrupted by the entrance of the other exalted personage from whom especially it was her wish to conceal it. After a hurried and vain endeavour to thrust it in a drawer, she was forced to place it, open as it was, upon a table. The address, however, was uppermost, and the contents thus unexposed, the letter escaped notice. At this juncture enters the Minister D——. His lynx eye immediately perceives the paper, recognises the handwriting of the address, observes the confusion of the personage addressed, and fathoms her secret. After some business transactions, hurried through in his ordinary manner, he produces a letter somewhat similar to the one in question, opens it, pretends to read it, and then places it in close juxtaposition to the other. Again he converses, for some fifteen minutes, upon the public affairs. At length, in taking leave, he takes also from the table the letter to which he had no claim. Its rightful owner saw, but, of course, dared not call attention to the act, in the presence of the third personage who stood at her elbow. The minister decamped; leaving his own letter—one of no importance—upon the table."

"Here, then," said Dupin to me, "you have precisely what you demand to make the ascendancy complete—the robber's knowledge of the loser's knowledge of the robber."

"Yes," replied the Prefect; "and the power thus attained has, for some months past, been wielded, for political purposes, to a very dangerous extent. The personage robbed is more thoroughly convinced, every day, of the necessity of reclaiming her letter. But this, of course, cannot be done openly. In fine, driven to despair, she has committed the matter to me."

"Than whom," said Dupin, amid a perfect whirlwind of smoke, "no more sagacious agent could, I suppose, be desired, or even imagined."

"You flatter me," replied the Prefect; "but it is possible that some such opinion may have been entertained."

"It is clear," said I, "as you observe, that the letter is still in possession of the minister; since it is this possession, and not any employment, of the letter, which bestows the power. With the employment the power departs."

"True," said G——; "and upon this conviction I proceeded. My first care was to make thorough search of the minister's hotel; and here my chief embarrassment lay in the necessity of searching without his knowledge. Beyond all things, I have been warned of the danger which would result from giving him reason to suspect our design."

"But," said I, "you are quite *au fait*[3] in these investigations. The Parisian police have done this thing often before."

"O yes; and for this reason I did not despair. The habits of the minister gave me, too, a great advantage. He is frequently absent from home all night. His servants are by no means numerous. They sleep at a distance from their master's apartments, and, being chiefly Neapolitans, are readily made drunk. I have keys, as you know, with which I can open any chamber or cabinet in Paris. For three months a night has not passed, during the greater part of which I have not been engaged, personally, in ransacking the D—— Hotel. My honour is interested, and, to mention a great secret, the reward is enor-

3. At home, expert (French).

mous. So I did not abandon the search until I had become fully satisfied that the thief is a more astute man than myself. I fancy that I have investigated every nook and corner of the premises in which it is possible that the paper can be concealed."

"But is it not possible," I suggested, "that although the letter may be in possession of the minister, as it unquestionably is, he may have concealed it elsewhere than upon his own premises?"

"This is barely possible," said Dupin. "The present peculiar condition of affairs at court, and especially of those intrigues in which D—— is known to be involved, would render the instant availability of the document—its susceptibility of being produced at a moment's notice—a point of nearly equal importance with its possession."

"Its susceptibility of being produced?" said I.

"That is to say, of being *destroyed*," said Dupin.

"True," I observed; "the paper is clearly then upon the premises. As for its being upon the person of the minister, we may consider that as out of the question."

"Entirely," said the Prefect. "He has been twice waylaid, as if by footpads, and his person rigorously searched under my own inspection."

"You might have spared yourself this trouble," said Dupin. "D——, I presume, is not altogether a fool, and, if not, must have anticipated these waylayings, as a matter of course."

"Not *altogether* a fool," said G——, "but then he's a poet, which I take to be only one remove from a fool."

"True;" said Dupin, after a long and thoughtful whiff from his meerschaum, "although I have been guilty of certain doggerel myself."

"Suppose you detail," said I, "the particulars of your search."

"Why the fact is, we took our time, and we searched *every where*. I have had long experience in these affairs. I took the entire building, room by room; devoting the nights of a whole week to each. We examined, first, the furniture of each apartment. We opened every possible drawer; and I presume you know that, to a properly trained police agent, such a thing as a *secret* drawer is impossible. Any man is a dolt who permits a 'secret' drawer to escape him in a search of this kind. The thing is *so* plain. There is a certain amount of bulk—of space—to be accounted for in every cabinet. Then we have accurate rules. The fiftieth part of a line could not escape us. After the cabinets we took the chairs. The cushions we probed with the fine long needles you have seen me employ. From the tables we removed the tops."

"Why so?"

"Sometimes the top of a table, or other similarly arranged piece of furniture, is removed by the person wishing to conceal an article; then the leg is excavated, the article deposited within the cavity, and the top replaced. The bottoms and tops of bed-posts are employed in the same way."

"But could not the cavity be detected by sounding?" I asked.

"By no means, if, when the article is deposited, a sufficient wadding of cotton be placed around it. Besides, in our case, we were obliged to proceed without noise."

"But you could not have removed—you could not have taken to pieces *all* articles of furniture in which it would have been possible to make a deposit in the manner you mention. A letter may be compressed into a thin spiral roll, not differing much in shape or bulk from a large knitting-needle, and in this form it might be inserted into the rung of a chair, for example. You did not take to pieces all the chairs?"

"Certainly not; but we did better—we examined the rungs of every chair in the hotel, and, indeed, the jointings of every description of furniture, by the aid of a most powerful microscope.[4] Had there been any traces of recent disturbance we should not have failed to detect it *instanter*.[5] A single grain of gimlet-dust, or sawdust, for example, would have been as obvious as an apple. Any disorder in the glueing—any unusual gaping in the joints—would have sufficed to insure detection."

"Of course you looked to the mirrors, between the boards and the plates, and you probed the beds and the bed-clothes, as well as the curtains and carpets."

"That of course; and when we had absolutely completed every particle of the furniture in this way, then we examined the house itself. We divided its entire surface into compartments, which we numbered, so that none might be missed; then we scrutinized each individual square inch throughout the premises, including the two houses immediately adjoining, with the microscope, as before."

"The two houses adjoining!" I exclaimed; "you must have had a great deal of trouble."

"We had; but the reward offered is prodigious."

"You include the *grounds* about the houses?"

"All the grounds are paved with brick. They gave us comparatively little trouble. We examined the moss between the bricks, and found it undisturbed."

"And the roofs?"

"We surveyed every inch of the external surface, and probed carefully beneath every tile."

"You looked among D——'s papers, of course, and into the books of the library?"

"Certainly; we opened every package and parcel; we not only opened every book, but we turned over every leaf in each volume, not contenting ourselves with a mere shake, according to the fashion of some of our police officers. We also measured the thickness of every book-*cover*, with the most accurate admeasurement, and applied to them the most jealous scrutiny of the microscope. Had any of the bindings been recently meddled with, it would have been utterly impossible that the fact should have escaped observation. Some five or six volumes, just from the hands of the binder, we carefully probed, longitudinally, with the needles."

"You explored the floors beneath the carpets?"

"Beyond doubt. We removed every carpet, and examined the boards with the microscope."

"And the paper on the walls?"

"Yes."

"You looked into the cellars?"

"We did; and, as time and labour were no objects, we dug up every one of them to the depth of four feet."

4. I.e., a powerful magnifying glass.          5. Instantly.

"Then," I said, "you have been making a miscalculation, and the letter is *not* upon the premises, as you suppose."

"I fear you are right there," said the Prefect. "And now, Dupin, what would you advise me to do?"

"To make a thorough re-search of the premises."

"That is absolutely needless," replied G——. "I am not more sure that I breathe than I am that the letter is not at the Hotel."

"I have no better advice to give you," said Dupin. "You have, of course, an accurate description of the letter?"

"Oh yes!"—And here the Prefect, producing a memorandum-book, proceeded to read aloud a minute account of the internal, and especially of the external, appearance of the missing document. Soon after finishing the perusal of this description, he took his departure, more entirely depressed in spirits than I had ever known the good gentleman before.

In about a month afterwards he paid us another visit, and found us occupied very nearly as before. He took a pipe and a chair, and entered into some ordinary conversation. At length I said,—

"Well, but G——, what of the purloined letter? I presume you have at last made up your mind that there is no such thing as overreaching the Minister?"

"Confound him, say I—yes; I made the re-examination, however, as Dupin suggested—but it was all labour lost, as I knew it would be."

"How much was the reward offered, did you say?" asked Dupin.

"Why, a very great deal—a *very* liberal reward—I don't like to say how much, precisely; but one thing I *will* say, that I wouldn't mind giving my individual check for fifty thousand francs to any one who could obtain me that letter. The fact is, it is becoming of more and more importance every day; and the reward has been lately doubled. If it were trebled, however, I could do no more than I have done."

"Why, yes," said Dupin, drawlingly, between the whiffs of his meerschaum, "I really—think, G——, you have not exerted yourself—to the utmost in this matter. You might—do a little more, I think, eh?"

"How?—in what way?"

"Why—puff, puff—you might—puff, puff—employ counsel in the matter, eh?—puff, puff, puff. Do you remember the story they tell of Abernethy?"

"No; hang Abernethy!"

"To be sure! hang him and welcome. But, once upon a time, a certain rich miser conceived the design of spunging upon this Abernethy for a medical opinion. Getting up, for this purpose, an ordinary conversation in a private company, he insinuated his case to the physician, as that of an imaginary individual.

" 'We will suppose,' said the miser, 'that his symptoms are such and such; now, doctor, what would *you* have directed him to take?'

" 'Take!' said Abernethy, 'why, take *advice*, to be sure.' "

"But," said the Prefect, a little discomposed, "I am *perfectly* willing to take advice, and to pay for it. I would *really* give fifty thousand francs, every *centime* of it, to any one who would aid me in the matter!"

"In that case," replied Dupin, opening a drawer, and producing a check-book, "you may as well fill me up a check for the amount mentioned. When you have signed it, I will hand you the letter."

I was astounded. The Prefect appeared absolutely thunder-stricken. For some minutes he remained speechless and motionless, looking incredulously at my friend with open mouth, and eyes that seemed starting from their sockets; then, apparently recovering himself in some measure, he seized a pen, and after several pauses and vacant stares, finally filled up and signed a check for fifty thousand francs, and handed it across the table to Dupin. The latter examined it carefully and deposited it in his pocket-book; then, unlocking an *escritoire*,[6] took thence a letter and gave it to the Prefect. This functionary grasped it in a perfect agony of joy; opened it with a trembling hand, cast a rapid glance at its contents, and then, scrambling and struggling to the door, rushed at length unceremoniously from the room and from the house, without having uttered a solitary syllable since Dupin had requested him to fill up the check.

When he had gone, my friend entered into some explanations.

"The Parisian police," he said, "are exceedingly able in their way. They are persevering, ingenious, cunning, and thoroughly versed in the knowledge which their duties seem chiefly to demand. Thus when G—— detailed to us his mode of searching the premises at the Hotel D——, I felt the entire confidence in his having made a satisfactory investigation—so far as his labours extended."

"So far as his labours extended?" said I.

"Yes," said Dupin. "The measures adopted were not only the best of their kind, but carried out to absolute perfection. Had the letter been deposited within the range of their search, these fellows would, beyond a question, have found it."

I merely laughed—but he seemed quite serious in all that he said.

"The measures, then," he continued, "were good in their kind, and well executed; their defect lay in their being inapplicable to the case, and to the man. A certain set of highly ingenious resources are, with the Prefect, a sort of Procrustean bed,[7] to which he forcibly adapts his designs. But he perpetually errs by being too deep or too shallow, for the matter in hand; and many a schoolboy is a better reasoner than he. I knew one about eight years of age, whose success at guessing in the game of 'even and odd' attracted universal admiration. This game is simple, and is played with marbles. One player holds in his hand a number of these toys; and demands of another whether that number is even or odd. If the guess is right, the guesser wins one; if wrong, he loses one. The boy to whom I allude won all the marbles of the school. Of course he had some principle of guessing; and this lay in mere observation and admeasurement of the astuteness of his opponents. For example, an arrant simpleton is his opponent, and, holding up his closed hand, asks, 'are they even or odd?' Our schoolboy replies 'odd,' and loses; but upon the second trial he wins, for he then says to himself, 'the simpleton had them even upon the first trial, and his amount of cunning is just sufficient to make him have them odd upon the second; I will therefore guess odd;'—he guesses odd, and wins. Now, with a simpleton a degree above the first, he would have reasoned thus: 'this fellow finds that in the first instance I guessed odd, and, in the second, he will propose to himself, upon the first impulse, a simple variation from even to odd, as did the first simpleton; but then a second thought will suggest

---

6. Writing desk (French) now spelled *écritoire*.
7. Procrustes, legendary Greek bandit, made his victims fit the bed he bound them to, either by stretching

them to the required length or by hacking off any surplus length in the feet and legs.

that this is too simple a variation, and finally he will decide upon putting it even as before. I will therefore guess even;'—he guesses even, and wins. Now this mode of reasoning in the schoolboy, whom his fellows termed 'lucky,'—what, in its last analysis, is it?"

"It is merely," I said, "an identification of the reasoner's intellect with that of his opponent."

"It is," said Dupin; "and, upon inquiring of the boy by what means he effected the *thorough* identification in which his success consisted, I received answer as follows: 'When I wish to find out how wise, or how stupid, or how good, or how wicked is any one, or what are his thoughts at the moment, I fashion the expression of my face, as accurately as possible, in accordance with the expression of his, and then wait to see what thoughts or sentiments arise in my mind or heart, as if to match or correspond with the expression.' This response of the schoolboy lies at the bottom of all the spurious profundity which has been attributed to Rochefoucault, to La Bruyère, to Machiavelli, and to Campanella."[8]

"And the identification," I said, "of the reasoner's intellect with that of his opponent, depends, if I understand you aright, upon the accuracy with which the opponent's intellect is admeasured."

"For its practical value it depends upon this," replied Dupin; "and the Prefect and his cohort fail so frequently, first, by default of this identification, and, secondly, by ill-admeasurement, or rather through non-admeasurement, of the intellect with which they are engaged. They consider only their *own* ideas of ingenuity; and, in searching for any thing hidden, advert only to the modes in which *they* would have hidden it. They are right in this much—that their own ingenuity is a faithful representative of that of *the mass*; but when the cunning of the individual felon is diverse in character from their own, the felon foils them, of course. This always happens when it is above their own, and very usually when it is below. They have no variation of principle in their investigations; at best, when urged by some unusual emergency—by some extraordinary reward—they extend or exaggerate their old modes of *practice*, without touching their principles. What, for example, in this case of D———, has been done to vary the principle of action? What is all this boring, and probing, and sounding, and scrutinizing with the microscope, and dividing the surface of the building into registered square inches—what is it all but an exaggeration *of the application* of the one principle or set of principles of search, which are based upon the one set of notions regarding human ingenuity, to which the Prefect, in the long routine of his duty, has been accustomed? Do you not see he has taken it for granted that *all* men proceed to conceal a letter,—not exactly in a gimlet-hole bored in a chair-leg—but, at least, in *some* out-of-the-way hole or corner suggested by the same tenor of thought which would urge a man to secrete a letter in a gimlet-hole bored in a chair-leg? And do you not see also, that such *recherches*[9] nooks for concealment are adapted only for ordinary occasions, and would be adopted only by ordinary intellects; for, in all cases of concealment, a disposal of the article concealed—a disposal of it in this *recherché* manner,—is, in the very first instance, presumed and presumable; and thus its discovery depends, not at all upon the

8. An oddly assorted group of moralists and political and religious philosophers, all denigrated by Dupin. The original reads "La Bougive," probably a printer's

error.

9. Out of the ordinary, esoteric (French) then permissible without the acute accent or with it, as just below.

acumen, but altogether upon the mere care, patience, and determination of the seekers; and where the case is of importance—or, what amounts to the same thing in the policial eyes, when the reward is of magnitude, the qualities in question have *never* been known to fail. You will now understand what I meant in suggesting that, had the purloined letter been hidden any where within the limits of the Prefect's examination—in other words, had the principle of its concealment been comprehended within the principles of the Prefect—its discovery would have been a matter altogether beyond question. This functionary, however, has been thoroughly mystified; and the remote source of his defeat lies in the supposition that the Minister is a fool, because he has acquired renown as a poet. All fools are poets; this the Prefect *feels*; and he is merely guilty of a *non distributio medii*[1] in thence inferring that all poets are fools."

"But is this really the poet?" I asked. "There are two brothers, I know; and both have attained reputation in letters. The Minister I believe has written learnedly on the Differential Calculus. He is a mathematician, and no poet."

"You are mistaken; I know him well; he is both. As poet *and* mathematician, he would reason well; as poet, profoundly; as mere mathematician, he could not have reasoned at all, and thus would have been at the mercy of the Prefect."

"You surprise me," I said, "by these opinions, which have been contradicted by the voice of the world. You do not mean to set at naught the well-digested idea of centuries. The mathematical reason has been long regarded as *the* reason *par excellence.*"

" 'Il y a à parièr,' replied Dupin, quoting from Chamfort, 'que toute idée publique, toute convention reçue, est une sottise, car elle a convenue au plus grand nombre.'[2] The mathematicians, I grant you, have done their best to promulgate the popular error to which you allude, and which is none the less an error for its promulgation as truth. With an art worthy a better cause, for example, they have insinuated the term 'analyis' into application to algebra. The French are the originators of this particular deception; but if a term is of any importance—if words derive any value from applicability—then 'analysis' conveys 'algebra' about as much as, in Latin, *'ambitus'* implies 'ambition,' *'religio'* 'religion,' or *'homines honesti,'* a set of *honourable* men."

"You have a quarrel on hand, I see," said I, "with some of the algebraists of Paris; but proceed."

"I dispute the availability, and thus the value, of that reason which is cultivated in any especial form other than the abstractly logical. I dispute, in particular, the reason educed by mathematical study. The mathematics are the science of form and quantity; mathematical reasoning is merely logic applied to observation upon form and quantity. The great error lies in supposing that even the truths of what is called *pure* algebra, are abstract or general truths. And this error is so egregious that I am confounded at the universality with which it has been received. Mathematical axioms are *not* axioms of general truth. What is true of *relation*—of form and quantity—is often grossly false in regard to morals, for example. In this latter science it is very usually *un*true

---

1. A fallacy in logic in which neither premise of a syllogism "distributes" (i.e., conveys information about every member of the class) the middle term. According to Dupin, the Prefect does not allow for the possibility that some poets are not fools.

2. The odds are that every common notion, every accepted convention, is nonsense, precisely because it has suited itself to the majority (French). Sébastian Roch Nicolas Chamfort (1741–1794), author of *Maximes et Pensées.*

that the aggregated parts are equal to the whole. In chemistry also the axiom fails. In the consideration of motive it fails; for two motives, each of a given value, have not, necessarily, a value when united, equal to the sum of their values apart. There are numerous other mathematical truths which are only truths within the limits of *relation*. But the mathematician argues, from his *finite truths*, through habit, as if they were of absolutely general applicability— as the world indeed imagines them to be. Bryant,[3] in his very learned 'Mythology,' mentions an analogous source of error, when he says that 'although the Pagan fables are not believed, yet we forget ourselves continually, and make inferences from them as existing realities.' With the algebraist, however, who are Pagans themselves, the 'Pagan fables' *are* believed, and the inferences are made, not so much through lapse of memory, as through an unaccountable addling of the brains. In short, I never yet encountered the mere mathematician who could be trusted out of equal roots, or one who did not clandestinely hold it as a point of his faith $x^2 + px$ was absolutely and unconditionally equal to $q$. Say to one of these gentlemen, by way of experiment, if you please, that you believe occasions may occur where $x^2 + px$ is *not* altogether equal to $q$, and, having made him understand what you mean, get out of his reach as speedily as convenient, for, beyond doubt, he will endeavour to knock you down.

"I mean to say," continued Dupin, while I merely laughed at his last observations, "that if the Minister had been no more than a mathematician, the Prefect would have been under no necessity of giving me this check. Had he been no more than a poet, I think it probable that he would have foiled us all. I knew him, however, as both mathematician and poet, and my measures were adapted to his capacity, with reference to the circumstances by which he was surrounded. I knew him as a courtier, too, and as a bold *intriguant*. Such a man, I considered, could not fail to be aware of the ordinary policial modes of action. He could not have failed to anticipate—and events have proved that he did not fail to anticipate—the waylayings to which he was subjected. He must have foreseen, I reflected, the secret investigations of his premises. His frequent absences from home at night, which were hailed by the Prefect as certain aids to his success, I regarded only as *ruses*, to afford opportunity for thorough search to the police, and thus the sooner to impress them with the conviction to which G——, in fact, did finally arrive—the conviction that the letter was not upon the premises. I felt, also, that the whole train of thought, which I was at some pains in detailing to you just now, concerning the invariable principle of policial action in searches for articles concealed—I felt that this whole train of thought would necessarily pass through the mind of the Minister. It would imperatively lead him to despise all the ordinary *nooks* of concealment. *He* could not, I reflected, be so weak as not to see that the most intricate and remote recess of his hotel would be as open as his commonest closets to the eyes, to the probes, to the gimlets, and to the microscopes of the Prefect. I saw, in fine, that he would be driven, as a matter of course, to *simplicity*, if not deliberately induced to it as a matter of choice. You will remember, perhaps how desperately the Prefect laughed when I suggested, upon our first interview, that it was just possible this mystery troubled him so much on account of its being so *very* self-evident."

---

3. Jacob Bryant (1715–1804), English scholar who wrote *A New System, or an Analysis of Antient Mythology* (1774–76).

"Yes," said I, "I remember his merriment well. I really thought he would have fallen into convulsions."

"The material world," continued Dupin, "abounds with very strict analogies to the immaterial; and thus some colour of truth has been given to the rhetorical dogma, that metaphor, or simile, may be made to strengthen an argument, as well as to embellish a description. The principle of the *vis inertiæ*,[4] for example, with the amount of *momentum* proportionate with it and consequent upon it, seems to be identical in physics and metaphysics. It is not more true in the former, that a large body is with more difficulty set in motion than a smaller one, and that its subsequent *impetus* is commensurate with this difficulty, than it is, in the latter, that intellects of the vaster capacity, while more forcible, more constant, and more eventful in their movements than those of inferior grade, are yet the less readily moved, and more embarrassed and full of hesitation in the first few steps of their progress. Again: have you ever noticed which of the street signs, over the shop-doors, are the most attractive of attention?"

"I have never given the matter a thought," I said.

"There is a game of puzzles," he resumed, "which is played upon a map. One party playing requires another to find a given word—the name of town, river, state, or empire—any word, in short, upon the motley and perplexed surface of the chart. A novice in the game generally seeks to embarrass his opponents by giving them the most minutely lettered names; but the adept selects such words as stretch, in large characters, from one end of the chart to the other. These, like the over-largely lettered signs and placards of the street, escape observation by dint of being excessively obvious; and here the physical oversight is precisely analogous with the moral inapprehension by which the intellect suffers to pass unnoticed those considerations which are too obtrusively and too palpably self-evident. But this is a point, it appears, somewhat above or beneath the understanding of the Prefect. He never once thought it probable, or possible, that the Minister had deposited the letter immediately beneath the nose of the whole world, by way of best preventing any portion of that world from perceiving it.

"But the more I reflected upon the daring, dashing, and discriminating ingenuity of D——; upon the fact that the document must always have been *at hand*, if he intended to use it to good purpose; and upon the decisive evidence, obtained by the Prefect, that it was not hidden within the limits of that dignitary's ordinary search—the more satisfied I became that, to conceal this letter, the Minister had resorted to the comprehensive and sagacious expedient of not attempting to conceal it at all.

"Full of these ideas, I prepared myself with a pair of green spectacles, and called one fine morning, quite by accident, at the ministerial hotel. I found D—— at home, yawning, lounging, and dawdling as usual, and pretending to be in the last extremity of *ennui*.[5] He is, perhaps, the most really energetic human being now alive—but that is only when nobody sees him.

"To be even with him, I complained of my weak eyes, and lamented the necessity of the spectacles, under cover of which I cautiously and thoroughly surveyed the whole apartment, while seemingly intent only upon the conversation of my host.

---

4. The power of inertia (Latin).                   5. Boredom (French).

"I paid especial attention to a large writing-table near which he sat, and upon which lay confusedly, some miscellanous letters and other papers, with one or two musical instruments and a few books. Here, however, after a long and very deliberate scrutiny, I saw nothing to excite particular suspicion.

"At length my eyes, in going the circuit of the room, fell upon a trumpery fillagree card-rack of pasteboard, that hung dangling by a dirty blue riband, from a little brass knob just beneath the middle of the mantel-piece. In this rack, which had three or four compartments, were five or six visiting-cards, and a solitary letter. This last was much soiled and crumpled. It was torn nearly in two, across the middle—as if a design, in the first instance, to tear it entirely up as worthless, had been altered, or stayed, in the second. It had a large black seal, bearing the D—— cipher *very* conspicuously, and was addressed, in a diminutive female hand, to D——, the minister himself. It was thrust carelessly, and even, as it seemed, contemptuously, into one of the uppermost divisions of the rack.

"No sooner had I glanced at this letter, than I concluded it to be that of which I was in search. To be sure, it was, to all appearance, radically different from the one of which the Prefect had read us so minute a description. Here the seal was large and black, with the D—— cipher; there, it was small and red, with the ducal arms of the S—— family. Here, the address, to the minister, was diminutive and feminine; there, the superscription, to a certain royal personage, was markedly bold and decided; the size alone formed a point of correspondence. But, then, the *radicalness* of these differences, which was excessive; the dirt, the soiled and torn condition of the paper, so inconsistent with the *true* methodical habits of D——, and so suggestive of a design to delude the beholder into an idea of the worthlessness of the document; these things, together with the hyper-obtrusive situation of this document, full in the view of every visiter, and thus exactly in accordance with the conclusions to which I had previously arrived; these things, I say, were strongly corroborative of suspicion, in one who came with the intention to suspect.

"I protracted my visit as long as possible, and, while I maintained a most animated discussion with the minister, upon a topic which I knew well had never failed to interest and excite him, I kept my attention really riveted upon the letter. In this examination, I committed to memory its external appearance and arrangement in the rack; and also fell, at length, upon a discovery which set at rest whatever trivial doubt I might have entertained. In scrutinizing the edges of the paper, I observed them to be more *chafed* than seemed necessary. They presented the *broken* appearance which is manifested when a stiff paper, having been once folded and pressed with a folder, is refolded in a reversed direction, in the same creases or edges which had formed the original fold. This discovery was sufficient. It was clear to me that the letter had been turned, as a glove, inside out, re-directed, and re-sealed. I bade the minister good morning and took my departure at once, leaving a gold snuff-box upon the table.

"The next morning I called for the snuff-box, when we resumed, quite eagerly, the conversation of the preceding day. While thus engaged, however, a loud report, as if of a pistol, was heard immediately beneath the windows of the hotel, and was succeeded by a series of fearful screams, and the shoutings of a terrified mob. D—— rushed to a casement, threw it open, and looked out. In the meantime, I stepped to the card-rack, took the letter, put it in my pocket, and replaced it by a *fac-simile*, which I had carefully prepared at my lodgings—imitating the D—— cipher, very readily, by means of a seal formed of bread.

"The disturbance in the street had been occasioned by the frantic behaviour of a man with a musket. He had fired it among a crowd of women and children. It proved, however, to have been without ball, and the fellow was suffered to go his way as a lunatic or a drunkard. When he had gone, D—— came from the window, whither I had followed him immediately upon securing the object in view. Soon afterwards I bade him farewell. The pretended lunatic was a man in my own pay."

"But what purpose had you," I asked, "in replacing the letter by a *fac-simile*? Would it not have been better, at the first visit, to have seized it openly, and departed?"

"D——," replied Dupin, "is a desperate man, and a man of nerve. His hotel, too, is not without attendants devoted to his interests. Had I made the wild attempt you suggest, I should never have left the ministerial presence alive. The good people of Paris would have heard of me no more. But I had an object apart from these considerations. You know my political prepossessions. In this matter, I act as a partisan of the lady concerned. For eighteen months the minister has had her in his power. She has now him in hers— since, being unaware that the letter is not in his possession, he will proceed with his exactions as if it was. Thus will he inevitably commit himself, at once, to his political destruction. His downfall, too, will not be more precipitate than awkward. It is all very well to talk about the *facilis descensus Averni*;[6] but in all kinds of climbing, as Catalini[7] said of singing, it is far more easy to get up than to come down. In the present instance I have no sympathy—at least no pity for him who descends. He is that *monstrum horrendum*,[8] an unprincipled man of genius. I confess, however, that I should like very well to know the precise character of his thoughts, when, being defied by her whom the Prefect terms 'a certain personage,' he is reduced to opening the letter which I left for him in the card-rack."

"How? did you put any thing particular in it?"

"Why—it did not seem altogether right to leave the interior blank—that would have been insulting. To be sure, D——, at Vienna once, did me an evil turn, which I told him, quite good-humouredly, that I should remember. So, as I knew he would feel some curiosity in regard to the identity of the person who had outwitted him, I thought it a pity not to give him a clue. He is well acquainted with my MS., and I just copied into the middle of the blank sheet the words—

" '——Un dessein si funeste,
S'il n'est digne d'Atrée, est digne de Thyeste.'

They are to be found in Crébillon's 'Atrée.' "[9]

1844

---

6. Slightly misquoted from Virgil's *Aeneid* book 6: "The descent to Avernus [Hell] is easy."
7. Angelica Catalani (1780-1849), Italian singer.
8. "Dreadful monstrosity" (Virgil's epithet for Polyphemus, the one-eyed man-eating giant).
9. Prosper Jolyot de Crébillon wrote *Atrée et Thyeste* (1707), in which Thyestes seduces the wife of his brother Atreus, the king of Mycenae; in revenge Atreus murders the sons of Thyestes and serves them to their father at a feast. The quotation reads: So baneful a scheme, if not worthy of Atreus, is worthy of Thyestes (French).

# The Cask of Amontillado[1]

The thousand injuries of Fortunato I had borne as I best could, but when he ventured upon insult I vowed revenge. You, who so well know the nature of my soul, will not suppose, however, that I gave utterance to a threat. At *length* I would be avenged; this was a point definitively settled—but the very definitiveness with which it was resolved precluded the idea of risk. I must not only punish but punish with impunity. A wrong is unredressed when retribution overtakes its redresser. It is equally unredressed when the avenger fails to make himself felt as such to him who has done the wrong.

It must be understood that neither by word nor deed had I given Fortunato cause to doubt my good will. I continued, as was my wont, to smile in his face, and he did not perceive that my smile *now* was at the thought of his immolation.

He had a weak point—this Fortunato—although in other regards he was a man to be respected and even feared. He prided himself upon his connoisseurship in wine. Few Italians have the true virtuoso spirit. For the most part their enthusiasm is adopted to suit the time and opportunity, to practice imposture upon the British and Austrian *millionaires*. In painting and gemmary, Fortunato, like his countrymen, was a quack, but in the matter of old wines he was sincere. In this respect I did not differ from him materially;—I was skilful in the Italian vintages myself, and bought largely whenever I could.

It was about dusk, one evening during the supreme madness of the carnival season, that I encountered my friend. He accosted me with excessive warmth, for he had been drinking much. The man wore motley.[2] He had on a tight-fitting parti-striped dress, and his head was surmounted by the conical cap and bells. I was so pleased to see him that I thought I should never have done wringing his hand.

I said to him—"My dear Fortunato, you are luckily met. How remarkably well you are looking to-day. But I have received a pipe of what passes for Amontillado,[3] and I have my doubts."

"How?" said he. "Amontillado? A pipe? Impossible! And in the middle of the carnival!"

"I have my doubts," I replied; "and I was silly enough to pay the full Amontillado price without consulting you in the matter. You were not to be found, and I was fearful of losing a bargain."

"Amontillado!"

"I have my doubts."

"Amontillado!"

"And I must satisfy them."

"Amontillado!"

"As you are engaged, I am on my way to Luchresi. If any one has a critical turn it is he. He will tell me——"

"Luchresi cannot tell Amontillado from Sherry."

"And yet some fools will have it that his taste is a match for your own."

"Come, let us go."

"Whither?"

"To your vaults."

---

1. The text is that of the first publication, in *Godey's Magazine and Lady's Book* 33 (November 1846).

2. Fool's varicolored costume.

3. A light Spanish sherry. "Pipe": a large barrel.

"My friend, no; I will not impose upon your good nature. I perceive you have an engagement. Luchresi——"

"I have no engagement;—come."

"My friend, no. It is not the engagement, but the severe cold with which I perceive you are afflicted. The vaults are insufferably damp. They are encrusted with nitre."[4]

"Let us go, nevertheless. The cold is merely nothing. Amontillado! You have been imposed upon. And as for Luchresi, he cannot distinguish Sherry from Amontillado."

Thus speaking, Fortunato possessed himself of my arm; and putting on a mask of black silk and drawing a *roquelaire*[5] closely about my person, I suffered him to hurry me to my palazzo.

There were no attendants at home; they had absconded to make merry in honour of the time. I had told them that I should not return until the morning, and had given them explicit orders not to stir from the house. These orders were sufficient, I well knew, to insure their immediate disappearance, one and all, as soon as my back was turned.

I took from their sconces two flambeaux, and giving one to Fortunato, bowed him through several suites of rooms to the archway that led into the vaults. I passed down a long and winding staircase, requesting him to be cautious as he followed. We came at length to the foot of the descent, and stood together upon the damp ground of the catacombs of the Montresors.

The gait of my friend was unsteady, and the bells upon his cap jingled as he strode.

"The pipe," said he.

"It is farther on," said I; "but observe the white web-work which gleams from these cavern walls."

He turned towards me, and looked into my eyes with two filmy orbs that distilled the rheum of intoxication.

"Nitre?" he asked, at length.

"Nitre," I replied. "How long have you had that cough?"

"Ugh! ugh! ugh!—ugh! ugh! ugh!—ugh! ugh !ugh!—ugh! ugh! ugh!—ugh! ugh! ugh!"

My poor friend found it impossible to reply for many minutes.

"It is nothing," he said, at last.

"Come," I said, with decision, "we will go back; your health is precious. You are rich, respected, admired, beloved; you are happy, as once I was. You are a man to be missed. For me it is no matter. We will go back; you will be ill, and I cannot be responsible. Besides, there is Luchresi——"

"Enough," he said; "the cough is a mere nothing; it will not kill me. I shall not die of a cough."

"True—true," I replied; "and, indeed, I had no intention of alarming you unneccessarily—but you should use all proper caution. A draught of this Medoc[6] will defend us from the damps."

Here I knocked off the neck of a bottle which I drew from a long row of its fellows that lay upon the mould.

"Drink," I said, presenting him the wine.

4. Saltpeter, the whitish mineral potassium nitrate.      6. A claret from near Bordeaux.
5. A knee-length cloak.

He raised it to his lips with a leer. He paused and nodded to me familiarly, while his bells jingled.

"I drink," he said, "to the buried that repose around us."

"And I to your long life."

He again took my arm, and we proceeded.

"These vaults," he said, "are extensive."

"The Montresors," I replied, "were a great and numerous family."

"I forget your arms."

"A huge human foot d'or, in a field azure; the foot crushes a serpent rampant whose fangs are imbedded in the heel."[7]

"And the motto?"

"*Nemo me impune lacessit.*"[8]

"Good!" he said.

The wine sparkled in his eyes and the bells jingled. My own fancy grew warm with the Medoc. We had passed through long walls of piled skeletons, with casks and puncheons intermingling, into the inmost recesses of the catacombs. I paused again, and this time I made bold to seize Fortunato by an arm above the elbow.

"The nitre!" I said; "see, it increases. It hangs like moss upon the vaults. We are below the river's bed. The drops of moisture trickle among the bones. Come, we will go back ere it is too late. Your cough——"

"It is nothing," he said; "let us go on. But first, another draught of the Medoc."

I broke and reached him a flaçon of De Grâve.[9] He emptied it at a breath. His eyes flashed with a fierce light. He laughed and threw the bottle upwards with a gesticulation I did not understand.

I looked at him in surprise. He repeated the movement—a grotesque one.

"You do not comprehend?" he said.

"Not I," I replied.

"Then you are not of the brotherhood."

"How?"

"You are not of the masons."

"Yes, yes," I said; "yes, yes."

"You? Impossible! A mason?"

"A mason," I replied.

"A sign," he said, "a sign."

"It is this," I answered, producing from beneath the folds of my *roquelaire* a trowel.

"You jest," he exclaimed, recoiling a few paces. "But let us proceed to the Amontillado."

"Be it so," I said, replacing the tool beneath the cloak and again offering him my arm. He leaned upon it heavily. We continued our rout in search of the Amontillado. We passed through a range of low arches, descended, passed on, and descending again, arrived at a deep crypt, in which the foulness of the air caused our flambeaux rather to glow than flame.

At the most remote end of the crypt there appeared another less spacious. Its walls had been lined with human remains, piled to the vault overhead, in

---

7. On the coat of arms the golden foot is in a blue background; the foot crushes a serpent whose head is reared up.　　8. No one insults me with impunity (Latin).　　9. A white Bordeaux wine.

the fashion of the great catacombs of Paris. Three sides of this interior crypt
were still ornamented in this manner. From the fourth side the bones had
been thrown down, and lay promiscuously upon the earth, forming at one
point a mound of some size. Within the wall thus exposed by the displacing
of the bones, we perceived a still interior crypt or recess, in depth about four
feet, in width three, in height six or seven. It seemed to have been constructed
for no especial use within itself, but formed merely the interval between two
of the colossal supports of the roof of the catacombs, and was backed by one
of their circumscribing walls of solid granite.

It was in vain that Fortunato, uplifting his dull torch, endeavoured to pry
into the depth of the recess. Its termination the feeble light did not enable us
to see.

"Proceed," I said; "herein is the Amontillado. As for Luchresi——"

"He is an ignoramus," interrupted my friend, as he stepped unsteadily forward, while I followed immediately at his heels. In an instant he had reached
the extremity of the niche, and finding his progress arrested by the rock, stood
stupidly bewildered. A moment more and I had fettered him to the granite.
In its surface were two iron staples, distant from each other about two feet,
horizontally. From one of these depended a short chain, from the other a
padlock. Throwing the links about his waist, it was but the work of a few
seconds to secure it. He was too much astounded to resist. Withdrawing the
key I stepped back from the recess.

"Pass your hand," I said, "over the wall; you cannot help feeling the nitre.
Indeed, it is *very* damp. Once more let me *implore* you to return. No? Then I
must positively leave you. But I will first render you all the little attentions in
my power."

"The Amontillado!" ejaculated my friend, not yet recovered from his
astonishment.

"True," I replied; "the Amontillado."

As I said these words I busied myself among the pile of bones of which I
have before spoken. Throwing them aside, I soon uncovered a quantity of
building stone and mortar. With these materials and with the aid of my trowel,
I began vigorously to wall up the entrance of the niche.

I had scarcely laid the first tier of the masonry when I discovered that the
intoxication of Fortunato had in great measure worn off. The earliest indication I had of this was a low moaning cry from the depth of the recess. It was
*not* the cry of a drunken man. There was then a long and obstinate silence. I
laid the second tier, and the third, and the fourth; and then I heard the furious
vibration of the chain. The noise lasted for several minutes, during which,
that I might hearken to it with the more satisfaction, I ceased my labours and
sat down upon the bones. When at last the clanking subsided, I resumed the
trowel, and finished without interruption the fifth, the sixth, and the seventh
tier. The wall was now nearly upon a level with my breast. I again paused,
and holding the flambeaux over the mason-work, threw a few feeble rays upon
the figure within.

A succession of loud and shrill screams, bursting suddenly from the throat
of the chained form, seemed to thrust me violently back. For a brief moment
I hesitated, I trembled. Unsheathing my rapier, I began to grope with it about
the recess; but the thought of an instant reassured me. I placed my hand upon
the solid fabric of the catacombs and felt satisfied. I reapproached the wall. I

replied to the yells of him who clamoured. I re-echoed, I aided, I surpassed them in volume and in strength. I did this, and the clamourer grew still. It was now midnight, and my task was drawing to a close. I had completed the eighth, the ninth and the tenth tier. I had finished a portion of the last and the eleventh; there remained but a single stone to be fitted and plastered in. I struggled with its weight; I placed it partially in its destined position. But now there came from out the niche a low laugh that erected the hairs upon my head. It was succeeded by a sad voice, which I had difficulty in recognizing as that of the noble Fortunato. The voice said—

"Ha! ha! ha!—he! he! he!—a very good joke, indeed—an excellent jest. We will have many a rich laugh about it at the palazzo—he! he! he!—over our wine—he! he! he!"

"The Amontillado!" I said.

"He! he! he!—he! he! he!—yes, the Amontillado. But is it not getting late? Will not they be awaiting us at the palazzo—the Lady Fortunato and the rest? Let us be gone."

"Yes," I said, "let us be gone."

"*For the love of God, Montresor!*"

"Yes," I said, "for the love of God!"

But to these words I hearkened in vain for a reply. I grew impatient. I called aloud—

"Fortunato!"

No answer. I called again—

"Fortunato!"

No answer still. I thrust a torch through the remaining aperture and let it fall within. There came forth in return only a jingling of the bells. My heart grew sick; it was the dampness of the catacombs that made it so. I hastened to make an end of my labour. I forced the last stone into its position; I plastered it up. Against the new masonry I re-erected the old rampart of bones. For the half of a century no mortal has disturbed them. *In pace requiescat!*[1]

1846

# [Reviews of Hawthorne's *Twice-Told Tales*][1]

## [*April*]

TWICE-TOLD TALES BY NATHANIEL HAWTHORNE.
JAMES MUNROE & CO.: BOSTON

We have always regarded the *Tale* (using this word in its popular acceptation) as affording the best prose opportunity for display of the highest talent. It has peculiar advantages which the novel does not admit. It is, of course, a far finer field than the essay. It has even points of superiority over the poem. An accident has deprived us, this month, of our customary space for review; and

1. May he rest in peace! (Latin).
1. Reprinted here are Poe's six-paragraph notice of *Twice-Told Tales* in *Graham's Magazine* 20 (April 1842), 254, and his longer essay in the same magazine the next month, 298–300. The second installment contains Poe's now-famous discussion of the way tales are or should be composed, with the desired effect chosen before incidents are invented. The theory as applied to poetry is exemplified in *The Philosophy of Composition*. A reworking of the *Graham's* material was published in *Godey's Lady's Book* for November 1847.

thus nipped in the bud a design long cherished of treating this subject in detail; taking Mr. Hawthorne's volumes as a text. In May we shall endeavor to carry out our intention. At present we are forced to be brief.

With rare exception—in the case of Mr. Irving's "Tales of a Traveller"[2] and a few other works of a like cast—we have had no American tales of high merit. We have had no skilful compositions—nothing which could bear examination as works of art. Of twattle called tale-making we have had, perhaps, more than enough. We have had a superabundance of the Rosa-Matilda effusions—gilt-edged papers all *couleur de rose:*[3] a full allowance of cut-and-thrust blue-blazing melodramaticisms; a nauseating surfeit of low miniature copying of low life, much in the manner, and with about half the merit, of the Dutch herrings and decayed cheeses of Van Tuyssel[4]—of all this, *eheu jam satis!*[5]

Mr. Hawthorne's volumes appear to us misnamed in two respects. In the first place they should not have been called "Twice-Told Tales"—for this is a title which will not bear *repetition.* If in the first collected edition they were twice-told, of course now they are thrice told.—May we live to hear them told a hundred times! In the second place, these compositions are by no means *all* "Tales." The most of them are essays properly so called. It would have been wise in their author to have modified his title, so as to have had reference to all included. This point could have been easily arranged.

But under whatever titular blunders we receive this book, it is most cordially welcome. We have seen no prose composition by any American which can compare with *some* of these articles in the higher merits, or indeed in the lower; while there is not a single piece which would do dishonor to the best of the British essayists.

"The Rill from the Town Pump" which, through the *ad captandum*[6] nature of its title, has attracted more of public notice than any one other of Mr. Hawthorne's compositions, is perhaps the *least* meritorious. Among his best, we may briefly mention "The Hollow of the Three Hills;" "The Minister's Black Veil;" "Wakefield;" "Mr. Higginbotham's Catastrophe;" "Fancy's Show-Box;" "Dr. Heidegger's Experiment;" "David Swan;" "The Wedding Knell;" and "The White Old Maid." It is remarkable that all these, with one exception, are from the first volume.

The style of Mr. Hawthorne is purity itself. His *tone* is singularly effective—wild, plaintive, thoughtful, and in full accordance with his themes. We have only to object that there is insufficient diversity in these themes themselves, or rather in their character. His *originality* both of incident and of reflection is very remarkable; and this trait alone would ensure him at least *our* warmest regard and commendation. We speak here chiefly of the tales; the essays are not so markedly novel. Upon the whole we look upon him as one of the few men of indisputable genius to whom our country has as yet given birth. As such, it will be our delight to do him honor; and lest, in these undigested and cursory remarks, without proof and without explanation, we should appear to do him *more* honor than is his due, we postpone all farther comment until a more favorable opportunity.

1842

2. This 1824 collection is normally thought inferior to Irving's earlier *Sketch Book* (1819–20) and *Bracebridge Hall* (1822), but its gothic stories such as *Adventure of the German Student* may have especially appealed to Poe.

3. Rose-colored (Latin).
4. A minor Dutch painter.
5. Ugh, enough of this!
6. Deliberately pleasing (Latin).

[*May*]

TWICE-TOLD TALES NATHANIEL HAWTHORNE. TWO VOLUMES.
BOSTON: JAMES MUNROE AND CO.

We said a few hurried words about Mr. Hawthorne in our last number, with the design of speaking more fully in the present. We are still, however, pressed for room, and must necessarily discuss his volumes more briefly and more at random than their high merits deserve.

The book professes to be a collection of *tales*, yet is, in two respects, misnamed. These pieces are now in their third republication, and, of course, are thrice-told. Moreover, they are by no means *all* tales, either in the ordinary or in the legitimate understanding of the term. Many of them are pure essays, for example, "Sights from a Steeple," "Sunday at Home," "Little Annie's Ramble," "A Rill from the Town-Pump," "The Toll-Gatherer's Day," "The Haunted Mind," "The Sister Years," "Snow-Flakes," "Night Sketches," and "Foot-Prints on the Sea-Shore." We mention these matters chiefly on account of their discrepancy with that marked precision and finish by which the body of the work is distinguished.

Of the Essays just named, we must be content to speak in brief. They are each and all beautiful, without being characterised by the polish and adaptation so visible in the tales proper. A painter would at once note their leading or predominant feature, and style it *repose*. There is no attempt at effect. All is quiet, thoughtful, subdued. Yet this repose may exist simultaneously with high originality of thought; and Mr. Hawthorne has demonstrated the fact. At every turn we meet with novel combinations; yet these combinations never surpass the limits of the quiet. We are soothed as we read; and withal is a calm astonishment that ideas so apparently obvious have never occurred or been presented to us before. Herein our author differs materially from Lamb or Hunt or Hazlitt—who, with vivid originality of manner and expression, have less of the true novelty of thought than is generally supposed, and whose originality, at best, has an uneasy and meretricious quaintness, replete with startling effects unfounded in nature, and inducing trains of reflection which lead to no satisfactory result. The Essays of Hawthorne have much of the character of Irving,[7] with more of originality, and less of finish; while, compared with the Spectator, they have a vast superiority at all points.[8] The Spectator, Mr. Irving, and Mr. Hawthorne have in common that tranquil and subdued manner which we have chosen to denominate *repose*; but, in the case of the two former, this repose is attained rather by the absence of novel combination, or of originality, than otherwise, and consists chiefly in the calm, quiet, unostentatious expression of commonplace thoughts, in an unambitious unadulterated Saxon. In them, by strong effort, we are made to conceive the absence of all. In the essays before us the absence of effort is too obvious to be mistaken, and a strong under-current of *suggestion* runs continuously beneath the upper stream of the tranquil thesis. In short, these effusions of Mr. Hawthorne are the product of a truly imaginative intellect, restrained, and in some measure repressed, by fastidiousness of taste, by constitutional melancholy and by indolence.

7. A good comparison is Irving's "Author's Account of Himself," prefatory to the *Sketch Book*.
8. Poe probably is thinking primarily of the essays of Joseph Addison (1672–1719) in the most admired of the 18th-century English periodicals, the *Spectator* (1711–14), although he may also mean to include Richard Steele (1672–1729), author of many of the *Spectator* essays either independently or in collaboration with Addison.

But it is of his tales that we desire principally to speak. The tale proper, in our opinion, affords unquestionably the fairest field for the exercise of the loftiest talent, which can be afforded by the wide domains of mere prose. Were we bidden to say how the highest genius could be most advantageously employed for the best display of its own powers, we should answer, without hesitation—in the composition of a rhymed poem, not to exceed in length what might be perused in an hour. Within this limit alone can the highest order of true poetry exist. We need only here say, upon this topic, that, in almost all classes of composition, the unity of effect or impression is a point of the greatest importance. It is clear, moreover, that this unity cannot be thoroughly preserved in productions whose perusal cannot be completed at one sitting. We may continue the reading of a prose composition, from the very nature of prose itself, much longer than we can persevere, to any good purpose, in the perusal of a poem. This latter, if truly fulfilling the demands of the poetic sentiment, induces an exaltation of the soul which cannot be long sustained. All high excitements are necessarily transient. Thus a long poem is a paradox. And, without unity of impression, the deepest effects cannot be brought about. Epics were the offspring of an imperfect sense of Art, and their reign is no more. A poem *too* brief may produce a vivid, but never an intense or enduring impression. Without a certain continuity of effort—without a certain duration or repetition of purpose—the soul is never deeply moved. There must be the dropping of the water upon the rock. De Béranger[9] has wrought brilliant things—pungent and spirit-stirring—but, like all immassive bodies, they lack *momentum*, and thus fail to satisfy the Poetic Sentiment. They sparkle and excite, but, from want of continuity, fail deeply to impress. Extreme brevity will degenerate into epigrammatism; but the sin of extreme length is even more unpardonable. *In medio tutissimus ibis.*[1]

Were we called upon however to designate that class of composition which, next to such a poem as we have suggested, should best fulfil the demands of high genius—should offer it the most advantageous field of exertion—we should unhesitatingly speak of the prose tale, as Mr. Hawthorne has here exemplified it. We allude to the short prose narrative, requiring from a half-hour to one or two hours in its perusal. The ordinary novel is objectionable, from its length, for reasons already stated in substance. As it cannot be read at one sitting, it deprives itself, of course, of the immense force derivable from *totality*. Worldly interests intervening during the pauses of perusal, modify, annul, or counteract, in a greater or less degree, the impressions of the book. But simple cessation in reading would, of itself, be sufficient to destroy the true unity. In the brief tale, however, the author is enabled to carry out the fulness of his intention, be it what it may. During the hour of perusal the soul of the reader is at the writer's control. There are no external or extrinsic influences—resulting from weariness or interruption.

A skilful literary artist has constructed a tale. If wise, he has not fashioned his thoughts to accommodate his incidents; but having conceived, with deliberate care, a certain unique or single *effect* to be wrought out, he then invents such incidents—he then combines such events as may best aid him in establishing this preconceived effect. If his very initial sentence tend not to the

9. Pierre Jean de Béranger (1780–1857), popular     1. You're safer in the middle (moderate) course
French poet and song writer.                        (Latin).

outbringing of this effect, then he has failed in his first step. In the whole composition there should be no word written, of which the tendency, direct or indirect, is not to the one pre-established design. And by such means, with such care and skill, a picture is at length painted which leaves in the mind of him who contemplates it with a kindred art, a sense of the fullest satisfaction. The idea of the tale has been presented unblemished, because undisturbed; and this is an end unattainable by the novel. Undue brevity is just as exceptionable here as in the poem; but undue length is yet more to be avoided.

We have said that the tale has a point of superiority even over the poem. In fact, while the *rhythm* of this latter is an essential aid in the development of the poem's highest idea—the idea of the Beautiful—the artificialities of this rhythm are an inseparable bar to the development of all points of thought or expression which have their basis in *Truth*. But Truth is often, and in very great degree, the aim of the tale. Some of the finest tales are tales of ratiocination. Thus the field of this species of composition, if not in so elevated a region on the mountain of Mind, is a table-land of far vaster extent than the domain of the mere poem. Its products are never so rich, but infinitely more numerous, and more appreciable by the mass of mankind. The writer of the prose tale, in short, may bring to his theme a vast variety of modes or inflections of thought and expression—(the ratiocinative, for example, the sarcastic or the humorous) which are not only antagonistical to the nature of the poem, but absolutely forbidden by one of its most peculiar and indispensable adjuncts; we allude of course, to rhythm. It may be added, here, *par parenthèse*, that the author who aims at the purely beautiful in a prose tale is laboring at great disadvantage. For Beauty can be better treated in the poem. Not so with terror, or passion, or horror, or a multitude of such other points. And here it will be seen how full of prejudice are the usual animadversions against those *tales of effect* many fine examples of which were found in the earlier numbers of Blackwood.[2] The impressions produced were wrought in a legitimate sphere of action, and constituted a legitimate although sometimes an exaggerated interest. They were relished by every man of genius: although there were found many men of genius who condemned them without just ground. The true critic will but demand that the design intended be accomplished, to the fullest extent, by the means most advantageously applicable.

We have very few American tales of real merit—we may say, indeed, none, with the exception of "The Tales of a Traveller" of Washington Irving, and these "Twice-Told Tales" of Mr. Hawthorne. Some of the pieces of Mr. John Neal[3] abound in vigor and originality; but in general, his compositions of this class are excessively diffuse, extravagant, and indicative of an imperfect sentiment of Art. Articles at random are, now and then, met with in our periodicals which might be advantageously compared with the best effusions of the British Magazines; but, upon the whole, we are far behind our progenitors in this department of literature.

Of Mr. Hawthorne's Tales we would say, emphatically, that they belong to the highest region of Art—an Art subservient to genius of a very lofty order. We had supposed, with good reason for so supposing, that he had been thrust into his present position by one of the impudent *cliques* which beset our litera-

---

2. The long-lived *Blackwood's Edinburgh Magazine*, founded in 1817. One of Poe's best satiric pieces is his loving tribute to the gothic excesses of this journal, *How to Write a Blackwood Article.*
3. John Neal (1793–1876), American literary man, more important as an editor.

ture, and whose pretensions it is our full purpose to expose at the earliest opportunity; but we have been most agreeably mistaken. We know of few compositions which the critic can more honestly commend than these "Twice-Told Tales." As Americans, we feel proud of the book.

Mr. Hawthorne's distinctive trait is invention, creation, imagination, originality—a trait which, in the literature of fiction, is positively worth all the rest. But the nature of originality, so far as regards its manifestation in letters, is but imperfectly understood. The inventive or original mind as frequently displays itself in novelty of *tone* as in novelty of matter. Mr. Hawthorne is original at *all* points.

It would be a matter of some difficulty to designate the best of these tales; we repeat that, without exception, they are beautiful. "Wakefield" is remarkable for the skill with which an old idea—a well-known incident—is worked up or discussed. A man of whims conceives the purpose of quitting his wife and residing *incognito*, for twenty years, in her immediate neighborhood. Something of this kind actually happened in London. The force of Mr. Hawthorne's tale lies in the analysis of the motives which must or might have impelled the husband to such folly, in the first instance, with the possible causes of his perseverance. Upon this thesis a sketch of singular power has been constructed.

"The Wedding Knell" is full of the boldest imagination—an imagination fully controlled by taste. The most captious critic could find no flaw in this production.

"The Minister's Black Veil" is a masterly composition of which the sole defect is that to the rabble its exquisite skill will be *caviare*. The *obvious* meaning of this article will be found to smother its insinuated one. The *moral* put into the mouth of the dying minister will be supposed to convey the *true* import of the narrative; and that a crime of dark dye, (having reference to the "young lady") has been committed, is a point which only minds congenial with that of the author will perceive.

"Mr. Higginbotham's Catastrophe" is vividly original and managed most dexterously.

"Dr. Heidegger's Experiment" is exceedingly well imagined, and executed with surpassing ability. The artist breathes in every line of it.

"The White Old Maid" is objectionable, even more than the "Minister's Black Veil," on the score of its mysticism. Even with the thoughtful and analytic, there will be much trouble in penetrating its entire import.

"The Hollow of the Three Hills" we would quote in full, had we space;— not as evincing higher talent than any of the other pieces, but as affording an excellent example of the author's peculiar ability. The subject is commonplace. A witch subjects the Distant and the Past to the view of a mourner. It has been the fashion to describe, in such cases, a mirror in which the images of the absent appear; or a cloud of smoke is made to arise, and thence the figures are gradually unfolded. Mr. Hawthorne has wonderfully heightened his effect by making the ear, in place of the eye, the medium by which the fantasy is conveyed. The head of the mourner is enveloped in the cloak of the witch, and within its magic folds there arise sounds which have an all-sufficient intelligence. Throughout this article also, the artist is conspicuous—not more in positive than in negative merits. Not only is all done that should be done, but (what perhaps is an end with more difficulty attained) there is nothing done which should not be. Every word *tells*, and there is not a word which does *not* tell.

In "Howe's Masquerade" we observe something which resembles a plagiarism—but which *may be* a very flattering coincidence of thought. We quote the passage in question.

> "*With a dark flush of wrath* upon his brow they saw the general *draw his sword* and *advance to meet* the figure *in the cloak* before the latter had stepped one pace upon the floor.
> '*Villain, unmuffle yourself*,' cried he, 'you pass no farther!'"
> "The figure, without blenching a hair's breadth from the sword which was pointed at his breast, made a solemn pause, and *lowered the cape of the cloak* from his face, yet not sufficiently for the spectators to catch a glimpse of it. But Sir William Howe had evidently seen enough. The sternness of his countenance gave place to a look of wild amazement, if not horror, while he recoiled several steps from the figure, *and let fall his sword* upon the floor.*"—See vol. 2, page 20.

The idea here is, that the figure in the cloak is the phantom or reduplication of Sir William Howe; but in an article called "William Wilson," one of the "Tales of the Grotesque and Arabesque," we have not only the same idea, but the same idea similarly presented in several respects. We quote two paragraphs, which our readers may compare with what has been already given. We have italicized, above, the immediate particulars of resemblance.

> "The brief moment in which I averted my eyes had been sufficient to produce, apparently, a material change in the arrangement at the upper or farther end of the room. A large mirror, it appeared to me, now stood where none had been perceptible before: and as I stepped up to it in extremity of terror, mine own image, but with features all pale and dabbled in blood, *advanced* with a feeble and tottering gait to meet me.
> "Thus it appeared I say, but was not. It was Wilson, who then stood before me in the agonies of dissolution. Not a line in all the marked and singular lineaments of that face which was not even identically mine own. *His mask and cloak lay where he had thrown them, upon the floor.*"—Vol. 2, p. 57.

Here it will be observed that, not only are the two general conceptions identical, but there are various *points* of similarity. In each case the figure seen is the wraith or duplication of the beholder. In each case the scene is a masquerade. In each case the figure is cloaked. In each, there is a quarrel— that is to say, angry words pass between the parties. In each the beholder is enraged. In each the cloak and sword fall upon the floor. The "villain, unmuffle yourself," of Mr. H. is precisely paralleled by a passage at page 56 of "William Wilson."

In the way of objection we have scarcely a word to say of these tales. There is, perhaps, a somewhat too general or prevalent *tone*—a tone of melancholy and mysticism. The subjects are insufficiently varied. There is not so much *versatility* evinced as we might well be warranted in expecting from the high powers of Mr. Hawthorne. But beyond these trivial exceptions we have really none to make. The style is purity itself. Force abounds. High imagination gleams from every page. Mr. Hawthorne is a man of the truest genius. We only regret that the limits of our Magazine will not permit us to pay him that full tribute of commendation, which, under other circumstances, we should be so eager to pay.

1842

# The Philosophy of Composition[1]

Charles Dickens, in a note now lying before me, alluding to an examination I once made of the mechanism of "Barnaby Rudge," says—"By the way, are you aware that Godwin wrote his 'Caleb Williams' backwards? He first involved his hero in a web of difficulties, forming the second volume, and then, for the first, cast about him for some mode of accounting for what had been done."[2]

I cannot think this the *precise* mode of procedure on the part of Godwin— and indeed what he himself acknowledges, is not altogether in accordance with Mr. Dickens' idea—but the author of "Caleb Williams" was too good an artist not to perceive the advantage derivable from at least a somewhat similar process. Nothing is more clear than that every plot, worth the name, must be elaborated to its *dénouement* before any thing be attempted with the pen. It is only with the *dénouement* constantly in view that we can give a plot its indispensable air of consequence, or causation, by making the incidents, and especially the tone at all points, tend to the development of the intention.

There is a radical error, I think, in the usual mode of constructing a story. Either history affords a thesis—or one is suggested by an incident of the day— or, at best, the author sets himself to work in the combination of striking events to form merely the basis of his narrative—designing, generally, to fill in with description, dialogue, or autorial comment, whatever crevices of fact, or action, may, from page to page, render themselves apparent.

I prefer commencing with the consideration of an *effect*. Keeping originality *always* in view—for he is false to himself who ventures to dispense with so obvious and so easily attainable a source of interest—I say to myself, in the first place, "Of the innumerable effects, or impressions, of which the heart, the intellect, or (more generally) the soul is susceptible, what one shall I, on the present occasion, select?" Having chosen a novel, first, and secondly a vivid effect, I consider whether it can best be wrought by incident or tone— whether by ordinary incidents and peculiar tone, or the converse, or by peculiarity both of incident and tone—afterward looking about me (or rather within) for such combinations of event, or tone, as shall best aid me in the construction of the effect.

I have often thought how interesting a magazine paper might be written by any author who would—that is to say, who could—detail, step by step, the processes by which any one of his compositions attained its ultimate point of completion. Why such a paper has never been given to the world, I am much

1. The title means something like "The Theory of Writing." Poe wrote the work as a lecture in hopes of capitalizing on the success of *The Raven*. For years in his reviews Poe had campaigned for deliberate artistry rather than uncontrolled effusions, and *The Philosophy of Composition* must be regarded as part of that campaign rather than a factual account of how Poe actually wrote *The Raven*. In a letter of August 9, 1846, Poe called the essay his "best specimen of analysis." The text here is that of the first printing, in *Graham's Magazine* 28 (April 1846), 163–67.
2. William Godwin makes this claim in his 1832 preface to *Caleb Williams* (first published in 1794).

at a loss to say—but, perhaps, the autorial vanity has had more to do with the omission than any one other cause. Most writers—poets in especial—prefer having it understood that they compose by a species of fine frenzy[3]—an ecstatic intuition—and would positively shudder at letting the public take a peep behind the scenes, at the elaborate and vacillating crudities of thought— at the true purposes seized only at the last moment—at the innumerable glimpses of idea that arrived not at the maturity of full view—at the fully matured fancies discarded in despair as unmanageable—at the cautious selections and rejections—at the painful erasures and interpolations—in a word, at the wheels and pinions—the tackle for scene-shifting—the step-ladders and demon-traps—the cock's feathers, the red paint and the black patches, which, in ninety-nine cases out of the hundred, constitute the properties of the literary *histrio*.[4]

I am aware, on the other hand, that the case is by no means common, in which an author is at all in condition to retrace the steps by which his conclusions have been attained. In general, suggestions, having arisen pell-mell, are pursued and forgotten in a similar manner.

For my own part, I have neither sympathy with the repugnance alluded to, nor, at any time, the least difficulty in recalling to mind the progressive steps of any of my compositions; and, since the interest of an analysis, or reconstruction, such as I have considered a *desideratum*,[5] is quite independent of any real or fancied interest in the thing analyzed, it will not be regarded as a breach of decorum on my part to show the *modus operandi*[6] by which some one of my own works was put together. I select "The Raven," as the most generally known. It is my design to render it manifest that no one point in its composition is referrible either to accident or intuition—that the work proceeded, step by step, to its completion with the precision and rigid consequence of a mathematical problem.

Let us dismiss, as irrelevant to the poem *per se*, the circumstance—or say the necessity—which, in the first place, gave rise to the intention of composing *a* poem that should suit at once the popular and the critical taste.

We commence, then, with this intention.

The initial consideration was that of extent. If any literary work is too long to be read at one sitting, we must be content to dispense with the immensely important effect derivable from unity of impression—for, if two sittings be required, the affairs of the world interfere, and every thing like totality is at once destroyed. But since, *ceteris paribus*,[7] no poet can afford to dispense with *any thing* that may advance his design, it but remains to be seen whether there is, in extent, any advantage to counterbalance the loss of unity which attends it. Here I say no, at once. What we term a long poem is, in fact, merely a succession of brief ones—that is to say, of brief poetical effects. It is needless to demonstrate that a poem is such, only inasmuch as it intensely excites, by elevating, the soul; and all intense excitements are, through a psychal necessity, brief. For this reason, at least one half of the "Paradise Lost"[8] is essentially

---

3. Shakespeare's *Midsummer Night's Dream* 5.1.12, in Theseus's description of the poet: "The poet's eye, in a fine frenzy rolling, / Doth glance from heaven to earth, from earth to heaven / And as imagination bodies forth / The forms of things unknown, the poet's pen / Turns them to shapes, and gives to airy nothing / A local habitation and a name."
4. Artist (Latin).

5. Something to be desired (Latin).
6. Method of procedure (Latin).
7. Other things being equal (Latin).
8. The twelve-book blank-verse epic by John Milton, which contains some 10,500 lines, more than a hundred times as many lines as Poe considered desirable in a poem.

prose—a succession of poetical excitements interspersed, *inevitably*, with corresponding depressions—the whole being deprived, through the extremeness of its length, of the vastly important artistic element, totality, or unity, of effect.

It appears evident, then, that there is a distinct limit, as regards length, to all works of literary art—the limit of a single sitting—and that, although in certain classes of prose composition, such as "Robinson Crusoe,"[9] (demanding no unity,) this limit may be advantageously overpassed, it can never properly be overpassed in a poem. Within this limit, the extent of a poem may be made to bear mathematical relation to its merit—in other words, to the excitement or elevation—again in other words, to the degree of the true poetical effect which it is capable of inducing; for it is clear that the brevity must be in direct ratio of the intensity of the intended effect:—this, with one proviso—that a certain degree of duration is absolutely requisite for the production of any effect at all.

Holding in view these considerations, as well as that degree of excitement which I deemed not above the popular, while not below the critical, taste, I reached at once what I conceived the proper *length* for my intended poem—a length of about one hundred lines. It is, in fact, a hundred and eight.

My next thought concerned the choice of an impression, or effect, to be conveyed: and here I may as well observe that, throughout the construction, I kept steadily in view the design of rendering the work *universally* appreciable. I should be carried too far out of my immediate topic were I to demonstrate a point upon which I have repeatedly insisted, and which, with the poetical, stands not in the slightest need of demonstration—the point, I mean, that Beauty is the sole legitimate province of the poem. A few words, however, in elucidation of my real meaning, which some of my friends have evinced a disposition to misrepresent. That pleasure which is at once the most intense, the most elevating, and the most pure, is, I believe, found in the contemplation of the beautiful. When, indeed, men speak of Beauty, they mean, precisely, not a quality, as is supposed, but an effect—they refer, in short, just to that intense and pure elevation of *soul*—not of intellect, or of heart—upon which I have commented, and which is experienced in consequence of contemplating "the beautiful." Now I designate Beauty as the province of the poem, merely because it is an obvious rule of Art that effects should be made to spring from direct causes—that objects should be attained through means best adapted for their attainment—no one as yet having been weak enough to deny that the peculiar elevation alluded to, is *most readily* attained in the poem. Now the object, Truth, or the satisfaction of the intellect, and the object, Passion, or the excitement of the heart, are, although attainable, to a certain extent, in poetry, far more readily attainable in prose. Truth, in fact, demands a precision, and Passion, a *homeliness* (the truly passionate will comprehend me) which are absolutely antagonistic to that Beauty which, I maintain, is the excitement, or pleasurable elevation, of the soul. It by no means follows from any thing here said, that passion, or even truth, may not be introduced, and even profitably introduced, into a poem—for they may serve in elucidation, or aid the general effect, as do discords in music, by contrast—but the true artist will always contrive, first, to tone them into proper subservi-

9. Daniel Defoe's novel of shipwreck in the Caribbean (1719), based on the experiences of Alexander Selkirk.

ence to the predominant aim, and, secondly, to enveil them, as far as possible, in that Beauty which is the atmosphere and the essence of the poem.

Regarding, then, Beauty as my province, my next question referred to the *tone* of its highest manifestation—and all experience has shown that this tone is one of *sadness*. Beauty of whatever kind, in its supreme development, invariably excites the sensitive soul to tears. Melancholy is thus the most legitimate of all the poetical tones.

The length, the province, and the tone, being thus determined, I betook myself to ordinary induction, with the view of obtaining some artistic piquancy which might serve me as a key-note in the construction of the poem—some pivot upon which the whole structure might turn. In carefully thinking over all the usual artistic effects—or more properly *points*, in the theatrical sense— I did not fail to perceive immediately that no one had been so universally employed as that of the *refrain*. The universality of its employment sufficed to assure me of its intrinsic value, and spared me the necessity of submitting it to analysis. I considered it, however, with regard to its susceptibility of improvement, and soon saw it to be in a primitive condition. As commonly used, the *refrain*, or burden, not only is limited to lyric verse, but depends for its impression upon the force of monotone—both in sound and thought. The pleasure is deduced solely from the sense of identity—of repetition. I resolved to diversify, and so vastly heighten, the effect, by adhering, in general, to the monotone of sound, while I continually varied that of thought: that is to say, I determined to produce continuously novel effects, by the variation *of the application* of the *refrain*—the *refrain* itself remaining, for the most part, unvaried.

These points being settled, I next bethought me of the *nature* of my *refrain*. Since its application was to be repeatedly varied, it was clear that the *refrain* itself must be brief, for there would have been an insurmountable difficulty in frequent variations of application in any sentence of length. In proportion to the brevity of the sentence, would, of course, be the facility of the variation. This led me at once to a single word as the best *refrain*.

The question now arose as to the *character* of the word. Having made up my mind to a *refrain*, the division of the poem into stanzas was, of course, a corollary: the *refrain* forming the close to each stanza. That such a close, to have force, must be sonorous and susceptible of protracted emphasis, admitted no doubt: and these considerations inevitably led me to the long *o* as the most sonorous vowel, in connection with *r* as the most producible consonant.

The sound of the *refrain* being thus determined, it became necessary to select a word embodying this sound, and at the same time in the fullest possible keeping with that melancholy which I had predetermined as the tone of the poem. In such a search it would have been absolutely impossible to overlook the word "Nevermore." In fact, it was the very first which presented itself.

The next *desideratum* was a pretext for the continuous use of the one word "nevermore." In observing the difficulty which I at once found in inventing a sufficiently plausible reason for its continuous repetition, I did not fail to perceive that this difficulty arose solely from the pre-assumption that the word was to be so continuously or monotonously spoken by *a human* being—I did not fail to perceive, in short, that the difficulty lay in the reconciliation of this monotony with the exercise of reason on the part of the creature repeating the word. Here, then, immediately arose the idea of a *non*-reasoning creature capable of speech; and, very naturally, a parrot, in the first instance, suggested itself, but was superseded forthwith by a Raven, as equally capable of speech, and infinitely more in keeping with the intended *tone*.

I had now gone so far as the conception of a Raven—the bird of ill omen—monotonously repeating the one word, "Nevermore," at the conclusion of each stanza, in a poem of melancholy tone, and in length about one hundred lines. Now, never losing sight of the object *supremeness*, or perfection, at all points, I asked myself—"Of all melancholy topics, what, according to the *universal* understanding of mankind, is the *most* melancholy?" Death—was the obvious reply. "And when," I said, "is this most melancholy of topics most poetical?" From what I have already explained at some length, the answer, here also, is obvious—"When it most closely allies itself to *Beauty*: the death, then, of a beautiful woman is, unquestionably, the most poetical topic in the world—and equally is it beyond doubt that the lips best suited for such topic are those of a bereaved lover."

I had now to combine the two ideas, of a lover lamenting his deceased mistress and a Raven continuously repeating the word "Nevermore"—I had to combine these, bearing in mind my design of varying, at every turn, the *application* of the word repeated; but the only intelligible model of such combination is that of imagining the Raven employing the word in answer to the queries of the lover. And here it was that I saw at once the opportunity afforded for the effect on which I had been depending—that is to say, the effect of the *variation of application*. I saw that I could make the first query propounded by the lover—the first query to which the Raven should reply "Nevermore"—that I could make this first query a commonplace one—the second less so—the third still less, and so on—until at length the lover, startled from his original *nonchalance* by the melancholy character of the word itself—by its frequent repetition—and by a consideration of the ominous reputation of the fowl that uttered it—is at length excited to superstition, and wildly propounds queries of a far different character—queries whose solution he has passionately at heart—propounds them half in superstition and half in that species of despair which delights in self-torture—propounds them not altogether because he believes in the prophetic or demoniac character of the bird (which, reason assures him, is merely repeating a lesson learned by rote) but because he experiences a phrenzied pleasure in so modeling his questions as to receive from the *expected* "Nevermore" the most delicious because the most intolerable of sorrow. Perceiving the opportunity thus afforded me—or, more strictly, thus forced upon me in the progress of the construction—I first established in mind the climax, or concluding query—that to which "Nevermore" should be in the last place an answer—that in reply to which this word "Nevermore" should involve the utmost conceivable amount of sorrow and despair.

Here then the poem may be said to have its beginning—at the end, where all works of art should begin—for it was here, at this point of my preconsiderations, that I first put pen to paper in the composition of the stanza:

> "Prophet," said I, "thing of evil! prophet still if bird or devil!
> By that heaven that bends above us—by that God we both adore,
> Tell this soul with sorrow laden, if within the distant Aidenn,
> It shall clasp a sainted maiden whom the angels name Lenore—
> Clasp a rare and radiant maiden whom the angels name Lenore."
>     Quoth the raven "Nevermore."

I composed this stanza, at this point, first that, by establishing the climax, I might the better vary and graduate, as regards seriousness and importance, the preceding queries of the lover—and, secondly, that I might definitely settle the rhythm, the metre, and the length and general arrangement of the stanza—as well as graduate the stanzas which were to precede, so that none of them might surpass this in rhythmical effect. Had I been able, in the subsequent composition, to construct more vigorous stanzas, I should, without scruple, have purposely enfeebled them, so as not to interfere with the climacteric effect.

And here I may as well say a few words of the versification. My first object (as usual) was originality. The extent to which this has been neglected, in versification, is one of the most unaccountable things in the world. Admitting that there is little possibility of variety in mere *rhythm*, it is still clear that the possible varieties of metre and stanza are absolutely infinite—and yet, *for centuries, no man, in verse, has ever done, or ever seemed to think of doing, an original thing.* The fact is, originality (unless in minds of very unusual force) is by no means a matter, as some suppose, of impulse or intuition. In general, to be found, it must be elaborately sought, and although a positive merit of the highest class, demands in its attainment less of invention than negation.

Of course, I pretend to no originality in either the rhythm or metre of the "Raven." The former is trochaic—the latter is octameter acatalectic, alternating with heptameter catalectic repeated in the *refrain* of the fifth verse, and terminating with tetrameter catalectic. Less pedantically—the feet employed throughout (trochees) consist of a long syllable followed by a short: the first line of the stanza consists of eight of these feet—the second of seven and a half (in effect two-thirds)—the third of eight—the fourth of seven and a half—the fifth the same—the sixth three and a half. Now, each of these lines, taken individually, has been employed before, and what originality the "Raven" has, is in their *combination into stanza*; nothing even remotely approaching this combination has ever been attempted. The effect of this originality of combination is aided by other unusual, and some altogether novel effects, arising from an extension of the application of the principles of rhyme and alliteration.

The next point to be considered was the mode of bringing together the lover and the Raven—and the first branch of this consideration was the *locale*. For this the most natural suggestion might seem to be a forest, or the fields—but it has always appeared to me that a close *circumscription of space* is absolutely necessary to the effect of insulated incident:—it has the force of a frame to a picture. It has an indisputable moral power in keeping concentrated the attention, and, of course, must not be confounded with mere unity of place.

I determined, then, to place the lover in his chamber—in a chamber rendered sacred to him by memories of her who had frequented it. The room is represented as richly furnished—this in mere pursuance of the ideas I have already explained on the subject of Beauty, as the sole true poetical thesis.

The *locale* being thus determined, I had now to introduce the bird—and the thought of introducing him through the window, was inevitable. The idea of making the lover suppose, in the first instance, that the flapping of the wings of the bird against the shutter, is a "tapping" at the door, originated in a wish to increase, by prolonging, the reader's curiosity, and in a desire to admit the incidental effect arising from the lover's throwing open the door, finding all dark, and thence adopting the half-fancy that it was the spirit of his mistress that knocked.

I made the night tempestuous, first, to account for the Raven's seeking admission, and secondly, for the effect of contrast with the (physical) serenity within the chamber.

I made the bird alight on the bust of Pallas,[1] also for the effect of contrast between the marble and the plumage—it being understood that the bust was absolutely *suggested* by the bird—the bust of *Pallas* being chosen, first, as most in keeping with the scholarship of the lover, and, secondly, for the sonorousness of the word, Pallas, itself.

About the middle of the poem, also, I have availed myself of the force of contrast, with a view of deepening the ultimate impression. For example, an air of the fantastic—approaching as nearly to the ludicrous as was admissible— is given to the Raven's entrance. He comes in "with many a flirt and flutter."

> Not the *least obeisance made he*—not a moment stopped or stayed he,
> *But with mien of lord or lady*, perched above my chamber door.

In the two stanzas which follow, the design is more obviously carried out:—

> Then this ebony bird beguiling my sad fancy into smiling
> By the *grave and stern decorum of the countenance it wore*,
> "Though thy *crest be shorn and shaven* thou," I said, "art sure no craven,
> Ghastly grim and ancient Raven wandering from the nightly shore—
> Tell me what thy lordly name is on the Night's Plutonian shore!"
>           Quoth the Raven "Nevermore."

> ———

> Much I marvelled *this ungainly fowl* to hear discourse so plainly,
> Though its answer little meaning—little relevancy bore;
> For we cannot help agreeing that no living human being
> *Ever yet was blessed with seeing bird above his chamber door*—
> *Bird or beast upon the sculptured bust above his chamber door*,
>           With such name as "Nevermore."

The effect of the *dénouement* being thus provided for, I immediately drop the fantastic for a tone of the most profound seriousness:—this tone commencing in the stanza directly following the one last quoted, with the line,

> But the Raven, sitting lonely on that placid bust, spoke only, etc.

From this epoch the lover no longer jests—no longer sees any thing even of the fantastic in the Raven's demeanor. He speaks of him as a "grim, ungainly, ghastly, gaunt, and ominous bird of yore," and feels the "fiery eyes" burning into his "bosom's core." This revolution of thought, or fancy, on the lover's part, is intended to induce a similar one on the part of the reader—to bring the mind into a proper frame for the *dénouement*—which is now brought about as rapidly and as *directly* as possible.

With the *dénouement* proper—with the Raven's reply, "Nevermore," to the lover's final demand if he shall meet his mistress in another world—the poem, in its obvious phase, that of a simple narrative, may be said to have its completion. So far, every thing is within the limits of the accountable—of the real. A raven, having learned by rote the single word "Nevermore," and having

---

1. Pallas Athena, the Greek goddess of wisdom and the arts.

escaped from the custody of its owner, is driven, at midnight, through the violence of a storm, to seek admission at a window from which a light still gleams—the chamber-window of a student, occupied half in poring over a volume, half in dreaming of a beloved mistress deceased. The casement being thrown open at the fluttering of the bird's wings, the bird itself perches on the most convenient seat out of the immediate reach of the student, who, amused by the incident and the oddity of the visiter's demeanor, demands of it, in jest and without looking for a reply, its name. The raven addressed, answers with its customary word, "Nevermore"—a word which finds immediate echo in the melancholy heart of the student, who, giving utterance aloud to certain thoughts suggested by the occasion, is again startled by the fowl's repetition of "Nevermore." The student now guesses the state of the case, but is impelled, as I have before explained, by the human thirst for self-torture, and in part by superstition, to propound such queries to the bird as will bring him, the lover, the most of the luxury of sorrow, through the anticipated answer "Nevermore." With the indulgence, to the utmost extreme, of this self-torture, the narration, in what I have termed its first or obvious phase, has a natural termination, and so far there has been no overstepping of the limits of the real.

But in subjects so handled, however skilfully, or with however vivid an array of incident, there is always a certain hardness or nakedness, which repels the artistical eye. Two things are invariably required—first, some amount of complexity, or more properly, adaptation; and, secondly, some amount of suggestiveness—some under current, however indefinite of meaning. It is this latter, in especial, which imparts to a work of art so much of that *richness* (to borrow from colloquy a forcible term) which we are too fond of confounding with *the ideal*. It is the *excess* of the suggested meaning—it is the rendering this the upper instead of the under current of the theme—which turns into prose (and that of the very flattest kind) the so called poetry of the so called transcendentalists.

Holding these opinions, I added the two concluding stanzas of the poem—their suggestiveness being thus made to pervade all the narrative which has preceded them. The under-current of meaning is rendered first apparent in the lines—

"Take thy beak from out *my heart*, and take thy form from off my door!"
Quoth the Raven "Nevermore!"

It will be observed that the words, "from out my heart," involve the first metaphorical expression in the poem. They, with the answer, "Nevermore," dispose the mind to seek a moral in all that has been previously narrated. The reader begins now to regard the Raven as emblematical—but it is not until the very last line of the very last stanza, that the intention of making him emblematical of *Mournful and Never-ending Remembrance* is permitted distinctly to be seen:

And the Raven, never flitting, still is sitting, still is sitting,
On the pallid bust of Pallas just above my chamber door;
And his eyes have all the seeming of a demon's that is dreaming,
And the lamplight o'er him streaming throws his shadow on the floor;
And my soul *from out that shadow* that lies floating on the floor
Shall be lifted—nevermore.

1846

## ABRAHAM LINCOLN
### 1809–1865

Abraham Lincoln's life and presidency can be seen as affirmative answers to the central question raised by the intellectual and political ferment of the late eighteenth century: Can individuals and nations rule themselves? Lincoln's career as self-made man is a paradigm of the possibilities of individual self-regulation and development within a context of freedom; his unshakable commitment to the preservation of the Union made possible the survival of a self-governing nation devoted to the principles of equality. Only by making himself independent and responsible could Lincoln be the Great Emancipator of others; only by surviving the test of civil war could the United States be the model and hope for democratic nations.

Lincoln was born on February 12, 1809, in a backwoods cabin in Hardin County, Kentucky, to nearly illiterate parents. He attended school only sporadically—probably for no more than a year all told—and was essentially self-taught. Although his access to books was limited, he absorbed and retained what he read of the King James Bible, *Aesop's Fables*, John Bunyan's *Pilgrim's Progress*, Daniel Defoe's *Robinson Crusoe*, and Mason Locke Weem's *A History of the Life and Death, Virtues, and Exploits of General George Washington*. Lincoln never lost his love of reading—adding Shakespeare, John Stuart Mill, Lord Byron, and Robert Burns to his list of favorite authors—and was always, in sensibility and by achievement, a great master of words.

Lincoln spent his impoverished youth in Kentucky and southern Indiana, where his father farmed for a living. His mother died when he was nine, but his stepmother, who soon joined the family with children of her own, seems to have singled out Abraham for special affection; he later spoke of her as his "angel mother." In 1830 the family moved to Illinois; after helping the family settle by splitting rails to fence in a new farm, young Lincoln set out on his own, making a trip to New Orleans as a flatboatman. He soon returned to settle in the tiny village of New Salem, Illinois, where he worked as storekeeper, postmaster, and surveyor. In 1832 he volunteered for service in the Black Hawk War; he was elected captain of his company but, as he later observed, saw more action against mosquitoes than he did against the Sac and Fox Indians.

Lincoln had considered blacksmithing as a trade, but decided instead in the early 1830s to prepare himself for a career in law. This he did by studying independently the basic law books of the time: Blackstone's *Commentaries*, Chitty's *Pleadings*, Greenleaf's *Evidence*, and Story's *Equity* and *Equity Pleadings*. In 1834 he was elected to the first of four terms in the state legislature, at that time a position of small influence and smaller salary. He passed the state bar examination in 1836 and moved the next year to the new state capital in Springfield. Here he entered a succession of law partnerships, the most enduring with William H. Herndon, later his biographer. By dint of hard work—which included twice-yearly sessions following the court on horseback or buggy as it moved from town to town to reach the people across the Illinois countryside—Lincoln prospered as a lawyer and earned a reputation as a shrewd, sensible, fair, and honest practitioner.

Much has been made of Lincoln's romance with Ann Rutledge, whom he had known in New Salem, but she died at nineteen years of age; so far as the records show, Lincoln's only love was Mary Todd. She came from a well-to-do Kentucky family, and the social aristocracy of Springfield to which she belonged advised her against marrying Lincoln despite his success as a lawyer and his obvious good qualities. He, too, apparently had misgivings about the prospects for the marriage, but they were married in the fall of 1842. The relationship between Mary Todd and Abraham Lincoln has been subject to endless speculation. She was witty and intense, and no doubt her temper and extravagance were often a trial to her husband, especially later in their marriage; but he was often absent from home, absorbed in his flourishing law practice, and was himself moody and sharp-tongued. On balance, the Lincolns seemed to have shared as much affection and pleasure in their union as one might reasonably expect. They certainly seem to have joined in affectionate concern for their four boys, only one of whom survived to adulthood.

The network of political and other historical events of the 1840s and 1850s that would result in Lincoln's election to the presidency in 1860 is complicated, but the central issue involved in these events is not. Very simply, the question was whether or not slavery would be permitted in the new territories, which eventually would become states. When he was elected to Congress in 1846, Lincoln voted against abolitionist measures but he insisted that the new territories must be kept free as "places for poor people to go and better their condition." He also joined in a vote of censure against President Polk for engaging in the war against Mexico (1848), a war he believed to be both unnecessary and unconstitutional. He did not run for reelection and it seemed that his political career had come to an end.

By 1854 the two major political parties of the time—the Whigs (to which Lincoln belonged) and the Democrats—had reached compromise on the extension of slavery into new territories and states. Strong antislavery elements in both parties established independent organizations, and when, in 1854, the Republican party was organized, Lincoln soon joined it. His new party lost the presidential election of 1856 to the Democrats, but in 1858 Lincoln reentered political life as the Republican candidate in the senatorial election. He opposed the Democrat Stephen A. Douglas, who had earlier sponsored the Kansas-Nebraska Bill, a bill that would have left it to new territories to establish their status as slave or free when they achieved statehood. Lincoln may have won the famous series of debates with Douglas, but he lost the election. More important for the future, though, he had gained national recognition and he found a theme commensurate with his rapidly intensifying powers of thought and expression. As the "House Divided" speech suggests, Lincoln now added to the often biting satirical humor, and to the logic and natural grace of his earlier utterances, a resonance and wisdom that mark his emergence as a national political leader and as a master of language.

This reputation was enhanced by the "Cooper Union Address" in 1860, and at the Republican convention he won nomination on the third ballot. Lincoln was elected sixteenth president of the United States in November 1860, but before he took office on March 4, 1861, seven states had seceded from the Union to form the Confederacy. Little more than a month after his inauguration, the Civil War had begun. He devoted himself to the preservation of the Union, without which, he believed, neither individuals nor the nation could live freely and decently. To preserve the Union he had to develop an overall war strategy, devise a workable command system, and find the right personnel to execute his plans. All of this he was to accomplish by trial and error in the early years of the war. At the same time he had to develop popular support for his purposes by using his extraordinary political skills in times of high passion and internal division. And when the war ended, leaving him and the country exhausted, he had immediately to face the monumental problems of healing a traumatized nation.

Only by degrees had Lincoln come to commit himself to the elimination of slavery throughout the country. Initially he wished only to stop the spread of slavery; then he saw that "a house divided against itself cannot stand," and finally, he took the leading role in the passage of the Thirteenth Amendment, which outlawed slavery everywhere and forever in the United States. Elected to a second term in 1864, he had served scarcely a month of his new term when he was assassinated, while attending a play, by the demented Shakespearean actor John Wilkes Booth. He died on April 15, 1865.

The texts of Lincoln's addresses are taken from Roy P. Basler's *Abraham Lincoln: His Speeches and Writings*, pp. 734 and 792–93. Lincoln's spellings have been retained throughout. The "Gettysburg Address" of November 19, 1863, is taken from the facsimiles reproduced in W. F. Barton's *Lincoln at Gettysburg* (1930); the "Second Inaugural" was delivered on March 4, 1865, and is based on photostats of the original manuscript owned by the Abraham Lincoln Association.

## Address Delivered at the Dedication of the Cemetery at Gettysburg November 19, 1863

Four score and seven years ago our fathers brought forth on this continent, a new nation, conceived in Liberty, and dedicated to the proposition that all men are created equal.

Now we are engaged in a great civil war, testing whether that nation, or any nation so conceived and so dedicated, can long endure. We are met on a great battle-field of that war. We have come to dedicate a portion of that field, as a final resting place for those who here gave their lives that that nation might live. It is altogether fitting and proper that we should do this.

But, in a larger sense, we can not dedicate—we can not consecrate—we can not hallow—this ground. The brave men, living and dead, who struggled here, have consecrated it, far above our poor power to add or detract. The world will little note, nor long remember what we say here, but it can never forget what they did here. It is for us the living, rather, to be dedicated here to the unfinished work which they who fought here have thus far so nobly advanced. It is rather for us to be here dedicated to the great task remaining before us—that from these honored dead we take increased devotion to that cause for which they gave the last full measure of devotion—that we here highly resolve that these dead shall not have died in vain—that this nation, under God, shall have a new birth of freedom—and that government of the people, by the people, for the people, shall not perish from the earth.

Abraham Lincoln

1863

## Second Inaugural Address March 4, 1865

At this second appearing to take the oath of the presidential office, there is less occasion for an extended address than there was at the first. Then a statement, somewhat in detail, of a course to be pursued, seemed fitting and proper. Now, at the expiration of four years, during which public declarations have been constantly called forth on every point and phase of the great contest which still absorbs the attention, and engrosses the energies of the nation, little that is new could be presented. The progress of our arms, upon which all else chiefly depends, is as well known to the public as to myself; and it is, I trust, reasonably satisfactory and encouraging to all. With high hope for the future, no prediction in regard to it is ventured.

On the occasion corresponding to this four years ago, all thoughts were anxiously directed to an impending civil war. All dreaded it—all sought to avert it. While the inaugural address was being delivered from this place, devoted altogether to *saving* the Union without war, insurgent agents were in the city seeking to *destroy* it without war—seeking to dissol[v]e the Union, and divide effects, by negotiation. Both parties deprecated war; but one of them would *make* war rather than let the nation survive; and the other would *accept* war rather than let it perish. And the war came.

One eighth of the whole population were colored slaves, not distributed generally over the Union, but localized in the Southern part of it. These slaves constituted a peculiar and powerful interest. All knew that this interest was, somehow, the cause of the war. To strengthen, perpetuate, and extend this interest was the object for which the insurgents would rend the Union, even by war; while the government claimed no right to do more than to restrict the territorial enlargement of it. Neither party expected for the war, the magnitude, or the duration, which it has already attained. Neither anticipated that the *cause* of the conflict might cease with, or even before, the conflict itself should cease. Each looked for an easier triumph, and a result less fundamental and astounding. Both read the same Bible, and pray to the same God; and each invokes His aid against the other. It may seem strange that any men should dare to ask a just God's assistance in wringing their bread from the sweat of other men's faces; but let us judge not that we be not judged. The prayers of both could not be answered; that of neither has been answered fully. The Almighty has his own purposes. "Woe unto the world because of offences! for it must needs be that offences come; but woe to that man by whom the offence cometh!" If we shall suppose that American Slavery is one of those offences which, in the providence of God, must needs come, but which, having continued through His appointed time, He now wills to remove, and that He gives to both North and South, this terrible war, as the woe due to those by whom the offence came, shall we discern therein any departure from those divine attributes which the believers in a Living God always ascribe to Him? Fondly do we hope—fervently do we pray—that this mighty scourge of war may speedily pass away. Yet, if God wills that it continue, until all the wealth piled by the bond-man's two hundred and fifty years of unrequited toil shall be sunk, and until every drop of blood drawn with the lash, shall be paid by another drawn with the sword, as was said three thousand years ago, so still it must be said "the judgments of the Lord, are true and righteous altogether."

With malice toward none; with charity for all; with firmness in the right, as God gives us to see the right, let us strive on to finish the work we are in; to bind up the nation's wounds; to care for him who shall have borne the battle, and for his widow, and his orphan—to do all which may achieve and cherish a just and lasting peace, among ourselves, and with all nations.

1865

## MARGARET FULLER
### 1810–1850

Sarah Margaret Fuller was born at Cambridgeport (now part of Cambridge), Massachusetts, on May 23, 1810. Her father supervised her education, making her a prodigy but depriving her of a childhood. After a brief, traumatic stay at a girls' school in her early teens, she returned to pursue her rigorous education at home, steeping herself in the classics and in modern languages and literatures, especially German. Accustomed to intense, lonely study, Fuller nevertheless formed lasting intellectual and emotional friendships with a few young Harvard scholars, among them her co-biographers James Freeman Clarke and W. H. Channing. A Cambridge lady, Eliza Farrar, undertook to instill some of the social graces into the father-taught Margaret. The death of her father in 1835 burdened Fuller with the education of younger brothers and sisters. Setting aside her own ambitions (including a planned trip to Europe), she taught for several years, in Boston and Providence. During this time the German novelist and dramatist Goethe became the chief influence on her religion and philosophy, and she tormented herself with the hope that she might have money, time, and ability to write his biography. In 1839 she began leading "Conversation" classes among an elite group of Boston women. Later, men participated also, and during the next years her topics included Greek mythology, the fine arts, ethics, education, demonology, creeds, and the ideal.

A close friend of Emerson's since she first sought him out in 1836, Fuller edited the Transcendentalists' magazine The Dial from 1840 to 1842, meanwhile continuing to translate works by and about Goethe. In 1844 Summer on the Lakes, an account of a trip to the Midwest, led Horace Greeley to hire her as literary critic for his New York Tribune, making her probably the first self-supporting American woman journalist. More than a literary reviewer, Fuller wrote a series of reports on public questions, among them the conditions of the blind, of the insane, and of female prisoners. In 1845 Greeley published her Woman in the Nineteenth Century, the title article of which was an expansion of a controversial Dial essay, The Great Lawsuit. This is one of the great neglected documents of American sexual liberation—not merely of feminism, for Fuller recognized that both men and women were imprisoned by social roles, although men at least had the power to make and enforce the definitions of those roles. In 1846 some of her Tribune pieces were collected in Papers on Literature and Art. In New York she fell in love with James Nathan, a German Jew who, a cosmopolite baffled by her mixture of sexual honesty and prudery, fled home in June 1845, letting the growing spaces between his letters persuade her gradually that he had rejected her.

Fuller sailed for Europe in August 1846, intending to support herself as foreign correspondent for the Tribune. In England one of her idols, Thomas Carlyle (then in his fifties), disappointed her by his reactionary political views and his insensitivity to the worth of others, especially the Italian revolutionary Joseph Mazzini, who had sought refuge in England. In Paris she met another idol, George Sand, who proved more satisfactory than Carlyle, and another political revolutionary, the exiled Polish poet Adam Mickiewicz. Sand's example of sexually liberated womanhood stirred Fuller profoundly, as did Mickiewicz's blunt speculation that she could not deeply respond to Europe while remaining a virgin—not the sort of comment men like Emerson and Greeley had accustomed her to. Fuller went on to Italy, then not a unified country but a collection of states—some controlled by the pope, others independent, and to the north, a third group controlled by Austria. Soon after her arrival in Rome she became the object of courtship by a Roman of the nobility, Giovanni Angelo Ossoli, almost eleven years younger than she.

When she returned from summering in northern Italy, Rome was undergoing antipapal ferment, and her dispatches to the *Tribune* became more and more political. Making use of her connections with varying factions, she began an earnest accumulation of documents concerning the forthcoming revolution—newspapers, pamphlets, leaflets.

And she began a love affair with Ossoli. In December she was pregnant, with no man or woman she could confide in, either in the United States or Europe. At the start of 1848 she wrote guardedly to a friend at home: "With this year I enter upon a sphere of my destiny so difficult that at present I see no way out except through the gate of death." Marriage seemed out of the question because of the certain opposition of Ossoli's family. Through a dismal rainy season, in which she lived on pennies a day, Fuller covered for the *Tribune* such events as the popular agitation against the Jesuits. She became intimate with the Princess Belgioioso, a leader of the anti-Austrian faction who drew her still more deeply into Italian politics. When cities of northern Italy revolted against the Austrians in March, Fuller described to her New York readers the joyous response of the Roman citizens. The revolutionaries Mickiewicz and Mazzini entered Italy; both kept in touch with Fuller out of their respect for her personal commitment to their goals and their sense of her value in shaping American opinion.

That spring, 1848, Emerson wrote from England urging her to return home with him before war broke out. Still keeping her secret, she withdrew instead to the Abruzzi region to wait out her pregnancy. Ossoli had become a member of the civic guard, but he managed to be with her for the birth of Angelo on September 5. Leaving the baby in Rieti with a wet nurse, Fuller returned to Rome late in November, in time to report the flight of the pope and, early in 1849, the arrival of the Italian nationalist Giuseppe Garibaldi and the proclamation of the Roman Republic. She shared the triumph of Mazzini's arrival in Rome, but the Republic was short-lived. Anticipating the intervention of the French on behalf of the pope, Princess Belgioioso urgently wrote Fuller on April 30, 1849: "You are named Regolatrice of the Hospital of the Fate Bene Fratelli"—on an island in the Tiber. Fuller ran the hospital heroically when the French laid siege, despite her concern for Ossoli, who was fighting with the Republican forces, and her uncertainty about the baby, whom she had hardly seen since he was two months old. After Rome fell to the French on the fourth of July she made her way to Rieti, only to find that the nurse, assuming the baby had been abandoned, was allowing him to starve. Retreating to Florence with Ossoli and the baby, Fuller faced down her shocked acquaintances, including Robert and Elizabeth Barrett Browning, and began work on her history of the Roman Republic. While at Florence she may have married Ossoli, as his sister later claimed. In May 1850, she sailed for the United States with Ossoli and the baby, full of forebodings about the ship and the way they would be received at home. All three died in a shipwreck off Fire Island, New York, on July 19. The body of the baby was washed ashore as well as a trunk that contained some of Fuller's papers but not the history. Thoreau sought in vain for her body.

Emerson, Clarke, and Channing edited Fuller's *Memoirs* (1852) in a way that sanitized her personal life, denigrated her accomplishments as a writer, and slighted her lifelong activism. In 1903 her friend Julia Ward Howe published her love letters to James Nathan, thereby sealing the image of Fuller as a would-be intellectual, willful and foolish in her personal entanglements. Hawthorne's old verdict seemed confirmed: "There never was such a tragedy as her whole story; the sadder and sterner, because so much of the ridiculous was mixed up with it, and because she could bear anything better than to be ridiculous."

Sexist ridicule dies hard, and in Fuller's case its death was retarded by the long inaccessibility of most of her writings. The Fuller bibliography included in this volume shows that her writings now, in the 1980s and the 1990s, are fast coming back into print—an excellent edition of her letters, a collection of her dispatches to the *Tribune* from Europe, an annotated edition of her *Woman in the Nineteenth Century*, and a generous anthology of her writings. The substantial "popular" biography of 1990 was followed in 1992 by the meticulously researched first volume of a projected two-volume scholarly biography. The evidence is at hand that may at last establish Fuller's candidacy for serious consideration as what Hawthorne said mockingly, "the greatest, wisest, best woman of the age."

## From The Great Lawsuit
## MAN versus MEN. WOMAN versus WOMEN[1]

### [Four Kinds of Equality]

Where the thought of equality has become pervasive, it shows itself in four kinds.

The household partnership. In our country the woman looks for a "smart but kind" husband, the man for a "capable, sweet-tempered" wife.

The man furnishes the house, the woman regulates it. Their relation is one of mutual esteem, mutual dependence. Their talk is of business, their affection shows itself by practical kindness. They know that life goes more smoothly and cheerfully to each for the other's aid; they are grateful and content. The wife praises her husband as a "good provider," the husband in return compliments her as a "capital housekeeper." This relation is good as far as it goes.

Next comes a closer tie which takes the two forms, either of intellectual companionship, or mutual idolatry. The last, we suppose, is to no one a pleasing subject of contemplation. The parties weaken and narrow one another; they lock the gate against all the glories of the universe that they may live in a cell together. To themselves they seem the only wise, to all others steeped in infatuation, the gods smile as they look forward to the crisis of cure, to men the woman seems an unlovely syren, to women the man an effeminate boy.

The other form, of intellectual companionship, has become more and more frequent. Men engaged in public life, literary men, and artists have often found in their wives companions and confidants in thought no less than in feeling. And, as in the course of things the intellectual development of woman has spread wider and risen higher, they have, not unfrequently, shared the same employment. As in the case of Roland and his wife, who were friends in the household and the nation's councils, read together, regulated home affairs, or prepared public documents together indifferently.

It is very pleasant, in letters begun by Roland and finished by his wife, to

---

1. Reprinted here from the Boston *Dial*, vol. 4 (July 1843). In 1844 Fuller published the revised, expanded version of this work under the title *Woman in the Nineteenth Century*, but the additions were hardly more than padding. This passage of her preliminary 1844 footnote makes clear her intentions for the original title of the essay: "Objections having been made to the former title, as not sufficiently easy to be understood, the present has been substituted as expressive of the main purpose of the essay; though, by myself, the other is preferred, partly for the reason others do not like it,— that is, that it requires some thought to see what it means, and might thus prepare the reader to meet me on my own ground. Besides, it offers a larger scope, and is, in that way, more just to my desire. I meant by that title to intimate the fact that, while it is the destiny of Man, in the course of the ages, to ascertain and fulfil the law of his being, so that his life shall be seen, as a whole, to be that of an angel or messenger, the action of prejudices and passions which attend, in the day, the growth of the individual, is continually obstructing the holy work that is to make earth a part of heaven. By Men I mean both man and woman; these are the two halves of one thought. I lay no especial stress on the welfare of either. I believe that the development of the one cannot be effected without that of the other. My highest wish is that this truth should be distinctly and rationally apprehended, and the conditions of life and freedom recognized as the same for the daughters and the sons of time; twin exponents of a divine thought." Fuller's relentlessly allusive style was typical of her time. A few of her more elusive references have had to remain unglossed in this anthology.

see the harmony of mind and the difference of nature, one thought, but various ways of treating it.

This is one of the best instances of a marriage of friendship. It was only friendship, whose basis was esteem; probably neither party knew love, except by name.

Roland was a good man, worthy to esteem and be esteemed, his wife as deserving of admiration as able to do without it. Madame Roland is the fairest specimen we have yet of her class, as clear to discern her aim, as valiant to pursue it, as Spenser's Britomart, austerely set apart from all that did not belong to her, whether as woman or as mind. She is an antetype of a class to which the coming time will afford a field, the Spartan matron, brought by the culture of a book-furnishing age to intellectual consciousness and expansion.

Self-sufficing strength and clear-sightedness were in her combined with a power of deep and calm affection. The page of her life is one of unsullied dignity.

Her appeal to posterity is one against the injustice of those who committed such crimes in the name of liberty. She makes it in behalf of herself and her husband. I would put beside it on the shelf a little volume, containing a similar appeal from the verdict of contemporaries to that of mankind, that of Godwin in behalf of his wife, the celebrated, the by most men detested Mary Wolstonecraft.[2] In his view it was an appeal from the injustice of those who did such wrong in the name of virtue.

Were this little book interesting for no other cause, it would be so for the generous affection evinced under the peculiar circumstances. This man had courage to love and honor this woman in the face of the world's verdict, and of all that was repulsive in her own past history. He believed he saw of what soul she was, and that the thoughts she had struggled to act out were noble. He loved her and he defended her for the meaning and intensity of her inner life. It was a good fact.

Mary Wolstonecraft, like Madame Dudevant[3] (commonly known as George Sand) in our day, was a woman whose existence better proved the need of some new interpretation of woman's rights, than anything she wrote. Such women as these, rich in genius, of most tender sympathies, and capable of high virtue and a chastened harmony, ought not to find themselves by birth in a place so narrow, that in breaking bonds they become outlaws. Were there as much room in the world for such, as in Spenser's poem for Britomart, they would not run their heads so wildly against its laws. They find their way at last to purer air, but the world will not take off the brand it has set upon them. The champion of the rights of woman found in Godwin one who would plead her own cause like a brother. George Sand smokes, wears male attire, wishes to be addressed as Mon frère;[4] perhaps, if she found those who were as brothers indeed, she would not care whether she were brother or sister.

We rejoice to see that she, who expresses such a painful contempt for men in most of her works, as shows she must have known great wrong from them, in La Roche Mauprat[5] depicting one raised, by the workings of love, from the

2. *Memoirs of the Author of "A Vindication of the Rights of Woman"* (1798) by William Godwin (1756–1836); Mary Wollstonecraft (1759–1797) married Godwin shortly before her death in childbirth.
3. Amandine Aurore Lucile Dudevant (1804–1876), French Romantic novelist, scandalous for her succession of lovers and mannish attire but admired by those like Fuller who saw her as crusader for the liberation of women.
4. Old friend and colleague (French); my brother (literal trans.).
5. Drama by George Sand.

depths of savage sensualism to a moral and intellectual life. It was love for a pure object, for a steadfast woman, one of those who, the Italian said, could make the stair to heaven.

Women like Sand will speak now, and cannot be silenced; their characters and their eloquence alike foretell an era when such as they shall easier learn to lead true lives. But though such forebode, not such shall be the parents of it. Those who would reform the world must show that they do not speak in the heat of wild impulse; their lives must be unstained by passionate error; they must be severe lawgivers to themselves. As to their transgressions and opinions, it may be observed, that the resolve of Eloisa to be only the mistress of Abelard, was that of one who saw the contract of marriage a seal of degradation.[6] Wherever abuses of this sort are seen, the timid will suffer, the bold protest. But society is in the right to outlaw them till she has revised her law, and she must be taught to do so, by one who speaks with authority, not in anger and haste.

If Godwin's choice of the calumniated authoress of the "Rights of Woman," for his honored wife, be a sign of a new era, no less so is an article of great learning and eloquence, published several years since in an English review, where the writer, in doing full justice to Eloisa, shows his bitter regret that she lives not now to love him, who might have known better how to prize her love than did the egotistical Abelard.

These marriages, these characters, with all their imperfections, express an onward tendency. They speak of aspiration of soul, of energy of mind, seeking clearness and freedom. Of a like promise are the tracts now publishing by Goodwyn Barmby[7] (the European Pariah as he calls himself) and his wife Catherine. Whatever we may think of their measures, we see them in wedlock, the two minds are wed by the only contract that can permanently avail, of a common faith, and a common purpose.

We might mention instances, nearer home, of minds, partners in work and in life, sharing together, on equal terms, public and private interests, and which have not on any side that aspect of offence which characterizes the attitude of the last named; persons who steer straight onward, and in our freer life have not been obliged to run their heads against any wall. But the principles which guide them might, under petrified or oppressive institutions, have made them warlike, paradoxical, or, in some sense, Pariahs. The phenomenon is different, the last the same, in all these cases. Men and women have been obliged to build their house from the very foundation. If they found stone ready in the quarry, they took it peaceably, otherwise they alarmed the country by pulling down old towers to get materials.

These are all instances of marriage as intellectual companionship. The parties meet mind to mind, and a mutual trust is excited which can buckler them against a million. They work together for a common purpose, and, in all these instances, with the same implement, the pen.

A pleasing expression in this kind is afforded by the union in the names of the Howitts.[8] William and Mary Howitt we heard named together for years, supposing them to be brother and sister; the equality of labors and reputation, even so, was auspicious, more so, now we find them man and wife. In his late work on Germany, Howitt mentions his wife with pride, as one among the

6. In her famous letters Eloisa steadfastly refused to marry Abelard, because marriage would force him to give up his teaching of theology within the church.

7. Minor British publisher.
8. William Howitt (1792–1879) and Mary Howitt (1799–1888), prolific British authors and translators.

constellation of distinguished English women, and in a graceful, simple manner.

In naming these instances we do not mean to imply that community of employment is an essential to union of this sort, more than to the union of friendship. Harmony exists no less in difference than in likeness, if only the same key-note govern both parts. Woman the poem, man the poet; woman the heart, man the head; such divisions are only important when they are never to be transcended. If nature is never bound down, nor the voice of inspiration stifled, that is enough. We are pleased that women should write and speak, if they feel the need of it, from having something to tell; but silence for a hundred years would be as well, if that silence be from divine command, and not from man's tradition.

While Goetz von Berlichingen[9] rides to battle, his wife is busy in the kitchen; but difference of occupation does not prevent that community of life, that perfect esteem, with which he says,

"Whom God loves, to him gives he such a wife!"

Manzoni thus dedicates his Adelchi.[1]

"To his beloved and venerated wife, Enrichetta Luigia Blondel, who, with conjugal affections and maternal wisdom, has preserved a virgin mind, the author dedicates this Adelchi, grieving that he could not, by a more splendid and more durable monument, honor the dear name and the memory of so many virtues."

The relation could not be fairer, nor more equal, if she too had written poems. Yet the position of the parties might have been the reverse as well; the woman might have sung the deeds, given voice to the life of the man, and beauty would have been the result, as we see in pictures of Arcadia[2] the nymph singing to the shepherds, or the shepherd with his pipe allures the nymphs, either makes a good picture. The sounding lyre requires not muscular strength, but energy of soul to animate the hand which can control it. Nature seems to delight in varying her arrangements, as if to show that she will be fettered by no rule, and we must admit the same varieties that she admits.

I have not spoken of the higher grade of marriage union, the religious, which may be expressed as pilgrimage towards a common shrine. This includes the others; home sympathies, and household wisdom, for these pilgrims must know how to assist one another to carry their burdens along the dusty way; intellectual communion, for how sad it would be on such a journey to have a companion to whom you could not communicate thoughts and aspirations, as they sprang to life, who would have no feeling for the more and more glorious prospects that open as we advance, who would never see the flowers that may be gathered by the most industrious traveler. It must include all these. Such a fellow pilgrim Count Zinzendorf[3] seems to have found in his countess of whom he thus writes:

9. German knight (1481–1562), a sort of Robin Hood, familiar to Fuller from Goethe's play *Göetz von Berlichingen*.
1. A tragedy (1822) by Alessandro Manzoni (1735–1873), Italian writer.
2. Pastoral district of the Peloponnesus in Greece, symbolic of rustic simplicity and contentment.

3. Nikolas Ludwig, Count von Zinzendorf (1700–1760) German leader of the Moravian church, or the Bohemian Brethren, a Protestant sect founded in Bohemia in 1457, influential both in Europe and in the Moravian settlements in the American colonies, which he visited.

"Twenty-five years' experience has shown me that just the help-mate whom I have is the only one that could suit my vocation, Who else could have so carried through my family affairs? Who lived so spotlessly before the world? Who so wisely aided me in my rejection of a dry morality? Who so clearly set aside the Pharisaism[4] which, as years passed, threatened to creep in among us? Who so deeply discerned as to the spirits of delusion which sought to bewilder us? Who would have governed my whole economy so wisely, richly, and hospitably when circumstances commanded? Who have taken indifferently the part of servant or mistress, without on the one side affecting an especial spirituality, on the other being sullied by any worldly pride? Who, in a community where all ranks are eager to be on a level, would, from wise and real causes, have known how to maintain inward and outward distinctions? Who, without a murmur, have seen her husband encounter such dangers by land and sea? Who undertaken with him and sustained such astonishing pilgrimages? Who amid such difficulties always held up her head, and supported me? Who found so many hundred thousands and acquitted them on her own credit? And, finally, who, of all human beings, would so well understand and interpret to others my inner and outer being as this one, of such nobleness in her way of thinking, such great intellectual capacity, and free from the theological perplexities that enveloped me?"

An observer[5] adds this testimony.

"We may in many marriages regard it as the best arrangement, if the man has so much advantage over his wife that she can, without much thought of her own, be, by him, led and directed, as by a father. But it was not so with the Count and his consort. She was not made to be a copy; she was an original; and, while she loved and honored him, she thought for herself on all subjects with so much intelligence, that he could and did look on her as a sister and friend also."

Such a woman is the sister and friend of all beings, as the worthy man is their brother and helper.

\* \* \*

## [The Great Radical Dualism]

For woman, if by a sympathy as to outward condition, she is led to aid the enfranchisement of the slave, must no less so, by inward tendency, to favor measures which promise to bring the world more thoroughly and deeply into harmony with her nature. When the lamb takes place of the lion as the emblem of nations, both women and men will be as children of one spirit, perpetual learners of the word and doers thereof, not hearers only.

A writer in a late number of the New York Pathfinder, in two articles headed "Femality," has uttered a still more pregnant word than any we have named. He views woman truly from the soul, and not from society, and the depth and leading of his thoughts is proportionably remarkable. He views the feminine

---

4. Self-righteous hypocrites, from the Jewish sect whom Jesus condemned as whitened sepulchres (Matthew 23.27), "which indeed appear beautiful outward, but are within full of dead men's bones, and of all uncleanness."

5. "Spangenberg" [Fuller's note]. August Gotlieb Spangenberg (1704–1792), successor to Count von Zinzendorf, bishop of the Moravian Brethren.

nature as a harmonizer of the vehement elements, and this has often been hinted elsewhere; but what he expresses more forcibly is the lyrical, the inspiring and inspired apprehensiveness of her being.

Had I room to dwell upon this topic, I could not say anything so precise, so near the heart of the matter, as may be found in that article; but, as it is, I can only indicate, not declare, my view.

There are two aspects of woman's nature, expressed by the ancients as Muse and Minerva.[6] It is the former to which the writer in the Pathfinder looks. It is the latter which Wordsworth has in mind, when he says,

> "With a placid brow,
> Which woman ne'er should forfeit, keep thy vow."[7]

The especial genius of woman I believe to be electrical[8] in movement, intuitive in function, spiritual in tendency. She is great not so easily in classification, or re-creation, as in an instinctive seizure of causes, and a simple breathing out of what she receives that has the singleness of life, rather than the selecting or energizing of art.

More native to her is it to be the living model of the artist, than to set apart from herself any one form in objective reality; more native to inspire and receive the poem than to create it. In so far as soul is in her completely developed, all soul is the same; but as far as it is modified in her as woman, it flows, it breathes, it sings, rather than deposits soil, or finishes work, and that which is especially feminine flushes in blossom the face of earth, and pervades like air and water all this seeming solid globe, daily renewing and purifying its life. Such may be the especially feminine element, spoken of as Femality. But it is no more the order of nature that it should be incarnated pure in any form, than that the masculine energy should exist unmingled with it in any form.

Male and female represent the two sides of the great radical dualism. But, in fact, they are perpetually passing into one another. Fluid hardens to solid, solid rushes to fluid. There is no wholly masculine man, no purely feminine woman.

History jeers at the attempts of physiologists to bind great original laws by the forms which flow from them. They make a rule; they say from observation what can and cannot be. In vain! Nature provides exceptions to every rule. She sends women to battle, and sets Hercules spinning;[9] she enables women to bear immense burdens, cold, and frost; she enables the man, who feels maternal love, to nourish his infant like a mother. Of late she plays still gayer pranks. Not only she deprives organizations, but organs, of a necessary end. She enables people to read with the top of the head, and see with the pit of the stomach. Presently she will make a female Newton, and a male Syren.[1]

Man partakes of the feminine in the Apollo, woman of the masculine as Minerva.

Let us be wise and not impede the soul. Let her work as she will. Let us

6. The poetical or artistic aspect, embodied in the Muses, goddesses of song and poetry and the arts and sciences, and the intellectually serene aspect, embodied in Minerva, goddess of wisdom.
7. Slightly misquoted from Liberty: Sequel to the Preceding, published 1835.
8. Darting in sparklike fashion; the root in New Latin, electricus, means "like amber," from the fact that

amber gives off sparks when rubbed.
9. I.e., sets the strongest men to domestic tasks.
1. In the inversion of sexual stereotypes, a male would be as alluring as the Syrens (or Sirens), Greek sea nymphs who lured mariners into shipwreck on the rocks surrounding their island. Isaac Newton (1642–1727), English mathematician.

have one creative energy, one incessant revelation. Let it take what form it will, and let us not bind it by the past to man or woman, black or white. Jove sprang from Rhea, Pallas from Jove.[2] So let it be.

If it has been the tendency of the past remarks to call woman rather to the Minerva side,—if I, unlike the more generous writer, have spoken from society no less than the soul,—let it be pardoned. It is love that has caused this, love for many incarcerated souls, that might be freed could the idea of religious self-dependence be established in them, could the weakening habit of dependence on others be broken up.

Every relation, every gradation of nature, is incalculably precious, but only to the soul which is poised upon itself, and to whom no loss, no change, can bring dull discord, for it is in harmony with the central soul.

If any individual live too much in relations, so that he becomes a stranger to the resources of his own nature, he falls after a while into a distraction, or imbecility, from which he can only be cured by a time of isolation, which gives the renovating fountains time to rise up. With a society it is the same. Many minds, deprived of the traditionary or instinctive means of passing a cheerful existence, must find help in self-impulse or perish. It is therefore that while any elevation, in the view of union, is to be hailed with joy, we shall not decline celibacy as the great fact of the time. It is one from which no vow, no arrangement, can at present save a thinking mind. For now the rowers are pausing on their oars, they wait a change before they can pull together. All tends to illustrate the thought of a wise contemporary. Union is only possible to those who are units. To be fit for relations in time, souls, whether of man or woman, must be able to do without them in the spirit.

It is therefore that I would have woman lay aside all thought, such as she habitually cherishes, of being taught and led by men. I would have her, like the Indian girl, dedicate herself to the Sun, the Sun of Truth, and go no where if his beams did not make clear the path. I would have her free from compromise, from complaisance, from helplessness, because I would have her good enough and strong enough to love one and all beings, from the fulness, not the poverty of being.

Men, as at present instructed, will not help this work, because they also are under the slavery of habit. I have seen with delight their poetic impulses. A sister is the fairest ideal and how nobly Wordsworth, and even Byron, have written of a sister.[3]

There is no sweeter sight than to see a father with his little daughter. Very vulgar men become refined to the eye when leading a little girl by the hand. At that moment the right relation between the sexes seems established, and you feel as if the man would aid in the noblest purpose, if you ask him in behalf of his little daughter. Once two fine figures stood before me, thus. The father of very intellectual aspect, his falcon eye softened by affection as he looked down on his fair child, she the image of himself, only more graceful and brilliant in expression. I was reminded of Southey's Kehama,[4] when lo, the dream was rudely broken. They were talking of education, and he said.

2. In Greek mythology, Rhea, the sister and wife of Cronus, bore Jove. Pallas Athena sprang from Jove's skull, fully grown and fully armed.
3. Fuller is thinking of the various tributes by William Wordsworth to his sister Dorothy and Lord Byron to his half-sister Augusta Leigh. Only later in the century was evidence presented of Byron's incest with Augusta,

and not until the late 20th century did scholars begin to debate the possibility that William and Dorothy Wordsworth might have committed incest. Fuller's examples are unfortunate, not deliberately ironic.
4. Robert Southey's *The Curse of Kehama* (1810), a rhymed Oriental tale.

"I shall not have Maria brought too forward. If she knows too much, she will never find a husband; superior women hardly ever can."

"Surely," said his wife, with a blush, "you wish Maria to be as good and wise as she can, whether it will help her to marriage or not."

"No," he persisted, "I want her to have a sphere and a home, and some one to protect her when I am gone."

It was a trifling incident, but made a deep impression. I felt that the holiest relations fail to instruct the unprepared and perverted mind. If this man, indeed, would have looked at it on the other side, he was the last that would have been willing to have been taken himself for the home and protection he could give, but would have been much more likely to repeat the tale of Alcibiades with his phials.

But men do *not* look at both sides, and women must leave off asking them and being influenced by them, but retire within themselves, and explore the groundwork of being till they find their peculiar secret. Then when they come forth again, renovated and baptized, they will know how to turn all dross to gold, and will be rich and free though they live in a hut, tranquil, if in a crowd. Then their sweet singing shall not be from passionate impulse, but the lyrical overflow of a divine rapture, and a new music shall be elucidated from this many-chorded world.

Grant her then for a while the armor and the javelin.[5] Let her put from her the press of other minds and meditate in virgin loneliness. The same idea shall reappear in due time as Muse, or Ceres,[6] the all-kindly, patient Earth-Spirit.

I tire every one with my Goethean illustrations. But it cannot be helped.

Goethe, the great mind which gave itself absolutely to the leadings of truth, and let rise through him the waves which are still advancing through the century, was its intellectual prophet. Those who know him, see, daily, his thought fulfilled more and more, and they must speak of it, till his name weary and even nauseate, as all great names have in their time. And I cannot spare the reader, if such there be, his wonderful sight as to the prospects and wants of women.

As his Wilhelm grows in life and advances in wisdom, he becomes acquainted with women of more and more character, rising from Mariana to Macaria.[7]

Macaria, bound with the heavenly bodies in fixed revolutions, the centre of all relations, herself unrelated, expresses the Minerva side.

Mignon, the electrical, inspired lyrical nature.

All these women, though we see them in relations, we can think of as unrelated. They all are very individual, yet seem nowhere restrained. They satisfy for the present, yet arouse an infinite expectation.

The economist Theresa, the benevolent Natalia, the fair Saint, have chosen a path, but their thoughts are not narrowed to it. The functions of life to them are not ends, but suggestions.

Thus to them all things are important, because none is necessary. Their different characters have fair play, and each is beautiful in its minute indications, for nothing is enforced or conventional, but everything, however slight, grows from the essential life of the being.

Mignon and Theresa wear male attire when they like, and it is graceful for

5. The weapons of Athena, Greek goddess of wisdom.
6. The Roman goddess of agriculture.
7. Feminine characters in Johann Wolfgang von

Goethe's *Wilhelm Meister's Apprenticeship*; other female characters from the same book are named just below.

them to do so, while Macaria is confined to her arm chair behind the green curtain, and the Fair Saint could not bear a speck of dust on her robe.

All things are in their places in this little world because all is natural and free, just as "there is room for everything out of doors." Yet all is rounded in by natural harmony which will always arise where Truth and Love are sought in the light of freedom.

Goethe's book bodes an era of freedom like its own, of "extraordinary generous seeking," and new revelations. New individualities shall be developed in the actual world, which shall advance upon it as gently as the figures come out upon his canvass.

A profound thinker has said "no married woman can represent the female world, for she belongs to her husband. The idea of woman must be represented by a virgin."

But that is the very fault of marriage, and of the present relation between the sexes, that the woman does belong to the man, instead of forming a whole with him. Were it otherwise there would be no such limitation to the thought.

Woman, self-centred, would never be absorbed by any relation; it would be only an experience to her as to man. It is a vulgar error that love, *a* love to woman is her whole existence; she also is born for Truth and Love in their universal energy. Would she but assume her inheritance, Mary would not be the only Virgin Mother. Not Manzoni[8] alone would celebrate in his wife the virgin mind with the maternal wisdom and conjugal affections. The soul is ever young, ever virgin.

And will not she soon appear? The woman who shall vindicate their birthright for all women; who shall teach them what to claim, and how to use what they obtain? Shall not her name be for her era Victoria, for her country and her life Virginia?[9] Yet predictions are rash; she herself must teach us to give her the fitting name.

1843

---

8. Another allusion to the preface to Manzoni's *Adelchi*.
9. I.e., shall not her character include both trium-

phant power (such as made Victoria so fit a name for a queen) and immaculateness (whether literally virginal or not)?

---

# HARRIET BEECHER STOWE
## 1811–1896

Harriet Beecher was born into a respectable family that was to become famous: her father, Lyman, was a renowned clergyman; two of her brothers, Henry Ward and Edward, were celebrated preachers; and her older sister, Catharine, pioneered in women's education. The family was dominated by the father, who ruled with the kind of wrathful severity that he imagined was the chief characteristic of the God he worshiped and feared. The boys were expected to become preachers, the girls to marry preachers.

Stowe began school in 1816 in Litchfield, Connecticut, and when Catharine established the Hartford Female Seminary in 1824, she joined her sister there. Their father became president of the recently founded Lane Theological Seminary in Cincinnati in 1832, and the sisters reluctantly rejoined the family in this "London of the West," as he described what was still a small, raw frontier town. Harriet

Stowe continued to work for her domineering older sister at the Western Female Institute she initiated, and seemed headed for a lifetime as an unknown, housebound spinster. She escaped this fate in part by converting, at great personal cost given her heavy domestic duties, her lifelong interest in writing into magazine stories that in the 1830s and 1840s earned her a few welcomed dollars. In 1836 she married Calvin Ellis Stowe, one of the leading professors at Lane, and bore the first four of their seven children within four years. The fees from her writing were useful in keeping the family on the respectable side of genteel poverty.

After eighteen years living across the Ohio River from slaveholding communities—and absorbing from fugitive slaves and visits to the South a personal knowledge of the institution of slavery—Stowe returned to New England in 1850 when her husband took a professorship at Bowdoin College in Brunswick, Maine. Partly inspired by the moral outrage that greeted the Fugitive Slave Act of 1850 (that allowed owners to pursue and recover their "property" in free states), partly liberated by her return to her New England roots, perhaps—as she claimed late in life—inspired by a God-sent image of a slave suffering, being beaten, yet forgiving his tormentors, *Uncle Tom's Cabin, or The Man That Was a Thing* (as it was originally titled) was conceived early in February 1851.

The novel began serially in the *National Era* on June 5, 1851, and the last installment appeared on April 1, 1852. The *National Era* was essentially, but not exclusively, devoted to promoting abolitionist principles, but it did so with less evangelical indignation than William Lloyd Garrison's *Liberator*. Even so, Stowe did not find a book publisher easily. When the novel did appear, however, it was an overnight success. It sold 350,000 copies during the first year, and since then has been published in some forty languages and has been read by millions of people around the world. The power of the novel unquestionably comes from the investment of the author's sense of her own suffering and oppression (as well as her determination to be free) in the characters of Tom and his fellow slave Eliza, the protagonists of the book's two main plots.

Stowe did not anticipate the sensation the novel created. To cope with Southern opposition and challenges to its accuracy, she wrote the nonfiction *A Key to Uncle Tom's Cabin*, with documented case histories to support what she had portrayed fictionally. *Dred: A Tale of the Great Dismal Swamp* (1856) was another antislavery novel, which may best be understood as an unsuccessful attempt to repeat the theme and extend the argument of her masterpiece: that a society resting on slavery could not long survive.

Because *Uncle Tom's Cabin* was such a phenomenal success, it is easy to forget that Stowe was a prolific writer for another thirty-five years, publishing regularly in *Atlantic Monthly* from the time of its founding in 1857 and in other leading periodicals on a wide variety of subjects and in a great many literary forms. Indeed, many critics feel that novels such as *The Pearl of Orr's Island* (1862), in which she depicts realistically rural life in Maine, and *Oldtown Folks* (1869), which details domestic life on the north shore of Massachusetts, constitute the true basis of her claim to our attention. There can be no question that her attention to local legends and dialects, her gift for creating humorous characters, and her capacity for compelling storytelling influenced many later regional writers, including Sarah Orne Jewett and Mary Wilkins Freeman.

Stowe's life was a sharply alternating mixture of success and notoriety and personal tragedy and pain. After *Uncle Tom's Cabin* broke upon the world, she traveled widely, met heads of state such as Abraham Lincoln and Queen Victoria, and lived among the rich and famous. At the same time, two sons died very young, another was an alcoholic, and she was deeply distressed by the scandal that touched her famous brother Henry Ward (who was tried for adultery). Her seventieth birthday was something of a national event, but her husband died a few years later and she ended her life an infirm recluse.

# *From* Uncle Tom's Cabin; or Life among the Lowly[1]

## Chapter VII. *The Mother's Struggle*

It is impossible to conceive of a human creature more wholly desolate and forlorn than Eliza, when she turned her footsteps from Uncle Tom's cabin.

Her husband's sufferings and dangers, the danger of her child, all blended in her mind with a confused and stunning sense of the risk she was running in leaving the only home she had ever known, and cutting loose from the protection of a friend whom she loved and revered. Then there was the parting from every familiar object—the place where she had grown up, the trees under which she had played, the groves where she had walked many an evening in happier days, by the side of her young husband—everything, as it lay in the clear frosty moonlight, seemed to speak reproachfully to her, and ask her whither could she go from a home like that?

But stronger than all was maternal love, wrought into a paroxysm of frenzy by the near approach of a fearful danger. Her boy was old enough to have walked by her side, and in an indifferent case she would only have led him by the hand; but now the bare thought of putting him out of her arms made her shudder, and she strained him to her bosom with a convulsive grasp as she went rapidly forward. The frosty ground creaked beneath her feet, and she trembled at the sound; every quaking leaf and fluttering shadow sent the blood backward to her heart, and quickened her footsteps. She wondered within herself at the strength that seemed to be come upon her, for she felt the weight of her boy as if it had been a feather, and every flutter of fear seemed to increase the supernatural strength that bore her on, while from her pale lips burst forth, in frequent ejaculations, the prayer to a Friend above—"Lord, help! Lord, save me!"

If it were *your* Harry, mother, or your Willie, that were going to be torn from you by a brutal trader, to-morrow morning—if you had seen the man, and heard that the papers were signed and delivered, and you had only from twelve o'clock till morning to make good your escape, how fast could *you* walk? How many miles could you make in those few brief hours, with the darling at your bosom—the little sleepy head on your shoulder—the small, soft arms trustingly holding on to your neck?

For the child slept; at first the novelty and alarm kept him waking; but his mother so hurriedly repressed every breath or sound, and so assured him that if he were only still, she would certainly save him, that he clung quietly round her neck, only asking, as he found himself sinking to sleep—

"Mother, I don't need to keep awake, do I?"

"No, my darling; sleep if you want to."

"But mother, if I do get asleep, you won't let him get me."

"No! so may God help me!" said his mother, with a paler cheek and a brighter light in her large dark eyes.

"You're sure, ain't you, mother?"

"Yes, *sure!*" said the mother, in a voice that startled herself, for it seemed to

---

1. *Uncle Tom's Cabin* was first published serially; the present chapter appeared in the *National Era* (July 19, 1851), the source of the present text. Before this selection opens, Mr. Shelby has sold his slaves Uncle Tom and Harry, young son of Eliza, to Dan Haley, a slave trader. A devout Christian, Tom accepts his fate as best he can, always hoping to return to his home in Kentucky. Eliza, however, flees across the Ohio River with her son.

her to come from a spirit within, that was no part of her; and the boy dropped his little weary head on her shoulder, and was soon asleep. How the touch of those warm arms, the gentle breathings that came in her neck, seemed to add fire and spirit to her movements. It seemed to her as if strength poured into her in electric streams, from every gentle touch and movement of her sleeping, confiding child. Sublime is the dominion of the mind over the body, that for a time can make flesh and nerve impregnable, and string the sinews, like steel, so that the weak become so mighty!

The boundaries of the farm, the grove, the wood-lot, passed by her dizzily as she passed on, and still she walked, leaving one familiar object after another, slacking not, pausing not, till reddening daylight found her many a long mile from all traces of any familiar objects upon the open highway.

She had often been with her mistress, to visit some connections in the little village of T———, not far from the Ohio river, and knew the road well. To go thither, to escape across the Ohio river, were the first hurried outlines of her plan of escape—beyond which she could only hope in God.

When horses and vehicles began to move along the highway, with that keen and alert perception peculiar to a state of excitement, and which seems to be a sort of inspiration, she became aware that her headlong pace and distracted air might bring on her remark and suspicion. She therefore put the boy on the ground, and, adjusting her dress and bonnet, she walked on at as rapid a pace as she thought consistent with the preservation of appearances. In her little bundle she had provided a store of cakes and apples, which she used as expedients for quickening the speed of the child—rolling the apple some yards before them, when the boy would run with all his might after it; and this ruse, often repeated, carried them over many a half mile.

After a while they came to a thick patch of woodland, through which murmured a clear brook. As the child complained of hunger and thirst, she climbed over the fence with him; and sitting down behind a large rock which concealed them from the road, she gave him a breakfast out of her little package. The boy wondered and grieved that she could not eat, and when, putting his arms around her neck, he tried to wedge some of his cake into her mouth, it seemed to her that the rising in her throat would choke her.

"No, no, Harry, darling, mother can't eat till you are safe. We must go on—on—till we come to the river." And she hurried again into the road, and again constrained herself to walk regularly and composedly forward.

She was many miles past any neighborhood where she was personally known. If she should chance to meet any who knew her, she reflected that the well-known kindness of the family would be of itself a blind to suspicion, as making it an unlikely supposition that she could be a fugitive. As she was also so white as not to be known as of colored lineage, without a critical survey, and her child was white also, it was much easier for her to pass on unsuspected.

On this presumption, she stopped at noon at a neat farm-house, to rest herself, and buy some dinner for her child and self—for as the danger decreased with the distance, the supernatural tension of the nervous system lessened, and she found herself both weary and hungry.

The good woman, kindly and gossiping, seemed rather pleased than otherwise, with having somebody come in to talk with, and accepted without examination Eliza's statement that she "was going on a little piece to spend a week with her friends"—all which she hoped in her heart might prove strictly true.

An hour before sunset she entered the village of T——, by the Ohio river, weary and footsore, but still strong in heart. Her first glance was at the river, which lay, like Jordan,[2] between her and the Canaan of liberty on the other side.

It was now early spring, and the river was swollen and turbulent; great cakes of floating ice were swinging heavily to and fro in the turbid waters. Owing to the peculiar form of the shore on the Kentucky side, the land bending far out into the water, the ice had been lodged and detained in great quantities, and the narrow channel which swept round the bend was full of ice, piled one cake over another—thus forming a temporary barrier to the descending ice, which lodged and formed a great undulating raft, filling up the whole river, and extending almost to the Kentucky shore.

Eliza stood for a moment contemplating this unfavorable aspect of things, which she saw at once must prevent the usual ferry-boat from running, and then turned into a small public house on the bank, to make a few inquiries.

The hostess, who was busy in various fizzing and stewing operations over the fire, preparatory to the evening meal, stopped, with a fork in her hand, as Eliza's sweet and plaintive voice arrested her.

"What is it?" she said.

"Isn't there any ferry or boat that takes people over to B—— now?" she said.

"No, indeed," said the woman, "the boats has stopped running."

Eliza's look of dismay and disappointment struck the woman, and she said, inquiringly—

"May be your wanting to get over?—anybody sick? ye seem mighty anxious."

"I've got a child that's very dangerous," said Eliza. "I never heard of it till last night, and I've walked quite a piece to-day, in hopes to get to the ferry."

"Well, now, that's onlucky," said the woman, whose motherly sympathies were much aroused; "I'm re'ely consarned for ye. Solomon!" she called, from the window, towards a small back building. A man in leather apron and very dirty hands appeared at the door.

"I say, Sol," said the woman, "is that ar man going to tote them bar'ls over to-night?"

"He said he should try, if twas any way prudent," said the man.

"There's a man a piece down here, that's going over with some truck this evening, if he durs'to; he'll be in here to supper to-night, so you'd better set down and wait. That's a sweet little fellow," added the woman, offering him a cake.

But the child, wholly exhausted, cried with weariness.

"Poor fellow! he isn't used to walking, and I've hurried him on so," said Eliza.

"Well, take him into this room," said the woman, opening into a small bed-room, where stood a comfortable bed. Eliza laid the weary boy upon it, and held his hands in hers till he was fast asleep. For her there was no rest. As a fire in her bones, the thought of the pursuer urged her on, and she gazed with longing eyes on the sullen, surging waters that lay between her and liberty.

2. The river in Palestine over which the Israelites crossed into Canaan, the land of milk and honey, after their forty-year exodus in the desert (Exodus 3.17).

Here we must take our leave of her for the present, to follow the course of her pursuers.

Though Mrs. Shelby had promised that the dinner should be hurried on table, yet it was soon seen, as the thing has often been seen before, that it required more than one to make a bargain. So, although the order was fairly given out in Haley's hearing, and carried to Aunt Chloe[3] by at least half a dozen juvenile messengers, that dignitary only gave certain very gruff snorts, and tosses of her head, and went on with every operation in an unusually leisurely and circumstantial manner. For some singular reason, an impression seemed to reign among the servants generally, that missis would not be particularly disobliged by delay, and it was wonderful what a number of counter accidents occurred constantly, to retard the course of things. One luckless wight contrived to upset the gravy, and then gravy had to be got up *de novo*,[4] with due care and formality, Aunt Chloe watching and stirring with dogged precision, answering shortly to all suggestions of haste, that she "warnt a going to have raw gravy on the table, to help nobody's catchings."[5] One tumbled down with the water, and had to go to the spring for more; and another precipitated the butter into the path of events, and there was from time to time giggling news brought into the kitchen that mass'r Haley was mighty oneasy, and that he couldn't sit in his cheer no ways, but was a walkin and stalkin to the winders and through the porch.

"Sarves him right!" said Aunt Chloe, indignantly. "He'll get wus nor oneasy one of these days, if he don't mend his ways. *His* master'll be sending for him, and then see how he'll look."

"He'll go to torment, and no mistake," said little Jake.

"He desarves it!" said Aunt Chloe, grimly, "he's broke a many many many hearts, I tell ye all!" she said, stopping, with a fork uplifted in her hands; "it's like what mass'r George reads in Ravelations—souls a callin under the altar! and a callin on the Lord for vengeance on sich! and by and by, the Lord he'll hear em—so he will!"[6]

Aunt Chloe, who was much revered in the kitchen, was listened to with open mouth; and the dinner being now fairly sent in, the whole kitchen was at leisure to gossip with her, and to listen to her remarks.

"Sich'll be burnt up forever, and no mistake! wont ther," said Andy.

"I'd be glad to see it, I'll be boun," said little Jake.

"Chil'en!" said a voice, that made them all start. It was Uncle Tom, who had come in, and stood listening to the conversation at the door.

"Chil'en!" he said, "I'm afeard you don't know what ye're sayin. Forever is a *dre'ful* word, chil'en; its awful to think on't. You oughtenter wish that ar to any human crittur!"

"We wouldn't to anybody but the soul-drivers,"[7] said Andy; "nobody can help wishing it to them, they's so awful wicked."

"Dont natur herself kinder cry out on em?" said Aunt Chloe. "Dont dey tear der suckin baby right off his mother's breast, and sell him, and der little children as is crying and holding on by her clothes; dont dey pull em off and

---

3. Uncle Tom's wife and Shelby's cook.
4. Anew (Latin).
5. Referring to Dan Haley's pursuit of Eliza and Harry.
6. "And when he had opened the fifth seal, I saw un-

der the altar the souls of them that were slain for the word of God, and for the testimony which they held" (Revelation 6.9).
7. A common term for clergymen, but here it apparently refers to the slave traders.

sells em? Dont dey tear wife and husband apart?" said Aunt Chloe, beginning
to cry—"when it's jest takin the very life on em—and all the while does they
feel one bit—dont dey drink and smoke, and take it oncommon easy? Lor, if
the devil don't get them, what's he good for?" And Aunt Chloe covered her
face with her checked apron, and began to sob in good earnest.

"Pray for them that 'spitefully use you, the good book says," says Tom.[8]

"Pray for 'em!" said Aunt Chloe; "Lor, it's too tough! I can't pray for 'em."

"It's natur, Chloe, and natur's strong," said Tom, "but the Lord's grace is
stronger; besides, you oughter think what an awful state a poor crittur's soul's
in that'll do them ar things—you oughter thank God that you aint *like* him,
Chloe, I'm sure I'd rather be sold ten thousand times over than to have all that
ar poor crittur's got to answer for."

"So'd I, a heap," said Jake. "Lor! *shouldn't* we cotch it, Andy?"

Andy shrugged his shoulders, and gave an acquiescent whistle.

"I'm glad mass'r didn't go off this morning as he looked to," said Tom; "that
ar hurt me more than the sellin—it did," said Tom. "Mebbe it might have
been natural for him, but 'twould have come desp't hard on me, as has known
him from a baby; but I've seen mass'r, and I begin ter feel sort o' reconciled to
the Lord's will now. Mass'r couldn't help hisself; he did right, but I'm feared
things will be kinder goin to rack when I'm gone. Mass'r can't be spected to be
a pryin round everywhar, as Joe done, a keepin up all the ends. The boys all
means well, but they's powerful careless! That ar troubles me."

The bell here rang, and Tom was summoned to the parlor.

"Tom," said his master, kindly, "I want you to notice that I give this gentleman bonds to forfeit a thousand dollars if you are not on the spot when he
wants you; he's going to-day to look after his other business, and you can have
the day to yourself. Go anywhere you like, boy."

"Thank you, mass'r," said Tom.

"And mind yerself," said the trader, "and don't come it over your master
with any o' yer nigger tricks, for I'll take every cent out of him if you aint thar.
If he'd hear to me, he wouldn't trust any on ye—slippery as eels!"

"Mass'r," said Tom—and he stood very straight—"I was just eight years old
when ole missis put you into my arms, and you wasn't a year old. 'Thar,' says
she, 'Tom, that's to be *your* young mass'r; take good care on him,' says she.
And now I jist ask you, mass'r, have I ever broke word to you, or gone contrary
to you, specially since I was a Christian?"

Mr. Shelby was fairly overcome, and the tears rose to his eyes.

"My good boy," said he, "the Lord knows you say but the truth! and if I was
able to help it, all the world shouldn't buy you."

"And sure as I am a Christian woman," said Mrs. Shelby, "you shall be
redeemed as soon as I can any way bring together means. Sir," she said to
Haley, "take good account of who you sell him to, and let me know."

"Lor, yes, for that matter," said the trader, "I may bring him up in a year,
not much the woss for wear, and trade him back."

"I'll trade with you then, and make it for your advantage," said Mrs. Shelby.

"Of course," said the trader, "all's equal with me; lives trade 'em up as
down! so I does a good business. All I want is a livin, you know, ma'am—
that's all any on us wants, I spose."

8. "Love your enemies, bless them that curse you, do good to them that hate you, and pray for them which
despitefully use you, and persecute you" (Matthew 5.44).

Mr. and Mrs. Shelby both felt annoyed and degraded by the familiar impudence of the trader, and yet both saw the absolute necessity of putting a constraint on their feelings. The more hopelessly sordid and insensible he appeared, the greater became Mrs. Shelby's dread his succeeding in recapturing Eliza and her child, and of course the greater her motive for detaining him by every female artifice. She therefore graciously smiled, assented, chatted familiarly, and did all she could to make time pass imperceptibly.

At two o'clock Sam and Andy brought the horses up to the posts, apparently greatly refreshed and invigorated by the scamper of the morning.

Sam was then new oiled from dinner, with an abundance of zealous and ready officiousness. As Haley approached, he was boasting in flourishing style to Andy of the evident and imminent success of the operation, now that he had "farly come to it."

"Your master, I spose, don't keep no dogs," said Haley, thoughtfully, as he prepared to mount.

"Heaps on 'em," said Sam, triumphantly; "thar's Bruno—he's a roarer! and besides that, bout every nigger on us keeps a pup o some natur ur uther."

"Poh!" said Haley—and he said something else, too, with regard to the said dogs, at which Sam muttered—

"I don't see no use cussin on 'em! no way."

"But your master don't keep no dogs (I pretty much know he don't) for trackin out niggers."

Sam knew exactly what he meant but he kept on a look of earnest and desperate simplicity.

"Our dogs all smells round considable sharp. I spect they's the kind, though they han't never had no practice. They's *far* dogs, though, at most anything, if you'd get 'em started. Here, Bruno," he called, whistling to the lumbering Newfoundland, who came pitching tumultuously toward them.

"You go hang!" said Haley, getting up. "Come, tumble up now."

Sam tumbled up accordingly, dexterously contriving to tickle Andy as he did so, which occasioned Andy to split out into a laugh, greatly to Haley's indignation, who made a cut at him with his riding whip.

"I's astonished at yer, Andy," said Sam, with awful gravity. "This yer's a seris bisness, Andy. Yer musn't be a makin game. Thus yer aint no way to help mass'r."

"I shall take the straight road to the river," said Haley, decidedly, after they had come to the boundaries of the estate. "I know the way of all of 'em—they makes tracks for the underground."[9]

"Sartin," said Sam, "dat's de idee. Mass'r Haley hits de thing right in de middle. Now, der's two roads to de river—de dirt road and der pike—which mass'r mean to take?"

Andy looked up innocently at Sam, surprised at hearing this new geographical fact, but instantly confirmed what he said by a vehement reiteration.

"Cause," said Sam, "I'd ruther be clined to magine that Lizy'd take de dirt road, bein it's the least travelled."

Haley, notwithstanding that he was a very old bird, and naturally inclined to be suspicious of chaff, was rather brought up by this view of the case.

9. Although many Northern sympathizers harbored runaway slaves from the South, the law strictly prohibited this practice. Therefore, the slaves fled to neutral Canada, by means of the "Underground Railroad," the clandestine organization of individuals whose homes were used as "stations" on the escape route.

"If yer warn't both on yer such cussed liars now!" he said, contemplatively, as he pondered a moment——

The pensive, reflecting tone in which this was spoken appeared to amuse Andy prodigiously, and he drew a little behind, and shook so as apparently to run a great risk of falling off his horse, while Sam's face was immovably composed into the most doleful gravity.

"Course," said Sam, "mass'r can do as he'd ruther; go the straight road, if mass'r thinks best—it's all one to us. Now, when I study pon it, I think de straight road de best, *decidedly.*"

"She would naturally go a lonesome way," said Haley, thinking aloud, and not minding Sam's remark.

"Dar aint no sayin!" said Sam; "gals is pecular; they never does nothin yer thinks they will; mose gen'lly the contrar. Gals is nat'lly made contrary; and so if you thinks they've gone one road, it is sartin you'd better go tother, and then you'll be sure to find 'em. Now, my private 'pinion is, Lizy took der dirt road, so I think we'd better take der straight one."

This profound generic view of the female sex did not seem to dispose Haley particularly to the straight road, and he announced decidedly that he should go the other, and asked Sam when they should come to it.

"A little piece ahead," said Sam, giving a wink to Andy with the eye which was on Andy's side of the head; and he added, gravely, "but I've studded on der matter, and I'm quite clar we ought not to go dat ar way. I nebber been over it no way. It's despit lonesome, and we might lose our way—whar we'd come to, de Lord only knows."

"Nevertheless," said Haley, "I shall go that way."

"Now I think on't, I think I hearn 'em tell that dat ar road was all fenced up down by der creek, and thar, an't it, Andy?"

Andy wasn't certain; he'd only "hearn tell" about that road, but never been over it. In short, he was strictly non-committal.

Haley, accustomed to strike the balance of probabilities between lies of greater or lesser magnitude, thought that it lay in favor of the dirt road aforesaid. The mention of the thing, he thought he perceived was involuntary on Sam's part at first, and his confused attempts to dissuade him he sat down to a desperate lying on second thoughts, as being unwilling to implicate Eliza.

When, therefore, Sam indicated the road, Haley plunged briskly into it, followed by Sam and Andy.

Now, the road in fact was an old one that had formerly been a thoroughfare to the river, but abandoned for many years after the laying of the new pike. It was open for about an hour's ride, and after that it was cut across by various farms and fences. Sam knew this fact perfectly well—indeed, the road had been so long closed up that Andy had never heard of it. He therefore rode along with an air of dutiful submission, only groaning and vociferating occasionally that 'twas "desp't rough, and bad for Jerry's foot."

"Now, I jest give yer warning," said Haley, "I know yer; yer won't get me to turn off this yer road with all yer fussin—so you shet up."

"Mass'r will go his own way," said Sam, with rueful submission, at the same time winking most portentously to Andy, whose delight was now very near the explosive point.

Sam was in wonderful spirits—professed to keep a very brisk lookout—at one time exclaiming that he saw "a gal's bonnet" on the top of some distant eminence, or calling to Andy "if that thar wasn't 'Lizy' down in the hollow," always making these exclamations in some rough or craggy part of the road, where the sudden quickening of speed was a special inconvenience to all parties concerned, and thus keeping Haley in a state of constant commotion.

After riding about an hour in this way, the whole party made a precipitate and tumultuous descent into a barn-yard belonging to a large farming establishment. Not a soul was in sight, all the hands being employed in the fields; but as the barn stood conspicuously and plainly square across the road, it was evident that their journey in that direction had reached a decided finale.

"Want dat ar what I telled mass'r," said Sam, with an air of injured innocence. "How does strange gentlemen spect to know more about a country dan der natives born and raised!"

"You rascal," said Haley, "you knew all about this."

"Didn't I tell yer I *knowd*, and yer wouldn't believe me. I telled mass'r 'twas all shet up, and fenced up, and I didn't spec we could get thro—Andy heard me."

It was all too true to be disputed, and the unlucky man had to pocket his wrath—with the best grace he was able, and all three faced to the right about, and took up their line of march for the highway.

In consequence of all the various delays, it was only about three-quarters of an hour after Eliza had laid her child to sleep in the village tavern, that the party came riding into the same place. Eliza was standing by the window, looking out in another direction, when Sam's quick eye caught a glimpse of her. Haley and Andy were two yards behind. At this crisis, Sam contrived to have his hat blown off, and uttered a loud and characteristic ejaculation, which startled her at once; she drew suddenly back; the whole train swept by the window, round to the front door.

A thousand lives seemed to be concentrated in that one moment to Eliza. Her room opened by a side door to the river. She caught her child, and sprang down the steps towards it. The trader caught a full glimpse of her just as she was disappearing down the bank, and, throwing himself from his horse, calling loudly to Sam and Andy, he was after her like a hound after a deer. In that dizzy moment her feet to her scarce seemed to touch the ground, and a moment brought her to the water's edge. Right on behind they came, and, nerved with strength such as God gives only to the desperate, with one wild cry, and flying leap, she vaulted sheer over the turbid current by the shore, on to the raft of ice beyond. It was a desperate leap, impossible to anything but madness and despair; and Haley, Sam, and Andy, instinctively cried out, and lifted up their hands as she did it.

The huge green fragment of ice on which she alighted pitched and creaked as her weight came on it, but she staid there not a moment—with wild cries and desperate energy she leaped to another and still another cake, stumbling, leaping, slipping, springing upwards again! Her shoes are gone, her stockings cut from her feet, while blood marked every step—but she saw nothing, felt nothing, till dimly as in a dream she saw the Ohio side, and a man helping her up the bank.

"Yer a brave gal, now, whoever ye ar," said the man, with an oath.

Eliza recognised the voice and face of a man who owned a farm not far from her old home.

"Oh, Mr. Symmes—save me—do save me—do hide me," said Eliza.
"Why, what's this?" said the man. "Why, if taint Shelby's gal."
"My child! this boy—he'd sold him! There is his mass'r," said she, pointing to the Kentucky shore. "Oh, Mr. Symmes, you've got a little boy."

"So I have," said the man, as he roughly, but kindly, drew her up the steep bank. "Besides, you'r a right brave gal. I like grit, wherever I see it."

When they had gained the top of the bank, the man paused.

"I'd be glad to do something for ye," said he, "but then there's nowhar I could take ye. The best I can do is to tell you to go *thar*," said he, pointing to a large white house which stood by itself, off the main street of the village. "Go thar; they'r kind folks. Thar's no kind'r danger but they'll help you—they'r up to all that sort o' thing."

"The Lord bless you," said Eliza earnestly.

"No casion, no casion in the world," said the man. "What I've done 's of no 'count."

"And, oh, surely, sir, you won't tell any one."

"Go to thunder, gal. What do you take a feller for? In course not," said the man. "Come, now, go along like a likely sensible gal, as you are. You've arnt your liberty, and you shall have it for all me."

The woman folded her child to her bosom, and walked firmly and swiftly away. The man stood and looked after her.

"Shelby, now, mebbe won't think this yer the most neighborly thing in the world, but what's a feller to do? If he catches one of my gals in the same fix, he's welcome to pay back. Somehow I never could see no kind of crittur a strivin' and pantin', and trying to clar theirselves with the dogs artur 'em, and go agin 'em. Besides, I don't see no kind of casion for me to be hunter and catcher for other folks, neither."

So spoke this poor, heathenish Kentuckian, who had not been enlightened on his constitutional relations, and consequently was betrayed into acting in a sort of Christianized manner, which, if he had been better situated and more enlightened, he would not have been left to do.

Haley had stood a perfectly amazed spectator of the scene, till Eliza had disappeared up the bank, when he turned a blank, inquiring look on Sam and Andy.

"That ar was a tolable fair stroke of business!" said Sam.

"The gal's got seven devils in her, I believe!" said Haley. "How like a wildcat she jumped!"

"Wal, now," said Sam, scratching his head, "I hope mass'r'll 'scuse us tryin dat ar road. Don't think I feels spry enough for dat ar, no way!" and Sam gave a hoarse chuckle.

"*You* laugh!" said the trader, with a growl.

"Lord bless ye, mass'r, I couldn't help it, now," said Sam, giving way to the long pent-up delight of his soul. She looked so curis—a leapin and springin, ice a crackin, and only to hear her, plump! ker chunk! kersplash! spring. Lord, how she goes it!" and Sam and Andy laughed till the tears rolled down their cheeks.

"I'll make ye laugh t'other side yer mouths," said the trader, laying about their heads with his riding whip.

Both ducked, and ran shouting up the bank, and were on their horses before he was up.

"Good evening, mass'r," said Sam, with much gravity. "I berry much spect missis be anxious bout Jerry. Mass'r Haley won't want us no longer. Missis wouldn't hear of our ridin the critturs over Lizy's bridge to-night," and, with a facetious poke into Andy's ribs, he started off, followed by the latter, at full speed—their shouts of laughter coming dimly on the wind.

1851, 1852

---

# HARRIET JACOBS
## c. 1813–1897

Harriet Jacobs was born in Edenton, North Carolina, the daughter of slaves and a slave herself. Her father was a skilled carpenter who was permitted to hire himself out, and her parents were permitted to live together even though they were "owned" by different masters; therefore, as a child Jacobs was unaware that she was a slave. Her mother's death and a change of owners for both Jacobs and her father brought her into the family of Dr. and Mrs. James Norcom in 1825. There, as she grew to adulthood, she was sexually harassed by the doctor and abused by his jealous wife. As a defense against this treatment, Jacobs involved herself with an unmarried white attorney, Samuel Tredwell Sawyer, by whom she had two children: Joseph, born in 1829, and Louisa Matilda, born in 1833. When Norcom sent her to a country plantation in 1835, she escaped back to Edenton, hiding for perhaps seven years in the home of her maternal grandmother, who had been emancipated some years earlier. While Jacobs was in hiding, Sawyer purchased, but did not emancipate, their two children. Jacobs finally escaped to the North in 1842, and later both her children came North also. Life in the North was insecure and perilous, however, because slave catchers were constantly hunting down escaped slaves to return them South, which they could do more aggressively after 1850 with the Fugitive Slave Law on their side.

For much of the next two decades Jacobs worked in the family of Nathaniel Parker Willis, one of the era's most popular writers and editors. She took care of his children and became particularly close to his second wife, Cornelia Grinnell Willis, a staunch abolitionist. In 1853 Cornelia Willis arranged to purchase Jacobs from Norcom's daughter, her legal owner; then she emancipated Jacobs.

Jacobs spent much of 1849 in Rochester, New York, working for the Anti-Slavery Office run by her younger brother, who had also escaped slavery. She read through a large body of antislavery writings and also came to know a number of abolitionists, including many white women, among them Emily Post, who became a mentor to her. Jacobs wanted to contribute her life story to the abolitionist cause in a way that would capture the attention of Northern white women in particular, to show them how slavery debased and demoralized women, at once subjecting them to white male lust and depriving them of the right to make homes for and with their children. Yet this topic was difficult to discuss in an era when extreme sexual prudery was the norm, when standards of female sexual "purity" could result in blaming the unmarried slave mother rather than sympathizing with her. In *Incidents in the Life of a Slave Girl* Jacobs tried to do more than create sympathy for her plight; she also sought to win the respect and admiration of her readers for the courage with which she forestalled abuse and for the independence with which she chose a lover rather than having one forced on her. Her description of hiding in the attic, her emphasis on family life and maternal values, and her account of the difficulties of fugitive slaves in the North also differentiate the book from the numerous slave narratives produced in the twenty years before the Civil War. *Incidents* is also distinguished by its awareness of the kinds of stories written by and about white women in the same era, for it self-consciously addresses women readers and carefully distinguishes the slave woman's experiences from theirs.

Free at last, and encouraged by the success of Harriet Beecher Stowe's *Uncle Tom's Cabin* (1852)—one of whose heroines is the slave concubine Cassy—Jacobs began work on her narrative around 1853 and finished it by 1858. She was not successful in finding a publisher for it, however, until Lydia Maria Child (1802–1880), a well-known woman of letters and abolitionist, agreed to write a preface for it. Child became very interested in the project, and when the contracted publishers went bankrupt, she arranged for its publication. The book came out under the pseudonym Linda Brent in 1861; it was sold at Anti-Slavery Offices around the country, published in England in 1862, and received several favorable reviews. The outbreak of the Civil War made its message less pressing, however, and it sank from notice until the 1980s, when interest in early writings by African-American women, and superb biographical scholarship by Jean Fagin Yellin, restored the book and its author to view.

During the war and its immediate aftermath Jacobs worked in the relief effort funded by Quaker organizations. Afterward she ran a boardinghouse in Cambridge, Massachusetts, and later moved to Washington, D.C., with her daughter. She is buried in Mount Auburn Cemetery in Cambridge.

Critics and students of *Incidents* agree that the book is a unique literary document but have wondered whether to regard it as truth or fiction and whether it is primarily Jacobs's work or Child's. Yellin has shown that all the characters and events in *Incidents* are based in reality, and Child's correspondence claims that as editor she added nothing and altered fewer than fifty words in the manuscript. But Child did take what she described as "much pains" with it, "transposing sentences and pages, so as to bring the story into continuous *order*, and the remarks into *appropriate* places," thereby making the story "much more clear and entertaining." She also asked Jacobs for instances of slave abuse apart from the author's own experiences, which Jacobs supplied. Lacking the manuscript of *Incidents*, one cannot speculate on Child's specific changes, but her work on the narrative involved precisely what editors in publishing houses do today as a matter of course. To the extent that Child's reorganization gave the book a more literary shape, *Incidents* is indeed a collaborative production. So, however, are T. S. Eliot's *The Waste Land*, Theodore Dreiser's *Sister Carrie*, and Thomas Wolfe's *Look Homeward, Angel*, to name only a few well-known examples. Jacobs expressed no dissatisfaction with Child's work and clearly regarded it as her own book, taking an active role in promoting and selling it. Not for another thirty years after *Incidents* would African-American women's writing emerge as a significant strand in American literature; when it did, many of the themes that Jacobs introduced would become central to such writing.

## *From* Incidents in the Life of a Slave Girl

### *I. Childhood*

I was born a slave; but I never knew it till six yeas of happy childhood had passed away. My father was a carpenter, and considered so intelligent and skilful in his trade, that, when buildings out of the common line were to be erected, he was sent for from long distances, to be head workman. On condition of paying his mistress two hundred dollars a year, and supporting himself, he was allowed to work at his trade, and manage his own affairs. His strongest wish was to purchase his children; but, though he several times offered his hard earnings for that purpose, he never succeeded. In complexion my parents were a light shade of brownish yellow, and were termed mulattoes. They lived together in a comfortable home; and, though we were all slaves, I was so fondly shielded that I never dreamed I was a piece of merchandise, trusted to them for safe keeping, and liable to be demanded of them at any moment. I had one brother, William, who was two years younger than myself—a bright, affectionate child. I had also a great treasure in my maternal grandmother, who was a remarkable woman in many respects. She was the daughter of a planter in South Carolina, who, at his death, left her mother and his three children free, with money to go to St. Augustine, where they had relatives. It was during the Revolutionary War; and they were captured on their passage, carried back, and sold to different purchasers. Such was the story my grandmother used to tell me; but I do not remember all the particulars. She was a little girl when she was captured and sold to the keeper of a large hotel. I have often heard her tell how hard she fared during childhood. But as she grew older she evinced so much intelligence, and was so faithful, that her master and mistress could not help seeing it was for their interest to take care of such a valuable piece of property. She became an indispensable personage in the household, officiating in all capacities, from cook and wet nurse to seamstress. She was much praised for her cooking; and her nice crackers became so famous in the neighborhood that many people were desirous of obtaining them. In consequence of numerous requests of this kind, she asked permission of her mistress to bake crackers at night, after all the household work was done; and she obtained leave to do it, provided she would clothe herself and her children from the profits. Upon these terms, after working hard all day for her mistress, she began her midnight bakings, assisted by her two oldest children. The business proved profitable; and each year she laid by a little, which was saved for a fund to purchase her children. Her master died, and the property was divided among his heirs. The widow had her dower in the hotel, which she continued to keep open. My grandmother remained in her service as a slave; but her children were divided among her master's children. As she had five, Benjamin, the youngest one, was sold, in order that each heir might have an equal portion of dollars and cents. There was so little difference in our ages that he seemed more like my brother than my uncle. He was a bright, handsome lad, nearly white; for he inherited the complexion my grandmother had derived from Anglo-Saxon ancestors. Though only ten years old, seven hundred and twenty dollars were paid for him. His sales was a terrible blow to my grandmother; but she was naturally hopeful, and she went to work with renewed energy, trusting in time to be able to purchase some of her children. She had laid up three hundred dollars, which her mistress one day begged as a loan, promising to pay her soon. The reader probably knows that no promise or writing given to a slave is legally binding; for, according to Southern laws, a slave, *being* property, can *hold* no property. When my grandmother lent her hard earnings to her mistress, she trusted solely to her honor. The honor of a slaveholder to a slave!

To this good grandmother I was indebted for many comforts. My brother Willie and I often received portions of the crackers, cakes, and preserves, she made to sell; and after we ceased to be children we were indebted to her for many more important services.

Such were the unusually fortunate circumstances of my early childhood. When I was six years old, my mother died, and then, for the first time, I learned, by the talk around me, that I was a slave. My mother's mistress was the daughter of my grandmother's mistress. She was the foster sister of my mother; they were both nourished at my grandmother's breast. In fact, my mother had been weaned at three months old, that the babe of the mistress might obtain sufficient food. They played together as children; and, when they became women, my mother was a most faithful servant to her whiter foster sister. On her death-bed her mistress promised that her children should never suffer for any thing; and during her lifetime she kept her word. They all spoke kindly of my dead mother, who had been a slave merely in name, but in nature was noble and womanly. I grieved for her, and my young mind was troubled with the thought who would now take care of me and my little brother. I was told that my home was now to be with her mistress; and I found it a happy one. No toilsome or disagreeable duties were imposed upon me. My mistress was so kind to me that I was always glad to do her bidding, and proud to labor for her as much as my young years would permit. I would sit by her side for hours, sewing diligently, with a heart as free from care as that of any free-born white child. When she thought I was tired, she would send me out to run and jump; and away I bounded, to gather berries or flowers to decorate her room. Those were happy days—too happy to last. The slave child had no thought for the morrow; but there came that blight, which too surely waits on every human being born to be a chattel.

When I was nearly twelve years old, my kind mistress sickened and died. As I saw the cheek grow paler, and the eye more glassy, how earnestly I prayed in my heart that she might live! I loved her; for she had been almost like a mother to me. My prayers were not answered. She died, and they buried her in the little churchyard, where, day after day, my tears fell upon her grave.

I was sent to spend a week with my grandmother. I was now old enough to begin to think of the future; and again and again I asked myself what they would do with me. I felt sure I should never find another mistress so kind as the one who was gone. She had promised my dying mother that her children should never suffer for any thing; and when I remembered that, and recalled her many proofs of attachment to me, I could not help having some hopes that she had left me free. My friends were almost certain it would be so. They thought she would be sure to do it, on account of my mother's love and faithful service. But, alas! we all know that the memory of a faithful slave does not avail much to save her children from the auction block.

After a brief period of suspense, the will of my mistress was read, and we learned that she had bequeathed me to her sister's daughter, a child of five years old. So vanished our hopes. My mistress had taught me the precepts of God's Word: "Thou shalt love thy neighbor as thyself."[1] Whatsoever ye would that men should do unto you, do ye even so unto them."[2] But I was her slave, and I suppose she did not recognize me as her neighbor. I would give much to blot out from my memory that one great wrong. As a child, I loved my mistress; and, looking back on the happy days I spent with her, I try to think with less bitterness of this act of injustice. While I was with her, she taught me to read and spell; and for this privilege, which so rarely falls to the lot of a slave, I bless her memory.

1. Mark 12.31.                    2. Matthew 7.12.

She possessed but few slaves; and at her death those were all distributed among her relatives. Five of them were my grandmother's children, and had shared the same milk that nourished her mother's children. Notwithstanding my grandmother's long and faithful service to her owners, not one of her children escaped the auction block. These God-breathing machines are no more, in the sight of their masters, than the cotton they plant, or the horses they tend.

## VII. The Lover

Why does the slave ever love? Why allow the tendrils of the heart to twine around objects which may at any moment be wrenched away by the hand of violence? When separations come by the hand of death, the pious soul can bow in resignation, and say, "Not my will, but thine be done, O Lord!"[3] But when the ruthless hand of man strikes the blow, regardless of the misery he causes, it is hard to be submissive. I did not reason thus when I was a young girl. Youth will be youth. I loved, and I indulged the hope that the dark clouds around me would turn out a bright lining. I forgot that in the land of my birth the shadows are too dense for light to penetrate. A land

"Where laughter is not mirth; nor thought the mind;
Nor words a language; no e'en men mankind.
Where cries reply to curses, shrieks to blows,
And each is tortured in his separate hell."[4]

There was in the neighborhood a young colored carpenter; a free born man. We had been well acquainted in childhood, and frequently met together afterwards. We became mutually attached, and he proposed to marry me. I loved him with all the ardor of a young girl's first love. But when I reflected that I was a slave, and that the laws gave no sanction to the marriage of such, my heart sank within me. My lover wanted to buy me; but I knew that Dr. Flint was too wilful and arbitrary a man to consent to that arrangement. From him, I was sure of experiencing all sorts of opposition, and I had nothing to hope from my mistress.[5] She would have been delighted to have got rid of me, but not in that way. It would have relieved her mind of a burden if she could have seen me sold to some distant state, but if I was married near home I should be just as much in her husband's power as I had previously been,—for the husband of a slave has no power to protect her.[6] Moreover, my mistress, like many others, seemed to think that slaves had no right to any family ties of their own; that they were created merely to wait upon the family of the mistress. I once heard her abuse a young slave girl, who told her that a colored man wanted to make her his wife. "I will have you peeled and pickled, my lady," said she, "if I ever hear you mention that subject again. Do you suppose that I will have you tending *my* children with the children of that nigger?" The girl to whom she said this had a mulatto child, of course not acknowledged by its father. The poor black man who loved her would have been proud to acknowledge his helpless offspring.

3. Cf. Matthew 26.39: "Nevertheless not as I will, but as thou wilt."
4. From *The Lament of Tasso* 4.7–10 (1817), by the English poet George Gordon, Lord Byron (1788–1824).
5. Dr. Flint was the father of Emily Flint, Linda

Brent's (i.e., Harriet Jacobs's) legal owner. Because Emily is a child at this time, her father and mother, whom Brent refers to as her mistress, have legal power over her slaves.
6. Dr. Flint has been harassing Brent for some time, apparently to coerce her into a sexual relationship.

Many and anxious were the thoughts I revolved in my mind. I was at a loss what to do. Above all things, I was desirous to spare my lover the insults that had cut so deeply into my own soul. I talked with my grandmother about it, and partly told her my fears. I did not dare to tell her the worst. She had long suspected all was not right, and if I confirmed her suspicions I knew a storm would rise that would prove the overthrow of all my hopes.

This love-dream had been my support through many trials; and I could not bear to run the risk of having it suddenly dissipated. There was a lady in the neighborhood, a particular friend of Dr. Flint's, who often visited the house. I had a great respect for her, and she had always manifested a friendly interest in me. Grandmother thought she would have great influence with the doctor. I went to this lady, and told her my story. I told her I was aware that my lover's being a free-born man would prove a great objection; but he wanted to buy me; and if Dr. Flint would consent to that arrangement, I felt sure he would be willing to pay any reasonable price. She knew that Mrs. Flint disliked me; therefore, I ventured to suggest that perhaps my mistress would approve of my being sold, as that would rid her of me. The lady listened with kindly sympathy, and promised to do her utmost to promote my wishes. She had an interview with the doctor, and I believe she pleaded my cause earnestly; but it was all to no purpose.

How I dreaded my master now! Every minute I expected to be summoned to his presence; but the day passed, and I heard nothing from him. The next morning, a message was brought to me: "Master wants you in his study." I found the door ajar, and I stood a moment gazing at the hateful man who claimed a right to rule me, body and soul. I entered, and tried to appear calm. I did not want him to know how my heart was bleeding. He looked fixedly at me, with an expression which seemed to say, "I have half a mind to kill you on the spot." At last he broke the silence, and that was a relief to both of us.

"So you want to be married, do you?" said he, "and to a free nigger."

"Yes, sir."

"Well, I'll soon convince you whether I am your master, or the nigger fellow you honor so highly. If you *must* have a husband, you may take up with one of my slaves."

What a situation I should be in, as the wife of one of *his* slaves, even if my heart had been interested!

I replied, "Don't you suppose, sir, that a slave can have some preference about marrying? Do you suppose that all men are alike to her?"

"Do you love this nigger?" said he, abruptly.

"Yes, sir."

"How dare you tell me so!" he exclaimed, in great wrath. After a slight pause, he added, "I supposed you thought more of yourself; that you felt above the insults of such puppies."

I replied, "If he is a puppy I am a puppy, for we are both of the negro race. It is right and honorable for us to love each other. The man you call a puppy never insulted me, sir; and he would not love me if he did not believe me to be a virtuous woman."

He sprang upon me like a tiger, and gave me a stunning blow. It was the first time he had ever struck me; and fear did not enable me to control my anger. When I had recovered a little from the effects, I exclaimed, "You have struck me for answering you honestly. How I despise you!"

There was silence for some minutes. Perhaps he was deciding what should be my punishment; or, perhaps, he wanted to give me time to reflect on what I had said, and to whom I had said it. Finally, he asked, "Do you know what you have said?"

"Yes, sir; but your treatment drove me to it."

"Do you know that I have a right to do as I like with you,—that I can kill you, if I please?"

"You have tried to kill me, and I wish you had; but you have no right to do as you like with me."

"Silence!" he exclaimed, in a thundering voice. "By heavens, girl, you forget yourself too far! Are you mad? If you are, I will soon bring you to your senses. Do you think any other master would bear what I have borne from you this morning? Many masters would have killed you on the spot. How would you like to be sent to jail for your insolence?"

"I know I have been disrespectful, sir," I replied; "but you drove me to it; I couldn't help it. As for the jail, there would be more peace for me there than there is here."

"You deserve to go there," he said, "and to be under such treatment, that you would forget the meaning of the word *peace*. It would do you good. It would take some of your high notions out of you. But I am not ready to send you there yet, notwithstanding your ingratitude for all my kindness and forbearance. You have been the plague of my life. I have wanted to make you happy, and I have been repaid with the basest ingratitude; but though you have proved yourself incapable of appreciating my kindness, I will be lenient towards you, Linda.[7] I will give you one more chance to redeem your character. If you behave yourself and do as I require, I will forgive you and treat you as I always have done; but if you disobey me, I will punish you as I would the meanest slave on my plantation. Never let me hear that fellow's name mentioned again. If I ever know of your speaking to him, I will cowhide you both; and if I catch him lurking about my premises, I will shoot him as soon as I would a dog. Do you hear what I say? I'll teach you a lesson about marriage and free niggers! Now go, and let this be the last time I have occasion to speak to you on this subject."

Reader, did you ever hate? I hope not. I never did but once; and I trust I never shall again. Somebody has called it "the atmosphere of hell;" and I believe it is so.

For a fortnight the doctor did not speak to me. He thought to mortify me; to make me feel that I had disgraced myself by receiving the honorable addresses of a respectable colored man, in preference to the base proposals of a white man. But though his lips disdained to address me, his eyes were very loquacious. No animal ever watched its prey more narrowly than he watched me. He knew that I could write, though he had failed to make me read his letters; and he was now troubled lest I should exchange letters with another man. After a while he became weary of silence; and I was sorry for it. One morning, as he passed through the hall, to leave the house, he contrived to thrust a note into my hand. I thought I had better read it, and spare myself the vexation of having him read it to me. It expressed regret for the blow he had given me, and reminded me that I myself was wholly to blame for it. He hoped

7. Linda Brent is the name Jacobs wrote under.

I had become convinced of the injury I was doing myself by incurring his displeasure. He wrote that he had made up his mind to go to Louisiana; that he should take several slaves with him, and intended I should be one of the number. My mistress would remain where she was; therefore I should have nothing to fear from that quarter. If I merited kindness from him, he assured me that it would be lavishly bestowed. He begged me to think over the matter, and answer the following day.

The next morning I was called to carry a pair of scissors to his room. I laid them on the table, with the letter beside them. He thought it was my answer, and did not call me back. I went as usual to attend my young mistress to and from school. He met me in the street, and ordered me to stop at his office on my way back. When I entered, he showed me his letter, and asked me why I had not answered it. I replied, "I am your daughter's property, and it is in your power to send me, or take me, wherever you please." He said he was very glad to find me so willing to go, and that we should start early in the autumn. He had a large practice in the town, and I rather thought he had made up the story merely to frighten me. However that might be, I was determined that I would never go to Louisiana with him.

Summer passed away, and early in the autumn, Dr. Flint's eldest son was sent to Louisiana to examine the country, with a view to emigrating. That news did not disturb me. I knew very well that I should not be sent with *him*. That I had not been taken to the plantation before this time, was owing to the fact that his son was there. He was jealous of his son; and jealousy of the overseer had kept him from punishing me by sending me into the fields to work. Is it strange that I was not proud of these protectors? As for the overseer, he was a man for whom I had less respect than I had for a bloodhound.

Young Mr. Flint did not bring back a favorable report of Louisiana, and I heard no more of that scheme. Soon after this, my lover met me at the corner of the street, and I stopped to speak to him. Looking up, I saw my master watching us from his window. I hurried home, trembling with fear. I was sent for, immediately, to go to his room. He met me with a blow. "When is mistress to be married?" said he, in a sneering tone. A shower o oaths and imprecations followed. How thankful I was that my lover was a free man! that my tyrant had no power to flog him for speaking to me in the street!

Again and again I revolved in my mind how all this would end. There was no hope that the doctor would consent to sell me on any terms. He had an iron will, and was determined to keep me, and to conquer me. My lover was an intelligent and religious man. Even if he could have obtained permission to marry me while I was a slave, the marriage would give him no power to protect me from my master. It would have made him miserable to witness the insults I should have been subjected to. And then, if we had children, I knew they must "follow the condition of the mother." What a terrible blight that would be on the heart of a free, intelligent father! For *his* sake, I felt that I ought not to link his fate with my own unhappy destiny. He was going to Savannah to see about a little property left him by an uncle; and had as it was to bring my feelings to it, I earnestly entreated him not to come back. I advised him to go to the Free States, where his tongue would not be tied, and where his intelligence would be of more avail to him. He left me, still hoping the day would come when I could be bought. With me the lamp of hope had gone out. The dream of my girlhood was over. I felt lonely and desolate.

Still I was not stripped of all. I still had my good grandmother, and my affectionate brother. When he put his arms round my neck, and looked into my eyes, as if to read there the troubles I dared not tell, I felt that I still had something to love. But even that pleasant emotion was chilled by the reflection that he might be torn from me at any moment, by some sudden freak of my master. If I had known how we love each other, I think he would have exulted in separating us. We often planned together how we could get to the north. But, as William remarked, such things are easier said than done. My movements were very closely watched, and we had no means of getting any money to defray our expenses. As for grandmother, she was strongly opposed to her children's undertaking any such project. She had not forgotten poor Benjamin's sufferings[8] and she was afraid that if another child tried to escape, he would have a similar or a worse fate. To me, nothing seemed more dreadful than my present life. I said to myself, "William *must* be free. He shall go to the north, and I will follow him." Many a slave sister has formed the same plans.

## X. A Perilous Passage in the Slave Girl's Life

After my lover went away, Dr. Flint contrived a new plan. He seemed to have an idea that my fear of my mistress was his greatest obstacle. In the blandest tones, he told me that he was going to build a small house for me, in a secluded place, four miles away from the town. I shuddered; but I was constrained to listen, while he talked of his intention to give me a home of my own, and to make a lady of me. Hitherto, I had escaped my dreaded fate, by being in the midst of people. My grandmother had already had high words with my master about me. She had told him pretty plainly what she thought of his character, and there was considerable gossip in the neighborhood about our affairs, to which the open-mouthed jealousy of Mrs. Flint contributed not a little. When my master said he was going to build a house for me, and that he could do it with little trouble and expense, I was in hopes something would happen to frustrate his scheme; but I soon heard that the house was actually begun. I vowed before my Maker that I would never enter it. I had rather toil on the plantation from dawn till dark; I had rather live and die in jail, than drag on, from day to day, though such a living death. I was determined that the master, whom I so hated and loathed, who had blighted the prospects of my youth, and made my life a desert, should not, after my long struggle with him, succeed at last in trampling his victim under his feet. I would do any thing, every thing, or the sake of defeating him. What *could* I do? I thought and thought, till I became desperate, and made a plunge into the abyss.

And now, reader, I come to a period in my unhappy life, which I would gladly forget if I could. The remembrance fills me with sorrow and shame. It pains me to tell you of it; but I have promised to tell you the truth, and I will do it honestly, let it cost me what it may. I will not try to screen myself behind the plea of compulsion from a master; for it was not so. Neither can I plead ignorance or thoughtlessness. For years, my master had done his utmost to pollute my mind with foul images, and to destroy the pure principles inculcated by my grandmother, and the good mistress of my childhood. The influences of slavery had had the same effect on me that they had on other young

---

8. One of Brent's uncles, who was caught in an escape attempt, jailed and mistreated for six months, and sold away to a trader. He eventually got to New York but never saw his mother again.

girls; they had made me prematurely knowing, concerning the evil ways of the world. I knew what I did, and I did it with deliberate calculation.

But, O, ye happy women, whose purity has been sheltered from childhood, who have been free to choose the objects of your affection, whose homes are protected by law, do not judge the poor desolate slave girl too severely! If slavery had been abolished, I, also, could have married the man of my choice; I could have had a home shielded by the laws; and I should have been spared the painful task of confessing what I am now about to relate; but all my prospects had been blighted by slavery. I wanted to keep myself pure; and, under the most adverse circumstances, I tried hard to preserve my self-respect; but I was struggling alone in the powerful grasp of the demon Slavery; and the monster proved too strong for me. I felt as if I was forsaken by God and man; as if all my efforts must be frustrated; and I became reckless in my despair.

I have told you that Dr. Flint's persecutions and his wife's jealousy had given rise to some gossip in the neighborhood. Among others, it chanced that a white unmarried gentleman had obtained some knowledge of the circumstances in which I was placed. He knew my grandmother, and often spoke to me in the street. He became interested for me, and asked questions about my master, which I answered in part. He expressed a great deal of sympathy, and a wish to aid me. He constantly sought opportunities to see me, and wrote to me frequently. I was a poor slave girl, only fifteen years old.

So much attention from a superior person was, of course, flattering; for human nature is the same in all. I also felt grateful for his sympathy, and encouraged by his kind words. It seemed to me a great thing to have such a friend. By degrees, a more tender feeling crept into my heart. He was an educated and eloquent gentleman; too eloquent, alas, for the poor slave girl who trusted in him. Of course I saw whither all this was tending. I knew the impassable gulf between us; but to be an object of interest to a man who is not married, and who is not her master, is agreeable to the pride and feelings of a slave, if her miserable situation has left her any pride or sentiment. It seems less degrading to give one's self, than to submit to compulsion. There is something akin to freedom in having a lover who has no control over you, except that which he gains by kindness and attachment. A master may treat you as rudely as he pleases, and you dare not speak; moreover, the wrong does not seem so great with an unmarried man, as with one who has a wife to be made unhappy. There may be sophistry in all this; but the condition of a slave confuses all principles of morality, and, in fact, renders the practice of them impossible.

When I found that my master had actually begun to build the lonely cottage, other feelings mixed with those I have described. Revenge, and calculations of interest, were added to flattered vanity and sincere gratitude for kindness. I knew nothing would enrage Dr. Flint so much as to know that I favored another; and it was something to triumph over my tyrant even in that small way. I thought he would revenge himself by selling me, and I was sure my friend, Mr. Sands, would buy me. He was a man of more generosity and feeling than my master, and I thought my freedom could be easily obtained from him. The crisis of my fate now came so near that I was desperate. I shuddered to think of being the mother of children that should be owned by my old tyrant. I knew that as soon as a new fancy took him, his victims were sold far off to get rid of them; especially if they had children. I had seen several women sold, with his babies at the breast. He never allowed his offspring by slaves to remain long in sight of himself and his wife. Of a man who was not my master I could ask to have my children well supported; and in this case, I felt confident I should obtain the boon. I also felt quite sure that they would be made free. With all these thoughts revolving in my mind, and seeing no other way of escaping the doom I so much dreaded, I made a headlong plunge. Pity me, and pardon me, O virtuous reader! You never knew what it is to be a slave; to be entirely unprotected by law or custom; to have the laws reduce you to the condition of a chattel, entirely subject to the will of another. You never exhausted your ingenuity in avoiding the snares, and eluding the power of a hated tyrant; you never shuddered at the sound of his footsteps, and trembled within hearing of his voice. I know I did wrong. No one can feel it more sensibly than I do. The painful and humiliating memory will haunt me to my dying day. Still, in looking back, calmly, on the events of my life, I feel that the slave woman ought not to be judged by the same standard as others.

The months passed on. I had many unhappy hours. I secretly mourned over the sorrow I was bringing on my grandmother, who had so tried to shield me from harm. I knew that I was the greatest comfort of her old age, and that it was a source of pride to her that I had not degraded myself, like most of the slaves. I wanted to confess to her that I was no longer worthy of her love; but I could not utter the dreaded words.

As for Dr. Flint, I had a feeling of satisfaction and triumph in the thought of telling *him*. From time to time he told me of his intended arrangements, and I was silent. At last, he came and told me the cottage was completed, and ordered me to go to it. I told him I would never enter it. He said, "I have heard enough of such talk as that. You shall go, if you are carried by force; and you shall remain there."

I replied, "I will never go there. In a few months I shall be a mother."

He stood and looked at me in dumb amazement, and left the house without a word. I thought I should be happy in my triumph over him. But now that the truth was out, and my relatives would hear of it, I felt wretched. Humble as were their circumstances, they had pride in my good character. Now, how could I look them in the face? My self-respect was gone! I had resolved that I would be virtuous, though I was a slave. I had said, "Let the storm beat! I will brave it till I die." And now, how humiliated I felt!

I went to my grandmother. My lips moved to make confession, but the words stuck in my throat. I sat down in the shade of a tree at her door and began to sew. I think she saw something unusual was the matter with me. The mother of slaves is very watchful. She knows there is no security for her children. After they have entered their teens she lives in daily expectation of trouble. This leads to many questions. If the girl is of a sensitive nature, timidity keeps her from answering truthfully, and this well-meant course has a tendency to drive her from maternal counsels. Presently, in came my mistress, like a mad woman, and accused me concerning her husband. My grandmother, whose suspicions had been previously awakened, believed what she said. She exclaimed, "O Linda! has it come to this? I had rather see you dead than to see you as you now are. You are a disgrace to your dead mother." She tore from my fingers my mother's wedding ring and her silver thimble. "Go away!" she exclaimed, "and never come to my house, again." Her reproaches fell so hot and heavy, that they left me no chance to answer. Bitter tears, such as the eyes never shed but once, were my only answer. I rose from my seat, but fell back again, sobbing. She did not speak to me; but the tears were running down her furrowed cheeks, and they scorched me like fire. She had always been so kind to me! So kind! How I longed to throw myself at her feet, and tell her all the truth! But she had ordered me to go, and never to come there again. After a few minutes, I mustered strength, and started to obey her. With what feelings did I now close that little gate, which I used to open with such an eager hand in my childhood! It closed upon me with a sound I never heard before.

Where could I go? I was afraid to return to my master's. I walked on recklessly, not caring where I went, or what would become of me. When I had gone four or five miles, fatigue compelled me to stop. I sat down on the stump of an old tree. The stars were shining through the boughs above me. How they mocked me, with their bright, calm light! The hours passed by, and as I sat there alone a chilliness and deadly sickness came over me. I sank on the ground. My mind was full of horrid thoughts. I prayed to die; but the prayer was not answered. At last, with great effort I roused myself, and walked some distance further, to the house of a woman who had been a friend of my mother. When I told her why I was there, she spoke soothingly to me; but I could not be comforted. I thought I could bear my shame if I could only be reconciled to my grandmother. I longed to open my heart to her. I thought if she could know the real state of the case, and all I had been bearing for years, she would perhaps judge me less harshly. My friend advised me to send for her. I did so; but days of agonizing suspense passed before she came. Had she utterly forsaken me? No. She came at last. I knelt before her, and told her the things that had poisoned my life; how long I had been persecuted; that I saw no way of escape; and in an hour of extremity I had become desperate. She listened in silence. I told her I would bear any thing and do any thing, if in time I had hopes of obtaining her forgiveness. I begged of her to pity me, for my dead mother's sake. And she did pity me. She did not say, "I forgive you;" but she looked at me lovingly, with her eyes full of tears. She laid her old hand gently on my head, and murmured, "Poor child! Poor child!"

## XIV. *Another Link to Life*

I had not returned to my master's house since the birth of my child. The old man raved to have me thus removed from his immediate power; but his wife vowed, by all that was good and great, she would kill me if I came back; and he did not doubt her word. Sometimes he would stay away for a season. Then he would come and renew the old threadbare discourse about his forbearance and my ingratitude. He labored, most unnecessarily, to convince me that I had lowered myself. The venomous old reprobate had no need of descanting on that theme. I felt humiliated enough. My unconscious babe was the ever-present witness of my shame. I listened with silent contempt when he talked about my having forfeited *his* good opinion; but I shed bitter tears that I was no longer worthy of being respected by the good and pure. Alas! slavery still held me in its poisonous grasp. There was no chance for me to be respectable. There was no prospect of being able to lead a better life.

Sometimes, when my master found that I still refused to accept what he called his kind offers, he would threaten to sell my child. "Perhaps that will humble you," said he.

Humble *me!* Was I not already in the dust?[9] But his threat lacerated my heart. I knew the law gave him power to fulfill it; for slaveholders have been cunning enough to enact that "the child shall follow the condition of the *mother,*" not of the *father;* thus taking care that licentiousness shall not interfere with avarice. This reflection made me clasp my innocent babe all the more firmly to my heart. Horrid visions passed through my mind when I thought of his liability to fall into the slave trader's hands. I wept over him, and said, "O my child! perhaps they will leave you in some cold cabin to die, and then throw you into a hole, as if you were a dog."

When Dr. Flint learned that I was again to be a mother, he was exasperated beyond measure. He rushed from the house, and returned with a pair of shears. I had a fine head of hair; and he often railed about my pride of arranging it nicely. He cut every hair close to my head, storming and swearing all the time. I replied to some of his abuse, and he struck me. Some months before, he had pitched me down stairs in a fit of passion; and the injury I received was so serious that I was unable to turn myself in bed for many days. He then said, "Linda, I swear by God I will never raise my hand against you again;" but I knew that he would forget his promise.

After he discovered my situation, he was like a restless spirit from the pit. He came every day; and I was subjected to such insults as no pen can describe. I would not describe them if I could; they were too low, too revolting. I tried to keep them from my grandmother's knowledge as much as I could. I knew she had enough to sadden her life, without having my troubles to bear. When she saw the doctor treat me with violence, and heard him utter oaths terrible enough to palsy a man's tongue, she could not always hold her peace. It was natural and motherlike that she should try to defend me; but it only made matters worse.

When they told me my new-born babe was a girl, my heart was heavier than it had ever been before. Slavery is terrible for men; but it is far more terrible for women. Superadded to the burden common to all, *they* have wrongs, and sufferings, and mortifications peculiarly their own.

Dr. Flint had sworn that he would make me suffer, to my last day, for this new crime against *him,* as he called it; and as long as he had me in his power he kept his word. On the fourth day after the birth of my babe, he entered my room suddenly, and commanded me to rise and bring my baby to him. The nurse who took care of me had gone out of the room to prepare some nourishment, and I was alone. There was no alternative. I rose, took up my babe, and crossed the room to where he sat. "Now stand there," said he, "till I tell you to go back!" My child bore a strong resemblance to her father, and to the deceased Mrs. Sands, her grandmother. He noticed this; and while I stood before him, trembling with weakness, he heaped upon me and my little one every vile epithet he could think of. Even the grandmother in her grave did not escape his curses. In the midst of his vituperations I fainted at his feet. This recalled him to his senses. He took the baby from my arms, laid it on the bed, dashed cold water in my face, took me up, and shook me violently, to restore my consciousness before any one entered the room. Just then my grandmother came in, and he hurried out of the house. I suffered in consequence of this treatment; but I begged my friends to let me die, rather than send for the doctor. There was nothing I dreaded so much as his presence. My

9. Cf. Job 42.6: "Wherefore I abhor myself, and repent in dust and ashes."

life was spared; and I was glad for the sake of my little ones. Had it not been
for these ties to life, I should have been glad to be released by death, though I
had lived only nineteen years.

Always it gave me a pang that my children had no lawful claim to a name.
Their father offered his; but, if I had wished to accept the offer, I dared not
while my master lived. Moreover, I knew it would not be accepted at their
baptism. A Christian name they were at least entitled to; and we resolved to
call my boy for our dear good Benjamin, who had gone far away from us.

My grandmother belonged to the church, and she was very desirous of having the children christened. I knew Dr. Flint would forbid it, and I did not
venture to attempt it. But chance favored me. He was called to visit a patient
out of town, and was obliged to be absent during Sunday. "Now is the time,"
said my grandmother; "we will take the children to church, and have them
christened."

When I entered the church, recollections of my mother came over me, and
I felt subdued in spirit. There she had presented me for baptism, without any
reason to feel ashamed. She had been married, and had such legal rights as
slavery allows a slave. The vows had at least been sacred to *her*, and she had
never violated them. I was glad she was not alive, to know under what different
circumstances her grandchildren were presented for baptism. Why had my lot
been so different from my mother's? *Her* master had died when she was a
child; and she remained with her mistress till she married. She was never in
the power of any master; and thus she escaped one class of the evils that generally fall upon slaves.

When my baby was about to be christened, the former mistress of my father
stepped up to me, and proposed to give it her Christian name. To this I added
the surname of my father, who had himself no legal right to it; for my grandfather on the paternal side was a white gentleman. What tangled skeins are the
genealogies of slavery! I loved my father; but it mortified me to be obliged to
bestow his name on my children.

When we left the church, my father's old mistress invited me to go home
with her. She clasped a gold chain around my baby's neck. I thanked her for
this kindness; but I did not like the emblem. I wanted no chain to be fastened
on my daughter, not even if its links were of gold. How earnestly I prayed that
she might never feel the weight of slavery's chain, whose iron entereth into
the soul.[1]

## XXI. The Loophole of Retreat[2]

A small shed had been added to my grandmother's house years ago. Some
boards were laid across the joists at the top, and between these boards and the
roof was a very small garret, never occupied by any thing but rats and mice. It
was a pent roof, covered with nothing but shingles, according to the southern
custom for such buildings. The garret was only nine feet long and seven wide.
The highest part was three feet high, and sloped down abruptly to the loose

1. Cf. Psalm 105.17–18: "He sent a man before them,
even Joseph, who was sold for a servant: Whose feet
they hurt with fetters: he was laid in iron." This and
other allusions identify Jacobs's family as Episcopa-
lians.
2. Cf. *The Task* 4.88–90, a popular long poem (1785)

by the English poet William Cowper (1731–1800). At
this point in the narrative Brent has escaped from the
Flint household and is hiding in her grandmother's
attic. The account states that she remains there for
seven years.

board floor. There was no admission for either light or air. My uncle Phillip, who was a carpenter, had very skilfully made a concealed trap-door, which communicated with the storeroom. He had been doing this while I was waiting in the swamp. The storeroom opened upon a piazza. To this hole I was conveyed as soon as I entered the house. The air was stifling; the darkness total. A bed had been spread on the floor. I could sleep quite comfortably on one side; but the slope was so sudden that I could not turn on the other without hitting the roof. The rats and mice ran over my bed; but I was weary, and I slept such sleep as the wretched may, when a tempest has passed over them. Morning came. I knew it only by the noises I heard; for in my small den day and night were all the same. I suffered for air even more than for light. But I was not comfortless. I heard the voices of my children. There was joy and there was sadness in the sound. It made my tears flow. How I longed to speak to them! I was eager to look on their faces; but there was no hole, no crack, through which I could peep. This continued darkness was oppressive. It seemed horrible to sit or lie in a cramped position day after day, without one gleam of light. Yet I would have chosen this, rather than my lot as a slave, though white people considered it an easy one; and it was so compared with the fate of others. I was never cruelly over-worked; I was never lacerated with the whip from head to foot; I was never so beaten and bruised that I could not turn from one side to the other; I never had my heel-strings cut to prevent my running away; I was never chained to a log and forced to drag it about, while I toiled in the fields from morning till night; I was never branded with hot iron, or torn by bloodhounds. On the contrary, I had always been kindly treated, and tenderly cared for, until I came into the hands of Dr. Flint. I had never wished for freedom till then. But though my life in slavery was comparatively devoid of hardships, God pity the woman who is compelled to lead such a life!

My food was passed up to me through the trap-door my uncle had contrived; and my grandmother, my uncle Phillip, and aunt Nancy would seize such opportunities as they could, to mount up there and chat with me at the opening. But of course this was not safe in the daytime. It must all be done in darkness. It was impossible or me to move in an erect position, but I crawled about my den for exercise. One day I hit my head against something, and found it was a gimlet. My uncle had left it sticking there when he made the trap-door. I was as rejoiced as Robinson Crusoe[3] could have been at finding such a treasure. It put a lucky thought into my head. I said to myself, "Now I will have some light. Now I will see my children." I did not dare to begin my work during the daytime, for fear of attracting attention. But I groped round; and having found the side next the street, where I could frequently see my children, I struck the gimlet in and waited for evening. I bored three rows of holes, one above another; then I bored out the interstices between. I thus succeeded in making one hole about an inch long and an inch broad. I sat by it till late into the night, to enjoy the little whiff of air that floated in. In the morning I watched for my children. The first person I saw in the street was Dr. Flint. I had a shuddering, superstitious feeling that it was a bad omen. Several familiar faces passed by. At last I heard the merry laugh of children, and presently two sweet little faces were looking up at me, as though they knew

---

3. Allusion to a popular novel (1719) by the English writer Daniel Defoe (1660–1731) about a man shipwrecked on a desert island.

I was there, and were conscious of the joy they imparted. How I longed to *tell* them I was there!

My condition was now a little improved. But for weeks I was tormented by hundreds of little red insects, fine as a needle's point, that pierced through my skin, and produced an intolerable burning. The good grandmother gave me herb teas and cooling medicines, and finally I got rid of them. The heat of my den was intense, for nothing but thin shingles protected me from the scorching summer's sun. But I had my consolations. Through my peeping-hole I could watch the children, and when they were near enough, I could hear their talk. Aunt Nancy brought me all the news she could hear at Dr. Flint's. From her I learned that the doctor had written to New York to a colored woman, who had been born and raised in our neighborhood, and had breathed his contaminating atmosphere. He offered her a reward if she could find out any thing about me. I know not what was the nature of her reply; but he soon after started for New York in haste, saying to his family that he had business of importance to transact. I peeped at him as he passed on his way to the steamboat. It was a satisfaction to have miles of land and water between us, even for a little while; and it was a still greater satisfaction to know that he believed me to be in the Free States. My little den seemed less dreary than it had done. He returned, as he did from his former journey to New York, without obtaining any satisfactory information. When he passed our house next morning, Benny was standing at the gate. He had heard them say that he had gone to find me, and he called out, "Dr. Flint, did you bring my mother home? I want to see her." The doctor stamped his foot at him in a rage, and exclaimed, "Get out of the way, you little damned rascal! If you don't, I'll cut off your head."

Benny ran terrified into the house, saying, "You can't put me in jail again. I don't belong to you now." It was well that the wind carried the words away from the doctor's ear. I told my grandmother of it, when we had our next conference at the trap-door; and begged of her not to allow the children to be impertinent to the irascible old man.

Autumn came, with a pleasant abatement of heat. My eyes had become accustomed to the dim light, and by holding my book or work in a certain position near the aperture I contrived to read and sew. That was a great relief to the tedious monotony of my life. But when winter came, the cold penetrated through the thin shingle roof, and I was dreadfully chilled. The winters there are not so long, or so severe, as in northern latitudes; but the houses are not built to shelter from cold, and my little den was peculiarly comfortless. The kind grandmother brought me bed-clothes and warm drinks. Often I was obliged to lie in bed all day to keep comfortable; but with all my precautions, my shoulders and feet were frostbitten. O, those long, gloomy days, with no object for my eye to rest upon, and no thoughts to occupy my mind, except the dreary past and the uncertain future! I was thankful when there came a day sufficiently mild for me to wrap myself up and sit at the loophole to watch the passers by. Southerners have the habit of stopping and talking in the streets, and I heard many conversations not intended to meet my ears. I heard slave-hunters planning how to catch some poor fugitive. Several times I heard allusions to Dr. Flint, myself, and the history of my children, who, perhaps, were playing near the gate. One would say, "I wouldn't move my little finger to catch her, as old Flint's property." Another would say, "I'll catch *any* nigger for the reward. A man ought to have what belongs to him, if he *is* a damned brute." The opinion was often expressed that I was in the Free States. Very rarely did any one suggest that I might be in the vicinity. Had the least suspicion rested on my grandmother's house, it would have been burned to the ground. But it was the last place they thought of. Yet there was no place, where slavery existed, that could have afforded me so good a place of concealment.

Dr. Flint and his family repeatedly tried to coax and bribe my children to tell something they had heard said about me. One day the doctor took them into a shop, and offered them some bright little silver pieces and gay handkerchiefs if they would tell where their mother was. Ellen shrank away from him, and would not speak; but Benny spoke up, and said, "Dr. Flint, I don't know where my mother is. I guess she's in New York; and when you go there again, I wish you'd ask her to come home, for I want to see her; but if you put her in jail, or tell her you'll cut her head off, I'll tell her to go right back."

## XLI. Free at Last[4]

Mrs. Bruce, and every member of her family, were exceedingly kind to me. I was thankful for the blessings of my lot, yet I could not always wear a cheerful countenance. I was doing harm to no one; on the contrary, I was doing all the good I could in my small way; yet I could never go out to breathe God's free air without trepidation at my heart. This seemed hard; and I could not think it was a right state of things in any civilized country.

From time to time I received news from my good old grandmother. She could not write; but she employed others to write for her. The following is an extract from one of her last letters:—

> "Dear Daughter: I cannot hope to see you again on earth; but I pray to God to unite us above, where pain will no more rack this feeble body of mine; where sorrow and parting from my children will be no more.[5] God has promised these things if we are faithful unto the end. My age and feeble health deprive me of going to church now; but God is with me here at home. Thank your brother for his kindness. Give much love to him, and tell him to remember the Creator in the days of his youth,[6] and strive to meet me in the Father's kingdom. Love to Ellen and Benjamin. Don't neglect him. Tell him for me, to be a good boy. Strive, my child, to train them for God's children. May he protect and provide for you, is the prayer of your loving old mother."

These letters both cheered and saddened me. I was always glad to have tidings from the kind, faithful old friend of my unhappy youth; but her messages of love made my heart yearn to see her before she died, and I mourned over the fact that it was impossible. Some months after I returned from my flight to New England, I received a letter from her, in which she wrote, "Dr.

---

4. This is the final chapter of *Incidents*. Brent has escaped to New York and found employment in the Bruce family, but the passage of the Fugitive Slave Law in 1850 means that she is not really free. The title alludes to a familiar spiritual.
5. Cf. Revelation 21.4: "And God shall wipe away all

tears from their eyes; and there shall be no more death, neither sorrow, nor crying, neither shall there be any more pain: for the former things are passed away."
6. Ecclesiastes 12.1. Throughout the narrative the grandmother is portrayed as a deeply pious woman with great knowledge of the Bible.

Flint is dead. He has left a distressed family. Poor old man! I hope he made his peace with God."

I remembered how he had defrauded my grandmother of the hard earnings she had loaned; how he had tried to cheat her out of the freedom her mistress had promised her, and how he had persecuted her children; and I thought to myself that she was a better Christian than I was, if she could entirely forgive him. I cannot say, with truth, that the news of my old master's death softened my feelings towards him. There are wrongs which even the grave does not bury. The man was odious to me while he lived, and his memory is odious now.

His departure from this world did not diminish my danger. He had threatened my grandmother that his heirs should hold me in slavery after he was gone; that I never should be free so long as a child of his survived. As for Mrs. Flint, I had seen her in deeper afflictions than I supposed the loss of her husband would be, for she had buried several children; yet I never saw any signs of softening in her heart. The doctor had died in embarrassed circumstances, and had little to will to his heirs, except such property as he was unable to grasp. I was well aware what I had to expect from the family of Flints; and my fears were confirmed by a letter from the south, warning me to be on my guard, because Mrs. Flint openly declared that her daughter could not afford to lose so valuable a slave as I was.

I kept close watch of the newspapers for arrivals; but one Saturday night, being much occupied, I forgot to examine the Evening Express as usual. I went down into the parlor for it, early in the morning, and found the boy about to kindle a fire with it. I took it from him and examined the list of arrivals. Reader, if you have never been a slave, you cannot imagine the acute sensation of suffering at my heart, when I read the names of Mr. and Mrs. Dodge,[7] at a hotel in Courtland Street. It was a third-rate hotel, and that circumstance convinced me of the truth of what I had heard, that they were short of funds and had need of my value, as *they* valued me; and that was by dollars and cents. I hastened with the paper to Mrs. Bruce. Her heart and hand were always open to every one in distress, and she always warmly sympathized with mine. It was impossible to tell how near the enemy was. He might have passed and repassed the house while we were sleeping. He might at that moment be waiting to pounce upon me if I ventured out of doors. I had never seen the husband of my young mistress, and therefore I could not distinguish him from any other stranger. A carriage was hastily ordered; and, closely veiled, I followed Mrs. Bruce, taking the baby again with me into exile. After various turnings and crossings, and returnings, the carriage stopped at the house of one of Mrs. Bruce's friends, where I was kindly received. Mrs. Bruce returned immediately, to instruct the domestics what to say if any one came to inquire for me.

It was lucky for me that the evening paper was not burned up before I had a chance to examine the list of arrivals. It was not long after Mrs. Bruce's return to her house, before several people came to inquire for me. One inquired for me, another asked for my daughter Ellen, and another said he had a letter from my grandmother, which he was requested to deliver in person. They were told, "She *has* lived here, but she has left."

7. Dodge is the married name of Emily Flint, Brent's legal owner.

"How long ago?"

"I don't know, sir."

"Do you know where she went?"

"I do not, sir." And the door was closed.

This Mr. Dodge, who claimed me as his property, was originally a Yankee pedler in the south; then he became a merchant, and finally a slaveholder. He managed to get introduced into what was called the first society, and married Miss Emily Flint. A quarrel arose between him and her brother, and the brother cowhided him. This led to a family feud, and he proposed to remove to Virginia. Dr. Flint left him no property, and his own means had become circumscribed, while a wife and children depended upon him for support. Under these circumstances, it was very natural that he should make an effort to put me into his pocket.

I had a colored friend, a man from my native place, in whom I had the most implicit confidence. I sent for him, and told him that Mr. and Mrs. Dodge had arrived in New York. I proposed that he should call upon them to make inquiries about his friends at the south, with whom Dr. Flint's family were well acquainted. He thought there was no impropriety in his doing so, and he consented. He went to the hotel, and knocked at the door of Mr. Dodge's room, which was opened by the gentleman himself, who gruffly inquired, "What brought you here? How came you to know I was in the city?"

"Your arrival was published in the evening papers, sir; and I called to ask Mrs. Dodge about my friends at home. I didn't suppose it would give any offence."

"Where's that negro girl, that belongs to my wife?"

"What girl, sir?"

"You know well enough. I mean Linda, that ran away from Dr. Flint's plantation, some years ago. I dare say you've seen her, and know where she is."

"Yes, sir, I've seen her, and know where she is. She is out of your reach, sir."

"Tell me where she is, or bring her to me, and I will give her a chance to buy her freedom."

"I don't think it would be of any use, sir. I have heard her say she would go to the ends of the earth, rather than pay any man or woman for her freedom, because she thinks she has a right to it. Besides, she couldn't do it, if she would, for she has spent her earnings to educate her children."

This made Mr. Dodge very angry, and some high words passed between them. My friend was afraid to come where I was; but in the course of the day I received a note from him. I supposed they had not come from the south, in the winter, for a pleasure excursion; and now the nature of their business was very plain.

Mrs. Bruce came to me and entreated me to leave the city the next morning. She said her house was watched, and it was possible that some clew to me might be obtained. I refused to take her advice. She pleaded with an earnest tenderness, that ought to have moved me; but I was in a bitter, disheartened mood. I was weary of flying from pillar to post. I had been chased during half my life, and it seemed as if the chase was never to end. There I sat, in that great city, guiltless of crime, yet not daring to worship God in any of the churches. I heard the bells ringing for afternoon service, and, with contemptuous sarcasm, I said, "Will the preachers take for their text, 'Proclaim liberty to the captive, and the opening of prison doors to them that are bound'?[8] or will they preach from the text, 'Do unto others as ye would they should do unto you'?"[9] Oppressed Poles and Hungarians could find a safe refuge in that city; John Mitchell[1] was free to proclaim in the City Hall his desire for "a plantation well stocked with slaves;" but there I sat, an oppressed American, not daring to show my face. "God forgive the black and bitter thoughts I indulged on that Sabbath day! The Scripture says, "Oppression makes even a wise man mad;"[2] and I was not wise.

I had been told that Mr. Dodge said his wife had never signed away her right to my children, and if he could not get me, he would take them. This it was, more than any thing else, that roused such a tempest in my soul. Benjamin was with his uncle William in California, but my innocent young daughter had come to spend a vacation with me. I thought of what I had suffered in slavery at her age, and my heart was like a tiger's when a hunter tries to seize her young.

Dear Mrs. Bruce! I seem to see the expression of her face, as she turned away discouraged by my obstinate mood. Finding her expostulations unavailing, she sent Ellen to entreat me. When ten o'clock in the evening arrived and Ellen had not returned, this watchful and unwearied friend became anxious. She came to us in a carriage, bringing a well-filled trunk for my journey—trusting that by this time I would listen to reason. I yielded to her, as I ought to have done before.

The next day, baby and I set out in a heavy snow storm, bound for New England again. I received letters from the City of Iniquity,[3] addressed to me under an assumed name. In a few days one came from Mrs. Bruce, informing me that my new master was still searching for me, and that she intended to put an end to this persecution by buying my freedom. I felt grateful for the kindness that prompted this offer, but the idea was not so pleasant to me as might have been expected. The more my mind had become enlightened, the more difficult it was for me to consider myself an article of property; and to pay money to those who had so grievously oppressed me seemed like taking from my sufferings the glory of triumph. I wrote to Mrs. Bruce, thanking her, but saying that being sold from one owner to another seemed too much like slavery; that such a great obligation could not be easily cancelled; and that I preferred to go to my brother in California.

Without my knowledge, Mrs. Bruce employed a gentleman in New York to enter into negotiations with Mr. Dodge. He proposed to pay three hundred dollars down, if Mr. Dodge would sell me, and enter into obligations to relinquish all claim to me or my children forever after. He who called himself my master said he scorned so small an offer for such a valuable servant. The gentleman replied, "You can do as you choose, sir. If you reject this offer you will never get any thing; for the woman has friends who will convey her and her children out of the country."

8. Isaiah 61.1.
9. Matthew 7.12.
1. Following the unsuccessful European revolutions of 1848, many Polish and Hungarian political refugees found homes in New York City and New England. John Mitchell (1815–1875), Irish-American founder of the New York City proslavery newspaper *The Citizen*. Throughout the pre–Civil War era, Irish-American

politicians tended to portray free blacks as competing for jobs that would otherwise go to the Irish; Mitchell indeed wrote what Jacobs attributes to him here.
2. Ecclesiastes 7.7: "Surely oppression maketh a wise man mad; and a gift destroyeth the heart.
3. Jacobs's term for New York City as the center of the business of returning fugitive slaves into bondage.

Mr. Dodge concluded that "half a loaf was better than no bread," and he agreed to the proffered terms. By the next mail I received this brief letter from Mrs. Bruce: "I am rejoiced to tell you that the money for your freedom has been paid to Mr. Dodge. Come home to-morrow. I long to see you and my sweet babe."

My brain reeled as I read these lines. A gentleman near me said, "It's true; I have seen the bill of sale." "The bill of sale!" Those words struck me like a blow. So I was *sold* at last! A human being *sold* in the free city of New York! The bill of sale is on record, and future generations will learn from it that women were articles of traffic in New York, late in the nineteenth century of the Christian religion. It may hereafter prove a useful document to antiquaries, who are seeking to measure the progress of civilization in the United States. I well know the value of that bit of paper; but much as I love freedom, I do not like to look upon it. I am deeply grateful to the generous friend who procured it, but I despise the miscreant who demanded payment for what never rightfully belonged to him or his.

I had objected to having my freedom bought, yet I must confess that when it was done I felt as if a heavy load had been lifted from my weary shoulders. When I rode home in the cars I was no longer afraid to unveil my face and look at people as they passed. I should have been glad to have met Daniel Dodge himself; to have had him seen me and known me, that he might have mourned over the untoward circumstances which compelled him to sell me for three hundred dollars.

When I reached home, the arms of my benefactress were thrown round me, and our tears mingled. As soon as she could speak, she said, "O Linda, I'm *so* glad it's all over! You wrote to me as if you thought you were going to be transferred from one owner to another. But I did not buy you for your services. I should have done just the same, if you had been going to sail for California tomorrow. I should, at least, have the satisfaction of knowing that you left me a free woman."

My heart was exceedingly full. I remembered how my poor father had tried to buy me, when I was a small child, and how he had been disappointed. I hoped his spirit was rejoicing over me now. I remembered how my good old grandmother had laid up her earnings to purchase me in later years, and how often her plans had been frustrated. How that faithful, loving old heart would leap for joy, if she could look on me and my children now that we were free! My relatives had been foiled in all their efforts, but God had raised me up a friend among strangers, who had bestowed on me the precious, long-desired boon. Friend! It is a common word, often lightly used. Like other good and beautiful things, it may be tarnished by careless handling; but when I speak of Mrs. Bruce as my friend, the word is sacred.

My grandmother lived to rejoice in my freedom; but not long after, a letter came with a black seal. She had gone "where the wicked cease from troubling, and the weary are at rest."[4]

Time passed on, and a paper came to me from the south, containing an obituary notice of my uncle Phillip. It was the only case I ever knew of such an honor conferred upon a colored person. It was written by one of his friends, and contained these words: "Now that death has laid him low, they call him a

---

4. Cf. Job 3.17: "There the wicked cease from troubling; and there the weary be at rest."

good man and a useful citizen; but what are eulogies to the black man, when the world has faded from his vision? It does not require man's praise to obtain rest in God's kingdom." So they called a colored man a *citizen!* Strange words to be uttered in that region![5]

Reader, my story ends with freedom; not in the usual way, with marriage.[6] I and my children are now free! We are as free from the power of slaveholders as are the white people of the north; and though that, according to my ideas, is not saying a great deal, it is a vast improvement in *my* condition. The dream of my life is not yet realized. I do not sit with my children in a home of my own. I still long for a hearthstone of my own, however humble. I wish it for my children's sake far more than for my own. But God so orders circumstances as to keep me with my friend Mrs. Bruce. Love, duty, gratitude, also bind me to her side. It is a privilege to serve her who pities my oppressed people, and who has bestowed the inestimable boon of freedom on me and my children.

It has been painful to me, in many ways, to recall the dreary years I passed in bondage. I would gladly forget them if I could. Yet the retrospection is not altogether without solace; for with those gloomy recollections come tender memories of my good old grandmother, like light, fleecy clouds floating over a dark and troubled sea.

5. The laws of North Carolina at this time denied the status of citizen to free blacks as well as to slaves.
6. Allusion to the fictional formula of women's nov-els, reminding readers that such novels are really about white women, because black women cannot share the same story while slavery threatens them.

---

# HENRY DAVID THOREAU
## 1817–1862

Henry David Thoreau Thoreau won his place in American literature by adventuring at home—traveling, as he put it, a good deal in Concord. With that kind of paradox he infuriated and inspired his Massachusetts neighbors and audiences while he lived; his writings have infuriated and inspired successive generations of readers since his death.

Of the men and women who made Concord the center of Transcendentalism, only Thoreau was born there. He lived in Concord all his life, except for a few years in early childhood, his college years at nearby Cambridge, and several months on Staten Island in 1843. He made numerous short excursions, including three to northern Maine, four to Cape Cod, others to New Hampshire, one to Quebec, and a last trip to Minnesota (1861) in a futile attempt to strengthen his tubercular lungs. Never marrying, and horrified by the one proposal that he received, his most complex personal relationship outside his family was with his older neighbor, Ralph Waldo Emerson, though the discrepancies between their rarefied ideals of friendship and the realities of social commerce finally left them frustrated with each other. Aside from Emerson, contemporary writers meant little to him except for Thomas Carlyle, whom he regarded as one of the great exhorting prophets of the generation, and Walt Whitman, although he was always a reader of any history of travel and exploration that could suggest possible ways of experimenting with life. He steeped himself in the classics—Greek, Roman, and English—and he knew in translation the sacred writings of the Hindus. He wrote constantly in his journals, which he began at Emerson's suggestion. Ultimately he made them a finished literary form, but in his early career he used them primarily as sources for his lectures, for his essays, and for both of the books that he published, A Week on the Concord and Merrimack Rivers (1849) and Walden (1854). Through his writings and lectures he attracted admirers, a few of whom must be called disciples. Much effort—and much unwonted tact—went into satisfying their demands on him while keeping them at an appropriate distance. In the 1850s, as his journals became more and more the record of his observations of nature, his scientific discoveries made him well known to important naturalists such as Louis Agassiz. During the same years, he became one of the most outspoken abolitionists. Although he was never one to affiliate himself with groups, he became known as a reliable abolitionist speaker—not as important as Wendell Phillips, William Lloyd Garrison, or Theodore Parker, but effective enough to be summoned to fill in for Frederick Douglass at a convention in Boston. Thoreau moved into the political forefront only with his defense of John Brown, immediately after the arrests at Harpers Ferry. He was forty-four when he died at Concord on May 6, 1862, in his mother's house. The little national fame he had achieved was as an eccentric Emersonian social experimenter and a firebrand champion of Brown. Emerson, himself famous as the sage of Concord, called Thoreau preeminently "the man of Concord," a sincere compliment that precisely delimited his sense of his younger friend as ultimately far more provincial than himself.

Thoreau's nonliterary neighbors, whom he taunted in Walden to compel their attention, knew him as an educated man without an occupation—an affront to a society in which few sons (and no daughters) had the privilege of going to Harvard College. Even Emerson thought that he had drifted into his odd way of life rather than choosing it deliberately. Thoreau might in fact have made a career of his first job as a Concord schoolteacher had he not quickly resigned rather than inflict corporal punishment on his students. He would have taken another teaching job, but in that depression year of 1837 could find none. He and his older brother John started their own progressive school in Concord, but it disbanded when John became ill. John died early in 1842, and Thoreau never went back to teaching. That year he became a handyman at Emerson's house in exchange for room and board, and stayed there intermittently during the 1840s, especially when Emerson was away on long trips. He tried tutoring at the Staten Island home of Emerson's brother William in 1843, but he grew miserably homesick. One long-term advantage was that the job had permitted him some contact with the New York publishing circle. He spent two years on Emerson's property at Walden Pond (1845–47) in a cabin he built himself. He first lectured at the Concord Lyceum in 1838; from the late 1840s onward he occasionally earned twenty-five dollars or so for lecturing in small towns such as New Bedford and Worcester and, less often, in Boston. Sometimes he charmed his audiences with woodlore and what reviewers called his "comical" and "highfalutin" variety of laconic Yankee wit; sometimes he infuriated them with righteous challenges to the way they lived. No critic, however friendly, claimed that Thoreau had much presence as a public speaker, except during the fury of some of his abolitionist addresses. After 1848 he earned some money now and then by surveying property. He sold a few magazine articles, but earned nothing from his two books. He worked at times in his father's pencil factory, and carried on the business when his father died in 1859, thereby aggravating his tuberculosis with the dust from graphite. His whole life, after the period of uncertainty about an occupation in his early manhood, became a calculated refusal to live by the materialistic values of the neighbors who provided him with a microcosm of the world. By simplifying his needs—an affront to what was already a consumer society devoted to arousing "artificial wants"—he succeeded, with minimal compromises, in living his life rather than wasting it, as he saw it, in earning a living.

Among Thoreau's literary acquaintances such as Bronson Alcott, Ellery Channing, and Margaret Fuller, Emerson was his first and most powerful champion. Emerson published many of Thoreau's early poems and essays in the Dial between 1842 and 1844, and tried to persuade publishers in Boston and New York to print Thoreau's first book. Emerson saw to it that Week and, later, Walden were known to his British friends, including Thomas Carlyle. Hawthorne, a sometime Concord resident, liked Thoreau although he thought him "the most unmalleable fellow alive." In 1845 Hawthorne discouraged Evert A. Duyckinck from looking for any popular book from Thoreau except perhaps "a book of simple observation of nature." Later, Hawthorne mentioned Thoreau in the prefaces to *Mosses from an Old Manse* (1846) and *The Scarlet Letter* (1850), and Elizabeth Peabody, Hawthorne's sister-in-law, printed *Resistance to Civil Government* in her *Aesthetic Papers* (1849). Horace Greeley, the vigorous editor of the New York *Tribune*, did more than anyone besides Emerson to make Thoreau a national figure, from 1843 onward mentioning his contributions to the *Dial*, reviewing his books, advertising his lectures, reprinting some of his writings, and aggressively forcing some of Thoreau's essays on magazine editors in New York and Philadelphia, then dunning them for payment. George William Curtis, who was one of the "raisers" of the Walden cabin, printed three parts of *A Yankee in Canada* (1866) in *Putnam's Monthly* (1853), but Thoreau withdrew the rest when Curtis wanted to modify what Greeley guessed were "very flagrant heresies (like your defiant Pantheism)." Curtis also accepted *Cape Cod* for *Putnam's Monthly*, but held it for three years before starting to print it in 1855, and even then Thoreau had to contend with Curtis's religious scruples. The *Atlantic Monthly*, founded in 1857 by men of abolitionist sympathies, ought to have become a regular outlet, but the editor, James Russell Lowell, had acquired a dislike for Thoreau, either at Harvard or during Lowell's enforced rustication at Concord. Lowell accepted part of what became *The Maine Woods* but deleted a climactic sentence about a pine tree: "It is as immortal as I am, and perchance will go to as high a heaven, there to tower above me still." Thoreau scathingly declared that the expurgation had been made in "a very mean and cowardly manner," and the *Atlantic Monthly* was closed to him until just before his death, when the new editors solicited manuscripts.

When he died, Thoreau was putting many of his works in shape for publication. His last audible words had to do with *The Maine Woods*: "moose" and "Indian." Although Thoreau had published only *Week* and *Walden* in book form, substantial sections of two posthumous books, *The Maine Woods* and *Cape Cod*, had appeared in magazines. Had they appeared as books, these two might have won Thoreau a wider reputation as a conservationist and an acute observer of people and places, but they would hardly have won him a loftier literary fame.

A *Week on the Concord and Merrimack Rivers* (1849) purports to be the record of a canoe excursion Thoreau and his brother took upriver. They leave Concord on a Saturday; by Thursday they are as far into New Hampshire as their canoe will go; and then they go back downstream to Concord on a Thursday and Friday (really of the next week). The book consists partly of descriptions of the fauna and flora that the brothers see, along with brief mention of people they encounter. Many pages are devoted to local history, plundered from gazetteers; Thoreau even includes a narrative of Indian captivity, which he ends with some Hawthornesque sensationalism. Poems by Thoreau and others and fragments of his translations from Greek epics and drama also take up space. The bulk of the small book, however, consists of numerous essays, spliced in hit or miss, on a variety of topics such as rivers, fish and fishing, fables, Christianity, poetry, reading, writing, reformers, Oriental scriptures, canal boats, Anacreon, quackery, pedestrian travel, Persius, the distinction between art and nature, the Concord Cattle Show, Ossian, and Chaucer. The longest essay is on friendship. Much of this, verse as well as prose, was fugitive material salvaged from issues of the *Dial*. First completed in the spring of 1846, *Week* was revised and expanded over the next years (the essay on friendship being added in 1848) before Thoreau published an edition of one thousand copies at his own expense in 1849; the true story of his having to accommodate some seven hundred unsold copies in his attic is one of the more grimly ironic episodes in the history of earning a living in America by writing. Emerson had generously assured one editor in 1846 that *Week* contained the results of years of study. That is even truer of the book in its final form, but it was never worked into a unified whole. Its great merit is that by its disastrous reception Thoreau was forced not to publish *Walden* right away (there were ads for it in *Week*). Instead, he kept the manuscript of *Walden* for several more years, reworking it many times. If *Week* had been even a modest success, *Walden* probably would not have been a literary classic.

As early as 1857, Thoreau made clear his intention to publish *The Maine Woods* as a book, though in his lifetime only the first two parts appeared. In this book there is very little satire and very little of the reflective writing shunned by magazines of the time. The most heightened passages of "Ktaadn" deal with Thoreau's realization that the Maine woods were "primeval, untamed, and forever untameable *Nature*," and his peroration would not have offended even the spoilers of nature, citing as it did the inviolable areas in America still left for exploration. Even passages on conservation are not in the voice of a nature-loving Jeremiah, though "Chesuncook" ends with the hope that we shall not, like villains, grub the forests all up, "poaching on our own national domains." These two sections, like almost all of the third, are largely straightforward descriptions of people, places, plants, and animals, with special attention paid to what woodlore could be picked up from lumbermen and American Indian guides. The book's modern editor aptly says that as Maine became a favorite hunting and resort area in the 1870s and 1880s *The Maine Woods* served as a backwoods Baedeker. The backwoods have retreated, but the book is a durable record of what a trained and resourceful observer could discover of primeval nature only a short way from Concord, a reminder that Thoreau was a frontiersman, an explorer of the primeval wilderness as well as of the higher latitudes to be found within oneself.

Thoreau also wrote *Cape Cod* as a book, but during his lifetime he was able to publish only the first four chapters. If he had managed to publish it in the early 1850s it might have gone some way toward making him a popular author. At this time Cape Cod was not fashionable, so Thoreau had a subject almost as exotic as Melville's "Encantadas" (which appeared in *Putnam's Monthly* a little earlier than the chapters from *Cape Cod*) with the added piquancy that Thoreau's unknown land was in the backyards of New York and Boston. Much of the book is vivid eyewitness reportage in the punning style of Thoreau's maturity and with a cheeriness none of his other works sustains. Many pages are openly cribbed from local histories; at best, such information is supplemented by fresh stories from the local inhabitants (who, to Thoreau's delight, often turned out to be even more cantankerous than himself) and by Thoreau's own observations. There is no rage in the book, even in the satire; much of the book is joyous tall talk. In the late twentieth century there is poignancy in reading Thoreau's concluding glance at the future of Cape Cod. The last sentence is a powerful image of Thoreau's repudiation of the worst aspects of his time: "A man may stand there [at Cape Cod] and put all America behind him."

None of the other books that Thoreau published or projected conveys anything like the image of the whole Thoreau that *Walden* does, and even his most representative short work, *Life without Principle*, contains little to suggest his cheerier humor or his love of nature. *Walden* has the meditativeness of *Week* without its diffuseness, the natural observation of *The Maine Woods* without its constriction to particular excursions, the attention to quaintnesses of person and place of *Cape Cod* without its sometimes smothering admixture of borrowed facts. The meandering of *Week* and the travelogue quality of both *The Maine Woods* and *Cape Cod* are replaced in *Walden* by an account that is both a factual record of a particular experience and a parable of all experience. The parables of *Week* are elaborated more richly and focused more memorably in *Walden*; in it the satiric verve of *Cape Cod* is focused on issues far more momentous; in it the nature study of *The Maine Woods* is infused with Thoreau's Transcendentalism. *Week* was the product of diverse impulses; *Cape Cod* and *The Maine Woods* were products of single but limited impulses—perfect of their kind but not belonging to the first order of aspiration or achievement. *Walden* was the product of a single impulse, but one of the strongest literary impulses ever felt: the determination to write a basic book on how to live wisely, a book so profoundly liberating that from the reading of it men and women would date new eras in their lives. In *Walden* Thoreau's whole character emerges. In it he becomes, in the highest sense, a public servant, offering the English-speaking public the fruits of his experience, thought, and artistic dedication.

Thoreau's early writing, even well after his college days, was undistinguished— mere educated prose, less individual, for the most part, than the thirdhand prose that Melville uneasily employed in *Typee*. Thoreau's prose ran to clichés even when the topics, such as love and friendship, were those that were to recur in memorable forms in his later writings. As late as *Week*, the writing was often pedestrianly learned, not up to the alertness of a profoundly educated walker like Thoreau. In *Walden* and a few other works of his mature years, however, Thoreau's style totally subserves his main purpose. Throughout *Walden* that purpose is to force his readers to evaluate the way they have been living and thinking. Whether with his famous aphoristic sentences, his brief fables or allegories, his thick-strewn puns, or many other rhetorical devices, Thoreau's intention always is to make the reader look beyond the obvious, routine sense of an expression to see what idea once vitalized it. He ultimately wants his readers to reevaluate any institution, from the Christian religion to the Constitution of the United States, but first he makes his readers work up their courage by reevaluating on a smaller scale. Thoreau's rhetorical devices afford the hard exercise by which a reader may learn to think freshly. The prose of *Walden*, in short, is designed as a practical course in the liberation of the reader.

Recognition of Thoreau as an important writer was slow in coming. Literary people of his own time knew well enough who he was, but the reading public did not until the publication of *Walden* occasioned comment in some widely read newspapers and magazines. What became Thoreau's most famous essay, *Resistance to Civil Government* (the posthumous title *On the Duty of Civil Disobedience*, now usually cut to the last two words, is apparently not authorial), was published anonymously and never attached to his name in print during his life, though such people as Emerson and Hawthorne knew Thoreau was the author; many decades passed before anyone explicitly acted on the essay's radical advice. Thoreau's early essays in magazines like the *Democratic Review* and *Graham's* were anonymous, and Greeley did not mention him by name when he printed in the *Tribune* for May 25, 1848, a remarkable quotation from a Thoreau letter that was to become part of the first chapter of *Walden*. Thoreau's *Putnam's Monthly* and *Atlantic Monthly* pieces were also anonymous, according to the custom, so that most of his readers probably never knew they were reading Thoreau. Ironically, his widest-read works published under his name during his lifetime were not *Week* or even *Walden*, but *Slavery in Massachusetts* (printed in William Lloyd Garrison's *Liberator* and copied in the *Tribune*) and *A Plea for Captain John Brown* (printed in the fast-selling *Echoes of Harper's Ferry*, 1860).

Between June 1862 (the month after Thoreau's death) and November 1863, the *Atlantic Monthly* published *Walking, Autumn Tints, Wild Apples, Life without Principle*, and *Night and Moonlight* anonymously, but publicized them as Thoreau's. Ticknor and Fields reissued *Week* and *Walden* and quickly got out five new books: *Excursions* (1863), *The Maine Woods* (1864), *Cape Cod* (1864), *Letters to Various Persons* (1865), and *A Yankee in Canada, with Anti-Slavery and Reform Papers* (1866). The expanded form of Emerson's funeral speech, published in the *Atlantic Monthly* for August 1863, confirmed Thoreau's growing reputation even while unnecessarily stressing some of his less attractive traits, especially his "habit of antagonism." In the *North American Review* for October 1865, James Russell Lowell—by then the foremost American critic—had his revenge for Thoreau's scorn for his censorship. Reviewing *Letters to Various Persons*, Lowell depicted Thoreau as a mere echoer of Emerson, "surly and stoic," with "a morbid self-consciousness that pronounces the world of men empty and worthless before trying it." Perhaps most damning, Thoreau was a man who "had no humor." Even Robert Louis Stevenson's description (1880) of Thoreau as a "skulker" had a less baneful effect. In American literary histories and classroom anthologies of the next sixty years, Lowell's words were endlessly quoted or paraphrased.

With Thoreau's credit as social philosopher so thoroughly squelched, his friends began emphasizing his role as a student of nature. Channing published *Thoreau: The Poet-Naturalist* (1873), and John Burroughs's essays followed in the 1880s. Capitalizing on this new attention, Thoreau's disciple H. G. O. Blake, who had inherited the journals from Thoreau's sister Sophia, published *Early Spring in Massachusetts* (1881), *Summer* (1884), *Winter* (1887), and *Autumn* (1892). British critics became interested in Thoreau, and in 1890 an important biography was published by the socialist H. S. Salt—just in time to introduce Thoreau to many Fabians and Labour party members. Thoreau was at last becoming widely recognized as a social philosopher as well as a naturalist. In 1906 Mahatma Gandhi, in his African exile, read *Civil Disobedience* and made it—and later *Life without Principle*—major documents in his struggle for Indian independence. The publication of the journals in 1906 in chronological order (Blake had plundered the journals for seasonal passages regardless of the years in which they occurred) gave readers for the first time a nearly full body of evidence for understanding and judging Thoreau. By the 1930s, when for many "Simplify!" had become not a whim but a necessity, Thoreau had attained the status of a major American voice. Scholarly attention in the next decades began to exalt him to a literary rank higher than Emerson's, even while civil-rights leaders such as Martin Luther King, Jr., tested his tactics of civil disobedience throughout the South and sometimes into the North. In the 1960s and 1970s the counterculture's concern with experiments in living and the general American concern for ecological sanity helped establish Thoreau more firmly than ever as a great American prophet, while his potential value to the radical left remains largely untested. Oddly enough, editors and publishers have kept much of his best work from being known by frequently reprinting *Walden* and *Civil Disobedience* together while ignoring his other works. Thoreau has yet to achieve his full recognition as a great prose stylist as well as a lover of nature, a New England mystic, and a powerful social philosopher. He remains the most challenging major writer America has produced. No good reader will ever be entirely pleased with himself or herself or with the current state of culture and civilization while reading any of Thoreau's best works.

# Resistance to Civil Government[1]

I heartily accept the motto,—"That government is best which governs least;"[2] and I should like to see it acted up to more rapidly and systematically.

1. *Resistance to Civil Government* is reprinted here from its first appearance, in *Aesthetic Papers* (1849); the editor and publisher, Elizabeth Peabody, was Hawthorne's sister-in-law. Thoreau had delivered the paper (or parts of it) as a lecture in January and again in February 1848 before the Concord Lyceum, under the title *The Rights and Duties of the Individual in Relation to Government*. After his death it was reprinted in *A Yankee in Canada, with Anti-Slavery and Reform Papers* (1866) as *Civil Disobedience*, the title by which it much later became world-famous. That title, although very commonly used, may well not be authorial, and Thoreauvians are accustoming themselves to the title of the first printing that, as Thoreau indicates, was a play on *Duty of Submission to Civil Government*, the title of one of the chapters in William Paley's *Principles of Moral and Political Philosophy* (1785). Ignored in its own time, in the 20th century the influence of the essay has been profound, most notably in Mahatma Gandhi's struggle for Indian independence and in the American civil rights movement under the leadership of Martin Luther King, Jr.

2. Associated with Jeffersonianism, these words appeared on the masthead of the *Democratic Review*, the New York magazine that had published two early Thoreau pieces in 1843.

Carried out, it finally amounts to this, which also I believe,—"That government is best which governs not at all;" and when men are prepared for it, that will be the kind of government which they will have. Government is at best but an expedient; but most governments are usually, and all governments are sometimes, inexpedient. The objections which have been brought against a standing army, and they are many and weighty, and deserve to prevail, may also at last be brought against a standing government. The standing army is only an arm of the standing government. The government itself, which is only the mode which the people have chosen to execute their will, is equally liable to be abused and perverted before the people can act through it. Witness the present Mexican war, the work of comparatively a few individuals using the standing government as their tool; for, in the outset, the people would not have consented to this measure.[3]

This American government,—what is it but a tradition, though a recent one, endeavoring to transmit itself unimpaired to posterity, but each instant losing some of its integrity? It has not the vitality and force of a single living man; for a single man can bend it to his will. It is a sort of wooden gun to the people themselves; and, if ever they should use it in earnest as a real one against each other, it will surely split. But it is not the less necessary for this; for the people must have some complicated machinery or other, and hear its din, to satisfy that idea of government which they have. Governments show thus how successfully men can be imposed on, even impose on themselves, for their own advantage. It is excellent, we must all allow; yet this government never of itself furthered any enterprise, but by the alacrity with which it got out of its way. *It* does not keep the country free. *It* does not settle the West. *It* does not educate. The character inherent in the American people has done all that has been accomplished; and it would have done somewhat more, if the government had not sometimes got in its way. For government is an expedient by which men would fain succeed in letting one another alone; and, as has been said, when it is most expedient, the governed are most let alone by it. Trade and commerce, if they were not made of India rubber, would never manage to bounce over the obstacles which legislators are continually putting in their way; and, if one were to judge these men wholly by the effects of their actions, and not partly by their intentions, they would deserve to be classed and punished with those mischievous persons who put obstructions on the railroads.

But, to speak practically and as a citizen, unlike those who call themselves no-government men, I ask for, not at once no government, but *at once* a better government. Let every man make known what kind of government would command his respect, and that will be one step toward obtaining it.

After all, the practical reason why, when the power is once in the hands of the people, a majority are permitted, and for a long period continue, to rule, is not because they are most likely to be in the right, nor because this seems fairest to the minority, but because they are physically the strongest. But a government in which the majority rule in all cases cannot be based on justice, even as far as men understand it. Can there not be a government in which

---

3. The Mexican War, widely criticized by Whigs and many Democrats as an "executive's war" because President Polk commenced hostilities without a congressional declaration of war, ended on February 2, 1848, just after Thoreau first delivered this essay as a lecture. He repeated the lecture after the official ending of the war (or perhaps gave another installment of it), and the next year let it go to press with the out-of-date reference.

majorities do not virtually decide right and wrong, but conscience?—in which majorities decide only those questions to which the rule of expediency is applicable? Must the citizen ever for a moment, or in the least degree, resign his conscience to the legislator? Why has every man a conscience, then? I think that we should be men first, and subjects afterward. It is not desirable to cultivate a respect for the law, so much as for the right. The only obligation which I have a right to assume, is to do at any time what I think right. It is truly enough said,[4] that a corporation has no conscience; but a corporation of conscientious men is a corporation *with* a conscience. Law never made men a whit more just; and, by means of their respect for it, even the well-disposed are daily made the agents of injustice. A common and natural result of an undue respect for law is, that you may see a file of soldiers, colonel, captain, corporal, privates, powder-monkeys and all, marching in admirable order over hill and dale to the wars, against their wills, aye, against their common sense and consciences, which makes it very steep marching indeed, and produces a palpitation of the heart. They have no doubt that it is a damnable business in which they are concerned; they are all peaceably inclined. Now, what are they? Men at all? or small moveable forts and magazines, at the service of some unscrupulous man in power? Visit the Navy Yard, and behold a marine, such a man as an American government can make, or such as it can make a man with its black arts, a mere shadow and reminiscence of humanity, a man laid out alive and standing, and already, as one may say, buried under arms with funeral accompaniments, though it may be

> "Not a drum was heard, nor a funeral note,
> As his corse to the ramparts we hurried;
> Not a soldier discharged his farewell shot
> O'er the grave where our hero we buried."[5]

The mass of men serve the State thus, not as men mainly, but as machines, with their bodies. They are the standing army, and the militia, jailers, constables, *posse comitatus,*[6] &c. In most cases there is no free exercise whatever of the judgment or of the moral sense; but they put themselves on a level with wood and earth and stones; and wooden men can perhaps be manufactured that will serve the purpose as well. Such command no more respect than men of straw, or a lump of dirt. They have the same sort of worth only as horses and dogs. Yet such as these even are commonly esteemed good citizens. Others, as most legislators, politicians, lawyers, ministers, and office-holders, serve the State chiefly with their heads; and, as they rarely make any moral distinctions, they are as likely to serve the devil, without intending it, as God. A very few, as heroes, patriots, martyrs, reformers in the great sense, and *men,* serve the State with their consciences also, and so necessarily resist it for the most part; and they are commonly treated by it as enemies. A wise man will only be useful as a man, and will not submit to be "clay," and "stop a hole to keep the wind away,"[7] but leave that office to his dust at least:—

> "I am too high-born to be propertied,
> To be a secondary at control,

---

4. By Sir Edward Coke, 1612, in a famous legal decision.
5. From Charles Wolfe's *Burial of Sir John Moore at*

*Corunna* (1817), a song Thoreau liked to sing.
6. Sheriff's posse (Latin).
7. Shakespeare's *Hamlet* 5.1.236–37.

Or useful serving-man and instrument
To any sovereign state throughout the world."[8]

He who gives himself entirely to his fellow-men appears to them useless and selfish; but he who gives himself partially to them is pronounced a benefactor and philanthropist.

How does it become a man to behave toward this American government to-day? I answer that he cannot without disgrace be associated with it. I cannot for an instant recognize that political organization as *my* government which is the *slave's* government also.

All men recognize the right of revolution; that is, the right to refuse allegiance to and to resist the government, when its tyranny or its inefficiency are great and unendurable. But almost all say that such is not the case now. But such was the case, they think, in the Revolution of '75. If one were to tell me that this was a bad government because it taxed certain foreign commodities brought to its ports, it is most probable that I should not make an ado about it, for I can do without them: all machines have their friction; and possibly this does enough good to counterbalance the evil. At any rate, it is a great evil to make a stir about it. But when the friction comes to have its machine, and oppression and robbery are organized, I say, let us not have such a machine any longer. In other words, when a sixth of the population of a nation which has undertaken to be the refuge of liberty are slaves, and a whole country is unjustly overrun and conquered by a foreign army, and subjected to military law, I think that it is not too soon for honest men to rebel and revolutionize. What makes this duty the more urgent is the fact, that the country so overrun is not our own, but ours is the invading army.

Paley, a common authority with many on moral questions, in his chapter on the "Duty of Submission to Civil Government,"[9] resolves all civil obligation into expediency; and he proceeds to say, "that so long as the interest of the whole society requires it, that is, so long as the established government cannot be resisted or changed without public inconveniency, it is the will of God that the established government be obeyed, and no longer."—"This principle being admitted, the justice of every particular case of resistance is reduced to a computation of the quantity of the danger and grievance on the one side, and of the probability and expense of redressing it on the other." Of this, he says, every man shall judge for himself. But Paley appears never to have contemplated those cases to which the rule of expediency does not apply, in which a people, as well as an individual, must do justice, cost what it may. If I have unjustly wrested a plank from a drowning man, I must restore it to him though I drown myself.[1] This, according to Paley, would be inconvenient. But he that would save his life, in such a case, shall lose it.[2] This people must cease to hold slaves, and to make war on Mexico, though it cost them their existence as a people.

In their practice, nations agree with Paley; but does any one think that Massachusetts does exactly what is right at the present crisis?

8. Shakespeare's *King John* 5.1.79–82.
9. The precise title of the chapter in William Paley's *Principles of Moral and Political Philosophy* (1785) is *The Duty of Submission to Civil Government Explained*. This book by Paley, English theologian and moralist (1743–1805), was one of Thoreau's Harvard textbooks.
1. A problem in situational ethics cited by Cicero in *De Officiis* 3, which Thoreau had studied.
2. Matthew 10.39; Luke 9.24.

"A drab of state, a cloth-o'-silver slut,
To have her train borne up, and her soul trail in the dirt."[3]

Practically speaking, the opponents to a reform in Massachusetts are not a hundred thousand politicians at the South, but a hundred thousand merchants and farmers here,[4] who are more interested in commerce and agriculture than they are in humanity, and are not prepared to do justice to the slave and to Mexico, *cost what it may*. I quarrel not with far-off foes, but with those who, near at home, co-operate with, and do the bidding of those far away, and without whom the latter would be harmless. We are accustomed to say, that the mass of men are unprepared; but improvement is slow, because the few are not materially wiser or better than the many. It is not so important that many should be as good as you, as that there be some absolute goodness somewhere; for that will leaven the whole lump.[5] There are thousands who are *in opinion* opposed to slavery and to the war, who yet in effect do nothing to put an end to them; who, esteeming themselves children of Washington and Franklin,[6] sit down with their hands in their pockets, and say that they know not what to do, and do nothing; who even postpone the question of freedom to the question of free-trade, and quietly read the prices-current along with the latest advices from Mexico, after dinner, and, it may be, fall asleep over them both. What is the price-current of an honest man and patriot to-day? They hesitate, and they regret, and sometimes they petition; but they do nothing in earnest and with effect. They will wait, well disposed, for others to remedy the evil, that they may no longer have it to regret. At most, they give only a cheap vote, and a feeble countenance and God-speed, to the right, as it goes by them. There are nine hundred and ninety-nine patrons of virtue to one virtuous man; but it is easier to deal with the real possessor of a thing than with the temporary guardian of it.

All voting is a sort of gaming, like chequers or backgammon, with a slight moral tinge to it, a playing with right and wrong, with moral questions; and betting naturally accompanies it. The character of the voters is not staked. I cast my vote, perchance, as I think right; but I am not vitally concerned that that right should prevail. I am willing to leave it to the majority. Its obligation, therefore, never exceeds that of expediency. Even voting *for the right* is *doing* nothing for it. It is only expressing to men feebly your desire that it should prevail. A wise man will not leave the right to the mercy of chance, nor wish it to prevail through the power of the majority. There is but little virtue in the action of masses of men. When the majority shall at length vote for the abolition of slavery, it will be because they are indifferent to slavery, or because there is but little slavery left to be abolished by their vote. *They* will then be the only slaves. Only *his* vote can hasten the abolition of slavery who asserts his own freedom by his vote.

I hear of a convention to be held at Baltimore, or elsewhere, for the selection of a candidate for the Presidency, made up chiefly of editors, and men who are politicians by profession; but I think, what is it to any independent, intelligent, and respectable man what decision they may come to, shall we not have the advantage of his wisdom and honesty, nevertheless? Can we not

3. Cyril Tourneur (1575?–1626), *The Revenger's Trag-edy* 3.4.

4. Thoreau refers to the economic alliance of South-ern cotton growers with Northern shippers and manufacturers.

5. 1 Corinthians 5.6: "Know ye not that a little leaven leaventh the whole lump?"

6. I.e., children of rebels and revolutionaries.

count upon some independent votes? Are there not many individuals in the country who do not attend conventions? But no: I find that the respectable man, so called, has immediately drifted from his position, and despairs of his country, when his country has more reason to despair of him. He forthwith adopts one of the candidates thus selected as the only *available* one, thus proving that he is himself *available* for any purposes of the demagogue. His vote is of no more worth than that of any unprincipled foreigner or hireling native, who may have been bought. Oh for a man who is a *man*, and, as my neighbor says, has a bone in his back which you cannot pass your hand through! Our statistics are at fault: the population has been returned too large. How many *men* are there to a square thousand miles in this country? Hardly one. Does not America offer any inducement for men to settle here? The American had dwindled into an Odd Fellow,—one who may be known by the development of his organ of gregariousness, and a manifest lack of intellect and cheerful self-reliance;[7] whose first and chief concern, on coming into the world, is to see that the alms-houses are in good repair; and, before yet he has lawfully donned the virile garb,[8] to collect a fund for the support of the widows and orphans that may be; who, in short, ventures to live only by the aid of the mutual insurance company, which has promised to bury him decently.

It is not a man's duty, as a matter of course, to devote himself to the eradication of any, even the most enormous wrong; he may still properly have other concerns to engage him; but it is his duty, at least, to wash his hands of it, and, if he gives it no thought longer, not to give it practically his support. If I devote myself to other pursuits and contemplations, I must first see, at least, that I do not pursue them sitting upon another man's shoulders. I must get off him first, that he may pursue his contemplations too. See what gross inconsistency is tolerated. I have heard some of my townsmen say, "I should like to have them order me out to help put down an insurrection of the slaves, or to march to Mexico,—see if I would go;" and yet these very men have each, directly by their allegiance, and so indirectly, at least, by their money, furnished a substitute. The soldier is applauded who refuses to serve in an unjust war by those who do not refuse to sustain the unjust government which makes the war; is applauded by those whose own act and authority he disregards and sets at nought; as if the State were penitent to that degree that it hired one to scourge it while it sinned, but not to that degree that it left off sinning for a moment. Thus, under the name of order and civil government, we are all made at last to pay homage to and support our own meanness. After the first blush of sin, comes its indifference; and from immoral it becomes, as it were, *un*moral, and not quite unnecessary to that life which we have made.

The broadest and most prevalent error requires the most disinterested virtue to sustain it. The slight reproach to which the virtue of patriotism is commonly liable, the noble are most likely to incur. Those who, while they disapprove of the character and measures of a government, yield to it their allegiance and support, are undoubtedly its most conscientious supporters, and so frequently the most serious obstacles to reform. Some are petitioning the State to dissolve the Union, to disregard the requisitions of the President. Why do they not

---

7. The Odd Fellows are a secret fraternal organization, chosen by Thoreau for the satirical value of its name: in his view the archetypal American is not the individualist, the genuine odd fellow, but the con-

formist.
8. Adult garb allowed a Roman boy on reaching fourteen.

dissolve it themselves,—the union between themselves and the State,—and refuse to pay their quota into its treasury? Do not they stand in the same relation to the State, that the State does to the Union? And have not the same reasons prevented the State from resisting the Union, which have prevented them from resisting the State?

How can a man be satisfied to entertain an opinion merely, and enjoy *it?* Is there any enjoyment in it, if his opinion is that he is aggrieved? If you are cheated out of a single dollar by your neighbor, you do not rest satisfied with knowing that you are cheated, or with saying that you are cheated, or even with petitioning him to pay you your due; but you take effectual steps at once to obtain the full amount, and see that you are never cheated again. Action from principle,—the perception and the performance of right,—changes things and relations; it is essentially revolutionary, and does not consist wholly with any thing which was. It not only divides states and churches, it divides families; aye, it divides the *individual*, separating the diabolical in him from the divine.

Unjust laws exist: shall we be content to obey them, or shall we endeavor to amend them, and obey them until we have succeeded, or shall we transgress them at once? Men generally, under such a government as this, think that they ought to wait until they have persuaded the majority to alter them. They think that, if they should resist, the remedy would be worse than the evil. But it is the fault of the government itself that the remedy *is* worse than the evil. *It* makes it worse. Why is it not more apt to anticipate and provide for reform? Why does it not cherish its wise minority? Why does it cry and resist before it is hurt? Why does it not encourage its citizens to be on the alert to point out its faults, and *do* better than it would have them? Why does it always crucify Christ, and excommunicate Copernicus and Luther,[9] and pronounce Washington and Franklin rebels?

One would think, that a deliberate and practical denial of its authority was the only offence never contemplated by government; else, why has it not assigned its definite, its suitable and proportionate penalty? If a man who has no property refuses but once to earn nine shillings[1] for the State, he is put in prison for a period unlimited by any law that I know, and determined only by the discretion of those who placed him there; but if I should steal ninety times nine shillings from the State, he is soon permitted to go at large again.

If the injustice is part of the necessary friction of the machine of government, let it go, let it go: perchance it will wear smooth,—certainly the machine will wear out. If the injustice has a spring, or a pulley, or a rope, or a crank, exclusively for itself, then perhaps you may consider whether the remedy will not be worse than the evil; but if it is of such a nature that it requires you to be the agent of injustice to another, then, I say, break the law. Let your life be a counter friction to stop the machine. What I have to do is to see, at any rate, that I do not lend myself to the wrong which I condemn.

As for adopting the ways which the State has provided for remedying the evil, I know not of such ways. They take too much time, and a man's life will be gone. I have other affairs to attend to. I came into this world, not chiefly to

9. Thoreau uses Copernicus (1473–1543), the Polish astronomer who died too soon after the publication of his new system of astronomy to be excommunicated from the Catholic Church for writing it, and Martin Luther (1483–1546), the German leader of the Protes-

tant Reformation who was excommunicated, as announcers of new truths.
1. The amount of the poll tax Thoreau had refused to pay.

make this a good place to live in, but to live in it, be it good or bad. A man has not every thing to do, but something; and because he cannot do *every thing*, it is not necessary that he should do *something* wrong. It is not my business to be petitioning the governor or the legislature any more than it is theirs to petition me; and, if they should not hear my petition, what should I do then? But in this case the State has provided no way: its very Constitution is the evil. This may seem to be harsh and stubborn and unconciliatory; but it is to treat with the utmost kindness and consideration the only spirit that can appreciate or deserves it. So is all change for the better, like birth and death which convulse the body.

I do not hesitate to say, that those who call themselves abolitionists should at once effectually withdraw their support, both in person and property, from the government of Massachusetts, and not wait till they constitute a majority of one, before they suffer the right to prevail through them. I think that it is enough if they have God on their side, without waiting for that other one. Moreover, any man more right than his neighbors, constitutes a majority of one already.[2]

I meet this American government, or its representative the State government, directly, and face to face, once a year, no more, in the person of its tax-gatherer; this is the only mode in which a man situated as I am necessarily meets it; and it then says distinctly, Recognize me; and the simplest, the most effectual, and, in the present posture of affairs, the indispensablest mode of treating with it on this head, of expressing your little satisfaction with and love for it, is to deny it then. My civil neighbor, the tax-gatherer,[3] is the very man I have to deal with,—for it is, after all, with men and not with parchment that I quarrel,—and he has voluntarily chosen to be an agent of the government. How shall he ever know well what he is and does as an officer of the government, or as a man, until he is obliged to consider whether he shall treat me, his neighbor, for whom he has respect, as a neighbor and well-disposed man, or as a maniac and disturber of the peace, and see if he can get over this obstruction to his neighborliness without a ruder and more impetuous thought or speech corresponding with his action? I know this well, that if one thousand, if one hundred, if ten men whom I could name,—if ten *honest* men only,—aye, if *one* HONEST man, in this State of Massachusetts, *ceasing to hold slaves*, were actually to withdraw from this copartnership, and be locked up in the county jail therefor, it would be the abolition of slavery in America. For it matters not how small the beginning may seem to be: what is once well done is done for ever. But we love better to talk about it: that we say is our mission. Reform keeps many scores of newspapers in its service, but not one man. If my esteemed neighbor, the State's ambassador,[4] who will devote his days to the settlement of the question of human rights in the Council Chamber, instead of being threatened with the prisons of Carolina, were to sit down the prisoner of Massachusetts, that State which is so anxious to foist the sin of slavery upon her sister,—though at present she can discover only an act of inhospitality to be the ground of a quarrel with her,—the Legislature would not wholly waive the subject the following winter.

2. John Knox (1505?–1572), the Scottish religious reformer, said that "a man with God is always in the majority."
3. Sam Staples, who sometimes assisted Thoreau in his surveying.
4. Samuel Hoar (1778–1856), local political figure who as agent of the state of Massachusetts had been expelled from Charleston, South Carolina, in 1844 while interceding on behalf of imprisoned black seamen from Massachusetts. The South Carolina legislature had voted to ask the governor to expel Hoar.

Under a government which imprisons any unjustly, the true place for a just man is also a prison. The proper place to-day, the only place which Massachusetts has provided for her freer and less desponding spirits, is in her prisons, to be put out and locked out of the State by her own act, as they have already put themselves out by their principles. It is there that the fugitive slave, and the Mexican prisoner on parole, and the Indian come to plead the wrongs of his race, should find them; on that separate, but more free and honorable ground, where the State places those who are not *with* her but *against* her,—the only house in a slave-state in which a free man can abide with honor. If any think that their influence would be lost there, and their voices no longer afflict the ear of the State, that they would not be as an enemy within its walls, they do not know by how much truth is stronger than error, nor how much more eloquently and effectively he can combat injustice who has experienced a little in his own person. Cast your whole vote, not a strip of paper merely, but your whole influence. A minority is powerless while it conforms to the majority; it is not even a minority then; but it is irresistible when it clogs by its whole weight. If the alternative is to keep all just men in prison, or give up war and slavery, the State will not hesitate which to choose. If a thousand men were not to pay their tax-bills this year, that would not be a violent and bloody measure, as it would be to pay them, and enable the State to commit violence and shed innocent blood. This is, in fact, the definition of a peaceable revolution, if any such is possible. If the tax-gatherer, or any other public officer, asks me, as one has done, "But what shall I do?" my answer is, "If you really wish to do any thing, resign your office." When the subject has refused allegiance, and the officer has resigned his office, then the revolution is accomplished. But even suppose blood should flow. Is there not a sort of blood shed when the conscience is wounded? Through this wound a man's real manhood and immortality flow out, and he bleeds to an everlasting death. I see this blood flowing now.

I have contemplated the imprisonment of the offender, rather than the seizure of his goods,—though both will serve the same purpose,—because they who assert the purest right, and consequently are most dangerous to a corrupt State, commonly have not spent much time in accumulating property. To such the State renders comparatively small service, and a slight tax is wont to appear exorbitant, particularly if they are obliged to earn it by special labor with their hands. If there were one who lived wholly without the use of money, the State itself would hesitate to demand it of him. But the rich man—not to make any invidious comparison—is always sold to the institution which makes him rich. Absolutely speaking, the more money, the less virtue; for money comes between a man and his objects, and obtains them for him; and it was certainly no great virtue to obtain it. It puts to rest many questions which he would otherwise be taxed to answer; while the only new question which it puts is the hard but superfluous one, how to spend it. Thus his moral ground is taken from under his feet. The opportunities of living are diminished in proportion as what are called the "means" are increased. The best thing a man can do for his culture when he is rich is to endeavour to carry out those schemes which he entertained when he was poor. Christ answered the Herodians according to their condition. "Show me the tribute-money," said he;—and one took a penny out of his pocket;—If you use money which has the image of Cæsar on it, and which he has made current and valuable, that is, *if you are men of the State*, and gladly enjoy the advantages of Cæsar's government, then pay him back some of his own when he demands it: "Render therefore to Cæsar that which is Cæsar's, and to God those things which are God's,"[5]—leaving them no wiser than before as to which was which; for they did not wish to know.

When I converse with the freest of my neighbors, I perceive that, whatever they may say about the magnitude and seriousness of the question, and their regard for the public tranquillity, the long and the short of the matter is, that they cannot spare the protection of the existing government, and they dread the consequences of disobedience to it to their property and families. For my own part, I should not like to think that I ever rely on the protection of the State. But, if I deny the authority of the State when it presents its tax-bill, it will soon take and waste all my property, and so harass me and my children without end. This is hard. This makes it impossible for a man to live honestly and at the same time comfortably in outward respects. It will not be worth the while to accumulate property; that would be sure to go again. You must hire or squat somewhere, and raise but a small crop, and eat that soon. You must live within yourself, and depend upon yourself, always tucked up and ready for a start, and not have many affairs. A man may grow rich in Turkey even, if he will be in all respects a good subject of the Turkish government. Confucious said,—"If a State is governed by the principles of reason, poverty and misery are subjects of shame; if a State is not governed by the principles of reason, riches and honors are the subjects of shame."[6] No: until I want the protection of Massachusetts to be extended to me in some distant southern port, where my liberty is endangered, or until I am bent solely on building up an estate at home by peaceful enterprise, I can afford to refuse allegiance to Massachusetts, and her right to my property and life. It costs me less in every sense to incur the penalty of disobedience to the State, than it would to obey. I should feel as if I were worth less in that case.

Some years ago, the State met me in behalf of the church, and commanded me to pay a certain sum toward the support of a clergyman whose preaching my father attended, but never I myself. "Pay it," it said, "or be locked up in the jail." I declined to pay. But, unfortunately, another man saw fit to pay it. I did not see why the schoolmaster should be taxed to support the priest, and not the priest the schoolmaster; for I was not the State's schoolmaster, but I supported myself by voluntary subscription. I did not see why the lyceum should not present its tax-bill, and have the State to back its demand, as well as the church. However, at the request of the selectmen, I condescended to make some such statement as this in writing:—"Know all men by these presents, that I, Henry Thoreau, do not wish to be regarded as a member of any incorporated society which I have not joined." This I gave to the town-clerk; and he has it. The State, having thus learned that I did not wish to be regarded as a member of that church, has never made a like demand on me since; though it said that it must adhere to its original presumption that time. If I had known how to name them, I should then have signed off in detail from all the societies which I never signed on to; but I did not know where to find a complete list.

I have paid no poll-tax for six years. I was put into a jail[7] once on this

---

5. Matthew 22.16–21. In their attempt to entrap Jesus, the Pharisees (a Jewish sect that held to Mosaic
law) were utilizing secular government functionaries of
Herod, the tetrarch or king of Judea.

6. *Analects* 8.13.
7. The Middlesex County jail in Concord, a large
three-story building. "Six years" would be since 1840.

account, for one night; and, as I stood considering the walls of solid stone, two or three feet thick, the door of wood and iron, a foot thick, and the iron grating which strained the light, I could not help being struck with the foolishness of that institution which treated me as if I were mere flesh and blood and bones, to be locked up. I wondered that it should have concluded at length that this was the best use it could put me to, and had never thought to avail itself of my services in some way. I saw that, if there was a wall of stone between me and my townsmen, there was a still more difficult one to climb or break through, before they could get to be as free as I was. I did not for a moment feel confined, and the walls seemed a great waste of stone and mortar. I felt as if I alone of all my townsmen had paid my tax. They plainly did not know how to treat me, but behaved like persons who are underbred. In every threat and in every compliment there was a blunder; for they thought that my chief desire was to stand the other side of that stone wall. I could not but smile to see how industriously they locked the door on my meditations, which followed them out again without let or hinderance, and *they* were really all that was dangerous. As they could not reach me, they had resolved to punish my body; just as boys, if they cannot come at some person against whom they have a spite, will abuse his dog. I saw that the State was half-witted, that it was timid as a lone woman with her silver spoons, and that it did not know its friends from its foes, and I lost all my remaining respect for it, and pitied it.

Thus the State never intentionally confronts a man's sense, intellectual or moral, but only his body, his senses. It is not armed with superior wit or honesty, but with superior physical strength. I was not born to be forced. I will breathe after my own fashion. Let us see who is the strongest. What force has a multitude? They only can force me who obey a higher law than I. They force me to become like themselves. I do not hear of *men* being *forced* to live this way or that by masses of men. What sort of live were that to live? When I meet a government which says to me, "Your money or your life,"[8] why should I be in haste to give it my money? It may be in a great strait, and not know what to do: I cannot help that. It must help itself; do as I do. It is not worth the while to snivel about it. I am not responsible for the successful working of the machinery of society. I am not the son of the engineer. I perceive that, when an acorn and a chestnut fall side by side, the one does not remain inert to make way for the other, but both obey their own laws, and spring and grow and flourish as best they can, till one, perchance, overshadows and destroys the other. If a plant cannot live according to its nature, it dies; and so a man.

The night in prison was novel and interesting enough. The prisoners in their shirt-sleeves were enjoying a chat and the evening air in the doorway, when I entered. But the jailer said, "Come, boys, it is time to lock up;" and so they dispersed, and I heard the sound of their steps returning into the hollow apartments. My room-mate was introduced to me by the jailer, as "a first-rate fellow and a clever man." When the door was locked, he showed me where to hang my hat, and how he managed matters there. The rooms were whitewashed once a month; and this one, at least, was the whitest, most simply furnished, and probably the neatest apartment in the town. He naturally wanted to know where I came from, and what brought me there; and, when I had told him, I asked him in my turn how he came there, presuming him to be an honest man, of

8. The cry of the highway robber.

course; and, as the world goes, I believe he was. "Why," said he, "they accuse me of burning a barn; but I never did it." As near as I could discover, he had probably gone to bed in a barn when drunk, and smoked his pipe there; and so a barn was burnt. He had the reputation of being a clever man, had been there some three months waiting for his trial to come on, and would have to wait as much longer; but he was quite domesticated and contented since he got his board for nothing, and thought that he was well treated.

He occupied one window, and I the other; and I saw, that, if one stayed there long, his principal business would be to look out the window. I had soon read all the tracts that were left there, and examined where former prisoners had broken out, and where a grate had been sawed off, and heard the history of the various occupants of that room; for I found that even here there was a history and a gossip which never circulated beyond the walls of the jail. Probably this is the only house in the town where verses are composed, which are afterward printed in a circular form, but not published. I was shown quite a long list of verses which were composed by some young men who had been detected in an attempt to escape, who avenged themselves by singing them.

I pumped my fellow-prisoner as dry as I could, for fear I should never see him again; but at length he showed me which was my bed, and left me to blow out the lamp.

It was like travelling into a far country, such as I had never expected to behold, to lie there for one night. It seemed to me that I never had heard the town-clock strike before, nor the evening sounds of the village; for we slept with the windows open, which were inside the grating. It was to see my native village in the light of the middle ages, and our Concord was turned into a Rhine stream, and visions of knights and castles passed before me. They were the voices of old burghers that I heard in the streets. I was an involuntary spectator and auditor of whatever was done and said in the kitchen of the adjacent village-inn,—a wholly new and rare experience to me. It was a closer view of my native town. I was fairly inside of it. I never had seen its institutions before. This is one of its peculiar institutions; for it is a shire town.[9] I began to comprehend what its inhabitants were about.

In the morning, our breakfasts were put through the hole in the door, in small oblong-square tin pans, made to fit, and holding a pint of chocolate, with brown bread, and an iron spoon. When they called for the vessels again, I was green enough to return what bread I had left; but my comrade seized it, and said that I should lay that up for lunch or dinner. Soon after, he was let out to work at haying in a neighboring field, whither he went every day, and would not be back till noon; so he bade me good-day, saying that he doubted if he should see me again.

When I came out of prison,—for some one interfered, and paid the tax,—I did not perceive that great changes had taken place on the common, such as he observed who went in a youth, and emerged a tottering and gray-headed man; and yet a change had to my eyes come over the scene,—the town, and State, and country,—greater than any that mere

9. Comparable to "county seat."

time could effect. I saw yet more distinctly the State in which I lived. I saw to what extent the people among whom I lived could be trusted as good neighbors and friends; that their friendship was for summer weather only; that they did not greatly purpose to do right; that they were a distinct race from me by their prejudices and superstitions, as the Chinamen and Malays are; that, in their sacrifices to humanity, they ran no risks, not even to their property; that, after all, they were not so noble but they treated the thief as he had treated them, and hoped, by a certain outward observance and a few prayers, and by walking in a particular straight though useless path from time to time, to save their souls. This may be to judge my neighbors harshly; for I believe that most of them are not aware that they have such an institution as the jail in their village.

It was formerly the custom in our village, when a poor debtor came out of jail, for his acquaintances to salute him, looking through their fingers, which were crossed to represent the grating of a jail window, "How do ye do?" My neighbors did not thus salute me, but first looked at me, and then at one another, as if I had returned from a long journey. I was put into jail as I was going to the shoemaker's to get a shoe which was mended. When I was let out the next morning, I proceeded to finish my errand, and, having put on my mended shoe, joined a huckleberry party, who were impatient to put themselves under my conduct; and in half an hour,—for the horse was soon tackled,[1]—was in the midst of a huckleberry field, on one of our highest hills, two miles off; and then the State was nowhere to be seen.

This is the whole history of "My Prisons."[2]

I have never declined paying the highway tax, because I am as desirous of being a good neighbor as I am of being a bad subject; and, as for supporting schools, I am doing my part to educate my fellow-countrymen now. It is for no particular item in the tax-bill that I refuse to pay it. I simply wish to refuse allegiance to the State, to withdraw and stand aloof from it effectually. I do not care to trace the course of my dollar, if I could, till it buys a man, or a musket to shoot one with,—the dollar is innocent,—but I am concerned to trace the effects of my allegiance. In fact, I quietly declare war with the State, after my fashion, though I will still make what use and get what advantage of her I can, as is usual in such cases.

If others pay the tax which is demanded of me, from a sympathy with the State, they do but what they have already done in their own case, or rather they abet injustice to a greater extent than the State requires. If they pay the tax from a mistaken interest in the individual taxed, to save his property or prevent his going to jail, it is because they have not considered wisely how far they let their private feelings interfere with the public good.

This, then, is my position at present. But one cannot be too much on his guard in such a case, lest his action be biassed by obstinacy, or an undue regard for the opinions of men. Let him see that he does only what belongs to himself and to the hour.

I think sometimes, Why, this people mean well; they are only ignorant; they would do better if they knew how; why give your neighbors this pain to treat

1. Harnessed.
2. A wry comparison to the title of a book (1832) by the Italian poet Silvio Pellico (1789–1854) on his years of hard labor in Austrian prisons.

you as they are not inclined to? But I think, again, this is no reason why I should do as they do, or permit others to suffer much greater pain of a different kind. Again, I sometimes say to myself, When many millions of men, without heat, without ill-will, without personal feeling of any kind, demand of you a few shillings only, without the possibility, such is their constitution, of retracting or altering their present demand, and without the possibility, on your side, of appeal to any other millions, why expose yourself to this overwhelming brute force? You do not resist cold and hunger, the winds and the waves, thus obstinately; you quietly submit to a thousand similar necessities. You do not put your head into the fire. But just in proportion as I regard this as not wholly a brute force, but partly a human force, and consider that I have relations to those millions as to so many millions of men, and not of mere brute or inanimate things, I see that appeal is possible, first and instantaneously, from them to the Maker of them, and, secondly, from them to themselves. But, if I put my head deliberately into the fire, there is no appeal to fire or to the Maker of fire, and I have only myself to blame. If I could convince myself that I have any right to be satisfied with men as they are, and to treat them accordingly, and not according, in some respects, to my requisitions and expectations of what they and I ought to be, then, like a good Mussulman[3] and fatalist, I should endeavor to be satisfied with things as they are, and say it is the will of God. And, above all, there is this difference between resisting this and a purely brute or natural force, that I can resist this with some effect; but I cannot expect, like Orpheus,[4] to change the nature of the rocks and trees and beasts.

I do not wish to quarrel with any man or nation. I do not wish to split hairs, to make fine distinctions, or set myself up as better than my neighbors. I seek rather, I may say, even an excuse for conforming to the laws of the land. I am but too ready to conform to them. Indeed I have reason to suspect myself on this head; and each year, as the tax-gatherer comes round, I find myself disposed to review the acts and position of the general and state governments, and the spirit of the people, to discover a pretext for conformity. I believe that the State will soon be able to take all my work of this sort out of my hands, and then I shall be no better a patriot than my fellow-countrymen. Seen from a lower point of view, the Constitution, with all its faults, is very good; the law and the courts are very respectable; even this State and this American government are, in many respects, very admirable and rare things, to be thankful for, such as a great many have described them; but seen from a point of view a little higher, they are what I have described them; seen from a higher still, and the highest, who shall say what they are, or that they are worth looking at or thinking of at all?

However, the government does not concern me much, and I shall bestow the fewest possible thoughts on it. It is not many moments that I live under a government, even in this world. If a man is thought-free, fancy-free, imagination-free, that which is not never for a long time appearing to be to him, unwise rulers or reformers cannot fatally interrupt him.

I know that most men think differently from myself; but those whose lives are by profession devoted to the study of these or kindred subjects, content me as little as any. Statesmen and legislators, standing so completely within the

3. Mohammedan.
4. The son of Calliope, one of the Muses, who gave him the gift of music. Trees and rocks moved to the playing of his lyre. He charmed the three-headed dog Cerberus in an unsuccessful attempt to bring his dead wife, Eurydice, up from the Underworld.

institution, never distinctly and nakedly behold it. They speak of moving society, but have no resting-place without it. They may be men of a certain experience and discrimination, and have no doubt invented ingenious and even useful systems, for which we sincerely thank them; but all their wit and usefulness lie within certain not very wide limits. They are wont to forget that the world is not governed by policy and expediency. Webster[5] never goes behind government, and so cannot speak with authority about it. His words are wisdom to those legislators who contemplate no essential reform in the existing government; but for thinkers, and those who legislate for all time, he never once glances at the subject. I know of those whose serene and wise speculations on this theme would soon reveal the limits of his mind's range and hospitality. Yet, compared with the cheap professions of most reformers, and the still cheaper wisdom and eloquence of politicians in general, his are almost the only sensible and valuable words, and we thank Heaven for him. Comparatively, he is always strong, original, and, above all, practical. Still his quality is not wisdom, but prudence. The lawyer's truth is not Truth, but consistency, or a consistent expediency. Truth is always in harmony with herself, and is not concerned chiefly to reveal the justice that may consist with wrong-doing. He well deserves to be called, as he has been called, the Defender of the Constitution. There are really no blows to be given by him but defensive ones. He is not a leader, but a follower. His leaders are the men of '87.[6] "I have never made an effort," he says, "and never propose to make an effort; I have never countenanced an effort, and never mean to countenance an effort, to disturb the arrangement as originally made, by which the various States came into the Union."[7] Still thinking of the sanction which the Constitution gives to slavery, he says, "Because it was a part of the original compact,—let it stand." Notwithstanding his special acuteness and ability, he is unable to take a fact out of its merely political relations, and behold it as it lies absolutely to be disposed of by the intellect,—what, for instance, it behoves a man to do here in America to-day with regard to slavery, but ventures, or is driven, to make some such desperate answer as the following, while professing to speak absolutely, and as a private man,—from which what new and singular code of social duties might be inferred?—"The manner," says he, "in which the government of those States where slavery exists are to regulate it, is for their own consideration, under their responsibility to their constituents, to the general laws of propriety, humanity, and justice, and to God. Associations formed elsewhere, springing from a feeling of humanity, or any other cause, having nothing whatever to do with it. They have never received any encouragement from me, and they never will."[8]

They who know of no purer sources of truth, who have traced up its stream no higher, stand, and wisely stand, by the Bible and the Constitution, and drink at it there with reverence and humility; but they who behold where it comes trickling into this lake or that pool, gird up their loins once more, and continue their pilgrimage toward its fountain-head.

No man with a genius for legislation has appeared in America. They are rare in the history of the world. There are orators, politicians, and eloquent men, by the thousand; but the speaker has not yet opened his mouth to speak,

5. Daniel Webster (1782–1852), prominent Whig politician of the second quarter of the 19th century.
6. The writers of the Constitution, who convened at Philadelphia in 1787.
7. From Webster's speech on *The Admission of Texas*

(December 22, 1845).
8. "These extracts have been inserted since the Lecture was read" [Thoreau's note]; he means the quotation beginning "The manner."

who is capable of settling the much-vexed questions of the day. We love eloquence for its own sake, and not for any truth which it may utter, or any
heroism it may inspire. Our legislators have not yet learned the comparative
value of free-trade and of freedom, of union, and of rectitude, to a nation.
They have no genius or talent for comparatively humble questions of taxation
and finance, commerce and manufactures and agriculture. If we were left
solely to the wordy wit of legislators in Congress for our guidance, uncorrected
by the seasonable experience and the effectual complaints of the people,
America would not long retain her rank among the nations. For eighteen
hundred years, though perchance I have no right to say it, the New Testament
has been written; yet where is the legislator who has wisdom and practical
talent enough to avail himself of the light which it sheds on the science of legislation?

The authority of government, even such as I am willing to submit to,—for
I will cheerfully obey those who know and can do better than I, and in many
things even those who neither know nor can do so well,—is still an impure
one: to be strictly just, it must have the sanction and consent of the governed.
It can have no pure right over my person and property but what I concede to
it. The progress from an absolute to a limited monarchy, from a limited monarchy to a democracy, is a progress toward a true respect for the individual. Is
a democracy, such as we know it, the last improvement possible in government? Is it not possible to take a step further towards recognizing and organizing the rights of man? There will never be a really free and enlightened State,
until the State comes to recognize the individual as a higher and independent
power, from which all its own power and authority are derived, and treats him
accordingly. I please myself with imagining a State at last which can afford to
be just to all men, and to treat the individual with respect as a neighbor; which
even would not think it inconsistent with its own repose, if a few were to live
aloof from it, not meddling with it, nor embraced by it, who fulfilled all the
duties of neighbors and fellow-men. A State which bore this kind of fruit, and
suffered it to drop off as fast as it ripened, would prepare the way for a still
more perfect and glorious State, which also I have imagined, but not yet anywhere seen.

1849, 1866

# Walden, or Life in the Woods[1]

I do not propose to write an ode to dejection, but to brag as lustily as chanticleer in the morning, standing on his roost, if only to wake my neighbors up.

## Economy[2]

When I wrote the following pages, or rather the bulk of them, I lived alone,
in the woods, a mile from any neighbor, in a house which I had built myself,

1. Thoreau began writing Walden early in 1846, some
months after he began living at Walden Pond, and by
late 1847, when he moved back into the village of Concord, he had drafted roughly half the book. Between
1852 and 1854 he rewrote the manuscript several times
and substantially enlarged it. The text printed here is
that of the 1st edition (1854), with a few printer's errors
corrected on the basis of Thoreau's set of marked
proofs, his corrections in his copy of Walden, and

scholars' comparisons of the printed book and the
manuscript drafts, especially the edition by J. Lyndon
Shanley (1971).

Any annotator of Walden is deeply indebted to Walter Harding, editor of The Variorum Walden (1962),
and Philip Van Doren Stern, editor of The Annotated
Walden (1970).
2. As Thoreau explains later in the chapter, the title
means something like "philosophy of living."

on the shore of Walden Pond, in Concord, Massachusetts, and earned my living by the labor of my hands only. I lived there two years and two months. At present I am a sojourner in civilized life again.

I should not obtrude my affairs so much on the notice of my readers if very particular inquiries had not been made by my townsmen concerning my mode of life, which some would call impertinent, though they do not appear to me at all impertinent, but, considering the circumstances, very natural and pertinent. Some have asked what I got to eat; if I did not feel lonesome; if I was not afraid; and the like. Others have been curious to learn what portion of my income I devoted to charitable purposes; and some, who have large families, how many poor children I maintained. I will therefore ask those of my readers who feel no particular interest in me to pardon me if I undertake to answer some of these questions in this book. In most books, the I, or first person, is omitted; in this it will be retained; that, in respect to egotism, is the main difference. We commonly do not remember that it is, after all, always the first person that is speaking. I should not talk so much about myself if there were any body else whom I knew as well. Unfortunately, I am confined to this theme by the narrowness of my experience. Moreover, I, on my side, require of every writer, first or last, a simple and sincere account of his own life, and not merely what he has heard of other men's lives; some such account as he would send to his kindred from a distant land; for if he has lived sincerely, it must have been in a distant land to me. Perhaps these pages are more particularly addressed to poor students. As for the rest of my readers, they will accept such portions as apply to them. I trust that none will stretch the seams in putting on the coat, for it may do good service to him whom it fits.

I would fain say something, not so much concerning the Chinese and Sandwich Islanders[3] as you who read these pages, who are said to live in New England; something about your condition, especially your outward condition or circumstances in this world, in this town, what it is, whether it is necessary that it be as bad as it is, whether it cannot be improved as well as not. I have travelled a good deal in Concord; and every where, in shops, and offices, and fields, the inhabitants have appeared to me to be doing penance in a thousand remarkable ways. What I have heard of Brahmins sitting exposed to four fires and looking in the face of the sun; or hanging suspended, with their heads downward, over flames; or looking at the heavens over their shoulders "until it becomes impossible for them to resume their natural position, while from the twist of the neck nothing but liquids can pass into the stomach;" or dwelling, chained for life, at the foot of a tree; or measuring with their bodies, like caterpillars, the breadth of vast empires; or standing on one leg on the tops of pillars,—even these forms of conscious penance are hardly more incredible and astonishing than the scenes which I daily witness.[4] The twelve labors of Hercules[5] were trifling in comparison with those which my neighbors have undertaken; for they were only twelve, and had an end; but I could never see that these men slew or captured any monster or finished any labor. They have

---

3. Hawaiians.
4. Thoreau's source has not been found for this depiction of the religious self-torture of high-caste Hindus in India.
5. Son of Zeus and Alcmene, this half mortal could become a god only by performing twelve labors, each apparently impossible. The second labor, the slaying of the Lernaean hydra, a many-headed sea monster, is

referred to just below. (Hercules' friend Iolas helped by searing the stump each time Hercules cut off one of the heads, which otherwise would have regenerated.) The seventh labor, mentioned in the following paragraph, was the cleansing of Augeas's pestilent stables in one day, a feat Hercules accomplished by diverting two nearby rivers through the stables.

no friend Iolas to burn with a hot iron the root of the hydra's head, but as soon as one head is crushed, two spring up.

I see young men, my townsmen, whose misfortune it is to have inherited farms, houses, barns, cattle, and farming tools; for these are more easily acquired than got rid of. Better if they had been born in the open pasture and suckled by a wolf, that they might have seen with clearer eyes what field they were called to labor in. Who made them serfs of the soil? Why should they eat their sixty acres, when man is condemned to eat only his peck of dirt? Why should they begin digging their graves as soon as they are born? They have got to live a man's life, pushing all these things before them, and get on as well as they can. How many a poor immortal soul have I met well nigh crushed and smothered under its load, creeping down the road of life, pushing before it a barn seventy-five feet by forty, its Augean stables never cleansed, and one hundred acres of land, tillage, mowing, pasture, and wood-lot! The portionless, who struggle with no such unnecessary inherited encumbrances, find it labor enough to subdue and cultivate a few cubic feet of flesh.

But men labor under a mistake. The better part of the man is soon ploughed into the soil for compost. By a seeming fate, commonly called necessity, they are employed, as it says in an old book, laying up treasures which moth and rust will corrupt and thieves break through and steal.[6] It is a fool's life, as they will find when they get to the end of it, if not before. It is said that Deucalion and Pyrrha created men by throwing stones over their heads behind them:[7]—

> Inde genus durum sumus, experiensque laborum,
> Et documenta damus quâ simus origine nati.

Or, as Raleigh rhymes it in his sonorous way,—

> "From thence our kind hard-hearted is, enduring pain and care,
> Approving that our bodies of a stony nature are."

So much for a blind obedience to a blundering oracle, throwing the stones over their heads behind them, and not seeing where they fell.

Most men, even in this comparatively free country, through mere ignorance and mistake, are so occupied with the factitious cares and superfluously coarse labors of life that its finer fruits cannot be plucked by them. Their fingers, from excessive toil, are too clumsy and tremble too much for that. Actually, the laboring man has not leisure for a true integrity day by day; he cannot afford to sustain the manliest relations to men; his labor would be depreciated in the market. He has no time to be any thing but a machine. How can he remember well his ignorance—which his growth requires—who has so often to use his knowledge? We should feed and clothe him gratuitously sometimes, and recruit him with our cordials, before we judge of him. The finest qualities of our nature, like the bloom on fruits, can be preserved only by the most delicate handling. Yet we do not treat ourselves nor one another thus tenderly.

Some of you, we all know, are poor, find it hard to live, are sometimes, as it were, gasping for breath. I have no doubt that some of you who read this book are unable to pay for all the dinners which you have actually eaten, or

6. Matthew 6.19.
7. Deucalion and Pyrrha, husband and wife in the Greek analogue to the biblical legend of Noah and the Flood, repopulated the earth by throwing stones behind them over their shoulders. The stones thrown by

Deucalion turned into men, and the stones thrown by Pyrrha turned into women. The quotation is from Ovid's *Metamorphoses* 1.414–15, as translated in Sir Walter Raleigh's *History of the World*.

for the coats and shoes which are fast wearing or are already worn out, and have come to this page to spend borrowed or stolen time, robbing your creditors of an hour. It is very evident what mean and sneaking lives many of you live, for my sight has been whetted by experience; always on the limits, trying to get into business and trying to get out of debt, a very ancient slough, called by the Latins, *æs alienum*, another's brass, for some of their coins were made of brass; still living, and dying, and buried by this other's brass; always promising to pay, promising to pay, to-morrow, and dying to-day, insolvent; seeking to curry favor, to get custom, by how many modes, only not state-prison offences; lying, flattering, voting, contracting yourselves into a nutshell of civility, or dilating into an atmosphere of thin and vaporous generosity, that you may persuade your neighbor to let you make his shoes, or his hat, or his coat, or his carriage, or import his groceries for him; making yourselves sick, that you may lay up something against a sick day, something to be tucked away in an old chest, or in a stocking behind the plastering, or, more safely, in the brick bank; no matter where, no matter how much or how little.

I sometimes wonder that we can be so frivolous, I may almost say, as to attend to the gross but somewhat foreign form of servitude called Negro Slavery, there are so many keen and subtle masters that enslave both north and south. It is hard to have a southern overseer; it is worse to have a northern one; but worst of all when you are the slave-driver of yourself. Talk of a divinity in man! Look at the teamster on the highway, wending to market by day or night; does any divinity stir within him? His highest duty to fodder and water his horses! What is his destiny to him compared with the shipping interests? Does not he drive for Squire Make-a-stir?[8] How godlike, how immortal, is he? See how he cowers and sneaks, how vaguely all the day he fears, not being immortal nor divine, but the slave and prisoner of his own opinion of himself, a fame won by his own deeds. Public opinion is a weak tyrant compared with our own private opinion. What a man thinks of himself, that it is which determines, or rather indicates, his fate. Self-emancipation even in the West Indian provinces of the fancy and imagination,—what Wilberforce[9] is there to bring that about? Think, also, of the ladies of the land weaving toilet cushions against the last day, not to betray too green an interest in their fates! As if you could kill time without injuring eternity.

The mass of men lead lives of quiet desperation. What is called resignation is confirmed desperation. From the desperate city you go into the desperate country, and have to console yourself with the bravery of minks and muskrats. A stereotyped but unconscious despair is concealed even under what are called the games and amusements of mankind. There is no play in them, for this comes after work. But it is a characteristic of wisdom not to do desperate things.

When we consider what, to use the words of the catechism, is the chief end of man,[1] and what are the true necessaries and means of life, it appears as if men had deliberately chosen the common mode of living because they preferred it to any other. Yet they honestly think there is no choice left. But alert and healthy natures remember that the sun rose clear. It is never too late to

8. An allegorical name modeled on those in John Bunyan's *Pilgrim's Progress*, familiar to almost any reader in Thoreau's time.
9. William Wilberforce (1759–1833), English philanthropist, leading opponent of the slave trade until its abolition in 1807.
1. From the Shorter Catechism in the *New England Primer*: "What is the chief end of man? Man's chief end is to glorify God and to enjoy him forever."

give up our prejudices. No way of thinking or doing, however ancient, can be trusted without proof. What every body echoes or in silence passes by as true to-day may turn out to be falsehood to-morrow, mere smoke of opinion, which some had trusted for a cloud that would sprinkle fertilizing rain on their fields. What old people say you cannot do you try and find that you can. Old deeds for old people, and new deeds for new. Old people did not know enough once, perchance, to fetch fresh fuel to keep the fire a-going; new people put a little dry wood under a pot, and are whirled round the globe with the speed of birds, in a way to kill old people, as the phrase is. Age is no better, hardly so well, qualified for an instructor as youth, for it has not profited so much as it has lost. One may almost doubt if the wisest man has learned any thing of absolute value by living. Practically, the old have no very important advice to give the young, their own experience has been so partial, and their lives have been such miserable failures, for private reasons, as they must believe; and it may be that they have some faith left which belies that experience, and they are only less young than they were. I have lived some thirty years on this planet, and I have yet to hear the first syllable of valuable or even earnest advice from my seniors. They have told me nothing, and probably cannot tell me any thing, to the purpose. Here is life, an experiment to a great extent untried by me; but it does not avail me that they have tried it. If I have any experience which I think valuable, I am sure to reflect that this my Mentors[2] said nothing about.

One farmer says to me, "You cannot live on vegetable food solely, for it furnishes nothing to make bones with;" and so he religiously devotes a part of his day to supplying his system with the raw material of bones; walking all the while he talks behind his oxen, which, with vegetable-made bones, jerk him and his lumbering plough along in spite of every obstacle. Some things are really necessaries of life in some circles, the most helpless and diseased, which in others are luxuries merely, and in others still are entirely unknown.

The whole ground of human life seems to some to have been gone over by their predecessors, both the heights and the valleys, and all things to have been cared for. According to Evelyn, "the wise Solomon prescribed ordinances for the very distances of trees; and the Roman prætors have decided how often you may go into your neighbor's land to gather the acorns which fall on it without trespass, and what share belongs to that neighbor."[3] Hippocrates[4] has even left directions how we should cut our nails; that is, even with the ends of the fingers, neither shorter nor longer. Undoubtedly the very tedium and ennui which presume to have exhausted the variety and the joys of life are as old as Adam. But man's capacities have never been measured; nor are we to judge of what he can do by any precedents, so little has been tried. Whatever have been thy failures hitherto, "be not afflicted, my child, for who shall assign to thee what thou hast left undone?"[5]

We might try our lives by a thousand simple tests; as, for instance, that the same sun which ripens my beans illumines at once a system of earths like ours. If I had remembered this it would have prevented some mistakes. This was not

---

2. From Mentor, in Homer's *Odyssey*: the friend whom Odysseus entrusted with the education of his son Telemachus.
3. *Silva: or, a Discourse of Forest-Trees*, by John Evelyn (1620–1706). "Prætors": in the Roman Republic, high elected magistrates.

4. Greek physician (460?–377? B.C.), known as the father of medicine.
5. "Be not afflicted, my child, for who shall efface what thou hast formerly done, or shall assign to thee what thou hast left undone?" H. H. Wilson's translation of the *Vishnu Purana* (1840).

the light in which I hoed them. The stars are the apexes of what wonderful triangles! What distant and different beings in the various mansions of the universe are contemplating the same one at the same moment! Nature and human life are as various as our several constitutions. Who shall say what prospect life offers to another? Could a greater miracle take place than for us to look through each other's eyes for an instant? We should live in all the ages of the world in an hour; ay, in all the worlds of the ages. History, Poetry, Mythology!—I know of no reading of another's experience so startling and informing as this would be.

The greater part of what my neighbors call good I believe in my soul to be bad, and if I repent of any thing, it is very likely to be my good behavior. What demon possessed me that I behaved so well? You may say the wisest thing you can old man,—you who have lived seventy years, not without honor of a kind,—I hear an irresistible voice which invites me away from all that. One generation abandons the enterprises of another like stranded vessels.

I think that we may safely trust a good deal more than we do. We may waive just so much care of ourselves as we honestly bestow elsewhere. Nature is as well adapted to our weakness as to our strength. The incessant anxiety and strain of some is a well nigh incurable form of disease. We are made to exaggerate the importance of what work we do; and yet how much is not done by us! or, what if we had been taken sick? How vigilant we are! determined not to live by faith if we can avoid it; all the day long on the alert, at night we unwillingly say our prayers and commit ourselves to uncertainties. So thoroughly and sincerely are we compelled to live, reverencing our life, and denying the possibility of change. This is the only way, we say; but there are as many ways as there can be drawn radii from one centre. All change is a miracle to contemplate; but it is a miracle which is taking place every instant. Confucius said, "To know that we know what we know, and that we do not know what we do not know, this is true knowledge."[6] When one man has reduced a fact of the imagination to be a fact to his understanding, I foresee that all men will at length establish their lives on that basis.

Let us consider for a moment what most of the trouble and anxiety which I have referred to is about, and how much it is necessary that we be troubled, or, at least, careful. It would be some advantage to live a primitive and frontier life, though in the midst of an outward civilization, if only to learn what are the gross necessaries of life and what methods have been taken to obtain them; or even to look over the old day-books of the merchants, to see what it was that men most commonly bought at the stores, what they stored, that is, what are the grossest groceries. For the improvements of ages have had but little influence on the essential laws of man's existence; as our skeletons, probably, are not to be distinguished from those of our ancestors.

By the words *necessary of life*, I mean whatever, of all that man obtains by his own exertions, has been from the first, or from long use has become, so important to human life that few, if any, whether from savageness, or poverty, or philosophy, ever attempt to do without it. To many creatures there is in this sense but one necessary of life, Food. To the bison of the prairie it is a few inches of palatable grass, with water to drink; unless he seeks the Shelter of the

6. *Analects* 2.17.

forest or the mountain's shadow. None of the brute creation requires more than Food and Shelter. The necessaries of life for man in this climate may, accurately enough, be distributed under the several heads of Food, Shelter, Clothing, and Fuel; for not till we have secured these are we prepared to entertain the true problems of life with freedom and a prospect of success. Man has invented, not only houses, but clothes and cooked food; and possibly from the accidental discovery of the warmth of fire, and the consequent use of it, at first a luxury, arose the present necessity to sit by it. We observe cats and dogs acquiring the same second nature. By proper Shelter and Clothing we legitimately retain our own internal heat; but with an excess of these, or of Fuel, that is, with an external heat greater than our own internal, may not cookery properly be said to begin? Darwin, the naturalist, says of the inhabitants of Tierra del Fuego, that while his own party, who were well clothed and sitting close to a fire, were far from too warm, these naked savages, who were farther off, were observed, to his great surprise, "to be streaming with perspiration at undergoing such a roasting."[7] So, we are told, the New Hollander[8] goes naked with impunity, while the European shivers in his clothes. Is it impossible to combine the hardiness of these savages with the intellectualness of the civilized man? According to Liebig,[9] man's body is a stove, and food the fuel which keeps up the internal combustion in the lungs. In cold weather we eat more, in warm less. The animal heat is the result of a slow combustion, and disease and death take place when this is too rapid; or for want of fuel, or from some defect in the draught, the fire goes out. Of course the vital heat is not to be confounded with fire; but so much for analogy. It appears, therefore, from the above list, that the expression, *animal life*, is nearly synonymous with the expression, *animal heat*; for while Food may be regarded as the Fuel which keeps up the fire within us,—and Fuel serves only to prepare that Food or to increase the warmth of our bodies by addition from without,—Shelter and Clothing also serve only to retain the *heat* thus generated and absorbed.

The grand necessity, then, for our bodies, is to keep warm, to keep the vital heat in us. What pains we accordingly take, not only with our Food, and Clothing, and Shelter, but with our beds, which are our night-clothes, robbing the nests and breasts of birds to prepare this shelter within a shelter, as the mole has its bed of grass and leaves at the end of its burrow! The poor man is wont to complain that this is a cold world; and to cold, no less physical than social, we refer directly a great part of our ails. The summer, in some climates, makes possible to man a sort of Elysian[1] life. Fuel, except to cook his Food, is then unnecessary; the sun is his fire, and many of the fruits are sufficiently cooked by its rays; while Food generally is more various, and more easily obtained, and Clothing and Shelter are wholly or half unnecessary. At the present day, and in this country, as I find by my own experience, a few implements, a knife, an axe, a spade, a wheelbarrow, &c., and for the studious, lamplight, stationery, and access to a few books, rank next to necessaries, and can all be obtained at a trifling cost. Yet some, not wise, go to the other side of the globe, to barbarous and unhealthy regions, and devote themselves to trade for ten or twenty years, in order that they may live,—that is, keep com-

7. Charles Darwin, *Journal of * * * the Various Countries Visited by H.M.S. Beagle* (1839).
8. I.e., Australian aborigine.
9. Justus, Baron von Liebig (1803–1873), German chemist, author of *Organic Chemistry*.
1. In Greek mythology, Elysium is the home of the blessed after death.

fortably warm,—and die in New England at last. The luxuriously rich are not simply kept comfortably warm, but unnaturally hot; as I implied before, they are cooked, of course *à la mode*.

Most of the luxuries, and many of the so called comforts of life, are not only not indispensable, but positive hinderances to the elevation of mankind. With respect to luxuries and comforts, the wisest have ever lived a more simple and meager life than the poor. The ancient philosophers, Chinese, Hindoo, Persian, and Greek, were a class than which none has been poorer in outward riches, none so rich in inward. We know not much about them. It is remarkable that *we* know so much of them as we do. The same is true of the more modern reformers and benefactors of their race. None can be an impartial or wise observer of human life but from the vantage ground of what *we* should call voluntary poverty. Of a life of luxury the fruit is luxury, whether in agriculture, or commerce, or literature, or art. There are nowadays professors of philosophy, but not philosophers. Yet it is admirable to profess because it was once admirable to live. To be a philosopher is not merely to have subtle thoughts, nor even to found a school, but so to love wisdom as to live according to its dictates, a life of simplicity, independence, magnanimity, and trust. It is to solve some of the problems of life, not only theoretically, but practically. The success of great scholars and thinkers is commonly a courtier-like success, not kingly, not manly. They make shift to live merely by conformity, practically as their fathers did, and are in no sense the progenitors of a nobler race of men. But why do men degenerate ever? What makes families run out? What is the nature of the luxury which enervates and destroys nations? Are we sure that there is none of it in our own lives? The philosopher is in advance of his age even in the outward form of his life. He is not fed, sheltered, clothed, warmed, like his contemporaries. How can a man be a philosopher and not maintain his vital heat by better methods than other men?

When a man is warmed by the several modes which I have described, what does he want next? Surely not more warmth of the same kind, as more and richer food, larger and more splendid houses, finer and more abundant clothing, more numerous incessant and hotter fires, and the like. When he has obtained those things which are necessary to life, there is another alternative than to obtain the superfluities; and that is, to adventure on life now, his vacation from humbler toil having commenced. The soil, it appears, is suited to the seed, for it has sent its radicle downward, and it may now send its shoot upward also with confidence. Why has man rooted himself thus firmly in the earth, but that he may rise in the same proportion into the heavens above?— for the nobler plants are valued for the fruit they bear at last in the air and light, far from the ground, and are not treated like the humbler esculents, which, though they may be biennials, are cultivated only till they have perfected their root, and often cut down at top for this purpose, so that most would not know them in their flowering season.

I do not mean to prescribe rules to strong and valiant natures, who will mind their own affairs whether in heaven or hell, and perchance build more magnificently and spend more lavishly than the richest, without ever impoverishing themselves, not knowing how they live,—if, indeed, there are any such, as has been dreamed; nor to those who find their encouragement and inspiration in precisely the present condition of things, and cherish it with the fondness and enthusiasm of lovers,—and, to some extent, I reckon myself in this number; I do not speak to those who are well employed, in whatever circumstances, and they know whether they are well employed or not;—but mainly to the mass of men who are discontented, and idly complaining of the hardness of their lot or of the times, when they might improve them. There are some who complain most energetically and inconsolably of any, because they are, as they say, doing their duty. I also have in my mind that seemingly wealthy, but most terribly impoverished class of all, who have accumulated dross, but know not how to use it, or get rid of it, and thus have forged their own golden or silver fetters.

If I should attempt to tell how I have desired to spend my life in years past, it would probably surprise those of my readers who are somewhat acquainted with its actual history; it would certainly astonish those who know nothing about it. I will only hint at some of the enterprises which I have cherished.

In any weather, at any hour of the day or night, I have been anxious to improve the nick of time, and notch it on my stick too; to stand on the meeting of two eternities, the past and future, which is precisely the present moment; to toe that line. You will pardon some obscurities, for there are more secrets in my trade than in most men's, and yet not voluntarily kept, but inseparable from its very nature. I would gladly tell all that I know about it, and never paint "No Admittance" on my gate.

I long ago lost a hound, a bay horse, and a turtle-dove, and am still on their trail.[2] Many are the travellers I have spoken concerning them, describing their tracks and what calls they answered to. I have met one or two who had heard the hound, and the tramp of the horse, and even seen the dove disappear behind a cloud, and they seemed as anxious to recover them as if they had lost them themselves.

To anticipate, not the sunrise and the dawn merely, but, if possible, Nature herself! How many mornings, summer and winter, before yet any neighbor was stirring about his business, have I been about mine! No doubt, many of my townsmen have met me returning from this enterprise, farmers starting for Boston in the twilight, or woodchoppers going to their work. It is true, I never assisted the sun materially in his rising, but, doubt not, it was of the last importance only to be present at it.

So many autumn, ay, and winter days, spent outside the town, trying to hear what was in the wind, to hear and carry it express! I well-nigh sunk all my capital in it, and lost my own breath into the bargain, running in the face of it. If it had concerned either of the political parties, depend upon it, it would have appeared in the Gazette with the earliest intelligence.[3] At other times watching from the observatory of some cliff or tree, to telegraph any new arrival; or waiting at evening on the hill-tops for the sky to fall, that I might catch something, though I never caught much, and that, manna-wise,[4] would dissolve again in the sun.

For a long time I was reporter to a journal, of no very wide circulation,

2. Thoreau's reply to B. B. Wiley, April 26, 1857, suggests something of the evocative way he wanted this passage interpreted: "If others have their losses, which they are busy repairing, so have I mine, & their hound & horse may perhaps be the symbols of some of them. But also I have lost, or am in danger of losing, a far finer & more etherial treasure, which commonly no loss of which they are conscious will symbolize—this I answer hastily & with some hesitation, according as I now understand my own words."
3. News. "Gazette": newspaper.
4. In Exodus 16 manna is the bread that God rained from heaven so the Israelites could survive in the desert on their way from Egypt to the Promised Land.

whose editor has never yet seen fit to print the bulk of my contributions, and, as is too common with writers, I got only my labor for my pains.[5] However, in this case my pains were their own reward.

For many years I was self-appointed inspector of snow storms and rain storms, and did my duty faithfully; surveyor, if not of highways, then of forest paths and all across-lot routes, keeping them open, and ravines bridged and passable at all seasons, where the public heel had testified to their utility.

I have looked after the wild stock of the town, which give a faithful herdsman a good deal of trouble by leaping fences; and I have had an eye to the unfrequented nooks and corners of the farm; though I did not always know whether Jonas or Solomon worked in a particular field to-day; that was none of my business. I have watered the red huckleberry, the sand cherry and the nettle tree, the red pine and the black ash, the white grape and the yellow violet, which might have withered else in dry seasons.

In short, I went on thus for a long time, I may say it without boasting, faithfully minding my business, till it became more and more evident that my townsmen would not after all admit me into the list of town officers, nor make my place a sinecure with a moderate allowance. My accounts, which I can swear to have kept faithfully, I have, indeed, never got audited, still less accepted, still less paid and settled. However, I have not set my heart on that.

Not long since, a strolling Indian went to sell baskets at the house of a well-known lawyer in my neighborhood. "Do you wish to buy any baskets?" he asked. "No, we do not want any," was the reply. "What!" exclaimed the Indian as he went out the gate, "do you mean to starve us?" Having seen his industrious white neighbors so well off,—that the lawyer had only to weave arguments, and by some magic wealth and standing followed, he had said to himself; I will go into business; I will weave baskets; it is a thing which I can do. Thinking that when he had made the baskets he would have done his part, and then it would be the white man's to buy them. He had not discovered that it was necessary for him to make it worth the other's while to buy them, or at least make him think that it was so, or to make something else which it would be worth his while to buy. I too had woven a kind of basket of a delicate texture, but I had not made it worth any one's while to buy them.[6] Yet not the less, in my case, did I think it worth my while to weave them, and instead of studying how to make it worth men's while to buy my baskets, I studied rather how to avoid the necessity of selling them. The life which men praise and regard as successful is but one kind. Why should we exaggerate any one kind at the expense of the others?

Finding that my fellow-citizens were not likely to offer me any room in the court house, or any curacy or living[7] any where else, but I must shift for myself, I turned my face more exclusively than ever to the woods, where I was better known. I determined to go into business at once, and not wait to acquire the usual capital, using such slender means as I had already got. My purpose in going to Walden Pond was not to live cheaply nor to live dearly there, but to transact some private business with the fewest obstacles; to be hindered from accomplishing which for want of a little common sense, a little enterprise and business talent, appeared not so sad as foolish.

5. Thoreau puns on the common usage of *journal* to mean a daily newspaper as well as a diary; Thoreau is the negligent or too demanding editor.

6. A reference to Thoreau's poorly selling first book, *A Week on the Concord and Merrimack Rivers* (1849).

7. A church office with a fixed, steady income.

I have always endeavored to acquire strict business habits; they are indispensable to every man. If your trade is with the Celestial Empire,[8] then some small counting house on the coast, in some Salem harbor, will be fixture enough. You will export such articles as the country affords, purely native products, much ice and pine timber and a little granite, always in native bottoms. These will be good ventures. To oversee all the details yourself in person; to be at once pilot and captain, and owner and underwriter; to buy and sell and keep the accounts; to read every letter received, and write or read every letter sent; to superintend the discharge of imports night and day; to be upon many parts of the coast almost at the same time;—often the richest freight will be discharged upon a Jersey shore,[9]—to be your own telegraph, unweariedly sweeping the horizon, speaking all passing vessels bound coastwise; to keep up a steady despatch of commodities, for the supply of such a distant and exorbitant market; to keep yourself informed of the state of the markets, prospects of war and peace every where, and anticipate the tendencies of trade and civilization,—taking advantage of the results of all exploring expeditions, using new passages and all improvements in navigation;—charts to be studied, the position of reefs and new lights and buoys to be ascertained, and ever, and ever, the logarithmic tables to be corrected, for by the error of some calculator the vessel often splits upon a rock that should have reached a friendly pier,— there is the untold fate of La Perouse;—universal science to be kept pace with, studying the lives of all great discoverers and navigators, great adventurers and merchants from Hanno[1] and the Phœnicians down to our day; in fine, account of stock to be taken from time to time, to know how you stand. It is a labor to task the faculties of a man,—such problems of profit and loss, of interest, of tare and tret,[2] and gauging of all kinds in it, as demand a universal knowledge.

I have thought that Walden Pond would be a good place for business, not solely on account of the railroad and the ice trade; it offers advantages which it may not be good policy to divulge; it is a good port and a good foundation. No Neva marshes to be filled; though you must every where build on piles of your own driving. It is said that a flood-tide, with a westerly wind, and ice in the Neva, would sweep St. Petersburg from the face of the earth.

As this business was to be entered into without the usual capital, it may not be easy to conjecture where those means, that will still be indispensable to every such undertaking, were to be obtained. As for Clothing, to come at once to the practical part of the question, perhaps we are led oftener by the love of novelty, and a regard for the opinions of men, in procuring it, than by a true utility. Let him who has work to do recollect that the object of clothing is, first, to retain the vital heat, and secondly, in this state of society, to cover nakedness, and he may judge how much of any necessary or important work may be accomplished without adding to his wardrobe. Kings and queens who wear a suit but once, though made by some tailor or dress-maker to their majesties, cannot know the comfort of wearing a suit that fits. They are no better than wooden horses to hang the clean clothes on. Every day our garments become more assimilated to ourselves, receiving the impress of the

8. China, from the belief that the Chinese Emperors were sons of heaven.
9. I.e., by shipwreck on the way to New York.
1. Carthaginian navigator (6th–5th centuries B.C.), credited with opening the coast of west Africa to trade. Jean François de Galaup (1741–1788), French ex-

plorer of the western Pacific.
2. An allowance to the purchase for waste or refuse in certain materials, 4 pounds being thrown in for every 104 pounds of suttle weight, or weight after the "tare" (the weight of the vehicle or smaller container) is deducted.

wearer's character, until we hesitate to lay them aside, without such delay and medical appliances and some such solemnity even as our bodies. No man ever stood the lower in my estimation for having a patch in his clothes; yet I am sure that there is greater anxiety, commonly, to have fashionable, or at least clean and unpatched clothes, than to have a sound conscience. But even if the rent is not mended, perhaps the worst vice betrayed is improvidence. I sometimes try my acquaintances by such tests as this;—who could wear a patch, or two extra seams only, over the knee? Most behave as if they believed that their prospects for life would be ruined if they should do it. It would be easier for them to hobble to town with a broken leg than with a broken pantaloon. Often if an accident happens to a gentleman's legs, they can be mended; but if a similar accident happens to the legs of his pantaloons, there is no help for it; for he considers, not what is truly respectable, but what is respected. We know but few men, a great many coats and breeches. Dress a scarecrow in your last shift, you standing shiftless by, who would not soonest salute the scarecrow? Passing a cornfield the other day, close by a hat and coat on a stake, I recognized the owner of the farm. He was only a little more weather-beaten than when I saw him last. I have heard of a dog that barked at every stranger who approached his master's premises with clothes on, but was easily quieted by a naked thief. It is an interesting question how far men would retain their relative rank if they were divested of their clothes. Could you, in such a case, tell surely of any company of civilized men, which belonged to the most respected class? When Madam Pfeiffer, in her adventurous travels round the world, from east to west, had got so near home as Asiatic Russia, she says that she felt the necessity of wearing other than a travelling dress, when she went to meet the authorities, for she "was now in a civilized country, where ——— –people are judged of by their clothes."[3] Even in our democratic New England towns the accidental possession of wealth, and its manifestation in dress and equipage alone, obtain for the possessor almost universal respect. But they who yield such respect, numerous as they are, are so far heathen, and need to have a missionary sent to them. Beside, clothes introduced sewing, a kind of work which you may call endless; a woman's dress, at least, is never done.[4]

A man who has at length found something to do will not need to get a new suit to do it in; for him the old will do, that has lain dusty in the garret for an indeterminate period. Old shoes will serve a hero longer than they have served his valet,—if a hero ever has a valet,—bare feet are older than shoes, and he can make them do. Only they who go to soirées and legislative halls must have new coats, coats to change as often as the man changes in them. But if my jacket and trousers, my hat and shoes, are fit to worship God in, they will do; will they not? Who ever saw his old clothes,—his old coat, actually worn out, resolved into its primitive elements, so that it was not a deed of charity to bestow it on some poor boy, by him perchance to be bestowed on some poorer still, or shall we say richer, who could do with less? I say, beware of all enterprises that require new clothes, and not rather a new wearer of clothes. If there is not a new man, how can the new clothes be made to fit? If you have any enterprise before you, try it in your old clothes. All men want, not something to *do with*, but something to *do*, or rather something to *be*. Perhaps we should never procure a new suit, however ragged or dirty the old, until we have so conducted, so enterprised or sailed in some way, that we feel like new men in

3. Ida Pfeiffer (1797–1858), A *Lady's Voyage round the World* (1852).

4. A play on the saying "Man may work from sun to sun, / But woman's work is never done."

the old, and that to retain it would be like keeping new wine in old bottles.[5] Our moulting season, like that of the fowls, must be a crisis in our lives. The loon retires to solitary ponds to spend it. Thus also the snake casts its slough, and the caterpillar its wormy coat, by an internal industry and expansion; for clothes are but our outmost cuticle and mortal coil. Otherwise we shall be found sailing under false colors, and be inevitably cashiered[6] at last by our own opinion, as well as that of mankind.

We don garment after garment, as if we grew like exogenous plants by addition without. Our outside and often thin and fanciful clothes are our epidermis or false skin, which partakes not of our life, and may be stripped off here and there without fatal injury; our thicker garments, constantly worn, are our cellular integument, or cortex; but our shirts are our liber[7] or true bark, which cannot be removed without girdling and so destroying the man. I believe that all races at some seasons wear something equivalent to the shirt. It is desirable that a man be clad so simply that he can lay his hands on himself in the dark, and that he live in all respects so compactly and preparedly, that, if an enemy take the town, he can, like the old philosopher, walk out the gate empty-handed without anxiety. While one thick garment is, for most purposes, as good as three thin ones, and cheap clothing can be obtained at prices really to suit customers; while a thick coat can be bought for five dollars, which will last as many years, thick pantaloons for two dollars, cowhide boots for a dollar and a half a pair, a summer hat for a quarter of a dollar, and a winter cap for sixty-two and a half cents, or a better be made at home at a nominal cost, where is he so poor that, clad in such a suit, *of his own earning*, there will not be found wise men to do him reverence?

When I ask for a garment of a particular form, my tailoress tells me gravely, "They do not make them so now," not emphasizing the "They" at all, as if she quoted an authority as impersonal as the Fates, and I find it difficult to get made what I want, simply because she cannot believe that I mean what I say, that I am so rash. When I hear this oracular sentence, I am for a moment absorbed in thought, emphasizing to myself each word separately that I may come at the meaning of it, that I may find out by what degree of consanguinity *They* are related to *me*, and what authority they may have in an affair which affects me so nearly; and, finally, I am inclined to answer her with equal mystery, and without any more emphasis of the "they,"—"It is true, they did not make them so recently, but they do now." Of what use this measuring of me if she does not measure my character, but only the breadth of my shoulders, as it were a peg to hang the coat on? We worship not the Graces, nor the Parcæ,[8] but Fashion. She spins and weaves and cuts with full authority. The head monkey at Paris puts on a traveller's cap, and all the monkeys in America do the same. I sometimes despair of getting any thing quite simple and honest done in this world by the help of men. They would have to be passed through a powerful press first, to squeeze their old notions out of them, so that they would not soon get upon their legs again, and then there would be some one in the company with a maggot in his head, hatched from an egg deposited there nobody knows when, for not even fire kills these things, and you would

---

5. "Neither do men put new wine into old bottles: else the bottles break, and the wine runneth out, and the bottles perish: but they put new wine into new bottles, and both are preserved" (Matthew 9.17).

6. Fired.
7. Inner bark.
8. In Roman mythology, the three Fates.

have lost your labor. Nevertheless, we will not forget that some Egyptian wheat
is said to have been handed down to us by a mummy.

On the whole, I think that it cannot be maintained that dressing has in this
or any country risen to the dignity of an art. At present men make shift to wear
what they can get. Like shipwrecked sailors, they put on what they can find
on the beach, and at a little distance, whether of space or time, laugh at each
other's masquerade. Every generation laighs at the old fashions, but follows
religiously the new. We are amused at beholding the costume of Henry VIII.,
or Queen Elizabeth, as much as if it was that of the King and Queen of the
Cannibal Islands. All costume off a man is pitiful or grotesque. It is only the
serious eye peering from and the sincere life passed within it, which restrain
laughter and consecrate the costume of any people. Let Harlequin[9] be taken
with a fit of the colic and his trappings will have to serve that mood too. When
the soldier is hit by a cannon ball rags are as becoming as purple.

The childish and savage taste of men and women for new patterns keeps
how many shaking and squinting through kaleidoscopes that they may discover
the particular figure which this generation requires to-day. The manufacturers
have learned that this taste is merely whimsical. Of two patterns which differ
only by a few threads more or less of a particular color, the one will be sold
readily, the other lie on the shelf, though it frequently happens that after the
lapse of a season the latter becomes the most fashionable. Comparatively,
tattooing is not the hideous custom which it is called. It is not barbarous
merely because the printing is skin-deep and unalterable.

I cannot believe that our factory system is the best mode by which men may
get clothing. The condition of the operatives is becoming every day more like
that of the English; and it cannot be wondered at, since, as far as I have heard
or observed, the principal object is, not that mankind may be well and honestly
clad, but, unquestionably, that the corporations may be enriched. In the long
run men hit only what they aim at. Therefore, though they should fail immediately, they had better aim at something high.

As for a Shelter, I will not deny that this is now a necessary of life, though
there are instances of men having done without it for long periods in colder
countries than this. Samuel Laing says that "The Laplander in his skin dress,
and in a skin bag which he puts over his head and shoulders, will sleep night
after night on the snow—in a degree of cold which would extinguish the life
of one exposed to it in any woollen clothing." He had seen them asleep thus.
Yet he adds, "They are not hardier than other people."[1] But, probably, man
did not live long on the earth without discovering the convenience which there
is in a house, the domestic comforts, which phrase may have originally signified the satisfactions of the house more than of the family; though these must
be extremely partial and occasional in those climates where the house is associated in our thoughts with winter or the rainy season chiefly, and two thirds of
the year, except for a parasol, is unnecessary. In our climate, in the summer,
it was formerly almost solely a covering at night. In the Indian gazettes[2] a
wigwam was the symbol of a day's march, and a row of them cut or painted
on the bark of a tree signified that so many times they had camped. Man was

9. A type of comic servant in *commedia dell'arte*,
dressed in mask and many-colored tights.
1. *Journal of a Residence in Norway* (1837).

2. In American Indian sign language (in messages
equivalent to gazettes or newspapers).

not made so large limbed and robust but that he must seek to narrow his world, and wall in a space such as fitted him. He was at first bare and out of doors; but though this was pleasant enough in serene and warm weather, by daylight, the rainy season and the winter, to say nothing of the torrid sun, would perhaps have nipped his race in the bud if he had not made haste to clothe himself with the shelter of a house. Adam and Eve, according to a fable, wore the bower before other clothes. Man wanted a home, a place of warmth, or comfort, first of physical warmth, then the warmth of the affections.

We may imagine a time when, in the infancy of the human race, some enterprising mortal crept into a hollow in a rock for shelter. Every child begins the world again, to some extent, and loves to stay out doors, even in wet and cold. It plays house, as well as horse, having an instinct for it. Who does not remember the interest with which when young he looked at shelving rocks, or any approach to a cave? It was the natural yearning of that portion of our most primitive ancestor which still survived in us. From the cave we have advanced to roofs of palm leaves, of bark and boughs, of linen woven and stretched, of grass and straw, of boards and shingles, of stones and tiles. At last, we know not what it is to live in the open air, and our lives are domestic in more senses than we think. From the hearth to the field is a great distance. It would be well perhaps if we were to spend more of our days and nights without any obstruction between us and the celestial bodies, if the poet did not speak so much from under a roof, or the saint dwell there so long. Birds do not sing in caves, nor do doves cherish their innocence in dovecots.

However, if one designs to construct a dwelling house, it behooves him to exercise a little Yankee shrewdness, lest after all he find himself in a workhouse, a labyrinth without a clew, a museum, an almshouse, a prison, or a splendid mausoleum instead. Consider first how slight a shelter is absolutely necessary. I have seen Penobscot Indians, in this town, living in tents of thin cotton cloth, while the snow was nearly a foot deep around them, and I thought that they would be glad to have it deeper to keep out the wind. Formerly, when how to get my living honestly, with freedom left for my proper pursuits, was a question which vexed me even more than it does now, for unfortunately I am become somewhat callous, I used to see a large box by the railroad, six feet long by three wide, in which the laborers locked up their tools at night, and it suggested to me that every man who was hard pushed might get such a one for a dollar, and, having bored a few auger holes in it, to admit the air at least, get into it when it rained and at night, and hook down the lid, and so have freedom in his love, and in his soul be free. This did not appear the worst, nor by any means a despicable alternative. You could sit up as late as you pleased, and, whenever you got up, go abroad without any landlord or house-lord dogging you for rent. Many a man is harassed to death to pay the rent of a larger and more luxurious box who would not have frozen to death in such a box as this. I am far from jesting. Economy is a subject which admits of being treated with levity, but it cannot so be disposed of. A comfortable house for a rude and hardy race, that lived mostly out of doors, was once made here almost entirely of such materials as Nature furnished ready to their hands. Gookin, who was superintendent of the Indians subject to the Massachusetts Colony, writing in 1674, says, "The best of their houses are covered very neatly, tight and warm, with barks of trees, slipped from their bodies at those seasons when the sap is up, and made into great flakes, with pressure of weighty timber, when they are green. . . . The meaner sort are covered with mats which they make of a kind of bulrush, and are also indifferently tight and warm, but not so good as the former. . . . Some I have seen, sixty or a hundred feet long and thirty feet broad. . . . I have often lodged in their wigwams, and found them as warm as the best English houses."[3] He adds, that they were commonly carpeted and lined within with well-wrought embroidered mats, and were furnished with various utensils. The Indians had advanced so far as to regulate the effect of the wind by a mat suspended over the hole in the roof and moved by a string. Such a lodge was in the first instance constructed in a day or two at most, and taken down and put up in a few hours; and every family owned one, or its apartment in one.

In the savage state every family owns a shelter as good as the best, and sufficient for its coarser and simpler wants; but I think that I speak within bounds when I say that, though the birds of the air have their nests, and the foxes their holes,[4] and the savages their wigwams, in modern civilized society not more than one half the families own a shelter. In the large towns and cities, where civilization especially prevails, the number of those who own a shelter is a very small fraction of the whole. The rest pay an annual tax for this outside garment of all, become indispensable summer and winter, which would buy a village of Indian wigwams, but now helps to keep them poor as long as they live. I do not mean to insist here on the disadvantage of hiring compared with owning, but it is evident that the savage owns his shelter because it costs so little, while the civilized man hires his commonly because he cannot afford to own it; nor can he, in the long run, any better afford to hire. But, answers one, by merely paying this tax the poor civilized man secures an abode which is a palace compared with the savage's. An annual rent of from twenty-five to a hundred dollars, these are the country rates, entitles him to the benefit of the improvements of centuries, spacious apartments, clean paint and paper, Rumford fireplace,[5] back plastering, Venetian blinds, copper pump, spring lock, a commodious cellar, and many other things. But how happens it that he who is said to enjoy these things is so commonly a *poor* civilized man, while the savage, who has them not, is rich as a savage? If it is asserted that civilization is a real advance in the condition of man,—and I think that it is, though only the wise improve their advantages,—it must be shown that it has produced better dwellings without making them more costly; and the cost of a thing is the amount of what I will call life which is required to be exchanged for it, immediately or in the long run. An average house in this neighborhood costs perhaps eight hundred dollars, and to lay up this sum will take from ten to fifteen years of the laborer's life, even if he is not encumbered with a family;—estimating the pecuniary value of every man's labor at one dollar a day, for if some receive more, others receive less;—so that he must have spent more than half his life commonly before *his* wigwam will be earned. If we suppose him to pay a rent instead, this is but a doubtful choice of evils. Would the savage have been wise to exchange his wigwam for a palace on these terms?

It may be guessed that I reduce almost the whole advantage of holding this

3. Daniel Gookin, *Historical Collections of the Indians in New England* (1792).
4. "The foxes have holes, and the birds of the air have nests; but the Son of man hath not where to lay his head" (Matthew 8.20).

5. Benjamin Thompson, Count Rumford (1753–1814), devised a shelf inside the chimney to prevent smoke from being carried back into a room by downdrafts.

superfluous property as a fund in store against the future, so far as the individual is concerned, mainly to the defraying of funeral expenses. But perhaps a man is not required to bury himself. Nevertheless this points to an important distinction between the civilized man and the savage; and, no doubt, they have designs on us for our benefit, in making the life of a civilized people an *institution*, in which the life of the individual is to a great extent absorbed, in order to preserve and perfect that of the race. But I wish to show at what a sacrifice this advantage is at present obtained, and to suggest that we may possibly so live as to secure all the advantage without suffering any of the disadvantage. What mean ye by saying that the poor ye have always with you, or that the fathers have eaten sour grapes, and the children's teeth are set on edge?[6]

"As I live, saith the Lord God, ye shall not have occasion any more to use this proverb in Israel."

"Behold all souls are mine; as the soul of the father, so also the soul of the son is mine: the soul that sinneth it shall die."[7]

When I consider my neighbors, the farmers of Concord, who are at least as well off as the other classes, I find that for the most part they have been toiling twenty, thirty, or forty years, that they may become the real owners of their farms, which commonly they have inherited with encumbrances, or else bought with hired money,—and we may regard one third of that toil as the cost of their houses,—but commonly they have not paid for them yet. It is true, the encumbrances sometimes outweigh the value of the farm, so that the farm itself becomes one great encumbrance, and still a man is found to inherit it, being well acquainted with it, as he says. On applying to the assessors, I am surprised to learn that they cannot at once name a dozen in the town who own their farms free and clear. If you would know the history of these homesteads, inquire at the bank where they are mortgaged. The man who has actually paid for his farm with labor on it is so rare that every neighbor can point to him. I doubt if there are three such men in Concord. What has been said of the merchants, that a very large majority, even ninety-seven in a hundred, are sure to fail, is equally true of the farmers. With regard to the merchants, however, one of them says pertinently that a great part of their failures are not genuine pecuniary failures, but merely failures to fulfil their engagements, because it is inconvenient; that is, it is the moral character that breaks down. But this puts an infinitely worse face on the matter, and suggests, beside, that probably not even the other three succeed in saving their souls, but are perchance bankrupt in a worse sense than they who fail honestly. Bankruptcy and repudiation are the spring-boards from which much of our civilization vaults and turns its somersets, but the savage stands on the unelastic plank of famine. Yet the Middlesex Cattle Show goes off here with *éclat* annually, as if all the joints of the agricultural machine were suent.[8]

The farmer is endeavoring to solve the problem of a livelihood by a formula more complicated than the problem itself. To get his shoestrings he speculates

---

6. Thoreau is repudiating Jesus' words to his disciples "For ye have the poor always with you; but me ye have not always" (Matthew 26.11) by combining it with God's reproof to Ezekiel for employing a negatively deterministic proverb: "What mean ye, that ye use this proverb concerning the land of Israel, saying, The fathers have eaten sour grapes, and the children's teeth are set on edge?" (Ezekiel 18.2).
7. These two verses are Ezekiel 18.3–4, but Thoreau so truncates the passage that the reader may find it hard to understand that the biblical intent (as well as Thoreau's own) is optimistic, to reject the notion that the sins of the fathers are visited unto their children.
8. In good working order, broken in.

in herds of cattle. With consummate skill he has set his trap with a hair spring to catch comfort and independence, and then, as he turned away, got his own leg into it. This is the reason he is poor; and for a similar reason we are all poor in respect to a thousand savage comforts, though surrounded by luxuries. As Chapman[9] sings,—

> "The false society of men—
> —for earthly greatness
> All heavenly comforts rarefies to air."

And when the farmer has got his house, he may not be the richer but the poorer for it, and it be the house that has got him. As I understand it, that was a valid objection urged by Momus[1] against the house which Minerva made, that she "had not made it movable, by which means a bad neighborhood might be avoided;" and it may still be urged, for our houses are such unwieldy property that we are often imprisoned rather than housed in them; and the bad neighborhood to be avoided is our own scurvy selves. I know one or two families, at least, in this town, who, for nearly a generation, have been wishing to sell their houses in the outskirts and move into the village, but have not been able to accomplish it, and only death will set them free.

Granted that the *majority* are able at last either to own or hire the modern house with all its improvements. While civilization has been improving our houses, it has not equally improved the men who are to inhabit them. It has created palaces, but it was not so easy to create noblemen and kings. And *if the civilized man's pursuits are no worthier than the savage's, if he is employed the greater part of his life in obtaining gross necessaries and comforts merely, why should he have a better dwelling than the former?*

But how do the poor *minority* fare? Perhaps it will be found, that just in proportion as some have been placed in outward circumstances above the savage, others have been degraded below him. The luxury of one class is counterbalanced by the indigence of another. On the one side is the palace, on the other are the almshouse and "silent poor."[2] The myriads who built the pyramids to be the tombs of the Pharaohs were fed on garlic, and it may be were not decently buried themselves. The mason who finishes the cornice of the palace returns at night perchance to a hut not so good as a wigwam. It is a mistake to suppose that, in a country where the usual evidences of civilization exist, the condition of a very large body of the inhabitants may not be as degraded as that of savages. I refer to the degraded poor, not now to the degraded rich. To know this I should not need to look farther than to the shanties which every where border our railroads, that last improvement in civilization; where I see in my daily walks human beings living in sties, and all winter with an open door, for the sake of light, without any visible, often imaginable, wood pile, and the forms of both old and young are permanently contracted by the long habit of shrinking from cold and misery, and the development of all their limbs and faculties is checked. It certainly is fair to look at that class by whose labor the works which distinguish the generation are accomplished. Such too, to a greater or less extent, is the condition of the operatives of every denomination in England, which is the great workhouse of

9. George Chapman (1559?–1634), *Caesar and Pompey* 5.2.
1. In Greek mythology, the god of pleasantry but also of carping criticism.

2. Harding identifies these as the poor of Concord who received public charity secretly to retain their dwellings and not go to the poorhouse.

the world. Or I could refer you to Ireland, which is marked as one of the white or enlightened spots on the map.[3] Contrast the physical condition of the Irish with that of the North American Indian, or the South Sea Islander, or any other savage race before it was degraded by contact with the civilized man. Yet I have no doubt that that people's rulers are as wise as the average of civilized rulers. Their condition only proves what squalidness may consist with civilization. I hardly need refer now to the laborers in our Southern States who produce the staple exports of this country, and are themselves a staple production of the South.[4] But to confine myself to those who are said to be in *moderate* circumstances.

Most men appear never to have considered what a house is, and are actually though needlessly poor all their lives because they think that they must have such a one as their neighbors have. As if one were to wear any sort of coat which the tailor might cut out for him, or, gradually leaving off palmleaf hat or cap of woodchuck skin, complain of hard times because he could not afford to buy him a crown! It is possible to invent a house still more convenient and luxurious than we have, which yet all would admit that man could not afford to pay for. Shall we always study to obtain more of these things, and not sometimes to be content with less? Shall the respectable citizen thus gravely teach, by precept and example, the necessity of the young man's providing a certain number of superfluous glow-shoes,[5] and umbrellas, and empty guest chambers for empty guests, before he dies? Why should not our furniture be as simple as the Arab's or the Indian's? When I think of the benefactors of the race, whom we have apotheosized as messengers from heaven, bearers of divine gifts to man, I do not see in my mind any retinue at their heels, any car-load of fashionable furniture. Or what if I were to allow—would it not be a singular allowance?—that our furniture should be more complex than the Arab's, in proportion as we are morally and intellectually his superiors! At present our houses are cluttered and defiled with it, and a good housewife would sweep out the greater part into the dust hole, and not leave her morning's work undone. Morning work! By the blushes of Aurora and the music of Memnon,[6] what should be man's *morning work* in this world? I had three pieces of limestone on my desk, but I was terrified to find that they required to be dusted daily, when the furniture of my mind was all undusted still, and I threw them out the window in disgust. How, then, could I have a furnished house? I would rather sit in the open air, for no dust gathers on the grass, unless where man has broken ground.

It is the luxurious and dissipated who set the fashions which the herd so diligently follow. The traveller who stops at the best houses, so called, soon discovers this, for the publicans presume him to be a Sardanapalus,[7] and if he resigned himself to their tender mercies he would soon be completely emasculated. I think that in the railroad car we are inclined to spend more on luxury than on safety and convenience, and it threatens without attaining these to become no better than a modern drawing room, with its divans, and ottomans,

3. Thoreau refers to the habit some cartographers had of leaving unexplored terrain in a dark color; other cartographers left unexplored areas white.
4. The accusation, denied by many historians, that some plantations, especially in Virginia, were run for the sole purpose of breeding slave children for sale.
5. Galoshes.

6. The Roman goddess of the dawn and her son, an Ethiopian prince who fought for Priam at Troy. Memnon is associated here with the Egyptian colossus near Thebes that in ancient times emitted a sound at dawn, presumably because of the warming of air currents.
7. Effeminate ruler of Assyria (9th century B.C.).

and sunshades, and a hundred other oriental things, which we are taking west with us, invented for the ladies of the harem and the effeminate natives of the Celestial Empire, which Jonathan[8] should be ashamed to know the names of. I would rather sit on a pumpkin and have it all to myself, than be crowded on a velvet cushion. I would rather ride on earth in an ox cart with a free circulation, than go to heaven in the fancy car of an excursion train and breathe a *malaria* all the way.

The very simplicity and nakedness of man's life in the primitive ages imply this advantage at least, that they left him still but a sojourner in nature. When he was refreshed with food and sleep he contemplated his journey again. He dwelt, as it were, in a tent in this world, and was either threading the valleys, or crossing the plains, or climbing the mountain tops. But lo! men have become the tools of their tools. The man who independently plucked the fruits when he was hungry is become a farmer; and he who stood under a tree for shelter, a housekeeper. We now no longer camp as for a night, but have settled down on earth and forgotten heaven. We have adopted Christianity merely as an improved method of *agri*-culture. We have built for this world a family mansion, and for the next a family tomb. The best works of art are the expression of man's struggle to free himself from this condition, but the effect of our art is merely to make this low state comfortable and that higher state to be forgotten. There is actually no place in this village for a work of *fine* art, if any had come down to us, to stand, for our lives, our houses and streets, furnish no proper pedestal for it. There is not a nail to hang a picture on, nor a shelf to receive the bust of a hero or a saint. When I consider how our houses are built and paid for, or not paid for, and their internal economy managed and sustained, I wonder that the floor does not give way under the visitor while he is admiring the gewgaws upon the mantel-piece, and let him through into the cellar, to some solid and honest though earthy foundation. I cannot but perceive that this so called rich and refined life is a thing jumped at, and I do not get on in the enjoyment of the *fine* arts which adorn it, my attention being wholly occupied with the jump; for I remember that the greatest genuine leap, due to human muscles alone, on record, is that of certain wandering Arabs, who are said to have cleared twenty-five feet on level ground. Without factitious support, man is sure to come to earth again beyond that distance. The first question which I am tempted to put to the proprietor of such great impropriety is, Who bolsters you? Are you one of the ninety-seven who fail? or of the three who succeed? Answer me these questions, and then perhaps I may look at your bawbles and find them ornamental. The cart before the horse is neither beautiful nor useful. Before we can adorn our houses with beautiful objects the walls must be stripped, and our lives must be stripped, and beautiful housekeeping and beautiful living be laid for a foundation: now, a taste for the beautiful is most cultivated out of doors, where there is no house and no housekeeper.

Old Johnson, in his "Wonder-Working Providence," speaking of the first settlers of this town, with whom he was contemporary, tells us that "they burrow themselves in the earth for their first shelter under some hillside, and, casting the soil aloft upon timber, they make a smoky fire against the earth, at the highest side." They did not "provide them houses," says he, "till the earth,

---

8. A type name at first applied to New Englanders, then later (as here) to the inhabitants of the entire United States.

by the Lord's blessing, brought forth bread to feed them," and the first year's crop was so light that "they were forced to cut their bread very thin for a long season."[9] The secretary of the Province of New Netherland, writing in Dutch, in 1650, for the information of those who wished to take up land there, states more particularly, that "those in New Netherland, and especially in New England, who have no means to build farm houses at first according to their wishes, dig a square pit in the ground, cellar fashion, six or seven feet deep, as long and as broad as they think proper, case the earth inside with wood all round the wall, and line the wood with the bark of trees or something else to prevent the caving in of the earth; floor this cellar with plank, and wainscot it overhead for a ceiling, raise a roof of spars clear up, and cover the spars with bark or green sods, so that they can live dry and warm in these houses with their entire families for two, three, and four years, it being understood that partitions are run through those cellars which are adapted to the size of the family. The wealthy and principal men in New England, in the beginning of the colonies, commenced their first dwelling houses in this fashion for two reasons; firstly, in order not to waste time in building, and not to want food the next season; secondly, in order not to discourage poor laboring people whom they brought over in numbers from Fatherland. In the course of three or four years, when the country became adapted to agriculture, they built themselves handsome houses, spending on them several thousands."[1]

In this course which our ancestors took there was a show of prudence at least, as if their principle were to satisfy the more pressing wants first. But are the more pressing wants satisfied now? When I think of acquiring for myself one of our luxurious dwellings, I am deterred, for, so to speak, the country is not yet adapted to *human* culture, and we are still forced to cut our *spiritual* bread far thinner than our forefathers did their wheaten. Not that all architectural ornament is to be neglected even in the rudest periods; but let our houses first be lined with beauty, where they come in contact with our lives, like the tenement of the shellfish, and not overlaid with it. But, alas! I have been inside one or two of them, and know what they are lined with.

Though we are not so degenerate but that we might possibly live in a cave or a wigwam or wear skins to-day, it certainly is better to accept the advantages, though so dearly bought, which the invention and industry of mankind offer. In such a neighborhood as this, boards and shingles, lime and bricks, are cheaper and more easily obtained than suitable caves, or whole logs, or bark in sufficient quantities, or even well-tempered clay or flat stones. I speak understandingly on this subject, for I have made myself acquainted with it both theoretically and practically. With a little more wit we might use these materials so as to become richer than the richest now are, and make our civilization a blessing. The civilized man is a more experienced and wiser savage. But to make haste to my own experiment.

Near the end of March, 1845, I borrowed an axe and went down to the woods by Walden Pond, nearest to where I intended to build my house, and began to cut down some tall arrowy white pines, still in their youth, for timber. It is difficult to begin without borrowing, but perhaps it is the most generous course thus to permit your fellow-men to have an interest in your enterprise.

9. Edward Johnson, *Wonder-working Providence of*      1. Edmund Bailey O'Callaghan, *Documentary His-*
*Sion's Saviour in New England* (1654).                            *tory of the State of New-York* (1851).

The owner of the axe, as he released his hold on it, said that it was the apple of his eye; but I returned it sharper than I received it. It was a pleasant hillside where I worked, covered with pine woods, through which I looked out on the pond, and a small open field in the woods where pines and hickories were springing up. The ice in the pond was not yet dissolved, though there were some open spaces, and it was all dark colored and saturated with water. There were some slight flurries of snow during the days that I worked there; but for the most part when I came out on to the railroad, on my way home, its yellow sand heap stretched away gleaming in the hazy atmosphere, and the rails shone in the spring sun, and I heard the lark and pewee and other birds already come to commence another year with us. They were pleasant spring days, in which the winter of man's discontent was thawing as well as the earth, and the life that had lain torpid began to stretch itself. One day, when my axe had come off and I had cut a green hickory for a wedge, driving it with a stone, and had placed the whole to soak in a pond hole in order to swell the wood, I saw a striped snake run into the water, and he lay on the bottom, apparently without inconvenience, as long as I staid there, or more than a quarter of an hour; perhaps because he had not yet fairly come out of the torpid state. It appeared to me that for a like reason men remain in their present low and primitive condition; but if they should feel the influence of the spring of springs arousing them, they would of necessity rise to a higher and more ethereal life. I had previously seen the snakes in frosty mornings in my path with portions of their bodies still numb and inflexible, waiting for the sun to thaw them. On the 1st of April it rained and melted the ice, and in the early part of the day, which was very foggy, I heard a stray goose groping about over the pond and cackling as if lost, or like the spirit of the fog.

So I went on for some days cutting and hewing timber, and also studs and rafters, all with my narrow axe, not having many communicable or scholar-like thoughts, singing to myself,—

> Men say they know many things;
> But lo! they have taken wings,—
> The arts and sciences,
> And a thousand appliances;
> The wind that blows
> Is all that any body knows.[2]

I hewed the main timbers six inches square, most of the studs on two sides only, and the rafters and floor timbers on one side, leaving the rest of the bark on, so that they were just as straight and much stronger than sawed ones. Each stick was carefully mortised or tenoned by its stump, for I had borrowed other tools by this time. My days in the woods were not very long ones; yet I usually carried my dinner of bread and butter, and read the newspaper in which it was wrapped, at noon, sitting amid the green pine boughs which I had cut off, and to my bread was imparted some of their fragrance, for my hands were covered with a thick coat of pitch. Before I had done I was more the friend than the foe of the pine tree, though I had cut down some of them, having become better acquainted with it. Sometimes a rambler in the wood was attracted by the sound of my axe, and we chatted pleasantly over the chips which I had made.

2. Like other poems in *Walden* not enclosed in quotation marks, this poem is Thoreau's.

By the middle of April, for I made no haste in my work, but rather made the most of it, my house was framed and ready for the raising. I had already bought the shanty of James Collins, an Irishman who worked on the Fitchburg Railroad, for boards. James Collins' shanty was considered an uncommonly fine one. When I called to see it he was not at home. I walked about the outside, at first unobserved from within, the window was so deep and high. It was of small dimensions, with a peaked cottage roof, and not much else to be seen, the dirt being raised five feet all around as if it were a compost heap. The roof was the soundest part, though a good deal warped and made brittle by the sun. Door-sill there was none, but a perennial passage for the hens under the door board. Mrs. C. came to the door and asked me to view it from the inside. The hens were driven in by my approach. It was dark, and had a dirt floor for the most part, dank, clammy, and aguish, only here a board and there a board which would not bear removal. She lighted a lamp to show me the inside of the roof and the walls, and also that the board floor extended under the bed, warning me not to step into the cellar, a sort of dust hole two feet deep. In her own words, they were "good boards overhead, good boards all around, and a good window,"—of two whole squares originally, only the cat had passed out that way lately. There was a stove, a bed, and a place to sit, an infant in the house where it was born, a silk parasol, gilt-framed looking-glass, and a patent new coffee mill nailed to an oak sapling, all told. The bargain was soon concluded, for James had in the mean while returned. I to pay four dollars and twenty-five cents to-night, he to vacate at five to-morrow morning, selling to nobody else meanwhile: I to take possession at six. It were well, he said, to be there early, and anticipate certain indistinct but wholly unjust claims on the score of ground rent and fuel. This he assured me was the only encumbrance. At six I passed him and his family on the road. One large bundle held their all,—bed, coffee-mill, looking-glass, hens,—all but the cat, she took to the woods and became a wild cat, and, as I learned afterward, trod in a trap set for woodchucks, and so became a dead cat at last.

I took down this dwelling the same morning, drawing the nails, and removed it to the pond side by small cartloads, spreading the boards on the grass there to bleach and warp back again in the sun. One early thrush gave me a note or two as I drove along the woodland path. I was informed treacherously by a young Patrick that neighbor Seeley, an Irishman, in the intervals of the carting, transferred the still tolerable, straight, and drivable nails, staples, and spikes to his pocket, and then stood when I came back to pass the time of day, and look freshly up, unconcerned, with spring thoughts, at the devastation; there being a dearth of work, as he said. He was there to represent spectatordom, and help make this seemingly insignificant event one with the removal of the gods of Troy.[3]

I dug my cellar in the side of a hill sloping to the south, where a woodchuck had formerly dug his burrow, down through sumach and blackberry roots, and the lowest stain of vegetation, six feet square by seven deep, to a fine sand where potatoes would not freeze in any winter. The sides were left shelving, and not stoned; but the sun having never shone on them, the sand still keeps its place. It was but two hours' work. I took particular pleasure in this breaking of ground, for in almost all latitudes men dig into the earth for an equable temperature. Under the most splendid house in the city is still to be found the

---

3. In Virgil's Aeneid, book 2, after the fall of Troy, Aeneas escapes with his father and son and his household gods.

cellar where they store their roots as of old, and long after the superstructure has disappeared posterity remark its dent in the earth. The house is still but a sort of porch at the entrance of a burrow.

At length, in the beginning of May, with the help of some of my acquaintances, rather to improve so good an occasion for neighborliness than from any necessity, I set up the frame of my house. No man was ever more honored in the character of his raisers[4] than I. They are destined, I trust, to assist at the raising of loftier structures one day. I began to occupy my house on the 4th of July, as soon as it was boarded and roofed, for the boards were carefully feather-edged and lapped, so that it was perfectly impervious to rain;[5] but before boarding I laid the foundation of a chimney at one end, bringing two cartloads of stones up the hill from the pond in my arms. I built the chimney after my hoeing in the fall, before a fire became necessary for warmth, doing my cooking in the mean while out of doors on the ground, early in the morning: which mode I still think is in some respects more convenient and agreeable than the usual one. When it stormed before my bread was baked, I fixed a few boards over the fire, and sat under them to watch my loaf, and passed some pleasant hours in that way. In those days, when my hands were much employed, I read but little, but the least scraps of paper which lay on the ground, my holder, or table-cloth, afforded me as much entertainment, in fact answered the same purpose as the Iliad.[6]

It would be worth the while to build still more deliberately than I did, considering, for instance, what foundation a door, a window, a cellar, a garret, have in the nature of man, and perchance never raising any superstructure until we found a better reason for it than our temporal necessities even. There is some of the same fitness in a man's building his own house that there is in a bird's building its own nest. Who knows but if men constructed their dwellings with their own hands, and provided food for themselves and families simply and honestly enough, the poetic faculty would be universally developed, as birds universally sing when they are so engaged? But alas! we do like cowbirds and cuckoos, which lay their eggs in nests which other birds have built, and cheer no traveller with their chattering and unmusical notes. Shall we forever resign the pleasure of construction to the carpenter? What does architecture amount to in the experience of the mass of men? I never in all my walks came across a man engaged in so simple and natural an occupation as building his house. We belong to the community. It is not the tailor alone who is the ninth part of a man; it is as much the preacher, and the merchant, and the farmer. Where is this division of labor to end? and what object does it finally serve? No doubt another *may* also think for me; but it is not therefore desirable that he should do so to the exclusion of my thinking for myself.

True, there are architects so called in this country, and I have heard of one at least possessed with the idea of making architectural ornaments have a core of truth, a necessity, and hence a beauty, as if it were a revelation to him.[7] All very well perhaps from his point of view, but only a little better than the

---

4. These "raisers" (a pun) included Emerson; Alcott; Ellery Channing; two young brothers who had studied at Brook Farm, Burrill and George William Curtis; and the Concord farmer Edmund Hosmer and his three sons.
5. I.e., on the boards to be nailed horizontally the top and bottom edges were cut at 45-degree angles and overlapped so as to shed rain.

6. Greek epic of the siege of Troy traditionally attributed to Homer.
7. The sculptor Horatio Greenough (1805–1852), whose theories Thoreau knew only imperfectly from a private letter of Greenough's to Emerson. The ideas attributed here are at variance with Greenough's published comments on architecture.

common dilettantism. A sentimental reformer in architecture, he began at the cornice, not at the foundation. It was only how to put a core of truth within the ornaments, that every sugar plum in fact might have an almond or caraway seed in it,—though I hold that almonds are most wholesome without the sugar,—and not how the inhabitant, the indweller, might build truly within and without, and let the ornaments take care of themselves. What reasonable man ever supposed that ornaments were something outward and in the skin merely,—that the tortoise got his spotted shell, or the shellfish its mother-o'-pearl tints, by such a contract as the inhabitants of Broadway their Trinity Church? But a man has no more to do with the style of architecture of his house than a tortoise with that of its shell: nor need the soldier be so idle as to try to paint the precise *color* of his virtue on his standard. The enemy will find it out. He may turn pale when the trial comes. This man seemed to me to lean over the cornice and timidly whisper his half truth to the rude occupants who really knew it better than he. What of architectural beauty I now see, I know has gradually grown from within outward, out of the necessities and character of the indweller, who is the only builder,—out of some unconscious truthfulness, and nobleness, without ever a thought for the appearance; and whatever additional beauty of this kind is destined to be produced will be preceded by a like unconscious beauty of life. The most interesting dwellings in this country, as the painter knows, are the most unpretending, humble log huts and cottages of the poor commonly; it is the life of the inhabitants whose shells they are, and not any peculiarity in their surfaces merely, which makes them *picturesque*; and equally interesting will be the citizen's suburban box, when his life shall be as simple and as agreeable to the imagination, and there is as little straining after effect in the style of his dwelling. A great proportion of architectural ornaments are literally hollow, and a September gale would strip them off, like borrowed plumes, without injury to the substantials. They can do without *architecture* who have no olives nor wines in the cellar. What if an equal ado were made about the ornaments of style in literature, and the architects of our bibles spent as much time about their cornices as the architects of our churches do? So are made the *belles-lettres* and the *beaux-arts* and their professors. Much it concerns a man, forsooth, how a few sticks are slanted over him or under him, and what colors are daubed upon his box. It would signify somewhat, if, in any earnest sense, *he* slanted them and daubed it; but the spirit having departed out of the tenant, it is of a piece with constructing his own coffin,—the architecture of the grave, and "carpenter" is but another name for "coffin-maker." One man says, in his despair or indifference to life, take up a handful of the earth at your feet, and paint your house that color. Is he thinking of his last and narrow house? Toss up a copper for it as well. What an abundance of leisure he must have! Why do you take up a handful of dirt? Better paint your house your own complexion; let it turn pale or blush for you. An enterprise to improve the style of cottage architecture! When you have got my ornaments ready I will wear them.

Before winter I built a chimney, and shingled the sides of my house, which were already impervious to rain, with imperfect and sappy shingles made of the first slice of the log, whose edges I was obliged to straighten with a plane.

I have thus a tight shingled and plastered house, ten feet wide by fifteen long, and eight-feet posts, with a garret and a closet, a large window on each side, two trap doors, one door at the end, and a brick fireplace opposite. The exact cost of my house, paying the usual price for such materials as I used, but not counting the work, all of which was done by myself, was as follows; and I give the details because very few are able to tell exactly what their houses cost, and fewer still, if any, the separate cost of the various materials which compose them:—

| | | |
|---|---|---|
| Boards, | $8 03½ | Mostly shanty boards |
| Refuse shingles for roof and sides, | 4 00 | |
| Laths, | 1 25 | |
| Two second-hand windows with glass, | 2 43 | |
| One thousand old brick, | 4 00 | |
| Two casks of lime, | 2 40 | That was high |
| Hair, | 0 31 | More than I needed |
| Mantle-tree iron, | 0 15 | |
| Nails, | 3 90 | |
| Hinges and screws, | 0 14 | |
| Latch, | 0 10 | |
| Chalk, | 0 01 | |
| Transportation, | 1 40 | I carried a good part on my back |
| In all, | $28 12½ | |

These are all the materials excepting the timber stones and sand, which I claimed by squatter's right. I have also a small wood-shed adjoining, made chiefly of the stuff which was left after building the house.

I intend to build me a house which will surpass any on the main street in Concord in grandeur and luxury, as soon as it pleases me as much and will cost me no more than my present one.

I thus found that the student who wishes for a shelter can obtain one for a lifetime at an expense not greater than the rent which he now pays annually. If I seem to boast more than is becoming, my excuse is that I brag for humanity rather than for myself; and my shortcomings and inconsistencies do not affect the truth of my statement. Notwithstanding much cant and hypocrisy,—chaff which I find it difficult to separate from my wheat, but for which I am as sorry as any man,—I will breathe freely and stretch myself in this respect, it is such a relief to both the moral and physical system; and I am resolved that I will not through humility become the devil's attorney. I will endeavor to speak a good word for the truth. At Cambridge College[8] the mere rent of a student's room, which is only a little larger than my own, is thirty dollars each year, though the corporation had the advantage of building thirty-two side by side and under one roof, and the occupant suffers the inconvenience of many and noisy neighbors, and perhaps a residence in the fourth story. I cannot but think that if we had more true wisdom in these respects, not only less education would be needed, because, forsooth, more would already have been acquired, but the pecuniary expense of getting an education would in a great measure vanish. Those conveniences which the student requires at Cambridge or elsewhere cost him or somebody else ten times as great a sacrifice of life as

8. Harvard University.

they would with proper management on both sides. Those things for which the most money is demanded are never the things which the student most wants. Tuition, for instance, is an important item in the term bill, while for the far more valuable education which he gets by associating with the most cultivated of his contemporaries no charge is made. The mode of founding a college is, commonly, to get up a subscription of dollars and cents, and then following blindly the principles of a division of labor to its extreme, a principle which should never be followed but with circumspection,—to call in a contractor who makes this a subject of speculation, and he employs Irishmen or other operatives actually to lay the foundations, while the students that are to be are said to be fitting themselves for it; and for these oversights successive generations have to pay. I think that it would be *better than this*, for the students, or those who desire to be benefited by it, even to lay the foundation themselves. The student who secures his coveted leisure and retirement by systematically shirking any labor necessary to man obtains but an ignoble and unprofitable leisure, defrauding himself of the experience which alone can make leisure fruitful. "But," says one, "you do not mean that the students should go to work with their hands instead of their heads?" I do not mean that exactly, but I mean something which he might think a good deal like that; I mean that they should not *play* life, or *study* it merely, while the community supports them at this expensive game, but earnestly *live* it from beginning to end. How could youths better learn to live than by at once trying the experiment of living? Methinks this would exercise their minds as much as mathematics. If I wished a boy to know something about the arts and sciences, for instance, I would not pursue the common course, which is merely to send him into the neighborhood of some professor, where any thing is professed and practised but the art of life;—to survey the world through a telescope or a microscope, and never with his natural eye; to study chemistry, and not learn how his bread is made, or mechanics, and not learn how it is earned; to discover new satellites to Neptune, and not detect the motes in his eyes, or to what vagabond he is a satellite himself; or to be devoured by the monsters that swarm all around him, while contemplating the monsters in a drop of vinegar. Which would have advanced the most at the end of the month,—the boy who had made his own jack-knife from the ore which he had dug and smelted, reading as much as would be necessary for this,—or the boy who had attended the lectures on metallurgy at the Institute in the mean while, and had received a Rodgers' penknife from his father? Which would be most likely to cut his fingers?—To my astonishment I was informed on leaving college that I had studied navigation!—why, if I had taken one turn down the harbor I should have known more about it. Even the *poor* student studies and is taught only *political* economy, while that economy of living which is synonymous with philosophy is not even sincerely professed in our colleges. The consequence is, that while he is reading Adam Smith, Ricardo, and Say,[9] he runs his father in debt irretrievably.

As with our colleges, so with a hundred "modern improvements"; there is an illusion about them; there is not always a positive advance. The devil goes on exacting compound interest to the last for his early share and numerous succeeding investments in them. Our inventions are wont to be pretty toys,

9. Three economists: the Scottish Adam Smith (1723–1790), the English David Ricardo (1772–1823), and the French Jean Baptiste Say (1767–1832).

which distract our attention from serious things. They are but improved means to an unimproved end, an end which it was already but too easy to arrive at; as railroads lead to Boston or New York. We are in great haste to construct a magnetic telegraph from Maine to Texas; but Maine and Texas, it may be, have nothing important to communicate. Either is in such a predicament as the man who was earnest to be introduced to a distinguished deaf woman, but when he was presented, and one end of her ear trumpet was put into his hand, had nothing to say. As if the main object were to talk fast and not to talk sensibly. We are eager to tunnel under the Atlantic and bring the old world some weeks nearer to the new; but perchance the first news that will leak through into the broad, flapping American ear will be that the Princess Adelaide has the whooping cough. After all, the man whose horse trots a mile in a minute does not carry the most important messages; he is not an evangelist, nor does he come round eating locusts and wild honey. I doubt if Flying Childers[1] ever carried a peck of corn to mill.

One says to me, "I wonder that you do not lay up money; you love to travel; you might take the cars and go to Fitchburg to-day and see the country." But I am wiser than that. I have learned that the swiftest traveller is he that goes afoot. I say to my friend, Suppose we try who will get there first. The distance is thirty miles; the fare ninety cents. That is almost a day's wages. I remember when wages were sixty cents a day for laborers on this very road. Well, I start now on foot, and get there before night; I have travelled at that rate by the week together. You will in the mean while have earned your fare, and arrive there some time to-morrow, or possibly this evening, if you are lucky enough to get a job in season. Instead of going to Fitchburg, you will be working here the greater part of the day. And so, if the railroad reached round the world, I think that I should keep ahead of you; and as for seeing the country and getting experience of that kind, I should have to cut your acquaintance altogether.

Such is the universal law, which no man can ever outwit, and with regard to the railroad even we may say it is as broad as it is long. To make a railroad round the world available to all mankind is equivalent to grading the whole surface of the planet. Men have an indistinct notion that if they keep up this activity of joint stocks and spades long enough all will at length ride somewhere, in next to no time, and for nothing; but though a crowd rushes to the depot, and the conductor shouts "All aboard!" when the smoke is blown away and the vapor condensed, it will be perceived that a few are riding, but the rest are run over,—and it will be called, and will be, "A melancholy accident." No doubt they can ride at last who shall have earned their fare, that is, if they survive so long, but they will probably have lost their elasticity and desire to travel by that time. This spending of the best part of one's life earning money in order to enjoy a questionable liberty during the least valuable part of it, reminds me of the Englishman who went to India to make a fortune first, in order that he might return to England and live the life of a poet. He should have gone up garret at once. "What!" exclaim a million Irishmen starting up from all the shanties in the land, "is not this railroad which we have built a good thing?" Yes, I answer, *comparatively* good, that is, you might have done worse; but I wish, as you are brothers of mine, that you could have spent your time better than digging in this dirt.

1. English racehorse.

Before I finished my house, wishing to earn ten or twelve dollars by some honest and agreeable method, in order to meet my unusual expenses, I planted about two acres and a half of light and sandy soil near it chiefly with beans, but also a small part with potatoes, corn, peas, and turnips. The whole lot contains eleven acres, mostly growing up to pines and hickories, and was sold the preceding season for eight dollars and eight cents an acre. One farmer said that it was "good for nothing but to raise cheeping squirrels on." I put no manure on this land, not being the owner, but merely a squatter, and not expecting to cultivate so much again, and I did not quite hoe it all once. I got out several cords of stumps in ploughing, which supplied me with fuel for a long time, and left small circles of virgin mould, easily distinguishable through the summer by the greater luxuriance of the beans there. The dead and for the most part unmerchantable wood behind my house, and the driftwood from the pond, have supplied the remainder of my fuel. I was obliged to hire a team and a man for the ploughing, though I held the plough myself. My farm outgoes for the first season were, for implements, seed, work, &c., $14 72½. The seed corn was given me. This never costs any thing to speak of, unless you plant more than enough. I got twelve bushels of beans, and eighteen bushels of potatoes, beside some peas and sweet corn. The yellow corn and formatn4turnips were too late to come to any thing. My whole income from the farm was

|  | $23 44. |
| Deducting the outgoes, | 14 72½ |
| there are left, | $ 8 71½, |

beside produce consumed and on hand at the time this estimate was made of the value of $4 50,—the amount on hand much more than balancing a little grass which I did not raise. All things considered, that is, considering the importance of a man's soul and of to-day, notwithstanding the short time occupied by my experiment, nay, partly even because of its transient character, I believe that that was doing better than any farmer in Concord did that year.

The next year I did better still, for I spaded up all the land which I required, about a third of an acre, and I learned from the experience of both years, not being in the least awed by many celebrated works on husbandry, Arthur Young[2] among the rest, that if one would live simply and eat only the crop which he raised, and raise no more than he ate, and not exchange it for an insufficient quantity of more luxurious and expensive things, he would need to cultivate only a few rods of ground, and that it would be cheaper to spade up that than to use oxen to plough it, and to select a fresh spot from time to time than to manure the old, and he could do all his necessary farm work as it were with his left hand at odd hours in the summer; and thus he would not be tied to an ox, or horse, or cow, or pig, as at present. I desire to speak impartially on this point, and as one not interested in the success or failure of the present economical and social arrangements. I was more independent than any farmer in Concord, for I was not anchored to a house or farm, but could follow the bent of my genius, which is a very crooked one, every moment. Beside being better off than they already, if my house had been burned or my

2. Author of *Rural Oeconomy, or Essays on the Practical Parts of Husbandry* (1773).

crops had failed, I should have been nearly as well off as before. I am wont to think that men are not so much the keepers of herds as herds are the keepers of men, the former are so much the freer. Men and oxen exchange work; but if we consider necessary work only, the oxen will be seen to have greatly the advantage, their farm is so much the larger. Man does some of his part of the exchange work in his six weeks of haying, and it is no boy's play. Certainly no nation that lived simply in all respects, that is, no nation of philosophers, would commit so great a blunder as to use the labor of animals. True, there never was and is not likely soon to be a nation of philosophers, nor am I certain it is desirable that there should be. However, *I* should never have broken a horse or bull and taken him to board for any work he might do for me, for fear I should become a horse-man or a herds-man merely; and if society seems to be the gainer by so doing, are we certain that what is one man's gain is not another's loss, and that the stable-boy has equal cause with his master to be satisfied? Granted that some public works would not have been constructed without this aid, and let man share the glory of such with the ox and horse; does is follow that he could not have accomplished works yet more worthy of himself in that case? When men begin to do, not merely unnecessary or artistic, but luxurious and idle work, with their assistance, it is inevitable that a few do all the exchange work with the oxen, or, in other words, become the slaves of the strongest. Man thus not only works for the animal within him, but, for a symbol of this, he works for the animal without him. Though we have many substantial houses of brick or stone, the prosperity of the farmer is still measured by the degree to which the barn overshadows the house. This town is said to have the largest houses for oxen cows and horses hereabouts, and it is not behindhand in its public buildings; but there are very few halls for free worship or free speech in this county. It should not be by their architecture, but why not even by their power of abstract thought, that nations should seek to commemorate themselves? How much more admirable the Bhagvat-Geeta[3] than all the ruins of the East! Towers and temples are the luxury of princes. A simple and independent mind does not toil at the bidding of any prince. Genius is not a retainer to any emperor, nor is its material silver, or gold, or marble, except to a trifling extent. To what end, pray, is so much stone hammered? In Arcadia,[4] when I was there, I did not see any hammering stone. Nations are possessed with an insane ambition to perpetuate the memory of themselves by the amount of hammered stone they leave. What if equal pains were taken to smooth and polish their manners? One piece of good sense would be more memorable than a monument as high as the moon. I love better to see stones in place. The grandeur of Thebes[5] was a vulgar grandeur. More sensible is a rod of stone wall that bounds an honest man's field than a hundred-gated Thebes that has wandered farther from the true end of life. The religion and civilization which are barbaric and heathenish build splendid temples; but what you might call Christianity does not. Most of the stone a nation hammers goes toward its tomb only. It buries itself alive. As for the Pyramids, there is nothing to wonder at in them so much as the fact that so many men could be found degraded enough to spend their lives constructing a tomb for some ambitious booby, whom it would have been

---

3. A sacred Hindu text.
4. Place epitomizing rustic simplicity and contentment, from the region in Greece celebrated by the bu-

colic poets.
5. Ancient city in Upper Egypt.

wiser and manlier to have drowned in the Nile, and then given his body to the dogs. I might possibly invent some excuse for them and him, but I have no time for it. As for the religion and love of art of the builders, it is much the same all the world over, whether the building be an Egyptian temple or the United States Bank. It costs more than it comes to. The mainspring is vanity, assisted by the love of garlic and bread and butter. Mr. Balcom, a promising young architect, designs it on the back of his Vitruvius,[6] with hard pencil and ruler, and the job is let out to Dobson & Sons, stonecutters. When the thirty centuries begin to look down on it, mankind begin to look up at it. As for your high towers and monuments, there was a crazy fellow once in this town who undertook to dig through to China, and he got so far that, as he said, he heard the Chinese pots and kettles rattle; but I think that I shall not go out of my way to admire the hole which he made. Many are concerned about the monuments of the West and the East,—to know who built them. For my part, I should like to know who in those days did not build them,—who were above such trifling. But to proceed with my statistics.

By surveying, carpentry, and day-labor of various other kinds in the village in the mean while, for I have as many trades as fingers, I had earned $13 34. The expense of food for eight months, namely, from July 4th to March 1st, the time when these estimates were made, though I lived there more than two years,—not counting potatoes, a little green corn, and some peas, which I had raised, nor considering the value of what was on hand at the last date, was

| | | |
|---|---|---|
| Rice, | 01 73½ | |
| Molasses, | 1 73 | Cheapest form of the saccharine. |
| Rye meal, | 1 04¾ | |
| Indian meal, | 0 99¾ | Cheaper than rye. |
| Pork, | 0 22 | |
| | | |
| Flour, | 0 88  } | Costs more than |
| | | Indian meal, |
| | | both money |
| Sugar, | 0 80 | and trouble. |
| Lard, | 0 65 | |
| Apples, | 0 25 | |
| Dried apple, | 0 22 | |
| Sweet potatoes, | 0 10 | |
| One pumpkin, | 0 6 | |
| One watermelon, | 0 2 | |
| Salt, | 0 3 | |

Yes, I did eat $8 74, all told; but I should not thus unblushingly publish my guilt, if I did not know that most of my readers were equally guilty with myself, and that their deeds would look no better in print. The next year I sometimes caught a mess of fish for my dinner, and once I went so far as to slaughter a woodchuck which ravaged my bean-field,—effect his transmigration, as a Tartar[7] would say,—and devour him, partly for experiment's sake; but though it

6. Vitruvius Pollio, Roman architect during the reigns of Julius Caesar and Augustus, author of De Architectura.

7. An inhabitant of Tartary, a broad area of Central Asia overrun by the Tatars (Tartars) in the 12th century.

afforded me a momentary enjoyment, notwithstanding a musky flavor, I saw that the longest use would not make that a good practice, however it might seem to have your woodchucks ready dressed by the village butcher.

Clothing and some incidental expenses within the same dates, though little can be inferred from this item, amounted to

$$\$8 \ 40\tfrac{3}{4}$$

Oil and some household utensils,   2  00

So that all the pecuniary outgoes, excepting for washing and mending, which for the most part were done out of the house, and their bills have not yet been received,—and these are all and more than all the ways by which money necessarily goes out in this part of the world,—were

| | |
|---|---|
| House, | $28 12½ |
| Farm one year, | 14 72½ |
| Food eight months, | 8 74 |
| Clothing, &c., eight months, | 8 40¾ |
| Oil, &c., eight months, | 2 00 |
| In all, | $61 99¾ |

I address myself now to those of my readers who have a living to get. And to meet this I have for farm produce sold

| | |
|---|---|
| | $23 44 |
| Earned by day-labor, | 13 34 |
| In all, | $36 78, |

which subtracted from the sum of the outgoes leaves a balance of $25 21¾ on the one side,—this being very nearly the means with which I started, and the measure of expenses to be incurred,—and on the other, beside the leisure and independence and health thus secured, a comfortable house for me as long as I choose to occupy it.

These statistics, however accidental and therefore uninstructive they may appear, as they have a certain completeness, have a certain value also. Nothing was given me of which I have not rendered some account. It appears from the above estimate, that my food alone cost me in money about twenty-seven cents a week. It was, for nearly two years after this, rye and Indian meal without yeast, potatoes, rice, a very little salt pork, molasses, and salt, and my drink water. It was fit that I should live on rice, mainly, who loved so well the philosophy of India. To meet the objections of some inveterate cavillers, I may as well state, that if I dined out occasionally, as I always had done, and I trust shall have opportunities to do again, it was frequently to the detriment of my domestic arrangements. But the dining out, being, as I have stated, a constant element, does not in the least affect a comparative statement like this.

I learned from my two years' experience that it would cost incredibly little trouble to obtain one's necessary food, even in this latitude; that a man may use as simple a diet as the animals, and yet retain health and strength. I have made a satisfactory dinner, satisfactory on several accounts, simply off a dish of purslane (*Portulaca oleracea*) which I gathered in my cornfield, boiled and salted. I give the Latin on account of the savoriness of the trivial name. And pray what more can a reasonable man desire, in peaceful times, in ordinary noons, than a sufficient number of ears of green sweet-corn boiled, with the addition of salt? Even the little variety which I used was a yielding to the demands of appetite, and not of health. Yet men have come to such a pass that they frequently starve, not for want of necessaries, but for want of luxuries; and I know a good woman who thinks that her son lost his life because he took to drinking water only.

The reader will perceive that I am treating the subject rather from an economic than a dietetic point of view, and he will not venture to put my abstemiousness to the test unless he has a well-stocked larder.

Bread I at first made of pure Indian meal and salt, genuine hoe-cakes, which I baked before my fire out of doors on a shingle or the end of a stick of timber sawed off in building my house; but it was wont to get smoked and to have a piny flavor. I tried flour also; but have at last found a mixture of rye and Indian meal most convenient and agreeable. In cold weather it was no little amusement to bake several small loaves of this in succession, tending and turning them as carefully as an Egyptian his hatching eggs.[8] They were a real cereal fruit which I ripened, and they had to my senses a fragrance like that of other noble fruits, which I kept in as long as possible by wrapping them in cloths. I made a study of the ancient and indispensable art of bread-making, consulting such authorities as offered, going back to the primitive days and first invention of the unleavened kind, when from the wildness of nuts and meats men first reached the mildness and refinement of this diet, and travelling gradually down in my studies through that accidental souring of the dough which, it is supposed, taught the leavening process, and through the various fermentations thereafter, till I came to "good, sweet, wholesome bread," the staff of life. Leaven, which some deem the soul of bread, the *spiritus* which fills its cellular tissue, which is religiously preserved like the vestal fire,—some precious bottle-full, I suppose, first brought over in the Mayflower, did the business for America, and its influence is still rising, swelling, spreading, in cerealian billows over the land,—this seed I regularly and faithfully procured from the village, till at length one morning I forgot the rules, and scalded my yeast; by which accident I discovered that even this was not indispensable,— for my discoveries were not by the synthetic but analytic process,—and I have gladly omitted it since, though most housewives earnestly assured me that safe and wholesome bread without yeast might not be, and elderly people prophesied a speedy decay of the vital forces. Yet I find it not to be an essential ingredient, and after going without it for a year am still in the land of the living; and I am glad to escape the trivialness of carrying a bottle-full in my pocket, which would sometimes pop and discharge its contents to my discomfiture. It is simpler and more respectable to omit it. Man is an animal who more than any other can adapt himself to all climates and circumstances. Neither did I put any sal soda, or other acid or alkali, into my bread. It would seem that I made it according to the recipe which Marcus Porcius Cato gave about two centuries before Christ. "Panem depsticium sic facito. Manus mortariumque bene lavato. Farinam in mortarium indito, aquæ paulatim addito, subigitoque pulchre. Ubi bene subegeris, defingito, coquitoque sub testu."[9]

---

8. Egyptians had devised incubators.          9. *De agri cultura*, 74.

Which I take to mean—"Make kneaded bread thus. Wash your hands and trough well. Put the meal into the trough, add water gradually, and knead it thoroughly. When you have kneaded it well, mould it, and bake it under a cover," that is, in a baking-kettle. Not a word about leaven. But I did not always use this staff of life. At one time, owing to the emptiness of my purse, I saw none of it for more than a month.

Every New Englander might easily raise all his own breadstuffs in this land of rye and Indian corn, and not depend on distant and fluctuating markets for them. Yet so far are we from simplicity and independence that, in Concord, fresh and sweet meal is rarely sold in the shops, and hominy and corn in a still coarser form are hardly used by any. For the most part the farmer gives to his cattle and hogs the grain of his own producing, and buys flour, which is at least no more wholesome, at a greater cost, at the store. I saw that I could easily raise my bushel or two of rye and Indian corn, for the former will grow on the poorest land, and the latter does not require the best, and grind them in a hand-mill, and so do without rice and pork; and if I must have some concentrated sweet, I found by experiment that I could make a very good molasses either of pumpkins or beets, and I knew that I needed only to set out a few maples to obtain it more easily still, and while these were growing I could use various substitutes beside those which I have named, "For," as the Forefathers sang,—

> "we can make liquor to sweeten our lips
> Of pumpkins and parsnips and walnut-tree chips."[1]

Finally, as for salt, that grossest of groceries, to obtain this might be a fit occasion for a visit to the seashore, or, if I did without it altogether, I should probably drink the less water. I do not learn that the Indians ever troubled themselves to go after it.

Thus I could avoid all trade and barter, so far as my food was concerned, and having a shelter already, it would only remain to get clothing and fuel. The pantaloons which I now wear were woven in a farmer's family,—thank Heaven there is so much virtue still in man; for I think the fall from the farmer to the operative as great and memorable as that from the man to the farmer;— and in a new country fuel is an encumbrance. As for a habitat, if I were not permitted still to squat, I might purchase one acre at the same price for which the land I cultivated was sold—namely, eight dollars and eight cents. But as it was, I considered that I enhanced the value of the land by squatting on it.

There is a certain class of unbelievers who sometimes ask me such questions as, if I think that I can live on vegetable food alone; and to strike at the root of the matter at once,—for the root is faith,—I am accustomed to answer such, that I can live on board nails. If they cannot understand that, they cannot understand much that I have to say. For my part, I am glad to hear of experiments of this kind being tried; as that a young man tried for a fortnight to live on hard raw corn on the ear, using his teeth for all mortar. The squirrel tribe tried the same and succeeded. The human race is interested in these experiments, though a few old women who are incapacitated for them, or who own their thirds in mills, may be alarmed.

---

1. From John Warner Barber's *Historical Collections* (1839).

My furniture, part of which I made myself, and the rest cost me nothing of which I have not rendered an account, consisted of a bed, a table, a desk, three chairs, a looking-glass three inches in diameter, a pair of tongs and andirons, a kettle, a skillet, and a frying-pan, a dipper, a wash-bowl, two knives and forks, three plates, one cup, one spoon, a jug for oil, a jug for molasses, and a japanned[2] lamp. None is so poor that he need sit on a pumpkin. That is shiftlessness. There is a plenty of such chairs as I like best in the village garrets to be had for taking them away. Furniture! Thank God, I can sit and I can stand without the aid of a furniture warehouse. What man but a philosopher would not be ashamed to see his furniture packed in a cart and going up country exposed to the light of heaven and the eyes of men, a beggarly account of empty boxes? That is Spaulding's furniture.[3] I could never tell from inspecting such a load whether it belonged to a so called rich man or a poor one; the owner always seemed poverty-stricken. Indeed, the more you have of such things the poorer you are. Each load looks as if it contained the contents of a dozen shanties; and if one shanty is poor, this is a dozen times as poor. Pray, for what do we *move* ever but to get rid of our furniture, our *exuviæ;*[4] at last to go from this world to another newly furnished, and leave this to be burned? It is the same as if all these traps were buckled to a man's belt, and he could not move over the rough country where our lines are cast without dragging them,—dragging his trap. He was a lucky fox that left his tail in the trap. The muskrat will gnaw his third leg off to be free. No wonder man has lost his elasticity. How often he is at a dead set! "Sir, if I may be so bold, what do you mean by a dead set?" If you are a seer, whenever you meet a man you will see all that he owns, ay, and much that he pretends to disown, behind him, even to his kitchen furniture and all the trumpery which he saves and will not burn, and he will appear to be harnessed to it and making what headway he can. I think that the man is at a dead set who has got through a knot hole or gateway where his sledge load of furniture cannot follow him. I cannot but feel compassion when I hear some trig, compact-looking man, seemingly free, all girded and ready, speak of his "furniture," as whether it is insured or not. "But what shall I do with my furniture?" My gay butterfly is entangled in a spider's web then. Even those who seem for a long while not to have any, if you inquire more narrowly you will find have some stored in somebody's barn. I look upon England to-day as an old gentleman who is travelling with a great deal of baggage, trumpery which has accumulated from long housekeeping, which he has not the courage to burn; great trunk, little trunk, bandbox and bundle. Throw away the first three at least. It would surpass the powers of a well man nowadays to take up his bed and walk, and I should certainly advise a sick one to lay down his bed and run. When I have met an immigrant tottering under a bundle which contained his all,—looking like an enormous wen which had grown out of the nape of his neck,—I have pitied him, not because that was his all, but because he had all *that* to carry. If I have got to drag my trap, I will take care that it be a light one and do not nip me in a vital part. But perchance it would be wisest never to put one's paw into it.

I would observe, by the way, that it costs me nothing for curtains, for I have no gazers to shut out but the sun and moon, and I am willing that they should look in. The moon will not sour milk nor taint meat of mine, nor will the sun

2. Lacquered with decorative scenes in the Japanese manner.

3. Unidentified.

4. Discarded objects (Latin).

injure my furniture or fade my carpet, and if he is sometimes too warm a friend, I find it still better economy to retreat behind some curtain which nature has provided, than to add a single item to the details of housekeeping. A lady once offered me a mat, but as I had no room to spare within the house, nor time to spare within or without to shake it, I declined it, preferring to wipe my feet on the sod before my door. It is best to avoid the beginnings of evil.

Not long since I was present at the auction of a deacon's effects, for his life had not been ineffectual:—

> "The evil that men do lives after them."[5]

As usual, a great proportion was trumpery which had begun to accumulate in his father's day. Among the rest was a dried tapeworm. And now, after lying half a century in his garret and other dust holes, these things were not burned; instead of a *bonfire*, or purifying destruction of them, there was an *auction*, or increasing of them.[6] The neighbors eagerly collected to view them, bought them all, and carefully transported them to their garrets and dust holes, to lie there till their estates are settled, when they will start again. When a man dies he kicks the dust.

The customs of some savage nations might, perchance, be profitably imitated by us, for they at least go through the semblance of casting their slough annually; they have the idea of the thing, whether they have the reality or not. Would it not be well if we were to celebrate such a "busk," or "feast of first fruits," as Bartram[7] describes to have been the custom of the Mucclasse Indians? "When a town celebrates the busk," says he, "having previously provided themselves with new clothes, new pots, pans, and other household utensils and furniture, they collect all their worn out clothes and other despicable things, sweep and cleanse their houses, squares, and the whole town, of their filth, which with all the remaining grain and other old provisions they cast together into one common heap, and consume it with fire. After having taken medicine, and fasted for three days, all the fire in the town is extinguished. During this fast they abstain from the gratification of every appetite and passion whatever. A general amnesty is proclaimed; all malefactors may return to their town.—"

"On the fourth morning, the high priest, by rubbing dry wood together, produces new fire in the public square, from whence every habitation in the town is supplied with the new and pure flame."

They then feast on the new corn and fruits and dance and sing for three days, "and the four following days they receive visits and rejoice with their friends from neighboring towns who have in like manner purified and prepared themselves."

The Mexicans also practised a similar purification at the end of every fifty-two years, in the belief that it was time for the world to come to an end.

I have scarcely heard of a truer sacrament, that is, as the dictionary defines it, "outward and visible sign of an inward and spiritual grace," than this, and I have no doubt that they were originally inspired directly from Heaven to do thus, though they have no biblical record of the revelation.

---

5. Tag from Antony's speech to the citizens, in Shakespeare's *Julius Caesar* 3.3.
6. Thoreau puns on the Latin root of *auction*, which means "to increase."
7. William Bartram, *Travels through North and South Carolina* (1791).

For more than five years I maintained myself thus solely by the labor of my hands, and I found, that by working about six weeks in a year, I could meet all the expenses of living. The whole of my winters, as well as most of my summers, I had free and clear for study. I have thoroughly tried school-keeping, and found that my expenses were in proportion, or rather out of proportion, to my income, for I was obliged to dress and train, not to say think and believe, accordingly, and I lost my time into the bargain. As I did not teach for the good of my fellow-men, but simply for a livelihood, this was a failure. I have tried trade; but I found that it would take ten years to get under way in that, and that then I should probably be on my way to the devil. I was actually afraid that I might by that time be doing what is called a good business. When formerly I was looking about to see what I could do for a living, some sad experience in conforming to the wishes of friends being fresh in my mind to tax my ingenuity, I thought often and seriously of picking huckleberries; that surely I could do, and its small profits might suffice,—for my greatest skill has been to want but little,—so little capital it required, so little distraction from my wonted moods, I foolishly thought. While my acquaintances went unhesitatingly into trade or the professions, I contemplated this occupation as most like theirs; ranging the hills all summer to pick the berries which came in my way, and thereafter carelessly dispose of them; so, to keep the flocks of Admetus.[8] I also dreamed that I might gather the wild herbs, or carry evergreens to such villagers as loved to be reminded of the woods, even to the city, by hay-cart loads. But I have since learned that trade curses every thing it handles; and though you trade in messages from heaven, the whole curse of trade attaches to the business.

As I preferred some things to others, and especially valued my freedom, as I could fare hard and yet succeed well, I did not wish to spend my time in earning rich carpets or other fine furniture, or delicate cookery, or a house in the Grecian or the Gothic style just yet. If there are any to whom it is no interruption to acquire these things, and who know how to use them when acquired, I relinquish to them the pursuit. Some are "industrious," and appear to love labor for its own sake, or perhaps because it keeps them out of worse mischief; to such I have at present nothing to say. Those who would not know what to do with more leisure than they now enjoy, I might advise to work twice as hard as they do,—work till they pay for themselves, and get their free papers. For myself I found that the occupation of a day-laborer was the most independent of any, especially as it required only thirty or forty days in a year to support one. The laborer's day ends with the going down of the sun, and he is then free to devote himself to his chosen pursuit, independent of his labor; but his employer, who speculates from month to month, has no respite from one end of the year to the other.

In short, I am convinced, both by faith and experience, that to maintain one's self on this earth is not a hardship but a pastime, if we will live simply and wisely; as the pursuits of the simpler nations are still the sports of the more artificial. It is not necessary that a man should earn his living by the sweat of his brow, unless he sweats easier than I do.

One young man of my acquaintance, who has inherited some acres, told me that he thought he should live as I did, *if he had the means.* I would not

---

8. Apollo, Greek god of poetry, tended the flocks of Admetus while banished from Olympus.

have any one adopt *my* mode of living on any account; for, beside that before he has fairly learned it I may have found out another for myself, I desire that there may be as many different persons in the world as possible; but I would have each one be very careful to find out and pursue *his own* way, and not his father's or his mother's or his neighbor's instead. The youth may build or plant or sail, only let him not be hindered from doing that which he tells me he would like to do. It is by a mathematical point only that we are wise, as the sailor or the fugitive slave keeps the polestar in his eye; but that is sufficient guidance for all our life. We may not arrive at our port within a calculable period, but we would preserve the true course.

Undoubtedly, in this case, what is true for one is truer still for a thousand, as a large house is not more expensive than a small one in proportion to its size, since one roof may cover, one cellar underlie, and one wall separate several apartments. But for my part, I preferred the solitary dwelling. Moreover, it will commonly be cheaper to build the whole yourself than to convince another of the advantage of the common wall; and when you have done this, the common partition, to be much cheaper, must be a thin one, and that other may prove a bad neighbor, and also not keep his side in repair. The only coöperation which is commonly possible is exceedingly partial and superficial; and what little true coöperation there is, is as if it were not, being a harmony inaudible to men. If a man has faith he will coöperate with equal faith every where; if he has not faith, he will continue to live like the rest of the world, whatever company he is joined to. To coöperate, in the highest as well as the lowest sense, means *to get our living together*. I heard it proposed lately that two young men should travel together over the world, the one without money, earning his means as he went, before the mast and behind the plough, the other carrying a bill of exchange in his pocket. It was easy to see that they could not long be companions or coöperate, since one would not *operate* at all. They would part at the first interesting crisis in their adventures. Above all, as I have implied, the man who goes alone can start today; but he who travels with another must wait till that other is ready, and it may be a long time before they get off.

But all this is very selfish, I have heard some of my townsmen say. I confess that I have hitherto indulged very little in philanthropic enterprises. I have made some sacrifices to a sense of duty, and among others have sacrificed this pleasure also. There are those who have used all their arts to persuade me to undertake the support of some poor family in the town; and if I had nothing to do,—for the devil finds employment for the idle,—I might try my hand at some such pastime as that. However, when I have thought to indulge myself in this respect, and lay their Heaven under an obligation by maintaining certain poor persons in all respects as comfortably as I maintain myself, and have even ventured so far as to make them the offer, they have one and all unhesitatingly preferred to remain poor. While my townsmen and women are devoted in so many ways to the good of their fellows, I trust that one at least may be spared to other and less humane pursuits. You must have a genius for charity as well as for any thing else. As for Doing-good, that is one of the professions which are full. Moreover, I have tried it fairly, and, strange as it may seem, am satisfied that it does not agree with my constitution. Probably I should not consciously and deliberately forsake my particular calling to do the good which society demands of me, to save the universe from annihilation; and I believe that a like but infinitely greater steadfastness elsewhere is all that now preserves it. But I would not stand between any man and his genius; and to him who does this work, which I decline, with his whole heart and soul and life, I would say, Persevere, even if the world call it doing evil, as it is most likely they will.

I am far from supposing that my case is a peculiar one; no doubt many of my readers would make a similar defence. At doing something,—I will not engage that my neighbors shall pronounce it good,—I do not hesitate to say that I should be a capital fellow to hire; but what that is, it is for my employer to find out. What *good* I do, in the common sense of that word, must be aside from my main path, and for the most part wholly unintended. Men say, practically, Begin where you are and such as you are, without aiming mainly to become of more worth, and with kindness aforethought go about doing good. If I were to preach at all in this strain, I should say rather, Set about being good. As if the sun should stop when he had kindled his fires up to the splendor of a moon or a star of the sixth magnitude, and go about like a Robin Goodfellow,[9] peeping in at every cottage window, inspiring lunatics, and tainting meats, and making darkness visible, instead of steadily increasing his genial heat and beneficence till he is of such brightness that no mortal can look him in the face, and then, and in the mean while too, going about the world in his own orbit, doing it good, or rather, as a truer philosophy has discovered, the world going about him getting good. When Phaeton,[1] wishing to prove his heavenly birth by his beneficence, had the sun's chariot but one day, and drove out of the beaten track, he burned several blocks of houses in the lower streets of heaven, and scorched the surface of the earth, and dried up every spring, and made the great desert of Sahara, till at length Jupiter hurled him headlong to the earth with a thunderbolt, and the sun, through grief at his death, did not shine for a year.

There is no odor so bad as that which arises from goodness tainted. It is human, it is divine, carrion. If I knew for a certainty that a man was coming to my house with the conscious design of doing me good, I should run for my life, as from that dry and parching wind of the African deserts called the simoom, which fills the mouth and nose and ears and eyes with dust till you are suffocated, for fear that I should get some of his good done to me,—some of its virus mingled with my blood. No,—in this case I would rather suffer evil the natural way. A man is not a good *man* to me because he will feed me if I should be starving, or warm me if I should be freezing, or pull me out of a ditch if I should ever fall into one. I can find you a Newfoundland dog that will do as much. Philanthropy is not love for one's fellow-man in the broadest sense. Howard[2] was no doubt an exceedingly kind and worthy man in his way, and has his reward; but, comparatively speaking, what are a hundred Howards to *us*, if their philanthropy do not help *us* in our best estate, when we are most worthy to be helped? I never heard of a philanthropic meeting in which it was sincerely proposed to do any good to me, or the like of me.

The Jesuits were quite balked by those Indians who, being burned at the

9. Mischievous fairy, known as Puck in Shakespeare's *A Midsummer Night's Dream*.
1. In Greek mythology, the son of Helios. He attempted to drive his father's chariot, the sun, with di-

sastrous consequences.
2. John Howard (1726?–1790), English prison reformer.

stake, suggested new modes of torture to their tormentors.[3] Being superior to physical suffering, it sometimes chanced that they were superior to any consolation which the missionaries could offer; and the law to do as you would be done by fell with less persuasiveness on the ears of those, who, for their part, did not care how they were done by, who loved their enemies after a new fashion, and came very near freely forgiving them all they did.

Be sure that you give the poor the aid they most need, though it be your example which leaves them far behind. If you give money, spend yourself with it, and do not merely abandon it to them. We make curious mistakes sometimes. Often the poor man is not so cold and hungry as he is dirty and ragged and gross. It is partly his taste, and not merely his misfortune. If you give him money, he will perhaps buy more rags with it. I was wont to pity the clumsy Irish laborers who cut ice on the pond, in such mean and ragged clothes, while I shivered in my more tidy and somewhat more fashionable garments, till, one bitter cold day, one who had slipped into the water came to my house to warm him, and I saw him strip off three pairs of pants and two pairs of stockings ere he got down to the skin, though they were dirty and ragged enough, it is true, and that he could afford to refuse the *extra* garments which I offered him, he had so many *intra* ones. This ducking was the very thing he needed. Then I began to pity myself, and I saw that it would be a greater charity to bestow on me a flannel shirt than a whole slop-shop on him. There are a thousand hacking at the branches of evil to one who is striking at the root, and it may be that he who bestows the largest amount of time and money on the needy is doing the most by his mode of life to produce that misery which he strives in vain to relieve. It is the pious slave-breeder devoting the proceeds of every tenth slave to buy a Sunday's liberty for the rest. Some show their kindness to the poor by employing them in their kitchens. Would they not be kinder if they employed themselves there? You boast of spending a tenth part of your income in charity; may be you should spend the nine tenths so, and done with it. Society recovers only a tenth part of the property then. Is this owing to the generosity of him in whose possession it is found, or to the remissness of the officers of justice?

Philanthropy is almost the only virtue which is sufficiently appreciated by mankind. Nay, it is greatly overrated; and it is our selfishness which overrates it. A robust poor man, one sunny day here in Concord, praised a fellow-townsman to me, because, as he said, he was kind to the poor; meaning himself. The kind uncles and aunts of the race are more esteemed than its true spiritual fathers and mothers. I once heard a reverend lecturer on England, a man of learning and intelligence, after enumerating her scientific, literary, and political worthies, Shakspeare, Bacon, Cromwell, Milton, Newton, and others, speak next of her Christian heroes, whom, as if his profession required it of him, he elevated to a place far above all the rest, as the greatest of the great. They were Penn, Howard, and Mrs. Fry.[4] Every one must feel the falsehood and cant of this. The last were not England's best men and women; only, perhaps, her best philanthropists.

I would not subtract any thing from the praise that is due to philanthropy,

3. Thoreau's source is unknown, but Harding cites comparable accounts in *The Jesuit Relations and Allied Documents* (1898), vol. 17.
4. Elizabeth Fry (1780–1845), English Quaker and prison reformer. William Penn (1644–1718), Quaker leader and proprietor of Pennsylvania. John Howard (see n. 2, p. 826).

but merely demand justice for all who by their lives and works are a blessing to mankind. I do not value chiefly a man's uprightness and benevolence, which are, as it were, his stem and leaves. Those plants of whose greenness withered we make herb tea for the sick, serve but a humble use, and are most employed by quacks. I want the flower and fruit of a man; that some fragrance be wafted over from him to me, and some ripeness flavor our intercourse. His goodness must not be a partial and transitory act, but a constant superfluity, which costs him nothing and of which he is unconscious. This is a charity that hides a multitude of sins. The philanthropist too often surrounds mankind with the remembrance of his own cast-off griefs as an atmosphere, and calls it sympathy. We should impart our courage, and not our despair, our health and ease, and not our disease, and take care that this does not spread by contagion. From what southern plains comes up the voice of wailing? Under what latitudes reside the heathen to whom we would send light? Who is that intemperate and brutal man whom we would redeem? If any thing ail a man, so that he does not perform his functions, if he have a pain in his bowels even,— for that is the seat of sympathy,—he forthwith sets about reforming—the world. Being a microcosm himself, he discovers, and it is a true discovery, and he is the man to make it,—that the world has been eating green apples; to his eyes, in fact, the globe itself is a great green apple, which there is danger awful to think of that the children of men will nibble before it is ripe; and straightway his drastic philanthropy seeks out the Esquimaux and the Patagonian, and embraces the populous Indian and Chinese villages; and thus, by a few years of philanthropic activity, the powers in the mean while using him for their own ends, no doubt, he cures himself of his dyspepsia, the globe acquires a faint blush on one or both of its cheeks, as if it were beginning to be ripe, and life loses its crudity and is once more sweet and wholesome to live. I never dreamed of any enormity greater than I have committed. I never knew, and never shall know, a worse man than myself.

I believe that what so saddens the reformer is not his sympathy with his fellows in distress, but, though he be the holiest son of God, is his private ail. Let this be righted, let the spring come to him, the morning rise over his couch, and he will forsake his generous companions without apology. My excuse for not lecturing against the use of tobacco is, that I never chewed it; that is a penalty which reformed tobacco-chewers have to pay; though there are things enough I have chewed, which I could lecture against. If you should ever be betrayed into any of these philanthropies, do not let your left hand know what your right hand does, for it is not worth knowing. Rescue the drowning and tie your shoe-strings. Take your time, and set about some free labor.

Our manners have been corrupted by communication with the saints. Our hymn-books resound with a melodious cursing of God and enduring him forever. One would say that even the prophets and redeemers had rather consoled the fears than confirmed the hopes of man. There is nowhere recorded a simple and irrepressible satisfaction with the gift of life, any memorable praise of God. All health and success does me good, however far off and withdrawn it may appear; all disease and failure helps to make me sad and does me evil, however much sympathy it may have with me or I with it. If, then, we would indeed restore mankind by truly Indian, botanic, magnetic, or natural means, let us first be as simple and well as Nature ourselves, dispel the clouds which hang over our own brows, and take up a little life into our pores. Do not stay to be an overseer of the poor, but endeavor to become one of the worthies of the world.

I read in the Gulistan, or Flower Garden, of Sheik Sadi of Shiraz, that "They asked a wise man, saying; Of the many celebrated trees which the Most High God has created lofty and umbrageous, they call none azad, or free, excepting the cypress, which bears no fruit; what mystery is there in this? He replied; Each has its appropriate produce, and appointed season, during the continuance of which it is fresh and blooming, and during their absence dry and withered; to neither of which states is the cypress exposed, being always flourishing; and of this nature are the azads, or religious independents.—Fix not thy heart on that which is transitory; for the Dijlah, or Tigris, will continue to flow through Bagdad after the race of caliphs is extinct: if thy hand has plenty, be liberal as the date tree; but if it affords nothing to give away, be an azad, or free man, like the cypress."[5]

## Complemental Verses[6]

### THE PRETENSIONS OF POVERTY

"Thou dost presume too much, poor needy wretch,
To claim a station in the firmament,
Because thy humble cottage, or thy tub,
Nurses some lazy or pedantic virtue
In the cheap sunshine or by shady springs,
With roots and pot-herbs; where thy right hand,
Tearing those humane passions from the mind,
Upon whose stocks fair blooming virtues flourish,
Degradeth nature, and benumbeth sense,
And, Gorgon-like, turns active men to stone.[7]
We not require the dull society
Of your necessitated temperance,
Or that unnatural stupidity
That knows nor joy nor sorrow; nor your forc'd
Falsely exalted passive fortitude
Above the active. This low abject brood,
That fix their seats in mediocrity,
Become your servile minds; but we advance
Such virtues only as admit excess,
Brave, bounteous acts, regal magnificence,
All-seeing prudence, magnanimity
That knows no bound, and that heroic virtue
For which antiquity hath left no name,
But patterns only, such as Hercules,
Achilles, Theseus. Back to thy loath'd cell;
And when thou seest the new enlightened sphere,
Study to know but what those worthies were."

—T. CAREW

5. Muslih-ud-Din (Saadi) (1184?–1291), *The Gulistan or Rose Garden*.
6. From *Coelum Britannicum* by the English Cavalier poet Thomas Carew (1595?–1645?), offered ironically as a retort to "Economy."
7. In Greek mythology the Gorgons were three sisters who, with snakes for hair and eyes, turned any beholder into stone.

## Where I Lived, and What I Lived For

At a certain season of our life we are accustomed to consider every spot as the possible site of a house. I have thus surveyed the country on every side within a dozen miles of where I live. In imagination I have bought all the farms in succession, for all were to be bought and I knew their price. I walked over each farmer's premises, tasted his wild apples, discoursed on husbandry with him, took his farm at his price, at any price, mortgaging it to him in my mind; even put a higher price on it,—took every thing but a deed of it,—took his word for his deed, for I dearly love to talk,—cultivated it, and him too to some extent, I trust, and withdrew when I had enjoyed it long enough, leaving him to carry it on. This experience entitled me to be regarded as a sort of real-estate broker by my friends. Wherever I sat, there I might live, and the landscape radiated from me accordingly. What is a house but a *sedes*, a seat?— better if a country seat. I discovered many a site for a house not likely to be soon improved, which some might have thought too far from the village, but to my eyes the village was too far from it. Well, there I might live, I said; and there I did live, for an hour, a summer and a winter life; saw how I could let the years run off, buffet the winter through, and see the spring come in. The future inhabitants of this region, wherever they may place their houses, may be sure that they have been anticipated. An afternoon sufficed to lay out the land into orchard woodlot and pasture, and to decide what fine oaks or pines should be left to stand before the door, and whence each blasted tree could be seen to the best advantage; and then I let it lie, fallow perchance, for a man is rich in proportion to the number of things which he can afford to let alone.

My imagination carried me so far that I even had the refusal of several farms,—the refusal was all I wanted,—but I never got my fingers burned by actual possession. The nearest that I came to actual possession was when I bought the Hollowell Place, and had begun to sort my seeds, and collected materials with which to make a wheelbarrow to carry it on or off with; but before the owner gave me a deed of it, his wife—every man has such a wife— changed her mind and wished to keep it, and he offered me ten dollars to release him. Now, to speak the truth, I had but ten cents in the world, and it surpassed my arithmetic to tell, if I was that man who had ten cents, or who had a farm, or ten dollars, or all together. However, I let him keep the ten dollars and the farm too, for I had carried it far enough; or rather, to be generous, I sold him the farm for just what I gave for it, and, as he was not a rich man, made him a present of ten dollars, and still had my ten cents, and seeds, and materials for a wheelbarrow left. I found thus that I had been a rich man without any damage to my poverty. But I retained the landscape, and I have since annually carried off what it yielded without a wheelbarrow. With respect to landscapes,—

> "I am monarch of all I *survey*,
> My right there is none to dispute."[8]

I have frequently seen a poet withdraw, having enjoyed the most valuable part of a farm, while the crusty farmer supposed that he had got a few wild apples only. Why, the owner does not know it for many years when a poet has

---

8. William Cowper's *Verses Supposed to Be Written by Alexander Selkirk*, with the pun italicized. Selkirk was Daniel Defoe's model for Robinson Crusoe.

put his farm in rhyme, the most admirable kind of invisible fence, has fairly impounded it, milked it, skimmed it, and got all the cream, and left the farmer only the skimmed milk.

The real attractions of the Hollowell farm, to me, were; its complete retirement, being about two miles from the village, half a mile from the nearest neighbor, and separated from the highway by a broad field; its bounding on the river, which the owner said protected it by its fogs from frosts in the spring, though that was nothing to me; the gray color and ruinous state of the house and barn, and the dilapidated fences, which put such an interval between me and the last occupant; the hollow and lichen-covered apple trees, gnawed by rabbits, showing what kind of neighbors I should have; but above all, the recollection I had of it from my earliest voyages up the river, when the house was concealed behind a dense grove of red maples, through which I heard the house-dog bark. I was in haste to buy it, before the proprietor finished getting out some rocks, cutting down the hollow apple trees, and grubbing up some young birches which had sprung up in the pasture, or, in short, had made any more of his improvements. To enjoy these advantages I was ready to carry it on; like Atlas,[9] to take the world on my shoulders,—I never heard what compensation he received for that,—and do all those things which had no other motive or excuse but that I might pay for it and be unmolested in my possession of it; for I knew all the while that it would yield the most abundant crop of the kind I wanted if I could only afford to let it alone. But it turned out as I have said.

All that I could say, then, with respect to farming on a large scale, (I have always cultivated a garden,) was, that I had had my seeds ready. Many think that seeds improve with age. I have no doubt that time discriminates between the good and the bad; and when at last I shall plant, I shall be less likely to be disappointed. But I would say to my fellows, once for all, As long as possible live free and uncommitted. It makes but little difference whether you are committed to a farm or the county jail.

Old Cato, whose "De Re Rusticâ" is my "Cultivator," says, and the only translation I have seen makes sheer nonsense of the passage, "When you think of getting a farm, turn it thus in your mind, not to buy greedily; nor spare your pains to look at it, and do not think it enough to go round it once. The oftener you go there the more it will please you, if it is good."[1] I think I shall not buy greedily, but go round and round it as long as I live, and be buried in it first, that it may please me the more at last.

The present was my next experiment of this kind, which I purpose to describe more at length; for convenience, putting the experience of two years into one. As I have said, I do not propose to write an ode to dejection, but to brag as lustily as chanticleer in the morning, standing on his roost, if only to wake my neighbors up.

When first I took up my abode in the woods, that is, began to spend my nights as well as days there, which, by accident, was on Independence Day, or the fourth of July, 1845, my house was not finished for winter, but was merely a defence against the rain, without plastering or chimney, the walls being of rough weather-stained boards, with wide chinks, which made it cool

9. A Titan whom Zeus forced to stand on the earth supporting the heavens on his head and in his hands as punishment for warring against the Olympian gods.
1. *De agri cultura*, 1.1.

at night. The upright white hewn studs and freshly planed door and window casings gave it a clean and airy look, especially in the morning, when its timbers were saturated with dew, so that I fancied that by noon some sweet gum would exude from them. To my imagination it retained throughout the day more or less of this auroral character, reminding me of a certain house on a mountain which I had visited the year before. This was an airy and unplastered cabin, fit to entertain a travelling god, and where a goddess might trail her garments. The winds which passed over my dwelling were such as sweep over the ridges of mountains, bearing the broken strains, or celestial parts only, of terrestrial music. The morning wind forever blows, the poem of creation is uninterrupted; but few are the ears that hear it. Olympus is but the outside of the earth every where.

The only house I had been the owner of before, if I except a boat, was a tent, which I used occasionally when making excursions in the summer, and this is still rolled up in my garret; but the boat, after passing from hand to hand, has gone down the stream of time. With this more substantial shelter about me, I had made some progress toward settling in the world. This frame, so slightly clad, was a sort of crystallization around me, and reacted on the builder. It was suggestive somewhat as a picture in outlines. I did not need to go out doors to take the air, for the atmosphere within had lost none of its freshness. It was not so much within doors as behind a door where I sat, even in the rainiest weather. The Harivansa[2] says, "An abode without birds is like a meat without seasoning." Such was not my abode, for I found myself suddenly neighbor to the birds; not by having imprisoned one, but having caged myself near them. I was not only nearer to some of those which commonly frequent the garden and the orchard, but to those wilder and more thrilling songsters of the forest which never, or rarely, serenade a villager,—the wood-thrush, the veery, the scarlet tanager, the field-sparrow, the whippoorwill, and many others.

I was seated by the shore of a small pond, about a mile and a half south of the village of Concord and somewhat higher than it, in the midst of an extensive wood between that town and Lincoln, and about two miles south of that our only field known to fame, Concord Battle Ground;[3] but I was so low in the woods that the opposite shore, half a mile off, like the rest, covered with wood, was my most distant horizon. For the first week, whenever I looked out on the pond it impressed me like a tarn[4] high up on the side of a mountain, its bottom far above the surface of other lakes, and, as the sun arose, I saw it throwing off its nightly clothing of mist, and here and there, by degrees, its soft ripples or its smooth reflecting surface was revealed, while the mists, like ghosts, were stealthily withdrawing in every direction into the woods, as at the breaking up of some nocturnal conventicle. The very dew seemed to hang upon the trees later into the day than usual, as on the sides of mountains.

This small lake was of most value as a neighbor in the intervals of a gentle rain storm in August, when, both air and water being perfectly still, but the sky overcast, mid-afternoon had all the serenity of evening, and the wood-thrush sang around, and was heard from shore to shore. A lake like this is never smoother than at such a time; and the clear portion of the air above it being shallow and darkened by clouds, the water, full of light and reflections,

2. A Hindu epic poem.                              Revolution, April 19, 1775.
3. The site of battle on the first day of the American        4. Lake.

becomes a lower heaven itself so much the more important. From a hill top near by, where the wood had been recently cut off, there was a pleasing vista southward across the pond, through a wide indentation in the hills which form the shore there, where their opposite sides sloping toward each other suggested a stream flowing out in that direction through a wooded valley, but stream there was none. That way I looked between and over the near green hills to some distant and higher ones in the horizon, tinged with blue. Indeed, by standing on tiptoe I could catch a glimpse of some of the peaks of the still bluer and more distant mountain ranges in the north-west, those true-blue coins from heaven's own mint, and also of some portion of the village. But in other directions, even from this point, I could not see over or beyond the woods which surrounded me. It is well to have some water in your neighborhood, to give buoyancy to and float the earth. One value even of the smallest well is, that when you look into it you see that earth is not continent but insular. This is as important as that it keeps butter cool. When I looked across the pond from this peak toward the Sudbury meadows, which in time of flood I distinguished elevated perhaps by a mirage in their seething valley, like a coin in a basin, all the earth beyond the pond appeared like a thin crust insulated and floated even by this small sheet of intervening water, and I was reminded that this on which I dwelt was but *dry land*.

Though the view from my door was still more contracted, I did not feel crowded or confined in the least. There was pasture enough for my imagination. The low shrub-oak plateau to which the opposite shore arose, stretched away toward the prairies of the West and the steppes of Tartary, affording ample room for all the roving families of men. "There are none happy in the world but beings who enjoy freely a vast horizon,"—said Damodara,[5] when his herds required new and larger pastures.

Both place and time were changed, and I dwelt nearer to those parts of the universe and to those eras in history which had most attracted me. Where I lived was as far off as many a region viewed nightly by astronomers. We are wont to imagine rare and delectable places in some remote and more celestial corner of the system, behind the constellation of Cassiopeia's Chair, far from noise and disturbance. I discovered that my house actually had its site in such a withdrawn, but forever new and unprofaned, part of the universe. If it were worth the while to settle in those parts near to the Pleiades or the Hyades, to Aldebaran or Altair,[6] then I was really there, or at an equal remoteness from the life which I had left behind, dwindled and twinkling with as fine a ray to my nearest neighbor, and to be seen only in moonless nights by him. Such was that part of creation where I had squatted;—

> "There was a shepherd that did live,
> And held his thoughts as high
> As were the mounts whereon his flocks
> Did hourly feed him by."[7]

What should we think of the shepherd's life if his flocks always wandered to higher pastures than his thoughts?

5. Another name for Krishna, the eighth avatar of Vishnu in Hindu mythology; Thoreau translates from a French edition of *Harivansa*.
6. The Pleiades and the Hyades are constellations; Aldebaran, in the constellation Taurus, is one of the

brightest stars; Altair is in the constellation Aquila.
7. Anonymous Jacobean verse set to music in *The Muses Garden* (1611) and probably found by Thoreau in Thomas Evans's *Old Ballads* (1810).

Every morning was a cheerful invitation to make my life of equal simplicity, and I may say innocence, with Nature herself. I have been as sincere a worshipper of Aurora as the Greeks. I got up early and bathed in the pond; that was a religious exercise, and one of the best things which I did. They say that characters were engraven on the bathing tub of king Tching-thang to this effect: "Renew thyself completely each day; do it again, and again, and forever again."[8] I can understand that. Morning brings back the heroic ages. I was as much affected by the faint hum of a mosquito making its invisible and unimaginable tour through my apartment at earliest dawn, when I was sitting with door and windows open, as I could be by any trumpet that ever sang of fame. It was Homer's requiem; itself an Iliad and Odyssey in the air, singing its own wrath and wanderings. There was something cosmical about it; a standing advertisement, till forbidden,[9] of the everlasting vigor and fertility of the world. The morning, which is the most memorable season of the day, is the awakening hour. Then there is least somnolence in us; and for an hour, at least, some part of us awakes which slumbers all the rest of the day and night. Little is to be expected of that day, if it can be called a day, to which we are not awakened by our Genius, but by the mechanical nudgings of some servitor, are not awakened by our own newly-acquired force and aspirations from within, accompanied by the undulations of celestial music, instead of factory bells, and a fragrance filling the air—to a higher life than we fell asleep from; and thus the darkness bear its fruit, and prove itself to be good, no less than the light. That man who does not believe that each day contains an earlier, more sacred, and auroral hour than he has yet profaned, has despaired of life, and is pursuing a descending and darkening way. After a partial cessation of his sensuous life, the soul of man, or its organs rather, are reinvigorated each day, and his Genius tries again what noble life it can make. All memorable events, I should say, transpire in morning time and in a morning atmosphere. The Vedas[1] say, "All intelligences awake with the morning." Poetry and art, and the fairest and most memorable of the actions of men, date from such an hour. All poets and heroes, like Memnon, are the children of Aurora, and emit their music at sunrise.[2] To him whose elastic and vigorous thought keeps pace with the sun, the day is a perpetual morning. It matters not what the clocks say or the attitudes and labors of men. Morning is when I am awake and there is a dawn in me. Moral reform is the effort to throw off sleep. Why is it that men give so poor an account of their day if they have not been slumbering? They are not such poor calculators. If they had not been overcome with drowsiness they would have performed something. The millions are awake enough for physical labor; but only one in a million is awake enough for effective intellectual exertion, only one in a hundred millions to a poetic or divine life. To be awake is to be alive. I have never yet met a man who was quite awake. How could I have looked him in the face?

We must learn to reawaken and keep ourselves awake, not by mechanical aids, but by an infinite expectation of the dawn, which does not forsake us in our soundest sleep. I know of no more encouraging fact than the unquestionable ability of man to elevate his life by a conscious endeavor. It is something

8. Confucius, The Great Learning, chap. 1.
9. In newspaper advertisements "TF" signaled to the compositor that an item was to be repeated daily "till forbidden."

1. The Vedas are Hindu scriptures; the quotation has not been located.
2. See n. 6, p. 806.

to be able to paint a particular picture, or to carve a statue, and so to make a few objects beautiful; but it is far more glorious to carve and paint the very atmosphere and medium through which we look, which morally we can do. To affect the quality of the day, that is the highest of arts. Every man is tasked to make his life, even in its details, worthy of the contemplation of his most elevated and critical hour. If we refused, or rather used up, such paltry information as we get, the oracles would distinctly inform us how this might be done.

I went to the woods because I wished to live deliberately, to front only the essential facts of life, and see if I could not learn what it had to teach, and not, when I came to die, discover that I had not lived. I did not wish to live what was not life, living is so dear; nor did I wish to practise resignation, unless it was quite necessary. I wanted to live deep and suck out all the marrow of life, to live so sturdily and Spartan-like as to put to rout all that was not life, to cut a broad swath and shave close, to drive life into a corner, and reduce it to its lowest terms, and, if it proved to be mean, why then to get the whole and genuine meanness of it, and publish its meanness to the world; or if it were sublime, to know it by experience, and be able to give a true account of it in my next excursion. For most men, it appears to me, are in a strange uncertainty about it, whether it is of the devil or of God, and have *somewhat hastily* concluded that it is the chief end of man here to "glorify God and enjoy him forever."[3]

Still we live meanly, like ants; though the fable tells us that we were long ago changed into men;[4] like pygmies we fight with cranes; it is error upon error, and clout upon clout, and our best virtue has for its occasion a superfluous and evitable wretchedness. Our life is frittered away by detail. An honest man has hardly need to count more than his ten fingers, or in extreme cases he may add his ten toes, and lump the rest. Simplicity, simplicity, simplicity! I say, let your affairs be as two or three, and not a hundred or a thousand; instead of a million count half a dozen, and keep your accounts on your thumb nail. In the midst of this chopping sea of civilized life, such are the clouds and storms and quicksands and thousand-and-one items to be allowed for, that a man has to live, if he would not founder and go to the bottom and not make his port at all, by dead reckoning, and he must be a great calculator indeed who succeeds. Simplify, simplify. Instead of three meals a day, if it be necessary eat but one; instead of a hundred dishes, five; and reduce other things in proportion. Our life is like a German Confederacy,[5] made up of petty states, with its boundary forever fluctuating, so that even a German cannot tell you how it is bounded at any moment. The nation itself, with all its so called internal improvements, which, by the way, are all external and superficial, is just such an unwieldy and overgrown establishment, cluttered with furniture and tripped up by its own traps, ruined by luxury and heedless expense, by want of calculation and a worthy aim, as the million households in the land; and the only cure for it as for them is in a rigid economy, a stern and more than Spartan simplicity of life and elevation of purpose. It lives too fast. Men think that it is essential that the *Nation* have commerce, and export ice, and

---

3. From the Shorter Catechism in the *New England Primer.*
4. In a Greek fable Aeacus persuaded Zeus to turn ants into men. The Trojans are compared to cranes fighting with pygmies (*Iliad*, book 3).
5. Later in the century Germany was unified under Prince Otto von Bismarck (1815–1898), first chancellor of the German Empire.

talk through a telegraph, and ride thirty miles an hour, without a doubt, whether *they* do or not; but whether we should live like baboons or like men, is a little uncertain. If we do not get out sleepers,[6] and forge rails, and devote days and nights to the work, but go to tinkering upon our *lives* to improve *them*, who will build railroads? And if railroads are not built, how shall we get to heaven in season? But if we stay at home and mind our business, who will want railroads? We do not ride on the railroad; it rides upon us. Did you ever think what those sleepers are that underlie the railroad? Each one is a man, an Irish-man, or a Yankee man. The rails are laid on them, and they are covered with sand, and the cars run smoothly over them. They are sound sleepers, I assure you. And every few years a new lot is laid down and run over; so that, if some have the pleasure of riding on a rail, others have the misfortune to be ridden upon. And when they run over a man that is walking in his sleep, a supernumerary sleeper in the wrong position, and wake him up, they suddenly stop the cars, and make a hue and cry about it, as if this were an exception. I am glad to know that it takes a gang of men for every five miles to keep the sleepers down and level in their beds as it is, for this is a sign that they may sometime get up again.

Why should we live with such hurry and waste of life? We are determined to be starved before we are hungry. Men say that a stitch in time saves nine, and so they take a thousand stitches to-day to save nine to-morrow. As for *work*, we haven't any of any consequence. We have the Saint Vitus' dance,[7] and cannot possibly keep our heads still. If I should only give a few pulls at the parish bell-rope, as for a fire, that is, without setting the bell, there is hardly a man on his farm in the outskirts of Concord, notwithstanding that press of engagements which was his excuse so many times this morning, nor a boy, nor a woman, I might almost say, but would forsake all and follow that sound, not mainly to save property from the flames, but, if we will confess the truth, much more to see it burn, since burn it must, and we, be it known, did not set it on fire,—or to see it put out, and have a hand in it, if that is done as handsomely; yes, even if it were the parish church itself. Hardly a man takes a half hour's nap after dinner, but when he wakes he holds up his head and asks, "What's the news?" as if the rest of mankind had stood his sentinels. Some give directions to be waked every half hour, doubtless for no other purpose; and then, to pay for it, they tell what they have dreamed. After a night's sleep the news is as indispensable as the breakfast. "Pray tell me any thing new that has happened to a man any where on this globe",—and he reads it over his coffee and rolls, that a man had had his eyes gouged out this morning on the Wachito River; never dreaming the while that he lives in the dark unfathomed mammoth cave of this world, and has but the rudiment of an eye himself.[8]

For my part, I could easily do without the post-office. I think that there are very few important communications made through it. To speak critically, I never received more than one or two letters in my life—I wrote this some years ago—that were worth the postage. The penny-post is, commonly, an institution through which you seriously offer a man that penny for his thoughts which is so often safely offered in jest. And I am sure that I never read any

6. Wooden railroad ties (another pun).
7. Chorea, a severe nervous disorder characterized by jerky motions.
8. Sightless fish had been found in Kentucky's Mam-

moth Cave. "Wachito": also spelled "Ouachita," a tributary of the Red River; Thoreau refers to a common-enough incident in backwoods brawling.

memorable news in a newspaper. If we read of one man robbed, or murdered, or killed by accident, or one house burned, or one vessel wrecked, or one steamboat blown up, or one cow run over on the Western Railroad, or one mad dog killed, or one lot of grasshoppers in the winter,—we never need read of another. One is enough. If you are acquainted with the principle, what do you care for a myriad instances and applications? To a philosopher all *news*, as it is called, is gossip, and they who edit and read it are old women over their tea. Yet not a few are greedy after this gossip. There was such a rush, as I hear, the other day at one of the offices to learn the foreign news by the last arrival, that several large squares of plate glass belonging to the establishment were broken by the pressure,—news which I seriously think a ready wit might write a twelvemonth or twelve years beforehand with sufficient accuracy. As for Spain, for instance, if you know how to throw in Don Carlos and the Infanta, and Don Pedro and Seville and Granada, from time to time in the right pro-portions,—they may have changed the names a little since I saw the papers,—and serve up a bull-fight when other entertainments fail, it will be true to the letter, and give us as good an idea of the exact state or ruin of things in Spain as the most succinct and lucid reports under this head in the newspapers: and as for England, almost the last significant scrap of news from that quarter was the revolution of 1649; and if you have learned the history of her crops for an average year, you never need attend to that thing again, unless your specula-tions are of a merely pecuniary character. If one may judge who rarely looks into the newspapers, nothing new does ever happen in foreign parts, a French revolution not excepted.

What news! how much more important to know what that is which was never old! "Kieou-pe-yu (great dignitary of the state of Wei) sent a man to Khoung-tseu to know his news. Khoung-tseu caused the messenger to be seated near him, and questioned him in these terms: What is your master doing? The messenger answered with respect: My master desires to diminish the number of his faults, but he cannot accomplish it. The messenger being gone, the philosopher remarked: What a worthy messenger! What a worthy messenger!"[9] The preacher, instead of vexing the ears of drowsy farmers on their day of rest at the end of the week,—for Sunday is the fit conclusion of an ill-spent week, and not the fresh and brave beginning of a new one,—with this one other draggle-tail of a sermon, should shout with thundering voice,—"Pause! Avast! Why so seeming fast, but deadly slow?"[1]

Shams and delusions are esteemed for soundest truths, while reality is fabu-lous. If men would steadily observe realities only, and not allow themselves to be deluded, life, to compare it with such things as we know, would be like a fairy tale and the Arabian Nights' Entertainments. If we respected only what is inevitable and has a right to be, music and poetry would resound along the streets. When we are unhurried and wise, we perceive that only great and worthy things have any permanent and absolute existence,—that petty fears and petty pleasures are but the shadow of the reality. This is always exhilarating and sublime. By closing the eyes and slumbering, and consenting to be deceived by shows, men establish and confirm their daily life of routine and habit every where, which still is built on purely illusory foundations. Children, who play life, discern its true law and relations more clearly than men, who

---

9. Confucius, *Analects* 14.
1. Father Taylor of the Seaman's Bethel in Boston was

one such preacher famous for the nautical cast of his sermons.

fail to live it worthily, but who think that they are wiser by experience, that is, by failure. I have read in a Hindoo book, that "there was a king's son, who, being expelled in infancy from his native city, was brought up by a forester, and, growing up to maturity in that state, imagined himself to belong to the barbarous race with which he lived. One of his father's ministers having discovered him, revealed to him what he was, and the misconception of his character was removed, and he knew himself to be a prince. So soul," continues the Hindoo philosopher, "from the circumstances in which it is placed, mistakes its own character, until the truth is revealed to it by some holy teacher, and then it knows itself to be *Brahme*."[2] I perceive that we inhabitants of New England live this mean life that we do because our vision does not penetrate the surface of things. We think that that *is* which *appears* to be. If a man should walk through this town and see only the reality, where, think you, would the "Mill-dam"[3] go to? If he should give us an account of the realities he beheld there, we should not recognize the place in his description. Look at a meeting-house, or a court-house, or a jail, or a shop, or a dwelling-house, and say what that thing really is before a true gaze, and they would all go to pieces in your account of them. Men esteem truth remote, in the outskirts of the system, behind the farthest star, before Adam and after the last man. In eternity there is indeed something true and sublime. But all these times and places and occasions are now and here. God himself culminates in the present moment, and will never be more divine in the lapse of all the ages. And we are enabled to apprehend at all what is sublime and noble only by the perpetual instilling and drenching of the reality which surrounds us. The universe constantly and obediently answers to our conceptions; whether we travel fast or slow, the track is laid for us. Let us spend our lives in conceiving them. The poet or the artist never yet had so fair and noble a design but some of his posterity at least could accomplish it.

Let us spend one day as deliberately as Nature, and not be thrown off the track by every nutshell and mosquito's wing that falls on the rails. Let us rise early and fast, or break fast, gently and without perturbation; let company come and let company go, let the bells ring and the children cry,—determined to make a day of it. Why should we knock under and go with the stream? Let us not be upset and overwhelmed in that terrible rapid and whirlpool called a dinner, situated in the meridian shallows. Weather this danger and you are safe, for the rest of the way is down hill. With unrelaxed nerves, with morning vigor, sail by it, looking another way, tied to the mast like Ulysses.[4] If the engine whistles, let it whistle till it is hoarse for its pains. If the bell rings, why should we run? We will consider what kind of music they are like. Let us settle ourselves, and work and wedge our feet downward through the mud and slush of opinion, and prejudice, and tradition, and delusion, and appearance, that alluvion[5] which covers the globe, through Paris and London, through New York and Boston and Concord, through church and state, through poetry and philosophy and religion, till we come to a hard bottom and rocks in place, which we can call *reality*, and say, This is, and no mistake; and then begin, having a *point d'appui*,[6] below freshet and frost and fire, a place where you

2. In the Hindu triad, Brahma is the divine reality in the aspect of creator; Vishnu is the preserver and Siva, the destroyer.
3. The business center of Concord.
4. A precaution Ulysses (Odysseus) took to prevent his yielding to the call of the Sirens, sea nymphs whose singing lured ships to destruction.
5. Sediment deposited by flowing water along a shore or bank.
6. Basis, leverage point (French).

might found a wall or a state, or set a lamp-post safely, or perhaps a gauge, not a Nilometer,[7] but a Realometer, that future ages might know how deep a freshet of shams and appearances had gathered from time to time. If you stand right fronting and face to face to a fact, you will see the sun glimmer on both its surfaces, as if it were a cimeter, and feel its sweet edge dividing you through the heart and marrow, and so you will happily conclude your mortal career. Be it life or death, we crave only reality. If we are really dying, let us hear the rattle in our throats and feel cold in the extremities; if we are alive, let us go about our business.

Time is but the stream I go a-fishing in. I drink at it; but while I drink I see the sandy bottom and detect how shallow it is. Its thin current slides away, but eternity remains. I would drink deeper; fish in the sky, whose bottom is pebbly with stars. I cannot count one. I know not the first letter of the alphabet. I have always been regretting that I was not as wise as the day I was born. The intellect is a cleaver; it discerns and rifts its way into the secret of things. I do not wish to be any more busy with my hands than is necessary. My head is hands and feet. I feel all my best faculties concentrated in it. My instinct tells me that my head is an organ for burrowing, as some creatures use their snout and fore-paws, and with it I would mine and burrow my way through these hills. I think that the richest vein is somewhere hereabouts; so by the divining rod and thin rising vapors I judge; and here I will begin to mine.

## Reading

With a little more deliberation in the choice of their pursuits, all men would perhaps become essentially students and observers, for certainly their nature and destiny are interesting to all alike. In accumulating property for ourselves or our posterity, in founding a family or a state, or acquiring fame even, we are mortal; but in dealing with truth we are immortal, and need fear no change nor accident. The oldest Egyptian or Hindoo philosopher raised a corner of the veil from the statue of the divinity; and still the trembling robe remains raised, and I gaze upon as fresh a glory as he did, since it was I in him that was then so bold, and it is he in me that now reviews the vision. No dust has settled on that robe; no time has elapsed since that divinity was revealed. That time which we really improve, or which is improvable, is neither past, present, nor future.

My residence was more favorable, not only to thought, but to serious reading, than a university; and though I was beyond the range of the ordinary circulating library, I had more than ever come within the influence of those books which circulate round the world, whose sentences were first written on bark, and are now merely copied from time to time on to linen paper. Says the poet Mîr Camar Uddîn Mast, "Being seated to run through the region of the spiritual world; I have had this advantage in books. To be intoxicated by a single glass of wine; I have experienced this pleasure when I have drunk the liquor of the esoteric doctrines."[8] I kept Homer's Iliad on my table through the summer, though I looked at his page only now and then. Incessant labor with my hands, at first, for I had my house to finish and my beans to hoe at the same time, made more study impossible. Yet I sustained myself by the

7. Gauge used at Memphis in ancient times for measuring the height of the Nile.

8. Thoreau knew this 18th-century Hindu poet from a French translation in a history of Hindu literature.

prospect of such reading in future. I read one or two shallow books of travel in the intervals of my work, till that employment made me ashamed of myself, and I asked where it was then that *I* lived.

The student may read Homer or Æschylus in the Greek without danger of dissipation or luxuriousness, for it implies that he in some measure emulate their heroes, and consecrate morning hours to their pages. The heroic books, even if printed in the character of our mother tongue, will always be in a language dead to degenerate times; and we must laboriously seek the meaning of each word and line, conjecturing a larger sense than common use permits out of what wisdom and valor and generosity we have. The modern cheap and fertile press, with all its translations, has done little to bring us nearer to the heroic writers of antiquity. They seem as solitary, and the letter in which they are printed as rare and curious, as ever. It is worth the expense of youthful days and costly hours, if you learn only some words of an ancient language, which are raised out of the trivialness of the street, to be perpetual suggestions and provocations. It is not in vain that the farmer remembers and repeats the few Latin words which he has heard. Men sometimes speak as if the study of the classics would at length make way for more modern and practical studies; but the adventurous student will always study classics, in whatever language they may be written and however ancient they may be. For what are the classics but the noblest recorded thoughts of man? They are the only oracles which are not decayed, and there are such answers to the most modern inquiry in them as Delphi and Dodona[9] never gave. We might as well omit to study Nature because she is old. To read well, that is, to read true books in a true spirit, is a noble exercise, and one that will task the reader more than any exercise which the customs of the day esteem. It requires a training such as the athletes underwent, the steady intention almost of the whole life to this object. Books must be read as deliberately and reservedly as they were written. It is not enough even to be able to speak the language of that nation by which they are written, for there is a memorable interval between the spoken and the written language, the language heard and the language read. The one is commonly transitory, a sound, a tongue, a dialect merely, almost brutish, and we learn it unconsciously, like the brutes, of our mothers. The other is the maturity and experience of that; if that is our mother tongue, this is our father tongue, a reserved and select expression, too significant to be heard by the ear, which we must be born again in order to speak. The crowds of men who merely *spoke* the Greek and Latin tongues in the middle ages were not entitled by the accident of birth to *read* the works of genius written in those languages; for these were not written in that Greek or Latin which they knew, but in the select language of literature. They had not learned the nobler dialects of Greece and Rome, but the very materials on which they were written were waste paper to them, and they prized instead a cheap contemporary literature. But when the several nations of Europe had acquired distinct though rude written languages of their own, sufficient for the purposes of their rising literatures, then first learning revived, and scholars were enabled to discern from that remoteness the treasures of antiquity. What the Roman and Grecian multitude could not *hear*, after the lapse of ages a few scholars *read*, and a few scholars only are still reading it.

However much we may admire the orator's occasional bursts of eloquence,

9. Oracles of ancient Greece.

the noblest written words are commonly as far behind or above the fleeting spoken language as the firmament with its stars is behind the clouds. *There* are the stars, and they who can may read them. The astronomers forever comment on and observe them. They are not exhalations like our daily colloquies and vaporous breath. What is called eloquence in the forum is commonly found to be rhetoric in the study. The orator yields to the inspiration of a transient occasion, and speaks to the mob before him, to those who can *hear* him; but the writer, whose more equable life is his occasion, and who would be distracted by the event and the crowd which inspire the orator, speaks to the intellect and heart of mankind, to all in any age who can *understand* him.

No wonder that Alexander carried the Iliad with him on his expeditions in a precious casket.[1] A written word is the choicest of relics. It is something at once more intimate with us and more universal than any other work of art. It is the work of art nearest to life itself. It may be translated into every language, and not only be read but actually breathed from all human lips;—not be represented on canvas or in marble only, but be carved out of the breath of life itself. The symbol of an ancient man's thought becomes a modern man's speech. Two thousand summers have imparted to the monuments of Grecian literature, as to her marbles, only a maturer golden and autumnal tint, for they have carried their own serene and celestial atmosphere into all lands to protect them against the corrosion of time. Books are the treasured wealth of the world and the fit inheritance of generations and nations. Books, the oldest and the best, stand naturally and rightfully on the shelves of every cottage. They have no cause of their own to plead, but while they enlighten and sustain the reader his common sense will not refuse them. Their authors are a natural and irresistible aristocracy in every society, and, more than kings or emperors, exert an influence on mankind. When the illiterate and perhaps scornful trader has earned by enterprise and industry his coveted leisure and independence, and is admitted to the circles of wealth and fashion, he turns inevitably at last to those still higher but yet inaccessible circles of intellect and genius, and is sensible only of the imperfection of his culture and the vanity and insufficiency of all his riches, and further proves his good sense by the pains which he takes to secure for his children that intellectual culture whose want he so keenly feels; and thus it is that he becomes the founder of a family.

Those who have not learned to read the ancient classics in the language in which they were written must have a very imperfect knowledge of the history of the human race; for it is remarkable that no transcript of them has ever been made into any modern tongue, unless our civilization itself may be regarded as such a transcript. Homer has never yet been printed in English, nor Æschylus, nor Virgil even,—works as refined, as solidly done, and as beautiful almost as the morning itself; for later writers, say what we will of their genius, have rarely, if ever, equalled the elaborate beauty and finish and the lifelong and heroic literary labors of the ancients. They only talk of forgetting them who never knew them. It will be soon enough to forget them when we have the learning and the genius which will enable us to attend to and appreciate them. That age will be rich indeed when those relics which we call Classics, and the still older and more than classic but even less known Scriptures of the nations, shall have still further accumulated, when the Vaticans[2] shall be filled with Vedas and Zendavestas and Bibles, with Homers and Dantes and Shak-

1. Plutarch attests to this in his biography of Alex-       2. I.e., libraries.
ander.

speares, and all the centuries to come shall have successively deposited their trophies in the forum of the world. By such a pile we may hope to scale heaven at last.

The works of the great poets have never yet been read by mankind, for only great poets can read them. They have only been read as the multitude read the stars, at most astrologically, not astronomically. Most men have learned to read to serve a paltry convenience, as they have learned to cipher in order to keep accounts and not be cheated in trade; but of reading as a noble intellectual exercise they know little or nothing; yet this only is reading, in a high sense, not that which lulls us as a luxury and suffers the nobler faculties to sleep the while, but what we have to stand on tiptoe to read and devote our most alert and wakeful hours to.

I think that having learned our letters we should read the best that is in literature, and not be forever repeating our a b abs, and words of one syllable, in the fourth or fifth classes, sitting on the lowest and foremost form all our lives.[3] Most men are satisfied if they read or hear read, and perchance have been convicted by the wisdom of one good book, the Bible, and for the rest of their lives vegetate and dissipate their faculties in what is called easy reading. There is a work in several volumes in our Circulating Library entitled Little Reading,[4] which I thought referred to a town of that name which I had not been to. There are those who, like cormorants and ostriches, can digest all sorts of this, even after the fullest dinner of meats and vegetables, for they suffer nothing to be wasted. If others are the machines to provide this provender, they are the machines to read it. They read the nine thousandth tale about Zebulon and Sephronia, and how they loved as none had ever loved before, and neither did the course of their true love run smooth,—at any rate, how it did run and stumble, and get up again and go on! how some poor unfortunate got up onto a steeple, who had better never have gone up as far as the belfry; and then, having needlessly got him up there, the happy novelist rings the bell for all the world to come together and hear, O dear! how he did get down again! For my part, I think that they had better metamorphose all such aspiring heroes of universal noveldom into man weathercocks, as they used to put heroes among the constellations, and let them swing round there till they are rusty, and not come down at all to bother honest men with their pranks. The next time the novelist rings the bell I will not stir though the meeting-house burn down. "The Skip of the Tip-Toe-Hop, a Romance of the Middle Ages, by the celebrated author of 'Title-Tol-Tan,'[5] to appear in monthly parts; a great rush; don't all come together." All this they read with saucer eyes, and erect and primitive curiosity, and with unwearied gizzard, whose corrugations even yet need no sharpening, just as some little four-year-old bencher[6] his two-cent gilt-covered edition of Cinderella,—without any improvement, that I can see, in the pronunciation, or accent, or emphasis, or any more skill in extracting or inserting the moral. The result is dulness of sight, a stagnation of the vital circulations, and a general deliquium and sloughing off of all the intellectual faculties. This sort of gingerbread is baked daily and more sedu-

3. I.e., with the youngest children at the front of a one-room schoolhouse.
4. Harding points out a basis for Thoreau's irony: a book called Much Instruction from Little Reading is included in the 1836 Catalogue of Concord Social Li-

brary.
5. Probably a play on James Fenimore Cooper's novel The Wept of the Wishton-Wish, which Thoreau would not have wasted his time reading.
6. A child too young to have graduated to a desk.

lously than pure wheat or rye-and-Indian in almost every oven, and finds a surer market.

The best books are not read even by those who are called good readers. What does our Concord culture amount to? There is in this town, with a very few exceptions, no taste for the best or for very good books even in English literature, whose words all can read and spell. Even the college-bred and so called liberally educated men here and elsewhere have really little or no acquaintance with the English classics; and as for the recorded wisdom of mankind, the ancient classics and Bibles, which are accessible to all who will know of them, there are the feeblest efforts any where made to become acquainted with them. I know a woodchopper, of middle age, who takes a French paper, not for news as he says, for he is above that, but to "keep himself in practice," he being a Canadian by birth; and when I ask him what he considers the best thing he can do in this world, he says, beside this, to keep up and add to his English. This is about as much as the college bred generally do or aspire to do, and they take an English paper for the purpose. One who has just come from reading perhaps one of the best English books will find how many with whom he can converse about it? Or suppose he comes from reading a Greek or Latin classic in the original, whose praises are familiar even to the so called illiterate; he will find nobody at all to speak to, but must keep silence about it. Indeed, there is hardly the professor in our colleges, who, if he has mastered the difficulties of the language, has proportionally mastered the difficulties of the wit and poetry of a Greek poet, and has any sympathy to impart to the alert and heroic reader; and as for the sacred Scriptures, or Bibles of mankind, who in this town can tell me even their titles? Most men do not know that any nation but the Hebrews have had a scripture. A man, any man, will go considerably out of his way to pick up a silver dollar; but here are golden words, which the wisest men of antiquity have uttered, and whose worth the wise of every succeeding age have assured us of;—and yet we learn to read only as far as Easy Reading, the primers and class-books, and when we leave school, the "Little Reading," and story books, which are for boys and beginners; and our reading, our conversation and thinking, are all on a very low level, worthy only of pygmies and manikens.

I aspire to be acquainted with wiser men than this our Concord soil has produced, whose names are hardly known here. Or shall I hear the name of Plato and never read his book? As if Plato were any townsman and I never saw him,—my next neighbor and I never heard him speak or attended to the wisdom of his words. But how actually is it? His Dialogues, which contain what was immortal in him, lie on the next shelf, and yet I never read them. We are under-bred and low-lived and illiterate; and in this respect I confess I do not make any very broad distinction between the illiterateness of my townsman who cannot read at all, and the illiterateness of him who has learned to read only what is for children and feeble intellects. We should be as good as the worthies of antiquity, but partly by first knowing how good they were. We are a race of tit-men,[7] and soar but little higher in our intellectual flights than the columns of the daily paper.

It is not all books that are as dull as their readers. There are probably words addressed to our condition exactly, which, if we could really hear and under-

7. Runts.

stand, would be more salutary than the morning or the spring to our lives, and possibly put a new aspect on the face of things for us. How many a man has dated a new era in his life from the reading of a book. The book exists for us perchance which will explain our miracles and reveal new ones. The at present unutterable things we may find somewhere uttered. These same questions that disturb and puzzle and confound us have in their turn occurred to all the wise men; not one has been omitted; and each has answered them, according to his ability, by his words and his life. Moreover, with wisdom we shall learn liberality. The solitary hired man on a farm in the outskirts of Concord, who has had his second birth and peculiar religious experience, and is driven as he believes into silent gravity and exclusiveness by his faith, may think it is not true; but Zoroaster, thousands of years ago, travelled the same road and had the same experience; but he, being wise, knew it to be universal, and treated his neighbors accordingly, and is even said to have invented and established worship among men. Let him humbly commune with Zoroaster then, and, through the liberalizing influence of all the worthies, with Jesus Christ himself, and let "our church" go by the board.

We boast that we belong to the nineteenth century and are making the most rapid strides of any nation. But consider how little this village does for its own culture. I do not wish to flatter my townsmen, nor to be flattered by them, for that will not advance either of us. We need to be provoked,—goaded like oxen, as we are, into a trot. We have a comparatively decent system of common schools, schools for infants only; but excepting the half-starved Lyceum[8] in the winter, and latterly the puny beginning of a library suggested by the state, no school for ourselves. We spend more on almost any article of bodily aliment or ailment than on our mental aliment. It is time that we had uncommon schools, that we did not leave off our education when we begin to be men and women. It is time that villages were universities, and their elder inhabitants the fellows of universities, with leisure—if they are indeed so well off—to pursue liberal studies the rest of their lives. Shall the world be confined to one Paris or one Oxford forever? Cannot students be boarded here and get a liberal education under the skies of Concord? Can we not hire some Abelard[9] to lecture us? Alas! what with foddering the cattle and tending the store, we are kept from school too long, and our education is sadly neglected. In this country, the village should in some respects take the place of the nobleman of Europe. It should be the patron of the fine arts. It is rich enough. It wants only the magnanimity and refinement. It can spend money enough on such things as farmers and traders value, but it is thought Utopian to propose spending money for things which more intelligent men know to be of far more worth. This town has spent seventeen thousand dollars on a town-house, thank fortune or politics, but probably it will not spend so much on living wit, the true meat to put into that shell, in a hundred years. The one hundred and twenty-five dollars annually subscribed for a Lyceum in the winter is better spent than any other equal sum raised in the town. If we live in the nineteenth century, why should we not enjoy the advantages which the nineteenth century offers? Why should our life be in any respect provincial? If we will read

8. Public hall where local citizens and others, often with national reputations, gave lectures on a great variety of topics. Thoreau was one of those in charge of lecture series at Concord for several years, and in 1844–45 divided the town by bringing Wendell Phil-

lips, the abolitionist, for a second controversial lecture. Concord Lyceum was in Thoreau's time one of the more liberal in the nation.
9. Peter Abelard (1079–1142) was a great teacher of philosophy and theology in medieval France.

newspapers, why not skip the gossip of Boston and take the best newspaper in the world at once?—not be sucking the pap of "neutral family" papers, or browsing "Olive-Branches" here in New England. Let the reports of all the learned societies come to us, and we will see if they know any thing. Why should we leave it to Harper & Brothers and Redding & Co.[1] to select our reading? As the nobleman of cultivated taste surrounds himself with whatever conduces to his culture,—genius—learning—wit—books—paintings—statuary—music—philosophical instruments, and the like; so let the village do,—not stop short at a pedagogue, a parson, a sexton, a parish library, and three selectmen, because our pilgrim forefathers got through a cold winter once on a bleak rock with these. To act collectively is according to the spirit of our institutions; and I am confident that, as our circumstances are more flourishing, our means are greater than the nobleman's. New England can hire all the wise men in the world to come and teach her, and board them round the while, and not be provincial at all. That is the *uncommon* school we want. Instead of noblemen, let us have noble villages of men. If it is necessary, omit one bridge over the river, go round a little there, and throw one arch at least over the darker gulf of ignorance which surrounds us.

*          *          *

## The Ponds

Sometimes, having had a surfeit of human society and gossip, and worn out all my village friends, I rambled still farther westward than I habitually dwell, into yet more unfrequented parts of the town, "to fresh woods and pastures new,"[2] or, while the sun was setting, made my supper of huckleberries and blueberries on Fair Haven Hill, and laid up a store for several days. The fruits do not yield their true flavor to the purchaser of them, nor to him who raises them for the market. There is but one way to obtain it, yet few take that way. If you would know the flavor of huckleberries, ask the cow-boy or the partridge. It is a vulgar error[3] to suppose that you have tasted huckleberries who never plucked them. A huckleberry never reaches Boston; they have not been known there since they grew on her three hills. The ambrosial and essential part of the fruit is lost with the bloom which is rubbed off in the market cart, and they become mere provender. As long as Eternal Justice reigns, not one innocent huckleberry can be transported thither from the country's hills.

Occasionally, after my hoeing was done for the day, I joined some impatient companion who had been fishing on the pond since morning, as silent and motionless as a duck or a floating leaf, and, after practising various kinds of philosophy, had concluded commonly, by the time I arrived, that he belonged to the ancient sect of Cœnobites.[4] There was one older man, an excellent fisher and skilled in all kinds of woodcraft, who was pleased to look upon my house as a building erected for the convenience of fishermen; and I was equally pleased when he sat in my doorway to arrange his lines. Once in a while we sat together on the pond, he at one end of the boat, and I at the other; but not many words passed between us, for he had grown deaf in his later years, but he occasionally hummed a psalm, which harmonized well enough with my

---

1. Major publishers and booksellers of New York City and Boston, respectively.
2. The last line of John Milton's *Lycidas*.
3. I.e., a common error (especially among the unedu-

cated); Thoreau recalls the English title of Sir Thomas Browne's *Pseudoxia Epidemica*.
4. As Harding points out, one of Thoreau's puns: "See, no bites."

philosophy. Our intercourse was thus altogether one of unbroken harmony, far more pleasing to remember than if it had been carried on by speech. When, as was commonly the case, I had none to commune with, I used to raise the echoes by striking with a paddle on the side of my boat, filling the surrounding woods with circling and dilating sound, stirring them up as the keeper of a menagerie his wild beasts, until I elicited a growl from every wooded vale and hill-side.

In warm evenings I frequently sat in the boat playing the flute, and saw the perch, which I seemed to have charmed, hovering around me, and the moon travelling over the ribbed bottom, which was strewed with the wrecks of the forest. Formerly I had come to this pond adventurously, from time to time, in dark summer nights, with a companion, and making a fire close to the water's edge, which we thought attracted the fishes, we caught pouts with a bunch of worms strung on a thread; and when we had done, far in the night, threw the burning brands high into the air like skyrockets, which, coming down into the pond, were quenched with a loud hissing, and we were suddenly groping in total darkness. Through this, whistling a tune, we took our way to the haunts of men again. But now I had made my home by the shore.

Sometimes, after staying in a village parlor till the family had all retired, I have returned to the woods, and, partly with a view to the next day's dinner, spent the hours of midnight fishing from a boat by moonlight, serenaded by owls and foxes, and hearing, from time to time, the creaking note of some unknown bird close at hand. These experiences were very memorable and valuable to me,—anchored in forty feet of water, and twenty or thirty rods from the shore, surrounded sometimes by thousands of small perch and shiners, dimpling the surface with their tails in the moonlight, and communicating by a long flaxen line with mysterious nocturnal fishes which had their dwelling forty feet below, or sometimes dragging sixty feet of line about the pond as I drifted in the gentle night breeze, now and then feeling a slight vibration along it, indicative of some life prowling about its extremity, of dull uncertain blundering purpose there, and slow to make up its mind. At length you slowly raise, pulling hand over hand, some horned pout squeaking and squirming to the upper air. It was very queer, especially in dark nights, when your thoughts had wandered to vast and cosmogonal themes in other spheres, to feel this faint jerk, which came to interrupt your dreams and link you to Nature again. It seemed as if I might next cast my line upward into the air, as well as downward into this element which was scarcely more dense. Thus I caught two fishes as it were with one hook.

The scenery of Walden is on a humble scale, and, though very beautiful, does not approach to grandeur, nor can it much concern one who has not long frequented it or lived by its shore; yet this pond is so remarkable for its depth and purity as to merit a particular description. It is a clear and deep green well, half a mile long and a mile and three quarters in circumference, and contains about sixty-one and a half acres; a perennial spring in the midst of pine and oak woods, without any visible inlet or outlet except by the clouds and evaporation. The surrounding hills rise abruptly from the water to the height of forty to eighty feet, though on the south-east and east they attain to about one hundred and one hundred and fifty feet respectively, within a quarter and a third of a mile. They are exclusively woodland. All our Concord waters have two colors at least, one when viewed at a distance, and another, more proper, close at hand. The first depends more on the light, and follows the sky. In clear weather, in summer, they appear blue at a little distance, especially if agitated, and at a great distance all appear alike. In stormy weather they are sometimes of a dark slate color. The sea, however, is said to be blue one day and green another without any perceptible change in the atmosphere. I have seen our river, when, the landscape being covered with snow, both water and ice were almost as green as grass. Some consider blue "to be the color of pure water, whether liquid or solid." But, looking directly down into our waters from a boat, they are seen to be of very different colors. Walden is blue at one time and green at another, even from the same point of view. Lying between the earth and the heavens, it partakes of the color of both. Viewed from a hill-top it reflects the color of the sky, but near at hand it is of a yellowish tint next the shore where you can see the sand, then a light green, which gradually deepens to a uniform dark green in the body of the pond. In some lights, viewed even from a hill-top, it is of a vivid green next the shore. Some have referred this to the reflection of the verdure; but it is equally green there against the railroad sand-bank, and in the spring, before the leaves are expanded, and it may be simply the result of the prevailing blue mixed with the yellow of the sand. Such is the color of its iris. This is that portion, also, where in the spring, the ice being warmed by the heat of the sun reflected from the bottom, and also transmitted through the earth, melts first and forms a narrow canal about the still frozen middle. Like the rest of our waters, when much agitated, in clear weather, so that the surface of the waves may reflect the sky at the right angle, or because there is more light mixed with it, it appears at a little distance of a darker blue than the sky itself; and at such a time, being on its surface, and looking with divided vision, so as to see the reflection, I have discerned a matchless and indescribable light blue, such as watered or changeable silks and sword blades suggest, more cerulean than the sky itself, alternating with the original dark green on the opposite sides of the waves, which last appeared but muddy in comparison. It is a vitreous greenish blue, as I remember it, like those patches of the winter sky seen through cloud vistas in the west before sundown. Yet a single glass of its water held up to the light is as colorless as an equal quantity of air. It is well known that a large plate of glass will have a green tint, owing, as the makers say, to its "body," but a small piece of the same will be colorless. How large a body of Walden water would be required to reflect a green tint I have never proved. The water of our river is black or a very dark brown to one looking directly down on it, and, like that of most ponds, imparts to the body of one bathing in it a yellow-ish tinge; but this water is of such crystalline purity that the body of the bather appears of an alabaster whiteness, still more unnatural, which, as the limbs are magnified and distorted withal, produces a monstrous effect, making fit studies for a Michael Angelo.

   The water is so transparent that the bottom can easily be discerned at the depth of twenty-five or thirty feet. Paddling over it, you may see many feet beneath the surface the schools of perch and shiners, perhaps only an inch long, yet the former easily distinguished by their transverse bars, and you think that they must be ascetic fish that find a subsistence there. Once, in the winter, many years ago, when I had been cutting holes through the ice in order to catch pickerel, as I stepped ashore I tossed my axe back on to the ice, but, as if some evil genius had directed it, it slid four or five rods directly into one of the holes, where the water was twenty-five feet deep. Out of curiosity, I lay down on the ice and looked through the hole, until I saw the axe a little on one side, standing on its head, with its helve erect and gently swaying to and fro with the pulse of the pond; and there it might have stood erect and swaying till in the course of time the handle rotted off, if I had not disturbed it. Making another hole directly over it with an ice chisel which I had, and cutting down the longest birch which I could find in the neighborhood with my knife, I made a slip-noose, which I attached to its end, and, letting it down carefully, passed it over the knob of the handle, and drew it by a line along the birch, and so pulled the axe out again.

The shore is composed of a belt of smooth rounded white stones like paving stones, excepting one or two short sand beaches, and is so steep that in many places a single leap will carry you into water over your head; and were it not for its remarkable transparency, that would be the last to be seen of its bottom till it rose on the opposite side. Some think it is bottomless. It is nowhere muddy, and a casual observer would say that there were no weeds at all in it; and of noticeable plants, except in the little meadows recently overflowed, which do not properly belong to it, a closer scrutiny does not detect a flag nor a bulrush, nor even a lily, yellow or white, but only a few small heart-leaves and potamogetons, and perhaps a water-target or two; all which however a bather might not perceive; and these plants are clean and bright like the element they grow in. The stones extend a rod or two into the water, and then the bottom is pure sand, except in the deepest parts, where there is usually a little sediment, probably from the decay of the leaves which have been wafted on to it so many successive falls, and a bright green weed is brought up on anchors even in midwinter.

We have one other pond just like this, White Pond in Nine Acre Corner, about two and a half miles westerly; but, though I am acquainted with most of the ponds within a dozen miles of this centre, I do not know a third of this pure and well-like character. Successive nations perchance have drank at, admired, and fathomed it, and passed away, and still its water is green and pellucid as ever. Not an intermitting spring! Perhaps on that spring morning when Adam and Eve were driven out of Eden Walden Pond was already in existence, and even then breaking up in a gentle spring rain accompanied with mist and a southerly wind, and covered with myriads of ducks and geese, which had not heard of the fall, when still such pure lakes sufficed them. Even then it had commenced to rise and fall, and had clarified its waters and colored them of the hue they now wear, and obtained a patent of heaven to be the only Walden Pond in the world and distiller of celestial dews. Who knows in how many unremembered nations' literatures this has been the Castalian Fountain?[5] or what nymphs presided over it in the Golden Age? It is a gem of the first water which Concord wears in her coronet.

Yet perchance the first who came to this well have left some trace of their footsteps. I have been surprised to detect encircling the pond, even where a thick wood has just been cut down on the shore, a narrow shelf-like path in the steep hill-side, alternately rising and falling, approaching and receding from the water's edge, as old probably as the race of man here, worn by the

---

5. In Greek mythology, a spring on Mount Parnassus, sacred to Apollo and the Muses.

feet of aboriginal hunters, and still from time to time unwittingly trodden by the present occupants of the land. This is particularly distinct to one standing on the middle of the pond in winter, just after a light snow has fallen, appearing as a clear undulating white line, unobscured by weeds and twigs, and very obvious a quarter of a mile off in many places where in summer it is hardly distinguishable close at hand. The snow reprints it, as it were, in clear white type alto-relievo.[6] The ornamented grounds of villas which will one day be built here may still preserve some trace of this.

The pond rises and falls, but whether regularly or not, and within what period, nobody knows, though, as usual, many pretend to know. It is commonly higher in the winter and lower in the summer, though not corresponding to the general wet and dryness. I can remember when it was a foot or two lower, and also when it was at least five feet higher, than when I lived by it. There is a narrow sandbar running into it, with very deep water on one side, on which I helped boil a kettle of chowder, some six rods from the main shore, about the year 1824, which it has not been possible to do for twenty-five years; and on the other hand, my friends used to listen with incredulity when I told them, that a few years later I was accustomed to fish from a boat in a secluded cove in the woods, fifteen rods from the only shore they knew, which place was long since converted into a meadow. But the pond has risen steadily for two years, and now, in the summer of '52, is just five feet higher than when I lived there, or as high as it was thirty years ago, and fishing goes on again in the meadow. This makes a difference of level, at the outside, of six or seven feet; and yet the water shed by the surrounding hills is insignificant in amount, and this overflow must be referred to causes which affect the deep springs. This same summer the pond has begun to fall again. It is remarkable that this fluctuation, whether periodical or not, appears thus to require many years for its accomplishment. I have observed one rise and a part of two falls, and I expect that a dozen or fifteen years hence the water will again be as low as I have ever known it. Flint's Pond, a mile eastward, allowing for the disturbance occasioned by its inlets and outlets, and the smaller intermediate ponds also, sympathize with Walden, and recently attained their greatest height at the same time with the latter. The same is true, as far as my observation goes, of White Pond.

This rise and fall of Walden at long intervals serves this use at least; the water standing at this great height for a year or more, though it makes it difficult to walk round it, kills the shrubs and trees which have sprung up about its edge since the last rise, pitch-pines, birches, alders, aspens, and others, and, falling again, leaves an unobstructed shore; for, unlike many ponds and all waters which are subject to a daily tide, its shore is cleanest when the water is lowest. On the side of the pond next my house, a row of pitch pines fifteen feet high has been killed and tipped over as if by a lever, and thus a stop put to their encroachments; and their size indicates how many years have elapsed since the last rise to this height. By this fluctuation the pond asserts its title to a shore, and thus the *shore* is *shorn*, and the trees cannot hold it by right of possession. These are the lips of the lake on which no beard grows. It licks its chaps from time to time. When the water is at its height, the alders, willows, and maples send forth a mass of fibrous red roots several feet long from all

6. High relief (Italian), so raised as to be partly detached from the background.

sides of their stems in the water, and to the height of three or four feet from the ground, in the effort to maintain themselves; and I have known the high-blueberry bushes about the shore, which commonly produce no fruit, bear an abundant crop under these circumstances.

Some have been puzzled to tell how the shore became so regularly paved. My townsmen have all heard the tradition, the oldest people tell me that they heard it in their youth, that anciently the Indians were holding a pow-wow upon a hill here, which rose as high into the heavens as the pond now sinks deep into the earth, and they used much profanity, as the story goes, though this vice is one of which the Indians were never guilty, and while they were thus engaged the hill shook and suddenly sank, and only one old squaw, named Walden, escaped, and from her the pond was named. It has been conjectured that when the hill shook these stones rolled down its side and became the present shore. It is very certain, at any rate, that once there was no pond here, and now there is one; and this Indian fable does not in any respect conflict with the account of that ancient settler whom I have mentioned, who remembers so well when he first came here with his divining rod, saw a thin vapor rising from the sward, and the hazel pointed steadily downward, and he concluded to dig a well here. As for the stones, many still think that they are hardly to be accounted for by the action of the waves on these hills; but I observe that the surrounding hills are remarkably full of the same kind of stones, so that they have been obliged to pile them up in walls on both sides of the railroad cut nearest the pond; and, moreover, there are most stones where the shore is most abrupt; so that, unfortunately, it is no longer a mystery to me. I detect the paver. If the name was not derived from that of some English locality,—Saffron Walden, for instance,—one might suppose that it was called, originally, Walled-in Pond.

The pond was my well ready dug. For four months in the year its water is as cold as it is pure at all times; and I think that it is then as good as any, if not the best, in the town. In the winter, all water which is exposed to the air is colder than springs and wells which are protected from it. The temperature of the pond water which had stood in the room where I sat from five o'clock in the afternoon till noon the next day, the sixth of March, 1846, the thermometer having been up to 65° or 70° some of the time, owing partly to the sun on the roof, was 42°, or one degree colder than the water of one of the coldest wells in the village just drawn. The temperature of the Boiling Spring the same day was 45°, or the warmest of any water tried, though it is the coldest that I know of in summer, when, beside, shallow and stagnant surface water is not mingled with it. Moreover, in summer, Walden never becomes so warm as most water which is exposed to the sun, on account of its depth. In the warmest weather I usually placed a pailful in my cellar, where it became cool in the night, and remained so during the day; though I also resorted to a spring in the neighborhood. It was as good when a week old as the day it was dipped, and had no taste of the pump. Whoever camps for a week in summer by the shore of a pond, needs only bury a pail of water a few feet deep in the shade of his camp to be independent of the luxury of ice.

There have been caught in Walden, pickerel, one weighing seven pounds, to say nothing of another which carried off a reel with great velocity, which the fisherman safely set down at eight pounds because he did not see him, perch and pouts, some of each weighing over two pounds, shiners, chivins or roach, (*Leuciscus pulchellus*,) a very few breams, (*Promotis obesus*,) and a couple of eels, one weighing four pounds,—I am thus particular because the weight of a fish is commonly its only title to fame, and these are the only eels I have heard of here;—also, I have a faint recollection of a little fish some five inches long, with silvery sides and a greenish back, somewhat dace[7]-like in its character, which I mention here chiefly to link my facts to fable. Nevertheless, this pond is not very fertile in fish. Its pickerel, though not abundant, are its chief boast. I have seen at one time lying on the ice pickerel of at least three different kinds; a long and shallow one, steel-colored, most like those caught in the river; a bright golden kind, with greenish reflections and remarkably deep, which is the most common here; and another, golden-colored, and shaped like the last, but peppered on the sides with small dark brown or black spots, intermixed with a few faint blood-red ones, very much like a trout. The specific name *reticulatus* would not apply to this; it should be *guttatus*[8] rather. These are all very firm fish, and weigh more than their size promises. The shiners, pouts, and perch also, and indeed all the fishes which inhabit this pond, are much cleaner, handsomer, and firmer fleshed than those in the river and most other ponds, as the water is purer, and they can easily be distinguished from them. Probably many ichthyologists would make new varieties of some of them. There are also a clean race of frogs and tortoises, and a few muscles in it; muskrats and minks leave their traces about it, and occasionally a travelling mud-turtle visits it. Sometimes, when I pushed off my boat in the morning, I disturbed a great mud-turtle which had secreted himself under the boat in the night. Ducks and geese frequent it in the spring and fall, the white-bellied swallows (*Hirundo bicolor*) skim over it, kingfishers dart away from its coves, and the peetweets (*Totanus macularius*) "teter" along its stony shores all summer. I have sometimes disturbed a fishhawk sitting on a white-pine over the water; but I doubt if it is ever profaned by the wing of a gull, like Fair Haven. At most, it tolerates one annual loon. These are all the animals of consequence which frequent it now.

You may see from a boat, in calm weather, near the sandy eastern shore, where the water is eight or ten feet deep, and also in some other parts of the pond, some circular heaps half a dozen feet in diameter by a foot in height, consisting of small stones less than a hen's egg in size, where all around is bare sand. At first you wonder if the Indians could have formed them on the ice for any purpose, and so, when the ice melted, they sank to the bottom; but they are too regular and some of them plainly too fresh for that. They are similar to those found in rivers; but as there are no suckers nor lampreys here, I know not by what fish they could be made. Perhaps they are the nests of the chivin.[9] These lend a pleasing mystery to the bottom.

The shore is irregular enough not to be monotonous. I have in my mind's eye the western indented with deep bays, the bolder northern, and the beautifully scolloped southern shore, where successive capes overlap each other and suggest unexplored coves between. The forest has never so good a setting, nor is so distinctly beautiful, as when seen from the middle of a small lake amid hills which rise from the water's edge; for the water in which it is reflected not only makes the best foreground in such a case, but, with its winding shore, the most natural and agreeable boundary to it. There is no rawness nor imper-

7. Small fresh-water fish.
8. Speckled. "*Reticulatus*": netlike.

9. What Thoreau saw has been confirmed to be heaps made by the chivin, a nest-building fish.

fection in its edge there, as where the axe has cleared a part, or a cultivated field abuts on it. The trees have ample room to expand on the water side, and each sends forth its most vigorous branch in that direction. There Nature has woven a natural selvage, and the eye rises by just gradations from the low shrubs of the shore to the highest trees. There are few traces of man's hand to be seen. The water laves the shore as it did a thousand years ago.

A lake is the landscape's most beautiful and expressive feature. It is earth's eye; looking into which the beholder measures the depth of his own nature. The fluviatile trees next the shore are the slender eyelashes which fringe it, and the wooded hills and cliffs around are its overhanging brows.

Standing on the smooth sandy beach at the east end of the pond, in a calm September afternoon, when a slight haze makes the opposite shore line indistinct, I have seen whence came the expression, "the glassy surface of a lake." When you invert your head, it looks like a thread of finest gossamer stretched across the valley, and gleaming against the distant pine woods, separating one stratum of the atmosphere from another. You would think that you could walk dry under it to the opposite hills, and that the swallows which skim over might perch on it. Indeed, they sometimes dive below the line, as it were by mistake, and are undeceived. As you look over the pond westward you are obliged to employ both your hands to defend your eyes against the reflected as well as the true sun, for they are equally bright; and if, between the two, you survey its surface critically, it is literally as smooth as glass, except where the skater insects, at equal intervals scattered over its whole extent, by their motions in the sun produce the finest imaginable sparkle on it, or, perchance, a duck plumes itself, or, as I have said, a swallow skims so low as to touch it. It may be that in the distance a fish describes an arc of three or four feet in the air, and there is one bright flash where it emerges, and another where it strikes the water; sometimes the whole silvery arc is revealed; or here and there, perhaps, is a thistle-down floating on its surface, which the fishes dart at and so dimple it again. It is like molten glass cooled but not congealed, and the few motes in it are pure and beautiful like the imperfections in glass. You may often detect a yet smoother and darker water, separated from the rest as if by an invisible cobweb, boom of the water nymphs, resting on it. From a hill-top you can see a fish leap in almost any part; for not a pickerel or shiner picks an insect from this smooth surface but it manifestly disturbs the equilibrium of the whole lake. It is wonderful with what elaborateness this simple fact is advertised,—this piscine murder will out,—and from my distant perch I distinguish the circling undulations when they are half a dozen rods in diameter. You can even detect a water-bug (*Gyrinus*) ceaselessly progressing over the smooth surface a quarter of a mile off; for they furrow the water slightly, making a conspicuous ripple bounded by two diverging lines, but the skaters glide over it without rippling it perceptibly. When the surface is considerably agitated there are no skaters nor water-bugs on it, but apparently, in calm days, they leave their havens and adventurously glide forth from the shore by short impulses till they completely cover it. It is a soothing employment, on one of those fine days in the fall when all the warmth of the sun is fully appreciated, to sit on a stump on such a height as this, overlooking the pond, and study the dimpling circles which are incessantly inscribed on its otherwise invisible surface amid the reflected skies and trees. Over this great expanse there is no disturbance but it is thus at once gently smoothed away and assuaged, as, when a vase of water is jarred, the trembling circles seek the shore and all is smooth again. Not a fish can leap or an insect fall on the pond but it is thus reported in circling dimples, in lines of beauty, as it were the constant welling up of its fountain, the gentle pulsing of its life, the heaving of its breast. The thrills of joy and thrills of pain are undistinguishable. How peaceful the phenomena of the lake! Again the works of man shine as in the spring. Ay, every leaf and twig and stone and cobweb sparkles now at mid-afternoon as when covered with dew in a spring morning. Every motion of an oar or an insect produces a flash of light; and if an oar falls, how sweet the echo!

In such a day, in September or October, Walden is a perfect forest mirror, set round with stones as precious to my eye as if fewer or rarer. Nothing so fair, so pure, and at the same time so large, as a lake, perchance, lies on the surface of the earth. Sky water. It needs no fence. Nations come and go without defiling it. It is a mirror which no stone can crack, whose quicksilver will never wear off, whose gilding Nature continually repairs; no storms, no dust, can dim its surface ever fresh;—a mirror in which all impurity presented to it sinks, swept and dusted by the sun's hazy brush,—this the light dust-cloth,—which retains no breath that is breathed on it, but sends its own to float as clouds high above its surface, and be reflected in its bosom still.

A field of water betrays the spirit that is in the air. It is continually receiving new life and motion from above. It is intermediate in its nature between land and sky. On land only the grass and trees wave, but the water itself is rippled by the wind. I see where the breeze dashes across it by the streaks or flakes of light. It is remarkable that we can look down on its surface. We shall, perhaps, look down thus on the surface of air at length, and mark where a still subtler spirit sweeps over it.

The skaters and water-bugs finally disappear in the latter part of October, when the severe frosts have come; and then and in November, usually, in a calm day, there is absolutely nothing to ripple the surface. One November afternoon, in the calm at the end of a rain storm of several days' duration, when the sky was still completely overcast and the air was full of mist, I observed that the pond was remarkably smooth, so that it was difficult to distinguish its surface; though it no longer reflected the bright tints of October, but the sombre November colors of the surrounding hills. Though I passed over it as gently as possible, the slight undulations produced by my boat extended almost as far as I could see, and gave a ribbed appearance to the reflections. But, as I was looking over the surface, I saw here and there at a distance a faint glimmer, as if some skater insects which had escaped the frosts might be collected there, or, perchance, the surface, being so smooth, betrayed where a spring welled up from the bottom. Paddling gently to one of these places, I was surprised to find myself surrounded by myriads of small perch, about five inches long, of a rich bronze color in the green water, sporting there and constantly rising to the surface and dimpling it, sometimes leaving bubbles on it. In such transparent and seemingly bottomless water, reflecting the clouds, I seemed to be floating through the air as in a balloon, and their swimming impressed me as a kind of flight or hovering, as if they were a compact flock of birds passing just beneath my level on the right or left, their fins, like sails, set all around them. There were many such schools in the pond, apparently improving the short season before winter would draw an icy shutter over their broad skylight, sometimes giving to the surface an appearance as if a slight

breeze struck it, or a few rain-drops fell there. When I approached carelessly
and alarmed them, they made a sudden plash and rippling with their tails, as
if one had struck the water with a brushy bough, and instantly took refuge in
the depths. At length the wind rose, the mist increased, and the waves began
to run, and the perch leaped much higher than before, half out of water, a
hundred black points, three inches long, at once above the surface. Even as
late as the fifth of December, one year, I saw some dimples on the surface,
and thinking it was going to rain hard immediately, the air being full of mist,
I made haste to take my place at the oars and row homeward; already the rain
seemed rapidly increasing, though I felt none on my cheek, and I anticipated
a thorough soaking. But suddenly the dimples ceased, for they were produced
by the perch, which the noise of my oars had scared into the depths, and I saw
their schools dimly disappearing; so I spent a dry afternoon after all.

An old man who used to frequent this pond nearly sixty years ago, when it
was dark with surrounding forests, tells me that in those days he sometimes
saw it all alive with ducks and other water fowl, and that there were many
eagles about it. He came here a-fishing, and used an old log canoe which he
found on the shore. It was made of two white-pine logs dug out and pinned
together, and was cut off square at the ends. It was very clumsy, but lasted a
great many years before it became water-logged and perhaps sank to the bottom. He did not know whose it was; it belonged to the pond. He used to make
a cable for his anchor of strips of hickory bark tied together. An old man, a
potter, who lived by the pond before the Revolution, told him once that there
was an iron chest at the bottom, and that he had seen it. Sometimes it would
come floating up to the shore; but when you went toward it, it would go back
into deep water and disappear. I was pleased to hear of the old log canoe,
which took the place of an Indian one of the same material but more graceful
construction, which perchance had first been a tree on the bank, and then, as
it were, fell into the water, to float there for a generation, the most proper
vessel for the lake. I remember that when I first looked into these depths there
were many large trunks to be seen indistinctly lying on the bottom, which had
either been blown over formerly, or left on the ice at the last cutting, when
wood was cheaper; but now they have mostly disappeared.

When I first paddled a boat on Walden, it was completely surrounded by
thick and lofty pine and oak woods, and in some of its coves grape vines had
run over the trees next the water and formed bowers under which a boat could
pass. The hills which form its shores are so steep, and the woods on them were
then so high, that, as you looked down from the west end, it had the appearance of an amphitheatre for some kind of sylvan spectacle. I have spent many
an hour, when I was younger, floating over its surface as the zephyr[1] willed,
having paddled my boat to the middle, and lying on my back across the seats,
in a summer forenoon, dreaming awake, until I was aroused by the boat touching the sand, and I arose to see what shore my fates had impelled me to; days
when idleness was the most attractive and productive industry. Many a forenoon have I stolen away, preferring to spend thus the most valued part of the
day; for I was rich, if not in money, in sunny hours and summer days, and
spent them lavishly; nor do I regret that I did not waste more of them in the
workshop or the teacher's desk. But since I left those shores the woodchoppers

1. The mild west wind.

have still further laid them waste, and now for many a year there will be no more rambling through the aisles of the wood, with occasional vistas through which you see the water. My Muse may be excused if she is silent henceforth. How can you expect the birds to sing when their groves are cut down?

Now the trunks of trees on the bottom, and the old log canoe, and the dark surrounding woods, are gone, and the villagers, who scarcely know where it lies, instead of going to the pond to bathe or drink, are thinking to bring its water, which should be as sacred as the Ganges at least, to the village in a pipe, to wash their dishes with!—to earn their Walden by the turning of a cock or drawing of a plug! That devilish Iron Horse, whose ear-rending neigh is heard throughout the town, has muddied the Boiling Spring with his foot, and he it is that has browsed off all the woods on Walden shore; that Trojan horse, with a thousand men in his belly, introduced by mercenary Greeks![2] Where is the country's champion, the Moore of Moore Hall,[3] to meet him at the Deep Cut and thrust an avenging lance between the ribs of the bloated pest?

Nevertheless, of all the characters I have known, perhaps Walden wears best, and best preserves its purity. Many men have been likened to it, but few deserve that honor. Though the woodchoppers have laid bare first this shore and then that, and the Irish have built their sties by it, and the railroad has infringed on its border, and the ice-men have skimmed it once, it is itself unchanged, the same water which my youthful eyes fell on; all the change is in me. It has not acquired one permanent wrinkle after all its ripples. It is perennially young, and I may stand and see a swallow dip apparently to pick an insect from its surface as of yore. It struck me again to-night, as if I had not seen it almost daily for more than twenty years,—Why, here is Walden, the same woodland lake that I discovered so many years ago; where a forest was cut down last winter another is springing up by its shore as lustily as ever; the same thought is welling up to its surface that was then; it is the same liquid joy and happiness to itself and its Maker, ay, and it *may* be to me. It is the work of a brave man surely, in whom there was no guile! He rounded this water with his hand, deepened and clarified it in his thought, and in his will bequeathed it to Concord. I see by its face that it is visited by the same reflection; and I can almost say, Walden, is it you?

> It is no dream of mine,
> To ornament a line;
> I cannot come nearer to God and Heaven
> Than I live to Walden even.
> I am its stony shore,
> And the breeze that passes o'er;
> In the hollow of my hand
> Are its water and its sand,
> And its deepest resort
> Lies high in my thought.

The cars never pause to look at it; yet I fancy that the engineers and firemen and brakemen, and those passengers who have a season ticket and see it often,

---

2. The stratagem by which the Greeks entered Troy.
3. From *The Dragon of Wantley* in Percy's *Reliques of Ancient English Poetry* (1765): "But More of More-

Hall, with nothing at all, / He slew the dragon of Wantley."

are better men for the sight. The engineer does not forget at night, or his
nature does not, that he has beheld this vision of serenity and purity once at
least during the day. Though seen but once, it helps to wash out State-street
and the engine's soot. One proposes that it be called "God's Drop."

I have said that Walden has no visible inlet nor outlet, but it is on the one
hand distantly and indirectly related to Flint's Pond, which is more elevated,
by a chain of small ponds coming from that quarter, and on the other directly
and manifestly to Concord River, which is lower, by a similar chain of ponds
through which in some other geological period it may have flowed, and by a
little digging, which God forbid, it can be made to flow thither again. If by
living thus reserved and austere, like a hermit in the woods, so long, it has
acquired such wonderful purity, who would not regret that the comparatively
impure waters of Flint's Pond should be mingled with it, or itself should ever
go to waste its sweetness in the ocean wave?

Flint's, or Sandy Pond, in Lincoln, our greatest lake and inland sea, lies
about a mile east of Walden. It is much larger, being said to contain one
hundred and ninety-seven acres, and is more fertile in fish, but it is comparatively shallow, and not remarkably pure. A walk through the woods thither
was often my recreation. It was worth the while, if only to feel the wind blow
on your cheek freely, and see the waves run, and remember the life of mariners. I went a-chestnutting there in the fall, on windy days, when the nuts
were dropping into the water and were washed to my feet; and one day, as I
crept along its sedgy shore, the fresh spray blowing in my face, I came upon
the mouldering wreck of a boat, the sides gone, and hardly more than the
impression of its flat bottom left amid the rushes; yet its model was sharply
defined, as if it were a large decayed pad, with its veins. It was as impressive a
wreck as one could imagine on the sea-shore, and had as good a moral. It is
by this time mere vegetable mould and undistinguishable pond shore, through
which rushes and flags have pushed up. I used to admire the ripple marks on
the sandy bottom, at the north end of this pond, made firm and hard to the
feet of the wader by the pressure of the water, and the rushes which grew in
Indian file, in waving lines, corresponding to these marks, rank behind rank,
as if the waves had planted them. There also I have found, in considerable
quantities, curious balls, composed apparently of fine grass or roots, of pipew-
ort perhaps, from half an inch to four inches in diameter, and perfectly spheri-
cal. These wash back and forth in shallow water on a sandy bottom, and are
sometimes cast on the shore. They are either solid grass, or have a little sand
in the middle. At first you would say that they were formed by the action of
the waves, like a pebble; yet the smallest are made of equally coarse materials,
half an inch long, and they are produced only at one season of the year.
Moreover, the waves, I suspect, do not so much construct as wear down a
material which has already acquired consistency. They preserve their form
when dry for an indefinite period.

Flint's Pond! Such is the poverty of our nomenclature. What right had the
unclean and stupid farmer, whose farm abutted on this sky water, whose shores
he has ruthlessly laid bare, to give his name to it? Some skin-flint, who loved
better the reflecting surface of a dollar, or a bright cent, in which he could see
his own brazen face; who regarded even the wild ducks which settled in it as
trespassers; his fingers grown into crooked and horny talons from the long habit

of grasping harpy-like;[4]—so it is not named for me. I go not there to see him nor to hear of him; who never *saw* it, who never bathed in it, who never loved it, who never protected it, who never spoke a good word for it, nor thanked God that he had made it. Rather let it be named from the fishes that swim in it, the wild fowl or quadrupeds which frequent it, the wild flowers which grow by its shores, or some wild man or child the thread of whose history is interwoven with its own; not from him who could show no title to it but the deed which a like-minded neighbor or legislature gave him,—him who thought only of its money value; whose presence perchance cursed all the shore; who exhausted the land around it, and would fain have exhausted the waters within it; who regretted only that it was not English hay or cranberry meadow,—there was nothing to redeem it, forsooth, in his eyes,—and would have drained and sold it for the mud at its bottom. It did not turn his mill, and it was no *privilege* to him to behold it. I respect not his labors, his farm where every thing has its price; who would carry the landscape, who would carry his God, to market, if he could get any thing for him; who goes to market *for* his god as it is; on whose farm nothing grows free, whose fields bear no crops, whose meadows no flowers, whose trees no fruits, but dollars; who loves not the beauty of his fruits, whose fruits are not ripe for him till they are turned to dollars. Give me the poverty that enjoys true wealth. Farmers are respectable and interesting to me in proportion as they are poor,—poor farmers. A model farm! where the house stands like a fungus in a muck-heap, chambers for men, horses, oxen, and swine, cleansed and uncleansed, all contiguous to one another! Stocked with men! A great grease-spot, redolent of manures and buttermilk! Under a high state of cultivation, being manured with the hearts and brains of men! As if you were to raise your potatoes in the church-yard! Such is a model farm.

No, no; if the fairest features of the landscape are to be named after men, let them be the noblest and worthiest men alone. Let our lakes receive as true names at least as the Icarian Sea, where "still the shore" a "brave attempt resounds."[5]

Goose Pond, of small extent, is on my way to Flint's; Fair-Haven, an expansion of Concord River, said to contain some seventy acres, is a mile southwest; and White Pond, of about forty acres, is a mile and a half beyond Fair-Haven. This is my lake country.[6] These, with Concord River, are my water privileges; and night and day, year in year out, they grind such grist as I carry to them.

Since the woodcutters, and the railroad, and I myself have profaned Walden, perhaps the most attractive, if not the most beautiful, of all our lakes, the gem of the woods, is White Pond;—a poor name from its commonness, whether derived from the remarkable purity of its waters or the color of its sands. In these as in other respects, however, it is a lesser twin of Walden. They are so much alike that you would say they must be connected under ground. It has the same stony shore, and its waters are of the same hue. As at Walden, in sultry dog-day weather, looking down through the woods on some of its bays which are not so deep but that the reflection from the bottom tinges

---

4. In Greek mythology, the Harpies were monsters with women's heads and birds' bodies who seized and carried off the soul at the moment of death.
5. From *Icarus* by William Drummond of Hawthorn-

den (1585–1649).
6. A New England equivalent of the English Lake District associated with Wordsworth and other Romantics.

them, its waters are of a misty bluish-green or glaucous color. Many years since I used to go there to collect the sand by cart-loads, to make sand-paper with, and I have continued to visit it ever since. One who frequents it proposes to call it Virid Lake.[7] Perhaps it might be called Yellow-Pine Lake, from the following circumstance. About fifteen years ago you could see the top of a pitch-pine, of the kind called yellow-pine hereabouts, though it is not a distinct species, projecting above the surface in deep water, many rods from the shore. It was even supposed by some that the pond had sunk, and this was one of the primitive forests that formerly stood there. I find that even so long ago as 1792, in a "Topographical Description of the Town of Concord," by one of its citizens, in the Collections of the Massachusetts Historical Society, the author, after speaking of Walden and White Ponds, adds: "In the middle of the latter may be seen, when the water is very low, a tree which appears as if it grew in the place where it now stands, although the roots are fifty feet below the surface of the water; the top of this tree is broken off, and at that place measures fourteen inches in diameter."[8] In the spring of '49 I talked with the man who lives nearest the pond in Sudbury, who told me that it was he who got out this tree ten or fifteen years before. As near as he could remember, it stood twelve or fifteen rods from the shore, where the water was thirty or forty feet deep. It was in the winter, and he had been getting out ice in the forenoon, and had resolved that in the afternoon, with the aid of his neighbors, he would take out the old yellow-pine. He sawed a channel in the ice toward the shore, and hauled it over and along and out on to the ice with oxen; but, before he had gone far in his work, he was surprised to find that it was wrong end upward, with the stumps of the branches pointing down, and the small end firmly fastened in the sandy bottom. It was about a foot in diameter at the big end, and he had expected to get a good saw-log, but it was so rotten as to be fit only for fuel, if for that. He had some of it in his shed then. There were marks of an axe and of woodpeckers on the but. He thought that it might have been a dead tree on the shore, but was finally blown over into the pond, and after the top had become waterlogged, while the but-end was still dry and light, had drifted out and sunk wrong end up. His father, eighty years old, could not remember when it was not there. Several pretty large logs may still be seen lying on the bottom, where, owing to the undulation of the surface, they look like huge water snakes in motion.

This pond has rarely been profaned by a boat, for there is little in it to tempt a fisherman. Instead of the white lily, which requires mud, or the common sweet flag, the blue flag (*Iris versicolor*) grows thinly in the pure water, rising from the stony bottom all around the shore, where it is visited by humming birds in June, and the color both of its bluish blades and its flowers, and especially their reflections, are in singular harmony with the glaucous water.

White Pond and Walden are great crystals on the surface of the earth, Lakes of Light. If they were permanently congealed, and small enough to be clutched, they would, perchance, be carried off by slaves, like precious stones, to adorn the heads of emperors; but being liquid, and ample, and secured to us and our successors forever, we disregard them, and run after the diamond of Kohinoor.[9] They are too pure to have a market value; they contain no

---

7. Green Lake.
8. William Jones, " 'A Topological Description of Concord,' " *Mass. Hist. Soc. Col.*, I (1792), 238 [Harding's note].

9. An enormous diamond found in India during the 18th century and added to the British crown jewels during the composition of *Walden*.

muck. How much more beautiful than our lives, how much more transparent than our characters, are they! We never learned meanness of them. How much fairer than the pool before the farmer's door, in which his ducks swim! Hither the clean wild ducks come. Nature has no human inhabitant who appreciates her. The birds with their plumage and their notes are in harmony with the flowers, but what youth or maiden conspires with the wild luxuriant beauty of Nature? She flourishes most alone, far from the towns where they reside. Talk of heaven! ye disgrace earth.

* * *

## Brute Neighbors

Sometimes I had a companion[1] in my fishing, who came through the village to my house from the other side of the town, and the catching of the dinner was as much a social exercise as the eating of it.

*Hermit.* I wonder what the world is doing now. I have not heard so much as a locust over the sweet-fern these three hours. The pigeons are all asleep upon their roosts,—no flutter from them. Was that a farmer's noon horn which sounded from beyond the woods just now? The hands are coming in to boiled salt beef and cider and Indian bread. Why will men worry themselves so? He that does not eat need not work. I wonder how much they have reaped. Who would live there where a body can never think for the barking of Bose?[2] And O, the housekeeping! to keep bright the devil's door-knobs, and scour his tubs this bright day! Better not keep a house. Say, some hollow tree; and then for morning calls and dinner-parties! Only a woodpecker tapping. O, they swarm; the sun is too warm there; they are born too far into life for me. I have water from the spring, and a loaf of brown bread on the shelf.—Hark! I hear a rustling of the leaves. Is it some ill-fed village hound yielding to the instinct of the chase? or the lost pig which is said to be in these woods, whose tracks I saw after the rain? It comes on apace; my sumachs and sweet-briars tremble.—Eh, Mr. Poet, is it you? How do you like the world to-day?

*Poet.* See those clouds; how they hang! That's the greatest thing I have seen to-day. There's nothing like it in old paintings, nothing like it in foreign lands,—unless when we were off the coast of Spain. That's a true Mediterranean sky. I thought, as I have my living to get, and have not eaten to-day, that I might go a-fishing. That's the true industry for poets. It is the only trade I have learned. Come, let's along.

*Hermit.* I cannot resist. My brown bread will soon be done. I will go with you gladly soon, but I am just concluding a serious meditation. I think that I am near the end of it. Leave me alone, then, for a while. But that we may not be delayed, you shall be digging the bait meanwhile. Angle-worms are rarely to be met with in these parts, where the soil was never fattened with manure; the race is nearly extinct. The sport of digging the bait is nearly equal to that of catching the fish, when one's appetite is not too keen; and this you may have all to yourself to-day. I would advise you to set in the spade down yonder among the ground-nuts, where you see the johnswort waving. I think that I may warrant you one worm to every three sods you turn up, if you look well in among the roots of the grass, as if you were weeding. Or, if you choose to

---

1. Channing, the "Poet" of the following dialogue.     2. Name for a dog, like "Fido."

go farther, it will not be unwise, for I have found the increase of fair bait to be
very nearly as the squares of the distances.

*Hermit alone.* Let me see; where was I? Methinks I was nearly in this frame
of mind; the world lay about at this angle. Shall I go to heaven or a-fishing? If
I should soon bring this meditation to an end, would another so sweet occasion
be likely to offer? I was as near being resolved into the essence of things as ever
I was in my life. I fear my thoughts will not come back to me. If it would do
any good, I would whistle for them. When they make us an offer, is it wise to
say, We will think of it? My thoughts have left no track, and I cannot find the
path again. What was it that I was thinking of? It was a very hazy day. I will
just try these three sentences of Con-fut-see;[3] they may fetch that state about
again. I know not whether it was the dumps or a budding ecstasy. Mem.[4]
There never is but one opportunity of a kind.

*Poet.* How now, Hermit, is it too soon? I have got just thirteen whole ones,
beside several which are imperfect or undersized; but they will do for the
smaller fry; they do not cover up the hook so much. Those village worms are
quite too large; a shiner may make a meal off one without finding the skewer.

*Hermit.* Well, then, let's be off. Shall we to the Concord? There's good
sport there if the water be not too high.

Why do precisely these objects which we behold make a world? Why has
man just these species of animals for his neighbors; as if nothing but a mouse
could have filled this crevice? I suspect that Pilpay & Co.[5] have put animals
to their best use, for they are all beasts of burden, in a sense, made to carry
some portion of our thoughts.

The mice which haunted my house were not the common ones, which
are said to have been introduced into the country, but a wild native kind
(*Musleucopus*) not found in the village. I sent one to a distinguished naturalist,[6] and it interested him much. When I was building, one of these had its
nest underneath the house, and before I had laid the second floor, and swept
out the shavings, would come out regularly at lunch time and pick up the
crumbs at my feet. It probably had never seen a man before; and it soon
became quite familiar, and would run over my shoes and up my clothes. It
could readily ascend the sides of the room by short impulses, like a squirrel,
which it resembled in its motions. At length, as I leaned with my elbow on
the bench one day, it ran up my clothes, and along my sleeve, and round and
round the paper which held my dinner, while I kept the latter close, and
dodged and played at bo-peep with it; and when at last I held still a piece of
cheese between my thumb and finger, it came and nibbled it, sitting in my
hand, and afterward cleaned its face and paws, like a fly, and walked away.

A phoebe soon built in my shed, and a robin for protection in a pine which
grew against the house. In June the partridge, (*Tetrao umbellus*,) which is so
shy a bird, led her brood past my windows, from the woods in the rear to the
front of my house, clucking and calling to them like a hen, and in all her
behavior proving herself the hen of the woods. The young suddenly disperse
on your approach, at a signal from the mother, as if a whirlwind had swept

3. Confucius.
4. Abbreviation for *memorandum*, used here as a self-
reminder.
5. I.e., all tellers of fables. Pilpay, or Bidpai, was credited with authorship of a collection of East Indian fa-

bles that Thoreau knew in Charles Wilkins's translation.
6. Louis Agassiz (1807–1873), Swiss-American naturalist, a teacher at Harvard, and an intimate of the
Cambridge literary circle.

them away, and they so exactly resemble the dried leaves and twigs that many a traveller has placed his foot in the midst of a brood, and heard the whir of the old bird as she flew off, and her anxious calls and mewing, or seen her trail her wings to attract his attention, without suspecting their neighborhood. The parent will sometimes roll and spin round before you in such a dishabille, that you cannot, for a few moments, detect what kind of creature it is. The young squat still and flat, often running their heads under a leaf, and mind only their mother's directions given from a distance, nor will your approach make them run again and betray themselves. You may even tread on them, or have your eyes on them for a minute, without discovering them. I have held them in my open hand at such a time, and still their only care, obedient to their mother and their instinct, was to squat there without fear or trembling. So perfect is this instinct, that once, when I had laid them on the leaves again, and one accidentally fell on its side, it was found with the rest in exactly the same position ten minutes afterward. They are not callow like the young of most birds, but more perfectly developed and precocious even than chickens. The remarkably adult yet innocent expression of their open and serene eyes is very memorable. An intelligence seems reflected in them. They suggest not merely the purity of infancy, but a wisdom clarified by experience. Such an eye was not born when the bird was, but is coeval with the sky it reflects. The woods do not yield another such a gem. The traveller does not often look into such a limpid well. The ignorant or reckless sportsman often shoots the parent at such a time, and leaves these innocents to fall a prey to some prowling beast or bird, or gradually mingle with the decaying leaves which they so much resemble. It is said that when hatched by a hen they will directly disperse on some alarm, and so are lost, for they never hear the mother's call which gathers them again. These were my hens and chickens.

It is remarkable how many creatures live wild and free though secret in the woods, and still sustain themselves in the neighborhood of towns, suspected by hunters only. How retired the otter manages to live here! He grows to be four feet long, as big as a small boy, perhaps without any human being getting a glimpse of him. I formerly saw the raccoon in the woods behind where my house is built, and probably still heard their whinnering at night. Commonly I rested an hour or two in the shade at noon, after planting, and ate my lunch, and read a little by a spring which was the source of a swamp and of a brook, oozing from under Brister's Hill, half a mile from my field. The approach to this was through a succession of descending grassy hollows, full of young pitch-pines, into a larger wood about the swamp. There, in a very secluded and shaded spot, under a spreading white-pine, there was yet a clean firm sward to sit on. I had dug out the spring and made a well of clear gray water, where I could dip up a pailful without roiling it, and thither I went for this purpose almost every day in midsummer, when the pond was warmest. Thither too the wood-cock led her brood, to probe the mud for worms, flying but a foot above them down the bank, while they ran in a troop beneath; but at last, spying me, she would leave her young and circle round and round me, nearer and nearer, till within four or five feet, pretending broken wings and legs, to attract my attention and get off her young, who would already have taken up their march, with faint wiry peep, single file through the swamp, as she directed. Or I heard the peep of the young when I could not see the parent bird. There too the turtle-doves sat over the spring, or fluttered from bough to bough of the soft white-pines over my head; or the red squirrel, coursing down the nearest bough, was particularly familiar and inquisitive. You only need sit still long enough in some attractive spot in the woods that all its inhabitants may exhibit themselves to you by turns. I was witness to events of a less peaceful character. One day when I went out to my wood-pile, or rather my pile of stumps, I observed two large ants, the one red, the other much larger, nearly half an inch long, and black, fiercely contending with one another. Having once got hold they never let go, but struggled and wrestled and rolled on the chips incessantly. Looking farther, I was surprised to find that the chips were covered with such combatants, that it was not a *duellum*, but a *bellum*, a war between two races of ants, the red always pitted against the black, and frequently two red ones to one black. The legions of these Myrmidons[7] covered all the hills and vales in my wood-yard, and the ground was already strewn with the dead and dying, both red and black. It was the only battle which I have ever witnessed, the only battle-field I ever trod while the battle was raging; internecine war; the red republicans on the one hand, and the black imperialists on the other. On every side they were engaged in deadly combat, yet without any noise that I could hear, and human soldiers never fought so resolutely. I watched a couple that were fast locked in each other's embraces, in a little sunny valley amid the chips, now at noon-day prepared to fight till the sun went down, or life went out. The smaller red champion had fastened himself like a vice to his adversary's front, and through all the tumblings on that field never for an instant ceased to gnaw at one of his feelers near the root, having already caused the other to go by the board; while the stronger black one dashed him from side to side, and, as I saw on looking nearer, had already divested him of several of his members. They fought with more pertinacity than bulldogs. Neither manifested the least disposition to retreat. It was evident that their battle-cry was Conquer or die. In the mean while there came along a single red ant on the hill-side of this valley, evidently full of excitement, who either had despatched his foe, or had not yet taken part in the battle; probably the latter, for he had lost none of his limbs; whose mother had charged him to return with his shield or upon it.[8] Or perchance he was some Achilles, who had nourished his wrath apart, and had now come to avenge or rescue his Patroclus.[9] He saw this unequal combat from afar,— for the blacks were nearly twice the size of the red,—he drew near with rapid pace till he stood on his guard within half an inch of the combatants; then, watching his opportunity, he sprang upon the black warrior, and commenced his operations near the root of his right fore-leg, leaving the foe to select among his own members; and so there were three united for life, as if a new kind of attraction had been invented which put all other locks and cements to shame. I should not have wondered by this time to find that they had their respective musical bands stationed on some eminent chip, and playing their national airs the while, to excite the slow and cheer the dying combatants. I was myself excited somewhat even as if they had been men. The more you think of it, the less the difference. And certainly there is not the fight recorded in Concord history, at least, if in the history of America, that will bear a moment's comparison with this, whether for the numbers engaged in it, or for the patriotism

---

7. The Myrmidons were warriors from southern Thessaly who went to fight at Troy under their chieftain Achilles.
8. What a Spartan mother was supposed to say to a son

going into battle.
9. In *The Iliad* Achilles sat out much of the Trojan War until the death of his friend Patroclus, which he revenged

and heroism displayed. For numbers and for carnage it was an Austerlitz or Dresden.[1] Concord Fight! Two killed on the patriots' side, and Luther Blanchard wounded! Why here every ant was a Buttrick,—"Fire! for God's sake fire!"—and thousands shared the fate of Davis and Hosmer.[2] There was not one hireling there. I have no doubt that it was a principle they fought for, as much as our ancestors, and not to avoid a three-penny tax on their tea; and the results of this battle will be as important and memorable to those whom it concerns as those of the battle of Bunker Hill, at least.

I took up the chip on which the three I have particularly described were struggling, carried it into my house, and placed it under a tumbler on my window-sill, in order to see the issue. Holding a microscope[3] to the first-mentioned red ant, I saw that, though he was assiduously gnawing at the near foreleg of his enemy, having severed his remaining feeler, his own breast was all torn away, exposing what vitals he had there to the jaws of the black warrior, whose breast-plate was apparently too thick for him to pierce; and the dark carbuncles of the sufferer's eyes shone with ferocity such as war only could excite. They struggled half an hour longer under the tumbler, and when I looked again the black soldier had severed the heads of his foes from their bodies, and the still living heads were hanging on either side of him like ghastly trophies at his saddle-bow, still apparently as firmly fastened as ever, and he was endeavoring with feeble struggles, being without feelers and with only the remnant of a leg, and I know not how many other wounds, to divest himself of them; which at length, after half an hour more, he accomplished. I raised the glass, and he went off over the windowsill in that crippled state. Whether he finally survived that combat, and spent the remainder of his days in some Hotel des Invalides,[4] I do not know; but I thought that his industry would not be worth much thereafter. I never learned which party was victorious, nor the cause of the war; but I felt for the rest of that day as if I had had my feelings excited and harrowed by witnessing the struggle, the ferocity and carnage, of a human battle before my door.

Kirby and Spence tell us that the battles of ants have long been celebrated and the date of them recorded, though they say that Huber[5] is the only modern author who appears to have witnessed them. "Æneas Sylvius," say they, "after giving a very circumstantial account of one contested with great obstinacy by a great and small species on the trunk of a pear tree," adds that " 'This action was fought in the pontificate of Eugenius the Fourth, in the presence of Nicholas Pistoriensis, an eminent lawyer, who related the whole history of the battle with the greatest fidelity.' A similar engagement between great and small ants is recorded by Olaus Magnus,[6] in which the small ones, being victorious, are said to have buried the bodies of their own soldiers, but left those of their giant enemies a prey to the birds. This event happened previous to the expulsion of the tyrant Christiern the Second from Sweden." The battle which I witnessed took place in the Presidency of Polk, five years before the passage of Webster's Fugitive-Slave Bill.[7]

Many a village Bose, fit only to course a mud-turtle in a victualling cellar,

1. Important battles of the Napoleonic Wars.
2. Davis and Hosmer were the only two colonists killed at Concord on April 19, 1775; the others named were participants in the battle, which Thoreau knew about in great detail.
3. Magnifying glass.
4. Old soldiers' home in Paris.

5. François Huber (1750–1831), Swiss entomologist.
6. From Kirby and Spence, Introduction to Entomology (1846): Æneas Sylvius (1405–1464) was Pope Pius II (1458–64) and Olaus Magnus (1490–1558) was archbishop of Uppsala.
7. That is, in 1845.

sported his heavy quarters in the woods, without the knowledge of his master, and ineffectually smelled at old fox burrows and woodchucks' holes; led perchance by some slight cur which nimbly threaded the wood, and might still inspire a natural terror in its denizens;—now far behind his guide, barking like a canine bull toward some small squirrel which had treed itself for scrutiny, then, cantering off, bending the bushes with his weight, imagining that he is on the track of some stray member of the gerbille family. Once I was surprised to see a cat walking along the stony shore of the pond, for they rarely wander so far from home. The surprise was mutual. Nevertheless the most domestic cat, which has lain on a rug all her days, appears quite at home in the woods, and, by her sly and stealthy behavior, proves herself more native there than the regular inhabitants. Once, when berrying, I met with a cat with young kittens in the woods, quite wild, and they all, like their mother, had their backs up and were fiercely spitting at me. A few years before I lived in the woods there was what was called a "winged cat" in one of the farm-houses in Lincoln nearest the pond, Mr. Gilian Baker's. When I called to see her in June, 1842, she was gone a-hunting in the woods, as was her wont, (I am not sure whether it was a male or female, and so use the more common pronoun,) but her mistress told me that she came into the neighborhood a little more than a year before, in April, and was finally taken into their house; that she was of a dark brownish-gray color, with a white spot on her throat, and white feet, and had a large bushy tail like a fox; that in the winter the fur grew thick and flatted out along her sides, forming strips ten or twelve inches long by two and a half wide, and under her chin like a muff, the upper side loose, the under matted like felt, and in the spring these appendages dropped off. They gave me a pair of her "wings," which I keep still. There is no appearance of a membrane about them. Some thought it was part flying-squirrel or some other wild animal, which is not impossible, for, according to naturalists, prolific hybrids[8] have been produced by the union of the marten and domestic cat. This would have been the right kind of cat for me to keep, if I had kept any; for why should not a poet's cat be winged as well as his horse?[9]

In the fall the loon (*Colymbus glacialis*) came, as usual, to moult and bathe in the pond, making the woods ring with his wild laughter before I had risen. At rumor of his arrival all the Mill-dam sportsmen are on the alert, in gigs and on foot, two by two and three by three, with patent rifles and conical balls and spy-glasses. They come rustling through the woods like autumn leaves, at least ten men to one loon. Some station themselves on this side of the pond, some on that, for the poor bird cannot be omnipresent; if he dive here he must come up there. But now the kind October wind rises, rustling the leaves and rippling the surface of the water, so that no loon can be heard or seen, though his foes sweep the pond with spy-glasses, and make the woods resound with their discharges. The waves generously rise and dash angrily, taking sides with all waterfowl, and our sportsmen must beat a retreat to town and shop and unfinished jobs. But they were too often successful. When I went to get a pail of water early in the morning I frequently saw this stately bird sailing out of my cove within a few rods. If I endeavored to overtake him in a boat, in order to see how he would manœuvre, he would dive and be completely lost, so that I did not discover him again, sometimes, till the latter part of the day. But I was

8. The important word is *prolific*, because hybrids (such as the mule) are often sterile.

9. During their flights of inspiration poets are supposed to ride on the winged horse Pegasus.

more than a match for him on the surface. He commonly went off in a rage.
As I was paddling along the north shore one very calm October afternoon,
for such days especially they settle on to the lakes, like the milkweed down,
having looked in vain over the pond for a loon, suddenly one, sailing out from
the shore toward the middle a few rods in front of me, set up his wild laugh
and betrayed himself. I pursued with a paddle and he dived, but when he
came up I was nearer than before. He dived again, but I miscalculated the
direction he would take, and we were fifty rods apart when he came to the
surface this time, for I had helped to widen the interval; and again he laughed
long and loud, and with more reason than before. He manœuvred so cunningly that I could not get within half a dozen rods of him. Each time, when
he came to the surface, turning his head this way and that, he coolly surveyed
the water and the land, and apparently chose his course so that he might come
up where there was the widest expanse of water and at the greatest distance
from the boat. It was surprising how quickly he made up his mind and put his
resolve into execution. He led me at once to the widest part of the pond, and
could not be driven from it. While he was thinking one thing in his brain, I
was endeavoring to divine his thought in mine. It was a pretty game, played
on the smooth surface of the pond, a man against a loon. Suddenly your
adversary's checker disappears beneath the board, and the problem is to place
yours nearest to where his will appear again. Sometimes he would come up
unexpectedly on the opposite side of me, having apparently passed directly
under the boat. So long-winded was he and so unweariable, that when he had
swum farthest he would immediately plunge again, nevertheless; and then no
wit could divine where in the deep pond, beneath the smooth surface, he
might be speeding his way like a fish, for he had time and ability to visit the
bottom of the pond in its deepest part. It is said that loons have been caught
in the New York lakes eighty feet beneath the surface, with hooks set for
trout,—though Walden is deeper than that. How surprised must the fishes be
to see this ungainly visitor from another sphere speeding his way amid their
schools! Yet he appeared to know his course as surely under water as on the
surface, and swam much faster there. Once or twice I saw a ripple where he
approached the surface, just put his head out to reconnoitre, and instantly
dived again. I found that it was as well for me to rest on my oars and wait his
reappearing as to endeavor to calculate where he would rise; for again and
again, when I was straining my eyes over the surface one way, I would suddenly be startled by his unearthly laugh behind me. But why, after displaying
so much cunning, did he invariably betray himself the moment he came up
by that loud laugh? Did not his white breast enough betray him? He was
indeed a silly loon, I thought. I could commonly hear the plash of the water
when he came up, and so also detected him. But after an hour he seemed as
fresh as ever, dived as willingly and swam yet farther than at first. It was surprising to see how serenely he sailed off with unruffled breast when he came
to the surface, doing all the work with his webbed feet beneath. His usual
note was this demoniac laughter, yet somewhat like that of a water-fowl; but
occasionally, when he had balked me most successfully and come up a long
way off, he uttered a long-drawn unearthly howl, probably more like that of a
wolf than any bird; as when a beast puts his muzzle to the ground and deliberately howls. This was his looning,—perhaps the wildest sound that is ever
heard here, making the woods ring far and wide. I concluded that he laughed

in derision of my efforts, confident of his own resources. Though the sky was by this time overcast, the pond was so smooth that I could see where he broke the surface when I did not hear him. His white breast, the stillness of the air, and the smoothness of the water were all against him. At length, having come up fifty rods off, he uttered one of those prolonged howls, as if calling on the god of loons to aid him, and immediately there came a wind from the east and rippled the surface, and filled the whole air with misty rain, and I was impressed as if it were the prayer of the loon answered, and his god was angry with me; and so I left him disappearing far away on the tumultuous surface.

For hours, in fall days, I watched the ducks cunningly tack and veer and hold the middle of the pond, far from the sportsman; tricks which they will have less need to practise in Louisiana bayous. When compelled to rise they would sometimes circle round and round and over the pond at a considerable height, from which they could easily see to other ponds and the river, like black motes in the sky; and, when I thought they had gone off thither long since, they would settle down by a slanting flight of a quarter of a mile on to a distant part which was left free; but what beside safety they got by sailing in the middle of Walden I do not know, unless they love its water for the same reason that I do.

\* \* \*

## Spring

The opening of large tracts by the ice-cutters commonly causes a pond to break up earlier; for the water, agitated by the wind, even in cold weather, wears away the surrounding ice. But such was not the effect on Walden that year, for she had soon got a thick new garment to take the place of the old. This pond never breaks up so soon as the others in this neighborhood, on account both of its grater depth and its having no stream passing through it to melt or wear away the ice. I never knew it to open in the course of a winter, not excepting that of '52–3, which gave the ponds so severe a trial. It commonly opens about the first of April, a week or ten days later than Flint's Pond and Fair-Haven, beginning to melt on the north side and in the shallower parts where it began to freeze. It indicates better than any water hereabouts the absolute progress of the season, being least affected by transient changes of temperature. A severe cold of a few days' duration in March may very much retard the opening of the former ponds, while the temperature of Walden increases almost uninterruptedly. A thermometer thrust into the middle of Walden on the 6th of March, 1847, stood at 32°, or freezing point; near the shore at 33°; in the middle of Flint's Pond, the same day, at 32½°; at a dozen rods from the shore, in shallow water, under ice a foot thick, at 36°. This difference of three and a half degrees between the temperature of the deep water and the shallow in the latter pond, and the fact that a great proportion of it is comparatively shallow, show why it should break up so much sooner than Walden. The ice in the shallowest part was at this time several inches thinner than in the middle. In mid-winter the middle had been the warmest and the ice thinnest there. So, also, every one who has waded about the shores of a pond in summer must have perceived how much warmer the water is close to the shore, where only three or four inches deep, than a little distance out, and on the surface where it is deep, than near the bottom. In spring the sun not only exerts an influence through the increased temperature of the air and earth, but its heat passes through ice a foot or more thick, and is reflected from the bottom in shallow water, and so also warms the water and melts the under side of the ice, at the same time that it is melting it more directly above, making it uneven, and causing the air bubbles which it contains to extend themselves upward and downward until it is completely honey-combed, and at last disappears suddenly in a single spring rain. Ice has its grain as well as wood, and when a cake begins to rot or "comb," that is, assume the appearance of honey-comb, whatever may be its position, the air cells are at right angles with what was the water surface. Where there is a rock or a log rising near to the surface the ice over it is much thinner, and is frequently quite dissolved by this reflected heat; and I have been told that in the experiment at Cambridge to freeze water in a shallow wooden pond, though the cold air circulated underneath, and so had access to both sides, the reflection of the sun from the bottom more than counterbalanced this advantage. When a warm rain in the middle of the winter melts off the snow-ice from Walden, and leaves a hard dark or transparent ice on the middle, there will be a strip of rotten though thicker white ice, a rod or more wide, about the shores, created by this reflected heat. Also, as I have said, the bubbles themselves within the ice operate as burning glasses to melt the ice beneath.

The phenomena of the year take place every day in a pond on a small scale. Every morning, generally speaking, the shallow water is being warmed more rapidly than the deep, though it may not be made so warm after all, and every evening it is being cooled more rapidly until the morning. The day is an epitome of the year. The night is the winter, the morning and evening are the spring and fall, and the noon is the summer. The cracking and booming of the ice indicate a change of temperature. One pleasant morning after a cold night, February 24th, 1850, having gone to Flint's Pond to spend the day, I noticed with surprise, that when I struck the ice with the head of my axe, it resounded like a gong for many rods around, or as if I had struck on a tight drum-head. The pond began to boom about an hour after sunrise, when it felt the influence of the sun's rays slanted upon it from the hills; it stretched itself and yawned like a waking man with a gradually increasing tumult, which was kept up three or four hours. It took a short siesta at noon, and boomed once more toward night, as the sun was withdrawing his influence. In the right stage of the weather a pond fires its evening gun with great regularity. But in the middle of the day, being full of cracks, and the air also being less elastic, it had completely lost its resonance, and probably fishes and muskrats could not then have been stunned by a blow on it. The fishermen say that the "thundering of the pond" scares the fishes and prevents their biting. The pond does not thunder every evening, and I cannot tell surely when to expect its thundering; but though I may perceive no difference in the weather, it does. Who would have suspected so large and cold and thick-skinned a thing to be so sensitive? Yet it has its law to which it thunders obedience when it should as surely as the buds expand in the spring. The earth is all alive and covered with papillæ. The largest pond is as sensitive to atmospheric changes as the globule of mercury in its tube.

One attraction in coming to the woods to live was that I should have leisure and opportunity to see the spring come in. The ice in the pond at length begins to be honey-combed, and I can set my heel in it as I walk. Fogs and rains and warmer suns are gradually melting the snow; the days have grown sensibly longer; and I see how I shall get through the winter without adding to my wood-pile, for large fires are no longer necessary. I am on the alert for the first signs of spring, to hear the chance note of some arriving bird, or the striped squirrel's chirp, for his stores must be now nearly exhausted, or see the woodchuck venture out of his winter quarters. On the 13th of March, after I had heard the bluebird, song-sparrow, and red-wing, the ice was still nearly a foot thick. As the weather grew warmer, it was not sensibly worn away by the water, nor broken up and floated off as in rivers, but, though it was completely melted for half a rod in width about the shore, the middle was merely honey-combed and saturated with water, so that you could put your foot through it when six inches thick; but by the next day evening, perhaps, after a warm rain followed by fog, it would have wholly disappeared, all gone off with the fog, spirited away. One year I went across the middle only five days before it disappeared entirely. In 1845 Walden was first completely open on the 1st of April; in '46, the 25th of March; in '47, the 8th of April; in '51, the 28th of March; in '52, the 18th of April; in '53, the 23rd of March; in '54, about the 7th of April.

Every incident connected with the breaking up of the rivers and ponds and the settling of the weather is particularly interesting to us who live in a climate of so great extremes. When the warmer days come, they who dwell near the river hear the ice crack at night with a startling whoop as loud as artillery, as if its icy fetters were rent from end to end, and within a few days see it rapidly going out. So the alligator comes out of the mud with quakings of the earth. One old man, who has been a close observer of Nature, and seems as thoroughly wise in regard to all her operations as if she had been put upon the stocks when he was a boy, and he had helped to lay her keel,—who has come to his growth, and can hardly acquire more of natural lore if he should live to the age of Methuselah[1]—told me, and I was surprised to hear him express wonder at any of Nature's operations, for I thought that there were no secrets between them, that one spring day he took his gun and boat, and thought that he would have a little sport with the ducks. There was ice still on the meadows, but it was all gone out of the river, and he dropped down without obstruction from Sudbury, where he lived, to Fair-Haven Pond, which he found, unexpectedly, covered for the most part with a firm field of ice. It was a warm day, and he was surprised to see so great a body of ice remaining. Not seeing any ducks, he hid his boat on the north or back side of an island in the pond, and then concealed himself in the bushes on the south side, to await them. The ice was melted for three or four rods from the shore, and there was a smooth and warm sheet of water, with a muddy bottom, such as the ducks love, within, and he thought it likely that some would be along pretty soon. After he had lain still there about an hour he heard a low and seemingly very distant sound, but singularly grand and impressive, unlike any thing he had ever heard, gradually swelling and increasing as if it would have a universal and memorable ending, a sullen rush and roar, which seemed to him all at once like the sound of a vast body of fowl coming in to settle there, and, seizing his gun, he started up in haste and excited; but he found, to his surprise, that the

1. "And the days of Methuselah were nine hundred sixty and nine years: and he died" (Genesis 5.27).

whole body of the ice had started while he lay there, and drifted in to the shore, and the sound he had heard was made by its edge grating on the shore,—at first gently nibbled and crumbled off, but at length heaving up and scattering its wrecks along the island to a considerable height before it came to a stand still.

At length the sun's rays have attained the right angle, and warm winds blow up mist and rain and melt the snow banks, and the sun dispersing the mist smiles on a checkered landscape of russet and white smoking with incense, through which the traveller picks his way from islet to islet, cheered by the music of a thousand tinkling rills and rivulets whose veins are filled with the blood of winter which they are bearing off.

Few phenomena gave me more delight than to observe the forms which thawing sand and clay assume in flowing down the sides of a deep cut on the railroad through which I passed on my way to the village, a phenomenon not very common on so large a scale, though the number of freshly exposed banks of the right material must have been greatly multiplied since railroads were invented. The material was sand of every degree of fineness and of various rich colors, commonly mixed with a little clay. When the frost comes out in the spring, and even in a thawing day in the winter, the sand begins to flow down the slopes like lava, sometimes bursting out through the snow and overflowing it where no sand was to be seen before. Innumerable little streams overlap and interlace one with another, exhibiting a sort of hybrid product, which obeys half way the law of currents, and half way that of vegetation. As it flows it takes the forms of sappy leaves or vines, making heaps of pulpy sprays a foot or more in depth, and resembling, as you look down on them, the laciniated lobed and imbricated[2] thalluses of some lichens; or you are reminded of coral, of leopards' paws or birds' feet, of brains or lungs or bowels, and excrements of all kinds. It is a truly *grotesque* vegetation, whose forms and color we see imitated in bronze, a sort of architectural foliage more ancient and typical than acanthus, chiccory, ivy, vine, or any vegetable leaves; destined perhaps, under some circumstances, to become a puzzle to future geologists. The whole cut impressed me as if it were a cave with its stalactites laid open to the light. The various shades of the sand are singularly rich and agreeable, embracing the different iron colors, brown, gray, yellowish, and reddish. When the flowing mass reaches the drain at the foot of the bank it spreads out flatter into *strands*, the separate streams losing their semi-cylindrical form and gradually becoming more flat and broad, running together as they are more moist, till they form an almost flat *sand*, still variously and beautifully shaded, but in which you can trace the original forms of vegetation; till at length, in the water itself, they are converted into *banks*, like those formed off the mouths of rivers, and the forms of vegetation are lost in the ripple marks on the bottom.

The whole bank, which is from twenty to forty feet high, is sometimes overlaid with a mass of this kind of foliage, or sandy rupture, for a quarter of a mile on one or both sides, the produce of one spring day. What makes this sand foliage remarkable is its springing into existence thus suddenly. When I see on the one side the inert bank,—for the sun acts on one side first,—and on the other this luxuriant foliage, the creation of an hour, I am affected as if in a peculiar sense I stood in the laboratory of the Artist who made the world

---

2. Lapped over in regular order like roof tiles. "Laciniated": deeply, irregularly lobed.

and me,—had come to where he was still at work, sporting on this bank, and
with excess of energy strewing his fresh designs about. I feel as if I were nearer
to the vitals of the globe, for this sandy overflow is something such a foliaceous
mass as the vitals of the animal body. You find thus in the very sands an
anticipation of the vegetable leaf. No wonder that the earth expresses itself
outwardly in leaves, it so labors with the idea inwardly. The atoms have
already learned this law, and are pregnant by it. The overhanging leaf sees
here its prototype. *Internally*, whether in the globe or animal body, it is a
moist thick *lobe*, a word especially applicable to the liver and lungs and the
*leaves* of fat. (λείβω, *labor, lapsus*, to flow or slip downward, a lapsing; λοβο.,
*globus*, lobe, globe; also lap, flap, and many other words,) *externally* a dry thin
*leaf*, even as the *f* and *v* are a pressed and dried *b*. The radicals of lobe are *lb*,
the soft mass of the *b* (single lobed, or B, double lobed,) with a liquid *l* behind
it pressing it forward. In globe, *glb*, the guttural *g* adds to the meaning the
capacity of the throat. The feathers and wings of birds are still drier and thinner
leaves. Thus, also, you pass from the lumpish grub in the earth to the airy and
fluttering butterfly. The very globe continually transcends and translates itself,
and becomes winged in its orbit. Even ice begins with delicate crystal leaves,
as if it had flowed into moulds which the fronds of water plants have impressed
on the watery mirror. The whole tree itself is but one leaf, and rivers are still
vaster leaves whose pulp is intervening earth, and towns and cities are the ova
of insects in their axils.

When the sun withdraws the sand ceases to flow, but in the morning the
streams will start once more and branch and branch again into a myriad of
others. You here see perchance how blood vessels are formed. If you look
closely you observe that first there pushes forward from the thawing mass a
stream of softened sand with a drop-like point, like the ball of the finger,
feeling its way slowly and blindly downward, until at last with more heat and
moisture, as the sun gets higher, the moist fluid portion, in its effort to obey
the law to which the most inert also yields, separates from the latter and forms
for itself a meandering channel or artery within that, in which is seen a little
silvery stream glancing like lightning from one stage of pulpy leaves or
branches to another, and ever and anon swallowed up in the sand. It is wonderful how rapidly yet perfectly the sand organizes itself as it flows, using the
best material its mass affords to form the sharp edges of its channel. Such are
the sources of rivers. In the silicious matter which the water deposits is perhaps
the bony system, and in the still finer soil and organic matter the fleshy fibre
or cellular tissue. What is man but a mass of thawing clay? The ball of the
human finger is but a drop congealed. The fingers and toes flow to their extent
from the thawing mass of the body. Who knows what the human body would
expand and flow out to under a more genial heaven? Is not the hand a spreading *palm* leaf with its lobes and veins? The ear may be regarded, fancifully, as
a lichen, *umbilicaria*, on the side of the head, with its lobe or drop. The lip
(*labium* from *labor* (?)) laps or lapses from the sides of the cavernous mouth.
The nose is a manifest congealed drop or stalactite. The chin is a still larger
drop, the confluent dripping of the face. The cheeks are a slide from the brows
into the valley of the face, opposed and diffused by the cheek bones. Each
rounded lobe of the vegetable leaf, too, is a thick and now loitering drop,
larger or smaller; the lobes are the fingers of the leaf; and as many lobes as it
has, in so many directions it tends to flow, and more heat or other genial
influences would have caused it to flow yet farther.

Thus it seemed that this one hillside illustrated the principle of all the operations of Nature. The Maker of this earth but patented a leaf. What Champollion[3] will decipher this hieroglyphic for us, that we may turn over a new leaf
at last? This phenomenon is more exhilarating to me than the luxuriance and
fertility of vineyards. True, it is somewhat excrementitious in its character,
and there is no end to the heaps of liver, lights and bowels, as if the globe were
turned wrong side outward; but this suggests at least that Nature has some
bowels, and there again is mother of humanity.[4] This is the frost coming out
of the ground; this is Spring. It precedes the green and flowery spring, as
mythology precedes regular poetry. I know of nothing more purgative of winter
fumes and indigestions. It convinces me that Earth is still in her swaddling
clothes, and stretches forth baby fingers on every side. Fresh curls spring from
the baldest brow. There is nothing inorganic. These foliaceous heaps lie along
the bank like the slag of a furnace, showing that Nature is "in full blast"
within. The earth is not a mere fragment of dead history, stratum upon stratum
like the leaves of a book, to be studied by geologists and antiquaries chiefly,
but living poetry like the leaves of a tree, which precede flowers and fruit,—
not a fossil earth, but a living earth; compared with whose great central life all
animal and vegetable life is merely parasitic. Its throes will heave our exuviæ
from their graves. You may melt your metals and cast them into the most
beautiful moulds you can; they will never excite me like the forms which this
molten earth flows out into. And not only it, but the institutions upon it, are
plastic like clay in the hands of the potter.

Ere long, not only on these banks, but on every hill and plain and in every
hollow, the frost comes out of the ground like a dormant quadruped from its
burrow, and seeks the sea with music, or migrates to other climes in clouds.
Thaw with his gentle persuasion is more powerful than Thor with his hammer.[5] The one melts, the other but breaks in pieces.

When the ground was partially bare of snow, and a few warm days had dried
its surface somewhat, it was pleasant to compare the first tender signs of the
infant year just peeping forth with the stately beauty of the withered vegetation
which had withstood the winter,—life-everlasting, golden-rods, pinweeds, and
graceful wild grasses, more obvious and interesting frequently than in summer
even, as if their beauty was not ripe till then; even cotton-grass, cat-tails, mul-
leins, johnswort, hard-hack, meadow-sweet, and other strong stemmed plants,
those unexhausted granaries which entertain the earliest birds,—decent
weeds,[6] at least, which widowed Nature wears. I am particularly attracted by
the arching and sheaf-like top of the wool-grass; it brings back the summer to
our winter memories, and is among the forms which art loves to copy, and
which, in the vegetable kingdom, have the same relation to types already in
the mind of man that astronomy has. It is an antique style older than Greek or
Egyptian. Many of the phenomena of Winter are suggestive of an inexpressible
tenderness and fragile delicacy. We are accustomed to hear this king described
as a rude and boisterous tyrant; but with the gentleness of a lover he adorns
the tresses of Summer.

At the approach of spring the red-squirrels got under my house, two at a

3. Jean François Champollion (1790–1832), French
archaeologist whose deciphering of the inscriptions on
the Rosetta stone fueled great popular interest in
Egyptology.
4. Thoreau puns on the sense of "bowels" as the seat

of compassion. "Lights": lungs.
5. As a New Englander, Thoreau apparently pronounced thaw to sound like Thor, the Norse god of
thunder.
6. Mourning garments.

time, directly under my feet as I sat reading or writing, and kept up the
queerest chuckling and chirruping and vocal pirouetting and gurgling sounds
that ever were heard; and when I stamped they only chirruped the louder, as
if past all fear and respect in their mad pranks, defying humanity to stop them.
No you don't—chickaree—chickaree. They were wholly deaf to my arguments, or failed to perceive their force, and fell into a strain of invective that
was irresistible.

The first sparrow of spring! The year beginning with younger hope than
ever! The faint silvery warblings heard over the partially bare and moist fields
from the blue-bird, the song-sparrow, and the red-wing, as if the last flakes of
winter tinkled as they fell! What at such a time are histories, chronologies,
traditions, and all written revelations? The brooks sing carols and glees to the
spring. The marsh-hawk sailing low over the meadow is already seeking the
first slimy life that awakes. The sinking sound of melting snow is heard in all
dells, and the ice dissolves apace in the ponds. The grass flames up on the
hillsides like a spring fire,—"et primitus oritur herba imbribus primoribus evo-
cata,"[7]—as if the earth sent forth an inward heat to greet the returning sun;
not yellow but green is the color of its flame;—the symbol of perpetual youth,
the grass-blade, like a long green ribbon, streams from the sod into the summer, checked indeed by the frost, but anon pushing on again, lifting its spear
of last year's hay with the fresh life below. It grows as steadily as the rill oozes
out of the ground. It is almost identical with that, for in the growing days of
June, when the rills are dry, the grass blades are their channels, and from year
to year the herds drink at this perennial green stream, and the mower draws
from it betimes their winter supply. So our human life but dies down to its
roots, and still puts forth its green blade to eternity.

Walden is melting apace. There is a canal two rods wide along the northerly
and westerly sides, and wider still at the east end. A great field of ice has
cracked off from the main body. I hear a song-sparrow singing from the bushes
on the shore,—*olit, olit, olit,—chip, chip, chip, che char,—che wiss, wiss,
wiss.* He too is helping to crack it. How handsome the great sweeping curves
in the edge of the ice, answering somewhat to those of the shore, but more
regular! It is unusually hard, owing to the recent severe but transient cold, and
all watered or waved like a palace floor. But the wind slides eastward over its
opaque surface in vain, till it reaches the living surface beyond. It is glorious
to behold this ribbon of water sparkling in the sun, the bare face of the pond
full of glee and youth, as if it spoke the joy of the fishes within it, and of the
sands on its shore,—a silvery sheen as from the scales of a *leuciscus*, as it were
all one active fish. Such is the contrast between winter and spring. Walden
was dead and is alive again. But this spring it broke up more steadily, as I
have said.

The change from storm and winter to serene and mild weather, from dark
and sluggish hours to bright and elastic ones, is a memorable crisis which all
things proclaim. It is seemingly instantaneous at last. Suddenly an influx of
light filled my house, though the evening was at hand, and the clouds of
winter still overhung it, and the eaves were dripping with sleety rain. I looked
out the window, and lo! where yesterday was cold gray ice there lay the transparent pond already calm and full of hope as on a summer evening, reflecting
a summer evening sky in its bosom, though none was visible overhead, as if it

7. Varro's *Rerum rusticarum* 2.2.14; Thoreau goes on to translate.

had intelligence with some remote horizon. I heard a robin in the distance, the first I had heard for many a thousand years, methought, whose note I shall not forget for many a thousand more,—the same sweet and powerful song of yore. O the evening robin, at the end of a New England summer day! If I could ever find the twig he sits upon! I mean *he*; I mean *the twig*. This at least is not the *Turdus migratorius*. The pitch-pines and shrub-oaks about my house, which had so long drooped, suddenly resumed their several characters, looked brighter, greener, and more erect and alive, as if effectually cleansed and restored by the rain. I knew that it would not rain any more. You may tell by looking at any twig of the forest, ay, at your very wood-pile, whether its winter is past or not. As it grew darker, I was startled by the *honking* of geese flying low over the woods, like weary travellers getting in late from southern lakes, and indulging at last in unrestrained complaint and mutual consolation. Standing at my door, I could hear the rush of their wings; when, driving toward my house, they suddenly spied my light, and with hushed clamor wheeled and settled in the pond. So I came in, and shut the door, and passed my first spring night in the woods.

In the morning I watched the geese from the door through the mist, sailing in the middle of the pond, fifty rods off, so large and tumultuous that Walden appeared like an aritifical pond for their amusement. But when I stood on the shore they at once rose up with a great flapping of wings at the signal of their commander, and when they had got into rank circled about over my head, twenty-nine of them, and then steered straight to Canada, with a regular *honk* from the leader at intervals, trusting to break their fast in muddier pools. A "plump" of ducks rose at the same time and took the route to the north in the wake of their noisier cousins.

For a week I heard the circling groping clangor of some solitary goose in the foggy mornings, seeking its companion, and still peopling the woods with the sound of a larger life than they could sustain. In April the pigeons were seen again flying express in small flocks, and in due time I heard the martins twittering over my clearing, though it had not seemed that the township contained so many that it could afford me any, and I fancied that they were peculiarly of the ancient race that dwelt in hollow trees ere white men came. In almost all climes the tortoise and the frog are among the precursors and heralds of this season, and birds fly with song and glancing plumage, and plants spring and bloom, and winds blow, to correct this slight oscillation of the poles and preserve the equilibrium of Nature.

As every season seems best to us in its turn, so the coming in of spring is like the creation of Cosmos out of Chaos and the realization of the Golden Age.—

> "Eurus ad Auroram, Nabathæaque regna recessit,
> Persidaque, et radiis juga subdita matutinis."

> "The East-Wind withdrew to Aurora and the Nabathæan kingdom,
> And the Persian, and the ridges placed under the morning rays.

> Man was born. Whether that Artificer of things,
> The origin of a better world, made him from the divine seed;
> Or the earth being recent and lately sundered from the high
> Ether, retained some seeds of cognate heaven."[8]

8. Ovid's *Metamorphoses* 1.61–62, 78–81.

A single gentle rain makes the grass many shades greener. So our prospects brighten on the influx of better thoughts. We should be blessed if we lived in the present always, and took advantage of every accident that befell us, like the grass which confesses the influence of the slightest dew that falls on it; and did not spend our time in atoning for the neglect of past opportunities, which we call doing our duty. We loiter in winter while it is already spring. In a pleasant spring morning all men's sins are forgiven. Such a day is a truce to vice. While such a sun holds out to burn, the vilest sinner may return. Through our own recovered innocence we discern the innocence of our neighbors. You may have known your neighbor yesterday for a thief, a drunkard, or a sensualist, and merely pitied or despised him, and despaired of the world; but the sun shines bright and warm this first spring morning, re-creating the world, and you meet him at some serene work, and see how his exhausted and debauched veins expand with still joy and bless the new day, feel the spring influence with the innocence of infancy, and all his faults are forgotten. There is not only an atmosphere of good will about him, but even a savor of holiness grop-ing for expression, blindly and ineffectually perhaps, like a new-born instinct, and for a short hour the south hill-side echoes to no vulgar jest. You see some innocent fair shoots preparing to burst from his gnarled rind and try another year's life, tender and fresh as the youngest plant. Even he has entered into the joy of his Lord. Why the jailer does not leave open his prison doors,—why the judge does not dismiss his case,—why the preacher does not dismiss his congregation! It is because they do not obey the hint which God gives them, nor accept the pardon which he freely offers to all.

"A return to goodness produced each day in the tranquil and beneficent breath of the morning, causes that in respect to the love of virtue and the hatred of vice, one approaches a little the primitive nature of man, as the sprouts of the forest which has been felled. In like manner the evil which one does in the interval of a day prevents the germs of virtues which began to spring up again from developing themselves and destroys them.

"After the germs of virtue have thus been prevented many times from devel-oping themselves, then the beneficent breath of evening does not suffice to preserve them. As soon as the breath of evening does not suffice longer to preserve them, then the nature of man does not differ much from that of the brute. Men seeing the nature of this man like that of the brute, think that he has never possessed the innate faculty of reason. Are those the true and natural sentiments of man?"[9]

> "The Golden Age was first created, which without any avenger
> Spontaneously without law cherished fidelity and rectitude.
> Punishment and fear were not; nor were threatening words read
> On suspended brass; nor did the suppliant crowd fear
> The words of their judge; but were safe without an avenger.
> Not yet the pine felled on its mountains had descended
> To the liquid waves that it might see a foreign world,
> And mortals knew no shore but their own.
>
>                    . . .
>
> There was eternal spring, and placid zephyrs with warm
> Blasts soothed the flowers born without seed."[1]

9. Mencius's (Meng-tzu's) Works 6.1.                    1. Ovid's Metamorphoses 1.89–96, 107–8.

On the 29th of April, as I was fishing from the bank of the river near the Nine-Acre-Corner bridge, standing on the quaking grass and willow roots, where the muskrats lurk, I heard a singular rattling sound, somewhat like that of the sticks which boys play with their fingers, when, looking up, I observed a very slight and graceful hawk, like a night-hawk, alternately soaring like a ripple and tumbling a rod or two over and over, showing the underside of its wings, which gleamed like a satin ribbon in the sun, or like the pearly inside of a shell. This sight reminded me of falconry and what nobleness and poetry are associated with that sport. The Merlin[2] it seemed to me it might be called: but I care not for its name. It was the most ethereal flight I had ever witnessed. It did not simply flutter like a butterfly, nor soar like the larger hawks, but it sported with proud reliance in the fields of air; mounting again and again with its strange chuckle, it repeated its free and beautiful fall, turning over and over like a kite, and then recovering from its lofty tumbling, as if it had never set its foot on *terra firma*. It appeared to have no companion in the universe,— sporting there alone,—and to need none but the morning and the ether with which it played. It was not lonely, but made all the earth lonely beneath it. Where was the parent which hatched it, its kindred, and its father in the heavens? The tenant of the air, it seemed related to the earth but by an egg hatched some time in the crevice of a crag;—or was its native nest made in the angle of a cloud, woven of the rainbow's trimmings and the sunset sky, and lined with some soft midsummer haze caught up from earth? Its eyry now some cliffy cloud.

Beside this I got a rare mess of golden and silver and bright cupreous[3] fishes, which looked like a string of jewels. Ah! I have penetrated to those meadows on the morning of many a first spring day, jumping from hummock to hummock, from willow root to willow root, when the wild river valley and the woods were bathed in so pure and bright a light as would have waked the dead, if they had been slumbering in their graves, as some suppose. There needs no stronger proof of immortality. All things must live in such a light. O Death, where was thy sting? O Grave, where was thy victory, then?[4]

Our village life would stagnate if it were not for the unexplored forests and meadows which surround it. We need the tonic of wildness,—to wade some-times in marshes where the bittern and the meadow-hen lurk, and hear the booming of the snipe; to smell the whispering sedge where only some wilder and more solitary fowl builds her nest, and the mink crawls with its belly close to the ground. At the same time that we are earnest to explore and learn all things, we require that all things be mysterious and unexplorable, that land and sea be infinitely wild, unsurveyed and unfathomed by us because unfath-omable. We can never have enough of Nature. We must be refreshed by the sight of inexhaustible vigor, vast and Titanic features, the sea-coast with its wrecks, the wilderness with its living and its decaying trees, the thunder cloud, and the rain which lasts three weeks and produces freshets. We need to witness our own limits transgressed, and some life pasturing freely where we never wander. We are cheered when we observe the vulture feeding on the carrion which disgusts and disheartens us and deriving health and strength from the

2. In Arthurian legend, Merlin is a magician and soothsayer, but Thoreau uses him as Emerson does in the poem *Merlin*, as a master poet. The hawk is usually taken as Thoreau's ideal image of himself. A merlin is

also a small falcon or pigeon hawk.
3. Coppery.
4. 1 Corinthians 15.55: "O death, where is thy sting? O grave, where is thy victory?"

repast. There was a dead horse in the hollow by the path to my house, which compelled me sometimes to go out of my way, especially in the night when the air was heavy, but the assurance it gave me of the strong appetite and inviolable health of Nature was my compensation for this. I love to see that Nature is so rife with life that myriads can be afforded to be sacrificed and suffered to prey on one another; that tender organizations can be so serenely squashed out of existence like pulp,—tadpoles which herons gobble up, and tortoises and toads run over in the road; and that sometimes it has rained flesh and blood! With the liability to accident, we must see how little account is to be made of it. The impression made on a wise man is that of universal innocence. Poison is not poisonous after all, nor are any wounds fatal. Compassion is a very untenable ground. It must be expeditious. Its pleadings will not bear to be stereotyped.

Early in May, the oaks, hickories, maples, and other trees, just putting out amidst the pine woods around the pond, imparted a brightness like sunshine to the landscape, especially in cloudy days, as if the sun were breaking through mists and shining faintly on the hill-sides here and there. On the third or fourth of May I saw a loon in the pond, and during the first week of the month I heard the whippoorwill, the brown-thrasher, the veery, the wood-pewee, the chewink, and other birds. I had heard the wood-thrush long before. The phœbe had already come once more and looked in at my door and window, to see if my house was cavern-like enough for her, sustaining herself on humming wings with clinched talons, as if she held by the air, while she surveyed the premises. The sulphur-like pollen of the pitch-pine soon covered the pond and the stones and rotten wood along the shore, so that you could have collected a barrel-ful. This is the "sulphur showers" we hear of. Even in Calidas' drama of Sacontala, we read of "rills dyed yellow with the golden dust of the lotus."[5] And so the seasons went rolling on into summer, as one rambles into higher and higher grass.

Thus was my first year's life in the woods completed; and the second year was similar to it. I finally left Walden September 6th, 1847.

## Conclusion

To the sick the doctors wisely recommend a change of air and scenery. Thank Heaven, here is not all the world. The buck-eye does not grow in New England, and the mocking-bird is rarely heard here. The wild-goose is more of a cosmopolite than we; he breaks his fast in Canada, takes a luncheon in the Ohio, and plumes himself for the night in a southern bayou. Even the bison, to some extent, keeps pace with the seasons, cropping the pastures of the Colorado only till a greener and sweeter grass awaits him by the Yellowstone. Yet we think that if rail-fences are pulled down, and stone-walls piled up on our farms, bounds are henceforth set to our lives and our fates decided. If you are chosen town-clerk, forsooth, you cannot go to Tierra del Fuego[6] this summer: but you may go to the land of infernal fire nevertheless. The universe is wider than our views of it.

Yet we should oftener look over the tafferel of our craft, like curious passen-

5. Sir William Jones's translation of *Sacontalá*, act 5, by Cálidás (5th century), Hindu writer.
6. Thoreau puns on the meaning of the name of the archipelago at the southern tip of South America: land of fire (Spanish).

gers, and not make the voyage like stupid sailors picking oakum.[7] The other side of the globe is but the home of our correspondent. Our voyaging is only great-circle sailing, and the doctors prescribe for diseases of the skin merely. One hastens to Southern Africa to chase the giraffe; but surely that is not the game he would be after. How long, pray, would a man hunt giraffes if he could? Snipes and woodcocks also may afford rare sport; but I trust it would be nobler game to shoot one's self.—

> "Direct your eye sight inward, and you'll find
> A thousand regions in your mind
> Yet undiscovered. Travel them, and be
> Expert in home-cosmography."[8]

What does Africa,—what does the West stand for? Is not our own interior white on the chart? black though it may prove, like the coast, when discovered. Is it the source of the Nile, or the Niger, or the Mississippi, or a North West Passage around this continent, that we would find? Are these the problems which most concern mankind? Is Franklin[9] the only man who is lost, that his wife should be so earnest to find him? Does Mr. Grinnell[1] know where he himself is? Be rather the Mungo Park, the Lewis and Clarke and Frobisher,[2] of your own streams and oceans; explore your own higher latitudes,—with shiploads of preserved meats to support you, if they be necessary; and pile the empty cans sky-high for a sign. Were preserved meats invented to preserve meat merely? Nay, be a Columbus to whole new continents and worlds within you, opening new channels, not of trade, but of thought. Every man is the lord of a realm beside which the earthly empire of the Czar is but a petty state, a hummock left by the ice. Yet some can be patriotic who have no *self*-respect, and sacrifice the greater to the less. They love the soil which makes their graves, but have no sympathy with the spirit which may still animate their clay. Patriotism is a maggot in their heads. What was the meaning of that South-Sea Exploring Expedition,[3] with all its parade and expense, but an indirect recognition of the fact, that there are continents and seas in the moral world, to which every man is an isthmus or an inlet, yet unexplored by him, but that it is easier to sail many thousand miles through cold and storm and cannibals, in a government ship, with five hundred men and boys to assist one, than it is to explore the private sea, the Atlantic and Pacific Ocean of one's being alone.—

> "Erret, et extremos alter scrutetur Iberos.
> Plus habet hic vitæ, plus habet ille viæ."[4]

7. Common nautical busywork: picking old rope apart so the pieces of hemp could be tarred and used for calking.
8. William Habington (1605–1654), *To My Honoured Friend Sir Ed. P. Knight.*
9. Sir John Franklin (1785–1847), lost on a British expedition to the Arctic.
1. Henry Grinnell (1799–1874), a rich New York whale-oil merchant from a New Bedford family who sponsored two attempts to rescue Sir Franklin, one in 1850 and another in 1853.
2. I.e., an explorer like Mungo Park (1771–1806), Scottish explorer of Africa; Meriwether Lewis (1774–1809) and William Clark (1770–1838), leaders of the American expedition into the Louisiana Territory

(1804–6); and Martin Frobisher (1535?–1594), English mariner.
3. The famous expedition to the Pacific Antarctic led by Charles Wilkes during 1838–42.
4. Thoreau's journal for May 10, 1841, begins: "A good warning to the restless tourists of these days is contained in the last verses of Claudian's 'Old Man of Verona.' " Claudius Claudianus was the last of the Latin classic poets (fl. A.D. 395) and author of *Epigrammata,* where Thoreau found the passage he loosely translates here. He changed *Spaniards* to "Australian," added "outlandish," and changed the pronouns. The last line would be better translated as "he [the traveler] may have more of a journey, but he who remains in Verona has more of a life."

Let them wander and scrutinize the outlandish Australians.
I have more of God, they more of the road.

It is not worth the while to go round the world to count the cats in Zanzibar.[5]
Yet do this even till you can do better, and you may perhaps find some "Symmes' Hole"[6] by which to get at the inside at last. England and France, Spain and Portugal, Gold Coast and Slave Coast, all front on this private sea; but no bark from them has ventured out of sight of land, though it is without doubt the direct way to India. If you would learn to speak all tongues and conform to the customs of all nations, if you would travel farther than all travellers, be naturalized in all climes, and cause the Sphinx to dash her head against a stone,[7] even obey the precept of the old philosopher, and Explore thyself. Herein are demanded the eye and the nerve. Only the defeated and deserters go to the wars, cowards that run away and enlist. Start now on that farthest western way, which does not pause at the Mississippi or the Pacific, nor conduct toward a worn-out China or Japan, but leads on direct a tangent to this sphere, summer and winter, day and night, sun down, moon down, and at last earth down too.

It is said that Mirabeau took to highway robbery "to ascertain what degree of resolution was necessary in order to place one's self in formal opposition to the most sacred laws of society." He declared that "a soldier who fights in the ranks does not require half so much courage as a foot-pad,"—"that honor and religion have never stood in the way of a well-considered and a firm resolve."[8] This was manly, as the world goes; and yet it was idle, if not desperate. A saner man would have found himself often enough "in formal opposition" to what are deemed "the most sacred laws of society," through obedience to yet more sacred laws, and so have tested his resolution without going out of his way. It is not for a man to put himself in such an attitude to society, but to maintain himself in whatever attitude he find himself through obedience to the laws of his being, which will never be one of opposition to a just government, if he should chance to meet with such.

I left the woods for as good a reason as I went there. Perhaps it seemed to me that I had several more lives to live, and could not spare any more time for that one. It is remarkable how easily and insensibly we fall into a particular route, and make a beaten track for ourselves. I had not lived there a week before my feet wore a path from my door to the pond-side; and though it is five or six years since I trod it, it is still quite distinct. It is true, I fear that others may have fallen into it, and so helped to keep it open. The surface of the earth is soft and impressible by the feet of men; and so with the paths which the mind travels. How worn and dusty, then, must be the highways of the world, how deep the ruts of tradition and conformity! I did not wish to take a cabin passage, but rather to go before the mast and on the deck of the world, for there I could best see the moonlight amid the mountains. I do not wish to go below now.

I learned this, at least, by my experiment; that if one advances confidently

---

5. Thoreau had read Charles Pickering's *The Races of Man* (1851), which reports on the domestic cats in Zanzibar [Harding's note].
6. In 1818 Captain John Symmes theorized that the earth was hollow with openings at both the North and South Poles.

7. As the Theban Sphinx did when Oedipus guessed her riddle. Thebes here is the ancient Greek city, not the Egyptian city Thoreau has previously referred to.
8. Thoreau encountered this passage by the Comte de Mirabeau (1749–1791) in *Harper's* 1 (1850).

in the direction of his dreams, and endeavors to live the life which he has imagined, he will meet with a success unexpected in common hours. He will put some things behind, will pass an invisible boundary; new, universal, and more liberal laws will begin to establish themselves around and within him; or the old laws be expanded, and interpreted in his favor in a more liberal sense, and he will live with the license of a higher order of beings. In proportion as he simplifies his life, the laws of the universe will appear less complex, and solitude will not be solitude, nor poverty poverty, nor weakness weakness. If you have built castles in the air, your work need not be lost; that is where they should be. Now put the foundations under them.

It is a ridiculous demand which England and America make, that you shall speak so that they can understand you. Neither men nor toad-stools grow so. As if that were important, and there were not enough to understand you without them. As if Nature could support but one order of understandings, could not sustain birds as well as quadrupeds, flying as well as creeping things, and *hush* and *who*, which Bright[9] can understand, were the best English. As if there were safety in stupidity alone. I fear chiefly lest my expression may not be *extra-vagant* enough, may not wander far enough beyond the narrow limits of my daily experience, so as to be adequate to the truth of which I have been convinced. *Extra vagance!* it depends on how you are yarded. The migrating buffalo, which seeks new pastures in another latitude, is not extravagant like the cow which kicks over the pail, leaps the cow-yard fence, and runs after her calf, in milking time. I desire to speak somewhere *without* bounds; like a man in a waking moment, to men in their waking moments; for I am convinced that I cannot exaggerate enough even to lay the foundation of a true expression. Who that has heard a strain of music feared then lest he should speak extravagantly any more forever? In view of the future or possible, we should live quite laxly and undefined in front, our outlines dim and misty on that side; as our shadows reveal an insensible perspiration toward the sun. The volatile truth of our words should continually betray the inadequacy of the residual statement. Their truth is instantly *translated*; its literal monument alone remains. The words which express our faith and piety are not definite; yet they are significant and fragrant like frankincense to superior natures.

Why level downward to our dullest perception always, and praise that as common sense? The commonest sense is the sense of men asleep, which they express by snoring. Sometimes we are inclined to class those who are once-and-a-half witted with the half-witted, because we appreciate only a third part of their wit. Some would find fault with the morning-red, if they ever got up early enough. "They pretend," as I hear, "that the verses of Kabir have four different senses; illusion, spirit, intellect, and the exoteric doctrine of the Vedas;"[1] but in this part of the world it is considered a ground for complaint if a man's writings admit of more than one interpretation. While England endeavors to cure the potato-rot, will not any endeavor to cure the brain-rot, which prevails so much more widely and fatally?

I do not suppose that I have attained to obscurity, but I should be proud if no more fatal fault were found with my pages on this score than was found with the Walden ice. Southern customers objected to its blue color, which is the evidence of its purity, as if it were muddy, and preferred the Cambridge

9. Name for an ox.
1. M. Garcin de Tassy's, *Histoire de la littérature hindoui* (1839).

ice, which is white, but tastes of weeds. The purity men love is like the mists which envelop the earth, and not like the azure ether beyond.

Some are dinning in our ears that we Americans, and moderns generally, are intellectual dwarfs compared with the ancients, or even the Elizabethan men.[2] But what is that to the purpose? A living dog is better than a dead lion.[3] Shall a man go and hang himself because he belongs to the race of pygmies, and not be the biggest pygmy that he can? Let every one mind his own business, and endeavor to be what he was made.

Why should we be in such desperate haste to succeed, and in such desperate enterprises? If a man does not keep pace with his companions, perhaps it is because he hears a different drummer. Let him step to the music which he hears, however measured or far away. It is not important that he should mature as soon as an apple-tree or an oak. Shall he turn his spring into summer? If the condition of things which we were made for is not yet, what were any reality which we can substitute? We will not be shipwrecked on a vain reality. Shall we with pains erect a heaven of blue glass over ourselves, though when it is done we shall be sure to gaze still at the true ethereal heaven far above, as if the former were not?

There was an artist in the city of Kouroo who was disposed to strive after perfection. One day it came into his mind to make a staff. Having considered that in an imperfect work time is an ingredient, but into a perfect work time does not enter, he said to himself, It shall be perfect in all respects, though I should do nothing else in my life. He proceeded instantly to the forest for wood, being resolved that it should not be made of unsuitable material; and as he searched for and rejected stick after stick, his friends gradually deserted him, for they grew old in their works and died, but he grew not older by a moment. His singleness of purpose and resolution, and his elevated piety, endowed him, without his knowledge, with perennial youth. As he made no compromise with Time, Time kept out of his way, and only sighed at a distance because he could not overcome him. Before he had found a stock in all respects suitable the city of Kouroo was a hoary ruin, and he sat on one of its mounds to peel the stick. Before he had given it the proper shape the dynasty of the Candahars was at an end, and with the point of the stick he wrote the name of the last of that race in the sand, and then resumed his work. By the time he had smoothed and polished the staff Kalpa was no longer the pole-star; and ere he had put on the ferule and the head adorned with precious stones, Brahma had awoke and slumbered many times. But why do I stay to mention these things? When the finishing stroke was put to his work, it suddenly expanded before the eyes of the astonished artist into the fairest of all the creations of Brahma. He had made a new system in making a staff, a world with full and fair proportions; in which, though the old cities and dynasties had passed away, fairer and more glorious ones had taken their places. And now he saw by the heap of shavings still fresh at his feet, that, for him and his work, the former lapse of time had been an illusion, and that no more time had elapsed than is required for a single scintillation from the brain of Brahma to fall on and inflame the tinder of a mortal brain. The material was pure, and his art was pure; how could the result be other than wonderful?

2. There had been serious as well as satirical specula-tion as to the debilitating effects of the American cli-mate, a continuation of the older question as to whether or not modern civilization could ever achieve the heights of ancient Greek and Roman civilization.
3. Ecclesiastes 9.4.

No face which we can give to a matter will stead us so well at last as the truth. This alone wears well. For the most part, we are not where we are, but in a false position. Through an infirmity of our natures, we suppose a case, and put ourselves into it, and hence are in two cases at the same time, and it is doubly difficult to get out. In sane moments we regard only the facts, the case that is. Say what you have to say, not what you ought. Any truth is better than make-believe. Tom Hyde, the tinker, standing on the gallows, was asked if he had any thing to say. "Tell the tailors," said he, "to remember to make a knot in their thread before they take the first stitch."[4] His companion's prayer is forgotten.

However mean your life is, meet it and live it; do not shun it and call it hard names. It is not so bad as you are. It looks poorest when you are richest. The fault-finder will find faults even in paradise. Love your life, poor as it is. You may perhaps have some pleasant, thrilling, glorious hours, even in a poor-house. The setting sun is reflected from the windows of the alms-house as brightly as from the rich man's abode; the snow melts before its door as early in the spring. I do not see but a quiet mind may live as contentedly there, and have as cheering thoughts, as in a palace. The town's poor seem to me often to live the most independent lives of any. May be they are simply great enough to receive without misgiving. Most think that they are above being supported by the town; but it oftener happens that they are not above supporting themselves by dishonest means, which should be more disreputable. Cultivate poverty like a garden herb, like sage. Do not trouble yourself much to get new things, whether clothes or friends. Turn the old; return to them. Things do not change; we change. Sell your clothes and keep your thoughts. God will see that you do not want society. If I were confined to a corner of a garret all my days, like a spider, the world would be just as large to me while I had my thoughts about me. The philosopher said: "From an army of three divisions one can take away its general, and put it in disorder; from the man the most abject and vulgar one cannot take away his thought."[5] Do not seek so anxiously to be developed, to subject yourself to many influences to be played on; it is all dissipation. Humility like darkness reveals the heavenly lights. The shadows of poverty and meanness gather around us, "and lo! creation widens to our view."[6] We are often reminded that if there were bestowed on us the wealth of Crœsus,[7] our aims must still be the same, and our means essentially the same. Moreover, if you are restricted in your range by poverty, if you cannot buy books and newspapers, for instance, you are but confined to the most significant and vital experiences; you are compelled to deal with the material which yields the most sugar and the most starch. It is life near the bone where it is sweetest. You are defended from being a trifler. No man loses ever on a lower level by magnanimity on a higher. Superfluous wealth can buy superfluities only. Money is not required to buy one necessary of the soul.

I live in the angle of a leaden wall, into whose composition was poured a little alloy of bell metal. Often, in the repose of my mid-day, there reaches my ears a confused *tintinnabulum*[8] from without. It is the noise of my contemporaries. My neighbors tell me of their adventures with famous gentlemen and

4. Presumably a reference to the tailors who will sew Hyde's shroud, although some custom may be involved such as that of making the last stitch through the nose in preparing a sailor for burial at sea.
5. Confucius's *Analects* 9.25.

6. From the sonnet *To Night* by the British writer Joseph Blanco White (1775–1841).
7. King of Lydia (d. 546 B.C.), fabled as the richest man on earth.
8. Tinkling.

ladies, what notabilities they met at the dinner-table; but I am no more interested in such things than in the contents of the Daily Times. The interest and the conversation are about costume and manners chiefly; but a goose is a goose still, dress it as you will. They tell me of California and Texas, of England and the Indies, of the Hon. Mr.———— of Georgia or of Massachusetts, all transient and fleeting phenomena, till I am ready to leap from their court-yard like the Mameluke bey.[9] I delight to come to my bearings,—not walk in procession with pomp and parade, in a conspicuous place, but to walk even with the Builder of the universe, if I may,—not to live in this restless, nervous, bustling, trivial Nineteenth Century, but stand or sit thoughtfully while it goes by. What are men celebrating? They are all on a committee of arrangements, and hourly expect a speech from somebody. God is only the president of the day, and Webster is his orator.[1] I love to weigh, to settle, to gravitate toward that which most strongly and rightfully attracts me;—not hang by the beam of the scale and try to weigh less,—not suppose a case, but take the case that is; to travel the only path I can, and that on which no power can resist me. It affords me no satisfaction to commence to spring an arch before I have got a solid foundation. Let us not play at kittlybenders.[2] There is a solid bottom every where. We read that the traveller asked the boy if the swamp before him had a hard bottom. The boy replied that it had. But presently the traveller's horse sank in up to the girths, and he observed to the boy, "I thought you said that this bog had a hard bottom." "So it has," answered the latter, "but you have not got half way to it yet." So it is with the bogs and quicksands of society; but he is an old boy that knows it. Only what is thought said or done at a certain rare coincidence is good. I would not be one of those who will foolishly drive a nail into mere lath and plastering; such a deed would keep me awake nights. Give me a hammer, and let me feel for the furring.[3] Do not depend on the putty. Drive a nail home and clinch it so faithfully that you can wake up in the night and think of your work with satisfaction,—a work at which you would not be ashamed to invoke the Muse. So will help you God, and so only. Every nail driven should be as another rivet in the machine of the universe, you carrying on the work.

Rather than love, than money, than fame, give me truth. I sat at a table where were rich food and wine in abundance, and obsequious attendance, but sincerity and truth were not; and I went away hungry from the inhospitable board. The hospitality was as cold as the ices. I thought that there was no need of ice to freeze them. They talked to me of the age of the wine and the fame of the vintage; but I thought of an older, a newer, and purer wine, of a more glorious vintage, which they had not got, and could not buy. The style, the house and grounds and "entertainment" pass for nothing with me. I called on the king, but he made me wait in his hall, and conducted like a man incapacitated for hospitality. There was a man in my neighborhood who lived in a hollow tree. His manners were truly regal. I should have done better had I called on him.

How long shall we sit in our porticoes practising idle and musty virtues,

---

9. A famous romantic exploit: in 1811 the Egyptian Mehemet Ali Pasha attempted to massacre the Mameluke caste, but one bey, or officer, escaped by leaping from a wall onto his horse.
1. Political meetings then had "presidents" (because they presided) rather than "chairpersons." Thoreau plays on the catch phrase from Mohammedanism "There is no other God than Allah, and Mohammed is his prophet." Thoreau regarded Daniel Webster with contempt.
2. Harding defines this as a "child's game of running out onto thin ice without breaking through."
3. Narrow lumber nailed as backing for lath. The first edition reads "furrowing," and one manuscript draft reads "stud."

which any work would make impertinent? As if one were to begin the day with long-suffering, and hire a man to hoe his potatoes; and in the afternoon go forth to practise Christian meekness and charity with goodness aforethought! Consider the China[4] pride and stagnant self-complacency of mankind. This generation reclines a little to congratulate itself on being the last of an illustrious line; and in Boston and London and Paris and Rome, thinking of its long descent, it speaks of its progress in art and science and literature with satisfaction. There are the Records of the Philosophical Societies, and the public Eulogies of *Great Men!* It is the good Adam contemplating his own virtue. "Yes, we have done great deeds, and sung divine songs, which shall never die,"—that is, as long as *we* can remember them. The learned societies and great men of Assyria,—where are they? What youthful philosophers and experimentalists we are! There is not one of my readers who has yet lived a whole human life. These may be but the spring months in the life of the race. If we have had the seven-years' itch, we have not seen the seventeen-year locust yet in Concord. We are acquainted with a mere pellicle of the globe on which we live. Most have not delved six feet beneath the surface, nor leaped as many above it. We know not where we are. Beside, we are sound asleep nearly half our time. Yet we esteem ourselves wise, and have an established order on the surface. Truly, we are deep thinkers, we are ambitious spirits! As I stand over the insect crawling amid the pine needles on the forest floor, and endeavoring to conceal itself from my sight, and ask myself why it will cherish those humble thoughts, and hide its head from me who might perhaps be its benefactor, and impart to its race some cheering information, I am reminded of the greater Benefactor and Intelligence that stands over me the human insect.

There is an incessant influx of novelty into the world, and yet we tolerate incredible dulness. I need only suggest what kind of sermons are still listened to in the most enlightened countries. There are such words as joy and sorrow, but they are only the burden of a psalm, sung with a nasal twang, while we believe in the ordinary and mean. We think that we can change our clothes only. It is said that the British Empire is very large and respectable, and that the United States are a first-rate power. We do not believe that a tide rises and falls behind every man which can float the British Empire like a chip, if he should ever harbor it in his mind. Who knows what sort of seventeen-year locust will next come out of the ground? The government of the world I live in was not framed, like that of Britain, in after-dinner conversations over the wine.

The life in us is like the water in the river. It may rise this year higher than man has ever known it, and flood the parched uplands; even this may be the eventful year, which will drown out all our muskrats. It was not always dry land where we dwell. I see far inland the banks which the stream anciently washed, before science began to record its freshets. Every one has heard the story which has gone the rounds of New England, of a strong and beautiful bug which came out of the dry leaf of an old table of apple-tree wood, which had stood in a farmer's kitchen for sixty years, first in Connecticut, and afterward in Massachusetts,—from an egg deposited in the living tree many years earlier still, as appeared by counting the annual layers beyond it; which was heard gnawing out for several weeks, hatched perchance by the heat of an

---

4. From China's lingering isolationism, despite the China trade so important to the New England economy.

urn.[5] Who does not feel his faith in a resurrection and immortality strengthened by hearing of this? Who knows what beautiful and winged life, whose egg has been buried for ages under many concentric layers of woodenness in the dead dry life of society, deposited at first in the alburnum of the green and living tree, which has been gradually converted into the semblance of its well-seasoned tomb,—heard perchance gnawing out now for years by the astonished family of man, as they sat round the festive board,—may unexpectedly come forth from amidst society's most trivial and handselled furniture, to enjoy its perfect summer life at last!

I do not say that John or Jonathan[6] will realize all this; but such is the character of that morrow which mere lapse of time can never make to dawn. The light which puts out our eyes is darkness to us. Only that day dawns to which we are awake. There is more day to dawn. The sun is but a morning star.

THE END

1846, 1850

5. A major account of the incident is in Timothy Dwight's *Travels in New England and New York* (1821), vol. 2.
6. John Bull or Brother Jonathan, i.e., England or America. Thoreau is now addressing not the restricted audience of the opening of "Economy" but all readers of the English language.

---

# FREDERICK DOUGLASS
## 1818–1895

Born a slave in Maryland, Frederick Douglass taught himself to read and write, escaped to Massachusetts by disguising himself as a sailor, and became one of the most effective orators of his day, an influential newspaper editor, a confidant of the radical abolitionist John Brown, a militant reformer, and a respected diplomat. The first two accounts of his experiences belong to the tradition of fugitive-slave narratives popular in the North before the Civil War; the final volume, published when Douglass was in his mid-sixties, reveals one of the most remarkable and successful lives of the nineteenth century.

*Narrative of the Life of Frederick Douglass, an American Slave, Written by Himself* (1845) told in 125 pages the story of his life from early childhood until he escaped from bondage (and changed his last name from Bailey to Douglass) in 1838. The vivid detail, the dignity of tone, and the sincerity of the writing left no doubt that Douglass had in fact suffered the horrors he had been describing in powerful lectures for several years.

There is ample evidence to support the view that Douglass was a powerful speaker. One of his admirers described him thus:

> He was more than six feet in height, and his majestic form, as he rose to speak, straight as an arrow, muscular, yet lithe and graceful, his flashing eye, and more than all, his voice, that rivaled [Daniel] Webster's in its richness, and in the depth and sonorousness of its cadences, made up such an ideal of an orator as the listeners never forgot.

Surely, no one in Rochester, New York, who heard Douglass's speech on the fifth of July 1852 was likely to have forgotten what his biographer William S. McFeely has characterized judiciously as "perhaps the greatest antislavery oration ever given." In moral intensity *The Meaning of July Fourth for the Negro* may be compared favorably with Thoreau's *A Plea for Captain John Brown*, in its range of reference with the best of Emerson's lectures, and in prophetic prescience with Whitman's shrewdest prefaces.

In 1855 he published a revised and enlarged version of the *Narrative* under the title *My Bondage and My Freedom.* This work balanced a more detailed account of his life as a slave with the impressive record of his intellectual growth and personal achievement since he had joined forces with the abolitionists in 1841. It told of his intimacy with the Garrisonian wing of the abolitionist movement (which demanded immediate freeing of all slaves on moral grounds), of his successful speaking tour of the British Isles, the purchase of his freedom for $700 by a group of his admirers, and his move to Rochester, New York, where he brought out in December 1847 the first issue of the increasingly outspoken weekly newspaper he published for the thirteen years (first as *The North Star*, later as *Frederick Douglass's Weekly* and *Monthly*). The third of Douglass's autobiographies, *The Life and Times of Frederick Douglass* (1881), subsumes the first two and adds to them the events of his career just before, during, and after the Civil War and traces the rising arc of his fame and influence and the ultimately honored recognition of his compatriots, black and white alike.

Wrongly accused of complicity in John Brown's raid on the arsenal at Harpers Ferry in 1859, Douglass was obliged to flee to Canada and thence to England. Once the Civil War began, he took an active role in the campaign to make black men eligible for Union service; he became a successful recruiter of black soldiers, whose ranks soon included two of his own sons. Having helped to enlist these men, Douglass was only acting in character when he took his protests over their unequal pay and treatment directly to President Lincoln.

It was also in character for Douglass to criticize Lincoln's successors over what Douglass believed was an insufficiently prompt and just Reconstruction policy once the war had been won. Douglass was particularly insistent on the necessity for swift passage of the Fifteenth Amendment guaranteeing suffrage to the newly emancipated slaves. Never satisfied with the grudging legal concessions the Civil War yielded, Douglass continued to object to every sign of discrimination—economic, gender, legal, and social. Even after he had been appointed U.S. marshal and then recorder of deeds for the District of Columbia, he continued to speak out on such matters as the exploitation of black sharecroppers in the South, to demand antilynching legislation, to protest the exclusion of black people from public accommodations. He also was active in suffrage movements for women, believing firmly in the power of the ballot as one of the necessities of freedom. It would be hard to exaggerate the importance for later black leaders such as Booker T. Washington and W. E. B. DuBois of Douglass's exemplary career as a champion of human rights. His life, in fact, has become the heroic paradigm for all oppressed people.

# Narrative of the Life of Frederick Douglass, an American Slave, Written by Himself[1]

## Chapter I

I was born in Tuckahoe, near Hillsborough, and about twelve miles from Easton, in Talbot county, Maryland. I have no accurate knowledge of my age,

---

1. First printed in May 1845 by the Anti-Slavery Office in Boston, the source of the present text. Punctuation and hyphenation have been slightly regularized and a few typographical emendations have also been made.

never having seen any authentic record containing it. By far the larger part of the slaves know as little of their ages as horses know of theirs, and it is the wish of most masters within my knowledge to keep their slaves thus ignorant. I do not remember to have ever met a slave who could tell of his birthday. They seldom come nearer to it than planting-time, harvest-time, cherry-time, spring-time, or fall-time. A want of information concerning my own was a source of unhappiness to me even during childhood. The white children could tell their ages. I could not tell why I ought to be deprived of the same privilege. I was not allowed to make any inquiries of my master concerning it. He deemed all such inquiries on the part of a slave improper and impertinent, and evidence of a restless spirit. The nearest estimate I can give makes me now between twenty-seven and twenty-eight years of age. I come to this, from hearing my master say, some time during 1835, I was about seventeen years old.

My mother was named Harriet Bailey. She was the daughter of Isaac and Betsey Bailey, both colored, and quite dark. My mother was of a darker complexion than either my grandmother or grandfather.

My father was a white man. He was admitted to be such by all I ever heard speak of my parentage. The opinion was also whispered that my master was my father; but of the correctness of this opinion, I know nothing; the means of knowing was withheld from me. My mother and I were separated when I was but an infant—before I knew her as my mother. It is a common custom, in the part of Maryland from which I ran away, to part children from their mothers at a very early age. Frequently, before the child has reached its twelfth month, its mother is taken from it, and hired out on some farm a considerable distance off, and the child is placed under the care of an old woman, too old for field labor. For what this separation is done, I do not know, unless it be to hinder the development of the child's affection toward its mother, and to blunt and destroy the natural affection of the mother for the child. This is the inevitable result.

I never saw my mother, to know her as such, more than four or five times in my life; and each of these times was very short in duration, and at night. She was hired by a Mr. Stewart, who lived about twelve miles from my home. She made her journeys to see me in the night, travelling the whole distance on foot, after the performance of her day's work. She was a field hand, and a whipping is the penalty of not being in the field at sunrise, unless a slave has special permission from his or her master to the contrary—a permission which they seldom get, and one that gives to him that gives it the proud name of being a kind master. I do not recollect of ever seeing my mother by the light of day. She was with me in the night. She would lie down with me, and get me to sleep, but long before I waked she was gone. Very little communication ever took place between us. Death soon ended what little we could have while she lived, and with it her hardships and suffering. She died when I was about seven years old, on one of my master's farms, near Lee's Mill. I was not allowed to be present during her illness, at her death, or burial. She was gone long before I knew any thing about it. Never having enjoyed, to any considerable extent, her soothing presence, her tender and watchful care, I received the tidings of her death with much the same emotions I should have probably felt at the death of a stranger.

Called thus suddenly away, she left me without the slightest intimation of who my father was. The whisper that my master was my father, may or may not be true; and, true or false, it is of but little consequence to my purpose whilst the fact remains, in all its glaring odiousness, that slaveholders have ordained, and by law established, that the children of slave women shall in all cases follow the condition of their mothers; and this is done too obviously to administer to their own lusts, and make a gratification of their wicked desires profitable as well as pleasurable; for by this cunning arrangement, the slaveholder, in cases not a few, sustains to his slaves the double relation of master and father.

I know of such cases; and it is worthy of remark that such slaves invariably suffer greater hardships, and have more to contend with, than others. They are, in the first place, a constant offence to their mistress. She is ever disposed to find fault with them; they can seldom do any thing to please her; she is never better pleased than when she sees them under the lash, especially when she suspects her husband of showing to his mulatto children favors which he withholds from his black slaves. The master is frequently compelled to sell this class of his slaves, out of deference to the feelings of his white wife; and, cruel as the deed may strike any one to be, for a man to sell his own children to human flesh-mongers, it is often the dictate of humanity for him to do so; for, unless he does this, he must not only whip them himself, but must stand by and see one white son tie up his brother, of but few shades darker complexion than himself, and ply the gory lash to his naked back; and if he lisp one word of disapproval, it is set down to his parental partiality, and only makes a bad matter worse, both for himself and the slave whom he would protect and defend.

Every year brings with it multitudes of this class of slaves. It was doubtless in consequence of a knowledge of this fact, that one great statesman of the south predicted the downfall of slavery by the inevitable laws of population. Whether this prophecy is ever fulfilled or not, it is nevertheless plain that a very different-looking class of people are springing up at the south, and are now held in slavery, from those originally brought to this country from Africa; and if their increase will do no other good, it will do away the force of the argument, that God cursed Ham,[2] and therefore American slavery is right. If the lineal descendants of Ham are alone to be scripturally enslaved, it is certain that slavery at the south must soon become unscriptural; for thousands are ushered into the world, annually, who, like myself, owe their existence to white fathers, and those fathers most frequently their own masters.

I have had two masters. My first master's name was Anthony. I do not remember his first name. He was generally called Captain Anthony—a title which, I presume, he acquired by sailing a craft on the Chesapeake Bay. He was not considered a rich slaveholder. He owned two or three farms, and about thirty slaves. His farms and slaves were under the care of an overseer. The overseer's name was Plummer. Mr. Plummer was a miserable drunkard, a profane swearer, and a savage monster. He always went armed with a cowskin[3] and a heavy cudgel. I have known him to cut and slash the women's heads so horribly, that even master would be enraged at his cruelty, and would threaten to whip him if he did not mind himself. Master, however, was not a humane slaveholder. It required extraordinary barbarity on the part of an overseer to

2. The specious argument referred to is based on an interpretation of Genesis 9.20–27, in which Noah curses his son Ham and condemns him to bondage to his brothers.

3. A whip made of raw cowhide.

affect him. He was a cruel man, hardened by a long life of slaveholding. He would at times seem to take great pleasure in whipping a slave. I have often been awakened at the dawn of day by the most heart-rending shrieks of an own aunt of mine, whom he used to tie up to a joist, and whip upon her naked back till she was literally covered with blood. No words, no tears, no prayers, from his gory victim, seemed to move his iron heart from its bloody purpose. The louder she screamed, the harder he whipped; and where the blood ran fastest, there he whipped longest. He would whip her to make her scream, and whip her to make her hush; and not until overcome by fatigue, would he cease to swing the blood-clotted cowskin. I remember the first time I ever witnessed this horrible exhibition. I was quite a child, but I well remember it. I never shall forget it whilst I remember any thing. It was the first of a long series of such outrages, of which I was doomed to be a witness and a participant. It struck me with awful force. It was the blood-stained gate, the entrance to the hell of slavery, through which I was about to pass. It was a most terrible spectacle. I wish I could commit to paper the feelings with which I beheld it.

This occurrence took place very soon after I went to live with my old master, and under the following circumstances. Aunt Hester went out one night,— where or for what I do not know,—and happened to be absent when my master desired her presence. He had ordered her not to go out evenings, and warned her that she must never let him catch her in company with a young man, who was paying attention to her, belonging to Colonel Lloyd. The young man's name was Ned Roberts, generally called Lloyd's Ned. Why master was so careful of her, may be safely left to conjecture. She was a woman of noble form, and of graceful proportions, having very few equals, and fewer superiors, in personal appearance, among the colored or white women of our neighborhood.

Aunt Hester had not only disobeyed his orders in going out, but had been found in company with Lloyd's Ned; which circumstance, I found, from what he said while whipping her, was the chief offence. Had he been a man of pure morals himself, he might have been thought interested in protecting the innocence of my aunt; but those who knew him will not suspect him of any such virtue. Before he commenced whipping Aunt Hester, he took her into the kitchen, and stripped her from neck to waist, leaving her neck, shoulders, and back, entirely naked. He then told her to cross her hands, calling her at the same time a d——d b——h. After crossing her hands, he tied them with a strong rope, and led her to a stool under a large hook in the joist, put in for the purpose. He made her get upon the stool, and tied her hands to the hook. She now stood fair for his infernal purpose. Her arms were stretched up at their full length, so that she stood upon the ends of her toes. He then said to her, "Now, you d——d b——h, I'll learn you how to disobey my orders!" and after rolling up his sleeves, he commenced to lay on the heavy cowskin, and soon the warm, red blood (amid heart-rending shrieks from her, and horrid oaths from him) came dripping to the floor. I was so terrified and horror-stricken at the sight, that I hid myself in a closet, and dared not venture out till long after the bloody transaction was over. I expected it would be my turn next. It was all new to me. I had never seen any thing like it before. I had always lived with my grandmother on the outskirts of the plantation, where she was put to raise the children of the younger women. I had therefore been, until now, out of the way of the bloody scenes that often occurred on the plantation.

## Chapter VI

My new mistress proved to be all she appeared when I first met her at the door,—a woman of the kindest heart and finest feelings. She had never had a slave under her control previously to myself, and prior to her marriage she had been dependent upon her own industry for a living. She was by trade a weaver; and by constant application to her business, she had been in a good degree preserved from the blighting and dehumanizing effects of slavery. I was utterly astonished at her goodness. I scarcely knew how to behave towards her. She was entirely unlike any other white woman I had ever seen. I could not approach her as I was accustomed to approach other white ladies. My early instruction was all out of place. The crouching servility, usually so acceptable a quality in a slave, did not answer when manifested toward her. Her favor was not gained by it; she seemed to be disturbed by it. She did not deem it impudent or unmannerly for a slave to look her in the face. The meanest slave was put fully at ease in her presence, and none left without feeling better for having seen her. Her face was made of heavenly smiles, and her voice of tranquil music.

But, alas! this kind heart had but a short time to remain such. The fatal poison of irresponsible power was already in her hands, and soon commenced its infernal work. That cheerful eye, under the influence of slavery, soon became red with rage; that voice, made all of sweet accord, changed to one of harsh and horrid discord; and that angelic face gave place to that of a demon.

Very soon after I went to live with Mr. and Mrs. Auld, she kindly commenced to teach me the A, B, C. After I had learned this, she assisted me in learning to spell words of three or four letters. Just at this point of my progress, Mr. Auld found out what was going on, and at once forbade Mrs. Auld to instruct me further, telling her, among other things, that it was unlawful, as well as unsafe, to teach a slave to read. To use his own words, further, he said, "If you give a nigger an inch, he will take an ell. A nigger should know nothing but to obey his master—to do as he is told to do. Learning would *spoil* the best nigger in the world. Now," said he, "if you teach that nigger (speaking of myself) how to read, there would be no keeping him. It would forever unfit him to be a slave. He would at once become unmanageable, and of no value to his master. As to himself, it could do him no good, but a great deal of harm. It would make him discontented and unhappy." These words sank deep into my heart, stirred up sentiments within that lay slumbering, and called into existence an entirely new train of thought. It was a new and special revelation, explaining dark and mysterious things, with which my youthful understanding had struggled, but struggled in vain. I now understood what had been to me a most perplexing difficulty—to wit, the white man's power to enslave the black man. It was a grand achievement, and I prized it highly. From that moment, I understood the pathway from slavery to freedom. It was just what I wanted, and I got it at a time when I the least expected it. Whilst I was saddened by the thought of losing the aid of my kind mistress, I was gladdened by the invaluable instruction which, by the merest accident, I had gained from my master. Though conscious of the difficulty of learning without a teacher, I set out with high hope, and a fixed purpose, at whatever cost of trouble, to learn how to read. The very decided manner with which he spoke, and strove to impress his wife with the evil consequences of giving me instruction, served to convince me that he was deeply sensible of the truths he was uttering. It gave me the best assurance that I might rely with the utmost confidence on the results which, he said, would flow from teaching me to read. What he most dreaded, that I most desired. What he most loved, that I most hated. That which to him was a great evil, to be carefully shunned, was to me a great good, to be diligently sought; and the argument which he so warmly urged, against my learning to read, only served to inspire me with a desire and determination to learn. In learning to read, I owe almost as much to the bitter opposition of my master, as to the kindly aid of my mistress. I acknowledge the benefit of both.

I had resided but a short time in Baltimore before I observed a marked difference, in the treatment of slaves, from that which I had witnessed in the country. A city slave is almost a freeman, compared with a slave on the plantation. He is much better fed and clothed, and enjoys privileges altogether unknown to the slave on the plantation. There is a vestige of decency, a sense of shame, that does much to curb and check those outbreaks of atrocious cruelty so commonly enacted upon the plantation. He is a desperate slaveholder, who will shock the humanity of his non-slaveholding neighbors with the cries of his lacerated slave. Few are willing to incur the odium attaching to the reputation of being a cruel master; and above all things, they would not be known as not giving a slave enough to eat. Every city slaveholder is anxious to have it known of him, that he feeds his slaves well; and it is due to them to say, that most of them do give their slaves enough to eat. There are, however, some painful exceptions to this rule. Directly opposite to us, on Philpot Street, lived Mr. Thomas Hamilton. He owned two slaves. Their names were Henrietta and Mary. Henrietta was about twenty-two years of age, Mary was about fourteen; and of all the mangled and emaciated creatures I ever looked upon, these two were the most so. His heart must be harder than stone, that could look upon these unmoved. The head, neck, and shoulders of Mary were literally cut to pieces. I have frequently felt her head, and found it nearly covered with festering sores, caused by the lash of her cruel mistress. I do not know that her master ever whipped her, but I have been an eye-witness to the cruelty of Mrs. Hamilton. I used to be in Mr. Hamilton's house nearly every day. Mrs. Hamilton used to sit in a large chair in the middle of the room, with a heavy cowskin always by her side, and scarce an hour passed during the day but was marked by the blood of one of these slaves. The girls seldom passed her without her saying, "Move faster, you *black gip!*" at the same time giving them a blow with the cowskin over the head or shoulders, often drawing the blood. She would then say, "Take that, you *black gip!*"—continuing, "If you don't move faster, I'll move you!" Added to the cruel lashings to which these slaves were subjected, they were kept nearly half-starved. They seldom knew what it was to eat a full meal. I have seen Mary contending with the pigs for the offal thrown into the street. So much was Mary kicked and cut to pieces, that she was oftener called "*pecked*" than by her name.

## Chapter VII

I lived in Master Hugh's family about seven years. During this time, I succeeded in learning to read and write. In accomplishing this, I was compelled to resort to various stratagems. I had no regular teacher. My mistress, who had kindly commenced to instruct me, had, in compliance with the advice and direction of her husband, not only ceased to instruct, but had set her face against my being instructed by any one else. It is due, however, to my mistress to say of her, that she did not adopt this course of treatment immediately. She at first lacked the depravity indispensable to shutting me up in mental darkness. It was at least necessary for her to have some training in the exercise of irresponsible power, to make her equal to the task of treating me as though I were a brute.

My mistress was, as I have said, a kind and tender-hearted woman; and in the simplicity of her soul she commenced, when I first went to live with her, to treat me as she supposed one human being ought to treat another. In entering upon the duties of a slaveholder, she did not seem to perceive that I sustained to her the relation of a mere chattel, and that for her to treat me as a human being was not only wrong, but dangerously so. Slavery proved as injurious to her as it did to me. When I went there, she was a pious, warm, and tender-hearted woman. There was no sorrow or suffering for which she had not a tear. She had bread for the hungry, clothes for the naked, and comfort for every mourner that came within her reach. Slavery soon proved its ability to divest her of these heavenly qualities. Under its influence, the tender heart became stone, and the lamblike disposition gave way to one of tiger-like fierceness. The first step in her downward course was in her ceasing to instruct me. She now commenced to practise her husband's precepts. She finally became even more violent in her opposition than her husband himself. She was not satisfied with simply doing as well as he had commanded; she seemed anxious to do better. Nothing seemed to make her more angry than to see me with a newspaper. She seemed to think that here lay the danger. I have had her rush at me with a face made all up of fury, and snatch from me a newspaper, in a manner that fully revealed her apprehension. She was an apt woman; and a little experience soon demonstrated, to her satisfaction, that education and slavery were incompatible with each other.

From this time I was most narrowly watched. If I was in a separate room any considerable length of time, I was sure to be suspected of having a book, and was at once called to give an account of myself. All this, however, was too late. The first step had been taken. Mistress, in teaching me the alphabet, had given me the *inch*, and no precaution could prevent me from taking the *ell*.

The plan which I adopted, and the one by which I was most successful, was that of making friends of all the little white boys whom I met in the street. As many of these as I could, I converted into teachers. With their kindly aid, obtained at different times and in different places, I finally succeeded in learning to read. When I was sent of errands, I always took my book with me, and by going one part of my errand quickly, I found time to get a lesson before my return. I used also to carry bread with me, enough of which was always in the house, and to which I was always welcome; for I was much better off in this regard than many of the poor white children in our neighborhood. This bread I used to bestow upon the hungry little urchins, who, in return, would give me that more valuable bread of knowledge. I am strongly tempted to give the names of two or three of those little boys, as a testimonial of the gratitude and affection I bear them; but prudence forbids;—not that it would injure me, but it might embarrass them; for it is almost an unpardonable offence to teach slaves to read in this Christian country. It is enough to say of the dear little fellows, that they lived on Philpot Street, very near Durgin and Bailey's ship-yard. I used to talk this matter of slavery over with them. I would sometimes say to them, I wished I could be as free as they would be when they got to be men. "You will be free as soon as you are twenty-one, *but I am a slave for life!* Have not I as good a right to be free as you have?" These words used to trouble them; they would express for me the liveliest sympathy, and console me with the hope that something would occur by which I might be free.

I was now about twelve years old, and the thought of being *a slave for life* began to bear heavily upon my heart. Just about this time, I got hold of a book entitled "The Columbian Orator."[4] Every opportunity I got, I used to read this book. Among much of other interesting matter, I found in it a dialogue between a master and his slave. The slave was represented as having run away from his master three times. The dialogue represented the conversation which took place between them, when the slave was retaken the third time. In this dialogue, the whole argument in behalf of slavery was brought forward by the master, all of which was disposed of by the slave. The slave was made to say some very smart as well as impressive things in reply to his master—things which had the desired though unexpected effect; for the conversation resulted in the voluntary emancipation of the slave on the part of the master.

In the same book, I met with one of Sheridan's[5] mighty speeches on and in behalf of Catholic emancipation. These were choice documents to me. I read them over and over again with unabated interest. They gave tongue to interesting thoughts of my own soul, which had frequently flashed through my mind, and died away for want of utterance. The moral which I gained from thedialogue was the power of truth over the conscience of even a slaveholder. What I got from Sheridan was a bold denunciation of slavery, and a powerful vindication of human rights. The reading of these documents enabled me to utter my thoughts, and to meet the arguments brought forward to sustain slavery; but while they relieved me of one difficulty, they brought on another even more painful than the one of which I was relieved. The more I read, the more I was led to abhor and detest my enslavers. I could regard them in no other light than a band of successful robbers, who had left their homes, and gone to Africa, and stolen us from our homes, and in a strange land reduced us to slavery. I loathed them as being the meanest as well as the most wicked of men. As I read and contemplated the subject, behold! that very discontentment which Master Hugh had predicted would follow my learning to read had already come, to torment and sting my soul to unutterable anguish. As I writhed under it, I would at times feel that learning to read had been a curse rather than a blessing. It had given me a view of my wretched condition, without the remedy. It opened my eyes to the horrible pit, but to no ladder upon which to get out. In moments of agony, I envied my fellow-slaves for their stupidity. I have often wished myself a beast. I preferred the condition of the meanest reptile to my own. Any thing, no matter what, to get rid of thinking! It was this everlasting thinking of my condition that tormented me. There was no getting rid of it. It was pressed upon me by every object within sight or hearing, animate or inanimate. The silver trump of freedom had roused my soul to eternal wakefulness. Freedom now appeared, to disappear no more forever. It was heard in every sound, and seen in every thing. It was ever

---

4. A popular collection of classic poems, dialogues, plays, and speeches that Douglass used as a model for his own speeches. "Columbian": American.

5. Richard Brinsley Sheridan (1751–1816), Irish dramatist and political leader.

present to torment me with a sense of my wretched condition. I saw nothing without seeing it, I heard nothing without hearing it, and felt nothing without feeling. It looked from every star, it smiled in every calm, breathed in every wind, and moved in every storm.

I often found myself regretting my own existence, and wishing myself dead; and but for the hope of being free, I have no doubt but that I should have killed myself, or done something for which I should have been killed. While in this state of mind, I was eager to hear any one speak of slavery. I was a ready listener. Every little while, I could hear something about the abolitionists. It was some time before I found what the word meant. It was always used in such connections as to make it an interesting word to me. If a slave ran away and succeeded in getting clear, or if a slave killed his master, set fire to a barn, or did any thing very wrong in the mind of a slaveholder, it was spoken of as the fruit of *abolition*. Hearing the word in this connection very often, I set about learning what it meant. The dictionary afforded me little or no help. I found it was "the act of abolishing;" but then I did not know what was to be abolished. Here I was perplexed. I did not dare to ask any one about its meaning, for I was satisfied that it was something they wanted me to know very little about. After a patient waiting, I got one of our city papers, containing an account of the number of petitions from the north, praying for the abolition of slavery in the District of Columbia, and of the slave trade between the States. From this time I understood the words *abolition* and *abolitionist*, and always drew near when that word was spoken, expecting to hear something of importance to myself and fellow-slaves. The light broke in upon me by degrees. I went one day down on the wharf of Mr. Waters; and seeing two Irishmen unloading a scow of stone, I went, unasked, and helped them. When we had finished, one of them came to me and asked me if I were a slave. I told him I was. He asked, "Are ye a slave for life?" I told him that I was. The good Irishman seemed to be deeply affected by the statement. He said to the other that it was a pity so fine a little fellow as myself should be a slave for life. He said it was a shame to hold me. They both advised me to run away to the north; that I should find friends there, and that I should be free. I pretended not to be interested in what they said, and treated them as if I did not understand them; for I feared they might be treacherous. White men have been known to encourage slaves to escape, and then, to get the reward, catch them and return them to their masters. I was afraid that these seemingly good men might use me so; but I nevertheless remembered their advice, and from that time I resolved to run away. I looked forward to a time at which it would be safe for me to escape. I was too young to think of doing so immediately; besides, I wished to learn how to write, as I might have occasion to write my own pass. I consoled myself with the hope that I should one day find a good chance. Meanwhile, I would learn to write.

The idea as to how I might learn to write was suggested to me by being in Durgin and Bailey's ship-yard, and frequently seeing the ship carpenters, after hewing, and getting a piece of timber ready for use, write on the timber the name of that part of the ship for which it was intended. When a piece of timber was intended for the larboard side, it would be marked thus—"L." When a piece was for the starboard side, it would be marked thus—"S." A piece for the larboard side forward, would be marked thus—"L. F." When a piece was for starboard side forward, it would be marked thus—"S. F." For larboard aft, it would be marked thus—"L. A." For starboard aft, it would be marked thus—"S. A." I soon learned the names of these letters, and for what they were intended when placed upon a piece of timber in the ship-yard. I immediately commenced copying them, and in a short time was able to make the four letters named. After that, when I met with any boy who I knew could write, I would tell him I could write as well as he. The next word would be, "I don't believe you. Let me see you try it." I would then make the letters which I had been so fortunate as to learn, and ask him to beat that. In this way I got a good many lessons in writing, which it is quite possible I should never have gotten in any other way. During this time, my copy-book was the board fence, brick wall, and pavement; my pen and ink was a lump of chalk. With these, I learned mainly how to write. I then commenced and continued copying the Italics in Webster's Spelling Book, until I could make them all without looking on the book. By this time, my little Master Thomas had gone to school, and learned how to write, and had written over a number of copy-books. These had been brought home, and shown to some of our near neighbors, and then laid aside. My mistress used to go to class meeting at the Wilk Street meetinghouse every Monday afternoon, and leave me to take care of the house. When left thus, I used to spend the time in writing in the spaces left in Master Thomas's copy-book, copying what he had written. I continued to do this until I could write a hand very similar to that of Master Thomas. Thus, after a long, tedious effort for years, I finally succeeded in learning how to write.

## Chapter IX

I have now reached a period of my life when I can give dates. I left Baltimore, and went to live with Master Thomas Auld, at St. Michael's, in March, 1832. It was now more than seven years since I lived with him in the family of my old master, on Colonel Lloyd's plantation. We of course were now almost entire strangers to each other. He was to me a new master, and I to him a new slave. I was ignorant of his temper and disposition; he was equally so of mine. A very short time, however brought us into full acquaintance with each other. I was made acquainted with his wife not less than with himself. They were well matched, being equally mean and cruel. I was now, for the first time during a space of more than seven years, made to feel the painful gnawings of hunger—a something which I had not experienced before since I left Colonel Lloyd's plantation. It went hard enough with me then, when I could look back to no period at which I had enjoyed a sufficiency. It was tenfold harder after living in Master Hugh's family, where I had always had enough to eat, and of that which was good. I have said Master Thomas was a mean man. He was so. Not to give a slave enough to eat, is regarded as the most aggravated development of meanness even among slaveholders. The rule is, no matter how coarse the food, only let there be enough of it. This is the theory; and in the part of Maryland from which I came, it is the general practice,—though there are many exceptions. Master Thomas gave us enough of neither coarse nor fine food. There were four slaves of us in the kitchen— my sister Eliza, my aunt Priscilla, Henny, and myself; and we were allowed less than half of a bushel of cornmeal per week, and very little else, either in the shape of meat or vegetables. It was not enough for us to subsist upon. We were therefore reduced to the wretched necessity of living at the expense of our neighbors. This we did by begging and stealing, whichever came handy in the time of need, the one being considered as legitimate as the other. A great many times have we poor creatures been nearly perishing with hunger, when food in abundance lay mouldering in the safe and smoke-house,[6] and our pious mistress was aware of the fact; and yet that mistress and her husband would kneel every morning, and pray that God would bless them in basket and store!

Bad as all slaveholders are, we seldom meet one destitute of every element of character commanding respect. My master was one of this rare sort. I do not know of one single noble act ever performed by him. The leading trait in his character was meanness; and if there were any other element in his nature, it was made subject to this. He was mean; and, like most other mean men, he lacked the ability to conceal his meanness. Captain Auld was not born a slaveholder. He had been a poor man, master only of a Bay craft. He came into possession of all his slaves by marriage; and of all men, adopted slaveholders are the worst. He was cruel, but cowardly. He commanded without firmness. In the enforcement of his rules he was at times rigid, and at times lax. At times, he spoke to his slaves with the firmness of Napoleon and the fury of a demon; at other times, he might well be mistaken for an inquirer who had lost his way. He did nothing of himself. He might have passed for a lion, but for his ears.[7] In all things noble which he attempted, his own meanness shone most conspicuous. His airs, words, and actions, were the airs, words, and actions of born slaveholders, and, being assumed, were awkward enough. He was not even a good imitator. He possessed all the disposition to deceive, but wanted the power. Having no resources within himself, he was compelled to be the copyist of many, and being such, he was forever the victim of inconsistency; and of consequence he was an object of contempt, and was held as such even by his slaves. The luxury of having slaves of his own to wait upon him was something new and unprepared for. He was a slaveholder without the ability to hold slaves. He found himself incapable of managing his slaves either by force, fear, or fraud. We seldom called him "master;" we generally called him "Captain Auld," and were hardly disposed to title him at all. I doubt not that our conduct had much to do with making him appear awkward, and of consequence fretful. Our want of reverence for him must have perplexed him greatly. He wished to have us call him master, but lacked the firmness necessary to command us to do so. His wife used to insist upon our calling him so, but to no purpose. In August, 1832, my master attended a Methodist camp-meeting held in the Bay-side, Talbot county, and there experienced religion. I indulged a faint hope that his conversion would lead him to emancipate his slaves, and that, if he did not do this, it would, at any rate, make him more kind and humane. I was disappointed in both these respects. It neither made him to be humane to his slaves, nor to emancipate them. If it had any effect on his character, it made him more cruel and hateful in all his ways; for I believe him to have been a much worse man after his conversion than before. Prior to his conversion, he relied upon his own depravity to shield and sustain him in his savage barbarity; but after his conversion, he found religious sanction and support for his slaveholding cruelty. He made the greatest pretensions

6. Used both to cure and to store meat and fish. "Safe": a meat safe is a structure for preserving food.
7. A mocking commentary on his master's inauthentic

display of nobility and strength, which can easily be seen to disguise meanness and weakness.

to piety. His house was the house of prayer. He prayed morning, noon, and night. He very soon distinguished himself among his brethren, and was soon made a class-leader and exhorter. His activity in revivals was great, and he proved himself an instrument in the hands of the church in converting many souls. His house was the preachers' home. They used to take great pleasure in coming there to put up; for while he starved us, he stuffed them. We have had three or four preachers there at a time. The names of those who used to come most frequently while I lived there, were Mr. Storks, Mr. Ewery, Mr. Humphry, and Mr. Hickey. I have also seen Mr. George Cookman at our house. We slaves loved Mr. Cookman. We believed him to be a good man. We thought him instrumental in getting Mr. Samuel Harrison, a very rich slaveholder, to emancipate his slaves; and by some means got the impression that he was laboring to effect the emancipation of all the slaves. When he was at our house, we were sure to be called in to prayers. When the others were there, we were sometimes called in and sometimes not. Mr. Cookman took more notice of us than either of the other ministers. He could not come among us with betraying his sympathy for us, and, stupid as we were, we had the sagacity to see it.

While I lived with my master in St. Michael's, there was a white young man, a Mr. Wilson, who proposed to keep a Sabbath school for the instruction of such slaves as might be disposed to learn to read the New Testament. We met but three times, when Mr. West and Mr. Fairbanks, both class-leaders, with many others, came upon with us with sticks and other missiles, drove us off, and forbade us to meet again. Thus ended our little Sabbath school in the pious town of St. Michael's.

I have said my master found religious sanction for his cruelty. As an example, I will state one of many facts going to prove the charge. I have seen him tie up a lame young woman, and whip her with a heavy cowskin upon her naked shoulders, causing the warm red blood to drip; and, in justification of the bloody deed, he would quote this passage of Scripture—"He that knoweth his master's will, and doeth it not, shall be beaten with many stripes."[8]

Master would keep this lacerated young woman tied up in this horrid situation four or five hours at a time. I have known him to tie her up early in the morning, and whip her before breakfast; leave her, go to his store, return at dinner, and whip her again, cutting her in the places already made raw with his cruel lash. The secret of master's cruelty toward "Henny" is found in the fact of her being almost helpless. When quite a child, she fell into the fire, and burned herself horribly. Her hands were so burnt that she never got the use of them. She could do very little but bear heavy burdens. She was to master a bill of expense; and as he was a mean man, she was a constant offence to him. He seemed desirous of getting the poor girl out of existence. He gave her away once to his sister; but, being a poor gift, she was not disposed to keep her. Finally, my benevolent master, to use his own words, "set her adrift to take care of herself." Here was a recently-converted man, holding on upon the mother, and at the same time turning out her helpless child, to starve and die! Master Thomas was one of the many pious slaveholders who hold slaves for the very charitable purpose of taking care of them.

My master and myself had quite a number of differences. He found me

---

8. Luke 12.47. Only those of his servants who have an unending faith in Christ are safe from all opposing forces in their lives.

unsuitable to his purpose. My city life, he said, had had a very pernicious effect upon me. It had almost ruined me for every good purpose, and fitted me for every thing which was bad. One of my greatest faults was that of letting his horse run away, and go down to his father-in-law's farm, which was about five miles from St. Michael's. I would then have to go after it. My reason for this kind of carelessness, or carefulness, was, that I could always get something to eat when I went there. Master William Hamilton, my master's father-in-law, always gave his slaves enough to eat. I never left there hungry, no matter how great the need of my speedy return. Master Thomas at length said he would stand it no longer. I had lived with him nine months, during which time he had given me a number of severe whippings, all to no good purpose. He resolved to put me out, as he said, to be broken; and, for this purpose, he let me for one year to a man named Edward Covey. Mr. Covey was a poor man, a farm-renter. He rented the place upon which he lived, as also the hands with which he tilled it. Mr. Covey had acquired a very high reputation for breaking young slaves, and this reputation was of immense value to him. It enabled him to get his farm tilled with much less expense to himself than he could have had it done without such a reputation. Some slaveholders thought it not much loss to allow Mr. Covey to have their slaves one year, for the sake of training to which they were subjected, without any other compensation. He could hire young help with great ease, in consequence of this reputation. Added to the natural good qualities of Mr. Covey, he was a professor of religion—a pious soul—a member and a class-leader in the Methodist church. All of this added weight to his reputation as a "nigger-breaker." I was aware of all the facts, having been made acquainted with them by a young man who had lived there. I nevertheless made the change gladly; for I was sure of getting enough to eat, which is not the smallest consideration to a hungry man.

## Chapter X

I left Master Thomas's house, and went to live with Mr. Covey, on the 1st of January, 1833. I was now, for the first time in my life, a field hand. In my new employment, I found myself even more awkward than a country boy appeared to be in a large city. I had been at my new home but one week before Mr. Covey gave me a very severe whipping, cutting my back, causing the blood to run, and raising ridges on my flesh as large as my little finger. The details of this affair are as follows: Mr. Covey sent me, very early in the morning of one of our coldest days in the month of January, to the woods, to get a load of wood. He gave me a team of unbroken oxen. He told me which was the in-hand ox, and which the off-hand one.[9] He then tied the end of a large rope around the horns of the in-hand-ox, and gave me the other end of it, and told me, if the oxen started to run, that I must hold on upon the rope. I had never driven oxen before, and of course I was very awkward. I, however, succeeded in getting to the edge of the woods with little difficulty; but I had got a very few rods into the woods, when the oxen took fright, and started full tilt, carrying the cart against trees, and over stumps, in the most frightful manner. I expected every moment that my brains would be dashed out against the

9. The one on the right of a pair hitched to a wagon. "In-hand ox": the one to the left.

trees. After running thus for a considerable distance, they finally upset the cart, dashing it with great force against a tree, and threw themselves into a dense thicket. How I escaped death, I do not know. There I was, entirely alone, in a thick wood, in a place new to me. My cart was upset and shattered, my oxen were entangled among the young trees, and there was none to help me. After a long spell of effort, I succeeded in getting my cart righted, my oxen disentangled, and again yoked to the cart. I now proceeded with my team to the place where I had, the day before, been chopping wood, and loaded my cart pretty heavily, thinking in this way to tame my oxen. I then proceeded on my way home. I had now consumed one half of the day. I got out of the woods safely, and now felt out of danger. I stopped my oxen to open the woods gate; and just as I did so, before I could get hold of my ox-rope, the oxen again started, rushed through the gate, catching it between the wheel and the body of the cart, tearing it to pieces, and coming within a few inches of crushing me against the gate-post. Thus twice, in one short day, I escaped death by the merest chance. On my return, I told Mr. Covey what had happened, and how it happened. He ordered me to return to the woods again immediately. I did so, and he followed on after me. Just as I got into the woods, he came up and told me to stop my cart, and that he would teach me how to trifle away my time, and break gates. He then went to a large gum-tree, and with his axe cut three large switches, and, after trimming them up neatly with his pocket-knife, he ordered me to take off my clothes. I made him no answer, but stood with my clothes on. He repeated his order. I still made him no answer, nor did I move to strip myself. Upon this he rushed at me with the fierceness of a tiger, tore off my clothes, and lashed me till he had worn out his switches, cutting me so savagely as to leave the marks visible for a long time after. This whipping was the first of a number just like it, and for similar offences.

I lived with Mr. Covey one year. During the first six months, of that year, scarce a week passed without his whipping me. I was seldom free from a sore back. My awkwardness was almost always his excuse for whipping me. We were worked fully up to the point of endurance. Long before day we were up, our horses fed, and by the first approach of day we were off to the field with our hoes and ploughing teams. Mr. Covey gave us enough to eat, but scarce time to eat it. We were often less than five minutes taking our meals. We were often in the field from the first approach of day till its last lingering ray had left us; and at saving-fodder time, midnight often caught us in the field binding blades.[1]

Covey would be out with us. The way he used to stand it, was this. He would spend the most of his afternoons in bed. He would then come out fresh in the evening, ready to urge us on with his words, example, and frequently with the whip. Mr. Covey was one of the few slaveholders who could and did work with his hands. He was a hard-working man. He knew by himself just what a man or a boy could do. There was no deceiving him. His work went on in his absence almost as well as in his presence; and he had the faculty of making us feel that he was ever present with us. This he did by surprising us. He seldom approached the spot where we were at work openly, if he could do it secretly. He always aimed at taking us by surprise. Such was his cunning, that we used to call him, among ourselves, "the snake." When we were at

---

1. I.e., of wheat or other plants. "Saving-fodder time": harvest time.

work in the cornfield, he would sometimes crawl on his hands and knees to avoid detection, and all at once he would rise nearly in our midst, and scream out, "Ha, ha! Come, come! Dash on, dash on!" This being his mode of attack, it was never safe to stop a single minute. His comings were like a thief in the night. He appeared to us as being ever at hand. He was under every tree, behind every stump, in every bush, and at every window, on the plantation. He would sometimes mount his horse, as if bound to St. Michael's, a distance of seven miles, and in half an hour afterwards you would see him coiled up in the corner of the wood-fence, watching every motion of the slaves. He would, for this purpose, leave his horse tied up in the woods. Again, he would sometimes walk up to us, and give us orders as though he was upon the point of starting on a long journey, turn his back upon us, and make as though he was going to the house to get ready; and, before he would get half way thither, he would turn short and crawl into a fence-corner, or behind some tree, and there watch us till the going down of the sun.

Mr. Covey's *forte* consisted in his power to deceive. His life was devoted to planning and perpetrating the grossest deceptions. Every thing he possessed in the shape of learning or religion, he made conform to his disposition to deceive. He seemed to think himself equal to deceiving the Almighty. He would make a short prayer in the morning, and a long prayer at night; and, strange as it may seem, few men would at times appear more devotional than he. The exercises of his family devotions were always commenced with singing; and, as he was a very poor singer himself, the duty of raising the hymn generally came upon me. He would read his hymn, and nod at me to commence. I would at times do so; at others, I would not. My non-compliance would almost always produce much confusion. To show himself independent of me, he would start and stagger through with his hymn in the most discordant manner. In this state of mind, he prayed with more than ordinary spirit. Poor man! such was his disposition, and success at deceiving, I do verily believe that he sometimes deceived himself into the solemn belief, that he was a sincere worshiper of the most high God; and this, too, at a time when he may be said to have been guilty of compelling his woman slave to commit the sin of adultery. The facts in the case are these: Mr. Covey was a poor man; he was just commencing in life; he was only able to buy one slave; and, shocking as is the fact, he bought her, as he said, for *a breeder*. This woman was named Caroline. Mr. Covey bought her from Mr. Thomas Lowe, about six miles from St. Michael's. She was a large, able-bodied woman, about twenty years old. She had already given birth to one child, which proved her to be just what he wanted. After buying her, he hired a married man of Mr. Samuel Harrison, to live with him one year; and him he used to fasten up with her every night! The result was, that, at the end of the year, the miserable woman gave birth to twins. At this result Mr. Covey seemed to be highly pleased, both with the man and the wretched woman. Such was his joy, and that of his wife, that nothing they could do for Caroline during her confinement was too good, or too hard, to be done. The children were regarded as being quite an addition to his wealth.

If at any one time of my life more than another, I was made to drink the bitterest dregs of slavery, that time was during the first six months of my stay with Mr. Covey. We were worked in all weathers. It was never too hot or too cold; it could never rain, blow, hail, or snow, too hard for us to work in the field. Work, work, work, was scarcely more the order of the day than of the night. The longest days were too short for him, and the shortest nights too long for him. I was somewhat unmanageable when I first went there, but a few months of this discipline tamed me. Mr. Covey succeeded in breaking me. I was broken in body, soul, and spirit. My natural elasticity was crushed, my intellect languished, the disposition to read departed, the cheerful spark that lingered about my eye died; the dark night of slavery closed in upon me; and behold a man transformed into a brute!

Sunday was my only leisure time. I spent this in a sort of beast-like stupor, between sleep and wake, under some large tree. At times I would rise up, a flash of energetic freedom would dart through my soul, accompanied with a faint beam of hope, that flickered for a moment, and then vanished. I sank down again, mourning over my wretched condition. I was sometimes prompted to take my life, and that of Covey, but was prevented by a combination of hope and fear. My sufferings on this plantation seem now like a dream rather than a stern reality.

Our house stood within a few rods of the Chesapeake Bay, whose broad bosom was ever white with sails from every quarter of the habitable globe. Those beautiful vessels, robed in purest white, so delightful to the eye of free-men, were to me so many shrouded ghosts, to terrify and torment me with thoughts of my wretched condition. I have often, in the deep stillness of a summer's Sabbath, stood all alone upon the lofty banks of that noble bay, and traced, with saddened heart and tearful eye, the countless number of sails moving off to the mighty ocean. The sight of these always affected me power-fully. My thoughts would compel utterance; and there, with no audience but the Almighty, I would pour out my soul's complaint, in my rude way, with an apostrophe to the moving multitude of ships:—

"You are loosed from your moorings, and are free; I am fast in my chains, and am a slave! You move merrily before the gentle gale, and I sadly before the bloody whip! You are freedom's swift-winged angels, that fly round the world; I am confined in bands of iron! O that I were free! Oh, that I were on one of your gallant decks, and under your protecting wing! Alas! betwixt me and you, the turbid waters roll. Go on, go on. O that I could also go! Could I but swim! If I could fly! O, why was I born a man, of whom to make a brute! The glad ship is gone; she hides in the dim distance. I am left in the hottest hell of unending slavery. O God, save me! God, deliver me! Let me be free! Is there any God? Why am I a slave? I will run away. I will not stand it. Get caught, or get clear, I'll try it. I had as well die with ague as the fever. I have only one life to lose. I had as well be killed running as die standing. Only think of it; one hundred miles straight north, and I am free! Try it? Yes! God helping me, I will. It cannot be that I shall live and die a slave. I will take to the water. This very bay shall yet bear me into freedom. The steamboats steered in a north-east course from North Point. I will do the same; and when I get to the head of the bay, I will turn my canoe adrift, and walk straight through Delaware into Pennsylvania. When I get there, I shall not be required to have a pass; I can travel without being disturbed. Let but the first opportu-nity offer, and, come what will, I am off. Meanwhile, I will try to bear up under the yoke. I am not the only slave in the world. Why should I fret? I can bear as much as any of them. Besides, I am but a boy, and all boys are bound to some one. It may be that my misery in slavery will only increase my happi-ness when I get free. There is a better day coming."

Thus I used to think, and thus I used to speak to myself; goaded almost to madness at one moment, and at the next reconciling myself to my wretched lot.

I have already intimated that my condition was much worse, during the first six months of my stay at Mr. Covey's, than in the last six. The circumstances leading to the change in Mr. Covey's course toward me form an epoch in my humble history. You have seen how a man was made a slave; you shall see how a slave was made a man. On one of the hottest days of the month of August, 1833, Bill Smith, William Hughes, a slave named Eli, and myself, were engaged in fanning wheat.[2] Hughes was clearing the fanned wheat from before the fan, Eli was turning, Smith was feeding, and I was carrying wheat to the fan. The work was simple, requiring strength rather than intellect; yet, to one entirely unused to such work, it came very hard. About three o'clock of that day, I broke down; my strength failed me; I was seized with a violent aching of the head, attended with extreme dizziness; I trembled in every limb. Finding what was coming, I nerved myself up, feeling it would never do to stop work. I stood as long as I could stagger to the hopper with grain. When I could stand no longer, I fell, and felt as if held down by an immense weight. The fan of course stopped; every one had his own work to do; and no one could do the work of the other, and have his own go on at the same time.

Mr. Covey was at the house, about one hundred yards from the treading-yard where we were fanning. On hearing the fan stop, he left immediately, and came to the spot where we were. He hastily inquired what the matter was. Bill answered that I was sick, and there was no one to bring wheat to the fan. I had by this time crawled away under the side of the post and rail-fence by which the yard was enclosed, hoping to find relief by getting out of the sun. He then asked where I was. He was told by one of the hands. He came to the spot, and, after looking at me awhile, asked me what was the matter. I told him as well as I could, for I scarce had strength to speak. He then gave me a savage kick in the side, and told me to get up. I tried to do so, but fell back in the attempt. He gave me another kick, and again told me to rise. I again tried, and succeeded in gaining my feet; but, stooping to get the tub with which I was feeding the fan, I again staggered and fell. While down in this situation, Mr. Covey took up the hickory slat with which Hughes had been striking off the half-bushel measure, and with it gave me a heavy blow upon the head, making a large wound, and the blood ran freely; and with this again told me to get up. I made no effort to comply, having now made up my mind to let him do his worst. In a short time after receiving this blow, my head grew better. Mr. Covey had now left me to my fate. At this moment I resolved, for the first time, to go to my master, enter a complaint, and ask his protection. In order to do this, I must that afternoon walk seven miles; and this, under the circumstances, was truly a severe undertaking. I was exceedingly feeble; made so as much by the kicks and blows which I received, as by the severe fit of sickness to which I had been subjected. I, however, watched my chance, while Covey was looking in an opposite direction, and started for St. Michael's. I succeeded in getting a considerable distance on my way to the woods, when Covey discovered me, and called after me to come back, threatening what he would do if I did not come. I disregarded both his calls and his threats, and made my way to the woods as fast as my feeble state would allow; and thinking

2. I.e., separating the wheat from the chaff.

I might be overhauled by him if I kept the road, I walked through the woods, keeping far enough from the road to avoid detection, and near enough to prevent losing my way. I had not gone far before my little strength again failed me. I could go no farther. I fell down, and lay for a considerable time. The blood was yet oozing from the wound on my head. For a time I thought I should bleed to death; and think now that I should have done so, but that the blood so matted my hair as to stop the wound. After lying there about three quarters of an hour, I nerved myself up again, and started on my way, through bogs and briers, barefooted and bareheaded, tearing my feet sometimes at nearly every step; and after a journey of about seven miles, occupying some five hours to perform it, I arrived at master's store. I then presented an appearance enough to affect any but a heart of iron. From the crown of my head to my feet, I was covered with blood. My hair was all clotted with dust and blood; my shirt was stiff with blood. My legs and feet were torn in sundry places with briers and thorns, and were also covered with blood. I suppose I looked like a man who had escaped a den of wild beasts, and barely escaped them. In this state I appeared before my master, humbly entreating him to interpose his authority for my protection. I told him all the circumstances as well as I could, and it seemed, as I spoke, at times to affect him. He would then walk the floor, and seek to justify Covey by saying he expected I deserved it. He asked me what I wanted. I told him, to let me get a new home; that as sure as I lived with Mr. Covey again, I should live with but to die with him; that Covey would surely kill me; he was in a fair way for it. Master Thomas ridiculed the idea that there was any danger of Mr. Covey's killing me, and said that he knew Mr. Covey; that he was a good man, and that he could not think of taking me from him; that, should he do so, he would lose the whole year's wages; that I belonged to Mr. Covey for one year, and that I must go back to him, come what might; and that I must not trouble him with any more stories, or that he would himself *get hold of me.* After threatening me thus, he gave me a very large dose of salts, telling me that I might remain in St. Michael's that night, (it being quite late,) but that I must be off back to Mr. Covey's early in the morning; and that if I did not, he would *get hold of me,* which meant that he would whip me. I remained all night, and, according to his orders, I started off to Covey's in the morning, (Saturday morning), wearied in body and broken in spirit. I got no supper that night, or breakfast that morning. I reached Covey's about nine o'clock; and just as I was getting over the fence that divided Mrs. Kemp's fields from ours, out ran Covey with his cowskin, to give me another whipping. Before he could reach me, I succeeded in getting to the cornfield; and as the corn was very high, it afforded me the means of hiding. He seemed very angry, and searched for me a long time. My behavior was altogether unaccountable. He finally gave up the chase, thinking, I suppose, that I must come home for something to eat; he would give himself no further trouble in looking for me. I spent that day mostly in the woods, having the alternative before me,—to go home and be whipped to death, or stay in the woods and be starved to death. That night, I fell in with Sandy Jenkins, a slave with whom I was somewhat acquainted. Sandy had a free wife[3] who lived about four miles from Mr. Covey's; and it being Saturday, he was on his way to see her. I told him my circumstances, and he very kindly invited me to go

---

3. I.e., his wife had been set free and was not legally a slave.

home with him. I went home with him, and talked this whole matter over, and got his advice as to what course it was best for me to pursue. I found Sandy an old adviser. He told me, with great solemnity, I must go back to Covey; but that before I went, I must go with him into another part of the woods, where there was a certain *root*, which, if I would take some of it with me, carrying it *always on my right side*, would render it impossible for Mr. Covey, or any other white man, to whip me. He said he had carried it for years; and since he had done so, he had never received a blow, and never expected to while he carried it. I at first rejected the idea, that the simple carrying of a root in my pocket would have any such effect as he had said, and was not disposed to take it; but Sandy impressed the necessity with much earnestness, telling me it could do no harm, if it did no good. To please him, I at length took the root, and, according to his direction, carried it upon my right side. This was Sunday morning. I immediately started for home; and upon entering the yard gate, out came Mr. Covey on his way to meeting. He spoke to me very kindly, bade me drive the pigs from a lot near by, and passed on towards the church. Now, this singular conduct of Mr. Covey really made me begin to think that there was something in the *root* which Sandy had given me; and had it been on any other day than Sunday, I could have attributed the conduct to no other cause then the influence of that root; and as it was, I was half inclined to think the *root* to be something more than I at first had taken it to be. All went well till Monday morning. On this morning, the virtue of the *root* was fully tested. Long before daylight, I was called to go and rub, curry, and feed, the horses. I obeyed, and was glad to obey. But whilst thus engaged, whilst in the act of throwing down some blades from the loft, Mr. Covey entered the stable with a long rope; and just as I was half out of the loft, he caught hold of my legs, and was about tying me. As soon as I found what he was up to, I gave a sudden spring, and as I did so, he holding to my legs, I was brought sprawling on the stable floor. Mr. Covey seemed now to think he had me, and could do what he pleased; but at this moment—from whence came the spirit I don't know— I resolved to fight; and, suiting my action to the resolution, I seized Covey hard by the throat; and as I did so, I rose. He held on to me, and I to him. My resistance was so entirely unexpected, that Covey seemed taken all aback. He trembled like a leaf. This gave me assurance, and I held him uneasy, causing the blood to run where I touched him with the ends of my fingers. Mr. Covey soon called out to Hughes for help. Hughes came, and, while Covey held me, attempted to tie my right hand. While he was in the act of doing so, I watched my chance, and gave him a heavy kick close under the ribs. This kick fairly sickened Hughes, so that he left me in the hands of Mr. Covey. This kick had the effect of not only weakening Hughes, but Covey also. When he saw Hughes bending over with pain, his courage quailed. He asked me if I meant to persist in my resistance. I told him I did, come what might; that he had used me like a brute for six months, and that I was determined to be used so no longer. With that, he strove to drag me to a stick that was lying just out of the stable door. He meant to knock me down. But just as he was leaning over to get the stick, I seized him with both hands by his collar, and brought him by a sudden snatch to the ground. By this time, Bill came. Covey called upon him for assistance. Bill wanted to know what he could do. Covey said, "Take hold of him, take hold of him!" Bill said his master hired him out to work, and not to help to whip me; so he left Covey and myself to fight our own battle out. We were at it for nearly two hours. Covey at length let me go, puffing and blowing at a great rate, saying that if I had not resisted, he would not have whipped me half so much. The truth was, that he had not whipped me at all. I considered him as getting entirely the worst end of the bargain; for he had drawn no blood from me, but I had from him. The whole six months afterwards, that I spent with Mr. Covey, he never laid the weight of his finger upon me in anger. He would occasionally say, he didn't want to get hold of me again. "No," thought I, "you need not; for you will come off worse than you did before."

This battle with Mr. Covey was the turning-point in my career as a slave. It rekindled the few expiring embers of freedom, and revived within me a sense of my own manhood. It recalled the departed self-confidence, and inspired me again with a determination to be free. The gratification afforded by the triumph was a full compensation for whatever else might follow, even death itself. He only can understand the deep satisfaction which I experienced, who has himself repelled by force the bloody arm of slavery. I felt as I never felt before. It was a glorious resurrection, from the tomb of slavery, to the heaven of freedom. My long-crushed spirit rose, cowardice departed, bold defiance took its place; and I now resolved that, however long I might remain a slave in form, the day had passed forever when I could be a slave in fact. I did not hesitate to let it be known of me, that the white man who expected to succeed in whipping, must also succeed in killing me.

From this time I was never again what might be called fairly whipped, though I remained a slave four years afterwards. I had several fights, but was never whipped.

It was for a long time a matter of surprise to me why Mr. Covey did not immediately have me taken by the constable to the whipping-post, and there regularly whipped for the crime of raising my hand against a white man in defence of myself. And the only explanation I can now think of does not entirely satisfy me; but such as it is, I will give it. Mr. Covey enjoyed the most unbounded reputation for being a first-rate overseer and negro-breaker. It was of considerable importance to him. That reputation was at stake; and had he sent me—a boy about sixteen years old—to the public whipping-post, his reputation would have been lost; so, to save his reputation, he suffered me to go unpunished.

My term of actual service to Mr. Edward Covey ended on Christmas day, 1833. The days between Christmas and New Year's day are allowed as holidays; and, accordingly, we were not required to perform any labor, more than to feed and take care of the stock. This time we regarded as our own, by the grace of our masters; and we therefore used or abused it nearly as we pleased. Those of us who had families at a distance, were generally allowed to spend the whole six days in their society. This time, however, was spent in various ways. The staid, sober, thinking and industrious ones of our number would employ themselves in making corn-brooms, mats, horse-collars, and baskets; and another class of us would spend the time hunting opossums, hares, and coons. But by far the larger part engaged in such sports and merriments as playing ball, wrestling, running foot-races, fiddling, dancing, and drinking whisky; and this latter mode of spending the time was by far the most agreeable to the feelings of our master. A slave who would work during the holidays was considered by our masters as scarcely deserving them. He was regarded as one who rejected the favor of his master. It was deemed a disgrace not to get drunk at Christmas; and he was regarded as lazy indeed, who had not provided himself with the necessary means, during the year, to get whisky enough to last him through Christmas.

From what I know of the effect of these holidays upon the slave, I believe them to be among the most effective means in the hands of the slaveholder in keeping down the spirit of insurrection. Were the slaveholders at once to abandon this practice, I have not the slightest doubt it would lead to an immediate insurrection among the slaves. These holidays serve as conductors, or safety-valves, to carry off the rebellious spirit of enslaved humanity. But for these, the slave would be forced up to the wildest desperation; and woe betide the slaveholder, the day he ventures to remove or hinder the operation of those conductors! I warn him that, in such an event, a spirit will go forth in their midst, more to be dreaded than the most appalling earthquake.

The holidays are part and parcel of the gross fraud, wrong, and inhumanity of slavery. They are professedly a custom established by the benevolence of the slaveholders; but I undertake to say, it is the result of selfishness, and one of the grossest frauds committed upon the down-trodden slave. They do not give the slaves this time because they would not like to have their work during its continuance, but because they know it would be unsafe to deprive them of it. This will be seen by the fact, that the slaveholders like to have their slaves spend those days just in such a manner as to make them as glad of their ending as of their beginning. Their object seems to be, to disgust their slaves with freedom, by plunging them into the lowest depths of dissipation. For instance, the slaveholders not only like to see the slave drink of his own accord, but will adopt various plans to make him drunk. One plan is, to make bets on their slaves, as to who can drink the most whisky without getting drunk; and in this way they succeed in getting whole multitudes to drink to excess. Thus, when the slave asks for virtuous freedom, the cunning slaveholder, knowing his ignorance, cheats him with a dose of vicious dissipation, artfully labelled with the name of liberty. The most of us used to drink it down, and the result was just what might be supposed: many of us were led to think that there was little to choose between liberty and slavery. We felt, and very properly too, that we had almost as well be slaves to man as to rum. So, when the holidays ended, we staggered up from the filth of our wallowing, took a long breath, and marched to the field,—feeling, upon the whole, rather glad to go, from what our master had deceived us into a belief was freedom, back to the arms of slavery.

I have said that this mode of treatment is a part of the whole system of fraud and inhumanity of slavery. It is so. The mode here adopted to disgust the slave with freedom, by allowing him to see only the abuse of it, is carried out in other things. For instance, a slave loves molasses; he steals some. His master, in many cases, goes off to town, and buys a large quantity; he returns, takes his whip, and commands the slave to eat the molasses, until the poor fellow is made sick at the very mention of it. The same mode is sometimes adopted to make the slaves refrain from asking for more food than their regular allowance. A slave runs through his allowance, and applies for more. His master is enraged at him; but, not willing to send him off without food, gives him more than is necessary, and compels him to eat it within a given time. Then, if he complains that he cannot eat it, he is said to be satisfied neither full nor fasting, and is whipped for being hard to please! I have an abundance of such illustrations of the same principle, drawn from my own observation, but think the cases I have cited sufficient. The practice is a very common one. On the first of January, 1834, I left Mr. Covey, and went to live with Mr. William Freeland, who lived about three miles from St. Michael's. I soon found Mr. Freeland a very different man from Mr. Covey. Though not rich, he was what would be called an educated southern gentleman. Mr. Covey, as I have shown, was a well-trained negro-breaker and slave-driver. The former (slaveholder though he was) seemed to possess some regard for honor, some reverence for justice, and some respect for humanity. The latter seemed totally insensible to all such sentiments. Mr. Freeland had many of the faults peculiar to slaveholders, such as being very passionate and fretful; but I must do him the justice to say, that he was exceedingly free from those degrading vices to which Mr. Covey was constantly addicted. The one was open and frank, and we always knew where to find him. The other was a most artful deceiver, and could be understood only by such as were skilful enough to detect his cunningly-devised frauds. Another advantage I gained in my new master was, he made no pretensions to, or profession of, religion; and this, in my opinion, was truly a great advantage. I assert most unhesitatingly, that the religion of the south is a mere covering for the most horrid crimes,—a justifier of the most appalling barbarity,—a sanctifier of the most hateful frauds,—and a dark shelter under, which the darkest, foulest, grossest, and most infernal deeds of slaveholders find the strongest protection. Were I to be again reduced to the chains of slavery, next to that enslavement, I should regard being the slave of a religious master the greatest calamity that could befall me. For of all slaveholders with whom I have ever met, religious slaveholders are the worst. I have ever found them the meanest and basest, the most cruel and cowardly, of all others. It was my unhappy lot not only to belong to a religious slaveholder, but to live in a community of such religionists. Very near Mr. Freeland lived the Rev. Daniel Weeden, and in the same neighborhood lived the Rev. Rigby Hopkins. These were members and ministers in the Reformed Methodist Church. Mr. Weeden owned, among others, a woman slave, whose name I have forgotten. This woman's back, for weeks, was kept literally raw, made so by the lash of this merciless, *religious* wretch. He used to hire hands. His maxim was, Behave well or behave ill, it is the duty of a master occasionally to whip a slave, to remind him of his master's authority. Such was his theory, and such his practice.

Mr. Hopkins was even worse than Mr. Weeden. His chief boast was his ability to manage slaves. The peculiar feature of his government was that of whipping slaves in advance of deserving it. He always managed to have one or more of his slaves to whip every Monday morning. He did this to alarm their fears, and strike terror into those who escaped. His plan was to whip for the smallest offences, to prevent the commission of large ones. Mr. Hopkins could always find some excuse for whipping a slave. It would astonish one, unaccustomed to a slaveholding life, to see with what wonderful ease a slaveholder can find things, of which to make occasion to whip a slave. A mere look, word, or motion,—a mistake, accident, or want of power,—are all matters for which a slave may be whipped at any time. Does a slave look dissatisfied? It is said, he has the devil in him, and it must be whipped out. Does he speak loudly when spoken to by his master? Then he is getting high-minded, and should be taken down a button-hole lower. Does he forget to pull off his hat at the approach of a white person? Then he is wanting in reverence, and should be whipped for it. Does he ever venture to vindicate his conduct, when censured for it? Then he is guilty of impudence,—one of the greatest crimes of which a slave can be guilty. Does he ever venture to suggest a different mode of doing things from that pointed out by his master? He is indeed presumptuous, and getting above himself; and nothing less than a flogging will do for him. Does he, while ploughing, break a plough,—or, while hoeing, break a hoe? It is owing to his carelessness, and for it a slave must always be whipped. Mr. Hopkins could always find something of this sort to justify the use of the lash, and he seldom failed to embrace such opportunities. There was not a man in the whole county, with whom the slaves who had the getting their own home, would not prefer to live, rather than with this Rev. Mr. Hopkins. And yet there was not a man any where round, who made higher professions of religion, or was more active in revivals—more attentive to the class, love-feast, prayer and preaching meetings, or more devotional in his family,—that prayed earlier, later, louder, and longer,—than this same reverend slave-driver, Rigby Hopkins.

But to return to Mr. Freeland, and to my experience while in his employment. He, like Mr. Covey, gave us enough to eat; but unlike Mr. Covey, he also gave us sufficient time to take our meals. He worked us hard, but always between sunrise and sunset. He required a good deal of work to be done, but gave us good tools with which to work. His farm was large, but he employed hands enough to work it, and with ease, compared with many of his neighbors. My treatment, while in his employment, was heavenly, compared with what I experienced at the hands of Mr. Edward Covey.

Mr. Freeland was himself the owner of but two slaves. Their names were Henry Harris and John Harris. The rest of his hands he hired. These consisted of myself, Sandy Jenkins[4] and Handy Caldwell. Henry and John were quite intelligent, and in a very little while after I went there, I succeeded in creating in them a strong desire to learn how to read. This desire soon sprang up in the others also. They very soon mustered up some old spelling-books, and nothing would do but that I must keep a Sabbath school. I agreed to do so, and accordingly devoted my Sundays to teaching these my loved fellow-slaves how to read. Neither of them knew his letters when I went there. Some of the slaves of the neighboring farms found what was going on, and also availed themselves of this little opportunity to learn to read. It was understood, among all who came, that there must be as little display about it as possible. It was necessary to keep our religious masters at St. Michael's unacquainted with the fact, that, instead of spending the Sabbath in wrestling, boxing, and drinking whisky, we were trying to learn how to read the will of God; for they had much rather see us engaged in those degrading sports, than to see us behaving like intellectual, moral, and accountable beings. My blood boils as I think of the bloody manner in which Messrs. Wright Fairbanks and Garrison West, both class-leaders, in connection with many others, rushed in upon us with sticks and stones, and broke up our virtuous little Sabbath school, at St. Michael's—all calling

---

4. "This is the same man who gave me the roots to prevent my being whipped by Mr. Covey. He was a 'clever soul.' We used frequently to talk about the fight with Covey, and as often as we did so, he would claim my success as the result of the roots he gave me. This superstition is very common among the more ignorant slaves. A slave seldom dies but that his death is attributed to trickery" [Douglass's note].

themselves Christians! humble followers of the Lord Jesus Christ! But I am again digressing.

I held my Sabbath school at the house of a free colored man, whose name I deem it imprudent to mention; for should it be known, it might embarrass him greatly, though the crime of holding the school was committed ten years ago. I had at one time over forty scholars, and those of the right sort, ardently desiring to learn. They were of all ages, though mostly men and women. I look back to those Sundays with an amount of pleasure not to be expressed. They were great days to my soul. The work of instructing my dear fellow-slaves was the sweetest engagement with which I was ever blessed. We loved each other, and to leave them at the close of the Sabbath was a severe cross indeed. When I think that those precious souls are to-day shut up in the prison-house of slavery, my feelings overcome me, and I am almost ready to ask, "Does a righteous God govern the universe? and for what does he hold the thunders in his right hand, if not to smite the oppressor, and deliver the spoiled out of the hand of the spoiler?" These dear souls came not to Sabbath school because it was popular to do so, nor did I teach them because it was reputable to be thus engaged. Every moment they spent in that school, they were liable to be taken up, and given thirty-nine lashes. They came because they wished to learn. Their minds had been starved by their cruel masters. They had been shut up in mental darkness. I taught them, because it was the delight of my soul to be doing something that looked like bettering the condition of my race. I kept up my school nearly the whole year I lived with Mr. Freeland; and, beside my Sabbath school, I devoted three evenings in the week, during the winter, to teaching the slaves at home. And I have the happiness to know, that several of those who came to Sabbath school learned how to read; and that one, at least, is now free through my agency.

The year passed off smoothly. It seemed only about half as long as the year which preceded it. I went through it without receiving a single blow. I will give Mr. Freeland the credit of being the best master I ever had, *till I became my own master.* For the ease with which I passed the year, I was, however, somewhat indebted to the society of my fellow-slaves. They were noble souls; they not only possessed loving hearts, but brave ones. We were linked and interlinked with each other. I loved them with a love stronger than any thing I have experienced since. It is sometimes said that we slaves do not love and confide in each other. In answer to this assertion, I can say, I never loved any or confided in any people more than my fellow-slaves, and especially those with whom I lived at Mr. Freeland's. I believe we would have died for each other. We never undertook to do any thing, of any importance, without a mutual consultation. We never moved separately. We were one; and as much so by our tempers and dispositions, as by the mutual hardships to which we were necessarily subjected by our condition as slaves.

At the close of the year 1834, Mr. Freeland again hired me of my master, for the year 1835. But, by this time, I began to want to live *upon free land* as well as *with Freeland*; and I was no longer content, therefore, to live with him or any other slaveholder. I began, with the commencement of the year, to prepare myself for a final struggle, which should decide my fate one way or the other. My tendency was upward. I was fast approaching manhood, and year after year had passed, and I was still a slave. These thoughts roused me— I must do something. I therefore resolved that 1835 should not pass without witnessing an attempt, on my part, to secure my liberty. But I was not willing to cherish this determination alone. My fellow-slaves were dear to me. I was anxious to have them participate with me in this, my life-giving determination. I therefore, though with great prudence, commenced early to ascertain their views and feelings in regard to their condition, and to imbue their minds with thoughts of freedom. I bent myself to devising ways and means for our escape, and meanwhile strove, on all fitting occasions, to impress them with the gross fraud and inhumanity of slavery. I went first to Henry, next to John, then to the others. I found, in them all, warm hearts and noble spirits. They were ready to hear, and ready to act when a feasible plan should be proposed. This was what I wanted. I talked to them of our want of manhood, if we submitted to our enslavement without at least one noble effort to be free. We met often, and consulted frequently, and told our hopes and fears, recounted the difficulties, real and imagined, which we should be called on to meet. At times we were almost disposed to give up, and try to content ourselves with our wretched lot; at others, we were firm and unbending in our determination to go. Whenever we suggested any plan, there was shrinking—the odds were fearful. Our path was beset with the greatest obstacles; and if we succeeded in gaining the end of it, our right to be free was yet questionable—we were yet liable to be returned to bondage. We could see no spot, this side of the ocean, where we could be free. We knew nothing about Canada. Our knowledge of the north did not extend farther than New York; and to go there, and be forever harassed with the frightful liability of being returned to slavery—with the certainty of being treated tenfold worse than before—the thought was truly a horrible one, and one which it was not easy to overcome. The case sometimes stood thus: At every gate through which we were to pass, we saw a watchman— at every ferry a guard—on every bridge a sentinel—and in every wood a patrol. We were hemmed in upon every side. Here were the difficulties, real or imagined—the good to be sought, and the evil to be shunned. On the one hand, there stood slavery, a stern reality, glaring frightfully upon us,—its robes already crimsoned with the blood of millions, and even now feasting itself greedily upon our own flesh. On the other hand, away back in the dim distance, under the flickering light of the north star, behind some craggy hill or snow-covered mountain, stood a doubtful freedom—half frozen—beckoning us to come and share its hospitality. This in itself was sometimes enough to stagger us; but when we permitted ourselves to survey the road, we were frequently appalled. Upon either side we saw grim death, assuming the most horrid shapes. Now it was starvation, causing us to eat our own flesh;—now we were contending with the waves, and were drowned;—now we were overtaken, and torn to pieces by the fangs of the terrible bloodhound. We were stung by scorpions, chased by wild beasts, bitten by snakes, and finally, after having nearly reached the desired spot,—after swimming rivers, encountering wild beasts, sleeping in the woods, suffering hunger and nakedness,—we were overtaken by our pursuers, and in our resistance, we were shot dead upon the spot! I say, this picture sometimes appalled us, and made us

> "rather bear those ills we had,
> Than fly to others, that we knew not of."[5]

5. Shakespeare's *Hamlet* 3.1.81–82.

In coming to a fixed determination to run away, we did more than Patrick Henry, when he resolved upon liberty or death. With us it was a doubtful liberty at most, and almost certain death if we failed. For my part, I should prefer death to hopeless bondage.

Sandy, one of our number, gave up the notion, but still encouraged us. Our company then consisted of Henry Harris, John Harris, Henry Bailey, Charles Roberts, and myself. Henry Bailey was my uncle, and belonged to my master. Charles married my aunt: he belonged to my master's father-in-law, Mr. William Hamilton.

The plan we finally concluded upon was, to get a large canoe belonging to Mr. Hamilton, and upon the Saturday night previous to Easter holidays, paddle directly up the Chesapeake Bay. On our arrival at the head of the bay, a distance of seventy or eighty miles from where we lived, it was our purpose to turn our canoe adrift, and follow the guidance of the north star till we got beyond the limits of Maryland. Our reason for taking the water route was, that we were less liable to be suspected as runaways; we hoped to be regarded as fishermen; whereas, if we should take the land route, we should be subjected to interruptions of almost every kind. Any one having a white face, and being so disposed, could stop us, and subject us to examination.

The week before our intended start, I wrote several protections, one for each of us. As well as I can remember, they were in the following words, to wit:—

> "This is to certify that I, the undersigned, have given the bearer, my servant, full liberty to go to Baltimore, and spend the Easter holidays. Written with mine own hand, &c., 1835.
>
> "WILLIAM HAMILTON,
> "Near St. Michael's, in Talbot county, Maryland."

We were not going to Baltimore; but, in going up the bay, we went toward Baltimore, and these protections were only intended to protect us while on the bay.

As the time drew near for our departure, our anxiety became more and more intense. It was truly a matter of life and death with us. The strength of our determination was about to be fully tested. At this time, I was very active in explaining every difficulty, removing every doubt, dispelling every fear, and inspiring all with the firmness indispensable to success in our undertaking; assuring them that half was gained the instant we made the move; we had talked long enough; we were now ready to move; if not now, we never should be; and if we did not intend to move now, we had as well fold our arms, sit down, and acknowledge ourselves fit only to be slaves. This, none of us were prepared to acknowledge. Every man stood firm; and at our last meeting, we pledged ourselves afresh, in the most solemn manner, that, at the time appointed, we would certainly start in pursuit of freedom. This was in the middle of the week, at the end of which we were to be off. We went, as usual, to our several fields of labor, but with bosoms highly agitated with thoughts of our truly hazardous undertaking. We tried to conceal our feelings as much as possible; and I think we succeeded very well.

After a painful waiting, the Saturday morning, whose night was to witness our departure, came. I hailed it with joy, bring what of sadness it might. Friday night was a sleepless one for me. I probably felt more anxious than the rest, because I was, by common consent, at the head of the whole affair. The responsibility of success or failure lay heavily upon me. The glory of the one, and the confusion of the other, were alike mine. The first two hours of that morning were such as I never experienced before, and hope never to again. Early in the morning, we went, as usual, to the field. We were spreading manure; and all at once, while thus engaged, I was overwhelmed with an indescribable feeling, in the fulness of which I turned to Sandy, who was near by, and said, "We are betrayed!" "Well," said he, "that thought has this moment struck me." We said no more. I was never more certain of any thing.

The horn was blown as usual, and we went up from the field to the house for breakfast. I went for the form, more than for want of any thing to eat that morning. Just as I got to the house, in looking out at the lane gate, I saw four white men, with two colored men. The white men were on horseback, and the colored ones were walking behind, as if tied. I watched them a few moments till they got up to our lane gate. Here they halted, and tied the colored men to the gate-post. I was not yet certain as to what the matter was. In a few moments, in rode Mr. Hamilton, with a speed betokening great excitement. He came to the door, and inquired if Master William was in. He was told he was at the barn. Mr. Hamilton, without dismounting, rode up to the barn with extraordinary speed. In a few moments, he and Mr. Freeland returned to the house. By this time, the three constables rode up, and in great haste dismounted, tied their horses, and met Master William and Mr. Hamilton returning from the barn; and after talking awhile, they all walked up to the kitchen door. There was no one in the kitchen but myself and John. Henry and Sandy were up at the barn. Mr. Freeland put his head in at the door, and called me by name, saying, there were some gentlemen at the door who wished to see me. I stepped to the door, and inquired what they wanted. They at once seized me, and, without giving me any satisfaction, tied me— lashing my hands closely together. I insisted upon knowing what the matter was. They at length said, that they had learned I had been in a "scrape," and that I was to be examined before my master; and if their information proved false, I should not be hurt.

In a few moments, they succeeded in tying John. They then turned to Henry, who had by this time returned, and commanded him to cross his hands. "I won't!" said Henry, in a firm tone, indicating his readiness to meet the consequences of his refusal. "Won't you?" said Tom Graham, the constable. "No, I won't!" said Henry, in a still stronger tone. With this, two of the constables pulled out their shining pistols, and swore, by their Creator, that they would make him cross his hands or kill him. Each cocked his pistol, and, with fingers on the trigger, walked up to Henry, saying, at the same time, if he did not cross his hands, they would blow his damned heart out. "Shoot me, shoot me!" said Henry; "you can't kill me but once. Shoot, shoot,—and be damned! *I won't be tied!*" This he said in a tone of loud defiance; and at the same time, with a motion as quick as lightning, he with one single stroke dashed the pistols from the hand of each constable. As he did this, all hands fell upon him, and, after beating him some time, they finally overpowered him, and got him tied.

During the scuffle, I managed, I know not how, to get my pass out, and, without being discovered, put it into the fire. We were all now tied; and just as we were to leave for Easton jail, Betsy Freeland, mother of William Freeland, came to the door with her hands full of biscuits, and divided them between Henry and John. She then delivered herself of a speech, to the following effect:—addressing herself to me, she said, "*You devil! You yellow devil!* it was you that put it into the heads of Henry and John to run away. But for you, you long-legged mulatto devil! Henry nor John would never have thought of such a thing." I made no reply, and was immediately hurried off towards St. Michael's. Just a moment previous to the scuffle with Henry, Mr. Hamilton suggested the propriety of making a search for the protections which he had understood Frederick had written for himself and the rest. But, just at the moment he was about carrying his proposal into effect, his aid was needed in helping to tie Henry; and the excitement attending the scuffle caused them either to forget, or to deem it unsafe, under the circumstances, to search. So we were not yet convicted of the intention to run away.

When we got about half way to St. Michael's, while the constables having us in charge were looking ahead, Henry inquired of me what he should do with his pass. I told him to eat it with his biscuit, and own nothing; and we passed the word around, "*Own nothing;*" and "*Own nothing!*" said we all. Our confidence in each other was unshaken. We were resolved to succeed or fail together, after the calamity had befallen us as much as before. We were now prepared for any thing. We were to be dragged that morning fifteen miles behind horses, and then to be placed in the Easton jail. When we reached St. Michael's, we underwent a sort of examination. We all denied that we ever intended to run away. We did this more to bring out the evidence against us, than from any hope of getting clear of being sold; for, as I have said, we were ready for that. The fact was, we cared but little where we went, so we went together. Our greatest concern was about separation. We dreaded that more than any thing this side of death. We found the evidence against us to be the testimony of one person; our master would not tell who it was; but we came to a unanimous decision among ourselves as to who their informant was. We were sent off to the jail at Easton. When we got there, we were delivered up to the sheriff, Mr. Joseph Graham, and by him placed in jail. Henry, John, and myself, were placed in one room together—Charles, and Henry Bailey, in another. Their object in separating us was to hinder concert.

We had been in jail scarcely twenty minutes, when a swarm of slave traders, and agents for slave traders, flocked into jail to look at us, and to ascertain if we were for sale. Such a set of beings I never saw before! I felt myself surrounded by so many fiends from perdition. A band of pirates never looked more like their father, the devil. They laughed and grinned over us, saying, "Ah, my boys! we have got you, haven't we?" And after taunting us in various ways, they one by one went into an examination of us, with intent to ascertain our value. They would impudently ask us if we would not like to have them for our masters. We would make them no answer, and leave them to find out as best they could. Then they would curse and swear at us, telling us that they could take the devil out of us in a very little while, if we were only in their hands.

While in jail, we found ourselves in much more comfortable quarters than we expected when we went there. We did not get much to eat, nor that which was very good; but we had a good clean room, from the windows of which we could see what was going on in the street, which was very much better than though we had been placed in one of the dark, damp cells. Upon the whole, we got along very well, so far as the jail and its keeper were concerned. Immediately after the holidays were over, contrary to all our expectations, Mr. Hamilton and Mr. Freeland came up to Easton, and took Charles, the two Henrys, and John, out of jail, and carried them home, leaving me alone. I regarded this separation as a final one. It caused me more pain than any thing else in the whole transaction. I was ready for any thing rather than separation. I supposed that they had consulted together, and had decided that, as I was the whole cause of the intention of the others to run away, it was hard to make the innocent suffer with the guilty; and that they had, therefore, concluded to take the others home, and sell me, as a warning to the others that remained. It is due to the noble Henry to say, he seemed almost as reluctant at leaving the prison as at leaving home to come to the prison. But we knew we should, in all probability, be separated, if we were sold; and since he was in their hands, he concluded to go peaceably home.

I was now left to my fate. I was all alone, and within the walls of a stone prison. But a few days before, and I was full of hope. I expected to have been safe in a land of freedom; but now I was covered with gloom, sunk down to the utmost despair. I thought the possibility of freedom was gone. I was kept in this way about one week, at the end of which, Captain Auld, my master, to my surprise and utter astonishment, came up, and took me out, with the intention of sending me, with a gentleman of his acquaintance, into Alabama. But, from some cause or other, he did not send me to Alabama, but concluded to send me back to Baltimore, to live again with his brother Hugh, and to learn a trade.

Thus, after an absence of three years and one month, I was once more permitted to return to my old home at Baltimore. My master sent me away, because there existed against me a very great prejudice in the community, and he feared I might be killed.

In a few weeks after I went to Baltimore, Master Hugh hired me to Mr. William Gardner, an extensive ship-builder, on Fell's Point. I was put there to learn how to calk. It, however, proved a very unfavorable place for the accomplishment of this object. Mr. Gardner was engaged that spring in building two large man-of-war brigs, professedly for the Mexican government. The vessels were to be launched in the July of that year, and in failure thereof, Mr. Gardner was to lose a considerable sum; so that when I entered, all was hurry. There was no time to learn any thing. Every man had to do that which he knew how to do. In entering the ship-yard, my orders from Mr. Gardner were, to do whatever the carpenters commanded me to do. This was placing me at the beck and call of about seventy-five men. I was to regard all these as masters. Their word was to be my law. My situation was a most trying one. At times I needed a dozen pair of hands. I was called a dozen ways in the space of a single minute. Three or four voices would strike my ear at the same moment. It was—"Fred., come help me to cant this timber here."—"Fred., come carry this timber yonder."—"Fred., bring that roller here."—"Fred., go get a fresh can of water."—"Fred., come help saw off the end of this timber."—"Fred., go quick, and get the crowbar."—"Fred., hold on the end of this fall."[6]—"Fred., go to the blacksmith's shop, and get a new punch."—"Hurra, Fred.! run and bring me a cold chisel."—"I say, Fred., bear a hand,

---

6. Nautical term for the free end of a rope of a tackle or hoisting device.

and get up a fire as quick as lightning under that steam-box."—"Halloo, nigger! come, turn this grindstone."—"Come, come! move, move! and *bowse*[7] this timber forward."—"I say, darky, blast your eyes, why don't you heat up some pitch?"—"Halloo! halloo! halloo!" (Three voices at the same time.) "Come here!—Go there!—Hold on where you are! Damn you, if you move, I'll knock your brains out!"

This was my school for eight months; and I might have remained there longer, but for a most horrid fight I had with four of the white apprentices, in which my left eye was nearly knocked out, and I was horribly mangled in other respects. The facts in the case were these: Until a very little while after I went there, white and black ship-carpenters worked side by side, and no one seemed to see any impropriety in it. All hands seemed to be very well satisfied. Many of the black carpenters were freemen. Things seemed to be going on very well. All at once, the white carpenters knocked off, and said they would not work with free colored workmen. Their reason for this, as alleged, was, that if free colored carpenters were encouraged, they would soon take the trade into their own hands, and poor white men would be thrown out of employment. They therefore felt called upon at once to put a stop to it. And, taking advantage of Mr. Gardner's necessities, they broke off, swearing they would work no longer, unless he would discharge his black carpenters. Now, though this did not extend to me in form, it did reach me in fact. My fellow-apprentices very soon began to feel it degrading to them to work with me. They began to put on airs, and talk about the "niggers" taking the country, saying we all ought to be killed; and, being encouraged by the journeymen, they commenced making my condition as hard as they could, by hectoring me around, and sometimes striking me. I, of course, kept the vow I made after the fight with Mr. Covey, and struck back again, regardless of consequences; and while I kept them from combining, I succeeded very well; for I could whip the whole of them, taking them separately. They, however, at length combined, and came upon me, armed with sticks, stones, and heavy handspikes. One came in front with a half brick. There was one at each side of me, and one behind me. While I was attending to those in front, and on either side, the one behind ran up with the handspike, and struck me a heavy blow upon the head. It stunned me. I fell, and with this they all ran upon me, and fell to beating me with their fists. I let them lay on for a while, gathering strength. In an instant, I gave a sudden surge, and rose to my hands and knees. Just as I did that, one of their number gave me, with his heavy boot, a powerful kick in the left eye. My eyeball seemed to have burst. When they saw my eye closed, and badly swollen, they left me. With this I seized the handspike, and for a time pursued them. But here the carpenters interfered, and I thought I might as well give it up. It was impossible to stand my hand against so many. All this took place in sight of not less than fifty white ship-carpenters, and not one interposed a friendly word; but some cried, "Kill the damned nigger! Kill him! kill him! He struck a white person." I found my only chance for life was in flight. I succeeded in getting away without an additional blow, and barely so; for to strike a white man is death by Lynch law,[8]—and that was the law in Mr. Gardner's ship-yard; nor is there much of any other out of Mr. Gardner's ship-yard.

I went directly home, and told the story of my wrongs to Master Hugh; and

7. To haul the timber by pulling on the rope.
8. I.e., to be subject to lynching, without benefit of legal procedures.

I am happy to say of him, irreligious as he was, his conduct was heavenly, compared with that of his brother Thomas under similar circumstances. He listened attentively to my narration of the circumstances leading to the savage outrage, and gave many proofs of his strong indignation at it. The heart of my once overkind mistress was again melted into pity. My puffed-out eye and blood-covered face moved her to tears. She took a chair by me, washed the blood from my face, and, with a mother's tenderness, bound up my head, covering the wounded eye with a lean piece of fresh beef. It was almost compensation for my suffering to witness, once more, a manifestation of kindness from this, my once affectionate old mistress. Master Hugh was very much enraged. He gave expression to his feelings by pouring out curses upon the heads of those who did the deed. As soon as I got a little the better of my bruises, he took me with him to Esquire Watson's, on Bond Street, to see what could be done about the matter. Mr. Watson inquired who saw the assault committed. Master Hugh told him it was done in Mr. Gardner's ship-yard, at midday, where there were a large company of men at work. "As to that," he said, "the deed was done, and there was no question as to who did it." His answer was, he could do nothing in the case, unless some white man would come forward and testify. He could issue no warrant on my word. If I had been killed in the presence of a thousand colored people, their testimony combined would have been insufficient to have arrested one of the murderers. Master Hugh, for once, was compelled to say this state of things was too bad. Of course, it was impossible to get any white man to volunteer his testimony in my behalf, and against the white young men. Even those who may have sympathized with me were not prepared to do this. It required a degree of courage unknown to them to do so; for just at that time, the slightest manifestation of humanity toward a colored person was denounced as abolitionism, and that name subjected its bearer to frightful liabilities. The watchwords of the bloody-minded in that region, and in those days, were, "Damn the abolitionists!" and "Damn the niggers!" There was nothing done, and probably nothing would have been done if I had been killed. Such was, and such remains, the state of things in the Christian city of Baltimore.

Master Hugh, finding he could get no redress, refused to let me go back again to Mr. Gardner. He kept me himself, and his wife dressed my wound till I was again restored to health. He then took me into the ship-yard of which he was foreman, in the employment of Mr. Walter Price. There I was immediately set to calking, and very soon learned the art of using my mallet and irons. In the course of one year from the time I left Mr. Gardner's, I was able to command the highest wages given to the most experienced calkers. I was now of some importance to my master. I was bringing him from six to seven dollars per week. I sometimes brought him nine dollars per week: my wages were a dollar and a half a day. After learning how to calk, I sought my own employment, made my own contracts, and collected the money which I earned. My pathway became much more smooth than before; my condition was now much more comfortable. When I could get no calking to do, I did nothing. During these leisure times, those old notions about freedom would steal over me again. When in Mr. Gardner's employment, I was kept in such a perpetual whirl of excitement, I could think of nothing, scarcely, but my life; and in thinking of my life, I almost forgot my liberty. I have observed this in my experience of slavery,—that whenever my condition was improved, instead of its increasing my contentment, it only increased my desire to be free, and set me to thinking of plans to gain my freedom. I have found that, to make a contented slave, it is necessary to make a thoughtless one. It is necessary to darken his moral and mental vision, and, as far as possible, to annihilate the power of reason. He must be able to detect no inconsistencies in slavery; he must be made to feel that slavery is right; and he can be brought to that only when he ceases to be a man.

I was now getting, as I have said, one dollar and fifty cents per day. I contracted for it; I earned it; it was paid to me; it was rightfully my own; yet, upon each returning Saturday night, I was compelled to deliver every cent of that money to Master Hugh. And why? Not because he earned it,—not because he had any hand in earning it,—not because I owed it to him,—nor because he possessed the slightest shadow of a right to it; but solely because he had the power to compel me to give it up. The right of the grim-visaged pirate upon the high seas is exactly the same.

---

# WALT WHITMAN
## 1819–1892

Walt Whitman was born on May 31, 1819, son of a Long Island farmer turned carpenter who moved the family into Brooklyn in 1823 during a building boom. The ancestors were undistinguished, but stories survived of some forceful characters among them, and Whitman's father was acquainted with powerful personalities like the aged Thomas Paine. Whitman left school at eleven to become an office boy in a law firm, then worked for a doctor; already he was enthralled with the novels of Sir Walter Scott. By twelve he was working in the printing office of a newspaper and contributing sentimental items. By fifteen, when his family moved back into the interior of Long Island, Whitman was on his own. Very early he reached full physical maturity and in his midteens was contributing "pieces"— probably correct, conventional poems—to one of the best Manhattan papers, the *Mirror*, and often crossing the ferry from Brooklyn to attend debating societies and to use his journalist's passes at theaters in Manhattan. His rich fantasy life was fueled by numberless romantic novels. By sixteen he was a compositor in Manhattan, a journeyman printer. But two great fires in 1835 disrupted the printing industry, and as he turned seventeen he rejoined his family. For five years he taught intermittently at country and small-town schools, interrupting teaching to start a newspaper of his own in 1838 and to work briefly on another Long Island paper. Although forced into the exile of Long Island, he refused to compromise further with the sort of life he wanted. During his visits home he outraged his father by refusing to do farm work. Although he was innovative in the classroom, he struck some of the farm families he boarded with as unwilling to fulfill his role of teacher outside school hours; the main charge against him was laziness. He was active in debating societies, however, and already thought of himself as a writer. By early 1840 he had started the series "Sun-Down Papers from the Desk of a School-Master" for the Long Island *Democrat* and was writing poems. One of his stories prophetically culminated with the dream of writing "a wonderful and ponderous book."

Just before he turned twenty-one he went back to Manhattan, his teaching days over, and began work on Park Benjamin's *New World*, a literary weekly that pirated

British novels; he also began a political career by speaking at Democratic rallies. Simultaneously, he was publishing stories in the *Democratic Review*, the foremost magazine of the Democratic party. Before he was twenty-three, he became editor of a Manhattan daily, the *Aurora*, and briefly transformed himself into a sartorial dandy while he spiked his editorial columns with his high democratic hopes. He exulted in the extremes of the city, where the violence of street gangs was countered by the lectures of Emerson and where even a young editor could get to know the poet Bryant (by livelihood, editor of the *Evening Post*). Fired from the *Aurora*, which publicly charged him with laziness, he wrote a temperance novel, *Franklin Evans, or the Inebriate*, for a one-issue extra of the *New World* late in 1842. For the next years he was journalist, hack writer, and a doughty minor politician. In 1845 he returned to Brooklyn, where he became a special contributor to the Long Island *Star*, assigned to Manhattan events, including musical and theatrical engagements. Just before he was twenty-seven he took over the editorship of the Brooklyn *Eagle*; for years he had kept to his eccentric daily routine of apparently purposeless walks in which he absorbed metropolitan sights and sounds, and now he formed the habit of a daily swim and shower at a bathhouse. On the *Eagle* he did most of the literary reviews, handling books by Carlyle, Emerson, Melville, Fuller, Sand, Goethe, and others. Like most Democrats, he was able to justify the Mexican War, and he hero-worshiped Zachary Taylor (on whom Melville was writing a series of satirical sketches). Linking territorial acquisition to personal and civic betterment, he was, in his nationalistic moods, capable of hailing the great American mission of "peopling the New World with a noble race." Yet by the beginning of 1848 he was fired from the *Eagle* because like Bryant he had become a Free-Soiler, opposed to the acquisition of more slave territory. Taking a chance offer of newspaper work, he made a brief but vivid trip to New Orleans, his only extensive journey until late in life, when he made a trip into the West.

By the summer of 1848, Whitman was back in New York, starting experiments with poetry and, in August, serving as delegate to the Buffalo Free-Soil convention. In the next years he was profoundly influenced by his association with a group of Brooklyn artists. All through the 1840s he had attended operas on his journalist's passes, hearing the greatest singers of the time. He went so far as to say that but for the "emotions, raptures, uplifts" of opera he could never have written *Leaves of Grass*. In an effort to control the disposition of his time, he became a "house builder" around 1851 or 1852, perhaps acting as contractor sometimes but also simply hiring out as a carpenter. By the early 1850s he had set a durable pattern of having discrete sets of friends simultaneously, the roughs and the artists, moving casually from one set to the other but seldom, if ever, mingling them. Living with his family, now back in Brooklyn, Whitman baffled and outraged them by ignoring regular mealtimes and appearing to loaf away his days in strolls, in reading at libraries, and in writing in the room he shared with a brother. Always self-taught, he undertook a more systematic plan of study. He became something of an expert on Egyptology through his trips to the Egyptian Museum on Broadway and his conversations with its proprietor. He became a student of astronomy, attending lectures and reading recent books; much of the information went into the cosmic concepts in *Song of Myself* and other poems. Cutting articles out of the great British quarterlies and monthlies, Whitman annotated them and argued with them in the margins, developing in the process clear ideas about aesthetics for the first time and formulating his notions about pantheism. By about 1853 he had arrived at something like his special poetic form in the little poem *Pictures*. He had given up newspaper work for carpentry; around the end of 1854 he gave up that also, and simply wrote. By the spring of 1855 he was seeing his "wonderful and ponderous book" through the press, probably setting some of the type himself. *Leaves of Grass* was on sale within a day or two of the Fourth of July of that year.

Facing the title page of this remarkable book was an engraving of a lounging working man, broad-hatted, bearded, shirt open at the neck to reveal a colored undershirt, the right arm akimbo, left hand in pants pocket, weight on the right leg. Such a man would hardly be expected to read verse, much less write it. The title page said simply "*Leaves of Grass*" and gave the place and date of publication as "Brooklyn, New York: 1855." The back of the title page named "Walter Whitman" as the man who had entered the work for copyright; that this was the author was confirmed by a line far down in the first poem (the one later retitled *Song of Myself*; here they were all titled *Leaves of Grass*).

Following the copyright page was an untitled essay running to ten pages, double column—an intimidating mass of type, most of it in long paragraphs punctuated by sets of what looked like ellipses. The essay was oracular in tone, sweeping in message, the outgrowth of Whitman's long musing on the place of art in American life. One of its starting points was pretty clearly Emerson's *The Poet*, especially the provocative list of some of the incomparable materials awaiting the tyrannous eye of the great American poet. It circled back to its major points much like Emerson's own essays, focusing primarily on the sort of poet America required and the sort of poetry that poet would write. The reader soon had every reason to suspect that the "Walter Whitman" of the copyright page might consider himself that poet and *Leaves of Grass* an example of that poetry.

Yet the prefatory essay did not quite prepare the reader for the poems that followed. The recitation of some of the incomparable materials awaiting the American poet suggested the comprehensiveness and brilliance of detail in some of the poetic catalogs (in fact, portions of the preface were later worked into poems); the declarations about science prepared for the sophisticated understanding the poems revealed of geology and astronomy, if not for the poetic uses of that knowledge; and the tributes to the American people partially suggested the profound tenderness that would be manifested toward all people in the poems. Yet not even the occasional ironic passages of the essay suggested that the poems that followed would include master strokes of comedy; nothing adequately prepared for the intense and explicit sexuality and the psychological complexity of the poems; and not even his comments on form suggested that Whitman had already achieved a new form splendidly appropriate to his democratic subject matter and had already become a supreme master of the English language.

The publication of *Leaves of Grass* did not immediately change Whitman's life. His father died just after it appeared, and support of his mother and a feebleminded brother devolved more and more on Whitman. He sent copies of his book out broadcast and got an immediate response from Emerson greeting him "at the beginning of a great career, which yet must have had a long foreground somewhere, for such a start." As weeks passed with few reviews, he wrote a few himself to be published anonymously, and in October he let Horace Greeley's *Tribune* print Emerson's letter. Unfazed by his own effrontery, he put clippings of the letter in presentation copies, to Longfellow among others. While Whitman was angling for reviews in England and working on an expansion of the book, Emerson visited him (in December of 1855), and in the fall of 1856 Bronson Alcott, Thoreau, and others came out to his house in Brooklyn. Whitman continued to do miscellaneous journalism, mainly for a weekly magazine called *Life Illustrated*, and wrote a long political tract—*The Eighteenth Presidency!*—which he never distributed. The excitement of the election year was reflected in the excessive nationalism of some of the new poems as well as the pomposity of titles, but among the new poems in the second edition (1856) was the great *Sun-Down Poem*, later called *Crossing Brooklyn Ferry*. Whitman flaunted Emerson's praise on the spine of the new edition and in the back printed the whole letter, following it with an open letter to the master at Concord in which Whitman announced his determination "to meet people and The States face to face, to confront them with an American rude tongue." As part of his campaign for a national identity, Whitman included a sexual "programme" based on "an avowed, empowered, unabashed development of sex," a manifesto notable for its nonsexist message: "Women in These States approach the day of that organic equality with men, without which, I see, men cannot have organic equality among themselves."

From 1857 to 1859 Whitman's main statements on the national crisis over slavery were contained in his editorials in the Brooklyn *Times*. During these years Whitman worked on a political, sexual, and poetic program that he could bring to the people of the States as a wandering lecturer, envisioning for himself a way of life that would fuse the tours of lecturers like Emerson with his own love of the open road and good comrades. He lectured locally, but nothing came of the grander scheme, and in some new poems he consciously turned away from the national situation to his private sexual concerns. Whitman wrote a group of twelve poems, *Live Oak, with Moss*, that seems to tell a straightforward story of his love for another man. Secure in that love, in one poem he reflects on the likelihood that other men throughout the world must have sexual longings like his own, and in another he dreams of an idealized city where nothing is greater than "manly love." In this sequence Whitman explicitly renounces his old role of public poet seeking knowledge and celebrating the American land and its heroes; instead, he chooses to be happy in private with his lover. If he had printed it, the sequence would have constituted a new and highly public sexual program, nothing short of an open homosexual manifesto.

Facing the impossibility of printing and distributing so direct a sexual statement of "adhesiveness" or "the passion of friendship" of man for man, Whitman chose a more covert way of expressing himself. In the next (1860) edition of *Leaves of Grass* Whitman included a cluster called *Enfans d'Adam*, for which he wrote fifteen counterbalancing poems that for the most part focus on the "amative" love of man for woman. Then, separated from *Enfans d'Adam* by several other poems, Whitman printed a cluster of forty-five poems about male love under the title *Calamus* (among which were versions of the *Live Oak* poems, reordered and altered); some of the new poems project future readers who will hold him "in hand" by holding his book and will "guess at" what he is only hinting. Whitman's placing the heterosexual section first muted the significance of the *Calamus* poems, the space between the two clusters muffled their relationship, and the dispersal of the *Live Oak* poems destroyed their original narrative impact. The two clusters as printed in 1860 differ markedly from the poems in the now-familiar 1892 *Children of Adam* (as *Efans d'Adam* was retitled in 1867) and *Calamus* section, for in intervening editions Whitman revised poems and moved some poems out of and into the clusters. The unavailability of texts of the various late editions of *Leaves of Grass* has made it difficult to study the two clusters in their various forms, but many readers have sensed perfunctoriness in many heterosexual passages in the *Children of Adam* poems (Whitman's biographer Gay Wilson Allen says they sound "theoretical and philosophical," unlike the "genuine love poems" in the *Calamus* section). By late 1859 Whitman had in hand the *Calamus* and *Enfans d'Adam* poems and others such as *A Child's Reminiscence* (*Out of the Cradle Endlessly Rocking*) in nearly final form. Early the next year he received an opportune letter from the Boston firm of Thayer & Eldridge: "We are young men. We 'celebrate' ourselves by acts. Try us. You can do us good. We can do you good—pecuniarily." For the first time, Whitman had a publisher.

Emerson welcomed him in Boston, arguing through a two-hour walk in the cold common that Whitman should not publish the *Children of Adam* poems. Whitman refused to compromise. When Emerson tried to introduce him into the Boston literary coterie, the Saturday Club, Longfellow, Holmes, and Lowell all objected, and apparently the families of Emerson, Thoreau, and Alcott refused to have him invited to Concord. Yet Whitman met a few kindred spirits during the weeks he labored over the proofs of his third edition, which was printed in May 1860. Besides the accustomed attacks, there were defenses, including one by the actress Adah Isaacks Menken, and for the first time, there were parodies, a sure

sign of public interest. But Thayer & Eldridge went bankrupt, and Whitman was
left again with the book on his own hands.

For society at the turn of the decade Whitman had, as usual, his separate groups
of friends, in one group stage drivers (i.e., drivers of the horse-pulled buses on
which he was an inveterate passenger) and in another literary, publishing, and
theatrical people, especially the bohemian habitués of the famous Pfaff's saloon on
lower Broadway. For years Whitman had paid cheering visits to prisoners and had
made regular visits to sick stage drivers. Almost imperceptibly, his role of visitor of
the sick merged into his Civil War services as hospital attendant. Just before Christmas 1862, Whitman went to Washington to find his brother George, who had
been reported wounded. The injury was slight, but Whitman stayed on with his
brother in camp (such was the casual fashion of the war), the two sharing a tent
with other soldiers. Returning to Washington, he rented a small room, found a
job as copyist in the paymaster's office, and began visiting Brooklyn soldiers in the
hospitals. Without premeditation, Whitman yielded to the irresistible appeal of the
occasion: his informality, gentleness, resourcefulness, and lack of preachiness were
uniquely required. Looking older than his age (only in his early forties), he could
serve as benevolent father to the men, and they returned his extraordinary sympathy and love; his friends became accustomed to seeing recovered soldiers stop him
in the street to hug and kiss him. It has been thought that the hospital experience
was a sublimation of Whitman's homosexual feelings, but Allen has shown that
those emotions permeate some of his correspondence with soldiers. Allen says that
the letters to Sergeant Tom Sawyer are "not easy for a modern critic to interpret,
for they were evidently motivated by a mixture of vicarious paternalism, longing for
companionship, and some rather confused erotic impulses that perhaps Whitman
himself did not clearly understand." Whitman may have understood his own emotions better than his biographers have done. Whatever Whitman's mixture of emotions, his role of wound dresser was heroic, and it eventually undercut his buoyant
physical health.

During the war, Whitman's deepest emotions and energies were reserved for his
hospital work, though he wrote a series of war poems designed to trace his own
varying attitudes toward the conflict, from his early near-mindless jingoism to
something quite rare in American poetry up to that time, a dedication to simple
realism. Whitman later wrote a section in *Specimen Days* called *The Real War
Will Never Get in the Books*, but to incorporate the real war into a book of poetry
became one of the dominant impulses of the *Drum-Taps* collection (1865). After
Lincoln's assassination Whitman delayed the new volume until it could include in
a "sequel" *When Lilacs Last in the Dooryard Bloom'd*, his masterpiece of the
1860s. Even as *Drum-Taps* was being published, Whitman was revising a copy of
the Boston edition of *Leaves of Grass* at his desk in the Department of the Interior.
The new secretary read the annotated copy and abruptly fired him. The consequences might have been minor: Whitman's friend William O'Connor quickly got
him a new post in the attorney general's office, and Whitman had been dismissed
before without catastrophic reactions, although this was the first time he had been
fired because of the sexual passages in *Leaves of Grass*. But the incident turned
O'Connor from a devoted friend into a disciple who quickly began writing a book
(with Whitman's help in supplying information and documents) called *The Good
Gray Poet* (1866). It was a piece of pure hagiography, in which Whitman was
identified with Jesus. O'Connor's book, coming out simultaneously with *Drum-
Taps*, polarized opinion, with negative immediate effects, but in the long run it
strengthened Whitman's determination not to yield to censorship or to apologize
for his earlier poems, and it set a pattern by which other remarkable men and
women would be drawn to Whitman as disciples, seeking to care for his few physical needs—minimal food and shelter—while working for his reputation as a great
poet.

For several years Whitman continued as a clerk in the attorney general's office, living most of the time in a bare, unheated room but gaining access to good lights for nighttime reading in his government office. He continued to rework *Leaves of Grass*, incorporating *Drum-Taps* into it in 1867, and with his friends' help continued to propagandize for its acceptance. After much correspondence involving Whitman, O'Connor, and a newer admirer (John Burroughs, the naturalist), William Michael Rossetti published a volume of Whitman's poems in London early in 1868. Though it was a selected and even an expurgated edition, it created many English admirers. As an ex-newspaperman, Whitman was accustomed to having immediate outlets for his political thoughts and general observations on the American scene. Such ruminations that in earlier years might have gone into editorials went into essays in the *Galaxy* during 1867 and 1868, then (in expanded form) into *Democratic Vistas* (1870), a passionate look to the future of democracy and democratic literature in America, based on his realistic appraisal of postwar culture. Another prose work, *Specimen Days*, published in book form in 1882, has affinities with Whitman's early editorial records of strolls through the city, but it is even more intensely personal, the record of representative days in the life of an American who had lived in the midst of great national events and who had kept alert to nature and his own mind and body. Through the late 1860s and early 1870s Whitman's compartmentalized life went on. He formed an emotional relationship with Peter Doyle, a young streetcar driver, about the time he was beginning in a small way to be treated as a literary lion. He was still jotting down notes on his devastating torments over his sexual drives.

The Washington years, a time of slow, faltering growth in reputation, marred by severe setbacks and complications, ended early in 1873, when Whitman suffered a paralytic stroke. His mother died a few months later, and Whitman joined his brother George's household in Camden, New Jersey, intending only a temporary move during his recuperation. His convalescence was bitterly lonely, for his well-meaning brother provided none of the intellectual companionship of a Burroughs or the emotional response of a Peter Doyle. During the second year of his illness, the government decided not to hold his job for him any longer, and he became dependent on occasional publication in newspapers and magazines—not an easy market, because his genteel enemies either ignored him in print or joined in a cabal to exclude him from some major publishing organs such as *Scribner's*. The 1867 edition of *Leaves of Grass* had involved much reworking and rearrangement, and the fifth edition (1871) continued that process, with many of the original *Drum-Taps* poems being distributed throughout the book and with an assemblage of old and new poems in a large new section, *Passage to India*. The "Centennial Edition" of 1876 was a reissue of the 1871 edition and was most notable for the way his English admirers got funds to him by having important literary people subscribe to it. American public opinion was gradually swayed by new evidences that the invalid in Camden could command the respect of Alfred, Lord Tennyson, the poet laureate, and many other famous British writers. Not even the most puritanic American critics could hold their ranks firm in the face of such extravagant admiration, however rough and outrageous his poetry. Yet in 1881, when the reputable Boston firm of James R. Osgood & Co. printed the sixth edition of *Leaves of Grass*, the Boston district attorney threatened to prosecute on the grounds of obscenity, and Whitman found himself with the plates on his hands and no publisher until he had impressions from the Osgood plates made by Philadelphia printers Rees Welsh & Co. in 1882 and David McKay thereafter. The "deathbed" edition of 1891–92 was in fact a reissue of the 1881 edition with the addition of two later groups of poems, *Sands at Seventy* (from *November Boughs*, which Whitman published in 1888) and *Good-bye My Fancy* (from the 1891 collection of that name).

Of all the American writers of the nineteenth century, Whitman offers the most inspiring example of fidelity to his art. While Hawthorne let marriage become his true career, and while Melville ceased writing for a public that would not accept him, Whitman persisted. (James persisted also, but he was equipped with material, educational, and social advantages Whitman lacked.) Outraging his employers and his family by his odd hours and the semblance of mere loafing, outraging his well-wishers by refusing to compromise on minor points that might have gained him fuller acceptance, finagling reviews, reviewing himself, writing admiring accounts of his work for others to sign, shocking some of his followers by refusing to give autographs gratis, Whitman kept on, like what he called some high-and-dry "hard-cased dilapidated grim ancient shell-fish or time-bang'd conch," uncompromising to the end, never bowing to the materialism and puerilities of nineteenth-century America. Appropriately, when he finally accumulated a few worldly belongings about him at Camden, he managed to give a nautical cast to his room, for eccentric as he seemed, crotchety, stubborn, Whitman was a literary equivalent of Melville's Bulkington in *Moby-Dick*, willing to renounce the comforts of the shore, all normal earthly felicity, for a life of the intellect and the imagination. He died at Camden on March 26, 1892, secure in the knowledge that he had held unwaveringly true to his art and to his role as an artist who had made that art prevail.

# Preface to *Leaves of Grass* (1855)[1]

America does not repel the past or what it has produced under its forms or amid other politics or the idea of castes or the old religions . . . accepts the lesson with calmness . . . is not so impatient as has been supposed that the slough still sticks to opinions and manners and literature while the life which served its requirements has passed into the new life of the new forms . . . perceives that the corpse is slowly borne from the eating and sleeping rooms of the house . . . perceives that it waits a little while in the door . . . that it was fittest for its days . . . that its action has descended to the stalwart and well-shaped heir who approaches . . . and that he shall be fittest for his days.

The Americans of all nations at any time upon the earth have probably the fullest poetical nature. The United States themselves are essentially the greatest poem. In the history of the earth hitherto the largest and most stirring appear tame and orderly to their ampler largeness and stir. Here at last is something in the doings of man that corresponds with the broadcast doings of the day and night. Here is not merely a nation but a teeming nation of nations. Here is action untied from strings necessarily blind to particulars and details magnificently moving in vast masses. Here is the hospitality which forever indicates heroes. . . . Here are the roughs and beards and space and rugged-ness and nonchalance that the soul loves. Here the performance disdaining the trivial unapproached in the tremendous audacity of its crowds and group-ings and the push of its perspective spreads with crampless and flowing breadth and showers its prolific and splendid extravagance. One sees it must indeed own the riches of the summer and winter, and need never be bankrupt while corn grows from the ground or the orchards drop apples or the bays contain fish or men beget children upon women.

Other states indicate themselves in their deputies . . . . but the genius of

1. This preface (reprinted here from the 1855 edition) has not yet attained its rightful place among the great American literary manifestoes. Like Emerson, Whit-man is celebrating the incomparable materials avail-able to the American poet, not simply physical re-sources but also the people themselves—the spirit of the place.

the United States is not best or most in its executives or legislatures, nor in its
ambassadors or authors or colleges or churches or parlors, nor even in its
newspapers or inventors . . . but always most in the common people. Their
manners speech dress friendships—the freshness and candor of their physiognomy—the picturesque looseness of their carriage . . . their deathless attachment to freedom—their aversion to anything indecorous or soft or mean—the
practical acknowledgment of the citizens of one state by the citizens of all
other states—the fierceness of their roused resentment—their curiosity and
welcome of novelty—their self-esteem and wonderful sympathy—their susceptibility to a slight—the air they have of persons who never knew how it felt to
stand in the presence of superiors—the fluency of their speech—their delight
in music, the sure symptom of manly tenderness and native elegance of soul
. . . their good temper and openhandedness—the terrible significance of their
elections—the President's taking off his hat to them not they to him—these
too are unrhymed poetry. It awaits the gigantic and generous treatment worthy
of it.

The largeness of nature or the nation were monstrous without a corresponding largeness and generosity of the spirit of the citizen. Not nature nor swarming states nor streets and steamships nor prosperous business nor farms nor
capital nor learning may suffice for the ideal of man . . . nor suffice the poet.
No reminiscences may suffice either. A live nation can always cut a deep mark
and can have the best authority the cheapest . . . namely from its own soul.
This is the sum of the profitable uses of individuals or states and of present
action and grandeur and of the subjects of poets.—As if it were necessary to
trot back generation after generation to the eastern records! As if the beauty
and sacredness of the demonstrable must fall behind that of the mythical! As
if men do not make their mark out of any times! As if the opening of the
western continent by discovery and what has transpired since in North and
South America were less than the small theatre of the antique or the aimless
sleepwalking of the middle ages! The pride of the United States leaves the
wealth and finesse of the cities and all returns of commerce and agriculture
and all the magnitude of geography or shows of exterior victory to enjoy the
breed of fullsized men or one fullsized man unconquerable and simple.

The American poets are to enclose old and new for America is the race of
races. Of them a bard[2] is to be commensurate with a people. To him the other
continents arrive as contributions . . . he gives them reception for their sake
and his own sake. His spirit responds to his country's spirit . . . . he incarnates
its geography and natural life and rivers and lakes. Mississippi with annual
freshets and changing chutes, Missouri and Columbia and Ohio and Saint
Lawrence with the falls and beautiful masculine Hudson, do not embouchure[3]
where they spend themselves more than they embouchure into him. The blue
breadth over the inland sea of Virginia and Maryland and the sea off Massachusetts and Maine and over Manhattan bay and over Champlain and Erie
and over Ontario and Huron and Michigan and Superior, and over the Texan
and Mexican and Floridian and Cuban seas and over the seas off California
and Oregon, is not tallied by the blue breadth of the waters below more than
the breadth of above and below is tallied by him. When the long Atlantic coast
stretches longer and the Pacific coast stretches longer he easily stretches with

2. The ideal national poet.          3. Pour.

them north or south. He spans between them also from east to west and reflects
what is between them. On him rise solid growths that offset the growths of
pine and cedar and hemlock and liveoak and locust and chestnut and cypress
and hickory and limetree and cottonwood and tuliptree and cactus and wild-
vine and tamarind and persimmon . . . . and tangles as tangled as any canebrake or swamp . . . . and forests coated with transparent ice and icicles
hanging from the boughs and crackling in the wind . . . . and sides and peaks
of mountains . . . . and pasturage sweet and free as savannah or upland or
prairie . . . . with flights and songs and screams that answer those of the wild
pigeon and highhold and orchard-oriole and coot and surf-duck and
redshouldered-hawk and fish-hawk and white-ibis and indian-hen and cat-owl
and water-pheasant and qua-bird and pied-sheldrake and blackbird and mockingbird and buzzard and condor and night-heron and eagle. To him the hereditary countenance descends both mother's and father's. To him enter the
essences of the real things and past and present events—of the enormous diversity of temperature and agriculture and mines—the tribes of red aborigines—
the weatherbeaten vessels entering new ports or making landings on rocky
coasts—the first settlements north or south—the rapid stature and muscle—
the haughty defiance of '76, and the war and peace and formation of the
constitution . . . . the union always surrounded by blatherers and always calm
and impregnable—the perpetual coming of immigrants—the wharf hem'd
cities and superior marine—the unsurveyed interior—the loghouses and clearings and wild animals and hunters and trappers . . . . the free commerce—
the fisheries and whaling and gold-digging—the endless gestation of new
states—the convening of Congress every December,[4] the members duly coming up from all climates and the uttermost parts . . . . the noble character of
the young mechanics and of all free American workmen and workwomen
. . . . the general ardor and friendliness and enterprise—the perfect equality
of the female with the male . . . . the large amativeness—the fluid movement
of the population—the factories and mercantile life and laborsaving machinery—the Yankee swap—the New-York firemen and the target excursion[5]—the
southern plantation life—the character of the northeast and of the northwest
and southwest—slavery and the tremulous spreading of hands to protect it, and
the stern opposition to it which shall never cease till it ceases or the speaking of
tongues and the moving of lips cease. For such the expression of the American
poet is to be transcendant and new. It is to be indirect and not direct or descriptive or epic. Its quality goes through these to much more. Let the age and wars
of other nations be chanted and their eras and characters be illustrated and
that finish the verse. Not so the great psalm of the republic. Here the theme is
creative and has vista. Here comes one among the wellbeloved stonecutters
and plans with decision and science and sees the solid and beautiful forms of
the future where there are now no solid forms.

Of all nations the United States with veins full of poetical stuff most need
poets and will doubtless have the greatest and use them the greatest. Their
Presidents shall not be their common referee so much as their poets shall. Of
all mankind the great poet is the equable man. Not in him but off from him
things are grotesque or eccentric or fail of their sanity. Nothing out of its place

4. Before the adoption of the Twentieth Amendment        Constitution.
in 1933, Congress convened on the first Monday in        5. Shooting contest.
December, according to Article 1, Section 4, of the

is good and nothing in its place is bad. He bestows on every object or quality its fit proportions neither more nor less. He is the arbiter of the diverse and he is the key. He is the equalizer of his age and land . . . . he supplies what wants supplying and checks what wants checking. If peace is the routine out of him speaks the spirit of peace, large, rich, thrifty, building vast and populous cities, encouraging agriculture and the arts and commerce—lighting the study of man, the soul, immortality—federal, state or municipal government, marriage, health, freetrade, intertravel by land and sea . . . . nothing too close, nothing too far off . . . the stars not too far off. In war he is the most deadly force of the war. Who recruits him recruits horse and foot . . . he fetches parks of artillery[6] the best that engineer ever knew. If the time becomes slothful and heavy he knows how to arouse it . . . he can make every word he speaks draw blood. Whatever stagnates in the flat of custom or obedience or legislation he never stagnates. Obedience does not master him, he masters it. High up out of reach he stands turning a concentrated light . . . he turns the pivot with his finger . . . he baffles the swiftest runners as he stands and easily overtakes and envelops them. The time straying toward infidelity and confections and persiflage he withholds by his steady faith . . . he spreads out his dishes . . . he offers the sweet firmfibred meat that grows men and women. His brain is the ultimate brain. He is no arguer . . . he is judgment. He judges not as the judge judges but as the sun falling around a helpless thing. As he sees the farthest he has the most faith. His thoughts are the hymns of the praise of things. In the talk on the soul and eternity and God off of his equal plane he is silent. He sees eternity less like a play with a prologue and denouement . . . . he sees eternity in men and women . . . he does not see men and women as dreams or dots. Faith is the antiseptic of the soul . . . it pervades the common people and preserves them . . . they never give up believing and expecting and trusting. There is that indescribable freshness and unconsciousness about an illiterate person that humbles and mocks the power of the noblest expressive genius. The poet sees for a certainty how one not a great artist may be just as sacred and perfect as the greatest artist . . . . . The power to destroy or remould is freely used by him but never the power of attack. What is past is past. If he does not expose superior models and prove himself by every step he takes he is not what is wanted. The presence of the greatest poet conquers . . . not parleying or struggling or any prepared attempts. Now he has passed that way see after him! there is not left any vestige of despair or misanthropy or cunning or exclusiveness or the ignominy of a nativity or color or delusion of hell or the necessity of hell . . . . . and no man thenceforward shall be degraded for ignorance or weakness or sin.

The greatest poet hardly knows pettiness or triviality. If he breathes into any thing that was before thought small it dilates with the grandeur and life of the universe. He is a seer . . . . he is individual . . . he is complete in himself . . . . the others are as good as he, only he sees it and they do not. He is not one of the chorus . . . . he does not stop for any regulation . . . he is the president of regulation. What the eyesight does to the rest he does to the rest. Who knows the curious mystery of the eyesight? The other senses corroborate themselves, but this is removed from any proof but its own and foreruns the identities of the spiritual world. A single glance of it mocks all the investiga-

---

6. I.e., parksful of artillery—from the custom of drilling and parading in civic parks.

tions of man and all the instruments and books of the earth and all reasoning. What is marvellous? what is unlikely? what is impossible or baseless or vague? after you have once just opened the space of a peachpit and given audience to far and near and to the sunset and had all things enter with electric swiftness softly and duly without confusion or jostling or jam.

The land and sea, the animals fishes and birds, the sky of heaven and the orbs, the forests mountains and rivers, are not small themes . . . but folks expect of the poet to indicate more than the beauty and dignity which always attach to dumb real objects . . . . they expect him to indicate the path between reality and their souls. Men and women perceive the beauty well enough . . probably as well as he. The passionate tenacity of hunters, woodmen, early risers, cultivators of gardens and orchards and fields, the love of healthy women for the manly form, sea-faring persons, drivers of horses, the passion for light and the open air, all is an old varied sign of the unfailing perception of beauty and of a residence of the poetic in outdoor people. They can never be assisted by poets to perceive . . . some may but they never can. The poetic quality is not marshalled in rhyme or uniformity or abstract addresses to things nor in melancholy complaints or good precepts, but is the life of these and much else and is in the soul. The profit of rhyme is that it drops seeds of a sweeter and more luxuriant rhyme, and of uniformity that it conveys itself into its own roots in the ground out of sight. The rhyme and uniformity of perfect poems show the free growth of metrical laws and bud from them as unerringly and loosely as lilacs or roses on a bush, and take shapes as compact as the shapes of chestnuts and oranges and melons and pears, and shed the perfume impalpable to form. The fluency and ornaments of the finest poems or music or orations or recitations are not independent but dependent. All beauty comes from beautiful blood and a beautiful brain. If the greatnesses are in conjunction in a man or woman it is enough . . . . the fact will prevail through the universe . . . . but the gaggery and gilt of a million years will not prevail. Who troubles himself about his ornaments or fluency is lost. This is what you shall do: Love the earth and sun and the animals, despise riches, give alms to every one that asks, stand up for the stupid and crazy, devote your income and labor to others, hate tyrants, argue not concerning God, have patience and indulgence toward the people, take off your hat to nothing known or unknown or to any man or number of men, go freely with powerful uneducated persons and with the young and with the mothers of families, read these leaves in the open air every season of every year of your life, reexamine all you have been told at school or church or in any book, dismiss whatever insults your own soul, and your very flesh shall be a great poem and have the richest fluency not only in its words but in the silent lines of its lips and face and between the lashes of your eyes and in every motion and joint of your body . . . . . . . The poet shall not spend his time in unneeded work. He shall know that the ground is always ready ploughed and manured . . . . others may not know it but he shall. He shall go directly to the creation. His trust shall master the trust of everything he touches . . . . and shall master all attachment.

The known universe has one complete lover and that is the greatest poet. He consumes an eternal passion and is indifferent which chance happens and which possible contingency of fortune or misfortune and persuades daily and hourly his delicious pay. What balks or breaks others is fuel for his burning progress to contact and amorous joy. Other proportions of the reception of pleasure dwindle to nothing to his proportions. All expected from heaven or from the highest he is rapport with in the sight of the daybreak or a scene of the winter woods or the presence of children playing or with his arm round the neck of a man or woman. His love above all love has leisure and expanse . . . . he leaves room ahead of himself. He is no irresolute or suspicious lover . . . he is sure . . . he scorns intervals. His experience and the showers and thrills are not for nothing. Nothing can jar him . . . . suffering and darkness cannot—death and fear cannot. To him complaint and jealousy and envy are corpses buried and rotten in the earth . . . . he saw them buried. The sea is not surer of the shore or the shore of the sea than he is of the fruition of his love and of all perfection and beauty.

The fruition of beauty is no chance of hit or miss . . . it is inevitable as life . . . . it is exact and plumb as gravitation. From the eyesight proceeds another eyesight and from the hearing proceeds another hearing and from the voice proceeds another voice eternally curious of the harmony of things with man. To these respond perfections not only in the committees that were supposed to stand for the rest but in the rest themselves just the same. These understand the law of perfection in masses and floods . . . that its finish is to each for itself and onward from itself . . . that it is profuse and impartial . . . that there is not a minute of the light or dark nor an acre of the earth or sea without it—nor any direction of the sky nor any trade or employment nor any turn of events. This is the reason that about the proper expression of beauty there is precision and balance . . . one part does not need to be thrust above another. The best singer is not the one who has the most lithe and powerful organ . . . the pleasure of poems is not in them that take the handsomest measure and similes and sound.

Without effort and without exposing in the least how it is done the greatest poet brings the spirit of any or all events and passions and scenes and persons some more and some less to bear on your individual character as you hear or read. To do this well is to compete with the laws that pursue and follow time. What is the purpose must surely be there and the clue of it must be there . . . . and the faintest indication is the indication of the best and then becomes the clearest indication. Past and present and future are not disjoined but joined. The greatest poet forms the consistence of what is to be from what has been and is. He drags the dead out of their coffins and stands them again on their feet . . . . he says to the past, Rise and walk before me that I may realize you. He learns the lesson . . . . he places himself where the future becomes present. The greatest poet does not only dazzle his rays over character and scenes and passions . . . he finally ascends and finishes all . . . he exhibits the pinnacles that no man can tell what they are for or what is beyond . . . . he glows a moment on the extremest verge. He is most wonderful in his last half-hidden smile or frown . . . by that flash of the moment of parting the one that sees it shall be encouraged or terrified afterward for many years. The greatest poet does not moralize or make applications of morals . . . he knows the soul. The soul has that measureless pride which consists in never acknowledging any lessons but its own. But it has sympathy as measureless as its pride and the one balances the other and neither can stretch too far while it stretches in company with the other. The inmost secrets of art sleep with the twain. The greatest poet has lain close betwixt both and they are vital in his style and thoughts.

WALT WHITMAN

The art of art, the glory of expression and the sunshine of the light of letters is simplicity. Nothing is better than simplicity . . . . nothing can make up for excess or for the lack of definiteness. To carry on the heave of impulse and pierce intellectual depths and give all subjects their articulations are powers neither common nor very uncommon. But to speak in literature with the perfect rectitude and insousiance of the movements of animals and the unimpeachableness of the sentiment of trees in the woods and grass by the roadside is the flawless triumph of art. If you have looked on him who has achieved it you have looked on one of the masters of the artists of all nations and times. You shall not contemplate the flight of the graygull over the bay or the mettlesome action of the blood horse or the tall leaning of sunflowers on their stalk or the appearance of the sun journeying through heaven or the appearance of the moon afterward with any more satisfaction than you shall contemplate him. The greatest poet has less a marked style and is more the channel of thoughts and things without increase or diminution, and is the free channel of himself. He swears to his art, I will not be meddlesome, I will not have in my writing any elegance or effect or originality to hang in the way between me and the rest like curtains. I will have nothing hang in the way, not the richest curtains. What I tell I tell for precisely what it is. Let who may exalt or startle or fascinate or sooth I will have purposes as health or heat or snow has and be as regardless of observation. What I experience or portray shall go from my composition without a shred of my composition. You shall stand by my side and look in the mirror with me.

The old red blood and stainless gentility of great poets will be proved by their unconstraint. A heroic person walks at his ease through and out of that custom or precedent or authority that suits him not. Of the traits of the brotherhood of writers savans[7] musicians inventors and artists nothing is finer than silent defiance advancing from new free forms. In the need of poems philosophy politics mechanism science behaviour, the craft of art, an appropriate native grand-opera, shipcraft, or any craft, he is greatest forever and forever who contributes the greatest original practical example. The cleanest expression is that which finds no sphere worthy of itself and makes one.

The messages of great poets to each man and woman are, Come to us on equal terms, Only then can you understand us, We are no better than you, What we enclose you enclose, What we enjoy you may enjoy. Did you suppose there could be only one Supreme? We affirm there can be unnumbered Supremes, and that one does not countervail another any more than one eyesight countervails another . . and that men can be good or grand only of the consciousness of their supremacy within them. What do you think is the grandeur of storms and dismemberments and the deadliest battles and wrecks and the wildest fury of the elements and the power of the sea and the motion of nature and of the throes of human desires and dignity and hate and love? It is that something in the soul which says, Rage on, Whirl on, I tread master here and everywhere, Master of the spasms of the sky and of the shatter of the sea, Master of nature and passion and death, And of all terror and all pain.

The American bards shall be marked for generosity and affection and for encouraging competitors . . They shall be kosmos[8] . . without monopoly or secresy . . glad to pass any thing to any one . . hungry for equals night and

---

7. Wise men, scientists.  8. I.e., a part of the one mind that is the world.

day. They shall not be careful of riches and privilege . . . . they shall be riches and privilege . . . . they shall perceive who the most affluent man is. The most affluent man is he that confronts all the shows he sees by equivalents out of the stronger wealth of himself. The American bard shall delineate no class of persons nor one or two out of the strata of interests nor love most nor truth most nor the soul most nor the body most . . . . and not be for the eastern states more than the western or the northern states more than the southern.

Exact science and its practical movements are no checks on the greatest poet but always his encouragement and support. The outset and remembrance are there . . there the arms that lifted him first and brace him best . . . . there he returns after all his goings and comings. The sailor and traveler. . . . the anatomist chemist astronomer geologist phrenologist spiritualist mathematician historian and lexicographer are not poets, but they are the lawgivers of poets and their construction underlies the structure of every perfect poem. No matter what rises or is uttered they sent the seed of the conception of it . . . of them and by them stand the visible proofs of souls . . . . . always of their fatherstuff must be begotten the sinewy races of bards. If there shall be love and content between the father and the son and if the greatness of the son is the exuding of the greatness of the father there shall be love between the poet and the man of demonstrable science. In the beauty of poems are the tuft and final applause of science.

Great is the faith of the flush of knowledge and of the investigation of the depths of qualities and things. Cleaving and circling here swells the soul of the poet yet it[9] president of itself always. The depths are fathomless and therefore calm. The innocence and nakedness are resumed . . . they are neither modest nor immodest. The whole theory of the special and supernatural and all that was twined with it or educed out of it departs as a dream. What has ever happened . . . . what happens and whatever may or shall happen, the vital laws enclose all . . . . they are sufficient for any case and for all cases . . . none to be hurried or retarded . . . . any miracle of affairs or persons inadmissible in the vast clear scheme where every motion and every spear of grass and the frames and spirits of men and women and all that concerns them are unspeakably perfect miracles all referring to all and each distinct and in its place. It is also not consistent with the reality of the soul to admit that there is anything in the known universe more divine than men and women.

Men and women and the earth and all upon it are simply to be taken as they are, and the investigation of their past and present and future shall be unintermitted and shall be done with perfect candor. Upon this basis philosophy speculates ever looking toward the poet, ever regarding the eternal tendencies of all toward happiness never inconsistent with what is clear to the senses and to the soul. For the eternal tendencies of all toward happiness make the only point of sane philosophy. Whatever comprehends less than that . . . whatever is less than the laws of light and of astronomical motion . . . or less than the laws that follow the thief the liar the glutton and the drunkard through this life and doubtless afterward . . . . . . or less than vast stretches of time or the slow formation of density or the patient upheaving of strata—is of no account. Whatever would put God in a poem or system of philosophy as contending against some being or influence is also of no account. Sanity and

---

9. Perhaps "remains" should be understood after "it," although "it" may simply be a typographical error for "is."

ensemble characterise the great master . . . spoilt in one principle all is spoilt.
The great master has nothing to do with miracles. He sees health for himself
in being one of the mass . . . . he sees the hiatus in singular eminence. To
the perfect shape comes common ground. To be under the general law is great
for that is to correspond with it. The master knows that he is unspeakably great
and that all are unspeakably great . . . . that nothing for instance is greater
than to conceive children and bring them up well . . . that to be is just as
great as to perceive or tell.

In the make of the great masters the idea of political liberty is indispensible.
Liberty takes the adherence of heroes wherever men and women exist . . . .
but never takes any adherence or welcome from the rest more than from poets.
They are the voice and exposition of liberty. They out of ages are worthy the
grand idea . . . . to them it is confided and they must sustain it. Nothing has
precedence of it and nothing can warp or degrade it. The attitude of great poets
is to cheer up slaves and horrify despots. The turn of their necks, the sound of
their feet, the motions of their wrists, are full of hazard to the one and hope to
the other. Come nigh them awhile and though they neither speak or advise
you shall learn the faithful American lesson. Liberty is poorly served by men
whose good intent is quelled from one failure or two failures or any number
of failures, or from the casual indifference or ingratitude of the people, or from
the sharp show of the tushes of power, or the bringing to bear soldiers and
cannon or any penal statutes. Liberty relies upon itself, invites no one, promises nothing, sits in calmness and light, is positive and composed, and knows
no discouragement. The battle rages with many a loud alarm and frequent
advance and retreat . . . . the enemy triumphs . . . . the prison, the handcuffs, the iron necklace and anklet, the scaffold, garrote and leadballs do their
work . . . . the cause is asleep . . . . the strong throats are choked with their
own blood . . . . the young men drop their eyelashes toward the ground when
they pass each other . . . . and is liberty gone out of that place? No never.
When liberty goes it is not the first to go nor the second or third to go . . it
waits for all the rest to go . . it is the last . . . When the memories of the old
martyrs are faded utterly away . . . . when the large names of patriots are
laughed at in the public halls from the lips of the orators . . . . when the boys
are no more christened after the same but christened after tyrants and traitors
instead . . . . when the laws of the free are grudgingly permitted and laws for
informers and bloodmoney are sweet to the taste of the people . . . . when I
and you walk abroad upon the earth stung with compassion at the sight of
numberless brothers answering our equal friendship and calling no man master—and when we are elated with noble joy at the sight of slaves . . . . when
the soul retires in the cool communion of the night and surveys its experience
and has much extasy over the word and deed that put back a helpless innocent
person into the gripe of the gripers or into any cruel inferiority . . . . when
those in all parts of these states who could easier realize the true American
character but do not yet—when the swarms of cringers, suckers, doughfaces,
lice of politics, planners of sly involutions for their own preferment to city
offices or state legislatures of the judiciary or congress or the presidency, obtain
a response of love and natural deference from the people whether they get the
offices or no . . . . when it is better to be a bound booby and rogue in office
at a high salary than the poorest free mechanic or farmer with his hat unmoved
from his head and firm eyes and a candid and generous heart . . . . and when

servility by town or state or the federal government or any oppression on a large scale or small scale can be tried on without its own punishment following duly after in exact proportion against the smallest chance of escape . . . . or rather when all life and all the souls of men and women are discharged from any part of the earth—then only shall the instinct of liberty be discharged from that part of the earth.

As the attributes of the poets of the kosmos concentre in the real body and soul and in the pleasure of things they possess the superiority of genuineness over all fiction and romance. As they emit themselves facts are showered over with light . . . . the daylight is lit with more volatile light . . . . also the deep between the setting and rising sun goes deeper many fold. Each precise object or condition or combination or process exhibits a beauty . . . . the multiplication table its—old age its—the carpenter's trade its—the grand-opera its . . . . the hugehulled cheanshaped New-York clipper at sea under steam or full sail gleams with unmatched beauty . . . . the American circles and large harmonies of government gleam with theirs . . . . and the commonest definite intentions and actions with theirs. The poets of the kosmos advance through all interpositions and coverings and turmoils and strategems to first principles. They are of use . . . . they dissolve poverty from its need and riches from its conceit. You large proprietor they say shall not realize or perceive more than any one else. The owner of the library is not he who holds a legal title to it having bought and paid for it. Any one and every one is owner of the library who can read the same through all the varieties of tongues and subjects and styles, and in whom they enter with ease and take residence and force toward paternity and maternity, and make supple and powerful and rich and large . . . . . . . . These American states strong and healthy and accomplished shall receive no pleasure from violations of natural models and must not permit them. In paintings or mouldings or carvings in mineral or wood, or in the illustrations of books or newspapers, or in any comic or tragic prints, or in the patterns of woven stuffs or any thing to beautify rooms or furniture or costumes, or to put upon cornices or monuments or on the prows or sterns of ships, or to put anywhere before the human eye indoors or out, that which distorts honest shapes or which creates unearthly beings or places or contingencies is a nuisance and revolt. Of the human form especially it is so great it must never be made ridiculous. Of ornaments to a work nothing outre[1] can be allowed . . but those ornaments can be allowed that conform to the perfect facts of the open air and that flow out of the nature of the work and come irrepressibly from it and are necessary to the completion of the work. Most works are most beautiful without ornament. . . Exaggerations will be revenged in human physiology. Clean and vigorous children are jetted and conceived only in those communities where the models of natural forms are public every day. . . . . Great genius and the people of these states must never be demeaned to romances. As soon as histories are properly told there is no more need of romances.

The great poets are also to be known by the absence in them of tricks and by the justification of perfect personal candor. Then folks echo a new cheap joy and a divine voice leaping from their brains: How beautiful is candor! All faults may be forgiven of him who has perfect candor. Henceforth let no man

---

1. Excessive, extravagant; an Americanization of the French *outré*.

of us lie, for we have seen that openness wins the inner and outer world and
that there is no single exception, and that never since our earth gathered itself
in a mass have deceit or subterfuge or prevarication attracted its smallest particle or the faintest tinge of a shade—and that through the enveloping wealth
and rank of a state or the whole republic of states a sneak or sly person shall be
discovered and despised . . . . and that the soul has never been once fooled
and never can be fooled . . . . and thrift without the loving nod of the soul is
only a fœtid puff . . . . and there never grew up in any of the continents of
the globe nor upon any planet or satellite or star, nor upon the asteroids, nor
in any part of ethereal space, nor in the midst of density, nor under the fluid
wet of the sea, nor in that condition which precedes the birth of babes, nor at
any time during the changes of life, nor in that condition that follows what we
term death, nor in any stretch of abeyance or action afterward of vitality, nor
in any process of formation or reformation anywhere, a being whose instinct
hated the truth.

Extreme caution or prudence, the soundest organic health, large hope and
comparison and fondness for women and children, large alimentiveness and
destructiveness and causality, with a perfect sense of the oneness of nature and
the propriety of the same spirit applied to human affairs . . these are called up
of the float of the brain of the world to be parts of the greatest poet from his
birth out of his mother's womb and from her birth out of her mother's. Caution seldom goes far enough. It has been thought that the prudent citizen was
the citizen who applied himself to solid gains and did well for himself and his
family and completed a lawful life without debt or crime. The greatest poet
sees and admits these economies as he sees the economies of food and sleep,
but has higher notions of prudence than to think he gives much when he gives
a few slight attentions at the latch of the gate. The premises of the prudence
of life are not the hospitality of it or the ripeness and harvest of it. Beyond the
independence of a little sum laid aside for burial-money, and of a few clap-
boards around and shingles overhead on a lot of American soil owned, and
the easy dollars that supply the year's plain clothing and meals, the melancholy
prudence of the abandonment of such a great being as a man is to the toss and
pallor of years of moneymaking with all their scorching days and icy nights
and all their stifling deceits and underhanded dodgings, or infinitessimals of
parlors, or shameless stuffing while others starve . . and all the loss of the
bloom and odor of the earth and of the flowers and atmosphere and of the sea
and of the true taste of the women and men you pass or have to do with in
youth or middle age, and the issuing sickness and desperate revolt at the close
of a life without elevation or naivete, and the ghastly chatter of a death without
serenity or majesty, is the great fraud upon modern civilization and forethought, blotching the surface and system which civilization undeniably
drafts, and moistening with tears the immense features it spreads and spreads
with such velocity before the reached kisses of the soul. . . Still the right explanation remains to be made about prudence. The prudence of the mere wealth
and respectability of the most esteemed life appears too faint for the eye to
observe at all when little and large alike drop quietly aside at the thought of
the prudence suitable for immortality. What is wisdom that fills the thinness
of a year or seventy or eighty years to wisdom spaced out by ages and coming
back at a certain time with strong reinforcements and rich presents and the
clear faces of wedding-guests as far as you can look in every direction running

gaily toward you? Only the soul is of itself . . . . all else has reference to what ensues. All that a person does or thinks is of consequence. Not a move can a man or woman make that affects him or her in a day or a month or any part of the direct lifetime or the hour of death but the same affects him or her onward afterward through the indirect lifetime. The indirect is always as great and real as the direct. The spirit receives from the body just as much as it gives to the body. Not one name of word or deed . . not of venereal sores or discolorations . . not the privacy of the onanist . . not of the putrid veins of gluttons or rumdrinkers . . . not peculation or cunning or betrayal or murder . . no serpentine poison of those that seduce women . . not the foolish yielding of women . . not prostitution . . not of any depravity of young men . . not of the attainment of gain by discreditable means . . not any nastiness of appetite . . not any harshness of officers to men or judges to prisoners or fathers to sons or sons to fathers or of husbands to wives or bosses to their boys . . not of greedy looks or malignant wishes . . . nor any of the wiles practised by people upon themselves . . . ever is or ever can be stamped on the programme but it is duly realized and returned, and that returned in further performances . . . and they returned again. Nor can the push of charity or personal force ever be any thing else than the profoundest reason, whether it brings arguments to hand or no. No specification is necessary . . to add or subtract or divide is in vain. Little or big, learned or unlearned, white or black, legal or illegal, sick or well, from the first inspiration down the windpipe to the last expiration out of it, all that a male or female does that is vigorous and benevolent and clean is so much sure profit to him or her in the unshakable order of the universe and through the whole scope of it forever. If the savage or felon is wise it is well . . . . if the greatest poet or savan is wise it is simply the same . . if the President or chief justice is wise it is the same . . . if the young mechanic or farmer is wise it is no more or less . . if the prostitute is wise it is no more nor less. The interest will come round . . all will come round. All the best actions of war and peace . . . all help given to relatives and strangers and the poor and old and sorrowful and young children and widows and the sick, and to all shunned persons . . all furtherance of fugitives and of the escape of slaves . . all the self-denial that stood steady and aloof on wrecks and saw others take the seats of the boats . . . all offering of substance or life for the good old cause, or for a friend's sake or opinion's sake . . . all pains of enthusiasts scoffed at by their neighbors . . all the vast sweet love and precious suffering of mothers . . . all honest men baffled in strifes recorded or unrecorded . . . . all the grandeur and good of the few ancient nations whose fragments of annals we inherit . . and all the good of the hundreds of far mightier and more ancient nations unknown to us by name or date or location . . . . all that was ever manfully begun, whether it succeeded or no . . . . all that has at any time been well suggested out of the divine heart of man or by the divinity of his mouth or by the shaping of his great hands . . and all that is well thought or done this day on any part of the surface of the globe . . or on any of the wandering stars or fixed stars by those there as we are here . . or that is henceforth to be well thought or done by you whoever you are, or by any one— these singly and wholly inured at their time and inure now and will inure always to the identities from which they sprung or shall spring . . . Did you guess any of them lived only its moment? The world does not so exist . . no parts palpable or impalpable so exist . . . no result exists now without being from its long antecedent result, and that from its antecedent, and so backward without the farthest mentionable spot coming a bit nearer the beginning than any other spot . . . . . Whatever satisfies the soul is truth. The prudence of the greatest poet answers at last the craving and glut of the soul, is not contemptuous of less ways of prudence if they conform to its ways, puts off nothing, permits no let-up for its own case or any case, has no particular sabbath or judgment-day, divides not the living from the dead or the righteous from the unrighteous, is satisfied with the present, matches every thought or act by its correlative, knows no possible forgiveness or deputed atonement . . knows that the young man who composedly periled his life and lost it has done exceeding well for himself, while the man who has not periled his life and retains it to old age in riches and ease has perhaps achieved nothing for himself worth mentioning . . and that only that person has no great prudence to learn who has learnt to prefer real longlived things, and favors body and soul the same, and perceives the indirect assuredly following the direct, and what evil or good he does leaping onward and waiting to meet him again—and who in his spirit in any emergency whatever neither hurries or avoids death.

The direct trial of him who would be the greatest poet is today. If he does not flood himself with the immediate age as with vast oceanic tides . . . . . and if he does not attract his own land body and soul to himself and hang on its neck with incomparable love and plunge his semitic[2] muscle into its merits and demerits . . . and if he be not himself the age transfigured . . . . and if to him is not opened the eternity which gives similitude to all periods and locations and processes and animate and inanimate forms, and which is the bond of time, and rises up from its inconceivable vagueness and infiniteness in the swimming shape of today, and is held by the ductile anchors of life, and makes the present spot the passage from what was to what shall be, and commits itself to the representation of this wave of an hour and this one of the sixty beautiful children of the wave—let him merge in the general run and wait his development . . . . . . . Still the final test of poems or any character or work remains. The prescient poet projects himself centuries ahead and judges performer or performance after the changes of time. Does it live through them? Does it still hold on untired? Will the same style and the direction of genius to similar points be satisfactory now? Has no new discovery in science or arrival at superior planes of thought and judgment and behaviour fixed him or his so that either can be looked down upon? Have the marches of tens and hundreds and thousands of years made willing detours to the right hand and the left hand for his sake? Is he beloved long and long after he is buried? Does the young man think often of him? and the young woman think often of him? and do the middleaged and the old think of him?

A great poem is for ages and ages in common and for all degrees and complexions and all departments and sects and for a woman as much as a man and a man as much as a woman. A great poem is no finish to a man or woman but rather a beginning. Has any one fancied he could sit at last under some due authority and rest satisfied with explanations and realize and be content and full? To no such terminus does the greatest poet bring . . . he brings neither cessation or sheltered fatness and ease. The touch of him tells in action. Whom he takes he takes with firm sure grasp into live regions pre-

---

2. Likely a sexual coinage meaning muscles through which semen passes, especially the muscles of the penis.

viously unattained . . . . . thenceforward is no rest . . . . they see the space and ineffable sheen that turn the old spots and lights into dead vacuums. The companion of him beholds the birth and progress of stars and learns one of the meanings. Now there shall be a man cohered out of tumult and chaos . . . . the elder encourages the younger and shows him how . . . they two shall launch off fearlessly together till the new world fits an orbit for itself and looks unabashed on the lesser orbits of the stars and sweeps through the ceaseless rings and shall never be quiet again.

There will soon be no more priests. Their work is done. They may wait awhile . . perhaps a generation or two . . dropping off by degrees. A superior breed shall take their place . . . . the gangs of kosmos and prophets en masse shall take their place. A new order shall arise and they shall be the priests of man, and every man shall be his own priest. The churches built under their umbrage[3] shall be the churches of men and women. Through the divinity of themselves shall the kosmos and the new breed of poets be interpreters of men and women and of all events and things. They shall find their inspiration in real objects today, symptoms of the past and future. . . . They shall not deign to defend immortality or God or the perfection of things or liberty or the exquisite beauty and reality of the soul. They shall arise in America and be responded to from the remainder of the earth.

The English language befriends the grand American expression . . . . it is brawny enough and limber and full enough. On the tough stock of a race who through all change of circumstance was never without the idea of political liberty, which is the animus of all liberty, it has attracted the terms of daintier and gayer and subtler and more elegant tongues. It is the powerful language of resistance . . . it is the dialect of common sense. It is the speech of the proud and melancholy races and of all who aspire. It is the chosen tongue to express growth faith self-esteem freedom justice equality friendliness amplitude prudence decision and courage. It is the medium that shall well nigh express the inexpressible.

No great literature nor any like style of behaviour or oratory or social intercourse or household arrangements or public institutions or the treatment by bosses of employed people, nor executive detail or detail of the army or navy, nor spirit of legislation or courts or police or tuition or architecture or songs or amusements or the costumes of young men, can long elude the jealous and passionate instinct of American standards. Whether or no the sign appears from the mouths of the people, it throbs a live interrogation in every freeman's and freewoman's heart after that which passes by or this built to remain. Is it uniform with my country? Are its disposals without ignominious distinctions? Is it for the evergrowing communes of brothers and lovers, large, well-united, proud beyond the old models, generous beyond all models? Is it something grown fresh out of the fields or drawn from the sea for use to me today here? I know that what answers for me an American must answer for any individual or nation that serves for a part of my materials. Does this answer? or is it without reference to universal needs? or sprung of the needs of the less developed society of special ranks? or old needs of pleasure overlaid by modern science and forms? Does this acknowledge liberty with audible and absolute acknowledgement, and set slavery at nought for life and death? Will it help

3. Shadow, protection.

breed one goodshaped and wellhung man, and a woman to be his perfect and independent mate? Does it improve manners? Is it for the nursing of the young of the republic? Does it solve readily with the sweet milk of the nipples of the breasts of the mother of many children? Has it too the old ever-fresh forbearance and impartiality? Does it look with the same love on the last born on those hardening toward stature, and on the errant, and on those who disdain all strength of assault outside of their own?

The poems distilled from other poems'will probably pass away. The coward will surely pass away. The expectation of the vital and great can only be satisfied by the demeanor of the vital and great. The swarms of the polished deprecating and reflectors and the polite float off and leave no remembrance. America prepares with composure and goodwill for the visitors that have sent word. It is not intellect that is to be their warrant and welcome. The talented, the artist, the ingenious, the editor, the statesman, the erudite . . they are not unappreciated . . they fall in their place and do their work. The soul of the nation also does its work. No disguise can pass on it . . no disguise can conceal from it. It rejects none, it permits all. Only toward as good as itself and toward the like of itself will it advance half-way. An individual is as superb as a nation when he has the qualities which make a superb nation. The soul of the largest and wealthiest and proudest nation may well go half-way to meet that of its poets. The signs are effectual. There is no fear of mistake. If the one is true the other is true. The proof of a poet is that his country absorbs him as affectionately as he has absorbed it.

1855

# Song of Myself[1]

*1*

I celebrate myself, and sing myself,
And what I assume you shall assume,
For every atom belonging to me as good belongs to you.

I loafe and invite my soul,
I lean and loafe at my ease observing a spear of summer grass.                    5

My tongue, every atom of my blood, form'd from this soil, this air,
Born here of parents born here from parents the same, and their parents
    the same,
I, now thirty-seven years old in perfect health begin,
Hoping to cease not till death.

---

1. Undeniably uncouth yet carefully fashioned, the poem was the outgrowth of years of labor; anticipatory notebook entries survive from the late 1840s and related poetic passages from the early 1850s. It first appeared in the 1855 *Leaves of Grass* without a title and with no internal divisions. In the second edition (1856), the title was *Poem of Walt Whitman, an American*; then it became *Walt Whitman* in 1860 and remained under that title until 1881, when it finally became *Song of Myself*. During all of this the poem itself was changed only slightly. Perhaps the most important changes made the purpose of the speaker's journeying more explicit: he is absorbing all that he sees to write the poem.

For textual information and guidance through Whitman's vocabulary, this edition has often drawn on the work of Harold W. Blodgett and Sculley Bradley in "*Leaves of Grass*": *Comprehensive Reader's Edition* (1965, 1968), reprinted with corrections and additions in the Bradley and Blodgett Norton Critical Edition of *Leaves of Grass* (1973). Unless otherwise indicated, all texts of Whitman's poems are those of the "deathbed" edition, the green hardbound issue of 1891–92.

Creeds and schools in abeyance,                                                    10
Retiring back a while sufficed at what they are, but never forgotten,
I harbor for good or bad, I permit to speak at every hazard,
Nature without check with original energy.


2


Houses and rooms are full of perfumes, the shelves are crowded with
        perfumes,
I breathe the fragrance myself and know it and like it,                            15
The distillation would intoxicate me also, but I shall not let it.

The atmosphere is not a perfume, it has no taste of the distillation, it is
        odorless,
It is for my mouth forever, I am in love with it,
I will go to the bank by the wood and become undisguised and naked,
I am mad for it to be in contact with me.                                          20

The smoke of my own breath,
Echoes, ripples, buzz'd whispers, love-root, silk-thread, crotch and vine,
My respiration and inspiration, the beating of my heart, the passing of blood
        and air through my lungs,
The sniff of green leaves and dry leaves, and of the shore and dark-color'd sea-
        rocks, and of hay in the barn,
The sound of the belch'd words of my voice loos'd to the eddies of the
        wind,                                                                      25
A few light kisses, a few embraces, a reaching around of arms,
The play of shine and shade on the trees as the supple boughs wag,
The delight alone or in the rush of the streets, or along the fields and hill-sides,
The feeling of health, the full-noon trill, the song of me rising from bed and
        meeting the sun.

Have you reckon'd a thousand acres much? have you reckon'd the earth
        much?                                                                      30
Have you practis'd so long to learn to read?
Have you felt so proud to get at the meaning of poems?

Stop this day and night with me and you shall possess the origin of all poems,
You shall possess the good of the earth and sun, (there are millions of suns
        left,)
You shall no longer take things at second or third hand, nor look through the
        eyes of the dead, nor feed on the spectres in books,                      35
You shall not look through my eyes either, nor take things from me,
You shall listen to all sides and filter them from your self.


3


I have heard what the talkers were talking, the talk of the beginning and the
        end,
But I do not talk of the beginning or the end.

There was never any more inception than there is now,                             40
Nor any more youth or age than there is now,

And will never be any more perfection than there is now,
Nor any more heaven or hell than there is now.

Urge and urge and urge,
Always the procreant urge of the world.                                    45

Out of the dimness opposite equals advance, always substance and increase,
    always sex,
Always a knit of identity, always distinction, always a breed of life.

To elaborate is no avail, learn'd and unlearn'd feel that it is so.

Sure as the most certain sure, plumb in the uprights, well entretied,[2] braced
    in the beams,
Stout as a horse, affectionate, haughty, electrical,                       50
I and this mystery here we stand.

Clear and sweet is my soul, and clear and sweet is all that is not my soul.

Lack one lacks both, and the unseen is proved by the seen,
Till that becomes unseen and receives proof in its turn.

Showing the best and dividing it from the worst age vexes age,             55
Knowing the perfect fitness and equanimity of things, while they discuss I am
    silent, and go bathe and admire myself.

Welcome is every organ and attribute of me, and of any man hearty and clean,
Not an inch nor a particle of an inch is vile, and none shall be less familiar
    than the rest.

I am satisfied—I see, dance, laugh, sing;
As the hugging and loving bed-fellow sleeps at my side through the night, and
    withdraws at the peep of the day with stealthy tread,                  60
Leaving me baskets cover'd with white towels swelling the house with their
    plenty,
Shall I postpone my acceptation and realization and scream at my eyes,
That they turn from gazing after and down the road,
And forthwith cipher[3] and show me to a cent,
Exactly the value of one and exactly the value of two, and which is ahead?  65

4

Trippers and askers surround me,
People I meet, the effect upon me of my early life or the ward and city I live
    in, or the nation,
The latest dates, discoveries, inventions, societies, authors old and new,
My dinner, dress, associates, looks, compliments, dues,
The real or fancied indifference of some man or woman I love,              70
The sickness of one of my folks or of myself, or ill-doing or loss or lack of
    money, or depressions or exaltations,
Battles, the horrors of fratricidal war, the fever of doubtful news, the fitful
    events;

---

2. Cross-braced.                          3. Calculate.

These come to me days and nights and go from me again,
But they are not the Me myself.

Apart from the pulling and hauling stands what I am,      75
Stands amused, complacent, compassionating, idle, unitary,
Looks down, is erect, or bends an arm on an impalpable certain rest,
Looking with side-curved head curious what will come next,
Both in and out of the game and watching and wondering at it.

Backward I see in my own days where I sweated through fog with linguists
     and contenders,      80
I have no mockings or arguments, I witness and wait.

### 5

I believe in you my soul, the other I am must not abase itself to you,
And you must not be abased to the other.

Loafe with me on the grass, loose the stop from your throat,
Not words, not music or rhyme I want, not custom or lecture, not even the
     best,      85
Only the lull I like, the hum of your valvèd voice.

I mind how once we lay such a transparent summer morning,
How you settled your head athwart my hips and gently turn'd over upon me,
And parted the shirt from my bosom-bone, and plunged your tongue to my
     bare-stript heart,
And reach'd till you felt my beard, and reach'd till you held my feet.      90

Swiftly arose and spread around me the peace and knowledge that pass all the
     argument of the earth,
And I know that the hand of God is the promise of my own,
And I know that the spirit of God is the brother of my own,
And that all the men ever born are also my brothers, and the women my sisters
     and lovers,
And that a kelson[4] of the creation is love,      95
And limitless are leaves stiff or drooping in the fields,
And brown ants in the little wells beneath them,
And mossy scabs of the worm fence, heap'd stones, elder, mullein and poke-
     weed.

### 6

A child said *What is the grass?* fetching it to me with full hands;
How could I answer the child? I do not know what it is any more than he.    100

I guess it must be the flag of my disposition, out of hopeful green stuff woven.

Or I guess it is the handkerchief of the Lord,
A scented gift and remembrancer designedly dropt,
Bearing the owner's name someway in the corners, that we may see and
     remark, and say *Whose?*

---

4. A basic structural unit; a reinforcing timber bolted to the keel (backbone) of a ship.

Or I guess the grass is itself a child, the produced babe of the vegetation.   105

Or I guess it is a uniform hieroglyphic,
And it means, Sprouting alike in broad zones and narrow zones,
Growing among black folks as among white,
Kanuck, Tuckahoe, Congressman, Cuff,[5] I give them the same, I receive
    them the same.

And now it seems to me the beautiful uncut hair of graves.   110

Tenderly will I use you curling grass,
It may be you transpire from the breasts of young men,
It may be if I had known them I would have loved them,
It may be you are from old people, or from offspring taken soon out of their
    mothers' laps,
And here you are the mothers' laps.   115

This grass is very dark to be from the white heads of old mothers,
Darker than the colorless beards of old men,
Dark to come from under the faint red roofs of mouths.

O I perceive after all so many uttering tongues,
And I perceive they do not come from the roofs of mouths for nothing.   120

I wish I could translate the hints about the dead young men and women,
And the hints about old men and mothers, and the offspring taken soon out of
    their laps.

What do you think has become of the young and old men?
And what do you think has become of the women and children?

They are alive and well somewhere,   125
The smallest sprout shows there is really no death,
And if ever there was it led forward life, and does not wait at the end
    to arrest it,
And ceas'd the moment life appear'd.

All goes onward and outward, nothing collapses,
And to die is different from what any one supposed, and luckier.   130

7

Has any one supposed it lucky to be born?
I hasten to inform him or her it is just as lucky to die, and I know it.

I pass death with the dying and birth with the new-wash'd babe, and am not
    contain'd between my hat and boots,

And peruse manifold objects, no two alike and every one good,
The earth good and the stars good, and their adjuncts all good.   135

5.  Black, from the African word *cuffee*. "Kanuck": French Canadian. "Tuckahoe": Virginian, from eaters of the
American Indian food plant tuckahoe.

I am not an earth nor an adjunct of an earth,
I am the mate and companion of people, all just as immortal and fathomless
    as myself,
(They do not know how immortal, but I know.)

Every kind for itself and its own, for me mine male and female,
For me those that have been boys and that love women,         140
For me the man that is proud and feels how it stings to be slighted,
For me the sweet-heart and the old maid, for me mothers and the mothers
    of mothers,
For me lips that have smiled, eyes that have shed tears,
For me children and the begetters of children.

Undrape! you are not guilty to me, nor stale nor discarded,      145
I see through the broadcloth and gingham whether or no,
And am around, tenacious, acquisitive, tireless, and cannot be shaken away.

### 8

The little one sleeps in its cradle,
I lift the gauze and look a long time, and silently brush away flies with my
    hand.

The youngster and the red-faced girl turn aside up the bushy hill,    150
I peeringly view them from the top.

The suicide sprawls on the bloody floor of the bedroom,
I witness the corpse with its dabbled hair, I note where the pistol has fallen.

The blab of the pave, tires of carts, sluff of boot-soles, talk of the promenaders,
The heavy omnibus, the driver with his interrogating thumb, the clank of the
    shod horses on the granite floor,    155
The snow-sleighs, clinking, shouted jokes, pelts of snow-balls,
The hurrahs for popular favorites, the fury of rous'd mobs,
The flap of the curtain'd litter, a sick man inside borne to the hospital,
The meeting of enemies, the sudden oath, the blows and fall,
The excited crowd, the policeman with his star quickly working his passage to
    the centre of the crowd,    160
The impassive stones that receive and return so many echoes,
What groans of over-fed or half-starv'd who fall sunstruck or in fits,
What exclamations of women taken suddenly who hurry home and give birth
    to babes,
What living and buried speech is always vibrating here, what howls restrain'd
    by decorum,
Arrests of criminals, slights, adulterous offers made, acceptances, rejections
    with convex lips,    165
I mind them or the show or resonance of them—I come and I depart.

### 9

The big doors of the country barn stand open and ready,
The dried grass of the harvest-time loads the slow-drawn wagon,

The clear light plays on the brown gray and green intertinged,
The armfuls are pack'd to the sagging mow.　　　　　　　　　170

I am there, I help, I came stretch'd atop of the load,
I felt its soft jolts, one leg reclined on the other,
I jump from the cross-beams and sieze the clover and timothy,
And roll head over heels and tangle my hair full of wisps.

10

Alone far in the wilds and mountains I hunt,　　　　　　　175
Wandering amazed at my own lightness and glee,
In the late afternoon choosing a safe spot to pass the night,
Kindling a fire and broiling the fresh-kill'd game,
Falling asleep on the gather'd leaves with my dog and gun by my side.

The Yankee clipper is under her sky-sails, she cuts the sparkle and scud,　180
My eyes settle the land, I bend at her prow or shout joyously from the deck.

The boatmen and clam-diggers arose early and stopt for me,
I tuck'd my trowser-ends in my boots and went and had a good time;
You should have been with us that day round the chowder-kettle.

I saw the marriage of the trapper in the open air in the far west, the bride was
　　a red girl,　　　　　　　　　　　　　　　　　　　　185
Her father and his friends sat near cross-legged and dumbly smoking, they had
　　moccasins to their feet and large thick blankets hanging from their
　　shoulders,
On a bank lounged the trapper, he was drest mostly in skins, his luxuriant
　　beard and curls protected his neck, he held his bride by the hand,
She had long eyelashes, her head was bare, her coarse straight locks descended
　　upon her voluptuous limbs and reach'd to her feet.

The runaway slave came to my house and stopt outside,
I heard his motions crackling the twigs of the woodpile,　　　　190
Through the swung half-door of the kitchen I saw him limpsy[6] and weak,
And went where he sat on a log and led him in and assured him,
And brought water and fill'd a tub for his sweated body and bruis'd feet,
And gave him a room that enter'd from my own, and gave him some coarse
　　clean clothes,
And remember perfectly well his revolving eyes and his awkwardness,　195
And remember putting plasters on the galls of his neck and ankles;
He staid with me a week before he was recuperated and pass'd north,
I had him sit next me at table, my fire-lock lean'd in the corner.

11

Twenty-eight young men bathe by the shore,
Twenty-eight young men and all so friendly;　　　　　　　200
Twenty-eight years of womanly life and all so lonesome.

---

6. Limping or swaying.

She owns the fine house by the rise of the bank,
She hides handsome and richly drest aft the blinds of the window.

Which of the young men does she like the best?
Ah the homeliest of them is beautiful to her.                   205

Where are you off to, lady? for I see you,
You splash in the water there, yet stay stock still in your room.

Dancing and laughing along the beach came the twenty-ninth bather,
The rest did not see her, but she saw them and loved them.

The beards of the young men glisten'd with wet, it ran from their
    long hair,                                                  210
Little streams pass'd over their bodies.

An unseen hand also pass'd over their bodies,
It descended tremblingly from their temples and ribs.

The young men float on their backs, their white bellies bulge to the sun, they
    do not ask who seizes fast to them,
They do not know who puffs and declines with pendant and bending arch, 215
They do not think whom they souse with spray.

### 12

The butcher-boy puts off his killing-clothes, or sharpens his knife at the stall
    in the market,
I loiter enjoying his repartee and his shuffle and break-down.[7]

Blacksmiths with grimed and hairy chests environ the anvil,
Each has his main-sledge, they are all out, there is a great heat in the fire. 220

From the cinder-strew'd threshold I follow their movements,
The lithe sheer of their waists plays even with their massive arms,
Overhand the hammers swing, overhand so slow, overhand so sure,
They do not hasten, each man hits in his place.

### 13

The negro holds firmly the reins of his four horses, the block swags underneath
    on its tied-over chain,                                     225
The negro that drives the long dray of the stone-yard, steady and tall he stands
    pois'd on one leg on the string-piece,[8]
His blue shirt exposes his ample neck and breast and loosens over his hip-band,
His glance is calm and commanding, he tosses the slouch of his hat away from
    his forehead,
The sun falls on his crispy hair and mustache, falls on the black of his polish'd
    and perfect limbs.

---

7. Two favorite minstrel-show dances: the "shuffle"
involves the sliding of feet across the floor and the
"break-down" is faster and noiser.
8. Long, heavy timber used to keep a load in place.

I behold the picturesque giant and love him, and I do not stop there,          230
I go with the team also.

In me the caresser of life wherever moving, backward as well as forward sluing,
To niches aside and junior[9] bending, not a person or object missing,
Absorbing all to myself and for this song.

Oxen that rattle the yoke and chain or halt in the leafy shade, what is that you
        express in your eyes?                                                    235
It seems to me more than all the print I have read in my life.

My tread scares the wood-drake and wood-duck on my distant and day-long
        ramble.
They rise together, they slowly circle around.

I believe in those wing'd purposes,
And acknowledge red, yellow, white, playing within me,                          240
And consider green and violet and the tufted crown[1] intentional,
And do not call the tortoise unworthy because she is not something else,
And the jay in the woods never studied the gamut,[2] yet trills pretty well to me,
And the look of the bay mare shames silliness out of me.


                                        14

The wild gander leads his flock through the cool night,                         245
Ya-honk he says, and sounds it down to me like an invitation,
The pert may suppose it meaningless, but I listening close,
Find its purpose and place up there toward the wintry sky.

The sharp-hoof'd moose of the north, the cat on the house-sill, the chickadee,
        the prairie-dog,
The litter of the grunting sow as they tug at her teats,                        250
The brood of the turkey-hen and she with her half-spread wings,
I see in them and myself the same old law.

The press of my foot to the earth springs a hundred affections,
They scorn the best I can do to relate them.

I am enamour'd of growing out-doors,                                            255
Of men that live among cattle or taste of the ocean or woods,
Of the builders and steerers of ships and the wielders of axes and mauls, and
        the drivers of horses,
I can eat and sleep with them week in and week out.

What is commonest, cheapest, nearest, easiest, is Me,
Me going in for my chances, spending for vast returns,                          260
Adorning myself to bestow myself on the first that will take me,
Not asking the sky to come down to my good will,
Scattering it freely forever.

---

9. Smaller.                                        2. The series of recognized musical notes.
1. Of the wood drake.

15

The pure contralto sings in the organ loft,
The carpenter dresses his plank, the tongue of his foreplane whistles its wild
    ascending lisp, 265
The married and unmarried children ride home to their Thanksgiving dinner,
The pilot seizes the king-pin, he heaves down with a strong arm,
The mate stands braced in the whale-boat, lance and harpoon are ready,
The duck-shooter walks by silent and cautious stretches,
The deacons are ordain'd with cross'd hands at the altar, 270
The spinning-girl retreats and advances to the hum of the big wheel,
The farmer stops by the bars as he walks on a First-day³ loafe and looks at the
    oats and rye,
The lunatic is carried at last to the asylum a confirm'd case,
(He will never sleep any more as he did in the cot in his mother's bed-room;)
The jour printer⁴ with gray head and gaunt jaws works at his case, 275
He turns his quid of tobacco while his eyes blurr with the manuscript;
The malform'd limbs are tied to the surgeon's table,
What is removed drops horribly in a pail;
The quadroon girl is sold at the auction-stand, the drunkard nods by the bar-
    room stove,
The machinist rolls up his sleeves, the policeman travels his beat, the gate-
    keeper marks who pass, 280
The young fellow drives the express-wagon, (I love him, though I do not
    know him;)
The half-breed straps on his light boots to compete in the race,
The western turkey-shooting draws old and young, some lean on their rifles,
    some sit on logs,
Out from the crowd steps the marksman, takes his position, levels his piece;
The groups of newly-come immigrants cover the wharf or levee, 285
As the woolly-pates hoe in the sugar-field, the overseer views them from his
    saddle,
The bugle calls in the ball-room, the gentlemen run for their partners, the
    dancers bow to each other,
The youth lies awake in the cedar-roof'd garret and harks to the musical rain,
The Wolverine⁵ sets traps on the creek that helps fill the Huron,
The squaw wrapt in her yellow-hemm'd cloth is offering moccasins and bead-
    bags for sale, 290
The connoisseur peers along the exhibition-gallery with half-shut eyes bent
    sideways,
As the deck-hands make fast the steamboat the plank is thrown for the shore-
    going passengers,
The young sister holds out the skein while the elder sister winds it off in a ball,
    and stops now and then for the knots,
The one-year wife is recovering and happy having a week ago borne her first
    child,
The clean-hair'd Yankee girl works with her sewing-machine or in the factory
    or mill, 295

3. Sunday. Whitman frequently uses the numerical
Quaker substitutes for the customary pagan names of
days and months. "Bars": i.e., of a rail fence.
4. I.e., a journeyman printer, or one who has passed

his apprenticeship and is fully qualified for all professional work. In this usage Whitman may imply that the
man works by the day, without a steady job.
5. Inhabitant of Michigan.

The paving-man[6] leans on his two-handed rammer, the reporter's lead flies
    swiftly over the note-book, the sign-painter is lettering with blue and gold,
The canal boy trots on the tow-path, the book-keeper counts at his desk, the
    shoemaker waxes his thread,
The conductor beats time for the band and all the performers follow him,
The child is baptized, the convert is making his first professions,
The regatta is spread on the bay, the race is begun, (how the white sails
    sparkle!)                                                                                          300
The drover watching his drove sings out to them that would stray,
The pedler sweats with his pack on his back, (the purchaser higgling about the
    odd cent;)
The bride unrumples her white dress, the minute-hand of the clock moves
    slowly,
The opium-eater reclines with rigid head and just-open'd lips,
The prostitute draggles her shawl, her bonnet bobs on her tipsy and pimpled
    neck,                                                                                              305
The crowd laugh at her blackguard oaths, the men jeer and wink to each other,


(Miserable! I do not laugh at your oaths nor jeer you;)
The President holding a cabinet council is surrounded by the great Secretaries,
On the piazza walk three matrons stately and friendly with twined arms,
The crew of the fish-smack pack repeated layers of halibut in the hold,          310
The Missourian crosses the plains toting his wares and his cattle,
As the fare-collector goes through the train he gives notice by the jingling of
    loose change,
The floor-men are laying the floor, the tinners are tinning the roof, the masons
    are calling for mortar,
In single file each shouldering his hod pass onward the laborers;
Seasons pursuing each other the indescribable crowd is gather'd, it is the fourth
    of Seventh-month, (what salutes of cannon and small arms!)                       315
Seasons pursuing each other the plougher ploughs, the mower mows, and the
    winter-grain falls in the ground;
Off on the lakes the pike-fisher watches and waits by the hole in the frozen
    surface,
The stumps stand thick round the clearing, the squatter strikes deep with his
    axe,
Flatboatmen make fast towards dusk near the cotton-wood or pecan-trees,
Coon-seekers go through the regions of the Red river or through those drain'd
    by the Tennessee, or through those of the Arkansas,                                 320
Torches shine in the dark that hangs on the Chattahooch or Altamahaw,[7]
Patriarchs sit at supper with sons and grandsons and great-grandsons around
    them,
In walls of adobie, in canvas tents, rest hunters and trappers after their day's
    sport,
The city sleeps and the country sleeps,
The living sleep for their time, the dead sleep for their time,                      325
The old husband sleeps by his wife and the young husband sleeps by his wife;
And these tend inward to me, and I tend outward to them,
And such as it is to be of these more or less I am,
And of these one and all I weave the song of myself.

6. Man building or repairing streets.                    7. Georgia rivers.

16

I am of old and young, of the foolish as much as the wise,                    330
Regardless of others, ever regardful of others,
Maternal as well as paternal, a child as well as a man,
Stuff'd with the stuff that is coarse and stuff'd with the stuff that is fine,
One of the Nation of many nations, the smallest the same and the largest
    the same,
A Southerner soon as a Northerner, a planter nonchalant and hospitable down
    by the Oconee[8] I live,                                                                  335
A Yankee bound my own way ready for trade, my joints the limberest joints
    on earth and the sternest joints on earth,
A Kentuckian walking the vale of the Elkhorn in my deer-skin leggings, a
    Louisianian or Georgian,
A boatman over lakes or bays or along coasts, a Hoosier, Badger, Buckeye;
At home on Kanadian[9] snow-shoes or up in the bush, or with fishermen off
    Newfoundland,
At home in the fleet of ice-boats, sailing with the rest and tacking,          340
At home on the hills of Vermont or in the woods of Maine, or the Texan
    ranch,
Comrade of Californians, comrade of free North-Westerners, (loving their
    big proportions,)
Comrade of raftsmen and coalmen, comrade of all who shake hands and wel-
    come to drink and meat,
A learner with the simplest, a teacher of the thoughtfullest,
A novice beginning yet experient of myriads of seasons,                        345
Of every hue and caste am I, of every rank and religion,
A farmer, mechanic, artist, gentleman, sailor, quaker,
Prisoner, fancy-man, rowdy, lawyer, physician, priest.

I resist any thing better than my own diversity,
Breathe the air but leave plenty after me,                                     350
And am not stuck up, and am in my place.

(The moth and the fish-eggs are in their place,
The bright suns I see and the dark suns I cannot see are in their place,
The palpable is in its place and the impalpable is in its place.)

17

These are really the thoughts of all men in all ages and lands, they are not
    original with me,                                                              355
If they are not yours as much as mine they are nothing, or next to nothing,
If they are not the riddle and the untying of the riddle they are nothing,
If they are not just as close as they are distant they are nothing.

This is the grass that grows wherever the land is and the water is,
This the common air that bathes the globe.                                     360

8. River in central Georgia.                        this spelling. "Hoosier, Badger, Buckeye": inhabitants
9. Apparently Whitman found something muscular in     of Indiana, Wisconsin, and Ohio, respectively.

18

With music strong I come, with my cornets and my drums,
I play not marches for accepted victors only, I play marches for conquer'd and
    slain persons.

Have you heard that it was good to gain the day?
I also say it is good to fall, battles are lost in the same spirit in which they
    are won.

I beat and pound for the dead,                                                          365
I blow through my embouchures[1] my loudest and gayest for them.

Vivas to those who have fail'd!
And to those whose war-vessels sank in the sea!
And to those themselves who sank in the sea!
And to all generals that lost engagements, and all overcome heroes!              370
And the numberless unknown heroes equal to the greatest heroes known!

19

This is the meal equally set, this the meat for natural hunger,
It is for the wicked just the same as the righteous, I make appointments with
    all,
I will not have a single person slighted or left away,
The kept-woman, sponger, thief, are hereby invited,                              375
The heavy-lipp'd slave is invited, the venerealee is invited;
There shall be no difference between them and the rest.

This is the press of a bashful hand, this the float and odor of hair,
This is the touch of my lips to yours, this the murmur of yearning,
This the far-off depth and height reflecting my own face,                        380
This the thoughtful merge of myself, and the outlet again.

Do you guess I have some intricate purpose?
Well I have, for the Fourth-month showers have, and the mica on the side of
    a rock has.

Do you take it I would astonish?
Does the daylight astonish? does the early redstart twittering through the
    woods?                                                                        385
Do I astonish more than they?

This hour I tell things in confidence,
I might not tell everybody, but I will tell you.

20

Who goes there? hankering, gross, mystical, nude;
How is it I extract strength from the beef I eat?                                 390

---

1. Mouthpieces of musical instruments such as the cornet, mentioned earlier.

What is a man anyhow? what am I? what are you?

All I mark as my own you shall offset it with your own,
Else it were time lost listening to me.

I do not snivel that snivel the world over,
That months are vacuums and the ground but wallow and filth.                      395

Whimpering and truckling fold with powders for invalids, conformity goes to
    the fourth-remov'd,[2]
I wear my hat as I please indoors or out.

Why should I pray? why should I venerate and be ceremonious?

Having pried through the strata, analyzed to a hair, counsel'd with doctors and
    calculated close,
I find no sweeter fat than sticks to my bones.                                     400

In all people I see myself, none more and not one a barley-corn[3] less,
And the good or bad I say of myself I say of them.

I know I am solid and sound,
To me the converging objects of the universe perpetually flow,
All are written to me, and I must get what the writing means.                      405

I know I am deathless,
I know this orbit of mine cannot be swept by a carpenter's compass,
I know I shall not pass like a child's carlacue[4] cut with a burnt stick at night.

I know I am august,
I do not trouble my spirit to vindicate itself or be understood,                   410
I see that the elementary laws never apologize,
(I reckon I behave no prouder than the level I plant my house by, after all.)

I exist as I am, that is enough,
If no other in the world be aware I sit content,
And if each and all be aware I sit content.                                        415

One world is aware and by far the largest to me, and that is myself,
And whether I come to my own to-day or in ten thousand or ten million years,
I can cheerfully take it now, or with equal cheerfulness I can wait.

My foothold is tenon'd and mortis'd[5] in granite,
I laugh at what you call dissolution,                                              420
And I know the amplitude of time.

---

2. Those very remote in relationship; from the genea-
logical use such as "third cousin, fourth removed."
"Fold with powders": a reference to the custom of a
physician's wrapping up a dose of medicine in a piece
of paper.
3. The seed or grain of barley, but also a unit of measure equal to about one-third inch.

4. Also spelled *curlicue*, a fancy flourish made with a
writing implement, here made in the dark with a
lighted stick, and so lasting only a moment.
5. Carpenter's terms for a particular way of joining two
boards together: a mortise is a cavity in a piece of wood
into which is placed the projection (tenon) from another piece of wood.

21

I am the poet of the Body and I am the poet of the Soul,
The pleasures of heaven are with me and the pains of hell are with me,
The first I graft and increase upon myself, the latter I translate into a new
   tongue.

I am the poet of the woman the same as the man,                    425
And I say it is as great to be a woman as to be a man,
And I say there is nothing greater than the mother of men.

I chant the chant of dilation or pride,
We have had ducking and deprecating about enough,
I show that size is only development.                               430

Have you outstript the rest? are you the President?
It is a trifle, they will more than arrive there every one, and still pass on.

I am he that walks with the tender and growing night,
I call to the earth and sea half-held by the night.

Press close bare-bosom'd night—press close magnetic nourishing night!   435
Night of south winds—night of the large few stars!
Still nodding night—mad naked summer night.

Smile O voluptuous cool-breath'd earth!
Earth of the slumbering and liquid trees!
Earth of departed sunset—earth of the mountains misty-topt!         440
Earth of the vitreous pour of the full moon just tinged with blue!
Earth of shine and dark mottling the tide of the river!
Earth of the limpid gray of clouds brighter and clearer for my sake!
Far-swooping elbow'd earth—rich apple-blossom'd earth!
Smile, for your lover comes.                                        445

Prodigal, you have given me love—therefore I to you give love!
O unspeakable passionate love.


22

You sea! I resign myself to you also—I guess what you mean,
I behold from the beach your crooked inviting fingers,
I believe you refuse to go back without feeling of me,              450
We must have a turn together, I undress, hurry me out of sight of the land,
Cushion me soft, rock me in billowy drowse,
Dash me with amorous wet, I can repay you.

Sea of stretch'd ground-swells,
Sea breathing broad and convulsive breaths,                        455
Sea of the brine of life and of unshovell'd yet always-ready graves,
Howler and scooper of storms, capricious and dainty sea,
I am integral with you, I too am of one phase and of all phases.

Partaker of influx and efflux I, extoller of hate and conciliation,
Extoller of amies[6] and those that sleep in each others' arms.              460

I am he attesting sympathy,
(Shall I make my list of things in the house and skip the house that supports
    them?)

I am not the poet of goodness only, I do not decline to be the poet of wick-
    edness also.

What blurt is this about virtue and about vice?
Evil propels me and reform of evil propels me, I stand indifferent,          465
My gait is no fault-finder's or rejecter's gait,
I moisten the roots of all that has grown.

Did you fear some scrofula out of the unflagging pregnancy?
Did you guess the celestial laws are yet to be work'd over and rectified?

I find one side a balance and the antipodal side a balance,                  470
Soft doctrine as steady help as stable doctrine,
Thoughts and deeds of the present our rouse and early start.

This minute that comes to me over the past decillions,
There is no better than it and now.

What behaved well in the past or behaves well to-day is not such a wonder,   475
The wonder is always and always how there can be a mean man or an infidel.

23

Endless unfolding of words of ages!
And mine a word of the modern, the word En-Masse.

A word of the faith that never balks,
Here or henceforward it is all the same to me, I accept Time absolutely.     480

It alone is without flaw, it alone rounds and completes all,
That mystic baffling wonder alone completes all.

I accept Reality and dare not question it.
Materialism first and last imbuing.

Hurrah for positive science! long live exact demonstration!                  485
Fetch stonecrop[7] mixt with cedar and branches of lilac,
This is the lexicographer, this the chemist, this made a grammar of the old car-
    touches,[8]
These mariners put the ship through dangerous unknown seas,
This is the geologist, this works with the scalpel, and this is a mathematician.

6. Friends (French), in Whitman's specialized sense
of comrades.
7. A fleshy-leafed plant of the genus *Sedum*.
8. Scroll-like tablet with space for an inscription.

Whitman knew the Egyptian cartouches with hieroglyphics, the deciphering of which contributed to
knowledge of ancient life.

Gentlemen, to you the first honors always!                                490
Your facts are useful, and yet they are not my dwelling,
I but enter by them to an area of my dwelling.

Less the reminders of properties told my words,
And more the reminders they of life untold, and of freedom and extrication,
And make short account of neuters and geldings, and favor men and women
    fully equipt,                                                          495
And beat the gong of revolt, and stop with fugitives and them that plot and
    conspire.

24

Walt Whitman, a kosmos, of Manhattan the son,
Turbulent, fleshy, sensual, eating, drinking and breeding,
No sentimentalist, no stander above men and women or apart from them,
No more modest than immodest.                                             500

Unscrews the locks from the doors!
Unscrews the doors themselves from their jambs!

Whoever degrades another degrades me,
And whatever is done or said returns at last to me.

Through me the afflatus[9] surging and surging, through me the current and
    index.                                                               505

I speak the pass-word primeval, I give the sign of democracy,
By God! I will accept nothing which all cannot have their counterpart of on
    the same terms.

Through me many long dumb voices,
Voices of the interminable generations of prisoners and slaves,
Voices of the diseas'd and despairing and of thieves and dwarfs,         510

Voices of cycles of preparation and accretion,
And of the threads that connect the stars, and of wombs and of the father-stuff,
And of the rights of them the others are down upon,
Of the deform'd, trivial, flat, foolish, despised,
Fog in the air, beetles rolling balls of dung.                           515

Through me forbidden voices,
Voices of sexes and lusts, voices veil'd and I remove the veil,
Voices indecent by me clarified and transfigur'd.

I do not press my fingers across my mouth,
I keep as delicate around the bowels as around the head and heart,       520
Copulation is no more rank to me than death is.

9. Divine wind or spirit.

I believe in the flesh and the appetites,
Seeing, hearing, feeling, are miracles, and each part and tag of me is a
    miracle.

Divine am I inside and out, and I make holy whatever I touch or am touch'd
    from,
The scent of these arm-pits aroma finer than prayer,                    525
This head more than churches, bibles, and all the creeds.

If I worship one thing more than another it shall be the spread of my own
    body, or any part of it,
Translucent mould of me it shall be you!
Shaded ledges and rests it shall be you!
Firm masculine colter¹ it shall be you!                    530
Whatever goes to the tilth² of me it shall be you!
You my rich blood! your milky stream pale strippings of my life!
Breast that presses against other breasts it shall be you!
My brain it shall be your occult convolutions!
Root of wash'd sweet-flag! timorous pond-snipe! nest of guarded duplicate eggs!
    it shall be you!                    535
Mix'd tussled hay of head, beard, brawn, it shall be you!
Trickling sap of maple, fibre of manly wheat, it shall be you!
Sun so generous it shall be you!
Vapors lighting and shading my face it shall be you!
You sweaty brooks and dews it shall be you!                    540
Winds whose soft-tickling genitals rub against me it shall be you!
Broad muscular fields, branches of live oak, loving lounger in my winding
    paths, it shall be you!
Hands I have taken, face I have kiss'd, mortal I have ever touch'd, it shall
    be you.

I dote on myself, there is that lot of me and all so luscious,
Each moment and whatever happens thrills me with joy,                    545
I cannot tell how my ankles bend, nor whence the cause of my faintest wish,
Nor the cause of the friendship I emit, nor the cause of the friendship I take
    again.

That I walk up my stoop, I pause to consider if it really be,
A morning-glory at my window satisfies me more than the metaphysics of
    books.

To behold the day-break!                    550
The little light fades the immense and diaphanous shadows,
The air tastes good to my palate.

Hefts³ of the moving world at innocent gambols silently rising freshly exuding,
Scooting obliquely high and low.

---

1. This phallic passage begins with reference to the    provement.
blade at the front of a plow.    3. Something being heaved or raised upward.
2. Plowing; here, any cultivation or personal im-

Something I cannot see puts upward libidinous prongs,                         555
Seas of bright juice suffuse heaven.

The earth by the sky staid with, the daily close of their junction,
The heav'd challenge from the east that moment over my head,
The mocking taunt, See then whether you shall be master!


### 25

Dazzling and tremendous how quick the sun-rise would kill me,                 560
If I could not now and always send sun-rise out of me.

We also ascend dazzling and tremendous as the sun,
We found our own O my soul in the calm and cool of the day-break.

My voice goes after what my eyes cannot reach,
With the twirl of my tongue I encompass worlds and volumes of worlds.         565

Speech is the twin of my vision, it is unequal to measure itself,
It provokes me forever, it says sarcastically,
*Walt you contain enough, why don't you let it out then?*

Come now I will not be tantalized, you conceive too much of articulation,
Do you not know O speech how the buds beneath you are folded?                 570
Waiting in gloom, protected by frost,
The dirt receding before my prophetical screams,
I underlying causes to balance them at last,
My knowledge my live parts, it keeping tally with the meaning of all things,
Happiness, (which whoever hears me let him or her set out in search of this
       day.)                                                                  575

My final merit I refuse you, I refuse putting from me what I really am,
Encompass worlds, but never try to encompass me.
I crowd your sleekest and best by simply looking toward you.

Writing and talk do not prove me,
I carry the plenum⁴ of proof and every thing else in my face,                 580
With the hush of my lips I wholly confound the skeptic.


### 26

Now I will do nothing but listen,
To accrue what I hear into this song, to let sounds contribute toward it.

I hear bravuras of birds, bustle of growing wheat, gossip of flames, clack of
       sticks cooking my meals,
I hear the sound I love, the sound of the human voice,                        585
I hear all sounds running together, combined, fused or following,
Sounds of the city and sounds out of the city, sounds of the day and night,
Talkative young ones to those that like them, the loud laugh of work-people at
       their meals,

4. Fullness.

The angry base of disjointed friendship, the faint tones of the sick,
The judge with hands tight to the desk, his pallid lips pronouncing a death-
    sentence,                                                                    590
The heave'e'yo of stevedores unlading ships by the wharves, the refrain of the
    anchor-lifters,
The ring of alarm-bells, the cry of fire, the whirr of swift-streaking engines and
    hose-carts with premonitory tinkles and color'd lights,
The steam-whistle, the solid roll of the train of approaching cars,
The slow march play'd at the head of the association marching two and two,
(They go to guard some corpse, the flag-tops are draped with black
    muslin.)                                                                     595

I hear the violoncello ('tis the young man's heart's complaint,)
I hear the key'd cornet, it glides quickly in through my ears,
It shakes mad-sweet pangs through my belly and breast.

I hear the chorus, it is a grand opera,
Ah this indeed is music—this suits me.                                           600

A tenor large and fresh as the creation fills me,
The orbic flex of his mouth is pouring and filling me full.

I hear the train'd soprano (what work with hers is this?)
The orchestra whirls me wider than Uranus[5] flies,
It wrenches such ardors from me I did not know I possess'd them,                 605
It sails me, I dab with bare feet, they are lick'd by the indolent waves,
I am cut by bitter and angry hail, I lose my breath,
Steep'd amid honey'd morphine, my windpipe throttled in fakes[6] of death,
At length let up again to feel the puzzle of puzzles,
And that we call Being.                                                          610


                                    27

To be in any form, what is that?
(Round and round we go, all of us, and ever come back thither,)
If nothing lay more develop'd the quahaug[7] in its callous shell were enough.

Mine is no callous shell,
I have instant conductors all over me whether I pass or stop,                    615
They seize every object and lead it harmlessly through me.

I merely stir, press, feel with my fingers, and am happy,
To touch my person to some one else's is about as much as I can stand.


                                    28

Is this then a touch? quivering me to a new identity,
Flames and ether making a rush for my veins,                                     620
Treacherous tip of me reaching and crowding to help them,

5. At that time Uranus (the seventh planet from the      6. Coils of rope.
sun) was thought to be the most remote planet in our     7. Edible clam of the Atlantic coast.
solar system.

My flesh and blood playing out lightning to strike what is hardly different
from myself,
On all sides prurient provokers stiffening my limbs,
Straining the udder of my heart for its withheld drip,
Behaving licentious toward me, taking no denial,                          625
Depriving me of my best as for a purpose,
Unbuttoning my clothes, holding me by the bare waist,
Deluding my confusion with the calm of the sunlight and pasture-fields,
Immodestly sliding the fellow-senses away,
They bribed to swap off with touch and go and graze at the edges of me,   630
No consideration, no regard for my draining strength or my anger,
Fetching the rest of the herd around to enjoy them a while,
Then all uniting to stand on a headland and worry me.

The sentries desert every other part of me,
They have left me helpless to a red marauder,                             635
They all come to the headland to witness and assist against me.

I am given up by traitors,
I talk wildly, I have lost my wits, I and nobody else am the greatest traitor,
I went myself first to the headland, my own hands carried me there.

You villain touch! what are you doing? my breath is tight in its throat,  640
Unclench your floodgates, you are too much for me.

### 29

Blind loving wrestling touch, sheath'd hooded sharp-tooth'd touch!
Did it make you ache so, leaving me?

Parting track'd by arriving, perpetual payment of perpetual loan,
Rich showering rain, and recompense richer afterward.                     645

Sprouts take and accumulate, stand by the curb prolific and vital,
Landscapes projected masculine, full-sized and golden.

### 30

All truths wait in all things,
They neither hasten their own delivery nor resist it,
They do not need the obstetric forceps of the surgeon,                    650
The insignificant is as big to me as any,
(What is less or more than a touch?)

Logic and sermons never convince,
The damp of the night drives deeper into my soul.

(Only what proves itself to every man and woman is so,                    655
Only what nobody denies is so.)

A minute and a drop of me settle my brain,
I believe the soggy clods shall become lovers and lamps,

And a compend[8] of compends is the meat of a man or woman,
And a summit and flower there is the feeling they have for each other,          660
And they are to branch boundlessly out of that lesson until it becomes omnific,[9]
And until one and all shall delight us, and we them.

### 31

I believe a leaf of grass is no less than the journey-work of the stars,
And the pismire[1] is equally perfect, and a grain of sand, and the egg of the
    wren,
And the tree-toad is a chief-d'œuvre for the highest,          665
And the running blackberry would adorn the parlors of heaven,
And the narrowest hinge in my hand puts to scorn all machinery,
And the cow crunching with depress'd head surpasses any statue,
And a mouse is miracle enough to stagger sextillions of infidels.

I find I incorporate gneiss,[2] coal, long-threaded moss, fruits, grains, esculent
    roots,          670
And am stucco'd with quadrupeds and birds all over,
And have distanced what is behind me for good reasons,
But call any thing back again when I desire it.

In vain the speeding or shyness,
In vain the plutonic rocks[3] send their old heat against my approach,          675
In vain the mastodon retreats beneath its own powder'd bones,
In vain objects stand leagues off and assume manifold shapes,
In vain the ocean settling in hollows and the great monsters lying low,
In vain the buzzard houses herself with the sky,
In vain the snake slides through the creepers and logs,          680
In vain the elk takes to the inner passes of the woods,
In vain the razor-bill'd auk sails far north to Labrador,
I follow quickly, I ascend to the nest in the fissure of the cliff.

### 32

I think I could turn and live with animals, they are so placid and self-contain'd,
I stand and look at them long and long.          685

They do not sweat and whine about their condition,
They do not lie awake in the dark and weep for their sins,
They do not make me sick discussing their duty to God,
Not one is dissatisfied, not one is demented with the mania of owning things,
Not one kneels to another, nor to his kind that lived thousands of years
    ago,          690
Not one is respectable or unhappy over the whole earth.

So they show their relations to me and I accept them,
They bring me tokens of myself, they evince them plainly in their possession.

---

8. I.e., a compendium, where something is reduced
to a short, essential summary.
9. All-encompassing.
1. Ant.

2. Metamorphic rock in which minerals are arranged
in layers.
3. Rock of igneus (fire created) or magmatic (molten)
origin (from Pluto, ruler of infernal regions).

I wonder where they get those tokens,
Did I pass that way huge times ago and negligently drop them?          695

Myself moving forward then and now and forever,
Gathering and showing more always and with velocity,
Infinite and omnigenous,[4] and the like of these among them,
Not too exclusive toward the reachers of my remembrancers,
Picking out here one that I love, and now go with him on brotherly terms.          700

A gigantic beauty of a stallion, fresh and responsive to my caresses,
Head high in the forehead, wide between the ears,
Limbs glossy and supple, tail dusting the ground,
Eyes full of sparkling wickedness, ears finely cut, flexibly moving.

His nostrils dilate as my heels embrace him,          705
His well-built limbs tremble with pleasure as we race around and return.

I but use you a minute, then I resign you, stallion,
Why do I need your paces when I myself out-gallop them?
Even as I stand or sit passing faster than you.

### 33

Space and Time! now I see it is true, what I guess'd at,          710
What I guess'd when I loaf'd on the grass,
What I guess'd while I lay alone in my bed,
And again as I walk'd the beach under the paling stars of the morning.

My ties and ballasts leave me, my elbows rest in sea-gaps,[5]
I skirt sierras, my palms cover continents,          715
I am afoot with my vision.

By the city's quadrangular houses—in log huts, camping with lumbermen,
Along the ruts of the turnpike, along the dry gulch and rivulet bed,
Weeding my onion-patch or hoeing rows of carrots and parsnips, crossing
          savannas,[6] trailing in forests,
Prospecting, gold-digging, girdling the trees of a new purchase,          720
Scorch'd ankle-deep by the hot sand, hauling my boat down the shallow river,
Where the panther walks to and fro on a limb overhead, where the buck turns
          furiously at the hunter,
Where the rattlesnake suns his flabby length on a rock, where the otter is
          feeding on fish,
Where the alligator in his tough pimples sleeps by the bayou,
Where the black bear is searching for roots or honey, where the beaver pats
          the mud with his paddle-shaped tail;          725
Over the growing sugar, over the yellow-flower'd cotton plant, over the rice in
          its low moist field,
Over the sharp-peak'd farm house, with its scallop'd scum and slender shoots
          from the gutters,[7]

---

4. Belonging to every form of life.
5. Estuaries or bays.
6. Flat, treeless, tropical grassland.

7. Presumably debris washed or blown down roofs,
settling into scalloplike shapes in the gutter and providing nutrients for grasses or weeds.

Over the western persimmon, over the long-leav'd corn, over the delicate blue-
flower flax,
Over the white and brown buckwheat, a hummer and buzzer there with the
rest,
Over the dusky green of the rye as it ripples and shades in the breeze;            730
Scaling mountains, pulling myself cautiously up, holding on by low scragged
limbs,
Walking the path worn in the grass and beat through the leaves of the brush,
Where the quail is whistling betwixt the woods and the wheat-lot,
Where the bat flies in the Seventh-month eve, where the great gold-bug drops
through the dark,
Where the brook puts out of the roots of the old tree and flows to the
meadow,                                              735
Where cattle stand and shake away flies with the tremulous shuddering of
their hides,
Where the cheese-cloth hangs in the kitchen, where andirons straddle the
hearth-slab, where cobwebs fall in festoons from the rafters;
Where trip-hammers crash, where the press is whirling its cylinders,
Wherever the human heart beats with terrible throes under its ribs,
Where the pear-shaped balloon is floating aloft, (floating in it myself and look-
ing composedly down,)                                   740
Where the life-car[8] is drawn on the slip-noose, where the heat hatches pale-
green eggs in the dented sand,
Where the she-whale swims with her calf and never forsakes it,
Where the steam-ship trails hind-ways its long pennant of smoke,
Where the fin of the shark cuts like a black chip out of the water,
Where the half-burn'd brig is riding on unknown currents,                       745
Where shells grow to her slimy deck, where the dead are corrupting below;
Where the dense-star'd flag is borne at the head of the regiments,
Approaching Manhattan up by the long-stretching island,
Under Niagara, the cataract falling like a veil over my countenance,
Upon a door-step, upon the horse-block of hard wood outside,                     750
Upon the race-course, or enjoying picnics or jigs or a good game of baseball,
At he-festivals, with blackguard gibes, ironical license, bull-dances,[9] drinking,
laughter,
At the cider-mill tasting the sweets of the brown mash, sucking the juice through
a straw,
At apple-peelings wanting kisses for all the red fruit I find,
At musters, beach-parties, friendly bees,[1] huskings, house-raisings;            755
Where the mocking-bird sounds his delicious gurgles, cackles, screams, weeps,
Where the hay-rick stands in the barn-yard, where the dry-stalks are scatter'd,
where the brood-cow waits in the hovel,
Where the bull advances to do his masculine work, where the stud to the
mare, where the cock is treading the hen,
Where the heifers browse, where geese nip their food with short jerks,
Where sun-down shadows lengthen over the limitless and lonesome
prairie,                                              760
Where herds of buffalo make a crawling spread of the square miles far and
near,

8. Watertight compartment for lowering passengers
from a ship when emergency evacuation is required.
9. Rowdy backwoods dances for which, in the absence
of women, men took male partners.

1. Gathering where people work while socializing with
their neighbors. "Musters": any assemblage of people,
but particularly a gathering of military troops for drill.

Where the humming-bird shimmers, where the neck of the long-lived swan is
    curving and winding,
Where the laughing-gull scoots by the shore, where she laughs her near-human
    laugh,
Where bee-hives range on a gray bench in the garden half hid by the high
    weeds,
Where band-neck'd partridges roost in a ring on the ground with their heads
    out,                                                                    765
Where burial coaches enter the arch'd gates of a cemetery,
Where winter wolves bark amid wastes of snow and icicled trees,
Where the yellow-crown'd heron comes to the edge of the marsh at night and
    feeds upon small crabs,
Where the splash of swimmers and divers cools the warm noon,
Where the katy-did works her chromatic[2] reed on the walnut-tree over the
    well,                                                                   770
Through patches of citrons and cucumbers with silver-wired leaves,
Through the salt-lick or orange glade, or under conical firs,
Through the gymnasium, through the curtain'd saloon, through the office or
    public hall;
Pleas'd with the native and pleas'd with the foreign, pleas'd with the new and
    old,
Pleas'd with the homely woman as well as the handsome,                     775
Pleas'd with the quakeress as she puts off her bonnet and talks melodiously,
Pleas'd with the tune of the choir of the whitewash'd church,
Pleas'd with the earnest words of the sweating Methodist preacher, impress'd
    seriously at the camp-meeting;
Looking in at the shop-windows of Broadway the whole forenoon, flatting the
    flesh of my nose on the thick plate glass,
Wandering the same afternoon with my face turn'd up to the clouds, or down
    a lane or along the beach,                                             780
My right and left arms round the sides of two friends, and I in the middle;
Coming home with the silent and dark-cheek'd bush-boy, (behind me he rides
    at the drape of the day,)
Far from the settlements studying the print of animals' feet, or the moccasin
    print,
By the cot in the hospital reaching lemonade to a feverish patient,
Nigh the coffin'd corpse when all is still, examining with a candle;       785
Voyaging to every port to dicker and adventure,
Hurrying with the modern crowd as eager and fickle as any,
Hot toward one I hate, ready in my madness to knife him,
Solitary at midnight in my back yard, my thoughts gone from me a long while,
Walking the old hills of Judæa with the beautiful gentle God by my side,    790
Speeding through space, speeding through heaven and the stars,
Speeding amid the seven satellites[3] and the broad ring, and the diameter of
    eighty thousand miles,
Speeding with tail'd meteors, throwing fire-balls like the rest,
Carrying the crescent child that carries its own full mother in its belly,
Storming, enjoying, planning, loving, cautioning,                          795
Backing and filling, appearing and disappearing,
I tread day and night such roads.

---

2. Consisting of chords or harmonies based on non-        3. The seven then-known satellites (moons) of Saturn.
harmonic tones.

I visit the orchards of spheres and look at the product,
And look at quintillions ripen'd and look at quintillions green.

I fly those flights of a fluid and swallowing soul,                              800
My course runs below the soundings of plummets.

I help myself to material and immaterial,
No guard can shut me off, no law prevent me.

I anchor my ship for a little while only,
My messengers continually cruise away or bring their returns to me.          805

I go hunting polar furs and the seal, leaping chasms with a pike-pointed staff,
    clinging to topples of brittle and blue.[4]

I ascend to the foretruck,
I take my place late at night in the crow's-nest,
We sail the arctic sea, it is plenty light enough,
Through the clear atmosphere I stretch around on the wonderful beauty,      810
The enormous masses of ice pass me and I pass them, the scenery is plain in
    all directions,
The white-topt mountains show in the distance, I fling out my fancies toward
    them,
We are approaching some great battle-field in which we are soon to be
    engaged,
We pass the colossal outposts of the encampment, we pass with still feet and
    caution,
Or we are entering by the suburbs some vast and ruin'd city,                  815
The blocks and fallen architecture more than all the living cities of the globe.

I am a free companion, I bivouac by invading watchfires,
I turn the bridegroom out of bed and stay with the bride myself,
I tighten her all night to my thighs and lips.

My voice is the wife's voice, the screech by the rail of the stairs,          820
They fetch my man's body up dripping and drown'd.

I understand the large hearts of heroes,
The courage of present times and all times,
How the skipper saw the crowded and rudderless wreck of the steam-ship, and
    Death chasing it up and down the storm,
How he knuckled tight and gave not back an inch, and was faithful of days
    and faithful of nights,                                                   825
And chalk'd in large letters on a board, *Be of good cheer, we will not desert you;*
How he follow'd with them and tack'd with them three days and would not
    give it up,
How he saved the drifting company at last,
How the lank loose-gown'd women look'd when boated from the side of their
    prepared graves,
How the silent old-faced infants and the lifted sick, and the sharp-lipp'd unshaved
    men;                                                                      830

4. Toppled pieces of ice.

All this I swallow, it tastes good, I like it well, it becomes mine,
I am the man, I suffer'd, I was there.

The disdain and calmness of martyrs,
The mother of old, condemn'd for a witch, burnt with dry wood, her children
    gazing on,
The hounded slave that flags in the race, leans by the fence, blowing, cover'd
    with sweat,                                                                   835
The twinges that sting like needles his legs and neck, the murderous buckshot
    and the bullets,
All these I feel or am.

I am the hounded slave, I wince at the bite of the dogs,
Hell and despair are upon me, crack and again crack the marksmen,
I clutch the rails of the fence, my gore dribs, thinn'd with the ooze of my
    skin,⁵                                                                        840
I fall on the weeds and stones,
The riders spur their unwilling horses, haul close,
Taunt my dizzy ears and beat me violently over the head with whip-stocks.

Agonies are one of my changes of garments,
I do not ask the wounded person how he feels, I myself become the wounded
    person,                                                                       845
My hurts turn livid upon me as I lean on a cane and observe.

I am the mash'd fireman with breast-bone broken,
Tumbling walls buried me in their debris,
Heat and smoke I inspired, I heard the yelling shouts of my comrades,
I heard the distant click of their picks and shovels,                            850
They have clear'd the beams away, they tenderly lift me forth.

I lie in the night air in my red shirt, the pervading hush is for my sake,
Painless after all I lie exhausted but not so unhappy,
White and beautiful are the faces around me, the heads are bared of their
    fire-caps,
The kneeling crowd fades with the light of the torches.                          855

Distant and dead resuscitate,
They show as the dial or move as the hands of me, I am the clock myself.

I am an old artillerist, I tell of my fort's bombardment,
I am there again.

Again the long roll of the drummers,                                             860
Again the attacking cannon, mortars,
Again to my listening ears the cannon responsive.

I take part, I see and hear the whole,
The cries, curses, roar, the plaudits of well-aim'd shots,
The ambulanza slowly passing trailing its red drip,                              865

---

5. Dribbles down, diluted with sweat.

Workmen searching after damages, making indispensable repairs,
The fall of grenades through the rent roof, the fan-shaped explosion,
The whizz of limbs, heads, stone, wood, iron, high in the air.

Again gurgles the mouth of my dying general, he furiously waves with his
    hand,
He gasps through the clot *Mind not me—mind—the entrenchments.*      870

## 34

Now I tell what I knew in Texas in my early youth,
(I tell not the fall of Alamo,
Not one escaped to tell the fall of Alamo,[6]
The hundred and fifty are dumb yet at Alamo,)
'Tis the tale of the murder in cold blood of four hundred and twelve young
    men.                                                                       875

Retreating they had form'd in a hollow square with their baggage for breast-
    works,
Nine hundred lives out of the surrounding enemy's, nine times their number,
    was the price they took in advance,
Their colonel was wounded and their ammunition gone,
They treated for an honorable capitulation, receiv'd writing and seal, gave up
    their arms and march'd back prisoners of war.

They were the glory of the race of rangers,                                    880
Matchless with horse, rifle, song, supper, courtship,
Large, turbulent, generous, handsome, proud, and affectionate,
Bearded, sunburnt, drest in the free costume of hunters,
Not a single one over thirty years of age.

The second First-day morning they were brought out in squads and massacred,
    it was beautiful early summer,                                             885
The work commenced about five o'clock and was over by eight.

None obey'd the command to kneel,
Some made a mad and helpless rush, some stood stark and straight,
A few fell at once, shot in the temple or heart, the living and dead lay together,
The maim'd and mangled dug in the dirt, the new-comers saw them there,        890
Some half-kill'd attempted to crawl away,
These were despatch'd with bayonets or batter'd with the blunts of muskets,
A youth not seventeen years old seiz'd his assassin till two more came to
    release him,
The three were all torn and cover'd with the boy's blood.

At eleven o'clock began the burning of the bodies;                            895
That is the tale of the murder of the four hundred and twelve young men.

6. The fall of the Alamo during the Mexican War was already well established in the American conscious-ness. Whitman here celebrates a lesser-known but bloodier massacre, the murder of some four hundred "Texans" (most of them new emigrants from southern states) after they surrendered to the Mexicans near Gol-iad (now in Texas) in late March 1836, three weeks after the fall of the Alamo (now in San Antonio, Texas).

## 35

Would you hear of an old-time sea-fight?[7]
Would you learn who won by the light of the moon and stars?
List to the yarn, as my grandmother's father the sailor told it to me.

Our foe was no skulk in his ship I tell you, (said he,)                                    900
His was the surly English pluck, and there is no tougher or truer, and never
     was, and never will be;
Along the lower'd eve he came horribly raking us.

We closed with him, the yards entangled, the cannon touch'd,
My captain lash'd fast with his own hands.

We had receiv'd some eighteen pound shots under the water,                   905
On our lower-gun-deck two large pieces had burst at the first fire, killing all
     around and blowing up overhead.

Fighting at sun-down, fighting at dark,
Ten o'clock at night, the full moon well up, our leaks on the gain, and five
     feet of water reported,
The master-at-arms loosing the prisoners confined in the after-hold to give
     them a chance for themselves.

The transit to and from the magazine[8] is now stopt by the sentinels,        910
They see so many strange faces they do not know whom to trust.

Our frigate takes fire,
The other asks if we demand quarter?
If our colors are struck and the fighting done?

Now I laugh content, for I hear the voice of my little captain,                     915
We have not struck, he composedly cries, we have just begun our part of the
     fighting.

Only three guns are in use,
One is directed by the captain himself against the enemy's mainmast,
Two well serv'd with grape and canister[9] silence his musketry and clear his
     decks.

The tops[1] alone second the fire of this little battery, especially the main-
     top,                                                                                                       920
They hold out bravely during the whole of the action.

Not a moment's cease,
The leaks gain fast on the pumps, the fire eats toward the powder-magazine.

7. The famous Revolutionary sea battle on September 23, 1779, between the American *BonHomme Richard*, commanded by John Paul Jones, and the British *Serapis* off the coast of Yorkshire. A brilliant account of the battle, based on naval histories, is in Melville's *Israel Potter*, chaps. 19 and 20.

8. Storeroom for ammunition.
9. Grapeshot ("grape"), clusters of small iron balls, was packed inside a metal cylinder ("canister") and used to charge a cannon.
1. Platforms enclosing the heads of each mast (here, the sailors manning the tops).

One of the pumps has been shot away, it is generally thought we are sinking.

Serene stands the little captain,                                                      925
He is not hurried, his voice is neither high nor low,
His eyes give more light to us than our battle-lanterns.

Toward twelve there in the beams of the moon they surrender to us.


### 36

Stretch'd and still lies the midnight,
Two great hulls motionless on the breast of the darkness,                930
Our vessel riddled and slowly sinking, preparations to pass to the one we have
 conquer'd,


The captain on the quarter-deck coldly giving his orders through a counte-
 nance white as a sheet,
Near by the corpse of the child that serv'd in the cabin,
The dead face of an old salt with long white hair and carefully curl'd whiskers,
The flames spite of all that can be done flickering aloft and below,         935
The husky voices of the two or three officers yet fit for duty,
Formless stacks of bodies and bodies by themselves, dabs of flesh upon the
 masts and spars,
Cut of cordage, dangle of rigging, slight shock of the soothe of waves,
Black and impassive guns, litter of powder-parcels, strong scent,
A few large stars overhead, silent and mournful shining,                      940
Delicate sniffs of sea-breeze, smells of sedgy grass and fields by the shore,
 death-messages given in charge to survivors,
The hiss of the surgeon's knife, the gnawing teeth of his saw,
Wheeze, cluck, swash of falling blood, short wild scream, and long, dull,
 tapering groan,
These so, these irretrievable.


### 37

You laggards there on guard! look to your arms!                              945
In at the conquer'd doors they crowd! I am possess'd!
Embody all presences outlaw'd or suffering,
See myself in prison shaped like another man,
And feel the dull unintermitted pain.

For me the keepers of convicts shoulder their carbines and keep watch,     950
It is I let out in the morning and barr'd at night.

Not a mutineer walks handcuff'd to jail but I am handcuff'd to him and walk
 by his side,
(I am less the jolly one there, and more the silent one with sweat on my
 twitching lips.)

Not a youngster is taken for larceny but I go up too, and am tried and
 sentenced.

Not a cholera patient lies at the last gasp but I also lie at the last gasp,      955
My face is ash-color'd, my sinews gnarl, away from me people retreat.

Askers embody themselves in me and I am embodied in them,
I project my hat, sit shame-faced, and beg.

### 38

Enough! enough! enough!
Somehow I have been stunn'd. Stand back!                                          960
Give me a little time beyond my cuff'd head, slumbers, dreams, gaping,
I discover myself on the verge of a usual mistake.

That I could forget the mockers and insults!
That I could forget the trickling tears and the blows of the bludgeons and
      hammers!
That I could look with a separate look on my own crucifixion and bloody
      crowning.                                                                   965

I remember now,
I resume the overstaid fraction,
The grave of rock multiplies what has been confided to it, or to any graves,
Corpses rise, gashes heal, fastenings roll from me.

I troop forth replenish'd with supreme power, one of an average unending
      procession,                                                                970
Inland and sea-coast we go, and pass all boundary lines,
Our swift ordinances on their way over the whole earth,
The blossoms we wear in our hats the growth of thousands of years.

Eleves,[2] I salute you! come forward!
Continue your annotations, continue your questionings.                           975

### 39

The friendly and flowing savage, who is he?
Is he waiting for civilization, or past it and mastering it?

Is he some Southwesterner rais'd out-doors? is he Kanadian?
Is he from the Mississippi country? Iowa, Oregon, California?
The mountains? prairie-life, bush-life? or sailor from the sea?                  980

Wherever he goes men and women accept and desire him,
They desire he should like them, touch them, speak to them, stay with them.

Behavior lawless as snow-flakes, words simple as grass, uncomb'd head, laugh-
      ter, and naivetè,
Slow-stepping feet, common features, common modes and emanations,
They descend in new forms from the tips of his fingers,                          985

---

2. From the French for "students," but Whitman's use carries some of the sense of "disciples" or "acolytes" as well.

They are wafted with the odor of his body or breath, they fly out of the glance
    of his eyes.

40

Flaunt of the sunshine I need not your bask—lie over!
You light surfaces only, I force surfaces and depths also.

Earth! you seem to look for something at my hands,
Say, old top-knot,[3] what do you want?       990

Man or woman, I might tell how I like you, but cannot,
And might tell what it is in me and what it is in you, but cannot,
And might tell that pining I have, that pulse of my nights and days.

Behold, I do not give lectures or a little charity,
When I give I give myself.       995

You there, impotent, loose in the knees,
Open your scarf'd chops[4] till I blow grit within you,
Spread your palms and lift the flaps of your pockets,
I am not to be denied, I compel, I have stores plenty and to spare,
And any thing I have I bestow.       1000

I do not ask who you are, that is not important to me,
You can do nothing and be nothing but what I will infold you.

To cotton-field drudge or cleaner of privies I lean,
On his right cheek I put the family kiss,
And in my soul I swear I never will deny him.       1005

On women fit for conception I start bigger and nimbler babes,
(This day I am jetting the stuff of far more arrogant republics.)

To any one dying, thither I speed and twist the knob of the door,
Turn the bed-clothes toward the foot of the bed,
Let the physician and the priest go home.       1010

I seize the descending man and raise him with resistless will,
O despairer, here is my neck,
By God, you shall not go down! hang your whole weight upon me.

I dilate you with tremendous breath, I buoy you up,
Every room of the house do I fill with an arm'd force,       1015
Lovers of me, bafflers of graves.

Sleep—I and they keep guard all night,
Not doubt, not decease shall dare to lay finger upon you,
I have embraced you, and henceforth possess you to myself,
And when you rise in the morning you will find what I tell you is so.    1020

3. As Blodgett and Bradley say in their note, this "epithet was familiar in frontier humor as a comic, half-
affectionate term for an Indian, whose tuft of hair or
ornament on top of the head was characteristic of certain tribes."
4. With chops (jaws) tied up in a scarf, as one might
do for a toothache, earache, or other ailment. See
line 1069.

### 41

I am he bringing help for the sick as they pant on their backs,
And for strong upright men I bring yet more needed help.

I heard what was said of the universe,
Heard it and heard it of several thousand years;
It is middling well as far as it goes—but is that all?                              1025

Magnifying and applying come I,
Outbidding at the start the old cautious hucksters,[5]
Taking myself the exact dimensions of Jehovah,
Lithographing Kronos, Zeus his son, and Hercules his grandson,
Buying drafts of Osiris, Isis, Belus, Brahma, Buddha,                              1030
In my portfolio placing Manito loose, Allah on a leaf, the crucifix engraved,
With Odin and the hideous-faced Mexitli[6] and every idol and image,
Taking them all for what they are worth and not a cent more,
Admitting they were alive and did the work of their days,
(They bore mites as for unfledg'd birds who have now to rise and fly and sing
    for themselves,)                                                                1035
Accepting the rough deific sketches to fill out better in myself, bestowing them
    freely on each man and woman I see,
Discovering as much or more in a framer framing a house,
Putting higher claims for him there with his roll'd-up sleeves driving the mallet
    and chisel,
Not objecting to special revelations, considering a curl of smoke or a hair on
    the back of my hand just as curious as any revelation,
Lads ahold of fire-engines and hook-and-ladder ropes no less to me than the
    gods of the antique wars,                                                       1040
Minding their voices peal through the crash of destruction,
Their brawny limbs passing safe over charr'd laths, their white foreheads whole
    and unhurt out of the flames;
By the mechanic's wife with her babe at her nipple interceding for every person
    born,
Three scythes at harvest whizzing in a row from three lusty angels with shirts
    bagg'd out at their waists,
The snag-tooth'd hostler with red hair redeeming sins past and to come,        1045
Selling all he possesses, traveling on foot to fee lawyers for his brother and sit
    by him while he is tried for forgery;
What was strewn in the amplest strewing the square rod about me, and not
    filling the square rod then,
The bull and the bug never worshipp'd half enough,[7]
Dung and dirt more admirable than was dream'd,

---

5. I.e., gods or priests who made too little of the divinity in human beings.
6. An Aztec war god. Jehovah was the God of the Jews and Christians. Kronos or Cronus, in Greek mythology, was the Titan who ruled the universe until dethroned by Zeus, his son, the chief of the Olympian gods. Hercules, son of Zeus and the mortal Alcmene, won immortality by performing twelve supposedly impossible feats. Osiris was the Egyptian god who annually died and was reborn, symbolizing the fertility of nature. Isis was the Egyptian goddess of fertility and the sister and wife of Osiris. Belus was a legendary god-

king of Assyria. Brahma, in Hinduism, was the divine reality in the role of creator. Buddha was the Indian philosopher Gautama Siddhartha, founder of Buddhism. Manito was the nature god of the Algonquian Indians. Allah was the supreme being in the Moslem religion. Odin was the chief Norse god.
7. As Whitman implies, the bull and the bug had in fact been worshiped in earlier religions, the bull in several, the scarab beetle as an Egyptian symbol of the soul; but they had been worshiped wrongly, as supernatural objects.

The supernatural of no account, myself waiting my time to be one of the
    supremes,                                                              1050
The day getting ready for me when I shall do as much good as the best, and
    be as prodigious;
By my life-lumps![8] becoming already a creator,
Putting myself here and now to the ambush'd womb of the shadows.


42


A call in the midst of the crowd,
My own voice, orotund sweeping and final.                                 1055


Come my children,
Come my boys and girls, my women, household and intimates,
Now the performer launches his nerve, he has pass'd his prelude on the reeds
    within.


Easily written loose-finger'd chords—I feel the thrum of your climax and close.


My head slues round on my neck,                                          1060
Music rolls, but not from the organ,
Folks are around me, but they are no household of mine.


Ever the hard unsunk ground,
Ever the eaters and drinkers, ever the upward and downward sun, ever the air
    and the ceaseless tides,
Ever myself and my neighbors, refreshing, wicked, real,                   1065
Ever the old inexplicable query, ever that thorn'd thumb, that breath of itches
    and thirsts,
Ever the vexer's *hoot! hoot!* till we find where the sly one hides and bring
    him forth,
Ever love, ever the sobbing liquid of life,
Ever the bandage under the chin, ever the trestles[9] of death.


Here and there with dimes on the eyes[1] walking,                         1070
To feed the greed of the belly the brains liberally spooning,
Tickets buying, taking, selling, but in to the feast never once going,
Many sweating, ploughing, thrashing, and then the chaff for payment receiving,
A few idly owning, and they the wheat continually claiming.


This is the city and I am one of the citizens,                           1075
Whatever interests the rest interests me, politics, wars, markets, newspapers,
    schools,
The mayor and councils, banks, tariffs, steamships, factories, stocks, stores,
    real estate and personal estate.


The little plentiful manikins skipping around in collars and tail'd coats,
I am aware who they are, (they are positively not worms or fleas,)


8. A felicitously comic way of referring to spurts of se-         1. Coins were placed on eyelids to hold them closed
men, here used figuratively.                                      until burial.
9. Sawhorses or similar supports holding up a coffin.

I acknowledge the duplicates of myself, the weakest and shallowest is deathless
    with me,         1080
What I do and say the same waits for them,
Every thought that flounders in me the same flounders in them.

I know perfectly well my own egotism,
Know my omnivorous lines and must not write any less,
And would fetch you whoever you are flush with myself.     1085

Not words of routine this song of mine,
But abruptly to question, to leap beyond yet nearer bring;
This printed and bound book—but the printer and the printing-office boy?
The well-taken photographs—but your wife or friend close and solid in your
    arms?
The black ship mail'd with iron, her mighty guns in her turrets—but the pluck
    of the captain and engineers?     1090
In the houses the dishes and fare and furniture—but the host and hostess, and
    the look out of their eyes?
The sky up there—yet here or next door, or across the way?
The saints and sages in history—but you yourself?
Sermons, creeds, theology—but the fathomless human brain,
And what is reason? and what is love? and what is life?     1095

### 43

I do not despise you priests, all time, the world over,
My faith is the greatest of faiths and the least of faiths,
Enclosing worship ancient and modern and all between ancient and modern,
Believing I shall come again upon the earth after five thousand years,
Waiting responses from oracles, honoring the gods, saluting the sun,     1100
Making a fetich of the first rock or stump, powowing with sticks in the circle
    of obis. [2]
Helping the llama or brahmin as he trims the lamps of the idols,
Dancing yet through the streets in a phallic procession, rapt and austere in the
    woods a gymnosophist,
Drinking mead from the skull-cup, to Shastas and Vedas admirant, minding
    the Koran,
Walking the teokallis, spotted with gore from the stone and knife, beating the
    serpent-skin drum,     1105
Accepting the Gospels, [3] accepting him that was crucified, knowing assuredly
    that he is divine,
To the mass kneeling or the puritan's prayer rising, or sitting patiently in a
    pew,
Ranting and frothing in my insane crisis, or waiting dead-like till my spirit
    arouses me,

2. Witch doctors, either in Africa or among blacks in the New World.
3. *Llama* is Whitman's spelling for lama, a Buddhist monk of Tibet or Mongolia. A brahmin here is also a Buddhist priest. Gymnosophists were members of an ancient Hindu ascetic sect, thought to have forgone clothing, as the name ("naked philosophers") implies. The other worshipers include old Teutonic drinkers of mead (an alcoholic beverage made of fermented honey), admiring or wondering readers of the sastras (or shastras or shasters, books of Hindu law) or of the Vedas (the oldest sacred writings of Hinduism), those attentive to the Koran (the sacred book of Islam, containing Allah's revelations to Mohammed), worshipers walking the teokallis (an ancient Central American temple built on a pyramidal mound), and believers in the New Testament Gospels.

Looking forth on pavement and land, or outside of pavement and land,
Belonging to the winders of the circuit of circuits.                1110

One of that centripetal and centrifugal gang I turn and talk like a man leaving
    charges before a journey.

Down-hearted doubters dull and excluded,
Frivolous, sullen, moping, angry, affected, dishearten'd, atheistical,
I know every one of you, I know the sea of torment, doubt, despair and
    unbelief.

How the flukes[4] splash!                1115
How they contort rapid as lightning, with spasms and spouts of blood!

Be at peace bloody flukes of doubters and sullen mopers,
I take my place among you as much as among any,
The past is the push of you, me, all, precisely the same,
And what is yet untried and afterward is for you, me, all, precisely the
    same.                1120

I do not know what is untried and afterward,
But I know it will in its turn prove sufficient, and cannot fail.

Each who passes is consider'd, each who stops is consider'd, not a single one
    can it fail.

It cannot fail the young man who died and was buried,
Nor the young woman who died and was put by his side,                1125
Nor the little child that peep'd in at the door, and then drew back and was
    never seen again,
Nor the old man who has lived without purpose, and feels it with bitterness
    worse than gall,
Nor him in the poor house tubercled by rum and the bad disorder,
Nor the numberless slaughter'd and wreck'd, nor the brutish koboo[5] call'd the
    ordure of humanity,
Nor the sacs merely floating with open mouths for food to slip in,                1130
Nor any thing in the earth, or down in the oldest graves of the earth,
Nor any thing in the myriads of spheres, nor the myriads of myriads that
    inhabit them,
Nor the present, nor the least wisp that is known.

44

It is time to explain myself—let us stand up.

What is known I strip away,                1135
I launch all men and women forward with me into the Unknown.

The clock indicates the moment—but what does eternity indicate?

---

4. The flat parts on either side of a whale's tail; here    5. Native of Sumatra.
used figuratively.

We have thus far exhausted trillions of winters and summers,
There are trillions ahead, and trillions ahead of them.

Births have brought us richness and variety,                                    1140
And other births will bring us richness and variety.

I do not call one greater and one smaller,
That which fills its period and place is equal to any.

Were mankind murderous or jealous upon you, my brother, my sister?
I am sorry for you, they are not murderous or jealous upon me,                  1145
All has been gentle with me, I keep no account with lamentation,
(What have I to do with lamentation?)

I am an acme of things accomplish'd, and I an encloser of things to be.

My feet strike an apex of the apices[6] of the stairs,
On every step bunches of ages, and larger bunches between the steps,           1150
All below duly travel'd, and still I mount and mount.

Rise after rise bow the phantoms behind me,
Afar down I see the huge first Nothing, I know I was even there,
I waited unseen and always, and slept through the lethargic mist,
And took my time, and took no hurt from the fetid carbon.[7]                    1155

Long I was hugg'd close—long and long.

Immense have been the preparations for me,
Faithful and friendly the arms that have help'd me.

Cycles[8] ferried my cradle, rowing and rowing like cheerful boatmen,
For room to me stars kept aside in their own rings,                            1160
They sent influences to look after what was to hold me.

Before I was born out of my mother generations guided me,
My embryo has never been torpid, nothing could overlay it.

For it the nebula cohered to an orb,
The long slow strata piled to rest it on,                                       1165
Vast vegetables gave it sustenance,
Monstrous sauroids transported it in their mouths and deposited it with care.

All forces have been steadily employ'd to complete and delight me,
Now on this spot I stand with my robust soul.


                                     45

O span of youth! ever-push'd elasticity!                                        1170
O manhood, balanced, florid and full.

6. The highest points (variant plural of *apex*).          probably ages far earlier than the period of the "mon-
7. Whitman knew a good deal about geology and pre-          strous sauroids" (line 1167).
Darwinian theories of evolution. Here the periods of       8. Centuries.
lethargic mist and fetid carbon are prehuman ages,

My lovers suffocate me,
Crowding my lips, thick in the pores of my skin,
Jostling me through streets and public halls, coming naked to me at night,
Crying by day *Ahoy!* from the rocks of the river, swinging and chirping over
    my head, 1175
Calling my name from flower-beds, vines, tangled underbrush,
Lighting on every moment of my life,
Bussing[9] my body with soft balsamic busses,
Noiselessly passing handfuls out of their hearts and giving them to be mine.

Old age superbly rising! O welcome, ineffable grace of dying days! 1180

Every condition promulges[1] not only itself, it promulges what grows after and
    out of itself,
And the dark hush promulges as much as any.

I open my scuttle at night and see the far-sprinkled systems,
And all I see multiplied as high as I can cipher edge but the rim of the farther
    systems.

Wider and wider they spread, expanding, always expanding, 1185
Outward and outward and forever outward.

My sun has his sun and round him obediently wheels,
He joins with his partners a group of superior circuit,
And greater sets follow, making specks of the greatest inside them.

There is no stoppage and never can be stoppage, 1190
If I, you, and the worlds, and all beneath or upon their surfaces, were this
    moment reduced back to a pallid float,[2] it would not avail in the long run,
We should surely bring up again where we now stand,
And surely go as much farther, and then farther and farther.

A few quadrillions of eras, a few octillions of cubic leagues, do not hazard[3] the
    span or make it impatient,
They are but parts, any thing is but a part. 1195

See ever so far, there is limitless space outside of that,
Count ever so much, there is limitless time around that.

My rendezvous is appointed, it is certain,
The Lord will be there and wait till I come on perfect terms,
The great Camerado, the lover true for whom I pine will be there. 1200

### 46

I know I have the best of time and space, and was never measured and never
    will be measured.

9. Kissing.
1. Promulgates, officially announces.
2. That period before the solar system had defined

itself.
3. Imperil, make hazardous.

I tramp a perpetual journey, (come listen all!)
My signs are a rain-proof coat, good shoes, and a staff cut from the woods,
No friend of mine takes his ease in my chair,
I have no chair, no church, no philosophy,                                      1205
I lead no man to a dinner-table, library, exchange,[4]
But each man and each woman of you I lead upon a knoll,
My left hand hooking you round the waist,
My right hand pointing to landscapes of continents and the public road.

Not I, not any one else can travel that road for you,                           1210
You must travel it for yourself.

It is not far, it is within reach,
Perhaps you have been on it since you were born and did not know,
Perhaps it is everywhere on water and on land.

Shoulder your duds dear son, and I will mine, and let us hasten forth,          1215
Wonderful cities and free nations we shall fetch as we go.

If you tire, give me both burdens, and rest the chuff[5] of your hand on my hip,
And in due time you shall repay the same service to me,
For after we start we never lie by again.

This day before dawn I ascended a hill and look'd at the crowded heaven,        1220
And I said to my spirit *When we become the enfolders of those orbs, and the
   pleasure and knowledge of every thing in them, shall we be fill'd and satisfied then?*
And my spirit said *No, we but level that lift to pass and continue beyond.*

You are also asking me questions and I hear you,
I answer that I cannot answer, you must find out for yourself.

Sit a while dear son,                                                           1225
Here are biscuits to eat and here is milk to drink,
But as soon as you sleep and renew yourself in sweet clothes, I kiss you with a
   good-by kiss and open the gate for your egress hence.

Long enough have you dream'd contemptible dreams,
Now I wash the gum from your eyes,
You must habit yourself to the dazzle of the light and of every moment of
   your life.                                                                   1230

Long have you timidly waded holding a plank by the shore,
Now I will you to be a bold swimmer,
To jump off in the midst of the sea, rise again, nod to me, shout, and laugh-
   ingly dash with your hair.

---

4. Stock exchange.                          5. The meaty part of the palm.

## 47

I am the teacher of athletes,
He that by me spreads a wider breast than my own proves the width of my
    own,                                                                    1235
He most honors my style who learns under it to destroy the teacher.

The boy I love, the same becomes a man not through derived power, but in
    his own right,
Wicked rather than virtuous out of conformity or fear,
Fond of his sweetheart, relishing well his steak,
Unrequited love or a slight cutting him worse than sharp steel cuts,        1240
First-rate to ride, to fight, to hit the bull's eye, to sail a skiff, to sing a song or
    play on the banjo,
Preferring scars and the beard and faces pitted with small-pox over all latherers,
And those well-tann'd to those that keep out of the sun.

I teach straying from me, yet who can stray from me?
I follow you whoever you are from the present hour,                         1245
My words itch at your ears till you understand them.

I do not say these things for a dollar or to fill up the time while I wait for a boat,
(It is you talking just as much as myself, I act as the tongue of you,
Tied in your mouth, in mine it begins to be loosen'd.)

I swear I will never again mention love or death inside a house,            1250
And I swear I will never translate myself at all, only to him or her who privately
    stays with me in the open air.

If you would understand me go to the heights or water-shore,
The nearest gnat is an explanation, and a drop or motion of waves a key,
The maul, the oar, the hand-saw, second my words.

No shutter'd room or school can commune with me,                           1255
But roughs and little children better than they.

The young mechanic is closest to me, he knows me well,
The woodman that takes his axe and jug with him shall take me with him
    all day,
The farm-boy ploughing in the field feels good at the sound of my voice,
In vessels that sail my words sail, I go with fishermen and seamen and love
    them.                                                                    1260

The soldier camp'd or upon the march is mine,
On the night ere the pending battle many seek me, and I do not fail them,
On that solemn night (it may be their last) those that know me seek me.

My face rubs to the hunter's face when he lies down alone in his blanket,
The driver thinking of me does not mind the jolt of his wagon,             1265
The young mother and old mother comprehend me,
The girl and the wife rest the needle a moment and forget where they are,
They and all would resume what I have told them.

## 48

I have said that the soul is not more than the body,
And I have said that the body is not more than the soul,                    1270
And nothing, not God, is greater to one than one's self is,
And whoever walks a furlong without sympathy walks to his own funeral drest
    in his shroud,
And I or you pocketless of a dime may purchase the pick of the earth,
And to glance with an eye or show a bean in its pod confounds the learning of
    all times,
And there is no trade or employment but the young man following it may
    become a hero,                                                1275
And there is no object so soft but it makes a hub for the wheel'd universe,
And I say to any man or woman, Let your soul stand cool and composed
    before a million universes.

And I say to mankind, Be not curious about God,
For I who am curious about each am not curious about God,
(No array of terms can say how much I am at peace about God and about
    death.)                                                      1280

I hear and behold God in every object, yet understand God not in the least,
Nor do I understand who there can be more wonderful than myself.

Why should I wish to see God better than this day?
I see something of God each hour of the twenty-four, and each moment then,
In the faces of men and women I see God, and in my own face in the
    glass,                                                        1285
I find letters from God dropt in the street, and every one is sign'd by God's
    name,
and I leave them where they are, for I know that wheresoe'er I go,
Others will punctually come for ever and ever.

## 49

And as to you Death, and you bitter hug of mortality, it is idle to try to alarm
    me.

To his work without flinching the accoucheur[6] comes,                      1290
I see the elder-hand pressing receiving supporting,
I recline by the sills of the exquisite flexible doors,
And mark the outlet, and mark the relief and escape.

And as to you Corpse I think you are good manure, but that does not offend
    me,
I smell the white roses sweet-scented and growing,                          1295
I reach to the leafy lips, I reach to the polish'd breasts of melons.

And as to you Life I reckon you are the leavings of many deaths,
(No doubt I have died myself ten thousand times before.)

---

6. Midwife.

I hear you whispering there O stars of heaven,
O suns—O grass of graves—O perpetual transfers and promotions,                1300
If you do not say any thing how can I say any thing?

Of the turbid pool that lies in the autumn forest,
Of the moon that descends the steeps of the soughing twilight,
Toss, sparkles of day and dusk—toss on the black stems that decay in the muck,
Toss to the moaning gibberish of the dry limbs.                               1305

I ascend from the moon, I ascend from the night,
I perceive that the ghastly glimmer is noonday sunbeams reflected,
And debouch[7] to the steady and central from the offspring great or small.

### 50

There is that in me—I do not know what it is—but I know it is in me.

Wrench'd and sweaty—calm and cool then my body becomes, I sleep —I sleep
     long.                                                                    1310

I do not know it—it is without name—it is a word unsaid,
It is not in any dictionary, utterance, symbol.

Something it swings on more than the earth I swing on,
To it the creation is the friend whose embracing awakes me.

Perhaps I might tell more. Outlines! I plead for my brothers and sisters.     1315

Do you see O my brothers and sisters?
It is not chaos or death—it is form, union, plan—it is eternal life—it is Happiness.

### 51

The past and present wilt—I have fill'd them, emptied them,
And proceed to fill my next fold of the future.

Listener up there! what have you to confide to me?                            1320
Look in my face while I snuff the sidle[8] of evening,
(Talk honestly, no one else hears you, and I stay only a minute longer.)

Do I contradict myself?
Very well then I contradict myself,
(I am large, I contain multitudes.)                                          1325

I concentrate toward them that are nigh, I wait on the door-slab.

Who has done his day's work? who will soonest be through with his supper?

7. Pour forth.
8. To snuff is to put out, as in extinguishing a candle;

here the light is the hesitant last light of day, sidling or
moving along edgeways.

Who wishes to walk with me?

Will you speak before I am gone? will you prove already too late?


52

The spotted hawk swoops by and accuses me, he complains of my gab and
    my loitering.                                                            1330

I too am not a bit tamed, I too am untranslatable,
I sound my barbaric yawp over the roofs of the world.

The last scud of day⁹ holds back for me,
It flings my likeness after the rest and true as any on the shadow'd wilds,
It coaxes me to the vapor and the dusk.                                      1335

I depart as air, I shake my white locks at the runaway sun,
I effuse my flesh in eddies, and drift it in lacy jags.

I bequeath myself to the dirt to grow from the grass I love,
If you want me again look for me under your boot-soles.

You will hardly know who I am or what I mean,                                1340
But I shall be good health to you nevertheless,
And filter and fibre your blood.

Failing to fetch me at first keep encouraged,
Missing me one place search another,
I stop somewhere waiting for you.                                            1345

                                                                   1855, 1881


# Letter to Ralph Waldo Emerson¹

## [Whitman's 1856 Manifesto]

                                                    BROOKLYN, AUGUST, 1856.
Here are thirty-two Poems, which I send you, dear Friend and Master, not
having found how I could satisfy myself with sending any usual acknowledgment of your letter. The first edition, on which you mailed me that till now

---

9. Wind-driven clouds, or merely the last rays of the
sun.
1. Having already in October 1855 "allowed" the *New
York Tribune* to print Emerson's 21 July 1855 letter to
him (after proudly carrying it around with him since
he received it), Whitman embellished the spine of the
1856 edition of *Leaves of Grass* with these words lettered in gold on a glued-on backstrip "I Greet You at
the / Beginning of A / Great Career / R. W. Emerson." In the back of the 1856 edition Whitman reprinted Emerson's letter in full (see p. 546) and followed it by this "Letter to Ralph Waldo Emerson"
dated Brooklyn, August 1856. The fuss about the in-
delicacy (or one might say hilariously self-conscious

vulgarity) of Whitman's unauthorized use of Emerson's letter has obscured the extraordinary virtues of
this 1856 "reply," which Sculley Bradley and Harold
W. Blodgett call a "preface" to the 1856 edition, despite its placement at the back of the volume.
    In *The New Walt Whitman Handbook*, Gay Wilson
Allen discusses the nature of the twenty new poems
Whitman added and his new focus on carrying on a
campaign against "asceticism and puritanism." Having
omitted the 1855 preface, Whitman was in the process
of turning some of it into poems. He added what Allen
calls "new sex poems" and, most notably, *Sun-Down
Poem*, later called *Crossing Brooklyn Ferry*.

unanswered letter, was twelve poems—I printed a thousand copies, and they readily sold; these thirty-two Poems I stereotype,[2] to print several thousand copies of. I much enjoy making poems. Other work I have set for myself to do, to meet people and The States face to face, to confront them with an American rude tongue; but the work of my life is making poems. I keep on till I make a hundred, and then several hundred—perhaps a thousand. The way is clear to me. A few years, and the average annual call for my Poems is ten or twenty thousand copies—more, quite likely. Why should I hurry or compromise? In poems or in speeches I say the word or two that has got to be said, adhere to the body, step with the countless common footsteps, and remind every man and woman of something.

Master, I am a man who has perfect faith. Master, we have not come through centuries, caste, heroisms, fables, to halt in this land today. Or I think it is to collect a ten-fold impetus that any halt is made. As nature, inexorable, onward, resistless, impassive amid the threats and screams of disputants, so America. Let all defer. Let all attend respectfully the leisure of These States, their politics, poems, literature, manners, and their free-handed modes of training their own offspring. Their own comes, just matured, certain, numerous and capable enough, with egotistical tongues, with sinewed wrists, seizing openly what belongs to them. They resume Personality, too long left out of mind. Their shadows are projected in employments, in books, in the cities, in trade; their feet are on the flights of the steps of the Capitol; they dilate, a large brawnier, more candid, more democratic, lawless, positive native to The States, sweet-bodied, completer, dauntless, flowing, masterful, beard-faced, new race of men.

Swiftly, on limitless foundations, the United States too are founding a literature. It is all as well done, in my opinion, as could be practicable. Each element here is in condition. Every day I go among the people of Manhattan Island, Brooklyn, and other cities, and among the young men, to discover the spirit of them, and to refresh myself. These are to be attended to; I am myself more drawn here than to those authors, publishers, importations, reprints, and so forth. I pass coolly through those, understanding them perfectly well, and that they do the indispensable service, outside of men like me, which nothing else could do. In poems, the young men of The States shall be represented, for they out-rival the best of the rest of the earth.

The lists of ready-made literature which America inherits by the mighty inheritance of the English language—all the rich repertoire of traditions, poems, histories, metaphysics, plays, classics, translations, have made, and still continue, magnificent preparations for that other plainly significant literature, to be our own, to be electric, fresh, lusty, to express the full-sized body, male and female—to give the modern meanings of things, to grow up beautiful, lasting, commensurate with America, with all the passions of home, with the inimitable sympathies of having been boys and girls together, and of parents who were with our parents.

What else can happen The States, even in their own despite? That huge English flow, so sweet, so undeniable, has done incalculable good here, and is to be spoken of for its own sake with generous praise and with gratitude. Yet

---

2. A printer's term before it became metaphorical, to stereotype was to make a mold of standing type, which could then be reused, while later printings could be made from the stereotyped plates. To go to the cost of stereotyping was evidence of optimism that future printings would be needed.

the price The States have had to lie under for the same has not been a small price. Payment prevails; a nation can never take the issues of the needs of other nations for nothing. America, grandest of lands in the theory of its politics, in popular reading, in hospitality, breadth, animal beauty, cities, ships, machines, money, credit, collapses quick as lightning at the repeated, admonishing, stern words. Where are any mental expressions from you, beyond what you have copied or stolen? Where the born throngs of poets, literats, orators, you promised? Will you but tag after other nations? They struggled long for their literature, painfully working their way, some with deficient languages, some with priest-craft, some in the endeavor just to live—yet achieved for their times, works, poems, perhaps the only solid consolation left to them through ages afterward of shame and decay. You are young, have the perfectest of dialects, a free press, a free government, the world forwarding its best to be with you. As justice has been strictly done to you, from this hour do strict justice to yourself. Strangle the singers who will not sing you loud and strong. Open the doors of The West. Call for new great masters to comprehend new arts, new perfections, new wants. Submit to the most robust bard till he remedy your barrenness. Then you will not need to adopt the heirs of others; you will have true heirs, begotten of yourself, blooded with your own blood.

With composure I see such propositions, seeing more and more every day of the answers that serve. Expressions do not yet serve, for sufficient reasons; but that is getting ready, beyond what the earth has hitherto known, to take home the expressions when they come, and to identify them with the populace of The States, which is the schooling cheaply procured by any outlay any number of years. Such schooling The States extract from the swarms of reprints, and from the current authors and editors. Such service and extract are done after enormous, reckless, free modes, characteristic of The States. Here are to be attained results never elsewhere thought possible; the modes are very grand too. The instincts of the American people are all perfect, and tend to make heroes. It is a rare thing in a man here to understand The States.

All current nourishments to literature serve. Of authors and editors I do not know how many there are in The States, but there are thousands, each one building his or her step to the stairs by which giants shall mount. Of the twenty-four modern mammoth two-double, three-double, and four-double cylinder presses now in the world, printing by steam, twenty-one of them are in These States. The twelve thousand large and small shops for dispensing books and newspapers—the same number of public libraries, any one of which has all the reading wanted to equip a man or woman for American reading—the three thousand different newspapers, the nutriment of the imperfect ones coming in just as usefully as any—the story papers, various, full of strong-flavored romances, widely circulated—the one cent and two-cent journals—the political ones, no matter what side—the weeklies in the country—the sporting and pictorial papers—the monthly magazines, with plentiful imported feed—the sentimental novels, numberless copies of them—the low-priced flaring tales, adventures, biographies—all are prophetic; all waft rapidly on. I see that they swell wide, for reasons. I am not troubled at the movement of them, but greatly pleased.[3] I see plying shuttles, the active ephemeral myriads of books also, faithfully weaving the garments of a generation of men, and a

3. Contrast Thoreau's disdain of "little reading" in *Walden, Reading* (p. 839).

generation of women, they do not perceive or know. What a progress popular reading and writing has made in fifty years! What a progress fifty years hence! The time is at hand when inherent literature will be a main part of These States, as general and real as steam-power, iron, corn, beef, fish. First-rate American persons are to be supplied. Our perennial materials for fresh thoughts, histories, poems, music, orations, religions, recitations, amusements, will then not be disregarded, any more than our perennial fields, mines, rivers, seas. Certain things are established, and are immovable; in those things millions of years stand justified. The mothers and fathers of whom modern centuries have come, have not existed for nothing; they too had brains and hearts. Of course all literature, in all nations and years, will share marked attributes in common, as we all, of all ages, share the common human attributes. America is to be kept coarse and broad. What is to be done is to withdraw from precedents, and be directed to men and women—also to The States in their federalness; for the union of the parts of the body is not more necessary to their life than the union of These States is to their life.

A profound person can easily know more of the people than they know of themselves. Always waiting untold in the souls of the armies of common people, is stuff better than anything that can possibly appear in the leadership of the same. That gives final verdicts. In every department of These States, he who travels with a coterie, or with selected persons, or with imitators, or with infidels, or with the owners of slaves, or with that which is ashamed of the body of a man, or with that which is ashamed of the body of a woman, or with any thing less than the bravest and the openest, travels straight for the slopes of dissolution. The genius of all foreign literature is clipped and cut small, compared to our genius, and is essentially insulting to our usages, and to the organic compacts of These States. Old forms, old poems, majestic and proper in their own lands here in this land are exiles; the air here is very strong. Much that stands well and has a little enough place provided for it in the small scales of European kingdoms, empires, and the like, here stands haggard, dwarfed, ludicrous, or has no place little enough provided for it. Authorities, poems, models, laws, names, imported into America, are useful to America today to destroy them, and so move disencumbered to great works, great days.

Just so long, in our country or any country, as no revolutionists advance, and are backed by the people, sweeping off the swarms of routine representatives, officers in power, book-makers, teachers, ecclesiastics; politicians, just so long, I perceive, do they who are in power fairly represent that country, and remain of use, probably of very great use. To supersede them, when it is the pleasure of These States, full provision is made; and I say the time has arrived to use it with a strong hand. Here also the souls of the armies have not only overtaken the souls of the officers, but passed on, and left the souls of the officers behind out of sight many weeks' journey; and the souls of the armies now go en-masse without officers. Here also formulas, glosses, blanks, minutiæ, are choking the throats of the spokesmen to death. Those things most listened for, certainly those are the things least said. There is not a single History of the World. There is not one of America, or of the organic compacts of These States, or of Washington, or of Jefferson, nor of Language, nor any Dictionary of the English Language. There is no great author; every one has demeaned himself to some etiquette or some impotence. There is no manhood or life-power in poems; there are shoats and geldings more like. Or literature will be dressed up, a fine gentleman, distasteful to our instincts, foreign to our soil. Its neck bends right and left wherever it goes. Its costumes and jewelry prove how little it knows Nature. Its flesh is soft; it shows less and less of the indefinable hard something that is Nature. Where is any thing but the shaved Nature of synods and schools? Where is a savage and luxuriant man? Where is an overseer? In lives, in poems, in codes of law, in Congress, in tuitions, theatres, conversations, argumentations, not a single head lifts itself clean out, with proof that it is their master, and has subordinated them to itself, and is ready to try their superiors. None believes in These States, boldly illustrating them in himself. Not a man faces round at the rest with terrible negative voice, refusing all terms to be bought off from his own eye-sight, or from the soul that he is, or from friendship, or from the body that he is, or from the soil and sea. To creeds, literature, art, the army, the navy, the executive, life is hardly proposed, but the sick and dying are proposed to cure the sick and dying. The churches are one vast lie; the people do not believe them, and they do not believe themselves; the priests are continually telling what they know well enough is not so, and keeping back what they know is so. The spectacle is a pitiful one. I think there can never be again upon the festive earth more bad-disordered persons deliberately taking seats, as of late in These States, at the heads of the public tables—such corpses' eyes for judges—such a rascal and thief in the Presidency.[4]

Up to the present, as helps best, the people, like a lot of large boys, have no determined tastes, are quite unaware of the grandeur of themselves, and of their destiny, and of their immense strides—accept with voracity whatever is presented them in novels, histories, newspapers, poems, schools, lectures, every thing. Pretty soon, through these and other means, their development makes the fibre that is capable of itself, and will assume determined tastes. The young men will be clear what they want, and will have it. They will follow none except him whose spirit leads them in the like spirit with themselves. Any such man will be welcome as the flowers of May. Others will be put out without ceremony. How much is there anyhow, to the young men of These States, in a parcel of helpless dandies, who can neither fight, work, shoot, ride, run, command—some of them devout, some quite insane, some castrated—all second-hand, or third, fourth, or fifth hand—waited upon by waiters, putting not this land first, but always other lands first, talking of art, doing the most ridiculous things for fear of being called ridiculous, smirking and skipping along, continually taking off their hats—no one behaving, dressing, writing, talking, loving, out of any natural and manly tastes of his own, but each one looking cautiously to see how the rest behave, dress, write, talk, love—pressing the noses of dead books upon themselves and upon their country—favoring no poets, philosophs, literats here, but dog-like danglers at the heels of the poets, philosophs, literats of enemies' lands—favoring mental expressions, models of gentlemen and ladies, social habitudes in These States, to grow up in sneaking defiance of the popular substratums of The States? Of course they and the likes of them can never justify the strong poems of America. Of course no feed of theirs is to stop and be made welcome to muscle the bodies, male and female, for Manhattan Island, Brooklyn, Boston, Worcester, Hartford, Portland, Montreal, Detroit, Buffalo, Cleaveland, Mil-

---

4. The proslavery sympathizer Franklin Pierce (president 1853–57).

waukee, St. Louis, Indianapolis, Chicago, Cincinnati, Iowa City, Philadelphia, Baltimore, Raleigh, Savannah, Charleston, Mobile, New Orleans, Galveston, Brownsville, San Francisco, Havana, and a thousand equal cities, present and to come. Of course what they and the likes of them have been used for, draws toward its close, after which they will all be discharged, and not one of them will ever be heard of any more.

America, having duly conceived, bears out of herself offspring of her own to do the workmanship wanted. To freedom, to strength, to poems, to personal greatness, it is never permitted to rest, not a generation or part of a generation. To be ripe beyond further increase is to prepare to die. The architects of These States laid their foundations, and passed to further spheres. What they laid is a work done; as much more remains. Now are needed other architects, whose duty is not less difficult, but perhaps more difficult. Each age forever needs architects. America is not finished, perhaps never will be; now America is a divine true sketch. There are Thirty-Two States sketched—the population thirty millions. In a few years there will be Fifty States. Again in a few years there will be A Hundred States, the population hundreds of millions, the freshest and freest of men. Of course such men stand to nothing less than the freshest and freest expression.

Poets here, literats here, are to rest on organic different bases from other countries; not a class set apart, circling only in the circle of themselves, modest and pretty, desperately scratching for rhymes, pallid with white paper, shut off, aware of the old pictures and traditions of the race, but unaware of the actual race around them—not breeding in and in among each other till they all have the scrofula. Lands of ensemble, bards of ensemble! Walking freely out from the old traditions, as our politics has walked out, American poets and literats recognize nothing behind them superior to what is present with them—recognize with joy the sturdy living forms of men and women of These States, the divinity of sex, the perfect eligibility of the female with the male, all The States, liberty and equality, real articles, the different trades, mechanics, the young fellows of Manhattan Island, customs, instincts, slang, Wisconsin, Georgia, the noble Southern heart, the hot blood, the spirit that will be nothing less than master, the filibuster spirit, the Western man, native-born perceptions, the eye for forms, the perfect models of made things, the wild smack of freedom, California, money, electric-telegraphs, free-trade, iron and the iron mines—recognize without demur those splendid resistless black poems, the steam-ships of the sea-board states, and those other resistless splendid poems, the locomotives, followed through the interior states by trains of railroad cars.

A word remains to be said, as of one ever present, not yet permitted to be acknowledged, discarded or made dumb by literature, and the results apparent. To the lack of an avowed, empowered, unabashed development of sex, (the only salvation for the same,) and to the fact of speakers and writers fraudulently assuming as always dead what every one knows to be always alive, is attributable the remarkable non-personality and indistinctness of modern productions in books, art, talk; also that in the scanned lives of men and women most of them appear to have been for some time past of the neuter gender; and also the stinging fact that in orthodox society today, if the dresses were changed, the men might easily pass for women and the women for men.

Infidelism usurps most with fœtid polite face; among the rest infidelism about sex. By silence or obedience the pens of savans, poets, historians, biographers, and the rest, have long connived at the filthy law, and books enslaved to it, that what makes the manhood of a man, that sex, womanhood, maternity, desires, lusty animations, organs, acts, are unmentionable and to be ashamed of, to be driven to skulk out of literature with whatever belongs to them. This filthy law has to be repealed—it stands in the way of great reforms. Of women just as much as men, it is the interest that there should not be infidelism about sex, but perfect faith. Women in These States approach the day of that organic equality with men, without which, I see, men cannot have organic equality among themselves. This empty dish, gallantry, will then be filled with something. This tepid wash, this diluted deferential love, as in songs, fictions, and so forth, is enough to make a man vomit; as to manly friendship, everywhere observed in The States, there is not the first breath of it to be observed in print. I say that the body of a man or woman, the main matter, is so far quite unexpressed in poems; but that the body is to be expressed, and sex is. Of bards for These States, if it come to a question, it is whether they shall celebrate in poems the eternal decency of the amativeness of Nature, the motherhood of all, or whether they shall be the bards of the fashionable delusion of the inherent nastiness of sex, and of the feeble and querulous modesty of deprivation. This is important in poems, because the whole of the other expressions of a nation are but flanges out of its great poems. To me, henceforth, that theory of any thing, no matter what, stagnates in its vitals, cowardly and rotten, while it cannot publicly accept, and publicly name, with specific words, the things on which all existence, all souls, all realization, all decency, all health, all that is worth being here for, all of woman and of man, all beauty, all purity, all sweetness, all friendship, all strength, all life, all immortality depend. The courageous soul, for a year or two to come, may be proved by faith in sex, and by disdaining concessions.

To poets and literats—to every woman and man, today or any day, the conditions of the present, needs, dangers, prejudices, and the like, are the perfect conditions on which we are here, and the conditions for wording the future with undissuadable words. These States, receivers of the stamina of past ages and lands, initiate the outlines of repayment a thousand fold. They fetch the American great masters, waited for by old words and new, who accept evil as well as good, ignorance as well as erudition, black as soon as white, foreign-born materials as well as home-born, reject none, force discrepancies into range, surround the whole, concentrate them on present periods and places, show the application to each and any one's body and soul, and show the true use of precedents. Always America will be agitated and turbulent. This day it is taking shape, not to be less so, but to be more so, stormily, capriciously, on native principles, with such vast proportions of parts! As for me, I love screaming, wrestling, boiling-hot days.

Of course, we shall have a national character, an identity. As it ought to be, and as soon as it ought to be, it will be. That, with much else, takes care of itself, is a result, and the cause of greater results. With Ohio, Illinois, Missouri, Oregon—with the states around the Mexican sea—with cheerfully welcomed immigrants form Europe, Asia, Africa—with Connecticut, Vermont, New Hampshire, Rhode Island—with all varied interests, facts, beliefs, parties, genesis—there is being fused a determined character, fit for the broadest use for the freewomen and freemen of The States, accomplished and to be

accomplished, without any exception whatever—each indeed free, each idiomatic, as becomes live states and men, but each adhering to one enclosing
general form of politics, manners, talk, personal style, as the plenteous varieties of the race adhere to one physical form. Such character is the brain and
spine to all, including literature, including poems. Such character, strong,
limber, just, open-mouthed, American-blooded, full of pride, full of ease, of
passionate friendliness, is to stand compact upon that vast basis of the supremacy of Individuality—that new moral American continent without which, I
see, the physical continent remained incomplete, may-be a carcass, a bloat—
that newer America, answering face to face with The States, with ever-satis-
fying and ever-unsurveyable seas and shores.

Those shores you found. I say you have led The States there—have led Me
there. I say that none has ever done, or ever can do, a greater deed for The
States, than your deed. Others may line out the lines, build cities, work mines,
break up farms; it is yours to have been the original true Captain who put to
sea, intuitive, positive, rendering the first report, to be told less by any report,
and more by the mariners of a thousand bays, in each tack of their arriving
and departing, many years after you.

Receive, dear Master, these statements and assurances through me, for all
the young men, and for an earnest that we know none before you, but the best
following you; and that we demand to take your name into our keeping, and
that we understand what you have indicated, and find the same indicated in
ourselves, and that we will stick to it and enlarge upon it through These States.

WALT WHITMAN.

1856

## LIVE OAK, WITH MOSS[1]

### I.

Not the heat flames up and consumes,
Not the sea-waves hurry in and out,
Not the air, delicious and dry, the air of the ripe summer, bears lightly along
    white down-balls of myriads of seeds, wafted, sailing gracefully, to drop
    where they may,
Not these—O none of these, more than the flames of me, consuming, burning
    for his love whom I love—O none, more than I, hurrying in and out;
Does the tide hurry, seeking something, and never give up?—O I, the same,
    to seek my life-long lover;                                                    5
O nor down-balls, nor perfumes, nor the high rain-emitting clouds, are borne
    through the open air, more than my copious soul is borne through the
    openair, wafted in all directions, for friendship, for love.—

1. In none of the editions did the *Calamus* poems
constitute so direct and coherent a sexual-poetic narrative as Whitman had made in the *Live Oak* sequence.
Whitman's original "programme" of "adhesiveness"—
what would now be termed a gay manifesto—is printed
here in its entirety. In 1953 Fredson Bowers first
printed the sequence in *Studies in Bibliography*, from
the manuscripts in the Valentine Collection in the Library of Clifton Waller Barrett. The texts here are
based on Mark Niemeyer's fresh collation from those
manuscripts.

## II.

I saw in Louisiana a live-oak growing,
All alone stood it, and the moss hung down from the branches,
Without any companion it grew there, glistening out joyous leaves of dark
　　green,
And its look, rude, unbending, lusty, made me think of myself;　　　　　　10
But I wondered how it could utter joyous leaves, standing alone there without
　　its friend, its lover—For I knew I could not;
And I plucked a twig with a certain number of leaves upon it, and twined
　　around it a little moss, and brought it away—And I have placed it in sight
　　in my room,
It is not needed to remind me as of my friends, (for I believe lately I think of
　　little else than of them,)
Yet it remains to me a curious token—it makes me think of manly love,
For all that, and though the live oak glistens there in Louisiana, solitary in a
　　wide flat space, uttering joyous leaves all its life, without a friend, a lover,
　　near—I know very well I could not.　　　　　　15

## III.

When I heard at the close of the day how I had been praised in the Capitol,
　　still it was not a happy night for me that followed;
Nor when I caroused—Nor when my favorite plans were accomplished—was
　　I really happy,
But that day I rose at dawn from the bed of perfect health, electric, inhaling
　　sweet breath,
When I saw the full moon in the west grow pale and disappear in the morn-
　　ing light,
When I wandered alone over the beach, and undressing, bathed, laughing
　　with the waters, and saw the sun rise,　　　　　　20
And when I thought how my friend, my lover, was coming, then O I was
　　happy;
Each breath tasted sweeter—and all that day my food nourished me more—
　　And the beautiful day passed well,
And the next came with equal joy—And with the next, at evening, came
　　my friend,
And that night, while all was still, I heard the waters roll slowly continually
　　up the shores
I heard the hissing rustle of the liquid and sands, as directed to me, whispering
　　to congratulate me,—For the friend I love lay sleeping by my side,　　　25
In the stillness his face was inclined towards me, while the moon's clear
　　beams shone,
And his arm lay lightly over my breast—And that night I was happy.

## IV.

This moment as I sit alone, yearning and pensive, it seems to me there are
　　other men, in other lands, yearning and pensive.
It seems to me I can look over and behold them, in Germany, France,
　　Spain—Or far away in China, India, or Russia—talking other dialects,

And it seems to me if I could know those men I should love them as I love
    men in my own lands,                                                    30
It seems to me they are as wise, beautiful, benevolent, as any in my own lands;
O I think we should be brethren—I think I should be happy with them.


## V.

Long I thought that knowledge alone would suffice me—O if I could but
    obtain knowledge!
Then the Land of the Prairies engrossed me—the south savannas engrossed
    me—For them I would live—I would be their orator;
Then I met the examples of old and new heroes—I heard of warriors, sailors,
    and all dauntless persons—And it seemed to me I too had it in me to be
    as dauntless as any, and would be so;                                    35
And then to finish all, it came to me to strike up the songs of the New World—
    And then I believed my life must be spent in singing;
But now take notice, Land of the prairies, Land of the south savannas,
    Ohio's land,
Take notice, you Kanuck woods—and you, Lake Huron—and all that with
    you roll toward Niagara—and you Niagara also,
And you, Californian mountains—that you all find some one else that he be
    your singer of songs,
For I can be your singer of songs no longer—I have ceased to enjoy them.  40
I have found him who loves me, as I him, in perfect love,
With the rest I dispense—I sever from all that I thought would suffice me, for
    it does not—it is now empty and tasteless to me,
I heed knowledge, and the grandeur of The States, and the examples of heroes,
    no more,
I am indifferent to my own songs—I am to go with him I love, and he is to go
    with me,
It is to be enough for each of us that we are together—We never separate
    again.—                                                                   45


## VI.

What think you I have taken my pen to record?
Not the battle-ship, perfect-model'd, majestic, that I saw to day arrive in the
    offing, under full sail,
Nor the splendors of the past day—nor the splendors of the night that enve-
    lopes me—Nor the glory and growth of the great city spread around me,
But the two men I saw to-day on the pier, parting the parting of dear friends.
The one to remain hung on the other's neck and passionately kissed him—
    while the one to depart tightly prest the one to remain in his arms.           50


## VII.

You bards of ages hence! when you refer to me, mind not so much my poems,
Nor speak of me that I prophesied of The States and led them the way of
    their glories,

But come, I will inform you who I was underneath that impassive exterior—I
    will tell you what to say of me,
Publish my name and hang up my picture as that of the tenderest lover,
The friend, the lover's portrait, of whom his friend, his lover, was fondest,   55
Who was not proud of his songs, but of the measureless ocean of love within
    him—and freely poured it forth,
Who often walked lonesome walks thinking of his dearest friends, his lovers,
Who pensive, away from one he loved, often lay sleepless and dissatisfied
    at night,
Who, dreading lest the one he loved might after all be indifferent to him, felt
    the sick feeling—O sick! sick!
Whose happiest days were those, far away through fields, in woods, on hills,
    he and another, wandering hand in hand, they twain, apart from other
    men.                                                                                          60
Who ever, as he sauntered the streets, curved with his arm the manly shoulder
    of his friend—while the curving arm of his friend rested upon him also.


## VIII.

Hours continuing long, sore and heavy-hearted,
Hours of the dusk, when I withdraw to a lonesome and unfrequented spot,
    seating myself, leaning my face in my hands,
Hours sleepless, deep in the night, when I go forth, speeding swiftly the coun-
    try roads, or through the city streets, or pacing miles and miles, stifling
    plaintive cries,
Hours discouraged, distracted,—For he, the one I cannot content myself with-
    out—soon I saw him content himself without me,                              65
Hours when I am forgotten—(O weeks and months are passing, but I believe
    I am never to forget!)
Sullen and suffering hours—(I am ashamed—but it is useless—I am what
    I am;)
Hours of torment—I wonder if other men ever have the like, out of the like
    feelings?
Is there even one other like me—distracted—his friend, his lover, lost to him?
Is he too as I am now? Does he still rise in the morning, dejected, thinking
    who is lost to him?                                                                        70
And at night, awaking, think who is lost?
Does he too harbor his friendship silent and endless? Harbor his anguish and
    passion?
Does some stray reminder, or the casual mention of a name, bring the fit back
    upon him, taciturn and deprest?
Does he see himself reflected in me? In these hours does he see the face of his
    hours reflected?


## IX.

I dreamed in a dream of a city where all the men were like brothers,         75
O I saw them tenderly love each other—I often saw them, in numbers, walk-
    ing hand in hand;

I dreamed that was the city of robust friends—Nothing was greater there than
    manly love—it led the rest,
It was seen every hour in the actions of the men of that city, and in all their
    looks and words.—

## X.

O you whom I often and silently come where you are, that I may be with you,
As I walk by your side, or sit near, or remain in the same room with you,     80
Little you know the subtle electric fire that for your sake is playing within
    me.—

## XI.

Earth! Though you look so impassive, ample and spheric there—I now suspect
    that is not all,
I now suspect there is something terrible in you, ready to break forth,
For an athlete loves me,—and I him—But toward him there is something
    fierce and terrible in me,
I dare not tell it in words—not even in these songs.     85

## XII.

To the young man, many things to absorb, to engraft, to develop, I teach, that
    he be my eleve,
But if through him speed not the blood of friendship, hot and red—If he be
    not silently selected by lovers, and do not silently select lovers—of what
    use were it for him to seek to become eleve of mine?

## From Children of Adam[1]

## Spontaneous Me

Spontaneous me, Nature,
The loving day, the mounting sun, the friend I am happy with,
The arm of my friend hanging idly over my shoulder,
The hillside whiten'd with blossoms of the mountain ash,
The same late in autumn, the hues of red, yellow, drab, purple, and light and
    dark green,     5

1. This group of poems celebrating sex first appeared
in the 1860 edition of Leaves of Grass as Enfans
d'Adam; later the contents and order were slightly altered until they reached final form in 1871. In their
edition Blodgett and Bradley quote a note in which
Whitman identifies the relationship of this group to the
Calamus poems: "Theory of a Cluster of Poems the
same to the passion of Woman-Love as the 'Calamus-
Leaves' are to adhesiveness, manly love. Full of ani-
mal-fire, tender, burning,—the tremulous ache, delicious, yet such a torment. The swelling elate and vehement, that will not be denied. Adam, as a central figure
and type. One piece presenting a vivid picture (in connection with the spirit) of a fully complete, well-devel-
oped man, eld, bearded, swart, fiery,—as a more than
rival of the youthful type-hero of novels and love
poems."

The rich coverlet of the grass, animals and birds, the private untrimm'd bank,
     the primitive apples, the pebble-stones,
Beautiful dripping fragments, the negligent list of one after another as I happen
     to call them to me or think of them,
The real poems, (what we call poems being merely pictures,)
The poems of the privacy of the night, and of men like me,
This poem drooping shy and unseen that I always carry, and that all men
     carry,                                                                    10
(Know once for all, avow'd on purpose, wherever are men like me, are our
     lusty lurking masculine poems,)
Love-thoughts, love-juice, love-odor, love-yielding, love-climbers, and the
     climbing sap,
Arms and hands of love, lips of love, phallic thumb of love, breasts of love,
     bellies press'd and glued together with love,
Earth of chaste love, life that is only life after love,
The body of my love, the body of the woman I love, the body of the man, the
     body of the earth,                                                        15
Soft forenoon airs that blow from the south-west,
The hairy wild-bee that murmurs and hankers up and down, that gripes the
     full-grown lady-flower, curves upon her with amorous firm legs, takes his
     will of her, and holds himself tremulous and tight till he is satisfied;
The wet of woods through the early hours,
Two sleepers at night lying close together as they sleep, one with an arm
     slanting down across and below the waist of the other,
The smell of apples, aromas from crush'd sage-plant, mint, birch-bark,     20
The boy's longings, the glow and pressure as he confides to me what he was
     dreaming,
The dead leaf whirling its spiral whirl and falling still and content to the ground,
The no-form'd stings that sights, people, objects, sting me with,
The hubb'd sting of myself, stinging me as much as it ever can any one,
The sensitive, orbic, underlapp'd brothers, that only privileged feelers may be
     intimate where they are,                                                  25
The curious roamer the hand roaming all over the body, the bashful withdraw-
     ing of flesh where the fingers soothingly pause and edge themselves,
The limpid liquid within the young man,
The vex'd corrosion so pensive and so painful,
The torment, the irritable tide that will not be at rest,
The like of the same I feel, the like of the same in others,               30
The young man that flushes and flushes, and the young woman that flushes
     and flushes,
The young man that wakes deep at night, the hot hand seeking to repress what
     would master him,
The mystic amorous night, the strange half-welcome pangs, visions, sweats,
The pulse pounding through palms and trembling encircling fingers, the
     young man all color'd, red, ashamed, angry;
The souse upon me of my lover the sea, as I lie willing and naked,         35
The merriment of the twin babes that crawl over the grass in the sun, the
     mother never turning her vigilant eyes from them,
The walnut-trunk, the walnut-husks, and the ripening or ripen'd long-round
     walnuts,
The continence of vegetables, birds, animals,
The consequent meanness of me should I skulk or find myself indecent, while

birds and animals never once skulk or find themselves indecent,
The great chastity of paternity, to match the great chastity of maternity,     40
The oath of procreation I have sworn, my Adamic and fresh daughters,
The greed that eats me day and night with hungry gnaw, till I saturate what
    shall produce boys to fill my place when I am through,
The wholesome relief, repose, content,
And this bunch pluck'd at random from myself,
It has done its work—I toss it carelessly to fall where it may.     45

1856, 1867

## Once I Pass'd through a Populous City[1]

Once I pass'd through a populous city imprinting my brain for future use with
    its shows, architecture, customs, traditions,
Yet now of all that city I remember only a woman I casually met there who
    detain'd me for love of me,
Day by day and night by night we were together—all else has long been forgot-
    ten by me,
I remember I say only that woman who passionately clung to me,
Again we wander, we love, we separate again,     5
Again she holds me by the hand, I must not go,
I see her close beside me with silent lips sad and tremulous.

1860, 1861

## Facing West from California's Shores

Facing west from California's shores,
Inquiring, tireless, seeking what is yet unfound,
I, a child, very old, over waves, towards the house of maternity, the land of
    migrations, look afar,
Look off the shores of my Western sea, the circle almost circled;
For starting westward from Hindustan, from the vales of Kashmere,     5
From Asia, from the north, from the God, the sage, and the hero,
From the south, from the flowery peninsulas and the spice islands,
Long having wander'd since, round the earth having wander'd,
Now I face home again, very pleas'd and joyous,
(But where is what I started for so long ago?     10
And why is it yet unfound?)

1860, 1867

---

1. Whitman revised this poem significantly for publication. Blodgett and Bradley quote from the manuscript, where the second line reads "But now of all that
city I remember only the man who wandered with me,
there, for love of me," and where the fourth line includes the words "—I remember, I say, only one rude
and ignorant man."

## FROM CALAMUS[1]

# Trickle Drops

Trickle drops! my blue veins leaving!
O drops of me! trickle, slow drops,
Candid from me falling, drip, bleeding drops,
From wounds made to free you whence you were prison'd,
From my face, from my forehead and lips,⁣ 5
From my breast, from within where I was conceal'd, press forth red drops,
⁣ confession drops,
Stain every page, stain every song I sing, every word I say, bloody drops,
Let them know your scarlet heat, let them glisten,
Saturate them with yourself all ashamed and wet,
Glow upon all I have written or shall write, bleeding drops, 10
Let it all be seen in your light, blushing drops.

1860, 1867

# Here the Frailest Leaves of Me

Here the frailest leaves of me and yet my strongest lasting,
Here I shade and hide my thoughts, I myself do not expose them,
And yet they expose me more than all my other poems.

1860, 1871

# Crossing Brooklyn Ferry[1]

1

Flood-tide below me! I see you face to face!
Clouds of the west—sun there half an hour high—I see you also face to face.

Crowds of men and women attired in the usual costumes, how curious you
⁣ are to me!
On the ferry-boats the hundreds and hundreds that cross, returning home, are
⁣ more curious to me than you suppose,
And you that shall cross from shore to shore years hence are more to me, and
⁣ more in my meditations, than you might suppose. 5

1. The Calamus group first appeared in the 3rd edition of Leaves of Grass (1860) and was given its final contents and order in 1881. Comparisons with the Children of Adam sequence are inevitable; Whitman himself saw the first as celebrating "amative" love of men and women and the Calamus poems as celebrating "adhesive" love of men for men. Blodgett and Bradley quote Whitman's insistence in Democratic Vistas that the adhesive love he celebrates was political in nature: "It is to the development, identification, and general prevalence of that fervid comradeship, (the adhesive love, at least rivaling the amative love hitherto possessing imaginative literature, if not going beyond it,) that I look for the counterbalance and offset of our materialistic and vulgar American democracy, and for the spiritualization thereof." For the 1876 preface to Leaves of Grass Whitman rewrote this passage as a direct comment on the Calamus poems.

1. Crossing Brooklyn Ferry is one of a dozen poems that follow the Calamus section and precede the Birds of Passage section; mostly longish poems, like this one, they have no section titles. Perhaps the clearest example of Whitman's desire to work by indirection, Crossing Brooklyn Ferry succeeds by alluring the reader without his or her quite knowing why. First published as Sun-Down Poem in the 2nd edition (1856), Crossing Brooklyn Ferry was given its final title in 1860.

2

The impalpable sustenance of me from all things at all hours of the day,
The simple, compact, well-join'd scheme, myself disintegrated, every one dis-
    integrated yet part of the scheme,
The similitudes of the past and those of the future,
The glories strung like beads on my smallest sights and hearings, on the walk
    in the street and the passage over the river,
The current rushing so swiftly and swimming with me far away,          10
The others that are to follow me, the ties between me and them,
The certainty of others, the life, love, sight, hearing of others.

Others will enter the gates of the ferry and cross from shore to shore,
Others will watch the run of the flood-tide,
Others will see the shipping of Manhattan north and west, and the heights of
    Brooklyn to the south and east,          15
Others will see the islands large and small;
Fifty years hence, others will see them as they cross, the sun half an hour high,
A hundred years hence, or ever so many hundred years hence, others will
    see them,
Will enjoy the sunset, the pouring-in of the flood-tide, the falling-back to the
    sea of the ebb-tide.

3

It avails not, time nor place—distance avails not,          20
I am with you, you men and women of a generation, or ever so many genera-
    tions hence,
Just as you feel when you look on the river and sky, so I felt,
Just as any of you is one of a living crowd, I was one of a crowd,
Just as you are refresh'd by the gladness of the river and the bright flow, I
    was refresh'd,
Just as you stand and lean on the rail, yet hurry with the swift current, I stood
    yet was hurried,          25
Just as you look on the numberless masts of ships and the thick-stemm'd pipes
    of steamboats, I look'd.

I too many and many a time cross'd the river of old,
Watched the Twelfth-month[2] sea-gulls, saw them high in the air floating with
    motionless wings, oscillating their bodies,
Saw how the glistening yellow lit up parts of their bodies and left the rest in
    strong shadow,
Saw the slow-wheeling circles and the gradual edging toward the south,          30
Saw the reflection of the summer sky in the water,
Had my eyes dazzled by the shimmering track of beams,
Look'd at the fine centrifugal spokes of light round the shape of my head in
    the sunlit water,
Look'd on the haze on the hills southward and south-westward,
Look'd on the vapor as it flew in fleeces tinged with violet,          35
Look'd toward the lower bay to notice the vessels arriving,
Saw their approach, saw aboard those that were near me,

2. December.

Saw the white sails of schooners and sloops, saw the ships at anchor,
The sailors at work in the rigging or out astride the spars,
The round masts, the swinging motion of the hulls, the slender serpentine
    pennants,                                                            40
The large and small steamers in motion, the pilots in their pilot-houses,
The white wake left by the passage, the quick tremulous whirl of the wheels,
The flags of all nations, the falling of them at sunset.
The scallop-edged waves in the twilight, the ladled cups, the frolicsome crests
    and glistening,
The stretch afar growing dimmer and dimmer, the gray walls of the granite
    storehouses by the docks,                                            45
On the river the shadowy group, the big steam-tug closely flank'd on each side
    by the barges, the hay-boat, the belated lighter,[3]
On the neighboring shore the fires from the foundry chimneys burning high
    and glaringly into the night,
Casting their flicker of black contrasted with wild red and yellow light over the
    tops of houses, and down into the clefts of streets.


                                    4

These and all else were to me the same as they are to you,
I loved well those cities, loved well the stately and rapid river,            50
The men and women I saw were all near to me,
Others the same—others who looked back on me because I look'd forward to
    them,
(The time will come, though I stop here to-day and to-night.)


                                    5

What is it then between us?
What is the count of the scores or hundreds of years between us?             55

Whatever it is, it avails not—distance avails not, and place avails not,
I too lived, Brooklyn of ample hills was mine,
I too walk'd the streets of Manhattan island, and bathed in the waters around
    it,
I too felt the curious abrupt questionings stir within me,
In the day among crowds of people sometimes they came upon me,              60
In my walks home late at night or as I lay in my bed they came upon me,
I too had been struck from the float forever held in solution,
I too had receiv'd identity by my body,
That I was I knew was of my body, and what I should be I knew I should be of
    my body.


                                    6

It is not upon you alone the dark patches fall,                            65
The dark threw its patches down upon me also,
The best I had done seem'd to me blank and suspicious,

3. Barge used to load or unload a cargo ship.

My great thoughts as I supposed them, were they not in reality meagre?
Nor is it you alone who know what it is to be evil,
I am he who knew what it was to be evil,                                    70
I too knitted the old knot of contrariety,
Blabb'd, blush'd, resented, lied, stole, grudg'd,
Had guile, anger, lust, hot wishes I dared not speak,
Was wayward, vain, greedy, shallow, sly, cowardly, malignant,
The wolf, the snake, the hog, not wanting in me,                           75
The cheating look, the frivolous word, the adulterous wish, not wanting,
Refusals, hates, postponements, meanness, laziness, none of these wanting,
Was one with the rest, the days and haps of the rest,
Was call'd by my nighest name by clear loud voices of young men as they
    saw me approaching or passing,
Felt their arms on my neck as I stood, or the negligent leaning of their flesh
    against me as I sat,                                                    80
Saw many I loved in the street or ferry-boat or public assembly, yet never
    told them a word,
Lived the same life with the rest, the same old laughing, gnawing, sleeping,
Play'd the part that still looks back on the actor or actress,
The same old role, the role that is what we make it, as great as we like,
Or as small as we like, or both great and small.                           85


                                    7

Closer yet I approach you,
What thought you have of me now, I had as much of you—I laid in my stores
    in advance,
I consider'd long and seriously of you before you were born.

Who was to know what should come home to me?
Who knows but I am enjoying this?                                           90
Who knows, for all the distance, but I am as good as looking at you now,
    for all you cannot see me?


                                    8

Ah, what can ever be more stately and admirable to me than mast-hemm'd
    Manhattan?
River and sunset and scallop-edg'd waves of flood-tide?
The sea-gulls oscillating their bodies, the hay-boat in the twilight, and the
    belated lighter?
What gods can exceed these that clasp me by the hand, and with voices I
    love call me promptly and loudly by my nighest name as I approach? 95
What is more subtle than this which ties me to the woman or man that looks
    in my face?
Which fuses me into you now, and pours my meaning into you?

We understand then do we not?
What I promis'd without mentioning it, have you not accepted?
What the study could not teach—what the preaching could not accomplish
    is accomplish'd, is it not?                                           100

9

Flow on, river! flow with the flood-tide, and ebb with the ebb-tide!
Frolic on, crested and scallop-edg'd waves!
Gorgeous clouds of the sunset! drench with your splendor me, or the men
    and women generations after me!
Cross from shore to shore, countless crowds of passengers!
Stand up, tall masts of Mannahatta![4] stand up, beautiful hills of Brooklyn! 105
Throb, baffled and curious brain! throw out questions and answers!
Suspend here and everywhere, eternal float of solution!
Gaze, loving and thirsting eyes, in the house or street or public assembly!
Sound out, voices of young men! loudly and musically call me by my nigh-
    est name!
Live, old life! play the part that looks back on the actor or actress!         110
Play the old role, the role that is great or small according as one makes it!
Consider, you who peruse me, whether I may not in unknown ways be
    looking upon you;
Be firm, rail over the river, to support those who lean idly, yet haste with
    the hasting current;
Fly on, sea-birds! fly sideways, or wheel in large circles high in the air;
Receive the summer sky, you water, and faithfully hold it till all downcast
    eyes have time to take it from you!                                        115
Diverge, fine spokes of light, from the shape of my head, or any one's head,
    in the sunlit water!
Come on, ships from the lower bay! pass up or down, white-sail'd schooners,
    sloops, lighters!
Flaunt away, flags of all nations! be duly lower'd at sunset!
Burn high your fires, foundry chimneys! cast black shadows at nightfall! cast
    red and yellow light over the tops of the houses!
Appearances, now or henceforth, indicate what you are,                         120
You necessary film, continue to envelop the soul,
About my body for me, and your body for you, be hung our divinest aromas,
Thrive, cities—bring your freight, bring your shows, ample and sufficient rivers,

Expand, being than which none else is perhaps more spiritual,
Keep your places, objects than which none else is more lasting.                125

You have waited, you always wait, you dumb, beautiful ministers,
We receive you with free sense at last, and are insatiate henceforward,
Not you any more shall be able to foil us, or withhold yourselves from us,
We use you, and do not cast you aside—we plant you permanently within
    us,
We fathom you not—we love you—there is perfection in you also,                 130
You furnish your parts toward eternity,
Great or small, you furnish your parts toward the soul.

1856, 1881

---

4. Variant for the American Indian word normally spelled "Manhattan."

## FROM SEA-DRIFT[1]

# Out of the Cradle Endlessly Rocking[2]

Out of the cradle endlessly rocking,
Out of the mocking-bird's throat, the musical shuttle,
Out of the Ninth-month midnight,
Over the sterile sands and the fields beyond, where the child leaving his bed
    wander'd alone, bareheaded, barefoot,
Down from the shower'd halo,                                                        5
Up from the mystic play of shadows twining and twisting as if they were alive,
Out from the patches of briers and blackberries,
From the memories of the bird that chanted to me,
From your memories sad brother, from the fitful risings and fallings I heard,
From under that yellow half-moon late-risen and swollen as if with tears,    10
From those beginning notes of yearning and love there in the mist,
From the thousand responses of my heart never to cease,
From the myriad thence-arous'd words,
From the word stronger and more delicious than any,
From such as now they start the scene revisiting,                              15
As a flock, twittering, rising, or overhead passing,
Borne hither, ere all eludes me, hurriedly,
A man, yet by these tears a little boy again,
Throwing myself on the sand, confronting the waves,
I, chanter of pains and joys, uniter of here and hereafter,                    20
Taking all hints to use them, but swiftly leaping beyond them,
A reminiscence sing.

Once Paumanok,[3]
When the lilac-scent was in the air and Fifth-month grass was growing,
Up this seashore in some briers,                                               25
Two feather'd guests from Alabama, two together,

And their nest, and four light-green eggs spotted with brown,
And every day the he-bird to and fro near at hand,
And every day the she-bird crouch'd on her nest, silent, with bright eyes,
And every day I, a curious boy, never too close, never disturbing them,       30
Cautiously peering, absorbing, translating.

*Shine! shine! shine!*
*Pour down your warmth, great sun!*
*While we bask, we two together.*

---

1. The *Sea-Drift* section of the 1881 edition of *Leaves of Grass* was made up of two new poems, seven poems from *Sea-Shore Memories* in the 1871 *Passage to India* section, and two poems from the 1876 *Two Rivulets* section.
2. First published as *A Child's Reminiscence* in the *New York Saturday Press* for December 24, 1859, this poem was incorporated into the 1860 *Leaves of Grass* as *A Word Out of the Sea*. Whitman continued to revise it until it reached the present form in the *Sea-Drift* section of the 1881 edition. *Out of the Cradle Endlessly*

*Rocking* had been the first of the *Sea-Shore Memories* group. The poem is about the way, at a crisis in his adult life, the poet remembers (and now fully comprehends) the boyhood experience of the annunciation of Whitman's role as a poet. On the most obvious level, the poem belongs to the Romantic tradition of poems about the revisiting of a spot important to the poet's earlier life: examples are Wordsworth's *Tintern Abbey* and *Wye Revisited* and Longfellow's *My Lost Youth.*
3. Long Island.

*Two together!*                                                    35
*Winds blow south, or winds blow north,*
*Day come white, or night come black,*
*Home, or rivers and mountains from home,*
*Singing all time, minding no time,*
*While we two keep together.*                                      40

Till of a sudden,
May-be kill'd, unknown to her mate,
One forenoon the she-bird crouch'd not on the nest,
Nor return'd that afternoon, nor the next
Nor ever appear'd again.                                           45

And thenceforward all summer in the sound of the sea,
And at night under the full of the moon in calmer weather,
Over the hoarse surging of the sea,
Or flitting from brier to brier by day,
I saw, I heard at intervals the remaining one, the he-bird,        50
The solitary guest from Alabama.

*Blow! blow! blow!*
*Blow up sea-winds along Paumanok's shore;*
*I wait and I wait till you blow my mate to me.*

Yes, when the stars glisten'd,                                     55
All night long on the prong of a moss-scallop'd stake,
Down almost amid the slapping waves,
Sat the lone singer wonderful causing tears.

He call'd on his mate,
He pour'd forth the meanings which I of all men know.              60

Yes my brother I know,
The rest might not, but I have treasur'd every note,
For more than once dimly down to the beach gliding,
Silent, avoiding the moonbeams, blending myself with the shadows,
Recalling now the obscure shapes, the echoes, the sounds and sights after their
    sorts,                                                         65
The white arms out in the breakers tirelessly tossing,
I, with bare feet, a child, the wind wafting my hair,
Listen'd long and long.

Listen'd to keep, to sing, now translating the notes.
Following you my brother.                                          70

*Soothe! soothe! soothe!*
*Close on its wave soothes the wave behind,*
*And again another behind embracing and lapping, every one close,*
*But my love soothes not me, not me.*

*Low hangs the moon, it rose late,*                                75
*It is lagging—O I think it is heavy with love, with love.*

O madly the sea pushes upon the land,
With love, with love.

O night! do I not see my love fluttering out among the breakers?
What is that little black thing I see there in the white? 80

Loud! loud! loud!
Loud I call to you, my love!

High and clear I shoot my voice over the waves,
Surely you must know who is here, is here,
You must know who I am, my love. 85

Low-hanging moon!
What is that dusky spot in your brown yellow?
O it is the shape, the shape of my mate!
O moon do not keep her from me any longer.

Land! land! O land! 90
Whichever way I turn, O I think you could give me my mate back again if you
    only would,
For I am almost sure I see her dimly whichever way I look.

O rising stars!
Perhaps the one I want so much will rise, will rise with some of you.

O throat! O trembling throat! 95
Sound clearer through the atmosphere!
Pierce the woods, the earth,
Somewhere listening to catch you must be the one I want.

Shake out carols!
Solitary here, the night's carols! 100
Carols of lonesome love! death's carols!
Carols under that lagging, yellow, waning moon!
O under that moon where she droops almost down into the sea!
O reckless despairing carols.

But soft! sink low! 105
Soft! let me just murmur,
And do you wait a moment you husky-nois'd sea,
For somewhere I believe I heard my mate responding to me,
So faint, I must be still, be still to listen,
But not altogether still, for then she might not come immediately to me. 110

Hither my love!
Here I am! here!
With this just-sustain'd note I announce myself to you,
This gentle call is for you my love, for you.

Do not be decoy'd elsewhere, 115
That is the whistle of the wind, it is not my voice,

*That is the fluttering, the fluttering of the spray,*
*Those are the shadows of leaves.*

*O darkness! O in vain!*
*O I am very sick and sorrowful.*                              120

*O brown halo in the sky near the moon, drooping upon the sea!*
*O troubled reflection in the sea!*
*O throat! O throbbing heart!*
*And I singing uselessly, uselessly all the night.*

*O past! O happy life! O songs of joy!*                        125
*In the air, in the woods, over fields,*
*Loved! loved! loved! loved! loved!*
*But my mate no more, no more with me!*
*We two together no more.*

The aria sinking,                                             130
All else continuing, the stars shining,
The winds blowing, the notes of the bird continuous echoing,
With angry moans the fierce old mother incessantly moaning,
On the sands of Paumanok's shore gray and rustling,
The yellow half-moon enlarged, sagging down, drooping, the face of the sea
      almost touching,                                        135
The boy ecstatic, with his bare feet the waves, with his hair the atmosphere
      dallying,
The love in the heart long pent, now loose, now at last tumultuously bursting,
The aria's meaning, the ears, the soul, swiftly depositing,
The strange tears down the cheeks coursing,
The colloquy there, the trio, each uttering,                  140
The undertone, the savage old mother incessantly crying,
To the boy's soul's questions sullenly timing, some drown'd secret hissing,
To the outsetting bard.

Demon or bird! (said the boy's soul,)
Is it indeed toward your mate you sing? or is it really to me?  145
For I, that was a child, my tongue's use sleeping, now I have heard you,
Now in a moment I know what I am for, I awake,
And already a thousand singers, a thousand songs, clearer, louder and more
      sorrowful than yours,
A thousand warbling echoes have started to life within me, never to die.

O you singer solitary, singing by yourself, projecting me,     150
O solitary me listening, never more shall I cease perpetuating you,
Never more shall I escape, never more the reverberations,
Never more the cries of unsatisfied love be absent from me,
Never again leave me to be the peaceful child I was before what there in
      the night,
By the sea under the yellow and sagging moon,                  155
The messenger there arous'd, the fire, the sweet hell within,
The unknown want, the destiny of me.

O give me the clew! (it lurks in the night here somewhere,)
O if I am to have so much, let me have more!

A word then, (for I will conquer it,)                                     160
The word final, superior to all,
Subtle, sent up—what is it?—I listen;
Are you whispering it, and have been all the time, you sea-waves?
Is that it from your liquid rims and wet sands?

Whereto answering, the sea,                                              165
Delaying not, hurrying not,
Whisper'd me through the night, and very plainly before daybreak,
Lisp'd to me the low and delicious word death,
And again death, death, death, death,
Hissing melodious, neither like the bird nor like my arous'd child's heart,   170
But edging near as privately for me rustling at my feet,
Creeping thence steadily up to my ears and laving me softly all over,
Death, death, death, death, death.

Which I do not forget,
But fuse the song of my dusky demon and brother,                         175
That he sang to me in the moonlight on Paumanok's gray beach,
With the thousand responsive songs at random,
My own songs awaked from that hour,
And with them the key, the word up from the waves,
The word of the sweetest song and all songs,                             180
That strong and delicious word which, creeping to my feet,
(Or like some old crone rocking the cradle, swathed in sweet garments, bend-
    ing aside,)
The sea whisper'd me.

                                                        1859, 1881


## As I Ebb'd with the Ocean of Life[1]

### 1

As I ebb'd with the ocean of life,
As I wended the shores I know,
As I walk'd where the ripples continually wash you Paumanok,[2]
Where they rustle up hoarse and sibilant,
Where the fierce old mother endlessly cries for her castaways,                5
I musing late in the autumn day, gazing off southward,
Held by this electric self out of the pride of which I utter poems,
Was seiz'd by the spirit that trails in the lines underfoot,

---

1. This poem was first published as *Bardic Symbols* in the *Atlantic* for April 1860, but only after James Russell Lowell had expurgated lines 59–60, which Whitman restored when he published the poem next in the 1860 edition of *Leaves of Grass*. Whitman gave it its final title and position as the second poem in *Sea-Drift* in the 1881 edition.
2. Long Island.

The rim, the sediment that stands for all the water and all the land of the globe.

Fascinated, my eyes reverting from the south, dropt, to follow those slender windrows, 10
Chaff, straw, splinters of wood, weeds, and the sea-gluten,[3]
Scum, scales from shining rocks, leaves of salt-lettuce, left by the tide,
Miles walking, the sound of breaking waves the other side of me,
Paumanok there and then as I thought the old thought of likenesses,
These you presented to me you fish-shaped island, 15
As I wended the shores I know,
As I walk'd with that electric self seeking types.[4]

2

As I wend to the shores I know not,
As I list to the dirge, the voices of men and women wreck'd,
As I inhale the impalpable breezes that set in upon me, 20
As the ocean so mysterious rolls toward me closer and closer,
I too but signify at the utmost a little wash'd-up drift,
A few sands and dead leaves to gather,
Gather, and merge myself as part of the sands and drift.

O baffled, balk'd, bent to the very earth, 25
Oppress'd with myself that I have dared to open my mouth,
Aware now that amid all that blab whose echoes recoil upon me I have not once had the least idea who or what I am,
But that before all my arrogant poems the real Me stands yet untouch'd, untold, altogether unreach'd,
Withdrawn far, mocking me with mock-congratulatory signs and bows,
With peals of distant ironical laughter at every word I have written, 30
Pointing in silence to these songs, and then to the sand beneath.

I perceive I have not really understood any thing, not a single object, and that no man ever can,
Nature here in sight of the sea taking advantage of me to dart upon me and sting me,
Because I have dared to open my mouth to sing at all.

3

You oceans both, I close with you, 35
We murmur alike reproachfully rolling sands and drift, knowing not why,
These little shreds indeed standing for you and me and all.

You friable[5] shore with trails of debris,
You fish-shaped island, I take what is underfoot,
What is yours is mine my father. 40

---

3. Gummy, viscid substance.
4. Types or likenesses of himself, in the debris left by
the receding tide.
5. Crumbling.

I too Paumanok,
I too have bubbled up, floated the measureless float, and been wash'd on
    your shores,
I too am but a trail of drift and debris,
I too leave little wrecks upon you, you fish-shaped island.

I throw myself upon your breast my father,                                              45
I cling to you so that you cannot unloose me,
I hold you so firm till you answer me something.

Kiss me my father,
Touch me with your lips as I touch those I love,
Breathe to me while I hold you close the secret of the murmuring I envy.      50

4

Ebb, ocean of life, (the flow will return,)
Cease not your moaning you fierce old mother,
Endlessly cry for your castaways, but fear not, deny not me,
Rustle not up so hoarse and angry against my feet as I touch you or gather
    from you.

I mean tenderly by you and all,                                                              55
I gather for myself and for this phantom looking down where we lead, and
    following me and mine.
Me and mine, loose windrows, little corpses,
Froth, snowy white, and bubbles,
(See, from my dead lips the ooze exuding at last,
See, the prismatic colors glistening and rolling,)                                          60
Tufts of straw, sands, fragments,
Buoy'd hither from many moods, one contradicting another,
From the storm, the long calm, the darkness, the swell,
Musing, pondering, a breath, a briny tear, a dab of liquid or soil,
Up just as much out of fathomless workings fermented and thrown,                    65
A limp blossom or two, torn, just as much over waves floating, drifted at
    random,
Just as much for us that sobbing dirge of Nature,
Just as much whence we come that blare of the cloud-trumpets,
We, capricious, brought hither we know not whence, spread out before you,
You up there walking or sitting,                                                              70
Whoever you are, we too lie in drifts at your feet.

1860, 1881

*FROM* BY THE ROADSIDE[1]

## When I Heard the Learn'd Astronomer

When I heard the learn'd astronomer,
When the proofs, the figures, were ranged in columns before me,
When I was shown the charts and diagrams, to add, divide, and measure
    them,
When I sitting heard the astronomer where he lectured with much applause
    in the lecture-room,
How soon unaccountable I became tired and sick,                   5
Till rising and gliding out I wander'd off by myself,
In the mystical moist night-air, and from time to time,
Look'd up in perfect silence at the stars.

                                          1865, 1865

## The Dalliance of the Eagles

Skirting the river road, (my forenoon walk, my rest,)
Skyward in air a sudden muffled sound, the dalliance of the eagles,
The rushing amorous contact high in space together,
The clinching interlocking claws, a living, fierce, gyrating wheel,
Four beating wings, two beaks, a swirling mass tight grappling,         5
In tumbling turning clustering loops, straight downward falling,
Till o'er the river pois'd, the twain yet one, a moment's lull,
A motionless still balance in the air, then parting, talons loosing,
Upward again on slow-firm pinions slanting, their separate diverse flight,
She hers, he his, pursuing.                                  10

                                          1880, 1881

*FROM* DRUM-TAPS[1]

## Beat! Beat! Drums!

Beat! beat! drums!—blow! bugles! blow!
Through the windows—through doors—burst like a ruthless force,

---

1. *By the Roadside* is the 1881 section title for around two dozen poems, most of which first appeared in the 1860 edition of *Leaves of Grass*. As Blodgett and Bradley say, "The group is truly a melange held together by the common bond of the poet's experience as roadside observer—passive, but alert and continually recording." Several of the poems are mere jottings of two, three, or four lines.
1. The contents of the original *Drum-Taps* (first printed in 1865 as a little book) differed considerably from the contents of the *Drum-Taps* section finally arrived at in the 1881 *Leaves of Grass*. In the final arrangement the poetic purpose shifts throughout, roughly reflecting the chronology of the Civil War and

the chronology of the composition of the poems. The first purpose is propagandistic. Indeed, *Beat! Beat! Drums!* served as a kind of recruiting poem when it was first printed (and reprinted) in the fall of 1861, having been composed after the Southern victory at the first battle of Bull Run. Later Whitman seems to have understood that the early jingoistic poems had a certain historical value that made them worth preserving. The dominant impulse of most of the later poems is realistic—a determination to record the war the way it was, and in the best of the poems the realistic record is achieved through elaborate technical subtleties. The stages of Whitman's own attitudes toward the war are well stated in the epigraph he gave the whole *Drum-*

Into the solemn church, and scatter the congregation,
Into the school where the scholar is studying;
Leave not the bridegroom quiet—no happiness must he have now with his
    bride,                                                                                                     5
Nor the peaceful farmer any peace, ploughing his field or gathering his grain,
So fierce you whirr and pound you drums—so shrill you bugles blow.

Beat! beat! drums!—blow! bugles! blow!
Over the traffic of cities—over the rumble of wheels in the streets;
Are beds prepared for sleepers at night in the houses? no sleepers must sleep
    in those beds,                                                                                     10
No bargainers' bargains by day—no brokers or speculators—would they con-
    tinue?
Would the talkers be talking? would the singer attempt to sing?
Would the lawyer rise in the court to state his case before the judge?
Then rattle quicker, heavier drums—you bugles wilder blow.

Beat! beat! drums!—blow! bugles! blow!                                                15
Make no parley—stop for no expostulation,
Mind not the timid—mind not the weeper or prayer,
Mind not the old man beseeching the young man,
Let not the child's voice be heard, nor the mother's entreaties,
Make even the trestles to shake the dead where they lie awaiting the
    hearses,                                                                                              20
So strong you thump O terrible drums—so loud you bugles blow.

                                                                                    1861, 1867


## Cavalry Crossing a Ford

A line in long array where they wind betwixt green islands,
They take a serpentine course, their arms flash in the sun—hark to the musical
    clank,
Behold the silvery river, in it the splashing horses loitering stop to drink,
Behold the brown-faced men, each group, each person a picture, the negligent
    rest on the saddles,
Some emerge on the opposite bank, others are just entering the ford—
    while,                                                                                                   5
Scarlet and blue and snowy white,
The guidon flags flutter gayly in the wind.

                                                                                    1865, 1871


## A Sight in Camp in the Daybreak Gray and Dim

A sight in camp in the daybreak gray and dim,
As from my tent I emerge so early sleepless,

---

*Taps* group in 1871 then inserted parenthetically into
*The Wound Dresser* in the 1881 edition: "Arous'd and
angry, I'd thought to beat the alarum, and urge relentless war, / But soon my fingers fail'd me, my face
droop'd and I resign'd myself / To sit by the wounded
and soothe them, or silently watch the dead.

As slow I walk in the cool fresh air the path near by the hospital tent,
Three forms I see on stretchers lying, brought out there untended lying,
Over each the blanket spread, ample brownish woolen blanket,     5
Gray and heavy blanket, folding, covering all.

Curious I halt and silent stand,
Then with light fingers I from the face of the nearest the first just lift the
    blanket;
Who are you elderly man so gaunt and grim, with well-gray'd hair, and flesh
    all sunken about the eyes?
Who are you my dear comrade?     10
Then to the second I step—and who are you my child and darling?


Who are you sweet boy with cheeks yet blooming?

Then to the third—a face nor child nor old, very calm, as of beautiful yellow-
    white ivory;
Young man I think I know you—I think this face is the face of the Christ
    himself,
Dead and divine and brother of all, and here again he lies.     15

1865, 1867

# The Wound-Dresser

### 1

An old man bending I come among new faces,
Years looking backward resuming in answer to children,
Come tell us old man, as from young men and maidens that love me,
(Arous'd and angry, I'd thought to beat the alarum, and urge relentless war,
But soon my fingers fail'd me, my face droop'd and I resign'd myself,     5
To sit by the wounded and soothe them, or silently watch the dead;)
Years hence of these scenes, of these furious passions, these chances,
Of unsurpass'd heroes, (was one side so brave? the other was equally brave;)
Now be witness again, paint the mightiest armies of earth,
Of those armies so rapid so wondrous what saw you to tell us?     10
What stays with you latest and deepest? of curious panics,
Of hard-fought engagements or sieges tremendous what deepest remains?

### 2

O maidens and young men I love and that love me,
What you ask of my days those the strangest and sudden your talking recalls,
Soldier alert I arrive after a long march cover'd with sweat and dust,     15
In the nick of time I come, plunge in the fight, loudly shout in the rush of
    successful charge,
Enter the captur'd works[1]—yet lo, like a swift-running river they fade,

---

1. Fortifications.

Pass and are gone they fade—I dwell not on soldiers' perils or soldiers' joys,
(Both I remember well—many the hardships, few the joys, yet I was content.)

But in silence in dreams' projections,                                    20
While the world of gain and appearance and mirth goes on,
So soon what is over forgotten, and waves wash the imprints off the sand,
With hinged knees returning I enter the doors, (while for you up there,
Whoever you are, follow without noise and be of strong heart.)

Bearing the bandages, water and sponge,                                    25
Straight and swift to my wounded I go,
Where they lie on the ground after the battle brought in,
Where their priceless blood reddens the grass the ground,
Or to the rows of the hospital tent, or under the roof'd hospital,
To the long rows of cots up and down each side I return,                  30
To each and all one after another I draw near, not one do I miss,
An attendant follows holding a tray, he carries a refuse pail,
Soon to be fill'd with clotted rags and blood, emptied, and fill'd again.

I onward go, I stop,
With hinged knees and steady hand to dress wounds,                        35
I am firm with each, the pangs are sharp yet unavoidable,
One turns to me his appealing eyes—poor boy! I never knew you,
Yet I think I could not refuse this moment to die for you, if that would save
    you.


3

On, on I go, (open doors of time! open hospital doors!)
The crush'd head I dress, (poor crazed hand tear not the bandage away,)    40
The neck of the cavalry-man with the bullet through and through I examine,
Hard the breathing rattles, quite glazed already the eye, yet life struggles hard,
(Come sweet death! be persuaded O beautiful death!
In mercy come quickly.)

From the stump of the arm, the amputated hand,                            45
I undo the clotted lint, remove the slough, wash off the matter and blood,
Back on his pillow the soldier bends with curv'd neck and side-falling head,
His eyes are closed, his face is pale, he dares not look on the bloody stump,
And has not yet look'd on it.

I dress a wound in the side, deep, deep,                                   50
But a day or two more, for see the frame all wasted and sinking,
And the yellow-blue countenance see.

I dress the perforated shoulder, the foot with the bullet-wound,
Cleanse the one with a gnawing and putrid gangrene, so sickening, so
    offensive,
While the attendant stands behind aside me holding the tray and pail.     55

I am faithful, I do not give out,
The fractur'd thigh, the knee, the wound in the abdomen,

These and more I dress with impassive hand, (yet deep in my breast a fire, a
   burning flame.)


                                           4

Thus in silence in dreams' projections,
Returning, resuming, I thread my way through the hospitals,                    60
The hurt and wounded I pacify with soothing hand,
I sit by the restless all the dark night, some are so young,
Some suffer so much, I recall the experience sweet and sad,
(Many a soldier's loving arms about this neck have cross'd and rested,
Many a soldier's kiss dwells on these bearded lips.)                          65

                                                                    1865, 1881


                                  Reconciliation

Word over all, beautiful as the sky,
Beautiful that war and all its deeds of carnage must in time be utterly lost,
That the hands of the sisters Death and Night incessantly softly wash again,
   and ever again, this soil'd world;
For my enemy is dead, a man divine as myself is dead,
I look where he lies white-faced and still in the coffin—I draw near,          5
Bend down and touch lightly with my lips the white face in the coffin.

                                                                  1865–66, 1881


                   FROM MEMORIES OF PRESIDENT LINCOLN[1]

              When Lilacs Last in the Dooryard Bloom'd


                                           1

When lilacs last in the dooryard bloom'd,
And the great star[2] early droop'd in the western sky in the night,
I mourn'd, and yet shall mourn with ever-returning spring.

Ever-returning spring, trinity sure to me you bring,
Lilac blooming perennial and drooping star in the west,                        5
And thought of him I love.


                                           2

O powerful western fallen star!
O shades of night—O moody, tearful night!

1. Composed in the months following Lincoln's assassination on April 14, 1865, this elegy was printed in
the fall of that year as an appendix to the recently published *Drum-Taps* volume. In the 1881 edition of
*Leaves of Grass* it and three lesser poems were joined
to make up the section *Memories of President Lincoln*.

Not simply a poem about the death of Lincoln, *When
Lilacs Last in the Dooryard Bloom'd* is about the stages
by which a poet transmutes his grief into poetry.
2. Literally Venus, although it becomes associated
with Lincoln himself.

O great star disappear'd—O the black murk that hides the star!
O cruel hands that hold me powerless—O helpless soul of me!     10
O harsh surrounding cloud that will not free my soul.

### 3

In the dooryard fronting an old farm-house near the white-wash'd palings,
Stands the lilac-bush tall-growing with heart-shaped leaves of rich green,
With many a pointed blossom rising delicate, with the perfume strong I
    love,
With every leaf a miracle—and from this bush in the dooryard,     15
With delicate-color'd blossoms and heart-shaped leaves of rich green,
A sprig with its flower I break.

### 4

In the swamp in secluded recesses,
A shy and hidden bird is warbling a song.

Solitary the thrush,     20
The hermit withdrawn to himself, avoiding the settlements,
Sings by himself a song.

Song of the bleeding throat,
Death's outlet song of life, (for well dear brother I know,
If thou wast not granted to sing thou would'st surely die.)     25

### 5

Over the breast of the spring, the land, amid cities,
Amid lanes and through old woods, where lately the violets peep'd from the
    ground, spotting the gray debris,
Amid the grass in the fields each side of the lanes, passing the endless grass,
Passing the yellow-spear'd wheat, every grain from its shroud in the dark-
    brown fields uprisen,
Passing the apple-tree blows[3] of white and pink in the orchards,     30
Carrying a corpse to where it shall rest in the grave,
Night and day journeys a coffin.

### 6

Coffin that passes through lanes and streets,
Through day and night with the great cloud darkening the land,
With the pomp of the inloop'd flags with the cities draped in black,     35
With the show of the States themselves as of crape-veil'd women standing,
With processions long and winding and the flambeaus[4] of the night,
With the countless torches lit, with the silent sea of faces and the unbared
    heads,
With the waiting depot, the arriving coffin, and the sombre faces,
With dirges through the night, with the thousand voices rising strong and
    solemn,     40

---

3. Blossoms.                         4. Torches.

With all the mournful voices of the dirges pour'd around the coffin,
The dim-lit churches and the shuddering organs—where amid these you
    journey,
With the tolling tolling bells' perpetual clang,
Here, coffin that slowly passes,
I give you my sprig of lilac.                                                    45

### 7

(Nor for you, for one alone,
Blossoms and branches green to coffins all I bring,
For fresh as the morning, thus would I chant a song for you O sane and
    sacred death.

All over bouquets of roses,
O death, I cover you over with roses and early lilies,                           50
But mostly and now the lilac that blooms the first,
Copious I break, I break the sprigs from the bushes,
With loaded arms I come, pouring for you,
For you and the coffins all of you O death.)

### 8

O western orb sailing the heaven,                                               55
Now I know what you must have meant as a month since I walk'd,
As I walk'd in silence the transparent shadowy night,
As I saw you had something to tell as you bent to me night after night,
As you droop'd from the sky low down as if to my side, (while the other
    stars all look'd on,)
As we wander'd together the solemn night, (for something I know not what
    kept me from sleep,)                                                          60

As the night advanced, and I saw on the rim of the west how full you were of
    woe,
As I stood on the rising ground in the breeze in the cool transparent night,
As I watch'd where you pass'd and was lost in the netherward black of the
    night,
As my soul in its trouble dissatisfied sank, as where you sad orb,
Concluded, dropt in the night, and was gone.                                    65

### 9

Sing on there in the swamp,
O singer bashful and tender, I hear your notes, I hear your call,
I hear, I come presently, I understand you,
But a moment I linger, for the lustrous star has detain'd me,
The star my departing comrade holds and detains me.                             70

### 10

O how shall I warble myself for the dead one there I loved?
And how shall I deck my song for the large sweet soul that has gone?
And what shall my perfume be for the grave of him I love?

Sea-winds blown from east and west,
Blown from the Eastern sea and blown from the Western sea, till there on the
    prairies meeting,                                                                                    75
These and with these and the breath of my chant,
I'll perfume the grave of him I love.

### 11

O what shall I hang on the chamber walls?
And what shall the pictures be that I hang on the walls,
To adorn the burial-house of him I love?                                                    80

Pictures of growing spring and farms and homes,
With the Fourth-month[5] eve at sundown, and the gray smoke lucid and
    bright,
With floods of the yellow gold of the gorgeous, indolent, sinking sun, burning,
    expanding the air,
With the fresh sweet herbage under foot, and the pale green leaves of the trees
    prolific,
In the distance the flowing glaze, the breast of the river, with a wind-dapple
    here and there,                                                                                          85
With ranging hills on the banks, with many a line against the sky, and
    shadows,
And the city at hand with dwellings so dense, and stacks of chimneys,
And all the scenes of life and the workshops, and the workmen homeward
    returning.

### 12

Lo, body and soul—this land,
My own Manhattan with spires, and the sparkling and hurrying tides, and the
    ships,                                                                                                        90
The varied and ample land, the South and the North in the light, Ohio's
    shores and flashing Missouri,
And ever the far-spreading prairies cover'd with grass and corn.

Lo, the most excellent sun so calm and haughty,
The violet and purple morn with just-felt breezes,
The gentle soft-born measureless light,                                                        95
The miracle spreading bathing all, the fulfill'd noon,
The coming eve delicious, the welcome night and the stars,
Over my cities shining all, enveloping man and land.

### 13

Sing on, sing on you gray-brown bird,
Sing from the swamps, the recesses, pour your chant from the bushes,      100
Limitless out of the dusk, out of the cedars and pines.

Sing on dearest brother, warble your reedy song,
Loud human song, with voice of uttermost woe.

_____

5. April.

O liquid and free and tender!
O wild and loose to my soul!—O wondrous singer!                    105
You only I hear—yet the star holds me, (but will soon depart,)
Yet the lilac with mastering odor holds me.


14

Now while I sat in the day and look'd forth,
In the close of the day with its light and the fields of spring, and the farmers
    preparing their crops,
In the large unconscious scenery of my land with its lakes and forests,                    110
In the heavenly aerial beauty, (after the perturb'd winds and the storms,)
Under the arching heavens of the afternoon swift passing, and the voices of
    children and women,
The many-moving sea-tides, and I saw the ships how they sail'd,
And the summer approaching with richness, and the fields all busy with labor,
And the infinite separate houses, how they all went on, each with its meals
    and minutia of daily usages,                    115
And the streets how their throbbings throbb'd, and the cities pent—lo, then
    and there,
Falling upon them all and among them all, enveloping me with the rest,
Appear'd the cloud, appear'd the long black trail,
And I knew death, its thought, and the sacred knowledge of death.

Then with the knowledge of death as walking one side of me,                    120
And the thought of death close-walking the other side of me,
And I in the middle as with companions, and as holding the hands of com-
    panions,
I fled forth to the hiding receiving night that talks not,
Down to the shores of the water, the path by the swamp in the dimness,
To the solemn shadowy cedars and ghostly pines so still.                    125

And the singer so shy to the rest receiv'd me,
The gray-brown bird I know receiv'd us comrades three,
And he sang the carol of death, and a verse for him I love.

From deep secluded recesses,
From the fragrant cedars and the ghostly pines so still,                    130
Came the carol of the bird.

And the charm of the carol rapt me,
As I held as if by their hands my comrades in the night,
And the voice of my spirit tallied the song of the bird.

*Come lovely and soothing death,*                    135
*Undulate round the world, serenely arriving, arriving,*
*In the day, in the night, to all, to each,*
*Sooner or later delicate death.*

*Prais'd be the fathomless universe,*
*For life and joy, and for objects and knowledge curious,*                    140
*And for love, sweet love—but praise! praise! praise!*
*For the sure-enwinding arms of cool-enfolding death.*

Dark mother always gliding near with soft feet,
Have none chanted for thee a chant of fullest welcome?
Then I chant it for thee, I glorify thee above all,                          145
I bring thee a song that when thou must indeed come, come unfalteringly.

Approach strong deliveress,
When it is so, when thou hast taken them I joyously sing the dead,
Lost in the loving floating ocean of thee,
Laved in the flood of thy bliss O death.                                     150

From me to thee glad serenades,
Dances for thee I propose saluting thee, adornments and feastings for thee,
And the sights of the open landscape and the high-spread sky are fitting,
And life and the fields, and the huge and thoughtful night.

The night in silence under many a star,                                      155
The ocean shore and the husky whispering wave whose voice I know,
And the soul turning to thee O vast and well-veil'd death,
And the body gratefully nestling close to thee.

Over the tree-tops I float thee a song,
Over the rising and sinking waves, over the myriad fields and the prairies
     wide,
Over the dense-pack'd cities all and the teeming wharves and ways,           160
I float this carol with joy, with joy to thee O death.

### 15

To the tally of my soul,
Loud and strong kept up the gray-brown bird,
With pure deliberate notes spreading filling the night.                      165

Loud in the pines and cedars dim,
Clear in the freshness moist and the swamp-perfume,
And I with my comrades there in the night.

While my sight that was bound in my eyes unclosed,
As to long panoramas of visions.                                             170

And I saw askant[6] the armies,
I saw as in noiseless dreams hundreds of battle-flags,
Borne through the smoke of the battles and pierc'd with missiles I saw them,
And carried hither and yon through the smoke, and torn and bloody,
And at last but a few shreds left on the staffs, (and all in silence,)       175
And the staffs all splinter'd and broken.

I saw battle-corpses, myriads of them,
And the white skeletons of young men, I saw them,
I saw the debris and debris of all the slain soldiers of the war,
But I saw they were not as was thought,                                      180
They themselves were fully at rest, they suffer'd not,

---

6. Sideways, aslant; an appropriate word for introducing a surrealistic vision.

The living remain'd and suffer'd, the mother suffer'd,
And the wife and the child and the musing comrade suffer'd,
And the armies that remain'd suffer'd.

### 16

Passing the visions, passing the night,                                          185
Passing, unloosing the hold of my comrades' hands,
Passing the song of the hermit bird and the tallying song of my soul,
Victorious song, death's outlet song, yet varying ever-altering song,
As low and wailing, yet clear the notes, rising and falling, flooding the night,
Sadly sinking and fainting, as warning and warning, and yet again bursting
    with joy,                                                                    190
Covering the earth and filling the spread of the heaven,
As that powerful psalm in the night I heard from recesses,
Passing, I leave thee lilac with heart-shaped leaves,
I leave thee there in the door-yard, blooming, returning with spring.

I cease from my song for thee,                                                   195
From my gaze on thee in the west, fronting the west, communing with thee,
O comrade lustrous with silver face in the night.

Yet each to keep and all, retrievements out of the night,
The song, the wondrous chant of the gray-brown bird,
And the tallying chant, the echo arous'd in my soul,                            200
With the lustrous and drooping star with the countenance full of woe,
With the holders holding my hand nearing the call of the bird,
Comrades mine and I in the midst, and their memory ever to keep, for the
    dead I loved so well,
For the sweetest, wisest soul of all my days and lands—and this for his dear
    sake,
Lilac and star and bird twined with the chant of my soul,                       205
There in the fragrant pines and the cedars dusk and dim.

                                                             1865–66, 1881

## FROM AUTUMN RIVULETS

# There Was a Child Went Forth[1]

There was a child went forth every day,
And the first object he look'd upon, that object he became,
And that object became part of him for the day or a certain part of the day,
Or for many years or stretching cycles of years.

---

1. This poem was first published in the 1856 edition
of *Leaves of Grass* as *Poem of the Child That Went
Forth, and Always Goes Forth, Forever and Forever,*
then subsequently published under other titles until the
present one was reached in the 1871 edition.

The early lilacs became part of this child, 5
And grass and white and red morning-glories, and white and red clover, and
the song of the phoebe-bird,
And the Third-month[2] lambs and the sow's pink-faint litter, and the mare's
foal and the cow's calf,
And the noisy brood of the barnyard or by the mire of the pond-side,
And the fish suspending themselves so curiously below there, and the beautiful
curious liquid,
And the water-plants with their graceful flat heads, all became part of him. 10

The field-sprouts of Fourth-month and Fifth-month became part of him,
Winter-grain sprouts and those of the light-yellow corn, and the esculent roots
of the garden,
And the apple-trees cover'd with blossoms and the fruit afterward, and wood-
berries, and the commonest weeds by the road,
And the old drunkard staggering home from the outhouse of the tavern whence
he had lately risen,
And the schoolmistress that pass'd on her way to the school, 15
And the friendly boys that pass'd, and the quarrelsome boys,
And the tidy and fresh-cheek'd girls, and the barefoot negro boy and girl,
And all the changes of city and country wherever he went.

His own parents, he that had father'd him and she that had conceiv'd him in
her womb and birth'd him,
They gave this child more of themselves than that, 20
They gave him afterward every day, they became part of him.

The mother at home quietly placing the dishes on the supper-table,
The mother with mild words, clean her cap and gown, a wholesome odor
falling off her person and clothes as she walks by,
The father, strong, self-sufficient, manly, mean, anger'd, unjust,
The blow, the quick loud word, the tight bargain, the crafty lure, 25
The family usages, the language, the company, the furniture, the yearning
and swelling heart,
Affection that will not be gainsay'd, the sense of what is real, the thought if
after all it should prove unreal,
The doubts of day-time and the doubts of night-time, the curious whether and
how,
Whether that which appears so is so, or is it all flashes and specks?
Men and women crowding fast in the streets, if they are not flashes and specks
what are they? 30
The streets themselves and the façades of houses, and goods in the windows,
Vehicles, teams, the heavy-plank'd wharves, the huge crossing at the ferries,
The village on the highland seen from afar at sunset, the river between,
Shadows, aureola and mist, the light falling on roofs and gables of white or
brown two miles off,
The schooner near by sleepily dropping down the tide, the little boat slack-
tow'd astern, 35
The hurrying tumbling waves, quick-broken crests, slapping,
The strata of color'd clouds, the long bar of maroon-tint away solitary by itself,
the spread of purity it lies motionless in,

2. I.e., March.

The horizon's edge, the flying sea-crow, the fragrance of salt marsh and shore
    mud,
These became part of that child who went forth every day, and who now goes,
    and will always go forth every day.

                                                                    1855, 1871


## This Compost

                                    1

Something startles me where I thought I was safest,
I withdraw from the still woods I loved,


I will not go now on the pastures to walk,
I will not strip the clothes from my body to meet my lover the sea,
I will not touch my flesh to the earth as to other flesh to renew me.        5

O how can it be that the ground itself does not sicken?
How can you be alive you growths of spring?
How can you furnish health you blood of herbs, roots, orchards, grain?
Are they not continually putting distemper'd corpses within you?
Is not every continent work'd over and over with sour dead?                   10

Where have you disposed of their carcasses?
Those drunkards and gluttons of so many generations?
Where have you drawn off all the foul liquid and meat?
I do not see any of it upon you to-day, or perhaps I am deceiv'd,
I will run a furrow with my plough, I will press my spade through the sod and
    turn it up underneath,                                                    15
I am sure I shall expose some of the foul meat.


                                    2

Behold this compost! behold it well!
Perhaps every mite has once form'd part of a sick person—yet behold!
The grass of spring covers the prairies,
The bean bursts noiselessly through the mould in the garden,                  20
The delicate spear of the onion pierces upward,
The apple-buds cluster together on the apple-branches,
The resurrection of the wheat appears with pale visage out of its graves,
The tinge awakes over the willow-tree and the mulberry-tree,
The he-birds carol mornings and evenings while the she-birds sit on their
    nests,                                                                    25
The young of poultry break through the hatch'd eggs,
The new-born of animals appear, the calf is dropt from the cow, the colt from
    the mare,
Out of its little hill faithfully rise the potato's dark green leaves,
Out of its hill rises the yellow maize-stalk, the lilacs bloom in the dooryards,
The summer growth is innocent and disdainful above all those strata of sour
    dead.                                                                     30

What chemistry!
That the winds are really not infectious,
That this is no cheat, this transparent green-wash of the sea which is so amo-
    rous after me,
That it is safe to allow it to lick my naked body all over with its tongues,
That it will not endanger me with the fevers that have deposited themselves in
    it,                                                                                    35
That all is clean forever and forever,
That the cool drink from the well tastes so good,
That blackberries are so flavorous and juicy,
That the fruits of the apple-orchard and the orange-orchard, that melons,
    grapes, peaches, plums, will none of them poison me,
That when I recline on the grass I do not catch any disease,                           40
Though probably every spear of grass rises out of what was once a catching
    disease.

Now I am terrified at the Earth, it is that calm and patient,
It grows such sweet things out of such corruptions,
It turns harmless and stainless on its axis, with such endless successions of
    diseas'd corpses,
It distills such exquisite winds out of such infused fetor,                            45
It renews with such unwitting looks its prodigal, annual, sumptuous crops,
It gives such divine materials to men, and accepts such leavings from them
    at last.

                                                                    1856, 1881


FROM WHISPERS OF HEAVENLY DEATH

## A Noiseless Patient Spider

A noiseless patient spider,
I mark'd where on a little promontory it stood isolated,
Mark'd how to explore the vacant vast surrounding,
It launch'd forth filament, filament, filament, out of itself,
Ever unreeling them, ever tirelessly speeding them.                                    5

And you O my soul where you stand,
Surrounded, detached, in measureless oceans of space,
Ceaselessly musing, venturing, throwing, seeking the spheres to connect
    them,
Till the bridge you will need be form'd, till the ductile anchor hold,
Till the gossamer thread you fling catch somewhere, O my soul.

                                                                    1868, 1881

FROM FROM NOON TO STARRY NIGHT

## To a Locomotive in Winter[1]

Thee for my recitative,
Thee in the driving storm even as now, the snow, the winter-day declining,
Thee in thy panoply,[2] thy measur'd dual throbbing and thy beat convulsive,
Thy black cylindric body, golden brass and silvery steel,
Thy ponderous side-bars, parallel and connecting rods, gyrating, shuttling at
    thy sides,                                       5
Thy metrical, now swelling pant and roar, now tapering in the distance,
Thy great protruding head-light fix'd in front,
Thy long, pale, floating vapor-pennants, tinged with delicate purple,
Thy dense and murky clouds out-belching from thy smoke-stack,
Thy knitted frame, thy springs and valves, the tremulous twinkle of thy
    wheels,                                         10
Thy train of cars behind, obedient, merrily following,
Through gale or calm, now swift, now slack, yet steadily careering;
Type of the modern—emblem of motion and power—pulse of the continent,
For once come serve the Muse and merge in verse, even as here I see thee,
With storm and buffeting gusts of wind and falling snow,          15
By day thy warning ringing bell to sound its notes,
By night thy silent signal lamps to swing.

Fierce-throated beauty!
Roll through my chant with all thy lawless music, thy swinging lamps at night,
Thy madly-whistled laughter, echoing, rumbling like an earthquake, rousing
    all,                                         20
Law of thyself complete, thine own track firmly holding,
(No sweetness debonair of tearful harp or glib piano thine,)
Thy trills of shrieks by rocks and hills return'd,
Launch'd o'er the prairies wide, across the lakes,
To the free skies unpent and glad and strong.              25

                                     1876, 1881

FROM SECOND ANNEX: GOOD-BYE MY FANCY[1]

## Good-bye My Fancy!

Good-bye my Fancy!
Farewell dear mate, dear love!
I'm going away, I know not where,
Or to what fortune, or whether I may ever see you again,
So Good-bye my Fancy.                             5

---

1. First printed in the *New York Tribune* on February 19, 1876, as a sample from the forthcoming *Two Rivulets*, this poem was moved to the *From Noon to Starry Night* group in the 1881 *Leaves of Grass*.
2. Suit of armor.

1. The poetic imagination. This, the second and final "annex" to *Leaves of Grass*, consisting of prose headnote and thirty-one poems, mostly new, was printed separately in 1891 as *Good-by My Fancy*, then added to *Leaves of Grass* in the 1891–92 edition.

Now for my last—let me look back a moment;
The slower fainter ticking of the clock is in me,
Exit, nightfall, and soon the heart-thud stopping.

Long have we lived, joy'd, caress'd together;
Delightful!—now separation—Good-bye my Fancy.      10

Yet let me not be too hasty,
Long indeed have we lived, slept, filter'd, become really blended into one;
Then if we die we die together, (yes, we'll remain one,)
If we go anywhere we'll go together to meet what happens,
May-be we'll be better off and blither, and learn something,      15
May-be it is yourself now really ushering me to the true songs, (who knows?)
May-be it is you the mortal knob really undoing, turning—so now finally,
Good-bye—and hail! my Fancy.

                                                     1891, 1891–92


## From Democratic Vistas[1]

### [American Literature]

\* \* \*

What, however, do we more definitely mean by New World literature? Are we not doing well enough here already? Are not the United States this day busily using, working, more printer's type, more presses, than any other country? uttering and absorbing more publications than any other? Do not our publishers fatten quicker and deeper? (helping themselves, under shelter of a delusive and sneaking law, or rather absence of law, to most of their forage, poetical, pictorial, historical, romantic, even comic without money and without price—and fiercely resisting the timidest proposal to pay for it.)[2]

Many will come under this delusion—but my purpose is to dispel it. I say that a nation may hold and circulate rivers and oceans of very readable print, journals, magazines, novels, library-books, "poetry," &c.—such as the States to-day possess and circulate—of unquestionable aid and value—hundreds of new volumes annually composed and brought out here, respectable enough, indeed unsurpass'd in smartness and erudition—with further hundreds, or rather millions, (as by free forage or theft aforemention'd,) also thrown into the market,—And yet, all the while, the said nation, land, strictly speaking, may possess no literature at all.

Repeating our inquiry, what, then, do we mean by real literature? especially the American literature of the future? Hard questions to meet. The clues are

1. The little book Democratic Vistas, published late in 1870 but dated 1871, was made up of three essays written for the Galaxy: Democracy appeared in December 1867 and Personalism in May 1868, but the magazine rejected the third, Literature, which was first published in the book form, the source of the present text. Democratic Vistas is one of the most neglected of major American literary, political, and philosophical documents.

2. From the founding of the United States until 1891, when Congress finally passed an international copyright law, American writers had been victimized by the fact that American publishers could reprint foreign books without payment to the authors: it cost a publisher only printing expenses to publish Dickens in this country, but Cooper or Melville or Clemens had to be paid royalties.

inferential, and turn us to the past. At best, we can only offer suggestions, comparisons, circuits.

It must still be reiterated, as, for the purpose of these memoranda, the deep lesson of history and time, that all else in the contributions of a nation or age, through its politics, materials, heroic personalities, military eclat, &c., remains crude, and defers, in any close and thorough-going estimate, until vitalized by national, original archetypes in literature. They only put the nation in form, finally tell anything—prove, complete anything—perpetuate anything. Without doubt, some of the richest and most powerful and populous communities of the antique world, and some of the grandest personalities and events, have, to after and present times, left themselves entirely unbequeath'd. Doubtless, greater than any that have come down to us, were among those lands, heroisms, persons, that have not come down to us at all, even by name, date, or location. Others have arrived safely, as from voyages over wide, century-stretching seas. The little ships, the miracles that have buoy'd them, and by incredible chances safely convey'd them, (or the best of them, their meaning and essence,) over long wastes, darkness, lethargy, ignorance, &c., have been a few inscriptions—a few immortal compositions, small in size, yet compassing what measureless values of reminiscence, contemporary portraitures, manners, idioms and beliefs, with deepest inference, hint and thought, to tie and touch forever the old, new body, and the old, new soul! These! and still these! bearing the freight so dear—dearer than pride—dearer than love. All the best experience of humanity folded, saved, freighted to us here. Some of these tiny ships we call Old and New Testament, Home Eschylus, Plato, Juvenal, &c. Precious minims![3] I think, if we were forced to choose, rather than have you, and the likes of you, and what belongs to, and has grown of you, blotted out and gone, we could better afford, appalling as that would be, to lose all actual ships, this day fasten'd by wharf, or floating on wave, and see them, with all their cargoes, scuttled and sent to the bottom.

Gather'd by geniuses of city, race or age, and put by them in highest of art's forms, namely, the literary form, the peculiar combinations and the outshows of that city, age, or race, its particular modes of the universal attributes and passions, its faiths, heroes, lovers and gods, wars, traditions, struggles, crimes, emotions, joys, (or the subtle spirit of these,) having been pass'd on to us to illumine our own selfhood, and its experiences—what they supply, indispensable and highest, if taken away, nothing else in all the world's boundless storehouses could make up to us, or ever again return.

For us, along the great highways of time, those monuments stand—those forms of majesty and beauty. For us those beacons burn though all the nights. Unknown Egyptians, graving hieroglyphs; Hindus, with hymn and apothegm and endless epic; Hebrew prophet, with spirituality, as in flashes of lightning, conscience like red-hot iron, plaintive songs and screams of vengeance for tyrannies and enslavement; Christ, with bent head, brooding love and peace, like a dove; Greek, creating eternal shapes of physical and esthetic proportion; Roman, lord of satire, the sword, and the codex;—of the figures, some far off and veil'd, others nearer and visible; Dante, stalking with lean form, nothing but fibre, not a grain of superfluous flesh; Angelo,[4] and the great painters,

3. In this sense, small containers, treasures being gathered into the small compass of a book.
4. Then an acceptable form of the name of Michel-angelo Buonarroti (1475–1564), Italian artist. Dante Alighieri (1265–1321), Italian poet, author of *The Divine Comedy*.

architects, musicians; rich Shakespeare, luxuriant as the sun, artist and singer of feudalism in its sunset, with all the gorgeous colors, owner thereof, and using them at will; and so to such as German Kant and Hegel,[5] where they, though near us, leaping over the ages, sit again, impassive, imperturbable, like the Egyptian gods. Of these, and the like of these, is it too much, indeed, to return to our favorite figure, and view them as orbs and systems of orbs, moving in free paths in the spaces of that other heaven, the kosmic intellect, the soul?

Ye powerful and resplendent ones! ye were, in your atmospheres, grown not for America, but rather for her foes, the feudal and the old—while our genius is democratic and modern. Yet could ye, indeed, but breathe your breath of life into our New World's nostrils—not to enslave us, as now, but, for our needs, to breed a spirit like your own—perhaps, (dare we to say it?) to dominate, even destroy, what you yourselves have left! On your plane, and no less, but even higher and wider, will I mete and measure for our wants to-day and here. I demand races of orbic bards, with unconditional uncompromising sway. Come forth, sweet democratic despots of the west!

By points and specimens like these we, in reflection, token what we mean by any land's or people's genuine literature. And thus compared and tested, judging amid the influence of loftiest products only, what do our current copious fields of print, covering in manifold forms, the United States, better, for an analogy, present, than, as in certain regions of the sea, those spreading, undulating masses of squid, through which the whale swimming, with head half out, feeds?

Not but that doubtless our current so-called literature, (like an endless supply of small coin,) performs a certain service, and may-be, too, the service needed for the time, (the preparation-service, as children learn to spell.) Everybody reads, and truly nearly everybody writes, either books, or for the magazines or journals. The matter has magnitude, too, after a sort. There is something impressive about the huge editions of the dailies and weeklies, the mountain-stacks of white paper piled in the press-vaults, and the proud, crashing, ten-cylinder presses, which I can stand and watch any time by the half hour. Then, (though the States in the field of imagination present not a single first-class work, not a single great literatus,) the main objects, to amuse, to titillate, to pass away time, to circulate the news, and rumors of news, to rhyme and read rhyme, are yet attain'd, and on a scale of infinity. To-day, in books, in the rivalry of writers, especially novelists, success, (so-call'd,) is for him or her who strikes the mean flat average, the sensational appetite for stimulus, incident,[6] &c., and depicts, to the common calibre, sensual, exterior life. To such, or the luckiest of them, as we see, the audiences are limitless and profitable; but they cease presently. While this day, or any day, to workmen portraying interior or spiritual life, the audiences were limited, and often laggard—but they last forever.

Compared with the past, our modern science soars, and our journals serve; but ideal and even ordinary romantic literature, does not, I think, substantially advance. Behold the prolific brood of the contemporary novel, magazine-tale,

5. Immanuel Kant (1724–1804) and George Wilhelm Friedrich Hegel (1770–1831), philosophers whose writings were familiar to Whitman.
6. In the reprinting of *Democratic Vistas* as part of

*Specimen Days & Collect* (1882), Whitman expanded the series to "the sensational appetite for stimulus, incident, persiflage, &c."

theatre-play, &c. The same endless thread of tangled and superlative love-story, inherited, apparently from the Amadises and Palmerins[7] of the 13th, 14th, and 15th centuries over there in Europe. The costumes and associations are brought down to date, the seasoning is hotter and more varied, the dragons and ogres are left out—but the *thing*, I should say, has not advanced—is just as sensational, just as strain'd—remains about the same, nor more, nor less.

What is the reason our time, our lands, that we see no fresh local courage, sanity, of our own—the Mississippi, stalwart Western men, real mental and physical facts, Southerners, &c., in the body of our literature? especially the poetic part of it. But always, instead, a parcel of dandies and ennuyees, dapper little gentlemen from abroad, who flood us with their thin sentiment of parlors, parasols, piano-songs, tinkling rhymes, the five-hundredth importation— or whimpering and crying about something, chasing one aborted conceit after another, and forever occupied in dyspeptic amours with dyspeptic women.

While, current and novel, the grandest events and revolutions, and stormiest passions of history, are crossing to-day with unparallel'd rapidity and magnificence over the stages of our own and all the continents, offering new materials, opening new vistas, with largest needs, inviting the daring launching forth of conceptions in literature, inspired by them, soaring in highest regions, serving art in its highest, (which is only the other name for serving God, and serving humanity,) where is the man of letters, where is the book, with any nobler aim than to follow in the old track, repeat what has been said before—and, as its utmost triumph, sell well, and be erudite or elegant?

✻　✻　✻

1870

---

7. Amadis de Gaul (with Gaul first meaning Wales, then being understood as meaning France) was the hero of various chivalric romances, as was Palmerin, the hero of *Palmerin of England*.

---

# HERMAN MELVILLE
## 1819–1891

Herman Melville began life with everything in his favor: heredity first of all, with two genuine Revolutionary heroes for grandfathers. The Melvill family (the *e* was added in the 1830s) was solidly established in Boston and the Gansevoorts were linked to the greatest Dutch patroon families of New York. Melville's much-traveled father, Allan Melvill, a dry-goods merchant in New York City, took inordinate pride in the genealogy of the Melvills, tracing the line past Scottish Renaissance courtiers to a queen of Hungary and tracing his mother's family, the Scollays, to the kings of Norway: "& so it appears we are of a royal line in both sides of the House—after all, it is not only an amusing but a just cause of pride, to resort back through the ages to such ancestry, & should produce a correspondent spirit of emulation in their descendants to the remotest posterity." As the third oldest of eight children born between 1815 and 1830, Herman Melville spent his early childhood in luxury. But Allan Melvill began borrowing from relatives in the 1820s, alternating between overenthusiasm about the future of business in America and dread of an inevitable recession. In 1832 he suddenly fell ill and died in a delirium that some in the family thought of as madness. He was many thousands of dollars in debt, and his family, then living in Albany, became dependent on the conscientious but finely calculated care of the Gansevoorts, especially Melville's uncle Peter.

Biographers justifiably hold that Melville's mature psychology is best understood as that of the decayed patrician. During his teens, he was distinctly a poor relation. The Princeton-educated Peter Gansevoort hobnobbed with the leading politicians of the day, entertaining President Van Buren at dinner during the years in which his widowed sister, Maria Melville, saw her brilliant oldest son Gansevoort and her more plodding second son Herman make do with what self-improvement they could derive from the Albany debating societies. Taken out of school when he was twelve, a few months after his father's death, Melville clerked for two years at a bank. Starting early in 1834 he worked two and a half years at his brother Gansevoort's fur-cap store in Albany. In 1837 he spent several months in nearby Pittsfield, Massachusetts, running his uncle Thomas Melvill's farm after his uncle left for Illinois. Just after he turned eighteen, he taught in a country school near Pittsfield, where he boarded with Yankee backwoods families. The next spring he took a course in surveying and engineering at the Lansingburgh Academy, near Albany, but in the aftermath of the Panic of 1837 found no work. He signed on a voyage to and from Liverpool in 1839, the summer he turned twenty, then the next year job-hunted fruitlessly around the Midwest. At twenty-one, in January 1841, he took the desperate measure of sailing on a whaler for the South Seas. His crucial experience had begun.

From Peru he wrote, in Gansevoort's paraphrase, that he was "not dissatisfied with his lot"—"The fact of his being one of a crew so much superior in morale and early advantages to the ordinary run of whaling crews affords him constant gratification." Nevertheless, in the summer of 1842 Melville and a shipmate, Toby Greene, jumped ship at Nukahiva, in the Marquesas, and for a few weeks Melville lived with a tribe quite untainted by Western civilization; late in life he felt he had lived in the world's last Eden. Picked up by an Australian whaler less than a month after he deserted, he took part in a comic opera mutiny and was imprisoned by the British consul in Tahiti, along with a learned friend (the "Dr. Long Ghost" of *Omoo*) who became his companion in exploring the flora and, especially, the fauna of Tahiti and Eimeo. Shipping on a Nantucket whaler at Eimeo, Melville was discharged in Lahaina, then knocked about Honolulu for a few months before signing on the frigate *United States* as an ordinary seaman. After a leisurely cruise in the Pacific, including a revisit to the Marquesas, the *United States* sailed for home, arriving at Boston in October 1844. On this ship Melville again encountered some remarkably literate, and even literary, sailors. No newspapers welcomed the young sailor home, but that month Democratic papers in New York were hailing the triumphant return of his brother Gansevoort from a splendidly histrionic stump-speaking tour in the West on behalf of Polk's campaign for the presidency. Herman Melville was twenty-five; he later said that from that year, beginning August 1, 1844, he dated his life. He apparently did not look for a job after his discharge from the navy in Boston on October 14; within two or three months he had begun writing *Typee* while staying with his lawyer brothers in New York City.

Circumstances were propitious. In the summer of 1845 Gansevoort was rewarded for his services to the Democrats with the secretaryship to the American Legation in London. When he sailed, he had with him the chaotic manuscript that Herman had just completed in Lansingburgh. It purported to be a straight autobiographical account of his detainment "in an indulgent captivity for about the space of four months" by an appealingly hedonistic, if also cannibalistic, tribe, but in fact Melville had quadrupled the time he had spent in the valley of the Typees. Gansevoort interested John Murray (the son of Lord Byron's friend and publisher) in the book for his Home and Colonial Library, and after it was eked out by new anthropological observations from Melville (many of which came from earlier books by sea captains and missionaries) and tidied up by a professional "reader," *Typee* was published early in 1846. As the earliest personal account of the South Seas to have the readability and suspense of adventure fiction, it made a great sensation, capturing the imagination of both the literary reviewers and the reading public with the surefire combination of anthropological novelty and what reviewers regularly tagged (remembering *Othello*) as "hair-breadth 'scapes." It was attended by vigorous, sales-stimulating controversy over its authenticity, capped by the emergence of Toby, the long-lost fellow runaway, in the person of Richard Tobias Greene, a house painter near Buffalo. G. P. Putnam of Wiley & Putnam (he was a cousin of Sophia Hawthorne's) had bought *Typee* in England at the urging of Washington Irving, but his partner, John Wiley, was appalled once he read closely the attacks on missionary operations in the South Seas. Although the American edition was already printed, Wiley demanded expurgations of sexual and political passages as well as of the attacks on the missionaries, and Melville agreed to excise a total of some thirty pages, contenting himself with exclaiming to the New York editor Evert Duyckinck that *expurgation* was an "odious" word. Melville followed the fortunes of *Typee* with zest and even wanted to manipulate the controversy through a planted newspaper review of his own. In the middle of the publicity over *Typee*, Gansevoort died suddenly at the age of thirty. In less than a year the unknown sailor, the unappreciated second son, had become a sensationally newsworthy writer and the head of his family.

Melville immediately turned to the composition of a sequel, *Omoo*, the account—more strictly autobiographical than *Typee*—of his beachcombing in Tahiti and Eimeo. Yet even as he was busily at work on *Omoo* at the end of 1846 he was trying to get a job in the Custom House in New York City—his notion of the ideal local job to provide a regular income and keep him among ships and sailors (as well as the necessary evil of bureaucrats) while, he must have hoped, giving him sufficient leisure for literary pursuits. When he offered *Omoo* to Murray, Melville wrote exuberantly that a "little experience in this art of book-craft has done wonders." He had in mind the condition of his manuscript, but he might well have said the same of his ability to manage a narrative. *Omoo* lacked the suspense of *Typee*, but it was a more polished performance of a writer far surer of himself. It is a fine, humorous production, full of vivid character sketches and memorable documentation of the evils wrought by the Christianizers. It delighted readers in 1847 and gave great pleasure to later South Sea wanderers like Robert Louis Stevenson and Henry Adams.

In the flush of his success with *Omoo*, Melville married Elizabeth Knapp Shaw on August 4, 1847, three days after his twenty-eighth birthday. Her father, Lemuel Shaw, the chief justice of Massachusetts, had been a school friend of Allan Melvill at the turn of the century and had been engaged to one of Allan's sisters who died early of tuberculosis. Allan had taken advantage of Shaw's friendship to borrow from him in the 1820s; Herman's uncle, Thomas Melvill, and Thomas's son Robert had further abused that friendship in the 1830s; then in the early 1840s Gansevoort Melville had sought Shaw out as patron. Melville dedicated *Typee* to Shaw, although it is not clear what their personal acquaintance had been; after the marriage Shaw provided several advances against his daughter's inheritance, the first being $2,000 toward the purchase of a house in New York, where Melville established himself with his bride, his younger brother Allan, Allan's own bride, his mother, four sisters, and his new manuscript. Melville was well on his way to becoming a literary fixture of New York City, a participant in projects of the Duyckinck literary clique such as the short-lived satirical *Yankee Doodle*, and for the longer-lived enterprise of the Duyckincks, *The Literary World*, a resident authority and reviewer of books on nautical matters and inland exploration, and a reliable dispenser of vigorous, humorous, authentic tales of exotic adventure.

Instead, the Polynesian adventurer discovered the world of the mind and the aesthetic range of the English language as he worked his way into his third book, *Mardi*, which was published in April 1849, just short of two years after he began it. His friends had some baffled inklings at the changes in Melville that could make him call the seventeenth-century writer Sir Thomas Browne a "cracked archangel" because of the speculations in the *Religio Medici* (Melville's new friend Evert Duyckinck wrote his brother, "Was ever any thing of this sort said before by a sailor?"), but for the most part the evidence of the transformation went into the manuscript of *Mardi*. It had begun as a South Sea adventure story like *Typee* and *Omoo*, or as they would have been if they had been written by a man intoxicated with his discovery of his powers. In the spring of 1848, after Melville thought he was through with *Mardi*, news of the new European revolutions led him to interpolate a long section of allegorical satire on European and American politics. Sometime in the last year of composition, he bade farewell to the New York literary cliques with another allegorical section on the great poet Lombardo's creation of a masterpiece that puzzled his small-minded contemporaries.

In his solitary expansion of mind Melville had become reckless, admitting in his book that he had "voyaged chartless," and he ultimately foundered in an attempt to persuade Murray that the work, though professedly fiction, would not retroactively impugn the much-challenged authenticity of the first two books. Another London publisher, Richard Bentley, promptly enough took the book, but Murray had been prescient. Many of the reviewers were appalled at the betrayal of their expectations of another *Typee* or *Omoo*, though a discriminating minority recognized what a valuable book they had in hand. It sold poorly, especially in the overpriced three-volume English edition, and deeply damaged Melville's growing reputation except with a few readers. *Mardi* is, in fact, almost unreadable, except for a rarely dedicated lover of antiquarian literary, philosophical, metaphysical, and political hodgepodge—the sort of eccentric scholar who loves Burton's *Anatomy of Melancholy* and Browne's *Vulgar Errors*. Melvilleans find it inexhaustibly fascinating, recognizing in it Melville's exuberant response to his realization that he was—or could become—a great literary genius. *Mardi* was his declaration of literary independence, though he did not fully achieve that independence until *Moby-Dick*, two books and two years later.

Early in 1849, during the interval between completing *Mardi* and its publication, Melville's first son, Malcolm, was born at the Shaw house in Boston, and Melville rested, went to the theater, heard Emerson lecture, and read Shakespeare with full attentiveness for the first time. He spoke hopefully of undertaking a work that would carry him beyond *Mardi*, but the first reviews of that book showed that he could not afford another such luxury. Accepting the responsibilities of a new father, he wrote *Redburn* (1849) and *White-Jacket* (1850) as acts of contrition, both ground out during one four-month period in the 1849 summer swelter of a cholera-ridden New York City. As he promised Richard Bentley, *Redburn* would contain no metaphysics, only cakes and ale. Written in the first person by the middle-aged, sentimental Wellingborough Redburn, it is the story of the narrator's first voyage, which like Melville's own was a summer voyage to and from Liverpool, though Redburn is hardly more than a boy while Melville was twenty. Often as good as *Huckleberry Finn*, better than such a twentieth-century rival as *Catcher in the Rye*, *Redburn* could have been a minor classic if Melville had sustained the point of view he had established—lovingly satiric toward the boy Redburn, more pointedly satiric toward the convention-bound narrator. But interest in his experiment with a limited character's first-person narrative flagged, and the second half of the book is only intermittently as compelling as the first. The reviewers and the readers liked it, especially the air of documentary convincingness that reminded them of *Robinson Crusoe* and other works by Daniel Defoe.

Long before *Redburn* was published, Melville had completed *White-Jacket*, which was based on his experiences on the man-of-war *United States* in 1843 and 1844, supplemented by lavish borrowings from earlier nautical literature. In *White-Jacket* Melville came into something like creative equilibrium, for his first-person narrator was once again, as in *Typee* and *Omoo*, at the same stage of development as the writer, capable of saying precisely what Melville might at that given moment be capable of saying. Overshadowed by *Moby-Dick*, slighted by most modern readers because of its unpromising—"unliterary"—subject matter, *White-Jacket* has been adequately praised only by its first readers. Melville himself never could quite regard it as much more than a product of forced labor, like *Redburn* (that "little nursery tale") the literary equivalent of "sawing wood."

Rather than bargaining with Bentley by mail (as he had just done for *Redburn*) and having the publisher again cite the new British ruling on copyright (which now was denied to books by American authors even if first printed in Great Britain), Melville sailed for London in October 1849, carrying with him proofs of the Harper edition of *White-Jacket*. An observer described him as wearily hawking his book "from Picadilly to Whitechapel, calling upon every publisher in his way," and in fact Melville repeatedly met refusal because of the copyright problem. He ultimately settled with Bentley on good terms—but not good enough to allow him to make his hoped-for tour of Europe and the Holy Land. He passed weeks in antiquarian book buying, sightseeing, library- and museum-going, and literary socializing, by his responses to these experiences confirming his sense of himself as a "pondering man." He made a brief excursion into France and Germany, then, homesick and guilty about his holiday, he cut short his trip. Leaving early meant refusing the duke of Rutland's "cordial invitation to visit him at his Castle," Melville's one chance to learn "what the highest English aristocracy really & practically is." Soon after his return to New York on February 1, 1850, enthusiastic reviews of *White-Jacket* began arriving from England, and in March the American edition was published to similar acclaim. In a buoyant mood, sure of his powers and sure of his ability to keep an audience, Melville began his whaling book. (By mid-1851 its working title was *The Whale*, which remained the title for the English edition; *Moby-Dick* was a last-minute substitute for the American edition.)

Like *Mardi*, *Moby-Dick* was luxury for Melville, an enormous, slowly written book. *Slowly* deserves qualification: Melville lived with the book some seventeen months, often writing very steadily for many weeks on end, but allowing several lengthy interruptions. By May 1, 1850, Melville was telling Richard Henry Dana, his well-known fellow sea writer, that he was "half way in the work." Critics have speculated that the book began as a matter-of-fact sea narrative, but Melville's letter makes it clear that from the start the challenge to his art lay in getting poetry from blubber and managing to "throw in a little fancy" without, as he said, resulting in gambols as ungainly as those of the whales. Furthermore, he meant "to give the truth of the thing." None of these intentions clashes with the book he finally completed, though whatever plans he had were later altered to accommodate new literary sources as well as his maturing philosophical and theological preoccupations.

One crucial event during the composition of *Moby-Dick* was Melville's vacation at his uncle Thomas's old place in the Berkshires (now occupied by his cousin Robert as a select boardinghouse where former President Tyler and the poet Longfellow had stayed). He had left the region as a teenage master of a backwoods school, and Pittsfield residents remembered him, if at all, as that lad or, from a few years before, as the orphan nephew of Thomas Melvill, a pretentious farmer in and out of debtor's prison until he moved to Illinois in 1837. Now this nephew was an author of international repute, and the collision of times and circumstances released a near-manic state in Melville. He was in this exalted mood when he met Nathaniel Hawthorne. Reading Hawthorne's *Mosses from an Old Manse* just after their meeting may have had some minor stylistic influence on a few passages in *Moby-Dick*; more important, Melville undertook for the Duyckinck brothers' *Liter-*

*ary World* a review of *Mosses* in which he articulated many of his deepest attitudes toward the problems and opportunities of American writers. Infusing the whole review is Melville's exultant sense that the day had come when American writers could rival Shakespeare; in praising Hawthorne's achievements, he was honoring what he knew lay in his own manuscript. Furthermore, Melville gave clearer hints at what sort of "truth" he might be trying to give in *Moby-Dick*—dark, "Shakespearean" truths about human nature and the universe that "in this world of lies" can be told only "covertly, and by snatches." Out of his failures with *Mardi* and the slave labor of the next two books, Melville had built a literary theory in which a writer writes simultaneously for two audiences, one composed of the mob, the other of "eagle-eyed" readers who perceive the true meaning of those passages that the author has "directly calculated to deceive—egregiously deceive—the superficial skimmer of pages." *Moby-Dick*, now reported by Evert Duyckinck to be "a new book mostly done—a romantic, fanciful & literal & most enjoyable presentment of the Whale Fishery—something quite new"—was to be such a book. It was the culmination of Melville's reading in great literature from the Bible through Rabelais, Burton, John Milton, Sterne, Lord Byron, Thomas De Quincey and Thomas Carlyle, yet anchored also in the nautical world of Baron Cuvier, Frederick Debell Bennett, William Scoresby, and Obed Macy, a fusion of aspects of Sir Thomas Browne and the American travel writer J. Ross Browne, with incidental hints from a multitude of quaint old encyclopedic volumes.

Still exultantly feeling his new powers, Melville moved his family to a farm near Pittsfield late in 1850. By December he had settled again into intense work on his book until the spring chores took him away from it. During 1851 the most stimulating fact of Melville's existence, other than the book he brought to completion and saw through the press, was Hawthorne's presence at Lenox, near enough for a few visits to be exchanged except during the worst of the Berkshire winter. On some of his visits he took the Old Lenox Road, passing by a rocky outcropping where years before, a futureless orphan, he had brooded on the natural landscape and the spires of Pittsfield. Small wonder if the collision of past and present heightened and perturbed his moods. Melville's intense friendship provided him with a desperately needed sense of literary community as well as a confidant for his metaphysical and philosophical speculations. His letters to Hawthorne, preserved now mostly in nineteenth-century transcripts and printings by Hawthorne's descendants, are among the glories of American literature and a priceless record of Melville's state of mind during his last months with *Moby-Dick*. Uppermost in them is his sense of kinship with the great writers and thinkers of the world—a sense that would seem megalomanic if his manuscript had not vindicated him. The recurrent themes of the letters—democracy and aristocracy, the ironic failure of Christians to be Christian, fame and immortality, the brotherhood of great-souled mortals, and in particular the Miltonic themes of "Providence, Foreknowledge, Will, and Fate, / Fixt Fate, free will, foreknowledge absolute"—were all recurrent themes of *Moby-Dick*. From his perception of himself as a descendant of kings abandoned to the universe, yet struggling back to reclaim his rightful majesty (a perception revealed in many of his scorings and underlinings in his two-volume set of Milton's poetry that surfaced in 1983 and was auctioned early in 1984 for $100,000), Melville created a hero who dared to turn God's lightning back against him and whose nature could only be explained by venturing deep below the antiquities of the earth to question a titanic captive god. For all Ahab's insanity, which was recognized by the narrator, Ishmael, Melville's emotional sympathies were with the defiant Ahab who rejected the slavish values of the shore to defy the malignancy in the universe. That was the world of the mind. But as he finished *Moby-Dick*, Melville was a family man whose household included his mother and sisters as well as a small child and a pregnant wife. He owed the Harpers $700 because they had advanced him more than his earlier books had earned, and in April 1851 they refused him an advance on his whaling book. On May 1, Melville borrowed $2,050 from T. D. Stewart, an old Lansingburgh acquaintance, and a few weeks later he painfully defined his literary-economic dilemma to Hawthorne: "What I feel most moved to write, that is banned.—it will not pay. Yet, altogether, write the *other* way I cannot. So the product is a final hash, and all my books are botches."

Late in 1851, about the time *Moby-Dick* was published, Melville tried once again to find a form in which he could write as profoundly as he could while retaining the popularity he had so easily won with his first two books. Settling on the gothic novel in its midcentury transmogrification as the sentimental psychological novel favored by women book buyers, he began *Pierre*, thinking he could express the agonies of the growth of a human psyche even while enthralling readers with the romantic and ethical perplexities attending on young Pierre Glendinning's discovery of a dark maiden who might be his unacknowledged half-sister. Melville was relentlessly analyzing both the tragic and the satiric implications of the impracticability of Christianity, for Pierre's calamitous decision was to obey his heart's idealism and attempt a life in imitation of the "divine unidentifiableness" of Jesus, who required of his followers the rejection of all worldly kith and kin. Melville took his manuscript to New York City around New Year's Day 1852, hoping to publish it as a taut 360-page book, little more than half the size of *Moby-Dick*. But despite the early sales of the whaling book, Melville was still in debt to the Harpers, who offered him a punitive contract for *Pierre*—twenty cents on the dollar after expenses rather than the old rate of fifty cents. Stung, Melville accepted, but his rage and shame over the contract mingled with pain from the reviews of *Moby-Dick* in the January periodicals: the *Southern Quarterly Review*, for instance, said a "writ *de lunatico*" was justified against Melville and his characters. Within days of coming to terms with Harpers, Melville began working into *Pierre* a sometimes wry, sometimes recklessly bitter account of his own literary career, ultimately enlarging the work by 150 printed pages and wrecking whatever chance he had of making the work what he had hoped—as much more profound than *Moby-Dick* as the legendary Krakens are larger than whales.

Pierre would probably have failed with its first readers even if it had been completed and published in its projected shorter form, for the subject matter even in the first half included atheism and incest and the language Melville created as a tool for psychological probing seemed hysterical and artificial to the reviewers. In any case, the *Pierre* that Harpers finally published late in July 1852 (giving Melville time for a fruitless negotiation with Bentley, who refused to publish it without expurgation) all but ended Melville's career. It was widely denounced as immoral, and one *Pierre*-inspired news account was captioned "HERMAN MELVILLE CRAZY." In panic the family made efforts to gain Melville some government post, preferably foreign, but nothing came of their attempts to call in old favors. Melville stayed on the farm with his expanding household (two daughters, Elizabeth and Frances, were born in 1853 and 1855). After *Pierre* Melville's career faltered. In May 1853 he completed *The Isle of the Cross*, a book about a patient Nantucket wife, but he was somehow "prevented" from publishing it, and he probably destroyed it. In 1853 and 1854 he wrote part of a book about tortoise hunting in the Galapagos Islands, then apparently diverted some of it into *The Encantadas* and destroyed the rest. Melville was undergoing a profound psychological crisis that left him more resigned to fate than defiant, and in addition to his older ailment of weak eyes he developed a new set of crippling afflictions diagnosed as sciatica and rheumatism.

Late in 1853 Melville began a new, low-keyed career as writer of short stories for the two major American monthlies, *Harper's* and *Putnam's*. All stories were anonymous, by magazine policy (though authorship was often leaked to editors of newspapers and other magazines), so what Melville published in the next years did not add greatly to his fame. One serial, the story of a Revolutionary exile named

Israel Potter, stretched out to book length. Offering it to the publisher, Melville promised that it would contain nothing "to shock the fastidious," and in fact he restrained his imagination and his metaphysical and theological compulsions. Straightforward novel that it is, *Israel Potter* contains passages of great historical interest, especially the complex portraits of Benjamin Franklin, John Paul Jones, and Ethan Allen. In 1856 Melville collected the *Putnam's* stories as *The Piazza Tales,* supplying a new prefatory sketch, "The Piazza," which marked his development past his earlier simple admiration for Hawthorne's subjects and techniques. Clear in all of Melville's writings in the mid-fifties is his growing tendency to brood less over his own career and his own relationship with cosmic forces and more over the American national character and the conditions in American life that would allow honest craftsmen like himself to be rejected. Self-pity tinges some of these writings, but more often a wry jocularity, an almost comfortable self-mockery. In them Melville achieved a new sureness of artistic control, even though the power of *Moby-Dick* and parts of *Pierre* was never regained. From this period of physical and psychic suffering and of financial distress emerged a new masterpiece, *The Confidence-Man,* a devastating indictment of national confidence in the form of mingled metaphysical satire and low comedy. It went almost unread in the United States; in England the reviews were more intelligent but the sales were also disappointing, and Melville did not earn a cent from either edition.

By the spring of 1856 Melville may have recovered from most of his mental, spiritual, and physical agonies, but his economic distress was greater than ever and he had composed *The Confidence-Man* (including a chapter on the catastrophic consequences of "a friendly loan") to the ticking of an economic time bomb. He was a year late in payment on the mortgage on the farm held by the previous owner; worse, he still owed the principal and the accumulating interest on the $2,050 he had borrowed in 1851, and the lender was pressing for full repayment. Melville was forced to sell part of the farm, but Judge Shaw met the family's anxieties about Herman's state of mind by providing funds for an extended trip to Europe and the Levant, from October 1856 to May 1857. In England Melville told Hawthorne, who had become consul at Liverpool, that he did not anticipate much pleasure in his rambles, since "the spirit of adventure" had gone out of him. For upwards of a decade, Melville's adventuring had been inward—philosophical, metaphysical, psychological, and artistic. As Hawthorne hoped, Melville brightened as he went onward, and after a few days he began to keep a journal. Melville's sightseeing and gallery-going were as compulsively American as Hawthorne's own. Many of Melville's observations were predictable responses to the places, palaces, and paintings given largest space in the guidebooks, but what he saw gradually led him to energetically original responses, as in his then unfashionable response to classical statuary, earlier Italian painters like Giotto, and the realistic Dutch and Flemish genre painters. As Howard Horsford, the editor of this journal, says, the entries show Melville's taste in the process of being formed. Horsford points out "the peculiar urgency, the sharpness, vividness, and freshness" of those entries where Melville was most deeply moved: "Many passages, such as those on the Pyramids, or the descriptions of the Jerusalem scene and the Palestinian landscape, are in his finest rhetorical style; many of his comments on people, places, and things display the most cutting edge of his irony and satire, as in his accounts of the Church of the Holy Sepulchre and of the missionaries in the Near East." Horsford also draws a precise contrast between the Melville of the late 1840s and the one of the mid-fifties. When Melville "had embarked on metaphysical speculation at the time of *Mardi,*" it had been "a welcome release, an escape into a new freedom from orthodoxy and dogmatism, a mental emancipation." Now Melville's metaphysical speculations had ended in "joyless skepticism." When he returned home, Melville was more than ever "a pondering man," but he told a young Gansevoort cousin that he was "not going to write any more at present."

That moment stretched on. Melville lectured in the East and Midwest for three seasons (1857–60) without much profit, speaking in successive years on "Statues in Rome," "The South Seas," and "Traveling." He prepared a volume of poems in 1860 but instead of trying to place it, he sailed on a voyage to San Francisco as passenger on a ship captained by his youngest brother, Thomas, leaving his wife and his brother Allan to seek fruitlessly for a publisher. Early in 1861, Melville attempted, once again, to "procure some foreign appointment under the new Administration—the consulship at Florence, for example"; once again, he failed to recognize that his refusal to take part in local politics would doom his chances, whatever famous statesmen spoke out for him. In Washington he attended Lincoln's second levee and "Old Abe," as he wrote home, shook his hand "like a good fellow." An urgent letter recalled him to Pittsfield, and he and his wife reached Boston too late to see Judge Shaw alive. The estate was slow in being settled, but promptly enough some stocks were in Mrs. Melville's possession, and their economic pressures began to ease. The Melvilles spent the winter of 1861–62 in Manhattan, then in April Melville returned to Arrowhead (which his brother Allan later bought) and moved the family into Pittsfield. A driver who on mountain excursions had been "daring to the point of recklessness" and who had derived some pleasure from terrifying his passengers while confident he would deliver them to "a safe landing place," Melville, while "driving at a moderate pace over a perfectly smooth and level road" at Pittsfield in November 1862, had a freak accident that left his right arm useless till the next spring and affected him emotionally, so that for a time he "shrank from entering a carriage" and perhaps never completely recovered from "the shock which his system had received." No longer a young man, Melville moved his family to New York in October 1863 and waited out the war, making a trip to the Virginia battlefields with Allan in 1864 to get sight of a Gansevoort cousin and (as Allan put it), like all literary men, to "have opportunities to see that they may describe": Battle-Pieces (1866), a volume of Civil War poems, was casually or disdainfully reviewed and quickly forgotten; now it ranks with Whitman's Drum-Taps as the best of hundreds of volumes of poetry to come out of the war. For all his front of nonchalance, Melville was devastated by the loss of his career and further rebuffs when he sought a government job in Washington in 1861. As the unemployed do, Melville took out his frustrations on his family, so much so that for years his wife's half-brothers considered him insane as well as financially incompetent, and by early 1867 Melville's wife was also convinced of his insanity. Her sense of loyalty to him and her horror of gossip, however, were strong enough to make her reject her minister's suggestion that she pretend to make a routine visit to Boston and then barricade herself in the Shaw house, but as her family realized, the law was on Melville's side, whatever unrecorded abuses he was guilty of. In 1866 Melville had at last obtained a political job—not as consul in some exotic capital but as a deputy inspector of customs in New York City; ironically, his beat during some years took him frequently to the pier on Gansevoort Street, named for his mother's heroic father. After Malcolm killed himself late in 1867 at the age of eighteen the Melvilles closed ranks.

As Melville had predicted to Hawthorne, he became known as the "man who lived among the cannibals," holding his place in encyclopedias and literary histories primarily as the author of Typee and Omoo, all but forgotten by the postbellum literary world. But for years through the early 1870s Melville worked on a poem about a motley group of American European pilgrims—and tourists—who talked their way through some of the same Palestinian scenes he had visited a decade and more earlier; apparently he carried about pocket-size slips of paper for writing in odd moments at work as well as during his evenings. This poem, Clarel, grew to 18,000 lines and lay unpublished for many months or perhaps even two years before it appeared in 1876, paid for by a specific bequest from the dying Peter Gansevoort. It is America's most thoughtful contribution to the conflict of religious faith and Darwinian skepticism that obsessed English contemporaries such as Matthew Arnold and Thomas Hardy. Like *Mardi* it is inexhaustible for what it reveals of Melville's mind and art, but unlike *Mardi* it is plotted with the surety of artistic control that he had learned in the 1850s; however, *Mardi* had been read and argued about, and *Clarel* was ignored.

Stanwix, the second Melville son, drifted away without a career, beachcombing for a time in Central America, finally dying in San Francisco in 1886. The first daughter, called Bessie, developed severe arthritis and never married, and died in 1908. Only Frances married, and she lived until 1934, unable to recognize her father in the words of twentieth-century admirers and flatly refusing to talk about him. But through the 1880s Melville and his wife drew closer together. An extraordinary series of legacies came to them in Melville's last years; ironically the wealth was too late to make much change in their lives, but it allowed him to retire from the Custom House at the beginning of 1886 and devote himself to his writing. From time to time after *Clarel* he had written poems that ultimately went into two volumes, which he printed privately shortly before his death, except for some that remained unpublished until the 1920s and later. Melville developed the habit of writing prose headnotes to poems, notably some dealing with an imaginary Burgundy Club in which he found consolation for his loneliness. He could relax with the intelligent good fellows of his imagination as he could never relax among the popular literary men of the 1870s and 1880s who now and then tried to patronize him. In the mid-1880s one poem about a British sailor evoked a headnote that, expanded and reexpanded, was left nearly finished at Melville's death as *Billy Budd, Sailor*, his final study of the ambiguous claims of authority and individuality.

Before Melville's death in 1891, something like a revival of his fame was in progress, especially in England. American newspapers became accustomed to reprinting and briefly commenting on extraordinary items in British periodicals, such as Robert Buchanan's footnote to Melville's name in a poetic tribute to Whitman (1885): "I sought everywhere for this Triton, who is still living somewhere in New York. No one seemed to know anything of the one great imaginative writer fit to stand shoulder to shoulder with Whitman on that continent." The recurrent imagery—used by Melville as well as journalists—was of burial and possible resurrection.

When he died, Melville had reason to think his reputation would ultimately be established. Just after his death, new editions of *Typee, Omoo, White-Jacket*, and *Moby-Dick* were published both in the United States and in England, and Mrs. Melville remained a loyal and alert custodian of his memory until her death in 1906, but interest sputtered away except for small cults of Melville lovers who, as an anonymous British writer said in 1922, came to use *Moby-Dick* (or *The Whale*) as the test of a worthy reader and friend, proffering it without special comment and staking all on the response of the reader. The true Melville revival began with articles on Melville's centennial in 1919. That revival, one of the most curious phenomena of American literary history, swept Melville from the ranks of the lesser American writers—lesser than James Fenimore Cooper and William Gilmore Simms—into the rarefied company of Shakespeare and a few fellow immortals of world literature so that only Whitman, James, and Faulkner are seen as his American equals. Many of the materials for a biography had by then been lost (Melville burned his letters from Hawthorne, family members censored their files from dangerous years like the 1860s), but scholars have found the study of Melville's life and works inexhaustible. Even during the mass consumption of Melville in the classroom and the spawning of the White Whale in comic books, cartoons, and seafood restaurants, even during Melville's inflated glory at the Postal Service (a stamped 6-cent envelope in 1970, with a white whale in a blue oval; a 20-cent stamp, no envelope, in 1984 with Melville's portrait), a few lonely cultists are still to be found, tracing his journeys in the South Seas and Manhattan Island, and visiting his grave in the Bronx, faithful to the Melville who speaks to them without the aid of an interpreter. That may be the true sign of the rarest literary immortality.

# Hawthorne and His Mosses

## By a Virginian Spending July in Vermont[1]

A papered chamber in a fine old farm-house—a mile from any other dwelling, and dipped to the eaves in foliage—surrounded by mountains, old woods, and Indian ponds,—this, surely, is the place to write of Hawthorne. Some charm is in this northern air, for love and duty seem both impelling to the task. A man of a deep and noble nature has seized me in this seclusion. His wild, witch voice rings through me; or, in softer cadences, I seem to hear it in the songs of the hill-side birds, that sing in the larch trees at my window.

Would that all excellent books were foundlings, without father or mother, that so it might be, we could glorify them, without including their ostensible authors. Nor would any true man take exception to this;—least of all, he who writes,—"When the Artist rises high enough to achieve the Beautiful, the symbol by which he makes it perceptible to mortal senses becomes of little value in his eyes, while his spirit possesses itself in the enjoyment of the reality."[2]

But more than this. I know not what would be the right name to put on the title-page of an excellent book, but this I feel, that the names of all fine authors are fictitious ones, far more so than that of Junius,—simply standing, as they do, for the mystical, ever-eluding Spirit of all Beauty, which ubiquitously possesses men of genius. Purely imaginative as this fancy may appear, it nevertheless seems to receive some warranty from the fact, that on a personal interview no great author has ever come up to the idea of his reader. But that dust of which our bodies are composed, how can it fitly express the nobler intelligences among us? With reverence be it spoken, that not even in the case of one deemed more than man, not even in our Saviour, did his visible frame betoken anything of the augustness of the nature within. Else, how could those Jewish eyewitnesses fail to see heaven in his glance.

It is curious, how a man may travel along a country road, and yet miss the grandest, or sweetest of prospects, by reason of an intervening hedge, so like all other hedges, as in no way to hint of the wide landscape beyond. So has it been with me concerning the enchanting landscape in the soul of this Hawthorne, this most excellent Man of Mosses. His "Old Manse" has been written now four years, but I never read it till a day or two since. I had seen it in the book-stores—heard of it often—even had it recommended to me by a tasteful friend, as a rare, quiet book, perhaps too deserving of popularity to be popular. But there are so many books called "excellent," and so much unpopular merit, that amid the thick stir of other things, the hint of my tasteful friend was disregarded; and for four years the Mosses on the Old Manse never refreshed

---

1. The manuscript shows that the pseudonymous "Virginian Spending July in Vermont" was an afterthought designed to account for the emotional outpouring that Melville had written in his own voice. Contrary to the assertion within the essay, Melville wrote the review after meeting Hawthorne during a lit- erary outing in the Berkshires on August 5, 1850. Several errors marred the first two-part publication in the New York *Literary World* for August 17 and 24, 1850; necessary spelling corrections are made, but the text printed here is based on the manuscript.
2. The conclusion of *The Artist of the Beautiful*.

me with their perennial green. It may be, however, that all this while, the book, like wine, was only improving in flavor and body. At any rate, it so chanced that this long procrastination eventuated in a happy result. At breakfast the other day, a mountain girl, a cousin of mine,[3] who for the last two weeks has every morning helped me to strawberries and raspberries,—which, like the roses and pearls in the fairy-tale, seemed to fall into the saucer from those strawberry-beds her cheeks,—this delightful creature, this charming Cherry says to me—"I see you spend your mornings in the hay-mow; and yesterday I found there 'Dwight's Travels in New England'.[4] Now I have something far better than that,—something more congenial to our summer on these hills. Take these raspberries, and then I will give you some moss."—"Moss!" said I.—"Yes, and you must take it to the barn with you, and good-bye to 'Dwight.' "

With that she left me, and soon returned with a volume, verdantly bound, and garnished with a curious frontispiece in green,—nothing less, than a fragment of real moss cunningly pressed to a flyleaf.—"Why this," said I, spilling my raspberries, "this is the 'Mosses from an Old Manse.'" "Yes," said cousin Cherry, "yes, it is that flowery Hawthorne."—"Hawthorne and Mosses," said I, "no more: it is morning: it is July in the country: and I am off for the barn."

Stretched on that new mown clover, the hill-side breeze blowing over me through the wide barn door, and soothed by the hum of the bees in the meadows around, how magically stole over me this Mossy Man! And how amply, how bountifully, did he redeem that delicious promise to his guests in the Old Manse, of whom it is written—"Others could give them pleasure, or amusement, or instruction—these could be picked up anywhere—but it was for me to give them rest. Rest, in a life of trouble! What better could be done for weary and world-worn spirits? what better could be done for anybody, who came within our magic circle, than to throw the spell of a magic spirit over him?"[5]—So all that day, half-buried in the new clover, I watched this Hawthorne's "Assyrian dawn, and Paphian sunset and moonrise, from the summit of our Eastern Hill."[6]

The soft ravishments of the man spun me round about in a web of dreams, and when the book was closed, when the spell was over, this wizard "dismissed me with but misty reminiscences, as if I had been dreaming of him."

What a mild moonlight of contemplative humor bathes that Old Manse!— the rich and rare distilment of a spicy and slowly-oozing heart. No rollicking rudeness, no gross fun fed on fat dinners, and bred in the lees of wine,—but a humor so spiritually gentle, so high, so deep, and yet so richly relishable, that it were hardly inappropriate in an angel. It is the very religion of mirth; for nothing so human but it may be advanced to that. The orchard of the Old

3. In fact, Melville's Aunt Mary Melvill gave him the book two weeks before he met Hawthorne.
4. I.e., Timothy Dwight's four-volume Travels in New-England and New-York (1821–22).
5. From Hawthorne's introductory essay, The Old Manse.
6. Also from The Old Manse, in the description of the "little nook of a study": "It was here that Emerson wrote 'Nature'; for he was then an inhabitant of the Manse, and used to watch the Assyrian dawn and the Paphian sunset and moonrise, from the summit of our

eastern hill." Hawthorne is paraphrasing chap. 3 of Nature: "Give me health and a day, and I will make the pomp of emperors ridiculous. The dawn is my Assyria; the sun-set and moon-rise my Paphos, and unimaginable realms of faerie; broad noon shall be my England of the senses and the understanding; the night shall be my Germany of mystic philosophy and dreams." Melville may not have understood that Hawthorne was paraphrasing Emerson: his first serious reading of 'Nature' apparently took place a few weeks later in the Hawthornes' house near Lenox.

Manse seems the visible type of the fine mind that has described it. Those twisted, and contorted old trees, "that stretch out their crooked branches, and take such hold of the imagination, that we remember them as humorists and odd-fellows." And then, as surrounded by these grotesque forms, and hushed in the noon-day repose of this Hawthorne's spell, how aptly might the still fall of his ruddy thoughts into your soul be symbolized by "the thump of a great apple, in the stillest afternoon, falling without a breath of wind, from the mere necessity of perfect ripeness"! For no less ripe than ruddy are the apples of the thoughts and fancies in this sweet Man of Mosses.

"Buds and Bird-Voices"—What a delicious thing is that!—"Will the world ever be so decayed, that Spring may not renew its greenness?"—And the "Fire-Worship." Was ever the hearth so glorified into an altar before? The mere title of that piece is better than any common work in fifty folio volumes. How exquisite is this:—"Nor did it lessen the charm of his soft, familiar courtesy and helpfulness, that the mighty spirit, were opportunity offered him, would run riot through the peaceful house, wrap its inmates in his terrible embrace, and leave nothing of them save their whitened bones. This possibility of mad destruction only made his domestic kindness the more beautiful and touching. It was so sweet of him, being endowed with such power, to dwell, day after day, and one long, lonesome night after another, on the dusky hearth, only now and then betraying his wild nature, by thrusting his red tongue out of the chimney-top! True, he had done much mischief in the world, and was pretty certain to do more, but his warm heart atoned for all. He was kindly to the race of man."

But he has still other apples, not quite so ruddy, though full as ripe:—apples, that have been left to wither on the tree, after the pleasant autumn gathering is past. The sketch of "The Old Apple Dealer" is conceived in the subtlest spirit of sadness; he whose "subdued and nerveless boyhood prefigured his abortive prime, which, likewise, contained within itself the prophecy and image of his lean and torpid age." Such touches as are in this piece can not proceed from any common heart. They argue such a depth of tenderness, such a boundless sympathy with all forms of being, such an omnipresent love, that we must needs say, that this Hawthorne is here almost alone in his genera-tion,—at least, in the artistic manifestation of these things. Still more. Such touches as these,—and many, very many similar ones, all through his chap-ters—furnish clews, whereby we enter a little way into the intricate, profound heart where they originated. And we see, that suffering, some time or other and in some shape or other,—this only can enable any man to depict it in others. All over him, Hawthorne's melancholy rests like an Indian Summer, which, though bathing a whole country in one softness, still reveals the dis-tinctive hue of every towering hill, and each far-winding vale.

But it is the least part of genius that attracts admiration. Where Hawthorne is known, he seems to be deemed a pleasant writer, with a pleasant style,—a sequestered, harmless man, from whom any deep and weighty thing would hardly be anticipated:—a man who means no meanings. But there is no man, in whom humor and love, like mountain peaks, soar to such a rapt height, as to receive the irradiations of the upper skies;—there is no man in whom humor and love are developed in that high form called genius; no such man can exist without also possessing, as the indispensable complement of these, a great, deep intellect, which drops down into the universe like a plummet. Or, love and humor are only the eyes, through which such an intellect views this world. The great beauty in such a mind is but the product of its strength. What, to all readers, can be more charming than the piece entitled "Monsieur du Miroir"; and to a reader at all capable of fully fathoming it, what, at the same time, can possess more mystical depth of meaning?—Yes, there he sits, and looks at me,—this "shape of mystery," this "identical Monsieur du Miroir."— "Methinks I should tremble now, were his wizard power of gliding through all impediments in search of me, to place him suddenly before my eyes."

How profound, nay appalling, is the moral evolved by the "Earth's Holocaust"; where—beginning with the hollow follies and affectations of the world,—all vanities and empty theories and forms, are, one after another, and by an admirably graduated, growing comprehensiveness, thrown into the allegorical fire, till, at length, nothing is left but the all-engendering heart of man; which remaining still unconsumed, the great conflagration is naught.

Of a piece with this, is the "Intelligence Office," a wondrous symbolizing of the secret workings in men's souls. There are other sketches, still more charged with ponderous import.

"The Christmas Banquet," and "The Bosom Serpent" would be fine subjects for a curious and elaborate analysis, touching the conjectural parts of the mind that produced them. For spite of all the Indian-summer sunlight on the hither side of Hawthorne's soul, the other side—like the dark half of the physical sphere—is shrouded in a blackness, ten times black. But this darkness but gives more effect to the evermoving dawn, that forever advances through it, and circumnavigates his world. Whether Hawthorne has simply availed himself of this mystical blackness as a means to the wondrous effects he makes it to produce in his lights and shades; or whether there really lurks in him, perhaps unknown to himself, a touch of Puritanic gloom,—this, I cannot altogether tell. Certain it is, however, that this great power of blackness in him derives its force from its appeals to that Calvinistic sense of Innate Depravity and Original Sin, from whose visitations, in some shape or other, no deeply thinking mind is always and wholly free. For, in certain moods, no man can weigh this world, without throwing in something, somehow like Original Sin, to strike the uneven balance. At all events, perhaps no writer has ever wielded this terrific thought with greater terror than this same harmless Hawthorne. Still more: this black conceit pervades him, through and through. You may be witched by his sunlight,—transported by the bright gildings in the skies he builds over you;—but there is the blackness of darkness beyond; and even his bright gildings but fringe, and play upon the edges of thunder-clouds.—In one word, the world is mistaken in this Nathaniel Hawthorne. He himself must often have smiled at its absurd misconception of him. He is immeasurably deeper than the plummet of the mere critic. For it is not the brain that can test such a man; it is only the heart. You cannot come to know greatness by inspecting it; there is no glimpse to be caught of it, except by intuition; you need not ring it, you but touch it, and you find it is gold.

Now it is that blackness in Hawthorne, of which I have spoken, that so fixes and fascinates me. It may be, nevertheless, that it is too largely developed in him. Perhaps he does not give us a ray of his light for every shade of his dark. But however this may be, this blackness it is that furnishes the infinite obscure of his background,—that background, against which Shakespeare plays his grandest conceits, the things that have made for Shakespeare his loftiest, but

most circumscribed renown, as the profoundest of thinkers. For by philosophers Shakespeare is not adored as the great man of tragedy and comedy.—
"Off with his head! so much for Buckingham!"[7] this sort of rant, interlined by
another hand, brings down the house,—those mistaken souls, who dream of
Shakespeare as a mere man of Richard-the-Third humps, and Macbeth daggers. But it is those deep far-away things in him; those occasional flashings-
forth of the intuitive Truth in him; those short, quick probings at the very axis
of reality:—these are the things that make Shakespeare, Shakespeare. Through
the mouths of the dark characters of Hamlet, Timon, Lear, and Iago, he
craftily says, or sometimes insinuates the things, which we feel to be so terrifi-
cally true, that it were all but madness for any good man, in his own proper
character, to utter, or even hint of them. Tormented into desperation, Lear
the frantic King tears off the mask, and speaks the sane madness of vital truth.
But, as I before said, it is the least part of genius that attracts admiration.
And so, much of the blind, unbridled admiration that has been heaped upon
Shakespeare, has been lavished upon the least part of him. And few of his
endless commentators and critics seem to have remembered, or even perceived, that the immediate products of a great mind are not so great, as that
undeveloped, (and sometimes undevelopable) yet dimly-discernible greatness,
to which these immediate products are but the infallible indices. In Shakespeare's tomb lies infinitely more than Shakespeare ever wrote. And if I magnify Shakespeare, it is not so much for what he did do, as for what he did not
do, or refrained from doing. For in this world of lies, Truth is forced to fly like
a scared white doe in the woodlands; and only by cunning glimpses will she
reveal herself, as in Shakespeare and other masters of the great Art of Telling
the Truth,—even though it be covertly, and by snatches.

But if this view of the all-popular Shakespeare be seldom taken by his readers, and if very few who extol him, have ever read him deeply, or, perhaps,
only have seen him on the tricky stage, (which alone made, and is still making
him his mere mob renown)—if few men have time, or patience, or palate, for
the spiritual truth as it is in that great genius;—it is, then, no matter of surprise
that in a contemporaneous age, Nathaniel Hawthorne is a man, as yet, almost
utterly mistaken among men. Here and there, in some quiet arm-chair in the
noisy town, or some deep nook among the noiseless mountains, he may be
appreciated for something of what he is. But unlike Shakespeare, who was
forced to the contrary course by circumstances. Hawthorne (either from simple
disinclination, or else from inaptitude) refrains from all the popularizing noise
and show of broad farce, and blood-besmeared tragedy; content with the still,
rich utterances of a great intellect in repose, and which sends few thoughts
into circulation, except they be arterialized at his large warm lungs, and
expanded in his honest heart.

Nor need you fix upon that blackness in him, if it suit you not. Nor, indeed,
will all readers discern it, for it is, mostly, insinuated to those who may best
understand it, and account for it; it is not obtruded upon every one alike.

Some may start to read of Shakespeare and Hawthorne on the same page.
They may say, that if an illustration were needed, a lesser light might have
sufficed to elucidate this Hawthorne, this small man of yesterday. But I am
not, willingly, one of those, who, as touching Shakespeare at least, exemplify

7. Line interpolated into Shakespeare's *Richard III* by Colley Cibber (1671–1757) in his revision of the play.

the maxim of Rochefoucauld,[8] that "we exalt the reputation of some, in order to depress that of others";—who, to teach all noble-souled aspirants that there is no hope for them, pronounce Shakespeare absolutely unapproachable. But Shakespeare has been approached. There are minds that have gone as far as Shakespeare into the universe. And hardly a mortal man, who, at some time or other, has not felt as great thoughts in him as any you will find in Hamlet. We must not inferentially malign mankind for the sake of any one man, who-ever he may be. This is too cheap a purchase of contentment for conscious mediocrity to make. Besides, this absolute and unconditional adoration of Shakespeare has grown to be a part of our Anglo-Saxon superstitions. The Thirty-Nine Articles[9] are now Forty. Intolerance has come to exist in this matter. You must believe in Shakespeare's unapproachability, or quit the country. But what sort of a belief is this for an American, a man who is bound to carry republican progressiveness into Literature, as well as into Life? Believe me, my friends, that men not very much inferior to Shakespeare, are this day being born on the banks of the Ohio. And the day will come, when you shall say who reads a book by an Englishman that is a modern?[1] The great mistake seems to be, that even with those Americans who look forward to the coming of a great literary genius among us, they somehow fancy he will come in the costume of Queen Elizabeth's day,—be a writer of dramas founded upon old English history, or the tales of Boccaccio. Whereas, great geniuses are parts of the times; they themselves are the times; and possess a correspondent coloring. It is of a piece with the Jews, who while their Shiloh[2] was meekly walking in their streets, were still praying for his magnificent coming; looking for him in a chariot, who was already among them on an ass. Nor must we forget, that, in his own life-time, Shakespeare was not Shakespeare, but only Master William Shakespeare of the shrewd, thriving business firm of Condell, Shakespeare & Co., proprietors of the Globe Theatre in London; and by a courtly author, of the name of Chettle,[3] was hooted at, as an "upstart crow" beautified "with other birds' feathers." For, mark it well, imitation is often the first charge brought against real originality. Why this is so, there is not space to set forth here. You must have plenty of sea-room to tell the Truth in; especially, when it seems to have an aspect of newness, as America did in 1492, though it was then just as old, and perhaps older than Asia, only those sagacious philoso-phers, the common sailors, had never seen it before; swearing it was all water and moonshine there.

Now, I do not say that Nathaniel of Salem is a greater than William of Avon, or as great. But the difference between the two men is by no means immeasurable. Not a very great deal more, and Nathaniel were verily William.

This, too, I mean, that if Shakespeare has not been equalled, give the world time, and he is sure to be surpassed, in one hemisphere or the other. Nor will it at all do to say, that the world is getting grey and grizzled now, and has lost that fresh charm which she wore of old, and by virtue of which the great poets

---

8. François de la Rochefoucauld (1613–1680), French moralist.
9. Doctrines of the Church of England; here, any national set of beliefs.
1. Reference to a famous insult by Sydney Smith, a Scottish critic, in the *Edinburgh Review*, vol. 33 (January 1820): "In the four quarters of the globe, who

reads an American book? Or goes to an American play? Or looks at an American picture or statue?"
2. Messiah, Christ.
3. Robert Greene (1558?–1592), not Henry Chettle (c. 1560–c. 1607), made these slurs against the young Shakespeare in *Groatsworth of Witte Bought with a Million of Repentance* (1592).

of past times made themselves what we esteem them to be. Not so. The world is as young today, as when it was created; and this Vermont morning dew is as wet to my feet, as Eden's dew to Adam's. Nor has Nature been all over ransacked by our progenitors, so that no new charms and mysteries remain for this latter generation to find. Far from it. The trillionth part has not yet been said; and all that has been said, but multiplies the avenues to what remains to be said. It is not so much paucity, as superabundance of material that seems to incapacitate modern authors.

Let America then prize and cherish her writers; yea, let her glorify them. They are not so many in number, as to exhaust her good-will. And while she has good kith and kin of her own, to take to her bosom, let her not lavish her embraces upon the household of an alien. For believe it or not England, after all, is, in many things, an alien to us. China has more bowels of real love for us than she. But even were there no Hawthorne, no Emerson, no Whittier, no Irving, no Bryant, no Dana, no Cooper, no Willis (not the author of the "Darter," but the author of the "Belfry Pigeon")—were there none of these, and others of like calibre,[4] nevertheless, let America first praise mediocrity even, in her own children, before she praises (for everywhere, merit demands acknowledgment from every one) the best excellence in the children of any other land. Let her own authors, I say, have the priority of appreciation. I was much pleased with a hot-headed Carolina cousin of mine, who once said,— "If there were no other American to stand by, in Literature,—why, then, I would stand by Pop Emmons and his 'Fredoniad,'[5] and till a better epic came along, swear it was not very far behind the 'Iliad'." Take away the words, and in spirit he was sound.

Not that American genius needs patronage in order to expand. For that explosive sort of stuff will expand though screwed up in a vice, and burst it, though it were triple steel. It is for the nation's sake, and not for her authors' sake, that I would have America be heedful of the increasing greatness among her writers. For how great the shame, if other nations should be before her, in crowning her heroes of the pen. But this is almost the case now. American authors have received more just and discriminating praise (however loftily and ridiculously given, in certain cases) even from some Englishmen, than from their own countrymen. There are hardly five critics in America; and several of them are asleep. As for patronage, it is the American author who now patronizes his country, and not his country him. And if at times some among them appeal to the people for more recognition, it is not always with selfish motives, but patriotic ones.

It is true, that but few of them as yet have evinced that decided originality which merits great praise. But that graceful writer,[6] who perhaps of all Americans has received the most plaudits from his own country for his productions,—that very popular and amiable writer, however good, and self-reliant in many things, perhaps owes his chief reputation to the self-acknowledged

---

4. Duyckinck deleted these names, replacing them with "But even were there no strong literary individualities among us, as there are some dozen at least"; probably he felt it prudent to avoid personalities. The contemporaries cited by Melville are included in this anthology except for his friend Richard Henry Dana, Jr. (1815–1882), author of *Two Years before the Mast*, and his (and his late brother Gansevoort's) friend Nathaniel Parker Willis (1806–1867), author of the prose

*Dashes at Life with a Free Pencil* and of poems, among them *The Belfry Pigeon*. Merton M. Sealts, Jr., was the first to work out Duyckink's responsibility for this major piece of toning down.
5. Richard Emmons (b. 1788) wrote the *Fredoniad; or Independence Preserved—an Epic Poem of the War of 1812*. The "hot-headed Carolina cousin" is invented to fit the persona of the vacationing Virginian.
6. Washington Irving.

imitation of a foreign model, and to the studied avoidance of all topics but smooth ones. But it is better to fail in originality, than to succeed in imitation. He who has never failed somewhere, that man can not be great. Failure is the true test of greatness. And if it be said, that continual success is a proof that a man wisely knows his powers,—it is only to be added, that, in that case, he knows them to be small. Let us believe it, then, once for all, that there is no hope for us in these smooth pleasing writers that know their powers. Without malice, but to speak the plain fact, they but furnish an appendix to Goldsmith,[7] and other English authors. And we want no American Goldsmiths; nay, we want no American Miltons. It were the vilest thing you could say of a true American author, that he were an American Tompkins.[8] Call him an American, and have done; for you can not say a nobler thing of him.—But it is not meant that all American writers should studiously cleave to nationality in their writings; only this, no American writer should write like an Englishman, or a Frenchman; let him write like a man, for then he will be sure to write like an American. Let us away with this leaven of literary flunkyism towards England. If either must play the flunky in this thing, let England do it, not us. While we are rapidly preparing for that political supremacy among the nations, which prophetically awaits us at the close of the present century; in a literary point of view, we are deplorably unprepared for it; and we seem studious to remain so. Hitherto, reasons might have existed why this should be; but no good reason exists now. And all that is requisite to amendment in this matter, is simply this: that, while freely acknowledging all excellence, everywhere, we should refrain from unduly lauding foreign writers, and, at the same time, duly recognize the meritorious writers that are our own;—those writers, who breathe that unshackled, democratic spirit of Christianity in all things, which now takes the practical lead in this world, though at the same time led by ourselves—us Americans. Let us boldly contemn all imitation, though it comes to us graceful and fragrant as the morning; and foster all originality, though, at first, it be crabbed and ugly as our own pine knots. And if any of our authors fail, or seem to fail, then, in the words of my enthusiastic Carolina cousin, let us clap him on the shoulder, and back him against all Europe for his second round. The truth is, that in our point of view, this matter of a national literature has come to such a pass with us, that in some sense we must turn bullies, else the day is lost, or superiority so far beyond us, that we can hardly say it will ever be ours.

And now, my countrymen, as an excellent author, of your own flesh and blood,—an unimitating, and, perhaps, in his way, an inimitable man—whom better can I commend to you, in the first place, than Nathaniel Hawthorne. He is one of the new, and far better generation of your writers. The smell of your beeches and hemlocks is upon him; your own broad prairies are in his soul; and if you travel away inland into his deep and noble nature, you will hear the far roar of his Niagara. Give not over to future generations the glad duty of acknowledging him for what he is. Take that joy to yourself, in your own generation; and so shall he feel those grateful impulses in him, that may possibly prompt him to the full flower of some still greater achievement in your eyes. And by confessing him, you thereby confess others; you brace the whole brotherhood. For genius, all over the world, stands hand in hand, and one shock of recognition runs the whole circle round.

---

7. Irving was often called the American Goldsmith.    8. Flunky, from the English type name for a butler.

In treating of Hawthorne, or rather of Hawthorne in his writings (for I never saw the man; and in the chances of a quiet plantation life, remote from his haunts, perhaps never shall) in treating of his works, I say, I have thus far omitted all mention of his "Twice Told Tales," and "Scarlet Letter."[9] Both are excellent; but full of such manifold, strange and diffusive beauties, that time would all but fail me, to point the half of them out. But there are things in those two books, which, had they been written in England a century ago, Nathaniel Hawthorne had utterly displaced many of the bright names we now revere on authority. But I am content to leave Hawthorne to himself, and to the infallible finding of posterity; and however great may be the praise I have bestowed upon him, I feel, that in so doing, I have more served and honored myself, than him. For, at bottom, great excellence is praise enough to itself; but the feeling of a sincere and appreciative love and admiration towards it, this is relieved by utterance; and warm, honest praise ever leaves a pleasant flavor in the mouth; and it is an honorable thing to confess to what is honorable in others.

But I cannot leave my subject yet. No man can read a fine author, and relish him to his very bones, while he reads, without subsequently fancying to himself some ideal image of the man and his mind. And if you rightly look for it, you will almost always find that the author himself has somewhere furnished you with his own picture. For poets (whether in prose or verse), being painters of Nature, are like their brethren of the pencil, the true portrait-painters, who, in the multitude of likenesses to be sketched, do not invariably omit their own; and in all high instances, they paint them without any vanity, though, at times, with a lurking something, that would take several pages to properly define.

I submit it, then, to those best acquainted with the man personally, whether the following is not Nathaniel Hawthorne;—and to himself, whether something involved in it does not express the temper of his mind,—that lasting temper of all true, candid men—a seeker, not a finder yet:—

"A man now entered, in neglected attire, with the aspect of a thinker, but somewhat too rough-hewn and brawny for a scholar. His face was full of sturdy vigor, with some finer and keener attribute beneath; though harsh at first, it was tempered with the glow of a large, warm heart, which had force enough to heat his powerful intellect through and through. He advanced to the Intelligencer, and looked at him with a glance of such stern sincerity, that perhaps few secrets were beyond its scope.

" 'I seek for Truth,' said he."[1]

Twenty-four hours have elapsed since writing the foregoing. I have just returned from the hay mow, charged more and more with love and admiration of Hawthorne. For I have just been gleaning through the "Mosses," picking up many things here and there that had previously escaped me. And I found that but to glean after this man, is better than to be in at the harvest of others. To be frank (though, perhaps, rather foolish), notwithstanding what I wrote yesterday of these Mosses, I had not then culled them all; but had, nevertheless, been sufficiently sensible of the subtle essence, in them, as to write as I did. To what infinite height of loving wonder and admiration I may yet be

9. Published in 1837 and 1850, respectively.
1. From *The Intelligence Office* (i.e., "the employment agency").

borne, when by repeatedly banquetting on these Mosses, I shall have thoroughly incorporated their whole stuff into my being,—that, I can not tell. But already I feel that this Hawthorne has dropped germinous seeds into my soul. He expands and deepens down, the more I contemplate him; and further, and further, shoots his strong New-England roots into the hot soil of my Southern soul.

By careful reference to the "Table of Contents," I now find, that I have gone through all the sketches; but that when I yesterday wrote, I had not at all read two particular pieces, to which I now desire to call special attention,—"A Select Party," and "Young Goodman Brown." Here, be it said to all those whom this poor fugitive scrawl of mine may tempt to the perusal of the "Mosses," that they must on no account suffer themselves to be trifled with, disappointed, or deceived by the triviality of many of the titles to these Sketches. For in more than one instance, the title utterly belies the piece. It is as if rustic demijohns containing the very best and costliest of Falernian and Tokay, were labeled "Cider," "Perry," and "Elder-berry Wine." The truth seems to be, that like many other geniuses, this Man of Mosses takes great delight in hoodwinking the world,—at least, with respect to himself. Personally, I doubt not, that he rather prefers to be generally esteemed but a so-so sort of author; being willing to reserve the thorough and acute appreciation of what he is, to that party most qualified to judge—that is, to himself. Besides, at the bottom of their natures, men like Hawthorne, in many things, deem the plaudits of the public such strong presumptive evidence of mediocrity in the object of them, that it would in some degree render them doubtful of their own powers, did they hear much and vociferous braying concerning them in the public pastures. True, I have been braying myself (if you please to be witty enough, to have it so) but then I claim to be the first that has so brayed in this particular matter; and therefore, while pleading guilty to the charge, still claim all the merit due to originality.

But with whatever motive, playful or profound, Nathaniel Hawthorne has chosen to entitle his pieces in the manner he has, it is certain, that some of them are directly calculated to deceive—egregiously deceive—the superficial skimmer of pages. To be downright and candid once more, let me cheerfully say, that two of these titles did dolefully dupe no less an eagle-eyed reader than myself; and that, too, after I had been impressed with a sense of the great depth and breadth of this American man. "Who in the name of thunder" (as the country-people say in this neighborhood), "who in the name of thunder," would anticipate any marvel in a piece entitled "Young Goodman Brown"? You would of course suppose that it was a simple little tale, intended as a supplement to "Goody Two Shoes." Whereas, it is deep as Dante; nor can you finish it, without addressing the author in his own words—"It is yours to penetrate, in every bosom, the deep mystery of sin." And with Young Goodman, too, in allegorical pursuit of his Puritan wife, you cry out in your anguish,—

"Faith!" shouted Goodman Brown, in a voice of agony and desperation; and the echoes of the forest mocked him, crying—"Faith! Faith!" as if bewildered wretches were seeking her all through the wilderness.

Now this same piece, entitled "Young Goodman Brown," is one of the two that I had not all read yesterday; and I allude to it now, because it is, in itself, such a strong positive illustration of that blackness in Hawthorne, which I had assumed from the mere occasional shadows of it, as revealed in several of the other sketches. But had I previously perused "Young Goodman Brown," I should have been at no pains to draw the conclusion, which I came to, at a time, when I was ignorant that the book contained one such direct and unqualified manifestation of it.

The other piece of the two referred to, is entitled "A Select Party," which, in my first simplicity upon originally taking hold of the book, I fancied must treat of some pumpkin-pie party in Old Salem, or some Chowder Party on Cape Cod. Whereas, by all the gods of Peedee![2] it is the sweetest and sublimest thing that has been written since Spenser wrote. Nay, there is nothing in Spenser that surpasses it, perhaps, nothing that equals it. And the test is this: read any canto in "The Faery Queen," and then read "A Select Party," and decide which pleases you the most,—that is, if you are qualified to judge. Do not be frightened at this; for when Spenser was alive, he was thought of very much as Hawthorne is now,—was generally accounted just such a "gentle" harmless man. It may be, that to common eyes, the sublimity of Hawthorne seems lost in his sweetness,—as perhaps in this same "Select Party" of his; for whom, he has builded so august a dome of sunset clouds, and served them on richer plate, than Belshazzar's when he banquetted his lords in Babylon.[3]

But my chief business now, is to point out a particular page in this piece, having reference to an honored guest, who under the name of "The Master Genius" but in the guise "of a young man of poor attire, with no insignia of rank or acknowledged eminence," is introduced to the Man of Fancy, who is the giver of the feast. Now the page having reference to this "Master Genius", so happily expresses much of what I yesterday wrote, touching the coming of the literary Shiloh of America, that I cannot but be charmed by the coincidence; especially, when it shows such a parity of ideas, at least, in this one point, between a man like Hawthorne and a man like me.

And here, let me throw out another conceit of mine touching this American Shiloh, or "Master Genius," as Hawthorne calls him. May it not be, that this commanding mind has not been, is not, and never will be, individually developed in any one man? And would it, indeed, appear so unreasonable to suppose, that this great fullness and overflowing may be, or may be destined to be, shared by a plurality of men of genius? Surely, to take the very greatest example on record, Shakespeare cannot be regarded as in himself the concretion of all the genius of his time; nor as so immeasurably beyond Marlowe, Webster, Ford, Beaumont, Jonson, that those great men can be said to share none of his power? For one, I conceive that there were dramatists in Elizabeth's day, between whom and Shakespeare the distance was by no means great. Let anyone, hitherto little acquainted with those neglected old authors, for the first time read them thoroughly, or even read Charles Lamb's Specimens of them, and he will be amazed at the wondrous ability of those Anaks[4] of men, and shocked at this renewed example of the fact, that Fortune has more to do with fame than merit,—though, without merit, lasting fame there can be none.

2. River in the Carolinas.
3. Daniel 5.1: "Belshazzar the king made a great feast to a thousand of his lords, and drank wine before the thousand."

4. Giants (Joshua 11.21). Charles Lamb (1775–1834), editor of Specimens of the English Dramatic Poets Who Lived about the Time of Shakespeare (1808).

Nevertheless, it would argue too illy of my country were this maxim to hold good concerning Nathaniel Hawthorne, a man, who already, in some few minds, has shed "such a light, as never illuminates the earth, save when a great heart burns as the household fire of a grand intellect."

The words are his,—in the "Select Party"; and they are a magnificent setting to a coincident sentiment of my own, but ramblingly expressed yesterday, in reference to himself. Gainsay it who will, as I now write, I am Posterity speaking by proxy—and after times will make it more than good, when I declare—that the American, who up to the present day, has evinced, in Literature, the largest brain with the largest heart, that man is Nathaniel Hawthorne. Moreover, that whatever Nathaniel Hawthorne may hereafter write, "The Mosses from an Old Manse" will be ultimately accounted his masterpiece. For there is a sure, though a secret sign in some works which proves the culmination of the powers (only the developable ones, however) that produced them. But I am by no means desirous of the glory of a prophet. I pray Heaven that Hawthorne may *yet* prove me an impostor in this prediction. Especially, as I somehow cling to the strange fancy, that, in all men, hiddenly reside certain wondrous, occult properties—as in some plants and minerals—which by some happy but very rare accident (as bronze was discovered by the melting of the iron and brass in the burning of Corinth) may chance to be called forth here on earth; not entirely waiting for their better discovery in the more congenial, blessed atmosphere of heaven.

Once more—for it is hard to be finite upon an infinite subject, and all subjects are infinite. By some people, this entire scrawl of mine may be esteemed altogether unnecessary, inasmuch, "as years ago" (they may say) "we found out the rich and rare stuff in this Hawthorne, whom you now parade forth, as if only *yourself* were the discoverer of this Portuguese diamond[5] in our Literature."—But even granting all this; and adding to it, the assumption that the books of Hawthorne have sold by the five-thousand,—what does that signify?—They should be sold by the hundred-thousand; and read by the million; and admired by every one who is capable of Admiration.

1850

# Bartleby, the Scrivener[1]

## A Story of Wall-Street

I am a rather elderly man. The nature of my avocations for the last thirty years has brought me into more than ordinary contact with what would seem an interesting and somewhat singular set of men, of whom as yet nothing that I know of has ever been written:—I mean the law-copyists or scriveners. I have known very many of them, professionally and privately, and if I pleased, could

5. A diamond cut according to an elaborate system— two rows of rhomboidal and three rows of triangular facets above and below the girdle (the widest part).
1. The text is from the first printing in the November and December 1853 issues of *Putnam's Monthly Magazine*, the first work by Melville's to be printed after the

disastrous reception of *Pierre* during the summer and fall of 1852. One work (*The Isle of the Cross*), probably the story of Agatha Robinson, a Nantucket woman who displayed patience, endurance, and resignedness, was apparently destroyed after being rejected by the Harpers.

relate divers histories, at which good-natured gentlemen might smile, and sentimental souls might weep. But I waive the biographies of all other scriveners for a few passages in the life of Bartleby, who was a scrivener the strangest I ever saw or heard of. While of other law-copyists I might write the complete life, of Bartleby nothing of that sort can be done. I believe that no materials exist for a full and satisfactory biography of this man. It is an irreparable loss to literature. Bartleby was one of those beings of whom nothing is ascertainable, except from the original sources, and in his case those are very small. What my own astonished eyes saw of Bartleby, *that* is all I know of him, except, indeed, one vague report which will appear in the sequel.

Ere introducing the scrivener, as he first appeared to me, it is fit I make some mention of myself, my *employées*, my business, my chambers, and general surroundings; because some such description is indispensable to an adequate understanding of the chief character about to be presented.

Imprimis: I am a man who, from his youth upwards, has been filled with a profound conviction that the easiest way of life is the best. Hence, though I belong to a profession proverbially energetic and nervous, even to turbulence, at times, yet nothing of that sort have I ever suffered to invade my peace. I am one of those unambitious lawyers who never addresses a jury, or in any way draws down public applause; but in the cool tranquillity of a snug retreat, do a snug business among rich men's bonds and mortgages and title-deeds. All who know me, consider me an eminently *safe* man. The late John Jacob Astor, a personage little given to poetic enthusiasm, had no hesitation in pronouncing my first grand point to be prudence; my next, method. I do not speak it in vanity, but simply record the fact, that I was not unemployed in my profession by the late John Jacob Astor; a name which, I admit, I love to repeat, for it hath a rounded and orbicular sound to it, and rings like unto bullion. I will freely add, that I was not insensible to the late John Jacob Astor's good opinion.

Some time prior to the period at which this little history begins, my avocations had been largely increased. The good old office, now extinct in the State of New-York, of a Master in Chancery,[2] had been conferred upon me. It was not a very arduous office, but very pleasantly remunerative. I seldom lose my temper; much more seldom indulge in dangerous indignation at wrongs and outrages; but I must be permitted to be rash here and declare, that I consider the sudden and violent abrogation of the office of Master in Chancery, by the new Constitution,[3] as a——premature act; inasmuch as I had counted upon a life-lease of the profits, whereas I only received those of a few short years. But this is by the way.

My chambers were up stairs at No.—Wall-street. At one end they looked upon the white wall of the interior of a spacious sky-light shaft, penetrating the building from top to bottom. This view might have been considered rather tame than otherwise, deficient in what landscape painters call "life." But if so, the view from the other end of my chambers offered, at least, a contrast, if nothing more. In that direction my windows commanded an unobstructed view of a lofty brick wall, black by age and everlasting shade; which wall

2. The narrator is understandably concerned about the abolition of a sinecure, but heirs had cause to rejoice, for chancery had kept estates tied up in prolonged litigation. In a poem written around the 1870s, *At the Hostelry*, Melville says that divided Italy, "Nigh para-lysed, by cowls misguided," was "Locked as in Chancery's numbing hand."
3. New York had adopted a "new Constitution" in 1846.

required no spy-glass to bring out its lurking beauties, but for the benefit of all near-sighted spectators, was pushed up to within ten feet of my window panes. Owing to the great height of the surrounding buildings, and my chambers being on the second floor, the interval between this wall and mine not a little resembled a huge square cistern.

At the period just preceding the advent of Bartleby, I had two persons as copyists in my employment, and a promising lad as an office-boy. First, Turkey; second, Nippers; third, Ginger Nut. These may seem names, the like of which are not usually found in the Directory. In truth they were nicknames, mutually conferred upon each other by my three clerks, and were deemed expressive of their respective persons or characters. Turkey was a short, pursy[4] Englishman of about my own age, that is, somewhere not far from sixty. In the morning, one might say, his face was of a fine florid hue, but after twelve o'clock, meridian—his dinner hour—it blazed like a grate full of Christmas coals; and continued blazing—but, as it were, with a gradual wane—till 6 o'clock, P.M. or thereabouts, after which I saw no more of the proprietor of the face, which gaining its meridian with the sun, seemed to set with it, to rise, culminate, and decline the following day, with the like regularity and undiminished glory. There are many singular coincidences I have known in the course of my life, not the least among which was the fact, that exactly when Turkey displayed his fullest beams from his red and radiant countenance, just then, too, at that critical moment, began the daily period when I considered his business capacities as seriously disturbed for the remainder of the twenty-four hours. Not that he was absolutely idle, or averse to business then; far from it. The difficulty was, he was apt to be altogether too energetic. There was a strange, inflamed, flurried, flighty recklessness of activity about him. He would be incautious in dipping his pen into his inkstand. All his blots upon my documents, were dropped there after twelve o'clock, meridian. Indeed, not only would he be reckless and sadly given to making blots in the afternoon, but some days he went further, and was rather noisy. At such times, too, his face flamed with augmented blazonry, as if cannel coal had been heaped on anthracite. He made an unpleasant racket with his chair; spilled his sand-box; in mending his pens, impatiently split them all to pieces, and threw them on the floor in a sudden passion; stood up and leaned over his table, boxing his papers about in a most indecorous manner, very sad to behold in an elderly man like him. Nevertheless, as he was in many ways a most valuable person to me, and all the time before twelve o'clock, meridian, was the quickest, steadiest creature too, accomplishing a great deal of work in a style not easy to be matched—for these reasons, I was willing to overlook his eccentricities, though indeed, occasionally, I remonstrated with him. I did this very gently, however, because, though the civilest, nay, the blandest and most reverential of men in the morning, yet in the afternoon he was disposed, upon provocation, to be slightly rash with his tongue, in fact, insolent. Now, valuing his morning services as I did, and resolved not to lose them; yet, at the same time made uncomfortable by his inflamed ways after twelve o'clock; and being a man of peace, unwilling by my admonitions to call forth unseemly retorts from him; I took upon me, one Saturday noon (he was always worse on Saturdays), to hint to him, very kindly, that perhaps now that he was growing old,

---

4. Shortwinded from obesity.

it might be well to abridge his labors; in short, he need not come to my chambers after twelve o'clock, but, dinner over, had best go home to his lodgings and rest himself till tea-time. But no; he insisted upon his afternoon devotions. His countenance became intolerably fervid, as he oratorically assured me— gesticulating with a long ruler at the other end of the room—that if his services in the morning were useful, how indispensable, then, in the afternoon?

"With submission, sir," said Turkey on this occasion, "I consider myself your right-hand man. In the morning I but marshal and deploy my columns; but in the afternoon I put myself at their head, and gallantly charge the foe, thus!"—and he made a violent thrust with the ruler.

"But the blots, Turkey," intimated I.

"True,—but, with submission, sir, behold these hairs! I am getting old. Surely, sir, a blot or two of a warm afternoon is not to be severely urged against gray hairs. Old age—even if it blot the page—is honorable. With submission, sir, we *both* are getting old."

This appeal to my fellow-feeling was hardly to be resisted. At all events, I saw that go he would not. So I made up my mind to let him stay, resolving, nevertheless, to see to it, that during the afternoon he had to do with my less important papers.

Nippers, the second on my list, was a whiskered, sallow, and, upon the whole, rather piratical-looking young man of about five and twenty. I always deemed him the victim of two evil powers—ambition and indigestion. The ambition was evinced by a certain impatience of the duties of a mere copyist, an unwarrantable usurpation of strictly professional affairs, such as the original drawing up of legal documents. The indigestion seemed betokened in an occasional nervous testiness and grinning irritability, causing the teeth to audibly grind together over mistakes committed in copying; unnecessary maledictions, hissed, rather than spoken, in the heat of business; and especially by a continual discontent with the height of the table where he worked. Though of a very ingenious mechanical turn, Nippers could never get this table to suit him. He put chips under it, blocks of various sorts, bits of pasteboard, and at last went so far as to attempt an exquisite adjustment by final pieces of folded blotting paper. But no invention would answer. If, for the sake of easing his back, he brought the table lid at a sharp angle well up towards his chin, and wrote there like a man using the steep roof of a Dutch house for his desk:—then he declared that it stopped the circulation in his arms. If now he lowered the table to his waistbands, and stooped over it in writing, then there was a sore aching in his back. In short, the truth of the matter was, Nippers knew not what he wanted. Or, if he wanted any thing, it was to be rid of a scrivener's table altogether. Among the manifestations of his diseased ambition was a fondness he had for receiving visits from certain ambiguous-looking fellows in seedy coats, whom he called his clients. Indeed I was aware that not only was he, at times, considerable of a ward-politician, but he occasionally did a little business at the Justices' courts, and was not unknown on the steps of the Tombs.[5] I have good reason to believe, however, that one individual who called upon him at my chambers, and who, with a grand air, he insisted was his client, was no other than a dun,[6] and the alleged title-deed, a bill. But with all his

5. I.e., Nippers is suspected of arranging bail for pris-    unseemly if not nefarious.
oners or other such activities that strike the narrator as    6. Bill collector.

failings, and the annoyances he caused me, Nippers, like his compatriot Turkey, was a very useful man to me; wrote a neat, swift hand; and, when he chose, was not deficient in a gentlemanly sort of deportment. Added to this, he always dressed in a gentlemanly sort of way; and so, incidentally, reflected credit upon my chambers. Whereas with respect to Turkey, I had much ado to keep him from being a reproach to me. His clothes were apt to look oily and smell of eating-houses. He wore his pantaloons very loose and baggy in summer. His coats were execrable; his hat not to be handled. But while the hat was a thing of indifference to me, inasmuch as his natural civility and deference, as a dependent Englishman, always led him to doff it the moment he entered the room, yet his coat was another matter. Concerning his coats, I reasoned with him; but with no effect. The truth was, I suppose, that a man with so small an income, could not afford to sport such a lustrous face and a lustrous coat at one and the same time. As Nippers once observed, Turkey's money went chiefly for red ink. One winter day I presented Turkey with a highly-respectable looking coat of my own, a padded gray coat, of a most comfortable warmth, and which buttoned straight up from the knee to the neck. I thought Turkey would appreciate the favor, and abate his rashness and obstreperousness of afternoons. But no. I verily believe that buttoning himself up in so downy and blanket-like a coat had a pernicious effect upon him; upon the same principle that too much oats are bad for horses. In fact, precisely as a rash, restive horse is said to feel his oats, so Turkey felt his coat. It made him insolent. He was a man whom prosperity harmed.

Though concerning the self-indulgent habits of Turkey I had my own private surmises, yet touching Nippers I was well persuaded that whatever might be his faults in other respects, he was, at least, a temperate young man. But indeed, nature herself seemed to have been his vintner, and at his birth charged him so thoroughly with an irritable, brandy-like disposition, that all subsequent potations were needless. When I consider how, amid the stillness of my chambers, Nippers would sometimes impatiently rise from his seat, and stooping over his table, spread his arms wide apart, seize the whole desk, and move it, and jerk it, with a grim, grinding motion on the floor, as if the table were a perverse voluntary agent, intent on thwarting and vexing him; I plainly perceive that for Nippers, brandy and water were altogether superfluous.

It was fortunate for me that, owing to its peculiar cause—indigestion—the irritability and consequent nervousness of Nippers, were mainly observable in the morning, while in the afternoon he was comparatively mild. So that Turkey's paroxysms only coming on about twelve o'clock, I never had to do with their eccentricities at one time. Their fits relieved each other like guards. When Nippers' was on, Turkey's was off; and *vice versa*. This was a good natural arrangement under the circumstances.

Ginger Nut, the third on my list, was a lad some twelve years old. His father was a carman,[7] ambitious of seeing his son on the bench instead of a cart, before he died. So he sent him to my office as student at law, errand boy, and cleaner and sweeper, at the rate of one dollar a week. He had a little desk to himself, but he did not use it much. Upon inspection, the drawer exhibited a great array of the shells of various sorts of nuts. Indeed, to this quick-witted youth the whole noble science of the law was contained in a nut-shell. Not

7. Driver, teamster.

the least among the employments of Ginger Nut, as well as one which he discharged with the most alacrity, was his duty as cake and apple purveyor for Turkey and Nippers. Copying law papers being proverbially a dry, husky sort of business, my two scriveners were fain to moisten their mouths very often with Spitzenbergs[8] to be had at the numerous stalls nigh the Custom House and Post Office. Also, they sent Ginger Nut very frequently for that peculiar cake—small, flat, round, and very spicy—after which he had been named by them. Of a cold morning when business was but dull, Turkey would gobble up scores of these cakes, as if they were mere wafers—indeed they sell them at the rate of six or eight for a penny—the scrape of his pen blending with the crunching of the crisp particles in his mouth. Of all the fiery afternoon blunders and flurried rashnesses of Turkey, was his once moistening a ginger-cake between his lips, and clapping it on to a mortgage for a seal.[9] I came within an ace of dismissing him then. But he mollified me by making an oriental bow, and saying—"With submission, sir, it was generous of me to find you in stationery on my own account."

Now my original business—that of a conveyancer[1] and title hunter, and drawer-up of recondite documents of all sorts—was considerably increased by receiving the master's office. There was now great work for scriveners. Not only must I push the clerks already with me, but I must have additional help. In answer to my advertisement, a motionless young man one morning, stood upon my office threshold, the door being open, for it was summer. I can see that figure now—pallidly neat, pitiably respectable, incurably forlorn! It was Bartleby.

After a few words touching his qualifications, I engaged him, glad to have among my corps of copyists a man of so singularly sedate an aspect, which I thought might operate beneficially upon the flighty temper of Turkey, and the fiery one of Nippers.

I should have stated before that ground glass folding-doors divided my premises into two parts, one of which was occupied by my scriveners, the other by myself. According to my humor I threw open these doors, or closed them. I resolved to assign Bartleby a corner by the folding-doors, but on my side of them, so as to have this quiet man within easy call, in case any trifling thing was to be done. I placed his desk close up to a small side-window in that part of the room, a window which originally had afforded a lateral view of certain grimy back-yards and bricks, but which, owing to subsequent erections, commanded at present no view at all, though it gave some light. Within three feet of the panes was a wall, and the light came down from far above, between two lofty buildings, as from a very small opening in a dome. Still further to a satisfactory arrangement, I procured a high green folding screen, which might entirely isolate Bartleby from my sight, though not remove him from my voice. And thus, in a manner, privacy and society were conjoined.

At first Bartleby did an extraordinary quantity of writing. As if long famishing for something to copy, he seemed to gorge himself on my documents. There was no pause for digestion. He ran a day and night line, copying by sun-light and by candle-light. I should have been quite delighted with his

---

8. Red-and-yellow New York apples.
9. The narrator is playing on the resemblance between thin cookies and wax wafers used for sealing documents.

1. Someone who checks records to be sure there are no encumbrances on the title of property to be transferred. "Conveyancer": someone who draws up deeds for transferring title to property.

application, had he been cheerfully industrious. But he wrote on silently, palely, mechanically.

It is, of course, an indispensable part of a scrivener's business to verify the accuracy of his copy, word by word. Where there are two or more scriveners in an office, they assist each other in this examination, one reading from the copy, the other holding the original. It is a very dull, wearisome, and lethargic affair. I can readily imagine that to some sanguine temperaments it would be altogether intolerable. For example, I cannot credit that the mettlesome poet Byron would have contentedly sat down with Bartleby to examine a law document of, say five hundred pages, closely written in a crimpy hand.

Now and then, in the haste of business, it had been my habit to assist in comparing some brief document myself, calling Turkey or Nippers for this purpose. One object I had in placing Bartleby so handy to me behind the screen, was to avail myself of his services on such trivial occasions. It was on the third day, I think, of his being with me, and before any necessity had arisen for having his own writing examined, that, being much hurried to complete a small affair I had in hand, I abruptly called to Bartleby. In my haste and natural expectancy of instant compliance, I sat with my head bent over the original on my desk, and my right hand sideways, and somewhat nervously extended with the copy, so that immediately upon emerging from his retreat, Bartleby might snatch it and proceed to business without the least delay.

In this very attitude did I sit when I called to him, rapidly stating what it was I wanted him to do—namely, to examine a small paper with me. Imagine my surprise, nay, my consternation, when without moving from his privacy, Bartleby in a singularly mild, firm voice, replied, "I would prefer not to."

I sat awhile in perfect silence, rallying my stunned faculties. Immediately it occurred to me that my ears had deceived me, or Bartleby had entirely misunderstood my meaning. I repeated my request in the clearest tone I could assume. in quite as clear a one came the previous reply, "I would prefer not to."

"Prefer not to," echoed I, rising in high excitement, and crossing the room with a stride. "What do you mean? Are you moon-struck? I want you to help me compare this sheet here—take it," and I thrust it towards him.

"I would prefer not to," said he.

I looked at him steadfastly. His face was leanly composed; his gray eye dimly calm. Not a wrinkle of agitation rippled him. Had there been the least uneasiness, anger, impatience or impertinence in his manner; in other words, had there been any thing ordinarily human about him, doubtless I should have violently dismissed him from the premises. But as it was, I should have as soon thought of turning my pale plaster-of-paris bust of Cicero[2] out of doors. I stood gazing at him awhile, as he went on with his own writing, and then reseated myself at my desk. This is very strange, thought I. What had one best do? But my business hurried me. I concluded to forget the matter for the present, reserving it for my future leisure. So calling Nippers from the other room, the paper was speedily examined.

A few days after this, Bartleby concluded four lengthy documents, being quadruplicates of a week's testimony taken before me in my High Court of Chancery. It became necessary to examine them. It was an important suit, and great accuracy was imperative. Having all things arranged I called Turkey,

2. Roman orator and statesman (106–42 B.C.).

Nippers and Ginger Nut from the next room, meaning to place the four copies
in the hands of my four clerks, while I should read from the original. Accordingly Turkey, Nippers and Ginger Nut had taken their seats in a row, each
with his document in hand, when I called to Bartleby to join this interesting
group.

"Bartleby! quick, I am waiting."

I heard a slow scrape of his chair legs on the uncarpeted floor, and soon he
appeared standing at the entrance of his hermitage.

"What is wanted?" said he mildly.

"The copies, the copies" said I hurriedly. "We are going to examine them.
There"—and I held towards him the fourth quadruplicate.

"I would prefer not to," he said, and gently disappeared behind the screen.

For a few moments I was turned into a pillar of salt,[3] standing at the head
of my seated column of clerks. Recovering myself, I advanced towards the
screen, and demanded the reason for such extraordinary conduct.

"Why do you refuse?"

"I would prefer not to."

With any other man I should have flown outright into a dreadful passion,
scorned all further words, and thrust him ignominiously from my presence.
But there was something about Bartleby that not only strangely disarmed me,
but in a wonderful manner touched and disconcerted me. I began to reason
with him.

"These are your own copies we are about to examine. It is labor saving to
you, because one examination will answer for your four papers. It is common
usage. Every copyist is bound to help examine his copy. Is it not so? Will you
not speak? Answer!"

"I prefer not to," he replied in a flute-like tone. It seemed to me that while
I had been addressing him, he carefully revolved every statement that I made;
fully comprehended the meaning; could not gainsay the irresistible conclusion;
but, at the same time, some paramount consideration prevailed with him to
reply as he did.

"You are decided, then, not to comply with my request—a request made
according to common usage and common sense?"

He briefly gave me to understand that on that point my judgment was
sound. Yes: his decision was irreversible.

It is not seldom the case that when a man is browbeaten in some unprecedented and violently unreasonable way, he begins to stagger in his own plainest
faith. He begins, as it were, vaguely to surmise that, wonderful as it may be,
all the justice and all the reason is on the other side. Accordingly, if any
disinterested persons are present, he turns to them for some reinforcement for
his own faltering mind.

"Turkey," said I, "what do you think of this? Am I not right?"

"With submission, sir," said Turkey, with his blandest tone, "I think that
you are."

"Nippers," said I, "what do you think of it?"

"I think I should kick him out of the office."

(The reader of nice perceptions will here perceive that, it being morning,
Turkey's answer is couched in polite and tranquil terms, but Nippers replies

3. The punishment of Lot's disobedient wife (Genesis 19.26).

in ill-tempered ones. Or, to repeat a previous sentence, Nippers's ugly mood was on duty, and Turkey's off.)

"Ginger Nut," said I, willing to enlist the smallest suffrage in my behalf, "what do *you* think of it?"

"I think, sir, he's a little *luny*," replied Ginger Nut, with a grin.

"You hear what they say," said I, turning towards the screen, "come forth and do your duty."

But he vouchsafed no reply. I pondered a moment in sore perplexity. But once more business hurried me. I determined again to postpone the consideration of this dilemma to my future leisure. With a little trouble we made out to examine the papers without Bartleby, though at every page or two, Turkey deferentially dropped his opinion that this proceeding was quite out of the common; while Nippers, twitching in his chair with a dyspeptic nervousness, ground out between his set teeth occasional hissing maledictions against the stubborn oaf behind the screen. And for his (Nippers's) part, this was the first and the last time he would do another man's business without pay.

Meanwhile Bartleby sat in his hermitage, oblivious to every thing but his own peculiar business there.

Some days passed, the scrivener being employed upon another lengthy work. His late remarkable conduct led me to regard his ways narrowly. I observed that he never went to dinner; indeed that he never went any where. As yet I had never of my personal knowledge known him to be outside of my office. He was a perpetual sentry in the corner. At about eleven o'clock though, in the morning, I noticed that Ginger Nut would advance toward the opening in Bartleby's screen, as if silently beckoned thither by a gesture invisible to me where I sat. The boy would then leave the office jingling a few pence, and reappear with a handful of ginger-nuts which he delivered in the hermitage, receiving two of the cakes for his trouble.

He lives, then, on ginger-nuts, thought I; never eats a dinner, properly speaking; he must be a vegetarian then; but no; he never eats even vegetables, he eats nothing but ginger-nuts. My mind then ran on in reveries concerning the probable effects upon the human constitution of living entirely on ginger-nuts. Ginger-nuts are so called because they contain ginger as one of their peculiar constituents, and the final flavoring one. Now what was ginger? A hot, spicy thing. Was Bartleby hot and spicy? Not at all. Ginger, then, had no effect upon Bartleby. Probably he preferred it should have none.

Nothing so aggravates an earnest person as a passive resistance. If the individual so resisted be of a not inhumane temper, and the resisting one perfectly harmless in his passivity; then, in the better moods of the former, he will endeavor charitably to construe to his imagination what proves impossible to be solved by his judgment. Even so, for the most part, I regarded Bartleby and his ways. Poor fellow! thought I, he means no mischief; it is plain he intends no insolence; his aspect sufficiently evinces that his eccentricities are involuntary. He is useful to me. I can get along with him. If I turn him away, the chances are he will fall in with some less indulgent employer, and then he will be rudely treated, and perhaps driven forth miserably to starve. Yes. Here I can cheaply purchase a delicious self-approval. To befriend Bartleby; to humor him in his strange wilfulness, will cost me little or nothing, while I lay up in my soul what will eventually prove a sweet morsel for my conscience. But this mood was not invariable with me. The passiveness of Bartleby some-

times irritated me. I felt strangely goaded on to encounter him in new opposition, to elicit some angry spark from him answerable to my own. But indeed I
might as well have essayed to strike fire with my knuckles against a bit of
Windsor soap.[4] But one afternoon the evil impulse in me mastered me, and
the following little scene ensued:

"Bartleby," said I, "when those papers are all copied, I will compare them
with you."

"I would prefer not to."

"How? Surely you do not mean to persist in that mulish vagary?"

No answer.

I threw open the folding-doors near by, and turning upon Turkey and Nippers, exclaimed in an excited manner—

"He says, a second time, he won't examine his papers. What do you think
of it, Turkey?"

It was afternoon, be it remembered. Turkey sat glowing like a brass boiler,
his bald head steaming, his hands reeling among his blotted papers.

"Think of it?" roared Turkey; "I think I'll just step behind his screen, and
black his eyes for him!"

So saying, Turkey rose to his feet and threw his arms into a pugilistic position. He was hurrying away to make good his promise, when I detained him,
alarmed at the effect of incautiously rousing Turkey's combativeness after
dinner.

"Sit down, Turkey," said I, "and hear what Nippers has to say. What do
you think of it, Nippers? Would I not be justified in immediately dismissing
Bartleby?"

"Excuse me, that is for you to decide, sir. I think his conduct quite unusual,
and indeed unjust, as regards Turkey and myself. But it may only be a passing whim."

"Ah," exclaimed I, "you have strangely changed your mind then—you
speak very gently of him now."

"All beer," cried Turkey; "gentleness is effects of beer—Nippers and I dined
together to-day. You see how gentle I am, sir. Shall I go and black his eyes?"

"You refer to Bartleby, I suppose. No, not to-day, Turkey," I replied; "pray,
put up your fists."

I closed the doors, and again advanced towards Bartleby. I felt additional
incentives tempting me to my fate. I burned to be rebelled against again. I
remembered that Bartleby never left the office.

"Bartleby," said I, "Ginger Nut is away; just step round to the Post Office,
won't you? ( it was but a three minutes' walk,) and see if there is any thing
for me."

"I would prefer not to."

"You *will* not?"

"I *prefer* not."

I staggered to my desk, and sat there in a deep study. My blind inveteracy
returned. Was there any other thing in which I could procure myself to be
ignominiously repulsed by this lean, penniless wight?—my hired clerk? What
added thing is there, perfectly reasonable, that he will be sure to refuse to do?

"Bartleby!"

4. Brown hand soap.

No answer.

"Bartleby," in a louder tone.

No answer.

"Bartleby," I roared.

Like a very ghost, agreeably to the laws of magical invocation, at the third summons, he appeared at the entrance of his hermitage.

"Go to the next room, and tell Nippers to come to me."

"I prefer not to," he respectfully and slowly said, and mildly disappeared.

"Very good, Bartleby," said I, in a quiet sort of serenely severe self-possessed tone, intimating the unalterable purpose of some terrible retribution very close at hand. At the moment I half intended something of the kind. But upon the whole, as it was drawing towards my dinner-hour, I thought it best to put on my hat and walk home for the day, suffering much from perplexity and distress of mind.

Shall I acknowledge it? The conclusion of this whole business was, that it soon became a fixed fact of my chambers, that a pale young scrivener, by the name of Bartleby, had a desk there; that he copied for me at the usual rate of four cents a folio (one hundred words); but he was permanently exempt from examining the work done by him, that duty being transferred to Turkey and Nippers, out of compliment doubtless to their superior acuteness; moreover, said Bartleby was never on any account to be dispatched on the most trivial errand of any sort; and that even if entreated to take upon him such a matter, it was generally understood that he would prefer not to—in other words, that he would refuse point-blank.

As days passed on, I became considerably reconciled to Bartleby. His steadiness, his freedom from all dissipation, his incessant industry (except when he chose to throw himself into a standing revery behind his screen), his great stillness, his unalterableness of demeanor under all circumstances, made him a valuable acquisition. One prime thing was this,—*he was always there;*—first in the morning, continually through the day, and the last at night. I had a singular confidence in his honesty. I felt my most precious papers perfectly safe in his hands. Sometimes to be sure I could not, for the very soul of me, avoid falling into sudden spasmodic passions with him. For it was exceeding difficult to bear in mind all the time those strange peculiarities, privileges, and unheard of exemptions, forming the tacit stipulations on Bartleby's part under which he remained in my office. Now and then, in the eagerness of dispatching pressing business, I would inadvertently summon Bartleby, in a short, rapid tone, to put his finger, say, on the incipient tie of a bit of red tape with which I was about compressing some papers. Of course, from behind the screen the usual answer, "I prefer not to," was sure to come; and then, how could a human creature with common infirmities of our nature, refrain from bitterly exclaiming upon such perverseness—such unreasonableness. However, every added repulse of this sort which I received only tended to lessen the probability of my repeating the inadvertence.

Here it must be said, that according to the customs of most legal gentlemen occupying chambers in densely-populated law buildings, there were several keys to my door. One was kept by a woman residing in the attic, which person weekly scrubbed and daily swept and dusted my apartments. Another was kept by Turkey for convenience sake. The third I sometimes carried in my own pocket. The fourth I knew not who had.

Now, one Sunday morning I happened to go to Trinity Church, to hear a celebrated preacher, and finding myself rather early on the ground, I thought I would walk round to my chambers for a while. Luckily I had my key with me; but upon applying it to the lock, I found it resisted by something inserted from the inside. Quite surprised, I called out; when to my consternation a key was turned from within; and thrusting his lean visage at me, and holding the door ajar, the apparition of Bartleby appeared, in his shirt sleeves, and otherwise in a strangely tattered dishabille, saying quietly that he was sorry, but he was deeply engaged just then, and—preferred not admitting me at present. In a brief word or two, he moreover added, that perhaps I had better walk round the block two or three times, and by that time he would probably have concluded his affairs.

Now, the utterly unsurmised appearance of Bartleby, tenanting my law-chambers of a Sunday morning, with his cadaverously gentlemanly *nonchalance*, yet withal firm and self-possessed, had such a strange effect upon me, that incontinently I slunk away from my own door, and did as desired. But not without sundry twinges of impotent rebellion against the mild effrontery of this unaccountable scrivener. Indeed, it was his wonderful mildness chiefly, which not only disarmed me, but unmanned me, as it were. For I consider that one, for the time, is a sort of unmanned when he tranquilly permits his hired clerk to dictate to him, and order him away from his own premises. Furthermore, I was full of uneasiness as to what Bartleby could possibly be doing in my office in his shirt sleeves, and in an otherwise dismantled condition of a Sunday morning. Was any thing amiss going on? Nay, that was out of the question. It was not to be thought of for a moment that Bartleby was an immoral person. But what could he be doing there?—copying? Nay again, whatever might be his eccentricities, Bartleby was an eminently decorous person. He would be the last man to sit down to his desk in any state approaching to nudity. Besides, it was Sunday; and there was something about Bartleby that forbade the supposition that he would by any secular occupation violate the proprieties of the day.

Nevertheless, my mind was not pacified; and full of a restless curiosity, at last I returned to the door. Without hindrance I inserted my key, opened it, and entered. Bartleby was not to be seen. I looked round anxiously, peeped behind his screen; but it was very plain that he was gone. Upon more closely examining the place, I surmised that for an indefinite period Bartleby must have ate, dressed, and slept in my office, and that too without plate, mirror, or bed. The cushioned seat of a ricketty old sofa in one corner bore the faint impress of a lean, reclining form. Rolled away under his desk, I found a blanket; under the empty grate, a blacking box and brush; on a chair, a tin basin, with soap and a ragged towel; in a newspaper a few crumbs of ginger-nuts and a morsel of cheese. Yes, thought I, it is evident enough that Bartleby has been making his home here, keeping bachelor's hall all by himself. Immediately then the thought came sweeping across me, What miserable friendlessness and loneliness are here revealed! His poverty is great; but his solitude, how horrible! Think of it. Of a Sunday, Wall-street is deserted as Petra;[5] and every night of every day it is an emptiness. This building too, which of week-days hums with industry and life, at nightfall echoes with sheer vacancy, and all through

---

5. Ancient city whose ruins are in Jordan, on a slope of Mount Hor.

Sunday is forlorn. And here Bartleby makes his home; sole spectator of a solitude which he has seen all populous—a sort of innocent and transformed
Marius[6] brooding among the ruins of Carthage!
For the first time in my life a feeling of overpowering stinging melancholy
seized me. Before, I had never experienced aught but a not-unpleasing sadness. The bond of a common humanity now drew me irresistibly to gloom. A
fraternal melancholy! For both I and Bartleby were sons of Adam. I remembered the bright silks and sparkling faces I had seen that day, in gala trim,
swan-like sailing down the Mississippi of Broadway; and I contrasted them
with the pallid copyist, and thought to myself, Ah, happiness courts the light,
so we deem the world is gay; but misery hides aloof, so we deem that misery
there is none. These sad fancyings—chimeras, doubtless, of a sick and silly
brain—led on to other and more special thoughts, concerning the eccentricities of Bartleby. Presentiments of strange discoveries hovered round me. The
scrivener's pale form appeared to me laid out, among uncaring strangers, in its
shivering winding sheet.
Suddenly I was attracted by Bartleby's closed desk, the key in open sight left
in the lock.
I mean no mischief, seek the gratification of no heartless curiosity, thought
I; besides, the desk is mine, and its contents too, so I will make bold to look
within. Every thing was methodically arranged, the papers smoothly placed.
The pigeon holes were deep, and removing the files of documents, I groped
into their recesses. Presently I felt something there, and dragged it out. It was
an old bandanna handkerchief, heavy and knotted. I opened it, and saw it was
a saving's bank.
I now recalled all the quiet mysteries which I had noted in the man. I
remembered that he never spoke but to answer; that though at intervals he had
considerable time to himself, yet I had never seen him reading—no, not even
a newspaper; that for long periods he would stand looking out, at his pale
window behind the screen, upon the dead brick wall; I was quite sure he never
visited any refectory or eating house; while his pale face clearly indicated that
he never drank beer like Turkey, or tea and coffee even, like other men; that
he never went any where in particular that I could learn; never went out for a
walk, unless indeed that was the case at present; that he had declined telling
who he was, or whence he came, or whether he had any relatives in the world;
that though so thin and pale, he never complained of ill health. And more
than all, I remembered a certain unconscious air of pallid—how shall I call
it?—of pallid haughtiness, say, or rather an austere reserve about him, which
had positively awed me into my tame compliance with his eccentricities, when
I had feared to ask him to do the slightest incidental thing for me, even though
I might know, from his long-continued motionlessness, that behind his screen
he must be standing in one of those dead-wall reveries of his.
Revolving all these things, and coupling them with the recently discovered
fact that he made my office his constant abiding place and home, and not
forgetful of his morbid moodiness; revolving all these things, a prudential feeling began to steal over me. My first emotions had been those of pure melancholy and sincerest pity; but just in proportion as the forlornness of Bartleby
grew and grew to my imagination, did that same melancholy merge into fear,

6. Gaius Marius (157–86 B.C.), Roman general who returned to power after exile.

that pity into repulsion. So true it is, and so terrible too, that up to a certain point the thought or sight of misery enlists our best affections; but, in certain special cases, beyond that point it does not. They err who would assert that invariably this is owing to the inherent selfishness of the human heart. It rather proceeds from a certain hopelessness of remedying excessive and organic ill. To a sensitive being, pity is not seldom pain. And when at last it is perceived that such pity cannot lead to effectual succor, common sense bids the soul be rid of it. What I saw that morning persuaded me that the scrivener was the victim of innate and incurable disorder. I might give alms to his body; but his body did not pain him; it was his soul that suffered, and his soul I could not reach.

I did not accomplish the purpose of going to Trinity Church that morning. Somehow, the things I had seen disqualified me for the time from church-going. I walked homeward, thinking what I would do with Bartleby. Finally, I resolved upon this;—I wold put certain calm questions to him the next morning, touching his history, &c., and if he declined to answer them openly and unreservedly (and I supposed he would prefer not), then to give him a twenty dollar bill over and above whatever I might owe him, and tell him his services were no longer required; but that if in any other way I could assist him, I would be happy to do so, especially if he desired to return to his native place, wherever that might be, I would willingly help to defray the expenses. More-over, if, after reaching home, he found himself at any time in want of aid, a letter from him would be sure of a reply.

The next morning came.

"Bartleby," said I, gently calling to him behind his screen.

No reply.

"Bartleby," said I, in a still gentler tone, "come here; I am not going to ask you to do any thing you would prefer not to do—I simply wish to speak to you."

Upon this he noiselessly slid into view.

"Will you tell me, Bartleby, where you were born?"

"I would prefer not to."

"Will you tell me *any thing* about yourself?"

"I would prefer not to."

"But what reasonable objection can you have to speak to me? I feel friendly towards you."

He did not look at me while I spoke, but kept his glance fixed upon my bust of Cicero, which as I then sat, was directly behind me, some six inches above my head.

"What is your answer, Bartleby?" said I, after waiting a considerable time for a reply, during which his countenance remained immovable, only there was the faintest conceivable tremor of the white attenuated mouth.

"At present I prefer to give no answer," he said, and retired into his hermitage.

It was rather weak in me I confess, but his manner on this occasion nettled me. Not only did there seem to lurk in it a certain calm disdain, but his perverseness seemed ungrateful, considering the undeniable good usage and indulgence he had received from me.

Again I sat ruminating what I should do. Mortified as I was at his behavior, and resolved as I had been to dismiss him when I entered my office, nevertheless I strangely felt something superstitious knocking at my heart, and forbidding me to carry out my purpose, and denouncing me for a villain if I dared to breathe one bitter word against this forlornest of mankind. At last, familiarly drawing my chair behind his screen, I sat down and said: "Bartleby, never mind then about revealing your history; but let me entreat you, as a friend, to comply as far as may be with the usages of this office. Say now you will help to examine papers to-morrow or next day: in short, say now that in a day or two you will begin to be a little reasonable:—say so, Bartleby."

"At present I would prefer not to be a little reasonable," was his mildly cadaverous reply.

Just then the folding-doors opened, and Nippers approached. He seemed suffering from an unusually bad night's rest, induced by severer indigestion than common. He overheard those final words of Bartleby.

"*Prefer not*, eh?" gritted Nippers—"I'd *prefer* him, if I were you, sir," addressing me—"I'd *prefer* him; I'd give him preferences, the stubborn mule! What is it, sir, pray, that he *prefers* not to do now?"

Bartleby moved not a limb.

"Mr. Nippers," said I, "I'd prefer that you would withdraw for the present."

Somehow, of late I had got into the way of involuntarily using this word "prefer" upon all sorts of not exactly suitable occasions. And I trembled to think that my contact with the scrivener had already and seriously affected me in a mental way. And what further and deeper aberration might it not yet produce? This apprehension had not been without efficacy in determining me to summary means.

As Nippers, looking very sour and sulky, was departing, Turkey blandly and deferentially approached.

"With submission, sir," said he, "yesterday I was thinking about Bartleby here, and I think that if he would but prefer to take a quart of good ale every day, it would do much towards mending him, and enabling him to assist in examining his papers."

"So you have got the word too," said I, slightly excited.

"With submission, what word, sir," asked Turkey, respectfully crowding himself into the contracted space behind the screen, and by so doing, making me jostle the scrivener. "What word, sir?"

"I would prefer to be left alone here," said Bartleby, as if offended at being mobbed in his privacy.

"*That's* the word, Turkey," said I—"*that's* it."

"Oh, *prefer?* oh yes—queer word. I never use it myself. But, sir, as I was saying, if he would but prefer—"

"Turkey," interrupted I, "you will please withdraw."

"Oh certainly, sir, if you prefer that I should."

As he opened the folding-door to retire, Nippers at his desk caught a glimpse of me, and asked whether I would prefer to have a certain paper copied on blue paper or white. He did not in the least roguishly accent the word prefer. It was plain that it involuntarily rolled from his tongue. I thought to myself, surely I must get rid of a demented man, who already has in some degree turned the tongues, if not the heads of myself and clerks. But I thought it prudent not to break the dismission at once.

The next day I noticed that Bartleby did nothing but stand at his window in his dead-wall revery. Upon asking him why he did not write, he said that he had decided upon doing no more writing.

"Why, how now? what next?" exclaimed I, "do no more writing?"

"No more."

"And what is the reason?"

"Do you not see the reason for yourself," he indifferently replied.

I looked steadfastly at him, and perceived that his eyes looked dull and glazed. Instantly it occurred to me, that his unexampled diligence in copying by his dim window for the first few weeks of his stay with me might have temporarily impaired his vision.

I was touched. I said something in condolence with him. I hinted that of course he did wisely in abstaining from writing for a while; and urged him to embrace that opportunity of taking wholesome exercise in the open air. This, however, he did not do. A few days after this, my other clerks being absent, and being in a great hurry to dispatch certain letters by the mail, I thought that, having nothing else earthly to do, Bartleby would surely be less inflexible than usual, and carry these letters to the post-office. But he blankly declined. So, much to my inconvenience, I went myself.

Still added days went by. Whether Bartleby's eyes improved or not, I could not say. To all appearance, I thought they did. But when I asked him if they did, he vouchsafed no answer. At all events, he would do no copying. At last, in reply to my urgings, he informed me that he had permanently given up copying.

"What!" exclaimed I; "suppose your eyes should get entirely well—better than ever before—would you not copy then?"

"I have given up copying," he answered, and slid aside.

He remained as ever, a fixture in my chamber. Nay—if that were possible—he became still more of a fixture than before. What was to be done? He would do nothing in the office: why should he stay there? In plain fact, he had now become a millstone to me, not only useless as a necklace, but afflictive to bear. Yet I was sorry for him. I speak less than truth when I say that, on his own account, he occasioned me uneasiness. If he would but have named a single relative or friend, I would instantly have written, and urged their taking the poor fellow away to some convenient retreat. But he seemed alone, absolutely alone in the universe. A bit of wreck in the mid Atlantic. At length, necessities connected with my business tyrannized over all other considerations. Decently as I could, I told Bartleby that in six days' time he must unconditionally leave the office. I warned him to take measures, in the interval, for procuring some other abode. I offered to assist him in this endeavor, if he himself would but take the first step towards a removal. "And when you finally quit me, Bartleby," added I, "I shall see that you go not away entirely unprovided. Six days from this hour, remember."

At the expiration of that period, I peeped behind the screen, and lo! Bartleby was there.

I buttoned up my coat, balanced myself; advanced slowly towards him, touched his shoulder, and said, "The time has come; you must quit this place; I am sorry for you; here is money; but you must go."

"I would prefer not," he replied, with his back still towards me.

"You *must*."

He remained silent.

Now I had an unbounded confidence in this man's common honesty. He had frequently restored to me sixpences and shillings carelessly dropped upon the floor, for I am apt to be very reckless in such shirt-button affairs. The proceeding then which followed will not be deemed extraordinary.

"Bartleby," said I, "I owe you twelve dollars on account; here are thirty-two; the odd twenty are yours.—Will you take it?" and I handed the bills towards him.

But he made no motion.

"I will leave them here then," putting them under a weight on the table. Then taking my hat and cane and going to the door I tranquilly turned and added—"After you have removed your things from these offices, Bartleby, you will of course lock the door—since every one is now gone for the day but you—and if you please, slip your key underneath the mat, so that I may have it in the morning. I shall not see you again; so good-bye to you. If hereafter in your new place of abode I can be of any service to you, do not fail to advise me by letter. Good-bye, Bartleby, and fare you well."

But he answered not a word; like the last column of some ruined temple, he remained standing mute and solitary in the middle of the otherwise deserted room.

As I walked home in a pensive mood, my vanity got the better of my pity. I could not but highly plume myself on my masterly management in getting rid of Bartleby. Masterly I call it, and such it must appear to any dispassionate thinker. The beauty of my procedure seemed to consist in its perfect quietness. There was no vulgar bullying, no bravado of any sort, no choleric hectoring, and striding to and fro across the apartment, jerking out vehement commands for Bartleby to bundle himself off with his beggarly traps. Nothing of the kind. Without loudly bidding Bartleby depart—as an inferior genius might have done—I *assumed* the ground that depart he must; and upon that assumption built all I had to say. The more I thought over my procedure, the more I was charmed with it. Nevertheless, next morning, upon awakening, I had my doubts,—I had somehow slept off the fumes of vanity. One of the coolest and wisest hours a man has, is just after he awakes in the morning. My procedure seemed as sagacious as ever,—but only in theory. How it would prove in practice—there was the rub. It was truly a beautiful thought to have assumed Bartleby's departure; but, after all, that assumption was simply my own, and none of Bartleby's. The great point was, not whether I had assumed that he would quit me, but whether he would prefer so to do. He was more a man of preferences than assumptions.

After breakfast, I walked down town, arguing the probabilities *pro* and *con*. One moment I thought it would prove a miserable failure, and Bartleby would be found all alive at my office as usual; the next moment it seemed certain that I should see his chair empty. And so I kept veering about. At the corner of Broadway and Canal-street, I saw quite an excited group of people standing in earnest conversation.

"I'll take odds he doesn't," said a voice as I passed.

"Doesn't go?—done!" said I, "put up your money."

I was instinctively putting my hand in my pocket to produce my own, when I remembered that this was an election day. The words I had overheard bore no reference to Bartleby, but to the success or non-success of some candidate for the mayoralty. In my intent frame of mind, I had, as it were, imagined that all Broadway shared in my excitement, and were debating the same question with me. I passed on, very thankful that the uproar of the street screened my momentary absent-mindedness.

As I had intended, I was earlier than usual at my office door. I stood listening for a moment. All was still. He must be gone. I tried the knob. The door was locked. Yes, my procedure had worked to a charm; he indeed must be vanished. Yet a certain melancholy mixed with this: I was almost sorry for my brilliant success. I was fumbling under the door mat for the key, which Bartleby was to have left there for me, when accidentally my knee knocked against a panel, producing a summoning sound, and in response a voice came to me from within—"Not yet; I am occupied."

It was Bartleby.

I was thunderstruck. For an instant I stood like the man who, pipe in mouth, was killed one cloudless afternoon long ago in Virginia, by summer lightning; at his own warm open window he was killed, and remained leaning out there upon the dreamy afternoon, till some one touched him, when he fell.

"Not gone!" I murmured at last. But again obeying that wondrous ascendancy which the inscrutable scrivener had over me, and from which ascendancy, for all my chafing, I could not completely escape, I slowly went down stairs and out into the street, and while walking round the block, considered what I should next do in this unheard-of perplexity. Turn the man out by an actual thrusting I could not; to drive him away by calling him hard names would not do; calling in the police was an unpleasant idea; and yet, permit him to enjoy his cadaverous triumph over me,—this too I could not think of. What was to be done? or, if nothing could be done, was there any thing further that I could *assume* in the matter? Yes, as before I had prospectively assumed that Bartleby would depart, so now I might retrospectively assume that departed he was. In the legitimate carrying out of this assumption, I might enter my office in a great hurry, and pretending not to see Bartleby at all, walk straight against him as if he were air. Such a proceeding would in a singular degree have the appearance of a home-thrust. It was hardly possible that Bartleby could withstand such an application of the doctrine of assumptions. But upon second thoughts the success of the plan seemed rather dubious. I resolved to argue the matter over with him again.

"Bartleby," said I, entering the office, with a quietly severe expression, "I am seriously displeased. I am pained, Bartleby. I had thought better of you. I had imagined you of such a gentlemanly organization, that in any delicate dilemma a slight hint would suffice—in short, an assumption. But it appears I am deceived. Why," I added, unaffectedly starting, "you have not even touched that money yet," pointing to it, just where I had left it the evening previous.

He answered nothing.

"Will you, or will you not, quit me?" I now demanded in a sudden passion, advancing close to him.

"I would prefer *not* to quit you," he replied, gently emphasizing the *not*.

"What earthly right have you to stay here? Do you pay any rent? Do you pay my taxes? Or is this property yours?"

He answered nothing.

"Are you ready to go on and write now? Are your eyes recovered? Could you copy a small paper for me this morning? or help examine a few lines? or

step round to the post-office? In a word, will you do any thing at all, to give a coloring to your refusal to depart the premises?"
He silently retired into his hermitage.
I was now in such a state of nervous resentment that I thought it but prudent to check myself at present from further demonstrations. Bartleby and I were alone. I remembered the tragedy of the unfortunate Adams and the still more unfortunate Colt in the solitary office of the latter; and how poor Colt, being dreadfully incensed by Adams,[7] and imprudently permitting himself to get wildly excited, was at unawares hurried into his fatal act—an act which certainly no man could possibly deplore more than the actor himself. Often it had occurred to me in my ponderings upon the subject, that had that altercation taken place in the public street, or at a private residence, it would not have terminated as it did. It was the circumstance of being alone in a solitary office, up stairs, of a building entirely unhallowed by humanizing domestic associations—an uncarpeted office, doubtless, of a dusty, haggard sort of appearance;—this it must have been, which greatly helped to enhance the irritable desperation of the hapless Colt.
But when this old Adam of resentment rose in me and tempted me concerning Bartleby, I grappled him and threw him. How? Why, simply by recalling the divine injunction: "A new commandment give I unto you, that ye love one another." Yes, this it was that saved me. Aside from higher considerations, charity often operates as a vastly wise and prudent principle—a great safeguard to its possessor. Men have committed murder for jealousy's sake, and anger's sake, and hatred's sake, and selfishness' sake, and spiritual pride's sake; but no man that ever I heard of, ever committed a diabolical murder for sweet charity's sake. Mere self-interest, then, if no better motive can be enlisted, should, especially with high-tempered men, prompt all beings to charity and philanthropy. At any rate, upon the occasion in question, I strove to drown my exasperated feelings towards the scrivener by benevolently constructing his conduct. Poor fellow, poor fellow! thought I, he don't mean any thing; and besides, he has seen hard.times, and ought to be indulged.
I endeavored also immediately to occupy myself, and at the same time to comfort my despondency. I tried to fancy that in the course of the morning, at such time as might prove agreeable to him, Bartleby, of his own free accord, would emerge from his hermitage, and take up some decided line of march in the direction of the door. But no. Half-past twelve o'clock came; Turkey began to glow in the face, overturn his inkstand, and become generally obstreperous; Nippers abated down into quietude and courtesy; Ginger Nut munched his noon apple; and Bartleby remained standing at his window in one of his profoundest dead-wall reveries. Will it be credited? Ought I to acknowledge it? That afternoon I left the office without saying one further word to him.
Some days now passed, during which, at leisure intervals I looked a little into "Edwards on the Will," and "Priestley on Necessity."[8] Under the circumstances, those books induced a salutary feeling. Gradually I slid into the per-

---

7. Notorious murder case that occurred while Melville was in the South Seas. In 1841 Samuel Adams, a printer, called on John C. Colt (brother of the inventor of the revolver) at Broadway and Chambers Street in lower Manhattan to collect a debt. Colt murdered Adams with a hatchet and crated the corpse for shipment to New Orleans. The body was found, and Colt was soon arrested. Despite his pleas of self-defense Colt was convicted the next year, amid continuing newspaper publicity, and stabbed himself to death just before he was to be hanged. The setting of Bartleby is not far from the scene of the murder.
8. Jonathan Edwards's Freedom of the Will (1754) and Joseph Priestley's Doctrine of Philosophical Necessity Illustrated (1777). The colonial minister and the English scientist agree that the will is not free.

suasion that these troubles of mine touching the scrivener, had been all predestinated from eternity, and Bartleby was billeted upon me for some mysterious purpose of an all-wise Providence, which it was not for a mere mortal like me to fathom. Yes, Bartleby, stay there behind your screen, thought I; I shall persecute you no more; you are harmless and noiseless as any of these old chairs; in short, I never feel so private as when I know you are here. At least I see it, I feel it; I penetrate to the predestinated purpose of my life. I am content. Others may have loftier parts to enact; but my mission in this world, Bartleby, is to furnish you with office-room for such period as you may see fit to remain.

I believe that this wise and blessed frame of mind would have continued with me, had it not been for the unsolicited and uncharitable remarks obtruded upon me by my professional friends who visited the rooms. But thus it often is, that the constant friction of illiberal minds wears out at last the best resolves of the more generous. Though to be sure, when I reflected upon it, it was not strange that people entering my office should be struck by the peculiar aspect of the unaccountable Bartleby, and so be tempted to throw out some sinister observations concerning him. Sometimes an attorney having business with me, and calling at my office, and finding no one but the scrivener there, would undertake to obtain some sort of precise information from him touching my whereabouts; but without heeding his idle talk, Bartleby would remain standing immovable in the middle of the room. So after contemplating him in that position for a time, the attorney would depart, no wiser than he came.

Also, when a Reference[9] was going on, and the room full of lawyers and witnesses and business was driving fast; some deeply occupied legal gentleman present, seeing Bartleby wholly unemployed, would request him to run round to his (the legal gentleman's) office and fetch some papers for him. Thereupon, Bartleby would tranquilly decline, and yet remain idle as before. Then the lawyer would give a great stare, and turn to me. And what could I say? At last I was made aware that all through the circle of my professional acquaintance, a whisper of wonder was running round, having reference to the strange creature I kept at my office. This worried me very much. And as the idea came upon me of his possibly turning out a long-lived man, and keep occupying my chambers, and denying my authority; and perplexing my visitors; and scandalizing my professional reputation; and casting a general gloom over the premises; keeping soul and body together to the last upon his savings (for doubtless he spent but half a dime a day), and in the end perhaps outlive me, and claim possession of my office by right of his perpetual occupancy: as all these dark anticipations crowded upon me more and more, and my friends continually intruded their relentless remarks upon the apparition in my room; a great change was wrought in me. I resolved to gather all my faculties together, and for ever rid me of this intolerable incubus.

Ere revolving any complicated project, however, adapted to this end, I first simply suggested to Bartleby the propriety of his permanent departure. In a calm and serious tone, I commended the idea to his careful and mature consideration. But having taken three days to meditate upon it, he apprised me that his original determination remained the same; in short, that he still preferred to abide with me.

9. The act of referring a disputed matter to referees.

What shall I do? I now said to myself, buttoning up my coat to the last button. What shall I do? what ought I to do? what does conscience say I *should* do with this man, or rather ghost. Rid myself of him, I must; go, he shall. But how? You will not thrust him, the poor, pale, passive mortal,—you will not thrust such a helpless creature out of your door? you will not dishonor yourself by such cruelty? No, I will not, I cannot do that. Rather would I let him live and die here, and then mason up his remains in the wall. What then will you do? For all your coaxing, he will not budge. Bribes he leaves under your own paper-weight on your table; in short, it is quite plain that he prefers to cling to you.

Then something severe, something unusual must be done. What! surely you will not have him collared by a constable, and commit his innocent pallor to the common jail? And upon what ground could you procure such a thing to be done?—a vagrant, is he? What! he a vagrant, a wanderer, who refuses to budge? It is because he will *not* be a vagrant, then, that you seek to count him *as* a vagrant. That is too absurd. No visible means of support: there I have him. Wrong again: for indubitably he *does* support himself, and that is the only unanswerable proof that any man can show of his possessing the means so to do. No more then. Since he will not quit me, I must quit him. I will change my offices; I will move elsewhere; and give him fair notice, that if I find him on my new premises I will then proceed against him as a common trespasser.

Acting accordingly, next day I thus addressed him: "I find these chambers too far from the City Hall; the air is unwholesome. In a word, I propose to remove my offices next week, and shall no longer require your services. I tell you this now, in order that you may seek another place."

He made no reply, and nothing more was said.

On the appointed day I engaged carts and men, proceeded to my chambers, and having but little furniture, every thing was removed in a few hours. Throughout, the scrivener remained standing behind the screen, which I directed to be removed the last thing. It was withdrawn; and being folded up like a huge folio, left him the motionless occupant of a naked room. I stood in the entry watching him a moment, while something from within me upbraided me.

I re-entered, with my hand in my pocket—and—and my heart in my mouth.

"Good-bye, Bartleby; I am going—good-bye, and God some way bless you; and take that," slipping something in his hand. But it dropped upon the floor, and then,—strange to say—I tore myself from him whom I had so longed to be rid of.

Established in my new quarters, for a day or two I kept the door locked, and started at every footfall in the passages. When I returned to my rooms after any little absence, I would pause at the threshold for an instant, and attentively listen, ere applying my key. But these fears were needless. Bartleby never came nigh me.

I thought all was going well, when a perturbed looking stranger visited me, inquiring whether I was the person who had recently occupied rooms at No.—Wall-street.

Full of forebodings, I replied that I was.

"Then sir," said the stranger, who proved a lawyer, "you are responsible for the man you left there. He refuses to do any copying; he refuses to do any thing; he says he prefers not to; and he refuses to quit the premises."

"I am very sorry, sir," said I, with assumed tranquillity, but an inward tremor, "but, really, the man you allude to is nothing to me—he is no relation or apprentice of mine, that you should hold me responsible for him."

"In mercy's name, who is he?"

"I certainly cannot inform you. I know nothing about him. Formerly I employed him as a copyist; but he has done nothing for me now for some time past."

"I shall settle him then,—good morning, sir."

Several days passed, and I heard nothing more; and though I often felt a charitable prompting to call at the place and see poor Bartleby, yet a certain squeamishness of I know not what withheld me.

All is over with him, by this time, thought I at last, when through another week no further intelligence reached me. But coming to my room the day after, I found several persons waiting at my door in a high state of nervous excitement.

"That's the man—here he comes," cried the foremost one, whom I recognized as the lawyer who had previously called upon me alone.

"You must take him away, sir, at once," cried a portly person among them, advancing upon me, and whom I knew to be the landlord of No.—Wall-street. "These gentlemen, my tenants, cannot stand it any longer; Mr. B——" pointing to the lawyer, "has turned him out of his room, and he now persists in haunting the building generally, sitting upon the banisters of the stairs by day, and sleeping in the entry by night. Every body is concerned; clients are leaving the offices; some fears are entertained of a mob; something you must do, and that without delay."

Aghast at this torrent, I fell back before it, and would fain have locked myself in my new quarters. In vain I persisted that Bartleby was nothing to me—no more than to any one else. In vain:—I was the last person known to have any thing to do with him, and they held me to the terrible account. Fearful then of being exposed in the papers (as one person present obscurely threatened) I considered the matter, and at length said, that if the lawyer would give me a confidential interview with the scrivener, in his (the lawyer's) own room, I would that afternoon strive my best to rid them of the nuisance they complained of.

Going up stairs to my old haunt, there was Bartleby silently sitting upon the banister at the landing.

"What are you doing here, Bartleby?" said I.

"Sitting upon the banister," he mildly replied.

I motioned him into the lawyer's room, who then left us.

"Bartleby," said I, "are you aware that you are the cause of great tribulation to me, by persisting in occupying the entry after being dismissed from the office?"

No answer.

"Now one of two things must take place. Either you must do something, or something must be done to you. Now what sort of business would you like to engage in? Would you like to re-engage in copying for some one?"

"No; I would prefer not to make any change."

"Would you like a clerkship in a dry-goods store?"

"There is too much confinement about that. No, I would not like a clerkship; but I am not particular."

"Too much confinement," I cried, "why you keep yourself confined all the time!"

"I would prefer not to take a clerkship," he rejoined, as if to settle that little item at once.

"How would a bar-tender's business suit you? There is no trying of the eyesight in that."

"I would not like it at all; though, as I said before, I am not particular."

His unwonted wordiness inspirited me. I returned to the charge.

"Well then, would you like to travel through the country collecting bills for the merchants? That would improve your health."

"No, I would prefer to be doing something else."

"How then would going as a companion to Europe, to entertain some young gentleman with your conversation,—how would that suit you?"

"Not at all. It does not strike me that there is any thing definite about that. I like to be stationary. But I am not particular."

"Stationary you shall be then," I cried, now losing all patience, and for the first time in all my exasperating connection with him fairly flying into a passion. "If you do not go away from these premises before night, I shall feel bound—indeed I *am* bound—to—to—to quit the premises myself!" I rather absurdly concluded, knowing not with what possible threat to try to frighten his immobility into compliance. Despairing of all further efforts, I was precipitately leaving him, when a final thought occurred to me—one which had not been wholly unindulged before.

"Bartleby," said I, in the kindest tone I could assume under such exciting circumstances, "will you go home with me now—not to my office, but my dwelling—and remain there till we can conclude upon some convenient arrangement for you at our leisure? Come, let us start now, right away."

"No: at present I would prefer not to make any change at all."

I answered nothing; but effectually dodging every one by the suddenness and rapidity of my flight, rushed from the building, ran up Wall-street towards Broadway, and jumping into the first omnibus was soon removed from pursuit. As soon as tranquillity returned I distinctly perceived that I had now done all that I possibly could, both in respect to the demands of the landlord and his tenants, and with regard to my own desire and sense of duty, to benefit Bartleby, and shield him from rude persecution. I now strove to be entirely carefree and quiescent; and my conscience justified me in the attempt; though indeed it was not so successful as I could have wished. So fearful was I of being again hunted out by the incensed landlord and his exasperated tenants, that, surrendering my business to Nippers, for a few days I drove about the upper part of the town and through the suburbs, in my rockaway; crossed over to Jersey City and Hoboken, and paid fugitive visits to Manhattanville and Astoria.[1] In fact I almost lived in my rockaway for the time.

When again I entered my office, lo, a note from the landlord lay upon the desk. I opened it with trembling hands. It informed me that the writer had sent to the police, and had Bartleby removed to the Tombs as a vagrant. More-

---

1. The narrator crossed the Hudson River to Jersey City and Hoboken, then drove far up unsettled Manhattan Island to the community of Manhattanville (Grant's Tomb is in what was Manhattanville), and finally crossed the East River to Astoria, on Long Island. "Rockaway": light open-sided carriage.

over, since I knew more about him than any one else, he wished me to appear at that place, and make a suitable statement of the facts. These tidings had a conflicting effect upon me. At first I was indignant; but at last almost approved. The landlord's energetic, summary disposition, had led him to adopt a procedure which I do not think I would have decided upon myself; and yet as a last resort, under such peculiar circumstances, it seemed the only plan.

As I afterwards learned, the poor scrivener, when told that he must be conducted to the Tombs, offered not the slightest obstacle, but in his pale unmoving way, silently acquiesced.

Some of the compassionate and curious bystanders joined the party; and headed by one of the constables arm in arm with Bartleby, the silent procession filed its way through all the noise, and heat, and joy of the roaring thoroughfares at noon.

The same day I received the note I went to the Tombs, or to speak more properly, the Halls of Justice. Seeking the right officer, I stated the purpose of my call, and was informed that the individual I described was indeed within. I then assured the functionary that Bartleby was a perfectly honest man, and greatly to be compassionated, however unaccountably eccentric. I narrated all I knew, and closed by suggesting the idea of letting him remain in as indulgent confinement as possible till something less harsh might be done—though indeed I hardly knew what. At all events, if nothing else could be decided upon, the alms-house must receive him. I then begged to have an interview.

Being under no disgraceful charge, and quite serene and harmless in all his ways, they had permitted him freely to wander about the prison, and especially in the inclosed grass-platted yards thereof. And so I found him there, standing all alone in the quietest of the yards, his face towards a high wall, while all around, from the narrow slits of the jail windows, I thought I saw peering out upon him the eyes of murderers and thieves.

"Bartleby!"

"I know you," he said, without looking round,—"and I want nothing to say to you."

"It was not I that brought you here, Bartleby," said I, keenly pained at his implied suspicion. "And to you, this should not be so vile a place. Nothing reproachful attaches to you by being here. And see, it is not so sad a place as one might think. Look, there is the sky, and here is the grass."

"I know where I am," he replied, but would say nothing more, and so I left him.

As I entered the corridor again, a broad meat-like man, in an apron, accosted me, and jerking his thumb over his shoulder said—"Is that your friend?"

"Yes."

"Does he want to starve? If he does, let him live on the prison fare, that's all."

"Who are you?" asked I, not knowing what to make of such an unofficially speaking person in such a place.

"I am the grub-man. Such gentlemen as have friends here, hire me to provide them with something good to eat."

"Is this so?" said I, turning to the turnkey.

He said it was.

"Well then," said I, slipping some silver into the grub-man's hands (for so they called him). "I want you to give particular attention to my friend there; let him have the best dinner you can get. And you must be as polite to him as possible."

"Introduce me, will you?" said the grub-man, looking at me with an expression which seemed to say he was all impatience for an opportunity to give a specimen of his breeding.

Thinking it would prove of benefit to the scrivener, I acquiesced; and asking the grub-man his name, went up with him to Bartleby.

"Bartleby, this is Mr. Cutlets; you will find him very useful to you."

"Your sarvant, sir, your sarvant," said the grub-man, making a low salutation behind his apron. "Hope you find it pleasant here, sir;—spacious grounds—cool apartments, sir—hope you'll stay with us some time—try to make it agreeable. May Mrs. Cutlets and I have the pleasure of your company to dinner, sir, in Mrs. Cutlets' private room?"

"I prefer not to dine to-day," said Bartleby, turning away. "It would disagree with me; I am unused to dinners." So saying he slowly moved to the other side of the inclosure, and took up a position fronting the dead-wall.

"How's this?" said the grub-man, addressing me with a stare of astonishment. "He's odd, aint he?"

"I think he is a little deranged," said I, sadly.

"Deranged? deranged is it? Well now, upon my word, I thought that friend of yourn was a gentleman forger; they are always pale and genteel-like, them forgers. I can't help pity 'em—can't help it, sir. Did you know Monroe Edwards?"[2] he added touchingly, and paused. Then, laying his hand pityingly on my shoulder, sighed, "he died of consumption at Sing-Sing.[3] So you weren't acquainted with Monroe?"

"No, I was never socially acquainted with any forgers. But I cannot stop longer. Look to my friend yonder. You will not lose by it. I will see you again."

Some few days after this, I again obtained admission to the Tombs, and went through the corridors in quest of Bartleby; but without finding him.

"I saw him coming from his cell not long ago," said a turnkey, "may be he's gone to loiter in the yards."

So I went in that direction.

"Are you looking for the silent man?" said another turnkey passing me. "Yonder he lies—sleeping in the yard there. 'Tis not twenty minutes since I saw him lie down."

The yard was entirely quiet. It was not accessible to the common prisoners. The surrounding walls, of amazing thickness, kept off all sounds behind them. The Egyptian character of the masonry weighed upon me with its gloom. But a soft imprisoned turf grew under foot. The heart of the eternal pyramids, it seemed, wherein, by some strange magic, through the clefts, grass-seed, dropped by birds, had sprung.

Strangely huddled at the base of the wall, his knees drawn up, and lying on his side, his head touching the cold stones, I saw the wasted Bartleby. But

2. Horace Greeley's *Tribune* called Col. Monroe Edwards (1808–1847) "the most distinguished financier since the days of Judas Iscariot"; his trial in New York City (lasting all the second week of June 1842) caused the greatest public excitement since the trial "of the murderer, Colt" (see n. 7, p. 1061). He was convicted of swindling two firms of $25,000 each through forged letters of credit, sending tremors through the "exchange banking and commission business"—like undermining our Security Exchange. Melville was then in the South Seas, but the case was sensational, and his brothers were in New York.

3. Prison at Ossining, New York, not far up the Hudson.

nothing stirred. I paused; then went close up to him; stooped over, and saw that his dim eyes were open; otherwise he seemed profoundly sleeping. Something prompted me to touch him. I felt his hand, when a tingling shiver ran up my arm and down my spine to my feet.

The round face of the grub-man peered upon me now. "His dinner is ready. Won't he dine to-day, either? Or does he live without dining?"

"Lives without dining," said I, and closed the eyes.

"Eh!—He's asleep, aint he?"

"With kings and counsellors,"[4] murmured I.

---

There would seem little need for proceeding further in this history. Imagination will readily supply the meagre recital of poor Bartleby's interment. But ere parting with the reader, let me say, that if this little narrative has sufficiently interested him, to awaken curiosity as to who Bartleby was, and what manner of life he led prior to the present narrator's making his acquaintance, I can only reply, that in such curiosity I fully share, but am wholly unable to gratify it. Yet here I hardly know whether I should divulge one little item of rumor, which came to my ear a few months after the scrivener's decease. Upon what basis it rested, I could never ascertain; and hence, how true it is I cannot now tell. But inasmuch as this vague report has not been without a certain strange suggestive interest to me, however sad, it may prove the same with some others; and so I will briefly mention it. The report was this: that Bartleby had been a subordinate clerk in the Dead Letter Office at Washington, from which he had been suddenly removed by a change in the administration. When I think over this rumor, I cannot adequately express the emotions which seize me. Dead letters! does it not sound like dead men? Conceive a man by nature and misfortune prone to a pallid hopelessness, can any business seem more fitted to heighten it than that of continually handling these dead letters, and assorting them for the flames? For by the cart-load they are annually burned. Sometimes from out the folded paper the pale clerk takes a ring:— the finger it was meant for, perhaps, moulders in the grave; a bank-note sent in swiftest charity:—he whom it would relieve, nor eats nor hungers any more; pardon for those who died despairing; hope for those who died unhoping; good tidings for those who died stifled by unrelieved calamities. On errands of life, these letters speed to death.

Ah Bartleby! Ah humanity!

1853

---

4. Job 3.14.

# Billy Budd, Sailor[1]

## (An Inside Narrative)

DEDICATED
TO
JACK CHASE
ENGLISHMAN
Wherever that great heart may now be
Here on Earth or harbored in Paradise
Captain of the Maintop
in the year 1843
in the U.S. Frigate
*United States*[2]

I

In the time before steamships, or then more frequently than now, a stroller along the docks of any considerable seaport would occasionally have his attention arrested by a group of bronzed mariners, man-of-war's men or merchant sailors in holiday attire, ashore on liberty. In certain instances they would flank, or like a bodyguard quite surround, some superior figure of their own class, moving along with them like Aldebaran[3] among the lesser lights of his constellation. That signal object was the "Handsome Sailor" of the less prosaic time alike of the military and merchant navies. With no perceptible trace of the vainglorious about him, rather with the offhand unaffectedness of natural regality, he seemed to accept the spontaneous homage of his shipmates.

A somewhat remarkable instance recurs to me. In Liverpool, now half a century ago, I saw under the shadow of the great dingy street-wall of Prince's Dock (an obstruction long since removed) a common sailor so intensely black that he must needs have been a native African of the unadulterate blood of Ham[4]—a symmetric figure much above the average height. The two ends of a gay silk handkerchief thrown loose about the neck danced upon the displayed ebony of his chest, in his ears were big hoops of gold, and a Highland bonnet with a tartan band set off his shapely head. It was a hot noon in July; and his face, lustrous with perspiration, beamed with barbaric good humor. In jovial sallies right and left, his white teeth flashing into view, he rollicked along, the center of a company of his shipmates. These were made up of such an assortment of tribes and complexions as would have well fitted them to be marched up by Anacharsis Cloots[5] before the bar of the first French Assembly as Repre-

---

1. Melville may have begun *Billy Budd* while he was still at the New York Custom House, but serious work on it began early in 1886, just after his retirement, and continued until his death in September 1891. It remained unpublished until 1924, when Raymond Weaver transcribed the manuscript for the Constable edition of Melville's works. The manuscript presented many difficulties, and Weaver did not surmount all of them; notably, he printed a discarded passage from a late chapter as a preface, having misread a query of Elizabeth Melville's. The best edition of the story, based on a careful study and fresh transcription of the manuscript, is that of Harrison Hayford and Merton

M. Sealts, Jr., first published in 1962. The Hayford-Sealts text is reprinted here, and the editors' explanatory notes have often been drawn on in the footnotes to this reprinting.
2. In the semiautobiographical *White-Jacket* Melville makes his actual shipmate a major character.
3. Brightest star in the constellation Taurus, the Bull, where it forms the animal's eye.
4. I.e., black, from the belief that God's curse in Genesis 9.25 made Ham and his descendants black.
5. Melville knew of the Prussian-born Baron de Cloots (1755–1794) from Thomas Carlyle's *The French Revolution*, part 2, book 1, chap. 10.

sentatives of the Human Race. At each spontaneous tribute rendered by the wayfarers to this black pagod[6] of a fellow—the tribute of a pause and stare, and less frequently an exclamation—the motley retinue showed that they took that sort of pride in the evoker of it which the Assyrian priests doubtless showed for their grand sculptured Bull when the faithful prostrated themselves.

To return. If in some cases a bit of a nautical Murat[7] in setting forth his person ashore, the Handsome Sailor of the period in question evinced nothing of the dandified Billy-be-Dam, an amusing character all but extinct now, but occasionally to be encountered, and in a form yet more amusing than the original, at the tiller of the boats on the tempestuous Erie Canal or, more likely, vaporing in the groggeries along the towpath.[8] Invariably a proficient in his perilous calling, he was also more or less of a mighty boxer or wrestler. It was strength and beauty. Tales of his prowess were recited. Ashore he was the champion; afloat the spokesman; on every suitable occasion always foremost. Close-reefing topsails in a gale, there he was, astride the weather yardarm-end, foot in the Flemish horse as stirrup, both hands tugging at the earing as at a bridle, in very much the attitude of young Alexander curbing the fiery Buceph-alus. A superb figure, tossed up as by the horns of Taurus[9] against the thunder-ous sky, cheerily hallooing to the strenuous file along the spar.

The moral nature was seldom out of keeping with the physical make. Indeed, except as toned by the former, the comeliness and power, always attractive in masculine conjunction, hardly could have drawn the sort of hon-est homage the Handsome Sailor in some examples received from his less gifted associates.

Such a cynosure, at least in aspect, and something such too in nature, though with important variations made apparent as the story proceeds, was welkin-eyed[1] Billy Budd—or Baby Budd, as more familiarly, under circum-stances hereafter to be given, he at last came to be called—aged twenty-one, a foretopman of the British fleet toward the close of the last decade of the eigh-teenth century. It was not very long prior to the time of the narration that follows that he had entered the King's service, having been impressed on the Narrow Seas from a homeward-bound English merchantman into a seventy-four outward bound, H.M.S. *Bellipotent*;[2] which ship, as was not unusual in those hurried days, having been obliged to put to sea short of her proper com-plement of men. Plump upon Billy at first sight in the gangway the boarding officer, Lieutenant Ratcliffe, pounced, even before the merchantman's crew was formally mustered on the quarter-deck for his deliberate inspection. And him only he elected. For whether it was because the other men when ranged before him showed to ill advantage after Billy, or whether he had some scru-ples in view of the merchantman's being rather short-handed, however it might be, the officer contented himself with his first spontaneous choice. To the surprise of the ship's company, though much to the lieutenant's satisfac-tion, Billy made no demur. But, indeed, any demur would have been as idle as the protest of a goldfinch popped into a cage.

6. An idol.
7. I.e., a dandy, like Joachim Murat (1767?–1815), whom Napoleon made king of Naples.
8. A joke, there being little danger from tempests on the canal.
9. Alexander the Great of Greece (356–323 B.C.) tamed the fierce horse Bucephalus ("bull-head"), thereby fulfilling the prophecy of an oracle. The horns

of Taurus are in the constellation.
1. Blue, like the heavens.
2. I.e., powerful in war; through most of the composi-tion the name of the ship was the *Indomitable* but at last Melville decided on *Bellipotent*. "Impressed": i.e., taken into naval service by force. "Narrow Seas": the English Channel and St. George's Channel. "Seventy-four": the number of guns on the ship.

Noting this uncomplaining acquiescence, all but cheerful, one might say, the shipmaster[3] turned a surprised glance of silent reproach at the sailor. The shipmaster was one of those worthy mortals found in every vocation, even the humbler ones—the sort of person whom everybody agrees in calling "a respectable man." And—nor so strange to report as it may appear to be—though a ploughman of the troubled waters, lifelong contending with the intractable elements, there was nothing this honest soul at heart loved better than simple peace and quiet. For the rest, he was fifty or thereabouts, a little inclined to corpulence, a prepossessing face, unwhiskered, and of an agreeable color—a rather full face, humanely intelligent in expression. On a fair day with a fair wind and all going well, a certain musical chime in his voice seemed to be the veritable unobstructed outcome of the innermost man. He had much prudence, much conscientiousness, and there were occasions when these virtues were the cause of overmuch disquietude in him. On a passage, so long as his craft was in any proximity to land, no sleep for Captain Graveling. He took to heart those serious responsibilities not so heavily borne by some shipmasters.

Now while Billy Budd was down in the forecastle getting his kit together, the *Bellipotent's* lieutenant, burly and bluff, nowise disconcerted by Captain Graveling's omitting to proffer the customary hospitalities on an occasion so unwelcome to him, an omission simply caused by preoccupation of thought, unceremoniously invited himself into the cabin, and also to a flask from the spirit locker, a receptacle which his experienced eye instantly discovered. In fact he was one of those sea dogs in whom all the hardship and peril of naval life in the great prolonged wars of his time never impaired the natural instinct for sensuous enjoyment. His duty he always faithfully did; but duty is sometimes a dry obligation, and he was for irrigating its aridity, whensoever possible, with a fertilizing decoction of strong waters. For the cabin's proprietor there was nothing left but to play the part of the enforced host with whatever grace and alacrity were practicable. As necessary adjuncts to the flask, he silently placed tumbler and water jug before the irrepressible guest. But excusing himself from partaking just then, he dismally watched the unembarrassed officer deliberately diluting his grog a little, then tossing it off in three swallows, pushing the empty tumbler away, yet not so far as to be beyond easy reach, at the same time settling himself in his seat and smacking his lips with high satisfaction, looking straight at the host.

These proceedings over, the master broke the silence; and there lurked a rueful reproach in the tone of his voice: "Lieutenant, you are going to take my best man from me, the jewel of 'em."

"Yes, I know," rejoined the other, immediately drawing back the tumbler preliminary to a replenishing. "Yes, I know. Sorry."

"Beg pardon, but you don't understand, Lieutenant. See here, now. Before I shipped that young fellow, my forecastle was a rat-pit of quarrels. It was black times, I tell you, aboard the *Rights* here. I was worried to that degree my pipe had no comfort for me. But Billy came; and it was like a Catholic priest striking peace in an Irish shindy.[4] Not that he preached to them or said or did anything in particular; but a virtue went out of him, sugaring the sour ones. They took to him like hornets to treacle; all but the buffer of the gang, the big shaggy chap with the fire-red whiskers. He indeed, out of envy, perhaps, of the new-

3. Captain.                              4. Brawl.

comer, and thinking such a "sweet and pleasant fellow," as he mockingly designated him to the others, could hardly have the spirit of a gamecock, must needs bestir himself in trying to get up an ugly row with him. Billy forebore with him and reasoned with him in a pleasant way—he is something like myself, Lieutenant, to whom aught like a quarrel is hateful—but nothing served. So, in the second dogwatch one day, the Red Whiskers in presence of the others, under pretense of showing Billy just whence a sirloin steak was cut—for the fellow had once been a butcher—insultingly gave him a dig under the ribs. Quick as lightning Billy let fly his arm. I dare say he never meant to do quite as much as he did, but anyhow he gave the burly fool a terrible drubbing. It took about half a minute, I should think. And, lord bless you, the lubber was astonished at the celerity. And will you believe it, Lieutenant, the Red Whiskers now really loves Billy—loves him, or is the biggest hypocrite that ever I heard of. But they all love him. Some of 'em do his washing, darn his old trousers for him; the carpenter is at odd times making a pretty little chest of drawers for him. Anybody will do anything for Billy Budd; and it's the happy family here. But now, Lieutenant, if that young fellow goes—I know how it will be aboard the *Rights*. Not again very soon shall I, coming up from dinner, lean over the capstan smoking a quiet pipe—no, not very soon again, I think. Ay, Lieutenant, you are going to take away the jewel of 'em; you are going to take away my peacemaker!" And with that the good soul had really some ado in checking a rising sob.

"Well," said the lieutenant, who had listened with amused interest to all this and now was waxing merry with his tipple; "well, blessed are the peacemakers, especially the fighting peacemakers. And such are the seventy-four beauties some of which you see poking their noses out of the portholes of yonder warship lying to for me," pointing through the cabin window at the *Bellipotent*. "But courage! Don't look so downhearted, man. Why, I pledge you in advance the royal approbation. Rest assured that His Majesty will be delighted to know that in a time when his hardtack is not sought for by sailors with such avidity as should be, a time also when some shipmasters privily resent the borrowing from them a tar or two for the service; His Majesty, I say, will be delighted to learn that *one* shipmaster at least cheerfully surrenders to the King the flower of his flock, a sailor who with equal loyalty makes no dissent.—But where's my beauty? Ah," looking through the cabin's open door "here he comes; and, by Jove, lugging along his chest—Apollo with his portmanteau!—My man," stepping out to him, "you can't take that big box aboard a warship. The boxes there are mostly shot boxes. Put your duds in a bag, lad. Boot and saddle for the cavalryman, bag and hammock for the man-of-war's man."

The transfer from chest to bag was made. And, after seeing his man into the cutter and then following him down, the lieutenant pushed off from the *Rights-of-Man*. That was the merchant ship's name, though by her master and crew abbreviated in sailor fashion into the *Rights*. The hardheaded Dundee owner was a staunch admirer of Thomas Paine, whose book in rejoinder to Burke's arraignment of the French Revolution had then been published for some time and had gone everywhere.[5] In christening his vessel after the title

5. *The Rights of Man* (1791), by the English-born American Thomas Paine (1737–1809) was a rejoinder to *Reflections on the Revolution in France* (1790) by the English statesman Edmund Burke (1729–1797). Burke's book made a classic case for the priority of social institutions, Paine's book for the primacy of natural human rights.

of Paine's volume the man of Dundee was something like his contemporary shipowner, Stephen Girard of Philadelphia, whose sympathies, alike with his native land and its liberal philosophers, he evinced by naming his ships after Voltaire, Diderot,[6] and so forth.

But now, when the boat swept under the merchantman's stern, and officer and oarsmen were noting—some bitterly and others with a grin—the name emblazoned there; just then it was that the new recruit jumped up from the bow where the coxswain[7] had directed him to sit, and waving hat to his silent shipmates sorrowfully looking over at him from the taffrail, bade the lads a genial good-bye. Then, making a salutation as to the ship herself, "And good-bye to you too, old *Rights-of-Man.*"

"Down, sir!" roared the lieutenant, instantly assuming all the rigor of his rank, though with difficulty repressing a smile.

To be sure, Billy's action was a terrible breach of naval decorum. But in that decorum he had never been instructed; in consideration of which the lieutenant would hardly have been so energetic in reproof but for the concluding farewell to the ship. This he rather took as meant to convey a covert sally on the new recruit's part, a sly slur at impressment in general, and that of himself in especial. And yet, more likely, if satire it was in effect, it was hardly so by intention, for Billy, though happily endowed with the gaiety of high health, youth, and a free heart, was yet by no means of a satirical turn. The will to it and the sinister dexterity[8] were alike wanting. To deal in double meanings and insinuations of any sort was quite foreign to his nature.

As to his enforced enlistment, that he seemed to take pretty much as he was wont to take any vicissitude of weather. Like the animals, though no philosopher, he was, without knowing it, practically a fatalist. And it may be that he rather liked this adventurous turn in his affairs, which promised an opening into novel scenes and martial excitements.

Aboard the *Bellipotent* our merchant sailor was forthwith rated as an able seaman and assigned to the starboard watch of the foretop.[9] He was soon at home in the service, not at all disliked for his unpretentious good looks and a sort of genial happy-go-lucky air. No merrier man in his mess:[1] in marked contrast to certain other individuals included like himself among the impressed portion of the ship's company; for these when not actively employed were sometimes, and more particularly in the last dogwatch[2] when the drawing near of twilight induced revery, apt to fall into a saddish mood which in some partook of sullenness. But they were not so young as our foretopman, and no few of them must have known a hearth of some sort, others may have had wives and children left, too probably, in uncertain circumstances, and hardly any but must have had acknowledged kith and kin, while for Billy, as will shortly be seen, his entire family was practically invested in himself.

2

Though our new-made foretopman was well received in the top and on the gun decks, hardly here was he that cynosure he had previously been among

6. Denis Diderot (1713–1784). Voltaire (1694–1778).
7. Steersman of the boat.
8. Ironic play on the Latin roots of the words: "sinister" meaning having to do with the left hand and "dexter" meaning having to do with the right hand.
9. Platform at the head of the foremast.
1. Group of sailors assigned to eat together.
2. From 6 to 8 P.M.

those minor ship's companies of the merchant marine, with which companies only had he hitherto consorted.

He was young; and despite his all but fully developed frame, in aspect looked even younger than he really was, owing to a lingering adolescent expression in the as yet smooth face all but feminine in purity of natural complexion but where, thanks to his seagoing, the lily was quite suppressed and the rose had some ado visibly to flush through the tan.

To one essentially such a novice in the complexities of factitious life, the abrupt transition from his former and simpler sphere to the ampler and more knowing world of a great warship; this might well have abashed him had there been any conceit or vanity in his composition. Among her miscellaneous multitude, the *Bellipotent* mustered several individuals who however inferior in grade were of no common natural stamp, sailors more signally susceptive of that air which continuous martial discipline and repeated presence in battle can in some degree impart even to the average man. As the Handsome Sailor, Billy Budd's position aboard the seventy-four was something analogous to that of a rustic beauty transplanted from the provinces and brought into competition with the highborn dames of the court. But this change of circumstances he scarce noted. As little did he observe that something about him provoked an ambiguous smile in one or two harder faces among the bluejackets. Nor less unaware was he of the peculiar favorable effect his person and demeanor had upon the more intelligent gentlemen of the quarter-deck. Nor could this well have been otherwise. Cast in a mold peculiar to the finest physical examples of those Englishmen in whom the Saxon strain would seem not at all to partake of any Norman or other admixture, he showed in face that humane look of reposeful good nature which the Greek sculptor in some instances gave to his heroic strong man, Hercules. But this again was subtly modified by another and pervasive quality. The ear, small and shapely, the arch of the foot, the curve in mouth and nostril, even the indurated hand dyed to the orange-tawny of the toucan's bill, a hand telling alike of the halyards and tar bucket; but, above all, something in the mobile expression, and every chance attitude and movement, something suggestive of a mother eminently favored by Love and the Graces; all this strangely indicated a lineage in direct contradiction to his lot. The mysteriousness here became less mysterious through a matter of fact elicited when Billy at the capstan was being formally mustered into the service. Asked by the officer, a small, brisk little gentleman as it chanced, among other questions, his place of birth, he replied, "Please, sir, I don't know."

"Don't know where you were born? Who was your father?"

"God knows, sir."

Struck by the straightforward simplicity of these replies, the officer next asked, "Do you know anything about your beginning?"

"No, sir. But I have heard that I was found in a pretty silk-lined basket hanging one morning from the knocker of a good man's door in Bristol."[3]

"*Found*, say you? Well," throwing back his head and looking up and down the new recruit; "well, it turns out to have been a pretty good find. Hope they'll find some more like you, my man; the fleet sadly needs them."

Yes, Billy Budd was a foundling, a presumable by-blow, and, evidently, no ignoble one. Noble descent was as evident in him as in a blood horse.

---

3. Seaport in the Bristol Channel in southwest England.

For the rest, with little or no sharpness of faculty or any trace of the wisdom of the serpent, nor yet quite a dove, he possessed that kind and degree of intelligence going along with the unconventional rectitude of a sound human creature, one to whom not yet has been proffered the questionable apple of knowledge. He was illiterate; he could not read, but he could sing, and like the illiterate nightingale was sometimes the composer of his own song.

Of self-consciousness he seemed to have little or none, or about as much as we may reasonably impute to a dog of Saint Bernard's breed.

Habitually living with the elements and knowing little more of the land than as a beach, or, rather, that portion of the terraqueous globe providentially set apart for dance-houses, doxies,[4] and tapsters, in short what sailors call a "fiddler's green," his simple nature remained unsophisticated by those moral obliquities which are not in every case incompatible with that manufacturable thing known as respectability. But are sailors, frequenters of fiddlers' greens, without vices? No; but less often than with landsmen do their vices, so called, partake of crookedness of heart, seeming less to proceed from viciousness than exuberance of vitality after long constraint: frank manifestations in accordance with natural law. By his original constitution aided by the co-operating influences of his lot, Billy in many respects was little more than a sort of upright barbarian, much such perhaps as Adam presumably might have been ere the urbane Serpent wriggled himself into his company.

And here be it submitted that apparently going to corroborate the doctrine of man's Fall, a doctrine now popularly ignored, it is observable that where certain virtues pristine and unadulterate peculiarly characterize anybody in the external uniform of civilization, they will upon scrutiny seem not to be derived from custom or convention, but rather to be out of keeping with these, as if indeed exceptionally transmitted from a period prior to Cain's city[5] and citified man. The character marked by such qualities has to an unvitiated taste an untampered-with flavor like that of berries, while the man thoroughly civilized, even in a fair specimen of the breed, has to the same moral palate a questionable smack as of a compounded wine. To any stray inheritor of these primitive qualities found, like Caspar Hauser,[6] wandering dazed in any Christian capital of our time, the good-natured poet's famous invocation, near two thousand years ago, of the good rustic out of his latitude in the Rome of the Caesars, still appropriately holds:

> Honest and poor, faithful in word and thought,
> What hath thee, Fabian, to the city brought?[7]

Though our Handsome Sailor had as much of masculine beauty as one can expect anywhere to see; nevertheless, like the beautiful woman in one of Hawthorne's minor tales,[8] there was just one thing amiss in him. No visible blemish indeed, as with the lady; no, but an occasional liability to a vocal defect. Though in the hour of elemental uproar or peril he was everything that a sailor should be, yet under sudden provocation of strong heart-feeling his voice, otherwise singularly musical, as if expressive of the harmony within, was apt to develop an organic hesitancy, in fact more or less of a stutter or even worse. In this particular Billy was a striking instance that the arch inter-

4. Whores.
5. Genesis 4.17.
6. Mysterious child (1812?–1833) who was found in Nuremberg in 1828 and claimed to have been kept in a hole; five years later he was given a mortal wound,

perhaps by his former captor.
7. The Roman poet Martial (1st century A.D.), *Epigrams* 1.4.1–2.
8. *The Birthmark*. "Minor": shorter.

ferer, the envious marplot of Eden,[9] still has more or less to do with every human consignment to this planet of Earth. In every case, one way or another he is sure to slip in his little card, as much as to remind us—I too have a hand here.

The avowal of such an imperfection in the Handsome Sailor should be evidence not alone that he is not presented as a conventional hero, but also that the story in which he is the main figure is no romance.

### 3

At the time of Billy Budd's arbitrary enlistment into the *Bellipotent* that ship was on her way to join the Mediterranean fleet. No long time elapsed before the junction was effected. As one of that fleet the seventy-four participated in its movements, though at times on account of her superior sailing qualities, in the absence of frigates, dispatched on separate duty as a scout and at times on less temporary service. But with all this the story has little concernment, restricted as it is to the inner life of one particular ship and the career of an individual sailor.

It was the summer of 1797. In the April of that year had occurred the commotion at Spithead followed in May by a second and yet more serious outbreak in the fleet at the Nore.[1] The latter is known, and without exaggeration in the epithet, as "the Great Mutiny." It was indeed a demonstration more menacing to England than the contemporary manifestoes and conquering and proselyting armies of the French Directory.[2] To the British Empire the Nore Mutiny was what a strike in the fire brigade would be to London threatened by general arson. In a crisis when the kingdom might well have anticipated the famous signal that some years later published along the naval line of battle what it was that upon occasion England expected of Englishmen;[3] *that* was the time when at the mastheads of the three-deckers and seventy-fours moored in her own roadstead[4]—a fleet the right arm of a Power then all but the sole free conservative one of the Old World—the bluejackets, to be numbered by thousands, ran up with huzzas the British colors with the union and cross wiped out; by that cancellation transmuting the flag of founded law and freedom defined, into the enemy's red meteor of unbridled and unbounded revolt. Reasonable discontent growing out of practical grievances in the fleet had been ignited into irrational combustion as by live cinders blown across the Channel from France in flames.[5]

The event converted into irony for a time those spirited strains of Dibdin[6]— as a song-writer no mean auxiliary to the English government at that European conjuncture—strains celebrating, among other things, the patriotic devotion of the British tar: "And as for my life, 'tis the King's!"

Such an episode in the Island's grand naval story her naval historians naturally abridge, one of them (William James)[7] candidly acknowledging that fain

9. Satan.
1. At the mouth of the Thames. Spithead is off the south of England, between Portsmouth and the Isle of Wight.
2. Body of five which held executive power in France 1795–99.
3. Lord Nelson's signal to his fleet at the Battle of Trafalgar (1805): "England expects that every man will do his duty."
4. Protected anchorage.
5. Especially during the Reign of Terror (1793–94) and its aftermath.
6. Charles Dibdin (1745–1814), English playwright and songwriter.
7. British historian (d. 1827), author of *Naval History of Great Britain.*

would he pass it over did not "impartiality forbid fastidiousness." And yet his mention is less a narration than a reference, having to do hardly at all with details. Nor are these readily to be found in the libraries. Like some other events in every age befalling states everywhere, including America, the Great Mutiny was of such character that national pride along with views of policy would fain shade it off into the historical background. Such events cannot be ignored, but there is a considerate way of historically treating them. If a well-constituted individual refrains from blazoning aught amiss or calamitous in his family, a nation in the like circumstance may without reproach be equally discreet.

Though after parleyings between government and the ring-leaders, and concessions by the former as to some glaring abuses, the first uprising—that at Spithead—with difficulty was put down, or matters for the time pacified; yet at the Nore the unforeseen renewal of insurrection on a yet larger scale, and emphasized in the conferences that ensued by demands deemed by the authorities not only inadmissible but aggressively insolent, indicated—if the Red Flag[8] did not sufficiently do so—what was the spirit animating the men. Final suppression, however, there was; but only made possible perhaps by the unswerving loyalty of the marine corps and a voluntary resumption of loyalty among influential sections of the crews.

To some extent the Nore Mutiny may be regarded as analogous to the distempering irruption of contagious fever in a frame constitutionally sound, and which anon throws it off.

At all events, of these thousands of mutineers were some of the tars who not so very long afterwards—whether wholly prompted thereto by patriotism, or pugnacious instinct, or by both—helped to win a coronet for Nelson at the Nile, and the naval crown of crowns for him at Trafalgar.[9] To the mutineers, those battles and especially Trafalgar were a plenary absolution and a grand one. For all that goes to make up scenic naval display and heroic magnificence in arms, those battles, especially Trafalgar, stand unmatched in human annals.

4

In this matter of writing, resolve as one may to keep to the main road, some bypaths have an enticement not readily to be withstood. I am going to err into such a bypath. If the reader will keep me company I shall be glad. At the least, we can promise ourselves that pleasure which is wickedly said to be in sinning, for a literary sin the divergence will be.

Very likely it is no new remark that the inventions of our time have at last brought about a change in sea warfare in degree corresponding to the revolution in all warfare effected by the original introduction from China into Europe of gunpowder. The first European firearm, a clumsy contrivance, was, as is well known, scouted by no few of the knights as a base implement, good enough peradventure for weavers too craven to stand up crossing steel with steel in frank fight. But as ashore knightly valor, though shorn of its blazonry, did not cease with the knights, neither on the seas—though nowadays in encounters there a certain kind of displayed gallantry be fallen out of date as

8. Signal of revolution—then of terrorism.
9. Nelson defeated the French at the Bay of Aboukir

near the mouth of the Nile in 1798, then died during his victory at Trafalgar in 1805.

hardly applicable under changed circumstances—did the nobler qualities of such naval magnates as Don John of Austria, Doria, Van Tromp, Jean Bart, the long line of British admirals, and the American Decaturs[1] of 1812 become obsolete with their wooden walls.

Nevertheless, to anybody who can hold the Present at its worth without being inappreciative of the Past, it may be forgiven, if to such an one the solitary old hulk at Portsmouth, Nelson's Victory, seems to float there, not alone as the decaying monument of a fame incorruptible, but also as a poetic reproach, softened by its picturesqueness, to the Monitors[2] and yet mightier hulls of the European ironclads. And this not altogether because such craft are unsightly, unavoidably lacking the symmetry and grand lines of the old battleships, but equally for other reasons.

There are some, perhaps, who while not altogether inaccessible to that poetic reproach just alluded to, may yet on behalf of the new order be disposed to parry it; and this to the extent of iconoclasm, if need be. For example, prompted by the sight of the star inserted in the Victory's quarter-deck designating the spot where the Great Sailor fell, these martial utilitarians may suggest considerations implying that Nelson's ornate publication of his person in battle was not only unnecessary, but not military, nay, savored of foolhardiness and vanity. They may add, too, that at Trafalgar it was in effect nothing less than a challenge to death; and death came; and that but for his bravado the victorious admiral might possibly have survived the battle, and so, instead of having his sagacious dying injunctions overruled by his immediate successor in command, he himself when the contest was decided might have brought his shattered fleet to anchor, a proceeding which might have averted the deplorable loss of life by shipwreck in the elemental tempest that followed the martial one.

Well, should we set aside the more than disputable point whether for various reasons it was possible to anchor the fleet, then plausibly enough the Benthamites[3] of war may urge the above. But the might-have-been is but boggy ground to build on. And, certainly, in foresight as to the larger issue of an encounter, and anxious preparations for it—buoying the deadly way and mapping it out, as at Copenhagen[4]—few commanders have been so painstakingly circumspect as this same reckless declarer of his person in fight.

Personal prudence, even when dictated by quite other than selfish considerations, surely is no special virtue in a military man; while an excessive love of glory, impassioning a less burning impulse, the honest sense of duty, is the first. If the name Wellington[5] is not so much of a trumpet to the blood as the simpler name Nelson, the reason for this may perhaps be inferred from the above. Alfred in his funeral ode[6] on the victor of Waterloo ventures not to call him the greatest soldier of all time, though in the same ode he invokes Nelson as "the greatest sailor since our world began."

1. Stephen Decatur (1779–1820) fought against the British in the War of 1812. Don John of Austria (1547–1578), commander for the Holy League at the Battle of Lepanto (1571). Andrea Doria (1468–1560), leader of the Genoese fleet against the Turks. Maarten Tromp (1597–1653) led the Dutch fleet against the Spanish. Jean Bart (1650–1702) commanded French privateers against the Dutch and British.
2. The Union ironclad Monitor engaged the Confederate ironclad Merrimack in 1862 off Virginia.
3. Those who weigh decisions only in terms of utility, from Jeremy Bentham (1748–1832), English philosopher, expounder of Utilitarianism.
4. In 1801 the Danes thought they had thwarted Nelson by removing the buoys near Copenhagen, but he took soundings and replaced the markers so he could navigate.
5. Arthur Wellesley, first duke of Wellington (1769–1852), British general in the Napoleonic Wars.
6. Alfred, Lord Tennyson (1809–1892), Ode on the Death of the Duke of Wellington (1852).

At Trafalgar Nelson on the brink of opening the fight sat down and wrote his last brief will and testament. If under the presentiment of the most magnificent of all victories to be crowned by his own glorious death, a sort of priestly motive led him to dress his person in the jewelled vouchers of his own shining deeds; if thus to have adorned himself for the altar and the sacrifice were indeed vainglory, then affectation and fustian is each more heroic line in the great epics and dramas, since in such lines the poet but embodies in verse those exaltations of sentiment that a nature like Nelson, the opportunity being given, vitalizes into acts.

5

Yes, the outbreak at the Nore was put down. But not every grievance was redressed. If the contractors, for example, were no longer permitted to ply some practices peculiar to their tribe everywhere, such as providing shoddy cloth, rations not sound, or false in the measure; not the less impressment, for one thing, went on. By custom sanctioned for centuries, and judicially maintained by a Lord Chancellor as late as Mansfield,[7] that mode of manning the fleet, a mode now fallen into a sort of abeyance but never formally renounced, it was not practicable to give up in those years. Its abrogation would have crippled the indispensable fleet, one wholly under canvas, no steam power, its innumerable sails and thousands of cannon, everything in short, worked by muscle alone; a fleet the more insatiate in demand for men, because then multiplying its ships of all grades against contingencies present and to come of the convulsed Continent.

Discontent foreran the Two Mutinies,[8] and more or less it lurkingly survived them. Hence it was not unreasonable to apprehend some return of trouble sporadic or general. One instance of such apprehensions: In the same year with this story, Nelson, then Rear Admiral Sir Horatio, being with the fleet off the Spanish coast, was directed by the admiral in command to shift his pennant from the *Captain* to the *Theseus*;[9] and for this reason: that the latter ship having newly arrived on the station from home, where it had taken part in the Great Mutiny, danger was apprehended from the temper of the men; and it was thought that an officer like Nelson was the one, not indeed to terrorize the crew into base subjection, but to win them, by force of his mere presence and heroic personality, back to an allegiance if not as enthusiastic as his own yet as true.

So it was that for a time, on more than one quarter-deck, anxiety did exist. At sea, precautionary vigilance was strained against relapse. At short notice an engagement might come on. When it did, the lieutenants assigned to batteries felt it incumbent on them, in some instances, to stand with drawn swords behind the men working the guns.

6

But on board the seventy-four in which Billy now swung his hammock, very little in the manner of the men and nothing obvious in the demeanor of the

---

7. William Murray, earl of Mansfield (1705–1793), lord chief justice of Britain.
8. At Spithead and the Nore.

9. To move bodily from the *Captain* to the *Theseus*, which then showed the flag of his office.

officers would have suggested to an ordinary observer that the Great Mutiny was a recent event. In their general bearing and conduct the commissioned officers of a warship naturally take their tone from the commander, that is if he have that ascendancy of character that ought to be his.

Captain the Honorable Edward Fairfax Vere, to give his full title, was a bachelor of forty or thereabouts, a sailor of distinction even in a time prolific of renowned seamen. Though allied to the higher nobility, his advancement had not been altogether owing to influences connected with that circumstance. He had seen much service, been in various engagements, always acquitting himself as an officer mindful of the welfare of his men, but never tolerating an infraction of discipline; thoroughly versed in the science of his profession, and intrepid to the verge of temerity, though never injudiciously so. For his gallantry in the West Indian waters as flag lieutenant under Rodney in that admiral's crowning victory over De Grasse,[1] he was made a post captain.

Ashore, in the garb of a civilian, scarce anyone would have taken him for a sailor, more especially that he never garnished unprofessional talk with nautical terms, and grave in his bearing, evinced little appreciation of mere humor. It was not out of keeping with these traits that on a passage when nothing demanded his paramount action, he was the most undemonstrative of men. Any landsman observing this gentleman not conspicuous by his stature and wearing no pronounced insignia, emerging from his cabin to the open deck, and noting the silent deference of the officers retiring to leeward, might have taken him for the King's guest, a civilian aboard the King's ship, some highly honorable discreet envoy on his way to an important post. But in fact this unobtrusiveness of demeanor may have proceeded from a certain unaffected modesty of manhood sometimes accompanying a resolute nature, a modesty evinced at all times not calling for pronounced action, which shown in any rank of life suggests a virtue aristocratic in kind. As with some others engaged in various departments of the world's more heroic activities, Captain Vere though practical enough upon occasion would at times betray a certain dreaminess of mood. Standing alone on the weather side of the quarter-deck, one hand holding by the rigging, he would absently gaze off at the blank sea. At the presentation to him then of some minor matter interrupting the current of his thoughts, he would show more or less irascibility; but instantly he would control it.

In the navy he was popularly known by the appellation "Starry Vere." How such a designation happened to fall upon one who whatever his sterling qualities was without any brilliant ones, was in this wise: A favorite kinsman, Lord Denton, a freehearted fellow, had been the first to meet and congratulate him upon his return to England from his West Indian cruise; and but the day previous turning over a copy of Andrew Marvell's[2] poems had lighted, not for the first time, however, upon the lines entitled "Appleton House," the name of one of the seats of their common ancestor, a hero in the German wars of the seventeenth century, in which poem occur the lines:

This 'tis to have been from the first
In a domestic heaven nursed,

1. The British Admiral George Brydges, Baron Rodney (1719–1792), defeated the French Admiral François de Grasse (1723–1788) off Dominica in 1782. 2. English poet (1621–1678).

Under the discipline severe
Of Fairfax and the starry Vere.

And so, upon embracing his cousin fresh from Rodney's great victory wherein he had played so gallant a part, brimming over with just family pride in the sailor of their house, he exuberantly exclaimed, "Give ye joy, Ed; give ye joy, my starry Vere!" This got currency, and the novel prefix serving in familiar parlance readily to distinguish the *Bellipotent's* captain from another Vere his senior, a distant relative, an officer of like rank in the navy, it remained permanently attached to the surname.

7

In view of the part that the commander of the *Bellipotent* plays in scenes shortly to follow, it may be well to fill out that sketch of him outlined in the previous chapter.

Aside from his qualities as a sea officer Captain Vere was an exceptional character. Unlike no few of England's renowned sailors, long and arduous service with signal devotion to it had not resulted in absorbing and *salting* the entire man. He had a marked leaning toward everything intellectual. He loved books, never going to sea without a newly replenished library, compact but of the best. The isolated leisure, in some cases so wearisome, falling at intervals to commanders even during a war cruise, never was tedious to Captain Vere. With nothing of that literary taste which less heeds the thing conveyed than the vehicle, his bias was toward those books to which every serious mind of superior order occupying any active post of authority in the world naturally inclines: books treating of actual men and events no matter of what era—history, biography, and unconventional writers like Montaigne,[3] who, free from cant and convention, honestly and in the spirit of common sense philosophize upon realities. In this line of reading he found confirmation of his own more reserved thoughts—confirmation which he had vainly sought in social converse, so that as touching most fundamental topics, there had got to be established in him some positive convictions which he forefelt would abide in him essentially unmodified so long as his intelligent part remained unimpaired. In view of the troubled period in which his lot was cast, this was well for him. His settled convictions were as a dike against those invading waters of novel opinion social, political, and otherwise, which carried away as in a torrent no few minds in those days, minds by nature not inferior to his own. While other members of that aristocracy to which by birth he belonged were incensed at the innovators mainly because their theories were inimical to the privileged classes. Captain Vere disinterestedly opposed them not alone because they seemed to him insusceptible of embodiment in lasting institutions, but at war with the peace of the world and the true welfare of mankind.

With minds less stored than his and less earnest, some officers of his rank, with whom at times he would necessarily consort, found him lacking in the companionable quality, a dry and bookish gentleman, as they deemed. Upon any chance withdrawal from their company one would be apt to say to another something like this: "Vere is a noble fellow, Starry Vere. 'Spite the gazettes,[4]

---

3. Michel de Montaigne (1533–1592), French politician and essayist.

4. Newspapers, or possibly the official publications
listing ranks, honors, etc.

Sir Horatio" (meaning him who became Lord Nelson) "is at bottom scarce a
better seaman or fighter. But between you and me now, don't you think there
is a queer streak of the pedantic running through him? Yes, like the King's
yarn in a coil of navy rope?"

Some apparent ground there was for this sort of confidential criticism; since
not only did the captain's discourse never fall into the jocosely familiar, but in
illustrating of any point touching the stirring personages and events of the time
he would be as apt to cite some historic character or incident of antiquity as
he would be to cite from the moderns. He seemed unmindful of the circumstance that to his bluff company such remote allusions, however pertinent they
might really be, were altogether alien to men whose reading was mainly confined to the journals.[5] But considerateness in such matters is not easy to
natures constituted like Captain Vere's. Their honesty prescribes to them
directness, sometimes far-reaching like that of a migratory fowl that in its flight
never heeds when it crosses a frontier.

<h2 style="text-align:center">8</h2>

The lieutenants and other commissioned gentlemen forming Captain Vere's
staff it is not necessary here to particularize, nor needs it to make any mention
of any of the warrant officers. But among the petty officers[6] was one who,
having much to do with the story, may as well be forthwith introduced. His
portrait I essay, but shall never hit it. This was John Claggart, the master-at-
arms. But that sea title may to landsmen seem somewhat equivocal. Originally, doubtless, that petty officer's function was the instruction of the men in
the use of arms, sword or cutlass. But very long ago, owing to the advance in
gunnery making hand-to-hand encounters less frequent and giving to niter and
sulphur the pre-eminence over steel, that function ceased; the master-at-arms
of a great warship becoming a sort of chief of police charged among other
matters with the duty of preserving order on the populous lower gun decks.

Claggart was a man about five-and-thirty, somewhat spare and tall, yet of
no ill figure upon the whole. His hand was too small and shapely to have been
accustomed to hard toil. The face was a notable one, the features all except
the chin cleanly cut as those on a Greek medallion; yet the chin, beardless as
Tecumseh's,[7] had something of strange protuberant broadness in its make that
recalled the prints of the Reverend Dr. Titus Oates, the historic deponent with
the clerical drawl in the time of Charles II and the fraud of the alleged Popish
Plot.[8] It served Claggart in his office that his eye could cast a tutoring glance.
His brow was of the sort phrenologically[9] associated with more than average
intellect; silken jet curls partly clustering over it, making a foil to the pallor
below, a pallor tinged with a faint shade of amber akin to the hue of time-
tinted marbles of old. This complexion, singularly contrasting with the red and
deeply bronzed visages of the sailors, and in part the result of his official seclusion from the sunlight, though it was not exactly displeasing, nevertheless
seemed to hint of something defective or abnormal in the constitution and

5. Newspapers.
6. Lesser officers appointed to their functions by the
commander, roughly equivalent to noncommissioned
officers in the army.
7. Shawnee chief (1768?–1813) who sided with the
British in the War of 1812 and was defeated at Tippeca-
noe by William Henry Harrison.

8. Oates (1649–1705) updated the Gunpowder Plot of
1605 into an imaginary Popish Plot (1678) to massacre
Protestants and burn London.
9. According to the pseudoscience of phrenology, in
which contours of the skull were thought to indicate
character.

blood. But his general aspect and manner were so suggestive of an education and career incongruous with his naval function that when not actively engaged in it he looked like a man of high quality, social and moral, who for reasons of his own was keeping incog.[1] Nothing was known of his former life. It might be that he was an Englishman; and yet there lurked a bit of accent in his speech suggesting that possibly he was not such by birth, but through natural-ization in early childhood. Among certain grizzled sea gossips of the gun decks and forecastle went a rumor perdue that the master-at-arms was a *chevalier*[2] who had volunteered into the King's navy by way of compounding for some mysterious swindle whereof he had been arraigned at the King's Bench.[3] The fact that nobody could substantiate this report was, of course, nothing against its secret currency. Such a rumor once started on the gun decks in reference to almost anyone below the rank of a commissioned officer would, during the period assigned to this narrative, have seemed not altogether wanting in credibility to the tarry old wiseacres of a man-of-war crew. And indeed a man of Claggart's accomplishments, without prior nautical experience entering the navy at mature life, as he did, and necessarily allotted at the start to the lowest grade in it; a man too who never made allusion to his previous life ashore; these were circumstances which in the dearth of exact knowledge as to his true antecedents opened to the invidious a vague field for unfavorable surmise.

But the sailors' dogwatch gossip concerning him derived a vague plausibility from the fact that now for some period the British navy could so little afford to be squeamish in the matter of keeping up the muster rolls, that not only were press gangs[4] notoriously abroad both afloat and ashore, but there was little or no secret about another matter, namely, that the London police were at liberty to capture any able-bodied suspect, any questionable fellow at large, and sum-marily ship him to the dockyard or fleet. Furthermore, even among voluntary enlistments there were instances where the motive thereto partook neither of patriotic impulse nor yet of a random desire to experience a bit of sea life and martial adventure. Insolvent debtors of minor grade, together with the promiscuous lame ducks of morality, found in the navy a convenient and secure refuge, secure because, once enlisted aboard a King's ship, they were as much in sanctuary as the transgressor of the Middle Ages harboring himself under the shadow of the altar. Such sanctioned irregularities, which for obvi-ous reasons the government would hardly think to parade at the time and which consequently, and as affecting the least influential class of mankind, have all but dropped into oblivion, lend color to something for the truth whereof I do not vouch, and hence have some scruple in stating; something I remember having seen in print though the book I cannot recall; but the same thing was personally communicated to me now more than forty years ago by an old pensioner in a cocked hat with whom I had a most interesting talk on the terrace at Greenwich, a Baltimore Negro, a Trafalgar man.[5] It was to this effect: In the case of a warship short of hands whose speedy sailing was impera-tive, the deficient quota, in lack of any other way of making it good, would be eked out by drafts culled direct from the jails. For reasons previously suggested it would not perhaps be easy at the present day directly to prove or disprove the allegation. But allowed as a verity, how significant would it be of England's

1. Incognito, with concealed identity.
2. Swindler, sharper. "Rumor perdue": reckless rumor.
3. I.e., in a court of law.

4. Gangs charged with rounding up men for ships, shanghaiing them if necessary. "Muster rolls": register of officers and men in a ship's company.
5. A veteran of the Battle of Trafalgar (1805).

straits at the time confronted by those wars which like a flight of harpies rose shrieking from the din and dust of the fallen Bastille.[6] That era appears measurably clear to us who look back at it, and but read of it. But to the grandfathers of us graybeards, the more thoughtful of them, the genius of it presented an aspect like that of Camoëns' Spirit of the Cape,[7] an eclipsing menace mysterious and prodigious. Not America was exempt from apprehension. At the height of Napoleon's unexampled conquests, there were Americans who had fought at Bunker Hill[8] who looked forward to the possibility that the Atlantic might prove no barrier against the ultimate schemes of this French portentous upstart from the revolutionary chaos who seemed in act of fulfilling judgment prefigured in the Apocalypse.[9]

But the less credence was to be given to the gun-deck talk touching Claggart, seeing that no man holding his office in a man-of-war can ever hope to be popular with the crew. Besides, in derogatory comments upon anyone against whom they have a grudge, or for any reason or no reason mislike, sailors are much like landsmen: they are apt to exaggerate or romance it.

About as much was really known to the *Bellipotent's* tars of the master-at-arms' career before entering the service as an astronomer knows about a comet's travels prior to its first observable appearance in the sky. The verdict of the sea quidnuncs[1] has been cited only by way of showing what sort of moral impression the man made upon rude uncultivated natures whose conceptions of human wickedness were necessarily of the narrowest, limited to ideas of vulgar rascality—a thief among the swinging hammocks during a night watch, or the man-brokers and land-sharks of the seaports.

It was no gossip, however, but fact that though, as before hinted, Claggart upon his entrance into the navy was, as a novice, assigned to the least honorable section[2] of a man-of-war's crew, embracing the drudgery, he did not long remain there. The superior capacity he immediately evinced, his constitutional sobriety, an ingratiating deference to superiors, together with a peculiar ferreting genius manifested on a singular occasion; all this, capped by a certain austere patriotism, abruptly advanced him to the position of master-at-arms.

Of this maritime chief of police the ship's corporals, so called, were the immediate subordinates, and compliant ones; and this, as is to be noted in some business departments ashore, almost to a degree inconsistent with entire moral volition. His place put various converging wires of underground influence under the chief's control, capable when astutely worked through his understrappers of operating to the mysterious discomfort, if nothing worse, of any of the sea commonalty.

## 9

Life in the foretop well agreed with Billy Budd. There, when not actually engaged on the yards yet higher aloft, the topmen, who as such had been picked out for youth and activity, constituted an aerial club lounging at ease

---

6. A 14th-century fortress in Paris, used as a prison when citizens demolished it on July 14, 1789, at the start of the French Revolution. "Harpies": rapacious mythological creatures.
7. In the *Lusiads* (1572), epic poem by the Portuguese Luiz de Camoëns (1524–1580), the spirit menaces Vasco da Gama as he rounds the Cape of Good Hope on his way to India.

8. Boston, Massachusetts, on June 17, 1775, where the British dislodged the colonialists.
9. I.e., the Book of Revelation.
1. Busybodies.
2. The waisters, charged with "attending to the drainage and sewerage below hatches," as Melville says in chap. 3 of *White-Jacket*.

against the smaller stun'sails rolled up into cushions, spinning yarns like the lazy gods, and frequently amused with what was going on in the busy world of the decks below. No wonder then that a young fellow of Billy's disposition was well content in such society. Giving no cause of offense to anybody, he was always alert at a call. So in the merchant service it had been with him. But now such a punctiliousness in duty was shown that his topmates would sometimes good-naturedly laugh at him for it. This heightened alacrity had its cause, namely, the impression made upon him by the first formal gangway-punishment he had ever witnessed, which befell the day following his impressment. It had been incurred by a little fellow, young, a novice after-guardsman[3] absent from his assigned post when the ship was being put about; a dereliction resulting in a rather serious hitch to that maneuver, one demanding instantaneous promptitude in letting go and making fast. When Billy saw the culprit's naked back under the scourge, gridironed with red welts and worse, when he marked the dire expression in the liberated man's face as with his woolen shirt flung over him by the executioner he rushed forward from the spot to bury himself in the crowd, Billy was horrified. He resolved that never through remissness would he make himself liable to such a visitation or do or omit aught that might merit even verbal reproof. What then was his surprise and concern when ultimately he found himself getting into petty trouble occasionally about such matters as the stowage of his bag or something amiss in his hammock, matters under the police oversight of the ship's corporals of the lower decks, and which brought down on him a vague threat from one of them.

So heedful in all things as he was, how could this be? He could not understand it, and it more than vexed him. When he spoke to his young topmates about it they were either lightly incredulous or found something comical in his unconcealed anxiety. "Is it your bag, Billy?" said one. "Well, sew yourself up in it, bully boy, and then you'll be sure to know if anybody meddles with it."

Now there was a veteran aboard who because his years began to disqualify him for more active work had been recently assigned duty as mainmastman in his watch, looking to the gear belayed at the rail roundabout that great spar near the deck.[4] At off-times the foretopman had picked up some acquaintance with him, and now in his trouble it occurred to him that he might be the sort of person to go to for wise counsel. He was an old Dansker[5] long anglicized in the service, of few words, many wrinkles, and some honorable scars. His wizened face, time-tinted and weather-stained to the complexion of an antique parchment, was here and there peppered blue by the chance explosion of a gun cartridge in action.

He was an *Agamemnon* man, some two years prior to the time of this story having served under Nelson when still captain in that ship immortal in naval memory, which dismantled and in part broken up to her bare ribs is seen a grand skeleton in Haden's etching.[6] As one of a boarding party from the *Aga-*

---

3. "Then, there is the *After-guard*, stationed on the Quarter-deck; who, under the Quarter-Masters and Quarter-Gunners, attend to the main-sail and spanker, and help haul the main-brace, and other ropes in the stern of the vessel. The duties assigned to the After-Guard's-Men being comparatively light and easy, and but little seamanship being expected from them, they are composed chiefly of landsmen; the least robust, least hardy, and least sailor-like of the crew" (*White-Jacket*, chap. 3).
4. Charged with duty pertaining to the mainmast but only from the mainyard to the deck, not higher.
5. Dane.
6. *Breaking Up of the "Agamemnon,"* by Sir Francis Seymour Haden (1818–1910).

*memnon* he had received a cut slantwise along one temple and cheek leaving a long pale scar like a streak of dawn's light falling athwart the dark visage. It was on account of that scar and the affair in which it was known that he had received it, as well as from his blue-peppered complexion, that the Dansker went among the *Bellipotent*'s crew by the name of "Board-Her-in-the-Smoke."

Now the first time that his small weasel eyes happened to light on Billy Budd, a certain grim internal merriment set all his ancient wrinkles into antic play. Was it that his eccentric unsentimental old sapience, primitive in its kind, saw or thought it saw something which in contrast with the warship's environment looked oddly incongruous in the Handsome Sailor? But after slyly studying him at intervals, the old Merlin's[7] equivocal merriment was modified; for now when the twain would meet, it would start in his face a quizzing sort of look, but it would be but momentary and sometimes replaced by an expression of speculative query as to what might eventually befall a nature like that, dropped into a world not without some mantraps and against whose subtleties simple courage lacking experience and address, and without any touch of defensive ugliness, is of little avail; and where such innocence as man is capable of does yet in a moral emergency not always sharpen the faculties or enlighten the will.

However it was, the Dansker in his ascetic way rather took to Billy. Nor was this only because of certain philosophic interest in such a character. There was another cause. While the old man's eccentricities, sometimes bordering on the ursine,[8] repelled the juniors, Billy, undeterred thereby, revering him as a salt hero, would make advances, never passing the old *Agamemnon* man without a salutation marked by that respect which is seldom lost on the aged, however crabbed at times or whatever their station in life.

There was a vein of dry humor, or what not, in the mastman; and, whether in freak of patriarchal irony touching Billy's youth and athletic frame, or for some other and more recondite reason, from the first in addressing him he always substituted *Baby* for Billy, the Dansker in fact being the originator of the name by which the foretopman eventually became known aboard ship.

Well then, in his mysterious little difficulty going in quest of the wrinkled one, Billy found him off duty in a dogwatch ruminating by himself, seated on a shot box of the upper gun deck, now and then surveying with a somewhat cynical regard certain of the more swaggering promenaders there. Billy recounted his trouble, again wondering how it all happened. The salt seer attentively listened, accompanying the foretopman's recital with queer twitchings of his wrinkles and problematical little sparkles of his small ferret eyes. Making an end of his story, the foretopman asked, "And now, Dansker, do tell me what you think of it."

The old man, shoving up the front of his tarpaulin and deliberately rubbing the long slant scar at the point where it entered the thin hair, laconically said, "Baby Budd, *Jemmy Legs*" (meaning the master-at-arms) "is down on you."

"*Jemmy Legs!*" ejaculated Billy, his welkin eyes expanding. "What for? Why, he calls me 'the sweet and pleasant young fellow,' they tell me."

"Does he so?" grinned the grizzled one; then said, "Ay, Baby lad, a sweet voice has Jemmy Legs."

---

7. Wizard or prophet, from the character in Arthurian legends.　　8. Bearlike.

"No, not always. But to me he has. I seldom pass him but there comes a pleasant word."

"And that's because he's down upon you, Baby Budd."

Such reiteration, along with the manner of it, incomprehensible to a novice, disturbed Billy almost as much as the mystery for which he had sought explanation. Something less unpleasingly oracular he tried to extract; but the old sea Chiron, thinking perhaps that for the nonce he had sufficiently instructed his young Achilles,[9] pursed his lips, gathered all his wrinkles together, and would commit himself to nothing further.

Years, and those experiences which befall certain shrewder men subordinated lifelong to the will of superiors, all this had developed in the Dansker the pithy guarded cynicism that was his leading characteristic.

## 10

The next day an incident served to confirm Billy Budd in his incredulity as to the Dansker's strange summing up of the case submitted. The ship at noon, going large before the wind, was rolling on her course,[1] and he below at dinner and engaged in some sportful talk with the members of his mess, chanced in a sudden lurch to spill the entire contents of his soup pan upon the new-scrubbed deck. Claggart, the master-at-arms, official rattan[2] in hand, happened to be passing along the battery in a bay of which the mess was lodged, and the greasy liquid streamed just across his path. Stepping over it, he was proceeding on his way without comment, since the matter was nothing to take notice of under the circumstances, when he happened to observe who it was that had done the spilling. His countenance changed. Pausing, he was about to ejaculate something hasty at the sailor, but checked himself, and pointing down to the streaming soup, playfully tapped him from behind with his rattan, saying in a low musical voice peculiar to him at times, "Handsomely done, my lad! And handsome is as handsome did it, too!" And with that passed on. Not noted by Billy as not coming within his view was the involuntary smile, or rather grimace, that accompanied Claggart's equivocal words. Aridly it drew down the thin corners of his shapely mouth. But everybody taking his remark as meant for humorous, and at which therefore as coming from a superior they were bound to laugh "with counterfeited glee,"[3] acted accordingly; and Billy, tickled, it may be, by the allusion to his being the Handsome Sailor, merrily joined in; then addressing his messmates exclaimed, "There now, who says that Jemmy Legs is down on me!"

"And who said he was, Beauty?" demanded one Donald with some surprise. Whereat the foretopman looked a little foolish, recalling that it was only one person, Board-Her-in-the-Smoke, who had suggested what to him was the smoky idea that this master-at-arms was in any peculiar way hostile to him. Meantime that functionary, resuming his path, must have momentarily worn some expression less guarded than that of the bitter smile, usurping the face from the heart—some distorting expression perhaps, for a drummer-boy heedlessly frolicking along from the opposite direction and chancing to come into

9. In Greek mythology, the centaur Chiron tutored Achilles.
1. With the wind behind her, was making good time.
2. Cane.

3. In Oliver Goldsmith's *The Deserted Village* the students laugh at the jokes of the tyrannical schoolmaster, but only "with counterfeited glee."

light collision with his person was strangely disconcerted by his aspect. Nor was the impression lessened when the official, impetuously giving him a sharp cut with the rattan, vehemently exclaimed, "Look where you go!"

## 11

What was the matter with the master-at-arms? And, be the matter what it might, how could it have direct relation to Billy Budd, with whom prior to the affair of the spilled soup he had never come into any special contact official or otherwise? What indeed could the trouble have to do with one so little inclined to give offense as the merchant-ship's "peacemaker," even him who in Claggart's own phrase was "the sweet and pleasant young fellow"? Yes, why should Jemmy Legs, to borrow the Dansker's expression, be "down" on the Handsome Sailor? But, at heart and not for nothing, as the late chance encounter may indicate to the discerning, down on him, secretly down on him, he assuredly was.

Now to invent something touching the more private career of Claggart, something involving Billy Budd, of which something the latter should be wholly ignorant, some romantic incident implying that Claggart's knowledge of the young bluejacket began at some period anterior to catching sight of him on board the seventy-four—all this, not so difficult to do, might avail in a way more or less interesting to account for whatever of enigma may appear to lurk in the case. But in fact there was nothing of the sort. And yet the cause necessarily to be assumed as the sole one assignable is in its very realism as much charged with that prime element of Radcliffian[4] romance, the mysterious, as any that the ingenuity of the author of *The Mysteries of Udolpho* could devise. For what can more partake of the mysterious than an antipathy spontaneous and profound such as is evoked in certain exceptional mortals by the mere aspect of some other mortal, however harmless he may be, if not called forth by this very harmlessness itself?

Now there can exist no irritating juxtaposition of dissimilar personalities comparable to that which is possible aboard a great warship fully manned and at sea. There, every day among all ranks, almost every man comes into more or less of contact with almost every other man. Wholly there to avoid even the sight of an aggravating object one must needs give it Jonah's toss[5] or jump overboard himself. Imagine how all this might eventually operate on some peculiar human creature the direct reverse of a saint!

But for the adequate comprehending of Claggart by a normal nature these hints are insufficient. To pass from a normal nature to him one must cross "the deadly space between." And this is best done by indirection.

Long ago an honest scholar, my senior,[6] said to me in reference to one who like himself is now no more, a man so unimpeachably respectable that against him nothing was ever openly said though among the few something was whispered, "Yes, X——is a nut not to be cracked by the tap of a lady's fan. You are aware that I am the adherent of no organized religion, much less of any philosophy built into a system. Well, for all that, I think that to try and get into X——, enter his labyrinth and get out again, without a clue derived from

---

4. Ann Radcliffe (1764–1823), British author of          5. Jonah 1.15.
Gothic fiction.                                           6. Melville himself.

some source other than what is known as 'knowledge of the world'—that were hardly possible, at least for me."

"Why," said I, "X——, however singular a study to some, is yet human, and knowledge of the world assuredly implies the knowledge of human nature, and in most of its varieties."

"Yes, but a superficial knowledge of it, serving ordinary purposes. But for anything deeper, I am not certain whether to know the world and to know human nature be not two distinct branches of knowledge, which while they may coexist in the same heart, yet either may exist with little or nothing of the other. Nay, in an average man of the world, his constant rubbing with it blunts that finer spiritual insight indispensable to the understanding of the essential in certain exceptional characters, whether evil ones or good. In a matter of some importance I have seen a girl wind an old lawyer about her little finger. Nor was it the dotage of senile love. Nothing of the sort. But he knew law better than he knew the girl's heart. Coke and Blackstone[7] hardly shed so much light into obscure spiritual places as the Hebrew prophets. And who were they? Mostly recluses."

At the time, my inexperience was such that I did not quite see the drift of all this. It may be that I see it now. And, indeed, if that lexicon which is based on Holy Writ were any longer popular, one might with less difficulty define and denominate certain phenomenal men. As it is, one must turn to some authority not liable to the charge of being tinctured with the biblical element.

In a list of definitions included in the authentic translation of Plato, a list attributed to him, occurs this: "Natural Depravity: a depravity according to nature,"[8] a definition which, though savoring of Calvinism, by no means involves Calvin's[9] dogma as to total mankind. Evidently its intent makes it applicable but to individuals. Not many are the examples of this depravity which the gallows and jail supply. At any rate, for notable instances, since these have no vulgar alloy of the brute in them, but invariably are dominated by intellectuality, one must go elsewhere. Civilization, especially if of the austerer sort, is auspicious to it. It folds itself in the mantle of respectability. It has its certain negative virtues serving as silent auxiliaries. It never allows wine to get within its guard. It is not going too far to say that it is without vices or small sins. There is a phenomenal pride in it that excludes them. It is never mercenary or avaricious. In short, the depravity here meant partakes nothing of the sordid or sensual. It is serious, but free from acerbity. Though no flatterer of mankind it never speaks ill of it.

But the thing which in eminent instances signalizes so exceptional a nature is this: Though the man's even temper and discreet bearing would seem to intimate a mind peculiarly subject to the law of reason, not the less in heart he would seem to riot in complete exemption from that law, having apparently little to do with reason further than to employ it as an ambidexter implement for effecting the irrational. That is to say: Toward the accomplishment of an aim which in wantonness of atrocity would seem to partake of the insane, he will direct a cool judgment sagacious and sound. These men are madmen, and of the most dangerous sort, for their lunacy is not continuous, but occa-

7. Sir Edward Coke (1552–1634) and Sir William Blackstone (1723–1780), British jurists.
8. Melville found this definition in the Bohn edition of Plato, vol. 6 (1854).

9. French theologian (1509–1564); he regarded all human beings as depraved, a consequence of the Fall of Man.

sional, evoked by some special object; it is protectively secretive, which is as much as to say it is self-contained, so that when, moreover most active it is to the average mind not distinguishable from sanity, and for the reason above suggested: that whatever its aims may be—and the aim is never declared—the method and the outward proceeding are always perfectly rational.

Now something such an one was Claggart, in whom was the mania of an evil nature, not engendered by vicious training or corrupting books or licentious living, but born with him and innate, in short "a depravity according to nature."

Dark sayings are these, some will say. But why? Is it because they somewhat savor of Holy Writ in its phrase "mystery of iniquity"? If they do, such savor was far enough from being intended, for little will it commend these pages to many a reader of today.

The point of the present story turning on the hidden nature of the master-at-arms has necessitated this chapter. With an added hint or two in connection with the incident at the mess, the resumed narrative must be left to vindicate, as it may, its own credibility.

## 12

That Claggart's figure was not amiss, and his face, save the chin, well molded, has already been said. Of these favorable points he seemed not insensible, for he was not only neat but careful in his dress. But the form of Billy Budd was heroic; and if his face was without the intellectual look of the pallid Claggart's, not the less was it lit, like his, from within, though from a different source. The bonfire in his heart made luminous the rose-tan in his cheek.

In view of the marked contrast between the persons of the twain, it is more than probable that when the master-at-arms in the scene last given applied to the sailor the proverb "Handsome is as handsome does," he there let escape an ironic inkling, not caught by the young sailors who heard it, as to what it was that had first moved him against Billy, namely, his significant personal beauty.

Now envy and antipathy, passions irreconcilable in reason, nevertheless in fact may spring conjoined like Chang and Eng[1] in one birth. Is Envy then such a monster? Well, though many an arraigned mortal has in hopes of mitigated penalty pleaded guilty to horrible actions, did ever anybody seriously confess to envy? Something there is in it universally felt to be more shameful than even felonious crime. And not only does everybody disown it, but the better sort are inclined to incredulity when it is in earnest imputed to an intelligent man. But since its lodgment is in the heart not the brain, no degree of intellect supplies a guarantee against it. But Claggart's was no vulgar form of the passion. Nor, as directed toward Billy Budd, did it partake of that streak of apprehensive jealousy that marred Saul's visage perturbedly brooding on the comely young David.[2] Claggart's envy struck deeper. If askance he eyed the good looks, cheery health, and frank enjoyment of young life in Billy Budd, it was because these went along with a nature that, as Claggart magnetically felt, had in its simplicity never willed malice or experienced the reactionary bite of that serpent. To him, the spirit lodged within Billy, and looking out from his

---

1. Famous Siamese twins (1811–1874), exhibited in     2. 1 Samuel 16.18, 18.9.
the United States by P. T. Barnum.

welkin eyes as from windows, that ineffability it was which made the dimple in his dyed cheek, suppled his joints, and dancing in his yellow curls made him pre-eminently the Handsome Sailor. One person excepted, the master-at-arms was perhaps the only man in the ship intellectually capable of adequately appreciating the moral phenomenon presented in Billy Budd. And the insight but intensified his passion, which assuming various secret forms within him, at times assumed that of cynic disdain, disdain of innocence—to be nothing more than innocent! Yet in an aesthetic way he saw the charm of it, the courageous free-and-easy temper of it, and fain would have shared it, but he despaired of it.

With no power to annul the elemental evil in him, though readily enough he could hide it; apprehending the good, but powerless to be it; a nature like Claggart's, surcharged with energy as such natures almost invariably are, what recourse is left to it but to recoil upon itself and, like the scorpion for which the Creator alone is responsible, act out to the end the part allotted it.

## 13

Passion, and passion in its profoundest, is not a thing demanding a palatial stage whereon to play its part. Down among the groundlings,[3] among the beggars and rakers of the garbage, profound passion is enacted. And the circumstances that provoke it, however trivial or mean, are no measure of its power. In the present instance the stage is a scrubbed gun deck, and one of the external provocations a man-of-war's man's spilled soup.

Now when the master-at-arms noticed whence came that greasy fluid streaming before his feet, he must have taken it—to some extent wilfully, perhaps—not for the mere accident it assuredly was, but for the sly escape of a spontaneous feeling on Billy's part more or less answering to the antipathy on his own. In effect a foolish demonstration, he must have thought, and very harmless, like the futile kick of a heifer, which yet were the heifer a shod stallion would not be so harmless. Even so was it that into the gall of Claggart's envy he infused the vitriol of his contempt. But the incident confirmed to him certain telltale reports purveyed to his ear by "Squeak," one of his more cunning corporals, a grizzled little man, so nicknamed by the sailors on account of his squeaky voice and sharp visage ferreting about the dark corners of the lower decks after interlopers, satirically suggesting to them the idea of a rat in a cellar.

From his chief's employing him as an implicit tool in laying little traps for the worriment of the foretopman—for it was from the master-at-arms that the petty persecutions heretofore adverted to had proceeded—the corporal, having naturally enough concluded that his master could have no love for the sailor, made it his business, faithful understrapper that he was, to foment the ill blood by perverting to his chief certain innocent frolics of the good-natured foretopman, besides inventing for his mouth sundry contumelious epithets he claimed to have overheard him let fall. The master-at-arms never suspected the veracity of these reports, more especially as to the epithets, for he well knew how secretly unpopular may become a master-at-arms, at least a master-at-arms of those days, zealous in his function, and how the bluejackets shoot

3. Spectators in the pit, the cheapest area of a theater.

at him in private their raillery and wit; the nickname by which he goes among them (Jemmy Legs) implying under the form of merriment their cherished disrespect and dislike. But in view of the greediness of hate for pabulum it hardly needed a purveyor to feed Claggart's passion.

An uncommon prudence is habitual with the subtler depravity, for it has everything to hide. And in case of an injury but suspected, its secretiveness voluntarily cuts it off from enlightenment or disillusion; and, not unreluctantly, action is taken upon surmise as upon certainty. And the retaliation is apt to be in monstrous disproportion to the supposed offense; for when in anybody was revenge in its exactions aught else but an inordinate usurer? But how with Claggart's conscience? For though consciences are unlike as foreheads, every intelligence, not excluding the scriptural devils who "believe and tremble,"[4] has one. But Claggart's conscience being but the lawyer to his will, made ogres of trifles, probably arguing that the motive imputed to Billy in spilling the soup just when he did, together with the epithets alleged, these, if nothing more, made a strong case against him; nay, justified animosity into a sort of retributive righteousness. The Pharisee is the Guy Fawkes[5] prowling in the hid chambers underlying some natures like Claggart's. And they can really form no conception of an unreciprocated malice. Probably the master-at-arms' clandestine persecution of Billy was started to try the temper of the man; but it had not developed any quality in him that enmity could make official use of or even pervert into plausible self-justification; so that the occurrence at the mess, petty if it were, was a welcome one to that peculiar conscience assigned to be the private mentor of Claggart; and, for the rest, not improbably it put him upon new experiments.

## 14

Not many days after the last incident narrated, something befell Billy Budd that more graveled him than aught that had previously occurred.

It was a warm night for the latitude; and the foretopman, whose watch at the time was properly below, was dozing on the uppermost deck whither he had ascended from his hot hammock, one of hundreds suspended so closely wedged together over a lower gun deck that there was little or no swing to them. He lay as in the shadow of a hillside, stretched under the lee[6] of the booms, a piled ridge of spare spars amidships between foremast and mainmast among which the ship's largest boat, the launch, was stowed. Alongside of three other slumberers from below, he lay near that end of the booms which approaches the foremast; his station aloft on duty as a foretopman being just over the deck-station of the forecastlemen, entitling him according to usage to make himself more or less at home in that neighborhood.

Presently he was stirred into semiconsciousness by somebody, who must have previously sounded the sleep of the others, touching his shoulder, and then, as the foretopman raised his head, breathing into his ear in a quick whisper, "Slip into the lee forechains,[7] Billy; there is something in the wind. Don't speak. Quick, I will meet you there," and disappearing.

4. James 2.19.
5. The Pharisee (the self-righteous hypocrite) is the Guy Fawkes (the treacherous terrorist), from the conspirers against Jesus (as in Matthew 22.15) and the Catholic who conspired to blow up the Houses of Parliament in 1605.
6. Shelter (away from the wind).
7. A hidden platform (as explained two paragraphs below).

Now Billy, like sundry other essentially good-natured ones, had some of the weaknesses inseparable from essential good nature; and among these was a reluctance, almost an incapacity of plumply saying *no* to an abrupt proposition not obviously absurd on the face of it, nor obviously unfriendly, nor iniquitous. And being of warm blood, he had not the phlegm tacitly to negative any proposition by unresponsive inaction. Like his sense of fear, his apprehension as to aught outside of the honest and natural was seldom very quick. Besides, upon the present occasion, the drowse from his sleep still hung upon him.

However it was, he mechanically rose and, sleepily wondering what could be in the wind, betook himself to the designated place, a narrow platform, one of six, outside of the high bulwarks and screened by the great deadeyes and multiple columned lanyards of the shrouds and backstays;[8] and, in a great warship of that time, of dimensions commensurate to the hull's magnitude; a tarry balcony in short, overhanging the sea, and so secluded that one mariner of the *Bellipotent*, a Nonconformist old tar of a serious turn, made it even in daytime his private oratory.[9]

In this retired nook the stranger soon joined Billy Budd. There was no moon as yet; a haze obscured the starlight. He could not distinctly see the stranger's face. Yet from something in the outline and carriage, Billy took him, and correctly, for one of the afterguard.

"Hist! Billy," said the man, in the same quick cautionary whisper as before. "You were impressed, weren't you? Well, so was I"; and he paused, as to mark the effect. But Billy, not knowing exactly what to make of this, said nothing. Then the other: "We are not the only impressed ones, Billy. There's a gang of us.—Couldn't you—help—at a pinch?"

"What do you mean?" demanded Billy, here thoroughly shaking off his drowse.

"Hist, hist!" the hurried whisper now growing husky. "See here," and the man held up two small objects faintly twinkling in the night-light; "see, they are yours, Billy, if you'll only——"

But Billy broke in, and in his resentful eagerness to deliver himself his vocal infirmity somewhat intruded. "D—d—damme, I don't know what you are d— d—driving at, or what you mean, but you had better g—g—go where you belong!" For the moment the fellow, as confounded, did not stir; and Billy, springing to his feet, said, "If you d—don't start, I'll t—t—toss you back over the r—rail!" There was no mistaking this, and the mysterious emissary decamped, disappearing in the direction of the mainmast in the shadow of the booms.

"Hallo, what's the matter?" here came growling from a forecastleman awakened from his deck-doze by Billy's raised voice. And as the foretopman reappeared and was recognized by him: "Ah, Beauty, is it you? Well, something must have been the matter, for you st—st—stuttered."

"Oh," rejoined Billy, now mastering the impediment, "I found an afterguardsman in our part of the ship here, and I bid him be off where he belongs."

"And is that all you did about it, Foretopman?" gruffly demanded another,

---

8. Help support the masts by extending from the mastheads to the sides of the ship, slanting a little aft. "Deadeyes": wooden blocks with holes through which ropes are run. "Lanyards": short ropes passing through deadeyes and used to extend shrouds or stays.

"Shrouds": ropes giving lateral support to the masts.
9. Prayer room. "Noncomformist": Protestant dissenter, refusing the religious policies and practices of the Church of England.

an irascible old fellow of brick-colored visage and hair who was known to his associate forecastlemen as "Red Pepper." "Such sneaks I should like to marry to the gunner's daughter!"—by that expression meaning that he would like to subject them to disciplinary castigation over a gun.

However, Billy's rendering of the matter satisfactorily accounted to these inquirers for the brief commotion, since of all the sections of a ship's company the forecastlemen, veterans for the most part and bigoted in their sea prejudices, are the most jealous in resenting territorial encroachments, especially on the part of any of the afterguard, of whom they have but a sorry opinion— chiefly landsmen, never going aloft except to reef or furl the mainsail, and in no wise competent to handle a marlinspike or turn in a deadeye, say.

## 15

This incident sorely puzzled Billy Budd. It was an entirely new experience, the first time in his life that he had ever been personally approached in underhand intriguing fashion. Prior to this encounter he had known nothing of the afterguardsman, the two men being stationed wide apart, one forward and aloft during his watch, the other on deck and aft.

What could it mean? And could they really be guineas,[1] those two glittering objects the interloper had held up to his (Billy's) eyes? Where could the fellow get guineas? Why, even spare buttons are not so plentiful at sea. The more he turned the matter over, the more he was nonplussed, and made uneasy and discomfited. In his disgustful recoil from an overture which, though he but ill comprehended, he instinctively knew must involve evil of some sort, Billy Budd was like a young horse fresh from the pasture suddenly inhaling a vile whiff from some chemical factory, and by repeated snortings trying to get it out of his nostrils and lungs. This frame of mind barred all desire of holding further parley with the fellow, even were it but for the purpose of gaining some enlightenment as to his design in approaching him. And yet he was not without natural curiosity to see how such a visitor in the dark would look in broad day.

He espied him the following afternoon in his first dogwatch below, one of the smokers on that forward part of the upper gun deck[2] allotted to the pipe. He recognized him by his general cut and build more than by his round freckled face and glassy eyes of pale blue, veiled with lashes all but white. And yet Billy was a bit uncertain whether indeed it were he—yonder chap about his own age chatting and laughing in freehearted way, leaning against a gun; a genial young fellow enough to look at, and something of a rattlebrain, to all appearance. Rather chubby too for a sailor, even an afterguardsman. In short, the last man in the world, one would think, to be overburdened with thoughts, especially those perilous thoughts that must needs belong to a conspirator in any serious project, or even to the underling of such a conspirator.

Although Billy was not aware of it, the fellow, with a side-long watchful glance, had perceived Billy first, and then noting that Billy was looking at him, thereupon nodded a familiar sort of friendly recognition as to an old acquaintance, without interrupting the talk he was engaged in with the group of smokers. A day or two afterwards, chancing in the evening promenade on a

---

1. Gold coins worth a little more than one pound.   2. The only place smoking was permitted to the crew.

gun deck to pass Billy, he offered a flying word of good-fellowship, as it were, which by its unexpectedness, and equivocalness under the circumstances, so embarrassed Billy that he knew not how to respond to it, and let it go unnoticed.

Billy was now left more at a loss than before. The ineffectual speculations into which he was led were so disturbingly alien to him that he did his best to smother them. It never entered his mind that here was a matter which, from its extreme questionableness, it was his duty as a loyal bluejacket to report in the proper quarter. And, probably, had such a step been suggested to him, he would have been deterred from taking it by the thought, one of novice magnanimity, that it would savor overmuch of the dirty work of a telltale. He kept the thing to himself. Yet upon one occasion he could not forbear a little disburdening himself to the old Dansker, tempted thereto perhaps by the influence of a balmy night when the ship lay becalmed; the twain, silent for the most part, sitting together on deck, their heads propped against the bulwarks. But it was only a partial and anonymous account that Billy gave, the unfounded scruples above referred to preventing full disclosure to anybody. Upon hearing Billy's version, the sage Dansker seemed to divine more than he was told; and after a little meditation, during which his wrinkles were pursed as into a point, quite effacing for the time that quizzing expression his face sometimes wore: "Didn't I say so, Baby Budd?"

"Say what?" demanded Billy.

"Why, *Jemmy Legs* is *down* on you."

"And what," rejoined Billy in amazement, "has *Jemmy Legs* to do with that cracked afterguardsman?"

"Ho, it was an afterguardsman, then. A cat's-paw, a cat's-paw!" And with that exclamation, whether it had reference to a light puff of air just then coming over the calm sea, or a subtler relation to the afterguardsman, there is no telling, the old Merlin gave a twisting wrench with his black teeth at his plug of tobacco, vouchsafing no reply to Billy's impetuous question, though now repeated, for it was his wont to relapse into grim silence when interrogated in skeptical sort as to any of his sententious oracles, not always very clear ones, rather partaking of that obscurity which invests most Delphic[3] deliverances from any quarter.

Long experience had very likely brought this old man to that bitter prudence which never interferes in aught and never gives advice.

16

Yes, despite the Dansker's pithy insistence as to the master-at-arms being at the bottom of these strange experiences of Billy on board the *Bellipotent*, the young sailor was ready to ascribe them to almost anybody but the man who, to use Billy's own expression, "always had a pleasant word for him." This is to be wondered at. Yet not so much to be wondered at. In certain matters, some sailors even in mature life remain unsophisticated enough. But a young seafarer of the disposition of our athletic foretopman is much of a child-man. And yet a child's utter innocence is but its blank ignorance, and the innocence more or less wanes as intelligence waxes. But in Billy Budd intelligence, such

3. Oracular.

as it was, had advanced while yet his simple-mindedness remained for the most part unaffected. Experience is a teacher indeed; yet did Billy's years make his experience small. Besides, he had none of that intuitive knowledge of the bad which in natures not good or incompletely so foreruns experience, and therefore may pertain, as in some instances it too clearly does pertain, even to youth.

And what could Billy know of man except of man as a mere sailor? And the old-fashioned sailor, the veritable man before the mast, the sailor from boyhood up, he, though indeed of the same species as a landsman, is in some respects singularly distinct from him. The sailor is frankness, the landsman is finesse. Life is not a game with the sailor, demanding the long head[4]—no intricate game of chess where few moves are made in straightforwardness and ends are attained by indirection, an oblique, tedious, barren game hardly worth that poor candle burnt out in playing it.

Yes, as a class, sailors are in character a juvenile race. Even their deviations are marked by juvenility, this more especially holding true with the sailors of Billy's time. Then too, certain things which apply to all sailors do more pointedly operate here and there upon the junior one. Every sailor, too, is accustomed to obey orders without debating them; his life afloat is externally ruled for him; he is not brought into that promiscuous commerce with mankind where unobstructed free agency on equal terms—equal superficially, at least—soon teaches one that unless upon occasion he exercise a distrust keen in proportion to the fairness of the appearance, some foul turn may be served him. A ruled undemonstrative distrustfulness is so habitual, not with businessmen so much as with men who know their kind in less shallow relations than business, namely, certain men of the world, that they come at last to employ it all but unconsciously; and some of them would very likely feel real surprise at being charged with it as one of their general characteristics.

### 17

But after the little matter at the mess Billy Budd no more found himself in strange trouble at times about his hammock or his clothes bag or what not. As to that smile that occasionally sunned him, and the pleasant passing word, these were, if not more frequent, yet if anything more pronounced than before.

But for all that, there were certain other demonstrations now. When Claggart's unobserved glance happened to light on belted Billy rolling along the upper gun deck in the leisure of the second dogwatch, exchanging passing broadsides of fun with other young promenaders in the crowd, that glance would follow the cheerful sea Hyperion[5] with a settled meditative and melancholy expression, his eyes strangely suffused with incipient feverish tears. Then would Claggart look like the man of sorrows. Yes, and sometimes the melancholy expression would have in it a touch of soft yearning, as if Claggart could even have loved Billy but for fate and ban. But this was an evanescence, and quickly repented of, as it were, by an immitigable look, pinching and shriveling the visage into the momentary semblance of a wrinkled walnut. But sometimes catching sight in advance of the foretopman coming in his direction, he

---

4. Foresight, sagacity.
5. A Titan, later identified with Apollo, god of manly beauty.

would, upon their nearing, step aside a little to let him pass, dwelling upon Billy for the moment with the glittering dental satire of a Guise.[6] But upon any abrupt unforeseen encounter a red light would flash forth from his eye like a spark from an anvil in a dusk smithy. That quick, fierce light was a strange one, darted from orbs which in repose were of a color nearest approaching a deeper violet, the softest of shades.

Though some of these caprices of the pit could not but be observed by their object, yet were they beyond the construing of such a nature. And the thews[7] of Billy were hardly compatible with that sort of sensitive spiritual organization which in some cases instinctively conveys to ignorant innocence an admonition of the proximity of the malign. He thought the master-at-arms acted in a manner rather queer at times. That was all. But the occasional frank air and pleasant word went for what they purported to be, the young sailor never having heard as yet of the "too fair-spoken man."

Had the foretopman been conscious of having done or said anything to provoke the ill will of the official, it would have been different with him, and his sight might have been purged if not sharpened. As it was, innocence was his blinder.

So was it with him in yet another matter. Two minor officers, the armorer and captain of the hold,[8] with whom he had never exchanged a word, his position in the ship not bringing him into contact with them, these men now for the first began to cast upon Billy, when they chanced to encounter him, that peculiar glance which evidences that the man from whom it comes has been some way tampered with, and to the prejudice of him upon whom the glance lights. Never did it occur to Billy as a thing to be noted or a thing suspicious, though he well knew the fact, that the armorer and captain of the hold, with the ship's yeoman, apothecary, and others of that grade, were by naval usage messmates of the master-at-arms, men with ears convenient to his confidential tongue.

But the general popularity that came from our Handsome Sailor's manly forwardness upon occasion and irresistible good nature, indicating no mental superiority tending to excite an invidious feeling, this good will on the part of most of his shipmates made him the less to concern himself about such mute aspects toward him as those whereto allusion has just been made, aspects he could not so fathom as to infer their whole import.

As to the afterguardsman, though Billy for reasons already given necessarily saw little of him, yet when the two did happen to meet, invariably came the fellow's offhand cheerful recognition, sometimes accompanied by a passing pleasant word or two. Whatever that equivocal young person's original design may really have been, or the design of which he might have been the deputy, certain it was from his manner upon these occasions that he had wholly dropped it.

It was as if his precocity of crookedness (and every vulgar villain is precocious) had for once deceived him, and the man he had sought to entrap as a simpleton had through his very simplicity ignominiously baffled him.

---

6. Henri de Guise (1550–1588) was one of those responsible for the treacherous massacre of French Huguenots that began on St. Bartholomew's Day (August 24) 1572. The idea is that of Shakespeare's *Hamlet* (1.5.108), that one may smile and smile and be a villain.
7. Muscles.
8. Petty officers in charge of caring for arms ("armorer") and of supervising the interior of a vessel below decks ("captain of the hold").

But shrewd ones may opine that it was hardly possible for Billy to refrain from going up to the afterguardsman and bluntly demanding to know his purpose in the initial interview so abruptly closed in the forechains. Shrewd ones may also think it but natural in Billy to set about sounding some of the other impressed men of the ship in order to discover what basis, if any, there was for the emissary's obscure suggestions as to plotting disaffection aboard. Yes, shrewd ones may so think. But something more, or rather something else than mere shrewdness is perhaps needful for the due understanding of such a character as Billy Budd's.

As to Claggart, the monomania in the man—if that indeed it were—as involuntarily disclosed by starts in the manifestations detailed, yet in general covered over by his self-contained and rational demeanor; this, like a subterranean fire, was eating its way deeper and deeper in him. Something decisive must come of it.

18

After the mysterious interview in the forechains, the one so abruptly ended there by Billy, nothing especially germane to the story occurred until the events now about to be narrated.

Elsewhere it has been said that in the lack of frigates (of course better sailers than line-of-battle ships) in the English squadron up the Straits at that period, the *Bellipotent* 74 was occasionally employed not only as an available substitute for a scout, but at times on detached service of more important kind. This was not alone because of her sailing qualities, not common in a ship of her rate, but quite as much, probably, that the character of her commander, it was thought, specially adapted him for any duty where under unforeseen difficulties a prompt initiative might have to be taken in some matter demanding knowledge and ability in addition to those qualities implied in good seamanship. It was on an expedition of the latter sort, a somewhat distant one, and when the *Bellipotent* was almost at her furthest remove from the fleet, that in the latter part of an afternoon watch she unexpectedly came in sight of a ship of the enemy. It proved to be a frigate. The latter, perceiving through the glass that the weight of men and metal would be heavily against her, invoking her light heels crowded sail to get away. After a chase urged almost against hope and lasting until about the middle of the first dogwatch, she signally succeeded in effecting her escape.

Not long after the pursuit had been given up, and ere the excitement incident thereto had altogether waned away, the master-at-arms, ascending from his cavernous sphere, made his appearance cap in hand by the mainmast respectfully waiting the notice of Captain Vere, then solitary walking the weather side of the quarter-deck, doubtless somewhat chafed at the failure of the pursuit. The spot where Claggart stood was the place allotted to men of lesser grades seeking some more particular interview either with the officer of the deck or the captain himself. But from the latter it was not often that a sailor or petty officer of those days would seek a hearing; only some exceptional cause would, according to established custom, have warranted that.

Presently, just as the commander, absorbed in his reflections, was on the point of turning aft in his promenade, he became sensible of Claggart's presence, and saw the doffed cap held in deferential expectancy. Here be it said that Captain Vere's personal knowledge of this petty officer had only begun at the time of the ship's last sailing from home, Claggart then for the first, in transfer from a ship detained for repairs, supplying on board the *Bellipotent* the place of a previous master-at-arms disabled and ashore.

No sooner did the commander observe who it was that now deferentially stood awaiting his notice than a peculiar expression came over him. It was not unlike that which uncontrollably will flit across the countenance of one at unawares encountering a person who, though known to him indeed, has hardly been long enough known for thorough knowledge, but something in whose aspect nevertheless now for the first provokes a vaguely repellent distaste. But coming to a stand and resuming much of his wonted official manner, save that a sort of impatience lurked in the intonation of the opening word, he said "Well? What is it, Master-at-arms?"

With the air of a subordinate grieved at the necessity of being a messenger of ill tidings, and while conscientiously determined to be frank yet equally resolved upon shunning overstatement, Claggart at this invitation, or rather summons to disburden, spoke up. What he said, conveyed in the language of no uneducated man, was to the effect following, if not altogether in these words, namely, that during the chase and preparations for the possible encounter he had seen enough to convince him that at least one sailor aboard was a dangerous character in a ship mustering some who not only had taken a guilty part in the late serious troubles, but others also who, like the man in question, had entered His Majesty's service under another form than enlistment.

At this point Captain Vere with some impatience interrupted him: "Be direct, man; say *impressed men.*"

Claggart made a gesture of subservience, and proceeded. Quite lately he (Claggart) had begun to suspect that on the gun decks some sort of movement prompted by the sailor in question was covertly going on, but he had not thought himself warranted in reporting the suspicion so long as it remained indistinct. But from what he had that afternoon observed in the man referred to, the suspicion of something clandestine going on had advanced to a point less removed from certainty. He deeply felt, he added, the serious responsibility assumed in making a report involving such possible consequences to the individual mainly concerned, besides tending to augment those natural anxieties which every naval commander must feel in view of extraordinary outbreaks so recent as those which, he sorrowfully said it, it needed not to name.

Now at the first broaching of the matter Captain Vere, taken by surprise, could not wholly dissemble his disquietude. But as Claggart went on, the former's aspect changed into restiveness under something in the testifier's manner in giving his testimony. However, he refrained from interrupting him. And Claggart, continuing, concluded with this: "God forbid, your honor, that the *Bellipotent's* should be the experience of the—"

"Never mind that!" here peremptorily broke in the superior, his face altering with anger, instinctively divining the ship that the other was about to name, one in which the Nore Mutiny had assumed a singularly tragical character that for a time jeopardized the life of its commander. Under the circumstances he was indignant at the purposed allusion. When the commissioned officers themselves were on all occasions very heedful how they referred to the recent events in the fleet, for a petty officer unnecessarily to allude to them in the presence of his captain, this struck him as a most immodest presumption.

Besides, to his quick sense of self-respect it even looked under the circum-stances something like an attempt to alarm him. Nor at first was he without some surprise that one who so far as he had hitherto come under his notice had shown considerable tact in his function should in this particular evince such lack of it.

But these thoughts and kindred dubious ones flitting across his mind were suddenly replaced by an intuitional surmise which, though as yet obscure in form, served practically to affect his reception of the ill tidings. Certain it is that, long versed in everything pertaining to the complicated gun-deck life, which like every other form of life has its secret mines and dubious side, the side popularly disclaimed, Captain Vere did not permit himself to be unduly disturbed by the general tenor of his subordinate's report.

Furthermore, if in view of recent events prompt action should be taken at the first palpable sign of recurring insubordination, for all that, not judicious would it be, he thought, to keep the idea of lingering disaffection alive by undue forwardness in crediting an informer, even if his own subordinate and charged among other things with police surveillance of the crew. This feeling would not perhaps have so prevailed with him were it not that upon a prior occasion the patriotic zeal officially evinced by Claggart had somewhat irri-tated him as appearing rather supersensible and strained. Furthermore, some-thing even in the official's self-possessed and somewhat ostentatious manner in making his specifications strangely reminded him of a bandsman,[9] a perjurous witness in a capital case before a court-martial ashore of which when a lieuten-ant he (Captain Vere) had been a member.

Now the peremptory check given to Claggart in the matter of the arrested allusion was quickly followed up by this: "You say that there is at least one dangerous man aboard. Name him."

"William Budd, a foretopman, your honor."

"William Budd!" repeated Captain Vere with unfeigned astonishment. "And mean you the man that Lieutenant Ratcliffe took from the merchantman not very long ago, the young fellow who seems to be so popular with the men—Billy, the Handsome Sailor, as they call him?"

"The same, your honor; but for all his youth and good looks, a deep one. Not for nothing does he insinuate himself into the good will of his shipmates, since at the least they will at a pinch say—all hands will—a good word for him, and at all hazards. Did Lieutenant Ratcliffe happen to tell your honor of that adroit fling of Budd's, jumping up in the cutter's bow under the mer-chantman's stern when he was being taken off? It is even masked by that sort of good-humored air that at heart he resents his impressment. You have but noted his fair cheek. A mantrap may be under the ruddy-tipped daisies."

Now the Handsome Sailor as a signal figure among the crew had naturally enough attracted the captain's attention from the first. Though in general not very demonstrative to his officers, he had congratulated Lieutenant Ratcliffe upon his good fortune in lighting on such a fine specimen of the *genus homo*,[1] who in the nude might have posed for a statue of young Adam before the Fall. As to Billy's adieu to the ship *Rights-of-Man*, which the boarding lieutenant had indeed reported to him, but, in a deferential way, more as a good story than aught else, Captain Vere, though mistakenly understanding it as a satiric

9. Hoist operator.                        1. Human race.

sally, had but thought so much the better of the impressed man for it; as a military sailor, admiring the spirit that could take an arbitrary enlistment so merrily and sensibly. The foretopman's conduct, too, so far as it had fallen under the captain's notice, had confirmed the first happy augury, while the new recruit's qualities as a "sailor-man" seemed to be such that he had thought of recommending him to the executive officer for promotion to a place that would more frequently bring him under his own observation, namely, the captaincy of the mizzentop,[2] replacing there in the starboard watch a man not so young whom partly for that reason he deemed less fitted for the post. Be it parenthesized here that since the mizzentopmen have not to handle such breadths of heavy canvas as the lower sails on the mainmast and foremast, a young man if of the right stuff not only seems best adapted to duty there, but in fact is generally selected for the captaincy of that top, and the company under him are light hands and often but striplings. In sum, Captain Vere had from the beginning deemed Billy Budd to be what in the naval parlance of the time was called a "King's bargain": that is to say, for His Britannic Majesty's navy a capital investment at small outlay or none at all.

After a brief pause, during which the reminiscences above mentioned passed vividly through his mind and he weighed the import of Claggart's last suggestion conveyed in the phrase "mantrap under the daisies," and the more he weighed it the less reliance he felt in the informer's good faith, suddenly he turned upon him and in a low voice demanded: "Do you come to me, Master-at-arms, with so foggy a tale? As to Budd, cite me an act or spoken word of his confirmatory of what you in general charge against him. Stay," drawing nearer to him; "heed what you speak. Just now, and in a case like this, there is a yardarm-end[3] for the false witness."

"Ah, your honor!" sighed Claggart, mildly shaking his shapely head as in sad deprecation of such unmerited severity of tone. Then, bridling—erecting himself as in virtuous self-assertion—he circumstantially alleged certain words and acts which collectively, if credited, led to presumptions mortally inculpating Budd. And for some of these averments, he added, substantiating proof was not far.

With gray eyes impatient and distrustful essaying to fathom to the bottom Claggart's calm violet ones, Captain Vere again heard him out; then for the moment stood ruminating. The mood he evinced, Claggart—himself for the time liberated from the other's scrutiny—steadily regarded with a look difficult to render: a look curious of the operation of his tactics, a look such as might have been that of the spokesman of the envious children of Jacob deceptively imposing upon the troubled patriarch the blood-dyed coat of young Joseph.[4]

Though something exceptional in the moral quality of Captain Vere made him, in earnest encounter with a fellow man, a veritable touchstone of that man's essential nature, yet now as to Claggart and what was really going on in him his feeling partook less of intuitional conviction than of strong suspicion clogged by strange dubieties. The perplexity he evinced proceeded less from aught touching the man informed against—as Claggart doubtless opined— than from considerations how best to act in regard to the informer. At first, indeed, he was naturally for summoning that substantiation of his allegations which Claggart said was at hand. But such a proceeding would result in the matter at once getting abroad, which in the present stage of it, he thought, might undesirably affect the ship's company. If Claggart was a false witness— that closed the affair. And therefore, before trying the accusation, he would first practically test the accuser; and he thought this could be done in a quiet, undemonstrative way.

The measure he determined upon involved a shifting of the scene, a transfer to a place less exposed to observation than the broad quarter-deck. For although the few gun-room officers there at the time had, in due observance of naval etiquette, withdrawn to leeward the moment Captain Vere had begun his promenade on the deck's weather side; and though during the colloquy with Claggart they of course ventured not to diminish the distance; and though throughout the interview Captain Vere's voice was far from high, and Claggart's silvery and low; and the wind in the cordage and the wash of the sea helped the more to put them beyond earshot; nevertheless, the interview's continuance already had attracted observation from some topmen aloft and other sailors in the waist or further forward.

Having determined upon his measures, Captain Vere forthwith took action. Abruptly turning to Claggart, he asked, "Master-at-arms, is it now Budd's watch aloft?"

"No, your honor."

Whereupon, "Mr. Wilkes!" summoning the nearest midshipman. "Tell Albert to come to me." Albert was the captain's hammock-boy, a sort of sea valet in whose discretion and fidelity his master had much confidence. The lad appeared.

"You know Budd, the foretopman?"

"I do, sir."

"Go find him. It is his watch off. Manage to tell him out of earshot that he is wanted aft. Contrive it that he speaks to nobody. Keep him in talk yourself. And not till you get well aft here, not till then let him know that the place where he is wanted is my cabin. You understand. Go.—Master-at-arms, show yourself on the decks below, and when you think it time for Albert to be coming with his man, stand by quietly to follow the sailor in."

### 19

Now when the foretopman found himself in the cabin, closeted there, as it were, with the captain and Claggart, he was surprised enough. But it was a surprise unaccompanied by apprehension or distrust. To an immature nature essentially honest and humane, forewarning intimations of subtler danger from one's kind come tardily if at all. The only thing that took shape in the young sailor's mind was this: Yes, the captain, I have always thought, looks kindly upon me. Wonder if he's going to make me his coxswain. I should like that. And may be now he is going to ask the master-at-arms about me.

"Shut the door there, sentry," said the commander; "stand without, and let nobody come in.—Now, Master-at-arms, tell this man to his face what you told of him to me," and stood prepared to scrutinize the mutually confronting visages.

With the measured step and calm collected air of an asylum physician approaching in the public hall some patient beginning to show indications of a coming paroxysm, Claggart deliberately advanced within short range of Billy and, mesmerically looking him in the eye, briefly recapitulated the accusation. Not at first did Billy take it in. When he did, the rose-tan of his cheek looked struck as by white leprosy. He stood like one impaled and gagged. Meanwhile the accuser's eyes, removing not as yet from the blue dilated ones, underwent a phenomenal change, their wonted rich violet color blurring into a muddy purple. Those lights of human intelligence, losing human expression, were gelidly protruding like the alien eyes of certain uncatalogued creatures of the deep. The first mesmeristic glance was one of serpent fascination; the last was as the paralyzing lurch of the torpedo fish.

"Speak, man!" said Captain Vere to the transfixed one, struck by his aspect even more than by Claggart's. "Speak! Defend yourself!" Which appeal caused but a strange dumb gesturing and gurgling in Billy; amazement at such an accusation so suddenly sprung on inexperienced nonage; this, and, it may be, horror of the accuser's eyes, serving to bring out his lurking defect and in this instance for the time intensifying it into a convulsed tongue-tie; while the intent head and entire form straining forward in an agony of ineffectual eagerness to obey the injunction to speak and defend himself, gave an expression to the face like that of a condemned vestal priestess in the moment of being buried alive, and in the first struggle against suffocation.[5]

Though at the time Captain Vere was quite ignorant of Billy's liability to vocal impediment, he now immediately divined it, since vividly Billy's aspect recalled to him that of a bright young schoolmate of his whom he had once seen struck by much the same startling impotence in the act of eagerly rising in the class to be foremost in response to a testing question put to it by the master. Going close up to the young sailor, and laying a soothing hand on his shoulder, he said, "There is no hurry, my boy. Take your time, take your time." Contrary to the effect intended, these words so fatherly in tone, doubtless touching Billy's heart to the quick, prompted yet more violent efforts at utterance—efforts soon ending for the time in confirming the paralysis, and bringing to his face an expression which was as a crucifixion to behold. The next instant, quick as the flame from a discharged cannon at night, his right arm shot out, and Claggart dropped to the deck. Whether intentionally or but owing to the young athlete's superior height, the blow had taken effect full upon the forehead, so shapely and intellectual-looking a feature in the master-at-arms; so that the body fell over lengthwise, like a heavy plank tilted from erectness. A gasp or two, and he lay motionless.

"Fated boy," breathed Captain Vere in tone so low as to be almost a whisper, "what have you done! But here, help me."

The twain raised the felled one from the loins up into a sitting position. The spare form flexibly acquiesced, but inertly. It was like handling a dead snake. They lowered it back. Regaining erectness, Captain Vere with one hand covering his face stood to all appearance as impassive as the object at his feet. Was he absorbed in taking in all the bearings of the event and what was best not only now at once to be done, but also in the sequel? Slowly he uncovered his face; and the effect was as if the moon emerging from eclipse should reappear with quite another aspect than that which had gone into hiding. The father in him, manifested towards Billy thus far in the scene, was replaced by the military disciplinarian. In his official tone he bade the foretopman retire to a state-room aft (pointing it out), and there remain till thence summoned. This order

5. The punishment of unchaste priestesses of the Roman goddess of the hearth, Vesta.

Billy in silence mechanically obeyed. Then going to the cabin door where it opened on the quarter-deck, Captain Vere said to the sentry without, "Tell somebody to send Albert here." When the lad appeared, his master so contrived it that he should not catch sight of the prone one. "Albert," he said to him, "tell the surgeon I wish to see him. You need not come back till called."

When the surgeon entered—a self-poised character of that grave sense and experience that hardly anything could take him aback—Captain Vere advanced to meet him, thus unconsciously intercepting his view of Claggart, and, interrupting the other's wonted ceremonious salutation, said, "Nay. Tell me how it is with yonder man," directing his attention to the prostrate one.

The surgeon looked, and for all his self-command somewhat started at the abrupt revelation. On Claggart's always pallid complexion, thick black blood was now oozing from nostril and ear. To the gazer's professional eye it was unmistakably no living man that he saw.

"Is it so, then?" said Captain Vere, intently watching him. "I thought it. But verify it." Whereupon the customary tests confirmed the surgeon's first glance, who now, looking up in unfeigned concern, cast a look of intense inquisitiveness upon his superior. But Captain Vere, with one hand to his brow, was standing motionless. Suddenly, catching the surgeon's arm convulsively, he exclaimed, pointing down to the body, "It is the divine judgment on Ananias![6] Look!"

Disturbed by the excited manner he had never before observed in the *Bellipont's* captain, and as yet wholly ignorant of the affair, the prudent surgeon nevertheless held his peace, only again looking an earnest interrogatory as to what it was that had resulted in such a tragedy.

But Captain Vere was now again motionless, standing absorbed in thought. Again starting, he vehemently exclaimed, "Struck dead by an angel of God! Yet the angel must hang!"

At these passionate interjections, mere incoherences to the listener as yet unapprised of the antecedents, the surgeon was profoundly discomposed. But now, as recollecting himself, Captain Vere in less passionate tone briefly related the circumstances leading up to the event. "But come; we must dispatch," he added. "Help me to remove him" (meaning the body) "to yonder compartment," designating one opposite that where the foretopman remained immured. Anew disturbed by a request that, as implying a desire for secrecy, seemed unaccountably strange to him, there was nothing for the subordinate to do but comply.

"Go now," said Captain Vere with something of his wonted manner. "Go now. I presently shall call a drumhead court.[7] Tell the lieutenants what has happened, and tell Mr. Mordant" (meaning the captain of marines),[8] "and charge them to keep the matter to themselves."

20

Full of disquietude and misgiving, the surgeon left the cabin. Was Captain Vere suddenly affected in his mind, or was it but a transient excitement,

---

6. Acts 5.3–5.
7. An emergency court (from the custom of using a drum for a table in an impromptu military or naval trial).

8. Captain of the soldiers stationed on shipboard; the mutual antipathy of marines and sailors was used as an aid to discipline.

brought about by so strange and extraordinary a tragedy? As to the drumhead court, it struck the surgeon as impolitic, if nothing more. The thing to do, he thought, was to place Billy Budd in confinement, and in a way dictated by usage, and postpone further action in so extraordinary a case to such time as they should rejoin the squadron, and then refer it to the admiral. He recalled the unwonted agitation of Captain Vere and his excited exclamations, so at variance with his normal manner. Was he unhinged?

But assuming that he is, it is not so susceptible of proof. What then can the surgeon do? No more trying situation is conceivable than that of an officer subordinate under a captain whom he suspects to be not mad, indeed, but yet not quite unaffected in his intellects. To argue his order to him would be insolence. To resist him would be mutiny.

In obedience to Captain Vere, he communicated what had happened to the lieutenants and captain of marines, saying nothing as to the captain's state. They fully shared his own surprise and concern. Like him too, they seemed to think that such a matter should be referred to the admiral.

21

Who in the rainbow can draw the line where the violet tint ends and the orange tint begins? Distinctly we see the difference of the colors, but where exactly does the one first blendingly enter into the other? So with sanity and insanity. In pronounced cases there is no question about them. But in some supposed cases, in various degrees supposedly less pronounced, to draw the exact line of demarcation few will undertake, though for a fee becoming considerate some professional experts will. There is nothing namable but that some men will, or undertake to, do it for pay.

Whether Captain Vere, as the surgeon professionally and privately surmised, was really the sudden victim of any degree of aberration, every one must determine for himself by such light as this narrative may afford.

That the unhappy event which has been narrated could not have happened at a worse juncture was but too true. For it was close on the heel of the suppressed insurrections, an aftertime very critical to naval authority, demanding from every English sea commander two qualities not readily interfusable—prudence and rigor. Moreover, there was something crucial in the case.

In the jugglery of circumstances preceding and attending the event on board the *Bellipotent*, and in the light of that martial code whereby it was formally to be judged, innocence and guilt personified in Claggart and Budd in effect changed places. In a legal view the apparent victim of the tragedy was he who had sought to victimize a man blameless; and the indisputable deed of the latter, navally regarded, constituted the most heinous of military crimes. Yet more. The essential right and wrong involved in the matter, the clearer that might be, so much the worse for the responsibility of a loyal sea commander, inasmuch as he was not authorized to determine the matter on that primitive basis.

Small wonder then that the *Bellipotent*'s captain, though in general a man of rapid decision, felt that circumspectness not less than promptitude was necessary. Until he could decide upon his course, and in each detail; and not only so, but until the concluding measure was upon the point of being enacted, he deemed it advisable, in view of all the circumstances, to guard as much as possible against publicity. Here he may or may not have erred. Certain it is, however, that subsequently in the confidential talk of more than one or two gun rooms and cabins he was not a little criticized by some officers, a fact imputed by his friends and vehemently by his cousin Jack Denton to professional jealousy of Starry Vere. Some imaginative ground for invidious comment there was. The maintenance of secrecy in the matter, the confining all knowledge of it for a time to the place where the homicide occurred, the quarter-deck cabin; in these particulars lurked some resemblance to the policy adopted in those tragedies of the palace which have occurred more than once in the capital founded by Peter the Barbarian.[9]

The case indeed was such that fain would the *Bellipotent's* captain have deferred taking any action whatever respecting it further than to keep the foretopman a close prisoner till the ship rejoined the squadron and then submitting the matter to the judgment of his admiral.

But a true military officer is in one particular like a true monk. Not with more of self-abnegation will the latter keep his vows of monastic obedience than the former his vows of allegiance to martial duty.

Feeling that unless quick action was taken on it, the deed of the foretopman, so soon as it should be known on the gun decks, would tend to awaken any slumbering embers of the Nore among the crew, a sense of the urgency of the case overruled in Captain Vere every other consideration. But though a conscientious disciplinarian, he was no lover of authority for mere authority's sake. Very far was he from embracing opportunities for monopolizing to himself the perils of moral responsibility, none at least that could properly be referred to an official superior or shared with him by his official equals or even subordinates. So thinking, he was glad it would not be at variance with usage to turn the matter over to a summary court of his own officers, reserving to himself, as the one on whom the ultimate accountability would rest, the right of maintaining a supervision of it, or formally or informally interposing at need. Accordingly a drumhead court was summarily convened, he electing the individuals composing it: the first lieutenant, the captain of marines, and the sailing master.[1]

In associating an officer of marines with the sea lieutenant and the sailing master in a case having to do with a sailor, the commander perhaps deviated from general custom. He was prompted thereto by the circumstance that he took that soldier to be a judicious person, thoughtful, and not altogether incapable of grappling with a difficult case unprecedented in his prior experience. Yet even as to him he was not without some latent misgiving, for withal he was an extremely good-natured man, an enjoyer of his dinner, a sound sleeper, and inclined to obesity—a man who though he would always maintain his manhood in battle might not prove altogether reliable in a moral dilemma involving aught of the tragic. As to the first lieutenant and the sailing master, Captain Vere could not but be aware that though honest natures, of approved gallantry upon occasion, their intelligence was mostly confined to the matter of active seamanship and the fighting demands of their profession.

The court was held in the same cabin where the unfortunate affair had taken place. This cabin, the commander's, embraced the entire area under

---

9. Peter the Great (1672–1725), czar of Russia.      1. Officer charged with navigating the ship.

the poop deck. Aft, and on either side, was a small stateroom, the one now temporarily a jail and the other a dead-house, and a yet smaller compartment, leaving a space between expanding forward into a goodly oblong of length coinciding with the ship's beam. A skylight of moderate dimension was overhead, and at each end of the oblong space were two sashed porthole windows easily convertible back into embrasures for short carronades.[2]

All being quickly in readiness, Billy Budd was arraigned, Captain Vere necessarily appearing as the sole witness in the case, and as such temporarily sinking his rank, though singularly maintaining it in a matter apparently trivial, namely, that he testified from the ship's weather side, with that object having caused the court to sit on the lee side.[3] Concisely he narrated all that had led up to the catastrophe, omitting nothing in Claggart's accusation and deposing as to the manner in which the prisoner had received it. At this testimony the three officers glanced with no little surprise at Billy Budd, the last man they would have suspected either of the mutinous design alleged by Claggart or the undeniable deed he himself had done. The first lieutenant, taking judicial primacy and turning toward the prisoner, said, "Captain Vere has spoken. Is it or is it not as Captain Vere says?"

In response came syllables not so much impeded in the utterance as might have been anticipated. They were these: "Captain Vere tells the truth. It is just as Captain Vere says, but it is not as the master-at-arms said. I have eaten the King's bread and I am true to the King."

"I believe you, my man," said the witness, his voice indicating a suppressed emotion not otherwise betrayed.

"God will bless you for that, your honor!" not without stammering said Billy, and all but broke down. But immediately he was recalled to self-control by another question, to which with the same emotional difficulty of utterance he said, "No, there was no malice between us. I never bore malice against the master-at-arms. I am sorry that he is dead. I did not mean to kill him. Could I have used my tongue I would not have struck him. But he foully lied to my face and in presence of my captain, and I had to say something, and I could only say it with a blow, God help me!"

In the impulsive aboveboard manner of the frank one the court saw confirmed all that was implied in words that just previously had perplexed them, coming as they did from the testifier to the tragedy and promptly following Billy's impassioned disclaimer of mutinous intent—Captain Vere's words, "I believe you, my man."

Next it was asked of him whether he knew of or suspected aught savoring of incipient trouble (meaning mutiny, though the explicit term was avoided) going on in any section of the ship's company.

The reply lingered. This was naturally imputed by the court to the same vocal embarrassment which had retarded or obstructed previous answers. But in main it was otherwise here, the question immediately recalling to Billy's mind the interview with the afterguardsman in the forechains. But an innate repugnance to playing a part at all approaching that of an informer against one's own shipmates—the same erring sense of uninstructed honor which had stood in the way of his reporting the matter at the time, though as a loyal man-

---

2. Light iron cannons (from Carron, Scotland, where they were first made). "Ship's beam": the widest point of the ship.

3. Vere testifies from the side from which the wind is blowing, so he looms higher than the officers.

of-war's man it was incumbent on him, and failure so to do, if charged against him and proven, would have subjected him to the heaviest of penalties; this, with the blind feeling now his that nothing really was being hatched, prevailed with him. When the answer came it was a negative.

"One question more," said the officer of marines, now first speaking and with a troubled earnestness. "You tell us that what the master-at-arms said against you was a lie. Now why should he have so lied, so maliciously lied, since you declare there was no malice between you?"

At that question, unintentionally touching on a spiritual sphere wholly obscure to Billy's thoughts, he was nonplussed, evincing a confusion indeed that some observers, such as can readily be imagined, would have construed into involuntary evidence of hidden guilt. Nevertheless, he strove some way to answer, but all at once relinquished the vain endeavor, at the same time turning an appealing glance towards Captain Vere as deeming him his best helper and friend. Captain Vere, who had been seated for a time, rose to his feet, addressing the interrogator. "The question you put to him comes naturally enough. But how can he rightly answer it?—or anybody else, unless indeed it be he who lies within there," designating the compartment where lay the corpse. "But the prone one there will not rise to our summons. In effect, though, as it seems to me, the point you make is hardly material. Quite aside from any conceivable motive actuating the master-at-arms, and irrespective of the provocation to the blow, a martial court must needs in the present case confine its attention to the blow's consequence, which consequence justly is to be deemed not otherwise than as the striker's deed."

This utterance, the full significance of which it was not at all likely that Billy took in, nevertheless caused him to turn a wistful interrogative look toward the speaker, a look in its dumb expressiveness not unlike that which a dog of generous breed might turn upon his master, seeking in his face some elucidation of a previous gesture ambiguous to the canine intelligence. Nor was the same utterance without marked effect upon the three officers, more especially the soldier. Couched in it seemed to them a meaning unanticipated, involving a prejudgment on the speaker's part. It served to augment a mental disturbance previously evident enough.

The soldier once more spoke, in a tone of suggestive dubiety addressing at once his associates and Captain Vere: "Nobody is present—none of the ship's company, I mean—who might shed lateral light, if any is to be had, upon what remains mysterious in this matter."

"That is thoughtfully put," said Captain Vere; "I see your drift. Ay, there is a mystery; but, to use a scriptural phrase, it is a 'mystery of iniquity,'[4] a matter for psychologic theologians to discuss. But what has a military court to do with it? Not to add that for us any possible investigation of it is cut off by the lasting tongue-tie of—him—in yonder," again designating the mortuary stateroom. "The prisoner's deed—with that alone we have to do."

To this, and particularly the closing reiteration, the marine soldier, knowing not how aptly to reply, sadly abstained from saying aught. The first lieutenant, who at the outset had not unnaturally assumed primacy in the court, now overrulingly instructed by a glance from Captain Vere, a glance more effective than words, resumed that primacy. Turning to the prisoner, "Budd," he said,

4. 2 Thessalonians 2.7.

and scarce in equable tones, "Budd, if you have aught further to say for yourself, say it now."

Upon this the young sailor turned another quick glance toward Captain Vere; then, as taking a hint from that aspect, a hint confirming his own instinct that silence was now best, replied to the lieutenant, "I have said all, sir."

The marine—the same who had been the sentinel without the cabin door at the time that the foretopman, followed by the master-at-arms, entered it— he, standing by the sailor throughout these judicial proceedings, was now directed to take him back to the after compartment originally assigned to the prisoner and his custodian. As the twain disappeared from view, the three officers, as partially liberated from some inward constraint associated with Billy's mere presence, simultaneously stirred in their seats. They exchanged looks of troubled indecision, yet feeling that decide they must and without long delay. For Captain Vere, he for the time stood—unconsciously with his back toward them, apparently in one of his absent fits—gazing out from a sashed porthole to windward upon the monotonous blank of the twilight sea. But the court's silence continuing, broken only at moments by brief consultations, in low earnest tones, this served to arouse him and energize him. Turning, he to-and-fro paced the cabin athwart; in the returning ascent to windward climbing the slant deck in the ship's lee roll,[5] without knowing it symbolizing thus in his action a mind resolute to surmount difficulties even if against primitive instincts strong as the wind and the sea. Presently he came to a stand before the three. After scanning their faces he stood less as mustering his thoughts for expression than as one inly deliberating how best to put them to well-meaning men not intellectually mature, men with whom it was necessary to demonstrate certain principles that were axioms to himself. Similar impatience as to talking is perhaps one reason that deters some minds from addressing any popular assemblies.

When speak he did, something, both in the substance of what he said and his manner of saying it, showed the influence of unshared studies modifying and tempering the practical training of an active career. This, along with his phraseology, now and then was suggestive of the grounds whereon rested that imputation of a certain pedantry socially alleged against him by certain naval men of wholly practical cast, captains who nevertheless would frankly concede that His Majesty's navy mustered no more efficient officer of their grade than Starry Vere.

What he said was to this effect: "Hitherto I have been but the witness, little more; and I should hardly think now to take another tone, that of your coadjutor for the time, did I not perceive in you—at the crisis too—a troubled hesitancy, proceeding, I doubt not, from the clash of military duty with moral scruple—scruple vitalized by compassion. For the compassion, how can I otherwise than share it? But, mindful of paramount obligations, I strive against scruples that may tend to enervate decision. Not, gentlemen, that I hide from myself that the case is an exceptional one. Speculatively regarded, it well might be referred to a jury of casuists.[6] But for us here, acting not as casuists or moralists, it is a case practical, and under martial law practically to be dealt with.

5. I.e., climbing as the ship rolled away from the wind.
6. Those who resolve matters of right and wrong by hairsplitting arguments, especially those who try to deduce principles of behavior from scriptural rules.

"But your scruples: do they move as in a dusk? Challenge them. Make them advance and declare themselves. Come now; do they import something like this: If, mindless of palliating circumstances, we are bound to regard the death of the master-at-arms as the prisoner's deed, then does that deed constitute a capital crime whereof the penalty is a mortal one. But in natural justice is nothing but the prisoner's overt act to be considered? How can we adjudge to summary and shameful death a fellow creature innocent before God, and whom we feel to be so?—Does that state it aright? You sign sad assent. Well, I too feel that, the full force of that. It is Nature. But do these buttons that we wear attest that our allegiance is to Nature? No, to the King. Though the ocean, which is inviolate Nature primeval, though this be the element where we move and have our being as sailors, yet as the King's officers lies our duty in a sphere correspondingly natural? So little is that true, that in receiving our commissions we in the most important regards ceased to be natural free agents. When war is declared are we the commissioned fighters previously consulted? We fight at command. If our judgments approve the war, that is but coincidence. So in other particulars. So now. For suppose condemnation to follow these present proceedings. Would it be so much we ourselves that would condemn as it would be martial law operating through us? For that law and the rigor of it, we are not responsible. Our vowed responsibility is in this: That however pitilessly that law may operate in any instances, we nevertheless adhere to it and administer it.

"But the exceptional in the matter moves the hearts within you. Even so too is mine moved. But let not warm hearts betray heads that should be cool. Ashore in a criminal case, will an upright judge allow himself off the bench to be waylaid by some tender kinswoman of the accused seeking to touch him with her tearful plea? Well, the heart here, sometimes the feminine in man, is as that piteous woman, and hard though it be, she must here be ruled out."

He paused, earnestly studying them for a moment; then resumed.

"But something in your aspect seems to urge that it is not solely the heart that moves in you, but also the conscience, the private conscience. But tell me whether or not, occupying the position we do, private conscience should not yield to that imperial one formulated in the code under which alone we officially proceed?"

Here the three men moved in their seats, less convinced than agitated by the course of an argument troubling but the more the spontaneous conflict within.

Perceiving which, the speaker paused for a moment; then abruptly changing his tone, went on.

"To steady us a bit, let us recur to the facts.—In wartime at sea a man-of-war's man strikes his superior in grade, and the blow kills. Apart from its effect the blow itself is, according to the Articles of War, a capital crime. Furthermore—"

"Ay, sir," emotionally broke in the officer of marines, "in one sense it was. But surely Budd purposed neither mutiny nor homicide."

"Surely not, my good man. And before a court less arbitrary and more merciful than a martial one, that plea would largely extenuate. At the Last Assizes[7] it shall acquit. But how here? We proceed under the law of the Mutiny Act. In feature no child can resemble his father more than that Act

7. The Last Judgment.

resembles in spirit the thing from which it derives—War. In His Majesty's service—in this ship, indeed—there are Englishmen forced to fight for the King against their will. Against their conscience, for aught we know. Though as their fellow creatures some of us may appreciate their position, yet as navy officers what reck we of it? Still less recks the enemy. Our impressed men he would fain cut down in the same swath with our volunteers. As regards the enemy's naval conscripts, some of whom may even share our own abhorrence of the regicidal French Directory, it is the same on our side. War looks but to the frontage, the appearance. And the Mutiny Act, War's child, takes after the father. Budd's intent or non-intent is nothing to the purpose.

"But while, put to it by those anxieties in you which I cannot but respect, I only repeat myself—while thus strangely we prolong proceedings that should be summary—the enemy may be sighted and an engagement result. We must do; and one of two things must we do—condemn or let go."

"Can we not convict and yet mitigate the penalty?" asked the sailing master, here speaking, and falteringly, for the first.

"Gentlemen, were that clearly lawful for us under the circumstances, consider the consequences of such clemency. The people" (meaning the ship's company) "have native sense; most of them are familiar with our naval usage and tradition; and how would they take it? Even could you explain to them— which our official position forbids—they, long molded by arbitrary discipline, have not that kind of intelligent responsiveness that might qualify them to comprehend and discriminate. No, to the people the foretopman's deed, however it be worded in the announcement, will be plain homicide committed in a flagrant act of mutiny. What penalty for that should follow, they know. But it does not follow. Why? they will ruminate. You know what sailors are. Will they not revert to the recent outbreak at the Nore? Ay. They know the well-founded alarm—the panic it struck throughout England. Your clement sentence they would account pusillanimous. They would think that we flinch, that we are afraid of them—afraid of practicing a lawful rigor singularly demanded at this juncture, lest it should provoke new troubles. What shame to us such a conjecture on their part, and how deadly to discipline. You see then, whither, prompted by duty and the law, I steadfastly drive. But I beseech you, my friends, do not take me amiss. I feel as you do for this unfortunate boy. But did he know our hearts, I take him to be of that generous nature that he would feel even for us on whom in this military necessity so heavy a compulsion is laid."

With that, crossing the deck he resumed his place by the sashed porthole, tacitly leaving the three to come to a decision. On the cabin's opposite side the troubled court sat silent. Loyal lieges, plain and practical, though at bottom they dissented from some points Captain Vere had put to them, they were without the faculty, hardly had the inclination, to gainsay one whom they felt to be an earnest man, one too not less their superior in mind than in naval rank. But it is not improbable that even such of his words as were not without influence over them, less came home to them than his closing appeal to their instinct as sea officers: in the forethought he threw out as to the practical consequences to discipline, considering the unconfirmed tone of the fleet at the time, should a man-of-war's man's violent killing at sea of a superior in grade be allowed to pass for aught else than a capital crime demanding prompt infliction of the penalty.

Not unlikely they were brought to something more or less akin to that harassed frame of mind which in the year 1842 actuated the commander of the U.S. brig-of-war *Somers* to resolve, under the so-called Articles of War, Articles modeled upon the English Mutiny Act, to resolve upon the execution at sea of a midshipman and two sailors as mutineers designing the seizure of the brig. Which resolution was carried out though in a time of peace and within not many days' sail of home. An act vindicated by a naval court of inquiry subsequently convened ashore. History, and here cited without comment. True, the circumstances on board the *Somers* were different from those on board the *Bellipotent*. But the urgency felt, well-warranted or otherwise, was much the same.

Says a writer[8] whom few know, "Forty years after a battle it is easy for a noncombatant to reason about how it ought to have been fought. It is another thing personally and under fire to have to direct the fighting while involved in the obscuring smoke of it. Much so with respect to other emergencies involving considerations both practical and moral, and when it is imperative promptly to act. The greater the fog the more it imperils the steamer, and speed is put on though at the hazard of running somebody down. Little ween the snug card players in the cabin of the responsibilities of the sleepless man on the bridge."

In brief, Billy Budd was formally convicted and sentenced to be hung at the yardarm in the early morning watch, it being now night. Otherwise, as is customary in such cases, the sentence would forthwith have been carried out. In wartime on the field or in the fleet, a mortal punishment decreed by a drumhead court—on the field sometimes decreed by but a nod from the general—follows without delay on the heel of conviction, without appeal.

22

It was Captain Vere himself who of his own motion communicated the finding of the court to the prisoner, for that purpose going to the compartment where he was in custody and bidding the marine there to withdraw for the time.

Beyond the communication of the sentence, what took place at this interview was never known. But in view of the character of the twain briefly closeted in that stateroom, each radically sharing in the rarer qualities of our nature—so rare indeed as to be all but incredible to average minds however much cultivated—some conjectures may be ventured.

It would have been in consonance with the spirit of Captain Vere should he on this occasion have concealed nothing from the condemned one—should he indeed have frankly disclosed to him the part he himself had played in bringing about the decision, at the same time revealing his actuating motives. On Billy's side it is not improbable that such a confession would have been received in much the same spirit that prompted it. Not without a sort of joy, indeed, he might have appreciated the brave opinion of him implied in his captain's making such a confidant of him. Nor, as to the sentence itself, could he have been insensible that it was imparted to him as to one not afraid to die. Even more may have been. Captain Vere in end may have developed the

8. Melville.

passion sometimes latent under an exterior stoical or indifferent. He was old enough to have been Billy's father. The austere devotee of military duty, letting himself melt back into what remains primeval in our formalized humanity, may in end have caught Billy to his heart, even as Abraham may have caught young Isaac on the brink of resolutely offering him up in obedience to the exacting behest.[9] But there is no telling the sacrament, seldom if in any case revealed to the gadding world, wherever under circumstances at all akin to those here attempted to be set forth two of great Nature's nobler order embrace. There is privacy at the time, inviolable to the survivor; and holy oblivion, the sequel to each diviner magnanimity, providentially covers all at last.

The first to encounter Captain Vere in act of leaving the compartment was the senior lieutenant. The face he beheld, for the moment one expressive of the agony of the strong, was to that officer, though a man of fifty, a startling revelation. That the condemned one suffered less than he who mainly had effected the condemnation was apparently indicated by the former's exclamation in the scene soon perforce to be touched upon.

## 23

Of a series of incidents within a brief term rapidly following each other, the adequate narration may take up a term less brief, especially if explanation or comment here and there seem requisite to the better understanding of such incidents. Between the entrance into the cabin of him who never left it alive, and him who when he did leave it left it as one condemned to die; between this and the closeted interview just given, less than an hour and a half had elapsed. It was an interval long enough, however, to awaken speculations among no few of the ship's company as to what it was that could be detaining in the cabin the master-at-arms and the sailor; for a rumor that both of them had been seen to enter it and neither of them had been seen to emerge, this rumor had got abroad upon the gun decks and in the tops, the people of a great warship being in one respect like villagers, taking microscopic note of every outward movement or non-movement going on. When therefore, in weather not at all tempestuous, all hands were called in the second dogwatch, a summons under such circumstances not usual in those hours, the crew were not wholly unprepared for some announcement extraordinary, one having connection too with the continued absence of the two men from their wonted haunts.

There was a moderate sea at the time; and the moon, newly risen and near to being at its full, silvered the white spar deck wherever not blotted by the clear-cut shadows horizontally thrown of fixtures and moving men. On either side the quarter-deck the marine guard under arms was drawn up; and Captain Vere, standing in his place surrounded by all the wardroom officers,[1] addressed his men. In so doing, his manner showed neither more nor less than that properly pertaining to his supreme position aboard his own ship. In clear terms and concise he told them what had taken place in the cabin: that the master-at-arms was dead, that he who had killed him had been already tried by a summary court and condemned to death, and that the execution would

9. Genesis 22.1–18.
1. The commissioned officers above the rank of ensign.

take place in the early morning watch. The word *mutiny* was not named in what he said. He refrained too from making the occasion an opportunity for any preachment as to the maintenance of discipline, thinking perhaps that under existing circumstances in the navy the consequence of violating discipline should be made to speak for itself.

Their captain's announcement was listened to by the throng of standing sailors in a dumbness like that of a seated congregation of believers in hell listening to the clergyman's announcement of his Calvinistic text.

At the close, however, a confused murmur went up. It began to wax. All but instantly, then, at a sign, it was pierced and suppressed by shrill whistles of the boatswain and his mates. The word was given to about ship.

To be prepared for burial Claggart's body was delivered to certain petty officers of his mess. And here, not to clog the sequel with lateral matters, it may be added that at a suitable hour, the master-at-arms was committed to the sea with every funeral honor properly belonging to his naval grade.

In this proceeding as in every public one growing out of the tragedy strict adherence to usage was observed. Nor in any point could it have been at all deviated from, either with respect to Claggart or Billy Budd, without begetting undesirable speculations in the ship's company, sailors, and more particularly men-of-war's men, being of all men the greatest sticklers for usage. For similar cause, all communication between Captain Vere and the condemned one ended with the closeted interview already given, the latter being now surrendered to the ordinary routine preliminary to the end. His transfer under guard from the captain's quarters was effected without unusual precautions—at least no visible ones. If possible, not to let the men so much as surmise that their officers anticipate aught amiss from them is the tacit rule in a military ship. And the more that some sort of trouble should really be apprehended, the more do the officers keep that apprehension to themselves, though not the less unostentatious vigilance may be augmented.. In the present instance, the sentry placed over the prisoner had strict orders to let no one have communication with him but the chaplain. And certain unobtrusive measures were taken absolutely to insure this point.

## 24

In a seventy-four of the old order the deck known as the upper gun deck was the one covered over by the spar deck, which last, though not without its armament, was for the most part exposed to the weather. In general it was at all hours free from hammocks; those of the crew swinging on the lower gun deck and berth deck, the latter being not only a dormitory but also the place for the stowing of the sailors' bags, and on both sides lined with the large chests or movable pantries of the many messes of the men.

On the starboard side of the *Bellipotent's* upper gun deck, behold Billy Budd under sentry lying prone in irons in one of the bays formed by the regular spacing of the guns comprising the batteries on either side. All these pieces were of the heavier caliber of that period. Mounted on lumbering wooden carriages, they were hampered with cumbersome harness of breeching and strong side-tackles for running them out. Guns and carriages, together with the long rammers and shorter linstocks[2] lodged in loops overhead—all these,

2. "Rammers" are rods for ramming home the charge of a gun, and "linstocks" are pointed forked staffs to hold a lighted match for firing cannon.

as customary, were painted black; and the heavy hempen breechings, tarred to the same tint, wore the like livery of the undertakers. In contrast with the funereal hue of these surroundings, the prone sailor's exterior apparel, white jumper and white duck trousers, each more or less soiled, dimly glimmered in the obscure light of the bay like a patch of discolored snow in early April lingering at some upland cave's black mouth. In effect he is already in his shroud, or the garments that shall serve him in lieu of one. Over him but scarce illuminating him, two battle lanterns swing from two massive beams of the deck above. Fed with the oil supplied by the war contractors (whose gains, honest or otherwise, are in every land an anticipated portion of the harvest of death), with flickering splashes of dirty yellow light they pollute the pale moonshine all but ineffectually struggling in obstructed flecks through the open ports from which the tampioned cannon protrude. Other lanterns at intervals serve but to bring out somewhat the obscurer bays which, like small confessionals or side-chapels in a cathedral, branch from the long dim-vistaed broad aisle between the two batteries of that covered tier.

Such was the deck where now lay the Handsome Sailor. Through the rosetan of his complexion no pallor could have shown. It would have taken days of sequestration from the winds and the sun to have brought about the effacement of that. But the skeleton in the cheekbone at the point of its angle was just beginning delicately to be defined under the warm-tinted skin. In fervid hearts self-contained, some brief experiences devour our human tissue as secret fire in a ship's hold consumes cotton in the bale.

But now lying between the two guns, as nipped in the vice of fate, Billy's agony, mainly proceeding from a generous young heart's virgin experience of the diabolical incarnate and effective in some men—the tension of that agony was over now. It survived not the something healing in the closeted interview with Captain Vere. Without movement, he lay as in a trance, that adolescent expression previously noted as his taking on something akin to the look of a slumbering child in the cradle when the warm hearth-glow of the still chamber at night plays on the dimples that at whiles mysteriously form in the cheek, silently coming and going there. For now and then in the gyved[3] one's trance a serene happy light born of some wandering reminiscence or dream would diffuse itself over his face, and then wane away only anew to return.

The chaplain, coming to see him and finding him thus, and perceiving no sign that he was conscious of his presence, attentively regarded him for a space, then slipping aside, withdrew for the time, peradventure feeling that even he, the minister of Christ though receiving his stipend from Mars,[4] had no consolation to proffer which could result in a peace transcending that which he beheld. But in the small hours he came again. And the prisoner, now awake to his surroundings, noticed his approach, and civilly, all but cheerfully, welcomed him. But it was to little purpose that in the interview following, the good man sought to bring Billy Budd to some godly understanding that he must die, and at dawn. True, Billy himself freely referred to his death as a thing close at hand; but it was something in the way that children will refer to death in general, who yet among their other sports will play a funeral with hearse and mourners.

Not that like children Billy was incapable of conceiving what death really is. No, but he was wholly without irrational fear of it, a fear more prevalent in

3. Shackled or chained.
4. The servant of the Prince of Peace being paid by the god of war.

highly civilized communities than those so-called barbarous ones which in all respects stand nearer to unadulterate Nature. And, as elsewhere said, a barbarian Billy radically was—as much so, for all the costume, as his countrymen the British captives, living trophies, made to march in the Roman triumph of Germanicus.[5] Quite as much so as those later barbarians, young men probably, and picked specimens among the earlier British converts to Christianity, at least nominally such, taken to Rome (as today converts from lesser isles of the sea may be taken to London), of whom the Pope of that time, admiring the strangeness of their personal beauty so unlike the Italian stamp, their clear ruddy complexion and curled flaxen locks, exclaimed, "Angles" (meaning *English*, the modern derivative), "Angles, do you call them? And is it because they look so like angels?"[6] Had it been later in time, one would think that the Pope had in mind Fra Angelico's seraphs, some of whom, plucking apples in gardens of the Hesperides,[7] have the faint rosebud complexion of the more beautiful English girls.

If in vain the good chaplain sought to impress the young barbarian with ideas of death akin to those conveyed in the skull, dial, and crossbones on old tombstones, equally futile to all appearance were his efforts to bring home to him the thought of salvation and a Savior. Billy listened, but less out of awe or reverence, perhaps, than from a certain natural politeness, doubtless at bottom regarding all that in much the same way that most mariners of his class take any discourse abstract or out of the common tone of the workaday world. And this sailor way of taking clerical discourse is not wholly unlike the way in which the primer of Christianity, full of transcendent miracles, was received long ago on tropic isles by any superior *savage*, so called—a Tahitian, say, of Captain Cook's time[8] or shortly after that time. Out of a natural courtesy he received, but did not appropriate. It was like a gift placed in the palm of an outreached hand upon which the fingers do not close.

But the *Bellipotent*'s chaplain was a discreet man possessing the good sense of a good heart. So he insisted not in his vocation here. At the instance of Captain Vere, a lieutenant had apprised him of pretty much everything as to Billy; and since he felt that innocence was even a better thing than religion wherewith to go to Judgment, he reluctantly withdrew; but in his emotion not without first performing an act strange enough in an Englishman, and under the circumstances yet more so in any regular priest. Stooping over, he kissed on the fair cheek his fellow man, a felon in martial law, one whom though on the confines of death he felt he could never convert to a dogma; nor for all that did he fear for his future.

Marvel not that having been made acquainted with the young sailor's essential innocence the worthy man lifted not a finger to avert the doom of such a martyr to martial discipline. So to do would not only have been as idle as invoking the desert, but would also have been an audacious transgression of the bounds of his function, one as exactly prescribed to him by military law as that of the boatswain or any other naval officer. Bluntly put, a chaplain is the minister of the Prince of Peace serving in the host of the God of War—Mars. As such, he is as incongruous as a musket would be on the altar at Christmas.

5. Germanicus Caesar (15 B.C.–A.D. 19), Roman general who fought Germanic tribes and was given a famous triumph in Rome (A.D. 17).
6. Pope Gregory (540?–604).
7. In Florence during 1857 Melville saw paintings by Giovanni da Fiesole (Fra Angelico) (1387–1455). In Greek mythology the Hesperides were islands where golden apples grew (guarded by a dragon).
8. Cook first visited Tahiti in 1769 and returned there a few years later.

Why, then, is he there? Because he indirectly subserves the purpose attested by the cannon; because too he lends the sanction of the religion of the meek to that which practically is the abrogation of everything but brute Force.

## 25

The night so luminous on the spar deck, but otherwise on the cavernous ones below, levels so like the tiered galleries in a coal mine—the luminous night passed away. But like the prophet in the chariot disappearing in heaven and dropping his mantle to Elisha,[9] the withdrawing night transferred its pale robe to the breaking day. A meek, shy light appeared in the East, where stretched a diaphanous fleece of white furrowed vapor. That light slowly waxed. Suddenly *eight bells* was struck aft, responded to by one louder metallic stroke from forward. It was four o'clock in the morning. Instantly the silver whistles were heard summoning all hands to witness punishment. Up through the great hatchways rimmed with racks of heavy shot the watch below came pouring, overspreading with the watch already on deck the space between the mainmast and foremast including that occupied by the capacious launch and the black booms tiered on either side of it, boat and booms making a summit of observation for the powder-boys and younger tars. A different group comprising one watch of topmen leaned over the rail of that sea balcony, no small one in a seventy-four, looking down on the crowd below. Man or boy, none spake but in whisper, and few spake at all. Captain Vere—as before, the central figure among the assembled commissioned officers—stood nigh the break of the poop deck facing forward. Just below him on the quarter-deck the marines in full equipment were drawn up much as at the scene of the promulgated sentence.

At sea in the old time, the execution by halter of a military sailor was generally from the foreyard. In the present instance, for special reasons the mainyard was assigned. Under an arm of that yard the prisoner was presently brought up, the chaplain attending him. It was noted at the time, and remarked upon afterwards, that in this final scene the good man evinced little or nothing of the perfunctory. Brief speech indeed he had with the condemned one, but the genuine Gospel was less on his tongue than in his aspect and manner towards him. The final preparations personal to the latter being speedily brought to an end by two boatswain's mates, the consummation impended. Billy stood facing aft. At the penultimate moment, his words, his only ones, words wholly unobstructed in the utterance, were these: "God bless Captain Vere!" Syllables so unanticipated coming from one with the ignominious hemp about his neck— a conventional felon's benediction directed aft towards the quarters of honor; syllables too delivered in the clear melody of a singing bird on the point of launching from the twig—had a phenomenal effect, not unenhanced by the rare personal beauty of the young sailor, spiritualized now through late experiences so poignantly profound.

Without volition, as it were, as if indeed the ship's populace were but the vehicles of some vocal current electric, with one voice from alow and aloft came a resonant sympathetic echo: "God bless Captain Vere!" And yet at that instant Billy alone must have been in their hearts, even as in their eyes.

9. 2 Kings 2.9–15.

At the pronounced words and the spontaneous echo that voluminously rebounded them, Captain Vere, either through stoic self-control or a sort of momentary paralysis induced by emotional shock, stood erectly rigid as a musket in the ship-armorer's rack.

The hull, deliberately recovering from the periodic roll to leeward, was just regaining an even keel when the last signal, a preconcerted dumb one, was given. At the same moment it chanced that the vapory fleece hanging low in the East was shot through with a soft glory as of the fleece of the Lamb of God seen in mystical vision,[1] and simultaneously therewith, watched by the wedged mass of upturned faces, Billy ascended; and, ascending, took the full rose of the dawn.

In the pinioned figure arrived at the yard-end, to the wonder of all no motion was apparent, none save that created by the slow roll of the hull in moderate weather, so majestic in a great ship ponderously cannoned.

## 26

When some days afterwards, in reference to the singularity just mentioned, the purser,[2] a rather ruddy, rotund person more accurate as an accountant than profound as a philosopher, said at mess to the surgeon, "What testimony to the force lodged in will power," the latter, saturnine, spare, and tall, one in whom a discreet causticity went along with a manner less genial than polite, replied, "Your pardon, Mr. Purser. In a hanging scientifically conducted— and under special orders I myself directed how Budd's was to be effected—any movement following the completed suspension and originating in the body suspended, such movement indicates mechanical spasm in the muscular system. Hence the absence of that is no more attributable to will power, as you call it, than to horsepower—begging your pardon."

"But this muscular spasm you speak of, is not that in a degree more or less invariable in these cases?"

"Assuredly so, Mr. Purser."

"How then, my good sir, do you account for its absence in this instance?"

"Mr. Purser, it is clear that your sense of the singularity in this matter equals not mine. You account for it by what you call will power—a term not yet included in the lexicon of science. For me, I do not, with my present knowledge, pretend to account for it at all. Even should we assume the hypothesis that at the first touch of the halyards the action of Budd's heart, intensified by extraordinary emotion at its climax, abruptly stopped—much like a watch when in carelessly winding it up you strain at the finish, thus snapping the chain—even under that hypothesis how account for the phenomenon that followed?"

"You admit, then, that the absence of spasmodic movement was phenomenal."

"It was phenomenal, Mr. Purser, in the sense that it was an appearance the cause of which is not immediately to be assigned."

"But tell me, my dear sir," pertinaciously continued the other, "was the man's death effected by the halter, or was it a species of euthanasia?"[3]

---

1. See Revelation 1.14.
2. Paymaster.
3. Not in our sense of a merciful death inflicted by someone else. Melville had read the definition of eu-

*thanasia* by the German philosopher Arthur Schopenhauer (1788–1860) as "an easy death, not ushered in by disease, and free from all pain and struggle."

"*Euthanasia*, Mr. Purser, is something like your *will power*: I doubt its authenticity as a scientific term—begging your pardon again. It is at once imaginative and metaphysical—in short, Greek.—But," abruptly changing his tone, "there is a case in the sick bay that I do not care to leave to my assistants. Beg your pardon, but excuse me." And rising from the mess he formally withdrew.

## 27

The silence at the moment of execution and for a moment or two continuing thereafter, a silence but emphasized by the regular wash of the sea against the hull or the flutter of a sail caused by the helmsman's eyes being tempted astray, this emphasized silence was gradually disturbed by a sound not easily to be verbally rendered. Whoever has heard the freshet-wave of a torrent suddenly swelled by pouring showers in tropical mountains, showers not shared by the plain; whoever has heard the first muffled murmur of its sloping advance through precipitous woods may form some conception of the sound now heard. The seeming remoteness of its source was because of its murmurous indistinctness, since it came from close by, even from the men massed on the ship's open deck. Being inarticulate, it was dubious in significance further than it seemed to indicate some capricious revulsion of thought or feeling such as mobs ashore are liable to, in the present instance possibly implying a sullen revocation on the men's part of their involuntary echoing of Billy's benediction. But ere the murmur had time to wax into clamor it was met by a strategic command, the more telling that it came with abrupt unexpectedness: "Pipe down the starboard watch, Boatswain, and see that they go."

Shrill as the shriek of the sea hawk, the silver whistles of the boatswain and his mates pierced that ominous low sound, dissipating it; and yielding to the mechanism of discipline the throng was thinned by one-half. For the remainder, most of them were set to temporary employments connected with trimming the yards and so forth, business readily to be got up to serve occasion by any officer of the deck.

Now each proceeding that follows a mortal sentence pronounced at sea by a drumhead court is characterized by promptitude not perceptibly merging into hurry, though bordering that. The hammock, the one which had been Billy's bed when alive, having already been ballasted with shot and otherwise prepared to serve for his canvas coffin, the last offices of the sea undertakers, the sailmaker's mates, were now speedily completed. When everything was in readiness a second call for all hands, made necessary by the strategic movement before mentioned, was sounded, now to witness burial.

The details of this closing formality it needs not to give. But when the tilted plank let slide its freight into the sea, a second strange human murmur was heard, blended now with another inarticulate sound proceeding from certain larger seafowl who, their attention having been attracted by the peculiar commotion in the water resulting from the heavy sloped dive of the shotted hammock into the sea, flew screaming to the spot. So near the hull did they come, that the stridor or bony creak of their gaunt double-jointed pinions was audible. As the ship under light airs passed on, leaving the burial spot astern, they still kept circling it low down with the moving shadow of their outstretched wings and the croaked requiem of their cries.

Upon sailors as superstitious as those of the age preceding ours, men-of-war's men too who had just beheld the prodigy of repose in the form suspended in air, and now foundering in the deeps; to such mariners the action of the seafowl, though dictated by mere animal greed for prey, was big with no prosaic significance. An uncertain movement began among them, in which some encroachment was made. It was tolerated but for a moment. For suddenly the drum beat to quarters, which familiar sound happening at least twice every day, had upon the present occasion a signal peremptoriness in it. True martial discipline long continued superinduces in average man a sort of impulse whose operation at the official word of command much resembles in its promptitude the effect of an instinct.

The drumbeat dissolved the multitude, distributing most of them along the batteries of the two covered gun decks. There, as wonted, the guns' crews stood by their respective cannon erect and silent. In due course the first officer, sword under arm and standing in his place on the quarter-deck, formally received the successive reports of the sworded lieutenants commanding the sections of batteries below; the last of which reports being made, the summed report he delivered with the customary salute to the commander. All this occupied time, which in the present case was the object in beating to quarters at an hour prior to the customary one. That such variance from usage was authorized by an officer like Captain Vere, a martinet as some deemed him, was evidence of the necessity for unusual action implied in what he deemed to be temporarily the mood of his men. "With mankind," he would say, "forms, measured forms, are everything; and that is the import couched in the story of Orpheus with his lyre spellbinding the wild denizens of the wood."[4] And this he once applied to the disruption of forms going on across the Channel and the consequences thereof.

At this unwonted muster at quarters, all proceeded as at the regular hour. The band on the quarter-deck played a sacred air, after which the chaplain went through the customary morning service. That done, the drum beat the retreat; and toned by music and religious rites subserving the discipline and purposes of war, the men in their wonted orderly manner dispersed to the places allotted them when not at the guns.

And now it was full day. The fleece of low-hanging vapor had vanished, licked up by the sun that late had so glorified it. And the circumambient air in the clearness of its serenity was like smooth white marble in the polished block not yet removed from the marble-dealer's yard.

## 28

The symmetry of form attainable in pure fiction cannot so readily be achieved in a narration essentially having less to do with fable than with fact. Truth uncompromisingly told will always have its ragged edges; hence the conclusion of such a narration is apt to be less finished than an architectural finial.[5]

How it fared with the Handsome Sailor during the year of the Great Mutiny has been faithfully given. But though properly the story ends with his life, something in way of sequel will not be amiss. Three brief chapters will suffice.

4. In Greek mythology Orpheus's music was so powerful that it bound the guardians of the Underworld so that his wife, Eurydice, was almost lured back to earth.

5. An ornament that forms the upper extremity of a post, pillar, or other architectural feature.

In the general rechristening under the Directory of the craft originally forming the navy of the French monarchy, the *St. Louis* line-of-battle ship was named the *Athée* (the *Atheist*). Such a name, like some other substituted ones in the Revolutionary fleet, while proclaiming the infidel audacity of the ruling power, was yet, though not so intended to be, the aptest name, if one consider it, ever given to a warship; far more so indeed than the *Devastation*, the *Erebus* (the *Hell*), and similar names bestowed upon fighting ships.

On the return passage to the English fleet from the detached cruise during which occurred the events already recorded, the *Bellipotent* fell in with the *Athée*. An engagement ensued, during which Captain Vere, in the act of putting his ship alongside the enemy with a view of throwing his boarders across her bulwarks, was hit by a musket ball from a porthole of the enemy's main cabin. More than disabled, he dropped to the deck and was carried below to the same cockpit where some of his men already lay. The senior lieutenant took command. Under him the enemy was finally captured, and though much crippled was by rare good fortune successfully taken into Gibraltar, an English port not very distant from the scene of the fight. There, Captain Vere with the rest of the wounded was put ashore. He lingered for some days, but the end came. Unhappily he was cut off too early for the Nile and Trafalgar. The spirit that 'spite its philosophic austerity may yet have indulged in the most secret of all passions, ambition, never attained to the fulness of fame.

Not long before death, while lying under the influence of that magical drug[6] which, soothing the physical frame, mysteriously operates on the subtler element in man, he was heard to murmur words inexplicable to his attendant: "Billy Budd, Billy Budd." That these were not the accents of remorse would seem clear from what the attendant said to the *Bellipotent*'s senior officer of marines, who, as the most reluctant to condemn of the members of the drumhead court, too well knew, though here he kept the knowledge to himself, who Billy Budd was.

### 29

Some few weeks after the execution, among other matters under the head of "News from the Mediterranean," there appeared in a naval chronicle of the time, an authorized weekly publication, an account of the affair. It was doubtless for the most part written in good faith, though the medium, partly rumor, through which the facts must have reached the writer served to deflect and in part falsify them. The account was as follows:

"On the tenth of the last month a deplorable occurrence took place on board H.M.S. *Bellipotent*. John Claggart, the ship's master-at-arms, discovering that some sort of plot was incipient among an inferior section of the ship's company, and that the ringleader was one William Budd; he, Claggart, in the act of arraigning the man before the captain, was vindictively stabbed to the heart by the suddenly drawn sheath knife of Budd.

"The deed and the implement employed sufficiently suggest that though mustered into the service under an English name the assassin was no Englishman, but one of those aliens adopting English cognomens whom the present extraordinary necessities of the service have caused to be admitted into it in considerable numbers.

6. Probably opium.

"The enormity of the crime and the extreme depravity of the criminal appear the greater in view of the character of the victim, a middle-aged man respectable and discreet, belonging to that minor official grade, the petty officers, upon whom, as none know better than the commissioned gentlemen, the efficiency of His Majesty's navy so largely depends. His function was a responsible one, at once onerous and thankless; and his fidelity in it the greater because of his strong patriotic impulse. In this instance as in so many other instances in these days, the character of this unfortunate man signally refutes, if refutation were needed, that peevish saying attributed to the late Dr. Johnson, that patriotism is the last refuge of a scoundrel.[7]

"The criminal paid the penalty of his crime. The promptitude of the punishment has proved salutary. Nothing amiss is now apprehended aboard H.M.S. Bellipotent."

The above, appearing in a publication now long ago superannuated and forgotten, is all that hitherto has stood in human record to attest what manner of men respectively were John Claggart and Billy Budd.

## 30

Everything is for a term venerated in navies. Any tangible object associated with some striking incident of the service is converted into a monument. The spar from which the foretopman was suspended was for some few years kept trace of by the bluejackets. Their knowledges followed it from ship to dockyard and again from dockyard to ship, still pursuing it even when at last reduced to a mere dockyard boom. To them a chip of it was as a piece of the Cross. Ignorant though they were of the secret facts of the tragedy, and not thinking but that the penalty was somehow unavoidably inflicted from the naval point of view, for all that, they instinctively felt that Billy was a sort of man as incapable of mutiny as of wilful murder. They recalled the fresh young image of the Handsome Sailor, that face never deformed by a sneer or subtler vile freak of the heart within. This impression of him was doubtless deepened by the fact that he was gone, and in a measure mysteriously gone. On the gun decks of the Bellipotent the general estimate of his nature and its unconscious simplicity eventually found rude utterance from another foretopman, one of his own watch, gifted, as some sailors are, with an artless poetic temperament. The tarry hand made some lines which, after circulating among the shipboard crews for a while, finally got rudely printed at Portsmouth as a ballad. The title given to it was the sailor's.

### BILLY IN THE DARBIES

Good of the chaplain to enter Lone Bay
And down on his marrowbones here and pray
For the likes just o'me, Billy Budd.—But, look:
Through the port comes the moonshine astray!
It tips the guard's cutlass and silvers this nook;
But 'twill die in the dawning of Billy's last day.
A jewel-block they'll make of me tomorrow,
Pendant pearl from the yardarm-end

---

7. Reported in Boswell's Life of Johnson (1791) as a pronouncement made on April 7, 1775.

Like the eardrop I gave to Bristol Molly—
O, 'tis me, not the sentence they'll suspend.
Ay, ay, all is up; and I must up too,
Early in the morning, aloft from alow.
On an empty stomach now never it would do.
They'll give me a nibble—bit o'biscuit ere I go.
Sure, a messmate will reach me the last parting cup;
But, turning heads away from the hoist and the belay,
Heaven knows who will have the running of me up!
No pipe to those halyards.—But aren't it all sham?
A blur's in my eyes; it is dreaming that I am.
A hatchet to my hawser? All adrift to go?
The drum roll to grog, and Billy never know?
But Donald he has promised to stand by the plank;
So I'll shake a friendly hand ere I sink.
But—no! It is dead then I'll be, come to think.
I remember Taff the Welshman when he sank.
And his cheek it was like the budding pink.
But me they'll lash in hammock, drop me deep.
Fathoms down, fathoms down, how I'll dream fast asleep.
I feel it stealing now. Sentry, are you there?
Just ease these darbies[8] at the wrist,
And roll me over fair!
I am sleepy, and the oozy weeds about me twist.

1886?–91                                                         1924, 1962

8. Handcuffs.

---

# EMILY DICKINSON
## 1830–1886

Emily Elizabeth Dickinson was born on December 10, 1830, in Amherst, Massachusetts, the second child of Edward (1803–1874) and Emily Norcross Dickinson (1804–1882). Dickinson lived in only two houses, the spacious but then-divided Dickinson family "Homestead" where she was born, then another large house nearby from 1840 until 1855, when her father bought back the entire Homestead. Thereafter she lived in the house where she was born, dying there, of Bright's disease, on May 15, 1886. Her closest friends and lifelong allies were her brother, William Austin (1829–1895), a year and a half older than she, and her sister, Lavinia (Vinnie), who was born in February 1833, and died in 1899. In 1856 when her brother, called Austin, married her school friend Susan Gilbert (1830–1913) the couple moved into the "Evergreens," next door to the Homestead, newly built for the couple by Edward Dickinson. Neither Emily Dickinson nor Lavinia married. Emily Dickinson seldom left Amherst. Her one lengthy absence was a year (1847–48) at Mt. Holyoke Female Seminary, at South Hadley, ten long miles away, where she was intensely homesick for her "*own* DEAR HOME," and once back in Amherst she beckoned her brother from his schoolteaching in Boston: "Walk away to freedom and the sunshine here at home." Undaunted by her powerful father's domestic tyrannies, cherishing her mother (who remains hard for biog-

raphers to characterize, a passive woman in a household of forceful personalities),
Dickinson declared home to be holy, "the definition of God," a place of "Infinite
power."

All the Dickinsons struck people as unusual, but Emily was identified as "the
climax of all the family oddity" and became known as the "Myth," the *character
of Amherst*," well before she died, according to the local gossip that the young
Mabel Loomis Todd passed on to her parents soon after moving to Amherst in
1881:

> She has not been outside of her own house in fifteen years, except once to see
> a new church, when she crept out at night, & viewed it by moonlight. No
> one who calls upon her mother & sister ever see her, but she allows little
> children once in a great while, & one at a time, to come in, when she gives
> them cake or candy, or some nicety, for she is very fond of little ones. But
> more often she lets down the sweetmeat by a string, out of a window, to them.
> She dresses wholly in white, & her mind is said to be perfectly wonderful.
> She writes finely, but no one *ever* sees her. Her sister . . . invited me to come
> & sing to her mother some time and I promised to go & if the performance
> pleases her [the "Myth"], a servant will enter with wine for me, or a flower,
> & perhaps her thanks; but just probably the token of approval will not come
> then, but a few days after, some dainty present will appear for me at twilight.
> People tell me that the *myth* will hear every note—she will be near, but
> unseen. . . . Isn't that like a book? So interesting.

"No one knows the cause of her isolation," Mabel Todd concluded, "but of course
there are dozens of reasons assigned." Many people have speculated about the
reasons for Dickinson's seclusion, but no single "cause of her isolation" has ever
been discovered.

Economically, politically, and intellectually, the Dickinsons were among
Amherst's most prominent families. Edward Dickinson was treasurer of Amherst
College for thirty-six years and served as a state representative and a state senator.
During his term in Congress (1853–54), Emily Dickinson visited him in Washington and stayed briefly in Philadelphia on her way home. A successful lawyer,
Austin became a justice of the peace in 1857 and followed his father, in 1873, as
treasurer of Amherst College. Emily Dickinson attended Amherst Academy from
1840 through 1846, years her biographer Richard B. Sewall calls "a blossoming
period in her life, full and joyous"; then she spent her year at Mt. Holyoke. At
eighteen she was formally educated far beyond the level then achieved by most
Americans, male or female.

Religion was an essential part of Dickinson's education, and Amherst was nearer
to Jonathan Edwards's Stockbridge of a century before than it was to the Boston of
the 1840s, where, for many of the educated classes, Unitarianism had disposed of
the idea of hell and the fear of the fiery pit. Dickinson was exposed to the sort of
terrorism from the pulpit that Harriet Beecher Stowe was soon to depict in her
realistic historical novels, and Dickinson seems to have experienced the psychological agonies that Stowe attributed to some of her delicate young female characters.
For Dickinson, being terrorized by old-fashioned sermons about damnation was
compounded by the closeness of death in that age of high infant and childhood
mortality and high mortality in childbirth. The death of her friend Sophia Holland
at fifteen in 1844 made Dickinson think she "should die too" and set her into "a
fixed melancholy." Soon afterward, swayed by the revivalistic fervor of the community, Dickinson felt that she had experienced an awakening in which she found
her "savior."

Dickinson's religious exaltation did not last, and as her girlhood friends married
and moved away, she gradually became estranged from the religious beliefs of
the community. For several years she dutifully attended church, but her terror

diminished, especially after 1852, when she became friends with Josiah Gilbert Holland, associate editor of the Springfield *Republican*, and his wife, Elizabeth; their liberal theology encouraged her to struggle against the influence of sermons threatening damnation for souls like her own. Her first religious rebellion was juvenile (the cocky irreverence of No. 61, "Papa above!" or the smug superiority of No. 324, "Some keep the Sabbath going to Church"), but later she could take ironic intellectual delight in her freedom from the tyrannical, arbitrary God (a "Mastiff" in No. 1317) worshipped by her townspeople. In her maturity, as a great poet, she understood that the feelings that distanced her from other people also enhanced her awareness of the seasonal rhythms of nature (No. 1068, "Further in Summer than the Birds"). Her introspection was unfailingly rigorous; while she triumphed at length in her rebellion against the theology of her town, to the extent that Cynthia Griffin Wolff refers to her as a "post-Christian artist," Dickinson remained a daughter of the Puritans, albeit a disobedient daughter.

Dickinson's slow triumph over religious fears was intricately involved in her seeing herself as a poet. Reading literature was a guilty pleasure in the Amherst of Dickinson's childhood, where there still reigned the antiartistic spirit that Harriet Beecher Stowe depicted as a common feature of late-eighteenth- and early-nineteenth-century New England households. Edward Hitchcock, the president of Amherst Academy, labeled much modern poetry "disastrous to religion," all the more insidious when the "poison" was "so interwoven with those fascinations of style, or thought, characteristic of genius, as to be unnoticed by the youthful mind, delighted with smartness and brilliancy." Dickinson's youthful mind, which delighted in smartness and brilliancy, chose rebellion. Once settled back at home from Mt. Holyoke, Dickinson embarked on a lifelong course of reading books that might "joggle the Mind"—the effect her father feared would result from the books he bought her.

Of contemporary American writing Dickinson knew the poetry of Longfellow, Holmes, and Lowell. She identified wryly with Hawthorne's isolated, gnarled, idiosyncratic characters, such as Hepzibah in *The House of the Seven Gables*. Ralph Waldo Emerson was an enduring favorite and a palpable presence, although she did not go next door to meet him when he stayed at the Evergreens on a lecture tour in 1857. By the early 1860s she loved Thoreau, recognizing a kindred spirit in the independent, nature-loving man who delighted in being the village crank of Concord. She also read a host of lesser American fiction writers and poets as lowly as the authors of what Richard B. Sewall calls "the endless string of fugitive verses in the periodicals (the *Republican*, the *Hampshire and Franklin Express*, the *Atlantic, Harper's*, and *Scribner's*)."

Dickinson's deepest literary debts were to the Bible and to British writers, dead and living. Her knowledge of Shakespeare was minute and extremely personal, and she knew line by line works of other older British poets, notably Milton. A favorite recent poet was Keats, and her reading of her English contemporaries started early. She read the novels of Charles Dickens year by year, as they appeared, made his characters part of her circle of acquaintances, and used his characters for coded messages with Samuel Bowles, who had met Dickens. She knew Robert Browning's poems well, although he was most valuable to her as an adjunct to Elizabeth Barrett Browning. She knew Tennyson, including poems now seldom read, such as *Maud*. In her maturity, through national magazines she subscribed to and books she ordered from Boston, she had access to the best British literature of her time within weeks or months, usually, of its publication.

The English contemporaries who mattered most to her career were Elizabeth Barrett Browning and the Brontë sisters. Browning was immensely important as an example of a successful contemporary female poet. Indeed (to judge from No. 593), she seems to have awakened Dickinson to her vocation when she was still "a sombre Girl," and Dickinson revered her. For Dickinson the Brontë sisters (or the "Yorkshire girls," especially "gigantic Emily") became not merely admired authors but daily presences in her life. Judith Farr (1992) has shown that Dickinson modeled her own epistolary and poetic persona on aspects of the Brontës' life and writings, especially on Charlotte Brontë's small independent heroine Jane Eyre. Dickinson subsequently had yet another English model, George Eliot, whose novels and poems she read as they appeared, and after whose death she eagerly awaited an announced biography. In her growing seclusion Dickinson became as familiar with Eliot's fictional characters as she was with many of the inhabitants of Amherst; only Dickens filled her mind with as many fictional acquaintances as Eliot did. The scandalous George Sand was a powerful example, not merely as a woman but, after her death, as a "queen"—like herself, a queen of a literary realm. Emily Brontë was a dead English queen. Elizabeth Browning and George Eliot reigned as dual English queens of poetry and (primarily) prose. And Emily Dickinson reigned unchallenged (in her own knowledge) as the queen of American poetry; humorously, she declared that every day she tried out ways of behaving " 'If I should be a Queen tomorrow' " (No. 373).

Richard B. Sewall showed that in her twenties Dickinson worked out a modus vivendi by which she could be private and independent and at the same time a loving and dutiful daughter. In the Dickinson house, where there were servants to empty chamber pots, scrub floors, dig potatoes, and care for the horses, Dickinson's chores were limited to those that a female in delicate health could perform, household duties that were reverential as well as practical, such as bread making for a small and much loved household, canning preserves, keeping flowers in bloom all year in the conservatory, and doing the finer sewing. According to her sister, it also became accepted that in the distribution of family tasks what Dickinson had to do was "to think." Her thought often came in the form of terse, striking definitions or propositions, used and reused in letters and poems, which she frequently wrote down, as Sewall says, thriftily, "on odds and ends of paper, on the back of recipes, invitations, shopping lists, clippings"; a young cousin recalled Dickinson composing poetry in the pantry as she skimmed the milk.

Edward Dickinson's financial security meant Emily never needed a husband to support her and never needed to think of taking a job—schoolteaching or millwork—then open to a young woman. Betsy Erkkila, building on evidence assembled by Jay Leyda and Richard B. Sewall, in *Emily Dickinson and Class* (1992) argues: "Within the domestic economy of the Dickinson household, as in the larger political economy of nineteenth-century America, Dickinson was the 'lady' and the intellectual whose leisure, freedom, and space 'to think' were made possible by the manual labor and proletarianization of others." In Erkkila's reading, "Dickinson's poems assert the ultimate and real value of an interior, mental, and spiritual economy against the instability of the new marketplace economy of wages, prices, contracts, merchants, securities, stocks, and reversals." It was Dickinson's economic dependence on her father that gave her the freedom to become a great poet.

No one has persuasively traced the precise stages of Dickinson's growth from a conventional schoolgirl verisfier to one of the greatest American poets. It seems, however, that her originality emerged in music before it emerged in verse. Through voice and piano lessons, she became a musician good enough to improvise for her family, but often alone, playing softly after the rest of the family had retired. Going beyond improvising original melodies on the piano, she began to improvise poetry that was not merely of her own authorship but was genuinely original, in Emerson's sense of adorning the world with a new thing. From her twenties until her death Dickinson was free to devote much of her life to poetry, and by the late 1850s, when she had become a true poet, Sewall explains, Dickinson "lived increasingly in her own chosen country, where she was free. Her home was the setting, with a family that learned not to intrude. Her companions were her Lexicon; the things of nature; her books; her letters, which became increasingly the measure of her fulfilled relationships; but especially her poems, in which she explored the truth of her fulfillments and her unfulfillments—with nature, man, and God." In 1862 she could write, "All men say 'What' to me." She disconcerted people, delighting in her peculiarities that by then were manifested not only in musical improvisations and brilliant conversation but also in great poems.

Dickinson found poetic freedom within the confines of the hymn meter familiar to her from earliest childhood; within that familiar form she multiplied aural possibilities by what a later audience called "off" rhymes or "slant" rhymes. Her precise syntactical allocations, which would run across the end of the conventional stopping place of a line or a stanza break, forced her reader to learn where to pause to collect the sense before reading on. Her ostensible subject matter, like her form, was familiar, a fact T. W. Higginson exploited when he devised rubrics under which he and Mabel Todd would group Dickinson's poems in the first (1890) edition: Life, Love, Nature, Time, and Eternity. Dickinson's treatment of these conventional themes could be commonplace, but more often she brought dazzling originality to the tritest topic. Her Nature poems, for example, delight with sharp, precise observations, but they are infused with mingled ecstasy and pain: her intense joy in the arrival of spring is tempered with the acute pain of knowing that summers in western Massachusetts may end when August burns "low."

She seized on the familiar genre of the "occasional poem," a poem suggested by some event or experience, as her way of responding to the events of the day, including many passages she encountered in her reading. Hers was often occasional poetry in which the occasion was tacit, not explicit. Leyda first identified a "major device" of her poems and letters, what he called the "omitted center":

> The riddle, the circumstance too well known to be repeated to the initiate, the deliberate skirting of the obvious—this was the means she used to increase the privacy of her communication; it has also increased our problems in piercing that privacy. With so much real background detail coming constantly to light, her poems and letters take on unexpectedly deep roots in national and community life, in family crises, and in her daily reading. . . . To ignore this central concealment in the letters (as in the poems), stripping them of nearly all their associations, is to divorce Emily Dickinson from her real, tangible surroundings. To read her writings only as "timeless" is to lose even that timelessness that derives strength from the passing real moment. The allusions and quotations of her letters also exploit this game of the omitted center. . . . To force her reader to "hear between the lines" was a method that, if unrecognized, made her messages puzzling to some contemporaries.

In his juxtapositions of documents in the *Years and Hours of Emily Dickinson* Leyda helped identify many such "omitted centers," and Sewall has pursued Leyda's insight with elaborate evidence that Dickinson made her own poems the means of having conversations with her real-life acquaintances and with writers as remote from her as the Apostle Paul and John the Evangelist.

Letters, in particular three drafts of letters to her "Master," and many dozens of love poems have convinced biographers that Dickinson experienced a number of passionate relationships, one of which may have been with the friend who became her sister-in-law, one or more of the most intense of which may have been with men already married. There is mystery about how she met some of the men whom she is said to have loved, mystery about which of the men loved her in return, mystery about where and how often she met them. One of these relationships was with a man who published a few of her poems and (had he been perceptive enough) could have published many more, the electric, startlingly handsome, married Samuel Bowles, editor of the Springfield *Republican*, who may have had Dickinson in mind when he insolently complained about the way "women-writers" take criticism: "they receive the unvarnished truth as if it were a red-hot bullet." Another possible object of her affections is the Reverend Charles Wadsworth, whom she met in Philadelphia in 1855 and who visited her in Amherst in 1860 and 1880. As a minister in Philadelphia, and in San Francisco after 1862, he lived a public life as minister and as husband and father. The last man she is known to have loved was Judge Otis Phillips Lord, two decades older than she, a conservative Whig who had outlived his party (much like her own father and Melville's father-in-law Lemuel Shaw, the "Shaw" of No. 116).

Like any genius, Dickinson knew how good she was, as such a poem as No. 326 makes plain. For some years she wanted fiercely to be published—on her own terms. She sent many poems to Mr. and Mrs. Bowles, privately, but in tacit hope that Samuel Bowles would see that they appeared in the *Republican;* he did publish a few, after whipping them into more conventional shape. She also sent poems to Josiah Holland, who did not publish them in *Scribner's* when he could have and who did not push Bowles to publish more in the *Republican.*

When Higginson's *Letter to a Young Contributor* appeared in the April 1862 *Atlantic Monthly,* a compendium of practical advice on preparing and placing manuscripts in a competitive literary marketplace, she found in the essay the assurance that "every editor is always hungering and thirsting after novelties," eager for the privilege of "bringing forward a new genius." In another passage Higginson encouragingly exalted "the magnificent mystery of words" over a style merely conventionally smooth and accurate. Ignoring other passages (such as a stern warning against premature individualism and "mannerism"), she copied out a few of her poems—plainly to see if he would publish them.

In her letter to Higginson on April 15, 1862, her first sentence was a naked plea for recognition: "Are you too deeply occupied to say if my Verse is alive?" If it was alive, plainly, it deserved to be in print. Higginson was incapable of responding as she hoped, and in the face of his disapproval of her formal imperfections she defensively disguised her desire to become a published poet. Higginson looms large in any Dickinson biography not because he recognized her as a great poet in time to nourish and prolong her intense creative years but because Mabel Todd much later enlisted him as a front man, whose literary stature would guarantee that attention would be paid to the 1890 volume of Dickinson's poetry she had edited with minimal help from him.

After Higginson's disappointing response to her poems, Dickinson built up an armor against rejection, proclaiming contemptuously that publication was "the Auction / Of the Mind of Man" and that she would go to her maker undefiled by commerce. But knowing she was great and having longed for public recognition, she continued for the rest of her life to function (in her own eyes) on equal footing with her great Victorian contemporaries.

The second half of Dickinson's life was marked not only by a succession of deaths (such as she had experienced all her life) but by tragedy being enacted next door at the Evergreens. Charmed with Susan Gilbert, Dickinson had urged Austin to marry her friend, a mistake that damned her brother and haunted her and Lavinia. Dickinson's seclusion may have owed as much to her desire to distance herself from strains in the marriage next door as anything else. In 1881 David Todd arrived in Amherst as director of the Amherst College Observatory. His young wife, Mabel, was taken up by Sue Gilbert for a time, and the subsequent sexual liaison between Austin and Mabel lasted until Austin's death. In recent years the story of this affair has been detailed by one of those wounded by it (Millicent Todd Bingham) and by more objective historians, such as Sewall and Polly Longsworth. The affair had no discernable effect on Dickinson's literary life, for she was then writing little poetry. It had, however, consequences of the most momentous sort for her reputation.

Several months before her death in 1882, Mrs. Dickinson read some of her daughter's poetry to Mabel Todd, who found them "full of power." Soon Mabel Todd and Dickinson had established "a very pleasant friendship" without meeting

(Mabel Todd saw Dickinson once, in her coffin), and Mabel Todd had decided that even though her neighbor reminded her of Dickens's Miss Havisham in *Great Expectations*, this Amherst eccentric was "in many respects a genius." Without the poet's overtures (a glass of sherry, flowers, and poems) to the newcomer, Dickinson would not be in this or any other anthology. She might have been wholly forgotten had not young Mabel Todd (at Lavinia's instigation) painstakingly transcribed many of Dickinson's poems. The subsequent preservation and publication of Dickinson's poems and letters was initiated and carried forth by Mabel Todd, almost single handedly. She persuaded the ever-cautious Higginson to help her see a collection of poems into print in 1890 and a "second series" of poems in 1891; she published a third series in 1896, without Higginson's involvement. Sewall estimates that only about a tenth of the letters Dickinson wrote have survived, and only a thousandth of those written to her. Mabel Todd could do nothing about the destruction of letters to Dickinson, but through her editing and her popular lectures she performed small miracles in alerting people, in time, to the preservation of Dickinson's letters, the first edition of which she published in 1894. In the 1890s some critics reacted with superiority toward what they saw as verse that violated the laws of meter, but the public loved the poems at once. After Mabel Todd's labors, Dickinson's survival as a popular minor poet was never long in doubt; and through her efforts, the documentary materials were preserved on which literary scholars and critics could later crown her as one of the great American poets, another "gigantic Emily."

The texts of the poems are from Thomas H. Johnson's three-volume variorum edition, *The Poems of Emily Dickinson* (1955). The letters are from vol. 2 of *The Letters of Emily Dickinson*, edited by Thomas H. Johnson and Theodora Ward (1958).

## 49

I never lost as much but twice,
And that was in the sod.
Twice have I stood a beggar
Before the door of God!

Angels—twice descending                                      5
Reimbursed my store—
Burglar! Banker—Father!
I am poor once more!

c. 1858                                                                      1890

## 67

Success is counted sweetest
By those who ne'er succeed.
To comprehend a nectar
Requires sorest need.

Not one of all the purple Host                                 5
Who took the Flag today
Can tell the definition
So clear of Victory

As he defeated—dying—
On whose forbidden ear                                          10
The distant strains of triumph
Burst agonized and clear!

c. 1859                                                                    1878


## 130

These are the days when Birds come back—
A very few—a Bird or two—
To take a backward look.

These are the days when skies resume
The old—old sophistries[1] of June—                              5
A blue and gold mistake.

Oh fraud that cannot cheat the Bee—
Almost thy plausibility
Induces my belief.

Till ranks of seeds their witness bear—                          10
And softly thro' the altered air
Hurries a timid leaf.

Of Sacrament of summer days,
Oh Last Communion[2] in the Haze—
Permit a child to join.                                          15

Thy sacred emblems to partake—
Thy consecrated bread to take
And thine immortal wine!

c. 1859                                                                    1890


## 131

Besides the Autumn poets sing
A few prosaic days
A little this side of the snow
And that side of the Haze—

A few incisive Mornings—                                         5
A few Ascetic Eves—
Gone—Mr Bryant's "Golden Rod"—
And Mr Thomson's "sheaves."[1]

---

1. Deceptively subtle reasonings.
2. I.e., the death of nature in late fall is compared to
the death of Christ commemorated by the Christian
sacrament of Communion.

1. James Thomson (1700–1748), British poet, published *The Seasons* in four parts, the last of which was
*Autumn* (1730).

Still, is the bustle in the Brook—
Sealed are the spicy valves— 10
Mesmeric fingers softly touch
The Eyes of many Elves—

Perhaps a squirrel may remain—
My sentiments to share—
Grant me, Oh Lord, a sunny mind— 15
Thy windy will to bear!

c. 1859                                                          1891


185

"Faith" is a fine invention
When Gentlemen can *see*—
But *Microscopes* are prudent
In an Emergency.

c. 1860                                                          1891


214

I taste a liquor never brewed—
From Tankards scooped in Pearl—
Not all the Vats upon the Rhine
Yield such an Alcohol!

Inebriate of Air—am I— 5
And Debauchee of Dew—
Reeling—thro endless summer days—
From inns of Molten Blue—

When "Landlords" turn the drunken Bee
Out of the Foxglove's door— 10
When Butterflies—renounce their "drams"—
I shall but drink the more!

Till Seraphs[2] swing their snowy Hats—
And Saints—to windows run—
To see the little Tippler 15
Leaning against the—Sun—

c. 1860                                                          1861


216

Safe in their Alabaster[1] Chambers—
Untouched by Morning

2. Six-winged angels believed to guard God's throne.    1. Translucent, white chalky material.

And untouched by Noon—
Sleep the meek members of the Resurrection—
Rafter of satin,                                                         5
And Roof of stone.

Light laughs the breeze
In her Castle above them—
Babbles the Bee in a stolid Ear,
Pipe the Sweet Birds in ignorant cadence—                               10
Ah, what sagacity perished here!

version of 1859                                                       1862

Safe in their Alabaster Chambers—
Untouched by Morning—
And untouched by Noon—
Lie the meek members of the Resurrection—
Rafter of Satin—and Roof of Stone!                                       5

Grand go the Years—in the Crescent—above them—
Worlds scoop their Arcs—
And Firmaments—row—
Diadems—drop—and Doges²—surrender—
Soundless as dots—on a Disc of Snow—                                    10

version of 1861                                                       1890


241

I like a look of Agony,
Because I know it's true—
Men do not sham Convulsion,
Nor simulate, a Throe—

The Eyes glaze once—and that is Death—                                   5
Impossible to feign
The Beads upon the Forehead
By homely Anguish strung.

c. 1861                                                               1890


249

Wild Nights—Wild Nights!
Were I with thee
Wild Nights should be
Our luxury!

2. Chief magistrates in the republics of Venice and Genoa from the 11th through the 16th centuries.

Futile—the Winds—                                    5
To a Heart in port—
Done with the Compass—
Done with the Chart!

Rowing in Eden—
Ah, the Sea!                                         10
Might I but moor—Tonight—
In Thee!

c. 1861                                              1891


## 258

There's a certain Slant of light,
Winter Afternoons—
That oppresses, like the Heft
Of Cathedral Tunes—

Heavenly Hurt, it gives us—                          5
We can find no scar,
But internal difference,
Where the Meanings, are—

None may teach it—Any—
'Tis the Seal[1] Despair—                            10
An imperial affliction
Sent us of the Air—

When it comes, the Landscape listens—
Shadows—hold their breath—
When it goes, 'tis like the Distance                 15
On the look of Death—

c. 1861                                              1890


## 287

A Clock stopped—
Not the Mantel's—
Geneva's[2] farthest skill
Cant put the puppet bowing—
That just now dangled still—                          5

An awe came on the Trinket!
The Figures hunched, with pain—
Then quivered out of Decimals—
Into Degreeless Noon—

---

1. In the double sense of a device used to imprint an    2. A city in Switzerland, famous for its clockmakers.
official mark and an official sign of confirmation.

It will not stir for Doctor's—                    10
This Pendulum of snow—
The Shopman importunes it—
While cool—concernless No—

Nods from the Gilded pointers—
Nods from the Seconds slim—                    15
Decades of Arrogance between
The Dial life—
And Him—

c. 1861                                    1896


### 303

The Soul selects her own Society—
Then—shuts the Door—
To her divine Majority—
Present no more—

Unmoved—she notes the Chariots—pausing—        5
At her low Gate—
Unmoved—an Emperor be kneeling
Upon her Mat—

I've known her—from an ample nation—
Choose One—                                    10
Then—close the Valves of her attention—
Like Stone—

c. 1862                                    1890


### 305

The difference between Despair
And Fear—is like the One
Between the instant of a Wreck—
And when the Wreck has been—

The Mind is smooth—no Motion—                  5
Contented as the Eye
Upon the Forehead of a Bust—
That knows—it cannot see—

c. 1862                                    1914


### 328

A Bird came down the Walk—
He did not know I saw—

He bit an Angleworm in halves
And ate the fellow, raw,

And then he drank a Dew                    5
From a convenient Grass—
And then hopped sidewise to the Wall
To let a Beetle pass—

He glanced with rapid eyes
That hurried all around—                   10
They looked like frightened Beads, I thought—
He stirred his Velvet Head

Like one in danger, Cautious,
I offered him a Crumb
And he unrolled his feathers               15
And rowed him softer home—

Than Oars divide the Ocean,
Too silver for a seam—
Or Butterflies, off Banks of Noon
Leap, plashless[1] as they swim.           20

c. 1862                                    1891

### 341

After great pain, a formal feeling comes—
The Nerves sit ceremonious, like Tombs—
The stiff Heart questions was it He, that bore,
And Yesterday, or Centuries before?

The Feet, mechanical, go round—            5
Of Ground, or Air, or Ought—
A Wooden way
Regardless grown,
A Quartz contentment, like a stone—

This is the Hour of Lead—                  10
Remembered, if outlived,
As Freezing persons, recollect the Snow—
First—Chill—then Stupor—then the letting go—

c. 1862                                    1929

### 348

I dreaded that first Robin, so,
But He is mastered, now,

---

1. I.e., splashless.

I'm some accustomed to Him grown,
He hurts a little, though—

I thought if I could only live                    5
Till that first Shout got by—
Not all Pianos in the Woods
Had power to mangle me—

I dared not meet the Daffodils—
For fear their Yellow Gown                        10
Would pierce me with a fashion
So foreign to my own—

I wished the Grass would hurry—
So—when 'twas time to see—
He'd be too tall, the tallest one                 15
Could stretch—to look at me—

I could not bear the Bees should come,
I wished they'd stay away
In those dim countries where they go,
What word had they, for me?                       20

They're here, though; not a creature failed—
No Blossom stayed away
In gentle deference to me—
The Queen of Calvary[1]—

Each one salutes me, as he goes,                  25
And I, my childish Plumes,
Lift, in bereaved acknowledgement
Of their unthinking Drums—

c. 1862                                           1891


### 435

Much Madness is divinest Sense—
To a discerning Eye—
Much Sense—the starkest Madness—
'Tis the Majority
In this, as All, prevail—                         5
Assent—and you are sane—
Demur—you're straightway dangerous—
And handled with a Chain—

c. 1862                                           1890

---

1. I.e., one who has experienced intense suffering.

## 441

This is my letter to the World
That never wrote to Me—
The simple News that Nature told—
With tender Majesty

Her Message is committed                                    5
To Hands I cannot see—
For love of Her—Sweet—countrymen—
Judge tenderly—of Me

c. 1862                                                    1890


## 448

This was a Poet—It is That
Distills amazing sense
From ordinary Meanings—
And Attar[1] so immense

From the familiar species                                  5
That perished by the Door—
We wonder it was not Ourselves
Arrested it—before—

Of Pictures, the Discloser'—
That Poet—it is He—                                        10
Entitles Us—by Contrast—
To ceaseless Poverty—

Of Portion—so unconscious—
The Robbing—could not harm—
Himself—to Him—a Fortune—                                  15
Exterior—to Time—

c. 1862                                                    1929


## 449

I died for Beauty—but was scarce
Adjusted in the tomb
When One who died for Truth, was lain
In an adjoining Room—

He questioned softly "Why I failed"?                       5
"For Beauty", I replied—
"And I—for Truth—Themself are One—
We Bretheren, are", He said—

1. Perfume obtained from flowers.

And so, as Kinsmen, met a Night—
We talked between the Rooms—                              10
Until the Moss had reached our lips—
And covered up—our names—

c. 1862                                                  1890


## 465

I heard a Fly buzz—when I died—
The Stillness in the Room
Was like the Stillness in the Air—
Between the Heaves of Storm—

The Eyes around—had wrung them dry—                      5
And Breaths were gathering firm
For that last Onset—when the King
Be witnessed—in the Room—

I willed my Keepsakes—Signed away
What portion of me be                                    10
Assignable—and then it was
There interposed a Fly—

With Blue—uncertain stumbling Buzz—
Between the light—and me—
And then the Windows failed—and then                     15
I could not see to see—

c. 1862                                                  1896


## 501

This World is not Conclusion.
A Species stands beyond—
Invisible, as Music—
But positive, as Sound—
It beckons, and it baffles—                              5
Philosophy—dont know—
And through a Riddle, at the last—
Sagacity, must go—
To guess it, puzzles scholars—
To gain it, Men have borne                               10
Contempt of Generations
And Crucifixion, shown—
Faith slips—and laughs, and rallies—
Blushes, if any see—
Plucks at a twig of Evidence—                            15
And asks a Vane, the way—
Much Gesture, from the Pulpit—

Strong Hallelujahs roll—
Narcotics cannot still the Tooth
That nibbles at the soul—                                     20

c. 1862                                                       1896

### 510

It was not Death, for I stood up,
And all the Dead, lie down—
It was not Night, for all the Bells
Put out their Tongues, for Noon.

It was not Frost, for on my Flesh                             5
I felt Siroccos[1]—crawl—
Nor Fire—for just my Marble feet
Could keep a Chancel,[2] cool—

And yet, it tasted, like them all,
The Figures I have seen                                       10
Set orderly, for Burial,
Reminded me, of mine—

As if my life were shaven,
And fitted to a frame,
And could not breathe without a key,                          15
And 'twas like Midnight, some—

When everything that ticked—has stopped—
And Space stares all around—
Or Grisly frosts—first Autumn morns,
Repeal the Beating Ground—                                    20

But, most, like Chaos—Stopless—cool—
Without a Chance, or Spar—
Or even a Report of Land—
To justify—Despair.

c. 1862                                                       1891

### 528

Mine—by the Right of the White Election!
Mine—by the Royal Seal!
Mine—by the Sign in the Scarlet prison—
Bars—cannot conceal!

1. Hot, oppressive winds from North Africa.
2. The part of the church that contains the choir and
sanctuary.

Mine—here—in Vision—and in Veto!                    5
Mine—by the Grave's Repeal—
Titled—Confirmed—
Delirious Charter!
Mine—long as Ages steal!

c. 1862                                                    1890


### 547

I've seen a Dying Eye
Run round and round a Room—
In search of Something—as it seemed—
Then Cloudier become—
And then—obscure with Fog—                           5
And then—be soldered down
Without disclosing what it be
'Twere blessed to have seen—

c. 1862                                                    1890


### 585

I like to see it lap the Miles—
And lick the Valleys up—
And stop to feed itself at Tanks—
And then—prodigious step

Around a Pile of Mountains—                           5
And supercilious peer
In Shanties—by the sides of Roads—
And then a Quarry pare

To fit its Ribs
And crawl between                                     10
Complaining all the while
In horrid—hooting stanza—
Then chase itself down Hill—

And neigh like Boanerges[1]—
Then—punctual as a Star                               15
Stop—docile and omnipotent
At its own stable door—

c. 1862                                                    1891


1. "Sons of thunder" (Mark 3.17); originally applied to the zealous apostles John and James; by extension, any vociferous orator.

### 632

The Brain—is wider than the Sky—
For—put them side by side—
The one the other will contain
With ease—and You—beside—

The Brain is deeper than the sea—                    5
For—hold them—Blue to Blue—
The one the other will absorb—
As Sponges—Buckets—do—

The Brain is just the weight of God—
For—Heft them—Pound for Pound—                    10
And they will differ—if they do—
As Syllable from Sound—

c. 1862                                            1896

### 640

I cannot live with You—
It would be Life—
And Life is over there—
Behind the Shelf

The Sexton[1] keeps the Key to—                      5
Putting up
Our Life—His Porcelain—
Like a Cup—

Discarded of the Housewife—
Quaint—or Broke—                                    10
A newer Sevres[2] pleases—
Old Ones crack—

I could not die—with You—
For One must wait
To shut the Other's Gaze down—                       15
You—could not—

And I—Could I stand by
And see You—freeze—
Without my Right of Frost—
Death's privilege?                                   20

Nor could I rise—with You—
Because Your Face

---

1. Church officer or employee who is custodian of    2. Fine, often elaborately decorated French porcelain.
church property, bellringer, and gravedigger.

Would put out Jesus'—
That New Grace

Glow plain—and foreign                    25
On my homesick Eye—
Except that You than He
Shone closer by—

They'd judge Us—How—
For You—served Heaven—You know,      30
Or sought to—
I could not—

Because You saturated Sight—
And I had no more Eyes
For sordid excellence               35
As Paradise

And were You lost, I would be—
Though My Name
Rang loudest
On the Heavenly fame—           40

And were You—saved—
And I—condemned to be
Where You were not—
That self—were Hell to Me—

So We must meet apart—         45
You there—I—here—
With just the Door ajar
That Oceans are—and Prayer—
And that White Sustenance—
Despair—         50

c. 1862                                      1890

## 650

Pain—has an Element of Blank—
It cannot recollect
When it begun—or if there were
A time when it was not—

It has no Future—but itself—       5
It's Infinite contain
It's Past—enlightened to perceive
New Periods—of Pain.

c. 1862                                      1890

## 664

Of all the Souls that stand create—
I have elected—One—
When Sense from Spirit—files away—
And Subterfuge—is done—
When that which is—and that which was—                5
Apart—intrinsic—stand—
And this brief Tragedy of Flesh—
Is shifted—like a Sand—
When Figures show their royal Front—
And Mists—are carved away,                             10
Behold the Atom—I preferred—
To all the lists of Clay!

c. 1862                                                1891


## 709

Publication—is the Auction
Of the Mind of Man—
Poverty—be justifying
For so foul a thing

Possibly—but We—would rather                          5
From Our Garret go
White—Unto the White Creator—
Than invest—Our Snow—

Thought belong to Him who gave it—
Then—to Him Who bear                                  10
It's Corporeal illustration—Sell
The Royal Air—

In the Parcel—Be the Merchant
Of the Heavenly Grace—
But reduce no Human Spirit                            15
To Disgrace of Price—

c. 1863                                                1929


## 712

Because I could not stop for Death—
He kindly stopped for me—
The Carriage held but just Ourselves—
And Immortality.

We slowly drove—He knew no haste                      5
And I had put away

My labor and my leisure too,
For His Civility—

We passed the School, where Children strove
At Recess—in the Ring—                                                    10
We passed the Fields of Gazing Grain—
We passed the Setting Sun—

Or rather—He passed Us—
The Dews drew quivering and chill—
For only Gossamer, my Gown—                                               15
My Tippet[1]—only Tulle—

We paused before a House that seemed
A Swelling of the Ground—
The Roof was scarcely visible—
The Cornice—in the Ground—                                                20

Since then—'tis Centuries—and yet
Feels shorter than the Day
I first surmised the Horses Heads
Were toward Eternity—

c. 1863                                                                  1890


## 732

She rose to His Requirement—dropt
The Playthings of Her Life
To take the honorable Work
Of Woman, and of Wife—

If ought She missed in Her new Day,                                        5
Of Amplitude, or Awe—
Or first Prospective—Or the Gold
In using, wear away,

It lay unmentioned—as the Sea
Develope Pearl, and Weed,                                                  10
But only to Himself—be known
The Fathoms they abide—

c. 1863                                                                  1890


## 744

Remorse—is Memory—awake—
Her Parties all astir—

---

1. Shoulder cape.

A Presence of Departed Acts—
At window—and at Door—

It's Past—set down before the Soul     5
And lighted with a Match—
Perusal—to facilitate—
And help Belief to stretch—

Remorse is cureless—the Disease
Not even God—can heal—     10
For 'tis His institution—and
The Adequate of Hell—

c. 1863                                                1891

## 754

My Life had stood—a Loaded Gun—
In Corners—till a Day
The Owner passed—identified—
And carried Me away—

And now We roam in Sovreign Woods—     5
And now We hunt the Doe—
And every time I speak for Him—
The Mountains straight reply—

And do I smile, such cordial light
Upon the Valley glow—     10
It is as a Vesuvian[1] face
Had let it's pleasure through—

And when at Night—Our good Day done—
I guard My Master's Head—
'Tis better than the Eider-Duck's     15
Deep Pillow—to have shared—

To foe of His—I'm deadly foe—
None stir the second time—
On whom I lay a Yellow Eye—
Or an emphatic Thumb—     20

Though I than He—may longer live
He longer must—than I—
For I have but the power to kill,
Without—the power to die—

c. 1863                                                1929

1. A face capable of erupting like Mount Vesuvius.

## 822

This Consciousness that is aware
Of Neighbors and the Sun
Will be the one aware of Death
And that itself alone

Is traversing the interval                                    5
Experience between
And most profound experiment
Appointed unto Men—

How adequate unto itself
It's properties shall be                                      10
Itself unto itself and none
Shall make discovery.

Adventure most unto itself
The Soul condemned to be—
Attended by a single Hound                                    15
It's own identity.

c. 1864                                                     1945


## 986

A narrow Fellow in the Grass
Occasionally rides—
You may have met Him—did you not
His notice sudden is—

The Grass divides as with a Comb—                             5
A spotted shaft is seen—
And then it closes at your feet
And opens further on—

He likes a Boggy Acre
A Floor too cool for Corn—                                    10
Yet when a Boy, and Barefoot—
I more than once at Noon
Have passed, I thought, a Whip lash
Unbraiding in the Sun
When stooping to secure it                                    15
It wrinkled, and was gone—

Several of Nature's People
I know, and they know me—
I feel for them a transport
Of cordiality—                                                20

But never met this Fellow
Attended, or alone

Without a tighter breathing
And Zero at the Bone—

c. 1865                                                    1866


### 1068

Further in Summer than the Birds
Pathetic from the Grass
A minor Nation celebrates
It's unobtrusive Mass.

No Ordinance be seen                                      5
So gradual the Grace
A pensive Custom it becomes
Enlarging Loneliness.

Antiquest felt at Noon
When August burning low                                  10
Arise this spectral Canticle
Repose to typify

Remit as yet no Grace
No Furrow on the Glow
Yet a Druidic Difference                                 15
Enhances Nature now

c. 1866                                                  1891


### 1072

Title divine—is mine!
The Wife—without the Sign!
Acute Degree—conferred on me—
Empress of Calvary!
Royal—all but the Crown!                                 5
Betrothed—without the swoon
God sends us Women—
When you—hold—Garnet to Garnet—
Gold—to Gold—
Born—Bridalled—Shrouded—                                10
In a Day—
Tri Victory
"My Husband"—women say—
Stroking the Melody—
Is *this*—the way?                                       15

c. 1862                                                  1924

## 1078

The Bustle in a House
The Morning after Death
Is solemnest of industries
Enacted upon Earth—

The Sweeping up the Heart                                    5
And putting Love away
We shall not want to use again
Until Eternity.

c. 1866                                                                    1890

## 1125

Oh Sumptuous moment
Slower go
That I may gloat on thee—
'Twill never be the same to starve
Now I abundance see—                                        5

Which was to famish, then or now—
The difference of Day
Ask him unto the Gallows led—
With morning in the sky

c. 1868                                                                    1945

## 1129

Tell all the Truth but tell it slant—
Success in Circuit lies
Too bright for our infirm Delight
The Truth's superb surprise
As Lightning to the Children eased                          5
With explanation kind
The Truth must dazzle gradually
Or every man be blind—

c. 1868                                                                    1945

## 1463

A Route of Evanescence
With a revolving Wheel—
A Resonance of Emerald—
A Rush of Cochineal¹—

1. Red dye.

And every Blossom on the Bush                    5
Adjusts it's tumbled Head—
The mail from Tunis,[2] probably,
An easy Morning's Ride—

c. 1879                                                        1891


## 1540

As imperceptibly as Grief
The Summer lapsed away—
Too imperceptible at last
To seem like Perfidy—

A Quietness distilled                             5
As Twilight long begun,
Or Nature spending with herself
Sequestered Afternoon—
The Dusk drew earlier in—
The Morning foreign shone—                       10
A courteous, yet harrowing Grace,
As Guest, that would be gone—
And thus, without a Wing
Or service of a Keel
Our Summer made her light escape                 15
Into the Beautiful.

c. 1865                                                        1891


## 1624

Apparently with no surprise
To any happy Flower
The Frost beheads it at it's play—
In accidental power—
The blonde Assassin passes on—                   5
The Sun proceeds unmoved
To measure off another Day
For an Approving God.

c. 1884                                                        1890


## 1651

A Word made Flesh is seldom
And tremblingly partook
Nor then perhaps reported
But have I not mistook

2. City on the northern coast of Africa.

Each one of us has tasted                              5
With ecstasies of stealth
The very food debated
To our specific strength—

A Word that breathes distinctly
Has not the power to die                               10
Cohesive as the Spirit
It may expire if He—
"Made Flesh and dwelt among us"[1]
Could condescension be
Like this consent of Language                          15
This loved Philology[2]

No Ms.                                                 1955


1670

In Winter in my Room
I came upon a Worm—
Pink, lank and warm—
But as he was a worm
And worms presume                                      5
Not quite with him at home—
Secured him by a string
To something neighboring
And went along.

A Trifle afterward                                     10
A thing occurred
I'd not believe it if I heard
But state with creeping blood—
A snake with mottles rare
Surveyed my chamber floor                              15
In feature as the worm before
But ringed with power—
The very string with which
I tied him—too
When he was mean and new                               20
That string was there—

I shrank—"How fair you are"!
Propitiation's claw—
"Afraid," he hissed
"Of me"?                                               25
"No cordiality"—
He fathomed me—

1. John 1.14.
2. I.e., literature and the disciplines that concern
themselves with words.

Then to a Rhythm *Slim*
Secreted in his Form
As Patterns swim                                         30
Projected him.

That time I flew
Both eyes his way
Lest he pursue
Nor ever ceased to run                                   35
Till in a distant Town
Towns on from mine
I set me down
This was a dream.

No Ms.                                                   1914


### 1732

My life closed twice before its close;
It yet remains to see
If Immortality unveil
A third event to me,

So huge, so hopeless to conceive                          5
As these that twice befel.
Parting is all we know of heaven,
And all we need of hell.

No Ms.                                                   1896


## Letters to Thomas Wentworth Higginson[1]

### [*Say If My Verse Is Alive?*]

15 April 1862

Mr higginson,
  Are you too deeply occupied to say if my Verse is alive?
  The Mind is so near itself—it cannot see, distinctly—and I have none to
ask—
  Should you think it breathed—and had you the leisure to tell me, I should
feel quick gratitude—
  If I make the mistake—that you dared to tell me—would give me sincerer
honor—toward you—

1. Thomas Wentworth Higginson had recently resigned his radically liberal church pastorate and was
beginning to make a name as a reform-minded essayist
and lecturer. Higginson's *Letter to a Young Contributor,* offering practical advice to beginning writers, was
published in the April *Atlantic Monthly.* This letter,
responding to that article, was accompanied by several
poems and marked the beginning of a correspondence—and a remarkable relationship—that lasted for
the rest of Dickinson's life. It should be noted that Higginson from the first was sensitive to the curious, original power of her poetry, but as a rather conventional
19th-century critic he found no way to judge its unorthodox formal qualities. For her part, Dickinson was
content to assume the ironic role of "scholar" to this
"Preceptor," content with his friendship and her own
"Barefoot-Rank."

I enclose my name—asking you, if you please—Sir—to tell me what is true? That you will not betray me—it is needless to ask—since Honor is it's own pawn[2]—

## [My Business Is Circumference]

July 1862

Could you believe me—without? I had no portrait, now, but am small, like the Wren, and my Hair is bold, like the Chestnut Bur—and my eyes, like the Sherry in the Glass, that the Guest leaves—Would this do just as well?

It often alarms Father—He says Death might occur, and he has Molds[3] of all the rest—but has no Mold of me, but I noticed the Quick wore off those things, in a few days, and forestall the dishonor—You will think no caprice of me—

You said "Dark." I know the Butterfly—and the Lizard—and the Orchis[4]— Are not those *your* Countrymen?

I am happy to be your scholar, and will deserve the kindness, I cannot repay.

If you truly consent, I recite, now—

Will you tell me my fault, frankly as to yourself, for I had rather wince, than die. Men do not call the surgeon, to commend—the Bone, but to set it, Sir, and fracture within, is more critical. And for this, Preceptor, I shall bring you—Obedience—the Blossom from my Garden, and every gratitude I know. Perhaps you smile at me. I could not stop for that—My Business is Circumference[5]—An ignorance, not of Customs, but if caught with the Dawn—or the Sunset see me—Myself the only Kangaroo among the Beauty, Sir, if you please, it afflicts me, and I thought that instruction would take it away.

Because you have much business, beside the growth of me—you will appoint, yourself, how often I shall come—without your inconvenience. And if at any time—you regret you received me, or I prove a different fabric to that you supposed—you must banish me—

When I state myself, as the Representative of the Verse—it does not mean— me—but a supposed person. You are true, about the "perfection."

Today, makes Yesterday mean.

You spoke of Pippa Passes[6]—I never heard anybody speak of Pippa Passes—before.

You see my posture is benighted.

To thank you, baffles me. Are you perfectly powerful? Had I a pleasure you had not, I could delight to bring it.

Your Scholar

2. In place of a signature, Emily Dickinson enclosed a signed card in its own envelope.
3. I.e., photographs or likenesses.
4. A small purplish or white orchid. Higginson wrote many nature essays with which she was familiar.
5. One of the crucial words in Dickinson's vocabulary; Johnson defines it as "a projection of her imagination into all relationships of man, nature, and spirit."
6. A dramatic poem by Robert Browning published in 1841.

# REBECCA HARDING DAVIS

## 1831–1910

Rebecca Harding was born in 1831 in Washington, Pennsylvania, her mother's hometown, then taken to Big Springs, Alabama, where her father, a book-loving English emigrant, was in business. Her earliest memories were of the Deep South, a landscape of tropical heat and beauty and a frontier society with extremes of wealth and poverty even among whites and based, for inextricable complications, on black slavery. As her recollections show, she learned in Alabama to see for herself, if not yet to think for herself. In 1836 her father moved the family to Wheeling, Virginia, still a jumping-off place for the West as well as a prosperous manufacturing center, in that anomalous fingerlike part of a slave state that reached far north between the free states of Ohio and Pennsylvania, a location fitted for the nurture of independent observation and judgment. Bookish like her father, Rebecca Harding at fourteen went to live with an aunt at her birthplace, across the Pennsylvania line to the east, to attend the female seminary. Back in Wheeling, alert in her young maturity to abolitionist agitation yet part of the slave society, she passed into what her era considered spinsterhood and was a serious-minded observer of the manners, morals, and machinations of people and a reticent and dutiful daughter, yet a woman of forthrightly independent views. She continued reading (we know she read John Bunyan, Sir Walter Scott, and Maria Edgeworth, and a few Hawthorne stories in a collection of *Moral Tales* affected her strongly). By her late twenties she had read English reform novels such as those by Charles Kingsley and Elizabeth Gaskell and had begun to publish anonymous reviews of new books in local papers. During the election year 1860, her mind more on the misery of the local mill workers than on the misery of slaves, she wrote *Life in the Iron-Mills*, apparently the first story she completed, and sent it to the *Atlantic Monthly*, the most prestigious magazine in the country, then under the editorship of James Fields.

As editor of the *Atlantic* James Russell Lowell had censored Thoreau and Whitman, and Fields himself was to censor Hawthorne's portrait of Lincoln (printed in this volume), but he recognized salable power in the new contributor and made no effort to alter the story, other than to suggest a more "taking" title (Harding's suggestions of *Beyond* or *The Korl-Woman* were not deemed "taking" enough either). The story was published (anonymously, by custom and by Harding's request) the month the Civil War broke out and Wheeling became capital of the new free state of West Virginia. The story's strength was recognized by many readers (Emily Dickinson among them), and with the author's name an open secret, Fields hoped to gain her as a regular contributor. Both he and his wife pressed her to come to Boston. She could not come at once because she was held by family duties and by the turmoil of a divided and embattled society, but she began a serial in the October 1861 *Atlantic—A Story of To-day*. It contained, in one of the character's words, not "a bit of hell" but "only a glimpse of the under-life of America." In her voice as narrator Harding offered a manifesto of realism before there was a literary movement so identified: "You want something . . . to lift you out of this crowded, tobacco-stained commonplace, to kindle and chafe and glow in you. I want you to dig into this commonplace, this vulgar American life, and see what is in it. Sometimes I think it has a raw and awful significance that we do not see." This work, which Fields published in book form as *Margret Howth* (1862), did not have the sustained power of her first story, yet much was expected of her, and when she made her pilgrimage to Boston in 1862 she was welcomed by the New England literary establishment. She delighted in Holmes and treasured her reception by Hawthorne. The more visionary Concordites like Bronson Alcott she regarded with a mixture of suspicion and disdain, and it was clear to her at once that Emerson had no notion at all of what war was like, however penetrating his insight might be once he paid attention to her or anyone else. Having formed a close friendship with Annie Fields, her hostess, and having made her presence felt (she astonished one group by the pronouncement that women had sexual desires), she had the chance to join the *Atlantic* circle (whom she called the Areopagites, from the Athenian hill where the high court had sat). Had she done so, she might have matured as a writer under the guidance of Holmes and others who were intensely interested in what she had to say, for her strong social criticisms were welcomed, not repelled.

Instead, she took the role of hack writer. Soon after the appearance of her first story, she had received a fan letter from an apprentice lawyer in Philadelphia, L. Clarke Davis, four years her junior, a man literary enough himself to have a connection with *Peterson's Magazine* and persuasive enough to interest her in meeting him. Before going to Boston she had arranged a stopover in Philadelphia on her way home; once they had met they soon decided to marry, and Davis persuaded her to contribute potboilers to *Peterson's*, though she was pledged to write only for the *Atlantic*. In her first years of marriage and even after her three children were born she continued her career as a magazine writer, creating an extensive body of hack work and a sizable body of more ambitious but flawed work. In the most massive as well as most ambitious of her later novels, *Waiting for the Verdict* (1868), as the sympathetic critic Tillie Olsen says, Harding posed "the basic question of the time": how was the nation going to redress the wrong of slavery, once the slaves were freed? In Olsen's words, Harding had conceived a great novel but "had failed to write it; had not given (had) the self and time (or always the knowledge) to write it."

Living out her life in Philadelphia, she never became fully a part of the local cultural establishment, but she was friendly not only with other writers but also (through her husband) with many actors, including the great theatrical families of the time such as the Drews and Barrymores. Long before her death in 1910 she was overshadowed first by the success of her husband as an editor and then by the astonishing success of her son, Richard Harding Davis. In 1890 she warned him about his "beginning to do hack work for money": "It is the beginning of decadence both in work and reputation for you. I know by my own and a thousand other people." Her son became the best-paid, most glamorous journalist and one of the most popular short-story writers of his generation, a celebrity as his mother had never been, but never the writer she had been.

Her first story was never forgotten, at least by a few readers and by literary historians, although the latter were sometimes uneasy about it. Fred Lewis Pattee in a chapter on the story in *The Cambridge History of American Literature* (1918) quoted the opening of that "grim" story and observed that the decades of the 1850s and 1860s "in America stand for the dawning of definiteness, of localized reality, of a feeling left on the reader of actuality and truth to human life." In *Literary History of the United States* (1948), Gordon S. Haight was disdainful: "In her effort to rouse pity in the manner of Dickens, Mrs. Stowe, and [Charles] Kingsley, Mrs. Davis violates her own rule of the commonplace. Few mill workers are hunchbacks, and except in a reformer's tract no consumptive could long be an iron puddler." In *Literature of the American People* (1951) Clarence Gohdes gave grudging praise: the story "is indeed a grim picture, and it has made its way into the anthologies as a specimen of realism of the times." In 1961 Gerald Langford was nearer the mark in calling the story "one of the revolutionary documents in American writing, although it came so prematurely that it was almost forgotten by the time the revolution in fiction caught up with it." He also speculated about the extent to which Harding anticipated the "theory and practice" of a later editor of the *Atlantic*, William Dean Howells. Davis's great story did indeed enter some anthologies, but not many, and Olsen, who edited the story for the Feminist Press with "A Biographical Interpretation," deserves credit for making it impossible again to ignore or to slight the story, the strongest criticism of American society that had been published since *Uncle Tom's Cabin*, an indictment of the exploitation of American free labor more concentrated in its power than the already classic indictment of slavery, the most sustained exposé in our literature between Stowe and the muckrakers.

Harding's story had no such repercussions on life in the iron mills as Stowe's book had had on freeing the slaves, and its effects on American literary realism are not fully established; ironically, later writers on working conditions in American factories—Thomas Bailey Aldrich (another editor of the *Atlantic*) in *The Stillwater Tragedy* (1880) and John Hay in the anonymous *The Bread-Winners* (1884)—sided with property rights rather than workers' rights, as Mary E. Wilkins (more ambivalently) did in *The Portion of Labor* (1901). The historical importance of *Life in the Iron-Mills* is partly as a record of the underside of American industrial prosperity, partly in what study of it and the rest of Davis's life and career can reveal about being both a writer and a woman in America. What finally counts is that the story affords one of the most overwhelming reading experiences in all American literature.

# Life in the Iron-Mills[1]

"Is this the end?
O Life, as futile, then, as frail!
What hope of answer or redress?"[2]

A cloudy day: do you know what that is in a town of iron-works?[3] The sky sank down before dawn, muddy, flat, immovable. The air is thick, clammy with the breath of crowded human beings. It stifles me. I open the window, and, looking out, can scarcely see through the rain the grocer's shop opposite, where a crowd of drunken Irishmen are puffing Lynchburg tobacco[4] in their pipes. I can detect the scent through all the foul smells ranging loose in the air.

The idiosyncrasy of this town is smoke. It rolls sullenly in slow folds from the great chimneys of the iron-foundries, and settles down in black, slimy pools on the muddy streets. Smoke on the wharves, smoke on the dingy boats, on the yellow river,—clinging in a coating of greasy soot to the house-front, the two faded poplars, the faces of the passers-by. The long train of mules, dragging masses of pig-iron[5] through the narrow street, have a foul vapor hanging to their reeking sides. Here, inside, is a little broken figure of an angel pointing upward from the mantel-shelf; but even its wings are covered with smoke, clotted and black. Smoke everywhere! A dirty canary chirps desolately in a cage beside me. Its dream of green fields and sunshine is a very old dream,—almost worn out, I think.

1. The text is that of the first printing in the *Atlantic Monthly*, 7 (April 1861).
2. Adapted from Alfred, Lord Tennyson's *In Memoriam A. H. H.* (1850), 12.4: " 'Is this the end of all my care?' . . . 'Is this the end? Is this the end?' " and from 56.7: "O Life, as futile, then, as frail! / O for thy voice to soothe and bless! / What hope of answer, or redress? / Behind the veil, behind the veil." In 13 the poet compares himself to a dove who springs up "To bear thro' Heaven a tale of woe / Some dolorous message knit be-

low." Through the epigraph (from this then-recent and enormously popular poem) Harding suggests that her own message is equally "dolorous."
3. The town is not named, but in its topography and other characteristics it is based on Harding's home-town, Wheeling, Virginia, on the banks of the Ohio River.
4. An inferior tobacco from south-central Virginia.
5. Oblong blocks of iron, hardened after being poured from a smelting furnace.

From the back-window I can see a narrow brick-yard sloping down to the river-side, strewed with rain-butts and tubs. The river, dull and tawny-colored, (*la belle rivière!*)[6] drags itself sluggishly along, tired of the heavy weight of boats and coal-barges. What wonder? When I was a child, I used to fancy a look of weary, dumb appeal upon the face of the negro-like river slavishly bearing its burden day after day. Something of the same idle notion comes to me to-day, when from the street-window I look on the slow stream of human life creeping past, night and morning, to the great mills. Masses of men, with dull, besotted faces bent to the ground, sharpened here and there by pain or cunning; skin and muscle and flesh begrimed with smoke and ashes; stooping all night over boiling caldrons of metal, laired by day in dens of drunkenness and infamy; breathing from infancy to death an air saturated with fog and grease and soot, vileness for soul and body. What do you make of a case like that, amateur psychologist? You call it an altogether serious thing to be alive: to these men it is a drunken jest, a joke,—horrible to angels perhaps, to them commonplace enough. My fancy about the river was an idle one: it is no type of such a life. What if it be stagnant and slimy here? It knows that beyond there waits for it odorous sunlight,—quaint old gardens, dusky with soft, green foliage of apple-trees, and flushing crimson with roses,—air, and fields, and mountains. The future of the Welsh puddler[7] passing just now is not so pleasant. To be stowed away, after his grimy work is done, in a hole in the muddy graveyard, and after that,——*not* air, nor green fields, nor curious roses.

Can you see how foggy the day is? As I stand here, idly tapping the window-pane, and looking out through the rain at the dirty back-yard and the coal-boats below, fragments of an old story float up before me,—a story of this house into which I happened to come to-day. You may think it a tiresome story enough, as foggy as the day, sharpened by no sudden flashes of pain or pleasure.—I know: only the outline of a dull life, that long since, with thou-sands of dull lives like its own, was vainly lived and lost: thousands of them,— massed, vile, slimy lives, like those of the torpid lizards in yonder stagnant water-butt.—Lost? There is a curious point for you to settle, my friend, who study psychology in a lazy, *dilettante* way. Stop a moment. I am going to be honest. This is what I want you to do. I want you to hide your disgust, take no heed to your clean clothes, and come right down with me,—here, into the thickest of the fog and mud and foul effluvia. I want you to hear this story. There is a secret down here, in this nightmare fog, that has lain dumb for centuries: I want to make it a real thing to you. You, Egoist, or Pantheist, or Arminian,[8] busy in making straight paths for your feet on the hills, do not see it clearly,—this terrible question which men here have gone mad and died trying to answer. I dare not put this secret into words. I told you it was dumb. These men, going by with drunken faces and brains full of unawakened power, do not ask it of Society or of God. Their lives ask it; their deaths ask it. There is no reply. I will tell you plainly that I have a great hope; and I bring it to you

6. The beautiful river (French); the phrase ironically recalls the purity of the Ohio when the French fur traders first saw it. "Rain-butts": large casks, around three or four barrels in capacity, used to catch rainwater for household and, here, industrial use.
7. Worker who stirs iron oxide into a molten vat of pig iron in order to make wrought iron or steel.
8. One who follows the teachings of Jacobus Arminius (1560–1607), Dutch theologian who opposed the Cal-

vinistic doctrine of absolute predestination. "Egoist": one devoted to his or her own interests and advance-ment, acting only according to self-interest. "Panthe-ist": one who identifies the deity with nature. The story is saturated with biblical language, as in the echo here of Hebrews 12.13: "And make straight paths for your feet, lest that which is lame be turned out of the way; but let it rather be healed."

to be tested. It is this: that this terrible dumb question is its own reply; that it is not the sentence of death we think it, but, from the very extremity of its darkness, the most solemn prophecy which the world has known of the Hope to come. I dare make my meaning no clearer, but will only tell my story. It will, perhaps, seem to you as foul and dark as this thick vapor about us, and as pregnant with death; but if your eyes are free as mine are to look deeper, no perfume-tinted dawn will be so fair with promise of the day that shall surely come.

My story is very simple,—only what I remember of the life of one of these men,—a furnace-tender in one of Kirby & John's rolling-mills,—Hugh Wolfe. You know the mills? They took the great order for the lower Virginia railroads there last winter; run usually with about a thousand men. I cannot tell why I choose the half-forgotten story of this Wolfe more than that of myriads of these furnace-hands. Perhaps because there is a secret, underlying sympathy between that story and this day with its impure fog and thwarted sunshine,—or perhaps simply for the reason that this house is the one where the Wolfes lived. There were the father and son,—both hands, as I said, in one of Kirby & John's mills for making railroad-iron,—and Deborah, their cousin, a picker[9] in some of the cotton-mills. The house was rented then to half a dozen families. The Wolfes had two of the cellar-rooms. The old man, like many of the puddlers and feeders[1] of the mills, was Welsh,—had spent half of his life in the Cornish tin-mines. You may pick the Welsh emigrants, Cornish miners, out of the throng passing the windows, any day. They are a trifle more filthy; their muscles are not so brawny; they stoop more. When they are drunk, they neither yell, nor shout, nor stagger, but skulk along like beaten hounds. A pure, unmixed blood, I fancy: shows itself in the slight angular bodies and sharply-cut facial lines. It is nearly thirty years since the Wolfes lived here. Their lives were like those of their class: incessant labor, sleeping in kennel-like rooms, eating rank pork and molasses, drinking—God and the distillers only know what; with an occasional night in jail, to atone for some drunken excess. Is that all of their lives?—of the portion given to them and these their duplicates swarming the streets to-day?—nothing beneath?—all? So many a political reformer will tell you,—and many a private reformer, too, who has gone among them with a heart tender with Christ's charity, and come out outraged, hardened.

One rainy night, about eleven o'clock, a crowd of half-clothed women stopped outside of the cellar-door. They were going home from the cotton-mill.

"Good-night, Deb," said one, a mulatto, steadying herself against the gas-post. She needed the post to steady her. So did more than one of them.

"Dah's a ball to Miss Potts' to-night. Ye'd best come."

"Inteet, Deb, if hur'll come, hur'll hef fun," said a shrill Welsh voice in the crowd.

Two or three dirty hands were thrust out to catch the gown of the woman, who was groping for the latch of the door.

"No."

<hr />

9. Worker in a cotton mill who operates the machine that pulls apart and separates cotton fibers; less often used to mean the one who throws the shuttle of a loom to put in the weft thread of a fabric. The men work for low wages in the iron mills; the women work for lower wages in the cotton mills.

1. Worker who feeds molten metal into the casting form while the iron is hardening and contracting (the purpose is to prevent the formation of air bubbles, which weaken the iron).

"No? Where 's Kit Small, then?"

"Begorra! on the spools.[2] Alleys behint, though we helped her, we dud. An wid ye! Let Deb alone! It's ondacent frettin' a quite body. Be the powers, an' we'll have a night of it! there'll be lashin's o' drink,—the Vargent[3] be blessed and praised for 't!"

They went on, the mulatto inclining for a moment to show fight, and drag the woman Wolfe off with them; but, being pacified, she staggered away.

Deborah groped her way into the cellar, and, after considerable stumbling, kindled a match, and lighted a tallow dip, that sent a yellow glimmer over the room. It was low, damp,—the earthen floor covered with a green, slimy moss,—a fetid air smothering the breath. Old Wolfe lay asleep on a heap of straw, wrapped in a torn horse-blanket. He was a pale, meek little man, with a white face and red rabbit-eyes. The woman Deborah was like him; only her face was even more ghastly, her lips bluer, her eyes more watery. She wore a faded cotton gown and a slouching bonnet. When she walked, one could see that she was deformed, almost a hunchback. She trod softly, so as not to waken him, and went through into the room beyond. There she found by the half-extinguished fire an iron saucepan filled with cold boiled potatoes, which she put upon a broken chair with a pint-cup of ale. Placing the old candlestick beside this dainty repast, she untied her bonnet, which hung limp and wet over her face, and prepared to eat her supper. It was the first food that had touched her lips since morning. There was enough of it, however: there is not always. She was hungry,—one could see that easily enough,—and not drunk, as most of her companions would have been found at this hour. She did not drink, this woman,—her face told that, too,—nothing stronger than ale. Perhaps the weak, flaccid wretch had some stimulant in her pale life to keep her up,—some love or hope, it might be, or urgent need. When that stimulant was gone, she would take to whiskey. Man cannot live by work alone. While she was skinning the potatoes, and munching them, a noise behind her made her stop.

"Janey!" she called, lifting the candle and peering into the darkness. "Janey, are you there?"

A heap of ragged coats was heaved up, and the face of a young girl emerged, staring sleepily at the woman.

"Deborah," she said, at last, "I'm here the night."

"Yes, child. Hur's welcome," she said, quietly eating on.

The girl's face was haggard and sickly; her eyes were heavy with sleep and hunger: real Milesian[4] eyes they were, dark, delicate blue, glooming out from black shadows with a pitiful fright.

"I was alone," she said, timidly.

"Where's the father?" asked Deborah, holding out a potato, which the girl greedily seized.

"He's beyant,—wid Haley,—in the stone house." (Did you ever hear the word *jail* from an Irish mouth?) "I came here. Hugh told me never to stay me-lone."

"Hugh?"

"Yes."

---

2. Spindles in the cotton mill on which the cotton is stretched and wound by the spinning machine. "Begorra!": a milder form of "By God!"

3. The Virgin Mary.

4. Irish.

A vexed frown crossed her face. The girl saw it, and added quickly,—
"I have not seen Hugh the day, Deb. The old man says his watch[5] lasts till the mornin'."

The woman sprang up, and hastily began to arrange some bread and flitch[6] in a tin pail, and to pour her own measure of ale into a bottle. Tying on her bonnet, she blew out the candle.

"Lay ye down, Janey dear," she said, gently, covering her with the old rags. "Hur can eat the potatoes, if hur's hungry."

"Where are ye goin', Deb? The rain's sharp."

"To the mill, with Hugh's supper."

"Let him bide till th' morn. Sit ye down."

"No, no,"—sharply pushing her off. "The boy'll starve."

She hurried from the cellar, while the child wearily coiled herself up for sleep. The rain was falling heavily, as the woman, pail in hand, emerged from the mouth of the alley, and turned down the narrow street, that stretched out, long and black, miles before her. Here and there a flicker of gas lighted an uncertain space of muddy footwalk and gutter; the long rows of houses, except an occasional lager-bier shop, were closed; now and then she met a band of millhands skulking to or from their work.

Not many even of the inhabitants of a manufacturing town know the vast machinery of system by which the bodies of workmen are governed, that goes on unceasingly from year to year. The hands of each mill are divided into watches that relieve each other as regularly as the sentinels of an army. By night and day the work goes on, the unsleeping engines groan and shriek, the fiery pools of metal boil and surge. Only for a day in the week, in half-courtesy to public censure, the fires are partially veiled; but as soon as the clock strikes midnight, the great furnaces break forth with renewed fury, the clamor begins with fresh, breathless vigor, the engines sob and shriek like "gods in pain."

As Deborah hurried down through the heavy rain, the noise of these thousand engines sounded through the sleep and shadow of the city like far-off thunder. The mill to which she was going lay on the river, a mile below the city-limits. It was far, and she was weak, aching from standing twelve hours at the spools. Yet it was her almost nightly walk to take this man his supper, though at every square she sat down to rest, and she knew she should receive small word of thanks.

Perhaps, if she had possessed an artist's eye, the picturesque oddity of the scene might have made her step stagger less, and the path seem shorter; but to her the mills were only "summat deilish[7] to look at by night."

The road leading to the mills had been quarried from the solid rock, which rose abrupt and bare on one side of the cinder-covered road, while the river, sluggish and black, crept past on the other. The mills for rolling[8] iron are simply immense tent-like roofs, covering acres of ground, open on every side. Beneath these roofs Deborah looked in on a city of fires, that burned hot and fiercely in the night. Fire in every horrible form: pits of flame waving in the wind; liquid metal-flames writhing in tortuous streams through the sand; wide caldrons filled with boiling fire, over which bent ghastly wretches stirring the strange brewing; and through all, crowds of half-clad men, looking like

5. Trick, work shift.
6. A rank form of salt pork.
7. Devilish.

8. Mill for flattening ingots into shapes, in this case rails for the expanding railroad system.

revengeful ghosts in the red light, hurried, throwing masses of glittering fire. It was like a street in Hell. Even Deborah muttered, as she crept through, " 'T looks like t' Devil's place!" It did,—in more ways than one.

She found the man she was looking for, at last, heaping coal on a furnace. He had not time to eat his supper; so she went behind the furnace,[9] and waited. Only a few men were with him, and they noticed her only by a "Hyur comes t' hunchback, Wolfe."

Deborah was stupid with sleep; her back pained her sharply; and her teeth chattered with cold, with the rain that soaked her clothes and dripped from her at every step. She stood, however, patiently holding the pail, and waiting.

"Hout, woman! ye look like a drowned cat. Come near to the fire,"—said one of the men, approaching to scrape away the ashes.

She shook her head. Wolfe had forgotten her. He turned, hearing the man, and came closer.

"I did no' think; gi' me my supper, woman."

She watched him eat with a painful eagerness. With a woman's quick instinct, she saw that he was not hungry,—was eating to please her. Her pale, watery eyes began to gather a strange light.

"Is't good, Hugh? T' ale was a bit sour, I feared."

"No, good enough." He hesitated a moment. "Ye 're tired, poor lass! Bide here till I go. Lay down there on that heap of ash, and go to sleep."

He threw her an old coat for a pillow, and turned to his work. The heap was the refuse of the burnt iron, and was not a hard bed; the half-smothered warmth, too, penetrated her limbs, dulling their pain and cold shiver.

Miserable enough she looked, lying there on the ashes like a limp, dirty rag,—yet not an unfitting figure to crown the scene of hopeless discomfort and veiled crime: more fitting, if one looked deeper into the heart of things,—at her thwarted woman's form, her colorless life, her waking stupor that smothered pain and hunger,—even more fit to be a type of her class. Deeper yet if one could look, was there nothing worth reading in this wet, faded thing, halfcovered with ashes? no story of a soul filled with groping passionate love, heroic unselfishness, fierce jealousy? of years of weary trying to please the one human being whom she loved, to gain one look of real heart-kindness from him? If anything like this were hidden beneath the pale, bleared eyes, and dull, washed-out-looking face, no one had ever taken the trouble to read its faint signs: not the half-clothed furnace-tender, Wolfe, certainly. Yet he was kind to her: it was his nature to be kind, even to the very rats that swarmed in the cellar: kind to her in just the same way. She knew that. And it might be that very knowledge had given to her face its apathy and vacancy more than her low, torpid life. One sees that dead, vacant look steal sometimes over the rarest, finest of women's faces,—in the very midst, it may be, of their warmest summer's day; and then one can guess at the secret of intolerable solitude that lies hid beneath the delicate laces and brilliant smile. There was no warmth, no brilliancy, no summer for this woman; so the stupor and vacancy had time to gnaw into her face perpetually. She was young, too, though no one guessed it; so the gnawing was the fiercer.

She lay quiet in the dark corner, listening, through the monotonous din and uncertain glare of the works, to the dull plash of the rain in the far distance,—shrinking back whenever the man Wolfe happened to look towards

9. I.e., away from some of the blinding glare.

her. She knew, in spite of all his kindness, that there was that in her face and form which made him loathe the sight of her. She felt by instinct, although she could not comprehend it, the finer nature of the man, which made him among his fellow-workmen something unique, set apart. She knew, that, down under all the vileness and coarseness of his life, there was a groping passion for whatever was beautiful and pure,—that his soul sickened with disgust at her deformity, even when his words were kindest. Through this dull consciousness, which never left her, came, like a sting, the recollection of the dark blue eyes and lithe figure of the little Irish girl she had left in the cellar. The recollection struck through even her stupid intellect with a vivid glow of beauty and of grace. Little Janey, timid, helpless, clinging to Hugh as her only friend: that was the sharp thought, the bitter thought, that drove into the glazed eyes a fierce light of pain. You laugh at it? Are pain and jealousy less savage realities down here in this place I am taking you to than in your own house or your own heart,—your heart, which they clutch at sometimes? The note is the same, I fancy, be the octave high or low.

If you could go into this mill where Deborah lay, and drag out from the hearts of these men the terrible tragedy of their lives, taking it as a symptom of the disease of their class, no ghost Horror would terrify you more. A reality of soul-starvation, of living death, that meets you every day under the besotted faces on the street,—I can paint nothing of this, only give you the outside outlines of a night, a crisis in the life of one man: whatever muddy depth of soul-history lies beneath you can read according to the eyes God has given you.

Wolfe, while Deborah watched him as a spaniel its master, bent over the furnace with his iron pole, unconscious of her scrutiny, only stopping to receive orders. Physically, Nature had promised the man but little. He had already lost the strength and instinct vigor of a man, his muscles were thin, his nerves weak, his face ( a meek, woman's face) haggard, yellow with consumption. In the mill he was known as one of the girl-men: "Molly Wolfe" was his *sobriquet.* He was never seen in the cockpit,[1] did not own a terrier, drank but seldom; when he did, desperately. He fought sometimes, but was always thrashed, pommelled to a jelly. The man was game enough, when his blood was up: but he was no favorite in the mill; he had the taint of school-learning on him,—not to a dangerous extent, only a quarter or so in the free-school in fact, but enough to ruin him as a good hand in a fight.

For other reasons, too, he was not popular. Not one of themselves, they felt that, though outwardly as filthy and ash-covered; silent, with foreign thoughts and longings breaking out through his quietness in innumerable curious ways: this one, for instance. In the neighboring furnace-buildings lay great heaps of the refuse from the ore after the pig-metal is run. *Korl* we call it here: a light, porous substance, of a delicate, waxen, flesh-colored tinge. Out of the blocks of this korl, Wolfe, in his off-hours from the furnace, had a habit of chipping and moulding figures,—hideous, fantastic enough, but sometimes strangely beautiful: even the mill-men saw that, while they jeered at him. It was a curious fancy in the man, almost a passion. The few hours for rest he spent hewing and hacking with his blunt knife, never speaking, until his watch came again,—working at one figure for months, and, when it was finished, breaking

---

1. Where fighting cocks are set against each other until one is severely injured or killed (or until they kill each other). The "sport" survives in the mid-Atlantic region, although repressed. Terriers were bred as hunting animals. "Sobriquet": nickname.

it to pieces perhaps, in a fit of disappointment. A morbid, gloomy man, untaught, unled, left to feed his soul in grossness and crime, and hard, grinding labor.

I want you to come down and look at this Wolfe, standing there among the lowest of his kind, and see him just as he is, that you may judge him justly when you hear the story of this night. I want you to look back, as he does every day, at his birth in vice, his starved infancy; to remember the heavy years he has groped through as boy and man,—the slow, heavy years of constant, hot work. So long ago he began, that he thinks sometimes he has worked there for ages. There is no hope that it will ever end. Think that God put into this man's soul a fierce thirst for beauty,—to know it, to create it; to *be*—something, he knows not what,—other than he is. There are moments when a passing cloud, the sun glinting on the purple thistles, a kindly smile, a child's face, will rouse him to a passion of pain,—when his nature starts up with a mad cry of rage against God, man, whoever it is that has forced this vile, slimy life upon him. With all this groping, this mad desire, a great blind intellect stumbling through wrong, a loving poet's heart, the man was by habit only a coarse, vulgar laborer, familiar with sights and words you would blush to name. Be just: when I tell you about this night, see him as he is. Be just,—not like man's law, which seizes on one isolated fact, but like God's judging angel, whose clear, sad eye saw all the countless cankering days of this man's life, all the countless nights, when, sick with starving, his soul fainted in him, before it judged him for this night, the saddest of all.

I called this night the crisis of his life. If it was, it stole on him unawares. These great turning-days of life cast no shadow before, slip by unconsciously. Only a trifle, a little turn of the rudder, and the ship goes to heaven or hell.

Wolfe, while Deborah watched him, dug into the furnace of melting iron with his pole, dully thinking only how many rails the lump would yield. It was late,—nearly Sunday morning; another hour, and the heavy work would be done,—only the furnaces to replenish and cover for the next day. The workmen were growing more noisy, shouting, as they had to do, to be heard over the deep clamor of the mills. Suddenly they grew less boisterous,—at the far end, entirely silent. Something unusual had happened. After a moment, the silence came nearer; the men stopped their jeers and drunken choruses. Deborah, stupidly lifting up her head, saw the cause of the quiet. A group of five or six men were slowly approaching, stopping to examine each furnace as they came. Visitors often came to see the mills after night: except by growing less noisy, the men took no notice of them. The furnace where Wolfe worked was near the bounds of the works; they halted there hot and tired: a walk over one of these great foundries is no trifling task. The woman, drawing out of sight, turned over to sleep. Wolfe, seeing them stop, suddenly roused from his indifferent stupor, and watched them keenly. He knew some of them: the overseer, Clarke,—a son of Kirby, one of the mill-owners,—and a Doctor May, one of the town-physicians. The other two were strangers. Wolfe came closer. He seized eagerly every chance that brought him into contact with this mysterious class that shone down on him perpetually with the glamour of another order of being. What made the difference between them? That was the mystery of his life. He had a vague notion that perhaps to-night he could find it out. One of the strangers sat down on a pile of bricks, and beckoned young Kirby to his side.

"This *is* hot, with a vengeance. A match, please?"—lighting his cigar. "But the walk is worth the trouble. If it were not that you must have heard it so often, Kirby, I would tell you that your works look like Dante's Inferno."[2] Kirby laughed.

"Yes. Yonder is Farinata himself[3] in the burning tomb,"—pointing to some figure in the shimmering shadows.

"Judging from some of the faces of your men," said the other, "they bid fair to try the reality of Dante's vision, some day."

Young Kirby looked curiously around, as if seeing the faces of his hands for the first time.

"They're bad enough, that's true. A desperate set, I fancy. Eh, Clarke?"

The overseer did not hear him. He was talking of net profits just then,— giving, in fact, a schedule of the annual business of the firm to a sharp peering little Yankee, who jotted down notes on a paper laid on the crown of his hat: a reporter for one of the city-papers, getting up a series of reviews of the leading manufactories. The other gentlemen had accompanied them merely for amusement. They were silent until the notes were finished, drying their feet at the furnaces, and sheltering their faces from the intolerable heat. At last the overseer concluded with—

"I believe that is a pretty fair estimate, Captain."

"Here, some of you men!" said Kirby, "bring up those boards. We may as well sit down, gentlemen, until the rain is over. It cannot last much longer at this rate."

"Pig-metal,"—mumbled the reporter,—"um!—coal facilities,—um!— hands employed, twelve hundred,—bitumen,—um!—all right, I believe, Mr. Clarke;—sinking-fund,—what did you say was your sinking-fund?"[4]

"Twelve hundred hands?" said the stranger, the young man who had first spoken. "Do you control their votes, Kirby?"

"Control? No." The young man smiled complacently. "But my father brought seven hundred votes to the polls for his candidate last November. No force-work, you understand,—only a speech or two, a hint to form themselves into a society, and a bit of red and blue bunting to make them a flag. The Invincible Roughs,—I believe that is their name. I forget the motto: 'Our country's hope,' I think."

There was a laugh. The young man talking to Kirby sat with an amused light in his cool gray eye, surveying critically the half-clothed figures of the puddlers, and the slow swing of their brawny muscles. He was a stranger in the city,—spending a couple of months in the borders of a Slave State,[5] to study the institutions of the South,—a brother-in-law of Kirby's,—Mitchell. He was an amateur gymnast,—hence his anatomical eye; a patron, in a *blasé* way, of the prize-ring; a man who sucked the essence out of a science or philosophy in an indifferent, gentlemanly way; who took Kant, Novalis, Humboldt,[6] for what they were worth in his own scales; accepting all, despising nothing, in heaven, earth, or hell, but one-idead men; with a temper yielding

2. *Hell*, the first part of *The Divine Comedy* by the Italian poet Dante Alighieri (1265–1321).
3. In Canto 10 of *The Inferno*, Farinata degli Uberti is one of the heretics, a leader of the Florentine faction opposed to Dante's own family.
4. Fund accumulated to pay off a corporate debt.
5. Part of Harding's irony is that, at the time she was writing, her slave-state setting was far north of the Mason-Dixon line, west, not south, of Pennsylvania.
6. Alexander von Humboldt (1769–1859), German naturalist and explorer of South America and Asia. Immanuel Kant (1724–1804), German philosopher. Novalis, pseudonym of Friedrich von Hardenberg (1772–1801), German poet.

and brilliant as summer water, until his Self was touched, when it was ice, though brilliant still. Such men are not rare in the States.

As he knocked the ashes from his cigar, Wolfe caught with a quick pleasure the contour of the white hand, the blood-glow of a red ring he wore. His voice, too, and that of Kirby's, touched him like music,—low, even, with chording cadences. About this man Mitchell hung the impalpable atmosphere belonging to the thoroughbred gentleman. Wolfe, scraping away the ashes beside him, was conscious of it, did obeisance to it with his artist sense, unconscious that he did so.

The rain did not cease. Clarke and the reporter left the mills; the others, comfortably seated near the furnace, lingered, smoking and talking in a desultory way. Greek would not have been more unintelligible to the furnace-tenders, whose presence they soon forgot entirely. Kirby drew out a newspaper from his pocket and read aloud some article, which they discussed eagerly. At every sentence, Wolfe listened more and more like a dumb, hopeless animal, with a duller, more stolid look creeping over his face, glancing now and then at Mitchell, marking acutely every smallest sign of refinement, then back to himself, seeing as in a mirror his filthy body, his more stained soul.

Never! He had no words for such a thought, but he knew now, in all the sharpness of the bitter certainty, that between them there was a great gulf[7] never to be passed. Never!

The bell of the mills rang for midnight. Sunday morning had dawned. Whatever hidden message lay in the tolling bells floated past these men unknown. Yet it was there. Veiled in the solemn music ushering the risen Saviour was a key-note to solve the darkest secrets of a world gone wrong,— even this social riddle which the brain of the grimy puddler grappled with madly to-night.

The men began to withdraw the metal from the caldrons. The mills were deserted on Sundays, except by the hands who fed the fires, and those who had no lodgings and slept usually on the ash-heaps. The three strangers sat still during the next hour, watching the men cover the furnaces, laughing now and then at some jest of Kirby's.

"Do you know," said Mitchell, "I like this view of the works better than when the glare was fiercest? These heavy shadows and the amphitheatre of smothered fires are ghostly, unreal. One could fancy these red smouldering lights to be the half-shut eyes of wild beasts, and the spectral figures their victims in the den."

Kirby laughed. "You are fanciful. Come, let us get out of the den. The spectral figures, as you call them, are a little too real for me to fancy a close proximity in the darkness,—unarmed, too."

The others rose, buttoning their overcoats, and lighting cigars.

"Raining, still," said Doctor May, "and hard. Where did we leave the coach, Mitchell?"

"At the other side of the works.—Kirby, what's that?"

Mitchell started back, half-frightened, as, suddenly turning a corner, the white figure of a woman faced him in the darkness,—a woman, white, of giant proportions, crouching on the ground, her arms flung out in some wild gesture of warning.

7. Words Jesus assigns to Abraham in the parable of the beggar Lazarus and the rich man, Luke 16.26: "And beside all this, between us and you there is a great gulf fixed"—the gulf between heaven, where Lazarus has found comfort, and hell, where the rich man is suffering.

"Stop! Make that fire burn there!" cried Kirby, stopping short. The flame burst out, flashing the gaunt figure into bold relief. Mitchell drew a long breath.

"I thought it was alive," he said, going up curiously. The others followed.

"Not marble, eh?" asked Kirby, touching it. One of the lower overseers stopped.

"Korl, Sir."

"Who did it?"

"Can't say. Some of the hands; chipped it out in off-hours."

"Chipped to some purpose, I should say. What a flesh-tint the stuff has! Do you see, Mitchell?"

"I see."

He had stepped aside where the light fell boldest on the figure, looking at it in silence. There was not one line of beauty or grace in it: a nude woman's form, muscular, grown coarse with labor, the powerful limbs instinct with some one poignant longing. One idea: there it was in the tense, rigid muscles, the clutching hands, the wild, eager face, like that of a starving wolf's. Kirby and Doctor May walked around it, critical, curious. Mitchell stood aloof, silent. The figure touched him strangely.

"Not badly done," said Doctor May. "Where did the fellow learn that sweep of the muscles in the arm and hand? Look at them! They are groping,—do you see?—clutching: the peculiar action of a man dying of thirst."

"They have ample facilities for studying anatomy," sneered Kirby, glancing at the half-naked figures.

"Look," continued the Doctor, "at this bony wrist, and the strained sinews of the instep! A working-woman,—the very type of her class."

"God forbid!" muttered Mitchell.

"Why?" demanded May. "What does the fellow intend by the figure? I cannot catch the meaning."

"Ask him," said the other, dryly. "There he stands,"—pointing to Wolfe, who stood with a group of men, leaning on his ash-rake.

The Doctor beckoned him with the affable smile which kind-hearted men put on, when talking to these people.

"Mr. Mitchell has picked you out as the man who did this,—I'm sure I don't know why. But what did you mean by it?"

"She be hungry."

Wolfe's eyes answered Mitchell, not the Doctor.

"Oh-h! But what a mistake you have made, my fine fellow! You have given no sign of starvation to the body. It is strong,—terribly strong. It has the mad, half-despairing gesture of drowning."

Wolfe stammered, glanced appealingly at Mitchell, who saw the soul of the thing, he knew. But the cool, probing eyes were turned on himself now,—mocking, cruel, relentless.

"Not hungry for meat," the furnace-tender said at last.

"What then? Whiskey?" jeered Kirby, with a coarse laugh.

Wolfe was silent a moment, thinking.

"I dunno," he said, with a bewildered look. "It mebbe. Summat to make her live, I think,—like you. Whiskey ull do it, in a way."

The young man laughed again. Mitchell flashed a look of disgust somewhere,—not at Wolfe.

"May," he broke out impatiently, "are you blind? Look at that woman's face! It asks questions of God, and says, 'I have a right to know.' Good God, how hungry it is!"

They looked a moment; then May turned to the mill-owner:—

"Have you many such hands as this? What are you going to do with them? Keep them at puddling iron?"

Kirby shrugged his shoulders. Mitchell's look had irritated him.

"*Ce n'est pas mon affaire.*[8] I have no fancy for nursing infant geniuses. I suppose there are some stray gleams of mind and soul among these wretches. The Lord will take care of his own; or else they can work out their own salvation. I have heard you call our American system a ladder which any man can scale. Do you doubt it? Or perhaps you want to banish all social ladders, and put us all on a flat table-land,—eh, May?"

The Doctor looked vexed, puzzled. Some terrible problem lay hid in this woman's face, and troubled these men. Kirby waited for an answer, and, receiving none, went on, warming with his subject.

"I tell you, there's something wrong that no talk of '*Liberté*' or '*Egalité*'[9] will do away. If I had the making of men, these men who do the lowest part of the world's work should be machines,—nothing more,—hands. It would be kindness. God help them! What are taste, reason, to creatures who must live such lives as that?" He pointed to Deborah, sleeping on the ash-heap. "So many nerves to sting them to pain. What if God had put your brain, with all its agony of touch, into your fingers, and bid you work and strike with that?"

"You think you could govern the world better?" laughed the Doctor.

"I do not think at all."

"That is true philosophy. Drift with the stream, because you cannot dive deep enough to find bottom, eh?"

"Exactly," rejoined Kirby. "I do not think. I wash my hands of all social problems,—slavery, caste, white or black. My duty to my operatives has a narrow limit,—the pay-hour on Saturday night.[1] Outside of that, if they cut korl, or cut each other's throats, (the more popular amusement of the two,) I am not responsible."

The Doctor sighed,—a good honest sigh, from the depths of his stomach.

"God help us! Who is responsible?"

"Not I, I tell you," said Kirby, testily. "What has the man who pays them money to do with their souls' concerns, more than the grocer or butcher who takes it?"

"And yet," said Mitchell's cynical voice, "look at her! How hungry she is!"

Kirby tapped his boot with his cane. No one spoke. Only the dumb face of the rough image looking into their faces with the awful question, "What shall we do to be saved?"[2] Only Wolfe's face, with its heavy weight of brain, its weak, uncertain mouth, its desperate eyes, out of which looked the soul of his class,—only Wolfe's face turned towards Kirby's. Mitchell laughed,—a cool, musical laugh.

---

8. It's none of my business (French).
9. Slogans of the French Revolution.
1. A bald statement of what Harding's Scot contemporary Thomas Carlyle was condemning as the "cash nexus," where monetary payment was the only connection between employer and worker. "Operatives":

workers.
2. The keeper of the prison in Philippi cries "Sirs, what must I do to be saved?" to Paul and Silas after an earthquake has opened the prison doors and loosed the prisoners' bonds (Acts 16.30).

"Money has spoken!" he said, seating himself lightly on a stone with the air of an amused spectator at a play. "Are you answered?"—turning to Wolfe his clear, magnetic face.

Bright and deep and cold as Arctic air, the soul of the man lay tranquil beneath. He looked at the furnace-tender as he had looked at a rare mosaic in the morning; only the man was the more amusing study of the two.

"Are you answered? Why, May, look at him! '*De profundis clamavi*.'[3] Or, to quote in English, 'Hungry and thirsty, his soul faints in him.' And so Money sends back its answer into the depths through you, Kirby! Very clear the answer, too!—I think I remember reading the same words somewhere:— washing your hands in Eau de Cologne, and saying, 'I am innocent of the blood of this man. See ye to it!' "[4]

Kirby flushed angrily.

"You quote Scripture freely."

"Do I not quote correctly? I think I remember another line, which may amend my meaning? 'Inasmuch as ye did it unto one of the least of these, ye did it unto me.' Deist?[5] Bless you, man, I was raised on the milk of the Word. Now, Doctor, the pocket of the world having uttered its voice, what has the heart to say? You are a philanthropist, in a small way,—*n'est ce pas?*[6] Here, boy, this gentleman can show you how to cut korl better,—or your destiny. Go on, May!"

"I think a mocking devil possesses you to-night," rejoined the Doctor, seri-ously.

He went to Wolfe and put his hand kindly on his arm. Something of a vague idea possessed the Doctor's brain that much good was to be done here by a friendly word or two: a latent genius to be warmed into life by a waited-for sunbeam. Here it was: he had brought it. So he went on complacently:—

"Do you know, boy, you have it in you to be a great sculptor, a great man?—do you understand?" (talking down to the capacity of his hearer: it is a way people have with children, and men like Wolfe,)—"to live a better, stronger life than I, or Mr. Kirby here? A man may make himself anything he chooses. God has given you stronger powers than many men,—me, for instance."

May stopped, heated, glowing with his own magnanimity. And it was mag-nanimous. The puddler had drunk in every word, looking through the Doc-tor's flurry, and generous heat, and self-approval, into his will, with those slow, absorbing eyes of his.

"Make yourself what you will. It is your right."

"I know," quietly. "Will you help me?"

Mitchell laughed again. The Doctor turned now, in a passion,—

"You know, Mitchell, I have not the means. You know, if I had, it is in my heart to take this boy and educate him for"—

"The glory of God, and the glory of John May."

3. The Latin version of Psalms 130.1: "Out of the depths have I cried unto thee, O Lord."
4. The Roman governor Pontius Pilate yielded to the mob's demand that Jesus be crucified but renounced responsibility for it: "When Pilate saw that he could prevail nothing, but that rather a tumult was made, he took water, and washed his hands before the multitude, saying, I am innocent of the blood of this just person:

see ye to it" (Matthew 27.24).
5. One who believes in a God who created the world but thereafter exercises no control over it. What Jesus says in Matthew 25.40: "Verily I say unto you, Inas-much as ye have done it unto one of the least of these my brethren, ye have done it unto me."
6. Aren't you? (French).

May did not speak for a moment; then, controlled, he said,—
"Why should one be raised, when myriads are left?—I have not the money,
boy," to Wolfe, shortly.

"Money?" He said it over slowly, as one repeats the guessed answer to a
riddle, doubtfully. "That is it? Money?"

"Yes, money,—that is it," said Mitchell, rising, and drawing his furred coat
about him. "You've found the cure for all the world's diseases.—Come, May,
find your good-humor, and come home. This damp wind chills my very
bones. Come and preach your Saint-Simonian doctrines[7] to-morrow to Kirby's
hands. Let them have a clear idea of the rights of the soul, and I'll venture
next week they'll strike for higher wages. That will be the end of it."

"Will you send the coach-driver to this side of the mills?" asked Kirby,
turning to Wolfe.

He spoke kindly: it was his habit to do so. Deborah, seeing the puddler go,
crept after him. The three men waited outside. Doctor May walked up and
down, chafed. Suddenly he stopped.

"Go back, Mitchell! You say the pocket and the heart of the world speak
without meaning to these people. What has its head to say? Taste, culture,
refinement? Go!"

Mitchell was leaning against a brick wall. He turned his head indolently,
and looked into the mills. There hung about the place a thick, unclean odor.
The slightest motion of his hand marked that he perceived it, and his insufferable disgust. That was all. May said nothing, only quickened his angry tramp.

"Besides," added Mitchell, giving a corollary to his answer, "it would be of
no use. I am not one of them."

"You do not mean"—said May, facing him.

"Yes, I mean just that. Reform is born of need, not pity. No vital movement
of the people's has worked down, for good or evil; fermented, instead, carried
up the heaving, cloggy mass. Think back through history, and you will know
it. What will this lowest deep—thieves, Magdalens,[8] negroes—do with the
light filtered through ponderous Church creeds, Baconian theories, Goethe
schemes?[9] Some day, out of their bitter need will be thrown up their own
light-bringer,—their Jean Paul, their Cromwell, their Messiah."[1]

"Bah!" was the Doctor's inward criticism. However, in practice, he adopted
the theory; for, when, night and morning, afterwards, he prayed that power
might be given these degraded souls to rise, he glowed at heart, recognizing
an accomplished duty.

Wolfe and the woman had stood in the shadow of the works as the coach
drove off. The Doctor had held out his hand in a frank, generous way, telling
him to "take care of himself, and to remember it was his right to rise." Mitchell had simply touched his hat, as to an equal, with a quiet look of thorough
recognition. Kirby had thrown Deborah some money, which she found, and
clutched eagerly enough. They were gone now, all of them. The man sat
down on the cinder-road, looking up into the murky sky.

7. Doctrines of the Count of Saint-Simon (1760–
1825), founder of French socialism.
8. Whores, from Mary Magdalene, out of whom Jesus
cast seven devils (Mark 16.9).
9. Abstract or fanciful theories such as the English essayist and statesman Francis Bacon (1561–1624) advanced in his New Atlantis (1627) or the visionary faith
in technological progress revealed by the German

writer Johann Wolfgang von Goethe (1749–1832) in
Wilhelm Meister's Travels (1821–29).
1. Not specifically Jesus whose return Christians await
or the Messiah whose coming Jews await. The German
novelist Jean Paul Richter (1763–1825), author of The
Titan. Oliver Cromwell (1599–1658), English military, political, and religious leader, dictator of England.

"'T be late, Hugh. Wunnot hur come?"

He shook his head doggedly, and the woman crouched out of his sight against the wall. Do you remember rare moments when a sudden light flashed over yourself, your world, God? when you stood on a mountain-peak, seeing your life as it might have been, as it is? one quick instant, when custom lost its force and every-day usage? when your friend, wife, brother, stood in a new light? your soul was bared, and the grave,—a foretaste of the nakedness of the Judgment-Day? So it came before him, his life, that night. The slow tides of pain he had borne gathered themselves up and surged against his soul. His squalid daily life, the brutal coarseness eating into his brain, as the ashes into his skin: before, these things had been a dull aching into his consciousness; to-night, they were reality. He griped the filthy red shirt that clung, stiff with soot, about him, and tore it savagely from his arm. The flesh beneath was muddy with grease and ashes,—and the heart beneath that! And the soul? God knows.

Then flashed before his vivid poetic sense the man who had left him,—the pure face, the delicate, sinewy limbs, in harmony with all he knew of beauty or truth. In his cloudy fancy he had pictured a Something like this. He had found it in this Mitchell, even when he idly scoffed at his pain: a Man all-knowing, all-seeing, crowned by Nature, reigning,—the keen glance of his eye falling like a sceptre on other men. And yet his instinct taught him that he too—He! He looked at himself with sudden loathing, sick, wrung his hands with a cry, and then was silent. With all the phantoms of his heated, ignorant fancy, Wolfe had not been vague in his ambitions. They were practical, slowly built up before him out of his knowledge of what he could do. Through years he had day by day made this hope a real thing to himself,—a clear, projected figure of himself, as he might become.

Able to speak, to know what was best, to raise these men and women working at his side up with him: sometimes he forgot this defined hope in the frantic anguish to escape,—only to escape,—out of the wet, the pain, the ashes, somewhere, anywhere,—only for one moment of free air on a hill-side, to lie down and let his sick soul throb itself out in the sunshine. But to-night he panted for life. The savage strength of his nature was roused; his cry was fierce to God for justice.

"Look at me!" he said to Deborah, with a low, bitter laugh, striking his puny chest savagely. "What am I worth, Deb? Is it my fault that I am no better? My fault? My fault?"

He stopped, stung with a sudden remorse, seeing her hunchback shape writhing with sobs. For Deborah was crying thankless tears, according to the fashion of women.

"God forgi' me, woman! Things go harder wi' you nor me. It's a worse share."

He got up and helped her to rise; and they went doggedly down the muddy street, side by side.

"It's all wrong," he muttered, slowly,—"all wrong! I dunnot understan'. But it'll end some day."

"Come home, Hugh!" she said, coaxingly; for he had stopped, looking around bewildered.

"Home,—and back to the mill!" He went on saying this over to himself, as if he would mutter down every pain in this dull despair.

She followed him through the fog, her blue lips chattering with cold. They reached the cellar at last. Old Wolfe had been drinking since she went out, and had crept nearer the door. The girl Janey slept heavily in the corner. He went up to her, touching softly the worn white arm with his fingers. Some bitterer thought stung him, as he stood there. He wiped the drops from his forehead, and went into the room beyond, livid, trembling. A hope, trifling, perhaps, but very dear, had died just then out of the poor puddler's life, as he looked at the sleeping, innocent girl,—some plan for the future, in which she had borne a part. He gave it up that moment, then and forever. Only a trifle, perhaps, to us: his face grew a shade paler,—that was all. But, somehow, the man's soul, as God and the angels looked down on it, never was the same afterwards.

Deborah followed him into the inner room. She carried a candle, which she placed on the floor, closing the door after her. She had seen the look on his face, as he turned away: her own grew deadly. Yet, as she came up to him, her eyes glowed. He was seated on an old chest, quiet, holding his face in his hands.

"Hugh!" she said, softly.

He did not speak.

"Hugh, did hur hear what the man said,—him with the clear voice? Did hur hear? Money, money,—that it wud do all?"

He pushed her away,—gently, but he was worn out; her rasping tone fretted him.

"Hugh!"

The candle flared a pale yellow light over the cobwebbed brick walls, and the woman standing there. He looked at her. She was young, in deadly earnest; her faded eyes, and wet, ragged figure caught from their frantic eagerness a power akin to beauty.

"Hugh, it is true! Money ull do it! Oh, Hugh, boy, listen till me! He said it true! It is money!"

"I know. Go back! I do not want you here."

"Hugh, it is t' last time. I'll never worrit hur again."

There were tears in her voice now, but she choked them back.

"Hear till me only to-night! If one of t' witch people wud come, them we heard of t' home, and gif hur all hur wants, what then? Say, Hugh!"

"What do you mean?"

"I mean money."

Her whisper shrilled through his brain.

"If one of t' witch dwarfs wud come from t' lane moors to-night, and gif hur money, to go out,—out, I say,—out, lad, where t' sun shines, and t' heath grows, and t' ladies walk in silken gownds, and God stays all t' time,—where t' man lives that talked to us to-night,—Hugh knows,—Hugh could walk there like a king!"

He thought the woman mad, tried to check her, but she went on, fierce in her eager haste.

"If I were t' witch dwarf, if I had t' money, wud hur thank me? Wud hur take me out o' this place wid hur and Janey? I wud not come into the gran' house hur wud build, to vex hur wid t' hunch,—only at night, when t' shadows were dark, stand far off to see hur."

Mad? Yes! Are many of us mad in this way?

"Poor Deb! poor Deb!" he said, soothingly.

"It is here," she said, suddenly, jerking into his hand a small roll. "I took it! I did it! Me, me!—not hur! I shall be hanged, I shall be burnt in hell, if anybody knows I took it! Out of his pocket, as he leaned against t' bricks. Hur knows?"

She thrust it into his hand, and then, her errand done, began to gather chips together to make a fire, choking down hysteric sobs.

"Has it come to this?"

That was all he said. The Welsh Wolfe blood was honest. The roll was a small green pocket-book containing one or two gold pieces, and a check for an incredible amount, as it seemed to the poor puddler. He laid it down, hiding his face again in his hands.

"Hugh, don't be angry wud me! It's only poor Deb,—hur knows?"

He took the long skinny fingers kindly in his.

"Angry? God help me, no! Let me sleep. I am tired."

He threw himself heavily down on the wooden bench, stunned with pain and weariness. She brought some old rags to cover him.

It was late on Sunday evening before he awoke. I tell God's truth, when I say he had then no thought of keeping this money. Deborah had hid it in his pocket. He found it there. She watched him eagerly, as he took it out.

"I must gif it to him," he said, reading her face.

"Hur knows," she said with a bitter sigh of disappointment. "But it is hur right to keep it."

His right! The word struck him. Doctor May had used the same. He washed himself, and went out to find this man Mitchell. His right! Why did this chance word cling to him so obstinately? Do you hear the fierce devils whisper in his ear, as he went slowly down the darkening street?

The evening came on, slow and calm. He seated himself at the end of an alley leading into one of the larger streets. His brain was clear to-night, keen, intent, mastering. It would not start back, cowardly, from any hellish temptation, but meet it face to face. Therefore the great temptation of his life came to him veiled by no sophistry, but bold, defiant, owning its own vile name, trusting to one bold blow for victory.

He did not deceive himself. Theft! That was it. At first the word sickened him; then he grappled with it. Sitting there on a broken cart-wheel, the fading day, the noisy groups, the church-bells' tolling passed before him like a panorama,[2] while the sharp struggle went on within. This money! He took it out, and looked at it. If he gave it back, what then? He was going to be cool about it.

People going by to church saw only a sickly mill-boy watching them quietly at the alley's mouth. They did not know that he was mad, or they would not have gone by so quietly: mad with hunger; stretching out his hands to the world, that had given so much to them, for leave to live the life God meant him to live. His soul within him was smothering to death; he wanted so much, thought so much, and knew—nothing. There was nothing of which he was certain, except the mill and things there. Of God and heaven he had heard so little, that they were to him what fairy-land is to a child: something real, but not here; very far off. His brain, greedy, dwarfed, full of thwarted energy and unused powers, questioned these men and women going by, coldly, bitterly, that night. Was it not his right to live as they,—a pure life, a good, true-

---

2. Like the continuous scenes painted on huge canvas and unrolled before audiences; attending a panorama was a popular mid-19th-century recreation, but probably too expensive for Harding's characters.

hearted life, full of beauty and kind words? He only wanted to know how to use the strength within him. His heart warmed, as he thought of it. He suffered himself to think of it longer. If he took the money?

Then he saw himself as he might be, strong, helpful, kindly. The night crept on, as this one image slowly evolved itself from the crowd of other thoughts and stood triumphant. He looked at it. As he might be! What wonder, if it blinded him to delirium,—the madness that underlies all revolution, all progress, and all fall?

You laugh at the shallow temptation? You see the error underlying its argument so clearly,—that to him a true life was one of full development rather than self-restraint? that he was deaf to the higher tone in a cry of voluntary suffering for truth's sake than in the fullest flow of spontaneous harmony? I do not plead his cause. I only want to show you the mote in my brother's eye: then you can see clearly to take it out.[3]

The money,—there it lay on his knee, a little blotted slip of paper, nothing in itself; used to raise him out of the pit, something straight from God's hand. A thief! Well, what was it to be a thief? He met the question at last, face to face, wiping the clammy drops of sweat from his forehead. God made this money—the fresh air, too—for his children's use. He never made the difference between poor and rich. The Something who looked down on him that moment through the cool gray sky had a kindly face, he knew,—loved his children alike. Oh, he knew that!

There were times when the soft floods of color in the crimson and purple flames, or the clear depth of amber in the water below the bridge, had somehow given him a glimpse of another world than this,—of an infinite depth of beauty and of quiet somewhere,—somewhere,—a depth of quiet and rest and love. Looking up now, it became strangely real. The sun had sunk quite below the hills, but his last rays struck upward, touching the zenith. The fog had risen, and the town and river were steeped in its thick, gray damp; but overhead, the sun-touched smoke-clouds opened like a cleft ocean,—shifting, rolling seas of crimson mist, waves of billowy silver veined with blood-scarlet, inner depths unfathomable of glancing light. Wolfe's artist-eye grew drunk with color. The gates of that other world! Fading, flashing before him now! What, in that world of Beauty, Content, and Right, were the petty laws, the mine and thine, of mill-owners and mill hands?

A consciousness of power stirred within him. He stood up. A man,—he thought, stretching out his hands,—free to work, to live, to love! Free! His right! He folded the scrap of paper in his hand. As his nervous fingers took it in, limp and blotted, so his soul took in the mean temptation, lapped it in fancied rights, in dreams of improved existences, drifting and endless as the cloud-seas of color. Clutching it, as if the tightness of his hold would strengthen his sense of possession, he went aimlessly down the street. It was his watch at the mill. He need not go, need never go again, thank God!— shaking off the thought with unspeakable loathing.

Shall I go over the history of the hours of that night? how the man wandered from one to another of his old haunts, with a half-consciousness of bidding

3. Jesus's words in the Sermon on the Mount (Matthew 7.3–4): "And why beholdest thou the mote that is in thy brother's eye, but considerest not the beam that is in thine own eye? Or how wilt thou say to thy brother, Let me pull out the mote out of thine eye; and behold, a beam is in thine own eye?" (Here a mote is a speck of dust and a beam is the large timber used to support a roof.)

them farewell,—lanes and alleys and back-yards where the mill-hands lodged,—noting, with a new eagerness, the filth and drunkenness, the pig-pens, the ash-heaps covered with potato-skins, the bloated, pimpled women at the doors,—with a new disgust, a new sense of sudden triumph, and, under all, a new, vague dread, unknown before, smothered down, kept under, but still there? It left him but once during the night, when, for the second time in his life, he entered a church. It was a sombre Gothic pile, where the stained light lost itself in far-retreating arches; built to meet the requirements and sympathies of a far other class than Wolfe's. Yet it touched, moved him uncontrollably. The distances, the shadows, the still, marble figures, the mass of silent kneeling worshippers, the mysterious music, thrilled, lifted his soul with a wonderful pain. Wolfe forgot himself, forgot the new life he was going to live, the mean terror gnawing underneath. The voice of the speaker strengthened the charm; it was clear, feeling, full, strong. An old man, who had lived much, suffered much; whose brain was keenly alive, dominant; whose heart was summer-warm with charity. He taught it to-night. He held up Humanity in its grand total; showed the great world-cancer to his people. Who could show it better? He was a Christian reformer; he had studied the age thoroughly; his outlook at man had been free, world-wide, over all time. His faith stood sublime upon the Rock of Ages; his fiery zeal guided vast schemes by which the Gospel was to be preached to all nations. How did he preach it to-night? In burning, light-laden words he painted Jesus, the incarnate Life, Love, the universal Man: words that became reality in the lives of these people,—that lived again in beautiful words and actions, trifling, but heroic. Sin, as he defined it, was a real foe to them; their trials, temptations, were his. His words passed far over the furnace-tender's grasp, toned to suit another class of culture; they sounded in his ears a very pleasant song in an unknown tongue. He meant to cure this world-cancer with a steady eye that had never glared with hunger, and a hand that neither poverty nor strychnine-whiskey[4] had taught to shake. In this morbid, distorted heart of the Welsh puddler he had failed.

Eighteen centuries ago, the Master of this man tried reform in the streets of a city as crowded and vile as this, and did not fail. His disciple, showing Him to-night to cultured hearers, showing the clearness of the God-power acting through Him, shrank back from one coarse fact; that in birth and habit the man Christ was thrown up from the lowest of the people: his flesh, their flesh; their blood, his blood; tempted like them, to brutalize day by day; to lie, to steal: the actual slime and want of their hourly life, and the wine-press he trod alone.

Yet, is there no meaning in this perpetually covered truth? If the son of the carpenter had stood in the church that night, as he stood with the fishermen and harlots by the sea of Galilee, before His Father and their Father, despised and rejected of men, without a place to lay His head, wounded for their iniquities, bruised for their transgressifons, would not that hungry mill-boy at least, in the back seat, have "known the man"? That Jesus did not stand there.

Wolfe rose at last, and turned from the church down the street. He looked up; the night had come on foggy, damp; the golden mists had vanished, and the sky lay dull and ash-colored. He wandered again aimlessly down the street,

---

4. Extremely dangerous whiskey (sometimes lethal) made from redistilling the mash along with various impurities.

idly wondering what had become of the cloud-sea of crimson and scarlet. The trial-day of this man's life was over, and he had lost the victory. What followed was mere drifting circumstance,—a quicker walking over the path,—that was all. Do you want to hear the end of it? You wish me to make a tragic story out of it? Why, in the police-reports of the morning paper you can find a dozen such tragedies: hints of shipwrecks unlike any that ever befell on the high seas; hints that here a power was lost to heaven,—that there a soul went down where no tide can ebb or flow. Commonplace enough the hints are,—jocose sometimes, done up in rhyme.

Doctor May, a month after the night I have told you of, was reading to his wife at breakfast from this fourth column of the morning-paper: an unusual thing,—these police-reports not being, in general, choice reading for ladies; but it was only one item he read.

"Oh, my dear! You remember that man I told you of, that we saw at Kirby's mill?—that was arrested for robbing Mitchell? Here he is; just listen:—'Circuit Court. Judge Day. Hugh Wolfe, operative in Kirby & John's Loudon Mills. Charge, grand larceny. Sentence, nineteen years hard labor in penitentiary.'— Scoundrel! Serves him right! After all our kindness that night! Picking Mitchell's pocket at the very time!"

His wife said something about the ingratitude of that kind of people, and then they began to talk of something else.

Nineteen years! How easy that was to read! What a simple word for Judge Day to utter! Nineteen years! Half a lifetime!

Hugh Wolfe sat on the window-ledge of his cell, looking out. His ankles were ironed. Not usual in such cases; but he had made two desperate efforts to escape. "Well," as Haley, the jailer, said, "small blame to him! Nineteen years' inprisonment was not a pleasant thing to look forward to." Haley was very good-natured about it, though Wolfe had fought him savagely.

"When he was first caught," the jailer said afterwards, in telling the story, "before the trial, the fellow was cut down at once,—laid there on that pallet like a dead man, with his hands over his eyes. Never saw a man so cut down in my life. Time of the trial, too, came the queerest dodge[5] of any customer I ever had. Would choose no lawyer. Judge gave him one, of course. Gibson it was. He tried to prove the fellow crazy; but it wouldn't go. Thing was plain as daylight: money found on him. 'T was a hard sentence,—all the law allows; but it was for 'xample's sake. These mill-hands are gettin' onbearable. When the sentence was read, he just looked up, and said the money was his by rights, and that all the world had gone wrong. That night, after the trial, a gentleman came to see him here, name of Mitchell,—him as he stole from. Talked to him for an hour. Thought he came for curiosity, like. After he was gone, thought Wolfe was remarkable quiet, and went into his cell. Found him very low; bed all bloody. Doctor said he had been bleeding at the lungs. He was as weak as a cat; yet if ye'll b'lieve me, he tried to get a-past me and get out. I just carried him like a baby, and threw him on the pallet. Three days after, he tried it again: that time reached the wall. Lord help you! he fought like a tiger,— giv' some terrible blows. Fightin' for life, you see; for he can't live long, shut up in the stone crib down yonder. Got a death-cough now. 'T took two of us to bring him down that day; so I just put the irons on his feet. There he sits, in there. Goin' to-morrow, with a batch more of 'em. That woman,

5. Trick, stratagem.

hunchback, tried with him,—you remember?—she's only got three years. 'Complice. But *she's* a woman, you know. He's been quiet ever since I put on irons: giv' up, I suppose. Looks white, sick-lookin'. It acts different on 'em, bein' sentenced. Most of 'em gets reckless, devilish-like. Some prays awful, and sings them vile songs of the mills, all in a breath. That woman, now, she's desper't'. Been beggin' to see Hugh, as she calls him, for three days. I'm a-goin' to let her in. She don't go with him. Here she is in this next cell. I'm a-goin' now to let her in."

He let her in. Wolfe did not see her. She crept into a corner of the cell, and stood watching him. He was scratching the iron bars of the window with a piece of tin which he had picked up, with an idle, uncertain, vacant stare, just as a child or idiot would do.

"Tryin' to get out, old boy?" laughed Haley. "Them irons will need a crow-bar beside your tin, before you can open 'em."

Wolfe laughed, too, in a senseless way.

"I think I'll get out," he said.

"I believe his brain's touched," said Haley, when he came out.

The puddler scraped away with the tin for half an hour. Still Deborah did not speak. At last she ventured nearer, and touched his arm.

"Blood?" she said, looking at some spots on his coat with a shudder.

He looked up at her. "Why, Deb!" he said, smiling,—such a bright, boyish smile, that it went to poor Deborah's heart directly, and she sobbed and cried out loud.

"Oh, Hugh, lad! Hugh! dunnot look at me, when it wur my fault! To think I brought hur to it! And I loved hur so! Oh lad, I dud!"

The confession, even in this wretch, came with the woman's blush through the sharp cry.

He did not seem to hear her,—scraping away diligently at the bars with the bit of tin.

Was he going mad? She peered closely into his face. Something she saw there made her draw suddenly back,—something which Haley had not seen, that lay beneath the pinched, vacant look it had caught since the trial, or the curious gray shadow that rested on it. That gray shadow,—yes, she knew what that meant. She had often seen it creeping over women's faces for months, who died at last of slow hunger or consumption. That meant death, distant, lingering: but this—Whatever it was the woman saw, or thought she saw, used as she was to crime and misery, seemed to make her sick with a new horror. Forgetting her fear of him, she caught his shoulders, and looked keenly, steadily, into his eyes.

"Hugh!" she cried, in a desperate whisper,—"oh, boy, not that! for God's sake, not *that!*"

The vacant laugh went off his face, and he answered her in a muttered word or two that drove her away. Yet the words were kindly enough. Sitting there on his pallet, she cried silently a hopeless sort of tears, but did not speak again. The man looked up furtively at her now and then. Whatever his own trouble was, her distress vexed him with a momentary sting.

It was market-day. The narrow window of the jail looked down directly on the carts and wagons drawn up in a long line, where they had unloaded. He could see, too, and hear distinctly the clink of money as it changed hands, the busy crowd of whites and blacks shoving, pushing one another, and the chaffering and swearing at the stalls. Somehow, the sound, more than anything else had done, wakened him up,—made the whole real to him. He was done with the world and the business of it. He let the tin fall, and looked out, pressing his face close to the rusty bars. How they crowded and pushed! And he,—he should never walk that pavement again! There came Neff Sanders, one of the feeders at the mill, with a basket on his arm. Sure enough, Neff was married the other week. He whistled, hoping he would look up; but he did not. He wondered if Neff remembered he was there,—if any of the boys thought of him up there, and thought that he never was to go down that old cinder-road again. Never again! He had not quite understood it before; but now he did. Not for days or years, but never!—that was it.

How clear the light fell on that stall in front of the market! and how like a picture it was, the dark-green heaps of corn, and the crimson beets, and golden melons! There was another with game: how the light flickered on that pheasant's breast, with the purplish blood dripping over the brown feathers! He could see the red shining of the drops, it was so near. In one minute he could be down there. It was just a step. So easy, as it seemed, so natural to go! Yet it could never be—not in all the thousands of years to come—that he should put his foot on that street again! He thought of himself with a sorrowful pity, as of some one else. There was a dog down in the market, walking after his master with such a stately, grave look!—only a dog, yet he could go backwards and forwards just as he pleased: he had good luck! Why, the very vilest cur, yelping there in the gutter, had not lived his life, had been free to act out whatever thought God had put into his brain; while he—No, he would not think of that! He tried to put the thought away, and to listen to a dispute between a countryman and a woman about some meat; but it would come back. He, what had he done to bear this?

Then came the sudden picture of what might have been, and now. He knew what it was to be in the penitentiary,—how it went with men there. He knew how in these long years he should slowly die, but not until soul and body had become corrupt and rotten,—how, when he came out, if he lived to come, even the lowest of the mill-hands would jeer him,—how his hands would be weak, and his brain senseless and stupid. He believed he was almost that now. He put his hand to his head, with a puzzled, weary look. It ached, his head, with thinking. He tried to quiet himself. It was only right, perhaps; he had done wrong. But was there right or wrong for such as he? What was right? And who had ever taught him? He thrust the whole matter away. A dark, cold quiet crept through his brain. It was all wrong; but let it be! It was nothing to him more than the others. Let it be!

The door grated, as Haley opened it.

"Come, my woman! Must lock up for t' night. Come, stir yerself!"

She went up and took Hugh's hand.

"Good-night, Deb," he said, carelessly.

She had not hoped he would say more; but the tired pain on her mouth just then was bitterer than death. She took his passive hand and kissed it.

"Hur'll never see Deb again!" she ventured, her lips growing colder and more bloodless.

What did she say that for? Did he not know it? Yet he would not be impatient with poor old Deb. She had trouble of her own, as well as he.

"No, never again," he said, trying to be cheerful.

She stood just a moment, looking at him. Do you laugh at her, standing there, with her hunchback, her rags, her bleared, withered face, and the great despised love tugging at her heart?

"Come, you!" called Haley, impatiently.

She did not move.

"Hugh!" she whispered.

It was to be her last word. What was it?

"Hugh, boy, not THAT!"

He did not answer. She wrung her hands, trying to be silent, looking in his face in an agony of entreaty. He smiled again, kindly.

"It is best, Deb. I cannot bear to be hurted any more."

"Hur knows," she said, humbly.

"Tell my father good-bye; and—and kiss little Janey."

She nodded, saying nothing, looked in his face again, and went out of the door. As she went, she staggered.

"Drinkin' to-day?" broke out Haley, pushing her before him. "Where the Devil did you get it? Here, in with ye!" and he shoved her into her cell, next to Wolfe's, and shut the door.

Along the wall of her cell there was a crack low down by the floor, through which she could see the light from Wolfe's. She had discovered it days before. She hurried in now, and, kneeling down by it, listened, hoping to hear some sound. Nothing but the rasping of the tin on the bars. He was at his old amusement again. Something in the noise jarred on her ear, for she shivered as she heard it. Hugh rasped away at the bars. A dull old bit of tin, not fit to cut korl with.

He looked out of the window again. People were leaving the market now. A tall mulatto girl, following her mistress, her basket on her head, crossed the street just below, and looked up. She was laughing; but, when she caught sight of the haggard face peering out through the bars, suddenly grew grave, and hurried by. A free, firm step, a clear-cut olive face, with a scarlet turban tied on one side, dark, shining eyes, and on the head the basket poised, filled with fruit and flowers, under which the scarlet turban and bright eyes looked out half-shadowed. The picture caught his eye. It was good to see a face like that. He would try to-morrow, and cut one like it. *To-morrow!* He threw down the tin, trembling, and covered his face with his hands. When he looked up again, the daylight was gone.

Deborah, crouching near by on the other side of the wall, heard no noise. He sat on the side of the low pallet, thinking. Whatever was the mystery which the woman had seen on his face, it came out now slowly, in the dark there, and became fixed,—a something never seen on his face before. The evening was darkening fast. The market had been over for an hour; the rumbling of the carts over the pavement grew more infrequent: he listened to each, as it passed, because he thought it was to be for the last time. For the same reason, it was, I suppose, that he strained his eyes to catch a glimpse of each passer-by, wondering who they were, what kind of homes they were going to, if they had children,—listening eagerly to every chance word in the street, as if— (God be merciful to the man! what strange fancy was this?)—as if he never should hear human voices again.

It was quite dark at last. The street was a lonely one. The last passenger, he thought, was gone. No,—there was a quick step: Joe Hill, lighting the lamps. Joe was a good old chap; never passed a fellow without some joke or other. He remembered once seeing the place where he lived with his wife. "Granny Hill" the boys called her. Bedridden she was; but so kind as Joe was to her! kept the room so clean!—and the old woman, when he was there, was laughing at "some of t' lad's foolishness." The step was far down the street; but he could see him place the ladder, run up, and light the gas. A longing seized him to be spoken to once more.

"Joe!" he called, out of the grating. "Good-bye, Joe!"

The old man stopped a moment, listening uncertainly; then hurried on. The prisoner thrust his hand out of the window, and called again, louder; but Joe was too far down the street. It was a little thing; but it hurt him,—this disappointment.

"Good-bye, Joe!" he called, sorrowfully enough.

"Be quiet!" said one of the jailers, passing the door, striking on it with his club.

Oh, that was the last, was it?

There was an inexpressible bitterness on his face, as he lay down on the bed, taking the bit of tin, which he had rasped to a tolerable degree of sharpness, in his hand,—to play with, it may be. He bared his arms, looking intently at their corded veins and sinews. Deborah, listening in the next cell, heard a slight clicking sound, often repeated. She shut her lips tightly, that she might not scream; the cold drops of sweat broke over her, in her dumb agony.

"Hur knows best," she muttered at last, fiercely clutching the boards where she lay.

If she could have seen Wolfe, there was nothing about him to frighten her. He lay quite still, his arms outstretched, looking at the pearly stream of moonlight coming into the window. I think in that one hour that came then he lived back over all the years that had gone before. I think that all the low, vile life, all his wrongs, all his starved hopes, came then, and stung him with a farewell poison that made him sick unto death. He made neither moan nor cry, only turned his worn face now and then to the pure light, that seemed so far off, as one that said, "How long, O Lord? how long?"

The hour was over at last. The moon, passing over her nightly path, slowly came nearer, and threw the light across his bed on his feet. He watched it steadily, as it crept up, inch by inch, slowly. It seemed to him to carry with it a great silence. He had been so hot and tired there always in the mills! The years had been so fierce and cruel! There was coming now quiet and coolness and sleep. His tense limbs relaxed, and settled in a calm languor. The blood ran fainter and slow from his heart. He did not think now with a savage anger of what might be and was not; he was conscious only of deep stillness creeping over him. At first he saw a sea of faces: the mill-men,—women he had known, drunken and bloated,—Janey's timid and pitiful—poor old Debs: then they floated together like a mist, and faded away, leaving only the clear, pearly moonlight.

Whether, as the pure light crept up the stretched-out figure, it brought with it calm and peace, who shall say? His dumb soul was alone with God in judgment. A Voice may have spoken for it from far-off Calvary, "Father, forgive them, for they know not what they do!"[6] Who dare say? Fainter and fainter the heart rose and fell, slower and slower the moon floated from behind a cloud, until, when at last its full tide of white splendor swept over the cell,

<hr />

6. Luke 23.34: "Father, forgive them: for they know not what they do" (Jesus' words from the cross).

it seemed to wrap and fold into a deeper stillness the dead figure that never should move again. Silence deeper than the Night! Nothing that moved, save the black, nauseous stream of blood dripping slowly from the pallet to the floor!

There was outcry and crowd enough in the cell the next day. The coroner and his jury, the local editors, Kirby himself, and boys with their hands thrust knowingly into their pockets and heads on one side, jammed into the corners. Coming and going all day. Only one woman. She came late, and outstayed them all. A Quaker, or Friend, as they call themselves. I think this woman was known by that name in heaven. A homely body, coarsely dressed in gray and white. Deborah (for Haley had let her in) took notice of her. She watched them all—sitting on the end of the pallet, holding his head in her arms—with the ferocity of a watch-dog, if any of them touched the body. There was no meekness, no sorrow, in her face; the stuff out of which murderers are made, instead. All the time Haley and the woman were laying straight the limbs and cleaning the cell, Deborah sat still, keenly watching the Quaker's face. Of all the crowd there that day, this woman alone had not spoken to her,—only once or twice had put some cordial to her lips. After they all were gone, the woman, in the same still, gentle way, brought a vase of wood-leaves and berries, and placed it by the pallet, then opened the narrow window. The fresh air blew in, and swept the woody fragrance over the dead face. Deborah looked up with a quick wonder.

"Did hur know my boy wud like it? Did hur know Hugh?"

"I know Hugh now."

The white fingers passed in a slow, pitiful way over the dead, worn face. There was a heavy shadow in the quiet eyes.

"Did hur know where they'll bury Hugh?" said Deborah in a shrill tone, catching her arm.

This had been the question hanging on her lips all day.

"In t' town-yard? Under t' mud and ash? T' lad 'll smother, woman! He wur born in t' lane moor, where t' air is frick[7] and strong. Take hur out, for God's sake, take hur out where t' air blows!"

The Quaker hesitated, but only for a moment. She put her strong arm around Deborah and led her to the window.

"Thee sees the hills, friend, over the river? Thee sees how the light lies warm there, and the winds of God blow all the day? I live there,—where the blue smoke is, by the trees. Look at me." She turned Deborah's face to her own, clear and earnest. "Thee will believe me? I will take Hugh and bury him there to-morrow."

Deborah did not doubt her. As the evening wore on, she leaned against the iron bars, looking at the hills that rose far off, through the thick sodden clouds, like a bright, unattainable calm. As she looked, a shadow of their solemn repose fell on her face; its fierce discontent faded into a pitiful, humble quiet. Slow, solemn tears gathered in her eyes: the poor weak eyes turned so hopelessly to the place where Hugh was to rest, the grave heights looking higher and brighter and more solemn than ever before. The Quaker watched her keenly. She came to her at last, and touched her arm.

"When thee comes back," she said, in a low, sorrowful tone, like one who speaks from a strong heart deeply moved with remorse or pity, "thee shall

7. Fresh.

begin thy life again,—there on the hills. I came too late; but not for thee,—
by God's help, it may be."

Not too late. Three years after, the Quaker began her work. I end my story
here. At evening-time it was light. There is no need to tire you with the long
years of sunshine, and fresh air, and slow, patient Christ-love, needed to make
healthy and hopeful this impure body and soul. There is a homely pine house,
on one of these hills, whose windows overlook broad, wooded slopes and clo-
ver-crimsoned meadows,—niched into the very place where the light is warmest, the air freest. It is the Friends'[8] meeting-house. Once a week they sit there,
in their grave, earnest way, waiting for the Spirit of Love to speak, opening
their simple hearts to receive His words. There is a woman, old, deformed,
who takes a humble place among them: waiting like them: in her gray dress,
her worn face, pure and meek, turned now and then to the sky. A woman
much loved by these silent, restful people; more silent than they, more humble, more loving. Waiting: with her eyes turned to hills higher and purer than
these on which she lives,—dim and far off now, but to be reached some day.
There may be in her heart some latent hope to meet there the love denied her
here,—that she shall find him whom she lost, and that then she will not be
all-unworthy. Who blames her? Something is lost in the passage of every soul
from one eternity to the other,—something pure and beautiful, which might
have been and was not: a hope, a talent, a love, over which the soul mourns,
like Esau deprived of his birthright.[9] What blame to the meek Quaker, if she
took her lost hope to make the hills of heaven more fair?

Nothing remains to tell that the poor Welsh puddler once lived, but this
figure of the mill-woman cut in korl. I have it here in a corner of my library.
I keep it hid behind a curtain,—it is such a rough, ungainly thing. Yet there
are about it touches, grand sweeps of outline, that show a master's hand.
Sometimes,—to-night, for instance,—the curtain is accidentally drawn back,
and I see a bare arm stretched out imploringly in the darkness, and an eager,
wolfish face watching mine: a wan, woful face, through which the spirit of the
dead korl-cutter looks out, with its thwarted life, its mighty hunger, its unfinished work. Its pale, vague lips seem to tremble with a terrible question. "Is
this the End?" they say,—"nothing beyond?—no more?" Why, you tell me
you have seen that look in the eyes of dumb brutes,—horses dying under the
lash. I know.

The deep of the night is passing while I write. The gas-light wakens from
the shadows here and there the objects which lie scattered through the room:
only faintly, though; for they belong to the open sunlight. As I glance at them,
they each recall some task or pleasure of the coming day. A half-moulded
child's head; Aphrodite;[1] a bough of forest-leaves; music; work; homely fragments, in which lie the secrets of all eternal truth and beauty. Prophetic all!
Only this dumb, woful face seems to belong to and end with the night. I turn
to look at it. Has the power of its desperate need commanded the darkness
away? While the room is yet steeped in heavy shadow, a cool, gray light suddenly touches its head like a blessing hand, and its groping arm points through
the broken cloud to the far East, where, in the flickering, nebulous crimson,
God has set the promise of the Dawn.

1861

8. Quakers.
9. Genesis 25 and 27 tell the story of Jacob's depriving

his elder twin brother Esau of his birthright.
1. Venus, the goddess of love.

# American Literature
## 1865-1914

THE TRANSFORMATION OF A NATION

In the second half of the nineteenth century, the fertile, mineral-rich American continent west of the Appalachians and Alleghenies was occupied, often by force, largely by Europeans, who exploited its resources freely. These new Americans, their numbers doubled by a continuous flow of immigrants, pushed westward to the Pacific coast, displacing the Native American cultures and the Spanish settlements when they stood in the way. Vast stands of timber were consumed; numberless herds of buffalo and other wild game gave way to cattle, sheep, farms, villages, and cities and the railroad that linked them to markets back east; various technologies converted the country's immense natural resources into industrial products both for its own burgeoning population and for foreign markets.

The result was that between the end of the Civil War and the beginning of World War I the country was wholly transformed. Before the Civil War, America had been essentially a rural, agrarian, isolated republic whose idealistic, confident, and self-reliant inhabitants for the most part believed in God; by the time the United States entered World War I as a world power, it was an industrialized, urbanized, continental nation whose people had been forced to come to terms with the implications of Darwin's theory of evolution as well as with profound changes in its own social institutions and cultural values. Increasingly, it would be obliged to acknowledge (if not to remedy) the legacy of racism left by slavery and the policy of Indian removal that were such prominent facts of its pre–Civil War life.

The Civil War cost some eight billion dollars and claimed six hundred thousand lives. It seems also to have left the country morally exhausted. Nonetheless, the country prospered materially over the five following decades, in part because the war had stimulated technological development and had served as an occasion to test new methods of organization and management that were required to move efficiently large numbers of men and matériel and that were then adapted to industrial modernization on a massive scale. The first transcontinental railroad was completed in 1869; industrial output grew at a geometric rate, and agricultural productivity increased dramatically; electricity was introduced on a large scale; new means of communication such as the telephone revolutionized many aspects of daily life; coal, oil, iron, gold, silver, and other kinds of mineral wealth were discovered and extracted to make large numbers of vast individual fortunes and to make the nation as a whole rich enough to capitalize for the first time on its own further development. By the end of the century, no longer a colony politically or economically, the United States could begin its own imperialist expansion (of which the Spanish-American War in 1898 was only one sign).

The central material fact of the period was industrialization, on a scale unprecedented in the earlier experiences of Great Britain and Europe. Between 1850 and 1880 capital invested in manufacturing industries more than quadrupled, while factory employment nearly doubled. By 1885 four transcontinental railroad lines were completed, using in their own construction and carrying to manufacturing centers in Pittsburgh, Cleveland, Detroit, and Chicago the nation's quintupled output of steel. This extensive railway system—and the invention of the refrigerated railway car—in turn made possible such economic developments as the centralization of the meat-packing industry in Chicago. Control over this enterprise as well as other industries passed to fewer and larger companies as time went on. In the two decades following the 1870s, a very small number of men controlled without significant competition the enormously profitable steel, railroad, oil, and meat-packing industries.

This group of men, known variously as buccaneers, captains of industry, self-made men, or robber barons, included Jay Gould, Jim Hill, Leland Stanford, Jim Fisk, Andrew Carnegie, J. P. Morgan, and John D. Rockefeller. However different in temperament and public behavior, all of these men successfully squeezed out their competitors and accumulated vast wealth and power. All were good examples of what the English novelist D. H. Lawrence described as "the lone hand and the huge success." These were the men who served as exemplars for Mark Twain's Colonel Beriah Sellers, a character who in turn epitomizes much of the spirit of acquisitiveness excoriated by Twain in The Gilded Age (1873; a novel written in collaboration with Charles Dudley Warner).

In this half century, as industry flourished, America's cities grew. When the Civil War broke out, America, except for the northeastern seaboard, was a country of farms, villages, and small towns. Most of its citizens were involved in agricultural pursuits and small family businesses. By the turn of the century only about one-third of the population lived on farms. New York had grown from a city of 500,000 in 1850 to a metropolis of nearly 3.5 million people by 1900, many of them recent immigrants from Central, Eastern, and Southern Europe. Chicago, at midcentury a raw town of 20,000, had more than 2 million inhabitants by 1910. By the end of World War I, one-half of the American population was concentrated in a dozen or so cities; the vast majority of all wage earners were employed by corporations and large enterprises, 8.5 million as factory workers. Millions of people participated in the prosperity that accompanied this explosive industrial expansion, but the social costs were immense.

The transformation of an entire continent, outlined above, was not accomplished without incalculable suffering. In the countryside increasing numbers of farmers, dependent for transportation of their crops on the monopolistic railroads, were squeezed off the land by what novelist Frank Norris characterized as the giant "octopus" that crisscrossed the continent. Everywhere independent farmers were placed "under the lion's paw" of land speculators and absentee landlords that Hamlin Garland's story made famous. For many, the great cities were also, as the radical novelist Upton Sinclair sensed, jungles where only the strongest, the most ruthless, and the luckiest survived. An oversupply of labor kept wages down and allowed the industrialists to maintain working conditions of notorious danger and discomfort for men, women, and children who competed for the scarce jobs. Neither farmers nor urban laborers were effectively organized to pursue their own interests, and neither group had any significant political leverage until the 1880s. Legislators essentially served the interests of business and industry, and the scandals of President Grant's administration, the looting of the New York City treasury by William Marcy ("Boss") Tweed in the 1870s, and the later horrors of municipal corruption exposed by journalist Lincoln Steffens and other "muckrakers" were symptomatic of what many writers of the time took to be the age of the "Great Barbecue." Early attempts by labor to organize were crude and often violent, and such groups as the notorious "Molly Maguires," which performed acts of terrorism in Pennsylvania, seemed to confirm the sense of the public and of the courts that labor organizations were "illegal conspiracies" and thus public enemies. Direct violence was probably, as young Emma Goldman believed, a necessary step toward establishing collective bargaining as a means of negotiating disputes between industrial workers and their employers; it was, in any event, not until such an alternative developed—really not until the 1930s—that labor acquired the unquestioned right to strike.

### MARK TWAIN, W. D. HOWELLS, AND HENRY JAMES

This rapid transcontinental settlement and these new urban industrial circumstances were accompanied by the development of a national literature of great abundance and variety. New themes, new forms, new subjects, new regions, new authors, new audiences all emerged in the literature of this half century. As a result, at the onset of World War I, the spirit and substance of American literature had evolved remarkably, just as its center of production had shifted from Boston to New York in the late 1880s and the sources of its energy to Chicago and the Midwest. No longer was it produced, at least in its popular forms, in the main by solemn, typically moralistic writers from New England and the Old South; no longer were polite well-dressed, grammatically correct, middle-class young people the only central characters in its narratives; no longer were these narratives to be set in exotic places and remote times; no longer, indeed, were fiction, poetry, drama, and formal history the chief acceptable forms of literary expression; no longer, finally, was literature read primarily by young, middle-class women. In sum, American literature in these years fulfilled in considerable measure the condition Whitman called for in 1867 in describing *Leaves of Grass*: it treats, he said of his own major work, each state and region as peers "and expands from them, and includes the world . . . connecting an American citizen with the citizens of all nations." Self-educated pioneers, adventurers, and journalists introduced industrial workers and the rural poor, ambitious business leaders and vagrants, prostitutes and unheroic soldiers as major characters in fiction. At the same time, these years saw the emergence of what the critic Warner Berthoff aptly designates "the literature of argument"—powerful works in sociology, philosophy, and psychology, many of them impelled by the spirit of exposure and reform. Just as America learned to play a role in this half century as an autonomous international political, economic, and military power, so did its literature establish itself as a producer of major works. In its new security, moreover, it welcomed (in translation) the leading European figures of the time—Tolstoy, Ibsen, Chekhov, Hardy, Zola, Galdós, Verga—often in the columns of Henry James and William Dean Howells, who reviewed their works enthusiastically in *Harper's Weekly* and *Harper's Monthly*, the *North American Review*, and other leading journals of the era. American writers in this period, like most writers of other times and places, wrote to earn money, earn fame, change the world, and—out of that mysterious compulsion to find the best order for the best words—express themselves in a permanent form and thus exorcise the demon that drove them.

The three figures who dominated prose fiction in the last quarter of the nineteenth century were Mark Twain, William Dean Howells, and Henry James. For half a century Howells was friend, editor, correspondent, and champion of both Twain and James. These latter two, however, knew each other little, and liked each other's work even less.

Twain was without doubt the most popular of the three, in part because of his unusual gift as a humorous public speaker. There is, indeed, much truth in the shrewd observation that Twain's art was in essence the art of the performer. Unlike many of his contemporaries who were successful on the platform, however, Twain had the even rarer ability to convert the humor of stage performance into written language. Twain is one of the few writers of any nationality who makes nearly all of his readers laugh out loud. He had flair; he shared the belief of one of his characters, that "you can't throw too much style into a miracle." To say this is not to deny Twain's skills as a craftsman, his consummate care with words. He was constitutionally incapable of writing—or speaking—a dull sentence. He was a master of style, and there is wide agreement among writers and literary historians alike that his masterpiece, *Adventures of Huckleberry Finn* (1885), is the fountainhead of American colloquial prose. Nor is there much dispute about Twain's ability to capture the enduring, archetypal, mythic images of America before the writer and the country came of age or to create some of the most memorable characters in all of American fiction—Colonel Beriah Sellers, Tom Sawyer, Huck Finn and his Pap, the king and the duke, and Miss Watson's slave Jim. Because of his "river" books—*The Adventures of Tom Sawyer* (1876), *Life on the Mississippi* (1883), and *Adventures of Huckleberry Finn* (1885)—we as Americans have a clearer (because it is mythic rather than historical) collective sense of life in the prewar Mississippi Valley than we do of any other region of America at any other time.

Huck Finn might, at the end of his adventures, imagine lighting out "for the territory," what he thought of as the still uncivilized frontier, but for Twain there was to be no escape; *Huck Finn* was his last "evasion." Obliged to confront the moral, mental, and material squalor of postwar industrialized America (and to deal with a succession of personal catastrophes), Twain's work became more cerebral, contrived, and embittered. Only when he began in the late 1890s to dictate his autobiography, as the critic Jay Martin observes, did he once again become invisible in his words. Freed of the need to be respectable or to make large coherent narrative structures, Twain once more could function as an artist.

If Twain was the most popular of these three major figures, his friend and adviser Howells was unquestionably the most influential American writer in the last quarter of the century. Relentlessly productive, Howells wrote and published the equivalent of one hundred books during his sixty-year professional career. He wrote novels, travel books, biographies, plays, criticism, essays, autobiography—and made them pay. He was the first American writer self-consciously to conceive, to cite the title of one of his essays, of *The Man of Letters as a Man of Business*. Howells was, however, no mere acquisitive hack. He wrote always with a sense of his genteel, largely female audience, but if he generally observed the proprieties, he often took real risks and opened new territories for fiction. In Marcia Gaylord of *A Modern Instance* (1881) he traces with great subtlety the moral decline of an overindulged country girl as she turns into a vindictively jealous woman. Nor can those who complain that Howells only wrote of the "smiling aspects" of life have read *The Landlord at Lion's Head* (1897), with its brutal Jeff Durgin, or *An Imperative Duty* (1892), a curious novel of miscegenation.

Starting with *The Rise of Silas Lapham* (1885), Howells addressed with deepening seriousness (and risk to his reputation) the relationship between the economic transformation of America and its moral condition. In *A Hazard of New Fortunes* (1890), written after his "conversion" to socialism by his reading of Tolstoy and what he described as the "civic murder" of the Haymarket anarchists in 1887, Howells offers his most extended interpretation of the decay of American life under the rule of competitive capitalism. Of the physical squalor and human misery he observes in the Bowery, his character Basil March (the central consciousness of the narrative) concludes:

> Accident and then exigency seemed the forces at work to this extraordinary effect; the play of energies as free and planless as those that force the forest from the soil to the sky; and then the fierce struggle for survival, with the stronger life persisting over the deformity, the mutilation, the destruction, the decay of the weaker. The whole at moments seemed to him lawless, Godless; the absence of intelligent, comprehensive purpose in the huge disorder, and the violent struggle to subordinate the result to the greater good, penetrated with its dumb appeal the consciousness of a man who had always been too self-inwrapt to perceive the chaos to which the individual selfishness must always lead.

Howells could see even more clearly in New York than he had in Boston that for the mass of their populations the cities had become infernos, the social environment degraded by the chasm that had opened between rich and poor, leaving the middle class trapped in their attitudes toward the poor between appalled sympathy and fear.

In his criticism, Howells had called for a literary realism that would treat commonplace Americans truthfully; "this truth given, the book *cannot* be wicked and cannot be weak; and without it all graces of style and feats of invention and cunning of construction are so many superfluities of naughtiness," he observed in *The Editor's Study* column of *Harper's Monthly* for April 1887. Critics are now pretty much in agreement that Howells's novels, especially those of the 1880s and 1890s, succeed in providing such a "truthful treatment." His lifelong friend Henry James observed in a letter on the occasion of Howells's seventy-fifth birthday: "Stroke by stroke and book by book your work was to become, for this exquisite notation of our whole democratic light and shade and give and take, in the highest degree *documentary*, so that none other . . . could approach it in value and amplitude." Whether Howells also had a truly "grasping imagination," the imagination to penetrate photographic surfaces, is the kind of question that finally each reader must decide; that it has become an active question at all is a sign of how far Howells's reputation has come since H. L. Mencken characterized him in 1919 as "an urbane and highly respectable old gentleman, a sitter on committees, an intimate of professors, . . . a placid conformist."

On his deathbed Howells was writing the essay *The American James*, an essay that apparently would have defended James against charges that in moving to England permanently in the mid-1870s he had cut himself off from the sources of his imaginative power as well as sacrificed any hope of having a large audience for his work. In view of the critical praise lavished on James since World War II, and in the light of the highly successful film and television adaptations of his fiction, the need for any such defense may seem puzzling. Yet it is true that during his lifetime few of James's books had much popular success and that he was not a favorite of the American people.

There is more of American life and spirit represented in his literary production than is often thought, but James early came to believe the literary artist should not simply hold a mirror to the surface of social life in particular times and places. Instead, the writer should use language to probe the deepest reaches of the psychological and moral nature of human beings. At a time when novels were widely conceived as mere popular entertainment, James believed that the best fiction illuminates life by revealing it as an immensely complex process, and he demonstrated in work after work what a superb literary sensibility can do to dignify both life and art. He is a realist of the inner life; a dramatizer, typically, to put it crudely, of the tensions that develop between the young, innocent, selfless, and free woman and the older, sophisticated, and convention-bound man. That he is always on the side of freedom, Ezra Pound was to be one of the first to note.

Twain, James, and Howells together brought to fulfillment native trends in the realistic portrayal of the landscape and social surfaces, brought to perfection the vernacular style, and explored and exploited the literary possibilities of the interior life. Among them they recorded and made permanent the essential life of the eastern third of the continent as it was lived in the last half of the nineteenth century on the vanishing frontier, in the village, small town, or turbulent metropolis, and in European watering places and capitals. Among them they established the literary identity of distinctively American protagonists, specifically the vernacular hero and the "American Girl," the baffled and strained middle-class family, the businessman, the psychologically complicated citizens of a new international culture. Together, in short, they set the example and charted the future course for the subjects, themes, techniques, and styles of fiction we still call modern.

OTHER REALISTS AND NATURALISTS

Terms like *realism*, *naturalism*, and *local color*, while useful shorthand for professors of literature trying to "cover" great numbers of books and long periods of time, probably do as much harm as they do good, especially for readers who are beginning their study of literature. The chief disservice these generalizing terms do to readers and authors is to divert attention from the distinctive quality of an author's sense of life to a general body of ideas. In a letter turning down one of the many professorships he was offered, Howells observed that the study of literature should begin and end in pleasure, and it is far more rewarding to establish, in Emerson's phrase, "an original relationship" to particular texts and authors than it is to attempt to fit them into movements. However, because these generalizations are still in currency, we need to examine some of them.

One of the most far-reaching intellectual events of the last half of the nineteenth century was the publication in 1859 of Charles Darwin's *The Origin of Species*. This book, together with Darwin's *Descent of Man* (1870), hypothesized that over the millennia humans had evolved from "lower" forms of life. Humans were special, not—as the Bible taught—because God had created them in His image, but because they had successfully adapted to changing environmental conditions and had passed on their survival-making characteristics genetically. Though few American authors wrote treatises in reaction to Darwinism, nearly every writer had to come to terms somehow with this challenge to traditional conceptions of humanity, nature, and the social order.

One response was to accept the more negative implications of evolutionary theory and to use it to account for the behavior of characters in literary works. That is, characters were conceived as more or less complex combinations of inherited attributes and habits conditioned by social and economic forces. As Émile Zola, the influential French theorist and novelist, put the matter in his essay *The Experimental Novel*:

> In short, we must operate with characters, passions, human and social data as the chemist and the physicist work on inert bodies, as the physiologist works on living bodies. Determinism governs everything. It is scientific investigation; it is experimental reasoning that combats one by one the hypotheses of the idealists and will replace novels of pure imagination by novels of observation and experiment.

Many American writers adopted this pessimistic form of realism, this so-called naturalistic view of humankind, though each writer, of course, incorporated this assumption, and many others, into his or her work in highly individual ways.

Stephen Crane is a case in point. Crane believed, as he said of *Maggie*, that environment counts for a great deal in determining human fate. Nature is not hostile, he observes in *The Open Boat*, only "indifferent, flatly indifferent." Indeed, the earth, in *The Blue Hotel*, is described in one of the most famous passages in naturalistic fiction as a "whirling, fire-smote, ice-locked, disease-stricken, space-lost bulb." In Crane's *The Red Badge of Courage* Henry Fleming responds to the very end to the world of chaos and violence that surrounds him with alternating surges of panic and self-congratulation, not as a man who has understood himself and his place in a world that reveals order below its confused surface.

But after we have granted this ostensibly "naturalistic" perspective to Crane, we are still left with his distinctiveness as a writer, with his "personal honesty" in reporting what he saw (and concomitant rejection of accepted literary conventions), and with his use of impressionistic literary techniques to present incomplete characters and a broken world—a world more random than scientifically predictable. We are also left with the hardly pessimistic implication of *The Open Boat*—that precisely because human beings are exposed to a savage world of chance where death is always imminent, they must learn the art of sympathetic identification with others and how to practice solidarity, often learned at the price of death. Without this deeply felt human connection, human experience is as meaningless as wind, sharks, and waves. It is Crane's power with words and his ability to live with paradox, then, that make him interesting, not his allegiance to philosophic or scientific theories.

Theodore Dreiser certainly did not share Crane's tendency to use words and images as if he were a composer or a painter. But he did share, at least early in his career, Crane's view that by and large human beings were more like moths drawn to flame than lords of creation. But, again, it is not Dreiser's beliefs that make him an enduring major figure in American letters: it is what his imagination and literary technique do with an extremely rich set of ideas, experiences, and emotions to create the "color of life" in his fictions that earns him an honored place. If Crane gave us through the personal honesty of his vision a new sense of the human consciousness under conditions of extreme pressure, Dreiser gave us for the first time in his unwieldy novels a sense of the fumbling, yearning, confused response to the simultaneously enchanting, exciting, ugly, and dangerous metropolis that had become the familiar residence for such large numbers of Americans by the turn of the century.

In sum, despite residual prohibitions that insisted on humanity's special place in the universe, and a status-conscious gentility that militated against the ugly as well as the "morally" unclean, America proved to be a fertile ground for naturalistic ideas and realistic literary technique, though the ideas were often undercut, and the technique, while commonly documentary, was adapted to highly individual uses. The country's democratic spirit (in any case, the principle of equality) and the harsh realities of country and urban life that accompanied industrialization and unbridled economic competitiveness made it receptive to a literature of familiar people and ordinary places keenly observed by eye and ear.

## REGIONAL WRITING

Regional writing, another expression of the realistic impulse, resulted from the desire both to preserve distinctive ways of life before industrialization dispersed or homogenized them and to come to terms with the harsh realities that seemed to replace these early times. At a more practical level, much of the writing was a response to the opportunities presented by the rapid growth of magazines, which created a new, largely female market for short fiction. By the end of the century, in any case, virtually every region of the country, from Maine to California, from the northern plains to the Louisiana bayous, had its "local colorist" (the implied comparison is to painters of so-called genre scenes) to immortalize its distinctive natural, social, and linguistic features. Though often suffused with nostalgia, the best work of these regionalists renders both a convincing surface of a particular time and location and penetrates below that surface to the depths that transform the local into the universal. This ambiguity of attitude may be seen even in an early example of local-color writing such as Bret Harte's *The Luck of Roaring Camp*, which made Harte a national celebrity in 1868. But Harte knew how to be entertaining, and the curiosity of the rest of the country about the Gold Rush country was satisfied in this and other myth-making stories Harte produced early in his career.

Hamlin Garland, rather than creating a myth, set out to destroy one. Like so many other writers of the time, Garland was encouraged by W. D. Howells to write about what he knew best—the bleak and exhausting life of farmers of the upper Midwest. As he later said, his purpose in writing his early stories was to show that the "mystic quality connected with free land . . . was a myth." Garland's farmers are not the vigorous, sensuous peasants of Brueghel's paintings, but bent, drab figures reminiscent of Millet's *Sowers* or Edwin Markham's *Man with a Hoe*.

*Under the Lion's Paw,* from the collection *Main-Travelled Roads* (1891), shows local color not as nostalgia but as realism in the service of social protest.

The work of Harriet Beecher Stowe, Sarah Orne Jewett, and Mary E. Wilkins Freeman may be seen as a less didactic form of social protest. That is, the regional fiction of each of them may be understood as an invitation to consider the world from the perspective of women awakening to, protesting against, and offering alternatives for a world dominated by men and male interests and values. Stowe, Jewett, and Freeman do more than lament the postwar economic and spiritual decline of New England; their female characters suggest the capacity of human beings to live independently and with dignity in the face of community pressures, patriarchal power, and material deprivation. Together with Alice Brown of New Hampshire and Rose Terry Cook of Connecticut—to mention only two others—these regional writers created not only places but themes that have assumed increasing importance in the twentieth century.

Chief among the southern local colorists are George Washington Cable, Joel Chandler Harris, Charles Waddell Chesnutt, and Kate Chopin. Like their Yankee counterparts, they become most universal when they are most faithfully particular. Harris's Georgia blacks live permanently in our imagination because he knew them well and from within. He did not exploit or demean them; and Kate Chopin did not exploit or demean the characters who people her stories of the Louisiana bayous.

### REALISM AS ARGUMENT

During these fifty years a vast body of nonfictional prose was devoted to the description, analysis, and critique of social, economic, and political institutions and to the unsolved social problems that were one consequence of the rapid growth and change of the time. Women's rights, political corruption, economic inequity, business deceptions, the exploitation of labor—these became the subjects of articles and books by a long list of journalists, historians, social critics, and economists. A surprising amount of this writing survives as literature, and much of it has genuine power that is often attributed only to the older, "purer" forms. Certainly in that most ambitious of all American works of moral instruction, *The Education of Henry Adams* (1918), Adams registers through a literary sensibility a sophisticated historian's sense of what we now recognize as the disorientation that accompanies rapid and continuous change. The result is one of the most essential books of and about the whole period, and it seems fitting that Adams should have the last— though surely not the conclusive—word about his own problematic times.

Of all the problems of the day, perhaps the most persistent and resistant to solution was the problem of racial inequality, more specifically what came to be known as the "Negro problem." Several of the selections in this anthology touch one aspect or another of the long, shameful history of white injustices to black Americans, but two items by major black writers and leaders have a special claim on our attention: the autobiography of Booker T. Washington, *Up from Slavery* (1900) and the brilliantly analytical essay on Washington in *The Souls of Black Folk* (1903) by W. E. B. Du Bois. The Washington-Du Bois controversy set the major terms of the continuing debate between black leaders and in the black community with respect to the future: which strategies will most effectively hasten complete equality educationally, socially, politically, and economically?

In this half century, material, intellectual, social, and psychological changes in the lives of many Americans went forward at such extreme speed and on such a massive scale that the enormously diverse writing of the time registers, at its core, degrees of shocked recognition of the human consequences of these radical transformations. Sometimes the shock is expressed in recoil and denial—thus the persistence, in the face of the ostensible triumph of realism, of the literature of diversion: nostalgic poetry, sentimental and melodramatic drama, and swashbuckling historical novels. The more enduring fictional and nonfictional prose forms of the era, however, come to terms imaginatively with the individual and collective dislocations and discontinuities associated with the closing out of the frontier, urbanization, intensified secularism, unprecedented immigration, the surge of national wealth unequally distributed, revised conceptions of human nature and destiny, the reordering of family and civil life, and the pervasive spread of mechanical and organizational technologies.

## NATIVE AMERICAN HISTORY AND LITERATURE

For the history of the native peoples of the United States, 1830 and 1890 mark the watershed moments within the nineteenth century: 1830 is the date of the passage by Congress of the Indian Removal Act, granting President Andrew Jackson permission to relocate eastern Indians to lands west of the Mississippi, and 1890 is both the year the census bureau anounced the closing of the frontier and the year of the massacre of Lakota people by U.S. troops at Wounded Knee, South Dakota. It was in the cold of Wounded Knee that Indian "history" seemed to come to an end.

In the years leading up to Wounded Knee, a familiar pattern of events had emerged: advancement by white settlers onto Indian lands contrary to treaty provisions, failure of the state and federal governments to take action against the settlers, exasperated retaliation by the Indians—and then the Indian wars, against Black Hawk and his Sauk and Fox (in 1832, the last Indian war fought east of the Mississippi) and then on to the Plains and into the Northwest and Southwest, against the Lakota and Cheyenne and Nez Percés, the Navajo and the Apache. Increasingly, in the wake of these conflicts, Indians were relegated to reservation lands west of the Mississippi River.

The haphazardly developed reservation system had its roots in the eighteenth century. Although the Indian peoples were dealt with as sovereign nations in the colonial period, some had already either agreed or been forced to restrict themselves to specific land areas by the colonies, whose obligations were taken over by the newly established states after the American Revolution. Established in 1789, the War Department was at first responsible for matters relating to the Native Americans. In 1824, the Bureau of Indian Affairs (BIA) was established under the jurisdiction of the War Department and was then transferred, in 1849, to the newly organized Interior Department. But despite the existence of a bureau devoted strictly to dealing with native peoples, by 1871 the government had abandoned the policy of treating the Indians as sovereign nations. With very little consultation or careful consideration, it now simply legislated Indians onto reservations that more often than not contained, as one commissioner of Indian affairs wrote, "ground unfitted for cultivation, but suited to the peculiar habits of the Indians." Management of the reservations was entrusted to federal employees called "Indian agents," whose motives and means were often somewhat questionable, and whose wages were poor. It was to improve the character of these agents—to get "God-fearing" persons of higher "morals" into the Indian service—that President Ulysses S. Grant, in the 1870s, turned reservation management over to the country's Christian denominations. That the agents were not generally successful in adjusting the native peoples to their fate was an economic as well as a moral fiasco for the United States: an 1870 estimate judged that each Indian killed in the frequent wars of the period had cost the government no less than one million dollars!

In an effort to address the problem of settling the native peoples on the reservations, so-called friends of the Indian succeeded in passing in 1887 the Dawes Allotment Act, which legislated the private rather than communal ownership of Indian lands: heads of families were each to receive 160 acres. At least Captain Richard Pratt, founder of the well-known Carlisle Indian School, was honest in his estimate of the benefit of the Dawes Act to the American Indians; he predicted that the Indians would quickly sell or waste their lands and be forced to go to work, a good thing for their moral, economic, and political development. Whether due to benign miscalculation or simple greed, the result of the Dawes Act by 1920 (it was overturned in 1934) was that the American Indians had lost more than 86 million of an estimated 138 million acres of land—and what remained to them was desert or semidesert, largely useless to the white population.

Thus by the time that Geronimo, the "last of the wild Indians," surrendered to the U.S. army in 1886, the plight of the native peoples was desperate, notwithstanding the dramatic defeat of Custer and his Seventh Cavalry detachment on the "Greasy Grass," or Little Bighorn, River by the Sioux and Cheyenne in 1876. For the most part, armed action against the settlers and U.S. troops had failed. So had attempts to leave the country and evade confinement to reservation lands, like the foiled flight to Canada of Chief Joseph and the Nez Percés in 1877. Not surprisingly, and consistent with native traditions, many American Indians turned to spiritual action as a means of bringing about desired ends. From this impulse arose what has been called the Ghost Dance religion.

On New Year's Day 1889, a Paiute from present-day Nevada, known by his adoptive name Jack Wilson or by his boyhood name Wovoka, experienced a powerful vision that was followed by a total eclipse of the sun. In his vision, Wovoka was transported to heaven, where God gave him a number of instructions to bring to his people. Interestingly, these were an amalgam of various American Indian traditions and Christian teachings: no lying, no stealing, no wars, and the performance of a set of dances that was to last (accounts vary) five or six nights. If the Indians performed the dances, sang the accompanying songs, and followed the teachings of Wovoka, the virtually extinct buffalo herds would return and the white invaders would miraculously (and, in Wovoka's Christian-influenced teaching, nonviolently) disappear. Although Wovoka's message was essentially pacific, some of the warrior groups of the Plains largely abandoned the Christian elements or altered them in accordance with their own cultural patterns. It was fear of the ghost dancers that brought the Seventh Cavalry—Custer's former command—to Wounded Knee in December 1890.

Whatever the key dates for Native American history, the key dates for Native American literary history are even harder to assign. Still, it is certain that 1865–1914 is one of the richest periods for which there are texts, from traditional oratory to Indian chants and songs to native writings within the genres of the Euro-American tradition. Because they regularly were a part of treaty negotiations, Native American oratorical performances—speeches—in translations of varying and largely unconfirmable accuracy had long been recorded (e.g., there is extant an English version of a 1609 speech by Powhatan). Such speeches continued to be recorded in the nineteenth century, although we know now that some of the most widely anthologized, in particular the one apparently delivered in 1855 by Chief Seatthl, are largely fabrications. (The most commonly reproduced version of Seatthl's speech was composed by the American writer William Arrowsmith in 1969!) Not surprisingly, anthropologists, rather than literary scholars, were the first to gain accurate insight into native verbal expression. In the 1880s and 1890s, amateur and professional anthropologists attached to the newly formed government bureaus (e.g., the Bureau of American Ethnology) did fieldwork among the different ethnic groups and began to record, in laborious shorthand, traditional native oral performances. Then, going far beyond these early fieldworkers in their linguistic and cultural competence, anthropologists of the decades around the turn of the century produced translations that conveyed something of the sophistication and beauty of an oral tradition that was not, as the Native American was supposed to be, "vanishing" but, indeed, persisting vigorously in spite of trying circumstances.

Not only early anthropologists but—as we now call them—ethnomusicologists like Alice Fletcher and Frances Densmore paid particular attention to the songs of native peoples. So did Natalie Curtis Burlin, whose curious compilation *The Indians' Book* appeared in 1907 with an approving endorsement by the great outdoorsman (and so admirer of the Indian!) former president Theodore Roosevelt. If many of these people viewed these literatures mainly as records of what was past or passing, still their publications had a current effect—on such people as Mary Austin, who, in an introduction to one of the first anthologies of American Indian poetry, George Cronyn's *The Path on the Rainbow* (1918), predicted that a relationship was "about to develop between Indian verse and the ultimate literary destiny of America," noting a similarity between the work of native "poets" and that of the latest "literary fashionables," the imagists.

Many native people who remained on reservations continued to sing songs and tell stories in the oral tradition; however, others who left the reservation began to use the written literary forms of Euro-Americans. From most of them, detailed contact with Euro-American culture came as a result of attendance—voluntary or otherwise—at one of the federal government's boarding schools. As has been painfully documented, these schools were sites of horror for most of their pupils. Upon arrival, Native American children had their long hair cut short and their clothes burned. The boys, dressed in stiff collars, woolen pants and coats, and the girls in long dresses, were forbidden to speak their own languages and were humiliated for not obeying instructions in a language they did not understand. Many of the Indian school boarders attempted to run away or commit suicide, clearly resisting the schools' mission, in the words of the Indian educator Richard Pratt, to "kill the Indian and save the man" or woman. Run by Catholics and Protestants of various denominations, these schools aimed to turn American Indians into people who would, like Booker T. Washington's modestly educated Negroes, take their decent but subordinate places in American society as blacksmiths, artisans, or for the women, domestic workers.

Other boarding-school cildren, like Zitkala Sa and the medical doctor Charles Alexander Eastman (Ohiyesa), both Lakota people, and the Cherokee John Milton Oskison, made adjustments to this harsh setting in order to pursue an education that, painful as it was to acquire, was of value to them. Not surprisingly, their writing makes use of the familiar Western genres of autobiography, personal memoir, and short story to convey varieties of native experience and value.

---

# SAMUEL CLEMENS

## 1835–1910

Samuel Langhorne Clemens, the third of five children, was born on November 30, 1835, in the village of Florida, Missouri, and grew up in the larger river town of Hannibal, that mixture of idyll and nightmare in and around which his two most famous characters, Tom Sawyer and Huck Finn, live out their adventure-filled summers. Clemens's father, an ambitious and respected but unsuccessful country lawyer and storekeeper, died when Clemens was twelve, and from that time on Clemens worked to support himself and the rest of the family. Perhaps, as more than one critic has remarked, the shortness of his boyhood made him value it the more.

Clemens was apprenticed to a printer after his father's death, and in 1851, when his brother Orion became a publisher in Hannibal, Clemens went to work for him. In 1853 he began a three-year period of restless travel, which took him to St. Louis,

New York, Philadelphia, Keokuk (Iowa), and Cincinnati, in each of which he earned his living as a printer hired by the day. In 1856 he set out by steamboat for New Orleans, intending to go to the Amazon, where he expected to find adventure and perhaps wealth and fame besides. This scheme fell through, and instead, he apprenticed himself to Horace Bixby, the pilot of the Mississippi riverboat. After a training period of eighteen months, Clemens satisfied a boyhood ambition when he became a pilot himself. Clemens practiced this lucrative and prestigious trade until the Civil War virtually ended commercial river traffic in 1861. During this period he began to write humorous accounts of his activities for the *Keokuk Saturday Post*; though only three of these articles were published (under the pseudonym Thomas Jefferson Snodgrass), they established the pattern of peripatetic journalism—the pattern for much of the next ten years of his life.

After brief and rather inglorious service in the Confederate militia, Clemens made the first of the trips that would take him farther west and toward his ultimate careers as humorist, lecturer, and writer. In 1861, he accompanied Orion to the Nevada Territory, to which the latter had been appointed secretary (chief record keeper for the territorial government) by President Lincoln. In *Roughing It*, written a decade later, Clemens told of the brothers' adventures on the way to Carson City and of the various schemes that, once there, Sam devised for getting rich quick on timber and silver. All of these schemes failed, however, and as usual Clemens was to get much more out of refining the ore of his experience into books than he was to earn from the actual experience of prospecting and claim staking. Soon enough Clemens was once again writing for newspapers, first for the *Territorial Enterprise* in Virginia City and then, after 1864, for the *Californian*. The fashion of the time called for a *nom de plume*, and Clemens used "Mark Twain," a term from his piloting days signifying "two fathoms deep" or "safe water." Twain's writing during these early years, while often distinctive and amusing, was largely imitative of the humorous journalism of the time and is important chiefly because it provided him with an opportunity to master the techniques of the short narrative and to try out a variety of subjects in a wide range of tones and modes. No less important than his writing during these formative western years were his friendships with three master storytellers: the writer Bret Harte, the famous professional lecturer Artemus Ward, and the obscure amateur raconteur Jim Gillis. Twain owed his earliest national audience and critical recognition to his performances as lecturer and to his skillful retelling of a well-known tall tale, *The Notorious Jumping Frog of Calaveras County*, first published in 1865.

In this same year Twain signed up with the *Sacramento Union* to cover in a series of amusing letters the newly opened passenger service between San Francisco and Honolulu. In these letters Twain used a fictitious character, Mr. Brown, to present inelegant ideas, attitudes, and information, sometimes in impolite language. In this series Twain discovered that he could say almost anything he wanted—provided he could convincingly claim that he was simply reporting what others said and did. The refinement of this technique—a written equivalent of "deadpan" lecturing—which allowed his fantasy a long leash and yet required him to anchor it in the circumstantial details of time and place, was to be his major technical accomplishment of the next two decades, the period of his best work.

The first book of this period—and still one of Twain's most popular—was *Innocents Abroad* (1869). It consists of a revised form of letters that Twain wrote for the *Alta California* and the *New York Tribune* during his 1867 excursion on the *Quaker City* to the Mediterranean and the Holy Land. The letters as they appeared in the newspaper—and later the book—were enormously popular, not only because they were exuberantly funny but also because the satire they leveled against a pretentious, decadent, and undemocratic Old World was especially relished by a young country about to enter a period of explosive economic growth and political consolidation.

Twain still had no literary aspirations or any clear plans for a career. Nor did he have a permanent base of operations. To record the second half of his life is to record his acquisition of status, the mature development of his literary powers, and his transformation into a living public legend. A wife came first. Twain courted and finally won the hand of Olivia Langdon, the physically delicate daughter of a wealthy industrialist in Elmira, New York. This unlikely marriage brought both husband and wife the special pleasure that the union of apparent opposites sometimes yields. She was his "Angel"; he was her "Youth." The charge leveled in the 1920s by the critic Van Wyck Brooks that Livy's gentility emasculated Twain as a writer is no longer given serious credence. The complex comfort that this ebullient, whiskey-drinking, cigar-smoking, wild humorist took in his wife is suggested in a letter that he wrote in 1870 to his childhood friend Will Bowen.

The letter also makes clear just how deep the rich material of his Mississippi boyhood ran in his memory and imagination. To get to it, Twain had, in effect, to work chronologically backward and psychically inward. He made a tentative probe of this material as early as 1870 in an early version of The Adventures of Tom Sawyer called A Boy's Manuscript. But it was not until 1875, when he wrote Old Times on the Mississippi in seven installments of the Atlantic Monthly (edited by his lifelong friend W. D. Howells), that Twain arrived at the place his deepest imagination called home. For in this work, an account of Twain's apprenticeship to the pilot Horace Bixby, he evokes not only "the great Mississippi, the majestic, the magnificent Mississippi, rolling its mile-wide tide along, shining in the sun" but also his most intimate ties to the life on its surface and shores. With Old Times Twain is no longer a writer exploiting material, rather he is a man expressing imaginatively a period of his life that he had deeply absorbed. The material he added to these installments to make the book Life on the Mississippi (1883) is often excellent, but it is clearly grafted on, not an organic development of the original story.

For all its charm and lasting appeal, The Adventures of Tom Sawyer (1876) is in certain respects a backward step. There is no mistaking its failure to integrate its self-consciously fine writing, addressed to adults, with its account in plain diction of thrilling adventures designed to appeal to young people. Twain had returned imaginatively to the Hannibal of his youth; before he could realize the deepest potential of this material he would have to put aside the psychological impediments of his civilized adulthood. Tom Sawyer creates a compelling myth of the endless summer of childhood pleasures mixed with terror, but as Twain hints in the opening sentence of Huck Finn, the earlier novel is important primarily as the place of origin of Huckleberry Finn—often described by critics and such writers as Hemingway as the greatest American character in the greatest American book.

Adventures of Huckleberry Finn took Twain eight years to write. He began it in 1876 and completed it, after several stops and starts, in 1883. The fact that he devoted seven months to subsequent revision suggests that Twain was aware of the novel's sometimes discordant tones and illogical shifts in narrative intention. Any real or imagined flaws in the novel, however, have not bothered most readers; Huck Finn has enjoyed extraordinary popularity since its publication more than one hundred years ago. Its unpretentious, colloquial, yet poetic style, its wide-ranging humor, its embodiment of the enduring and universally shared dream of perfect innocence and freedom, its recording of a vanished way of life in the pre–Civil War Mississippi Valley have moved millions of people of all ages and conditions, and all over the world. It is one of those rare works that reveals to us the discrepancy between appearance and reality without leading us to despair of ourselves or others.

Though Twain made a number of attempts to return to the characters, themes, settings, and points of view of Tom and Huck, Old Times, Tom Sawyer, and Huck Finn had exhausted the rich themes of river and boyhood. Twain would live to write successful—even memorable—books, but the critical consensus is that his creative time had passed when he turned fifty. A Connecticut Yankee at King

*Arthur's Court* (1889), for instance, is vividly imagined and very entertaining, but the satire, burlesque, moral outrage, and comic invention remain unintegrated. A similar mood of despair informs and flaws *The Tragedy of Pudd'nhead Wilson* (1894). The book shows the disastrous effects of slavery on victimizer and victim alike—the unearned pride of whites and the undeserved self-hate of blacks. Satire turns to scorn, and beneath the drollery and fun one senses angry contempt for what Twain would soon refer to regularly as the "damned human race."

The decline of Twain's achievement as a writer between *Huck Finn* in 1884 and *Pudd'nhead Wilson* ten years later, however, is not nearly so precipitous as it turned out to be in the next decade, a decade that saw Twain's physical, economic, familial, and psychological supports collapse in a series of calamitous events. For forty years Twain had been fortune's favorite. Now, suddenly, his health was broken, his speculative investments in such enterprises as the Paige typesetting machine bankrupted him in the panic of 1893, his youngest daughter, Jean, was diagnosed as an epileptic, his oldest daughter, Susy, died of meningitis while he and Livy were in Europe, his wife began her decline into permanent invalidism, and Twain's grief for a time threatened his own sanity. For several years, as the critic Bernard DeVoto has shown, writing became both agonized labor and necessary therapy. The result of these circumstances was a dull book, *Following the Equator* (1897), which records Twain's round-the-world lecture tour undertaken to pay off debts; a sardonically preachy story, *The Man That Corrupted Hadleyburg* (1900); an embittered treatise on humanity's foibles, follies, and venality, *What Is Man?* (1906); and the bleakly despairing *The Mysterious Stranger*, first published in an "edited" version by Albert Bigelow Paine in 1916. Though the continuing study of the large bulk of Twain's unfinished (and, until recently, unpublished) work reveals much that is of interest to students of Twain, no one has come forward to claim that his final fifteen years represent a Henry Jamesian "major phase."

Unlike James, however, Twain in his last years became a revered public institution; his opinions were sought by the press on every subject of general interest. Though his opinions on many of these subjects—political, military, and social—were often tinged with vitriol, it was only to his best friends—who understood the complex roots of his despair and anger at the human race in general—that he vented his blackest rages. Much of this bitterness nonetheless informs such works, unpublished in his lifetime, as *The War Prayer* and *Letters from the Earth*.

But early and late Twain maintained his magical power with language. What he said of one of his characters is a large part of his permanent appeal: "He could curl his tongue around the bulliest words in the language when he was a mind to, and lay them before you without a jint started, anywheres." His love of words and command over their arrangement, his mastery at distilling the rhythms and metaphors of oral speech into written prose, his vivid personality, his identification with the deepest centers of humanity's emotional and moral condition—all of these made Twain unique. As his friend Howells observed, he was unlike any of his contemporaries in American letters: "Emerson, Longfellow, Lowell, Holmes—I knew them all and all the rest of our sages, poets, seers, critics, humorists; they were like one another and like other literary men; but Clemens was sole, incomparable, the Lincoln of our literature." Like Lincoln, Clemens spoke to and for the common person of the American heartland that had nourished them both. And like Lincoln, who transcended the local political traditions in which he was trained to become the first great president of a continental nation, Clemens made out of the frontier humor and storytelling conventions of his journalistic influences a body of work of enduring value to the world of letters.

The editor is indebted to Frederick Anderson, late editor of the Mark Twain Papers at the Bancroft Library, University of California, Berkeley, for textual advice and general counsel in preparing the Clemens materials.

# The Notorious Jumping Frog of Calaveras County[1]

In compliance with the request of a friend of mine, who wrote me from the East, I called on good-natured, garrulous old Simon Wheeler, and inquired after my friend's friend, Leonidas W. Smiley, as requested to do, and I hereunto append the result. I have a lurking suspicion that Leonidas W. Smiley is a myth; that my friend never knew such a personage; and that he only conjectured that if I asked old Wheeler about him, it would remind him of his infamous Jim Smiley, and he would go to work and bore me to death with some exasperating reminiscence of him as long and as tedious as it should be useless to me. If that was the design, it succeeded.

I found Simon Wheeler dozing comfortably by the barroom stove of the dilapidated tavern in the decayed mining camp of Angel's, and I noticed that he was fat and bald-headed, and had an expression of winning gentleness and simplicity upon his tranquil countenance. He roused up, and gave me good-day. I told him a friend of mine had commissioned me to make some inquiries about a cherished companion of his boyhood named Leonidas W. Smiley—Rev. Leonidas W. Smiley, a young minister of the Gospel, who he had heard was at one time a resident of Angel's Camp. I added that if Mr. Wheeler could tell me anything about this Rev. Leonidas W. Smiley, I would feel under many obligations to him.

Simon Wheeler backed me into a corner and blockaded me there with his chair, and then sat down and reeled off the monotonous narrative which follows this paragraph. He never smiled, he never frowned, he never changed his voice from the gentle-flowing key to which he tuned his initial sentence, he never betrayed the slightest suspicion of enthusiasm; but all through the interminable narrative there ran a vein of impressive earnestness and sincerity, which showed me plainly that, so far from his imagining that there was anything ridiculous or funny about his story, he regarded it as a really important matter, and admired its two heroes as men of transcendent genius in *finesse*. I let him go on in his own way, and never interrupted him once.

Rev. Leonidas W. H'm, Reverend Le—well, there was a feller here once by the name of *Jim* Smiley, in the winter of '49—or may be it was the spring of '50—I don't recollect exactly, somehow, though what makes me think it was one or the other is because I remember the big flume warn't finished when he first come to the camp; but any way, he was the curiosest man about always betting on anything that turned up you ever see, if he could get anybody to bet on the other side; and if he couldn't he'd change sides. Any way that suited the other man would suit *him*—any way just so's he got a bet, *he* was satisfied. But still he was lucky, uncommon lucky; he most always come out winner. He was always ready and laying for a chance; there couldn't be no solit'ry thing mentioned but that feller'd offer to bet on it, and take ary side you please, as I was just telling you. If there was a horse-race, you'd find him flush or you'd find him busted at the end of it; if there was a dog-fight, he'd bet on it; if there was a cat-fight, he'd bet on it; if there was a chicken-fight, he'd bet on it; why, if there was two birds setting on a fence, he would bet you which one would fly first; or if there was a camp-meeting, he would be there reg'lar to bet on

1. The story first appeared in the New York *Saturday Press* for November 18, 1865, and was subsequently revised several times. The source of the present text is the version published in *Mark Twain's Sketches, New and Old* (1875). In a note, Twain instructs his readers that "Calaveras" is pronounced *Cal-e-va'-ras*.

Parson Walker, which he judged to be the best exhorter about here, and so he
was too, and a good man. If he even see a straddle-bug start to go anywheres,
he would bet you how long it would take him to get to—to wherever he was
going to, and if you took him up, he would foller that straddle-bug to Mexico
but what he would find out where he was bound for and how long he was on
the road. Lots of the boys here has seen that Smiley, and can tell you about
him. Why, it never made no difference to *him*—he'd bet on *any* thing—the
dangdest feller. Parson Walker's wife laid very sick once, for a good while, and
it seemed as if they warn't going to save her; but one morning he come in, and
Smiley up and asked him how she was, and he said she was considable better—
thank the Lord for his inf'nite mercy—and coming on so smart that with the
blessing of Prov'dence she'd get well yet; and Smiley, before he thought says,
"Well, I'll resk two-and-a-half she don't anyway."

Thish-yer Smiley had a mare—the boys called her the fifteen-minute nag,
but that was only in fun, you know, because of course she was faster than
that—and he used to win money on that horse, for all she was so slow and
always had the asthma, or the distemper, or the consumption, or something
of that kind. They used to give her two or three hundred yards start, and then
pass her under way; but always at the fag end of the race she'd get excited and
desperate-like, and come cavorting and straddling up, and scattering her legs
around limber, sometimes in the air, and sometimes out to one side among
the fences, and kicking up m-o-r-e dust and raising m-o-r-e racket with her
coughing and sneezing and blowing her nose—and *always* fetch up at the
stand just about a neck ahead, as near as you could cipher it down.

And he had a little small bull-pup, that to look at him you'd think he warn't
worth a cent but to set around and look ornery and lay for a chance to steal
something. But as soon as money was up on him he was a different dog; his
under-jaw'd begin to stick out like the fo'castle of a steamboat, and his teeth
would uncover and shine like the furnaces. And a dog might tackle him and
bully-rag him, and bite him, and throw him over his shoulder two or three
times, and Andrew Jackson—which was the name of the pup—Andrew Jackson would never let on but what *he* was satisfied, and hadn't expected nothing
else—and the bets being doubled and doubled on the other side all the time,
till the money was all up; and then all of a sudden he would grab that other
dog jest by the j'int of his hind leg and freeze to it—not chaw, you understand,
but only just grip and hang on till they throwed up the sponge, if it was a year.
Smiley always come out winner on that pup, till he harnessed a dog once that
didn't have no hind legs, because they'd been sawed off in a circular saw, and
when the thing had gone along far enough, and the money was all up, and he
come to make a snatch for his pet holt, he see in a minute how he's been
imposed on, and how the other dog had him in the door, so to speak, and he
'peared surprised, and then he looked sorter discouraged-like, and didn't try
no more to win the fight, and so he got shucked out bad. He give Smiley a
look, as much as to say his heart was broke, and it was *his* fault, for putting up
a dog that hadn't no hind legs for him to take holt of, which was his main
dependence in a fight, and then he limped off a piece and laid down and died.
It was a good pup, was that Andrew Jackson, and would have made a name
for hisself if he'd lived, for the stuff was in him and he had genius—I know it,
because he hadn't no opportunities to speak of, and it don't stand to reason
that a dog could make such a fight as he could under them circumstances if

he hadn't no talent. It always makes me feel sorry when I think of that last fight of his'n, and the way it turned out.

Well, thish-yer Smiley had rat-tarriers, and chicken cocks, and tomcats and all them kind of things, till you couldn't rest, and you couldn't fetch nothing for him to bet on but he'd match you. He ketched a frog one day, and took him home, and said he cal'lated to educate him; and so he never done nothing for three months but set in his back yard and learn that frog to jump. And you bet you he *did* learn him, too. He'd give him a little punch behind, and the next minute you'd see that frog whirling in the air like a doughnut—see him turn one summerset, or may be a couple, if he got a good start, and come down flat-footed and all right, like a cat. He got him up so in the matter of ketching flies, and kep' him in practice so constant, that he'd nail a fly every time as fur as he could see him. Smiley said all a frog wanted was education, and he could do 'most anything—and I believe him. Why, I've seen him set Dan'l Webster down here on this floor—Dan'l Webster was the name of the frog—and sing out, "Flies, Dan'l, flies!" and quicker'n you could wink he'd spring straight up and snake a fly off'n the counter there, and flop down on the floor ag'in as solid as a gob of mud, and fall to scratching the side of his head with his hind foot as indifferent as if he hadn't no idea he'd been doin' any more'n any frog might do. You never see a frog so modest and straightfor'ard as he was, for all he was so gifted. And when it come to fair and square jumping on a dead level, he could get over more ground at one straddle than any animal of his breed you ever see. Jumping on a dead level was his strong suit, you understand; and when it come to that, Smiley would ante up money on him as long as he had a red. Smiley was monstrous proud of his frog, and well he might be, for fellers that had traveled and been everywheres all said he laid over any frog that ever *they* see.

Well, Smiley kep' the beast in a little lattice box, and he used to fetch him down town sometimes and lay for a bet. One day a feller—a stranger in the camp, he was—come acrost him with his box, and says:

"What might it be that you've got in the box?"

And Smiley says, sorter indifferent-like, "It might be a parrot, or it might be a canary, maybe, but it ain't—it's only just a frog."

And the feller took it, and looked at it careful, and turned it round this way and that, and says, "H'm—so 'tis. Well, what's *he* good for?"

"Well," Smiley says, easy and careless, "he's good enough for *one* thing, I should judge—he can outjump any frog in Calaveras county."

The feller took the box again, and took another long, particular look, and give it back to Smiley, and says, very deliberate, "Well," he says, "I don't see no p'ints about that frog that's any better'n any other frog."

"Maybe you don't," Smiley says. "Maybe you understand frogs and maybe you don't understand 'em; maybe you've had experience, and maybe you ain't only an amature, as it were. Anyways, I've got *my* opinion and I'll resk forty dollars that he can outjump any frog in Calaveras county."

And the feller studied a minute, and then says, kinder sad like, "Well, I'm only a stranger here, and I ain't got no frog; but if I had a frog, I'd bet you."

And then Smiley says, "That's all right—that's all right—if you'll hold my box a minute, I'll go and get you a frog." And so the feller took the box, and put up his forty dollars along with Smiley's, and set down to wait.

So he set there a good while thinking and thinking to hisself, and then he got the frog out and prized his mouth open and took a teaspoon and filled him full of quail shot—filled him pretty near up to his chin—and set him on the floor. Smiley he went to the swamp and slopped around in the mud for a long time, and finally he ketched a frog, and fetched him in, and give him to this feller, and says:

"Now, if you're ready, set him alongside of Dan'l, with his forepaws just even with Dan'l's, and I'll give the word." Then he says, "One—two—three-git!" and him and the feller touched up the frogs from behind, and the new frog hopped off lively, but Dan'l give a heave, and hysted up his shoulders—so—like a Frenchman, but it warn't no use—he couldn't budge; he was planted as solid as a church, and he couldn't no more stir than if he was anchored out. Smiley was a good deal surprised, and he was disgusted too, but he didn't have no idea what the matter was, of course.

The feller took the money and started away; and when he was going out at the door, he sorter jerked his thumb over his shoulder—so—at Dan'l, and says again, very deliberate, "Well," he says, "*I* don't see no p'ints about that frog that's any better'n any other frog."

Smiley he stood scratching his head and looking down at Dan'l a long time, and at last he says, "I do wonder what in the nation that frog throw'd off for— I wonder if there ain't something the matter with him—he 'pears to look mighty baggy, somehow." And he ketched Dan'l by the nap of the neck, and hefted him, and says, "Why blame my cats if he don't weigh five pound!" and turned him upside down and he belched out a double handful of shot. And then he see how it was, and he was the maddest man—he set the frog down and took out after that feller, but he never ketched him. And——"

[Here Simon Wheeler heard his name called from the front yard, and got up to see what was wanted.] And turning to me as he moved away, he said: "Just set where you are, stranger, and rest easy—I ain't going to be gone a second."

But, by your leave, I did not think that a continuation of the history of the enterprising vagabond *Jim* Smiley would be likely to afford me much information concerning the *Rev. Leonidas W.* Smiley, and so I started away.

At the door I met the sociable Wheeler returning, and he button-holed me and recommenced:

"Well, thish-yer Smiley had a yaller one-eyed cow that didn't have no tail, only jest a short stump like a bannanner, and——"

However, lacking both time and inclination, I did not wait to hear about the afflicted cow, but took my leave.

1865, 1867

# *From* Roughing It[1]

## [The Story of the Old Ram]

Every now and then, in these days, the boys used to tell me I ought to get one Jim Blaine to tell me the stirring story of his grandfather's old ram—but

---

1. The source of the present text is that of the 1872 edition. The story of the composition and publication of this episodic work is told fully by Franklin R. Rogers in the introduction to *The Works of Mark Twain*, Vol.

2 (1972); the basis for the present text is Chap. 53. The time is 1863 in Virginia City; the "boys" are the local roughs. Clemens was twenty-eight at the time of this "incident."

they always added that I must not mention the matter unless Jim was drunk at the time—just comfortably and sociably drunk. They kept this up until my curiosity was on the rack to hear the story. I got to haunting Blaine; but it was of no use, the boys always found fault with his condition; he was often moderately but never satisfactorily drunk. I never watched a man's condition with such absorbing interest, such anxious solicitude; I never so pined to see a man uncompromisingly drunk before. At last, one evening I hurried to his cabin, for I learned that this time his situation was such that even the most fastidious could find no fault with it—he was tranquilly, serenely, symmetrically drunk—not a hiccup to mar his voice, not a cloud upon his brain thick enough to obscure his memory. As I entered, he was sitting upon an empty powder-keg, with a clay pipe in one hand and the other raised to command silence. His face was round, red, and very serious; his throat was bare and his hair tumbled; in general appearance and costume he was a stalwart miner of the period. On the pine table stood a candle, and its dim light revealed "the boys" sitting here and there on bunks, candle-boxes, powder-kegs, etc. They said:

"Sh—! Don't speak—he's going to commence."

### THE STORY OF THE OLD RAM

I found a seat at once, and Blaine said:

"I don't reckon them times will ever come again. There never was a more bullier old ram than what he was. Grandfather fetched him from Illinois—got him of a man by the name of Yates—Bill Yates—maybe you might have heard of him; his father was a deacon—Baptist—and he was a rustler, too; a man had to get up ruther early to get the start of old Thankful Yates; it was him that put the Greens up to jining teams with my grandfather when he moved west. Seth Green was prob'ly the pick of the flock; he married a Wilkerson—Sarah Wilkerson—good cretur, she was—one of the likeliest heifers that was ever raised in old Stoddard, everybody said that knowed her. She could heft a bar'l of flour as easy as I can flirt a flapjack. And spin? Don't mention it! Independent? Humph! When Sile Hawkins come a-browsing around her, she let him know that for all his tin he couldn't trot in harness alongside of her. You see, Sile Hawkins was—no, it warn't Sile Hawkins, after all—it was a galoot by the name of Filkins—I disremember his first name; but he was a stump—come into pra'r meeting drunk, one night, hooraying for Nixon, becuz he thought it was a primary; and old deacon Ferguson up and scooted him through the window and he lit on old Miss Jefferson's head, poor old filly. She was a good soul—had a glass eye and used to lend it to old Miss Wagner, that hadn't any, to receive company in; it warn't big enough, and when Miss Wagner warn't noticing, it would get twisted around in the socket, and look up, maybe, or out to one side, and every which way, while t'other one was looking as straight ahead as a spy-glass. Grown people didn't mind it, but it most always made the children cry, it was so sort of scary. She tried packing it in raw cotton, but it wouldn't work, somehow—the cotton would get loose and stick out and look so kind of awful that the children couldn't stand it no way. She was always dropping it out, and turning up her old dead-light on the company empty, and making them oncomfortable, becuz she never could tell when it hopped out, being blind on that side, you see. So somebody would have to hunch her and say, 'Your game eye has fetched loose, Miss Wagner dear'—and then all of them would have to sit and wait till she jammed it in again—wrong side before, as a general thing, and green as a bird's egg, being a bashful cretur and easy sot back before company. But being wrong side before warn't much difference, anyway, becuz her own eye was sky-blue and the glass one was yaller on the front side, so whichever way she turned it it didn't match nohow. Old Miss Wagner was considerable on the borrow, she was. When she had a quilting, or Dorcas S'iety[2] at her house she gen'ally borrowed Miss Higgins's wooden leg to stump around on; it was considerable shorter than her other pin, but much *she* minded that. She said she couldn't abide crutches when she had company, becuz they were so slow; said when she had company and things had to be done, she wanted to get up and hump herself. She was as bald as a jug, and so she used to borrow Miss Jacops's wig—Miss Jacops was the coffin-peddler's wife—a ratty old buzzard, he was, that used to go roosting around where people was sick, waiting for 'em; and there that old rip would sit all day, in the shade, on a coffin that he judged would fit the can'idate; and if it was a slow customer and kind of uncertain, he'd fetch his rations and a blanket along and sleep in the coffin nights. He was anchored out that way, in frosty weather, for about three weeks, once, before old Robbins's place, waiting for him; and after that, for as much as two years, Jacops was not on speaking terms with the old man, on account of his disapp'inting him. He got one of his feet froze, and lost money, too, becuz old Robbins took a favorable turn and got well. The next time Robbins got sick, Jacops tried to make up with him, and varnished up the same old coffin and fetched it along; but old Robbins was too many for him; he had him in, and 'peared to be powerful weak; he bought the coffin for ten dollars and Jacops was to pay it back and twenty-five more besides if Robbins didn't like the coffin after he'd tried it. And then Robbins died, and at the funeral he bursted off the lid and riz up in his shroud and told the parson to let up on the performances, becuz he could *not* stand such a coffin as that. You see he had been in a trance once before, when he was young, and he took the chances on another, cal'lating that if he made the trip it was money in his pocket, and if he missed fire he couldn't lose a cent. And by George he sued Jacops for the rhino[3] and got jedgment; and he set up the coffin in his back parlor and said he 'lowed to take his time, now. It was always an aggravation to Jacops, the way that miserable old thing acted. He moved back to Indiany pretty soon—went to Wellsville—Wellsville was the place the Hogadorns was from. Mighty fine family. Old Maryland stock. Old Squire Hogadorn could carry around more mixed licker, and cuss better than most any man I ever see. His second wife was the widder Billings—she that was Becky Martin; her dam was deacon Dunlap's first wife. Her oldest child, Maria, married a missionary and died in grace—et up by the savages. They et *him*, too, poor feller—biled him. It warn't the custom, so they say, but they explained to friends of his'n that went down there to bring away his things, that they'd tried missionaries every other way and never could get any good out of 'em—and so it annoyed all his relations to find out that that man's life was fooled away just out of a dern'd experiment, so to speak. But mind you, there ain't anything ever reely lost; everything that people can't understand and don't see the reason of does good if you only hold on and give it a fair shake; Prov'dence don't fire no blank ca'tridges, boys. That there missionary's

2. Dorcas Society; common name for charitable church societies. From the biblical Dorcas (Acts 9. 36–42), who performed charitable deeds, particularly sew-ing clothes for the poor.
3. Slang for cash, money.

substance, unbeknowns to himself, actu'ly converted every last one of them heathens that took a chance at the barbacue. Nothing ever fetched them but that. Don't tell *me* it was an accident that he was biled. There ain't no such thing as an accident. When my uncle Lem was leaning up agin a scaffolding once, sick, or drunk, or suthin, an Irishman with a hod full of bricks fell on him out of the third story and broke the old man's back in two places. People said it was an accident. Much accident there was about that. He didn't know what he was there for, but he was there for a good object. If he hadn't been there the Irishman would have been killed. Nobody can ever make me believe anything different from that. Uncle Lem's dog was there. Why didn't the Irishman fall on the dog? Becuz the dog would a seen him a-coming and stood from under. That's the reason the dog warn't appinted. A dog can't be depended on to carry out a special providence. Mark my words it was a put-up thing. Accidents don't happen, boys. Uncle Lem's dog—I wish you could a seen that dog. He was a reglar shepherd—or ruther he was part bull and part shepherd—splendid animal; belonged to parson Hagar before Uncle Lem got him. Parson Hagar belonged to the Western Reserve Hagars; prime family; his mother was a Watson; one of his sisters married a Wheeler; they settled in Morgan county, and he got nipped by the machinery in a carpet factory and went through in less than a quarter of a minute; his widder bought the piece of carpet that had his remains wove in, and people come a hundred mile to 'tend the funeral. There was fourteen yards in the piece. She wouldn't let them roll him up, but planted him just so—full length. The church was middling small where they preached the funeral, and they had to let one end of the coffin stick out the window. They didn't bury him—they planted one end, and let him stand up, same as a monument. And they nailed a sign on it and put—put on—put on it—sacred to—the m-e-m-o-r-y—of fourteen y-a-r-d-s— of three-ply—car - - - pet—containing all that was—m-o-r-t-a-l—of—of— W-i-l-l-i-a-m—W-h-e—"

Jim Blaine had been growing gradually drowsy and drowsier—his head nodded, once, twice, three times—dropped peacefully upon his breast, and he fell tranquilly asleep. The tears were running down the boys' cheeks—they were suffocating with suppressed laughter—and had been from the start, though I had never noticed it. I perceived that I was "sold." I learned then that Jim Blaine's peculiarity was that whenever he reached a certain stage of intoxication, no human power could keep him from setting out, with impressive unction, to tell about a wonderful adventure which he had once had with his grandfather's old ram—and the mention of the ram in the first sentence was as far as any man had ever heard him get, concerning it. He always maundered off, interminably, from one thing to another, till his whisky got the best of him and he fell asleep. What the thing was that happened to him and his grandfather's old ram is a dark mystery to this day, for nobody has ever yet found out.

1872

# Adventures of Huckleberry Finn[1]

*(Tom Sawyer's Comrade)*

Scene: *The Mississippi Valley*

Time: *Forty to Fifty Years Ago*[2]

---

NOTICE

Persons attempting to find a motive in this narrative
will be prosecuted; persons attempting to find a moral in
it will be banished; persons attempting to find a plot in
it will be shot.

BY ORDER OF THE AUTHOR
PER G. G., CHIEF OF ORDNANCE.

---

*Explanatory*

In this book a number of dialects are used, to wit: the Missouri negro dialect;
the extremest form of the backwoods South-Western dialect; the ordinary
"Pike-County"[3] dialect; and four modified varieties of this last. The shadings
have not been done in a hap-hazard fashion, or by guess-work; but painstakingly, and with the trustworthy guidance and support of personal familiarity
with these several forms of speech.

I make this explanation for the reason that without it many readers would
suppose that all these characters were trying to talk alike and not succeeding.

THE AUTHOR

## Chapter I

You don't know about me, without you have read a book by the name of
"The Adventures of Tom Sawyer,"[4] but that ain't no matter. That book was
made by Mr. Mark Twain, and he told the truth, mainly. There was things
which he stretched, but mainly he told the truth. That is nothing. I never seen
anybody but lied, one time or another, without it was Aunt Polly, or the
widow, or maybe Mary. Aunt Polly—Tom's Aunt Polly, she is—and Mary,
and the Widow Douglas, is all told about in that book—which is mostly a true
book; with some stretchers, as I said before.

Now the way that the book winds up, is this: Tom and me found the money
that the robbers hid in the cave, and it made us rich. We got six thousand
dollars apiece—all gold. It was an awful sight of money when it was piled up.
Well, Judge Thatcher, he took it and put it out at interest, and it fetched us a
dollar a day apiece, all the year round—more than a body could tell what to
do with. The Widow Douglas, she took me for her son, and allowed she would
sivilize me; but it was rough living in the house all the time, considering how

---

1. *Adventures of Huckleberry Finn* was first published
in England in December 1884. The present text is a
corrected version of the first American edition of 1885.

2. That is, in 1835 or 1845—well before the Civil War.
3. Pike County, Missouri.
4. Published in 1876.

dismal regular and decent the widow was in all her ways; and so when I couldn't stand it no longer, I lit out. I got into my old rags, and my sugar-hogshead[5] again, and was free and satisfied. But Tom Sawyer, he hunted me up and said he was going to start a band of robbers, and I might join if I would go back to the widow and be respectable. So I went back.

The widow she cried over me, and called me a poor lost lamb, and she called me a lot of other names, too, but she never meant no harm by it. She put me in them new clothes again, and I couldn't do nothing but sweat and sweat, and feel all cramped up. Well, then, the old thing commenced again. The widow rung a bell for supper, and you had to come to time. When you got to the table you couldn't go right to eating, but you had to wait for the widow to tuck down her head and grumble a little over the victuals, though there warn't really anything the matter with them. That is, nothing only every-thing was cooked by itself. In a barrel of odds and ends it is different; things get mixed up, and the juice kind of swaps around, and the things go better.

After supper she got out her book and learned me about Moses and the Bulrushers;[6] and I was in a sweat to find out all about him; but by-and-by she let it out that Moses had been dead a considerable long time; so then I didn't care no more about him; because I don't take no stock in dead people.

Pretty soon I wanted to smoke, and asked the widow to let me. But she wouldn't. She said it was a mean practice and wasn't clean, and I must try to not do it any more. That is just the way with some people. They get down on a thing when they don't know nothing about it. Here she was a bothering about Moses, which was no kin to her, and no use to anybody, being gone, you see, yet finding a power of fault with me for doing a thing that had some good in it. And she took snuff too; of course that was all right, because she done it herself.

Her sister, Miss Watson, a tolerable slim old maid, with goggles on, had just come to live with her, and took a set at me now, with a spelling-book. She worked me middling hard for about an hour, and then the widow made her ease up. I couldn't stood it much longer. Then for an hour it was deadly dull, and I was fidgety. Miss Watson would say, "Don't put your feet up there, Huckleberry"; and "don't scrunch up like that, Huckleberry—set up straight"; and pretty soon she would say, "Don't gap and stretch like that, Huckleberry— why don't you try to behave?" Then she told me all about the bad place, and I said I wished I was there. She got mad, then, but I didn't mean no harm. All I wanted was to go somewheres; all I wanted was a change, I warn't particu-lar. She said it was wicked to say what I said; said she wouldn't say it for the whole world; *she* was going to live so as to go to the good place. Well, I couldn't see no advantage in going where she was going, so I made up my mind I wouldn't try for it. But I never said so, because it would only make trouble, and wouldn't do no good.

Now she had got a start, and she went on and told me all about the good place. She said all a body would have to do there was to go around all day long with a harp and sing, forever and ever.[7] So I didn't think much of it. But I never said so. I asked her if she reckoned Tom Sawyer would go there, and,

---

5. A large barrel.
6. Pharoah's daughter discovered the infant Moses floating in the Nile in a basket woven from bulrushes (Exodus 2). She adopted him into the royal family just as the widow has adopted Huck.
7. Conventional conceptions of the Christian heaven were satirized early and late in Clemens's writings.

she said, not by a considerable sight. I was glad about that, because I wanted him and me to be together.

Miss Watson she kept pecking at me, and it got tiresome and lonesome. By-and-by they fetched the niggers[8] in and had prayers, and then everybody was off to bed. I went up to my room with a piece of candle and put it on the table. Then I set down in a chair by the window and tried to think of something cheerful, but it warn't no use. I felt so lonesome I most wished I was dead. The stars was shining, and the leaves rustled in the woods ever so mournful; and I heard an owl, away off, who-whooing about somebody that was dead, and a whippowill and a dog crying about somebody that was going to die; and the wind was trying to whisper something to me and I couldn't make out what it was, and so it made the cold shivers run over me. Then away out in the woods I heard that kind of a sound that a ghost makes when it wants to tell about something that's on its mind and can't make itself understood, and so can't rest easy in its grave and has to go about that way every night grieving. I got so down-hearted and scared, I did wish I had some company. Pretty soon a spider went crawling up my shoulder, and I flipped it off and it lit in the candle; and before I could budge it was all shriveled up. I didn't need anybody to tell me that that was an awful bad sign and would fetch me some bad luck, so I was scared and most shook the clothes off of me. I got up and turned around in my tracks three times and crossed my breast every time; and then I tied up a little lock of my hair with a thread to keep witches away. But I hadn't no confidence. You do that when you've lost a horse-shoe that you've found, instead of nailing it up over the door, but I hadn't ever heard anybody say it was any way to keep off bad luck when you'd killed a spider.

I set down again, a shaking all over, and got out my pipe for a smoke; for the house was all as still as death, now, and so the widow wouldn't know. Well, after a long time I heard the clock away off in the town go boom—boom—boom—twelve licks—and all still again—stiller than ever. Pretty soon I heard a twig snap, down in the dark amongst the trees—something was a stirring. I set still and listened. Directly I could just barely hear a "me-yow! me-yow!" down there. That was good! Says I, "me-yow! me-yow!" as soft as I could, and then I put out the light and scrambled out of the window onto the shed. Then I slipped down to the ground and crawled in amongst the trees, and sure enough there was Tom Sawyer waiting for me.

## Chapter II

We went tip-toeing along a path amongst the trees back towards the end of the widow's garden, stooping down so as the branches wouldn't scrape our heads. When we was passing by the kitchen I fell over a root and made a noise. We scrouched down and laid still. Miss Watson's big nigger, named Jim, was setting in the kitchen door; we could see him pretty clear, because there was a light behind him. He got up and stretched his neck out about a minute, listening. Then he says,

"Who dah?"

He listened some more; then he come tip-toeing down and stood right between

---

8. Huck appropriately speaks the colloquial word used in the South to describe black slaves; it is not used derisively or contemptuously.

us; we could a touched him, nearly. Well, likely it was minutes and minutes that there warn't a sound, and we all there so close together. There was a place on my ankle that got to itching; but I dasn't scratch it; and then my ear begun to itch; and next my back, right between my shoulders. Seemed like I'd die if I couldn't scratch. Well, I've noticed that thing plenty of times since. If you are with the quality, or at a funeral, or trying to go to sleep when you ain't sleepy—if you are anywheres where it won't do for you to scratch, why you will itch all over in upwards of a thousand places. Pretty soon Jim says:

"Say—who is you? Whar is you? Dog my cats ef I didn' hear sumf'n. Well, I knows what I's gwyne to do. I's gwyne to set down here and listen tell I hears it agin."

So he set down on the ground betwixt me and Tom. He leaned his back up against a tree, and stretched his legs out till one of them most touched one of mine. My nose begun to itch. It itched till the tears come into my eyes. But I dasn't scratch. Then it begun to itch on the inside. Next I got to itching underneath. I didn't know how I was going to set still. This miserableness went on as much as six or seven minutes; but it seemed a sight longer than that. I was itching in eleven different places now. I reckoned I couldn't stand it more'n a minute longer, but I set my teeth hard and got ready to try. Just then Jim begun to breathe heavy; next he begun to snore—and then I was pretty soon comfortable again.

Tom he made a sign to me—kind of a little noise with his mouth—and we went creeping away on our hands and knees. When we was ten foot off, Tom whispered to me and wanted to tie Jim to the tree for fun; but I said no; he might wake and make a disturbance, and then they'd find out I warn't in. Then Tom said he hadn't got candles enough, and he would slip in the kitchen and get some more. I didn't want him to try. I said Jim might wake up and come. But Tom wanted to resk it; so we slid in there and got three candles, and Tom laid five cents on the table for pay. Then we got out, and I was in a sweat to get away; but nothing would do Tom but he must crawl to where Jim was, on his hands and knees, and play something on him. I waited, and it seemed a good while, everything was so still and lonesome.

As soon as Tom was back, we cut along the path, around the garden fence, and by-and-by fetched up on the steep top of the hill the other side of the house. Tom said he slipped Jim's hat off of his head and hung it on a limb right over him, and Jim stirred a little, but he didn't wake. Afterwards Jim said the witches bewitched him and put him in a trance, and rode him all over the State, and then set him under the trees again and hung his hat on a limb to show who done it. And next time Jim told it he said they rode him down to New Orleans; and after that, every time he told it he spread it more and more, till by-and-by he said they rode him all over the world, and tired him most to death, and his back was all over saddle-boils. Jim was monstrous proud about it, and he got so he wouldn't hardly notice the other niggers. Niggers would come miles to hear Jim tell about it, and he was more looked up to than any nigger in that country. Strange niggers[9] would stand with their mouths open and look him all over, same as if he was a wonder. Niggers is always talking about witches in the dark by the kitchen fire; but whenever one was talking and letting on to know all about such things, Jim would happen in and say,

9. Those who did not live in the immediate area.

"Hm! What you know 'bout witches?" and that nigger was corked up and had to take a back seat. Jim always kept that five-center piece around his neck with a string and said it was a charm the devil give to him with his own hands and told him he could cure anybody with it and fetch witches whenever he wanted to, just by saying something to it; but he never told what it was he said to it. Niggers would come from all around there and give Jim anything they had, just for a sight of the five-center piece; but they wouldn't touch it, because the devil had had his hands on it. Jim was most ruined, for a servant, because he got so stuck up on account of having seen the devil and been rode by witches.

Well, when Tom and me got to the edge of the hill-top, we looked away down into the village[1] and could see three or four lights twinkling, where there was sick folks, may be; and the stars over us was sparkling ever so fine; and down by the village was the river, a whole mile broad, and awful still and grand. We went down the hill and found Jo Harper, and Ben Rogers, and two or three more of the boys, hid in the old tanyard. So we unhitched a skiff and pulled down the river two mile and a half, to the big scar on the hillside, and went ashore.

We went to a clump of bushes, and Tom made everybody swear to keep the secret, and then showed them a hole in the hill, right in the thickest part of the bushes. Then we lit the candles and crawled in on our hands and knees. We went about two hundred yards, and then the cave opened up. Tom poked about amongst the passages and pretty soon ducked under a wall where you wouldn't a noticed that there was a hole. We went along a narrow place and got into a kind of room, all damp and sweaty and cold, and there we stopped. Tom says:

"Now we'll start this band of robbers and call it Tom Sawyer's Gang. Everybody that wants to join has got to take an oath, and write his name in blood."

Everybody was willing. So Tom got out a sheet of paper that he had wrote the oath on, and read it. It swore every boy to stick to the band, and never tell any of the secrets; and if anybody done anything to any boy in the band, whichever boy was ordered to kill that person and his family must do it, and he mustn't eat and he mustn't sleep till he had killed them and hacked a cross in their breasts, which was the sign of the band. And nobody that didn't belong to the band could use that mark, and if he did he must be sued; and if he done it again he must be killed. And if anybody that belonged to the band told the secrets, he must have his throat cut, and then have his carcass burnt up and the ashes scattered all around, and his name blotted off of the list with blood and never mentioned again by the gang, but have a curse put on it and be forgot, forever.

Everybody said it was a real beautiful oath, and asked Tom if he got it out of his own head. He said, some of it, but the rest was out of pirate books, and robber books, and every gang that was high-toned had it.

Some thought it would be good to kill the *families* of boys that told the secrets. Tom said it was a good idea, so he took a pencil and wrote it in. Then Ben Rogers says:

"Here's Huck Finn, he hain't got no family—what you going to do 'bout him?"

"Well, hain't he got a father?" says Tom Sawyer.

---

1. The village, called St. Petersburg here and in *Tom Sawyer*, is modeled on Hannibal, Missouri.

"Yes, he's got a father, but you can't never find him, these days. He used to lay drunk with the hogs in the tanyard, but he hain't been seen in these parts for a year or more."

They talked it over, and they was going to rule me out, because they said every boy must have a family or somebody to kill, or else it wouldn't be fair and square for the others. Well, nobody could think of anything to do—everybody was stumped, and set still. I was most ready to cry; but all at once I thought of a way, and so I offered them Miss Watson—they could kill her. Everybody said:

"Oh, she'll do, she'll do. That's all right. Huck can come in."

Then they all stuck a pin in their fingers to get blood to sign with, and I made my mark on the paper.

"Now," says Ben Rogers, "what's the line of business of this Gang?"

"Nothing only robbery and murder," Tom said.

"But who are we going to rob? houses—or cattle—or—"

"Stuff! stealing cattle and such things ain't robbery, it's burglary," says Tom Sawyer. "We ain't burglars. That ain't no sort of style. We are highwaymen. We stop stages and carriages on the road, with masks on, and kill the people and take their watches and money."

"Must we always kill the people?"

"Oh, certainly. It's best. Some authorities think different, but mostly it's considered best to kill them. Except some that you bring to the cave here and keep them till they're ransomed."

"Ransomed? What's that?"

"I don't know. But that's what they do. I've seen it in books; and so of course that's what we've got to do."

"But how can we do it if we don't know what it is?"

"Why blame it all, we've *got* to do it. Don't I tell you it's in the books? Do you want to go to doing different from what's in the books, and get things all muddled up?"

"Oh, that's all very fine to *say*, Tom Sawyer, but how in the nation[2] are these fellows going to be ransomed if we don't know how to do it to them? that's the thing *I* want to get at. Now what do you *reckon* it is?"

"Well I don't know. But per'aps if we keep them till they're ransomed, it means that we keep them till they're dead."

"Now, that's something *like*. That'll answer. Why couldn't you said that before? We'll keep them till they're ransomed to death—and a bothersome lot they'll be, too, eating up everything and always trying to get loose."

"How you talk, Ben Rogers. How can they get loose when there's a guard over them, ready to shoot them down if they move a peg?"

"A guard. Well, that *is* good. So somebody's got to set up all night and never get any sleep, just so as to watch them. I think that's foolishness. Why can't a body take a club and ransom them as soon as they get here?"

"Because it ain't in the books so—that's why. Now Ben Rogers, do you want to do things regular, or don't you?—that's the idea. Don't you reckon that the people that made the books knows what's the correct thing to do? Do you reckon *you* can learn 'em anything? Not by a good deal. No, sir, we'll just go on and ransom them in the regular way."

2. Damnation.

"All right. I don't mind; but I say it's a fool way, anyhow. Say—do we kill the women, too?"

"Well, Ben Rogers, if I was as ignorant as you I wouldn't let on. Kill the women? No—nobody ever saw anything in the books like that. You fetch them to the cave, and you're always as polite as pie to them; and by-and-by they fall in love with you and never want to go home any more."

"Well, if that's the way, I'm agreed, but I don't take no stock in it. Mighty soon we'll have the cave so cluttered up with women, and fellows waiting to be ransomed, that there won't be no place for the robbers. But go ahead, I ain't got nothing to say."

Little Tommy Barnes was asleep, now, and when they waked him up he was scared, and cried, and said he wanted to go home to his ma, and didn't want to be a robber any more.

So they all made fun of him, and called him cry-baby, and that made him mad, and he said he would go straight and tell all the secrets. But Tom give him five cents to keep quiet, and said we would all go home and meet next week and rob somebody and kill some people.

Ben Rogers said he couldn't get out much, only Sundays, and so he wanted to begin next Sunday; but all the boys said it would be wicked to do it on Sunday, and that settled the thing. They agreed to get together and fix a day as soon as they could, and then we elected Tom Sawyer first captain and Jo Harper second captain of the Gang, and so started home.

I clumb up the shed and crept into my window just before day was breaking. My new clothes was all greased up and clayey, and I was dog-tired.

## Chapter III

Well, I got a good going-over in the morning, from old Miss Watson, on account of my clothes; but the widow she didn't scold, but only cleaned off the grease and clay and looked so sorry that I thought I would behave a while if I could. Then Miss Watson she took me in the closet[3] and prayed, but nothing come of it. She told me to pray every day, and whatever I asked for I would get it. But it warn't so. I tried it. Once I got a fish-line, but no hooks. It warn't any good to me without hooks. I tried for the hooks three or four times, but somehow I couldn't make it work. By-and-by, one day, I asked Miss Watson to try for me, but she said I was a fool. She never told me why, and I couldn't make it out no way.

I set down, one time, back in the woods, and had a long think about it. I says to myself, if a body can get anything they pray for, why don't Deacon Winn get back the money he lost on pork? Why can't the widow get back her silver snuff-box that was stole? Why can't Miss Watson fat up? No, says I to myself, there ain't nothing in it. I went and told the widow about it, and she said the thing a body could get by praying for it was "spiritual gifts." This was too many for me, but she told me what she meant—I must help other people, and do everything I could for other people, and look out for them all the time, and never think about myself. This was including Miss Watson, as I took it. I went out in the woods and turned it over in my mind a long time, but I couldn't see no advantage about it—except for the other people—so at last I

3. "But thou, when thou prayest, enter into thy closet" (Matthew 6.6) is apparently the admonition Miss Watson has in mind.

reckoned I wouldn't worry about it any more, but just let it go. Sometimes the widow would take me one side and talk about Providence in a way to make a boy's mouth water; but maybe next day Miss Watson would take hold and knock it all down again. I judged I could see that there was two Providences, and a poor chap would stand considerable show with the widow's Providence, but if Miss Watson's got him there warn't no help for him any more. I thought it all out, and reckoned I would belong to the widow's, if he wanted me, though I couldn't make out how he was agoing to be any better off then than what he was before, seeing I was so ignorant and so kind of low-down and ornery.

Pap he hadn't been seen for more than a year, and that was comfortable for me; I didn't want to see him no more. He used to always whale me when he was sober and could get his hands on me; though I used to take to the woods most of the time when he was around. Well, about this time he was found in the river drowned, about twelve mile above town, so people said. They judged it was him, anyway; said this drowned man was just his size, and was ragged, and had uncommon long hair—which was all like pap—but they couldn't make nothing out of the face, because it had been in the water so long it warn't much like a face at all. They said he was floating on his back in the water. They took him and buried him on the bank. But I warn't comfortable long, because I happened to think of something. I knowed mighty well that a drownded man don't float on his back, but on his face. So I knowed, then, that this warn't pap, but a woman dressed up in a man's clothes. So I was uncomfortable again. I judged the old man would turn up again by-and-by, though I wished he wouldn't.

We played robber now and then about a month, and then I resigned. All the boys did. We hadn't robbed nobody, we hadn't killed any people, but only just pretended. We used to hop out of the woods and go charging down on hog-drovers and women in carts taking garden stuff to market, but we never hived[4] any of them. Tom Sawyer called the hogs "ingots," and he called the turnips and stuff "julery" and we would go to the cave and pow-wow over what we had done and how many people we had killed and marked. But I couldn't see no profit in it. One time Tom sent a boy to run about town with a blazing stick, which he called a slogan (which was the sign for the Gang to get together), and then he said he had got secret news by his spies that next day a whole parcel of Spanish merchants and rich A-rabs was going to camp in Cave Hollow with two hundred elephants, and six hundred camels, and over a thousand "sumter" mules,[5] all loaded with di'monds, and they didn't have only a guard of four hundred soldiers, and so we would lay in ambuscade, as he called it, and kill the lot and scoop the things. He said we must slick up our swords and guns, and get ready. He never could go after even a turnip-cart but he must have the swords and guns all scoured up for it; though they was only lath and broom-sticks, and you might scour at them till you rotted and then they warn't worth a mouthful of ashes more than what they was before. I didn't believe we could lick such a crowd of Spaniards and A-rabs, but I wanted to see the camels and elephants, so I was on hand next day, Saturday, in the ambuscade; and when we got the word, we rushed out of the woods and down the hill. But there warn't no Spaniards and A-rabs, and there warn't no

---

4. Captured, secured.     5. Pack mules.

camels nor no elephants. It warn't anything but a Sunday-school picnic, and only a primer-class at that. We busted it up, and chased the children up the hollow; but we never got anything but some doughnuts and jam, though Ben Rogers got a rag doll, and Jo Harper got a hymn-book and a tract; and then the teacher charged in and made us drop everything and cut. I didn't see no di'monds, and I told Tom Sawyer so. He said there was loads of them there, anyway; and he said there was A-rabs there, too, and elephants and things. I said, why couldn't we see them, then? He said if I warn't so ignorant, but had read a book called "Don Quixote,"[6] I would know without asking. He said it was all done by enchantment. He said there was hundreds of soldiers there, and elephants and treasure, and so on, but we had enemies which he called magicians, and they had turned the whole thing into an infant Sunday school, just out of spite. I said, all right, then the thing for us to do was to go for the magicians. Tom Sawyer said I was a numskull.

"Why," says he, "a magician could call up a lot of genies, and they would hash you up like nothing before you could say Jack Robinson. They are as tall as a tree and as big around as a church."

"Well," I says, "s'pose we got some genies to help us—can't we lick the other crowd then?"

"How you going to get them?"

"I don't know. How do they get them?"

"Why they rub an old tin lamp or an iron ring, and then the genies come tearing in, with the thunder and lightning a-ripping around and the smoke a-rolling, and everything they're told to do they up and do it. They don't think nothing of pulling a shot tower[7] up by the roots, and belting a Sunday-school superintendent over the head with it—or any other man."

"Who makes them tear around so?"

"Why, whoever rubs the lamp or the ring. They belong to whoever rubs the lamp or the ring, and they've got to do whatever he says. If he tells them to build a palace forty miles long, out of di'monds, and fill it full of chewing gum, or whatever you want, and fetch an emperor's daughter from China for you to marry, they've got to do it—and they've got to do it before sun-up next morning, too. And more—they've got to waltz that palace around over the country whenever you want it, you understand."

"Well," says I, "I think they are a pack of flatheads for not keeping the palace themselves 'stead of fooling them away like that. And what's more—if I was one of them I would see a man in Jericho before I would drop my business and come to him for the rubbing of an old tin lamp."

"How you talk, Huck Finn. Why, you'd have to come when he rubbed it, whether you wanted to or not."

"What, and I as high as a tree and as big as a church? All right, then; I would come; but I lay I'd make that man climb the highest tree there was in the country."

"Shucks, it ain't no use to talk to you, Huck Finn. You don't seem to know anything, somehow—perfect sap-head."

I thought all this over for two or three days, and then I reckoned I would see if there was anything in it. I got an old tin lamp and an iron ring and went

---

6. Tom is here alluding to stories in *The Arabian Nights Entertainments* (1838–41) and to the hero in Cervantes' *Don Quixote* (1605).

7. A device in which gunshot was formed by dripping molten lead into water.

out in the woods and rubbed and rubbed till I sweat like an Injun, calculating to build a palace and sell it; but it warn't no use, none of the genies come. So then I judged that all that stuff was only just one of Tom Sawyer's lies. I reckoned he believed in the A-rabs and the elephants, but as for me I think different. It had all the marks of a Sunday school.

## Chapter IV

Well, three or four months run along, and it was well into the winter, now. I had been to school most all the time, and could spell, and read, and write just a little, and could say the multiplication table up to six times seven is thirty-five, and I don't reckon I could ever get any further than that if I was to live forever. I don't take no stock in mathematics, anyway.

At first I hated the school, but by-and-by I got so I could stand it. Whenever I got uncommon tired I played hookey, and the hiding I got next day done me good and cheered me up. So the longer I went to school the easier it got to be. I was getting sort of used to the widow's ways, too, and they warn't so raspy on me. Living in a house, and sleeping in a bed, pulled on me pretty tight, mostly, but before the cold weather I used to slide out and sleep in the woods, sometimes, and so that was a rest to me. I liked the old ways best, but I was getting so I liked the new ones, too, a little bit. The widow said I was coming along slow but sure, and doing very satisfactory. She said she warn't ashamed of me.

One morning I happened to turn over the salt-cellar at breakfast. I reached for some of it as quick as I could, to throw over my left shoulder and keep off the bad luck, but Miss Watson was in ahead of me, and crossed me off. She says, "Take your hands away, Huckleberry—what a mess you are always making." The widow put in a good word for me, but that warn't going to keep off the bad luck, I knowed that well enough. I started out, after breakfast, feeling worried and shaky, and wondering where it was going to fall on me, and what it was going to be. There is ways to keep off some kinds of bad luck, but this wasn't one of them kind; so I never tried to do anything, but just poked along low-spirited and on the watch-out.

I went down the front garden and clumb over the stile,[8] where you go through the high board fence. There was an inch of new snow on the ground, and I seen somebody's tracks. They had come up from the quarry and stood around the stile a while, and then went on around the garden fence. It was funny they hadn't come in, after standing around so. I couldn't make it out. It was very curious, somehow. I was going to follow around, but I stooped down to look at the tracks first. I didn't notice anything at first, but next I did. There was a cross in the left boot-heel made with big nails, to keep off the devil.

I was up in a second and shinning down the hill. I looked over my shoulder every now and then, but I didn't see nobody. I was at Judge Thatcher's as quick as I could get there. He said:

"Why, my boy, you are all out of breath. Did you come for your interest?"

"No sir," I says; "is there some for me?"

"Oh, yes, a half-yearly is in, last night. Over a hundred and fifty dollars.

---

8. Steps that flank and straddle a fence.

Quite a fortune for you. You better let me invest it along with your six thousand, because if you take it you'll spend it."

"No sir," I says, "I don't want to spend it. I don't want it at all—nor the six thousand, nuther. I want you to take it; I want to give it to you—the six thousand and all."

He looked surprised. He couldn't seem to make it out. He says:

"Why, what can you mean, my boy?"

I says, "Don't you ask me no questions about it, please. You'll take it—won't you?"

He says:

"Well I'm puzzled. Is something the matter?"

"Please take it," says I, "and don't ask me nothing—then I won't have to tell no lies."

He studied a while, and then he says:

"Oho-o. I think I see. You want to *sell* all your property to me—not give it. That's the correct idea."

Then he wrote something on a paper and read it over, and says:

"There—you see it says 'for a consideration.' That means I have bought it of you and paid you for it. Here's a dollar for you. Now, you sign it."

So I signed it, and left.

Miss Watson's nigger, Jim, had a hair-ball as big as your fist, which had been took out of the fourth stomach of an ox, and he used to do magic with it.[9] He said there was a spirit inside of it, and it knowed everything. So I went to him that night and told him pap was here again, for I found his tracks in the snow. What I wanted to know, was, what he was going to do, and was he going to stay? Jim got out his hair-ball, and said something over it, and then he held it up and dropped it on the floor. It fell pretty solid, and only rolled about an inch. Jim tried it again, and then another time, and it acted just the same. Jim got down on his knees and put his ear against it and listened. But it warn't no use; he said it wouldn't talk. He said sometimes it wouldn't talk without money. I told him I had an old slick counterfeit quarter that warn't no good because the brass showed through the silver a little, and it wouldn't pass nohow, even if the brass didn't show, because it was so slick it felt greasy, and so that would tell on it every time. (I reckoned I wouldn't say nothing about the dollar I got from the judge.) I said it was pretty bad money, but maybe the hair-ball would take it, because maybe it wouldn't know the difference. Jim smelt it, and bit it, and rubbed it, and said he would manage so the hair-ball would think it was good. He said he would split open a raw Irish potato and stick the quarter in between and keep it there all night, and next morning you couldn't see no brass, and it wouldn't feel greasy no more, and so anybody in town would take it in a minute, let alone a hair-ball. Well, I knowed a potato would do that, before, but I had forgot it.

Jim put the quarter under the hair-ball and got down and listened again. This time he said the hair-ball was all right. He said it would tell my whole fortune if I wanted it to. I says, go on. So the hair-ball talked to Jim, and Jim told it to me. He says:

"Yo' ole father doan' know, yit, what he's a-gwyne to do. Sometimes he

9. Though most of the superstitions in *Tom Sawyer* and *Huck Finn* have been traced to European sources, the belief in the magical powers of the hair ball found in the stomachs of oxen seems to be African-American in origin.

spec he'll go 'way, en den agin he spec he'll stay. De bes' way is to res' easy en let de ole man take his own way. Dey's two angels hoverin' roun' 'bout him. One uv 'em is white en shiny, en 'tother one is black. De white one gits him to go right, a little while, den de black one sail in en bust it all up. A body can't tell, yit, which one gwyne to fetch him at de las'. But you is all right. You gwyne to have considable trouble in yo' life, en considable joy. Sometimes you gwyne to git hurt, en sometimes you gwyne to git sick; but every time you's gwyne to git well agin. Dey's two gals flyin' 'bout you in yo' life. One uv 'em's light en 'tother one is dark. One is rich en 'tother is po'. You's gwyne to marry de po' one fust en de rich one by-en-by. You wants to keep 'way fum de water as much as you kin, en don't run no resk, 'kase it's down in de bills dat you's gwyne to git hung."

When I lit my candle and went up to my room that night, there set pap, his own self!

## Chapter V

I had shut the door to. Then I turned around, and there he was. I used to be scared of him all the time, he tanned me so much. I reckoned I was scared now, too; but in a minute I see I was mistaken. That is, after the first jolt, as you may say, when my breath sort of hitched—he being so unexpected; but right away after, I see I warn't scared of him worth bothering about.

He was most fifty, and he looked it. His hair was long and tangled and greasy, and hung down, and you could see his eyes shining through like he was behind vines. It was all black, no gray; so was his long, mixed-up whiskers. There warn't no color in his face, where his face showed; it was white; not like another man's white, but a white to make a body sick, a white to make a body's flesh crawl—a tree-toad white, a fish-belly white. As for his clothes—just rags, that was all. He had one ankle resting on 'tother knee; the boot on that foot was busted, and two of his toes stuck through, and he worked them now and then. His hat was laying on the floor; an old black slouch with the top caved in, like a lid.

I stood a-looking at him; he set there a-looking at me, with his chair tilted back a little. I set the candle down. I noticed the window was up; so he had clumb in by the shed. He kept a-looking me all over. By-and-by he says:

"Starchy clothes—very. You think you're a good deal of a big-bug, *don't* you?"

"Maybe I am, maybe I ain't," I says.

"Don't you give me none o' your lip," says he. "You've put on considerble many frills since I been away. I'll take you down a peg before I get done with you. You're educated, too, they say; can read and write. You think you're better'n your father, now, don't you, because he can't? *I'll* take it out of you. Who told you you might meddle with such hifalut'n foolishness, hey?—who told you you could?"

"The widow. She told me."

"The widow, hey?—and who told the widow she could put in her shovel about a thing that ain't none of her business?"

"Nobody never told her."

"Well, I'll learn her how to meddle. And looky here—you drop that school, you hear? I'll learn people to bring up a boy to put on airs over his own father and let on to be better'n what *he* is. You lemme catch you fooling around that school again, you hear? Your mother couldn't read, and she couldn't write, nuther, before she died. None of the family couldn't, before *they* died. I can't; and here you're a-swelling yourself up like this. I ain't the man to stand it— you hear? Say—lemme hear you read."

I took up a book and begun something about General Washington and the wars. When I'd read about a half a minute, he fetched the book a whack with his hand and knocked it across the house. He says:

"It's so. You can do it. I had my doubts when you told me. Now looky here; you stop that putting on frills. I won't have it. I'll lay for you, my smarty; and if I catch you about that school I'll tan you good. First you know you'll get religion, too. I never see such a son."

He took up a little blue and yaller picture of some cows and a boy, and says: "What's this?"

"It's something they give me for learning my lessons good."

He tore it up, and says—

"I'll give you something better—I'll give you a cowhide."[1]

He set there a-mumbling and a-growling a minute, and then he says—

"*Ain't* you a sweet-scented dandy, though? A bed; and bedclothes; and a look'n-glass; and a piece of carpet on the floor—and your own father got to sleep with the hogs in the tanyard. I never see such a son. I bet I'll take some o' these frills out o' you before I'm done with you. Why there ain't no end to your airs—they say you're rich. Hey?—how's that?"

"They lie—that's how."

"Looky here—mind how you talk to me; I'm a-standing about all I can stand, now—so don't gimme no sass. I've been in town two days, and I hain't heard nothing but about you bein' rich. I heard about it away down the river, too. That's why I come. You git me that money to-morrow—I want it."

"I hain't got no money."

"It's a lie. Judge Thatcher's got it. You git it. I want it."

"I hain't got no money, I tell you. You ask Judge Thatcher; he'll tell you the same."

"All right. I'll ask him; and I'll make him pungle,[2] too, or I'll know the reason why. Say—how much you got in your pocket? I want it."

"I hain't got only a dollar, and I want that to—"

"It don't make no difference what you want it for—you just shell it out."

He took it and bit it to see if it was good, and then he said he was going down town to get some whiskey; said he hadn't had a drink all day. When he had got out on the shed, he put his head in again, and cussed me for putting on frills and trying to be better than him; and when I reckoned he was gone, he come back and put his head in again, and told me to mind about that school, because he was going to lay for me and lick me if I didn't drop that.

Next day he was drunk, and he went to Judge Thatcher's and bullyragged him and tried to make him give up the money, but he couldn't, and then he swore he'd make the law force him.

The judge and the widow went to law to get the court to take me away from him and let one of them be my guardian; but it was a new judge that had just come, and he didn't know the old man; so he said courts mustn't interfere and

---

1. A strapping with a cowhide whip.    2. Turn over the money.

separate families if they could help it; said he'd druther not take a child away from its father. So Judge Thatcher and the widow had to quit on the business. That pleased the old man till he couldn't rest. He said he'd cowhide me till I was black and blue if I didn't raise some money for him. I borrowed three dollars from Judge Thatcher, and pap took it and got drunk and went a-blowing around and cussing and whooping and carrying on; and he kept it up all over town, with a tin pan, till most midnight; then they jailed him, and next day they had him before court, and jailed him again for a week. But he said *he* was satisfied; said he was boss of his son, and he'd make it warm for *him*.

When he got out the new judge said he was agoing to make a man of him. So he took him to his own house, and dressed him up clean and nice, and had him to breakfast and dinner and supper with the family, and was just old pie to him, so to speak. And after supper he talked to him about temperance and such things till the old man cried, and said he'd been a fool, and fooled away his life; but now he was agoing to turn over a new leaf and be a man nobody wouldn't be ashamed of, and he hoped the judge would help him and not look down on him. The judge said he could hug him for them words; so *he* cried, and his wife she cried again; pap said he'd been a man that had always been misunderstood before, and the judge said he believed it. The old man said that what a man wanted that was down, was sympathy; and the judge said it was so; so they cried again. And when it was bedtime, the old man rose up and held out his hand, and says:

"Look at it gentlemen, and ladies all; take ahold of it; shake it. There's a hand that was the hand of a hog; but it ain't so no more; it's the hand of a man that's started in on a new life, and 'll die before he'll go back. You mark them words—don't forget I said them. It's a clean hand now; shake it—don't be afeard."

So they shook it, one after the other, all around, and cried. The judge's wife she kissed it. Then the old man he signed a pledge—made his mark. The judge said it was the holiest time on record, or something like that. Then they tucked the old man into a beautiful room, which was the spare room, and in the night sometime he got powerful thirsty and clumb out onto the porch-roof and slid down a stanchion and traded his new coat for a jug of forty-rod,[3] and clumb back again and had a good old time; and towards daylight he crawled out again, drunk as a fiddler, and rolled off the porch and broke his left arm in two places and was almost froze to death when somebody found him after sun-up. And when they come to look at that spare room, they had to take soundings before they could navigate it.

The judge he felt kind of sore. He said he reckoned a body could reform the ole man with a shot-gun, maybe, but he didn't know no other way.

## Chapter VI

Well, pretty soon the old man was up and around again, and then he went for Judge Thatcher in the courts to make him give up that money, and he went for me, too, for not stopping school. He catched me a couple of times and thrashed me, but I went to school just the same, and dodged him or outrun him most of the time. I didn't want to go to school much, before, but I

---

3. Home-distilled whiskey strong enough to knock a person forty rods, or 220 yards.

reckoned I'd go now to spite pap. That law trial was a slow business; appeared like they warn't ever going to get started on it; so every now and then I'd borrow two or three dollars off of the judge for him, to keep from getting a cowhiding. Every time he got money he got drunk; and every time he got drunk he raised Cain around town; and every time he raised Cain he got jailed. He was just suited—this kind of thing was right in his line.

He got to hanging around the widow's too much, and so she told him at last, that if he didn't quit using around there she would make trouble for him. Well, *wasn't* he mad? He said he would show who was Huck Finn's boss. So he watched out for me one day in the spring, and catched me, and took me up the river about three mile, in a skiff, and crossed over to the Illinois shore where it was woody and there warn't no houses but an old log hut in a place where the timber was so thick you couldn't find it if you didn't know where it was.

He kept me with him all the time, and I never got a chance to run off. We lived in that old cabin, and he always locked the door and put the key under his head, nights. He had a gun which he had stole, I reckon, and we fished and hunted, and that was what we lived on. Every little while he locked me in and went down to the store, three miles, to the ferry, and traded fish and game for whisky and fetched it home and got drunk and had a good time, and licked me. The widow she found out where I was, by-and-by, and she sent a man over to try to get hold of me, but pap drove him off with the gun, and it warn't long after that till I was used to being where I was, and liked it, all but the cowhide part.

It was kind of lazy and jolly, laying off comfortable all day, smoking and fishing, and no books nor study. Two months or more run along, and my clothes got to be all rags and dirt, and I didn't see how I'd ever got to like it so well at the widow's, where you had to wash, and eat on a plate, and comb up, and go to bed and get up regular, and be forever bothering over a book and have old Miss Watson pecking at you all the time. I didn't want to go back no more. I had stopped cussing, because the widow didn't like it; but now I took to it again because pap hadn't no objections. It was pretty good times up in the woods there, take it all around.

But by-and-by pap got too handy with his hick'ry, and I couldn't stand it. I was all over welts. He got to going away so much, too, and locking me in. Once he locked me in and was gone three days. It was dreadful lonesome. I judged he had got drowned and I wasn't ever going to get out any more. I was scared. I made up my mind I would fix up some way to leave there. I had tried to get out of that cabin many a time, but I couldn't find no way. There warn't a window to it big enough for a dog to get through. I couldn't get up the chimbly, it was too narrow. The door was thick solid oak slabs. Pap was pretty careful not to leave a knife or anything in the cabin when he was away; I reckon I had hunted the place over as much as a hundred times; well, I was 'most all the time at it, because it was about the only way to put in the time. But this time I found something at last; I found an old rusty wood-saw without any handle; it was laid in between a rafter and the clapboards of the roof. I greased it up and went to work. There was an old horse-blanket nailed against the logs at the far end of the cabin behind the table, to keep the wind from blowing through the chinks and putting the candle out. I got under the table and raised the blanket and went to work to saw a section of the big bottom log out, big enough to let me through. Well, it was a good long job, but I was getting towards the end of it when I heard pap's gun in the woods. I got rid of the signs of my work, and dropped the blanket and hid my saw, and pretty soon pap come in.

Pap warn't in a good humor—so he was his natural self. He said he was down to town, and everything was going wrong. His lawyer said he reckoned he would win his lawsuit and get the money, if they ever got started on the trial; but then there was ways to put it off a long time, and Judge Thatcher knowed how to do it. And he said people allowed there'd be another trial to get me away from him and give me to the widow for my guardian, and they guessed it would win, this time. This shook me up considerable, because I didn't want to go back to the widow's any more and be so cramped up and sivilized, as they called it. Then the old man got to cussing, and cussed everything and everybody he could think of, and then cussed them all over again to make sure he hadn't skipped any, and after that he polished off with a kind of general cuss all round, including a considerable parcel of people which he didn't know the names of, and so called them what's-his-name, when he got to them, and went right along with his cussing.

He said he would like to see the widow get me. He said he would watch out, and if they tried to come any such game on him he knowed of a place six or seven mile off, to stow me in, where they might hunt till they dropped and they couldn't find me. That made me pretty uneasy again, but only for a minute; I reckoned I wouldn't stay on hand till he got that chance.

The old man made me go to the skiff and fetch the things he had got. There was a fifty-pound sack of corn meal, and a side of bacon, ammunition, and a four-gallon jug of whisky,and an old book and two newspapers for wadding, besides some tow.[4] I toted up a load, and went back and set down on the bow of the skiff to rest. I thought it all over, and I reckoned I would walk off with the gun and some lines, and take to the woods when I run away. I guessed I wouldn't stay in one place, but just tramp right across the country, mostly night times, and hunt and fish to keep alive, and so get so far away that the old man nor the widow couldn't ever find me any more. I judged I would saw out and leave that night if pap got drunk enough, and I reckoned he would. I got so full of it I didn't notice how long I was staying, till the old man hollered and asked me whether I was asleep or drownded.

I got the things all up to the cabin, and then it was about dark. While I was cooking supper the old man took a swig or two and got sort of warmed up, and went to ripping again. He had been drunk over in town, and laid in the gutter all night, and he was a sight to look at. A body would a thought he was Adam, he was just all mud.[5] Whenever his liquor begun to work, he most always went for the govment. This time he says:

"Call this a govment! why, just look at it and see what it's like. Here's the law a-standing ready to take a man's son away from him—a man's own son, which he has had all the trouble and all the anxiety and all the expense of raising. Yes, just as that man has got that son raised at last, and ready to go to work and begin to do suthin' for *him* and give him a rest, the law up and goes for him. And they call *that* govment! That ain't all, nuther. The law backs that old Judge Thatcher up and helps him to keep me out o' my property.

4. Cheap rope. "Wadding": material (here paper) used to pack the gunpowder in a rifle.    5. God created Adam from earth in Genesis 2.7.

Here's what the law does. The law takes a man worth six thousand dollars and upards, and jams him into an old trap of a cabin like this, and lets him go round in clothes that ain't fitten for a hog. They call that govment! A man can't get his rights in a govment like this. Sometimes I've a mighty notion to just leave the country for good and all. Yes, and I *told* 'em so: I told old Thatcher so to his face. Lots of 'em heard me, and can tell what I said. Says I, for two cents I'd leave the blamed country and never come anear it agin. Them's the very words. I says, look at my hat—if you call it a hat—but the lid raises up and the rest of it goes down till it's below my chin, and then it ain't rightly a hat at all, but more like my head was shoved up through a jint o' stove-pipe. Look at it, says I—such a hat for me to wear—one of the wealthiest men in this town, if I could git my rights.

"Oh, yes, this is a wonderful govment, wonderful. Why, looky here. There was a free nigger there, from Ohio; a mulatter,[6] most as white as a white man. He had the whitest shirt on you ever see, too, and the shiniest hat; and there ain't a man in that town that's got as fine clothes as what he had; and he had a gold watch and chain and a silver-headed cane—the awfulest old gray-headed nabob in the State. And what do you think? they said he was a p'fessor in a college, and could talk all kinds of languages, and knowed everything. And that ain't the wust. They said he could *vote*, when he was at home. Well, that let me out. Thinks I, what is the country a-coming to? It was 'lection day, and I was just about to go and vote, myself, if I warn't too drunk to get there; but when they told me there was a State in this country where they'd let that nigger vote, I drawed out. I says I'll never vote agin. Them's the very words I said; they all heard me; and the country may rot for all me—I'll never vote agin as long as I live. And to see the cool way of that nigger—why, he wouldn't a give me the road if I hadn't shoved him out o' the way. I says to the people, why ain't this nigger put up at auction and sold?—that's what I want to know. And what do you reckon they said? Why, they said he couldn't be sold till he'd been in the State six months, and he hadn't been there that long yet. There, now—that's a specimen. They call that a govment that can't sell a free nigger till he's been in the State six months. Here's a govment that calls itself a govment, and lets on to be a govment, and thinks it is a govment, and yet's got to set stock-still for six whole months before it can take ahold of a prowling, thieving, infernal, white-shirted free nigger, and[7]—"

Pap was agoing on so, he never noticed where his old limber legs was taking him to, so he went head over heels over the tub of salt pork, and barked both shins, and the rest of his speech was all the hottest kind of language—mostly hove at the nigger and the govment, though he give the tub some, too, all along, here and there. He hopped around the cabin considerble, first on one leg and then on the other, holding first one shin and then the other one, and at last he let out with his left foot all of a sudden and fetched the tub a rattling kick. But it warn't good judgment, because that was the boot that had a couple of his toes leaking out of the front end of it; so now he raised a howl that fairly made a body's hair raise, and down he went in the dirt, and rolled there, and

---

6. Person of mixed white and black ancestry.
7. Missouri's original constitution prohibited the entrance of freed slaves and mulattoes into the state, but the "second Missouri Compromise" of 1820 deleted the provision. In the 1830s and 1840s, however, in-

creasingly strict antiblack laws were passed, and by 1850 a black without freedom papers could be sold downriver with a mere sworn statement of ownership from a white man.

held his toes; and the cussing he done then laid over anything he had ever done previous. He said so his own self, afterwards. He had heard old Sowberry Hagan in his best days, and he said it laid over him, too; but I reckon that was sort of piling it on, maybe.

After supper pap took the jug, and said he had enough whiskey there for two drunks and one delirium tremens. That was always his word. I judged he would be blind drunk in about an hour, an then I would steal the key, or saw myself out, one or 'tother. He drank, and drank, and tumbled down on his blankets, by-and-by; but luck didn't run my way. He didn't go sound asleep, but was uneasy. He groaned, and moaned, and thrashed around this way and that, for a long time. At last I got so sleepy I couldn't keep my eyes open, all I could do, and so before I knowed what I was about I was sound asleep, and the candle burning.

I don't know how long I was asleep, but all of a sudden there was an awful scream and I was up. There was pap, looking wild and skipping around every which way and yelling about snakes. He said they was crawling up his legs; and then he would give a jump and scream, and say one had bit him on the cheek—but I couldn't see no snakes. He started to run round and round the cabin, hollering "take him off! take him off! he's biting me on the neck!" I never see a man look so wild in the eyes. Pretty soon he was all fagged out, and fell down panting; then he rolled over and over, wonderful fast, kicking things every which way, and striking and grabbing at the air with his hands, and screaming, and saying there was devils ahold of him. He wore out, by-and-by, and laid still a while, moaning. Then he laid stiller, and didn't make a sound. I could hear the owls and the wolves, away off in the woods, and it seemed terrible still. He was laying over by the corner. By-and-by he raised up, part way, and listened, with his head to one side. He says very low:

"Tramp—tramp—tramp; that's the dead; tramp—tramp—tramp; they're coming after me; but I won't go— Oh, they're here! don't touch me—don't! hands off—they're cold; let go— Oh, let a poor devil alone!"

Then he went down on all fours and crawled off begging them to let him alone, and he rolled himself up in his blanket and wallowed in under the old pine table, still a-begging; and then he went to crying. I could hear him through the blanket.

By-and-by he rolled out and jumped up on his feet looking wild, and he see me and went for me. He chased me round and round the place, with a clasp-knife, calling me the Angel of Death and saying he would kill me and then I couldn't come for him no more. I begged, and told him I was only Huck, but he laughed *such* a screechy laugh, and roared and cussed, and kept on chasing me up. Once when I turned short and dodged under his arm he made a grab and got me by the jacket between my shoulders, and I thought I was gone; but I skid out of the jacket quick as lightning, and saved myself. Pretty soon he was all tired out, and dropped down with his back against the door, and said he would rest a minute and then kill me. He put his knife under him, and said he would sleep and get strong, and then he would see who was who.

So he dozed off, pretty soon. By-and-by I got the old split bottom[8] chair and clumb up, as easy as I could, not to make any noise, and got down the gun. I slipped the ramrod down it to make sure it was loaded, and then I laid it across

---

8. I.e., splint-bottom, made by weaving thin strips of wood.

the turnip barrel, pointing towards pap, and set down behind it to wait for him to stir. And how slow and still the time did drag along.

## Chapter VII

"Git up! what you 'bout!"

I opened my eyes and looked around, trying to make out where I was. It was after sun-up, and I had been sound asleep. Pap was standing over me, looking sour—and sick, too. He says—

"What you doin' with this gun?"

I judged he didn't know nothing about what he had been doing, so I says:

"Somebody tried to get in, so I was laying for him."

"Why didn't you roust me out?"

"Well I tried to, but I couldn't; I couldn't budge you."

"Well, all right. Don't stand there palavering all day, but out with you and see if there's a fish on the lines for breakfast. I'll be along in a minute."

He unlocked the door and I cleared out, up the river bank. I noticed some pieces of limbs and such things floating down, and a sprinkling of bark; so I knowed the river had begun to rise. I reckoned I would have great times, now, if I was over at the town. The June rise used to be always luck for me; because as soon as that rise begins, here comes cord-wood floating down, and pieces of log rafts—sometimes a dozen logs together; so all you have to do is to catch them and sell them to the wood yards and the sawmill.

I went along up the bank with one eye out for pap and 'tother one out for what the rise might fetch along. Well, all at once, here comes a canoe; just a beauty, too, about thirteen or fourteen foot long, riding high like a duck. I shot head first off of the bank, like a frog, clothes and all on, and struck out for the canoe. I just expected there'd be somebody laying down in it, because people often done that to fool folks, and when a chap had pulled a skiff out most to it they'd raise up and laugh at him. But it warn't so this time. It was a drift-canoe, sure enough, and I clumb in and paddled her ashore. Thinks I, the old man will be glad when he sees this—she's worth ten dollars. But when I got to shore pap wasn't in sight yet, and as I was running her into a little creek like a gully, all hung over with vines and willows, I struck another idea; I judged I'd hide her good, and then, stead of taking to the woods when I run off, I'd go down the river about fifty mile and camp in one place for good, and not have such a rough time tramping on foot.

It was pretty close to the shanty, and I thought I heard the old man coming, all the time; but I got her hid; and then I out and looked around a bunch of willows, and there was the old man down the path apiece just drawing a bead on a bird with his gun. So he hadn't seen anything.

When he got along, I was hard at it taking up a "trot" line.[9] He abused me a little for being so slow, but I told him I fell in the river and that was what made me so long. I knowed he would see I was wet, and then he would be asking questions. We got five catfish off of the lines and went home.

While we laid off, after breakfast, to sleep up, both of us being about wore out, I got to thinking that if I could fix up some way to keep pap and the widow from trying to follow me, it would be a certainer thing than trusting to luck to

---

9. A long fishing line fastened across a stream; to this line several shorter baited lines are attached.

get far enough off before they missed me; you see, all kinds of things might happen. Well, I didn't see no way for a while, but by-and-by pap raised up a minute, to drink another barrel of water, and he says:

"Another time a man comes a-prowling round here, you roust me out, you hear? That man warn't here for no good. I'd a shot him. Next time, you roust me out, you hear?"

Then he dropped down and went to sleep again—but what he had been saying give me the very idea I wanted. I says to myself, I can fix it now so nobody won't think of following me.

About twelve o'clock we turned out and went along up the bank. The river was coming up pretty fast, and lots of drift-wood going by on the rise. By-and-by, along comes part of a log raft—nine logs fast together. We went out with the skiff and towed it ashore. Then we had dinner. Anybody but pap would a waited and seen the day through, so as to catch more stuff; but that warn't pap's style. Nine logs was enough for one time; he must shove right over to town and sell. So he locked me in and took the skiff and started off towing the raft about half-past three. I judged he wouldn't come back that night. I waited till I reckoned he had got a good start, then I out with my saw and went to work on that log again. Before he was 'tother side of the river I was out of the hole; him and his raft was just a speck on the water away off yonder.

I took the sack of corn meal and took it to where the canoe was hid, and shoved the vines and branches apart and put it in; then I done the same with the side of bacon; then the whiskey jug; I took all the coffee and sugar there was, and all the ammunition; I took the wadding; I took the bucket and gourd, I took a dipper and a tin cup, and my old saw and two blankets, and the skillet and the coffee-pot. I took fish-lines and matches and other things—everything that was worth a cent. I cleaned out the place. I wanted an axe, but there wasn't any, only the one out at the wood pile, and I knowed why I was going to leave that. I fetched out the gun, and now I was done.

I had wore the ground a good deal, crawling out of the hole and dragging out so many things. So I fixed that as good as I could from the outside by scattering dust on the place, which covered up the smoothness and the saw-dust. Then I fixed the piece of log back into its place, and put two rocks under it and one against it to hold it there,—for it was bent up at the place, and didn't quite touch ground. If you stood four or five foot away and didn't know it was sawed, you wouldn't ever notice it; and besides, this was the back of the cabin and it warn't likely anybody would go fooling around there.

It was all grass clear to the canoe; so I hadn't left a track. I followed around to see. I stood on the bank and looked out over the river. All safe. So I took the gun and went up a piece into the woods and was hunting around for some birds, when I see a wild pig; hogs soon went wild in them bottoms after they had got away from the prairie farms. I shot this fellow and took him into camp.

I took the axe and smashed in the door—I beat it and hacked it considerable, a-doing it. I fetched the pig in and took him back nearly to the table and hacked into his throat with the ax, and laid him down on the ground to bleed—I say ground, because it *was* ground—hard packed, and no boards. Well, next I took an old sack and put a lot of big rocks in it,—all I could drag—and I started it from the pig and dragged it to the door and through the woods down to the river and dumped it in, and down it sunk, out of sight. You could easy see that something had been dragged over the ground. I did wish Tom Sawyer was there, I knowed he would take an interest in this kind of business, and throw in the fancy touches. Nobody could spread himself like Tom Sawyer in such a thing as that.

Well, last I pulled out some of my hair, and bloodied the ax good, and stuck it on the back side, and slung the ax in the corner. Then I took up the pig and held him to my breast with my jacket (so he couldn't drip) till I got a good piece below the house and then dumped him into the river. Now I thought of something else. So I went and got the bag of meal and my old saw out of the canoe and fetched them to the house. I took the bag to where it used to stand, and ripped a hole in the bottom of it with the saw, for there warn't no knives and forks on the place—pap done everything with his clasp-knife, about the cooking. Then I carried the sack about a hundred yards across the grass and through the willows east of the house, to a shallow lake that was five mile wide and full of rushes—and ducks too, you might say, in the season. There was a slough or a creek leading out of it on the other side, that went miles away, I don't know where, but it didn't go to the river. The meal sifted out and made a little track all the way to the lake. I dropped pap's whetstone there too, so as to look like it had been done by accident. Then I tied up the rip in the meal sack with a string, so it wouldn't leak no more, and took it and my saw to the canoe again.

It was about dark, now; so I dropped the canoe down the river under some willows that hung over the bank, and waited for the moon to rise. I made fast to a willow; then I took a bite to eat, and by-and-by laid down in the canoe to smoke a pipe and lay out a plan. I says to myself, they'll follow the track of that sackful of rocks to the shore and then drag the river for me. And they'll follow that meal track to the lake and go browsing down the creek that leads out of it to find the robbers that killed me and took the things. They won't ever hunt the river for anything but my dead carcass. They'll soon get tired of that, and won't bother no more about me. All right; I can stop anywhere I want to. Jackson's Island[1] is good enough for me; I know that island pretty well, and nobody ever comes there. And then I can paddle over to town, nights, and slink around and pick up things I want. Jackson's Island's the place.

I was pretty tired, and the first thing I knowed, I was asleep. When I woke up I didn't know where I was, for a minute. I set up and looked around, a little scared. Then I remembered. The river looked miles and miles across. The moon was so bright I could a counted the drift logs that went a slipping along, black and still, hundreds of yards out from shore. Everything was dead quiet, and it looked late, and *smelt* late. You know what I mean—I don't know the words to put it in.

I took a good gap and a stretch, and was just going to unhitch and start, when I heard a sound away over the water. I listened. Pretty soon I made it out. It was that dull kind of a regular sound that comes from oars working in rowlocks when it's a still night. I peeped out through the willow branches, and there it was—a skiff, away across the water. I couldn't tell how many was in it. It kept a-coming, and when it was abreast of me I see there warn't but one man in it. Thinks I, maybe it's pap, though I warn't expecting him. He dropped below me, with the current, and by-and-by he come a-swinging up shore in the easy water, and he went by so close I could a reached out the gun

1. The same island that serves for an adventure in *Tom Sawyer* (Chap. 13); actually known as Glasscock's Island, it has now been washed away.

and touched him. Well, it *was* pap, sure enough—and sober, too, by the way he laid to his oars.

I didn't lose no time. The next minute I was a-spinning down stream soft but quick in the shade of the bank. I made two mile and a half, and then struck out a quarter of a mile or more towards the middle of the river, because pretty soon I would be passing the ferry landing and people might see me and hail me. I got out amongst the drift-wood and then laid down in the bottom of the canoe and let her float. I laid there and had a good rest and a smoke out of my pipe, looking away into the sky, not a cloud in it. The sky looks ever so deep when you lay down on your back in the moonshine; I never knowed it before. And how far a body can hear on the water such nights! I heard people talking at the ferry landing. I heard what they said, too, every word of it. One man said it was getting towards the long days and the short nights, now. 'Tother one said *this* warn't one of the short ones, he reckoned—and then they laughed, and he said it over again and they laughed again; then they waked up another fellow and told him, and laughed, but he didn't laugh; he ripped out something brisk and said let him alone. The first fellow said he 'lowed to tell it to his old woman—she would think it was pretty good; but he said that warn't nothing to some things he had said in his time. I heard one man say it was nearly three o'clock, and he hoped daylight wouldn't wait more than about a week longer. After that, the talk got further and further away, and I couldn't make out the words any more, but I could hear the mumble; and now and then a laugh, too, but it seemed a long ways off.

I was away below the ferry now. I rose up and there was Jackson's Island, about two mile and a half down stream, heavy-timbered and standing up out of the middle of the river, big and dark and solid, like a steamboat without any lights. There warn't any signs of the bar at the head—it was all under water, now.

It didn't take me long to get there. I shot past the head at a ripping rate, the current was so swift, and then I got into the dead water and landed on the side towards the Illinois shore. I run the canoe into a deep dent in the bank that I knowed about; I had to part the willow branches to get in; and when I made fast nobody could a seen the canoe from the outside.

I went up and set down on a log at the head of the island and looked out on the big river and the black driftwood, and away over to the town, three mile away, where there was three or four lights twinkling. A monstrous big lumber raft was about a mile up stream, coming along down, with a lantern in the middle of it. I watched it come creeping down, and when it was most abreast of where I stood I heard a man say, "Stern oars, there! heave her head to stabboard!"[2] I heard that just as plain as if the man was by my side.

There was a little gray in the sky, now; so I stepped into the woods and laid down for a nap before breakfast.

## Chapter VIII

The sun was up so high when I waked, that I judged it was after eight o'clock. I laid there in the grass and the cool shade, thinking about things and feeling rested and ruther comfortable and satisfied. I could see the sun out at

---

2. Starboard, the right-hand side of a boat, facing forward.

one or two holes, but mostly it was big trees all about, and gloomy in there amongst them. There was freckled places on the ground where the light sifted down through the leaves, and the freckled places swapped about a little, showing there was a little breeze up there. A couple of squirrels set on a limb and jabbered at me very friendly.

I was powerful lazy and comfortable—didn't want to get up and cook breakfast. Well, I was dozing off again, when I thinks I hears a deep sound of "boom!" away up the river. I rouses up and rests on my elbow and listens; pretty soon I hears it again. I hopped up and went and looked out at a hole in the leaves, and I see a bunch of smoke laying on the water a long ways up—about abreast the ferry. And there was the ferry-boat full of people, floating along down. I knowed what was the matter, now. "Boom!" I see the white smoke squirt out of the ferry-boat's side. You see, they was firing cannon over the water, trying to make my carcass come to the top.

I was pretty hungry, but it warn't going to do for me to start a fire, because they might see the smoke. So I set there and watched the cannon-smoke and listened to the boom. The river was a mile wide, there, and it always looks pretty on a summer morning—so I was having a good enough time seeing them hunt for my remainders, if I only had a bite to eat. Well, then I happened to think how they always put quicksilver in loaves of bread and float them off because they always go right to the drownded carcass and stop there. So says I, I'll keep a lookout, and if any of them's floating around after me, I'll give them a show. I changed to the Illinois edge of the island to see what luck I could have, and I warn't disappointed. A big double loaf come along, and I most got it, with a long stick, but my foot slipped and she floated out further. Of course I was where the current set in the closest to the shore—I knowed enough for that. But by-and-by along comes another one, and this time I won. I took out the plug and shook out the little dab of quicksilver, and set my teeth in. It was "baker's bread"—what the quality eat—none of your low-down corn-pone.[3]

I got a good place amongst the leaves, and set there on a log, munching the bread and watching the ferry-boat, and very well satisfied. And then something struck me. I says, now I reckon the widow or the parson or somebody prayed that this bread would find me, and here it has gone and done it. So there ain't no doubt but there is something in that thing. That is, there's something in it when a body like the widow or the parson prays, but it don't work for me, and I reckon it don't work for only just the right kind.

I lit a pipe and had a good long smoke and went on watching. The ferry-boat was floating with the current, and I allowed I'd have a chance to see who was aboard when she come along, because she would come in close, where the bread did. When she'd got pretty well along down towards me, I put out my pipe and went to where I fished out the bread, and laid down behind a log on the bank in a little open place. Where the log forked I could peep through.

By-and-by she came along, and she drifted in so close that they could a run out a plank and walked ashore. Most everybody was on the boat. Pap, and Judge Thatcher, and Bessie Thatcher, and Jo Harper, and Tom Sawyer, and his old Aunt Polly, and Sid and Mary, and plenty more. Everybody was talking about the murder, but the captain broke in and says:

"Look sharp, now; the current sets in the closest here, and maybe he's

3. A simple corn bread.

washed ashore and got tangled amongst the brush at the water's edge. I hope
so, anyway."

I didn't hope so. They all crowded up and leaned over the rails, nearly in
my face, and kept still, watching with all their might. I could see them first-
rate, but they couldn't see me. Then the captain sung out:

"Stand away!" and the cannon let off such a blast right before me that it
made me deef with the noise and pretty near blind with the smoke, and I
judged I was gone. If they'd a had some bullets in, I reckon they'd a got the
corpse they was after. Well, I see I warn't hurt, thanks to goodness. The boat
floated on and went out of sight around the shoulder of the island. I could
hear the booming, now and then, further and further off, and by-and-by after
an hour, I didn't hear it no more. The island was three mile long. I judged
they had got to the foot, and was giving it up. But they didn't yet a while.
They turned around the foot of the island and started up the channel on the
Missouri side, under steam, and booming once in a while as they went. I
crossed over to that side and watched them. When they got abreast the head
of the island they quit shooting and dropped over to the Missouri shore and
went home to the town.

I knowed I was all right now. Nobody else would come a-hunting after me.
I got my traps out of the canoe and made me a nice camp in the thick woods.
I made a kind of a tent out of my blankets to put my things under so the rain
couldn't get at them. I catched a cat fish and haggled him open with my saw,
and towards sundown I started my camp fire and had supper. Then I set out a
line to catch some fish for breakfast.

When it was dark I set by my camp fire smoking, and feeling pretty satisfied;
but by-and-by it got sort of lonesome, and so I went and set on the bank and
listened to the currents washing along, and counted the stars and drift-logs and
rafts that come down, and then went to bed; there ain't no better way to put in
time when you are lonesome; you can't stay so, you soon get over it.

And so for three days and nights. No difference—just the same thing. But
the next day I went exploring around down through the island. I was boss of
it; it all belonged to me, so to say, and I wanted to know all about it; but
mainly I wanted to put in the time. I found plenty strawberries, ripe and prime;
and green summer-grapes, and green razberries; and the green blackberries
was just beginning to show. They would all come handy by-and-by, I judged.

Well, I went fooling along in the deep woods till I judged I warn't far from
the foot of the island. I had my gun along, but I hadn't shot nothing; it was
for protection; thought I would kill some game nigh home. About this time I
mighty near stepped on a good sized snake, and it went sliding off through the
grass and flowers, and I after it, trying to get a shot at it. I clipped along,
and all of sudden I bounded right on to the ashes of a camp fire that was
still smoking.

My heart jumped up amongst my lungs. I never waited for to look further,
but uncocked my gun and went sneaking back on my tip-toes as fast as ever I
could. Every now and then I stopped a second, amongst the thick leaves, and
listened; but my breath come so hard I couldn't hear nothing else. I slunk
along another piece further, then listened again; and so on, and so on; if I see
a stump, I took it for a man; if I trod on a stick and broke it, it made me feel
like a person had cut one of my breaths in two and I only got half, and the
short half, too.

When I got to camp I warn't feeling very brash, there warn't much sand in my craw;[4] but I says, this ain't no time to be fooling around. So I got all my traps into my canoe again so as to have them out of sight, and I put out the fire and scattered the ashes around to look like an old last year's camp, and then clumb a tree.

I reckon I was up in the tree two hours; but I didn't see nothing, I didn't hear nothing—I only *thought* I heard and seen as much as a thousand things. Well, I couldn't stay up there forever; so at last I got down, but I kept in the thick woods and on the lookout all the time. All I could get to eat was berries and what was left over from breakfast.

By the time it was night I was pretty hungry. So when it was good and dark, I slid out from shore before moonrise and paddled over to the Illinois bank— about a quarter of a mile. I went out in the woods and cooked a supper, and I had about made up my mind I would stay there all night, when I hear a *plunkety-plunk, plunkety-plunk,* and says to myself, horses coming; and next I hear people's voices. I got everything into the canoe as quick as I could, and then went creeping through the woods to see what I could find out. I hadn't got far when I hear a man say:

"We'd better camp here, if we can find a good place; the horses is about beat out. Let's look around."[5]

I didn't wait, but shoved out and paddled away easy. I tied up in the old place, and reckoned I would sleep in the canoe.

I didn't sleep much. I couldn't, somehow, for thinking. And every time I waked up I thought somebody had me by the neck. So the sleep didn't do me no good. By-and-by I says to myself, I can't live this way; I'm agoing to find out who it is that's here on the island with me; I'll find it out or bust. Well, I felt better, right off.

So I took my paddle and slid out from shore just a step or two, and then let the canoe drop along down amongst the shadows. The moon was shining, and outside of the shadows it made it most as light as day. I poked along well onto an hour, everything still as rocks and sound asleep. Well by this time I was most down to the foot of the island. A little ripply, cool breeze begun to blow, and that was as good as saying the night was about done. I give her a turn with the paddle and brung her nose to shore; then I got my gun and slipped out and into the edge of the woods. I set down there on a log and looked out through the leaves. I see the moon go off watch and the darkness begin to blanket the river. But in a little while I see a pale streak over the tree-tops, and knowed the day was coming. So I took my gun and slipped off towards where I had run across that camp fire, stopping every minute or two to listen. But I hadn't no luck, somehow; I couldn't seem to find the place. But by-and-by, sure enough, I catched a glimpse of fire, away through the trees. I went for it, cautious and slow. By-and-by I was close enough to have a look, and there laid a man on the ground. It most give me the fan-tods.[6] He had a blanket around his head, and his head was nearly in the fire. I set there behind a clump of bushes, in about six foot of him, and kept my eyes on him steady. It was getting gray daylight, now. Pretty soon he gapped, and stretched himself, and hove off the blanket, and it was Miss Watson's Jim! I bet I was glad to see him. I says:

---

4. Slang for not feeling very brave.
5. Apparently this episode is a vestige of an early conception of the novel involving Pap in a murder plot

and court trial.
6. Slang for the hallucinatory state associated with delirium tremens.

"Hello, Jim!" and skipped out.

He bounced up and stared at me wild. Then he drops down on his knees, and puts his hands together and says:

"Doan' hurt me—don't! I hain't ever done no harm to a ghos'. I awluz liked dead people, en done all I could for 'em. You go en git in de river agin, whah you b'longs, en doan' do nuffn to Ole Jim, 'at 'uz awluz yo' fren'."

Well, I warn't long making him understand I warn't dead. I was ever so glad to see Jim. I warn't lonesome, now. I told him I warn't afraid of *him* telling the people where I was. I talked along, but he only set there and looked at me; never said nothing. Then I says:

"It's good daylight. Let's get breakfast. Make up your camp fire good."

"What's de use er makin' up de camp fire to cook strawbries en sich truck? But you got a gun, hain't you? Den we kin git sumfn better den strawbries."

"Strawberries and such truck," I says. "Is that what you live on?"

"I couldn' git nuffn else," he says.

"Why, how long you been on the island, Jim?"

"I come heah de night arter you's killed."

"What, all that time?"

"Yes-indeedy."

"And ain't you had nothing but that kind of rubbage to eat?"

"No, sah—nuffn else."

"Well, you must be most starved, ain't you?"

"I reck'n I could eat a hoss. I think I could. How long you ben on de islan'?"

"Since the night I got killed."

"No! W'y, what has you lived on? But you got a gun. Oh, yes, you got a gun. Dat's good. Now you kill sumfn en I'll make up de fire."

So we went over to where the canoe was, and while he built a fire in a grassy open place amongst the trees, I fetched meal and bacon and coffee, and coffee-pot and frying-pan, and sugar and tin cups, and the nigger was set back considerable, because he reckoned it was all done with witchcraft. I catched a good big cat-fish, too, and Jim cleaned him with his knife, and fried him.

When breakfast was ready, we lolled on the grass and eat it smoking hot. Jim laid it in with all his might, for he was most about starved. Then when we had got pretty well stuffed, we laid off and lazied.

By-and-by Jim says:

"But looky here, Huck, who wuz it dat 'uz killed in dat shanty, ef it warn't you?"

Then I told him the whole thing, and he said it was smart. He said Tom Sawyer couldn't get up no better plan than what I had. Then I says:

"How do you come to be here, Jim, and how'd you get here?"

He looked pretty uneasy, and didn't say nothing for a minute. Then he says:

"Maybe I better not tell."

"Why, Jim?"

"Well, dey's reasons. But you wouldn' tell on me ef I 'uz to tell you, would you, Huck?"

"Blamed if I would, Jim."

"Well, I b'lieve you, Huck. I—I *run off*."

"Jim!"

"But mind, you said you wouldn't tell—you know you said you wouldn't tell, Huck."

"Well, I did. I said I wouldn't, and I'll stick to it. Honest *injun* I will. People would call me a low down Ablitionist and despise me for keeping mum—but that don't make no difference. I ain't agoing to tell, and I ain't agoing back there anyways. So now, le's know all about it."

"Well, you see, it 'uz dis way. Ole Missus—dat's Miss Watson—she pecks on me all de time, en treats me pooty rough, but she awluz said she wouldn' sell me down to Orleans. But I noticed dey wuz a nigger trader roun' de place considable, lately, en I begin to git oneasy. Well, one night I creeps to de do', pooty late, en de do' warn't quite shet, en I hear ole missus tell de widder she gwyne to sell me down to Orleans, but she didn' want to, but she could git eight hund'd dollars for me,[7] en it 'uz sich a big stack o' money she couldn' resis'. De widder she try to git her to say she wouldn' do it, but I never waited to hear de res'. I lit out mighty quick, I tell you.

"I tuck out en shin down de hill en 'spec to steal a skift 'long de sho' som'ers 'bove de town, but dey wuz people a-stirrin' yit, so I hid in de ole tumble-down cooper shop on de bank to wait for everybody to go 'way. Well, I wuz dah all night. Dey wuz somebody roun' all de time. 'Long 'bout six in de mawnin', skifts begin to go by, en 'bout eight or nine every skift dat went 'long wuz talkin' 'bout how yo' pap come over to de town en say you's killed. Dese las' skifts wuz full o' ladies en genlmen agoin' over for to see de place. Sometimes dey'd pull up at de sho' en take a res' b'fo' dey started acrost, so by de talk I got to know all 'bout de killin'. I 'uz powerful sorry you's killed, Huck, but I ain't no mo', now.

"I laid dah under de shavins all day. I 'uz hungry, but I warn't afeared; bekase I knowed ole missus en de widder wuz goin' to start to de camp-meetn' right arter breakfas' en be gone all day, en dey knows I goes off wid de cattle 'bout daylight, so dey wouldn' 'spec to see me roun' de place, en so dey wouldn' miss me tell arter dark in de evenin'. De yuther servants wouldn' miss me, kase dey'd shin out en take holiday, soon as de ole folks 'uz out'n de way.

"Well, when it come dark I tuck out up de river road, en went 'bout two mile er more to whah dey warn't no houses. I'd made up my mind 'bout what I's agwyne to do. You see ef I kep' on tryin' to git away afoot, de dogs 'ud track me; ef I stole a skift to cross over, dey'd miss dat skift, you see, en dey'd know 'bout whah I'd lan' on de yuther side en whah to pick up my track. So I says, a raff is what I's arter; it doan' *make* no track.

"I see a light a-comin' roun' de p'int, bymeby, so I wade' in en shove' a log ahead o' me, en swum more'n half-way acrost de river, en got in 'mongst de drift-wood, en kep' my head down low, en kinder swum agin de current tell de raff come along. Den I swum to de stern uv it, en tuck aholt. It clouded up en 'uz pooty dark for a little while. So I clumb up en laid down on de planks. De men 'uz all 'way yonder in de middle,[8] whah de lantern wuz. De river wuz arisin' en dey wuz a good current; so I reck'n'd 'at by fo' in de mawnin' I'd be twenty-five mile down de river, en den I'd slip in, jis' b'fo' daylight, en swim asho' en take to de woods on de Illinoi side.[9]

"But I didn' have no luck. When we 'uz mos' down to de head er de islan', a man begin to come aft wid de lantern. I see it warn't no use fer to wait, so I

---

7. A realistic price for a healthy male slave in the 1840s.
8. A river raft would be large enough to make this easily possible.
9. Though Illinois was not a slave state, by state law any black person without freedom papers could be arrested and subjected to forced labor. Jim's chances for escape would be improved if he went down the Mississippi and then up the Ohio.

slid overboad, en struck out fer de islan'. Well, I had a notion I could lan' mos' anywhers, but I couldn'—bank too bluff. I 'uz mos' to de foot er de islan' b'fo' I foun' a good place. I went into de woods en jedged I wouldn' fool wid raffs no mo', long as dey move de lantern roun' so. I had my pipe en a plug er dog-leg,[1] en some matches in my cap, en dey warn't wet, so I 'uz all right."

"And so you ain't had no meat nor bread to eat all this time? Why didn't you get mud-turkles?"

"How you gwyne to git'm? You can't slip up on um en grab um; en how's a body gwyne to hit um wid a rock? How could a body do it in de night? en I warn't gwyne to show myself on de bank in de daytime."

"Well, that's so. You've had to keep in the woods all the time, of course. Did you hear 'em shooting the cannon?"

"Oh, yes. I knowed dey was arter you. I see um go by heah; watched um thoo de bushes."

Some young birds come along, flying a yard or two at a time and lighting. Jim said it was a sign it was going to rain. He said it was a sign when young chickens flew that way, and so he reckoned it was the same way when young birds done it. I was going to catch some of them, but Jim wouldn't let me. He said it was death. He said his father laid mighty sick once, and some of them catched a bird, and his old granny said his father would die, and he did.

And Jim said you mustn't count the things you are going to cook for dinner, because that would bring bad luck. The same if you shook the table-cloth after sundown. And he said if a man owned a bee-hive, and that man died, the bees must be told about it before sun-up next morning, or else the bees would all weaken down and quit work and die. Jim said bees wouldn't sting idiots; but I didn't believe that, because I had tried them lots of times myself, and they wouldn't sting me.

I had heard about some of these things before, but not all of them. Jim knowed all kinds of signs. He said he knowed most everything. I said it looked to me like all the signs was about bad luck, and so I asked him if there warn't any good-luck signs. He says:

"Mighty few—an' *dey* ain' no use to a body. What you want to know when good luck's a-comin' for? want to keep it off?" And he said: "Ef you's got hairy arms en a hairy breas', it's a sign dat you's agwyne to be rich. Well, dey's some use in a sign like dat, 'kase it's so fur ahead. You see, maybe you's got to be po' a long time fust, en so you might git discourage' en kill yo'sef 'f you didn' know by de sign dat you gwyne to be rich bymeby."

"Have you got hairy arms and a hairy breast, Jim?"

"What's de use to ax dat question? don' you see I has?"

"Well, are you rich?"

"No, but I ben rich wunst, and gwyne to be rich agin. Wunst I had foteen dollars, but I tuck to specalat'n', en got busted out."

"What did you speculate in, Jim?"

"Well, fust I tackled stock."

"What kind of stock?"

"Why, live stock. Cattle, you know. I put ten dollars in a cow. But I ain't gwyne to resk no mo' money in stock. De cow up 'n' died on my han's."

"So you lost the ten dollars."

---

1. Cheap tobacco.

"No, I didn' lose it all. I on'y los' 'bout nine of it. I sole de hide en taller for a dollar en ten cents."

"You had five dollars and ten cents left. Did you speculate any more?"

"Yes. You know dat one-laigged nigger dat b'longs to old Misto Bradish? well, he sot up a bank, en say anybody dat put in a dollar would git fo' dollars mo' at de en' er de year. Well, all de niggers went in, but dey didn' have much. I wuz de on'y one dat had much. So I stuck out for mo' dan fo' dollars, en I said 'f I didn' git it I'd start a bank myself. Well o' course dat nigger want' to keep me out er de business, bekase he say dey warn't business 'nough for two banks, so he say I could put in my five dollars en he pay me thirty-five at de en' er de year.

"So I done it. Den I reck'n'd I'd inves' de thirty-five dollars right off en keep things a-movin'. Dey wuz a nigger name' Bob, dat had ketched a wood-flat,[2] en his marster didn' know it; en I bought it off'n him en told him to take de thirty-five dollars when de en' er de year come; but somebody stole de wood-flat dat night, en nex' day de one-laigged nigger say de bank 's busted. So dey didn' none uv us git no money."

"What did you do with the ten cents, Jim?"

"Well, I 'uz gwyne to spen' it, but I had a dream, en de dream tole me to give it to a nigger name' Balum—Balum's Ass[3] dey call him for short, he's one er dem chuckle-heads, you know. But he's lucky, dey say, en I see I warn't lucky. De dream say let Balum inves' de ten cents en he'd make a raise for me. Well, Balum he tuck de money, en when he wuz in church he hear de preacher say dat whoever give to de po' len' to de Lord, en boun' to git his money back a hund'd times. So Balum he tuck en give de ten cents to de po', en laid low to see what wuz gwyne to come of it."

"Well, what did come of it, Jim?"

"Nuffn never come of it. I couldn' manage to k'leck dat money no way; en Balum he couldn'. I ain' gwyne to len' no mo' money 'dout I see de security. Boun' to git yo' money back a hund'd times, de preacher says! Ef I could git de ten *cents* back, I'd call it squah, en be glad er de chanst."

"Well, it's all right anyway, Jim, long as you're going to be rich again some time or other."

"Yes—en I's rich now, come to look at it. I owns mysef, en I's wuth eight hund'd dollars. I wisht I had de money, I wouldn' want no mo'."

## Chapter IX

I wanted to go and look at a place right about the middle of the island, that I'd found when I was exploring; so we started, and soon got to it, because the island was only three miles long and a quarter of a mile wide.

This place was a tolerable long steep hill or ridge, about forty foot high. We had a rough time getting to the top, the sides was so steep and the bushes so thick. We tramped and clumb around all over it, and by-and-by found a good big cavern in the rock, most up to the top on the side towards Illinois. The cavern was as big as two or three rooms bunched together, and Jim could stand

---

2. A flat-bottomed boat used to transport timber.
3. Balaam, Old Testament prophet. God's avenging angel interrupted this prophet's journey to curse the Israelites by standing in the path of his progress. Ba-laam was blind to the angel's presence, but his ass saw the angel clearly and swerved off the road, much to Balaam's chagrin (Numbers 22).

up straight in it. It was cool in there. Jim was for putting our traps in there, right away, but I said we didn't want to be climbing up and down there all the time.

Jim said if we had the canoe hid in a good place, and had all the traps in the cavern, we could rush there if anybody was to come to the island, and they would never find us without dogs. And besides, he said them little birds had said it was going to rain, and did I want the things to get wet?

So we went back and got the canoe and paddled up abreast the cavern, and lugged all the traps up there. Then we hunted up a place close by to hide the canoe in, amongst the thick willows. We took some fish off of the lines and set them again, and begun to get ready for dinner.

The door of the cavern was big enough to roll a hogshead in, and on one side of the door the floor stuck out a little bit and was flat and a good place to build a fire on. So we built it there and cooked dinner.

We spread the blankets inside for a carpet, and eat our dinner in there. We put all the other things handy at the back of the cavern. Pretty soon it darkened up and begun to thunder and lighten; so the birds was right about it. Directly it begun to rain, and it rained like all fury, too, and I never see the wind blow so. It was one of these regular summer storms. It would get so dark that it looked all blue-black outside, and lovely; and the rain would thrash along by so thick that the trees off a little ways looked dim and spider-webby; and here would come a blast of wind that would bend the trees down and turn up the pale underside of the leaves; and then a perfect ripper of a gust would follow along and set the branches to tossing their arms as if they was just wild; and next, when it was just about the bluest and blackest—*fst!* it was as bright as glory and you'd have a little glimpse of tree-tops a-plunging about, away off yonder in the storm, hundreds of yards further than you could see before; dark as sin again in a second, and now you'd hear the thunder let go with an awful crash and then go rumbling, grumbling, tumbling down the sky towards the under side of the world, like rolling empty barrels down stairs, where it's long stairs and they bounce a good deal, you know.

"Jim, this is nice," I says. "I wouldn't want to be nowhere else but here. Pass me along another hunk of fish and some hot cornbread."

"Well, you wouldn' a ben here, 'f it hadn' a ben for Jim. You'd a ben down dah in de woods widout any dinner, en gittn' mos' drownded, too, dat you would, honey. Chickens knows when its gwyne to rain, en so do de birds, chile."

The river went on raising and raising for ten or twelve days, till at last it was over the banks. The water was three or four foot deep on the island in the low places and on the Illinois bottom. On that side it was a good many miles wide; but on the Missouri side it was the same old distance across—a half a mile—because the Missouri shore was just a wall of high bluffs.

Daytimes we paddled all over the island in the canoe. It was mighty cool and shady in the deep woods even if the sun was blazing outside. We went winding in and out amongst the trees; and sometimes the vines hung so thick we had to back away and go some other way. Well, on every old broken-down tree, you could see rabbits, and snakes, and such things; and when the island had been overflowed a day or two, they got so tame, on account of being hungry, that you could paddle right up and put your hand on them if you wanted to; but not the snakes and turtles—they would slide off in the water.

The ridge our cavern was in, was full of them. We could a had pets enough if we'd wanted them.

One night we catched a little section of a lumber raft—nice pine planks. It was twelve foot wide and about fifteen or sixteen foot long, and the top stood above water six or seven inches, a solid level floor. We could see saw-logs go by in the daylight, sometimes, but we let them go; we didn't show ourselves in daylight.

Another night, when we was up at the head of the island, just before daylight, here comes a frame house down, on the west side. She was a two-story, and tilted over, considerable. We paddled out and got aboard—clumb in at an up-stairs window. But it was too dark to see yet, so we made the canoe fast and set in her to wait for daylight.

The light begun to come before we got to the foot of the island. Then we looked in at the window. We could make out a bed, and a table, and two old chairs, and lots of things around about on the floor; and there was clothes hanging against the wall. There was something laying on the floor in the far corner that looked like a man. So Jim says.

"Hello, you!"

But it didn't budge. So I hollered again, and then Jim says:

"De man ain' asleep—he's dead. You hold still—I'll go en see."

He went and bent down and looked, and says:

"It's a dead man. Yes, indeedy; naked, too. He's ben shot in de back. I reck'n he's ben dead two er three days. Come in, Huck, but doan' look at his face—it's too gashly."

I didn't look at him at all. Jim throwed some old rags over him, but he needn't done it; I didn't want to see him. There was heaps of old greasy cards scattered around over the floor, and old whisky bottles, and a couple of masks made out of black cloth; and all over the walls was the ignorantest kind of words and pictures, made with charcoal. There was two old dirty calico dresses, and a sun-bonnet, and some women's under-clothes, hanging against the wall, and some men's clothing, too. We put the lot into the canoe; it might come good. There was a boy's old speckled straw hat on the floor; I took that too. And there was a bottle that had had milk in it; and it had a rag stopper for a baby to suck. We would a took the bottle, but it was broke. There was a seedy old chest, and an old hair trunk with the hinges broke. They stood open, but there warn't nothing left in them that was any account. The way things was scattered about, we reckoned the people left in a hurry and warn't fixed so as to carry off most of their stuff.

We got an old tin lantern, and a butcher-knife without any handle, and a bran-new Barlow knife[4] worth two bits in any store, and a lot of tallow candles, and a tin candlestick, and a gourd, and a tin cup, and a ratty old bed-quilt off the bed, and a reticule with needles and pins and beeswax and buttons and thread and all such truck in it, and a hatchet and some nails, and a fish-line as thick as my little finger, with some monstrous hooks on it, and a roll of buckskin, and a leather dog-collar, and a horse-shoe, and some vials of medicine that didn't have no label on them; and just as we was leaving I found a tolerable good curry-comb, and Jim he found a ratty old fiddle-bow, and a wooden leg. The straps was broke off of it, but barring that, it was a good

---

4. Pocketknife with one blade, named for the inventor.

enough leg, though it was too long for me and not long enough for Jim, and we couldn't find the other one, though we hunted all around. And so, take it all around, we made a good haul. When we was ready to shove off, we was a quarter of a mile below the island, and it was pretty broad day; so I made Jim lay down in the canoe and cover up with the quilt, because if he set up, people could tell he was a nigger a good ways off. I paddled over to the Illinois shore, and drifted down most a half a mile doing it. I crept up the dead water under the bank, and hadn't no accidents and didn't see nobody. We got home all safe.

## Chapter X

After breakfast I wanted to talk about the dead man and guess out how he come to be killed, but Jim didn't want to. He said it would fetch bad luck; and besides, he said, he might come and ha'nt us; he said a man that warn't buried was more likely to go a-ha'nting around than one that was planted and comfortable. That sounded pretty reasonable, so I didn't say no more; but I couldn't keep from studying over it and wishing I knowed who shot the man, and what they done it for.

We rummaged the clothes we'd got, and found eight dollars in silver sewed up in the lining of an old blanket overcoat. Jim said he reckoned the people in that house stole the coat, because if they'd a knowed the money was there they wouldn't a left it. I said I reckoned they killed him, too; but Jim didn't want to talk about that. I says:

"Now, you think it's bad luck; but what did you say when I fetched in the snake-skin that I found on the top of the ridge day before yesterday? You said it was the worst bad luck in the world to touch a snake-skin with my hands. Well, here's your bad luck! We've raked in all this truck and eight dollars besides. I wish we could have some bad luck like this every day, Jim."

"Never you mind, honey, never you mind. Don't you git too peart. It's a-comin'. Mind I tell you, it's a-comin'."

It did come, too. It was Tuesday that we had that talk. Well, after dinner Friday, we was laying around in the grass at the upper end of the ridge, and got out of tobacco. I went to the cavern to get some, and found a rattlesnake in there. I killed him, and curled him up on the foot of Jim's blanket, ever so natural, thinking there'd be some fun when Jim found him there. Well, by night I forgot all about the snake, and when Jim flung himself down on the blanket while I struck a light, the snake's mate was there, and bit him.

He jumped up yelling, and the first thing the light showed was the varmint curled up and ready for another spring. I laid him out in a second with a stick, and Jim grabbed pap's whiskey jug and began to pour it down.

He was barefooted, and the snake bit him right on the heel. That all comes of my being such a fool as to not remember that whenever you leave a dead snake its mate always comes there and curls around it. Jim told me to chop off the snake's head and throw it away, and then skin the body and roast a piece of it. I done it, and he eat it and said it would help cure him.[5] He made me take off the rattles and tie them around his wrist, too. He said that that would help. Then I slid out quiet and throwed the snakes clear away amongst the

---

5. Jim's homeopathic remedy is a common folk-medical practice.

bushes; for I warn't going to let Jim find out it was all my fault, not if I could help it.

Jim sucked and sucked at the jug, and now and then he got out of his head and pitched around and yelled; but every time he come to himself he went to sucking at the jug again. His foot swelled up pretty big, and so did his leg; but by-and-by the drunk begun to come, and so I judged he was all right; but I'd druther been bit with a snake than pap's whiskey.

Jim was laid up for four days and nights. Then the swelling was all gone and he was around again. I made up my mind I wouldn't ever take aholt of a snake-skin again with my hands, now that I see what had come of it. Jim said he reckoned I would believe him next time. And he said that handling a snake-skin was such awful bad luck that maybe we hadn't got to the end of it yet. He said he druther see the new moon over his left shoulder as much as a thousand times than take up a snake-skin in his hand. Well, I was getting to feel that way myself, though I've always reckoned that looking at the new moon over your left shoulder is one of the carelessest and foolishest things a body can do. Old Hank Bunker done it once, and bragged about it; and in less than two years he got drunk and fell off of the shot tower and spread himself out so that he was just a kind of layer, as you may say; and they slid him edgeways between two barn doors for a coffin, and buried him so, so they say, but I didn't see it. Pap told me. But anyway, it all come of looking at the moon that way, like a fool.

Well, the days went along, and the river went down between its banks again; and about the first thing we done was to bait one of the big hooks with a skinned rabbit and set it and catch a cat-fish that was as big as a man, being six foot two inches long, and weighed over two hundred pounds. We couldn't handle him, of course; he would a flung us into Illinois. We just set there and watched him rip and tear around till he drowned. We found a brass button in his stomach, and a round ball, and lots of rubbage. We split the ball open with the hatchet, and there was a spool in it. Jim said he'd had it there a long time, to coat it over so and make a ball of it. It was as big a fish as was ever catched in the Mississippi, I reckon. Jim said he hadn't ever seen a bigger one. He would a been worth a good deal over at the village. They peddle out such a fish as that by the pound in the market house there; everybody buys some of him; his meat's as white as snow and makes a good fry.

Next morning I said it was getting slow and dull, and I wanted to get a stirring up, some way. I said I reckoned I would slip over the river and find out what was going on. Jim liked that notion; but he said I must go in the dark and look sharp. Then he studied it over and said, couldn't I put on some of them old things and dress up like a girl? That was a good notion, too. So we shortened up one of the calico gowns and I turned up my trowser-legs to my knees and got into it. Jim hitched it behind with the hooks, and it was a fair fit. I put on the sun-bonnet and tied it under my chin, and then for a body to look in and see my face was like looking down a joint of stove-pipe. Jim said nobody would know me, even in the daytime, hardly. I practiced around all day to get the hang of the things, and by-and-by I could do pretty well in them, only Jim said I didn't walk like a girl; and he said I must quit pulling up my gown to get at my britches pocket. I took notice, and done better.

I started up the Illinois shore in the canoe just after dark.

I started across to the town from a little below the ferry landing, and the drift of the current fetched me in at the bottom of the town. I tied up and started along the bank. There was a light burning in a little shanty that hadn't been lived in for a long time, and I wondered who had took up quarters there. I slipped up and peeped in at the window. There was a woman about forty year old in there, knitting by a candle that was on a pine table. I didn't know her face; she was a stranger, for you couldn't start a face in that town that I didn't know. Now this was lucky, because I was weakening; I was getting afraid I had come; people might know my voice and find me out. But if this woman had been in such a little town two days she could tell me all I wanted to know; so I knocked at the door, and made up my mind I wouldn't forget I was a girl.

## Chapter XI

"Come in," says the woman, and I did. She says:

"Take a cheer."

I done it. She looked me all over with her little shiny eyes, and says:

"What might your name be?"

"Sarah Williams."

"Where 'bouts do you live? In this neighborhood?"

"No'm. In Hookerville, seven mile below. I've walked all the way and I'm all tired out."

"Hungry, too, I reckon. I'll find you something."

"No'm, I ain't hungry. I was so hungry I had to stop two mile below here at a farm; so I ain't hungry no more. It's what makes me so late. My mother's down sick, and out of money and everything, and I come to tell my uncle Abner Moore. He lives at the upper end of the town, she says. I hain't ever been here before. Do you know him?"

"No; but I don't know everybody yet. I haven't lived here quite two weeks. It's a considerable ways to the upper end of the town. You better stay here all night. Take off your bonnet."

"No," I says, "I'll rest a while, I reckon, and go on. I ain't afeard of the dark."

She said she wouldn't let me go by myself, but her husband would be in by-and-by, maybe in a hour and a half, and she'd send him along with me. Then she got to talking about her husband, and about her relations up the river, and her relations down the river, and how much better off they used to was, and how they didn't know but they'd made a mistake coming to our town, instead of letting well alone—and so on and so on, till I was afeard I had made a mistake coming to her to find out what was going on in the town; but by-and-by she dropped onto pap and the murder, and then I was pretty willing to let her clatter right along. She told about me and Tom Sawyer finding the six thousand dollars (only she got it ten) and all about pap and what a hard lot he was, and what a hard lot I was, and at last she got down to where I was murdered. I says:

"Who done it? We've heard considerable about these goings on, down in Hookerville, but we don't know who 'twas that killed Huck Finn."

"Well, I reckon there's a right smart chance of people here that'd like to know who killed him. Some thinks old Finn done it himself."

"No—is that so?"

"Most everybody thought it at first. He'll never know how nigh he come to getting lynched. But before night they changed around and judged it was done by a runaway nigger named Jim."

"Why he—"

I stopped. I reckoned I better keep still. She run on, and never noticed I had put in at all.

"The nigger run off the very night Huck Finn was killed. So there's a reward out for him—three hundred dollars. And there's a reward out for old Finn too—two hundred dollars. You see, he come to town the morning after the murder, and told about it, and was out with 'em on the ferry-boat hunt, and right away after he up and left. Before night they wanted to lynch him, but he was gone, you see. Well, next day they found out the nigger was gone; they found out he hadn't ben seen sence ten o'clock the night the murder was done. So then they put it on him, you see, and while they was full of it, next day back comes old Finn and went boohooing to Judge Thatcher to get money to hunt for the nigger all over Illinois with. The judge give him some, and that evening he got drunk and was around till after midnight with a couple of mighty hard looking strangers, and then went off with them. Well, he hain't come back sence, and they ain't looking for him back till this thing blows over a little, for people thinks now that he killed his boy and fixed things so folks would think robbers done it, and then he'd get Huck's money without having to bother a long time with a lawsuit. People do say he warn't any too good to do it. Oh, he's sly, I reckon. If he don't come back for a year, he'll be all right. You can't prove anything on him, you know; everything will be quieted down then, and he'll walk into Huck's money as easy as nothing."

"Yes, I reckon so, 'm. I don't see nothing in the way of it. Has everybody quit thinking the nigger done it?"

"Oh no, not everybody. A good many thinks he done it. But they'll get the nigger pretty soon, now, and maybe they can scare it out of him."

"Why, are they after him yet?"

"Well, you're innocent, ain't you! Does three hundred dollars lay round every day for people to pick up? Some folks thinks the nigger ain't far from here. I'm one of them—but I hain't talked it around. A few days ago I was talking with an old couple that lives next door in the log shanty, and they happened to say hardly anybody ever goes to that island over yonder that they call Jackson's Island. Don't anybody live there? says I. No, nobody, says they. I didn't say any more, but I done some thinking. I was pretty near certain I'd seen smoke over there, about the head of the island, a day or two before that, so I says to myself, like as not that nigger's hiding over there; anyway, says I, it's worth the trouble to give the place a hunt. I hain't seen any smoke sence, so I reckon maybe he's gone, if it was him; but husband's going over to see— him and another man. He was gone up the river; but he got back to-day and I told him as soon as he got here two hours ago."

I had got so uneasy I couldn't set still. I had to do something with my hands; so I took up a needle off of the table and went to threading it. My hands shook and I was making a bad job of it. When the woman stopped talking, I looked up, and she was looking at me pretty curious, and smiling a little. I put down the needle and thread and let on to be interested—and I was, too—and says:

"Three hundred dollars is a power of money. I wish my mother could get it. Is your husband going over there to-night?"

"Oh, yes. He went up town with the man I was telling you of, to get a boat and see if they could borrow another gun. They'll go over after midnight."

"Couldn't they see better if they was to wait till daytime?"

"Yes. And couldn't the nigger see better too? After midnight he'll likely be asleep, and they can slip around through the woods and hunt up his camp fire all the better for the dark, if he's got one."

"I didn't think of that."

The woman kept looking at me pretty curious, and I didn't feel a bit comfortable. Pretty soon she says:

"What did you say your name was, honey?"

"M—Mary Williams."

Somehow it didn't seem to me that I said it was Mary before, so I didn't look up; seemed to me I said it was Sarah; so I felt sort of cornered, and was afeared maybe I was looking it, too. I wished the woman would say something more; the longer she set still, the uneasier I was. But now she says:

"Honey, I thought you said it was Sarah when you first come in?"

"Oh, yes'm, I did. Sarah Mary Williams. Sarah's my first name. Some calls me Sarah, some calls me Mary."

"Oh, that's the way of it?"

"Yes'm."

I was feeling better, then, but I wished I was out of there, anyway. I couldn't look up yet.

Well, the woman fell to talking about how hard times was, and how poor they had to live, and how the rats was as free as if they owned the place, and so forth, and so on, and then I got easy again. She was right about the rats. You'd see one stick his nose out of a hole in the corner every little while. She said she had to have things handy to throw at them when she was alone, or they wouldn't give her no peace. She showed me a bar of lead, twisted up into a knot, and she said she was a good shot with it generly, but she'd wrenched her arm a day or two ago, and didn't know whether she could throw true, now. But she watched for a chance, and directly she banged away at a rat, but she missed him wide, and said "Ouch!" it hurt her arm so. Then she told me to try for the next one. I wanted to be getting away before the old man got back, but of course I didn't let on. I got the thing, and the first rat that showed his nose I let drive, and if he'd a stayed where he was he'd a been a tolerable sick rat. She said that that was first-rate, and she reckoned I would hive[6] the next one. She went and got the lump of lead and fetched it back and brought along a hank of yarn, which she wanted me to help her with. I held up my two hands and she put the hank over them and went on talking about her and her husband's matters. But she broke off to say:

"Keep your eye on the rats. You better have the lead in your lap, handy."

So she dropped the lump into my lap, just at that moment, and I clapped my legs together on it and she went on talking. But only about a minute. Then she took off the hank and looked me straight in the face, but very pleasant, and says:

"Come, now—what's your real name?"

"Wh-what, mum?"

"What's your real name? Is it Bill, or Tom, or Bob?—or what is it?"

I reckon I shook like a leaf, and I didn't know hardly what to do. But I says:

6. Get, in the sense of hit and kill.

"Please to don't poke fun at a poor girl like me, mum. If I'm in the way, here I'll—"

"No, you won't. Set down and stay where you are. I ain't going to hurt you, and I ain't going to tell on you, nuther. You just tell me your secret, and trust me. I'll keep it; and what's more, I'll help you. So'll my old man, if you want him to. You see, you're a run-away 'prentice—that's all. It ain't anything. There ain't any harm in it. You've been treated bad, and you made up your mind to cut. Bless you, child, I wouldn't tell on you. Tell me all about it, now—that's a good boy.

So I said it wouldn't be no use to try to play it any longer, and I would just make a clean breast and tell her everything, but she mustn't go back on her promise. Then I told her my father and mother was dead, and the law had bound me out to a mean old farmer in the country thirty mile back from the river, and he treated me so bad I couldn't stand it no longer; he went away to be gone a couple of days, and so I took my chance and stole some of his daughter's old clothes, and cleared out, and I had been three nights coming the thirty miles; I traveled nights, and hid daytimes and slept, and the bag of bread and meat I carried from home lasted me all the way and I had a plenty. I said I believed my uncle Abner Moore would take care of me, and so that was why I struck out for this town of Goshen.

"Goshen, child? This ain't Goshen. This is St. Petersburg. Goshen's ten mile further up the river. Who told you this was Goshen?"

"Why, a man I met at day-break this morning, just as I was going to turn into the woods for my regular sleep. He told me when the roads forked I must take the right hand, and five mile would fetch me to Goshen."

"He was drunk I reckon. He told you just exactly wrong."

"Well, he did act like he was drunk, but it ain't no matter now. I got to be moving along. I'll fetch Goshen before day-light."

"Hold on a minute. I'll put you up a snack to eat. You might want it."

So she put me up a snack, and says:

"Say—when a cow's laying down, which end of her gets up first? Answer up prompt, now—don't stop to study over it. Which end gets up first?"

"The hind end, mum."

"Well, then, a horse?"

"The for'rard end, mum."

"Which side of a tree does the most moss grow on?"

"North side."

"If fifteen cows is browsing on a hillside, how many of them eats with their heads pointed the same direction?"

"The whole fifteen, mum."

"Well, I reckon you *have* lived in the country. I thought maybe you was trying to hocus me again. What's your real name, now?"

"George Peters, mum."

"Well, try to remember it, George. Don't forget and tell me it's Elexander before you go, and then get out by saying it's George Elexander when I catch you. And don't go about women in that old calico. You do a girl tolerable poor, but you might fool men, maybe. Bless you, child, when you set out to thread a needle, don't hold the thread still and fetch the needle up to it; hold the needle still and poke the thread at it—that's the way a woman most always does; but a man always does 'tother way. And when you throw at a rat or anything, hitch yourself up a tip-toe, and fetch your hand up over your head as awkard as you can, and miss your rat about six or seven foot. Throw stiff-armed from the shoulder, like there was a pivot there for it to turn on—like a girl; not from the wrist and elbow, with your arm out to one side, like a boy. And mind you, when a girl tries to catch anything in her lap, she throws her knees apart; she don't clap them together, the way you did when you catched the lump of lead. Why, I spotted you for a boy when you was threading the needle; and I contrived the other things just to make certain. Now trot along to your uncle, Sarah Mary Williams George Elexander Peters, and if you get into trouble you send word to Mrs. Judith Loftus, which is me, and I'll do what I can to get you out of it. Keep the river road, all the way, and next time you tramp, take shoes and socks with you. The river road's a rocky one, and your feet 'll be in a condition when you get to Goshen, I reckon."

I went up the bank about fifty yards, and then I doubled on my tracks and slipped back to where my canoe was, a good piece below the house. I jumped in and was off in a hurry. I went up stream far enough to make the head of the island, and then started across. I took off the sun-bonnet, for I didn't want no blinders on, then. When I was about the middle, I hear the clock begin to strike; so I stops and listens; the sound come faint over the water, but clear—eleven. When I struck the head of the island I never waited to blow, though I was most winded, but I shoved right into the timber where my old camp used to be, and started a good fire there on a high-and-dry spot.

Then I jumped in the canoe and dug out for our place a mile and a half below, as hard as I could go. I landed, and slopped through the timber and up the ridge and into the cavern. There Jim laid, sound asleep on the ground. I roused him out and says.

"Git up and hump yourself, Jim! There ain't a minute to lose. They're after us!"

Jim never asked no questions, he never said a word; but the way he worked for the next half an hour showed about how he was scared. By that time everything we had in the world was on our raft and she was ready to be shoved out from the willow cove where she was hid. We put out the camp fire at the cavern the first thing, and didn't show a candle outside after that.

I took the canoe out from shore a little piece and took a look, but if there was a boat around I couldn't see it, for stars and shadows ain't good to see by. Then we got out the raft and slipped along down in the shade, past the foot of the island dead still, never saying a word.

## Chapter XII

It must a been close onto one o'clock when we got below the island at last, and the raft did seem to go mighty slow. If a boat was to come along, we was going to take to the canoe and break for the Illinois shore; and it was well a boat didn't come, for we hadn't ever thought to put the gun into the canoe, or a fishing-line or anything to eat. We was in ruther too much of a sweat to think of so many things. It warn't good judgment to put *everything* on the raft.

If the men went to the island, I just expect they found the camp fire I built, and watched it all night for Jim to come. Anyways, they stayed away from us, and if my building the fire never fooled them it warn't no fault of mine. I played it as low-down on them as I could.

When the first streak of day begun to show, we tied up to a tow-head in a big bend on the Illinois side, and hacked off cotton-wood branches with the hatchet and covered up the raft with them so she looked like there had been a cave-in in the bank there. A tow-head is a sand-bar that has cotton-woods on it as thick as harrow-teeth.

We had mountains on the Missouri shore and heavy timber on the Illinois side, and the channel was down the Missouri shore at that place, so we warn't afraid of anybody running across us. We laid there all day and watched the rafts and steamboats spin down the Missouri shore, and up-bound steamboats fight the big river in the middle. I told Jim all about the time I had jabbering with that woman; and Jim said she was a smart one, and if she was to start after us herself she wouldn't set down and watch a camp fire—no, sir, she'd fetch a dog. Well, then, I said, why couldn't she tell her husband to fetch a dog? Jim said he bet she did think of it by the time the men was ready to start, and he believed they must a gone up town to get a dog and so they lost all that time, or else we wouldn't be here on a tow-head sixteen or seventeen mile below the village—no, indeedy, we would be in that same old town again. So I said I didn't care what was the reason they didn't get us, as long as they didn't.

When it was beginning to come on dark, we poked our heads out of the cottonwood thicket and looked up, and down, and across; nothing in sight; so Jim took up some of the top planks of the raft and built a snug wigwam to get under in blazing weather and rainy, and to keep the things dry. Jim made a floor for the wigwam, and raised it a foot or more above the level of the raft, so now the blankets and all the traps was out of the reach of steamboat waves. Right in the middle of the wigwam we made a layer of dirt about five or six inches deep with a frame around it for to hold it to its place; this was to build a fire on in sloppy weather or chilly; the wigwam would keep it from being seen. We made an extra steering oar, too, because one of the others might get broke, on a snag or something. We fixed up a short forked stick to hang the old lantern on; because we must always light the lantern whenever we see a steamboat coming down stream, to keep from getting run over; but we wouldn't have to light it up for upstream boats unless we see we was in what they call "crossing;" for the river was pretty high yet, very low banks being still a little under water; so up-bound boats didn't always run the channel, but hunted easy water.

This second night we run between seven and eight hours, with a current that was making over four mile an hour. We catched fish, and talked, and we took a swim now and then to keep off sleepiness. It was kind of solemn, drifting down the big still river, laying on our backs looking up at the stars, and we didn't ever feel like talking loud, and it warn't often that we laughed, only a little kind of a low chuckle. We had mighty good weather, as a general thing, and nothing ever happened to us at all, that night, nor the next, nor the next.

Every night we passed towns, some of them away up on black hillsides, nothing but just a shiny bed of lights, not a house could you see. The fifth night we passed St. Louis, and it was like the whole world lit up. In St. Petersburg they used to say there was twenty or thirty thousand people in St. Louis,[7] but I never believed it till I see that wonderful spread of lights at two o'clock that still night. There warn't a sound there; everybody was asleep.

---

7. St. Louis is 170 miles down the Mississippi from Hannibal.

Every night now, I used to slip ashore, towards ten o'clock, at some little village, and buy ten or fifteen cents' worth of meal or bacon or other stuff to eat; and sometimes I lifted a chicken that warn't roosting comfortable, and took him along. Pap always said, take a chicken when you get a chance, because if you don't want him yourself you can easy find somebody that does, and a good deed ain't ever forgot. I never see pap when he didn't want the chicken himself, but that is what he used to say, anyway.

Mornings, before daylight, I slipped into corn fields and borrowed a watermelon, or a mushmelon, or a punkin, or some new corn, or things of that kind. Pap always said it warn't no harm to borrow things, if you was meaning to pay them back, sometime; but the widow said it warn't anything but a soft name for stealing, and no decent body would do it. Jim said he reckoned the widow was partly right and pap was partly right; so the best way would be for us to pick out two or three things from the list and say we wouldn't borrow them any more—then he reckoned it wouldn't be no harm to borrow the others. So we talked it over all one night, drifting along down the river, trying to make up our minds whether to drop the watermelons, or the cantelopes, or the mushmelons, or what. But towards daylight we got it all settled satisfactory, and concluded to drop crabapples and p'simmons. We warn't feeling just right, before that, but it was all comfortable now. I was glad the way it come out, too, because crabapples ain't ever good, and the p'simmons wouldn't be ripe for two or three months yet.

We shot a water-fowl, now and then, that got up too early in the morning or didn't go to bed early enough in the evening. Take it all around, we lived pretty high.

The fifth night below St. Louis we had a big storm after midnight, with a power of thunder and lightning, and the rain poured down in a solid sheet. We stayed in the wigwam and let the raft take care of itself. When the lightning glared out we could see a big straight river ahead, and high rocky bluffs on both sides. By-and-by says I, "Hel-*lo* Jim, looky yonder!" It was a steamboat that had killed herself on a rock. We was drifting straight down for her. The lightning showed her very distinct. She was leaning over, with part of her upper deck above water, and you could see every little chimbly-guy[8] clean and clear, and a chair by the big bell, with an old slouch hat hanging on the back of it when the flashes come.

Well, it being away in the night, and stormy, and all so mysterious-like, I felt just the way any other boy would a felt when I see that wreck laying there so mournful and lonesome in the middle of the river. I wanted to get aboard of her and slink around a little, and see what there was there. So I says:

"Le's land on her, Jim."

But Jim was dead against it, at first. He says:

"I doan' want to go fool'n 'long er no wrack. We's doin' blame' well, en we better let blame' well alone, as de good book says. Like as not dey's a watchman on dat wrack."

"Watchman your grandmother," I says; "there ain't nothing to watch but the texas[9] and the pilot-house; and do you reckon anybody's going to resk his life for a texas and a pilot-house such a night as this, when it's likely to break up and wash off down the river any minute?" Jim couldn't say nothing to that,

8. Wires used to steady the chimney stacks.
9. The large cabin on the top deck located just behind or beneath the pilothouse; it serves as officers' quarters.

so he didn't try. "And besides," I says, "we might borrow something worth having, out of the captain's stateroom. Seegars, *I* bet you—and cost five cents apiece, solid cash. Steamboat captains is always rich, and get sixty dollars a month, and *they* don't care a cent what a thing costs, you know, long as they want it. Stick a candle in your pocket; I can't rest, Jim, till we give her a rummaging. Do you reckon Tom Sawyer would ever go by this thing? Not for pie, he wouldn't. He'd call it an adventure—that's what he'd call it; and he'd land on that wreck if it was his last act. And wouldn't he throw style into it?— wouldn't he spread himself, nor nothing? Why, you'd think it was Christopher C'lumbus discovering Kingdom-Come. I wish Tom Sawyer *was* here."

Jim he grumbled a little, but give in. He said we mustn't talk any more than we could help, and then talk mighty low. The lightning showed us the wreck again, just in time, and we fetched the starboard derrick,[1] and made fast there.

The deck was high out, here. We went sneaking down the slope of it to labboard, in the dark, towards the texas, feeling our way slow with our feet, and spreading our hands out to fend off the guys, for it was so dark we couldn't see no sign of them. Pretty soon we struck the forward end of the skylight, and clumb onto it; and the next step fetched us in front of the captain's door, which was open, and by Jimminy, away down through the texas-hall we see a light! and all in the same second we seem to hear low voices in yonder!

Jim whispered and said he was feeling powerful sick, and told me to come along. I says, all right; and was going to start for the raft; but just then I heard a voice wail out and say:

"Oh, please don't, boys; I swear I won't ever tell!"

Another voice said, pretty loud:

"It's a lie, Jim Turner. You've acted this way before. You always want more'n your share of the truck and you've always got it, too, because you've swore 't if you didn't you'd tell. But this time you've said it jest one time too many. You're the meanest, treacherousest hound in this country."

By this time Jim was gone for the raft. I was just a-biling with curiosity; and I says to myself, Tom Sawyer wouldn't back out now, and so I won't either; I'm agoing to see what's going on here. So I dropped on my hands and knees, in the little passage, and crept aft in the dark, till there warn't but about one stateroom betwixt me and the cross-hall of the texas. Then, in there I see a man stretched on the floor and tied hand and foot, and two men standing over him, and one of them had a dim lantern in his hand, and the other one had a pistol. This one kept pointing the pistol at the man's head on the floor and saying—

"I'd *like* to! And I orter, too, a mean skunk!"

The man on the floor would shrivel up, and say: "Oh, please don't, Bill— I hain't ever goin' to tell."

And every time he said that, the man with the lantern would laugh and say:

" 'Deed you *ain't!* You never said no truer thing 'n that, you bet you." And once he said, "Hear him beg! and yit if we hadn't got the best of him and tied him, he'd a killed us both. And what *for?* Jist for noth'n. Jist because we stood on our *rights*—that's what for. But I lay you ain't agoin' to threaten nobody any more, Jim Turner. Put *up* that pistol, Bill."

Bill says:

---

1. Boom for lifting cargo.

"I don't want to, Jake Packard. I'm for killin' him—and didn't he kill old Hatfield jist the same way—and don't he deserve it?"

"But I don't *want* him killed, and I've got my reasons for it."

"Bless yo' heart for them words, Jake Packard! I'll never forgit you, long's I live!" says the man on the floor, sort of blubbering.

Packard didn't take no notice of that, but hung up his lantern on a nail, and started towards where I was, there in the dark, and motioned Bill to come. I crawfished[2] as fast as I could, about two yards, but the boat slanted so that Icouldn't make very good time; so to keep from getting run over and catched I crawled into a stateroom on the upper side. The man come a-pawing along in the dark, and when Packard got to my stateroom, he says:

"Here—come in here."

And in he come, and Bill after him. But before they got in, I was up in the upper berth, cornered, and sorry I come. Then they stood there, with their hands on the ledge of the berth, and talked. I couldn't see them, but I could tell where they was, by the whisky they'd been having. I was glad I didn't drink whisky; but it wouldn't made much difference, anyway, because most of the time they couldn't a treed me because I didn't breathe. I was too scared. And besides, a body *couldn't* breathe, and hear such talk. They talked low and earnest. Bill wanted to kill Turner. He says:

"He's said he'll tell, and he will. If we was to give both our shares to him *now*, it wouldn't make no difference after the row, and the way we've served him. Shore's you're born, he'll turn State's evidence; now you hear *me*. I'm for putting him out of his troubles."

"So'm I," says Packard, very quiet.

"Blame it, I'd sorter begun to think you wasn't. Well, then, that's all right. Les' go and do it."

"Hold on a minute; I hain't had my say yit. You listen to me. Shooting's good, but there's quieter ways if the thing's *got* to be done. But what I say, is this; it ain't good sense to go court'n around after a halter,[3] if you can git at what you're up to in some way that's jist as good and at the same time don't bring you into no resks. Ain't that so?"

"You bet it is. But how you goin' to manage it this time?"

"Well, my idea is this: we'll rustle around and gether up whatever pickins we've overlooked in the staterooms, and shove for shore and hide the truck. Then we'll wait. Now I say it ain't agoin' to be more 'n two hours befo' this wrack breaks up and washes off down the river. See? He'll be drownded, and won't have nobody to blame for it but his own self. I reckon that's a considerble sight better'n killin' of him. I'm unfavorable to killin' a man as long as you can git around it; it ain't good sense, it ain't good morals. Ain't I right?"

"Yes—I reck'n you are. But s'pose she *don't* break up and wash off?"

"Well, we can wait the two hours, anyway, and see, can't we?"

"All right, then; come along."

So they started, and I lit out, all in a cold sweat, and scrambled forward. It was dark as pitch there; but I said in a kind of a coarse whisper, "Jim!" and he answered up, right at my elbow, with a sort of a moan, and I says:

"Quick, Jim, it ain't no time for fooling around and moaning; there's a gang of murderers in yonder, and if we don't hunt up their boat and set her drifting

---

2. Crept backward on all fours.          3. Hangman's noose.

down the river so these fellows can't get away from the wreck, there's one of 'em going to be in a bad fix. But if we find their boat we can put *all* of 'em in a bad fix—for the Sheriff 'll get 'em. Quick—hurry! I'll hunt the labboard side, you hunt the stabboard. You start at the raft, and—"

"Oh, my lordy, lordy! *Raf?* Dey ain' no raf no mo', she done broke loose en gone!—'en here we is!"

## Chapter XIII

Well, I catched my breath and most fainted. Shut up on a wreck with such a gang as that! But it warn't no time to be sentimentering. We'd *got* to find that boat, now—had to have it for ourselves. So we went a-quaking and shaking down the stabboard side, and slow work it was, too—seemed a week before we got to the stern. No sign of a boat. Jim said he didn't believe he could go any further—so scared he hadn't hardly any strength left, he said. But I said come on, if we get left on this wreck, we are in a fix, sure. So on we prowled, again. We struck for the stern of the texas, and found it, and then scrabbled along forwards on the skylight, hanging on from shutter to shutter, for the edge of the skylight was in the water. When we got pretty close to the cross-hall door there was the skiff, sure enough! I could just barely see her. I felt ever so thankful. In another second I would a been aboard of her; but just then the door opened. One of the men stuck his head out, only about a couple of foot from me, and I thought I was gone; but he jerked it in again, and says:

"Heave that blame lantern out o' sight, Bill!"

He flung a bag of something into the boat, and then got in himself, and set down. It was Packard. Then Bill *he* come out and got in. Packard says, in a low voice:

"All ready—shove off!"

I couldn't hardly hang onto the shutters, I was so weak. But Bill says:

"Hold on—'d you go through him?"

"No. Didn't you?"

"No. So he's got his share o' the cash, yet."

"Well, then, come along—no use to take truck and leave money."

"Say—won't he suspicion what we're up to?"

"Maybe he won't. But we got to have it anyway. Come along." So they got out and went in.

The door slammed to, because it was on the careened side; and in a half second I was in the boat, and Jim come a tumbling after me. I out with my knife and cut the rope, and away we went!

We didn't touch an oar, and we didn't speak nor whisper, nor hardly even breathe. We went gliding swift along, dead silent, past the tip of the paddle-box, and past the stern; then in a second or two more we was a hundred yards below the wreck, and the darkness soaked her up, every last sign of her, and we was safe, and knowed it.

When we was three or four hundred yards down stream, we see the lantern show like a little spark at the texas door, for a second, and we knowed by that that the rascals had missed their boat, and was beginning to understand that they was in just as much trouble, now, as Jim Turner was.

Then Jim manned the oars, and we took out after our raft. Now was the first time that I begun to worry about the men—I reckon I hadn't had time to before. I begun to think how dreadful it was, even for murderers, to be in such a fix. I says to myself, there ain't no telling but I might come to be a murderer myself, yet, and then how would *I* like it? So says I to Jim:

"The first light we see, we'll land a hundred yards below it or above it, in a place where it's a good hiding-place for you and the skiff, and then I'll go and fix up some kind of a yarn, and get somebody to go for that gang and get them out of their scrape, so they can be hung when their time comes."

But that idea was a failure; for pretty soon it begun to storm again, and this time worse than ever. The rain poured down, and never a light showed; everybody in bed, I reckon. We boomed along down the river, watching for lights and watching for our raft. After a long time the rain let up, but the clouds staid, and the lightning kept whimpering, and by-and-by a flash showed us a black thing ahead, floating, and we made for it.

It was the raft, and mighty glad was we to get aboard of it again. We seen a light, now, away down to the right, on shore. So I said I would go for it. The skiff was half full of plunder which that gang had stole, there on the wreck. We hustled it onto the raft in a pile, and I told Jim to float along down, and show a light when he judged he had gone about two mile, and keep it burning till I come; then I manned my oars and shoved for the light. As I got down towards it, three or four more showed—up on a hillside. It was a village. I closed in above the shore-light, and laid on my oars and floated. As I went by, I see it was a lantern hanging on the jackstaff of a double-hull ferry-boat. I skimmed around for the watchman, a-wondering whereabouts he slept; and by-and-by I found him roosting on the bitts,[4] forward, with his head down between his knees. I give his shoulder two or three little shoves, and begun to cry.

He stirred up, in a kind of startlish way; but when he see it was only me, he took a good gap and stretch, and then he says:

"Hello, what's up? Don't cry, bub. What's the trouble?"

I says:

"Pap, and mam, and sis, and—"

Then I broke down. He says:

"Oh, dang it, now, *don't* take on so, we all has to have our troubles and this'n 'll come out all right. What's the matter with 'em?"

"They're—they're—are you the watchman of the boat?"

"Yes," he says, kind of pretty-well-satisfied like. "I'm the captain and the owner, and the mate, and the pilot, and watchman, and head deck-hand; and sometimes I'm the freight and passengers. I ain't as rich as old Jim Hornback, and I can't be so blame' generous and good to Tom, Dick and Harry as what he is, and slam around money the way he does; but I've told him a many a time 't I wouldn't trade places with him; for, says I, a sailor's life's the life for me, and I'm derned if I'd live two mile out o' town, where there ain't nothing ever goin' on, not for all his spondulicks and as much more on top of it. Says I—"

I broke in and says:

"They're in an awful peck of trouble, and—"

"*Who* is?"

"Why, pap, and mam, and sis, and Miss Hooker; and if you'd take your ferry-boat and go up there—"

"Up where? Where are they?"

---

4. Vertical wooden posts to which cables can be secured.

"On the wreck."

"What wreck?"

"Why, there ain't but one."

"What, you don't mean the *Walter Scott?*"[5]

"Yes."

"Good land! what are they doin' *there,* for gracious sakes?"

"Well, they didn't go there a-purpose."

"I bet they didn't! Why, great goodness, there ain't no chance for 'em if they don't git off mighty quick! Why, how in the nation did they ever git into such a scrape?"

"Easy enough. Miss Hooker was a-visiting, up there to the town—"

"Yes, Booth's Landing—go on."

"She was a-visiting, there at Booth's Landing, and just in the edge of the evening she started over with her nigger woman in the horse-ferry,[6] to stay all night at her friend's house, Miss What-you-may-call her, I disremember her name, and they lost their steering-oar, and swung around and went a-floating down, stern-first, about two mile, and saddle-baggsed[7] on the wreck, and the ferry man and the nigger woman and the horses was all lost, but Miss Hooker she made a grab and got aboard the wreck. Well, about an hour after dark, we come along down in our trading-scow, and it was so dark we didn't notice the wreck till we was right on it; and so *we* saddle-baggsed; but all of us was saved but Bill Whipple—and oh, he *was* the best cretur!—I most wish't it had been me, I do."

"My George! It's the beatenest thing I ever struck. And *then* what did you all do?"

"Well, we hollered and took on, but it's so wide there, we couldn't make nobody hear. So pap said somebody got to get ashore and get help somehow. I was the only one that could swim, so I made a dash for it, and Miss Hooker she said if I didn't strike help sooner, come here and hunt up her uncle, and he'd fix the thing. I made the land about a mile below, and been fooling along ever since, trying to get people to do something, but they said, 'What, in such a night and such a current? there ain't no sense in it; go for the steam-ferry.' Now if you'll go, and—"

"By Jackson, I'd *like* to, and blame it I don't know but I will; but who in the dingnation's agoin' to *pay* for it? Do you reckon your pap—"

"Why *that's* all right. Miss Hooker she told me, *particular,* that her uncle Hornback—"

"Great guns! is *he* her uncle? Look here, you break for that light over yonder-way, and turn out west when you git there, and about a quarter of a mile out you'll come to the tavern; tell 'em to dart you out to Jim Hornback's and he'll foot the bill. And don't you fool around any, because he'll want to know the news. Tell him I'll have his niece all safe before he can get to town. Hump yourself, now; I'm agoing up around the corner here, to roust out my engineer."

I struck for the light, but as soon as he turned the corner I went back and

<hr />

5. Clemens held Sir Walter Scott's romantic adventure novels set in feudal England responsible for the distorted antidemocratic notions held by so many southerners and thus for the false ideology they were willing to fight and die for in the Civil War. Clemens expressed himself most vividly on this subject in *Life*

on the Mississippi (Chap. 46), where he observes: "Sir Walter had so large a hand in making Southern character, as it existed before the war, that he is in great measure responsible for the war."

6. A ferry large enough to take horses and wagons.

7. Broken and doubled around the wreck.

got into my skiff and bailed her out and then pulled up shore in the easy water about six hundred yards, and tucked myself in among some woodboats; for I couldn't rest easy till I could see the ferry-boat start. But take it all around, I was feeling ruther comfortable on accounts of taking all this trouble for that gang, for not many would a done it. I wished the widow knowed about it. I judged she would be proud of me for helping these rapscallions, because rapscallions and dead beats is the kind the widow and good people takes the most interest in.

Well, before long, here comes the wreck, dim and dusky, sliding along down! A kind of cold shiver went through me, and then I struck out for her. She was very deep, and I see in a minute there warn't much chance for anybody being alive in her. I pulled all around her and hollered a little, but there wasn't any answer; all dead still. I felt a little bit heavy-hearted about the gang, but not much, for I reckoned if they could stand it, I could.

Then here comes the ferry-boat; so I shoved for the middle of the river on a long down-stream slant; and when I judged I was out of eye-reach, I laid on my oars, and looked back and see her go and smell around the wreck for Miss Hooker's remainders, because the captain would know her uncle Hornback would want them; and then pretty soon the ferry-boat give it up and went for shore, and I laid into my work and went a-booming down the river.

It did seem a powerful long time before Jim's light showed up; and when it did show, it looked like it was a thousand mile off. By the time I got there the sky was beginning to get a little gray in the east; so we struck for an island, and hid the raft, and sunk the skiff, and turned in and slept like dead people.

## Chapter XIV

By-and-by, when we got up, we turned over the truck the gang had stole off of the wreck, and found boots, and blankets, and clothes, and all sorts of other things, and a lot of books, and a spyglass, and three boxes of seegars. We hadn't ever been this rich before, in neither of our lives. The seegars was prime. We laid off all the afternoon in the woods talking, and me reading the books, and having a general good time. I told Jim all about what happened inside the wreck, and at the ferry-boat; and I said these kinds of things was adventures; but he said he didn't want no more adventures. He said that when I went in the texas and he crawled back to get on the raft and found her gone, he nearly died; because he judged it was all up with *him*, anyway it could be fixed; for if he didn't get saved he would get drownded; and if he did get saved, whoever saved him would send him back home so as to get the reward, and then Miss Watson would sell him South, sure. Well, he was right; he was most always right; he had an uncommon level head, for a nigger.

I read considerable to Jim about kings, and dukes, and earls, and such, and how gaudy they dressed, and how much style they put on, and called each other your majesty, and your grace, and your lordship, and so on, 'stead of mister; and Jim's eyes bugged out, and he was interested. He says:

"I didn't know dey was so many un um. I hain't hearn 'bout none un um, skasely, but ole King Sollermun, onless you counts dem kings dat's in a pack er k'yards. How much do a king git?"

"Get?" I says; "why, they get a thousand dollars a month if they want it; they can have just as much as they want; everything belongs to them."

"*Ain'* dat gay? En what dey got to do, Huck?"

"*They* don't do nothing! Why how you talk. They just set around."

"No—is dat so?"

"Of course it is. They just set around. Except maybe when there 's a war; then they go to the war. But other times they just lazy around; or go hawking— just hawking and sp— Sh!—d' you hear a noise?"

We skipped out and looked; but it warn't nothing but the flutter of a steamboat's wheel, away down coming around the point; so we come back.

"Yes," says I, "and other times, when things is dull, they fuss with the parlyment; and if everybody don't go just so he whacks their heads off. But mostly they hang round the harem."

"Roun' de which?"

"Harem."

"What's de harem?"

"The place where he keep his wives. Don't you know about the harem? Solomon had one; he had about a million wives."

"Why, yes, dat's so; I—I'd done forgot it. A harem's a bo'd'n-house, I reck'n. Mos' likely dey has rackety times in de nussery. En I reck'n de wives quarrels considable; en dat 'crease de racket. Yit dey say Sollermun de wises' man dat ever live.' I doan' take no stock in dat. Bekase why: would a wise man want to live in de mids' er sich a blimblammin' all de time? No—'deed he wouldn't. A wise man 'ud take en buil' a biler-factry; en den he could shet *down* de bilerfactry when he want to res'."

"Well, but he *was* the wisest man, anyway; because the widow she told me so, her own self."

"I doan k'yer what de widder say, he *warn'* no wise man, nuther. He had some er de dad-fetchedes' ways I ever see. Does you know 'bout dat chile dat he 'uz gwyne to chop in two?"[8]

"Yes, the widow told me all about it."

"*Well*, den! Warn' dat de beatenes' notion in de worl'? You jes' take en look at it a minute. Dah's de stump, dah—dat's one er de women; heah's you— dat's de yuther one; I's Sollermun; en dish-yer dollar bill's de chile. Bofe un you claims it. What does I do? Does I shin aroun' mongs' de neighbors en fine out which un you de bill do b'long to, en han' it over to de right one, all safe en soun', de way dat anybody dat had any gumption would? No—I take en whack de bill in *two*, en give half un it to you, en de yuther half to de yuther woman. Dat's de way Sollermun was gwyne to do wid de chile. Now I want to ask you: what's de use er dat half a bill?—can't buy noth'n wid it. En what use is a half a chile? I wouldn' give a dern for a million un um."

"But hang it, Jim, you've clean missed the point—blame it, you've missed it a thousand mile."

"Who? Me? Go 'long. Doan' talk to *me* 'bout yo' pints. I reck'n I knows sense when I sees it; en dey ain' no sense in sich doin's as dat. De 'spute warn't 'bout a half a chile, de 'spute was 'bout a whole chile; en de man dat think he kin settle a 'spute 'bout a whole chile wid a half a chile, doan' know enough to come in out'n de rain. Doan' talk to me 'bout Sollermun, Huck, I knows him by de back."

"But I tell you you don't get the point."

---

8. In 1 Kings 3.16–28. When two women appeared before him claiming to be the mother of the same infant, Solomon ordered the child cut in two. The child's real mother pleaded with him to save the baby and to give it to the other woman, who maliciously agreed to Solomon's original plan.

"Blame de pint! I reck'n I knows what I knows. En mine you, de *real* pint is down furder—it's down deeper. It lays in de way Sollermun was raised. You take a man dat's got on'y one er two children; is dat man gwyne to be waseful o' chillen? No, he ain't; he can't 'ford it. *He* know how to value 'em. But you take a man dat's got 'bout five million chillen runnin' roun' de house, en it's diffunt. *He* as soon chop a chile in two as a cat. Dey's plenty mo'. A chile er two, mo' er less, warn't no consekens to Sollermun, dad fetch him!"

I never see such a nigger. If he got a notion in his head once, there warn't no getting it out again. He was the most down on Solomon of any nigger I ever see. So I went to talking about other kings, and let Solomon slide. I told about Louis Sixteenth that got his head cut off in France long time ago; and about his little boy the dolphin,[9] that would a been a king, but they took and shut him up in jail, and some say he died there.

"Po' little chap."

"But some says he got out and got away, and come to America."

"Dat's good! But he'll be pooty lonesome—dey ain' no kings here, is dey, Huck?"

"No."

"Den he cain't git no situation. What he gwyne to do?"

"Well, I don't know. Some of them gets on the police, and some of them learns people how to talk French."

"Why, Huck, doan' de French people talk de same way we does?"

"No, Jim; you couldn't understand a word they said—not a single word."

"Well now, I be ding-busted! How do dat come?"

"I don't know; but it's so. I got some of their jabber out of a book. Spose a man was to come to you and say *Polly-voo-franzy*—what would you think?"

"I wouldn' think nuff'n; I'd take en bust him over de head. Dat is, if he warn't white. I wouldn't 'low no nigger to call me dat."

"Shucks, it ain't calling you anything. It's only saying do you know how to talk French?"

"Well, den, why couldn't he *say* it?"

"Why, he *is* a-saying it. That's a Frenchman's *way* of saying it."

"Well, it's a blame' ridicklous way, en I doan' want to hear no mo' 'bout it. Dey ain' no sense in it."

"Looky here, Jim; does a cat talk like we do?"

"No, a cat don't."

"Well, does a cow?"

"No, a cow don't, nuther."

"Does a cat talk like a cow, or a cow talk like a cat?"

"No, dey don't."

"It's natural and right for 'em to talk different from each other, ain't it?"

"'Course."

"And ain't it natural and right for a cat and a cow to talk different from *us*?"

"Why, mos' sholy it is."

"Well, then, why ain't it natural and right for a *Frenchman* to talk different from us? You answer me that."

"Is a cat a man, Huck?"

9. The Dauphin, Louis Charles, next in line of the succession to the throne, was eight years old when his father, Louis XVI, was beheaded (1793). Though the boy died in prison, probably in 1795, legends of his escape to America (and elsewhere) persisted, and Clemens owned a book on the subject by Horace W. Fuller: *Imposters and Adventurers, Noted French Trials* (1882).

"No."

"Well, den, dey ain't no sense in a cat talkin' like a man. Is a cow a man?—er is a cow a cat?"

"No, she ain't either of them."

"Well, den, she ain' got no business to talk like either one er the yuther of 'em. Is a Frenchman a man?"

"Yes."

"*Well*, den! Dad blame it, why doan' he *talk* like a man? You answer me *dat!*"

I see it warn't no use wasting words—you can't learn a nigger to argue. So I quit.

## Chapter XV

We judged that three nights more would fetch us to Cairo,[1] at the bottom of Illinois, where the Ohio River comes in, and that was what we was after. We would sell the raft and get on a steamboat and go way up the Ohio amongst the free States, and then be out of trouble.[2]

Well, the second night a fog begun to come on, and we made for a tow-head to tie to, for it wouldn't do to try to run in fog; but when I paddled ahead in the canoe, with the line, to make fast, there warn't anything but little sap-lings to tie to. I passed the line around one of them right on the edge of the cut bank, but there was a stiff current, and the raft come booming down so lively she tore it out by the roots and away she went. I see the fog closing down, and it made me so sick and scared I couldn't budge for most a half a minute it seemed to me—and then there warn't no raft in sight; you couldn't see twenty yards. I jumped into the canoe and run back to the stern and grabbed the paddle and set her back a stroke. But she didn't come. I was in such a hurry I hadn't untied her. I got up and tried to untie her, but I was so excited my hands shook so I couldn't hardly do anything with them.

As soon as I got started I took out after the raft, hot and heavy, right down the tow-head. That was all right as far as it went, but the tow-head warn't sixty yards long, and the minute I flew by the foot of it I shot out into the solid white fog, and hadn't no more idea which way I was going than a dead man.

Thinks I, it won't do to paddle; first I know I'll run into the bank or a tow-head or something; I got to set still and float, and yet it's mighty fidgety busi-ness to have to hold your hands still at such a time. I whooped and listened. Away down there, somewheres, I hears a small whoop, and up comes my spirits. I went tearing after it, listening sharp to hear it again. The next time it come, I see I warn't heading for it but heading away to the right of it. And the next time, I was heading away to the left of it—and not gaining on it much, either, for I was flying around, this way and that and 'tother, but it was going straight ahead all the time.

I did wish the fool would think to beat a tin pan, and beat it all the time, but he never did, and it was the still places between the whoops that was

---

1. Pronounced *Cair-ō*, the town is 364 miles from Hannibal, 194 miles from St. Louis.
2. Southern Illinois was proslavery in sentiment. The state, moreover, had a system of indentured labor not unlike slavery to which a black without proof of free

status might be subjected. Although even among the "free" states there were similar dangers for Jim, the chances of his making his way to freedom and safety in Canada from Ohio or Pennsylvania would be much greater.

making the trouble for me. Well, I fought along, and directly I hears the whoops *behind* me. I was tangled good, now. That was somebody's else's whoop, or else I was turned around.

I throwed the paddle down. I heard the whoop again; it was behind me yet, but in a different place; it kept coming, and kept changing its place, and I kept answering, till by-and-by it was in front of me again and I knowed the current had swung the canoe's head down stream and I was all right, if that was Jim and not some other raftsman hollering. I couldn't tell nothing about voices in a fog, for nothing don't look natural nor sound natural in a fog.

The whooping went on, and in about a minute I come a booming down on a cut bank[3] with smoky ghosts of big trees on it, and the current throwed me off to the left and shot by, amongst a lot of snags that fairly roared, the current was tearing by them so swift.

In another second or two it was solid white and still again. I set perfectly still, then, listening to my heart thump, and I reckon I didn't draw a breath while it thumped a hundred.

I just give up, then. I knowed what the matter was. That cut bank was an island, and Jim had gone down 'tother side of it. It warn't no tow-head, that you could float by in ten minutes. It had the big timber of a regular island; it might be five or six mile long and more than a half a mile wide.

I kept quiet, with my ears cocked, about fifteen minutes, I reckon. I was floating along, of course, four or five mile an hour; but you don't ever think of that. No, you *feel* like you are laying dead still on the water; and if a little glimpse of a snag slips by, you don't think to yourself how fast *you're* going, but you catch your breath and think, my! how that snag's tearing along. If you think it ain't dismal and lonesome out in a fog that way, by yourself, in the night, you try it once—you'll see.

Next, for about a half an hour, I whoops now and then; at last I hears the answer a long ways off, and tries to follow it, but I couldn't do it, and directly I judged I'd got into a nest of tow-heads, for I had little dim glimpses of them on both sides of me, sometimes just a narrow channel between; and some that I couldn't see, I knowed was there, because I'd hear the wash of the current against the old dead brush and trash that hung over the banks. Well, I warn't long losing the whoops, down amongst the tow-heads; and I only tried to chase them a little while, anyway, because it was worse than chasing a Jack-o-lantern. You never knowed a sound dodge around so, and swap places so quick and so much.

I had to claw away from the bank pretty lively, four or five times, to keep from knocking the islands out of the river; and so I judged the raft must be butting into the bank every now and then, or else it would get further ahead and clear out of hearing—it was floating a little faster than what I was.

Well, I seemed to be in the open river again, by-and-by, but I couldn't hear no sign of a whoop nowheres. I reckoned Jim had fetched up on a snag, maybe, and it was all up with him. I was good and tired, so I laid down in the canoe and said I wouldn't bother no more. I didn't want to go to sleep, of course; but I was so sleepy I couldn't help it; so I thought I would take just one little cat-nap.

But I reckon it was more than a cat-nap, for when I waked up the stars was

---

3. Steep bank carved out by the force of the current.

shining bright, the fog was all gone, and I was spinning down a big bend stern first. First I didn't know where I was; I thought I was dreaming; and when things begun to come back to me, they seemed to come up dim out of last week.

It was a monstrous big river here, with the tallest and the thickest kind of timber on both banks; just a solid wall, as well as I could see, by the stars. I looked away down stream, and seen a black speck on the water. I took out after it; but when I got to it it warn't nothing but a couple of saw-logs made fast together. Then I see another speck, and chased that; then another, and this time I was right. It was the raft.

When I got to it Jim was setting there with his head down between his knees, asleep, with his right arm hanging over the steering oar. The other oar was smashed off, and the raft was littered up with leaves and branches and dirt. So she'd had a rough time.

I made fast and laid down under Jim's nose on the raft, and begun to gap, and stretch my fists out against Jim, and says:

"Hello, Jim, have I been asleep? Why didn't you stir me up?"

"Goodness gracious, is dat you, Huck? En you ain' dead—you ain' drownded—you's back agin? It's too good for true, honey, it's too good for true. Lemme look at you, chile, lemme feel o' you. No, you ain' dead? you's back agin, 'live en soun', jis de same ole Huck—de same ole Huck, thanks to goodness!"

"What's the matter with you, Jim? You been a drinking?"

"Drinkin'? Has I ben a drinkin'? Has I had a chance to be a drinkin'?"

"Well, then, what makes you talk so wild?"

"How does I talk wild?"

"How? why, haint you been talking about my coming back, and all that stuff, as if I'd been gone away?"

"Huck—Huck Finn, you look me in de eye; look me in de eye. *Hain't* you ben gone away?"

"Gone away? Why, what in the nation do you mean? *I* hain't been gone anywhere. Where would I go to?"

"Well, looky here, boss, dey's sumf'n wrong, dey is. Is I *me*, or who *is* I? Is I heah, or whah *is* I? Now dat's what I wants to know?"

"Well, I think you're here, plain enough, but I think you're a tangle-headed old fool, Jim."

"I is, is I? Well you answer me dis. Didn't you tote out de line in de canoe, fer to make fas' to de tow-head?"

"No, I didn't. What tow-head? I hain't seen no tow-head."

"You hain't seen no tow-head? Looky here—didn't de line pull loose en de raf' go a hummin' down de river, en leave you en de canoe behine in de fog?"

"What fog?"

"Why *de* fog. De fog dat's ben aroun' all night. En didn't you whoop, en didn't I whoop, tell we got mix' up in de islands en one un us got 'los' en 'tother one was jis' as good as los', 'kase he didn' know whah he wuz? En didn't I bust up agin a lot er dem islands en have a turrible time en mos' git drownded? Now ain' dat so, boss—ain't it so? You answer me dat."

"Well, this is too many for me, Jim. I hain't seen no fog, nor no islands, nor no troubles, nor nothing. I been setting here talking with you all night till you went to sleep about ten minutes ago, and I reckon I done the same. You couldn't a got drunk in that time, so of course you've been dreaming."

"Dad fetch it, how is I gwyne to dream all dat in ten minutes?"

"Well, hang it all, you did dream it, because there didn't any of it happen."

"But Huck, it's all jis' as plain to me as—"

"It don't make no difference how plain it is, there ain't nothing in it. I know, because I've been here all the time."

Jim didn't say nothing for about five minutes, but set there studying over it. Then he says:

"Well, den, I reck'n I did dream it, Huck; but dog my cats ef it ain't de powerfullest dream I ever see. En I hain't ever had no dream b'fo' dat's tired me like dis one."

"Oh, well, that's all right, because a dream does tire a body like everything, sometimes. But this one was a staving[4] dream—tell me all about it, Jim."

So Jim went to work and told me the whole thing right through, just as it happened, only he painted it up considerable. Then he said he must start in and " 'terpret" it, because it was sent for a warning. He said the first tow-head stood for a man that would try to do us some good, but the current was another man that would get us away from him. The whoops was warnings that would come to us every now and then, and if we didn't try hard to make out to understand them they'd just take us into bad luck, 'stead of keeping us out of it. The lot of tow-heads was troubles we was going to get into with quarrelsome people and all kinds of mean folks, but if we minded our business and didn't talk back and aggravate them, we would pull through and get out of the fog and into the big clear river, which was the free States, and wouldn't have no more trouble.

It had clouded up pretty dark just after I got onto the raft, but it was clearing up again, now.

"Oh, well, that's all interpreted well enough, as far as it goes, Jim," I says; "but what does *these* things stand for?"

It was the leaves and rubbish on the raft, and the smashed oar. You could see them first rate, now.

Jim looked at the trash, and then looked at me, and back at the trash again. He had got the dream fixed so strong in his head that he couldn't seem to shake it loose and get the facts back into its place again, right away. But when he did get the thing straightened around, he looked at me steady, without ever smiling, and says:

"What do dey stan' for? I's gwyne to tell you. When I got all wore out wid work, en wid de callin' for you, en went to sleep, my heart wuz mos' broke bekase you wuz los', en I didn' k'yer no mo' what become er me en de raf'. En when I wake up en fine you back agin', all safe en soun', de tears come en I could a got down on my knees en kiss' yo' foot I's so thankful. En all you wuz thinkin' 'bout wuz how you could make a fool uv ole Jim wid a lie. Dat truck dah is *trash*; en trash is what people is dat puts dirt on de head er dey fren's en makes 'em ashamed."

Then he got up slow, and walked to the wigwam, and went in there, without saying anything but that. But that was enough. It made me feel so mean I could almost kissed *his* foot to get him to take it back.

It was fifteen minutes before I could work myself up to go and humble

---

4. Vivid, compelling.

myself to a nigger—but I done it, and I warn't ever sorry for it afterwards, neither. I didn't do him no more mean tricks, and I wouldn't done that one if I'd a knowed it would make him feel that way.

## Chapter XVI

We slept most all day, and started out at night, a little ways behind a monstrous long raft that was as long going by as a procession. She had four long sweeps[5] at each end, so we judged she carried as many as thirty men, likely. She had five big wigwams aboard, wide apart, and an open camp fire in the middle, and a tall flagpole at each end. There was a power of style about her. It *amounted* to something being a raftsman on such a craft as that.

We went drifting down into a big bend, and the night clouded up and got hot. The river was very wide, and was walled with solid timber on both sides; you couldn't see a break in it hardly ever, or a light. We talked about Cairo, and wondered whether we would know it when we got to it. I said likely we wouldn't, because I had heard say there warn't but about a dozen houses there, and if they didn't happen to have them lit up, how was we going to know we was passing a town? Jim said if the two big rivers joined together there, that would show. But I said maybe we might think we was passing the foot of an island and coming into the same old river again. That disturbed Jim—and me too. So the question was, what to do? I said, paddle ashore the first time a light showed, and tell them pap was behind, coming along with a trading-scow, and was a green hand at the business, and wanted to know how far it was to Cairo. Jim thought it was a good idea, so we took a smoke on it and waited.[6]

But you know a young person can't wait very well when he is impatient to find a thing out. We talked it over, and by and by Jim said it was such a black night, now, that it wouldn't be no risk to swim down to the big raft and crawl aboard and listen—they would talk about Cairo, because they would be calculating to go ashore there for a spree, maybe; or anyway they would send boats ashore to buy whisky or fresh meat or something. Jim had a wonderful level head, for a nigger: he could most always start a good plan when you wanted one.

I stood up and shook my rags off and jumped into the river, and struck out for the raft's light. By and by, when I got down nearly to her, I eased up and went slow and cautious. But everything was all right—nobody at the sweeps. So I swum down along the raft till I was most abreast the camp fire in the middle, then I crawled aboard and inched along and got in among some bundles of shingles on the weather side of the fire. There was thirteen men there—they was the watch on deck of course. And a mighty rough-looking lot, too. They had a jug, and tin cups, and they kept the jug moving. One man was singing—roaring, you may say; and it wasn't a nice song—for a parlor, anyway. He roared through his nose, and strung out the last word of every line

5. Long oars used chiefly for steering.
6. The passage that follows was part of the final autograph manuscript for *Huck Finn* that Clemens sent to his nephew-publisher Charles L. Webster in April 1884. Though Clemens acquiesced to the cutting of this "Raft Passage" (on a suggestion made initially by W. D. Howells), the cut was made to save space and not on literary or aesthetic grounds, and the passage is, therefore, reinstated in this text. The raft material had already appeared—with an introductory note explaining that it was part of a book in progress—as part of Chap. 3 of *Life on the Mississippi* (1883). For a further discussion of this textual crux see Walter Blair, *Mark Twain and "Huck Finn"* (1960), and Peter G. Beidler, "The Raft Episode in Huckleberry Finn," *Modern Fiction Studies* 14, no. 1 (Spring 1965), 11–20.

very long. When he was done they all fetched a kind of Injun war-whoop, and then another was sung. It begun:

> "There was a woman in our towdn,
> In our towdn did dwed'l [dwell],
> She loved her husband dear-i-lee,
> But another man twyste as wed'l.

> "Singing too, riloo, riloo, riloo,
> Ri-too, riloo, rilay——e,
> She loved her husband dear-i-lee,
> But another man twyste as wed'l."

And so on—fourteen verses. It was kind of poor, and when he was going to start on the next verse one of them said it was the tune the old cow died on; and another one said: "Oh, give us a rest!" And another one told him to take a walk. They made fun of him till he got mad and jumped up and begun to cuss the crowd, and said he could lam any thief in the lot.

They was all about to make a break for him, but the biggest man there jumped up and says:

"Set whar you are, gentlemen. Leave him to me; he's my meat."

Then he jumped up in the air three times, and cracked his heels together every time. He flung off a buckskin coat that was all hung with fringes, and says, "You lay thar tell the chawin-up's done"; and flung his hat down, which was all over ribbons, and says, "You lay thar tell his sufferin's is over."

Then he jumped up in the air and cracked his heels together again, and shouted out:

"Whoo-oop! I'm the old original iron-jawed, brass-mounted, copper-bellied corpse-maker from the wilds of Arkansaw. Look at me! I'm the man they call Sudden Death and General Desolation! Sired by a hurricane, dam'd by an earthquake, half-brother to the cholera, nearly related to the smallpox on the mother's side! Look at me! I take nineteen alligators and a bar'l of whisky for breakfast when I'm in robust health, and a bushel of rattlesnakes and a dead body when I'm ailing. I split the everlasting rocks with my glance, and I squench[7] the thunder when I speak! Whoo-oop! Stand back and give me room according to my strength! Blood's my natural drink, and the wails of the dying is music to my ear. Cast your eye on me, gentlemen! and lay low and hold your breath, for I'm 'bout to turn myself loose![8]

All the time he was getting this off, he was shaking his head and looking fierce, and kind of swelling around in a little circle, tucking up his wristbands, and now and then straightening up and beating his breast with his fist, saying, "Look at me, gentlemen!" When he got through, he jumped up and cracked his heels together three times, and let off a roaring "Whoo-oop! I'm the blood-iest son of a wildcat that lives!"

Then the man that had started the row tilted his old slouch hat down over his right eye; then he bent stooping forward, with his back sagged and his south end sticking out far, and his fists a-shoving out and drawing in in front of him, and so went around in a little circle about three times, swelling himself up and breathing hard. Then he straightened, and jumped up and cracked his

---

7. Outdo, overpower.
8. Clemens here immortalizes the ritual boasting of the "ring-tailed roarers," chiefly associated with Ken-
tucky but familiar both in the oral traditions of the frontier and in the writings of the southwestern humorists, in whose tradition Clemens follows.

heels together three times before he lit again (that made them cheer), and he began to shout like this:

"Whoo-oop! bow you neck and spread, for the kingdom of sorrow's a-coming! Hold me down to the earth, for I feel my powers a-working! whoo-oop! I'm a child of sin, *don't* let me get a start! Smoked glass, here, for all! Don't attempt to look at me with the naked eye, gentlemen! When I'm playful I use the meridians of longitude and parallels of latitude for a seine, and drag the Atlantic Ocean for whales! I scratch my head with the lightning and purr myself to sleep with the thunder! When I'm cold, I bile the Gulf of Mexico and bathe in it; when I'm hot I fan myself with an equinoctial storm; when I'm thirsty I reach up and suck a cloud dry like a sponge; when I range the earth hungry, famine follows in my tracks! Whoo-oop! Bow your neck and spread! I put my hand on the sun's face and make it night in the earth; I bite a piece out of the moon and hurry the seasons; I shake myself and crumble the mountains! Contemplate me through leather—*don't* use the naked eye! I'm the man with a petrified heart and biler-iron bowels! The massacre of isolated communities is the pastime of my idle moments, the destruction of nationalities the serious business of my life! The boundless vastness of the great American desert is my inclosed property, and I bury my dead on my own premises!" He jumped up and cracked his heels together three times before he lit (they cheered him again), and as he come down he shouted out: "Whoo-oop! bow your neck and spread, for the Pet Child of Calamity's a-coming!"

Then the other one went to swelling around and blowing again—the first one—the one they called Bob; next, the Child of Calamity chipped in again, bigger than ever; then they both got at it at the same time, swelling round and round each other and punching their fists most into each other's faces, and whooping and jawing like Injuns; then Bob called the Child names, and the Child called him names back again; next, Bob called him a heap rougher names, and the Child come back at him with the very worst kind of language; next, Bob knocked the Child's hat off, and the Child picked it up and kicked Bob's ribbony hat about six foot; Bob went and got it and said never mind, this warn't going to be the last of this thing, because he was a man that never forgot and never forgive, and so the Child better look out, for there was a time a-coming, just as sure as he was a living man, that he would have to answer to him with the best blood in his body. The Child said no man was willinger than he for that time to come, and he would give Bob fair warning, *now*, never to cross his path again, for he could never rest till he had waded in his blood, for such was his nature, though he was sparing him now on account of his family, if he had one.

Both of them was edging away in different directions, growling and shaking their heads and going on about what they was going to do; but a little black-whiskered chap skipped up and says:

"Come back here, you couple of chicken-livered cowards, and I'll thrash the two of ye!"

And he done it, too. He snatched them, he jerked them his way and that, he booted them around, he knocked them sprawling faster than they could get up. Why, it warn't two minutes till they begged like dogs—and how the other lot did yell and laugh and clap their hands all the way through, and shout "Sail in, Corpse-Maker!" "Hit at him again, Child of Calamity!" "Bully for you, little Davy!" Well, it was a perfect pow-wow for a while. Bob and the

Child had red noses and black eyes when they got through. Little Davy made them own up that they were sneaks and cowards and not fit to eat with a dog or drink with a nigger; then Bob and the Child shook hands with each other, very solemn, and said they had always respected each other and was willing to let bygones be bygones. So then they washed their faces in the river; and just then there was a loud order to stand by for a crossing, and some of them went forward to man the sweeps there, and the rest went aft to handle the after sweeps.

I laid still and waited for fifteen minutes, and had a smoke out of a pipe that one of them left in reach; then the crossing was finished, and they stumped back and had a drink around and went to talking and singing again. Next they got out an old fiddle, and one played, and another patted juba, and the rest turned themselves loose on a regular old-fashioned keelboat breakdown.[9] They couldn't keep that up very long without getting winded, so by and by they settled around the jug again.

They sung "Jolly, Jolly Raftsman's the Life for Me," with a rousing chorus, and then they got to talking about differences betwixt hogs, and their different kind of habits, and next about women and their different ways; and next about the best ways to put out houses that was afire; and next about what ought to be done with the Injuns; and next about what a king had to do, and how much he got; and next about how to make cats fight; and next about what to do when a man has fits; and next about differences betwixt clear-water rivers and muddy-water ones. The man they called Ed said the muddy Mississippi water was wholesomer to drink than the clear water of the Ohio; he said if you let a pint of this yaller Mississippi water settle, you would have about a half to three-quarters of an inch of mud in the bottom, according to the stage of the river, and then it warn't no better than Ohio water—what you wanted to do was to keep it stirred up—and when the river was low, keep mud on hand to put in and thicken the water up the way it ought to be.

The Child of Calamity said that was so; he said there was nutritiousness in the mud, and a man that drunk Mississippi water could grow corn in his stomach if he wanted to. He says:

"You look at the graveyards; that tells the tale. Trees won't grow worth shucks in a Cincinnati graveyard, but in a Sent Louis graveyard they grow upwards of eight hundred foot high. It's all on account of the water the people drunk before they laid up. A Cincinnati corpse don't richen a soil any."

And they talked about how Ohio water didn't like to mix with Mississippi water. Ed said if you take the Mississippi on a rise when the Ohio is low, you'll find a wide band of clear water all the way down the east side of the Mississippi for a hundred miles or more, and the minute you get out a quarter of a mile from shore and pass the line, it is all thick and yaller the rest of the way across. Then they talked about how to keep tobacco from getting moldy, and from that they went into ghosts and told about a lot that other folks had seen; but Ed says:

"Why don't you tell something that you've seen yourselves? Now let me have a say. Five years ago I was on a raft as big as this, and right along here it was a bright moonshiny night, and I was on watch and boss of the stabboard

---

9. As the name suggests, a wild dance with a rapid rhythm. The "juba" is a strongly rhythmical dance that originated among southern blacks about 1830; to "pat a juba" would be to clap the hands or tap the feet to make the rhythm.

oar forrard, and one of my pards was a man named Dick Allbright, and he come along to where I was sitting, forrard—gaping and stretching, he was— and stooped down on the edge of the raft and washed his face in the river, and come and set down by me and got out his pipe, and had just got it filled, when he looks up and says:

"'Why looky-here,' he says, 'ain't that Buck Miller's place, over yander in the bend?"

"'Yes,' says I, 'it is—why?' He laid his pipe down and leaned his head on his hand, and says:

"'I thought we'd be furder down.' I says:

"'I thought it, too, when I went off watch'—we was standing six hours on and six off—'but the boys told me,' I says, 'that the raft didn't seem to hardly move, for the last hour,' says I, 'though she's a-slipping along all right now,' says I. He give a kind of a groan, and says:

"'I've seed a raft act so before, along here,' he says. 'Pears to me the current has most quit above the head of this bend durin' the last two years,' he says.

"Well, he raised up two or three times, and looked away off and around on the water. That started me at it, too. A body is always doing what he sees somebody else doing, though there mayn't be no sense in it. Pretty soon I see a black something floating on the water away off to stabboard and quartering behind us. I see he was looking at it, too. I says:

"'What's that?' He says, sort of pettish:

"' 'Tain't nothing but an old empty bar'l.'

"'An empty bar'l!' says I, 'why,' says I, 'a spy-glass is a fool to *your* eyes. How can you tell it's an empty bar'l?' He says:

"'I don't know; I reckon it ain't a bar'l, but I thought it might be,' says he.

"'Yes,' I says, 'so it might be, and it might be anything else too; a body can't tell nothing about it, such a distance as that,' I says.

"We hadn't nothing else to do, so we kept on watching it. By and by I says:

"'Why, looky-here, Dick Allbright, that thing's a-gaining on us, I believe.'

"He never said nothing. The thing gained and gained, and I judged it must be a dog that was about tired out. Well, we swung down into the crossing, and the thing floated across the bright streak of the moonshine, and by George, it *was* a bar'l. Says I:

"'Dick Allbright, what made you think that thing was a bar'l, when it was half a mile off?' says I. Says he:

"'I don't know.' Says I:

"'You tell me, Dick Allbright.' Says he:

"'Well, I knowed it was a bar'l; I've seen it before; lots has seen it; they says it's a ha'nted bar'l.'

"I called the rest of the watch, and they come and stood there, and I told them what Dick said. It floated right along abreast, now, and didn't gain any more. It was about twenty foot off. Some was for having it aboard, but the rest didn't want to. Dick Allbright said rafts that had fooled with it had got bad luck by it. The captain of the watch said he didn't believe in it. He said he reckoned the bar'l gained on us because it was in a little better current than what we was. He said it would leave by and by.

"So then we went to talking about other things, and we had a song, and then a breakdown; and after that the captain of the watch called for another song; but it was clouding up now, and the bar'l stuck right thar in the same place, and the song didn't seem to have much warm-up to it, somehow, and so they didn't finish it, and there warn't any cheers, but it sort of dropped flat, and nobody said anything for a minute. Then everybody tried to talk at once, and one chap got off a joke, but it warn't no use, they didn't laugh, and even the chap that made the joke didn't laugh at it, which ain't usual. We all just settled down glum, and watched the bar'l, and was oneasy and oncomfortable. Well, sir, it shut down black and still, and then the wind began to moan around, and next the lightning began to play and the thunder to grumble. And pretty soon there was a regular storm, and in the middle of it a man that was running aft stumbled and fell and sprained his ankle so that he had to lay up. This made the boys shake their heads. And every time the lightning come, there was that bar'l, with the blue lights winking around it. We was always on the lookout for it. But by and by, toward dawn, she was gone. When the day come we couldn't see her anywhere, and we warn't sorry, either.

"But next night about half-past nine, when there was songs and high jinks going on, here she comes again, and took her old roost on the stabboard side. There warn't no more high jinks. Everybody got solemn; nobody talked; you couldn't get anybody to do anything but set around moody and look at the bar'l. It begun to cloud up again. When the watch changed, the off watch stayed up, 'stead of turning in. The storm ripped and roared around all night, and in the middle of it another man tripped and sprained his ankle, and had to knock off. The bar'l left toward day, and nobody see it go.

"Everybody was sober and down in the mouth all day. I don't mean the kind of sober that comes of leaving liquor alone—not that. They was quiet, but they all drunk more than usual—not together, but each man sidled off and took it private, by himself.

"After dark the off watch didn't turn in; nobody sung, nobody talked; the boys didn't scatter around, neither; they sort of huddled together, forrard; and for two hours they set there, perfectly still, looking steady in the one direction, and heaving a sigh once in a while. And then, here comes the bar'l again. She took up her old place. She stayed there all night; nobody turned in. The storm come on again, after midnight. It got awful dark; the rain poured down; hail, too; the thunder boomed and roared and bellowed; the wind blowed a hurricane; and the lightning spread over everything in big sheets of glare, and showed the whole raft as plain as day; and the river lashed up white as milk as far as you could see for miles, and there was that bar'l jiggering along, same as ever. The captain ordered the watch to man the after sweeps for a crossing, and nobody would go—no more sprained ankles for them, they said. They wouldn't even *walk* aft. Well, then, just then the sky split wide open, with a crash, and the lightning killed two men of the after watch, and crippled two more. Crippled them how, say you? Why, *sprained their ankles!*

"The bar'l left in the dark betwixt lightnings, toward dawn. Well, not a body eat a bite at breakfast that morning. After that the men loafed around, in twos and threes, and talked low together. But none of them herded with Dick Allbright. They all give him the cold shake. If he come around where any of the men was, they split up and sidled away. They wouldn't man the sweeps with him. The captain had all the skiffs hauled up on the raft, alongside of his wigwam, and wouldn't let the dead men be took ashore to be planted; he didn't believe a man that got ashore would come back: and he was right.

"After night come, you could see pretty plain that there was going to be trouble if that bar'l come again; there was such a muttering going on. A good many wanted to kill Dick Allbright, because he'd seen the bar'l on other trips, and that had an ugly look. Some wanted to put him ashore. Some said: 'Let's all go ashore in a pile, if the bar'l comes again.'

"This kind of whispers was still going on, the men being bunched together forrard watching for the bar'l, when lo and behold you! here she comes again. Down she comes, slow and steady, and settles into her old tracks. You could 'a' heard a pin drop. Then up comes the captain, and says:

" 'Boys, don't be a pack of children and fools; I don't want this bar'l to be dogging us all the way to Orleans, and you don't: Well, then, how's the best way to stop it? Burn it up—that's the way. I'm going to fetch it aboard,' he says. And before anybody could say a word, in he went.

"He swum to it, and as he come pushing it to the raft, the men spread to one side. But the old man got it aboard and busted in the head, and there was a baby in it! Yes, sir; a stark-naked baby. It was Dick Allbright's baby; he owned up and said so.

" 'Yes,' he says, a-leaning over it, 'yes, it is my own lamented darling, my poor lost Charles William Allbright deceased,' says he—for he could curl his tongue around the bulliest words in the language when he was a mind to, and lay them before you without a jint started anywheres. [1] Yes, he said, he used to live up at the head of this bend, and one night he choked his child, which was crying, not intending to kill it—which was prob'ly a lie—and then he was scared, and buried it in a bar'l, before his wife got home, and off he went, and struck the northern trail and went to rafting; and this was the third year that the bar'l had chased him. He said the bad luck always begun light, and lasted till four men was killed, and then the bar'l didn't come any more after that. He said if the men would stand it one more night—and was a-going on like that—but the men had got enough. They started to get out a boat to take him ashore and lynch him, but he grabbed the little child all of a sudden and jumped overboard with it, hugged up to his breast and shedding tears, and we never see him again in this life, poor old suffering soul, nor Charles William neither."

"Who was shedding tears?" says Bob; "was it Allbright or the baby?"

"Why, Allbright, of course; didn't I tell you the baby was dead? Been dead three years—how could it cry?"

"Well, never mind how it could cry—how could it keep all that time?" says Davy. "You answer me that."

"I don't know how it done it," says Ed. "It done it, though—that's all I know about it."

"Say—what did they do with the bar'l?" says the Child of Calamity.

"Why, they hove it overboard, and it sunk like a chunk of lead."

"Edward, did the child look like it was choked?" says one.

"Did it have its hair parted?" says another.

"What was the brand on that bar'l, Eddy?" says a fellow they called Bill.

"Have you got the papers for them statistics, Edmund?" says Jimmy.

"Say, Edwin, was you one of the men that was killed by the lightning?" says Davy.

"Hm? Oh, no! he was both of 'em," says Bob. Then they all haw-hawed.

---

1. Without cracking open joints; i.e., perfectly smoothly and eloquently.

"Say, Edward, don't you reckon you'd better take a pill? You look bad—don't you feel pale?" says the Child of Calamity.

"Oh, come now, Eddy," says Jimmy, "show up; you must 'a' kept part of that bar'l to prove the thing by. Show us the bung-hole—*do*—and we'll all believe you."

"Say, boys," says Bill, "less divide it up. Thar's thirteen of us. I can swaller a thirteenth of the yarn, if you can worry down the rest."

Ed got up mad and said they could all go to some place which he ripped out pretty savage, and then walked off aft, cussing to himself, and they yelling and jeering at him, and roaring and laughing so you could hear them a mile.

"Boys, we'll split a watermelon on that," says the Child of Calamity; and he came rummaging around in the dark amongst the shingle bundles where I was, and put his hand on me. I was warm and soft and naked; so he says "Ouch!" and jumped back.

"Fetch a lantern or a chunk of fire here, boys—there's a snake here as big as a cow!"

So they run there with a lantern, and crowded up and looked in on me.

"Come out of that, you beggar!" says one.

"Who are you?" says another.

"What are you after here? Speak up prompt, or overboard you go."

"Snake him out, boys. Snatch him out by the heels."

I began to beg, and crept out amongst them trembling. They looked me over, wondering, and the Child of Calamity says:

"A cussed thief! Lend a hand and less heave him overboard!"

"No," says Big Bob, "less get out the paint-pot and paint him a sky-blue all over from head to heel, and *then* heave him over."

"Good! that's it. Go for the paint, Jimmy."

When the paint come, and Bob took the brush and was just going to begin, the others laughing and rubbing their hands, I begun to cry, and that sort of worked on Davy, and he says:

" 'Vast there. He's nothing but a cub. I'll paint the man that teches him!"

So I looked around on them, and some of them grumbled and growled, and Bob put down the paint, and the others didn't take it up.

"Come here to the fire, and less see what you're up to here," says Davy. "Now set down there and give an account of yourself. How long have you been aboard here?"

"Not over a quarter of a minute, sir," says I.

"How did you get dry so quick?"

"I don't know, sir. I'm always that way, mostly."

"Oh, you are, are you? What's your name?"

I warn't going to tell my name. I didn't know what to say, so I just says:

"Charles William Allbright, sir."

Then they roared—the whole crowd; and I was mighty glad I said that, because, maybe, laughing would get them in a better humor.

When they got done laughing, Davy says:

"It won't hardly do, Charles William. You couldn't have growed this much in five year, and you was a baby when you come out of the bar'l, you know, and dead at that. Come, now, tell a straight story, and nobody'll hurt you, if you ain't up to anything wrong. What is your name?"

"Aleck Hopkins, sir. Aleck James Hopkins."

"Well, Aleck, where did you come from, here?"

"From a trading-scow. She lays up the bend yonder. I was born on her. Pap has traded up and down here all his life; and he told me to swim off here, because when you went by he said he would like to get some of you to speak to a Mr. Jonas Turner, in Cairo, and tell him—"

"Oh, come!"

"Yes, sir, it's as true as the world. Pap he says—"

"Oh, your grandmother!"

They all laughed, and I tried again to talk, but they broke in on me and stopped me.

"Now, looky-here," says Davy; "you're scared, and so you talk wild. Honest, now, do you live in a scow, or is it a lie?"

"Yes, sir, in a trading-scow. She lays up at the head of the bend. But I warn't born in her. It's our first trip."

"Now you're talking! What did you come aboard here for? To steal?"

"No sir, I didn't. It was only to get a ride on the raft. All boys does that."

"Well, I know that. But what did you hide for?"

"Sometimes they drive the boys off."

"So they do. They might steal. Looky-here; if we let you off this time, will you keep out of these kind of scrapes hereafter?"

" 'Deed I will, boss. You try me."

"All right, then. You ain't but little ways from shore. Overboard with you, and don't you make a fool of yourself another time this way. Blast it, boy, some raftsmen would rawhide you till you were black and blue!"

I didn't wait to kiss good-by, but went overboard and broke for shore. When Jim come along by and by, the big raft was away out of sight around the point. I swum out and got aboard, and was mighty glad to see home again.[2]

There warn't nothing to do, now, but to look out sharp for the town, and not pass it without seeing it. He said he'd be mighty sure to see it, because he'd be a free man the minute he seen it, but if he missed it he'd be in the slave country again and no more show for freedom. Every little while he jumps up and says:

"Dah she is!"

But it warn't. It was Jack-o-lanterns, or lightning-bugs; so he set down again, and went to watching, same as before. Jim said it made him all over trembly and feverish to be so close to freedom. Well, I can tell you it made me all over trembly and feverish, too, to hear him, because I begun to get it through my head that he *was* most free—and who was to blame for it? Why, *me*. I couldn't get that out of my conscience, no how nor no way. It got to troubling me so I couldn't rest; I couldn't stay still in one place. It hadn't ever come home to me before, what this thing was that I was doing. But now it did; and it staid with me, and scorched me more and more. I tried to make out to myself that *I* warn't to blame, because I didn't run Jim off from his rightful owner; but it warn't no use, conscience up and says, every time, "But you knowed he was running for his freedom, and you could a paddled ashore and told somebody." That was so—I couldn't get around that, noway. That was where it pinched. Conscience says to me, "What had poor Miss Watson done to you, that you could see her nigger go off right under your eyes and never say one single word? What did that poor old woman do to you, that you could treat her so mean? Why, she tried to learn you your book, she tried to learn you your manners, she tried to be good to you every way she knowed how. *That's* what she done."

I got to feeling so mean and so miserable I most wished I was dead. I fidgeted up and down the raft, abusing myself to myself, and Jim was fidgeting up and down past me. We neither of us could keep still. Every time he danced around and says, "Dah's Cairo!" it went through me like a shot, and I thought if it *was* Cairo I reckoned I would die of miserableness.

Jim talked out loud all the time while I was talking to myself. He was saying how the first thing he would do when he got to a free State he would go to saving up money and never spend a single cent, and when he got enough he would buy his wife, which was owned on a farm close to where Miss Watson lived; and then they would both work to buy the two children, and if their master wouldn't sell them, they'd get an Ab'litionist to go and steal them.

It most froze me to hear such talk. He wouldn't ever dared to talk such talk in his life before. Just see what a difference it made in him the minute he judged he was about free. It was according to the old saying, "give a nigger an inch and he'll take an ell." Thinks I, this is what comes of my not thinking. Here was this nigger which I had as good as helped to run away, coming right out flat-footed and saying he would steal his children—children that belonged to a man I didn't even know; a man that hadn't ever done me no harm.

I was sorry to hear Jim say that, it was such a lowering of him. My conscience got to stirring me up hotter than ever, until at last I says to it, "Let up on me—it ain't too late, yet—I'll paddle ashore at the first light, and tell." I felt easy, and happy, and light as a feather, right off. All my troubles was gone. I went to looking out sharp for a light, and sort of singing to myself. By-and-by one showed. Jim sings out:

"We's safe, Huck, we's safe! Jump up and crack yo' heels, dat's de good ole Cairo at las', I jis knows it!"

I says:

"I'll take the canoe and go see, Jim. It mightn't be, you know."

He jumped and got the canoe ready, and put his old coat in the bottom for me to set on, and give me the paddle; and as I shoved off, he says:

"Pooty soon I'll be a-shout'n for joy, en I'll say, it's all on accounts o' Huck; I's a free man, en I couldn't ever ben free ef it hadn' ben for Huck; Huck done it. Jim won't ever forget you, Huck; you's de bes' fren' Jim's ever had; en you's de *only* fren' ole Jim's got now."

I was paddling off, all in a sweat to tell on him; but when he says this, it seemed to kind of take the tuck all out of me. I went along slow then, and I warn't right down certain whether I was glad I started or whether I warn't. When I was fifty yards off, Jim says:

"Dah you goes, de ole true Huck; de on'y white genlman dat ever kep' his promise to ole Jim."

Well, I just felt sick. But I says, I *got* to do it—I can't get *out* of it. Right then, along comes a skiff with two men in it, with guns, and they stopped and I stopped. One of them says:

"What's that, yonder?"

"A piece of raft," I says.

"Do you belong on it?"

"Yes, sir."

"Any men on it?"

"Only one, sir."

"Well, there's five niggers run off to-night, up yonder above the head of the bend. Is your man white or black?"

I didn't answer up prompt. I tried to, but the words wouldn't come. I tried, for a second or two, to brace up and out with it, but I warn't man enough—hadn't the spunk of a rabbit. I see I was weakening; so I just give up trying, and up and says—

"He's white."

"I reckon we'll go and see for ourselves."

"I wish you would," says I, "because it's pap that's there, and maybe you'd help me tow the raft ashore where the light is. He's sick—and so is mam and Mary Ann."

"Oh, the devil! we're in a hurry, boy. But I s'pose we've got to. Come—buckle to your paddle, and let's get along."

I buckled to my paddle and they laid to their oars. When we had made a stroke or two, I says:

"Pap'll be mighty much obleeged to you, I can tell you. Everybody goes away when I want them to help me tow the raft ashore, and I can't do it myself."

"Well, that's infernal mean. Odd, too. Say, boy, what's the matter with your father?"

"It's the—a—the—well, it ain't anything, much."

They stopped pulling. It warn't but a mighty little ways to the raft, now. One says:

"Boy, that's a lie. What *is* the matter with your pap? Answer up square, now, and it'll be the better for you."

"I will, sir, I will, honest—but don't leave us, please. It's the—the—gentlemen, if you'll only pull ahead, and let me heave you the head-line you won't have to come a-near the raft—please do."

"Set her back, John, set her back!" says one. They backed water. "Keep away, boy—keep to looard.[3] Confound it, I just expect the wind has blowed it to us. Your pap's got the small-pox,[4] and you know it precious well. Why didn't you come out and say so? Do you want to spread it all over?"

"Well," says I, a-blubbering, "I've told everybody before, and then they just went away and left us."

"Poor devil, there's something in that. We are right down sorry for you, but we—well, hang it, we don't want the small-pox, you see. Look here, I'll tell you what to do. Don't you try to land by yourself, or you'll smash everything to pieces. You float along down about twenty miles and you'll come to a town on the left-hand side of the river. It will be long after sun-up, then, and when you ask for help, you tell them your folks are all down with chills and fever. Don't be a fool again, and let people guess what is the matter. Now we're trying to do you a kindness; so you just put twenty miles between us, that's a good boy. It wouldn't do any good to land yonder where the light is—it's only a wood-yard. Say—I reckon your father's poor, and I'm bound to say he's in pretty hard luck. Here—I'll put a twenty dollar gold piece on this board, and

---

3. I.e., leeward.                        4. At the time a highly infectious, often fatal disease.

you get it when it floats by. I feel mighty mean to leave you, but my kingdom! it won't do to fool with small-pox, don't you see?"

"Hold on, Parker," says the other man, "here's a twenty to put on the board for me. Good-bye boy, you do as Mr. Parker told you, and you'll be all right."

"That's so, my boy—good-bye, good-bye. If you see any runaway niggers, you get help and nab them, and you can make some money by it."

"Good-bye, sir," says I, "I won't let no runaway niggers get by me if I can help it."

They went off, and I got aboard the raft, feeling bad and low, because I knowed very well I had done wrong, and I see it warn't no use for me to try to learn to do right; a body that don't get *started* right when he's little, ain't got no show—when the pinch comes there ain't nothing to back him up and keep him to his work, and so he gets beat. Then I thought a minute, and says to myself, hold on,—s'pose you'd a done right and give Jim up; would you felt better than what you do now? No, says I, I'd feel bad—I'd feel just the same way I do now. Well, then, says I, what's the use you learning to do right, when it's troublesome to do right and ain't no trouble to do wrong, and the wages is just the same? I was stuck. I couldn't answer that. So I reckoned I wouldn't bother no more about it, but after this always do whichever come handiest at the time.

I went into the wigwam; Jim warn't there. I looked all around; he warn't anywhere. I says:

"Jim!"

"Here I is, Huck. Is dey out o' sight yit? Don't talk loud."

He was in the river, under the stern oar, with just his nose out. I told him they was out of sight, so he come aboard. He says:

"I was a-listenin' to all de talk, en I slips into de river en was gwyne to shove for sho' if dey come aboard. Den I was gwyne to swim to de raf' agin when dey was gone. But lawsy, how you did fool 'em, Huck! Dat *wuz* de smartes' dodge! I tell you, chile, I 'speck it save' ole Jim—ole Jim ain' gwyne to forgit you for dat, honey."

Then we talked about the money. It was a pretty good raise, twenty dollars apiece. Jim said we could take deck passage on a steamboat now, and the money would last us as far as we wanted to go in the free States. He said twenty mile more warn't far for the raft to go, but he wished we was already there.

Towards daybreak we tied up, and Jim was mighty particular about hiding the raft good. Then he worked all day fixing things in bundles, and getting all ready to quit rafting.

That night about ten we hove in sight of the lights of a town away down in a left-hand bend.

I went off in the canoe, to ask about it. Pretty soon I found a man out in the river with a skiff, setting a trot-line. I ranged up and says:

"Mister, is that town Cairo?"

"Cairo? no. You must be a blame' fool."

"What town is it, mister?"

"If you want to know, go and find out. If you stay here botherin' around me for about a half a minute longer, you'll get something you won't want."

I paddled to the raft. Jim was awful disappointed, but I said never mind, Cairo would be the next place, I reckoned.

We passed another town before daylight, and I was going out again; but it was high ground, so I didn't go. No high ground about Cairo, Jim said. I had forgot it. We laid up for the day, on a tow-head tolerable close to the left-hand bank. I begun to suspicion something. So did Jim. I says:

"Maybe we went by Cairo in the fog that night."

He says:

"Doan' less' talk about it, Huck. Po' niggers can't have no luck. I awluz 'spected dat rattle-snake skin warn't done wid it's work."

"I wish I'd never seen that snake-skin, Jim—I do wish I'd never laid eyes on it."

"It ain't yo' fault, Huck; you didn't know. Don't you blame yo'sef 'bout it."

When it was daylight, here was the clear Ohio water in shore, sure enough, and outside was the old regular Muddy! So it was all up with Cairo.[5]

We talked it all over. It wouldn't do to take to the shore; we couldn't take the raft up the stream, of course. There warn't no way but to wait for dark, and start back in the canoe and take the chances. So we slept all day amongst the cotton-wood thicket, so as to be fresh for the work, and when we went back to the raft about dark the canoe was gone!

We didn't say a word for a good while. There warn't anything to say. We both knowed well enough it was some more work of the rattle-snake skin; so what was the use to talk about it? It would only look like we was finding fault, and that would be bound to fetch more bad luck—and keep on fetching it, too, till we knowed enough to keep still.

By-and-by we talked about what we better do, and found there warn't no way but just to go along down with the raft till we got a chance to buy a canoe to go back in. We warn't going to borrow it when there warn't anybody around, the way pap would do, for that might set people after us.

So we shoved out, after dark, on the raft.[6]

Anybody that don't believe yet, that it's foolishness to handle a snake-skin, after all that that snake-skin done for us, will believe it now, if they read on and see what more it done for us.

The place to buy canoes is off of rafts laying up at shore. But we didn't see no rafts laying up; so we went along during three hours and more. Well, the night got gray, and ruther thick, which is the next meanest thing to fog. You can't tell the shape of the river, and you can't see no distance. It got to be very late and still, and then along comes a steamboat up the river. We lit the lantern, and judged she would see it. Up-stream boats didn't generly come close to us; they go out and follow the bars and hunt for easy water under the reefs; but nights like this they bull right up the channel against the whole river.

We could hear her pounding along, but we didn't see her good till she was close. She aimed right for us. Often they do that and try to see how close they can come without touching; sometimes the wheel bites off a sweep, and then the pilot sticks his head out and laughs, and thinks he's mighty start. Well, here she comes, and we said she was going to try to shave us; but she didn't

---

5. Because Cairo is located at the confluence of the Ohio and Mississippi rivers, which in turn lies below the confluence of the Missouri (Big Muddy) and Mississippi, they know that they have passed Cairo and lost the opportunity to sell the raft and travel up the Ohio by steamboat to freedom.
6. Clemens was "stuck" at this point in the writing of the novel and put the four-hundred-page manuscript aside for approximately three years. In the winter of

1879–80 he added the two chapters dealing with the feud (XVII and XVIII) and then the three chapters (XIX–XXI) in which the king and duke enter the story and for a time dominate the action. The novel was not completed until 1883, when Clemens wrote the last half of the novel in a few months of concentrated writing. As late as 1882, he was not confident he would ever complete the book. See Walter Blair, *Mark Twain and "Huck Finn"* (1960).

seem to be sheering off a bit. She was a big one, and she was coming in a hurry, too, looking like a black cloud with rows of glow-worms around it; but all of a sudden she bulged out, big and scary, with a long row of wide-open furnace doors shining like red-hot teeth, and her monstrous bows and guards hanging right over us. There was a yell at us, and a jingling of bells to stop the engines, a pow-wow of cussing, and whistling of steam—and as Jim went overboard on one side and I on the other, she come smashing straight through the raft.

I dived—and I aimed to find the bottom, too, for a thirty-foot wheel had got to go over me, and I wanted it to have plenty of room. I could always stay under water a minute; this time I reckon I staid under water a minute and a half. Then I bounced for the top in a hurry, for I was nearly busting. I popped out to my arm-pits and blowed the water out of my nose, and puffed a bit. Of course there was a booming current; and of course that boat started her engines again ten seconds after she stopped them, for they never cared much for rafts-men; so now she was churning along up the river, out of sight in the thick weather, though I could hear her.

I sung out for Jim about a dozen times, but I didn't get any answer; so I grabbed a plank that touched me while I was "treading water," and struck out for shore, shoving it ahead of me. But I made out to see that the drift of the current was towards the left-hand shore,[7] which meant that I was in a crossing; so I changed off and went that way.

It was one of these long, slanting, two-mile crossings; so I was a good long time in getting over. I made a safe landing, and clum up the bank. I couldn't see but a little ways, but I went poking along over rough ground for a quarter of a mile or more, and then I run across a big old-fashioned double log house before I noticed it. I was going to rush by and get away, but a lot of dogs jumped out and went to howling and barking at me, and I knowed better than to move another peg.

## Chapter XVII

In about half a minute somebody spoke out of a window, without putting his head out, and says:

"Be done, boys! Who's there?"

I says:

"It's me."

"Who's me?"

"George Jackson, sir."

"What do you want?"

"I don't want nothing, sir. I only want to go along by, but the dogs won't let me."

"What are you prowling around here this time of night, for—hey?"

"I warn't prowling around, sir; I fell overboard off of the steamboat."

"Oh, you did, did you? Strike a light there, somebody. What did you say your name was?"

"George Jackson, sir. I'm only a boy."

"Look here; if you're telling the truth, you needn't be afraid—nobody'll hurt

7. Kentucky, where the feud in Chaps. XVII and XVIII is set.

you. But don't try to budge; stand right where you are. Rouse our Bob and Tom, some of you, and fetch the guns. George Jackson, is there anybody with you?"

"No, sir, nobody."

I heard the people stirring around in the house, now, and see a light. The man sung out:

"Snatch that light away, Betsy, you old fool—ain't you got any sense? Put it on the floor behind the front door. Bob, if you and Tom are ready, take your places."

"All ready."

"Now, George Jackson, do you know the Shepherdsons?"

"No, sir—I never heard of them."

"Well, that may be so, and it mayn't. Now, all ready. Step forward, George Jackson. And mind, don't you hurry—come mighty slow. If there's anybody with you, let him keep back—if he shows himself he'll be shot. Come along, now. Come slow; push the door open, yourself—just enough to squeeze in, d' you hear?"

I didn't hurry, I couldn't if I'd a wanted to. I took one slow step at a time, and there warn't a sound, only I thought I could hear my heart. The dogs were as still as the humans, but they followed a little behind me. When I got to the three log door-steps, I heard them unlocking and unbarring and unbolting. I put my hand on the door and pushed it a little and a little more, till somebody said, "There, that's enough—put your head in." I done it, but I judged they would take it off.

The candle was on the floor, and there they all was, looking at me, and me at them, for about a quarter of a minute. Three big men with guns pointed at me, which made me wince, I tell you; the oldest, gray and about sixty, the other two thirty or more—all of them fine and handsome—and the sweetest old gray-headed lady, and back of her two young women which I couldn't see right well. The old gentleman says:

"There—I reckon it's all right. Come in."

As soon as I was in, the old gentleman he locked the door and barred it and bolted it, and told the young men to come in with their guns, and they all went in a big parlor that had a new rag carpet on the floor, and got together in a corner that was out of range of the front windows—there warn't none on the side. They held the candle, and took a good look at me, and all said, "Why *he* ain't a Shepherdson—no, there ain't any Shepherdson about him." Then the old man said he hoped I wouldn't mind being searched for arms, because he didn't mean no harm by it—it was only to make sure. So he didn't pry into my pockets, but only felt outside with his hands, and said it was all right. He told me to make myself easy and at home, and tell all about myself; but the old lady says:

"Why bless you, Saul, the poor thing's as wet as he can be; and don't you reckon it may be he's hungry?"

"True for you, Rachel—I forgot."

So the old lady says:

"Betsy" (this was a nigger woman), "you fly around and get him something to eat, as quick as you can, poor thing; and one of you girls go and wake up Buck and tell him— Oh, here he is himself. Buck, take this little stranger and get the wet clothes off from him and dress him up in some of yours that's dry."

Buck looked about as old as me—thirteen or fourteen[8] or along there, though he was a little bigger than me. He hadn't on anything but a shirt, and he was very frowsy-headed. He come in gaping and digging one fist into his eyes, and he was dragging a gun along with the other one. He says:

"Ain't they no Shepherdsons around?"

They said, no, 'twas a false alarm.

"Well," he says, "if they'd a ben some, I reckon I'd a got one."

They all laughed, and Bob says:

"Why, Buck, they might have scalped us all, you've been so slow in coming."

"Well, nobody come after me, and it ain't right. I'm always kep' down; I don't get no show."

"Never mind, Buck, my boy," says the old man, "you'll have show enough, all in good time, don't you fret about that. Go 'long with you now, and do as your mother told you."

When we got up stairs to his room, he got me a coarse shirt and a round-about[9] and pants of his, and I put them on. While I was at it he asked me what my name was, but before I could tell him, he started to telling me about a blue jay and a young rabbit he had catched in the woods day before yester-day, and he asked me where Moses was when the candle went out. I said I didn't know; I hadn't heard about it before, no way.

"Well, guess," he says.

"How'm I going to guess," says I, "when I never heard tell about it before?"

"But you can guess, can't you? It's just as easy."

"Which candle?" I says.

"Why, any candle," he says.

"I don't know where he was," says I; "where was he?"

"Why he was in the *dark!* That's where he was!"

"Well, if you knowed where he was, what did you ask me for?"

"Why, blame it, it's a riddle, don't you see? Say, how long are you going to stay here? You got to stay always. We can just have booming times—they don't have no school now. Do you own a dog? I've got a dog—and he'll go in the river and bring out chips that you throw in. Do you like to comb up, Sundays, and all that kind of foolishness? You bet I don't, but ma she makes me. Confound these ole britches, I reckon I'd better put 'em on, but I'd ruther not, it's so warm. Are you all ready? All right—come along, old hoss."

Cold corn-pone, cold corn-beef, butter and butter-milk—that is what they had for me down there, and there ain't nothing better that ever I've come across yet. Buck and his ma and all of them smoked cob pipes, except the nigger woman, which was gone, and the two young women. They all smoked and talked, and I eat and talked. The young women had quilts around them, and their hair down their backs. They all asked me questions, and I told them how pap and me and all the family was living on a little farm down at the bottom of Arkansaw, and my sister Mary Ann run off and got married and never was heard of no more, and Bill went to hunt them and he warn't heard of no more, and Tom and Mort died, and then there warn't nobody but just me and pap left, and he was just trimmed down to nothing, on account of his

---

8. Clemens identifies Huck as "a boy of 14" in a notebook.   9. Short, close-fitting jacket.

troubles; so when he died I took what there was left, because the farm didn't belong to us, and started up the river, deck passage, and fell overboard; and that was how I come to be here. So they said I could have a home there as long as I wanted it. Then it was most daylight, and everybody went to bed, and I went to bed with Buck, and when I waked up in the morning, drat it all, I had forgot what my name was. So I laid there about an hour trying to think and when Buck waked up, I says:

"Can you spell, Buck?"

"Yes," he says.

"I bet you can't spell my name," says I.

"I bet you what you dare I can," says he.

"All right," says I, "go ahead."

"G-o-r-g-e J-a-x-o-n—there now," he says.

"Well," says I, "you done it, but I didn't think you could. It ain't no slouch of a name to spell—right off without studying."

I set it down, private, because somebody might want *me* to spell it, next, and so I wanted to be handy with it and rattle it off like I was used to it.

It was a mighty nice family, and a mighty nice house, too. I hadn't seen no house out in the country before that was so nice and had so much style.[1] It didn't have an iron latch on the front door, nor a wooden one with a buckskin string, but a brass knob to turn, the same as houses in a town. There warn't no bed in the parlor, not a sign of a bed; but heaps of parlors in towns has beds in them. There was a big fireplace that was bricked on the bottom, and the bricks was kept clean and red by pouring water on them and scrubbing them with another brick; sometimes they washed them over with red water-paint that they call Spanish-brown, same as they do in town. They had big brass dog-irons that could hold up a saw-log.[2] There was a clock on the middle of the mantel-piece, with a picture of a town painted on the bottom half of the glass front, and a round place in the middle of it for the sun, and you could see the pendulum swing behind it. It was beautiful to hear that clock tick; and sometimes when one of these peddlers had been along and scoured her up and got her in good shape, she would start in and strike a hundred and fifty before she got tuckered out. They wouldn't took any money for her.

Well, there was a big outlandish parrot on each side of the clock, made out of something like chalk, and painted up gaudy. By one of the parrots was a cat made of crockery, and a crockery dog by the other; and when you pressed down on them they squeaked, but didn't open their mouths nor look different nor interested. They squeaked through underneath. There was a couple of big wild-turkey-wing fans spread out behind those things. On a table in the middle of the room was a kind of a lovely crockery basket that had apples and orangesand peaches and grapes piled up in it which was much redder and yellower and prettier than real ones is, but they warn't real because you could see where pieces had got chipped off and showed the white chalk or whatever it was, underneath.

This table had a cover made out of beautiful oil-cloth, with a red and blue spread-eagle painted on it, and a painted border all around. It come all the way from Philadelphia, they said. There was some books too, piled up per-

---

1. Every detail of the furniture, furnishing, and decorations as well as the dress, speech, manners, and mores of the Grangerford household is carefully selected to epitomize satirically pre–Civil War culture of the lower Mississippi Valley.

2. A log large enough to be sawed into planks.

fectly exact, on each corner of the table. One was a big family Bible, full of pictures. One was "Pilgrim's Progress," about a man that left his family it didn't say why. I read considerable in it now and then. The statements was interesting, but tough. Another was "Friendship's Offering," full of beautiful stuff and poetry; but I didn't read the poetry. Another was Henry Clay's Speeches, and another was Dr. Gunn's Family Medicine, which told you all about what to do if a body was sick or dead. There was a Hymn Book, and a lot of other books.[3] And there was nice split-bottom chairs, and perfectly sound, too—not bagged down in the middle and busted, like an old basket.

They had pictures hung on the walls—mainly Washingtons and Lafayettes, and battles, and Highland Marys,[4] and one called "Signing the Declaration." There was some that they called crayons, which one of the daughters which was dead made her own self when she was only fifteen years old. They was different from any pictures I ever see before; blacker, mostly, than is common. One was a woman in a slim black dress, belted small under the armpits, with bulges like a cabbage in the middle of the sleeves, and a large black scoop-shovel bonnet with a black veil, and white slim ankles crossed about with black tape, and very wee black slippers, like a chisel, and she was leaning pensive on a tombstone on her right elbow, under a weeping willow, and her other hand hanging down her side holding a white handkerchief and a reticule, and underneath the picture it said "Shall I Never See Thee More Alas." Another one was a young lady with her hair all combed up straight to the top of her head, and knotted there in front of a comb like a chair-back, and she was crying into a handkerchief and had a dead bird laying on its back in her other hand with its heels up, and underneath the picture it said "I Shall Never Hear Thy Sweet Chirrup More Alas." There was one where a young lady was at a window looking up at the moon, and tears running down her cheeks; and she had an open letter in one hand with black sealing-wax showing on one edge of it, and she was mashing a locket with a chain to it against her mouth, and underneath the picture it said "And Art Thou Gone Yes Thou Art Gone Alas." These was all nice pictures, I reckon, but I didn't somehow seem to take to them, because if ever I was down a little, they always give me the fan-tods. Everybody was sorry she died, because she had laid out a lot more of these pictures to do, and a body could see by what she had done what they had lost. But I reckoned, that with her disposition, she was having a better time in the graveyard. She was at work on what they said was her greatest picture when she took sick, and every day and every night it was her prayer to be allowed to live till she got it done, but she never got the chance. It was a picture of a young woman in a long white gown, standing on the rail of a bridge all ready to jump off, with her hair all down her back, and looking up to the moon, with the tears running down her face, and she had two arms folded across her breast, and two arms stretched out in front, and two more reaching up towards the moon—and the idea was, to see which pair would look best and then scratch out all the other arms; but, as I was saying, she died before she got her mind made up, and now they kept this picture over the head of the bed in her

3. The neatly stacked, unread books are meant to define the values and tastes of the time and place: the Bible, Bunyan's *Pilgrim's Progress*, and the hymn book establish Calvinistic piety; Clay's speeches suggest political orthodoxy; Gunn's *Domestic Medicine* suggests popular notions of science and medical practice;

*Friendship's Offering* was a popular gift book.
4. The pictures similarly typify the culture of the region in the 1840s and 1850s. "Highland Mary" depicts poet Robert Burns's first love, who died a few months after they met. He memorialized her in several poems, especially *To Mary in Heaven*.

room, and every time her birthday come they hung flowers on it. Other times
it was hid with a little curtain. The young woman in the picture had a kind of
a nice sweet face, but there was so many arms it made her look too spidery,
seemed to me.

This young girl kept a scrap-book when she was alive, and used to paste
obituaries and accidents and cases of patient suffering in it out of the *Presbyterian Observer*, and write poetry after them out of her own head. It was very
good poetry.[5] This is what she wrote about a boy by the name of Stephen
Dowling Bots that fell down a well and was drownded:

ODE TO STEPHEN DOWLING BOTS, DEC'D

And did young Stephen sicken,
   And did young Stephen die?
And did the sad hearts thicken,
   And did the mourners cry?

No; such was not the fate of
   Young Stephen Dowling Bots;
Though sad hearts round him thickened,
   'Twas not from sickness' shots.

No whooping-cough did rack his frame,
   Nor measles drear, with spots;
Not these impaired the sacred name
   Of Stephen Dowling Bots.

Despised love struck not with woe
   That head of curly knots,
Nor stomach troubles laid him low,
   Young Stephen Dowling Bots.

O no. Then list with tearful eye,
   Whilst I his fate do tell.
His soul did from this cold world fly,
   By falling down a well.

They got him out and emptied him;
   Alas it was too late;
His spirit was gone for to sport aloft
   In the realms of the good and great.

If Emmeline Grangerford could make poetry like that before she was fourteen, there ain't no telling what she could a done by-and-by. Buck said she
could rattle off poetry like nothing. She didn't ever have to stop to think. He
said she would slap down a line, and if she couldn't find anything to rhyme
with it she would just scratch it out and slap down another one, and go ahead.
She warn't particular, she could write about anything you choose to give her

5. This parody derives in particular from two poems
by "The Sweet Singer of Michigan," Julia A. Moore
(1847–1920), whose sentimental poetry was popular at
the time Clemens was writing *Huck Finn*. In one of
the two poems, *Little Libbie*, the heroine "was choken
on a piece of beef." The graveyard and obituary (or
"sadful") schools of popular poetry are much older and
widespread. See Walter Blair, *Mark Twain and "Huck
Finn"* (1960).

to write about, just so it was sadful. Every time a man died, or a woman died, or a child died, she would be on hand with her "tribute" before he was cold. She called them tributes. The neighbors said it was the doctor first, then Emmeline, then the undertaker—the undertaker never got in ahead of Emmeline but once, and then she hung fire on a rhyme for the dead person's name, which was Whistler. She warn't ever the same, after that; she never complained, but she kind of pined away and did not live long. Poor thing, many's the time I made myself go up to the little room that used to be hers and get out her poor old scrapbook and read in it when her pictures had been aggravating me and I had soured on her a little. I liked all the family, dead ones and all, and warn't going to let anything come between us. Poor Emmeline made poetry about all the dead people when she was alive, and it didn't seem right that there warn't nobody to make some about her, now she was gone; so I tried to sweat out a verse or two myself, but I couldn't seem to make it go, somehow. They kept Emmeline's room trim and nice and all the things fixed in it just the way she liked to have them when she was alive, and nobody ever slept there. The old lady took care of the room herself, though there was plenty of niggers, and she sewed there a good deal and read her Bible there, mostly.

Well, as I was saying about the parlor, there was beautiful curtains on the windows: white, with pictures painted on them, of castles with vines all down the walls, and cattle coming down to drink. There was a little old piano, too, that had tin pans in it, I reckon, and nothing was ever so lovely as to hear the young ladies sing, "The Last Link is Broken" and play "The Battle of Prague"[6] on it. The walls of all the rooms was plastered, and most had carpets on the floors, and the whole house was whitewashed on the outside.

It was a double house, and the big open place betwixt them was roofed and floored, and sometimes the table was set there in the middle of the day, and it was a cool, comfortable place. Nothing couldn't be better. And warn't the cooking good, and just bushels of it too!

## Chapter XVIII

Col. Grangerford was a gentleman, you see. He was a gentleman all over; and so was his family. He was well born, as the saying is, and that's worth as much in a man as it is in a horse, so the Widow Douglas said, and nobody ever denied that she was of the first aristocracy in our town; and pap he always said it, too, though he warn't no more quality than a mudcat,[7] himself. Col. Grangerford was very tall and very slim, and had a darkish-paly complexion, not a sign of red in it anywheres; he was clean-shaved every morning, all over his thin face, and he had the thinnest kind of lips, and the thinnest kind of nostrils, and a high nose, and heavy eyebrows, and the blackest kind of eyes, sunk so deep back that they seemed like they was looking out of caverns at you, as you may say. His forehead was high, and his hair was black and straight, and hung to his shoulders. His hands was long and thin, and every day of his life he put on a clean shirt and a full suit from head to foot made out of linen so white it hurt your eyes to look at it; and on Sundays he wore a blue tail-coat

---

6. William Clifton's *The Last Link Is Broken* was published about 1840; it is the musical equivalent of Moore's poetry. *The Battle of Prague*, written by Czech composer Franz Kotswara about 1788, is a bloody story told in clichéd style. Clemens first heard it in 1878.
7. General term for a number of species of catfish; in this context the lowliest and least esteemed.

with brass buttons on it. He carried a mahogany cane with a silver head to it. There warn't no frivolishness about him, not a bit, and he warn't ever loud. He was as kind as he could be—you could feel that, you know, and so you had confidence. Sometimes he smiled, and it was good to see; but when he straightened himself up like a liberty-pole,[8] and the lightning begun to flicker out from under his eyebrows you wanted to climb a tree first, and find out what the matter was afterwards. He didn't ever have to tell anybody to mind their manners—everybody was always good mannered where he was. Everybody loved to have him around, too; he was sunshine most always—I mean he made it seem like good weather. When he turned into a cloud-bank it was awful dark for a half a minute and that was enough; there wouldn't nothing go wrong again for a week.

When him and the old lady come down in the morning, all the family got up out of their chairs and give them good-day, and didn't set down again till they had set down. Then Tom and Bob went to the sideboard where the decanters was, and mixed a glass of bitters and handed it to him, and he held it in his hand and waited till Tom's and Bob's was mixed, and then they bowed and said "Our duty to you, sir, and madam;" and *they* bowed the least bit in the world and said thank you, and so they drank, all three, and Bob and Tom poured a spoonful of water on the sugar and the mite of whisky or apple brandy in the bottom of their tumblers, and give it to me and Buck, and we drank to the old people too.

Bob was the oldest, and Tom next. Tall, beautiful men with very broad shoulders and brown faces, and long black hair and black eyes. They dressed in white linen from head to foot, like the old gentleman, and wore broad Panama hats.

Then there was Miss Charlotte, she was twenty-five, and tall and proud and grand, but as good as she could be, when she warn't stirred up; but when she was, she had a look that would make you wilt in your tracks, like her father. She was beautiful.

So was her sister, Miss Sophia, but it was a different kind. She was gentle and sweet, like a dove, and she was only twenty.

Each person had their own nigger to wait on them—Buck, too. My nigger had a monstrous easy time, because I warn't used to having anybody do anything for me, but Buck's was on the jump most of the time.

This was all there was of the family, now; but there used to be more—three sons; they got killed; and Emmeline that died.

The old gentleman owned a lot of farms, and over a hundred niggers. Sometimes a stack of people would come there, horseback, from ten or fifteen miles around, and stay five or six days, and have such junketings round about and on the river, and dances and picnics in the woods, day-times, and balls at the house, nights. These people was mostly kin-folks of the family. The men brought their guns with them. It was a handsome lot of quality, I tell you.

There was another clan of aristocracy around there—five or six families— mostly of the name of Shepherdson. They was as high-toned, and well born, and rich and grand, as the tribe of Grangerfords. The Shepherdsons and the Grangerfords used the same steamboat landing, which was about two mile above our house; so sometimes when I went up there with a lot of our folks I used to see a lot of Shepherdsons there, on their fine horses.

8. Flagpole.

One day Buck and me was away out in the woods, hunting, and heard a horse coming. We was crossing the road. Buck says:

"Quick! Jump for the woods!"

We done it, and then peeped down the woods through the leaves. Pretty soon a splendid young man come galloping down the road, setting his horse easy and looking like a soldier. He had his gun across his pommel. I had seen him before. It was young Harney Shepherdson. I heard Buck's gun go off at my ear, and Harney's hat tumbled off from his head. He grabbed his gun and rode straight to the place where we was hid. But we didn't wait. We started through the woods on a run. The woods warn't thick, so I looked over my shoulder, to dodge the bullet, and twice I seen Harney cover Buck with his gun; and then he rode away the way he come—to get his hat, I reckon, but I couldn't see. We never stopped running till we got home. The old gentleman's eyes blazed a minute—'twas pleasure, mainly, I judged—then his face sort of smoothed down, and he says, kind of gentle:

"I don't like that shooting from behind a bush. Why didn't you step into the road, my boy?"

"The Shepherdsons don't, father. They always take advantage."

Miss Charlotte she held her head up like a queen while Buck was telling his tale, and her nostrils spread and her eyes snapped. The two young men looked dark, but never said nothing. Miss Sophia she turned pale, but the color come back when she found the man warn't hurt.

Soon as I could get Buck down by the corn-cribs under the trees by ourselves, I says:

"Did you want to kill him, Buck?"

"Well, I bet I did."

"What did he do to you?"

"Him? He never done nothing to me."

"Well, then, what did you want to kill him for?"

"Why nothing—only it's on account of the feud."

"What's a feud?"

"Why, where was you raised? Don't you know what a feud is?"

"Never heard of it before—tell me about it."

"Well," says Buck, "a feud is this way. A man has a quarrel with another man, and kills him; then that other man's brother kills *him*; then the other brothers, on both sides, goes for one another; then the *cousins* chip in—and by-and-by everybody's killed off, and there ain't no more feud. But it's kind of slow, and takes a long time."

"Has this one been going on long, Buck?"

"Well I should *reckon!* it started thirty year ago, or som'ers along there. There was trouble 'bout something and then a lawsuit to settle it; and the suit went agin one of the men, and so he up and shot the man that won the suit—which he would naturally do, of course. Anybody would."

"What was the trouble about, Buck?—land?"

"I reckon maybe—I don't know."

"Well, who done the shooting?—was it a Grangerford or a Shepherdson?"

"Laws, how do *I* know? it was so long ago."

"Don't anybody know?"

"Oh, yes, pa knows, I reckon, and some of the other old folks; but they don't know, now, what the row was about in the first place."

"Has there been many killed, Buck?"

"Yes—right smart chance of funerals. But they don't always kill. Pa's got a few buck-shot in him; but he don't mind it 'cuz he don't weigh much anyway. Bob's been carved up some with a bowie, and Tom's been hurt once or twice."

"Has anybody been killed this year, Buck?"

"Yes, we got one and they got one. 'Bout three months ago, my cousin Bud, fourteen year old, was riding through the woods, on t'other side of the river, and didn't have no weapon with him, which was blame' foolishness, and in a lonesome place he hears a horse a-coming behind him, and sees old Baldy Shepherdson a-linkin' after him with his gun in his hand and his white hair a-flying in the wind; and 'stead of jumping off and taking to the brush, Bud 'lowed he could outrun him; so they had it, nip and tuck, for five mile or more, the old man a-gaining all the time; so at last Bud seen it warn't any use, so he stopped and faced around so as to have the bullet holes in front, you know, and the old man he rode up and shot him down. But he didn't git much chance to enjoy his luck, for inside of a week our folks laid *him* out."

"I reckon that old man was a coward, Buck."

"I reckon he *warn't* a coward. Not by a blame' sight. There ain't a coward amongst them Shepherdsons—not a one. And there ain't no cowards amongst the Grangerfords, either. Why, that old man kep' up his end in a fight one day, for a half an hour, against three Grangerfords, and come out winner. They was all a-horseback; he lit off of his horse and got behind a little wood-pile, and kep' his horse before him to stop the bullets; but the Grangerfords staid on their horses and capered around the old man, and peppered away at him, and he peppered away at them. Him and his horse both went home pretty leaky and crippled, but the Grangerfords had to be *fetched* home—and one of 'em was dead, and another died the next day. No, sir, if a body's out hunting for cowards, he don't want to fool away any time amongst them Shepherdsons, becuz they don't breed any of that *kind*."

Next Sunday we all went to church, about three mile, everybody a-horse-back. The men took their guns along, so did Buck, and kept them between their knees or stood them handy against the wall. The Shepherdsons done the same. It was pretty ornery preaching—all about brotherly love, and such-like tiresomeness; but everybody said it was a good sermon, and they all talked it over going home, and had such a powerful lot to say about faith, and good works, and free grace, and preforeordestination,[9] and I don't know what all, that it did seem to me to be one of the roughest Sundays I had run across yet.

About an hour after dinner everybody was dozing around, some in their chairs and some in their rooms, and it got to be pretty dull. Buck and a dog was stretched out on the grass in the sun, sound asleep. I went up to our room, and judged I would take a nap myself. I found that sweet Miss Sophia standing in her door, which was next to ours, and she took me in her room and shut the door very soft, and asked me if I liked her, and I said I did; and she asked me if I would do something for her and not tell anybody, and I said I would. Then she said she'd forgot her Testament, and left it in the seat at church, between two other books and would I slip out quiet and go there and fetch it to her, and not say nothing to nobody. I said I would. So I slid out and slipped off up the road, and there warn't anybody at the church, except maybe a hog or two, for there warn't any lock on the door, and hogs like a puncheon floor[1]

9. Huck combines the closely related Presbyterian terms *predestination* and *foreordination*.

1. A crude floor made from log slabs in which the flat side is turned up and the rounded side is set in the dirt.

in summer-time because it's cool. If you notice, most folks don't go to church only when they've got to; but a hog is different. Says I to myself something's up—it ain't natural for a girl to be in such a sweat about a Testament; so I give it a shake, and out drops a little piece of paper with "Half-past two" wrote on it with a pencil. I ransacked it, but couldn't find anything else. I couldn't make anything out of that, so I put the paper in the book again, and when I got home and up stairs, there was Miss Sophia in her door waiting for me. She pulled me in and shut the door; then she looked in the Testament till she found the paper, and as soon as she read it she looked glad; and before a body could think, she grabbed me and give me a squeeze, and said I was the best boy in the world, and not to tell anybody. She was mighty red in the face, for a minute, and her eyes lighted up and it made her powerful pretty. I was a good deal astonished, but when I got my breath I asked her what the paper was about, and she asked me if I had read it, and I said no, and she asked me if I could read writing, and I told her "no, only coarse-hand,"[2] and then she said the paper warn't anything but a book-mark to keep her place, and I might go and play now.

I went off down to the river, studying over this thing, and pretty soon I noticed that my nigger was following along behind. When we was out of sight of the house, he looked back and around a second, and then comes a-running, and says:

"Mars Jawge, if you'll come down into de swamp, I'll show you a whole stack o' water-moccasins."

Thinks I, that's mighty curious; he said that yesterday. He oughter know a body don't love water-moccasins enough to go around hunting for them. What is he up to anyway? So I says—

"All right, trot ahead."

I followed a half a mile, then he struck out over the swamp and waded ankle deep as much as another half mile. We come to a little flat piece of land which was dry and very thick with trees and bushes and vines, and he says—

"You shove right in dah, jist a few steps, Mars Jawge, dah's whah dey is. I's seed 'm befo', I don't k'yer to see 'em no mo'."

Then he slopped right along and went away, and pretty soon the trees hid him. I poked into the place a-ways, and come to a little open patch as big as a bedroom, all hung around with vines, and found a man laying there asleep—and by jings it was my old Jim!

I waked him up, and I reckoned it was going to be a grand surprise to him to see me again, but it warn't. He nearly cried, he was so glad, but he warn't surprised. Said he swum along behind me, that night, and heard me yell every time, but dasn't answer, because he didn't want nobody to pick *him* up, and take him into slavery again. Says he—

"I got hurt a little, en couldn't swim fas', so I wuz a considable ways behine you, towards de las'; when you landed I reck'ned I could ketch up wid you on de lan' 'dout havin' to shout at you; but when I see dat house I begin to go slow. I 'uz off too fur to hear what dey say to you—I wuz 'fraid o' de dogs—but when it 'uz all quiet again, I knowed you's in de house, so I struck out for de woods to wait for day. Early in de mawnin' some er de niggers come along, gwyne to de fields, en dey tuck me en showed me dis place, whah de dogs

2. Block printing.

can't track me on accounts o' de water, en dey brings me truck to eat every night, en tells me how you's a gitt'n along."

"Why didn't you tell my Jack to fetch me here sooner, Jim?"

"Well, 'twarn't no use to 'sturb you, Huck, tell we could do sumfn—but we's all right, now. I ben a-buyin' pots en pans en vittles, as I got a chanst, en a patchin' up de raf', nights, when—"

"*What* raft, Jim?"

"Our ole raf'."

"You mean to say our old raft warn't smashed all to flinders?"

"No, she warn't. She was tore up a good deal—one en' of her was—but dey warn't no great harm done, on'y our traps was mos' all los'. Ef we hadn' dive' so deep en swum so fur under water, en de night hadn' ben so dark, en we warn't so sk'yerd, en ben sich punkin-heads, as de sayin' is, we'd a seed de raf'. But it's jis' as well we didn't, 'kase now she's all fixed up agin mos' as good as new, en we's got a new lot o' stuff, too, in de place o' what 'uz los'."

"Why, how did you get hold of the raft again, Jim—did you catch her?"

"How I gwyne to ketch her, en I out in de woods? No, some er de niggers foun' her ketched on a snag, along heah in de ben', en dey hid her in a crick, 'mongst de willows, en dey wuz so much jawin' 'bout which un 'um she b'long to de mos', dat I come to heah 'bout it pooty soon, so I ups en settles de trouble by tellin' um she don't b'long to none uv um, but to you en me; en I ast 'm if dey gwyne to grab a young white genlman's propaty, en git a hid'n for it? Den I gin 'm ten cents apiece, en dey 'uz mighty well satisfied, en wisht some mo' raf's 'ud come along en make 'm rich agin. Dey's mighty good to me, dese niggers is, en whatever I wants 'm to do fur me, I doan' have to ast 'm twice, honey. Dat Jack's a good nigger, en pooty smart."

"Yes, he is. He ain't ever told me you was here; told me to come, and he'd show me a lot of water-moccasins. If anything happens, *he* ain't mixed up in it. He can say he never seen us together, and it'll be the truth."

I don't want to talk much about the next day. I reckon I'll cut it pretty short. I waked up about dawn, and was agoing to turn over and go to sleep again, when I noticed how still it was—didn't seem to be anybody stirring. That warn't usual. Next I noticed that Buck was up and gone. Well, I gets up, a-wondering, and goes down stairs—nobody around; everything as still as a mouse. Just the same outside; thinks I, what does it mean? Down by the wood-pile I comes across my Jack, and says:

"What's it all about?"

Says he:

"Don't you know, Mars Jawge?"

"No," says I, "I don't."

"Well, den, Miss Sophia's run off! 'deed she has. She run off in de night, sometime—nobody don't know jis' when—run off to git married to dat young Harney Shepherdson, you know—leastways, so dey 'spec. De fambly foun' it out, 'bout half an hour ago—maybe a little mo'—en' I *tell* you dey warn't no time los'. Sich another hurryin' up guns en hosses *you* never see! De women folks has gone for to stir up de relations, en ole Mars Saul en de boys tuck dey guns en rode up de river road for to try to ketch dat young man en kill him 'fo' he kin git acrost de river wid Miss Sophia. I reck'n dey's gwyne to be mighty rough times."

"Buck went off 'thout waking me up."

"Well I reck'n he *did!* Dey warn't gwyne to mix you up in it. Mars Buck he loaded up his gun en 'lowed he's gwyne to fetch home a Shepherdson or bust. Well, dey'll be plenty un 'm dah, I reck'n, en you bet you he'll fetch one ef he gits a chanst."

I took up the river road as hard as I could put. By-and-by I begin to hear guns a good ways off. When I come in sight of the log store and the wood-pile where the steamboats lands, I worked along under the trees and brush till I got to a good place, and then I clumb up into the forks of a cotton-wood that was out of reach, and watched. There was a wood-rank four foot high,[3] a little ways in front of the tree, and first I was going to hide behind that; but maybe it was luckier I didn't.

There was four or five men cavorting around on their horses in the open place before the log store, cussing and yelling, and trying to get at a couple of young chaps that was behind the wood-rank alongside of the steamboat landing—but they couldn't come it. Every time one of them showed himself on the river side of the wood-pile he got shot at. The two boys was squatting back to back behind the pile, so they could watch both ways.

By-and-by the men stopped cavorting around and yelling. They started riding towards the store; then up gets one of the boys, draws a steady bead over the wood-rank, and drops one of them out of his saddle. All the men jumped off of their horses and grabbed the hurt one and started to carry him to the store; and that minute the two boys started on the run. They got half-way to the tree I was in before the men noticed. Then the men see them, and jumped on their horses and took out after them. They gained on the boys, but it didn't do no good, the boys had too good a start; they got to the wood-pile that was in front of my tree, and slipped in behind it, and so they had the bulge[4] on the men again. One of the boys was Buck, and the other was a slim young chap about nineteen years old.

The men ripped around awhile, and then rode away. As soon as they was out of sight, I sung out to Buck and told him. He didn't know what to make of my voice coming out of the tree, at first. He was awful surprised. He told me to watch out sharp and let him know when the men come in sight again; said they was up to some devilment or other—wouldn't be gone long. I wished I was out of that tree, but I dasn't come down. Buck began to cry and rip, and 'lowed that him and his cousin Joe (that was the other young chap) would make up for this day, yet. He said his father and his two brothers was killed, and two or three of the enemy. Said the Shepherdsons laid for them, in ambush. Buck said his father and brothers ought to waited for their relations— the Shepherdsons was too strong for them. I asked him what was become of young Harney and Miss Sophia. He said they'd got across the river and was safe. I was glad of that; but the way Buck did take on because he didn't manage to kill Harney that day he shot at him—I hain't ever heard anything like it.

All of a sudden, bang! bang! bang! goes three or four guns—the men had slipped around through the woods and come in from behind without their horses! The boys jumped for the river—both of them hurt—and as they swum down the current the men run along the bank shooting at them and singing out, "Kill them, kill them!" It made me so sick I most fell out of the tree. I ain't agoing to tell *all* that happened!—it would make me sick again if I was to do that. I wished I hadn't ever come ashore that night, to see such things. I ain't ever going to get shut of them—lots of times I dream about them.

---

3. Half a cord of stacked firewood.    4. Upper hand.

I staid in the tree till it begun to get dark, afraid to come down. Some- times I heard guns away off in the woods; and twice I seen little gangs of men gallop past the log store with guns; so I reckoned the trouble was still agoing on. I was mighty downhearted; so I made up my mind I wouldn't ever go anear that house again, because I reckoned I was to blame, somehow. I judged that that piece of paper meant that Miss Sophia was to meet Harney somewheres at half-past two and run off; and I judged I ought to told her father about that paper and the curious way she acted, and then maybe he would a locked her up and this awful mess wouldn't ever happened.

When I got down out of the tree, I crept along down the river bank a piece, and found the two bodies laying in the edge of the water, and tugged at them till I got them ashore; then I covered up their faces, and got away as quick as I could. I cried a little when I was covering up Buck's face, for he was mighty good to me.

It was just dark, now. I never went near the house, but struck through the woods and made for the swamp. Jim warn't on his island, so I tramped off in a hurry for the crick, and crowded through the willows, red-hot to jump aboard and get out of that awful country—the raft was gone! My souls, but I was scared! I couldn't get my breath for most a minute. Then I raised a yell. A voice not twenty-five foot from me, says—

"Good lan'! is dat you, honey? Doan' make no noise."

It was Jim's voice—nothing ever sounded so good before. I run along the bank a piece and got aboard, and Jim he grabbed me and hugged me, he was so glad to see me. He says—

"Laws bless you, chile, I 'uz right down sho' you's dead agin. Jack's been heah, he say he reck'n you's ben shot, kase you didn' come home no mo'; so I's jes' dis minute a startin' de raf' down towards de mouf er de crick, so's to be all ready for to shove out en leave soon as Jack comes agin en tells me for certain you *is* dead. Lawsy, I's mighty glad to git you back agin, honey."

I says—

"All right—that's mighty good; they won't find me, and they'll think I've been killed, and floated down the river—there's something up there that'll help them to think so—so don't you lose no time, Jim, but just shove off for the big water as fast as ever you can."

I never felt easy till the raft was two mile below there and out in the middle of the Mississippi. Then we hung up our signal lantern, and judged that we was free and safe once more. I hadn't had a bite to eat since yesterday; so Jim he got out some corn-dodgers[5] and buttermilk, and pork and cabbage, and greens—there ain't nothing in the world so good, when it's cooked right—and whilst I eat my supper we talked, and had a good time. I was powerful glad to get away from the feuds, and so was Jim to get away from the swamp. We said there warn't no home like a raft, after all. Other places do seem so cramped up and smothery, but a raft don't. You feel mighty free and easy and comfort- able on a raft.

## Chapter XIX

Two or three days and nights went by; I reckon I might say they swum by, they slid along so quiet and smooth and lovely. Here is the way we put in the

---

5. Hard cornmeal rolls or cakes.

time. It was a monstrous big river down there—sometimes a mile and a half wide; we run nights, and laid up and hid day-times; soon as night was most gone, we stopped navigating and tied up—nearly always in the dead water under a tow-head; and then cut young cottonwoods and willows and hid the raft with them. Then we set out the lines. Next we slid into the river and had a swim, so as to freshen up and cool off; then we set down on the sandy bottom where the water was about knee deep, and watched the daylight come. Not a sound, anywheres—perfectly still—just like the whole world was asleep, only sometimes the bull-frogs a-cluttering, maybe. The first thing to see, looking away over the water, was a kind of dull line—that was the woods on t'other side—you couldn't make nothing else out; then a pale place in the sky; then more paleness, spreading around; then the river softened up, away off, and warn't black any more, but gray; you could see little dark spots drifting along, ever so far away—trading scows, and such things; and long black streaks—rafts; sometimes you could hear a sweep screaking; or jumbled up voices, it was so still, and sounds come so far; and by-and-by you could see a streak on the water which you know by the look of the streak that there's a snag there in a swift current which breaks on it and makes that streak look that way; and you see the mist curl up off of the water, and the east reddens up, and the river, and you make out a log cabin in the edge of the woods, away on the bank on t'other side of the river, being a wood-yard, likely, and piled by them cheats so you can throw a dog through it anywheres;[6] then the nice breeze springs up, and comes fanning you from over there, so cool and fresh, and sweet to smell, on account of the woods and the flowers; but sometimes not that way, because they've left dead fish laying around, gars, and such, and they do get pretty rank; and next you've got the full day, and everything smiling in the sun, and the song-birds just going it!

A little smoke couldn't be noticed, now, so we would take some fish off of the lines, and cook up a hot breakfast. And afterwards we would watch the lonesomeness of the river, and kind of lazy along, and by-and-by lazy off to sleep. Wake up, by-and-by, and look to see what done it, and maybe see a steamboat coughing along up stream, so far off towards the other side you couldn't tell nothing about her only whether she was stern-wheel or side-wheel; then for about an hour there wouldn't be nothing to hear nor nothing to see—just solid lonesomeness. Next you'd see a raft sliding by, away off yonder, and maybe a galoot on it chopping, because they're almost always doing it on a raft; you'd see the ax flash, and come down—you don't hear nothing; you see that ax go up again, and by the time it's above the man's head, then you hear the *k'chunk!*—it had took all that time to come over the water. So we would put in the day, lazying around, listening to the stillness. Once there was a thick fog, and the rafts and things that went by was beating tin pans so the steamboats wouldn't run over them. A scow or a raft went by so close we could hear them talking and cussing and laughing—heard them plain; but we couldn't see no sign of them; it made you feel crawly, it was like spirits carrying on that way in the air. Jim said he believed it was spirits; but I says:

"No, spirits wouldn't say, 'dern the dern fog.' "

Soon as it was night, out we shoved; when we got her out to about the middle, we let her alone, and let her float wherever the current wanted her to;

---

6. Stacks of wood in this yard were sold by their volume, gappage included.

then we lit the pipes, and dangled our legs in the water and talked about all kinds of things—we was always naked, day and night, whenever the mosquitoes would let us—the new clothes Buck's folks made for me was too good to be comfortable, and besides I didn't go much on clothes, nohow.

Sometimes we'd have that whole river all to ourselves for the longest time. Yonder was the banks and the islands, across the water; and maybe a spark—which was a candle in a cabin window—and sometimes on the water you could see a spark or two—on a raft or a scow, you know; and maybe you could hear a fiddle or a song coming over from one of them crafts. It's lovely to live on a raft. We had the sky, up there, all speckled with stars, and we used to lay on our backs and look up at them, and discuss about whether they was made, or only just happened—Jim he allowed they was made, but I allowed they happened; I judged it would have took too long to *make* so many. Jim said the moon could a *laid* them; well, that looked kind of reasonable, so I didn't say nothing against it, because I've seen a frog lay most as many, so of course it could be done. We used to watch the stars that fell, too, and see them streak down. Jim allowed they'd got spoiled and was hove out of the nest.

Once or twice of a night we would see a steamboat slipping along in the dark, and now and then she would belch a whole world of sparks up out of her chimbleys, and they would rain down in the river and look awful pretty; then she would turn a corner and her lights would wink out and her pow-wow shut off and leave the river still again; and by-and-by her waves would get to us, a long time after she was gone, and joggle the raft a bit, and after that you wouldn't hear nothing for you couldn't tell how long, except maybe frogs or something.

After midnight the people on shore went to bed, and then for two or three hours the shores was black—no more sparks in the cabin windows. These sparks was our clock—the first one that showed again meant morning was coming, so we hunted a place to hide and tie up, right away.

One morning about day-break, I found a canoe and crossed over a chute[7] to the main shore—it was only two hundred yards—and paddled about a mile up a crick amongst the cypress woods, to see if I couldn't get some berries. Just as I was passing a place where a kind of a cow-path crossed the crick, here comes a couple of men tearing up the path as tight as they could foot it. I thought I was a goner, for whenever anybody was after anybody I judged it was *me*—or maybe Jim. I was about to dig out from there in a hurry, but they was pretty close to me then, and sung out and begged me to save their lives—said they hadn't been doing nothing, and was being chased for it—said there was men and dogs a-coming. They wanted to jump right in, but I says—

"Don't you do it. I don't hear the dogs and horses yet; you've got time to crowd through the brush and get up the crick a little ways; then you take to the water and wade down to me and get in—that'll throw the dogs off the scent."

They done it, and soon as they was aboard I lit out for our tow-head, and in about five or ten minutes we heard the dogs and the men away off, shouting. We heard them come along towards the crick, but couldn't see them; they seemed to stop and fool around a while; then, as we got further and further away all the time, we couldn't hardly hear them at all; by the time we had left

---

7. A narrow channel with swift-flowing water.

a mile of woods behind us and struck the river, everything was quiet, and we paddled over to the tow-head and hid in the cotton-woods and was safe.

One of these fellows was about seventy, or upwards, and had a bald head and very gray whiskers. He had an old battered-up slouch hat on, and a greasy blue woolen shirt, and ragged old blue jeans britches stuffed into his boot tops, and home-knit galluses[8]—no, he only had one. He had an old long-tailed blue jeans coat with slick brass buttons, flung over his arm, and both of them had big fat ratty-looking carpet-bags.

The other fellow was about thirty and dressed about as ornery. After breakfast we all laid off and talked, and the first thing that come out was that these chaps didn't know one another.

"What got you into trouble?" says the baldhead to t'other chap.

"Well, I'd been selling an article to take the tartar off the teeth—and it does take it off, too, and generly the enamel along with it—but I staid about one night longer than I ought to, and was just in the act of sliding out when I ran across you on the trail this side of town, and you told me they were coming, and begged me to help you to get off. So I told you I was expecting trouble myself and would scatter out *with* you. That's the whole yarn—what's yourn?"

"Well, I'd ben a-runnin' a little temperance revival thar, 'bout a week, and was the pet of the women-folks, big and little, for I was makin' it mighty warm for the rummies, I *tell* you, and takin' as much as five or six dollars a night— ten cents a head, children and niggers free—and business a growin' all the time; when somehow or another a little report got around, last night, that I had a way of puttin' in my time with a private jug, on the sly. A nigger rousted me out this mornin', and told me the people was getherin' on the quiet, with their dogs and horses, and they'd be along pretty soon and give me 'bout half an hour's start, and then run me down, if they could; and if they got me they'd tar and feather me and ride me on a rail, sure. I didn't wait for no breakfast— I warn't hungry."

"Old man," says the young one, "I reckon we might double-team it together; what do you think?"

"I ain't undisposed. What's your line—mainly?"

"Jour printer,[9] by trade; do a little in patent medicines; theatre-actor—tragedy, you know; take a turn at mesmerism and phrenology,[1] when there's a chance; teach singing-geography school for a change; sling a lecture, sometimes—oh, I do lots of things—most anything that comes handy, so it ain't work. What's your lay?"[2]

"I've done considerable in the doctoring way in my time. Layin' on o' hands is my best holt—for cancer, and paralysis, and sich things; and I k'n tell a fortune pretty good, when I've got somebody along to find out the facts for me. Preachin's my line, too; and workin' camp-meetin's; and missionaryin' around."

Nobody never said anything for a while; then the young man hove a sigh and says—

"Alas!"

---

8. Suspenders.
9. A journeyman-printer, not yet a salaried master-printer, who worked by the day.
1. The study of the shape of the skull as an indicator of

mental acumen and character. "Mesmerism": hypnotic induction involving animal magnetism.
2. Work, in the sense here of hustle or scheme.

"What 're you alassin' about?" says the baldhead.

"To think I should have lived to be leading such a life, and be degraded down into such company." And he begun to wipe the corner of his eye with a rag.

"Dern your skin, ain't the company good enough for you?" says the baldhead, pretty pert and uppish.

"Yes, it *is* good enough for me; it's as good as I deserve; for who fetched me so low, when I was so high? *I* did myself. I don't blame *you*, gentlemen—far from it; I don't blame anybody. I deserve it all. Let the cold world do its worst; one thing I know—there's a grave somewhere for me. The world may go on just as its always done, and take everything from me—loved ones, property, everything—but it can't take that. Some day I'll lie down in it and forget it all, and my poor broken heart will be at rest." He went on a-wiping.

"Drot your pore broken heart," says the baldhead; "what are you heaving your pore broken heart at *us* f'r? *We* hain't done nothing."

"No, I know you haven't. I ain't blaming you, gentlemen. I brought myself down—yes, I did it myself. It's right I should suffer—perfectly right—I don't make any moan."

"Brought you down from whar? Whar was you brought down from?"

"Ah, you would not believe me; the world never believes—let it pass—'tis no matter. The secret of my birth—"

"The secret of your birth? Do you mean to say—"

"Gentlemen," says the young man, very solemn, "I will reveal it to you, for I feel I may have confidence in you. By rights I am a duke!"

Jim's eyes bugged out when he heard that; and I reckon mine did, too. Then the baldhead says: "No! you can't mean it?"

"Yes. My great-grandfather, eldest son of the Duke of Bridgewater, fled to this country about the end of the last century, to breathe the pure air of freedom; married here, and died, leaving a son, his own father dying about the same time. The second son of the late duke seized the title and estates—the infant real duke was ignored. I am the lineal descendant of that infant—I am the rightful Duke of Bridgewater; and here am I, forlorn, torn from my high estate, hunted of men, despised by the cold world, ragged, worn, heart-broken, and degraded to the companionship of felons on a raft!"

Jim pitied him ever so much, and so did I. We tried to comfort him, but he said it warn't much use, he couldn't be much comforted; said if we was a mind to acknowledge him, that would do him more good than most anything else; so we said we would, if he would tell us how. He said we ought to bow, when we spoke to him, and say "Your Grace," or "My Lord," or "Your Lordship"— and he wouldn't mind it if we called him plain "Bridgewater," which he said was a title, anyway, and not a name; and one of us ought to wait on him at dinner, and do any little thing for him he wanted done.

Well, that was all easy, so we done it. All through dinner Jim stood around and waited on him, and says, "Will yo' Grace have some o' dis, or some o' dat?" and so on, and a body could see it was mighty pleasing to him.

But the old man got pretty silent, by-and-by—didn't have much to say, and didn't look pretty comfortable over all that petting that was going on around that duke. He seemed to have something on his mind. So, along in the afternoon, he says:

"Looky here, Bilgewater," he says, "I'm nation sorry for you, but you ain't the only person that's had troubles like that."

"No?"

"No, you ain't. You ain't the only person that's ben snaked down wrongfully out'n a high place."

"Alas!"

"No, you ain't the only person that's had a secret of his birth." And by jings, *he* begins to cry.

"Hold! What do you mean?"

"Bilgewater, kin I trust you?" says the old man, still sort of sobbing.

"To the bitter death!" He took the old man by the hand and squeezed it, and says, "The secret of your being: speak!"

"Bilgewater, I am the late Dauphin!"[3]

You bet you Jim and me stared, this time. Then the duke says:

"You are what?"

"Yes, my friend, it is too true—your eyes is lookin' at this very moment on the pore disappeared Dauphin, Looy the Seventeen, son of Looy the Sixteen and Marry Antonette."

"You! At your age! No! You mean you're the late Charlemagne;[4] you must be six or seven hundred years old, at the very least."

"Trouble has done it, Bilgewater, trouble has done it; trouble has brung these gray hairs and this premature balditude. Yes, gentlemen, you see before you, in blue jeans and misery, the wanderin', exiled, trampled-on and sufferin' rightful King of France."

Well, he cried and took on so, that me and Jim didn't know hardly what to do, we was so sorry—and so glad and proud we'd got him with us, too. So we set in, like we done before with the duke, and tried to comfort *him*. But he said it warn't no use, nothing but to be dead and done with it all could do him any good; though he said it often made him feel easier and better for a while if people treated him according to his rights, and got down on one knee to speak to him, and always called him "Your Majesty," and waited on him first at meals, and didn't set down in his presence till he asked them. So Jim and me set to majestying him, and doing this and that and t'other for him, and standing up till he told us we might set down. This done him heaps of good, and so he got cheerful and comfortable. But the duke kind of soured on him, and didn't look a bit satisfied with the way things was going; still, the king acted real friendly towards him, and said the duke's great-grandfather and all the other Dukes of Bilgewater was a good deal thought of by *his* father and was allowed to come to the palace considerable; but the duke staid huffy a good while, till by-and-by the king says:

"Like as not we got to be together a blamed long time, on this h-yer raft, Bilgewater, and so what's the use o' your bein' sour? It'll only make things oncomfortable. It ain't my fault I warn't born a duke, it ain't your fault you warn't born a king—so what's the use to worry? Make the best o' things the way you find 'em, says I—that's my motto. This ain't no bad thing that we've struck here—plenty grub and an easy life—come, give us your hand, Duke, and less all be friends."

The duke done it, and Jim and me was pretty glad to see it. It took away all the uncomfortableness, and we felt mighty good over it, because it would a been a miserable business to have any unfriendliness on the raft; for what you

---

3. The Dauphin, born in 1785, would have been in his mid-fifties or sixties had he survived.

4. Charlemagne (742–814) established the Holy Roman Empire.

want, above all things, on a raft, is for everybody to be satisfied, and feel right and kind towards the others.

It didn't take me long to make up my mind that these liars warn't no kings nor dukes, at all, but just low-down humbugs and frauds. But I never said nothing, never let on; kept it to myself; it's the best way; then you don't have no quarrels, and don't get into no trouble. If they wanted us to call them kings and dukes, I hadn't no objections, 'long as it would keep peace in the family; and it warn't no use to tell Jim, so I didn't tell him. If I never learnt nothing else out of pap, I learnt that the best way to get along with his kind of people is to let them have their own way.

## Chapter XX

They asked us considerable many questions; wanted to know what we covered up the raft that way for, and laid by in the daytime instead of running—was Jim a runaway nigger? Says I—

"Goodness sakes, would a runaway nigger run *south?*"

No, they allowed he wouldn't. I had to account for things some way, so I says:

"My folks was living in Pike County, in Missouri, where I was born, and they all died off but me and pa and my brother Ike. Pa, he 'lowed he'd break up and go down and live with Uncle Ben, who's got a little one-horse place on the river, forty-four mile below Orleans. Pa was pretty poor, and had some debts; so when he'd squared up there warn't nothing left but sixteen dollars and our nigger, Jim. That warn't enough to take us fourteen hundred mile, deck passage nor no other way. Well, when the river rose, pa had a streak of luck one day; he ketched this piece of a raft; so we reckoned we'd go down to Orleans on it. Pa's luck didn't hold out; a steamboat run over the forrard corner of the raft, one night, and we all went overboard and dove under the wheel; Jim and me come up, all right, but pa was drunk, and Ike was only four years old, so they never come up no more. Well, for the next day or two we had considerable trouble, because people was always coming out in skiffs and trying to take Jim away from me, saying they believed he was a runaway nigger. We don't run day-times no more, now; nights they don't bother us."

The duke says—

"Leave me alone to cipher out a way so we can run in the daytime if we want to. I'll think the thing over—I'll invent a plan that'll fix it. We'll let it alone for to-day, because of course we don't want to go by that town yonder in daylight—it mightn't be healthy."

Towards night it begun to darken up and look like rain; the heat lightning was squirting around, low down in the sky, and the leaves was beginning to shiver—it was going to be pretty ugly, it was easy to see that. So the duke and the king went to overhauling our wigwam, to see what the beds was like. My bed was a straw tick[5]—better than Jim's, which was a corn-shuck tick; there's always cobs around about in a shuck tick, and they poke into you and hurt; and when you roll over, the dry shucks sound like you was rolling over in a pile of dead leaves; it makes such a rustling that you wake up. Well, the duke

5. Mattress.

allowed he would take my bed; but the king allowed he wouldn't. He says—
"I should a reckoned the difference in rank would a sejested to you that a corn-shuck bed warn't just fitten for me to sleep on. Your Grace'll take the shuck bed yourself."

Jim and me was in a sweat again, for a minute, being afraid there was going to be some more trouble amongst them; so we was pretty glad when the duke says—

" 'Tis my fate to be always ground into the mire under the iron heel of oppression. Misfortune has broken my once haughty spirit; I yield, I submit; 'tis my fate. I am alone in the world—let me suffer; I can bear it."

We got away as soon as it was good and dark. The king told us to stand well out towards the middle of the river, and not show a light till we got a long ways below the town. We come in sight of the little bunch of lights by-and-by—that was the town, you know—and slid by, about a half a mile out, all right. When we was three-quarters of a mile below, we hoisted up our signal lantern; and about ten o'clock it come on to rain and blow and thunder and lighten like everything; so the king told us to both stay on watch till the weather got better; then him and the duke crawled into the wigwam and turned in for the night. It was my watch below, till twelve, but I wouldn't a turned in, anyway, if I'd had a bed; because a body don't see such a storm as that every day in the week, not by a long sight. My souls, how the wind did scream along! And every second or two there'd come a glare that lit up the white-caps for a half a mile around, and you'd see the islands looking dusty through the rain, and the trees thrashing around in the wind; then comes a *h-wack!*—bum! bum! bumble-umble-um-bum-bum-bum-bum—and the thunder would go rumbling and grumbling away, and quit—and then *rip* comes another flash and another sock-dolager.[6] The waves most washed me off the raft, sometimes, but I hadn't any clothes on, and didn't mind. We didn't have no trouble about snags; the lightning was glaring and flittering around so constant that we could see them plenty soon enough to throw her head this way or that and miss them.

I had the middle watch, you know, but I was pretty sleepy by that time, so Jim he said he would stand the first half of it for me; he was always mighty good, that way, Jim was. I crawled into the wigwam, but the king and the duke had their legs sprawled around so there warn't no show for me; so I laid outside—I didn't mind the rain, because it was warm, and the waves warn't running so high, now. About two they come up again, though, and Jim was going to call me, but he changed his mind because he reckoned they warn't high enough yet to do any harm; but he was mistaken about that, for pretty soon all of a sudden along comes a regular ripper, and washed me overboard. It most killed Jim a-laughing. He was the easiest nigger to laugh that ever was, anyway.

I took the watch, and Jim he laid down and snored away; and by-and-by the storm let up for good and all; and the first cabin-light that showed, I rousted him out and we slid the raft into hiding-quarters for the day.

The king got out an old ratty deck of cards, after breakfast, and him and the duke played seven-up a while, five cents a game. Then they got tired of it, and allowed they would "lay out a campaign," as they called it. The duke went

6. Something exceptionally strong or climactic.

down into his carpet-bag and fetched up a lot of little printed bills, and read them out loud. One bill said "The celebrated Dr. Armand de Montalban of Paris," would "lecture on the Science of Phrenology" at such and such a place, on the blank day of blank, at ten cents admission, and "furnish charts of character at twenty-five cents apiece." The duke said that was *him*. In another bill he was the "world renowned Shaksperean tragedian, Garrick the Younger,[7] of Drury Lane, London." In other bills he had a lot of other names and done other wonderful things, like finding water and gold with a "divining rod," "dissipating witch-spells," and so on. By-and-by he says—

"But the histrionic muse is the darling. Have you ever trod the boards, Royalty?"

"No," says the king.

"You shall, then, before you're three days older, Fallen Grandeur," says the duke. "The first good town we come to, we'll hire a hall and do the sword-fight in Richard III. and the balcony scene in Romeo and Juliet. How does that strike you?"

"I'm in, up to the hub, for anything that will pay, Bilgewater, but you see I don't know nothing about play-actn', and hain't ever seen much of it. I was too small when pap used to have 'em at the palace. Do you reckon you can learn me?"

"Easy!"

"All right. I'm jist a-freezn' for something fresh, anyway. Less commence, right away."

So the duke he told him all about who Romeo was, and who Juliet was, and said he was used to being Romeo, so the king could be Juliet.

"But if Juliet's such a young gal, Duke, my peeled head and my white whiskers is goin' to look oncommon odd on her, maybe."

"No, don't you worry—these country jakes won't ever think of that. Besides, you know, you'll be in costume, and that makes all the difference in the world; Juliet's in a balcony, enjoying the moonlight before she goes to bed, and she's got on her night-gown and her ruffled night-cap. Here are the costumes for the parts."

He got out two or three curtain-calico suits, which he said was meedyevil armor for Richard III. and t'other chap, and a long white cotton night-shirt and a ruffled night-cap to match. The king was satisfied; so the duke got out his book and read the parts over in the most splendid spread-eagle way, prancing around and acting at the same time, to show how it had got to be done; then he give the book to the king and told him to get his part by heart.

There was a little one-horse town about three mile down the bend, and after dinner the duke said he had ciphered out his idea about how to run in daylight without it being dangersome for Jim; so he allowed he would go down to the town and fix that thing. The king allowed he would go too, and see if he couldn't strike something. We was out of coffee, so Jim said I better go along with them in the canoe and get some.

When we got there, there warn't nobody stirring; streets empty, and perfectly dead and still, like Sunday. We found a sick nigger sunning himself in a back yard, and he said everybody that warn't too young or too sick or too old, was gone to camp-meeting, about two mile back in the woods. The king got the

---

7. David Garrick (1717–1779) was a famous tragedian at the Theatre Royal in Drury Lane, London.

directions, and allowed he'd go and work that camp-meeting for all it was worth, and I might go, too.[8]

The duke said what he was after was a printing office. We found it; a little bit of a concern, up over a carpenter shop—carpenters and printers all gone to the meeting, and no doors locked. It was a dirty, littered-up place, and had ink marks, and handbills with pictures of horses and runaway niggers on them, all over the walls. The duke shed his coat and said he was all right, now. So me and the king lit out for the camp-meeting.

We got there in about a half an hour, fairly dripping, for it was a most awful hot day. There was as much as a thousand people there, from twenty mile around. The woods was full of teams and wagons, hitched everywheres, feeding out of the wagon troughs and stomping to keep off the flies. There was sheds made out of poles and roofed over with branches, where they had lemonade and gingerbread to sell, and piles of watermelons and green corn and such-like truck.

The preaching was going on under the same kinds of sheds, only they was bigger and held crowds of people. The benches was made out of outside slabs of logs, with holes bored in the round side to drive sticks into for legs. They didn't have no backs. The preachers had high platforms to stand on, at one end of the sheds. The women had on sunbonnets; and some had linsey-woolsey frocks, some gingham ones, and a few of the young ones had on calico. Some of the young men was barefooted, and some of the children didn't have on any clothes but just a tow-linen[9] shirt. Some of the old women was knitting, and some of the young folks was courting on the sly.

The first shed we come to, the preacher was lining out a hymn. He lined out two lines, everybody sung it, and it was kind of grand to hear it, there was so many of them and they done it in such a rousing way; then he lined out two more for them to sing—and so on. The people woke up more and more, and sung louder and louder; and towards the end, some begun to groan, and some begun to shout. Then the preacher begun to preach; and begun in earnest, too; and went weaving first to one side of the platform and then the other, and then a leaning down over the front of it, with his arms and his body going all the time, and shouting his words out with all his might; and every now and then he would hold up his Bible and spread it open, and kind of pass it around this way and that, shouting, "It's the brazen serpent in the wilderness! Look upon it and live!" And people would shout out, "Glory!—A-a-men!" And so he went on, and the people groaning and crying and saying amen:

"Oh, come to the mourners' bench![1] come, black with sin! (amen!) come, sick and sore! (amen!) come, lame and halt, and blind! (amen!) come, pore and needy, sunk in shame! (a-a-men!) come all that's worn, and soiled, and suffering!—come with a broken spirit! come with a contrite heart! come in your rags and sin and dirt! the waters that cleanse is free, the door of heaven stands open—oh, enter in and be at rest!" (a-a-men! glory, glory hallelujah!)

And so on. You couldn't make out what the preacher said, any more, on account of the shouting and crying. Folks got up, everywheres in the crowd,

---

8. Notoriously easy pickings for confidence men, camp meetings are extended evangelical meetings held in the open air. Families camp nearby for the duration of the event. One of the best-known literary renderings of this stock situation was Johnson J. Hooper's *The Captain Attends a Camp-Meeting*.

9. Coarse linen cloth. "Linsey-woolsey": cheap, often homespun, unpatterned cloth composed of wool and flax. "Gingham" and "Calico" are inexpensive, store-bought printed cotton.

1. Front-row pews filled by penitents.

and worked their way, just by main strength, to the mourners' bench, with the tears running down their faces; and when all the mourners had got up there to the front benches in a crowd, they sung, and shouted, and flung themselves down on the straw, just crazy and wild.

Well, the first I knowed, the king got agoing; and you could hear him over everybody; and next he went a-charging up on to the platform and the preacher he begged him to speak to the people, and he done it. He told them he was a pirate—been a pirate for thirty years, out in the Indian Ocean, and his crew was thinned out considerable, last spring, in a fight, and he was home now, to take out some fresh men, and thanks to goodness he'd been robbed last night, and put ashore off of a steamboat without a cent, and he was glad of it, it was the blessedest thing that ever happened to him, because he was a changed man now, and happy for the first time in his life; and poor as he was, he was going to start right off and work his way back to the Indian Ocean and put in the rest of his life trying to turn the pirates into the true path; for he could do it better than anybody else, being acquainted with all the pirate crews in that ocean; and though it would take him a long time to get there, without money, he would get there anyway, and every time he convinced a pirate he would say to him, "Don't you thank me, don't you give me no credit, it all belongs to them dear people in Pokeville camp-meeting, natural brothers and benefactors of the race—and that dear preacher there, the truest friend a pirate ever had!"

And then he busted into tears, and so did everybody. Then somebody sings out, "Take up a collection for him, take up a collection!" Well, a half a dozen made a jump to do it, but somebody sings out, "Let *him* pass the hat around!" Then everybody said it, the preacher too.

So the king went all through the crowd with his hat, swabbing his eyes, and blessing the people and praising them and thanking them for being so good to the poor pirates away off there; and every little while the prettiest kind of girls, with the tears running down their cheeks, would up and ask him would he let them kiss him, for to remember him by; and he always done it; and some of them he hugged and kissed as many as five or six times—and he was invited to stay a week; and everybody wanted him to live in their houses, and said they'd think it was an honor; but he said as this was the last day of the camp-meeting he couldn't do no good, and besides he was in a sweat to get to the Indian Ocean right off and go to work on the pirates.

When we got back to the raft and he come to count up, he found he had collected eighty-seven dollars and seventy-five cents. And then he had fetched away a three-gallon jug of whisky, too, that he found under a wagon when we was starting home through the woods. The king said, take it all around, it laid over any day he'd ever put in in the missionarying line. He said it warn't no use talking, heathens don't amount to shucks, alongside of pirates, to work a camp-meeting with.

The duke was thinking *he'd* been doing pretty well, till the king come to show up, but after that he didn't think so so much. He had set up and printed off two little jobs for farmers, in that printing office—horse bills—and took the money, four dollars. And he had got in ten dollars worth of advertisements for the paper, which he said he would put in for four dollars if they would pay in advance—so they done it. The price of the paper was two dollars a year, but he took in three subscriptions for half a dollar apiece on condition of them paying him in advance; they were going to pay in cord-wood and onions, as usual, but he said he had just bought the concern and knocked down the price as low as he could afford it, and was going to run it for cash. He set up a little piece of poetry, which he made, himself, out of his own head—three verses—kind of sweet and saddish—the name of it was, "Yes, crush, cold world, this breaking heart"—and he left that all set up and ready to print in the paper and didn't charge nothing for it. Well, he took in nine dollars and a half, and said he'd done a pretty square day's work for it.

Then he showed us another little job he'd printed and hadn't charged for, because it was for us. It had a picture of a runaway nigger, with a bundle on a stick, over his shoulder, and "$200 reward" under it. The reading was all about Jim, and just described him to a dot. It said he run away from St. Jacques' plantation, forty mile below New Orleans, last winter, and likely went north, and whoever would catch him and send him back, he could have the reward and expenses.

"Now," says the duke, "after to-night we can run in the daytime if we want to. Whenever we see anybody coming, we can tie Jim hand and foot with a rope, and lay him in the wigwam and show this handbill and say we captured him up the river, and were too poor to travel on a steamboat, so we got this little raft on credit from our friends and are going down to get the reward. Handcuffs and chains would look still better on Jim, but it wouldn't go well with the story of us being so poor. Too much like jewelry. Ropes are the correct thing—we must preserve the unities,[2] as we say on the boards."

We all said the duke was pretty smart, and there couldn't be no trouble about running daytimes. We judged we could make miles enough that night to get out of the reach of the pow-wow we reckoned the duke's work in the printing office was going to make in that little town—then we could boom right along, if we wanted to.

We laid low and kept still, and never shoved out till nearly ten o'clock; then we slid by, pretty wide away from the town, and didn't hoist our lantern till we was clear out of sight of it.

When Jim called me to take the watch at four in the morning, he says—

"Huck, does you reck'n we gwyne to run acrost any mo' kings on dis trip?"

"No," I says, "I reckon not."

"Well," says he, "dat's all right, den. I doan' mine one er two kings, but dat's enough. Dis one's powerful drunk, en de duke ain' much better."

I found Jim had been trying to get him to talk French, so he could hear what it was like; but he said he had been in this country so long, and had so much trouble, he'd forgot it.

## Chapter XXI

It was after sun-up, now, but we went right on, and didn't tie up. The king and the duke turned out, by-and-by, looking pretty rusty; but after they'd jumped overboard and took a swim, it chippered them up a good deal. After breakfast the king he took a seat on a corner of the raft, and pulled off his boots and rolled up his britches, and let his legs dangle in the water, so as to be comfortable, and lit his pipe, and went to getting his Romeo and Juliet by

2. Of time, place, and action in classical drama; here the duke is using the term to mean "consistent with the rest of our story."

heart. When he had got it pretty good, him and the duke begun to practice it together. The duke had to learn him over and over again, how to say every speech; and he made him sigh, and put his hand on his heart, and after while he said he done it pretty well; "only," he says, "you mustn't bellow out *Romeo!* that way, like a bull—you must say it soft, and sick, and languishy, so—R-o-o-meo! that is the idea; for Juliet's a dear sweet mere child of a girl, you know, and she don't bray like a jackass."

Well, next they got out a couple of long swords that the duke made out of oak laths, and begun to practice the sword-fight—the duke called himself Richard III.; and the way they laid on, and pranced around the raft was grand to see. But by-and-by the king tripped and fell overboard, and after that they took a rest, and had a talk about all kinds of adventures they'd had in other times along the river.

After dinner, the duke says:

"Well, Capet,[3] we'll want to make this a first-class show, you know, so I guess we'll add a little more to it. We want a little something to answer encores with, anyway."

"What's onkores, Bilgewater?"

The duke told him, and then says:

"I'll answer by doing the Highland fling or the sailor's hornpipe; and you—well, let me see—oh, I've got it—you can do Hamlet's soliloquy."

"Hamlet's which?"

"Hamlet's soliloquy, you know; the most celebrated thing in Shakespeare. Ah, it's sublime, sublime! Always fetches the house. I haven't got it in the book—I've only got one volume—but I reckon I can piece it out from memory. I'll just walk up and down a minute, and see if I can call it back from recollection's vaults."

So he went to marching up and down, thinking, and frowning horrible every now and then; then he would hoist up his eyebrows; next he would squeeze his hand on his forehead and stagger back and kind of moan; next he would sigh, and next he'd let on to drop a tear. It was beautiful to see him. By-and-by he got it. He told us to give attention. Then he strikes a most noble attitude, with one leg shoved forwards, and his arms stretched away up, and his head tilted back, looking up at the sky; and then he begins to rip and rave and grit his teeth; and after that, all through his speech he howled, and spread around, and swelled up his chest, and just knocked the spots out of any acting ever *I* see before. This is the speech—I learned it, easy enough, while he was learning it to the king:[4]

To be, or not to be; that is the bare bodkin
That makes calamity of so long life;
For who would fardels bear, till Birnam Wood do come to Dunsinane,
But that the fear of something after death
Murders the innocent sleep,
Great nature's second course,
And makes us rather sling the arrows of outrageous fortune
Than fly to others that we know not of.
There's the respect must give us pause:
Wake Duncan with thy knocking! I would thou couldst;

3. The family name of Louis XVI.
4. The comical garbling of Shakespeare was another stock-in-trade of the southwestern humorists in whose

tradition Clemens follows. The soliloquy is composed chiefly of phrases from *Hamlet* and *Macbeth*; but several other plays are also drawn upon.

For who would bear the whips and scorns of time,
The oppressor's wrong, the proud man's contumely,
The law's delay, and the quietus which his pangs might take,
In the dead waste and middle of the night, when churchyards yawn
In customary suits of solemn black,
But that the undiscovered country from whose bourne no traveler returns,
Breathes forth contagion on the world,
And thus the native hue of resolution, like the poor cat i' the adage,
Is sicklied o'er with care,
And all the clouds that lowered o'er our housetops,
With this regard their currents turn awry,
And lose the name of action.
'Tis a consummation devoutly to be wished. But soft you, the fair Ophelia:
Ope not thy ponderous and marble jaws,
But get thee to a nunnery—go!

Well, the old man he liked that speech, and he mighty soon got it so he could do it first rate. It seemed like he was just born for it; and when he had his hand in and was excited, it was perfectly lovely the way he would rip and tear and rair up behind when he was getting it off.

The first chance we got, the duke he had some show bills printed; and after that, for two or three days as we floated along, the raft was a most uncommon lively place, for there warn't nothing but sword-fighting and rehearsing—as the duke called it—going on all the time. One morning, when we was pretty well down the State of Arkansaw, we come in sight of a little one-horse town[5] in a big bend; so we tied up about three-quarters of a mile above it, in the mouth of a crick which was shut in like a tunnel by the cypress trees, and all of us but Jim took the canoe and went down there to see if there was any chance in that place for our show.

We struck it mighty lucky; there was going to be a circus there that afternoon, and the country people was already beginning to come in, in all kinds of old shackly wagons, and on horses. The circus would leave before night, so our show would have a pretty good chance. The duke he hired the court house, and we went around and stuck up our bills. They read like this:

Shaksperean Revival! ! !
Wonderful Attraction!
For One Night Only!
The world renowned tragedians,
David Garrick the younger, of Drury Lane Theatre, London,
and
Edmund Kean the elder,[6] of the Royal Haymarket Theatre, White-
chapel, Pudding Lane, Piccadilly, London, and the
Royal Continental Theatres, in their sublime
Shaksperean Spectacle entitled
The Balcony Scene
in
Romeo and Juliet! ! !

---

5. Clemens's Bricksville is apparently modeled after Napoleon, Arkansas, although certain unattractive elements of this river town and its inhabitants were common to most—including Hannibal.

6. Here, as elsewhere, the duke garbles the facts. Garrick, Edmund Kean (1787–1833), and Charles John Kean (1811–1868) were all famous tragedians at the Theatre Royal in Drury Lane, London.

Romeo ...................................................................... Mr. Garrick.
Juliet........................................................................... Mr. Kean.
Assisted by the whole strength of the company!
New costumes, new scenery, new appointments!
Also:
The thrilling, masterly, and blood-curdling
Broad-sword conflict
In Richard III.!!!
Richard III............................................................... Mr. Garrick.
Richmond ................................................................. Mr. Kean.
also:
(by special request,)
Hamlet's Immortal Soliloquy! !
By the Illustrious Kean!
Done by him 300 consecutive nights in Paris!
For One Night Only,
On account of imperative European engagements!
Admission 25 cents; children and servants, 10 cents.

Then we went loafing around the town. The stores and houses was most all old shackly dried-up frame concerns that hadn't ever been painted; they was set up three or four foot above ground on stilts, so as to be out of reach of the water when the river was overflowed. The houses had little gardens around them, but they didn't seem to raise hardly anything in them but jimpson weeds, and sunflowers, and ash-piles, and old curled-up boots and shoes, and pieces of bottles, and rags, and played-out tin-ware. The fences was made of different kinds of boards, nailed on at different times; and they leaned every which-way, and had gates that didn't generly have but one hinge—a leather one. Some of the fences had been whitewashed, some time or another, but the duke said it was in Clumbus's time, like enough. There was generly hogs in the garden, and people driving them out.

All the stores was along one street. They had white-domestic awnings[7] in front, and the country people hitched their horses to the awning-posts. There was empty dry-goods boxes under the awnings, and loafers roosting on them all day long, whittling them with their Barlow knives; and chawing tobacco, and gaping and yawning and stretching—a mighty ornery lot. They generly had on yellow straw hats most as wide as an umbrella, but didn't wear no coats nor waistcoats; they called one another Bill, and Buck, and Hank, and Joe, and Andy, and talked lazy and drawly, and used considerable many cuss-words. There was as many as one loafer leaning up against every awning-post, and he most always had his hands in his britches pockets, except when he fetched them out to lend a chaw of tobacco or scratch. What a body was hearing amongst them, all the time was—

"Gimme a chaw 'v tobacker, Hank."

"Cain't—I hain't got but one chaw left. Ask Bill."

Maybe Bill he gives him a chaw; maybe he lies and says he ain't got none. Some of them kinds of loafers never has a cent in the world, nor a chaw of tobacco of their own. They get all their chawing by borrowing—they say to a fellow, "I wisht you'd len' me a chaw, Jack, I jist this minute give Ben Thomp-

---

7. Awnings made from crude canvas.

son the last chaw I had"—which is a lie, pretty much every time; it don't fool anybody but a stranger; but Jack ain't no stranger, so he says—

"*You* give him a chaw, did you? so did your sister's cat's grandmother. You pay me back the chaws you've awready borry'd off'n me, Lafe Buckner, then I'll loan you one or two ton of it, and won't charge you no back intrust, nuther."

"Well, I *did* pay you back some of it wunst."

"Yes, you did—'bout six chaws. You borry'd store tobacker and paid back nigger-head."

Store tobacco is flat black plug, but these fellows mostly chaws the natural leaf twisted. When they borrow a chaw, they don't generly cut it off with a knife, but they set the plug in between their teeth, and gnaw with their teeth and tug at the plug with their hands till they get it in two—then sometimes the one that owns the tobacco looks mournful at it when it's handed back, and says, sarcastic—

"Here, gimme the *chaw*, and you take the *plug*."

All the streets and lanes was just mud, they warn't nothing else *but* mud—as black as tar, and nigh about a foot deep in some places; and two or three inches deep in *all* the places. The hogs loafed and grunted around, everywheres. You'd see a muddy sow and a litter of pigs come lazying along the street and whollop herself right down in the way, where folks had to walk around her, and she'd stretch out, and shut her eyes, and wave her ears, whilst the pigs was milking her, and look as happy as if she was on salary. And pretty soon you'd hear a loafer sing out, "Hi! *so* boy! sick him, Tige!" and away the sow would go, squealing most horrible, with a dog or two swinging to each ear, and three or four dozen more a-coming; and then you would see all the loafers get up and watch the thing out of sight, and laugh at the fun and look grateful for the noise. Then they'd settle back again till there was a dog-fight. There couldn't anything wake them up all over, and make them happy all over, like a dog-fight—unless it might be putting turpentine on a stray dog and setting fire to him, or tying a tin pan to his tail and see him run himself to death.

On the river front some of the houses was sticking out over the bank, and they was bowed and bent, and about ready to tumble in. The people had moved out of them. The bank was caved away under one corner of some others, and that corner was hanging over. People lived in them yet, but it was dangersome, because sometimes a strip of land as wide as a house caves in at a time. Sometimes a belt of land a quarter of a mile deep will start in and cave along and cave along till it all caves into the river in one summer. Such a town as that has to be always moving back, and back, and back, because the river's always gnawing at it.

The nearer it got to noon that day, the thicker and thicker was the wagons and horses in the streets, and more coming all the time. Families fetched their dinners with them, from the country, and eat them in the wagons. There was considerable whiskey drinking going on, and I seen three fights. By-and-by somebody sings out—

"Here comes old Boggs!—in from the country for his little old monthly drunk—here he comes, boys!"

All the loafers looked glad—I reckoned they was used to having fun out of Boggs. One of them says—

"Wonder who he's a gwyne to chaw up this time. If he'd a chawed up all the men he's ben a gwyne to chaw up in the last twenty year, he'd have considerable ruputation, now."

Another one says, "I wisht old Boggs'd threaten me, 'cuz then I'd know I warn't gwyne to die for a thousan' year."

Boggs comes a-tearing along on his horse, whooping and yelling like an Injun, and singing out—

"Cler the track, thar. I'm on the war-path, and the price uv coffins is a gwyne to raise."

He was drunk, and weaving about in his saddle; he was over fifty year old, and had a very red face. Everybody yelled at him, and laughed at him, and sassed him, and he sassed back, and said he'd attend to them and lay them out in their regular turns, but he couldn't wait now, because he'd come to town to kill old Colonel Sherburn, and his motto was, "meat first, and spoon vittles to top off on."

He see me, and rode up and says—

"Whar'd you come f'm, boy? You prepared to die?"

Then he rode on. I was scared; but a man says—

"He don't mean nothing; he's always a carryin' on like that, when he's drunk. He's the best-naturedest old fool in Arkansaw—never hurt nobody, drunk nor sober."

Boggs rode up before the biggest store in town and bent his head down so he could see under the curtain of the awning, and yells—

"Come out here, Sherburn! Come out and meet the man you've swindled. You're the houn' I'm after, and I'm a gwyne to have you, too!"

And so he went on, calling Sherburn everything he could lay his tongue to, and the whole street packed with people listening and laughing and going on. By-and-by a proud-looking man about fifty-five—and he was a heap the best dressed man in that town, too—steps out of the store, and the crowd drops back on each side to let him come. He says to Boggs, mighty ca'm and slow— he says:

"I'm tired of this; but I'll endure it till one o'clock. Till one o'clock, mind— no longer. If you open your mouth against me only once, after that time, you can't travel so far but I will find you."

Then he turns and goes in. The crowd looked mighty sober; nobody stirred, and there warn't no more laughing. Boggs rode off blackguarding Sherburn as loud as he could yell, all down the street; and pretty soon back he comes and stops before the store, still keeping it up. Some men crowded around him and tried to get him to shut up, but he wouldn't; they told him it would be one o'clock in about fifteen minutes, and so he *must* go home—he must go right away. But it didn't do no good. He cussed away, with all his might, and throwed his hat down in the mud and rode over it, and pretty soon away he went a-raging down the street again, with his gray hair a-flying. Everybody that could get a chance at him tried their best to coax him off of his horse so they could lock him up and get him sober; but it warn't no use—up the street he would tear again, and give Sherburn another cussing. By-and-by somebody says—

"Go for his daughter!—quick, go for his daughter; sometimes he'll listen to her. If anybody can persuade him, she can."

So somebody started on a run. I walked down street a ways, and stopped. In about five or ten minutes, here comes Boggs again—but not on his horse. He was a-reeling across the street towards me, bareheaded, with a friend on both sides of him aholt of his arms and hurrying him along. He was quiet, and looked uneasy; and he warn't hanging back any, but was doing some of the hurrying himself. Somebody sings out—

"Boggs!"

I looked over there to see who said it, and it was that Colonel Sherburn. He was standing perfectly still, in the street, and had a pistol raised in his right hand—not aiming it, but holding it out with the barrel tilted up towards the sky. The same second I see a young girl coming on the run, and two men with her. Boggs and the men turned round, to see who called him, and when they see the pistol the men jumped to one side, and the pistol barrel come down slow and steady to a level—both barrels cocked. Boggs throws up both of his hands, and says, "O Lord, don't shoot!" Bang! goes the first shot, and he staggers back clawing at the air—bang! goes the second one, and he tumbles backwards onto the ground, heavy and solid, with his arms spread out. That young girl screamed out, and comes rushing, and down she throws herself on her father, crying, and saying, "Oh, he's killed him, he's killed him!" The crowd closed up around them, and shouldered and jammed one another, with their necks stretched, trying to see, and people on the inside trying to shove them back, and shouting, "Back, back! give him air, give him air!"

Colonel Sherburn he tossed his pistol onto the ground, and turned around on his heels and walked off.

They took Boggs to a little drug store, the crowd pressing around, just the same, and the whole town following, and I rushed and got a good place at the window, where I was close to him and could see in. They laid him on the floor, and put one large Bible under his head, and opened another one and spread it on his breast—but they tore open his shirt first, and I seen where one of the bullets went in. He made about a dozen long gasps, his breast lifting the Bible up when he drawed in his breath, and letting it down again when he breathed it out—and after that he laid still; he was dead.[8] Then they pulled his daughter away from him, screaming and crying, and took her off. She was about sixteen, and very sweet and gentle-looking, but awful pale and scared.

Well, pretty soon the whole town was there, squirming and scrouging and pushing and shoving to get at the window and have a look, but people that had the places wouldn't give them up, and folks behind them was saying all the time, "Say, now, you've looked enough, you fellows; 'taint right and 'taint fair, for you to stay thar all the time, and never give nobody a chance; other folks has their rights as well as you."

There was considerable jawing back, so I slid out, thinking maybe there was going to be trouble. The streets was full, and everybody was excited. Everybody that seen the shooting was telling how it happened, and there was a big crowd packed around each one of these fellows, stretching their necks and listening. One long lanky man, with long hair and a big white fur stove-pipe hat on the back of his head, and a crooked-handled cane, marked out the places on the ground where Boggs stood, and where Sherburn stood, and the people follow-

8. Clemens had witnessed a shooting very much like this one when he was ten years old. His father was judge at the trial, which ended in acquittal. Only the Bibles under the victim's head and on his chest seem to have been added by Clemens, who seldom could resist ironies at the expense of institutionalized religion.

ing him around from one place to t'other and watching everything he done, and bobbing their heads to show they understood, and stooping a little and resting their hands on their thighs to watch him mark the places on the ground with his cane; and then he stood up straight and stiff where Sherburn had stood, frowning and having his hat-brim down over his eyes, and sung out, "Boggs!" and then fetched his cane down slow to a level, and says "Bang!" staggered backwards, says "Bang!" again, and fell down flat on his back. The people that had seen the thing said he done it perfect; said it was just exactly the way it all happened. Then as much as a dozen people got out their bottles and treated him.

Well, by-and-by somebody said Sherburn ought to be lynched. In about a minute everybody was saying it; so away they went, mad and yelling, and snatching down every clothes-line they come to, to do the hanging with.

## Chapter XXII

They swarmed up the street towards Sherburn's house, a-whooping and yelling and raging like Injuns, and everything had to clear the way or get run over and tromped to mush, and it was awful to see. Children was heeling it ahead of the mob, screaming and trying to get out of the way; and every window along the road was full of women's heads, and there was nigger boys in every tree, and bucks and wenches looking over every fence; and as soon as the mob would get nearly to them they would break and skaddle back out of reach. Lots of the women and girls was crying and taking on, scared most to death.

They swarmed up in front of Sherburn's palings as thick as they could jam together, and you couldn't hear yourself think for the noise. It was a little twenty-foot yard. Some sung out "Tear down the fence! tear down the fence!" Then there was a racket of ripping and tearing and smashing, and down she goes, and the front wall of the crowd begins to roll in like a wave.

Just then Sherburn steps out on to the roof of his little front porch, with a double-barrel gun in his hand, and takes his stand, perfectly ca'm and deliberate, not saying a word. The racket stopped, and the wave sucked back.

Sherburn never said a word—just stood there, looking down. The stillness was awful creepy and uncomfortable. Sherburn run his eye slow along the crowd; and wherever it struck, the people tried a little to outgaze him, but they couldn't; they dropped their eyes and looked sneaky. Then pretty soon Sherburn sort of laughed; not the pleasant kind, but the kind that makes you feel like when you are eating bread that's got sand in it.

Then he says, slow and scornful:

"The idea of you lynching anybody! It's amusing. The idea of you thinking you had pluck enough to lynch a *man*! Because you're brave enough to tar and feather poor friendless cast-out women that come along here, did that make you think you had grit enough to lay your hands on a *man*? Why, a *man's* safe in the hands of ten thousand of your kind—as long as it's day-time and you're not behind him.

"Do I know you? I know you clear through. I was born and raised in the South, and I've lived in the North; so I know the average all around. The average man's a coward. In the North he lets anybody walk over him that wants to, and goes home and prays for a humble spirit to bear it. In the South one man, all by himself, has stopped a stage full of men, in the day-time, and robbed the lot. Your newspapers call you a brave people so much that you think you *are* braver than any other people—whereas you're just *as* brave, and no braver. Why don't your juries hang murderers? Because they're afraid the man's friends will shoot them in the back, in the dark—and it's just what they *would* do.

"So they always acquit; and then a *man* goes in the night, with a hundred masked cowards at his back, and lynches the rascal. Your mistake is, that you didn't bring a man with you; that's one mistake, and the other is that you didn't come in the dark, and fetch your masks. You brought *part* of a man— Buck Harkness, there—and if you hadn't had him to start you, you'd a taken it out in blowing.

"You didn't want to come. The average man don't like trouble and danger. *You* don't like trouble and danger. But if only *half* a man—like Buck Harkness, there—shouts 'Lynch him, lynch him!' you're afraid to back down—afraid you'll be found out to be what you are—*cowards*—and so you raise a yell, and hang yourselves onto that half-a-man's coat tail, and come raging up here, swearing what big things you're going to do. The pitifulest thing out is a mob; that's what an army is—a mob; they don't fight with courage that's born in them, but with courage that's borrowed from their mass, and from their officers. But a mob without any *man* at the head of it, is *beneath* pitifulness. Now the thing for *you* to do, is to droop your tails and go home and crawl in a hole. If any real lynching's going to be done, it will be done in the dark, Southern fashion; and when they come they'll bring their masks, and fetch a *man* along. Now *leave*—and take your half-a-man with you"—tossing his gun up across his left arm and cocking it, when he says this.

The crowd washed back sudden, and then broke all apart and went tearing off every which way, and Buck Harkness he heeled it after them, looking tolerable cheap. I could a staid, if I'd a wanted to, but I didn't want to.

I went to the circus, and loafed around the back side till the watchman went by, and then dived in under the tent. I had my twenty-dollar gold piece and some other money, but I reckoned I better save it, because there ain't no telling how soon you are going to need it, away from home and amongst strangers, that way. You can't be too careful. I ain't opposed to spending money on circuses, when there ain't no other way, but there ain't no use in *wasting* it on them.

It was a real bully circus. It was the splendidest sight that ever was, when they all come riding in, two and two, a gentleman and lady, side by side, the men just in their drawers and under-shirts, and no shoes nor stirrups, and resting their hands on their thighs, easy and comfortable—there must a' been twenty of them—and every lady with a lovely complexion, and perfectly beautiful, and looking just like a gang of real sure-enough queens, and dressed in clothes that cost millions of dollars, and just littered with diamonds. It was a powerful fine sight; I never see anything so lovely. And then one by one they got up and stood, and went a-weaving around the ring so gentle and wavy and graceful, the men looking ever so tall and airy and straight, with their heads bobbing and skimming along, away up there under the tent-roof, and every lady's rose-leafy dress flapping soft and silky around her hips, and she looking like the most loveliest parasol.

And then faster and faster they went, all of them dancing, first one foot stuck out in the air and then the other, the horses leaning more and more, and the ring-master going round and round the centre-pole, cracking his whip and shouting "hi!—hi!" and the clown cracking jokes behind him; and by-and-by all hands dropped the reins, and every lady put her knuckles on her hips and every gentlemen folded his arms, and then how the horses did lean over and hump themselves! And so, one after the other they all skipped off into the ring, and made the sweetest bow I ever see, and then scampered out, and everybody clapped their hands and went just about wild.

Well, all through the circus they done the most astonishing things; and all the time that clown carried on so it most killed the people. The ring-master couldn't ever say a word to him but he was back at him quick as a wink with the funniest things a body ever said; and how he ever *could* think of so many of them, and so sudden and so pat, was what I couldn't noway understand. Why, I couldn't a thought of them in a year. And by-and-by a drunk man tried to get into the ring—said he wanted to ride; said he could ride as well as anybody that ever was. They argued and tried to keep him out, but he wouldn't listen, and the whole show come to a standstill. Then the people begun to holler at him and make fun of him, and that made him mad, and he begun to rip and tear; so that stirred up the people, and a lot of men began to pile down off of the benches and swarm towards the ring, saying "Knock him down! throw him out!" and one or two women begun to scream. So, then, the ring-master he made a little speech, and said he hoped there wouldn't be no disturbance, and if the man would promise he wouldn't make no more trouble, he would let him ride, if he thought he could stay on the horse. So everybody laughed and said all right, and the man got on. The minute he was on, the horse begun to rip and tear and jump and cavort around, with two circus men hanging onto his bridle trying to hold him, and the drunk man hanging onto his neck, and his heels flying in the air every jump, and the whole crowd of people standing up shouting and laughing till the tears rolled down. And at last, sure enough, all the circus men could do, the horse broke loose, and away he went like the very nation, round and round the ring, with that sot laying down on him and hanging to his neck, with first one leg hanging most to the ground on one side, and then t'other one on t'other side, and the people just crazy. It warn't funny to me, though; I was all of a tremble to see his danger. But pretty soon he struggled up astraddle and grabbed the bridle, a-reeling this way and that; and the next minute he sprung up and dropped the bridle and stood! and the horse agoing like a house afire too. He just stood up there, a-sailing around as easy and comfortable as if he warn't ever drunk in his life—and then he begun to pull off his clothes and sling them. He shed them so thick they kind of clogged up the air, and altogether he shed seventeen suits. And then, there he was, slim and handsome, and dressed the gaudiest and prettiest you ever saw, and he lit into that horse with his whip and made him fairly hum—and finally skipped off, and made his bow and danced off to the dressing-room, and everybody just a-howling with pleasure and astonishment.

Then the ring-master he see how he had been fooled, and he *was* the sickest ring-master you ever see, I reckon. Why, it was one of his own men! He had got up that joke all out of his own head, and never let on to nobody. Well, I felt sheepish enough, to be took in so, but I wouldn't a been in that ring-master's place, not for a thousand dollars. I don't know; there may be bullier circuses than what that one was, but I never struck them yet. Anyways it was plenty good enough for *me*; and wherever I run across it, it can have all of *my* custom, everytime.

Well, that night we had *our* show; but there warn't only about twelve people there; just enough to pay expenses. And they laughed all the time, and that made the duke mad; and everybody left, anyway, before the show was over, but one boy which was asleep. So the duke said these Arkansaw lunkheads couldn't come up to Shakspeare; what they wanted was low comedy—and may be something ruther worse than low comedy, he reckoned. He said he could size their style. So next morning he got some big sheets of wrapping-paper and some black paint, and drawed off some handbills and stuck them up all over the village. The bills said:

AT THE COURT HOUSE!

FOR 3 NIGHTS ONLY!

The World-Renowned Tragedians
DAVID GARRICK THE YOUNGER
AND
EDMUND KEAN THE ELDER!
*Of the London and Continental
Theatres,*
In their Thrilling Tragedy of
THE KING'S CAMELOPARD[9]
OR
THE ROYAL NONESUCH! ! !
*Admission 50 cents.*

Then at the bottom was the biggest line of all—which said:

LADIES AND CHILDREN NOT ADMITTED.

"There," says he, "if that line don't fetch them, I don't know Arkansaw!"

## Chapter XXIII

Well, all day him and the king was hard at it, rigging up a stage, and a curtain, and a row of candles for footlights; and that night the house was jam full of men in no time. When the place couldn't hold no more, the duke he quit tending door and went around the back way and come onto the stage and stood up before the curtain, and made a little speech, and praised up this tragedy, and said it was the most thrillingest one that ever was; and so he went on a-bragging about the tragedy and about Edmund Kean the Elder, which was to play the main principal part in it; and at last when he'd got everybody's expectations up high enough, he rolled up the curtain, and the next minute the king come a-prancing out on all fours, naked; and he was painted all over, ring-streaked-and-striped, all sorts of colors, as splendid as a rainbow. And— but never mind the rest of his outfit, it was just wild, but it was awful funny. The people most killed themselves laughing; and when the king got done

9. An archaic name for a giraffe, but also describes a legendary spotted beast the size of a camel. This hoax performance was a popular subject of comic stories, and Clemens had heard a version he referred to as *The Burning Shame* from his friend Jim Gillis in his California newspaper days.

capering, and capered off behind the scenes, they roared and clapped and stormed and haw-hawed till he come back and done it over again; and after that, they made him do it another time. Well, it would a made a cow laugh to see the shines that old idiot cut.

Then the duke he lets the curtain down, and bows to the people, and says the great tragedy will be performed only two nights more, on accounts of pressing London engagements, where the seats is all sold aready for it in Drury Lane; and then he makes them another bow, and says if he has succeeded in pleasing them and instructing them, he will be deeply obleeged if they will mention it to their friends and get them to come and see it.

Twenty people sings out:

"What, is it over? Is that *all?*"

The duke says yes. Then there was a fine time. Everybody sings out "sold," and rose up mad, and was agoing for that stage and them tragedians. But a big fine-looking man jumps up on a bench, and shouts:

"Hold on! Just a word, gentlemen." They stopped to listen. "We are sold— mighty badly sold. But we don't want to be the laughing-stock of this whole town, I reckon, and never hear the last of this thing as long as we live. No. What we want, is to go out of here quiet, and talk this show up, and sell the *rest* of the town! Then we'll all be in the same boat. Ain't that sensible?" ("You bet it is!—the jedge is right!" everybody sings out.) "All right, then—not a word about any sell. Go along home, and advise everybody to come and see the tragedy."

Next day you couldn't hear nothing around that town but how splendid that show was. House was jammed again, that night, and we sold this crowd the same way. When me and the king and the duke got home to the raft, we all had a supper; and by-and-by, about midnight, they made Jim and me back her out and float her down the middle of the river and fetch her in and hide her about two mile below town.

The third night the house was crammed again—and they warn't new-comers, this time, but people that was at the show the other two nights. I stood by the duke at the door, and I see that every man that went in had his pockets bulging, or something muffled up under his coat—and I see it warn't no perfumery neither, not by a long sight. I smelt sickly eggs by the barrel, and rotten cabbages, and such things; and if I know the signs of a dead cat being around, and I bet I do, there was sixty-four of them went in. I shoved in there for a minute, but it was too various for me, I couldn't stand it. Well, when the place couldn't hold no more people, the duke he give a fellow a quarter and told him to tend door for him a minute, and then he started around for the stage door, I after him; but the minute we turned the corner and was in the dark, he says:

"Walk fast, now, till you get away from the houses, and then shin for the raft like the dickens was after you!"

I done it, and he done the same. We struck the raft at the same time, and in less than two seconds we was gliding down stream, all dark and still, and edging towards the middle of the river, nobody saying a word. I reckoned the poor king was in for a gaudy time of it with the audience; but nothing of the sort; pretty soon he crawls out from under the wigwam, and says:

"Well, how'd the old thing pan out this time, Duke?"

He hadn't been up town at all.

We never showed a light till we was about ten mile below that village. Then we lit up and had a supper, and the king and the duke fairly laughed their bones loose over the way they'd served them people. The duke says:

"Greenhorns, flatheads! *I* knew the first house would keep mum and let the rest of the town get roped in; and I knew they'd lay for us the third night, and consider it was *their* turn now. Well, it *is* their turn, and I'd give something to know how much they'd take for it. I *would* just like to know how they're putting in their opportunity. They can turn it into a picnic, if they want to— they brought plenty provisions."

Them rapscallions took in four hundred and sixty-five dollars in that three nights. I never see money hauled in by the wagon-load like that, before.

By-and-by, when they was asleep and snoring, Jim says:

"Don't it 'sprise you, de way dem kings carries on, Huck?"

"No," I says, "it don't."

"Why don't it, Huck?"

"Well, it don't, because it's in the breed. I reckon they're all alike."

"But, Huck, dese kings o' ourn is reglar rapscallions; dat's jist what dey is; dey's reglar rapscallions."

"Well, that's what I'm a-saying; all kings is mostly rapscallions, as fur as I can make out."

"Is dat so?"

"You read about them once—you'll see. Look at Henry the Eight; this'n 's a Sunday-School Superintendent to *him*. And look at Charles Second, and LouisFourteen, and Louis Fifteen, and James Second, and Edward Second, and Richard Third, and forty more; besides all them Saxon heptarchies that used to rip around so in old times and raise Cain. My, you ought to seen old Henry the Eight when he was in bloom. He *was* a blossom. He used to marry a new wife every day, and chop off her head next morning. And he would do it just as indifferent as if he was ordering up eggs. 'Fetch up Nell Gwynn,' he says. They fetch her up. Next morning, 'Chop off her head!' And they chop it off. 'Fetch up Jane Shore,' he says; and up she comes. Next morning 'Chop off her head'—and they chop it off. 'Ring up Fair Rosamun.' Fair Rosamun answers the bell. Next morning, 'Chop off her head.' And he made every one of them tell him a tale every night; and he kept that up till he had hogged a thousand and one tales that way, and then he put them all in a book, and called it Domesday Book—which was a good name and stated the case. You don't know kings, Jim, but I know them; and this old rip of ourn is one of the cleanest I've struck in history. Well, Henry he takes a notion he wants to get up some trouble with this country. How does he go at it—give notice?—give the country a show? No. All of sudden he heaves all the tea in Boston Harbor overboard, and whacks out a declaration of independence, and dares them to come on. That was *his* style—he never give anybody a chance. He had suspicions of his father, the Duke of Wellington. Well, what did he do?—ask him to show up? No—drownded him in a butt of mamsey, like a cat. Spose people left money laying around where he was—what did he do? He collared it. Spose he contracted to do a thing; and you paid him, and didn't set down there and see that he done it—what did he do? He always done the other thing. Spose he opened his mouth—what then? If he didn't shut it up powerful quick, he'd lose a lie, every time. That's the kind of a bug Henry was; and if we'd a had him along 'stead of our kings, he'd a fooled that town a heap worse than ourn done.[1] I don't say that ourn is lambs, because they ain't, when you come right down to the cold facts; but they ain't nothing to *that* old ram, anyway. All I say is, kings is kings, and you got to make allowances. Take them all around, they're a mighty ornery lot. It's the way they're raised."

"But dis one do *smell* so like de nation, Huck."

"Well, they all do, Jim. We can't help the way a king smells; history don't tell no way."

"Now de duke, he's a tolerable likely man, in some ways."

"Yes, a duke's different. But not very different. This one's a middling hard lot, for a duke. When he's drunk, there ain't no near-sighted man could tell him from a king."

"Well, anyways, I doan' hanker for no mo' un um, Huck. Dese is all I kin stan'."

"It's the way I feel, too, Jim. But we've got them on our hands, and we got to remember what they are, and make allowances. Sometimes I wish we could hear of a country that's out of kings."

What was the use to tell Jim these warn't real kings and dukes? It wouldn't a done no good; and besides, it was just as I said; you couldn't tell them from the real kind.

I went to sleep, and Jim didn't call me when it was my turn. He often done that. When I waked up, just at day-break, he was setting there with his head down betwixt his knees, moaning and mourning to himself. I didn't take notice, nor let on. I knowed what it was about. He was thinking about his wife and his children, away up yonder, and he was low and homesick; because he hadn't ever been away from home before in his life; and I do believe he cared just as much for his people as white folks does for their'n. It don't seem natural, but I reckon it's so. He was often moaning and mourning that way, nights, when he judged I was asleep, and saying "Po' little 'Lizabeth! po' little Johnny! its mighty hard; I spec' I ain't ever gwyne to see you no mo', no mo'!" He was a mighty good nigger, Jim was.

But this time I somehow got to talking to him about his wife and young ones; and by-and-by he says:

"What makes me feel so bad dis time, 'uz bekase I hear sumpn over yonder on de bank like a whack, er a slam, while ago, en it mine me er de time I treat my little 'Lizabeth so ornery. She warn't on'y 'bout fo' year ole, en she tuck de sk'yarlet-fever, en had a powful rough spell; but she got well, en one day she was a-stannin' aroun', en I says to her, I says:

" 'Shet de do'.'

"She never done it; jis' stood dar, kiner smilin' up at me. It make me mad; en I says agin, mighty loud, I says:

" 'Doan' you hear me?—shet de do'!'

"She jis' stood de same way, kiner smilin' up. I was a-bilin'! I says:

---

1. Huck's "history" of kingly behavior is a farrago of fact and fiction. Henry VIII, king of England from 1509 to 1547, did execute two of his wives and divorced two others. Nell Gwynn, however, was the mistress of Charles II (reigned 1669–85). Jane Shore was mistress to Edward IV (who reigned in the 15th century). Rosamund Clifford was mistress to Henry II in the 12th century. The Anglo-Saxon heptarchy (seven friendly kingdoms) ruled England 449–829. The Domesday Book, in which William the Conqueror of England had recorded all landowners and the value of their holdings, was completed in 1086; Huck confuses it with the stories in the *Arabian Nights*. The duke of Wellington is a 19th-century personage. The duke of Clarence was reportedly drowned in a wine butt in the early 16th century. The Boston Tea Party took place in 1773, and the Declaration of Independence was adopted in 1776; neither event, of course, has any connection with Henry VIII.

" 'I lay I *make* you mine!'

"En wid dat I fetch' her a slap side de head dat sont her a-sprawlin'. Den I went into de yuther room, en 'uz gone 'bout ten minutes; en when I come back, dah was dat do' a-stannin' open *yit*, en dat chile stannin' mos' right in it, a-lookin' down and mournin', en de tears runnin' down. My, but I *wuz* mad, I was agwyne for de chile, but jis' den—it was a do' dat open innerds—jis' den, 'long come de wind en slam it to, behine de chile, *ker-blam!*—en my lan', de chile never move'! My breff mos' hop outer me; en I feel so—so—I doan' know *how* I feel. I crope out, all a-tremblin', en crope aroun' en open de do' easy en slow, en poke my head in behine de chile, sof' en still, en all uv a sudden, I says *pow!* jis' as loud as I could yell. *She never budge!* Oh, Huck, I bust out a-cryin' en grab her up in my arms, en say, 'Oh, de po' little thing! de Lord God Amighty fogive po' ole Jim, kaze he never gwyne to fogive hisself as long's he live!' Oh, she was plumb deef en dumb, Huck, plumb deef en dumb—en I'd ben a'treat'n her so!"

## Chapter XXIV

Next day, towards night, we laid up under a little willow tow-head out in the middle, where there was a village on each side of the river, and the duke and the king begun to lay out a plan for working them towns. Jim he spoke to the duke, and said he hoped it wouldn't take but a few hours, because it got mighty heavy and tiresome to him when he had to lay all day in the wigwam tied with the rope. You see, when we left him all alone we had to tie him, because if anybody happened on him all by himself and not tied, it wouldn't look much like he was a runaway nigger, you know. So the duke said it *was* kind of hard to have to lay roped all day, and he'd cipher out some way to get around it.

He was uncommon bright, the duke was, and he soon struck it. He dressed Jim up in King Lear's outfit—it was a long curtain-calico gown, and a white horse-hair wig and whiskers; and then he took his theatre-paint and painted Jim's face and hands and ears and neck all over a dead dull solid blue, like a man that's been drownded nine days. Blamed if he warn't the horriblest looking outrage I ever see. Then the duke took and wrote out a sign on a shingle so—

*Sick Arab—but harmless when not out of his head.*

And he nailed that shingle to a lath, and stood the lath up four or five foot in front of the wigwam. Jim was satisfied. He said it was a sight better than laying tied a couple of years every day, and trembling all over every time there was a sound. The duke told him to make himself free and easy, and if anybody ever come meddling around, he must hop out of the wigwam, and carry on a little, and fetch a howl or two like a wild beast, and he reckoned they would light out and leave him alone. Which was sound enough judgment; but you take the average man, and he wouldn't wait for him to howl. Why, he didn't only look like he was dead, he looked considerable more than that.

These rapscallions wanted to try the Nonesuch again, because there was so much money in it, but they judged it wouldn't be safe, because maybe the news might a worked along down by this time. They couldn't hit no project that suited, exactly; so at last the duke said he reckoned he'd lay off and work his brains an hour or two and see if he couldn't put up something on the Arkansaw village; and the king he allowed he would drop over to t'other village, without any plan, but just trust in Providence to lead him the profitable way—meaning the devil, I reckon. We had all bought store clothes where we stopped last; and now the king put his'n on, and he told me to put mine on. I done it, of course. The king's duds was all black, and he did look real swell and starchy. I never knowed how clothes could change a body before. Why, before, he looked like the orneriest old rip that ever was; but now, when he'd take off his new white beaver and make a bow and do a smile, he looked that grand and good and pious that you'd say he had walked right out of the ark, and maybe was old Leviticus[2] himself. Jim cleaned up the canoe, and I got my paddle ready. There was a big steamboat laying at the shore away up under the point, about three mile above town—been there a couple of hours, taking on freight. Says the king:

"Seein' how I'm dressed, I reckon maybe I better arrive down from St. Louis or Cincinnati, or some other big place. Go for the steamboat, Huckleberry; we'll come down to the village on her."

I didn't have to be ordered twice, to go and take a steamboat ride. I fetched the shore a half a mile above the village, and then went scooting along the bluff bank in the easy water. Pretty soon we come to a nice innocent-looking young country jake setting on a log swabbing the sweat off of his face, for it was powerful warm weather; and he had a couple of big carpet-bags by him.

"Run her nose in shore," says the king. I done it. "Wher' you bound for, young man?"

"For the steamboat; going to Orleans."

"Git aboard," says the king. "Hold on a minute, my servant 'll he'p you with them bags. Jump out and he'p the gentleman, Adolphus"—meaning me, I see.

I done so, and then we all three started on again. The young chap was mighty thankful; said it was tough work toting his baggage such weather. He asked the king where he was going, and the king told him he'd come down the river and landed at the other village this morning, and now he was going up a few mile to see an old friend on a farm up there. The young fellow says:

"When I first see you, I says to myself, 'It's Mr. Wilks, sure, and he come mighty near getting here in time.' But then I says again, 'No, I reckon it ain't him, or else he wouldn't be paddling up the river.' You ain't him, are you?"

"No, my name's Blodgett—Elexander Blodgett—Reverend Elexander Blodgett, I spose I must say, as I'm one o' the Lord's poor servants. But still I'm jist as able to be sorry for Mr. Wilks for not arriving in time, all the same, if he's missed anything by it—which I hope he hasn't."

"Well, he don't miss any property by it, because he'll get that all right; but he's missed seeing his brother Peter die—which he mayn't mind, nobody can tell as to that—but his brother would a give anything in this world to see him before he died; never talked about nothing else all these three weeks; hadn't seen him since they was boys together—and hadn't ever seen his brother William at all—that's the deef and dumb one—William ain't more than thirty or thirty-five. Peter and George was the only ones that come out here; George was the married brother; him and his wife both died last year. Harvey and

2. The third book of the Old Testament is here confused with Noah.

William's the only ones that's left now; and, as I was saying, they haven't got here in time."

"Did anybody send 'em word?"

"Oh, yes; a month or two ago, when Peter was first took; because Peter said then that he sorter felt like he warn't going to get well this time. You see, he was pretty old, and George's g'yirls was too young to be much company for him, except Mary Jane the red-headed one; and so he was kinder lonesome after George and his wife died, and didn't seem to care much to live. He most desperately wanted to see Harvey—and William too, for that matter—because he was one of them kind that can't bear to make a will. He left a letter behind for Harvey, and said he'd told in it where his money was hid, and how he wanted the rest of the property divided up so George's g'yirls would be all right—for George didn't leave nothing. And that letter was all they could get him to put a pen to."

"Why do you reckon Harvey don't come? Wher' does he live?"

"Oh, he lives in England—Sheffield—preaches there—hasn't ever been in this country. He hasn't had any too much time—and besides he mightn't a got the letter at all, you know."

"Too bad, too bad he couldn't a lived to see his brothers, poor soul. You going to Orleans, you say?"

"Yes, but that ain't only a part of it. I'm going in a ship, next Wednesday, for Ryo Janeero, where my uncle lives."

"It's a pretty long journey. But it'll be lovely; I wisht I was agoing. Is Mary Jane the oldest? How old is the others?"

"Mary Jane's nineteen, Susan's fifteen, and Joanna's about fourteen—that's the one that gives herself to good works and has a hare-lip."

"Poor things! to be left alone in the cold world so."

"Well, they could be worse off. Old Peter had friends, and they ain't going to let them come to no harm. There's Hobson, the Babtis' preacher; and Deacon Lot Hovey, and Ben Rucker, and Abner Shackleford, and Levi Bell, the lawyer; and Dr. Robinson, and their wives, and the widow Bartley, and—well, there's a lot of them; but these are the ones that Peter was thickest with, and used to write about sometimes, when he wrote home; so Harvey'll know where to look for friends when he gets here."

Well, the old man he went on asking questions till he just fairly emptied that young fellow. Blamed if he didn't inquire about everybody and everything in that blessed town, and all about all the Wilkses; and about Peter's business—which was a tanner; and about George's—which was a carpenter; and about Harvey's—which was a dissentering[3] minister, and so on, and so on. Then he says:

"What did you want to walk all the way up to the steamboat for?"

"Because she's a big Orleans boat, and I was afeard she mightn't stop there. When they're deep they won't stop for a hail. A Cincinnati boat will, but this is a St. Louis one."

"Was Peter Wilks well off?"

"Oh, yes, pretty well off. He had houses and land, and it's reckoned he left three or four thousand in cash hid up som'ers."

"When did you say he died?"

3. Dissenting.

"I didn't say, but it was last night."

"Funeral to-morrow, likely?"

"Yes, 'bout the middle of the day."

"Well, it's all terrible sad; but we've all got to go, one time or another. So what we want to do is to be prepared; then we're all right."

"Yes, sir, it's the best way. Ma used to always say that."

When we struck the boat, she was about done loading, and pretty soon she got off. The king never said nothing about going aboard, so I lost my ride, after all. When the boat was gone, the king made me paddle up another mile to a lonesome place, and then he got ashore, and says:

"Now hustle back, right off, and fetch the duke up here, and the new carpet-bags. And if he's gone over to t'other side, go over there and git him. And tell him to git himself up regardless. Shove along, now."

I see what *he* was up to; but I never said nothing, of course. When I got back with the duke, we hid the canoe and then they set down on a log, and the king told him everything, just like the young fellow had said it—every last word of it. And all the time he was a doing it, he tried to talk like an Englishman; and he done it pretty well too, for a slouch. I can't imitate him, and so I ain't agoing to try to; but he really done it pretty good. Then he says:

"How are you on the deef and dumb, Bilgewater?"

The duke said, leave him alone for that; said he had played a deef and dumb person on the histrionic boards. So then they waited for a steamboat.

About the middle of the afternoon a couple of little boats come along, but they didn't come from high enough up the river; but at last there was a big one, and they hailed her. She sent out her yawl, and we went aboard, and she was from Cincinnati; and when they found we only wanted to go four or five mile, they was booming mad, and give us a cussing, and said they wouldn't land us. But the king was ca'm. He says:

"If gentlemen kin afford to pay a dollar a mile apiece, to be took on and put off in a yawl, a steamboat kin afford to carry 'em, can't it?"

So they softened down and said it was all right; and when we got to the village, they yawled us ashore. About two dozen men flocked down, when they see the yawl a coming; and when the king says—

"Kin any of you gentlemen tell me wher' Mr. Peter Wilks lives?" they give a glance at one another, and nodded their heads, as much as to say, "What d' I tell you?" Then one of them says, kind of soft and gentle:

"I'm sorry, sir, but the best we can do is to tell you where he *did* live yesterday evening."

Sudden as winking, the ornery old cretur went all to smash, and fell up against the man, and put his chin on his shoulder, and cried down his back, and says:

"Alas, alas, our poor brother—gone, and we never got to see him; oh, it's too, *too* hard!"

Then he turns around, blubbering, and makes a lot of idiotic signs to the duke on his hands, and blamed if *he* didn't drop a carpet-bag and bust out a-crying. If they warn't the beatenest lot, them two frauds, that ever I struck.

Well, the men gethered around, and sympathized with them, and said all sorts of kind things to them, and carried their carpet-bags up the hill for them, and let them lean on them and cry, and told the king all about his brother's last moments, and the king he told it all over again on his hands to the duke, and both of them took on about that dead tanner like they'd lost the twelve disciples. Well, if ever I struck anything like it, I'm a nigger. It was enough to make a body ashamed of the human race.

## Chapter XXV

The news was all over town in two minutes, and you could see the people tearing down on the run, from every which way, some of them putting on their coats as they come. Pretty soon we was in the middle of a crowd, and the noise of the tramping was like a soldier-march. The windows and dooryards was full; and every minute somebody would say, over a fence:

"Is it *them!*"

And somebody trotting along with the gang would answer back and say.

"You bet it is."

When we got to the house, the street in front of it was packed, and the three girls was standing in the door. Mary Jane *was* red-headed, and that don't make no difference, she was most awful beautiful, and her face and her eyes was all lit up like glory, she was so glad her uncles was come. The king he spread his arms, and Mary Jane she jumped for them, and the hare-lip jumped for the duke, and there they *had* it! Everybody most, leastways women, cried for joy to see them meet again at last and have such good times.

Then the king he hunched the duke, private—I see him do it—and then he looked around and see the coffin, over in the corner on two chairs; so then, him and the duke, with a hand across each other's shoulder, and t'other hand to their eyes, walked slow and solemn over there, everybody dropping back to give them room, and all the talk and noise stopping, people saying "Sh!" and all the men taking their hats off and drooping their heads, so you could a heard a pin fall. And when they got there, they bent over and looked in the coffin, and took one sight, and then they bust out a crying so you could a heard them to Orleans, most; and then they put their arms around each other's necks, and hung their chins over each other's shoulders; and then for three minutes, or maybe four, I never see two men leak the way they done. And mind you, everybody was doing the same; and the place was that damp I never see any-thing like it. Then one of them got on one side of the coffin, and t'other on t'other side, and they kneeled down and rested their foreheads on the coffin, and let on to pray all to theirselves. Well, when it come to that, it worked the crowd like you never see anything like it, and so everybody broke down and went to sobbing right out loud—the poor girls, too; and every woman, nearly, went up to the girls, without saying a word, and kissed them, solemn, on the forehead, and then put their hand on their head, and looked up towards the sky, with the tears running down, and then busted out and went off sobbing and swabbing, and give the next woman a show. I never see anything so dis-gusting.

Well, by-and-by the king he gets up and comes forward a little, and works himself up and slobbers out a speech, all full of tears and flapdoodle about its being a sore trial for him and his poor brother to lose the diseased, and to miss seeing diseased alive, after the long journey of four thousand mile, but it's a trial that's sweetened and sanctified to us by this dear sympathy and these holy tears, and so he thanks them out of his heart and out of his brother's heart, because out of their mouths they can't, words being too weak and cold, and all that kind of rot and slush, till it was just sickening; and then he blubbers out a pious goody-goody Amen, and turns himself loose and goes to crying fit to bust.

And the minute the words was out of his mouth somebody over in the crowd struck up the doxolojer,[4] and everybody joined in with all their might, and it just warmed you up and made you feel as good as church letting out. Music *is* a good thing; and after all that soul-butter and hogwash, I never see it freshen up things so, and sound so honest and bully.

Then the king begins to work his jaw again, and says how him and his nieces would be glad if a few of the main principal friends of the family would take supper here with them this evening, and help set up with the ashes of the diseased; and says if his poor brother laying yonder could speak, he knows who he would name, for they was names that was very dear to him, and mentioned often in his letters; and so he will name the same, to-wit, as follows, vizz:— Rev. Mr. Hobson, and Deacon Lot Hovey, and Mr. Ben Rucker, and Abner Shackleford, and Levi Bell, and Dr. Robinson, and their wives, and the widow Bartley.

Rev. Hobson and Dr. Robinson was down to the end of the town, a-hunting together; that is, I mean the doctor was shipping a sick man to t'other world, and the preacher was pinting him right. Lawyer Bell was away up to Louisville on some business. But the rest was on hand, and so they all come and shook hands with the king and thanked him and talked to him; and then they shook hands with the duke, and didn't say nothing but just kept a-smiling and bobbing their heads like a passel of sapheads whilst he made all sorts of signs with his hands and said "Goo-goo—goo-goo-goo," all the time, like a baby that can't talk.

So the king he blatted along, and managed to inquire about pretty much everybody and dog in town, by his name, and mentioned all sorts of little things that happened one time or another in the town, or to George's family, or to Peter; and he always let on that Peter wrote him the things, but that was a lie, he got every blessed one of them out of that young flathead that we canoed up to the steamboat.

Then Mary Jane she fetched the letter her father left behind, and the king he read it out loud and cried over it. It give the dwelling-house and three thousand dollars, gold, to the girls; and it give the tanyard (which was doing a good business), along with some other houses and land (worth about seven thousand), and three thousand dollars in gold to Harvey and William, and told where the six thousand cash was hid, down cellar. So these two frauds said they'd go and fetch it up, and have everything square and above-board; and told me to come with a candle. We shut the cellar door behind us, and when they found the bag they spilt it out on the floor, and it was a lovely sight, all them yallerboys.[5] My, the way the king's eyes did shine! He slaps the duke on the shoulder, and says:

"Oh, *this* ain't bully, nor noth'n! Oh, no, I reckon not! Why, Biljy, it beats the Nonesuch, *don't* it!"

The duke allowed it did. They pawed the yaller-boys, and sifted them through their fingers and let them jingle down on the floor; and the king says:

"It ain't no use talkin'; bein' brothers to a rich dead man, and representatives

---

4. I.e., doxology, or hymn of praise to God. The particular doxology referred to here begins "Praise God, from whom all blessings flow."

5. Gold coins.

of furrin heirs that's got left, is the line for you and me, Bilge. Thish-yer comes of trust'n to Providence. It's the best way, in the long run. I've tried 'em all, and ther' ain't no better way."

Most everybody would a been satisfied with the pile, and took it on trust; but no, they must count it. So they counts it, and it comes out four hundred and fifteen dollars short. Says the king:

"Dern him, I wonder what he done with that four hundred and fifteen dollars?"

They worried over that a while, and ransacked all around for it. Then the duke says:

"Well, he was a pretty sick man, and likely he made a mistake—I reckon that's the way of it. The best way's to let it go, and keep still about it. We can spare it."

"Oh, shucks, yes, we can *spare* it. I don't k'yer noth'n 'bout that—it's the *count* I'm thinkin' about. We want to be awful square and open and above-board, here, you know. We want to lug this h'yer money up stairs and count it before everybody—then ther' ain't noth'n suspicious. But when the dead man says ther's six thous'n dollars, you know, we don't want to—"

"Hold on," says the duke. "Less make up the deffisit"—and he begun to haul out yallerboys out of his pocket.

"It's a most amaz'n good idea, duke—you *have* got a rattlin' clever head on you," says the king. "Blest if the old Nonesuch ain't a heppin' us out agin"— and *he* begun to haul out yallerjackets and stack them up.

It most busted them, but they made up the six thousand clean and clear.

"Say," says the duke, "I got another idea. Le's go up stairs and count this money, and then take and *give it to the girls.*"

"Good land, duke, lemme hug you! It's the most dazzling idea 'at ever a man struck. You have cert'nly got the most astonishin' head I ever see. Oh, this is the boss dodge,[6] ther' ain't no mistake 'bout it. Let 'em fetch along their suspicions now, if they want to—this'll lay 'em out."

When we got up stairs, everybody gathered around the table, and the king he counted it and stacked it up, three hundred dollars in a pile—twenty elegant little piles. Everybody looked hungry at it, and licked their chops. Then they raked it into the bag again, and I see the king begin to swell himself up for another speech. He says:

"Friends all, my poor brother that lays yonder, has done generous by them that's left behind in the vale of sorrers. He has done generous by these-yer poor little lambs that he loved and sheltered, and that's left fatherless and mother-less. Yes, and we that knowed him, knows that he would a done *more* generous by 'em if he hadn't been afeard o' woundin' his dear William and me. Now, *wouldn't* he? Ther' ain't no question 'bout it, in *my* mind. Well, then—what kind o' brothers would it be, that 'd stand in his way at sech a time? And what kind o' uncles would it be that 'd rob—yes, *rob*—sech poor sweet lambs as these 'at he loved so, at sech a time? If I know William—and I *think* I do— he—well, I'll jest ask him." He turns around and beings to make a lot of signs to the duke with his hands; and the duke he looks at him stupid and leather-headed a while, then all of sudden he seems to catch his meaning, and jumps for the king, goo-gooing with all his might for joy, and hugs him about fifteen

6. Best confidence trick.

times before he lets up. Then the king says, "I knowed it; I reckon *that* 'll convince anybody the way *he* feels about it. Here, Mary Jane, Susan, Joanner, take the money—take it *all*. It's the gift of him that lays yonder, cold but joyful."

Mary Jane she went for him, Susan and the hare-lip went for the duke, and then such another hugging and kissing I never see yet. And everybody crowded up with the tears in their eyes, and most shook the hands off of them frauds, saying all the time:

"You *dear* good souls!—how *lovely!*—how *could* you!"

Well, then, pretty soon all hands got to talking about the diseased again, and how good he was, and what a loss he was, and all that; and before long a big iron-jawed man worked himself in there from outside, and stood a listening and looking, and not saying anything; and nobody saying anything to him either, because the king was talking and they was all busy listening. The king was saying—in the middle of something he'd started in on—

"—they bein' partickler friends o' the diseased. That's why they're invited here this evenin'; but to-morrow we want *all* to come—everybody; for he respected everybody, he liked everybody, and so it's fitten that his funeral orgies sh'd be public."

And so he went a-mooning on and on, liking to hear himself talk, and every little while he fetched in his funeral orgies again, till the duke he couldn't stand it no more; so he writes on a little scrap of paper, "*obsequies*, you old fool," and folds it up and goes to goo-gooing and reaching it over people's heads to him. The king he reads it, and puts it in his pocket, and says:

"Poor William, afflicted as he is, his *heart's* aluz right. Asks me to invite everybody to come to the funeral—wants me to make 'em all welcome. But he needn't a worried—it was jest what I was at."

Then he weaves along again, perfectly ca'm, and goes to dropping in his funeral orgies again every now and then, just like he done before. And when he done it the third time, he says:

"I say orgies, not because it's the common term, because it ain't—obsequies bein' the common term—but because orgies is the right term. Obsequies ain't used in England no more, now—it's gone out. We say orgies now, in England. Orgies is better, because it means the thing you're after, more exact. It's a word that's made up out'n the Greek *orgo*, outside, open, abroad; and the Hebrew *jeesum*, to plant, cover up; hence in*ter*. So, you see, funeral orgies is an open er public funeral."[7]

He was the *worst* I ever struck. Well, the iron-jawed man he laughed right in his face. Everybody was shocked. Everybody says, "Why *doctor!*" and Abner Shackleford says:

"Why, Robinson, hain't you heard the news? This is Harvey Wilks."

The king he smiled eager, and shoved out his flapper, and says:

"*Is* it my poor brother's dear good friend and physician? I—"

"Keep your hands off of me!" says the doctor. "*You* talk like an Englishman—*don't* you? It's the worse imitation I ever heard. *You* Peter Wilks's brother. You're a fraud, that's what you are!"

Well, how they all took on! They crowded around the doctor, and tried to

---

7. The comic etymology was a stock-in-trade of the southwestern humorists and is still popular in comedy routines.

quiet him down, and tried to explain to him, and tell him how Harvey'd showed in forty ways that he *was* Harvey, and knowed everybody by name, and the names of the very dogs, and begged and *begged* him not to hurt Harvey's feelings and the poor girls' feelings, and all that; but it warn't no use, he stormed right along, and said any man that pretended to be an Englishman and couldn't imitate the lingo no better than what he did, was a fraud and a liar. The poor girls was hanging to the king and crying; and all of a sudden the doctor ups and turns on *them.* He says:

"I was your father's friend, and I'm your friend; and I warn you *as* a friend, and an honest one, that wants to protect you and keep you out of harm and trouble, to turn your backs on that scoundrel, and have nothing to do with him, the ignorant tramp, with his idiotic Greek and Hebrew as he calls it. He is the thinnest kind of an impostor—has come here with a lot of empty names and facts which he has picked up somewheres, and you take them for *proofs,* and are helped to fool yourselves by these foolish friends here, who ought to know better. Mary Jane Wilks, you know me for your friend, and for your unselfish friend, too. Now listen to me; turn this pitiful rascal out—I *beg* you to do it. Will you?"

Mary Jane straightened herself up, and my, but she was handsome! She says: "*Here* is my answer." She hove up the bag of money and put it in the king's hands, and says, "Take this six thousand dollars, and invest it for me and my sisters any way you want to, and don't give us no receipt for it."

Then she put her arm around the king on one side, and Susan and the harelip done the same on the other. Everybody clapped their hands and stomped on the floor like a perfect storm, whilst the king held up his head and smiled proud. The doctor says:

"All right, I wash *my* hands of the matter. But I warn you all that a time's coming when you're going to feel sick whenever you think of this day"—and away he went.

"All right, doctor," says the king, kinder mocking him, "we'll try and get 'em to send for you"—which made them all laugh, and they said it was a prime good hit.

## Chapter XXVI

Well, when they was all gone, the king he asks Mary Jane how they was off for spare rooms, and she said she had one spare room, which would do for Uncle William, and she'd give her own room to Uncle Harvey, which was a little bigger, and she would turn into the room with her sisters and sleep on a cot; and up garret was a little cubby, with a pallet in it. The king said the cubby would do for his valley—meaning me.

So Mary Jane took us up, and she showed them their rooms, which was plain but nice. She said she'd have her frocks and a lot of other traps took out of her room if they was in Uncle Harvey's way, but he said they warn't. The frocks was hung along the wall, and before them was a curtain made out of calico that hung down to the floor. There was an old hair trunk in one corner, and a guitar box in another, and all sorts of little knickknacks and jimcracks around, like girls brisken up a room with. The king said it was all the more homely and more pleasanter for these fixings, and so don't disturb them. The duke's room was pretty small, but plenty good enough, and so was my cubby.

That night they had a big supper, and all them men and women was there, and I stood behind the king and the duke's chairs and waited on them, and the niggers waited on the rest. Mary Jane she set at the head of the table, with Susan along side of her, and said how bad the biscuits was, and how mean the preserves was, and how ornery and tough the fried chickens was—and all that kind of rot, the way women always do for to force out compliments; and the people all knowed everything was tip-top, and said so—said "How *do* you get biscuits to brown so nice?" and "Where, for the land's sake *did* you get these amaz'n pickles?" and all that kind of humbug talky-talk, just the way people always does at a supper, you know.

And when it was all done, me and the hare-lip had supper in the kitchen off of the leavings, whilst the others was helping the niggers clean up the things. The hare-lip she got to pumping me about England, and blest if I didn't think the ice was getting mighty thin, sometimes. She says:

"Did you ever see the king?"

"Who? William Fourth? Well, I bet I have—he goes to our church." I knowed he was dead years ago, but I never let on. So when I says he goes to our church, she says:

"What—regular?"

"Yes—regular. His pew's right over opposite ourn—on 'tother side the pulpit."

"I thought he lived in London?"

"Well, he does. Where *would* he live?"

"But I thought *you* lived in Sheffield?"

I see I was up a stump. I had to let on to get choked with a chicken bone, so as to get time to think how to get down again. Then I says:

"I mean he goes to our church regular when he's in Sheffield. That's only in the summer-time, when he comes there to take the sea baths."

"Why, how you talk—Sheffield ain't on the sea."

"Well, who said it was?"

"Why, you did."

"I *didn't*, nuther."

"You did!"

"I didn't."

"You did."

"I never said nothing of the kind."

"Well, what *did* you say, then?"

"Said he come to take the sea *baths*—that's what I said."

"Well, then! how's he going to take the sea baths if it ain't on the sea?"

"Looky here," I says, "did you ever see any Congress water?"[8]

"Yes."

"Well, did you have to go to Congress to get it?"

"Why, no."

"Well, neither does William Fourth have to go to the sea to get a sea bath."

"How does he get it, then?"

"Gets it the way people down here gets Congress water—in barrels. There in the palace at Sheffield they've got furnaces, and he wants his water hot. They can't bile that amount of water away off there at the sea. They haven't got no conveniences for it."

8. Famous mineral water from the Congress Spring in Saratoga, New York.

"Oh, I see, now. You might a said that in the first place and saved time."
When she said that, I see I was out of the woods again, and so I was comfortable and glad. Next, she says:
"Do you go to church, too?"
"Yes—regular."
"Where do you set?"
"Why, in our pew."
"*Whose* pew?"
"Why, ourn—your Uncle Harvey's."
"His'n? What does *he* want with a pew?"
"Wants it to set in. What did you *reckon* he wanted with it?"
"Why, I thought he'd be in the pulpit."
Rot him, I forgot he was a preacher. I see I was up a stump again, so I played another chicken bone and got another think. Then I says:
"Blame it, do you suppose there ain't but one preacher to a church?"
"Why, what do they want with more?"
"What!—to preach before a king? I never see such a girl as you. They don't have no less than seventeen."
"Seventeen! My land! Why, I wouldn't set out such a string as that, not if I *never* got to glory. It must take 'em a week."
"Shucks, they don't *all* of 'em preach the same day—only *one* of 'em."
"Well, then, what does the rest of 'em do?"
"Oh, nothing much. Loll around, pass the plate—and one thing or another. But mainly they don't do nothing."
"Well, then, what are they *for?*"
"Why, they're for *style*. Don't you know nothing?"
"Well, I don't *want* to know no such foolishness as that. How is servants treated in England? Do they treat 'em better 'n we treat our niggers?"
"*No!* A servant ain't nobody there. They treat them worse than dogs."
"Don't they give 'em holidays, the way we do, Christmas and New Year's week, and Fourth of July?"
"Oh, just listen! A body could tell *you* hain't ever been to England, by that. Why, Hare-l—why, Joanna, they never see a holiday from year's end to year's end; never go to the circus, nor theatre, nor nigger shows, nor nowheres."
"Nor church?"
"Nor church."
"But *you* always went to church."
Well, I was gone up again. I forgot I was the old man's servant. But next minute I whirled in on a kind of an explanation how a valley was different from a common servant, and *had* to go to church whether he wanted to or not, and set with the family, on account of it's being the law. But I didn't do it pretty good, and when I got done I see she warn't satisfied. She says:
"Honest injun, now, hain't you been telling me a lot of lies?"
"Honest injun," says I.
"None of it at all?"
"None of it at all. Not a lie in it," says I.
"Lay your hand on this book and say it."
I see it warn't nothing but a dictionary, so I laid my hand on it and said it. So then she looked a little better satisfied, and says:
"Well, then, I'll believe some of it; but I hope to gracious if I'll believe the rest."

"What is it you won't believe, Joe?" says Mary Jane, stepping in with Susan behind her. "It ain't right nor kind for you to talk so to him, and him a stranger and so far from his people. How would you like to be treated so?"

"That's always your way, Maim—always sailing in to help somebody before they're hurt. I hain't done nothing to him. He's told some stretchers, I reckon; and I said I wouldn't swallow it all; and that's every bit and grain I *did* say. I reckon he can stand a little thing like that, can't he?"

"I don't care whether 'twas little or whether 'twas big, he's here in our house and a stranger, and it wasn't good of you to say it. If you was in his place, it would make you feel ashamed; and so you ought'nt to say a thing to another person that will make *them* feel ashamed."

"Why, Maim, he said—"

"It don't make no difference what he *said*—that ain't the thing. The thing is for you to treat him *kind*, and not be saying things to make him remember he ain't in his own country and amongst his own folks."

I says to myself, *this* is a girl that I'm letting that old reptle rob her of her money!

Then Susan *she* waltzed in; and if you'll believe me, she did give Hare-lip hark from the tomb![9]

Says I to myself, And this is *another* one that I'm letting him rob her of her money!

Then Mary Jane she took another inning, and went in sweet and lovely again—which was her way—but when she got done there warn't hardly anything left o' poor Hare-lip. So she hollered.

"All right, then," says the other girls, "you just ask his pardon."

She done it, too. And she done it beautiful. She done it so beautiful it was good to hear; and I wished I could tell her a thousand lies, so she could do it again.

I says to myself, this is *another* one that I'm letting him rob her of her money. And when she got through, they all jest laid theirselves out to make me feel at home and know I was amongst friends. I felt so ornery and low down and mean, that I says to myself, My mind's made up; I'll hive that money for them or bust.

So then I lit out—for bed, I said, meaning some time or another. When I got by myself, I went to thinking the thing over. I says to myself, shall I go to that doctor, private, and blow on these frauds? No—that won't do. He might tell who told him; then the king and the duke would make it warm for me. Shall I go, private, and tell Mary Jane? No—I dasn't do it. Her face would give them a hint, sure; they've got the money, and they'd slide right out and get away with it. If she was to fetch in help, I'd get mixed up in the business, before it was done with, I judge. No, there ain't no good way but one. I got to steal that money, somehow; and I got to steal it some way that they won't suspicion that I done it. They've got a good thing, here; and they ain't agoing to leave till they've played this family and this town for all they're worth, so I'll find a chance time enough. I'll steal it, and hide it; and by-and-by, when I'm away down the river, I'll write a letter and tell Mary Jane where it's hid. But I better hive it to-night, if I can, because the doctor maybe hasn't let up as much as he lets on he has; he might scare them out of here, yet.

So, thinks I, I'll go and search them rooms. Up stairs the hall was dark, but

9. A chewing out.

I found the duke's room, and started to paw around it with my hands; but I recollected it wouldn't be much like the king to let anybody else take care of that money but his own self; so then I went to his room and begun to paw around there. But I see I couldn't do nothing without a candle, and I dasn't light one, of course. So I judged I'd got to do the other thing—lay for them, and eavesdrop. About that time, I hears their footsteps coming, and was going to skip under the bed; I reached for it, but it wasn't where I thought it would be; but I touched the curtain that hid Mary Jane's frocks, so I jumped in behind that and snuggled in amongst the gowns, and stood there perfectly still.

They come in and shut the door; and the first thing the duke done was to get down and look under the bed. Then I was glad I hadn't found the bed when I wanted it. And yet, you know, it's kind of natural to hide under the bed when you are up to anything private. They sets down, then, and the king says:

"Well, what is it? and cut it middlin' short, because it's better for us to be down there a whoopin'-up the mournin', than up here givin' 'em a chance to talk us over."

"Well, this is it, Capet. I ain't easy; I ain't comfortable. That doctor lays on my mind. I wanted to know your plans. I've got a notion, and I think it's a sound one."

"What is it, duke?"

"That we better glide out of this, before three in the morning, and clip it down the river with what we've got. Specially, seeing we got it so easy—*given* back to us, flung at our heads, as you may say, when of course we allowed to have to steal it back. I'm for knocking off and lighting out."

That made me feel pretty bad. About an hour or two ago, it would a been a little different, but now it made me feel bad and disappointed. The king rips out and says:

"What! And not sell out the rest o' the property? March off like a passel o' fools and leave eight or nine thous'n dollars' worth o' property layin' around jest sufferin' to be scooped in?—and all good salable stuff, too."

The duke he grumbled; said the bag of gold was enough, and he didn't want to go no deeper—didn't want to rob a lot of orphans of *everything* they had.

"Why, how you talk!" says the king. "We shan't rob 'em of nothing at all but jest this money. The people that *buys* the property is the suff'rers; because as soon's it's found out 'at we didn't own it—which won't be long after we've slid—the sale won't be valid, and it'll all go back to the estate. These-yer orphans 'll git their house back agin, and that's enough for *them*; they're young and spry, and k'n easy earn a livin'. *They* ain't agoing to suffer. Why, jest think—there's thous'n's and thous'n's that ain't nigh so well off. Bless you, *they* ain't got noth'n to complain of."

Well, the king he talked him blind; so at last he give in, and said all right, but said he believed it was blame foolishness to stay, and that doctor hanging over them. But the king says:

"Cuss the doctor! What do we k'yer for *him?* Hain't we got all the fools in town on our side? and ain't that a big enough majority in any town?"

So they got ready to go down stairs again. The duke says:

"I don't think we put that money in a good place."

That cheered me up. I'd begun to think I warn't going to get a hint of no kind to help me. The king says:

"Why?"

"Because Mary Jane 'll be in mourning from this out; and first you know the nigger that does up the rooms will get an order to box these duds up and put 'em away; and do you reckon a nigger can run across money and not borrow some of it?"

"Your head's level, agin, duke," says the king; and he come a fumbling under the curtain two or three foot from where I was. I stuck tight to the wall, and kept mighty still, though quivery; and I wondered what them fellows would say to me if they catched me; and I tried to think what I'd better do if they did catch me. But the king he got the bag before I could think more than about a half a thought, and he never suspicioned I was around. They took and shoved the bag through a rip in the straw tick that was under the feather bed, and crammed it in a foot or two amongst the straw and said it was all right, now, because a nigger only makes up the feather bed, and don't turn over the straw tick only about twice a year, and so it warn't in no danger of getting stole, now.

But I knowed better. I had it out of there before they was halfway down stairs. I groped along up to my cubby, and hid it there till I could get a chance to do better. I judged I better hide it outside of the house somewheres, because if they missed it they would give the house a good ransacking. I knowed that very well. Then I turned in, with my clothes all on; but I couldn't a gone to sleep, if I'd a wanted to, I was in such a sweat to get through with the business. By-and-by I heard the king and the duke come up; so I rolled off of my pallet and laid with my chin at the top of my ladder and waited to see if anything was going to happen. But nothing did.

So I held on till all the late sounds had quit and the early ones hadn't begun, yet; and then I slipped down the ladder.

## Chapter XXVII

I crept to their doors and listened; they was snoring, so I tip-toed along, and got down stairs all right. There warn't a sound anywheres. I peeped through a crack of the dining-room door, and see the men that was watching the corpse all sound asleep on their chairs. The door was open into the parlor, where the corpse was laying, and there was a candle in both rooms. I passed along, and the parlor door was open; but I see there warn't nobody in there but the remainders of Peter; so I shoved on by; but the front door was locked, and the key wasn't there. Just then I heard somebody coming down the stairs, back behind me. I run in the parlor, and took a swift look around, and the only place I see to hide the bag was in the coffin. The lid was shoved along about a foot, showing the dead man's face down in there, with a wet cloth over it, and his shroud on. I tucked the money-bag in under the lid, just down beyond where his hands was crossed, which made me creep, they was so cold, and then I run back across the room and in behind the door.

The person coming was Mary Jane. She went to the coffin, very soft, and kneeled down and looked in; then she put up her handkerchief and I see she begun to cry, though I couldn't hear her, and her back was to me. I slid out, and as I passed the dining-room I thought I'd make sure them watchers hadn't seen me; so I looked through the crack and everything was all right. They hadn't stirred.

I slipped up to bed, feeling ruther blue, on accounts of the thing playing out that way after I had took so much trouble and run so much resk about it. Says I, if it could stay where it is, all right; because when we get down the river a hundred mile or two, I could write back to Mary Jane, and she could dig him up again and get it; but that ain't the thing that's going to happen; the thing that's going to happen is, the money 'll be found when they come to screw on the lid. Then the king 'll get it again, and it 'll be a long day before he gives anybody another chance to smouch it from him. Of course I *wanted* to slide down and get it out of there, but I dasn't try it. Every minute it was getting earlier, now, and pretty soon some of them watchers would begin to stir, and I might get catched—catched with six thousand dollars in my hands that nobody hadn't hired me to take care of. I don't wish to be mixed up in no such business as that, I says to myself.

When I got down stairs in the morning, the parlor was shut up, and the watchers was gone. There warn't nobody around but the family and the widow Bartley and our tribe. I watched their faces to see if anything had been happening, but I couldn't tell.

Towards the middle of the day the undertaker come, with his man, and they set the coffin in the middle of the room on a couple of chairs, and then set all our chairs in rows, and borrowed more from the neighbors till the hall and the parlor and the dining-room was full. I see the coffin lid was the way it was before, but I dasn't go to look in under it, with folks around.

Then the people begun to flock in, and the beats and the girls took seats in the front row at the head of the coffin, and for a half an hour the people filed around slow, in single rank, and looked down at the dead man's face a minute, and some dropped in a tear, and it was all very still and solemn, only the girls and the beats holding handkerchiefs to their eyes and keeping their heads bent, and sobbing a little. There warn't no other sound but the scraping of the feet on the floor, and blowing noses—because people always blows them more at a funeral than they do at other places except church.

When the place was packed full, the undertaker he slid around in his black gloves with his softy soothering ways, putting on the last touches, and getting people and things all shipshape and comfortable, and making no more sound than a cat. He never spoke; he moved people around, he squeezed in late ones, he opened up passage-ways, and done it all with nods, and signs with his hands. Then he took his place over against the wall. He was the softest, glidingest, stealthiest man I ever see; and there warn't no more smile to him than there is to a ham.

They had borrowed a melodeum[1]—a sick one; and when everything was ready, a young woman set down and worked it, and it was pretty skreeky and colicky, and everybody joined in and sung, and Peter was the only one that had a good thing, according to my notion. Then the Reverend Hobson opened up, slow and solemn, and begun to talk; and straight off the most outrageous row busted out in the cellar a body ever heard; it was only one dog, but he made a most powerful racket, and he kept it up, right along; the parson he had to stand there, over the coffin, and wait—you couldn't hear yourself think. It was right down awkward, and nobody didn't seem to know what to do. But pretty soon they see that long-legged undertaker make a sign to the preacher as much as to say, "Don't you worry—just depend on me." Then he stooped

---

1. A melodeon, small keyboard organ.

down and begun to glide along the wall, just his shoulders showing over the people's heads. So he glided along, and the pow-wow and racket getting more and more outrageous all the time; and at last, when he had gone around two sides of the room, he disappears down cellar. Then, in about two seconds we heard a whack, and the dog he finished up with a most amazing howl or two, and then everything was dead still, and the parson begun his solemn talk where he left off. In a minute or two here comes this undertaker's back and shoulders gliding along the wall again; and so he glided, and glided, around three sides of the room, and then rose up, and shaded his mouth with his hands, and stretched his neck out towards the preacher, over the people's heads, and says, in a kind of a coarse whisper, *"He had a rat!"* Then he drooped down and glided along the wall again to his place. You could see it was a great satisfaction to the people, because naturally they wanted to know. A little thing like that don't cost nothing, and it's just the little things that makes a man to be looked up to and liked. There warn't no more popular man in town than what that undertaker was.

Well, the funeral sermon was very good, but pison long and tiresome; and then the king he shoved in and got off some of his usual rubbage, and at last the job was through, and the undertaker begun to sneak up on the coffin with his screw-driver. I was in a sweat then, and watched him pretty keen. But he never meddled at all; just slid the lid along, as soft as mush, and screwed it down tight and fast. So there I was! I didn't know whether the money was in there, or not. So, says I, spose somebody has hogged that bag on the sly?— now how do *I* know whether to write to Mary Jane or not? 'Spose she dug him up and didn't find nothing—what would she think of me? Blame it, I says, I might get hunted up and jailed; I'd better lay low and keep dark, and not write at all; the thing's awful mixed, now; trying to better it, I've worsened it a hundred times, and I wish to goodness I'd just let it alone, dad fetch the whole business!

They buried him, and we come back home, and I went to watching faces again—I couldn't help it, and I couldn't rest easy. But nothing come of it; the faces didn't tell me nothing.

The king he visited around, in the evening, and sweetened every body up, and made himself ever so friendly; and he give out the idea that his congregation over in England would be in a sweat about him, so he must hurry and settle up the estate right away, and leave for home. He was very sorry he was so pushed, and so was everybody; they wished he could stay longer, but they said they could see it couldn't be done. And he said of course him and William would take the girls home with them; and that pleased everybody too, because then the girls would be well fixed, and amongst their own relations; and it pleased the girls, too—tickled them so they clean forgot they ever had a trouble in the world; and told him to sell out as quick as he wanted to, they would be ready. Them poor things was that glad and happy it made my heart ache to see them getting fooled and lied to so, but I didn't see no safe way for me to chip in and change the general tune.

Well, blamed if the king didn't bill the house and the niggers and all the property for auction straight off—sale two days after the funeral; but anybody could buy private beforehand if they wanted to.

So the next day after the funeral, along about noontime, the girls' joy got the first jolt; a couple of nigger traders come along, and the king sold them the niggers reasonable, for three-day drafts[2] as they called it, and away they went, the two sons up the river to Memphis, and their mother down the river to Orleans. I thought them poor girls and them niggers would break their hearts for grief; they cried around each other, and took on so it most made me down sick to see it. The girls said they hadn't ever dreamed of seeing the family separated or sold away from the town. I can't ever get it out of my memory, the sight of them poor miserable girls and niggers hanging around each other's necks and crying; and I reckon I couldn't a stood it all but would a had to bust out and tell on our gang if I hadn't knowed the sale warn't no account and the niggers would be back home in a week or two.

The thing made a big stir in the town, too, and a good many come out flatfooted and said it was scandalous to separate the mother and the children that way. It injured the frauds some; but the old fool he bulled right along, spite of all the duke could say or do, and I tell you the duke was powerful uneasy.

Next day was auction day. About broad-day in the morning, the king and the duke come up in the garret and woke me up, and I see by their look that there was trouble. The king says:

"Was you in my room night before last?"

"No, your majesty"—which was the way I always called him when nobody but our gang warn't around.

"Was you in there yesterday er last night?"

"No, your majesty."

"Honor bright, now—no lies."

"Honor bright, your majesty, I'm telling you the truth. I hain't been anear your room since Miss Mary Jane took you and the duke and showed it to you."

The duke says:

"Have you seen anybody else go in there?"

"No, your grace, not as I remember, I believe."

"Stop and think."

I studied a while, and see my chance, then I says:

"Well, I see the niggers go in there several times."

Both of them give a little jump; and looked like they hadn't ever expected it, and then like they *had*. Then the duke says:

"What, *all* of them?"

"No—leastways not all at once. That is, I don't think I ever see them all come *out* at once but just one time."

"Hello—when was that?"

"It was the day we had the funeral. In the morning. It warn't early, because I overslept. I was just starting down the ladder, and I see them."

"Well, go on, *go* on—what did they do? How'd they act?"

"They didn't do nothing. And they didn't act anyway, much, as fur as I see. They tip-toed away; so I seen, easy enough, that they'd shoved in there to do up your majesty's room, or something, sposing you was up; and found you *warn't* up, and so they was hoping to slide out of the way of trouble without waking you up, if they hadn't already waked you up."

"Great guns, *this* is a go!" says the king; and both of them looked pretty sick, and tolerable silly. They stood there a thinking and scratching their heads,

2. Bank drafts or checks payable three days later.

a minute, and then the duke he bust into a kind of a little raspy chuckle, and says:

"It does beat all, how neat the niggers played their hand. They let on to be *sorry* they was going out of this region! and I believed they *was* sorry. And so did you, and so did everybody. Don't ever tell *me* any more that a nigger ain't got any histrionic talent. Why, the way they played that thing, it would fool *anybody*. In my opinion there's a fortune in 'em. If I had capital and a theatre, I wouldn't want a better lay out than that—and here we've gone and sold 'em for a song. Yes, and ain't privileged to sing the song, yet. Say, where *is* that song?—that draft."

"In the bank for to be collected. Where *would* it be?"

"Well, *that's* all right then, thank goodness."

Says I, kind of timid-like:

"Is something gone wrong?"

The king whirls on me and rips out:

"None o' your business! You keep your head shet, and mind y'r own affairs—if you got any. Long as you're in this town, don't you forget *that*, you hear?" Then he says to the duke, "We got to jest swaller it, and say noth'n: mum's the word for *us*."

As they was starting down the ladder, the duke he chuckles again, and says:

"Quick sales *and* small profits! It's a good business—yes."

The king snarls around on him and says,

"I was trying to do for the best, in sellin' 'm out so quick. If the profits has turned out to be none, lackin' considable, and none to carry, is it my fault any more'n it's yourn?"

"Well, *they'd* be in this house yet, and we *wouldn't* if I could a got my advice listened to."

The king sassed back, as much as was safe for him, and then swapped around and lit into *me* again. He give me down the banks[3] for not coming and *telling* him I see the niggers come out of his room acting that way—said any fool would a *knowed* something was up. And then waltzed in and cussed *himself* a while; and said it all come of him not laying late and taking his natural rest that morning, and he'd be blamed if he'd ever do it again. So they went off a jawing; and I felt dreadful glad I'd worked it all off onto the niggers and yet hadn't done the niggers no harm by it.

## Chapter XXVIII

By-and-by it was getting-up time; so I come down the ladder and started for down stairs, but as I come to the girls' room, the door was open, and I see Mary Jane setting by her old hair trunk, which was open and she'd been packing things in it—getting ready to go to England. But she had stopped now, with a folded gown in her lap, and had her face in her hands, crying. I felt awful bad to see it; of course anybody would. I went in there, and says:

"Miss Mary Jane, you can't abear to see people in trouble, and *I* can't—most always. Tell me about it."

So she done it. And it was the niggers—I just expected it. She said the beautiful trip to England was most about spoiled for her; she didn't know *how*

3. A cussing out.

she was ever going to be happy there, knowing the mother and the children warn't ever going to see each other no more—and then busted out bitterer than ever, and flung up her hands, and says

"Oh, dear, dear, to think they ain't *ever* going to see each other any more!"

"But they *will*—and inside of two weeks—and I *know* it!" says I.

Laws it was out before I could think!—and before I could budge, she throws her arms around my neck, and told me to say it *again*, say it *again*, say it *again!*

I see I had spoke too sudden, and said too much, and was in a close place. I asked her to let me think a minute; and she set there, very impatient and excited, and handsome, but looking kind of happy and eased-up, like a person that's had a tooth pulled out. So I went to studying it out. I says to myself, I reckon a body that ups and tells the truth when he is in a tight place, is taking considerable many resks, though I ain't had no experience, and can't say for certain; but it looks so to me, anyway; and yet here's a case where I'm blest if it don't look to me like the truth is better, and actuly *safer*, than a lie. I must lay it by in my mind, and think it over some time or other, it's so kind of strange and unregular. I never see nothing like it. Well, I says to myself at last, I'm agoing to chance it; I'll up and tell the truth this time, though it does seem most like setting down on a kag of powder and touching it off just to see where you'll go to. Then I says:

"Miss Mary Jane, is there any place out of town a little ways, where you could go and stay three or four days?"

"Yes—Mr. Lothrop's. Why?"

"Never mind why, yet. If I'll tell you how I know the niggers will see each other again—inside of two weeks—here in this house—and *prove* how I know it—will you go to Mr. Lothrop's and stay four days?"

"Four days!" she says; "I'll stay a year!"

"All right," I says, "I don't want nothing more out of *you* than just your word—I druther have it than another man's kiss-the-Bible." She smiled, and reddened up very sweet, and I says, "If you don't mind it, I'll shut the door—and bolt it."

Then I come back and set down again, and says:

"Don't you holler. Just set still, and take it like a man. I got to tell the truth, and you want to brace up, Miss Mary, because it's a bad kind, and going to be hard to take, but there ain't no help for it. These uncles of yourn ain't no uncles at all—they're a couple of frauds—regular dead-beats. There, now we're over the worst of it—you can stand the rest middling easy."

It jolted her up like everything, of course; but I was over the shoal water now, so I went right along, her eyes a blazing higher and higher all the time, and told her every blame thing, from where we first struck that young fool going up to the steamboat, clear through to where she flung herself onto the king's breast at the front door and he kissed her sixteen or seventeen times—and then up she jumps, with her face afire like sunset, and says:

"The brute! Come—don't waste a minute—not a *second*—we'll have them tarred and feathered, and flung in the river!"[4]

Says I;

---

4. The victim of this fairly commonplace mob punishment was tied to a rail, smeared with hot tar, and covered with feathers. Then the victim would be ridden out of town on the rail to the jeers of the mob.

"Cert'nly. But do you mean, *before* you go to Mr. Lothrop's, or—"

"Oh," she says, "what am I *thinking* about!" she says, and set right down again. "Don't mind what I said—please don't—you *won't*, now, *will* you?" Laying her silky hand on mine in that kind of a way that I said I would die first. "I never thought, I was so stirred up," she says; "now go on, and I won't do so any more. You tell me what to do, and whatever you say, I'll do it."

"Well," I says, "it's a rough gang, them two frauds, and I'm fixed so I got to travel with them a while longer, whether I want to or not—I druther not tell you why—and if you was to blow on them this town would get me out of their claws, and I'd be all right, but there'd be another person that you don't know about who'd be in big trouble. Well, we got to save *him*, hain't we? Of course. Well, then, we won't blow on them."

Saying them words put a good idea in my head. I see how maybe I could get me and Jim rid of the frauds; get them jailed here, and then leave. But I didn't want to run the raft in day-time, without anybody aboard to answer questions but me; so I didn't want the plan to begin working till pretty late to-night. I says:

"Miss Mary Jane, I'll tell you what we'll do—and you won't have to stay at Mr. Lothrop's so long, nuther. How fur is it?"

"A little short of four miles—right out in the country, back here."

"Well, that'll answer. Now you go along out there, and lay low till nine or half-past, to-night, and then get them to fetch you home again—tell them you've thought of something. If you get here before eleven, put a candle in this window, and if I don't turn up, wait *till* eleven, and *then* if I don't turn up it means I'm gone, and out of the way, and safe. Then you come out and spread the news around, and get these beats jailed."

"Good," she says, "I'll do it."

"And if it just happens so that I don't get away, but get took up along with them, you must up and say I told you the whole thing beforehand, and you must stand by me all you can."

"Stand by you, indeed I will. They sha'n't touch a hair of your head!" she says, and I see her nostrils spread and her eyes snap when she said it, too.

"If I get away, I sha'n't be here," I says, "to prove these rapscallions ain't your uncles, and I couldn't do it if I *was* here. I could swear they was beats and bummers, that's all; though that's worth something. Well, there's others can do that better than what I can—and they're people that ain't going to be doubted as quick as I'd be. I'll tell you how to find them. Gimme a pencil and a piece of paper. There—'*Royal Nonesuch, Bricksville.*' Put it away, and don't lose it. When the court wants to find out something about these two, let them send up to Bricksville and say they've got the men that played the Royal Nonesuch, and ask for some witnesses—why, you'll have that entire town down here before you can hardly wink, Miss Mary. And they'll come a-biling, too."

I judged we had got everything fixed about right, now. So I says:

"Just let the auction go right along, and don't worry. Nobody don't have to pay for the things they buy till a whole day after the auction, on accounts of the short notice, and they ain't going out of this till they get that money—and the way we've fixed it the sale ain't going to count, and they ain't going to *get* no money. It's just like the way it was with the niggers—it warn't no sale, and the niggers will be back before long. Why, they can't collect the money for the *niggers*, yet—they're in the worst kind of a fix, Miss Mary."

"Well," she says, "I'll run down to breakfast now, and then I'll start straight for Mr. Lothrop's."

" 'Deed, *that* ain't the ticket, Miss Mary Jane," I says, "by no manner of means; go *before* breakfast."

"Why?"

"What did you reckon I wanted you to go at all for, Miss Mary?"

"Well, I never thought—and come to think, I don't know. What was it?"

"Why, it's because you ain't one of these leather-face people. I don't want no better book than what your face is. A body can set down and read it off like coarse paint. Do you reckon you can go and face your uncles, when they come to kiss you good-morning, and never—"

"There, there, don't! Yes, I'll go before breakfast—I'll be glad to. And leave my sisters with them?"

"Yes—never mind about them. They've got to stand it yet a while. They might suspicion something if all of you was to go. I don't want you to see them, nor your sisters, nor nobody in this town—if a neighbor was to ask how is your uncles this morning, your face would tell something. No, you go right along, Miss Mary Jane, and I'll fix it with all of them. I'll tell Miss Susan to give your love to your uncles and say you've went away for a few hours for to get a little rest and change, or to see a friend, and you'll be back to-night or early in the morning."

"Gone to see a friend is all right, but I won't have my love given to them."

"Well, then, it sha'n't be." It was well enough to tell *her* so—no harm in it. It was only a little thing to do, and no trouble; and it's the little things that smoothes people's roads the most, down here below; it would make Mary Jane comfortable, and it wouldn't cost nothing. Then I says: "There's one more thing—that bag of money."

"Well, they've got that; and it makes me feel pretty silly to think *how* they got it."

"No, you're out, there. They hain't got it."

"Why, who's got it?"

"I wish I knowed, but I don't. I *had* it, because I stole it from them: and I stole it to give to you; and I know where I hid it, but I'm afraid it ain't there no more. I'm awful sorry, Miss Mary Jane, I'm just as sorry as I can be; but I done the best I could; I did, honest. I come nigh getting caught, and I had to shove it into the first place I come to, and run—and it warn't a good place."

"Oh, stop blaming yourself—it's too bad to do it, and I won't allow it—you couldn't help it; it wasn't your fault. Where did you hide it?"

I didn't want to set her to thinking about her troubles again; and I couldn't seem to get my mouth to tell her what would make her see that corpse laying in the coffin with that bag of money on his stomach. So for a minute I didn't say nothing—then I says:

"I'd ruther not *tell* you where I put it, Miss Mary Jane, if you don't mind letting me off; but I'll write it for you on a piece of paper, and you can read it along the road to Mr. Lothrop's; if you want to. Do you reckon that'll do?"

"Oh, yes."

So I wrote: "I put it in the coffin. It was in there when you was crying there, away in the night. I was behind the door, and I was mighty sorry for you, Miss Mary Jane."

It made my eyes water a little, to remember her crying there all by herself in the night, and them devils laying there right under her own roof, shaming her and robbing her; and when I folded it up and give it to her, I see the water come into her eyes, too; and she shook me by the hand, hard, and says:

"Good-bye—I'm going to do everything just as you've told me; and if I don't ever see you again, I sha'n't ever forget you, and I'll think of you a many and a many a time, and I'll *pray* for you, too!"—and she was gone.

Pray for me! I reckoned if she knowed me she'd take a job that was more nearer her size. But I bet she done it, just the same—she was just that kind. She had the grit to pray for Judus if she took the notion—there warn't no backdown to her, I judge. You may say what you want to, but in my opinion she had more sand in her than any girl I ever see; in my opinion she was just full of sand.[5] It sounds like flattery, but it ain't no flattery. And when it comes to beauty—and goodness too—she lays over them all. I hain't ever seen her since that time that I see her go out of that door; no, I hain't ever seen her since, but I reckon I've thought of her a many and a many a million times, and of her saying she would pray for me; and if ever I'd a thought it would do any good for me to pray for *her*, blamed if I wouldn't a done it or bust.

Well, Mary Jane she lit out the back way, I reckon; because nobody see her go. When I struck Susan and the hare-lip, I says:

"What's the name of them people over on t'other side of the river that you all goes to see sometimes?"

They says:

"There's several; but it's the Proctors, mainly."

"That's the name," I says; "I most forgot it. Well, Miss Mary Jane she told me to tell you she's gone over there in a dreadful hurry—one of them's sick."

"Which one?"

"I don't know; leastways I kinder forget; but I think it's—"

"Sakes alive, I hope it ain't *Hanner?*"

"I'm sorry to say it," I says, "but Hanner's the very one."

"My goodness—and she so well only last week! Is she took bad?"

"It ain't no name for it. They set up with her all night, Miss Mary Jane said, and they don't think she'll last many hours."

"Only think of that, now! What's the matter with her!"

I couldn't think of anything reasonable, right off that way, so I says:

"Mumps."

"Mumps your granny! They don't set up with people that's got the mumps."

"They don't, don't they? You better bet they do with *these* mumps. These mumps is different. It's a new kind, Miss Mary Jane said."

"How's it a new kind?"

"Because it's mixed up with other things."

"What other things?"

"Well, measles, and whooping-cough, and erysiplas, and consumption, and yaller janders, and brain fever, and I don't know what all."

"My land! And they call it the *mumps?*"

"That's what Miss Mary Jane said."

"Well, what in the nation do they call it the *mumps* for?"

"Why, because it *is* the mumps. That's what it starts with."

"Well, ther' ain't no sense in it. A body might stump his toe, and take

5. Courage, guts.

pison, and fall down the well, and break his neck, and bust his brains out, and somebody come along and ask what killed him, and some numskull up and say, 'Why, he stumped his *toe.*' Would ther' be any sense in that? No. And ther' ain't no sense in *this*, nuther. Is it ketching?"

"Is it *ketching*? Why, how you talk. Is a *harrow* catching?—in the dark? If you don't hitch onto one tooth, you're bound to on another, ain't you? And you can't get away with that tooth without fetching the whole harrow along, can you? Well, these kind of mumps is a kind of a harrow, as you may say— and it ain't no slouch of a harrow, nuther, you come to get it hitched on good."

"Well, it's awful, *I* think," says the hare-lip. "I'll go to Uncle Harvey and—"

"Oh, yes," I says, "I *would*. Of *course* I would. I wouldn't lose no time."

"Well, why wouldn't you?"

"Just look at it a minute, and maybe you can see. Hain't your uncles obleeged to get along home to England as fast as they can? And do you reckon they'd be mean enough to go off and leave you to go all that journey by yourselves? *You* know they'll wait for you. So fur, so good. Your uncle Harvey's a preacher, ain't he? Very well, then; is a *preacher* going to deceive a steamboat clerk? is he going to deceive a *ship clerk?*—so as to get them to let Miss Mary Jane go aboard? Now *you* know he ain't. What *will* he do, then? Why, he'll say, 'It's a great pity, but my church matters has got to get along the best way they can; for my niece has been exposed to the dreadful pluribus-unum[6] mumps, and so it's my bounden duty to set down here and wait the three months it takes to show on her if she's got it.' But never mind, if you think it's best to tell your uncle Harvey—"

"Shucks, and stay fooling around here when we could all be having good times in England whilst we was waiting to find out whether Mary Jane's got it or not? Why, you talk like a muggins."[7]

"Well, anyway, maybe you better tell some of the neighbors."

"Listen at that, now. You do beat all, for natural stupidness. Can't you *see* that *they'd* go and tell? Ther' ain't no way but just to not tell anybody at *all*."

"Well, maybe you're right—yes, I judge you *are* right."

"But I reckon we ought to tell Uncle Harvey she's gone out a while, anyway, so he wont be uneasy about her?"

"Yes, Miss Mary Jane she wanted you to do that. She says, 'Tell them to give Uncle Harvey and William my love and a kiss, and say I've run over the river to see Mr.—Mr.—what *is* the name of that rich family your uncle Peter used to think so much of?—I mean the one that—"

"Why, you must mean the Apthorps, ain't it?"

"Of course; bother them kind of names, a body can't ever seem to remember them, half the time, somehow. Yes, she said, say she has run over for to ask the Apthorps to be sure and come to the auction and buy this house, because she allowed her uncle Peter would ruther they had it than anybody else; and she's going to stick to them till they say they'll come, and then, if she ain't too tired, she's coming home; and if she is, she'll be home in the morning anyway. She said, don't say nothing about the Proctors, but only about the Apthorps— which'll be perfectly true, because she *is* going there to speak about their buy-ing the house; I know it, because she told me so, herself."

6. Huck reaches for the handiest Latin phrase he could be expected to know; meaning "many-in-one,"  the phrase is appropriate.  7. A fool.

"All right," they said, and cleared out to lay for their uncles, and give them the love and the kisses, and tell them the message.

Everything was all right now. The girls wouldn't say nothing because they wanted to go to England; and the king and the duke would ruther Mary Jane was off working for the auction than around in reach of Doctor Robinson. I felt very good; I judged I had done it pretty neat—I reckoned Tom Sawyer couldn't a done it no neater himself. Of course he would a throwed more style into it, but I can't do that very handy, not being brung up to it.

Well, they held the auction in the public square, along towards the end of the afternoon, and it strung along, and strung along, and the old man he was on hand and looking his level piousest, up there longside of the auctioneer, and chipping in a little Scripture, now and then, or a little goody-goody saying, of some kind, and the duke he was around goo-gooing for sympathy all he knowed how, and just spreading himself generly.

But by-and-by the thing dragged through, and everything was sold. Everything but a little old trifling lot in the graveyard. So they'd got to work *that* off—I never see such a giraff as the king was for wanting to swallow *everything*. Well, whilst they was at it, a steamboat landed, and in about two minutes up comes a crowd a whooping and yelling and laughing and carrying on, and singing out:

"*Here's* your opposition line! here's your two sets o' heirs to old Peter Wilks—and you pays your money and you takes your choice!"

## Chapter XXIX

They was fetching a very nice looking old gentleman along, and a nice looking younger one, with his right arm in a sling. And my souls, how the people yelled, and laughed, and kept it up. But I didn't see no joke about it, and I judged it would strain the duke and the king some to see any. I reckoned they'd turn pale. But no, nary a pale did *they* turn. The duke he never let on he suspicioned what was up, but just went a goo-gooing around, happy and satisfied, like a jug that's googling out buttermilk; and as for the king, he just gazed and gazed down sorrowful on them newcomers like it give him the stomach-ache in his very heart to think there could be such frauds and rascals in the world. Oh, he done it admirable. Lots of the principal people gethered around the king, to let him see they was on his side. That old gentleman that had just come looked all puzzled to death. Pretty soon he begun to speak, and I see, straight off, he pronounced *like* an Englishman, not the king's way, though the king's *was* pretty good, for an imitation. I can't give the old gent's words, nor I can't imitate him; but he turned around to the crowd, and says, about like this:

"This is a surprise to me which I wasn't looking for; and I'll acknowledge, candid and frank, I ain't very well fixed to meet it and answer it; for my brother and me has had misfortunes, he's broke his arm, and our baggage got put off at a town above here, last night in the night by a mistake. I am Peter Wilks's brother Harvey, and this is his brother William, which can't hear nor speak—and can't even make signs to amount to much, now 't he's only got one hand to work them with. We are who we say we are; and in a day or two, when I get the baggage, I can prove it. But, up till then, I won't say nothing more, but go to the hotel and wait."

So him and the new dummy started off; and the king he laughs, and blethers out:

"Broke his arm—*very* likely *ain't* it?—and very convenient, too, for a fraud that's got to make signs, and hain't learnt how. Lost their baggage! That's *mighty* good!—and mighty ingenious—under the *circumstances!*"

So he laughed again; and so did everybody else, except three or four, or maybe half a dozen. One of these was that doctor; another one was a sharp looking gentleman, with a carpet-bag of the old-fashioned kind made out of carpet-stuff, that had just come off of the steamboat and was talking to him in a low voice, and glancing towards the king now and then and nodding their heads—it was Levi Bell, the lawyer that was gone up to Louisville; and another one was a big rough husky that come along and listened to all the old gentleman said, and was listening to the king now. And when the king got done, this husky up and says:

"Say, looky here; if you are Harvey Wilks, when'd you come to this town?"

"The day before the funeral, friend," says the king.

"But what time o' day?"

"In the evenin'—'bout an hour er two before sundown."

"*How'd* you come?"

"I come down on the *Susan Powell*, from Cincinnati."

"Well, then, how'd you come to be up at the Pint in the *mornin'*—in a canoe?"

"I warn't up at the Pint in the mornin'."

"It's a lie."

Several of them jumped for him and begged him not to talk that way to an old man and a preacher.

"Preacher be hanged, he's a fraud and a lair. He was up at the Pint that mornin'. I live up there, don't I? Well, I was up there, and he was up there. I *see* him there. He come in a canoe, along with Tim Collins and a boy."

The doctor he up and says:

"Would you know the boy again if you was to see him, Hines?"

"I reckon I would, but I don't know. Why, yonder he is, now. I know him perfectly easy."

It was me he pointed at. The doctor says:

"Neighbors. I don't know whether the new couple is frauds or not; but if *these* two ain't frauds, I am an idiot, that's all. I think it's our duty to see that they don't get away from here till we've looked into this thing. Come along, Hines; come along, the rest of you. We'll take these fellows to the tavern and affront them with t'other couple, and I reckon we'll find out *something* before we get through."

It was nuts for the crowd, though maybe not for the king's friends; so we all started. It was about sundown. The doctor he led me along by the hand, and was plenty kind enough, but he never let *go* my hand.

We all got in a big room in the hotel, and lit up some candles, and fetched in the new couple. First, the doctor says:

"I don't wish to be too hard on these two men, but *I* think they're frauds, and they may have complices that we don't know nothing about. If they have, won't the complices get away with that bag of gold Peter Wilks left? It ain't unlikely. If these men ain't frauds, they won't object to sending for that money and letting us keep it till they prove they're all right—ain't that so?"

Everybody agreed to that. So I judged they had our gang in a pretty tight place, right at the outstart. But the king he only looked sorrowful, and says:

"Gentlemen, I wish the money was there, for I ain't got no disposition to throw anything in the way of a fair, open, out-and-out investigation o' this misable business; but alas, the money ain't there; you k'n send and see, if you want to."

"Where is it, then?"

"Well, when my niece give it to me to keep for her, I took and hid it inside o' the straw tick o' my bed, not wishin' to bank it for the few days we'd be here, and considerin' the bed a safe place, we not bein' used to niggers, and suppos'n' 'em honest, like servants in England. The niggers stole it the very next mornin' after I had went down stairs; and when I sold 'em, I hadn't missed the money yit, so they got clean away with it. My servant here k'n tell you 'bout it gentlemen."

The doctor and several said "Shucks!" and I see nobody didn't altogether believe him. One man asked me if I see the niggers steal it. I said no, but I see them sneaking out of the room and hustling away, and I never thought nothing, only I reckoned they was afraid they had waked up my master and was trying to get away before he made trouble with them. That was all they asked me. Then the doctor whirls on me and says:

"Are *you* English too?"

I says yes; and him and some others laughed, and said, "Stuff!"

Well, then they sailed in on the general investigation, and there we had it, up and down, hour in, hour out, and nobody never said a word about supper, nor ever seemed to think about it—and so they kept it up, and kept it up; and it *was* the worst mixed-up thing you ever see. They made the king tell his yarn, and they made the old gentleman tell his'n; and anybody but a lot of prejudiced chuckleheads would a *seen* that the old gentleman was spinning truth and t'other one lies. And by-and-by they had me up to tell what I knowed. The king he give me a left-handed look out of the corner of his eye, and so I knowed enough to talk on the right side. I begun to tell about Sheffield, and how we lived there, and all about the English Wilkses, and so on; but I didn't get pretty fur till the doctor begun to laugh; and Levi Bell, the lawyer says:

"Set down, my boy, I wouldn't strain myself, if I was you. I reckon you ain't used to lying, it don't seem to come handy; what you want is practice. You do it pretty awkward."

I didn't care nothing for the compliment, but I was glad to be let off, anyway.

The doctor he started to say something, and turns and says:

"If you'd been in town at first, Levi Bell—"

The king broke in and reached out his hand, and says:

"Why, is this my poor dead brother's old friend that he's wrote so often about?"

The lawyer and him shook hands, and the lawyer smiled and looked pleased, and they talked right along a while, and then got to one side and talked low; and at last the lawyer speaks up and says:

"That'll fix it. I'll take the order and send it, along with your brother's, and then they'll know it's all right."

So they got some paper and a pen, and the king he set down and twisted his

head to one side, and chawed his tongue, and scrawled off something; and
then they give the pen to the duke—and then for the first time, the duke
looked sick. But he took the pen and wrote. So then the lawyer turns to the
new old gentleman and says:
"You and your brother please write a line or two and sign your names."
The old gentleman wrote, but nobody couldn't read it. The lawyer looked
powerful astonished, and says:
"Well, it beats *me*"—and snaked a lot of old letters out of his pocket, and
examined them, and then examined the old man's writing, and then *them*
again; and then says: "These old letters is from Harvey Wilks; and here's *these*
two's handwritings, and anybody can see *they* didn't write them" (the king and
the duke looked sold and foolish, I tell you, to see how the lawyer had took
them in), "and here's *this* old gentleman's handwriting, and anybody can tell,
easy enough, *he* didn't write them—fact is, the scratches he makes ain't properly *writing*, at all. Now here's some letters from—"
The new old gentleman says:
"If you please, let me explain. Nobody can read my hand but my brother
there—so he copies for me. It's *his* hand you've got there, not mine."
"*Well!*" says the lawyer, "this *is* a state of things. I've got some of William's
letters too; so if you'll get him to write a line or so we can com—"
"He *can't* write with his left hand," says the old gentleman. "If he could use
his right hand, you would see that he wrote his own letters and mine too. Look
at both, please—they're by the same hand."
The lawyer done it, and says:
"I believe it's so—and if it ain't so, there's a heap stronger resemblance than
I'd noticed before, anyway. Well, well, well! I thought we was right on the
track of a slution, but it's gone to grass, partly. But anyway, *one* thing is
proved—*these* two ain't either of 'em Wilkses"—and he wagged his head
towards the king and the duke.
Well, what do you think?—that muleheaded old fool wouldn't give in *then!*
Indeed he wouldn't. Said it warn't no fair test. Said his brother William was
the cussedest joker in the world, and hadn't *tried* to write—*he* see William was
going to play one of his jokes the minute he put the pen to paper. And so he
warmed up and went warbling and warbling right along, till he was actuly
beginning to believe what he was saying, *himself*—but pretty soon the new old
gentleman broke in, and says:
"I've thought of something. Is there anybody here that helped to lay out my
br—helped to lay out the late Peter Wilks for burying?"
"Yes," says somebody, "me and Ab Turner done it. We're both here."
Then the old man turns towards the king, and says:
"Peraps this gentleman can tell me what was tatooed on his breast?"
Blamed if the king didn't have to brace up mighty quick, or he'd a squshed
down like a bluff bank that the river has cut under, it took him so sudden—
and mind you, it was a thing that was calculated to make most *anybody* sqush
to get fetched such a solid one as that without any notice—because how was
*he* going to know what was tatooed on the man? He whitened a little; he
couldn't help it; and it was mighty still in there, and everybody bending a little
forwards and gazing at him. Says I to myself, Now he'll throw up the sponge—
there ain't no more use. Well, did he? A body can't hardly believe it, but he
didn't. I reckon he thought he'd keep the thing up till he tired them people

out, so they'd thin out, and him and the duke could break loose and get away.
Anyway, he set there, and pretty soon he begun to smile, and says:

"Mf! It's a *very* tough question, *ain't* it! Yes, sir, I k'n tell you what's tatooed
on his breast. It's jest a small, thin, blue arrow—that's what it is; and if you
don't look clost, you can't see it. *Now* what do you say—hey?"

Well, *I* never see anything like that old blister for clean out-and-out cheek.

The new old gentleman turns brisk towards Ab Turner and his pard, and
his eye lights up like he judged he'd got the king *this* time, and says:

"There—you've heard what he said! Was there any such mark on Peter
Wilks's breast?"

Both of them spoke up and says:

"We didn't see no such mark."

"Good!" says the old gentleman. "Now, what you *did* see on his breast was
a small dim P, and a B (which is an initial he dropped when he was young),
and a W, with dashes between them, so: P—B—W"—and he marked them
that way on a piece of paper. "Come—ain't that what you saw?"

Both of them spoke up again, and says:

"No, we *didn't.* We never seen any marks at all."

Well, everybody *was* in a state of mind, now; and they sings out:

"The whole *bilin'* of 'm 's frauds! Le's duck 'em! le's drown 'em! le's ride
'em on a rail!" and everybody was whooping at once, and there was a rattling
pow-wow. But the lawyer he jumps on the table and yells, and says:

"Gentlemen—gentle*men!* Hear me just a word—just a *single* word—if you
PLEASE! There's one way yet—let's go and dig up the corpse and look."

That took them.

"Hooray!" they all shouted, and was starting right off; but the lawyer and
the doctor sung out:

"Hold on, hold on! Collar all these four men and the boy, and fetch *them*
along, too!"

"We'll do it!" they all shouted: "and if we don't find them marks we'll lynch
the whole gang!"

I *was* scared, now, I tell you. But there warn't no getting away, you know.
They gripped us all, and marched us right along, straight for the graveyard,
which was a mile and a half down the river, and the whole town at our heels,
for we made noise enough, and it was only nine in the evening.

As we went by our house I wished I hadn't sent Mary Jane out of town;
because now if I could tip her the wink, she'd light out and save me, and blow
on our dead-beats.

Well, we swarmed along down the river road, just carrying on like wild-
cats; and to make it more scary, the sky was darking up, and the lightning
beginning to wink and flitter, and the wind to shiver amongst the leaves. This
was the most awful trouble and most dangersome I ever was in; and I was
kinder stunned; everything was going so different from what I had allowed for;
stead of being fixed so I could take my own time, if I wanted to, and see all
the fun, and have Mary Jane at my back to save me and set me free when the
close-fit come, here was nothing in the world betwixt me and sudden death
but just them tatoo-marks. If they didn't find them—

I couldn't bear to think about it; and yet, somehow, I couldn't think about
nothing else. It got darker and darker, and it was a beautiful time to give the
crowd the slip; but that big husky had me by the wrist—Hines—and a body

might as well try to give Goliar[8] the slip. He dragged me right along, he was so excited; and I had to run to keep up.

When they got there they swarmed into the graveyard and washed over it like an overflow. And when they got to the grave, they found they had about a hundred times as many shovels as they wanted, but nobody hadn't thought to fetch a lantern. But they sailed into digging, anyway, by the flicker of the lightning, and sent a man to the nearest house a half a mile off, to borrow one.

So they dug and dug, like everything; and it got awful dark, and the rain started, and the wind swished and swushed along, and the lightning come brisker and brisker, and the thunder boomed; but them people never took no notice of it, they was so full of this business; and one minute you could see everything and every face in that big crowd, and the shovelfuls of dirt sailing up out of the grave, and the next second the dark wiped it all out, and you couldn't see nothing at all.

At last they got out the coffin, and begun to unscrew the lid, and then such another crowding, and shouldering, and shoving as there was, to scrouge in and get a sight, you never see; and in the dark, that way, it was awful. Hines he hurt my wrist dreadful, pulling and tugging so, and I reckon he clean forgot I was in the world, he was so excited and panting.

All of a sudden the lightning let go a perfect sluice of white glare, and somebody sings out:

"By the living jingo, here's the bag of gold on his breast!"

Hines let out a whoop, like everybody else, and dropped my wrist and give a big surge to bust his way in and get a look, and the way I lit out and shinned for the road in the dark, there ain't nobody can tell.

I had the road all to myself, and I fairly flew—leastways I had it all to myself except the solid dark, and the now-and-then glares, and the buzzing of the rain, and the thrashing of the wind, and the splitting of the thunder; and sure as you are born I did clip it along!

When I struck the town, I see there warn't nobody out in the storm, so I never hunted for no back streets, but humped it straight through the main one; and when I begun to get towards our house I aimed my eye and set it. No light there; the house all dark—which made me feel sorry and disappointed, I didn't know why. But at last, just as I was sailing by, *flash* comes the light in Mary Jane's window! and my heart swelled up sudden, like to bust; and the same second the house and all was behind me in the dark, and wasn't ever going to be before me no more in this world. She *was* the best girl I ever see, and had the most sand.

The minute I was far enough above the town to see I could make the tow-head, I begun to look sharp for a boat to borrow; and the first time the lightning showed me one that wasn't chained, I snatched it and shoved. It was a canoe, and warn't fastened with nothing but a rope. The tow-head was a rattling big distance off, away out there in the middle of the river, but I didn't lose no time; and when I struck the raft at last, I was so fagged I would a just laid down to blow and gasp if I could afforded it. But I didn't. As I sprung aboard I sung out:

"Out with you Jim, and set her loose! Glory be to goodness, we're shut of them!"

8. Goliath, a Philistine giant who challenged the Israelites. David, a young shepherd boy, accepted his challenge and killed him with a stone thrown from a sling.

Jim lit out, and was a coming for me with both arms spread, he was so full of joy; but when I glimpsed him in the lightning, my heart shot up in my mouth, and I went overboard backwards; for I forgot he was old King Lear and a drownded A-rab all in one, and it most scared the livers and lights out of me. But Jim fished me out, and was going to hug me and bless me, and so on, he was so glad I was back and we was shut of the king and the duke, but I says:

"Not now—have it for breakfast, have it for breakfast! Cut loose and let her slide!"

So, in two seconds, away we went, a sliding down the river, and it *did* seem so good to be free again and all by ourselves on the big river and nobody to bother us. I had to skip around a bit, and jump up and crack my heels a few times, I couldn't help it; but about the third crack, I noticed a sound that I knowed mighty well—and held my breath and listened and waited—and sure enough, when the next flash busted out over the water, here they come!—and just a laying to their oars and making their skiff hum! It was the king and the duke.

So I wilted right down onto the planks, then, and give up; and it was all I could do to keep from crying.

## Chapter XXX

When they got aboard, the king went for me, and shook me by the collar, and says:

"Tryin' to give us the slip, was ye, you pup! Tired of our company—hey!"

I says:

"No, your majesty, we warn't—*please* don't, your majesty!"

"Quick, then, and tell us what *was* your idea, or I'll shake the insides out o' you!"

"Honest, I'll tell you everything, just as it happened, your majesty. The man that had aholt of me was very good to me, and kept saying he had a boy about as big as me that died last year, and he was sorry to see a boy in such a dangerous fix; and when they was all took by surprise by finding the gold, and made a rush for the coffin, he lets go of me and whispers, 'Heel it, now, or they'll hang ye, sure!' and I lit out. It didn't seem no good for *me* to stay—I couldn't do nothing, and I didn't want to be hung if I could get away. So I never stopped running till I found the canoe; and when I got here I told Jim to hurry, or they'd catch me and hang me yet, and said I was afeard you and the duke wasn't alive, now, and I was awful sorry, and so was Jim, and was awful glad when we see you coming, you may ask Jim if I didn't."

Jim said it was so; and the king told him to shut up, and said, "Oh, yes, it's *mighty* likely!" and shook me up again, and said he reckoned he'd drownded me. But the duke says:

"Leggo the boy, you old idiot! Would *you* a done any different? Did you inquire around for *him*, when you got loose? *I* don't remember it."

So the king let go of me, and begun to cuss that town and everybody in it. But the duke says:

"You better a blame sight give *yourself* a good cussing, for you're the one that's entitled to it most. You hain't done a thing, from the start, that had any sense in it, except coming out so cool and cheeky with that imaginary blue-arrow mark. That *was* bright—it was right down bully; and it was the thing that saved us. For if it hadn't been for that, they'd a jailed us till them Englishmen's baggage come—and then—the penitentiary, you bet! But that trick took 'em to the graveyard, and the gold done us a still bigger kindness; for if the excited fools hadn't let go all holts and made that rush to get a look, we'd a slept in our cravats to-night—cravats warranted to *wear*, too—longer than *we'd* need 'em."

They was still a minute—thinking—then the king says, kind of absent-minded like:

"Mf! And we reckoned the *niggers* stole it!"

That made me squirm!

"Yes," says the duke, kinder slow, and deliberate, and sarcastic, "We did."

After about a half a minute, the king drawls out:

"Leastways—*I* did."

The duke says, the same way:

"On the contrary—*I* did."

The king kind of ruffles up, and says:

"Looky here, Bilgewater, what'r you referrin' to?"

The duke says, pretty brisk:

"When it comes to that, maybe you'll let me ask, what was *you* referring to?"

"Shucks!" says the king, very sarcastic; "but *I* don't know—maybe you was asleep, and didn't know what you was about."

The duke bristles right up, now, and says:

"Oh, let *up* on this cussed nonsense—do you take me for a blame' fool? Don't you reckon *I* know who hid that money in that coffin?"

"*Yes*, sir! I know you *do* know—because you done it yourself!"

"It's a lie!"—and the duke went for him. The king sings out:

"Take y'r hands off!—leggo my throat!—I take it all back!"

The duke says:

"Well, you just own up, first, that you *did* hide that money there, intending to give me the slip one of these days, and come back and dig it up, and have it all to yourself."

"Wait jest a minute, duke—answer me this one question, honest and fair; if you didn't put the money there, say it, and I'll b'lieve you, and take back everything I said."

"You old scoundrel, I didn't, and you know I didn't. There, now!"

"Well, then, I b'lieve you. But answer me only jest this one more—now *don't* git mad; didn't you have it in your *mind* to hook the money and hide it?"

The duke never said nothing for a little bit; then he says:

"Well—I don't care if I *did*, I didn't *do* it, anyway. But you not only had it in mind to do it, but you *done* it."

"I wisht I may never die if I done it, duke, and that's honest. I won't say I warn't *goin'* to do it, because I *was*; but you—I mean somebody—got in ahead o' me."

"It's a lie! You done it, and you got to *say* you done it, or—"

The king begun to gurgle, and then he gasps out:

" 'Nough!—I *own up!*"

I was very glad to hear him say that, it made me feel much more easier than what I was feeling before. So the duke took his hands off, and says:

"If you ever deny it again, I'll drown you. It's *well* for you to set there and blubber like a baby—it's fitten for you, after the way you've acted. I never see such an old ostrich for wanting to gobble everything—and I a trusting you all the time, like you was my own father. You ought to be ashamed of yourself to stand by and hear it saddled onto a lot of poor niggers and you never say a word for 'em. It makes me feel ridiculous to think I was soft enough to *believe* that rubbage. Cuss you, I can see, now, why you was so anxious to make up the deffesit—you wanted to get what money I'd got out of the Nonesuch and one thing or another, and scoop it *all!*"

The king says, timid, and still a snuffling:

"Why, duke, it was you that said make up the deffersit, it warn't me."

"Dry up! I don't want to hear no more *out* of you!" says the duke. "And *now* you see what you *got* by it. They've got all their own money back, and all of *ourn* but a shekel or two, *besides.* G'long to bed—and don't you deffersit *me* no more deffersits, long 's *you* live!"

So the king sneaked into the wigwam, and took to his bottle for comfort; and before long the duke tackled *his* bottle; and so in about a half an hour they was as thick as thieves again, and the tighter they got, the lovinger they got; and went off a snoring in each other's arms. They both got powerful mellow, but I noticed the king didn't get mellow enough to forget to remember to not deny about hiding the money-bag again. That made me feel easy and satisfied. Of course when they got to snoring, we had a long gabble, and I told Jim everything.

## Chapter XXXI

We dasn't stop again at any town, for days and days; kept right along down the river. We was down south in the warm weather, now, and a mighty long ways from home. We begun to come to trees with Spanish moss on them, hanging down from the limbs like long gray beards. It was the first I ever see it growing, and it made the woods look solemn and dismal. So now the frauds reckoned they was out of danger, and they begun to work the villages again.

First they done a lecture on temperance; but they didn't make enough for them both to get drunk on. Then in another village they started a dancing school; but they didn't know no more how to dance than a kangaroo does; so the first prance they made, the general public jumped in and pranced them out of town. Another time they tried a go at yellocution; but they didn't yellocute long till the audience got up and give them a solid good cussing and made them skip out. They tackled missionarying, and mesmerizering, and doctoring, and telling fortunes, and a little of everything; but they couldn't seem to have no luck. So at last they got just about dead broke, and laid around the raft, as she floated along, thinking, and thinking, and never saying nothing, by the half a day at a time, and dreadful blue and desperate.

And at last they took a change, and begun to lay their heads together in the wigwam and talk low and confidential two or three hours at a time. Jim and me got uneasy. We didn't like the look of it. We judged they was studying up some kind of worse deviltry than ever. We turned it over and over, and at last we made up our minds they was going to break into somebody's house or store, or was going into the counterfeit-money business, or something. So then we was pretty scared, and made up an agreement that we wouldn't have nothing in the world to do with such actions, and if we ever got the least show we would give them the cold shake, and clear out and leave them behind. Well, early one morning we hid the raft in a good safe place about two mile below a little bit of a shabby village, named Pikesville, and the king he went ashore, and told us all to stay hid whilst he went up to town and smelt around to see if anybody had got any wind of the Royal Nonesuch there yet. ("House to rob, you *mean*," says I to myself; "and when you get through robbing it you'll come back here and wonder what's become of me and Jim and the raft—and you'll have to take it out in wondering.") And he said if he warn't back by midday, the duke and me would know it was all right, and we was to come along.

So we staid where we was. The duke he fretted and sweated around, and was in a mighty sour way. He scolded us for everything, and we couldn't seem to do nothing right; he found fault with every little thing. Something was a-brewing, sure. I was good and glad when midday come and no king; we could have a change, anyway—and maybe a chance for *the* change, on top of it. So me and the duke went up to the village, and hunted around there for the king, and by-and-by we found him in the back room of a little low doggery,[9] very tight, and a lot of loafers bullyragging him for sport, and he a cussing and threatening with all his might, and so tight he couldn't walk, and couldn't do nothing to them. The duke he begun to abuse him for an old fool, and the king begun to sass back; and the minute they was fairly at it, I lit out, and shook the reefs out of my hind legs, and spun down the river road like a deer— for I see our chance; and I made up my mind that it would be a long day before they ever see me and Jim again. I got down there all out of breath but loaded up with joy, and sung out—

"Set her loose, Jim, we're all right, now!"

But there warn't no answer, and nobody come out of the wigwam. Jim was gone! I set up a shout—and then another—and then another one; and run this way and that in the woods, whooping and screeching; but it warn't no use— old Jim was gone. Then I set down and cried; I couldn't help it. But I couldn't set still long. Pretty soon I went out on the road, trying to think what I better do, and I run across a boy walking, and asked him if he'd seen a strange nigger, dressed so and so, and he says:

"Yes."

"Whereabouts?" says I.

"Down to Silas Phelps's place, two mile below here. He's a runaway nigger, and they've got him. Was you looking for him?"

"You bet I ain't! I run across him in the woods about an hour or two ago, and he said if I hollered he'd cut my livers out—and told me to lay down and stay where I was; and I done it. Been there ever since; afeard to come out."

"Well," he says, "you needn't be afraid no more, becuz they've got him. He run off f'm down South, som'ers."

"It's a good job they got him."

"Well, I *reckon*! There's two hundred dollars reward on him. It's like picking up money out'n the road."

"Yes, it is—and I could a had it if I'd been big enough; I see him *first.* Who nailed him?"

"It was an old fellow—a stranger—and he sold out his chance in him for

9. Cheap barroom.

forty dollars, becuz he's got to go up the river and can't wait. Think o' that, now! You bet I'd wait, if it was seven year."

"That's me, every time," says I. "But maybe his chance ain't worth no more than that, if he'll sell it so cheap. Maybe there's something ain't straight about it."

"But it *is*, though—straight as a string. I see the handbill myself. It tells all about him, to a dot—paints him like a picture, and tells the plantation he's frum, below New*rleans*. No-siree-*bob*, they ain't no trouble 'bout *that* speculation, you bet you. Say, gimme a chaw tobacker, won't ye?"

I didn't have none, so he left. I went to the raft, and set down in the wigwam to think. But I couldn't come to nothing. I thought till I wore my head sore, but I couldn't see no way out of the trouble. After all this long journey, and after all we'd done for them scoundrels, here was it all come to nothing, everything all busted up and ruined, because they could have the heart to serve Jim such a trick as that, and make him a slave again all his life, and amongst strangers, too, for forty dirty dollars.

Once I said to myself it would be a thousand times better for Jim to be a slave at home where his family was, as long as he'd *got* to be a slave, and so I'd better write a letter to Tom Sawyer and tell him to tell Miss Watson where he was. But I soon give up that notion, for two things: she'd be mad and disgusted at his rascality and ungratefulness for leaving her, and so she'd sell him straight down the river again; and if she didn't, everybody naturally despises an ungrateful nigger, and they'd make Jim feel it all the time, and so he'd feel ornery and disgraced. And then think of *me!* It would get all around, that Huck Finn helped a nigger to get his freedom; and if I was to ever see anybody from that town again, I'd be ready to get down and lick his boots for shame. That's just the way: a person does a low-down thing, and then he don't want to take no consequences of it. Thinks as long as he can hide it, it ain't no disgrace. That was my fix exactly. The more I studied about this, the more my conscience went to grinding me, and the more wicked and low-down and ornery I got to feeling. And at last, when it hit me all of a sudden that here was the plain hand of Providence slapping me in the face and letting me know my wickedness was being watched all the time from up there in heaven, whilst I was stealing a poor old woman's nigger that hadn't ever done me no harm, and now was showing me there's One that's always on the lookout, and ain't agoing to allow no such miserable doings to go only just so fur and no further, I most dropped in my tracks I was so scared. Well, I tried the best I could to kinder soften it up somehow for myself, by saying I was brung up wicked, and so I warn't so much to blame; but something inside of me kept saying, "There was the Sunday school, you could a gone to it; and if you'd a done it they'd a learnt you, there, that people that acts as I'd been acting about the nigger goes to everlasting fire."

It made me shiver. And I about made up my mind to pray; and see if I couldn't try to quit being the kind of a boy I was, and be better. So I kneeled down. But the words wouldn't come. Why wouldn't they? It warn't no use to try and hide it from Him. Nor from *me*, neither. I knowed very well why they wouldn't come. It was because my heart warn't right; it was because I warn't square; it was because I was playing double. I was letting *on* to give up sin, but away inside of me I was holding on to the biggest one of all. I was trying to make my mouth *say* I would do the right thing and the clean thing, and go and write to that nigger's owner and tell where he was; but deep down in me I knowed it was a lie—and He knowed it. You can't pray a lie—I found that out. So I was full of trouble, full as I could be; and didn't know what to do. At last I had an idea; and I says, I'll go and write the letter—and *then* see if I can pray. Why, it was astonishing, the way I felt as light as a feather, right straight off, and my troubles all gone. So I got a piece of paper and a pencil, all glad and excited, and set down and wrote:

> Miss Watson your runaway nigger Jim is down here two mile below Pikesville and Mr. Phelps has got him and he will give him up for the reward if you send.
>
> HUCK FINN.

I felt good and all washed clean of sin for the first time I had ever felt so in my life, and I knowed I could pray now. But I didn't do it straight off, but laid the paper down and set there thinking—thinking how good it was all this happened so, and how near I come to being lost and going to hell. And went on thinking. And got to thinking over our trip down the river; and I see Jim before me, all the time, in the day, and in the night-time, sometimes moonlight, sometimes storms, and we a floating along, talking, and singing, and laughing. But somehow I couldn't seem to strike no places to harden me against him, but only the other kind. I'd see him standing my watch on top of his'n, stead of calling me, so I could go on sleeping; and see him how glad he was when I come back out of the fog; and when I come to him again in the swamp, up there where the feud was; and such-like times; and would always call me honey, and pet me, and do everything he could think of for me, and how good he always was; and at last I struck the time I saved him by telling the men we had small-pox aboard, and he was so grateful, and said I was the best friend old Jim ever had in the world, and the *only* one he's got now; and then I happened to look around, and see that paper.

It was a close place. I took it up, and held it in my hand. I was a trembling, because I'd got to decide, forever, betwixt two things, and I knowed it. I studied a minute, sort of holding my breath, and then says to myself:

"All right, then, I'll *go* to hell"—and tore it up.

It was awful thoughts, and awful words, but they was said. And I let them stay said; and never thought no more about reforming. I shoved the whole thing out of my head; and said I would take up wickedness again, which was in my line, being brung up to it, and the other warn't. And for a starter, I would go to work and steal Jim out of slavery again; and if I could think up anything worse, I would do that, too; because as long as I was in, and in for good, I might as well go the whole hog.

Then I set to thinking over how to get at it, and turned over considerable many ways in my mind; and at last fixed up a plan that suited me. So then I took the bearings of a woody island that was down the river a piece, and as soon as it was fairly dark I crept out with my raft and went for it, and hid it there, and then turned in. I slept the night through, and got up before it was light, and had my breakfast, and put on my store clothes, and tied up some others and one thing or another in a bundle, and took the canoe and cleared for shore. I landed below where I judged was Phelps's place, and hid my bundle in the woods, and then filled up the canoe with water, and loaded rocks into her and sunk her where I could find her again when I wanted her, about a quarter of a mile below a little steam sawmill that was on the bank.

Then I struck up the road, and when I passed the mill I see a sign on it, "Phelps's Sawmill," and when I come to the farmhouses, two or three hundred yards further along, I kept my eyes peeled, but didn't see nobody around, though it was good daylight, now. But I didn't mind, because I didn't want to see nobody just yet—I only wanted to get the lay of the land. According to my plan, I was going to turn up there from the village, not from below. So I just took a look, and shoved along, straight for town. Well, the very first man I see, when I got there, was the duke. He was sticking up a bill for the Royal Nonesuch—three-night performance—like that other time. *They* had the cheek, them frauds! I was right on him, before I could shirk. He looked astonished, and says:

"Hel-*lo!* Where'd *you* come from?" Then he says, kind of glad and eager, "Where's the raft?—got her in a good place?"

I says:

"Why, that's just what I was agoing to ask your grace."

Then he didn't look so joyful—and says:

"What was your idea for asking *me?*" he says.

"Well," I says, "when I see the king in that doggery yesterday, I says to myself, we can't get him home for hours, till he's soberer; so I went a loafing around town to put in the time, and wait. A man up and offered me ten cents to help him pull a skiff over the river and back to fetch a sheep, and so I went along; but when we was dragging him to the boat, and the man left me aholt of the rope and went behind him to shove him along, he was too strong for me, and jerked loose and run, and we after him. We didn't have no dog, and so we had to chase him all over the country till we tired him out. We never got him till dark, then we fetched him over, and I started down for the raft. When I got there and see it was gone, I says to myself, 'they've got into trouble and had to leave; and they've took my nigger, which is the only nigger I've got in the world, and now I'm in a strange country, and ain't got no property no more, nor nothing, and no way to make my living;' so I set down and cried. I slept in the woods all night. But what *did* become of the raft then?—and Jim, poor Jim!"

"Blamed if *I* know—that is, what's become of the raft. That old fool had made a trade and got forty dollars, and when we found him in the doggery the loafers had matched half dollars with him and got every cent but what he'd spent for whisky; and when I got him home late last night and found the raft gone, we said, 'That little rascal has stole our raft and shook us, and run off down the river.' "

"I wouldn't shake my *nigger*, would I?—the only nigger I had in the world, and the only property."

"We never thought of that. Fact is, I reckon we'd come to consider him *our* nigger; yes, we did consider him so—goodness knows we had trouble enough for him. So when we see the raft was gone, and we flat broke, there warn't anything for it but to try the Royal Nonesuch another shake. And I've pegged along ever since, dry as a powderhorn. Where's that ten cents? Give it here."

I had considerable money, so I give him ten cents, but begged him to spend it for something to eat, and give me some, because it was all the money I had, and I hadn't had nothing to eat since yesterday. He never said nothing. The next minute he whirls on me and says:

"Do you reckon that nigger would blow on us? We'd skin him if he done that!"

"How can be blow? Hain't he run off?"

"No! That old fool sold him, and never divided with me, and the money's gone."

"Sold him?" I says, and begun to cry; "why, he was *my* nigger, and that was my money. Where is he?—I want my nigger."

"Well, you can't *get* your nigger, that's all—so dry up your blubbering. Looky here—do you think you'd venture to blow on us? Blamed if I think I'd trust you. Why, if you *was* to blow on us—"

He stopped, but I never see the duke look so ugly out of his eyes before. I went on a-whimpering, and says:

"I don't want to blow on nobody; and I ain't got no time to blow, nohow. I got to turn out and find my nigger."

He looked kinder bothered, and stood there with his bills fluttering on his arm, thinking, and wrinkling up his forehead. At last he says:

"I'll tell you something. We got to be here three days. If you'll promise you won't blow, and won't let the nigger blow, I'll tell you where to find him."

So I promised, and he says:

"A farmer by the name of Silas Ph—" and then he stopped. You see he started to tell me the truth; but when he stopped, that way, and begun to study and think again, I reckoned he was changing his mind. And so he was. He wouldn't trust me; he wanted to make sure of having me out of the way the whole three days. So pretty soon he says: "The man that bought him is named Abram Foster—Abram G. Foster—and he lives forty mile back here in the country, on the road to Lafayette."

"All right," I says, "I can walk it in three days. And I'll start this very afternoon."

"No you won't, you'll start *now*; and don't you lose any time about it, neither, nor do any gabbling by the way. Just keep a tight tongue in your head and move right along, and then you won't get into trouble with *us*, d'ye hear?"

That was the order I wanted, and that was the one I played for. I wanted to be left free to work my plans.

"So clear out," he says; "and you can tell Mr. Foster whatever you want to. Maybe you can get him to believe that Jim *is* your nigger—some idiots don't require documents—leastways I've heard there's such down South here. And when you tell him the handbill and the reward's bogus, maybe he'll believe you when you explain to him what the idea was for getting 'em out. Go 'long, now, and tell him anything you want to; but mind you don't work your jaw any *between* here and there."

So I left, and struck for the back country. I didn't look around, but I kinder felt like he was watching me. But I knowed I could tire him out at that. I went straight out in the country as much as a mile, before I stopped; then I doubled back through the woods towards Phelps's. I reckoned I better start in on my plan straight off, without fooling around, because I wanted to stop Jim's mouth till these fellows could get away. I didn't want no trouble with their kind. I'd seen all I wanted to of them, and wanted to get entirely shut of them.

## Chapter XXXII

When I got there it was all still and Sunday-like, and hot and sunshiny—the hands was gone to the fields; and there was them kind of faint dronings of bugs and flies in the air that makes it seem so lonesome and like everybody's dead and gone; and if a breeze fans along and quivers the leaves, it makes you feel mournful, because you feel like it's spirits whispering—spirits that's been dead ever so many years—and you always think they're talking about *you*. As a general thing it makes a body wish *he* was dead, too, and done with it all.

Phelps's was one of these little one-horse cotton plantations; and they all look alike. A rail fence round a two-acre yard; a stile, made out of logs sawed off and up-ended, in steps, like barrels of a different length, to climb over the fence with, and for the women to stand on when they are going to jump onto a horse; some sickly grass-patches in the big yard, but mostly it was bare and smooth, like an old hat with the nap rubbed off; big double log house for the white folks—hewed logs, with the chinks stopped up with mud or mortar, and these mud-stripes been whitewashed some time or another; round-log kitchen, with a big broad, open but roofed passage joining it to the house; log smoke-house back of the kitchen; three little log nigger-cabins in a row t'other side the smokehouse; one little hut all by itself away down against the back fence, and some outbuildings down a piece the other side; ash-hopper,[1] and big kettle to bile soap in, by the little hut; bench by the kitchen door, with bucket of water and a gourd; hound asleep there, in the sun; more hounds asleep, round about; about three shade-trees away off in a corner; some currant bushes and gooseberry bushes in one place by the fence; outside of the fence a garden and a water-melon patch; then the cotton fields begins; and after the fields, the woods.

I went around and clumb over the back stile by the ash-hopper, and started for the kitchen. When I got a little ways, I heard the dim hum of a spinning-wheel wailing along up and sinking along down again; and then I knowed for certain I wished I was dead—for that *is* the lonesomest sound in the whole world.[2]

I went right along, not fixing up any particular plan, but just trusting to Providence to put the right words in my mouth when the time come; for I'd noticed that Providence always did put the right words in my mouth, if I left it alone.

When I got half-way, first one hound and then another got up and went for me, and of course I stopped and faced them, and kept still. And such another pow-wow as they made! In a quarter of a minute I was a kind of a hub of a wheel, as you may say—spokes made out of dogs—circle of fifteen of them packed together around me, with their necks and noses stretched up towards me, a barking and howling; and more a coming; you could see them sailing over fences and around corners from everywheres.

A nigger woman come tearing out of the kitchen with a rolling-pin in her hand, singing out, "Begone! *you* Tige! you Spot! begone, sah!" and she fetched first one and then another of them a clip and sent him howling, and then the rest followed; and the next second, half of them come back, wagging their tails

---

1. A container for lye used in making soap.
2. For the details of the Phelps plantation Clemens drew on his memories of vacations at his Uncle John

Quarles's farm near Hannibal. See Clemens's *Autobiography* for his vivid evocation of the farm.

around me and making friends with me. There ain't no harm in a hound, nohow.

And behind the woman comes a little nigger girl and two little nigger boys, without anything on but tow-linen shirts, and they hung onto their mother's gown, and peeped out from behind her at me, bashful, the way they always do. And here comes the white woman running from the house, about forty-five or fifty year old, bare-headed, and her spinning-stick in her hand; and behind her comes her little white children, acting the same way the little niggers was doing. She was smiling all over so she could hardly stand—and says:

"It's *you*, at last!—*ain't* it?"

I out with a "Yes'm," before I thought.

She grabbed me and hugged me tight; and then gripped me by both hands and shook and shook; and the tears come in her eyes, and run down over; and she couldn't seem to hug and shake enough, and kept saying, "You don't look as much like your mother as I reckoned you would, but law sakes, I don't care for that, I'm *so* glad to see you! Dear, dear, it does seem like I could eat you up! Children, it's your cousin Tom!—tell him howdy."

But they ducked their heads, and put their fingers in their mouths, and hid behind her. So she run on:

"Lize, hurry up and get him a hot breakfast, right away—or did you get your breakfast on the boat?"

I said I had got it on the boat. So then she started for the house, leading me by the hand, and the children tagging after. When we got there, she set me down in a split-bottomed chair, and set herself down on a little low stool in front of me, holding both of my hands, and says:

"Now I can have a *good* look at you; and laws-a-me, I've been hungry for it a many and a many a time, all these long years, and it's come at last! We been expecting you a couple of days and more. What's kep' you?—boat get aground?"

"Yes'm—she—"

"Don't say yes'm—say Aunt Sally. Where'd she get aground?"

I didn't rightly know what to say, because I didn't know whether the boat would be coming up the river or down. But I go a good deal on instinct; and my instinct said she would be coming up—from down toward Orleans. That didn't help me much, though; for I didn't know the names of bars down that way. I see I'd got to invent a bar, or forget the name of the one we got aground on—or—Now I struck an idea, and fetched it out:

"It warn't the grounding—that didn't keep us back but a little. We blowed out a cylinder-head."

"Good gracious! anybody hurt?"

"No'm. Killed a nigger."

"Well, it's lucky; because sometimes people do get hurt. Two years ago last Christmas, your uncle Silas was coming up from Newrleans on the old *Lally Rook*,[3] and she blowed out a cylinder-head and crippled a man. And I think he died afterwards. He was a Babtist. Your uncle Silas knowed a family in Baton Rouge that knowed his people very well. Yes, I remember, now he *did* die. Mortification[4] set in, and they had to amputate him. But it didn't save

3. *Lalla Rookh* (1817) is a popular Romantic poem by     4. Gangrene.
Thomas Moore.

him. Yes, it was mortification—that was it. He turned blue all over, and died in the hope of a glorious resurrection. They say he was a sight to look at. Your uncle's been up to the town every day to fetch you. And he's gone again, not more'n an hour ago; he'll be back any minute, now. You must a met him on the road, didn't you?—oldish man, with a—"

"No, I didn't see nobody, Aunt Sally. The boat landed just at daylight, and I left my baggage on the wharf-boat and went looking around the town and out a piece in the country, to put in the time and not get here too soon; and so I come down the back way."

"Who'd you give the baggage to?"

"Nobody."

"Why, child, it'll be stole!"

"Not where I hid it I reckon it won't," I says.

"How'd you get your breakfast so early on the boat?"

It was kinder thin ice, but I says:

"The captain see me standing around, and told me I better have something to eat before I went ashore; so he took me in the texas to the officers' lunch, and give me all I wanted."

I was getting so uneasy I couldn't listen good. I had my mind on the children all the time; I wanted to get them out to one side, and pump them a little, and find out who I was. But I couldn't get no show, Mrs. Phelps kept it up and run on so. Pretty soon she made the cold chills streak all down my back, because she says:

"But here we're a running on this way, and you hain't told me a word about Sis, nor any of them. Now I'll rest my works a little, and you start up yourn; just tell me *everything*— tell me all about 'm all—every one of 'm; and how they are, and what they're doing, and what they told you to tell me; and every last thing you can think of."

Well, I see I was up a stump—and up it good. Providence had stood by me this fur, all right, but I was hard and tight aground, now. I see it warn't a bit of use to try to go ahead—I'd *got* to throw up my hand. So I says to myself, here's another place where I got to resk the truth. I opened my mouth to begin; but she grabbed me and hustled me in behind the bed, and says:

"Here he comes! stick your head down lower—there, that'll do; you can't be seen, now. Don't you let on you're here. I'll play a joke on him. Children, don't you say a word."

I see I was in a fix, now. But it warn't no use to worry; there warn't nothing to do but just hold still, and try to be ready to stand from under when the lightning struck.

I had just one little glimpse of the old gentleman when he come in, then the bed hid him. Mrs. Phelps she jumps for him and says:

"Has he come?"

"No," says her husband.

"Good-*ness* gracious!" she says, "what in the world *can* have become of him?"

"I can't imagine," says the old gentleman; "and I must say, it makes me dreadful uneasy."

"Uneasy!" she says, "I'm ready to go distracted! He *must* a come; and you've missed him along the road. I *know* it's so—something *tells* me so."

"Why Sally, I *couldn't* miss him along the road—*you* know that."

"But oh, dear, dear, what *will* Sis say! He must a come! You must a missed him. He—"

"Oh, don't distress me any more'n I'm already distressed. I don't know what in the world to make of it. I'm at my wit's end, and I don't mind acknowledging 't I'm right down scared. But there's no hope that he's come; for he *couldn't* come and me miss him. Sally, it's terrible—just terrible—something's happened to the boat, sure!"

"Why, Silas! Look yonder!—up the road!—ain't that somebody coming?"

He sprung to the window at the head of the bed, and that give Mrs. Phelps the chance she wanted. She stooped down quick, at the foot of the bed, and give me a pull, and out I come; and when he turned back from the window, there she stood, a-beaming and a-smiling like a house afire, and I standing pretty meek and sweaty alongside. The old gentleman stared, and says:

"Why, who's that?"

"Who do you reckon 't is?"

"I hain't no idea. Who *is* it?"

"It's *Tom Sawyer!*"

By jings, I most slumped through the floor. But there warn't no time to swap knives;[5] the old man grabbed me by the hand and shook, and kept on shaking; and all the time, how the woman did dance around and laugh and cry; and then how they both did fire off questions about Sid, and Mary, and the rest of the tribe.

But if they was joyful, it warn't nothing to what I was; for it was like being born again, I was so glad to find out who I was. Well, they froze to me for two hours; and at last when my chin was so tired it couldn't hardly go, any more, I had told them more about my family—I mean the Sawyer family—than ever happened to any six Sawyer families. And I explained all about how we blowed out a cylinder-head at the mouth of the White River and it took us three days to fix it. Which was all right, and worked first rate; because *they* didn't know but what it would take three days to fix it. If I'd a called it a bolt-head it would a done just as well.

Now I was feeling pretty comfortable all down one side, and pretty uncomfortable all up the other. Being Tom Sawyer was easy and comfortable; and it stayed easy and comfortable till by-and-by I hear a steamboat coughing along down the river—then I says to myself, spose Tom Sawyer come down on that boat?—and spose he steps in here, any minute, and sings out my name before I can throw him a wink to keep quiet? Well, I couldn't *have* it that way—it wouldn't do at all. I must go up the road and waylay him. So I told the folks I reckoned I would go up to the town and fetch down my baggage. The old gentleman was for going along with me, but I said no, I could drive the horse myself, and I druther he wouldn't take no trouble about me.

## Chapter XXXIII

So I started for town, in the wagon, and when I was half-way I see a wagon coming, and sure enough it was Tom Sawyer, and I stopped and waited till he come along. I says "Hold on!" and it stopped alongside, and his mouth opened

5. Change plans.

up like a trunk, and staid so; and he swallowed two or three times like a person that's got a dry throat, and then says:

"I hain't ever done you no harm. You know that. So then, what you want to come back and ha'nt *me* for?"

I says:

"I hain't come back—I hain't been *gone.*"

When he heard my voice, it righted him up some, but he warn't quite satisfied yet. He says:

"Don't you play nothing on me, because I wouldn't on you. Honest injun, now, you ain't a ghost?"

"Honest injun, I ain't," I says.

"Well—I—I—well, that ought to settle it, of course; but I can't somehow seem to understand it, no way. Looky here, warn't you ever murdered *at all?*"

"No. I warn't ever murdered at all—I played it on them. You come in here and feel of me if you don't believe me."

So he done it; and it satisfied him; and he was that glad to see me again, he didn't know what to do. And he wanted to know all about it right off; because it was a grand adventure, and mysterious, and so it hit him where he lived. But I said, leave it along till by-and-by; and told his driver to wait, and we drove off a little piece, and I told him the kind of a fix I was in, and what did he reckon we better do? He said, let him alone a minute, and don't disturb him. So he thought and thought, and pretty soon he says:

"It's all right, I've got it. Take my trunk in your wagon, and let on it's your'n; and you turn back and fool along slow, so as to get to the house about the time you ought to; and I'll go towards town a piece, and take a fresh start, and get there a quarter or a half an hour after you; and you needn't let on to know me, at first."

I says:

"All right; but wait a minute. There's one more thing—a thing that *nobody* don't know but me. And that is, there's a nigger here that I'm trying to steal out of slavery—and his name is *Jim*—old Miss Watson's Jim."

He says:

"What! Why Jim is—"

He stopped and went to studying. I says:

"*I* know what you'll say. You'll say it's dirty low-down business; but what if it is?—*I'm* low down; and I'm agoing to steal him, and I want you to keep mum and not let on. Will you?"

His eye lit up, and he says:

"I'll *help* you steal him!"

Well, I let go all holts then, like I was shot. It was the most astonishing speech I ever heard—and I'm bound to say Tom Sawyer fell, considerable, in my estimation. Only I couldn't believe it. Tom Sawyer a *nigger stealer!*

"Oh, shucks," I says, "you're joking."

"I ain't joking, either."

"Well, then," I says, "joking or no joking, if you hear anything said about a runaway nigger, don't forget to remember that *you* don't know nothing about him, and *I* don't know nothing about him."

Then we took the trunk and put it in my wagon, and he drove off his way, and I drove mine. But of course I forgot all about driving slow, on accounts of being glad and full of thinking; so I got home a heap too quick for that length of trip. The old gentleman was at the door, and he says:

"Why, this is wonderful. Who ever would a thought it was in that mare to do it. I wish we'd a timed her. And she hain't sweated a hair—not a hair. It's wonderful. Why, I wouldn't take a hundred dollars for that horse now; I wouldn't, honest; and yet I'd a sold her for fifteen before, and thought 'twas all she was worth."

That's all he said. He was the innocentest, best old soul I ever see. But it warn't surprising; because he warn't only just a farmer, he was a preacher, too, and had a little one-horse log church down back of the plantation, which he built it himself at his own expense, for a church and school-house, and never charged nothing for his preaching, and it was worth it, too. There was plenty other farmer-preachers like that, and done the same way, down South.

In about half an hour Tom's wagon drove up to the front stile, and Aunt Sally she see it through the window because it was only about fifty yards, and says:

"Why, there's somebody come! I wonder who 'tis? Why, I do believe it's a stranger. Jimmy" (that's one of the children), "run and tell Lize to put on another plate for dinner."

Everybody made a rush for the front door, because, of course, a stranger don't come *every* year, and so he lays over the yaller fever, for interest, when he does come. Tom was over the stile and starting for the house; the wagon was spinning up the road for the village, and we was all bunched in the front door. Tom had his store clothes on, and an audience—and that was always nuts for Tom Sawyer. In them circumstances it warn't no trouble to him to throw in an amount of style that was suitable. He warn't a boy to meeky along up that yard like a sheep; no, he come ca'm and important, like the ram. When he got afront of us, he lifts his hat ever so gracious and dainty, like it was the lid of a box that had butterflies asleep in it and he didn't want to disturb them, and says:

"Mr. Archibald Nichols, I presume?"

"No, my boy," says the old gentleman, "I'm sorry to say 't your driver has deceived you; Nichols's place is down a matter of three mile more. Come in, come in."

Tom he took a look back over his shoulder, and says, "Too late—he's out of sight."

"Yes, he's gone, my son, and you must come in and eat your dinner with us; and then we'll hitch up and take you down to Nichols's."

"Oh, I *can't* make you so much trouble; I couldn't think of it. I'll walk—I don't mind the distance."

"But we won't *let* you walk—it wouldn't be Southern hospitality to do it. Come right in."

"Oh, *do*," says Aunt Sally; "it ain't a bit of trouble to us, not a bit in the world. You *must* stay. It's a long, dusty three mile, and we *can't* let you walk. And besides, I've already told 'em to put on another plate, when I see you coming; so you mustn't disappoint us. Come right in, and make yourself at home."

So Tom he thanked them very hearty and handsome, and let himself be persuaded, and come in; and when he was in, he said he was a stranger from Hicksville, Ohio, and his name was William Thompson—and he made another bow.

Well, he run on, and on, and on, making up stuff about Hicksville and everybody in it he could invent, and I getting a little nervous, and wondering how this was going to help me out of my scrape; and at last, still talking along, he reached over and kissed Aunt Sally right on the mouth, and then settled back again in his chair, comfortable, and was going on talking; but she jumped up and wiped it off with the back of her hand, and says:

"You owdacious puppy!"

He looked kind of hurt, and says:

"I'm surprised at you, m'am."

"You're s'rp— Why, what do you reckon *I* am? I've a good notion to take and—say, what do you mean by kissing me?"

He looked kind of humble, and says:

"I didn't mean nothing, m'am. I didn't mean no harm. I—I—thought you'd like it."

"Why, you born fool!" She took up the spinning-stick, and it looked like it was all she could do to keep from giving him a crack with it. "What made you think I'd like it?"

"Well, I don't know. Only, they—they—told me you would."

"*They* told you I would. Whoever told you's *another* lunatic. I never heard the beat of it. Who's *they?*"

"Why—everybody. They all said so, m'am."

It was all she could do to hold in; and her eyes snapped, and her fingers worked like she wanted to scratch him; and she says:

"Who's everybody?' Out with their names—or ther'll be an idiot short."

He got up and looked distressed, and fumbled his hat, and says:

"I'm sorry, and I warn't expecting it. They told me to. They all told me to. They all said kiss her; and said she'll like it. They all said it—every one of them. But I'm sorry, m'am, and I won't do it no more—I won't, honest."

"You won't, won't you? Well, I sh'd *reckon* you won't!"

"No'm, I'm honest about it; I won't ever do it again. Till you ask me."

"Till I *ask* you! Well, I never see the beat of it in my born days! I lay you'll be the Methusalem-numskull[6] of creation before ever *I* ask you—or the likes of you."

"Well," he says, "it does surprise me so. I can't make it out, somehow. They said you would, and I thought you would. But—" He stopped and looked around slow, like he wished he could run across a friendly eye, somewhere's; and fetched up on the old gentleman's, and says, "Didn't *you* think she'd like me to kiss her, sir?"

"Why, no, I—I—well, no, I b'lieve I didn't."

Then he looks on around, the same way, to me—and says:

"Tom, didn't *you* think Aunt Sally 'd open out her arms and say, 'Sid Sawyer—' "

"My land!" she says, breaking in and jumping for him, "you impudent young rascal, to fool a body so—" and was going to hug him, but he fended her off, and says:

"No, not till you've asked me, first."

So she didn't lose no time, but asked him; and hugged him and kissed him, over and over again, and then turned him over to the old man, and he took what was left. And after they got a little quiet again, she says:

"Why, dear me, I never see such a surprise. We warn't looking for *you*, at all, but only Tom. Sis never wrote to me about anybody coming but him."

---

6. Methuselah was a biblical patriarch said to have lived 969 years.

"It's because it warn't *intended* for any of us to come but Tom," he says; "but I begged and begged, and at the last minute she let me come, too; so, coming down the river, me and Tom thought it would be a first-rate surprise for him to come here to the house first, and for me to by-and-by tag along and drop in and let on to be a stranger. But it was a mistake, Aunt Sally. This ain't no healthy place for a stranger to come."

"No—not impudent whelps, Sid. You ought to had your jaws boxed; I hain't been so put out since I don't know when. But I don't care, I don't mind the terms—I'd be willing to stand a thousand such jokes to have you here. Well, to think of that performance! I don't deny it, I was most putrified[7] with astonishment when you give me that smack."

We had dinner out in that broad open passage betwixt the house and the kitchen; and there was things enough on that table for seven families—and all hot, too; none of your flabby tough meat that's laid in a cupboard in a damp cellar all night and tastes like a hunk of old cold cannibal in the morning. Uncle Silas he asked a pretty long blessing over it, but it was worth it; and it didn't cool it a bit, neither, the way I've seen them kind of interruptions do, lots of times.

There was a considerable good deal of talk, all the afternoon, and me and Tom was on the lookout all the time, but it warn't no use, they didn't happen to say nothing about any runaway nigger, and we was afraid to try to work up to it. But at supper, at night, one of the little boys says:

"Pa, mayn't Tom and Sid and me go to the show?"

"No," says the old man, "I reckon there ain't going to be any; and you couldn't go if there was; because the runaway nigger told Burton and me all about that scandalous show, and Burton said he would tell the people; so I reckon they've drove the owdacious loafers out of town before this time."

So there it was!—but *I* couldn't help it. Tom and me was to sleep in the same room and bed; so, being tired, we bid good-night and went up to bed, right after supper, and clumb out of the window and down the lightning-rod, and shoved for the town; for I didn't believe anybody was going to give the king and the duke a hint, and so, if I didn't hurry up and give them one they'd get into trouble sure.

On the road Tom he told me all about how it was reckoned I was murdered, and how pap disappeared, pretty soon, and didn't come back no more, and what a stir there was when Jim run away; and I told Tom all about our Royal Nonesuch rapscallions, and as much of the raft-voyage as I had time to; and as we struck into the town and up through the middle of it—it was as much as half-after eight, then—here comes a raging rush of people, with torches, and an awful whooping and yelling, and banging tin pans and blowing horns; and we jumped to one side to let them go by; and as they went by, I see they had the king and the duke astraddle of a rail—that is, I knowed it *was* the king and the duke, though they was all over tar and feathers, and didn't look like nothing in the world that was human—just looked like a couple of monstrous big soldier-plumes. Well, it made me sick to see it; and I was sorry for them poor pitiful rascals, it seemed like I couldn't ever feel any hardness against them any more in the world. It was a dreadful thing to see. Human beings *can* be awful cruel to one another.

We see we was too late—couldn't do no good. We asked some stragglers

---

7. Petrified or stunned.

about it, and they said everybody went to the show looking very innocent; and laid low and kept dark till the poor old king was in the middle of his cavortings on the stage; then somebody give a signal, and the house rose up and went for them.

So we poked along back home, and I warn't feeling so brash as I was before, but kind of ornery, and humble, and to blame, somehow—though *I* hadn't done anything. But that's always the way; it don't make no difference whether you do right or wrong, a person's conscience ain't got no sense, and just goes for him *anyway*. If I had a yaller dog that didn't know no more than a person's conscience does, I would pison him. It takes up more room than all the rest of a person's insides, and yet ain't no good, nohow. Tom Sawyer he says the same.

## Chapter XXXIV

We stopped talking, and got to thinking. By-and-by Tom says:

"Looky here, Huck, what fools we are, to not think of it before! I bet I know where Jim is."

"No! Where?"

"In that hut down by the ash-hopper. Why, looky here. When we was at dinner, didn't you see a nigger man go in there with some vittles?"

"Yes."

"What did you think the vittles was for?"

"For a dog."

"So'd I. Well, it wasn't for a dog."

"Why?"

"Because part of it was watermelon."

"So it was—I noticed it. Well, it does beat all, that I never thought about a dog not eating watermelon. It shows how a body can see and don't see at the same time."

"Well, the nigger unlocked the padlock when he went in, and he locked it again when he come out. He fetched uncle a key, about the time we got up from table—same key, I bet. Watermelon shows man, lock shows prisoner; and it ain't likely there's two prisoners on such a little plantation, and where the people's all so kind and good. Jim's the prisoner. All right—I'm glad we found it out detective fashion; I wouldn't give shucks for any other way. Now you work your mind and study out a plan to steal Jim, and I will study out one, too; and we'll take the one we like the best."

What a head for just a boy to have! If I had Tom Sawyer's head, I wouldn't trade it off to be a duke, nor mate of a steamboat, nor clown in a circus, nor nothing I can think of. I went to thinking out a plan, but only just to be doing something; I knowed very well where the right plan was going to come from. Pretty soon, Tom says:

"Ready?"

"Yes," I says.

"All right—bring it out."

"My plan is this," I says. "We can easy find out if it's Jim in there. Then get up my canoe to-morrow night, and fetch my raft over from the island. Then the first dark night that comes, steal the key out of the old man's britches, after he goes to bed, and shove off down the river on the raft, with Jim, hiding daytimes and running nights, the way me and Jim used to do before. Wouldn't that plan work?"

"Work? Why cert'nly, it would work, like rats a fighting. But it's too blame' simple; there ain't nothing to it. What's the good of a plan that ain't no more trouble than that? It's as mild as goose-milk. Why, Huck, it wouldn't make no more talk than breaking into a soap factory."

I never said nothing, because I warn't expecting nothing different; but I knowed mighty well that whenever he got *his* plan ready it wouldn't have none of them objections to it.

And it didn't. He told me what it was, and I see in a minute it was worth fifteen of mine, for style, and would make Jim just as free a man as mine would, and maybe get us all killed besides. So I was satisfied, and said we would waltz in on it. I needn't tell what it was, here, because I knowed it wouldn't stay the way it was. I knowed he would be changing it around, every which way, as we went along, and heaving in new bullinesses wherever he got a chance. And that is what he done.

Well, one thing was dead sure; and that was, that Tom Sawyer was in earnest and was actly going to help steal that nigger out of slavery. That was the thing that was too many for me. Here was a boy that was respectable, and well brung up; and had a character to lose; and folks at home that had characters; and he was bright and not leather-headed; and knowing and not ignorant; and not mean, but kind; and yet here he was, without any more pride, or rightness, or feeling, than to stoop to this business, and make himself a shame, and his family a shame, before everybody. I *couldn't* understand it, no way at all. It was outrageous, and I knowed I ought to just up and tell him so; and so be his true friend, and let him quit the thing right where he was, and save himself. And I *did* start to tell him; but he shut me up, and says:

"Don't you reckon I know what I'm about? Don't I generly know what I'm about?"

"Yes."

"Didn't I *say* I was going to help steal the nigger?"

"Yes."

"*Well* then."

That's all he said, and that's all I said. It warn't no use to say any more; because when he said he'd do a thing, he always done it. But *I* couldn't make out how he was willing to go into this thing; so I just let it go, and never bothered no more about it. If he was bound to have it so, I couldn't help it.

When we got home, the house was all dark and still; so we went on down to the hut by the ash-hopper, for to examine it. We went through the yard, so as to see what the hounds would do. They knowed us, and didn't make no more noise than country dogs is always doing when anything comes by in the night. When we got to the cabin, we took a look at the front and the two sides; and on the side I warn't acquainted with—which was the north side—we found a square window-hole, up tolerable high, with just one stout board nailed across it. I says:

"Here's the ticket. This hole's big enough for Jim to get through, if we wrench off the board."

Tom says:

"It's as simple as tit-tat-toe, three-in-a-row, and as easy as playing hooky. I should *hope* we can find a way that's a little more complicated than *that*, Huck Finn."

"Well, then," I says, "how'll it do to saw him out, the way I done before I was murdered, that time?"

"That's more *like*," he says, "It's real mysterious, and troublesome, and good," he says; "but I bet we can find a way that's twice as long. There ain't no hurry; le's keep on looking around."

Betwixt the hut and the fence, on the back side, was a lean-to, that joined the hut at the eaves, and was made out of plank. It was as long as the hut, but narrow—only about six foot wide. The door to it was at the south end, and was padlocked. Tom he went to the soap kettle, and searched around and fetched back the iron thing they lift the lid with; so he took it and prized out one of the staples. The chain fell down, and we opened the door and went in, and shut it, and struck a match, and see the shed was only built against the cabin and hadn't no connection with it; and there warn't no floor to the shed, nor nothing in it but some old rusty played-out hoes, and spades, and picks, and a crippled plow. The match went out, and so did we, and shoved in the in the staple again, and the door was locked as good as ever. Tom was joyful. He says:

"Now we're all right. We'll *dig* him out. It'll take about a week!"

Then we started for the house, and I went in the back door—you only have to pull a buckskin latch-string, they don't fasten the doors—but that warn't romantical enough for Tom Sawyer: no way would do him but he must climb up the lightning-rod. But after he got up half-way about three times, and missed fire and fell every time, and the last time most busted his brains out, he thought he'd got to give it up; but after he rested, he allowed he would give her one more turn for luck, and this time he made the trip.

In the morning we was up at break of day, and down to the nigger cabins to pet the dogs and make friends with the nigger that fed Jim—if it *was* Jim that was being fed. The niggers was just getting through breakfast and starting for the fields; and Jim's nigger was piling up a tin pan with bread and meat and things; and whilst the other was leaving, the key come from the house.

This nigger had a good-natured, chuckle-headed face, and his wool was all tied up in little bunches with thread. That was to keep witches off. He said the witches was pestering him awful, these nights, and making him see all kinds of strange things, and hear all kinds of strange words and noises, and he didn't believe he was ever witched so long, before, in his life. He got so worked up, and got to running on so about his troubles, he forgot all about what he'd been agoing to do. So Tom says:

"What's the vittles for? Going to feed the dogs?"

The nigger kind of smiled around graduly over his face, like when you heave a brickbat in a mud puddle, and he says:

"Yes, Mars Sid, *a* dog. Cur'us dog too. Does you want to go en look at 'im?"

"Yes."

I hunched Tom, and whispers:

"You going, right here in the day-break? *That* warn't the plan."

"No, it warn't—but it's the plan *now*."

So, drat him, we went along, but I didn't like it much. When we got in, we couldn't hardly see anything, it was so dark; but Jim was there, sure enough, and could see us; and he sings out:

"Why, *Huck!* En good *lan'!* ain' dat Misto Tom?"

I just knowed how it would be; I just expected it. *I* didn't know nothing to do; and if I had, I couldn't done it; because that nigger busted in and says:

"Why, de gracious sakes! do he know you genlmen?"

We could see pretty well, now. Tom he looked at the nigger, steady and kind of wondering, and says:

"Does *who* know us?"

"Why, dish-yer runaway nigger."

"I don't reckon he does; but what put that into your head?"

"What *put* it dar? Didn' he jis' dis minute sing out like he knowed you?"

Tom says, in a puzzled-up kind of way:

"Well, that's mighty curious. *Who* sung out? *When* did he sing out. *What* did he sing out?" And turns to me, perfectly ca'm, and says, "Did *you* hear anybody sing out?"

Of course there warn't nothing to be said but the one thing; so I says:

"No; *I* ain't heard nobody say nothing."

Then he turns to Jim, and looks him over like he never see him before; and says:

"Did you sing out?"

"No, sah," says Jim; "*I* hain't said nothing, sah."

"Not a word?"

"No, sah, I hain't said a word."

"Did you ever see us before?"

"No, sah; not as *I* knows on."

So Tom turns to the nigger, which was looking wild and distressed, and says, kind of severe:

"What do you reckon's the matter with you, anyway? What made you think somebody sung out?"

"Oh, it's de dad-blame' witches, sah, en I wisht I was dead, I do. Dey's awluz at it, sah, en dey do mos' kill me, dey sk'yers me so. Please to don't tell nobody 'bout it sah, er old Mars Silas he'll scole me; 'kase he say dey *ain't* no witches. I jis' wish to goodness he was heah now—*den* what would he say! I jis' bet he couldn' fine no way to git aroun' it *dis* time. But it's awluz jis' so; people dat's *sot*, stays sot; dey won't look into nothn' en fine it out fr deyselves, en when *you* fine it out en tell um 'bout it, dey doan' b'lieve you."

Tom give him a dime, and said we wouldn't tell nobody; and told him to buy some more thread to tie up his wool with; and then looks at Jim, and says:

"I wonder if Uncle Silas is going to hang this nigger. If I was to catch a nigger that was ungrateful enough to run away, *I* wouldn't give him up, I'd hang him." And whilst the nigger stepped to the door to look at the dime and bite it to see if it was good, he whispers to Jim and says:

"Don't ever let on to know us. And if you hear any digging going on nights, it's us: we're going to set you free."

Jim only had time to grab us by the hand and squeeze it, then the nigger come back, and we said we'd come again some time if the nigger wanted us to; and he said he would, more particular if it was dark, because the witches went for him mostly in the dark, and it was good to have folks around then.

## Chapter XXXV

It would be most an hour, yet, till breakfast, so we left, and struck down into the woods; because Tom said we got to have *some* light to see how to dig by, and a lantern makes too much, and might get us into trouble; what we must have was a lot of them rotten chunks that's called fox-fire[8] and just makes a soft kind of a glow when you lay them in a dark place. We fetched an armful and hid it in the weeds, and set down to rest, and Tom says, kind of dissatisfied:

"Blame it, this whole thing is just as easy and awkard as it can be. And so it makes it so rotten difficult to get up a difficult plan. There ain't no watchman to be drugged—now there *ought* to be a watchman. There ain't even a dog to give a sleeping-mixture to. And there's Jim chained by one leg, with a ten-foot chain, to the leg of his bed; why, all you got to do is to lift up the bedstead and slip off the chain. And Uncle Silas he trusts everybody; sends the key to thepunkin-headed nigger, and don't send nobody to watch the nigger. Jim could a got out of that window hole before this, only there wouldn't be no use trying to travel with a ten-foot chain on his leg. Why, drat it, Huck, it's the stupidest arrangement I ever see. You got to invent *all* the difficulties. Well, we can't help it, we got to do the best we can with the materials we've got. Anyhow, there's one thing—there's more honor in getting him out through a lot of difficulties and dangers, where there warn't one of them furnished to you by the people who it was their duty to furnish them, and you had to contrive them all out of your own head. Now look at just that one thing of the lantern. When you come down to the cold facts, we simply got to *let on* that a lantern's resky. Why, we could work with a torchlight procession if we wanted to, *I* believe. Now, whilst I think of it, we got to hunt up something to make a saw out of, the first chance we get."

"What do we want of a saw?"

"What do we *want* of it? Hain't we got to saw the leg of Jim's bed off, so as to get the chain loose?"

"Why, you just said a body could lift up the bedstead and slip the chain off."

"Well, if that ain't just like you, Huck Finn. You *can* get up the infant-schooliest ways of going at a thing. Why, hain't you ever read any books at all?—Baron Trenck, nor Casanova, nor Benvenuto Chelleeny, nor Henri IV.,[9] nor none of them heroes? Whoever heard of getting a prisoner loose in such an old-maidy way as that? No; the way all the best authorities does, is to saw the bedleg in two, and leave it just so, and swallow the sawdust, so it can't be found, and put some dirt and grease around the sawed place so the very keenest seneskal[1] can't see no sign of it's being sawed, and thinks the bed-leg is perfectly sound. Then, the night you're ready, fetch the leg a kick, down she goes; slip off your chain, and there you are. Nothing to do but hitch your rope-ladder to the battlements, shin down it, break your leg in the moat—because a rope-ladder is nineteen foot too short, you know—and there's your horses and your trusty vassles, and they scoop you up and fling you across a saddle and away you go, to your native Langudoc, or Navarre,[2] or wherever it

---

8. Phosphorescent glow of fungus on rotting wood.
9. Baron Friedrich von der Trenck (1726–1794), an Austrian soldier, and Henry IV of France (1553–1610) were military heroes. Benvenuto Cellini (1500–1571), an artist, and Giovanni Jacopo Casanova (1725–1798)

were both famous lovers. All four were involved in daring escape attempts.
1. Seneschal, powerful official in the service of medieval nobles.
2. Provinces in France and Spain, respectively.

is. It's gaudy, Huck. I wish there was a moat to this cabin. If we get time, the night of the escape, we'll dig one."

I says:

"What do we want of a moat, when we're going to snake him out from under the cabin?"

But he never heard me. He had forgot me and everything else. He had his chin in his hand, thinking. Pretty soon, he sighs, and shakes his head; then sighs again, and says:

"No, it wouldn't do—there ain't necessity enough for it."

"For what?" I says.

"Why, to saw Jim's leg off," he says.

"Good land!" I says, "why, there ain't *no* necessity for it. And what would you want to saw his leg off for, anyway?"

"Well, some of the best authorities has done it. They couldn't get the chain off, so they just cut their hand off, and shoved. And a leg would be better still. But we got to let that go. There ain't necessity enough in this case; and besides, Jim's a nigger and wouldn't understand the reasons for it, and how it's the custom in Europe, so we'll let it go. But there's one thing—he can have a rope-ladder; we can tear up our sheets and make him a rope-ladder easy enough. And we can send it to him in a pie; it's mostly done that way. And I've et worse pies."

"Why, Tom Sawyer, how you talk," I says; "Jim ain't got no use for a rope-ladder."

"He *has* got use for it. How *you* talk, you better say; you don't know nothing about it. He's *got* to have a rope ladder; they all do."

"What in the nation can he *do* with it?"

"*Do* with it? He can hide it in his bed, can't he? That's what they all do; and he's got to, too. Huck, you don't ever seem to want to do anything that's regular; you want to be starting something fresh all the time. Spose he *don't* do nothing with it? ain't it there in his bed, for a clew, after he's gone? and don't you reckon they'll want clews? Of course they will. And you wouldn't leave them any? That would be a *pretty* howdy-do *wouldn't* it! I never heard of such a thing."

"Well," I says, "if it's in the regulations, and he's got to have it, all right, let him have it; because I don't wish to go back on no regulations; but there's one thing, Tom Sawyer—if we go tearing up our sheets to make Jim a rope-ladder, we're going to get into trouble with Aunt Sally, just as sure as you're born. Now, the way I look at it, a hickry-bark ladder don't cost nothing, and don't waste nothing, and is just as good to load up a pie with, and hide in a straw tick, as any rag ladder you can start; and as for Jim, he hain't had no experience, and so he don't care what kind of a—"

"Oh, shucks, Huck Finn, if I was as ignorant as you, I'd keep still—that's what I'd do. Who ever heard of a state prisoner escaping by a hickry-bark ladder? Why, it's perfectly ridiculous."

"Well, all right, Tom, fix it your own way; but if you'll take my advice, you'll let me borrow a sheet off of the clothes-line."

He said that would do. And that give him another idea, and he says:

"Borrow a shirt, too."

"What do we want of a shirt, Tom?"

"Want it for Jim to keep a journal on."

"Journal your granny—*Jim* can't write."

"Spose he *can't* write—he can make marks on the shirt, can't he, if we make him a pen out of an old pewter spoon or a piece of an old iron barrel-hoop?"

"Why, Tom, we can pull a feather out of a goose and make him a better one; and quicker, too."

"*Prisoners* don't have geese running around the donjon-keep to pull pens out of, you muggins. They *always* make their pens out of the hardest, toughest, troublesomest piece of old brass candlestick or something like that they can get their hands on; and it takes them weeks and weeks, and months and months to file it out, too, because they've got to do it by rubbing it on the wall. *They* wouldn't use a goose-quill if they had it. It ain't regular."

"Well, then, what'll we make him the ink out of?"

"Many makes it out of iron-rust and tears; but that's the common sort and women; the best authorities uses their own blood. Jim can do that; and when he wants to send any little common ordinary mysterious message to let the world know where he's captivated, he can write it on the bottom of a tin plate with a fork and throw it out of the window. The Iron Mask[3] always done that, and it's a blame' good way, too."

"Jim ain't got no tin plates. They feed him in a pan."

"That ain't anything; we can get him some."

"Can't nobody *read* his plates."

"That ain't got nothing to *do* with it, Huck Finn. All *he's* got to do is to write on the plate and throw it out. You don't *have* to be able to read it. Why, half the time you can't read anything a prisoner writes on a tin plate, or anywhere else."

"Well, then, what's the sense in wasting the plates?"

"Why, blame it all, it ain't the *prisoner's* plates."

"But it's *somebody's* plates, ain't it?"

"Well, spos'n it is? What does the *prisoner* care whose—"

He broke off there, because we heard the breakfast-horn blowing. So we cleared out for the house.

Along during that morning I borrowed a sheet and a white shirt off of the clothes-line; and I found an old sack and put them in it, and we went down and got the fox-fire, and put that in too. I called it borrowing, because that was what pap always called it; but Tom said it warn't borrowing, it was stealing. He said we was representing prisoners; and prisoners don't care how they get a thing so they get it, and nobody don't blame them for it, either. It ain't no crime in a prisoner to steal the thing he needs to get away with, Tom said; it's his right; and so, as long as we was representing a prisoner, we had a perfect right to steal anything on this place we had the least use for, to get ourselves out of prison with. He said if we warn't prisoners it would be a very different thing, and nobody but a mean ornery person would steal when he warn't a prisoner. So we allowed we would steal everything there was that come handy. And yet he made a mighty fuss, one day, after that, when I stole a watermelon out of the nigger patch and eat it; and he made me go and give the niggers a dime, without telling them what it was for. Tom said that what he meant was, we could steal anything we *needed*. Well, I says, I needed the watermelon.

---

3. The chief character in Alexandre Dumas's novel *Le Vicomte de Bragelonne* (1848–50), part of which was soon after translated into English as *The Man in the Iron Mask*.

But he said I didn't need it to get out of prison with, there's where the difference was. He said if I'd a wanted it to hide a knife in, and smuggle it to Jim to
kill the seneskal with, it would a been all right. So I let it go at that, though I
couldn't see no advantage in my representing a prisoner, if I got to set down
and chaw over a lot of gold-leaf distinctions like that, every time I see a chance
to hog a watermelon.

Well, as I was saying, we waited that morning till everybody was settled
down to business, and nobody in sight around the yard; then Tom he carried
the sack into the lean-to whilst I stood off a piece to keep watch. By-and-by he
come out, and we went and set down on the wood-pile, to talk. He says:

"Everything's all right, now, except tools; and that's easy fixed."

"Tools?" I says.

"Yes."

"Tools for what?"

"Why, to dig with. We ain't agoing to *gnaw* him out, are we?"

"Ain't them old crippled picks and things in there good enough to dig a
nigger out with?" I says.

He turns on me looking pitying enough to make a body cry, and says:

"Huck Finn, did you *ever* hear of a prisoner having picks and shovels, and
all the modern conveniences in his wardrobe to dig himself out with? Now I
want to ask you—if you got any reasonableness in you at all—what kind of a
show would *that* give him to be a hero? Why, they might as well lend him the
key, and done with it. Picks and shovels—why they wouldn't furnish 'em to
a king."

"Well, then," I says, "if we don't want the picks and shovels, what do we
want?"

"A couple of case-knives."[4]

"To dig the foundations out from under that cabin with?"

"Yes."

"Confound it, it's foolish, Tom."

"It don't make no difference how foolish it is, it's the *right* way—and it's the
regular way. And there ain't no *other* way, that ever *I* heard of, and I've read
all the books that gives any information about these things. They always dig
out with a case-knife—and not through dirt, mind you; generly it's through
solid rock. And it takes them weeks and weeks and weeks, and for ever and
ever. Why, look at one of them prisoners in the bottom dungeon of the Castle
Deef,[5] in the harbor of Marseilles, that dug himself out that way; how long
was *he* at it, you reckon?"

"I don't know."

"Well, guess."

"I don't know. A month and a half?"

"*Thirty-seven year*— and he come out in China. *That's* the kind. I wish the
bottom of *this* fortress was solid rock."

"*Jim* don't know nobody in China."

"What's *that* got to do with it? Neither did that other fellow. But you're
always a-wandering off on a side issue. Why can't you stick to the main point?"

"All right—*I* don't care where he comes out, so he *comes* out; and Jim don't,

---

4. Ordinary kitchen knives.
5. The hero of Alexandre Dumas's popular Romantic
novel *The Count of Monte Cristo* (1844) was held prisoner at the Chateau d'If, a castle built by Francis I in
1524 on a small island in Marseilles harbor and used
for many years as a state prison.

either, I reckon. But there's one thing, anyway—Jim's too old to be dug out with a case-knife. He won't last."

"Yes he will *last*, too. You don't reckon it's going to take thirty-seven years to dig out through a *dirt* foundation, do you?"

"How long will it take, Tom?"

"Well, we can't resk being as long as we ought to, because it mayn't take very long for Uncle Silas to hear from down there by New Orleans. He'll hear Jim ain't from there. Then his next move will be to advertise Jim, or something like that. So we can't resk being as long digging him out as we ought to. By rights I reckon we ought to be a couple of years; but we can't. Things being so uncertain, what I recommend is this: that we really dig right in, as quick as we can; and after that, we can *let on*, to ourselves, that we was at it thirty-seven years. Then we can snatch him out and rush him away the first time there's an alarm. Yes, I reckon that'll be the best way."

"Now, there's *sense* in that," I says. "Letting on don't cost nothing; letting on ain't no trouble; and if it's any object, I don't mind letting on we was at it a hundred and fifty year. It wouldn't strain me none, after I got my hand in. So I'll mosey along now, and smouch a couple of case-knives."

"Smouch three," he says; "we want one to make a saw out of."

"Tom, if it ain't unregular and irreligious to sejest it," I says, "there's an old rusty saw-blade around yonder sticking under the weatherboarding behind the smoke-house."

He looked kind of weary and discouraged-like, and says:

"It ain't no use to try to learn you nothing, Huck. Run along and smouch the knives—three of them." So I done it.

## Chapter XXXVI

As soon as we reckoned everybody was asleep, that night, we went down the lightning-rod, and shut ourselves up in the lean-to, and got out our pile of fox-fire, and went to work. We cleared everything out of the way, about four or five foot along the middle of the bottom log. Tom said he was right behind Jim's bed now, and we'd dig in under it, and when we got through there couldn't nobody in the cabin ever know there was any hole there, because Jim's counterpin[6] hung down most to the ground, and you'd have to raise it up and look under to see the hole. So we dug and dug, with case-knives, till most midnight; and then we was dog-tired, and our hands was blistered, and yet you couldn't see we'd done anything, hardly. At last I says:

"This ain't no thirty-seven year job, this is a thirty-eight year job, Tom Sawyer."

He never said nothing. But he sighed, and pretty soon he stopped digging, and then for a good little while I knowed he was thinking. Then he says:

"It ain't no use, Huck, it ain't agoing to work. If we was prisoners it would, because then we'd have as many years as we wanted, and no hurry; and we wouldn't get but a few minutes to dig, every day, while they was changing watches, and so our hands wouldn't get blistered, and we could keep it up right along, year in and year out, and do it right, and the way it ought to be done. But *we* can't fool along, we got to rush; we ain't got no time to spare. If

---

6. Counterpane or bedspread.

we was to put in another night this way, we'd have to knock off for a week to let our hands get well—couldn't touch a case-knife with them sooner."

"Well, then, what we going to do, Tom?"

"I'll tell you. It ain't right, and it ain't moral, and I wouldn't like it to get out—but there ain't only just the one way; we got to dig him out with the picks, and *let on* it's case-knives."

"*Now* you're *talking!*" I says; "your head gets leveler and leveler all the time, Tom Sawyer," I says. "Picks is the thing, moral or no moral; and as for me, I don't care shucks for the morality of it, nohow. When I start in to steal a nigger, or a watermelon, or a Sunday-school book, I ain't no ways particular how it's done so it's done. What I want is my nigger; or what I want is my watermelon; or what I want is my Sunday-school book; and if a pick's the handiest thing, that's the thing I'm agoing to dig that nigger or that watermelon or that Sunday-school book out with; and I don't give a dead rat what the authorities thinks about it nuther."

"Well," he says, "there's excuse for picks and letting-on in a case like this; if it warn't so, I wouldn't approve of it, nor I wouldn't stand by and see the rules broke—because right is right, and wrong is wrong, and a body ain't got no business doing wrong when he ain't ignorant and knows better. It might answer for *you* to dig Jim out with a pick, *without* any letting-on, because you don't know no better; but it wouldn't for me, because I do know better. Gimme a case-knife."

He had his own by him, but I handed him mine. He flung it down, and says:

"Gimme a *case-knife.*"

I didn't know just what to do—but then I thought. I scratched around amongst the old tools, and got a pick-ax and give it to him, and he took it and went to work, and never said a word.

He was always just that particular. Full of principle.

So then I got a shovel, and then we picked and shoveled, turn about, and made the fur fly. We stuck to it about a half an hour, which was as long as we could stand up; but we had a good deal of a hole to show for it. When I got up stairs, I looked out at the window and see Tom doing his level best with the lightning-rod, but he couldn't come it, his hands was so sore. At last he says:

"It ain't no use, it can't be done. What you reckon I better do? Can't you think up no way?"

"Yes," I says, "but I reckon it ain't regular. Come up the stairs, and let on it's a lightning-rod."

So he done it.

Next day Tom stole a pewter spoon and a brass candlestick in the house, for to make some pens for Jim out of, and six tallow candles; and I hung around the nigger cabins, and laid for a chance, and stole three tin plates. Tom said it wasn't enough; but I said nobody wouldn't ever see the plates that Jim throwed out, because they'd fall in the dog-fennel and jimpson weeds under the window-hole—then we could tote them back and he could use them over again. So Tom was satisfied. Then he says:

"Now, the thing to study out is, how to get the things to Jim."

"Take them in through the hole," I says, "when we get it done."

He only just looked scornful, and said something about nobody ever heard of such an idiotic idea, and then he went to studying. By-and-by he said he had ciphered out two or three ways, but there warn't no need to decide on any of them yet. Said we'd got to post Jim first.

That night we went down the lightning-rod a little after ten, and took one of the candles along, and listened under the window-hole, and heard Jim snoring; so we pitched it in, and it didn't wake him. Then we whirled in with the pick and shovel, and in about two hours and a half the job was done. We crept in under Jim's bed and into the cabin, and pawed around and found the candle and lit it, and stood over Jim a while, and found him looking hearty and healthy, and then we woke him up gentle and gradual. He was so glad to see us he most cried; and called us honey, and all the pet names he could think of; and was for having us hunt up a cold chisel to cut the chain off of his leg with, right away, and clearing out without losing any time. But Tom he showed him how unregular it would be, and set down and told him all about our plans, and how we could alter them in a minute any time there was an alarm; and not to be the least afraid, because we would see he got away, *sure*. So Jim he said it was all right, and we set there and talked over old times a while, and then Tom asked a lot of questions, and when Jim told him Uncle Silas come in every day or two to pray with him, and Aunt Sally come in to see if he was comfortable and had plenty to eat, and both of them was kind as they could be, Tom says:

"Now I know how to fix it. We'll send you some things by them."

I said, "Don't do nothing of the kind; it's one of the most jackass ideas I ever struck;" but he never paid no attention to me; went right on. It was his way when he'd got his plans set.

So he told Jim how we'd have to smuggle in the rope-ladder pie, and other large things, by Nat, the nigger that fed him, and he must be on the lookout, and not be surprised, and not let Nat see him open them; and we would put small things in uncle's coat pockets and he must steal them out; and we would tie things to aunt's apron strings or put them in her apron pocket, if we got a chance; and told him what they would be and what they was for. And told him how to keep a journal on the shirt with his blood, and all that. He told him everything. Jim he couldn't see no sense in the most of it, but he allowed we was white folks and knowed better than him; so he was satisfied, and said he would do it all just as Tom said.

Jim had plenty corn-cob pipes and tobacco; so we had a right down good sociable time; then we crawled out through the hole, and so home to bed, with hands that looked like they'd been chawed. Tom was in high spirits. He said it was the best fun he ever had in his life, and the most intellectural; and said if he only could see his way to it we would keep it up all the rest of our lives and leave Jim to our children to get out; for he believed Jim would come to like it better and better the more he got used to it. He said that in that way it could be strung out to as much as eighty year, and would be the best time on record. And he said it would make us all celebrated that had a hand in it.

In the morning we went out to the wood-pile and chopped up the brass candlestick into handy sizes, and Tom put them and the pewter spoon in his pocket. Then we went to the nigger cabins, and while I got Nat's notice off, Tom shoved a piece of candlestick into the middle of a corn-pone that was in Jim's pan, and we went along with Nat to see how it would work, and it just worked noble; when Jim bit into it it most mashed all his teeth out; and there warn't ever anything could a worked better. Tom said so himself. Jim he never let on but what it was only just a piece of rock or something like that that's always getting into bread, you know; but after that he never bit into nothing but what he jabbed his fork into it in three or four places, first.

And whilst we was a standing there in the dimmish light, here comes a couple of the hounds bulging in, from under Jim's bed; and they kept on piling in till there was eleven of them, and there warn't hardly room in there to get your breath. By jings, we forgot to fasten that lean-to door. The nigger Nat he only just hollered "witches!" once, and kneeled over onto the floor amongst the dogs, and begun to groan like he was dying. Tom jerked the door open and flung out a slab of Jim's meat, and the dogs went for it, and in two seconds he was out himself and back again and shut the door, and I knowed he'd fixed the other door too. Then he went to work on the nigger, coaxing him and petting him, and asking him if he'd been imagining he saw something again. He raised up, and blinked his eyes around, and says:

"Mars Sid, you'll say I's a fool, but if I didn't b'lieve I see most a million dogs, er devils, er some'n, I wisht I may die right heah in dese tracks. I did, mos' sholy. Mars Sid, I *felt* um—I *felt* um, sah; dey was all over me. Dad fetch it, I jis' wisht I could git my han's on one er dem witches jis' wunst— on'y jis' wunst—it's all I'd ast. But mos'ly I wisht dey'd lemme 'lone, I does."

Tom says:

"Well, I tell you what *I* think. What makes them come here just at this runaway nigger's breakfast-time? It's because they're hungry; that's the reason. You make them a witch pie; that's the thing for *you* to do."

"But my lan', Mars Sid, how's I gwyne to make 'm a witch pie? I doan' know how to make it. I hain't ever hearn er sich a thing b'fo.' "

"Well, then, I'll have to make it myself."

"Will you do it, honey?—will you? I'll wusshup de groun' und' yo' foot, I will!"

"All right, I'll do it, seeing it's you, and you've been good to us and showed us the runaway nigger. But you got to be mighty careful. When we come around, you turn your back; and then whatever we've put in the pan, don't you let on you see it at all. And don't you look, when Jim unloads the pan— something might happen, I don't know what. And above all, don't you *handle* the witch-things."

"*Hannel* 'm Mars Sid? What *is* you a talkin' 'bout? I wouldn' lay de weight er my finger on um, not fr ten hund'd thous'n' billion dollars, I wouldn't."

## Chapter XXXVII

That was all fixed. So then we went away and went to the rubbage-pile in the back yard where they keep the old boots, and rags, and pieces of bottles, and wore-out tin things, and all such truck, and scratched around and found an old tin washpan and stopped up the holes as well as we could, to bake the pie in, and took it down cellar and stole it full of flour, and started for breakfast and found a couple of shingle-nails that Tom said would be handy for a pris-oner to scrabble his name and sorrows on the dungeon walls with, and dropped one of them in Aunt Sally's apron pocket which was hanging on a chair, and t'other we stuck in the band of Uncle Silas's hat, which was on the bureau, because we heard the children say their pa and ma was going to the runaway nigger's house this morning, and then went to breakfast, and Tom dropped the pewter spoon in Uncle Silas's coat pocket, and Aunt Sally wasn't come yet, so we had to wait a little while.

And when she come she was hot, and red, and cross, and couldn't hardly wait for the blessing; and then she went to sluicing out coffee with one hand and cracking the handiest child's head with her thimble with the other, and says:

"I've hunted high, and I've hunted low, and it does beat all, what *has* become of your other shirt."

My heart fell down amongst my lungs and livers and things, and a hard piece of corn-crust started down my throat after it and got met on the road with a cough and was shot across the table and took one of the children in the eye and curled him up like a fishing-worm, and let a cry out of him the size of a war-whoop, and Tom he turned kinder blue around the gills, and it all amounted to a considerable state of things for about a quarter of a minute or as much as that, and I would a sold out for half price if there was a bidder. But after that we was all right again—it was the sudden surprise of it that knocked us so kind of cold. Uncle Silas he says:

"It's most uncommon curious, I can't understand it. I know perfectly well I took it *off*, because——"

"Because you hain't got but one on. Just *listen* at the man! *I* know you took it off, and know it by a better way than your wool-gethering memory, too, because it was on the clo'es-line yesterday—I see it there myself. But it's gone—that's the long and the short of it, and you'll just have to change to a red flann'l one till I can get time to make a new one. And it'll be the third I've made in two years; it just keeps a body on the jump to keep you in shirts; and whatever you do manage to *do* with 'm all, is more'n *I* can make out. A body'd think you *would* learn to take some sort of care of 'em, at your time of life."

"I know it, Sally, and I do try all I can. But it oughtn't to be altogether my fault, because you know I don't see them nor have nothing to do with them except when they're on me; and I don't believe I've ever lost one of them *off* of me."

"Well, it ain't *your* fault if you haven't, Silas—you'd a done it if you could, I reckon. And the shirt ain't all that's gone, nuther. Ther's a spoon gone; and *that* ain't all. There was ten, and now ther's only nine. The calf got the shirt I reckon, but the calf never took the spoon, *that's* certain."

"Why, what else is gone, Sally?"

"Ther's six *candles* gone—that's what. The rats could a got the candles, and I reckon they did; I wonder they don't walk off with the whole place, the way you're always going to stop their holes and don't do it; and if they warn't fools they'd sleep in your hair, Silas—*you'd* never find it out; but you can't lay the *spoon* on the rats, and that I *know*."

"Well, Sally, I'm in fault, and I acknowledge it; I've been remiss; but I won't let to-morrow go by without stopping up them holes."

"Oh, I wouldn't hurry, next year'll do. Matilda Angelina Araminta *Phelps!*"

Whack comes the thimble, and the child snatches her claws out of the sugar-bowl without fooling around any. Just then, the nigger woman steps onto the passage, and says:

"Missus, dey's a sheet gone."

"A *sheet* gone! Well, for land's sake!"

"I'll stop up them holes *to-day*," says Uncle Silas, looking sorrowful.

"Oh, *do* shet up!—spose the rats took the *sheet*? *Where's* it gone, Lize?"

"Clah to goodness I hain't no notion, Miss Sally. She wuz on de clo's-line yistiddy, but she done gone; she ain' dah no mo', now."

"I reckon the world *is* coming to an end. I *never* see the beat of it, in all my born days. A shirt, and a sheet, and a spoon, and six can—"

"Missus," comes a young yaller wench, "dey's a brass candlestick miss'n."

"Cler out from here, you hussy, er I'll take a skillet to ye!"

Well, she was just a biling. I begun to lay for a chance; I reckoned I would sneak out and go for the woods till the weather moderated. She kept a raging right along, running her insurrection all by herself, and everybody else mighty meek and quiet; and at last Uncle Silas, looking kind of foolish, fishes up that spoon out of his pocket. She stopped, with her mouth open and her hands up, and as for me, I wished I was in Jeruslem or somewheres. But not long; because she says:

"It's *just* as I expected. So you had it in your pocket all the time; and like as not you've got the other things there, too. How'd it get there?"

"I reely don't know, Sally," he says, kind of apologizing, "or you know I would tell. I was a-studying over my text in Acts Seventeen, before breakfast, and I reckon I put it in there, not noticing, meaning to put my Testament in, and it must be so, because my Testament ain't in, but I'll go and see, and if the Testament is where I had it, I'll know I didn't put it in, and that will show that I laid the Testament down and took up the spoon, and——"

"Oh, for the land's sake! Give a body a rest! Go 'long now, the whole kit and biling of ye; and don't come nigh me again till I've got back my peace of mind."

I'd a heard her, if she'd a said it to herself, let alone speaking it out; and I'd a got up and obeyed her, if I'd a been dead. As we was passing through the setting-room, the old man he took up his hat, and the shingle-nail fell out on the floor, and he just merely picked it up and laid it on the mantel-shelf, and never said nothing, and went out. Tom see him do it, and remembered about the spoon, and says:

"Well, it ain't no use to send things by *him* no more, he ain't reliable." Then he says: "But he done us a good turn with the spoon, anyway, without knowing it, and so we'll go and do him one without *him* knowing it—stop up his rat-holes."

There was a noble good lot of them, down cellar, and it took us a whole hour, but we done the job tight and good, and ship-shape. Then we heard steps on the stairs, and blowed out our light, and hid; and here comes the old man, with a candle in one hand and a bundle of stuff in t'other, looking as absent-minded as year before last. He went a mooning around, first to one rat-hole and then another, till he'd been to them all. Then he stood about five minutes, picking tallow-drip off of his candle and thinking. Then he turns off slow and dreamy towards the stairs, saying:

"Well, for the life of me I can't remember when I done it. I could show her now that I warn't to blame on account of the rats. But never mind—let it go. I reckon it wouldn't do no good."

And so he went on a mumbling up stairs, and then we left. He was a mighty nice old man. And always is.

Tom was a good deal bothered about what to do for a spoon, but he said we'd got to have it; so he took a think. When he had ciphered it out, he told me how we was to do; then we went and waited around the spoon-basket till we see Aunt Sally coming, and then Tom went to counting the spoons and laying them out to one side, and I slip one of them up my sleeve, and Tom says:

"Why, Aunt Sally, there ain't but nine spoons, yet."

She says:

"Go 'long to your play, and don't bother me. I know better, I counted 'm myself."

"Well, I've counted them twice, Aunty, and I can't make but nine."

She looked out of all patience, but of course she come to count—anybody would.

"I declare to gracious ther' ain't but nine!" she says. "Why, what in the world—plague take the things, I'll count 'm again."

So I slipped back the one I had, and when she got done counting, she says:

"Hang the troublesome rubbage, ther's ten now!" and she looked huffy and bothered both. But Tom says:

"Why, Aunty I don't think there's ten."

"You numskull, didn't you see me count 'm?"

"I know, but—"

"Well, I'll count 'm again."

So I smouched one, and they come out nine same as the other time. Well, she was in a tearing way—just a trembling all over, she was so mad. But she counted and counted, till she got that addled she'd start to count-in the basket for a spoon, sometimes; and so, three times they come out right, and three times they come out wrong. Then she grabbed up the basket and slammed it across the house and knocked the cat galley-west;[7] and she said cle'r out and let her have some peace, and if we come bothering around her again betwixt that and dinner, she'd skin us. So we had the odd spoon; and dropped it in her apron pocket whilst she was giving us our sailing-orders, and Jim got it all right, along with her shingle-nail, before noon. We was very well satisfied with the business, and Tom allowed it was worth twice the trouble it took, because he said now she couldn't ever count them spoons twice alike again to save her life; and wouldn't believe she'd counted them right, if she did; and said that after she'd about counted her head off, for the last three days, he judged she'd give it up and offer to kill anybody that wanted her to ever count them any more.

So we put the sheet back on the line, that night, and stole one out of her closet; and kept on putting it back and stealing it again, for a couple of days, till she didn't know how many sheets she had, any more, and said she didn't care, and warn't agoing to bullyrag[8] the rest of her soul out about it, and wouldn't count them again not to save her life, she druther die first.

So we was all right now, as to the shirt and the sheet and the spoon and the candles, by the help of the calf and the rats and the mixed-up counting; and as to the candlestick, it warn't no consequence, it would blow over by-and-by.

But that pie was a job; we had no end of trouble with that pie. We fixed it up away down in the woods, and cooked it there; and we got it done at last, and very satisfactory, too; but not all in one day; and we had to use up three

7. Knocked out completely.                    8. To nag mercilessly.

washpans full of flour, before we got through, and we got burnt pretty much all over, in places, and eyes put out with the smoke; because, you see, we didn't want nothing but a crust, and we couldn't prop it up right, and she would always cave in. But of course we thought of the right way at last; which was to cook the ladder, too, in the pie. So then we laid in with Jim, the second night, and tore up the sheet all in little strings, and twisted them together, and long before daylight we had a lovely rope, that you could a hung a person with. We let on it took nine months to make it.

And in the forenoon we took it down to the woods, but it wouldn't go in the pie. Being made of a whole sheet, that way, there was rope enough for forty pies, if we'd a wanted them, and plenty left over for soup, or sausage, or anything you choose. We could a had a whole dinner.

But we didn't need it. All we needed was just enough for the pie, and so we throwed the rest away. We didn't cook none of the pies in the washpan, afraid the solder would melt; but Uncle Silas he had a noble brass warming-pan which he thought considerable of, because it belonged to one of his ancestors with a long wooden handle that come over from England with William the Conqueror in the *Mayflower*[9] or one of them early ships and was hid away up garret with a lot of other old pots and things that was valuable, not on account of being any account because they warn't, but on account of them being relicts, you know, and we snaked her out, private, and took her down there, but she failed on the first pies, because we didn't know how, but she come up smiling on the last one. We took and lined her with dough, and set her in the coals, and loaded her up with rag-rope, and put on a dough roof, and shut down the lid, and put hot embers on top, and stood off five foot, with the long handle, cool and comfortable, and in fifteen minutes she turned out a pie that was a satisfaction to look at. But the person that et it would want to fetch a couple of kags of toothpicks along, for if that rope-ladder wouldn't cramp him down to business, I don't know nothing what I'm talking about, and lay him in enough stomach-ache to last him till next time, too.

Nat didn't look, when we put the witch-pie in Jim's pan; and we put the three tin plates in the bottom of the pan under the vittles; and so Jim got everything all right, and as soon as he was by himself he busted into the pie and hid the rope-ladder inside of his straw tick, and scratched some marks on a tin plate and throwed it out of the window-hole.

## Chapter XXXVIII

Making them pens was a distressid-tough job, and so was the saw; and Jim allowed the inscription was going to be the toughest of all. That's the one which the prisoner has to scrabble on the wall. But we had to have it; Tom said we'd *got* to; there warn't no case of a state prisoner not scrabbling his inscription to leave behind, and his coat of arms.

"Look at Lady Jane Grey," he says; "look at Gilford Dudley; look at old Northumberland![1] Why, Huck, spose it *is* considerable trouble?—what you

9. William the Conqueror lived in the 11th century. The *Mayflower* made its historic crossing in 1620.
1. The story of Lady Jane Grey (1537–1554), her husband Guildford Dudley, and his father the duke of Northumberland was told in W. H. Ainsworth's romance *The Tower of London* (1840). The duke was at work carving a poem on the wall of his cell when the executioners came for him.

going to do?—how you going to get around it? Jim's *got* to do his inscription and coat of arms. They all do."

Jim says:

"Why, Mars Tom, I hain't got no coat o' arms; I hain't got nuffn but dish-yer old shirt, en you knows I got to keep de journal on dat."

"Oh, you don't understand, Jim; a coat of arms is very different."

"Well," I says, "Jim's right, anyway, when he says he hain't got no coat of arms, because he hain't."

"I reckon *I* knowed that," Tom says, "but you bet he'll have one before he goes out of this—because he's going out *right*, and there ain't going to be no flaws in his record."

So whilst me and Jim filed away at the pens on a brickbat[2] apiece, Jim a making his'n out of the brass and I making mine out of the spoon, Tom set to work to think out the coat of arms. By-and-by he said he'd struck so many good ones he didn't hardly know which to take, but there was one which he reckoned he'd decide on. He says:

"On the scutcheon[3] we'll have a bend *or* in the dexter base, a saltire *murrey* in the fess, with a dog, couchant, for common charge, and under his foot a chain embattled, for slavery, with a chevron *vert* in a chief engrailed, and three invected lines on a field *azure*, with the nombril points rampant on a dancette indented; crest, a runaway nigger, *sable*, with his bundle over his shoulder on a bar sinister: and a couple of gules for supporters, which is you and me; motto, *Maggiore fretta, minore atto.* Got it out of a book—means, the more haste, the less speed."

"Geewhillikins," I says, "but what does the rest of it mean?"

"We ain't got no time to bother over that," he says, "we got to dig in like all git-out."

"Well, anyway," I says, "what's *some* of it? What's a fess?"

"A fess—a fess is—*you* don't need to know what a fess is. I'll show him how to make it when he gets to it."

"Shucks, Tom," I says, "I think you might tell a person. What's a bar sinister?"

"Oh, *I* don't know. But he's got to have it. All the nobility does."

That was just his way. If it didn't suit him to explain a thing to you, he wouldn't do it. You might pump at him a week, it wouldn't make no difference.

He'd got all that coat of arms business fixed, so now he started in to finish up the rest of that part of the work, which was to plan out a mournful inscription—said Jim got to have one, like they all done. He made up a lot, and wrote them out on a paper, and read them off, so:

1. *Here a captive heart busted.*

2. *Here a poor prisoner, forsook by the world and friends, fretted out his sorrowful life.*

3. *Here a lonely heart broke, and a worn spirit went to its rest, after thirty-seven years of solitary captivity.*

4. *Here, homeless and friendless, after thirty-seven years of bitter captivity, perished a noble stranger, natural son of Louis XIV.*

2. A fragment of brick.
3. An escutcheon is the shield-shaped surface on

which the coat of arms is inscribed. The details are expressed in the technical argot of heraldry.

Tom's voice trembled, whilst he was reading them, and he most broke down. When he got done, he couldn't no way make up his mind which one for Jim to scrabble onto the wall, they was all so good; but at last he allowed he would let him scrabble them all on. Jim said it would take him a year to scrabble such a lot of truck onto the logs with a nail, and he didn't know how to make letters, besides; but Tom said he would block them out for him, and then he wouldn't have nothing to do but just follow the lines. Then pretty soon he says:

"Come to think, the logs ain't agoing to do; they don't have log walls in a dungeon: we got to dig the inscriptions into a rock. We'll fetch a rock."

Jim said the rock was worse than the logs; he said it would take him such a pison long time to dig them into a rock, he wouldn't ever get out. But Tom said he would let me help him do it. Then he took a look to see how me and Jim was getting along with the pens. It was most pesky tedious hard work and slow, and didn't give my hands no show to get well of the sores, and we didn't seem to make no headway, hardly. So Tom says:

"I know how to fix it. We got to have a rock for the coat of arms and mournful inscriptions, and we can kill two birds with that same rock. There's a gaudy big grindstone down at the mill, and we'll smouch it, and carve the things on it, and file out the pens and the saw on it, too."

It warn't no slouch of an idea; and it warn't no slouch of a grindstone nuther; but we allowed we'd tackle it. It warn't quite midnight, yet, so we cleared out for the mill, leaving Jim at work. We smouched the grindstone, and set out to roll her home, but it was a most nation tough job. Sometimes, do what we could, we couldn't keep her from falling over, and she come mighty near mashing us, every time. Tom said she was going to get one of us, sure, before we got through. We got her half way; and then we was plumb played out, and most drownded with sweat. We see it warn't no use, we got to go and fetch Jim. So he raised up his bed and slid the chain off of the bed-leg, and wrapt it round and round his neck, and we crawled out through our hole and down there, and Jim and me laid into that grindstone and walked her along like nothing; and Tom superintended. He could out-superintend any boy I ever see. He knowed how to do everything.

Our hole was pretty big, but it warn't big enough to get the grindstone through; but Jim he took the pick and soon made it big enough. Then Tom marked out them things on it with the nail, and set Jim to work on them, with the nail for a chisel and an iron bolt from the rubbage in the lean-to for a hammer, and told him to work till the rest of his candle quit on him, and then he could go to bed, and hide the grindstone under his straw tick and sleep on it. Then we helped him fix his chain back on the bed-leg, and was ready for bed ourselves. But Tom thought of something, and says:

"You got any spiders in here, Jim?"

"No, sah, thanks to goodness I hain't, Mars Tom."

"All right, we'll get you some."

"But bless you, honey, I doan' *want* none. I's afeard un um. I jis' 's soon have rattlesnakes aroun'."

Tom thought a minute or two, and says:

"It's a good ida. And I reckon it's been done. It *must* a been done; it stands to reason. Yes, it's a prime good idea. Where could you keep it?"

"Keep what, Mars Tom?"

"Why, a rattlesnake."

"De goodness gracious alive, Mars Tom! Why, if dey was a rattlesnake to come in heah, I'd take en bust right out thoo dat log wall, I would, wid my head."

"Why, Jim, you wouldn't be afraid of it, after a little. You could tame it."

"*Tame* it!"

"Yes—easy enough. Every animal is grateful for kindness and petting, and they wouldn't *think* of hurting a person that pets them. Any book will tell you that. You try—that's all I ask; just try for two or three days. Why, you can get him so, in a little while, that he'll love you; and sleep with you; and won't stay away from you a minute; and will let you wrap him round your neck and put his head in your mouth."

"Please, Mars Tom—*doan'* talk so! I can't *stan'* it! He'd *let* me shove his head in my mouf—fer a favor, hain't it? I lay he'd wait a pow'ful long time 'fo' I *ast* him. En mo' en dat, I doan' *want* him to sleep wid me."

"Jim, don't act so foolish. A prisoner's *got* to have some kind of a dumb pet, and if a rattlesnake hain't ever been tried, why, there's more glory to be gained in your being the first to ever try it than any other way you could ever think of to save your life."

"Why, Mars Tom, I doan' *want* no sich glory. Snake take 'n bite Jim's chin off, den *whah* is de glory? No, sah, I doan' want no sich doin's."

"Blame it, can't you *try?* I only *want* you to try—you needn't keep it up if it don't work."

"But de trouble all *done,* ef de snake bite me while I's a tryin' him. Mars Tom, I's willin' to tackle mos' anything 'at ain't onreasonable, but ef you en Huck fetches a rattlesnake in heah for me to tame, I's gwyne to *leave,* dat's *shore.*"

"Well, then, let it go, let it go, if you're so bullheaded about it. We can get you some garter-snakes and you can tie some buttons on their tails, and let on they're rattlesnakes, and I reckon that'll have to do."

"I k'n stan' *dem,* Mars Tom, but blame' 'f I couldn't get along widout um, I tell you dat. I never knowed b'fo', 't was so much bother and trouble to be a prisoner."

"Well, it *always* is, when it's done right. You got any rats around here?"

"No, sah, I hain't seed none."

"Well, we'll get you some rats."

"Why, Mars Tom, I doan' *want* no rats. Dey's de dad-blamedest creturs to sturb a body, en rustle roun' over 'im, en bite his feet, when he's tryin' to sleep, I ever see. So, sah, gimme g'yarter-snakes, 'f I's got to have 'm, but doan' gimme no rats. I ain' got not use f'r um, skasely."

"But Jim, you *got* to have 'em—they all do. So don't make no more fuss about it. Prisoners ain't ever without rats. There ain't no instance of it. And they train them, and pet them, and learn them tricks, and they get to be as sociable as flies. But you got to play music to them. You got anything to play music on?"

"I ain't got nuffn but a coase comb en a piece o' paper, en a juice-harp; but I reck'n dey wouldn't take no stock in a juice-harp."

"Yes, they would. *They* don't care what kind of music 'tis. A jews-harp's plenty good enough for a rat. All animals likes music—in a prison they dote on it. Specially, painful music; and you can't get no other kind out of a jews-harp. It always interests them; they come out to see what's the matter with you. Yes, you're all right; you're fixed very well. You want to set on your bed, nights, before you go to sleep, and early in the mornings, and play your jews-harp; play The Last Link is Broken—that's the thing that'll scoop a rat, quicker'n anything else: and when you've played about two minutes, you'll see all the rats, and the snakes, and spiders, and things begin to feel worried about you, and come. And they'll just fairly swarm over you, and have a noble good time."

"Yes, *dey* will, I reck'n, Mars Tom, but what kine er time is *Jim* havin'? Blest if I kin see de pint. But I'll do it ef I got to. I reck'n I better keep de animals satisfied, en not have no trouble in de house."

Tom waited to think over, and see if there wasn't nothing else; and pretty soon he says:

"Oh—there's one thing I forgot. Could you raise a flower here, do you reckon?"

"I doan' know but maybe I could, Mars Tom; but it's tolable dark in heah, en I ain' got no use f'r no flower, nohow, en she'd be a pow'ful sight o' trouble."

"Well, you try it, anyway. Some other prisoners has done it."

"One er dem big cat-tail-lookin' mullen-stalks would grow in heah, Mars Tom, I reck'n, but she wouldn' be wuth half de trouble she'd coss."

"Don't you believe it. We'll fetch you a little one, and you plant it in the corner, over there, and raise it. And don't call it mullen, call it Pitchiola—that's its right name, when it's in a prison.[4] And you want to water it with your tears."

"Why, I got plenty spring water, Mars Tom."

"You don't *want* spring water; you want to water it with your tears. It's the way they always do."

"Why, Mars Tom, I lay I kin raise one er dem mullen-stalks twyste wid spring water whiles another man's a *start'n* one wid tears."

"That ain't the idea. You *got* to do it with tears."

"She'll die on my han's, Mars Tom, she sholy will; kase I doan' skasely ever cry."

So Tom was stumped. But he studied it over, and then said Jim would have to worry along the best he could with an onion. He promised he would go to the nigger cabins and drop one, private, in Jim's coffee-pot, in the morning. Jim said he would "jis' 's soon have tobacker in his coffee;" and found so much fault with it, and with the work and bother of raising the mullen, and jews-harping the rats, and petting and flattering up the snakes and spiders and things, on top of all the other work he had to do on pens, and inscriptions, and journals, and things, which made it more trouble and worry and responsi-bility to be a prisoner than anything he ever undertook, that Tom most lost all patience with him; and said he was just loadened down with more gaudier chances than a prisoner ever had in the world to make a name for himself, and yet he didn't know enough to appreciate them, and they was just about wasted on him. So Jim he was sorry, and said he wouldn't behave so no more, and then me and Tom shoved for bed.

---

4. *Picciola* (1836) was a popular romantic story by Xavier Saintine (pseudonym for Joseph Xavier Boniface, 1798–1865), in which a plant helps sustain a prisoner.

## Chapter XXXIX

In the morning we went up to the village and bought a wire rat trap and
fetched it down, and unstopped the best rat hole, and in about an hour we
had fifteen of the bulliest kind of ones; and then we took it and put it in a safe
place under Aunt Sally's bed. But while we was gone for spiders, little Thomas
Franklin Benjamin Jefferson Elexander Phelps found it there, and opened the
door of it to see if the rats would come out, and they did; and Aunt Sally she
come in, and when we got back she was standing on top of the bed raising
Cain, and the rats was doing what they could to keep off the dull times for
her. So she took and dusted us both with the hickry, and we was as much as
two hours catching another fifteen or sixteen, drat that meddlesome cub, and
they warn't the likeliest, nuther, because the first haul was the pick of the
flock. I never see a likelier lot of rats than what that first haul was.

We got a splendid stock of sorted spiders, and bugs, and frogs, and caterpillars, and one thing or another; and we like-to got a hornet's nest, but we didn't.
The family was at home. We didn't give it right up, but staid with them as
long as we could; because we allowed we'd tire them out or they'd got to tire
us out, and they done it. Then we got allycumpain[5] and rubbed on the places,
and was pretty near all right again, but couldn't set down convenient. And so
we went for the snakes, and grabbed a couple of dozen garters and house-
snakes, and put them in a bag, and put it in our room, and by that time it was
supper time, and a rattling good honest day's work; and hungry?—oh, no I
reckon not! And there warn't a blessed snake up there, when we went back—
we didn't half tie the sack, and they worked out, somehow, and left. But it
didn't matter much, because they was still on the premises somewheres. So
we judged we could get some of them again. No, there warn't no real scarcity
of snakes about the house for a considerble spell. You'd see them dripping
from the rafters and places, every now and then; and they generly landed in
your plate, or down the back of your neck, and most of the time where you
didn't want them. Well, they was handsome, and striped, and there warn't no
harm in a million of them; but that never made no difference to Aunt Sally,
she despised snakes, be the breed what they might, and she couldn't stand
them no way you could fix it; and every time one of them flopped down on
her, it didn't make no difference what she was doing, she would just lay that
work down and light out. I never see such a woman. And you could hear her
whoop to Jericho. You couldn't get her to take aholt of one of them with the
tongs. And if she turned over and found one in bed, she would scramble out
and lift a howl that you would think the house was afire. She disturbed the old
man so, that he said he could most wish there hadn't ever been no snakes
created. Why, after every last snake had been gone clear out of the house for
as much as a week, Aunt Sally warn't over it yet; she warn't near over it; when
she was setting thinking about something, you could touch her on the back of
her neck with a feather and she would jump right out of her stockings. It was
very curious. But Tom said all women was just so. He said they was made that
way; for some reason or other.

We got a licking every time one of our snakes come in her way; and she
allowed these lickings warn't nothing to what she would do if we ever loaded

---

5. Elecampane is an herb to relieve the pain of the hornet sting.

up the place again with them. I didn't mind the lickings, because they didn't amount to nothing; but I minded the trouble we had, to lay in another lot. But we got them laid in, and all the other things; and you never see a cabin as blithesome as Jim's was when they'd all swarm out for music and go for him. Jim didn't like the spiders, and the spiders didn't like Jim; and so they'd lay for him and make it mighty warm for him. And he said that between the rats, and the snakes, and the grindstone, there warn't no room in bed for him, skasely; and when there was, a body couldn't sleep, it was so lively, and it was always lively, he said, because *they* never all slept at one time, but took turn about, so when the snakes was asleep the rats was on deck, and when the rats turned in the snakes come on watch, so he always had one gang under him, in his way, and t'other gang having a circus over him, and if he got up to hunt a new place, the spiders would take a chance at him as he crossed over. He said if he ever got out, this time, he wouldn't ever be a prisoner again, not for a salary.

Well, by the end of three weeks, everything was in pretty good shape. The shirt was sent in early, in a pie, and every time a rat bit Jim he would get up and write a little in his journal whilst the ink was fresh; the pens was made, the inscriptions and so on was all carved on the grindstone; the bed-leg was sawed in two, and we had et up the sawdust, and it give us a most amazing stomach-ache. We reckoned we was all going to die, but didn't. It was the most undigestible sawdust I ever see; and Tom said the same. But as I was saying, we'd got all the work done, now, at last; and we was all pretty much fagged out, too, but mainly Jim. The old man had wrote a couple of times to the plantation below Orleans to come and get their runaway nigger, but hadn't got no answer, because there warn't no such plantation; so he allowed he would advertise Jim in the St. Louis and New Orleans papers; and when he mentioned the St. Louis ones, it give me the cold shivers, and I see we hadn't no time to lose. So Tom said, now for the nonnamous letters.

"What's them?" I says.

"Warnings to the people that something is up. Sometimes it's done one way, sometimes another. But there's always somebody spying around, that gives notice to the governor of the castle. When Louis XVI was going to light out of the Tooleries,[6] a servant girl done it. It's a very good way, and so is the nonnamous letters. We'll use them both. And it's usual for the prisoner's mother to change clothes with him, and she stays in, and he slides out in her clothes. We'll do that too."

"But looky here, Tom, what do we want to *warn* anybody for, that something's up? Let them find it out for themselves—it's their lookout."

"Yes, I know; but you can't depend on them. It's the way they've acted from the very start—left us to do *everything*. They're so confiding and mullet-headed they don't take notice of nothing at all. So if we don't *give* them notice, there won't be nobody nor nothing to interfere with us, and so after all our hard work and trouble this escape 'll go off perfectly flat: won't amount to nothing—won't be nothing *to* it."

"Well, as for me, Tom, that's the way I'd like."

"Shucks," he says, and looked disgusted. So I says:

"But I ain't going to make no complaint. Anyway that suits you suits me. What you going to do about the servant-girl?"

---

6. Clemens probably read this episode of the Tuileries, a palace in Paris, in Thomas Carlyle's *French Revolution* (1837).

"You'll be her. You slide in, in the middle of the night, and hook that yaller girl's frock."

"Why, Tom, that'll make trouble next morning; because of course she prob'bly hain't got any but that one."

"I know; but you don't want it but fifteen minutes, to carry the nonnamous letter and shove it under the front door."

"All right, then, I'll do it; but I could carry it just as handy in my own togs."

"You wouldn't look like a servant-girl *then*, would you?"

"No, but there won't be nobody to see what I look like, *anyway.*"

"That ain't got nothing to do with it. The thing for us to do, is just to do our *duty,* and not worry about whether anybody *sees* us do it or not. Hain't you got no principle at all?"

"All right, I ain't saying nothing; I'm the servant-girl. Who's Jim's mother?"

"I'm his mother. I'll hook a gown from Aunt Sally."

"Well, then, you'll have to stay in the cabin when me and Jim leaves."

"Not much. I'll stuff Jim's clothes full of straw and lay it on his bed to represent his mother in disguise: and Jim 'll take Aunt Sally's gown off of me and wear it, and we'll all evade together. When a prisoner of style escapes, it's called an evasion. It's always called so when a king escapes, f'rinstance. And the same with a king's son; it don't make no difference whether he's a natural one or an unnatural one."

So Tom he wrote the nonnamous letter, and I smouched the yaller wench's frock, that night, and put it on, and shoved it under the front door, the way Tom told me to. It said:

> Beware, Trouble is brewing. Keep a sharp lookout.
>
> UNKNOWN FRIEND.

Next night we stuck a picture which Tom drawed in blood, of a skull and crossbones, on the front door; and next night another one of a coffin, on the back door. I never see a family in such a sweat. They couldn't a been worse scared if the place had a been full of ghosts laying for them behind everything and under the beds and shivering through the air. If a door banged, Aunt Sally she jumped, and said "ouch!" if anything fell, she jumped and said "ouch!" if you happened to touch her, when she warn't noticing, she done the same; she couldn't face noway and be satisfied, because she allowed there was something behind her every time—so she was always a whirling around, sudden, and saying "ouch," and before she'd get two-thirds around, she'd whirl back again, and say it again; and she was afraid to go to bed, but she dasn't set up. So the thing was working very well, Tom said; he said he never see a thing work more satisfactory. He said it showed it was done right.

So he said, now for the grand bulge! So the very next morning at the streak of dawn we got another letter ready, and was wondering what we better do with it, because we heard them say at supper they was going to have a nigger on watch at both doors all night. Tom he went down the lightning-rod to spy around; and the nigger at the back door was asleep, and he stuck it in the back of his neck and come back. This letter said:

> Don't betray me, I wish to be your friend. There is a desprate gang of cut-throats from over in the Ingean Territory[7] going to steal your runaway nigger

7. The area now the state of Oklahoma was granted to the Indians and became a base of operations for outlaws for most of the 19th century.

*to-night, and they have been trying to scare you so as you will stay in the house
and not bother them. I am one of the gang, but have got religgion and wish to
quit it and lead a honest life again, and will betray the helish design. They will
sneak down from northards, along the fence, at midnight exact, with a false
key, and go in the nigger's cabin to get him. I am to be off a piece and blow a
tin horn if I see any danger; but stead of that, I will* BA *like a sheep soon as they
get in and not blow at all; then whilst they are getting his chains loose, you slip
there and lock them in, and can kill them at your leasure. Don't do anything
but just the way I am telling you, if you do they will suspicion something and
raise whoopjamboreehoo. I do not wish any reward but to know I have done the
right thing.*

UNKNOWN FRIEND.

## Chapter XL

We was feeling pretty good, after breakfast, and took my canoe and went
over the river a fishing, with a lunch, and had a good time, and took a look at
the raft and found her all right, and got home late to supper, and found them
in such a sweat and worry they didn't know which end they was standing on,
and made us go right off to bed the minute we was done supper, and wouldn't
tell us what the trouble was, and never let on a word about the new letter, but
didn't need to, because we knowed as much about it as anybody did, and as
soon as we was half up stairs and her back was turned, we slid for the cellar
cupboard and loaded up a good lunch and took it up to our room and went to
bed, and got up about half-past eleven, and Tom put on Aunt Sally's dress
that he stole and was going to start with the lunch, but says:

"Where's the butter?"

"I laid out a hunk of it," I says, "on a piece of a corn-pone."

"Well, you *left* it laid out, then—it ain't here."

"We can get along without it," I says.

"We can get along *with* it, too," he says; "just you slide down cellar and
fetch it. And then mosey right down the lightning-rod and come along. I'll go
and stuff the straw into Jim's clothes to represent his mother in disguise, and
be ready to *ba* like a sheep and shove soon as you get there."

So out he went, and down cellar went I. The hunk of butter, big as a
person's fist, was where I had left it, so I took up the slab of corn-pone with it
on, and blowed out my light, and started up stairs, very stealthy, and got up to
the main floor all right, but here comes Aunt Sally with a candle, and I
clapped the truck in my hat, and clapped my hat on my head, and the next
second she see me; and she says:

"You been down cellar?"

"Yes'm."

"What you been doing down there?"

"Noth'n."

"*Noth'n!*"

"No'm."

"Well, then, what possessed you to go down there, this time of night?"

"I don't know'm."

"You don't *know?* Don't answer me that way, Tom, I want to know what
you been *doing* down there?"

"I hain't been doing a single thing, Aunt Sally, I hope to gracious if I have."

I reckoned she'd let me go, now, and as a generl thing she would; but I spose there was so many strange things going on she was just in a sweat about every little thing that warn't yard-stick straight; so she says, very decided:

"You just march into that setting-room and stay there till I come. You been up to something you no business to, and I lay I'll find out what it is before I'm done with you."

So she went away as I opened the door and walked into the setting-room. My, but there was a crowd there! Fifteen farmers, and every one of them had a gun. I was most powerful sick, and slunk to a chair and set down. They was setting around, some of them talking a little, in a low voice, and all of them fidgety and uneasy, but trying to look like they warn't; but I knowed they was, because they was always taking off their hats, and putting them on, and scratching their heads, and changing their seats, and fumbling with their buttons. I warn't easy myself, but I didn't take my hat off, all the same.

I did wish Aunt Sally would come, and get done with me, and lick me, if she wanted to, and let me get away and tell Tom how we'd overdone this thing, and what a thundering hornet's nest we'd got ourselves into, so we could stop fooling around, straight off, and clear out with Jim before these rips got out of patience and come for us.

At last she come, and begun to ask me questions, but I *couldn't* answer them straight, I didn't know which end of me was up; because these men was in such a fidget now, that some was wanting to start right *now* and lay for them desperadoes, and saying it warn't but a few minutes to midnight; and others was trying to get them to hold on and wait for the sheep-signal; and here was aunty pegging away at the questions, and me a shaking all over and ready to sink down in my tracks I was that scared; and the place getting hotter and hotter, and the butter beginning to melt and run down my neck and behind my ears: and pretty soon, when one of them says, "*I'm* for going and getting in the cabin *first*, and right *now*, and catching them when they come," I most dropped; and a streak of butter came a trickling down my forehead, and Aunt Sally she see it, and turns white as a sheet, and says:

"For the land's sake what *is* the matter with the child!—he's got the brain fever as shore as you're born, and they're oozing out!"

And everybody runs to see, and she snatches off my hat, and out comes the bread, and what was left of the butter, and she grabbed me, and hugged me, and says:

"Oh, what a turn you did give me! and how glad and grateful I am it ain't no worse; for luck's against us, and it never rains but it pours, and when I see that truck I thought we'd lost you, for I knowed by the color and all, it was just like your brains would be if—Dear, dear, whyd'nt you *tell* me that was what you'd been down there for, *I* wouldn't a cared. Now cler out to bed, and don't lemme see no more of you till morning!"

I was up stairs in a second, and down the lightning-rod in another one, and shinning through the dark for the lean-to. I couldn't hardly get my words out, I was so anxious; but I told Tom as quick as I could, we must jump for it, now, and not a minute to lose—the house full of men, yonder, with guns!

His eyes just blazed; and he says:

"No!—is that so? *Ain't* it bully! Why, Huck, if it was to do over again, I bet I could fetch two hundred! If we could put it off till—"

"Hurry! *hurry!*" I says. "Where's Jim?"

"Right at your elbow; if you reach out your arm you can touch him. He's dressed, and everything's ready. Now we'll slide out and give the sheep-signal."

But then we heard the tramp of men, coming to the door, and heard them begin to fumble with the padlock; and heard a man say:

"I *told* you we'd be too soon; they haven't come—the door is locked. Here, I'll lock some of you into the cabin and you lay for 'em in the dark and kill 'em when they come; and the rest scatter around a piece, and listen if you can hear 'em coming."

So in they come, but couldn't see us in the dark, and most trod on us whilst we was hustling to get under the bed. But we got under all right, and out through the hole, swift but soft—Jim first, me next, and Tom last, which was according to Tom's orders. Now we was in the lean-to, and heard trampings close by outside. So we crept to the door, and Tom stopped us there and put his eye to the crack, but couldn't make out nothing, it was so dark; and whispered and said he would listen for the steps to get further, and when he nudged us Jim must glide out first, and him last. So he set his ear to the crack and listened, and listened, and listened, and the steps a scraping around, out there, all the time; and at last he nudged us, and we slid out, and stooped down, not breathing, and not making the least noise, and slipped stealthy towards the fence, in Injun file, and got to it, all right, and me and Jim over it; but Tom's britches catched fast on a splinter on the top rail, and then he hear the steps coming, so he had to pull loose, which snapped the splinter and made a noise; and as he dropped in our tracks and started, somebody sings out:

"Who's that? Answer, or I'll shoot!"

But we didn't answer; we just unfurled our heels and shoved. Then there was a rush, and a *bang, bang, bang!* and the bullets fairly whizzed around us! We heard them sing out:

"Here they are! They've broke for the river! after 'em, boys! And turn loose the dogs!"

So here they come, full tilt. We could hear them, because they wore boots, and yelled, but we didn't wear no boots, and didn't yell. We was in the path to the mill; and when they got pretty close onto us, we dodged into the bush and let them go by, and then dropped in behind them. They'd had all the dogs shut up, so they wouldn't scare off the robbers; but by this time somebody had let them loose, and here they come, making pow-wow enough for a million; but they was our dogs; so we stopped in our tracks till they catched up; and when they see it warn't nobody but us, and no excitement to offer them, they only just said howdy, and tore right ahead towards the shouting and clattering; and then we up steam again and whizzed along after them till we was nearly to the mill, and then struck up through the bush to where my canoe was tied, and hopped in and pulled for dear life towards the middle of the river, but didn't make no more noise than we was obleeged to. Then we struck out, easy and comfortable, for the island where my raft was; and we could hear them yelling and barking at each other all up and down the bank, till we was so far away the sounds got dim and died out. And when we stepped onto the raft, I says:

"*Now*, old Jim, you're a free man *again*, and I bet you won't ever be a slave no more."

"En a mighty good job it wuz, too, Huck. It 'uz planned beautiful, en it 'uz *done* beautiful; en dey aint' *nobody* kin git up a plan dat's mo' mixed-up en splendid den what dat one wuz."

We was all as glad as we could be, but Tom was the gladdest of all, because he had a bullet in the calf of his leg.

When me and Jim heard that, we didn't feel so brash as what we did before. It was hurting him considerble, and bleeding; so we laid him in the wigwam and tore up one of the duke's shirts for to bandage him, but he says:

"Gimme the rags, I can do it myself. Don't stop, now; don't fool around here, and the evasion booming along so handsome; man the sweeps, and set her loose! Boys, we done it elegant!—'deed we did. I wish *we'd* a had the handling of Louis XVI, there wouldn't a been no 'Son of Saint Louis, ascend to heaven!'[8] wrote down in *his* biography: no, sir, we'd a whooped him over the *border*—that's what we'd a done with *him*—and done it just as slick as nothing at all, too. Man the sweeps—man the sweeps!"

But me and Jim was consulting—and thinking. And after we'd thought a minute, I says:

"Say it, Jim."

So he says:

"Well, den, dis is de way it look to me, Huck. Ef it wuz *him* dat 'uz bein' sot free, en one er de boys wuz to git shot, would he say, 'Go on en save me, nemmine 'bout a doctor f'r to save dis one?' Is dat like Mars Tom Sawyer? Would he say dat? You *bet* he wouldn't! *Well*, den, is *Jim* gwyne to say it? No, sah—I doan' budge a step out'n dis place, 'dout a *doctor*; not if its forty year!"

I knowed he was white inside, and I reckoned he'd say what he did say—so it was all right, now, and I told Tom I was agoing for a doctor. He raised considerble row about it, but me and Jim stuck to it and wouldn't budge; so he was for crawling out and setting the raft loose himself; but we wouldn't let him. Then he give us a piece of his mind—but it didn't do no good.

So when he see me getting the canoe ready, he says:

"Well, then, if you're bound to go, I'll tell you the way to do, when you get to the village. Shut the door, and blindfold the doctor tight and fast, and make him swear to be silent as the grave, and put a purse full of gold in his hand, and then take and lead him all around the back alleys and everywheres, in the dark, and then fetch him here in the canoe, in a roundabout way amongst the islands, and search him and take his chalk away from him, and don't give it back to him till you get him back to the village, or else he will chalk this raft so he can find it again. It's the way they all do."

So I said I would, and left, and Jim was to hide in the woods when he see the doctor coming, till he was gone again.

## Chapter XLI

The doctor was an old man; a very nice, kind-looking old man, when I got him up. I told him me and my brother was over on Spanish Island hunting, yesterday afternoon, and camped on a piece of a raft we found, and about midnight he must a kicked his gun in his dreams, for it went off and shot him in the leg, and we wanted him to go over there and fix it and not say nothing

---

8. Taken from Carlyle's rendering of the king's execution in his *French Revolution* (1837).

about it, nor let anybody know, because we wanted to come home this evening, and surprise the folks.

"Who is your folks?" he says.

"The Phelpses, down yonder."

"Oh," he says. And after a minute, he says: "How'd you say he got shot?"

"He had a dream," I says, "and it shot him."

"Singlular dream," he says.

So he lit up his lantern, and got his saddle-bags, and we started. But when he see the canoe, he didn't like the look of her—said she was big enough for one, but didn't look pretty safe for two. I says:

"Oh, you needn't be afeard, sir, she carried the three of us, easy enough."

"What three?"

"Why, me and Sid, and—and—and *the guns*; that's what I mean."

"Oh," he says.

But he put his foot on the gunnel, and rocked her; and shook his head, and said he reckoned he'd look around for a bigger one. But they was all locked and chained; so he took my canoe, and said for me to wait till he come back, or I could hunt around further, or maybe I better go down home and get them ready for the surprise, if I wanted to. But I said I didn't; so I told him just how to find the raft, and then he started.

I struck an idea, pretty soon. I says to myself, spos'n he can't fix that leg just in three shakes of a sheep's tail, as the saying is? spos'n it takes him three or four days? What are we going to do?—lay around there till he lets the cat out of the bag? No, sir, I know what *I'll* do. I'll wait, and when he comes back, if he says he's got to go any more, I'll get him down there, too, if I swim; and we'll take and tie him, and keep him, and shove out down the river; and when Tom's done with him, we'll give him what it's worth, or all we got, and then let him get shore.

So then I crept into a lumber pile to get some sleep; and next time I waked up the sun was away up over my head! I shot out and went for the doctor's house, but they told me he'd gone away in the night, some time or other, and warn't back yet. Well, thinks I, that looks powerful bad for Tom, and I'll dig out for the island, right off. So away I shoved, and turned the corner, and nearly rammed my head into Uncle Silas's stomach! He says:

"Why, Tom! Where you been, all this time, you rascal?"

"*I* hain't been nowheres," I says, "only just hunting for the runaway nigger—me and Sid."

"Why, where ever did you go?" he says. "Your aunt's been mighty uneasy."

"She needn't," I says, "because we was all right. We followed the men and the dogs, but they out-run us, and we lost them; but we thought we heard them on the water, so we got a canoe and took out after them, and crossed over but couldn't find nothing of them; so we cruised along up-shore till we got kind of tired and beat out; and tied up the canoe and went to sleep, and never waked up till about an hour ago, then we paddled over here to hear the news, and Sid's at the post-office to see what he can hear, and I'm a branching out to get something to eat for us, and then we're going home."

So then we went to the post-office to get "Sid"; but just as I suspicioned, he warn't there; so the old man he got a letter out of the office, and we waited a while longer but Sid didn't come; so the old man said come along, let Sid foot it home, or canoe-it, when he got done fooling around—but we would ride. I couldn't get him to let me stay and wait for Sid; and he said there warn't no use in it, and I must come along, and let Aunt Sally see we was all right.

When we got home, Aunt Sally was that glad to see me she laughed and cried both, and hugged me, and give me one of them lickings of hern that don't amount to shucks, and said she'd serve Sid the same when he come.

And the place was plumb full of farmers and farmers' wives, to dinner; and such another clack a body never heard. Old Mrs. Hotchkiss was the worst; her tongue was agoing all the time. She says:

"Well, Sister Phelps, I've ransacked that-air cabin over an' I b'lieve the nigger was crazy. I says so to Sister Damrell—didn't I, Sister Damrell?—s'I, he's crazy, s'I—them's the very words I said. You all hearn me: he's crazy, s'I; everything shows it, s'I. Look at that-air grindstone, s'I; want to tell *me*'t any cretur 'ts in his right mind 's agoin' to scrabble all them crazy things onto a grindstone, s'I? Here sich 'n' sich a person busted his heart; 'n' here so 'n' so pegged along for thirty-seven year, 'n' all that—natcherl son o' Louis some-body, 'n' sich everlast'n rubbage. He's plumb crazy, s'I; it's what I says in the fust place, it's what I says in the middle, 'n' it's what I says last 'n' all the time—the nigger's crazy—crazy's Nebokoodneezer,[9] s'I."

"An' look at that-air ladder made out'n rags, Sister Hotchkiss," says old Mrs. Damrell, "what in the name o'goodness *could* he ever want of—"

"The very words I was a-sayin' no longer ago th'n this minute to Sister Utterback, 'n' she'll tell you so herself. Sh-she, look at that-air rag ladder, sh-she; 'n' s'I, yes, *look* at it, s'I—what *could* he a wanted of it, s'I. Sh-she, Sister Hotchkiss, sh-she—"

"But how in the nation'd they ever *git* that grindstone *in* there, *anyway?* 'n' who dug that-air *hole?* 'n' who—"

"My very *words*, Brer Penrod! I was a-sayin'—pass that-air sasser o' m'lasses, won't ye?—I was a-sayin' to Sister Dunlap, jist this minute, how *did* they git that grindstone in there, s'I. Without *help*, mind you—'thout *help! That's* wher' tis. Don't tell *me*, s'I; there *wuz* help, s'I; 'n' ther' wuz a *plenty* help, too, s'I; ther's ben a *dozen* a-helpin' that nigger, 'n' I lay I'd skin every last nigger on this place, but *I'd* find out who done it, s'I; 'n' moreover, s'I—"

"A *dozen* says you!—*forty* couldn't a done everything that's been done. Look at them case-knife saws and things, how tedious they've been made; look at that bed-leg sawed off with 'em, a week's work for six men; look at that nigger made out'n straw on the bed; and look at—"

"You may *well* say it, Brer Hightower! It's jist as I was a-sayin' to Brer Phelps, his own self. S'e, what do *you* think of it, Sister Hotchkiss, s'e? think o' what, Brer Phelps, s'I? think o' that bed-leg sawed off that a way, s'e? *think* of it, s'I? I lay it never sawed *itself* off, s'I—somebody sawed it, s'I; that's my opinion, take it or leave it, it mayn't be no 'count, s'I, but sich as 't is, it's my opinion, s'I, 'n' if anybody k'n start a better one, s'I, let him *do* it, s'I, that's all. I says to Sister Dunlap, s'I—"

"Why, dog my cats, they must a ben a house-full o' niggers in there every night for four weeks, to a done all that work, Sister Phelps. Look at that shirt— every last inch of it kivered over with secret African writ'n done with blood! Must a ben a raft uv 'm at it right along, all the time, amost. Why, I'd give two dollars to have it read to me; 'n' as for the niggers that wrote it, I 'low I'd take 'n' lash 'm t'll—"

9. Nebuchadnezzar (605–562 B.C.), king of Babylon, is described in Daniel 4.33 as going mad and eating grass.

"People to *help* him, Brother Marples! Well, I reckon you'd *think* so, if you'd a been in this house for a while back. Why, they've stole everything they could lay their hands on—and we a watching, all the time, mind you. They stole that shirt right off o' the line! and as for that sheet they made the rag ladder out of ther' ain't no telling how many times they *didn't* steal that; and flour, and candles, and candlesticks, and spoons, and the old-warming-pan, and most a thousand things that I disremember, now, and my new calico dress; and me, and Silas, and my Sid and Tom on the constant watch day *and* night, as I was a telling you, and not a one of us could catch hide nor hair, nor sight nor sound of them; and here at the last minute, lo and behold you, they slides right in under our noses, and fools us, and not only fools *us* but the Injun Territory robbers too, and actuly gets *away* with that nigger, safe and sound, and that with sixteen men and twenty-two dogs right on their very heels at that very time! I tell you, it just bangs anything I ever *heard* of. Why, *spirits* couldn't a done better, and been no smarter. And I reckon they must a *been* sperits—because, *you* know our dogs, and ther' ain't no better; well, them dogs never even got on the *track* of 'm, once! You explain *that* to me, if you can!—*any* of you!"

"Well, it does beat—"

"Laws alive, I never—"

"So help me, I wouldn't a be—"

"*House* thieves as well as—"

"Goodnessgracioussakes, I'd a ben afeard to *live* in sich a—"

" 'Fraid to *live!*—why, I was that scared I dasn't hardly go to bed, or get up, or lay down, or *set* down, Sister Ridgeway. Why, they'd steal the very—why, goodness sakes, you can guess what kind of a fluster *I* was in by the time midnight come, last night. I hope to gracious if I warn't afraid they'd steal some o' the family! I was just to that pass, I didn't have no reasoning faculties no more. It looks foolish enough, *now*, in the day-time; but I says to myself, there's my two poor boys asleep, 'way up stairs in that lonesome room, and I declare to goodness I was that uneasy 't I crep' up there and locked 'em in! I *did*. And anybody would. Because, you know, when you get scared, that way, and it keeps running on, and getting worse and worse, all the time, and your wits gets to addling, and you get to doing all sorts o' wild things, and by-and-by you think to yourself, spos'n *I* was a boy, and was away up there, and the door ain't locked, and you—" She stopped, looking kind of wondering, and then she turned her head around slow, and when her eye lit on me—I got up and took a walk.

Says I to myself, I can explain better how we come to not be in that room this morning, if I go out to one side and study over it a little. So I done it. But I dasn't go fur, or she'd a sent for me. And when it was late in the day, the people all went, and then I come in and told her the noise and shooting waked up me and "Sid," and the door was locked, and we wanted to see the fun, so we went down the lightning-rod, and both of us got hurt a little, and we didn't never want to try *that* no more. And then I went on and told her all what I told Uncle Silas before; and then she said she'd forgive us, and maybe it was all right enough anyway, and about what a body might expect of boys, for all boys was a pretty harum-scarum lot, as fur as she could see; and so, as long as no harm hadn't come of it, she judged she better put in her time being grateful we was alive and well and she had us still, stead of fretting over what was past and done. So then she kissed me, and patted me on the head, and dropped into a kind of a brown study; and pretty soon jumps up, and says:

"Why, lawsamercy, it's most night, and Sid not come yet! What *has* become of that boy?"

I see my chance; so I skips up and says:

"I'll run right up to town and get him," I says.

"No, you won't," she says. "You'll stay right wher' you are; *one's* enough to be lost at a time. If he ain't here to supper, your uncle 'll go."

Well, he warn't there to supper; so right after supper uncle went.

He come back about ten, a little bit uneasy; hadn't run across Tom's track. Aunt Sally was a good *deal* uneasy; but Uncle Silas he said there warn't no occasion to be—boys will be boys, he said, and you'll see this one turn up in the morning, all sound and right. So she had to be satisfied. But she said she'd set up for him a while, anyway, and keep a light burning, so he could see it.

And then when I went up to bed she come up with me and fetched her candle, and tucked me in, and mothered me so good I felt mean, and like I couldn't look her in the face; and she set down on the bed and talked with me a long time, and said what a splendid boy Sid was, and didn't seem to want to ever stop talking about him; and kept asking me every now and then, if I reckoned he could a got lost, or hurt, or maybe drownded, and might be laying at this minute, somewheres, suffering or dead, and she not by him to help him, and so the tears would drip down, silent, and I would tell her that Sid was all right, and would be home in the morning, sure; and she would squeeze my hand, or maybe kiss me, and tell me to say it again, and keep on saying it, because it done her good, and she was in so much trouble. And when she was going away, she looked down in my eyes, so steady and gentle, and says:

"The door ain't going to be locked, Tom; and there's the window and the rod; but you'll be good, *won't* you? And you won't go? For *my* sake."

Laws knows I *wanted* to go, bad enough, to see about Tom, and was all intending to go; but after that, I wouldn't a went, not for kingdoms.

But she was on my mind, and Tom was on my mind; so I slept very restless. And twice I went down the rod, away in the night, and slipped around front, and see her setting there by her candle in the window with her eyes towards the road and the tears in them; and I wished I could do something for her, but I couldn't, only to swear that I wouldn't never do nothing to grieve her any more. And the third time, I waked up at dawn, and slid down, and she was there yet, and her candle was most out, and her old gray head was resting on her hand, and she was asleep.

## Chapter XLII

The old man was up town again, before breakfast, but couldn't get no track of Tom; and both of them set at the table, thinking, and not saying nothing, and looking mournful, and their coffee getting cold, and not eating anything. And by-and-by the old man says:

"Did I give you the letter?"

"What letter?"

"The one I got yesterday out of the post-office."

"No, you didn't give me no letter."

"Well, I must a forgot it."

So he rummaged his pockets, and then went off somewheres where he had laid it down, and fetched it, and give it to her. She says:

"Why, it's from St. Petersburg—it's from Sis."

I allowed another walk would do me good; but I couldn't stir. But before she could break it open, she dropped it and run—for she see something. And so did I. It was Tom Sawyer on a mattress; and that old doctor; and Jim, in *her* calico dress, with his hands tied behind him; and a lot of people. I hid the letter behind the first thing that come handy, and rushed. She flung herself at Tom, crying, and says:

"Oh, he's dead, he's dead, I know he's dead!"

And Tom he turned his head a little, and muttered something or other, which showed he warn't in his right mind; then she flung up her hands and says:

"He's alive, thank God! And that's enough!" and she snatched a kiss of him, and flew for the house to get the bed ready, and scattering orders right and left at the niggers and everybody else, as fast as her tongue could go, every jump of the way.

I followed the men to see what they was going to do with Jim; and the old doctor and Uncle Silas followed after Tom into the house. The men was very huffy, and some of them wanted to hang Jim, for an example to all the other niggers around there, so they wouldn't be trying to run away, like Jim done, and making such a raft of trouble, and keeping a whole family scared most to death for days and nights. But the others said, don't do it, it wouldn't answer at all, he ain't our nigger, and his owner would turn up and make us pay for him, sure. So that cooled them down a little, because the people that's always the most anxious for to hang a nigger that hain't done just right, is always the very ones that ain't the most anxious to pay for him when they've got their satisfaction out of him.

They cussed Jim considerble, though, and give him a cuff or two, side the head, once in a while, but Jim never said nothing, and he never let on to know me, and they took him to the same cabin, and put his own clothes on him, and chained him again, and not to no bed-leg, this time, but to a big staple drove into the bottom log, and chained his hands, too, and both legs, and said he warn't to have nothing but bread and water to eat, after this, till his owner come or he was sold at auction, because he didn't come in a certain length of time, and filled up our hole, and said a couple of farmers with guns must stand watch around about the cabin every night, and a bull-dog tied to the door in the day time; and about this time they was through with the job and was tapering off with a kind of generl good-bye cussing, and then the old doctor comes and takes a look and says:

"Don't be no rougher on him than you're obleeged to, because he ain't a bad nigger. When I got to where I found the boy, I see I couldn't cut the bullet out without some help, and he warn't in no condition for me to leave, to go and get help; and he got a little worse and a little worse, and after a long time he went out of his head, and wouldn't let me come anigh him, any more, and said if I chalked his raft he'd kill me, and no end of wild foolishness like that, and I see I couldn't do anything at all with him; so I says, I got to have *help*, somehow; and the minute I says it, out crawls this nigger from somewheres, and says he'll help, and he done it, too, and done it very well. Of course I judged he must be a runaway nigger, and there I *was!* and there I had to stick, right straight along all the rest of the day, and all night. It was a fix, I tell you! I had a couple of patients with the chills, and of course I'd of liked to run up to town and see them, but I dasn't, because the nigger might get away, and then I'd be to blame; and yet never a skiff come close enough for me to hail. So there I had to stick, plumb till daylight this morning; and I never see a nigger that was a better nuss or faithfuller, and yet he was resking his freedom to do it, and was all tired out, too, and I see plain enough he'd been worked main hard, lately. I liked the nigger for that; I tell you, gentlemen, a nigger like that is worth a thousand dollars—and kind treatment, too. I had everything I needed, and the boy was doing as well there as he would a done at home— better, maybe, because it was so quiet; but there I *was*, with both of 'm on my hands; and there I had to stick, till about dawn this morning; then some men in a skiff come by, and as good luck would have it, the nigger was setting by the pallet with his head propped on his knees, sound asleep; so I motioned them in, quiet, and they slipped up on him and grabbed him and tied him before he knowed what he was about, and we never had no trouble. And the boy being in a kind of a flighty sleep, too, we muffled the oars and hitched the raft on, and towed her over very nice and quiet, and the nigger never made the least row nor said a word, from the start. He ain't no bad nigger, gentlemen; that's what I think about him."

Somebody says:

"Well, it sounds very good, doctor, I'm obleeged to say."

Then the others softened up a little, too, and I was mighty thankful to that old doctor for doing Jim that good turn; and I was glad it was according to my judgment of him, too; because I thought he had a good heart in him and was a good man, the first time I see him. Then they all agreed that Jim had acted very well, and was deserving to have some notice took of it, and reward. So every one of them promised, right out and hearty, that they wouldn't cuss him no more.

Then they come out and locked him up. I hoped they was going to say he could have one or two of the chains took off, because they was rotten heavy, or could have meat and greens with his bread and water, but they didn't think of it, and I reckoned it warn't best for me to mix in, but I judged I'd get the doctor's yarn to Aunt Sally, somehow or other, as soon as I'd got through the breakers that was laying just ahead of me. Explanations, I mean, of how I forgot to mention about Sid being shot, when I was telling how him and me put in that dratted night paddling around hunting the runaway nigger.

But I had plenty time. Aunt Sally she stuck to the sick-room all day and all night; and every time I see Uncle Silas mooning around, I dodged him.

Next morning I heard Tom was a good deal better, and they said Aunt Sally was gone to get a nap. So I slips to the sick-room, and if I found him awake I reckoned we could put up a yarn for the family that would wash. But he was sleeping, and sleeping very peaceful, too; and pale, not fire-faced the way he was when he come. So I set down and laid for him to wake. In about a half an hour, Aunt Sally comes gliding in, and there I was, up a stump again! She motioned me to be still, and set down by me, and begun to whisper, and said we could all be joyful now, because all the symptoms was first rate, and he'd been sleeping like that for ever so long, and looking better and peacefuller all the time, and ten to one he'd wake up in his right mind.

So we set there watching, and by-and-by he stirs a bit, and opened his eyes very natural, and takes a look, and says:

"Hello, why I'm at *home!* How's that? Where's the raft?"

"It's all right," I says.

"And *Jim?*"

"The same," I says, but couldn't say it pretty brash. But he never noticed, but says:

"Good! Splendid! *Now* we're all right and safe! Did you tell Aunty?"

I was about to say yes; but she chipped in and says:

"About what, Sid?"

"Why, about the way the whole thing was done."

"What whole thing?"

"Why, *the* whole thing. There ain't but one; how we set the runaway nigger free—me and Tom."

"Good land! Set the run— What *is* the child talking about! Dear, dear, out of his head again!"

"No, I ain't out of my HEAD; I know all what I'm talking about. We *did* set him free—me and Tom. We laid out to do it, and we *done* it. And we done it elegant, too." He'd got a start, and she never checked him up, just set and stared and stared, and let him clip along, and I see it warn't no use for *me* to put in. "Why, Aunty, it cost us a power of work—weeks of it—hours and hours, every night, whilst you was all asleep. And we had to steal candles, and the sheet, and the shirt, and your dress, and spoons, and tin plates, and case-knives, and the warming-pan, and the grindstone, and flour, and just no end of things, and you can't think what work it was to make the saws, and pens, and inscriptions, and one thing or another, and you can't think *half* the fun it was. And we had to make up the pictures of coffins and things, and nonna-mous letters from the robbers, and get up and down the lightning-rod, and dig the hole into the cabin, and make the rope-ladder and send it in cooked up in a pie, and send in spoons and things to work with, in your apron pocket"—

"Mercy sakes!"

—"and load up the cabin with rats and snakes and so on, for company for Jim; and then you kept Tom here so long with the butter in his hat that you come near spiling the whole business, because the men come before we was out of the cabin, and we had to rush, and they heard us and let drive at us, and I got my share, and we dodged out of the path and let them go by, and when the dogs come they warn't interested in us, but went for the most noise, and we got our canoe, and made for the raft, and was all safe, and Jim was a free man, and we done it all by ourselves, and *wasn't* it bully, Aunty!"

"Well, I never heard the likes of it in all my born days! So it was *you*, you little rapscallions, that's been making all this trouble, and turn everybody's wits clean inside out and scared us all most to death. I've as good a notion as ever I had in my life, to take it out o' you this very minute. To think, here I've been, night after night, a—*you* just get well once, you young scamp, and I lay I'll tan the Old Harry out o' both o' ye!"

But Tom, he *was* so proud and joyful, he just *couldn't* hold in, and his tongue just *went* it—she a-chipping in, and spitting fire all along, and both of them going it at once, like a cat-convention; and she says:

"*Well*, you get all the enjoyment you can out of it *now*, for mind I tell you if I catch you meddling with him again—"

"Meddling with *who?*" Tom says, dropping his smile and looking surprised.

"With *who?* Why, the runaway nigger, of course. Who'd you reckon?"

Tom looks at me very grave, and says:

"Tom, didn't you just tell me he was all right? Hasn't he got away?"

"*Him?*" says Aunt Sally; "the runaway nigger? 'Deed he hasn't. They've got him back, safe and sound, and he's in that cabin again, on bread and water, and loaded down with chains, till he's claimed or sold!"

Tom rose square up in bed, with his eye hot, and his nostrils opening and shutting like gills, and sings out to me:

"They hain't no *right* to shut him up! *Shove!*—and don't you lose a minute. Turn him loose! he ain't no slave; he's as free as any cretur that walks this earth!"

"What *does* the child mean?"

"I mean every word I *say*, Aunt Sally, and if somebody don't go, *I'll* go. I've knowed him all his life, and so has Tom, there. Old Miss Watson died two months ago, and she was ashamed she ever was going to sell him down the river, and *said* so; and she set him free in her will."

"Then what on earth did *you* want to set him free for, seeing he was already free?"

"Well, that *is* a question, I must say; and *just* like women! Why, I wanted the *adventure* of it; and I'd a waded neck-deep in blood to—goodness alive, AUNT POLLY!"[1]

If she warn't standing right there, just inside the door, looking as sweet and contented as an angel half-full of pie, I wish I may never!

Aunt Sally jumped for her, and most hugged the head off of her, and cried over her, and I found a good enough place for me under the bed, for it was getting pretty sultry for *us*, seemed to me. And I peeped out, and in a little while Tom's Aunt Polly shook herself loose and stood there looking across at Tom over her spectacles—kind of grinding him into the earth, you know. And then she says:

"Yes, you *better* turn y'r head away—I would if I was you, Tom."

"Oh, deary me!" says Aunt Sally; "*is* he changed so? Why, that ain't *Tom* it's Sid; Tom's—Tom's—why, where is Tom? He was here a minute ago."

"You mean where's Huck *Finn*—that's what you mean! I reckon I hain't raised such a scamp as my Tom all these years, not to know him when I *see* him. That *would* be a pretty howdy-do. Come out from under the bed, Huck Finn."

So I done it. But not feeling brash.

Aunt Sally she was one of the mixed-upest looking persons I ever see; except one, and that was Uncle Silas, when he come in, and they told it all to him. It kind of made him drunk, as you may say, and he didn't know nothing at all the rest of the day, and preached a prayer-meeting sermon that night that give him a rattling ruputation, because the oldest man in the world couldn't a understood it. So Tom's Aunt Polly, she told all about who I was, and what; and I had to up and tell how I was in such a tight place that when Mrs. Phelps took me for Tom Sawyer—she chipped in and says, "Oh, go on and call me Aunt Sally, I'm used to it, now, and 'tain't no need to change"—that when Aunt Sally took me for Tom Sawyer, I had to stand it—that warn't no other way, and I knowed he wouldn't mind, because it would be nuts for him, being a mystery, and he'd make an adventure out of it and be perfectly satisfied. And so it turned out, and he let on to be Sid, and made things as soft as he could for me.

---

1. Tom Sawyer's aunt and guardian.

And his Aunt Polly she said Tom was right about old Miss Watson setting Jim free in her will; and so, sure enough, Tom Sawyer had gone and took all that trouble and bother to set a free nigger free! and I couldn't ever understand, before, until that minute and that talk, how he *could* help a body set a nigger free, with his bringing-up.

Well, Aunt Polly she said that when Aunt Sally wrote to her that Tom and *Sid* had come, all right and safe, she says to herself:

"Look at that, now! I might have expected it, letting him go off that way without anybody to watch him. So now I got to go and trapse all the way down the river, eleven hundred mile,[2] and find out what that creetur's up to, *this* time; as long as I couldn't seem to get any answer out of you about it."

"Why, I never heard nothing from you," says Aunt Sally.

"Well, I wonder! Why, I wrote to you twice, to ask you what you could mean by Sid being here."

"Well, I never got 'em, Sis."

Aunt Polly, she turns around slow and severe, and says:

"You, Tom!"

"Well—*what?*" he says, kind of pettish.

"Don't you what *me*, you impudent thing—hand out them letters."

"What letters?"

"*Them* letters. I be bound, if I have to take aholt of you I'll—"

"They're in the trunk. There, now. And they're just the same as they was when I got them out of the office. I hain't looked into them, I hain't touched them. But I knowed they'd make trouble, and I thought if you warn't in no hurry, I'd—"

"Well, you *do* need skinning, there ain't no mistake about it. And I wrote another one to tell you I was coming; and I spose he—"

"No, it come yesterday; I hain't read it yet, but *it's* all right, I've got that one."

I wanted to offer to bet two dollars she hadn't, but I reckoned maybe it was just as safe to not to. So I never said nothing.

## Chapter the Last

The first time I catched Tom, private, I asked him what was his idea, time of the evasion?—what it was he'd planned to do if the evasion worked all right and he managed to set a nigger free that was already free before? And he said, what he had planned in his head, from the start, if we got Jim out all safe, was for us to run him down the river, on the raft, and have adventures plumb to the mouth of the river, and then tell him about his being free, and take him back up home on a steamboat, in style, and pay him for his lost time, and write word ahead and get out all the niggers around, and have them waltz him into town with a torchlight procession and a brass band, and then he would be a hero, and so would we. But I reckoned it was about as well the way it was.

We had Jim out of the chains in no time, and when Aunt Polly and Uncle Silas and Aunt Sally found out how good he helped the doctor nurse Tom, they made a heap of fuss over him, and fixed him up prime, and give him all he wanted to eat, and a good time, and nothing to do. And we had him up to the sickroom; and had a high talk; and Tom give Jim forty dollars for being

---

2. This distance from Hannibal would place the Phelps plantation in northern Louisiana.

prisoner for us so patient, and doing it up so good, and Jim was pleased most to death, and busted out, and says:

"*Dah*, now, Huck, what I tell you?—what I tell you up dah on Jackson islan'? I *tole* you I got a hairy breas', en what's de sign un it; en I *tole* you I ben rich wunst, en gwineter to be rich *agin*; en it's come true; en heah she *is*! *Dah*, now! doan' talk to *me*—signs is *signs*, mine I tell you; en I knowed jis' 's well 'at I 'uz gwineter be rich agin as I's a stannin' heah dis minute!"

And then Tom he talked along, and talked along, and says, le's all three slide out of here, one of these nights, and get an outfit, and go for howling adventures amongst the Injuns, over in the Territory, for a couple of weeks or two; and I says, all right, that suits me, but I ain't got no money for to buy the outfit, and I reckon I couldn't get none from home, because it's likely pap's been back before now, and got it all away from Judge Thatcher and drunk it up.

"No he hain't," Tom says; "it's all there, yet—six thousand dollars and more; and your pap hain't ever been back since. Hadn't when I come away, anyhow."

Jim says, kind of solemn:

"He ain't a comin' back no mo', Huck."

I says:

"Why, Jim?"

"Nemmine why, Huck—but he ain't comin' back no mo'."

But I kept at him; so at last he says:

"Doan' you 'member de house dat was float'n down de river, en dey wuz a man in dah, kivered up, en I went in en unkivered him and didn' let you come in? Well, den, you k'n git yo' money when you wants it; kase dat wuz him."

Tom's most well, now, and got his bullet around his neck on a watch-guard for a watch, and is always seeing what time it is, and so there ain't nothing more to write about, and I am rotten glad of it, because if I'd a knowed what a trouble it was to make a book I wouldn't a tackled it and ain't agoing to no more. But I reckon I got to light out for the Territory ahead of the rest, because Aunt Sally she's going to adopt me and sivilize me and I can't stand it. I been there before.

THE END. YOURS TRULY, HUCK FINN.

1876–83                                                                 1884

# [The Art of Authorship][1]

Your inquiry has set me thinking, but, so far, my thought fails to materialize. I mean that, upon consideration, I am not sure that I have methods in composition. I do suppose I have—I suppose I must have—but they somehow refuse to take shape in my mind; their details refuse to separate and submit to classification and description; they remain a jumble—visible, like the fragments of glass when you look in at the wrong end of a kaleidoscope, but still a jumble. If I could turn the whole thing around and look in at the other end,

---

1. This reflection on literary method was prompted by an inquiry from George Bainton, who edited and published Clemens's reply together with those of many of his contemporaries under the title *The Art of Authorship* (1890).

why then the figures would flash into form out of the chaos, and I shouldn't have any more trouble. But my head isn't right for that today, apparently. It might have been, maybe, if I had slept last night.

However, let us try guessing. Let us guess that whenever we read a sentence and like it, we unconsciously store it away in our model-chamber; and it goes with a myriad of its fellows to the building, brick, by brick, of the eventual edifice which we call our style. And let us guess that whenever we run across other forms—bricks—whose color, or some other defect, offends us, we unconsciously reject these, and so one never finds them in our edifice.

If I have subjected myself to any training processes, and no doubt I have, it must have been in this unconscious or half-conscious fashion. I think it unlikely that deliberate and consciously methodical training is usual with the craft. I think it likely that the training most in use is of this unconscious sort, and is guided and governed and made by-and-by unconsciously systematic, by an automatically-working taste—a taste which selects and rejects without asking you for any help, and patiently and steadily improves itself without troubling you to approve or applaud. Yes, and likely enough when the structure is at last pretty well up, and attracts attention, YOU feel complimented, whereas you didn't build it, and didn't even consciously superintend.

Yes; one notices, for instance, that long, involved sentences confuse him, and that he is obliged to re-read them to get the sense. Unconsciously, then, he rejects that brick. Unconsciously he accustoms himself to writing short sentences as a rule. At times he may indulge himself with a long one, but he will make sure that there are no folds in it, no vaguenesses, no parenthetical interruptions of its view as a whole; when he is done with it, it won't be a sea-serpent, with half its arches under the water, it will be a torchlight procession.

Well, also he will notice in the course of time, as his reading goes on, that the difference between the almost right word and the right word is really a large matter—'tis the difference between the lightning-bug and the lightning. After that, of course, that exceedingly important brick, the exact word—however, this is running into an essay, and I beg pardon. So I seemed to have arrived at this: doubtless I have methods, but they begot themselves, in which case I am only their proprietor, not their father.

1890

# How to Tell a Story[1]

The Humorous Story an American Development.—Its
Difference from Comic and Witty Stories.

I do not claim that I can tell a story as it ought to be told. I only claim to know how a story ought to be told, for I have been almost daily in the company of the most expert story-tellers for many years.

There are several kinds of stories, but only one difficult kind—the humorous. I will talk mainly about that one. The humorous story is American, the comic story is English, the witty story is French. The humorous story depends for its effect upon the *manner* of the telling; the comic story and the witty story upon the *matter*.

1. First published in *Youth's Companion*, October 3, 1895, the basis of the present text.

The humorous story may be spun out to great length, and may wander around as much as it pleases, and arrive nowhere in particular; but the comic and witty stories must be brief and end with a point. The humorous story bubbles gently along, the others burst.

The humorous story is strictly a work of art—high and delicate art—and only an artist can tell it; but no art is necessary in telling the comic and the witty story; anybody can do it. The art of telling a humorous story—understand, I mean by word of mouth, not print—was created in America, and has remained at home.

The humorous story is told gravely; the teller does his best to conceal the fact that he even dimly suspects that there is anything funny about it; but the teller of the comic story tells you beforehand that it is one of the funniest things he has ever heard, then tells it with eager delight, and is the first person to laugh when he gets through. And sometimes, if he has had good success, he is so glad and happy that he will repeat the "nub" of it and glance around from fact to face, collecting applause, and then repeat it again. It is a pathetic thing to see.

Very often, of course, the rambling and disjointed humorous story finishes with a nub, point, snapper, or whatever you like to call it. Then the listener must be alert, for in many cases the teller will divert attention from that nub by dropping it in a carefully casual and indifferent way, with the pretence that he does not know it is a nub.

Artemus Ward[2] used that trick a good deal; then when the belated audience presently caught the joke he would look up with innocent surprise, as if wondering what they had found to laugh at. Dan Setchell used it before him, Nye and Riley[3] and others use it to-day.

But the teller of the comic story does not slur the nub; he shouts it at you—every time. And when he prints it, in England, France, Germany, and Italy, he italicizes it, puts some whooping exclamation-points after it, and sometimes explains it in a parenthesis. All of which is very depressing, and makes one want to renounce joking and lead a better life.

Let me set down an instance of the comic method, using an anecdote which has been popular all over the world for twelve or fifteen hundred years. The teller tells it in this way:

### The Wounded Soldier

In the course of a certain battle a soldier whose leg had been shot off appealed to another soldier who was hurrying by to carry him to the rear, informing him at the same time of the loss which he had sustained; whereupon the generous son of Mars, shouldering the unfortunate, proceeded to carry out his desire. The bullets and cannon-balls were flying in all directions, and presently one of the latter took the wounded man's head off—without, however, his deliverer being aware of it. In no long time he was hailed by an officer, who said:

2. Artemus Ward, pseudonym of Charles Farrar Browne (1834–1867), journalist and humorous lecturer.
3. Dan Setchell (apparently a humorous lecturer) has not been identified. He is not listed in Will M. Clemens's *Famous Funny Fellows* (1882), which provides thirty-five brief biographical sketches of American humorists of the late 19th century. Edgar Wilson (Bill) Nye (1850–1896), editor, journalist, humorous lecturer. James Whitcomb Riley (1849–1916), journalist, popular dialect versifier, and lecturer.

"Where are you going with that carcass?"

"To the rear, sir—he's lost his leg!"

"His leg, forsooth?" responded the astonished officer; "you mean his head, you booby."

Whereupon the soldier dispossessed himself of his burden, and stood looking down upon it in great perplexity. At length he said:

"It is true, sir, just as you have said." Then after a pause he added, "*But he* TOLD *me* IT WAS HIS LEG! ! ! ! !"

---

Here the narrator bursts into explosion after explosion of thunderous horse-laughter, repeating that nub from time to time through his gaspings and shriekings and suffocatings.

It takes only a minute and a half to tell that in its comic-story form; and isn't worth the telling, after all. Put into the humorous-story form it takes ten minutes, and is about the funniest thing I have ever listened to—as James Whitcomb Riley tells it.

He tells it in the character of a dull-witted old farmer who has just heard it for the first time, thinks it is unspeakably funny, and is trying to repeat it to a neighbor. But he can't remember it; so he gets all mixed up and wanders helplessly round and round, putting in tedious details that don't belong in the tale and only retard it; taking them out conscientiously and putting in others that are just as useless; making minor mistakes now and then and stopping to correct them and explain how he came to make them; remembering things which he forgot to put in in their proper place and going back to put them in there; stopping his narrative a good while in order to try to recall the name of the soldier that was hurt, and finally remembering that the soldier's name was not mentioned, and remarking placidly that the name is of no real importance, anyway—better, of course, if one knew it, but not essential, after all—and so on, and so on, and so on.

The teller is innocent and happy and pleased with himself, and has to stop every little while to hold himself in and keep from laughing outright; and does hold in, but his body quakes in a jelly-like way with interior chuckles; and at the end of the ten minutes the audience have laughed until they are exhausted, and the tears are running down their faces.

The simplicity and innocence and sincerity and unconsciousness of the old farmer are perfectly simulated, and the result is a performance which is thoroughly charming and delicious. This is art—and fine and beautiful, and only a master can compass it; but a machine could tell the other story.

To string incongruities and absurdities together in a wandering and sometimes purposeless way, and seem innocently unaware that they are absurdities, is the basis of the American art, if my position is correct. Another feature is the slurring of the point. A third is the dropping of a studied remark apparently without knowing it, as if one were thinking aloud. The fourth and last is the pause.

Artemus Ward dealt in numbers three and four a good deal. He would begin to tell with great animation something which he seemed to think was wonderful; then lose confidence, and after an apparently absent-minded pause add an incongruous remark in a soliloquizing way; and that was the remark intended to explode the mine—and it did.

For instance, he would say eagerly, excitedly, "I once knew a man in New

Zealand who hadn't a tooth in his head"—here his animation would die out; a silent, reflective pause would follow, then he would say dreamily, and as if to himself, "and yet that man could beat a drum better than any man I ever saw."

The pause is an exceedingly important feature in any kind of story, and a frequently recurring feature, too. It is a dainty thing, and delicate, and also uncertain and treacherous; for it must be exactly the right length—no more and no less—or it fails of its purpose and makes trouble. If the pause is too short the impressive point is passed, and the audience have had time to divine that a surprise is intended—and then you can't surprise them, of course.

On the platform I used to tell a negro ghost story that had a pause in front of the snapper on the end, and that pause was the most important thing in the whole story. If I got it the right length precisely, I could spring the finishing ejaculation with effect enough to make some impressible girl deliver a startled little yelp and jump out of her seat—and that was what I was after. This story was called "The Golden Arm," and was told in this fashion. You can practise with it yourself—and mind you look out for the pause and get it right.

## The Golden Arm

Once 'pon a time dey wuz a monsus mean man, en he live 'way out in de prairie all 'lone by hisself, 'cep'n he had a wife. En bimeby she died, en he tuck en toted her way out dah in de prairie en buried her. Well, she had a golden arm—all solid gold, fum de shoulder down. He wuz pow'ful mean— pow'ful; en dat night he couldn't sleep, caze he want dat golden arm so bad.

When it come midnight he couldn't stan' it no mo'; so he git up, he did, en tuck his lantern en shoved out thoo de storm en dug her up en got de golden arm; en he bent his head down 'gin de win', en plowed en plowed en plowed thoo de snow. Den all on a sudden he stop (make a considerable pause here, and look startled, and take a listening attitude) en say: "My *lan'*, what's dat!"

En he listen—en listen—en de win' say (set your teeth together and imitate the wailing and wheezing singsong of the wind), "Bzzz-z-zzz"—en den, way back yonder whah de grave is, he hear a *voice!*—he hear a voice all mix' up in de win'—can't hardly tell 'em 'part—"Bzzz-zzz—W-h-o—g-o-t—m-y— g-o-l-d-e-n *arm?*—zzz—zzz—W-h-o g-o-t m-y g-o-l-d-e-n *arm?* (You must begin to shiver violently now.)

En he begin to shiver en shake, en say, "Oh, my! *Oh,* my lan'!" en de win' blow de lantern out, en de snow en sleet blow in his face en mos' choke him, en he start a-plowin' knee-deep towards home mos' dead, he so sk'yerd—en pooty soon he hear de voice agin, en (pause) it 'us comin' *after* him! "Bzzz— zzz—zzz—W-h-o—g-o-t—m-y—g-o-l-d-e-n—*arm?*"

When he git to de pasture he hear it agin—closter now, en a-*comin'!*—a-comin' back dah in de dark en de storm—(repeat the wind and the voice). When he git to de house he rush upstairs en jump in de bed en kiver up, head and years, en lay dah shiverin' en shakin'—en den way out dah he hear it *agin!*—en a-*comin'!* En bimeby he hear (pause—awed, listening attitude)— pat—pat—pat—*hit's* a-*comin'* up-stairs! Den he hear de latch, en he *know* it's in de room!

Den pooty soon he know it's a-*stannin'* by de bed! (Pause.) Den—he know it's a-*bendin' down over him*—en he cain't skasely git his breath! Den—den—

he seem to feel someth'n *c-o-l-d*, right down 'most agin his head! (Pause.)

Den de voice say, *right at his year*—"W-h-o—g-o-t—m-y—g-o-l-d-e-n *arm?*" (You must wait it out very plaintively and accusingly; then you stare steadily and impressively into the face of the farthest-gone auditor—a girl, preferably—and let that awe-inspiring pause begin to build itself in the deep hush. When it has reached exactly the right length, jump suddenly at that girl and yell, "*You've* got it!"

If you've got the *pause* right, she'll fetch a dear little yelp and spring right out of her shoes. But you *must* get the pause right; and you will find it the most troublesome and aggravating and uncertain thing you ever undertook.)

1895

# *From* Letters from the Earth[1]

## *Letter IV*

I have told you nothing about man that is not true. You must pardon me if I repeat that remark now and then in these letters; I want you to take seriously the things I am telling you, and I feel that if I were in your place and you in mine, I should need that reminder from time to time, to keep my credulity from flagging.

For there is nothing about Man that is not strange to an Immortal. He looks at nothing as we look at it, his sense of proportion is quite different from ours, and his sense of values is so widely divergent from ours, that with all our large intellectual powers it is not likely that even the most gifted among us would ever be quite able to understand it.

For instance, take this sample: he has imagined a heaven, and has left entirely out of it the supremest of all his delights, the one ecstasy that stands first and foremost in the heart of every individual of his race—and of ours—sexual intercourse!

It is as if a lost and perishing person in a roasting desert should be told by a rescuer he might choose and have all longed-for things but one, and he should elect to leave out water!

His heaven is like himself: strange, interesting, astonishing, grotesque. I give you my word, it has not a single feature in it that he *actually values*. It consists—utterly and entirely—of diversions which he cares next to nothing about, here in the earth, yet is quite sure he will like in heaven. Isn't it curious? Isn't it interesting? You must not think I am exaggerating, for it is not so. I will give you details.

Most men do not sing, most men cannot sing, most men will not stay where others are singing if it be continued more than two hours. Note that.

---

1. *Letters from the Earth* was written in late 1909 and is one of Clemens's last substantial works. He considered it too controversial for general distribution, but did not forbid publication. Occasional passages were quoted, but publication of the whole manuscript was not considered until 1937, when Bernard de Voto succeeded Albert Bigelow Paine as executor of the Mark Twain Papers. It was not until 1962, however, that de Voto's texts were published posthumously through the agency of Henry Nash Smith, then literary editor of the Mark Twain Papers. Our text is from Vol. 19 of the *Works of Mark Twain*, edited by Paul Baender in 1973, under the title *What is Man? and Other Philosophical Writings*, pp. 406–12. The "Letters" are written by the yet unfallen archangel Satan. Following temporary banishment from heaven for too frequent and too vocal criticism of the celestial establishment, he decides to visit earth as an observer. His findings are related in his letters to his friends, the saints Michael and Gabriel.

Only about two men in a hundred can play upon a musical instrument, and not four in a hundred have any wish to learn how. Set that down.

Many men pray, not many of them like to do it. A few pray long, the others make a short cut.

More men go to church than want to.

To forty-nine men in fifty the Sabbath Day is a dreary, dreary bore.

Of all the men in a church on a Sunday, two-thirds are tired when the service is half over, and the rest before it is finished.

The gladdest moment for all of them is when the preacher uplifts his hands for the benediction. You can hear the soft rustle of relief that sweeps the house, and you recognize that it is eloquent with gratitude.

All nations look down upon all other nations.

All nations dislike all other nations.

All white nations despise all colored nations, of whatever hue, and oppress them when they can.

White men will not associate with "niggers," nor marry them.

They will not allow them in their schools and churches.

All the world hates the Jew, and will not endure him except when he is rich.

I ask you to note all those particulars.

Further. All sane people detest noise.

All sane people, sane or insane, like to have variety in their life. Monotony quickly wearies them.

Every man, according to the mental equipment that has fallen to his share, exercises his intellect constantly, ceaselessly, and this exercise makes up a vast and valued and essential part of his life. The lowest intellect, like the highest, possesses a skill of some kind and takes a keen pleasure in testing it, proving it, perfecting it. The urchin who is his comrade's superior in games is as diligent and as enthusiastic in his practice as are the sculptor, the painter, the pianist, the mathematician and the rest. Not one of them could be happy if his talent were put under an interdict.

Now then, you have the facts. You know what the human race enjoys, and what it doesn't enjoy. It has invented a heaven, out of its own head, all by itself: guess what it is like! In fifteen hundred eternities you couldn't do it. The ablest mind known to you or me in fifty million aeons couldn't do it. Very well, I will tell you about it.

## II

1. First of all, I recall to your attention the extraordinary fact with which I began. To-wit, that the human being, like the immortals, naturally places sexual intercourse far and away above all other joys—yet he has left it out of his heaven! The very thought of it excites him; opportunity sets him wild; in this state he will risk life, reputation, everything—even his queer heaven itself—to make good that opportunity and ride it to the overwhelming climax. From youth to middle age all men and all women prize copulation above all other pleasures combined, yet it is actually as I have said: it is not in their heaven, prayer takes its place.

They prize it thus highly; yet, like all their so-called "boons," it is a poor thing. At its very best and longest the act is brief beyond imagination—the imagination of an immortal, I mean. In the matter of repetition the man is limited—oh, quite beyond immortal conception. We who continue the act *and* its supremest ecstasies unbroken and without withdrawal for centuries, will never be able to understand or adequately pity the awful poverty of these people in that rich gift which, possessed as we possess it, makes all other possessions trivial and not worth the trouble of invoicing.

2. In man's heaven *everybody sings!* There are no exceptions. The man who did not sing on earth, sings there; the man who could not sing on earth is able to do it there. This universal singing is not casual, not occasional, not relieved by intervals of quiet, it goes on, all day long, and every day, during a stretch of twelve hours. And *everybody stays;* whereas in the earth the place would be empty in two hours. The singing is of hymns alone. Nay, it is of *one* hymn alone. The words are always the same, in number they are only about a dozen, there is no rhyme, there is no poetry: "Hosannah, hosannah, hosannah, Lord God of Sabaoth, 'rah! 'rah! 'rah!—ssht!—boom! . . . . . a-a-ah!"

3. Meantime, *every person* is playing on a harp—those millions and millions! whereas not more than twenty in the thousand of them could play an instrument in the earth, or ever *wanted* to.

Consider the deafening hurricane of sound—millions and millions of voices screaming at once, and millions and millions of harps gritting their teeth at the same time! I ask you—is it hideous, is it odious, is it horrible?

Consider further: it is a *praise* service; a service of compliment, of flattery, of adulation! Do you ask who it is that is willing to endure this strange compliment, this insane compliment; and who not only endures it but likes it, enjoys it, requires it, *commands* it? Hold your breath!

It is God! This race's God, I mean. He sits on his throne, attended by his four and twenty elders and some other dignitaries pertaining to his court, and looks out over his miles and miles of tempestuous worshippers, and smiles, and purrs, and nods his satisfaction northward, eastward, southward; as quaint and naif a spectacle as has yet been imagined in this universe, I take it.

It is easy to see that the inventor of the heaven did not originate the idea, but copied it from the show-ceremonies of some sorry little sovereign State up in the back settlements of the Orient somewhere.

All sane white people *hate noise;* yet they have tranquilly accepted this kind of a heaven—without thinking, without reflection, without examination—and they actually want to go to it! Profoundly devout old gray-headed men put in a large part of their time dreaming of the happy day when they will lay down the cares of this life and enter into the joys of that place. Yet you can see how unreal it is to them, and how little it takes a grip upon them as being *fact,* for they make no practical preparation for the great change: you never see one of them with a harp, you never hear one of them sing.

As you have seen, that singular show is a service of divine worship—a service of praise: praise by hymn, praise by instrumental ecstasies, praise by prostration. It takes the place of "church." Now then, in the earth these people cannot stand much church—an hour and a quarter is the limit, and they draw the line at once a week. That is to say, Sunday. One day in seven; and even then they do not look forward to it with longing. And so—consider what their heaven provides for them: "church" that lasts forever, and a *Sabbath that has no end!* They quickly weary of this brief hebdomadal[2] Sabbath here, yet they long for that eternal one; they dream of it, they talk about it, they

---

2. I.e., once every seven days.

*think* they think they are going to enjoy it—with all their simple hearts they
think they think they are going to be happy in it!

It is because they do not think *at all*; they only think they think. Whereas
they can't think; not two human beings in ten thousand have anything to think
with. And as to imagination—oh, well, look at their heaven! They accept it,
they approve it, they admire it. That gives you their intellectual measure.

4. The inventor of their heaven empties into it all the nations of the earth,
in one common jumble. All are on an equality absolute, no one of them
ranking another; they have to be "brothers"; they have to mix together, pray
together, harp together, hosannah together—whites, niggers, Jews, everybody—there's no distinction. Here in the earth all nations hate each other,
every one of them hates the Jew. Yet every pious person adores that heaven
and wants to get into it. He really does. And when he is in a holy rapture he
thinks he thinks that if he were only there he would take all the populace to
his heart, and hug, and hug, and hug!

He is a marvel—man is! I would I knew who invented him.

5. Every man on earth possesses some share of intellect, large or small; and
be it large or be it small he takes a pride in it. Also his heart swells at mention
of the names of the majestic intellectual chiefs of his race, and he loves the
tale of their splendid achievements. For he is of their blood, and in honoring
themselves they have honored him. Lo, what the mind of man can do! he
cries; and calls the roll of the illustrious of all the ages; and points to the
imperishable literatures they have given to the world, and the mechanical
wonders they have invented, and the glories wherewith they have clothed science and the arts; and to them he uncovers, as to kings, and gives to them the
profoundest homage and the sincerest his exultant heart can furnish—thus
exalting intellect above all things else in his world, and enthroning it there
under the arching skies in a supremacy unapproachable. And then he contrives a heaven that hasn't a rag of intellectuality in it anywhere!

Is it odd, is it curious, is it puzzling? It is exactly as I have said, incredible
as it may sound. This sincere adorer of intellect and prodigal rewarder of its
mighty services here in the earth has invented a religion and a heaven which
pay no compliments to intellect, offer it no distinctions, fling to it no largess:
in fact, never even mention it.

By this time you will have noticed that the human being's heaven has been
thought out and constructed upon an absolutely definite plan; and that this
plan is, that it shall contain, in labored detail, each and every imaginable
thing that is repulsive to a man, and not a single thing he likes!

Very well, the further we proceed the more will this curious fact be
apparent.

Make a note of it: in man's heaven there are no exercises for the intellect,
nothing for it to live upon. It would rot there in a year—rot and stink. Rot and
stink—and at that stage become holy. A blessed thing; for only the holy can
stand the joys of that bedlam.

1909                                                                    1962, 1973

# W. D. HOWELLS

## 1837–1920

No other American writer dominated the literary scene the way William Dean Howells did in his prime. As a steadily productive novelist, playwright, critic, essayist, reviewer, and editor, Howells was always in the public eye, and his influence during the 1880s and 1890s on a growing, serious middle-class readership was incalculable. He made that emerging middle class aware of itself: in his writings an entire generation discovered, through his faithful description of familiar places, his dramatizations of ordinary lives, and his shrewd analyses of shared moral issues, its tastes, its social behavior, its values, and its problems. Howells was by temperament genial and modest, but he was also forthright and tough minded. He was, as critic Lionel Trilling has observed, a deeply civil man with a balanced sense of life. Perhaps that is why when he died, in 1920, the spontaneous outpouring of sorrow and admiration was the kind reserved for national heroes.

Howells's eminence had its roots in humble beginnings. He was born, one of eight children, in the postfrontier village of Martin's Ferry, Ohio, on March 1, 1837, to a poor, respectable, proud, and culturally informed family. Like his contemporary Mark Twain and their predecessor Ben Franklin, Howells went to school at the printer's office, setting type for the series of unsuccessful newspapers that his good-natured, somewhat impractical father owned. Though the family moved around a good deal in Ohio, Howells's youth was secure and, on the whole, happy. His mother, he observed, had the gift of making each child feel that he or she was the center of the world.

From his earliest years Howells had both literary passions and literary ambitions. When he was not setting type or reading Goldsmith, Irving, Shakespeare, Dickens, Thackeray, or other favorites, he was teaching himself several foreign languages. Howells tried his hand at a number of literary forms in his teens, but his first regular jobs involved writing for newspapers in Columbus and Cincinnati. It was as a journalist that he made his first pilgrimage to New England in 1860, where he was treated with remarkable generosity by such literary leaders as Lowell, Holmes, Emerson, and Hawthorne, who must have recognized that he possessed talent and the will to succeed as well as courtesy and deference.

A campaign biography of Lincoln, his first significant book, won for Howells the consulship at Venice in 1861. There he wrote the series of travel letters that eventually became *Venetian Life* (1866); more important, they made his name known in eastern literary circles. When he returned to America in 1866, he went to work in New York briefly for the *Nation* until James T. Fields offered him the assistant editorship of the enormously prestigious and influential *Atlantic Monthly*, to which he had contributed some of his earliest verse before the war. In effect, Howells assumed active control of the magazine from the very beginning, and he succeeded officially to the editorship in 1871, a position he held until he resigned in 1881 to have more time to write fiction. Because the *Atlantic* was the preeminent literary magazine of the day, Howells had, as a young man, the power to make or break careers, a power he exercised tactfully and responsibly.

Howells had been finding his way as a novelist during his ten years as editor, publishing seven novels in this period, beginning with *Their Wedding Journey* (1872) and concluding with *The Undiscovered Country* (1880). These first novels are short, uncomplicated linear narratives that deliberately eschew the passionate, heroic, action-packed, and exciting adventures that were the staple of American fiction of the time, a fiction read chiefly by middle-class women.

In the 1880s Howells came into his own as novelist and critic. A *Modern*

*Instance* (1882) examines psychic, familial, and social disintegration under the pressure of the secularization and urbanization of post–Civil War America, the disintegration that is Howells's central and deepest subject. Three years later Howells published his most famous novel, *The Rise of Silas Lapham* (1885). Within a year of its publication Howells, who was ostensibly successful and financially secure, suddenly felt that the bottom had dropped out of his life; he had been profoundly affected by Tolstoy's Christian socialism and publicly defended the "Haymarket Anarchists," a group of Chicago workers, several of whom were executed without clear proof of their complicity in a dynamiting at a public demonstration. After *Lapham*, Howells offered more direct, ethical criticism of social and economic anomalies and inequities in such succeeding novels as the popular, large-canvassed *A Hazard of New Fortunes* (1890) and the utopian romance *A Traveller from Altruria* (1894). In these same years Howells also penetrated more deeply into individual consciousness, particularly in two short novels, *The Shadow of a Dream* (1890) and *An Imperative Duty* (1892). In *Editha* (1905), Howells characteristically explores the double moral failure of a society and of an individual who has been corrupted by its worst values.

In his later years Howells sustained and deepened his varied literary output. Among his novels of consequence in this period are the naturalistic *The Landlord at Lion's Head* (1897) and the elegiac *The Vacation of the Kelwyns* (published posthumously, 1920). He also wrote charming and vivid autobiography and reminiscence in *A Boy's Town* (1890) and *Years of My Youth* (1916), and as he had since the 1870s, Howells continued to produce plays and farces, which served, as one critic has remarked, as "finger exercises for his novels."

In the mid-1880s Howells had aggressively argued the case for realism and against the "romanticistic," promoting Henry James in particular at the expense of such English novelists as Scott, Dickens, and Thackeray. In *The Editor's Study* essays he wrote for *Harper's Monthly* starting in 1886 (some of which in 1891 he made into *Criticism and Fiction*), Howells attacked sentimentality of thought and feeling and the falsification of moral nature and ethical options wherever he found them in fiction. He believed that realism "was nothing more or less than the truthful treatment of material," especially the motives and actions of *ordinary* men and women. He insisted, sooner and more vigorously than any other American critic, that the novel be objective or dramatic in point of view, solidly based in convincingly motivated characters speaking the language of actual men and women, free of contrived events or melodramatic effects, true to the particulars of a recent time and specific place, and ethically and aesthetically a seamless piece. Indeed, perhaps the polemical nature of his critical stance in the 1880s did as much as anything to obscure until recently the flexibility and range of his sensibility. Certainly *Novel-Writing and Novel-Reading*, first delivered as a lecture in 1899, suggests more accurately than *Criticism and Fiction* (1891) the shrewdness, common sense, and penetrating thoughtfulness that characterize his criticism at its best.

In the course of his lifelong career as literary arbiter, Howells was remarkably international in outlook, and promoted in his diverse critical writings such non-American contemporaries as Ivan Turgenev, Benito Pérez Galdós, Björnstjerne Björnson, Leo Tolstoy, Henrik Ibsen, Émile Zola, George Eliot, and Thomas Hardy. Howells also championed many younger American writers and early recognized many talented women writers in the relentless stream of reviews he wrote over six decades—among them Sarah Orne Jewett, Mary E. Wilkins Freeman, Edith Wharton, and Emily Dickinson. He is even better known for actively promoting the careers of such emerging realists and naturalists as Stephen Crane, Hamlin Garland, and Frank Norris. His chief fault as critic—if it is one—was excessive generosity, though he never falsely flattered or encouraged anyone.

The two contemporaries in whom Howells had the greatest critical confidence were Henry James and Mark Twain, both of whom he served from the 1860s on as editor and with both of whom he also sustained a personal friendship of forty years and more. In the late 1860s, Howells had walked the Cambridge streets with James, discussing the present state and future prospects for the substance and techniques of fiction. As editor of *Atlantic Monthly*, Howells had accepted a number of James's early tales. Throughout his career he wrote essays and reviews in praise of James's work; on his deathbed Howells was working on an essay, *The American James*. He genuinely admired and was friendly with the patrician James, but he clearly loved and was more intimate with the rough-textured Twain. *My Mark Twain*, written immediately after his friend's death in 1910, records that affection in one of the enduring memoirs of our literary history.

By the time Howells died, he had served for thirteen years as first president of the American Academy of Arts and Letters, the organization that seeks to identify and honor the most distinguished work in these fields, and was himself a national institution. For rebels and iconoclasts like H. L. Mencken, Sinclair Lewis, and a young Van Wyck Brooks, he epitomized the dead hand of the past, the genteel, Victorian enemy. Since the 1930s, however, Howells's reputation has slowly recovered from these charges. The courage of his liberal—at times radical—perspective in his own time has been acknowledged; his steady, masterful style has been given its due; and his intelligent civility has been commended.

# Editha[1]

The air was thick with the war feeling,[2] like the electricity of a storm which has not yet burst. Editha sat looking out into the hot spring afternoon, with her lips parted, and panting with the intensity of the question whether she could let him go. She had decided that she could not let him stay, when she saw him at the end of the still leafless avenue, making slowly up towards the house, with his head down and his figure relaxed. She ran impatiently out on the veranda, to the edge of the steps, and imperatively demanded greater haste of him with her will before she called aloud to him: "George!"

He had quickened his pace in mystical response to her mystical urgence, before he could have heard her; now he looked up and answered, "Well?"

"Oh, how united we are!" she exulted, and then she swooped down the steps to him. "What is it?" she cried.

"It's war," he said, and he pulled her up to him and kissed her.

She kissed him back intensely, but irrelevantly, as to their passion, and uttered from deep in her throat. "How glorious!"

"It's war," he repeated, without consenting to her sense of it; and she did not know just what to think at first. She never knew what to think of him; that made his mystery, his charm. All through their courtship, which was contemporaneous with the growth of the war feeling, she had been puzzled by his want of seriousness about it. He seemed to despise it even more than he abhorred it. She could have understood his abhorring any sort of bloodshed; that would have been a survival of his old life when he thought he would be a minister, and before he changed and took up the law. But making light of a cause so high and noble seemed to show a want of earnestness at the core of his being. Not but that she felt herself able to cope with a congenital defect of that sort, and make his love for her save him from himself. Now perhaps the miracle was already wrought in him. In the presence of the tremendous fact that he announced, all triviality seemed to have gone out of him; she began to

1. First printed in *Harper's Monthly* for January 1905, the source of the present text. Published first in book form in *Between the Dark and the Daylight: Ro-* *mances* (1907).

2. I.e., "war fever," the excessive patriotism or "jingoism" preceding the Spanish-American War (1898).

feel that. He sank down on the top step, and wiped his forehead with his handkerchief, while she poured out upon him her question of the origin and authenticity of his news.

All the while, in her duplex emotioning, she was aware that now at the very beginning she must put a guard upon herself against urging him, by any word or act, to take the part that her whole soul willed him to take, for the completion of her ideal of him. He was very nearly perfect as he was, and he must be allowed to perfect himself. But he was peculiar, and he might very well be reasoned out of his peculiarity. Before her reasoning went her emotioning: her nature pulling upon his nature, her womanhood upon his manhood, without her knowing the means she was using to the end she was willing. She had always supposed that the man who won her would have done something to win her; she did not know what, but something. George Gearson had simply asked her for her love, on the way home from a concert, and she gave her love to him, without, as it were, thinking. But now, it flashed upon her, if he could do something worthy to *have* won her—be a hero, *her* hero—it would be even better than if he had done it before asking her; it would be grander. Besides, she had believed in the war from the beginning.

"But don't you see, dearest," she said, "that it wouldn't have come to this, if it hadn't been in the order of Providence? And I call any war glorious that is for the liberation of people who have been struggling for years against the cruelest oppression. Don't you think so, too?"

"I suppose so," he returned, languidly. "But war! Is it glorious to break the peace of the world?"

"That ignoble peace! It was no peace at all, with that crime and shame at our very gates." She was conscious of parroting the current phrases of the newspapers, but it was no time to pick and choose her words. She must sacrifice anything to the high ideal she had for him, and after a good deal of rapid argument she ended with the climax: "But now it doesn't matter about the how or why. Since the war has come, all that is gone. There are no two sides, any more. There is nothing now but our country."

He sat with his eyes closed and his head leant back against the veranda, and he said with a vague smile, as if musing aloud, "Our country—right or wrong."[3]

"Yes, right or wrong!" she returned, fervidly. "I'll go and get you some lemonade." She rose rustling, and whisked away; when she came back with two tall glasses of clouded liquid, on a tray, and the ice clucking in them, he still sat as she had left him, and she said as if there had been no interruption: "But there is no question of wrong in this case. I call it a sacred war. A war for liberty, and humanity, if ever there was one. And I know you will see it just as I do, yet."

He took half the lemonade at a gulp, and he answered as he set the glass down: "I know you always have the highest ideal. When I differ from you, I ought to doubt myself."

A generous sob rose in Editha's throat for the humility of a man, so very nearly perfect, who was willing to put himself below her.

Besides, she felt, more subliminally, that he was never so near slipping through her fingers as when he took that meek way.

3. "Our country! In her intercourse with foreign nations may she always be in the right; but our country right or wrong." Part of a toast given by the American naval officer Stephen Decatur (1779–1820).

"You shall not say that! Only, for once I happen to be right." She seized his hand in her two hands, and poured her soul from her eyes into his. "Don't you think so?" she entreated him.

He released his hand and drank the rest of his lemonade, and she added, "Have mine, too," but he shook his head in answering, "I've no business to think so, unless I act so, too."

Her heart stopped a beat before it pulsed on with leaps that she felt in her neck. She had noticed that strange thing in men: they seemed to feel bound to do what they believed, and not think a thing was finished when they said it, as girls did. She knew what was in his mind, but she pretended not, and she said, "Oh, I am not sure," and then faltered.

He went on as if to himself without apparently heeding her. "There's only one way of proving one's faith in a thing like this."

She could not say that she understood, but she did understand.

He went on again. "If I believed—if I felt as you do about this war— Do you wish me to feel as you do?"

Now she was really not sure; so she said, "George, I don't know what you mean."

He seemed to muse away from her as before. "There is a sort of fascination in it. I suppose that at the bottom of his heart every man would like at times to have his courage tested, to see how he would act."

"How can you talk in that ghastly way?"

"It *is* rather morbid. Still, that's what it comes to, unless you're swept away by ambition, or driven by conviction. I haven't the conviction or the ambition, and the other thing is what it comes to with me. I ought to have been a preacher, after all; then I couldn't have asked it of myself, as I must, now I'm a lawyer. And you believe it's a holy war, Editha?" he suddenly addressed her. "Oh, I know you do! But you wish me to believe so, too?"

She hardly knew whether he was mocking or not, in the ironical way he always had with her plainer mind. But the only thing was to be outspoken with him.

"George, I wish you to believe whatever you think is true, at any and every cost. If I've tried to talk you into anything, I take it all back."

"Oh, I know that, Editha. I know how sincere you are, and how— I wish I had your undoubting spirit! I'll think it over; I'd like to believe as you do. But I don't, now; I don't, indeed. It isn't this war alone; though this seems peculiarly wanton and needless; but it's every war—so stupid; it makes me sick. Why shouldn't this thing have been settled reasonably?"

"Because," she said, very throatily again, "God meant it to be war."

"You think it was God? Yes, I suppose that is what people will say."

"Do you suppose it would have been war if God hadn't meant it?"

"I don't know. Sometimes it seems as if God had put this world into men's keeping to work it as they pleased."

"Now, George, that is blasphemy."

"Well, I won't blaspheme. I'll try to believe in your pocket Providence," he said, and then he rose to go.

"Why don't you stay to dinner?" Dinner at Balcom's Works was at one o'clock.

"I'll come back to supper, if you'll let me. Perhaps I shall bring you a convert."

"Well, you may come back, on that condition."

"All right. If I don't come, you'll understand."

He went away without kissing her, and she felt it a suspension of their engagement. It all interested her intensely; she was undergoing a tremendous experience, and she was being equal to it. While she stood looking after him, her mother came out through one of the long windows, on to the veranda, with a catlike softness and vagueness.

"Why didn't he stay to dinner?"

"Because—because—war has been declared," Editha pronounced, without turning.

Her mother said, "Oh, my!" and then said nothing more until she had sat down in one of the large Shaker chairs[4] and rocked herself for some time. Then she closed whatever tacit passage of thought there had been in her mind with the spoken words: "Well, I hope *he* won't go."

"And *I* hope he *will*," the girl said, and confronted her mother with a stormy exaltation that would have frightened any creature less unimpressionable than a cat.

Her mother rocked herself again for an interval of cogitation. What she arrived at in speech was: "Well, I guess you've done a wicked thing, Editha Balcom."

The girl said, as she passed indoors through the same window her mother had come out by: "I haven't done anything—yet."

In her room, she put together all her letters and gifts from Gearson, down to the withered petals of the first flower he had offered, with that timidity of his veiled in that irony of his. In the heart of the packet she enshrined her engagement ring which she had restored to the pretty box he had brought it her in. Then she sat down, if not calmly yet strongly, and wrote:

> "GEORGE:—I understood—when you left me. But I think we had better emphasize your meaning that if we cannot be one in everything we had better be one in nothing. So I am sending these things for your keeping till you have made up your mind.
>
> "I shall always love you, and therefore I shall never marry any one else. But the man I marry must love his country first of all, and be able to say to me,
>
> > "'I could not love thee, dear, so much,
> > Loved I not honor more.'[5]
>
> "There is no honor above America with me. In this great hour there is no other honor.
>
> "Your heart will make my words clear to you. I had never expected to say so much, but it has come upon me that I must say the utmost.
>
> > EDITHA."

She thought she had worded her letter well, worded it in a way that could not be bettered; all had been implied and nothing expressed.

She had it ready to send with the packet she had tied with red, white, and

---

4. Sturdy, simple, unadorned chairs made by the Shaker sect.　　5. Lines from Richard Lovelace's (1618–1658) poem *To Lucasta, on Going to the Wars.*

blue ribbon, when it occurred to her that she was not just to him, that she was not giving him a fair chance. He had said he would go and think it over, and she was not waiting. She was pushing, threatening, compelling. That was not a woman's part. She must leave him free, free, free. She could not accept for her country or herself a forced sacrifice.

In writing her letter she had satisfied the impulse from which it sprang; she could well afford to wait till he had thought it over. She put the packet and the letter by, and rested serene in the consciousness of having done what was laid upon her by her love itself to do, and yet used patience, mercy, justice.

She had her reward. Gearson did not come to tea, but she had given him till morning, when, late at night there came up from the village the sound of a fife and drum with a tumult of voices, in shouting, singing, and laughing. The noise drew nearer and nearer; it reached the street end of the avenue; there it silenced itself, and one voice, the voice she knew best, rose over the silence. It fell; the air was filled with cheers; the fife and drum struck up, with the shouting, singing, and laughing again, but now retreating; and a single figure came hurrying up the avenue.

She ran down to meet her lover and clung to him. He was very gay, and he put his arm round her with a boisterous laugh. "Well, you must call me Captain, now; or Cap, if you prefer; that's what the boys call me. Yes, we've had a meeting at the town hall, and everybody has volunteered; and they selected me for captain, and I'm going to the war, the big war, the glorious war, the holy war ordained by the pocket Providence that blesses butchery. Come along; let's tell the whole family about it. Call them from their downy beds, father, mother, Aunt Hitty, and all the folks!"

But when they mounted the veranda steps he did not wait for a larger audience; he poured the story out upon Editha alone.

"There was a lot of speaking, and then some of the fools set up a shout for me. It was all going one way, and I thought it would be a good joke to sprinkle a little cold water on them. But you can't do that with a crowd that adores you. The first thing I knew I was sprinkling hell-fire on them. 'Cry havoc, and let slip the dogs of war.'[6] That was the style. Now that it had come to the fight, there were no two parties; there was one country, and the thing was to fight the fight to a finish as quick as possible. I suggested volunteering then and there, and I wrote my name first of all on the roster. Then they elected me— that's all. I wish I had some ice-water!"

She left him walking up and down the veranda, while she ran for the ice-pitcher and a goblet, and when she came back he was still walking up and down, shouting the story he had told her to her father and mother, who had come out more sketchily dressed than they commonly were by day. He drank goblet after goblet of the ice-water without noticing who was giving it, and kept on talking, and laughing through his talk wildly. "It's astonishing," he said, "how well the worse reason looks when you try to make it appear the better. Why, I believe I was the first convert to the war in that crowd to-night! I never thought I should like to kill a man; but now, I shouldn't care; and the smokeless powder lets you see the man drop that you kill. It's all for the country! What a thing it is to have a country that *can't* be wrong, but if it is, is right, anyway!"

---

6. From Antony's soliloquy after the murder of Caesar, in Shakespeare's *Julius Caesar* (3.1.274).

Editha had a great, vital thought, an inspiration. She set down the ice-pitcher on the veranda floor, and ran up-stairs and got the letter she had written him. When at last he noisily bade her father and mother, "Well, good night. I forgot I woke you up; I sha'n't want any sleep myself," she followed him down the avenue to the gate. There, after the whirling words that seemed to fly away from her thoughts and refuse to serve them, she made a last effort to solemnize the moment that seemed so crazy, and pressed the letter she had written upon him.

"What's this?" he said. "Want me to mail it?"

"No, no. It's for you. I wrote it after you went this morning. Keep it—keep it—and read it sometime—" She thought, and then her inspiration came: "Read it if ever you doubt what you've done, or fear that I regret your having done it. Read it after you've started."

They strained each other in embraces that seemed as ineffective as their words, and he kissed her face with quick, hot breaths that were so unlike him, that made her feel as if she had lost her old lover and found a stranger in his place. The stranger said: "What a gorgeous flower you are, with your red hair, and your blue eyes that look black now, and your face with the color painted out by the white moonshine! Let me hold you under my chin, to see whether I love blood, you tiger-lily!" Then he laughed Gearson's laugh, and released her, scared and giddy. Within her wilfulness she had been frightened by a sense of subtler force in him, and mystically mastered as she had never been before.

She ran all the way back to the house, and mounted the steps panting. Her mother and father were talking of the great affair. Her mother said: "Wa'n't Mr. Gearson in rather of an excited state of mind? Didn't you think he acted curious?"

"Well, not for a man who'd just been elected captain and had to set 'em up for the whole of Company A," her father chuckled back.

"What in the world do you mean, Mr. Balcom? Oh! There's Editha!" She offered to follow the girl indoors.

"Don't come, mother!" Editha called, vanishing.

Mrs. Balcom remained to reproach her husband. "I don't see much of anything to laugh at."

"Well, it's catching. Caught it from Gearson. I guess it won't be much of a war, and I guess Gearson don't think so, either. The other fellows will back down as soon as they see we mean it. I wouldn't lose any sleep over it. I'm going back to bed, myself."

Gearson came again next afternoon, looking pale, and rather sick, but quite himself, even to his languid irony. "I guess I'd better tell you, Editha, that I consecrated myself to your god of battles last night by pouring too many libations to him down my own throat. But I'm all right now. One has to carry off the excitement, somehow."

"Promise me," she commanded, "that you'll never touch it again!"

"What! Not let the cannikin clink? Not let the soldier drink?[7] Well, I promise."

"You don't belong to yourself now; you don't even belong to *me*. You belong

---

7. Allusion to Shakespeare's *Othello* (2.3.64–68), in which Iago sings a soldier's drinking song.

to your country, and you have a sacred charge to keep yourself strong and well for your country's sake. I have been thinking, thinking all night and all day long."

"You look as if you had been crying a little, too," he said with his queer smile.

"That's all past. I've been thinking, and worshipping *you*. Don't you suppose I know all that you've been through, to come to this? I've followed you every step from your old theories and opinions."

"Well, you've had a long row to hoe."

"And I know you've done this from the highest motives—"

"'Oh, there won't be much pettifogging to do till this cruel war is—"

"And you haven't simply done it for my sake. I couldn't respect you if you had."

"Well, then we'll say I haven't. A man that hasn't got his own respect intact wants the respect of all the other people he can corner. But we won't go into that. I'm in for the thing now, and we've got to face our future. My idea is that this isn't going to be a very protracted struggle; we shall just scare the enemy to death before it comes to a fight at all. But we must provide for contingencies, Editha. If anything happens to me—"

"Oh, George!" She clung to him sobbing.

"I don't want you to feel foolishly bound to my memory. I should hate that, wherever I happened to be."

"I am yours, for time and eternity—time and eternity." She liked the words; they satisfied her famine for phrases.

"Well, say eternity; that's all right; but time's another thing; and I'm talking about time. But there is something! My mother ! If anything happens—"

She winced, and he laughed. "You're not the bold soldier-girl of yesterday!" Then he sobered. "If anything happens, I want you to help my mother out. She won't like my doing this thing. She brought me up to think war a fool thing as well as a bad thing. My father was in the civil war, all through it; lost his arm in it." She thrilled with the sense of the arm round her; what if that should be lost? He laughed as if divining her: "Oh, it doesn't run in the family, as far as I know!" Then he added, gravely: "He came home with misgivings about war, and they grew on him. I guess he and mother agreed between them that I was to be brought up in his final mind about it; but that was before my time. I only knew him from my mother's report of him and his opinions; I don't know whether they were hers first; but they were hers last. This will be a blow to her. I shall have to write and tell her—"

He stopped, and she asked: "Would you like me to write too, George?"

"I don't believe that would do. No, I'll do the writing. She'll understand a little if I say that I thought the way to minimize it was to make war on the largest possible scale at once—that I felt I must have been helping on the war somehow if I hadn't helped keep it from coming, and I knew I hadn't; when it came, I had no right to stay out of it."

Whether his sophistries satisfied him or not, they satisfied her. She clung to his breast, and whispered, with closed eyes and quivering lips: "Yes, yes, yes!"

"But if anything should happen, you might go to her, and see what you could do for her. You know? It's rather far off; she can't leave her chair—"

"Oh, I'll go, if it's the ends of the earth! But nothing will happen! Nothing *can!* I—"

She felt herself lifted with his rising, and Gearson was saying, with his arm still round her, to her father: "Well, we're off at once, Mr. Balcom. We're to be formally accepted at the capital, and then bunched up with the rest somehow, and sent into camp somewhere, and got to the front as soon as possible. We all want to be in the van,[8] of course; we're the first company to report to the Governor. I came to tell Editha, but I hadn't got round to it."

She saw him again for a moment at the capital, in the station, just before the train started southward with his regiment. He looked well, in his uniform, and very soldierly, but somehow girlish, too, with his clean-shaven face and slim figure. The manly eyes and the strong voice satisfied her, and his preoccupation with some unexpected details of duty flattered her. Other girls were weeping and bemoaning themselves, but she felt a sort of noble distinction in the abstraction, the almost unconsciousness, with which they parted. Only at the last moment he said: "Don't forget my mother. It mayn't be such a walk-over as I supposed," and he laughed at the notion.

He waved his hand to her as the train moved off—she knew it among a score of hands that were waved to other girls from the platform of the car, for it held a letter which she knew was hers. Then he went inside the car to read it, doubtless, and she did not see him again. But she felt safe for him through the strength of what she called her love. What she called her God, always speaking the name in a deep voice and with the implication of a mutual understanding, would watch over him and keep him and bring him back to her. If with an empty sleeve, then he should have three arms instead of two, for both of hers should be his for life. She did not see, though, why she should always be thinking of the arm his father had lost.

There were not many letters from him, but they were such as she could have wished, and she put her whole strength into making hers such as she imagined he could have wished, glorifying and supporting him. She wrote to his mother glorifying him as their hero, but the brief answer she got was merely to the effect that Mrs. Gearson was not well enough to write herself, and thanking her for her letter by the hand of someone who called herself "Yrs truly, Mrs. W. J. Andrews."

Editha determined not to be hurt, but to write again quite as if the answer had been all she expected. But before it seemed as if she could have written, there came news of the first skirmish, and in the list of the killed, which was telegraphed as a trifling loss on our side, was Gearson's name. There was a frantic time of trying to make out that it might be, must be, some other Gearson; but the name and the company and the regiment, and the State were too definitely given.

Then there was a lapse into depths out of which it seemed as if she never could rise again; then a lift into clouds far above all grief, black clouds, that blotted out the sun, but where she soared with him, with George, George! She had the fever that she expected of herself, but she did not die in it; she was not even delirious, and it did not last long. When she was well enough to leave her bed, her one thought was of George's mother, of his strangely worded wish that she should go to her and see what she could do for her. In the exaltation of the duty laid upon her—it buoyed her up instead of burdening her—she rapidly recovered.

8. Short for vanguard, the foremost division of an army.

Her father went with her on the long railroad journey from northern New York to western Iowa; he had business out at Davenport, and he said he could just as well go then as any other time; and he went with her to the little country town where George's mother lived in a little house on the edge of illimitable corn-fields, under trees pushed to a top of the rolling prairie. George's father had settled there after the civil war, as so many other old soldiers had done; but they were Eastern people, and Editha fancied touches of the East in the June rose overhanging the front door, and the garden with early summer flowers stretching from the gate of the paling fence.

It was very low inside the house, and so dim, with the closed blinds, that they could scarcely see one another: Editha tall and black in her crapes which filled the air with the smell of their dyes; her father standing decorously apart with his hat on his forearm, as at funerals; a woman rested in a deep arm-chair, and the woman who had let the strangers in stood behind the chair.

The seated woman turned her head round and up, and asked the woman behind her chair: "*Who* did you say?"

Editha, if she had done what she expected of herself, would have gone down on her knees at the feet of the seated figure and said, "I am George's Editha," for answer.

But instead of her own voice she heard that other woman's voice, saying: "Well, I don't know as I *did* get the name just right. I guess I'll have to make a little more light in here," and she went and pushed two of the shutters ajar.

Then Editha's father said, in his public will-now-address-a-few-remarks tone: "My name is Balcom, ma'am—Junius H. Balcom, of Balcom's Works, New York; my daughter—"

"Oh!" the seated woman broke in, with a powerful voice, the voice that always surprised Editha from Gearson's slender frame. "Let me see you! Stand round where the light can strike on your face," and Editha dumbly obeyed. "So, you're Editha Balcom," she sighed.

"Yes," Editha said, more like a culprit than a comforter.

"What did you come for?" Mrs. Gearson asked.

Editha's face quivered and her knees shook. "I came—because—because George—" She could go no further.

"Yes," the mother said, "he told me he had asked you to come if he got killed. You didn't expect that, I suppose, when you sent him."

"I would rather have died myself than done it!" Editha said with more truth in her deep voice than she ordinarily found in it. "I tried to leave him free—"

"Yes, that letter of yours, that came back with his other things, left him free."

Editha saw now where George's irony came from.

"It was not to be read before—unless—until— I told him so," she faltered.

"Of course, he wouldn't read a letter of yours, under the circumstances, till he thought you wanted him to. Been sick?" the woman abruptly demanded.

"Very sick." Editha said, with self-pity.

"Daughter's life," her father interposed, "was almost despaired of, at one time."

Mrs. Gearson gave him no heed. "I suppose you would have been glad to die, such a brave person as you! I don't believe *he* was glad to die. He was always a timid boy, that way; he was afraid of a good many things; but if he was afraid he did what he made up his mind to. I suppose he made up his mind to go, but I knew what it cost him, by what it cost me when I heard of

it. I had been through *one* war before. When you sent him you didn't expect
he would get killed."

The voice seemed to compassionate Editha, and it was time. "No," she
huskily murmured.

"No, girls don't; women don't, when they give their men up to their country. They think they'll come marching back, somehow, just as gay as they
went, or if it's an empty sleeve, or even an empty pantaloon, it's all the more
glory, and they're so much the prouder of them, poor things!"

The tears began to run down Editha's face; she had not wept till then; but it
was now such a relief to be understood that the tears came.

"No, you didn't expect him to get killed," Mrs. Gearson repeated in a voice
which was startlingly like George's again. "You just expected him to kill some
one else, some of those foreigners, that weren't there because they had any say
about it, but because they had to be there, poor wretches—conscripts, or whatever they call 'em. You thought it would be all right for my George, *your*
George, to kill the sons of those miserable mothers and the husbands of those
girls that you would never see the faces of." The woman lifted her powerful
voice in a psalmlike note. "I thank my God he didn't live to do it! I thank my
God they killed him first, and that he ain't livin' with their blood on his
hands!" She dropped her eyes, which she had raised with her voice, and glared
at Editha. "What you got that black on for?" She lifted herself by her powerful
arms so high that her helpless body seemed to hang limp its full length. "Take
it off, take it off, before I tear it from your back!"

The lady who was passing the summer near Balcom's Works was sketching
Editha's beauty, which lent itself wonderfully to the effects of a colorist. It had
come to that confidence which is rather apt to grow between artist and sitter,
and Editha told her everything.

"To think of your having such a tragedy in your life!" the lady said. She
added: "I suppose there are people who feel that way about war. But when you
consider the good this war has done—how much it has done for the count I
can't understand such people, for my part. And when you had come all the
way out there to console her—got up out of a sick-bed! Well!"

"I think," Editha said, magnanimously, "she wasn't quite in her right mind;
and so did papa."

"Yes," the lady said, looking at Editha's lips in nature and then at her lips
in art, and giving an empirical touch to them in the picture. "But how dreadful
of her! How perfectly—excuse me—how *vulgar!*"

A light broke upon Editha in the darkness which she felt had been without
a gleam of brightness for weeks and months. The mystery that had bewildered
her was solved by the word; and from that moment she rose from grovelling in
shame and self-pity, and began to live again in the ideal.

1907

# AMBROSE BIERCE
## 1842–1914?

Ambrose Gwinnett Bierce was born on June 24, 1842, in Meigs County, Ohio, the last of nine children of strongly religious parents. He led an unhappy childhood, and as an adult he cut himself off from his parents and all but one of his brothers and sisters. Perhaps his fascination with the supernatural in his fiction is similarly an attempt to escape the ordinary society of humanity he observed closely and claimed to detest. In any case, from his earliest days "Bitter Bierce," as he came to be called, seemed disappointed with what had been, displeased with his present condition, and pessimistic about what lay ahead.

Not long after he had spent one year at a military academy in Kentucky—his only formal schooling—the Civil War broke out and Bierce volunteered for the Union Army. He was involved in several battles, and was mustered out a lieutenant. Bierce later defined war (in his *Devil's Dictionary*) as a "by-product of the arts of peace" and peace as "a period of cheating between two periods of fighting," and it is hard to accept his own testimony that, even while a soldier, he had been a zealous military man. The Civil War experience, however, was an important source of some of his best fiction, including the spare and shocking *Chickamauga* and *An Occurence at Owl Creek Bridge*.

After the war, Bierce moved to San Francisco. By 1866 he had secured a job as a journalist, the career he pursued for the rest of his life. He began as a columnist for the *News Letter* and in 1868 became its editor. Among his writer friends in San Francisco were Mark Twain, Bret Harte, Joaquin Miller, and George Sterling, all of whom were involved as journalists, lecturers, and writers in establishing San Francisco as a literary center. Bierce married in 1872 and took his bride to England, where they lived until 1876. There, under the influence of literary sophisticates such as George Augustus Sala and Thomas Hood, he developed from a crude western humorist into a satirist of elegance and bite. His best early work appeared in the *Prattler* column written first for the *Argonaut* (1877–79), and then for the *Wasp* until 1886. In that year the popular column was picked up by William Randolph Hearst's *San Francisco Sunday Examiner*, where it continued until 1896. A mixture of reviews, gossip, and political and social commentary, the *Prattler* also served as outlet for a number of Bierce's best short stories.

Bierce's personal life was a series of disasters. His definition of marriage—"the state or condition of a community consisting of a master, a mistress, and two slaves, making in all, two"—reflected his views on his own marriage (which ended in divorce in 1891). In 1889 his elder son was shot to death during a fight over a girl; in 1901 his younger son died of alcoholism. In 1913, he went to Mexico and disappeared without a trace, although there is a story that he was killed in the revolutionary war, which pitted Pancho Villa and Venustiano Carranza against General Victoriano Huerta.

Bierce's pessimism, cynicism, nihilism, and gallows humor are in the American tradition of no-saying, which runs from Herman Melville to Thomas Pynchon. It is not the mordant wit of *The Devil's Dictionary* (first published in 1906 as *The Cynic's Word Book*) or Bierce's penchant for the grotesque, however, that finally makes him significant. In his best work, such as *Tales of Soldiers and Civilians* (1891; later retitled *In the Midst of Life*), Bierce, like Stephen Crane, Ernest Hemingway, and Norman Mailer after him, converted the disordered experience of war into resonant and dramatic fictional revelations.

# Chickamauga[1]

One sunny autumn afternoon a child strayed away from its rude home in a small field and entered a forest unobserved. It was happy in a new sense of freedom from control, happy in the opportunity of exploration and adventure; for this child's spirit, in bodies of its ancestors, had for thousands of years been trained to memorable feats of discovery and conquest—victories in battles whose critical moments were centuries, whose victors' camps were cities of hewn stone. From the cradle of its race it had conquered its way through two continents and passing a great sea had penetrated a third, there to be born to war and dominion as a heritage.

The child was a boy aged about six years, the son of a poor planter. In his younger manhood the father had been a soldier, had fought against naked savages and followed the flag of his country into the capital of a civilized race[2] to the far South. In the peaceful life of a planter the warrior-fire survived; once kindled, it is never extinguished. The man loved military books and pictures and the boy had understood enough to make himself a wooden sword, though even the eye of his father would hardly have known it for what it was. This weapon he now bore bravely, as became the son of an heroic race, and pausing now and again in the sunny space of the forest assumed, with some exaggeration, the postures of aggression and defense that he had been taught by the engraver's art. Made reckless by the ease with which he overcame invisible foes attempting to stay his advance, he committed the common enough military error of pushing the pursuit to a dangerous extreme, until he found himself upon the margin of a wide but shallow brook, whose rapid waters barred his direct advance against the flying foe that had crossed with illogical ease. But the intrepid victor was not to be baffled; the spirit of the race which had passed the great sea burned unconquerable in that small breast and would not be denied. Finding a place where some bowlders in the bed of the stream lay but a step or a leap apart, he made his way across and fell again upon the rear-guard of his imaginary foe, putting all to the sword.

Now that the battle had been won, prudence required that he withdraw to his base of operations. Alas; like many a mightier conqueror, and like one, the mightiest, he could not

> curb the lust for war,
> Nor learn that tempted Fate will leave the loftiest star.[3]

Advancing from the bank of the creek he suddenly found himself confronted with a new and more formidable enemy: in the path that he was following, sat, bolt upright, with ears erect and paws suspended before it, a rabbit! With a startled cry the child turned and fled, he knew not in what direction, calling with inarticulate cries for his mother, weeping, stumbling, his tender skin cruelly torn by brambles, his little heart beating hard with terror—breathless, blind with tears—lost in the forest! Then, for more than an hour, he wandered

---

1. First published in the *San Francisco Examiner* on January 20, 1889, this story was subsequently reprinted as part of *Tales of Soldiers and Civilians* (1891; retitled *In the Midst of Life* in 1898) and in Vol. 2 of the *Collected Works of Ambrose Bierce* (1909–12), the source of the present text. In the Civil War, the Battle of Chickamauga Creek (Tennessee) was fought on September 19–20, 1863. The thirty-four thousand casual-

ties made this one of the bloodiest engagements of the war.
2. Refers to Mexico, against which the United States warred from 1846 to 1848; Mexico City fell in 1847. The "naked savages" are American Indians.
3. Lord Byron's (1788–1824) *Childe Harold's Pilgrimage* (3.38.8–9). The "mightiest" conqueror is an allusion to Napoleon.

with erring feet through the tangled undergrowth, till at last, overcome by
fatigue, he lay down in a narrow space between two rocks, within a few yards
of the stream and still grasping his toy sword, no longer a weapon but a companion, sobbed himself to sleep. The wood birds sang merrily above his head;
the squirrels, whisking their bravery of tail, ran barking from tree to tree,
unconscious of the pity of it, and somewhere far away was a strange, muffled
thunder, as if the partridges were drumming in celebration of nature's victory
over the son of her immemorial enslavers. And back at the little plantation,
where white men and black were hastily searching the fields and hedges in
alarm, a mother's heart was breaking for her missing child.

Hours passed, and then the little sleeper rose to his feet. The chill of the
evening was in his limbs, the fear of the gloom in his heart. But he had rested,
and he no longer wept. With some blind instinct which impelled to action he
struggled through the undergrowth about him and came to a more open
ground—on his right the brook, to the left a gentle acclivity studded with
infrequent trees; over all, the gathering gloom of twilight. A thin, ghostly mist
rose along the water. It frightened and repelled him; instead of recrossing, in
the direction whence he had come, he turned his back upon it, and went
forward toward the dark inclosing wood. Suddenly he saw before him a strange
moving object which he took to be some large animal—a dog, a pig—he could
not name it; perhaps it was a bear. He had seen pictures of bears, but he knew
of nothing to their discredit and had vaguely wished to meet one. But something in form or movement of this object—something in the awkwardness of
its approach—told him that it was not a bear, and curiosity was stayed by fear.
He stood still and as it came slowly on gained courage every moment, for he
saw that at least it had not the long, menacing ears of the rabbit. Possibly his
impressionable mind was half conscious of something familiar in its sham-
bling, awkward gait. Before it had approached near enough to resolve his
doubts he saw that it was followed by another and another. To right and to left
were many more; the whole open space about him was alive with them—all
moving toward the brook.

They were men. They crept upon their hands and knees. They used their
hands only, dragging their legs. They used their knees only, their arms hanging idle at their sides. They strove to rise to their feet, but fell prone in the
attempt. They did nothing naturally, and nothing alike, save only to advance
foot by foot in the same direction. Singly, in pairs and in little groups, they
came on through the gloom, some halting now and again while others crept
slowly past them, then resuming their movement. They came by dozens and
by hundreds; as far on either hand as one could see in the deepening gloom
they extended and the black wood behind them appeared to be inexhaustible.
The very ground seemed in motion toward the creek. Occasionally one who
had paused did not again go on, but lay motionless. He was dead. Some,
pausing, made strange gestures with their hands, erected their arms and lowered them again, clasped their heads; spread palms upward, as men are sometimes seen to do in public prayer.

Not all of this did the child note; it is what would have been noted by an
elder observer; he saw little but that these were men, yet crept like babes. Being
men, they were not terrible, though unfamiliarly clad. He moved among them
freely, going from one to another and peering into their faces with childish
curiosity. All their faces were singularly white and many were streaked and

gouted[4] with red. Something in this—something too, perhaps, in their grotesque attitudes and movements—reminded him of the painted clown whom
he had seen last summer in the circus, and he laughed as he watched them.
But on and ever on they crept, these maimed and bleeding men, as heedless
as he of the dramatic contrast between his laughter and their own ghastly
gravity. To him it was a merry spectacle. He had seen his father's negroes
creep upon their hands and knees for his amusement—had ridden them so,
"making believe" they were his horses. He now approached one of these crawling figures from behind and with an agile movement mounted it astride. The
man sank upon his breast, recovered, flung the small boy fiercely to the ground
as an unbroken colt might have done, then turned upon him a face that lacked
a lower jaw—from the upper teeth to the throat was a great red gap fringed
with hanging shreds of flesh and splinters of bone. The unnatural prominence
of nose, the absence of chin, the fierce eyes, gave this man the appearance of
a great bird of prey crimsoned in throat and breast by the blood of its quarry.
The man rose to his knees, the child to his feet. The man shook his fist at the
child; the child, terrified at last, ran to a tree near by, got upon the farther side
of it and took a more serious view of the situation. And so the clumsy multitude dragged itself slowly and painfully along in hideous pantomime—moved
forward down the slope like a swarm of great black beetles, with never a sound
of going—in silence profound, absolute.

Instead of darkening, the haunted landscape began to brighten. Through
the belt of trees beyond the brook shone a strange red light, the trunks and
branches of the trees making a black lacework against it. It struck the creeping
figures and gave them monstrous shadows, which caricatured their movements
on the lit grass. It fell upon their faces, touching their whiteness with a ruddy
tinge, accentuating the stains with which so many of them were freaked and
maculated.[5] It sparkled on buttons and bits of metal in their clothing. Instinctively the child turned toward the growing splendor and moved down the slope
with his horrible companions; in a few moments had passed the foremost of
the throng—not much of a feat, considering his advantages. He placed himself
in the lead, his wooden sword still in hand, and solemnly directed the march,
conforming his pace to theirs and occasionally turning as if to see that his
forces did not straggle. Surely such a leader never before had such a following.

Scattered about upon the ground now slowly narrowing by the encroachment of this awful march to water, were certain articles to which, in the
leader's mind, were coupled no significant associations: an occasional blanket,
tightly rolled lengthwise, doubled and the ends bound together with a string; a
heavy knapsack here, and there a broken rifle—such things, in short, as are
found in the rear of retreating troops, the "spoor" of men flying from their
hunters. Everywhere near the creek, which here had a margin of lowland, the
earth was trodden into mud by the feet of men and horses. An observer of
better experience in the use of his eyes would have noticed that these footprints
pointed in both directions; the ground had been twice passed over—in advance
and in retreat. A few hours before, these desperate, stricken men, with their
more fortunate and now distant comrades, had penetrated the forest in thousands. Their successive battalions, breaking into swarms and re-forming in
lines, had passed the child on every side—had almost trodden on him as he

---

4. Clotted.                        5. Flecked and stained.

slept. The rustle and murmur of their march had not awakened him. Almost within a stone's throw of where he lay they had fought a battle; but all unheard by him were the roar of the musketry, the shock of the cannon, "the thunder of the captains and the shouting."[6] He had slept through it all, grasping his little wooden sword with perhaps a tighter clutch in unconscious sympathy with his martial environment, but as heedless of the grandeur of the struggle as the dead who had died to make the glory.

The fire beyond the belt of woods on the farther side of the creek, reflected to earth from the canopy of its own smoke, was now suffusing the whole landscape. It transformed the sinuous line of mist to the vapor of gold. The water gleamed with dashes of red, and red, too, were many of the stones protruding above the surface. But that was blood; the less desperately wounded had stained them in crossing. On them, too, the child now crossed with eager steps; he was going to the fire. As he stood upon the farther bank he turned about to look at the companions of his march. The advance was arriving at the creek. The stronger had already drawn themselves to the brink and plunged their faces into the flood. Three or four who lay without motion appeared to have no heads. At this the child's eyes expanded with wonder; even his hospitable understanding could not accept a phenomenon implying such vitality as that. After slaking their thirst these men had not had the strength to back away from the water, nor to keep their heads above it. They were drowned. In rear of these, the open spaces of the forest showed the leader as many formless figures of his grim command as at first; but not nearly so many were in motion. He waved his cap for their encouragement and smilingly pointed with his weapon in the direction of the guiding light—a pillar of fire to this strange exodus.[7]

Confident of the fidelity of his forces, he now entered the belt of woods, passed through it easily in the red illumination, climbed a fence, ran across a field, turning now and again to coquet with his responsive shadow, and so approached the blazing ruin of a dwelling. Desolation everywhere! In all the wide glare not a living thing was visible. He cared nothing for that; the spectacle pleased, and he danced with glee in imitation of the wavering flames. He ran about, collecting fuel, but every object that he found was too heavy for him to cast in from the distance to which the heat limited his approach. In despair he flung in his sword—a surrender to the superior forces of nature. His military career was at an end.

Shifting his position, his eyes fell upon some outbuildings which had an oddly familiar appearance, as if he had dreamed of them. He stood considering them with wonder, when suddenly the entire plantation, with its inclosing forest, seemed to turn as if upon a pivot. His little world swung half around; the points of the compass were reversed. He recognized the blazing building as his own home!

For a moment he stood stupefied by the power of the revelation, then ran with stumbling feet, making a half-circuit of the ruin. There, conspicuous in the light of the conflagration, lay the dead body of a woman—the white face turned upward, the hands thrown out and clutched full of grass, the clothing deranged, the long dark hair in tangles and full of clotted blood. The greater part of the forehead was torn away, and from the jagged hole the brain pro-

---

6. "He [a horse] saith among the trumpets, Ha, Ha; and he smelleth the battle afar off, the thunder of the captains, and the shouting" (Job 39.25).

7. During the flight from Egypt the Israelites were led by God in the form of a pillar of clouds during the day, a pillar of fire by night (Exodus 13.21).

truded, overflowing the temple, a frothy mass of gray, crowned with clusters of crimson bubbles—the work of a shell.

The child moved his little hands, making wild, uncertain gestures. He uttered a series of inarticulate and indescribable cries—something between the chattering of an ape and the gobbling of a turkey—a startling, soulless, unholy sound, the language of a devil. The child was a deaf mute.

Then he stood motionless, with quivering lips, looking down upon the wreck.

1889, 1892

---

# NATIVE AMERICAN ORATORY

American Indian oratory in its sacred forms marked significant occasions fixed in the calendrical and ceremonial year. In its secular forms (these distinctions are Western not native), it responded to notable events in daily life. Speeches might be given to greet a victorious war party or, as in the case of Hopi chants, addressed to the people of the village to mobilize participation in a house-building project. Today, traditional rhetorical practices continue to govern formal speeches given, for example, to dedicate a new local fish hatchery or gaming casino or to bless a museum exhibit of Indian art and craftswork.

While cultural differences among tribal groups make it difficult to generalize about native oratorical practices, it is fair to say that the conventions of American Indian oratory place it somewhere between the casualness of indigenous narrative genres like stories or jokes and the highly formalized diction of some song genres. In oratorical performance, the speaker is more constrained in the choice of vocabulary, pronunciation, pauses, and repetitions than is a storyteller but has far more freedom of choice than singers of ritual or ceremonial songs. For all of that, it must again be noted that oratorical practices—like the practices of traditional storytelling or singing—differ considerably from group to group.

The native oratory described above is Indian speech for Indian communities. But there is little textual record of this speech. What there is much of is Indian speech for (and to) whites who provoked occasions for oratory and then transcribed in translation what they thought the native person had said. Often it is impossible to tell how accurate these English versions are. We do know that Chief Seatthl's celebrated speech of 1855 is largely fabricated. For the speeches included here, materials exist to suggest that each text is fairly close to what must have been said by the speaker in his own Native American language, or in some cases in English or Spanish.

The great theme of recorded American Indian oratory is *land*, from John Smith's 1609 version of a speech by the Algonquin leader Powhatan to the present. As the settlers advanced and claimed "ownership" of America from its original inhabitants, again and again the red people and the white met to discuss conditions of cession and then, when almost all had been ceded, conditions of survival. For native peoples, these speeches are traditional responses to untraditional occasions, attempts to employ old and familiar culture-specific practices to deal with the new and unfamiliar demands of another culture. The selections that follow reflect the varieties of native oratory from 1865 to 1914, a period of intense pressure on the Indians by settlers in fevered pursuit of their "manifest destiny."

# COCHISE

## c. 1812–1874

Cochise was a Chiricahua Apache leader, grandson of a renowned warrior known as Cuchillo Negro, or Black Knife, and son-in-law to Mangas Coloradas, a leader of the Mimbreño Apache (a subdivision of the Chiricahua, itself one of four main Apache groups, along with the Mescalero, the Lipan, and the Jicarilla). Relative newcomers to the Southwest, arriving probably no more than five or six hundred years ago, the Apache lived by raiding sheep, cattle, and horses from their neighbors—the Pueblo peoples, the Mexicans, and after the end of the Mexican War in 1848, the Americans. With the increased movement into Apache lands by the ever-advancing whites, a series of "wars" between the settlers and the various Apache bands broke out around 1860. Cochise first came into conflict with the whites in 1861, when he was accused by Lieutenant George Bascom, the officer in charge of the garrison at Fort Buchanan, in present-day Arizona, of stealing farm animals. Cochise protested his innocence; still, Bascom attempted to arrest him. Cochise resisted, was wounded, but managed to escape. Thus began the Apache wars that would last until Geronimo's surrender in 1886.

Cochise and his followers successfully resisted the government soldiers, reduced in number in the Southwest during the Civil War, to the extent that Apache raids threatened to drive both Mexicans and Euro-Americans out of Arizona. Some years after the end of the Civil War, in 1871, Colonel George Crook, an experienced Indian fighter, assumed command of the army in Arizona. Employing a number of native scouts, Crook managed to track Cochise down and persuade him to negotiate a peace settlement. But when Cochise learned that his people were to be placed on a harsh and dismal reservation at Fort Tularosa, New Mexico, he renounced the agreement.

General Oliver Howard, another seasoned Indian fighter, was then sent as President Grant's envoy to the Apache. Howard enlisted the aid of Thomas Jeffords (or Jefferds), a former captain of the California volunteer cavalry who had established a friendship with Cochise, to arrange a meeting in 1872 between Cochise and General Gordon Granger, commander of the district of New Mexico. After eleven days of negotiations, it was agreed that Cochise and his people might live on a reservation along Apache Pass, in southeastern Arizona, where Jeffords would serve as Indian agent.

It was during these negotiations that Cochise made a speech to the Americans that has since been anthologized (though incorrectly dated) in three important collections of Native American oratory. One of these accounts, all of which are based on A. N. Ellis's *Recollections of an Interview with Cochise* (1913), mentions another account, "presumably of the same occasion, by Henry Stuart Turrill," a retired brigadier general of the U.S. Army, who, as a young soldier, was present at the parley between Cochise, Granger, and Jeffords.

In an extraordinary talk called *A Vanished Race of Aboriginal Founders*, delivered on February 14, 1907, to the New York Society of the Founders and Patriots of America, at the Hotel Manhattan, Turrill gives the history of the Apaches and the Southwest and calls Cochise "the strongest Indian I had ever seen"—no small praise inasmuch as Turrill had encountered the eminent Lakota warriors Red Cloud, Spotted Tail, and Gall, and the illustrious Chief Joseph of the Nez Percés. Much as he admired these men, said Turrill, "I do not hesitate in naming Cochise as the greatest Indian that I have ever met."

While he admits that he can do no more than attempt to recreate Cochise's speech "after a lapse of thirty-five years," Turrill offers the account of a witness aware of the complexity of the communication he was hearing. Cochise, according to Turrill, began in Apache and then shifted to Spanish, in which he was quite fluent. While the A. N. Ellis version conventionally anthologized is more "poetic" than Turrill's, Turrill conveys more sharply the historical and political basis of Cochise's bargain with "your great father in Washington."

# [I am alone][1]

This for a very long time has been the home of my people; they came from the darkness, few in numbers and feeble. The country was held by a much stronger and more numerous people, and from their stone houses[2] we were quickly driven. We were a hunting people, living on the animals that we could kill. We came to these mountains about us; no one lived here, and so we took them for our home and country. Here we grew from the first feeble band to be a great people, and covered the whole country as the clouds cover the mountains. Many people came to our country. First the Spanish, with their horses and their iron shirts, their long knives[3] and guns, great wonders to my simple people. We fought some, but they never tried to drive us from our homes in these mountains. After many years the Spanish soldiers were driven away and the Mexican ruled the land. With these little wars came, but we were now a strong people and we did not fear them. At last in my youth came the white man, your people. Under the counsels of my grandfather, who had for a very long time been the head of the Apaches, they were received with friendship.[4] Soon their numbers increased and many passed through my country to the great waters of the setting sun.[5] Your soldiers came and their strong houses[6] were all through my country. I received favors from your people and did all that I could in return and we lived at peace. At last your soldiers did me a very great wrong,[7] and I and my whole people went to war with them. At first we were successful and your soldiers were driven away and your people killed and we again possessed our land. Soon many soldiers came from the north and from the west, and my people were driven to the mountain hiding places; but these did not protect us, and soon my people were flying from one mountain to another, driven by the soldiers, even as the wind is now driving the clouds. I have fought long and as best I could against you. I have destroyed many of your people, but where I have destroyed one white man many have come in his place; but where an Indian has been killed, there has been none to come in his place, so that the great people that welcomed you with acts of kindness to this land are now but a feeble band that fly before your soldiers as the deer

---

1. From Brigadier General Henry Stuart Turrill, *A Vanished Race of Aboriginal Founders*, address delivered before the New York Society of the Order of the Founders and Patriots of America (1907).
2. In keeping with the early-20th-century belief that the most substantial archaeological ruins of the Southwest were remnants of the Aztec civilization, Turrill believed the people of the stone houses were Aztecs. This belief was guided by disbelief that the ancestors of the Pueblo peoples native to the region could have been the architects of such substantial constructions. But the "stone house" people, according to archaeological data, were indeed the ancestors of the contemporary Pueblo peoples.

3. I.e., swords. The horse was introduced in the Americas by the Spaniards. "Iron shirts": the breast armor of the Spanish.
4. If the "grandfather" referred to is Cuchillo Negro, any "friendship" on his part toward the whites seems purely invented.
5. I.e., the Pacific Ocean. Cochise is referring to the westward migration in the wake of the discovery of gold in California in 1848.
6. The military forts established throughout the Southwest.
7. This is almost surely Lt. George Bascom's attempt to arrest Cochise in spite of his protestation of innocence.

before the hunter, and must all perish if this war continues. I have come to you, not from any love for you or for your great father in Washington, or from any regard for his or your wishes, but as a conquered chief, to try to save alive the few people that still remain to me. I am the last of my family, a family that for very many years have been the leaders of this people, and on me depends their future, whether they shall utterly vanish from the land or that a small remnant remain for a few years to see the sun rise over these mountains, their home. I here pledge my word, a word that has never been broken, that if your great father will set aside a part of my own country, where I and my little band can live, we will remain at peace with your people forever. If from his abundance he will give food for my women and children, whose protectors his soldiers have killed, with blankets to cover their nakedness, I will receive them with gratitude. If not, I will do my best to feed and clothe them, in peace with the white man. I have spoken.

1907                                                                       1872

# CHARLOT
## c. 1831–1900

Slemhakkah, or Bear Claw, known as Charlot, succeeded his father as a principal chief of the Kalispel band of the Flathead Indians, whose traditional homelands were in present-day Idaho, northeast Montana, and northwest Washington.

In 1855, Charlot's father signed a treaty with the federal government ceding a large portion of Flathead land on the condition that the Bitterroot Valley in western Montana be the site of his people's reservation. The government, however, assigned them land elsewhere. Some Flathead people agreed to settle on the Kalispel and Colville reservations in Washington and the Jocko reservation in Montana. Charlot refused and continued to live with his people in the Bitterroot region. In 1872, under government pressure, some of the Bitterroot Kalispels moved to the Jocko reservation, but Charlot continued to resist nonviolently. Federal agents then declared that Arlee, a more cooperative subchief, would now be the official representative of the Kalispel people. Atlhough Arlee was able to lead some seventy people to Jocko, several hundred Kalispels remained with Charlot in their traditional homelands. Charlot held out peacefully against the whites until 1890, when troops were sent in to force the last of his band onto the Jocko reservation, where Charlot died ten years later.

In 1876, it was proposed that reservation Indians in Montana be required to pay taxes. Charlot spoke to this issue, and his speech, a strong condemnation of the white people's greed, was reported in the Missoula (Montana) Missoulian. The text below is the entirety of Charlot's speech (translated, with what accuracy it is not possible to say, from the Salish language) as reported under the headline "Indian Taxation, Recent Speech of a Flathead Chief Presenting the Question from an Indian Standpoint." That this powerful critique of the white people's ways found its way into print on the western frontier in the year of the centennial celebration of American independence (and two months short of the defeat of Custer on the Little Bighorn) is in itself extraordinary.

# [He has filled graves with our bones][1]

Yes, my people, the white man wants us to pay him. He comes in his intent, and says we must pay him—pay him for our own—for the things we have from our God and our forefathers; for things he never owned, and never gave us. What law or right is that? What shame or what charity? The Indian says that a woman is more shameless than a man;[2] but the white man has less shame than our women. Since our forefathers first beheld him, more than seven times ten winters have snowed and melted. Most of them like those snows have dissolved away. Their spirits went whither they came; his, they say, go there too. Do they meet and see us here[?] Can he blush before his Maker, or is he forever dead[?] Is his prayer his promise—a trust of the wind? Is it a sound without sense? Is it a thing whose life is a foul thing? And is he not foul? He has filled graves with our bones. His horses, his cattle, his sheep, his men, his women have a rot. Does not his breath, his gums, stink? His jaws lose their teeth, and he stamps them with false ones; yet he is not ashamed. No, no; his course is destruction; he spoils what the Spirit who gave us this country made beautiful and clean. But that is not enough; he wants us to pay him besides his enslaving our country. Yes, and our people, besides, that degradation of a tribe who never were his enemies. What is he? Who sent him here? We were happy when he first came; since then we often saw him, always heard him and of him. We first thought he came from the light;[3] but he comes like the dusk of the evening now, not like the dawn of the morning. He comes like a day that has passed, and night enters our future with him.

To take and to lie should be burnt on his forehead, as he burns the sides of my stolen horses with his own name. Had Heaven's Chief burnt him with some mark[4] to refuse him, we might have refused him[.] No; we did not refuse him in his weakness; in his poverty we fed, we cherished him—yes, befriended him, and showed [him] the fords and defiles of our lands. Yet we did think his face was concealed with hair, and that he often smiled like a rabbit in his own beard. A long-tailed, skulking thing, fond of flat lands, and soft grass and woods.

Did he not feast us with our own cattle, on our own land, yes, on our own plain by the cold spring? Did he not invite our hands to his papers;[5] did he not promise before the sun, and before the eye that put fire in it,[6] and to the name of both, and in the name of his own Chief,[7] promise us what he promised—to give us what he has not given; to do what he knew he would never do. Now, because he lied, and because he yet lies, without friendship, manhood, justice, or charity, he wants us to give him money—pay him more. When shall he be satisfied? A roving skulk,[8] first; a natural liar, next; and, withal, a murderer, a tyrant.

To confirm his purpose; to make the trees and stones and his own people

---

1. From the *Missoula* (Montana) *Missoulian* (1876).
2. A statement fairly typical of male-centered cultures, Indian and non-Indian, vaguely parallel to such Western proverbial wisdom as "Vanity thy name is woman."
3. I.e., from the east, where the sun rises.
4. References both to the Euro-American practice of branding horses and cattle and, perhaps, to Cain, who bore a mark that would identify him as a murderer (of his brother Abel).
5. Ask that the Flatheads make their mark on treaties.

6. Possibly a reference to the God of Genesis, who created the sun.
7. Probably the president of the United States, the "chief" of the whites.
8. One who "skulked" about Indian lands. In violation of treaties, settlers encroached on Indian lands, and when the Native Americans retaliated, the state and/or federal government intervened to protect the settlers who were violating laws negotiated and passed by that same government.

hear him, he whispers soldiers, lock houses and iron chains.[9] My people, we
are poor; we are fatherless. The white man fathers this doom—yes, this curse
on us and on the few that may yet see a few days more. He, the cause of our
ruin, is his own snake, which he says stole on his mother in her own country
to lie to her.[1] He says his story is that man was rejected and cast off. Why did
we not reject him forever? He says one of his virgins had a son nailed to death
on two cross sticks to save him. Were all of them dead then when that young
man died, we would be all safe now and our country our own.

But he lives to persist; yes, the rascal is also an unsatisfied beggar, and his
hangman and swine[2] follow his walk. Pay him money! Did he inquire, how?
No, no; his meanness ropes his charity, his avarice wives[3] his envy, his race
breeds to extort. Did he speak at all like a friend? He saw a few horses and
some cows, and many tens of rails,[4] with the few of us that own them. His
envy thereon baited to the quick. Why thus? Because he himself says he is in
a big debt, and wants us to help him pay it. His avarice put him in debt, and
he wants us to pay him for it and be his fools. Did he ask how many a helpless
widow, how many a fatherless child, how many a blind and naked thing fare
a little of that little we have[?] Did he—in a destroying night when the mountains and the firmaments [sic] put their faces together to freeze us—did he
inquire if we had a spare rag of a blanket to save his lost and perishing steps to
our fires? No, no; cold he is, you know, and merciless. Four times in one
shivering night I last winter knew the old one-eyed Indian, Keneth [sic], that
gray man of full seven tens of winters, was refused shelter in four of the white
man's houses on his way in that bad night; yet the aged, blinded man was
turned out to his fate. No, no; he is cold and merciless, haughty and overbearing. Look at him, and he looks at you—how? His fishy eye scans you as the
why-oops[5] do the shelled blue cock. He is cold, and stealth and envy are with
him, and fit him as do his hands and feet. We owe him nothing; he owes us
more than he will pay, yet says there is a God.

I know another aged Indian, with his only daughter and wife alone in their
lodge. He had a few beaver skins and four or five poor horses—all he had. The
light [? print unclear] was bad, and held every stream in thick ice; the earth
was white; the stars burned nearer us as if to pity us, but the more they burned
the more stood the hair of the deer on end with cold, nor heeded they the
frost-bursting barks of the willows. Two of the white man's people came to the
lodge, lost and freezing pitifully. They fared well inside that lodge. The old
wife and only daughter unbound and put [? print unclear] off their frozen
shoes; gave them new ones, and crushed sage bark rind to put therein to keep
their feet smooth and warm. She gave them warm soup; boiled deer meat, and
boiled beaver. They were saved; their safety returned to make them live. After
a while they would not stop; they would go. They went away. Mind you;
remember well: at midnight they returned. [M]urdered the old father, and his
daughter and her mother asleep, took the beaver skins and horses, and left.

---

9. I.e., the white people threaten by hinting at the intervention of soldiers and of imprisonment in chains.
1. Reference to the story of Eve's temptation in the
Garden of Eden.
2. Pig farming, a practice introduced by the Euro-
Americans, was apparently as strange and repugnant
to some American Indians as death by hanging, also

introduced by Euro-Americans. Many frontier towns
counted among their first constructions a jailhouse
and gallows.
3. I.e., is married to. "Ropes": constrains.
4. Fence rails.
5. Unidentified, but undoubtedly a Salish word for an
animal that preys on the blue cock.

Next day, the first and only Indian they met, a fine young man, they killed, put his body under the ice and rode away on his horse.

Yet, they say we are not good. Will he tell his own crimes? No, no; his crimes to us are left untold. But the Desolator bawls and cries the dangers of the country from us, the few left of us. Other tribes kill and ravish his women and stake his children, and eat his steers, and he gives them blankets and sugar for it. We, the poor Flatheads, who never troubled him, he wants now to distress and make poorer.

I have more to say, my people; but this much I have said, and chose [close?] to hear your minds about this payment. We never begot laws or rights to ask it. His laws never gave us a blade nor a tree, nor a duck; nor a grouse, nor a trout. No; like the wolverine that steals your *cache*, how often does he come: You know he comes as long as he lives, and takes more and more, and dirties what he leaves.

1876

# WOVOKA
## c. 1856–1932

Quoitze Ow, known most commonly by his boyhood name Wovoka (the Wood Cutter) or his adoptive name Jack Wilson, was a Numu (Paiute) Indian, born in 1856 or 1857 at Walker Lake in present-day Nevada. Although he had earlier experienced trancelike states and revelations, Wovoka's formative vision seems to have come on New Year's Day 1889, when he fell into a coma while suffering from scarlet fever, an event that was followed by a total solar eclipse. In this vision, Wovoka was transported to heaven, where he spoke to God, who assured him that the Messiah—Jesus, it would seem, although Wovoka himself began to assume the role of Messiah to many American Indians, particularly after the fulfillment of his prediction of rain to drought-stricken Nevada—was already on earth and that soon the buffalo would return (this was of particular importance to the Plains Indians), game animals would abound, and the Indian dead would be reunited with their kin in an earthly paradise. As for the whites, they would either disappear or somehow be assimilated into the native new world order.

The Ghost Dance itself was a form of the traditional round dance that was to be performed for five or six nights. Men and women, hand in hand, moved sideways and in a circular motion around a fire, singing songs that varied from group to group. Followers of the Ghost Dance religion believed that performing this dance, along with carrying out specifically peaceful, thoroughly Christian behaviors, would ensure the realization of Wovoka's vision of paradise. Also assumed by some, particularly the Plains Indians, who early on stripped away the religion's pacific aspects, was the impermeability to bullets of the dyed and painted, fringed muslin or buckskin garments known as Ghost Dance shirts. When asked about this belief, Wovoka himself called it a joke. But it was no joke when the Seventh Cavalry trained its guns on a band of starving Sioux, at Wounded Knee on the Pine Ridge reservation, called there because the government's Indian agent had become panicky about the activities of the Ghost Dancers.

A Minneconjou Sioux named Kicking Bear and his brother-in-law Short Bull made the trip southwest to the land of the Fish Eaters (the Paiutes) to find out about this new religion, word of which had spread even to the Plains. They met the Paiute Messiah, learned the songs and dances of the Ghost Dance religion and, upon their return, introduced them to the Sioux on the Rosebud, Cheyenne River, and Pine Ridge reservations. Sitting Bull, one of the most notable of the Sioux chiefs and a principal participant in the defeat of Custer at the Little Bighorn River, had his doubts about the power of the Ghost Dance. He was, however, willing to have the religion introduced among his people at Standing Rock reservation— although he had heard that government Indian agents had called for soldiers to stop the dances. James McLaughlin, a Catholic who was in charge of Standing Rock reservation, was particularly upset about the Ghost Dance, which he called a "pernicious system of religion," for all that its main tenets were deeply Christian. By November 1890 the agent at Pine Ridge reservation had telegraphed Washington: "Indians are dancing in the snow and are wild and crazy. . . . We need protection and we need it now." Sitting Bull, as one of the most visible and eminent of the Sioux, was singled out by those fearful of the Ghost Dance.

Shortly before dawn on December 15, 1890, Sitting Bull's cabin was surrounded by Indian police under the command of Lieutenant Bull Head, who attempted to take the old chief prisoner. Although Sitting Bull cooperated, outside the cabin a crowd of Ghost Dancers urged him to resist arrest. A man named Catch-the-Bear pulled out a rifle and shot at Bull Head, who, as he fell, attempted to shoot back at Catch-the-Bear. His bullet struck Sitting Bull instead; Red Tomahawk, another of the Indian police, then shot the old chief in the head, killing him.

Less than ten days after Sitting Bull's murder the call came for the arrest of Big Foot, an elderly Minneconjou Sioux, who was suffering, in the cold, from pneumonia. His people, too, had been participants in the Ghost Dance, and with little resistance possible, Big Foot led them to surrender at Wounded Knee, on the Pine Ridge reservation. Surrounded by cavalry, the Indians were halted and counted: 120 men and 230 women and children. The next morning Colonel James W. Forsyth of the Seventh Cavalry ordered the men outside and announced that they were to be disarmed. Some weapons were given up, but the soldiers persisted in their search. A young man named Black Coyote, who may have been deaf, refused to hand over his Winchester rifle. The soldiers seized him; Black Coyote's rifle discharged or was fired, and the violence began. Soldiers shot indiscriminately at the assembled men and the women who, at the sound of gunfire, had run to the scene. Then the big Hotchkiss guns positioned on the surrounding hills began to fire, and in a short time, the massacre was complete. Big Foot and most of his people, the majority women and children, were dead.

Later in the day, the soldiers returned to the scene and loaded the wounded Sioux into wagons: four men and forty-seven women and children. Because a blizzard was approaching, the Indian dead were left where they had fallen. After the storm had passed, on New Year's Day of 1891, white settlers, who were paid two dollars a corpse, gathered the Sioux dead, frozen, photographs show, into grotesque shapes, and threw them into a mass grave.

In what follows, we give two versions of Wovoka's teachings, instances of native oratory addressed to native peoples. First, we have a Cheyenne version (many of the tribes sent emissaries to visit the Paiute prophet), dictated, in English, by Black Short Nose to his daughter around 1891, following his visit with Wovoka. We have left uncorrected the grammatical and spelling errors in this account in the belief that Black Short Nose's hybrid English is, however different from the standard, of potentially literary interest. Next follows Wovoka's own version of his message, as given in 1892 to James Mooney (1861–1921), the "Indian man" of the Bureau of American Ethnology. Mooney produced this free rendering, which he titles *The Messiah Letter*, as part of his detailed study of the Ghost Dance religion.

## The Messiah Letter: Cheyenne Version[1]

When you get home you have to make dance. You must dance for four nights and one day time. You will take bath in the same morning before you go to yours home, for every body, and give you all the same as this. Jackson Wilson[2] likes you all, he is glad to get good many things. His heart satting fully of gladness, after you get home, I will give you a good cloud and give you chance to make you feel good. I give you a good spirit, and give you all good paint, I want you people to come here again, want them in three months any tribs of you from there. There will be a good deal snow this year. Some time rains, in fall this year some rain, never give you any thing like that, grandfather, said, when they were die never cry, no hurt anybody, do any harm for it, not to fight. Be a good behave always. It will give a satisfaction in your life. This young man is a good father and mother. Do not tell the white people about this, Juses is on the ground, he just like cloud. Every body is a live again. I don't know when he will be here, may be will be this fall or in spring. When it happen it may be this. There will be no sickness and return to young again. Do not refuse to work for white man or do not make any trouble with them until you leave them. When the earth shakes do not be afraid it will not hurt you. I want you to make dance for six weeks. Eat and wash good clean yourselves.[3]

## The Messiah Letter: Mooney's Free Rendering[1]

When you get home you must make a dance to continue five days. Dance four successive nights, and the last night keep up the dance until the morning of the fifth day, when all must bathe in the river and then disperse to their homes. You must all do in the same way.

I, Jack Wilson,[2] love you all, and my heart is full of gladness for the gifts you have brought me. When you get home I shall give you a good cloud[3] which will make you feel good. I give you a good spirit and give you all good paint. I want you to come again in three months, some from each tribe there.[4]

There will be a good deal of snow this year and some rain. In the fall there will be such a rain as I have never given you before.

Grandfather[5] says, when your friends die you must not cry. You must not hurt anybody or do harm to anyone. You must not fight. Do right always. It will give you satisfaction in life. This young man has a good father and mother.[6]

Do not tell the white people about this. Jesus is now upon the earth. He appears like a cloud. The dead are all alive again. I do not know when they will be here; maybe this fall or in the spring. When the time comes there will be no more sickness and everyone will be young again.

1. From James Mooney's *The Ghost-Dance Religion and the Sioux Outbreak of 1890* (1893, 1965).
2. Wovoka.
3. "The rest of the letter had been erased" [Mooney's note].
1. From James Mooney's *The Ghost-Dance Religion and the Sioux Outbreak of 1890* (1893, 1965).
2. Wovoka.
3. "Rain?" [Mooney's note].
4. "The Indian Territory" [Mooney's note].
5. "A universal title of reverence among Indians and here meaning the messiah" [Mooney's note].
6. "Possibly refers to Casper Edson, the young Arapaho who transcribed this message for the delegation" [Mooney's note].

Do not refuse to work for the whites and do not make any trouble with them until you leave them. When the earth shakes[7] do not be afraid. It will not hurt you.

I want everyone to dance every six weeks. Make a feast at the dance and have food that everybody may eat. Then bathe in the water. That is all. You will receive good words again from me some time. Do not tell lies.

7. "At the coming of the new world" [Mooney's note].

---

# HENRY JAMES
## 1843–1916

Henry James was the first American writer to conceive his career in international terms; he set out, that is, to be a "literary master" in the European sense. Partly because of this grandiose self-conception, partly because he spent most of his adult life in England, and partly because his intricate style and choices of cultivated characters ran counter to the dominant vernacular tradition initiated by Mark Twain, James attracted, in his own lifetime, only a select company of admirers. The recognition of his intrinsic importance as well as his wide influence as novelist and critic did not emerge until the years between the world wars, when American literary taste reached a new level of sophistication. Only quite recently has his playful prediction that "some day all my buried prose will kick off its various tombstones at once" largely come to pass. James is now firmly established as one of America's major novelists and critics and as a psychological realist of unsurpassed subtlety.

James was born in New York City on April 15, 1843. His father was an eccentric, independently wealthy philosopher and religious visionary; his slightly older brother, William, was the first notable American psychologist and perhaps our country's most influential philosopher; two younger brothers and a sister completed one of the most remarkable of American families. First taken to Europe as an infant, James spent his boyhood in a still almost bucolic New York City before the family once again left for the Continent when he was twelve. His father wanted the children to have a rich, "sensuous education," and during the next four years, with stays in England, Switzerland, and France, they were endlessly exposed to galleries, libraries, museums, and (of special interest to Henry) theaters. Henry's formal schooling was unsystematic, but he mastered French well enough to begin his lifelong study of its literature, and he thoroughly absorbed the ambiance of the Old World. From childhood on he was aware of the intricate network of institutions and traditions that he later lamented (in his study of Hawthorne and elsewhere) American novelists had to do without.

James early developed what he described in A Small Boy and Others (1913) as the "practice of wondering and dawdling and gaping." In that same memoir he also relates how he suffered the "obscure hurt" to his back that disqualified him from service in the Civil War and that must have helped to reinforce his inclination to be an observer rather than a participator. In his later teens his interest in literature and in writing intensified, and by the time he reached his majority he was publishing reviews and stories in some of the leading American journals—Atlantic Monthly, North American Review, Galaxy, and Nation. Though the crucial decision to establish his base of operations in England in 1876 remained to be made (after much shuttling back and forth between America and Europe, and after trial residence in France and Italy), the direction of James's single-minded career as man of letters was clearly marked in his early manhood. James never married. He maintained close ties with his family, kept up a large correspondence, was extremely sociable and a famous diner-out, knew most of his great contemporaries in the arts, many intimately—but he lived and worked alone. His emotional life and prodigious creative energy were invested for fifty years in what he called the "sacred rage" of his art.

Leon Edel, James's biographer, divides the writer's mature career into three parts. In the first, which culminated with *The Portrait of a Lady* (1881), he felt his way toward and appropriated the so-called international theme—the drama, comic and tragic, of Americans in Europe and Europeans in America. In the tripartite second period, he experimented with diverse themes and forms—first with novels dealing explicitly with strong social and political currents of the 1870s and 1880s, then with writing for the theater, and finally with shorter fictions that explore the relationship of artists to society and the troubled psychology of oppressed children and haunted or obsessed men and women such as those depicted in *The Turn of the Screw*. In James's last period—the so-called major phase—he returned to international or cosmopolitan subjects in an extraordinary series of elaborately developed novels, shorter fiction, and criticism.

Three of his earliest books—*A Passionate Pilgrim*, a collection of stories; *Transatlantic Sketches*, a collection of travel pieces; and *Roderick Hudson*, a novel— were all published in 1875. *The American* (1877) was his first successful and extended treatment of the naive young American (Christopher Newman) from the New World in tension with the traditions, customs, and values of the Old. *Daisy Miller* (1878) was the work with which he first achieved widespread popularity. In this "study," as it was originally subtitled, the dangerously naive young American girl (a subject to be treated often by James and his friend W. D. Howells) pays for her innocence of European social mores—and her willfulness—with her life. These stories make it clear that James was neither a chauvinist nor a resentful émigré but a cosmopolitan whose concern was to explore the moral qualities of men and women forced to deal with the dilemmas of cultural displacement.

Despite their appeal, the characters of Daisy Miller and Christopher Newman are simple, and this makes romance, melodrama, and pathos (whatever their charms) more likely than psychological complexity and genuine tragedy, which require, especially for James, a broad canvas. In the character and career of Isabel Archer—for which he drew on the tragically blighted life of his beloved cousin, Mary Temple, who died of tuberculosis in 1870 at the age of twenty-four—he found the focus for his first masterpiece on the international theme, *The Portrait of a Lady*. Here, for the first time, the complex inner life of his characters— compounded of desire, will, thought, impulse—is fully and realistically projected. All the same, even in a relatively short work like *Daisy Miller*, James's essential themes and procedures are evident.

From 1885 to 1890 James was largely occupied writing three novels in the naturalistic mode—*The Bostonians* (1886), *The Princess Casamassima* (1886), and *The Tragic Muse* (1889). James may have been right to put aside temporarily the "American-European legend" as subject, but he could not finally accept philosophic determinism of his characters' behavior or render his materials in documentary detail or depend for interest and effect on violent, physical action. These three novels have their virtues, but they are not the virtues of the mode as practiced by Zola, Norris, or Dreiser. For better *and* for worse, the English novelist Joseph Conrad observed, James was the "historian of fine consciences."

These stories of reformers, radicals, and revolutionaries, better appreciated in our time than in his, alienated James's hard-won audience. Out of a sense of artistic challenge as well as financial need (he was never rich), James attempted to regain popularity and earn money by turning dramatist. Between 1890 and 1895 he wrote seven plays; two were produced, neither was a success. Humiliated by the boos and hooting of a hostile first-night crowd for *Guy Domville* (1895), James gave up the attempt to master his new form.

Between 1895 and 1900 James returned to fiction, especially to experiment in shorter works with three dominant subjects, which he often combined: misunderstood or troubled writers and artists, ghosts and apparitions, and doomed or threatened children and adolescents. *The Real Thing* is an excellent example of a special kind of artistic dilemma that fascinated James, whereas *The Turn of the Screw* (1898), in which a whole household, including two young children, is terrorized by "ghosts," is the most powerful and famous of those stories in which, as James put it, "the strange and sinister is embroidered on the very type of the normal and the easy." Almost as well known, *The Beast in the Jungle* (1903) projects the pathetic career of a man who allows his obsessive imagination of personal disaster in the future to destroy his chances for love and life in the present.

Following his own advice to other novelists to "dramatize, dramatize, dramatize," James increasingly removed himself as controlling narrator—became "invisible," in T. S. Eliot's phrase—from the reader's awareness. The benefits of this heightened emphasis on showing rather than telling were compression or intensification and enhanced opportunity for ambiguity. The more the author withdrew, the more the reader was forced to enter the process of creating meaning. We are accustomed now to having our fiction thus "objectified," but it is James who is largely responsible for this development in narrative technique.

*The Wings of the Dove* (1902), *The Ambassadors* (1903), which James thought was "the best 'all round'" of his productions, and *The Golden Bowl* (1904) are demanding novels. The first two deal with subjects he had treated earlier in *The American* and *The Portrait of a Lady*, and all three concern themselves with James's grand theme of freedom through perception: only awareness of one's own character and others' provides the wisdom to live well. The treatment of this theme in these books, however, is characterized by richness of syntax, characterization, point of view, symbolic resonance, metaphoric texture, and organizing rhythms. The world of these novels is, as a critic has remarked, like the very atmosphere of the mind. These dramas of perception are widely considered to be James's most influential contribution to the craft of fiction.

When James was not writing fiction, he was most often writing about it—either his own or others. He was, as he noted in one of his letters, "a critical, a non-naif, a questioning, worrying reader." If he was somewhat narrow in his reading—restricting himself chiefly to nineteenth-century fiction—he made his limited experience count for as much in criticism as it did in fiction. His inquiries into the achievement of other writers—preserved in such volumes as *French Poets and Novelists* (1878), *Partial Portraits* (1888), and *Notes on Novelists* (1914)—are remarkable for their breadth, balance, and acuteness. His taste and judgments have been largely confirmed by time.

More broadly philosophic than the reviews or even the essays on individual writers, *The Art of Fiction* (1884) fairly represents James's central aesthetic conceptions. Calling attention to the unparalleled opportunities open to the artist of fiction and the beauty of the novel that creates a new form, James also insists that "the deepest quality of a work of art will always be the quality of the mind of the producer" and that "no good novel will ever proceed from a superficial mind." James left no better record than this essay of his always twinned concerns over the moral and formal qualities of fiction, of the relationship between aesthetic and moral perception.

James was an extremely self-conscious writer, and his *Notebooks* (published in 1947) reveal a subtle, intense mind in the act of discovering subjects, methods, and principles. The prefaces he wrote for the definitive New York Edition of his extensively revised novels and tales (gathered and published in 1934 as *The Art of the Novel*) contain James's final study of the works that he considered best represented his achievement. As the culmination of an entire lifetime of reflection on the craft of fiction, they provide extraordinary accounts of the origins and growth of his major writings and exquisite analyses of the fictional problems that each work posed. Despite their occasional opacity, they also serve, as he wrote Howells he hoped they would, as a "sort of comprehensive manual or *vade-mecum* for aspirants in our arduous profession." These prefaces provided both vocabulary and example for the close textual analysis of prose fiction in the "New Criticism" that was dominant in America in the generation following World War II.

While James was in the United States arranging for Scribner's New York Edition of his novels and tales, he also took the occasion to travel extensively and to lecture in his native land and Canada. The chief fruit of this experience was *The American Scene* (1907), which carried the art of travel writing to the same sophisticated level he had carried the art of fiction in *The Ambassadors*, *The Wings of the Dove*, and *The Golden Bowl*. This "absolutely personal" book is perhaps the most vividly particular account we have of the vast and profound changes that occurred in America between the Civil War and World War I, the period James later characterized as the "Age of the Mistake."

The same intricate, ruminative richness marks the three autobiographical reminiscences he wrote late in life: *A Small Boy and Others* (1913), *Notes of a Son and Brother* (1914), and the fragmentary and posthumously published *The Middle Years* (1917). Henry James died in 1916; a year after he became a naturalized British subject out of impatience with America's reluctance to enter World War I.

At one time or another James has been characterized as a snob, a deserter from his native land, an old maid, a mere aesthete; his fiction has been deprecated as narrowly concerned with the rich, the bloodless, and the sexless; as needlessly elaborate and long-winded; and as excessively introspective and autobiographical. But James, who always believed in his own genius, has been vindicated because he understood the mixed nature of men and women profoundly, because he judged them humanely, and because he gave enduring and compelling shape to his sense of life.

# Daisy Miller: A Study[1]

## *I*

At the little town of Vevey, in Switzerland, there is a particularly comfortable hotel. There are, indeed, many hotels; for the entertainment of tourists is the business of the place, which, as many travelers will remember, is seated upon the edge of a remarkably blue lake[2]—a lake that it behoves every tourist to visit. The shore of the lake presents an unbroken array of establishments of this order, of every category, from the "grand hotel" of the newest fashion, with a chalk-white front, a hundred balconies, and a dozen flags flying from its roof, to the little Swiss *pension* of an elder day, with its name inscribed in German-looking lettering upon a pink or yellow wall, and an awkward summer-house in the angle of the garden. One of the hotels at Vevey, however, is famous, even classical, being distinguished from many of its upstart neighbors by an air both of luxury and of maturity. In this region, in the month of June, American travelers are extremely numerous; it may be said, indeed, that Vevey

---

1. First published in the *Cornhill Magazine* 37 (June–July 1878). The text reprinted here follows the 1st British book edition, published by Macmillan in 1879. Punctuation and spelling have been Americanized.
2. Lac Léman, or Lake of Geneva.

assumes at this period some of the characteristics of an American watering-place. There are sights and sounds which evoke a vision, an echo, of Newport and Saratoga.[3] There is a flitting hither and thither of "stylish" young girls, a rustling of muslin flounces, a rattle of dance-music in the morning hours, a sound of high-pitched voices at all times. You receive an impression of these things at the excellent inn of the "Trois Couronnes,"[4] and are transported in fancy to the Ocean House or to Congress Hall. But at the "Trois Couronnes," it must be added, there are other features that are much at variance with these suggestions: neat German waiters, who look like secretaries of legation; Russian princesses sitting in the garden; little Polish boys walking about, held by the hand, with their governors; a view of the snowy crest of the Dent du Midi[5] and the picturesque towers of the Castle of Chillon.

I hardly know whether it was the analogies or the differences that were uppermost in the mind of a young American, who, two or three years ago, sat in the garden of the "Trois Couronnes," looking about him, rather idly, at some of the graceful objects I have mentioned. It was a beautiful summer morning, and in whatever fashion the young American looked at things, they must have seemed to him charming. He had come from Geneva the day before, by the little steamer, to see his aunt, who was staying at the hotel—Geneva having been for a long time his place of residence. But his aunt had a headache—his aunt had almost always a headache—and now she was shut up in her room, smelling camphor, so that he was at liberty to wander about. He was some seven-and-twenty years of age; when his friends spoke of him, they usually said that he was at Geneva, "studying." When his enemies spoke of him they said—but, after all, he had no enemies; he was an extremely amiable fellow, and universally liked. What I should say is, simply, that when certain persons spoke of him they affirmed that the reason of his spending so much time at Geneva was that he was extremely devoted to a lady who lived there—a foreign lady—a person older than himself. Very few Americans—indeed I think none—had ever seen this lady, about whom there were some singular stories. But Winterbourne had an old attachment for the little metropolis of Calvinism;[6] he had been put to school there as a boy, and he had afterwards gone to college there—circumstances which had led to his forming a great many youthful friendships. Many of these he had kept, and they were a source of great satisfaction to him.

After knocking at his aunt's door and learning that she was indisposed, he had taken a walk about the town, and then he had come in to his breakfast. He had now finished his breakfast, but he was drinking a small cup of coffee, which had been served to him on a little table in the garden by one of the waiters who looked like an *attaché*.[7] At last he finished his coffee and lit a cigarette. Presently a small boy came walking along the path—an urchin of nine or ten. The child, who was diminutive for his years, had an aged expression of countenance, a pale complexion, and sharp little features. He was dressed in knickerbockers, with red stockings, which displayed his poor little spindleshanks; he also wore a brilliant red cravat. He carried in his hand a long alpenstock, the sharp point of which he thrust into everything that he

---

3. Newport, Rhode Island, and Saratoga, New York, resort areas for the rich, where the Ocean House and Congress Hall (below) are located.
4. Three Crowns (French).
5. The highest peak in the Dents du Midi, a mountain group in the Alps in southwest Switzerland.
6. Geneva, where John Calvin (1509–1564) centered his Protestant regime.
7. I.e., like a member of the diplomatic corps.

approached—the flower-beds, the garden-benches, the trains of the ladies' dresses. In front of Winterbourne he paused, looking at him with a pair of bright, penetrating little eyes.

"Will you give me a lump of sugar?" he asked, in a sharp, hard little voice— a voice immature, and yet, somehow, not young.

Winterbourne glanced at the small table near him, on which his coffee-service rested, and saw that several morsels of sugar remained. "Yes, you may take one," he answered; "but I don't think sugar is good for little boys."

This little boy stepped forward and carefully selected three of the coveted fragments, two of which he buried in the pocket to his knickerbockers, depositing the other as promptly in another place. He poked his alpenstock, lance-fashion, into Winterbourne's bench, and tried to crack the lump of sugar with his teeth.

"Oh, blazes; it's har-r-d!" he exclaimed, pronouncing the adjective in a peculiar manner.

Winterbourne had immediately perceived that he might have the honor of claiming him as a fellow-countryman. "Take care you don't hurt your teeth," he said, paternally.

"I haven't got any teeth to hurt. They have all come out. I have only got seven teeth. My mother counted them last night, and one came out right afterwards. She said she'd slap me if any more came out. I can't help it. It's this old Europe. It's the climate that makes them come out. In America they didn't come out. It's these hotels."

Winterbourne was much amused. "If you eat three lumps of sugar, your mother will certainly slap you." he said.

"She's got to give me some candy, then," rejoined his young interlocutor. "I can't get any candy here—any American candy. American candy's the best candy."

"And are American little boys the best little boys?" asked Winterbourne.

"I don't know. I'm an American boy," said the child.

"I see you are one of the best!" laughed Winterbourne.

"Are you an American man?" pursued this vivacious infant. And then, on Winterbourne's affirmative reply—"American men are the best," he declared.

His companion thanked him for the compliment; and the child, who had now got astride of his alpenstock, stood looking about him, while he attacked a second lump of sugar. Winterbourne wondered if he himself had been like this in his infancy, for he had been brought to Europe at about this age.

"Here comes my sister!" cried the child, in a moment. "She's an American girl."

Winterbourne looked along the path and saw a beautiful young lady advancing. "American girls are the best girls," he said, cheerfully, to his young companion.

"My sister ain't the best!" the child declared, "She's always blowing at me."

"I imagine that is your fault, not hers," said Winterbourne. The young lady meanwhile had drawn near. She was dressed in white muslin, with a hundred frills and flounces, and knots of pale-colored ribbon. She was bare-headed; but she balanced in her hand a large parasol, with a deep border of embroidery; and she was strikingly, admirably pretty. "How pretty they are!" thought Winterbourne, straightening himself in his seat, as if he were prepared to rise.

The young lady paused in front of his bench, near the parapet of the garden,

which overlooked the lake. The little boy had now converted his alpenstock
into a vaulting-pole, by the aid of which he was springing about in the gravel,
and kicking it up not a little.

"Randolph," said the young lady, "what *are* you doing?"

"I'm going up the Alps," replied Randolph. "This is the way!" And he gave
another little jump, scattering the pebbles about Winterbourne's ears.

"That's the way they come down," said Winterbourne.

"He's an American man!" cried Randolph, in his little hard voice.

The young lady gave no heed to this announcement, but looked straight at
her brother. "Well, I guess you had better be quiet," she simply observed.

It seemed to Winterbourne that he had been in a manner presented. He got
up and stepped slowly towards the young girl, throwing away his cigarette.
"This little boy and I have made acquaintance," he said, with great civility. In
Geneva, as he had been perfectly aware, a young man was not at liberty to
speak to a young unmarried lady except under certain rarely-occurring conditions; but here at Vevey, what conditions could be better than these?—a pretty
American girl coming and standing in front of you in a garden.—This pretty
American girl, however, on hearing Winterbourne's observation, simply
glanced at him; she then turned her head and looked over the parapet, at the
lake and the opposite mountains. He wondered whether he had gone too far;
but he decided that he must advance farther, rather than retreat. While he was
thinking of something else to say, the young lady turned to the little boy again.

"I should like to know where you got that pole," she said.

"I bought it!" responded Randolph.

"You don't mean to say you're going to take it to Italy!"

"Yes, I am going to take it to Italy!" the child declared.

The young girl glanced over the front of her dress, and smoothed out a knot
or two of ribbon. Then she rested her eyes upon the prospect again. "Well, I
guess you had better leave it somewhere," she said, after a moment.

"Are you going to Italy?" Winterbourne inquired, in a tone of great respect.

The young lady glanced at him again.

"Yes, sir," she replied. And she said nothing more.

"Are you—a—going over the Simplon?"[8] Winterbourne pursued, a little
embarrassed.

"I don't know," she said, "I suppose it's some mountain. Randolph, what
mountain are we going over?"

"Going where?" the child demanded.

"To Italy," Winterbourne explained.

"I don't know," said Randolph. "I don't want to go to Italy. I want to go
to America."

"Oh, Italy is a beautiful place!" rejoined the young man.

"Can you get candy there?" Randolph loudly inquired.

"I hope not," said his sister. "I guess you have had enough candy, and
mother thinks so too."

"I haven't had any for ever so long—for a hundred weeks!" cried the boy,
still jumping about.

The young lady inspected her flounces and smoothed her ribbons again;
and Winterbourne presently risked an observation upon the beauty of the view.

8. A pass in the Alps between Switzerland and Italy.

He was ceasing to be embarrassed, for he had begun to perceive that she was not in the least embarrassed herself. There had not been the slightest alteration in her charming complexion; she was evidently neither offended nor fluttered. If she looked another way when he spoke to her, and seemed not particularly to hear him, this was simply her habit, her manner. Yet, as he talked a little more, and pointed out some of the objects of interest in the view, with which she appeared quite unacquainted, she gradually gave him more of the benefit of her glance; and then he saw that this glance was perfectly direct and unshrinking. It was not, however, what would have been called an immodest glance, for the young girls' eyes were singularly honest and fresh. They were wonderfully pretty eyes; and, indeed, Winterbourne had not seen for a long time anything prettier than his fair countrywoman's various features—her complexion, her nose, her ears, her teeth. He had a great relish for feminine beauty; he was addicted to observing and analyzing it; and as regards this young lady's face he made several observations. It was not at all insipid, but it was not exactly expressive; and though it was eminently delicate, Winterbourne mentally accused it—very forgivingly—of a want of finish. He thought it very possible that Master Randolph's sister was a coquette; he was sure she had a spirit of her own; but in her bright, sweet, superficial little visage there was no mockery, no irony. Before long it became obvious that she was much disposed towards conversation. She told him that they were going to Rome for the winter—she and her mother and Randolph. She asked him if he was a "real American"; she wouldn't have taken him for one; he seemed more like a German—this was said after a little hesitation, especially when he spoke. Winterbourne, laughing, answered that he had met Germans who spoke like Americans; but that he had not, so far as he remembered, met an American who spoke like a German. Then he asked her if she would not be more comfortable in sitting upon the bench which he had just quitted. She answered that she liked standing up and walking about; but she presently sat down. She told him she was from New York State—"if you know where that is." Winterbourne learned more about her by catching hold of her small, slippery brother and making him stand a few minutes by his side.

"Tell me your name, my boy," he said.

"Randolph C. Miller," said the boy, sharply. "And I'll tell you her name"; and he leveled his alpenstock at his sister.

"You had better wait till you are asked!" said this young lady, calmly.

"I should like very much to know your name," said Winterbourne.

"Her name is Daisy Miller!" cried the child. "But that isn't her real name; that isn't her name on her cards."

"It's a pity you haven't got one of my cards!" said Miss Miller.

"Her real name is Annie P. Miller," the boy went on.

"Ask him *his* name," said his sister, indicating Winterbourne.

But on this point Randolph seemed perfectly indifferent; he continued to supply information with regard to his own family. "My father's name is Ezra B. Miller," he announced. "My father ain't in Europe; my father's in a better place than Europe."

Winterbourne imagined for a moment that this was the manner in which the child had been taught to intimate that Mr. Miller had been removed to the sphere of celestial rewards. But Randolph immediately added, "My father's in Schenectady. He's got a big business. My father's rich, you bet."

"Well!" ejaculated Miss Miller, lowering her parasol and looking at the embroidered border. Winterbourne presently released the child, who departed, dragging his alpenstock along the path. "He doesn't like Europe," said the young girl. "He wants to go back."

"To Schenectady, you mean?"

"Yes; he wants to go right home. He hasn't got any boys here. There is one boy here, but he always goes round with a teacher; they won't let him play."

"And your brother hasn't any teacher?" Winterbourne inquired.

"Mother thought of getting him one, to travel round with us. There was a lady told her of a very good teacher; an American lady—perhaps you know her—Mrs. Sanders. I think she came from Boston. She told her of this teacher, and we thought of getting him to travel round with us. But Randolph said he didn't want a teacher traveling round with us. He said he wouldn't have lessons when he was in the cars.[9] And we *are* in the cars about half the time. There was an English lady we met in the cars—I think her name was Miss Featherstone; perhaps you know her. She wanted to know why I didn't give Randolph lessons—give him 'instruction,' she called it. I guess he could give me more instruction than I could give him. He's very smart."

"Yes," said Winterbourne; "he seems very smart."

"Mother's going to get a teacher for him as soon as we get to Italy. Can you get good teachers in Italy?"

"Very good, I should think," said Winterbourne.

"Or else she's going to find some school. He ought to learn some more. He's only nine. He's going to college." And in this way Miss Miller continued to converse upon the affairs of her family, and upon other topics. She sat there with her extremely pretty hands, ornamented with very brilliant rings, folded in her lap, and with her pretty eyes now resting upon those of Winterbourne, now wandering over the garden, the people who passed by, and the beautiful view. She talked to Winterbourne as if she had known him a long time. He found it very pleasant. It was many years since he heard a young girl talk so much. It might have been said of this unknown young lady, who had come and sat down beside him upon a bench, that she chattered. She was very quiet, she sat in a charming tranquil attitude; but her lips and her eyes were constantly moving. She had a soft, slender, agreeable voice, and her tone was decidedly sociable. She gave Winterbourne a history of her movements and intentions, and those of her mother and brother, in Europe, and enumerated, in particular, the various hotels at which they had stopped. "That English lady in the cars," she said—"Miss Featherstone—asked me if we didn't all live in hotels in America. I told her I had never been in so many hotels in my life as since I came to Europe. I have never seen so many—it's nothing but hotels." But Miss Miller did not make this remark with a querulous accent; she appeared to be in the best humor with everything. She declared that the hotels were very good, when once you got used to their ways, and that Europe was perfectly sweet. She was not disappointed—not a bit. Perhaps it was because she had heard so much about it before. She had ever so many intimate friends that had been there ever so many times. And then she had had ever so many dresses and things from Paris. Whenever she put on a Paris dress she felt as if she were in Europe.

9. Railway cars.

"It was a kind of wishing-cap," said Winterbourne.

"Yes," said Miss Miller, without examining this analogy; "it always made me wish I was here. But I needn't have done that for dresses. I am sure they send all the pretty ones to America; you see the most frightful things here. The only thing I don't like," she proceeded, "is the society. There isn't any society; or, if there is, I don't know where it keeps itself. Do you? I suppose there is some society somewhere, but I haven't seen anything of it. I'm very fond of society, and I have always had a great deal of it. I don't mean only in Schenectady, but in New York. I used to go to New York every winter. In New York I had lots of society. Last winter I had seventeen dinners given me; and three of them were by gentlemen," added Daisy Miller. "I have more friends in New York than in Schenectady—more gentlemen friends; and more young lady friends too," she resumed in a moment. She paused again for an instant; she was looking at Winterbourne with all her prettiness in her lively eyes and in her light, slightly monotonous smile, "I have always had," she said, "a great deal of gentlemen's society."

Poor Winterbourne was amused, perplexed, and decidedly charmed. He had never yet heard a young girl express herself in just this fashion; never, at least, save in cases where to say such things seemed a kind of demonstrative evidence of a certain laxity of deportment. And yet was he to accuse Miss Daisy Miller of actual or potential *inconduite*,[1] as they said at Geneva? He felt that he had lived at Geneva so long that he had lost a good deal; he had become dishabituated to the American tone. Never, indeed, since he had grown old enough to appreciate things, had he encountered a young American girl of so pronounced a type as this. Certainly she was very charming; but how deucedly sociable! Was she simply a pretty girl from New York State—were they all like that, the pretty girls who had a good deal of gentlemen's society? Or was she also a designing, an audacious, an unscrupulous young person? Winterbourne had lost his instinct in this matter, and his reason could not help him. Miss Daisy Miller looked extremely innocent. Some people had told him that, after all, American girls were exceedingly innocent; and others had told him that, after all, they were not. He was inclined to think Miss Daisy Miller was a flirt—a pretty American flirt. He had never, as yet, had any relations with young ladies of this category. He had known, here in Europe, two or three women—persons older than Miss Daisy Miller, and provided, for respectability's sake, with husbands—who were great coquettes—dangerous, terrible women, with whom one's relations were liable to take a serious turn. But this young girl was not a coquette in that sense; she was very unsophisticated; she was only a pretty American flirt. Winterbourne was almost grateful for having found the formula that applied to Miss Daisy Miller. He leaned back in his seat; he remarked to himself that she had the most charming nose he had ever seen; he wondered what were the regular conditions and limitations of one's intercourse with a pretty American flirt. It presently became apparent that he was on the way to learn.

"Have you been to that old castle?" asked the young girl, pointing with her parasol to the far-gleaming walls of the Château de Chillon.

"Yes, formerly, more than once," said Winterbourne. "You too, I suppose, have seen it?"

1. Misconduct (French).

"No; we haven't been there. I want to go there dreadfully. Of course I mean to go there. I wouldn't go away from here without having seen that old castle."

"It's a very pretty excursion," said Winterbourne, "and very easy to make. You can drive, you know, or you can go by the little steamer."

"You can go in the cars," said Miss Miller.

"Yes; you can go in the cars," Winterbourne assented.

"Our courier[2] says they take you right up to the castle," the young girl continued. "We were going last week; but my mother gave out. She suffers dreadfully from dyspepsia. She said she couldn't go. Randolph wouldn't go either; he says he doesn't think much of old castles. But I guess we'll go this week, if we can get Randolph."

"Your brother is not interested in ancient monuments?" Winterbourne inquired, smiling.

"He says he don't care much about old castles. He's only nine. He wants to stay at the hotel. Mother's afraid to leave him alone, and the courier won't stay with him; so we haven't been to many places. But it will be too bad if we don't go up there." And Miss Miller pointed again at the Château de Chillon.

"I should think it might be arranged," said Winterbourne. "Couldn't you get some one to stay—for the afternoon—with Randolph?"

Miss Miller looked at him a moment; and then, very placidly—"I wish *you* would stay with him!" she said.

Winterbourne hesitated a moment. "I would much rather go to Chillon with you."

"With me?" asked the young girl, with the same placidity.

She didn't rise, blushing, as a young girl at Geneva would have done; and yet Winterbourne, conscious that he had been very bold, thought it possible she was offended. "With your mother," he answered very respectfully.

But it seemed that both his audacity and his respect were lost upon Miss Daisy Miller. "I guess my mother won't go, after all," she said. "She don't like to ride round in the afternoon. But did you really mean what you said just now; that you would like to go up there?"

"Most earnestly," Winterbourne declared.

"Then we may arrange it. If mother will stay with Randolph, I guess Eugenio will."

"Eugenio?" the young man inquired.

"Eugenio's our courier. He doesn't like to stay with Randolph; he's the most fastidious man I ever saw. But he's a splendid courier. I guess he'll stay at home with Randolph if mother does, and then we can go to the castle."

Winterbourne reflected for an instant as lucidly as possible—"we" could only mean Miss Daisy Miller and himself. This programme seemed almost too agreeable for credence; he felt as if he ought to kiss the young lady's hand. Possibly he would have done so—and quite spoiled the project; but at this moment another person—presumably Eugenio—appeared. A tall, handsome man, with superb whiskers, wearing a velvet morning-coat and a brilliant watch-chain, approached Miss Miller, looking sharply at her companion. "Oh, Eugenio!" said Miss Miller, with the friendliest accent.

Eugenio had looked at Winterbourne from head to foot; he now bowed

2. Social guide.

gravely to the young lady. "I have the honor to inform mademoiselle that luncheon is upon the table."

Miss Miller slowly rose. "See here, Eugenio," she said. "I'm going to that old castle, any way."

"To the Château de Chillon, mademoiselle?" the courier inquired. "Mademoiselle had made arrangements?" he added, in a tone which struck Winterbourne as very impertinent.

Eugenio's tone apparently threw, even to Miss Miller's own apprehension, a slightly ironical light upon the young girl's situation. She turned to Winterbourne, blushing a little—a very little. "You won't back out?" she said.

"I shall not be happy till we go!" he protested.

"And you are staying in this hotel?" she went on. "And you are really an American?"

The courier stood looking at Winterbourne, offensively. The young man, at least, thought his manner of looking an offence to Miss Miller; it conveyed an imputation that she "picked up" acquaintances. "I shall have the honor of presenting to you a person who will tell you all about me," he said smiling, and referring to his aunt.

"Oh well, we'll go some day," said Miss Miller. And she gave him a smile and turned away. She put up her parasol and walked back to the inn beside Eugenio. Winterbourne stood looking after her; and as she moved away, drawing her muslin furbelows over the gravel, said to himself that she had the *tournure* of a princess.

## II

He had, however, engaged to do more than proved feasible, in promising to present his aunt, Mrs. Costello, to Miss Daisy Miller. As soon as the former lady had got better of her headache he waited upon her in her apartment; and, after the proper inquiries in regard to her health, he asked her if she had observed, in the hotel, an American family—a mamma, a daughter, and a little boy.

"And a courier?" said Mrs. Costello. "Oh, yes, I have observed them. Seen them—heard them—and kept out of their way." Mrs. Costello was a widow with a fortune; a person of much distinction, who frequently intimated that, if she were not so dreadfully liable to sick-headaches, she would probably have left a deeper impress upon her time. She had a long pale face, a high nose, and a great deal of very striking white hair, which she wore in large puffs and *rouleaux* over the top of her head. She had two sons married in New York, and another who was now in Europe. This young man was amusing himself at Homburg,[3] and, though he was on his travels, was rarely perceived to visit any particular city at the moment selected by his mother for her own appearance there. Her nephew, who had come up to Vevey expressly to see her, was therefore more attentive than those who, as she said, were nearer to her. He had imbibed at Geneva the idea that one must always be attentive to one's aunt. Mrs. Costello had not seen him for many years, and she was greatly pleased with him, manifesting her approbation by initiating him into many of the secrets of that social sway which, as she gave him to understand, she

---

3. A resort in Germany.

exerted in the American capital. She admitted that she was very exclusive; but, if he were acquainted with New York, he would see that one had to be. And her picture of the minutely hierarchical constitution of the society of that city, which she presented to him in many different lights, was, to Winterbourne's imagination, almost oppressively striking.

He immediately perceived, from her tone, that Miss Daisy Miller's place in the social scale was low. "I am afraid you don't approve of them," he said.

"They are very common," Mrs. Costello declared. "They are the sort of Americans that one does one's duty by not—not accepting."

"Ah, you don't accept them?" said the young man.

"I can't, my dear Frederick. I would if I could, but I can't."

"The young girl is very pretty," said Winterbourne, in a moment.

"Of course she's pretty. But she is very common."

"I see what you mean, of course," said Winterbourne, after another pause.

"She has that charming look that they all have," his aunt resumed. "I can't think where they pick it up; and she dresses in perfection—no, you don't know how well she dresses. I can't think where they get their taste."

"But, my dear aunt, she is not, after all, a Comanche savage."

"She is a young lady," said Mrs. Costello, "who has an intimacy with her mamma's courier?"

"An intimacy with the courier?" the young man demanded.

"Oh, the mother is just as bad! They treat the courier like a familiar friend—like a gentleman. I shouldn't wonder if he dines with them. Very likely they have never seen a man with such good manners, such fine clothes, so like a gentleman. He probably corresponds to the young lady's idea of a Count. He sits with them in the garden, in the evening. I think he smokes."

Winterbourne listened with interest to these disclosures; they helped him to make up his mind about Miss Daisy. Evidently she was rather wild. "Well," he said, "I am not a courier, and yet she was very charming to me."

"You had better have said at first," said Mrs. Costello with dignity, "that you had made her acquaintance."

"We simply met in the garden, and we talked a bit."

"*Tout bonnement!* And pray what did you say?"

"I said I should take the liberty of introducing her to my admirable aunt."

"I am much obliged to you."

"It was to guarantee my respectability," said Winterbourne.

"And pray who is to guarantee hers?"

"Ah, you are cruel!" said the young man. "She's a very nice girl."

"You don't say that as if you believed it," Mrs. Costello observed.

"She is completely uncultivated," Winterbourne went on. "But she is wonderfully pretty, and, in short, she is very nice. To prove that I believe it, I am going to take her to the Château de Chillon."

"You two are going off there together? I should say it proved just the contrary. How long had you known her, may I ask, when this interesting project was formed. You haven't been twenty-four hours in the house."

"I had known her half-an-hour!" said Winterbourne, smiling.

"Dear me!" cried Mrs Costello. "What a dreadful girl!"

Her nephew was silent for some moments.

"You really think, then," he began earnestly, and with a desire for trustworthy information—"you really think that—" But he paused again.

"Think what, sir," said his aunt.

"That she is the sort of young lady who expects a man—sooner or later—to carry her off?"

"I haven't the least idea what such young ladies expect a man to do. But I really think that you had better not meddle with little American girls that are uncultivated, as you call them. You have lived too long out of the country. You will be sure to make some great mistake. You are too innocent."

"My dear aunt, I am not so innocent," said Winterbourne, smiling and curling his moustache.

"You are too guilty, then?"

Winterbourne continued to curl his moustache, meditatively. "You won't let the poor girl know you then?" he asked at last.

"Is it literally true that she is going to the Château de Chillon with you?"

"I think that she fully intends it."

"Then, my dear Frederick," said Mrs. Costello, "I must decline the honor of her acquaintance. I am an old woman, but I am not too old—thank Heaven—to be shocked!"

"But don't they all do these things—the young girls in America?" Winterbourne inquired.

Mrs. Costello stared a moment. "I should like to see my granddaughters do them!" she declared, grimly.

This seemed to throw some light upon the matter, for Winterbourne remembered to have heard that his pretty cousins in New York were "tremendous flirts." If, therefore, Miss Daisy Miller exceeded the liberal license allowed to these young ladies, it was probable that anything might be expected of her. Winterbourne was impatient to see her again, and he was vexed with himself that, by instinct, he should not appreciate her justly.

Though he was impatient to see her, he hardly knew what he should say to her about his aunt's refusal to become acquainted with her; but he discovered, promptly enough, that with Miss Daisy Miller there was no great need of walking on tiptoe. He found her that evening in the garden, wandering about in the warm starlight, like an indolent sylph, and swinging to and fro the largest fan he had ever beheld. It was ten o'clock. He had dined with his aunt, had been sitting with her since dinner, and had just taken leave of her till the morrow. Miss Daisy Miller seemed very glad to see him; she declared it was the longest evening she had ever passed.

"Have you been all alone?" he asked.

"I have been walking round with mother. But mother gets tired walking round," she answered.

"Has she gone to bed?"

"No; she doesn't like to go to bed," said the young girl. "She doesn't sleep—not three hours. She says she doesn't know how she lives. She's dreadfully nervous. I guess she sleeps more than she thinks. She's gone somewhere after Randolph; she wants to try to get him to go to bed. He doesn't like to go to bed."

"Let us hope she will persuade him," observed Winterbourne.

"She will talk to him all she can; but he doesn't like her to talk to him," said Miss Daisy, opening her fan. "She's going to try to get Eugenio to talk to him. But he isn't afraid of Eugenio. Eugenio's a splendid courier, but he can't make much impression on Randolph! I don't believe he'll go to bed before eleven."

It appeared that Randolph's vigil was in fact triumphantly prolonged, for Winterbourne strolled about with the young girl for some time without meeting her mother. "I have been looking round for that lady you want to introduce me to," his companion resumed. "She's your aunt." Then, on Winterbourne's admitting the fact, and expressing some curiosity as to how she had learned it, she said she had heard all about Mrs. Costello from the chambermaid. She wasvery quiet and very *comme il faut;*[4] she wore white puffs; she spoke to no one, and she never dined at the *table d'hôte*. Every two days she had a headache. "Ithink that's a lovely description, headache and all!" said Miss Daisy, chattering along in her thin, gay voice. "I want to know her ever so much. I know just what *your* aunt would be; I know I should like her. She would be very exclusive. I like a lady to be exclusive; I'm dying to be exclusive myself. Well, we *are* exclusive, mother and I. We don't speak to every one—or they don't speak to us. I suppose it's about the same thing. Any way, I shall be ever so glad to know your aunt."

Winterbourne was embarrassed. "She would be most happy," he said, "but I am afraid those headaches will interfere."

The young girl looked at him through the dusk. "But I suppose she doesn't have a headache every day," she said, sympathetically.

Winterbourne was silent a moment. "She tells me she does," he answered at last—not knowing what to say.

Miss Daisy Miller stopped and stood looking at him. Her prettiness was still visible in the darkness; she was opening and closing her enormous fan. "She doesn't want to know me!" she said suddenly. "Why don't you say so? You needn't be afraid. I'm not afraid!" And she gave a little laugh.

Winterbourne fancied there was a tremor in her voice; he was touched, shocked, mortified by it. "My dear young lady," he protested, "she knows no one. It's her wretched health."

The young girl walked on a few steps, laughing still. "You needn't be afraid," she repeated. "Why should she want to know me?" Then she paused again; she was close to the parapet of the garden, and in front of her was the starlit lake. There was a vague sheen upon its surface, and in the distance were dimly-seen mountain forms. Daisy Miller looked out upon the mysterious prospect, and then she gave another little laugh. "Gracious! she *is* exclusive!" she said. Winterbourne wondered whether she was seriously wounded, and for a moment almost wished that her sense of injury might be such as to make it becoming in him to attempt to reassure and comfort her. He had a pleasant sense that she would be very approachable for consolatory purposes. He felt then, for the instant, quite ready to sacrifice his aunt, conversationally; to admit that she was a proud, rude woman, and to declare that they needn't mind her. But before he had time to commit himself to this perilous mixture of gallantry and impiety, the young lady, resuming her walk, gave an exclamation in quite another tone. "Well; here's mother! I guess she hasn't got Randolph to go to bed." The figure of a lady appeared, at a distance, very indistinct in the darkness, and advancing with a slow and wavering movement. Suddenly it seemed to pause.

"Are you sure it is your mother? Can you distinguish her in this thick dusk?" Winterbourne asked.

4. Well mannered (French).

"Well!" cried Miss Daisy Miller, with a laugh, "I guess I know my own mother. And when she has got on my shawl, too! She is always wearing my things."

The lady in question, ceasing to advance, hovered vaguely about the spot at which she had checked her steps.

"I am afraid your mother doesn't see you," said Winterbourne. "Or perhaps," he added—thinking, with Miss Miller, the joke permissible—"perhaps she feels guilty about your shawl."

"Oh, it's a fearful old thing!" the young girl replied, serenely. "I told her she could wear it. She won't come here, because she sees you."

"Ah, then," said Winterbourne, "I had better leave you."

"Oh, no; come on!" urged Miss Daisy Miller.

"I'm afraid your mother doesn't approve of my walking with you."

Miss Miller gave him a serious glance. "It isn't for me; it's for you—that is, it's for her. Well; I don't know who it's for! But mother doesn't like any of my gentlemen friends. She's right down timid. She always makes a fuss if I introduce a gentleman. But I do introduce them—almost always. If I didn't introduce my gentlemen friends to mother," the young girl added, in her little soft, flat monotone, "I shouldn't think I was natural." .

"To introduce me," said Winterbourne, "you must know my name." And he proceeded to pronounce it.

"Oh, dear; I can't say all that!" said his companion, with a laugh. But by this time they had come up to Mrs. Miller, who, as they drew near, walked to the parapet of the garden and leaned upon it, looking intently at the lake and turning her back upon them. "Mother!" said the young girl, in a tone of decision. Upon this the elderly lady turned round. "Mr. Winterbourne," said Miss Daisy Miller, introducing the young man very frankly and prettily. "Common" she was, as Mrs. Costello had pronounced her; yet it was a wonder to Winterbourne that, with her commonness, she had a singularly delicate grace.

Her mother was a small, spare, light person, with a wandering eye, a very exiguous nose, and a large forehead, decorated with a certain amount of thin, much-frizzled hair. Like her daughter, Mrs. Miller was dressed with extreme elegance; she had enormous diamonds in her ears. So far as Winterbourne could observe, she gave him no greeting—she certainly was not looking at him. Daisy was near her, pulling her shawl straight. "What are you doing, poking round here?" this young lady inquired; but by no means with that harshness of accent which her choice of words may imply.

"I don't know," said her mother, turning towards the lake again.

"I shouldn't think you'd want that shawl!" Daisy exclaimed.

"Well—I do!" her mother answered, with a little laugh.

"Did you get Randolph to go to bed?" asked the young girl.

"No; I couldn't induce him," said Mrs. Miller, very gently. "He wants to talk to the waiter. He likes to talk to that waiter."

"I was telling Mr. Winterbourne," the young girl went on; and to the young man's ear her tone might have indicated that she had been uttering his name all her life.

"Oh, yes!" said Winterbourne; "I have the pleasure of knowing your son."

Randolph's mamma was silent; she turned her attention to the lake. But at last she spoke. "Well, I don't see how he lives!"

"Anyhow, it isn't so bad as it was at Dover," said Daisy Miller.

"And what occurred at Dover?" Winterbourne asked.

"He wouldn't go to bed at all. I guess he sat up all night—in the public parlour. He wasn't in bed at twelve o'clock: I know that."

"It was half-past twelve," declared Mrs. Miller, with mild emphasis.

"Does he sleep much during the day?" Winterbourne demanded.

"I guess he doesn't sleep much," Daisy rejoined.

"I wish he would!" said her mother. "It seems as if he couldn't."

"I think he's real tiresome," Daisy pursued.

Then, for some moments, there was silence. "Well, Daisy Miller," said the elder lady, presently, "I shouldn't think you'd want to talk against your own brother!"

"Well, he *is* tiresome, mother," said Daisy, quite without the asperity of a retort.

"He's only nine," urged Mrs. Miller.

"Well, he wouldn't go to that castle," said the young girl. "I'm going there with Mr. Winterbourne."

To this announcement, very placidly made, Daisy's mamma offered no response. Winterbourne took for granted that she deeply disapproved of the projected excursion; but he said to himself that she was a simple, easily managed person, and that a few deferential protestations would take the edge from her displeasure. "Yes," he began; "your daughter has kindly allowed me the honor of being her guide."

Mrs. Miller's wandering eyes attached themselves, with a sort of appealing air, to Daisy, who, however, strolled a few steps farther, gently humming to herself. "I presume you will go in the cars," said her mother.

"Yes; or in the boat," said Winterbourne.

"Well, of course, I don't know," Mrs. Miller rejoined. "I have never been to that castle."

"It is a pity you shouldn't go," said Winterbourne, beginning to feel reassured as to her opposition. And yet he was quite prepared to find that, as a matter of course, she meant to accompany her daughter.

"We've been thinking ever so much about going," she pursued; "but it seems as if we couldn't. Of course Daisy—she wants to go round. But there's a lady here—I don't know her name—she says she shouldn't think we'd want to go to see castles *here*; she should think we'd want to wait till we got to Italy. It seems as if there would be so many there," continued Mrs. Miller, with an air of increasing confidence. "Of course, we only want to see the principal ones. We visited several in England," she presently added.

"Ah, yes! in England there are beautiful castles," said Winterbourne. "But Chillon, here, is very well worth seeing."

"Well, if Daisy feels up to it—," said Mrs. Miller, in a tone impregnated with a sense of the magnitude of the enterprise. "It seems as if there was nothing she wouldn't undertake."

"Oh, I think she'll enjoy it!" Winterbourne declared. And he desired more and more to make it a certainty that he was to have the privilege of a tête-à-tête with the young lady, who was still strolling along in front of them, softly vocalizing. "You are not disposed, madam," he inquired, "to undertake it yourself?"

Daisy's mother looked at him, an instant, askance, and then walked forward in silence. Then—"I guess she had better go alone," she said, simply.

Winterbourne observed to himself that this was a very different type of maternity from that of the vigilant matrons who massed themselves in the forefront of social intercourse in the dark old city at the other end of the lake. But his meditations were interrupted by hearing his name very distinctly pronounced by Mrs. Miller's unprotected daughter.

"Mr. Winterbourne!" murmured Daisy.

"Mademoiselle!" said the young man.

"Don't you want to take me out in a boat?"

"At present?" he asked.

"Of course!" said Daisy.

"Well, Annie Miller!" exclaimed her mother.

"I beg you, madam, to let her go," said Winterbourne, ardently; for he had never yet enjoyed the sensation of guiding through the summer starlight a skiff freighted with a fresh and beautiful young girl.

"I shouldn't think she'd want to," said her mother. "I should think she'd rather go indoors."

"I'm sure Mr. Winterbourne wants to take me," Daisy declared. "He's so awfully devoted!"

"I will row you over to Chillon, in the starlight."

"I don't believe it!" said Daisy.

"Well!" ejaculated the elderly lady again.

"You haven't spoken to me for half-an-hour," her daughter went on.

"I have been having some very pleasant conversation with your mother," said Winterbourne.

"Well; I want you to take me out in a boat!" Daisy repeated. They had all stopped, and she had turned round and was looking at Winterbourne. Her face wore a charming smile, her pretty eyes were gleaming, she was swinging her great fan about. No; it's impossible to be prettier than that, thought Winterbourne.

"There are half-a-dozen boats moored at that landing-place," he said, pointing to certain steps which descended from the garden to the lake. "If you will do me the honor to accept my arm, we will go and select one of them."

Daisy stood there smiling; she threw back her head and gave a little light laugh. "I like a gentleman to be formal!" she declared.

"I assure you it's a formal offer."

"I was bound I would make you say something," Daisy went on.

"You see it's not very difficult," said Winterbourne. "But I am afraid you are chaffing me."

"I think not, sir," remarked Mrs. Miller, very gently.

"Do, then, let me give you a row," he said to the young girl.

"It's quite lovely, the way you say that!" said Daisy.

"It will be still more lovely to do it."

"Yes, it would be lovely!" said Daisy. But she made no movement to accompany him; she only stood there laughing.

"I should think you had better find out what time it is," interposed her mother.

"It is eleven o'clock, madam," said a voice, with a foreign accent, out of the neighboring darkness; and Winterbourne, turning, perceived the florid personage who was in attendance upon the two ladies. He had apparently just approached.

"Oh, Eugenio," said Daisy, "I am going out in a boat!"

Eugenio bowed. "At eleven o'clock, mademoiselle?"

"I am going with Mr. Winterbourne. This very minute."

"Do tell her she can't," said Mrs. Miller to the courier.

"I think you had better not go out in a boat, mademoiselle," Eugenio declared.

Winterbourne wished to Heaven this pretty girl were not so familiar with her courier; but he said nothing.

"I suppose you don't think it's proper!" Daisy exclaimed, "Eugenio doesn't think anything's proper."

"I am at your service," said Winterbourne.

"Does mademoiselle propose to go alone?" asked Eugenio of Mrs. Miller.

"Oh, no; with this gentleman!" answered Daisy's mamma.

The courier looked for a moment at Winterbourne—the latter thought he was smiling—and then, solemnly, with a bow, "As mademoiselle pleases!" he said.

"Oh, I hoped you would make a fuss!" said Daisy. "I don't care to go now."

"I myself shall make a fuss if you don't go," said Winterbourne.

"That's all I want—a little fuss!" And the young girl began to laugh again.

"Mr. Randolph has gone to bed!" the courier announced, frigidly.

"Oh, Daisy; now we can go!" said Mrs. Miller.

Daisy turned away from Winterbourne, looking at him, smiling and fanning herself. "Good night," she said; "I hope you are disappointed, or disgusted, or something!"

He looked at her, taking the hand she offered him. "I am puzzled," he answered.

"Well; I hope it won't keep you awake!" she said, very smartly; and, under the escort of the privileged Eugenio, the two ladies passed towards the house.

Winterbourne stood looking after them; he was indeed puzzled. He lingered beside the lake for a quarter of an hour, turning over the mystery of the young girl's sudden familiarities and caprices. But the only very definite conclusion he came to was that he should enjoy deucedly "going off" with her somewhere.

Two days afterwards he went off with her to the Castle of Chillon. He waited for her in the large hall of the hotel, where the couriers, the servants, the foreign tourists were lounging about and staring. It was not the place he would have chosen, but she had appointed it. She came tripping downstairs, buttoning her long gloves, squeezing her folded parasol against her pretty figure, dressed in the perfection of a soberly elegant travelling-costume. Winterbourne was a man of imagination and, as our ancestors used to say, of sensibility; as he looked at her dress and, on the great staircase, her little rapid, confiding step, he felt as if there were something romantic going forward. He could have believed he was going to elope with her. He passed out with her among all the idle people that were assembled there; they were all looking at her very hard; she had begun to chatter as soon as she joined him. Winterbourne's preference had been that they should be conveyed to Chillon in a carriage; but she expressed a lively wish to go in the little steamer; she declared that she had a passion for steamboats. There was always such a lovely breeze upon the water, and you saw such lots of people. The sail was not long, but Winterbourne's companion found time to say a great many things. To the young man himself their little excursion was so much of an escapade—an adventure—that, even allowing for her habitual sense of freedom, he had some expectation of seeing her regard it in the same way. But it must be confessed that, in this particular, he was disappointed. Daisy Miller was extremely animated, she was in charming spirits; but she was apparently not at all excited; she was not fluttered; she avoided neither his eyes nor those of any one else; she blushed neither when she looked at him nor when she saw that people were looking at her. People continued to look at her a great deal, and Winterbourne took much satisfaction in his pretty companion's distinguished air. He had been a little afraid that she would talk loud, laugh overmuch, and even, perhaps, desire to move about the boat a good deal. But he quite forgot his fears; he sat smiling, with his eyes upon her face, while, without moving from her place, she delivered herself of a great number of original reflections. It was the most charming garrulity he had ever heard. He had assented to the idea that she was "common"; but was she so, after all, or was he simply getting used to her commonness? Her conversation was chiefly of what metaphysicans term the objective cast; but every now and then it took a subjective turn.

"What on *earth* are you so grave about?" she suddenly demanded, fixing her agreeable eyes upon Winterbourne's.

"Am I grave?" he asked. "I had an idea I was grinning from ear to ear."

"You look as if you were taking me to a funeral. If that's a grin, your ears are very near together."

"Should you like me to dance a hornpipe on the deck?"

"Pray do, and I'll carry round your hat. It will pay the expenses of our journey."

"I never was better pleased in my life," murmured Winterbourne.

She looked at him a moment, and then burst into a little laugh. "I like to make you say those things! You're a queer mixture!"

In the castle, after they had landed, the subjective element decidedly prevailed. Daisy tripped about the vaulted chambers, rustled her skirts in the corkscrew staircases, flirted back with a pretty little cry and a shudder from the edge of the *oubliettes*,[5] and turned a singularly well-shaped ear to everything that Winterbourne told her about the place. But he saw that she cared very little for feudal antiquities, and that the dusky traditions of Chillon made but a slight impression upon her. They had the good fortune to have been able to walk about without other companionship than that of the custodian; and Winterbourne arranged with this functionary that they should not be hurried—that they should linger and pause wherever they chose. The custodian interpreted the bargain generously—Winterbourne, on his side, had been generous—and ended by leaving them quite to themselves. Miss Miller's observations were not remarkable for logical consistency; for anything she wanted to say she was sure to find a pretext. She found a great many pretexts in the rugged embrasures of Chillon for asking Winterbourne sudden questions about himself—his family, his previous history, his tastes, his habits, his intentions—and for supplying information upon corresponding points in her own personality. Of her own tastes, habits, and intentions Miss Miller was prepared to give the most definite, and indeed the most favourable, account.

"Well; I hope you know enough!" she said to her companion, after he had told her the history of the unhappy Bonivard.[6] "I never saw a man that knew so much!" The history of Bonivard had evidently, as they say, gone into one

5. Secret pitlike dungeons with an opening only at the top; places where one is forgotten (French).
6. Hero of Byron's poem *The Prisoner of Chillon;*

François de Bonivard (1496–1570), Swiss patriot and martyr, was confined for seven years in the Castle of Chillon.

ear and out of the other. But Daisy went on to say that she wished Winterbourne would travel with them and "go round" with them; they might know something, in that case. "Don't you want to come and teach Randolph?" she asked. Winterbourne said that nothing could possibly please him so much; but that he had unfortunately other occupations. "Other occupations? I don't believe it!" said Miss Daisy . "What do you mean? You are not in business." The young man admitted that he was not in business; but he had engagements which, even within a day or two, would force him to go back to Geneva. "Oh, bother!" she said. "I don't believe it!" and she began to talk about something else. But a few moments later, when he was pointing out to her the pretty design of an antique fireplace, she broke out irrelevantly, "You don't mean to say you are going back to Geneva?"

"It is a melancholy fact that I shall have to return to Geneva to-morrow."

"Well, Mr. Winterbourne," said Daisy; "I think you're horrid!"

"Oh, don't say such dreadful things!" said Winterbourne— "just at the last."

"The last!" cried the young girl; "I call it the first. I have half a mind to leave you here and go straight back to the hotel alone." And for the next ten minutes she did nothing but call him horrid. Poor Winterbourne was fairly bewildered; no young lady had as yet done him the honor to be so agitated by the announcement of his movements. His companion, after this, ceased to pay any attention to the curiosities of Chillon or the beauties of the lake; she opened fire upon the mysterious charmer in Geneva, whom she appeared to have instantly taken it for granted that he was hurrying back to see. How did Miss Daisy Miller know that there was a charmer in Geneva? Winterbourne, who denied the existence of such a person, was quite unable to discover; and he was divided between amazement at the rapidity of her induction and amusement at the frankness of her *persiflage*. She seemed to him, in all this, an extraordinary mixture of innocence and crudity. "Does she never allow you more than three days at a time?" asked Daisy, ironically. "Doesn't she give you a vacation in summer? There's no one so hard worked but they can get leave to go off somewhere at this season. I suppose, if you stay another day, she'll come after you in the boat. Do wait over till Friday, and I will go down to the landing to see her arrive!" Winterbourne began to think he had been wrong to feel disappointed in the temper in which the young lady had embarked. If he had missed the personal accent, the personal accent was now making its appearance. It sounded very distinctly, at last, in her telling him she would stop "teasing" him if he would promise her solemnly to come down to Rome in the winter.

"That's not a difficult promise to make," said Winterbourne. "My aunt has taken an apartment in Rome for the winter, and has already asked me to come and see her."

"I don't want you to come for your aunt," said Daisy; "I want you to come for me." And this was the only allusion that the young man was ever to hear her make to his invidious kinswoman. He declared that, at any rate, he would certainly come. After this Daisy stopped teasing. Winterbourne took a carriage, and they drove back to Vevey in the dusk; the young girl was very quiet.

In the evening Winterbourne mentioned to Mrs. Costello that he had spent the afternoon at Chillon, with Miss Daisy Miller.

"The Americans—of the courier?" asked this lady.

"Ah, happily," said Winterbourne, "the courier stayed at home."

"She went with you all alone?"

"All alone."

Mrs. Costello sniffed a little at her smelling-bottle. "And that," she exclaimed, "is the young person you wanted me to know!"

## III

Winterbourne, who had returned to Geneva the day after his excursion to Chillon, went to Rome towards the end of January. His aunt had been established there for several weeks, and he had received a couple of letters from her. "Those people you were so devoted to last summer at Vevey have turned up here, courier and all," she wrote. "They seem to have made several acquaintances, but the courier continues to be the most *intime*. The young lady, however, is also very intimate with some third-rate Italians, with whom she rackets about in a way that makes much talk. Bring me that pretty novel of Cherbuliez's[7]—'Paule Méré'—and don't come later than the 23rd."

In the natural course of events, Winterbourne, on arriving in Rome, would presently have ascertained Mrs. Miller's address at the American banker's and have gone to pay his compliments to Miss Daisy. "After what happened at Vevey I certainly think I may call upon them," he said to Mrs. Costello.

"If, after what happens—at Vevey and everywhere—you desire to keep up the acquaintance, you are very welcome. Of course a man may know every one. Men are welcome to the privilege!"

"Pray what is it that happens—here, for instance?" Winterbourne demanded.

"The girl goes about alone with her foreigners. As to what happens farther, you must apply elsewhere for information. She has picked up half-a-dozen of the regular Roman fortune-hunters, and she takes them about to people's houses. When she comes to a party she brings with her a gentleman with a good deal of manner and a wonderful moustache."

"And where is the mother?"

"I haven't the least idea. They are very dreadful people."

Winterbourne meditated a moment. "They are very ignorant—very innocent only. Depend upon it they are not bad."

"They are hopelessly vulgar," said Mrs. Costello. "Whether or no being hopelessly vulgar is being 'bad' is a question for the metaphysicians. They are bad enough to dislike, at any rate; and for this short life that is quite enough."

The news that Daisy Miller was surrounded by half-a-dozen wonderful moustaches checked Winterbourne's impulse to go straightway to see her. He had perhaps not definitely flattered himself that he had made an ineffaceable impression upon her heart, but he was annoyed at hearing of a state of affairs so little in harmony with an image that had lately flitted in and out of his own meditations; the image of a very pretty girl looking out of an old Roman window and asking herself urgently when Mr. Winterbourne would arrive. If, however, he determined to wait a little before reminding Miss Miller of his claims to her consideration, he went very soon to call upon two or three other friends. One of these friends was an American lady who had spent several

---

7. Victor Cherbuliez (1829–1899), which James spelled "Cherbuliex," a minor French novelist of Swiss origin.

winters at Geneva, when she had placed her children at school. She was a very accomplished woman and she lived in the Via Gregoriana. Winterbourne found her in a little crimson drawing-room, on a third floor; the room was filled with southern sunshine. He had not been there ten minutes when the servant came in, announcing "Madame Mila!" This announcement was presently followed by the entrance of little Randolph Miller, who stopped in the middle of the room and stood staring at Winterbourne. An instant later his pretty sister crossed the threshold; and then, after a considerable interval, Mrs. Miller slowly advanced.

"I know you!" said Randolph.

"I'm sure you know a great many things," exclaimed Winterbourne, taking him by the hand. "How is your education coming on?"

Daisy was exchanging greetings very prettily with her hostess; but when she heard Winterbourne's voice she quickly turned her head. "Well, I declare!" she said.

"I told you I should come, you know," Winterbourne rejoined smiling.

"Well—I didn't believe it," said Miss Daisy.

"I am much obliged to you," laughed the young man.

"You might have come to see me!" said Daisy.

"I arrived only yesterday."

"I don't believe that!" the young girl declared.

Winterbourne turned with a protesting smile to her mother; but this lady evaded his glance, and seating herself, fixed her eyes upon her son. "We've got a bigger place than this," said Randolph. "It's all gold on the walls."

Mrs. Miller turned uneasily in her chair. "I told you if I were to bring you, you would say something!" she murmured.

"I told *you*!" Randolph exclaimed. "I tell *you*, sir!" he added jocosely, giving Winterbourne a thump on the knee. "It *is* bigger, too!"

Daisy had entered upon a lively conversation with her hostess; Winterbourne judged it becoming to address a few words to her mother. "I hope you have been well since we parted at Vevey," he said.

Mrs. Miller now certainly looked at him—at his chin. "Not very well, sir," she answered.

"She's got the dyspepsia," said Randolph. "I've got it too. Father's got it. I've got it worst!"

This announcement, instead of embarrassing Mrs. Miller, seemed to relieve her. "I suffer from the liver," she said. "I think it's the climate; it's less bracing than Schenectady, especially in the winter season. I don't know whether you know we reside at Schenectady. I was saying to Daisy that I certainly hadn't found any one like Dr. Davis, and I didn't believe I should. Oh, at Schenectady, he stands first; they think everything of him. He has so much to do, and yet there was nothing he wouldn't do for me. He said he never saw anything like my dyspepsia, but he was bound to cure it. I'm sure there was nothing he wouldn't try. He was just going to try something new when we came off. Mr. Miller wanted Daisy to see Europe for herself. But I wrote to Mr. Miller that it seems as if I couldn't get on without Dr. Davis. At Schenectady he stands at the very top; and there's a great deal of sickness there, too. It affects my sleep."

Winterbourne had a good deal of pathological gossip with Dr. Davis's patient, during which Daisy chattered unremittingly to her own companion. The young man asked Mrs. Miller how she was pleased with Rome. "Well, I must say I am disappointed," she answered. "We had heard so much about it; I suppose we had heard too much. But we couldn't help that. We had been led to expect something different."

"Ah, wait a little, and you will become very fond of it," said Winterbourne.

"I hate it worse and worse every day!" cried Randolph.

"You are like the infant Hannibal,"[8] said Winterbourne.

"No, I ain't!" Randolph declared, at a venture.

"You are not much like an infant," said his mother. "But we have seen places," she resumed, "that I should put a long way before Rome." And in reply to Winterbourne's interrogation, "There's Zurich," she observed; "I think Zurich is lovely; and we hadn't heard half so much about it."

"The best place we've seen is the City of Richmond!" said Randolph.

"He means the ship," his mother explained. "We crossed in that ship. Randolph had a good time on the City of Richmond."

"It's the best place I've seen," the child repeated. "Only it was turned the wrong way."

"Well, we've got to turn the right way some time," said Mrs. Miller, with a little laugh. Winterbourne expressed the hope that her daughter at least found some gratification in Rome, and she declared that Daisy was quite carried away. "It's on account of the society—the society's splendid. She goes round everywhere; she has made a great number of acquaintances. Of course she goes round more than I do. I must say they have been very sociable; they have taken her right in. And then she knows a great many gentlemen. Oh, she thinks there's nothing like Rome. Of course, it's a great deal pleasanter for a young lady if she knows plenty of gentlemen."

By this time Daisy had turned her attention again to Winterbourne. "I've been telling Mrs. Walker how mean you were!" the young girl announced.

"And what is the evidence you have offered?" asked Winterbourne, rather annoyed at Miss Miller's want of appreciation of the zeal of an admirer who on his way down to Rome had stopped neither at Bologna nor at Florence, simply because of a certain sentimental impatience. He remembered that a cynical compatriot had once told him that American women—the pretty ones, and this gave a largeness to the axiom—were at once the most exacting in the world and the least endowed with a sense of indebtedness.

"Why, you were awfully mean at Vevey," said Daisy. "You wouldn't do anything. You wouldn't stay there when I asked you."

"My dearest young lady," cried Winterbourne, with eloquence, "have I come all the way to Rome to encounter your reproaches?"

"Just hear him say that!" said Daisy to her hostess, giving a twist to a bow on this lady's dress. "Did you ever hear anything so quaint?"

"So quaint, my dear?" murmured Mrs. Walker, in the tone of a partisan of Winterbourne.

"Well, I don't know," said Daisy, fingering Mrs. Walker's ribbons. "Mrs. Walker, I want to tell you something."

"Motherr," interposed Randolph, with his rough ends to his words, "I tell you you've got to go. Eugenio'll raise something!"

"I'm not afraid of Eugenio," said Daisy, with a toss of her head. "Look here, Mrs. Walker," she went on, "you know I'm coming to your party."

8. The Carthaginian general (247–183 B.C.) was sworn at his birth to an eternal hatred of Rome.

"I am delighted to hear it."

"I've got a lovely dress."

"I am very sure of that."

"But I want to ask a favor—permission to bring a friend."

"I shall be happy to see any of your friends," said Mrs. Walker, turning with a smile to Mrs. Miller.

"Oh, they are not my friends," answered Daisy's mamma, smiling shyly, in her own fashion. "I never spoke to them!"

"It's an intimate friend of mine—Mr. Giovanelli," said Daisy, without a tremor in her clear little voice or a shadow on her brilliant little face.

Mrs. Walker was silent a moment, she gave a rapid glance at Winterbourne. "I shall be glad to see Mr. Giovanelli," she then said.

"He's an Italian," Daisy pursued, with the prettiest serenity. "He's a great friend of mine—he's the handsomest man in the world—except Mr. Winterbourne! He knows plenty of Italians, but he wants to know some Americans. He thinks ever so much of Americans. He's tremendously clever. He's perfectly lovely!"

It was settled that this brilliant personage should be brought to Mrs. Walker's party, and then Mrs. Miller prepared to take her leave. "I guess we'll go back to the hotel," she said.

"You may go back to the hotel, mother, but I'm going to take a walk," said Daisy.

"She's going to walk with Mr. Giovanelli," Randolph proclaimed.

"I am going to the Pincio," said Daisy, smiling.

"Alone, my dear at this hour?" Mrs. Walker asked. The afternoon was drawing to a close—it was the hour for the throng of carriages and of contemplative pedestrians. "I don't think it's safe, my dear," said Mrs. Walker.

"Neither do I," subjoined Mrs. Miller. "You'll get the fever as sure as you live. Remember what Dr. Davis told you!"

"Give her some medicine before she goes," said Randolph.

The company had risen to its feet; Daisy, still showing her pretty teeth, bent over and kissed her hostess. "Mrs. Walker, you are too perfect," she said. "I'm not going alone; I am going to meet a friend."

"Your friend won't keep you from getting the fever," Mrs. Miller observed.

"Is it Mr. Giovanelli?" asked the hostess.

Winterbourne was watching the girl; at this question his attention quickened. She stood there smiling and smoothing her bonnet-ribbons; she glanced at Winterbourne. Then, while she glanced and smiled, she answered without a shade of hesitation, "Mr. Giovanelli—the beautiful Giovanelli."

"My dear young friend," said Mrs. Walker, taking her hand, pleadingly, "don't walk off to the Pincio at this hour to meet a beautiful Italian."

"Well, he speaks English," said Mrs. Miller.

"Gracious me!" Daisy exclaimed, "I don't want to do anything improper. There's an easy way to settle it." She continued to glance at Winterbourne. "The Pincio is only a hundred yards distant, and if Mr. Winterbourne were as polite as he pretends he would offer to walk with me!"

Winterbourne's politeness hastened to affirm itself, and the young girl gave him gracious leave to accompany her. They passed downstairs before her mother, and at the door Winterbourne perceived Mrs. Miller's carriage drawn up, with the ornamental courier whose acquaintance he had made at Vevey seated within. "Good-bye, Eugenio!" cried Daisy, "I'm going to take a walk." The distance from the Via Gregoriana to the beautiful garden at the other end of the Pincian Hill is, in fact, rapidly traversed. As the day was splendid, however, and the concourse of vehicles, walkers, and loungers numerous, the young Americans found their progress much delayed. This fact was highly agreeable to Winterbourne, in spite of his consciousness of his singular situation. The slow-moving, idly-gazing Roman crowd bestowed much attention upon the extremely pretty young foreign lady who was passing through it upon his arm; and he wondered what on earth had been in Daisy's mind when she proposed to expose herself, unattended, to its appreciation. His own mission, to her sense, apparently, was to consign her to the hands of Mr. Giovanelli; but Winterbourne, at once annoyed and gratified, resolved that he would do no such thing.

"Why haven't you been to see me?" asked Daisy. "You can't get out of that."

"I have had the honor of telling you that I have only just stepped out of the train."

"You must have stayed in the train a good while after it stopped!" cried the young girl, with her little laugh. "I suppose you were asleep. You have had time to go to see Mrs. Walker."

"I knew Mrs. Walker—" Winterbourne began to explain.

"I knew where you knew her. You knew her at Geneva. She told me so. Well, you knew me at Vevey. That's just as good. So you ought to have come." She asked him no other question than this; she began to prattle about her own affairs. "We've got splendid rooms at the hotel; Eugenio says they're the best rooms in Rome. We are going to stay all winter—if we don't die of the fever; and I guess we'll stay then. It's a great deal nicer than I thought; I thought it would be fearfully quiet; I was sure it would be awfully poky. I was sure we should be going round all the time with one of those dreadful old men that explain about the pictures and things. But we only had about a week of that, and now I'm enjoying myself. I know ever so many people, and they are all so charming. The society's extremely select. There are all kinds—English, and Germans, and Italians. I think I like the English best. I like their style of conversation. But there are some lovely Americans. I never saw anything so hospitable. There's something or other every day. There's not much dancing; but I must say I never thought dancing was everything. I was always fond of conversation. I guess I shall have plenty at Mrs. Walker's—her rooms are so small." When they had passed the gate of the Pincian Gardens, Miss Miller began to wonder where Mr. Giovanelli might be. "We had better go straight to that place in front," she said, "where you look at the view."

"I certainly shall not help you to find him," Winterbourne declared.

"Then I shall find him without you," said Miss Daisy.

"You certainly won't leave me!" cried Winterbourne.

She burst into her little laugh. "Are you afraid you'll get lost—or run over? But there's Giovanelli, leaning against that tree. He's staring at the women in the carriages: did you ever see anything so cool?"

Winterbourne perceived at some distance a little man standing with folded arms, nursing his cane. He had a handsome face, an artfully poised hat, a glass in one eye, and a nosegay in his button-hole. Winterbourne looked at him a moment and then said, "Do you mean to speak to that man?"

"Do I mean to speak to him? Why, you don't suppose I mean to communicate by signs?"

"Pray understand, then," said Winterbourne, "that I intend to remain with you."

Daisy stopped and looked at him, without a sign of troubled consciousness in her face; with nothing but the presence of her charming eyes and her happy dimples. "Well, she's a cool one!" thought the young man.

"I don't like the way you say that," said Daisy. "It's too imperious."

"I beg your pardon if I say it wrong. The main point is to give you an idea of my meaning."

The young girl looked at him more gravely, but with eyes that were prettier than ever. "I have never allowed a gentleman to dictate to me, or to interfere with anything I do."

"I think you have made a mistake," said Winterbourne. "You should sometimes listen to a gentleman—the right one?"

Daisy began to laugh again, "I do nothing but listen to gentlemen!" she exclaimed. "Tell me if Mr. Giovanelli is the right one?"

The gentleman with the nosegay in his bosom had now perceived our two friends, and was approaching the young girl with obsequious rapidity. He bowed to Winterbourne as well as to the latter's companion; he had a brilliant smile, an intelligent eye; Winterbourne thought him not a bad-looking fellow. But he nevertheless said to Daisy—"No, he's not the right one."

Daisy evidently had a natural talent for performing introductions; she mentioned the name of each of her companions to the other. She strolled along with one of them on each side of her; Mr. Giovanelli, who spoke English very cleverly—Winterbourne afterwards learned that he had practiced the idiom upon a great many American heiresses—addressed her a great deal of very polite nonsense; he was extremely urbane, and the young American, who said nothing, reflected upon that profundity of Italian cleverness which enables people to appear more gracious in proportion as they are more acutely disappointed. Giovanelli, of course, had counted upon something more intimate; he had not bargained for a party of three. But he kept his temper in a manner which suggested far-stretching intentions. Winterbourne flattered himself that he had taken his measure. "He is not a gentleman," said the young American; "he is only a clever imitation of one. He is a music-master, or a penny-a-liner, or a third-rate artist. Damn his good looks!" Mr. Giovanelli had certainly a very pretty face; but Winterbourne felt a superior indignation at his own lovely fellow-countrywoman's not knowing the difference between a spurious gentleman and a real one. Giovanelli chattered and jested and made himself wonderfully agreeable. It was true that if he was an imitation the imitation was very skillful. "Nevertheless," Winterbourne said to himself, "a nice girl ought to know!" And then he came back to the question whether this was in fact a nice girl. Would a nice girl—even allowing for her being a little American flirt—make a rendezvous with a presumably low-lived foreigner? The rendezvous in this case, indeed, had been in broad daylight, and in the most crowded corner of Rome; but was it not impossible to regard the choice of these circumstances as a proof of extreme cynicism? Singular though it may seem, Winterbourne was vexed that the young girl, in joining her *amoroso*,[9] should not appear more impatient of his own company, and he was vexed because of his inclination. It was impossible to regard her as a perfectly well-conducted young lady; she was wanting in a certain indispensable delicacy. It would therefore

9. Lover (Italian).

simplify matters greatly to be able to treat her as the object of one of those sentiments which are called by romancers "lawless passions." That she should seem to wish to get rid of him would help him to think more lightly of her, and to be able to think more lightly of her would make her much less perplexing. But Daisy, on this occasion, continued to present herself as an inscrutable combination of audacity and innocence.

She had been walking some quarter of an hour, attended by her two cavaliers, and responding in a tone of very childish gaiety, as it seemed to Winterbourne, to the pretty speeches of Mr. Giovanelli, when a carriage that had detached itself from the revolving train drew up beside the path. At the same moment Winterbourne perceived that his friend Mrs. Walker—the lady whose house he had lately left—was seated in the vehicle and was beckoning to him. Leaving Miss Miller's side, he hastened to obey her summons. Mrs. Walker was flushed; she wore an excited air. "It is really too dreadful," she said. "That girl must not do this sort of thing. She must not walk here with you two men. Fifty people have noticed her."

Winterbourne raised his eyebrows. "I think it's a pity to make too much fuss about it."

"It's a pity to let the girl ruin herself!"

"She is very innocent," said Winterbourne.

"She's very crazy!" cried Mrs. Walker. "Did you ever see anything so imbecile as her mother? After you had all left me, just now, I could not sit still for thinking of it. It seemed too pitiful, not even to attempt to save her. I ordered the carriage and put on my bonnet, and came here as quickly as possible. Thank heaven I have found you!"

"What do you propose to do with us?" asked Winterbourne, smiling.

"To ask her to get in, to drive her about here for half-an-hour, so that the world may see she is not running absolutely wild, and then to take her safely home."

"I don't think it's a very happy thought," said Winterbourne; "but you can try."

Mrs. Walker tried. The young man went in pursuit of Miss Miller, who had simply nodded and smiled at his interlocutrix in the carriage and had gone her way with her own companion. Daisy, on learning that Mrs. Walker wished to speak to her, retraced her steps with a perfect good grace and with Mr. Giovanelli at her side. She declared that she was delighted to have a chance to present this gentleman to Mrs. Walker. She immediately achieved the introduction, and declared that she had never in her life seen anything so lovely as Mrs. Walker's carriage-rug.

"I am glad you admire it," said this lady, smiling sweetly. "Will you get in and let me put it over you?"

"Oh, no, thank you," said Daisy. "I shall admire it much more as I see you driving round with it."

"Do get in and drive with me," said Mrs. Walker.

"That would be charming, but it's so enchanting just as I am!" and Daisy gave a brilliant glance at the gentlemen on either side of her.

"It may be enchanting, dear child, but it is not the custom here," urged Mrs. Walker, leaning forward in her victoria[1] with her hands devoutly clasped.

"Well, it ought to be, then!" said Daisy. "If I didn't walk I should expire."

---

1. A horse-drawn carriage for two with a raised seat in front for the driver.

"You should walk with your mother, dear," cried the lady from Geneva, losing patience.

"With my mother dear!" exclaimed the young girl. Winterbourne saw that she scented interference. "My mother never walked ten steps in her life. And then, you know," she added with a laugh, "I am more than five years old."

"You are old enough to be more reasonable. You are old enough, dear Miss Miller, to be talked about."

Daisy looked at Mrs. Walker, smiling intensely. "Talked about? What do you mean?"

"Come into my carriage and I will tell you."

Daisy turned her quickened glance again from one of the gentlemen beside her to the other. Mr. Giovanelli was bowing to and fro, rubbing down his gloves and laughing very agreeably; Winterbourne thought it a most unpleasant scene. "I don't think I want to know what you mean," said Daisy presently. "I don't think I should like it."

Winterbourne wished that Mrs. Walker would tuck in her carriage-rug and drive away; but this lady did not enjoy being defied, as she afterwards told him. "Should you prefer being thought a very reckless girl?" she demanded.

"Gracious me!" exclaimed Daisy. She looked again at Mr. Giovanelli, then she turned to Winterbourne. There was a little pink flush in her check; she was tremendously pretty. "Does Mr. Winterbourne think," she asked slowly, smiling, throwing back her head and glancing at him from head to foot, "that—to save my reputation—I ought to get into the carriage?"

Winterbourne colored; for an instant he hesitated greatly. It seemed so strange to hear her speak that way of her "reputation." But he himself, in fact, must speak in accordance with gallantry. The finest gallantry, here, was simply to tell her the truth; and the truth, for Winterbourne, as the few indications I have been able to give have made him known to the reader, was that Daisy Miller should take Mrs. Walker's advice. He looked at her exquisite prettiness; and then he said very gently, "I think you should get into the carriage."

Daisy gave a violent laugh. "I never heard anything so stiff! If this is improper, Mrs. Walker," she pursued, "then I am all improper, and you must give me up. Good-bye; I hope you'll have a lovely ride!" and, with Mr. Giovanelli, who made a triumphantly obsequious salute, she turned away.

Mrs. Walker sat looking after her, and there were tears in Mrs. Walker's eyes. "Get in here, sir," she said to Winterbourne, indicating the place beside her. The young man answered that he felt bound to accompany Miss Miller; whereupon Mrs. Walker declared that if he refused her this favor she would never speak to him again. She was evidently in earnest. Winterbourne overtook Daisy and her companion and, offering the young girl his hand, told her that Mrs. Walker had made an imperious claim upon his society. He expected that in answer she would say something rather free, something to commit herself still farther to that "recklessness" from which Mrs. Walker had so charitably endeavored to dissuade her. But she only shook his hand, hardly looking at him, while Mr. Giovanelli bade him farewell with a too emphatic flourish of the hat.

Winterbourne was not in the best possible humor as he took his seat in Mrs. Walker's victoria. "That was not clever of you," he said candidly, while the vehicle mingled again with the throng of carriages.

"In such a case," his companion answered, "I don't wish to be clever, I wish to be *earnest!*"

"Well, your earnestness has only offended her and put her off."

"It has happened very well," said Mrs. Walker. "If she is so perfectly determined to compromise herself, the sooner one knows it the better; one can act accordingly."

"I suspect she meant no harm," Winterbourne rejoined.

"So I thought a month ago. But she has been going too far."

"What has she been doing?"

"Everything that is not done here. Flirting with any man she could pick up; sitting in corners with mysterious Italians; dancing all the evening with the same partners; receiving visits at eleven o'clock at night. Her mother goes away when visitors come."

"But her brother," said Winterbourne, laughing, "sits up till midnight."

"He must be edified by what he sees. I'm told that at their hotel every one is talking about her, and that a smile goes round among the servants when a gentleman comes and asks for Miss Miller."

"The servants be hanged!" said Winterbourne angrily. "The poor girl's only fault," he presently added, "is that she is very uncultivated."

"She is naturally indelicate," Mrs. Walker declared. "Take that example this morning. How long had you known her at Vevey?"

"A couple of days."

"Fancy, then, her making it a personal matter that you should have left the place!"

Winterbourne was silent for some moments; then he said, "I suspect, Mrs. Walker, that you and I have lived too long at Geneva!" And he added a request that she should inform him with what particular design she had made him enter her carriage.

"I wished to beg you to cease your relations with Miss Miller—not to flirt with her—to give her no farther opportunity to expose herself—to let her alone, in short."

"I'm afraid I can't do that," said Winterbourne. "I like her extremely."

"All the more reason that you shouldn't help her to make a scandal."

"There shall be nothing scandalous in my attentions to her."

"There certainly will be in the way she takes them. But I have said what I had on my conscience," Mrs. Walker pursued. "If you wish to rejoin the young lady I will put you down. Here, by-the-way, you have a chance."

The carriage was traversing that part of the Pincian Garden which overhangs the wall of Rome and overlooks the beautiful Villa Borghese. It is bordered by a large parapet, near which there are several seats. One of the seats, at a distance, was occupied by a gentleman and a lady, towards whom Mrs. Walker gave a toss of her head. At the same moment these persons rose and walked towards the parapet. Winterbourne had asked the coachman to stop; he now descended from the carriage. His companion looked at him a moment in silence; then, while he raised his hat, she drove majestically away. Winterbourne stood there; he had turned his eyes towards Daisy and her cavalier. They evidently saw no one; they were too deeply occupied with each other. When they reached the low garden-wall they stood a moment looking off at the great flat-topped pine-clusters of the Villa Borghese; then Giovanelli seated himself familiarly upon the broad ledge of the wall. The western sun in the opposite sky sent out a brilliant shaft through a couple of cloud-bars; whereupon Daisy's companion took her parasol out of her hands and opened it. She came a little nearer and he held the parasol over her; then, still holding it, he let it rest upon her shoulder, so that both of their heads were hidden from Winterbourne. This young man lingered a moment, then he began to walk. But he walked—not towards the couple with the parasol; towards the residence of his aunt, Mrs. Costello.

## IV

He flattered himself on the following day that there was no smiling among the servants when he, at least, asked for Mrs. Miller at her hotel. This lady and her daughter, however, were not at home; and on the next day, after repeating his visit, Winterbourne again had the misfortune not to find them. Mrs. Walker's party took place on the evening of the third day, and in spite of the frigidity of his last interview with the hostess, Winterbourne was among the guests. Mrs. Walker was one of those American ladies who, while residing abroad, make a point, in their own phrase, of studying European society; and she had on this occasion collected several specimens of her diversely-born fellow-mortals to serve, as it were, as text-books. When Winterbourne arrived Daisy Miller was not there; but in a few moments he saw her mother come in alone, very shyly and ruefully. Mrs. Miller's hair, above her exposed-looking temples, was more frizzled than ever. As she approached Mrs. Walker, Winterbourne also drew near.

"You see I've come all alone," said poor Mrs. Miller. "I'm so frightened; I don't know what to do; it's the first time I've ever been to a party alone—especially in this country. I wanted to bring Randolph or Eugenio, or someone, but Daisy just pushed me off by myself. I ain't used to going round alone."

"And does not your daughter intend to favor us with her society?" demanded Mrs. Walker, impressively.

"Well, Daisy's all dressed," said Mrs. Miller, with that accent of the dispassionate, if not of the philosophic, historian with which she always recorded the current incidents of her daughter's career. "She's got dressed on purpose before dinner. But she's got a friend of hers there; that gentleman—the Italian—that she wanted to bring. They've got going at the piano; it seems as if they couldn't leave off. Mr. Giovanelli sings splendidly. But I guess they'll come before very long," concluded Mrs. Miller hopefully.

"I'm sorry she should come—in that way," said Mrs. Walker.

"Well, I told her that there was no use in her getting dressed before dinner if she was going to wait three hours," responded Daisy's mamma. "I didn't see the use of her putting on such a dress as that to sit round with Mr. Giovanelli."

"This is most horrible!" said Mrs. Walker, turning away and addressing herself to Winterbourne. "*Elle s'affiche.*[2] It's her revenge for my having ventured to remonstrate with her. When she comes I shall not speak to her."

Daisy came after eleven o'clock, but she was not, on such an occasion, a young lady to wait to be spoken to. She rustled forward in radiant loveliness, smiling and chattering, carrying a large bouquet and attended by Mr. Giovanelli. Every one stopped talking, and turned and looked at her. She came straight to Mrs. Walker. "I'm afraid you thought I never was coming, so I sent mother off to tell you. I wanted to make Mr. Giovanelli practice some things before he came; you know he sings beautifully, and I want you to ask him to

2. She's making a spectacle of herself (French).

sing. This is Mr. Giovanelli; you know I introduced him to you; he's got the most lovely voice and he knows the most charming set of songs. I made him go over them this evening, on purpose; we had the greatest time at the hotel." Of all this Daisy delivered herself with the sweetest, brightest audibleness, looking now at her hostess and now round the room, while she gave a series of little pats, round her shoulders, to the edges of her dress. "Is there anyone I know?" she asked.

"I think every one knows you!" said Mrs. Walker pregnantly, and she gave a very cursory greeting to Mr. Giovanelli. This gentleman bore himself gallantly. He smiled and bowed and showed his white teeth, he curled his moustaches and rolled his eyes, and performed all the proper functions of a handsome Italian at an evening party. He sang, very prettily, half-a-dozen songs, though Mrs. Walker afterwards declared that she had been quite unable to find out who asked him. It was apparently not Daisy who had given him his orders. Daisy sat at a distance from the piano, and though she had publicly, as it were, professed a high admiration for his singing, talked, not inaudibly, while it was going on.

"It's a pity these rooms are so small; we can't dance," she said to Winterbourne, as if she had seen him five minutes before.

"I am not sorry we can't dance," Winterbourne answered; "I don't dance."

"Of course you don't dance; you're too stiff," said Miss Daisy. "I hope you enjoyed your drive with Mrs. Walker."

"No, I didn't enjoy it; I preferred walking with you."

"We paired off, that was much better," said Daisy. "But did you ever hear anything so cool as Mrs. Walker's wanting me to get into her carriage and drop poor Mr. Giovanelli; and under the pretext that it was proper? People have different ideas! It would have been most unkind; he had been talking about that walk for ten days."

"He should not have talked about it at all," said Winterbourne; "he would never have proposed to a young lady of this country to walk about the streets with him."

"About the streets?" cried Daisy, with her pretty stare. "Where then would he have proposed to her to walk? The Pincio is not the streets, either; and I, thank goodness, am not a young lady of this country. The young ladies of this country have a dreadfully pokey time of it, so far as I can learn; I don't see why I should change my habits for *them*."

"I am afraid your habits are those of a flirt," said Winterbourne gravely.

"Of course they are," she cried, giving him her little smiling stare again. "I'm a fearful, frightful flirt! Did you ever hear of a nice girl that was not? But I suppose you will tell me now that I am not a nice girl."

"You're a very nice girl, but I wish you would flirt with me, and me only," said Winterbourne.

"Ah! thank you, thank you very much; you are the last man I should think of flirting with. As I have had the pleasure of informing you, you are too stiff."

"You say that too often," said Winterbourne.

Daisy gave a delighted laugh. "If I could have the sweet hope of making you angry, I would say it again."

"Don't do that; when I am angry I'm stiffer than ever. But if you won't flirt with me, do cease at least to flirt with your friend at the piano; they don't understand that sort of thing here."

"I thought they understood nothing else!" exclaimed Daisy.

"Not in young unmarried women."

"It seems to me much more proper in young unmarried women than in old married ones," Daisy declared.

"Well," said Winterbourne, "when you deal with natives you must go by the custom of the place. Flirting is a purely American custom; it doesn't exist here. So when you show yourself in public with Mr. Giovanelli and without your mother—"

"Gracious! Poor mother!" interposed Daisy.

"Though you may be flirting, Mr. Giovanelli is not; he means something else."

"He isn't preaching, at any rate," said Daisy with vivacity. "And if you want very much to know, we are neither of us flirting; we are too good friends for that; we are very intimate friends."

"Ah," rejoined Winterbourne, "if you are in love with each other it is another affair."

She had allowed him up to this point to talk so frankly that he had no expectation of shocking her by this ejaculation; but she immediately got up, blushing visibly, and leaving him to exclaim mentally that little American flirts were the queerest creatures in the world. "Mr. Giovanelli, at least," she said, giving her interlocutor a single glance, "never says such very disagreeable things to me."

Winterbourne was bewildered; he stood staring. Mr. Giovanelli had finished singing; he left the piano and came over to Daisy. "Won't you come into the other room and have some tea?" he asked, bending before her with his decorative smile.

Daisy turned to Winterbourne, beginning to smile again. He was still more perplexed, for this inconsequent smile made nothing clear, though it seemed to prove, indeed, that she had a sweetness and softness that reverted instinctively to the pardon of offences. "It has never occurred to Mr. Winterbourne to offer me any tea," she said, with her little tormenting manner.

"I have offered you advice," Winterbourne rejoined.

"I prefer weak tea!" cried Daisy, and she went off with the brilliant Giovanelli. She sat with him in the adjoining room, in the embrasure of the window, for the rest of the evening. There was an interesting performance at the piano, but neither of these young people gave heed to it. When Daisy came to take leave of Mrs. Walker, this lady conscientiously repaired the weakness of which she had been guilty at the moment of the young girl's arrival. She turned her back straight upon Miss Miller and left her to depart with what grace she might. Winterbourne was standing near the door; he saw it all. Daisy turned very pale and looked at her mother, but Mrs. Miller was humbly unconscious of any violation of the usual social forms. She appeared, indeed, to have felt an incongruous impulse to draw attention to her own striking observance of them. "Good night, Mrs. Walker," she said; "we've had a beautiful evening. You see if I let Daisy come to parties without me, I don't want her to go away without me." Daisy turned away, looking with a pale, grave face at the circle near the door; Winterbourne saw that, for the first moment, she was too much shocked and puzzled even for indignation. He on his side was greatly touched.

"That was very cruel," he said to Mrs. Walker.

"She never enters my drawing-room again," replied his hostess.

Since Winterbourne was not to meet her in Mrs. Walker's drawing-room, he went as often as possible to Mrs. Miller's hotel. The ladies were rarely at home, but when he found them the devoted Giovanelli was always present. Very often the polished little Roman was in the drawing-room with Daisy alone, Mrs. Miller being apparently constantly of the opinion that discretion is the better part of surveillance. Winterbourne noted, at first with surprise, that Daisy on these occasions was never embarrassed or annoyed by his own entrance; but he very presently began to feel that she had no more surprises for him; the unexpected in her behavior was the only thing to expect. She showed no displeasure at her *tête-à-tête* with Giovanelli being interrupted; she could chatter as freshly and freely with two gentlemen as with one; there was always, in her conversation, the same odd mixture of audacity and puerility. Winterbourne remarked to himself that if she was seriously interested in Giovanelli it was very singular that she should not take more trouble to preserve the sanctity of their interviews, and he liked her the more for her innocent-looking indifference and her apparently inexhaustible good humor. He could hardly have said why, but she seemed to him a girl who would never be jealous. At the risk of exciting a somewhat derisive smile on the reader's part, I may affirm that with regard to the women who had hitherto interested him it very often seemed to Winterbourne among the possibilities that, given certain contingencies, he should be afraid—literally afraid—of these ladies. He had a pleasant sense that he should never be afraid of Daisy Miller. It must be added that this sentiment was not altogether flattering to Daisy; it was part of his conviction, or rather of his apprehension, that she would prove a very light young person.

But she was evidently very much interested in Giovanelli. She looked at him whenever he spoke; she was perpetually telling him to do this and to do that; she was constantly "chaffing" and abusing him. She appeared completely to have forgotten that Winterbourne had said anything to displease her at Mrs. Walker's little party. One Sunday afternoon, having gone to St. Peter's with his aunt, Winterbourne perceived Daisy strolling about the great church in company with the inevitable Giovanelli. Presently he pointed out the young girl and her cavalier to Mrs. Costello. This lady looked at them a moment through her eyeglasses, and then she said:

"That's what makes you so pensive in these days, eh?"

"I had not the least idea I was pensive," said the young man.

"You are very much pre occupied, you are thinking of something."

"And what is it," he asked, "that you accuse me of thinking of?"

"Of that young lady's, Miss Baker's, Miss Chandler's—what's her name?— Miss Miller's intrigue with that little barber's block."

"Do you call it an intrigue," Winterbourne asked—"an affair that goes on with such peculiar publicity?"

"That's their folly," said Mrs. Costello, "it's not their merit."

"No," rejoined Winterbourne, with something of that pensiveness to which his aunt had alluded. "I don't believe that there is anything to be called an intrigue."

"I have heard a dozen people speak of it; they say she is quite carried away by him."

"They are certainly very intimate," said Winterbourne.

Mrs. Costello inspected the young couple again with her optical instrument. "He is very handsome. One easily sees how it is. She thinks him the most elegant man in the world, the finest gentleman. She has never seen anything like him; he is better even than the courier. It was the courier probably who introduced him, and if he succeeds in marrying the young lady, the courier will come in for a magnificent commission."

"I don't believe she thinks of marrying him," said Winterbourne, "and I don't believe he hopes to marry her."

"You may be very sure she thinks of nothing. She goes on from day to day, from hour to hour, as they did in the Golden Age. I can imagine nothing more vulgar. And at the same time," added Mrs. Costello, "depend upon it that she may tell you any moment that she is 'engaged.' "

"I think that is more than Giovanelli expects," said Winterbourne.

"Who is Giovanelli?"

"The little Italian. I have asked questions about him and learned something. He is apparently a perfectly respectable little man. I believe he is in a small way a *cavaliere avvocato*.[3] But he doesn't move in what are called the first circles. I think it is really not absolutely impossible that the courier introduced him. He is evidently immensely charmed with Miss Miller. If she thinks him the finest gentleman in the world, he, on his side, has never found himself in personal contact with such splendor, such opulence, such expensiveness, as this young lady's. And then she must seem to him wonderfully pretty and interesting. I rather doubt whether he dreams of marrying her. That must appear to him too impossible a piece of luck. He has nothing but his handsome face to offer, and there is a substantial Mr. Miller in that mysterious land of dollars. Giovanelli knows that he hasn't a title to offer. If he were only a count or a *marchese*![4] He must wonder at his luck at the way they have taken him up."

"He accounts for it by his handsome face, and thinks Miss Miller a young lady *qui se passe ses fantaisies*![5]" said Mrs. Costello.

"It is very true," Winterbourne pursued, "that Daisy and her mamma have not yet risen to that stage of—what shall I call it?—of culture, at which the idea of catching a count or a *marchese* begins. I believe that they are intellectually incapable of that conception."

"Ah! but the *cavalier* can't believe it," said Mrs. Costello.

Of the observation excited by Daisy's "intrigue," Winterbourne gathered that day at St. Peter's sufficient evidence. A dozen of the American colonists in Rome came to talk with Mrs. Costello, who sat on a little portable stool at the base of one of the great pilasters. The vesper-service was going forward in splendid chants and organ-tones in the adjacent choir, and meanwhile, between Mrs. Costello and her friends, there was a great deal said about poor little Miss Miller's going really "too far." Winterbourne was not pleased with what he heard; but when, coming out upon the great steps of the church, he saw Daisy, who had emerged before him, get into an open cab with her accomplice and roll away through the cynical streets of Rome, he could not deny to himself that she was going very far indeed. He felt very sorry for her— not exactly that he believed that she had completely lost her head, but because it was painful to hear so much that was pretty and undefended and natural

3. Lawyer (Italian). *Cavaliere* is merely honorific.     5. Who is indulging her whims (French).
4. Marquis (Italian).

assigned to a vulgar place among the categories of disorder. He made an attempt after this to give a hint to Mrs. Miller. He met one day in the Corso a friend—a tourist like himself—who had just come out of the Doria Palace, where he had been walking through the beautiful gallery. His friend talked for a moment about the superb portrait of Innocent X. by Velasquez,[6] which hangs in one of the cabinets of the palace, and then said, "And in the same cabinet, by-the-way, I had the pleasure of contemplating a picture of a different kind—that pretty American girl whom you pointed out to me last week." In answer to Winterbourne's inquiries, his friend narrated that the pretty American girl—prettier than ever—was seated with a companion in the secluded nook in which the great papal portrait is enshrined.

"Who was her companion?" asked Winterbourne.

"A little Italian with a bouquet in his button hole. The girl is delightfully pretty, but I thought I understood from you the other day that she was a young lady du meilleur monde."[7]

"So she is!" answered Winterbourne; and having assured himself that his informant had seen Daisy and her companion but five minutes before, he jumped into a cab and went to call on Mrs. Miller. She was at home; but she apologized to him for receiving him in Daisy's absence.

"She's gone out somewhere with Mr. Giovanelli," said Mrs. Miller. "She's always going round with Mr. Giovanelli."

"I have noticed that they are very intimate," Winterbourne observed.

"Oh! it seems as if they couldn't live without each other!" said Mrs. Miller. "Well, he's a real gentleman, anyhow. I keep telling Daisy she's engaged!"

"And what does Daisy say?"

"Oh, she says she isn't engaged. But she might as well be!" this impartial parent resumed. "She goes on as if she was. But I've made Mr. Giovanelli promise to tell me, if she doesn't. I should want to write to Mr. Miller about it—shouldn't you?"

Winterbourne replied that he certainly should; and the state of mind of Daisy's mamma struck him as so unprecedented in the annals of parental vigilance that he gave up as utterly irrelevant the attempt to place her upon her guard.

After this Daisy was never at home, and Winterbourne ceased to meet her at the houses of their common acquaintances, because, as he perceived, these shrewd people had quite made up their minds that she was going too far. They ceased to invite her, and they intimated that they desired to express to observant Europeans the great truth that, though Miss Daisy Miller was a young American lady, her behavior was not representative—was regarded by her compatriots as abnormal. Winterbourne wondered how she felt about all the cold shoulders that were turned towards her, and sometimes it annoyed him to suspect that she did not feel at all. He said to himself that she was too light and childish, too uncultivated and unreasoning, too provincial, to have reflected upon her ostracism or even to have perceived it. Then at other moments he believed that she carried about in her elegant and irresponsible little organism a defiant, passionate, perfectly observant consciousness of the impression she produced. He asked himself whether Daisy's defiance came from the consciousness of innocence or from her being, essentially, a young person of the reckless class. It must be admitted that holding oneself to a belief

6. Diego Rodríguez de Silva y Velázquez (1599–        7. Of the better society (French).
1660), Spanish painter.

in Daisy's "innocence" came to seem to Winterbourne more and more a matter of fine-spun gallantry. As I have already had occasion to relate, he was angry at finding himself reduced to chopping logic about this young lady; he was vexed at his want of instinctive certitude as to how far her eccentricities were generic, national, and how far they were personal. From either view of them he had somehow missed her, and now it was too late. She was "carried away" by Mr. Giovanelli.

A few days after his brief interview with her mother, he encountered her in that beautiful abode of flowering desolation known as the Palace of the Cæsars. The early Roman spring had filled the air with bloom and perfume, and the rugged surface of the Palatine was muffled with tender verdure. Daisy was strolling along the top of one of those great mounds of ruin that are embanked with mossy marble and paved with monumental inscriptions. It seemed to him that Rome had never been so lovely as just then. He stood looking off at the enchanting harmony of line and color that remotely encircles the city, inhaling the softly humid odors and feeling the freshness of the year and the antiquity of the place reaffirm themselves in mysterious interfusion. It seemed to him also that Daisy had never looked so pretty; but this had been an observation of his whenever he met her. Giovanelli was at her side, and Giovanelli, too, wore an aspect of even unwonted brilliancy.

"Well," said Daisy, "I should think you would be lonesome!"

"Lonesome?" asked Winterbourne.

"You are always going round by yourself. Can't you get any one to walk with you?"

"I am not so fortunate," said Winterbourne, "as your companion."

Giovanelli, from the first, had treated Winterbourne with distinguished politeness; he listened with a deferential air to his remarks; he laughed, punctiliously, at his pleasantries; he seemed disposed to testify to his belief that Winterbourne was a superior young man. He carried himself in no degree like a jealous wooer; he had obviously a great deal of tact; he had no objection to your expecting a little humility of him. It even seemed to Winterbourne at times that Giovanelli would find a certain mental relief in being able to have a private understanding with him—to say to him, as an intelligent man, that, bless you, *he* knew how extraordinary was this young lady, and didn't flatter himself with delusive—or at least *too* delusive—hopes of matrimony and dollars. On this occasion he strolled away from his companion to pluck a sprig of almond blossom, which he carefully arranged in his button-hole.

"I know why you say that," said Daisy, watching Giovanelli, "Because you think I go round too much with *him*!" And she nodded at her attendant.

"Everyone thinks so—if you care to know," said Winterbourne.

"Of course I care to know!" Daisy exclaimed seriously. "But I don't believe it. They are only pretending to be shocked. They don't really care a straw what I do. Besides, I don't go round so much."

"I think you will find they do care. They will show it—disagreeably."

Daisy looked at him a moment. "How—disagreeably?"

"Haven't you noticed anything?" Winterbourne asked.

"I have noticed you. But I noticed you were as stiff as an umbrella the first time I saw you."

"You will find I am not so stiff as several others," said Winterbourne, smiling.

"How shall I find it?"

"By going to see the others."

"What will they do to me?"

"They will give you the cold shoulder. Do you know what that means?"

Daisy was looking at him intently; she began to color. "Do you mean as Mrs. Walker did the other night?"

"Exactly!" said Winterbourne.

She looked away at Giovanelli, who was decorating himself with his almond-blossom. Then looking back at Winterbourne—"I shouldn't think you would let people be so unkind!" she said.

"How can I help it?" he asked.

"I should think you would say something."

"I do say something"; and he paused a moment. "I say that your mother tells me that she believes you are engaged."

"Well, she does," said Daisy very simply.

Winterbourne began to laugh. "And does Randolph believe it?" he asked.

"I guess Randolph doesn't believe anything," said Daisy. Randolph's scepticism excited Winterbourne to farther hilarity, and he observed that Giovanelli was coming back to them. Daisy, observing it too, addressed herself again to her countryman. "Since you have mentioned it," she said, "I *am* engaged." . . . Winterbourne looked at her; he had stopped laughing. "You don't believe it!" she added.

He was silent a moment; and then, "Yes, I believe it!" he said.

"Oh, no, you don't," she answered. "Well, then—I am not!"

The young girl and her cicerone were on their way to the gate of the enclosure, so that Winterbourne, who had but lately entered, presently took leave of them. A week afterwards he went to dine at a beautiful villa on the Cælian Hill, and, on arriving, dismissed his hired vehicle. The evening was charming, and he promised himself the satisfaction of walking home beneath the Arch of Constantine and past the vaguely-lighted monuments of the Forum. There was a waning moon in the sky, and her radiance was not brilliant, but she was veiled in a thin cloud-curtain which seemed to diffuse and equalize it. When, on his return from the villa (it was eleven o'clock), Winterbourne approached the dusky circle of the Colosseum, it occurred to him, as a lover of the picturesque, that the interior, in the pale moonshine, would be well worth a glance. He turned aside and walked to one of the empty arches, near which, as he observed, an open carriage—one of the little Roman street-cabs—was stationed. Then he passed in among the cavernous shadows of the great structure, and emerged upon the clear and silent arena. The place had never seemed to him more impressive. One-half of the gigantic circus was in deep shade; the other was sleeping in the luminous dusk. As he stood there he began to murmur Byron's famous lines, out of "Manfred"; but before he had finished his quotation he remembered that if nocturnal meditations in the Colosseum are recommended by the poets, they are deprecated by the doctors. The historic atmosphere was there, certainly; but the historic atmosphere, scientifically considered, was not better than a villainous miasma. Winterbourne walked to the middle of the arena, to take a more general glance, intending thereafter to make a hasty retreat. The great cross in the center was covered with shadow; it was only as he drew near it that he made it out distinctly. Then he saw that two persons were stationed upon the low steps which formed its base. One of these was a woman, seated; her companion was standing in front of her.

Presently the sound of the woman's voice came to him distinctly in the warm night air. "Well, he looks at us as one of the old lions or tigers may have looked at the Christian martyrs!" These were the words he heard, in the familiar accent of Miss Daisy Miller.

"Let us hope he is not very hungry," responded the ingenious Giovanelli. "He will have to take me first; you will serve for dessert!"

Winterbourne stopped, with a sort of horror; and, it must be added, with a sort of relief. It was as if a sudden illumination had been flashed upon the ambiguity of Daisy's behavior and the riddle had become easy to read. She was a young lady whom a gentleman need no longer be at pains to respect. He stood there looking at her—looking at her companion, and not reflecting that though he saw them vaguely, he himself must have been more brightly visible. He felt angry with himself that he had bothered so much about the right way of regarding Miss Daisy Miller. Then, as he was going to advance again, he checked himself; not from the fear that he was doing her injustice, but from a sense of the danger of appearing unbecomingly exhilarated by this sudden revulsion from cautious criticism. He turned away towards the entrance of the place; but as he did so he heard Daisy speak again.

"Why, it was Mr. Winterbourne! He saw me—and he cuts me!"

What a clever little reprobate she was, and how smartly she played an injured innocence! But he wouldn't cut her. Winterbourne came forward again, and went towards the great cross. Daisy had got up; Giovanelli lifted his hat. Winterbourne had now begun to think simply of the craziness, from a sanitary point of view, of a delicate young girl lounging away the evening in this nest of malaria. What if she *were* a clever little reprobate? that was no reason for her dying of the *perniciosa*.[8] "How long have you been there?" he asked, almost brutally.

Daisy, lovely in the flattering moonlight, looked at him a moment. Then— "All the evening," she answered gently. . . . . "I never saw anything so pretty."

"I am afraid," said Winterbourne, "that you will not think Roman fever very pretty. This is the way people catch it. I wonder," he added, turning to Giovanelli, "that you, a native Roman, should countenance such a terrible indiscretion."

"Ah," said the handsome native, "for myself, I am not afraid."

"Neither am I—for you! I am speaking for this young lady."

Giovanelli lifted his well-shaped eyebrows and showed his brilliant teeth. But he took Winterbourne's rebuke with docility. "I told the Signorina it was a grave indiscretion; but when was the Signorina ever prudent?"

"I never was sick, and I don't mean to be!" the Signorina declared. "I don't look like much, but I'm healthy! I was bound to see the Colosseum by moonlight; I shouldn't have wanted to go home without that; and we have had the most beautiful time, haven't we, Mr. Giovanelli! If there has been any danger, Eugenio can give me some pills. He has got some splendid pills."

"I should advise you," said Winterbourne, "to drive home as fast as possible and take one!"

"What you say is very wise," Giovanelli rejoined. "I will go and make sure the carriage is at hand." And he went forward rapidly.

Daisy followed with Winterbourne. He kept looking at her; she seemed not

8. Malaria (Italian).

in the least embarrassed. Winterbourne said nothing; Daisy chattered about the beauty of the place. "Well, I *have* seen the Colosseum by moonlight!" she exclaimed. "That's one good thing." Then, noticing Winterbourne's silence, she asked him why he didn't speak. He made no answer; he only began to laugh. They passed under one of the dark archways; Giovanelli was in front with the carriage. Here Daisy stopped a moment, looking at the young American. "*Did* you believe I was engaged the other day?" she asked.

"It doesn't matter what I believed the other day," said Winterbourne, still laughing.

"Well, what do you believe now?"

"I believe that it makes very little difference whether you are engaged or not!"

He felt the young girl's pretty eyes fixed upon him through the thick gloom of the archway; she was apparently going to answer. But Giovanelli hurried her forward. "Quick, quick," he said; "if we get in by midnight we are quite safe."

Daisy took her seat in the carriage, and the fortunate Italian placed himself beside her. "Don't forget Eugenio's pills!" said Winterbourne, as he lifted his hat.

"I don't care," said Daisy, in a little strange tone, "whether I have Roman fever or not!" Upon this the cab-driver cracked his whip, and they rolled away over the desultory patches of the antique pavement.

Winterbourne—to do him justice, as it were—mentioned to no one that he had encountered Miss Miller, at midnight, in the Colosseum with a gentleman; but nevertheless, a couple of days later, the fact of her having been there under these circumstances was known to every member of the little American circle, and commented accordingly. Winterbourne reflected that they had of course known it at the hotel, and that, after Daisy's return, there had been an exchange of jokes between the porter and the cab-driver. But the young man was conscious at the same moment that it had ceased to be a matter of serious regret to him that the little American flirt should be "talked about" by low-minded menials. These people, a day or two later, had serious information to give: the little American flirt was alarmingly ill. Winterbourne, when the rumor came to him, immediately went to the hotel for more news. He found that two or three charitable friends had preceded him, and that they were being entertained in Mrs. Miller's salon by Randolph.

"It's going round at night," said Randolph—"that's what made her sick. She's always going round at midnight. I shouldn't think she'd want to—it's so plaguey dark. You can't see anything here at night, except when there's a moon. In America there's always a moon!" Mrs. Miller was invisible; she was now, at least, giving her daughter the advantage of her society. It was evident that Daisy was dangerously ill.

Winterbourne went often to ask for news of her, and once he saw Mrs. Miller, who, though deeply alarmed, was—rather to his surprise—perfectly composed, and, as it appeared, a most efficient and judicious nurse. She talked a good deal about Dr. Davis, but Winterbourne paid her the compliment of saying to himself that she was not, after all, such a monstrous goose. "Daisy spoke of you the other day," she said to him. "Half the time she doesn't know what she's saying, but that time I think she did. She gave me a message: she told me to tell you. She told me to tell you that she never was engaged to that handsome Italian. I am sure I am very glad; Mr. Giovanelli hasn't been near us since she was taken ill. I thought he was so much of a gentleman; but I don't call that very polite! A lady told me that he was afraid I was angry with him for taking Daisy round at night. Well, so I am; but I suppose he knows I'm a lady. I would scorn to scold him. Any way, she says she's not engaged. I don't know why she wanted you to know; but she said to me three times— 'Mind you tell Mr. Winterbourne.' And then she told me to ask if you remembered the time you went to that castle, in Switzerland. But I said I wouldn't give any such messages as that. Only, if she is not engaged, I'm sure I'm glad to know it."

But, as Winterbourne had said, it mattered very little. A week after this the poor girl died; it had been a terrible case of the fever. Daisy's grave was in the little Protestant cemetery, in an angle of the wall of imperial Rome, beneath the cypresses and the thick spring-flowers. Winterbourne stood there beside it, with a number of other mourners; a number larger than the scandal excited by the young lady's career would have led you to expect. Near him stood Giovanelli, who came nearer still before Winterbourne turned away. Giovanelli was very pale; on this occasion he had no flower in his button-hole; he seemed to wish to say something. At last he said, "She was the most beautiful young lady I ever saw, and the most amiable." And then he added in a moment, "And she was the most innocent."

Winterbourne looked at him, and presently repeated his words, "And the most innocent?"

"The most innocent!"

Winterbourne felt sore and angry. "Why the devil," he asked, "did you take her to that fatal place?"

Mr. Giovanelli's urbanity was apparently imperturbable. He looked on the ground a moment, and then he said, "For myself, I had no fear; and she wanted to go."

"That was no reason!" Winterbourne declared.

The subtle Roman again dropped his eyes. "If she had lived, I should have got nothing. She would never have married me, I am sure."

"She would never have married you?"

"For a moment I hoped so. But no, I am sure."

Winterbourne listened to him; he stood staring at the raw protuberance among the April daisies. When he turned away again Mr. Giovanelli, with his light slow step, had retired.

Winterbourne almost immediately left Rome; but the following summer he again met his aunt, Mrs. Costello, at Vevey. Mrs. Costello was fond of Vevey. In the interval Winterbourne had often thought of Daisy Miller and her mystifying manners. One day he spoke of her to his aunt—said it was on his conscience that he had done her injustice.

"I am sure I don't know," said Mrs. Costello. "How did your injustice affect her?"

"She sent me a message before her death which I didn't understand at the time. But I have understood it since. She would have appreciated one's esteem."

"Is that a modest way," asked Mrs. Costello, "of saying that she would have reciprocated one's affection?"

Winterbourne offered no answer to this question; but he presently said, "You were right in that remark that you made last summer. I was booked to make a mistake. I have lived too long in foreign parts."

Nevertheless, he went back to live at Geneva, whence there continue to come the most contradictory accounts of his motives of sojourn: a report that he is "studying" hard—an intimation that he is much interested in a very clever foreign lady.

1878, 1879

# The Real Thing[1]

## I

When the porter's wife, who used to answer the house-bell, announced "A gentleman and a lady, sir" I had, as I often had in those days—the wish being father to the thought—an immediate vision of sitters. Sitters my visitors in this case proved to be; but not in the sense I should have preferred. There was nothing at first however to indicate that they mightn't have come for a portrait. The gentleman, a man of fifty, very high and very straight, with a moustache slightly grizzled and a dark grey walking-coat admirably fitted, both of which I noted professionally—I don't mean as a barber or yet as a tailor—would have struck me as a celebrity if celebrities often were striking. It was a truth of which I had for some time been conscious that a figure with a good deal of frontage was, as one might say, almost never a public institution. A glance at the lady helped to remind me of this paradoxical law: she also looked too distinguished to be a "personality." Moreover one would scarcely come across two variations together.

Neither of the pair immediately spoke—they only prolonged the preliminary gaze suggesting that each wished to give the other a chance. They were visibly shy; they stood there letting me take them in—which, as I afterwards perceived, was the most practical thing they could have done. In this way their embarrassment served their cause. I had seen people painfully reluctant to mention that they desired anything so gross as to be represented on canvas; but the scruples of my new friends appeared almost insurmountable. Yet the gentleman might have said "I should like a portrait of my wife," and the lady might have said "I should like a portrait of my husband." Perhaps they weren't husband and wife—this naturally would make the matter more delicate. Perhaps they wished to be done together—in which case they ought to have brought a third person to break the news.

"We come from Mr. Rivet," the lady finally said with a dim smile that had the effect of a moist sponge passed over a "sunk"[2] piece of painting, as well as of a vague allusion to vanished beauty. She was as tall and straight, in her degree, as her companion, and with ten years less to carry. She looked as sad as a woman could look whose face was not charged with expression; that is her tinted oval mask showed waste as an exposed surface shows friction. The hand of time had played over her freely, but to an effect of elimination. She was slim and stiff, and so well-dressed, in dark blue cloth, with lappets and pockets and buttons, that it was clear she employed the same tailor as her husband.

1. This "little gem of bright, quick vivid form," as James called it, first appeared in *Black and White* on April 16, 1892; in *The Real Thing and Other Tales* (1893); and finally in Vol. 18 (1909) of the New York Edition, the source of the present text.
2. When colors lose their brilliance after they have dried on the canvas, they are said to have "sunk in."

The couple had an indefinable air of prosperous thrift—they evidently got a good deal of luxury for their money. If I was to be one of their luxuries it would behove me to consider my terms.

"Ah Claude Rivet recommended me?" I echoed; and I added that it was very kind of him, though I could reflect that, as he only painted landscape, this wasn't a sacrifice.

The lady looked very hard at the gentleman, and the gentleman looked round the room. Then staring at the floor a moment and stroking his moustache, he rested his pleasant eyes on me with the remark: "He said you were the right one."

"I try to be, when people want to sit."

"Yes, we should like to," said the lady anxiously.

"Do you mean together?"

My visitors exchanged a glance. "If you could do anything with *me* I suppose it would be double," the gentleman stammered.

"Oh yes, there's naturally a higher charge for two figures than for one."

"We should like to make it pay," the husband confessed.

"That's very good of you," I returned, appreciating so unwonted a sympathy—for I supposed he meant pay the artist.

A sense of strangeness seemed to draw on the lady.

"We mean for the illustrations—Mr. Rivet said you might put one in."

"Put in—an illustration?" I was equally confused.

"Sketch her off, you know," said the gentleman, colouring.

It was only then that I understood the service Claude Rivet had rendered me; he had told them how I worked in black-and-white, for magazines, for storybooks, for sketches of contemporary life, and consequently had copious employment for models. These things were true, but it was not less true—I may confess it now; whether because the aspiration was to lead to everything or to nothing I leave the reader to guess—that I couldn't get the honours, to say nothing of the emoluments, of a great painter of portraits out of my head. My "illustrations" were my pot-boilers; I looked to a different branch of art— far and away the most interesting it had always seemed to me—to perpetuate my fame. There was no shame in looking to it also to make my fortune; but that fortune was by so much further from being made from the moment my visitors wished to be "done" for nothing. I was disappointed; for in the pictorial sense I had immediately *seen* them. I had seized their type—I had already settled what I would do with it. Something that wouldn't absolutely have pleased them, I afterwards reflected.

"Ah you're—you're—a—?" I began as soon as I had mastered my surprise. I couldn't bring out the dingy word "models": it seemed so little to fit the case.

"We haven't had much practice," said the lady.

"We've got to *do* something, and we've thought that an artist in your line might perhaps make something of us," her husband threw off. He further mentioned that they didn't know many artists and that they had gone first, on the off-chance—he painted views of course, but sometimes put in figures; perhaps I remembered—to Mr. Rivet, whom they had met a few years before at a place in Norfolk where he was sketching.

"We used to sketch a little ourselves," the lady hinted.

"It's very awkward, but we absolutely *must* do something," her husband went on.

"Of course we're not so *very* young," she admitted with a wan smile.

With the remark that I might as well know something more about them the husband had handed me a card extracted from a neat new pocket-book—their appurtenances were all of the freshest—and inscribed with the words "Major Monarch." Impressive as these words were they didn't carry my knowledge much further; but my visitor presently added: "I've left the army and we've had the misfortune to lose our money. In fact our means are dreadfully small."

"It's awfully trying—a regular strain," said Mrs. Monarch.

They evidently wished to be discreet—to take care not to swagger because they were gentlefolk. I felt them willing to recognise this as something of a drawback, at the same time that I guessed at an underlying sense—their consolation in adversity—that they *had* their points. They certainly had; but these advantages struck me as preponderantly social; such for instance as would help to make a drawing-room look well. However, a drawing-room was always, or ought to be, a picture.

In consequence of his wife's allusion to their age Major Monarch observed: "Naturally it's more for the figure that we thought of going in. We can still hold ourselves up." On the instant I saw that the figure was indeed their strong point. His "naturally" didn't sound vain, but it lighted up the question. "*She* has the best one," he continued, nodding at his wife with a pleasant after-dinner absence of circumlocution. I could only reply, as if we were in fact sitting over our wine, that this didn't prevent his own from being very good; which led him in turn to make answer: "We thought that if you ever have to do people like us we might be something like it. *She* particularly—for a lady in a book, you know."

I was so amused by them that, to get more of it, I did my best to take their point of view; and though it was an embarrassment to find myself appraising physically, as if they were animals on hire or useful blacks, a pair whom I should have expected to meet only in one of the relations in which criticism is tacit, I looked at Mrs. Monarch judicially enough to be able to exclaim after a moment with conviction: "Oh yes, a lady in a book!" She was singularly like a bad illustration.

"We'll stand up, if you like," said the Major; and he raised himself before me with a really grand air.

I could take his measure at a glance—he was six feet two and a perfect gentleman. It would have paid any club in process of formation and in want of a stamp to engage him at a salary to stand in the principal window. What struck me at once was that in coming to me they had rather missed their vocation; they could surely have been turned to better account for advertising purposes. I couldn't of course see the thing in detail, but I could see them make somebody's fortune—I don't mean their own. There was something in them for a waistcoat-maker, an hotel-keeper or a soap-vendor. I could imagine "We always use it" pinned on their bosoms with the greatest effect; I had a vision of the brilliancy with which they would launch a table d'hôte.[3]

Mrs. Monarch sat still, not from pride but from shyness, and presently her husband said to her; "Get up, my dear, and show how smart you are." She obeyed, but she had no need to get up to show it. She walked to the end of the studio and then came back blushing, her fluttered eyes on the partner of

---

3. A common table for guests at a hotel.

her appeal. I was reminded of an incident I had accidentally had a glimpse of
in Paris—being with a friend there, a dramatist about to produce a play, when
an actress came to him to ask to be entrusted with a part. She went through
her paces before him, walked up and down as Mrs. Monarch was doing. Mrs.
Monarch did it quite as well, but I abstained from applauding. It was very odd
to see such people apply for such poor pay. She looked as if she had ten
thousand a year. Her husband had used the word that described her: she was
in the London current jargon essentially and typically "smart." Her figure was,
in the same order of ideas, conspicuously and irreproachably "good." For a
woman of her age her waist was surprisingly small; her elbow moreover had
the orthodox crook. She held her head at the conventional angle, but why did
she come to *me*? She ought to have tried on jackets at a big shop. I feared my
visitors were not only destitute but "artistic"—which would be a great complication. When she sat down again I thanked her, observing that what a
draughtsman most valued in his model was the faculty of keeping quiet.

"Oh *she* can keep quiet," said Major Monarch. Then he added jocosely:
"I've always kept her quiet."

"I'm not a nasty fidget, am I?" It was going to wring tears from me, I felt,
the way she hid her head, ostrich-like, in the other broad bosom.

The owner of this expanse addressed his answer to me. "Perhaps it isn't out
of place to mention—because we ought to be quite business-like, oughtn't
we?—that when I married her she was known as the Beautiful Statue."

"Oh dear!" said Mrs. Monarch ruefully.

"Of course I should want a certain amount of expression," I rejoined.

"Of *course*!"—and I had never heard such unanimity.

"And then I suppose you know that you'll get awfully tired."

"Oh we *never* get tired!" they eagerly cried.

"Have you had any kind of practice?"

They hesitated—they looked at each other. "We've been photographed—
*immensely*," said Mrs. Monarch.

"She means the fellows have asked us themselves," added the Major.

"I see—because you're so good-looking."

"I don't know what they thought, but they were always after us."

"We always got our photographs for nothing," smiled Mrs. Monarch.

"We might have brought some, my dear," her husband remarked.

"I'm not sure we have any left. We've given quantities away," she explained
to me.

"With our autographs and that sort of thing," said the Major.

"Are they to be got in the shops?" I enquired as a harmless pleasantry.

"Oh yes, *hers*—they used to be."

"Not now," said Mrs. Monarch with her eyes on the floor.

## II

I could fancy the "sort of thing" they put on the presentation copies of their
photographs, and I was sure they wrote a beautiful hand. It was odd
how quickly I was sure of everything that concerned them. If they were now
so poor as to have to earn shillings and pence they could never have had much
of a margin. Their good looks had been their capital, and they had good-
humouredly made the most of the career that this resource marked out for

them. It was in their faces, the blankness, the deep intellectual repose of the twenty years of country-house visiting that had given them pleasant intonations. I could see the sunny drawing-rooms, sprinkled with periodicals she didn't read, in which Mrs. Monarch had continuously sat; I could see the wet shrubberies in which she had walked, equipped to admiration for either exercise. I could see the rich covers[4] the Major had helped to shoot and the wonderful garments in which, late at night, he repaired to the smoking-room to talk about them. I could imagine their leggings and waterproofs, their knowing tweeds and rugs, their rolls of sticks and cases of tackle and neat umbrellas; and I could evoke the exact appearance of their servants and the compact variety of their luggage on the platforms of country stations.

They gave small tips, but they were liked; they didn't do anything themselves, but they were welcome. They looked so well everywhere; they gratified the general relish for stature, complexion and "form." They knew it without fatuity or vulgarity, and they respected themselves in consequence. They weren't superficial; they were thorough and kept themselves up—it had been their line. People with such a taste for activity had to have some line. I could feel how even in a dull house they could have been counted on for the joy of life. At present something had happened—it didn't matter what, their little income had grown less, it had grown least—and they had to do something for pocket-money. Their friends could like them, I made out, without liking to support them. There was something about them that represented credit—their clothes, their manners, their type; but if credit is a large empty pocket in which an occasional chink reverberates, the chink at least must be audible. What they wanted of me was to help to make it so. Fortunately they had no children—I soon divined that. They would also perhaps wish our relations to be kept secret: this was why it was "for the figure"— the reproduction of the face would betray them.

I liked them—I felt, quite as their friends must have done—they were so simple; and I had no objection to them if they would suit. But somehow with all their perfections I didn't easily believe in them. After all they were amateurs, and the ruling passion of my life was the detestation of the amateur. Combined with this was another perversity—an innate preference for the represented subject over the real one: the defect of the real one was so apt to be a lack of representation. I liked things that appeared; then one was sure. Whether they *were* or not was a subordinate and almost always a profitless question. There were other considerations, the first of which was that I already had two or three recruits in use, notably a young person with big feet, in alpaca, from Kilburn, who for a couple of years had come to me regularly for my illustrations and with whom I was still—perhaps ignobly—satisfied. I frankly explained to my visitors how the case stood, but they had taken more precautions than I supposed. They had reasoned out their opportunity, for Claude Rivet had told them of the projected *édition de luxe* of one of the writers of our day—the rarest of the novelists—who, long neglected by the multitudinous vulgar and dearly prized by the attentive (need I mention Philip Vincent?)[5] had had the happy fortune of seeing, late in life, the dawn and then the full light of a higher criticism; an estimate in which on the part of the public there was something really of expiation. The edition preparing, planned by a publisher of taste, was practically an act of high reparation; the wood-cuts

---

4. I.e., successful bagging of game birds.
5. Obviously James, here indulging in some good-

natured complaining and fantasizing.

with which it was to be enriched were the homage of English art to one of the most independent representatives of English letters. Major and Mrs. Monarch confessed to me they had hoped I might be able to work *them* into my branch of the enterprise. They knew I was to do the first of the books, "Rutland Ramsay," but I had to make clear to them that my participation in the rest of the affair—this first book was to be a test—must depend on the satisfaction I should give. If this should be limited my employers would drop me with scarce common forms. It was therefore a crisis for me, and naturally I was making special preparations, looking about for new people, should they be necessary, and securing the best types. I admitted however that I should like to settle down to two or three good models who would do for everything.

"Should we have often to—a—put on special clothes?" Mrs. Monarch timidly demanded.

"Dear yes—that's half the business."

"And should we be expected to supply our own costumes?"

"Oh no; I've got a lot of things. A painter's models put on—or put off— anything he likes."

"And you mean—a—the same?"

"The same?"

Mrs. Monarch looked at her husband again.

"Oh she was just wondering," he explained, "if the costumes are in *general* use." I had to confess that they were, and I mentioned further that some of them—I had a lot of genuine greasy last-century things—had served their time, a hundred years ago, on living world-stained men and women; on figures not perhaps so far removed, in that vanished world, from *their* type, the Monarchs', *quoi!*[6] of a breeched and bewigged age. "We'll put on anything that *fits*," said the Major.

"Oh I arrange that—they fit in the pictures."

"I'm afraid I should do better for the modern books. I'd come as you like," said Mrs. Monarch.

"She has got a lot of clothes at home: they might do for contemporary life," her husband continued.

"Oh I can fancy scenes in which you'd be quite natural." And indeed I could see the slipshod rearrangements of stale properties—the stories I tried to produce pictures for without the exasperation of reading them—whose sandy tracts the good lady might help to people. But I had to return to the fact that for this sort of work—the daily mechanical grind—I was already equipped: the people I was working with were fully adequate.

"We only thought we might be more like *some* characters," said Mrs. Monarch mildly, getting up.

Her husband also rose; he stood looking at me with a dim wistfulness that was touching in so fine a man. "Wouldn't it be rather a pull sometimes to have—a—to have—?" He hung fire; he wanted me to help him by phrasing what he meant. But I couldn't—I didn't know. So he brought it out awkwardly: "The *real* thing; a gentleman, you know, or a lady." I was quite ready to give a general assent—I admitted that there was a great deal in that. This encouraged Major Monarch to say, following up his appeal with an unacted gulp: "It's awfully hard—we've tried everything." The gulp was communicative; it proved too much for his wife. Before I knew it Mrs. Monarch had dropped

6. What! (French).

again upon a divan and burst into tears. Her husband sat down beside her, holding one of her hands; whereupon she quickly dried her eyes with the other, while I felt embarrassed as she looked up at me. "There isn't a confounded job I haven't applied for—waited for—prayed for. You can fancy we'd be pretty bad first. Secretaryships and that sort of thing? You might as well ask for a peerage. I'd be *anything*—I'm strong; a messenger or a coalheaver. I'd put on a gold-laced cap and open carriage-doors in front of the haberdasher's; I'd hang about a station to carry portmanteaux; I'd be a postman. But they won't *look* at you; there are thousands as good as yourself already on the ground. Gentlemen, poor beggars, who've drunk their wine, who've kept their hunters!"

I was as reassuring as I knew how to be, and my visitors were presently on their feet again while, for the experiment, we agreed on an hour. We were discussing it when the door opened and Miss Churm came in with a wet umbrella. Miss Churm had to take the omnibus to Maida Vale and then walk half a mile. She looked a trifle blowsy and slightly splashed. I scarcely ever saw her come in without thinking afresh how odd it was that, being so little in herself, she should yet be so much in others. She was a meagre little Miss Churm, but was such an ample heroine of romance. She was only a freckled cockney,[7] but she could represent everything, from a fine lady to a shepherdess; she had the faculty as she might have had a fine voice or long hair. She couldn't spell and she loved beer, but she had two or three "points," and practice, and a knack, and mother-wit, and a whimsical sensibility, and a love of the theatre, and seven sisters, and not an ounce of respect, especially for the *h*. The first thing my visitors saw was that her umbrella was wet, and in their spotless perfection they visibly winced at it. The rain had come on since their arrival.

"I'm all in a soak; there *was* a mess of people in the 'bus. I wish you lived near a stytion," said Miss Churm. I requested her to get ready as quickly as possible, and she passed into the room in which she always changed her dress. But before going out she asked me what she was to get into this time.

"It's the Russian princess, don't you know?" I answered; "the one with the 'golden eyes,' in black velvet, for the long thing in the *Cheapside*."[8]

"Golden eyes? I *say!*" cried Miss Churm, while my companions watched her with intensity as she withdrew. She always arranged herself, when she was late, before I could turn around; and I kept my visitors a little on purpose, so that they might get an idea, from seeing her, what would be expected of themselves. I mentioned that she was quite my notion of an excellent model—she was really very clever.

"Do you think she looks like a Russian princess?" Major Monarch asked with lurking alarm.

"When I make her, yes."

"Oh if you have to *make* her—!" he reasoned, not without point.

"That's the most you can ask. There are so many who are not makeable."

"Well now, *here's* a lady"—and with a persuasive smile he passed his arm into his wife's—"who's already made!"

"Oh I'm not a Russian princess," Mrs. Monarch protested a little coldly. I

---

7. Native of London, especially the East End. The cockney dialect is known for dropping *h*'s; e.g., *hair* would be pronounced *air*.

8. Imaginary magazine named after a main business street in London.

could see she had known some and didn't like them. There at once was a complication of a kind I never had to fear with Miss Churm.

This young lady came back in black velvet—the gown was rather rusty and very low on her lean shoulders—and with a Japanese fan in her red hands. I reminded her that in the scene I was doing she had to look over some one's head. "I forget whose it is; but it doesn't matter. Just look over a head."

"I'd rather look over a stove," said Miss Churm; and she took her station near the fire. She fell into position, settled herself into a tall attitude, gave a certain backward inclination to her head and a certain forward droop to her fan, and looked, at least to my prejudiced sense, distinguished and charming, foreign and dangerous. We left her looking so while I went downstairs with Major and Mrs. Monarch.

"I believe I could come about as near it as that," said Mrs. Monarch.

"Oh, you think she's shabby, but you must allow for the alchemy of art."

However, they went off with an evident increase of comfort founded on their demonstrable advantage in being the real thing. I could fancy them shuddering over Miss Churm. She was very droll about them when I went back, for I told her what they wanted.

"Well, if she can sit I'll tyke to bookkeeping," said my model.

"She's very ladylike," I replied as an innocent form of aggravation.

"So much the worse for you. That means she can't turn round."

"She'll do for the fashionable novels."

"Oh yes, she'll do for them!" my model humorously declared. "Ain't they bad enough without her?" I had often sociably denounced them to Miss Churm.

### III

It was for the elucidation of a mystery in one of these works that I first tried Mrs. Monarch. Her husband came with her, to be useful if necessary—it was sufficiently clear that as a general thing he would prefer to come with her. At first I wondered if this were for "propriety's" sake—if he were going to be jealous and meddling. The idea was too tiresome, and if it had been confirmed it would speedily have brought our acquaintance to a close. But I soon saw there was nothing in it and that if he accompanied Mrs. Monarch it was—in addition to the chance of being wanted—simply because he had nothing else to do. When they were separate his occupation was gone and they never had been separate. I judged rightly that in their awkward situation their close union was their main comfort and that this union had no weak spot. It was a real marriage, an encouragement to the hesitating, a nut for pessimists to crack. Their address was humble—I remember afterwards thinking it had been the only thing about them that was really professional—and I could fancy the lamentable lodgings in which the Major would have been left alone. He could sit there more or less grimly with his wife—he couldn't sit there anyhow without her.

He had too much tact to try and make himself agreeable when he couldn't be useful; so when I was too absorbed in my work to talk he simply sat and waited. But I liked to hear him talk—it made my work, when not interrupting it, less mechanical, less special. To listen to him was to combine the excitement of going out with the economy of staying at home. There was only one hindrance—that I seemed not to know any of the people this brilliant couple had known. I think he wondered extremely, during the term of our intercourse, whom the deuce I *did* know. He hadn't a stray sixpence of an idea to fumble for, so we didn't spin it very fine; we confined ourselves to questions of leather and even of liquor—saddlers and breeches-makers and how to get excellent claret cheap—and matters like "good trains" and the habits of small game. His lore on these last subjects was astonishing—he managed to interweave the station-master with the ornithologist. When he couldn't talk about greater things he could talk cheerfully about smaller, and since I couldn't accompany him into reminiscences of the fashionable world he could lower the conversation without a visible effort to my level.

So earnest a desire to please was touching in a man who could so easily have knocked one down. He looked after the fire and had an opinion on the draught of the stove without my asking him, and I could see that he thought many of my arrangements not half knowing. I remember telling him that if I were only rich I'd offer him a salary to come and teach me how to live. Sometimes he gave a random sigh of which the essence might have been: "Give me even such a bare old barrack as *this*, and I'd do something with it!" When I wanted to use him he came alone; which was an illustration of the superior courage of women. His wife could bear her solitary second floor, and she was in general more discreet; showing by various small reserves that she was alive to the propriety of keeping our relations markedly professional—not letting them slide into sociability. She wished it to remain clear that she and the Major were employed, not cultivated, and if she approved of me as a superior, who could be kept in his place, she never thought me quite good enough for an equal.

She sat with great intensity, giving the whole of her mind to it, and was capable of remaining for an hour almost as motionless as before a photographer's lens. I could see she had been photographed often, but somehow the very habit that made her good for that purpose unfitted her for mine. At first I was extremely pleased with her ladylike air, and it was a satisfaction, on coming to follow her lines, to see how good they were and how far they could lead the pencil. But after a little skirmishing I began to find her too insurmountably stiff; do what I would with it my drawing looked like a photograph or a copy of a photograph. Her figure had no variety of expression—she herself had no sense of variety. You may say that this was my business and was only a question of placing her. Yet I placed her in every conceivable position and she managed to obliterate their differences. She was always a lady certainly, and into the bargain was always the same lady. She was the real thing, but always the same thing. There were moments when I rather writhed under the serenity of her confidence that she *was* the real thing. All her dealings with me and all her husband's were an implication that this was lucky for *me*. Meanwhile I found myself trying to invent types that approached her own, instead of making her own transform itself—in the clever way that was not impossible for instance to poor Miss Churm. Arrange as I would and take the precautions I would, she always came out, in my pictures, too tall—landing me in the dilemma of having represented a fascinating woman as seven feet high, which (out of respect perhaps to my own very much scantier inches) was far from my idea of such a personage.

The case was worse with the Major—nothing I could do would keep *him* down, so that he became useful only for representation of brawny giants. I adored variety and range, I cherished human accidents, the illustrative note; I wanted to characterise closely, and the thing in the world I most hated was the danger of being ridden by a type. I had quarrelled with some of my friends about it; I had parted company with them for maintaining that one *had* to be, and that if the type was beautiful—witness Raphael and Leonardo[9]—the servitude was only a gain. I was neither Leonardo nor Raphael—I might only be a presumptuous young modern searcher; but I held that everything was to be sacrificed sooner than character. When they claimed that the obsessional form could easily *be* character I retorted, perhaps superficially, "Whose?" It couldn't be everybody's—it might end in being nobody's.

After I had drawn Mrs. Monarch a dozen times I felt surer even than before that the value of such a model as Miss Churm resided precisely in the fact that she had no positive stamp, combined of course with the other fact that what she did have was a curious and inexplicable talent for imitation. Her usual appearance was like a curtain which she could draw up at request for a capital performance. This performance was simply suggestive; but it was a word to the wise—it was vivid and pretty. Sometimes even I thought it, though she was plain herself, too insipidly pretty; I made it a reproach to her that the figures drawn from her were monotonously *(bêtement,*[1] as we used to say) graceful. Nothing made her more angry: it was so much her pride to feel she could sit for characters that had nothing in common with each other. She would accuse me at such moments of taking away her "reputytion."

It suffered a certain shrinkage, this queer quantity, from the repeated visits of my new friends. Miss Churm was greatly in demand, never in want of employment, so I had no scruple in putting her off occasionally, to try them more at my ease. It was certainly amusing at first to do the real thing—it was amusing to do Major Monarch's trousers. There *were* the real thing, even if he did come out colossal. It was amusing to do his wife's back hair—it was so mathematically neat—and the particular "smart" tension of her tight stays. She lent herself especially to positions in which the face was somewhat averted or blurred; she abounded in ladylike back views and *profils perdus.*[2] When she stood erect she took naturally one of the attitudes in which court-painters represent queens and princesses; so that I found myself wondering whether, to draw out this accomplishment, I couldn't get the editor of the *Cheapside* to publish a really royal romance, "A Tale of Buckingham Palace." Sometimes however the real thing and the make-believe came into contact; by which I mean that Miss Churm, keeping an appointment or coming to make one on days when I had much work in hand, encountered her invidious rivals. The encounter was not on their part, for they noticed her no more than if she had been the housemaid; not from intentional loftiness, but simply because as yet, professionally, they didn't know how to fraternise, as I could imagine they would have liked—or at least that the Major would. They couldn't talk about the omnibus—they always walked; and they didn't know what else to try—she wasn't interested in good trains or cheap claret. Besides, they must have felt— in the air—that she was amused at them, secretly derisive of their ever knowing how. She wasn't a person to conceal the limits of her faith if she had had a

9. Raffaello Santi or Sanzio (1483–1520), Italian painter. Leonardo da Vinci (1452–1519), Florentine painter, sculptor, architect, and engineer.

1. Foolishly (French).
2. Averted glances (French).

chance to show them. On the other hand Mrs. Monarch didn't think her tidy; for why else did she take pains to say to me—it was going out of the way, for Mrs. Monarch—that she didn't like dirty women?

One day when my young lady happened to be present with my other sitters—she even dropped in, when it was convenient, for a chat—I asked her to be so good as to lend a hand in getting tea, a service with which she was familiar and which was one of a class that, living as I did in a small way, with slender domestic resources, I often appealed to my models to render. They liked to lay hands on my property, to break the sitting, and sometimes the china—it made them feel Bohemian. The next time I saw Miss Churm after this incident she surprised me greatly by making a scene about it—she accused me of having wished to humiliate her. She hadn't resented the outrage at the time, but had seemed obliging and amused, enjoying the comedy of asking Mrs. Monarch, who sat vague and silent, whether she would have cream and sugar, and putting an exaggerated simper into the question. She had tried intonations—as if she too wished to pass for the real thing—till I was afraid my other visitors would take offence.

Oh they were determined no to do this, and their touching patience was the measure of their great need. They would sit by the hour, uncomplaining, till I was ready to use them; they would come back on the chance of being wanted and would walk away cheerfully if it failed. I used to go to the door with them to see in what magnificent order they retreated. I tried to find other employment for them—I introduced them to several artists. But they didn't "take," for reasons I could appreciate, and I became rather anxiously aware that after such disappointments they fell back upon me with a heavier weight. They did me the honour to think me most *their* form. They weren't romantic enough for the painters, and in those days there were few serious workers in black-and-white. Besides, they had an eye to the great job I had mentioned to them— they had secretly set their hearts on supplying the right essence for my pictorial vindication of our fine novelist. They knew that for this undertaking I should want no costume-effects, none of the frippery of past ages—that it was a case in which everything would be contemporary and satirical and presumably genteel. If I could work them into it their future would be assured, for the labour would of course be long and the occupation steady.

One day Mrs. Monarch came without her husband—she explained his absence by his having had to go to the City.[3] While she sat there in her usual relaxed majesty there came at the door a knock which I immediately recognised as the subdued appeal of a model out of work. It was followed by the entrance of a young man whom I at once saw to be a foreigner and who proved in fact an Italian acquainted with no English word but my name, which he uttered in a way that made it seem to include all others. I hadn't then visited his country, nor was I proficient in his tongue; but as he was not so meanly constituted—what Italian is?—as to depend only on that member for expression he conveyed to me, in familiar but graceful mimicry, that he was in search of exactly the employment in which the lady before me was engaged. I was not struck with him at first, and while I continued to draw I dropped few signs of interest or encouragement. He stood his ground however—not importunately, but with a dumb dog-like fidelity in his eyes that amounted to

3. London.

innocent impudence, the manner of a devoted servant—he might have been in the house for years—unjustly suspected. Suddenly it struck me that this very attitude and expression made a picture; whereupon I told him to sit down and wait till I should be free. There was another picture in the way he obeyed me, and I observed as I worked that there were others still in the way he looked wonderingly, with his head thrown back, about the high studio. He might have been crossing himself in Saint Peter's. Before I finished I said to myself "The fellow's a bankrupt orange-monger, but a treasure."

When Mrs. Monarch withdrew he passed across the room like a flash to open the door for her, standing there with the rapt pure gaze of the young Dante spellbound by the young Beatrice.[4] As I never insisted, in such situations, on the blankness of the British domestic, I reflected that he had the making of a servant—and I needed one, but couldn't pay him to be only that—as well as of a model; in short I resolved to adopt my bright adventurer if he would agree to officiate in the double capacity. He jumped at my offer, and in the event my rashness—for I had really known nothing about him—wasn't brought home to me. He proved a sympathetic though a desultory ministrant, and had in a wonderful degree the *sentiment de la pose*.[5] It was uncultivated, instinctive, a part of the happy instinct that had guided him to my door and helped him to spell out my name on the card nailed to it. He had had no other introduction to me than a guess, from the shape of my high north window, seen outside, that my place was a studio and that as a studio it would contain an artist. He had wandered to England in search of fortune, like other itinerants, and had embarked, with a partner and a small green hand-cart, on the sale of penny ices. The ices had melted away and the partner had dissolved in their train. My young man wore tight yellow trousers with reddish stripes and his name was Oronte. He was sallow but fair, and when I put him into some old clothes of my own he looked like an Englishman. He was as good as Miss Churm, who could look, when requested, like an Italian.

## IV

I thought Mrs. Monarch's face slightly convulsed when, on her coming back with her husband, she found Oronte installed. It was strange to have to recognise in a scrap of a lazzarone[6] a competitor to her magnificent Major. It was she who scented danger first, for the Major was anecdotically unconscious. But Oronte gave us tea, with a hundred eager confusions—he had never been concerned in so queer a process—and I think she thought better of me for having at last an "establishment." They saw a couple of drawings that I had made of the establishment, and Mrs. Monarch hinted that it never would have struck her he had sat for them. "Now the drawings you make from *us*, they look exactly like us," she reminded me, smiling in triumph; and I recognised that this was indeed just their defect. When I drew the Monarchs I couldn't anyhow get away from them—get into the character I wanted to represent; and I hadn't the least desire my model should be discoverable in my picture. Miss Churm never was, and Mrs. Monarch thought I hid her, very properly,

4. Dante Alighieri (1265–1321), Italian poet, first saw Beatrice Portinari when they were both nine. Though he saw her only a few times, she made a lasting impression on him and became his ideal, his life's inspiration, and the direct agent of his salvation (as his greatest work, *The Divine Comedy*, makes clear).
5. Instinct for striking poses (French).
6. Beggar.

because she was vulgar; whereas if she was lost it was only as the dead who go to heaven are lost—in the gain of an angel the more.

By this time I had got a certain start with "Rutland Ramsay," the first novel in the great projected series; that is I had produced a dozen drawings, several with the help of the Major and his wife, and I had sent them in for approval. My understanding with the publishers, as I have already hinted, had been that I was to be left to do my work, in this particular case, as I liked, with the whole book committed to me; but my connexion with the rest of the series was only contingent. There were moments when, frankly, it *was* a comfort to have the real thing under one's hand; for there were characters in "Rutland Ramsay" that were very much like it. There were people presumably as erect as the Major and women of as good a fashion as Mrs. Monarch. There was a great deal of country-house life—treated, it is true, in a fine fanciful ironical gener- alised way—and there was a considerable implication of knickerbockers and kilts.[7] There were certain things I had to settle at the outset; such things for instance as the exact appearance of the hero and the particular bloom and figure of the heroine. The author of course gave me a lead, but there was a margin for interpretation. I took the Monarchs into my confidence, I told them frankly what I was about, I mentioned my embarrassments and alterna- tives. "Oh take *him!*" Mrs. Monarch murmured sweetly, looking at her hus- band; and "What could you want better than my wife?" the Major enquired with the comfortable candour that now prevailed between us.

I wasn't obliged to answer these remarks—I was only obliged to place my sitters. I wasn't easy in mind, and I postponed a little timidly perhaps the solving of my question. The book was a large canvas, the other figures were numerous, and I worked off at first some of the episodes in which the hero and the heroine were not concerned. When once I had set *them* up I should have to stick to them—I couldn't make my young man seven feet high in one place and five feet nine in another. I inclined on the whole to the latter measurement, though the Major more than once reminded me that *he* looked about as young as any one. It was indeed quite possible to arrange him, for the figure, so that it would have been difficult to detect his age. After the spontane- ous Oronte had been with me a month, and after I had given him to under- stand several times over that his native exuberance would presently constitute an insurmountable barrier to our further intercourse, I waked to a sense of his heroic capacity. He was only five feet seven, but the remaining inches were latent. I tried him almost secretly at first, for I was really rather afraid of the judgment my other models would pass on such a choice. If they regarded Miss Churm as little better than a snare what would they think of the representation by a person so little the real thing as an Italian street-vendor of a protagonist formed by a public school?

If I went a little in fear of them it wasn't because they bullied me, because they had got an oppressive foothold, but because in their really pathetic deco- rum and mysteriously permanent newness they counted on me so intensely. I was therefore very glad when Jack Hawley came home: he was always of such good counsel. He painted badly himself, but there was no one like him for putting his finger on the place. He had been absent from England for a year; he had been somewhere—I don't remember where—to get a fresh eye. I was

7. Knickerbockers (close-fitting short pants gathered at the knee) and kilts (a knee-length pleated skirt, usually of tartan, worn by Scottish men) are suggestive of rural, outdoor attire.

in a good deal of dread of any such organ, but we were old friends; he had been away for months and a sense of emptiness was creeping into my life. I hadn't dodged a missile for a year.

He came back with a fresh eye, but with the same old black velvet blouse, and the first evening he spent in my studio we smoked cigarettes till the small hours. He had done no work himself, he had only got the eye; so the field was clear for the production of my little things. He wanted to see what I had produced for the *Cheapside*, but he was disappointed in the exhibition. That at least seemed the meaning of two or three comprehensive groans which, as he lounged on my big divan, his leg folded under him, looking at my latest drawings, issued from his lips with the smoke of the cigarette.

"What's the matter with you?" I asked.

"What's the matter with *you?*"

"Nothing save that I'm mystified."

"You are indeed. You're quite off the hinge. What's the meaning of this new fad?" And he tossed me, with visible irreverence, a drawing in which I happened to have depicted both my elegant models. I asked if he didn't think it good, and he replied that it struck him as execrable, given the sort of thing I had always represented myself to him as wishing to arrive at; but I let that pass—I was so anxious to see exactly what he meant. The two figures in the picture looked colossal, but I supposed this was *not* what he meant, inasmuch as, for aught he knew the contrary, I might have been trying for some such effect. I maintained that I was working exactly in the same way as when he last had done me the honour to tell me I might do something some day. "Well, there's a screw loose somewhere," he answered; "wait a bit and I'll discover it." I depended upon him to do so: where else was the fresh eye? But he produced at last nothing more luminous than "I don't know—I don't like your types." This was lame for a critic who had never consented to discuss with me anything but the question of execution, the direction of strokes and the mystery of values.

"In the drawings you've been looking at I think my types are very handsome."

"Oh they won't do!"

"I've been working with new models."

"I see you have. *They* won't do."

"Are you very sure of that?"

"Absolutely—they're stupid."

"You mean *I* am—for I ought to get round that."

"You *can't*—with such people. Who are they?"

I told him, so far as was necessary, and he concluded heartlessly: "Ce sont des gens qu'il faut mettre à la porte."[8]

"You've never seen them; they're awfully good"—I flew to their defence.

"Not seen them? Why all this recent work of yours drops to pieces with them. It's all I want to see of them."

"No one else has said anything against it—the *Cheapside* people are pleased."

"Everyone else is an ass, and the *Cheapside* people the biggest asses of all. Come, don't pretend at this time of day to have pretty illusions about the

---

8. Such people should be shown the door (French).

public, especially about publishers and editors. It's not for *such* animals you work—it's for those who know, *coloro che sanno;*[9] so keep straight for *me* if you can't keep straight for yourself. There was a certain sort of thing you used to try for—and a very good thing it was. But this twaddle isn't *in* it." When I talked with Hawley later about "Rutland Ramsay" and its possible successors he declared that I must get back into my boat again or I should go to the bottom. His voice in short was the voice of warning.

I noted the warning, but I didn't turn my friends out of doors. They bored me a good deal; but the very fact that they bored me admonished me not to sacrifice them—if there was anything to be done with them—simply to irritation. As I look back at this phase they seem to me to have pervaded my life not a little. I have a vision of them as most of the time in my studio, seated against the wall on an old velvet bench to be out of the way, and resembling the while a pair of patient courtiers in a royal ante-chamber. I'm convinced that during the coldest weeks of the winter they held their ground because it saved them fire. Their newness was losing its gloss, and it was impossible not to feel them objects of charity. Whenever Miss Churm arrived they went away, and after I was fairly launched in "Rutland Ramsay" Miss Churm arrived pretty often. They managed to express to me tacitly that they supposed I wanted her for the low life of the book, and I let them suppose it, since they had attempted to study the work—it was lying about the studio—without discovering that it dealt only with the highest circles. They had dipped into the most brilliant of our novelists without deciphering many passages. I still took an hour from them, now and again, in spite of Jack Hawley's warning: it would be time enough to dismiss them, if dismissal should be necessary, when the rigour of the season was over. Hawley had made their acquaintance—he had met them at my fireside—and thought them a ridiculous pair. Learning that he was a painter they tried to approach him, to show him too that they were the real thing; but he looked at them, across the big room, as if they were miles away: they were a compendium of everything he most objected to in the social system of his country. Such people as that, all convention and patent-leather, with ejaculations that stopped conversation, had no business in a studio. A studio was a place to learn to see, and how could you see through a pair of feather-beds?

The main inconvenience I suffered at their hands was that at first I was shy of letting it break upon them that my artful little servant had begun to sit to me for "Rutland Ramsay." They knew I had been odd enough—they were prepared by this time to allow oddity to artists—to pick a foreign vagabond out of the streets when I might have had a person with whiskers and credentials, but it was some time before they learned how high I rated his accomplishments. They found him in an attitude more than once, but they never doubted I was doing him as an organ-grinder. There were several things they never guessed, and one of them was that for a striking scene in the novel, in which a footman briefly figured, it occurred to me to make use of Major Monarch as the menial. I kept putting this off, I didn't like to ask him to don the livery—besides the difficulty of finding a livery to fit him. At last, one day late in the winter, when I was at work on the despised Oronte, who caught one's idea on the wing, and was in the glow of feeling myself go very straight, they came in, the Major and his wife, with their society laugh about nothing (there was less

9. A misquotation of a phrase Dante applied to Aristotle in *The Divine Comedy*, "Inferno," 4.131, which reads, "*el maestro di color che sanno,*" literally, "the master of those who know."

and less to laugh at); came in like country-callers—they always reminded me of that—who have walked across the park after church and are presently persuaded to stay to luncheon. Luncheon was over, but they could stay to tea—I knew they wanted it. The fit was on me, however, and I couldn't let my ardour cool and my work wait, with the fading daylight, while my model prepared it. So I asked Mrs. Monarch if she would mind laying it out—a request which for an instant brought all the blood to her face. Her eyes were on her husband's for a second, and some mute telegraphy passed between them. Their folly was over the next instant; his cheerful shrewdness put an end to it. So far from pitying their wounded pride, I must add, I was moved to give it as complete a lesson as I could. They bustled about together and got out the cups and saucers and made the kettle boil. I know they felt as if they were waiting on my servant, and when the tea was prepared I said: "He'll have a cup, please—he's tired." Mrs. Monarch brought him one where he stood, and he took it from her as if had been a gentleman at a party squeezing a crush-hat with an elbow.

Then it came over me that she had made a great effort for me—made it with a kind of nobleness—and that I owed her a compensation. Each time I saw her after this I wondered what the compensation could be. I couldn't go on doing the wrong thing to oblige them. Oh it *was* the wrong thing, the stamp of the work for which they sat—Hawley was not the only person to say it now. I sent in a large number of the drawings I had made for "Rutland Ramsay," and I received a warning that was more to the point than Hawley's. The artistic adviser of the house for which I was working was of opinion that many of my illustrations were not what had been looked for. Most of these illustrations were the subjects in which the Monarchs had figured. Without going into the question of what *had* been looked for, I had to face the fact that at this rate I shouldn't get the other books to do. I hurled myself in despair on Miss Churm—I put her through all her paces. I not only adopted Oronte publicly as my hero, but one morning when the Major looked in to see if I didn't require him to finish a *Cheapside* figure for which he had begun to sit the week before, I told him I had changed my mind—I'd do the drawing from my man. At this my visitor turned pale and stood looking at me. "Is *he* your idea of an English gentlemen?" he asked.

I was disappointed, I was nervous, I wanted to get on with my work; so I replied with irritation: "Oh my dear Major—I can't be ruined for *you!*"

It was a horrid speech, but he stood another moment—after which, without a word, he quitted the studio. I drew a long breath, for I said to myself that I shouldn't see him again. I hadn't told him definitely that I was in danger of having my work rejected, but I was vexed at his not having felt the catastrophe in the air, read with me the moral of our fruitless collaboration, the lesson that in the deceptive atmosphere of art even the highest respectability may fail of being plastic.

I didn't owe my friends money, but I did see them again. They reappeared together three days later, and, given all the other facts, there was something tragic in that one. It was a clear proof they could find nothing else in life to do. They had threshed the matter out in a dismal conference—they had digested the bad news that they were not in for the series. If they weren't useful to me even for the *Cheapside* their function seemed difficult to determine, and I could only judge at first that they had come, forgivingly, decorously, to take a last leave. This made me rejoice in secret that I had little leisure for a scene;

for I had placed both my other models in position together and I was pegging away at a drawing from which I hoped to derive glory. It had been suggested by the passage in which Rutland Ramsay, drawing up a chair to Artemisia's piano-stool, says extraordinary things to her while she ostensibly fingers out a difficult piece of music. I had done Miss Churm at the piano before—it was an attitude in which she knew how to take on an absolutely poetic grace. I wished the two figures to "compose" together with intensity, and my little Italian had entered perfectly into my conception. The pair were vividly before me, the piano had been pulled out; it was a charming show of blended youth and murmured love, which I had only to catch and keep. My visitors stood and looked at it, and I was friendly to them over my shoulder.

They made no response, but I was used to silent company and went on with my work, only a little disconcerted—even though exhilarated by the sense that *this* was at least the ideal thing—at not having got rid of them after all. Presently I heard Mrs. Monarch's sweet voice beside or rather above me: "I wish her hair were a little better done." I looked up and she was staring with a strange fixedness at Miss Churm, whose back was turned to her. "Do you mind my just touching it?" she went on—a question which made me spring up for an instant as with the instinctive fear that she might do the young lady a harm. But she quieted me with a glance I shall never forget—I confess I should like to have been able to paint *that*—and went for a moment to my model. She spoke to her softly, laying a hand on her shoulder and bending over her; and as the girl, understanding, gratefully assented, she disposed her rough curls, with a few quick passes, in such a way as to make Miss Churm's head twice as charming. It was one of the most heroic personal services I've ever seen rendered. Then Mrs. Monarch turned away with a low sigh and, looking about her as if for something to do, stooped to the floor with a noble humility and picked up a dirty rag that had dropped out of my paint-box.

The Major meanwhile had also been looking for something to do, and, wandering to the other end of the studio, saw before him my breakfast-things neglected, unremoved. "I say, can't I be useful *here*?" he called out to me with an irrepressible quaver. I assented with a laugh that I fear was awkward, and for the next ten minutes, while I worked, I heard the light clatter of china and the tinkle of spoons and glass. Mrs. Monarch assisted her husband—they washed up my crockery, they put it away. They wandered off into my little scullery, and I afterwards found that they had cleaned my knives and that my slender stock of plate had an unprecedented surface. When it came over me, the latent eloquence of what they were doing, I confess that my drawing was blurred for a moment—the picture swam. They had accepted their failure, but they couldn't accept their fate. They had bowed their heads in bewilderment to the perverse and cruel law in virtue of which the real thing could be so much less precious than the unreal; but they didn't want to starve. If my servants were my models; then my models might be my servants. They would reverse the parts—the others would sit for the ladies and gentlemen and *they* would do the work. They would still be in the studio—it was an intense dumb appeal to me not to turn them out. "Take us on," they wanted to say—"we'll do *anything*."

My pencil dropped from my hand; my sitting was spoiled and I got rid of my sitters, who were also evidently rather mystified and awestruck. Then, alone with the Major and his wife I had a most uncomfortable moment. He put their prayer into a single sentence: "I say, you know—just let *us* do for you, can't you?" I couldn't—it was dreadful to see them emptying my slops; but I pretended I could, to oblige them, for about a week. Then I gave them a sum of money to go away, and I never saw them again. I obtained the remaining books, but my friend Hawley repeats that Major and Mrs. Monarch did me a permanent harm, got me into false ways. If it be true I'm content to have paid the price—for the memory.

1892, 1909

# The Beast in the Jungle[1]

## I

What determined the speech that startled him in the course of their encounter scarcely matters, being probably but some words spoken by himself quite without intention—spoken as they lingered and slowly moved together after their renewal of acquaintance. He had been conveyed by friends an hour or two before to the house at which she was staying; the party of visitors at the other house, of whom he was one, and thanks to whom it was his theory, as always, that he was lost in the crowd, had been invited over to luncheon. There had been after luncheon much dispersal, all in the interest of the original motive, a view of Weatherend itself and the fine things, intrinsic features, pictures, heirlooms, treasures of all the arts, that made the place almost famous; and the great rooms were so numerous that guests could wander at their will, hang back from the principal group and in cases where they took such matters with the last seriousness give themselves up to mysterious appreciations and measurements. There were persons to be observed, singly or in couples, bending toward objects in out-of-the-way corners with their hands on their knees and their heads nodding quite as with the emphasis of an excited sense of smell. When they were two they either mingled their sounds of ecstasy or melted into silences of even deeper import, so that there were aspects of the occasion that gave it for Marcher much the air of the "look round," previous to a sale highly advertised, that excites or quenches, as may be, the dream of acquisition. The dream of acquisition at Weatherend would have had to be wild indeed, and John Marcher found himself, among such suggestions, disconcerted almost equally by the presence of those who knew too much and by that of those who knew nothing. The great rooms caused so much poetry and history to press upon him that he needed some straying apart to feel in a proper relation with them, though this impulse was not, as happened, like the gloating of some of his companions, to be compared to the movements of a dog sniffing a cupboard. It had an issue promptly enough in a direction that was not to have been calculated.

It led, briefly, in the course of the October afternoon, to his closer meeting with May Bartram, whose face, a reminder, yet not quite a remembrance, as they sat much separated at a very long table, had begun merely by troubling

---

1. James initially recorded the germ for this story in 1895, but it first appeared in the collection *The Better Sort* (1903). It was reprinted, with minor revisions, in the *Altar of the Dead* volume of the New York Edition, Vol. 17 (1909), the source of the present text.

him rather pleasantly. It affected him as the sequel of something of which he had lost the beginning. He knew it, and for the time quite welcomed it, as a continuation, but didn't know what it continued, which was an interest or an amusement the greater as he was also somehow aware—yet without a direct sign from her—that the young woman herself hadn't lost the thread. She hadn't lost it, but she wouldn't give it back to him, he saw, without some putting forth of his hand for it; and he not only saw that, but saw several things more, things odd enough in the light of the fact that at the moment some accident of grouping brought them face to face he was still merely fumbling with the idea that any contact between them in the past would have had no importance. If it had had no importance he scarcely knew why his actual impression of her should so seem to have so much; the answer to which, however, was that in such a life as they all appeared to be leading for the moment one could but take things as they came. He was satisfied, without in the least being able to say why, that this young lady might roughly have ranked in the house as a poor relation; satisfied also that she was not there on a brief visit, but was more or less a part of the establishment—almost a working, a remunerated part. Didn't she enjoy at periods a protection that she paid for by helping, among other services, to show the place and explain it, deal with the tiresome people, answer questions about the dates of the building, the styles of the furniture, the authorship of the pictures, the favourite haunts of the ghost? It wasn't that she looked as if you could have given her shillings—it was impossible to look less so. Yet when she finally drifted toward him, distinctly handsome, though ever so much older—older than when he had seen her before—it might have been as an effect of her guessing that he had, within the couple of hours, devoted more imagination to her than to all the others put together, and had thereby penetrated to a kind of truth that the others were too stupid for. She *was* there on harder terms than any one; she was there as a consequence of things suffered, one way and another, in the interval of years; and she remembered him very much as she was remembered—only a good deal better.

By the time they at last thus came to speech they were alone in one of the rooms—remarkable for a fine portrait over the chimney-place—out of which their friends had passed, and the charm of it was that even before they had spoken they had practically arranged with each other to stay behind for talk. The charm, happily, was in other things too—partly in there being scarce a spot at Weatherend without something to stay behind for. It was in the way the autumn day looked into the high windows as it waned; the way the red light, breaking at the close from under a low sombre sky, reached out in a long shaft and played over old wainscots, old tapestry, old gold, old colour. It was most of all perhaps in the way she came to him as if, since she had been turned on to deal with the simpler sort, he might, should he choose to keep the whole thing down, just take her mild attention for a part of her general business. As soon as he heard her voice, however, the gap was filled up and the missing link supplied; the slight irony he divined in her attitude lost its advantage. He almost jumped at it to get there before her. "I met you years and years ago in Rome. I remember all about it." She confessed to disappointment—she had been so sure he didn't; and to prove how well he did he began to pour forth the particular recollections that popped up as he called for them. Her face and her voice, all at his service now, worked the miracle—the impression operating like the torch of a lamplighter who touches into flame, one by one, a long row of gas-jets. Marcher flattered himself the illumination was brilliant, yet he was really still more pleased on her showing him, with amusement, that in his haste to make everything right he had got most things rather wrong. It hadn't been at Rome—it had been at Naples; and it hadn't been eight years before—it had been more nearly ten. She hadn't been, either, with her uncle and aunt, but with her mother and her brother; in addition to which it was not with the Pembles *he* had been, but with the Boyers, coming down in their company from Rome—a point on which she insisted, a little to his confusion, and as to which she had her evidence in hand. The Boyers she had known, but didn't know the Pembles, though she had heard of them, and it was the people he was with who had made them acquainted. The incident of the thunderstorm that had raged round them with such violence as to drive them for refuge into an excavation—this incident had not occurred at the Palace of the Cæsars, but at Pompeii,[2] on an occasion when they had been present there at an important find.

He accepted her amendments, he enjoyed her corrections, though the moral of them was, she pointed out, that he *really* didn't remember the least thing about her; and he only felt it as a drawback that when all was made strictly historic there didn't appear much of anything left. They lingered together still, she neglecting her office—for from the moment he was so clever she had no proper right to him—and both neglecting the house, just waiting as to see if a memory or two more wouldn't again breathe on them. It hadn't taken them many minutes, after all, to put down on the table, like the cards of a pack, those that constituted their respective hands; only what came out was that the pack was unfortunately not perfect—that the past, invoked, invited, encouraged, could give them, naturally, no more than it had. It had made them anciently meet—her at twenty, him at twenty-five; but nothing was so strange, they seemed to say to each other, as that, while so occupied, it hadn't done a little more for them. They looked at each other as with the feeling of an occasion missed; the present would have been so much better if the other, in the far distance, in the foreign land, hadn't been so stupidly meagre. There weren't apparently, all counted, more than a dozen little old things that had succeeded in coming to pass between them; trivialities of youth, simplicities of freshness, stupidities of ignorance, small possible germs, but too deeply buried—too deeply (didn't it seem?) to sprout after so many years. Marcher could only feel he ought to have rendered her some service—saved her from a capsized boat in the Bay or at least recovered her dressing-bag, filched from her cab in the streets of Naples by a lazzarone[3] with a stiletto. Or it would have been nice if he could have been taken with fever all alone at his hotel, and she could have come to look after him, to write to his people, to drive him out in convalescence. *Then* they would be in possession of the something or other that their actual show seemed to lack. It yet somehow presented itself, this show, as too good to be spoiled; so that they were reduced for a few minutes more to wondering a little helplessly why—since they seemed to know a certain number of the same people—their reunion had been so long averted. They didn't use that name for it, but their delay from minute to minute to join the others was a kind of confession that they didn't quite want it to be a

2. Pompeii is near Naples, not Rome.                    3. Beggar.

failure. Their attempted supposition of reasons for their not having met but showed how little they knew of each other. There came in fact a moment when Marcher felt a positive pang. It was vain to pretend she was an old friend, for all the communities were wanting, in spite of which it was as an old friend that he saw she would have suited him. He had new ones enough—was surrounded with them for instance on the stage of the other house; as a new one he probably wouldn't have so much as noticed her. He would have liked to invent something, get her to make-believe with him that some passage of a romantic or critical kind *had* originally occurred. He was really almost reaching out in imagination—as against time—for something that would do, and saying to himself that if it didn't come this sketch of a fresh start would show for quite awkwardly bungled. They would separate, and now for no second or no third chance. They would have tried and not succeeded. Then it was, just at the turn, as he afterwards made it out to himself, that, everything else failing, she herself decided to take up the case and, as it were, save the situation. He felt as soon as she spoke that she had been consciously keeping back what she said and hoping to get on without it; a scruple in her that immensely touched him when, by the end of three or four minutes more, he was able to measure it. What she brought out, at any rate, quite cleared the air and supplied the link—the link it was so odd he should frivolously have managed to lose.

"You know you told me something I've never forgotten and that again and again has made me think of you since; it was that tremendously hot day when we went to Sorrento,[4] across the bay, for the breeze. What I allude to was what you said to me, on the way back, as we sat under the awning of the boat enjoying the cool. Have you forgotten?"

He had forgotten and was even more surprised than ashamed. But the great thing was that he saw in this no vulgar reminder of any "sweet" speech. The vanity of women had long memories, but she was making no claim on him of a compliment or a mistake. With another woman, a totally different one, he might have feared the recall possibly of even some imbecile "offer." So, in having to say that he had indeed forgotten, he was conscious rather of a loss than of a gain; he already saw an interest in the matter of her mention. "I try to think—but I give it up. Yet I remember the Sorrento day."

"I'm not very sure you do," May Bartram after a moment said; "and I'm not very sure I ought to want you to. It's dreadful to bring a person back at any time to what he was ten years before. If you've lived away from it," she smiled, "so much the better."

"Ah if *you* haven't why should I?" he asked.

"Lived away, you mean, from what I myself was?"

"From what *I* was. I was of course an ass," Marcher went on; "but I would rather know from you just the sort of ass I was than—from the moment you have something in your mind—not know anything."

Still, however, she hesitated. "But if you've completely ceased to be that sort—?"

"Why I can then all the more bear to know. Besides, perhaps I haven't."

"Perhaps. Yet if you haven't," she added, "I should suppose you'd remember. Not indeed that *I* in the least connect with my impression the invidious

---

4. Across the bay from Naples.

name you use. If I had only thought you foolish," she explained, "the thing I speak of wouldn't so have remained with me. It was about yourself." She waited as if it might come to him; but as, only meeting her eyes in wonder, he gave no sign, she burnt her ships. "Has it ever happened?"

Then it was that, while he continued to stare, a light broke for him and the blood slowly came to his face, which began to burn with recognition. "Do you mean I told you—?" But he faltered, lest what came to him shouldn't be right, lest he should only give himself away.

"It was something about yourself that it was natural one shouldn't forget—that is if one remembered you at all. That's why I ask you," she smiled, "if the thing you then spoke of has ever come to pass?"

Oh then he saw, but he was lost in wonder and found himself embarrassed. This, he also saw, made her sorry for him, as if her allusion had been a mistake. It took him but a moment, however, to feel it hadn't been, much as it had been a surprise. After the first little shock of it her knowledge on the contrary began, even if rather strangely, to taste sweet to him. She was the only other person in the world then who would have it, and she had had it all these years, while the fact of his having so breathed his secret had unaccountably faded from him. No wonder they couldn't have met as if nothing had happened. "I judge," he finally said, "that I know what you mean. Only I had strangely enough lost any sense of having taken you so far into my confidence."

"Is it because you've taken so many others as well?"

"I've taken nobody. Not a creature since then."

"So that I'm the only person who knows?"

"The only person in the world."

"Well," she quickly replied, "I myself have never spoken. I've never, never repeated of you what you told me." She looked at him so that he perfectly believed her. Their eyes met over it in such a way that he was without a doubt. "And I never will."

She spoke with an earnestness that, as if almost excessive, put him at ease about her possible derision. Somehow the whole question was a new luxury to him—that is from the moment she was in possession. If she didn't take the sarcastic view she clearly took the sympathetic, and that was what he had had, in all the long time, from no one whomsoever. What he felt was that he couldn't at present have begun to tell her, and yet could profit perhaps exquisitely by the accident of having done so of old. "Please don't then. We're just right as it is."

"Oh I am," she laughed, "if you are!" To which she added: "Then you do still feel in the same way?"

It was impossible he shouldn't take to himself that she was really interested, though it all kept coming as perfect surprise. He had thought of himself so long as abominably alone, and lo he wasn't alone a bit. He hadn't been, it appeared, for an hour—since those moments on the Sorrento boat. It was *she* who had been, he seemed to see as he looked at her—she who had been made so by the graceless fact of his lapse of fidelity. To tell her what he had told her—what had it been but to ask something of her? something that she had given, in her charity, without his having, by a remembrance, by a return of the spirit, failing another encounter, so much as thanked her. What he had asked of her had been simply at first not to laugh at him. She had beautifully not done so for ten years, and she was not doing so now. So he had endless gratitude to make up. Only for that he must see just how he had figured to her. "What, exactly, was the account I gave—?"

"Of the way you did feel? Well, it was very simple. You said you had had from your earliest time, as the deepest thing within you, the sense of being kept for something rare and strange, possibly prodigious and terrible, that was sooner or later to happen to you, that you had in your bones the foreboding and the conviction of, and that would perhaps overwhelm you."

"Do you call that very simple?" John Marcher asked.

She thought a moment. "It was perhaps because I seemed, as you spoke, to understand it."

"You do understand it?" he eagerly asked.

Again she kept her kind eyes on him. "You still have the belief?"

"Oh!" he exclaimed helplessly. There was too much to say.

"Whatever it's to be," she clearly made out, "it hasn't yet come."

He shook his head in complete surrender now. "It hasn't yet come. Only, you know, it isn't anything I'm to *do*, to achieve in the world, to be distinguished or admired for. I'm not such an ass as *that*. It would be much better, no doubt, if I were."

"It's to be something you're merely to suffer?"

"Well, say to wait for—to have to meet, to face, to see suddenly break out in my life; possibly destroying all further consciousness, possibly annihilating me; possibly, on the other hand, only altering everything, striking at the root of all my world and leaving me to the consequences, however they shape themselves."

She took this in, but the light in her eyes continued for him not to be that of mockery. "Isn't what you describe perhaps but the expectation—or at any rate the sense of danger, familiar to so many people—of falling in love?"

John Marcher wondered. "Did you ask me that before?"

"No—I wasn't so free-and-easy then. But it's what strikes me now."

"Of course," he said after a moment, "it strikes you. Of course it strikes *me*. Of course what's in store for me may be no more than that. The only thing is," he went on, "that I think if it had been that I should by this time know."

"Do you mean because you've *been* in love?" And then as he but looked at her in silence: "You've been in love, and it hasn't meant such a cataclysm, hasn't proved the great affair?"

"Here I am, you see. It hasn't been overwhelming."

"Then it hasn't been love," said May Bartram.

"Well, I at least thought it was. I took it for that—I've taken it till now. It was agreeable, it was delightful, it was miserable," he explained. "But it wasn't strange. It wasn't what *my* affair's to be."

"You want something all to yourself—something that nobody else knows or *has* known?"

"It isn't a question of what I 'want'—God knows I don't want anything. It's only a question of the apprehension that haunts me—that I live with day by day."

He said this so lucidly and consistently that he could see it further impose itself. If she hadn't been interested before she'd have been interested now. "Is it a sense of coming violence?"

Evidently now too again he liked to talk of it. "I don't think of it as—when it does come—necessarily violent. I only think of it as natural and as of course above all unmistakeable. I think of it simply as *the* thing. *The* thing will of itself appear natural."

"Then how will it appear strange?"

Marcher bethought himself. "It won't—to *me*."

"To whom then?"

"Well," he replied, smiling at last, "say to you."

"Oh then I'm to be present?"

"Why you *are* present—since you know."

"I see." She turned it over. "But I mean at the catastrophe."

At this, for a minute, their lightness gave way to their gravity; it was as if the long look they exchanged held them together. "It will only depend on yourself—if you'll watch with me."

"Are you afraid?" she asked.

"Don't leave me *now*," he went on.

"Are you afraid?" she repeated.

"Do you think me simply out of my mind?" he pursued instead of answering. "Do I merely strike you as a harmless lunatic?"

"No," said May Bartram. "I understand you. I believe you."

"You mean you feel how my obsession—poor old thing!—may correspond to some possible reality?"

"To some possible reality."

"Then you *will* watch with me?"

She hesitated, then for the third time put her question. "Are you afraid?"

"Did I tell you I was—at Naples?"

"No, you said nothing about it."

"Then I don't know. And I should *like* to know," said John Marcher. "You'll tell me yourself whether you think so. If you'll watch with me you'll see."

"Very good then." They had been moving by this time across the room, and at the door, before passing out, they paused as for the full wind-up of their understanding. "I'll watch with you," said May Bartram.

## II

The fact that she "knew"—knew and yet neither chaffed him nor betrayed him—had in a short time begun to constitute between them a goodly bond, which became more marked when, within the year that followed their afternoon at Weatherend, the opportunities for meeting multiplied. The event that thus promoted these occasions was the death of the ancient lady her great-aunt, under whose wing, since losing her mother, she had to such an extent found shelter, and who, though but the widowed mother of the new successor to the property, had succeeded—thanks to a high tone and a high temper—in not forfeiting the supreme position at the great house. The deposition of this personage arrived but with her death, which, followed by many changes, made in particular a difference for the young woman in whom Marcher's expert attention had recognised from the first a dependent with a pride that might ache though it didn't bristle. Nothing for a long time had made him easier than the thought that the aching must have been much soothed by Miss Bartram's now finding herself able to set up a small home in London. She had acquired property, to an amount that made that luxury just possible, under her aunt's extremely complicated will, and when the whole matter began to be straightened out, which indeed took time, she let him know that the happy issue was at last in view. He had seen her again before that day, both because she had more than once accompanied the ancient lady to town and because he had paid another visit to the friends who so conveniently made of Weatherend one of the charms of their own hospitality. These friends had taken him back there; he had achieved there again with Miss Bartram some quiet detachment; and he had in London succeeded in persuading her to more than one brief absence from her aunt. They went together, on these latter occasions, to the National Gallery and the South Kensington Museum, where, among vivid reminders, they talked of Italy at large—not now attempting to recover, as at first, the taste of their youth and their ignorance. That recovery, the first day at Weatherend, had served its purpose well, had given them quite enough; so that they were, to Marcher's sense, no longer hovering about the headwaters of their stream, but had felt their boat pushed sharply off and down the current.

They were literally afloat together; for our gentleman this was marked, quite as marked as that the fortunate cause of it was just the buried treasure of her knowledge. He had with his own hands dug up this little hoard, brought to light—that is to within reach of the dim day constituted by their discretions and privacies—the object of value the hiding-place of which he had, after putting it into the ground himself, so strangely, so long forgotten. The rare luck of his having again just stumbled on the spot made him indifferent to any other question; he would doubtless have devoted more time to the odd accident of his lapse of memory if he hadn't been moved to devote so much to the sweetness, the comfort, as he felt, for the future, that this accident itself had helped to keep fresh. It had never entered into his plan that any one should "know," and mainly for the reason that it wasn't in him to tell any one. That would have been impossible, for nothing but the amusement of a cold world would have waited on it. Since, however, a mysterious fate had opened his mouth betimes, in spite of him, he would count that a compensation and profit by it to the utmost. That the right person *should* know tempered the asperity of his secret more even than his shyness had permitted him to imagine; and May Bartram was clearly right, because—well, because there she was. Her knowledge simply settled it; he would have been sure enough by this time had she been wrong. There was that in his situation, no doubt, that disposed him too much to see her as a mere confidant, taking all her light for him from the fact—the fact only—of her interest in his predicament; from her mercy, sympathy, seriousness, her consent not to regard him as the funniest of the funny. Aware, in fine, that her price for him was just in her giving him this constant sense of his being admirably spared, he was careful to remember that she had also a life of her own, with things that might happen to *her*, things that in friendship one should likewise take account of. Something fairly remarkable came to pass with him, for that matter, in this connexion—something represented by a certain passage of his consciousness, in the suddenest way, from one extreme to the other.

He had thought himself, so long as nobody knew, the most disinterested person in the world, carrying his concentrated burden, his perpetual suspense, ever so quietly, holding his tongue about it, giving others no glimpse of it nor of its effect upon his life, asking of them no allowance and only making on his side all those that were asked. He hadn't disturbed people with the queerness of their having to know a haunted man, though he had had moments of rather special temptation on hearing them say they were forsooth "unsettled." If they were as unsettled as he was—he who had never been settled for an hour in his life—they would know what it meant. Yet it wasn't, all the same, for him to make them, and he listened to them civilly enough. This was why he had such good—though possibly such rather colourless—manners; this was why, above all, he could regard himself, in a greedy world, as decently—as in fact perhaps even a little sublimely—unselfish. Our point is accordingly that he valued this character quite sufficiently to measure his present danger of letting it lapse, against which he promised himself to be much on his guard. He was quite ready, none the less, to be selfish just a little, since surely no more charming occasion for it had come to him. "Just a little," in a word, was just as much as Miss Bartram, taking one day with another, would let him. He never would be in the least coercive, and would keep well before him the lines on which consideration for her—the very highest—ought to proceed. He would thoroughly establish the heads under which her affairs, her require-ments, her peculiarities—he went so far as to give them the latitude of that name—would come into their intercourse. All this naturally was a sign of how much he took the intercourse itself for granted. There was nothing more to be done about *that*. It simply existed; had sprung into being with her first pene-trating question to him in the autumn light there at Weatherend. The real form it should have taken on the basis that stood out large was the form of their marrying. But the devil in this was that the very basis itself put marrying out of the question. His conviction, his apprehension, his obsession, in short, wasn't a privilege he could invite a woman to share; and that consequence of it was precisely what was the matter with him. Something or other lay in wait for him, amid the twists and the turns of the months and the years, like a crouching beast in the jungle. It signified little whether the crouching beast were destined to slay him or to be slain. The definite point was the inevitable spring of the creature; and the definite lesson from that was that a man of feeling didn't cause himself to be accompanied by a lady on a tiger-hunt. Such was the image under which he had ended by figuring his life.

They had at first, none the less, in the scattered hours spent together, made no allusion to that view of it; which was a sign he was handsomely alert to give that he didn't expect, that he in fact didn't care, always to be talking about it. Such a feature in one's outlook was really like a hump on one's back. The difference it made every minute of the day existed quite independently of dis-cussion. One discussed of course *like* a hunchback, for there was always, if nothing else, the hunchback face. That remained, and she was watching him; but people watched best, as a general thing, in silence, so that such would be predominantly the manner of their vigil. Yet he didn't want, at the same time, to be tense and solemn; tense and solemn was what he imagined he too much showed for with other people. The thing to be, with the one person who knew, was easy and natural—to make the reference rather than be seeming to avoid it, to avoid it rather than be seeming to make it, and to keep it, in any case, familiar, facetious even, rather than pedantic and portentous. Some such con-sideration as the latter was doubtless in his mind for instance when he wrote pleasantly to Miss Bartram that perhaps the great thing he had so long felt as in the lap of the gods was no more than this circumstance, which touched him so nearly, of her acquiring a house in London. It was the first allusion they had yet again made, needing any other hitherto so little; but when she replied, after having given him the news, that she was by no means satisfied with such a trifle as the climax to so special a suspense, she almost set him wondering if she hadn't even a larger conception of singularity for him than he had for himself. He was at all events destined to become aware little by little, as time went by, that she was all the while looking at his life, judging it, measuring it, in the light of the thing she knew, which grew to be at last, with the consecration of the years, never mentioned between them save as "the real truth" about him. That had always been his own form of reference to it, but she adopted the form so quietly that, looking back at the end of a period, he knew there was no moment at which it was traceable that she had, as he might say, got inside his idea, or exchanged the attitude of beautifully indulging for that of still more beautifully believing him.

It was always open to him to accuse her of seeing him but as the most harmless of maniacs, and this, in the long run—since it covered so much ground—was his easiest description of their friendship. He had a screw loose for her, but she liked him in spite of it and was practically, against the rest of the world, his kind wise keeper, unremunerated but fairly amused and, in the absence of other near ties, not disreputably occupied. The rest of the world of course thought him queer, but she, she only, knew how, and above all why, queer; which was precisely what enabled her to dispose the concealing veil in the right folds. She took his gaiety from him—since it had to pass with them for gaiety—as she took everything else; but she certainly so far justified by her unerring touch his finer sense of the degree to which he had ended by convincing her. *She* at least never spoke of the secret of his life except as "the real truth about you," and she had in fact a wonderful way of making it seem, as such, the secret of her own life too. That was in fine how he so constantly felt her as allowing for him; he couldn't on the whole call it anything else. He allowed for himself, but she, exactly, allowed still more; partly because, better placed for a sight of the matter, she traced his unhappy perversion through reaches of its course into which he could scarce follow it. He knew how he felt, but, besides knowing that, she knew how he *looked* as well; he knew each of the things of importance he was insidiously kept from doing, but she could add up the amount they made, understand how much, with a lighter weight on his spirit, he might have done, and thereby establish how, clever as he was, he fell short. Above all she was in the secret of the difference between the forms he went through—those of his little office under Government, those of caring for his modest patrimony, for his library, for his garden in the country, for the people in London whose invitations he accepted and repaid—and the detachment that reigned beneath them and that made of all behaviour, all that could in the least be called behaviour, a long act of dissimulation. What it had come to was that he wore a mask painted with the social simper, out of the eyeholes of which there looked eyes of an expression not in the least matching the other features. This the stupid world, even after years, had never more than half-discovered. It was only May Bartram who had, and she achieved, by an art indescribable, the feat of at once—or perhaps it was only alternately—meeting the eyes from in front and mingling her own vision, as from over his shoulder, with their peep through the apertures.

So while they grew older together she did watch with him, and so she let this association give shape and colour to her own existence. Beneath *her* forms as well detachment had learned to sit, and behaviour had become for her, in the social sense, a false account of herself. There was but one account of her that would have been true all the while and that she could give straight to nobody, least of all to John Marcher. Her whole attitude was a virtual statement, but the perception of that only seemed called to take its place for him as one of the many things necessarily crowded out of his consciousness. If she had moreover, like himself, to make sacrifices to their real truth, it was to be granted that her compensation might have affected her as more prompt and more natural. They had long periods, in this London time, during which, when they were together, a stranger might have listened to them without in the least pricking up his ears; on the other hand the real truth was equally liable at any moment to rise to the surface, and the auditor would then have wondered indeed what they were talking about. They had from an early hour made up their mind that society was, luckily, unintelligent, and the margin allowed them by this had fairly become one of their commonplaces. Yet there were still moments when the situation turned almost fresh—usually under the effect of some expression drawn from herself. Her expressions doubtless repeated themselves, but her intervals were generous. "What saves us, you know, is that we answer so completely to so usual an appearance: that of the man and woman whose friendship has become such a daily habit—or almost—as to be at last indispensable." That for instance was a remark she had frequently enough had occasion to make, though she had given it at different times different developments. What we are especially concerned with is the turn it happened to take from her one afternoon when he had come to see her in honour of her birthday. This anniversary had fallen on a Sunday, at a season of thick fog and general outward gloom; but he had brought her his customary offering, having known her now long enough to have established a hundred small traditions. It was one of his proofs to himself, the present he made her on her birthday, that he hadn't sunk into real selfishness. It was mostly nothing more than a small trinket, but it was always fine of its kind, and he was regularly careful to pay for it more than he thought he could afford. "Our habit saves you at least, don't you see? because it makes you, after all, for the vulgar, indistinguishable from other men. What's the most inveterate mark of men in general? Why the capacity to spend endless time with dull women—to spend it I won't say without being bored, but without minding that they are, without being driven off at a tangent by it; which comes to the same thing. I'm your dull woman, a part of the daily bread for which you pray at church. That covers your tracks more than anything."

"And what covers yours?" asked Marcher, whom his dull woman could mostly to this extent amuse. "I see of course what you mean by your saving me, in this way and that, so far as other people are concerned—I've seen it all along. Only what is it that saves you? I often think, you know, of that."

She looked as if she sometimes thought of that too, but rather in a different way. "Where other people, you mean, are concerned?"

"Well, you're really so in with me, you know—as a sort of result of my being so in with yourself. I mean of my having such an immense regard for you, being so tremendously mindful of all you've done for me. I sometimes ask myself if it's quite fair. Fair I mean to have so involved and—since one may say it—interested you. I almost feel as if you hadn't really had time to do anything else."

"Anything else but be interested?" she asked. "Ah what else does one ever want to be? If I've been 'watching' with you, as we long ago agreed I was to do, watching's always in itself an absorption."

"Oh certainly," John Marcher said, "if you hadn't had your curiosity—! Only doesn't it sometimes come to you as time goes on that your curiosity isn't being particularly repaid?"

May Bartram had a pause. "Do you ask that, by any chance, because you feel at all that yours isn't? I mean because you have to wait so long."

Oh he understood what she meant! "For the thing to happen that never does happen? For the beast to jump out? No, I'm just where I was about it. It isn't a matter as to which I can *choose*, I can decide for a change. It isn't one as to which there *can* be a change. It's in the lap of the gods. One's in the hands of one's law—there one is. As to the form the law will take, the way it will operate, that's its own affair."

"Yes," Miss Bartram replied; "of course one's fate's coming, of course it *has* come in its own form and its own way, all the while. Only, you know, the form and the way in your case were to have been—well, something so exceptional and, as one may say, so particularly *your* own."

Something in this made him look at her with suspicion. "You say 'were to *have* been,' as if in your heart you had begun to doubt."

"Oh!" she vaguely protested.

"As if you believed," he went on, "that nothing will now take place."

She shook her head slowly but rather inscrutably. "You're far from my thought."

He continued to look at her. "What then is the matter with you?"

"Well," she said after another wait, "the matter with me is simply that I'm more sure than ever my curiosity, as you call it, will be but too well repaid."

They were frankly grave now; he had got up from his seat, had turned once more about the little drawing-room to which, year after year, he brought his inevitable topic; in which he had, as he might have said, tasted their intimate community with every sauce, where every object was as familiar to him as the things of his own house and the very carpets were worn with his fitful walk very much as the desks in old counting-houses are worn by the elbows of generations of clerks. The generations of his nervous moods had been at work there, and the place was the written history of his whole middle life. Under the impression of what his friend had just said he knew himself, for some reason, more aware of these things; which made him, after a moment, stop again before her. "Is it possibly that you've grown afraid?"

"Afraid?" He thought, as she repeated the word, that his question had made her, a little, change colour; so that, lest he should have touched on a truth, he explained very kindly: "You remember that that was what you asked *me* long ago—that first day at Weatherend."

"Oh yes, and you told me you didn't know—that I was to see for myself. We've said little about it since, even in so long a time."

"Precisely," Marcher interposed—"quite as if it were too delicate a matter for us to make free with. Quite as if we might find, on pressure, that I *am* afraid. For then," he said, "we shouldn't, should we? quite know what to do."

She had for the time no answer to his question. "There have been days when I thought you were. Only, of course," she added, "there have been days when we have thought almost anything."

"Everything. Oh!" Marcher softly groaned as with a gasp, half-spent, at the face, more uncovered just then than it had been for a long while, of the imagination always with them. It had always had its incalculable moments of glaring out, quite as with the very eyes of the very Beast, and, used as he was to them, they could still draw from him the tribute of a sigh that rose from the depths of his being. All they had thought, first and last, rolled over him; the past seemed to have been reduced to mere barren speculation. This in fact was what the place had just struck him as so full of—the simplification of every-thing but the state of suspense. That remained only by seeming to hang in the void surrounding it. Even his original fear, if fear it had been, had lost itself in the desert. "I judge, however," he continued, "that you see I'm not afraid now."

"What I see, as I make it out, is that you've achieved something almost unprecedented in the way of getting used to danger. Living with it so long and so closely you've lost your sense of it; you know it's there, but you're indiffer-ent, and you cease even, as of old, to have to whistle in the dark. Considering what the danger is," May Bartram wound up, "I'm bound to say I don't think your attitude could well be surpassed."

John Marcher faintly smiled. "It's heroic?"

"Certainly—call it that."

It was what he would have liked indeed to call it. "I *am* then a man of courage?"

"That's what you were to show me."

He still, however, wondered. "But doesn't the man of courage know what he's afraid of—or *not* afraid of? I don't know *that*, you see. I don't focus it. I can't name it. I only know I'm exposed."

"Yes, but exposed—how shall I say?—so directly. So intimately. That's surely enough."

"Enough to make you feel then—as what we may call the end and the upshot of our watch—that I'm not afraid?"

"You're not afraid. But it isn't," she said, "the end of our watch. That is it isn't the end of yours. You've everything still to see."

"Then why haven't *you?*" he asked. He had had, all along, to-day, the sense of her keeping something back, and he still had it. As this was his first impres-sion of that it quite made a date. The case was the more marked as she didn't at first answer; which in turn made him go on. "You know something I don't." Then his voice, for that of a man of courage, trembled a little. "You know what's to happen." Her silence, with the face she showed, was almost a confes-sion—it made him sure. "You know, and you're afraid to tell me. It's so bad that you're afraid I'll find out."

All this might be true, for she did look as if, unexpectedly to her, he had crossed some mystic line that she had secretly drawn round her. Yet she might, after all, not have worried; and the real climax was that he himself, at all events, needn't. "You'll never find out."

## III

It was all to have made, none the less, as I have said, a date; which came out in the fact that again and again, even after long intervals, other things that passed between them wore in relation to this hour but the character of recalls and results. Its immediate effect had been indeed rather to lighten insistence—

almost to provoke a reaction; as if their topic had dropped by its own weight and as if moreover, for that matter, Marcher had been visited by one of his occasional warnings against egotism. He had kept up, he felt, and very decently on the whole, his consciousness of the importance of not being selfish, and it was true that he had never sinned in that direction without promptly enough trying to press the scales the other way. He often repaired his fault, the season permitting, by inviting his friend to accompany him to the opera; and it not infrequently thus happened that, to show he didn't wish her to have but one sort of food for her mind, he was the cause of her appearing there with him a dozen nights in the month. It even happened that, seeing her home at such times, he occasionally went in with her to finish, as he called it, the evening, and, the better to make his point, sat down to the frugal but always careful little supper that awaited his pleasure. His point was made, he thought, by his not eternally insisting with her on himself; made for instance, at such hours, when it befell that, her piano at hand and each of them familiar with it, they went over passages of the opera together. It chanced to be on one of these occasions, however, that he reminded her of her not having answered a certain question he had put to her during the talk that had taken place between them on her last birthday. "What is it that saves *you?*"—saved her, he meant, from that appearance of variation from the usual human type. If he had practically escaped remark, as she pretended, by doing, in the most important particular, what most men do—find the answer to life in patching up an alliance of a sort with a woman no better than himself—how had she escaped it, and how could the alliance, such as it was, since they must suppose it had been more or less noticed, have failed to make her rather positively talked about?

"I never said," May Bartram replied, "that it hadn't made me a good deal talked about."

"Ah well then you're not 'saved.' "

"It hasn't been a question for me. If you've had your woman I've had," she said, "my man."

"And you mean that makes you all right?"

Oh it was always as if there were so much to say! "I don't know why it shouldn't make me—humanly, which is what we're speaking of—as right as it makes you."

"I see," Marcher returned. " 'Humanly,' no doubt, as showing that you're living for something. Not, that is, just for me and my secret."

May Bartram smiled. "I don't pretend it exactly shows that I'm not living for you. It's my intimacy with you that's in question."

He laughed as he saw what she meant. "Yes, but since, as you say, I'm only, so far as people make out, ordinary, you're—aren't you?—no more than ordinary either. You help me to pass for a man like another. So if I *am*, as I understand you, you're not compromised. Is that it?"

She had another of her waits, but she spoke clearly enough. "That's it. It's all that concerns me—to help you to pass for a man like another."

He was careful to acknowledge the remark handsomely. "How kind, how beautiful, you are to me! How shall I ever repay you?"

She had her last grave pause, as if there might be a choice of ways. But she chose. "By going on as you are."

It was into this going on as he was that they relapsed, and really for so long a time that the day inevitably came for a further sounding of their depths. These depths, constantly bridged over by a structure firm enough in spite of its lightness and of its occasional oscillation in the somewhat vertiginous air, invited on occasion, in the interest of their nerves, a dropping of the plummet and a measurement of the abyss. A difference had been made moreover, once for all, by the fact that she had all the while not appeared to feel the need of rebutting his charge of an idea within her that she didn't dare to express—a charge uttered just before one of the fullest of their later discussions ended. It had come up for him then that she "knew" something and that what she knew was bad—too bad to tell him. When he had spoken of it as visibly so bad that she was afraid he might find it out, her reply had left the matter too equivocal to be let alone and yet, for Marcher's special sensibility, almost too formidable again to touch. He circled about it at a distance that alternately narrowed and widened and that still wasn't much affected by the consciousness in him that there was nothing she could "know," after all, any better than he did. She had no source of knowledge he hadn't equally—except of course that she might have finer nerves. That was what women had where they were interested; they made out things, where people were concerned, that the people often couldn't have made out for themselves. Their nerves, their sensibility, their imagination, were conductors and revealers, and the beauty of May Bartram was in particular that she had given herself so to his case. He felt in these days what, oddly enough, he had never felt before, the growth of a dread of losing her by some catastrophe—some catastrophe that yet wouldn't at all be *the* catastrophe: partly because she had almost of a sudden begun to strike him as more useful to him than ever yet, and partly by reason of an appearance of uncertainty in her health, coincident and equally new. It was characteristic of the inner detachment he had hitherto so successfully cultivated and to which our whole account of him is a reference, it was characteristic that his complications, such as they were, had never yet seemed so as at this crisis to thicken about him, even to the point of making him ask himself if he were, by any chance, of a truth, within sight or sound, within touch or reach, within the immediate jurisdiction, of the thing that waited.

When the day came, as come it had to, that his friend confessed to him her fear of a deep disorder in her blood, he felt somehow the shadow of a change and the chill of a shock. He immediately began to imagine aggravations and disasters, and above all to think of her peril as the direct menace for himself of personal privation. This indeed gave him one of those partial recoveries of equanimity that were agreeable to him—it showed him that what was still first in his mind was the loss she herself might suffer. "What if she should have to die before knowing, before seeing—?" It would have been brutal, in the early stages of her trouble, to put that question to her; but it had immediately sounded for him to his own concern, and the possibility was what most made him sorry for her. If she did "know," moreover, in the sense of her having had some—what should he think?—mystical irresistible light, this would make the matter not better, but worse, inasmuch as her original adoption of his own curiosity had quite become the basis of her life. She had been living to see what would *be* to be seen, and it would quite lacerate her to have to give up before the accomplishment of the vision. These reflexions, as I say, quickened his generosity; yet, make them as he might, he saw himself, with the lapse of the period, more and more disconcerted. It lapsed for him with a strange steady sweep, and the oddest oddity was that it gave him, independently of the threat of much inconvenience, almost the only positive surprise his career, if career it could be called, had yet offered him. She kept the house as she had never done; he had to go to her to see her—she could meet him nowhere now, though there was scarce a corner of their loved old London in which she hadn't in the past, at one time or another, done so; and he found her always seated by her fire in the deep old-fashioned chair she was less and less able to leave. He had been struck one day, after an absence exceeding his usual measure, with her suddenly looking much older to him than he had ever thought of her being; then he recognised that the suddenness was all on his side—he had just simply and suddenly noticed. She looked older because inevitably, after so many years, she *was* old, or almost; which was of course true in still greater measure of her companion. If she was old, or almost, John Marcher assuredly was, and yet it was her showing of the lesson, not his own, that brought the truth home to him. His surprises began here; when once they had begun they multiplied; they came rather with a rush: it was as if, in the oddest way in the world, they had all been kept back, sown in a thick cluster, for the late afternoon of life, the time at which for people in general the unexpected has died out.

One of them was that he should have caught himself—for he *had* so done—*really* wondering if the great accident would take form now as nothing more than his being condemned to see this charming woman, this admirable friend, pass away from him. He had never so unreservedly qualified her as while confronted in thought with such a possibility; in spite of which there was small doubt for him that as an answer to his long riddle the mere effacement of even so fine a feature of his situation would be an abject anti-climax. It would represent, as connected with his past attitude, a drop of dignity under the shadow of which his existence could only become the most grotesque of failures. He had been far from holding it a failure—long as he had waited for the appearance that was to make it a success. He had waited for quite another thing, not for such a thing as that. The breath of his good faith came short, however, as he recognised how long he had waited, or how long at least his companion had. That she, at all events, might be recorded as having waited in vain—this affected him sharply, and all the more because of his at first having done little more than amuse himself with the idea. It grew more grave as the gravity of her condition grew, and the state of mind it produced in him, which he himself ended by watching as if it had been some definite disfigurement of his outer person, may pass for another of his surprises. This conjoined itself still with another, the really stupefying consciousness of a question that he would have allowed to shape itself had he dared. What did everything mean—what, that is, did *she* mean, she and her vain waiting and her probable death and the soundless admonition of it all—unless that, at this time of day, it was simply, it was overwhelmingly too late? He had never at any stage of his queer consciousness admitted the whisper of such a correction; he had never till within these last few months been so false to his conviction as not to hold that what was to come to him had time, whether *he* struck himself as having it or not. That at last, at last, he certainly hadn't it, to speak of, or had it but in the scantiest measure—such, soon enough, as things went with him, became the inference with which his old obsession had to reckon: and this it was not helped to do by the more and more confirmed appearance that the great vagueness casting the long shadow in which he had lived had, to attest itself, almost no margin left. Since it was in Time that he was to have met his fate, so it was in Time that his fate was to have acted; and as he waked up to the sense of no longer being young, which was exactly the sense of being stale, just as that, in turn, was the sense of being weak, he waked up to another matter beside. It all hung together; they were subject, he and the great vagueness, to an equal and indivisible law. When the possibilities themselves had accordingly turned stale, when the secret of the gods had grown faint, had perhaps even quite evaporated, that, and that only, was failure. It wouldn't have been failure to be bankrupt, dishonoured, pilloried, hanged; it was failure not to be anything. And so, in the dark valley into which his path had taken its unlooked-for twist, he wondered not a little as he groped. He didn't care what awful crash might overtake him, with what ignominy or what monstrosity he might yet be associated—since he wasn't after all too utterly old to suffer— if it would only be decently proportionate to the posture he had kept, all his life, in the threatened presence of it. He had but one desire left—that he shouldn't have been "sold."

## IV

Then it was that, one afternoon, while the spring of the year was young and new she met all in her own way his frankest betrayal of these alarms. He had gone in late to see her, but evening hadn't settled and she was presented to him in that long fresh light of waning April days which affects us often with a sadness sharper than the greyest hours of autumn. The week had been warm, the spring was supposed to have begun early, and May Bartram sat, for the first time in the year, without a fire; a fact that, to Marcher's sense, gave the scene of which she formed part a smooth and ultimate look, an air of knowing, in its immaculate order and cold meaningless cheer, that it would never see a fire again. Her own aspect—he could scarce have said why—intensified this note. Almost as white as wax, with the marks and signs in her face as numerous and as fine as if they had been etched by a needle, with soft white draperies relieved by a faded green scarf on the delicate tone of which the years had further refined, she was the picture of a serene and exquisite but impenetrable sphinx, whose head, or indeed all whose person, might have been powdered with silver. She was a sphinx, yet with her white petals and green fronds she might have been a lily too—only an artificial lily, wonderfully imitated and constantly kept, without dust or stain, though not exempt from a slight droop and a complexity of faint creases, under some clear glass bell. The perfection of household care, of high polish and finish, always reigned in her rooms, but they now looked most as if everything had been wound up, tucked in, put away, so that she might sit with folded hands and with nothing more to do. She was "out of it," to Marcher's vision; her work was over; she communicated with him as across some gulf or from some island of rest that she had already reached, and it made him feel strangely abandoned. Was it—or rather wasn't it—that if for so long she had been watching with him the answer to their question must have swum into her ken and taken on its name, so that her occupation was verily gone? He had as much as charged her with this in saying to her, many months before, that she even then knew something she was keeping from him. It was a point he had never since ventured to press, vaguely fearing as he did that it might become a difference, perhaps a disagreement, between them. He had in this later time turned nervous, which was what he in all the other years had never been; and the oddity was that his nervousness should have waited till he had begun to doubt, should have held off so long as he was sure. There was something, it seemed to him, that the wrong word would bring down on his head, something that would so at least ease off his tension. But he wanted not to speak the wrong word; that would make every-thing ugly. He wanted the knowledge he lacked to drop on him, if drop it could, by its own august weight. If she was to forsake him it was surely for her to take leave. This was why he didn't directly ask her again what she knew; but it was also why, approaching the matter from another side, he said to her in the course of his visit: "What do you regard as the very worst that at this time of day *can* happen to me?"

He had asked her that in the past often enough; they had, with the odd irregular rhythm of their intensities and avoidances, exchanged ideas about it and then had seen the ideas washed away by cool intervals, washed like figures traced in sea-sand. It had ever been the mark of their talk that the oldest allusions in it required but a little dismissal and reaction to come out again, sounding for the hour as new. She could thus at present meet his enquiry quite freshly and patiently. "Oh yes, I've repeatedly thought, only it always seemed to me of old that I couldn't quite make up my mind. I thought of dreadful things, between which it was difficult to choose; and so must you have done."

"Rather! I feel now as if I had scarce done anything else. I appear to myself to have spent my life in thinking of nothing *but* dreadful things. A great many of them I've at different times named to you, but there were others I couldn't name."

"They were too, too dreadful?"

"Too, too dreadful—some of them."

She looked at him a minute, and there came to him as he met it an inconse-quent sense that her eyes, when one got their full clearness, were still as beauti-ful as they had been in youth, only beautiful with a strange cold light—a light that somehow was a part of the effect, if it wasn't rather a part of the cause, of the pale hard sweetness of the season and the hour. "And yet," she said at last, "there are horrors we've mentioned."

It deepened the strangeness to see her, as such a figure in such a picture, talk of "horrors," but she was to do in a few minutes something stranger yet—though even of this he was to take the full measure but afterwards—and the note of it already trembled. It was, for the matter of that, one of the signs that her eyes were having again the high flicker of their prime. He had to admit, however, what she said. "Oh yes, there were times when we did go far." He caught himself in the act of speaking as if it all were over. Well, he wished it were; and the consummation depended for him clearly more and more on his friend.

But she had now a soft smile. "Oh far—!"

It was oddly ironic. "Do you mean you're prepared to go further?"

She was frail and ancient and charming as she continued to look at him, yet it was rather as if she had lost the thread. "Do you consider that we went far?"

"Why I thought it the point you were just making—that we *had* looked most things in the face."

"Including each other?" She still smiled. "But you're quite right. We've had together great imaginations, often great fears; but some of them have been unspoken."

"Then the worst—we haven't faced that. I *could* face it, I believe, if I knew what you think it. I feel," he explained, "as if I had lost my power to conceive such things." And he wondered if he looked as blank as he sounded. "It's spent."

"Then why do you assume," she asked, "that mine isn't?"

"Because you've given me signs to the contrary. It isn't a question for you of conceiving, imagining, comparing. It isn't a question now of choosing." At last he came out with it. "You know something I don't. You've shown me that before."

These last words had affected her, he made out in a moment, exceedingly, and she spoke with firmness. "I've shown you, my dear, nothing."

He shook his head. "You can't hide it."

"Oh, oh!" May Bartram sounded over what she couldn't hide. It was almost a smothered groan.

"You admitted it months ago, when I spoke of it to you as of something you were afraid I should find out. Your answer was that I couldn't, that I wouldn't, and I don't pretend I have. But you had something therefore in mind, and I now see how it must have been, how it still is, the possibility that, of all possibilities, has settled itself for you as the worst. This," he went on, "is why I appeal to you. I'm only afraid of ignorance to-day—I'm not afraid of knowledge." And then as for a while she said nothing: "What makes me sure is that I see in your face and feel here, in this air and amid these appearances, that you're out of it. You've done. You've had your experience. You leave me to my fate."

Well, she listened, motionless and white in her chair, as on a decision to be made, so that her manner was fairly an avowal, though still, with a small fine inner stiffness, an imperfect surrender. "It *would* be the worst," she finally let herself say. "I mean the thing I've never said."

It hushed him a moment. "More monstrous than all the monstrosities we've named?"

"More monstrous. Isn't that what you sufficiently express," she asked, "in calling it the worst?"

Marcher thought. "Assuredly—if you mean, as I do, something that includes all the loss and all the shame that are thinkable."

"It would if it *should* happen," said May Bartram. "What we're speaking of, remember, is only my idea."

"It's your belief," Marcher returned. "That's enough for me. I feel your beliefs are right. Therefore if, having this one, you give me no more light on it, you abandon me."

"No, no!" she repeated. "I'm with you—don't you see?—still." And as to make it more vivid to him she rose from her chair—a movement she seldom risked in these days—and showed herself, all draped and all soft, in her fairness and slimness. "I haven't forsaken you."

It was really, in its effort against weakness, a generous assurance, and had the success of the impulse not, happily, been great, it would have touched him to pain more than to pleasure. But the cold charm in her eyes had spread, as she hovered before him, to all the rest of her person, so that it was for the minute almost a recovery of youth. He couldn't pity her for that; he could only take her as she showed—as capable even yet of helping him. It was as if, at the same time, her light might at any instant go out; wherefore he must make the most of it. There passed before him with intensity the three or four things he wanted most to know; but the question that came of itself to his lips really covered the others. "Then tell me if I shall consciously suffer."

She promptly shook her head. "Never!"

It confirmed the authority he imputed to her, and it produced on him an extraordinary effect. "Well, what's better than that? Do you call that the worst?"

"You think nothing is better?" she asked.

She seemed to mean something so special that he again sharply wondered, though still with the dawn of a prospect of relief. "Why not, if one doesn't know?" After which, as their eyes, over his question, met in a silence, the dawn deepened and something to his purpose came prodigiously out of her very face. His own, as he took it in, suddenly flushed to the forehead, and he gasped with the force of a perception to which, on the instant, everything fitted. The sound of his gasp filled the air; then he became articulate. "I see— if I don't suffer!"

In her own look, however, was doubt. "You see what?"

"Why what you mean—what you've always meant."

She again shook her head. "What I mean isn't what I've always meant. It's different."

"It's something new?"

She hung back from it a little. "Something new. It's not what you think. I see what you think."

His divination drew breath then; only her correction might be wrong. "It isn't that I am a blockhead?" he asked between faintness and grimness. "It isn't that it's all a mistake."

"A mistake?" she pityingly echoed. That possibility, for her, he saw, would be monstrous; and if she guaranteed him the immunity from pain it would accordingly not be what she had in mind. "Oh no," she declared; "it's nothing of that sort. You've been right."

Yet he couldn't help asking himself if she weren't, thus pressed, speaking but to save him. It seemed to him he should be most in a hole if his history should prove all a platitude. "Are you telling me the truth, so that I shan't have been a bigger idiot than I can bear to know? I *haven't* lived with a vain imagination, in the most besotted illusion? I haven't waited but to see the door shut in my face?"

She shook her head again. "However the case stands *that* isn't the truth. Whatever the reality, it *is* a reality. The door isn't shut. The door's open," said May Bartram.

"Then something's to come?"

She waited once again, always with her cold sweet eyes on him. "It's never too late." She had, with her gliding step, diminished the distance between them, and she stood nearer to him, close to him, a minute, as if still charged with the unspoken. Her movement might have been for some finer emphasis of what she was at once hesitating and deciding to say. He had been standing by the chimney-piece, fireless and sparely adorned, a small perfect old French clock and two morsels of rosy Dresden constituting all its furniture; and her hand grasped the shelf while she kept him waiting, grasped it a little as for support and encouragement. She only kept him waiting, however; that is he only waited. It had become suddenly, from her movement and attitude, beautiful and vivid to him that she had something more to give him; her wasted face delicately shone with it—it glittered almost as with the white lustre of silver in her expression. She was right, incontestably, for what he saw in her face was the truth, and strangely, without consequence, while their talk of it as dreadful was still in the air, she appeared to present it as inordinately soft. This, prompting bewilderment, made him but gape the more gratefully for her revelation, so that they continued for some minutes silent, her face shining at him, her contact imponderably pressing, and his stare all kind but all expectant. The end, none the less, was that what he had expected failed to come to him. Something else took place instead, which seemed to consist at first in the mere closing of her eyes. She gave way at the same instant to a slow fine shudder, and though he remained staring—though he stared in fact but the harder—turned off and regained her chair. It was the end of what she had been intending, but it left him thinking only of that.

"Well, you don't say—?"

She had touched in her passage a bell near the chimney and had sunk back strangely pale. "I'm afraid I'm too ill."

"Too ill to tell me?" It sprang up sharp to him, and almost to his lips, the fear she might die without giving him light. He checked himself in time from so expressing his question, but she answered as if she had heard the words.

"Don't you know—now?"

" 'Now'—?" She had spoken as if some difference had been made within the moment. But her maid, quickly obedient to her bell, was already with them. "I know nothing." And he was afterwards to say to himself that he must have spoken with odious impatience, such an impatience as to show that, supremely disconcerted, he washed his hands of the whole question.

"Oh!" said May Bartram.

"Are you in pain?" he asked as the woman went to her.

"No," said May Bartram.

Her maid, who had put an arm round her as if to take her to her room, fixed on him eyes that appealingly contradicted her; in spite of which, however, he showed once more his mystification. "What then has happened?"

She was once more, with her companion's help, on her feet, and, feeling withdrawal imposed on him, he had blankly found his hat and gloves and had reached the door. Yet he waited for her answer. "What *was* to," she said.

V

He came back the next day, but she was then unable to see him, and as it was literally the first time this had occurred in the long stretch of their acquaintance he turned away, defeated and sore, almost angry—or feeling at least that such a break in their custom was really the beginning of the end—and wandered alone with his thoughts, especially with the one he was least able to keep down. She was dying and he would lose her; she was dying and his life would end. He stopped in the Park, into which he had passed, and stared before him at his recurrent doubt. Away from her the doubt pressed again; in her presence he had believed her, but as he felt his forlornness he threw himself into the explanation that, nearest at hand, had most of a miserable warmth for him and least of a cold torment. She had deceived him to save him—to put him off with something in which he should be able to rest. What could the thing that was to happen to him be, after all, but just this thing that had begun to happen? Her dying, her death, his consequent solitude—*that* was what he had figured as the Beast in the Jungle, that was what had been in the lap of the gods. He had had her word for it as he left her—what else on earth could she have meant? It wasn't a thing of a monstrous order; not a fate rare and distinguished; not a stroke of fortune that overwhelmed and immortalised; it had only the stamp of the common doom. But poor Marcher at this hour judged the common doom sufficient. It would serve his turn, and even as the consummation of infinite waiting he would bend his pride to accept it. He sat down on a bench in the twilight. He hadn't been a fool. Something had *been*, as she had said, to come. Before he rose indeed it had quite struck him that the final fact really matched with the long avenue through which he had had to reach it. As sharing his suspense and as giving herself all, giving her life, to bring it to an end, she had come with him every step of the way. He had lived by her aid, and to leave her behind would be cruelly, damnably to miss her. What could be more overwhelming than that?

Well, he was to know within the week, for though she kept him a while at bay, left him restless and wretched during a series of days on each of which he asked about her only again to have to turn away, she ended his trial by receiving him where she had always received him. Yet she had been brought out at some hazard into the presence of so many of the things that were, consciously, vainly, half their past, and there was scant service left in the gentleness of her mere desire, all too visible, to check his obsession and wind up his long trouble. That was clearly what she wanted, the one thing more for her own peace while she could still put out her hand. He was so affected by her state that, once seated by her chair, he was moved to let everything go; it was she herself therefore who brought him back, took up again, before she dismissed him, her last word of the other time. She showed how she wished to leave their business in order. "I'm not sure you understood. You've nothing to wait for more. It *has* come."

Oh how he looked at her! "Really?"

"Really."

"The thing that, as you said, *was* to?"

"The thing that we began in our youth to watch for."

Face to face with her once more he believed her; it was a claim to which he had so abjectly little to oppose. "You mean that it has come as a positive definite occurrence, with a name and a date?"

"Positive. Definite. I don't know about the 'name,' but oh with a date!"

He found himself again too helplessly at sea. "But come in the night—come and passed me by?"

May Bartram had her strange faint smile. "Oh no, it hasn't passed you by!"

"But if I haven't been aware of it and it hasn't touched me—?"

"Ah your not being aware of it"—and she seemed to hesitate an instant to deal with this—"your not being aware of it is the strangeness *in* the strangeness. It's the wonder *of* the wonder." She spoke as with the softness almost of a sick child, yet now at last, at the end of all, with the perfect straightness of a sibyl. She visibly knew that she knew, and the effect on him was of something co-ordinate, in its high character, with the law that had ruled him. It was the true voice of the law; so on her lips would the law itself have sounded. "It *has* touched you," she went on. "It has done its office. It has made you all its own."

"So utterly without my knowing it?"

"So utterly without your knowing it." His hand, as he leaned to her, was on the arm of her chair, and, dimly smiling always now, she placed her own on it. "It's enough if *I* know it."

"Oh!" he confusedly breathed, as she herself of late so often had done.

"What I long ago said is true. You'll never know now, and I think you ought to be content. You've *had* it," said May Bartram.

"But had what?"

"Why what was to have marked you out. The proof of your law. It has acted. I'm too glad," she then bravely added, "to have been able to see what it's *not*."

He continued to attach his eyes to her, and with the sense that it was all beyond him, and that *she* was too, he would still have sharply challenged her hadn't he so felt it an abuse of her weakness to do more than take devoutly what she gave him, take it hushed as to a revelation. If he did speak, it was out of the foreknowledge of his loneliness to come. "If you're glad of what it's 'not' it might then have been worse?"

She turned her eyes away, she looked straight before her; with which after a moment: "Well, you know our fears."

He wondered. "It's something then we never feared?"

On this slowly she turned to him. "Did we ever dream, with all our dreams, that we should sit and talk of it thus?"

He tried for a little to make out that they had; but it was as if their dreams, numberless enough, were in solution in some thick cold mist through which thought lost itself. "It might have been that we couldn't talk?"

"Well"—she did her best for him—"not from this side. This, you see," she said, "is the *other* side."

"I think," poor Marcher returned, "that all sides are the same to me." Then, however, as she gently shook her head in correction: "We mightn't, as it were, have got across—?"

"To where we are—no. We're *here*"—she made her weak emphasis.

"And much good does it do us!" was her friend's frank comment.

"It does us the good it can. It does us the good that *it* isn't here. It's past. It's behind," said May Bartram. "Before—" but her voice dropped.

He had got up, not to tire her, but it was hard to combat his yearning. She after all told him nothing but that his light had failed—which he knew well enough without her. "Before—?" he blankly echoed.

"Before, you see, it was always to *come*. That kept it present."

"Oh I don't care what comes now! Besides," Marcher added, "it seems to me I liked it better present, as you say, than I can like it absent with *your* absence."

"Oh mine!"—and her pale hands made light of it.

"With the absence of everything." He had a dreadful sense of standing there before her for—so far as anything but this proved, this bottomless drop was concerned—the last time of their life. It rested on him with a weight he felt he could scarce bear, and this weight it apparently was that still pressed out what remained in him of speakable protest. "I believe you; but I can't begin to pretend I understand. *Nothing*, for me, is past; nothing *will* pass till I pass myself, which I pray my stars may be as soon as possible. Say, however," he added, "that I've eaten my cake, as you contend, to the last crumb—how can the thing I've never felt at all be the thing I was marked out to feel?"

She met him perhaps less directly, but she met him unperturbed. "You take your 'feelings' for granted. You were to suffer your fate. That was not necessarily to know it."

"How in the world—when what is such knowledge but suffering?"

She looked up at him a while in silence. "No—you don't understand."

"I suffer," said John Marcher.

"Don't, don't!

"How can I help at least *that?*"

"*Don't!*" May Bartram repeated.

She spoke it in a tone so special, in spite of her weakness, that he stared an instant—stared as if some light, hitherto hidden, had shimmered across his vision. Darkness again closed over it, but the gleam had already become for him an idea. "Because I haven't the right—?"

"Don't *know*—when you needn't," she mercifully urged. "You needn't—for we shouldn't."

"Shouldn't?" If he could but know what she meant!

"No—it's too much."

"Too much?" he still asked but, with a mystification that was the next moment of a sudden to give way. Her words, if they meant something, affected him in this light—the light also of her wasted face—as meaning *all*, and the sense of what knowledge had been for herself came over him with a rush which broke through into a question. "Is it of that then you're dying?"

She but watched him, gravely at first, as to see, with this, where he was, and she might have seen something or feared something that moved her sympathy. "I would live for you still—if I could." Her eyes closed for a little, as if, withdrawn into herself, she were for a last time trying. "But I can't!" she said as she raised them again to take leave of him.

She couldn't indeed, as but too promptly and sharply appeared, and he had no vision of her after this that was anything, but darkness and doom. They had parted for ever in that strange talk; access to her chamber of pain, rigidly guarded, was almost wholly forbidden him; he was feeling now moreover, in the face of doctors, nurses, the two or three relatives attracted doubtless by the presumption of what she had to "leave," how few were the rights, as they were called in such cases, that he had to put forward, and how odd it might even seem that their intimacy shouldn't have given him more of them. The stupidest fourth cousin had more, even though she had been nothing in such a person's life. She had been a feature of features in *his*, for what else was it to have been so indispensable? Strange beyond saying were the ways of existence, baffling for him the anomaly of his lack, as he felt it to be, of producible claim. A woman might have been, as it were, everything to him, and it might yet present him in no connexion that any one seemed held to recognise. If this was the case in these closing weeks it was the case more sharply on the occasion of the last offices rendered, in the great grey London cemetery, to what had been mortal, to what had been precious, in his friend. The concourse at her grave was not numerous, but he saw himself treated as scarce more nearly concerned with it than if there had been a thousand others. He was in short from this moment face to face with the fact that he was to profit extraordinarily little by the interest May Bartram had taken in him. He couldn't quite have said what he expected, but he hadn't surely expected this approach to a double privation. Not only had her interest failed him, but he seemed to feel himself unattended—and for a reason he couldn't seize—by the distinction, the dignity, the propriety, if nothing else, of the man markedly bereaved. It was as if in the view of society he had not *been* markedly bereaved, as if there still failed some sign or proof of it, and as if none the less his character could never be affirmed nor the deficiency ever made up. There were moments as the weeks went by when he would have liked, by some almost aggressive act, to take his stand on the intimacy of his loss, in order that it *might* be questioned and his retort, to the relief of his spirit, so recorded; but the moments of an irritation more helpless followed fast on these, the moments during which, turning things over with a good conscience but with a bare horizon, he found himself wondering if he oughtn't to have begun, so to speak, further back.

He found himself wondering at many things, and this last speculation had others to keep it company. What could he have done, after all, in her lifetime, without giving them both, as it were, away? He couldn't have made known she was watching him, for that would have published the superstition of the Beast. This was what closed his mouth now—now that the Jungle had been threshed to vacancy and that the Beast had stolen away. It sounded too foolish and too flat; the difference for him in this particular, the extinction in his life of the element of suspense, was such as in fact to surprise him. He could scarce have said what the effect resembled; the abrupt cessation, the positive prohibition, of music perhaps, more than anything else, in some place all adjusted and all accustomed to sonority and to attention. If he could at any rate have conceived lifting the veil from his image at some moment of the past (what had he done, after all, if not lift it to *her?*) so to do this to-day, to talk to people at large of the Jungle cleared and confide to them that he now felt it as safe, would have been not only to see them listen as to a goodwife's tale, but really to hear himself tell one. What it presently came to in truth was that poor Marcher waded through his beaten grass, where no life stirred, where no breath sounded, where no evil eye seemed to gleam from a possible lair, very much as if vaguely looking for the Beast, and still more as if acutely missing it. He walked about in an existence that had grown strangely more spacious and, stopping fitfully in places where the undergrowth of life struck him as closer, asked himself yearningly, wondered secretly and sorely, if it would have lurked here or there. It would have at all events *sprung;* what was at least complete was his belief in the truth of the assurance given him. The change from his old sense to his new was absolute and final: what was to happen *had* so abso- lutely and finally happened that he was as little able to know a fear for his future as to know a hope; so absent in short was any question of anything still to come. He was to live entirely with the other question, that of his unidentified past, that of his having to see his fortune impenetrably muffled and masked.

The torment of this vision became then his occupation; he couldn't perhaps have consented to live but for the possibility of guessing. She had told him, his friend, not to guess; she had forbidden him, so far as he might, to know, and she had even in a sort denied the power in him to learn: which were so many things, precisely, to deprive him of rest. It wasn't that he wanted, he argued for fairness, that anything past and done should repeat itself; it was only that he shouldn't, as an anticlimax, have been taken sleeping so sound as not to be able to win back by an effort of thought the lost stuff of consciousness. He declared to himself at moments that he would either win it back or have done with consciousness for ever; he made this idea his one motive in fine, made it so much his passion that none other, to compare with it, seemed ever to have touched him. The lost stuff of consciousness became thus for him as a strayed or stolen child to an unappeasable father; he hunted it up and down very much as if he were knocking at doors and enquiring of the police. This was the spirit in which, inevitably, he set himself to travel; he started on a journey that was to be as long as he could make it; it danced before him that, as the other side of the globe couldn't possibly have less to say to him, it might, by a possibility of suggestion, have more. Before he quitted London, however, he made a pilgrimage to May Bartram's grave, took his way to it through the endless avenues of the grim suburban metropolis, sought it out in the wilderness of tombs, and, though he had come but for the renewal of the act of farewell, found himself, when he had at last stood by it, beguiled into long intensities. He stood for an hour, powerless to turn away and yet powerless to penetrate the darkness of death; fixing with his eyes her inscribed name and date, beating his forehead against the fact of the secret they kept, drawing his breath, while he waited, as if some sense would in pity of him rise from the stones. He kneeled on the stones, however, in vain; they kept what they concealed; and if the face of the tomb did become a face for him it was because her two names became a pair of eyes that didn't know him. He gave them a last long look, but no palest light broke.

## VI

He stayed away, after this, for a year; he visited the depths of Asia, spending himself on scenes of romantic interest, of superlative sanctity; but what was present to him everywhere was that for a man who had known what *he* had known the world was vulgar and vain. The state of mind in which he had lived for so many years shone out to him, in reflexion, as a light that coloured and refined, a light beside which the glow of the East was garish cheap and thin. The terrible truth was that he had lost—with everything else—a distinction as well; the things he saw couldn't help being common when he had become common to look at them. He was simply now one of them himself—he was in the dust, without a peg for the sense of difference; and there were hours when, before the temples of gods and the sepulchres of kings, his spirit turned for nobleness of association to the barely discriminated slab in the London suburb. That had become for him, and more intensely with time and distance, his one witness of a past glory. It was all that was left to him for proof or pride, yet the past glories of Pharaohs were nothing to him as he thought of it. Small wonder then that he came back to it on the morrow of his return. He was drawn there this time as irresistibly as the other, yet with a confidence, almost, that was doubtless the effect of the many months that had elapsed. He had lived, in spite of himself, into his change of feeling, and in wandering over the earth had wandered, as might be said, from the circumference to the centre of his desert. He had settled to his safety and accepted perforce his extinction; figuring to himself, with some colour, in the likeness of certain little old men he remembered to have seen, of whom, all meagre and wizened as they might look, it was related that they had in their time fought twenty duels or been loved by ten princesses. They indeed had been wondrous for others while he was but wondrous for himself; which, however, was exactly the cause of his haste to renew the wonder by getting back, as he might put it, into his own presence. That had quickened his steps and checked his delay. If his visit was prompt it was because he had been separated so long from the part of himself that alone he now valued.

It's accordingly not false to say that he reached his goal with a certain elation and stood there again with a certain assurance. The creature beneath the sod *knew* of his rare experience, so that, strangely now, the place had lost for him its mere blankness of expression. It met him in mildness—not, as before, in mockery; it wore for him the air of conscious greeting that we find, after absence, in things that have closely belonged to us and which seem to confess of themselves to the connexion. The plot of ground, the graven tablet, the tended flowers affected him so as belonging to him that he resembled for the hour a contented landlord reviewing a piece of property. Whatever had happened—well, had happened. He had not come back this time with the vanity of that question, his former worrying "What, *what?*" now practically so spent. Yet he would none the less never again so cut himself off from the spot; he would come back to it every month, for if he did nothing else by its aid he at least held up his head. It thus grew for him, in the oddest way, a positive resource; he carried out his idea of periodical returns, which took their place at last among the most inveterate of his habits. What it all amounted to, oddly enough, was that in his finally so simplified world this garden of death gave him the few square feet of earth on which he could still most live. It was as if, being nothing anywhere else for any one, nothing even for himself, he were just everything here, and if not for a crowd of witnesses or indeed for any witness but John Marcher, then by clear right of the register that he could scan like an open page. The open page was the tomb of his friend, and *there* were the facts of the past, there the truth of his life, there the backward reaches in which he could lose himself. He did this from time to time with such effect that he seemed to wander through the old years with his hand in the arm of a companion who was, in the most extraordinary manner, his other, his younger self; and to wander, which was more extraordinary yet, round and round a third presence—not wandering she, but stationary, still, whose eyes, turning with his revolution, never ceased to follow him, and whose seat was his point, so to speak, of orientation. Thus in short he settled to live—feeding all on the sense that he once *had* lived, and dependent on it not alone for a support but for an identity.

It sufficed him in its way for months and the year elapsed; it would doubtless even have carried him further but for an accident, superficially slight, which moved him, quite in another direction, with a force beyond any of his impressions of Egypt or of India. It was a thing of the merest chance—the turn, as he afterwards felt, of a hair, though he was indeed to live to believe that if light hadn't come to him in this particular fashion it would still have come in another. He was to live to believe this, I say, though he was not to live, I may not less definitely mention, to do much else. We allow him at any rate the benefit of the conviction, struggling up for him at the end, that, whatever might have happened or not happened, he would have come round of himself to the light. The incident of an autumn day had put the match to the train laid from of old by his misery. With the light before him he knew that even of late his ache had only been smothered. It was strangely drugged, but it throbbed; at the touch it began to bleed. And the touch, in the event, was the face of a fellow mortal. This face, one grey afternoon when the leaves were thick in the alleys, looked into Marcher's own, at the cemetery, with an expression like the cut of a blade. He felt it, that is, so deep down that he winced at the steady thrust. The person who so mutely assaulted him was a figure he had noticed, on reaching his own goal, absorbed by a grave a short distance away, a grave apparently fresh, so that the emotion of the visitor would probably match it for frankness. This face alone forbade further attention, though during the time he stayed he remained vaguely conscious of his neighbour, a middle-aged man apparently, in mourning, whose bowed back, among the clustered monuments and mortuary yews, was constantly presented. Marcher's theory that these were elements in contact with which he himself revived, had suffered, on this occasion, it may be granted, a marked, an excessive check. The autumn day was dire for him as none had recently been, and he rested with a heaviness he had not yet known on the low stone table that bore May Bartram's name. He rested without power to move, as if some spring in him, some spell vouchsafed, had suddenly been broken for ever. If he could have done that moment as he wanted he would simply have stretched himself on the slab that was ready to take him, treating it as a place prepared to receive his last sleep. What in all the wide world had he now to keep awake for? He stared before him with the question, and it was then that, as one of the cemetery walks passed near him, he caught the shock of the face.

His neighbour at the other grave had withdrawn, as he himself, with force enough in him, would have done by now, and was advancing along the path on his way to one of the gates. This brought him close, and his pace was slow, so that—and all the more as there was a kind of hunger in his look—the two men were for a minute directly confronted. Marcher knew him at once for one of the deeply stricken—a perception so sharp that nothing else in the picture comparatively lived, neither his dress, his age, nor his presumable character and class; nothing lived but the deep ravage of the features he showed. He *showed* them—that was the point; he was moved, as he passed, by some impulse that was either a signal for sympathy or, more possibly, a challenge to an opposed sorrow. He might already have been aware of our friend, might at some previous hour have noticed in him the smooth habit of the scene, with which the state of his own senses so scantly consorted, and might thereby have been stirred as by an overt discord. What Marcher was at all events conscious of was in the first place that the image of scarred passion presented to him was conscious too—of something that profaned the air; and in the second that, roused, startled, shocked, he was yet the next moment looking after it, as it went, with envy. The most extraordinary thing that had happened to him—though he had given that name to other matters as well— took place, after his immediate vague stare, as a consequence of this impression. The stranger passed, but the raw glare of his grief remained, making our friend wonder in pity what wrong, what wound it expressed, what injury not to be healed. What had the man *had*, to make him by the loss of it so bleed and yet live?

Something—and this reached him with a pang—that *he*, John Marcher, hadn't; the proof of which was precisely John Marcher's arid end. No passion had ever touched him, for this was what passion meant; he had survived and maundered and pined, but where had been *his* deep ravage? The extraordinary thing we speak of was the sudden rush of the result of this question. The sight that had just met his eyes named to him, as in letters of quick flame, something he had utterly, insanely missed, and what he had missed made these things a train of fire, made them mark themselves in an anguish of inward throbs. He had seen *outside* of his life, not learned it within, the way a woman was mourned when she had been loved for herself: such was the force of his conviction of the meaning of the stranger's face, which still flared for him as a smoky torch. It hadn't come to him, the knowledge, on the wings of experience; it had brushed him, jostled him, upset him, with the disrespect of chance, the insolence of accident. Now that the illumination had begun, however, it blazed to the zenith, and what he presently stood there gazing at was the sounded void of his life. He gazed, he drew breath, in pain; he turned in his dismay, and, turning, he had before him in sharper incision than ever the open page of his story. The name on the table smote him as the passage of his neighbour had done, and what it said to him, full in the face, was that *she* was what he had missed. This was the awful thought, the answer to all the past, the vision at the dread clearness of which he grew as cold as the stone beneath him. Everything fell together, confessed, explained, overwhelmed; leaving him most of all stupefied at the blindness he had cherished. The fate he had been marked for he had met with a vengeance—he had emptied the cup to the lees; he had been the man of his time, *the* man, to whom nothing on earth was to have happened. That was the rare stroke—that was his visitation. So he saw it, as we say, in pale horror, while the pieces fitted and fitted. So *she* had seen it while he didn't, and so she served at this hour to drive the truth home. It was the truth, vivid and monstrous, that all the while he had waited the wait was itself his portion. This companion of his vigil had at a given moment made out, and she had then offered him the chance to baffle his doom. One's doom, however, was never baffled, and on the day she told him his own had come down she had seen him but stupidly stare at the escape she offered him.

The escape would have been to love her; then, *then* he would have lived. *She* had lived—who could say now with what passion?—since she had loved him for himself; whereas he had never thought of her (ah, how it hugely glared at him!) but in the chill of his egotism and the light of her use. Her spoken words came back to him—the chain stretched and stretched. The Beast had lurked indeed, and the Beast, at its hour, had sprung; it had sprung in that twilight of the cold April when, pale, ill, wasted, but all beautiful, and perhaps even then recoverable, she had risen from her chair to stand before him and let him imaginably guess. It had sprung as he didn't guess; it had sprung as she hopelessly turned from him, and the mark, by the time he left her, had fallen where it *was* to fall. He had justified his fear and achieved his fate; he had failed, with the last exactitude, of all he was to fail of; and a moan now rose to his lips as he remembered she had prayed he mightn't know. This horror of waking—*this* was knowledge, knowledge under the breath of which the very tears in his eyes seemed to freeze. Through them, none the less, he tried to fix it and hold it; he kept it there before him so that he might feel the pain. That at least, belated and bitter, had something of the taste of life. But the bitterness suddenly sickened him, and it was as if, horribly, he saw, in the truth, in the cruelty of his image, what had been appointed and done. He saw the Jungle of his life and saw the lurking Beast; then, while he looked, perceived it, as by a stir of the air, rise, huge and hideous, for the leap that was to settle him. His eyes darkened—it was close; and, instinctively turning, in his hallucination, to avoid it, he flung himself, face down, on the tomb.

1901                                                                    1903, 1909

# The Art of Fiction[1]

I should not have affixed so comprehensive a title to these few remarks, necessarily wanting in any completeness upon a subject the full consideration of which would carry us far, did I not seem to discover a pretext for my temerity in the interesting pamphlet lately published under this name by Mr. Walter Besant. Mr. Besant's lecture at the Royal Institution—the original form of his pamphlet—appears to indicate that many persons are interested in the art of fiction, and are not indifferent to such remarks, as those who practise it may attempt to make about it. I am therefore anxious not to lose the benefit of this favourable association, and to edge in a few words under cover of the attention which Mr. Besant is sure to have excited. There is something very encouraging in his having put into form certain of his ideas on the mystery of story-telling.

It is a proof of life and curiosity—curiosity on the part of the brotherhood of novelists as well as on the part of their readers. Only a short time ago it might have been supposed that the English novel was not what the French call *discutable*.[2] It had no air of having a theory, a conviction, a consciousness of itself behind it—of being the expression of an artistic faith, the result of choice and comparison. I do not say it was necessarily the worse for that: it would take much more courage than I possess to intimate that the form of the novel as Dickens and Thackeray (for instance) saw it had any taint of incompleteness. It was, however, *naïf* (if I may help myself out with another French word); and evidently if it be destined to suffer in any way for having lost its *naïveté* it has now an idea of making sure of the corresponding advantages. During the period I have alluded to there was a comfortable, good-humoured feeling abroad that a novel is a novel, as a pudding is a pudding, and that our only business with it could be to swallow it. But within a year or two, for some reason or other, there have been signs of returning animation—the era of discussion would appear to have been to a certain extent opened. Art lives upon discussion, upon experiment, upon curiosity, upon variety of attempt, upon the exchange of views and the comparison of standpoints; and there is a presumption that those times when no one has anything particular to say about it, and has no reason to give for practice or preference, though they may be times of honour, are not times of development—are times, possibly even, a little of dulness. The successful application of any art is a delightful spectacle, but the theory too is interesting; and though there is a great deal of the latter without the former I suspect there has never been a genuine success that has not had a latent core of conviction. Discussion, suggestion, formulation, these

---

1. James's most famous (and influential) critical essay was written in response to a lecture on fiction delivered by the English novelist and historian Walter Besant (1836–1901) at the Royal Institution (London) on April 25, 1884. First published in *Longman's Magazine* for September 1884, the essay was reprinted in book form the next year and in *Partial Portraits* (1888), the source of the present text.
2. Debatable.

things are fertilising when they are frank and sincere. Mr. Besant has set an excellent example in saying what he thinks, for his part, about the way in which fiction should be written, as well as about the way in which it should be published; for his view of the "art," carried on into an appendix, covers that too. Other labourers in the same field will doubtless take up the argument, they will give it the light of their experience, and the effect will surely be to make our interest in the novel a little more what it had for some time threatened to fail to be—a serious, active, inquiring interest, under protection of which this delightful study may, in moments of confidence, venture to say a little more what it thinks of itself.

It must take itself seriously for the public to take it so. The old superstition about fiction being "wicked" has doubtless died out in England; but the spirit of it lingers in a certain oblique regard directed toward any story which does not more or less admit that it is only a joke. Even the most jocular novel feels in some degree the weight of the proscription that was formerly directed against literary levity: the jocularity does not always succeed in passing for orthodoxy. It is still expected, though perhaps people are ashamed to say it, that a production which is after all only a "make-believe" (for what else is a "story"?) shall be in some degree apologetic—shall renounce the pretension of attempting really to represent life. This, of course, any sensible, wide-awake story declines to do, for it quickly perceives that the tolerance granted to it on such a condition is only an attempt to stifle it disguised in the form of generosity. The evangelical hostility to the novel, which was as explicit as it was narrow, and which regarded it as little less favourable to our immortal part than a stage-play, was in reality far less insulting. The only reason for the existence of a novel is that it does attempt to represent life. When it relinquishes this attempt, the same attempt that we see on the canvas of the painter, it will have arrived at a very strange pass. It is not expected of the picture that it will make itself humble in order to be forgiven; and the analogy between the art of the painter and the art of the novelist is, so far as I am able to see, complete. Their inspiration is the same, their process (allowing for the different quality of the vehicle), is the same, their success is the same. They may learn from each other, they may explain and sustain each other. Their cause is the same, and the honour of one is the honour of another. The Mahometans think a picture an unholy thing, but it is a long time since any Christian did, and it is therefore the more odd that in the Christian mind the traces (dissimulated though they may be) of a suspicion of the sister art should linger to this day. The only effectual way to lay it to rest is to emphasise the analogy to which I just alluded—to insist on the fact that as the picture is reality, so the novel is history. That is the only general description (which does it justice) that we may give of the novel. But history also is allowed to represent life; it is not, any more than painting, expected to apologise. The subject-matter of fiction is stored up likewise in documents and records, and if it will not give itself away, as they say in California, it must speak with assurance, with the tone of the historian. Certain accomplished novelists have a habit of giving themselves away which must often bring tears to the eyes of people who take their fiction seriously. I was lately struck, in reading over many pages of Anthony Trollope,[3] with his want of discretion in this particular. In a digression, a parenthe-

---

3. English novelist (1815–1882).

sis or an aside, he concedes to the reader that he and this trusting friend are only "making believe." He admits that the events he narrates have not really happened, and that he can give his narrative any turn the reader may like best. Such a betrayal of a sacred office seems to me, I confess, a terrible crime; it is what I mean by the attitude of apology, and it shocks me every whit as much in Trollope as it would have shocked me in Gibbon or Macaulay.[4] It implies that the novelist is less occupied in looking for the truth (the truth, of course I mean, that he assumes, the premises that we must grant him, whatever they may be), than the historian, and in doing so it deprives him at a stroke of all his standing-room. To represent and illustrate the past, the actions of men, is the task of either writer, and the only difference that I can see is, in proportion as he succeeds, to the honour of the novelist, consisting as it does in his having more difficulty in collecting his evidence, which is so far from being purely literary. It seems to me to give him a great character, the fact that he has at once so much in common with the philosopher and the painter; this double analogy is a magnificent heritage.

It is of all this evidently that Mr. Besant is full when he insists upon the fact that fiction is one of the *fine* arts, deserving in its turn of all the honours and emoluments that have hitherto been reserved for the successful profession of music, poetry, painting, architecture. It is impossible to insist too much on so important a truth, and the place that Mr. Besant demands for the work of the novelist may be represented, a trifle less abstractly, by saying that he demands not only that it shall be reputed artistic, but that it shall be reputed very artistic indeed. It is excellent that he should have struck this note, for his doing so indicates that there was need of it, that his proposition may be to many people a novelty. One rubs one's eyes at the thought; but the rest of Mr. Besant's essay confirms the revelation. I suspect in truth that it would be possible to confirm it still further, and that one would not be far wrong in saying that in addition to the people to whom it has never occurred that a novel ought to be artistic, there are a great many others who, if this principle were urged upon them, would be filled with an indefinable mistrust. They would find it difficult to explain their repugnance, but it would operate strongly to put them on their guard. "Art," in our Protestant communities, where so many things have got so strangely twisted about, is supposed in certain circles to have some vaguely injurious effect upon those who make it an important consideration, who let it weigh in the balance. It is assumed to be opposed in some mysterous manner to morality, to amusement, to instruction. When it is embodied in the work of the painter (the sculptor is another affair!) you know what it is: it stands there before you, in the honesty of pink and green and a gilt frame; you can see the worst of it at a glance, and you can be on your guard. But when it is introduced into literature it becomes more insidious—there is danger of its hurting you before you know it. Literature should be either instructive or amusing, and there is in many minds an impression that these artistic preoccu- pations, the search for form, contribute to neither end, interfere indeed with both. They are too frivolous to be edifying, and too serious to be diverting; and they are moreover priggish and paradoxical and superfluous. That, I think, represents the manner in which the latent thought of many people who read novels as an exercise in skipping would explain itself if it were to become

4. Edward Gibbon (1737–1794) and Thomas Babington Macaulay (1800–1859), English historians.

articulate. They would argue, of course, that a novel ought to be "good," but they would interpret this term in a fashion of their own, which indeed would vary considerably from one critic to another. One would say that being good means representing virtuous and aspiring characters, placed in prominent positions; another would say that it depends on a "happy ending," on a distribution at the last of prizes, pensions, husbands, wives, babies, millions, appended paragraphs, and cheerful remarks. Another still would say that it means being full of incident and movement, so that we shall wish to jump ahead, to see who was the mysterious stranger, and if the stolen will was ever found, and shall not be distracted from this pleasure by any tiresome analysis or "description." But they would all agree that the "artistic" idea would spoil some of their fun. One would hold it accountable for all the description, another would see it revealed in the absence of sympathy. Its hostility to a happy ending would be evident, and it might even in some cases render any ending at all impossible. The "ending" of a novel is, for many persons, like that of a good dinner, a course of dessert and ices, and the artist in fiction is regarded as a sort of meddlesome doctor who forbids agreeable aftertastes. It is therefore true that this conception of Mr. Besant's of the novel as a superior form encounters not only a negative but a positive indifference. It matters little that as a work of art it should really be as little or as much of its essence to supply happy endings, sympathetic characters, and an objective tone, as if it were a work of mechanics: the association of ideas, however incongruous, might easily be too much for it if an eloquent voice were not sometimes raised to call attention to the fact that it is at once as free and as serious a branch of literature as any other.

Certainly this might sometimes be doubted in presence of the enormous number of works of fiction that appeal to the credulity of our generation, for it might easily seem that there could be no great character in a commodity so quickly and easily produced. It must be admitted that good novels are much compromised by bad ones, and that the field at large suffers discredit from overcrowding. I think, however, that this injury is only superficial, and that the superabundance of written fiction proves nothing against the principle itself. It has been vulgarised, like all other kinds of literature, like everything else to-day, and it has proved more than some kinds accessible to vulgarisation. But there is as much difference as there ever was between a good novel and a bad one: the bad is swept with all the daubed canvases and spoiled marble into some unvisited limbo, or infinite rubbish-yard beneath the back-windows of the world, and the good subsists and emits its light and stimulates our desire for perfection. As I shall take the liberty of making but a single criticism of Mr. Besant, whose tone is so full of the love of his art, I may as well have done with it at once. He seems to me to mistake in attempting to say so definitely beforehand what sort of an affair the good novel will be. To indicate the danger of such an error as that has been the purpose of these few pages; to suggest that certain traditions on the subject, applied a priori, have already had much to answer for, and that the good health of an art which undertakes so immediately to reproduce life must demand that it be perfectly free. It lives upon exercise, and the very meaning of exercise is freedom. The only obligation to which in advance we may hold a novel, without incurring the accusation of being arbitrary, is that it be interesting. That general responsibility rests upon it, but it is the only one I can think of. The ways in which it is at liberty to accomplish this result (of interesting us) strike me as innumerable, and such as can only suffer from being marked out or fenced in by prescription. They are as various as the temperament of man, and they are successful in proportion as they reveal a particular mind, different from others. A novel is in its broadest definition a personal, a direct impression of life: that, to begin with, constitutes its value, which is greater or less according to the intensity of the impression. But there will be no intensity at all, and therefore no value, unless there is freedom to feel and say. The tracing of a line to be followed, of a tone to be taken, of a form to be filled out, is a limitation of that freedom and a suppression of the very thing that we are most curious about. The form, it seems to me, is to be appreciated after the fact: then the author's choice has been made, his standard has been indicated; then we can follow lines and directions and compare tones and resemblances. Then in a word we can enjoy one of the most charming of pleasures, we can estimate quality, we can apply the test of execution. The execution belongs to the author alone; it is what is most personal to him, and we measure him by that. The advantage, the luxury, as well as the torment and responsibility of the novelist, is that there is no limit to what he may attempt as an executant—no limit to his possible experiments, efforts, discoveries, successes. Here it is especially that he works, step by step, like his brother of the brush, of whom we may always say that he has painted his picture in a manner best known to himself. His manner is his secret, not necessarily a jealous one. He cannot disclose it as a general thing if he would; he would be at a loss to teach it to others. I say this with a due recollection of having insisted on the community of method of the artist who paints a picture and the artist who writes a novel. The painter *is* able to teach the rudiments of his practice, and it is possible, from the study of good work (granted the aptitude), both to learn how to paint and to learn how to write. Yet it remains true, without injury to the *rapprochement*, that the literary artist would be obliged to say to his pupil much more than the other, "Ah, well, you must do it as you can!" It is a question of degree, a matter of delicacy. If there are exact sciences, there are also exact arts, and the grammar of painting is so much more definite that it makes the difference.

I ought to add, however, that if Mr. Besant says at the beginning of his essay that the "laws of fiction may be laid down and taught with as much precision and exactness as the laws of harmony, perspective, and proportion," he mitigates what might appear to be an extravagance by applying his remark to "general" laws, and by expressing most of these rules in a manner with which it would certainly be unaccommodating to disagree. That the novelist must write from his experience, that his "characters must be real and such as might be met with in actual life"; that "a young lady brought up in a quiet country village should avoid descriptions of garrison life," and "a writer whose friends and personal experiences belong to the lower middle-class should carefully avoid introducing his characters into society"; that one should enter one's notes in a common-place book; that one's figures should be clear in outline; that making them clear by some trick of speech or of carriage is a bad method, and "describing them at length" is a worse one; that English Fiction should have a "conscious moral purpose"; that "it is almost impossible to estimate too highly the value of careful workmanship—that is, of style"; that "the most important point of all is the story," that "the story is everything": these are principles with most of which it is surely impossible not to sympathise. That remark about the lower middle-class writer and his knowing his place is perhaps rather chilling;

but for the rest I should find it difficult to dissent from any one of these recommendations. At the same time, I should find it difficult positively to assent to them, with the exception, perhaps, of the injunction as to entering one's notes in a common-place book. They scarcely seem to me to have the quality that Mr. Besant attributes to the rules of the novelist—the "precision and exactness" of "the laws of harmony, perspective, and proportion." They are suggestive, they are even inspiring, but they are not exact, though they are doubtless as much so as the case admits of: which is a proof of that liberty of interpretation for which I just contended. For the value of these different injunctions—so beautiful and so vague—is wholly in the meaning one attaches to them. The characters, the situation, which strike one as real will be those that touch and interest one most, but the measure of reality is very difficult to fix. The reality of Don Quixote or of Mr. Micawber[5] is a very delicate shade; it is a reality so coloured by the author's vision that, vivid as it may be, one would hesitate to propose it as a model: one would expose one's self to some very embarrassing questions on the part of a pupil. It goes without saying that you will not write a good novel unless you possess the sense of reality; but it will be difficult to give you a recipe for calling that sense into being. Humanity is immense, and reality has a myriad forms; the most one can affirm is that some of the flowers of fiction have the odour of it, and others have not; as for telling you in advance how your nosegay should be composed, that is another affair. It is equally excellent and inconclusive to say that one must write from experience; to our supposititious aspirant such a declaration might savour of mockery. What kind of experience is intended, and where does it begin and end? Experience is never limited, and it is never complete; it is an immense sensibility, a kind of huge spiderweb of the finest silken threads suspended in the chamber of consciousness, and catching every airborne particle in its tissue. It is the very atmosphere of the mind; and when the mind is imaginative—much more when it happens to be that of a man of genius—it takes to itself the faintest hints of life, it converts the very pulses of the air into revelations. The young lady living in a village has only to be a damsel upon whom nothing is lost to make it quite unfair (as it seems to me) to declare to her that she shall have nothing to say about the military. Greater miracles have been seen than that, imagination assisting, she should speak the truth about some of these gentlemen. I remember an English novelist, a woman of genius,[6] telling me that she was much commended for the impression she had managed to give in one of her tales of the nature and way of life of the French Protestant youth. She had been asked where she learned so much about this recondite being, she had been congratulated on her peculiar opportunities. These opportunities consisted in her having once, in Paris, as she ascended a staircase, passed an open door where, in the household of a *pasteur*,[7] some of the young Protestants were seated at table round a finished meal. The glimpse made a picture; it lasted only a moment, but that moment was experience. She had got her direct personal impression, and she turned out her type. She knew what youth was, and what Protestantism; she also had the advantage of having seen what it was to be French, so that she converted these ideas into a concrete image and produced a reality. Above all, however, she was blessed with the faculty

5. Main characters in the novel by Cervantes and in Dickens's *David Copperfield*.
6. Leon Edel identifies her as novelist Thackeray's daughter Anne, whose first novel contains many of the elements of James's description.
7. Pastor, minister (French).

which when you give it an inch takes an ell, and which for the artist is a much greater source of strength than any accident of residence or of place in the social scale. The power to guess the unseen from the seen, to trace the implication of things, to judge the whole piece by the pattern, the condition of feeling life in general so completely that you are well on your way to knowing any particular corner of it—this cluster of gifts may almost be said to constitute experience, and they occur in country and in town, and in the most differing stages of education. If experience consists of impressions, it may be said that impressions *are* experience, just as (have we not seen it?) they are the very air we breathe. Therefore, if I should certainly say to a novice, "Write from experience and experience only," I should feel that this was rather a tantalising monition if I were not careful immediately to add, "Try to be one of the people on whom nothing is lost!"

I am far from intending by this to minimise the importance of exactness—of truth of detail. One can speak best from one's own taste, and I may therefore venture to say that the air of reality (solidity of specification) seems to me to be the supreme virtue of a novel—the merit on which all its other merits (including that conscious moral purpose of which Mr. Besant speaks) helplessly and submissively depend. If it be not there they are all as nothing, and if these be there, they owe their effect to the success with which the author has produced the illusion of life. The cultivation of this success, the study of this exquisite process, form, to my taste, the beginning and the end of the art of the novelist. They are his inspiration, his despair, his reward, his torment, his delight. It is here in very truth that he competes with life; it is here that he competes with his brother the painter in *his* attempt to render the look of things, the look that conveys their meaning, to catch the colour, the relief, the expression, the surface, the substance of the human spectacle. It is in regard to this that Mr. Besant is well inspired when he bids him take notes. He cannot possibly take too many, he cannot possibly take enough. All life solicits him, and to "render" the simplest surface, to produce the most momentary illusion, is a very complicated business. His case would be easier, and the rule would be more exact, if Mr. Besant had been able to tell him what notes to take. But this, I fear, he can never learn in any manual; it is the business of his life. He has to take a great many in order to select a few, he has to work them up as he can, and even the guides and philosophers who might have most to say to him must leave him alone when it comes to the application of precepts, as we leave the painter in communion with his palette. That his characters "must be clear in outline," as Mr. Besant says—he feels that down to his boots; but how he shall make them so is a secret between his good angel and himself. It would be absurdly simple if he could be taught that a great deal of "description" would make them so, or that on the contrary the absence of description and the cultivation of dialogue, or the absence of dialogue and the multiplication of "incident," would rescue him from his difficulties. Nothing, for instance, is more possible than that he be of a turn of mind for which this odd, literal opposition of description and dialogue, incident and description, has little meaning and light. People often talk of these things as if they had a kind of internecine distinctness, instead of melting into each other at every breath, and being intimately associated parts of one general effort of expression. I cannot imagine composition existing in a series of blocks, nor conceive, in any novel worth discussing at all, of a passage of description that is not in its intention narrative, a passage of dialogue that is not in its intention descriptive, a touch of truth of any sort that does not partake of the nature of incident, or an incident that derives its interest from any other source than the general and only source of the success of a work of art—that of being illustrative. A novel is a living thing, all one and continuous, like any other organism, and in proportion as it lives will it be found, I think, that in each of the parts there is something of each of the other parts. The critic who over the close texture of a finished work shall pretend to trace a geography of items will mark some frontiers as artificial, I fear, as any that have been known to history. There is an old-fashioned distinction between the novel of character and the novel of incident which must have cost many a smile to the intending fabulist who was keen about his work. It appears to me as little to the point as the equally celebrated distinction between the novel and the romance—to answer as little to any reality. There are bad novels and good novels, as there are bad pictures and good pictures; but that is the only distinction in which I see any meaning, and I can as little imagine speaking of a novel of character as I can imagine speaking of a picture of character. When one says picture one says of character, when one says novel one says of incident, and the terms may be transposed at will. What is character but the determination of incident? What is incident but the illustration of character? What is either a picture or a novel that is *not* of character? What else do we seek in it and find in it? It is an incident for a woman to stand up with her hand resting on a table and look out at you in a certain way; or if it be not an incident I think it will be hard to say what it is. At the same time it is an expression of character. If you say you don't see it (character in *that—allons donc!*[8]), this is exactly what the artist who has reasons of his own for thinking he *does* see it undertakes to show you. When a young man makes up his mind that he has not faith enough after all to enter the church as he intended, that is an incident, though you may not hurry to the end of the chapter to see whether perhaps he doesn't change once more. I do not say that these are extraordinary or startling incidents. I do not pretend to estimate the degree of interest proceeding from them, for this will depend upon the skill of the painter. It sounds almost puerile to say that some incidents are intrinsically much more important than others, and I need not take this precaution after having professed my sympathy for the major ones in remarking that the only classification of the novel that I can understand is into that which has life and that which has it not.

The novel and the romance, the novel of incident and that of character— these clumsy separations appear to me to have been made by critics and readers for their own convenience, and to help them out of some of their occasional queer predicaments, but to have little reality or interest for the producer, from whose point of view it is of course that we are attempting to consider the art of fiction. The case is the same with another shadowy category which Mr. Besant apparently is disposed to set up—that of the "modern English novel"; unless indeed it be that in this matter he has fallen into an accidental confusion of standpoints. It is not quite clear whether he intends the remarks in which he alludes to it to be didactic or historical. It is as difficult to suppose a person intending to write a modern English as to suppose him writing an ancient English novel: that is a label which begs the question. One writes the novel,

8. Come now! (French); i.e., nonsense!

one paints the picture, of one's language and of one's time, and calling it
modern English will not, alas! make the difficult task any easier. No more,
unfortunately, will calling this or that work of one's fellow-artist a romance—
unless it be, of course, simply for the pleasantness of the thing, as for instance
when Hawthorne gave this heading to his story of *Blithedale*.[9] The French,
who have brought the theory of fiction to remarkable completeness, have but
one name for the novel, and have not attempted smaller things in it, that I
can see, for that. I can think of no obligation to which the "romancer" would
not be held equally with the novelist; the standard of execution is equally high
for each. Of course it is of execution that we are talking—that being the only
point of a novel that is open to contention. This is perhaps too often lost sight
of, only to produce interminable confusions and cross-purposes. We must
grant the artist his subject, his idea, his *donnée:*[1] our criticism is applied only
to what he makes of it. Naturally I do not mean that we are bound to like it or
find it interesting: in case we do not our course is perfectly simple—to let it
alone. We may believe that of a certain idea even the most sincere novelist
can make nothing at all, and the event may perfectly justify our belief; but the
failure will have been a failure to execute, and it is in the execution that the
fatal weakness is recorded. If we pretend to respect the artist at all, we must
allow him his freedom of choice, in the face, in particular cases, of innumerable presumptions that the choice will not fructify. Art derives a considerable
part of its beneficial exercise from flying in the face of presumptions, and some
of the most interesting experiments of which it is capable are hidden in the
bosom of common things. Gustave Flaubert has written a story about the
devotion of a servant-girl to a parrot,[2] and the production, highly finished as it
is, cannot on the whole be called a success. We are perfectly free to find it
flat, but I think it might have been interesting; and I, for my part, am
extremely glad he should have written it; it is a contribution to our knowledge
of what can be done—or what cannot. Ivan Turgénieff has written a tale about
a deaf and dumb serf and a lap-dog,[3] and the thing is touching, loving, a little
masterpiece. He struck the note of life where Gustave Flaubert missed it—he
flew in the face of a presumption and achieved a victory.

Nothing, of course, will ever take the place of the good old fashion of "liking" a work of art or not liking it: the most improved criticism will not abolish
that primitive, that ultimate test. I mention this to guard myself from the
accusation of intimating that the idea, the subject, of a novel or a picture,
does not matter. It matters, to my sense, in the highest degree, and if I might
put up a prayer it would be that artists should select none but the richest.
Some, as I have already hastened to admit, are much more remunerative than
others, and it would be a world happily arranged in which persons intending
to treat them should be exempt from confusions and mistakes. This fortunate
condition will arrive only, I fear, on the same day that critics become purged
from error. Meanwhile, I repeat, we do not judge the artist with fairness unless
we say to him, "Oh, I grant you your starting-point, because if I did not I
should seem to prescribe to you, and heaven forbid I should take that responsibility. If I pretend to tell you what you must not take, you will call upon me
to tell you then what you must take; in which case I shall be prettily caught.
Moreover, it isn't till I have accepted your data that I can begin to measure

---

9. *The Blithedale Romance* was published in 1852.   2. *A Simple Soul*, by Flaubert (1821–1880).
1. That which is given (French).                      3. *Mumu*, by Ivan Turgenev (1818–1883).

you. I have the standard, the pitch; I have no right to tamper with your flute and then criticise your music. Of course I may not care for your idea at all; I may think it silly, or stale, or unclean; in which case I wash my hands of you altogether. I may content myself with believing that you will not have succeeded in being interesting, but I shall, of course, not attempt to demonstrate it, and you will be as indifferent to me as I am to you. I needn't remind you that there are all sorts of tastes: who can know it better? Some people, for excellent reasons, don't like to read about carpenters; others, for reasons even better, don't like to read about courtesans. Many object to Americans. Others (I believe they are mainly editors and publishers) won't look at Italians. Some readers don't like quiet subjects; others don't like bustling ones. Some enjoy a complete illusion, others the consciousness of large concessions. They choose their novels accordingly, and if they don't care about your idea they won't, *a fortiori*,[4] care about your treatment."

So that it comes back very quickly, as I have said, to the liking: in spite of M. Zola,[5] who reasons less powerfully than he represents, and who will not reconcile himself to this absoluteness of taste, thinking that there are certain things that people ought to like, and that they can be made to like. I am quite at a loss to imagine anything (at any rate in this matter of fiction) that people *ought* to like or to dislike. Selection will be sure to take care of itself, for it has a constant motive behind it. That motive is simply experience. As people feel life, so they will feel the art that is most closely related to it. This closeness of relation is what we should never forget in talking of the effort of the novel. Many people speak of it as a factitious, artificial form, a product of ingenuity, the business of which is to alter and arrange the things that surround us, to translate them into conventional, traditional moulds. This however, is a view of the matter which carries us but a very short way, condemns the art to an eternal repetition of a few familiar *clichés*, cuts short its development, and leads us straight up to a dead wall. Catching the very note and trick, the strange irregular rhythm of life, that is the attempt whose strenuous forces keeps Fiction upon her feet. In proportion as in what she offers us we see life *without* rearrangement do we feel that we are touching the truth; in proportion as we see it *with* rearrangement do we feel that we are being put off with a substitute, a compromise and convention. It is not uncommon to hear an extraordinary assurance of remark in regard to this matter of rearranging, which is often spoken of as if it were the last word of art. Mr. Besant seems to me in danger of falling into the great error with his rather unguarded talk about "selection." Art is essentially selection, but it is a selection whose main care is to be typical, to be inclusive. For many people art means rose-coloured window-panes, and selection means picking a bouquet for Mrs. Grundy.[6] They will tell you glibly that artistic considerations have nothing to do with the disagreeable, with the ugly; they will rattle off shallow commonplaces about the province of art and the limits of art till you are moved to some wonder in return as to the province and the limits of ignorance. It appears to me that no one can ever have made a seriously artistic attempt without becoming conscious of an immense increase—a kind of revelation—of freedom. One perceives in that case—by

4. All the more reason (Latin).
5. Émile Zola (1840–1902), French naturalistic novelist and literary theorist who argued that people should like best what was represented with the greatest mea-

sure of scientific objectivity.
6. A stock character marked by prudishness who is alluded to in Thomas Morton's *Speed the Plough* (1798).

the light of a heavenly ray—that the province of art is all life, all feeling, all observation, all vision. As Mr. Besant so justly intimates, it is all experience. That is a sufficient answer to those who maintain that it must not touch the sad things of life, who stick into its divine unconscious bosom little prohibitory inscriptions on the end of sticks, such as we see in public gardens—"It is forbidden to walk on the grass; it is forbidden to touch the flowers; it is not allowed to introduce dogs or to remain after dark; it is requested to keep to the right." The young aspirant in the line of fiction whom we continue to imagine will do nothing without taste, for in that case his freedom would be of little use to him; but the first advantage of his taste will be to reveal to him the absurdity of the little sticks and tickets. If he have taste, I must add, of course he will have ingenuity, and my disrespectful reference to that quality just now was not meant to imply that it is useless in fiction. But it is only a secondary aid; the first is a capacity for receiving straight impressions.

Mr. Besant has some remarks on the question of "the story" which I shall not attempt to criticise, though they seem to me to contain a singular ambiguity, because I do not think I understand them. I cannot see what is meant by talking as if there were a part of a novel which is the story and part of it which for mystical reasons is not—unless indeed the distinction be made in a sense in which it is difficult to suppose that any one should attempt to convey anything. "The story," if it represents anything, represents the subject, the idea, the *donnée* of the novel; and there is surely no "school"—Mr. Besant speaks of a school—which urges that a novel should be all treatment and no subject. There must assuredly be something to treat; every school is intimately conscious of that. This sense of the story being the idea, the starting-point, of the novel, is the only one that I see in which it can be spoken of as something different from its organic whole; and since in proportion as the work is successful the idea permeates and penetrates it, informs and animates it, so that every word and every punctuation-point contribute directly to the expression, in that proportion do we lose our sense of the story being a blade which may be drawn more or less out of its sheath. The story and the novel, the idea and the form, are the needle and thread, and I never heard of a guild of tailors who recommended the use of the thread without the needle, or the needle without the thread. Mr. Besant is not the only critic who may be observed to have spoken as if there were certain things in life which constitute stories, and certain others which do not. I find the same odd implication in an entertaining article in the *Pall Mall Gazette*, devoted, as it happens, to Mr. Besant's lecture. "The story is the thing!" says this graceful writer, as if with a tone of opposition to some other idea. I should think it was, as every painter who, as the time for "sending in"[7] his picture looms in the distance, finds himself still in quest of a subject—as every belated artist not fixed about his theme will heartily agree. There are some subjects which speak to us and others which do not, but he would be a clever man who should undertake to give a rule—an index expurgatorius[8]—by which the story and the no-story should be known apart. It is impossible (to me at least) to imagine any such rule which shall not be altogether arbitrary. The writer in the *Pall Mall* opposes the delightful (as I suppose) novel of *Margot la Balafrée*[9] to certain tales in which "Bostonian

---

7. I.e., at the time of shipping his painting to a Royal Academy exhibit.
8. The list of books from which condemned passages must be removed before the book could be read by

Catholics.
9. *Margot the Scarred Woman* (1884) by Fortuné du Boisgobey.

nymphs" appear to have "rejected English dukes for psychological reasons." I am not acquainted with the romance just designated, and can scarcely forgive the *Pall Mall* critic for not mentioning the name of the author, but the title appears to refer to a lady who may have received a scar in some heroic adventure. I am inconsolable at not being acquainted with this episode,[1] but am utterly at a loss to see why it is a story when the rejection (or acceptance) of a duke is not, and why a reason, psychological or other, is not a subject when a cicatrix[2] is. They are all particles of the multitudinous life with which the novel deals, and surely no dogma which pretends to make it lawful to touch the one and unlawful to touch the other will stand for a moment on its feet. It is the special picture that must stand or fall, according as it seem to possess truth or to lack it. Mr. Besant does not, to my sense, light up the subject by intimating that a story must, under penalty of not being a story, consist of "adventures." Why of adventures more than of green spectacles? He mentions a category of impossible things, and among them he places "fiction without adventure." Why without adventure, more than without matrimony, or celibacy, or parturition, or cholera, or hydropathy, or Jansenism?[3] This seems to me to bring the novel back to the hapless little *rôle* of being an artificial, ingenious thing—bring it down from its large, free character of an immense and exquisite correspondence with life. And what *is* adventure, when it comes to that, and by what sign is the listening pupil to recognise it? It is an adventure—an immense one—for me to write this little article; and for a Bostonian nymph to reject an English duke is an adventure only less stirring, I should say, than for an English duke to be rejected by a Bostonian nymph. I see dramas within dramas in that, and innumerable points of view. A psychological reason is, to my imagination, an object adorably pictorial; to catch the tint of its complexion—I feel as if that idea might inspire one to Titianesque[4] efforts. There are few things more exciting to me, in short, than a psychological reason, and yet, I protest, the novel seems to me the most magnificent form of art. I have just been reading, at the same time, the delightful story of *Treasure Island*, by Mr. Robert Louis Stevenson and, in a manner less consecutive, the last tale from M. Edmond de Goncourt, which is entitled *Chérie*.[5] One of these works treats of murders, mysteries, islands of dreadful renown, hairbreadth escapes, miraculous coincidences and buried doubloons. The other treats of a little French girl who lived in a fine house in Paris, and died of wounded sensibility because no one would marry her. I call *Treasure Island* delightful, because it appears to me to have succeeded wonderfully in what it attempts; and I venture to bestow no epithet upon *Chérie*, which strikes me as having failed deplorably in what it attempts—that is in tracing the development of the moral consciousness of a child. But one of these productions strikes me as exactly as much of a novel as the other, and as having a "story" quite as much. The moral consciousness of a child is as much a part of life as the islands of the Spanish Main, and the one sort of geography seems to me to have those "surprises"—of which Mr. Besant speaks quite as much as the other. For myself (since it comes back in the last resort, as I say, to the preference of the individual), the picture of the child's experience has the advantage

1. I.e., with Boisgobey's novel.
2. Scar.
3. A theological doctrine named after Cornelis Jansen (1585–1638), Dutch theologian who emphasized predestination and the necessity of belonging to the Catholic Church for salvation. "Hydropathy": the use of wa-

ter in the treatment of disease.
4. Titian (1477–1576), Italian painter highly regarded for his use of color.
5. *Treasure Island* was published in 1883, *Chérie* in 1884.

that I can at successive steps (an immense luxury, near to the "sensual plea-sure" of which Mr. Besant's critic in the *Pall Mall* speaks) say Yes or No, as it may be, to what the artist puts before me. I have been a child in fact, but I have been on a quest for a buried treasure only in supposition, and it is a simple accident that with M. de Goncourt I should have for the most part to say No. With George Eliot, when she painted that country[6] with a far other intelligence, I always said Yes.

The most interesting part of Mr. Besant's lecture is unfortunately the briefest passage—his very cursory allusion to the "conscious moral purpose" of the novel. Here again it is not very clear whether he be recording a fact or laying down a principle; it is a great pity that in the latter case he should not have developed his idea. This branch of the subject is of immense importance, and Mr. Besant's few words point to considerations of the widest reach, not to be lightly disposed of. He will have treated the art of fiction but superficially who is not prepared to go every inch of the way that these considerations will carry him. It is for this reason that at the beginning of these remarks I was careful to notify the reader that my reflections on so large a theme have no pretension to be exhaustive. Like Mr. Besant, I have left the question of the morality of the novel till the last, and at the last I find I have used up my space. It is a question surrounded with difficulties, as witness the very first that meets us, in the form of a definite question, on the threshold. Vagueness, in such a discussion, is fatal, and what is the meaning of your morality and your conscious moral purpose? Will you not define your terms and explain how (a novel being a picture) a picture can be either moral or immoral? You wish to paint a moral picture or carve a moral statue: will you not tell us how you would set about it? We are discussing the Art of Fiction; questions of art are questions (in the widest sense) of execution; questions of morality are quite another affair, and will you not let us see how it is that you find it so easy to mix them up? These things are so clear to Mr. Besant that he has deduced from them a law which he sees embodied in English Fiction, and which is "a truly admirable thing and a great cause for congratulation." It is a great cause for congratulation indeed when such thorny problems become as smooth as silk. I may add that in so far as Mr. Besant perceives that in point of fact English Fiction has addressed itself preponderantly to these delicate questions he will appear to many people to have made a vain discovery. They will have been positively struck, on the contrary, with the moral timidity of the usual English novelist; with his (or with her) aversion to face the difficulties with which on every side the treatment of reality bristles. He is apt to be extremely shy (whereas the picture that Mr. Besant draws is a picture of boldness), and the sign of his work, for the most part, is a cautious silence on certain subjects. In the English novel (by which of course I mean the American as well), more than in any other, there is a traditional difference·between that which people know and that which they agree to admit that they know, that which they see and that which they speak of, that which they feel to be a part of life and that which they allow to enter into literature. There is the great difference, in short, between what they talk of in conversation and what they talk of in print. The essence of moral energy is to survey the whole field, and I should directly reverse Mr. Besant's remark and say not that the English novel has a purpose,

---

6. Geography of a child's moral consciousness. George Eliot is the pseudonym for Marian Evans (1819–1880), English novelist.

but that it has a diffidence. To what degree a purpose in a work of art is a source of corruption I shall not attempt to inquire; the one that seems to me least dangerous is the purpose of making a perfect work. As for our novel, I may say lastly on this score that as we find it in England to-day it strikes me as addressed in a large degree to "young people," and that this in itself constitutes a presumption that it will be rather shy. There are certain things which it is generally agreed not to discuss, not even to mention, before young people. That is very well, but the absence of discussion is not a symptom of the moral passion. The purpose of the English novel—"a truly admirable thing, and a great cause for congratulation"—strikes me therefore as rather negative.

There is one point at which the moral sense and the artistic sense lie very near together; that is in the light of the very obvious truth that the deepest quality of a work of art will always be the quality of the mind of the producer. In proportion as that intelligence is fine will the novel, the picture, the statue partake of the substance of beauty and truth. To be constituted of such elements is, to my vision, to have purpose enough. No good novel will ever proceed from a superficial mind; that seems to me an axiom which, for the artist in fiction, will cover all needful moral ground: if the youthful aspirant take it to heart it will illuminate for him many of the mysteries of "purpose." There are many other useful things that might be said to him, but I have come to the end of my article, and can only touch them as I pass. The critic in the *Pall Mall Gazette*, whom I have already quoted, draws attention to the danger, in speaking of the art of fiction, of generalising. The danger that he has in mind is rather, I imagine, that of particularising, for there are some comprehensive remarks which, in addition to those embodied in Mr. Besant's suggestive lecture, might without fear of misleading him be addressed to the ingenuous student. I should remind him first of the magnificence of the form that is open to him, which offers to sight so few restrictions and such innumerable opportunities. The other arts, in comparison, appear confined and hampered; the various conditions under which they are exercised are so rigid and definite. But the only condition that I can think of attaching to the composition of the novel is, as I have already said, that it be sincere. This freedom is a splendid privilege, and the first lesson of the young novelist is to learn to be worthy of it. "Enjoy it as it deserves," I should say to him; "take possession of it, explore it to its utmost extent, publish it, rejoice in it. All life belongs to you, and do not listen either to those who would shut you up into corners of it and tell you that it is only here and there that art inhabits, or to those who would persuade you that this heavenly messenger wings her way outside of life altogether, breathing a superfine air, and turning away her head from the truth of things. There is no impression of life, no manner of seeing it and feeling it, to which the plan of the novelist may not offer a place; you have only to remember that talents so dissimilar as those of Alexandre Dumas and Jane Austen, Charles Dickens and Gustave Flaubert have worked in this field with equal glory. Do not think too much about optimism and pessimism; try and catch the colour of life itself. In France to-day we see a prodigious effort (that of Emile Zola, to whose solid and serious work no explorer of the capacity of the novel can allude without respect), we see an extraordinary effort vitiated by a spirit of pessimism on a narrow basis. M. Zola is magnificent, but he strikes an English reader as ignorant; he has an air of working in the dark; if he had as much light as energy, his results would be of the highest value. As for

the aberrations of a shallow optimism, the ground (of English fiction especially) is strewn with their brittle particles as with broken glass. If you must
indulge in conclusions, let them have the taste of a wide knowledge. Remember that your first duty is to be as complete as possible—to make as perfect a
work. Be generous and delicate and pursue the prize."

1884, 1888

---

# SARAH ORNE JEWETT
## 1849–1909

When Sarah Orne Jewett was born in South Berwick, Maine, in 1849, the town
and region she was to memorialize in her fiction were already changing rapidly.
Her grandfather had been a sea captain, shipowner, and merchant, and as a child
she was exposed to the bustle of this small inland port. By the end of the Civil
War, however, textile mills and a cannery had largely replaced agriculture, shipbuilding, and logging as the economic base of the community, and the arrival of
new French-Canadian and Irish immigrants signaled a change in the ethnic character of the town from English to a more heterogeneous mixture. The stable,
secure, and remote small town she knew and loved as a child was yielding to the
economic, technological, and demographic pressures that transformed America in
her lifetime.

Jewett's family life was stable and affectionate; she and her two sisters led happy
and generally carefree childhoods. Their father was a kindly, hardworking obstetri-
cian who indulged all three of his daughters, but Sarah most of all. He encouraged
her reading, and even as a small child she accompanied him on his horse-and-
buggy rounds, meeting the rural people who would later populate her fiction.
Jewett loved her father deeply, and some of her strong feelings for him are invested
in the novel A Country Doctor (1884), a novel that at the same time celebrates the
competence and independence of its female protagonist.

In part inspired by Harriet Beecher Stowe's novel about Maine seacoast life, The
Pearl of Orr's Island (1862), Jewett began to write and publish verse and stories
while still in her teens. One of her first efforts was accepted in 1869 by the influential editor W. D. Howells for publication in the prestigious Atlantic Monthly. In
her early twenties, encouraged by Howells, she wrote a group of stories and
sketches about a fictional coastal town in Maine to which she gave the name Deephaven; under that title she published her first collection of short pieces in 1877.
With the publication of this book, she entered the company of Mark Twain, Bret
Harte, George Washington Cable, Harriet Beecher Stowe, and other regional writers who were depicting realistically the settings, people, speech patterns, and modes
of life of many distinctive regions of the country. At their best, though, the "regionalists" created works whose themes are universally appealing and valid. Certainly
Jewett's depiction of the courageous response of women to frustration and loneliness is a case in point.

Jewett reached maturity with the publication of the collection A White Heron in
1886; later collections of sketches and stories include The King of Folly Island
(1888), A Native of Winby (1893), and The Life of Nancy (1895). In these works
the careful documentary record of landscape, people, and dialect is suffused with
a ripe understanding and sympathy that adds dimension to these fragments of
remembered life. Jewett's most enduring work is The Country of the Pointed Firs

(1896). What most distinguishes it and *The Foreigner* from *Deephaven*, published two decades earlier, is the resonance—not quite tragic—that comes from a mature lifetime of conscious and subconscious mulling over of familiar material. In this work, bits and pieces of the lives of a small group of various blighted men and nurturing women are converted by Jewett's art into a quasimythic total community.

# The Foreigner[1]

## I

One evening, at the end of August, in Dunnet Landing, I heard Mrs. Todd's firm footstep crossing the small front entry outside my door, and her conventional cough which served as a herald's trumpet, or a plain New England knock, in the harmony of our fellowship.

"Oh, please come in!" I cried, for it had been so still in the house that I supposed my friend and hostess had gone to see one of her neighbors. The first cold northeasterly storm of the season was blowing hard outside. Now and then there was a dash of great raindrops and a flick of wet lilac leaves against the window, but I could hear that the sea was already stirred to its dark depths, and the great rollers were coming in heavily against the shore. One might well believe that Summer was coming to a sad end that night, in the darkness and rain and sudden access of autumnal cold. It seemed as if there must be danger offshore among the outer islands.

"Oh, there!" exclaimed Mrs. Todd, as she entered. "I know nothing ain't ever happened out to Green Island since the world began, but I always do worry about mother in these great gales. You know those tidal waves occur sometimes down to the West Indies, and I get dwellin' on 'em so I can't set still in my chair, nor knit a common row to a stocking. William might get mooning, out in his small bo't, and not observe how the sea was making, an' meet with some accident. Yes, I thought I'd come in and set with you if you wa'n't busy. No, I never feel any concern about 'em in winter 'cause then they're prepared, and all ashore and everything snug. William ought to keep help, as I tell him; yes, he ought to keep help."

I hastened to reassure my anxious guest by saying that Elijah Tilley had told me in the afternoon, when I came along the shore past the fish houses, that Johnny Bowden and the Captain were out at Green Island; he had seen them beating up the bay, and thought they must have put into Burnt Island cove, but one of the lobstermen brought word later that he saw them hauling out at Green Island as he came by, and Captain Bowden pointed ashore and shook his head to say that he did not mean to try to get in. "The old Miranda just managed it, but she will have to stay at home a day or two and put new patches in her sail," I ended, not without pride in so much circumstantial evidence.

Mrs. Todd was alert in a moment. "Then they'll all have a very pleasant evening," she assured me, apparently dismissing all fears of tidal waves and other sea-going disasters. "I was urging Alick Bowden to go ashore some day and see mother before cold weather. He's her own nephew; she sets a great deal by him. And Johnny's a great chum o' William's; don't you know the first

---

1. *The Foreigner* was first published in the *Atlantic Monthly* 86 (1900), the source of the present text. Jewett never incorporated the story into a collection, but the story draws on the setting (Dunnet Landing), ambience, and some characters—especially Almira Todd— of *The Country of the Pointed Firs*.

day we had Johnny out 'long of us, he took an' give William his money to keep for him that he'd been a-savin', and William showed it to me an' was so affected I thought he was goin' to shed tears? 'Twas a dollar an' eighty cents; yes, they'll have a beautiful evenin' all together, and like's not the sea'll be flat as a doorstep come morning."

I had drawn a large wooden rocking-chair before the fire, and Mrs. Todd was sitting there jogging herself a little, knitting fast, and wonderfully placid of countenance. There came a fresh gust of wind and rain, and we could feel the small wooden house rock and hear it creak as if it were a ship at sea.

"Lord, hear the great breakers!" exclaimed Mrs. Todd. "How they pound!— there, there! I always run of an idea that the sea knows anger these nights and gets full o' fight. I can hear the rote² o' them old black ledges way down the thoroughfare. Calls up all those stormy verses in the Book o' Psalms; David he knew how old sea-goin' folks have to quake at the heart."

I thought as I had never thought before of such anxieties. The families of sailors and coastwise adventurers by sea must always be worrying about somebody, this side of the world or the other. There was hardly one of Mrs. Todd's elder acquaintances, men or women, who had not at some time or other made a sea voyage, and there was often no news until the voyagers themselves came back to bring it.

"There's a roaring high overhead, and a roaring in the deep sea," said Mrs. Todd solemnly, "and they battle together nights like this. No, I couldn't sleep; some women folks always goes right to bed an' to sleep, so's to forget, but 'taint my way. Well, it's a blessin' we don't all feel alike; there's hardly any of our folks at sea to worry about, nowadays, but I can't help my feelin's, an' I got thinking of mother all alone, if William had happened to be out lobsterin' and couldn't make the cove gettin' back."

"They will have a pleasant evening," I repeated. "Captain Bowden is the best of good company."

"Mother'll make him some pancakes for his supper, like's not," said Mrs. Todd, clicking her knitting needles and giving a pull at her yarn. Just then the old cat pushed open the unlatched door and came straight toward her mistress's lap. She was regarded severely as she stepped about and turned on the broad expanse, and then made herself into a round cushion of fur, but was not openly admonished. There was another great blast of wind overhead, and a puff of smoke came down the chimney.

"This makes me think o' the night Mis' Cap'n Tolland died," said Mrs. Todd, half to herself. "Folks used to say these gales only blew when somebody's a-dyin', or the devil was a-comin' for his own, but the worst man I ever knew died a real pretty mornin' in June."

"You have never told me any ghost stories," said I; and such was the gloomy weather and the influence of the night that I was instantly filled with reluctance to have this suggestion followed. I had not chosen the best of moments; just before I spoke we had begun to feel as cheerful as possible. Mrs. Todd glanced doubtfully at the cat and then at me, with a strange absent look, and I was really afraid that she was going to tell me something that would haunt my thoughts on every dark stormy night as long as I lived.

"Never mind now; tell me to-morrow by daylight, Mrs. Todd," I hastened to say, but she still looked at me full of doubt and deliberation.

---

2. Noise of the surf on the shore.

"Ghost stories!" she answered. "Yes, I don't know but I've heard a plenty of 'em first an' last. I was just sayin' to myself that this is like the night Mis' Cap'n Tolland died. 'Twas the great line storm in September all of thirty, or maybe forty, year ago. I ain't one that keeps much account o' time."

"Tolland? That's a name I have never heard in Dunnet," I said.

"Then you haven't looked well about the old part o' the buryin' ground, no'theast corner," replied Mrs. Todd. "All their women folks lies there; the sea's got most o' the men. They were a known family o' shipmasters in early times. Mother had a mate, Ellen Tolland, that she mourns to this day; died right in her bloom with quick consumption, but the rest o' that family was all boys but one, and older than she, an' they lived hard seafarin' lives an' all died hard. They were called very smart seamen. I've heard that when the youngest went into one o' the old shippin' houses in Boston, the head o' the firm called out to him: 'Did you say Tolland from Dunnet? That's recommendation enough for any vessel!' There was some o' them old shipmasters as tough as iron, an' they had the name o' usin' their crews very severe, but there wa'n't a man that wouldn't rather sign with 'em an' take his chances, than with the slack ones that didn't know how to meet accidents."

## II

There was so long a pause, and Mrs. Todd still looked so absentminded, that I was afraid she and the cat were growing drowsy together before the fire, and I should have no reminiscences at all. The wind struck the house again, so that we both started in our chairs and Mrs. Todd gave a curious, startled look at me. The cat lifted her head and listened too, in the silence that followed, while after the wind sank we were more conscious than ever of the awful roar of the sea. The house jarred now and then, in a strange, disturbing way.

"Yes, they'll have a beautiful evening out to the island," said Mrs. Todd again; but she did not say it gayly. I had not seen her before in her weaker moments.

"Who was Mrs. Captain Tolland?" I asked eagerly, to change the current of our thoughts.

"I never knew her maiden name; if I ever heard it, I've gone an' forgot; 'twould mean nothing to me," answered Mrs. Todd.

"She was a foreigner, an' he met with her out in the Island o' Jamaica. They said she'd been left a widow with property. Land knows what become of it; she was French born, an' her first husband was a Portugee, or somethin'."

I kept silence now, a poor and insufficient question being worse than none.

"Cap'n John Tolland was the least smartest of any of 'em, but he was full smart enough, an' commanded a good brig at the time, in the sugar trade; he'd taken out a cargo o' pine lumber to the islands from somewheres up the river, an' had been loadin' for home in the port o' Kingston, an' had gone ashore that afternoon for his papers, an' remained afterwards 'long of three friends o' his, shipmasters. They was havin' their suppers together in a tavern; 'twas late in the evenin' an' they was more lively than usual, an' felt boyish; and over opposite was another house full o' company, real bright and pleasant lookin', with a lot o' lights, an' they heard somebody singin' very pretty to a guitar. They wa'n't in no go-to-meetin' condition, an' one of 'em, he slapped the table an' said, 'Le' 's go over, an' hear that lady sing!" an' over they all went, good honest sailors, but three sheets in the wind, and stepped in as if they was invited, an' made their bows inside the door, an' asked if they could hear the music; they were all respectable well-dressed men. They saw the woman that had the guitar, an' there was a company a-listenin', regular highbinders all of 'em; an' there was a long table all spread out with big candlesticks like little trees o' light, and a sight o' glass an' silver ware; an' part o' the men was young officers in uniform, an' the colored folks was steppin' round servin' 'em, an' they had the lady singin'. 'Twas a wasteful scene, an' a loud talkin' company, an' though they was three sheets in the wind themselves there wa'n't one o' them cap'ns but had sense to perceive it. The others had pushed back their chairs, an' their decanters an' glasses was standin' thick about, an' they was teasin' the one that was singin' as if they'd just got her in to amuse 'em. But they quieted down; one o' the young officers had beautiful manners, an' invited the four cap'ns to join 'em, very polite; 'twas a kind of public house, and after they'd all heard another song, he come to consult with 'em whether they wouldn't git up and dance a hornpipe or somethin' to the lady's music.

"They was all elderly men an' shipmasters, and owned property; two of 'em was church members in good standin'," continued Mrs. Todd loftily, "an' they wouldn't lend theirselves to no such kick shows as that, an' spite o' bein' three sheets in the wind, as I have once observed; they waved aside the tumblers of wine the young officer was pourin' out for 'em so freehanded, and said they should rather be excused. An' when they all rose, still very dignified, as I've been well informed, and made their partin' bows and was goin' out, them young sports got round 'em an' tried to prevent 'em, and they had to push an' strive considerable, but out they come. There was this Cap'n Tolland and two Cap'n Bowdens, and the fourth was my own father." (Mrs. Todd spoke slowly, as if to impress the value of her authority.) "Two of them was very religious, upright men, but they would have their night off sometimes, all 'o them old-fashioned cap'ns, when they was free of business and ready to leave port.

"An' they went back to their tavern an' got their bills paid, an' set down kind o' mad with everybody by the front windows, mistrusting some o' their tavern charges, like's not, by that time, an' when they got tempered down, they watched the house over across, where the party was.

"There was a kind of a grove o' trees between the house an' the road, an' they heard the guitar a-goin' an' a-stoppin' short by turns, and pretty soon somebody began to screech, an' they saw a white dress come runnin' out through the bushes, an' tumbled over each other in their haste to offer help; an' out she come, with the guitar, cryin' into the street, and they just walked off four square with her amongst 'em, down toward the wharves where they felt more to home. They couldn't make out at first what 'twas she spoke,— Cap'n Lorenzo Bowden was well acquainted in Havre an' Bordeaux,[3] an' spoke a poor quality o' French, an' she knew a little mite o' English, but not much; and they come somehow or other to discern that she was in real distress. Her husband and her children had died o' yellow fever; they'd all come up to Kingston from one o' the far Wind'ard Islands to get passage on a steamer to France, an' a negro had stole their money off her husband while he lay sick o' the fever, an' she had been befriended some, but the folks that knew about her had died too; it had been a dreadful run o' the fever that season, an' she fell at

---

3. French seaport cities.

last to playin' an' singin' for hire, and for what money they'd throw to her round them harbor houses.

" 'Twas a real hard case, an' when them cap'ns made out about it, there wa'n't one that meant to take leave without helpin' of her. They was pretty mellow, an' whatever they might lack o' prudence they more'n made up with charity: they didn't want to see nobody abused, an' she was sort of a pretty woman, an' they stopped in the street then an' there an' drew lots who should take her aboard, bein' all bound home. An' the lot fell to Cap'n Jonathan Bowden who did act discouraged; his vessel had but small accommodations, though he could stow a big freight, an' she was a dreadful slow sailer through bein' square as a box, an' his first wife, that was livin' then, was a dreadful jealous woman. He threw himself right onto the mercy o' Cap'n Tolland."

Mrs. Todd indulged herself for a short time in a season of calm reflection.

"I always thought they'd have done better, and more reasonable, to give her some money to pay her passage home to France, or wherever she may have wanted to go," she continued.

I nodded and looked for the rest of the story.

"Father told mother," said Mrs. Todd confidentially, "that Cap'n Jonathan Bowden an' Cap'n John Tolland had both taken a little more than usual; I wouldn't have you think, either, that they both wasn't the best o' men, an' they was solemn as owls, and argued the matter between 'em, an' waved aside the other two when they tried to put their oars in. An' spite o' Cap'n Tolland's bein' a settled old bachelor they fixed it that he was to take the prize on his brig; she was a fast sailer, and there was a good spare cabin or two where he'd sometimes carried passengers, but he'd filled 'em with bags o' sugar on his own account an' was loaded very heavy beside. He said he'd shift the sugar an' get along somehow, an' the last the other three cap'ns saw of the party was Cap'n John handing the lady into his bo't, guitar and all, an' off they all set tow'ds their ships with their men rowin' 'em in the bright moonlight down to Port Royal where the anchorage was, an' where they all lay, goin' out with the tide an' mornin' wind at break o' day. An' the others thought they heard music of the guitar, two o' the bo'ts kept well together, but it may have come from another source."

"Well; and then?" I asked eagerly after a pause. Mrs. Todd was almost laughing aloud over her knitting and nodding emphatically. We had forgotten all about the noise of the wind and sea.

"Lord bless you! he come sailing into Portland with his sugar, all in good time, an' they stepped right afore a justice o' the peace, and Cap'n John Tolland come paradin' home to Dunnet Landin' a married man. He owned one o' them thin, narrow-lookin' houses with one room each side o' the front door, and two slim black spruces spindlin' up against the front windows to make it gloomy inside. There was no horse nor cattle of course, though he owned pasture land, an' you could see rifts o' light right through the barn as you drove by. And there was a good excellent kitchen, but his sister reigned over that; she had a right to two rooms, and took the kitchen an' a bedroom that led out of it; an' bein' given no rights in the kitchen had angered the cap'n so they weren't on no kind o' speakin' terms. He preferred his old brig for comfort, but now and then, between voyages, he'd come home for a few days, just to show he was master over his part o' the house, and show Eliza she couldn't commit no trespass.

"They stayed a little while; 'twas pretty spring weather, an' I used to see Cap'n John rollin' by with his arms full o' bundles from the store, lookin' as pleased and important as a boy; an' then they went right off to sea again, an' was gone a good many months. Next time he left her to live there alone, after they'd stopped at home together some weeks, an' they said she suffered from bein' at sea, but some said that the owners wouldn't have a woman aboard. 'Twas before father was lost on that last voyage of his, an' he and mother went up once or twice to see them. Father said there wa'n't a mite o' harm in her, but somehow or other a sight o' prejudice arose; it may have been caused by the remarks of Eliza an' her feelin's tow'ds her brother. Even my mother had no regard for Eliza Tolland. But mother asked the cap'n's wife to come with her one evenin' to a social circle that was down to the meetin'-house vestry, so she'd get acquainted a little, an' she appeared very pretty until they started to have some singin' to the melodeon. Mari' Harris an' one o' the younger Caplin girls undertook to sing a duet, an' they sort o' flatted, an' she put her hands right up to her ears, and gave a little squeal, an' went quick as could be an' give 'em the right notes, for she could read the music like plain print, an' made 'em try it over again. She was real willin' an' pleasant, but that didn't suit, an' she made faces when they got it wrong. An' then there fell a dead calm, an' we was all settin' round prim as dishes, an' my mother, that never expects ill feelin',' asked her if she wouldn't sing somethin,' an' up she got,— poor creatur', it all seems so different to me now,—an' sung a lovely little song standin' in the floor; it seemed to have something gay about it that kept a-repeatin', an' nobody could help keepin' time, an' all of sudden she looked round at the tables and caught up a tin plate that somebody'd fetched a Washin'ton pie in, an' she begun to drum on it with her fingers like one o' them tambourines, an' went right on singin' faster an' faster, and next minute she began to dance a little pretty dance between the verses, just as light and pleasant as a child. You couldn't help seein' how pretty 'twas; we all got to trottin' a foot, an' some o' the men clapped their hands quite loud, a-keepin' time, 'twas so catchin', an' seemed so natural to her. There wa'n't one of 'em but enjoyed it; she just tried to do her part, an' some urged her on, till she stopped with a little twirl of her skirts an' went to her place again by mother. And I can see mother now, reachin' over an' smilin' and pattin' her hand.

"But next day there was an awful scandal goin' in the parish, an' Mari' Harris reproached my mother to her face, an' I never wanted to see her since, but I've had to a good many times. I said Mis' Tolland didn't intend no impropriety,—I reminded her of David's dancin' before the Lord; but she said such a man as David never would have thought o' dancin' right there in the Ortho-dox vestry, and she felt I spoke with irreverence.

"And next Sunday Mis' Tolland come walkin' into our meeting, but I must say she acted like a cat in a strange garret, and went right out down the aisle with her head in air, from the pew Deacon Caplin had showed her into. 'Twas just in the beginning of the long prayer. I wished she'd stayed through, what-ever her reasons were. Whether she'd expected somethin' different, or misun-derstood some o' the pastor's remarks, or what 'twas, I don't really feel able to explain, but she kind o' declared war, at least folks thought so, an' war 'twas from that time. I see she was cryin', or had been, as she passed by me; perhaps bein' in meetin' was what had power to make her feel homesick and strange.

"Cap'n John Tolland was away fittin' out; that next week he come home to see her and say farewell. He was lost with his ship in the Straits of Malacca, and she lived there alone in the old house a few months longer till she died. He left her well off; 'twas said he hid his money about the house and she knew where 'twas. Oh, I expect you've heard that story told over an' over twenty times, since you've been here at the Landin'?"

"Never one word," I insisted.

"It was a good while ago," explained Mrs. Todd, with reassurance. "Yes, it all happened a great while ago."

## III

At this moment, with a sudden flaw of the wind, some wet twigs outside blew against the window panes and made a noise like a distressed creature trying to get in. I started with sudden fear, and so did the cat, but Mrs. Todd knitted away and did not even look over her shoulder.

"She was a good-looking woman; yes, I always thought Mis' Tolland was good-looking, though she had, as was reasonable, a sort of foreign cast, and she spoke very broken English, no better than a child. She was always at work about her house, or settin' at a front window with her sewing; she was a beautiful hand to embroider. Sometimes, summer evenings, when the windows was open, she'd set an' drum on her guitar, but I don't know as I ever heard her sing but once after the cap'n went away. She appeared very happy about havin' him, and took on dreadful at partin' when he was down here on the wharf, going back to Portland by boat to take ship for that last v'y'ge. He acted kind of ashamed, Cap'n John did; folks about here ain't so much accustomed to show their feelings. The whistle had blown an' they was waitin' for him to get aboard, an' he was put to it to know what to do and treated her very affectionate in spite of all impatience; but mother happened to be there and she went an' spoke, and I remember what a comfort she seemed to be. Mis' Tolland clung to her then, and she wouldn't give a glance after the boat when it had started, though the captain was very eager a-wavin' to her. She wanted mother to come home with her an' wouldn't let go her hand, and mother had just come in to stop all night with me an' had plenty o' time ashore, which didn't always happen, so they walked off together, an' 'twas some considerable time before she got back.

" 'I want you to neighbor with that poor lonesome creatur',' says mother to me, lookin' reproachful. 'She's a stranger in a strange land,' says mother. 'I want you to make her have a sense that somebody feels kind to her.'

" 'Why, since that time she flaunted out o' meetin', folks have felt she liked other ways better'n our'n,' says I. I was provoked, because I'd had a nice supper ready, an' mother'd let it wait so long 'twas spoiled. 'I hope you'll like your supper!' I told her. I was dreadful ashamed afterward of speakin' so to mother.

" 'What consequence is my supper?' says she to me; mother can be very stern,—'or your comfort or mine, beside letting a foreign person an' a stranger feel so desolate; she's done the best a woman could do in her lonesome place, and she asks nothing of anybody except a little common kindness. Think if 'twas you in a foreign land!'

"And mother set down to drink her tea, an' I set down humbled enough over by the wall to wait till she finished. An' I did think it all over, an' next day I never said nothin', but I put on my bonnet, and went to see Mis' Cap'n

Tolland, if 'twas only for mother's sake. 'Twas about three quarters of a mile up the road here, beyond the school-house. I forgot to tell you that the cap'n had bought out his sister's right at three or four times what 'twas worth, to save trouble, so they'd got clear o' her, an' I went round into the side yard sort o' friendly an' sociable, rather than stop an' deal with the knocker an' the front door. It looked so pleasant an' pretty I was glad I come; she had set a little table for supper, though 'twas still early, with a white cloth on it, right out under an old apple tree close by the house. I noticed 'twas same as with me at home, there was only one plate. She was just coming out with a dish; you couldn't see the door nor the table from the road.

"In the few weeks she'd been there she'd got some bloomin' pinks an' other flowers next the doorstep. Somehow it looked as if she'd known how to make it homelike for the cap'n. She asked me to set down' she was very polite, but she looked very mournful, and I spoke of mother, an' she put down her dish and caught holt o' me with both hands an' said my mother was an angel. When I see the tears in her eyes 'twas all right between us, and we were always friendly after that, and mother had us come out and make a little visit that summer; but she come a foreigner and she went a foreigner, and never was anything but a stranger among our folks. She taught me a sight o' things about herbs I never knew before nor since; she was well acquainted with the virtues o' plants. She'd act awful secret about some things too, an' used to work charms for herself sometimes, an' some o' the neighbors told to an' fro after she died that they knew enough not to provoke her, but 'twas all nonsense; 'tis the believin' in such things that causes 'em to be any harm, an' so I told 'em," confided Mrs. Todd contemptuously. "That first night I stopped to tea with her she'd cooked some eggs with some herb or other sprinkled all through, and 'twas she that first led me to discern mushrooms; an' she went right down on her knees in my garden here when she saw I had my different officious herbs. Yes, 'twas she that learned me the proper use o' parsley too; she was a beautiful cook."

Mrs. Todd stopped talking, and rose, putting the cat gently in the chair, while she went away to get another stick of apple-tree wood. It was not an evening when one wished to let the fire go down, and we had a splendid bank of bright coals. I had always wondered where Mrs. Todd had got such an unusual knowledge of cookery, of the varieties of mushrooms, and the use of sorrel as a vegetable, and other blessings of that sort. I had long ago learned that she could vary her omelettes like a child of France, which was indeed a surprise in Dunnet Landing.

## IV

All these revelations were of the deepest interest, and I was ready with a question as soon as Mrs. Todd came in and had well settled the fire and herself and the cat again.

"I wonder why she never went back to France, after she was left alone?"

"She come here from the French islands," explained Mrs. Todd. "I asked her once about her folks, an' she said they were all dead; 'twas the fever took 'em. She made this her home, lonesome as 'twas; she told me she hadn't been in France since she was 'so small,' and measured me off a child o' six. She'd lived right out in the country before, so that part wa'n't unusual to her. Oh yes, there was something very strange about her, and she hadn't been brought up in high circles nor nothing o' that kind. I think she'd been really pleased to have the cap'n marry her an' give her a good home, after all she'd passed through, and leave her free with his money an' all that. An' she got over bein' so strange-looking to me after a while, but 'twas a very singular expression: she wore a fixed smile that wa'n't a smile; there wa'n't no light behind it, same's a lamp can't shine if it ain't lit. I don't know just how to express it, 'twas a sort of made countenance."

One could not help thinking of Sir Philip Sidney's phrase, "A made countenance, between simpering and smiling."[4]

"She took it hard, havin' the captain go off on that last voyage," Mrs. Todd went on. "She said somethin' told her when they was partin' that he would never come back. He was lucky to speak a home-bound ship this side o' the Cape o' Good Hope, an' got a chance to send her a letter, an' that cheered her up. You often felt as if you was dealin' with a child's mind, for all she had so much information that other folks hadn't. I was a sight younger than I be now, and she made me imagine new things, and I got interested watchin' her an' findin' out what she had to say, but you couldn't get to no affectionateness with her. I used to blame me sometimes; we used to be real good comrades goin' off for an afternoon, but I never give her a kiss till the day she laid in her coffin and it come to my heart there wa'n't no one else to do it."

"And Captain Tolland died," I suggested after a while.

"Yes, the cap'n was lost," said Mrs. Todd, "and of course word didn't come for a good while after it happened. The letter come from the owners to my uncle, Cap'n Lorenzo Bowden, who was in charge of Cap'n Tolland's affairs at home, and he come right up for me an' said I must go with him to the house. I had known what it was to be a widow, myself, for near a year, an' there was plenty o' widow women along this coast that the sea had made desolate, but I never saw a heart break as I did then.

" 'Twas this way: we walked together along the road, me an' uncle Lorenzo. You know how it leads straight from just above the schoolhouse to the brook bridge, and their house was just this side o' the brook bridge on the left hand; the cellar's there now, and a couple or three good-sized gray birches growin' in it. And when we come near enough I saw that the best room, this way, where she most never set, was all lighted up, and the curtains up so that the light shone bright down the road, and as we walked, those lights would dazzle and dazzle in my eyes, and I could hear the guitar a-goin', an' she was singin'. She heard our steps with her quick ears and come running to the door with her eyes a-shinin', an' all that set look gone out of her face, an' begun to talk French, gay as a bird, an' shook hands and behaved very pretty an' girlish, sayin' 'twas her fête day. I didn't know what she meant then. And she had gone an' put a wreath o' flowers on her hair an' wore a handsome gold chain that the cap'n had given her; an' there she was, poor creatur', makin' believe have a party all alone in her best room; 'twas prim enough to discourage a person, with too many chairs set close to the walls, just as the cap'n's mother had left it, but she had put sort o' long garlands on the walls, droopin' very graceful, and a sight of green boughs in the corners, till it looked lovely, and all lit up with a lot o' candles."

"Oh dear!" I sighed. "Oh, Mrs. Todd, what did you do?"

4. From *The Countess of Pembroke's Arcadia*, book 1, chap. 16. The quotation actually reads "with a made countenance about her mouth, betweene simpering and smyling" in the 1590 quarto edition. The 1593 folio and following editions read "a made countenance."

"She beheld our countenances," answered Mrs. Todd solemnly. "I expect they was telling everything plain enough, but Cap'n Lorenzo spoke the sad words to her as if he had been her father; and she wavered a minute and then over she went on the floor before we could catch hold of her, and then we tried to bring her to herself and failed, and at last we carried her upstairs, an' I told uncle to run down and put out the lights, and then go fast as he could for Mrs. Begg, being very experienced in sickness, an' he so did. I got off her clothes and her poor wreath, and I cried as I done it. We both stayed there that night, and the doctor said 'twas a shock when he come in the morning; he'd been over to Black Island an' had to stay all night with a very sick child."

"You said that she lived alone some time after the news came," I reminded Mrs. Todd then.

"Oh yes, dear," answered my friend sadly, "but it wa'n't what you'd call livin'; no, it was only dyin', though at a snail's pace. She never went out again those few months, but for a while she could manage to get about the house a little, and do what was needed, an' I never let two days go by without seein' her or hearin' from her. She never took much notice as I came an' went except to answer if I asked her anything. Mother was the one who gave her the only comfort."

"What was that?" I asked softly.

"She said that anybody in such trouble ought to see their minister, mother did, and one day she spoke to Mis' Tolland, and found that the poor soul had been believin' all the time that there weren't any priests here. We'd come to know she was a Catholic by her beads and all, and that had set some narrow minds against her. And mother explained it just as she would to a child; and uncle Lorenzo sent word right off somewhere up river by a packet that was bound up the bay, and the first o' the week a priest come by the boat, an' uncle Lorenzo was on the wharf 'tendin' to some business; so they just come up for me, and I walked with him to show him the house. He was a kind-hearted old man; he looked so benevolent an' fatherly I could ha' stopped an' told him my own troubles; yes, I was satisfied when I first saw his face, an' when poor Mis' Tolland beheld him enter the room, she went right down on her knees and clapsed her hands together to him as if he'd come to save her life, and he lifted her up and blessed her, an' I left 'em together, and slipped out into the open field and walked there in sight so if they needed to call me, and I had my own thoughts. At last I saw him at the door; he had to catch the return boat. I meant to walk back with him and offer him some supper, but he said no, and said he was comin' again if needed, and signed me to go into the house to her, and shook his head in a way that meant he understood everything. I can see him now; he walked with a cane, rather tired and feeble; I wished somebody would come along, so's to carry him down to the shore.

"Mis' Tolland looked up at me with a new look when I went in, an' she even took hold o' my hand and kept it. He had put some oil on her forehead, but nothing anybody could do would keep her alive very long; 'twas his medicine for the soul rather 'n the body. I helped her to bed, and next morning she couldn't get up to dress her, and that was Monday, and she began to fail, and 't was Friday night she died." (Mrs. Todd spoke with unusual haste and lack of detail.) "Mrs. Begg and I watched with her, and made everything nice and proper, and after all the ill will there was a good number gathered to the funeral. 'Twas in Reverend Mr. Bascom's day, and he done very well in his prayer, considering he couldn't fill in with mentioning all the near connections by name as was his habit. He spoke very feeling about her being a stranger and twice widowed, and all he said about her being reared among the heathen was to observe that there might be roads leadin' up to the New Jerusalem from various points. I says to myself that I guessed quite a number must ha' reached there that wa'n't able to set out from Dunnet Landin'!"

Mrs. Todd gave an odd little laugh as she bent toward the firelight to pick up a dropped stitch in her knitting, and then I heard a heartfelt sigh.

" 'Twas most forty years ago," she said; "most everybody's gone a'ready that was there that day."

## V

Suddenly Mrs. Todd gave an energetic shrug of her shoulders, and a quick look at me, and I saw that the sails of her narrative were filled with a fresh breeze.

"Uncle Lorenzo, Cap'n Bowden that I have referred to"—

"Certainly!" I agreed with eager expectation.

"He was the one that had been left in charge of Cap'n John Tolland's affairs, and had now come to be of unforeseen importance.

"Mrs. Begg an' I had stayed in the house both before an' after Mis' Tolland's decease, and she was now in haste to be gone, having affairs to call her home; but uncle come to me as the exercises was beginning, and said he thought I'd better remain at the house while they went to the buryin' ground. I couldn't understand his reasons, an' I felt disappointed, bein' as near to her as most anybody; 'twas rough weather, so mother couldn't get in, and didn't even hear Mis' Tolland was gone till next day. I just nodded to satisfy him, 't wa'n't no time to discuss anything. Uncle seemed flustered; he'd gone out deep-sea fishin' the day she died, and the storm I told you of rose very sudden, so they got blown off way down the coast beyond Monhegan, and he'd just got back in time to dress himself and come.

"I set there in the house after I'd watched her away down the straight road far's I could see from the door; 'twas a little short walkin' funeral an' a cloudy sky, so everything looked dull an' gray, an' it crawled along all in one piece, same's walking funerals do, an' I wondered how it ever come to the Lord's mind to let her begin down among them gay islands all heat and sun, and end up here among the rocks with a north wind blowin'. 'Twas a gale that begun the afternoon before she died, and had kept blowin' off an' on ever since. I'd thought more than once how glad I should be to get home an' out o' sound o' them black spruces a-beatin' an' scratchin' at the front windows.

"I set to work pretty soon to put the chairs back, an' set outdoors some that was borrowed, an' I went out in the kitchen, an' I made up a good fire in case somebody come an' wanted a cup o' tea; but I didn't expect any one to travel way back to the house unless 'twas uncle Lorenzo. 'Twas growin' so chilly that I fetched some kindlin' wood and made fires in both the fore rooms. Then I set down an' begun to feel as usual, and I got my knittin' out of a drawer. You can't be sorry for a poor creatur' that's come to the end o' all her troubles; my only discomfort was I thought I'd ought to feel worse at losin' her than I did; I was younger then than I be now. And as I set there, I begun to hear some long notes o' dronin' music from upstairs that chilled me to the bone."

Mrs. Todd gave a hasty glance at me.

"Quick's I could gather me, I went right upstairs to see what 'twas," she added eagerly, "an' 'twas just what I might ha' known. She'd always kept her guitar hangin' right against the wall in her room; 'twas tied by a blue ribbon, and there was a window left wide open; the wind was veerin' a good deal, an' it slanted in and searched the room. The strings was jarrin' yet.

" 'Twas growin' pretty late in the afternoon, an' I begun to feel lonesome as I shouldn't now, and I was disappointed at having to stay there, the more I thought it over, but after a while I saw Cap'n Lorenzo polin' back up the road all alone, and when he come nearer I could see he had a bundle under his arm and had shifted his best black clothes for his everyday ones. I run out and put some tea into the teapot and set it back on the stove to draw, an' when he come in I reached down a little jug o' spirits,—Cap'n Tolland had left his house well provisioned as if his wife was goin' to put to sea same's himself, an' there she'd gone an' left it. There was some cake that Mis' Begg an' I had made the day before. I thought that uncle an' me had a good right to the funeral supper, even if there wa'n't any one to join us. I was lookin' forward to my cup o' tea; 'twas beautiful tea out of a green lacquered chest that I've got now."

"You must have felt very tired," said I, eagerly listening.

"I was 'most beat out, with watchin' an' tendin' and all," answered Mrs. Todd, with as much sympathy in her voice as if she were speaking of another person. "But I called out to uncle as he came in, 'Well, I expect it's all over now, an' we've all done what we could. I thought we'd better have some tea or somethin' before we go home. Come right out in the kitchen, sir,' says I, never thinking but we only had to let the fires out and lock up everything safe an' eat our refreshment, an' go home.

" 'I want both of us to stop here tonight,' says uncle, looking at me very important.

" 'Oh, what for?' says I, kind o' fretful.

" 'I've got my proper reasons,' says uncle. 'I'll see you well satisfied, Almira. Your tongue ain't so easy-goin' as some o' the women folks, an' there's property here to take charge of that you don't know nothin' at all about.'

" 'What do you mean?' says I.

" 'Cap'n Tolland acquainted me with his affairs; he hadn't no sort o' confidence in nobody but me an' his wife, after he was tricked into signin' that Portland note, an' lost money. An' she didn't know nothin' about business; but what he didn't take to sea to be sunk with him he's hid somewhere in this house. I expect Mis' Tolland may have told you where she kept things?' said uncle.

"I see he was dependin' a good deal on my answer," said Mrs. Todd, "but I had to disappoint him; no, she had never said nothin' to me.

" 'Well, then, we've got to make a search,' says he, with considerable relish; but he was all tired and worked up, and we set down to the table, an' he had somethin,' an' I took my desired cup o' tea, and then I begun to feel more interested.

" 'Where you goin' to look first?' says I, but he give me a short look an' made no answer, an begun to mix me a very small portion out of the jug, in another glass. I took it to please him; he said I looked tired, speakin' real fatherly, and I did feel better for it, and we set talkin' a few minutes, an' then he started for the cellar, carrying an old ship's lantern he fetched out o' the stairway an' lit.

" 'What are you lookin' for, some kind of a chist?" I inquired, and he said yes. All of a sudden it come to me to ask who was the heirs; Eliza Tolland, Cap'n John's own sister, had never demeaned herself to come near the funeral, and uncle Lorenzo faced right about and begun to laugh, sort o' pleased. I thought queer of it; 't wa'n't what he'd taken, which would be nothin' to an old weathered sailor like him.

" 'Who's the heir?' " says I the second time.

" 'Why, it's *you*, Almiry,' says he; and I was so took aback I set right down on the turn o' the cellar stairs.

" 'Yes 'tis,' said uncle Lorenzo. 'I'm glad of it too. Some thought she didn't have no sense but foreign sense, an' a poor stock o' that, but she said you was friendly to her, an' one day after she got news of Tolland's death, an' I had fetched up his will that left everything to her, she said she was goin' to make a writin', so's you could have things after she was gone, an' she give five hundred to me for bein' executor. Square[5] Pease fixed up the paper, an' she signed it; it's all accordin' to law.' There, I begun to cry," said Mrs. Todd; "I couldn't help it. I wished I had her back again to do somethin' for, an' to make her know I felt sisterly to her more'n I'd ever showed, an' it come over me 'twas all too late, an' I cried the more, till uncle showed impatience, an' I got up an' stumbled along down cellar with my apern to my eyes the greater part of the time.

" 'I'm goin' to have a clean search,' says he; 'you hold the light.' An' I held it and he rummaged in the arches an' under the stairs, an' over in some old closet where he reached out bottles an' stone jugs an' canted[6] some kags an' one or two casks, an' chuckled well when he heard there was somethin' inside,—but there wa'n't nothin' to find but things usual in a cellar, an' then the old lantern was givin' out an' we come away.

" 'He spoke to me of a chist, Cap'n Tolland did,' says uncle in a whisper. 'He said a good sound chist was as safe a bank as there was, an' I beat him out of such nonsense, 'count o' fire an' other risks.' 'There's no chist in the rooms above,' says I; 'no, uncle, there ain't no sea-chist, for I've been here long enough to see what there was to be seen.' Yet he wouldn't feel contented till he'd mounted up into the toploft; 'twas one o' them single, hip-roofed houses that don't give proper accommodation for a real garret, like Cap'n Littlepage's down here at the Landin'. There was broken furniture and rubbish, an' he let down a terrible sight o' dust into the front entry, but sure enough there wasn't no chist. I had it all to sweep up next day.

" 'He must have took it away to sea,' says I to the cap'n, an' even then he didn't want to agree, but we was both beat out. I told him where I'd always seen Mis' Tolland get her money from, and we found much as a hundred dollars there in an old red morocco wallet. Cap'n John had been gone a good while a'ready, and she had spent what she needed. 'Twas in an old desk o' his in the settin' room that we found the wallet."

"At the last minute he may have taken his money to sea," I suggested.

"Oh yes," agreed Mrs. Todd. "He did take considerable to make his venture to bring home, as was customary, an' that was drowned with him as uncle

---

5. I.e., Squire.     6. Tipped or tilted.

agreed; but he had other property in shipping, and a thousand dollars invested in Portland in a cordage shop, but 'twas about the time shipping begun to decay, and the cordage shop failed, and in the end I wa'n't so rich as I thought I was goin' to be for those few minutes on the cellar stairs. There was an auction that accumulated something. Old Mis' Tolland, the cap'n's mother, had heired some good furniture from a sister: there was above thirty chairs in all, and they're apt to sell well. I got over a thousand dollars when we come to settle up, and I made uncle take his five hundred; he was getting along in years and had met with losses in navigation, and he left it back to me when he died, so I had a real good lift. It all lays in the bank over to Rockland, and I draw my interest fall an' spring, with the little Mr. Todd was able to leave me; but that's kind o' sacred money; 'twas earnt and saved with the hope o' youth, an' I'm very particular what I spend it for. Oh yes, what with ownin' my house, I've been enabled to get along very well, with prudence!" said Mrs. Todd contentedly.

"But there was the house and land," I asked,—"what became of that part of the property?"

Mrs. Todd looked into the fire, and a shadow of disapproval flitted over her face.

"Poor old uncle!" she said, "he got childish about the matter. I was hoping to sell at first, and I had an offer, but he always run of an idea that there was more money hid away, and kept wanting me to delay; an' he used to go up there all alone and search, and dig in the cellar, empty an' bleak as 'twas in winter weather or any time. An' he'd come and tell me he'd dreamed he found gold behind a stone in the cellar wall, or somethin.' And one night we all see the light o' fire up that way, an' the whole Landin' took the road, and run to look, and the Tolland property was all in a light blaze. I expect the old gentleman had dropped fire about; he said he'd been up there to see if everything was safe in the afternoon. As for the land, 'twas so poor that everybody used to have a joke that the Tolland boys preferred to farm the sea instead. It's 'most all grown up to bushes now, where it ain't poor water grass in the low places. There's some upland that has a pretty view, after you cross the brook bridge. Years an' years after she died, there was some o' her flowers used to come up an' bloom in the door garden. I brought two or three that was unusual down here; they always come up and remind me of her, constant as the spring. But I never did want to fetch home that guitar, some way or 'nother; I wouldn't let it go at the auction, either. It was hangin' right there in the house when the fire took place. I've got some o' her other little things scattered about the house: that picture on the mantelpiece belonged to her."

I had often wondered where such a picture had come from, and why Mrs. Todd had chosen it; it was a French print of the statue of the Empress Josephine in the Savane at old Fort Royal, in Martinique.[7]

## VI

Mrs. Todd drew her chair closer to mine; she held the cat and her knitting with one hand as she moved, but the cat was so warm and so sound asleep

---

7. A statue of the Empress Josephine (1763–1814) stands in the public gardens of Fort-de-France in Martinique, an island in the West Indies.

that she only stretched a lazy paw in spite of what must have felt like a slight earthquake. Mrs. Todd began to speak almost in a whisper.

"I ain't told you all," she continued; "no, I haven't spoken of all to but very few. The way it came was this," she said solemnly, and then stopped to listen to the wind, and sat for a moment in deferential silence, as if she waited for the wind to speak first. The cat suddenly lifted her head with quick excitement and gleaming eyes, and her mistress was leaning forward toward the fire with an arm laid on either knee, as if they were consulting the glowing coals for some augury. Mrs. Todd looked like an old prophetess as she sat there with the firelight shining on her strong face; she was posed for some great painter. The woman with the cat was as unconscious and as mysterious as any sibyl of the Sistine Chapel.

"There, that's the last struggle o' the gale," said Mrs. Todd, nodding her head with impressive certainty and still looking into the bright embers of the fire. "You'll see!" She gave me another quick glance, and spoke in a low tone as if we might be overheard.

" 'Twas such a gale as this the night Mis' Tolland died. She appeared more comfortable the first o' the evenin'; and Mrs. Begg was more spent than I, bein' older, and a beautiful nurse that was the first to see and think of everything, but perfectly quiet an' never asked a useless question. You remember her funeral when you first come to the Landing? And she consented to goin' an' havin' a good sleep while she could, and left me one o' those good little pewter lamps that burnt whale oil an' made plenty o' light in the room, but not too bright to be disturbin'.'

"Poor Mis' Tolland had been distressed the night before, an' all that day, but as night came on she grew more and more easy, an' was layin' there asleep; 'twas like setting' by any sleepin' person, and I had none but usual thoughts. When the wind lulled and the rain, I could hear the seas, though more distant than this, and I don' know's I observed any other sound than what the weather made: 'twas a very solemn feelin' night. I set close by the bed; there was times she looked to find somebody when she was awake. The light was on her face, so I could see her plain; there was always times when she wore a look that made her seem a stranger you'd never set eyes on before. I did think what a world it was that her an' me should have come together so, and she have nobody but Dunnet Landin' folks about her in her extremity. 'You're one o' the stray ones, poor creatur',' I said. I remember those very words passin' through my mind, but I saw reason to be glad she had some comforts, and didn't lack friends at the last, though she'd seen misery an' pain. I was glad she was quiet; all day she'd been restless, and we couldn't understand what she wanted from her French speech. We had the window open to give her air, an' now an' then a gust would strike that guitar that was on the wall and set it swinging by the blue ribbon, and soundin' as if somebody begun to play it. I come near takin' it down, but you never know what'll fret a sick person an' put 'em on the rack, an' that guitar was one o' the few things she'd brought with her."

I nodded assent, and Mrs. Todd spoke still lower.

"I set there close by the bed; I'd been through a good deal for some days back, and I thought I might's well be droppin' asleep too, bein' a quick person to wake. She looked to me as if she might last a day longer, certain, now she'd got more comfortable, but I was real tired, an' sort o' cramped as watchers will get, an' a fretful feeling begun to creep over me such as they often do have. If you give way, there ain't no support for the sick person; they can't count on no composure o' their own. Mis' Tolland moved then, a little restless, an' I forgot me quick enough, an' begun to hum out a little part of a hymn tune just to make her feel everything was as usual an' not wake up into a poor uncertainty. All of a sudden she set right up in bed with her eyes wide open, an' I stood an' put my arm behind her; she hadn't moved like that for days. And she reached out both her arms toward the door, an' I looked the way she was lookin', an' I see some one was standin' there against the dark. No, 't wa'n't Mis' Begg; 'twas somebody a good deal shorter than Mis' Begg. The lamplight struck across the room between us. I couldn't tell the shape, but 'twas a woman's dark face lookin' right at us; 't wa'n't but an instant I could see. I felt dreadful cold, and my head begun to swim; I thought the light went out; 't wa'n't but an instant, as I say, an' when my sight come back I couldn't see nothing there. I was one that didn't know what it was to faint away, no matter what happened; time was I felt above it in others, but 'twas somethin' that made poor human natur' quail. I saw very plain while I could see; 'twas a pleasant enough face, shaped somethin' like Mis' Tolland's, and a kind of expectin' look.

"No, I don't expect I was asleep," Mrs. Todd assured me quietly, after a moment's pause, though I had not spoken. She gave a heavy sigh before she went on. I could see that the recollection moved her in the deepest way.

"I suppose if I hadn't been so spent an' quavery with long watchin', I might have kept my head an' observed much better," she added humbly; 'but I see all I could bear. I did try to act calm, an' I laid Mis' Tolland down on her pillow, an' I was a-shakin' as I done it. All she did was to look up to me so satisfied and sort o' questioning, an' I looked back to her.

" 'You saw her, didn't you?' she says to me, speakin' perfectly reasonable. ' 'Tis my mother,' she says again, very feeble, but lookin' straight up at me, kind of surprised with the pleasure, and smiling as if she saw I was overcome, an' would have said more if she could, but we had hold of hands. I see then her change was comin', but I didn't call Mis' Begg, nor make no uproar. I felt calm then, an' lifted to somethin' different as I never was since. She opened her eyes just as she was goin'—

" 'You saw her, didn't you?' she said the second time, an' I says, 'Yes, *dear, I did; you ain't never goin' to feel strange an' lonesome no more.'* An' then in a few quiet minutes 'twas all over. I felt they'd gone away together. No, I wa'n't alarmed afterward; 'twas just that one moment I couldn't live under, but I never called it beyond reason I should see the other watcher. I saw plain enough there was somebody there with me in the room.

## VII

" 'Twas just such a night as this Mis' Tolland died," repeated Mrs. Todd, returning to her usual tone and leaning back comfortably in her chair as she took up her knitting. " 'Twas just such a night as this. I've told the circumstances to but very few; but I don't call it beyond reason. When folks is goin' 'tis all natural, and only common things can jar upon the mind. You know plain enough there's somethin' beyond this world; the doors stand wide open. There's somethin' of us that must still live on; we've got to join both worlds together an' live in one but for the other.' The doctor said that to me one day, an' I never could forget it; he said 'twas in one o' his old doctor's books."

We sat together in silence in the warm little room; the rain dropped heavily from the eaves, and the sea still roared, but the high wind had done blowing. We heard the far complaining fog horn of a steamer up the Bay.

"There goes the Boston boat out, pretty near on time," said Mrs. Todd with satisfaction. "Sometimes these late August storms'll sound a good deal worse than they really be. I do hate to hear the poor steamers callin' when they're bewildered in thick nights in winter, comin' on the coast. Yes, there goes the boat; they'll find it rough at sea, but the storm's all over."

1900

---

# KATE CHOPIN
## 1850–1904

Katherine O'Flaherty did not appear to be destined for a literary career, certainly not one that would end with the overtones of scandal. Her father was a successful businessman; the family enjoyed a high place in St. Louis society; and her mother, grandmother, and great-grandmother were active, pious Catholics. But in part under the influence of her strong-willed great-grandmother (who was also a compelling and tireless storyteller), and long before she began to compose and submit stories in the late 1880s for publication, the young woman asserted her independence by smoking in company and going about the streets without a companion of either sex—both rather daring acts for the time.

At the age of twenty she married Oscar Chopin (who pronounced his name *Show-pan*) and spent the next decade in New Orleans, where her husband first prospered, then failed, in the cotton business. After spending a few years in Cloutierville in northwest Louisiana, where her husband had opened a general store and taken over the management of a family cotton plantation, she returned to St. Louis in 1884, a year after her husband's sudden death from swamp fever. A year later her mother died, and at the age of thirty-five Chopin was left essentially alone to raise her children and to fashion a literary career out of her experience of Louisiana life and her reading of such French contemporary realists as Émile Zola and Guy de Maupassant. Chopin's subtle understanding of Cajun and Creole life and the nonjudgmental narrative stance she adopted from her French fictional influences come together brilliantly in *At the 'Cadian Ball* and its daring sequel, *The Storm* (so daring that it was not published until 1969).

Chopin wrote on a lapboard in the midst of a busy household. She claimed, moreover, that she wrote on impulse, that she was "completely at the mercy of unconscious selection" of subject, and that "the polishing up process . . . always proved disastrous." This method, although it ensured freshness and sincerity, made some of her stories seem anecdotal, and sometimes too loose or thin. In the relatively few years of her writing career—scarcely more than a decade—she completed three novels; more than 150 stories and sketches; and a substantial body of poetry, reviews, and criticism. A first novel, *At Fault*, was published in 1890, but it was her early stories of Louisiana rural life, especially the collection *Bayou Folk* (1894), that won her national recognition as a leading practitioner of local-color fiction. She made the Catholic Creoles with their old-fashioned European customs, their polyglot, witty speech, and the rich agricultural landscape of picturesque Natchitoches Parish as familiar to Americans as Sarah Orne Jewett (whom she admired) was making the townspeople of the coastal region of Maine. A second collection of her stories, *A Night in Acadie*, was published three years later and increased that reputation.

Chopin's major work, *The Awakening*, was published in 1899. The novel, which traces the psychological and sexual coming to consciousness of a young woman, predictably aroused hostility among contemporary reviewers, just as Whitman's *Leaves of Grass*, which she admired, had done half a century earlier. The "new woman" of the time—demanding social, economic, and political equality—was already a common topic of public discussion and subject for fiction. But the depiction of such an unrepentant sensualist as Edna Pontellier was more than the critics of the time could allow to pass. The book was described as "trite and sordid," "essentially vulgar," and "unhealthily introspective and morbid in feeling." Chopin was hurt by this criticism and the social ostracism that accompanied it. Her only published response, however, was to claim, tongue in cheek, "I never dreamed of Mrs. Pontellier making such a mess of things and working out her own damnation as she did. If I had had the slightest intimation of such a thing I would have excluded her from the company." Though the book and its author fell into obscurity for half a century, they have now secured an honored place in American literary history.

In *The Awakening*, more impressively because on a grander scale than in a number of her shorter fictions, Chopin demonstrates her unusual capacity to make the alien, somewhat exotic world of New Orleans and the Gulf islands real, and to people it with complex and often baffled men and women whose humanity she confirms by refusing to use it to support a thesis or to judge it.

# At the 'Cadian Ball[1]

Bobinôt, that big, brown, good-natured Bobinôt, had no intention of going to the ball, even though he knew Calixta would be there. For what came of those balls but heartache, and a sickening disinclination for work the whole week through, till Saturday night came again and his tortures began afresh? Why could he not love Ozéina, who would marry him tomorrow; or Fronie, or any one of a dozen others, rather than that little Spanish vixen? Calixta's slender foot had never touched Cuban soil; but her mother's had, and the Spanish was in her blood all the same. For that reason the prairie people forgave her much that they would not have overlooked in their own daughters or sisters.

Her eyes,—Bobinôt thought of her eyes, and weakened,—the bluest, the drowsiest, most tantalizing that ever looked into a man's; he thought of her flaxen hair that kinked worse than a mulatto's close to her head; that broad, smiling mouth and tiptilted nose, that full figure; that voice like a rich contralto song, with cadences in it that must have been taught by Satan, for there was no one else to teach her tricks on that 'Cadian prairie. Bobinôt thought of them all as he plowed his rows of cane.

There had even been a breath of scandal whispered about her a year ago, when she went to Assumption,[2]—but why talk of it? No one did now. "C'est Espagnol, ça,"[3] most of them said with lenient shoulder-shrugs. "Bon chien

---

1. First published in *Two Tales* (October 1892); first published in book form in *Bayou Folk* (1894), the source of the present text.

2. I.e., Assumption Parish, Louisiana.

3. That's a Spaniard for you (French).

tient de race,"[4] the old men mumbled over their pipes, stirred by recollections. Nothing was made of it, except that Fronie threw it up to Calixta when the two quarreled and fought on the church steps after mass one Sunday, about a lover. Calixta swore roundly in fine 'Cadian French and with true Spanish spirit, and slapped Fronie's face. Fronie had slapped her back; "Tiens, cocotte, va!"[5] "Espèce de lionèse; prends ça, et ça!"[6] till the curé himself was obliged to hasten and make peace between them. Bobinôt thought of it all, and would not go to the ball,

But in the afternoon, over at Friedheimer's store, where he was buying a trace-chain,[7] he heard some one say that Alcée Laballière would be there. Then wild horses could not have kept him away. He knew how it would be—or rather he did not know how it would be—if the handsome young planter came over to the ball as he sometimes did. If Alcée happened to be in a serious mood, he might only go to the card-room and play a round or two; or he might stand out on the galleries talking crops and politics with the old people. But there was no telling. A drink or two could put the devil in his head,—that was what Bobinôt said to himself, as he wiped the sweat from his brow with his red bandanna; a gleam from Calixta's eyes, a flash of her ankle, a twirl of her skirts could do the same. Yes, Bobinôt would go to the ball.

That was the year Alcée Laballière put nine hundred acres in rice. It was putting a good deal of money into the ground, but the returns promised to be glorious. Old Madame Laballière, sailing about the spacious galleries in her white *volante*,[8] figured it all out in her head. Clarisse, her goddaughter, helped her a little, and together they built more air-castles than enough. Alcée worked like a mule that time; and if he did not kill himself, it was because his constitution was an iron one. It was an every-day affair for him to come in from the field well-nigh exhausted, and wet to the waist. He did not mind if there were visitors; he left them to his mother and Clarisse. There were often guests: young men and women who came up from the city, which was but a few hours away, to visit his beautiful kinswoman. She was worth going a good deal farther than that to see. Dainty as a lily; hardy as a sunflower; slim, tall, graceful, like one of the reeds that grew in the marsh. Cold and kind and cruel by turn, and everything that was aggravating to Alcée.

He would have liked to sweep the place of those visitors, often. Of the men, above all, with their ways and their manners; their swaying of fans like women, and dandling about hammocks. He could have pitched them over the levee into the river, if it hadn't meant murder. That was Alcée. But he must have been crazy the day he came in from the rice-field, and, toil-stained as he was, clasped Clarisse by the arms and panted a volley of hot, blistering love-words into her face. No man had ever spoken love to her like that.

"Monsieur!" she exclaimed, looking him full in the eyes, without a quiver. Alcée's hands dropped and his glance wavered before the chill of her calm, clear eyes.

"*Par exemple!*"[9] she muttered disdainfully, as she turned from him, deftly adjusting the careful toilet that he had so brutally disarranged.

That happened a day or two before the cyclone came that cut into the rice

---

4. Just like her mother (French).
5. Listen you flirt, get out of here! (French).
6. You bitch; take that and that! (French).
7. Equipment used to harness horses.

8. A flowing garment.
9. For example (French, literal trans.); here, "Get a hold of yourself!"

like fine steel. It was an awful thing, coming so swiftly, without a moment's warning in which to light a holy candle or set a piece of blessed palm burning. Old Madame wept openly and said her beads, just as her son Didier, the New Orleans one, would have done. If such a thing had happened to Alphonse, the Laballière planting cotton up in Natchitoches,[1] he would have raved and stormed like a second cyclone, and made his surroundings unbearable for a day or two. But Alcée took the misfortune differently. He looked ill and gray after it, and said nothing. His speechlessness was frightful. Clarisse's heart melted with tenderness; but when she offered her soft, purring words of condolence, he accepted them with mute indifference. Then she and her nénaine[2] wept afresh in each other's arms.

A night or two later, when Clarisse went to her window to kneel there in the moonlight and say her prayers before retiring, she saw that Bruce, Alcée's negro servant, had led his master's saddle-horse noiselessly along the edge of the sward that bordered the gravel-path, and stood holding him near by. Presently, she heard Alcée quit his room, which was beneath her own, and traverse the lower portico. As he emerged from the shadow and crossed the strip of moonlight, she perceived that he carried a pair of well-filled saddle-bags which he at once flung across the animal's back. He then lost no time in mounting, and after a brief exchange of words with Bruce, went cantering away, taking no precaution to avoid the noisy gravel as the negro had done.

Clarisse had never suspected that it might be Alcée's custom to sally forth from the plantation secretly, and at such an hour; for it was nearly midnight. And had it not been for the telltale saddle-bags, she would only have crept to bed, to wonder, to fret and dream unpleasant dreams. But her impatience and anxiety would not be held in check. Hastily unbolting the shutters of her door that opened upon the gallery, she stepped outside and called softly to the old negro.

"Gre't Peter! Miss Clarisse. I was n' sho it was a ghos' o' w'at, stan'in' up dah, plumb in de night, dataway."

He mounted halfway up the long, broad flight of stairs. She was standing at the top.

"Bruce, w'ere has Monsieur Alcée gone?" she asked.

"W'y, he gone 'bout he business, I reckin," replied Bruce, striving to be non-committal at the outset.

"W'ere has Monsieur Alcée gone?" she reiterated, stamping her bare foot. "I won't stan' any nonsense or any lies; mine, Bruce."

"I don' ric'lic ez I eva tole you lie yit, Miss Clarisse. Mista Alcée, he all broke up, sho."

"W'ere—has—he gone? Ah, Sainte Vierge! faut de la patience! butor, va!"[3]

"W'en I was in he room, a-breshin' off he clo'es to-day," the darkey began, settling himself against the stair-rail, "he look dat speechless an' down, I say, 'you 'pear to me like some pussun w'at gwine have a spell o' sickness, Mista Alcée.' He say, 'You reckin?' 'I dat he git up, go look hisse'f stiddy in de glass. Den he go to de chimbly an' jerk up de quinine bottle an' po' a gre't hoss-dose on to he han'. An' he swalla dat mess in a wink, an' wash hit down wid a big dram o'w'iskey w'at he keep in he room, aginst he come all soppin' wet outen de fiel'.

"He 'lows, 'No, I ain' gwine be sick, Bruce.' Den he square off. He say, 'I

---

1. Parish in northwest Louisiana.
2. Female attendant, in this case his mother.

3. Ah, Blessed Virgin! Give me patience! Lout, get out of here! (French).

kin mak out to stan' up an' gi' an' take wid any man I knows, lessen hit's John
L. Sulvun.[4] But w'en God A'mighty an' a 'oman jines fo'ces agin me, dat's
one too many fur me.' I tell 'im, 'Jis so,' whils' I 'se makin' out to bresh a spot
off w'at ain' dah, on he coat colla. I tell 'im, 'You wants li'le res', suh.' He
say, 'No, I wants li'le fling; dat w'at I wants; an' I gwine git it. Pitch me a fis'ful
o' clo'es in dem 'ar saddlebags.' Dat w'at he say. Don't you bodda, missy. He
jis' gone a-caperin' yonda to de Cajun ball. Uh—uh—de skeeters is fair' a-
swarmin' like bees roun' yo' foots!"

The mosquitoes were indeed attacking Clarisse's white feet savagely. She
had unconsciously been alternately rubbing one foot over the other during the
darkey's recital.

"The 'Cadian ball," she repeated contemptuously. "Humph! *Par exemple!*[5]
Nice conduc' for a Laballière. An' he needs a saddle-bag, fill' with clothes, to
go to the 'Cadian ball!"

"Oh, Miss Clarisse; you go on to bed, chile; git yo' soun' sleep. He 'low he
come back in couple weeks o' so. I kiarn be repeatin' lot o' truck w'at young
mans say, out heah face o' young gal."

Clarisse said no more, but turned and abruptly reëntered the house.

"You done talk too much wid yo' mouf a'ready, you ole fool nigga, you,"
muttered Bruce to himself as he walked away.

Alcée reached the ball very late, of course—too late for the chicken gumbo
which had been served at midnight.

The big, low-ceiled room—they called it a hall—was packed with men and
women dancing to the music of three fiddles. There were broad galleries all
around it. There was a room at one side where sober-faced men were playing
cards. Another, in which babies were sleeping, was called *le parc aux petits.*[6]
Any one who is white may go to a 'Cadian ball, but he must pay for his
lemonade, his coffee and chicken gumbo. And he must behave himself like a
'Cadian. Grosbœuf was giving this ball. He had been giving them since he
was a young man, and he was a middle-aged one, now. In that time he could
recall but one disturbance, and that was caused by American railroaders, who
were not in touch with their surroundings and had no business there. "Ces
maudits gens du raiderode,"[7] Grosbœuf called them.

Alcée Laballière's presence at the ball caused a flutter even among the men,
who could not but admire his "nerve" after such misfortune befalling him. To
be sure, they knew the Laballières were rich—that there were resources East,
and more again in the city. But they felt it took a *brave homme*[8] to stand a
blow like that philosophically. One old gentleman, who was in the habit of
reading a Paris newspaper and knew things, chuckled gleefully to everybody
that Alcée's conduct was altogether *chic, mais chic.* That he had more
*panache*[9] than Boulanger. Well, perhaps he had.

But what he did not show outwardly was that he was in a mood for ugly
things to-night. Poor Bobinôt alone felt it vaguely. He discerned a gleam of it
in Alcée's handsome eyes, as the young planter stood in the doorway, looking
with rather feverish glance upon the assembly, while he laughed and talked
with a 'Cadian farmer who was beside him.

Bobinôt himself was dull-looking and clumsy. Most of the men were. But

---

4. American heavyweight boxing champion (1855–       7. Those cursed railroad people (French).
1918).                                              8. Sturdy fellow (French).
5. Here, "Quite an example!"                        9. Style.
6. Playroom (French).

the young women were very beautiful. The eyes that glanced into Alcée's as they passed him were big, dark, soft as those of the young heifers standing out in the cool prairie grass.

But the belle was Calixta. Her white dress was not nearly so handsome or well made as Fronie's (she and Fronie had quite forgotten the battle on the church steps, and were friends again), nor were her slippers so stylish as those of Ozéina; and she fanned herself with a handkerchief, since she had broken her red fan at the last ball, and her aunts and uncles were not willing to give her another. But all the men agreed she was at her best to-night. Such animation! and abandon! such flashes of wit!

"Hé, Bobinôt! *Mais* w'at's the matta? W'at you standin' *planté là*[1] like ole Ma'ame Tina's cow in the bog, you!"

That was good. That was an excellent thrust at Bobinôt, who had forgotten the figure[2] of the dance with his mind bent on other things, and it started a clamor of laughter at his expense. He joined good-naturedly. It was better to receive even such notice as that from Calixta than none at all. But Madame Suzonne, sitting in a corner, whispered to her neighbor that if Ozéina were to conduct herself in a like manner, she should immediately be taken out to the mule-cart and driven home. The women did not always approve of Calixta.

Now and then were short lulls in the dance, when couples flocked out upon the galleries for a brief respite and fresh air. The moon had gone down pale in the west, and in the east was yet no promise of day. After such an interval, when the dancers again assembled to resume the interrupted quadrille, Calixta was not among them.

She was sitting upon a bench out in the shadow, with Alcée beside her. They were acting like fools. He had attempted to take a little gold ring from her finger; just for the fun of it, for there was nothing he could have done with the ring but replace it again. But she clinched her hand tight. He pretended that it was a very difficult matter to open it. Then he kept the hand in his. They seemed to forget about it. He played with her earring, a thin crescent of gold hanging from her small brown ear. He caught a wisp of the kinky hair that had escaped its fastening, and rubbed the ends of it against his shaven cheek.

"You know, last year in Assumption, Calixta?" They belonged to the younger generation, so preferred to speak English.

"Don't come say Assumption to me, M'sieur Alcée. I done yeard Assumption till I'm plumb sick."

"Yes, I know. The idiots! Because you were in Assumption, and I happened to go to Assumption, they must have it that we went together. But it was nice—*hein*,[3] Calixta?—in Assumption?"

They saw Bobinôt emerge from the hall and stand a moment outside the lighted doorway, peering uneasily and searchingly into the darkness. He did not see them, and went slowly back.

"There is Bobinôt looking for you. You are going to set poor Bobinôt crazy. You'll marry him some day; *hein*, Calixta?"

"I don't say no, me," she replied, striving to withdraw her hand, which he held more firmly for the attempt.

"But come, Calixta; you know you said you would go back to Assumption, just to spite them."

1. Rooted there (French).                    3. Huh.
2. The pattern of steps.

"No, I neva said that, me. You mus' dreamt that."

"Oh, I thought you did. You know I'm going down to the city."

"W'en?"

"To-night."

"Betta make has'e, then; it's mos' day."

"Well, to-morrow'll do."

"W'at you goin' do, yonda?"

"I don't know. Drown myself in the lake, maybe; unless you go down there to visit your uncle."

Calixta's senses were reeling; and they well-nigh left her when she felt Alcée's lips brush her ear like the touch of a rose.

"Mista Alcée! Is dat Mista Alcée?" the thick voice of a negro was asking; he stood on the ground, holding to the banister-rails near which the couple sat.

"W'at do you want now?" cried Alcée impatiently. "Can't I have a moment of peace?"

"I ben huntin' you high an' low, suh," answered the man. "Dey—dey some one in de road, onda de mulbare-tree, want see you a minute."

"I wouldn't go out to the road to see the Angel Gabriel. And if you come back here with any more talk, I'll have to break your neck." The negro turned mumbling away.

Alcée and Calixta laughed softly about it. Her boisterousness was all gone. They talked low, and laughed softly, as lovers do.

"Alcée! Alcée Laballière!"

It was not the negro's voice this time; but one that went through Alcée's body like an electric shock, bringing him to his feet.

Clarisse was standing there in her riding-habit, where the negro had stood. For an instant confusion reigned in Alcée's thoughts, as with one who awakes suddenly from a dream. But he felt that something of serious import had brought his cousin to the ball in the dead of night.

"W'at does this mean, Clarisse?" he asked.

"It means something has happen' at home. You mus' come."

"Happened to maman?" he questioned, in alarm.

"No; nénaine is well, and asleep. It is something else. Not to frighten you. But you mus' come. Come with me, Alcée."

There was no need for the imploring note. He would have followed the voice anywhere.

She had now recognized the girl sitting back on the bench.

"Ah, c'est vous, Calixta? Comment ça va, mon enfant?"[4]

"Tcha va b'en; et vous, mam'zélle?"[5]

Alcée swung himself over the low rail and started to follow Clarisse, without a word, without a glance back at the girl. He had forgotten he was leaving her there. But Clarisse whispered something to him, and he turned back to say "Good-night, Calixta," and offer his hand to press through the railing. She pretended not to see it.

"How come that? You settin' yere by yo'se'f, Calixta?" It was Bobinôt who had found her there alone. The dancers had not yet come out. She looked ghastly in the faint, gray light struggling out of the east.

4. Ah, is it you, Calixta? How's it going my little   5. Everything's fine; and with you, Miss? (French).
one? (French).

"Yes, that's me. Go yonda in the *parc aux petits* an' ask Aunt Olisse fu' my hat. She knows w'ere 't is. I want to go home, me."

"How you came?"

"I come afoot, with the Cateaus. But I'm goin' now. I ent goin' wait fu' 'em. I'm plumb wo' out, me."

"Kin I go with you, Calixta?"

"I don' care."

They went together across the open prairie and along the edge of the fields, stumbling in the uncertain light. He told her to lift her dress that was getting wet and bedraggled; for she was pulling at the weeds and grasses with her hands.

"I don' care; it's got to go in the tub, anyway. You been sayin' all along you want to marry me, Bobinôt. Well, if you want, yet, I don' care, me."

The glow of a sudden and overwhelming happiness shone out in the brown, rugged face of the young Acadian. He could not speak, for very joy. It choked him.

"Oh well, if you don' want," snapped Calixta, flippantly, pretending to be piqued at his silence.

"*Bon Dieu!*[6] You know that makes me crazy, w'at you sayin'. You mean that, Calixta? You ent goin' turn roun' agin?"

"I neva tole you that much *yet*, Bobinôt. I mean that. *Tiens,*"[7] and she held out her hand in the business-like manner of a man who clinches a bargain with a hand-clasp. Bobinôt grew bold with happiness and asked Calixta to kiss him. She turned her face, that was almost ugly after the night's dissipation, and looked steadily into his.

"I don' want to kiss you, Bobinôt," she said, turning away again, "not to-day. Some other time. *Bonté divine!*[8] ent you satisfy, *yet!*"

"Oh, I'm satisfy, Calixta," he said.

Riding through a patch of wood, Clarisse's saddle became ungirted, and she and Alcée dismounted to readjust it.

For the twentieth time he asked her what had happened at home.

"But, Clarisse, w'at is it? Is it a misfortune?"

"Ah Dieu sait![9] It's only something that happen' to me."

"To you!"

"I saw you go away las' night, Alcée, with those saddle-bags," she said, haltingly, striving to arrange something about the saddle, "an' I made Bruce tell me. He said you had gone to the ball, an' wouldn' be home for weeks an' weeks. I thought, Alcée—maybe you were going to—to Assumption. I got wild. An' then I knew if you didn't come back, *now*, tonight, I couldn't stan' it,—again."

She had her face hidden in her arm that she was resting against the saddle when she said that.

He began to wonder if this meant love. But she had to tell him so, before he believed it. And when she told him, he thought the face of the Universe was changed—just like Bobinôt. Was it last week the cyclone had well-nigh ruined him? The cyclone seemed a huge joke, now. It was he, then, who, an hour ago was kissing little Calixta's ear and whispering nonsense into it.

6. Good God! (French).
7. Well (French).

8. Goodness gracious! (French).
9. God knows! (French).

Calixta was like a myth, now. The one, only, great reality in the world was Clarisse standing before him, telling him that she loved him.

In the distance they heard the rapid discharge of pistol-shots; but it did not disturb them. They knew it was only the negro musicians who had gone into the yard to fire their pistols into the air, as the custom is, and to announce "*le bal est fini.*"[1]

1892, 1894

# The Storm

## A Sequel to "The 'Cadian Ball"[1]

### I

The leaves were so still that even Bibi thought it was going to rain. Bobinôt, who was accustomed to converse on terms of perfect equality with his little son, called the child's attention to certain sombre clouds that were rolling with sinister intention from the west, accompanied by a sullen, threatening roar. They were at Friedheimer's store and decided to remain there till the storm had passed. They sat within the door on two empty kegs. Bibi was four years old and looked very wise.

"Mama'll be 'fraid, yes," he suggested with blinking eyes.

"She'll shut the house. Maybe she got Sylvie helpin' her this evenin'," Bobinôt responded reassuringly.

"No; she ent got Sylvie. Sylvie was helpin' her yistiday," piped Bibi.

Bobinôt arose and going across to the counter purchased a can of shrimps, of which Calixta was very fond. Then he returned to his perch on the keg and sat stolidly holding the can of shrimps while the storm burst. It shook the wooden store and seemed to be ripping furrows in the distant field. Bibi laid his little hand on his father's knee and was not afraid.

### II

Calixta, at home, felt no uneasiness for their safety. She sat at a side window sewing furiously on a sewing machine. She was greatly occupied and did not notice the approaching storm. But she felt very warm and often stopped to mop her face on which the perspiration gathered in beads. She unfastened her white sacque at the throat. It began to grow dark, and suddenly realizing the situation she got up hurriedly and went about closing windows and doors.

Out on the small front gallery she had hung Bobinôt's Sunday clothes to dry and she hastened out to gather them before the rain fell. As she stepped outside, Alcée Laballière rode in at the gate. She had not seen him very often since her marriage, and never alone. She stood there with Bobinôt's coat in her hands, and the big rain drops began to fall. Alcée rode his horse under the

---

1. The ball is over (French).
1. Chopin's notebooks show that this story was written on July 18, 1898, just six months after she had submitted *The Awakening* to a publisher. As its subtitle indicates, it was intended as a sequel to *At the 'Cadian Ball. The Storm* was apparently never submitted for publication and did not see print until the publication of Per Seyersted's edition of *The Complete Works of Kate Chopin* in 1969, the basis for the present text.

shelter of a side projection where the chickens had huddled and there were plows and a harrow piled up in the corner.

"May I come and wait on your gallery till the storm is over, Calixta?" he asked.

"Come 'long in, M'sieur Alcée."

His voice and her own startled her as if from a trance, and she seized Bobinôt's vest. Alcée, mounting to the porch, grabbed the trousers and snatched Bibi's braided jacket that was about to be carried away by a sudden gust of wind. He expressed an intention to remain outside, but it was soon apparent that he might as well have been out in the open: the water beat in upon the boards in driving sheets, and he went inside, closing the door after him. It was even necessary to put something beneath the door to keep the water out.

"My! what a rain! It's good two years sence it rain' like that," exclaimed Calixta as she rolled up a piece of bagging and Alcée helped her to thrust it beneath the crack.

She was a little fuller of figure than five years before when she married; but she had lost nothing of her vivacity. Her blue eyes still retained their melting quality; and her yellow hair, disheveled by the wind and rain, kinked more stubbornly than ever about her ears and temples.

The rain beat upon the low, shingled roof with a force and clatter that threatened to break an entrance and deluge them there. They were in the dining room—the sitting room—the general utility room. Adjoining was her bed room, with Bibi's couch along side her own. The door stood open, and the room with its white, monumental bed, its closed shutters, looked dim and mysterious.

Alcée flung himself into a rocker and Calixta nervously began to gather up from the floor the lengths of a cotton sheet which she had been sewing.

"If this keeps up, *Dieu sait* if the levees[2] goin' to stan' it!" she exclaimed.

"What have you got to do with the levees?"

"I got enough to do! An' there's Bobinôt with Bibi out in that storm—if he only didn' left Friedheimer's!"

"Let us hope, Calixta, that Bobinôt's got sense enough to come in out of a cyclone."

She went and stood at the window with a greatly disturbed look on her face. She wiped the frame that was clouded with moisture. It was stiflingly hot. Alcée got up and joined her at the window, looking over her shoulder. The rain was coming down in sheets obscuring the view of far-off cabins and enveloping the distant wood in a gray mist. The playing of the lightning was incessant. A bolt struck a tall chinaberry tree at the edge of the field. It filled all visible space with a blinding glare and the crash seemed to invade the very boards they stood upon.

Calixta put her hands to her eyes, and with a cry, staggered backward. Alcée's arm encircled her, and for an instant he drew her close and spasmodically to him.

"*Bonté!*"[3] she cried, releasing herself from his encircling arm and retreating from the window, "the house'll go next! If I only knew w'ere Bibi was!" She would not compose herself; she would not be seated. Alcée clasped her shoulders and looked into her face. The contact of her warm, palpitating body when

2. Built-up earth banks designed to keep the river (in this case the Red River) from flooding the surrounding     land. "*Dieu sait*": God only knows (French).
3. Goodness! (French).

he had unthinkingly drawn her into his arms, had aroused all the old-time infatuation and desire for her flesh.

"Calixta," he said, "don't be frightened. Nothing can happen. The house is too low to be struck, with so many tall trees standing about. There! aren't you going to be quiet? say, aren't you?" He pushed her hair back from her face that was warm and steaming. Her lips were as red and moist as pomegranate seed. Her white neck and a glimpse of her full, firm bosom disturbed him powerfully. As she glanced up at him the fear in her liquid blue eyes had given place to a drowsy gleam that unconsciously betrayed a sensuous desire. He looked down into her eyes and there was nothing for him to do but to gather her lips in a kiss. It reminded him of Assumption.[4]

"Do you remember—in Assumption, Calixta?" he asked in a low voice broken by passion. Oh! she remembered; for in Assumption he had kissed her and kissed and kissed her; until his senses would well nigh fail, and to save her he would resort to a desperate flight. If she was not an immaculate dove in those days, she was still inviolate; a passionate creature whose very defenselessness had made her defense, against which his honor forbade him to prevail. Now— well, now—her lips seemed in a manner free to be tasted, as well as her round, white throat and her whiter breasts.

They did not heed the crashing torrents, and the roar of the elements made her laugh as she lay in his arms. She was a revelation in that dim, mysterious chamber; as white as the couch she lay upon. Her firm, elastic flesh that was knowing for the first time its birthright, was like a creamy lily that the sun invites to contribute its breath and perfume to the undying life of the world.

The generous abundance of her passion, without guile or trickery, was like a white flame which penetrated and found response in depths of his own sensuous nature that had never yet been reached.

When he touched her breasts they gave themselves up in quivering ecstasy, inviting his lips. Her mouth was a fountain of delight. And when he possessed her, they seemed to swoon together at the very borderland of life's mystery.

He stayed cushioned upon her, breathless, dazed, enervated, with his heart beating like a hammer upon her. With one hand she clasped his head, her lips lightly touching his forehead. The other hand stroked with a soothing rhythm his muscular shoulders.

The growl of the thunder was distant and passing away. The rain beat softly upon the shingles, inviting them to drowsiness and sleep. But they dared not yield.

III

The rain was over; and the sun was turning the glistening green world into a palace of gems. Calixta, on the gallery, watched Alcée ride away. He turned and smiled at her with a beaming face; and she lifted her pretty chin in the air and laughed aloud.

Bobinôt and Bibi, trudging home, stopped without at the cistern to make themselves presentable.

"My! Bibi, w'at will yo' mama say! You ought to be ashame'. You oughta' put on those good pants. Look at 'em! An' that mud on yo' collar! How you

4. I.e., Assumption Parish, Louisiana, the setting for "The Cadian Ball."

got that mud on yo' collar, Bibi? I never saw such a boy!" Bibi was the picture of pathetic resignation. Bobinôt was the embodiment of serious solicitude as he strove to remove from his own person and his son's the signs of their tramp over heavy roads and through wet fields. He scraped the mud off Bibi's bare legs and feet with a stick and carefully removed all traces from his heavy brogans. Then, prepared for the worst—the meeting with an over-scrupulous housewife, they entered cautiously at the back door.

Calixta was preparing supper. She had set the table and was dripping coffee at the hearth. She sprang up as they came in.

"Oh, Bobinôt! You back! My! but I was uneasy. W'ere you been during the rain? An' Bibi? he ain't wet? he ain't hurt?" She had clasped Bibi and was kissing him effusively. Bobinôt's explanations and apologies which he had been composing all along the way, died on his lips as Calixta felt him to see if he were dry, and seemed to express nothing but satisfaction at their safe return.

"I brought you some shrimps, Calixta," offered Bobinôt, hauling the can from his ample side pocket and laying it on the table.

"Shrimps! Oh, Bobinôt! you too good fo' anything!" and she gave him a smacking kiss on the cheek that resounded, "*J'vous réponds*,[5] we'll have a feas' to night! umph-umph!"

Bobinôt and Bibi began to relax and enjoy themselves, and when the three seated themselves at table they laughed much and so loud that anyone might have heard them as far away as Laballière's.

IV

Alcée Laballière wrote to his wife, Clarisse, that night. It was a loving letter, full of tender solicitude. He told her not to hurry back, but if she and the babies liked it at Biloxi, to stay a month longer. He was getting on nicely; and though he missed them, he was willing to bear the separation a while longer— realizing that their health and pleasure were the first things to be considered.

V

As for Clarisse, she was charmed upon receiving her husband's letter. She and the babies were doing well. The society was agreeable; many of her old friends and acquaintances were at the bay. And the first free breath since her marriage seemed to restore the pleasant liberty of her maiden days. Devoted as she was to her husband, their intimate conjugal life was something which she was more than willing to forego for a while.

So the storm passed and every one was happy.

1898                                                                          1969

_____

5. I promise you (French).

# MARY E. WILKINS FREEMAN
## 1852–1930

Mary E. Wilkins Freeman, best known for her depiction of New England village life, was born on October 31, 1852, in Randolph, Massachusetts, a small town south of Boston. She was not a strong child, and two other Wilkins children died before they reached three years of age; the only other child, Anne, lived to be seventeen. Young Freeman, as a result, may have been somewhat spoiled at home and at school, but her parents were orthodox Congregationalists and she was subject to a strict code of behavior. The constraints of religious belief and the effect of these constraints on character is, indeed, one of her chief subjects.

In 1867 Freeman's father became part owner of a dry-goods store in Brattleboro, Vermont, where she graduated from high school. In 1870, she entered Mount Holyoke Female Seminary, which Emily Dickinson had attended two decades earlier. Like Dickinson, Freeman left after a year because the school's pressure on all students to offer public testimony as to their Christian commitment was a strain on her health. She finished her formal education with a year at West Brattleboro Seminary, though the reading and discussion with her friend Evelyn Sawyer of Goethe, Emerson, Thoreau, Dickens, Thackeray, Poe, Hawthorne, Stowe, and Jewett was probably more important than her schoolwork in developing her literary taste.

After the death of her sister Anne and the failure of her father's business in 1876, Freeman's family moved into the home of the Reverend Thomas Pickman Tyler where her mother became housekeeper. Poverty was hard to bear for the Wilkinses, especially because their Puritan heritage led them to believe that poverty was a punishment for sin. Freeman's mother died in 1880, her father three years later. Freeman was thus left alone at twenty-eight years of age, with a legacy of less than one thousand dollars.

Fortunately, Freeman had by this time begun to sell her poems and stories to such leading magazines of the day as *Harper's Bazaar*, and by the mid-1880s she had a ready market for her work. As soon as she achieved a measure of economic independence she returned to her birthplace, where she lived with her childhood friend Mary Wales. Her early stories, most notably those gathered and published in *A Humble Romance* (1887), are set in the Vermont countryside, but the characters are amalgams of the people she knew as a youngster in Massachusetts and those she came to understand during her twenties in Vermont. As she put it in a preface to an edition of these stories published in Edinburgh, these characters are "studies of the descendants of the Massachusetts Bay colonists, in whom can still be seen traces of those features of will and conscience, so strong as to be almost exaggerations and deformities, which characterized their ancestors." More specifically, the title story dramatizes a theme Freeman was to return to frequently: the potentiality for unpredictable revolt in ostensibly meek and downtrodden natures, such as the sisters in *A Mistaken Charity*.

*A New England Nun and Other Stories* appeared in 1891; the quality of the stories is not as consistently high as in the earlier collection, but the volume does contain several of her best stories, most notably the title story, which treats the pervasive theme of psychic oppression and rebellion of women with particular dramatic success. It also offers an example of the way in which Freeman's art raises her above the school of regional realism so widely practiced at the time. Although she does provide a vivid sense of place, local dialect, and personality type, she also gives us in her best work an insight into the individual psychology and interior life produced when confining, inherited codes of village life are subjected to the pressure of a rapidly changing secular and urban world. This is a world in which, as the critic Marjorie Pryse has argued, women begin to assert, individually and collectively, their vision and power against those of an exhausted Puritan patriarchy.

Freeman continued to write for another three decades, steadily producing stories, plays, and a substantial number of novels, the best of which are *Pembroke* (1894) and *The Shoulders of Atlas* (1908). She married Dr. Charles Freeman in 1902 when she was forty-nine; after a few happy years, her husband's drinking turned into destructive alcoholism, and he finally had to be institutionalized in 1920. When she was awarded the W. D. Howells medal for fiction by the American Academy of Arts and Letters in 1926, she had long since ceased producing first-rate work.

# A New England Nun[1]

It was late in the afternoon, and the light was waning. There was a difference in the look of the tree shadows out in the yard. Somewhere in the distance cows were lowing and a little bell was tinkling; now and then a farm-wagon tilted by, and the dust flew; some blue-shirted laborers with shovels over their shoulders plodded past; little swarms of flies were dancing up and down before the peoples' faces in the soft air. There seemed to be a gentle stir arising over everything for the mere sake of subsidence—a very premonition of rest and hush and night.

This soft diurnal commotion was over Louisa Ellis also. She had been peacefully sewing at her sitting-room window all the afternoon. Now she quilted her needle carefully into her work, which she folded precisely, and laid in a basket with her thimble and thread and scissors. Louisa Ellis could not remember that ever in her life she had mislaid one of these little feminine appurtenances, which had become, from long use and constant association, a very part of her personality.

Louisa tied a green apron round her waist, and got out a flat straw hat with a green ribbon. Then she went into the garden with a little blue crockery bowl, to pick some currants for her tea. After the currants were picked she sat on the back door-step and stemmed them, collecting the stems carefully in her apron, and afterwards throwing them into the hen-coop. She looked sharply at the grass beside the step to see if any had fallen there.

Louisa was slow and still in her movements; it took her a long time to prepare her tea; but when ready it was set forth with as much grace as if she had been a veritable guest to her own self. The little square table stood exactly in the centre of the kitchen, and was covered with a starched linen cloth whose border pattern of flowers glistened. Louisa had a damask napkin on her tea-tray, where were arranged a cut-glass tumbler full of teaspoons, a silver cream-pitcher, a china sugar-bowl, and one pink china cup and saucer. Louisa used china every day—something which none of her neighbors did. They whispered about it among themselves. Their daily tables were laid with common crockery, their sets of best china stayed in the parlor closet, and Louisa Ellis was no richer nor better bred than they. Still she would use the china. She had for her supper a glass dish full of sugared currants, a plate of little cakes,

---

1. From *A New England Nun and Other Stories* (1891), the source of the present text.

and one of light white biscuits. Also a leaf or two of lettuce, which she cut up daintily. Louisa was very fond of lettuce, which she raised to perfection in her little garden. She ate quite heartily, though in a delicate, pecking way; it seemed almost surprising that any considerable bulk of the food should vanish.

After tea she filled a plate with nicely baked thin corn-cakes, and carried them out into the back-yard.

"Cæsar!" she called. "Cæsar! Cæsar!"

There was a little rush, and the clank of a chain, and a large yellow-and-white dog appeared at the door of his tiny hut, which was half hidden among the tall grasses and flowers. Louisa patted him and gave him the corn-cakes. Then she returned to the house and washed the tea-things, polishing the china carefully. The twilight had deepened; the chorus of the frogs floated in at the open window wonderfully loud and shrill, and once in a while a long sharp drone from a tree-toad pierced it. Louisa took off her green gingham apron, disclosing a shorter one of pink and white print. She lighted her lamp, and sat down again with her sewing.

In about half an hour Joe Dagget came. She heard his heavy step on the walk, and rose and took off her pink-and-white apron. Under that was still another—white linen with a little cambric edging on the bottom; that was Louisa's company apron. She never wore it without her calico sewing apron over it unless she had a guest. She had barely folded the pink and white one with methodical haste and laid it in a table-drawer when the door opened and Joe Dagget entered.

He seemed to fill up the whole room. A little yellow canary that had been asleep in his green cage at the south window woke up and fluttered wildly, beating his little yellow wings against the wires. He always did so when Joe Dagget came into the room.

"Good-evening," said Louisa. She extended her hand with a kind of solemn cordiality.

"Good-evening, Louisa," returned the man, in a loud voice.

She placed a chair for him, and they sat facing each other, with the table between them. He sat bolt-upright, toeing out his heavy feet squarely, glancing with a good-humored uneasiness around the room. She sat gently erect, folding her slender hands in her white-linen lap.

"Been a pleasant day," remarked Dagget.

"Real pleasant," Louisa assented, softly. "Have you been haying?" she asked, after a little while.

"Yes, I've been haying all day, down in the ten-acre lot. Pretty hot work."

"It must be."

"Yes, it's pretty hot work in the sun."

"Is your mother well to-day?"

"Yes, mother's pretty well."

"I suppose Lily Dyer's with her now?"

Dagget colored. "Yes, she's with her," he answered, slowly.

He was not very young, but there was a boyish look about his large face. Louisa was not quite as old as he, her face was fairer and smoother, but she gave people the impression of being older.

"I suppose she's a good deal of help to your mother," she said, further.

"I guess she is; I don't know how mother'd get along without her," said Dagget, with a sort of embarrassed warmth.

"She looks like a real capable girl. She's pretty-looking too," remarked Louisa.

"Yes, she is pretty fair looking."

Presently Dagget began fingering the books on the table. There was a square red autograph album, and a Young Lady's Gift-Book[2] which had belonged to Louisa's mother. He took them up one after the other and opened them; then laid them down again, the album on the Gift-Book.

Louisa kept eying them with mild uneasiness. Finally she rose and changed the position of the books, putting the album underneath. That was the way they had been arranged in the first place.

Dagget gave an awkward little laugh. "Now what difference did it make which book was on top?" said he.

Louisa looked at him with a deprecating smile. "I always keep them that way," murmured she.

"You do beat everything," said Dagget, trying to laugh again. His large face was flushed.

He remained about an hour longer, then rose to take leave. Going out, he stumbled over a rug, and trying to recover himself, hit Louisa's work-basket on the table, and knocked it on the floor.

He looked at Louisa, then at the rolling spools; he ducked himself awkwardly toward them, but she stopped him. "Never mind," said she; "I'll pick them up after you're gone."

She spoke with a mild stiffness. Either she was a little disturbed, or his nervousness affected her, and made her seem constrained in her effort to reassure him.

When Joe Dagget was outside he drew in the sweet evening air with a sigh, and felt much as an innocent and perfectly well-intentioned bear might after his exit from a china shop.

Louisa, on her part, felt much as the kind-hearted, long-suffering owner of the china shop might have done after the exit of the bear.

She tied on the pink, then the green apron, picked up all the scattered treasures and replaced them in her work-basket, and straightened the rug. Then she set the lamp on the floor, and began sharply examining the carpet. She even rubbed her fingers over it, and looked at them.

"He's tracked in a good deal of dust," she murmured. "I thought he must have."

Louisa got a dust-pan and brush, and swept Joe Dagget's track carefully.

If he could have known it, it would have increased his perplexity and uneasiness, although it would not have disturbed his loyalty in the least. He came twice a week to see Louisa Ellis, and every time, sitting there in her delicately sweet room, he felt as if surrounded by a hedge of lace. He was afraid to stir lest he should put a clumsy foot or hand through the fairy web, and he had always the consciousness that Louisa was watching fearfully lest he should.

Still the lace and Louisa commanded perforce his perfect respect and patience and loyalty. They were to be married in a month, after a singular courtship which had lasted for a matter of fifteen years. For fourteen out of the fifteen years the two had not once seen each other, and they had seldom

2. Gift books (c. 1825–65) were popular annual miscellanies, containing stories, essays, and poems, usually with a polite or moral tone. They were lavishly printed and decorated for use as Christmas or New Year's gifts.

exchanged letters. Joe had been all those years in Australia, where he had gone to make his fortune, and where he had stayed until he made it. He would have stayed fifty years if it had taken so long, and come home feeble and tottering, or never come home at all, to marry Louisa.

But the fortune had been made in the fourteen years, and he had come home now to marry the woman who had been patiently and unquestioningly waiting for him all that time.

Shortly after they were engaged he had announced to Louisa his determination to strike out into new fields, and secure a competency before they should be married. She had listened and assented with the sweet serenity which never failed her, not even when her lover set forth on that long and uncertain journey. Joe, buoyed up as he was by his sturdy determination, broke down a little at the last, but Louisa kissed him with a mild blush, and said good-by.

"It won't be for long," poor Joe had said, huskily; but it was for fourteen years.

In that length of time much had happened. Louisa's mother and brother had died, and she was all alone in the world. But greatest happening of all—a subtle happening which both were too simple to understand—Louisa's feet had turned into a path, smooth maybe under a calm, serene sky, but so straight and unswerving that it could only meet a check at her grave, and so narrow that there was no room for any one at her side.

Louisa's first emotion when Joe Dagget came home (he had not apprised her of his coming) was consternation, although she would not admit it to herself, and he never dreamed of it. Fifteen years ago she had been in love with him—at least she considered herself to be. Just at that time, gently acquiescing with and falling into the natural drift of girlhood, she had seen marriage ahead as a reasonable feature and a probable desirability of life. She had listened with calm docility to her mother's views upon the subject. Her mother was remarkable for her cool sense and sweet, even temperament. She talked wisely to her daughter when Joe Dagget presented himself, and Louisa accepted him with no hesitation. He was the first lover she had ever had.

She had been faithful to him all these years. She had never dreamed of the possibility of marrying any one else. Her life, especially for the last seven years, had been full of a pleasant peace, she had never felt discontented nor impatient over her lover's absence; still she had always looked forward to his return and their marriage as the inevitable conclusion of things. However, she had fallen into a way of placing it so far in the future that it was almost equal to placing it over the boundaries of another life.

When Joe came she had been expecting him, and expecting to be married for fourteen years, but she was as much surprised and taken aback as if she had never thought of it.

Joe's consternation came later. He eyed Louisa with an instant confirmation of his old admiration. She had changed but little. She still kept her pretty manner and soft grace, and was, he considered, every whit as attractive as ever. As for himself, his stent was done; he had turned his face away from fortune-seeking, and the old winds of romance whistled as loud and sweet as ever through his ears. All the song which he had been wont to hear in them was Louisa; he had for a long time a loyal belief that he heard it still, but finally it seemed to him that although the winds sang always that one song, it had another name. But for Louisa the wind had never more than murmured;

now it had gone down, and everything was still. She listened for a little while with half-wistful attention; then she turned quietly away and went to work on her wedding clothes.

Joe had made some extensive and quite magnificent alterations in his house. It was the old homestead; the newly-married couple would live there, for Joe could not desert his mother, who refused to leave her old home. So Louisa must leave hers. Every morning, rising and going about among her neat maidenly possessions, she felt as one looking her last upon the faces of dear friends. It was true that in a measure she could take them with her, but, robbed of their old environments, they would appear in such new guises that they would almost cease to be themselves. Then there were some peculiar features of her happy solitary life which she would probably be obliged to relinquish altogether. Sterner tasks than these graceful but half-needless ones would probably devolve upon her. There would be a large house to care for; there would be company to entertain; there would be Joe's rigours and feeble old mother to wait upon; and it would be contrary to all thrifty village traditions for her to keep more than one servant. Louisa had a little still, and she used to occupy herself pleasantly in summer weather with distilling the sweet and aromatic essences from roses and peppermint and spearmint. By-and-by her still must be laid away. Her store of essences was already considerable, and there would be no time for her to distil for the mere pleasure of it. Then Joe's mother would think it foolishness; she had already hinted her opinion in the matter. Louisa dearly loved to sew a linen seam, not always for use, but for the simple, mild pleasure which she took in it. She would have been loath to confess how more than once she had ripped a seam for the mere delight of sewing it together again. Sitting at her window during long sweet afternoons, drawing her needle gently through the dainty fabric, she was peace itself. But there was small chance of such foolish comfort in the future. Joe's mother, domineering, shrewd old matron that she was even in her old age, and very likely even Joe himself, with his honest masculine rudeness, would laugh and frown down all these pretty but senseless old maiden ways.

Louisa had almost the enthusiasm of an artist over the mere order and cleanliness of her solitary home. She had throbs of genuine triumph at the sight of the window-panes which she had polished until they shone like jewels. She gloated gently over her orderly bureau-drawers, with their exquisitely folded contents redolent with lavender and sweet clover and very purity. Could she be sure of the endurance of even this? She had visions, so startling that she half repudiated them as indelicate, of coarse masculine belongings strewn about in endless litter; of dust and disorder arising necessarily from a coarse masculine presence in the midst of all this delicate harmony.

Among her forebodings of disturbance, not the least was with regard to Cæsar. Cæsar was a veritable hermit of a dog. For the greater part of his life he had dwelt in his secluded hut, shut out from the society of his kind and all innocent canine joys. Never had Cæsar since his early youth watched at a woodchuck's hole; never had he known the delights of a stray bone at a neighbor's kitchen door. And it was all on account of a sin committed when hardly out of his puppyhood. No one knew the possible depth of remorse of which this mild-visaged, altogether innocent-looking old dog might be capable; but whether or not he had encountered remorse, he had encountered a full measure of righteous retribution. Old Cæsar seldom lifted up his voice in a growl or a bark; he was fat and sleepy; there were yellow rings which looked like spectacles around his dim old eyes; but there was a neighbor who bore on his hand the imprint of several of Cæsar's sharp white youthful teeth, and for that he had lived at the end of a chain, all alone in a little hut, for fourteen years. The neighbor, who was choleric and smarting with the pain of his wound, had demanded either Cæsar's death or complete ostracism. So Louisa's brother, to whom the dog had belonged, had built him his little kennel and tied him up. It was now fourteen years since, in a flood of youthful spirits, he had inflicted that memorable bite, and with the exception of short excursions, always at the end of the chain, under the strict guardianship of his master or Louisa, the old dog had remained a close prisoner. It is doubtful if, with his limited ambition, he took much pride in the fact, but it is certain that he was possessed of considerable cheap fame. He was regarded by all the children in the village and by many adults as a very monster of ferocity. St. George's dragon[3] could hardly have surpassed in evil repute Louisa Ellis's old yellow dog. Mothers charged their children with solemn emphasis not to go too near him, and the children listened and believed greedily, with a fascinated appetite for terror, and ran by Louisa's house stealthily, with many sidelong and backward glances at the terrible dog. If perchance he sounded a hoarse bark, there was a panic. Wayfarers chancing into Louisa's yard eyed him with respect, and inquired if the chain were stout. Cæsar at large might have seemed a very ordinary dog, and excited no comment whatever; chained, his reputation overshadowed him, so that he lost his own proper outlines and looked darkly vague and enormous. Joe Dagget, however, with his good-humored sense and shrewdness, saw him as he was. He strode valiantly up to him and patted him on the head, in spite of Louisa's soft clamor of warning, and even attempted to set him loose. Louisa grew so alarmed that he desisted, but kept announcing his opinion in the matter quite forcibly at intervals. "There ain't a better-natured dog in town," he would say, "and it's downright cruel to keep him tied up there. Some day I'm going to take him out."

Louisa had very little hope that he would not, one of these days, when their interests and possessions should be more completely fused in one. She pictured to herself Cæsar on the rampage through the quiet and unguarded village. She saw innocent children bleeding in his path. She was herself very fond of the old dog, because he had belonged to her dead brother, and he was always very gentle with her; still she had great faith in his ferocity. She always warned people not to go too near him. She fed him on ascetic fare of corn-mush and cakes, and never fired his dangerous temper with heating and sanguinary diet of flesh and bones. Louisa looked at the old dog munching his simple fare, and thought of her approaching marriage and trembled. Still no anticipation of disorder and confusion in lieu of sweet peace and harmony, no forebodings of Cæsar on the rampage, no wild fluttering of her little yellow canary, were sufficient to turn her a hair's-breadth. Joe Dagget had been fond of her and working for her all these years. It was not for her, whatever came to pass, to prove untrue and break his heart. She put the exquisite little stitches into her wedding-garments, and the time went on until it was only a week before her wedding-day. It was a Tuesday evening, and the wedding was to be a week from Wednesday.

3. St. George (patron saint of England) and the Dragon are an allegorical expression of the triumph of the Christian hero over evil.

There was a full moon that night. About nine o'clock Louisa strolled down the road a little way. There were harvest-fields on either hand, bordered by low stone walls. Luxuriant clumps of bushes grew beside the wall, and trees— wild cherry and old apple-trees—at intervals. Presently Louisa sat down on the wall and looked about her with mildly sorrowful reflectiveness. Tall shrubs of blueberry and meadow-sweet, all woven together and tangled with blackberry vines and horsebriers, shut her in on either side. She had a little clear space between. Opposite her, on the other side of the road, was a spreading tree; the moon shone between its boughs, and the leaves twinkled like silver. The road was bespread with a beautiful shifting dapple of silver and shadow; the air was full of a mysterious sweetness. "I wonder if it's wild grapes?" murmured Louisa. She sat there some time. She was just thinking of rising, when she heard footsteps and low voices, and remained quiet. It was a lonely place, and she felt a little timid. She thought she would keep still in the shadow and let the persons, whoever they might be, pass her.

But just before they reached her the voices ceased, and the footsteps. She understood that their owners had also found seats upon the stone wall. She was wondering if she could not steal away unobserved, when the voice broke the stillness. It was Joe Dagget's. She sat still and listened.

The voice was announced by a loud sigh, which was as familiar as itself. "Well," said Dagget, "you've made up your mind, then, I suppose?"

"Yes," returned another voice; "I'm going day after to-morrow."

"That's Lily Dyer," thought Louisa to herself. The voice embodied itself in her mind. She saw a girl tall and full-figured, with a firm, fair face, looking fairer and firmer in the moonlight, her strong yellow hair braided in a close knot. A girl full of a calm rustic strength and bloom, with a masterful way which might have beseemed a princess. Lily Dyer was a favorite with the village folk; she had just the qualities to arouse the admiration. She was good and handsome and smart. Louisa had often heard her praises sounded.

"Well," said Joe Dagget, "I ain't got a word to say."

"I don't know what you could say," returned Lily Dyer.

"Not a word to say," repeated Joe, drawing out the words heavily. Then there was silence. "I ain't sorry," he began at last, "that that happened yesterday—that we kind of let on how we felt to each other. I guess it's just as well we knew. Of course I can't do anything any different. I'm going right on an' get married next week. I ain't going back on a woman that's waited for me fourteen years, an' break her heart."

"If you should jilt her to-morrow, I wouldn't have you," spoke up the girl, with sudden vehemence.

"Well, I ain't going to give you the chance," said he; "but I don't believe you would, either."

"You'd see I wouldn't. Honor's honor, an' right's right. An' I'd never think anything of any man that went against 'em for me or any other girl; you'd find that out, Joe Dagget."

"Well, you'll find out fast enough that I ain't going against 'em for you or any other girl," returned he. Their voices sounded almost as if they were angry with each other. Louisa was listening eagerly.

"I'm sorry you feel as if you must go away," said Joe, "but I don't know but it's best."

"Of course it's best. I hope you and I have got common-sense."

"Well, I suppose you're right." Suddenly Joe's voice got an undertone of tenderness. "Say, Lily," said he, "I'll get along well enough myself, but I can't bear to think—You don't suppose you're going to fret much over it?"

"I guess you'll find out I sha'n't fret much over a married man."

"Well, I hope you won't—I hope you won't, Lily. God knows I do. And—I hope—one of these days—you'll—come across somebody else—"

"I don't see any reason why I shouldn't." Suddenly her tone changed. She spoke in a sweet, clear voice, so loud that she could have been heard across the street. "No, Joe Dagget," said she, "I'll never marry any other man as long as I live. I've got good sense, an' I ain't going to break my heart nor make a fool of myself; but I'm never going to be married, you can be sure of that. I ain't that sort of a girl to feel this way twice."

Louisa heard an exclamation and a soft commotion behind the bushes; then Lily spoke again—the voice sounded as if she had risen. "This must be put a stop to," said she. "We've stayed here long enough. I'm going home."

Louisa sat there in a daze, listening to their retreating steps. After a while she got up and slunk softly home herself. The next day she did her housework methodically; that was as much a matter of course as breathing; but she did not sew on her wedding-clothes. She sat at her window and meditated. In the evening Joe came. Louisa Ellis had never known that she had any diplomacy in her, but when she came to look for it that night she found it, although meek of its kind, among her little feminine weapons. Even now she could hardly believe that she had heard aright, and that she would not do Joe a terrible injury should she break her troth-plight. She wanted to sound him without betraying too soon her own inclinations in the matter. She did it successfully, and they finally came to an understanding; but it was a difficult thing, for he was as afraid of betraying himself as she.

She never mentioned Lily Dyer. She simply said that while she had no cause of complaint against him, she had lived so long in one way that she shrank from making a change.

"Well, I never shrank, Louisa," said Dagget. "I'm going to be honest enough to say that I think maybe it's better this way; but if you'd wanted to keep on, I'd have stuck to you till my dying day. I hope you know that."

"Yes, I do," said she.

That night she and Joe parted more tenderly than they had done for a long time. Standing in the door, holding each other's hands, a last great wave of regretful memory swept over them.

"Well, this ain't the way we've thought it was all going to end, is it, Louisa?" said Joe.

She shook her head. There was a little quiver on her placid face.

"You let me know if there's ever anything I can do for you," said he. "I ain't ever going to forget you, Louisa." Then he kissed her, and went down the path.

Louisa, all alone by herself that night, wept a little, she hardly knew why; but the next morning, on waking, she felt like a queen who, after fearing lest her domain be wrested away from her, sees it firmly insured in her possession.

Now the tall weeds and grasses might cluster around Cæsar's little hermit hut, the snow might fall on its roof year in and year out, but he never would go on a rampage through the unguarded village. Now the little canary might turn itself into a peaceful yellow ball night after night, and have no need to wake and flutter with wild terror against its bars. Louisa could sew linen seams, and distil roses, and dust and polish and fold away in lavender, as long as she listed. That afternoon she sat with her needle-work at the window, and felt fairly steeped in peace. Lily Dyer, tall and erect and blooming, went past; but she felt no qualm. If Louisa Ellis had sold her birthright she did not know it, the taste of the pottage[4] was so delicious, and had been her sole satisfaction for so long. Serenity and placid narrowness had become to her as the birthright itself. She gazed ahead through a long reach of future days strung together like pearls in a rosary, every one like the others, and all smooth and flawless and innocent, and her heart went up in thankfulness. Outside was the fervid summer afternoon; the air was filled with the sounds of the busy harvest of men and birds and bees; there were halloos, metallic clatterings, sweet calls, and long hummings. Louisa sat, prayerfully numbering her days, like an uncloistered nun.

1891

4. In Genesis 25, Esau sells his birthright as oldest son of Isaac and Rebekah to his younger brother Jacob for a bowl of lentil stew.

---

# BOOKER T. WASHINGTON
## 1856?–1915

Between the end of the Civil War and the beginning of the World War I, no one exercised more influence over the course of race relations in the United States than did Booker T. Washington. Washington lacked the personal dynamism and militancy of Frederick Douglass and did not have the keen intellectual gifts and fierce independence of W. E. B. DuBois, but Washington was a shrewder politician than either and was able to institutionalize his power in such measure that the period from 1895 to 1915 is called by historians of black America the "Era of Booker T. Washington." No small part of that power he owed to his extraordinary rhetorical skill with written and spoken language.

Washington's exact birth date is uncertain, but as an adult he settled on April 5, 1856. His mother was a slave in Hale's Ford, Virginia; his father was a white man whose identity is unknown. As a boy, Booker had, like most slaves, only a first name, and it was not until he entered school that he adopted his stepfather's first name as his last name.

Washington's early life is a catalog of deprivation and daily struggle. At the end of the war, he accompanied his mother to Malden, West Virginia, to join his stepfather, who had found work there in a salt furnace. There he attended makeshift schools in odd hours while he held jobs as a salt packer, coal miner, and houseboy and thus began to satisfy his "intense longing" to learn to read and write. Several years later, his desire for learning still unsatisfied, he set out on a month-long journey by rail, by cart, and on foot for Hampton Normal and Agricultural Institute in Virginia, some five hundred miles from Malden. The institute had been established by the American Missionary Association a few years earlier to train black teachers and to prepare students for agriculture and such trades as harness making. Washington earned his way at Hampton by serving as a janitor, and in three years graduated with honors and with a certificate to teach trade school. He had also learned, in the quasimilitary atmosphere of the school, the Puritan work ethic and the virtues of cleanliness, thrift, and hard work that later would be so central to his life and educational philosophy.

In 1881, having taught in an experimental program for American Indian students at Hampton with success, Washington was offered the position as first principal of what was to become Tuskegee Institute, a school established by the Alabama legislature to train black men and women in the agricultural and mechanical trades and for teaching. Tuskegee began with thirty students, but by practicing the Christian virtues and the simple, disciplined living he preached (and obliged others to follow) and by exercising his considerable powers as a conciliator and fund-raiser, Washington soon established a thriving institution in rural Alabama.

It was not until 1895, however, that he emerged as a national figure as the result of a short address, reprinted below (Chapter 14 of *Up from Slavery*), to a crowd of two thousand people at the Atlanta Exposition of 1895. Popularly known as the "Atlanta Compromise," the speech seemed to offer to trade black civil, social, and political rights for low-level economic opportunity and nonviolent relations with whites, an offer that appealed to the vast majority of southern blacks as well as to most whites in the North and the South. It is easy in retrospect to condemn Washington for his lack of principle and failure to assume a militant stance, but if one remembers that between 1885 and 1910, approximately 3,500 blacks were lynched in America and that most southern states had by this time disenfranchised blacks anyway, the attractiveness to most African-Americans of peaceful coexistence and the desire to have the opportunity for economic self-development are understandable. Even such militant black leaders as the editor T. Thomas Fortune and W. E. B. DuBois joined in praising the speech and in supporting the philosophy of conciliation that was its pragmatic basis; their opposition to Washington did not develop until several years later.

In the years following the Atlanta speech, Washington consolidated his position as the "Moses of his race." Nothing did more to create this mythic stature than his own brilliant, simple autobiography, *Up from Slavery*, a masterpiece of the genre. In these years, he was given an honorary degree by Harvard University, was invited to dine with President Theodore Roosevelt, was widely consulted on policy questions by white political and business leaders, effectively manipulated the black and white press, and controlled public and private patronage as it concerned blacks. He was, in short, a major power broker of his time, and the debate over his life and the book that reveals it is likely to continue.

*From* Up from Slavery [1]

*Chapter XIV. The Atlanta Exposition Address*

The Atlanta Exposition, at which I had been asked to make an address as a representative of the Negro race, as stated in the last chapter, was opened with a short address from Governor Bullock. After other interesting exercises, including an invocation from Bishop Nelson, of Georgia, a dedicatory ode by Albert Howell, Jr., and addresses by the President of the Exposition and Mrs. Joseph Thompson, the President of the Woman's Board, Governor Bullock introduced me with the words, "We have with us to-day a representative of Negro enterprise and Negro civilization."

When I arose to speak, there was considerable cheering, especially from the

1. Originally published serially in *Outlook* from November 3, 1900, to February 23, 1901, *Up from Slavery* was first published in book form by Doubleday, Page and Company (1901), the source of the present text.

coloured people. As I remember it now, the thing that was uppermost in my mind was the desire to say something that would cement the friendship of the races and bring about hearty coöperation between them. So far as my outward surroundings were concerned, the only thing that I recall distinctly now is that when I got up, I saw thousands of eyes looking intently into my face. The following is the address which I delivered:—

Mr. President and Gentlemen of the Board of Directors and Citizens:
One-third of the population of the South is of the Negro race. No enterprise seeking the material, civil, or moral welfare of this section can disregard this element of our population and reach the highest success. I but convey to you, Mr. President and Directors, the sentiment of the masses of my race when I say that in no way have the value and manhood of the American Negro been more fittingly and generously recognized than by the managers of this magnificent Exposition at every stage of its progress. It is a recognition that will do more to cement the friendship of the two races than any occurrence since the dawn of our freedom.

Not only this, but the opportunity here afforded will awaken among us a new era of industrial progress. Ignorant and inexperienced, it is not strange that in the first years of our new life we began at the top instead of at the bottom; that a seat in Congress or the state legislature was more sought than real estate or industrial skill; that the political convention or stump speaking had more attractions than starting a dairy farm or truck garden.

A ship lost at sea for many days suddenly sighted a friendly vessel. From the mast of the unfortunate vessel was seen a signal, "Water, water; we die of thirst!" The answer from the friendly vessel at once came back, "Cast down your bucket where you are." A second time the signal, "Water, water; send us water!" ran up from the distressed vessel, and was answered, "Cast down your bucket where you are." And a third and fourth signal for water was answered, "Cast down your bucket where you are." The captain of the distressed vessel, at last heeding the injunction, cast down his bucket, and it came up full of fresh, sparkling water from the mouth of the Amazon River. To those of my race who depend on bettering their condition in a foreign land or who underestimate the importance of cultivating friendly relations with the Southern white man, who is their next-door neighbour, I would say: "Cast down your bucket where you are"—cast it down in making friends in every manly way of the people of all races by whom we are surrounded.

Cast it down in agriculture, mechanics, in commerce, in domestic service, and in the professions. And in this connection it is well to bear in mind that whatever other sins the South may be called to bear, when it comes to business, pure and simple, it is in the South that the Negro is given a man's chance in the commercial world, and in nothing is this Exposition more eloquent than in emphasizing this chance. Our greatest danger is that in the great leap from slavery to freedom we may overlook the fact that the masses of us are to live by the productions of our hands, and fail to keep in mind that we shall prosper in proportion as we learn to dignify and glorify common labour and put brains and skill into the common occupations of life; shall prosper in proportion as we learn to draw the line between the superficial and the substantial, the ornamental gewgaws of life and the useful. No race can prosper till it learns that there is as much dignity in tilling a field as in writing a poem. It is at the bottom of life we must begin, and not at the top. Nor should we permit our grievances to overshadow our opportunities.

To those of the white race who look to the incoming of those of foreign birth and strange tongue and habits for the prosperity of the South, were I permitted I would repeat what I say to my own race, "Cast down your bucket where you are." Cast it down among the eight millions of Negroes whose habits you know, whose fidelity and love you have tested in days when to have proved treacherous meant the ruin of your firesides. Cast down your bucket among these people who have, without strikes and labour wars, tilled your fields, cleared your forests, builded your railroads and cities, and brought forth treasures from the bowels of the earth, and helped make possible this magnificent representation of the progress of the South. Casting down your bucket among my people, helping and encouraging them as you are doing on these grounds, and to education of head, hand, and heart, and you will find that they will buy your surplus land, make blossom the waste places in your fields, and run your factories. While doing this, you can be sure in the future, as in the past, that you and your families will be surrounded by the most patient, faithful, law-abiding, and unresentful people that the world has seen. As we have proved our loyalty to you in the past, in nursing your children, watching by the sick-bed of your mothers and fathers, and often following them with tear-dimmed eyes to their graves, so in the future, in our humble way, we shall stand by you with a devotion that no foreigner can approach, ready to lay down our lives, if need be, in defence of yours, interlacing our industrial, commercial, civil, and religious life with yours in a way that shall make the interests of both races one. In all things that are purely social we can be as separate as the fingers, yet one as the hand in all things essential to mutual progress.

There is no defence or security for any of us except in the highest intelligence and development of all. If anywhere there are efforts tending to curtail the fullest growth of the Negro, let these efforts be turned into stimulating, encouraging, and making him the most useful and intelligent citizen. Effort or means so invested will pay a thousand per cent interest. These efforts will be twice blessed—"blessing him that gives and him that takes."[2]

There is no escape through law of man or God from the inevitable:—

> "The laws of changeless justice bind
> Oppressor with oppressed;
> And close as sin and suffering joined
> We march to fate abreast."[3]

Nearly sixteen millions of hands will aid you in pulling the load upward, or they will pull against you the load downward. We shall constitute one-third and more of the ignorance and crime of the South, or one-third its intelligence and progress; we shall contribute one-third to the business and industrial prosperity of the South, or we shall prove a verita-

---

2. "It blesseth him that gives and him that takes" (Shakespeare, *The Merchant of Venice* 3.1.167).    3. John Greenleaf Whittier (1807–1892), *Song of Negro Boatmen*.

ble body of death, stagnating, depressing, retarding every effort to advance the body politic.

Gentlemen of the Exposition, as we present to you our humble effort at an exhibition of our progress, you must not expect overmuch. Starting thirty years ago with ownership here and there in a few quilts and pumpkins and chickens (gathered from miscellaneous sources), remember the path that has led from these to the inventions and production of agricultural implements, buggies, steam-engines, newspapers, books, statuary, carving, paintings, the management of drug-stores and banks, has not been trodden without contact with thorns and thistles. While we take pride in what we exhibit as a result of our independent efforts, we do not for a moment forget that our part in this exhibition would fall far short of your expectations but for the constant help that has come to our educational life, not only from the Southern states, but especially from Northern philanthropists, who have made their gifts a constant stream of blessing and encouragement.

The wisest among my race understand that the agitation of questions of social equality is the extremest folly, and that progress in the enjoyment of all the privileges that will come to us must be the result of severe and constant struggle rather than of artificial forcing. No race that has anything to contribute to the markets of the world is long in any degree ostracized. It is important and right that all privileges of the law be ours, but it is vastly more important that we be prepared for the exercises of these privileges. The opportunity to earn a dollar in a factory just now is worth infinitely more than the opportunity to spend a dollar in an opera-house.

In conclusion, may I repeat that nothing in thirty years has given us more hope and encouragement, and drawn us so near to you of the white race, as this opportunity offered by the Exposition; and here bending, as it were, over the altar that represents the results of the struggles of your race and mine, both starting practically empty-handed three decades ago, I pledge that in your effort to work out the great and intricate problem which God has laid at the doors of the South, you shall have at all times the patient, sympathetic help of my race; only let this be constantly in mind, that, while from representations in these buildings of the product of field, of forest, of mine, of factory, letters, and art, much good will come, yet far above and beyond material benefits will be that higher good, that, let us pray God, will come, in a blotting out of sectional differences and racial animosities and suspicions, in a determination to administer absolute justice, in a willing obedience among all classes to the mandates of law. This, this, coupled with our material prosperity, will bring into our beloved South a new heaven and a new earth.

The first thing that I remember, after I had finished speaking, was that Governor Bullock rushed across the platform and took me by the hand, and that others did the same. I received so many and such hearty congratulations that I found it difficult to get out of the building. I did not appreciate to any degree, however, the impression which my address seemed to have made, until the next morning, when I went into the business part of the city. As soon as I was recognized, I was surprised to find myself pointed out and surrounded by a crowd of men who wished to shake hands with me. This was kept up on every street on to which I went, to an extent which embarrassed me so much that I went back to my boarding-place. The next morning I returned to Tuskegee. At the station in Atlanta, and at almost all of the stations at which the train stopped between the city and Tuskegee, I found a crowd of people anxious to shake hands with me.

The papers in all the parts of the United States published the address in full, and for months afterward there were complimentary editorial references to it. Mr. Clark Howell, the editor of the Atlanta *Constitution*, telegraphed to a New York paper, among other words, the following, "I do not exaggerate when I say that Professor Booker T. Washington's address yesterday was one of the most notable speeches, both as to character and as to the warmth of its reception, ever delivered to a Southern audience. The address was a revelation. The whole speech is a platform upon which blacks and whites can stand with full justice to each other."

The Boston *Transcript* said editorially: "The speech of Booker T. Washington at the Atlanta Exposition, this week, seems to have dwarfed all the other proceedings and the Exposition itself. The sensation that it has caused in the press has never been equalled."

I very soon began receiving all kinds of propositions from lecture bureaus, and editors of magazines and papers, to take the lecture platform, and to write articles. One lecture bureau offered me fifty thousand dollars, or two hundred dollars a night and expenses, if I would place my services at its disposal for a given period. To all these communications I replied that my life-work was at Tuskegee; and that whenever I spoke it must be in the interests of the Tuskegee school and my race, and that I would enter into no arrangements that seemed to place a mere commercial value upon my services.

Some days after its delivery I sent a copy of my address to the President of the United States, the Hon. Grover Cleveland.[4] I received from him the following autograph reply:—

> Gray Gables
> Buzzard's Bay, Mass., October 6, 1895
>
> Booker T. Washington, Esq.:
>
> My Dear Sir: I thank you for sending me a copy of your address delivered at the Atlanta Exposition.
>
> I thank you with much enthusiasm for making the address. I have read it with intense interest, and I think the Exposition would be fully justified if it did not do more than furnish the opportunity for its delivery. Your words cannot fail to delight and encourage all who wish well for your race; and if our coloured fellow-citizens do not from your utterances father new hope and form new determinations to gain every valuable advantage offered them by their citizenship, it will be strange indeed. Yours very truly,
>
> Grover Cleveland

Later I met Mr. Cleveland, for the first time, when, as President, he visited the Atlanta Exposition. At the request of myself and others he consented to spend an hour in the Negro Building, for the purpose of inspecting the Negro

4. Grover Cleveland (1837–1908), twenty-second (1885–89) and twenty-fourth (1893–97) president of the United States.

exhibit and of giving the coloured people in attendance an opportunity to shake hands with him. As soon as I met Mr. Cleveland I became impressed with his simplicity, greatness, and rugged honesty. I have met him many times since then, both at public functions and at his private residence in Princeton, and the more I see of him the more I admire him. When he visited the Negro Building in Atlanta he seemed to give himself up wholly, for that hour, to the coloured people. He seemed to be as careful to shake hands with some old coloured "auntie" clad partially in rags, and to take as much pleasure in doing so, as if he were greeting some millionaire. Many of the coloured people took advantage of the occasion to get him to write his name in a book or on a slip of paper. He was as careful and patient in doing this as if he were putting his signature to some great state document.

Mr. Cleveland has not only shown his friendship for me in many personal ways, but has always consented to do anything I have asked of him for our school. This he has done, whether it was to make a personal donation or to use his influence in securing the donations of others. Judging from my personal acquaintance with Mr. Cleveland, I do not believe that he is conscious of possessing any colour prejudice. He is too great for that. In my contact with people I find that, as a rule, it is only the little, narrow people who live for themselves, who never read good books, who do not travel, who never open up their souls in a way to permit them to come into contact with other souls—with the great outside world. No man whose vision is bounded by colour can come into contact with what is highest and best in the world. In meeting men, in many places, I have found that the happiest people are those who do the most for others; the most miserable are those who do the least. I have also found that few things, if any, are capable of making one so blind and narrow as race prejudice. I often say to our students, in the course of my talks to them on Sunday evenings in the chapel, that the longer I live and the more experience I have of the world, the more I am convinced that, after all, the one thing that is most worth living for—and dying for, if need be—is the opportunity of making some one else more happy and more useful.

The coloured people and the coloured newspapers at first seemed to be greatly pleased with the character of my Atlanta address, as well as with its reception. But after the first burst of enthusiasm began to die away, and the coloured people began reading the speech in cold type, some of them seemed to feel that they had been hypnotized. They seemed to feel that I had been too liberal in my remarks toward the Southern whites, and that I had not spoken out strongly enough for what they termed the "rights" of the race. For a while there was a reaction, so far as a certain element of my own race was concerned, but later these reactionary ones seemed to have been won over to my way of believing and acting.

While speaking of changes in public sentiment, I recall that about ten years after the school at Tuskegee was established, I had an experience that I shall never forget. Dr. Lyman Abbott, then the pastor of Plymouth Church, and also editor of the *Outlook* (then the *Christian Union*), asked me to write a letter for his paper giving my opinion of the exact condition, mental and moral of the coloured ministers in the South, as based upon my observations. I wrote the letter, giving the exact facts as I conceived them to be. The picture painted was a rather black one—or, since I am black, shall I say "white"? It could not be otherwise with a race but a few years out of slavery, a race which had not had time or opportunity to produce a competent ministry.

What I said soon reached every Negro minister in the country, I think, and the letters of condemnation which I received from them were not few. I think that for a year after the publication of this article every association and every conference or religious body of any kind, of my race, that met, did not fail before adjourning to pass a resolution condemning me, or calling upon me to retract or modify what I had said. Many of these organizations went so far in their resolutions as to advise parents to cease sending their children to Tuskegee. One association even appointed a "missionary" whose duty it was to warn the people against sending their children to Tuskegee. This missionary had a son in the school, and I noticed that, whatever the "missionary" might have said or done with regard to others, he was careful not to take his son away from the institution. Many of the coloured papers, especially those that were the organs of religious bodies, joined in the general chorus of condemnation or demands for retraction.

During the whole time of the excitement, and through all the criticism, I did not utter a word of explanation or retraction. I knew that I was right, and that time and the sober second thought of the people would vindicate me. It was not long before the bishops and other church leaders began to make a careful investigation of the conditions of the ministry, and they found out that I was right. In fact, the oldest and most influential bishop in one branch of the Methodist Church said that my words were far too mild. Very soon public sentiment began making itself felt, in demanding a purifying of the ministry. While this is not yet complete by any means, I think I may say, without egotism, and I have been told by many of our most influential ministers, that my words had much to do with starting a demand for the placing of a higher type of men in the pulpit. I have had the satisfaction of having many who once condemned me thank me heartily for my frank words.

The change of the attitude of the Negro ministry, so far as regards myself, is so complete that at the present time I have no warmer friends among any class than I have among the clergymen. The improvement in the character and life of the Negro ministers is one of the most gratifying evidences of the progress of the race. My experience with them, as well as other events in my life, convince me that the thing to do, when one feels sure that he has said or done the right thing, and is condemned, is to stand still and keep quiet. If he is right, time will show it.

In the midst of the discussion which was going on concerning my Atlanta speech, I received a letter which I give below, from Dr. Gilman, the President of Johns Hopkins University, who had been made chairman of the judges of award in connection with the Atlanta Exposition:—

Johns Hopkins University, Baltimore
President's Office, September 30, 1895
Dear Mr. Washington: Would it be agreeable to you to be one of the Judges of Award in the Department of Education at Atlanta? If so, I shall be glad to place your name upon the list. A line by telegraph will be welcomed. Yours very truly,

D. C. Gilman

I think I was even more surprised to receive this invitation than I had been to receive the invitation to speak at the opening of the Exposition. It was to be a part of my duty, as one of the jurors, to pass not only upon the exhibits of the coloured schools, but also upon those of the white schools. I accepted the position, and spent a month in Atlanta in performance of the duties which it entailed. The board of jurors was a large one, consisting in all of sixty members. It was about equally divided between Southern white people and Northern white people. Among them were college presidents, leading scientists and men of letters, and specialists in many subjects. When the group of jurors to which I was assigned met for organization, Mr. Thomas Nelson Page,[5] who was one of the number, moved that I be made secretary of that division, and the motion was unanimously adopted. Nearly half of our division were Southern people. In performing my duties in the inspection of the exhibits of white schools I was in every case treated with respect, and at the close of our labours I parted from my associates with regret.

I am often asked to express myself more freely than I do upon the political condition and the political future of my race. These recollections of my experience in Atlanta give me the opportunity to do so briefly. My own belief is, although I have never before said so in so many words, that the time will come when the Negro in the South will be accorded all the political rights which his ability, character, and material possessions entitle him to. I think, though, that the opportunity to freely exercise such political rights will not come in any large degree through outside or artificial forcing, but will be accorded to the Negro by the Southern white people themselves, and that they will protect him in the exercise of those rights. Just as soon as the South gets over the old feeling that it is being forced by "foreigners," or "aliens," to do something which it does not want to do, I believe that the change in the direction that I have indicated is going to begin. In fact, there are indications that it is already beginning in a slight degree.

Let me illustrate my meaning. Suppose that some months before the opening of the Atlanta Exposition there had been a general demand from the press and public platform outside the South that a Negro be given a place on the opening programme, and that a Negro be placed upon the board of jurors of award. Would any such recognition of the race have taken place? I do not think so. The Atlanta officials went as far as they did because they felt it to be a pleasure, as well as a duty, to reward what they considered merit in the Negro race. Say what we will, there is something in human nature which we cannot blot out, which makes one man, in the end, recognize and reward merit in another, regardless of colour or race.

I believe it is the duty of the Negro—as the greater part of the race is already doing—to deport himself modestly in regard to political claims, depending upon the slow but sure influences that proceed from the possession of property, intelligence, and high character for the full recognition of his political rights. I think that the according of the full exercise of political rights is going to be a matter of natural, slow growth, not an over-night, gourd-vine affair. I do not believe that the Negro should cease voting, for a man cannot learn the exercise of self-government by ceasing to vote, any more than a boy can learn to swim by keeping out of the water, but I do believe that in his voting he should more and more be influenced by those of intelligence and character who are his next-door neighbours.

I know coloured men who, through the encouragement, help, and advice of Southern white people, have accumulated thousands of dollars' worth of

5. Thomas Nelson Page (1853–1922), American author and diplomat.

property, but who, at the same time, would never think of going to those same persons for advice concerning the casting of their ballots. This, it seems to me, is unwise and unreasonable, and should cease. In saying this I do not mean that the Negro should truckle, or not vote from principle, for the instant he ceases to vote from principle he loses the confidence and respect of the Southern white man even.

I do not believe that any state should make a law that permits an ignorant and poverty-stricken white man to vote, and prevents a black man in the same condition from voting. Such a law is not only unjust, but it will react, as all unjust laws do, in time; for the effect of such a law is to encourage the Negro to secure education and property, and at the same time it encourages the white man to remain in ignorance and poverty. I believe that in time, through the operation of intelligence and friendly race relations, all cheating at the ballot-box in the South will cease. It will become apparent that the white man who begins by cheating a Negro out of his ballot soon learns to cheat a white man out of his, and that the man who does this ends his career of dishonesty by the theft of property or by some equally serious crime. In my opinion, the time will come when the South will encourage all of its citizens to vote. It will see that it pays better, from every standpoint, to have healthy, vigorous life than to have that political stagnation which always results when one-half of the population has no share and no interest in the Government.

As a rule, I believe in universal, free suffrage, but I believe that in the South we are confronted with peculiar conditions that justify the protection of the ballot in many of the states, for a while at least, either by an educational test, a property test, or by both combined; but whatever tests are required, they should be made to apply with equal and exact justice to both races.

1901

---

# CHARLOTTE PERKINS GILMAN
## 1860–1935

Charlotte Perkins Gilman lived her life, for the most part, on the margins of a society whose economic assumptions and social definitions of women she vigorously repudiated. Out of this resistance to conventional values and what she later characterized as "masculinist" ideals, Gilman produced the large body of polemical work and self-consciously feminist fiction that made her the leading feminist theoretician and writer of her time.

Charlotte Anna Perkins was born in Hartford, Connecticut, on July 3, 1860. Her father, Frederic Beecher Perkins, was a minor literary figure, grandson of the theologian Lyman Beecher and nephew of the preacher Henry Ward Beecher and Harriet Beecher Stowe. Her mother was Mary A. Fitch, whose family had lived in Rhode Island since the middle of the seventeenth century. Gilman's father deserted his family shortly after her birth, and she spent many years trying, without success, to establish some intimacy with him. About all she got from him were occasional letters with lists of books she should read. Her mother supported herself and her two children with great difficulty; she withheld from them all the physical expressions of love, hoping to prevent their later disillusionment over broken relationships. It is easy to understand why in her autobiography Gilman described her childhood as painful and lonely.

Before her marriage in 1884 to Charles Stetson, a promising artist, Gilman had supported herself as a governess, art teacher, and as a designer of greeting cards. During those years she had increasingly become aware of the injustices inflicted on women, and she had begun to write poems—one in defense of prostitutes—in which she developed her own views on women's suffrage. She entered into the marriage reluctantly, anticipating the difficulties of reconciling her ambition to be a writer with the demands of being a wife, housekeeper, and mother.

Within nine months, their only child, Katherine, was born, and Gilman became increasingly despondent. Her husband was convinced that what she needed was more rest and greater willpower to bring her out of her depression, and he convinced his wife to put herself in the hands of Dr. S. Weir Mitchell, the most famous American neurologist of the day, who specialized in women's nervous disorders. He prescribed the standard rest cure for her and, as she put it in *Why I Wrote "The Yellow Wallpaper"?* (1913): "sent me home with the solemn advice to 'live as domestic a life as . . . possible,' to 'have but two hours' intellectual life a day,' and 'never to touch pen, brush, or pencil again' as long as I lived." The patient returned home and obeyed these instructions for three months "and came so near the borderline of utter mental ruin that I could see over." She drew back from the edge of madness by resuming her normal life and a few years later wrote her most famous story. As she concluded: "It was not intended to drive people crazy, but to save people from being driven crazy, and it worked." Writing *The Yellow Wallpaper,* however, did not keep Gilman from suffering all her life with often extended periods of depression.

In 1888, convinced that her marriage threatened her sanity, Gilman moved with her daughter to Pasadena, California, and in 1892 was granted a divorce. Her former husband promptly married her best friend, the writer Grace Ellery Channing, and not long thereafter Gilman sent her daughter, Katherine, east to live with them. Such actions generated much publicity and hostile criticism in the press, but nothing kept Gilman from pursuing her double career as writer and lecturer on women, labor, and social organization. In these years she was particularly influenced by the sociologist Lester Ward and the utopian novelist Edward Bellamy.

In 1898 Gilman published *Women and Economics,* the book that earned her immediate celebrity and that is still considered her most important nonfiction work. This powerful "feminist manifesto" argues a thesis Gilman was to develop and refine for the rest of her life: women's economic dependency on men stunts not only the growth of women but that of the whole human species. More particularly, she argued that because of the dependency of women on men for food and shelter, the sexual and maternal aspects of their personalities had been developed excessively and to the detriment of their other productive capacities. To free women to develop in a more balanced and socially constructive way, Gilman urged such reforms as centralized (in *Concerning Children,* 1900) and professionally staffed collective kitchens (in *The Home,* 1904).

In 1911 she published *Man-Made World,* which contrasted the competitiveness and aggressiveness of men with the cooperativeness and nurturance of women and posited that, until women played a larger part in national and international life, social injustice and war would continue to characterize societies. Similarly, in *His Religion and Hers* (1923) Gilman predicted that only when women influenced theology would death and punishment cease to be central to religious institutions and practices.

Gilman's fiction, mostly written when she was well past forty, must be seen, as the critic Ann J. Lane observed, as "part of her ideological world view, and therein lies its interest and power." Therein, also, lies its limits, for as Lane also says: "She wrote quickly, carelessly, to make a point." Still, many of Gilman's stories and her utopian novels—such as *Moving the Mountain* (1911), *Herland* (1915), and *With Her in Ourland* (1916)—offer vivid dramatizations of the social ills (and their potential remedies) that result from a competitive economic system in which women are subordinate to men and accept their subordination.

In 1900, after a long courtship (much of it preserved in an extraordinary correspondence), she married her first cousin George Houghton Gilman. They lived together happily, first in New York, then in Norwich, Connecticut, until he died suddenly in 1934. Gilman moved to Pasadena to live with her daughter's family. The next year, suffering from breast cancer and convinced that her productive life was over, she committed suicide with chloroform she had long been accumulating.

Gilman was an important force in the feminist movement at the turn of the century and an effective writer, editor, lecturer, and organizer. As her work is recovered and made available again, we also are able to see the size of her contribution to that critical idealist tradition in America which includes women as well as men of good hope.

# The Yellow Wallpaper[1]

It is very seldom that mere ordinary people like John and myself secure ancestral halls for the summer.

A colonial mansion, a hereditary estate, I would say a haunted house and reach the height of romantic felicity—but that would be asking too much of fate!

Still I will proudly declare that there is something queer about it.

Else, why should it be let so cheaply? And why have stood so long untenanted?

John laughs at me, of course, but one expects that.

John is practical in the extreme. He has no patience with faith, an intense horror of superstition, and he scoffs openly at any talk of things not to be felt and seen and put down in figures.

John is a physician, and *perhaps*—(I would not say it to a living soul, of course, but this is dead paper and a great relief to my mind)—*perhaps* that is one reason I do not get well faster.

You see, he does not believe I am sick! And what can one do?

If a physician of high standing, and one's own husband, assures friends and relatives that there is really nothing the matter with one but temporary nervous depression—a slight hysterical tendency[2]—what is one to do?

My brother is also a physician, and also of high standing, and he says the same thing.

So I take phosphates or phosphites—whichever it is—and tonics, and air and exercise, and journeys, and am absolutely forbidden to "work" until I am well again.

Personally, I disagree with their ideas.

---

1. This story was first published in the *New England Magazine* in January 1892. Alfred Bendixen, to whom we are indebted for information concerning the publication history of this story, is preparing a version using the manuscript as copy text. The only change we have made in the magazine text is to make *wallpaper* one word; in the magazine it appears both as one word and as a hyphenated compound.

2. At the time this story was written, *hysteria* was a term used loosely to describe a wide variety of symptoms, thought to be particularly prevalent among women, that indicated emotional disturbance or dysfunction. Depression, anxiety, excitability, and vague somatic complaints were among the conditions treated as "hysteria."

Personally, I believe that congenial work, with excitement and change, would do me good.

But what is one to do?

I did write for a while in spite of them; but it *does* exhaust me a good deal—having to be so sly about it, or else meet with heavy opposition.

I sometimes fancy that in my condition, if I had less opposition and more society and stimulus—but John says the very worst thing I can do is to think about my condition, and I confess it always makes me feel bad.

So I will let it alone and talk about the house.

The most beautiful place! It is quite alone, standing well back from the road, quite three miles from the village. It makes me think of English places that you read about, for there are hedges and walls and gates that lock, and lots of separate little houses for the gardeners and people.

There is a *delicious* garden! I never saw such a garden—large and shady, full of box-bordered paths, and lined with long grape-covered arbors with seats under them.

There were greenhouses, but they are all broken now.

There was some legal trouble, I believe, something about the heirs and co-heirs; anyhow, the place has been empty for years.

That spoils my ghostliness, I am afraid, but I don't care—there is something strange about the house—I can feel it.

I even said so to John one moonlight evening, but he said what I felt was a draught, and shut the window.

I get unreasonably angry with John sometimes. I'm sure I never used to be so sensitive. I think it is due to this nervous condition.

But John says if I feel so, I shall neglect proper self-control; so I take pains to control myself—before him, at least, and that makes me very tired.

I don't like our room a bit. I wanted one downstairs that opened on the piazza and had roses all over the window, and such pretty old-fashioned chintz hangings! But John would not hear of it.

He said there was only one window and not room for two beds, and no near room for him if he took another.

He is very careful and loving, and hardly lets me stir without special direction.

I have a schedule prescription for each hour in the day; he takes all care from me, and so I feel basely ungrateful not to value it more.

He said we came here solely on my account, that I was to have perfect rest and all the air I could get. "Your exercise depends on your strength, my dear," said he, "and your food somewhat on your appetite; but air you can absorb all the time." So we took the nursery at the top of the house.

It is a big, airy room, the whole floor nearly, with windows that look all ways, and air and sunshine galore. It was nursery first and then playroom and gymnasium, I should judge; for the windows are barred for little children, and there are rings and things in the walls.

The paint and paper look as if a boys' school had used it. It is stripped off—the paper—in great patches all around the head of my bed, about as far as I can reach, and in a great place on the other side of the room low down. I never saw a worse paper in my life. One of those sprawling flamboyant patterns committing every artistic sin.

It is dull enough to confuse the eye in following, pronounced enough to constantly irritate and provoke study, and when you follow the lame uncertain curves for a little distance they suddenly commit suicide—plunge off at outrageous angles, destroy themselves in unheard-of contradictions.

The color is repellant, almost revolting; a smouldering unclean yellow, strangely faded by the slow-turning sunlight. It is a dull yet lurid orange in some places, a sickly sulphur tint in others.

No wonder the children hated it! I should hate it myself if I had to live in this room long.

There comes John, and I must put this away—he hates to have me write a word.

*     *     *     *     *     *

We have been here two weeks, and I haven't felt like writing before, since that first day.

I am sitting by the window now, up in this atrocious nursery, and there is nothing to hinder my writing as much as I please, save lack of strength.

John is away all day, and even some nights when his cases are serious.

I am glad my case is not serious!

But these nervous troubles are dreadfully depressing.

John does not know how much I really suffer. He knows there is no reason to suffer, and that satisfies him.

Of course it is only nervousness. It does weigh on me so not to do my duty in any way!

I mean to be such a help to John, such a real rest and comfort, and here I am a comparative burden already!

Nobody would believe what an effort it is to do what little I am able—to dress and entertain, and order things.

It is fortunate Mary is so good with the baby. Such a dear baby!

And yet I *cannot* be with him, it makes me so nervous.

I suppose John never was nervous in his life. He laughs at me so about this wallpaper!

At first he meant to repaper the room, but afterwards he said that I was letting it get the better of me, and that nothing was worse for a nervous patient than to give way to such fancies.

He said that after the wallpaper was changed it would be the heavy bedstead, and then the barred windows, and then that gate at the head of the stairs, and so on.

"You know the place is doing you good," he said, "and really, dear, I don't care to renovate the house just for a three months' rental."

"Then do let us go downstairs," I said. "There are such pretty rooms there."

Then he took me in his arms and called me a blessed little goose, and said he would go down cellar, if I wished, and have it whitewashed into the bargain.

But he is right enough about the beds and windows and things.

It is as airy and comfortable a room as anyone need wish, and, of course, I would not be so silly as to make him uncomfortable just for a whim.

I'm really getting quite fond of the big room, all but that horrid paper.

Out of one window I can see the garden—those mysterious deep-shaded arbors, the riotous old-fashioned flowers, and bushes and gnarly trees.

Out of another I get a lovely view of the bay and a little private wharf belonging to the estate. There is a beautiful shaded lane that runs down there from the house. I always fancy I see people walking in these numerous paths and arbors, but John has cautioned me not to give way to fancy in the least. He says that with my imaginative power and habit of story-making, a nervous weakness like mine is sure to lead to all manner of excited fancies, and that I ought to use my will and good sense to check the tendency. So I try.

I think sometimes that if I were only well enough to write a little it would relieve the press of ideas and rest me.

But I find I get pretty tired when I try.

It is so discouraging not to have any advice and companionship about my work. When I get really well, John says we will ask Cousin Henry and Julia down for a long visit; but he says he would as soon put fireworks in my pillow-case as to let me have those stimulating people about now.

I wish I could get well faster.

But I must not think about that. This paper looks to me as if it *knew* what a vicious influence it had!

There is a recurrent spot where the pattern lolls like a broken neck and two bulbous eyes stare at you upside down.

I get positively angry with the impertinence of it and the everlastingness. Up and down and sideways they crawl, and those absurd unblinking eyes are everywhere. There is one place where two breadths didn't match, and the eyes go all up and down the line, one a little higher than the other.

I never saw so much expression in an inanimate thing before, and we all know how much expression they have! I used to lie awake as a child and get more entertainment and terror out of blank walls and plain furniture than most children could find in a toy-store.

I remember what a kindly wink the knobs of our big old bureau used to have, and there was one chair that always seemed like a strong friend.

I used to feel that if any of the other things looked too fierce I could always hop into that chair and be safe.

The furniture in this room is no worse than inharmonious, however, for we had to bring it all from downstairs. I suppose when this was used as a playroom they had to take the nursery things out, and no wonder! I never saw such ravages as the children have made here.

The wallpaper, as I said before, is torn off in spots, and it sticketh closer than a brother—they must have had perseverance as well as hatred.

Then the floor is scratched and gouged and splintered, the plaster itself is dug out here and there, and this great heavy bed which is all we found in the room, looks as if it had been through the wars.

But I don't mind it a bit—only the paper.

There comes John's sister. Such a dear girl as she is, and so careful of me! I must not let her find me writing.

She is a perfect and enthusiastic housekeeper, and hopes for no better profession. I verily believe she thinks it is the writing which made me sick!

But I can write when she is out, and see her a long way off from these windows.

There is one that commands the road, a lovely shaded winding road, and one that just looks off over the country. A lovely country, too, full of great elms and velvet meadows.

This wallpaper has a kind of sub-pattern in a different shade, a particularly irritating one, for you can only see it in certain lights, and not clearly then.

But in the places where it isn't faded and where the sun is just so—I can see a strange, provoking, formless sort of figure that seems to skulk about behind that silly and conspicuous front design.

There's sister on the stairs!

• • • • • •

Well, the Fourth of July is over! The people are all gone, and I am tired out. John thought it might do me good to see a little company, so we just had Mother and Nellie and the children down for a week.

Of course I didn't do a thing. Jennie sees to everything now.

But it tired me all the same.

John says if I don't pick up faster he shall send me to Weir Mitchell[3] in the fall.

But I don't want to go there at all. I had a friend who was in his hands once, and she says he is just like John and my brother, only more so!

Besides, it is such an undertaking to go so far.

I don't feel as if it was worthwhile to turn my hand over for anything, and I'm getting dreadfully fretful and querulous.

I cry at nothing, and cry most of the time.

Of course I don't when John is here, or anybody else, but when I am alone.

And I am alone a good deal just now. John is kept in town very often by serious cases, and Jennie is good and lets me alone when I want her to.

So I walk a little in the garden or down that lovely lane, sit on the porch under the roses, and lie down up here a good deal.

I'm getting really fond of the room in spite of the wallpaper. Perhaps *because* of the wallpaper.

It dwells in my mind so!

I lie here on this great immovable bed—it is nailed down, I believe—and follow that pattern about by the hour. It is as good as gymnastics, I assure you. I start, we'll say, at the bottom, down in the corner over there where it has not been touched, and I determine for the thousandth time that I *will* follow that pointless pattern to some sort of conclusion.

I know a little of the principle of design, and I know this thing was not arranged on any laws of radiation, or alternation, or repetition, or symmetry, or anything else that I ever heard of.

It is repeated, of course, by the breadths, but not otherwise.

Looked at in one way, each breadth stands alone; the bloated curves and flourishes—a kind of "debased Romanesque"[4] with delirium tremens—go waddling up and down in isolated columns of fatuity.

But, on the other hand, they connect diagonally, and the sprawling outlines run off in great slanting waves of optic horror, like a lot of wallowing sea-weeds in full chase.

The whole thing goes horizontally, too, at least it seems so, and I exhaust myself trying to distinguish the order of its going in that direction.

They have used a horizontal breadth for a frieze,[5] and that adds wonderfully to the confusion.

---

3. Silas Weir Mitchell (1829–1914), American physician, novelist, and specialist in nerve disorders, popularized the "rest cure" in the management of hysteria, nervous breakdowns, and related disorders. A friend of W. D. Howells (1837–1920), he was the model for the nerve specialist in Howells's *The Shadow of a Dream*

(1890).
4. Romanesque style is here associated with ornamental complexity and repeated motifs and figures.
5. An ornamental band used as a border at the top of the wall.

There is one end of the room where it is almost intact, and there, when the crosslights fade and the low sun shines directly upon it, I can almost fancy radiation after all—the interminable grotesque seems to form around a common center and rush off in headlong plunges of equal distraction.

It makes me tired to follow it. I will take a nap, I guess.

•   •   •   •   •   •

I don't know why I should write this.

I don't want to.

I don't feel able.

And I know John would think it absurd. But I *must* say what I feel and think in some way—it is such a relief!

But the effort is getting to be greater than the relief.

Half the time now I am awfully lazy, and lie down ever so much.

John says I mustn't lose my strength, and has me take cod liver oil and lots of tonics and things, to say nothing of ale and wine and rare meat.

Dear John! He loves me very dearly, and hates to have me sick. I tried to have a real earnest reasonable talk with him the other day, and tell him how I wish he would let me go and make a visit to Cousin Henry and Julia.

But he said I wasn't able to go, nor able to stand it after I got there; and I did not make out a very good case for myself, for I was crying before I had finished.

It is getting to be a great effort for me to think straight. Just this nervous weakness, I suppose.

And dear John gathered me up in his arms, and just carried me upstairs and laid me on the bed, and sat by me and read to me till it tired my head.

He said I was his darling and his comfort and all he had, and that I must take care of myself for his sake, and keep well.

He says no one but myself can help me out of it, that I must use my will and self-control and not let any silly fancies run away with me.

There's one comfort—the baby is well and happy, and does not have to occupy this nursery with the horrid wallpaper.

If we had not used it, that blessed child would have! What a fortunate escape! Why, I wouldn't have a child of mine, an impressionable little thing, live in such a room for worlds.

I never thought of it before, but it is lucky that John kept me here after all, I can stand it so much easier than a baby, you see.

Of course I never mention it to them any more—I am too wise—but I keep watch for it all the same.

There are things in that paper that nobody knows about but me, or ever will.

Behind that outside pattern the dim shapes get clearer every day.

It is always the same shape, only very numerous.

And it is like a woman stooping down and creeping about behind that pattern. I don't like it a bit. I wonder—I begin to think—I wish John would take me away from here!

•   •   •   •   •   •

It is so hard to talk with John about my case, because he is so wise, and because he loves me so.

But I tried it last night.

It was moonlight. The moon shines in all around just as the sun does.

I hate to see it sometimes, it creeps so slowly, and always comes in by one window or another.

John was asleep and I hated to waken him, so I kept still and watched the moonlight on that undulating wallpaper till I felt creepy.

The faint figure behind seemed to shake the pattern, just as if she wanted to get out.

I got up softly and went to feel and see if the paper *did* move, and when I came back John was awake.

"What is it, little girl?" he said. "Don't go walking about like that—you'll get cold."

I thought it was a good time to talk, so I told him that I really was not gaining here, and that I wished he would take me away.

"Why, darling!" said he. "Our lease will be up in three weeks, and I can't see how to leave before.

"The repairs are not done at home, and I cannot possibly leave town just now. Of course if you were in any danger, I could and would, but you really are better, dear, whether you can see it or not. I am a doctor, dear, and I know. You are gaining flesh and color, your appetite is better, I feel really much easier about you."

"I don't weigh a bit more," said I, "nor as much; and my appetite may be better in the evening when you are here but it is worse in the morning when you are away!"

"Bless her little heart!" said he with a big hug. "She shall be as sick as she pleases! But now let's improve the shining hours by going to sleep, and talk about it in the morning!"

"And you won't go away?" I asked gloomily.

"Why, how can I, dear? It is only three weeks more and then we will take a nice little trip of a few days while Jennie is getting the house ready. Really, dear, you are better!"

"Better in body perhaps—" I began, and stopped short, for he sat up straight and looked at me with such a stern, reproachful look that I could not say another word.

"My darling," said he, "I beg of you, for my sake and for our child's sake, as well as for your own, that you will never for one instant let that idea enter your mind! There is nothing so dangerous, so fascinating, to a temperament like yours. It is a false and foolish fancy. Can you not trust me as a physician when I tell you so?"

So of course I said no more on that score, and we went to sleep before long. He thought I was asleep first, but I wasn't, and lay there for hours trying to decide whether that front pattern and the back pattern really did move together or separately.

• • • • • •

On a pattern like this, by daylight, there is a lack of sequence, a defiance of law, that is a constant irritant to a normal mind.

The color is hideous enough, and unreliable enough, and infuriating enough, but the pattern is torturing.

You think you have mastered it, but just as you get well under way in following, it turns a back-somersault and there you are. It slaps you in the face, knocks you down, and tramples upon you. It is like a bad dream.

The outside pattern is a florid arabesque, reminding one of a fungus. If you can imagine a toadstool in joints, an interminable string of toadstools, budding and sprouting in endless convolutions—why, that is something like it.

That is, sometimes!

There is one marked peculiarity about this paper, a thing nobody seems to notice but myself, and that is that it changes as the light changes.

When the sun shoots in through the east window—I always watch for that first long, straight ray—it changes so quickly that I never can quite believe it.

That is why I watch it always.

By moonlight—the moon shines in all night when there is a moon—I wouldn't know it was the same paper.

At night in any kind of light, in twilight, candlelight, lamplight, and worst of all by moonlight, it becomes bars! The outside pattern, I mean, and the woman behind it is as plain as can be.

I didn't realize for a long time what the thing was that showed behind, that dim sub-pattern, but now I am quite sure it is a woman.

By daylight she is subdued, quiet. I fancy it is the pattern that keeps her so still. It is so puzzling. It keeps me quiet by the hour.

I lie down ever so much now. John says it is good for me, and to sleep all I can.

Indeed he started the habit by making me lie down for an hour after each meal.

It is a very bad habit I am convinced, for you see, I don't sleep.

And that cultivates deceit, for I don't tell them I'm awake—O no!

The fact is I am getting a little afraid of John.

He seems very queer sometimes, and even Jennie has an inexplicable look.

It strikes me occasionally, just as a scientific hypothesis, that perhaps it is the paper!

I have watched John when he did not know I was looking, and come into the room suddenly on the most innocent excuses, and I've caught him several times *looking at the paper!* And Jennie too. I caught Jennie with her hand on it once.

She didn't know I was in the room, and when I asked her in a quiet, a very quiet voice, with the most restrained manner possible, what she was doing with the paper—she turned around as if she had been caught stealing, and looked quite angry—asked me why I should frighten her so!

Then she said that the paper stained everything it touched, that she had found yellow smooches on all my clothes and John's, and she wished we would be more careful!

Did not that sound innocent? But I know she was studying that pattern, and I am determined that nobody shall find it out but myself!

·   ·   ·   ·   ·   ·

Life is very much more exciting now than it used to be. You see I have something more to expect, to look forward to, to watch. I really do eat better, and am more quiet than I was.

John is so pleased to see me improve! He laughed a little the other day, and said I seemed to be flourishing in spite of my wallpaper.

I turned it off with a laugh. I had no intention of telling him it was *because* of the wallpaper—he would make fun of me. He might even want to take me away.

I don't want to leave now until I have found it out. There is a week more, and I think that will be enough.

· · · · · · ·

I'm feeling so much better!

I don't sleep much at night, for it is so interesting to watch developments; but I sleep a good deal during the daytime.

In the daytime it is tiresome and perplexing.

There are always new shoots on the fungus, and new shades of yellow all over it. I cannot keep count of them, though I have tried conscientiously.

It is the strangest yellow, that wallpaper! It makes me think of all the yellow things I ever saw—not beautiful ones like buttercups, but old, foul, bad yellow things.

But there is something else about that paper—the smell! I noticed it the moment we came into the room, but with so much air and sun it was not bad. Now we have had a week of fog and rain, and whether the windows are open or not, the smell is here.

It creeps all over the house.

I find it hovering in the dining-room, skulking in the parlor, hiding in the hall, lying in wait for me on the stairs.

It gets into my hair.

Even when I go to ride, if I turn my head suddenly and surprise it—there is that smell!

Such a peculiar odor, too! I have spent hours in trying to analyze it, to find what it smelled like.

It is not bad—at first—and very gentle, but quite the subtlest, most enduring odor I ever met.

In this damp weather it is awful, I wake up in the night and find it hanging over me.

It used to disturb me at first. I thought seriously of burning the house—to reach the smell.

But now I am used to it. The only thing I can think of that it is like is the *color* of the paper! A yellow smell.

There is a very funny mark on this wall, low down, near the mopboard. A streak that runs round the room. It goes behind every piece of furniture, except the bed, a long, straight, even *smooch*, as if it had been rubbed over and over.

I wonder how it was done and who did it, and what they did it for. Round and round and round—round and round and round—it makes me dizzy!

· · · · · · ·

I really have discovered something at last.

Through watching so much at night, when it changes so, I have finally found out.

The front pattern *does* move—and no wonder! The woman behind shakes it!

Sometimes I think there are a great many women behind, and sometimes only one, and she crawls around fast, and her crawling shakes it all over.

Then in the very bright spots she keeps still, and in the very shady spots she just takes hold of the bars and shakes them hard.

And she is all the time trying to climb through. But nobody could climb through that pattern—it strangles so; I think that is why it has so many heads.

They get through, and then the pattern strangles them off and turns them upside down, and makes their eyes white!

If those heads were covered or taken off it would not be half so bad.

· · · · · ·

I think that woman gets out in the daytime!

And I'll tell you why—privately—I've seen her!

I can see her out of every one of my windows!

It is the same woman, I know, for she is always creeping, and most women do not creep by daylight.

I see her in that long shaded lane, creeping up and down. I see her in those dark grape arbors, creeping all around the garden.

I see her on that long road under the trees, creeping along, and when a carriage comes she hides under the blackberry vines.

I don't blame her a bit. It must be very humiliating to be caught creeping by daylight!

I always lock the door when I creep by daylight. I can't do it at night, for I know John would suspect something at once.

And John is so queer now that I don't want to irritate him. I wish he would take another room! Besides, I don't want anybody to get that woman out at night but myself.

I often wonder if I could see her out of all the windows at once.

But, turn as fast as I can, I can only see out of one at one time.

And though I always see her, she *may* be able to creep faster than I can turn! I have watched her sometimes away off in the open country, creeping as fast as a cloud shadow in a wind.

· · · · · ·

If only that top pattern could be gotten off from the under one! I mean to try it, little by little.

I have found out another funny thing, but I shan't tell it this time! It does not do to trust people too much.

There are only two more days to get this paper off, and I believe John is beginning to notice. I don't like the look in his eyes.

And I heard him ask Jennie a lot of professional questions about me. She had a very good report to give.

She said I slept a good deal in the daytime.

John knows I don't sleep very well at night, for all I'm so quiet!

He asked me all sorts of questions, too, and pretended to be very loving and kind.

As if I couldn't see through him!

Still, I don't wonder he acts so, sleeping under this paper for three months.

It only interests me, but I feel sure John and Jennie are affected by it.

· · · · · ·

Hurrah! This is the last day, but it is enough. John is to stay in town over night, and won't be out until this evening.

Jennie wanted to sleep with me—the sly thing; but I told her I should undoubtedly rest better for a night all alone.

That was clever, for really I wasn't alone a bit! As soon as it was moonlight and that poor thing began to crawl and shake the pattern, I got up and ran to help her.

I pulled and she shook, I shook and she pulled, and before morning we had peeled off yards of that paper.

A strip about as high as my head and half around the room.

And then when the sun came and that awful pattern began to laugh at me, I declared I would finish it today!

We go away tomorrow, and they are moving all my furniture down again to leave things as they were before.

Jennie looked at the wall in amazement, but I told her merrily that I did it out of pure spite at the vicious thing.

She laughed and said she wouldn't mind doing it herself, but I must not get tired.

How she betrayed herself that time!

But I am here, and no person touches this paper but Me—not *alive*!

She tried to get me out of the room—it was too patent! But I said it was so quiet and empty and clean now that I believed I would lie down again and sleep all I could; and not to wake me even for dinner—I would call when I woke.

So now she is gone, and the servants are gone, and the things are gone, and there is nothing left but that great bedstead nailed down, with the canvas mattress we found on it.

We shall sleep downstairs tonight, and take the boat home tomorrow.

I quite enjoy the room, now it is bare again.

How those children did tear about here!

This bedstead is fairly gnawed!

But I must get to work.

I have locked the door and thrown the key down into the front path.

I don't want to go out, and I don't want to have anybody come in, till John comes.

I want to astonish him.

I've got a rope up here that even Jennie did not find. If that woman does get out, and tries to get away, I can tie her!

But I forgot I could not reach far without anything to stand on!

This bed will *not* move!

I tried to lift and push it until I was lame, and then I got so angry I bit off a little piece at one corner—but it hurt my teeth.

Then I peeled off all the paper I could reach standing on the floor. It sticks horribly and the pattern just enjoys it! All those strangled heads and bulbous eyes and waddling fungus growths just shriek with derision!

I am getting angry enough to do something desperate. To jump out of the window would be admirable exercise, but the bars are too strong even to try.

Besides I wouldn't do it. Of course not. I know well enough that a step like that is improper and might be misconstrued.

I don't like to *look* out of the windows even—there are so many of those creeping women, and they creep so fast.

I wonder if they all come out of that wallpaper as I did?

But I am securely fastened now by my well-hidden rope—you don't get *me* out in the road there!

I suppose I shall have to get back behind the pattern when it comes night, and that is hard!

It is so pleasant to be out in this great room and creep around as I please!

I don't want to go outside. I won't, even if Jennie asks me to.

For outside you have to creep on the ground, and everything is green instead of yellow.

But here I can creep smoothly on the floor, and my shoulder just fits in that long smooch around the wall, so I cannot lose my way.

Why there's John at the door!

It is no use, young man, you can't open it!

How he does call and pound!

Now he's crying to Jennie for an axe.

It would be a shame to break down that beautiful door!

"John dear!" said I in the gentlest voice. "The key is down by the front steps, under a plantain leaf!"

That silenced him for a few moments.

Then he said—very quietly indeed, "Open the door, my darling!"

"I can't," said I. "The key is down by the front door under a plantain leaf!"

And then I said it again, several times, very gently and slowly, and said it so often that he had to go and see, and he got it of course, and came in. He stopped short by the door.

"What is the matter?" he cried. "For God's sake, what are you doing!"

I kept on creeping just the same, but I looked at him over my shoulder.

"I've got out at last," said I, "in spite of you and Jane? And I've pulled off most of the paper, so you can't put me back!"

Now why should that man have fainted? But he did, and right across my path by the wall, so that I had to creep over him every time!

1892

---

# EDITH WHARTON

## 1862–1937

Edith Wharton's patrician background, troubled marriage, and international social life are all of interest; above all else, however, she was a prolific and successful writer. She began to write as a very young woman, published some fifty varied volumes in her lifetime, and left a number of unpublished manuscripts and a voluminous correspondence at her death. *The House of Mirth* (1905), her second novel, was a best-seller; another novel, *The Age of Innocence* (1920), won the Pulitzer Prize; in 1930 she was awarded the gold medal of the National Institute of Arts and Letters, the first woman to be so honored.

Edith Newbold Jones was born in New York City on January 24, 1862, into a patriarchal, monied, cultivated, and rather rigid family that, like others in its small circle, disdained and feared the drastic social, cultural, and economic changes brought on by post–Civil War expansionism. It is small wonder, then, that her work at its best deals with what she described as the tragic psychic and moral effects on its members of a frivolous society under pressure. She was educated by tutors and governesses, much of the time while the family resided in Europe. In 1885 she married the Bostonian Edward Wharton, a social equal thirteen years her senior. Though they lived together (in New York, Newport, Lenox, and Paris) for twenty-eight years, most of those years were unhappy because of the nervous ill-nessess they each suffered. That she did not seek a divorce until 1913 (on grounds of her husband's adultery) is more a tribute to what her biographer R. W. B. Lewis characterized as her "moral conservatism and her devotion to family ties and the sanctities of tradition" than to personal affection.

*Souls Belated* (1899) is one of Wharton's earliest and most successful efforts to convert her personal tension over divorce into art. In another early story, *The Other Two* (1904), divorce is presented more humorously, though just below the surface is a profounder exploration of the ways social values and gender roles subtly corrupt consciousness and threaten a woman's identity.

In 1905, with the publication of *The House of Mirth*, Wharton confirmed her unconventional choice of role as writer and immediately found a wide public. Although she was later to write about other subjects, she discovered in it her central settings, plots, and themes; the old aristocracy of New York in conflict with the nouveau riche; and the futile struggle of central characters trapped by social forces larger and individuals morally smaller than themselves. This same fundamental situation informs her most popular book, the novel *Ethan Frome* (1911), although this grim work is set in symbolically named Starkfield, Massachusetts, and the central character, a farmer, is emotionally cannibalized by two narrow, selfish countrywomen. In *The Custom of the Country* (1913), considered by many of her critics to be her most forceful and successful novel, she confronts the effects of cultural dislocation in the Gilded Age on a beautiful and rather vicious adventurer.

There is general agreement that the rest of Wharton's literary career was less distinguished. Much of her best work seems to have been completed under pressure of great personal strain and crisis. In any case, after her divorce in 1913 her work, even when successful—as it surely was in the novel *The Age of Innocence* (1920), in a number of her stories, and in the charming reminiscence *A Backward Glance* (1934)—was softer and more nostalgic than her biting, satiric earlier writings. In these later years, more and more of her time was given to the company of an impressive international circle of diplomats, artists, and intellectuals as various in age, personality, and interests as Henry James (whose style and person she admired greatly), Jean Cocteau, and Sinclair Lewis (who dedicated *Babbitt* to her). During the last thirty years of her life, her periodic visits to America became more widely spaced; she died in August 1937 in one of the two homes she maintained in France.

# The Other Two[1]

## I

Waythorn, on the drawing-room hearth, waited for his wife to come down to dinner.

It was their first night under his own roof, and he was surprised at his thrill of boyish agitation. He was not so old, to be sure—his glass gave him little more than the five-and-thirty years to which his wife confessed—but he had fancied himself already in the temperate zone; yet here he was listening for her step with a tender sense of all it symbolised, with some old trail of verse

1. First published by Scribner's in the 1904 collection *The Descent of Man and Other Stories*, the source of the present text.

about the garlanded nuptial door-posts floating through his enjoyment of the pleasant room and the good dinner just beyond it.

They had been hastily recalled from their honeymoon by the illness of Lily Haskett, the child of Mrs. Waythorn's first marriage. The little girl, at Waythorn's desire, had been transferred to his house on the day of her mother's wedding, and the doctor, on their arrival, broke the news that she was ill with typhoid, but declared that all the symptoms were favourable. Lily could show twelve years of unblemished health, and the case promised to be a light one. The nurse spoke as reassuringly, and after a moment of alarm Mrs. Waythorn had adjusted herself to the situation. She was very fond of Lily—her affection for the child had perhaps been her decisive charm in Waythorn's eyes—but she had the perfectly balanced nerves which her little girl had inherited, and no woman ever wasted less tissue in unproductive worry. Waythorn was therefore quite prepared to see her come in presently, a little late because of a last look at Lily, but as serene and well-appointed as if her goodnight kiss had been laid on the brow of health. Her composure was restful to him; it acted as ballast to his somewhat unstable sensibilities. As he pictured her bending over the child's bed he thought how soothing her presence must be in illness: her very step would prognosticate recovery.

His own life had been a gray one, from temperament rather than circumstance, and he had been drawn to her by the unperturbed gaiety which kept her fresh and elastic at an age when most woman's activities are growing either slack or febrile. He knew what was said about her; for, popular as she was, there had always been a faint undercurrent of detraction. When she had appeared in New York, nine or ten years earlier, as the pretty Mrs. Haskett whom Gus Varick had unearthed somewhere—was it in Pittsburg or Utica?—society, while promptly accepting her, had reserved the right to cast a doubt on its own indiscrimination. Enquiry, however, established her undoubted connection with a socially reigning family, and explained her recent divorce as the natural result of a runaway match at seventeen; and as nothing was known of Mr. Haskett it was easy to believe the worst of him.

Alice Haskett's remarriage with Gus Varick was a passport to the set whose recognition she coveted, and for a few years the Varicks were the most popular couple in town. Unfortunately the alliance was brief and stormy, and this time the husband had his champions. Still, even Varick's stanchest supporters admitted that he was not meant for matrimony, and Mrs. Varick's grievances were of a nature to bear the inspection of the New York courts.[2] A New York divorce is in itself a diploma of virtue, and in the semi-widowhood of this second separation Mrs. Varick took on an air of sanctity, and was allowed to confide her wrongs to some of the most scrupulous ears in town. But when it was known that she was to marry Waythorn there was a momentary reaction. Her best friends would have preferred to see her remain in the rôle of the injured wife, which was as becoming to her as crape to a rosy complexion. True, a decent time had elapsed, and it was not even suggested that Waythorn had supplanted his predecessor. People shook their heads over him, however, and one grudging friend, to whom he affirmed that he took the step with his eyes open, replied oracularly: "Yes—and with your ears shut."

Waythorn could afford to smile at these innuendoes. In the Wall Street

2. Divorce in New York State could then be granted only on the grounds of adultery.

phrase, he had "discounted" them. He knew that society has not yet adapted itself to the consequences of divorce, and that till the adaptation takes place every woman who uses the freedom the law accords her must be her own social justification. Waythorn had an amused confidence in his wife's ability to justify herself. His expectations were fulfilled, and before the wedding took place Alice Varick's group had rallied openly to her support. She took it all imperturbably: she had a way of surmounting obstacles without seeming to be aware of them, and Waythorn looked back with wonder at the trivialities over which he had worn his nerves thin. He had the sense of having found refuge in a richer, warmer nature than his own, and his satisfaction, at the moment, was humourously summed up in the thought that his wife, when she had done all she could for Lily, would not be ashamed to come down and enjoy a good dinner.

The anticipation of such enjoyment was not, however, the sentiment expressed by Mrs. Waythorn's charming face when she presently joined him. Though she had put on her most engaging teagown she had neglected to assume the smile that went with it, and Waythorn thought he had never seen her look so nearly worried.

"What is it?" he asked. "Is anything wrong with Lily?"

"No; I've just been in and she's still sleeping." Mrs. Waythorn hesitated. "But something tiresome has happened."

He had taken her two hands, and now perceived that he was crushing a paper between them.

"This letter?"

"Yes—Mr. Haskett has written—I mean his lawyer has written."

Waythorn felt himself flush uncomfortably. He dropped his wife's hands.

"What about?"

"About seeing Lily. You know the courts—"

"Yes, yes," he interrupted nervously.

Nothing was known about Haskett in New York. He was vaguely supposed to have remained in the outer darkness from which his wife had been rescued, and Waythorn was one of the few who were aware that he had given up his business in Utica and followed her to New York in order to be near his little girl. In the days of his wooing, Waythorn had often met Lily on the doorstep, rosy and smiling, on her way "to see papa."

"I am so sorry," Mrs. Waythorn murmured.

He roused himself. "What does he want?"

"He wants to see her. You know she goes to him once a week."

"Well—he doesn't expect her to go to him now, does he?"

"No—he has heard of her illness; but he expects to come here."

"*Here?*"

Mrs. Waythorn reddened under his gaze. They looked away from each other.

"I'm afraid he has the right. . . . You'll see. . . ." She made a proffer of the letter.

Waythorn moved away with a gesture of refusal. He stood staring about the softly lighted room, which a moment before had seemed so full of bridal intimacy.

"I'm so sorry," she repeated. "If Lily could have been moved—"

"That's out of the question," he returned impatiently.

"I suppose so."

Her lip was beginning to tremble, and he felt himself a brute.

"He must come, of course," he said. "When is—his day?"

"I'm afraid—to-morrow."

"Very well. Send a note in the morning."

The butler entered to announce dinner.

Waythorn turned to his wife. "Come—you must be tired. It's beastly, but try to forget about it," he said, drawing her hand through his arm.

"You're so good, dear. I'll try," she whispered back.

Her face cleared at once, and as she looked at him across the flowers, between the rosy candle-shades, he saw her lips waver back into a smile.

"How pretty everything is!" she sighed luxuriously.

He turned to the butler. "The champagne at once, please. Mrs. Waythorn is tired."

In a moment or two their eyes met above the sparkling glasses. Her own were quite clear and untroubled: he saw that she had obeyed his injunction and forgotten.

## II

Waythorn, the next morning, went down town earlier than usual. Haskett was not likely to come till the afternoon, but the instinct of flight drove him forth. He meant to stay away all day—he had thoughts of dining at his club. As his door closed behind him he reflected that before he opened it again it would have admitted another man who had as much right to enter it as himself, and the thought filled him with a physical repugnance.

He caught the "elevated"[3] at the employés' hour, and found himself crushed between two layers of pendulous humanity. At Eighth Street the man facing him wriggled out, and another took his place. Waythorn glanced up and saw that it was Gus Varick. The men were so close together that it was impossible to ignore the smile of recognition on Varick's handsome overblown face. And after all—why not? They had always been on good terms, and Varick had been divorced before Waythorn's attentions to his wife began. The two exchanged a word on the perennial grievance of the congested trains, and when a seat at their side was miraculously left empty the instinct of self-preservation made Waythorn slip into it after Varick.

The latter drew the stout man's breath of relief. "Lord—I was beginning to feel like a pressed flower." He leaned back, looking unconcernedly at Waythorn. "Sorry to hear that Sellers is knocked out again."

"Sellers?" echoed Waythorn, starting at his partner's name.

Varick looked surprised. "You didn't know he was laid up with the gout?"

"No. I've been away—I only got back last night." Waythorn felt himself reddening in anticipation of the other's smile.

"Ah—yes; to be sure. And Seller's attack came on two days ago. I'm afraid he's pretty bad. Very awkward for me, as it happens, because he was just putting through a rather important thing for me."

"Ah?" Waythorn wondered vaguely since when Varick had been dealing in "important things." Hitherto he had dabbled only in the shallow pools of

3. Elevated railway.

speculation, with which Waythorn's office did not usually concern itself.

It occurred to him that Varick might be talking at random, to relieve the strain of their propinquity. That strain was becoming momentarily more apparent to Waythorn, and when, at Cortlandt Street, he caught sight of an acquaintance and had a sudden vision of the picture he and Varick must present to an initiated eye, he jumped up with a muttered excuse.

"I hope you'll find Sellers better," said Varick civilly, and he stammered back: "If I can be of any use to you—" and let the departing crowd sweep him to the platform.

At his office he heard that Sellers was in fact ill with the gout, and would probably not be able to leave the house for some weeks.

"I'm sorry it should have happened so, Mr. Waythorn," the senior clerk said with affable significance. "Mr. Sellers was very much upset at the idea of giving you such a lot of extra work just now."

"Oh, that's no matter," said Waythorn hastily. He secretly welcomed the pressure of additional business, and was glad to think that, when the day's work was over, he would have to call at his partner's on the way home.

He was late for luncheon, and turned in at the nearest restaurant instead of going to his club. The place was full, and the waiter hurried him to the back of the room to capture the only vacant table. In the cloud of cigar-smoke Waythorn did not at once distinguish his neighbours: but presently, looking about him, he saw Varick seated a few feet off. This time, luckily, they were too far apart for conversation, and Varick, who faced another way, had probably not even seen him; but there was an irony in their renewed nearness.

Varick was said to be fond of good living, and as Waythorn sat despatching his hurried luncheon he looked across half enviously at the other's leisurely degustation of his meal. When Waythorn first saw him he had been helping himself with critical deliberation to a bit of Camembert at the ideal point of liquefaction, and now, the cheese removed, he was just pouring his *café double* from its little two-storied earthen pot. He poured slowly, his ruddy profile bent above the task, and one beringed white hand steadying the lid of the coffee-pot; then he stretched his other hand to the decanter of cognac at his elbow, filled a liqueur-glass, took a tentative sip, and poured the brandy into his coffee-cup.

Waythorn watched him in a kind of fascination. What was he thinking of—only of the flavour of the coffee and the liqueur? Had the morning's meeting left no more trace in his thoughts than on his face? Had his wife so completely passed out of his life that even this odd encounter with her present husband, within a week after her remarriage, was no more than an incident in his day? And as Waythorn mused, another idea struck him: had Haskett ever met Varick as Varick and he had just met? The recollection of Haskett perturbed him, and he rose and left the restaurant, taking a circuitous way out to escape the placid irony of Varick's nod.

It was after seven when Waythorn reached home. He thought the footman who opened the door looked at him oddly.

"How is Miss Lily?" he asked in haste.

"Doing very well, sir. A gentleman—"

"Tell Barlow to put off dinner for half an hour," Waythorn cut him off, hurrying upstairs.

He went straight to his room and dressed without seeing his wife. When he reached the drawing-room she was there, fresh and radiant. Lily's day had been good; the doctor was not coming back that evening.

At dinner Waythorn told her of Sellers's illness and of the resulting complications. She listened sympathetically, adjuring him not to let himself be overworked, and asking vague feminine questions about the routine of the office. Then she gave him the chronicle of Lily's day; quoted the nurse and doctor, and told him who had called to inquire. He had never seen her more serene and unruffled. It struck him, with a curious pang, that she was very happy in being with him, so happy that she found a childish pleasure in rehearsing the trivial incidents of her day.

After dinner they went to the library, and the servant put the coffee and liqueurs on a low table before her and left the room. She looked singularly soft and girlish in her rosy pale dress, against the dark leather of one of his bachelor armchairs. A day earlier the contrast would have charmed him.

He turned away now, choosing a cigar with affected deliberation.

"Did Haskett come?" he asked, with his back to her.

"Oh, yes—he came."

"You didn't see him, of course?"

She hesitated a moment. "I let the nurse see him."

That was all. There was nothing more to ask. He swung round toward her, applying a match to his cigar. Well, the thing was over for a week, at any rate. He would try not to think of it. She looked up at him, a trifle rosier than usual, with a smile in her eyes.

"Ready for your coffee, dear?"

He leaned against the mantelpiece, watching her as she lifted the coffee-pot. The lamplight struck a gleam from her bracelets and tipped her soft hair with brightness. How light and slender she was, and how each gesture flowed into the next! She seemed a creature all compact of harmonies. As the thought of Haskett receded, Waythorn felt himself yielding again to the joy of possessorship. They were his, those white hands with their flitting motions, his the light haze of hair, the lips and eyes. . . .

She set down the coffee-pot, and reaching for the decanter of cognac, measured off a liqueur-glass and poured it into his cup.

Waythorn uttered a sudden exclamation.

"What is the matter?" she said, startled.

"Nothing; only—I don't take cognac in my coffee."

"Oh, how stupid of me," she cried.

Their eyes met, and she blushed a sudden agonised red.

## III

Ten days later, Mr. Sellers, still house-bound, asked Waythorn to call on his way down town.

The senior partner, with his swaddled foot propped up by the fire, greeted his associate with an air of embarrassment.

"I'm sorry, my dear fellow; I've got to ask you to do an awkward thing for me."

Waythorn waited, and the other went on, after a pause apparently given to the arrangement of his phrases: "The fact is, when I was knocked out I had just gone into a rather complicated piece of business for—Gus Varick."

"Well?" said Waythorn, with an attempt to put him at his ease.

"Well—it's this way: Varick came to me the day before my attack. He had evidently had an inside tip from somebody, and had made about a hundred thousand. He came to me for advice, and I suggested his going in with Vanderlyn."

"Oh, the deuce!" Waythorn exclaimed. He saw in a flash what had happened. The investment was an alluring one, but required negotiation. He listened quietly while Sellers put the case before him, and, the statement ended, he said: "You think I ought to see Varick?"

"I'm afraid I can't as yet. The doctor is obdurate. And this thing can't wait. I hate to ask you, but no one else in the office knows the ins and outs of it."

Waythorn stood silent. He did not care a farthing for the success of Varick's venture, but the honour of the office was to be considered, and he could hardly refuse to oblige his partner.

"Very well," he said, "I'll do it."

That afternoon, apprised by telephone, Varick called at the office. Waythorn, waiting in his private room, wondered what the others thought of it. The newspapers, at the time of Mrs. Waythorn's marriage, had acquainted their readers with every detail of her previous matrimonial ventures, and Waythorn could fancy the clerks smiling behind Varick's back as he was ushered in.

Varick bore himself admirably. He was easy without being undignified, and Waythorn was conscious of cutting a much less impressive figure. Varick had no experience of business, and the talk prolonged itself for nearly an hour while Waythorn set forth with scrupulous precision the details of the proposed transaction.

"I'm awfully obliged to you," Varick said as he rose. "The fact is I'm not used to having much money to look after, and I don't want to make an ass of myself—" He smiled, and Waythorn could not help noticing that there was something pleasant about his smile. "It feels uncommonly queer to have enough cash to pay one's bills. I'd have sold my soul for it a few years ago!"

Waythorn winced at the allusion. He had heard it rumoured that a lack of funds had been one of the determining causes of the Varick separation, but it did not occur to him that Varick's words were intentional. It seemed more likely that the desire to keep clear of embarrassing topics had fatally drawn him into one. Waythorn did not wish to be outdone in civility.

"We'll do the best we can for you," he said. "I think this is a good thing you're in."

"Oh, I'm sure it's immense. It's awfully good of you—" Varick broke off, embarrassed. "I suppose the thing's settled now—but if—"

"If anything happens before Sellers is about, I'll see you again," said Waythorn quietly. He was glad, in the end, to appear the more self-possessed of the two.

• • •

The course of Lily's illness ran smooth, and as the days passed Waythorn grew used to the idea of Haskett's weekly visit. The first time the day came round, he stayed out late, and questioned his wife as to the visit on his return. She replied at once that Haskett had merely seen the nurse downstairs, as the doctor did not wish any one in the child's sick-room till after the crisis.

The following week Waythorn was again conscious of the recurrence of the

day, but had forgotten it by the time he came home to dinner. The crisis of
the disease came a few days later, with a rapid decline of fever, and the little
girl was pronounced out of danger. In the rejoicing which ensued the thought
of Haskett passed out of Waythorn's mind, and one afternoon, letting himself
into the house with a latch-key, he went straight to his library without noticing
a shabby hat and umbrella in the hall.

In the library he found a small effaced-looking man with a thinnish gray
beard sitting on the edge of a chair. The stranger might have been a piano-
tuner, or one of those mysteriously efficient persons who are summoned in
emergencies to adjust some detail of the domestic machinery. He blinked at
Waythorn through a pair of gold-rimmed spectacles and said mildly: "Mr.
Waythorn, I presume? I am Lily's father."

Waythorn flushed. "Oh—" he stammered uncomfortably. He broke off,
disliking to appear rude. Inwardly he was trying to adjust the actual Haskett to
the image of him projected by his wife's reminiscences. Waythorn had been
allowed to infer that Alice's first husband was a brute.

"I am sorry to intrude," said Haskett, with his over-the-counter politeness.

"Don't mention it," returned Waythorn, collecting himself. "I suppose the
nurse has been told?"

"I presume so. I can wait," said Haskett. He had a resigned way of speaking,
as though life had worn down his natural powers of resistance.

Waythorn stood on the threshold, nervously pulling off his gloves.

"I'm sorry you've been detained. I will send for the nurse," he said; and as
he opened the door he added with an effort: "I'm glad we can give you a good
report of Lily." He winced as the *we* slipped out, but Haskett seemed not to
notice it.

"Thank you, Mr. Waythorn. It's been an anxious time for me."

"Ah, well, that's past. Soon she'll be able to go to you." Waythorn nodded
and passed out.

In his own room he flung himself down with a groan. He hated the womanish sensibility which made him suffer so acutely from the grotesque chances
of life. He had known when he married that his wife's former husbands were
both living, and that amid the multiplied contacts of modern existence there
were a thousand chances to one that he would run against one or the other,
yet he found himself as much disturbed by his brief encounter with Haskett
as though the law had not obligingly removed all difficulties in the way of
their meeting.

Waythorn sprang up and began to pace the room nervously. He had not
suffered half as much from his two meetings with Varick. It was Haskett's
presence in his own house that made the situation so intolerable. He stood
still, hearing steps in the passage.

"This way, please," he heard the nurse say. Haskett was being taken upstairs,
then: not a corner of the house but was open to him. Waythorn dropped into
another chair, staring vaguely ahead of him. On his dressing-table stood a
photograph of Alice, taken when he had first known her. She was Alice Varick
then—how fine and exquisite he had thought her! Those were Varick's pearls
about her neck. At Waythorn's instance they had been returned before her
marriage. Had Haskett ever given her any trinkets—and what had become of
them, Waythorn wondered? He realised suddenly that he knew very little of
Haskett's past or present situation; but from the man's appearance and manner

of speech he could reconstruct with curious precision the surroundings of
Alice's first marriage. And it startled him to think that she had, in the background of her life, a phase of existence so different from anything with which
he had connected her. Varick, whatever his faults, was a gentleman, in the
conventional, traditional sense of the term: the sense which at that moment
seemed, oddly enough, to have most meaning to Waythorn. He and Varick
had the same social habits, spoke the same language, understood the same
allusions. But this other man . . . it was grotesquely uppermost in Waythorn's
mind that Haskett had worn a made-up tie attached with an elastic. Why
should that ridiculous detail symbolise the whole man? Waythorn was exasperated by his own paltriness, but the fact of the tie expanded, forced itself on
him, became as it were the key to Alice's past. He could see her, as Mrs.
Haskett, sitting in a "front parlour" furnished in plush, with a pianola, and a
copy of "Ben Hur"[4] on the centre-table. He could see her going to the theatre
with Haskett—or perhaps even to a "Church Sociable"—she in a "picture hat"
and Haskett in a black frock coat, a little creased, with the made-up tie on an
elastic. On the way home they would stop and look at the illuminated shop-
windows, lingering over the photographs of New York actresses. On Sunday
afternoons Haskett would take her for a walk, pushing Lily ahead of them in a
white enamelled perambulator, and Waythorn had a vision of the people they
would stop and talk to. He could fancy how pretty Alice must have looked, in
a dress adroitly constructed from the hints of a New York fashion-paper, and
how she must have looked down on the other women, chafing at her life, and
secretly feeling that she belonged in a bigger place.

For the moment his foremost thought was one of wonder at the way in
which she had shed the phase of existence which her marriage with Haskett
implied. It was as if her whole aspect, every gesture, every inflection, every
allusion, were a studied negation of that period of her life. If she had denied
being married to Haskett she could hardly have stood more convicted of
duplicity than in this obliteration of the self which had been his wife.

Waythorn started up, checking himself in the analysis of her motives. What
right had he to create a fantastic effigy of her and then pass judgment on it?
She had spoken vaguely of her first marriage as unhappy, had hinted, with
becoming reticence, that Haskett had wrought havoc among her young illusions. . . . It was a pity for Waythorn's peace of mind that Haskett's very
inoffensiveness shed a new light on the nature of those illusions. A man would
rather think that his wife has been brutalised by her first husband than that the
process has been reversed.

## IV

"Mr. Waythorn, I don't like that French governess of Lily's."

Haskett, subdued and apologetic, stood before Waythorn in the library,
revolving his shabby hat in his hand.

Waythorn, surprised in his armchair over the evening paper, stared back
perplexedly at his visitor.

"You'll excuse me asking to see you," Haskett continued. "But this is my

---

4. *Ben Hur, A Tale of the Christ* (1880), an immensely popular, rather melodramatic romance by Lew Wallace
(1827–1905).

last visit, and I thought if I could have a word with you it would be a better way than writing to Mrs. Waythorn's lawyer."

Waythorn rose uneasily. He did not like the French governess either; but that was irrelevant.

"I am not so sure of that," he returned stiffly; "but since you wish it I will give your message to—my wife." He always hesitated over the possessive pronoun in addressing Haskett.

The latter sighed. "I don't know as that will help much. She didn't like it when I spoke to her."

Waythorn turned red. "When did you see her?" he asked.

"Not since the first day I came to see Lily—right after she was taken sick. I remarked to her then that I didn't like the governess."

Waythorn made no answer. He remembered distinctly that, after the first visit, he had asked his wife if she had seen Haskett. She had lied to him then, but she had respected his wishes since; and the incident cast a curious light on her character. He was sure she would not have seen Haskett the first day if she had divined that Waythorn would object, and the fact that she did not divine it was almost as disagreeable to the latter as the discovery that she had lied to him.

"I don't like the woman," Haskett was repeating with mild persistency. "She ain't straight, Mr. Waythorn—she'll teach the child to be underhand. I've noticed a change in Lily—she's too anxious to please—and she don't always tell the truth. She used to be the straightest child, Mr. Waythorn—" He broke off, his voice a little thick. "Not but what I want her to have a stylish education," he ended.

Waythorn was touched. "I'm sorry, Mr. Haskett; but frankly, I don't quite see what I can do."

Haskett hesitated. Then he laid his hat on the table, and advanced to the hearth-rug, on which Waythorn was standing. There was nothing aggressive in his manner, but he had the solemnity of a timid man resolved on a decisive measure.

"There's just one thing you can do, Mr. Waythorn," he said. "You can remind Mrs. Waythorn that, by the decree of the courts, I am entitled to have a voice in Lily's bringing up." He paused, and went on more deprecatingly: "I'm not the kind to talk about enforcing my rights, Mr. Waythorn. I don't know as I think a man is entitled to rights he hasn't known how to hold on to; but this business of the child is different. I've never let go there—and I never mean to."

• • •

The scene left Waythorn deeply shaken. Shamefacedly, in indirect ways, he had been finding out about Haskett; and all that he learned was favourable. The little man, in order to be near his daughter, had sold out his share in a profitable business in Utica, and accepted a modest clerkship in a New York manufacturing house. He boarded in a shabby street and had few acquaintances. His passion for Lily filled his life. Waythorn felt that this exploration of Haskett was like groping about with a dark-lantern in his wife's past; but he saw now that there were recesses his lantern had not explored. He had never enquired into the exact circumstances of his wife's first matrimonial rupture. On the surface all had been fair. It was she who had obtained the divorce, and the court had given her the child. But Waythorn knew how many ambiguities such a verdict might cover. The mere fact that Haskett retained a right over his daughter implied an unsuspected compromise. Waythorn was an idealist. He always refused to recognise unpleasant contingencies till he found himself confronted with them, and then he saw them followed by a spectral train of consequences. His next days were thus haunted, and he determined to try to lay the ghosts by conjuring them up in his wife's presence.

When he repeated Haskett's request a flame of anger passed over her face; but she subdued it instantly and spoke with a slight quiver of outraged motherhood.

"It is very ungentlemanly of him," she said.

The word grated on Waythorn. "That is neither here nor there. It's a bare question of rights."

She murmured: "It's not as if he could ever be a help to Lily—"

Waythorn flushed. This was even less to his taste. "The question is," he repeated, "what authority has he over her?"

She looked downward, twisting herself a little in her seat. "I am willing to see him—I thought you objected," she faltered.

In a flash he understood that she knew the extent of Haskett's claims. Perhaps it was not the first time she had resisted them.

"My objecting has nothing to do with it," he said coldly; "if Haskett has a right to be consulted you must consult him."

She burst into tears, and he saw that she expected him to regard her as a victim.

Haskett did not abuse his rights. Waythorn had felt miserably sure that he would not. But the governess was dismissed, and from time to time the little man demanded an interview with Alice. After the first outburst she accepted the situation with her usual adaptability. Haskett had once reminded Waythorn of the piano-tuner, and Mrs. Waythorn, after a month or two, appeared to class him with that domestic familiar. Waythorn could not but respect the father's tenacity. At first he had tried to cultivate the suspicion that Haskett might be "up to" something, that he had an object in securing a foothold in the house. But in his heart Waythorn was sure of Haskett's single-mindedness; he even guessed in the latter a mild contempt for such advantages as his relation with the Waythorns might offer. Haskett's sincerity of purpose made him invulnerable, and his successor had to accept him as a lien on the property.

• • •

Mr. Sellers was sent to Europe to recover from his gout, and Varick's affairs hung on Waythorn's hands. The negotiations were prolonged and complicated; they necessitated frequent conferences between the two men, and the interests of the firm forbade Waythorn's suggesting that his client should transfer his business to another office.

Varick appeared well in the transaction. In moments of relaxation his coarse streak appeared, and Waythorn dreaded his geniality; but in the office he was concise and clear-headed, with a flattering deference to Waythorn's judgment. Their business relations being so affably established, it would have been absurd for the two men to ignore each other in society. The first time they met in a drawing-room, Varick took up their intercourse in the same easy key, and his hostess's grateful glance obliged Waythorn to respond to it. After that they ran

across each other frequently, and one evening at a ball Waythorn, wandering
through the remoter rooms, came upon Varick seated beside his wife. She
coloured a little, and faltered in what she was saying; but Varick nodded to
Waythorn without rising, and the latter strolled on.

In the carriage, on the way home, he broke out nervously: "I didn't know
you spoke to Varick."

Her voice trembled a little. "It's the first time—he happened to be standing
near me; I didn't know what to do. It's so awkward, meeting everywhere—and
he said you had been very kind about some business."

"That's different," said Waythorn.

She paused a moment. "I'll do just as you wish," she returned pliantly. "I
thought it would be less awkward to speak to him when we meet."

Her pliancy was beginning to sicken him. Had she really no will of her
own—no theory about her relation to these men? She had accepted Haskett—
did she mean to accept Varick? It was "less awkward," as she had said, and her
instinct was to evade difficulties or to circumvent them. With sudden vividness
Waythorn saw how the instinct had developed. She was "as easy as an old
shoe"—a shoe that too many feet had worn. Her elasticity was the result of
tension in too many different directions. Alice Haskett—Alice Varick—Alice
Waythorn—she had been each in turn, and had left hanging to each name a
little of her privacy, a little of her personality, a little of the inmost self where
the unknown god abides.

"Yes—it's better to speak to Varick," said Waythorn wearily.


                                    V

The winter wore on, and society took advantage of the Waythorns' acceptance of Varick. Harassed hostesses were grateful to them for bridging over a
social difficulty, and Mrs. Waythorn was held up as a miracle of good taste.
Some experimental spirits could not resist the diversion of throwing Varick
and his former wife together, and there were those who thought he found a
zest in the propinquity. But Mrs. Waythorn's conduct remained irreproachable. She neither avoided Varick nor sought him out. Even Waythorn could
not but admit that she had discovered the solution of the newest social
problem.

He had married her without giving much thought to that problem. He had
fancied that a woman can shed her past like a man. But now he saw that Alice
was bound to hers both by the circumstances which forced her into continued
relation with it, and by the traces it had left on her nature. With grim irony
Waythorn compared himself to a member of a syndicate. He held so many
shares in his wife's personality and his predecessors were his partners in the
business. If there had been any element of passion in the transaction he would
have felt less deteriorated by it. The fact that Alice took her change of husbands
like a change of weather reduced the situation to mediocrity. He could have
forgiven her for blunders, for excesses; for resisting Haskett, for yielding to
Varick; for anything but her acquiescence and her tact. She reminded him of
a juggler tossing knives; but the knives were blunt and she knew they would
never cut her.

And then, gradually, habit formed a protecting surface for his sensibilities.
If he paid for each day's comfort with the small change of his illusions, he

grew daily to value the comfort more and set less store upon the coin. He had drifted into a dulling propinquity with Haskett and Varick and he took refuge in the cheap revenge of satirising the situation. He even began to reckon up the advantages which accrued from it, to ask himself if it were not better to own a third of a wife who knew how to make a man happy than a whole one who had lacked opportunity to acquire the art. For it *was* an art, and made up, like all others, of concessions, eliminations and embellishments; of lights judiciously thrown and shadows skilfully softened. His wife knew exactly how to manage the lights, and he knew exactly to what training she owed her skill. He even tried to trace the source of his obligations, to discriminate between the influences which had combined to produce his domestic happiness: he perceived that Haskett's commonness had made Alice worship good breeding, while Varick's liberal construction of the marriage bond had taught her to value the conjugal virtues; so that he was directly indebted to his predecessors for the devotion which made his life easy if not inspiring.

From this phase he passed into that of complete acceptance. He ceased to satirise himself because time dulled the irony of the situation and the joke lost its humour with its sting. Even the sight of Haskett's hat on the hall table had ceased to touch the springs of epigram. The hat was often seen there now, for it had been decided that it was better for Lily's father to visit her than for the little girl to go to his boarding-house. Waythorn, having acquiesced in this arrangement, had been surprised to find how little difference it made. Haskett was never obtrusive, and the few visitors who met him on the stairs were unaware of his identity. Waythorn did not know how often he saw Alice, but with himself Haskett was seldom in contact.

One afternoon, however, he learned on entering that Lily's father was waiting to see him. In the library he found Haskett occupying a chair in his usual provisional way. Waythorn always felt grateful to him for not leaning back.

"I hope you'll excuse me, Mr. Waythorn," he said rising. "I wanted to see Mrs. Waythorn about Lily, and your man asked me to wait here till she came in."

"Of course," said Waythorn, remembering that a sudden leak had that morning given over the drawing-room to the plumbers.

He opened his cigar-case and held it out to his visitor, and Haskett's acceptance seemed to mark a fresh stage in their intercourse. The spring evening was chilly, and Waythorn invited his guest to draw up his chair to the fire. He meant to find an excuse to leave Haskett in a moment; but he was tired and cold, and after all the little man no longer jarred on him.

The two were enclosed in the intimacy of their blended cigar smoke when the door opened and Varick walked into the room. Waythorn rose abruptly. It was the first time that Varick had come to the house, and the surprise of seeing him, combined with the singular inopportuneness of his arrival, gave a new edge to Waythorn's blunted sensibilities. He stared at his visitor without speaking.

Varick seemed too preoccupied to notice his host's embarrassment.

"My dear fellow," he exclaimed in his most expansive tone, "I must apologize for tumbling in on you in this way, but I was too late to catch you down town, and so I thought—"

He stopped short, catching sight of Haskett, and his sanguine colour deepened to a flush which spread vividly under his scant blond hair. But in a moment he recovered himself and nodded slightly. Haskett returned the bow in silence, and Waythorn was still groping for speech when the footman came in carrying a tea-table.

The intrusion offered a welcome vent to Waythorn's nerves. "What the deuce are you bringing this here for?" he said sharply.

"I beg your pardon, sir, but the plumbers are still in the drawing-room, and Mrs. Waythorn said she would have tea in the library." The footman's perfectly respectful tone implied a reflection on Waythorn's reasonableness.

"Oh, very well," said the latter resignedly, and the footman proceeded to open the folding tea-table and set out its complicated appointments. While this interminable process continued the three men stood motionless, watching it with a fascinated stare, till Waythorn, to break the silence, said to Varick: "Won't you have a cigar?"

He held out the case he had just tendered to Haskett, and Varick helped himself with a smile. Waythorn looked about for a match, and finding none, proffered a light from his own cigar. Haskett, in the background, held his ground mildly, examining his cigar-tip now and then, and stepping forward at the right moment to knock its ashes into the fire.

The footman at last withdrew, and Varick immediately began: "If I could just say half a word to you about this business—"

"Certainly," stammered Waythorn; "in the dining-room—"

But as he placed his hand on the door it opened from without, and his wife appeared on the threshold.

She came in fresh and smiling, in her street dress and hat, shedding a fragrance from the boa which she loosened in advancing.

"Shall we have tea in here, dear?" she began; and then she caught sight of Varick. Her smile deepened, veiling a slight tremor of surprise.

"Why, how do you do?" she said with a distinct note of pleasure.

As she shook hands with Varick she saw Haskett standing behind him. Her smile faded for a moment, but she recalled it quickly, with a scarcely perceptible side-glance at Waythorn.

"How do you do, Mr. Haskett?" she said, and shook hands with him a shade less cordially.

The three men stood awkwardly before her, till Varick, always the most self-possessed, dashed into an explanatory phrase.

"We—I had to see Waythorn a moment on business," he stammered, brick-red from chin to nape.

Haskett stepped forward with his air of mild obstinacy. "I am sorry to intrude; but you appointed five o'clock—" he directed his resigned glance to the timepiece on the mantel.

She swept aside their embarrassment with a charming gesture of hospitality.

"I'm so sorry—I'm always late; but the afternoon was so lovely." She stood drawing off her gloves, propitiatory and graceful, diffusing about her a sense of ease and familiarity in which the situation lost its grotesqueness. "But before talking business," she added brightly, "I'm sure every one wants a cup of tea."

She dropped into her low chair by the tea-table, and the two visitors, as if drawn by her smile, advanced to receive the cups she held out.

She glanced about for Waythorn, and he took the third cup with a laugh.

1904

# W. E. B. DU BOIS

## 1868–1963

William Edward Burghardt Du Bois was born on February 23, 1868, in Great Barrington, Massachusetts. His childhood was happy, but with the approach of adolescence Du Bois discovered that what made him different from his schoolmates was not so much his superior academic achievement as his brown skin. Looking back on his rejection by a white girl in grade school, "it dawned on me with a certain suddenness," Du Bois wrote, "that I was . . . shut out from their world by a vast veil," a veil he claimed to have no desire to force his way behind. Du Bois's entire career, nonetheless, may be understood as an attempt to lift that veil all over the world so that all races might see each other in the clear light of historical fact.

Du Bois was educated at Fisk, Harvard, and the University of Berlin. His doctoral dissertation, *The Suppression of the African Slave Trade to the United States of America, 1638–1870*, was published as the first volume in the Harvard Historical Studies series. By the time Du Bois completed his graduate studies his accomplishments were already considerable, but he could not secure an appointment at a major university. He taught first instead at Wilberforce College in Ohio, then a small, poor, provincial black college. There he offered Greek, Latin, German, and English—subjects far removed from his real interest in the relatively new field of sociology.

After spending a year at the University of Pennsylvania, where he produced his first major work, *The Philadelphia Negro*, Du Bois moved to Atlanta University in 1897. There, over the next thirteen years, he produced a steady stream of important studies of African-American life. Dedicated to the rigorous, scholarly examination of the so-called Negro problem, Du Bois soon had to face up to the violent emotional realities of the lives he proposed to study. On his way to present an appeal for reason in the case of a black man accused of murder and rape, Du Bois was met by the news that a lynch mob had dismembered and burned the man at the stake and that "his knuckles were on exhibition at a grocery store." Though Du Bois never ceased being a scholar, from this time on he increasingly became an activist and sought a wider audience for his writings.

Du Bois first came to national attention with the publication of *The Souls of Black Folk* (1903). Several essay-chapters explore the implications of this extraordinary book's dramatic and prophetic announcement that "the problem of the Twentieth Century is the problem of the color line." The chapter that particularly caused a stir was the one that challenged—coolly and without rancor—the enormous authority and power that had accumulated in the hands of one black spokesman, Booker T. Washington. Washington had founded Tuskegee Institute in Alabama to train blacks in basic agricultural and mechanical skills and had gained national prominence with his Atlanta Exposition speech in 1895. His address in effect accepted disenfranchisement and segregation and settled for a low level of education in exchange for white "toleration" and economic cooperation. Although Du Bois had initially joined in the general approval of this "separate and unequal" philosophy, by the early 1900s he had begun to reject Washington's position, and with the publication of *Souls of Black Folk*, his defiance of Washington amounted to a declaration of war. The almost immediate result of the controversy was to reinforce Du Bois's emerging radicalism and to make him become a leader in the Niagara Movement, a movement aggressively devoted to demanding for black people the same civil rights enjoyed by white Americans.

In 1910 Du Bois left Atlanta for New York, where he served for the next quarter of a century as editor of *Crisis*, the official publication of the newly formed NAACP, an organization he helped to create. Through this publication Du Bois reached an increasingly large audience—100,000 by 1919—with powerful messages that argued the need for black development and white enlightenment.

Frustrated by the lack of fundamental change and progress in the condition of African-Americans, from 1920 on Du Bois increasingly shifted his attention away from the attempt to reform race relations in America through research and political legislation and toward the search for longer-range worldwide economic solutions to the international problems of inequity among the races. He began a steady movement toward Pan-African and socialist perspectives that led to his joining the Communist party of the United States in 1961 and, in the year of his death, becoming a citizen of Ghana. During these forty years he was extremely active as politician, organizer, and diplomat, and he also sustained his extraordinary productiveness as a powerful writer of poetry, fiction, autobiography, essays, and scholarly works. When, in his last major speech, Martin Luther King, Jr., spoke of Du Bois as "one of the most remarkable men of our time," he was uttering the verdict of history.

## From The Souls of Black Folk

### III. Of Mr. Booker T. Washington and Others[1]

*From birth till death enslaved; in word, in deed, unmanned!*

*Hereditary bondsmen! Know ye not*
*Who would be free themselves must strike the blow?*

                                —Byron

Easily the most striking thing in the history of the American Negro since 1876[3] is the ascendancy of Mr. Booker T. Washington. It began at the time when war memories and ideals were rapidly passing; a day of astonishing commercial development was dawning; a sense of doubt and hesitation overtook the freedmen's sons,—then it was that his leading began. Mr. Washington came, with a simple definite programme, at the psychological moment when the nation was a little ashamed of having bestowed so much sentiment on

1. *Of Mr. Booker T. Washington and Others* was first published in *Guardian*, July 27, 1902, and collected in *The Souls of Black Folk* (1903), which was otherwise a compilation of seven previously published and five unpublished essays. The source of the present text is the first book edition. Booker T. Washington (1856?–1915) founded and helped build with his own hands Tuskegee Institute, a black college in Alabama, and became a powerful leader of and spokesman for black Americans especially after his address at the Atlanta Exposition in 1895.
2. *Childe Harold's Pilgrimage*, Canto 11, 74.710,

76.720–21. The music is from the refrain of a black spiritual titled *A Great Camp-Meetin' in de Promised Land* (also called *There's a Great Camp Meeting* and *Walk Together Children*). The words of the refrain set to this music are

   Going to mourn and never tire—
   mourn and never tire, mourn and never tire.

3. Reconstruction effectively ended in 1876; federal troops were withdrawn from the South, and black political power was essentially destroyed.

Negroes, and was concentrating its energies on Dollars. His programme of industrial education, conciliation of the South, and submission and silence as to civil and political rights, was not wholly original; the Free Negroes from 1830 up to war-time had striven to build industrial schools, and the American Missionary Association had from the first taught various trades; and Price[4] and others had sought a way of honorable alliance with the best of the Southerners. But Mr. Washington first indissolubly linked these things; he put enthusiasm, unlimited energy, and perfect faith into this programme, and changed it from a by-path into a veritable Way of Life. And the tale of the methods by which he did this is a fascinating study of human life.

It startled the nation to hear a Negro advocating such a programme after many decades of bitter complaint; it startled and won the applause of the South, it interested and won the admiration of the North; and after a confused murmur of protest, it silenced if it did not convert the Negroes themselves.

To gain the sympathy and cooperation of the various elements comprising the white South was Mr. Washington's first task; and this, at the time Tuskegee was founded, seemed, for a black man, well-nigh impossible. And yet ten years later it was done in the word spoken at Atlanta: "In all things purely social we can be as separate as the five fingers, and yet one as the hand in all things essential to mutual progress." This "Atlanta Compromise"[5] is by all odds the most notable thing in Mr. Washington's career. The South interpreted it in different ways: the radicals received it as a complete surrender of the demand for civil and political equality; the conservatives, as a generously conceived working basis for mutual understanding. So both approved it, and to-day its author is certainly the most distinguished Southerner since Jefferson Davis, and the one with the largest personal following.

Next to this achievement comes Mr. Washington's work in gaining place and consideration in the North. Others less shrewd and tactful had formerly essayed to sit on these two stools and had fallen between them; but as Mr. Washington knew the heart of the South from birth and training, so by singular insight he intuitively grasped the spirit of the age which was dominating the North. And so thoroughly did he learn the speech and thought of triumphant commercialism, and the ideals of material prosperity, that the picture of a lone black boy poring over a French grammar amid the weeds and dirt of a neglected home soon seemed to him the acme of absurdities.[6] One wonders what Socrates and St. Francis of Assisi would say to this.

And yet this very singleness of vision and thorough oneness with his age is a mark of the successful man. It is as though Nature must needs make men narrow in order to give them force. So Mr. Washington's cult has gained unquestioning followers, his work has wonderfully prospered, his friends are legion, and his enemies are confounded. To-day he stands as the one recog-

4. Thomas Frederick Price (1860–1919), American editor, missionary, and Roman Catholic priest; one of the founders of the American Missionary Association.
5. In a speech at the Atlanta Exposition of 1895, Washington in effect traded political, civil, and social rights for blacks for the promise of vocational-training schools and jobs. His purpose was to reduce racial tension in the South while providing a stable black labor force whose skills would provide some hope for job security.
6. In Washington's extremely popular *Up from Slav-*

*ery: An Autobiography* (1901), chap. 8, "Teaching School in a Stable and a Hen-House," there is a passage on the absurdity of knowledge not practically useful:

In fact, one of the saddest things I saw during the month of travel which I have described was a young man, who had attended some high school, sitting down in a one-room cabin, with grease on his clothing, filth all around him, and weeds in the yard and garden, engaged in studying French grammar.

nized spokesman of his ten million fellows, and one of the most notable figures
in a nation of seventy millions. One hesitates, therefore, to criticise a life
which, beginning with so little, has done so much. And yet the time is come
when one may speak in all sincerity and utter courtesy of the mistakes and
shortcomings of Mr. Washington's career, as well as of his triumphs, without
being thought captious or envious, and without forgetting that it is easier to do
ill than well in the world.

The criticism that has hitherto met Mr. Washington has not always been of
this broad character. In the South especially has he had to walk warily to
avoid the harshest judgments,—and naturally so, for he is dealing with the
one subject of deepest sensitiveness to that section. Twice—once when at the
Chicago celebration of the Spanish-American War he alluded to the color-
prejudice that is "eating away the vitals of the South," and once when he
dined with President Roosevelt[7]—has the resulting Southern criticism been
violent enough to threaten seriously his popularity. In the North the feeling
has several times forced itself into words, that Mr. Washington's counsels of
submission overlooked certain elements of true manhood, and that his educational programme was unnecessarily narrow. Usually, however, such criticism
has not found open expression, although, too, the spiritual sons of the Abolitionists have not been prepared to acknowledge that the schools founded before
Tuskegee, by men of broad ideals and self-sacrificing spirit, were wholly failures or worthy of ridicule. While, then, criticism has not failed to follow Mr.
Washington, yet the prevailing public opinion of the land has been but too
willing to deliver the solution of a wearisome problem into his hands, and say,
"If that is all you and your race ask, take it."

Among his own people, however, Mr. Washington has encountered the
strongest and most lasting opposition, amounting at times to bitterness, and
even to-day continuing strong and insistent even though largely silenced in
outward expression by the public opinion of the nation. Some of this opposition is, of course, mere envy; the disappointment of displaced demagogues and
the spite of narrow minds. But aside from this, there is among educated and
thoughtful colored men in all parts of the land a feeling of deep regret, sorrow,
and apprehension at the wide currency and ascendancy which some of Mr.
Washington's theories have gained. These same men admire his sincerity of
purpose, and are willing to forgive much to honest endeavor which is doing
something worth the doing. They co;auoperate with Mr. Washington as far as
they conscientiously can; and, indeed, it is no ordinary tribute to this man's
tact and power that, steering as he must between so many diverse interests and
opinions, he so largely retains the respect of all.

But the hushing of the criticism of honest opponents is a dangerous thing.
It leads some of the best of the critics to unfortunate silence and paralysis of
effort, and others to burst into speech so passionately and intemperately as to
lose listeners. Honest and earnest criticism from those whose interests are most
nearly touched,—criticism of writers by readers, of government by those governed, of leaders by those led,—this is the soul of democracy and the safeguard
of modern society. If the best of the American Negroes receive by outer pressure a leader whom they had not recognized before, manifestly there is here a
certain palpable gain. Yet there is also irreparable loss,—a loss of that peculiarly valuable education which a group receives when by search and criticism

7. Theodore Roosevelt (1858–1919), twenty-sixth    dining with him in 1901 caused a storm of criticism
president of the United States (1901–9). Washington's    around the country.

it finds and commissions its own leaders. The way in which this is done is at once the most elementary and the nicest problem of social growth. History is but the record of such group-leadership; and yet how infinitely changeful is its type and character! And of all types and kinds, what can be more instructive than the leadership of a group within a group?—that curious double movement where real progress may be negative and actual advance be relative retrogression. All this is the social student's inspiration and despair.

Now in the past the American Negro has had instructive experience in the choosing of group leaders, founding thus a peculiar dynasty which in the light of present conditions is worth while studying. When sticks and stones and beasts form the sole environment of a people, their attitude is largely one of determined opposition to and conquest of natural forces. But when to earth and brute is added an environment of men and ideas, then the attitude of the imprisoned group may take three main forms,—a feeling of revolt and revenge; an attempt to adjust all thought and action to the will of the greater group; or, finally, a determined effort at self-realization and self-development despite environing opinion. The influence of all of these attitudes at various times can be traced in the history of the American Negro, and in the evolution of his successive leaders.

Before 1750, while the fire of African freedom still burned in the veins of the slaves, there was in all leadership or attempted leadership but the one motive of revolt and revenge,—typified in the terrible Maroons, the Danish blacks, and Cato of Stono,[8] and veiling all the Americas in fear of insurrection. The liberalizing tendencies of the latter half of the eighteenth century brought, along with kindlier relations between black and white, thoughts of ultimate adjustment and assimilation. Such aspiration was especially voiced in the earnest songs of Phyllis, in the martyrdom of Attucks, the fighting of Salem and Poor, the intellectual accomplishments of Banneker and Derham, and the political demands of the Cuffes.[9]

Stern financial and social stress after the war cooled much of the previous humanitarian ardor. The disappointment and impatience of the Negroes at the persistence of slavery and serfdom voiced itself in two movements. The slaves in the South, aroused undoubtedly by vague rumors of the Haytian revolt, made three fierce attempts at insurrection,—in 1800 under Gabriel in Virginia, in 1822 under Vesey in Carolina, and in 1831 again in Virginia under the terrible Nat Turner.[1] In the Free States, on the other hand, a new and curious attempt at self-development was made. In Philadelphia and New

8. The leader of the Stono, South Carolina, slave revolt of September 9, 1739, in which twenty-five whites were killed before the insurrection was put down. "Maroons": fugitive slaves from the West Indies and Guiana in the 17th and 18th centuries or their descendants. Many of the slaves in the Danish West Indies revolted in 1733 because of the lack of sufficient food.
9. Paul Cuffe (1759–1817) organized to resettle free blacks in African colonies. A champion of civil rights for free blacks in Massachusetts, he took thirty-eight blacks to Africa in 1815 at his own expense. Phyllis (or Phillis) Wheatley (c. 1753–1784), black slave and poet. Crispus Attucks (c. 1723–1770), the leader of the Boston Massacre against British troops, was killed in the massacre. Peter Salem (d. 1816), black patriot who killed Major Pitcairn in the battle of Bunker Hill. Salem Poor (1747–?), a black soldier who fought at Bunker Hill, Valley Forge, and White Plains. Benjamin

Banneker (1731–1806), a black mathematician who also studied astronomy. James Derham (1762–?), the first recognized black physician in America; born a slave, he learned medicine from his physician master, bought his freedom in 1783, and by 1788 was one of the foremost physicians of New Orleans.
1. A slave (1800–1831), he led the Southampton insurrection in 1831, during which sixty-one whites and more than a hundred slaves were killed or executed. Gabriel (1775?–1800) conspired to attack Richmond, Virginia, with a thousand other slaves on August 30, 1800, but a storm forced a suspension of the mission and two slaves betrayed the conspiracy. On October 7, Gabriel and fifteen others were hanged. Denmark Vesey (c. 1767–1822), a mulatto rebel, purchased his freedom in 1800; he led an unsuccessful uprising in 1822 and was hanged.

York color-prescription led to a withdrawal of Negro communicants from white churches and the formation of a peculiar socio-religious institution among the Negroes known as the African Church,—an organization still living and controlling in its various branches over a million of men.

Walker's wild appeal[2] against the trend of the times showed how the world was changing after the coming of the cotton-gin. By 1830 slavery seemed hopelessly fastened on the South, and the slaves thoroughly cowed into submission. The free Negroes of the North, inspired by the mulatto immigrants from the West Indies, began to change the basis of their demands; they recognized the slavery of slaves, but insisted that they themselves were freemen, and sought assimilation and amalgamation with the nation on the same terms with other men. Thus, Forten and Purvis of Philadelphia, Shad of Wilmington, Du Bois of New Haven, Barbadoes[3] of Boston, and others, strove singly and together as men, they said, not as slaves; as "people of color," not as "Negroes." The trend of the times, however, refused them recognition save in individual and exceptional cases, considered them as one with all the despised blacks, and they soon found themselves striving to keep even the rights they formerly had of voting and working and moving as freemen. Schemes of migration and colonization arose among them; but these they refused to entertain, and they eventually turned to the Abolition movement as a final refuge.

Here, led by Remond, Nell, Wells-Brown, and Douglass,[4] a new period of self-assertion and self-development dawned. To be sure, ultimate freedom and assimilation was the ideal before the leaders, but the assertion of the manhood rights of the Negro by himself was the main reliance, and John Brown's raid was the extreme of its logic. After the war and emancipation, the great form of Frederick Douglass, the greatest of American Negro leaders, still led the host. Self-assertion, especially in political lines, was the main programme, and behind Douglass came Elliot, Bruce, and Langston, and the Reconstruction politicians, and, less conspicuous but of greater social significance Alexander Crummell and Bishop Daniel Payne.[5]

Then came the Revolution of 1876, the suppression of the Negro votes, the changing and shifting of ideals, and the seeking of new lights in the great night. Douglass, in his old age, still bravely stood for the ideals of his early manhood,—ultimate assimilation *through* self-assertion, and on no other

2. The "wild appeal" was a militant, inflammatory, eloquent antislavery pamphlet by David Walker (1785–1830), black leader.
3. James G. Barbadoes was one of those present at the first National Negro Convention along with Forten, Purvis, Shadd, and others. James Forten (1766–1842), black civic leader and philanthropist. Robert Purvis (1810–1898), abolitionist, helped found the American Anti-Slavery Society in 1833 and was the president of the Underground Railway. Abraham Shadd, abolitionist, was on the first board of managers of the American Anti-Slavery Society, a delegate from Delaware for the first National Negro Convention (1830), and president of the third one in 1833. Alexander Du Bois (1803–1887), paternal grandfather of W. E. B. Du Bois, helped form the Negro Episcopal Parish of St. Luke in 1847 and was the senior warden there.
4. Frederick Douglass (1817–1895), abolitionist and orator and born a slave, was U.S. minister to Haiti and U.S. marshal of the District of Columbia. Charles Lenox Remond (1810–1873), black leader. William

Cooper Nell (1816–1874), abolitionist, writer, and first African-American to hold office under the government of the United States (clerk in the post office). Through his efforts equal school privileges were obtained for black children in Boston. William Wells Brown (1816?–1884), black writer, published *Clotel* in 1853, the first novel by a black American, and *The Escape* in 1858, the first play by a black American.
5. Daniel Alexander Payne (1811–1893), bishop of the African Methodist Episcopal church and president of Wilberforce University (1863–76). Robert Brown Elliot (1842–84), black politician, graduate of Eton, South Carolina congressman in the U.S. House of Representatives. Blanche K. Bruce (1841–1898), born a slave, first black man to serve a full term in the U.S. Senate (1875–81). John Mercer Langston (1829–1897), congressman, lawyer, diplomat, educator, born a slave. Crummell (1819–1898), clergyman of the Protestant Episcopal church, missionary in Liberia for twenty years and then in Washington, D.C.

terms. For a time Price arose as a new leader, destined, it seemed, not to give up, but to re-state the old ideals in a form less repugnant to the white South. But he passed away in his prime. Then came the new leader. Nearly all the former ones had become leaders by the silent suffrage of their fellows, had sought to lead their own people alone, and were usually, save Douglass, little known outside their race. But Booker T. Washington arose as essentially the leader not of one race but of two,—a compromiser between the South, the North, and the Negro. Naturally the Negroes resented, at first bitterly, signs of compromise which surrendered their civil and political rights, even though this was to be exchanged for larger chances of economic development. The rich and dominating North, however, was not only weary of the race problem, but was investing largely in Southern enterprises, and welcomed any method of peaceful coöperation. Thus, by national opinion, the Negroes began to recognize Mr. Washington's leadership; and the voice of criticism was hushed.

Mr. Washington represents in Negro thought the old attitude of adjustment and submission; but adjustment at such a peculiar time as to make his programme unique. This is an age of unusual economic development, and Mr. Washington's programme naturally takes an economic cast, becoming a gospel of Work and Money to such an extent as apparently almost completely to overshadow the higher aims of life. Moreover, this is an age when the more advanced races are coming in closer contact with the less developed races, and the race-feeling is therefore intensified; and Mr. Washington's programme practically accepts the alleged inferiority of the Negro races. Again, in our own land, the reaction from the sentiment of war time has given impetus to race-prejudice against Negroes, and Mr. Washington withdraws many of the high demands of Negroes as men and American citizens. In other periods of intensified prejudice all the Negro's tendency to self-assertion has been called forth; at this period a policy of submission is advocated. In the history of nearly all other races and peoples the doctrine preached at such crises has been that manly self-respect is worth more than lands and houses, and that a people who voluntarily surrender such respect, or cease striving for it, are not worth civilizing.

In answer to this, it has been claimed that the Negro can survive only through submission. Mr. Washington distinctly asks that black people give up, at least for the present, three things,—

First, political power,

Second, insistence on civil rights,

Third, higher education of Negro youth,—

and concentrate all their energies on industrial education, the accumulation of wealth, and the conciliation of the South. This policy has been courageously and insistently advocated for over fifteen years, and has been triumphant for perhaps ten years. As a result of this tender of the palm-branch, what has been the return? In these years there have occurred:

1. The disfranchisement of the Negro.

2. The legal creation of a distinct status of civil inferiority for the Negro.

3. The steady withdrawal of aid from institutions for the higher training of the Negro.

These movements are not, to be sure, direct results of Mr. Washington's teachings; but his propaganda has, without a shadow of doubt, helped their speedier accomplishment. The question then comes: Is it possible, and prob-

able, that nine millions of men can make effective progress in economic lines
if they are deprived of political rights, made a servile caste, and allowed only
the most meagre chance for developing their exceptional men? If history and
reason give any distinct answer to these questions, it is an emphatic No. And
Mr. Washington thus faces the triple paradox of his career:

1. He is striving nobly to make Negro artisans business men and property-
owners; but it is utterly impossible, under modern competitive methods, for
workingmen and property-owners to defend their rights and exist without the
right of suffrage.

2. He insists on thrift and self-respect, but at the same time counsels a silent
submission to civic inferiority such as is bound to sap the manhood of any race
in the long run.

3. He advocates common-school[6] and industrial training, and depreciates
institutions of higher learning; but neither the Negro common-schools, nor
Tuskegee itself, could remain open a day were it not for teachers trained in
Negro colleges, or trained by their graduates.

This triple paradox in Mr. Washington's position is the object of criticism
by two classes of colored Americans. One class is spiritually descended from
Toussaint the Savior,[7] through Gabriel, Vesey, and Turner, and they represent the attitude of revolt and revenge; they hate the white South blindly and
distrust the white race generally, and so far as they agree on definite action,
think that the Negro's only hope lies in emigration beyond the borders of the
United States. And yet, by the irony of fate, nothing has more effectually
made this programme seem hopeless than the recent course of the United
States toward weaker and darker peoples in the West Indies, Hawaii, and the
Philippines,—for where in the world may we go and be safe from lying and
brute force?

The other class of Negroes who cannot agree with Mr. Washington has
hitherto said little aloud. They deprecate the sight of scattered counsels, of
internal disagreement; and especially they dislike making their just criticism of
a useful and earnest man an excuse for a general discharge of venom from
small-minded opponents. Nevertheless, the questions involved are so fundamental and serious that it is difficult to see how men like the Grimkes, Kelly
Miller, J. W. E. Bowen,[8] and other representatives of this group, can much
longer be silent. Such men feel in conscience bound to ask of this nation
three things:

1. The right to vote.
2. Civic equality.
3. The education of youth according to ability.

They acknowledge Mr. Washington's invaluable service in counselling
patience and courtesy in such demands; they do not ask that ignorant black
men vote when ignorant whites are debarred, or that any reasonable restrictions in the suffrage should not be applied; they know that the low social level
of the mass of the race is responsible for much discrimination against it, but

---

6. A free public school offering courses at precollege
level.
7. Pierre Dominique Toussaint (1743–1803), later
called L'Ouverture, black Haitian leader of the slave
insurrection that led eventually to Haitian independence even though Toussaint died in France as a result
of Napoleon's treachery.

8. John Wesley Edward Bowen (1855–?), Methodist
clergyman and educator, president of Gammon Theological Seminary of Atlanta. Archibald Grimké (1849–
1930) and Francis Grimké (1850–1937), American
civic leaders concerned with African-American affairs.
Miller (1863–1939), dean of Howard University, lectured on the race problem.

they also know, and the nation knows, that relentless color-prejudice is more often a cause than a result of the Negro's degradation; they seek the abatement of this relic of barbarism, and not its systematic encouragement and pampering by all agencies of social power from the Associated Press to the Church of Christ. They advocate, with Mr. Washington, a broad system of Negro common schools supplemented by thorough industrial training; but they are surprised that a man of Mr. Washington's insight cannot see that no such educational system ever has rested or can rest on any other basis than that of the well-equipped college and university, and they insist that there is a demand for a few such institutions throughout the South to train the best of the Negro youth as teachers, professional men, and leaders.

This group of men honor Mr. Washington for his attitude of conciliation toward the white South; they accept the "Atlanta Compromise" in its broadest interpretation; they recognize, with him, many signs of promise, many men of high purpose and fair judgment, in this section; they know that no easy task has been laid upon a region already tottering under heavy burdens. But, nevertheless, they insist that the way to truth and right lies in straightforward honesty, not in indiscriminate flattery; in praising those of the South who do well and criticising uncompromisingly those who do ill; in taking advantage of the opportunities at hand and urging their fellows to do the same, but at the same time in remembering that only a firm adherence to their higher ideals and aspirations will ever keep those ideals within the realm of possibility. They do not expect that the free right to vote, to enjoy civic rights, and to be educated, will come in a moment; they do not expect to see the bias and prejudices of years disappear at the blast of a trumpet; but they are absolutely certain that the way for a people to gain their reasonable rights is not by voluntarily throwing them away and insisting that they do not want them; that the way for a people to gain respect is not by continually belittling and ridiculing themselves; that, on the contrary, Negroes must insist continually, in season and out of season, that voting is necessary to modern manhood, that color discrimination is barbarism, and that black boys need education as well as white boys.

In failing thus to state plainly and unequivocally the legitimate demands of their people, even at the cost of opposing an honored leader, the thinking classes of American Negroes would shirk a heavy responsibility,—a responsibility to themselves, a responsibility to the struggling masses, a responsibility to the darker races of men whose future depends so largely on this American experiment, but especially a responsibility to this nation,—this common Fatherland. It is wrong to encourage a man or a people in evil-doing; it is wrong to aid and abet a national crime simply because it is unpopular not to do so. The growing spirit of kindliness and reconciliation between the North and South after the frightful differences of a generation ago ought to be a source of deep congratulation to all, and especially to those whose mistreatment caused the war; but if that reconciliation is to be marked by the industrial slavery and civic death of those same black men, with permanent legislation into a position of inferiority, then those black men, if they are really men, are called upon by every consideration of patriotism and loyalty to oppose such a course by all civilized methods, even though such opposition involves disagreement with Mr. Booker T. Washington. We have no right to sit silently by while the inevitable seeds are sown for a harvest of disaster to our children, black and white.

First, it is the duty of black men to judge the South discriminatingly. The present generation of Southerners are not responsible for the past, and they should not be blindly hated or blamed for it. Furthermore, to no class is the indiscriminate endorsement of the recent course of the South toward Negroes more nauseating than to the best thought of the South. The South is not "solid"; it is a land in the ferment of social change, wherein forces of all kinds are fighting for supremacy; and to praise the ill the South is to-day perpetrating is just as wrong as to condemn the good. Discriminating and broad-minded criticism is what the South needs,—needs it for the sake of her own white sons and daughters, and for the insurance of robust, healthy mental and moral development.

To-day even the attitude of the Southern whites toward the blacks is not, as so many assume, in all cases the same; the ignorant Southerner hates the Negro, the workingmen fear his competition, the money-makers wish to use him as a laborer, some of the educated see a menace in his upward development, while others—usually the sons of the masters—wish to help him to rise. National opinion has enabled this last class to maintain the Negro common schools, and to protect the Negro partially in property, life, and limb. Through the pressure of the money-makers, the Negro is in danger of being reduced to semi-slavery, especially in the country districts; the workingmen, and those of the educated who fear the Negro, have united to disfranchise him, and some have urged his deportation; while the passions of the ignorant are easily aroused to lynch and abuse any black man. To praise this intricate whirl of thought and prejudice is nonsense; to inveigh indiscriminately against "the South" is unjust; but to use the same breath in praising Governor Aycock, exposing Senator Morgan, arguing with Mr. Thomas Nelson Page, and denouncing Senator Ben Tillman,[9] is not only sane, but the imperative duty of thinking black men.

It would be unjust to Mr. Washington not to acknowledge that in several instances he has opposed movements in the South which were unjust to the Negro; he sent memorials to the Louisiana and Alabama constitutional conventions, he has spoken against lynching, and in other ways has openly or silently set his influence against sinister schemes and unfortunate happenings. Notwithstanding this, it is equally true to assert that on the whole the distinct impression left by Mr. Washington's propaganda is, first, that the South is justified in its present attitude toward the Negro because of the Negro's degradation; secondly, that the prime cause of the Negro's failure to rise more quickly is his wrong education in the past; and, thirdly, that his future rise depends primarily on his own efforts. Each of these propositions is a dangerous half-truth. The supplementary truths must never be lost sight of: first, slavery and race-prejudice are potent if not sufficient causes of the Negro's position; second, industrial and common-school training were necessarily slow in planting because they had to await the black teachers trained by higher institu-

9. Benjamin Ryan Tillman (1847–1918), governor of South Carolina (1890–94) and U.S. Senator (1895–1918), served as the chairman on the committee on suffrage (during the South Carolina constitutional convention) and framed the article providing for an educational and property qualification for voting, thus eliminating the black vote. He presenred the views of the southern extremists on the race question, justified lynching in cases of rape and the repeal of the Fifteenth Amendment. Charles Brantly Aycock (1859–1912), governor of North Carolina (1901–5). Edwin Denison Morgan (1811–1883), governor of New York (1859–63) and U.S. Senator (1863–69), voted with the minority in President Johnson's veto of the Freedman's Bureau bill and for Johnson's conviction. Page (1853–1922), American novelist and diplomat, did much to build up romantic legends of the southern plantation.

tions,—it being extremely doubtful if any essentially different development was possible, and certainly a Tuskegee was unthinkable before 1880; and, third, while it is a great truth to say that the Negro must strive and strive mightily to help himself, it is equally true that unless his striving be not simply seconded, but rather aroused and encouraged, by the initiative of the richer and wiser environing group, he cannot hope for great success.

In his failure to realize and impress this last point, Mr. Washington is especially to be criticised. His doctrine has tended to make the whites, North and South, shift the burden of the Negro problem to the Negro's shoulders and stand aside as critical and rather pessimistic spectators; when in fact the burden belongs to the nation, and the hands of none of us are clean if we bend not our energies to righting these great wrongs.

The South ought to be led, by candid and honest criticism, to assert her better self and do her full duty to the race she has cruelly wronged and is still wronging. The North—her co-partner in guilt—cannot salve her conscience by plastering it with gold. We cannot settle this problem by diplomacy and suaveness, by "policy" alone. If worse come to worst, can the moral fibre of this country survive the slow throttling and murder of nine millions of men?

The black men of America have a duty to perform, a duty stern and delicate,—a forward movement to oppose a part of the work of their greatest leader. So far as Mr. Washington preaches Thrift, Patience, and Industrial Training for the masses, we must hold up his hands and strive with him, rejoicing in his honors and glorying in the strength of this Joshua called of God and of man to lead the headless host. But so far as Mr. Washington apologizes for injustice, North or South, does not rightly value the privilege and duty of voting, belittles the emasculating effects of caste distinctions, and opposes the higher training and ambition of our brighter minds,—so far as he, the South, or the Nation, does this,—we must unceasingly and firmly oppose them. By every civilized and peaceful method we must strive for the rights which the world accords to men, clinging unwaveringly to those great words which the sons of the Fathers would fain forget: "We hold these truths to be self-evident: That all men are created equal; that they are endowed by their Creator with certain unalienable rights; that among these are life, liberty, and the pursuit of happiness."

1902                                                                    1903

---

# STEPHEN CRANE
## 1871–1900

Stephen Crane was born November 1, 1871, and died on June 5, 1900. By the age of twenty-eight he had published enough material to fill a dozen volumes of a collected edition and had lived a legendary life that has grown in complexity and interest to scholars and readers the more the facts have come to light. His family settled in America in the mid-seventeenth century. He himself was the son of a Methodist minister, but he systematically rejected religious and social traditions, indentified with the urban poor, and "married" the mistress of one "of the better houses of ill-fame" in Jacksonville, Florida. Although he was temperamentally a gentle man, Crane was attracted to—even obsessed by—war and other forms of physical and psychic violence. He frequently lived the down-and-out life of a penniless artist; he was also ambitious and something of a snob; he was a poet and an impressionist: a journalist, a social critic, and a realist. In short, there is much about Crane's life and writing that is paradoxical; he is an original and not easy to be right about.

Crane once explained to an editor: "After all, I cannot help vanishing and disappearing and dissolving. It is my foremost trait." This distinctively restless, peripatetic quality of Crane's life began early. The last of fourteen children, Crane moved with his family at least three times before he entered school at age seven in the small town of Port Jervis, New York. His father died in 1880, and after a tentative return to Paterson the family settled in the coastal resort town of Asbury Park, New Jersey, three years later. The next five years, as his biographer and critic Edwin H. Cady has observed, "confirmed in the sensitive, vulnerable, fatherless preacher's kid his fate as isolato." Crane never took to schooling. At Syracuse University he distinguished himself as a baseball player but was unable to accept the routine of academic life and after one semester left with no intention of returning. He was not sure what he would do with himself, but by 1891 he had begun to write for newspapers, and he hungered for immersion in life of the kind that his early journalistic assignments caused him to witness at close hand.

New York City was the inevitable destination for a young man with literary ambitions and a desire to experience the fullness of life. A couple of jobs with New York newspapers proved abortive, and Crane spent much of the next two years shuttling between the seedy apartments of his artist friends and his brother Edmund's house in nearby Lake View, New Jersey. In these years of extreme privation, Crane developed his powers as an observer of psychological and social reality; an early example of these powers may be seen in *An Experiment in Misery*, written in 1893. Crane was encouraged by the realist credo of Hamlin Garland, whom he had heard lecture in 1891. Crane wrote and then—after it had been rejected by several New York editors—published in 1893, at his own expense, a work he had begun while at Syracuse: *Maggie, A Girl of the Streets.* Although Garland admired the short novel and the powerful literary arbiter W. D. Howells promoted Crane and his book (and continued to think it his best work), the book did not sell. The mass audience of the time sought from literature what *Maggie* denied: escape, distraction, and easy pleasure in romances that falsified and obscured the social, emotional, and moral nature of life.

Just why Crane turned next to the Civil War as a subject for *The Red Badge of Courage* is not clear. He may have wished to appeal to a popular audience and make some money; he later described the book as a "pot-boiler." Or he may have been compelled by a half-recognized need to test himself imaginatively by placing his young protagonist-counterpart in a psychological and philosophical pressure cooker. In any case, in 1893 Crane began his best-known work, *The Red Badge of Courage: An Episode of the American Civil War.* The narrative, which depicts the education of a young man in the context of struggle, is as old as Homer's *Odyssey* and is a dominant story-type in American literature from Benjamin Franklin through Melville, Hemingway, Malcolm X, and Saul Bellow. Crane was not so much working within or against this tradition as he was departing sharply from it. That is, Crane is distinctively modern in conceiving personal identity as complex and ambiguous and in obliging his readers to judge for themselves the adequacy of Henry's responses to his experiences.

When *Red Badge* was first published as a syndicated newspaper story in December 1894, Crane's fortunes began to improve. The same syndicate that took *Red Badge* hired him early in 1895 as a roving reporter in the American West and Mexico, an experience that would give him the material for several of his finest tales—*The Bride Comes to Yellow Sky* and *The Blue Hotel* among them. Early in 1895 an established New York publisher agreed to issue *Red Badge* in book form. In the spring of that year, *The Black Riders and Other Lines*, his first volume of poetry, was published. Predictably, Garland and Howells responded intelligently to Crane's spare, original, unflinchingly honest poetry, but it was too experimental in form and too unconventional in philosophic outlook to win wide acceptance. *The Red Badge of Courage* appeared in the fall as a book and became the first widely successful American work to be realistic in the modern way. It won Crane international acclaim at the age of twenty-four.

In all of his poetry, journalism, and fiction Crane clearly demonstrated his religious, social, and literary rebelliousness; his alienated, unconventional stance also led him to direct action. After challenging the New York police force on behalf of a prostitute who claimed harassment at its hands, Crane left the city in the winter of 1896–97 to cover the insurrection against Spain in Cuba. On his way to Cuba he met Cora Howorth Taylor, the proprietor of the aptly named Hotel de Dream in Jacksonville, Florida, with whom he lived for the last three years of his life. On January 2, 1897, Crane's ship *The Commodore* sank off the coast of Florida. His report of this harrowing adventure was published a few days later in the *New York Press*. He promptly converted this event into *The Open Boat*. This story, like *Red Badge*, reveals Crane's characteristic subject matter—the physical, emotional, and intellectual responses of people under extreme pressure—and the dominant themes of nature's indifference to humanity's fate and the consequent need for compassionate collective action. These are not Crane's only themes, however, and it is well to remember that in stories like *An Episode of War* no cheerful moral can be drawn. In the late stories *The Open Boat* and *The Blue Hotel*, Crane achieved his mature style. In both of these works we can observe his tough-minded irony and his essential vision: a sympathetic but unflinching demand for courage, integrity, grace, and generosity in the face of a universe in which human beings, to quote from *The Blue Hotel*, are so many lice clinging "to a whirling, fire-smote, ice-locked, disease-stricken, space-lost bulb."

In the summer of 1897 Crane covered the Greco-Turkish War and later that year settled in England, where he made friends with the English writers Joseph Conrad, H. G. Wells, and Ford Maddox Hueffer (later Ford) and the American writers Henry James and Harold Frederic. The following year he covered the Spanish-American War for Joseph Pulitzer's *New York World*. When he wrote *The Red Badge of Courage*, he had never observed battle at firsthand, but his experiences during the Greco-Turkish and Spanish-American wars confirmed his sense that he had recorded, with more than literal accuracy, the realities of battle.

In the last months of his life Crane's situation became desperate; he was suffering from tuberculosis and was hopelessly in debt. He wrote furiously in a doomed attempt to earn money, but the effort only worsened his health. In 1899 he drafted thirteen stories set in the fictional town Whilomville for *Harper's* magazine and published his second volume of poetry, *War Is Kind*, the weak novel *Active Service*, and the American edition of *The Monster and Other Stories*. During a Christmas party that year Crane nearly died of a lung hemorrhage. Surviving only a few months, he somehow summoned the strength to write a series of nine articles on great battles and complete the first twenty-five chapters of the novel *The O'Ruddy*. In spite of Cora's hopes for a miraculous cure and the generous assistance of Henry James and others, Crane died, at Badenweiler, Germany, on June 5, 1900.

# The Open Boat[1]

A TALE INTENDED TO BE AFTER THE FACT, BEING THE EXPERIENCE OF
FOUR MEN FROM THE SUNK STEAMER COMMODORE

## I

None of them knew the color of the sky. Their eyes glanced level, and were fastened upon the waves that swept toward them. These waves were of the hue of slate, save for the tops, which were of foaming white, and all of the men knew the colors of the sea. The horizon narrowed and widened, and dipped and rose, and at all times its edge was jagged with waves that seemed thrust up in points like rocks.

Many a man ought to have a bath-tub larger than the boat which here rode upon the sea. These waves were most wrongfully and barbarously abrupt and tall, and each froth-top was a problem in small boat navigation.

The cook squatted in the bottom and looked with both eyes at the six inches of gunwale which separated him from the ocean. His sleeves were rolled over his fat forearms, and the two flaps of his unbuttoned vest dangled as he bent to bail out the boat. Often he said: "Gawd! That was a narrow clip." As he remarked it he invariably gazed eastward over the broken sea.

The oiler,[2] steering with one of the two oars in the boat, sometimes raised himself suddenly to keep clear of water that swirled in over the stern. It was a thin little oar and it seemed often ready to snap.

The correspondent, pulling at the other oar, watched the waves and wondered why he was there.

The injured captain, lying in the bow, was at this time buried in that profound dejection and indifference which comes, temporarily at least, to even the bravest and most enduring when, willy nilly, the firm fails, the army loses, the ship goes down. The mind of the master of a vessel is rooted deep in the timbers of her, though he command for a day or a decade, and this captain had on him the stern impression of a scene in the grays of dawn of seven turned faces, and later a stump of a top-mast with a white ball on it that slashed to and fro at the waves, went low and lower, and down. Thereafter there was something strange in his voice. Although steady, it was deep with mourning, and of a quality beyond oration or tears.

"Keep'er a little more south, Billie," said he.

" 'A little more south,' sir," said the oiler in the stern.

A seat in his boat was not unlike a seat upon a bucking broncho, and, by the same token, a broncho is not much smaller. The craft pranced and reared, and plunged like an animal. As each wave came, and she rose for it, she seemed like a horse making at a fence outrageously high. The manner of her scramble over these walls of water is a mystic thing, and, moreover, at the top of them were ordinarily these problems in white water, the foam racing down

1. Crane sailed as a correspondent on the steamer *Commodore*, which on January 1, 1897, left Jacksonville, Florida, with munitions for the Cuban insurrectionists. Early on the morning of January 2, the steamer sank. With three others, Crane reached Daytona Beach in a ten-foot dinghy on the following morning. Under the title "Stephen Crane's Own Story," the *New York Press* on January 7 carried the details of his nearly fatal experience. In June 1897, he published his fictional account, *The Open Boat*, in *Scribner's Magazine*. The story gave the title to *The Open Boat and Other Tales of Adventure* (1898). The present text reprints that established for the University of Virginia edition of *The Works of Stephen Crane*, Vol. 5, *Tales of Adventure* (1970).

2. One who oils machinery in the engine room of a ship.

from the summit of each wave, requiring a new leap, and a leap from the air. Then, after scornfully bumping a crest, she would slide, and race, and splash down a long incline and arrive bobbing and nodding in front of the next menace.

A singular disadvantage of the sea lies in the fact that after successfully surmounting one wave you discover that there is another behind it just as important and just as nervously anxious to do something effective in the way of swamping boats. In a ten-foot dingey one can get an idea of the resources of the sea in the line of waves that is not probable to the average experience, which is never at sea in a dingey. As each slaty wall of water approached, it shut all else from the view of the men in the boat, and it was not difficult to imagine that this particular wave was the final outburst of the ocean, the last effort of the grim water. There was a terrible grace in the move of the waves, and they came in silence, save for the snarling of the crests.

In the wan light, the faces of the men must have been gray. Their eyes must have glinted in strange ways as they gazed steadily astern. Viewed from a balcony, the whole thing would doubtlessly have been weirdly picturesque. But the men in the boat had no time to see it, and if they had had leisure there were other things to occupy their minds. The sun swung steadily up the sky, and they knew it was broad day because the color of the sea changed from slate to emerald-green, streaked with amber lights, and the foam was like tumbling snow. The process of the breaking day was unknown to them. They were aware only of this effect upon the color of the waves that rolled toward them.

In disjointed sentences the cook and the correspondent argued as to the difference between a life-saving station and a house of refuge. The cook had said: "There's a house of refuge just north of the Mosquito Inlet Light, and as soon as they see us, they'll come off in their boat and pick us up."

"As soon as who see us?" said the correspondent.

"The crew," said the cook.

"Houses of refuge don't have crews," said the correspondent. "As I understand them, they are only places where clothes and grub are stored for the benefit of shipwrecked people. They don't carry crews."

"Oh, yes, they do," said the cook.

"No, they don't," said the correspondent.

"Well, we're not there yet, anyhow," said the oiler, in the stern.

"Well," said the cook, "perhaps it's not a house of refuge that I'm thinking of as being near Mosquito Inlet Light. Perhaps it's a life-saving station."

"We're not there yet," said the oiler, in the stern.

## II

As the boat bounced from the top of each wave, the wind tore through the hair of the hatless men, and as the craft plopped her stern down again the spray slashed past them. The crest of each of these waves was a hill, from the top of which the men surveyed, for a moment, a broad tumultuous expanse, shining and wind-riven. It was probably splendid. It was probably glorious, this play of the free sea, wild with lights of emerald and white and amber.

"Bully good thing it's an on-shore wind," said the cook. "If not, where would we be? Wouldn't have a show."

"That's right," said the correspondent.

The busy oiler nodded his assent.

Then the captain, in the bow, chuckled in a way that expressed humor, contempt, tragedy, all in one. "Do you think we've got much of a show, now, boys?" said he.

Whereupon the three were silent, save for a trifle of hemming and hawing. To express any particular optimism at this time they felt to be childish and stupid, but they all doubtless possessed this sense of the situation in their mind. A young man thinks doggedly at such times. On the other hand, the ethics of their condition was decidedly against any open suggestion of hopelessness. So they were silent.

"Oh, well," said the captain, soothing his children, "we'll get ashore all right."

But there was that in his tone which made them think, so the oiler quoth: "Yes! If this wind holds!"

The cook was bailing. "Yes! If we don't catch hell in the surf."

Canton flannel[3] gulls flew near and far. Sometimes they sat down on the sea, near patches of brown sea-weed that rolled over the waves with a movement like carpets on a line in a gale. The birds sat comfortably in groups, and they were envied by some in the dingey, for the wrath of the sea was no more to them than it was to a covey of prairie chickens a thousand miles inland. Often they came very close and stared at the men with black bead-like eyes. At these times they were uncanny and sinister in their unblinking scrutiny, and the men hooted angrily at them, telling them to be gone. One came, and evidently decided to alight on the top of the captain's head. The bird flew parallel to the boat and did not circle, but made short sidelong jumps in the air in chicken-fashion. His black eyes were wistfully fixed upon the captain's head. "Ugly brute," said the oiler to the bird. "You look as if you were made with a jack-knife." The cook and the correspondent swore darkly at the creature. The captain naturally wished to knock it away with the end of the heavy painter, but he did not dare do it, because anything resembling an emphatic gesture would have capsized this freighted boat, and so with his open hand, the captain gently and carefully waved the gull away. After it had been discouraged from the pursuit the captain breathed easier on account of his hair, and others breathed easier because the bird struck their minds at this time as being somehow grewsome and ominous.

In the meantime the oiler and the correspondent rowed. And also they rowed.

They sat together in the same seat, and each rowed an oar. Then the oiler took both oars; then the correspondent took both oars; then the oiler; then the correspondent. They rowed and they rowed. The very ticklish part of the business was when the time came for the reclining one in the stern to take his turn at the oars. By the very last star of truth, it is easier to steal eggs from under a hen than it was to change seats in the dingey. First the man in the stern slid his hand along the thwart and moved with care, as if he were of Sèvres.[4] Then the man in the rowing seat slid his hand along the other thwart. It was all done with the most extraordinary care. As the two sidled past each other, the whole party kept watchful eyes on the coming wave, and the captain cried: "Look out now! Steady there!"

The brown mats of sea-weed that appeared from time to time were like

---

3. Stout cotton fabric.                    4. Fine, often ornately decorated, French porcelain.

islands, bits of earth. They were travelling, apparently, neither one way nor the other. They were, to all intents, stationary. They informed the men in the boat that it was making progress slowly toward the land.

The captain, rearing cautiously in the bow, after the dingey soared on a great swell, said that he had seen the light-house at Mosquito Inlet. Presently the cook remarked that he had seen it. The correspondent was at the oars, then, and for some reason he too wished to look at the light-house, but his back was toward the far shore and the waves were important, and for some time he could not seize an opportunity to turn his head. But at last there came a wave more gentle than the others, and when at the crest of it he swiftly scoured the western horizon.

"See it?" said the captain.

"No," said the correspondent, slowly, "I didn't see anything."

"Look again," said the captain. He pointed. "It's exactly in that direction."

At the top of another wave, the correspondent did as he was bid, and this time his eyes chanced on a small still thing on the edge of the swaying horizon. It was precisely like the point of a pin. It took an anxious eye to find a light-house so tiny.

"Think we'll make it, Captain?"

"If this wind holds and the boat don't swamp, we can't do much else," said the captain.

The little boat, lifted by each towering sea, and splashed viciously by the crests, made progress that in the absence of sea-weed was not apparent to those in her. She seemed just a wee thing wallowing, miraculously, top-up, at the mercy of five oceans. Occasionally, a great spread of water, like white flames, swarmed into her.

"Bail her, cook," said the captain, serenely.

"All right, Captain," said the cheerful cook.

### III

It would be difficult to describe the subtle brotherhood of men that was here established on the seas. No one said that it was so. No one mentioned it. But it dwelt in the boat, and each man felt it warm him. They were a captain, an oiler, a cook, and a correspondent, and they were friends, friends in a more curiously iron-bound degree than may be common. The hurt captain, lying against the water-jar in the bow, spoke always in a low voice and calmly, but he could never command a more ready and swiftly obedient crew than the motley three of the dingey. It was more than a mere recognition of what was best for the common safety. There was surely in it a quality that was personal and heartfelt. And after this devotion to the commander of the boat there was this comradeship that the correspondent, for instance, who had been taught to be cynical of men, knew even at the time was the best experience of his life. But no one said that it was so. No one mentioned it.

"I wish we had a sail," remarked the captain. "We might try my overcoat on the end of an oar and give you two boys a chance to rest." So the cook and the correspondent held the mast and spread wide the overcoat. The oiler steered, and the little boat made good way with her new rig. Sometimes the oiler had to scull sharply to keep a sea from breaking into the boat, but otherwise sailing was a success.

Meanwhile the light-house had been growing slowly larger. It had now almost assumed color, and appeared like a little gray shadow on the sky. The man at the oars could not be prevented from turning his head rather often to try for a glimpse of this little gray shadow.

At last, from the top of each wave the men in the tossing boat could see land. Even as the light-house was an upright shadow on the sky, this land seemed but a long black shadow on the sea. It certainly was thinner than paper. "We must be about opposite New Smyrna," said the cook, who had coasted this shore often in schooners. "Captain, by the way, I believe they abandoned that life-saving station there about a year ago."

"Did they?" said the captain.

The wind slowly died away. The cook and the correspondent were not now obliged to slave in order to hold high the oar. But the waves continued their old impetuous swooping at the dingey, and the little craft, no longer under way, struggled woundily over them. The oiler or the correspondent took the oars again.

Shipwrecks are *apropos* of nothing. If men could only train for them and have them occur when the men had reached pink condition, there would be less drowning at sea. Of the four in the dingey none had slept any time worth mentioning for two days and two nights previous to embarking in the dingey, and in the excitement of clambering about the deck of a foundering ship they had also forgotten to eat heartily.

For these reasons, and for others, neither the oiler nor the correspondent was fond of rowing at this time. The correspondent wondered ingenuously how in the name of all that was sane could there be people who thought it amusing to row a boat. It was not an amusement; it was a diabolical punishment, and even a genius of mental aberrations could never conclude that it was anything but a horror to the muscles and a crime against the back. He mentioned to the boat in general how the amusement of rowing struck him, and the weary-faced oiler smiled in full sympathy. Previously to the foundering, by the way, the oiler had worked double-watch in the engine-room of the ship.

"Take her easy, now, boys," said the captain. "Don't spend yourselves. If we have to run a surf you'll need all your strength, because we'll sure have to swim for it. Take your time."

Slowly the land arose from the sea. From a black line it became a line of black and a line of white—trees and sand. Finally, the captain said that he could make out a house on the shore. "That's the house of refuge, sure," said the cook. "They'll see us before long, and come out after us."

The distant light-house reared high. "The keeper ought to be able to make us out now, if he's looking through a glass," said the captain. "He'll notify the life-saving people."

"None of those other boats could have got ashore to give word of the wreck," said the oiler, in a low voice. "Else the life-boat would be out hunting us."

Slowly and beautifully the land loomed out of the sea. The wind came again. It had veered from the northeast to the southeast. Finally, a new sound struck the ears of the men in the boat. It was the low thunder of the surf on the shore. "We'll never be able to make the light-house now," said the captain. "Swing her head a little more north, Billie."

" 'A little more north,' sir," said the oiler.

Whereupon the little boat turned her nose once more down the wind, and all but the oarsman watched the shore grow. Under the influence of this expansion doubt and direful apprehension was leaving the minds of the men. The management of the boat was still most absorbing, but it could not prevent a quiet cheerfulness. In an hour, perhaps, they would be ashore.

Their back-bones had become thoroughly used to balancing in the boat and they now rode this wild colt of a dingey like circus men. The correspondent thought that he had been drenched to the skin, but happening to feel in the top pocket of his coat, he found therein eight cigars. Four of them were soaked with seawater; four were perfectly scatheless. After a search, somebody produced three dry matches, and thereupon the four waifs rode impudently in their little boat, and with an assurance of an impending rescue shining in their eyes, puffed at the big cigars and judged well and ill of all men. Everybody took a drink of water.

## IV

"Cook," remarked the captain, "there don't seem to be any signs of life about your house of refuge."

"No," replied the cook. "Funny they don't see us!"

A broad stretch of lowly coast lay before the eyes of the men. It was of dunes topped with dark vegetation. The roar of the surf was plain, and sometimes they could see the white lip of a wave as it spun up the beach. A tiny house was blocked out black upon the sky. Southward, the slim light-house lifted its little gray length.

Tide, wind, and waves were swinging the dingey northward. "Funny they don't see us," said the men.

The surf's roar was here dulled, but its tone was, nevertheless, thunderous and mighty. As the boat swam over the great rollers, the men sat listening to this roar. "We'll swamp sure," said everybody.

It is fair to say here that there was not a life-saving station within twenty miles in either direction, but the men did not know this fact and in consequence they made dark and opprobrious remarks concerning the eyesight of the nation's life-savers. Four scowling men sat in the dingey and surpassed records in the invention of epithets.

"Funny they don't see us."

The light-heartedness of a former time had completely faded. To their sharpened minds it was easy to conjure pictures of all kinds of incompetency and blindness and, indeed, cowardice. There was the shore of the populous land, and it was bitter and bitter to them that from it came no sign.

"Well," said the captain, ultimately, "I suppose we'll have to make a try for ourselves. If we stay out here too long, we'll none of us have strength left to swim after the boat swamps."

And so the oiler, who was at the oars, turned the boat straight for the shore. There was a sudden tightening of muscles. There was some thinking.

"If we don't all get ashore—" said the captain. "If we don't all get ashore, I suppose you fellows know where to send news of my finish?"

They then briefly exchanged some addresses and admonitions. As for the reflections of the men, there was a great deal of rage in them. Perchance they might be formulated thus: "If I am going to be drowned—if I am going to be drowned—if I am going to be drowned, why, in the name of the seven mad gods who rule the sea, was I allowed to come thus far and contemplate sand and trees? Was I brought here merely to have my nose dragged away as I was about to nibble the sacred cheese of life? It is preposterous. If this old ninny-woman, Fate, cannot do better than this, she should be deprived of the management of men's fortunes. She is an old hen who knows not her intention. If she has decided to drown me, why did she not do it in the beginning and save me all this trouble. The whole affair is absurd. . . . But, no, she cannot mean to drown me. She dare not drown me. She cannot drown me. Not after all this work." Afterward the man might have had an impulse to shake his fist at the clouds. "Just you drown me, now, and then hear what I call you!"

The billows that came at this time were more formidable. They seemed always just about to break and roll over the little boat in a turmoil of foam. There was a preparatory and long growl in the speech of them. No mind unused to the sea would have concluded that the dingey could ascend these sheer heights in time. The shore was still afar. The oiler was a wily surfman. "Boys," he said, swiftly, "she won't live three minutes more and we're too far out to swim. Shall I take her to sea again, Captain?"

"Yes! Go ahead!" said the captain.

This oiler, by a series of quick miracles, and fast and steady oarsmanship, turned the boat in the middle of the surf and took her safely to sea again.

There was a considerable silence as the boat bumped over the furrowed sea to deeper water. Then somebody in gloom spoke. "Well, anyhow, they must have seen us from the shore by now."

The gulls went in slanting flight up the wind toward the gray desolate east. A squall, marked by dingy clouds, and clouds brick-red, like smoke from a burning building, appeared from the southeast.

"What do you think of those life-saving people? Ain't they peaches?"

"Funny they haven't seen us."

"Maybe they think we're out here for sport! Maybe they think we're fishin'. Maybe they think we're damned fools."

It was a long afternoon. A changed tide tried to force them southward, but wind and wave said northward. Far ahead, where coast-line, sea, and sky formed their mighty angle, there were little dots which seemed to indicate a city on the shore.

"St. Augustine?"

The captain shook his head. "Too near Mosquito Inlet."

And the oiler rowed, and then the correspondent rowed. Then the oiler rowed. It was a weary business. The human back can become the seat of more aches and pains than are registered in books for the composite anatomy of a regiment. It is a limited area, but it can become the theatre of innumerable muscular conflicts, tangles, wrenches, knots, and other comforts.

"Did you ever like to row, Billie?" asked the correspondent.

"No," said the oiler. "Hang it."

When one exchanged the rowing-seat for a place in the bottom of the boat, he suffered a bodily depression that caused him to be careless of everything save an obligation to wiggle one finger. There was cold sea-water swashing to and fro in the boat, and he lay in it. His head, pillowed on a thwart, was within an inch of the swirl of a wave crest, and sometimes a particularly obstreperous sea came inboard and drenched him once more. But these matters did not annoy him. It is almost certain that if the boat had capsized he would have tumbled comfortably out upon the ocean as if he felt sure that it was a great soft mattress.

"Look! There's a man on the shore!"

"Where?"

"There? See 'im? See 'im?"

"Yes, sure! He's walking along."

"Now he's stopped. Look! He's facing us!"

"He's waving at us!"

"So he is! By thunder!"

"Ah, now, we're all right! Now we're all right! There'll be a boat out here for us in half an hour."

"He's going on. He's running. He's going up to that house there."

The remote beach seemed lower than the sea, and it required a searching glance to discern the little black figure. The captain saw a floating stick and they rowed to it. A bath-towel was by some weird chance in the boat, and, tying this on the stick, the captain waved it. The oarsman did not dare turn his head, so he was obliged to ask questions.

"What's he doing now?"

"He's standing still again. He's looking, I think. . . . There he goes again. Toward the house. . . . Now he's stopped again."

"Is he waving at us?"

"No, not now! he was, though."

"Look! There comes another man!"

"He's running."

"Look at him go, would you."

"Why, he's on a bicycle. Now he's met the other man. They're both waving at us. Look!"

"There comes something up the beach."

"What the devil is that thing?"

"Why, it looks like a boat."

"Why, certainly it's a boat."

"No, it's on wheels."

"Yes, so it is. Well, that must be the life-boat. They drag them along shore on a wagon."

"That's the life-boat, sure."

"No, by——, it's—it's an omnibus."

"I tell you it's a life-boat."

"It is not! It's an omnibus. I can see it plain. See? One of those big hotel omnibuses."

"By thunder, you're right. It's an omnibus, sure as fate. What do you suppose they are doing with an omnibus? Maybe they are going around collecting the life-crew, hey?"

"That's it, likely. Look! There's a fellow waving a little black flag. He's standing on the steps of the omnibus. There come those other two fellows. Now they're all talking together. Look at the fellow with the flag. Maybe he ain't waving it!"

"That ain't a flag, is it? That's his coat. Why, certainly, that's his coat."

"So it is. It's his coat. He's taken it off and is waving it around his head. But would you look at him swing it!"

"Oh, say, there isn't any life-saving station there. That's just a winter resort hotel omnibus that has brought over some of the boarders to see us drown."

"What's that idiot with the coat mean? What's he signaling, anyhow?"

"It looks as if he were trying to tell us to go north. There must be a life-saving station up there."

"No! He thinks we're fishing. Just giving us a merry hand. See? Ah, there, Willie."

"Well, I wish I could make something out of those signals. What do you suppose he means?"

"He don't mean anything. He's just playing."

"Well, if he'd just signal us to try the surf again, or to go to sea and wait, or go north, or go south, or go to hell—there would be some reason in it. But look at him. He just stands there and keeps his coat revolving like a wheel. The ass!"

"There come more people."

"Now there's quite a mob. Look! Isn't that a boat?"

"Where? Oh, I see where you mean. No, that's no boat."

"That fellow is still waving his coat."

"He must think we like to see him do that. Why don't he quit it. It don't mean anything."

"I don't know. I think he is trying to make us go north. It must be that there's a life-saving station there somewhere."

"Say, he ain't tired yet. Look at 'im wave."

"Wonder how long he can keep that up. He's been revolving his coat ever since he caught sight of us. He's an idiot. Why aren't they getting men to bring a boat out. A fishing boat—one of those big yawls—could come out here all right. Why don't he do something?"

"Oh, it's all right, now."

"They'll have a boat out here for us in less than no time, now that they've seen us."

A faint yellow tone came into the sky over the low land. The shadows on the sea slowly deepened. The wind bore coldness with it, and the men began to shiver.

"Holy smoke!" said one, allowing his voice to express his impious mood, "if we keep on monkeying out here! If we've got to flounder out here all night!"

"Oh, we'll never have to stay here all night! Don't you worry. They've seen us now, and it won't be long before they'll come chasing out after us."

The shore grew dusky. The man waving a coat blended gradually into this gloom, and it swallowed in the same manner the omnibus and the group of people. The spray, when it dashed uproariously over the side, made the voyagers shrink and swear like men who were being branded.

"I'd like to catch the chump who waved the coat. I feel like socking him one, just for luck."

"Why? What did he do?"

"Oh, nothing, but then he seemed so damned cheerful."

In the meantime the oiler rowed, and then the correspondent rowed, and then the oiler rowed. Gray-faced and bowed forward, they mechanically, turn by turn, plied the leaden oars. The form of the light-house had vanished from the southern horizon, but finally a pale star appeared, just lifting from the sea. The streaked saffron in the west passed before the all-merging darkness, and the sea to the east was black. The land had vanished, and was expressed only by the low and drear thunder of the surf.

"If I am going to be drowned—if I am going to be drowned—if I am going to be drowned, why, in the name of the seven mad gods who rule the sea, was I allowed to come thus far and contemplate sand and trees? Was I brought here merely to have my nose dragged away as I was about to nibble the sacred cheese of life?"

The patient captain, drooped over the water-jar, was sometimes obliged to speak to the oarsman.

"Keep her head up! Keep her head up!"

" 'Keep her head up,' sir." The voices were weary and low.

This was surely a quiet evening. All save the oarsman lay heavily and listlessly in the boat's bottom. As for him, his eyes were just capable of noting the tall black waves that swept forward in a most sinister silence, save for an occasional subdued growl of a crest.

The cook's head was on a thwart, and he looked without interest at the water under his nose. He was deep in other scenes. Finally he spoke. "Billie," he murmured, dreamfully, "what kind of pie do you like best?"

## V

"Pie," said the oiler and the correspondent, agitatedly. "Don't talk about those things, blast you!"

"Well," said the cook, "I was just thinking about ham sandwiches, and——"

A night on the sea in an open boat is a long night. As darkness settled finally, the shine of the light, lifting from the sea in the south, changed to full gold. On the northern horizon a new light appeared, a small bluish gleam on the edge of the waters. These two lights were the furniture of the world. Otherwise there was nothing but waves.

Two men huddled in the stern, and distances were so magnificent in the dingey that the rower was enabled to keep his feet partly warmed by thrusting them under his companions. Their legs indeed extended far under the rowing-seat until they touched the feet of the captain forward. Sometimes, despite the efforts of the tired oarsman, a wave came piling into the boat, an icy wave of the night, and the chilling water soaked them anew. They would twist their bodies for a moment and groan, and sleep the dead sleep once more, while the water in the boat gurgled about them as the craft rocked.

The plan of the oiler and the correspondent was for one to row until he lost the ability, and then arouse the other from his sea-water couch in the bottom of the boat.

The oiler plied the oars until his head drooped forward, and the overpowering sleep blinded him. And he rowed yet afterward. Then he touched a man in the bottom of the boat, and called his name. "Will you spell me for a little while?" he said meekly.

"Sure, Billie," said the correspondent, awakening and dragging himself to a sitting position. They exchanged places carefully, and the oiler, cuddling down in the sea-water at the cook's side, seemed to go to sleep instantly.

The particular violence of the sea had ceased. The waves came without snarling. The obligation of the man at the oars was to keep the boat headed so that the tilt of the rollers would not capsize her, and to preserve her from filling when the crests rushed past. The black waves were silent and hard to be seen in the darkness. Often one was almost upon the boat before the oarsman was aware.

In a low voice the correspondent addressed the captain. He was not sure that the captain was awake, although this iron man seemed to be always awake. "Captain, shall I keep her making for that light north, sir?"

The same steady voice answered him. "Yes. Keep it about two points off the port bow."

The cook had tied a life-belt around himself in order to get even the warmth which this clumsy cork contrivance could donate, and he seemed almost stove-like when a rower, whose teeth invariably chattered wildly as soon as he ceased his labor, dropped down to sleep.

The correspondent, as he rowed, looked down at the two men sleeping under foot. The cook's arm was around the oiler's shoulders, and, with their fragmentary clothing and haggard faces, they were the babes of the sea, a grotesque rendering of the old babes in the wood.

Later he must have grown stupid at his work, for suddenly there was a growling of water, and a crest came with a roar and a swash into the boat, and it was a wonder that it did not set the cook afloat in his life-belt. The cook continued to sleep, but the oiler sat up, blinking his eyes and shaking with the new cold.

"Oh, I'm awful sorry, Billie," said the correspondent, contritely.

"That's all right, old boy," said the oiler, and lay down again and was asleep.

Presently it seemed that even the captain dozed, and the correspondent thought that he was the one man afloat on all the oceans. The wind had a voice as it came over the waves, and it was sadder than the end.

There was a long, loud swishing astern of the boat, and a gleaming trail of phosphorescence, like blue flame, was furrowed on the black waters. It might have been made by a monstrous knife.

Then there came a stillness, while the correspondent breathed with the open mouth and looked at the sea.

Suddenly there was another swish and another long flash of bluish light, and this time it was alongside the boat, and might almost have been reached with an oar. The correspondent saw an enormous fin speed like a shadow through the water, hurling the crystalline spray and leaving the long glowing trail.

The correspondent looked over his shoulder at the captain. His face was hidden, and he seemed to be asleep. He looked at the babes of the sea. They certainly were asleep. So, being bereft of sympathy, he leaned a little way to one side and swore softly into the sea.

But the thing did not then leave the vicinity of the boat. Ahead or astern, on one side or the other, at intervals long or short, fled the long sparkling streak, and there was to be heard the whiroo of the dark fin. The speed and power of the thing was greatly to be admired. It cut the water like a gigantic and keen projectile.

The presence of this biding thing did not affect the man with the same horror that it would if he had been a picnicker. He simply looked at the sea dully and swore in an undertone.

Nevertheless, it is true that he did not wish to be alone with the thing. He wished one of his companions to awaken by chance and keep him company with it. But the captain hung motionless over the water-jar and the oiler and the cook in the bottom of the boat were plunged in slumber.

## VI

"If I am going to be drowned—if I am going to be drowned—if I am going to be drowned, why, in the name of the seven mad gods who rule the sea, was I allowed to come thus far and contemplate sand and trees?"

During this dismal night, it may be remarked that a man would conclude that it was really the intention of the seven mad gods to drown him, despite the abominable injustice of it. For it was certainly an abominable injustice to drown a man who had worked so hard, so hard. The man felt it would be a crime most unnatural. Other people had drowned at sea since galleys swarmed with painted sails, but still——

When it occurs to a man that nature does not regard him as important, and that she feels she would not maim the universe by disposing of him, he at first wishes to throw bricks at the temple, and he hates deeply the fact that there are no bricks and no temples. Any visible expression of nature would surely be pelleted with his jeers.

Then, if there be no tangible thing to hoot he feels, perhaps, the desire to confront a personification and indulge in pleas, bowed to one knee, and with hands supplicant, saying: "Yes, but I love myself."

A high cold star on a winter's night is the word he feels that she says to him. Thereafter he knows the pathos of his situation.

The men in the dingey had not discussed these matters, but each had, no doubt, reflected upon them in silence and according to his mind. There was seldom any expression upon their faces save the general one of complete weariness. Speech was devoted to the business of the boat.

To chime the notes of his emotion, a verse mysteriously entered the correspondent's head. He had even forgotten that he had forgotten this verse, but it suddenly was in his mind.

> A soldier of the Legion lay dying in Algiers,
> There was lack of woman's nursing, there was dearth of woman's tears;
> But a comrade stood beside him, and he took that comrade's hand,
> And he said: "I never more shall see my own, my native land.[5]

In his childhood, the correspondent had been made acquainted with the fact that a soldier of the Legion lay dying in Algiers, but he had never regarded it as important. Myriads of his school-fellows had informed him of the soldier's plight, but the dinning had naturally ended by making him perfectly indifferent. He had never considered it his affair that a soldier of the Legion lay dying in Algiers, nor had it appeared to him as a matter for sorrow. It was less to him than the breaking of a pencil's point.

Now, however, it quaintly came to him as a human, living thing. It was no longer merely a picture of a few throes in the breast of a poet, meanwhile drinking tea and warming his feet at the grate; it was an actuality—stern, mournful, and fine.

The correspondent plainly saw the soldier. He lay on the sand with his feet

---

5. The lines are incorrectly quoted from Caroline E. S. Norton's poem *Bingen on the Rhine* (1883).

out straight and still. While his pale left hand was upon his chest in an attempt to thwart the going of his life, the blood came between his fingers. In the far Algerian distance, a city of low square forms was set against a sky that was faint with the last sunset hues. The correspondent, plying the oars and dreaming of the slow and slower movements of the lips of the soldier, was moved by a profound and perfectly impersonal comprehension. He was sorry for the soldier of the Legion who lay dying in Algiers.

The thing which had followed the boat and waited had evidently grown bored at the delay. There was no longer to be heard the slash of the cut-water, and there was no longer the flame of the long trail. The light in the north still glimmered, but it was apparently no nearer to the boat. Sometimes the boom of the surf rang in the correspondent's ears, and he turned the craft seaward then and rowed harder. Southward, some one had evidently built a watch-fire on the beach. It was too low and too far to be seen, but it made a shimmering, roseate reflection upon the bluff back of it, and this could be discerned from the boat. The wind came stronger, and sometimes a wave suddenly raged out like a mountain-cat and there was to be seen the sheen and sparkle of a broken crest.

The captain, in the bow, moved on his water-jar and sat erect. "Pretty long night," he observed to the correspondent. He looked at the shore. "Those life-saving people take their time."

"Did you see that shark playing around?"

"Yes, I saw him. He was a big fellow, all right."

"Wish I had known you were awake."

Later the correspondent spoke into the bottom of the boat.

"Billie!" There was a slow and gradual disentanglement. "Billie, will you spell me?"

"Sure," said the oiler.

As soon as the correspondent touched the cold comfortable seawater in the bottom of the boat, and had huddled close to the cook's life-belt he was deep in sleep, despite the fact that his teeth played all the popular airs. This sleep was so good to him that it was but a moment before he heard a voice call his name in a tone that demonstrated the last stages of exhaustion. "Will you spell me?"

"Sure, Billie."

The light in the north had mysteriously vanished, but the correspondent took his course from the wide-awake captain.

Later in the night they took the boat farther out to sea, and the captain directed the cook to take one oar at the stern and keep the boat facing the seas. He was to call out if he should hear the thunder of the surf. This plan enabled the oiler and the correspondent to get respite together. "We'll give those boys a chance to get into shape again," said the captain. They curled down and, after a few preliminary chatterings and trembles, slept once more the dead sleep. Neither knew they had bequeathed to the cook the company of another shark, or perhaps the same shark.

As the boat caroused on the waves, spray occasionally bumped over the side and gave them a fresh soaking, but this had no power to break their repose. The ominous slash of the wind and the water affected them as it would have affected mummies.

"Boys," said the cook, with the notes of every reluctance in his voice, "she's drifted in pretty close. I guess one of you had better take her to sea again." The correspondent, aroused, heard the crash of the toppled crests.

As he was rowing, the captain gave him some whiskey and water, and this steadied the chills out of him. "If I ever get ashore and anybody shows me even a photograph of an oar——"

At last there was a short conversation.

"Billie. . . . Billie, will you spell me?"

"Sure," said the oiler.

## VII

When the correspondent again opened his eyes, the sea and the sky were each of the gray hue of the dawning. Later, carmine and gold was painted upon the waters. The morning appeared finally, in its splendor, with a sky of pure blue, and the sunlight flamed on the tips of the waves.

On the distant dunes were set many little black cottages, and a tall white wind-mill reared above them. No man, nor dog, nor bicycle appeared on the beach. The cottages might have formed a deserted village.

The voyagers scanned the shore. A conference was held in the boat. "Well," said the captain, "if no help is coming, we might better try a run through the surf right away. If we stay out here much longer we will be too weak to do anything for ourselves at all." The others silently acquiesced in this reasoning. The boat was headed for the beach. The correspondent wondered if none ever ascended the tall wind-tower, and if then they never looked seaward. This tower was a giant, standing with its back to the plight of the ants. It represented in a degree, to the correspondent, the serenity of nature amid the struggles of the individual—nature in the wind, and nature in the vision of men. She did not seem cruel to him then, nor beneficent, nor treacherous, nor wise. But she was indifferent, flatly indifferent. It is, perhaps, plausible that a man in this situation, impressed with the unconcern of the universe, should see the innumerable flaws of his life and have them taste wickedly in his mind and wish for another chance. A distinction between right and wrong seems absurdly clear to him, then, in this new ignorance of the grave-edge, and he understands that if he were given another opportunity he would mend his conduct and his words, and be better and brighter during an introduction, or at a tea.

"Now, boys," said the captain, "she is going to swamp sure. All we can do is to work her in as far as possible, and then when she swamps, pile out and scramble for the beach. Keep cool now, and don't jump until she swamps sure."

The oiler took the oars. Over his shoulders he scanned the surf. "Captain," he said, "I think I'd better bring her about, and keep her head-on to the seas and back her in."

"All right, Billie," said the captain. "Back her in." The oiler swung the boat then and, seated in the stern, the cook and the correspondent were obliged to look over their shoulders to contemplate the lonely and indifferent shore.

The monstrous inshore rollers heaved the boat high until the men were again enabled to see the white sheets of water scudding up the slanted beach. "We won't get in very close," said the captain. Each time a man could wrest his attention from the rollers, he turned his glance toward the shore, and in the expression of the eyes during this contemplation there was a singular quality. The correspondent, observing the others, knew that they were not afraid, but the full meaning of their glances was shrouded.

As for himself, he was too tired to grapple fundamentally with the fact. He tried to coerce his mind into thinking of it, but the mind was dominated at this time by the muscles, and the muscles said they did not care. It merely occurred to him that if he should drown it would be a shame.

There were no hurried words, no pallor, no plain agitation. The men simply looked at the shore. "Now, remember to get well clear of the boat when you jump," said the captain.

Seaward the crest of a roller suddenly fell with a thunderous crash, and the long white comber came roaring down upon the boat.

"Steady now," said the captain. The men were silent. They turned their eyes from the shore to the comber and waited. The boat slid up the incline, leaped at the furious top, bounced over it, and swung down the long back of the wave. Some water had been shipped and the cook bailed it out.

But the next crest crashed also. The tumbling boiling flood of white water caught the boat and whirled it almost perpendicular. Water swarmed in from all sides. The correspondent had his hands on the gunwale at this time, and when the water entered at that place he swiftly withdrew his fingers, as if he objected to wetting them.

The little boat, drunken with this weight of water, reeled and snuggled deeper into the sea.

"Bail her out, cook! Bail her out," said the captain.

"All right, Captain," said the cook.

"Now, boys, the next one will do for us, sure," said the oiler. "Mind to jump clear of the boat."

The third wave moved forward, huge, furious, implacable. It fairly swallowed the dingey, and almost simultaneously the men tumbled into the sea. A piece of life-belt had lain in the bottom of the boat, and as the correspondent went overboard he held this to his chest with his left hand.

The January water was icy, and he reflected immediately that it was colder than he had expected to find it off the coast of Florida. This appeared to his dazed mind as a fact important enough to be noted at the time. The coldness of the water was sad; it was tragic. This fact was somehow so mixed and confused with his opinion of his own situation that it seemed almost a proper reason for tears. The water was cold.

When he came to the surface he was conscious of little but the noisy water. Afterward he saw his companions in the sea. The oiler was ahead in the race. He was swimming strongly and rapidly. Off to the correspondent's left, the cook's great white and corked back bulged out of the water, and in the rear the captain was hanging with his one good hand to the keel of the overturned dingey.

There is a certain immovable quality to a shore, and the correspondent wondered at it amid the confusion of the sea.

It seemed also very attractive, but the correspondent knew that it was a long journey, and he paddled leisurely. The piece of life preserver lay under him, and sometimes he whirled down the incline of a wave as if he were on a hand-sled.

But finally he arrived at a place in the sea where travel was beset with difficulty. He did not pause swimming to inquire what manner of current had caught him, but there his progress ceased. The shore was set before him like a bit of scenery on a stage, and he looked at it and understood with his eyes each detail of it.

As the cook passed, much farther to the left, the captain was calling to him, "Turn over on your back, cook! Turn over on your back and use the oar."

"All right, sir." The cook turned on his back, and, paddling with an oar, went ahead as if he were a canoe.

Presently the boat also passed to the left of the correspondent with the captain clinging with one hand to the keel. He would have appeared like a man raising himself to look over a board fence, if it were not for the extraordinary gymnastics of the boat. The correspondent marvelled that the captain could still hold to it.

They passed on, nearer to the shore—the oiler, the cook, the captain—and following them went the water-jar, bouncing gayly over the seas.

The correspondent remained in the grip of this strange new enemy—a current. The shore, with its white slope of sand and its green bluff, topped with little silent cottages, was spread like a picture before him. It was very near to him then, but he was impressed as one who in a gallery looks at a scene from Brittany or Holland.

He thought: "I am going to drown? Can it be possible? Can it be possible? Can it be possible?" Perhaps an individual must consider his own death to be the final phenomenon of nature.

But later a wave perhaps whirled him out of this small deadly current, for he found suddenly that he could again make progress toward the shore. Later still, he was aware that the captain, clinging with one hand to the keel of the dingey, had his face turned away from the shore and toward him, and was calling his name. "Come to the boat! Come to the boat!"

In his struggle to reach the captain and the boat, he reflected that when one gets properly wearied, drowning must really be a comfortable arrangement, a cessation of hostilities accompanied by a large degree of relief, and he was glad of it, for the main thing in his mind for some moments had been horror of the temporary agony. He did not wish to be hurt.

Presently he saw a man running along the shore. He was undressing with most remarkable speed. Coat, trousers, shirt, everything flew magically off him.

"Come to the boat," called the captain.

"All right, Captain." As the correspondent paddled, he saw the captain let himself down to bottom and leave the boat. Then the correspondent performed his one little marvel of the voyage. A large wave caught him and flung him with ease and supreme speed completely over the boat and far beyond it. It struck him even then as an event in gymnastics, and a true miracle of the sea. An overturned boat in the surf is not a plaything to a swimming man.

The correspondent arrived in water that reached only to his waist, but his condition did not enable him to stand for more than a moment. Each wave knocked him into a heap, and the under-tow pulled at him.

Then he saw the man who had been running and undressing, and undressing and running, come bounding into the water. He dragged ashore the cook, and then waded toward the captain, but the captain waved him away, and sent him to the correspondent. He was naked, naked as a tree in winter, but a halo was about his head, and he shone like a saint. He gave a strong pull, and a long drag, and a bully heave at the correspondent's hand. The correspondent schooled in the minor formulæ, said: "Thanks, old man." But suddenly the man cried: "What's that?" He pointed a swift finger. The correspondent said: "Go."

In the shallows, face downward, lay the oiler. His forehead touched sand that was periodically, between each wave, clear of the sea.

The correspondent did not know all that transpired afterward. When he achieved safe ground he fell, striking the sand with each particular part of his body. It was as if he had dropped from a roof, but the thud was grateful to him.

It seems that instantly the beach was populated with men with blankets, clothes, and flasks, and women with coffee-pots and all the remedies sacred to their minds. The welcome of the land to the men from the sea was warm and generous, but a still and dripping shape was carried slowly up the beach, and the land's welcome for it could only be the different and sinister hospitality of the grave.

When it came night, the white waves paced to and fro in the moonlight, and the wind brought the sound of the great sea's voice to the men on shore, and they felt that they could then be interpreters.

1897, 1898

## The Blue Hotel[1]

### I

The Palace Hotel at Fort Romper was painted a light blue, a shade that is on the legs of a kind of heron, causing the bird to declare its position against any background. The Palace Hotel, then, was always screaming and howling in a way that made the dazzling winter landscape of Nebraska seem only a gay swampish hush. It stood alone on the prairie, and when the snow was falling the town two hundred yards away was not visible. But when the traveler alighted at the railway station he was obliged to pass the Palace Hotel before he could come upon the company of low clap-board houses which composed Fort Romper, and it was not to be thought that any traveler could pass the Palace Hotel without looking at it. Pat Scully, the proprietor, had proved himself a master of strategy when he chose his paints. It is true that on clear days, when the great trans-continental expresses, long lines of swaying Pullmans, swept through Fort Romper, passengers were overcome at the sight, and the cult that knows the brown-reds and the subdivisions of the dark greens of the East expressed shame, pity, horror, in a laugh. But to the citizens of this prairie town, and to the people who would naturally stop there, Pat Scully had performed a feat. With this opulence and splendor, these creeds, classes, egotisms, that streamed through Romper on the rails day after day, they had no color in common.

As if the displayed delights of such a blue hotel were not sufficiently entic-

---

1. The story was first published in two installments in *Collier's Weekly* for November 26 and December 3, 1898, then in *The Monster and Other Stories* (1899). The present text reprints that established for the University of Virginia edition of *The Works of Stephen Crane*, Vol. 5, *Tales of Adventure* (1970).

ing, it was Scully's habit to go every morning and evening to meet the leisurely trains that stopped at Romper and work his seductions upon any man that he might see wavering, gripsack in hand.

One morning, when a snow-crusted engine dragged its long string of freight cars and its one passenger coach to the station, Scully performed the marvel of catching three men. One was a shaky and quick-eyed Swede, with a great shining cheap valise; one was a tall bronzed cowboy, who was on his way to a ranch near the Dakota line; one was a little silent man from the East, who didn't look it, and didn't announce it. Scully practically made them prisoners. He was so nimble and merry and kindly that each probably felt it would be the height of brutality to try to escape. They trudged off over the creaking board sidewalks in the wake of the eager little Irishman. He wore a heavy fur cap squeezed tightly down on his head. It caused his two red ears to stick out stiffly, as if they were made of tin.

At last, Scully, elaborately, with boisterous hospitality, conducted them through the portals of the blue hotel. The room which they entered was small. It seemed to be merely a proper temple for an enormous stove, which, in the center, was humming with god-like violence. At various points on its surface the iron had become luminous and glowed yellow from the heat. Beside the stove Scully's son Johnnie was playing High-Five[2] with an old farmer who had whiskers both gray and sandy. They were quarreling. Frequently the old farmer turned his face toward a box of sawdust—colored brown from tobacco juice—that was behind the stove, and spat with an air of great impatience and irritation. With a loud flourish of words Scully destroyed the game of cards, and bustled his son upstairs with part of the baggage of the new guests. He himself conducted them to three basins of the coldest water in the world. The cowboy and the Easterner burnished themselves fiery red with this water, until it seemed to be some kind of a metal polish. The Swede, however, merely dipped his fingers gingerly and with trepidation. It was notable that throughout this series of small ceremonies the three travelers were made to feel that Scully was very benevolent. He was conferring great favors upon them. He handed the towel from one to the other with an air of philanthropic impulse.

Afterward they went to the first room, and, sitting about the stove, listened to Scully's officious clamor at his daughters, who were preparing the midday meal. They reflected in the silence of experienced men who tread carefully amid new people. Nevertheless, the old farmer, stationary, invincible in his chair near the warmest part of the stove, turned his face from the sawdust box frequently and addressed a glowing commonplace to the strangers. Usually he was answered in short but adequate sentences by either the cowboy or the Easterner. The Swede said nothing. He seemed to be occupied in making furtive estimates of each man in the room. One might have thought that he had the sense of silly suspicion which comes to guilt. He resembled a badly frightened man.

Later, at dinner, he spoke a little, addressing his conversation entirely to Scully. He volunteered that he had come from New York, where for ten years he had worked as a tailor. These facts seemed to strike Scully as fascinating, and afterward he volunteered that he had lived at Romper for fourteen years. The Swede asked about the crops and the price of labor. He seemed barely

2. I.e., cinch, a card game.

to listen to Scully's extended replies. His eyes continued to rove from man to man.

Finally, with a laugh and a wink, he said that some of these Western communities were very dangerous; and after his statement he straightened his legs under the table, tilted his head, and laughed again, loudly. It was plain that the demonstration had no meaning to the others. They looked at him wondering and in silence.

## II

As the men trooped heavily back into the front room, the two little windows presented views of a turmoiling sea of snow. The huge arms of the wind were making attempts—mighty, circular, futile—to embrace the flakes as they sped. A gate-post like a still man with a blanched face stood aghast amid this profligate fury. In a hearty voice Scully announced the presence of a blizzard. The guests of the blue hotel, lighting their pipes, assented with grunts of lazy masculine contentment. No island of the sea could be exempt in the degree of this little room with its humming stove. Johnnie, son of Scully, in a tone which defined his opinion of his ability as a card-player, challenged the old farmer of both gray and sandy whiskers to a game of High-Five. The farmer agreed with a contemptuous and bitter scoff. They sat close to the stove, and squared their knees under a wide board. The cowboy and the Easterner watched the game with interest. The Swede remained near the window, aloof, but with a countenance that showed signs of an inexplicable excitement.

The play of Johnnie and the gray-beard was suddenly ended by another quarrel. The old man arose while casting a look of heated scorn at his adversary. He slowly buttoned his coat, and then stalked with fabulous dignity from the room. In the discreet silence of all other men the Swede laughed. His laughter rang somehow childish. Men by this time had begun to look at him askance, as if they wished to inquire what ailed him.

A new game was formed jocosely. The cowboy volunteered to become the partner of Johnnie, and they all then turned to ask the Swede to throw in his lot with the little Easterner. He asked some questions about the game, and learning that it wore many names, and that he had played it when it was under an alias, he accepted the invitation. He strode toward the men nervously, as if he expected to be assaulted. Finally, seated, he gazed from face to face and laughed shrilly. This laugh was so strange that the Easterner looked up quickly, the cowboy sat intent and with his mouth open, and Johnnie paused, holding the cards with still fingers.

Afterward there was a short silence. Then Johnnie said: "Well, let's get at it. Come on now!" They pulled their chairs forward until their knees were bunched under the board. They began to play, and their interest in the game caused the others to forget the manner of the Swede.

The cowboy was a board-whacker. Each time that he held superior cards he whanged them, one by one, with exceeding force, down upon the improvised table, and took the tricks with a glowing air of prowess and pride that sent thrills of indignation into the hearts of his opponents. A game with a board-whacker in it is sure to become intense. The countenances of the Easterner and the Swede were miserable whenever the cowboy thundered down his aces and kings, while Johnnie, his eyes gleaming with joy, chuckled and chuckled.

Because of the absorbing play none considered the strange ways of the

Swede. They paid strict heed to the game. Finally, during a lull caused by a new deal, the Swede suddenly addressed Johnnie: "I suppose there have been a good many men killed in this room." The jaws of the others dropped and they looked at him.

"What in hell are you talking about?" asked Johnnie.

The Swede laughed again his blatant laugh, full of a kind of false courage and defiance. "Oh, you know what I mean all right," he answered.

"I'm a liar if I do!" Johnnie protested. The card was halted, and the men stared at the Swede. Johnnie evidently felt that as the son of the proprietor he should make a direct inquiry. "Now, what might you be drivin' at, mister?" he asked. The Swede winked at him. It was a wink full of cunning. His fingers shook on the edge of the board. "Oh, maybe you think I have been to nowheres. Maybe you think I'm a tenderfoot?"

"I don't know nothin' about you," answered Johnnie, "and I don't give a damn where you've been. All I got to say is that I don't know what you're driving at. There hain't never been nobody killed in this room."

The cowboy, who had been steadily gazing at the Swede, then spoke. "What's wrong with you, mister?"

Apparently it seemed to the Swede that he was formidably menaced. He shivered and turned white near the corners of his mouth. He sent an appealing glance in the direction of the little Easterner. During these moments he did not forget to wear his air of advanced pot-valor.[3] "They say they don't know what I mean," he remarked mockingly to the Easterner.

The latter answered after prolonged and cautious reflection. "I don't understand you," he said, impassively.

The Swede made a movement then which announced that he thought he had encountered treachery from the only quarter where he had expected sympathy if not help. "Oh, I see you are all against me. I see——"

The cowboy was in a state of deep stupefaction. "Say," he cried, as he tumbled the deck violently down upon the board. "Say, what are you gittin' at, hey?"

The Swede sprang up with the celerity of a man escaping from a snake on the floor. "I don't want to fight!" he shouted. "I don't want to fight!"

The cowboy stretched his long legs indolently and deliberately. His hands were in his pockets. He spat into the sawdust box. "Well, who the hell thought you did?" he inquired.

The Swede backed rapidly toward a corner of the room. His hands were out protectingly in front of his chest, but he was making an obvious struggle to control his fright. "Gentlemen," he quavered, "I suppose I am going to be killed before I can leave this house! I suppose I am going to be killed before I can leave this house!" In his eyes was the dying swan look. Through the windows could be seen the snow turning blue in the shadow of dusk. The wind tore at the house and some loose thing beat regularly against the clap-boards like a spirit tapping.

A door opened, and Scully himself entered. He paused in surprise as he noted the tragic attitude of the Swede. Then he said: "What's the matter here?"

The Swede answered him swiftly and eagerly: "These men are going to kill me."

"Kill you!" ejaculated Scully. "Kill you! What are you talkin'?"

3. Drunken bravado.

The Swede made the gesture of a martyr.

Scully wheeled sternly upon his son. "What is this, Johnnie?"

The lad had grown sullen. "Damned if I know," he answered. "I can't make no sense to it." He began to shuffle the cards, fluttering them together with an angry snap. "He says a good many men have been killed in this room, or something like that. And he says he's goin' to be killed here too. I don't know what ails him. He's crazy, I shouldn't wonder."

Scully then looked for explanation to the cowboy, but the cowboy simply shrugged his shoulders.

"Kill you?" said Scully again to the Swede. "Kill you? Man, you're off your nut."

"Oh, I know," burst out the Swede. "I know what will happen. Yes, I'm crazy—yes. Yes, of course, I'm crazy—yes. But I know one thing——" There was a sort of sweat of misery and terror upon his face. "I know I won't get out of here alive."

The cowboy drew a deep breath, as if his mind was passing into the last stages of dissolution. "Well, I'm dog-goned," he whispered to himself.

Scully wheeled suddenly and faced his son. "You've been troublin' this man!"

Johnnie's voice was loud with its burden of grievance. "Why, good Gawd, I ain't done nothin' to 'im."

The Swede broke in. "Gentlemen, do not disturb yourselves. I will leave this house. I will go 'way because——" He accused them dramatically with his glance. "Because I do not want to be killed."

Scully was furious with his son. "Will you tell me what is the matter, you young divil? What's the matter, anyhow? Speak out!"

"Blame it," cried Johnnie in despair, "don't I tell you I don't know. He—he says we want to kill him, and that's all I know. I can't tell what ails him."

The Swede continued to repeat: "Never mind, Mr. Scully, never mind. I will leave this house. I will go away, because I do not wish to be killed. Yes, of course, I am crazy—yes. But I know one thing! I will go away. I will leave this house. Never mind, Mr. Scully, never mind. I will go away."

"You will not go 'way," said Scully. "You will not go 'way until I hear the reason of this business. If anybody has troubled you I will take care of him. This is my house. You are under my roof, and I will not allow any peaceable man to be troubled here." He cast a terrible eye upon Johnnie, the cowboy, and the Easterner.

"Never mind, Mr. Scully, never mind. I will go 'way. I do not wish to be killed." The Swede moved toward the door, which opened upon the stairs. It was evidently his intention to go at once for his baggage.

"No, no," shouted Scully peremptorily; but the white-faced man slid by him and disappeared. "Now," said Scully severely, "what does this mean?"

Johnnie and the cowboy cried together: "Why, we didn't do nothin' to 'im!"

Scully's eyes were cold. "No," he said, "you didn't?"

Johnnie swore a deep oath. "Why, this is the wildest loon I ever see. We didn't do nothin' at all. We were jest sittin' here playin' cards and he——"

The father suddenly spoke to the Easterner. "Mr. Blanc," he asked, "what has these boys been doin'?"

The Easterner reflected again. "I didn't see anything wrong at all," he said at last slowly.

Scully began to howl. "But what does it mane?" He stared ferociously at his son. "I have a mind to lather you for this, me boy." Johnnie was frantic. "Well, what have I done?" he bawled at his father.

### III

"I think you are tongue-tied," said Scully finally to his son, the cowboy and the Easterner, and at the end of this scornful sentence he left the room.

Upstairs the Swede was swiftly fastening the straps of his great valise. Once his back happened to be half-turned toward the door, and hearing a noise there, he wheeled and sprang up, uttering a loud cry. Scully's wrinkled visage showed grimly in the light of the small lamp he carried. This yellow effulgence, streaming upward, colored only his prominent features, and left his eyes, for instance, in mysterious shadow. He resembled a murderer.

"Man, man!" he exclaimed, "have you gone daffy?"

"Oh, no! Oh, no!" rejoined the other. "There are people in this world who know pretty nearly as much as you do—understand?"

For a moment they stood gazing at each other. Upon the Swede's deathly pale cheeks were two spots brightly crimson and sharply edged, as if they had been carefully painted. Scully placed the light on the table and sat himself on the edge of the bed. He spoke ruminatively. "By cracky, I never heard of such a thing in my life. It's a complete muddle. I can't for the soul of me think how you ever got this idea into your head." Presently he lifted his eyes and asked: "And did you sure think they were going to kill you?"

The Swede scanned the old man as if he wished to see into his mind. "I did," he said at last. He obviously suspected that this answer might precipitate an outbreak. As he pulled on a strap his whole arm shook, the elbow wavering like a bit of paper.

Scully banged his hand impressively on the foot-board of the bed. "Why, man, we're goin' to have a line of ilictric street-cars in this town next spring."

" 'A line of electric street-cars,' " repeated the Swede stupidly.

"And," said Scully, "there's a new railroad goin' to be built down from Broken Arm to here. Not to mintion the four churches and the smashin' big brick school-house. Then there's the big factory, too. Why, in two years Romper'll be a met-tro-*pol*-is."

Having finished the preparation of his baggage, the Swede straightened himself. "Mr. Scully," he said with sudden hardihood, "how much do I owe you?"

"You don't owe me anythin'," said the old man angrily.

"Yes, I do," retorted the Swede. He took seventy-five cents from his pocket and tendered it to Scully; but the latter snapped his fingers in disdainful refusal. However, it happened that they both stood gazing in a strange fashion at three silver pieces on the Swede's open palm.

"I'll not take your money," said Scully at last. "Not after what's been goin' on here." Then a plan seemed to strike him. "Here," he cried, picking up his lamp and moving toward the door. "Here! Come with me a minute."

"No," said the Swede in overwhelming alarm.

"Yes," urged the old man. "Come on! I want you to come and see a picter— just across the hall—in my room."

The Swede must have concluded that his hour was come. His jaw dropped and his teeth showed like a dead man's. He ultimately followed Scully across the corridor, but he had the step of one hung in chains.

Scully flashed the light high on the wall of his own chamber. There was revealed a ridiculous photograph of a little girl. She was leaning against a balustrade of gorgeous decoration, and the formidable bang to her hair was prominent. The figure was as graceful as an upright sled-stake, and, withal, it was the hue of lead. "There," said Scully tenderly. "That's the picter of my little girl that died. Her name was Carrie. She had the purtiest hair you ever saw! I was that fond of her, she——"

Turning then he saw that the Swede was not contemplating the picture at all, but, instead, was keeping keen watch on the gloom in the rear.

"Look, man!" shouted Scully heartily. "That's the picter of my little gal that died. Her name was Carrie. And then here's the picter of my oldest boy, Michael. He's a lawyer in Lincoln an' doin' well. I gave that boy a grand eddycation, and I'm glad for it now. He's a fine boy. Look at 'im now. Ain't he bold as blazes, him there in Lincoln, an honored an' respicted gintleman. An honored an' respicted gintleman," concluded Scully with a flourish. And so saying, he smote the Swede jovially on the back.

The Swede faintly smiled.

"Now," said the old man, "there's only one more thing." He dropped suddenly to the floor and thrust his head beneath the bed. The Swede could hear his muffled voice. "I'd keep it under me piller if it wasn't for that boy Johnnie. Then there's the old woman——Where is it now? I never put it twice in the same place. Ah, now come out with you!"

Presently he backed clumsily from under the bed, dragging with him an old coat rolled into a bundle. "I've fetched him," he muttered. Kneeling on the floor he unrolled the coat and extracted from its heart a large yellow-brown whisky bottle.

His first maneuver was to hold the bottle up to the light. Reassured, apparently, that nobody had been tampering with it, he thrust it with a generous movement toward the Swede.

The weak-kneed Swede was about to eagerly clutch this element of strength, but he suddenly jerked his hand away and cast a look of horror upon Scully.

"Drink," said the old man affectionately. He had arisen to his feet, and now stood facing the Swede.

There was a silence. Then again Scully said: "Drink!"

The Swede laughed wildly. He grabbed the bottle, put it to his mouth, and as his lips curled absurdly around the opening and his throat worked, he kept his glance burning with hatred upon the old man's face.

## IV

After the departure of Scully the three men, with the cardboard still upon their knees, preserved for a long time an astounded silence. Then Johnnie said: "That's the dod-dangest Swede I ever see."

"He ain't no Swede," said the cowboy scornfully.

"Well, what is he then?" cried Johnnie. "What is he then?"

"It's my opinion," replied the cowboy deliberately, "he's some kind of a Dutchman." It was a venerable custom of the country to entitle as Swedes all light-haired men who spoke with a heavy tongue. In consequence the idea of the cowboy was not without its daring. "Yes, sir," he repeated. "It's my opinion this feller is some kind of a Dutchman."

"Well, he says he's a Swede, anyhow," muttered Johnnie sulkily. He turned to the Easterner: "What do you think, Mr. Blanc?"

"Oh, I don't know," replied the Easterner.

"Well, what do you think makes him act that way?" asked the cowboy.

"Why, he's frightened!" The Easterner knocked his pipe against a rim of the stove. "He's clear frightened out of his boots."

"What at?" cried Johnnie and cowboy together.

The Easterner reflected over his answer.

"What at?" cried the others again.

"Oh, I don't know, but it seems to me this man has been reading dime-novels, and he thinks he's right out in the middle of it—the shootin' and stabbin' and all."

"But," said the cowboy, deeply scandalized, "this ain't Wyoming, ner none of them places. This is Nebrasker."

"Yes," added Johnnie, "an' why don't he wait till he gits *out West?*"

The traveled Easterner laughed. "It isn't different there even—not in these days. But he thinks he's right in the middle of hell."

Johnnie and the cowboy mused long.

"It's awful funny," remarked Johnnie at last.

"Yes," said the cowboy. "This is a queer game. I hope we don't git snowed in, because then we'd have to stand this here man bein' around with us all the time. That wouldn't be no good."

"I wish pop would throw him out," said Johnnie.

Presently they heard a loud stamping on the stairs, accompanied by ringing jokes in the voice of old Scully, and laughter, evidently from the Swede. The men around the stove stared vacantly at each other. "Gosh," said the cowboy. The door flew open, and old Scully, flushed and anecdotal, came into the room. He was jabbering at the Swede, who followed him, laughing bravely. It was the entry of two roysterers from a banquet ball.

"Come now," said Scully sharply to the three seated men, "move up and give us a chance at the stove." The cowboy and the Easterner obediently sidled their chairs to make room for the newcomers. Johnnie, however, simply arranged himself in a more indolent attitude, and then remained motionless.

"Come! Git over, there," said Scully.

"Plenty of room on the other side of the stove," said Johnnie.

"Do you think we want to sit in the draught?" roared the father.

But the Swede here interposed with a grandeur of confidence. "No, no. Let the boy sit where he likes," he cried in a bullying voice to the father.

"All right! All right!" said Scully deferentially. The cowboy and the Easterner exchanged glances of wonder.

The five chairs were formed in a crescent about one side of the stove. The Swede began to talk; he talked arrogantly, profanely, angrily. Johnnie, the cowboy and the Easterner maintained a morose silence, while old Scully appeared to be receptive and eager, breaking in constantly with sympathetic ejaculations.

Finally, the Swede announced that he was thirsty. He moved in his chair, and said that he would go for a drink of water.

"I'll git it for you," cried Scully at once.

"No," said the Swede contemptuously. "I'll get it for myself." He arose and stalked with the air of an owner off into the executive parts of the hotel.

As soon as the Swede was out of hearing Scully sprang to his feet and whispered intensely to the others. "Upstairs he thought I was tryin' to poison 'im."

"Say," said Johnnie, "this makes me sick. Why don't you throw 'im out in the snow?"

"Why, he's all right now," declared Scully. "It was only that he was from the East and he thought this was a tough place. That's all. He's all right now."

The cowboy looked with admiration upon the Easterner. "You were straight," he said. "You were on to that there Dutchman."

"Well," said Johnnie to his father, "he may be all right now, but I don't see it. Other time he was scared, and now he's too fresh."

Scully's speech was always a combination of Irish brogue and idiom, Western twang and idiom, and scraps of curiously formal diction taken from the story-books and newspapers. He now hurled a strange mass of language at the head of his son. "What do I keep? What do I keep? What do I keep?" he demanded in a voice of thunder. He slapped his knee impressively, to indicate that he himself was going to make reply, and that all should heed. "I keep a hotel," he shouted. "A hotel, do you mind? A guest under my roof has sacred privileges. He is to be intimidated by none. Not one word shall he hear that would prijudice him in favor of goin' away. I'll not have it. There's no place in this here town where they can say they iver took in a guest of mine because he was afraid to stay here." He wheeled suddenly upon the cowboy and the Easterner "Am I right?"

"Yes, Mr. Scully," said the cowboy, "I think you're right."

"Yes, Mr. Scully," said the Easterner, "I think you're right."

## V

At six-o'clock supper, the Swede fizzed like a fire-wheel. He sometimes seemed on the point of bursting into riotous song, and in all his madness he was encouraged by old Scully. The Easterner was incased in reserve; the cowboy sat in wide-mouthed amazement, forgetting to eat, while Johnnie wrathily demolished great plates of food. The daughters of the house when they were obliged to replenish the biscuits approached as warily as Indians, and, having succeeded in their purposes, fled with ill-concealed trepidation. The Swede domineered the whole feast, and he gave it the appearance of a cruel bacchanal. He seemed to have grown suddenly taller; he gazed, brutally disdainful, into every face. His voice rang through the room. Once when he jabbed out harpoon-fashion with his fork to pinion a biscuit the weapon nearly impaled the hand of the Easterner which had been stretched quietly out for the same biscuit.

After supper, as the men filed toward the other room, the Swede smote Scully ruthlessly on the shoulder. "Well, old boy, that was a good square meal." Johnnie looked hopefully at his father; he knew that shoulder was tender from an old fall; and indeed it appeared for a moment as if Scully was going to flame out over the matter, but in the end he smiled a sickly smile and remained silent. The others understood from his manner that he was admitting his responsibility for the Swede's new viewpoint.

Johnnie, however, addressed his parent in an aside. "Why don't you license somebody to kick you downstairs?" Scully scowled darkly by way of reply.

When they were gathered about the stove, the Swede insisted on another game of High-Five. Scully gently deprecated the plan at first, but the Swede turned a wolfish glare upon him. The old man subsided, and the Swede canvassed the others. In his tone there was always a great threat. The cowboy and the Easterner both remarked indifferently that they would play. Scully said that he would presently have to go to meet the 6.58 train, and so the Swede turned menacingly upon Johnnie. For a moment their glances crossed like blades, and then Johnnie smiled and said: "Yes, I'll play."

They formed a square with the little board on their knees. The Easterner and the Swede were again partners. As the play went on, it was noticeable that the cowboy was not board-whacking as usual. Meanwhile, Scully, near the lamp, had put on his spectacles and, with an appearance curiously like an old priest, was reading a newspaper. In time he went out to meet the 6.58 train, and, despite his precautions, a gust of polar wind whirled into the room as he opened the door. Besides scattering the cards, it chilled the players to the marrow. The Swede cursed frightfully. When Scully returned, his entrance disturbed a cozy and friendly scene. The Swede again cursed. But presently they were once more intent, their heads bent forward and their hands moving swiftly. The Swede had adopted the fashion of board-whacking.

Scully took up his paper and for a long time remained immersed in matters which were extraordinarily remote from him. The lamp burned badly, and once he stopped to adjust the wick. The newspaper as he turned from page to page rustled with a slow and comfortable sound. Then suddenly he heard three terrible words: "You are cheatin'!"

Such scenes often prove that there can be little of dramatic import in environment. Any room can present a tragic front; any room can be comic. This little den was now hideous as a torture-chamber. The new faces of the men themselves had changed it upon the instant. The Swede held a huge fist in front of Johnnie's face, while the latter looked steadily over it into the blazing orbs of his accuser. The Easterner had grown pallid; the cowboy's jaw had dropped in that expression of bovine amazement which was one of his important mannerisms. After the three words, the first sound in the room was made by Scully's paper as it floated forgotten to his feet. His spectacles had also fallen from his nose, but by a clutch he had saved them in air. His hand, grasping the spectacles, now remained poised awkwardly and near his shoulder. He stared at the card-players.

Probably the silence was while a second elapsed. Then, if the floor had been suddenly twitched out from under the men they could not have moved quicker. The five had projected themselves headlong toward a common point. It happened that Johnnie in rising to hurl himself upon the Swede had stumbled slightly because of his curiously instinctive care for the cards and the board. The loss of the moment allowed time for the arrival of Scully, and also allowed the cowboy time to give the Swede a great push which sent him staggering back. The men found tongue together, and hoarse shouts of rage, appeal or fear burst from every throat. The cowboy pushed and jostled feverishly at the Swede, and the Easterner and Scully clung wildly to Johnnie; but, through the smoky air, above the swaying bodies of the peace-compellers, the eyes of the two warriors ever sought each other in glances of challenge that were at once hot and steely.

Of course the board had been overturned, and now the whole company of cards was scattered over the floor, where the boots of the men trampled the fat and painted kings and queens as they gazed with their silly eyes at the war that was waging above them.

Scully's voice was dominating the yells. "Stop now! Stop, I say! Stop, now——"

Johnnie, as he struggled to burst through the rank formed by Scully and the Easterner, was crying: "Well, he says I cheated! He says I cheated! I won't allow no man to say I cheated! If he says I cheated, he's a—— ——!"

The cowboy was telling the Swede: "Quit, now! Quit, d'ye hear——"

The screams of the Swede never ceased. "He did cheat! I saw him! I saw him——"

As for the Easterner, he was importuning in a voice that was not heeded. "Wait a moment, can't you? Oh, wait a moment. What's the good of a fight over a game of cards? Wait a moment——"

In this tumult no complete sentences were clear. "Cheat"—"Quit"—"He says"—These fragments pierced the uproar and rang out sharply. It was remarkable that whereas Scully undoubtedly made the most noise, he was the least heard of any of the riotous band.

Then suddenly there was a great cessation. It was as if each man had paused for breath, and although the room was still lighted with the anger of men, it could be seen that there was no danger of immediate conflict, and at once Johnnie, shouldering his way forward, almost succeeded in confronting the Swede. "What did you say I cheated for? What did you say I cheated for? I don't cheat and I won't let no man say I do!"

The Swede said: "I saw you! I saw you!"

"Well," cried Johnnie, "I'll fight any man what says I cheat!"

"No, you won't," said the cowboy. "Not here."

"Ah, be still, can't you?" said Scully, coming between them.

The quiet was sufficient to allow the Easterner's voice to be heard. He was repeating: "Oh, wait a moment, can't you? What's the good of a fight over a game of cards? Wait a moment."

Johnnie, his red face appearing above his father's shoulder, hailed the Swede again. "Did you say I cheated?"

The Swede showed his teeth. "Yes."

"Then," said Johnnie, "we must fight."

"Yes, fight," roared the Swede. He was like a demoniac. "Yes, fight! I'll show you what kind of a man I am! I'll show you who you want to fight! Maybe you think I can't fight! Maybe you think I can't! I'll show you, you skin,[4] you card-sharp! Yes, you cheated! You cheated! You cheated!"

"Well, let's git at it, then, mister," said Johnnie coolly.

The cowboy's brow was beaded with sweat from his efforts in intercepting all sorts of raids. He turned in despair to Scully. "What are you goin' to do now?"

A change had come over the Celtic visage of the old man. He now seemed all eagerness; his eyes glowed.

"We'll let them fight," he answered stalwartly. "I can't put up with it any longer. I've stood this damned Swede till I'm sick. We'll let them fight."

4. Cheat (colloquial).

## VI

The men prepared to go out of doors. The Easterner was so nervous that he had great difficulty in getting his arms into the sleeves of his new leather-coat. As the cowboy drew his fur-cap down over his ears his hands trembled. In fact, Johnnie and old Scully were the only ones who displayed no agitation. These preliminaries were conducted without words.

Scully threw open the door. "Well, come on," he said. Instantly a terrific wind caused the flame of the lamp to struggle at its wick, while a puff of black smoke sprang from the chimney-top. The stove was in mid-current of the blast, and its voice swelled to equal the roar of the storm. Some of the scarred and bedabbled cards were caught up from the floor and dashed helplessly against the further wall. The men lowered their heads and plunged into the tempest as into a sea.

No snow was falling, but great whirls and clouds of flakes, swept up from the ground by the frantic winds, were streaming southward with the speed of bullets. The covered land was blue with the sheen of an unearthly satin, and there was no other hue save where at the low black railway station—which seemed incredibly distant—one light gleamed like a tiny jewel. As the men floundered into a thigh-deep drift, it was known that the Swede was bawling out something. Scully went to him, put a hand on his shoulder and projected an ear. "What's that you say?" he shouted.

"I say," bawled the Swede again, "I won't stand much show against this gang. I know you'll all pitch on me."

Scully smote him reproachfully on the arm. "Tut, man," he yelled. The wind tore the words from Scully's lips and scattered them far a-lee.

"You are all a gang of——" boomed the Swede, but the storm also seized the remainder of this sentence.

Immediately turning their backs upon the wind, the men had swung around a corner to the sheltered side of the hotel. It was the function of the little house to preserve here, amid this great devastation of snow, an irregular V-shape of heavily-incrusted grass, which crackled beneath the feet. One could imagine the great drifts piled against the windward side. When the party reached the comparative peace of this spot it was found that the Swede was still bellowing.

"Oh, I know what kind of a thing this is! I know you'll all pitch on me. I can't lick you all!"

Scully turned upon him panther-fashion. "You'll not have to whip all of us. You'll have to whip my son Johnnie. An' the man what troubles you durin' that time will have me to dale with."

The arrangements were swiftly made. The two men faced each other, obedient to the harsh commands of Scully, whose face, in the subtly luminous gloom, could be seen set in the austere impersonal lines that are pictured on the countenances of the Roman veterans. The Easterner's teeth were chattering, and he was hopping up and down like a mechanical toy. The cowboy stood rock-like.

The contestants had not stripped off any clothing. Each was in his ordinary attire. Their fists were up, and they eyed each other in a calm that had the elements of leonine cruelty in it.

During this pause, the Easterner's mind, like a film, took lasting impressions of three men—the iron-nerved master of the ceremony; the Swede, pale, motionless, terrible; and Johnnie, serene yet ferocious, brutish yet heroic. The entire prelude had in it a tragedy greater than the tragedy of action, and this aspect was accentuated by the long mellow cry of the blizzard, as it sped the tumbling and wailing flakes into the black abyss of the south.

"Now!" said Scully.

The two combatants leaped forward and crashed together like bullocks. There was heard the cushioned sound of blows, and a curse squeezing out from between the tight teeth of one.

As for the spectators, the Easterner's pent-up breath exploded from him with a pop of relief, absolute relief from the tension of the preliminaries. The cowboy bounded into the air with a yowl. Scully was immovable as from supreme amazement and fear at the fury of the fight which he himself had permitted and arranged.

For a time the encounter in the darkness was such a perplexity of flying arms that it presented no more detail than would a swiftly-revolving wheel. Occasionally a face, as if illumined by a flash of light, would shine out, ghastly and marked with pink spots. A moment later, the men might have been known as shadows, if it were not for the involuntary utterance of oaths that came from them in whispers.

Suddenly a holocaust of warlike desire caught the cowboy, and he bolted forward with the speed of a broncho. "Go it, Johnnie; go it! Kill him! Kill him!"

Scully confronted him. "Kape back," he said; and by his glance the cowboy could tell that this man was Johnnie's father.

To the Easterner there was a monotony of unchangeable fighting that was an abomination. This confused mingling was eternal to his sense, which was concentrated in a longing for the end, the priceless end. Once the fighters lurched near him, and as he scrambled hastily backward, he heard them breathe like men on the rack.

"Kill him, Johnnie! Kill him! Kill him!" The cowboy's face was contorted like one of those agony-masks in museums.

"Keep still," said Scully icily.

Then there was a sudden loud grunt, incomplete, cut-short, and Johnnie's body swung away from the Swede and fell with sickening heaviness to the grass. The cowboy was barely in time to prevent the mad Swede from flinging himself upon his prone adversary. "No, you don't," said the cowboy, interposing an arm. "Wait a second."

Scully was at his son's side. "Johnnie! Johnnie, me boy?" His voice had a quality of melancholy tenderness. "Johnnie? Can you go on with it?" He looked anxiously down into the bloody pulpy face of his son.

There was a moment of silence, and then Johnnie answered in his ordinary voice: "Yes, I—it—yes."

Assisted by his father he struggled to his feet. "Wait a bit now till you git your wind," said the old man.

A few paces away the cowboy was lecturing the Swede. "No, you don't! Wait a second!"

The Easterner was plucking at Scully's sleeve. "Oh, this is enough," he pleaded. "This is enough! Let it go as it stands. This is enough!"

"Bill," said Scully, "git out of the road." The cowboy stepped aside. "Now." The combatants were actuated by a new caution as they advanced toward collision. They glared at each other, and then the Swede aimed a lightning blow that carried with it his entire weight. Johnnie was evidently half-stupid from weakness, but he miraculously dodged, and his fist sent the over-balanced Swede sprawling.

The cowboy, Scully and the Easterner burst into a cheer that was like a chorus of triumphant soldiery, but before its conclusion the Swede had scuf-fled agilely to his feet and come in berserk abandon at his foe. There was another perplexity of flying arms, and Johnnie's body again swung away and fell, even as a bundle might fall from a roof. The Swede instantly staggered to a little wind-waved tree and leaned upon it, breathing like an engine, while his savage and flame-lit eyes roamed from face to face as the men bent over Johnnie. There was a splendor of isolation in his situation at this time which the Easterner felt once when, lifting his eyes from the man on the ground, he beheld that mysterious and lonely figure, waiting.

"Are you any good yet, Johnnie?" asked Scully in a broken voice.

The son gasped and opened his eyes languidly. After a moment he answered: "No—I ain't—any good—any—more." Then, from shame and bodily ill, he began to weep, the tears furrowing down through the blood-stains on his face. "He was too—too—too heavy for me."

Scully straightened and addressed the waiting figure. "Stranger," he said, evenly, "it's all up with our side." Then his voice changed into that vibrant huskiness which is commonly the tone of the most simple and deadly announcements. "Johnnie is whipped."

Without replying, the victor moved off on the route to the front door of the hotel.

The cowboy was formulating new and unspellable blasphemies. The East-erner was startled to find that they were out in a wind that seemed to come direct from the shadowed arctic floes. He heard again the wail of the snow as it was flung to its grave in the south. He knew now that all this time the cold had been sinking into him deeper and deeper, and he wondered that he had not perished. He felt indifferent to the condition of the vanquished man.

"Johnnie, can you walk?" asked Scully.

"Did I hurt—hurt him any?" asked the son.

"Can you walk, boy? Can you walk?"

Johnnie's voice was suddenly strong. There was a robust impatience in it. "I asked you whether I hurt him any!"

"Yes, yes, Johnnie," answered the cowboy consolingly; "he's hurt a good deal."

They raised him from the ground, and as soon as he was on his feet he went tottering off, rebuffing all attempts at assistance. When the party rounded the corner they were fairly blinded by the pelting of the snow. It burned their faces like fire. The cowboy carried Johnnie through the drift to the door. As they entered some cards again rose from the floor and beat against the wall.

The Easterner rushed to the stove. He was so profoundly chilled that he almost dared to embrace the glowing iron. The Swede was not in the room. Johnnie sank into a chair, and folding his arms on his knees, buried his face in them. Scully, warming one foot and then the other at a rim of the stove, muttered to himself with Celtic mournfulness. The cowboy had removed his fur-cap, and with a dazed and rueful air he was now running one hand through his tousled locks. From overhead they could hear the creaking of boards, as the Swede tramped here and there in his room.

The sad quiet was broken by the sudden flinging open of a door that led toward the kitchen. It was instantly followed by an inrush of women. They precipitated themselves upon Johnnie amid a chorus of lamentation. Before they carried their prey off to the kitchen, there to be bathed and harangued with that mixture of sympathy and abuse which is a feat of their sex, the mother straightened herself and fixed old Scully with an eye of stern reproach. "Shame be upon you, Patrick Scully!" she cried. "Your own son, too. Shame be upon you!"

"There, now! Be quiet, now!" said the old man weakly.

"Shame be upon you, Patrick Scully!" The girls, rallying to this slogan, sniffed disdainfully in the direction of those trembling accomplices, the cowboy and the Easterner. Presently they bore Johnnie away, and left the three men to dismal reflection.

## VII

"I'd like to fight this here Dutchman myself," said the cowboy, breaking a long silence.

Scully wagged his head sadly. "No, that wouldn't do. It wouldn't be right. It wouldn't be right."

"Well, why wouldn't it?" argued the cowboy. "I don't see no harm in it."

"No," answered Scully with mournful heroism. "It wouldn't be right. It was Johnnie's fight, and now we mustn't whip the man just because he whipped Johnnie."

"Yes, that's true enough," said the cowboy; "but—he better not get fresh with me, because I couldn't stand no more of it."

"You'll not say a word to him," commanded Scully, and even then they heard the tread of the Swede on the stairs. His entrance was made theatric. He swept the door back with a bang and swaggered to the middle of the room. No one looked at him. "Well," he cried, insolently, at Scully. "I s'pose you'll tell me now how much I owe you?"

The old man remained stolid. "You don't owe me nothin'."

"Huh!" cried the Swede, "huh! Don't owe 'im nothin'."

The cowboy addressed the Swede. "Stranger, I don't see how you come to be so gay around here."

Old Scully was instantly alert. "Stop!" he shouted, holding his hand forth, fingers upward. "Bill, you shut up!"

The cowboy spat carelessly into the sawdust box. "I didn't say a word, did I?" he asked.

"Mr. Scully," called the Swede, "how much do I owe you?" It was seen that he was attired for departure, and that he had his valise in his hand.

"You don't owe me nothin'," repeated Scully in his same imperturbable way.

"Huh!" said the Swede. "I guess you're right. I guess if it was any way at all, you'd owe me somethin'. That's what I guess." He turned to the cowboy. " 'Kill him! Kill him! Kill him!' " he mimicked, and then guffawed victoriously. " 'Kill him!' " He was convulsed with ironical humor.

But he might have been jeering the dead. The three men were immovable and silent, staring with glassy eyes at the stove.

The Swede opened the door and passed into the storm, giving one derisive glance backward at the still group.

As soon as the door was closed, Scully and the cowboy leaped to their feet
and began to curse. They trampled to and fro, waving their arms and smashing
into the air with their fists. "Oh, but that was a hard minute!" wailed Scully.
"That was a hard minute! Him there leerin' and scoffin'! One bang at his nose
was worth forty dollars to me that minute! How did you stand it, Bill?"

"How did I stand it?" cried the cowboy in a quivering voice. "How did I
stand it? Oh!"

The old man burst into sudden brogue. "I'd loike to take that Swade," he
wailed, "and hould 'im down on a shtone flure and bate 'im to a jelly wid
a shtick!"

The cowboy groaned in sympathy. "I'd like to git him by the neck and hammer him"—he brought his hand down on a chair with a noise like a pistol-
shot—"hammer that there Dutchman until he couldn't tell himself from a
dead coyote!"

"I'd bate 'im until he——"

"I'd show *him* some things——"

And then together they raised a yearning fanatic cry. "Oh-o-oh! if we only
could——"

"Yes!"

"Yes!"

"And then I'd——"

"O-o-oh!"


## VIII

The Swede, tightly gripping his valise, tacked across the face of the storm as
if he carried sails. He was following a line of little naked gasping trees, which
he knew must mark the way of the road. His face, fresh from the pounding of
Johnnie's fists, felt more pleasure than pain in the wind and the driving snow.
A number of square shapes loomed upon him finally, and he knew them as
the houses of the main body of the town. He found a street and made travel
along it, leaning heavily upon the wind whenever, at a corner, a terrific blast
caught him.

He might have been in a deserted village. We picture the world as thick
with conquering and elate humanity, but here, with the bugles of the tempest
pealing, it was hard to imagine a peopled earth. One viewed the existence of
man then as a marvel, and conceded a glamour of wonder to these lice which
were caused to cling to a whirling, fire-smote, ice-locked, disease-stricken,
space-lost bulb. The conceit of man was explained by this storm to be the very
engine of life. One was a coxcomb not to die in it. However, the Swede found
a saloon.

In front of it an indomitable red light was burning, and the snow-flakes were
made blood-color as they flew through the circumscribed territory of the
lamp's shining. The Swede pushed open the door of the saloon and entered.
A sanded expanse was before him, and at the end of it four men sat about a
table drinking. Down one side of the room extended a radiant bar, and its
guardian was leaning upon his elbows listening to the talk of the men at the
table. The Swede dropped his valise upon the floor, and, smiling fraternally
upon the barkeeper, said: "Gimme some whisky, will you?" The man placed

a bottle, a whisky-glass, and a glass of ice-thick water upon the bar. The Swede poured himself an abnormal portion of whisky and drank it in three gulps. "Pretty bad night," remarked the bartender indifferently. He was making the pretension of blindness, which is usually a distinction of his class; but it could have been seen that he was furtively studying the half-erased blood-stains on the face of the Swede. "Bad night," he said again.

"Oh, it's good enough for me," replied the Swede, hardily, as he poured himself more whisky. The barkeeper took his coin and maneuvered it through its reception by the highly-nickeled cash-machine. A bell rang; a card labeled "20 cts." had appeared.

"No," continued the Swede, "this isn't too bad weather. It's good enough for me."

"So?" murmured the barkeeper languidly.

The copious drams made the Swede's eyes swim, and he breathed a trifle heavier. "Yes, I like this weather. I like it. It suits me." It was apparently his design to impart a deep significance to these words.

"So?" murmured the bartender again. He turned to gaze dreamily at the scroll-like birds and bird-like scrolls which had been drawn with soap upon the mirrors back of the bar.

"Well, I guess I'll take another drink," said the Swede presently. "Have something?"

"No, thanks; I'm not drinkin'," answered the bartender. Afterward he asked: "How did you hurt your face?"

The Swede immediately began to boast loudly. "Why, in a fight. I thumped the soul out of a man down here at Scully's hotel."

The interest of the four men at the table was at last aroused.

"Who was it?" said one.

"Johnnie Scully," blustered the Swede. "Son of the man what runs it. He will be pretty near dead for some weeks, I can tell you. I made a nice thing of him, I did. He couldn't get up. They carried him in the house. Have a drink?"

Instantly the men in some subtle way incased themselves in reserve. "No, thanks," said one. The group was of curious formation. Two were prominent local business men; one was the district-attorney; and one was a professional gambler of the kind known as "square." But a scrutiny of the group would not have enabled an observer to pick the gambler from the men of more reputable pursuits. He was, in fact, a man so delicate in manner, when among people of fair class, and so judicious in his choice of victims, that in the strictly masculine part of the town's life he had come to be explicitly trusted and admired. People called him a thoroughbred. The fear and contempt with which his craft was regarded was undoubtedly the reason that his quiet dignity shone conspicuous above the quiet dignity of men who might be merely hatters, billiard-markers[5] or grocery clerks. Beyond an occasional unwary traveler, who came by rail, this gambler was supposed to prey solely upon reckless and senile farmers, who, when flush with good crops, drove into town in all the pride and confidence of an absolutely invulnerable stupidity. Hearing at times in circuitous fashion of the despoilment of such a farmer, the important men of Romper invariably laughed in contempt of the victim, and if they thought of the wolf at all, it was a kind of pride at the knowledge that he would never

---

5. Scorekeepers at billiards matches.

dare think of attacking their wisdom and courage. Besides, it was popular that this gambler had a real wife and two real children in a neat cottage in a suburb, where he led an exemplary home life, and when any one even suggested a discrepancy in his character, the crowd immediately vociferated descriptions of this virtuous family circle. Then men who led exemplary home lives, and men who did not lead exemplary home lives, all subsided in a bunch, remarking that there was nothing more to be said.

However, when a restriction was placed upon him—as, for instance, when a strong clique of members of the new Pollywog Club refused to permit him, even as a spectator, to appear in the rooms of the organization—the candor and gentleness with which he accepted the judgment disarmed many of his foes and made his friends more desperately partisan. He invariably distinguished between himself and a respectable Romper man so quickly and frankly that his manner actually appeared to be a continual broadcast compliment.

And one must not forget to declare the fundamental fact of his entire position in Romper. It is irrefutable that in all affairs outside of his business, in all matters that occur eternally and commonly between man and man, this thieving card-player was so generous, so just, so moral, that, in a contest, he could have put to flight the consciences of nine-tenths of the citizens of Romper.

And so it happened that he was seated in this saloon with the two prominent local merchants and the district-attorney.

The Swede continued to drink raw whisky, meanwhile babbling at the barkeeper and trying to induce him to indulge in potations. "Come on. Have a drink. Come on. What—no? Well, have a little one then. By gawd, I've whipped a man to-night, and I want to celebrate. I whipped him good, too. Gentlemen," the Swede cried to the men at the table, "have a drink?"

"Ssh!" said the barkeeper.

The group at the table, although furtively attentive, had been pretending to be deep in talk, but now a man lifted his eyes toward the Swede and said shortly: "Thanks. We don't want any more."

At this reply the Swede ruffled out his chest like a rooster. "Well," he exploded, "it seems I can't get anybody to drink with me in this town. Seems so, don't it? Well!"

"Ssh!" said the barkeeper.

"Say," snarled the Swede, "don't you try to shut me up. I won't have it. I'm a gentleman, and I want people to drink with me. And I want 'em to drink with me now. Now—do you understand?" He rapped the bar with his knuckles.

Years of experience had calloused the bartender. He merely grew sulky. "I hear you," he answered.

"Well," cried the Swede, "listen hard then. See those men over there? Well, they're going to drink with me, and don't you forget it. Now you watch."

"Hi!" yelled the barkeeper, "this won't do!"

"Why won't it?" demanded the Swede. He stalked over to the table, and by chance laid his hand upon the shoulder of the gambler. "How about this?" he asked, wrathfully. "I asked you to drink with me."

The gambler simply twisted his head and spoke over his shoulder. "My friend, I don't know you."

"Oh, hell!" answered the Swede, "come and have a drink."

"Now, my boy," advised the gambler kindly, "take your hand off my shoulder and go 'way and mind your own business." He was a little slim man, and it seemed strange to hear him use this tone of heroic patronage to the burly Swede. The other men at the table said nothing.

"What? You won't drink with me, you little dude! I'll make you then! I'll make you!" The Swede had grasped the gambler frenziedly at the throat, and was dragging him from his chair. The other men sprang up. The barkeeper dashed around the corner of his bar. There was a great tumult, and then was seen a long blade in the hand of the gambler. It shot forward, and a human body, this citadel of virtue, wisdom, power, was pierced as easily as if it had been a melon. The Swede fell with a cry of supreme astonishment.

The prominent merchants and the district-attorney must have at once tumbled out of the place backward. The bartender found himself hanging limply to the arm of a chair and gazing into the eyes of a murderer.

"Henry," said the latter, as he wiped his knife on one of the towels that hung beneath the bar-rail, "you tell 'em where to find me. I'll be home, waiting for 'em." Then he vanished. A moment afterward the barkeeper was in the street dinning through the storm for help, and, moreover, companionship.

The corpse of the Swede, alone in the saloon, had its eyes fixed upon a dreadful legend that dwelt a-top of the cash-machine. "This registers the amount of your purchase."

IX

Months later, the cowboy was frying pork over the stove of a little ranch near the Dakota line, when there was a quick thud of hoofs outside, and, presently, the Easterner entered with the letters and the papers.

"Well," said the Easterner at once, "the chap that killed the Swede has got three years. Wasn't much, was it?"

"He has? Three years?" The cowboy poised his pan of pork, while he ruminated upon the news. "Three years. That ain't much."

"No. It was a light sentence," replied the Easterner as he unbuckled his spurs. "Seems there was a good deal of sympathy for him in Romper."

"If the bartender had been any good," observed the cowboy thoughtfully, "he would have gone in and cracked that there Dutchman on the head with a bottle in the beginnin' of it and stopped all this here murderin'."

"Yes, a thousand things might have happened," said the Easterner tartly.

The cowboy returned his pan of pork to the fire, but his philosophy continued. "It's funny, ain't it? If he hadn't said Johnnie was cheatin' he'd be alive this minute. He was an awful fool. Game played for fun, too. Not for money. I believe he was crazy."

"I feel sorry for that gambler," said the Easterner.

"Oh, so do I," said the cowboy. "He don't deserve none of it for killin' who he did."

"The Swede might not have been killed if everything had been square."

"Might not have been killed?" exclaimed the cowboy. "Everythin' square? Why, when he said that Johnnie was cheatin' and acted like such a jackass? And then in the saloon he fairly walked up to git hurt?" With these arguments the cowboy browbeat the Easterner and reduced him to rage.

"You're a fool!" cried the Easterner viciously. "You're a bigger jackass than the Swede by a million majority. Now let me tell you one thing. Let me tell you something. Listen! Johnnie *was* cheating!"

" 'Johnnie,' " said the cowboy blankly. There was a minute of silence, and then he said robustly: "Why, no. The game was only for fun."

"Fun or not," said the Easterner, "Johnnie was cheating. I saw him. I know it. I saw him. And I refused to stand up and be a man. I let the Swede fight it out alone. And you—you were simply puffing around the place and wanting to fight. And then old Scully himself! We are all in it! This poor gambler isn't even a noun. He is kind of an adverb. Every sin is the result of a collaboration. We, five of us, have collaborated in the murder of this Swede. Usually there are from a dozen to forty women really involved in every murder, but in this case it seems to be only five men—you, I, Johnnie, old Scully, and that fool of an unfortunate gambler came merely as a culmination, the apex of a human movement, and gets all the punishment."

The cowboy, injured and rebellious, cried out blindly into this fog of mysterious theory. "Well, I didn't do anythin', did I?"

1898, 1902

## An Episode of War[1]

The lieutenant's rubber blanket lay on the ground, and upon it he had poured the company's supply of coffee. Corporals and other representatives of the grimy and hot-throated men who lined the breastwork had come for each squad's portion.

The lieutenant was frowning and serious at this task of division. His lips pursed as he drew with his sword various crevices in the heap until brown squares of coffee, astoundingly equal in size, appeared on the blanket. He was on the verge of a great triumph in mathematics and the corporals were thronging forward, each to reap a little square, when suddenly the lieutenant cried out and looked quickly at a man near him as if he suspected it was a case of personal assault. The others cried out also when they saw blood upon the lieutenant's sleeve.

He had winced like a man stung, swayed dangerously, and then straightened. The sound of his hoarse breathing was plainly audible. He looked sadly, mystically, over the breastwork at the green face of a wood where now were many little puffs of white smoke. During this moment, the men about him gazed statue-like and silent, astonished and awed by this catastrophe which had happened when catastrophes were not expected—when they had leisure to observe it.

As the lieutenant stared at the wood, they too swung their heads so that for another moment all hands, still silent, contemplated the distant forest as if their minds were fixed upon the mystery of a bullet's journey.

The officer had, of course, been compelled to take his sword at once into his left hand. He did not hold it by the hilt. He gripped it at the middle of the blade, awkwardly. Turning his eyes from the hostile wood, he looked at the sword as he held it there, and seemed puzzled as to what to do with it, where to put it. In short this weapon had of a sudden become a strange thing to him.

---

1. *An Episode of War* was first published in the English magazine *The Gentlewoman* (December 1899). The source of the present text is Vol. 6 of the University of Virginia edition of *The Works of Stephen Crane*.

He looked at it in a kind of stupefaction, as if he had been miraculously endowed with a trident, a sceptre, or a spade.

Finally, he tried to sheath it. To sheath a sword held by the left hand, at the middle of the blade, in a scabbard hung at the left hip, is a feat worthy of a sawdust ring. This wounded officer engaged in a desperate struggle with the sword and the wobbling scabbard, and during the time of it, he breathed like a wrestler.

But at this instant the men, the spectators, awoke from their stone-like poses and crowded forward sympathetically. The orderly-sergeant took the sword and tenderly placed it in the scabbard. At the time, he leaned nervously backward, and did not allow even his finger to brush the body of the lieutenant. A wound gives strange dignity to him who bears it. Well men shy from this new and terrible majesty. It is as if the wounded man's hand is upon the curtain which hangs before the revelations of all existence, the meaning of ants, potentates, wars, cities, sunshine, snow, a feather dropped from a bird's wing, and the power of it sheds radiance upon a bloody form, and makes the other men understand sometimes that they are little. His comrades look at him with large eyes thoughtfully. Moreover, they fear vaguely that the weight of a finger upon him might send him headlong, precipitate the tragedy, hurl him at once into the dim grey unknown. And so the orderly-sergeant while sheathing the sword leaned nervously backward.

There were others who proffered assistance. One timidly presented his shoulder and asked the lieutenant if he cared to lean upon it, but the latter waved them away mournfully. He wore the look of one who knows he is the victim of a terrible disease and understands his helplessness. He again stared over the breastwork at the forest, and then turning went slowly rearward. He held his right wrist tenderly in his left hand, as if the wounded arm was made of very brittle glass.

And the men in silence stared at the wood, then at the departing lieutenant—then at the wood, then at the lieutenant.

As the wounded officer passed from the line of battle, he was enabled to see many things which as a participant in the fight were unknown to him. He saw a general on a black horse gazing over the lines of blue infantry at the green woods which veiled his problems. An aide galloped furiously, dragged his horse suddenly to a halt, saluted, and presented a paper. It was, for a wonder, precisely like an historical painting.

To the rear of the general and his staff, a group, composed of a bugler, two or three orderlies, and the bearer of the corps standard, all upon maniacal horses, were working like slaves to hold their ground, preserve their respectful interval, while the shells bloomed in the air about them, and caused their chargers to make furious quivering leaps.

A battery, a tumultuous and shining mass, was swirling toward the right. The wild thud of hoofs, the cries of the riders shouting blame and praise, menace and encouragement, and, last, the roar of the wheels, the slant of the glistening guns, brought the lieutenant to an intent pause. The battery swept in curves that stirred the heart; it made halts as dramatic as the crash of a wave on the rocks, and when it fled onward, this aggregation of wheels, levers, motors, had a beautiful unity, as if it were a missle. The sound of it was a war-chorus that reached into the depths of man's emotion.

The lieutenant, still holding his arm as if it were of glass, stood watching this battery until all detail of it was lost, save the figures of the riders, which rose and fell and waved lashes over the black mass.

Later he turned his eyes toward the battle where the shooting sometimes crackled like bush-fires, sometimes sputtered with exasperating irregularity, and sometimes reverberated like the thunder. He saw the smoke rolling upward and saw crowds of men who ran and cheered, or stood and blazed away at the inscrutable distance.

He came upon some stragglers and they told him how to find the field hospital. They described its exact location. In fact these men, no longer having part in the battle, knew more of it than others. They told the performance of every corps, every division, the opinion of every general. The lieutenant, carrying his wounded arm rearward, looked upon them with wonder.

At the roadside a brigade was making coffee and buzzing with talk like a girls' boarding-school. Several officers came out to him and inquired concerning things of which he knew nothing. One, seeing his arm, began to scold. "Why, man, that's no way to do. You want to fix that thing." He appropriated the lieutenant and the lieutenant's wound. He cut the sleeve and laid bare the arm, every nerve of which softly fluttered under his touch. He bound his handkerchief over the wound, scolding away in the meantime. His tone allowed one to think that he was in the habit of being wounded every day. The lieutenant hung his head, feeling, in this presence, that he did not know how to be correctly wounded.

The low white tents of the hospital were grouped around an old school-house. There was here a singular commotion. In the foreground two ambulances interlocked wheels in the deep mud. The drivers were tossing the blame of it back and forth, gesticulating and berating, while from the ambulances, both crammed with wounded, there came an occasional groan. An interminable crowd of bandaged men were coming and going. Great numbers sat under the trees nursing heads or arms or legs. There was a dispute of some kind raging on the steps of the school-house. Sitting with his back against a tree a man with a face as grey as a new army blanket was serenely smoking a corn-cob pipe. The lieutenant wished to rush forward and inform him that he was dying.

A busy surgeon was passing near the lieutenant. "Good morning," he said with a friendly smile. Then he caught sight of the lieutenant's arm and his face at once changed. "Well, let's have a look at it." He seemed possessed suddenly of a great contempt for the lieutenant. This wound evidently placed the latter on a very low social plane. The doctor cried out impatiently. What-mutton-head had tied it up that way anyhow. The lieutenant answered: "Oh, a man."

When the wound was disclosed the doctor fingered it disdainfully. "Humph," he said. "You come along with me and I'll 'tend to you." His voice contained the same scorn as if he were saying: "You will have to go to jail."

The lieutenant had been very meek but now his face flushed, and he looked into the doctor's eyes. "I guess I won't have it amputated," he said.

"Nonsense, man! nonsense! nonsense!" cried the doctor. "Come along, now. I won't amputate it. Come along. Don't be a baby."

"Let go of me," said the lieutenant, holding back wrathfully. His glance fixed upon the door of the old school-house, as sinister to him as the portals of death.

And this is the story of how the lieutenant lost his arm. When he reached home his sisters, his mother, his wife, sobbed for a long time at the sight of the flat sleeve. "Oh, well," he said, standing shamefaced amid these tears. "I don't suppose it matters so much as all that."

1899

## FROM THE BLACK RIDERS AND OTHER LINES[1]

### 1

Black riders came from the sea.
There was clang and clang of spear and shield,
And clash and clash of hoof and heel,
Wild shouts and the wave of hair
In the rush upon the wind:                                              5
Thus the ride of Sin.

### 27

A youth in apparel that glittered
Went to walk in a grim forest.
There he met an assassin
Attired all in garb of old days;
He, scowling through the thickets,                                      5
And dagger poised quivering,
Rushed upon the youth.
"Sir," said this latter,
"I am enchanted, believe me,
To die, thus,                                                          10
In this medieval fashion,
According to the best legends;
Ah, what joy!"
Then took he the wound, smiling,
And died, content.                                                     15

## FROM WAR IS KIND[1]

### 76

Do not weep, maiden, for war is kind.
Because your lover threw wild hands toward the sky
And the affrighted steed ran on alone,
Do not weep.
War is kind.                                                            5

---

1. These poems from *The Black Riders and Other Lines* (1895), together with their numbering, are reprinted from Joseph Katz's *The Poems of Stephen Crane* (1966).

1. These poems from *War Is Kind* (1899) are reprinted from Joseph Katz's critical edition of *The Poems of Stephen Crane* (1966).

Hoarse, booming drums of the regiment,
Little souls who thirst for fight,
These men were born to drill and die.
The unexplained glory flies above them,
Great is the Battle-God, great, and his Kingdom—                10
A field where a thousand corpses lie.

Do not weep, babe, for war is kind.
Because your father tumbled in the yellow trenches,
Raged at his breast, gulped and died,
Do not weep.                                                    15
War is kind.

Swift blazing flag of the regiment,
Eagle with crest of red and gold,
These men were born to drill and die.
Point for them the virtue of slaughter,                         20
Make plain to them the excellence of killing
And a field where a thousand corpses lie.

Mother whose heart hung humble as a button
On the bright splendid shroud of your son,
Do not weep.                                                    25
War is kind.

1896                                                            1899


## 96

A man said to the universe:
"Sir, I exist!"
"However," replied the universe,
"The fact has not created in me
A sense of obligation."                                         5

1899


## FROM POSTHUMOUSLY PUBLISHED POEMS[1]

### 113

A man adrift on a slim spar
A horizon smaller than the rim of a bottle
Tented waves rearing lashy dark points
The near whine of froth in circles.
                    God is cold.                                5

---

1. The poem, first published in *The Bookman* (April 1929), is reprinted from Joseph Katz's critical edition of *The Poems of Stephen Crane* (1966).

The incessant raise and swing of the sea
And growl after growl of crest
The sinkings, green, seething, endless
The upheaval half-completed.
                God is cold.                                    10

The seas are in the hollow of The Hand;
Oceans may be turned to a spray
Raining down through the stars
Because of a gesture of pity toward a babe.
Oceans may become grey ashes,                                   15
Die with a long moan and a roar
Amid the tumult of the fishes
And the cries of the ships,
Because The Hand beckons the mice.

A horizon smaller than a doomed assassin's cap,                20
Inky, surging tumults
A reeling, drunken sky and no sky
A pale hand sliding from a polished spar.
                God is cold.

The puff of a coat imprisoning air:                            25
A face kissing the water-death
A weary slow sway of a lost hand
And the sea, the moving sea, the sea.
                God is cold.

c. 1898                                                       1929

---

# THEODORE DREISER

## 1871–1945

Theodore Herman Albert Dreiser was born in Terre Haute, Indiana, on August
17, 1871, the twelfth of thirteen children. His gentle and devoted mother was
illiterate; his German immigrant father was severe and distant. From the former
he seems to have absorbed a quality of compassionate wonder; from the latter he
seems to have inherited moral earnestness and the capacity to persist in the face of
failure, disappointment, and despair.

Dreiser's childhood was decidedly unhappy. The large family moved from house
to house in Indiana dogged by poverty, insecurity, and internal division. One of
his brothers became a famous popular songwriter under the name of Paul Dresser,
but other brothers and sisters drifted into drunkenness, promiscuity, and squalor.
Dreiser as a youth was as ungainly, confused, shy, and full of vague yearnings as
most of his fictional protagonists, male and female. In this as in many other ways,
Dreiser's novels are direct projections of his inner life as well as careful transcriptions of his experiences.

From the age of fifteen Dreiser was essentially on his own, earning meager
support from a variety of menial jobs. A high-school teacher staked him to a year

at Indiana University in 1889, but Dreiser's education was to come from experience and from independent reading and thinking. This education began in 1892 when he wangled his first newspaper job with the *Chicago Globe*. Over the next decade as an itinerant journalist Dreiser slowly groped his way to authorship, testing what he knew from direct experience against what he was learning from reading Charles Darwin, Ernst Haeckel, Thomas Huxley, and Herbert Spencer, those late-nineteenth-century scientists and social scientists who lent support to the view that nature and society had no divine sanction.

*Sister Carrie* (1900), which traces the material rise of Carrie Meeber and the tragic decline of G. W. Hurstwood, was Dreiser's first novel. Because it depicted social transgressions by characters who felt no remorse and largely escaped punishment, and because it used "strong" language and used names of living persons, it was virtually suppressed by its publisher, who printed but refused to promote the book. Since its reissue in 1907 it has steadily risen in popularity and scholarly acceptance as one of the key works in the Dreiser canon. Indeed, though turn-of-the-century readers found Dreiser's point of view crude and immoral, his influence on the fiction of the first quarter of the century is perhaps greater than any other writer's. In this early period some of his best short fictions were written, among them *Nigger Jeff* and *Old Rogaum and His Theresa*. The best of his short stories— like all of Dreiser's fiction—have the unusual power to compel our sympathy for and wonder over characters whose minds and inner life we never really enter, but the urgency of whose desire we are made to feel. For Theresa there is at least a temporary rescue from the potentially dangerous consequences of her strong sexual and imaginative awakening in the beguiling city streets; for Emily, there is only prostitution and a ghastly death.

In the first years of the century Dreiser suffered a breakdown. With the help of his brother Paul, however, he eventually recovered and by 1904 was on the way to several successful years as an editor, the last of them as editorial director of the Butterick Publishing Company. In 1910 he resigned to write *Jennie Gerhardt* (1911), one of his best novels and the first of a long succession of books that marked his turn to writing as a full-time career.

In *The Financier* (1912), *The Titan* (1914), and *The Stoic* (not published until 1947), Dreiser shifted from the pathos of helpless protagonists to the power of those unusual individuals who assume dominant roles in business and society. The protagonist of this "Trilogy of Desire" (as Dreiser described it), Frank Cowperwood, is modeled after the Chicago speculator Charles T. Yerkes. These novels of the businessman as buccaneer introduced, even more explicitly than had *Sister Carrie*, the notion that men of high sexual energy were financially successful, a theme that is carried over into the rather weak autobiographical novel *The "Genius"* (1915).

The identification of potency with money is at the heart of Dreiser's greatest and most successful novel, *An American Tragedy* (1925). The center of this immense novel's thick texture of biographical circumstance, social fact, and industrial detail is a young man who acts as if the only way he can be truly fulfilled is by acquiring wealth—through marriage if necessary.

During the last two decades of his life Dreiser turned entirely away from fiction and toward political activism and polemical writing. He visited the Soviet Union in 1927 and published *Dreiser Looks at Russia* the following year. In the 1930s, like many other American intellectuals and writers, Dreiser was increasingly attracted by the philosophical program of the Communist party. Unable to believe in traditional religious credos, yet unable to give up his strong sense of justice, he continued to seek a way to reconcile his determinism with his compassionate sense of the mystery of life.

In his lifetime Dreiser was controversial as a man and as a writer. He was accused, with some justice by conventional standards, of being immoral in his personal behavior, a poor thinker, and a dangerous political radical; his style was said (by critics more than by authors) to be ponderous and his narrative sense weak. As time has passed, however, Dreiser has become recognized as a profound and prescient critic of debased American values and as a powerful novelist.

# Old Rogaum and His Theresa[1]

In all Bleecker Street[2] was no more comfortable doorway than that of the butcher Rogaum, even if the first floor was given over to meat market purposes. It was to one side of the main entrance, which gave ingress to the butcher shop, and from it led up a flight of steps, at least five feet wide, to the living rooms above. A little portico stood out in front of it, railed on either side, and within was a second or final door, forming, with the outer or storm door, a little area, where Mrs. Rogaum and her children frequently sat of a summer's evening. The outer door was never locked, owing to the inconvenience it would inflict on Mr. Rogaum, who had no other way of getting upstairs. In winter, when all had gone to bed, there had been cases in which belated travelers had taken refuge there from the snow or sleet. One or two newsboys occasionally slept there, until routed out by Officer Maguire, who, seeing it half open one morning at two o'clock, took occasion to look in. He jogged the newsboys sharply with his stick, and then, when they were gone, tried the inner door, which was locked.

"You ought to keep that outer door locked, Rogaum," he observed to the phlegmatic butcher the next evening, as he was passing, "people might get in. A couple o' kids was sleepin' in there last night."

"Ach, dot iss no difference," answered Rogaum pleasantly. "I haf der inner door locked, yet. Let dem sleep. Dot iss no difference."

"Better lock it," said the officer, more to vindicate his authority than anything else. "Something will happen there yet."

The door was never locked, however, and now of a summer evening Mrs. Rogaum and the children made pleasant use of its recess, watching the rout of street cars and occasionally belated trucks go by. The children played on the sidewalk, all except the budding Theresa (eighteen just turning), who, with one companion of the neighborhood, the pretty Kenrihan girl, walked up and down the block, laughing, glancing, watching the boys. Old Mrs. Kenrihan lived in the next block, and there, sometimes, the two stopped. There, also, they most frequently pretended to be when talking with the boys in the intervening side street. Young "Connie" Almerting and George Goujon were the bright particular mashers[3] who held the attention of the maidens in this block. These two made their acquaintance in the customary bold, boyish way, and thereafter the girls had an urgent desire to be out in the street together after eight, and to linger where the boys could see and overtake them.

Old Mrs. Rogaum never knew. She was a particularly fat, old German lady, completely dominated by her liege and portly lord, and at nine o'clock regu-

1. First published as *Butcher Rogaum's Door* in *Reedy's Mirror* 2 (December 12, 1901). Dreiser revised it, as *Old Rogaum and His Theresa*, for inclusion in *Free and Other Stories* (1918), the source of the present text.
2. A street in Greenwich Village in New York City.

Dreiser lived in Greenwich Village during the years 1917–18 while he revised this story.
3. Male flirts. Charles Drouet in *Sister Carrie* is initially described as a masher, a man "whose dress or manners are calculated to elicit the admiration of susceptible young women."

larly, as he had long ago deemed meet and fit, she was wont to betake her way upward and so to bed. Old Rogaum himself, at that hour, closed the market and went to his chamber.

Before that all the children were called sharply, once from the doorstep below and once from the window above, only Mrs. Rogaum did it first and Rogaum last. It had come, because of a shade of lenience, not wholly apparent in the father's nature, that the older of the children needed two callings and sometimes three. Theresa, now that she had "got in" with the Kenrihan maiden, needed that many calls and even more.

She was just at that age for which mere thoughtless, sensory life holds its greatest charm. She loved to walk up and down in the as yet bright street where were voices and laughter, and occasionally moonlight streaming down. What a nuisance it was to be called at nine, anyhow. Why should one have to go in then, anyhow. What old fogies her parents were, wishing to go to bed so early. Mrs. Kenrihan was not so strict with her daughter. It made her pettish when Rogaum insisted, calling as he often did, in German, "Come you now," in a very hoarse and belligerent voice.

She came, eventually, frowning and wretched, all the moonlight calling her, all the voices of the night urging her to come back. Her innate opposition due to her urgent youth made her coming later and later, however, until now, by August of this, her eighteenth year, it was nearly ten when she entered, and Rogaum was almost invariably angry.

"I vill lock you oudt," he declared, in strongly accented English, while she tried to slip by him each time. "I vill show you. Du sollst[4] come ven I say, yet. Hear now."

"I'll not," answered Theresa, but it was always under her breath.

Poor Mrs. Rogaum troubled at hearing the wrath in her husband's voice. It spoke of harder and fiercer times which had been with her. Still she was not powerful enough in the family councils to put in a weighty word. So Rogaum fumed unrestricted.

There were other nights, however, many of them, and now that the young sparks of the neighborhood had enlisted the girls' attention, it was a more trying time than ever. Never did a street seem more beautiful. Its shabby red walls, dusty pavements and protruding store steps and iron railings seemed bits of the ornamental paraphernalia of heaven itself. These lights, the cars, the moon, the street lamps! Theresa had a tender eye for the dashing Almerting, a young idler and loafer of the district, the son of a stationer farther up the street. What a fine fellow he was, indeed! What a handsome nose and chin! What eyes! What authority! His cigarette was always cocked at a high angle, in her presence, and his hat had the least suggestion of being set to one side. He had a shrewd way of winking one eye, taking her boldly by the arm, hailing her as, "Hey, Pretty!" and was strong and athletic and worked (when he worked) in a tobacco factory. His was a trade, indeed, nearly acquired, as he said, and his jingling pockets attested that he had money of his own. Altogether he was very captivating.

"Aw, whaddy ya want to go in for?" he used to say to her, tossing his head gayly on one side to listen and holding her by the arm, as old Rogaum called. "Tell him yuh didn't hear."

4. You shall (German).

"No, I've got to go," said the girl, who was soft and plump and fair—a Rhine maiden type.

"Well, yuh don't have to go just yet. Stay another minute. George, what was that fellow's name that tried to sass us the other day?"

"Theresa!" roared old Rogaum forcefully. "If you do not now come! Ve vill see!"

"I've got to go," repeated Theresa with a faint effort at starting. "Can't you hear? Don't hold me. I haf to."

"Aw, whaddy ya want to be such a coward for? Y' don't have to go. He won't do nothin' tuh yuh. My old man was always hollerin' like that up tuh a coupla years ago. Let him holler! Say, kid, but yuh got sweet eyes! They're as blue! An' your mouth——"

"Now stop! You hear me!" Theresa would protest softly, as, swiftly, he would slip an arm about her waist and draw her to him, sometimes in a vain, sometimes in a successful effort to kiss her.

As a rule she managed to interpose an elbow between her face and his, but even then he would manage to touch an ear or a cheek or her neck—sometimes her mouth, full and warm—before she would develop sufficient energy to push him away and herself free. Then she would protest mock earnestly or sometimes run away.

"Now, I'll never speak to you any more, if that's the way you're going to do. My father don't allow me to kiss boys, anyhow," and then she would run, half ashamed, half smiling to herself as he would stare after her, or if she lingered, develop a kind of anger and even rage.

"Aw, cut it! Whaddy ya want to be so shy for? Dontcha like me? What's gettin' into yuh, anyhow? Hey?"

In the meantime George Goujon and Myrtle Kenrihan, their companions, might be sweeting and going through a similar contest, perhaps a hundred feet up the street or near at hand. The quality of old Rogaum's voice would by now have become so raucous, however, that Theresa would have lost all comfort in the scene and, becoming frightened, hurry away. Then it was often that both Almerting and Goujon as well as Myrtle Kenrihan would follow her to the corner, almost in sight of the irate old butcher.

"Let him call," young Almerting would insist, laying a final hold on her soft white fingers and causing her to quiver thereby.

"Oh, no," she would gasp nervously. "I can't."

"Well, go on, then," he would say, and with a flip of his heel would turn back, leaving Theresa to wonder whether she had alienated him forever or no. Then she would hurry to her father's door.

"Muss ich all my time spenden calling, mit you on de streeds oudt?" old Rogaum would roar wrathfully, the while his fat hand would descend on her back. "Take dot now. Vy don'd you come ven I call? In now. I vill show you. Und come you yussed vunce more at dis time—ve vill see if I am boss in my own house, aber! Komst du vun minute nach[5] ten to-morrow und you vill see vot you vill get. I vill der door lock. Du sollst not in kommen. Mark! Oudt sollst du stayen—oudt!" and he would glare wrathfully at her retreating figure.

Sometimes Theresa would whimper, sometimes cry or sulk. She almost hated her father for his cruelty, "the big, fat, rough thing," and just because

5. After (German).

she wanted to stay out in the bright streets, too! Because he was old and stout and wanted to go to bed at ten, he thought every one else did. And outside was the dark sky with its stars, the street lamps, the cars, the tinkle and laughter of eternal life!

"Oh!" she would sigh as she undressed and crawled into her small neat bed. To think that she had to live like this all her days! At the same time old Rogaum was angry and equally determined. It was not so much that he imagined that his Theresa was in bad company as yet, but he wished to forefend against possible danger. This was not a good neighborhood by any means. The boys around here were tough. He wanted Theresa to pick some nice sober youth from among the other Germans he and his wife knew here and there—at the Lutheran Church, for instance. Otherwise she shouldn't marry. He knew she only walked from his shop to the door of the Kenrihans and back again. Had not his wife told him so? If he had thought upon what far pilgrimage her feet had already ventured, or had even seen the dashing Almerting hanging near, then had there been wrath indeed. As it was, his mind was more or less at ease.

On many, many evenings it was much the same. Sometimes she got in on time, sometimes not, but more and more "Connie" Almerting claimed her for his "steady," and bought her ice-cream. In the range of the short block and its confining corners it was all done, lingering by the curbstone and strolling a half block either way in the side streets, until she had offended seriously at home, and the threat was repeated anew. He often tried to persuade her to go on picnics or outings of various kinds, but this, somehow, was not to be thought of at her age—at least with him. She knew her father would never endure the thought, and never even had the courage to mention it, let alone run away. Mere lingering with him at the adjacent street corners brought stronger and stronger admonishments—even more blows and the threat that she should not get in at all.

Well enough she meant to obey, but on one radiant night late in June the time fled too fast. The moon was so bright, the air so soft. The feel of far summer things was in the wind and even in this dusty street. Theresa, in a newly starched white summer dress, had been loitering up and down with Myrtle when as usual they encountered Almerting and Goujon. Now it was ten, and the regular calls were beginning.

"Aw, wait a minute," said "Connie." "Stand still. He won't lock yuh out."

"But he will, though," said Theresa. "You don't know him."

"Well, if he does, come on back to me. I'll take care of yuh. I'll be here. But he won't though. If you stayed out a little while he'd letcha in all right. That's the way my old man used to try to do me but it didn't work with me. I stayed out an' he let me in, just the same. Don'tcha let him kidja." He jingled some loose change in his pocket.

Never in his life had he had a girl on his hands at any unseasonable hour, but it was nice to talk big, and there was a club to which he belonged. The Varick Street Roosters, and to which he had a key. It would be closed and empty at this hour, and she could stay there until morning, if need be or with Myrtle Kenrihan. He would take her there if she insisted. There was a sinister grin on the youth's face.

By now Theresa's affections had carried her far. This youth with his slim body, his delicate strong hands, his fine chin, straight mouth and hard dark eyes—how wonderful he seemed! He was but nineteen to her eighteen but cold, shrewd, daring. Yet how tender he seemed to her, how well worth having! Always, when he kissed her now, she trembled in the balance. There was something in the iron grasp of his fingers that went through her like fire. His glance held hers at times when she could scarcely endure it.

"I'll wait, anyhow," he insisted.

Longer and longer she lingered, but now for once no voice came.

She began to feel that something was wrong—a greater strain than if old Rogaum's voice had been filling the whole neighborhood.

"I've got to go," she said.

"Gee, but you're a coward, yuh are!" said he derisively. "What 'r yuh always so scared about? He always says he'll lock yuh out, but he never does."

"Yes, but he will," she insisted nervously. "I think he has this time. You don't know him. He's something awful when he gets real mad. Oh, Connie, I must go!" For the sixth or seventh time she moved, and once more he caught her arm and waist and tried to kiss her, but she slipped away from him.

"Ah, yuh!" he exclaimed. "I wish he would lock yuh out!"

At her own doorstep she paused momentarily, more to soften her progress than anything. The outer door was open as usual, but not the inner. She tried it, but it would not give. It was locked! For a moment she paused, cold fear racing over her body, and then knocked.

No answer.

Again she rattled the door, this time nervously, and was about to cry out. Still no answer.

At last she heard her father's voice, hoarse and indifferent, not addressed to her at all, but to her mother.

"Let her go, now," it said savagely, from the front room where he supposed she could not hear. "I vill her a lesson teach."

"Hadn't you better let her in now, yet?" pleaded Mrs. Rogaum faintly.

"No," insisted Mr. Rogaum. "Nefer! Let her go now. If she vill alvays stay oudt, let her stay now. Ve vill see how she likes dot."

His voice was rich in wrath, and he was saving up a good beating for her into the bargain, that she knew. She would have to wait and wait and plead, and when she was thoroughly wretched and subdued he would let her in and beat her—such a beating as she had never received in all her born days.

Again the door rattled, and still she got no answer. Not even her call brought a sound.

Now, strangely, a new element, not heretofore apparent in her nature but nevertheless wholly there, was called into life, springing in action as Diana,[6] full formed. Why should he always be so harsh? She hadn't done anything but stay out a little later than usual. He was always so anxious to keep her in and subdue her. For once the cold chill of her girlish fears left her, and she wavered angrily.

"All right," she said, some old German stubbornness springing up, "I won't knock. You don't need to let me in, then."

A suggestion of tears was in her eyes, but she backed firmly out onto the stoop and sat down, hesitating. Old Rogaum saw her, lowering down from the lattice, but said nothing. He would teach her for once what were proper hours!

---

6. A Roman deity, goddess of the moon, hunting, and women in childbirth.

At the corner, standing, Almerting also saw her. He recognized the simple white dress, and paused steadily, a strange thrill racing over him. Really they had locked her out! Gee, this was new. It was great, in a way. There she was, white, quiet, shut out, waiting at her father's doorstep.

Sitting thus, Theresa pondered a moment, her girlish rashness and anger dominating her. Her pride was hurt and she felt revengeful. They would shut her out, would they? All right, she would go out and they should look to it how they would get her back—the old curmudgeons. For the moment the home of Myrtle Kenrihan came to her as a possible refuge, but she decided that she need not go there yet. She had better wait about awhile and see—or walk and frighten them. He would beat her, would he? Well, maybe he would and maybe he wouldn't. She might come back, but still that was a thing afar off. Just now it didn't matter so much. "Connie" was still there on the corner. He loved her dearly. She felt it.

Getting up, she stepped to the now quieting sidewalk and strolled up the street. It was a rather nervous procedure, however. There were street cars still, and stores lighted and people passing, but soon these would not be, and she was locked out. The side streets were already little more than long silent walks and gleaming rows of lamps.

At the corner her youthful lover almost pounced upon her.

"Locked out, are yuh?" he asked, his eyes shining.

For the moment she was delighted to see him, for a nameless dread had already laid hold of her. Home meant so much. Up to now it had been her whole life.

"Yes," she answered feebly.

"Well, let's stroll on a little," said the boy. He had not as yet quite made up his mind what to do, but the night was young. It was so fine to have her with him—his.

At the farther corner they passed Officers Maguire and Delahanty, idly swinging their clubs and discussing politics.

" 'Tis a shame," Officer Delahanty was saying, "the way things are run now," but he paused to add, "Ain't that old Rogaum's girl over there with young Almerting?"

"It is," replied Maguire, looking after.

"Well, I'm thinkin' he'd better be keepin' an eye on her," said the former. "She's too young to be runnin' around with the likes o' him."

Maguire agreed. "He's a young tough," he observed. "I never liked him. He's too fresh. He works over here in Myer's tobacco factory, and belongs to The Roosters. He's up to no good, I'll warrant that."

"Teach 'em a lesson, I would," Almerting was saying to Theresa as they strolled on. "We'll walk around a while an' make 'em think yuh mean business. They won't lock yuh out any more. If they don't let yuh in when we come back I'll find yuh a place, all right."

His sharp eyes were gleaming as he looked around into her own. Already he had made up his mind that she should not go back if he could help it. He knew a better place than home for this night, anyhow—the club room of the Roosters, if nowhere else. They could stay there for a time, anyhow.

By now old Rogaum, who had seen her walking up the street alone, was marveling at her audacity, but thought she would soon come back. It was amazing that she should exhibit such temerity, but he would teach her! Such a whipping! At half-past ten, however, he stuck his head out of the open window and saw nothing of her. At eleven, the same. Then he walked the floor.

At first wrathful, then nervous, then nervous and wrathful, he finally ended all nervous, without a scintilla of wrath. His stout wife sat up in bed and began to wring her hands.

"Lie down!" he commanded. "You make me sick. I know vot I am doing!"

"Is she still at der door?" pleaded the mother.

"No," he said. "I don't tink so. She should come ven I call."

His nerves were weakening, however, and now they finally collapsed.

"She vent de stread up," he said anxiously after a time. "I vill go after."

Slipping on his coat, he went down the stairs and out into the night. It was growing late, and the stillness and gloom of midnight were nearing. Nowhere in sight was his Theresa. First one way and then another he went, looking here, there, everywhere, finally groaning.

"Ach, Gott!" he said, the sweat bursting out on his brow, "vot in Teufel's[7] name iss dis?"

He thought he would seek a policeman, but there was none. Officer Maguire had long since gone for a quiet game in one of the neighboring saloons. His partner had temporarily returned to his own beat. Still old Rogaum hunted on, worrying more and more.

Finally he bethought him to hasten home again, for she must have got back. Mrs. Rogaum, too, would be frantic if she had not. If she were not there he must go to the police. Such a night! And his Theresa——This thing could not go on.

As he turned into his own corner he almost ran, coming up to the little portico wet and panting. At a puffing step he turned, and almost fell over a white body at his feet, a prone and writhing woman.

"Ach, Gott!" he cried aloud, almost shouting in his distress and excitement. "Theresa, vot iss dis? Wilhelmina, a light now. Bring a light now, I say, for himmel's sake! Theresa hat sich *umgebracht*.[8] Help!"

He had fallen to his knees and was turning over the writhing, groaning figure. By the pale light of the street, however, he could make out that it was not his Theresa, fortunately, as he had at first feared, but another and yet there was something very like her in the figure.

"Um!" said the stranger weakly. "Ah!"

The dress was gray, not white as was his Theresa's, but the body was round and plump. It cut the fiercest cords of his intensity, this thought of death to a young woman, but there was something else about the situation which made him forget his own troubles.

Mrs. Rogaum, loudly admonished, almost tumbled down the stairs. At the foot she held the light she had brought—a small glass oil-lamp—and then nearly dropped it. A fairly attractive figure, more girl than woman, rich in all the physical charms that characterize a certain type, lay near to dying. Her soft hair had fallen back over a good forehead, now quite white. Her pretty hands, well decked with rings, were clutched tightly in an agonized grip. At her neck a blue silk shirtwaist and light lace collar were torn away where she had clutched herself, and on the white flesh was a yellow stain as of one who had

---

7. The Devil's.

8. Theresa has killed herself (German).

OLD ROGAUM AND HIS THERESA 1659

been burned. A strange odor reeked in the area, and in one corner was a spilled bottle.

"Ach, Gott!" exclaimed Mrs. Rogaum. "It iss a vooman! She haf herself gekilt. Run for der police! Oh, my! oh, my!"

Rogaum did not kneel for more than a moment. Somehow, this creature's fate seemed in some psychic way identified with that of his own daughter. He bounded up, and jumping out his front door, began to call lustily for the police. Officer Maguire, at his social game nearby, heard the very first cry and came running.

"What's the matter here, now?" he exclaimed, rushing up full and ready for murder, robbery, fire, or, indeed, anything in the whole roster of human calamities.

"A vooman!" said Rogaum excitedly. "She haf herself *umgebracht*. She iss dying. Ach, Gott! in my own doorstep, yet!"

"Vere iss der hospital?" put in Mrs. Rogaum, thinking clearly of an ambulance, but not being able to express it. "She iss gekilt, sure. Oh! Oh!" and banding over her the poor old motherly soul stroked the tightened hands, and trickled tears upon the blue shirtwaist. "Ach, vy did you do dot?" she said. "Ach, for vy?"

Officer Maguire was essentially a man of action. He jumped to the sidewalk, amid the gathering company, and beat loudly with his club upon the stone flagging. Then he ran to the nearest police phone, returning to aid in any other way he might. A milk wagon passing on its way from the Jersey ferry with a few tons of fresh milk aboard, he held it up and demanded a helping.

"Give us a quart there, will you?" he said authoritatively. "A woman's swallowed acid in here."

"Sure," said the driver, anxious to learn the cause of the excitement. "Got a glass, anybody?"

Maguire ran back and returned, bearing a measure. Mrs. Rogaum stood looking nervously on, while the stocky officer raised the golden head and poured the milk.

"Here, now, drink this," he said. "Come on. Try an' swallow it."

The girl, a blonde of the type the world too well knows, opened her eyes, and looked, groaning a little.

"Drink it," shouted the officer fiercely. "Do you want to die? Open your mouth!"

Used to a fear of the law in all her days, she obeyed now, even in death. The lips parted, the fresh milk was drained to the end, some spilling on neck and cheek.

While they were working old Rogaum came back and stood looking on, by the side of his wife. Also Officer Delahanty, having heard the peculiar wooden ring of the stick upon the stone in the night, had come up.

"Ach, ach," exclaimed Rogaum rather distractedly, "und she iss oudt yet. I could not find her. Oh, oh!"

There was a clang of a gong up the street as the racing ambulance turned rapidly in. A young hospital surgeon dismounted, and seeing the woman's condition, ordered immediate removal. Both officers and Rogaum, as well as the surgeon, helped place her in the ambulance. After a moment the lone bell, ringing wildly in the night, was all the evidence remaining that a tragedy had been here.

"Do you know how she came here?" asked Officer Delahanty, coming back to get Rogaum's testimony for the police.

"No, no," answered Rogaum wretchedly. "She vass here alretty. I vass for my daughter loog. Ach, himmel, I haf my daughter lost. She iss avay."

Mrs. Rogaum also chattered, the significance of Theresa's absence all the more painfully emphasized by this.

The officer did not at first get the import of this. He was only interested in the facts of the present case.

"You say she was here when you come? Where was you?"

"I say I vass for my daughter loog. I come here, und der vooman vass here now alretty."

"Yes. What time was this?"

"Only now yet. Yussed a half-hour."

Officer Maguire had strolled up, after chasing away a small crowd that had gathered with fierce and unholy threats. For the first time now he noticed the peculiar perturbation of the usually placid German couple.

"What about your daughter?" he asked, catching a word as to that.

Both old people raised their voices at once.

"She haf gone. She haf run avay. Ach, himmel, ve must for her loog. Quick—she could not get in. Ve had der door shut."

"Locked her out, eh?" inquired Maguire after a time, hearing much of the rest of the story.

"Yes," explained Rogaum. "It was to schkare her a liddle. She vould not come ven I called."

"Sure, that's the girl we saw walkin' with young Almerting, do ye mind? The one in the white dress," said Delahanty to Maguire.

"White dress, yah!" echoed Rogaum, and then the fact of her walking with some one came home like a blow.

"Did you hear dot?" he exclaimed even as Mrs. Rogaum did likewise. "*Mein Gott, hast du das gehoert?*"[9]

He fairly jumped as he said it. His hands flew up to his stout and ruddy head.

"Whaddy ya want to let her out for nights?" asked Maguire roughly, catching the drift of the situation. "That's no time for young girls to be out, anyhow, and with these toughs around here. Sure, I saw her, nearly two hours ago."

"Ach," groaned Rogaum. "Two hours yet. Ho, ho, ho!" His voice was quite hysteric.

"Well, go on in," said Officer Delahanty. "There's no use yellin' out here. Give us a description of her an' we'll send out an alarm. You won't be able to find her walkin' around."

Her parents described her exactly. The two men turned to the nearest police box and then disappeared, leaving the old German couple in the throes of distress. A time-worn old church-clock nearby now chimed out one and then two. The notes cut like knives. Mrs. Rogaum began fearfully to cry. Rogaum walked and blustered to himself.

"It's a queer case, that," said Officer Delahanty to Maguire after having reported the matter of Theresa, but referring solely to the outcast of the door-

9. My God, did you hear that? (German).

way so recently sent away and in whose fate they were much more interested. She being a part of the commercialized vice of the city, they were curious as to the cause of her suicide. "I think I know that woman. I think I know where she came from. You do, too—Adele's, around the corner, eh? She didn't come into that doorway by herself, either. She was put there. You know how they do."

"You're right," said Maguire. "She was put there, all right, and that's just where she come from, too."

The two of them now tipped up their noses and cocked their eyes significantly.

"Let's go around," added Maguire.

They went, the significant red light over the transom at 68 telling its own story. Strolling leisurely up, they knocked. At the very first sound a painted denizen of the half-world opened the door.

"Where's Adele?" asked Maguire as the two, hats on as usual, stepped in.

"She's gone to bed."

"Tell her to come down."

They seated themselves deliberately in the gaudy mirrored parlor and waited, conversing between themselves in whispers. Presently a sleepy-looking woman of forty in a gaudy robe of heavy texture, and slippered in red, appeared.

"We're here about that suicide case you had tonight. What about it? Who was she? How'd she come to be in that doorway around the corner? Come, now," Maguire added, as the madam assumed an air of mingled injured and ignorant innocence, "you know. Can that stuff! How did she come to take poison?"

"I don't know what you're talking about," said the woman with the utmost air of innocence. "I never heard of any suicide."

"Aw, come now," insisted Delahanty, "the girl around the corner. You know. We know you've got a pull, but we've got to know about this case, just the same. Come across now. It won't be published. What made her take the poison?"

Under the steady eyes of the officers the woman hesitated, but finally weakened.

"Why—why—her lover went back on her—that's all. She got so blue we just couldn't do anything with her. I tried to, but she wouldn't listen."

"Lover, eh?" put in Maguire as though that were the most unheard-of thing in the world. "What was his name?"

"I don't know. You never can tell that."

"What was her name—Annie?" asked Delahanty wisely, as though he knew but was merely inquiring for form's sake.

"No—Emily."

"Well, how did she come to get over there, anyhow?" inquired Maguire most pleasantly.

"George took her," she replied, referring to a man-of-all-work about the place.

Then little by little as they sat there the whole miserable story came out, miserable as all the wilfulness and error and suffering of the world.

"How old was she?"

"Oh, twenty-one."

"Well, where'd she come from?"

"Oh, here in New York. Her family locked her out one night, I think."

Something in the way the woman said this last brought old Rogaum and his daughter back to the policemen's minds. They had forgotten all about her by now, although they had turned in an alarm. Fearing to interfere too much with this well-known and politically controlled institution, the two men left, but outside they fell to talking of the other case.

"We ought to tell old Rogaum about her some time," said Maguire to Delahanty cynically. "He locked his kid out to-night."

"Yes, it might be a good thing for him to hear that," replied the other. "We'd better go round there an' see if his girl's back yet. She may be back by now," and so they returned but little disturbed by the joint miseries.

At Rogaum's door they once more knocked loudly.

"Is your daughter back again?" asked Maguire when a reply was had.

"Ach, no," replied the hysterical Mrs. Rogaum, who was quite alone now. "My husband he haf gone oudt again to loog vunce more. Oh, my! Oh, my!"

"Well, that's what you get for lockin' her out," returned Maguire loftily, the other story fresh in his mind. "That other girl downstairs here tonight was locked out too, once." He chanced to have a girl-child of his own and somehow he was in the mood for pointing a moral. "You oughtn't to do anything like that. Where d'yuh expect she's goin' to if you lock her out?"

Mrs. Rogaum groaned. She explained that it was not her fault, but anyhow it was carrying coals to Newcastle to talk to her so. The advice was better for her husband.

The pair finally returned to the station to see if the call had been attended to.

"Sure," said the sergeant, "certainly. Whaddy ya think?" and he read from the blotter before him:

" 'Look out for girl, Theresa Rogaum. Aged 18; height, about 5, 3; light hair, blue eyes, white cotton dress, trimmed with blue ribbon. Last seen with lad named Almerting, about 19 years of age, about 5, 9; weight 135 pounds.' "

There were other details even more pointed and conclusive. For over an hour now, supposedly, policemen from the Battery to Harlem, and far beyond, had been scanning long streets and dim shadows for a girl in a white dress with a youth of nineteen,—supposedly.

Officer Halsey, another of this region, which took in a portion of Washington Square, had seen a good many couples this pleasant summer evening since the description of Theresa and Almerting had been read to him over the telephone, but none that answered to these. Like Maguire and Delahanty, he was more or less indifferent to all such cases, but idling on a corner near the park at about three a.m., a brother officer, one Paisly by name, came up and casually mentioned the missing pair also.

"I bet I saw that couple, not over an hour ago. She was dressed in white, and looked to me as if she didn't want to be out. I didn't happen to think at the time, but now I remember. They acted sort o' funny. She did, anyhow. They went in this park down at the Fourth Street end there."

"Supposing we beat it, then," suggested Halsey, weary for something to do.

"Sure," said the other quickly, and together they began a careful search, kicking around in the moonlight under the trees. The moon was leaning moderately toward the west, and all the branches were silvered with light and dew.

Among the flowers, past clumps of bushes, near the fountain, they searched, each one going his way alone. At last, the wandering Halsey pushed beside a thick clump of flaming bushes, ruddy, slightly, even in the light. A murmur of voices greeted him, and something very much like the sound of a sob.

"What's that?" he said mentally, drawing near and listening.

"Why don't you come on now?" said the first of the voices heard. "They won't let you in any more. You're with me, ain't you? What's the use cryin'?"

No answer to this, but no sobs. She must have been crying silently.

"Come on. I can take care of yuh. We can live in Hoboken.[1] I know a place where we can go to-night. That's all right."

There was a movement as if the speaker were patting her on the shoulder.

"What's the use cryin'? Don't you believe I love yuh?"

The officer who had stolen quietly around to get a better view now came closer. He wanted to see for himself. In the moonlight, from a comfortable distance, he could see them seated. The tall bushes were almost all about the bench. In the arms of the youth was the girl in white, held very close. Leaning over to get a better view, he saw him kiss her and hold her—hold her in such a way that she could but yield to him, whatever her slight disinclination.

It was a common affair at earlier hours, but rather interesting now. The officer was interested. He crept nearer.

"What are you two doin' here?" he suddenly inquired, rising before them, as though he had not seen.

The girl tumbled out of her compromising position, speechless and blushing violently. The young man stood up, nervous, but still defiant.

"Aw, we were just sittin' here," he replied.

"Yes? Well, say, what's your name? I think we're lookin' for you two, any-how. Almerting?"

"That's me," said the youth.

"And yours?" he added, addressing Theresa.

"Theresa Rogaum," replied the latter brokenly, beginning to cry.

"Well, you two'll have to come along with me," he added laconically. "The Captain wants to see both of you," and he marched them solemnly away.

"What for?" young Almerting ventured to inquire after a time, blanched with fright.

"Never mind," replied the policeman irritably. "Come along, you'll find out at the station house. We want you both. That's enough."

At the other end of the park Paisly joined them, and, at the station-house, the girl was given a chair. She was all tears and melancholy with a modicum possibly of relief at being thus rescued from the world. Her companion, for all his youth, was defiant if circumspect, a natural animal defeated of its aim.

"Better go for her father," commented the sergeant, and by four in the morning old Rogaum, who had still been up and walking the floor, was rushing stationward. From an earlier rage he had passed to an almost killing grief, but now at the thought that he might possibly see his daughter alive and well once more he was overflowing with a mingled emotion which contained rage, fear, sorrow, and a number of other things. What should he do to her if she were alive? Beat her? Kiss her? Or what? Arrived at the station, however, and seeing his fair Theresa in the hands of the police, and this young stranger

---

1. A seaport in northeastern New Jersey, opposite New York City.

lingering near, also detained, he was beside himself with fear, rage, affection.

"You! You!" he exclaimed at once, glaring at the imperturbable Almerting, when told that this was the young man who was found with his girl. Then, seized with a sudden horror, he added, turning to Theresa, "Vot haf you done? Oh, oh! You! You!" he repeated again to Almerting angrily, now that he felt that his daughter was safe. "Come not near my tochter any more! I vill preak your effery pone, du teufel, du!"

He made a move toward the incarcerated lover, but here the sergeant interfered.

"Stop that, now," he said calmly. "Take your daughter out of here and go home, or I'll lock you both up. We don't want any fighting in here. D'ye hear? Keep your daughter off the streets hereafter, then she won't get into trouble. Don't let her run around with such young toughs as this." Almerting winced. "Then there won't anything happen to her. We'll do whatever punishing's to be done."

"Aw, what's eatin' him!" commented Almerting dourly, now that he felt himself reasonably safe from a personal encounter. "What have I done? He locked her out, didn't he? I was just keepin' her company till morning."

"Yes, we know all about that," said the sergeant, "and about you, too. You shut up, or you'll go downtown to Special Sessions. I want no guff out o' you." Still he ordered the butcher angrily to be gone.

Old Rogaum heard nothing. He had his daughter. He was taking her home. She was not dead—not even morally injured in so far as he could learn. He was a compound of wondrous feelings. What to do was beyond him.

At the corner near the butcher shop they encountered the wakeful Maguire, still idling, as they passed. He was pleased to see that Rogaum had his Theresa once more. It raised him to a high, moralizing height.

"Don't lock her out any more," he called significantly. "That's what brought the other girl to your door, you know!"

"Vot iss dot?" said Rogaum.

"I say the other girl was locked out. That's why she committed suicide."

"Ach, I know," said the husky German under his breath, but he had no intention of locking her out. He did not know what he would do until they were in the presence of his crying wife, who fell upon Theresa, weeping. Then he decided to be reasonably lenient.

"She vass like you," said the old mother to the wandering Theresa, ignorant of the seeming lesson brought to their very door. "She vass loog like you."

"I vill not vip you now," said the old butcher solemnly, too delighted to think of punishment after having feared every horror under the sun, "aber, go not oudt any more. Keep off de streads so late. I von't haf it. Dot loafer, aber— let him yussed come here some more! I fix him!"

"No, no," said the fat mother tearfully, smoothing her daughter's hair. "She vouldn't run avay no more yet, no, no." Old Mrs. Rogaum was all mother.

"Well, you wouldn't let me in," insisted Theresa, "and I didn't have any place to go. What do you want me to do? I'm not going to stay in the house all the time."

"I fix him!" roared Rogaum, unloading all his rage now on the recreant lover freely. "Yussed let him come some more! Der penitentiary he should haf!"

"Oh, he's not so bad," Theresa told her mother, almost a heroine now that she was home and safe. "He's Mr. Almerting, the stationer's boy. They live here in the next block."

"Don't you ever bother that girl again," the sergeant was saying to young Almerting as he turned him loose an hour later. "If you do, we'll get you, and you won't get off under six months. Y' hear me, do you?"

"Aw, I don't want 'er," replied the boy truculently and cynically. "Let him have his old daughter. What'd he want to lock 'er out for? They'd better not lock 'er out again though, that's all I say. I don't want 'er."

"Beat it!" replied the sergeant, and away he went.

1901, 1918

---

# JACK LONDON
## 1876–1916

John Griffith London was born on January 12, 1876, the illegitimate son of W. H. Chaney, a talented and self-taught man who became an astrologer, and Flora Wellman, an eccentric woman from a wealthy Ohio family who was both a spiritualist and music teacher. London, who never saw his real father, took the name of his stepfather. London may have exaggerated his early poverty, but from earliest youth he supported himself with menial and dangerous jobs, experiencing profoundly the struggle for survival that most other writers and intellectuals knew only from observation or books. By the time he was eighteen he had worked in a cannery and as an oyster pirate, seaman, jute-mill worker, and coal shoveler. After crossing much of the continent as a member of "Kelly's Army" (which was supposed to join with "Coxey's Army," an organized group of unemployed who, following the panic of 1893, carried their call for economic reform to Washington, D.C.), he was jailed for thirty days for vagrancy. At this point he determined to educate himself to improve his own condition and that of others.

With an intellectual energy that matched his physical strength, London quickly completed high school and spent a semester reading prodigiously as a special student at the University of California. Temperament rather than logic led him to embrace the hopeful socialism of Marx on the one hand and the rather darker views of Nietzsche and Darwinism on the other. That is, London believed at the same time in the inevitable triumph of the working class and in the evolutionary necessity of the survival of the strongest individuals. London's sincere intellectual and personal involvement in that socialist movement is recorded in such novels and polemical works as *The People of the Abyss* (1903), *The Iron Heel* (1908), *War of the Classes* (1905), and *Revolution* (1910); his competing, deeply felt commitment to the fundamental reality of the law of survival and the will to power is dramatized in his most popular novels, *The Call of the Wild* (1903) and *The Sea-Wolf* (1904). Wolf Larsen, the ruthless, amoral protagonist of the latter book, best realizes the ideal of the "superman." The contradiction between these competing beliefs is most vividly projected in the patently autobiographical novel *Martin Eden* (1909), a central document for the London scholar.

London had been writing sporadically for five years, but his professional career began after he spent the winter of 1897–98 in the Klondike in a futile search for gold. Within two years, by the time he published his first collection of stories, *The Son of the Wolf* (1900), he was on his way to becoming the highest paid author of his time. By his twenty-eighth birthday *The Call of the Wild* had made him famous.

London said he disliked his profession and claimed that he wrote for money, but he was also a methodical and careful craftsman who produced a minimum of a thousand publishable words a day six days a week. He wrote on many subjects, from agronomy to penal reform, from astral projection to warfare. The most enduringly popular of his stories involved the primitive (and melodramatic) struggle of strong and weak individuals in the context of irresistible natural forces such as the wild sea or the Arctic wastes. At a time when America's frontier was closing and President Theodore Roosevelt was urging the strenuous life, London adapted the physical ruggedness and psychological independence of Rudyard Kipling's heroes to the American experience in *The Call of the Wild*, *The Sea-Wolf*, and *White Fang* (1906). Like his contemporaries Stephen Crane and Frank Norris (and like Hemingway a generation later), London was fascinated by the way violence tested and defined human character, though he was much more interested in ideas than Crane and less sentimental than Norris. Thus, in *The Law of Life*, the tribal patriarch's death is depicted both as an illustration of the law that all living things die and in terms of the particular psychological state of the individual facing his end.

London continued to write until his death in 1916 from a "gastrointestinal type of uraemia," widely supposed to have been suicide. But the bulk of his best work had been done by 1910. He had written too much too fast, with too little concern for the stylistic and formal refinement and subtlety of characterization that rank high with critics. He had not, moreover, reconciled his contradictory views of humanity's nature and destiny. But London's stories of humanity in and against nature continue to be popular all over the world. In them, London strips everything down to the symbolic starkness of dream, to a primordial simplicity that has the strange and compelling power of ancient myth.

# The Law of Life[1]

Old Koskoosh listened greedily. Though his sight had long since faded, his hearing was still acute, and the slightest sound penetrated to the glimmering intelligence which yet abode behind the withered forehead, but which no longer gazed forth upon the things of the world. Ah! that was Sit-cum-to-ha, shrilly anathematizing the dogs as she cuffed and beat them into the harnesses. Sit-cum-to-ha was his daughter's daughter, but she was too busy to waste a thought upon her broken grandfather, sitting alone there in the snow, forlorn and helpless. Camp must be broken. The long trail waited while the short day refused to linger. Life called her, and the duties of life, not death. And he was very close to death now.

The thought made the old man panicky for the moment, and he stretched forth a palsied hand which wandered tremblingly over the small heap of dry wood beside him. Reassured that it was indeed there, his hand returned to the shelter of his mangy furs, and he again fell to listening. The sulky crackling of half-frozen hides told him that the chief's moose-skin lodge had been struck, and even then was being rammed and jammed into portable compass. The chief was his son, stalwart and strong, head man of the tribesmen, and a mighty hunter. As the women toiled with the camp luggage, his voice rose, chiding them for their slowness. Old Koskoosh strained his ears. It was the last

---

1. This story was first printed in *McClure's Magazine* (March 1901) and was included in the collection *Children of the Frost* (1902); the present text is a reprint from *McClure's*.

time he would hear that voice. There went Geehow's lodge! And Tusken's! Seven, eight, nine; only the Shaman's could be still standing. There! They were at work upon it now. He could hear the Shaman grunt as he piled it on the sled. A child whimpered, and a woman soothed it with soft, crooning gutturals. Little Koo-tee, the old man thought, a fretful child, and not over strong. It would die soon, perhaps, and they would burn a hole through the frozen tundra and pile rocks above to keep the wolverines away. Well, what did it matter? A few years at best, and as many an empty belly as a full one. And in the end, Death waited, ever-hungry and hungriest of them all.

What was that? Oh, the men lashing the sleds and drawing tight the thongs. He listened, who would listen no more. The whip-lashes snarled and bit among the dogs. Hear them whine! How they hated the work and the trail! They were off! Sled after sled churned slowly away into the silence. They were gone. They had passed out of his life, and he faced the last bitter hour alone. No. The snow crunched beneath a moccasin; a man stood beside him; upon his head a hand rested gently. His son was good to do this thing. He remembered other old men whose sons had not waited after the tribe. But his son had. He wandered away into the past, till the young man's voice brought him back.

"Is it well with you?" he asked.

And the old man answered, "It is well."

"There be wood beside you," the younger man continued, "and the fire burns bright. The morning is gray, and the cold has broken. It will snow presently. Even now is it snowing."

"Ay, even now is it snowing."

"The tribesmen hurry. Their bales are heavy, and their bellies flat with lack of feasting. The trail is long and they travel fast. I go now. It is well?"

"It is well. I am as a last year's leaf, clinging lightly to the stem. The first breath that blows, and I fall. My voice is become like an old woman's. My eyes no longer show me the way of my feet, and my feet are heavy, and I am tired. It is well."

He bowed his head in content till the last noise of the complaining snow had died away, and he knew his son was beyond recall. Then his hand crept out in haste to the wood. It alone stood betwixt him and the eternity which yawned in upon him. At last the measure of his life was a handful of fagots. One by one they would go to feed the fire, and just so, step by step, death would creep upon him. When the last stick had surrendered up its heat, the frost would begin to gather strength. First his feet would yield, then his hands; and the numbness would travel, slowly, from the extremities to the body. His head would fall forward upon his knees, and he would rest. It was easy. All men must die.

He did not complain. It was the way of life, and it was just. He had been born close to the earth, close to the earth had he lived, and the law thereof was not new to him. It was the law of all flesh. Nature was not kindly to the flesh. She had no concern for that concrete thing called the individual. Her interest lay in the species, the race. This was the deepest abstraction old Koskoosh's barbaric mind was capable of, but he grasped it firmly. He saw it exemplified in all life. The rise of the sap, the bursting greenness of the willow bud, the fall of the yellow leaf—in this alone was told the whole history. But one task did nature set the individual. Did he not perform it, he died. Did he perform it, it was all the same, he died. Nature did not care; there were plenty who were obedient, and it was only the obedience in this matter, not the obedient, which lived and lived always. The tribe of Koskoosh was very old. The old men he had known when a boy, had known old men before them. Therefore it was true that the tribe lived, that it stood for the obedience of all its members, way down into the forgotten past, whose very resting places were unremembered. They did not count; they were episodes. They had passed away like clouds from a summer sky. He also was an episode, and would pass away. Nature did not care. To life she set one task, gave one law. To perpetuate was the task of life, its law was death. A maiden was a good creature to look upon, full-breasted and strong, with spring to her step and light in her eyes. But her task was yet before her. The light in her eyes brightened, her step quickened, she was now bold with the young men, now timid, and she gave them of her own unrest. And ever she grew fairer and yet fairer to look upon, till some hunter, able no longer to withhold himself, took her to his lodge to cook and toil for him and to become the mother of his children. And with the coming of her offspring her looks left her. Her limbs dragged and shuffled, her eyes dimmed and bleared, and only the little children found joy against the withered cheek of the old squaw by the fire. Her task was done. But a little while, on the first pinch of famine or the first long trail, and she would be left, even as he had been left, in the snow, with a little pile of wood. Such was the law.

He placed a stick carefully upon the fire and resumed his meditations. It was the same everywhere, with all things. The mosquitos vanished with the first frost. The little tree-squirrel crawled away to die. When age settled upon the rabbit it became slow and heavy, and could no longer outfoot its enemies. Even the big bald-face grew clumsy and blind and quarrelsome, in the end to be dragged down by a handful of yelping huskies. He remembered how he had abandoned his own father on an upper reach of the Klondike one winter, the winter before the missionary came with his talk-books and his box of medicines. Many a time had Koskoosh smacked his lips over the recollection of that box, though now his mouth refused to moisten. The "painkiller" had been especially good. But the missionary was a bother after all, for he brought no meat into the camp, and he ate heartily, and the hunters grumbled. But he chilled his lungs on the divide by the Mayo, and the dogs afterwards nosed the stones away and fought over his bones.

Koskoosh placed another stick on the fire and harked back deeper into the past. There was the time of the Great Famine, when the old men crouched empty-bellied to the fire, and from their lips fell dim traditions of the ancient day when the Yukon ran wide open for three winters, and then lay frozen for three summers. He had lost his mother in that famine. In the summer the salmon run had failed, and the tribe looked forward to the winter and the coming of the caribou. Then the winter came, but with it there were no caribou. Never had the like been known, not even in the lives of the old men. But the caribou did not come, and it was the seventh year, and the rabbits had not replenished, and the dogs were naught but bundles of bones. And through the long darkness the children wailed and died, and the women, and the old men; and not one in ten of the tribe lived to meet the sun when it came back in the spring. That *was* a famine!

But he had seen times of plenty, too, when the meat spoiled on their hands, and the dogs were fat and worthless with over-eating—times when they let the game go unkilled, and the women were fertile, and the lodges were cluttered with sprawling men-children and women-children. Then it was the men became high-stomached, and revived ancient quarrels, and crossed the divides to the south to kill the Pellys, and to the west that they might sit by the dead fires of the Tananas. He remembered, when a boy, during a time of plenty, when he saw a moose pulled down by the wolves. Zing-ha lay with him in the snow and watched—Zing-ha, who later became the craftiest of hunters, and who, in the end, fell through an air-hole on the Yukon. They found him, a month afterward, just as he had crawled half-way out and frozen stiff to the ice.

But the moose. Zing-ha and he had gone out that day to play at hunting after the manner of their fathers. On the bed of the creek they struck the fresh track of a moose, and with it the tracks of many wolves. "An old one," Zing-ha, who was quicker at reading the sign, said—"an old one who cannot keep up with the herd. The wolves have cut him out from his brothers, and they will never leave him." And it was so. It was their way. By day and by night, never resting, snarling on his heels, snapping at his nose, they would stay by him to the end. How Zing-ha and he felt the blood-lust quicken! The finish would be a sight to see!

Eager-footed, they took the trail, and even he, Koskoosh, slow of sight and an unversed tracker, could have followed it blind, it was so wide. Hot were they on the heels of the chase, reading the grim tragedy, fresh-written, at every step. Now they came to where the moose had made a stand. Thrice the length of a grown man's body, in every direction, had the snow been stamped about and uptossed. In the midst were the deep impressions of the splay-hoofed game, and all about, everywhere, were the lighter footmarks of the wolves. Some, while their brothers harried the kill, had lain to one side and rested. The full-stretched impress of their bodies in the snow was as perfect as though made the moment before. One wolf had been caught in a wild lunge of the maddened victim and trampled to death. A few bones, well picked, bore witness.

Again, they ceased the uplift of their snowshoes at a second stand. Here the great animal had fought desperately. Twice had he been dragged down, as the snow attested, and twice had he shaken his assailants clear and gained footing once more. He had done his task long since, but none the less was life dear to him. Zing-ha said it was a strange thing, a moose once down to get free again; but this one certainly had. The Shaman would see signs and wonders in this when they told him.

And yet again, they came to where the moose had made to mount the bank and gain the timber. But his foes had laid on from behind, till he reared and fell back upon them, crushing two deep into the snow. It was plain the kill was at hand, for their brothers had left them untouched. Two more stands were hurried past, brief in time-length and very close together. The trail was red now, and the clean stride of the great beast had grown short and slovenly. Then they heard the first sounds of the battle—not the full-throated chorus of the chase, but the short, snappy bark which spoke of close quarters and teeth to flesh. Crawling up the wind, Zing-ha bellied it through the snow, and with him crept he, Koskoosh, who was to be chief of the tribesmen in the years to come. Together they shoved aside the under branches of a young spruce and peered forth. It was the end they saw.

The picture, like all of youth's impressions, was still strong with him, and his dim eyes watched the end played out as vividly as in that far-off time. Koskoosh marveled at this, for in the days which followed, when he was a leader of men and a head of councilors, he had done great deeds and made his name a curse in the mouths of the Pellys, to say naught of the strange white man he had killed, knife to knife, in open fight.

For long he pondered on the days of his youth, till the fire died down and the frost bit deeper. He replenished it with two sticks this time, and gauged his grip on life by what remained. If Sit-cum-to-ha had only remembered her grandfather, and gathered a larger armful, his hours would have been longer. It would have been easy. But she was ever a careless child, and honored not her ancestors from the time the Beaver, son of the son of Zing-ha, first cast eyes upon her. Well, what mattered it? Had he not done likewise in his own quick youth? For a while he listened to the silence. Perhaps the heart of his son might soften, and he would come back with the dogs to take his old father on with the tribe to where the caribou ran thick and the fat hung heavy upon them.

He strained his ears, his restless brain for the moment stilled. Not a stir, nothing. He alone took breath in the midst of the great silence. It was very lonely. Hark! What was that? A chill passed over his body. The familiar, long-drawn howl broke the void, and it was close at hand. Then on his darkened eyes was projected the vision of the moose—the old bull moose—the torn flanks and bloody sides, the riddled mane, and the great branching horns, down low and tossing to the last. He saw the flashing forms of gray, the gleaming eyes, the lolling tongues, the slavered fangs. And he saw the inexorable circle close in till it became a dark point in the midst of the stamped snow.

A cold muzzle thrust against his cheek, and at its touch his soul leaped back to the present. His hand shot into the fire and dragged out a burning fagot. Overcome for the nonce by his hereditary fear of man, the brute retreated, raising a prolonged call to his brothers; and greedily they answered, till a ring of crouching, jaw-slobbered gray was stretched round about. The old man listened to the drawing in of this circle. He waved his brand wildly, and sniffs turned to snarls; but the panting brutes refused to scatter. Now one wormed his chest forward, dragging his haunches after, now a second, now a third; but never a one drew back. Why should he cling to life? he asked, and dropped the blazing stick into the snow. It sizzled and went out. The circle grunted uneasily, but held its own. Again he saw the last stand of the old bull moose, and Koskoosh dropped his head warily upon his knees. What did it matter after all? Was it not the law of life?

1901, 1902

# NATIVE AMERICAN CHANTS AND SONGS

## THE NAVAJO NIGHT CHANT

The Navajo migrated to the American Southwest from points further north somewhere between A.D. 1000–1300. Once settled, the Navajo learned farming and weaving from the Pueblo peoples; they later acquired livestock from the Spanish and developed silver-working skills from contact with the Mexicans. When the United States took possession of the southwestern territories in 1848 after the Mexican war, it inherited the problem of raiding Navajos. In 1863, the government hired the well-known scout Kit Carson to subdue the Navajo by destroying their crops and livestock. One year later starving Navajo people began to make their way into Fort Defiance. Later that year, some eight thousand Navajo were forced to make the Long Walk from Fort Defiance in western Arizona three hundred miles to Fort Sumner in east-central New Mexico, where they were imprisoned. This traumatic event is remembered by the Navajo as the Trail of Tears is remembered by the Cherokee and Wounded Knee by the Sioux. In 1868 a new treaty established a three-million-acre reservation for the Navajo in New Mexico and Arizona—and the people began to return to their homes. Despite food shortages, drought, and further land cessions, the Navajo gradually grew in number. Today they are the most populous American Indian group in the United States.

Ceremonies are a central part of Navajo culture. They are used to enhance life—to promote a successful hunt and good crops—to cure physical illness, and to remedy misfortunes of all kinds—a fire or miscarriage, lightning striking sheep. Although songs, dances, and sand paintings are important parts of Navajo ceremonies, it was the intoning of long, complex prayers that led the first recorders of these ceremonies to call them chants. An individual desiring that a ceremony be performed first consults with a seer, a ritual diagnostician who determines which chant is likely to address the problem at hand. The initiator of the ceremony is referred to as the "patient," regardless of whether she or he is sick in the Western sense. The chants may last from one to nine nights. They are conducted by an expert in a particular ceremonial, a person endowed not so much with special power (as is the seer) as with special knowledge. Each ceremonial requires elaborate preparation by the chanter and the patient's family. The chanter must renew or refresh ritual objects to be used during the ceremony—masks, prayer sticks, and the like—and the family must provide such things as the baskets used as drums that the chanter will require and food for the many invited guests.

The Night Chant is one of the most elaborate of Navajo ceremonials, taking a full nine nights to perform. It begins at sunset, when the chanter enters the house of the patient and a crier, standing at the door, calls, Biké hatáli hakú ("Come on the trail of song"), enjoining both the patient and the guests to participate. The patient seats himself or herself west of a fire that has been kindled for the ceremony: the place of honor. At sunrise on the ninth day, after an elaborate series of songs, dances, and chanted prayers, the patient is invited to look eastward and greet the dawn in newfound health and wholeness.

The earliest and still most detailed version of the Navajo Night Chant was published in 1902 by Washington Matthews (1843–1905), an army surgeon assigned to Fort Wingate, New Mexico, in the 1880s. Drawn to the culture of the Navajo, Matthews learned their language and published his first study of a Navajo ceremonial, The Mountain Chant, in 1887. After witnessing a Night Chant in the fall of 1884, Matthews devoted the last twenty years of his life to its study. Although he worked with many priests of the Night Chant, one in particular, Hatali Natloi (Laughing Chanter), contributed to the version Matthews published in 1902.

Today, the chants are commonly referred to in English as *ways:* Night Way, Mountain Way, Enemy Way, Blessing Way, the Red Ant Way, and so on. The change of name points to the fact that these are dramatic *acts* not limited to chanting alone. We retain the name Night Chant, originally used by Matthews and still used by John Bierhorst, whose edition of Matthews's version we print here.

# The Night Chant[1]

## Concluding Rite, First Day

### THE SACRED MOUNTAINS

Sprinkling dry pigments on the floor of the lodge, the chanter prepares a small sand painting featuring the four sacred mountains of the Navajo world; a trail leads into their midst. At the doorway the crier issues his usual call: *Biké hatáli hakú.*[2] The patient enters, walking slowly along the "trail" to the "mountains," followed by Hastshéyalti.[3] The singers begin:

> In a holy place with a god I walk,
> In a holy place with a god I walk,
> On Tsisnadzhíni with a god I walk,
> On a chief of mountains with a god I walk,
> In old age wandering with a god I walk,                                   5
> On a trail of beauty with a god I walk.

The stanza is repeated three times, changing the name of the mountain, in turn, to Tsótsil, Dokoslíd, and Depéntsa. The patient reaches the center of the picture; the chanter recites:

> From the base of the east.
> From the base of Tsisnadzhíni.[4]
> From the house made of mirage,
> From the story[5] made of mirage,
> From the doorway of rainbow,                                             10
> The path out of which is the rainbow,
> The rainbow passed out with me.
> The rainbow raised up with me
> Through the middle of broad fields,
> The rainbow returned with me.                                           15
> To where my house is visible,
> The rainbow returned with me.
> To the roof of my house,
> The rainbow returned with me.
> To the entrance of my house,                                            20

---

1. From John Bierhorst's *Four Masterworks of American Indian Literature: Quetzalcoatl, The Ritual of Condolence, Cuceb, The Night Chant* (1974, 1984). Bierhorst's version of Washington Matthews's text condenses it somewhat and slightly alters the original spelling. The descriptions of ritual procedure are also condensed from Matthews.
2. Come on the trail of song (Navajo).
3. The Talking God, principal figure of the Night Chant.
4. "[Tsisnadzhíni is] probably Pelado Peak, New Mex-

ico, the mountain marking the eastern point of the Navajo world. Tsótil is Mt. Taylor, NM, and marks the south; Dokoslíd is Humphrey's Peak, Arizona, and marks the west; while Depéntsa is probably Hesperus Peak, Colorado, and marks the north. The patient symbolically follows a holy trail that takes him to each of these mountains, homes of the gods" [Bierhorst's note].
5. "Matthews's poetic 'story' is misleading. 'Base,' or 'lower part,' would be more correct" [Bierhorst's note].

The rainbow returned with me.
To just within my house,
The rainbow returned with me.
To my fireside,
The rainbow returned with me.                                    25
To the center of my house,
The rainbow returned with me.
At the fore part of my house with the dawn,[6]
The Talking God sits with me.
The House God sits with me.                                      30
Pollen Boy sits with me.
Grasshopper Girl sits with me.
In beauty Estsánatlehi, my mother, for her I return.[7]
Beautifully my fire to me is restored.
Beautifully my possessions are to me restored.                  35
Beautifully my soft goods to me are restored.
Beautifully my hard goods to me are restored.
Beautifully my horses to me are restored.
Beautifully my sheep to me are restored.
Beautifully my old men to me are restored.                      40
Beautifully my old women to me are restored.
Beautifully my young men to me are restored.
Beautifully my young women to me are restored.
Beautifully my children to me are restored.
Beautifully my wife to me is restored.                          45
Beautifully my chiefs to me are restored.
Beautifully my country to me is restored.
Beautifully my fields to me are restored.
Beautifully my house to me is restored.
Talking God sits with me.                                       50
House God sits with me.
Pollen Boy sits with me.
Grasshopper Girl sits with me.
Beautifully white corn to me is restored.
Beautifully yellow corn to me is restored.                      55
Beautifully blue corn to me is restored.
Beautifully corn of all kinds to me is restored.
In beauty may I walk.
All day long may I walk.
Through the returning seasons may I walk.                       60
[*line untranslated*][8]
Beautifully . . . will I possess again.
[*line untranslated*]
Beautifully birds . . .
Beautifully joyful birds . . .                                  65
On the trail marked with pollen may I walk.
With grasshoppers about my feet may I walk.
With dew about my feet may I walk.

6. I.e., the front ("forepart") of all Navajo houses, or
hogans, faces east.
7. Estsánatlehi is Changing Woman, a personification
of the earth. The return to the mother (or grandmother) is a motif typical of Navajo as of many other
myths. Pollen Boy symbolizes male generative power

and Grasshopper Girl, female generative power
[adapted from Bierhorst's note].
8. Matthews's 1902 publication gives the Navajo for
these lines, because he could not arrive at a satisfactory
translation of them.

With beauty may I walk.
With beauty before me, may I walk.                                    70
With beauty behind me, may I walk.
With beauty above me, may I walk.
With beauty below me, may I walk.
With beauty all around me, may I walk.
In old age wandering on a trail of beauty, lively, may I walk.        75
In old age wandering on a trail of beauty, living again, may I walk.
It is finished in beauty.
It is finished in beauty.

The prayer is thrice repeated, substituting in turn the names of the other three directions (south, west, north) and their corresponding mountains (Tsótsil, Dokoslíd, Depéntsa). Kneeling, Hastshéyalti takes sand from each of the "mountains" and applies it to the patient. The patient kneels: coals are removed from the fire and placed before him; over these the chanter sprinkles a powder of feathers and resin, giving rise to an incense inhaled by the patient. The coals are extinguished, the picture obliterated. The party withdraws.

## Concluding Rite, Ninth Day

Four great fires are kindled on either side of the level space, or "dancing ground," in front of the lodge. Facing the lodge at a distance of some hundred paces stands the newly constructed "arbor," a circle of evergreen boughs to be used as the performers' changing room. Spectators, numbering in the hundreds, gather just beyond the fires along both sides of the dancing ground.

### DANCE OF THE ATSÁLEI, OR THUNDERBIRDS

The chanter's assistants paint with white earth the bodies of dancers who will represent the four thunderbirds (of corn, of child-rain, of vegetation, and of pollen). The chanter sings:

Now the holy one paints his form,
The Wind Boy,[9] the holy one, paints his form,
All over his body, he paints his form,
With the dark cloud he paints his form,
With the misty rain he paints his form,                               5
With the rainy bubbles he paints his form,
To the ends of his toes he paints his form,
To fingers and rattle he paints his form,
To the plume on his head he paints his form.

As the dancers repair to the arbor, the basket is turned down [overturned, used as a drum] and singing begins anew. Fully costumed, the thunderbirds, led by Hastshéyalti, approach the dancing ground. A crier calls: Come on the trail of song [Biké hatáli hakú]. The patient emerges from the lodge and sprinkles the dancers with meal. (Singing within the lodge continues unabated.) Addressing the thunderbird of pollen, the patient recites after the chanter, line by line:[1]

---

9. "Wind is the precursor of rain. Before he becomes rain, the dancer must be wind (or 'Wind Boy,' emphasizing his youthfulness)" [Bierhorst's note].

1. "In the great prayer that follows, the Night Chant reaches its climax; the prayer for rain is the prayer for salvation" [Bierhorst's note].

In Tsegíhi,[2]                                                          10
In the house made of the dawn,
In the house made of the evening twilight,
In the house made of the dark cloud,
In the house made of the he-rain,
In the house made of the dark mist,                                    15
In the house made of the she-rain,
In the house made of pollen,
In the house made of grasshoppers,
Where the dark mist curtains the doorway,
The path to which is on the rainbow,                                   20
Where the zigzag lightning stands high on top,
Where the he-rain stands high on top,
Oh, male divinity!
With your moccasins of dark cloud, come to us.
With your leggings of dark cloud, come to us.                          25
With your shirt of dark cloud, come to us.
With your headdress of dark cloud, come to us.
With your mind enveloped in dark cloud, come to us.
With the dark thunder above you, come to us soaring.
With the shapen cloud at your feet, come to us soaring.                30
With the far darkness made of the dark cloud
    over your head, come to us soaring.
With the far darkness made of the he-rain
    over your head, come to us soaring.
With the far darkness made of the dark mist
    over your head, come to us asoaring.
With the far darkness made of the she-rain
    over your head, some to us soaring.
With the zigzag lightning flung out on high
    over your head, come to us soaring.                                35
With the rainbow hanging high over your head,
    come to us soaring.
With the far darkness made of the dark cloud on
    the ends of your wings, come to us soaring.
With the far darkness made of the he-rain on
    the ends of your wings, come to us soaring.
With the far darkness made of the dark mist on
    the ends of your wings, come to us soaring.
With the far darkness made of the she-rain on
    the ends of your wings, come to us soaring.                        40
With the zigzag lightning flung out on high on
    the ends of your wings, come to us soaring.
With the rainbow hanging high on the ends of
    your wings, come to us soaring.
With the near darkness made of the dark cloud, of
    the he-rain, of the dark mist, and of the
    she-rain, come to us.
With the darkness on the earth, come to us.
With these I wish the foam floating on the
    flowing water over the roots of the great corn.                    45

---

2. Tseglíhi is a distant canyon, site of the shrine known as House Made of Dawn (cf. N. Scott Momaday's novel of that name), considered to be the dwelling place of the sun on earth.

I have made your sacrifice.
I have prepared a smoke for you.
My feet restore for me.
My limbs restore for me.
My body restore for me.                                              50
My mind restore for me.
My voice restore for me.
Today, take out your spell for me.
Today, take away your spell for me.
Away from me you have taken it.                                      55
Far off from me it is taken.
Far off you have done it.
Happily I recover.
Happily my interior becomes cool.
Happily my eyes regain their power.                                 60
Happily my head becomes cool.
Happily my limbs regain their power.
Happily I hear again.
Happily for me *the spell* is taken off.
Happily may I walk.                                                  65
Impervious to pain, may I walk.
Feeling light within, may I walk.
With lively feelings, may I walk.
Happily abundant dark clouds I desire.
Happily abundant dark mists I desire.                               70
Happily abundant passing showers I desire.
Happily an abundance of vegetation I desire.
Happily an abundance of pollen I desire.
Happily abundant dew I desire.
Happily may fair white corn, to the ends of the
    earth, come with you.                                           75
Happily may fair yellow corn, to the end of the
    earth, come with you.
Happily may fair blue corn, to the ends of the
    earth, come with you.
Happily may fair corn of all kinds, to the ends
    of the earth, come with you.
Happily may fair plants of all kinds, to the ends
    of the earth, come with you.
Happily may fair goods of all kinds, to the ends
    of the earth, come with you.                                    80
Happily may fair jewels of all kinds, to the ends
    of the earth, come with you.
With these before you, happily may they come
    with you.
With these behind you, happily may they come
    with you.
With these below you, happily may they come
    with you.
With these above you, happily may they come
    with you.                                                       85
With these all around you, happily may they
    come with you.

Thus happily you accomplish your tasks.
Happily the old men will regard you.
Happily the old women will regard you.
Happily the young men will regard you.                    90
Happily the young women will regard you.
Happily the boys will regard you.
Happily the girls will regard you.
Happily the children will regard you.
Happily the chiefs will regard you.                       95
Happily, as they scatter in different directions,
    they will regard you.
Happily, as they approach their homes, they will
    regard you.
Happily may their roads home be on the trail of
    pollen.
Happily may they all get back.
In beauty I walk.                                        100
With beauty before me, I walk.
With beauty behind me, I walk.
With beauty below me, I walk.
With beauty above me, I walk.
With beauty all around me, I walk.                       105
It is finished in beauty,
It is finished in beauty,
It is finished in beauty,
It is finished in beauty.

\*   \*   \*

The grand ceremonial concludes: The basket [used as a drum] is turned up and the drumstick (of twisted yucca leaves) taken outside by an assistant, who pulls it apart, sprinkling pollen on the shreds, repeating in a low voice the benediction:

Thus will it be beautiful,
Thus walk in beauty, my grandchild.

The patient, facing east, inhales the breath of dawn.[3]

3. The description of the patient's gesture as the very last action of the Night Chant, Bierhorst notes, is *not* from Matthews, who probably never witnessed it in the late-19th- and early-20th-century performances he at-tended. Later writers note the patient's inhalation of the breath of dawn as typical of the Night Chant's conclusion.

# CHIPPEWA SONGS

The Chippewa, one of the largest Indian groups in North America, are also known as the Ojibwe or, in their own Algonquian language, the Anishinabe. Their territories once ranged along the shores of Lake Huron and Lake Superior, across Minnesota, and west to the Turtle Mountains of North Dakota. In summer Chippewa bands gathered into villages where they fished, planted small gardens, and collected wild foods. In fall Chippewa living on the lakes cultivated large wild rice fields, paddling the lakes in their canoes and harvesting the rice by striking the plants with a stick. In winter bands moved to their hunting grounds in pursuit of deer, moose, bear, and small animals like rabbits, otter, and beaver. The most important ceremonial organization of the Woodlands Chippewa was the Mide'wiwin, or Medicine Lodge Society, whose central ritual, the Medicine Dance, like the Navajo Night Chant, lasted several days and was predominantly a curing ceremony.

Frances Densmore (1867–1957) was born in Chippewa country, in the small town of Red Wing, Minnesota. At an early age, she became interested in a wide range of American Indian music, eventually devoting her life to its study and publishing on Chippewa, Teton Sioux, Mandan, Northern Ute, Papago, Yaqui, Nootka, Quileute, and Seminole music. Deeply interested in the importance of the Mide'wiwin to the Chippewa, Densmore published in 1910 an elaborate account of the Mide', or Medicine Society songs, and in 1913 issued the second part of her study of Chippewa music. The songs anthologized here were collected by Densmore between 1907 and 1909 on the White Earth, Leech Lake, and Red Lake reservations, all west of Lake Superior in Minnesota.

"Every phase of Chippewa life," Densmore wrote, "is expressed in music." Many Chippewa songs offer an individual yet culturally patterned response to the concerns of Chippewa life—love, war, a change in the weather, and the like; these often pass, with great interest and respect, from reservation to reservation. Traditionally, the songs were said to be "given" in dreams by some spirit power or animal. Singers frequently prefaced their performances with short speeches announcing the origin of the song and its relation to other songs. The usual accompaniment for Mide' and other medicine songs was the drum and rattle; love songs would often include the music of a flute. As will be apparent, Chippewa songs are quite short, with few words and brief melodies. But phrases could be repeated many times, with the drum sometimes continuing during the pauses in between the sets of repetitions. In the *Love-Charm Song* of the Mide'wiwin sung by Na'waji'bigo'kwe, printed here, the first word, translated as "What are you saying to me?" is repeated seven times before the second word, translated as "I am arrayed like the roses," is sung. The third word, translated as "And beautiful as they," does not conclude the song, as the translation seems to suggest, because another five repetitions of the first word follow.

These songs may be read simply as poems; recently, the Chippewa writer Gerald Vizenor has compared them with Japanese haiku. Nonetheless, because the Chippewa songs were meant to be sung, we have in two cases included the music. Also included here are the Chippewa language texts as transcribed by Densmore.

## Song of the Crows[1]

### Sung by Henry Selkirk

Be'bani'gani'
Nin'digog'
Binĕsiwûg'
Nin'wĕndjigi'miwûñ'
Andeg'nindigo'

TRANSLATION

The first to come
I am called
Among the birds
I bring the rain
Crow is my name

1. From *Chippewa Music* (1910). Densmore notes that crows are said to have given this song to a young man who was fasting. The crow then became his *man-* *ido*, or spirit power. As crows are the first birds to return to the Chippewa lands in spring, they are thought to bring the welcome spring rains.

# My Love Has Departed[2]

### Sung by Mrs. Mary English

VOICE ♭ = 132; RECORDED WITHOUT DRUM

Man-go-dŭg - win    nĭn - dĭ - nĕn-dŭm man-go-dŭg-win nĭn - dĭ - nĕn-dŭm,

mi-gwe - na-wĭn    nĭn - I - mu-ce ĕ-ui-wa-wa - sa- bo - ye-zud.

Ba - wi-tĭŭ    gi - nĭ - ma-dja    nĭn-I-mu-ce   a - ni - ma-dja

ka - wĭn-i-na-wa nĭn-da-wa-ba-ma — si    Sĭ   Man-go-dŭg - win

nĭu   dĭ - nĕn-dum    man-go-dŭg - win   nĭu - dĭ - nĕn-dum,

mi-gwe - na-wĭn ka - wĭn-i-mu-ce,    ĕ-ni-wa-wa - sa - bo - ye-zud.

TRANSLATION

1
A loon
I thought it was
But it was
My love's
Splashing oar     5

2
To Sault Ste. Marie[3]
He has departed
My love
Has gone on before me
Never again     10
Can I see him

---

2. From *Chippewa Music* (1910). Densmore notes that the song recalls a time when the city of Duluth, Minnesota, at the western end of Lake Superior, was a camping ground for the Chippewa.
3. Sault Ste. Marie marks the eastern end of Lake Superior.

# Love-Charm Song[4]

*Sung by Na'waji'bigo'kwe*

VOICE ♭ = 88; RECORDED WITHOUT DRUM

A - ni - na - ji - a - ne    a - ni - na - ji - a - ne

a - ni - na - ji - a - ne    a - ni - na - ji - a - ne

a - ni - na - ji - a - ne    a - ni - na - ji - a - ne

a - ni - na - ji - a - ne    o - gĭ - ni - ba - uň    e

a - ji - na - go - o - yăn    a - ni - na - ji - a - ne

a - ni - na - ji - a - ne    a - ni - na - ji - a - ne

a - ni - na - ji - a - ne    a - ni - na - ji - a - ne

TRANSLATION

What are you saying to me?
I am arrayed like the roses
And beautiful as they

---

4. From *Chippewa Music* (1910) by Frances Densmore. Densmore notes that love-charm songs were considered very powerful. The woman who sang this song used the tenor range, because, Densmore guesses, the lower register was adopted generally by women who sang Mide' songs in unison with men.

# The Approach of the Storm[5]

*Sung by Ga'Gandac'*

Abitû'
Gicĭguñ'
Ebigwēn'
Kabide'bwewiduñ'

TRANSLATION

From the half of the sky
That which lives there
Is coming, and makes a noise

# The Sioux Women Gather Up Their Wounded[6]

*Sung by Odjĭb'we*

Oma'mikweg'
Paba'made'mowûg'
Ona'djida'bamawûn'
O'dinini'miwûn
Ani'mûde'mûwug'

TRANSLATION

The Sioux women
Pass to and fro wailing
As they gather up
Their wounded men
The voice of their weeping comes back to us

# The Sioux Woman Defends Her Children[7]

*Sung by Odjib'we*

Neta'gica'wasosig'
Wape'toñ[8]
Biäpi'sika'dug
Go'cawin'
Bigica'wasud'

5. From *Chippewa Music* (1910). The thunder, understood as a *manido*, or spirit, of the storm, is imagined to make its noise to warn people that severe weather is on the way. Upon hearing thunder, the Chippewa would put tobacco on the fire, offering the smoke in peace to the *manido*, in gratitude for the warning [adapted from Densmore's note].

6. From *Chippewa Music—II* (1913) by Frances Densmore. The Sioux were traditional enemies of the Chippewa, and there are many war songs relating to engagements with the Sioux.

7. From *Chippewa Music—II* (1913). Densmore notes that "the following two songs were composed about a war expedition which occurred when Odjib'we [the singer] was a young man." This song and the next refer to a hard-fought battle between the Chippewa and the Sioux a few miles north of present-day St. Cloud, Minnesota. The first song, composed by Odjib'we's father, recalls a Sioux woman who seized an ax to protect her children from the attacking Chippewa. She and all her children were nonetheless killed.

8. A Sioux word.

TRANSLATION

Once careless of her children[9]
She of the Wapeton Sioux
Now comes in haste
Surely
To their defense

## Song of the Captive Sioux Woman[1]

*Sung by Odjib'we*

Kaka'tawû[2]
Waya'bamagin'
Nin'gaödji'ma
Kegēt'
Nin'jawe'nimīg'

TRANSLATION

Any Chippewa
Whenever I see
I will greet with a kiss
Truly
He pities me

9. This may reflect Chippewa views of Sioux child care in general.
1. From *Chippewa Music—II* (1913). The woman referred to was taken captive in the battle referred to in n. 7 and was to be shot. First, she was given the opportunity to sing. The song she sang is not known, but as Densmore notes, "It moved the elder brother of Odjib'we so strongly that he rushed forward and rescued her." Later, the captive woman thanked the warriors for sparing her and sang this song.
2. The Sioux word for "Chippewa."

# GHOST DANCE SONGS

The songs that various groups of Native American people composed to accompany the dances of the Ghost Dance religion resembled the songs that had traditionally accompanied "round dances," communal dances in which, as the following drawings from the Comanche and Sioux indicate, the dancers held hands and moved in a loose circle. Ghost Dance songs would originate when a dancer fell into a trancelike state and upon regaining consciousness expressed in a song what he or she had seen in the spirit world. As each dance would almost surely give rise to new songs, each tribe's repertoire was constantly changing—although some particularly appealing songs were repeated again and again, and in some cases made their way to other Indian groups.

Ghost Dance songs embodied what each tribe took to be the teachings of the Indian Messiah, Wovoka, but the songs also made mention of aspects of the daily lives and traditional customs and ceremonies of the various native peoples. Thus references to important berries; to gambling wheels and gambling sticks involved in various games; to the sacred pipe, the crow, or the eagle; and to specific activities of the men or the women all appear in the Ghost Dance songs.

James Mooney (1861–1921) of the Bureau of American Ethnology studied the Ghost Dance religion and, in 1896, published a massive work titled *The Ghost Dance Religion and the Sioux Outbreak of 1890.* Mooney not only interviewed

Wovoka but conducted extensive interviews with people from many Indian groups who had participated in the Ghost Dance. An accomplished ethnographic observer familiar with Sioux languages (he had published *Siouan Tribes of the East* in 1894), Mooney is an extremely sympathetic observer and his commentary is richly descriptive and explanatory.

Anthologized here are ghost songs from the Arapaho and Sioux. We have provided examples of musical notation as a reminder that these were songs sung as a circle of dancers moved slowly hand in hand. All the selections printed here are from James Mooney's *The Ghost-Dance Religion and the Sioux Outbreak of 1890*, edited and abridged by Anthony F. C. Wallace (1965).

## Songs of the Arapaho[1]

### [*Father, have pity on me*][2]

TRANSLATION

Father, have pity on me,
Father, have pity on me;
I am crying for thirst,
I am crying for thirst;
All is gone—I have nothing to eat,
All is gone—I have nothing to eat.

### [*When I met him approaching*][3]

1. The Arapaho are an Algonquian-speaking people whose northern branch occupied the present state of Wyoming and whose southern branch lived in present-day Arkansas. They were traditionally a nomadic hunting and gathering group. The Arapaho share many of the traits of the Plains Indians and were particularly close to the Cheyenne. Unlike the Cheyenne, however, the Arapaho maintained generally friendly relations with the whites.
2. "This is the most pathetic of the Ghost-dance songs.

It is sung to a plaintive tune, sometimes with tears rolling down the cheeks of the dancers as the words would bring up thoughts of their present miserable and dependent condition" [Mooney's note].
3. "This song was brought from the north to the southern Arapaho by Sitting Bull. It refers to the trance vision of a dancer, who saw the messiah advancing at the head of all the spirit army. It is an old favorite, and is sung with vigor and animation" [Mooney's note].

TRANSLATION

*He!* When I met him approaching—
*He!* When I met him approaching—
My children, my children—
I then saw the multitude plainly,
I then saw the multitude plainly.

Native drawings of the Ghost Dance. A, Comanche; B, Sioux.

## Songs of the Sioux

*[The father says so]*[1]

A'te he'ye e'yayo!
A'te he'ye e'yayo!
A'te he'ye lo,
A'te he'ye lo.
Nitu'ñkañshi'la wa'ñiyegala'ke—kta' e'yayo'!      5
Nitu'ñkañshi'la wa'ñiyegala'ke—kta' e'yayo'!
A'te he'ye lo,
A'te he'ye lo.
Ni'takuye wañye'gāla'ke—kta e'yayo'!
Ni'takuye wañye'gāla'ke—kta e'yayo'!      10
A'te he'ye lo,
A'te he'ye lo.

1. "This is the opening song of the dance. While sing- ing it, all the dancers stand motionless with hands stretched out toward the west, the country of the mes- siah and the quarter whence the new spirit world is to come. When it is ended, all cry together, after which they join hands and begin to circle around to the left. 'Grandfather,' as well as 'father,' is a reverential term applied to the messiah" [Mooney's note].

### TRANSLATION

The father says so—*E'yayo!*
The father says so—*E'yayo!*
The father says so,
The father says so.
You shall see your grandfather—*E'yayo'!*          5
You shall see your grandfather—*E'yayo'!*
The father says so,
The father says so.
You shall see your kindred—*E'yayo'!*
You shall see your kindred—*E'yayo'!*             10
The father says so,
The father says so.

### [*Give me my knife*]²

Mila kiñ hiyu'michi'chiyana,
Mila kiñ hiyu'michi'chiyana.
Wa'waka'bla-kte—Ye'ye'!
Wa'waka'bla-kte—Ye'ye'!
Oñchi he'ye lo—Yo'yo'!                             5
Oñchi he'ye lo—Yo'yo'!
Puye chiñyi wa'sna wakaghiñyiñ-kte,
Puye chiñyi wa'sna wakaghiñyiñ-kte,
Oñchi heye lo—Yo'yo!
Oñchi heye lo—Yo'yo!                              10

### TRANSLATION

Give me my knife,
Give me my knife,
I shall hang up the meat to dry—*Ye'ye'!*
I shall hang up the meat to dry—*Ye'ye'!*
Says grandmother—*Yo'yo'!*                         5
Says grandmother—*Yo'yo'!*
When it is dry I shall make pemmican,³
When it is dry I shall make pemmican,
Says grandmother—*Yo'yo!*
Says grandmother—*Yo'yo!*                          10

### [*The whole world is coming*]⁴

Maka' sito'maniyañ ukiye,
Oya'te uki'ye, oya'te uki'ye,

2. "This song brings up a vivid picture of the old Indian life. In her trance vision the old grandmother whose experience it relates came upon her friends in the spirit world just as all the women of the camp were engaged in cutting up the meat for drying after a successful buffalo hunt. In her joy she calls for her knife to assist in the work, and says that as soon as the meat is dry she will make some pemmican" [Mooney's note].
3. Dried beef, which is toasted and then pounded into a hash; it may be eaten with sugar, fruit, or mesquite pods.
4. "This fine song summarizes the whole hope of the Ghost dance—the return of the buffalo and the departed dead, the message being brought to the people by the sacred birds, the Eagle and the Crow. The eagle known as *wañ'bali* is the war eagle, from which feathers are procured as war bonnets" [Mooney's note].

Wa'ñbali oya'te wañ hoshi'hi-ye lo,
Ate heye lo, ate heye lo,
Maka o'wañcha'ya uki'ye.                                              5
Pte kiñ ukiye, pte kiñ ukiye,
Kañghi oya'te wañ hoshi'hi-ye, lo,
A'te he'ye lo, a'te he'ye lo.

### TRANSLATION

The whole world is coming,
A nation is coming, a nation is coming,
The Eagle has brought the message to the tribe.
The father says so, the father says so.
Over the whole earth they are coming.                               5
The buffalo are coming, the buffalo are coming,
The Crow has brought the message to the tribe,
The father says so, the father says so.

---

# GERTRUDE SIMMONS BONNIN (Zitkala Ša)
## 1876–1938

Born Gertrude Simmons on February 22, 1876, Zitkala Ša, or Red Bird, as she also called herself, became a writer and reformer of considerable importance in spite of extraordinary obstacles: she was a Sioux, a woman, born on a reservation, and thus poor. According to stereotypes, she was supposed to be invisible, silent, segregated, and submissive; instead she became visible, vocal, intrusive, and aggressive in pursuit of her own development and the legal, economic, and cultural rights of other Native Americans.

Brought up as a Yankton Sioux in South Dakota until she was eight years old, Bonnin left the reservation to attend a Quaker missionary school for American Indians in Wabash, Indiana. The contrast between her secure and happy life as a Sioux child and her painful and confusing initiation into a Christian work ethic is the subject of the autobiographical essay included here and requires no elaborate explanation or interpretation (although it is rich in symbolic detail). In two other essays, *The School Days of an Indian Girl* and *An Indian Teacher among Indians*, Bonnin narrates the devastating disorientation experienced by someone who has left one culture behind and who has been unable to enter another one.

Bonnin's autobiography, in short, satisfies none of the conventional expectations of male autobiographies (typically narratives of individual triumphs of the will) or of female autobiographies (typically narratives of victories of love and domesticity). What we get instead is a peculiarly modern story of a multiple outsider who has made the painful passage from one culture to another and who is left angry and indignant but without self-pity. Bonnin has abandoned both her mother and the Great White Father, and she must make her way alone.

Although she doesn't mention it in her autobiographical pieces, Bonnin left her teaching to study violin at the Boston Conservatory of Music. In 1900, she appeared as violin soloist with the Carlisle Indian Band during its visit to the Paris Exposition. (In 1913, with William Hanson, she wrote an opera, *Sun Dance*, selected in 1937 as the American opera of the year by the New York Light Opera Guild.) In this same period she was writing the autobiographical material as well as stories for *Harper's Monthly*. In 1901, she published *Old Indian Legends*. In 1902, she married Raymond Talesfase Bonnin, a Sioux who worked for the Indian Service; they settled on the Uintah and Ouray Reservation in Utah, where they spent the next fourteen years. Their son, Raymond, was born there, apparently in 1903.

Sometime after 1911, when the Society of American Indians was established, Bonnin became involved in the activities of this group. This society was the first of its kind to be managed exclusively by Native Americans, and it engaged in efforts of reform and promoted legislation designed to change the federal government's treatment of Native Americans. Of course, Native Americans differed among themselves as to which reforms should be undertaken.

She was elected secretary of the society in 1916 and moved to Washington, D.C., where she and her husband spent their remaining years. In 1926 she organized the National Council of American Indians, which she served as president until her death in 1938.

As Mary Young observes in her excellent critical biography of Bonnin in *Notable American Women*, her most effective work was done with the General Federation of Women's Clubs, which Bonnin persuaded in 1921 to establish an Indian Welfare Committee. In cooperation with the influential Indian Rights Association and other groups, the federation was successful in improving treatment of American Indians and in preserving Native American cultures. Organizational work, lobbying, lecturing, and other obligations associated with her relentless promoting of Native American causes left her little time for writing, and her second book, *American Indian Stories* (1921), was her last.

# Impressions of an Indian Childhood[1]

## I. My Mother

A wigwam of weather-stained canvas stood at the base of some irregularly ascending hills. A footpath wound its way gently down the sloping land till it reached the broad river bottom; creeping through the long swamp grasses that bent over it on either side, it came out on the edge of the Missouri.

Here, morning, noon, and evening, my mother came to draw water from the muddy stream for our household use. Always, when my mother started for the river, I stopped my play to run along with her. She was only of medium height. Often she was sad and silent, at which times her full arched lips were compressed into hard and bitter lines, and shadows fell under her black eyes. Then I clung to her hand and begged to know what made the tears fall.

"Hush; my little daughter must never talk about my tears;" and smiling through them, she patted my head and said, "Now let me see how fast you can run to-day." Whereupon I tore away at my highest possible speed, with my long black hair blowing in the breeze.

I was a wild little girl of seven. Loosely clad in a slip of brown buckskin, and light-footed with a pair of soft moccasins on my feet, I was as free as the wind that blew my hair, and no less spirited than a bounding deer. These were my mother's pride,—my wild freedom and overflowing spirits. She taught me no fear save that of intruding myself upon others.

Having gone many paces ahead I stopped, panting for breath, and laughing

---

1. *Impressions of an Indian Childhood* first appeared in the *Atlantic Monthly* for January of 1900.

with glee as my mother watched my every movement. I was not wholly conscious of myself, but was more keenly alive to the fire within. It was as if I were the activity, and my hands and feet were only experiments for my spirit to work upon.

Returning from the river, I tugged beside my mother, with my hand upon the bucket I believed I was carrying. One time, on such a return, I remember a bit of conversation we had. My grown-up cousin, Warca-Ziwin (Sunflower), who was then seventeen, always went to the river alone for water for her mother. Their wigwam was not far from ours; and I saw her daily going to and from the river. I admired my cousin greatly. So I said: "Mother, when I am tall as my cousin Warca-Ziwin, you shall not have to come for water. I will do it for you."

With a strange tremor in her voice which I could not understand, she answered, "If the paleface does not take away from us the river we drink."

"Mother, who is this bad paleface?" I asked.

"My little daughter, he is a sham,—a sickly sham! The bronzed Dakota is the only real man."

I looked up into my mother's face while she spoke; and seeing her bite her lips, I knew she was unhappy. This aroused revenge in my small soul. Stamping my foot on the earth, I cried aloud, "I hate the paleface that makes my mother cry!"

Setting the pail of water on the ground, my mother stooped, and stretching her left hand out on the level with my eyes, she placed her other arm about me; she pointed to the hill where my uncle and my only sister lay buried.

"There is what the paleface has done! Since then your father too has been buried in a hill nearer the rising sun. We were once very happy. But the paleface has stolen our lands and driven us hither. Having defrauded us of our land, the paleface forced us away.

"Well, it happened on the day we moved camp that your sister and uncle were both very sick. Many others were ailing, but there seemed to be no help. We traveled many days and nights; not in the grand happy way that we moved camp when I was a little girl, but we were driven, my child, driven like a herd of buffalo. With every step, your sister, who was not as large as you are now, shrieked with the painful jar until she was hoarse with crying. She grew more and more feverish. Her little hands and cheeks were burning hot. Her little lips were parched and dry, but she would not drink the water I gave her. Then I discovered that her throat was swollen and red. My poor child, how I cried with her because the Great Spirit had forgotten us!

"At last, when we reached this western country, on the first weary night your sister died. And soon your uncle died also, leaving a widow and an orphan daughter, your cousin Warca-Ziwin. Both your sister and uncle might have been happy with us to-day, had it not been for the heartless paleface."

My mother was silent the rest of the way to our wigwam. Though I saw no tears in her eyes, I knew that was because I was with her. She seldom wept before me.

## II. The Legends

During the summer days, my mother built her fire in the shadow of our wigwam.

In the early morning our simple breakfast was spread upon the grass west of our tepee. At the farthest point of the shade my mother sat beside her fire, toasting a savory piece of dried meat. Near her, I sat upon my feet, eating my dried meat with unleavened bread, and drinking strong black coffee.

The morning meal was our quiet hour, when we two were entirely alone. At noon, several who chanced to be passing by stopped to rest, and to share our luncheon with us, for they were sure of our hospitality.

My uncle, whose death my mother ever lamented, was one of our nation's bravest warriors. His name was on the lips of old men when talking of the proud feats of valor; and it was mentioned by younger men, too, in connection with deeds of gallantry. Old women praised him for his kindness toward them; young women held him up as an ideal to their sweethearts. Every one loved him, and my mother worshiped his memory. Thus it happened that even strangers were sure of welcome in our lodge, if they but asked a favor in my uncle's name.

Though I heard many strange experiences related by these wayfarers, I loved best the evening meal, for that was the time old legends were told. I was always glad when the sun hung low in the west, for then my mother sent me to invite the neighboring old men and women to eat supper with us. Running all the way to the wigwams, I halted shyly at the entrances. Sometimes I stood long moments without saying a word. It was not any fear that made me so dumb when out upon such a happy errand; nor was it that I wished to withhold the invitation, for it was all I could do to observe this very proper silence. But it was a sensing of the atmosphere, to assure myself that I should not hinder other plans. My mother used to say to me, as I was almost bounding away for the old people: "Wait a moment before you invite any one. If other plans are being discussed, do not interfere, but go elsewhere."

The old folks knew the meaning of my pauses; and often they coaxed my confidence by asking, "What do you seek, little granddaughter?"

"My mother says you are to come to our tepee this evening," I instantly exploded, and breathed the freer afterwards.

"Yes, yes, gladly, gladly I shall come!" each replied. Rising at once and carrying their blankets across one shoulder, they flocked leisurely from their various wigwams toward our dwelling.

My mission done, I ran back, skipping and jumping with delight. All out of breath, I told my mother almost the exact words of the answers to my invitation. Frequently she asked, "What were they doing when you entered their tepee?" This taught me to remember all I saw at a single glance. Often I told my mother my impressions without being questioned.

While in the neighboring wigwams sometimes an old Indian woman asked me, "What is your mother doing?" Unless my mother had cautioned me not to tell, I generally answered her questions without reserve.

At the arrival of our guests I sat close to my mother, and did not leave her side without first asking her consent. I ate my supper in quiet, listening patiently to the talk of the old people, wishing all the time that they would begin the stories I loved best. At last, when I could not wait any longer, I whispered in my mother's ear, "Ask them to tell an Iktomi[2] story, mother."

Soothing my impatience, my mother said aloud, "My little daughter is anx-

---

2. Spider (Sioux, literal trans.); sometimes used to mean trickster.

ious to hear your legends." By this time all were through eating, and the evening was fast deepening into twilight.

As each in turn began to tell a legend, I pillowed my head in my mother's lap; and lying flat upon my back, I watched the stars as they peeped down upon me, one by one. The increasing interest of the tale aroused me, and I sat up eagerly listening for every word. The old women made funny remarks, and laughed so heartily that I could not help joining them.

The distant howling of a pack of wolves or the hooting of an owl in the river bottom frightened me, and I nestled into my mother's lap. She added some dry sticks to the fire, and the bright flames heaped up into the faces of the old folks as they sat around in a great circle.

On such an evening, I remember the glare of the fire shone on a tattooed star upon the brow of the old warrior who was telling a story. I watched him curiously as he made his unconscious gestures. The blue star upon his bronzed forehead was a puzzle to me. Looking about, I saw two parallel lines on the chin of one of the old women. The rest had none. I examined my mother's face, but found no sign there.

After the warrior's story was finished, I asked the old woman the meaning of the blue lines on her chin, looking all the while out of the corners of my eyes at the warrior with the star on his forehead. I was a little afraid that he would rebuke me for my boldness.

Here the old woman began: "Why, my grandchild, they are signs,—secret signs I dare not tell you. I shall, however, tell you a wonderful story about a woman who had a cross tattooed upon each of her cheeks."

It was a long story of a woman whose magic power lay hidden behind the marks upon her face. I fell asleep before the story was completed.

Ever after that night I felt suspicious of tattooed people. Wherever I saw one I glanced furtively at the mark and round about it, wondering what terrible magic power was covered there.

It was rarely that such a fearful story as this one was told by the camp fire. Its impression was so acute that the picture still remains vividly clear and pronounced.

### III.  The Beadwork

Soon after breakfast, mother sometimes began her beadwork. On a bright clear day, she pulled out the wooden pegs that pinned the skirt of our wigwam to the ground, and rolled the canvas part way up on its frame of slender poles. Then the cool morning breezes swept freely through our dwelling, now and then wafting the perfume of sweet grasses from newly burnt prairie.

Untying the long tasseled strings that bound a small brown buckskin bag, my mother spread upon a mat beside her bunches of colored beads, just as an artist arranges the paints upon his palette. On a lapboard she smoothed out a double sheet of soft white buckskin; and drawing from a beaded case that hung on the left of her wide belt a long, narrow blade, she trimmed the buckskin into shape. Often she worked upon small moccasins for her small daughter. Then I became intensely interested in her designing. With a proud, beaming face, I watched her work. In imagination, I saw myself walking in a new pair of snugly fitting moccasins. I felt the envious eyes of my playmates upon the pretty red beads decorating my feet.

Close beside my mother I sat on a rug, with a scrap of buckskin in one hand and an awl in the other. This was the beginning of my practical observation lessons in the art of beadwork. From a skein of finely twisted threads of silvery sinews my mother pulled out a single one. With an awl she pierced the buckskin, and skillfully threaded it with the white sinew. Picking up the tiny beads one by one, she strung them with the point of her thread, always twisting it carefully after every stitch.

It took many trials before I learned how to knot my sinew thread on the point of my finger, as I saw her do. Then the next difficulty was in keeping my thread stiffly twisted, so that I could easily string my beads upon it. My mother required of me original designs for my lessons in beading. At first I frequently ensnared many a sunny hour into working a long design. Soon I learned from self-inflicted punishment to refrain from drawing complex patterns, for I had to finish whatever I began.

After some experience I usually drew easy and simple crosses and squares. These were some of the set forms. My original designs were not always symmetrical nor sufficiently characteristic, two faults with which my mother had little patience. The quietness of her oversight made me feel strongly responsible and dependent upon my own judgment. She treated me as a dignified little individual as long as I was on my good behavior; and how humiliated I was when some boldness of mine drew forth a rebuke from her!

In the choice of colors she left me to my own taste. I was pleased with an outline of yellow upon a background of dark blue, or a combination of red and myrtle-green. There was another of red with a bluish gray that was more conventionally used. When I became a little familiar with designing and the various pleasing combinations of color, a harder lesson was given me. It was the sewing on, instead of beads, some tinted porcupine quills, moistened and flattened between the nails of the thumb and forefinger. My mother cut off the prickly ends and burned them at once in the centre fire. These sharp points were poisonous, and worked into the flesh wherever they lodged. For this reason, my mother said, I should not do much alone in quills until I was as tall as my cousin Warca-Ziwin.

Always after these confining lessons I was wild with surplus spirits, and found joyous relief in running loose in the open again. Many a summer afternoon, a party of four or five of my playmates roamed over the hills with me. We each carried a light sharpened rod about four feet long, with which we pried up certain sweet roots. When we had eaten all the choice roots we chanced upon, we shouldered our rods and strayed off into patches of a stalky plant under whose yellow blossoms we found little crystal drops of gum. Drop by drop we gathered this nature's rockcandy, until each of us could boast of a lump the size of a small bird's egg. Soon satiated with its woody flavor, we tossed away our gum, to return again to the sweet roots.

I remember well how we used to exchange our necklaces, beaded belts, and sometimes even our moccasins. We pretended to offer them as gifts to one another. We delighted in impersonating our own mothers. We talked of things we had heard them say in their conversations. We imitated their various manners, even to the inflection of their voices. In the lap of the prairie we seated ourselves upon our feet; and leaning our painted cheeks in the palms of our hands, we rested our elbows on our knees, and bent forward as old women were most accustomed to do.

While one was telling of some heroic deed recently done by a near relative, the rest of us listened attentively, and exclaimed in undertones, "Han! han!" (yes! yes!) whenever the speaker paused for breath, or sometimes for our sympathy. As the discourse became more thrilling, according to our ideas, we raised our voices in these interjections. In these impersonations our parents were led to say only those things that were in common favor.

No matter how exciting a tale we might be rehearsing, the mere shifting of a cloud shadow in the landscape near by was sufficient to change our impulses; and soon we were all chasing the great shadows that played among the hills. We shouted and whooped in the chase; laughing and calling to one another, we were like little sportive nymphs on that Dakota sea of rolling green.

On one occasion, I forgot the cloud shadow in a strange notion to catch up with my own shadow. Standing straight and still, I began to glide after it, putting out one foot cautiously. When, with the greatest care, I set my foot in advance of myself, my shadow crept onward too. Then again I tried it; this time with the other foot. Still again my shadow escaped me. I began to run; and away flew my shadow, always just a step beyond me. Faster and faster I ran, setting my teeth and clenching my fists, determined to overtake my own fleet shadow. But ever swifter it glided before me, while I was growing breathless and hot. Slackening my speed, I was greatly vexed that my shadow should check its pace also. Daring it to the utmost, as I thought, I sat down upon a rock imbedded in the hillside.

So! my shadow had the impudence to sit down beside me!

Now my comrades caught up with me, and began to ask why I was running away so fast.

"Oh, I was chasing my shadow! Didn't you ever do that?" I inquired, surprised that they should not understand.

They planted their moccasined feet firmly upon my shadow to stay it, and I arose. Again my shadow slipped away, and moved as often as I did. Then we gave up trying to catch my shadow.

Before this peculiar experience I have no distinct memory of having recognized any vital bond between myself and my own shadow. I never gave it an afterthought.

Returning our borrowed belts and trinkets, we rambled homeward. That evening, as on other evenings, I went to sleep over my legends.

## IV. The Coffee-Making

One summer afternoon, my mother left me alone in our wigwam, while she went across the way to my aunt's dwelling.

I did not much like to stay alone in our tepee, for I feared a tall, broadshouldered crazy man, some forty years old, who walked loose among the hills. Wiyaka-Napbina (Wearer of a Feather Necklace) was harmless, and whenever he came into a wigwam he was driven there by extreme hunger. He went nude except for the half of a red blanket he girdled around his waist. In one tawny arm he used to carry a heavy bunch of wild sunflowers that he gathered in his aimless ramblings. His black hair was matted by the winds, and scorched into a dry red by the constant summer sun. As he took great strides, placing one brown bare foot directly in front of the other, he swung his long lean arm to and fro.

Frequently he paused in his walk and gazed far backward, shading his eyes with his hand. He was under the belief that an evil spirit was haunting his steps. This was what my mother told me once, when I sneered at such a silly big man. I was brave when my mother was near by, and Wiyaka-Napbina walking farther and farther away.

"Pity the man, my child. I knew him when he was a brave and handsome youth. He was overtaken by a malicious spirit among the hills, one day, when he went hither and thither after his ponies. Since then he cannot stay away from the hills," she said.

I felt so sorry for the man in his misfortune that I prayed to the Great Spirit to restore him. But though I pitied him at a distance, I was still afraid of him when he appeared near our wigwam.

Thus, when my mother left me by myself that afternoon, I sat in a fearful mood within our tepee. I recalled all I had ever heard about Wiyaka-Napbina; and I tried to assure myself that though he might pass near by, he would not come to our wigwam because there was no little girl around our grounds.

Just then, from without a hand lifted the canvas covering of the entrance; the shadow of a man fell within the wigwam, and a large roughly moccasined foot was planted inside.

For a moment I did not dare to breathe or stir, for I thought that could be no other than Wiyaka-Napbina. The next instant I sighed aloud in relief. It was an old grandfather who had often told me Iktomi legends.

"Where is your mother, my little grandchild?" were his first words.

"My mother is soon coming back from my aunt's tepee," I replied.

"Then I shall wait awhile for her return," he said, crossing his feet and seating himself upon a mat.

At once I began to play the part of a generous hostess. I turned to my mother's coffeepot.

Lifting the lid, I found nothing but coffee grounds in the bottom. I set the pot on a heap of cold ashes in the centre, and filled it half full of warm Missouri River water. During this performance I felt conscious of being watched. Then breaking off a small piece of our unleavened bread, I placed it in a bowl. Turning soon to the coffeepot, which would never have boiled on a dead fire had I waited forever, I poured out a cup of worse than muddy warm water. Carrying the bowl in one hand and cup in the other, I handed the light luncheon to the old warrior. I offered them to him with the air of bestowing generous hospitality.

"How! how!"[3] he said, and placed the dishes on the ground in front of his crossed feet. He nibbled at the bread and sipped from the cup. I sat back against a pole watching him. I was proud to have succeeded so well in serving refreshments to a guest all by myself. Before the old warrior had finished eating, my mother entered. Immediately she wondered where I had found coffee, for she knew I had never made any, and that she had left the coffeepot empty. Answering the question in my mother's eyes, the warrior remarked, "My granddaughter made coffee on a heap of dead ashes, and served me the moment I came."

They both laughed, and mother said, "Wait a little longer, and I shall build a fire." She meant to make some real coffee. But neither she nor the warrior,

---

3. Or *hao* (*hau*), American Indian greeting.

whom the law of our custom had compelled to partake of my insipid hospitality, said anything to embarrass me. They treated my best judgment, poor as it was, with the utmost respect. It was not till long years afterward that I learned how ridiculous a thing I had done.

## V. The Dead Man's Plum Bush

One autumn afternoon, many people came streaming toward the dwelling of our near neighbor. With painted faces, and wearing broad white bosoms of elk's teeth, they hurried down the narrow footpath to Haraka Wambdi's wigwam. Young mothers held their children by the hand, and half pulled them along in their haste. They overtook and passed by the bent old grandmothers who were trudging along with crooked canes toward the centre of excitement. Most of the young braves galloped hither on their ponies. Toothless warriors, like the old women, came more slowly, though mounted on lively ponies. They sat proudly erect on their horses. They wore their eagle plumes, and waved their various trophies of former wars.

In front of the wigwam a great fire was built, and several large black kettles of venison were suspended over it. The crowd were seated about it on the grass in a great circle. Behind them some of the braves stood leaning against the necks of their ponies, their tall figures draped in loose robes which were well drawn over their eyes.

Young girls, with their faces glowing like bright red autumn leaves, their glossy braids falling over each ear, sat coquettishly beside their chaperons. It was a custom for young Indian women to invite some older relative to escort them to the public feasts. Though it was not an iron law, it was generally observed.

Haraka Wambdi was a strong young brave, who had just returned from his first battle, a warrior. His near relatives, to celebrate his new rank, were spreading a feast to which the whole of the Indian village was invited.

Holding my pretty striped blanket in readiness to throw over my shoulders, I grew more and more restless as I watched the gay throng assembling. My mother was busily broiling a wild duck that my aunt had that morning brought over.

"Mother, mother, why do you stop to cook a small meal when we are invited to a feast?" I asked, with a snarl in my voice.

"My child, learn to wait. On our way to the celebration we are going to stop at Chanyu's wigwam. His aged mother-in-law is lying very ill, and I think she would like a taste of this small game."

Having once seen the suffering on the thin, pinched features of this dying woman, I felt a momentary shame that I had not remembered her before.

On our way, I ran ahead of my mother, and was reaching out my hand to pick some purple plums that grew on a small bush, when I was checked by a low "Sh!" from my mother.

"Why, mother, I want to taste the plums!" I exclaimed, as I dropped my hand to my side in disappointment.

"Never pluck a single plum from this bush, my child, for its roots are wrapped around an Indian's skeleton. A brave is buried here. While he lived, he was so fond of playing the game of striped plum seeds that, at his death, his set of plum seeds were buried in his hands. From them sprang up this little bush."

Eyeing the forbidden fruit, I trod lightly on the sacred ground, and dared to speak only in whispers, until we had gone many paces from it. After that time, I halted in my ramblings whenever I came in sight of the plum bush. I grew sober with awe, and was alert to hear a long-drawn-out whistle rise from the roots of it. Though I had never heard with my own ears this strange whistle of departed spirits, yet I had listened so frequently to hear the old folks describe it that I knew I should recognize it at once.

The lasting impression of that day, as I recall it now, is what my mother told me about the dead man's plum bush.

## VI. *The Ground Squirrel*

In the busy autumn days, my cousin Warca-Ziwin's mother came to our wigwam to help my mother preserve foods for our winter use. I was very fond of my aunt, because she was not so quiet as my mother. Though she was older, she was more jovial and less reserved. She was slender and remarkably erect. While my mother's hair was heavy and black, my aunt had unusually thin locks.

Ever since I knew her, she wore a string of large blue beads around her neck,—beads that were precious because my uncle had given them to her when she was a younger woman. She had a peculiar swing in her gait, caused by a long stride rarely natural to so slight a figure. It was during my aunt's visit with us that my mother forgot her accustomed quietness, often laughing heartily at some of my aunt's witty remarks.

I loved my aunt threefold: for her hearty laughter, for the cheerfulness she caused my mother, and most of all for the times she dried my tears and held me in her lap, when my mother had reproved me.

Early in the cool mornings, just as the yellow rim of the sun rose above the hills, we were up and eating our breakfast. We awoke so early that we saw the sacred hour when a misty smoke hung over a pit surrounded by an impassable sinking mire. This strange smoke appeared every morning, both winter and summer; but most visibly in midwinter it rose immediately above the marshy spot. By the time the full face of the sun appeared above the eastern horizon, the smoke vanished. Even very old men, who had known this country the longest, said that the smoke from this pit had never failed a single day to rise heavenward.

As I frolicked about our dwelling, I used to stop suddenly, and with a fearful awe watch the smoking of the unknown fires. While the vapor was visible, I was afraid to go very far from our wigwam unless I went with my mother.

From a field in the fertile river bottom my mother and aunt gathered an abundant supply of corn. Near our tepee, they spread a large canvas upon the grass, and dried their sweet corn in it. I was left to watch the corn, that nothing should disturb it. I played around it with dolls made of ears of corn. I braided their soft fine silk for hair, and gave them blankets as various as the scraps I found in my mother's workbag.

There was a little stranger with a black-and-yellow-striped coat that used to come to the drying corn. It was a little ground squirrel, who was so fearless of me that he came to one corner of the canvas and carried away as much of the sweet corn as he could hold. I wanted very much to catch him, and rub his pretty fur back, but my mother said he would be so frightened if I caught him that he would bite my fingers. So I was as content as he to keep the corn between us. Every morning he came for more corn. Some evenings I have seen him creeping about our grounds; and when I gave a sudden whoop of recognition, he ran quickly out of sight.

When mother had dried all the corn she wished, then she sliced great pumpkins into thin rings; and these she doubled and linked together into long chains. She hung them on a pole that stretched between two forked posts. The wind and sun soon thoroughly dried the chains of pumpkin. Then she packed them away in a case of thick and stiff buckskin.

In the sun and wind she also dried many wild fruits,—cherries, berries, and plums. But chiefest among my early recollections of autumn is that one of the corn drying and the ground squirrel.

I have few memories of winter days, at this period of my life, though many of the summer. There is one only which I can recall.

Some missionaries gave me a little bag of marbles. They were all sizes and colors. Among them were some of colored glass. Walking with my mother to the river, on a late winter day, we found great chunks of ice piled all along the bank. The ice on the river was floating in huge pieces. As I stood beside one large block, I noticed for the first time the colors of the rainbow in the crystal ice. Immediately I thought of my glass marbles at home. With my bare fingers I tried to pick out some of the colors, for they seemed so near the surface. But my fingers began to sting with the intense cold, and I had to bite them hard to keep from crying.

From that day on, for many a moon, I believed that glass marbles had river ice inside of them.

### VII. The Big Red Apples

The first turning away from the easy, natural flow of my life occurred in an early spring. It was in my eighth year; in the month of March, I afterward learned. At this age I knew but one language, and that was my mother's native tongue.

From some of my playmates I heard that two paleface missionaries were in our village. They were from that class of white men who wore big hats and carried large hearts, they said. Running direct to my mother, I began to question her why these two strangers were among us. She told me, after I had teased much, that they had come to take away Indian boys and girls to the East. My mother did not seem to want me to talk about them. But in a day or two, I gleaned many wonderful stories from my playfellows concerning the strangers.

"Mother, my friend Judéwin is going home with the missionaries. She is going to a more beautiful country than ours; the palefaces told her so!" I said wistfully, wishing in my heart that I too might go.

Mother sat in a chair, and I was hanging on her knee. Within the last two seasons my big brother Dawée had returned from a three years' education in the East, and his coming back influenced my mother to take a farther step from her native way of living. First it was a change from the buffalo skin to the white man's canvas that covered our wigwam. Now she had given up her wigwam of slender poles, to live, a foreigner, in a home of clumsy logs.

"Yes, my child, several others besides Judéwin are going away with the palefaces. Your brother said the missionaries had inquired about his little sister," she said, watching my face very closely.

My heart thumped so hard against my breast, I wondered if she could hear it.

"Did he tell them to take me, mother?" I asked, fearing lest Dawée had forbidden the palefaces to see me, and that my hope of going to the Wonderland would be entirely blighted.

With a sad, slow smile, she answered: "There! I knew you were wishing to go, because Judéwin has filled your ears with the white men's lies. Don't believe a word they say! Their words are sweet, but, my child, their deeds are bitter. You will cry for me, but they will not even soothe you. Stay with me, my little one! Your brother Dawée says that going East, away from your mother, is too hard an experience for his baby sister."

Thus my mother discouraged my curiosity about the lands beyond our eastern horizon; for it was not yet an ambition for Letters that was stirring me. But on the following day the missionaries did come to our very house. I spied them coming up the footpath leading to our cottage. A third man was with them, but he was not my brother Dawée. It was another, a young interpreter, a paleface who had a smattering of the Indian language. I was ready to run out to meet them, but I did not dare to displease my mother. With great glee, I jumped up and down on our ground floor. I begged my mother to open the door, that they would be sure to come to us. Alas! They came, they saw, and they conquered!

Judéwin had told me of the great tree where grew red, red apples; and how we could reach out our hands and pick all the red apples we could eat. I had never seen apple trees. I had never tasted more than a dozen red apples in my life; and when I heard of the orchards of the East, I was eager to roam among them. The missionaries smiled into my eyes, and patted my head. I wondered how mother could say such hard words against them.

"Mother, ask them if little girls may have all the red apples they want, when they go East," I whispered aloud, in my excitement.

The interpreter heard me, and answered: "Yes, little girl, the nice red apples are for those who pick them; and you will have a ride on the iron horse if you go with these good people."

I had never seen a train, and he knew it.

"Mother, I'm going East! I like big red apples, and I want to ride on the iron horse! Mother, say yes!" I pleaded.

My mother said nothing. The missionaries waited in silence; and my eyes began to blur with tears, though I struggled to choke them back. The corners of my mouth twitched, and my mother saw me.

"I am not ready to give you any word," she said to them. "To-morrow I shall send you my answer by my son."

With this they left us. Alone with my mother, I yielded to my tears, and cried aloud, shaking my head so as not to hear what she was saying to me. This was the first time I had ever been so unwilling to give up my own desire that I refused to hearken to my mother's voice.

There was a solemn silence in our home that night. Before I went to bed I begged the Great Spirit to make my mother willing I should go with the missionaries.

The next morning came, and my mother called me to her side. "My daughter, do you still persist in wishing to leave your mother?" she asked.

"Oh, mother, it is not that I wish to leave you, but I want to see the wonderful Eastern land," I answered.

My dear old aunt came to our house that morning, and I heard her say, "Let her try it."

I hoped that, as usual, my aunt was pleading on my side. My brother Dawée came for mother's decision. I dropped my play, and crept close to my aunt.

"Yes, Dawée, my daughter, though she does not understand what it all means, is anxious to go. She will need an education when she is grown, for then there will be fewer real Dakotas, and many more palefaces. This tearing her away, so young, from her mother is necessary, if I would have her an educated woman. The palefaces, who owe us a large debt for stolen lands, have begun to pay a tardy justice in offering some education to our children. But I know my daughter must suffer keenly in this experiment. For her sake, I dread to tell you my reply to the missionaries. Go, tell them that they may take my little daughter, and that the Great Spirit shall not fail to reward them according to their hearts."

Wrapped in my heavy blanket, I walked with my mother to the carriage that was soon to take us to the iron horse. I was happy. I met my playmates, who were also wearing their best thick blankets. We showed one another our new beaded moccasins, and the width of the belts that girdled our new dresses. Soon we were being drawn rapidly away by the white man's horses. When I saw the lonely figure of my mother vanish in the distance, a sense of regret settled heavily upon me. I felt suddenly weak, as if I might fall limp to the ground. I was in the hands of strangers whom my mother did not fully trust. I no longer felt free to be myself, or to voice my own feelings. The tears trickled down my cheeks, and I buried my face in the folds of my blanket. Now the first step, parting me from my mother, was taken, and all my belated tears availed nothing.

Having driven thirty miles to the ferryboat, we crossed the Missouri in the evening. Then riding again a few miles eastward, we stopped before a massive brick building. I looked at it in amazement, and with a vague misgiving, for in our village I had never seen so large a house. Trembling with fear and distrust of the palefaces, my teeth chattering from the chilly ride, I crept noiselessly in my soft moccasins along the narrow hall, keeping very close to the bare wall. I was as frightened and bewildered as the captured young of a wild creature.

1900

---

# HENRY ADAMS
## 1838–1918

Henry Adams's great-grandfather John was second president of the United States, his grandfather John Quincy was sixth president, and his father Charles Francis was a distinguished political leader and diplomat. Despite Henry's lifelong penchant for self-deprecation, his own achievements as scholar, teacher, novelist, editor, and cultural historian are worthy of his eminent forebears, for they earn him an important place in American intellectual and literary history.

Adams was born in Boston, on Beacon Hill, and spent his happy childhood in the constant presence of renowned politicians, artists, and intellectuals; the index to his autobiography, *The Education of Henry Adams*, is virtually an "International Who Was Who" of the time. He was to claim that his studies at Harvard College of the 1850s prepared him neither for a career nor for the extraordinary intellectual, technological, and social transformations of the last half of the century, but the records reveal that he was a good student and his disparagement of his college experience should be understood as an example of Adams's persistent self-irony. After graduation, he studied and traveled in Europe before he returned to America in 1860 to become private secretary to his father, a position he held for nine years, first in Washington when the elder Adams was elected to Congress, then in London, where his father served as foreign minister during the Civil War years.

In 1870, after a brief career as a free-lance journalist, he rather reluctantly accepted a position as assistant professor of medieval history at Harvard, doubting his own fitness for the position; he observed later that the entire educational system of the college was "fallacious from the beginning to the end," and that "the lecture-room was futile enough, but the faculty-room was worse." In the same period he undertook the editorship of the prestigious *North American Review*, using this position to criticize both of the major political parties in this period concerning uncontrolled expansion and widespread government corruption. He sardonically remarked of his two vocations that "a professor commonly became a pedagogue or a pedant; an editor an authority on advertising." By all accounts other than his own, however, he served the college and the journal well before he gave up both positions in the late 1870s to settle in Washington to devote full time to historical research.

Adams's new career as historian did not begin auspiciously. His biography (1879) of Albert Gallatin, Thomas Jefferson's secretary of the treasury, and his subsequent biography of the flamboyant congressman John Randolph, were successful neither with his professional colleagues nor with the public. The research in original documents Adams had undertaken to write these biographies, however, brought him to the grander subject of which they were a part: *The History of the United States of America during the Administrations of Thomas Jefferson and James Madison* (1889–91). The nine-volume work (which took almost nine years to complete) is still a standard account of this crucial period of transition from Old to New World dominance. During these years Adams also published two novels rich in social detail: *Democracy* in 1880, and *Esther* in 1884. Both novels stirred considerable interest when they were published and continue to attract readers who seek, in the first novel, a contemporary account of the corruption of government by business interests and, in the second, a representation of the effect of scientific thought on traditional religious belief.

Adams's life was profoundly changed by the suicide, in 1885, of his charming and seemingly contented wife, Marian Hooper. The publication of *The History* also left Adams physically drained and intellectually depleted. For a time it seemed that he would occupy himself with nothing more serious than travel to familiar places in Europe and to more exotic places in the Pacific and Middle East. But a trip to nothern France in the summer of 1895 with Mrs. Henry Cabot Lodge, the wife of his friend the senator from Massachusetts, stirred his intellectual curiosity and ignited his creative energies once again.

What most struck the world-weary Adams that summer was the severe and majestic harmony of the twelfth- and thirteenth-century Norman and Gothic cathedrals they visited, particularly the one at Chartres. *Mont-Saint-Michel and Chartres* (privately printed in 1904; published 1913) not only provided illuminating discussions of the literary and architectural monuments of the period but penetrated to the powerful spiritual forces that lay behind those achievements. Paradoxically, the insights that allowed Adams to represent what he considered a straight-line historical decline from this medieval unity to his own period of confusion and immanent disaster served to renew his own spirits and brought his mind and work to the attention of a wider public.

The Education of Henry Adams, begun as a kind of sequel to Mont-Saint-Michel, was privately printed early in 1907 and distributed to nearly one hundred friends and prominent personages mentioned in the text. In it, Adams rehearses his own miseducation by his family, by schools, and by his experience of various social institutions; ironically offers his own "failures" as a negative example to young men of the time; and describes the increasingly rapid collapse of Western culture in the era after the twelfth century, during which the Virgin Mary (the spiritually unifying) gave way to the Industrial Dynamo (the scientifically disunifying) as the object of humankind's worship.

The Virgin and the Dynamo were not presented simply as historical facts but to serve as symbols. In fact, The Education is primarily a literary, not a biographical or historical, work. This book, because it shows imaginatively how all the major intellectual, social, political, military, and economic issues and developments of Adams's day are interrelated, is now considered by many critics to be the one indispensable text for students seeking to understand the period between the Civil War and World War I. The perspective taken by Adams in The Education used to seem excessively pessimistic; its final chapter (dated 1905) prophesied that the disintegrative forces unleashed by science threatened to effect the destruction of the world within a generation. This prophecy has not been borne out literally, but the sense of imminent global disaster has come to be widely shared. "Naturally," as Adams went on to observe in this chapter, "such an attitude of an umpire is apt to infuriate the spectators. Above all, it was profoundly unmoral, and tended to discourage effort. On the other hand, it tended to encourage foresight and to economize waste of mind. If this was not itself education, it pointed out the economies necessary for the education of the new American. There, the duty stopped."

The Education has grown in interest in recent years for two major reasons: for what it tells us about its complex, elusive, and paradoxical author and for what it tells us about the technology-dominated, dehumanized world whose major power alignments, political and material, he foresaw so clearly. As a prophet, he was, as social analyst Daniel Bell observed, the first American writer who "caught a sense of the quickening change of pace that drives all our lives." As a historian of his own time, he was also, as historian Richard Hofstadter noted, "singular not only for the quality of his prose and the sophistication of his mind but also for the unparalleled mixture of his detachment and involvement." Adams, like many of us, was fascinated with the past, horrified by the present, and skeptical about the future; thus, more than half a century after his death, Adams and his most complex book speak with renewed pertinence to his dilemmas and ours.

# From The Education of Henry Adams

## Chapter XXV. The Dynamo and the Virgin (1900)[1]

Until the Great Exposition of 1900[2] closed its doors in November, Adams haunted it, aching to absorb knowledge, and helpless to find it. He would have

1. This selection from The Education reprints Houghton Mifflin Company's Riverside Edition text established by Ernest Samuels. For the notes we are indebted to Samuels's annotation for that volume. The

Education was begun in 1903, essentially completed in 1905, and privately printed in 1907.
2. The World's Fair held in Paris from April through November.

liked to know how much of it could have been grasped by the best-informed man in the world. While he was thus meditating chaos, Langley[3] came by, and showed it to him. At Langley's behest, the Exhibition dropped its superfluous rags and stripped itself to the skin, for Langley knew what to study, and why, and how; while Adams might as well have stood outside in the night, staring at the Milky Way. Yet Langley said nothing new, and taught nothing that one might not have learned from Lord Bacon,[4] three hundred years before; but though one should have known the "Advancement of Science" as well as one knew the "Comedy of Errors,"[5] the literary knowledge counted for nothing until some teacher should show how to apply it. Bacon took a vast deal of trouble in teaching King James I[6] and his subjects, American or other, towards the year 1620, that true science was the development or economy of forces; yet an elderly American in 1900 knew neither the formula nor the forces; or even so much as to say to himself that his historical business in the Exposition concerned only the economics or developments of force since 1893, when he began to study at Chicago.[7]

Nothing in education is so astonishing as the amount of ignorance it accumulates in the form of inert facts. Adams had looked at most of the accumulations of art in the storehouses called Art Museums; yet he did not know how to look at the art exhibits of 1900. He had studied Karl Marx[8] and his doctrines of history with profound attention, yet he could not apply them at Paris. Langley, with the ease of a great master of experiment, threw out of the field every exhibit that did not reveal a new application of force, and naturally threw out, to begin with, almost the whole art exhibit. Equally, he ignored almost the whole industrial exhibit. He led his pupil directly to the forces. His chief interest was in new motors to make his airship feasible, and he taught Adams the astonishing complexities of the new Daimler[9] motor, and of the automobile, which, since 1893, had become a nightmare at a hundred kilometres an hour, almost as destructive as the electric tram which was only ten years older; and threatening to become as terrible as the locomotive steam-engine itself, which was almost exactly Adams's own age.

Then he showed his scholar the great hall of dynamos, and explained how little he knew about electricity or force of any kind, even of his own special sun, which spouted heat in inconceivable volume, but which, as far as he knew, might spout less or more, at any time, for all the certainty he felt in it. To him, the dynamo itself was but an ingenious channel for conveying somewhere the heat latent in a few tons of poor coal hidden in a dirty engine-house carefully kept out of sight; but to Adams the dynamo became a symbol of infinity. As he grew accustomed to the great gallery of machines, he began to feel the forty-foot dynamos as a moral force, much as the early Christians felt the Cross. The planet itself seemed less impressive, in its old-fashioned, deliberate, annual or daily revolution, than this huge wheel, revolving within arm's-length at some vertiginous speed, and barely murmuring—scarcely

---

3. Samuel P. Langley (1834–1906), American astronomer and inventor, in 1896, of the first airplane to fly successfully.
4. Sir Francis Bacon (1561–1626), English natural philosopher, author of The Advancement of Learning (1605).
5. Early Shakespearean comedy (1594).
6. King of England (1603–25).
7. The subject of Chap. 22 of the Education. The Chicago Exposition of 1893 first stimulated Adams's interest in the "economy of forces."
8. German social philosopher (1818–1883) and architect of modern socialism and communism; he formulated his theories on the principle of "dialectical materialism."
9. Gottlieb Daimler (1834–1900), German engineer, inventor of the high-speed internal combusion engine and an early developer of the automobile.

humming an audible warning to stand a hair's-breadth further for respect of power—while it would not wake the baby lying close against its frame. Before the end, one began to pray to it; inherited instinct taught the national expression of man before silent and infinite force. Among the thousand symbols of ultimate energy, the dynamo was not so human as some, but it was the most expressive.

Yet the dynamo, next to the steam-engine, was the most familiar of exhibits. For Adams's object its value lay chiefly in its occult mechanism. Between the dynamo in the gallery of machines and the engine-house outside, the break of continuity amounted to abysmal fracture for a historian's objects. No more relation could he discover between the steam and the electric current than between the Cross and the cathedral. The forces were interchangeable if not reversible, but he could see only an absolute *fiat* in electricity as in faith. Langley could not help him. Indeed, Langley seemed to be worried by the same trouble, for he constantly repeated that the new forces were anarchical, and especially that he was not responsible for the new rays, that were little short of parricidal in their wicked spirit towards science. His own rays,[1] with which he had doubled the solar spectrum, were altogether harmless and beneficent; but Radium denied its God[2]—or, what was to Langley the same thing, denied the truths of his Science. The force was wholly new.

A historian who asked only to learn enough to be as futile as Langley or Kelvin,[3] made rapid progress under this teaching, and mixed himself up in the tangle of ideas until he achieved a sort of Paradise of ignorance vastly consoling to his fatigued senses. He wrapped himself in vibrations and rays which were new, and he would have hugged Marconi and Branly[4] had he met them, as he hugged the dynamo; while he lost his arithmetic in trying to figure out the equation between the discoveries and the economies of force. The economies, like the discoveries, were absolute, supersensual, occult; incapable of expression in horse-power. What mathematical equivalent could he suggest as the value of a Branly coherer? Frozen air, or the electric furnace, had some scale of measurement, no doubt, if somebody could invent a thermometer adequate to the purpose; but X-rays[5] had played no part whatever in man's consciousness, and the atom itself had figured only as a fiction of thought. In these seven years man had translated himself into a new universe which had no common scale of measurement with the old. He had entered a supersensual world, in which he could measure nothing except by chance collisions of movements imperceptible to his senses, perhaps even imperceptible to his instruments, but perceptible to each other, and so to some known ray at the end of the scale. Langley seemed prepared for anything, even for an indeterminable number of universes interfused—physics stark mad in metaphysics.

Historians undertake to arrange sequences,—called stories, or histories—assuming in silence a relation of cause and effect. These assumptions, hidden in the depths of dusty libraries, have been astounding, but commonly unconscious and childlike; so much so, that if any captious critic were to drag them

---

1. Langley had invented the bolometer, with which he was able to measure intensities of invisible heat rays in the infrared spectrum.
2. Because radium, first isolated by the Curies in 1898, underwent spontaneous transformation through radioactive emission, it did not fit prevailing scientific distinctions between matter and energy.
3. William Thomson, Baron Kelvin (1824–1907),

English mathematician and physicist known especially for his work in thermodynamics and electrodynamics.
4. Édouard Branly (1844–1940), French physicist and inventor, in 1890, of the Branly "coherer" for detecting radio waves. Guglielmo Marconi (1874–1937), Italian inventor of radio telegraphy in 1895.
5. Wilhelm Roentgen (1845–1923) discovered x rays in 1895.

to light, historians would probably reply, with one voice, that they had never supposed themselves required to know what they were talking about. Adams, for one, had toiled in vain to find out what he meant. He had even published a dozen volumes of American history for no other purpose than to satisfy himself whether, by the severest process of stating, with the least possible comment, such facts as seemed sure, in such order as seemed rigorously consequent, he could fix for a familiar moment a necessary sequence of human movement. The result had satisfied him as little as at Harvard College. Where he saw sequence, other men saw something quite different, and no one saw the same unit of measure. He cared little about his experiments and less about his statesmen, who seemed to him quite as ignorant as himself and, as a rule, no more honest; but he insisted on a relation of sequence, and if he could not reach it by one method, he would try as many methods as science knew. Satisfied that the sequence of men led to nothing and that the sequence of their society could lead no further, while the mere sequence of time was artificial, and the sequence of thought was chaos, he turned at last to the sequence of force; and thus it happened that, after ten years' pursuit, he found himself lying in the Gallery of Machines at the Great Exposition of 1900, his historical neck broken by the sudden irruption of forces totally new.

Since no one else showed much concern, an elderly person without other cares had no need to betray alarm. The year 1900 was not the first to upset schoolmasters. Copernicus and Galileo[6] had broken many professorial necks about 1600; Columbus had stood the world on its head towards 1500; but the nearest approach to the revolution of 1900 was that of 310, when Constantine set up the Cross.[7] The rays that Langley disowned, as well as those which he fathered, were occult, supersensual, irrational; they were a revelation of mysterious energy like that of the Cross; they were what, in terms of mediæval science, were called immediate modes of the divine substance.

The historian was thus reduced to his last resources. Clearly if he was bound to reduce all these forces to a common value, this common value could have no measure but that of their attraction on his own mind. He must treat them as they had been felt; as convertible, reversible, interchangeable attractions on thought. He made up his mind to venture it; he would risk translating rays into faith. Such a reversible process would vastly amuse a chemist, but the chemist could not deny that he, or some of his fellow physicists, could feel the force of both. When Adams was a boy in Boston, the best chemist in the place had probably never heard of Venus except by way of scandal, or of the Virgin except as idolatry;[8] neither had he heard of dynamos or automobiles or radium; yet his mind was ready to feel the force of all, thought the rays were unborn and the women were dead.

Here opened another totally new education, which promised to be by far the most hazardous of all. The knife-edge along which he must crawl, like Sir Lancelot[9] in the twelfth century, divided two kingdoms of force which had nothing in common but attraction. They were as different as a magnet is from

6. Galileo (1564–1642), Italian astronomer and developer of the refracting telescope, was condemned by the Inquisition for espousing Copernican heliocentric theory. Copernicus (1473–1543), Polish astronomer, proved that the earth rotated around the sun and not vice versa.
7. Constantine the Great (288?–337), Roman emperor, issued the Edict of Milan in 313 proclaiming toleration of Christians, which paved the way for the ascendancy of Christianity.
8. That is, the druggist knew of Venus only through selling medication for venereal disease, and because Boston was largely Protestant, he would only have heard of the Virgin as the object of idolatrous worship.
9. In Chrétien de Troyes's *Lancelot*, the hero was obliged to crawl across a bridge composed of a knife to enter a castle and rescue Guinevere.

gravitation, supposing one knew what a magnet was, or gravitation, or love. The force of the Virgin was still felt at Lourdes,[1] and seemed to be as potent as X-rays; but in America neither Venus nor Virgin ever had value as force— at most as sentiment. No American had ever been truly afraid of either.

This problem in dynamics gravely perplexed an American historian. The Woman had once been supreme; in France she still seemed potent, not merely as a sentiment, but as a force. Why was she unknown in America? For evidently America was ashamed of her, and she was ashamed of herself, otherwise they would not have strewn fig-leaves so profusely all over her.[2] When she was a true force, she was ignorant of fig-leaves, but the monthly-magazine-made American female had not a feature that would have been recognized by Adam. The trait was notorious, and often humorous, but any one brought up among Puritans knew that sex was sin. In any previous age, sex was strength. Neither art nor beauty was needed. Every one, even among Puritans, knew that neither Diana of the Ephesians[3] nor any of the Oriental goddesses was worshipped for her beauty. She was goddess because of her force; she was the animated dynamo; she was reproduction—the greatest and most mysterious of all energies; all she needed was to be fecund. Singularly enough, not one of Adams's many schools of education had ever drawn his attention to the opening lines of Lucretius,[4] though they were perhaps the finest in all Latin literature, where the poet invoked Venus exactly as Dante invoked the Virgin:—

"Quae quoniam rerum naturam *sola* gubernas."

The Venus of Epicurean philosophy survived in the Virgin of the Schools:—

"Donna, sei tanto grande, e tanto vali,
Che qual vuol grazia, e a te non ricorre,
Sua disianza vuol volar senz' ali."[5]

All this was to American thought as though it had never existed. The true American knew something of the facts, but nothing of the feelings; he read the letter, but he never felt the law. Before this historical chasm, a mind like that of Adams felt itself helpless; he turned from the Virgin to the Dynamo as though he were a Branly coherer. On one side, at the Louvre and at Chartres, as he knew by the record of work actually done and still before his eyes, was the highest energy ever known to man, the creator of four-fifths of his noblest art, exercising vastly more attraction over the human mind than all the steam-engines and dynamos ever dreamed of; and yet this energy was unknown to the American mind. An American Virgin would never dare command; an American Venus would never dare exist.

The question, which to any plain American of the nineteenth century seemed as remote as it did to Adams, drew him almost violently to study, once it was posed; and on this point Langleys were as useless as though they were

---

1. A famous shrine in France known for its miraculous cures; the Virgin Mary was said to have appeared to a peasant girl there in 1858.
2. I.e., to conceal sexual organs and sensuality.
3. The shrine at Ephesus on the west coast of Asia Minor was dedicated to Artemis, a virgin goddess and mother figure.
4. Lucretius (c. 99–55 B.C.), in On the Nature of Things, 1.21: "And since 'tis thou / Venus alone /

Guidest the Cosmos" (trans. W. E. Leonard).
5. The Virgin of the Schools is a reference to medieval scholastic philosophers. The lines from Dante translate as follows:
Lady, thou art so great and hath such worth, that if there be who would have grace yet betaketh not himself to thee, his longing seeketh to fly without wings (Paradiso, 33, trans. Carlyle-Wicksteed).

Herbert Spencers[6] or dynamos. The idea survived only as art. There one turned as naturally as though the artist were himself a woman. Adams began to ponder, asking himself whether he knew of any American artist who had ever insisted on the power of sex, as every classic had always done; but he could think only of Walt Whitman; Bret Harte,[7] as far as the magazines would let him venture; and one or two painters, for the flesh-tones. All the rest had used sex for sentiment, never for force; to them, Eve was a tender flower, and Herodias[8] an unfeminine horror. American art, like the American language and American education, was as far as possible sexless.[9] Society regarded this victory over sex as its greatest triumph, and the historian readily admitted it, since the moral issue, for the moment, did not concern one who was studying the relations of unmoral force. He cared nothing for the sex of the dynamo until he could measure its energy.

Vaguely seeking a clue, he wandered through the art exhibit, and, in his stroll, stopped almost every day before St. Gaudens's[1] General Sherman, which had been given the central post of honor. St. Gaudens himself was in Paris, putting on the work his usual interminable last touches, and listening to the usual contradictory suggestions of brother sculptors. Of all the American artists who gave to American art whatever life it breathed in the seventies, St. Gaudens was perhaps the most sympathetic, but certainly the most inarticulate. General Grant or Don Cameron[2] had scarcely less instinct of rhetoric than he. All the others—the Hunts, Richardson, John La Farge, Stanford White[3]—were exuberant; only St. Gaudens could never discuss or dilate on an emotion, or suggest artistic arguments for giving to his work the forms that he felt. He never laid down the law, or affected the despot, or became brutalized like Whistler[4] by the brutalities of his world. He required no incense; he was no egoist; his simplicity of thought was excessive; he could not imitate, or give any form but his own to the creations of his hand. No one felt more strongly than he the strength of other men, but the idea that they could affect him never stirred an image in his mind.

This summer his health was poor and his spirits were low. For such a temper, Adams was not the best companion, since his own gaiety was not folle;[5] but he risked going now and then to the studio on Mont Parnasse to draw him out for a stroll in the Bois de Boulogne,[6] or dinner as pleased his moods, and in return St. Gaudens sometimes let Adams go about in his company.

Once St. Gaudens took him down to Amiens, with a party of Frenchmen, to see the cathedral. Not until they found themselves actually studying the sculpture of the western portal, did it dawn on Adams's mind that, for his purposes, St. Gaudens on the spot had more interest to him than the cathedral

6. English philosopher and popularizer of Darwinian evolutionary principles (1820–1893). Adams ironically suggests that Spencer's explanations were too general and abstract to explain this primal force.
7. Harte (1836–1902) sympathetically portrayed prostitutes in such stories as *The Outcasts of Poker Flat.* Whitman's (1819–1892) *Leaves of Grass* (1855) treated sex boldly and was much criticized on that account.
8. The wife of King Herod who collaborated with her daughter Salome in arranging the beheading of John the Baptist.
9. Just as the American language had no genders, American education was coeducational and in Adams's day entirely excluded sex as a subject from the curriculum.
1. Augustus Saint-Gaudens (1848–1907), American

sculptor.
2. Senator James Donald Cameron (1833–1918), secretary of war (1876) under President Grant.
3. Architect (1853–1906). William Morris Hunt (1824–1879), noted painter, and his younger brother Richard Morris Hunt (1828–1895), noted architect. Henry Hobson Richardson (1838–1886), architect. La Farge (1835–1910), muralist and maker of stained-glass windows.
4. James Abbott McNeill Whistler (1834–1903), American painter and lithographer.
5. Excessive (French).
6. A large wooded park on the outskirts of Paris. "Mont Parnasse": a Paris Left Bank district frequented by artists and writers.

itself. Great men before great monuments express great truths, provided they are not taken too solemnly. Adams never tired of quoting the supreme phrase of his idol Gibbon, before the Gothic cathedrals: "I darted a contemptuous look on the stately monuments of superstition."[7] Even in the footnotes of his history, Gibbon had never inserted a bit of humor more human than this, and one would have paid largely for a photograph of the fat little historian, on the background of Notre Dame of Amiens, trying to persuade his readers—perhaps himself—that he was darting a contemptuous look on the stately monument, for which he felt in fact the respect which every man of his vast study and active mind always feels before objects worthy of it; but besides the humor, one felt also the relation. Gibbon ignored the Virgin, because in 1789 religious monuments were out of fashion. In 1900 his remark sounded fresh and simple as the green fields to ears that had heard a hundred years of other remarks, mostly no more fresh and certainly less simple. Without malice, one might find it more instructive than a whole lecture of Ruskin.[8] One sees what one brings, and at that moment Gibbon brought the French Revolution. Ruskin brought reaction against the Revolution. St. Gaudens had passed beyond all. He liked the Stately monuments much more than he liked Gibbon or Ruskin; he loved their dignity; their unity; their scale; their lines; their lights and shadows; their decorative sculpture; but he was even less conscious than they of the force that created it all—the Virgin, the Woman—by whose genius "the stately monuments of superstition" were built, through which she was expressed. He would have seen more meaning in Isis[9] with the cow's horns, at Edfoo, who expressed the same thought. The art remained, but the energy was lost even upon the artist.

Yet in mind and person St. Gaudens was a survival of the 1500s; he bore the stamp of the Renaissance, and should have carried an image of the Virgin round his neck, or stuck in his hat, like Louis XI.[1] In mere time he was a lost soul that had strayed by chance into the twentieth century, and forgotten where it came from. He writhed and cursed at his ignorance, much as Adams did at his own, but in the opposite sense. St. Gaudens was a child of Benvenuto Cellini,[2] smothered in an American cradle. Adams was a quintessence of Boston, devoured by curiosity to think like Benvenuto. St. Gaudens's art was starved from birth, and Adams's instinct was blighted from babyhood. Each had but half of a nature, and when they came together before the Virgin of Amiens they ought both to have felt in her the force that made them one; but it was not so. To Adams she became more than ever a channel of force; to St Gaudens she remained as before a channel of taste.

For a symbol of power St. Gaudens instinctively preferred the horse, as was plain in his horse and Victory of the Sherman monument. Doubtless Sherman also felt it so. The attitude was so American that, for at least forty years, Adams had never realized that any other could be in sound taste. How many years had he taken to admit a notion of what Michael Angelo and Rubens[3] were

7. Apparently Adams's adaptation of a passage in Gibbon's French journal for February 21, 1763.
8. John Ruskin (1819–1900), English art critic and social reformer, famous for his highly imaginative interpretations of great works of the Italian Renaissance.
9. Egyptian earth-mother goddess. Adams visited Edfu, the site of the best-preserved temple in Egypt, in 1872–73 and in 1893.
1. A pious French king (1423–1483) who often dis-

guised himself as a pilgrim and wore an old felt hat decorated with the lead statuette of a saint.
2. Flamboyant Italian sculptor and goldsmith (1500–1571), author of a famous autobiography.
3. Peter Paul Rubens (1577–1640), 17th-century Flemish painter. Michelangelo Buonarroti (1475–1564), Italian sculptor, painter, architect, and poet of the High Renaissance. Both are known for their exceptional renderings of the human body.

driving at? He could not say; but he knew that only since 1895 had he begun to feel the Virgin or Venus as force, and not everywhere even so. At Chartres—perhaps at Lourdes—possibly at Cnidos[4] if one could still find there the divinely naked Aphrodite of Praxiteles—but otherwise one must look for force to the goddesses of Indian mythology. The idea died out long ago in the German and English stock. St. Gaudens at Amiens was hardly less sensitive to the force of the female energy than Matthew Arnold at the Grande Chartreuse.[5] Neither of them felt goddesses as power—only as reflected emotion, human expression, beauty, purity, taste, scarcely even as sympathy. They felt a railway train as power; yet they, and all other artists, constantly complained that the power embodied in a railway train could never be embodied in art. All the steam in the world could not, like the Virgin, build Chartres.

Yet in mechanics, whatever the mechanicians might think, both energies acted as interchangeable forces on man, and by action on man all known force may be measured. Indeed, few men of science measured force in any other way. After once admitting that a straight line was the shortest distance between two points, no serious mathematician cared to deny anything that suited his convenience, and rejected no symbol, unproved or unproveable, that helped him to accomplish work. The symbol was force, as a compass-needle or a triangle was force, as the mechanist might prove by losing it, and nothing could be gained by ignoring their value. Symbol or energy, the Virgin had acted as the greatest force the Western world ever felt, and had drawn man's activities to herself more strongly than any other power, natural or supernatural, had ever done; the historian's business was to follow the track of the energy; to find where it came from and where it went to; its complex source and shifting channels; its values, equivalents, conversions. It could scarcely be more complex than radium; it could hardly be deflected, diverted, polarized, absorbed more perplexingly than other radiant matter. Adams knew nothing about any of them, but as a mathematical problem of influence on human progress, though all were occult, all reacted on his mind, and he rather inclined to think the Virgin easiest to handle.

The pursuit turned out to be long and tortuous, leading at last into the vast forests of scholastic science. From Zeno to Descartes, hand in hand with Thomas Aquinas, Montaigne, and Pascal,[6] one stumbled as stupidly as though one were still a German student of 1860. Only with the instinct of despair could one force one's self into this old thicket of ignorance after having been repulsed at a score of entrances more promising and more popular. Thus far, no path had led anywhere, unless perhaps to an exceedingly modest living. Forty-five years of study had proved to be quite futile for the pursuit of power; one controlled no more force in 1900 than in 1850, although the amount of force controlled by society had enormously increased. The secret of education still hid itself somewhere behind ignorance, and one fumbled over it as feebly as ever. In such labyrinths, the staff is a force almost more necessary than the

---

4. Cnidos, or Cnidus, is an ancient city in Asia Minor, site of the most famous of the statues of Aphrodite by Praxiteles (c. 370–330 B.C.); only a copy survives, in the Vatican.
5. Arnold's (1822–1888) poem *Stanzas from the GrandeChartreuse* invokes the Virgin Mary in mourning the loss of faith formerly held by ascetic Carthusian monks.

6. Blaise Pascal (1623–1662), French philosopher. Probably Zeno of Citium (c. 366–264 B.C.), Greek philosopher. René Descartes (1596–1650), French philosopher. Aquinas (1225?–1274), Italian philosopher and theologian who is the subject of the last chapter of Adams's *Mont-Saint-Michel and Chartres*. Michel Eyquem de Montaigne (1533–1592), French essayist and skeptical philosopher.

legs; the pen becomes a sort of blind-man's dog, to keep him from falling into the gutters. The pen works for itself, and acts like a hand, modelling the plastic material over and over again to the form that suits it best. The form is never arbitrary, but is a sort of growth like crystallization, as any artist knows too well; for often the pencil or pen runs into side-paths and shapelessness, loses its relations, stops or is bogged. Then it has to return on its trail, and recover, if it can, its line of force. The result of a year's work depends more on what is struck out than on what is left in; on the sequence of the main lines of thought, than on their play or variety. Compelled once more to lean heavily on this support, Adams covered more thousands of pages with figures as formal as though they were algebra, laboriously striking out, altering, burning, experimenting, until the year had expired, the Exposition had long been closed, and winter drawing to its end, before he sailed from Cherbourg, on January 19, 1901, for home.

1907, 1918

# American Literature
# between the Wars
# 1914–1945

Although World War I began in 1914, the United States did not enter that war until 1917. Both the long delay and eventual entry expressed sides of a continuing debate over the desirability of American involvement in European affairs. For some Americans, the nation had its own special mission to pursue and could only be contaminated by engagement with the Old World. For others, America was so inextricably tied to Europe that a major European war was inevitably an American war too. The participation of the United States in World War I did not end this debate, which was complicated by the success of the Russian revolution in 1918 and the related formation of international Communist and labor movements dedicated to the demise of capitalism worldwide. In response to these developments, the so-called red scare in America immediately after the war (red was the color of the Soviet flag) led to the deportation of many American radical agitators of foreign birth. Some native-born Americans resented immigrants who criticized American policies, and there were profound antagonisms between white-collar, management-class Americans and people of the working classes. This turbulence produced a highly restrictive immigration act in 1924 and underlay the continual labor violence that marked the period right up to the outbreak of World War II. There were bloody strikes in Colorado, Massachusetts, North Carolina, and elsewhere. Simultaneously, as German armies invaded one European country after another in the late 1930s, Americans remained divided about whether to fight against Hitler or turn their backs on the plight of Europe. Not until the Japanese bombed the American fleet at Pearl Harbor, in Hawaii, on December 7, 1941, did the United States enter this war, and even then it entered the European theater only because Germany and Japan were allies.

Nevertheless, U.S. participation in World War I marked a crucial stage in the nation's evolution to a world power. More narrowly but more immediately, it involved American artists and thinkers with the brutal actualities of large-scale modern war, so different from imaginary heroism. American losses were not great in "absolute" terms—more men had been killed in the Civil War—and there was no fighting on American ground. Ironically, more soldiers were killed by disease than in battle, and in the fall of 1918, after the war had officially ended, but before many soldiers were discharged, a worldwide flu epidemic struck army camps with particular intensity. But the senses of a great civilization being destroyed or destroying itself, of social breakdown, and of individual powerlessness became part of the American experience as a result of its participation in World War I, with resulting feelings of fear, disorientation, and, on occasion, liberation. Certainty that an old order had ended (whether one regretted or rejoiced at this fact) and uncertainty as to what might arise (whether one looked ahead with fear or anticipation) marked what more than one social critic called the "modern temper."

Other forces making for rapid social change and resulting disorientation had been at work in the country for some time. Urbanization, industrialization, and immigration had been altering the appearance and character of the United States since the end of the Civil War and they continued apace after World War I. New technology evolved as well. The telephone and electricity, both nineteenth-century inventions, now expanded into American homes at large. The phonograph record and the record player, the motion picture (which acquired sound in 1929), and the radio made possible and perhaps inevitable a new kind of connectedness and a new kind of culture, neither elite nor regional, which we call mass or popular culture. This culture—verbal, visual, musical—quickly overpowered both "high" and "folk" culture in its influences. Many writers criticized the commercialism and manipulativeness of this culture. But no artist could escape it; nobody could grow up in America between the wars without listening to the radio, hearing records, and going to the movies. Talented writers were recruited by Hollywood; the possibility of selling one's book to the movies promised new levels of wealth; and various cinematic techniques—the flashback, intercutting, and the like—gave writers new ideas about literary form.

By far the most powerful technological influence in America between the wars was the automobile. Automobiles came into existence just before the turn of the twentieth century; thanks to Henry Ford's development of the assembly-line technique for producing them, after 1920 they became cheap enough for most Americans to buy. They drastically reshaped the American occupational structure; literally millions of jobs—in automobile plants, steel mills, highway construction, gas stations, roadside restaurants, and motels—became dependent, in one way or another, on the automobile. The appearance of the countryside and the shape of American cities changed as highways were constructed, as rings of development around urban cores expanded, and as the suburbs came into being. Individual Americans acquired a mobility unimaginable to previous generations. There is no detail of American life that the automobile did not affect. Yet, considered historically, it can be said merely to have intensified qualities of American life that the French social commentator Alexis de Tocqueville pointed to as early as the 1830s: continual movement, lack of tradition, and rootlessness.

To divide history into decades is to simplify; yet to those living in the era, America in the 1930s seemed very different from America in the 1920s, because of the depression brought on by the stock market crash of 1929. The 1920s saw a great struggle over such concerns as personal freedom, social permissiveness, the pursuit of pleasure, and the results of new affluence. Traditionalist Americans—believing in the work ethic, social conformity, duty, and respectability—attempted to control social and private behavior according to a model of white, Protestant, small-town virtues; arrayed against them were newly articulate groups: immigrants, minorities, youth, women, and of course, artists, arguing for a diversity of styles of life. Much energy focused on the issue of Prohibition. The Eighteenth Amendment to the U.S. Constitution, forbidding the "manufacture, sale or transportation of intoxicating liquors" was ratified in January 1919. It was widely and openly ignored. Some historians believe that Prohibition opened the door to organized crime, and certainly the phenomenon of the "gangster" arose in the 1920s in connection with bootleg liquor, which organized crime was ready to transport and supply to otherwise law-abiding citizens. The amendment was finally perceived to be unenforceable and was repealed in 1933. The gangster, however, persisted in American life and became a central figure, sometimes a hero, sometimes a villain, in the movies and in the hard-boiled fiction of the 1930s.

The 1920s also saw a significant relaxation of sexual mores. Because the double standard had always granted sexual freedom to men, the sexual revolution of the

1920s consisted chiefly in increased freedom for women and increased openness of sexual behavior. The wide-awake yet innocent American girl whose fresh femininity had been celebrated by such writers as Henry James (for example, in *Daisy Miller*) gave way to the wise-cracking, free-wheeling, independent "flapper" of the Jazz Age, as the 1920s were widely called.

The condition of women improved in other areas of life as well. The Nineteenth Amendment to the Constitution, giving women the right to vote, was ratified in August 1920 after more than seventy years of activity on behalf of female suffrage. During the 1920s women began to enter the workforce in much larger numbers than before and in a wider range of occupations than the domestic service and factory work that had previously been their chief options outside of marriage. Primary- and secondary-school teaching and clerical and sales positions became almost exclusively female occupations, while women began to enter the higher professions as well—academia, law, medicine, and journalism—although in very small numbers. The numbers of women attending college increased, as did the numbers living alone, traveling on their own, and generally forging independent lives for themselves—notwithstanding that the great majority still looked to marriage and family as their chief goals. Ironically, many of the American male writers who spoke up for self-expression and individualism did not extend their ideas of freedom to women; indeed, Ezra Pound, F. Scott Fitzgerald, Ernest Hemingway, William Carlos Williams, and T. S. Eliot all interpreted the "New Woman" as an ominous sign of social breakdown.

Although the lives of African-Americans also changed significantly, the deeply segregated structure of American society still resisted integration or respect for black culture. Beginning around 1915, the growth of urban and industrial centers in the North brought millions of blacks out of the rural South and into northern cities. Although this transition turned many black Americans into urban wage earners, the available jobs were at the bottom of the occupational hierarchy. They were forced to live in segregated neighborhoods and attend segregated schools.

The most important intellectual development in the period between the wars was certainly the growth of modern science. But because scientific thought and practice remained obscure to most Americans—even American intellectuals—science entered the public domain through the metaphors it provided for organizing nonscientific realms of reality. Without understanding the precise scientific implications of Albert Einstein's special and general theories of relativity, Werner Heisenberg's uncertainty principle, and Niels Bohr's quantum mechanics theories, people could tell from their very names that scientists saw less certainty and more chance in the universe than had nineteenth-century science, whose procedures of labeling and classifying had assumed stability in nature. Distinctions between matter and energy, between observer and observed, and between time and space were blurred at the frontiers of scientific thinking.

For many literary intellectuals, especially the more conservative, the chief problem raised by the expansion of scientific authority was the corresponding loss of authority for traditional, humanistic explanations of the real world and human life. Such southern writers as John Crowe Ransom, John Peale Bishop, and Allen Tate, as well as poets Ezra Pound, T. S. Eliot, Wallace Stevens, and William Carlos Williams, reacted spiritedly to the increasingly prevalent assumption that nonscientific thinking, because it was imprecise and value-laden, could not explain anything. They belittled the capacity of science to provide accounts of the things that matter, like subjective experience and moral issues. Art, to them, became the repository of a way of experiencing the world other than that offered by science, an alternative worldview. Their approach put a heavy burden of "meaning" on art and was a sign, if not a contributing cause, of the increased specialization of intellectual activity and the division of educated people into what the British novelist and physicist C. P. Snow was later to call the "two cultures"—science versus letters.

The two thinkers whose ideas had the greatest impact on the period were the Austrian Sigmund Freud (1856–1939) and the German Karl Marx (1818–1883). Freud, who invented the practice of psychoanalysis, propounded an idea of the self as grounded in an "unconscious" that controlled a great deal of overt behavior. Hidden in this unconscious were experiences that one had repressed: traumas, forbidden desires, unacceptable emotions—most of these of a sexual nature and many deriving from earliest childhood. Freud believed that human development— at least human male development—was universally marked by what he called an "Oedipus complex," a name borrowed from the classic story of King Oedipus, who had, in a series of dreadful mistakes, killed his father and married his mother. Freud theorized that the story represented the disguised childhood wish of most boys to eliminate the father as a rival and to possess the mother. The forbidden and impossible nature of these wishes left lifelong scars on the adult personality. Freud hypothesized that the process of analysis would help patients understand these emotions and that understanding in turn would enable them to recover the ability to function as productive adults. In popularized form, these ideas were extended to support the relaxation of sexual mores as well as permissiveness in childrearing, and they underlay the larger trend toward openness and informality in American behavior.

Marx was a social thinker who believed that the root cause of all behavior was economic and that the leading feature of economic life was the division of society into antagonistic classes based on a relation to the means of production. The Industrial Revolution, according to him, depended on the accumulation of surplus capital by industrialists who paid the least possible amount to workers. The ideas and ideals of any particular society represented the interests of its dominant class; thus individualism was a middle-class or "bourgeois" value because it opposed group movements such as unions or communes. Marx provided an analysis of human behavior directly opposed to Freud's, since for Marx people were controlled by forces outside the self. Yet both seemed to espouse a kind of determinism that, although counter to long-standing American beliefs in free will and free choice, also seemed better able to explain the terrible things that were happening in the twentieth century.

Marxism can be either a theoretical way of describing society and history or a justification for radical political action. Russian Communists adapted it to their revolutionary aims in 1917. Americans who thought of themselves as Marxists in the 1920s and 1930s were interested in identifying themselves with the world's workers and with advancing the cause of a society in which the workers would control the means of production. Of course, these ideas went counter to traditional American beliefs in free enterprise and competition in the marketplace. The growth of labor movements in the 1920s, therefore, was contested by industrialists, and because Marxism was of "foreign" origin, the popularity of radical ideas in the decade was often attributed to foreign influences. In the 1920s American Marxists, Socialists, anarchists, and radicals, along with union organizers, were subject to great hostility. The most dramatic instance of this hostility was the so-called Sacco-Vanzetti case. Nicola Sacco and Bartolomeo Vanzetti were two Italian immigrants, both avowed anarchists, who were arrested near Boston after a paymaster and his guard were murdered during a robbery on April 15, 1920. They were tried for this crime and condemned to death in 1921, but it was widely felt that they had not received a fair trial, that their political beliefs had been held against them. There were a number of appeals but eventually, in 1927, they were executed, maintaining to the end that they were innocent. Many literary and public figures became involved in their defense, and several were arrested and jailed during demonstrations. It is estimated that well over a hundred poems as well as six plays and eight novels of the time treated the incident.

The Great Depression made political and economic issues even more salient in

American life. If the leading theme of the 1920s was social and personal, then that of the 1930s was economic and political. The justification of free-enterprise capitalism, that it ensured a better life for all, seemed disproved by the massive bank and business failures of the decade, along with unprecedented unemployment. In the worst years of the Depression, more than 25 percent of the labor force was unemployed; because most families had only one breadwinner and because there was no help from welfare or social security benefits, the extent of the hardship was enormous. The suicides of millionaire bankers and stockbrokers made the headlines, but more compelling was the enormous toll among ordinary people who lost homes, jobs, farms, and life savings in the crash. Conservatives advised waiting until things got better; radicals espoused immediate restructuring of the economy. In this atmosphere, the election of Franklin Delano Roosevelt to the presidency in 1932 was a victory for American pragmatism; his series of liberal reforms—social security, acts creating jobs in the public sector, welfare, and unemployment insurance—cushioned the worst effects of the Depression and avoided the revolution that many had thought inevitable. Real prosperity did not return, however, until World War II created a great expansion in industry. The Depression was a worldwide phenomenon, and social unrest led to the rise of fascist dictatorships in Europe, among which were those of Generalissimo Francisco Franco in Spain, Benito Mussolini in Italy, and Adolf Hitler in Germany. Hitler's program, which was to make Germany rich and strong by conquering the rest of Europe, led inexorably to World War II.

Given the terrible situation in the United States, the Communist party enjoyed a significant increase in membership and prestige in the 1930s. Numerous intellectuals allied themselves with its causes even if they did not become party members. An old radical journal, *The Masses*, later *The New Masses*, became the official literary voice of the party, and various other radical groups founded journals to represent their viewpoints. Visitors to the Soviet Union returned with glowing reports about a true workers' democracy and prosperity for all. The appeal of communism was significantly enhanced by its claim to be an opponent of fascism. Communists fought against Franco in the Spanish Civil War of 1936 and 1937. Hitler's nightmare policies of genocide and racial superiority and his plans for a general European war to secure more room for the superior German "folk" to live became increasingly evident as European refugees began to flee to the United States in the 1930s, and many believed that the U.S.S.R. would be the only country able to withstand the German war machine. But Soviet communism showed another side to Americans when Josef Stalin, the Soviet dictator, instituted a series of brutal purges in the Soviet Union beginning in 1936 and then in 1939 signed a pact promising not to go to war against Germany. The senses of disillusionment and betrayal felt by many radicals over these acts led, after the end of World War II, to many 1930s left-wing activists' becoming staunch anti-Communists.

### LITERATURE AND THE TIMES

Despite the dramatic social changes of the period between World War I and II, American literature was not completely separated from its roots. The influences of such great nineteenth-century figures as Ralph Waldo Emerson and Walt Whitman remained strong, while those of other, newly recognized, writers like Herman Melville and Emily Dickinson were also felt. The teaching of American literature in colleges became established in the 1920s on the premise that these earlier writers constituted a true American literary tradition worthy of study alongside the British. Many writers of the post–Civil War period were still active in the 1920s and 1930s: for example, Hamlin Garland, the spokesman for literary naturalism, wrote his four-volume autobiography between 1917 and 1930; Edith Wharton published her masterpiece, *The Age of Innocence*, in 1920; and Theodore Dreiser's best novel, *An American Tragedy*, appeared in 1925. A number of writers who achieved eminence after 1914—Gertrude Stein, Ezra Pound, Robert Frost, Sherwood Anderson, H. D., Edwin Arlington Robinson, Carl Sandburg, and Willa Cather—had begun to publish before the beginning of World War I. Finally, writers like Edmund Wilson, Richard Wright, Eudora Welty, Tennessee Williams, and others who achieved their greatest recognition after World War II began their careers before 1945.

Nevertheless, we are justified in seeing coherence in the work written between the two world wars and in relating that coherence to historical pressures. Put in the most general terms, much serious literature written between 1914 and 1945 attempted to convey a vision of social decay through appropriate techniques or offered radical critiques of American society on behalf of working people or tried to develop a conservative literature that could counter social breakdown. In contrast, literature created before World War I reflected a sense of society as something stable, whose repetitions and predictability enabled one to chronicle a universal human situation through accurate representation of particulars. And in contrast again, writers after World War II tended to lack the faith that literature could reflect *any* reality, even a disintegrating one; they also had much less confidence in literary art than did writers working in the 1920s and 1930s. To simplify: writers before World War I had faith in society and in art, writers between 1914 and 1945 had faith in art, and writers after 1945 had lost even that sustaining faith and hence the faith in themselves that had inspired and sustained writers between the wars.

*Modernism* is the name of the major artistic movement responding to the sense of social breakdown in the early twentieth century. It was an international movement shared by many art forms. The poetry of William Butler Yeats, James Joyce's *Ulysses* (1922), Marcel Proust's *Remembrance of Things Past* (1913–27), Thomas Mann's novels and short stories, including *The Magic Mountain* (1927)—these were only a few of the literary products of this movement in England and on the Continent. In painting, artists like Pablo Picasso, Juan Gris, and Georges Braque invented cubism; in the twenties the surrealistic movement known as dadaism emerged. The American public was introduced to modern art at the famous New York Armory Show of 1913, which featured cubist paintings and caused an uproar. Marcel Duchamp's *Nude Descending a Staircase*, which, to the untrained eye, looked like no more than a mass of crudely drawn rectangles, was especially provocative. Composers like Igor Stravinsky similarly produced music in a "modern" mode, featuring dissonance and discontinuity rather than neat formal structure and appealing tonal harmonies. His composition *The Rite of Spring* provoked a riot in the Paris concert hall where it was premiered.

At the heart of the modernist aesthetic lay the conviction that the previously sustaining structures of human life, whether social, political, religious, or artistic, had been either destroyed or shown up as falsehoods or fantasies. To the extent that art incorporated such a false order, it had to be renovated. Order, sequence, and unity in works of art might well be considered only expressions of a desire for coherence rather than actual reflections of reality. Generalization, abstraction, and high-flown writing might conceal rather than convey the real. The form of a story, with its beginnings, complications, and resolutions, might be mere artifice imposed on the flux and fragmentation of experience.

Thus the defining formal characteristic of the modernist work, whether a painting, a sculpture, or a musical composition, is its construction out of fragments. The long work is an assemblage of fragments, the short work a carefully realized fragment. Compared with earlier writing, modernist literature is notable for what it omits—the explanations, interpretations, connections, summaries, and distancing that provide continuity, perspective, and security in traditional literature. A typical modernist work will seem to begin arbitrarily, to advance without explanation, and to end without resolution, consisting of vivid segments juxtaposed without cushioning or integrating transitions. There will be shifts in perspective, voice, and tone. Its rhetoric will be understated, ironic. It will suggest rather than assert, making use of symbols and images instead of statements. Fragments will be drawn from diverse areas of experience. The effect will be surprising, shocking, and unsettling; the experience of reading will be challenging and difficult.

In practice, as opposed to theory, most modernist literature retains a degree of coherence, but its dynamic pattern is beneath the surface. The reader has to dig the structure out. This is why the reader of a modernist work is often said to participate in the actual work of making the poem or story. Often, the modernist work is structured as a quest for the very coherence that, on its surface, it seems to lack. Because patterns of searching appear in most of the world's mythologies, many modernist works are unified by reference to myth. Christianity appears among world myths as the basis of Western civilization, and the modern world for some comes into being when circumstances seem to show Christianity to be only a myth, a merely human construction for creating order out of, and finding purpose in, meaningless flux.

The search for meaning, even if it does not succeed, becomes meaningful in itself. Literature, especially poetry, becomes the place where the one meaningful activity, the search for meaning, is carried out, and therefore literature is, or should be, vitally important to society. The subject matter of modernist writing often became, by extension, the poem or literary work itself. Ironically—because this subject matter was motivated by deep concern about the interrelation of literature and life—this subject often had the effect of limiting the audience for a modernist work. The difficulty of this new type of writing also limited the appeal of modernism: clearly, difficult works about poetry are not candidates for best-sellers. Nevertheless, over time, the principles of modernism became increasingly influential.

The content of the modernist work may be as varied as the interests and observations of the writer; indeed, with a stable external world in question, subjectivity was ever more valued and accepted in literature. Modernists in general, however, emphasized the concrete sensory image or detail as the direct conveyer of experience. They also relied on the reference (allusion) to literary, historical, philosophical, or religious details of the past as a way of reminding readers of the old, lost coherence. Vignettes of contemporary life, chunks of popular culture, dream imagery, and symbolism drawn from the author's private repertory of life experiences are also important. A work built from these various levels and kinds of material may move across time and space, shift from the public to the personal, and open literature as a field for every sort of concern. The inclusion of all sorts of material previously deemed "unliterary" in works of high seriousness involved the use of language that would also previously have been thought improper, including representations of the speech of the uneducated and the inarticulate, the colloquial, slangy, and the popular. The traditional educated literary voice, conveying truth and culture, lost its authority; this is what Ernest Hemingway had in mind when he asserted that the American literary tradition began with *Huckleberry Finn*.

Though modernist techniques and manifestos were initiated by poets, they entered and transformed fiction in this period as well. Prose writers strove for directness, compression, and vividness. They were sparing of words. The average novel became quite a bit shorter than it had been in the nineteenth century, when a novel was expected to fill two or even three volumes. The modernist aesthetic gave new significance to the short story, which had previously been thought of as a relatively slight artistic form. (Poems, too, became shorter; modernist poets struggled to write long poems but the principles of unity or organization that had enabled long poems to be written in previous eras were not available to them.) Victorian or realistic fiction achieved its effects by accumulation and saturation; modern fiction preferred suggestion. Victorian fiction featured an authoritative narrator; modern fiction tended to be written in the first person or to limit the reader to one character's point of view on the action. This limitation accorded with the modernist sense that "truth" does not exist objectively but is the product of a personal interaction with reality. The selected point of view was often that of a naive or marginal person—a child or an outsider—so as to convey better the reality of confusion rather than the myth of certainty.

"Serious" literature between the two world wars found itself in a curious relationship with the culture at large. For if it was attacking the old-style idea of traditional literature, it felt itself attacked in turn by the ever-growing industry of popular literature. The reading audience in America was vast, but it preferred a kind of book quite different from that turned out by literary modernists: tales of romance or adventure, historical novels, crime fiction, and westerns became popular modes that enjoyed a success the serious writer could only dream of. The problem was that often he or she *did* dream of it; unrealistically, perhaps, the Ezra Pounds of the era imagined themselves with an audience of millions. When, on occasion, this dream came true—as it did for F. Scott Fitzgerald and Ernest Hemingway—writers often accused themselves of having sold out.

Nevertheless, serious writers in these years were, in fact, being published and read as writers had not been in earlier times. The number of so-called little magazines—that is, magazines of very small circulations devoted to the publication of works for a small audience (sometimes the works of a specific group of authors)— was in the hundreds. *Poetry: A Magazine of Verse* began in 1912. The *Little Review* followed in 1914. Then came the *Seven Arts* in 1916, the *Dial* in 1917, the *Frontier* in 1920, *Reviewer* and *Broom* in 1921, *Fugitive* in 1922, *This Quarter* in 1925, *Transition* and *Hound and Horn* in 1927, and many more. The culture that did not listen to serious writers or make them rich still gave them plenty of opportunity to be read and allowed them (in such neighborhoods as Greenwich Village in New York City) a freedom in style of life that was quite new in American history. In addition, such major publishers as New Directions, Random House, Scribner, and Harper were actively looking for serious fiction and poetry to feature along with best-sellers like *Gone with the Wind* and *Anthony Adverse*.

### TRADITIONALISM

The profession of authorship in the United States has always defined itself in part as a patriotic enterprise, whose aims were to help develop a cultural life for the nation and embody national values. From these aims, a powerful tradition of regionally based literature emerged after the Civil War. Because modernism was an international movement, it seemed to some to conflict with the American tradition in literature and hence was by no means automatically accepted by American writers. To some, the frequent pessimism, nostalgia, and conservatism of the movement made it essentially unsuited to the progressive, dynamic culture that they believed to be distinctive of this nation. To many others, modernist techniques were exciting and indispensable but required adaptation to specifically American topics and to the goal of contributing to a uniquely American literature. Thus artists who may be thought of as modernists in one context—Hart Crane or William Carlos Williams, for example—must be thought of as traditional American writers in another, since they wanted to write "American" works as such. And a profoundly modern writer like William Faulkner cannot be extricated from his commitment to writing about his native South.

The leading American exponents of a "pure" modernism tended to be permanent expatriates like Gertrude Stein, Ezra Pound, H. D., and T. S. Eliot. (But two important exceptions to this generalization are Marianne Moore and Wallace Stevens.) These writers left the United States because they found the country singularly lacking in a tradition of high culture and indifferent, if not downright hostile, to artistic achievement. They also believed that a national culture could never be more than parochial. In London in the first two decades of the twentieth century, and in Paris during the 1920s, they found a vibrant community of dedicated artists and a society that respected them and allowed them a great deal of personal freedom. Yet they seldom thought of themselves as deserting their nation and none of them gave up American citizenship. They thought of themselves as bringing the United States into the larger context of European culture. The ranks of these permanent expatriates were swelled by American writers who lived abroad for some part of the period: Ernest Hemingway, Sherwood Anderson, F. Scott Fitzgerald, Katherine Anne Porter, Robert Frost, Eugene O'Neill, and Dorothy Parker all did so, as did many others including Sinclair Lewis and Djuna Barnes.

Those writers who came back, however, and those who never left took very seriously the task of integrating modernist ideas and methods with American subject matter. Many writers chose to identity themselves with the American scene and to root their work in a specific region. The treatment of the regions in such works was sometimes celebratory and sometimes critical. Carl Sandburg, Edgar Lee Masters, Sherwood Anderson, and Willa Cather worked with the Midwest; Cather grounded her later work in the Southwest; Robinson Jeffers and John Steinbeck wrote about California; and Edwin Arlington Robinson and Robert Frost identified their work with New England.

An especially strong center of regional literary activity emerged in the South, which had a weak literary tradition up to the Civil War. Critics and poets centered at Vanderbilt University in Nashville, Tennessee, produced a group manifesto in 1929 called *I'll Take My Stand*, a collection of essays that advocated some traditional southern values—the gracious, stable, leisurely, ritualized, hierarchical plantation civilization—as a cultural alternative to the social fragmentation they perceived in the urban North. Among these "Southern Agrarians" were John Crowe Ransom, Allen Tate, and Robert Penn Warren, all writing an elegant, learned verse in which they tried to revivify what they took as the ideals of an earlier time. The influence of these writers, especially in academia, sometimes tended to conceal the fact that the South spoke with many voices during this period. Ellen Glasgow wrote about a South made up of cities and small farmers; Thomas Wolfe's was an Appalachian South of hardy mountain people; Katherine Anne Porter wrote about her native Texas as a heterogeneous combination of frontier, plantation, and Latin cultures. Above all, William Faulkner depicted a decaying Deep South anguished by racial and historical conflict.

Some writers—as the title of John Dos Passos's *U.S.A.* clearly shows—attempted to speak for the nation as a whole. Hart Crane's long poem *The Bridge* and William Carlos Williams's *Paterson* both take an American place as symbol and expand it to a vision for all America, following the model established by Walt Whitman. F. Scott Fitzgerald's *The Great Gatsby* is similarly ambitious, and many writers addressed the whole nation in individual works—for example, E. E. Cummings's *next to of course god america i* and Robinson Jeffers's *Shine, Perishing Republic*.

Something akin to regionalism can be seen in the new literary articulateness of black Americans. In the 1920s the area of New York City called Harlem, whose population had been swelled both by black New Yorkers moving "uptown" and by southern newcomers, became a center for black cultural activities. The so-called Harlem Renaissance involved the attempt of African-American artists in many media to develop a strong cultural presence in America, both to demonstrate that black artists could equal white artists in their achievements and to articulate their own cultural traditions and values. Writers like Countee Cullen, Langston Hughes, and Zora Neale Hurston attained prominence. The Harlem Renaissance, though it expressed protest and anger, was deliberately upbeat, avoiding the rage and despair characteristic of African-American writing after World War II. The note of pure anger was not expressed until Richard Wright, who had come to literary maturity in Chicago, not Harlem, published *Native Son* in 1940. A more pervasive black influence on American culture came through music, which was also concentrated in the Harlem setting, although it had its origins in the South: jazz and blues, both originally black forms, are felt by many to be the most authentically American art forms the nation has ever produced. African-American singers and musicians in this period achieved worldwide reputations and were often much more highly regarded abroad than in the United States.

Many American writers of the period between the wars were women, both white and black. Women were associated with all the important literary trends of the era: H. D. and Amy Lowell with imagism, Marianne Moore with high modernism, Willa Cather with regionalism, Zora Neale Hurston and Angelina Grimké with the Harlem Renaissance, Katherine Anne Porter with psychological fiction; Edna St. Vincent Millay and Dorothy Parker with social and sexual liberation, Genevieve Taggard and Muriel Rukeyser with proletarian and radical literature. Although many of these women concentrated on depictions of women characters or women's thoughts and experiences, including their own, few labeled themselves feminists. The passage of the suffrage amendment in 1920 had taken some of the energy out of feminism that would not return until the 1960s. Some women writers perceived feminism as a constraint on individual artistic expression, whereas others found social causes like labor and racism more important than women's rights. Nevertheless, these literary women were clearly pushing back the boundaries of the permissible, demanding new cultural freedom for women. Equally important, they were operating as public figures and taking positions on public causes.

### PROSE, POETRY, AND POLITICS

Many of the modernists met the social challenges of the postwar era by producing severely pessimistic cultural criticism or by loftily rejecting social issues altogether. Imaginative vision was thought by many to give access to an ideal world, apart from and above reality, or to contain alternative, higher values than those reigning in the statehouse and the marketplace, which could enrich life. Others maintained that literature was an independent domain, with its own subjects and rewards, whose independence would be undermined by nonliterary goals. And still others maintained that literature had to be a sanctuary of free artistic expression, so that its ultimate meaning was precisely the value of the individual, a meaning that would be compromised by social platforms and party politics. Because poetry had always been thought of as the purest and highest form of literature, arguments of this nature tended to center on poetry not prose.

Many poets rejected these arguments, and the idea of literature itself was hotly contested during this period. Writers following the Communist party line insisted that art should celebrate the working classes, attack capitalism, and forward the revolutionary goals articulated in Moscow. Less doctrinaire social-minded writers argued that poetry, with its historical origins in public ritual, could continue to play a role in the public domain without sacrificing artistic quality. Moreover, they held that defenses of artistic freedom should extend to artists who chose to write for political or social ends. Some maintained that unlike prose, which could at best only reflect and analyze social conditions, poetry could change the world. Thus along with the social realist and proletarian prose of the 1920s and 1930s came a significant outpouring of political and protest poetry. Few poets did this kind of work exclusively, but almost every writer of the period produced some of it, with politics ranging from the libertarian conservatism of Robinson Jeffers and the fascism of Ezra Pound through the liberalism of Edna St. Vincent Millay to the radicalism of Langston Hughes and Genevieve Taggard. With the coming of World War II, many poets who had previously held themselves aloof from social activism—like Marianne Moore—felt the need to put their writing to public service. For several reasons, however, the political poetry of many modernist writers slipped out of view in the 1950s and early 1960s. College literature classes, dominated by a view of good literature as necessarily disengaged from specific social issues, ignored this engaged, partisan work entirely. Moreover, in the atmosphere of the McCarthy era, many writers suppressed or revised their earlier radical poetry. Finally, recognition of the repressive and brutal aspects of Soviet communism was deeply disillusioning to many writers; the more idealistic they had been to start, the greater their later cynicism.

### AMERICAN DRAMA IN THE TWENTIETH CENTURY

Drama in America was slow to develop as a self-conscious literary form. It was not until 1920—the year of Eugene O'Neill's *Beyond the Horizon*—that America produced a playwright. This is not to say that *theater*—productions and performances—was new to American life. After the American Revolution theaters—at first with itinerant English actors and companies, then with American—opened throughout the East; among early centers were Boston and Philadelphia as well as New York City. As the country expanded westward, so did its theater, together with other kinds of performance: burlesques, showboats on the Mississippi, minstrel shows, pantomimes. As the nineteenth century went on, the activity became centered more and more in New York—indeed, within a few blocks, known as "Broadway." Managers originated plays there, and then sent them out to tour through the rest of the country, as Eugene O'Neill's father did with his *Count of Monte Cristo*.

Healthy changes in American theater are often in reaction against Broadway, a pattern observable as early as 1915 with the formation of the Washington Square Players and the Provincetown Players, both located in New York's Greenwich Village and both dedicated to the production of plays that more conservative managers refused. The Provincetown Players would shortly be producing the first works of Eugene O'Neill. These fledgling companies, and others like them, knew better what they opposed than what they wanted. European influence was strong. By 1915, Henrik Ibsen in Europe and George Bernard Shaw in England had shown that the theater could be an arena for serious ideas, while the psychological dramas of August Strindberg, the symbolic work of Maurice Maeterlinck, and the sophisticated cynicism of Arthur Schnitzler provided other models. The American tours of European companies, in particular the Moscow Art Theatre in 1923, further exposed Americans to the theatrical avant-garde. American playwrights in the 1920s and 1930s were united not so much by a common cause of ideas, European or American, as by the new assumption that drama could be a branch of contemporary literature.

The era's leading playwright, if not the most successful in all his experiments, was Eugene O'Neill. Just as his contemporaries in poetry and fiction were changing and questioning their forms, so O'Neill—although not under their influence—sought to redefine his. He experimented less in language than in dramatic structure and in new production methods available through technology (e.g., lighting) or borrowed from the stylized realism of German expressionism. Almost as famous at the time was Maxwell Anderson, whose best plays—the tragic *Winterset* (1935) and the romantic comedy *High Tor* (1937)—embody a stylized blank verse, a language attempted by few modern dramatists. Playwrights such as Sidney Howard, Lillian Hellman, and Robert Sherwood explored problems of the modern character in serious realistic plays. George Kaufman and his many collaborators, especially Moss Hart, invented a distinctively American form, the wisecracking domestic and social comedy, while S. N. Behrman and Philip Barry wrote higher comedies of ideas. The musical comedy was another distinctively American invention: beginning as an amalgam of jokes, songs, and dances, it progressed steadily toward an integration of its various elements.

Social commentary and satire had been a thread in the bright weave of American drama since the early twenties, beginning, perhaps, with Elmer Rice's fiercely expressionistic play about a rebellious nonentity, *The Adding Machine* (1923). After the Depression social criticism became a much more important dramatic theme. Propaganda plays were performed by many radical groups. Perhaps the most significant was Clifford Odets's *Waiting for Lefty* (1935), which dramatized a taxidrivers' strike meeting and turned the stage into a platform for argument.

The year 1945 saw the first successful production of a play by Tennessee Williams, *The Glass Menagerie*, while Arthur Miller's *All My Sons* was produced in 1947. Each play introduced its audience to themes and emphases that its author would pursue in future works—for Williams a heightened "poetic realism" in the study of troubled characters of a "fugitive kind," and for Miller more intellectualized examinations of ordinary people under social pressure. In the 1940s and 1950s, as in the 1910s, experimental productions that could not exist in the conservative and expensive atmosphere of Broadway were done "off-Broadway," usually in Greenwich Village. Off-Broadway became the alternative center for both new and established playwrights. The Circle in the Square, for example, had a remarkable success with its premiere of O'Neill's *The Iceman Cometh* (1956), a production that did much to revive flagging interest in the playwright. The Circle also hosted the first public production of Adrienne Kennedy's *Funnyhouse of a Negro* (1964).

The same experimental impulse surfaced again in the 1960s, this time as "off-off-Broadway." The movement was in part a reaction to the rising costs of off-Broadway, but was also part of the American counterculture. "The plays of Off Off," wrote the theater historians Albert Poland and Bruce Mailman, "have a common language that is built on a new set of symbols. The new symbols are a function of the new audience, for Off Off is an audience-oriented theatre." The venues were often not conventional theaters, but "performance spaces," such as those at the Caffe Cino and the La Mama Experimental Theater. Sam Shepard was among the playwrights who served an apprenticeship in this heady atmosphere.

Moreover, theatrical activity outside New York has strongly increased: a number of cities support regional theaters, as do universities. What is noteworthy about these theaters is their support of new work. David Mamet, for example, for years had his plays produced in Chicago theaters; some of Shepard's plays were written for San Francisco's Magic Theater; and August Wilson, the most powerful African-American playwright in recent years, has his plays mounted at the Yale Repertory Theatre. Indeed, the plays of the Broadway year 1987–88 almost all originated elsewhere, for, as the critic Gerald Weales has remarked, "Broadway . . . is now a merchandiser of pretested goods."

The Asian-American playwright David Henry Hwang, winner of a Tony award in 1988 for *M. Butterfly*, has noted that "American theater is beginning to discover Americans. Black theater, women's theater, gay theater, Asian-American theater, Hispanic theater." Thus although Lorraine Hansberry's early death prevented her from fulfilling the strong promise of *A Raisin in the Sun* (1959), she has been followed by such tough-minded but lyrical writers as LeRoi Jones (later Imamu Amiri Baraka), Ed Bullins, Ntozake Shange, and Wilson. A generation of younger women have written warmly and incisively—and not only on women's themes— among them Tina Howe and Beth Henley; Marsha Norman's *'Night, Mother* (1982) won the Pulitzer Prize.

Many of the poets and fictionists of this century have written plays—among them Saul Bellow, E. E. Cummings, William Carlos Williams, William Faulkner, Frank O'Hara, Edna St. Vincent Millay, Angelina Grimké, T. S. Eliot, John Steinbeck, and Robert Lowell. Such work indicates that drama has moved decisively into the American literary mainstream.

# BLACK ELK

1863–1950

# JOHN G. NEIHARDT

1881–1973

"The land was ours before we were the land's," Robert Frost intoned at the inauguration of President John F. Kennedy in 1961, conveniently forgetting (like most of his compatriots) that the first European settlers of North America had arrived on a soil already supporting more than eighteen million occupants. Dispersed across the continent, representing at least three hundred different cultural groups, speaking over two hundred languages and many more dialects, these diverse peoples were dubbed "Indians" by the newcomers who, more or less systematically over the next two and a half centuries, displaced and decimated them. These peoples, in the European imagination confronting them, were merely noble or barbaric "savages" whose destiny it was to give way before the march of civilization.

Within the first century of European settlement, northeastern Native American populations were drastically reduced, more by such imported diseases as smallpox and tuberculosis than by warfare. During the 1830s, under the administration of Andrew Jackson—the president celebrated as democratic champion of "the common man"—the U.S. government instituted an "Indian removal" policy that forced southeastern tribes to relocate on the plains west of the Mississippi. Those who survived the marches had to live on unfamiliar terrain and mingle uncomfortably with resentful Plains tribes. As the pressures of immigration and land hunger increased, all the tribes were pushed farther and farther west and required to live under the eye of U.S. government officials. When the arid lands to which they had been driven were found to contain precious metals and minerals, Native Americans were subjected to yet more pressure. Beginning around 1860, desperate for land and freedom, they intensified their ongoing struggle against the encroaching whites. They were victorious over General Custer in 1876 at the battle of the Little Bighorn, but in 1890 the massacre at Wounded Knee brought American Indian resistance to an end.

Black Elk, an Oglala Lakota (one of the many branches of the Sioux), was born in 1863, on tribal lands that are now probably within the borders of Wyoming. A year later, the cutting of the Bozeman trail opened this region to white passage and settlement. Thus Black Elk never knew a time when his tribe's traditional ways of life were not threatened. When he was nine years old, he had a vision—an event not uncommon to Lakota boys, part of whose rites of passage to manhood involved a formal quest for visions that would show them the future and their place in it. Black Elk's childhood vision showed that he was to be a holy man, his social role to heal and conduct religious ceremonies. Black Elk did not reveal his vision to tribal elders and practice his calling until he was almost seventeen years old. By this time his people had returned from Canada, where they had fled following the defeat of Custer, and were living on the Sioux reservation in what has since become South Dakota.

In 1886 Black Elk joined Buffalo Bill's Wild West Show, traveling in the eastern United States and Europe for the next three years. His motive was to find out the nature of the white's power so that he could appropriate it in ways that would regenerate the Lakota. Returning to the Sioux reservation, he witnessed the massacre at Wounded Knee, an event that he interpreted as a call to responsibility to contribute to the health and renewal of the tribe. He married in 1892, took the name "Nicholas Black Elk," and settled down on the reservation to raise a family, to ranch, and to farm. In 1904 he became a Catholic and in 1907, a catechist, authorized to travel around the reservation and give instruction in Catholic rites and doctrine.

By the time the poet John Neihardt met him, in the spring of 1931, Black Elk seemed adjusted to the new ways, his days as a holy man long forgotten. But Neihardt's questions, in connection with research for the final volume of his epic poem, Cycle of the West, touched a chord. In May of 1931, over a period of weeks, Black Elk, along with several elders of the tribe, formally described their memories of early days. Some of these older men—Standing Bear, Holy Black Tail Deer, Chase in the Morning, and Iron Hawk—could remember events like the Battle of the Little Bighorn better than could Black Elk himself, and their reports went into the making of Black Elk Speaks. But only Black Elk could describe his vision and his conduct of ritual ceremonies.

The procedures followed in these interviews were laborious; Black Elk spoke almost no English and could not read or write it at all, while Neihardt could not speak the Lakota language. The two therefore used an interpreter, Black Elk's son Ben, who translated Neihardt's questions into Lakota and Black Elk's answers into English. Since Ben spoke a nonstandard "Reservation" English, Neihardt rephrased it aloud until Ben felt that the sense of his father's words had been captured. Sometimes Neihardt asked additional questions of Black Elk. Finally, a sentence was agreed on, which Neihardt then dictated to his daughter, Enid, who took it down in shorthand. Later, she made a typescript of her shorthand and from this typescript—relying also on his memory of their conversations—Neihardt built the book Black Elk Speaks.

Black Elk lived until 1950. After Black Elk Speaks was published, he became a central actor in an Indian tourist pageant performed during the summers near Mount Rushmore. His purpose here was not commercial; he saw these spectacles as opportunities to preserve and publicize his people's heritage. He gave a second set of interviews to Neihardt in 1944, which were incorporated into Neihardt's novel When the Tree Flowered (1951); he was also interviewed in 1947, 1948, and 1949 by Joseph Epes Brown, whose book partly based on this material, The Sacred Pipe, appeared in 1953.

Bicultural collaboration in the telling of Native American stories had been standard practice since the eighteenth century. Understandably, questions are raised about how authentic these stories can be. According to anthropologist Raymond DeMallie, "In most respects, Black Elk's religious experiences were entirely representative of late nineteenth-century Lakota culture." At the same time, however, one must remember that neither Neihardt nor Black Elk was aiming for an accurate life story or an anthropological study. They wanted to convey Black Elk's religious worldview with convincing dignity to an English-speaking and -reading public. Neihardt devised a chronological narrative of Black Elk's years up to Wounded Knee. As much as possible, he removed the traces of Black Elk's later life from the account, thereby giving readers the full impact of the horror of Wounded Knee, rather than the long story of Black Elk's survival after it. He also cut out some of the militarism of Black Elk's rhetoric, in line, perhaps, with a desire to stress Sioux peacefulness.

When published in 1932, the book was very favorably reviewed but attracted little public attention. When reissued in 1961, Black Elk Speaks not only attracted the wide "white" reading audience it had originally aimed for but also became a focal point, a basic text, for the generation of young American Indians who were then beginning to write prose and poetry in remarkable quantity and quality. For these writers, it is both Black Elk's vision and his history that authorize them to claim a specifically Native American identity that transcends tribal diversity.

# From Black Elk Speaks

## XVI. Heyoka[1] Ceremony

Twenty days passed, and it was time to perform the dog vision with heyokas. But before I tell you how we did it, I will say something about heyokas and the heyoka ceremony, which seems to be very foolish, but is not so.

Only those who have had visions of the thunder beings of the west can act as heyokas. They have sacred power and they share some of this with all the people, but they do it through funny actions. When a vision comes from the thunder beings of the west, it comes with terror like a thunder storm; but when the storm of vision has passed, the world is greener and happier; for wherever the truth of vision comes upon the world, it is like a rain. The world, you see, is happier after the terror of the storm.

But in the heyoka ceremony, everything is backwards, and it is planned that the people shall be made to feel jolly and happy first, so that it may be easier for the power to come to them. You have noticed that the truth comes into this world with two faces. One is sad with suffering, and the other laughs; but it is the same face, laughing or weeping. When people are already in despair, maybe the laughing face is better for them; and when they feel too good and are too sure of being safe, maybe the weeping face is better for them to see. And so I think that is what the heyoka ceremony is for.

There was a man by the name of Wachpanne (Poor) who took charge of this ceremony for me, because he had acted as a heyoka many times and knew all about it. First he told all the people to gather in a circle on the flat near Pine Ridge, and in the center, near a sacred tepee that was set there, he placed a pot of water which was made to boil by dropping hot stones from a fire into it. First, he had to make an offering of sweet grass to the west. He sat beside the fire with some sweet grass in his hand, and said: "To the Great Spirit's day, to that day grown old and wise, I will make an offering." Then, as he sprinkled the grass upon the fire and the sweet smoke arose, he sang:

> "This I burn as an offering.
> Behold it!
> A sacred praise I am making.
> A sacred praise I am making.
> My nation, behold it in kindness!
> The day of the sun has been my strength.
> The path of the moon shall be my robe.
> A sacred praise I am making.
> A sacred praise I am making."

Then the dog had to be killed quickly and without making any scar, as lightning kills, for it is the power of the lightning that heyokas have.

Over the smoke of the sweet grass a rawhide rope was held to make it sacred. Then two heyokas tied a slip noose in the rope and put this over the neck of the dog. Three times they pulled the rope gently, one at each end of the rope, and the fourth time they jerked it hard, breaking the neck. Then Wachpanne singed the dog and washed it well, and after that he cut away everything but

---

1. Lakota word for clown, but also a contrary—that is, in this ceremony the clowning is a ritual reversal of expectations. Black Elk is trying to explain how a serious religious ceremony can be presided over by comic figures.

the head, the spine and the tail. Now walking six steps away from the pot, one for each of the Powers,[2] he turned to the west, offering the head and spine to the thunder beings, then to the north, the east and the south, then to the Spirit above and to Mother Earth.

After this, standing where he was, six steps away, he faced the pot and said: "In a sacred manner I thus boil this dog." Three times he swung it, and the fourth time he threw it so that it fell head first into the boiling water. Then he took the heart of the dog and did with it just what he had done with the head and spine.

During all this time, thirty heyokas, one for each day of a moon,[3] were doing foolish tricks among the people to make them feel jolly. They were all dressed and painted in such funny ways that everybody who saw them had to laugh. One Side and I were fellow clowns. We had our bodies painted red all over and streaked with black lightning. The right sides of our heads were shaved, and the hair on the left side was left hanging long. This looked very funny, but it had a meaning; for when we looked toward where you are always facing (the south) the bare sides of our heads were toward the west, which showed that we were humble before the thunder beings who had given us power. Each of us carried a very long bow, so long that nobody could use it, and it was very crooked too. The arrows that we carried were very long and very crooked, so that it looked crazy to have them. We were riding sorrels[4] with streaks of black lightning all over them, for we were to represent the two men of my dog vision.

Wachpanne now went into the sacred tepee, where he sang about the heyokas:

> "These are sacred,
> These are sacred,
> They have said,
> They have said.
> These are sacred,
> They have said."

Twelve times he sang this, once for each of the moons.

Afterwards, while the pot was boiling, One Side and I, sitting on our painted sorrels, faced the west and sang:

> "In a sacred manner they have sent voices.
> Half the universe has sent voices.
> In a sacred manner they have sent voices to you."

Even while we were singing thus, the heyokas were doing foolish things and making laughter. For instance, two heyokas with long crooked bows and arrows painted in a funny way would come to a little shallow puddle of water. They would act as though they thought it was a wide, deep river that they had to cross; so, making motions, but saying nothing, they would decide to see how deep the river was. Taking their long crooked arrows, they would thrust these into the water, not downwards, but flat-wise just under the surface. This

---

2. There are six Powers (also called Grandfathers), one for each direction: North, South, East, West, Above, and Below (earth direction). Black Elk's vision identified him with the sixth Grandfather, the earth, and

hence with humankind.
3. Month.
4. Chestnut-colored horses. The ceremony combines traditional ritual with Black Elk's particular vision.

would make the whole arrow wet. Standing the arrows up beside them, they would show that the water was far over their heads in depth, so they would get ready to swim. One would then plunge into the shallow puddle head first, getting his face in the mud and fighting the water wildly as though he were drowning. Then the other one would plunge in to save his comrade, and there would be more funny antics in the water to make the people laugh.

After One Side and I had sung to the west, we faced the pot, where the heart and the head of the dog had been boiling. With sharp pointed arrows, we charged on horseback upon the pot and past it. I had to catch the head upon my arrow and One Side had to catch the heart, for we were representing the two men I had seen in the vision. After we had done this, the heyokas all chased us, trying to get a piece of the meat, and the people rushed to the pot, trying to get a piece of the sacred flesh. Ever so little of it would be good for them, for the power of the west was in it now. It was like giving them medicine to make them happier and stronger.

When the ceremony was over, everybody felt a great deal better, for it had been a day of fun. They were better able now to see the greenness of the world, the wideness of the sacred day, the colors of the earth, and to set these in their minds.

The Six Grandfathers have placed in this world many things, all of which should be happy. Every little thing is sent for something, and in that thing there should be happiness and the power to make happy. Like the grasses showing tender faces to each other, thus we should do, for this was the wish of the Grandfathers of the World.

## XXIV. *The Butchering at Wounded Knee*

That evening before it happened, I went in to Pine Ridge and heard these things, and while I was there, soldiers started for where the Big Foots[5] were. These made about five hundred soldiers that were there next morning. When I saw them starting I felt that something terrible was going to happen. That night I could hardly sleep at all. I walked around most of the night.

In the morning I went out after my horses, and while I was out I heard shooting off toward the east, and I knew from the sound that it must be wagon-guns (cannon) going off. The sounds went right through my body, and I felt that something terrible would happen.

When I reached camp with the horses, a man rode up to me and said: "Hey-hey-hey! The people that are coming are fired on! I know it!"

I saddled up my buckskin and put on my sacred shirt. It was one I had made to be worn by no one but myself. It had a spotted eagle outstretched on the back of it, and the daybreak star was on the left shoulder, because when facing south that shoulder is toward the east. Across the breast, from the left shoulder to the right hip, was the flaming rainbow, and there was another rainbow around the neck, like a necklace, with a star at the bottom. At each shoulder, elbow, and wrist was an eagle feather; and over the whole shirt were red streaks of lightning. You will see that this was from my great vision, and you will know how it protected me that day.

5. Band of Minneconjou Sioux under the leadership of Big Foot.

I painted my face all red, and in my hair I put one eagle feather for the One Above.

It did not take me long to get ready, for I could still hear the shooting over there.

I started out alone on the old road that ran across the hills to Wounded Knee. I had no gun. I carried only the sacred bow of the west that I had seen in my great vision. I had gone only a little way when a band of young men came galloping after me. The first two who came up were Loves War and Iron Wasichu. I asked what they were going to do, and they said they were just going to see where the shooting was. Then others were coming up, and some older men.

We rode fast, and there were about twenty of us now. The shooting was getting louder. A horseback from over there came galloping very fast toward us, and he said: "Hey-hey-hey! They have murdered them!" Then he whipped his horse and rode away faster toward Pine Ridge.

In a little while we had come to the top of the ridge where, looking to the east, you can see for the first time the monument and the burying ground on the little hill where the church is. That is where the terrible thing started. Just south of the burying ground on the little hill a deep dry gulch runs east and west, very crooked, and it rises westward to nearly the top of the ridge where we were. It had no name, but the Wasichus sometimes call it Battle Creek now. We stopped on the ridge not far from the head of the dry gulch. Wagon guns were still going off over there on the little hill, and they were going off again where they hit along the gulch. There was much shooting down yonder, and there were many cries, and we could see cavalrymen scattered over the hills ahead of us. Cavalrymen were riding along the gulch and shooting into it, where the women and children were running away and trying to hide in the gullies and the stunted pines.

A little way ahead of us, just below the head of the dry gulch, there were some women and children who were huddled under a clay bank, and some cavalrymen were there pointing guns at them.

We stopped back behind the ridge, and I said to the others: "Take courage. These are our relatives. We will try to get them back." Then we all sang a song which went like this:

> "A thunder being nation I am, I have said.
> A thunder being nation I am, I have said.
> You shall live.
> You shall live.
> You shall live.
> You shall live."

Then I rode over the ridge and the others after me, and we were crying: "Take courage! It is time to fight!" The soldiers who were guarding our relatives shot at us and then ran away fast, and some more cavalrymen on the other side of the gulch did too. We got our relatives and sent them across the ridge to the northwest where they would be safe.

I had no gun, and when we were charging, I just held the sacred bow out in front of me with my right hand. The bullets did not hit us at all.

We found a little baby lying all alone near the head of the gulch. I could not pick her up just then, but I got her later and some of my people adopted her. I just wrapped her up tighter in a shawl that was around her and left her there. It was a safe place, and I had other work to do.

The soldiers had run eastward over the hills where there were some more soldiers, and they were off their horses and lying down. I told the others to stay back, and I charged upon them holding the sacred bow out toward them with my right hand. They all shot at me, and I could hear bullets all around me, but I ran my horse right close to them, and then swung around. Some soldiers across the gulch began shooting at me too, but I got back to the others and was not hurt at all.

By now many other Lakotas, who had heard the shooting, were coming up from Pine Ridge, and we all charged on the soldiers. They ran eastward toward where the trouble began. We followed down along the dry gulch, and what we saw was terrible. Dead and wounded women and children and little babies were scattered all along there where they had been trying to run away. The soldiers had followed along the gulch, as they ran, and murdered them in there. Sometimes they were in heaps because they had huddled together,.and some were scattered all along. Sometimes bunches of them had been killed and torn to pieces where the wagon-guns hit them. I saw a little baby trying to suck its mother, but she was bloody and dead.

There were two little boys at one place in this gulch. They had guns and they had been killing soldiers all by themselves. We could see the soldiers they had killed. The boys were all alone there, and they were not hurt. These were very brave little boys.

When we drove the soldiers back, they dug themselves in, and we were not enough people to drive them out from there. In the evening they marched off up Wounded Knee Creek, and then we saw all that they had done there.

Men and women and children were heaped and scattered all over the flat at the bottom of the little hill where the soldiers had their wagon-guns, and westward up the dry gulch all the way to the high ridge, the dead women and children and babies were scattered.

When I saw this I wished that I had died too, but I was not sorry for the women and children. It was better for them to be happy in the other world, and I wanted to be there too. But before I went there I wanted to have revenge. I thought there might be a day, and we should have revenge.

After the soldiers marched away, I heard from my friend, Dog Chief, how the trouble started, and he was right there by Yellow Bird when it happened. This is the way it was:

In the morning the soldiers began to take all the guns away from the Big Foots, who were camped in the flat below the little hill where the monument and burying ground are now. The people had stacked most of their guns, and even their knives, by the tepee where Big Foot was lying sick. Soldiers were on the little hill and all around, and there were soldiers across the dry gulch to the south and over east along Wounded Knee Creek too. The people were nearly surrounded, and the wagon-guns were pointing at them.

Some had not yet given up their guns, and so the soldiers were searching all the tepees, throwing things around and poking into everything. There was a man called Yellow Bird, and he and another man were standing in front of the tepee where Big Foot was lying sick. They had white sheets around and over them, with eyeholes to look through, and they had guns under these. An officer came to search them. He took the other man's gun, and then started to take Yellow Bird's. But Yellow Bird would not let go. He wrestled with the officer, and while they were wrestling, the gun went off and killed the officer. Wasichus and some others have said he meant to do this, but Dog Chief was standing right there, and he told me it was not so. As soon as the gun went off, Dog Chief told me, an officer shot and killed Big Foot who was lying sick inside the tepee.

Then suddenly nobody knew what was happening, except that the soldiers were all shooting and the wagon-guns began going off right in among the people.

Many were shot down right there. The women and children ran into the gulch and up west, dropping all the time, for the soldiers shot them as they ran. There were only about a hundred warriors and there were nearly five hundred soldiers. The warriors rushed to where they had piled their guns and knives. They fought soldiers with only their hands until they got their guns.

Dog Chief saw Yellow Bird run into a tepee with his gun, and from there he killed soldiers until the tepee caught fire. Then he died full of bullets.

It was a good winter day when all this happened. The sun was shining. But after the soldiers marched away from their dirty work, a heavy snow began to fall. The wind came up in the night. There was a big blizzard, and it grew very cold. The snow drifted deep in the crooked gulch, and it was one long grave of butchered women and children and babies, who had never done any harm and were only trying to run away.

1932, 1961

---

# EDWIN ARLINGTON ROBINSON
## 1869–1935

Like his own Miniver Cheevy, Edwin Arlington Robinson felt himself born too late. He turned to poetry as to an alternative world of elegance and beauty, but wrote his best poems about wasted, blighted, or impoverished lives. His brief story and portrait poems are in traditional form with metrically regular verse, rhymes, and elevated diction. Such techniques dignify the subject matter and also provide a contrast, where his subject is unpoetic according to traditional standards, that emphasizes its sadness and banality.

Robinson was raised in Gardiner, Maine, the *Tilbury Town* of such poems as *Miniver Cheevy* and *Richard Cory*. His father's lumber business and land speculations failed during the Great Panic of 1893. One of his brothers, a physician, became a drug addict; the other, a businessman, became an alcoholic. Robinson, by nature a scholar and book lover, was able to afford just two years at Harvard. Returning to Gardiner and trying to become a professional poet, he had to depend for support on friends and patrons, until a Pulitzer Prize in 1922 brought him some financial security. But by this time he was over fifty.

Robinson studied alone and with friends long after his formal schooling ended. He read classic works in many languages as well as such American writers as Hawthorne, Whitman, Emerson, and Henry James, who conveyed to him the individualistic idealism of the American tradition. He was drawn to the bleak, tragic vision of the British novelist Thomas Hardy and to the narrative realism of the eighteenth-century English poet George Crabbe. All these influences were distilled in the gloomy, austere, yet sonorous verse of his second book, *Children of the Night* (1897—*The Torrent and the Night Before* had been published the previous year, at his own expense). Celebrating the pain of isolated lives, Robinson worked through to a residue of affirmation, an occasional "light" or "word" that is glimpsed in the "night" of these poems.

Robinson moved to New York City around the turn of the century. *The Town Down the River* (1910) and *The Man against the Sky* (1916) won increasing numbers of readers and critics' awards. *Avon's Harvest* and *Collected Poems* (both 1922) were successful, as was a trilogy of long narrative poems, beginning with *Merlin* (1917). The last of these, *Tristram* (1927), brought a third Pulitzer Prize. Yet to some of the tougher-minded critics of the 1920s, the escapism of the later work (precisely what seemed to make it attractive to a larger audience), uncorrected by the somber wit and sustained irony of the Tilbury poems, seemed pleasant but sentimental. The prizes and honors represented, to a large extent, their belated recognition of his earlier poetry.

Although in that earlier work Robinson was a New England regional poet like Robert Frost and a chronicler of small-town life like Edgar Lee Masters and Sherwood Anderson, he always saw himself as estranged both from his time and from the practices of other poets. The difference between him and these others lay in his ever-present sense of a lost, glorious past.

The text of the poems included here is that of *Collected Poems of Edwin Arlington Robinson* (1921, 1937).

## Luke Havergal

Go to the western gate,[1] Luke Havergal,—
There where the vines cling crimson on the wall,—
And in the twilight wait for what will come.
The wind will moan, the leaves will whisper some,—
Whisper of her, and strike you as they fall;                              5
But go, and if you trust her she will call.
Go to the western gate, Luke Havergal—
Luke Havergal.

No, there is not a dawn in eastern skies
To rift the fiery night that's in your eyes;                            10
But there, where western glooms are gathering,
The dark will end the dark, if anything:
God slays Himself with every leaf that flies,
And hell is more than half of paradise.
No, there is not a dawn in eastern skies—                              15
In eastern skies.

Out of a grave I come to tell you this,—
Out of a grave I come to quench the kiss
That flames upon your forehead with a glow
That blinds you to the way that you must go.                            20
Yes, there is yet one way to where she is,—
Bitter, but one that faith may never miss.

---

1. The natural symbolism of nightfall and autumn associates "the western gate" with the end of life.

Out of a grave I come to tell you this—
To tell you this.

There is the western gate, Luke Havergal,    25
There are the crimson leaves upon the wall.
Go,—for the winds are tearing them away,—
Nor think to riddle the dead words they say,
Nor any more to feel them as they fall;
But go! and if you trust her she will call.    30
There is the western gate, Luke Havergal—
Luke Havergal.

           1896


## Richard Cory

Whenever Richard Cory went down town,
We people on the pavement looked at him:
He was a gentleman from sole to crown,
Clean favored, and imperially slim.

And he was always quietly arrayed,    5
And he was always human when he talked;
But still he fluttered pulses when he said,
"Good-morning," and he glittered when he walked.

And he was rich—yes, richer than a king,—
And admirably schooled in every grace:    10
In fine, we thought that he was everything
To make us wish that we were in his place.

So on we worked, and waited for the light,
And went without the meat, and cursed the bread;
And Richard Cory, one calm summer night,    15
Went home and put a bullet through his head.

           1896


## Miniver Cheevy

Miniver Cheevy, child of scorn,
 Grew lean while he assailed the seasons;
He wept that he was ever born,
 And he had reasons.

Miniver loved the days of old    5
 When swords were bright and steeds were prancing;
The vision of a warrior bold
 Would set him dancing.

Miniver sighed for what was not,
 And dreamed, and rested from his labors;    10

He dreamed of Thebes and Camelot,
  And Priam's neighbors.[1]

Miniver mourned the ripe renown
  That made so many a name so fragrant;
He mourned Romance, now on the town,                    15
  And Art, a vagrant.

Miniver loved the Medici,[2]
  Albeit he had never seen one;
He would have sinned incessantly
  Could he have been one.                    20

Miniver cursed the commonplace
  And eyed a khaki suit with loathing;
He missed the mediæval grace
  Of iron clothing.

Miniver scorned the gold he sought,                    25
  But sore annoyed was he without it;
Miniver thought, and thought, and thought,
  And thought about it.

Miniver Cheevy, born too late,
  Scratched his head and kept on thinking;                    30
Miniver coughed, and called it fate,
  And kept on drinking.

                                                   1910


# The Mill

  The miller's wife had waited long,
    The tea was cold, the fire was dead;
  And there might yet be nothing wrong
    In how he went and what he said:
  "There are no millers any more,"                    5
    Was all that she had heard him say;
  And he had lingered at the door
    So long that it seemed yesterday.

  Sick with a fear that had no form
    She knew that she was there at last;                    10
  And in the mill there was a warm
    And mealy fragrance of the past.
  What else there was would only seem
    To say again what he had meant;

---

1. The neighbors of King Priam in Homer's *Iliad* are his heroic compatriots in the doomed city of Troy. Thebes was an ancient city in Boeotia, rival of Athens and Sparta for supremacy in Greece and the setting of Sophocles' tragedies about Oedipus. Camelot is the legendary court of King Arthur and the knights of the Round Table.
2. Family of wealthy merchants, politicians, and art patrons in Renaissance Florence.

And what was hanging from a beam          15
Would not have heeded where she went.

And if she thought it followed her,
    She may have reasoned in the dark
That one way of the few there were
    Would hide her and would leave no mark:          20
Black water, smooth above the weir
    Like starry velvet in the night,
Though ruffled once, would soon appear
    The same as ever to the sight.

                                                    1920

# Mr. Flood's Party

Old Eben Flood, climbing alone one night
Over the hill between the town below
And the forsaken upland hermitage
That held as much as he should ever know
On earth again of home, paused warily.          5
The road was his with not a native near;
And Eben, having leisure, said aloud,
For no man else in Tilbury Town[1] to hear:

"Well, Mr. Flood, we have the harvest moon
Again, and we may not have many more;          10
The bird is on the wing, the poet says,[2]
And you and I have said it here before.
Drink to the bird." He raised up to the light
The jug that he had gone so far to fill,
And answered huskily: "Well, Mr. Flood,          15
Since you propose it, I believe I will."

Alone, as if enduring to the end
A valiant armor of scarred hopes outworn,
He stood there in the middle of the road
Like Roland's ghost winding a silent horn.[3]          20
Below him, in the town among the trees,
Where friends of other days had honored him,
A phantom salutation of the dead
Rang thinly till old Eben's eyes were dim.

Then, as a mother lays her sleeping child          25
Down tenderly, fearing it may awake,

---

1. The fictive town in a number of Robinson's poems, modeled on Gardiner, Maine.
2. Flood paraphrases stanza 7 of the Persian poem *The Rubáiyát of Omar Khayyám* in the 1859 translation by the English poet Edward FitzGerald (1809–1883): "Come, fill the Cup, and in the Fire of Spring / Your Winter-garment of Repentance fling: / The Bird of

Time has but a little way / To flutter—and the Bird is on the Wing."
3. King Charlemagne's nephew, celebrated in the medieval *Chanson de Roland* (Song of Roland, c. 1000). Just before dying in the battle of Roncevalles (A.D. 778), he sounded his horn for help.

He set the jug down slowly at his feet
With trembling care, knowing that most things break;
And only when assured that on firm earth
It stood, as the uncertain lives of men                            30
Assuredly did not, he paced away,
And with his hand extended paused again:

"Well, Mr. Flood, we have not met like this
In a long time; and many a change has come
To both of us, I fear, since last it was                          35
We had a drop together. Welcome home!"
Convivially returning with himself,
Again he raised the jug up to the light;
And with an acquiescent quaver said:
"Well, Mr. Flood, if you insist, I might.                          40

"Only a very little, Mr. Flood—
For auld lang syne.[4] No more, sir; that will do."
So, for the time, apparently it did,
And Eben evidently thought so too;
For soon amid the silver loneliness                               45
Of night he lifted up his voice and sang,
Secure, with only two moons listening,
Until the whole harmonious landscape rang—

"For auld lang syne." The weary throat gave out,
The last word wavered, and the song was done.                     50
He raised again the jug regretfully
And shook his head, and was again alone.
There was not much that was ahead of him,
And there was nothing in the town below—
Where strangers would have shut the many doors                    55
That many friends had opened long ago.

                                                                1921

4. Old long since (Scottish, literal trans.); hence "the days of long ago," the title and refrain of a famous song by
the Scottish poet Robert Burns (1759–1796).

---

# WILLA CATHER
## 1873–1947

Through her stories of the Nebraska prairie, Willa Cather became famous for her
depictions of the pioneers who settled the American West. But any person who
forges ahead of the crowd is a pioneer. Over a long writing career the heart of
Cather's writing was a study of pioneers in this broader sense—their achievements,
their motivations, and their problematic relation to those who follow. Her work
also portrayed accomplished, strongly individual, independent women who, to
her, were pioneers in societies that expected female submissiveness.
    Born in Virginia, she moved with her family at the age of ten to Red Cloud,

Nebraska, where her father became a mortgage and loan broker. Red Cloud was then a small town in the midst of a rough prairie, which Scandinavian as well as Bohemian and French immigrants were trying to cultivate; "Americans" were a minority. This childhood oriented Cather toward the land, the immigrant, and Europe. She attended the University of Nebraska in Lincoln, graduating in 1895, one of a tiny fraction of women at that time to achieve a college education. While in school she composed naturalistic short stories and worked for the Nebraska Journal, reviewing books, plays, and music. She insisted on applying what she considered professional standards even to the performances of traveling theater groups, because she saw no reason why cultural life in America had to be second best.

After graduating, Cather took an editorial job on a magazine in Pittsburgh, Pennsylvania; five years later she turned to teaching high school English; in 1906 she went to New York City as managing editor of the famous muckraking journal, McClure's magazine. In 1908 she met and became friends with the New England regional writer Sarah Orne Jewett, whose quiet celebrations of life on the land were probably the main influence on Cather's artistic practice. She hoped to devote herself fully to imaginative writing, and after the publication of her novel Alexander's Bridge in 1912, she felt ready to do so. Close to forty years old, she had up until then published only a book of poetry, April Twilights (1903), and a collection of short stories, The Troll Garden (1905).

Her next three novels established her position firmly on the literary scene. O Pioneers! (1913) tells the story of Alexandra Bergson, daughter of Swedish immigrants, one of the few with enough strength and vision to succeed as a farmer on the vast plains, so unlike the comfortable farms of Europe. Her lonely struggle with the land is compounded because as an independent woman she evokes fear and resentment from other settlers, especially her own brothers. The Song of the Lark (1915) concerns the struggle of the gifted Thea Kronberg to realize her talents as an opera singer; she succeeds, but at the price of alienation from her midwestern small-town origins, where people approve of women who sing in the church choir but not of women who are artists. My Antonia (1918) chronicles and celebrates the simple heroism of a woman who survives childhood poverty and adolescent seduction to marry and settle down as wife and mother on a Nebraska farm. Critics praised the artistry of all these novels: their efficient evocation of setting and the clear, measured, unsentimental narrative voice.

Willa Cather never had any romantic interest in men; her emotional life centered on women. Whether her works encode a lesbian sensibility has been a matter of much critical debate. Certainly estrangement from conventional sexuality and sex roles is typical of her main characters. In 1908 she began to share an apartment with Edith Lewis, another Nebraskan whom she had met in 1903. They lived together until Cather's death. Despite literary success and this happy relationship, Cather suffered from a combination of poor health, dissatisfaction with her publisher, and distress at the increasing mechanization and mass-produced quality of American society. Around 1922, she wrote, the world broke in two for her. She joined the Episcopal church, after which her novels took a new direction, concerning themselves with finding and asserting alternative values to the materialistic life she saw around her. The theme of heroic womanhood receded. Books from her "middle period" include A Lost Lady (1923) and The Professor's House (1925); both deal with spiritual and cultural crises in the lives of their main characters.

In 1926 Cather published Death Comes for the Archbishop, a work that initiates her third stage. She had visited and become entranced with the American Southwest; as early as The Song of the Lark she showed Thea Kronberg finding spiritual renewal in its strange, beautiful landscapes. Death Comes for the Archbishop is set in nineteenth-century New Mexico and describes the experiences of two well-bred European priests sent there to establish Catholicism in Santa Fe. Shadows on the Rock is set further back in time, in seventeenth-century Quebec. These books, evoking the solidity of a vanished past, oppose nature and Christianity to the trivia of modern life. Like many other modernists, her view of the present was highly critical, and it became more severe as she grew older.

The short story *Neighbour Rosicky* recapitulates Cather's earlier interest in the pioneers. Cather's focus is character rather than plot; a life story unfolds through a steady but loose accumulation of conversation and internal reminiscence with minimal intrusion by a narrator. Often, Cather chose to use narrative vantage points that keep the reader at a distance from the character. She preferred to evoke rather than to explain a character and distrusted all psychological theories that purported to account for human behavior. Indeed, to be evocative rather than explanatory was her general literary aim. She once described her work as "unfurnished," meaning that it contained only those details necessary to provoke the reader into imagining her fictional world. "Suggestion rather than enumeration" was another way she described her goal. She believed in art as a high calling and strove to create works of beauty. This commitment to culture and aesthetics set her apart from the social movements of the day but won her considerable critical praise.

# Neighbour Rosicky[1]

## I

When Doctor Burleigh told neighbour Rosicky he had a bad heart, Rosicky protested.

"So? No, I guess my heart was always pretty good. I got a little asthma, maybe. Just a awful short breath when I was pitchin' hay last summer, dat's all."

"Well, now, Rosicky, if you know more about it than I do, what did you come to me for? It's your heart that makes you short of breath, I tell you. You're sixty-five years old, and you've always worked hard, and your heart's tired. You've got to be careful from now on, and you can't do heavy work any more. You've got five boys at home to do it for you."

The old farmer looked up at the Doctor with a gleam of amusement in his queer triangular-shaped eyes. His eyes were large and lively, but the lids were caught up in the middle in a curious way, so that they formed a triangle. He did not look like a sick man. His brown face was creased but not wrinkled, he had a ruddy colour in his smooth-shaven cheeks and in his lips, under his long brown moustache. His hair was thin and ragged around his ears, but very little grey. His forehead, naturally high and crossed by deep parallel lines, now ran all the way up to his pointed crown. Rosicky's face had the habit of looking interested,—suggested a contented disposition and a reflective quality that was gay rather than grave. This gave him a certain detachment, the easy manner of an onlooker and observer.

"Well, I guess you ain't got no pills fur a bad heart, Doctor Ed. I guess the only thing is fur me to git me a new one."

Doctor Burleigh swung round in his desk-chair and frowned at the old farmer.

"I think if I were you I'd take a little care of the old one, Rosicky."

Rosicky shrugged. "Maybe I don't know how. I expect you mean fur me not to drink my coffee no more."

"I wouldn't, in your place. But you'll do as you choose about that. I've

1. The text is that of *Obscure Destinies* (1932).

never yet been able to separate a Bohemian[2] from his coffee or his pipe. I've quit trying. But the sure thing is you've got to cut out farm work. You can feed the stock and do chores about the barn, but you can't do anything in the fields that makes you short of breath."

"How about shelling corn?"

"Of course not!"

Rosicky considered with puckered brows.

"I can't make my heart go no longer'n it wants to, can I, Doctor Ed?"

"I think it's good for five or six years yet, maybe more, if you'll take the strain off it. Sit around the house and help Mary. If I had a good wife like yours, I'd want to stay around the house."

His patient chuckled. "It ain't no place fur a man. I don't like no old man hanging round the kitchen too much. An' my wife, she's a awful hard worker her own self."

"That's it; you can help her a little. My Lord, Rosicky, you are one of the few men I know who has a family he can get some comfort out of; happy dispositions, never quarrel among themselves, and they treat you right. I want to see you live a few years and enjoy them."

"Oh, they're good kids, all right," Rosicky assented.

The Doctor wrote him a prescription and asked him how his oldest son, Rudolph, who had married in the spring, was getting on. Rudolph had struck out for himself, on rented land. "And how's Polly? I was afraid Mary mightn't like an American daughter-in-law, but it seems to be working out all right."

"Yes, she's a fine girl. Dat widder woman bring her daughters up very nice. Polly got lots of spunk, an' she got some style, too. Da's nice, for young folks to have some style." Rosicky inclined his head gallantly. His voice and his twinkly smile were an affectionate compliment to his daughter-in-law.

"It looks like a storm, and you'd better be getting home before it comes. In town in the car?" Doctor Burleigh rose.

"No, I'm in de wagon. When you got five boys, you ain't got much chance to ride round in de Ford. I ain't much for cars, noway."

"Well, it's a good road out to your place; but I don't want you bumping around in a wagon much. And never again on a hay-rake, remember!"

Rosicky placed the Doctor's fee delicately behind the desk-telephone, looking the other way, as if this were an absent-minded gesture. He put on his plush cap and his corduroy jacket with a sheepskin collar, and went out.

The Doctor picked up his stethoscope and frowned at it as if he were seriously annoyed with the instrument. He wished it had been telling tales about some other man's heart, some old man who didn't look the Doctor in the eye so knowingly, or hold out such a warm brown hand when he said good-bye. Doctor Burleigh had been a poor boy in the country before he went away to medical school; he had known Rosicky almost ever since he could remember, and he had a deep affection for Mrs. Rosicky.

Only last winter he had had such a good breakfast at Rosicky's, and that when he needed it. He had been out all night on a long, hard confinement case at Tom Marshall's—a big rich farm where there was plenty of stock and plenty of feed and a great deal of expensive farm machinery of the newest model, and no comfort whatever. The woman had too many children and too

2. Native of Bohemia, in the Czech Republic.

much work, and she was no manager. When the baby was born at last, and handed over to the assisting neighbour woman, and the mother was properly attended to, Burleigh refused any breakfast in that slovenly house, and drove his buggy—the snow was too deep for a car—eight miles to Anton Rosicky's place. He didn't know another farm-house where a man could get such a warm welcome, and such good strong coffee with rich cream. No wonder the old chap didn't want to give up his coffee!

He had driven in just when the boys had come back from the barn and were washing up for breakfast. The long table, covered with a bright oilcloth, was set out with dishes waiting for them, and the warm kitchen was full of the smell of coffee and hot biscuit and sausage. Five big handsome boys, running from twenty to twelve, all with what Burleigh called natural good manners— they hadn't a bit of the painful self-consciousness he himself had to struggle with when he was a lad. One ran to put his horse away, another helped him off with his fur coat and hung it up, and Josephine, the youngest child and the only daughter, quickly set another place under her mother's direction.

With Mary, to feed creatures was the natural expression of affection—her chickens, the calves, her big hungry boys. It was a rare pleasure to feed a young man whom she seldom saw and of whom she was as proud as if he belonged to her. Some country housekeepers would have stopped to spread a white cloth over the oilcloth, to change the thick cups and plates for their best china, and the wooden-handled knives for plated ones. But not Mary.

"You must take us as you find us, Doctor Ed. I'd be glad to put out my good things for you if you was expected, but I'm glad to get you any way at all."

He knew she was glad—she threw back her head and spoke out as if she were announcing him to the whole prairie. Rosicky hadn't said anything at all; he merely smiled his twinkling smile, put some more coal on the fire, and went into his own room to pour the Doctor a little drink in a medicine glass. When they were all seated, he watched his wife's face from his end of the table and spoke to her in Czech. Then, with the instinct of politeness which seldom failed him, he turned to the doctor and said slyly: "I was just tellin' her not to ask you no questions about Mrs. Marshall till you eat some breakfast. My wife, she's terrible fur to ask questions."

The boys laughed, and so did Mary. She watched the Doctor devour her biscuit and sausage, too much excited to eat anything herself. She drank her coffee and sat taking in everything about her visitor. She had known him when he was a poor country boy, and was boastfully proud of his success, always saying: "What do people go to Omaha for, to see a doctor, when we got the best one in the State right here?" If Mary liked people at all, she felt physical pleasure in the sight of them, personal exultation in any good fortune that came to them. Burleigh didn't know many women like that, but he knew she was like that.

When his hunger was satisfied, he did, of course, have to tell them about Mrs. Marshall, and he noticed what a friendly interest the boys took in the matter.

Rudolph, the oldest one (he was still living at home then), said: "The last time I was over there, she was lifting them big heavy milk-cans, and I knew she oughtn't to be doing it."

"Yes, Rudolph told me about that when he come home, and I said it wasn't right," Mary put in warmly. "It was all right for me to do them things up to the last, for I was terrible strong, but that woman's weakly. And do you think she'll be able to nurse it, Ed?" She sometimes forgot to give him the title she was so proud of. "And to think of your being up all night and then not able to get a decent breakfast! I don't know what's the matter with such people."

"Why, Mother," said one of the boys, "if Doctor Ed had got breakfast there, we wouldn't have him here. So you ought to be glad."

"He knows I'm glad to have him, John, any time. But I'm sorry for that poor woman, how bad she'll feel the Doctor had to go away in the cold without his breakfast."

"I wish I had been in practice when these were getting born." The Doctor looked down the row of close-clipped heads. "I missed some good breakfasts by not being."

The boys began to laugh at their mother because she flushed so red, but she stood her ground and threw up her head. "I don't care, you wouldn't have got away from this house without breakfast. No doctor ever did. I'd have had something ready fixed that Anton could warm up for you."

The boys laughed harder than ever, and exclaimed at her: "I'll bet you would!" "She would, that!"

"Father, did you get breakfast for the Doctor when we were born?"

"Yes, and he used to bring me my breakfast, too, mighty nice. I was always awful hungry!" Mary admitted with a guilty laugh.

While the boys were getting the Doctor's horse, he went to the window to examine the house plants. "What do you do to your geraniums to keep them blooming all winter, Mary? I never pass this house that from the road I don't see your windows full of flowers."

She snapped off a dark red one, and a ruffled new green leaf, and put them in his buttonhole. "There, that looks better. You look too solemn for a young man, Ed. Why don't you git married? I'm worried about you. Settin' at breakfast, I looked at you real hard, and I seen you've got some grey hairs already."

"Oh, yes! They're coming. Maybe they'd come faster if I married."

"Don't talk so. You'll ruin your health eating at the hotel. I could send your wife a nice loaf of nut bread, if you only had one. I don't like to see a young man getting grey. I'll tell you something, Ed; you make some strong black tea and keep it handy in a bowl, and every morning just brush it into your hair, an' it'll keep the grey from showin' much. That's the way I do!"

Sometimes the Doctor heard the gossipers in the drug-store wondering why Rosicky didn't get on faster. He was industrious, and so were his boys, but they were rather free and easy, weren't pushers, and they didn't always show good judgment. They were comfortable, they were out of debt, but they didn't get much ahead. Maybe, Doctor Burleigh reflected, people as generous and warm-hearted and affectionate as the Rosickys never got ahead much; maybe you couldn't enjoy your life and put it into the bank, too.

## II

When Rosicky left Doctor Burleigh's office, he went into the farm-implement store to light his pipe and put on his glasses and read over the list Mary had given him. Then he went into the general merchandise place next door and stood about until the pretty girl with the plucked eyebrows, who always waited on him, was free. Those eyebrows, two thin India-ink strokes, amused him, because he remembered how they used to be. Rosicky always prolonged his shopping by a little joking; the girl knew the old fellow admired her, and she liked to chaff with him.

"Seems to me about every other week you buy ticking, Mr. Rosicky, and always the best quality," she remarked as she measured off the heavy bolt with red stripes.

"You see, my wife is always makin' goose-fedder pillows, an' de thin stuff don't hold in dem little down-fedders."

"You must have lots of pillows at your home."

"Sure. She makes quilts of dem, too. We sleeps easy. Now she's makin' a fedder quilt for my son's wife. You know Polly, that married my Rudolph. How much my bill, Miss Pearl?"

"Eight eighty-five."

"Chust make it nine, and put in some candy fur de women."

"As usual. I never did see a man buy so much candy for his wife. First thing you know, she'll be getting too fat."

"I'd like dat. I ain't much fur all dem slim women like what de style is now."

"That's one for me, I suppose, Mr. Bohunk!"[3] Pearl sniffed and elevated her India-ink strokes.

When Rosicky went out to his wagon, it was beginning to snow,—the first snow of the season, and he was glad to see it. He rattled out of town and along the highway through a wonderfully rich stretch of country, the finest farms in the county. He admired this High Prairie, as it was called, and always liked to drive through it. His own place lay in a rougher territory, where there was some clay in the soil and it was not so productive. When he bought his land, he hadn't the money to buy on High Prairie; so he told his boys, when they grumbled, that if their land hadn't some clay in it, they wouldn't own it at all. All the same, he enjoyed looking at these fine farms, as he enjoyed looking at a prize bull.

After he had gone eight miles, he came to the graveyard, which lay just at the edge of his own hay-land. There he stopped his horses and sat still on his wagon seat, looking about at the snowfall. Over yonder on the hill he could see his own house, crouching low, with the clump of orchard behind and the windmill before, and all down the gentle hill-slope the rows of pale gold corn-stalks stood out against the white field. The snow was falling over the cornfield and the pasture and the hay-land, steadily, with very little wind—a nice dry snow. The graveyard had only a light wire fence about it and was all overgrown with long red grass. The fine snow, settling into this red grass and upon the few little evergreens and the headstones, looked very pretty.

It was a nice graveyard, Rosicky reflected, sort of snug and homelike, not cramped or mournful,—a big sweep all round it. A man could lie down in the long grass and see the complete arch of the sky over him, hear the wagons go by; in summer the mowing-machine rattled right up to the wire fence. And it was so near home. Over there across the cornstalks his own roof and windmill looked so good to him that he promised himself to mind the Doctor and take care of himself. He was awful fond of his place, he admitted. He wasn't anx-

---

3. Slang for "Bohemian," here used affectionately.

ious to leave it. And it was a comfort to think that he would never have to go farther than the edge of his own hayfield. The snow, falling over his barnyard and the graveyard, seemed to draw things together like. And they were all old neighbours in the graveyard, most of them friends; there was nothing to feel awkward or embarrassed about. Embarrassment was the most disagreeable feeling Rosicky knew. He didn't often have it,—only with certain people whom he didn't understand at all.

Well, it was a nice snowstorm; a fine sight to see the snow falling so quietly and graciously over so much open country. On his cap and shoulders, on the horses' backs and manes, light, delicate, mysterious it fell; and with it a dry cool fragrance was released into the air. It meant rest for vegetation and men and beasts, for the ground itself; a season of long nights for sleep, leisurely breakfasts, peace by the fire. This and much more went through Rosicky's mind, but he merely told himself that winter was coming, clucked to his horses, and drove on.

When he reached home, John, the youngest boy, ran out to put away his team for him, and he met Mary coming up from the outside cellar with her apron full of carrots. They went into the house together. On the table, covered with oilcloth figured with clusters of blue grapes, a place was set, and he smelled hot coffee-cake of some kind. Anton never lunched in town; he thought that extravagant, and anyhow he didn't like the food. So Mary always had something ready for him when he got home.

After he was settled in his chair, stirring his coffee in a big cup, Mary took out of the oven a pan of *kolache*[4] stuffed with apricots, examined them anxiously to see whether they had got too dry, put them beside his plate, and then sat down opposite him.

Rosicky asked her in Czech if she wasn't going to have any coffee.

She replied in English, as being somehow the right language for transacting business: "Now what did Doctor Ed say, Anton? You tell me just what."

"He said I was to tell you some compliments, but I forgot 'em." Rosicky's eyes twinkled.

"About you, I mean. What did he say about your asthma?"

"He says I ain't got no asthma." Rosicky took one of the little rolls in his broad brown fingers. The thickened nail of his right thumb told the story of his past.

"Well, what is the matter? And don't try to put me off."

"He don't say nothing much, only I'm a little older, and my heart ain't so good like it used to be."

Mary started and brushed her hair back from her temples with both hands as if she were a little out of her mind. From the way she glared, she might have been in a rage with him.

"He says there's something the matter with your heart? Doctor Ed says so?"

"Now don't yell at me like I was a hog in de garden, Mary. You know I always did like to hear a woman talk soft. He didn't say anything de matter wid my heart, only it ain't so young like it used to be, an' he tell me not to pitch hay or run de corn-sheller."

Mary wanted to jump up, but she sat still. She admired the way he never under any circumstances raised his voice or spoke roughly. He was city-bred,

---

4. Or "kolacky," a sweet bun with fruit filling.

and she was country-bred; she often said she wanted her boys to have their papa's nice ways.

"You never have no pain there, do you? It's your breathing and your stomach that's been wrong. I wouldn't believe nobody but Doctor Ed about it. I guess I'll go see him myself. Didn't he give you no advice?"

"Chust to take it easy like, an' stay round de house dis winter. I guess you got some carpenter work for me to do. I kin make some new shelves for you, and I want dis long time to build a closet in de boys' room and make dem two little fellers keep dere clo'es hung up."

Rosicky drank his coffee from time to time, while he considered. His moustache was of the soft long variety and came down over his mouth like the teeth of a buggy-rake over a bundle of hay. Each time he put down his cup, he ran his blue handkerchief over his lips. When he took a drink of water, he managed very neatly with the back of his hand.

Mary sat watching him intently, trying to find any change in his face. It is hard to see anyone who has become like your own body to you. Yes, his hair had got thin, and his high forehead had deep lines running from left to right. But his neck, always clean-shaved except in the busiest seasons, was not loose or baggy. It was burned a dark reddish brown, and there were deep creases in it, but it looked firm and full of blood. His cheeks had a good colour. On either side of his mouth there was a half-moon down the length of his cheek, not wrinkles, but two lines that had come there from his habitual expression. He was shorter and broader than when she married him; his back had grown broad and curved, a good deal like the shell on an old turtle, and his arms and legs were short.

He was fifteen years older than Mary, but she had hardly ever thought about it before. He was her man, and the kind of man she liked. She was rough, and he was gentle—city-bred, as she always said. They had been shipmates on a rough voyage and had stood by each other in trying times. Life had gone well with them because, at bottom, they had the same ideas about life. They agreed, without discussion, as to what was most important and what was secondary. They didn't often exchange opinions, even in Czech—it was as if they had thought the same thought together. A good deal had to be sacrificed and thrown overboard in a hard life like theirs, and they had never disagreed as to the things that could go. It had been a hard life, and a soft life, too. There wasn't anything brutal in the short, broad-backed man with the three-cornered eyes and the forehead that went on to the top of his skull. He was a city man, a gentle man, and though he had married a rough farm girl, he had never touched her without gentleness.

They had been at one accord not to hurry through life, not to be always skimping and saving. They saw their neighbours buy more land and feed more stock than they did, without discontent. Once when the creamery agent came to the Rosickys to persuade them to sell him their cream, he told them how much money the Fasslers, their nearest neighbours, had made on their cream last year.

"Yes," said Mary, "and look at them Fassler children! Pale, pinched little things, they look like skimmed milk. I had rather put some colour into my children's faces than put money into the bank."

The agent shrugged and turned to Anton.

"I guess we'll do like she says," said Rosicky.

## III

Mary very soon got into town to see Doctor Ed, and then she had a talk with her boys and set a guard over Rosicky. Even John, the youngest, had his father on his mind. If Rosicky went to throw hay down from the loft, one of the boys ran up the ladder and took the fork from him. He sometimes complained that though he was getting to be an old man, he wasn't an old woman yet.

That winter he stayed in the house in the afternoons and carpentered, or sat in the chair between the window full of plants and the wooden bench where the two pails of drinking-water stood. This spot was called "Father's corner," though it was not a corner at all. He had a shelf there, where he kept his Bohemian papers and his pipes and tobacco, and his shears and needles and thread and tailor's thimble. Having been a tailor in his youth, he couldn't bear to see a woman patching at his clothes, or at the boys'. He liked tailoring, and always patched all the overalls and jackets and work shirts. Occasionally he made over a pair of pants one of the older boys had outgrown, for the little fellow.

While he sewed, he let his mind run back over his life. He had a good deal to remember, really; life in three countries. The only part of his youth he didn't like to remember was the two years he had spent in London, in Cheapside, working for a German tailor who was wretchedly poor. Those days, when he was nearly always hungry, when his clothes were dropping off him for dirt, and the sound of a strange language kept him in continual bewilderment, had left a sore spot in his mind that wouldn't bear touching.

He was twenty when he landed at Castle Garden in New York, and he had a protector who got him work in a tailor shop in Vesey Street, down near the Washington Market. He looked upon that part of his life as very happy. He became a good workman, he was industrious, and his wages were increased from time to time. He minded his own business and envied nobody's good fortune. He went to night school and learned to read English. He often did overtime work and was well paid for it, but somehow he never saved anything. He couldn't refuse a loan to a friend, and he was self-indulgent. He liked a good dinner, and a little went for beer, a little for tobacco; a good deal went to the girls. He often stood through an opera on Saturday nights; he could get standing-room for a dollar. Those were the great days of opera in New York, and it gave a fellow something to think about for the rest of the week. Rosicky had a quick ear, and a childish love of all the stage splendour; the scenery, the costumes, the ballet. He usually went with a chum, and after the performance they had beer and maybe some oysters somewhere. It was a fine life; for the first five years or so it satisfied him completely. He was never hungry or cold or dirty, and everything amused him: a fire, a dog fight, a parade, a storm, a ferry ride. He thought New York the finest, richest, friendliest city in the world.

Moreover, he had what he called a happy home life. Very near the tailor shop was a small furniture-factory, where an old Austrian, Loeffler, employed a few skilled men and made unusual furniture, most of it to order, for the rich German housewives uptown. The top floor of Loeffler's five-storey factory was a loft, where he kept his choice lumber and stored the old pieces of furniture left on his hands. One of the young workmen he employed was a Czech, and he and Rosicky became fast friends. They persuaded Loeffler to let them have a sleeping-room in one corner of the loft. They bought good beds and bedding and had their pick of the furniture kept up there. The loft was low-pitched, but light and airy, full of windows, and good-smelling by reason of the fine lumber put up there to season. Old Loeffler used to go down to the docks and buy wood from South America and the East from the sea captains. The young men were as foolish about their house as a bridal pair. Zichec, the young cabinet-maker, devised every sort of convenience, and Rosicky kept their clothes in order. At night and on Sundays, when the quiver of machinery underneath was still, it was the quietest place in the world, and on summer nights all the sea winds blew in. Zichec often practised on his flute in the evening. They were both fond of music and went to the opera together. Rosicky thought he wanted to live like that for ever.

But as the years passed, all alike, he began to get a little restless. When spring came round, he would begin to feel fretted, and he got to drinking. He was likely to drink too much of a Saturday night. On Sunday he was languid and heavy, getting over his spree. On Monday he plunged into work again. So he never had time to figure out what ailed him, although he knew something did. When the grass turned green in Park Place, and the lilac hedge at the back of Trinity churchyard put out its blossoms, he was tormented by a longing to run away. That was why he drank too much; to get a temporary illusion of freedom and wide horizons.

Rosicky, the old Rosicky, could remember as if it were yesterday the day when the young Rosicky found out what was the matter with him. It was on a Fourth of July afternoon, and he was sitting in Park Place in the sun. The lower part of New York was empty. Wall Street, Liberty Street, Broadway, all empty. So much stone and asphalt with nothing going on, so many empty windows. The emptiness was intense, like the stillness in a great factory when the machinery stops and the belts and bands cease running. It was too great a change, it took all the strength out of one. Those blank buildings, without the stream of life pouring through them, were like empty jails. It struck young Rosicky that this was the trouble with big cities; they built you in from the earth itself, cemented you away from any contact with the ground. You lived in an unnatural world, like the fish in an aquarium, who were probably much more comfortable than they ever were in the sea.

On that very day he began to think seriously about the articles he had read in the Bohemian papers, describing prosperous Czech farming communities in the West. He believed he would like to go out there as a farm hand; it was hardly possible that he could ever have land of his own. His people had always been workmen, his father and grandfather had worked in shops. His mother's parents had lived in the country, but they rented their farm and had a hard time to get along. Nobody in his family had ever owned any land,—that belonged to a different station of life altogether. Anton's mother died when he was little, and he was sent into the country to her parents. He stayed with them until he was twelve, and formed those ties with the earth and the farm animals and growing things which are never made at all unless they are made early. After his grandfather died, he went back to live with his father and stepmother, but she was very hard on him, and his father helped him to get passage to London.

After that Fourth of July day in Park Place, the desire to return to the country never left him. To work on another man's farm would be all he asked; to see the sun rise and set and to plant things and watch them grow. He was a very simple man. He was like a tree that has not many roots, but one tap-root that goes down deep. He subscribed for a Bohemian paper printed in Chicago, then for one printed in Omaha. His mind got farther and farther west. He began to save a little money to buy his liberty. When he was thirty-five, there was a great meeting in New York of Bohemian athletic societies, and Rosicky left the tailor shop and went home with the Omaha delegates to try his fortune in another part of the world.

## IV

Perhaps the fact that his own youth was well over before he began to have a family was one reason why Rosicky was so fond of his boys. He had almost a grandfather's indulgence for them. He had never had to worry about any of them—except, just now, a little about Rudolph.

On Saturday night the boys always piled into the Ford, took little Josephine, and went to town to the moving-picture show. One Saturday morning they were talking at the breakfast table about starting early that evening, so that they would have an hour or so to see the Christmas things in the stores before the show began. Rosicky looked down the table.

"I hope you boys ain't disappointed, but I want you to let me have de car tonight. Maybe some of you can go in with de neighbours."

Their faces fell. They worked hard all week, and they were still like children. A new jack-knife or a box of candy pleased the older ones as much as the little fellow.

"If you and mother are going to town," Frank said, "maybe you could take a couple of us along with you, anyway.'"

"No, I want to take de car down to Rudolph's, and let him an' Polly go in to de show. She don't git into town enough, an' I'm afraid she's gettin' lonesome, an' he can't afford no car yet."

That settled it. The boys were a good deal dashed. Their father took another piece of apple-cake and went on: "Maybe next Saturday night de two little fellers can go along wid dem."

"Oh, is Rudolph going to have the car every Saturday night?"

Rosicky did not reply at once; then he began to speak seriously: "Listen, boys; Polly ain't lookin' so good. I don't like to see nobody lookin' sad. It comes hard fur a town girl to be a farmer's wife. I don't want no trouble to start in Rudolph's family. When it starts, it ain't so easy to stop. An American girl don't git used to our ways all at once. I like to tell Polly she and Rudolph can have the car every Saturday night till after New Year's, if it's all right with you boys."

"Sure, it's all right, papa," Mary cut in. "And it's good you thought about that. Town girls is used to more than country girls. I lay awake nights, scared she'll make Rudolph discontented with the farm."

The boys put as good a face on it as they could. They surely looked forward to their Saturday nights in town. That evening Rosicky drove the car the half-mile down to Rudolph's new, bare little house.

Polly was in a short-sleeved gingham dress, clearing away the supper dishes. She was a trim, slim little thing, with blue eyes and shingled yellow hair, and her eyebrows were reduced to a mere brush-stroke, like Miss Pearl's. "Good-evening, Mr. Rosicky. Rudolph's at the barn, I guess." She never called him father, or Mary mother. She was sensitive about having married a foreigner. She never in the world would have done it if Rudolph hadn't been such a handsome, persuasive fellow and such a gallant lover. He had graduated in her class in the high school in town, and their friendship began in the ninth grade.

Rosicky went in, though he wasn't exactly asked. "My boys ain't goin' to town tonight, an' I brought de car over fur you two to go in to de picture show."

Polly, carrying dishes to the sink, looked over her shoulder at him. "Thank you. But I'm late with my work tonight, and pretty tired. Maybe Rudolph would like to go in with you."

"Oh, I don't go to de shows! I'm too old-fashioned. You won't feel so tired after you ride in de air a ways. It's a nice clear night, an' it ain't cold. You go an' fix yourself up, Polly, an' I'll wash de dishes an' leave everything nice fur you."

Polly blushed and tossed her bob. "I couldn't let you do that, Mr. Rosicky, I wouldn't think of it."

Rosicky said nothing. He found a bib apron on a nail behind the kitchen door. He slipped it over his head and then took Polly by her two elbows and pushed her gently toward the door of her own room. "I washed up de kitchen many times for my wife, when de babies was sick or somethin'. You go an' make yourself look nice. I like you to look prettier'n any of dem town girls when you go in. De young folks must have some fun, an' I'm goin' to look out fur you, Polly."

That kind, reassuring grip on her elbows, the old man's funny bright eyes, made Polly want to drop her head on his shoulder for a second. She restrained herself, but she lingered in his grasp at the door of her room, murmuring tearfully: "You always lived in the city when you were young, didn't you? Don't you ever get lonesome out here?"

As she turned round to him, her hand fell naturally into his, and he stood holding it and smiling into her face with his peculiar, knowing, indulgent smile without a shadow of reproach in it. "Dem big cities is all right fur de rich, but dey is terrible hard fur de poor."

"I don't know. Sometimes I think I'd like to take a chance. You lived in New York, didn't you?"

"An' London. Da's bigger still. I learned my trade dere. Here's Rudolph comin', you better hurry."

"Will you tell me about London some time?"

"Maybe. Only I ain't no talker, Polly. Run an' dress yourself up."

The bedroom door closed behind her, and Rudolph came in from the outside, looking anxious. He had seen the car and was sorry any of his family should come just then. Supper hadn't been a very pleasant occasion. Halting in the doorway, he saw his father in a kitchen apron, carrying dishes to the sink. He flushed crimson and something flashed in his eye. Rosicky held up a warning finger.

"I brought de car over fur you an' Polly to go to de picture show, an' I made her let me finish here so you won't be late. You go put on a clean shirt, quick!"

"But don't the boys want the car, Father?"

"Not tonight dey don't." Rosicky fumbled under his apron and found his pants pocket. He took out a silver dollar and said in a hurried whisper: "You go an' buy dat girl some ice cream an' candy tonight, like you was courtin'. She's awful good friends wid me."

Rudolph was very short of cash, but he took the money as if it hurt him. There had been a crop failure all over the county. He had more than once been sorry he'd married this year.

In a few minutes the young people came out, looking clean and a little stiff. Rosicky hurried them off, and then he took his own time with the dishes. He scoured the pots and pans and put away the milk and swept the kitchen. He put some coal in the stove and shut off the draughts, so the place would be warm for them when they got home late at night. Then he sat down and had a pipe and listened to the clock tick.

Generally speaking, marrying an American girl was certainly a risk. A Czech should marry a Czech. It was lucky that Polly was the daughter of a poor widow woman; Rudolph was proud, and if she had a prosperous family to throw up at him, they could never make it go. Polly was one of four sisters, and they all worked; one was book-keeper in the bank, one taught music, and Polly and her younger sister had been clerks, like Miss Pearl. All four of them were musical, had pretty voices, and sang in the Methodist choir, which the eldest sister directed.

Polly missed the sociability of a store position. She missed the choir, and the company of her sisters. She didn't dislike housework, but she disliked so much of it. Rosicky was a little anxious about this pair. He was afraid Polly would grow so discontented that Rudy would quit the farm and take a factory job in Omaha. He had worked for a winter up there, two years ago, to get money to marry on. He had done very well, and they would always take him back at the stockyards. But to Rosicky that meant the end of everything for his son. To be a landless man was to be a wage-earner, a slave, all your life; to have nothing, to be nothing.

Rosicky thought he would come over and do a little carpentering for Polly after the New Year. He guessed she needed jollying. Rudolph was a serious sort of chap, serious in love and serious about his work.

Rosicky shook out his pipe and walked home across the fields. Ahead of him the lamplight shone from his kitchen windows. Suppose he were still in a tailor shop on Vesey Street, with a bunch of pale, narrow-chested sons working on machines, all coming home tired and sullen to eat supper in a kitchen that was a parlour also; with another crowded, angry family quarrelling just across the dumb-waiter shaft, and squeaking pulleys at the windows where dirty washings hung on dirty lines above a court full of old brooms and mops and ash-cans . . .

He stopped by the windmill to look up at the frosty winter stars and draw a long breath before he went inside. That kitchen with the shining windows was dear to him; but the sleeping fields and bright stars and the noble darkness were dearer still.

## V

On the day before Christmas the weather set in very cold; no snow, but a bitter, biting wind that whistled and sang over the flat land and lashed one's face like fine wires. There was baking going on in the Rosicky kitchen all day, and Rosicky sat inside, making over a coat that Albert had outgrown into an overcoat for John. Mary had a big red geranium in bloom for Christmas, and a row of Jerusalem cherry trees, full of berries. It was the first year she had ever grown these; Doctor Ed brought her the seeds from Omaha when he went to some medical convention. They reminded Rosicky of plants he had seen in England; and all afternoon, as he stitched, he sat thinking about those two years in London, which his mind usually shrank from even after all this while.

He was a lad of eighteen when he dropped down into London, with no money and no connexions except the address of a cousin who was supposed to be working at a confectioner's. When he went to the pastry shop, however, he found that the cousin had gone to America. Anton tramped the streets for several days, sleeping in doorways and on the Embankment, until he was in utter despair. He knew no English, and the sound of the strange language all about him confused him. By chance he met a poor German tailor who had learned his trade in Vienna, and could speak a little Czech. This tailor, Lifschnitz, kept a repair shop in a Cheapside basement, underneath a cobbler. He didn't much need an apprentice, but he was sorry for the boy and took him in for no wages but his keep and what he could pick up. The pickings were supposed to be coppers given you when you took work home to a customer. But most of the customers called for their clothes themselves, and the coppers that came Anton's way were very few. He had, however, a place to sleep. The tailor's family lived upstairs in three rooms; a kitchen, a bedroom, where Lifschnitz and his wife and five children slept, and a living-room. Two corners of this living room were curtained off for lodgers; in one Rosicky slept on an old horsehair sofa, with a feather quilt to wrap himself in. The other corner was rented to a wretched, dirty boy, who was studying the violin. He actually practised there. Rosicky was dirty, too. There was no way to be anything else. Mrs. Lifschnitz got the water she cooked and washed with from a pump in a brick court, four flights down. There were bugs in the place, and multitudes of fleas, though the poor woman did the best she could. Rosicky knew she often went empty to give another potato or a spoonful of dripping to the two hungry, sad-eyed boys who lodged with her. He used to think he would never get out of there, never get a clean shirt to his back again. What would he do, he wondered, when his clothes actually dropped to pieces and the worn cloth wouldn't hold patches any longer?

It was still early when the old farmer put aside his sewing and his recollections. The sky had been a dark grey all day, with not a gleam of sun, and the light failed at four o'clock. He went to shave and change his shirt while the turkey was roasting. Rudolph and Polly were coming over for supper.

After supper they sat round in the kitchen, and the younger boys were saying how sorry they were it hadn't snowed. Everybody was sorry. They wanted a deep snow that would lie long and keep the wheat warm, and leave the ground soaked when it melted.

"Yes, sir!" Rudolph broke out fiercely; "if we have another dry year like last year, there's going to be hard times in this country."

Rosicky filled his pipe. "You boys don't know what hard times is. You don't owe nobody, you got plenty to eat an' keep warm, an' plenty water to keep clean. When you got them, you can't have it very hard."

Rudolph frowned, opened and shut his big right hand, and dropped it clenched upon his knee. "I've got to have a good deal more than that, father, or I'll quit this farming gamble. I can always make good wages railroading, or at the packing house, and be sure of my money."

"Maybe so," his father answered dryly.

Mary, who had just come in from the pantry and was wiping her hands on the roller towel, thought Rudy and his father were getting too serious. She brought her darning-basket and sat down in the middle of the group.

"I ain't much afraid of hard times, Rudy," she said heartily. "We've had a plenty, but we've always come through. Your father wouldn't never take nothing very hard, not even hard times. I got a mind to tell you a story on him. Maybe you boys can't hardly remember the year we had that terrible hot wind, that burned everything up on the Fourth of July? All the corn an' the gardens. An' that was in the days when we didn't have alfalfa yet,—I guess it wasn't invented.

"Well, that very day your father was out cultivatin' corn, and I was here in the kitchen makin' plum preserves. We had bushels of plums that year. I noticed it was terrible hot, but it's always hot in the kitchen when you're preservin', an' I was too busy with my plums to mind. Anton come in from the field about three o'clock, an' I asked him what was the matter.

" 'Nothin',' he says, 'but it's pretty hot an' I think I won't work no more to-day.' He stood round for a few minutes, an' then he says: 'Ain't you near through? I want you should git up a nice supper for us tonight. It's Fourth of July.'

"I told him to git along, that I was right in the middle of preservin', but the plums would taste good on hot biscuit. 'I'm goin' to have fried chicken, too,' he says, and he went off an' killed a couple. You three oldest boys was little fellers, playin' round outside, real hot an' sweaty, an' your father took you to the horse tank down by the windmill an' took off your clothes an' put you in. Them two box-elder trees were little then, but they made shade over the tank. Then he took off all his own clothes, an' got in with you. While he was playin' in the water with you, the Methodist preacher drove into our place to say how all the neighbours was goin' to meet at the schoolhouse that night, to pray for rain. He drove right to the windmill, of course, and there was your father and you three with no clothes on. I was in the kitchen door, an' I had to laugh, for the preacher acted like he ain't never seen a naked man before. He surely was embarrassed, an' your father couldn't git to his clothes; they was all hangin' up on the windmill to let the sweat dry out of 'em. So he laid in the tank where he was, an' put one of you boys on top of him to cover him up a little, an' talked to the preacher.

"When you got through playin' in the water, he put clean clothes on you and a clean shirt on himself, an' by that time I'd begun to get supper. He says: 'It's too hot in here to eat comfortable. Let's have a picnic in the orchard. We'll eat our supper behind the mulberry hedge, under them linden trees.'

"So he carried our supper down, an' a bottle of my wild-grape wine, an' everything tasted good, I can tell you. The wind got cooler as the sun was goin' down, and it turned out pleasant, only I noticed how the leaves was curled up on the linden trees. That made me think, an' I asked your father if that hot wind all day hadn't been terrible hard on the gardens an' the corn.

" 'Corn,' he says, 'there ain't no corn.'

" 'What you talkin' about?' I said. 'Ain't we got forty acres?'

" 'We ain't got an ear,' he says, 'nor nobody else ain't got none. All the corn in this country was cooked by three o'clock today, like you'd roasted it in an oven.'

" 'You mean you won't get no crop at all?' I asked him. I couldn't believe it, after he'd worked so hard.

" 'No crop this year,' he says. 'That's why we're havin' a picnic. We might as well enjoy what we got.'

"An' that's how your father behaved, when all the neighbours was so discouraged they couldn't look you in the face. An' we enjoyed ourselves that year, poor as we was, an' our neighbours wasn't a bit better off for bein' miserable. Some of 'em grieved till they got poor digestions and couldn't relish what they did have."

The younger boys said they thought their father had the best of it. But Rudolph was thinking that, all the same, the neighbours had managed to get ahead more, in the fifteen years since that time. There must be something wrong about his father's way of doing things. He wished he knew what was going on in the back of Polly's mind. He knew she liked his father, but he knew, too, that she was afraid of something. When his mother sent over coffee-cake or prune tarts or a loaf of fresh bread, Polly seemed to regard them with a certain suspicion. When she observed to him that his brothers had nice manners, her tone implied that it was remarkable they should have. With his mother she was stiff and on her guard. Mary's hearty frankness and gusts of good humour irritated her. Polly was afraid of being unusual or conspicuous in any way, of being 'ordinary' as she said!

When Mary had finished her story, Rosicky laid aside his pipe.

"You boys like me to tell you about some of dem hard times I been through in London?" Warmly encouraged, he sat rubbing his forehead along the deep creases. It was bothersome to tell a long story in English (he nearly always talked to the boys in Czech), but he wanted Polly to hear this one.

"Well, you know about dat tailor shop I worked in in London? I had one Christmas dere I ain't never forgot. Times was awful bad before Christmas; de boss ain't got much work, an' have it awful hard to pay his rent. It ain't so much fun, bein' poor in a big city like London, I'll say! All de windows is full of good t'ings to eat, an' all de pushcarts in de streets is full, an' you smell 'em all de time, an' you ain't got no money—not a damn bit. I didn't mind de cold so much, though I didn't have no overcoat, chust a short jacket I'd outgrowed so it wouldn't meet on me, an' my hands was chapped raw. But I always had a good appetite, like you all know, an' de sight of dem pork pies in de windows was awful fur me!

"Day before Christmas was terrible foggy dat year, an' dat fog gits into your bones and makes you all damp like. Mrs. Lifschnitz didn't give us nothin' but a little bread an' drippin' for supper, because she was savin' to try for to give us a good dinner on Christmas Day. After supper de boss say I go an' enjoy myself, so I went into de streets to listen to de Christmas singers. Dey sing old songs an' make very nice music, an' I run round after dem a good ways, till I got awful hungry. I t'ink maybe if I go home, I can sleep till morning an' forgit my belly.

"I went into my corner real quiet, and roll up in my fedder quilt. But I ain't got my head down, till I smell somet'ing good. Seem like it git stronger an' stronger, an' I can't git to sleep noway. I can't understand dat smell. Dere was a gas light in a hall across de court, dat always shine in at my window a little. I got up an' look round. I got a little wooden box in my corner fur a stool, 'cause I ain't got no chair. I picks up dat box, and under it dere is a roast goose on a platter! I can't believe my eyes. I carry it to de window where de light comes in, an' touch it and smell it to find out, an' den I taste it to be sure. I say, I will eat chust one little bite of dat goose, so I can go to sleep, and to-morrow I won't eat none at all. But I tell you, boys, when I stop, one half of dat goose was gone!"

The narrator bowed his head, and the boys shouted. But little Josephine slipped behind his chair and kissed him on the neck beneath his ear.

"Poor little Papa, I don't want him to be hungry!"

"Da's long ago, child. I ain't never been hungry since I had your mudder to cook fur me."

"Go on and tell us the rest, please," said Polly.

"Well, when I come to realize what I done, of course, I felt terrible. I felt better in de stomach, but very bad in de heart. I set on my bed wid dat platter on my knees, an' it all come to me; how hard dat poor woman save to buy dat goose, and how she get some neighbour to cook it dat got more fire, an' how she put it in my corner to keep it away from dem hungry children. Dere was a old carpet hung up to shut my corner off, an' de children wasn't allowed to go in dere. An' I know she put it in my corner because she trust me more'n she did de violin boy. I can't stand it to face her after I spoil de Christmas. So I put on my shoes and go out into de city. I tell myself I better throw myself in de river; but I guess I ain't dat kind of a boy.

"It was after twelve o'clock, an' terrible cold, an' I start out to walk about London all night. I walk along de river awhile, but dey was lots of drunks all along; men, and women too. I chust move along to keep away from de police. I git onto de Strand, an' den over to New Oxford Street, where dere was a big German restaurant on de ground floor, wid big windows all fixed up fine, an' I could see de people havin' parties inside. While I was lookin' in, two men and two ladies come out, laughin' and talkin' and feelin' happy about all dey been eatin' an' drinkin', an' dey was speakin' Czech—not like de Austrians, but like de home folks talk it.

"I guess I went crazy, an' I done what I ain't never done before nor since. I went right up to dem gay people an' begun to beg dem: 'Fellow countrymen, for God's sake give me money enough to buy a goose!'

"Dey laugh, of course, but de ladies speak awful kind to me, an' dey take me back into de restaurant and give me hot coffee and cakes, an' make me tell all about how I happened to come to London, an' what I was doin' dere. Dey take my name and where I work down on paper, an' both of dem ladies give me ten shillings.

"De big market at Covent Garden[5] ain't very far away, an' by dat time it was open. I go dere an buy a big goose an' some pork pies, an' potatoes and onions, an' cakes an' oranges fur de children—all I could carry! When I git home, everybody is still asleep. I pile all I bought on de kitchen table, an' go in an' lay down on my bed, an I ain't waken up till I hear dat woman scream when she come out into her kitchen. My goodness, but she was surprise! She laugh an' cry at de same time, an' hug me and waken all de children. She ain't stop

5. Square in London, site of a famous flower and vegetable market and of the Covent Garden opera house.

fur no breakfast; she git de Christmas dinner ready dat morning, and we all sit down an' eat all we can hold. I ain't never seen dat violin boy have all he can hold before.

"Two-three days after dat, de two men come to hunt me up, an' dey ask my boss, and he give me a good report an' tell dem I was a steady boy all right. One of dem Bohemians was very smart an' run a Bohemian newspaper in New York, an' de odder was a rich man, in de importing business, an' dey been travelling togedder. Dey told me how t'ings was easier in New York, an' offered to pay my passage when dey was goin' home soon on a boat. My boss say to me: 'You go. You ain't got no chance here, an' I like to see you git ahead, fur you always been a good boy to my woman, and fur dat fine Christmas dinner you give us all.' An' da's how I got to New York."

That night when Rudolph and Polly, arm in arm, were running home across the fields with the bitter wind at their backs, his heart leaped for joy when she said she thought they might have his family come over for supper on New Year's Eve. "Let's get up a nice supper, and not let your mother help at all; make her be company for once."

"That would be lovely of you, Polly," he said humbly. He was a very simple, modest boy, and he, too, felt vaguely that Polly and her sisters were more experienced and worldly than his people.

The winter turned out badly for farmers. It was bitterly cold, and after the first light snows before Christmas there was no snow at all—and no rain. March was as bitter as February. On those days when the wind fairly punished the country, Rosicky sat by his window. In the fall he and the boys had put in a big wheat planting, and now the seed had frozen in the ground. All that land would have to be ploughed up and planted over again, planted in corn. It had happened before, but he was younger then, and he never worried about what had to be. He was sure of himself and of Mary; he knew they could bear what they had to bear, that they would always pull through somehow. But he was not so sure about the young ones, and he felt troubled because Rudolph and Polly were having such a hard start.

Sitting beside his flowering window while the panes rattled and the wind blew in under the door, Rosicky gave himself to reflection as he had not done since those Sundays in the loft of the furniture factory in New York, long ago. Then he was trying to find what he wanted in life for himself; now he was trying to find what he wanted for his boys, and why it was he so hungered to feel sure they would be here, working this very land, after he was gone.

They would have to work hard on the farm, and probably they would never do much more than make a living. But if he could think of them as staying here on the land, he wouldn't have to fear any great unkindness for them. Hardships, certainly; it was a hardship to have the wheat freeze in the ground when seed was so high; and to have to sell your stock because you had no feed. But there would be other years when everything came along right, and you caught up. And what you had was your own. You didn't have to choose between bosses and strikers, and go wrong either way. You didn't have to do with dishonest and cruel people. They were the only things in his experience he had found terrifying and horrible: the look in the eyes of a dishonest and crafty man, of a scheming and rapacious woman.

In the country, if you had a mean neighbour, you could keep off his land and make him keep off yours. But in the city, all the foulness and misery and brutality of your neighbours was part of your life. The worst things he had come upon in his journey through the world were human,—depraved and poisonous specimens of man. To this day he could recall certain terrible faces in the London streets. There were mean people everywhere, to be sure, even in their own country town here. But they weren't tempered, hardened, sharpened, like the treacherous people in cities who live by grinding or cheating or poisoning their fellow-men. He had helped to bury two of his fellow-workmen in the tailoring trade, and he was distrustful of the organized industries that see one out of the world in big cities. Here, if you were sick, you had Doctor Ed to look after you; and if you died, fat Mr. Haycock, the kindest man in the world, buried you.

It seemed to Rosicky that for good, honest boys like his, the worst they could do on the farm was better than the best they would be likely to do in the city. If he'd had a mean boy, now, one who was crooked and sharp and tried to put anything over on his brothers, then town would be the place for him. But he had no such boy. As for Rudolph, the discontented one, he would give the shirt off his back to anyone who touched his heart. What Rosicky really hoped for his boys was that they could get through the world without ever knowing much about the cruelty of human beings. "Their mother and me ain't prepared them for that," he sometimes said to himself.

These thoughts brought him back to a grateful consideration of his own case. What an escape he had had, to be sure! He, too, in his time, had had to take money for repair work from the hand of a hungry child who let it go so wistfully; because it was money due his boss. And now, in all these years, he had never had to take a cent from anyone in bitter need—never had to look at the face of a woman become like a wolf's from struggle and famine. When he thought of these things, Rosicky would put on his cap and jacket and slip down to the barn and give his work-horses a little extra oats, letting them eat it out of his hand in their slobbery fashion. It was his way of expressing what he felt, and made him chuckle with pleasure.

The spring came warm, with blue skies,—but dry, dry as bone. The boys began ploughing up the wheat-fields to plant them over in corn. Rosicky would stand at the fence corner and watch them, and the earth was so dry it blew up in clouds of brown dust that hid the horses and the sulky plough and the driver. It was a bad outlook.

The big alfalfa-field that lay between the home place and Rudolph's came up green, but Rosicky was worried because during that open windy winter a great many Russian thistle plants had blown in there and lodged. He kept asking the boys to rake them out; he was afraid their seed would root and "take the alfalfa." Rudolph said that was nonsense. The boys were working so hard planting corn, their father felt he couldn't insist about the thistles, but he set great store by that big alfalfa-field. It was a feed you could depend on,—and there was some deeper reason, vague, but strong. The peculiar green of that clover woke early memories in old Rosicky, went back to something in his childhood in the old world. When he was a little boy, he had played in fields of that strong blue-green colour.

One morning, when Rudolph had gone to town in the car, leaving a work-team idle in his barn, Rosicky went over to his son's place, put the horses to the buggy-rake, and set about quietly taking up those thistles. He behaved with guilty caution, and rather enjoyed stealing a march on Doctor Ed, who was just then taking his first vacation in seven years of practice and was attending a clinic in Chicago. Rosicky got the thistles raked up, but did not stop to burn them. That would take some time, and his breath was pretty short, so he thought he had better get the horses back to the barn.

He got them into the barn and to their stalls, but the pain had come on so sharp in his chest that he didn't try to take the harness off. He started for the house, bending lower with every step. The cramp in his chest was shutting him up like a jack-knife. When he reached the windmill, he swayed and caught at the ladder. He saw Polly coming down the hill, running with the swiftness of a slim greyhound. In a flash she had her shoulder under his armpit.

"Lean on me, Father, hard! Don't be afraid. We can get to the house all right."

Somehow they did, though Rosicky became blind with pain; he could keep on his legs, but he couldn't steer his course. The next thing he was conscious of was lying on Polly's bed, and Polly bending over him wringing out bathtowels in hot water and putting them on his chest. She stopped only to throw coal into the stove, and she kept the tea-kettle and the black pot going. She put these hot applications on him for nearly an hour, she told him afterwards, and all that time he was drawn up stiff and blue, with the sweat pouring off him.

As the pain gradually loosed its grip, the stiffness went out of his jaws, the black circles round his eyes disappeared, and a little of his natural colour came back. When his daughter-in-law buttoned his shirt over his chest at last, he sighed.

"Da's fine, de way I feel now, Polly. It was a awful bad spell, an' I was so sorry it all come on you like it did."

Polly was flushed and excited. "Is the pain really gone? Can I leave you long enough to telephone over to your place?"

Rosicky's eyelids fluttered. "Don't telephone, Polly. It ain't no use to scare my wife. It's nice and quiet here, an' if I ain't too much trouble to you, just let me lay still till I feel like myself. I ain't got no pain now. It's nice here."

Polly bent over him and wiped the moisture from his face. "Oh, I'm so glad it's over!" she broke out impulsively. "It just broke my heart to see you suffer so, Father."

Rosicky motioned her to sit down on the chair where the tea-kettle had been, and looked up at her with that lively affectionate gleam in his eyes. "You was awful good to me, I won't never forget dat. I hate it to be sick on you like dis. Down at de barn I say to myself, dat young girl ain't had much experience in sickness, I don't want to scare her, an' maybe she's got a baby comin' or somet'ing."

Polly took his hand. He was looking at her so intently and affectionately and confidingly; his eyes seemed to caress her face, to regard it with pleasure. She frowned with her funny streaks of eyebrows, and then smiled back at him.

"I guess maybe there is something of that kind going to happen. But I haven't told anyone yet, not my mother or Rudolph. You'll be the first to know."

His hand pressed hers. She noticed that it was warm again. The twinkle in his yellow-brown eyes seemed to come nearer.

"I like mighty well to see dat little child, Polly," was all he said. Then he closed his eyes and lay half-smiling. But Polly sat still, thinking hard. She had a sudden feeling that nobody in the world, not her mother, not Rudolph, or anyone, really loved her as much as old Rosicky did. It perplexed her. She sat frowning and trying to puzzle it out. It was as if Rosicky had a special gift for loving people, something that was like an ear for music or an eye for colour. It was quiet, unobtrusive; it was merely there. You saw it in his eyes,—perhaps that was why they were merry. You felt it in his hands, too. After he dropped off to sleep, she sat holding his warm, broad, flexible brown hand. She had never seen another in the least like it. She wondered if it wasn't a kind of gipsy hand, it was so alive and quick and light in its communications,—very strange in a farmer. Nearly all the farmers she knew had huge lumps of fists, like mauls, or they were knotty and bony and uncomfortable-looking, with stiff fingers. But Rosicky's was like quicksilver, flexible, muscular, about the colour of a pale cigar, with deep, deep creases across the palm. It wasn't nervous, it wasn't a stupid lump; it was a warm brown human hand, with some cleverness in it, a great deal of generosity, and something else which Polly could only call "gypsy-like"—something nimble and lively and sure, in the way that animals are.

Polly remembered that hour long afterwards; it had been like an awakening to her. It seemed to her that she had never learned so much about life from anything as from old Rosicky's hand. It brought her to herself; it communicated some direct and untranslatable message.

When she heard Rudolph coming in the car, she ran out to meet him.

"Oh, Rudy, your father's been awful sick! He raked up those thistles he's been worrying about, and afterward he could hardly get to the house. He suffered so I was afraid he was going to die."

Rudolph jumped to the ground. "Where is he now?"

"On the bed. He's asleep. I was terribly scared, because, you know, I'm so fond of your father." She slipped her arm through his and they went into the house. That afternoon they took Rosicky home and put him to bed, though he protested that he was quite well again.

The next morning he got up and dressed and sat down to breakfast with his family. He told Mary that his coffee tasted better than usual to him, and he warned the boys not to bear any tales to Doctor Ed when he got home. After breakfast he sat down by his window to do some patching and asked Mary to thread several needles for him before she went to feed her chickens,—her eyes were better than his, and her hands steadier. He lit his pipe and took up John's overalls. Mary had been watching him anxiously all morning, and as she went out of the door with her bucket of scraps, she saw that he was smiling. He was thinking, indeed, about Polly, and how he might never have known what a tender heart she had if he hadn't got sick over there. Girls nowadays didn't wear their heart on their sleeve. But now he knew Polly would make a fine woman after the foolishness wore off. Either a woman had that sweetness at her heart or she hadn't. You couldn't always tell by the look of them; but if they had that, everything came out right in the end.

After he had taken a few stitches, the cramp began in his chest, like yesterday. He put his pipe cautiously down on the window-sill and bent over to ease the pull. No use,—he had better try to get to his bed if he could. He rose and groped his way across the familiar floor, which was rising and falling like the deck of a ship. At the door he fell. When Mary came in, she found him lying there, and the moment she touched him she knew that he was gone.

Doctor Ed was away when Rosicky died, and for the first few weeks after he got home he was harddriven. Every day he said to himself that he must get out to see that family that had lost their father. One soft, warm moonlight night in early summer he started for the farm. His mind was on other things, and not until his road ran by the graveyard did he realize that Rosicky wasn't over there on the hill where the red lamplight shone, but here, in the moonlight. He stopped his car, shut off the engine, and sat there for a while.

A sudden hush had fallen on his soul. Everything here seemed strangely moving and significant, though signifying what, he did not know. Close by the wire fence stood Rosicky's mowing-machine, where one of the boys had been cutting hay that afternoon; his own work-horses had been going up and down there. The new-cut hay perfumed all the night air. The moonlight silvered the long, billowy grass that grew over the graves and hid the fence; the few little evergreens stood out black in it, like shadows in a pool. The sky was very blue and soft, the stars rather faint because the moon was full.

For the first time it struck Doctor Ed that this was really a beautiful graveyard. He thought of city cemeteries; acres of shrubbery and heavy stone, so arranged and lonely and unlike anything in the living world. Cities of the dead, indeed; cities of the forgotten, of the "put away." But this was open and free, this little square of long grass which the wind for ever stirred. Nothing but the sky overhead, and the many-coloured fields running on until they met that sky. The horses worked here in summer; the neighbours passed on their way to town; and over yonder, in the cornfield, Rosicky's own cattle would be eating fodder as winter came on. Nothing could be more undeathlike than this place; nothing could be more right for a man who had helped to do the work of great cities and had always longed for the open country and had got to it at last. Rosicky's life seemed to him complete and beautiful.

1928, 1932

---

# AMY LOWELL
## 1874–1925

Born in Brookline, Massachusetts, the fifth and last child, twelve years younger than her nearest sibling, Amy Lowell hailed from one of Boston's wealthiest and most prestigious and powerful families. The first Lowell arrived at Massachusetts Bay Colony in 1639; from the revolutionary years on, when a Lowell was made a judge by George Washington, no era was without one or more Lowells prominent in the intellectual, religious, political, philanthropic, and commercial life of New England. In the early nineteenth century her paternal grandfather and his brothers established the Lowell textile mills in Lowell, Massachusetts—the town had been established by the first Lowell immigrant in 1653. The success of these mills changed the economy of New England. Profits were invested in utilities, highways, railroads, and banks. In the same generation her maternal grandfather, Abbot Lawrence, established a second New England textile dynasty. All the Lowell men went to Harvard. Traditionally, those who were not in business turned to the Unitarian church or to scholarship—the poet James Russell Lowell was her great-uncle, her father, Augustus, was important to the founding of the Massachusetts Institute of Technology, her brother Percival was a pioneering scholar of Japanese and Korean civilization and astronomer (he founded the Lowell Observatory and discovered the planet Pluto), her brother Abbot Lawrence was president of Harvard from 1909 to 1933.

In her background, then, were millionaires, manufacturers, philanthropists, statesmen, ambassadors, judges, and scholars—none of whom, however, being men, gave the energetic and unusually intelligent young woman a model that she could easily follow, even though she understood the importance of being a Lowell and shared the self-confidence and drive to contribute notably to public life that characterized the family. As for the Lowell women, their roles were to raise children with a strong sense of family loyalty, to maintain smoothly several understatedly luxurious domestic establishments, and to take a prominent part in the social activities of Boston's upper class. None of this interested Amy Lowell.

She resisted formal education, attending school only between the ages of ten and seventeen; in the main she educated herself through the use of her family's extensive private library as well as the resources of the Boston Athenaeum, a dues-paying library club founded by a Lowell early in the nineteenth century. Attracted to the theater, she was denied even the possibility of a stage career by a weight problem that was glandular in origin. She had also enjoyed writing since childhood, yet did little to further a public literary career until she was well into her thirties. When, in 1912, at the age of thirty-eight, she finally brought out a book of poems—*A Dome of Many-Coloured Glass*—her work was critically well received and immediately popular.

The year 1912 was the year that Harriet Monroe launched her influential little magazine, *Poetry*, and when in January 1913 Lowell read H. D.'s imagistic poetry she was converted to this new style of poetic writing. She decided to put her popularity and social prominence to the service of imagism, and with characteristic energy and self-confidence journeyed to England to meet H. D., Ezra Pound, D. H. Lawrence, Richard Aldington, and other participants in the informal movement. When Pound abandoned imagism for vorticism, Lowell became the chief spokesperson for the movement, editing several imagist anthologies. Two volumes of original criticism by Lowell—*Six French Poets* (1915) and *Tendencies in Modern American Poetry* (1917)—also forwarded the cause. Pound, upstaged as a publicist, enviously renamed the movement "Amygism." Lowell retorted that "it was not until I entered the arena and Ezra dropped out that Imagism had to be considered seriously."

Lowell's own poetry—published in *Sword Blades and Poppy Seed* (1914), *Men, Women, and Ghosts* (1916), *Can Grande's Castle* (1918), *Pictures of the Floating World* (1919), and *Legends* (1921)—was never exclusively imagistic but included long historical narrative poems and journalistic prose poems and utilized standard verse patterns, blank verse, and a Whitmanesque free verse resembling the open line developed by Carl Sandburg. Her best poems tend to enclose sharp imagistic representation within this relatively fluid line, thereby achieving an effect of simultaneous compactness and flexibility. Like many women poets, she worked with a symbolic vocabulary of flowers and color.

Lowell enjoyed her success and cheerfully went on the lecture circuit as a celebrity, making innumerable close friendships as a result of her warmth and generosity. Despite a variety of health problems that plagued her for most of her life, she remained full of energy and zest. She depended for support on the companionship of Ada Dwyer Russell, a former actress, for whom she wrote many of her most moving appreciations of female beauty. Although she traveled widely in Europe, she was ultimately committed to New England and the Lowell heritage, both of which fused in an attachment to her home, Sevenels, in Brookline. A devotee of Romantic poetry and especially of Keats, she had begun to collect Keats manuscripts in 1905; these now form the basis of the great collection at Harvard University. In addition to all her other activities in the 1920s, she worked on a two-volume biography of Keats that greatly extended the published information

about the poet when it appeared in 1925, although its psychological approach
outraged many traditional critics.

Lowell was just fifty-one when she died. Despite continued sniping from the
high modernist poets who thought her work was too accessible, her poetry continued to be both popular and critically esteemed until the 1950s, when scholars
focused the canon on a very small number of writers. The efforts of feminists to
rediscover and republicize the work of neglected women authors as well as the
researches of literary historians into the whole picture of American literary achievement have together brought her work back into the spotlight that it occupied during
her lifetime

## Madonna of the Evening Flowers

All day long I have been working,
Now I am tired.
I call: "Where are you?"
But there is only the oak tree rustling in the wind.
The house is very quiet,                                                    5
The sun shines in on your books,
On your scissors and thimble just put down,
But you are not there.
Suddenly I am lonely:
Where are you?                                                              10
I go about searching.

Then I see you,
Standing under a spire of pale blue larkspur,
With a basket of roses on your arm.
You are cool, like silver,                                                  15
And you smile.
I think the Canterbury bells[1] are playing little tunes.

You tell me that the peonies need spraying,
That the columbines have overrun all bounds,
That the pyrus japonica should be cut back and rounded.                      20
You tell me these things.
But I look at you, heart of silver,
White heart-flame of polished silver,
Burning beneath the blue steeples of the larkspur,
And I long to kneel instantly at your feet,                                  25
While all about us peal the loud, sweet *Te Deums* of the
    Canterbury bells.

                                                                        1919

## The Weather-Cock Points South

I put your leaves aside,
One by one:

---

1. Little bell-shaped blue flowers; Lowell puns on the bells of Canterbury Cathedral in England pealing out
religious music.

The stiff, broad outer leaves;
The smaller ones,
Pleasant to touch, veined with purple;                    5
The glazed inner leaves.
One by one
I parted you from your leaves,
Until you stood up like a white flower
Swaying slightly in the evening wind.                    10

White flower,
Flower of wax, of jade, of unstreaked agate;
Flower with surfaces of ice,
With shadows faintly crimson.
Where in all the garden is there such a flower?          15
The stars crowd through the lilac leaves
To look at you.
The low moon brightens you with silver.

The bud is more than the calyx.
There is nothing to equal a white bud,                   20
Of no colour, and of all,
Burnished by moonlight,
Thrust upon by a softly-swinging wind.

                                              1919


## Penumbra

As I sit here in the quiet Summer night,
Suddenly, from the distant road, there comes
The grind and rush of an electric car.
And, from still farther off,
An engine puffs sharply,                                  5
Followed by the drawn-out shunting scrape of a freight train.
These are the sounds that men make
In the long business of living.
They will always make such sounds,
Years after I am dead and cannot hear them.              10

Sitting here in the Summer night,
I think of my death.
What will it be like for you then?
You will see my chair
With its bright chintz covering                          15
Standing in the afternoon sunshine,
As now.
You will see my narrow table
At which I have written so many hours.
My dogs will push their noses into your hand,            20
And ask—ask—
Clinging to you with puzzled eyes.

The old house will still be here,
The old house which has known me since the beginning.
The walls which have watched me while I played:                    25
Soldiers, marbles, paper-dolls,
Which have protected me and my books.
The front-door will gaze down among the old trees
Where, as a child, I hunted ghosts and Indians;
It will look out on the wide gravel sweep                    30
Where I rolled my hoop,
And at the rhododendron bushes
Where I caught black-spotted butterflies.

The old house will guard you,
As I have done.                    35
Its walls and rooms will hold you,
And I shall whisper my thoughts and fancies
As always,
From the pages of my books.

You will sit here, some quiet Summer night,                    40
Listening to the puffing trains,
But you will not be lonely,
For these things are a part of me.
And my love will go on speaking to you
Through the chairs, and the tables, and the pictures,                    45
As it does now through my voice,
And the quick, necessary touch of my hand.

                                                      1919


## In the Stadium

Marshall Joffre Reviewing The
Harvard Regiment, May 12, 1917[1]

A little old man
Huddled up in a corner of a carriage,
Rapidly driven in front of throngs of people
With his hand held to a perpetual salute.
The people cheer,                    5
But he has heard so much cheering.
On his breast is a row of decorations.
He feels his body recoil before attacks of pain.

They are all like this:
Napoleon,                    10
Hannibal,

---

1. Joseph Jacques Césaire Joffre (1852–1931), marshal of France, was appointed commander in chief in 1911; he oversaw the fighting in France during World War I. The Harvard Regiment, made up of students from the university, was departing to join the troops in France fighting against Germany.

Great Caesar[2] even,
But that he died out of time.
Sick old men,
Driving rapidly before a concourse of people,     15
Gay with decorations,
Crumpled with pain.

The drum-major lifts his silver-headed stick,
And the silver trumpets and tubas,
The great round drums,     20
Each with an H on them,
Crash out martial music.
Heavily rhythmed march music
For the stepping of a regiment.

Slant lines of rifles,     25
A twinkle of stepping,
The regiment comes.
The young regiment,
Boys in khaki
With slanted rifles.     30
The young bodies of boys
Bulwarked in front of us.
The white bodies of young men
Heaped like sandbags
Against the German guns.     35

This is war:
Boys flung into a breach
Like shoveled earth;
And old men,
Broken,     40
Driving rapidly before crowds of people
In a glitter of silly decorations.

Behind the boys
And the old men,
Life weeps,     45
And shreds her garments
To the blowing winds.

                 1919

# September, 1918

This afternoon was the colour of water falling through sunlight;
The trees glittered with the tumbling of leaves;
The sidewalks shone like alleys of dropped maple leaves;

---

2. Three famous generals. Napoleon Bonaparte (1769–1821), made emperor of France in 1804. Hannibal (247 B.C.–182? B.C.), Carthaginian who success-fully battled the legions of the Roman empire. Julius Caesar (102? B.C.–44 B.C.), assassinated head of the Roman republic.

And the houses ran along them laughing out of square, open windows.
Under a tree in the park,                                                    5
Two little boys, lying flat on their faces,
Were carefully gathering red berries
To put in a pasteboard box.

Some day there will be no war.
Then I shall take out this afternoon                                         10
And turn it in my fingers,
And remark the sweet taste of it upon my palate,
And note the crisp variety of its flights of leaves.
To-day I can only gather it
And put it into my lunch-box,                                                15
For I have time for nothing
But the endeavour to balance myself
Upon a broken world.

                                                                    1919

## St. Louis

### *June*

Flat,
Flat,
Long as sight
Either way,
An immense country,                                                         5
With a great river
Steaming it full of moist, unbearable heat.
The orchards are little quincunxes of Noah's Ark trees,
The plows and horses are children's toys tracing amusingly shallow lines
    upon an illimitable surface.
Great chunks of life to match the country,                                  10
Great lungs to breathe this hot, wet air.

But it is not mine.
Mine is a land of hills
Lying couchant in the angles of heraldic beasts
About white villages.                                                       15
A land of singing elms and pine-trees.
A restless up and down land
Always mounting, dipping, slipping into a different contour,
Where the roads turn every hundred yards or so,
Where brooks rattle forgotten Indian names to tired farm-houses,            20
And faint spires of old meeting-houses
Flaunt their golden weather-cocks in a brave show of challenge at a sunset sky.

Here the heat stuffs down with the thickness of boiled feathers,
The river runs in steam.
There, lilacs are in bloom,                                                  25

Cool blue-purples, wine-reds, whites,
Flying colour to quiet dooryards.
Grown year on year to a suddenness of old perfection,
Saying "Before! Before!" to each new Spring.
Here is "Now,"                                                              30
But "Before" is mine with the lilacs,
With the white sea of everywhither,
With the heraldic, story-telling hills.

                                                                    1927

---

# ROBERT FROST
## 1874–1963

Robert Frost was forty before his poetry "caught on" with the American public, but from 1914 to his death, he was probably the nation's best-known and best-loved serious poet. It was a sign of his unique position in American letters that president-elect John F. Kennedy invited him to read a poem—*The Gift Outright*—at the inauguration in 1961.

Although he identified himself with New England, Frost was actually born in California and lived there in early childhood. His father died when Frost was eleven; the family then moved to New England where his mother supported them by teaching school. He graduated from high school in 1891 in Lawrence, Massachusetts, sharing the post of valedictorian with Elinor White, whom he married three years later. Occasional attendance at Dartmouth College and Harvard, and a variety of different jobs including an attempt to run a farm in Derry, New Hampshire, marked the next twenty years. His family was augmented by the births of four children and hard pressed by poverty. He made a new start in 1912, taking his family to England, where he worked on his poetry and found a publisher for his first book, *A Boy's Will* (1913). Ezra Pound reviewed it favorably, excited (as he put it in a letter) by this "VURRY Amur'k'n talent." He recommended Frost's poems to American editors and helped get his second book, *North of Boston*, published in 1914.

*North of Boston* was widely praised by critics in America and England when it appeared; the favorable reception persuaded Frost to return home. He bought another farm in New Hampshire and attained financial stability through sales of his books and papers, along with teaching and lecturing at various colleges. The success he enjoyed for the rest of his life, however, came too late to cancel the bitterness left by his earlier struggles. Moreover, he endured personal tragedy: a son committed suicide, and a daughter had a complete mental collapse. To the end of his life friends and acquaintances would express surprise at the gap between the calm, wise, cordial speaker in Frost's poetry and the man himself.

The clarity of Frost's diction, the colloquial rhythms, the simplicity of his images, and above all the folksy speaker—these are intended to make the poems look natural, unplanned. In the context of the modernist movement, however, they can be seen as a thoughtful reply to modernism's fondness for obscurity and difficulty. Although Frost's ruralism affirmed the modernist distaste for cities, he was writing the kind of traditional poetry that modernists thought could no longer be written. In addition, by investing in the New England terrain, he rejected modernist internationalism and revitalized the tradition of New England regionalism. Readers who accepted Frost's persona and his setting as typically American accepted the powerful myth that rural New England was the heart of America. Because Frost was originally from California—where there are no snowfields and trees do not shed their leaves in autumn—he was evidently choosing to align himself with, and so to affirm, that myth.

Frost achieved an internal dynamic in his poems by playing the rhythms of ordinary speech against formal patterns of line and verse and containing them within traditional forms. To Frost traditional forms were the essence of poetry, material with which poets responded to flux and disorder (what, adopting scientific terminology, he called "decay") by forging something permanent. Poetry, he wrote, was "one step backward taken," resisting time—a "momentary stay against confusion."

Throughout the 1920s Frost's poetic practice changed very little; later books—including *Mountain Interval* (1916), *New Hampshire* (1923), and *West-Running Brook* (1928)—affirmed the essential impression he had established in *North of Boston*. Most of his poems fall into a few types. Nature lyrics describing and commenting on a scene or event—like *Stopping by Woods on a Snowy Evening*, *Birches*, and *After Apple-Picking*,—are probably the best known and the most popular. There are also dramatic narrative poems about the lives of country people, like *The Death of the Hired Man*, and poems of commentary or generalization, like *The Gift Outright*; he could also be humorous or sardonic, as in *Fire and Ice*. In the nature lyrics, a comparison often emerges between the outer scene and the psyche, a comparison of what Frost in one poem called "outer and inner weather."

Because he worked so much with nature, and because he presented himself as a New Englander, Frost is often interpreted as an ideological descendant of the nineteenth-century American Transcendentalists. But he is far less affirmative about the universe than they; for where they, looking at nature, discerned a benign creator, he saw "no expression, nothing to express." Frost did share with Emerson and Thoreau, however, the belief that everybody was a separate individuality and that collective enterprises could do nothing but weaken the self. Politically conservative, therefore, he avoided movements of the left and the right precisely because they were movements, group undertakings. In the 1930s when writers tended to be political activists, he was seen as one whose old-fashioned values were inappropriate, even dangerous, in modern times. Frost deeply resented this criticism, and responded to it with a newly hortatory, didactic kind of poetry. In the last twenty years of his life, Frost made a second reputation as a teacher and lecturer—at Amherst, at Dartmouth, at Harvard, at the Bread Loaf School of English at Middlebury College in Vermont, and in poetry readings and talks around the country.

The text of the poems included here is that of *The Poetry of Robert Frost* (1969).


## The Pasture

I'm going out to clean the pasture spring;
I'll only stop to rake the leaves away
(And wait to watch the water clear, I may):
I shan't be gone long.—You come too.

I'm going out to fetch the little calf                                    5
That's standing by the mother. It's so young
It totters when she licks it with her tongue.
I shan't be gone long.—You come too.

1913

# Mowing

There was never a sound beside the wood but one,
And that was my long scythe whispering to the ground.
What was it it whispered? I knew not well myself;
Perhaps it was something about the heat of the sun,
Something, perhaps, about the lack of sound—                        5
And that was why it whispered and did not speak.
It was no dream of the gift of idle hours,
Or easy gold at the hand of fay or elf:
Anything more than the truth would have seemed too weak
To the earnest love that laid the swale[1] in rows,              10
Not without feeble-pointed spikes of flowers
(Pale orchises), and scared a bright green snake.
The fact is the sweetest dream that labor knows.
My long scythe whispered and left the hay to make.

1913

# Mending Wall

Something there is that doesn't love a wall,
That sends the frozen-ground-swell under it,
And spills the upper boulders in the sun,
And makes gaps even two can pass abreast.
The work of hunters is another thing:                               5
I have come after them and made repair
Where they have left not one stone on a stone,
But they would have the rabbit out of hiding,
To please the yelping dogs. The gaps I mean,
No one has seen them made or heard them made,                      10
But at spring mending-time we find them there.
I let my neighbor know beyond the hill;
And on a day we meet to walk the line
And set the wall between us once again.
We keep the wall between us as we go.                               15
To each the boulders that have fallen to each.
And some are loaves and some so nearly balls
We have to use a spell to make them balance:
"Stay where you are until our backs are turned!"
We wear our fingers rough with handling them.                      20
Oh, just another kind of outdoor game,
One on a side. It comes to little more:
There where it is we do not need the wall:
He is all pine and I am apple orchard.
My apple trees will never get across                               25
And eat the cones under his pines, I tell him.
He only says, "Good fences make good neighbors."
Spring is the mischief in me, and I wonder
If I could put a notion in his head:

1. Grasses in a marshy meadow.

"*Why* do they make good neighbors? Isn't it          30
Where there are cows? But here there are no cows.
Before I built a wall I'd ask to know
What I was walling in or walling out,
And to whom I was like to give offense.
Something there is that doesn't love a wall,          35
That wants it down." I could say "Elves" to him,
But it's not elves exactly, and I'd rather
He said it for himself. I see him there
Bringing a stone grasped firmly by the top
In each hand, like an old-stone savage armed.         40
He moves in darkness as it seems to me,
Not of woods only and the shade of trees.
He will not go behind his father's saying,
And he likes having thought of it so well
He says again, "Good fences make good neighbors."     45

                                            1914


# The Death of the Hired Man

Mary sat musing on the lamp-flame at the table
Waiting for Warren. When she heard his step,
She ran on tip-toe down the darkened passage
To meet him in the doorway with the news
And put him on his guard. "Silas is back."            5
She pushed him outward with her through the door
And shut it after her. "Be kind," she said.
She took the market things from Warren's arms
And set them on the porch, then drew him down
To sit beside her on the wooden steps.                10

"When was I ever anything but kind to him?
But I'll not have the fellow back," he said.
"I told him so last haying, didn't I?
If he left then, I said, that ended it.
What good is he? Who else will harbor him             15
At his age for the little he can do?
What help he is there's no depending on.
Off he goes always when I need him most.
He thinks he ought to earn a little pay,
Enough at least to buy tobacco with,                  20
So he won't have to beg and be beholden.
'All right,' I say, 'I can't afford to pay
Any fixed wages, though I wish I could.'
'Someone else can.' 'Then someone else will have to.'
I shouldn't mind his bettering himself                25
If that was what it was. You can be certain,
When he begins like that, there's someone at him
Trying to coax him off with pocket-money,—
In haying time, when any help is scarce.
In winter he comes back to us. I'm done."             30

"Sh! not so loud: he'll hear you," Mary said.

"I want him to: he'll have to soon or late."

"He's worn out. He's asleep beside the stove.
When I came up from Rowe's I found him here,
Huddled against the barn-door fast asleep,               35
A miserable sight, and frightening, too—
You needn't smile—I didn't recognize him—
I wasn't looking for him—and he's changed.
Wait till you see."

                "Where did you say he'd been?"      40

"He didn't say. I dragged him to the house,
And gave him tea and tried to make him smoke.
I tried to make him talk about his travels.
Nothing would do: he just kept nodding off."

"What did he say? Did he say anything?"      45

"But little."

          "Anything? Mary, confess
He said he'd come to ditch the meadow for me."

"Warren!"

          "But did he? I just want to know."      50

"Of course he did. What would you have him say?
Surely you wouldn't grudge the poor old man
Some humble way to save his self-respect.
He added, if you really care to know,
He meant to clear the upper pasture, too.      55
That sounds like something you have heard before?
Warren, I wish you could have heard the way
He jumbled everything. I stopped to look
Two or three times—he made me feel so queer—
To see if he was talking in his sleep.      60
He ran on Harold Wilson—you remember—
The boy you had in haying four years since.
He's finished school, and teaching in his college.
Silas declares you'll have to get him back.
He says they two will make a team for work:      65
Between them they will lay this farm as smooth!
The way he mixed that in with other things.
He thinks young Wilson a likely lad, though daft
On education—you know how they fought
All through July under the blazing sun,      70
Silas up on the cart to build the load,
Harold along beside to pitch it on."

"Yes, I took care to keep well out of earshot."

"Well, those days trouble Silas like a dream.
You wouldn't think they would. How some things linger!          75
Harold's young college-boy's assurance piqued him.
After so many years he still keeps finding
Good arguments he sees he might have used.
I sympathize. I know just how it feels
To think of the right thing to say too late.          80
Harold's associated in his mind with Latin.
He asked me what I thought of Harold's saying
He studied Latin, like the violin,
Because he liked it—that an argument!
He said he couldn't make the boy believe          85
He could find water with a hazel prong—
Which showed how much good school had ever done him.
He wanted to go over that. But most of all
He thinks if he could have another chance
To teach him how to build a load of hay—"          90

"I know, that's Silas' one accomplishment.
He bundles every forkful in its place,
And tags and numbers it for future reference,
So he can find and easily dislodge it
In the unloading. Silas does that well.          95
He takes it out in bunches like big birds' nests.
You never see him standing on the hay
He's trying to lift, straining to lift himself."

"He thinks if he could teach him that, he'd be
Some good perhaps to someone in the world.          100
He hates to see a boy the fool of books.
Poor Silas, so concerned for other folk,
And nothing to look backward to with pride,
And nothing to look forward to with hope,
So now and never any different."          105

Part of a moon was falling down the west,
Dragging the whole sky with it to the hills.
Its light poured softly in her lap. She saw it
And spread her apron to it. She put out her hand
Among the harplike morning-glory strings,          110
Taut with the dew from garden bed to eaves,
As if she played unheard some tenderness
That wrought on him beside her in the night.
"Warren," she said, "he has come home to die:
You needn't be afraid he'll leave you this time."          115

"Home," he mocked gently.

                              "Yes, what else but home?
It all depends on what you mean by home.
Of course he's nothing to us, any more
Than was the hound that came a stranger to us          120
Out of the woods, worn out upon the trail."

"Home is the place where, when you have to go there,
They have to take you in."

                              "I should have called it
Something you somehow haven't to deserve."                    125

Warren leaned out and took a step or two,
Picked up a little stick, and brought it back
And broke it in his hand and tossed it by.
"Silas has better claim on us you think
Than on his brother? Thirteen little miles                    130
As the road winds would bring him to his door.
Silas has walked that far no doubt today.
Why doesn't he go there? His brother's rich,
A somebody—director in the bank."

"He never told us that."                                      135

                    "We know it though."

"I think his brother ought to help, of course.
I'll see to that if there is need. He ought of right
To take him in, and might be willing to—
He may be better than appearances.                            140
But have some pity on Silas. Do you think
If he had any pride in claiming kin
Or anything he looked for from his brother,
He'd keep so still about him all this time?"

"I wonder what's between them."                               145

                              "I can tell you.
Silas is what he is—we wouldn't mind him—
But just the kind that kinsfolk can't abide.
He never did a thing so very bad.
He don't know why he isn't quite as good                      150
As anybody. Worthless though he is,
He won't be made ashamed to please his brother."

"I can't think Si ever hurt anyone."

"No, but he hurt my heart the way he lay
And rolled his old head on that sharp-edged chair-back.       155
He wouldn't let me put him on the lounge.
You must go in and see what you can do.
I made the bed up for him there tonight.
You'll be surprised at him—how much he's broken.
His working days are done; I'm sure of it."                   160

"I'd not be in a hurry to say that."

"I haven't been. Go, look, see for yourself.
But, Warren, please remember how it is:

He's come to help you ditch the meadow.
He has a plan. You mustn't laugh at him.                165
He may not speak of it, and then he may.
I'll sit and see if that small sailing cloud
Will hit or miss the moon."

                    It hit the moon.
Then there were three there, making a dim row,          170
The moon, the little silver cloud, and she.

Warren returned—too soon, it seemed to her,
Slipped to her side, caught up her hand and waited.

"Warren?" she questioned.

                    "Dead," was all he answered.       175

                                            1914


## After Apple-Picking

My long two-pointed ladder's sticking through a tree
Toward heaven still,
And there's a barrel that I didn't fill
Beside it, and there may be two or three
Apples I didn't pick upon some bough.                   5
But I am done with apple-picking now.
Essence of winter sleep is on the night,
The scent of apples: I am drowsing off.
I cannot rub the strangeness from my sight
I got from looking through a pane of glass              10
I skimmed this morning from the drinking trough
And held against the world of hoary grass.
It melted, and I let it fall and break.
But I was well
Upon my way to sleep before it fell,                    15
And I could tell
What form my dreaming was about to take.
Magnified apples appear and disappear,
Stem end and blossom end,
And every fleck of russet showing clear.                20
My instep arch not only keeps the ache,
It keeps the pressure of a ladder-round.
I feel the ladder sway as the boughs bend.
And I keep hearing from the cellar bin
The rumbling sound                                      25
Of load on load of apples coming in.
For I have had too much
Of apple-picking: I am overtired
Of the great harvest I myself desired.
There were ten thousand thousand fruit to touch,        30
Cherish in hand, lift down, and not let fall.

For all
That struck the earth,
No matter if not bruised or spiked with stubble,
Went surely to the cider-apple heap                              35
As of no worth.
One can see what will trouble
This sleep of mine, whatever sleep it is.
Were he not gone,
The woodchuck could say whether it's like his               40
Long sleep, as I describe its coming on,
Or just some human sleep.

                                                             1914


## The Wood-Pile

Out walking in the frozen swamp one gray day,
I paused and said, "I will turn back from here.
No, I will go on farther—and we shall see."
The hard snow held me, save where now and then
One foot went through. The view was all in lines              5
Straight up and down of tall slim trees
Too much alike to mark or name a place by
So as to say for certain I was here
Or somewhere else: I was just far from home.
A small bird flew before me. He was careful                  10
To put a tree between us when he lighted,
And say no word to tell me who he was
Who was so foolish as to think what *he* thought.
He thought that I was after him for a feather—
The white one in his tail; like one who takes                15
Everything said as personal to himself.
One flight out sideways would have undeceived him.
And then there was a pile of wood for which
I forgot him and let his little fear
Carry him off the way I might have gone,                     20
Without so much as wishing him good-night.
He went behind it to make his last stand.
It was a cord of maple, cut and split
And piled—and measured, four by four by eight.
And not another like it could I see.                         25
No runner tracks in this year's snow looped near it.
And it was older sure than this year's cutting,
Or even last year's or the year's before.
The wood was gray and the bark warping off it
And the pile somewhat sunken. Clematis                       30
Had wound strings round and round it like a bundle.
What held it, though, on one side was a tree
Still growing, and on one a stake and prop,
These latter about to fall. I thought that only
Someone who lived in turning to fresh tasks                  35

Could so forget his handiwork on which
He spent himself, the labor of his ax,
And leave it there far from a useful fireplace
To warm the frozen swamp as best it could
With the slow smokeless burning of decay.     40

1914

## The Road Not Taken

Two roads diverged in a yellow wood,
And sorry I could not travel both
And be one traveler, long I stood
And looked down one as far as I could
To where it bent in the undergrowth;     5

Then took the other, as just as fair,
And having perhaps the better claim,
Because it was grassy and wanted wear;
Though as for that, the passing there
Had worn them really about the same,     10

And both that morning equally lay
In leaves no step had trodden black.
Oh, I kept the first for another day!
Yet knowing how way leads on to way,
I doubted if I should ever come back.     15

I shall be telling this with a sigh
Somewhere ages and ages hence:
Two roads diverged in a wood, and I—
I took the one less traveled by,
And that has made all the difference.     20

1916

## An Old Man's Winter Night

All out-of-doors looked darkly in at him
Through the thin frost, almost in separate stars,
That gathers on the pane in empty rooms.
What kept his eyes from giving back the gaze
Was the lamp tilted near them in his hand.     5
What kept him from remembering what it was
That brought him to that creaking room was age.
He stood with barrels round him—at a loss.
And having scared the cellar under him
In clomping here, he scared it once again     10
In clomping off—and scared the outer night,
Which has its sounds, familiar, like the roar

Of trees and crack of branches, common things,
But nothing so like beating on a box.
A light he was to no one but himself                                    15
Where now he sat, concerned with he knew what,
A quiet light, and then not even that.
He consigned to the moon—such as she was,
So late-arising—to the broken moon,
As better than the sun in any case                                     20
For such a charge, his snow upon the roof,
His icicles along the wall to keep;
And slept. The log that shifted with a jolt
Once in the stove, disturbed him and he shifted,
And eased his heavy breathing, but still slept.                        25
One aged man—one man—can't keep a house,
A farm, a countryside, or if he can,
It's thus he does it of a winter night.

1916

## The Oven Bird

There is a singer everyone has heard,
Loud, a mid-summer and a mid-wood bird,
Who makes the solid tree trunks sound again.
He says that leaves are old and that for flowers
Mid-summer is to spring as one to ten.                                  5
He says the early petal-fall is past,
When pear and cherry bloom went down in showers
On sunny days a moment overcast;
And comes that other fall we name the fall.
He says the highway dust is over all.                                  10
The bird would cease and be as other birds
But that he knows in singing not to sing.
The question that he frames in all but words
Is what to make of a diminished thing.

1916

## Birches

When I see birches bend to left and right
Across the lines of straighter darker trees,
I like to think some boy's been swinging them.
But swinging doesn't bend them down to stay
As ice storms do. Often you must have seen them                         5
Loaded with ice a sunny winter morning
After a rain. They click upon themselves
As the breeze rises, and turn many-colored
As the stir cracks and crazes their enamel.
Soon the sun's warmth makes them shed crystal shells                   10

Shattering and avalanching on the snow crust—
Such heaps of broken glass to sweep away
You'd think the inner dome of heaven had fallen.
They are dragged to the withered bracken by the load,
And they seem not to break; though once they are bowed      15
So low for long, they never right themselves:
You may see their trunks arching in the woods
Years afterwards, trailing their leaves on the ground
Like girls on hands and knees that throw their hair
Before them over their heads to dry in the sun.              20
But I was going to say when Truth broke in
With all her matter of fact about the ice storm,
I should prefer to have some boy bend them
As he went out and in to fetch the cows—
Some boy too far from town to learn baseball,               25
Whose only play was what he found himself,
Summer or winter, and could play alone.
One by one he subdued his father's trees
By riding them down over and over again
Until he took the stiffness out of them,                     30
And not one but hung limp, not one was left
For him to conquer. He learned all there was
To learn about not launching out too soon
And so not carrying the tree away
Clear to the ground. He always kept his poise               35
To the top branches, climbing carefully
With the same pains you use to fill a cup
Up to the brim, and even above the brim.
Then he flung outward, feet first, with a swish,
Kicking his way down through the air to the ground.          40
So was I once myself a swinger of birches.
And so I dream of going back to be.
It's when I'm weary of considerations,
And life is too much like a pathless wood
Where your face burns and tickles with the cobwebs          45
Broken across it, and one eye is weeping
From a twig's having lashed across it open.
I'd like to get away from earth awhile
And then come back to it and begin over.
May no fate willfully misunderstand me                      50
And half grant what I wish and snatch me away
Not to return. Earth's the right place for love:
I don't know where it's likely to go better.
I'd like to go by climbing a birch tree,
And climb black branches up a snow-white trunk              55
*Toward* heaven, till the tree could bear no more,
But dipped its top and set me down again.
That would be good both going and coming back.
One could do worse than be a swinger of birches.

1916

## "Out, Out—"[1]

The buzz saw snarled and rattled in the yard
And made dust and dropped stove-length sticks of wood,
Sweet-scented stuff when the breeze drew across it.
And from there those that lifted eyes could count
Five mountain ranges one behind the other     5
Under the sunset far into Vermont.
And the saw snarled and rattled, snarled and rattled,
As it ran light, or had to bear a load.
And nothing happened: day was all but done.
Call it a day, I wish they might have said     10
To please the boy by giving him the half hour
That a boy counts so much when saved from work.
His sister stood beside them in her apron
To tell them "Supper." At the word, the saw,
As if to prove saws knew what supper meant,     15
Leaped out at the boy's hand, or seemed to leap—
He must have given the hand. However it was,
Neither refused the meeting. But the hand!
The boy's first outcry was a rueful laugh,
As he swung toward them holding up the hand,     20
Half in appeal, but half as if to keep
The life from spilling. Then the boy saw all—
Since he was old enough to know, big boy
Doing a man's work, though a child at heart—
He saw all spoiled. "Don't let him cut my hand off—     25
The doctor, when he comes. Don't let him, sister!"
So. But the hand was gone already.
The doctor put him in the dark of ether.
He lay and puffed his lips out with his breath.
And then—the watcher at his pulse took fright.     30
No one believed. They listened at his heart.
Little—less—nothing!—and that ended it.
No more to build on there. And they, since they
Were not the one dead, turned to their affairs.

1916

## Fire and Ice

Some say the world will end in fire,
Some say in ice.
From what I've tasted of desire
I hold with those who favor fire.
But if it had to perish twice,     5
I think I know enough of hate
To say that for destruction ice

---

1. A quotation from Shakespeare's *Macbeth* (5.5.23–24): "Out, out, brief candle! / Life's but a walking shadow."

Is also great
And would suffice.

1923

## Nothing Gold Can Stay

Nature's first green is gold,
Her hardest hue to hold.
Her early leaf's a flower;
But only so an hour.
Then leaf subsides to leaf.                              5
So Eden sank to grief,
So dawn goes down to day.
Nothing gold can stay.

1923

## Stopping by Woods on a Snowy Evening

Whose woods these are I think I know.
His house is in the village, though;
He will not see me stopping here
To watch his woods fill up with snow.

My little horse must think it queer                     5
To stop without a farmhouse near
Between the woods and frozen lake
The darkest evening of the year.

He gives his harness bells a shake
To ask if there is some mistake.                        10
The only other sound's the sweep
Of easy wind and downy flake.

The woods are lovely, dark, and deep,
But I have promises to keep,
And miles to go before I sleep.                         15
And miles to go before I sleep.

1923

## Once by the Pacific

The shattered water made a misty din.
Great waves looked over others coming in,
And thought of doing something to the shore
That water never did to land before.
The clouds were low and hairy in the skies,             5

Like locks blown forward in the gleam of eyes.
You could not tell, and yet it looked as if
The shore was lucky in being backed by cliff,
The cliff in being backed by continent;
It looked as if a night of dark intent      10
Was coming, and not only a night, an age.
Someone had better be prepared for rage.
There would be more than ocean-water broken
Before God's last *Put out the Light* was spoken.[1]

1928

## Departmental

An ant on the tablecloth
Ran into a dormant moth
Of many times his size.
He showed not the least surprise.
His business wasn't with such.      5
He gave it scarcely a touch,
And was off on his duty run.
Yet if he encountered one
Of the hive's enquiry squad
Whose work is to find out God      10
And the nature of time and space,
He would put him onto the case.
Ants are a curious race;
One crossing with hurried tread
The body of one of their dead      15
Isn't given a moment's arrest—
Seems not even impressed.
But he no doubt reports to any
With whom he crosses antennae,
And they no doubt report      20
To the higher-up at court.
Then word goes forth in Formic:[1]
"Death's come to Jerry McCormic,
Our selfless forager Jerry.
Will the special Janizary[2]      25
Whose office it is to bury
The dead of the commissary
Go bring him home to his people.
Lay him in state on a sepal.
Wrap him for shroud in a petal.      30
Embalm him with ichor of nettle.
This is the word of your Queen."
And presently on the scene
Appears a solemn mortician;

---

1. Ironic reversal of God's creation of the world in
Genesis 1.3: "And God said, Let there be light."

1. Acid emitted by ants.
2. Troop of Turkish infantry soldiers.

And taking formal position                                35
With feelers calmly atwiddle,
Seizes the dead by the middle,
And heaving him high in air,
Carries him out of there.
No one stands round to stare.                              40
It is nobody else's affair.

It couldn't be called ungentle.
But how thoroughly departmental.

1936

## Desert Places

Snow falling and night falling fast, oh, fast
In a field I looked into going past,
And the ground almost covered smooth in snow,
But a few weeds and stubble showing last.

The woods around it have it—it is theirs.                  5
All animals are smothered in their lairs.
I am too absent-spirited to count;
The loneliness includes me unawares.

And lonely as it is, that loneliness
Will be more lonely ere it will be less—                   10
A blanker whiteness of benighted snow
With no expression, nothing to express.

They cannot scare me with their empty spaces
Between stars—on stars where no human race is.
I have it in me so much nearer home                        15
To scare myself with my own desert places.

1936

## Design

I found a dimpled spider, fat and white,
On a white heal-all,[1] holding up a moth
Like a white piece of rigid satin cloth—
Assorted characters of death and blight
Mixed ready to begin the morning right,                    5
Like the ingredients of a witches' broth—
A snow-drop spider, a flower like a froth,
And dead wings carried like a paper kite.

1. An albino version of the common field flower *Prunella vulgaris*, whose hooded blossom is normally violet
or blue.

What had that flower to do with being white,
The wayside blue and innocent heal-all?                    10
What brought the kindred spider to that height,
Then steered the white moth thither in the night?
What but design of darkness to appall?—
If design govern in a thing so small.

                                                    1922, 1936


## Neither out Far nor in Deep

The people along the sand
All turn and look one way.
They turn their back on the land.
They look at the sea all day.

As long as it takes to pass                                5
A ship keeps raising its hull;
The wetter ground like glass
Reflects a standing gull.

The land may vary more;
But wherever the truth may be—                            10
The water comes ashore,
And the people look at the sea.

They cannot look out far.
They cannot look in deep.
But when was that ever a bar                               15
To any watch they keep?

                                                    1936


## Provide, Provide

The witch that came (the withered hag)
To wash the steps with pail and rag
Was once the beauty Abishag,[1]

The picture pride of Hollywood.
Too many fall from great and good                          5
For you to doubt the likelihood.

Die early and avoid the fate.
Or if predestined to die late,
Make up your mind to die in state.

---

1. A beautiful maiden brought to comfort King David in his old age (1 Kings 1.2–4).

Make the whole stock exchange your own!                    10
If need be occupy a throne,
Where nobody can call *you* crone.

Some have relied on what they knew,
Others on being simply true.
What worked for them might work for you.                    15

No memory of having starred
Atones for later disregard
Or keeps the end from being hard.

Better to go down dignified
With boughten friendship at your side                    20
Than none at all. Provide, provide!

                                        1934, 1936


## The Gift Outright

The land was ours before we were the land's.
She was our land more than a hundred years
Before we were her people. She was ours
In Massachusetts, in Virginia,
But we were England's, still colonials,                    5
Possessing what we still were unpossessed by,
Possessed by what we now no more possessed.
Something we were withholding made us weak
Until we found out that it was ourselves
We were withholding from our land of living,                    10
And forthwith found salvation in surrender.
Such as we were we gave ourselves outright
(The deed of gift was many deeds of war)
To the land vaguely realizing westward,
But still unstoried, artless, unenhanced,                    15
Such as she was, such as she would become.

                                        1942


## Directive

Back out of all this now too much for us,
Back in a time made simple by the loss
Of detail, burned, dissolved, and broken off
Like graveyard marble sculpture in the weather,
There is a house that is no more a house                    5
Upon a farm that is no more a farm
And in a town that is no more a town.
The road there, if you'll let a guide direct you
Who only has at heart your getting lost,
May seem as if it should have been a quarry—                    10

Great monolithic knees the former town
Long since gave up pretense of keeping covered.
And there's a story in a book about it:
Besides the wear of iron wagon wheels
The ledges show lines ruled southeast-northwest,                    15
The chisel work of an enormous Glacier
That braced his feet against the Arctic Pole.
You must not mind a certain coolness from him
Still said to haunt this side of Panther Mountain.
Nor need you mind the serial ordeal                                 20
Of being watched from forty cellar holes
As if by eye pairs out of forty firkins.[1]
As for the woods' excitement over you
That sends light rustle rushes to their leaves,
Charge that to upstart inexperience.                               25
Where were they all not twenty years ago?
They think too much of having shaded out
A few old pecker-fretted[2] apple trees.
Make yourself up a cheering song of how
Someone's road home from work this once was,                       30
Who may be just ahead of you on foot
Or creaking with a buggy load of grain.
The height of the adventure is the height
Of country where two village cultures faded
Into each other. Both of them are lost.                            35
And if you're lost enough to find yourself
By now, pull in your ladder road behind you
And put a sign up CLOSED to all but me.
Then make yourself at home. The only field
Now left's no bigger than a harness gall.[3]                       40
First there's the children's house of make-believe,
Some shattered dishes underneath a pine,
The playthings in the playhouse of the children.
Weep for what little things could make them glad.
Then for the house that is no more a house,                        45
But only a belilaced cellar hole,
Now slowly closing like a dent in dough.
This was no playhouse but a house in earnest.
Your destination and your destiny's
A brook that was the water of the house,                           50
Cold as a spring as yet so near its source,
Too lofty and original to rage.
(We know the valley streams that when aroused
Will leave their tatters hung on barb and thorn.)
I have kept hidden in the instep arch                              55
Of an old cedar at the waterside
A broken drinking goblet like the Grail[4]
Under a spell so the wrong ones can't find it,

1. Small wooden tub for butter or lard.
2. Apple trees marked up with small holes by woodpeckers.
3. Sore on a horse's skin caused by the rubbing of the
harness.
4. The cup used by Jesus at the Last Supper. Accord-

ing to legend, the Grail later disappeared from its keepers because of their moral impurity, and various
knights, including those of King Arthur's Round Table, went in quest of it. From this, the quest for the
Grail has come to symbolize any spiritual search.

So can't get saved, as Saint Mark[5] says they mustn't.
(I stole the goblet from the children's playhouse.)                    60
Here are your waters and your watering place.
Drink and be whole again beyond confusion.

                                                                       194

5. The Gospel according to Mark (16.16) notes that those who are not baptized cannot be saved.

---

# SHERWOOD ANDERSON
## 1876–1941

Sherwood Anderson was approaching middle age when, giving in to long-deferred ambitions, he left a successful business career to become a writer. Living in Chicago, New Orleans, and Paris, meeting literary people, he worked furiously to make up for his late start, producing novels, short stories, essays, and an autobiography. His short fiction provided a model for younger writers, whose careers he encouraged by literary advice and by practical help in getting published as well. *Winesburg, Ohio*, which appeared in 1919 when he was forty-three years old, remains a major work of experimental fiction and was in its time a bold treatment of small-town life in the American Midwest in the tradition of Edgar Lee Masters's *Spoon River Anthology*.

Anderson was born in southern Ohio, the third of seven children in a family headed by a father whose training and skill as a harness maker were becoming useless in the new world of the automobile. A heavy drinker and gifted storyteller, Anderson's father kept his family on the move in search of work; the stamina and tenderness of his mother supplied whatever coherence and security there was in this nomadic life. Not until 1894, when Anderson was sixteen, did they settle down in the town of Clyde, Ohio, which became the model for Winesburg. Anderson's schooling was irregular and he never finished high school. He held a variety of jobs, living in Chicago with an older brother in 1896 and again in 1900 when he worked as an advertising copywriter.

His first wife came from a successful Ohio business family; the couple settled in Ohio where Anderson managed a mail-order house as well as two paint firms. But in secret he wrote fiction and found increasingly that the need to write conflicted with his career. In 1912 he abandoned his business and his marriage. He returned to Chicago, and met the writers and artists whose activities were creating the Chicago Renaissance: the novelists Floyd Dell and Theodore Dreiser; the poets Edgar Lee Masters, Vachel Lindsay, and Carl Sandburg; the editors Harriet Monroe of *Poetry* and Margaret C. Anderson of the *Little Review*. His first major publication was *Windy McPherson's Son* (1916), the story of a man who runs away from a small Iowa town in futile search for life's meaning; his second was *Marching Men* (1917), about a charismatic lawyer who tries—unsuccessfully—to reorganize the factory system in a small town. These books reveal three of Anderson's preoccupations: the individual quest for self and social betterment, the small-town environment, and the distrust of modern industrial society. Missing, however, is the interest in human psychology and the sense of conflict between inner and outer worlds that appear in *Winesburg* and later works.

In 1916 Anderson began writing and publishing the tales that were brought together in *Winesburg, Ohio*. The formal achievement of the book lay in its articulation of individual tales to a loose but coherent structure. The lives of a number of people living in the town of Winesburg are observed by the naive adolescent George Willard, a reporter for the local newspaper. Their stories contribute to his understanding of life and to his preparation for an adult career as a writer. The book ends with the death of George's mother and his departure from Winesburg. With the help of the narrator, whose vision is larger than that of George Willard, the reader can see how the lives of the characters have been profoundly distorted by the frustration and suppression of so many of their desires. (Anderson's treatment of sexual motivation was outspoken for its day.) Anderson calls these characters "grotesques," but the intention of *Winesburg, Ohio* is to show that life in all American small towns is grotesque in the same way. Anderson's attitude toward the characters mixes compassion for the individual with dismay at a social order that can do so much damage. His criticism is not specifically political, however; he is measuring society by a utopian standard of free emotional and sensual expression.

Stylistically Anderson strove for the simplest possible prose, using brief or at least uncomplex sentences and an unsophisticated vocabulary appropriate to the muffled awareness and limited resources of his typical characters. The model behind his work was Mark Twain masking himself as Huckleberry Finn. But he lacked Twain's brilliant humor and ferocious anger. Structurally, Anderson's stories build toward a moment when the character, frustrated beyond endurance, breaks out in some frenzied gesture of release that is revelatory of a hidden inner life. In both style and structure Anderson's works were important influences on other writers: he encouraged simplicity and directness of style, made attractive the use of the point of view of outsider characters as a way of criticizing conventional society, and gave the craft of the short story a decided push toward stories presenting a slice of life or a significant moment as opposed to panorama and summary. He never was able, however, to forge the complex unity readers expect in longer fiction.

*Winesburg, Ohio* appeared near the beginning of Anderson's literary career, and although he continued writing for two decades, he never repeated the success of that book. His best later work was in short stories, published in three volumes: *The Triumph of the Egg* (1921), *Horses and Men* (1923), and *Death in the Woods and Other Stories* (1933). He also wrote a number of novels, including *Poor White* (1920), *Many Marriages* (1923), *Beyond Desire* (1932), and *Kit Brandon* (1936), as well as free verse, prose poems, plays, and essays. A series of autobiographical volumes advertised his career, attempted to define the writer's vocation in America, and discussed his impact on other writers. The more he claimed, however, the less other writers were willing to allow him; both Hemingway and Faulkner, for example, whom he had met in Paris and New Orleans, respectively, satirized his cult of the simple and thereby disclaimed his influence. (In fact, he *had* stimulated and helped both of them—stimulated Hemingway in his quest for stylistic simplicity, Faulkner in his search for the proper subject matter.) During the 1930s Anderson, along with many other writers, was active in liberal causes, and he died at sea on the way to South America while on a goodwill mission for the State Department.

## FROM WINESBURG, OHIO[1]

# Mother

Elizabeth Willard, the mother of George Willard, was tall and gaunt and her face was marked with smallpox scars. Although she was but forty-five, some obscure disease had taken the fire out of her figure. Listlessly she went about the disorderly old hotel looking at the faded wall-paper and the ragged

1. The text is that of *Winesburg, Ohio* (1919).

MOTHER                                   1783

carpets and, when she was able to be about, doing the work of a chambermaid among beds soiled by the slumbers of fat traveling men. Her husband, Tom Willard, a slender, graceful man with square shoulders, a quick military step, and a black mustache, trained to turn sharply up at the ends, tried to put the wife out of his mind. The presence of the tall ghostly figure, moving slowly through the halls, he took as a reproach to himself. When he thought of her he grew angry and swore. The hotel was unprofitable and forever on the edge of failure and he wished himself out of it. He thought of the old house and the woman who lived there with him as things defeated and done for. The hotel in which he had begun life so hopefully was now a mere ghost of what a hotel should be. As he went spruce and businesslike through the streets of Winesburg, he sometimes stopped and turned quickly about as though fearing that the spirit of the hotel and of the woman would follow him even into the streets. "Damn such a life, damn it!" he sputtered aimlessly.

Tom Willard had a passion for village politics and for years had been the leading Democrat in a strongly Republican community. Some day, he told himself, the tide of things political will turn in my favor and the years of ineffectual service count big in the bestowal of rewards. He dreamed of going to Congress and even of becoming governor. Once when a younger member of the party arose at a political conference and began to boast of his faithful service, Tom Willard grew white with fury. "Shut up, you," he roared, glaring about. "What do you know of service? What are you but a boy? Look at what I've done here! I was a Democrat here in Winesburg when it was a crime to be a Democrat. In the old days they fairly hunted us with guns."

Between Elizabeth and her one son George there was a deep unexpressed bond of sympathy, based on a girlhood dream that had long ago died. In the son's presence she was timid and reserved, but sometimes while he hurried about town intent upon his duties as a reporter, she went into his room and closing the door knelt by a little desk, made of a kitchen table, that sat near a window. In the room by the desk she went through a ceremony that was half a prayer, half a demand, addressed to the skies. In the boyish figure she yearned to see something half forgotten that had once been a part of herself recreated. The prayer concerned that. "Even though I die, I will in some way keep defeat from you," she cried, and so deep was her determination that her whole body shook. Her eyes glowed and she clenched her fists. "If I am dead and see him becoming a meaningless drab figure like myself, I will come back," she declared. "I ask God now to give me that privilege. I demand it. I will pay for it. God may beat me with his fists. I will take any blow that may befall if but this my boy be allowed to express something for us both." Pausing uncertainly, the woman stared about the boy's room. "And do not let him become smart and successful either," she added vaguely.

The communion between George Willard and his mother was outwardly a formal thing without meaning. When she was ill and sat by the window in her room he sometimes went in the evening to make her a visit. They sat by a window that looked over the roof of a small frame building into Main Street. By turning their heads they could see, through another window, along an alleyway that ran behind the Main Street stores and into the back door of Abner Groff's bakery. Sometimes as they sat thus a picture of village life presented itself to them. At the back door of his shop appeared Abner Groff with a stick or an empty milk bottle in his hand. For a long time there was a feud between the baker and a grey cat that belonged to Sylvester West, the druggist. The boy and his mother saw the cat creep into the door of the bakery and presently emerge followed by the baker who swore and waved his arms about. The baker's eyes were small and red and his black hair and beard were filled with flour dust. Sometimes he was so angry that, although the cat had disappeared, he hurled sticks, bits of broken glass, and even some of the tools of his trade about. Once he broke a window at the back of Sinning's Hardware Store. In the alley the grey cat crouched behind barrels filled with torn paper and broken bottles above which flew a black swarm of flies. Once when she was alone, and after watching a prolonged and ineffectual outburst on the part of the baker, Elizabeth Willard put her head down on her long white hands and wept. After that she did not look along the alleyway any more, but tried to forget the contest between the bearded man and the cat. It seemed like a rehearsal of her own life, terrible in its vividness.

In the evening when the son sat in the room with his mother, the silence made them both feel awkward. Darkness came on and the evening train came in at the station. In the street below feet tramped up and down upon a board sidewalk. In the station yard, after the evening train had gone, there was a heavy silence. Perhaps Skinner Leason, the express agent, moved a truck the length of the station platform. Over on Main Street sounded a man's voice, laughing. The door of the express office banged. George Willard arose and crossing the room fumbled for the doorknob. Sometimes he knocked against a chair, making it scrape along the floor. By the window sat the sick woman, perfectly still, listless. Her long hands, white and bloodless, could be seen drooping over the ends of the arms of the chair. "I think you had better be out among the boys. You are too much indoors," she said, striving to relieve the embarrassment of the departure. "I thought I would take a walk," replied George Willard, who felt awkward and confused.

One evening in July, when the transient guests who made the New Willard House their temporary homes had become scarce, and the hallways, lighted only by kerosene lamps turned low, were plunged in gloom, Elizabeth Willard had an adventure. She had been ill in bed for several days and her son had not come to visit her. She was alarmed. The feeble blaze of life that remained in her body was blown into a flame by her anxiety and she crept out of bed, dressed and hurried along the hallway toward her son's room, shaking with exaggerated fears. As she went along she steadied herself with her hand, slipped along the papered walls of the hall and breathed with difficulty. The air whistled through her teeth. As she hurried forward she thought how foolish she was. "He is concerned with boyish affairs," she told herself. "Perhaps he has now begun to walk about in the evening with girls."

Elizabeth Willard had a dread of being seen by guests in the hotel that had once belonged to her father and the ownership of which still stood recorded in her name in the county courthouse. The hotel was continually losing patronage because of its shabbiness and she thought of herself as also shabby. Her own room was in an obscure corner and when she felt able to work she voluntarily worked among the beds, preferring the labor that could be done when the guests were abroad seeking trade among the merchants of Winesburg.

By the door of her son's room the mother knelt upon the floor and listened for some sound from within. When she heard the boy moving about and talking in low tones a smile came to her lips. George Willard had a habit of

talking aloud to himself and to hear him doing so had always given his mother
a peculiar pleasure. The habit in him, she felt, strengthened the secret bond
that existed between them. A thousand times she had whispered to herself of
the matter. "He is groping about, trying to find himself," she thought. "He is
not a dull clod, all words and smartness. Within him there is a secret something that is striving to grow. It is the thing I let be killed in myself."

In the darkness in the hallway by the door the sick woman arose and started
again toward her own room. She was afraid that the door would open and the
boy come upon her. When she had reached a safe distance and was about to
turn a corner into a second hallway she stopped and bracing herself with her
hands waited, thinking to shake off a trembling fit of weakness that had come
upon her. The presence of the boy in the room had made her happy. In her
bed, during the long hours alone, the little fears that had visited her had
become giants. Now they were all gone. "When I get back to my room I shall
sleep," she murmured gratefully.

But Elizabeth Willard was not to return to her bed and to sleep. As she
stood trembling in the darkness the door of her son's room opened and the
boy's father, Tom Willard, stepped out. In the light that streamed out at the
door he stood with the knob in his hand and talked. What he said infuriated
the woman.

Tom Willard was ambitious for his son. He had always thought of himself
as a successful man, although nothing he had ever done had turned out successfully. However, when he was out of sight of the New Willard House and
had no fear of coming upon his wife, he swaggered and began to dramatize
himself as one of the chief men of the town. He wanted his son to succeed.
He it was who had secured for the boy the position on the *Winesburg Eagle*.
Now, with a ring of earnestness in his voice, he was advising concerning some
course of conduct. "I tell you what, George, you've got to wake up," he said
sharply. "Will Henderson has spoken to me three times concerning the matter.
He says you go along for hours not hearing when you are spoken to and acting
like a gawky girl. What ails you?" Tom Willard laughed good-naturedly.
"Well, I guess you'll get over it," he said. "I told Will that. You're not a fool
and you're not a woman. You're Tom Willard's son and you'll wake up. I'm
not afraid. What you say clears things up. If being a newspaper man had put
the notion of becoming a writer into your mind that's all right. Only I guess
you'll have to wake up to do that too, eh?"

Tom Willard went briskly along the hallway and down a flight of stairs to
the office. The woman in the darkness could hear him laughing and talking
with a guest who was striving to wear away a dull evening by dozing in a chair
by the office door. She returned to the door of her son's room. The weakness
had passed from her body as by a miracle and she stepped boldly along. A
thousand ideas raced through her head. When she heard the scraping of a
chair and the sound of a pen scratching upon paper, she again turned and
went back along the hallway to her own room.

A definite determination had come into the mind of the defeated wife of the
Winesburg Hotel keeper. The determination was the result of long years of
quiet and rather ineffectual thinking. "Now," she told herself, "I will act.
There is something threatening my boy and I will ward it off." The fact that
the conversation between Tom Willard and his son had been rather quiet and
natural, as though an understanding existed between them, maddened her.

Although for years she had hated her husband, her hatred had always before been a quite impersonal thing. He had been merely a part of something else that she hated. Now, and by the few words at the door, he had become the thing personified. In the darkness of her own room she clenched her fists and glared about. Going to a cloth bag that hung on a nail by the wall she took out a long pair of sewing scissors and held them in her hand like a dagger. "I will stab him," she said aloud. "He has chosen to be the voice of evil and I will kill him. When I have killed him something will snap within myself and I will die also. It will be a release for all of us."

In her girlhood and before her marriage with Tom Willard, Elizabeth had borne a somewhat shaky reputation in Winesburg. For years she had been what is called "stage-struck" and had paraded through the streets with traveling men guests at her father's hotel, wearing loud clothes and urging them to tell her of life in the cities out of which they had come. Once she startled the town by putting on men's clothes and riding a bicycle down Main Street.

In her own mind the tall girl had been in those days much confused. A great restlessness was in her and it expressed itself in two ways. First there was an uneasy desire for change, for some big definite movement to her life. It was this feeling that had turned her mind to the stage. She dreamed of joining some company and wandering over the world, seeing always new faces and giving something out of herself to all people. Sometimes at night she was quite beside herself with the thought, but when she tried to talk of the matter to the members of the theatrical companies that came to Winesburg and stopped at her father's hotel, she got nowhere. They did not seem to know what she meant, or if she did get something of her passion expressed, they only laughed. "It's not like that," they said. "It's as dull and uninteresting as this here. Nothing comes of it."

With the traveling men when she walked about with them, and later with Tom Willard, it was quite different. Always they seemed to understand and sympathize with her. On the side streets of the village, in the darkness under the trees, they took hold of her hand and she thought that something unexpressed in herself came forth and became a part of an unexpressed something in them.

And then there was the second expression of her restlessness. When that came she felt for a time released and happy. She did not blame the men who walked with her and later she did not blame Tom Willard. It was always the same, beginning with kisses and ending, after strange wild emotions, with peace and then sobbing repentance. When she sobbed she put her hand upon the face of the man and had always the same thought. Even though he were large and bearded she thought he had become suddenly a little boy. She wondered why he did not sob also.

In her room, tucked away in a corner of the old Willard House, Elizabeth Willard lighted a lamp and put it on a dressing table that stood by the door. A thought had come into her mind and she went to a closet and brought out a small square box and set it on the table. The box contained material for make-up and had been left with other things by a theatrical company that had once been stranded in Winesburg. Elizabeth Willard had decided that she would be beautiful. Her hair was still black and there was a great mass of it braided and coiled about her head. The scene that was to take place in the office below began to grow in her mind. No ghostly worn-out figure should confront Tom

Willard, but something quite unexpected and startling. Tall and with dusky cheeks and hair that fell in a mass from her shoulders, a figure should come striding down the stairway before the startled loungers in the hotel office. The figure would be silent—it would be swift and terrible. As a tigress whose cub had been threatened would she appear, coming out of the shadows, stealing noiselessly along and holding the long wicked scissors in her hand.

With a little broken sob in her throat Elizabeth Willard blew out the light that stood upon the table and stood weak and trembling in the darkness. The strength that had been a miracle in her body left and she half reeled across the floor, clutching at the back of the chair in which she had spent so many long days staring out over the tin roofs into the main street of Winesburg. In the hallway there was the sound of footsteps and George Willard came in at the door. Sitting in a chair beside his mother he began to talk. "I'm going to get out of here," he said. "I don't know where I shall go or what I shall do but I am going away."

The woman in the chair waited and trembled. An impulse came to her. "I suppose you had better wake up," she said. "You think that? You will go to the city and make money, eh? It will be better for you, you think, to be a business man, to be brisk and smart and alive?" She waited and trembled.

The son shook his head. "I suppose I can't make you understand, but oh, I wish I could," he said earnestly. "I can't even talk to father about it. I don't try. There isn't any use. I don't know what I shall do. I just want to go away and look at people and think."

Silence fell upon the room where the boy and woman sat together. Again, as on the other evenings, they were embarrassed. After a time the boy tried again to talk. "I suppose it won't be for a year or two but I've been thinking about it," he said, rising and going toward the door. "Something father said makes it sure that I shall have to go away." He fumbled with the door knob. In the room the silence became unbearable to the woman. She wanted to cry out with joy because of the words that had come from the lips of her son, but the expression of joy had become impossible to her. "I think you had better go out among the boys. You are too much indoors," she said. "I thought I would go for a little walk," replied the son stepping awkwardly out of the room and closing the door.

# The Egg[1]

My father was, I am sure, intended by nature to be a cheerful, kindly man. Until he was thirty-four years old he worked as a farm-hand for a man named Thomas Butterworth whose place lay near the town of Bidwell, Ohio. He had then a horse of his own and on Saturday evenings drove into town to spend a few hours in social intercourse with other farm-hands. In town he drank several glasses of beer and stood about in Ben Head's saloon—crowded on Saturday evenings with visiting farm-hands. Songs were sung and glasses thumped on the bar. At ten o'clock father drove home along a lonely country road, made his horse comfortable for the night and himself went to bed, quite happy

---

1. The text is that of *The Triumph of the Egg* (1921).

in his position in life. He had at that time no notion of trying to rise in the world.

It was in the spring of his thirty-fifth year that father married my mother, then a country school-teacher, and in the following spring I came wriggling and crying into the world. Something happened to the two people. They became ambitious. The American passion for getting up in the world took possession of them.

It may have been that mother was responsible. Being a school-teacher she had no doubt read books and magazines. She had, I presume, read of how Garfield, Lincoln,[2] and other Americans rose from poverty to fame and greatness and as I lay beside her—in the days of her lying-in—she may have dreamed that I would some day rule men and cities. At any rate she induced father to give up his place as a farm-hand, sell his horse and embark on an independent enterprise of his own. She was a tall silent woman with a long nose and troubled grey eyes. For herself she wanted nothing. For father and myself she was incurably ambitious.

The first venture into which the two people went turned out badly. They rented ten acres of poor stony land on Griggs's Road, eight miles from Bidwell, and launched into chicken raising. I grew into boyhood on the place and got my first impressions of life there. From the beginning they were impressions of disaster and if, in my turn, I am a gloomy man inclined to see the darker side of life, I attribute it to the fact that what should have been for me the happy joyous days of childhood were spent on a chicken farm.

One unversed in such matters can have no notion of the many and tragic things that can happen to a chicken. It is born out of an egg, lives for a few weeks as a tiny fluffy thing such as you will see pictured on Easter cards, then becomes hideously naked, eats quantities of corn and meal bought by the sweat of your father's brow, gets diseases called pip, cholera, and other names, stands looking with stupid eyes at the sun, becomes sick and dies. A few hens and now and then a rooster, intended to serve God's mysterious ends, struggle through to maturity. The hens lay eggs out of which come other chickens and the dreadful cycle is thus made complete. It is all unbelievably complex. Most philosophers must have been raised on chicken farms. One hopes for so much from a chicken and is so dreadfully disillusioned. Small chickens, just setting out on the journey of life, look so bright and alert and they are in fact so dreadfully stupid. They are so much like people they mix one up in one's judgments of life. If disease does not kill them they wait until your expectations are thoroughly aroused and then walk under the wheels of a wagon—to go squashed and dead back to their maker. Vermin infest their youth, and fortunes must be spent for curative powders. In later life I have seen how a literature has been built up on the subject of fortunes to be made out of the raising of chickens. It is intended to be read by the gods who have just eaten of the tree of the knowledge of good and evil. It is a hopeful literature and declares that much may be done by simple ambitious people who own a few hens. Do not be led astray by it. It was not written for you. Go hunt for gold on the frozen hills of Alaska, put your faith in the honesty of a politician, believe if you will that the world is daily growing better and that good will triumph over

2. James Garfield (1831–1881), twentieth president of the United States. Abraham Lincoln (1809–1865), sixteenth president of the United States.

evil, but do not read and believe the literature that is written concerning the hen. It was not written for you.

I, however, digress. My tale does not primarily concern itself with the hen. If correctly told it will centre on the egg. For ten years my father and mother struggled to make our chicken farm pay and then they gave up that struggle and began another. They moved into the town of Bidwell, Ohio and embarked in the restaurant business. After ten years of worry with incubators that did not hatch, and with tiny—and in their own way lovely—balls of fluff that passed on into semi-naked pullethood and from that into dead henhood, we threw all aside and packing our belongings on a wagon drove down Griggs's Road toward Bidwell, a tiny caravan of hope looking for a new place from which to start on our upward journey through life.

We must have been a sad looking lot, not, I fancy, unlike refugees fleeing from a battlefield. Mother and I walked in the road. The wagon that contained our goods had been borrowed for the day from Mr. Albert Griggs, a neighbor. Out of its sides stuck the legs of cheap chairs and at the back of the pile of beds, tables, and boxes filled with kitchen utensils was a crate of live chickens, and on top of that the baby carriage in which I had been wheeled about in my infancy. Why we stuck to the baby carriage I don't know. It was unlikely other children would be born and the wheels were broken. People who have few possessions cling tightly to those they have. That is one of the facts that make life so discouraging.

Father rode on top of the wagon. He was then a bald-headed man of forty-five, a little fat and from long association with mother and the chickens he had become habitually silent and discouraged. All during our ten years on the chicken farm he had worked as a laborer on neighboring farms and most of the money he had earned had been spent for remedies to cure chicken diseases, on Wilmer's White Wonder Cholera Cure or Professor Bidlow's Egg Producer or some other preparations that mother found advertised in the poultry papers. There were two little patches of hair on father's head just above his ears. I remember that as a child I used to sit looking at him when he had gone to sleep in a chair before the stove on Sunday afternoons in the winter. I had at that time already begun to read books and have notions of my own and the bald path that led over the top of his head was, I fancied, something like a broad road, such a road as Caesar might have made on which to lead his legions out of Rome[3] and into the wonders of an unknown world. The tufts of hair that grew above father's ears were, I thought, like forests. I fell into a half-sleeping, half-waking state and dreamed I was a tiny thing going along the road into a far beautiful place where there were no chicken farms and where life was a happy eggless affair.

One might write a book concerning our flight from the chicken farm into town. Mother and I walked the entire eight miles—she to be sure that nothing fell from the wagon and I to see the wonders of the world. On the seat of the wagon beside father was his greatest treasure. I will tell you of that.

On a chicken farm where hundreds and even thousands of chickens come out of eggs surprising things sometimes happen. Grotesques are born out of eggs as out of people. The accident does not often occur—perhaps once in a thousand births. A chicken is, you see, born that has four legs, two pairs of

---

3. Alluding to the system of roads built by the Caesars, or "emperors," of the Roman empire.

wings, two heads or what not. The things do not live. They go quickly back to the hand of their maker that has for a moment trembled. The fact that the poor little things could not live was one of the tragedies of life to father. He had some sort of notion that if he could but bring into henhood or roosterhood a five-legged hen or a two-headed rooster his fortune would be made. He dreamed of taking the wonder about to county fairs and of growing rich by exhibiting it to other farm-hands.

At any rate he saved all the little monstrous things that had been born on our chicken farm. They were preserved in alcohol and put each in its own glass bottle. These he had carefully put into a box and on our journey into town it was carried on the wagon seat beside him. He drove the horses with one hand and with the other clung to the box. When we got to our destination the box was taken down at once and the bottles removed. All during our days as keepers of a restaurant in the town of Bidwell, Ohio, the grotesques in their little glass bottles sat on a shelf back of the counter. Mother sometimes protested but father was a rock on the subject of his treasure. The grotesques were, he declared, valuable. People, he said, liked to look at strange and wonderful things.

Did I say that we embarked in the restaurant business in the town of Bidwell, Ohio? I exaggerated a little. The town itself lay at the foot of a low hill and on the shore of a small river. The railroad did not run through the town and the station was a mile away to the north at a place called Pickleville. There had been a cider mill and pickle factory at the station, but before the time of our coming they had both gone out of business. In the morning and in the evening busses came down to the station along a road called Turner's Pike from the hotel on the main street of Bidwell. Our going to the out of the way place to embark in the restaurant business was mother's idea. She talked of it for a year and then one day went off and rented an empty store building opposite the railroad station. It was her idea that the restaurant would be profitable. Traveling men, she said, would be always waiting around to take trains out of town and town people would come to the station to await incoming trains. They would come to the restaurant to buy pieces of pie and drink coffee. Now that I am older I know that she had another motive in going. She was ambitious for me. She wanted me to rise in the world, to get into a town school and become a man of the towns.

At Pickleville father and mother worked hard as they always had done. At first there was the necessity of putting our place into shape to be a restaurant. That took a month. Father built a shelf on which he put tins of vegetables. He painted a sign on which he put his name in large red letters. Below his name was the sharp command—"EAT HERE"—that was so seldom obeyed. A show case was bought and filled with cigars and tobacco. Mother scrubbed the floor and the walls of the room. I went to school in the town and was glad to be away from the farm and from the presence of the discouraged, sad-looking chickens. Still I was not very joyous. In the evening I walked home from school along Turner's Pike and remembered the children I had seen playing in the town school yard. A troop of little girls had gone hopping about and singing. I tried that. Down along the frozen road I went hopping solemnly on one leg. "Hippity Hop to the Barber Shop," I sang shrilly. Then I stopped and looked doubtfully about. I was afraid of being seen in my gay mood. It must have seemed to me that I was doing a thing that should not be done by one who, like myself, had been raised on a chicken farm where death was a daily visitor.

Mother decided that our restaurant should remain open at night. At ten in the evening a passenger train went north past our door followed by a local freight. The freight crew had switching to do in Pickleville and when the work was done they came to our restaurant for hot coffee and food. Sometimes one of them ordered a fried egg. In the morning at four they returned north-bound and again visited us. A little trade began to grow up. Mother slept at night and during the day tended the restaurant and fed our boarders while father slept. He slept in the same bed mother had occupied during the night and I went off to the town of Bidwell and to school. During the long nights, while mother and I slept, father cooked meats that were to go into sandwiches for the lunch baskets of our boarders. Then an idea in regard to getting up in the world came into his head. The American spirit took hold of him. He also became ambitious.

In the long nights when there was little to do father had time to think. That was his undoing. He decided that he had in the past been an unsuccessful man because he had not been cheerful enough and that in the future he would adopt a cheerful outlook on life. In the early morning he came upstairs and got into bed with mother. She woke and the two talked. From my bed in the corner I listened.

It was father's idea that both he and mother should try to entertain the people who came to eat at our restaurant. I cannot now remember his words, but he gave the impression of one about to become in some obscure way a kind of public entertainer. When people, particularly young people from the town of Bidwell, came into our place, as on very rare occasions they did, bright entertaining conversation was to be made. From father's words I gathered that something of the jolly inn-keeper effect was to be sought. Mother must have been doubtful from the first, but she said nothing discouraging. It was father's notion that a passion for the company of himself and mother would spring up in the breasts of the younger people of the town of Bidwell. In the evening bright happy groups would come singing down Turner's Pike. They would troop shouting with joy and laughter into our place. There would be song and festivity. I do not mean to give the impression that father spoke so elaborately of the matter. He was as I have said an uncommunicative man. "They want some place to go. I tell you they want some place to go," he said over and over. That was as far as he got. My own imagination has filled in the blanks.

For two or three weeks this notion of father's invaded our house. We did not talk much, but in our daily lives tried earnestly to make smiles take the place of glum looks. Mother smiled at the boarders and I, catching the infection, smiled at our cat. Father became a little feverish in his anxiety to please. There was no doubt, lurking somewhere in him, a touch of the spirit of the showman. He did not waste much of his ammunition on the railroad men he served at night but seemed to be waiting for a young man or woman from Bidwell to come in to show what he could do. On the counter in the restaurant there was a wire basket kept always filled with eggs, and it must have been before his eyes when the idea of being entertaining was born in his brain. There was something pre-natal about the way eggs kept themselves connected with the development of his idea. At any rate an egg ruined his new impulse in life. Late one night I was awakened by a roar of anger coming from father's throat. Both mother and I sat upright in our beds. With trembling hands she lighted a lamp that stood on a table by her head. Downstairs the front door of our restaurant went shut with a bang and in a few minutes father tramped up the stairs. He held an egg in his hand and his hand trembled as though he were having a chill. There was a half insane light in his eyes. As he stood glaring at us I was sure he intended throwing the egg at either mother or me. Then he laid it gently on the table beside the lamp and dropped on his knees beside mother's bed. He began to cry like a boy and I, carried away by his grief, cried with him. The two of us filled the little upstairs room with our wailing voices. It is ridiculous, but of the picture we made I can remember only the fact that mother's hand continually stroked the bald path that ran across the top of his head. I have forgotten what mother said to him and how she induced him to tell her of what had happened downstairs. His explanation also has gone out of my mind. I remember only my own grief and fright and the shiny path over father's head glowing in the lamp light as he knelt by the bed.

As to what happened downstairs. For some unexplainable reason I know the story as well as though I had been a witness to my father's discomfiture. One in time gets to know many unexplainable things. On that evening young Joe Kane, son of a merchant of Bidwell, came to Pickleville to meet his father, who was expected on the ten o'clock evening train from the South. The train was three hours late and Joe came into our place to loaf about and to wait for its arrival. The local freight train came in and the freight crew were fed. Joe was left alone in the restaurant with father.

From the moment he came into our place the Bidwell young man must have been puzzled by my father's actions. It was his notion that father was angry at him for hanging around. He noticed that the restaurant keeper was apparently disturbed by his presence and he thought of going out. However, it began to rain and he did not fancy the long walk to town and back. He bought a five-cent cigar and ordered a cup of coffee. He had a newspaper in his pocket and took it out and began to read. "I'm waiting for the evening train. It's late," he said apologetically.

For a long time father, whom Joe Kane had never seen before, remained silently gazing at his visitor. He was no doubt suffering from an attack of stage fright. As so often happens in life he had thought so much and so often of the situation that now confronted him that he was somewhat nervous in its presence.

For one thing, he did not know what to do with his hands. He thrust one of them nervously over the counter and shook hands with Joe Kane. "How-de-do," he said. Joe Kane put his newspaper down and stared at him. Father's eye lighted on the basket of eggs that sat on the counter and he began to talk. "Well," he began hesitatingly, "well, you have heard of Christopher Columbus, eh?" He seemed to be angry. "That Christopher Columbus was a cheat," he declared emphatically. "He talked of making an egg stand on its end.[4] He talked, he did, and then he went and broke the end of the egg."

My father seemed to his visitor to be beside himself at the duplicity of Christopher Columbus. He muttered and swore. He declared it was wrong to teach children that Christopher Columbus was a great man when, after all, he

---

4. Christopher Columbus (1446?–1506) is said to have used an egg to help argue his theory that sailing west across a round world would take one to the East.

cheated at the critical moment. He had declared he would make an egg stand
on end and then when his bluff had been called he had done a trick. Still
grumbling at Columbus, father took an egg from the basket on the counter
and began to walk up and down. He rolled the egg between the palms of his
hands. He smiled genially. He began to mumble words regarding the effect to
be produced on an egg by the electricity that comes out of the human body.
He declared that without breaking its shell and by virtue of rolling it back and
forth on his hands he could stand the egg on its end. He explained that the
warmth of his hands and the gentle rolling movement he gave the egg created
a new centre of gravity, and Joe Kane was mildly interested. "I have handled
thousands of eggs," father said. "No one knows more about eggs than I do."

He stood the egg on the counter and it fell on its side. He tried the trick
again and again, each time rolling the egg between the palms of his hands and
saying the words regarding the wonders of electricity and the laws of gravity.
When after a half hour's effort he did succeed in making the egg stand for a
moment he looked up to find that his visitor was no longer watching. By the
time he had succeeded in calling Joe Kane's attention to the success of his
effort the egg had again rolled over and lay on its side.

Afire with the showman's passion and at the same time a good deal disconcerted by the failure of his first effort, father now took the bottles containing
the poultry monstrosities down from their place on the shelf and began to show
them to his visitor. "How would you like to have seven legs and two heads like
this fellow?" he asked, exhibiting the most remarkable of his treasures. A
cheerful smile played over his face. He reached over the counter and tried to
slap Joe Kane on the shoulder as he had seen men do in Ben Head's saloon
when he was a young farm-hand and drove to town on Saturday evenings. His
visitor was made a little ill by the sight of the body of the terribly deformed
bird floating in the alcohol in the bottle and got up to go. Coming from behind
the counter father took hold of the young man's arm and led him back to his
seat. He grew a little angry and for a moment had to turn his face away and
force himself to smile. Then he put the bottles back on the shelf. In an outburst of generosity he fairly compelled Joe Kane to have a fresh cup of coffee
and another cigar at his expense. Then he took a pan and filling it with vinegar, taken from a jug that sat beneath the counter, he declared himself about
to do a new trick. "I will heat this egg in this pan of vinegar," he said. "Then
I will put it through the neck of a bottle without breaking the shell. When the
egg is inside the bottle it will resume its normal shape and the shell will
become hard again. Then I will give the bottle with the egg in it to you. You
can take it about with you wherever you go. People will want to know how
you got the egg in the bottle. Don't tell them. Keep them guessing. That is
the way to have fun with this trick."

Father grinned and winked at his visitor. Joe Kane decided that the man
who confronted him was mildly insane but harmless. He drank the cup of
coffee that had been given him and began to read his paper again. When the
egg had been heated in vinegar father carried it on a spoon to the counter and
going into a back room got an empty bottle. He was angry because his visitor
did not watch him as he began to do his trick, but nevertheless went cheerfully
to work. For a long time he struggled, trying to get the egg to go through the
neck of the bottle. He put the pan of vinegar back on the stove, intending to
reheat the egg, then picked it up and burned his fingers. After a second bath

in the hot vinegar the shell of the egg had been softened a little but not enough for his purpose. He worked and worked and a spirit of desperate determination took possession of him. When he thought that at last the trick was about to be consummated the delayed train came in at the station and Joe Kane started to go nonchalantly out at the door. Father made a last desperate effort to conquer the egg and make it do the thing that would establish his reputation as one who knew how to entertain guests who came into his restaurant. He worried the egg. He attempted to be somewhat rough with it. He swore and the sweat stood out on his forehead. The egg broke under his hand. When the contents spurted over his clothes, Joe Kane, who had stopped at the door, turned and laughed.

A roar of anger rose from my father's throat. He danced and shouted a string of inarticulate words. Grabbing another egg from the basket on the counter, he threw it, just missing the head of the young man as he dodged through the door and escaped.

Father came upstairs to mother and me with an egg in his hand. I do not know what he intended to do. I imagine he had some idea of destroying it, of destroying all eggs, and that he intended to let mother and me see him begin. When, however, he got into the presence of mother something happened to him. He laid the egg gently on the table and dropped on his knees by the bed as I have already explained. He later decided to close the restaurant for the night and to come upstairs and get into bed. When he did so he blew out the light and after much muttered conversation both he and mother went to sleep. I suppose I went to sleep also, but my sleep was troubled. I awoke at dawn and for a long time looked at the egg that lay on the table. I wondered why eggs had to be and why from the egg came the hen who again laid the egg. The question got into my blood. It has stayed there, I imagine, because I am the son of my father. At any rate, the problem remains unsolved in my mind. And that, I conclude, is but another evidence of the complete and final triumph of the egg—at least as far as my family is concerned.

1921

---

# CARL SANDBURG
## 1878–1967

Son of an immigrant Swedish blacksmith who had settled in Galesburg, Illinois, Carl Sandburg was an active populist and socialist, a journalist, and an important figure in the Chicago Renaissance of arts and letters. During the 1920s and 1930s he was one of the best-known and most widely read poets in the nation. His poetic aim was to celebrate the working people of America in poems that they could understand. He wrote sympathetically and affirmatively of the masses in simple language, using a long verse line unfettered by rhyme or regular meter, a line deriving from Whitman but with cadences closer to the rhythms of ordinary speech. "Simple poems for simple people," he said.

Sandburg's irregular schooling included four full years at Lombard College, but he was too restless to work through to a degree. He loved the open road, holding a variety of jobs before moving to Chicago in 1913; he was in the army during the Spanish-American War, contributed details about the war to the Galesburg *Evening Mail*, worked for the Social Democratic party in Wisconsin, was secretary to the Socialist mayor of Milwaukee, and wrote editorials for the Milwaukee *Leader*. He had long been writing poetry but achieved his first success—and it was a lasting one—with the 1914 publication of his poem *Chicago* in *Poetry* magazine.

*Poetry* was one element in a surge of artistic activity in Chicago following the 1893 World's Fair. Such midwesterners as the architect Frank Lloyd Wright; the novelists Theodore Dreiser, Henry Blake Fuller, and Floyd Dell; and the poets Edgar Lee Masters and Vachel Lindsay believed not only that Chicago was a great city but that since the Midwest was America's heartland, it was in this region that the cultural life of the nation ought to center. Two literary magazines—*Poetry*, founded in 1912 by Harriet Monroe, and the *Little Review*, founded by Margaret C. Anderson in 1914—helped bring this informal movement to international attention. Nothing could be more apt to local interests than a celebratory poem called *Chicago*.

Four volumes of poetry by Sandburg appeared in the next ten years: *Chicago Poems* (1916), *Cornhuskers* (1918), *Smoke and Steel* (1920), and *Slabs of the Sunburnt West* (1922). These present a panorama of all America, concentrating on the prairies and cities of the Midwest. Like Whitman, Sandburg was aware that American life was increasingly urban, and he had little interest in the small town and its conventional middle class. In the cities of the Midwest the urban spectacle seemed to display both the vitality of the masses and their exploitation in an inequitable class system. Unlike many radicals whose politics were formed after the turn of the twentieth century, Sandburg believed that the people themselves, rather than a cadre of intellectuals acting on behalf of the people, would ultimately shape their own destiny. His political poems express appreciation for the people's energy and outrage at the injustices they suffer. They also balance strong declarative statements with passages of precise description. Other poems show Sandburg working in more lyrical or purely imagistic modes.

If the early *Chicago* is his best-known poem, his most ambitious is the book-length *The People, Yes* (1936), a collage of prose vignettes, anecdotes, and poetry, making use of his researches into American folk song. Sandburg had published these researches in *The American Songbag* in 1927, and he also composed a multivolume biography of Abraham Lincoln between 1926 and 1939. The purpose of this painstaking work was to present Lincoln as an authentic folk hero, a great man who had risen from among the people of the American heartland and represented its best values. He wrote features, editorials, and columns for the *Chicago Daily News* between 1917 and 1932, and pursued other literary projects as well. As early as 1920, before it was common for poets to read their works at campuses around the country, he enjoyed bringing his old-style populist radicalism to college students.

The text of the poems included here is that of *The Complete Poems of Carl Sandburg* (1970).

# Chicago

Hog Butcher for the World,
Tool Maker, Stacker of Wheat,
Player with Railroads and the Nation's Freight Handler;
Stormy, husky, brawling,
City of the Big Shoulders:

They tell me you are wicked and I believe them, for I have seen your painted
　　women under the gas lamps luring the farm boys.
And they tell me you are crooked and I answer: Yes, it is true I have seen the
　　gunman kill and go free to kill again.
And they tell me you are brutal and my reply is: On the faces of women and
　　children I have seen the marks of wanton hunger.
And having answered so I turn once more to those who sneer at this my city,
　　and I give them back the sneer and say to them:
Come and show me another city with lifted head singing so proud to be alive
　　and coarse and strong and cunning.　　　　　　　　　　　　　　　　10
Flinging magnetic curses amid the toil of piling job on job, here is a tall bold
　　slugger set vivid against the little soft cities;
Fierce as a dog with tongue lapping for action, cunning as a savage pitted
　　against the wilderness,
　　　　Bareheaded,
　　　　Shoveling,
　　　　Wrecking,　　　　　　　　　　　　　　　　　　　　　　　15
　　　　Planning,
　　　　Building, breaking, rebuilding,
Under the smoke, dust all over his mouth, laughing with white teeth,
Under the terrible burden of destiny laughing as a young man laughs,
Laughing even as an ignorant fighter laughs who has never lost a battle,　　20
Bragging and laughing that under his wrist is the pulse, and under his ribs the
　　heart of the people,
　　　　Laughing!
Laughing the stormy, husky, brawling laughter of Youth, half-naked, sweat-
　　ing, proud to be Hog Butcher, Tool Maker, Stacker of Wheat, Player
　　with Railroads and Freight Handler to the Nation.

　　　　　　　　　　　　　　　　　　　　　　　　　　1914, 1916


# Fog

The fog comes
on little cat feet.

It sits looking
over harbor and city
on silent haunches　　　　　　　　　　　　　　　　　　5
and then moves on.

　　　　　　　　　　　　　　　　　　　　　　　　　　1916


# Grass[1]

Pile the bodies high at Austerlitz and Waterloo.
Shovel them under and let me work—
　　　　　I am the grass; I cover all.

---

1. The proper names in this poem are all famous battlefields in, respectively, the Napoleonic Wars, the American
Civil War, and World War I.

And pile them high at Gettysburg
And pile them high at Ypres and Verdun.                                    5
Shovel them under and let me work.
Two years, ten years, and passengers ask the conductor:
        What place is this?
        Where are we now?

        I am the grass.                                              10
        Let me work.

1918

---

# WALLACE STEVENS

## 1879–1955

Throughout Wallace Stevens's poetry we meet three agents: the real world, the imagination, and poetry. A real world exists, in splendor and sordidness, but it exists only because it is experienced in the imagination. Imagination, however, cannot "invent" reality: "The pears are not seen / As the observer wills." Stevens wanted "not ideas about the thing, but the thing itself," as the title of another poem expresses it. When human beings see what is really there, they are at one with the universe and liberated from everyday cares. Poetry, which is the record of the human search for such insight, is the highest form of human expression. The author of poetry written from so profound a conviction of the sacredness of art was also the vice president of an insurance company. Most of his business associates knew nothing about his writing. This doubleness may look like inconsistency; it may also imply Stevens's belief that the inner and outer lives have little connection to each other.

Stevens, raised in Reading, Pennsylvania, went to Harvard for three years but left school in 1897 in pursuit of a literary career. Determined, however, that he would never "make a petty struggle for existence," he also looked for a well-paying job. After briefly trying journalism, he went to law school. In 1916 he began to work for the Hartford Accident and Indemnity Company and moved with his wife to Hartford, Connecticut. They made Hartford their lifelong home, Stevens writing his poetry at night and during summers. Visiting Florida frequently on business, he found the contrast between the South's lush vegetation and tropical climate and the chilly austerity of New England a useful metaphor for opposing ways of imagining the world, as poems like *The Snow Man* and *Gubbinal* show.

Stevens began to publish his poetry in little magazines around 1914. In the early years of his career, he frequented literary gatherings in New York City, becoming friends with William Carlos Williams and Marianne Moore, among others. Because his concern was with the private interaction of the observed and the observer, however, he had little interest in artistic causes—less still in politics— and after moving to Hartford, he dropped out of literary circles, although he maintained an active correspondence with his friends. A good businessman, by the mid-1930s Stevens was prosperous. He continued to work for the same company until his death.

His first volume of poetry, *Harmonium*, appeared in 1923. The poems in this book, mostly brief lyrics, are technical triumphs, dazzling in their wit, imagery, and color; they established Stevens as one of the most accomplished poets of his era, although some critics found in them so much display as to make their "seriousness" questionable. But Stevens's purpose in part was to show that display was a valid poetic exercise—that poetry existed to illuminate the world's surfaces as well as its depths. He brought a newly perceived but real world before the reader, authenticating both the beauty of reality and the dependence of that beauty on the eye that perceives it. The two repeated activities are (1) looking at things—the self as active observer of reality—and (2) playing musical instruments or singing—the self as creator of reality (as in *The Idea of Order at Key West*). In this concern with the role of the perceiver in the creation of what is nevertheless real—the sense of an inescapable subjectivity in everything we know—Stevens clearly shared a modernist ideology; his idea, increasingly expressed in the later poems, that with the fading of religious belief poetry might become the forger of new faiths also coincides with the convictions of such poets as T. S. Eliot (in his earlier phase) and Ezra Pound.

His poems feature the continually unexpected in diction and imagery. They abound in allusions to music and painting; are packed with sense images, especially of sound and color; and are elegant and funny. Consider the surprise and humor in the titles of our selections as well as these: *Floral Decorations for Bananas; Anatomy of Monotony; The Bird with the Coppery, Keen Claws; Frogs Eat Butterflies, Snakes Eat Frogs, Hogs Eat Snakes, Men Eat Hogs*. Stevens's line is simple—either blank verse or brief stanzas, usually unrhymed—so that the reader's attention is directed to vocabulary rather than prosody. Invented words are frequent, some employed simply for sound effects. Multilayered puns that ingeniously convey many important meanings serve to thicken and lighten the poetic texture.

Among the poems in *Harmonium* at least three have become touchstones for critics: *Sunday Morning, The Comedian as the Letter C*, and *Peter Quince at the Clavier*. *The Comedian as the Letter C* establishes a contrast between an idealistic would-be poet with his empty imaginings and the same poet enmeshed in the rich reality of the senses and human affections. *Peter Quince at the Clavier*, again, opposes an idea of beauty in the mind with the reality of beauty in the flesh—paradoxically, it is beauty in the flesh that is immortal. *Sunday Morning* opens with a woman taking her ease at home on the day traditionally reserved for churchgoing, and mentally contrasting a fearful, death-obsessed Christianity with her own celebration of earthly pleasure. She would like to think that her behavior is a religion—a celebration—of life, yet death too is real and to some extent she knows that her behavior is as partial as the Christianity she cannot accept. She wonders whether there might ever be a religion that would take the real world rather than another world as its ground, accepting death and change as inevitable and beautiful. The poem, in the form of a meditation deriving from this opening situation, attempts to sketch out the resolution that the woman desires.

In the six years following the appearance of *Harmonium* Stevens published little new work. With the 1930s came a surge of creativity, beginning with the republication of *Harmonium* in an expanded version in 1931. New volumes and major works appeared regularly thereafter: *Ideas of Order* in 1935, *Owl's Clover* in 1936, *The Man with a Blue Guitar* in 1937, *Parts of a World* in 1942, *Transport to Summer* in 1947, and *The Auroras of Autumn* in 1950. A book collecting his occasional lectures appeared as *The Necessary Angel* in 1951; its gist was that poetry was "the supreme fiction" that enabled human beings to apprehend reality as a whole instead of in fragmentary flashes of insight. Stevens's poetry can be usefully thought of as reconceiving and expressing the ideas of the nineteenth-century American Transcendentalists in modernist terms, for they too located the individual at the center of the world while defining that individual chiefly as a perceiver rather than a doer or defining perceiving as the most important human activity. The difference is that the Transcendentalists confidently assumed that their perceptions were guaranteed by God. Stevens was not sure of this.

In his poetry of the 1930s and after, Stevens became increasingly abstract and theoretical; the dazzling effects diminished, the diction became plainer. Major, long poems from these years were *Notes toward a Supreme Fiction* (from *Transport to Summer*) and *An Ordinary Evening in New Haven* (from *The Auroras of Autumn*). In these later poems Stevens was more concerned about what active role poetry might play in the world than he had been in earlier work. These expository and discursive poems should have been easier to follow than the earlier compressed and elliptical poetry, but critics generally agree that the difficulty and abstractness of their ideas make them much more difficult. And to some readers the absence of the earlier specificity and sparkle also makes the later work less rewarding. But those who enjoyed a taxing poetry of ideas saw the late work as an advance. Although critics may argue about the relative value of particular poems, all agree that Stevens's complete *Collected Poems* (1954) is one of the most important books of poetry written in the twentieth century.

The text of the poems included here is that of *The Collected Poems of Wallace Stevens* (1954).

## The Snow Man

One must have a mind of winter
To regard the frost and the boughs
Of the pine-trees crusted with snow;

And have been cold a long time
To behold the junipers shagged with ice,                                  5
The spruces rough in the distant glitter

Of the January sun; and not to think
Of any misery in the sound of the wind,
In the sound of a few leaves,

Which is the sound of the land                                            10
Full of the same wind
That is blowing in the same bare place

For the listener, who listens in the snow,
And, nothing himself, beholds
Nothing that is not there and the nothing that is.                        15

1931

## A High-Toned Old Christian Woman

Poetry is the supreme fiction, madame.
Take the moral law and make a nave[1] of it
And from the nave build haunted heaven. Thus,
The conscience is converted into palms,
Like windy citherns[2] hankering for hymns.                               5

---

1. Main body of a church building, especially the   2. Variation of "cittern," a pear-shaped guitar.
vaulted central portion of a Christian Gothic church.

We agree in principle. That's clear. But take
The opposing law and make a peristyle,[3]
And from the peristyle project a masque[4]
Beyond the planets. Thus, our bawdiness,
Unpurged by epitaph, indulged at last,                    10
Is equally converted into palms,
Squiggling like saxophones. And palm for palm,
Madame, we are where we began. Allow,
Therefore, that in the planetary scene
Your disaffected flagellants, well-stuffed,               15
Smacking their muzzy[5] bellies in parade,
Proud of such novelties of the sublime,
Such tink and tank and tunk-a-tunk-tunk,
May, merely may, madame, whip from themselves
A jovial hullabaloo among the spheres.                    20
This will make widows wince. But fictive things
Wink as they will. Wink most when widows wince.

1923


## The Emperor of Ice-Cream

Call the roller of big cigars,
The muscular one, and bid him whip
In kitchen cups concupiscent curds.
Let the wenches dawdle in such dress
As they are used to wear, and let the boys            5
Bring flowers in last month's newspapers.
Let be be finale of seem.
The only emperor is the emperor of ice-cream.

Take from the dresser of deal,[1]
Lacking the three glass knobs, that sheet             10
On which she embroidered fantails[2] once
And spread it so as to cover her face.
If her horny feet protrude, they come
To show how cold she is, and dumb.
Let the lamp affix its beam.                          15
The only emperor is the emperor of ice-cream.

1923


## Disillusionment of Ten O'Clock

The houses are haunted
By white night-gowns.

---

3. Colonnade surrounding a building, especially the cells or main chamber of an ancient Greek temple—an "opposing law" to a Christian church.
4. Spectacle or entertainment consisting of music, dancing, mime, and often poetry.

5. Sodden with drunkenness.
1. Plain, unfinished wood.
2. Stevens explained that "the word fantails does not mean fan, but fantail pigeons."

None are green,
Or purple with green rings,
Or green with yellow rings,                              5
Or yellow with blue rings.
None of them are strange,
With socks of lace
And beaded ceintures.
People are not going                                     10
To dream of baboons and periwinkles.
Only, here and there, an old sailor,
Drunk and asleep in his boots,
Catches tigers
In red weather.                                          15

1931

# Sunday Morning[1]

### I

Complacencies of the peignoir, and late
Coffee and oranges in a sunny chair,
And the green freedom of a cockatoo
Upon a rug mingle to dissipate
The holy hush of ancient sacrifice.                      5
She dreams a little, and she feels the dark
Encroachment of that old catastrophe,
As a calm darkens among water-lights.
The pungent oranges and bright, green wings
Seem things in some procession of the dead,             10
Winding across wide water, without sound.
The day is like wide water, without sound,
Stilled for the passing of her dreaming feet
Over the seas, to silent Palestine,
Dominion of the blood and sepulchre.                     15

### II

Why should she give her bounty to the dead?
What is divinity if it can come
Only in silent shadows and in dreams?
Shall she not find in comforts of the sun,
In pungent fruit and bright, green wings, or else        20
In any balm or beauty of the earth,
Things to be cherished like the thought of heaven?
Divinity must live within herself:
Passions of rain, or moods in falling snow;
Grievings in loneliness, or unsubdued                    25
Elations when the forest blooms; gusty
Emotions on wet roads on autumn nights;
All pleasures and all pains, remembering

---

1. This poem was first published in *Poetry* magazine in 1915; the editor Harriet Monroe printed only five of its eight stanzas but arranged them in the order Stevens suggested when consenting to the deletions (I, VIII, IV, V, and VII); he restored the deletions and the original sequence in subsequent printings.

The bough of summer and the winter branch.
These are the measures destined for her soul.                    30

### III

Jove[2] in the clouds had his inhuman birth.
No mother suckled him, no sweet land gave
Large-mannered motions to his mythy mind.
He moved among us, as a muttering king,
Magnificent, would move among his hinds,                         35
Until our blood, commingling, virginal,
With heaven, brought such requital to desire
The very hinds[3] discerned it, in a star.
Shall our blood fail? Or shall it come to be
The blood of paradise? And shall the earth                       40
Seem all of paradise that we shall know?
The sky will be much friendlier then than now,
A part of labor and a part of pain,
And next in glory to enduring love,
Not this dividing and indifferent blue.                          45

### IV

She says, "I am content when wakened birds,
Before they fly, test the reality
Of misty fields, by their sweet questionings;
But when the birds are gone, and their warm fields
Return no more, where, then, is paradise?"                       50
There is not any haunt of prophecy,
Nor any old chimera[4] of the grave,
Neither the golden underground, nor isle
Melodious, where spirits gat them home,
Nor visionary south, nor cloudy palm                             55
Remote on heaven's hill, that has endured
As April's green endures; or will endure
Like her remembrance of awakened birds,
Or her desire for June and evening, tipped
By the consummation of the swallow's wings.                      60

### V

She says, "But in contentment I still feel
The need of some imperishable bliss."
Death is the mother of beauty; hence from her,
Alone, shall come fulfillment to our dreams
And our desires. Although she strews the leaves                  65
Of sure obliteration on our paths,
The path sick sorrow took, the many paths
Where triumph rang its brassy phrase, or love
Whispered a little out of tenderness,
She makes the willow shiver in the sun                           70
For maidens who were wont to sit and gaze
Upon the grass, relinquished to their feet.
She causes boys to pile new plums and pears
On disregarded plate. The maidens taste
And stray impassioned in the littering leaves.                   75

2. Supreme god in Roman mythology.                    the star of Bethlehem that signaled the birth of Jesus.
3. Farmhands; an allusion to the shepherds who saw    4. Monster with lion's head.

VI
Is there no change of death in paradise?
Does ripe fruit never fall? Or do the boughs
Hang always heavy in that perfect sky,
Unchanging, yet so like our perishing earth,
With rivers like our own that seek for seas          80
They never find, the same receding shores
That never touch with inarticulate pang?
Why set the pear upon those river-banks
Or spice the shores with odors of the plum?
Alas, that they should wear our colors there,          85
The silken weavings of our afternoons,
And pick the strings of our insipid lutes!
Death is the mother of beauty, mystical,
Within whose burning bosom we devise
Our earthly mothers waiting, sleeplessly.          90
VII
Supple and turbulent, a ring of men
Shall chant in orgy on a summer morn
Their boisterous devotion to the sun,
Not as a god, but as a god might be,
Naked among them, like a savage source.          95
Their chant shall be a chant of paradise,
Out of their blood, returning to the sky;
And in their chant shall enter, voice by voice,
The windy lake wherein their lord delights,
The trees, like serafin,[5] and echoing hills,          100
That choir among themselves long afterward.
They shall know well the heavenly fellowship
Of men that perish and of summer morn.
And whence they came and whither they shall go
The dew upon their feet shall manifest.          105
VIII
She hears, upon that water without sound,
A voice that cries, "The tomb in Palestine
Is not the porch of spirits lingering.
It is the grave of Jesus, where he lay."
We live in an old chaos of the sun,          110
Or old dependency of day and night,
Or island solitude, unsponsored, free,
Of that wide water, inescapable.
Deer walk upon our mountains, and the quail
Whistle about us their spontaneous cries;          115
Sweet berries ripen in the wilderness;
And, in the isolation of the sky,
At evening, casual flocks of pigeons make
Ambiguous undulations as they sink,
Downward to darkness, on extended wings.          120

1915, 1923

5. Seraphim: angels.

# Anecdote of the Jar

I placed a jar in Tennessee,
And round it was, upon a hill.
It made the slovenly wilderness
Surround that hill.

The wilderness rose up to it,                              5
And sprawled around, no longer wild.
The jar was round upon the ground
And tall and of a port in air.

It took dominion everywhere.
The jar was gray and bare.                                10
It did not give of bird or bush,
Like nothing else in Tennessee.

1923

# Peter Quince[1] at the Clavier

## I

Just as my fingers on these keys
Make music, so the selfsame sounds
On my spirit make a music, too.

Music is feeling, then, not sound;
And thus it is that what I feel,                           5
Here in this room, desiring you,

Thinking of your blue-shadowed silk,
Is music. It is like the strain
Waked in the elders by Susanna.[2]

Of a green evening, clear and warm,                       10
She bathed in her still garden, while
The red-eyed elders watching, felt

The basses of their beings throb
In witching chords, and their thin blood
Pulse pizzicati of Hosanna.[3]                            15

1. Stage manager of the rustic actors in A *Midsummer
Night's Dream* by William Shakespeare; the name calls
up images of pastoral innocence and pleasure. There is
an echo of the poem "Quince to Lilac: to G. H." from
the once-popular *More Songs from Vagabondia* by
Bliss Carman and Richard Hovey (1895). Stevens was
very fond of this book and its predecessor, *Songs from
Vagabondia*, which appeared in the same year.
2. Central character in chapter 13 of the Book of Daniel in the Apocrypha. She rejects two elders who attempt to seduce her; they retaliate by falsely accusing
her of sexual immorality. She is saved from punishment by Daniel, who exposes discrepancies in the elders' testimony. The implied contrast is between the
innocent beauty of Susanna's body and the lustful
thoughts that perceive her beauty as immorality.
3. Expression of great praise. "Pizzicati": notes or passages played by plucking strings.

## II

In the green water, clear and warm,
Susanna lay.
She searched
The touch of springs,
And found                                                                    20
Concealed imaginings.
She sighed,
For so much melody.

Upon the bank, she stood
In the cool                                                                  25
Of spent emotions.
She felt, among the leaves,
The dew
Of old devotions.

She walked upon the grass,                                                   30
Still quavering.
The winds were like her maids,
On timid feet,
Fetching her woven scarves,
Yet wavering.                                                                35

A breath upon her hand
Muted the night.
She turned—
A cymbal crashed,
And roaring horns.                                                           40

## III

Soon, with a noise like tambourines,
Came her attendant Byzantines.

They wondered why Susanna cried
Against the elders by her side;

And as they whispered, the refrain                                          45
Was like a willow swept by rain.

Anon, their lamps' uplifted flame
Revealed Susanna and her shame.

And then, the simpering Byzantines
Fled, with a noise like tambourines.                                        50

## IV

Beauty is momentary in the mind—
The fitful tracing of a portal;

But in the flesh it is immortal.
The body dies; the body's beauty lives.
So evenings die, in their green going,        55
A wave, interminably flowing.
So gardens die, their meek breath scenting
The cowl of winter, done repenting.
So maidens die, to the auroral
Celebration of a maiden's choral.        60
Susanna's music touched the bawdy strings
Of those white elders; but, escaping,
Left only Death's ironic scraping.
Now, in its immortality, it plays
On the clear viol of her memory,        65
And makes a constant sacrament of praise.

1923, 1931

# Thirteen Ways of Looking at a Blackbird

### I
Among twenty snowy mountains,
The only moving thing
Was the eye of the blackbird.

### II
I was of three minds,
Like a tree        5
In which there are three blackbirds.

### III
The blackbird whirled in the autumn winds.
It was a small part of the pantomime.

### IV
A man and a woman
Are one.        10
A man and a woman and a blackbird
Are one.

### V
I do not know which to prefer,
The beauty of inflections
Or the beauty of innuendoes,        15
The blackbird whistling
Or just after.

### VI
Icicles filled the long window
With barbaric glass.
The shadow of the blackbird        20
Crossed it, to and fro.
The mood
Traced in the shadow
An indecipherable cause.

#### VII

O thin men of Haddam,[1]                                        25
Why do you imagine golden birds?
Do you not see how the blackbird
Walks around the feet
Of the women about you?

#### VIII

I know noble accents                                            30
And lucid, inescapable rhythms;
But I know, too,
That the blackbird is involved
In what I know.

#### IX

When the blackbird flew out of sight,                           35
It marked the edge
Of one of many circles.

#### X

At the sight of blackbirds
Flying in a green light,
Even the bawds of euphony                                       40
Would cry out sharply.

#### XI

He rode over Connecticut
In a glass coach.
Once, a fear pierced him,
In that he mistook                                              45
The shadow of his equipage
For blackbirds.

#### XII

The river is moving.
The blackbird must be flying.

#### XIII

It was evening all afternoon.                                   50
It was snowing
And it was going to snow.
The blackbird sat
In the cedar-limbs.

                                                          1931

## The Death of a Soldier

Life contracts and death is expected,
    As in a season of autumn.
    The soldier falls.

He does not become a three-days personage,
    Imposing his separation,                                     5
    Calling for pomp.

---

1. A city in Connecticut.

Death is absolute and without memorial,
As in a season of autumn,
When the wind stops,

When the wind stops and, over the heavens,                    10
The clouds go, nevertheless,
In their direction.

1931


## The Idea of Order at Key West[1]

She sang beyond the genius of the sea.
The water never formed to mind or voice,
Like a body wholly body, fluttering
Its empty sleeves; and yet its mimic motion
Made constant cry, caused constantly a cry,              5
That was not ours although we understood,
Inhuman, of the veritable ocean.

The sea was not a mask. No more was she.
The song and water were not medleyed sound
Even if what she sang was what she heard,                10
Since what she sang was uttered word by word.
It may be that in all her phrases stirred
The grinding water and the gasping wind;
But it was she and not the sea we heard.

For she was the maker of the song she sang.              15
The ever-hooded, tragic-gestured sea
Was merely a place by which she walked to sing.
Whose spirit is this? we said, because we knew
It was the spirit that we sought and knew
That we should ask this often as she sang.               20

If it was only the dark voice of the sea
That rose, or even colored by many waves;
If it was only the outer voice of sky
And cloud, of the sunken coral water-walled,
However clear, it would have been deep air,              25
The heaving speech of air, a summer sound
Repeated in a summer without end
And sound alone. But it was more than that,
More even than her voice, and ours, among
The meaningless plungings of water and the wind,         30
Theatrical distances, bronze shadows heaped
On high horizons, mountainous atmospheres
Of sky and sea.
                    It was her voice that made

---

1. One of the semitropical islands off the tip of Florida. The poem begins with a scene leading to reflection, the scene of a woman walking by the sea on a summer's evening and singing.

The sky acutest at its vanishing.                                        35
She measured to the hour its solitude.
She was the single artificer of the world
In which she sang. And when she sang, the sea,
Whatever self it had, became the self
That was her song, for she was the maker. Then we,          40
As we beheld her striding there alone,
Knew that there never was a world for her
Except the one she sang and, singing, made.

Ramon Fernandez,[2] tell me, if you know,
Why, when the singing ended and we turned                   45
Toward the town, tell why the glassy lights,
The lights in the fishing boats at anchor there,
As the night descended, tilting in the air,
Mastered the night and portioned out the sea,
Fixing emblazoned zones and fiery poles,                    50
Arranging, deepening, enchanting night.

Oh! Blessed rage for order, pale Ramon,
The maker's rage to order words of the sea,
Words of the fragrant portals, dimly-starred,
And of ourselves and of our origins,                        55
In ghostlier demarcations, keener sounds.

                                                            1936


## A Postcard from the Volcano

Children picking up our bones
Will never know that these were once
As quick as foxes on the hill;

And that in autumn, when the grapes
Made sharp air sharper by their smell                        5
These had a being, breathing frost;

And least will guess that with our bones
We left much more, left what still is
The look of things, left what we felt

At what we saw. The spring clouds blow                      10
Above the shuttered mansion-house,
Beyond our gate and the windy sky

Cries out a literate despair.
We knew for long the mansion's look
And what we said of it became                               15

---

2. A French literary critic and essayist (1894–1944). Stevens claimed that he had invented the name and that its coincidence with a real person was accidental.

A part of what it is . . . Children,
Still weaving budded aureoles,[1]
Will speak our speech and never know,

Will say of the mansion that it seems
As if he that lived there left behind                    20
A spirit storming in blank walls,

A dirty house in a gutted world,
A tatter of shadows peaked to white,
Smeared with the gold of the opulent sun.

1936

# The Sense of the Sleight-of-hand Man

One's grand flights, one's Sunday baths,
One's tootings at the weddings of the soul
Occur as they occur. So bluish clouds
Occurred above the empty house and the leaves
Of the rhododendrons rattled their gold,                    5
As if someone lived there. Such floods of white
Came bursting from the clouds. So the wind
Threw its contorted strength around the sky.

Could you have said the bluejay suddenly
Would swoop to earth? It is a wheel, the rays             10
Around the sun. The wheel survives the myths.
The fire eye in the clouds survives the gods.
To think of a dove with an eye of grenadine
And pines that are cornets, so it occurs,
And a little island full of geese and stars:            15
It may be that the ignorant man, alone,
Has any chance to mate his life with life
That is the sensual, pearly spouse, the life
That is fluent in even the wintriest bronze.

1942

# Of Modern Poetry

The poem of the mind in the act of finding
What will suffice. It has not always had
To find: the scene was set; it repeated what
Was in the script.
                    Then the theatre was changed              5
To something else. Its past was a souvenir.
It has to be living, to learn the speech of the place.
It has to face the men of the time and to meet

1. Haloes, radiances.

The women of the time. It has to think about war
And it has to find what will suffice. It has                    10
To construct a new stage. It has to be on that stage
And, like an insatiable actor, slowly and
With meditation, speak words that in the ear,
In the delicatest ear of the mind, repeat,
Exactly, that which it wants to hear, at the sound          15
Of which, an invisible audience listens,
Not to the play, but to itself, expressed
In an emotion as of two people, as of two
Emotions becoming one. The actor is
A metaphysician in the dark, twanging                       20
An instrument, twanging a wiry string that gives
Sounds passing through sudden rightnesses, wholly
Containing the mind, below which it cannot descend,
Beyond which it has no will to rise.
                              It must                        25
Be the finding of a satisfaction, and may
Be of a man skating, a woman dancing, a woman
Combing. The poem of the act of the mind.

                                              1942


## Asides on the Oboe

The prologues are over. It is a question, now,
Of final belief. So, say that final belief
Must be in a fiction. It is time to choose.
                    I
That obsolete fiction of the wide river[1] in
An empty land; the gods that Boucher[2] killed;            5
And the metal heroes that time granulates—
The philosophers' man alone still walks in dew,
Still by the sea-side mutters milky lines
Concerning an immaculate imagery.
If you say on the hautboy[3] man is not enough,            10
Can never stand as god, is ever wrong
In the end, however naked, tall, there is still
The impossible possible philosophers' man,
The man who has had the time to think enough,
The central man, the human globe, responsive              15
As a mirror with a voice, the man of glass,
Who in a million diamonds sums us up.
                    II
He is the transparence of the place in which
He is and in his poems we find peace.

1. In Greek mythology, the river that the souls of the
dead had to cross on their journey from the realm of
the living. The land is "empty" because only the dead
live there.
2. Jacques Boucher de Crèvecoeur de Perthes (1788–
1868), French writer and archaeologist who, as the first
to show that humans had existed in prehistoric times,
suggested that the biblical Creation story was a myth.
3. An old French word for "oboe," but *haut* means
"high" or "tall," the "hautboy man" can also be the
hero, the central man, the philosopher. As in other
Stevens poems, the playing of musical instruments is
identified with imagination and poetry.

He sets this peddler's pie and cries in summer,                    20
The glass man, cold and numbered, dewily cries,
"Thou art not August unless I make thee so."
Clandestine steps upon imagined stairs
Climb through the night, because his cuckoos call.

### III

One year, death and war prevented the jasmine scent          25
And the jasmine islands were bloody martyrdoms.
How was it then with the central man? Did we
Find peace? We found the sum of men. We found,
If we found the central evil, the central good.
We buried the fallen without jasmine crowns.                 30
There was nothing he did not suffer, no; nor we.

It was not as if the jasmine ever returned.
But we and the diamond globe at last were one.
We had always been partly one. It was as we came
To see him, that we were wholly one, as we heard           35
Him chanting for those buried in their blood,
In the jasmine haunted forests, that we knew
The glass man, without external reference.

1942

## The Plain Sense of Things

After the leaves have fallen, we return
To a plain sense of things. It is as if
We had come to an end of the imagination,
Inanimate in an inert savoir.[1]

It is difficult even to choose the adjective                       5
For this blank cold, this sadness without cause.
The great structure has become a minor house.
No turban walks across the lessened floors.

The greenhouse never so badly needed paint.
The chimney is fifty years old and slants to one side.        10
A fantastic effort has failed, a repetition
In a repetitiousness of men and flies.

Yet the absence of the imagination had
Itself to be imagined. The great pond,
The plain sense of it, without reflections, leaves,           15
Mud, water like dirty glass, expressing silence

Of a sort, silence of a rat come out to see,
The great pond and its waste of the lilies, all this

---

1. To know (French, literal trans.); here, knowledge.

Had to be imagined as an inevitable knowledge,
Required, as a necessity requires.                                    20

                                                                    1954


## A Quiet Normal Life

His place, as he sat and as he thought, was not
In anything that he constructed, so frail,
So barely lit, so shadowed over and naught,

As, for example, a world in which, like snow,
He became an inhabitant, obedient                                      5
To gallant notions on the part of cold.

It was here. This was the setting and the time
Of Year. Here in his house and in his room,
In his chair, the most tranquil thought grew peaked

And the oldest and the warmest heart was cut                          10
By gallant notions on the part of night—
Both late and alone, above the crickets' chords,

Babbling, each one, the uniqueness of its sound.
There was no fury in transcendent forms.
But his actual candle blazed with artifice.                           15

                                                                    1954

---

# ANGELINA WELD GRIMKÉ
## 1880–1958

Like many other African-American writers who became known in the 1920s, Angelina Grimké was not a resident of Harlem even though she was associated with the Harlem Renaissance movement. Rather, she was a New Englander whose approach to issues of race was shaped by her mainly white ancestry as well as by the ideology of "racial uplift" prevalent in the 1890s. This ideology held that better-off and more-educated American blacks, the so-called talented tenth, should dedicate their talents to the good of the race, helping the less fortunate to advance socially and intellectually. Grimké's father, Archibald, was the son of Henry Grimké—a wealthy white South Carolinian—and Nancy Weston, a slave who bore two other children by Henry as well. Henry's two sisters, Angelina Grimké Weld and Sarah M. Grimké, were outspoken abolitionists who left the South in anger and frustration before the Civil War. When they learned about Archibald after the War, the sisters acknowledged him as their nephew and helped him attend Harvard Law School, where he took a degree in 1874. In 1879 Archibald married Sarah E. Stanley, a white woman from a prominent Boston family. For unknown reasons Sarah left her husband and child and rejoined her parents; Angelina, named after her abolitionist great-aunt, was raised by her father. While Sarah continued to correspond with her daughter until her death in 1897, she apparently never saw her even though she expressed the wish for an eventual reunion. In the relatively liberal atmosphere of Boston, Angelina Grimké enjoyed a privileged upbringing. Her great-uncle Theodore Weld left a bequest to support her education, and she attended prestigious schools in Boston and Washington, D.C. (where her father was attached to the diplomatic service), often as the only African-American student. After graduating from the Boston Normal School of Gymnastics (now Wellesley College) with a degree in physical education in 1902, she took a job as a gym teacher at a vocational school in Washington, D.C. It is not clear why she made this choice, but she was unhappy in her work, transferring in 1907 to the more academic M Street High School (later Dunbar High School), where she taught English for close to twenty years. She retired in 1926 to care for her ailing father. After he died in 1930, she moved to New York and stopped writing, seemingly content to slip into total obscurity.

As a young girl she had pledged in her diary to forego marriage and children and devote her life to writing and her father, a pledge that she fulfilled. Grimké's many love poems to women suggest that marriage did not interest her; yet the recurring theme in her work of black women renouncing motherhood also suggests that Grimké found race attitudes in America so destructive to personal identity that she resolved not to bring children into a world where they would be legally defined as black. This is the choice made by the heroine of Rachel, Grimké's play first staged in Washington, D.C., in 1916 by amateur actors and published in 1920. Grimké explained that in Rachel she wanted "to show how a refined, sensitive, highly-strung girl, a dreamer and an idealist, the strongest instinct in whose nature is a love for children and a desire some day to be a mother herself" would react to race prejudice. While it is not realistic to imagine that Rachel, an African-American woman, could escape awareness of racism until she reached adulthood, Grimké was less interested in realism than in the effect of the play on a white audience; she hoped to make racism personally meaningful to whites through the experiences of a character with whom they could identify. A second play, Mara, is about lynching—a subtopic in Rachel—and was never published.

Grimké wrote most of her stories and poems before 1920, but published mainly after that date, when the Harlem Renaissance movement opened up publishing venues and created new audiences for African-American writings. Her strongest abilities lay in poetry. Her poems were published in the two leading Harlem Renaissance journals, Opportunity and The Crisis, as well as in other periodicals and were reprinted in anthologies like Alain Locke's The New Negro (1925) and Countee Cullen's Caroling Dusk (1927). Most of her writing, however, was never published in her lifetime. A 1991 collection still omits about two-thirds of her poetry and half of her short stories, which exist in manuscript among her papers at Howard University.

Critic Gloria T. Hull divides Grimké's poetry into five general categories—elegies, love lyrics, nature lyrics, race poems, and poems about the human condition. She stresses that a majority of the poems are nature lyrics, with love lyrics next in quantity, whereas the powerful race poems are few in number. In the nature poems, Grimké negotiates smoothly between traditional, relatively simple verse patterns and a more modern stress on economical use of vivid imagery. Grimké does not approach nature philosophically, but rather describes it to enable readers to visualize a scene and sense a correlated mood. The race poems build on this imagistic foundation; they are subdued, well-crafted lyrics in which ominous imagery suddenly disrupts the calm surface with startling glimpses of anger and violence.

Some of Grimké's love poems are addressed to particular women, others are more generalized, but all of them clearly represent a woman's love and longing for other women. Critics theorize that Grimké was troubled by her sexuality and suppressed these poems out of guilt or concern over their public reception—a reasonable hypothesis for the 1920s. But in fact some of these love poems were published, and it is worth remembering that strong, expressively emotional friendships among women were readily accepted in the 1890s when Grimké was growing up. Overall, the published and unpublished poems show a writer dedicated to private expression and personal feelings but not inclined to extended self-analysis in poetry. Race and blackness, always present, are felt in the psyche and registered on the individual body rather than encountered as generalized social truths.

## El Beso [1]

Twilight—and you
Quiet—the stars;
Snare of the shine of your teeth,
Your provocative laughter,
The gloom of your hair;                                              5
Lure of you, eye and lip;
Yearning, yearning,
Languor, surrender;
    Your mouth,
And madness, madness,                                              10
Tremulous, breathless, flaming,
The space of a sigh;
Then awakening—remembrance,
Pain, regret—your sobbing;
And again, quiet—the stars,                                        15
Twilight—and you.

                                                          1923

## The Black Finger

I have just seen a most beautiful thing:
    Slim and still,
    Against a gold, gold sky,
    A straight, black cypress
        Sensitive                                                   5
        Exquisite
        A black finger
        Pointing upwards.
Why, beautiful still finger, are you black?
And why are you pointing upwards?                                   10

                                                    1923, 1925

## The Eyes of My Regret

Always at dusk, the same tearless experience,
The same dragging of feet up the same well-worn path
To the same well-worn rock;

1. The Kiss (Spanish).

The same crimson or gold dropping away of the sun,
The same tints—rose, saffron, violet, lavender, grey,                    5
Meeting, mingling, mixing mistily;
Before me the same blue black cedar rising jaggedly to a point;
Over it, the same slow unlidding of twin stars,
Two eyes unfathomable, soul-searing,
Watching, watching—watching me;                                          10
The same two eyes that draw me forth, against my will dusk after dusk;
The same two eyes that keep me sitting late into the night, chin on knees,
Keep me there lonely, rigid, tearless, numbly miserable,
    —The eyes of my Regret.

1927

## Tenebris

There is a tree, by day,
That, at night,
Has a shadow,
A hand huge and black,
With fingers long and black.                                             5
    All through the dark,
Against the white man's house,
    In the little wind,
The black hand plucks and plucks
    At the bricks.                                                       10
The bricks are the color of blood and very small.
    Is it a black hand,
    Or is it a shadow?

1927

## To
## Clarissa Scott Delaney

1
She has not found herself a hard pillow
    And a long hard bed,
A chilling cypress, a wan willow
    For her gay young head . . . . .
    These are for the dead.                                             5
2
Does the violet-lidded twilight die
    And the piercing dawn
And the white clear noon and the night-blue sky . . . .
    When they are gone?
3
Does the shimmering note                                                10
In the shy, shy throat
Of the swaying bird?

4
O, does children's laughter
Live not after
It is heard?                                                                    15

5
Does the dear, dear shine upon dear, dear things
In the eyes, on the hair,
On waters, on wings . . . .
Live no more anywhere?

6
Does the tang of the sea, the breath of frail flowers,                          20
    Of fern crushed, of clover,
Of grasses at dark, of the earth after showers
    Not linger, not hover?

7
Does the beryl in tarns, the soft orchid in haze,
The primrose through tree-tops, the unclouded jade                              25
Of the north sky, all earth's flamings and russets and grays
    Simply smudge out and fade?

8
And all loveliness, all sweetness, all grace,
All the gay questing, all wonder, all dreaming,
They that cup beauty that veiled opaled vase,                                    30
Are they only the soul of a seeming?

9
O, hasn't she found just a little, thin door
And passed through and closed it between?
O, aren't those her light feet upon that light floor,
. . . . . . . . That her laughter . . . . . . O, doesn't she lean               35
As we do to listen? . . . . . . . O, doesn't it mean
    She is only unseen, unseen?

                                                                              1991


## At April

    Toss your gay heads,
        Brown girl trees;
    Toss your gay lovely heads;
    Shake your downy russet curls
    All about your brown faces;                                                  5
    Stretch your brown slim bodies;
    Stretch your brown slim arms;
    Stretch your brown slim toes.
    Who knows better than we,
    With the dark, dark bodies,                                                 10
    What it means
    When April comes alaughing and aweeping
    Once again
    At our hearts?

                                                                              1991

## Trees

God made them very beautiful, the trees:
He spoke and gnarled of bole or silken sleek
They grew; majestic bowed or very meek;
Huge-bodied, slim; sedate and full of glees.
And He had pleasure deep in all of these.　　　　　　5
And to them soft and little tongues to speak
Of Him to us, He gave, wherefore they seek
From dawn to dawn to bring us to our knees.
. . . . . . .

Yet here amid the wistful sounds of leaves,
A black-hued gruesome something swings and swings,　　　10
Laughter it knew and joy in little things
Till man's hate ended all.——And so man weaves,
And God, how slow, how very slow weaves He—
Was Christ Himself not nailéd to a tree?

1991

---

# WILLIAM CARLOS WILLIAMS
## 1883–1963

A modernist known for his disagreements with all the other modernists, William Carlos Williams thought of himself as the most underrated poet of his generation. His reputation has risen dramatically since World War II as a younger generation of poets testified to the influence of his work on their idea of what poetry should be. The simplicity of his verse forms, the matter-of-factness of both his subject matter and his means of describing it, seemed to bring poetry into natural relation with everyday life. He is now judged to be among the most important poets writing between the wars. His career continued into the 1960s, taking new directions as he produced, along with shorter lyrics, his epic five-part poem *Paterson*.

He was born in 1883 in Rutherford, New Jersey, a town near the city of Paterson. His maternal grandmother, an Englishwoman deserted by her husband, had come to America with her son, married again, and moved to Puerto Rico. Her son—Williams's father—married a woman descended on one side from French Basque people, on the other from Dutch Jews. This mix of origins always fascinated Williams and made him feel that he was different from mainstream Americans, i.e., northeasterners or midwesterners of English descent. After the family moved to New Jersey, Williams's father worked as a salesman for a perfume company; in childhood his father was often away from home, and the two women—mother and grandmother—were the most important adults to him. Throughout Williams's poetry the figure of woman as an earth mother, whom men require for completion and whose reason for being is to supply that completeness, appears, perhaps reflecting that early experience.

Except for a year in Europe, Williams attended local schools. He entered the School of Dentistry at the University of Pennsylvania directly after graduating from high school. He soon switched to medicine, however. In college he met and became friends with Ezra Pound, two years younger than he but much more self-assured; Hilda Doolittle, later to become known as the poet H. D.; and the painter Charles Demuth. These friendships did much to intensify an interest in writing poetry, and even as he completed his medical work, interned in New York City, and did postgraduate study in Leipzig, Germany, he was reconceiving his commitment to medicine as a means of self-support in the more important enterprise of becoming a poet. Although he never lost his sense that he was a doctor in order to be a poet, his patients knew him as a dedicated old-fashioned physician, who made house calls, listened to people's problems, and helped them through life's crises. Pediatrics was his specialty, and in the course of his career, he delivered more than two thousand babies.

In 1912, after internship and study abroad, Williams married his fiancée of several years, Florence Herman. Despite strains in their relationship caused by Williams's continuing interest in other women, the marriage lasted and became, toward the end of Williams's life, the subject of some beautiful love poetry, including *Asphodel, that Greeny Flower*. In the meantime, women and the mixed belittlement-adoration accorded them by men (including the poet) were persistent themes. The couple settled in Rutherford, where Williams opened his practice. Except for a trip to Europe in 1924, when he saw Pound and met James Joyce, among others, and trips for lectures and poetry readings later in his career, Williams remained in Rutherford all his life, continuing his medical practice until poor health forced him to retire. Involved in his medical practice by day, he wrote at night, and spent weekends in New York City with friends who were writers and artists—the avant-garde painters Marcel Duchamp and Francis Picabia, the poets Marianne Moore and Wallace Stevens, and others. At their gatherings he acquired a reputation for his outspoken hostility to most of the "-isms" of the day.

The characteristic Williams style emerged clearly in the landmark volume of mixed prose and poetry *Spring and All* (1923). One can see in this book that the gesture of staying at home was more for him than a practical assessment of his chances of self-support. Interested, like his friend Ezra Pound, in making a new kind of poetry, Williams was also vigorously nationalistic in his aims as Pound was not. He wanted always to speak as an American within an American context. One can observe this bias in the title of one of his books of essays, *In the American Grain* (1925), and in his choice of his own region as the setting and subject of *Paterson*. He can thus be seen as a bridge between the regional approach of Robert Frost and the European focus of T. S. Eliot. In fact, Williams detested *The Waste Land* and thought that its popularity was a "catastrophe," deploring not only its internationalism but its despondency and obscurity as well.

On the other hand, he felt that Frost's poetry was rather an American stereotype than an American re-visioning. His America was an America of small cities, immigrants, industry, and working people, not farmers and rural landscape. Williams was not, however, a celebratory poet; like the expatriate poets he saw modern American life as ugly and superficial. Yet at the same time he believed that social custom should be presented in an American idiom, because social criticism was an American tradition. Traditionally, he wanted a vocabulary drawn from up-to-date American speech and, even more important, a poetic line derived from the cadences of contemporary American life. The idea of "free verse" he considered absurd; rhythm within the line, and connecting line to line, was the very essence of poetry to him. The poet's art should lie in making rhythmical entities out of the unpromising materials of modern talk and the everyday experience that such talk reflected. At different points in his career he espoused one or another line as the solution to his poetic problem. While working on early parts of *Paterson* he invented the "triadic" or "stepped line," a long line broken into three segments, which for a while seemed to him the poetic solution he had been seeking for so long, but eventually he decided that the discovery of the line that would remake poetry still lay in the future. Nevertheless, the success of his enterprise is reflected in the effect his work has: it makes poetry look easy—until one tries to write like Williams and discovers how much care has gone into the choice of words and the placement of emphasis.

Williams also opposed making general statements or expressing abstract ideas in poetry, either overtly or by implication, as both Pound and Eliot did in their works about the decline of Western civilization. His poetry stayed at the surface of life, presenting details of the urban, ordinary scene around him without comment. It drew frankly on his own experience but again avoided the generalizations typical of autobiographical writing. Much like Hemingway's work, Williams's treats significance as something inherent in an object that the poet need not and should not point out. "No ideas but in things," he wrote in several places, meaning that the poet's job was to deal with concrete particulars and let ideas take care of themselves. His earthy plainness is fruitfully contrasted in this context with the elegant fastidiousness of Stevens, who shared his goal of writing a poetry of things rather than ideas. Although Williams's approach to abstractions may seem to conflict with his Whitmanesque project of writing like an American, and thus to remake the poetry of his country, the very distrust of the general can be seen as an aspect of American practicality and intellectual insecurity.

Williams published fiction and essays as well as poetry, especially during the 1930s. Books of short stories (*The Edge of the Knife*, 1932, and *Life Along the Passaic River*, 1938) and novels (*White Mule*, 1937, and *In the Money*, 1940) appeared in these years. He was also involved with others in the establishment of several little magazines, each designed to promulgate counterstatements to the powerful influences of Pound, Eliot, and the New Critics. All the time he remained active in his community and in political events; in the 1930s and 1940s he aligned himself with liberal Democratic and, on occasion, leftist issues but always from the vantage point of an unreconstructed individualism. Some of his affiliations were held against him in the McCarthy era and to his great distress he was deprived in 1948 of the post of consultant in poetry at the Library of Congress.

It was also in 1948 that he had a heart attack, and in 1951 the first of a series of strokes required him to turn over his medical practice to one of his two sons and made writing increasingly difficult. Nevertheless, he persevered in his work on *Paterson*, whose five books were published in 1946, 1948, 1949, 1951, and 1958. *The Desert Music* (1954) and *Pictures from Brueghel* (1962), containing new poetry, also appeared, but by 1961 Williams finally had to stop writing. By the time of his death a host of younger poets, including Allen Ginsberg, Denise Levertov, Charles Olson, and Robert Creeley, had been inspired by his example. He won the National Book Award in 1950, the Bollingen Prize in 1953, and the Pulitzer Prize in 1962.

The texts of the poems included here are those of *The Collected Earlier Poems of William Carlos Williams*, Volume 1: 1909–1939, edited by A. Walton Litz and Christopher MacGowan (1986); *The Collected Earlier Poems of William Carlos Williams*, Volume 2: 1939–1962, edited by Christopher MacGowan (1988); *Collected Later Poems of William Carlos Williams* (1950); and *Pictures from Brueghel* (1962).

## The Young Housewife

At ten A.M. the young housewife
moves about in negligee behind
the wooden walls of her husband's house.
I pass solitary in my car.

Then again she comes to the curb                                    5
to call the ice-man, fish-man, and stands
shy, uncorseted, tucking in
stray ends of hair, and I compare her
to a fallen leaf.

The noiseless wheels of my car                                     10
rush with a crackling sound over
dried leaves as I bow and pass smiling.

                                                    1916, 1917

## Portrait of a Lady

Your thighs are appletrees
whose blossoms touch the sky.
Which sky? The sky
where Watteau[1] hung a lady's
slipper. Your knees                                                 5
are a southern breeze—or
a gust of snow. Agh! what
sort of man was Fragonard?[2]
—as if that answered
anything. Ah, yes—below                                            10
the knees, since the tune
drops that way, it is
one of those white summer days,
the tall grass of your ankles
flickers upon the shore—                                           15
Which shore?—
the sand clings to my lips—
Which shore?
Agh, petals maybe. How
should I know?                                                     20
Which shore? Which shore?
I said petals from an appletree.

                                                    1920, 1934

## Queen-Anne's-Lace[1]

Her body is not so white as
anemone petals nor so smooth—nor
so remote a thing. It is a field
of the wild carrot taking

1. Jean Antoine Watteau (1684–1721), French rococo
artist. He painted sensuous, refined love scenes, with
elegantly dressed lovers in idealized rustic settings.
2. Jean Honoré Fragonard (1732–1806), French
painter, depicted fashionable lovers in paintings more
wittily and openly erotic than Watteau's. Fragonard's

*The Swing* depicts a girl who has kicked her slipper into
the air.
1. A common white field flower composed of a multitude of minute blossoms, each with a dark spot at the
center, joined to the stalk by fibrous stems.

the field by force; the grass 5
does not raise above it.
Here is no question of whiteness,
white as can be, with a purple mole
at the center of each flower.
Each flower is a hand's span 10
of her whiteness. Wherever
his hand has lain there is
a tiny purple blemish. Each part
is a blossom under his touch
to which the fibres of her being 15
stem one by one, each to its end,
until the whole field is a
white desire, empty, a single stem,
a cluster, flower by flower,
a pious wish to whiteness gone over— 20
or nothing.

1921

## The Widow's Lament in Springtime

Sorrow is my own yard
where the new grass
flames as it has flamed
often before but not
with the cold fire 5
that closes round me this year.
Thirtyfive years
I lived with my husband.
The plumtree is white today
with masses of flowers. 10
Masses of flowers
load the cherry branches
and color some bushes
yellow and some red
but the grief in my heart 15
is stronger than they
for though they were my joy
formerly, today I notice them
and turn away forgetting.
Today my son told me 20
that in the meadows,
at the edge of the heavy woods
in the distance, he saw
trees of white flowers.
I feel that I would like 25
to go there
and fall into those flowers
and sink into the marsh near them.

1921

## Spring and All[1]

By the road to the contagious hospital[2]
under the surge of the blue
mottled clouds driven from the
northeast—a cold wind. Beyond, the
waste of broad, muddy fields                              5
brown with dried weeds, standing and fallen

patches of standing water
the scattering of tall trees

All along the road the reddish
purplish, forked, upstanding, twiggy                     10
stuff of bushes and small trees
with dead, brown leaves under them
leafless vines—

Lifeless in appearance, sluggish
dazed spring approaches—                                 15

They enter the new world naked,
cold, uncertain of all
save that they enter. All about them
the cold, familiar wind—

Now the grass, tomorrow                                  20
the stiff curl of wildcarrot leaf

One by one objects are defined—
It quickens: clarity, outline of leaf

But now the stark dignity of
entrance—Still, the profound change                      25
has come upon them: rooted, they
grip down and begin to awaken

                                                    1923

## To Elsie[1]

The pure products of America
go crazy—
mountain folk from Kentucky

---

1. In the volume *Spring and All* (as originally published, 1923), prose statements were interspersed
through the poems and the poems were identified by
roman numerals. Williams added titles later and used
the volume's title for the opening poem.

2. A hospital for treating contagious diseases.
1. In *Spring and All*, this poem was originally numbered XVIII. Elsie was a "retarded nursemaid from the
State Orphanage who worked for the Williams family"
[Litz and MacGowan's note].

or the ribbed north end of
Jersey                                                          5
with its isolate lakes and

valleys, its deaf-mutes, thieves
old names
and promiscuity between

devil-may-care men who have taken          10
to railroading
out of sheer lust of adventure—

and young slatterns, bathed
in filth
from Monday to Saturday                          15

to be tricked out that night
with gauds
from imaginations which have no

peasant traditions to give them
character                                                    20
but flutter and flaunt

sheer rags—succumbing without
emotion
save numbed terror

under some hedge of choke-cherry          25
or viburnum—
which they cannot express—

Unless it be that marriage
perhaps
with a dash of Indian blood                      30

will throw up a girl so desolate
so hemmed round
with disease or murder

that she'll be rescued by an
agent—                                                         35
reared by the state and

sent out at fifteen to work in
some hard-pressed
house in the suburbs—

some doctor's family, some Elsie—        40
voluptuous water
expressing with broken

brain the truth about us—
her great
ungainly hips and flopping breasts                    45

addressed to cheap
jewelry
and rich young men with fine eyes

as if the earth under our feet
were                                                  50
an excrement of some sky

and we degraded prisoners
destined
to hunger until we eat filth

while the imagination strains                         55
after deer
going by fields of goldenrod in

the stifling heat of September
Somehow
it seems to destroy us                                60

It is only in isolate flecks that
something
is given off

No one
to witness                                            65
and adjust, no one to drive the car

                                                    1923


# The Red Wheelbarrow[1]

so much depends
upon

a red wheel
barrow

glazed with rain                                      5
water

beside the white
chickens

                                                    1923

---

1. Numbered XXII in *Spring and All*.

# This Is Just to Say

I have eaten
the plums
that were in
the icebox

and which                                          5
you were probably
saving
for breakfast

Forgive me
they were delicious                                10
so sweet
and so cold

1934

# A Sort of a Song

Let the snake wait under
his weed
and the writing
be of words, slow and quick, sharp
to strike, quiet to wait,                           5
sleepless.

—through metaphor to reconcile
the people and the stones.
Compose. (No ideas
but in things) Invent!                              10
Saxifrage is my flower that splits
the rocks.

1944

# The Dance

In Brueghel's great picture, The Kermess,[1]
the dancers go round, they go round and
around, the squeal and the blare and the
tweedle of bagpipes, a bugle and fiddles
tipping their bellies (round as the thick-          5
sided glasses whose wash they impound)
their hips and their bellies off balance
to turn them. Kicking and rolling about
the Fair Grounds, swinging their butts, those

---

1. *The Wedding Dance* by the Flemish painter Pieter Brueghel (or Breughel) the Elder (c. 1525–1569).

shanks must be sound to bear up under such          10
rollicking measures, prance as they dance
in Brueghel's great picture, The Kermess.

1944

## Burning the Christmas Greens

Their time past, pulled down
cracked and flung to the fire
—go up in a roar

All recognition lost, burnt clean
clean in the flame, the green          5
dispersed, a living red,
flame red, red as blood wakes
on the ash—

and ebbs to a steady burning
the rekindled bed become          10
a landscape of flame

At the winter's midnight
we went to the trees, the coarse
holly, the balsam and
the hemlock for their green          15

At the thick of the dark
the moment of the cold's
deepest plunge we brought branches
cut from the green trees

to fill our need, and over          20
doorways, about paper Christmas
bells covered with tinfoil
and fastened by red ribbons

we stuck the green prongs
in the windows hung          25
woven wreaths and above pictures
the living green. On the

mantle we built a green forest
and among those hemlock
sprays put a herd of small          30
white deer as if they

were walking there. All this!
and it seemed gentle and good
to us. Their time past,
relief! The room bare. We          35

stuffed the dead grate
with them upon the half burnt out
log's smoldering eye, opening
red and closing under them

and we stood there looking down.                    40
Green is a solace
a promise of peace, a fort
against the cold (though we

did not say so) a challenge
above the snow's                                    45
hard shell. Green (we might
have said) that, where

small birds hide and dodge
and lift their plaintive
rallying cries, blocks for them                     50
and knocks down

the unseeing bullets of
the storm. Green spruce boughs
pulled down by a weight of
snow—Transformed!                                   55

Violence leaped and appeared.
Recreant! roared to life
as the flame rose through and
our eyes recoiled from it.

In the jagged flames green                          60
to red, instant and alive. Green!
those sure abutments . . . Gone!
lost to mind

and quick in the contracting
tunnel of the grate                                 65
appeared a world! Black
mountains, black and red—as

yet uncolored—and ash white,
an infant landscape of shimmering
ash and flame and we, in                            70
that instant, lost,

breathless to be witnesses,
as if we stood
ourselves refreshed among
the shining fauna of that fire.                     75

1944

# Lear[1]

When the world takes over for us
and the storm in the trees
replaces our brittle consciences
(like ships, female to all seas)
when the few last yellow leaves                                    5
stand out like flags on tossed ships
at anchor—our minds are rested

Yesterday we sweated and dreamed
or sweated in our dreams walking
at a loss through the bulk of figures                              10
that appeared solid, men or women,
but as we approached down the paved
corridor, melted—Was it I?—like
smoke from bonfires blowing away

Today the storm, inescapable, has                                  15
taken the scene and we return
our hearts to it, however made, made
wives by it and though we secure
ourselves for a dry skin from the drench
of its passionate approaches we                                    20
yield and are made quiet by its fury

Pitiful Lear, not even you could
outshout the storm—to make a fool
cry! Wife to its power might you not
better have yielded sooner? as on ships                            25
facing the seas were carried once
the figures of women at repose to
signify the strength of the waves' lash.

                                                            1948


# Landscape with the Fall of Icarus[1]

According to Brueghel[2]
when Icarus fell
it was spring

a farmer was ploughing
his field                                                          5
the whole pageantry

1. The aging king whose madness reaches its height
during a storm on the heath in Shakespeare's tragedy
*King Lear* (1606).
1. In Greek mythology, a young man whose father
made wings for him whose feathers were held together
by wax. Icarus flew too close to the sun, the wax

melted, and he fell into the sea and drowned. His story
is used to symbolize daring or foolhardy attempts.
2. A landscape by Brueghel in which Icarus is depicted
by a tiny leg sticking out of the sea in one corner of the
picture (see n. 1, p. 1826).

of the year was
awake tingling
near

the edge of the sea                                        10
concerned
with itself

sweating in the sun
that melted
the wings' wax                                             15

unsignificantly
off the coast
there was

a splash quite unnoticed
this was                                                   20
Icarus drowning

                                                        1962

# The Dance

When the snow falls the flakes
spin upon the long axis
that concerns them most intimately
two and two to make a dance

the mind dances with itself,                                5
taking you by the hand,
your lover follows
there are always two,

yourself and the other,
the point of your shoe setting the pace,                   10
if you break away and run
the dance is over

Breathlessly you will take
another partner
better or worse who will keep                              15
at your side, at your stops

whirls and glides until he too
leaves off
on his way down as if
there were another direction                               20

gayer, more carefree
spinning face to face but always down

with each other secure
only in each other's arms

But only the dance is sure!                25
make it your own.
Who can tell
what is to come of it?

in the woods of your
own nature whatever                        30
twig interposes, and bare twigs
have an actuality of their own

this flurry of the storm
that holds us,
plays with us and discards us              35
dancing, dancing as may be credible.

1962

---

# EZRA POUND
## 1885–1972

Ambitious for himself, poetry, and Western civilization, Ezra Pound followed a path that led to exile, well-founded charges of treason, a diagnosis of insanity, and a long imprisonment. To defend and appreciate his poetry, critics try to separate it from his life and especially his obstreperous anti-Semitism. Yet Pound himself insisted that his work, life, and ideas were all of a piece. It is highly ironic that this most political of poets has been critically refashioned a spokesman for pure aestheticism.

Ezra Loomis Pound was born in Hailey, Idaho. When he was still an infant his parents settled in a comfortable suburb near Philadelphia where his father was an assayer at the regional branch of the U.S. Mint. In high school, the study of Latin inspired him to become a poet. He had this goal in mind as an undergraduate at the University of Pennsylvania (where he met and became lifelong friends with William Carlos Williams and had a romance with Hilda Doolittle, who was later to be come the poet H. D.) and at Hamilton College; it also motivated his graduate studies in languages—French, Italian, Old English, and Latin—at the University of Pennsylvania, where he received an M.A. in 1906. He planned to support himself as a college teacher while writing.

The poetry that he had in mind in these early years was in vogue at the turn of the twentieth century—melodious in versification and diction, romantic in themes, world-weary in tone—poetry for which the term *decadent* was used. A particular image of the poet went with such poetry: the poet committed to art for its own sake, careless of convention, and continually shocking the respectable middle class, who were thought to appreciate only art with conventional moral messages. A rebellious and colorful personality, Pound delighted in this role but quickly found that it was not compatible with the sober behavior expected from professors of language. He lost his first teaching job, at Wabash College in Indiana, in fewer than six months.

Convinced that his country had no place for him—and that a country with no place for him had no place for art—he went to Europe in 1908. He settled in London and quickly became involved in its literary life, and especially in movements to revolutionize poetry. He supported himself by teaching and reviewing for several journals. For a while he acted as secretary to the great Irish poet William Butler Yeats. He married Dorothy Shakespear, daughter of a close friend of Yeats, in 1914. Ten years later he became involved with the American expatriate Olga Rudge and maintained relationships with both women thereafter.

Ironically, as an advocate of the new, he found himself propagandizing against the very poetry that had made him want to be a poet at the start, and this contradiction remained throughout his life: on the one hand, a desire to "make it new"; on the other, a deep attachment to the old. Many of his critical essays were later collected and published in books such as *Make It New* (1934), *The ABC of Reading* (1934), *Polite Essays* (1937), and *Literary Essays* (1954). He was generous in his efforts to assist other writers in their work and in their attempts to get published; it was on account of this that so many rallied around him in his time of public disgrace. He was helpful to H. D., T. S. Eliot, James Joyce, William Carlos Williams, Robert Frost, Ernest Hemingway, and Marianne Moore, to name just a few.

Pound first campaigned for "imagism," a name he coined for a new kind of poetry. Rather than describing something—an object or situation—and then generalizing about it, imagist poets attempted to present the object directly. In doing so, they had to avoid the ornate diction and complex but predictable verse forms of traditional poetry, elements that distracted the reader from the impact of the pure image. Any significance to be derived from the image had to appear inherent in its spare, clean presentation. "Go in fear of abstraction," Pound wrote. The rules of grammar seemed too artificial, and hence this new poetry tended to work in nonsyntactical fragments. Although imagism as a formal movement lasted only briefly, most subsequent twentieth-century poetry shows its influence. Pound soon moved on to "vorticism," which, although still espousing direct and bare presentation, sought for some principle of dynamism and energy in the image. In his imagist phase Pound was connected with H. D. and Richard Aldington, a British poet who became H. D.'s husband; as a vorticist he was allied with the iconoclastic writer and artist Wyndham Lewis.

Pound's major works during his London years consisted of free translations of languages unknown to modern Westerners: Provençal, Chinese, Japanese. He also experimented with the dramatic monologue form developed by the English Victorian poet Robert Browning. Poems from these years appeared in his volumes *A Lume Spento* (Italian, "by the spent light"), which appeared in 1908, *A Quinzaine for This Yule* (1908), and *Personae* (1910). *Persona* means "mask," and the poems in this last volume developed the dramatic monologue as a means for the poet to assume various identities and to engage in acts of historical reconstruction and empathy.

Although his view of poetry would seem to exclude the long poem as a workable form, Pound could not overcome the traditional belief that a really great poem had to be long. He hoped to write such a poem himself, a poem for his time, which would unite biography and history by representing the total content of his mind and memory. To this end he began working on his *Cantos* in 1915. The cantos were separate poems of varying lengths, combining reminiscence, meditation, description, and transcriptions from books Pound was reading, all of which were to be forged into unity by the heat of the poet's imagination. Ultimately, he produced 116 cantos, whose intricate obscurities continue to fascinate and challenge critics. The London period came to a close with two poems of disillusionment, *Hugh Selwyn Mauberley: Life and Contacts* and *Mauberley*, which described the demise of Western civilization in the Great War and its aftermath.

Looking for an explanation of what had gone wrong, Pound came upon the

reactionary "social credit" theories of Major Clifford Hugh Douglas, a social economist who attributed all the ills of civilization to the interposition of money
between human exchanges of goods. Once and for all, poetry and politics fused in
Pound's work, as he began to search for a society in which art was protected from
money and to record this search in poems and essays. Leaving England for good
in 1920, he lived in Paris for a time and then settled in the small Mediterranean
town of Rapallo in 1925. His survey of history having persuaded him that the ideal
society was a hierarchy with a strong leader and an agricultural economy, he
greeted the Italian fascist dictator Benito Mussolini as a deliverer. After World War
II broke out, he voluntarily served the Italian government by making numerous
English-language broadcasts aimed at American soldiers in which he vilified the
Jews (whom he identified with a money economy), American president Franklin
D. Roosevelt, and American society in general. When the Americans occupied
Italy, Pound was arrested, held for weeks in an open-air cage at the prison camp
near Pisa, and finally brought back to the United States to be tried for treason. The
trial did not take place, however, because the court accepted a psychiatric report to
the effect that Pound was "insane and mentally unfit to be tried." From 1946 to
1958 he was a patient and a prisoner in St. Elizabeth's Hospital for the criminally
insane in Washington, D.C. During these years he received visits, wrote letters,
composed cantos, and continued his polemic against American society.

In 1948 the *Pisan Cantos* (lxxiv–lxxxiv) won the Library of Congress's newly
established Bollingen Prize for poetry, an event that provoked tremendous debate
about Pound's stature as a poet as well as a citizen. Ten years later the efforts of a
committee of writers succeeded in winning Pound's release, and he returned to
Italy, where he died at the age of eighty-seven.

The texts of the poems included here are those of *Personae: The Collected Poems*
(rev., 1949) and *The Cantos* (1976).

# Portrait d'une Femme[1]

Your mind and you are our Sargasso Sea,[2]
London has swept about you this score years
And bright ships left you this or that in fee:
Ideas, old gossip, oddments of all things,
Strange spars of knowledge and dimmed wares of price.            5
Great minds have sought you—lacking someone else.
You have been second always. Tragical?
No. You preferred it to the usual thing:
One dull man, dulling and uxorious,
One average mind—with one thought less, each year.            10
Oh, you are patient, I have seen you sit
Hours, where something might have floated up.
And now you pay one. Yes, you richly pay.
You are a person of some interest, one comes to you
And takes strange gain away:            15
Trophies fished up; some curious suggestion;
Fact that leads nowhere; and a tale or two,
Pregnant with mandrakes,[3] or with something else
That might prove useful and yet never proves,
That never fits a corner or shows use,            20

---

1. Portrait of a lady (French).
2. Sea in the North Atlantic where boats were becalmed; named for its large masses of floating seaweed.

3. Herb, used as a cathartic; believed in legend to have
human properties, to shriek when pinched, and to promote pregnancy.

Or finds its hour upon the loom of days:
The tarnished, gaudy, wonderful old work;
Idols and ambergris and rare inlays,
These are your riches, your great store; and yet
For all this sea-hoard of deciduous things,                    25
Strange woods half sodden, and new brighter stuff:
In the slow float of differing light and deep,
No! there is nothing! In the whole and all,
Nothing that's quite your own.
                    Yet this is you.                           30

                                                            1912

# A Virginal[1]

No, no! Go from me. I have left her lately.
I will not spoil my sheath with lesser brightness,
For my surrounding air hath a new lightness;
Slight are her arms, yet they have bound me straitly
And left me cloaked as with a gauze of æther;                   5
As with sweet leaves; as with subtle clearness.
Oh, I have picked up magic in her nearness
To sheathe me half in half the things that sheathe her.
No, no! Go from me. I have still the flavour,
Soft as spring wind that's come from birchen bowers.          10
Green come the shoots, aye April in the branches,
As winter's wound with her sleight hand she staunches,
Hath of the trees a likeness of the savour:
As white their bark, so white this lady's hours.

                                                            1912

# A Pact

I make a pact with you, Walt Whitman—
I have detested you long enough.
I come to you as a grown child
Who has had a pig-headed father;
I am old enough now to make friends.                           5
It was you that broke the new wood,
Now is a time for carving.
We have one sap and one root—
Let there be commerce between us.

                                                        1913, 1916

# The Rest

O helpless few in my country,
O remnant enslaved!

---

1. A small spinet, a musical instrument popular in the 16th and 17th centuries.

Artists broken against her,
A-stray, lost in the villages,
Mistrusted, spoken-against,                                              5

Lovers of beauty, starved,
Thwarted with systems,
Helpless against the control;

You who can not wear yourselves out
By persisting to successes,                                            10
You who can only speak,
Who can not steel yourselves into reiteration;

You of the finer sense,
Broken against false knowledge,
You who can know at first hand,                                        15
Hated, shut in, mistrusted:

Take thought:
I have weathered the storm,
I have beaten out my exile.

                                                      1913, 1916


# In a Station of the Metro[1]

The apparition of these faces in the crowd;
Petals on a wet, black bough.

                                                      1913, 1916


# The River-Merchant's Wife: A Letter[2]

While my hair was still cut straight across my forehead
I played about the front gate, pulling flowers.
You came by on bamboo stilts, playing horse,
You walked about my seat, playing with blue plums.
And we went on living in the village of Chōkan:                         5
Two small people, without dislike or suspicion.

At fourteen I married My Lord you.
I never laughed, being bashful.
Lowering my head, I looked at the wall.
Called to, a thousand times, I never looked back.                      10

At fifteen I stopped scowling,
I desired my dust to be mingled with yours
Forever and forever and forever.
Why should I climb the look out?

1. Paris subway.
2. Adaptation from the Chinese of Li Po (701–762),
named Rihaku in Japanese, from the papers of Ernest
Fenollosa, an American scholar whose widow gave his
papers on Japan and China to Pound.

At sixteen you departed,　　　　　　　　　　　　　　　　15
You went into far Ku-tō-en, by the river of swirling eddies,
And you have been gone five months.
The monkeys make sorrowful noise overhead.

You dragged your feet when you went out.
By the gate now, the moss is grown, the different mosses,　　20
Too deep to clear them away!
The leaves fall early this autumn, in wind.
The paired butterflies are already yellow with August
Over the grass in the West garden;
They hurt me. I grow older.　　　　　　　　　　　　　　25
If you are coming down through the narrows of the river Kiang,
Please let me know beforehand,
And I will come out to meet you
　　　　　As far as Chō-fū-Sa.

　　　　　　　　　　　　　　　　　　　*By Rihaku*
　　　　　　　　　　　　　　　　　　　1915

# Hugh Selwyn Mauberley[1]
# (Life and Contacts)[2]

*"Vocat æstus in umbram"*[3]
　　　　　　　　　—Nemesianus, *Ec. IV*

### E. P. *Ode pour l'election de Son Sepulchre*[4]

For three years, out of key with his time,
He strove to resuscitate the dead art
Of poetry; to maintain "the sublime"
In the old sense. Wrong from the start—

No, hardly, but seeing he had been born　　　　　　　　5
In a half savage country, out of date;

---

1. This poem was published in 1920 when Pound was on the verge of leaving London. It measures both the validity and the limitations of his aesthetic practices. At the same time it diagnoses the social, economic, and cultural ills of England. Pound declared that the poem was modeled partly on the technique of Henry James's prose fiction: it presents its subject through the medium of a character's mind or voice, a "center of consciousness" whose mind and standards are also part of the subject being treated and are exposed themselves to scrutiny and assessment. In *Hugh Selwyn Mauberley*, the first thirteen lyrics are presented through "E.P.," a persona through which Pound expresses some of his own ambitions and tastes; cultural conditions in London and representative literary figures (some clearly opposed, some more closely linked to Pound's own aims and associations) are surveyed through the mind of "E.P.," and reactions to them are expressed in his voice. In the next section, titled "Mauberley" (I through "Medallion"), the persona of "E.P." is absorbed in his attention to the fictitious poet Mauberley, a second persona through whom Pound subtly mocks while simultaneously pursuing his own attempt to explore experience and resuscitate poetry in sculptured forms. Pound attempts by tender but pointed irony to exorcise the nostalgia, isolation, and cult of durable form that impels his own poetic practice but threatens to enervate it and reduce it to an aesthete's "overblotted / Series / Of intermittences."
2. Ironic echo of a conventional subtitle of literary biographies, "Life and Letters." In a subsequent edition of 1957, Pound reversed the sequence, claiming that "Contacts and Life" followed the "order of the subject matter." To the American edition of *Personae* in 1926, Pound added the following note: "The sequence is so distinctly a farewell to London that the reader who chooses to regard this as an exclusively American edition may as well omit it and turn at once to page 205."
3. The heat calls us into the shade (Latin); from the *Eclogues* (4.38) of the 3rd-century Carthaginian poet Nemesianus.
4. Adaptation of the title of an ode by Pierre de Ronsard (1524–1585), *On the Selection of His Tomb* (*Odes* 4.5).

Bent resolutely on wringing lilies from the acorn;
Capaneus,[5] trout for factitious bait;

Ἴδμεν γάρ τοι πάνθ', ὅσ' ἐνὶ Τροίῃ[6]
Caught in the unstopped ear;                                     10
Giving the rocks small lee-way
The chopped seas held him, therefore, that year.

His true Penelope[7] was Flaubert,[8]
He fished by obstinate isles;
Observed the elegance of Circe's[9] hair                          15
Rather than the mottoes on sun-dials.

Unaffected by "the march of events,"
He passed from men's memory in *l'an trentuniesme*
*De son eage*,[1] the case presents
No adjunct to the Muses' diadem.                                  20

## II[2]

The age demanded an image
Of its accelerated grimace,
Something for the modern stage,
Not, at any rate, an Attic grace;

Not, not certainly, the obscure reveries                          25
Of the inward gaze;
Better mendacities
Than the classics in paraphrase!

The "age demanded" chiefly a mould in plaster,
Made with no loss of time,                                        30
A prose kinema,[3] not, not assuredly, alabaster
Or the "sculpture" of rhyme.

## III

The tea-rose tea-gown, etc.
Supplants the mousseline of Cos,[4]
The pianola "replaces"                                            35
Sappho's barbitos.[5]

5. One of the seven champions who attack Thebes in Aeschylus's tragedy *The Seven Against Thebes* (476 B.C.) and who is struck down by Zeus.
6. For we know all the toils [endured] in wide Troy (Greek). In Homer's *Odyssey* (12.189) part of the sirens' song to detain Odysseus. Odysseus stopped his comrades' ears with wax to prevent their succumbing to the lure.
7. Odysseus's wife, who remained faithful during his long absence despite appeals from many suitors.
8. Gustave Flaubert (1821–1880), French novelist who cultivated form and stylistic precision.
9. Enchantress with whom Odysseus dallied for a year before returning home.
1. The thirtieth year of his age (French); adapted from

*The Testament* by the 15th-century French poet François Villon. Since the turning point Pound had in mind was the publication of his *Lustra* in 1916, he later changed the line to *trentunieme* or "thirty-first," to conform to his age at that time.
2. The ironies of this poem derive from three senses of the word *demanded*: what the age wanted and liked, what by contrast it needed, and what it "asked for" in the sense of deserved to get.
3. Movement (Greek) and early spelling of *cinema*, "motion pictures."
4. Gauzelike fabric for which the Aegean island Cos was famous.
5. Lyrelike instrument used by the Greek poet Sappho (fl. 600 B.C.).

Christ follows Dionysus,[6]
Phallic and ambrosial
Made way for macerations;[7]
Caliban casts out Ariel.[8]                                              40

All things are a flowing,
Sage Heracleitus[9] says;
But a tawdry cheapness
Shall outlast our days.

Even the Christian beauty                                               45
Defects—after Samothrace;[1]
We see τὸ καλόν[2]
Decreed in the market place.

Faun's flesh is not to us,
Nor the saint's vision.                                                 50
We have the press for wafer;
Franchise for circumcision.

All men, in law, are equals.
Free of Pisistratus,[3]
We choose a knave or an eunuch                                          55
To rule over us.

O bright Apollo,
τίν᾽ ἄνδρα, τίν᾽ ἥρωα, τινα θεόν,[4]

What god, man, or hero
Shall I place a tin wreath upon!                                        60

## IV

These fought in any case,
and some believing,
                pro domo,[5] in any case . . .

Some quick to arm,
some for adventure,                                                     65
some from fear of weakness,
some from fear of censure,
some for love of slaughter, in imagination,

6. Greek god of fertility, regenerative suffering, wine, and poetic inspiration; his worshipers were known for destructive frenzies and consuming ecstasies; his festivals included sexual rites, wine tasting, and dramatic performances.
7. Wasting, fasting. Pound contrasts Christian asceticism to Dionysian rites.
8. In Shakespeare's *Tempest*, as Pound interprets it here, Caliban is earthbound and Ariel is imaginative.
9. Greek philosopher (fl. 500 B.C.) who taught that all reality is flux or a "flowing."

1. North Aegean island, center of religious mystery cults, site of the famous statue *Winged Victory*.
2. The beautiful (Greek).
3. Athenian tyrant and art patron (fl. 6th century B.C.).
4. What man, what hero, what god (Greek); Pound's version of Pindar's "What god, what hero, what man shall we loudly praise" (*Olympian Odes* 2.2).
5. For the home (Latin); adapted from Cicero's *De Domo Sua*.

learning later . . .
some in fear, learning love of slaughter; 70

Died some, pro patria,
     non "dulce" non "et decor"[6] . . .
walked eye-deep in hell
believing in old men's lies, then unbelieving
came home, home to a lie, 75
home to many deceits,
home to old lies and new infamy;
usury age-old and age-thick
and liars in public places.

Daring as never before, wastage as never before. 80
Young blood and high blood,
fair cheeks, and fine bodies;

fortitude as never before

frankness as never before,
disillusions as never told in the old days, 85
hysterias, trench confessions,
laughter out of dead bellies.

V

There died a myriad,
And of the best, among them,
For an old bitch gone in the teeth, 90
For a botched civilization,

Charm, smiling at the good mouth,
Quick eyes gone under earth's lid,

For two gross of broken statues,
For a few thousand battered books. 95

### Yeux Glauques

Gladstone was still respected,
When John Ruskin produced
"King's Treasuries"; Swinburne
And Rossetti still abused.

Fœtid Buchanan lifted up his voice 100
When that faun's head of hers
Became a pastime for
Painters and adulterers.

---

6. For one's native land, not sweetly, not gloriously (Latin); adapted from Horace, "it is sweet and glorious to die for one's fatherland" (*Odes* 3.2.13).

The Burne-Jones cartoons[7]
Have preserved her eyes;                                              105
Still, at the Tate, they teach
Cophetua to rhapsodize;

Thin like brook-water,
With a vacant gaze.
The English Rubaiyat was still-born[8]                                110
In those days.

The thin, clear gaze, the same
Still darts out faun-like from the half-ruin'd face,
Questing and passive. . . .
"Ah, poor Jenny's[9] case" . . .                                     115

Bewildered that a world
Shows no surprise
At her last maquero's[1]
Adulteries.

*"Siena mi fe'; Disfecemi Maremma"*[2]

Among the pickled fœtuses and bottled bones,                         120
Engaged in perfecting the catalogue,
I found the last scion of the
Senatorial families of Strasbourg, Monsieur Verog.[3]

For two hours he talked of Gallifet;[4]
Of Dowson; of the Rhymers' Club;                                     125
Told me how Johnson (Lionel)[5] died
By falling from a high stool in a pub . . .

But showed no trace of alcohol
At the autopsy, privately performed—
Tissue preserved—the pure mind                                       130
Arose toward Newman[6] as the whiskey warmed.

---

7. Drawings. *"Yeux Glauques"*: The brilliant yellow-green eyes of Elizabeth Siddal, the seamstress who became the favorite model of the Pre-Raphaelite painters and later the wife of the painter and poet Dante Gabriel Rossetti (1828–1882). She was the model for the beggar maid in *Cophetua and the Beggar Maid* (now hanging in the Tate Gallery, London), by Sir Edward Burne-Jones (1833–1898). The Pre-Raphaelites, including the poet Algernon Swinburne (1837–1909), were attacked as "The Fleshly School of Poetry" by Robert W. Buchanan (1841–1901) in 1871 and were defended by the critic John Ruskin (1819–1900), whose *Sesame and Lilies* (1865) contains a chapter titled "Kings' Treasuries," calling for the diffusion of literature and the improvement of English tastes in the arts. William E. Gladstone (1809–1898) was a politician and three times prime minister of Britain.
8. Edward Fitzgerald (1809–1883) translated *The Rubáiyát of Omar Khayyám* in 1859, but it was not read ("still-born") until discovered later by the Pre-Raphaelites.

9. Prostitute, heroine of a poem by Rossetti.
1. Or *maquereau*: sexual exploiter, pimp.
2. Siena made me, Maremma unmade me (Medieval Italian); spoken by a Sienese woman, condemned by her husband to die in Maremma marshes for her infidelity, in Dante's *Purgatory* (5.134).
3. Victor Plarr (1863–1929), French poet (*In the Dorian Mood*, 1896) and raconteur from Strasbourg, later librarian of the Royal College of Surgeons and member of the Rhymer's Club.
4. Marquis de Galliffet (1830–1909), French general at the battle of Sedan, which the French lost, in the Franco-Prussian War.
5. Two members of the Rhymer's Club were Roman Catholic poets and heavy drinkers: Ernest Dowson (1867–1900), of whom Plarr published a memoir, and Lionel Johnson (1867–1902), whose *Poetical Works* Pound edited in 1915.
6. John Henry Newman (1801–1890), editor and Roman Catholic convert and intellectual, later cardinal.

Dowson found harlots cheaper than hotels;
Headlam for uplift; Image[7] impartially imbued
With raptures for Bacchus, Terpsichore[8] and the Church
So spoke the author of "The Dorian Mood,"                    135

M. Verog, out of step with the decade,
Detached from his contemporaries,
Neglected by the young,
Because of these reveries.

### Brennbaum

The sky-like limpid eyes,                                    140
The circular infant's face,
The stiffness from spats to collar
Never relaxing into grace;

The heavy memories of Horeb, Sinai and the forty years,[9]
Showed only when the daylight fell                           145
Level across the face
Of Brennbaum "The Impeccable."

### Mr. Nixon

In the cream gilded cabin of his steam yacht
Mr. Nixon advised me kindly, to advance with fewer
Dangers of delay. "Consider                                  150
        "Carefully the reviewer.

"I was as poor as you are;
"When I began I got, of course,
"Advance on royalties, fifty at first," said Mr. Nixon,
"Follow me, and take a column,                               155
"Even if you have to work free.

"Butter reviewers. From fifty to three hundred
"I rose in eighteen months;
"The hardest nut I had to crack
"Was Dr. Dundas.                                             160

"I never mentioned a man but with the view
"Of selling my own works.
"The tip's a good one, as for literature
"It gives no man a sinecure.

"And no one knows, at sight, a masterpiece.                  165
"And give up verse, my boy,
"There's nothing in it."

7. Two more members of the Rhymer's Club: the Reverend Stewart D. Headlam (1847–1924), forced to resign his curacy for lecturing on the dance to workers'
clubs, and Selwyn Image (1849–1930), founder with
Headlam of the Church and Stage Guild.

8. Greek Muse of the dance.
9. The children of Israel wandered in the wilderness
for forty years. Moses saw the burning bush at Horeb
(Exodus 3.2); he received the Ten Commandments at
Sinai (Exodus 19.20ff.).

. . . . . . . . . . . . . .

Likewise a friend of Blougram's once advised me:[1]
Don't kick against the pricks,[2]
Accept opinion. The "Nineties" tried your game                    170
And died, there's nothing in it.

### X

Beneath the sagging roof
The stylist has taken shelter,
Unpaid, uncelebrated,
At last from the world's welter                    175

Nature receives him;
With a placid and uneducated mistress
He exercises his talents
And the soil meets his distress.

The haven from sophistications and contentions                    180
Leaks through its thatch;
He offers succulent cooking;
The door has a creaking latch.

### XI

"Conservatrix of Milésien"[3]
Habits of mind and feeling,                    185
Possibly. But in Ealing[4]
With the most bank-clerky of Englishmen?

No, "Milésian" is an exaggeration.
No instinct has survived in her
Older than those her grandmother                    190
Told her would fit her station.

### XII

"Daphne with her thighs in bark
Stretches toward me her leafy hands,"[5]
Subjectively. In the stuffed-satin drawing-room
I await The Lady Valentine's commands,                    195

Knowing my coat has never been
Of precisely the fashion
To stimulate, in her,
A durable passion;

1. In Browning's *Bishop Bloughram's Apology*, the bishop rationalized this doctrinal laxity.
2. Ironic echo of Christ's statement to Saul: "It is hard for you to kick against the pricks" (Acts 9.5).
3. I.e., conservator of the erotic indulgence for which the Ionian city of Miletus and Aristides' *Milesian Tales*

(2nd century B.C.) were known.
4. London suburb.
5. The metamorphosis of the nymph Daphne into a laurel tree to escape the embrace of Apollo; Pound's lines are a translation of Théophile Gautier's version of Ovid's story in *Le Château de Souvenir*.

Doubtful, somewhat, of the value 200
Of well-gowned approbation
Of literary effort,
But never of The Lady Valentine's vocation:

Poetry, her border of ideas,
The edge, uncertain, but a means of blending 205
With other strata
Where the lower and higher have ending;

A hook to catch the Lady Jane's attention,
A modulation toward the theatre,
Also, in the case of revolution, 210
A possible friend and comforter.

.     .     .     .     .     .     .     .     .     .     .

Conduct, on the other hand, the soul
"Which the highest cultures have nourished"[6]
To Fleet St. where
Dr. Johnson flourished;[7] 215

Beside this thoroughfare
The sale of half-hose has
Long since superseded the cultivation
Of Pierian roses.[8]

Envoi (1919)[9]

*Go, dumb-born book,* 220
*Tell her that sang me once that song of Lawes:*
*Hadst thou but song*
*As thou hast subjects known,*
*Then were there cause in thee that should condone*
*Even my faults that heavy upon me lie,* 225
*And build her glories their longevity.*

*Tell her that sheds*
*Such treasure in the air,*
*Recking naught else but that her graces give*
*Life to the moment,* 230
*I would bid them live*
*As roses might, in magic amber laid,*
*Red overwrought with orange and all made*
*One substance and one colour*
*Braving time.* 235

---

6. A translation of two lines from *Complainte de Pi-anos* by French poet Jules Laforgue (1860–1887).
7. Samuel Johnson (1709–1784), journalist, poet, critic, and moral essayist, the reigning man of letters in mid-18th-century London. "Fleet St.": newspaper publishing center in London.

8. Roses of Pieria, place near Mount Olympus where the Muses were worshiped.
9. This poem is modeled on the rhetoric and cadences of *Go, Lovely Rose* by Edmund Waller (1606–1687), whose poems were set to music by Henry Lawes (1596–1662).

*Tell her that goes*
*With song upon her lips*
*But sings not out the song, nor knows*
*The maker of it, some other mouth,*
*May be as fair as hers,*                                    240
*Might, in new ages, gain her worshippers,*
*When our two dusts with Waller's shall be laid,*
*Siftings on siftings in oblivion,*
*Till change hath broken down*
*All things save Beauty alone.*                              245

1920

## FROM THE CANTOS

# I[1]

And then went down to the ship,
Set keel to breakers, forth on the godly sea, and
We set up mast and sail on that swart ship,
Bore sheep aboard her, and our bodies also
Heavy with weeping, and winds from sternward            5
Bore us out onward with bellying canvas,
Circe's this craft, the trim-coifed goddess.[2]
Then sat we amidships, wind jamming the tiller,
Thus with stretched sail, we went over sea till day's end.
Sun to his slumber, shadows o'er all the ocean,        10
Came we then to the bounds of deepest water,
To the Kimmerian lands,[3] and peopled cities
Covered with close-webbed mist, unpierced ever
With glitter of sun-rays
Nor with stars stretched, nor looking back from heaven  15
Swartest night stretched over wretched men there
The ocean flowing backward, came we then to the place
Aforesaid by Circe.
Here did they rites, Perimedes and Eurylochus,[4]
And drawing sword from my hip                           20
I dug the ell-square pitkin;[5]
Poured we libations unto each the dead,
First mead then sweet wine, water mixed with white flour.
Then prayed I many a prayer to the sickly death's-heads;
As set in Ithaca, sterile bulls of the best            25
For sacrifice, heaping the pyre with goods,
A sheep to Tiresias only, black and a bell-sheep.[6]
Dark blood flowed in the fosse,[7]

---

1. Lines 1–68 are an adaptation of book 11 of Homer's *Odyssey*, which recounts Odysseus's voyage to Hades, the underworld of the dead.
2. Odysseus lived for a year with the enchantress Circe until he determined to return home to Ithaca. She instructed him to get directions for his trip home by first visiting the Theban prophet Tiresias in the underworld.
3. Mythical people living in a foggy region at the edge of the earth.
4. Two of Odysseus's companions.
5. Small pit, one ell on each side.
6. The prophet Tiresias is likened to a sheep that leads the herd.
7. Ditch, trench.

Souls out of Erebus,[8] cadaverous dead, of brides
Of youths and of the old who had borne much;                    30
Souls stained with recent tears, girls tender,
Men many, mauled with bronze lance heads,
Battle spoil, bearing yet dreory[9] arms,
These many crowded about me; with shouting,
Pallor upon me, cried to my men for more beasts;               35
Slaughtered the herds, sheep slain of bronze;
Poured ointment, cried to the gods,
To Pluto the strong, and praised Proserpine;[1]
Unsheathed the narrow sword,
I sat to keep off the impetuous impotent dead,                  40
Till I should hear Tiresias.
But first Elpenor[2] came, our friend Elpenor,
Unburied, cast on the wide earth,
Limbs that we left in the house of Circe,
Unwept, unwrapped in sepulchre, since toils urged other.        45
Pitiful spirit. And I cried in hurried speech:
"Elpenor, how art thou come to this dark coast?
"Cam'st thou afoot, outstripping seamen?"
        And he in heavy speech:
"Ill fate and abundant wine. I slept in Circe's ingle.[3]        50
"Going down the long ladder unguarded,
"I fell against the buttress,
"Shattered the nape-nerve, the soul sought Avernus.[4]
"But thou, O King, I bid remember me, unwept, unburied,
"Heap up mine arms, be tomb by sea-bord, and inscribed:          55
"A *man of no fortune, and with a name to come.*
"And set my oar up, that I swung mid fellows."


And Anticlea[5] came, whom I beat off, and then Tiresias Theban,
Holding his golden wand, knew me, and spoke first:
"A second time?[6] why? man of ill star,                         60
"Facing the sunless dead and this joyless region?
"Stand from the fosse, leave me my bloody bever[7]
"For soothsay."
        And I stepped back,
And he strong with the blood, said then: "Odysseus               65
"Shalt return through spiteful Neptune,[8] over dark seas,
"Lose all companions." And then Anticlea came.
Lie quiet Divus. I mean, that is Andreas Divus,
In officina Wecheli, 1538, out of Homer.[9]
And he sailed, by Sirens and thence outward and away             70
And unto Circe.

8. Land of the dead, Hades.
9. Bloody.
1. Goddess of regeneration and wife of Pluto, god of the underworld.
2. Odysseus's companion who fell to his death from the roof of Circe's house and was left unburied by his friends.
3. Corner, house.
4. Lake near Naples, the entrance to Hades.
5. Odysseus's mother. In the *Odyssey*, Odysseus weeps at the sight of her but obeys Circe's instructions to speak to no one until Tiresias has first drunk the libation of blood that will enable him to speak.
6. They met once before on earth.
7. Libation.
8. God of the sea, who was to delay Odysseus's return by a storm at sea.
9. Pound acknowledges using the Renaissance Latin translation of Homer, produced in the workshop ("officina") of Wechel in Paris in 1538, by Andreas Divus.

Venerandam,[1]
In the Cretan's phrase, with the golden crown, Aphrodite,
Cypri munimenta sortita est,[2] mirthful, orichalchi,[3] with golden
Girdles and breast bands, thou with dark eyelids                                    75
Bearing the golden bough of Argicida.[4] So that:

                                                                                    1925

# XLV

With *Usura*[1]

With usura hath no man a house of good stone
each block cut smooth and well fitting
that design might cover their face,
with usura                                                                          5
hath no man a painted paradise on his church wall
*harpes et luz*[2]
or where virgin receiveth message
and halo projects from incision,[3]
with usura                                                                          10
seeth no man Gonzaga[4] his heirs and his concubines
no picture is made to endure nor to live with
but it is made to sell and sell quickly
with usura, sin against nature,
is thy bread ever more of stale rags                                                15
is thy bread dry as paper,
with no mountain wheat, no strong flour
with usura the line grows thick
with usura is no clear demarcation
and no man can find site for his dwelling.                                           20
Stonecutter is kept from his stone
weaver is kept from his loom
WITH USURA
wool comes not to market
sheep bringeth no gain with usura                                                   25
Usura is a murrain,[5] usura
blunteth the needle in the maid's hand

---

1. Commanding reverence; a phrase describing
Aphrodite, the goddess of love, in the Latin translation
of the second Homeric Hymn by Georgius Dartona
Cretensis (the "Cretan" in the next line).
2. The fortresses of Cyprus were her appointed realm
(Latin).
3. Of copper (Latin); a reference to gifts presented to
Aphrodite in the second Homeric Hymn.
4. Aeneas offered the Golden Bough to Proserpina before descending to the underworld. Pound apparently
associated Persephone, goddess of regeneration, with
Aphrodite, goddess of love and slayer of the Greeks
(Argi) during the Trojan War; and the Golden Bough,
sacred to the goddess Diana, with the magic wand of
the god Hermes, slayer of the many-eyed Argus ("Argicida") and liberator of Io.

1. Usury, or lending money at interest (Latin). Pound
interpreted this practice as the root of all corruption in
the modern world, the cause of the separation of the
worker—whether farmer, laborer, or artist—from the
work.
2. Harps and lutes (Latin). In medieval and Renaissance depictions of Paradise, the angels are shown
playing on such instruments.
3. Description of scenes in religious paintings, especially the Annunciation, where the Virgin Mary is informed that she is to be the mother of Christ.
4. Luigi Gonzaga (1267–1360), prince of Mantua and
founder of a dynasty that ruled that Italian city until
the 18th century.
5. A plague (archaic).

and stoppeth the spinner's cunning. Pietro Lombardo
came not by usura
Duccio came not by usura                                         30
nor Pier della Francesca; Zuan Bellin' not by usura
nor was 'La Calumnia' painted.[6]
Came not by usura Angelico; came not Ambrogio Praedis,[7]
Came no church of cut stone signed: *Adamo me fecit.*[8]
Not by usura St Trophime                                         35
Not by usura Saint Hilaire,[9]
Usura rusteth the chisel
It rusteth the craft and the craftsman
It gnaweth the thread in the loom
None learneth to weave gold in her pattern;                     40
Azure hath a canker by usura; cramoisi[1] is unbroidered
Emerald findeth no Memling[2]
Usura slayeth the child in the womb
It stayeth the young man's courting
It hath brought palsey to bed, lyeth                             45
between the young bride and her bridegroom
                CONTRA NATURAM[3]
They have brought whores for Eleusis[4]
Corpses are set to banquet
at behest of usura.                                              50

N.B. Usury: A charge for the use of purchasing power, levied without regard
to production; often without regard to the possibilities of production. (Hence
the failure of the Medici bank.[5])

                                                                1937

6. Pietro Lombardo (1435–1515), Italian sculptor.
Duccio di Buoninsegna (1260?–1318?), Piero della
Francesca (1420?–1492), and Giovanni Bellini
(1430?–1516) were Italian painters from Florence and
nearby towns; *La Calumnia* (Rumor), allegorical
painting by Sandro Botticelli (1445–1510), one of the
greatest of the Italian Renaissance painters.
7. Fra Angelico (1387?–1455) and Ambrogio Praedis
(1455?–1506) were Italian painters.
8. Adam made me (Latin); words carved into the
church of San Zeno Maggiore in Verona, Italy; to
Pound, a symbol of the architect's pride in and feeling
of connection with his work.
9. Medieval churches in the French cities of Arles and

Poitiers, respectively.
1. Heavy crimson cloth (French).
2. Hans Memling (1430?–1495), Flemish painter.
3. Against nature (Latin).
4. City in ancient Greece, northwest of Athens, where
secret religious rites in honor of Demeter and Persephone, the goddess of fertility and her daughter, were celebrated by priestesses every spring. The substitution of
whores for priestesses represents the degradation of ancient rituals.
5. A bank operated from 1397 to 1494 by the Medici
family of Florence; it anticipated modern banking
techniques.

---

# H. D. (Hilda Doolittle)
## 1886–1961

In January 1913, Harriet Monroe's influential little magazine, *Poetry*, printed three
vivid poems by an unknown "H. D., Imagiste." These spare, elegant lyrics were
among the first important products of the "imagist movement": poems devoid of
explanation and declamation, unrhymed and lacking regular beat, depending on
the power of an image to arrest attention and convey emotion. The poet's pen

name, the movement's name, and the submission to the magazine were all the work of Ezra Pound, poet and tireless publicist for anything new in the world of poetry. The poems themselves had been written by his friend Hilda Doolittle. In later years, H. D. would look back at these events as epitomizing her dilemma: how to be a woman poet speaking in a world where women were spoken for and about by men. It is, perhaps, a symbol of her sense of difficulty that, though she strove for a voice that could be recognized as clearly feminine, she continued to publish under the name that Pound had devised for her.

She had been born in Bethlehem, Pennsylvania, one girl in a family of five boys. Her mother—who was her father's second wife—was a musician and music teacher, active in the Moravian church to which many in Bethlehem belonged. The symbols and rituals of this group, along with its tradition of secrecy created in response to centuries of oppression, had much to do with H. D.'s interest in images and her attraction in later life to occult and other symbol systems: the cabala, numerology, the tarot, and psychoanalysis.

When her father, an astronomer and mathematician, was appointed director of the observatory at the University of Pennsylvania, the family moved to a suburb of Philadelphia. There, when she was fifteen years old, H. D. met Ezra Pound, a student at the university, already dedicated to poetry and acting the poet's role with dramatic intensity. The two were engaged for a while, but Pound's influence continued long after each had gone on to other partners. H. D. attended college at Bryn Mawr for two years; in 1911 she made a bold move to London, where Pound had gone some years earlier. She married a member of his circle, the English poet Richard Aldington, in 1913. With Aldington she studied Greek and read the classics, but the marriage was not a success and was destroyed by their separation during World War I when Aldington went into the army and served in France.

The year 1919 was a terrible one for H. D.: her brother Gilbert was killed in the fighting in France, her father died soon thereafter, her marriage officially broke up, close friendships with Pound and with D. H. Lawrence came to an end, she had a nearly fatal case of flu, and amid all this gave birth to a daughter whom Aldington said was not his child. Aftereffects of all these traumas haunted her for the rest of her life. But she was rescued from the worst of her emotional and financial troubles by Winifred Ellerman, whose father, a shipping magnate, was one of the wealthiest men in England. Ellerman, a writer who had adopted the pen name Bryher, had initially been attracted by H. D.'s poetry; their relationship developed first as a love affair and then into a lifelong friendship.

In 1923, H. D. settled in Switzerland. With Bryher's financial help she raised her daughter and cared for her ailing mother who had joined her household. During 1933 and 1934 she spent some time in Vienna, where she underwent analysis by Sigmund Freud. Freud's theory of the unconscious and the disguised ways in which it reaches surface expression accorded well with H. D.'s understanding of how the unexplained images in a poem could be significant; the images were a code, carrying personal meanings in disguise. Freud and H. D. had many arguments, especially over the destiny of women, for H. D. by this time had become a feminist, and Freud believed that woman's nature was determined entirely by biology; still, H. D. felt strong affection for him, and was instrumental (with Bryher's help) in getting him safely to London when the Nazi regime took over in Austria. When World War II broke out H. D. went back to London to share England's fate in crisis.

Like many of the major poets of the era, H. D. came in time to feel the need to write longer works. During the 1930s she worked mostly in prose forms and composed several autobiographical pieces (some of which remain unpublished); the bombardment of London inspired three long related poems about World War II, *The Walls Do Not Fall* (1944), *Tribute to the Angels* (1945), and *The Flowering of the Rod* (1946), which appeared together as *Trilogy*. In them she combined layers of historical and personal experience; wars going back to the Trojan War all came together in one image of humankind forever imposing and enduring violence.

The personal and the historical had always been one to her, and now she became increasingly attracted to the image of Helen, the so-called cause of the Trojan War, as an image of herself. According to Homer's *Iliad*, Helen's beauty led Paris, a Trojan prince, to steal her from her Greek husband Menelaus, and all the Greek warriors made common cause to get her back. After ten years encamped before the walls of Troy, they found a devious way to enter the city and destroy it. H. D. was struck by the fact that the legend was related entirely from the male point of view; Helen never had a chance to speak. The object of man's acts and the subject of their poems, she was herself always silent. If Helen tried to speak, would she even have a voice or a point of view? Out of these broodings, and helped by her study of symbols, H. D. wrote her meditative epic of more than fourteen hundred lines, *Helen in Egypt*. The poem, composed between 1951 and 1955, consists of three books of interspersed verse and prose commentary, which follow Helen's quest. "She herself is the writing" that she seeks to understand, the poet observes.

H. D.'s imagist poetry, for which she was known during her lifetime, represents the imagist credo with its vivid phrasing, compelling imagery, free verse, short poetic line, and avoidance of abstraction and generalization. She followed Pound's example in producing many translations of poetry from older literature, choosing her favorite Greek poets for the exercise. Her images come chiefly from nature: austere landscapes of sea, wind, and sand are contrasted with exotic figures of flowers, jewelry, and shells. This contrast can be understood in many ways: it is sterility versus fruitfulness, intellect versus passion, control versus abandon, grief versus joy. H. D. lived a liberated life for a woman of her time, but experienced too much grief to be an exponent of self-abandon. The austere landscapes were as attractive to her as the luscious jewels and flowers that decorated her poetry. Her poetry, although centered on her experience as a woman, was also entirely modernist in its representation of the psyche—anybody's psyche—adrift in a violent, fragmented, alien, and insecure reality.

The texts of the poems included here are those of *Collected Poems 1912–1944*, edited by Louis L. Martz (1983).

# Mid-day

The light beats upon me.
I am startled—
a split leaf crackles on the paved floor—
I am anguished—defeated.

A slight wind shakes the seed-pods—      5
my thoughts are spent
as the black seeds.
My thoughts tear me,
I dread their fever.
I am scattered in its whirl.      10
I am scattered like
the hot shrivelled seeds.

The shrivelled seeds
are split on the path—
the grass bends with dust,      15
the grape slips

under its crackled leaf:
yet far beyond the spent seed-pods,
and the blackened stalks of mint,
the poplar is bright on the hill,                    20
the poplar spreads out,
deep-rooted among trees.

O poplar, you are great
among the hill-stones,
while I perish on the path                           25
among the crevices of the rocks.

1916

## Oread[1]

Whirl up, sea—
whirl your pointed pines,
splash your great pines
on our rocks,
hurl your green over us,                             5
cover us with your pools of fir.

1914, 1924

## Helen[2]

All Greece hates
the still eyes in the white face,
the lustre as of olives
where she stands,
and the white hands.                                 5

All Greece reviles
the wan face when she smiles,
hating it deeper still
when it grows wan and white,
remembering past enchantments                        10
and past ills.

Greece sees unmoved,
God's daughter, born of love,
the beauty of cool feet
and slenderest knees,                                15
could love indeed the maid,
only if she were laid,
white ash amid funereal cypresses.

1924

---

1. A nymph of mountains and hills.
2. In Greek legend, the wife of Menelaus; her abduction by the Trojan prince Paris started the Trojan War.

She was the daughter of the god Zeus, the product of his rape, when disguised as a swan, of the mortal Leda.

# *From* The Walls Do Not Fall

### To Bryher

FOR KARNAK 1923
FROM LONDON 1942

### 1

An incident here and there,
and rails gone (for guns)
from your (and my) old town square:

mist and mist-grey, no colour,
still the Luxor bee, chick and hare[1]          5
pursue unalterable purpose

in green, rose-red, lapis;
they continue to prophesy
from the stone papyrus:
there, as here, ruin opens          10
the tomb, the temple; enter,
there as here, there are no doors:

the shrine lies open to the sky,
the rain falls, here, there
sand drifts; eternity endures:          15

ruin everywhere, yet as the fallen roof
leaves the sealed room
open to the air,

so, through our desolation,
thoughts stir, inspiration stalks us          20
through gloom:

unaware, Spirit announces the Presence;
shivering overtakes us,
as of old, Samuel:[2]

trembling at a known street-corner,          25
we know not nor are known;
the Pythian[3] pronounces—we pass on

to another cellar, to another sliced wall
where poor utensils show
like rare objects in a museum;          30

1. Luxor is a town on the Nile River in Egypt, close
to the ruins of the ancient city of Thebes, where the
Temple of Karnak is located. The bee, chick, and hare
are carved symbols appearing on the temple.
2. An Old Testament seer and prophet.
3. Pythia is another name for Delphi, Greek town famous because the Oracle of Apollo was located there.
The Pythian is the high priestess of that oracle, who
was possessed by the Delphic spirit and prophesied.
The poem's movement from one seer-prophet to another in different religious traditions is meant to unify
all religions.

Pompeii[4] has nothing to teach us,
we know crack of volcanic fissure,
slow flow of terrible lava,

pressure on heart, lungs, the brain
about to burst its brittle case                                    35
(what the skull can endure!):

over us, Apocryphal fire,[5]
under us, the earth sway, dip of a floor,
slope of a pavement

where men roll, drunk                                              40
with a new bewilderment,
sorcery, bedevilment:

the bone-frame was made for
no such shock knit within terror,
yet the skeleton stood up to it:                                   45

the flesh? it was melted away,
the heart burnt out, dead ember,
tendons, muscles shattered, outer husk dismembered,

yet the frame held:
we passed the flame: we wonder                                     50
what saved us? what for?

2

Evil was active in the land,
Good was impoverished and sad;

Ill promised adventure,
Good was smug and fat;                                             55

Dev-ill was after us,
tricked up like Jehovah;

Good was the tasteless pod,
stripped from the manna-beans, pulse, lentils:

they were angry when we were so hungry                             60
for the nourishment, God;

they snatched off our amulets,
charms are not, they said, grace;

but gods always face two-ways,
so let us search the old highways                                  65

---

4. Ancient Italian city near Naples, burned and buried          5. The Apocrypha are books rejected from the Bible
in a matter of hours by the eruption of Mount Vesuvius          because of doubtful authenticity.
in A.D. 79.

for the true-rune, the right-spell,
recover old values;

nor listen if they shout out,
your beauty, Isis, Aset or Astarte,[6]

is a harlot; you are retrogressive,                                    70
zealot, hankering after old flesh-pots;

your heart, moreover,
is a dead canker,

they continue, and
your rhythm is the devil's hymn,                                       75

your stylus is dipped in corrosive sublimate,
how can you scratch out

indelible ink of the palimpsest[7]
of past misadventure?

### 3

Let us, however, recover the Sceptre,                                  80
the rod of power:

it is crowned with the lily-head
or the lily-bud:

it is Caduceus;[8] among the dying
it bears healing:                                                      85

or evoking the dead,
it brings life to the living.

### 4

There is a spell, for instance,
in every sea-shell:

continuous, the sea-thrust                                             90
is powerless against coral,

bone, stone, marble
hewn from within by that craftsman,

the shell-fish:
oyster, clam, mollusc                                                  95

6. Three goddesses of fertility from Egyptian and
Phoenician mythologies.
7. A parchment or tablet that has been written on
more than once, with the underlying texts only partly
erased and hence still visible: H. D.'s symbol for human history.
8. Name of the winged staff with two serpents twined
around it carried by Mercury (Hermes), Greco-Roman
messenger god and god of healing.

is master-mason planning
the stone marvel:

yet that flabby, amorphous hermit
within, like the planet

senses the finite,                                    100
it limits its orbit

of being, its house,
temple, fane, shrine:

it unlocks the portals
at stated intervals:                                  105

prompted by hunger,
it opens to the tide-flow:

but infinity? no,
of nothing-too-much:

I sense my own limit,                                 110
my shell-jaws snap shut

at invasion of the limitless,
ocean-weight; infinite water

can not crack me, egg in egg-shell;
closed in, complete, immortal                         115

full-circle, I know the pull
of the tide, the lull

as well as the moon;
the octopus-darkness

is powerless against                                  120
her cold immortality;

so I in my own way know
that the whale

can not digest me:[9]
be firm in your own small, static, limited            125

orbit and the shark-jaws
of outer circumstance

will spit you forth:
be indigestible, hard, ungiving.

9. Allusion to the Old Testament story of Jonah, who was swallowed by a whale when he disobeyed God's orders, preserved in the whale's belly until he repented, and then cast up on dry land.

so that, living within,                                          130
yet beget, self-out-of-self,

selfless,
that pearl-of-great-price.

*     *     *

21

Splintered the crystal of identity,
shattered the vessel of integrity,                               445

till the Lord *Amen*,
paw-er of the ground,

bearer of the curled horns,
bellows from the horizon:

here am I, Amen-Ra,                                              450
*Amen*, Aries, the Ram;[1]

time, time for you to begin a new spiral,
see—I toss you into the star-whirlpool;

till pitying, pitying,
snuffing the ground,                                             455

here am I, Amen-Ra whispers,
*Amen*, Aries, the Ram,

be cocoon, smothered in wool,
be Lamb,[2] mothered again.

22

Now my right hand,                                               460
now my left hand

clutch your curled fleece;
take me home, take me home,

my voice wails from the ground;
take me home, Father:                                            465

pale as the worm in the grass,
yet I am a spark

struck by your hoof from a rock:
*Amen*, you are so warm,

---

1. Latin name for a constellation, one of the signs of
the zodiac. "Amen-Ra": Egyptian god of life and reproduction. "*Amen*": Hebrew for "may it be so, certainly,
truly," said at the end of a prayer. Here is a good example of how H. D. uses similar-sounding words to pull
together many mythologies and religions.
2. Traditional reference to Christ; H. D. links it by
association with Aries, the Ram.

hide me in your fleece,                                              470
crop me up with the new-grass;

let your teeth devour me,
let me be warm in your belly,

the sun-disk,
the re-born Sun.                                                     475


23

Take me home
where canals

flow
between iris-banks:

where the heron                                                     480
has her nest:

where the mantis
prays on the river-reed:

where the grasshopper says
*Amen, Amen, Amen.*                                                 485


24

Or anywhere
where stars blaze through clear air,

where we may greet individually,
Sirius, Vega, Arcturus,[3]

where these separate entities                                       490
are intimately concerned with us,

where each, with its particular attribute,
may be invoked

with accurate charm, spell, prayer,
which will reveal unquestionably,                                   495

whatever healing or inspirational essence
is necessary for whatever particular ill

the inquiring soul is heir to:
O stars, little jars of that indisputable

and absolute Healer, Apothecary,                                    500
wrought, faceted, jewelled

---

3. Three bright stars.

boxes, very precious, to hold further
unguent, myrrh, incense:

jasper, beryl, sapphire
that, as we draw them nearer                                    505

by prayer, spell,
litany, incantation,

will reveal their individual fragrance,
personal magnetic influence,

become, as they once were,                                      510
personified messengers,

healers, helpers
of the One, *Amen*, All-father.

*   *   *

41

*Sirius:*
*what mystery is this?*                                         820

you are seed,
corn near the sand,
enclosed in black-lead,
ploughed land.

*Sirius:*                                                       825
*what mystery is this?*

you are drowned
in the river;
the spring freshets
push open the water-gates.                                      830

*Sirius:*
*what mystery is this?*

where heat breaks and cracks
the sand-waste,
you are a mist                                                  835
of snow: white, little flowers.

42

O, Sire, is this the path?
over sedge, over dune-grass,

silently
sledge-runners pass.                                            840

O, Sire, is this the waste?
unbelievably,

sand glistens like ice,
cold, cold;

drawn to the temple gate, O, Sire,                    845
is this union at last?


43

*Still the walls do not fall,*
*I do not know why;*

*there is zrr-hiss,*
*lightning in a not-known,*                    850

*unregistered dimension;*
*we are powerless,*

*dust and powder fill our lungs*
*our bodies blunder*

*through doors twisted on hinges,*                    855
*and the lintels slant*

*cross-wise;*
*we walk continually*

*on thin air*
*that thickens to a blind fog,*                    860

*then step swiftly aside,*
*for even the air*

*is independable,*
*thick where it should be fine*

*and tenuous*                    865
*where wings separate and open,*

*and the ether*
*is heavier than the floor,*

*and the floor sags*
*like a ship floundering;*                    870

*we know no rule*
*of procedure,*

*we are voyagers, discoverers*
*of the not-known,*

*the unrecorded;*                                              875
*we have no map;*

*possibly we will reach haven,*
*heaven.*

1944

---

# ROBINSON JEFFERS
## 1887–1962

As American poets between the wars strove together to find a place for poetry in the modern world, Robinson Jeffers stood aloof. He wanted nothing to do with movements or controversy. Like a nineteenth-century American frontiersman, he identified the essence of the nation in the possibilities it afforded for solitude. Even rural America was too crowded, and as the country became ever more populous and urban in the twentieth century, he looked away from land and out into the Pacific Ocean for the wilderness and wildness he could not find elsewhere.

He was born on January 10, 1887, in Pittsburgh. His father, who was forty-seven when he was born, was a minister and professor of Old Testament literature. The family, which included Jeffers's mother, twenty years younger than her husband, and a brother seven years younger than he, traveled often to Europe. When the family settled in northern California in 1903, at that time a sparsely settled and beautifully rugged region, Jeffers found his roots.

Jeffers received his B.A. at Occidental College in Los Angeles in 1905. He attended graduate school at the University of Southern California (USC) in medicine and at the University of Washington in Seattle in forestry between 1906 and 1910. At USC he met Una Kall Custer, a married woman; they fell deeply in love and their commitment persisted through eight years until a divorce was finally obtained and they were married in 1913. Their thoroughly happy union lasted until her death in 1950. The couple had one daughter (who died in infancy) and twin sons.

In 1914 they moved to Carmel, on the Pacific coast south of San Francisco. Jeffers built a stone tower near their home, a symbol of his self, and dedicated himself to writing poetry, something he had wished to do since his student days. His first volume, *Flagons and Apples*, had been published at his own expense in 1912. Not until the 1920s, with the publication of *Tamar* (1924) and *Roan Stallion* (1925), did he attract critical attention; at this time he became one of America's best-known—and one of its few financially successful—poets. His reputation rose steadily until about the mid-1930s when the public began to tire of his relentless misanthropy.

Over the years Jeffers became more self-aware, and more conscious of his poetic aims, but his practice and his goals changed very little. Because he saw the modern world as a falling away from the American past, he had no interest in finding new forms to suit the age. He wrote brief lyrics and long narrative poems, the former in free verse and the latter in a traditional blank verse. Unlike the modernist poets who rejected narrative, Jeffers wrote many long heroic story poems: *Candor* (1928), *Dear Judas* (1929), *Thurso's Landing* (1932), *Give Your Heart to the Hawks* (1933), and *Solstice* (1935), among others. These were the basis of his popularity during years when the modernists had little audience. In the last two decades of his life he wrote several verse plays based on Greek myths, a logical development from the narrative poems of the 1920s and 1930s.

For his short lyrics Jeffers turned for his subject to the landscape and to wild animals, whom he admired more for their strength and ferocity than for their peacefulness. Adopting a Whitmanesque prophetic tone in many lyrics, he berated rather than celebrated American democracy, expressing his rage at the careless destruction of irrecoverable natural beauty. Where the modernists were mourning the loss of civilization, Jeffers was deploring its triumph.

The text of the poems included here is that of *Selected Poetry* (1963).

# To the Stone-Cutters

Stone-cutters fighting time with marble, you foredefeated
Challengers of oblivion
Eat cynical earnings, knowing rock splits, records fall down,
The square-limbed Roman letters
Scale in the thaws, wear in the rain. The poet as well                    5
Builds his monument mockingly;
For man will be blotted out, the blithe earth die, the brave sun
Die blind and blacken to the heart:
Yet stones have stood for a thousand years, and pained thoughts found
The honey of peace in old poems.                                          10

                                                                      1924

# Shine, Perishing Republic

While this America settles in the mould of its vulgarity, heavily thickening
    to empire,
And protest, only a bubble in the molten mass, pops and sighs out, and the
    mass hardens,

I sadly smiling remember that the flower fades to make fruit, the fruit rots to
    make earth.
Out of the mother; and through the spring exultances, ripeness and decadence;
    and home to the mother.

You making haste haste on decay: not blameworthy; life is good, be it
    stubbornly long or suddenly                                           5
A mortal splendor: meteors are not needed less than mountains: shine, perish-
    ing republic.

But for my children, I would have them keep their distance from the thicken-
    ing center; corruption
Never has been compulsory, when the cities lie at the monster's feet there are
    left the mountains.

And boys, be in nothing so moderate as in love of man, a clever servant,
    insufferable master.

There is the trap that catches noblest spirits, that caught—they say—God,
     when he walked on earth.                                                10

                                                                          1925


# Carmel Point

The extraordinary patience of things!
This beautiful place defaced with a crop of suburban houses—
How beautiful when we first beheld it,
Unbroken field of poppy and lupin walled with clean cliffs;
No intrusion but two or three horses pasturing,                              5
Or a few milch cows rubbing their flanks on the outcrop rockheads—
Now the spoiler has come: does it care? 
Not faintly. It has all time. It knows the people are a tide
That swells and in time will ebb, and all
Their works dissolve. Meanwhile the image of the pristine beauty            10
Lives in the very grain of the granite,
Safe as the endless ocean that climbs our cliff.—As for us:
We must uncenter our minds from ourselves;
We must unhumanize our views a little, and become confident
As the rock and ocean that we were made from.                              15

                                                                          1951


# Birds and Fishes

Every October millions of little fish come along the shore,
Coasting this granite edge of the continent
On their lawful occasions: but what a festival for the seafowl.
What a witches' sabbath of wings
Hides the dark water. The heavy pelicans shout "Haw!" like Job's friend's
     warhorse[1]                                                            5
And dive from the high air, the cormorants
Slip their long black bodies under the water and hunt like wolves
Through the green half-light. Screaming, the gulls watch,
Wild with envy and malice, cursing and snatching. What hysterical greed!
What a filling of pouches! the mob                                          10
Hysteria is nearly human—these decent birds!—as if they were finding
Gold in the street. It is better than gold,
It can be eaten: and which one in all this fury of wildfowl pities the fish?
No one certainly. Justice and mercy
Are human dreams, they do not concern the birds nor the fish nor
     eternal God.
However—look again before you go.                                          15
The wings and the wild hungers, the wave-worn skerries, the bright
     quick minnows
Living in terror to die in torment—

---

1. In Job 39.25, the horse "saith among the trumpets, Ha, ha."

Man's fate and theirs—and the island rocks and immense ocean
    beyond, and Lobos[2]
Darkening above the bay: they are beautiful?                        20
That is their quality: not mercy, not mind, not goodness, but the
    beauty of God.

1963

2. Rocky promontory jutting out into the Pacific Ocean near Carmel, California.

---

# MARIANNE MOORE
## 1887–1972

In her style of life Marianne Moore seemed more like a nineteenth-century than a modern woman, residing lifelong, quietly and unmarried, with her mother and brother. But in her poetry she was a radically inventive modernist, greatly admired by other poets of her generation, and a powerful influence on such later writers as Robert Lowell, Randall Jarrell, and Richard Wilbur. Like her forerunner Emily Dickinson, she made of the traditional and constraining "woman's place" a protected space to do her own work, but unlike Emily Dickinson, she was a deliberate professional, publishing her poems regularly, in touch with the movements and artists of her time. She was famous for the statement that poetry, though departing from the real world, recreated that world within its forms: poems were "imaginary gardens with real toads in them." Her earlier work is distinguished by great precision of observation and language, ornate diction, and complex stanza and prosodic patterns. Her later work is much less ornate, and in revising her poetry, she tended to simplify and shorten.

She was born in Kirkwood, Missouri, a suburb of St. Louis. In her childhood, the family was abandoned by her father; they moved to Carlisle, Pennsylvania, where—in a pattern curiously common among both men and women writers of this period—her mother supported them by teaching school. She went to Bryn Mawr College, graduating in 1909, traveled with her mother in England and France in 1911, and taught at the U.S. Indian School in Carlisle, Pennsylvania, between 1911 and 1915. Having begun to write poetry in college, she was first published in 1915 and 1916 in such little magazines as the *Egoist* (an English magazine with which Ezra Pound was associated), *Poetry*, and *Others* (a journal for experimental writing with which William Carlos Williams was associated, founded by Alfred Kreymbourg, a New York poet and playwright). Through these magazines she entered the avant-garde and modernist world. In 1916 she and her mother merged their household with that of Moore's brother, a Presbyterian minister; they moved with him to a parish in Brooklyn, New York. There Moore was close to literary circles and (as a lifelong Dodger fan) Ebbets Field.

While holding various jobs in schools and libraries, Moore worked at her poetry. A volume called simply *Poems* was brought out in London in 1921 without her knowledge through the efforts of two women friends who were writers, H.D. (whom she had met at Bryn Mawr) and Bryher. Another book, *Observations*, appeared in 1924 and won the Dial Award. In 1925 she began to work as editor of the *Dial*, continuing in this influential position until the magazine was disbanded in 1929. Her reviews and editorial judgments were greatly respected, although her preference for elegance and decorum over sexual frankness was not shared by some of the writers—Hart Crane and James Joyce among them—whose work she rejected or published only after they revised it.

As a critic of poetry Moore wrote numerous essays—her collected prose makes a larger book than her collected poetry. She believed that poets usually undervalued prose; "precision, economy of statement, logic" were features of good prose that could "liberate" the imagination, she wrote. In writing about animals she was able to take advantage of two different prose modes that attracted her—scientific and historical description; the unfamiliar subject matter, because it aroused no prior expectations in readers about its treatment in poetry, gave her something of the freedom of a scientist in the laboratory. Her poems were an amalgam of her own observation and her readings, which she acknowledged by quotation marks and often by footnotes as well. In Moore's writings, the reader almost never finds the conventional poetic allusions that invoke a great tradition and assert the present poet's place in it. Like other modernists, Moore was trying to break with tradition and attach poetry to the world in a new way; unlike them, however, she had no large social mission and did not think of her poetry as necessarily reflecting or commenting on the state of modern civilization.

Against the exactitude and "unbearable accuracy" (as she put it) of her language, Moore counterpointed a complex texture of stanza form and versification. Pound worked with the clause, Williams with the line, H. D. with the image, Stevens and Stein with the word; Moore, unlike these modernist contemporaries, used the entire stanza as the unit of her poetry. Her stanza is composed of regular lines counted by syllables, instead of by stress, which are connected in an elaborate verse pattern, and in which rhymes often occur at unaccented syllables and even in the middle of a word. The effects she achieves are complex and subtle; she was often called the "poet's poet" of her day because the reader needed expert technical understanding to recognize what she was doing.

Nevertheless, this poetry also had a thematic, declarative edge that other modernists tended to ignore. The outbreak of World War II led her to enhance this aspect of her writing. The sentiments expressed in this later verse are the need for human decency and the desirability of a political and social system in which dignity is accorded to all. Moore received the Bollingen, National Book, and Pulitzer awards for *Collected Poems* in 1951, and thereafter was a more public figure. Throughout her lifetime she continued to revise, expand, cut, and select, so that from volume to volume a poem with the same name may become a very different work. Her *Complete Poems* of 1967 represented her poetry as she wanted it remembered, but a full understanding of Moore calls for reading all the versions of her changing work.

# Poetry[1]

I, too, dislike it: there are things that are important beyond all
    this fiddle.
Reading it, however, with a perfect contempt for it, one
    discovers in
it after all, a place for the genuine.                                    5
    Hands that can grasp, eyes
    that can dilate, hair that can rise
      if it must, these things are important not because a

---

1. The version printed here follows the text and format of *Selected Poems* (1935).

high-sounding interpretation can be put upon them but because
     they are                                                                    10
useful. When they become so derivative as to become
     unintelligible,
the same thing may be said for all of us, that we
     do not admire what
     we cannot understand: the bat                                               15
          holding on upside down or in quest of something to

eat, elephants pushing, a wild horse taking a roll, a tireless wolf
     under
a tree, the immovable critic twitching his skin like a horse
     that feels a flea, the base-                                                20
ball fan, the statistician—
     nor is it valid
          to discriminate against "business documents and

school-books";[2] all these phenomena are important. One must
     make a distinction                                                          25
however: when dragged into prominence by half poets, the
     result is not poetry,
nor till the poets among us can be
     "literalists of
     the imagination"[3]— above                                                  30
          insolence and triviality and can present

for inspection, "imaginary gardens with real toads in them," shall
     we have
it. In the meantime, if you demand on the one hand,
     the raw material of poetry in                                               35
     all its rawness and
     that which is on the other hand
          genuine, then you are interested in poetry.

                                                             1921, 1935


## To a Snail[1]

If "compression is the first grace of style,"[2]
you have it. Contractility is a virtue
as modesty is a virtue.
It is not the acquisition of any one thing
that is able to adorn,                                                           5
or the incidental quality that occurs

2. "Diary of Tolstoy (Dutton), p. 84. 'Where the boundary between prose and poetry lies, I shall never be able to understand. The question is raised in manuals of style, yet the answer to it lies beyond me. Poetry is verse; prose is not verse. Or else poetry is everything with the exception of business documents and school books' " [Moore's note].
3. "Yeats' *Ideas of Good and Evil* (A. H. Bullen), p. 182. 'The limitation of his view was from the very intensity of his vision; he was a too literal realist of imagi-

nation, as others are of nature; and because he believed that the figures seen by the mind's eye, when exalted by inspiration, were "eternal existences," symbols of divine essences, he hated every grace of style that might obscure their lineaments' " [Moore's note].
1. The text is from *Complete Poems* (1967).
2. " 'The very first grace of style is that which comes from compression.' *Demetrius on Style* translated by W. Hamilton Fyfe. Heinemann, 1932" [Moore's note].

as a concomitant of something well said,
that we value in style,
but the principle that is hid:
in the absence of feet, "a method of conclusions";          10
"a knowledge of principles,"
in the curious phenomenon of your occipital horn.

1924

## The Mind Is an Enchanting Thing[1]

is an enchanted thing
          like the glaze on a
katydid-wing
                    subdivided by sun
                    till the nettings are legion.          5
Like Gieseking playing Scarlatti;[2]

like the apteryx-awl
          as a beak, or the
kiwi's[3] rain-shawl
                    of haired feathers, the mind          10
                    feeling its way as though blind,
walks along with its eyes on the ground.

It has memory's ear
          that can hear without
having to hear.          15
                    Like the gyroscope's fall,
                    truly unequivocal
because trued by regnant certainty,

it is a power of
          strong enchantment. It          20
is like the dove-
                    neck animated by
                    sun; it is memory's eye;
it's conscientious inconsistency.

It tears off the veil; tears          25
          the temptation, the
mist the heart wears,
                    from its eye—if the heart
                    has a face; it takes apart
dejection. It's fire in the dove-neck's          30

iridescence; in the
          inconsistencies
of Scarlatti.

1. The text is from *Complete Poems* (1967).
2. Walter Wilhelm Gieseking (1895–1956), French-
born German pianist, known for his renditions of compositions by the Italian composer Domenico Scarlatti

(1685–1757).
3. Apteryx, a flightless New Zealand bird, related to
the kiwi, with a beak shaped like an awl.

> Unconfusion submits
> its confusion to proof; it's                                    35
> not a Herod's oath that cannot change.[4]

1944

## "Keeping Their World Large"[1]

*All too literally, their flesh and their spirit are our shield.*
New York Times, June 7, 1944

I should like to see that country's tiles, bedrooms,
stone patios
    and ancient wells: Rinaldo
Caramonica's the cobbler's, Frank Sblendorio's
    and Dominick Angelastro's country—                    5
        the grocer's, the iceman's, the dancer's—the
beautiful Miss Damiano's;[2] wisdom's

and all angels' Italy, this Christmas Day
this Christmas year.
        A noiseless piano, an                         10
innocent war, the heart that can act against itself, Here,
    each unlike and all alike, could
        so many—stumbling, falling, multiplied
till bodies lay as ground to walk on—

"If Christ and the apostles died in vain,                         15
I'll die in vain with them"
        against this way of victory.
That forest of white crosses!
    My eyes won't close to it.

All laid like animals for sacrifice—                             20
like Isaac on the mount,
        were their own sacrifice.

Marching to death, marching to life?
"Keeping their world large,"
        whose spirits and whose bodies                    25
all too literally were our shield,
    are still our shield.

They fought the enemy,
we fight fat living and self-pity.
        Shine, o shine,                               30
unfalsifying sun, on this sick scene.

1951, 1967

4. Herod Antipas (d. A.D. 39), ruler of Judea under the Romans. He had John the Baptist beheaded in fulfillment of a promise to Salome (Mark 6.22–27). 1. The poem refers to the destruction of Italy by the retreating German forces toward the end of World War II. 2. The names are of Italian-Americans living in Moore's neighborhood.

## O to Be a Dragon

If I, like Solomon, . . .
could have my wish—

    my wish . . . O to be a dragon,
a symbol of the power of Heaven—of silkworm
size or immense; at times invisible.      5
Felicitous phenomenon!

                    1959, 1967

---

# T. S. ELIOT
## 1888–1965

The publication in 1922 of *The Waste Land* in the British little magazine *Criterion* and the American *Dial* was a cultural and literary event. The poem's title and the view it incorporated of modern civilization seemed, to many, to catch precisely the state of culture and society after World War I. The war, supposedly fought to save European civilization, had been the most brutal and destructive in history: what kind of civilization, after all, could have allowed it to take place? The long, fragmented structure of *The Waste Land*, too, contained so many technical innovations that ideas of what poetry was and how it worked seemed fundamentally changed. A generation of poets either imitated or resisted it.

The author of this poem was an American living in London, T. S. Eliot. He had a comfortable upbringing in St. Louis: his mother involved herself in cultural and charitable activities and wrote poetry; his father was a successful businessman. His grandfather Eliot had been a New England Unitarian minister who, moving to St. Louis, had founded Washington University. Eliot was thus a product of that New England–based "genteel tradition" that shaped the nation's cultural life after the Civil War. He attended Harvard for both undergraduate and graduate work (1906–10, 1911–14). He studied at the Sorbonne in Paris from 1910 to 1911 and at Oxford from 1915 to 1916, writing a dissertation on the idealistic philosophy of the English logician and metaphysician F. H. Bradley (1846–1924). The war prevented Eliot from returning to Harvard for the oral defense required for the Ph.D. degree, and this delay became the occasion of his turning to a life in poetry and letters rather than in academics.

Eliot had begun writing traditional poetry as a college student. In 1908, however, he read Arthur Symons's *The Symbolist Movement in Literature* and learned about Jules LaForgue and other French Symbolist poets. Symons's book altered Eliot's view of poetry, as *The Love Song of J. Alfred Prufrock* (published in *Poetry* in 1915) and *Preludes* (published in *Blast* in the same year) clearly showed. Ezra Pound, reading this work, began enthusiastically introducing Eliot in literary circles as a young American who had "trained himself *and* modernized himself *on his own*." Pound helped Eliot over several years to get financially established. In addition, he was a perceptive reader and critic of Eliot's draft poems.

Eliot now settled in England, marrying Vivian Haigh-Wood in 1915. The marriage was not a success. Separated in 1932, they never divorced; Haigh-Wood died in an institution in 1947. After marrying, Eliot worked in London, first as a teacher and then from 1917 to 1925 in the foreign department of Lloyd's Bank, hoping to find time to write poetry and literary essays. His criticism was published in the *Egoist* and then in the little magazine that he founded, *Criterion*, which was published from 1922 to 1939. His persuasive style, a mixture of advocacy and judiciousness, effectively counterpointed Pound's "battering ram" approach; the two together had a tremendous effect on how poetry of the day was written and how poetry of the past was evaluated.

Eliot began working on *The Waste Land* in 1921 and finished it in a Swiss sanatorium while recovering from a mental collapse brought on by overwork, marital problems, and general depression. He accepted some alterations suggested by his wife and cut huge chunks out of the poem on Pound's advice. Indeed, although Pound's work on the poem was all excision, study of the manuscript before and after Pound's suggestions were incorporated has led some critics to suggest that we should think of *The Waste Land* as jointly authored. The poem as published in *Criterion* and the *Dial* had no footnotes; these were added for its publication in book form and added yet another layer (possibly self-mocking) to the complex texture of the poem.

*The Waste Land* consists of five discontinuous segments, each composed of fragments incorporating multiple voices and characters, literary and historical allusions, bits and pieces of contemporary life, myths and legends. "These fragments I have shored against my ruins," the poet writes, asking whether he can form any coherent structure from the splinters of civilization. Lacking narrative and expository shape, the poem is organized by recurrent allusions to the myth of seasonal death and rebirth that, according to much anthropological thinking of the time, underlay all religions. In Sir James Frazer's *The Golden Bough* and Jessie Weston's *From Ritual to Romance* Eliot found a repertory of myths through which he could invoke, without specifically naming any religion, the story of a desert land brought to life by a king's sacrifice. Although it gestured toward religious belief, *The Waste Land* was not an affirmative or religious poem; the desperate quest for regeneration in a cacaphonous, desolate landscape remains unfulfilled.

Many readers saw *The Waste Land* as the definitive cultural statement of its time, but it was not definitive for Eliot. In fact, for Eliot himself the poem may have been much less broadly conceived and, above all, an indirect confession of personal discord. Whatever the fate of culture, the individual needed to work for personal certainty. In a preface to the collection of essays *For Lancelot Andrewes* (1928) he declared himself a "classicist in literature, royalist in politics, and anglo-catholic in religion." After *The Hollow Men* and the *Sweeney* poems, which continue *The Waste Land*'s critique of modern civilization, he turned increasingly to poems of religious doubt and reconciliation. *The Journey of the Magi* and *Ash Wednesday* are poems about the search for a faith that is desperately needed, yet difficult to sustain. The *Four Quartets*, begun with *Burnt Norton* in 1934 and completed in 1943, are poems written after his conversion to Christian faith; they are not so much reports of a faith already secure as dramatizations of the continual process of arriving at belief. In this process Eliot found a center for his own life as well as for his later poetry. The *Four Quartets* incorporate a good deal of the discursive and expository, elements that he had objected to in his earlier essays and rejected from his earlier poems.

An emphasis on "order," "hierarchy," and racial homogeneity emerged in his social essays of the late 1920s and 1930s, and nasty instances of anti-Semitism had appeared earlier in the *Sweeney* poems. It is clear that for Eliot and other poets who saw upheaval and breakdown in the modern world, the stability promised by hierarchical authoritarian regimes was often appealing. They did not form a unified group, however; Eliot's versions of a better future involved an orthodox Christian faith in opposition to Pound's secularism and the more or less ad hoc religious eclecticism of a poet like John Crowe Ransom. When World War II began, Eliot—again in contrast to Pound—retreated from politics. In the world of the little magazine as well as in academia, Eliot's conservative critical essays tended to carry as much weight as his poetry. His influential *Tradition and the Individual Talent* defined the Western poetic tradition as an organic, elastic equilibrium that constantly reformed itself as major new poets entered in. The essay argued that the proper context for understanding poems and poets was not social, historical, or political circumstances; it was entirely the context of other poems and poets. Literature was a world of its own. Other essays denigrated didactic, expository, or narrative poets like Milton and the Victorians while applauding the verbally complex, ironic, indirect, symbolic work of seventeenth-century Metaphysical poets like Donne and Herbert.

For the New Criticism, which approached each poem as a self-contained verbal artifact demanding careful analysis for imagery, allusion, ambiguity, and the like, Eliot's essays provided theory, his poetry opportunities for practical criticism. But when critics used Eliot's standards of difficult indirection to judge literary quality and made interpretation the main task of readers, they often overlooked the simple lyricism, obvious didacticism, and straightforward humor of Eliot's own poetry. And they failed to see the poems' specific cultural and autobiographical content.

However elitist his pronouncements, however hostile to modernity he claimed to be, Eliot actually drew very heavily on popular forms and longed to have wide cultural influence. There are vaudeville turns throughout *The Waste Land.* He admired Charlie Chaplin and longed to write "for as large and miscellaneous an audience as possible." He pursued this ambition by writing verse plays. *Murder in the Cathedral* (1935) was a church pageant; *The Family Reunion* (1939), *The Cocktail Party* (1949), *The Confidential Clerk* (1953), and *The Elder Statesman* (1959), all religious in theme (though their symbolism was often hidden), were successfully produced in London and on Broadway. Although Eliot remained a resident of England, he returned to the United States frequently in the 1930s and 1940s to lecture and to give readings of his poems. On these visits he played the role of aloof English gentleman as though he had never known a city called St. Louis. He married his assistant, Valerie Fletcher, in 1957. By the time of his death he had become a social and cultural institution.

The text of the poems included here is that of *The Complete Poems and Plays of T. S. Eliot* (1969).

# The Love Song of J. Alfred Prufrock

S'io credessi che mia risposta fosse
a persona che mai tornasse al mondo,
questa fiamma staria senza più scosse.
Ma per ciò che giammai di questo fondo
non tornò vivo alcun, s'i'odo il vero,
senza tema d'infamia ti rispondo.[1]

Let us go then, you and I,
When the evening is spread out against the sky
Like a patient etherised upon a table;
Let us go, through certain half-deserted streets,

1. If I thought that my reply would be to one who would ever return to the world, this flame would stay without further movement; but since none has ever returned alive from this depth, if what I hear is true, I answer you without fear of infamy (Dante, *Inferno* 27.61–66). The speaker, Guido da Montefeltro, consumed in flame as punishment for giving false counsel, confesses his shame without fear of its being reported since he believes Dante cannot return to earth.

The muttering retreats                                                         5
Of restless nights in one-night cheap hotels
And sawdust restaurants with oyster-shells:
Streets that follow like a tedious argument
Of insidious intent
To lead you to an overwhelming question . . .                                  10
Oh, do not ask, 'What is it?'
Let us go and make our visit.

In the room the women come and go
Talking of Michelangelo.

The yellow fog that rubs its back upon the window-panes,                       15
The yellow smoke that rubs its muzzle on the window-panes,
Licked its tongue into the corners of the evening,
Lingered upon the pools that stand in drains,
Let fall upon its back the soot that falls from chimneys,
Slipped by the terrace, made a sudden leap,                                    20
And seeing that it was a soft October night,
Curled once about the house, and fell asleep.

And indeed there will be time²
For the yellow smoke that slides along the street
Rubbing its back upon the window-panes;                                        25
There will be time, there will be time
To prepare a face to meet the faces that you meet;
There will be time to murder and create,
And time for all the works and days³ of hands
That lift and drop a question on your plate;                                   30
Time for you and time for me,
And time yet for a hundred indecisions,
And for a hundred visions and revisions,
Before the taking of a toast and tea.

In the room the women come and go                                             35
Talking of Michelangelo.

And indeed there will be time
To wonder, 'Do I dare?' and, 'Do I dare?'
Time to turn back and descend the stair,
With a bald spot in the middle of my hair—                                    40
(They will say: 'How his hair is growing thin!')
My morning coat, my collar mounting firmly to the chin,
My necktie rich and modest, but asserted by a simple pin—
(They will say: 'But how his arms and legs are thin!')
Do I dare                                                                      45
Disturb the universe?
In a minute there is time
For decisions and revisions which a minute will reverse.

2. An echo of Andrew Marvell, *To His Coy Mistress* (1681): "Had we but world enough and time."

3. *Works and Days* is a didactic poem about farming by the Greek poet Hesiod (8th century B.C.).

For I have known them all already, known them all—
Have known the evenings, mornings, afternoons,                               50
I have measured out my life with coffee spoons;
I know the voices dying with a dying fall[4]
Beneath the music from a farther room.
    So how should I presume?

And I have known the eyes already, known them all—                          55
The eyes that fix you in a formulated phrase,
And when I am formulated, sprawling on a pin,
When I am pinned and wriggling on the wall,
Then how should I begin
To spit out all the butt-ends of my days and ways?                          60
    And how should I presume?

And I have known the arms already, known them all—
Arms that are braceleted and white and bare
(But in the lamplight, downed with light brown hair!)
Is it perfume from a dress                                                    65
That makes me so digress?
Arms that lie along a table, or wrap about a shawl.
    And should I then presume?
    And how should I begin?

. . . . . .
Shall I say, I have gone at dusk through narrow streets                       70
And watched the smoke that rises from the pipes
Of lonely men in shirt-sleeves, leaning out of windows? . . .

I should have been a pair of ragged claws
Scuttling across the floors of silent seas.

. . . . . .
And the afternoon, the evening, sleeps so peacefully!                         75
Smoothed by long fingers,
Asleep . . . tired . . . or it malingers,
Stretched on the floor, here beside you and me.
Should I, after tea and cakes and ices,
Have the strength to force the moment to its crisis?                          80
But though I have wept and fasted, wept and prayed,
Though I have seen my head (grown slightly bald) brought in upon a platter,[5]
I am no prophet—and here's no great matter;
I have seen the moment of my greatness flicker,
And I have seen the eternal Footman hold my coat, and snicker,               85
And in short, I was afraid.

And would it have been worth it, after all,
After the cups, the marmalade, the tea,
Among the porcelain, among some talk of you and me,
Would it have been worth while,                                              90

---

4. Echo of Duke Orsino's invocation of music in
Shakespeare's *Twelfth Night* (1.1.4): "If music be the
food of love, play on . . . That strain again! It had a
dying fall."

5. The head of the prophet John the Baptist, who was
killed at the behest of Princess Salome, was brought to
her on a platter (see Mark 6.17–20, Matthew 14.3–11,
and Oscar Wilde's play *Salome*, 1894).

To have bitten off the matter with a smile,
To have squeezed the universe into a ball
To roll it towards some overwhelming question,
To say: 'I am Lazarus,[6] come from the dead,
Come back to tell you all, I shall tell you all'—                    95
If one, settling a pillow by her head,
    Should say: 'That is not what I meant at all.
    That is not it, at all.'

And would it have been worth it, after all,
Would it have been worth while,                                      100
After the sunsets and the dooryards and the sprinkled streets,
After the novels, after the teacups, after the skirts that trail along the floor—
And this, and so much more?—
It is impossible to say just what I mean!
But as if a magic lantern threw the nerves in patterns on a screen:   105
Would it have been worth while
If one, settling a pillow or throwing off a shawl,
And turning toward the window, should say:
    'That is not it at all,
    That is not what I meant, at all.'                               110
    .   .   .   .   .
No! I am not Prince Hamlet, nor was meant to be;
Am an attendant lord, one that will do
To swell a progress,[7] start a scene or two,
Advise the prince; no doubt, an easy tool,
Deferential, glad to be of use,                                      115
Politic, cautious, and meticulous;
Full of high sentence,[8] but a bit obtuse;
At times, indeed, almost ridiculous—
Almost, at times, the Fool.

I grow old . . . I grow old . . .                                    120
I shall wear the bottoms of my trousers rolled.

Shall I part my hair behind? Do I dare to eat a peach?
I shall wear white flannel trousers, and walk upon the beach.
I have heard the mermaids singing, each to each.

I do not think that they will sing to me.                            125

I have seen them riding seaward on the waves
Combing the white hair of the waves blown back
When the wind blows the water white and black.

We have lingered in the chambers of the sea
By sea-girls wreathed with seaweed red and brown                     130
Till human voices wake us, and we drown.

                                                    1915, 1917

---

6. The resurrection of Lazarus is recounted in John          often portrayed on Elizabethan stages.
11.1–44.                                                      8. Opinions, sententiousness.
7. A journey or procession made by royal courts and

# Sweeney among the Nightingales[1]

*ὦμοι, πέπληγμαι καιρίαν πληγὴν ἔσω.*[2]

Apeneck Sweeney spreads his knees
Letting his arms hang down to laugh,
The zebra stripes along his jaw
Swelling to maculate giraffe.

The circles of the stormy moon      5
Slide westward toward the River Plate,[3]
Death and the Raven drift above
And Sweeney guards the hornèd gate.[4]

Gloomy Orion and the Dog[5]
Are veiled; and hushed the shrunken seas;     10
The person in the Spanish cape
Tries to sit on Sweeney's knees

Slips and pulls the table cloth
Overturns a coffee-cup,
Reorganised upon the floor     15
She yawns and draws a stocking up;

The silent man in mocha brown
Sprawls at the window-sill and gapes;
The waiter brings in oranges
Bananas figs and hothouse grapes;     20

The silent vertebrate in brown
Contracts and concentrates, withdraws;
Rachel *née* Rabinovitch
Tears at the grapes with murderous paws;

She and the lady in the cape     25
Are suspect, thought to be in league;
Therefore the man with heavy eyes
Declines the gambit, shows fatigue,

Leaves the room and reappears
Outside the window, leaning in,     30
Branches of wistaria
Circumscribe a golden grin;

1. This poem, dramatizing a tragicomic conspiracy, employs a regular stanza pattern (rhyming quatrains), inspired by the *Emaux et Camées* (Enamels and cameos, 1852) of the French writer Théophile Gautier (1811–1872). The poem juxtaposes the imminent death of Sweeney in a grubby and nonheroic present, the ritual sacrifice of Christ enacted in a convent, the murder (by his wife and her lover) of heroic Agamemnon in Aeschylus's tragedy, and the tragedy of the mythological Philomela. Raped by her sister's husband, who then cut out her tongue, Philomela was transformed into a nightingale whose song springs from the violation she has suffered but cannot report.
2. Alas, I am struck a mortal blow within (Greek; Aeschylus, *Agamemnon*); this is Agamemnon's cry when he is murdered.
3. Estuary between Argentina and Uruguay.
4. The Gates of Horn, in the Greek underworld; dreams pass through them to the upper world.
5. Orion in mythology was a handsome hunter, slain by Diana, then immortalized as a constellation of stars. "Dog": the brilliant Dog Star, Sirius, who in mythology sired the Sphinx and, in Homer, was Orion's dog.

The host with someone indistinct
Converses at the door apart,
The nightingales are singing near                                      35
The Convent of the Sacred Heart,

And sang within the bloody wood
When Agamemnon cried aloud
And let their liquid siftings fall
To stain the stiff dishonoured shroud.                                 40

1918, 1919

## *From* Tradition and the Individual Talent[1]

In English writing we seldom speak of tradition, though we occasionally apply its name in deploring its absence. We cannot refer to 'the tradition' or to 'a tradition'; at most, we employ the adjective in saying that the poetry of So-and-so is 'traditional' or even 'too traditional.' Seldom, perhaps, does the word appear except in a phrase of censure. If otherwise, it is vaguely approbative, with the implication, as to the work approved, of some pleasing archaeological reconstruction. You can hardly make the word agreeable to English ears without this comfortable reference to the reassuring science of archaeology.

Certainly the word is not likely to appear in our appreciations of living or dead writers. Every nation, every race, has not only its own creative, but its own critical turn of mind; and is even more oblivious of the shortcomings and limitations of its critical habits than of those of its creative genius. We know, or think we know, from the enormous mass of critical writing that has appeared in the French language the critical method or habit of the French; we only conclude (we are such unconscious people) that the French are 'more critical' than we, and sometimes even plume ourselves a little with the fact, as if the French were the less spontaneous. Perhaps they are; but we might remind ourselves that criticism is as inevitable as breathing, and that we should be none the worse for articulating what passes in our minds when we read a book and feel an emotion about it, for criticizing our own minds in their work of criticism. One of the facts that might come to light in this process is our tendency to insist, when we praise a poet, upon those aspects of his work in which he least resembles anyone else. In these aspects or parts of his work we pretend to find what is individual, what is the peculiar essence of the man. We dwell with satisfaction upon the poet's difference from his predecessors, especially his immediate predecessors; we endeavour to find something that can be isolated in order to be enjoyed. Whereas if we approach a poet without this prejudice we shall often find that not only the best, but the most individual parts of his work may be those in which the dead poets, his ancestors, assert their immortality most vigorously. And I do not mean the impressionable period of adolescence, but the period of full maturity.

Yet if the only form of tradition, of handing down, consisted in following the ways of the immediate generation before us in a blind or timid adherence to its successes, 'tradition' should positively be discouraged. We have seen

1. From *The Sacred Wood* (1920), first published in the *Egoist* (1919). The text is that of *Selected Essays* (1951).

many such simple currents soon lost in the sand; and novelty is better than repetition. Tradition is a matter of much wider significance. It cannot be inherited, and if you want it you must obtain it by great labour. It involves, in the first place, the historical sense, which we may call nearly indispensable to anyone who would continue to be a poet beyond his twenty-fifth year; and the historical sense involves a perception, not only of the pastness of the past, but of its presence; the historical sense compels a man to write not merely with his own generation in his bones, but with a feeling that the whole of the literature of Europe from Homer and within it the whole of the literature of his own country has a simultaneous existence and composes a simultaneous order. This historical sense, which is a sense of the timeless as well as of the temporal and of the timeless and of the temporal together, is what makes a writer traditional. And it is at the same time what makes a writer most acutely conscious of his place in time, of his own contemporaneity.

No poet, no artist of any art, has his complete meaning alone. His significance, his appreciation is the appreciation of his relation to the dead poets and artists. You cannot value him alone; you must set him, for contrast and comparison, among the dead. I mean this as a principle of aesthetic, not merely historical, criticism. The necessity that he shall conform, that he shall cohere, is not onesided; what happens when a new work of art is created is something that happens simultaneously to all the works of art which preceded it. The existing monuments form an ideal order among themselves, which is modified by the introduction of the new (the really new) work of art among them. The existing order is complete before the new work arrives; for order to persist after the supervention of novelty, the *whole* existing order must be, if ever so slightly, altered; and so the relations, proportions, values of each work of art toward the whole are readjusted; and this is conformity between the old and the new. Whoever has approved this idea of order, of the form of European, of English literature will not find it preposterous that the past should be altered by the present as much as the present is directed by the past. And the poet who is aware of this will be aware of great difficulties and responsibilities.

\* \* \*

## II

Honest criticism and sensitive appreciation are directed not upon the poet but upon the poetry. If we attend to the confused cries of the newspaper critics and the susurrus[2] of popular repetition that follows, we shall hear the names of poets in great numbers; if we seek not Blue-book[3] knowledge but the enjoyment of poetry, and ask for a poem, we shall seldom find it. I have tried to point out the importance of the relation of the poem to other poems by other authors, and suggested the conception of poetry as a living whole of all the poetry that has ever been written. The other aspect of this Impersonal theory of poetry is the relation of the poem to its author. And I hinted, by an analogy, that the mind of the mature poet differs from that of the immature one not precisely in any valuation of 'personality,' not being necessarily more interesting, or having 'more to say,' but rather by being a more finely perfected medium in which special, or very varied, feelings are at liberty to enter into new combinations.

---

2. Murmuring, buzzing (Latin).　　　　3. Official British government publication.

The analogy was that of the catalyst. When the two gases previously mentioned are mixed in the presence of a filament of platinum, they form sulphurous acid. This combination takes place only if the platinum is present; nevertheless the newly formed acid contains no trace of platinum, and the platinum itself is apparently unaffected: has remained inert, neutral, and unchanged. The mind of the poet is the shred of platinum. It may partly or exclusively operate upon the experience of the man himself; but, the more perfect the artist, the more completely separate in him will be the man who suffers and the mind which creates; the more perfectly will the mind digest and transmute the passions which are its material.

*   *   *

It is not in his personal emotions, the emotions provoked by particular events in his life, that the poet is in any way remarkable or interesting. His particular emotions may be simple, or crude, or flat. The emotion in his poetry will be a very complex thing, but not with the complexity of the emotions of people who have very complex or unusual emotions in life. One error, in fact, of eccentricity in poetry is to seek for new human emotions to express, and in this search for novelty in the wrong place it discovers the perverse. The business of the poet is not to find new emotions, but to use the ordinary ones and, in working them up into poetry, to express feelings which are not in actual emotions at all. And emotions which he has never experienced will serve his turn as well as those familiar to him. Consequently, we must believe that 'emotion recollected in tranquillity'[4] is an inexact formula. For it is neither emotion, nor recollection, nor, without distortion of meaning, tranquillity. It is a concentration, and a new thing resulting from the concentration, of a very great number of experiences which to the practical and active person would not seem to be experiences at all; it is a concentration which does not happen consciously or of deliberation. These experiences are not 'recollected,' and they finally unite in an atmosphere which is 'tranquil' only in that it is a passive attending upon the event. Of course this is not quite the whole story. There is a great deal, in the writing of poetry, which must be conscious and deliberate. In fact, the bad poet is usually unconscious where he ought to be conscious, and conscious where he ought to be unconscious. Both errors tend to make him 'personal.' Poetry is not a turning loose of emotion, but an escape from emotion; it is not the expression of personality, but an escape from personality. But, of course, only those who have personality and emotions know what it means to want to escape from these things.

III

ὁ δὲ νοῦς ἴσως θειότερόν τι χαὶ ἀπαθές ἐστιν.[5]

This essay proposes to halt at the frontiers of metaphysics or mysticism, and confine itself to such practical conclusions as can be applied by the responsible person interested in poetry. To divert interest from the poet to the poetry is a laudable aim: for it would conduce to a juster estimation of actual poetry, good

---

4. In his Preface to *Lyrical Ballads* (2d ed., 1800), William Wordsworth (1770–1850) declared that "poetry takes its origin from emotion recollected in tranquility."

5. No doubt the mind is something divine and not subject to external impressions (Greek; Aristotle, *De Anima* [On the soul] 1.4).

and bad. There are many people who appreciate the expression of sincere emotion in verse, and there is a smaller number of people who can appreciate technical excellence. But very few know when there is an expression of *significant* emotion, emotion which has its life in the poem and not in the history of the poet. The emotion of art is impersonal. And the poet cannot reach this impersonality without surrendering himself wholly to the work to be done. And he is not likely to know what is to be done unless he lives in what is not merely the present, but the present moment of the past, unless he is conscious, not of what is dead, but of what is already living.

1919, 1920

# The Waste Land[1]

'Nam Sibyllam quidem Cumis ego ipse oculis meis vidi in ampulla pendere, et cum illi pueri dicerent: Σίβυλλα τί θέλεις; respondebat illa: ἀποθανεῖν θέλω.'[2]

FOR EZRA POUND
IL MIGLIOR FABBRO.[3]

## I. The Burial of the Dead[4]

April is the cruellest month, breeding
Lilacs out of the dead land, mixing
Memory and desire, stirring
Dull roots with spring rain.
Winter kept us warm, covering                        5
Earth in forgetful snow, feeding
A little life with dried tubers.
Summer surprised us, coming over the Starnbergersee[5]
With a shower of rain; we stopped in the colonnade,
And went on in sunlight, into the Hofgarten,[6]          10
And drank coffee, and talked for an hour.
Bin gar keine Russin, stamm' aus Litauen, echt deutsch.[7]
And when we were children, staying at the arch-duke's,
My cousin's, he took me out on a sled,
And I was frightened. He said, Marie,                   15

1. Eliot's notes for the first hardcover edition of *The Waste Land* opened with his acknowledgment that "not only the title, but the plan and a good deal of the incidental symbolism of the poem" were suggested by Miss Jessie L. Weston's book on the Grail Legend: *From Ritual to Romance* (1920) and that he was indebted also to James G. Frazer's *The Golden Bough* (1890–1915), "especially the two volumes *Adonis, Attis, Osiris*," which deal with vegetation myths and fertility rites. Eliot's notes are incorporated in the footnotes to this text. Many critics believe that the notes were added in a spirit of parody. The numerous and extensive literary quotations add to the multivocal effect of the poem and constitute a sort of anthology of works that influenced Eliot.
2. A quotation from Petronius's *Satyricon* (1st century

A.D.) and about the Sibyl (prophetess) of Cumae, blessed with eternal life by Apollo but doomed to perpetual old age, who guided Aeneas though Hades in Virgil's *Aeneid*: "For once I myself saw with my own eyes the Sibyl at Cumae hanging in a cage, and when the boys said to her 'Sibyl, what do you want?' she replied, 'I want to die.' "
3. "The better maker," the tribute in Dante's *Purgatorio* 26.117 to the Provençal poet Arnaut Daniel.
4. The title of the Anglican burial service.
5. A lake near Munich. Lines 8–16 were suggested by the Countess Marie Larisch's memoir, *My Past* (1913).
6. A public park in Munich, with cafés; former grounds of a Bavarian palace.
7. I am certainly not Russian; I come from Lithuania, a true German (German).

Marie, hold on tight. And down we went.
In the mountains, there you feel free.
I read, much of the night, and go south in the winter.

What are the roots that clutch, what branches grow
Out of this stony rubbish? Son of man,[8]      20
You cannot say, or guess, for you know only
A heap of broken images, where the sun beats,
And the dead tree gives no shelter, the cricket no relief,[9]
And the dry stone no sound of water. Only
There is shadow under this red rock,[1]      25
(Come in under the shadow of this red rock),
And I will show you something different from either
Your shadow at morning striding behind you
Or your shadow at evening rising to meet you;
I will show you fear in a handful of dust.      30
> *Frisch weht der Wind*
> *Der Heimat zu*
> *Mein Irisch Kind,*
> *Wo weilest du?*[2]
'You gave me hyacinths first a year ago;      35
'They called me the hyacinth girl.'
—Yet when we came back, late, from the hyacinth garden,
Your arms full, and your hair wet, I could not
Speak, and my eyes failed, I was neither
Living nor dead, and I knew nothing,      40
Looking into the heart of light, the silence.
*Oed' und leer das Meer.*[3]

Madame Sosostris,[4] famous clairvoyante,
Had a bad cold, nevertheless
Is known to be the wisest woman in Europe,      45
With a wicked pack of cards.[5] Here, said she,
Is your card, the drowned Phoenician Sailor,[6]

---

8. "Cf. Ezekiel II, i" [Eliot's note], where God addresses the prophet Ezekiel as "Son of man" and declares: "Stand upon thy feet, and I will speak unto thee."

9. "Cf. Ecclesiastes XII, v" [Eliot's note], where the preacher describes the bleakness of old age when "the grasshopper shall be a burden, and desire shall fail."

1. Cf. Isaiah 32.1–2 and the prophecy that the reign of the Messiah "shall be . . . as rivers of water in a dry place, as the shadow of a great rock in a weary land."

2. "V. [see] *Tristan und Isolde,* I, verses 5–8" [Eliot's note]. In Wagner's opera, a carefree sailor aboard Tristan's ship recalls his girlfriend in Ireland: "Fresh blows the wind to the homeland; my Irish child, where are you waiting?" The young boy Hyacinth (below), in Ovid's *Metamorphoses* 10, was beloved by Apollo but slain by a jealous rival. The Greeks celebrated his festival in May.

3. In *Tristan* "III, verse 24" [Eliot's note] the dying Tristan, awaiting the ship that carries his beloved Isolde, is told that "Empty and barren is the sea."

4. Eliot derived the name from "Sesostris, the Sorceress of Ectabana," the pseudo-Egyptian name assumed by a woman who tells fortunes in Aldous Huxley's novel *Chrome Yellow* (1921). Sesostris was a twelfth-dynasty Egyptian king.

5. The tarot deck of cards. Eliot's note to this passage reads: "I am not familiar with the exact constitution of the Tarot pack of cards, from which I have obviously departed to suit my own convenience. The Hanged Man, a member of the traditional pack, fits my purpose in two ways: because he is associated in my mind with the Hanged God of Frazer, and because I associate him with the hooded figure in the passage of the disciples to Emmaus in Part V. The Phoenician Sailor and the Merchant appear later; also the 'crowds of people,' and Death by Water is executed in Part IV. The Man with Three Staves (an authentic member of the Tarot pack) I associate, quite arbitrarily, with the Fisher King himself."

6. The Phoenician Sailor is a symbolic figure that includes "Mr. Eugenides, the Smyrna merchant" in Part III and "Phlebas the Phoenician" in Part IV. The ancient Phoenicians were seagoing merchants whose crews spread Egyptian fertility cults throughout the Mediterranean.

(Those are pearls that were in his eyes.[7] Look!)
Here is Belladonna, the Lady of the Rocks,[8]
The lady of situations.                                                    50
Here is the man with three staves, and here the Wheel,
And here is the one-eyed merchant,[9] and this card,
Which is blank, is something he carries on his back,
Which I am forbidden to see. I do not find
The Hanged Man. Fear death by water.                                       55
I see crowds of people, walking round in a ring.
Thank you. If you see dear Mrs. Equitone,
Tell her I bring the horoscope myself:
One must be so careful these days.

Unreal City,[1]                                                            60
Under the brown fog of a winter dawn,
A crowd flowed over London Bridge, so many,
I had not thought death had undone so many.[2]
Sighs, short and infrequent, were exhaled,[3]
And each man fixed his eyes before his feet.                               65
Flowed up the hill and down King William Street,
To where Saint Mary Woolnoth kept the hours
With a dead sound on the final stroke of nine.[4]
There I saw one I knew, and stopped him, crying: 'Stetson!
'You who were with me in the ships at Mylae![5]                            70
'That corpse you planted last year in your garden,
'Has it begun to sprout? Will it bloom this year?
'Or has the sudden frost disturbed its bed?
'O keep the Dog far hence, that's friend to men,
'Or with his nails he'll dig it up again![6]                               75
'You! hypocrite lecteur!—mon semblable,—mon frère!'[7]

---

7. The line is a quotation from Ariel's song in Shake-speare, *The Tempest* 1.2.398. Prince Ferdinand, disconsolate because he thinks his father has drowned in the storm, is consoled when Ariel sings of a miraculous "sea change" that has transformed death into "something rich and strange." Fear of drowning and the sea as an agent of purification and possible resurrection are important throughout the poem.
8. Belladonna, literally meaning "beautiful lady," is the name of both the poisonous plant deadly nightshade and a cosmetic. It suggests also the Christian madonna or Virgin Mary, particularly, in context, the painting *Madonna of the Rocks* by Leonardo da Vinci.
9. These three figures are taken from the Tarot deck.
1. "Cf. Baudelaire: 'Fourmillante cité, cité pleine de rêves, / Où le spectre en plein jour raccroche le passant" [Eliot's note]. The lines are quoted from *Les Sept Vieillards* (The seven old men), poem 93 of *Les Fleurs du Mal* (The flowers of evil, 1857) by the French Symbolist Charles Baudelaire (1821–1867), and may be translated from the French: "Swarming city, city full of dreams, / Where the specter in broad daylight accosts the passerby."
2. "Cf. *Inferno* III, 55–57" [Eliot's note]. The note continues to quote Dante's lines, which may be translated: "So long a train of people, / That I should never have believed / That death had undone so many."

3. "Cf. *Inferno* IV, 25–27" [Eliot's note]. Dante describes, in Limbo, the virtuous but pagan dead, who, living before Christ, could not achieve the hope of embracing the Christian God. The lines read: "Here, so far as I could tell by listening, / There was no lamentation except sighs, / Which caused the eternal air to tremble."
4. "A phenomenon which I have often noticed" [Eliot's note]. The church named is in the financial district of London.
5. The battle of Mylae (260 B.C.) was a victory for Rome against Carthage. "Stetson": a hat manufacturer.
6. "Cf. the dirge in Webster's *White Devil*" [Eliot's note]: in the play by John Webster (d. 1625), a crazed matron fears that the corpses of her decadent and murdered relatives might be disinterred: "But keep the wolf far thence, that's foe to men, / For with his nails he'll dig them up again." In echoing the lines Eliot altered "foe" to "friend" and the "wolf" to "Dog," invoking the brilliant Dog Star Sirius, whose rise in the heavens accompanied the flooding of the Nile and promised the return of fertility to Egypt.
7. "V. Baudelaire, Preface to *Fleurs du Mal*" [Eliot's note]: the last line of the introductory poem to *Les Fleurs du Mal*. "Au Lecteur" (To the Reader) may be translated from the French: "Hypocrite reader!—my likeness—my brother!"

## II.　A Game of Chess[8]

The Chair she sat in, like a burnished throne,[9]
Glowed on the marble, where the glass
Held up by standards wrought with fruited vines
From which a golden Cupidon peeped out　　　　　　　　　80
(Another hid his eyes behind his wing)
Doubled the flames of sevenbranched candelabra
Reflecting light upon the table as
The glitter of her jewels rose to meet it,
From satin cases poured in rich profusion.　　　　　　　　85
In vials of ivory and coloured glass
Unstoppered, lurked her strange synthetic perfumes,
Unguent, powdered, or liquid—troubled, confused
And drowned the sense in odours; stirred by the air
That freshened from the window, these ascended　　　　　　90
In fattening the prolonged candle-flames,
Flung their smoke into the laquearia,[1]
Stirring the pattern on the coffered ceiling.
Huge sea-wood fed with copper
Burned green and orange, framed by the coloured stone,　　95
In which sad light a carvèd dolphin swam.
Above the antique mantel was displayed
As though a window gave upon the sylvan scene[2]
The change of Philomel, by the barbarous king
So rudely forced; yet there the nightingale　　　　　　　100
Filled all the desert with inviolable voice
And still she cried, and still the world pursues,
'Jug Jug'[3] to dirty ears.
And other withered stumps of time
Were told upon the walls; staring forms　　　　　　　　105
Leaned out, leaning, hushing the room enclosed.
Footsteps shuffled on the stair.
Under the firelight, under the brush, her hair
Spread out in fiery points
Glowed into words, then would be savagely still.　　　　110

'My nerves are bad to-night. Yes, bad. Stay with me.
'Speak to me. Why do you never speak. Speak.

8. The title suggests two plays by Thomas Middleton:
*A Game of Chess* (1627), about a marriage of political
expediency, and *Women Beware Women* (1657), containing a scene in which a mother-in-law is engrossed
in a chess game while her daughter-in-law is seduced
nearby. Eliot's note to line 137 below refers readers to
this play. It is now believed that much of this section
reflects Eliot's disintegrating marriage.
9. "Cf. *Antony and Cleopatra*, II,ii. 190" [Eliot's
note]. In Shakespeare's play, Enobarbus's description
of Cleopatra begins: "The barge she sat in, like a bur-
nish'd throne, / Burn'd on the water."
1. "Laquearia, V. *Aeneid*, I, 726." [Eliot's note]. Eliot
quotes the passage containing the term *laquearia* ("paneled ceiling") and describing the banquet hall where
Queen Dido welcomed Aeneas to Carthage. It reads:
"Blazing torches hang from the gilded paneled ceiling,

and torches conquer the night with flames." Aeneas
became Dido's lover but abandoned her to continue
his journey to found Rome, and she committed
suicide.
2. Eliot's notes for lines 98–99 refer the reader to
"Milton, *Paradise Lost*, IV, 140" for the phrase "sylvan
scene" and to "Ovid, *Metamorphoses*, VI, Philomela."
The lines ironically splice the setting of Eve's temptation in the Garden of Eden, first described through Satan's eyes, with the rape of Philomela by her sister's
husband, King Tereus, and her transformation into the
nightingale. Eliot's note for line 100 refers the reader
ahead to the nightingale's song as rendered in Part III,
line 204, of his own poem. The myth of Philomela
suggests the transformation of suffering into art.
3. The conventional rendering of the nightingale's
song in Elizabethan poetry.

'What are you thinking of? What thinking? What?
'I never know what you are thinking. Think.'

I think we are in rats' alley[4]                                    115
Where the dead men lost their bones.

'What is that noise?'
                    The wind under the door.[5]
'What is that noise now? What is the wind doing?'
                    Nothing again nothing.                      120
                                        'Do
'You know nothing? Do you see nothing? Do you remember
'Nothing?'

        I remember
Those are pearls that were his eyes.                        125
'Are you alive, or not? Is there nothing in your head?'
                                        But
O O O O that Shakespeherian Rag—
It's so elegant
So intelligent                                              130
'What shall I do now? What shall I do?'
'I shall rush out as I am, and walk the street
'With my hair down, so. What shall we do tomorrow?
'What shall we ever do?'
                    The hot water at ten.                   135
And if it rains, a closed car at four.
And we shall play a game of chess,
Pressing lidless eyes and waiting for a knock upon the door.

When Lil's husband got demobbed,[6] I said—
I didn't mince my words, I said to her myself,               140
HURRY UP PLEASE ITS TIME[7]
Now Albert's coming back, make yourself a bit smart.
He'll want to know what you done with that money he gave you
To get yourself some teeth. He did, I was there.
You have them all out, Lil, and get a nice set,             145
He said, I swear, I can't bear to look at you.
And no more can't I, I said, and think of poor Albert,
He's been in the army four years, he wants a good time,
And if you don't give it him, there's others will, I said.
Oh is there, she said. Something o' that, I said.          150
Then I'll know who to thank, she said, and give me a straight look.
HURRY UP PLEASE ITS TIME
If you don't like it you can get on with it, I said.
Others can pick and choose if you can't.
But if Albert makes off, it won't be for lack of telling.    155

4. Eliot's note refers readers to "Part III,l.195."
5. "Cf. Webster: 'Is the wind in that door still?' " [El-
iot's note]. In The Devil's Law Case (1623) 3.2.162, by
John Webster (d. 1625), a duke is cured of an infection
by a wound intended to kill him; a surprised surgeon
asks the quoted question, meaning, "Is he still alive?"
6. Slang for "demobilized," discharged from the army.
7. Routine call of British bartenders to clear the pub
at closing time.

You ought to be ashamed, I said, to look so antique.
(And her only thirty-one.)
I can't help it, she said, pulling a long face,
It's them pills I took, to bring it off, she said.
(She's had five already, and nearly died of young George.)        160
The chemist[8] said it would be all right, but I've never been the same.
You *are* a proper fool, I said.
Well, if Albert won't leave you alone, there it is, I said,
What you get married for if you don't want children?
HURRY UP PLEASE ITS TIME                                          165
Well, that Sunday Albert was home, they had a hot gammon,[9]
And they asked me in to dinner, to get the beauty of it hot—
HURRY UP PLEASE ITS TIME
HURRY UP PLEASE ITS TIME
Goonight Bill, Goonight Lou. Goonight May. Goonight.            170
Ta ta. Goonight. Goonight.
Good night, ladies, good night, sweet ladies, good night, good night.[1]

### III.  The Fire Sermon[2]

The river's tent is broken; the last fingers of leaf
Clutch and sink into the wet bank. The wind
Crosses the brown land, unheard. The nymphs are departed.        175
Sweet Thames, run softly, till I end my song.[3]
The river bears no empty bottles, sandwich papers,
Silk handkerchiefs, cardboard boxes, cigarette ends
Or other testimony of summer nights. The nymphs are
        departed.
And their friends, the loitering heirs of City directors;        180
Departed, have left no addresses.
By the waters of Leman I sat down and wept[4] . . .
Sweet Thames, run softly till I end my song,
Sweet Thames, run softly, for I speak not loud or long.
But at my back in a cold blast I hear[5]                          185
The rattle of the bones, and chuckle spread from ear to ear.

A rat crept softly through the vegetation
Dragging its slimy belly on the bank
While I was fishing in the dull canal
On a winter evening round behind the gashouse                    190
Musing upon the king my brother's wreck[6]

8. Druggist.
9. Ham or bacon.
1. A double echo of the popular song "Good night ladies, we're going to leave you now" and mad Ophelia's
pathetic farewell before drowning, in Shakespeare,
*Hamlet* 4.5.72.
2. I.e., Buddha's Fire Sermon. See note to lines
307–9.
3. "V. Spenser, *Prothalamion*" [Eliot's note]. The line
is the refrain of the marriage song by Edmund Spenser
(d. 1599), a pastoral celebration of marriage set along
the Thames River near London.
4. The phrasing recalls Psalm 137.1 where the exiled
Jews mourn for their homeland: "By the rivers of Babylon, there we sat down, yea, we wept, when we re-

membered Zion." Lake Leman is another name for
Lake Geneva, location of the sanatorium where Eliot
wrote the bulk of *The Waste Land*. The archaic term
*leman*, for "illicit mistress," led to the phrase "waters of
leman" signifying lusts.
5. This line and line 196 echo Andrew Marvell
(1621–1678), *To His Coy Mistress*, lines 21–24: "But
at my back I always hear / Time's wingèd chariot hurrying near; / And yonder all before us lie / Deserts of
vast eternity."
6. "Cf. *The Tempest*, I,ii" [Eliot's note]. An allusion
to Shakespeare's play, 1.2.389–90, where Prince Ferdinand, thinking his father dead, describes himself as
"Sitting on a bank, / Weeping again the King my father's wrack."

And on the king my father's death before him.
White bodies naked on the low damp ground
And bones cast in a little low dry garret,
Rattled by the rat's foot only, year to year. 195
But at my back from time to time I hear
The sound of horns and motors, which shall bring
Sweeney to Mrs. Porter in the spring.[7]
O the moon shone bright on Mrs. Porter
And on her daughter 200
They wash their feet in soda water[8]
Et, O ces voix d'enfants, chantant dans la coupole![9]

Twit twit twit
Jug jug jug jug jug jug
So rudely forc'd. 205
Tereu[1]

Unreal City
Under the brown fog of a winter noon
Mr. Eugenides, the Smyrna merchant
Unshaven, with a pocket full of currants 210
C.i.f.[2] London: documents at sight,
Asked me in demotic French
To luncheon at the Cannon Street Hotel
Followed by a weekend at the Metropole.

At the violet hour, when the eyes and back 215
Turn upward from the desk, when the human engine waits
Like a taxi throbbing waiting,
I Tiresias,[3] though blind, throbbing between two lives,
Old man with wrinkled female breasts, can see

7. "Cf. Day, *Parliament of Bees*: 'When of the sudden, listening, you shall hear, / A noise of horns and hunting, which shall bring / Actaeon to Diana in the spring, / Where all shall see her naked skin' " [Eliot's note]. Actaeon was changed into a stag and hunted to death as punishment for seeing Diana, goddess of chastity, bathing. John Day (1574–c. 1640), English poet.
8. "I do not know the origin of the ballad from which these lines are taken: it was reported to me from Sydney, Australia" [Eliot's note]. The bawdy song was popular among World War I troops.
9. "V. Verlaine, *Parsifal*" [Eliot's note]. The last line of the sonnet *Parsifal* by the French Symbolist Paul Verlaine (1844–96) reads: "And O those children's voices singing in the cupola." In Wagner's opera, the feet of Parsifal, the questing knight, are washed before he enters the sanctuary of the Grail.
1. Alludes to Tereus, who raped Philomela, and like *jug* is a conventional Elizabethan term for the nightingale's song. It is also a slang pronunciation of *true*.
2. "The currants were quoted at a price 'carriage and insurance free to London'; and the Bill of Lading, etc. were to be handed to the buyer upon payment of the sight draft" [Eliot's note]. His second wife has corrected the phrase "carriage and insurance free" to read "cost, insurance and freight."
3. Eliot's note reads: "Tiresias, although a mere spectator and not indeed a 'character,' is yet the most im-portant personage in the poem, uniting all the rest. Just as the one-eyed merchant, seller of currants, melts into the Phoenician Sailor, and the latter is not wholly distinct from Ferdinand Prince of Naples, so all the women are one woman, and the two sexes meet in Tiresias. What Tiresias *sees*, in fact, is the substance of the poem. The whole passage from Ovid is of great anthropological interest." The note quotes the Latin passage from Ovid, *Metamorphoses* 3.320–38, which may be translated: "Jove [very drunk] said jokingly to Juno: 'You women have greater pleasure in love than that enjoyed by men.' She denied it. So they decided to refer the question to wise Tiresias who knew love from both points of view. For once, with a blow of his staff, he had separated two huge snakes who were copulating in the forest, and miraculously was changed instantly from a man into a woman and remained so for seven years. In the eighth year he saw the snakes again and said: 'If a blow against you is so powerful that it changes the sex of the author of it, now I shall strike you again.' With these words he struck them, and his former shape and masculinity were restored. As referee in the sportive quarrel, he supported Jove's claim. Juno, overly upset by the decision, condemned the arbitrator to eternal blindness. But the all-powerful father (inasmuch as no god can undo what has been done by another god) gave him the power of prophecy, with this honor compensating him for the loss of sight."

At the violet hour, the evening hour that strives          220
Homeward, and brings the sailor home from sea,[4]
The typist home at teatime, clears her breakfast, lights
Her stove, and lays out food in tins.
Out of the window perilously spread
Her drying combinations touched by the sun's last rays,     225
On the divan are piled (at night her bed)
Stockings, slippers, camisoles, and stays.
I Tiresias, old man with wrinkled dugs
Perceived the scene, and foretold the rest—
I too awaited the expected guest.                           230
He, the young man carbuncular, arrives,
A small house agent's clerk, with one bold stare,
One of the low on whom assurance sits
As a silk hat on a Bradford[5] millionaire.
The time is now propitious, as he guesses,                  235
The meal is ended, she is bored and tired,
Endeavours to engage her in caresses
Which still are unreproved, if undesired.
Flushed and decided, he assaults at once;
Exploring hands encounter no defence;                       240
His vanity requires no response,
And makes a welcome of indifference.
(And I Tiresias have foresuffered all
Enacted on this same divan or bed;
I who have sat by Thebes below the wall[6]                  245
And walked among the lowest of the dead.)
Bestows one final patronising kiss,
And gropes his way, finding the stairs unlit . . .

She turns and looks a moment in the glass,
Hardly aware of her departed lover;                         250
Her brain allows one half-formed thought to pass:
'Well now that's done: and I'm glad it's over.'
When lovely woman stoops to folly and
Paces about her room again, alone,
She smoothes her hair with automatic hand,                  255
And puts a record on the gramophone.[7]

'This music crept by me upon the waters'[8]
And along the Strand, up Queen Victoria Street.

4. "This may not appear as exact as Sappho's lines, but
I had in mind the 'longshore' or 'dory' fisherman, who
returns at nightfall" [Eliot's note]. Fragment 149, by
the Greek woman poet Sappho (fl. 600 B.C.), celebrates
the Evening Star who "brings homeward all those /
Scattered by the dawn, / The sheep to fold . . . / The
children to their mother's side." A more familiar echo
is "Home is the sailor, home from sea" in *Requiem* by
the Scottish poet Robert Louis Stevenson (1850–1894).
5. A Yorkshire, England, manufacturing town where
fortunes were made during World War I.
6. Tiresias prophesied in the marketplace below the
wall of Thebes, witnessed the tragedies of Oedipus and
Creon in that city, and retained his prophetic powers
in the Underworld.

7. Eliot's note refers to the novel *The Vicar of Wakefield* (1766) by Oliver Goldsmith (1728–1774) and the
song sung by Olivia when she revisits the scene of her
seduction: "When lovely woman stoops to folly / And
finds too late that men betray / What charm can soothe
her melancholy, / What art can wash her guilt away? /
The only art her guilt to cover, / To hide her shame
from every eye, / To give repentance to her lover / And
wring his bosom—is to die."
8. Eliot's note refers to Shakespeare's *The Tempest*, the
scene where Ferdinand listens to Ariel's song telling of
his father's miraculous sea-change: "This music crept
by me on the waters, / Allaying both their fury and my
passion / With its sweet air" (1.2.391–93).

O City city, I can sometimes hear
Beside a public bar in Lower Thames Street,                    260
The pleasant whining of a mandoline
And a clatter and a chatter from within
Where fishmen lounge at noon: where the walls
Of Magnus Martyr⁹ hold
Inexplicable splendour of Ionian white and gold.              265

       The river sweats¹
       Oil and tar
       The barges drift
       With the turning tide
       Red sails                                      270
       Wide
       To leeward, swing on the heavy spar.
       The barges wash
       Drifting logs
       Down Greenwich reach                           275
       Past the Isle of Dogs.²
               Weialala leia
               Wallala leialala

       Elizabeth and Leicester³
       Beating oars                                   280
       The stern was formed
       A gilded shell
       Red and gold
       The brisk swell
       Rippled both shores                            285
       Southwest wind
       Carried down stream
       The peal of bells
       White towers
               Weialala leia                   290
               Wallala leialala

'Trams and dusty trees.
Highbury bore me. Richmond and Kew
Undid me.⁴ By Richmond I raised my knees
Supine on the floor of a narrow canoe.'                        295

9. "The interior of St. Magnus Martyr is to my mind one of the finest among [Christopher] Wren's interiors" [Eliot's note].
1. "The Song of the (three) Thames-daughters begins here. From line 292 to 306 inclusive they speak in turn. V. *Götterdämmerung*, III, i: the Rhine-daughters" [Eliot's note]. Lines 277–78 and 290–91 are from the lament of the Rhine maidens for the lost beauty of the Rhine River in the opera by Richard Wagner (1813–1883), *Die Götterdämmerung* (The twilight of the gods, 1876).
2. A peninsula in the Thames opposite Greenwich, a borough of London and the birthplace of Queen Elizabeth. Throughout this section Eliot has named places along the Thames River.

3. Reference to the love affair of Queen Elizabeth and the earl of Leicester (Robert Dudley). Eliot's note refers to the historian James A. Froude, *"Elizabeth*, Vol. I. ch. iv, letter of [bishop] De Quadra [the ambassador] to Philip of Spain: 'In the afternoon we were in a barge, watching the games on the river. (The queen) was alone with Lord Robert and myself on the poop, when they began to talk nonsense, and went so far that Lord Robert at last said, as I was on the spot there was no reason why they should not be married if the queen pleased.' "
4. "Cf. *Purgatorio*, V, 133" [Eliot's note]. Eliot quotes Dante's lines, which he parodied; they may be translated: "Remember me, who am La Pia. / Siena made me, Maremma undid me."

'My feet are at Moorgate, and my heart
Under my feet. After the event
He wept. He promised "a new start."
I made no comment. What should I resent?'

'On Margate Sands,                    300
I can connect
Nothing with nothing.
The broken fingernails of dirty hands.
My people humble people who expect
Nothing.'                                305
        la la

To Carthage then I came[5]

Burning burning burning burning[6]
O Lord Thou pluckest me out[7]
O Lord Thou pluckest                 310

burning

## IV. Death by Water

Phlebas the Phoenician, a fortnight dead,
Forgot the cry of gulls, and the deep sea swell
And the profit and loss.
                 A current under sea        315
Picked his bones in whispers. As he rose and fell
He passed the stages of his age and youth
Entering the whirlpool.
                 Gentile or Jew
O you who turn the wheel and look to windward,       320
Consider Phlebas, who was once handsome and tall as you.

## V. What the Thunder Said[8]

After the torchlight red on sweaty faces
After the frosty silence in the gardens
After the agony in stony places
The shouting and the crying                  325
Prison and palace and reverberation
Of thunder of spring over distant mountains
He who was living is now dead

---

5. "V. St. Augustine's *Confessions:* 'to Carthage then I came, where a cauldron of unholy loves sang all about mine ears' " [Eliot's note]. Augustine here recounts his licentious youth.
6. Eliot's note to lines 307–9 refer to "Buddha's Fire Sermon (which corresponds in importance to the Sermon on the Mount)" and "St. Augustine's Confessions." The "collocation of these two representatives of eastern and western asceticism, as the culmination of this part of the poem, is not an accident."
7. The line is from Augustine's *Confessions* and ech-

oes also Zechariah 3.2, where Jehovah, rebuking Satan, calls the high priest Joshua "a brand plucked out of the fire."
8. "In the first part of Part V three themes are employed: the journey to Emmaus, the approach to the Chapel Perilous (see Miss Weston's book) and the present decay of eastern Europe" [Eliot's note]. During his disciples' journey to Emmaus, after his Crucifixion and Resurrection, Jesus walked alongside and conversed with them, but they thought him a stranger until he revealed his identity (Luke 24.13–34).

We who were living are now dying
With a little patience⁹                                          330

Here is no water but only rock
Rock and no water and the sandy road
The road winding above among the mountains
Which are mountains of rock without water
If there were water we should stop and drink          335
Amongst the rock one cannot stop or think
Sweat is dry and feet are in the sand
If there were only water amongst the rock
Dead mountain mouth of carious teeth that cannot spit
Here one can neither stand nor lie nor sit              340
There is not even silence in the mountains
But dry sterile thunder without rain
There is not even solitude in the mountains
But red sullen faces sneer and snarl
From doors of mudcracked houses                         345
                    If there were water
    And no rock
    If there were rock
    And also water
    And water                                            350
    A spring
    A pool among the rock
    If there were the sound of water only
    Not the cicada¹
    And dry grass singing                                355
    But sound of water over a rock
    Where the hermit-thrush² sings in the pine trees
    Drip drop drip drop drop drop drop
    But there is no water

Who is the third who walks always beside you?³          360
When I count, there are only you and I together
But when I look ahead up the white road
There is always another one walking beside you
Gliding wrapt in a brown mantle, hooded
I do not know whether a man or a woman                 365
—But who is that on the other side of you?

What is that sound high in the air⁴
Murmur of maternal lamentation

9. The opening nine lines allude to Christ's imprisonment and trial, to his agony in the garden of Geth-
semane, and to his Crucifixion on Golgotha (Calvary)
and burial; they suggest the despair during the days between the Crucifixion and the Resurrection on Easter.
1. Grasshopper. Cf. line 23 and Ecclesiastes 12.5: "the
grasshopper shall be a burden, and desire shall fail."
2. "This is . . . the hermit-thrush which I have heard
in Quebec Province. Chapman says (*Handbook of
Birds of Eastern North America*) 'it is most at home in
secluded woodland and thickety retreats.' . . . Its 'water
dripping song' is justly celebrated" [Eliot's note].

3. "The following lines were stimulated by the account of one of the Antarctic expeditions (I forget
which, but I think one of Shackleton's): it was related
that the party of explorers, at the extremity of their
strength, had the constant delusion that there was *one
more member* than could actually be counted" [Eliot's
note]. The reminiscence is associated with Christ's un-
recognized presence on the journey to Emmaus.
4. Eliot's note quotes a passage in German from *Blick
ins Chaos* (1920) by Hermann Hesse (1877–1962),
which may be translated: "Already half of Europe, already at least half of Eastern Europe, on the way to

Who are those hooded hordes swarming
Over endless plains, stumbling in cracked earth                    370
Ringed by the flat horizon only
What is the city over the mountains
Cracks and reforms and bursts in the violet air
Falling towers
Jerusalem Athens Alexandria                                        375
Vienna London
Unreal

A woman drew her long black hair out tight
And fiddled whisper music on those strings
And bats with baby faces in the violet light                       380
Whistled, and beat their wings
And crawled head downward down a blackened wall
And upside down in air were towers
Tolling reminiscent bells, that kept the hours
And voices singing out of empty cisterns and exhausted wells.      385

In this decayed hole among the mountains
In the faint moonlight, the grass is singing
Over the tumbled graves, about the chapel
There is the empty chapel, only the wind's home.
It has no windows, and the door swings,                            390
Dry bones can harm no one.
Only a cock stood on the rooftree
Co co rico co co rico[5]
In a flash of lightning. Then a damp gust
Bringing rain                                                      395

Ganga[6] was sunken, and the limp leaves
Waited for rain, while the black clouds
Gathered far distant, over Himavant.[7]
The jungle crouched, humped in silence.
Then spoke the thunder                                             400
DA[8]          .
Datta: what have we given?
My friend, blood shaking my heart
The awful daring of a moment's surrender
Which an age of prudence can never retract                         405
By this, and this only, we have existed
Which is not to be found in our obituaries

---

Chaos, drives drunk in sacred infatuation along the edge of the precipice, since drunkenly, as though hymn-singing, as Dimitri Karamazov sang in [the novel] The Brothers Karamazov [1882] by Feodor Dostoevsky [1821–1881]. The offended bourgeois laughs at the songs; the saint and the seer hear them with tears."
5. A cock's crow in folklore signaled the departure of ghosts (as in Shakespeare's Hamlet 1.1.157ff); in Matthew 26.34 and 74 a cock crowed, as Christ predicted, when Peter denied him three times.
6. The Indian river Ganges, sacred to Hindus.
7. A mountain in the Himalayas.

8. " 'Datta, dayadhvam, damyata' (Give, sympathise, control). The fable of the meaning of the Thunder is found in the Brihadaranyaka—Upanishad, 5, 1" [Eliot's note]. In the Hindu legend, the injunction of Prajapati (supreme deity) is Da, which is interpreted in three different ways by gods, men, and demons, to mean "control ourselves," "give alms," and "have compassion." Prajapati assures them that when "the devine voice, The Thunder," repeats the syllable it means all three things and that therefore "one should practice . . . Self-Control, Alms-giving, and Compassion."

Or in memories draped by the beneficient spider[9]
Or under seals broken by the lean solicitor
In our empty rooms                                                      410
DA
Dayadhvam: I have heard the key[1]
Turn in the door once and turn once only
We think of the key, each in his prison
Thinking of the key, each confirms a prison             415
Only at nightfall, aethereal rumours
Revive for a moment a broken Coriolanus[2]
DA
Damyata: The boat responded
Gaily, to the hand expert with sail and oar              420
The sea was calm, your heart would have responded
Gaily, when invited, beating obedient
To controlling hands

                              I sat upon the shore
Fishing,[3] with the arid plain behind me                 425
Shall I at least set my lands in order?[4]
London Bridge is falling down falling down falling down
Poi s'ascose nel foco che gli affina[5]
Quando fiam uti chelidon[6]—O swallow swallow
Le Prince d'Aquitaine à la tour abolie[7]                    430
These fragments I have shored against my ruins
Why then Ile fit you. Hieronymo's mad againe.[8]
Datta. Dayadhvam. Damyata.
               Shantih    shantih    shantih[9]

1921                                                                        1922

9. Eliot's note refers to The White Devil (1612) by the English playwright John Webster (d. 1625) 5.6: ". . . they'll remarry / Ere the worm pierce your winding-sheet, ere the spider / Make a thin curtain for your epitaphs."
1. "Cf. Inferno, XXXIII, 46" [Eliot's note]. At this point Ugolino recalls his imprisonment with his children, where they starved to death: "And I heard below the door of the horrible tower being locked up." Eliot's note continues: "Also F. H. Bradley, Appearance and Reality, p. 346. 'My external sensations are no less private to myself than are my thoughts or my feelings. In either case my experience falls within my own circle, a circle closed on the outside; and, with all its elements alike, every sphere is opaque to the others which surround it. . . . In brief, regarded as an existence which appears in a soul, the whole world for each is peculiar and private to that soul.' "
2. The Roman patrician Coriolanus defiantly chose self-exile when threatened with banishment by the leaders of the populace. He is the tragic protagonist in Shakespeare's Coriolanus (1608).
3. "V. Weston: From Ritual to Romance; chapter on the Fisher King" [Eliot's note].
4. Cf. Isaiah 38.1: "Thus saith the Lord, Set thine house in order: for thou shalt die, and not live."
5. Eliot's note to Purgatorio 26 quotes in Italian the passage (lines 145–48) where the Provençal poet Arnaut Daniel, recalling his lusts, addresses Dante: "I pray you now, by the Goodness that guides you to the

summit of this staircase, reflect in due season on my suffering." Then, in the line quoted in The Waste Land, "he hid himself in the fire that refines them."
6. Eliot's note refers to the Pervigilium Veneris (The vigil of Venus), an anonymous Latin poem, and suggests a comparison with "Philomela in Parts II and III" of The Waste Land. The last stanzas of the Pervigilium recreate the myth of the nightingale in the image of a swallow, and the poet listening to the bird speaks the quoted line, "When shall I be as the swallow," and adds: "that I may cease to be silent." "O Swallow, Swallow" are the opening words of one of the songs interspersed in Tennyson's narrative poem The Princess (1847).
7. "V. Gerard de Nerval, Sonnet El Desdichado" [Eliot's note]. The line reads: "The Prince of Aquitaine in the ruined tower."
8. Eliot's note refers to Thomas Kyd's revenge play, The Spanish Tragedy, subtitled Hieronymo's Mad Againe (1594). In it Hieronymo is asked to write a court play and he answers, "I'll fit you," in the double sense of "oblige" and "get even." He manages, although mad, to kill the murderers of his son by acting in the play and assigning parts appropriately, then commits suicide.
9. "Shantih. Repeated as here, a formal ending to an Upanishad [Vedic treatise, sacred Hindu text]. 'The peace which passeth understanding' is our equivalent to this word" [Eliot's note].

# The Hollow Men

*Mistah Kurtz—he dead.*[1]

### I

A *penny for the Old Guy*[2]

We are the hollow men
We are the stuffed men
Leaning together
Headpiece filled with straw. Alas!
Our dried voices, when                                        5
We whisper together
Are quiet and meaningless
As wind in dry grass
Or rats' feet over broken glass
In our dry cellar                                             10

Shape without form, shade without colour,
Paralysed force, gesture without motion;

Those who have crossed
With direct eyes, to death's other Kingdom
Remember us—if at all—not as lost                            15
Violent souls, but only
As the hollow men
The stuffed men.

### II

Eyes I dare not meet in dreams
In death's dream kingdom                                      20
These do not appear:
There, the eyes are
Sunlight on a broken column
There, is a tree swinging
And voices are                                                25
In the wind's singing
More distant and more solemn
Than a fading star.

Let me be no nearer
In death's dream kingdom                                      30
Let me also wear
Such deliberate disguises
Rat's coat, crowskin, crossed staves
In a field
Behaving as the wind behaves                                  35
No nearer—

---

1. Quotation from *Heart of Darkness*, a story by the English writer Joseph Conrad (1857–1924). Kurtz went into the African jungle as an official of a trading company and there degenerated into an evil, tryannical man. His dying words were "the horror!"
2. Guy Fawkes was leader of a group of conspirators who planned to blow up the English House of Commons in 1605; he was caught and executed before the plan was carried out, and the day of his execution (November 5) is celebrated in England in a way similar to Halloween in the United States. Children make straw effigies of the "guy" and beg for pennies for fireworks.

Not that final meeting
In the twilight kingdom

## III

This is the dead land
This is cactus land                                                    40
Here the stone images
Are raised, here they receive
The supplication of a dead man's hand
Under the twinkle of a fading star.

Is it like this                                                        45
In death's other kingdom
Waking alone
At the hour when we are
Trembling with tenderness
Lips that would kiss                                                   50
Form prayers to broken stone.

## IV

The eyes are not here
There are no eyes here
In this valley of dying stars
In this hollow valley                                                  55
This broken jaw of our lost kingdoms

In this last of meeting places
We grope together
And avoid speech
Gathered on this beach of the tumid river                             60

Sightless, unless
The eyes reappear
As the perpetual star
Multifoliate rose[3]
Of death's twilight kingdom                                           65
The hope only
Of empty men.

## V

*Here we go round the prickly pear*
*Prickly pear prickly pear*
*Here we go round the prickly pear*                                   70
*At five o'clock in the morning.*[4]

3. Part 3 of *The Divine Comedy*, by Dante Alighieri (1265–1321), is a vision of Paradise. The souls of the saved in heaven range themselves around the Diety in the figure of a "multifoliate rose" (*Paradiso* 28.30).
4. Sardonic allusion to a children's rhyming game,

"Here we go round the mulberry bush." Substituting a prickly pear cactus for the mulberry bush, Eliot meshes this image with others of the modern world as a "cactus land."

Between the idea
And the reality
Between the motion
And the act                                                              75
Falls the Shadow
                    *For Thine is the Kingdom*[5]

Between the conception
And the creation
Between the emotion                                                       80
And the response
Falls the Shadow
                    *Life is very long*

Between the desire
And the spasm                                                            85
Between the potency
And the existence
Between the essence
And the descent
Falls the Shadow                                                         90
                    *For Thine is the Kingdom*

For Thine is
Life is
For Thine is the

*This is the way the world ends*                                         95
*This is the way the world ends*
*This is the way the world ends*
*Not with a bang but a whimper.*

                                                                  1925

# Journey of the Magi[1]

'A cold coming we had of it,
Just the worst time of the year
For a journey, and such a long journey:
The ways deep and the weather sharp,
The very dead of winter.'[2]                                             5
And the camels galled, sore-footed, refractory,
Lying down in the melting snow.
There were times we regretted
The summer palaces on slopes, the terraces,
And the silken girls bringing sherbet.                                   10
Then the camel men cursing and grumbling
And running away, and wanting their liquor and women,

---

5. Part of a line from the Lord's Prayer.
1. The three wise men, or kings, who followed the star
of Bethlehem, bringing gifts to the newly born Christ.

2. These lines are adapted from the sermon preached
at Christmas, in 1622, by Bishop Lancelot Andrewes.

And the night-fires going out, and the lack of shelters,
And the cities hostile and the towns unfriendly
And the villages dirty and charging high prices:                        15
A hard time we had of it.
At the end we preferred to travel all night,
Sleeping in snatches,
With the voices singing in our ears, saying
That this was all folly.                                                20

Then at dawn we came down to a temperate valley,
Wet, below the snow line, smelling of vegetation,
With a running stream and a water-mill beating the darkness,
And three trees on the low sky.
And an old white horse galloped away in the meadow.                     25
Then we came to a tavern with vine-leaves over the lintel,
Six hands at an open door dicing for pieces of silver,
And feet kicking the empty wine-skins.
But there was no information, and so we continued
And arrived at evening, not a moment too soon                           30
Finding the place; it was (you may say) satisfactory.

All this was a long time ago, I remember,
And I would do it again, but set down
This set down
This: were we led all that way for                                      35
Birth or Death? There was a Birth, certainly,
We had evidence and no doubt. I had seen birth and death,
But had thought they were different; this Birth was
Hard and bitter agony for us, like Death, our death.
We returned to our places, these Kingdoms,                              40
But no longer at ease here, in the old dispensation,
With an alien people clutching their gods.
I should be glad of another death.

                                                                1935

## FROM FOUR QUARTETS

# Burnt Norton[1]

τοῦ λόγον δ'ἐόντος ξυνοῦ ζώουσιν οἱ πολλοί
ὡς ἰδίαν ἔχοντες φρόνησιν.
I. p. 77. Fr. 2.
ὁδὸς ἄνω κάτω μία καὶ ὡυτή.
I. p. 89. Fr. 60.

—Diels: *Die Fragmente der Vorsokratiker* (Herakleitos)

## I[2]

Time present and time past
Are both perhaps present in time future,
And time future contained in time past.
If all time is eternally present
All time is unredeemable.                                                    5
What might have been is an abstraction
Remaining a perpetual possibility
Only in a world of speculation.
What might have been and what has been
Point to one end, which is always present.                                  10
Footfalls echo in the memory
Down the passage which we did not take
Towards the door we never opened
Into the rose-garden.[3] My words echo
Thus, in your mind.
                          But to what purpose                               15
Disturbing the dust on a bowl of rose-leaves
I do not know.
                  Other echoes
Inhabit the garden. Shall we follow?
Quick, said the bird, find them, find them,
Round the corner. Through the first gate,                                   20
Into our first world, shall we follow
The deception of the thrush? Into our first world.
There they were, dignified, invisible,

1. Eliot made *Burnt Norton*, published originally as a separate poem, the basis and formal model for *East Coker* (1940), *The Dry Salvages* (1941), and *Little Gidding* (1942). Together they comprise *Four Quartets* (1943). The *Quartets* seeks to capture those rare moments when eternity "intersects" the temporal continuum, while treating also the relations between those moments and the flux of time. The series and each quartet in it recapitulate the central theme through contrapuntal variations while moving gradually (through often tentative and enigmatic sequences) toward the explicit naming and more full revelation of its Christian content (the "Word" at the end of *Burnt Norton*, the "purgatorial fires" and "Annunciation" in subsequent quartets, the coalescence of religious symbols at the end of *Little Gidding*). Central to its structure, and particularly in *Burnt Norton*, is the idea of the Spanish mystic St. John of the Cross (1542–1591) that the ascent of a soul to union with God is facilitated by memory and disciplined meditation but that medita-

tion is superseded by a "dark night of the soul," a passive surrender of the will to God, an emptying of the senses and the self, a descent into darkness that is deepened paradoxically the nearer one approaches the light of God. The Greek epigraphs are from the pre-Socratic philosopher Heraclitus (540?–475 B.C.) and may be translated: "But although the Word is common to all, the majority of people live as though they had each an understanding peculiarly his own" and "The way up and the way down are one and the same."
2. Burnt Norton is a manor house in Gloucestershire, England. The opening lines echo Ecclesiastes 3.15: "That which hath been is now; and that which is to be hath already been."
3. The rose is a symbol of sexual and spiritual love; in Christian traditions it is associated with the harmony of religious truth and with the Virgin Mary, her bower being depicted often as a rose garden. The memory may be personal as well.

Moving without pressure, over the dead leaves,
In the autumn heat, through the vibrant air,                              25
And the bird called, in response to
The unheard music hidden in the shrubbery,
And the unseen eyebeam crossed, for the roses
Had the look of flowers that are looked at.
There they were as our guests, accepted and accepting.                   30
So we moved, and they, in a formal pattern,
Along the empty alley, into the box circle,[4]
To look down into the drained pool.
Dry the pool, dry concrete, brown edged,
And the pool was filled with water out of sunlight,                      35
And the lotos rose, quietly, quietly,
The surface glittered out of heart of light,[5]
And they were behind us, reflected in the pool.
Then a cloud passed, and the pool was empty.
Go, said the bird, for the leaves were full of children,                 40
Hidden excitedly, containing laughter.
Go, go, go, said the bird: human kind
Cannot bear very much reality.
Time past and time future
What might have been and what has been.                                   45
Point to one end, which is always present.

## II

Garlic and sapphires in the mud
Clot the bedded axle-tree.
The trilling wire in the blood
Sings below inveterate scars                                              50
Appeasing long forgotten wars.
The dance along the artery
The circulation of the lymph
Are figured in the drift of stars
Ascend to summer in the tree                                             55
We move above the moving tree
In light upon the figured leaf[6]
And hear upon the sodden floor
Below, the boarhound and the boar
Pursue their pattern as before                                           60
But reconciled among the stars.

At the still point of the turning world. Neither flesh nor fleshless;
Neither from nor towards; at the still point, there the dance is,
But neither arrest nor movement. And do not call it fixity,
Where past and future are gathered. Neither movement from
    nor towards,                                       65
Neither ascent nor decline. Except for the point, the still point,

4. Evergreen boxwood shrubs, planted in a circle.
5. An echo of Dante, *Paradiso* 12.28–29: "From out
of the heart of one of the new lights there moved a
voice."

6. An echo of the description of death in Tennyson,
*In Memoriam* (1850) 43.10–12: "So that still garden of
the souls / In many a figured leaf enrolls / The total
world since life began."

There would be no dance and there is only the dance.
I can only say, *there* we have been: but I cannot say where.
And I cannot say, how long, for that is to place it in time.

The inner freedom from the practical desire,                                    70
The release from action and suffering, release from the inner
And the outer compulsion, yet surrounded
By a grace of sense, a white light still and moving,
*Erhebung*[7] without motion, concentration
Without elimination, both a new world                                          75
And the old made explicit, understood
In the completion of its partial ecstasy,
The resolution of its partial horror.
Yet the enchainment of past and future
Woven in the weakness of the changing body,                                    80
Protects mankind from heaven and damnation
Which flesh cannot endure.
                          Time past and time future
Allow but a little consciousness.
To be conscious is not to be in time                                           85
But only in time can the moment in the rose-garden,
The moment in the arbour where the rain beat,
The moment in the draughty church at smokefall
Be remembered; involved with past and future.
Only through time time is conquered.                                           90

*III*

Here is a place of disaffection
Time before and time after
In a dim light: neither daylight
Investing form with lucid stillness
Turning shadow into transient beauty                                           95
With slow rotation suggesting permanence
Nor darkness to purify the soul
Emptying the sensual with deprivation
Cleansing affection from the temporal.
Neither plenitude nor vacancy. Only a flicker                                  100
Over the strained time-ridden faces
Distracted from distraction by distraction
Filled with fancies and empty of meaning
Tumid apathy with no concentration
Men and bits of paper, whirled by the cold wind                               105
That blows before and after time,
Wind in and out of unwholesome lungs
Time before and time after.
Eructation of unhealthy souls
Into the faded air, the torpid                                                 110
Driven on the wind that sweeps the gloomy hills of London,
Hampstead and Clerkenwell, Campden and Putney,

7. Exaltation (German).

Highgate, Primrose and Ludgate.[8] Not here
Not here the darkness, in this twittering world.

Descend lower, descend only                                            115
Into the world of perpetual solitude,
World not world, but that which is not world,
Internal darkness, deprivation
And destitution of all property,
Desiccation of the world of sense,                                     120
Evacuation of the world of fancy,
Inoperancy of the world of spirit;
This is the one way, and the other
Is the same, not in movement
But abstention from movement; while the world moves                    125
In appetency, on its metalled ways
Of time past and time future.


IV

Time and the bell have buried the day,
The black cloud carries the sun away.
Will the sunflower turn to us, will the clematis                       130
Stray down, bend to us; tendril and spray
Clutch and cling?
Chill
Fingers of yew be curled
Down on us? After the kingfisher's wing                                135
Has answered light to light, and is silent, the light is still
At the still point of the turning world.

V

Words move, music moves
Only in time; but that which is only living
Can only die. Words, after speech, reach                               140
Into the silence. Only by the form, the pattern,
Can words or music reach
The stillness, as a Chinese jar still
Moves perpetually in its stillness.
Not the stillness of the violin, while the note lasts,                 145
Not that only, but the co-existence,
Or say that the end precedes the beginning,
And the end and the beginning were always there
Before the beginning and after the end.
And all is always now. Words strain,                                   150
Crack and sometimes break, under the burden,
Under the tension, slip, slide, perish,
Decay with imprecision, will not stay in place,
Will not stay still. Shrieking voices

8. Districts and neighborhoods in London.

Scolding, mocking, or merely chattering,      155
Always assail them. The Word in the desert[9]
Is most attacked by voices of temptation,
The crying shadow in the funeral dance,
The loud lament of the disconsolate chimera.[1]

The detail of the pattern is movement,      160
As in the figure of the ten stairs.[2]
Desire itself is movement
Not in itself desirable;
Love is itself unmoving,
Only the cause and end of movement,      165
Timeless, and undesiring
Except in the aspect of time
Caught in the form of limitation
Between un-being and being.
Sudden in a shaft of sunlight      170
Even while the dust moves
There rises the hidden laughter
Of children in the foliage
Quick, now, here, now always—
Ridiculous the waste sad time      175
Stretching before and after.

1936, 1943

9. An allusion to Christ's temptation in the wilderness (Luke 4.1–4).
1. A monster in Greek mythology and a symbol of fantasies and delusions.

2. An allusion to St. John of the Cross's figure for the soul's ascent to God: "The Ten Degrees of the Mystical Ladder of Divine Love."

---

# EUGENE O'NEILL
## 1888–1953

Although the theater had an active history in the United States before the twentieth century, most of the plays produced were by Europeans, the great majority melodrama and spectacle, vehicles for bombastic performances by actors and actresses who were the great celebrities of the pre-cinema era. Eugene O'Neill was the nation's first major playwright, the first to explore serious themes in the theater and to experiment with theatrical conventions. His many plays were translated and staged all over the world; he won the Pulitzer Prize four times and is still the only dramatist to win a Nobel Prize (1936).

He was born on October 16, 1888, son of James O'Neill, an actor who made a fortune playing the lead role in a dramatization of Alexander Dumas's swashbuckling novel, *The Count of Monte Cristo*. The father's dream of becoming a major serious actor was sacrificed to that one role: he played it on tour more than five thousand times. O'Neill's mother, Ella Quinlan, was the daughter of a successful Irish immigrant businessman in Cincinnati. She loved her husband but hated backstage life and escaped her private misery by taking morphine. An older brother, James, Jr., was born in 1878 and during most of Eugene's childhood was away at various boarding schools. Later "Jamie," his brother's idol, became an actor and an alcoholic.

During O'Neill's childhood, his parents toured for part of every year, lived in New York City hotels for another part, and spent summers at their home in New London, Connecticut. O'Neill went to good preparatory schools and started college at Princeton in 1906. He quit after a year. For the next five years he drank and drifted—he eloped but the marriage was quickly terminated, he shipped out to sea for a year, and he searched for gold in South America. Most of the time he spent among the homeless, the outcasts, the artists, and the radicals who were sharing Greenwich Village—an area of lower Manhattan that was becoming a favorite place for Bohemians. After a bout with tuberculosis nearly killed him in 1912, O'Neill decided to stay sober and write plays. His Greenwich Village friends helped him: he joined a new experimental theater group that called itself the Provincetown Players, because in the summer its members staged plays on a dilapidated wharf in Provincetown, Massachusetts. For the rest of the year they used a small theater in the Village. They did O'Neill's one-act play *Thirst* in the summer of 1917.

The Provincetown group gave O'Neill his forum, and he gave them a place in American theater history. Play followed play in these early years; in 1913–14, he wrote nine plays; in 1916–17, six; in 1918, four. The works that had likely appeal for general audiences were moved uptown from the Village to Broadway, where their stagings made O'Neill both famous and financially successful. Many of O'Neill's first plays were grim one-acters based on his experiences at sea. In these, the dialogue was a striking departure from stage eloquence: crude, natural, and slangy. Instead of the elegant parlors of drawing-room comedy, audiences were faced with ships' holds and sailors' bars. An exaggerated realism, veering toward expressionism, was the mode of these earliest works.

Around 1920, his plays became longer and his aims more ambitious. His first works have been stark and naturalistic; now he began to experiment with techniques to convey inner emotions that usually were not openly expressed in dramatizable action—the world of the mind, of memories and fears. He ignored normal play divisions of scenes and acts; paid no attention to the expected length of plays (the *Mourning Becomes Electra* sequence ran for nine hours); made his characters wear masks; split one character between two actors; and reintroduced ghosts, choruses, and Shakespearean-style monologue and direct addresses to the audience. He employed sets, lighting, and sounds to enhance emotion rather than to represent a real place. Having chosen the theater as his form, he seemed determined to work at its limits, to redefine it. Important works from this period include *The Emperor Jones* (1920), in which, under stress, civilized veneer gives way to primitive fear; *The Hairy Ape* (1922), where a sailor, becoming aware of how he is viewed by the upper class, degenerates into what he is perceived to be; *Desire under the Elms* (1924), about family conflict and desire; *The Great God Brown* (1926), exposing the inner life of a business magnate; and *Strange Interlude* (1928), similarly uncovering the hidden life of a beautiful woman. In different forms, all these plays subject their leading characters to experiences so intense that their "characters" disintegrate, exposing the chaotic or primitive interior self.

O'Neill's father had died in 1920, his mother in 1921, his brother in 1923. During the mid-1920s O'Neill became interested in dramatizing the complicated pattern of his family's life. He was influenced by the popularization of certain ideas of the Viennese psychoanalyst Sigmund Freud: the power of irrational drives; the existence of a subconscious; the roles of repression, suppression, and inhibition in the formation of personality and in adult suffering; the importance of sex; and above all the lifelong influence of parents. But where Freud posited a universal dynamic in the relation between children and parents and rooted development in biology, O'Neill saw each child's experiences as uniquely determined by particular parents. His strongly felt individualism came to focus on the family, rather than the person, as the fundamental human unit. He found inspiration and confirmation for this approach in classical Greek drama, which had always centered on families. His 1931 *Mourning Becomes Electra*, based on the *Oresteia* cycle of Aeschylus, situated the ancient story of family murder and divine retribution in Civil War America with great success.

Twice-married after the annulment of his early elopement, O'Neill began to suffer from Parkinson's disease in the 1930s and lived in relative seclusion for the last twenty years of his life. Following the production of *Mourning Becomes Electra*, his output slowed noticeably. Much of his work of the 1930s and 1940s remained in manuscript until after his death, and there was a twelve-year gap in the staging of his plays—between *Days without End* (1934), which failed on Broadway, and *The Iceman Cometh*, in 1946, which also did poorly. As a young man, he had been much attracted to socialists, communists, and anarchists, but it was more on account of their rebelliousness and energetic nonconformity than their political doctrines. When his play about an interracial marriage appeared (*All God's Chillun Got Wings*, 1924), he insisted that it was not about race but about "the special lives of individual human beings. It is primarily a study of the two principal characters and their tragic struggle for happiness." Although, as the Edmund character who stands for O'Neill in *Long Day's Journey* shows, he did experience his Irishness partly in class terms, deeply resenting those whose backgrounds raised them above most Americans, his radicalism was based on a sense that individual merit should be the human measure, not on a belief in class solidarity. In the 1930s, the persistent commitment to individual experience did not accord with the main currents of drama on the American stage, which may be one reason that he kept these biographical plays out of production.

Three years after his death, however, *Iceman* was successfully revived with Jason Robards, Jr., in the main role, and O'Neill's work reattained prominence. His widow released other plays, which were widely acclaimed in posthumous productions. Among such stagings were parts of a projected nine- or eleven-play sequence (critics differ in their interpretation of the surviving manuscript material) about an Irish family in America named the Melody family and some obviously autobiographical dramas about a family named the Tyrones. The Melody plays produced after O'Neill's death include *A Touch of the Poet*, produced in 1957, and *More Stately Mansions*, which was staged in 1967; the Tyrone plays include *Long Day's Journey into Night*, produced in 1956, and *A Moon for the Misbegotten* produced in 1957.

In inscribing the manuscript of *Long Day's Journey* to his wife, O'Neill wrote that he had faced his dead in this play, writing "with deep pity and understanding and forgiveness for *all* the four haunted Tyrones." By this he seemed to mean that his treatment made it impossible to blame any of the characters for the suffering they inflicted on the others; each Tyrone was both a victim and an oppressor, and none of them could escape. O'Neill's characters could neither help nor understand what they did; the word *haunted* catches his sense that the Tyrones are at the mercy of the past—their psyches are the dwelling places of ghosts, and the word *ghosts* recurs throughout the play: ghosts of those they remember, those who influenced them, their younger selves, their dreams and ambitions, and their disappointments. A spectator in the theater, or a first-time reader of the play, may experience *Long Day's Journey* simply as unabating raw emotion, but study shows that O'Neill designed the play as a series of encounters—each character is placed with one, two, or three of the others, until every combination is worked through. At the same time that these various configurations are staged, the family is followed through one day, from the simulacrum of conventional family life in the morning to the tragic truth of their night. It is thus a literal day in the lives of the Tyrones, and also the Tyrones' journey through life toward death, that we witness.

Romantic, realistic, naturalistic, melodramatic, sentimental, cynical, poetic— the family dramas, indeed O'Neill's work in general, are all of these. We can see in retrospect that even while he made his characters espouse philosophical positions,

O'Neill was not trying to write philosophical drama. Nor was he designing plays to fit into a familiar dramatic type: tragedy, comedy, and the like. He wanted to make plays conveying emotions of such intensity and complexity that the theater would become a vital force in American life. In all his works, the spectacle of emotional intensity was meant to produce emotional response in an audience—what Aristotle, in his *Poetics*, had called "catharsis." As one critic wrote, "The meaning and unity of his work lies not in any controlling intellectual idea and certainly not in a 'message,' but merely in the fact that each play is an experience of extraordinary intensity."

# Long Day's Journey into Night[1]

## CHARACTERS

JAMES TYRONE
MARY CAVAN TYRONE, *his wife*
JAMES TYRONE, JR., *their elder son*
EDMUND TYRONE, *their younger son*
CATHLEEN, *second girl*[2]

## SCENES

ACT 1    *Living room of the Tyrones' summer home* 8:30 A.M. *of a day in August, 1912*
ACT 2   SCENE 1   *The same, around* 12:45
         SCENE 2   *The same, about a half hour later*
ACT 3    *The same, around* 6:30 *that evening*
ACT 4    *The same, around midnight*

## Act One

SCENE—*Living room of* JAMES TYRONE's *summer home on a morning in August,* 1912.

*At rear are two double doorways with portieres. The one at right leads into a front parlor with the formally arranged, set appearance of a room rarely occupied. The other opens on a dark, windowless back parlor, never used except as a passage from living room to dining room. Against the wall between the doorways is a small bookcase, with a picture of Shakespeare above it, containing novels by Balzac, Zola, Stendhal, philosophical and sociological works by Schopenhauer, Nietzsche, Marx, Engels, Kropotkin, Max Sterner, plays by Ibsen, Shaw, Strindberg, poetry by Swinburne, Rossetti, Wilde, Ernest Dowson, Kipling, etc.*[3]

*In the right wall, rear, is a screen door leading out on the porch which extends halfway around the house. Farther forward, a series of three windows looks over the front lawn to the harbor and the avenue that runs along the water front. A small wicker table and an ordinary oak desk are against the wall, flanking the windows.*

---

1. The text is that of the Yale University Press edition (1956).
2. A servant.
3. A variety of 19th-century (especially late-19th-century) authors are cited. Nobody in the audience would be able to read the titles and authors on these books—an example of O'Neill's novelistic approach to theatrical detail, also to be seen in the minute physical descriptions he provides of the actors' appearance and behavior throughout the play.

In the left wall, a similar series of windows looks out on the grounds in back of the house. Beneath them is a wicker couch with cushions, its head toward rear. Farther back is a large, glassed-in bookcase with sets of Dumas, Victor Hugo, Charles Lever, three sets of Shakespeare, The World's Best Literature in fifty large volumes, Hume's History of England, Thiers' History of the Consulate and Empire, Smollett's History of England, Gibbon's Roman Empire and miscellaneous volumes of old plays, poetry, and several histories of Ireland. The astonishing thing about these sets is that all the volumes have the look of having been read and reread.

The hardwood floor is nearly covered by a rug, inoffensive in design and color. At center is a round table with a green shaded reading lamp, the cord plugged in one of the four sockets in the chandelier above. Around the table within reading-light range are four chairs, three of them wicker armchairs, the fourth (at right front of table) a varnished oak rocker with leather bottom.

It is around 8:30. Sunshine comes through the windows at right.

As the curtain rises, the family have just finished breakfast. MARY TYRONE and her husband enter together from the back parlor, coming from the dining room.

MARY is fifty-four, about medium height. She still has a young, graceful figure, a trifle plump, but showing little evidence of middle-aged waist and hips, although she is not tightly corseted. Her face is distinctly Irish in type. It must once have been extremely pretty, and is still striking. It does not match her healthy figure but is thin and pale with the bone structure prominent. Her nose is long and straight, her mouth wide with full, sensitive lips. She uses no rouge or any sort of make-up. Her high forehead is framed by thick, pure white hair. Accentuated by her pallor and white hair, her dark brown eyes appear black. They are unusually large and beautiful, with black brows and long curling lashes.

What strikes one immediately is her extreme nervousness. Her hands are never still. They were once beautiful hands, with long, tapering fingers, but rheumatism has knotted the joints and warped the fingers, so that now they have an ugly crippled look. One avoids looking at them, the more so because one is conscious she is sensitive about their appearance and humiliated by her inability to control the nervousness which draws attention to them.

She is dressed simply but with a sure sense of what becomes her. Her hair is arranged with fastidious care. Her voice is soft and attractive. When she is merry, there is a touch of Irish lilt in it.

Her most appealing quality is the simple, unaffected charm of a shy convent-girl youthfulness she has never lost—an innate unworldly innocence.

JAMES TYRONE is sixty-five but looks ten years younger. About five feet eight, broad-shouldered and deep-chested, he seems taller and slenderer because of his bearing, which has a soldierly quality of head up, chest out, stomach in, shoulders squared. His face has begun to break down but he is still remarkably good looking—a big, finely shaped head, a handsome profile, deep-set light-brown eyes. His grey hair is thin with a bald spot like a monk's tonsure.

The stamp of his profession is unmistakably on him. Not that he indulges in any of the deliberate temperamental posturings of the stage star. He is by nature and preference a simple, unpretentious man, whose inclinations are still close to his humble beginnings and his Irish farmer forebears. But the actor shows in all his unconscious habits of speech, movement and gesture. These have the quality of belonging to a studied technique. His voice is remarkably fine, resonant and flexible, and he takes great pride in it.

*His clothes, assuredly, do not costume any romantic part. He wears a thread-bare, ready-made, grey sack suit and shineless black shoes, a collar-less shirt with a thick white handkerchief knotted loosely around his throat. There is nothing picturesquely careless about this get-up. It is commonplace shabby. He believes in wearing his clothes to the limit of usefulness, is dressed now for gardening, and doesn't give a damn how he looks.*

*He has never been really sick a day in his life. He has no nerves. There is a lot of stolid, earthy peasant in him, mixed with streaks of sentimental melancholy and rare flashes of intuitive sensibility.*

TYRONE*'s arm is around his wife's waist as they appear from the back parlor. Entering the living room he gives her a playful hug.*

TYRONE    You're a fine armful now, Mary, with those twenty pounds you've gained.

MARY [*smiles affectionately*]    I've gotten too fat, you mean, dear. I really ought to reduce.

TYRONE    None of that, my lady! You're just right. We'll have no talk of reducing. Is that why you ate so little breakfast?

MARY    So little? I thought I ate a lot.

TYRONE    You didn't. Not as much as I'd like to see, anyway.

MARY [*teasingly*]    Oh you! You expect everyone to eat the enormous breakfast you do. No one else in the world could without dying of indigestion. [*She comes forward to stand by the right of table.*]

TYRONE [ *following her*]    I hope I'm not as big a glutton as that sounds. [*with hearty satisfaction*] But thank God, I've kept my appetite and I've the digestion of a young man of twenty, if I am sixty-five.

MARY    You surely have, James. No one could deny that.

[*She laughs and sits in the wicker armchair at right rear of table. He comes around in back of her and selects a cigar from a box on the table and cuts off the end with a little clipper. From the dining room* JAMIE*'s and* EDMUND*'s voices are heard. Mary turns her head that way.*]

Why did the boys stay in the dining room, I wonder? Cathleen must be waiting to clear the table.

TYRONE [ *jokingly but with an undercurrent of resentment*]    It's a secret confab they don't want me to hear, I suppose. I'll bet they're cooking up some new scheme to touch the Old Man.

[*She is silent on this, keeping her head turned toward their voices. Her hands appear on the table top, moving restlessly. He lights his cigar and sits down in the rocker at right of table, which is his chair, and puffs contentedly.*]

There's nothing like the first after-breakfast cigar, if it's a good one, and this new lot have the right mellow flavor. They're a great bargain, too. I got them dead cheap. It was McGuire put me on to them.

MARY [*a trifle acidly*]    I hope he didn't put you on to any new piece of property at the same time. His real estate bargains don't work out so well.

TYRONE [*defensively*]    I wouldn't say that, Mary. After all, he was the one who advised me to buy that place on Chestnut Street and I made a quick turnover on it for a fine profit.

MARY [*smiles now with teasing affection*]    I know. The famous one stroke of good luck. I'm sure McGuire never dreamed— [*Then she pats his hand.*] Never mind, James. I know it's a waste of breath trying to convince you you're not a cunning real estate speculator.

TYRONE [*huffily*] I've no such idea. But land is land, and it's safer than the stocks and bonds of Wall Street swindlers. [*then placatingly*] But let's not argue about business this early in the morning.

    [*A pause. The boys' voices are again heard and one of them has a fit of coughing.* MARY *listens worriedly. Her fingers play nervously on the table top.*]

MARY James, it's Edmund you ought to scold for not eating enough. He hardly touched anything except coffee. He needs to eat to keep up his strength. I keep telling him that but he says he simply has no appetite. Of course, there's nothing takes away your appetite like a bad summer cold.

TYRONE Yes, it's only natural. So don't let yourself get worried—

MARY [*quickly*] Oh, I'm not. I know he'll be all right in a few days if he takes care of himself. [*as if she wanted to dismiss the subject but can't*] But it does seem a shame he should have to be sick right now.

TYRONE Yes, it is bad luck. [*He gives her a quick, worried look.*] But you mustn't let it upset you, Mary. Remember, you've got to take care of yourself, too.

MARY [*quickly*] I'm not upset. There's nothing to be upset about. What makes you think I'm upset?

TYRONE Why, nothing, except you've seemed a bit high-strung the past few days.

MARY [*forcing a smile*] I have? Nonsense, dear. It's your imagination. [*with sudden tenseness*] You really must not watch me all the time, James. I mean, it makes me self-conscious.

TYRONE [*putting a hand over one of her nervously playing ones*] Now, now, Mary. That's your imagination. If I've watched you it was to admire how fat and beautiful you looked. [*His voice is suddenly moved by deep feeling.*] I can't tell you the deep happiness it gives me, darling, to see you as you've been since you came back to us, your dear old self again. [*He leans over and kisses her cheek impulsively—then turning back adds with a constrained air*] So keep up the good work, Mary.

MARY [*has turned her head away*] I will, dear. [*She gets up restlessly and goes to the windows at right.*] Thank heavens, the fog is gone. [*She turns back.*] I do feel out of sorts this morning. I wasn't able to get much sleep with that awful foghorn going all night long.

TYRONE Yes, it's like having a sick whale in the back yard. It kept me awake, too.

MARY [*affectionately amused*] Did it? You had a strange way of showing your restlessness. You were snoring so hard I couldn't tell which was the foghorn! [*She comes to him, laughing, and pats his cheek playfully.*] Ten foghorns couldn't disturb you. You haven't a nerve in you. You've never had.

TYRONE [*his vanity piqued—testily*] Nonsense. You always exaggerate about my snoring.

MARY I couldn't. If you could only hear yourself once—

    [*A burst of laughter comes from the dining room. She turns her head, smiling.*]

What's the joke, I wonder?

TYRONE [*grumpily*] It's on me. I'll bet that much. It's always on the Old Man.

MARY [*teasingly*] Yes, it's terrible the way we all pick on you, isn't it? You're so abused! [*She laughs—then with a pleased, relieved air*] Well, no matter what the joke is about, it's a relief to hear Edmund laugh. He's been so down in the mouth lately.

TYRONE [*ignoring this—resentfully*]  Some joke of Jamie's, I'll wager. He's forever making sneering fun of somebody, that one.

MARY  Now don't start in on poor Jamie, dear. [*without conviction*] He'll turn out all right in the end, you wait and see.

TYRONE  He'd better start soon, then. He's nearly thirty-four.

MARY [*ignoring this*]  Good heavens, are they going to stay in the dining room all day? [*She goes to the back parlor doorway and calls*] Jamie! Edmund! Come in the living room and give Cathleen a chance to clear the table.

   [EDMUND *calls back, "We're coming, Mama." She goes back to the table.*]

TYRONE [*grumbling*]  You'd find excuses for him no matter what he did.

MARY [*sitting down beside him, pats his hand*]  Shush.

   *Their sons* JAMES, JR., *and* EDMUND *enter together from the back parlor. They are both grinning, still chuckling over what had caused their laughter, and as they come forward they glance at their father and their grins grow broader.*

   JAMIE, *the elder, is thirty-three. He has his father's broad-shouldered, deep-chested physique, is an inch taller and weighs less, but appears shorter and stouter because he lacks* TYRONE's *bearing and graceful carriage. He also lacks his father's vitality. The signs of premature disintegration are on him. His face is still good looking, despite marks of dissipation, but it has never been handsome like* TYRONE's, *although* JAMIE *resembles him rather than his mother. He has fine brown eyes, their color midway between his father's lighter and his mother's darker ones. His hair is thinning and already there is indication of a bald spot like* TYRONE's. *His nose is unlike that of any other member of the family, pronouncedly aquiline. Combined with his habitual expression of cynicism it gives his countenance a Mephistophelian cast. But on the rare occasions when he smiles without sneering, his personality possesses the remnant of a humorous, romantic, irresponsible Irish charm—that of the beguiling ne'er-do-well, with a strain of the sentimentally poetic, attractive to women and popular with men.*

   *He is dressed in an old sack suit, not as shabby as* TYRONE's, *and wears a collar and tie. His fair skin is sunburned a reddish, freckled tan.*

   EDMUND *is ten years younger than his brother, a couple of inches taller, thin and wiry. Where* JAMIE *takes after his father, with little resemblance to his mother,* EDMUND *looks like both his parents, but is more like his mother. Her big, dark eyes are the dominant feature in his long, narrow Irish face. His mouth has the same quality of hypersensitiveness hers possesses. His high forehead is hers accentuated, with dark brown hair, sunbleached to red at the ends, brushed straight back from it. But his nose is his father's and his face in profile recalls* TYRONE's. EDMUND's *hands are noticeably like his mother's, with the same exceptionally long fingers. They even have to a minor degree the same nervousness. It is in the quality of extreme nervous sensibility that the likeness of* EDMUND *to his mother is most marked.*

   *He is plainly in bad health. Much thinner than he should be, his eyes appear feverish and his cheeks are sunken. His skin, in spite of being sunburned a deep brown, has a parched sallowness. He wears a shirt, collar and tie, no coat, old flannel trousers, brown sneakers.*

MARY [*turns smilingly to them, in a merry tone that is a bit forced*]  I've been teasing your father about his snoring. [*to* TYRONE] I'll leave it to the boys, James. They must have heard you. No, not you, Jamie. I could hear you down the hall almost as bad as your father. You're like him. As soon as your head touches the pillow you're off and ten foghorns couldn't wake you. [*She stops abruptly, catching* JAMIE's *eyes regarding her with an uneasy, probing look. Her smile vanishes and her manner becomes self-conscious.*] *Why* are you staring, Jamie? [*Her hands flutter up to her hair.*] Is my hair coming down? It's hard for me to do it up properly now. My eyes are getting so bad and I never can find my glasses.

JAMIE [*looks away guiltily*]　Your hair's all right, Mama. I was only thinking how well you look.

TYRONE [*heartily*]　Just what I've been telling her, Jamie. She's so fat and sassy, there'll soon be no holding her.

EDMUND　Yes, you certainly look grand, Mama. [*She is reassured and smiles at him lovingly. He winks with a kidding grin.*] I'll back you up about Papa's snoring. Gosh, what a racket!

JAMIE　I heard him, too. [*He quotes, putting on a ham-actor manner*] "The Moor, I know his trumpet."[4]

[*His mother and brother laugh.*]

TYRONE [*scathingly*]　If it takes my snoring to make you remember Shakespeare instead of the dope sheet on the ponies, I hope I'll keep on with it.

MARY　Now, James! You mustn't be so touchy.

[JAMIE *shrugs his shoulders and sits down in the chair on her right.*]

EDMUND [*irritably*]　Yes, for Pete's sake, Papa! The first thing after breakfast! Give it a rest, can't you? [*He slumps down in the chair at left of table next to his brother. His father ignores him.*]

MARY [*reprovingly*]　Your father wasn't finding fault with you. You don't have to always take Jamie's part. You'd think you were the one ten years older.

JAMIE [*boredly*]　What's all the fuss about? Let's forget it.

TYRONE [*contemptuously*]　Yes, forget! Forget everything and face nothing! It's a convenient philosophy if you've no ambition in life except to—

MARY　James, do be quiet. [*She puts an arm around his shoulder—coaxingly*] You must have gotten out of the wrong side of the bed this morning. [*to the boys, changing the subject*] What were you two grinning about like Cheshire cats when you came in? What was the joke?

TYRONE [*with a painful effort to be a good sport*]　Yes, let us in on it, lads. I told your mother I knew damned well it would be one on me, but never mind that, I'm used to it.

JAMIE [*dryly*]　Don't look at me. This is the Kid's story.

EDMUND [*grins*]　I meant to tell you last night, Papa, and forgot it. Yesterday when I went for a walk I dropped in at the Inn—

MARY [*worriedly*]　You shouldn't drink now, Edmund.

EDMUND [*ignoring this*]　And who do you think I met there, with a beautiful bun on,[5] but Shaughnessy, the tenant on that farm of yours.

MARY [*smiling*]　That dreadful man! But he is funny.

TYRONE [*scowling*]　He's not so funny when you're his landlord. He's a wily Shanty Mick, that one. He could hide behind a corkscrew. What's he complaining about now, Edmund—for I'm damned sure he's complaining. I suppose he wants his rent lowered. I let him have the place for almost nothing, just to keep someone on it, and he never pays that till I threaten to evict him.

EDMUND　No, he didn't beef about anything. He was so pleased with life he even bought a drink, and that's practically unheard of. He was delighted

4. Shakespeare, *Othello* 2.1.180.　　　　　5. I.e., drunk.

because he'd had a fight with your friend, Harker, the Standard Oil millionaire, and won a glorious victory.

MARY [with amused dismay]   Oh, Lord! James, you'll really have to do something—

TYRONE   Bad luck to Shaughnessy, anyway!

JAMIE [maliciously]   I'll bet the next time you see Harker at the Club and give
him the old respectful bow, he won't see you.

EDMUND   Yes. Harker will think you're no gentleman for harboring a tenant
who isn't humble in the presence of a king of America.

TYRONE   Never mind the Socialist gabble. I don't care to listen—

MARY [tactfully]   Go on with your story, Edmund.

EDMUND [grins at his father provocatively]   Well, you remember, Papa, the
ice pond on Harker's estate is right next to the farm, and you remember
Shaughnessy keeps pigs. Well, it seems there's a break in the fence and the
pigs have been bathing in the millionaire's ice pond, and Harker's foreman
told him he was sure Shaughnessy had broken the fence on purpose to give
his pigs a free wallow.

MARY [shocked and amused]   Good heavens!

TYRONE [sourly, but with a trace of admiration]   I'm sure he did, too, the
dirty scallywag. It's like him.

EDMUND   So Harker came in person to rebuke Shaughnessy. [He chuckles.] A
very bonehead play! If I needed any further proof that our ruling plutocrats,
especially the ones who inherited their boodle, are not mental giants, that
would clinch it.

TYRONE [with appreciation, before he thinks]   Yes, he'd be no match for
Shaughnessy. [then he growls] Keep your damned anarchist remarks to your-
self. I won't have them in my house. [But he is full of eager anticipation.]
What happened?

EDMUND   Harker had as much chance as I would with Jack Johnson.[6]
Shaughnessy got a few drinks under his belt and was waiting at the gate to
welcome him. He told me he never gave Harker a chance to open his
mouth. He began by shouting that he was no slave Standard Oil could
trample on. He was a King of Ireland, if he had his rights, and scum was
scum to him, no matter how much money it had stolen from the poor.

MARY   Oh, Lord! [But she can't help laughing.]

EDMUND   Then he accused Harker of making his foreman break down the
fence to entice the pigs into the ice pond in order to destroy them. The poor
pigs, Shaughnessy yelled, had caught their death of cold. Many of them
were dying of pneumonia, and several others had been taken down with
cholera from drinking the poisoned water. He told Harker he was hiring a
lawyer to sue him for damages. And he wound up by saying that he had to
put up with poison ivy, ticks, potato bugs, snakes and skunks on his farm,
but he was an honest man who drew the line somewhere, and he'd be
damned if he'd stand for a Standard Oil thief trespassing. So would Harker
kindly remove his dirty feet from the premises before he sicked the dog on
him. And Harker did! [He and JAMIE laugh.]

MARY [shocked but giggling]   Heavens, what a terrible tongue that man has!

TYRONE [admiringly before he thinks]   The damned old scoundrel! By God,
you can't beat him! [He laughs—then stops abruptly and scowls.] The dirty

6. Famous prizefighter.

blackguard! He'll get me in serious trouble yet. I hope you told him I'd be mad as hell—

EDMUND    I told him you'd be tickled to death over the great Irish victory, and so you are. Stop faking, Papa.

TYRONE    Well, I'm not tickled to death.

MARY [*teasingly*]    You are, too, James. You're simply delighted!

TYRONE    No, Mary, a joke is a joke, but—

EDMUND    I told Shaughnessy he should have reminded Harker that a Standard Oil millionaire ought to welcome the flavor of hog in his ice water as an appropriate touch.

TYRONE    The devil you did! [ *frowning*] Keep your damned Socialist anarchist sentiments out of my affairs!

EDMUND    Shaughnessy almost wept because he hadn't thought of that one, but he said he'd include it in a letter he's writing to Harker, along with a few other insults he'd overlooked. [*He and* JAMIE *laugh.*]

TYRONE    What are you laughing at? There's nothing funny—A fine son you are to help that blackguard get me into a lawsuit!

MARY    Now, James, don't lose your temper.

TYRONE [*turns on* JAMIE]    And you're worse than he is, encouraging him. I suppose you're regretting you weren't there to prompt Shaughnessy with a few nastier insults. You've a fine talent for that, if for nothing else.

MARY    James! There's no reason to scold Jamie.

[ JAMIE *is about to make some sneering remark to his father, but he shrugs his shoulders.*]

EDMUND [*with sudden nervous exasperation*]    Oh, for God's sake, Papa! If you're starting that stuff again, I'll beat it. [*He jumps up.*] I left my book upstairs, anyway. [*He goes to the front parlor, saying disgustedly*] God, Papa, I should think you'd get sick of hearing yourself—

[*He disappears.* TYRONE *looks after him angrily.*]

MARY    You mustn't mind Edmund, James. Remember he isn't well.

[EDMUND *can be heard coughing as he goes upstairs. She adds nervously*]

A summer cold makes anyone irritable.

JAMIE [*genuinely concerned*]    It's not just a cold he's got. The Kid is damned sick.

[*His father gives him a sharp warning look but he doesn't see it.*]

MARY [*turns on him resentfully*]    Why do you say that? It *is* just a cold! Anyone can tell that! You always imagine things!

TYRONE [*with another warning glance at* JAMIE—*easily*]    All Jamie meant was Edmund might have a touch of something else, too, which makes his cold worse.

JAMIE    Sure, Mama. That's all I meant.

TYRONE    Doctor Hardy thinks it might be a bit of malarial fever he caught when he was in the tropics. If it is, quinine will soon cure it.

MARY [*a look of contemptuous hostility flashes across her face*]    Doctor Hardy! I wouldn't believe a thing he said, if he swore on a stack of Bibles! I know what doctors are. They're all alike. Anything, they don't care what, to keep you coming to them. [*She stops short, overcome by a fit of acute self-consciousness as she catches their eyes fixed on her. Her hands jerk nervously to her hair. She forces a smile.*] What is it? What are you looking at? Is my hair—?

TYRONE [*puts his arm around her—with guilty heartiness, giving her a playful hug*] There's nothing wrong with your hair. The healthier and fatter you get, the vainer you become. You'll soon spend half the day primping before the mirror.

MARY [*half reassured*] I really should have new glasses. My eyes are so bad now.

TYRONE [*with Irish blarney*] Your eyes are beautiful, and well you know it. [*He gives her a kiss. Her face lights up with a charming, shy embarrassment. Suddenly and startlingly one sees in her face the girl she had once been, not a ghost of the dead, but still a living part of her.*]

MARY You mustn't be so silly, James. Right in front of Jamie!

TYRONE Oh, he's on to you, too. He knows this fuss about eyes and hair is only fishing for compliments. Eh, Jamie?

JAMIE [*his face has cleared, too, and there is an old boyish charm in his loving smile at his mother*] Yes, You can't kid us, Mama.

MARY [*laughs and an Irish lilt comes into her voice*] Go along with both of you! [*then she speaks with a girlish gravity*] But I did truly have beautiful hair once, didn't I, James?

TYRONE The most beautiful in the world!

MARY It was a rare shade of reddish brown and so long it came down below my knees. You ought to remember it, too, Jamie. It wasn't until after Edmund was born that I had a single grey hair. Then it began to turn white. [*The girlishness fades from her face.*]

TYRONE [*quickly*] And that made it prettier than ever.

MARY [*again embarrassed and pleased*] Will you listen to your father, Jamie—after thirty-five years of marriage! He isn't a great actor for nothing, is he? What's come over you, James? Are you pouring coals of fire on my head for teasing you about snoring? Well, then, I take it all back. It must have been only the foghorn I heard. [*She laughs, and they laugh with her. Then she changes to a brisk businesslike air.*] But I can't stay with you any longer, even to hear compliments. I must see the cook about dinner and the day's marketing. [*She gets up and sighs with humorous exaggeration.*] Bridget is so lazy. And so sly. She begins telling me about her relatives so I can't get a word in edgeways and scold her. Well, I might as well get it over. [*She goes to the back-parlor doorway, then turns, her face worried again.*] You mustn't make Edmund work on the grounds with you, James, remember. [*again with the strange obstinate set to her face*] Not that he isn't strong enough, but he'd perspire and he might catch more cold. [*She disappears through the back parlor. Tyrone turns on JAMIE condemningly.*]

TYRONE You're a fine lunkhead! Haven't you any sense? The one thing to avoid is saying anything that would get her more upset over Edmund.

JAMIE [*shrugging his shoulders*] All right. Have it your way. I think it's the wrong idea to let Mama go on kidding yourself. It will only make the shock worse when she has to face it. Anyway, you can see she's deliberately fooling herself with that summer cold talk. She knows better.

TYRONE Knows? Nobody knows yet.

JAMIE Well, I do. I was with Edmund when he went to Doc Hardy on Monday. I heard him pull that touch of malaria stuff. He was stalling. That isn't what he thinks any more. You know it as well as I do. You talked to him when you went uptown yesterday, didn't you?

TYRONE He couldn't say anything for sure yet. He's to phone me today before Edmund goes to him.

JAMIE [*slowly*]   He thinks it's consumption,[7] doesn't he, Papa?

TYRONE [*reluctantly*]   He said it might be.

JAMIE [*moved, his love for his brother coming out*]   Poor kid! God damn it! [*He turns on his father accusingly.*] It might never have happened if you'd sent him to a real doctor when he first got sick.

TYRONE   What's the matter with Hardy? He's always been our doctor up here.

JAMIE   Everything's the matter with him! Even in this hick burg he's rated third class! He's a cheap old quack!

TYRONE   That's right! Run him down! Run down everybody! Everyone is a fake to you!

JAMIE [*contemptuously*]   Hardy only charges a dollar. That's what makes you think he's a fine doctor!

TYRONE [*stung*]   That's enough! You're not drunk now! There's no excuse— [*He controls himself—a bit defensively*] If you mean I can't afford one of the fine society doctors who prey on the rich summer people—

JAMIE   Can't afford? You're one of the biggest property owners around here.

TYRONE   That doesn't mean I'm rich. It's all mortgaged—

JAMIE   Because you always buy more instead of paying off mortgages. If Edmund was a lousy acre of land you wanted, the sky would be the limit!

TYRONE   That's a lie! And your sneers against Doctor Hardy are lies! He doesn't put on frills, or have an office in a fashionable location, or drive around in an expensive automobile. That's what you pay for with those other five-dollars-to-look-at-your-tongue fellows, not their skill.

JAMIE [*with a scornful shrug of his shoulders*]   Oh, all right. I'm a fool to argue. You can't change the leopard's spots.

TYRONE [*with rising anger*]   No, you can't. You've taught me that lesson only too well. I've lost all hope you will ever change yours. You dare tell me what I can afford? You've never known the value of a dollar and never will! You've never saved a dollar in your life! At the end of each season you're penniless! You've thrown your salary away every week on whores and whiskey!

JAMIE   My salary! Christ!

TYRONE   It's more than you're worth, and you couldn't get that if it wasn't for me. If you weren't my son, there isn't a manager in the business who would give you a part, your reputation stinks so. As it is, I have to humble my pride and beg for you, saying you've turned over a new leaf, although I know it's a lie!

JAMIE   I never wanted to be an actor. You forced me on the stage.

TYRONE   That's a lie! You made no effort to find anything else to do. You left it to me to get you a job and I have no influence except in the theater. Forced you! You never wanted to do anything except loaf in barrooms! You'd have been content to sit back like a lazy lunk and sponge on me for the rest of your life! After all the money I'd wasted on your education, and all you did was get fired in disgrace from every college you went to!

JAMIE   Oh, for God's sake, don't drag up that ancient history!

TYRONE   It's not ancient history that you have to come home every summer to live on me.

JAMIE   I earn my board and lodging working on the grounds. It saves you hiring a man.

TYRONE   Bah! You have to be driven to do even that much! [*His anger ebbs*

---

7. I.e., tuberculosis.

*into a weary complaint.*] I wouldn't give a damn if you ever displayed the slightest sign of gratitude. The only thanks is to have you sneer at me for a dirty miser, sneer at my profession, sneer at every damned thing in the world—except yourself.

JAMIE [*wryly*] That's not true, Papa. You can't hear me talking to myself, that's all.

TYRONE [*stares at him puzzledly, then quotes mechanically*] "Ingratitude, the vilest weed that grows"![8]

JAMIE I could see that line coming! God, how many thousand times—! [*He stops, bored with their quarrel, and shrugs his shoulders.*] All right, Papa. I'm a bum. Anything you like, so long as it stops the argument.

TYRONE [*with indignant appeal now*] If you'd get ambition in your head instead of folly! You're young yet. You could still make your mark. You had the talent to become a fine actor! You have it still. You're my son—!

JAMIE [*boredly*] Let's forget me. I'm not interested in the subject. Neither are you. [TYRONE *gives up.* JAMIE *goes on casually.*] What started us on this? Oh, Doc Hardy. When is he going to call you up about Edmund?

TYRONE Around lunch time. [*He pauses—then defensively*] I couldn't have sent Edmund to a better doctor. Hardy's treated him whenever he was sick up here, since he was knee high. He knows his constitution as no other doctor could. It's not a question of my being miserly, as you'd like to make out. [*bitterly*] And what could the finest specialist in America do for Edmund, after he's deliberately ruined his health by the mad life he's led ever since he was fired from college? Even before that when he was in prep school, he began dissipating and playing the Broadway sport to imitate you, when he's never had your constitution to stand it. You're a healthy hulk like me—or you were at his age—but he's always been a bundle of nerves like his mother. I've warned him for years his body couldn't stand it, but he wouldn't heed me, and now it's too late.

JAMIE [*sharply*] What do you mean, too late? You talk as if you thought—

TYRONE [*guiltily explosive*] Don't be a damned fool! I meant nothing but what's plain to anyone! His health has broken down and he may be an invalid for a long time.

JAMIE [*stares at his father, ignoring his explanation*] I know it's an Irish peasant idea consumption is fatal. It probably is when you live in a hovel on a bog, but over here, with modern treatment—

TYRONE Don't I know that! What are you gabbing about, anyway? And keep your dirty tongue off Ireland, with your sneers about peasants and bogs and hovels! [*accusingly*] The less you say about Edmund's sickness, the better for your conscience! You're more responsible than anyone!

JAMIE [*stung*] That's a lie! I won't stand for that, Papa!

TYRONE It's the truth! You've been the worst influence for him. He grew up admiring you as a hero! A fine example you set him! If you ever gave him advice except in the ways of rottenness, I've never heard of it! You made him old before his time, pumping him full of what you consider worldly wisdom, when he was too young to see that your mind was so poisoned by your own failure in life, you wanted to believe every man was a knave with his soul for sale, and every woman who wasn't a whore was a fool!

JAMIE [*with a defensive air of weary indifference again*] All right. I did put Edmund wise to things, but not until I saw he'd started to raise hell, and

---

8. Shakespeare, *King Lear* 1.4.

knew he'd laugh at me if I tried the good advice, older brother stuff. All I did was make a pal of him and be absolutely frank so he'd learn from my mistakes that—[*He shrugs his shoulders—cynically*] Well, that if you can't be good you can at least be careful.

[*His father snorts contemptuously. Suddenly* JAMIE *becomes really moved.*] That's a rotten accusation, Papa. You know how much the Kid means to me, and how close we've always been—not like the usual brothers! I'd do anything for him.

TYRONE [*impressed—mollifyingly*]   I know you may have thought it was for the best, Jamie. I didn't say you did it deliberately to harm him.

JAMIE   Besides it's damned rot! I'd like to see anyone influence Edmund more than he wants to be. His quietness fools people into thinking they can do what they like with him. But he's stubborn as hell inside and what he does is what he wants to do, and to hell with anyone else! What had I to do with all the crazy stunts he's pulled in the last few years—working his way all over the map as a sailor and all that stuff. I thought that was a damned fool idea, and I told him so. You can't imagine me getting fun out of being on the beach in South America, or living in filthy dives, drinking rotgut, can you? No, thanks! I'll stick to Broadway, and a room with a bath, and bars that serve bonded Bourbon.

TYRONE   You and Broadway! It's made you what you are! [*with a touch of pride*] Whatever Edmund's done, he's had the guts to go off on his own, where he couldn't come whining to me the minute he was broke.

JAMIE [*stung into sneering jealousy*]   He's always come home broke finally, hasn't he? And what did his going away get him? Look at him now! [*He is suddenly shamefaced.*] Christ! That's a lousy thing to say. I don't mean that.

TYRONE [*decides to ignore this*]   He's been doing well on the paper. I was hoping he'd found the work he wants to do at last.

JAMIE [*sneering jealously again*]   A hick town rag! Whatever bull they hand you, they tell me he's a pretty bum reporter. If he weren't your son— [*ashamed again*] No, that's not true! They're glad to have him, but it's the special stuff that gets him by. Some of the poems and parodies he's written are damned good. [*grudgingly again*] Not that they'd ever get him anywhere on the big time. [*hastily*] But he's certainly made a damned good start.

TYRONE   Yes. He's made a start. You used to talk about wanting to become a newspaper man but you were never willing to start at the bottom. You expected—

JAMIE   Oh, for Christ's sake, Papa! Can't you lay off me!

TYRONE [*stares at him—then looks away—after a pause*]   It's damnable luck Edmund should be sick right now. It couldn't have come at a worse time for him. [*He adds, unable to conceal an almost furtive uneasiness*] Or for your mother. It's damnable she should have this to upset her, just when she needs peace and freedom from worry. She's been so well in the two months since she came home. [*His voice grows husky and trembles a little.*] It's been heaven to me. This home has been a home again. But I needn't tell you, Jamie.

[*His son looks at him, for the first time with an understanding sympathy. It is as if suddenly a deep bond of common feeling existed between them in which their antagonisms could be forgotten.*]

JAMIE [*almost gently*]   I've felt the same way, Papa.

TYRONE   Yes, this time you can see how strong and sure of herself she is.

She's a different woman entirely from the other times. She has control of
her nerves—or she had until Edmund got sick. Now you can feel her growing tense and frightened underneath. I wish to God we could keep the truth
from her, but we can't if he has to be sent to a sanatorium. What makes it
worse is her father died of consumption. She worshiped him and she's never
forgotten. Yes, it will be hard for her. But she can do it! She has the will
power now! We must help her, Jamie, in every way we can!

JAMIE [moved]   Of course, Papa. [hesitantly] Outside of nerves, she seems
perfectly all right this morning.

TYRONE [with hearty confidence now]   Never better. She's full of fun and mischief. [Suddenly he frowns at JAMIE suspiciously.] Why do you say, seems?
Why shouldn't she be all right? What the hell do you mean?

JAMIE   Don't start jumping down my throat! God, Papa, this ought to be one
thing we can talk over frankly without a battle.

TYRONE   I'm sorry, Jamie. [tensely] But go on and tell me—

JAMIE   There's nothing to tell. I was all wrong. It's just that last night—Well,
you know how it is, I can't forget the past. I can't help being suspicious.
Any more than you can. [bitterly] That's the hell of it. And it makes it hell
for Mama! She watches us watching her—

TYRONE [sadly]   I know. [tensely] Well, what was it! Can't you speak out!

JAMIE   Nothing, I tell you. Just my damned foolishness. Around three o'clock
this morning, I woke up and heard her moving around in the spare room.
Then she went to the bathroom. I pretended to be asleep. She stopped in
the hall to listen, as if she wanted to make sure I was.

TYRONE [with forced scorn]   For God's sake, is that all? She told me herself
the foghorn kept her awake all night, and every night since Edmund's been
sick she's been up and down, going to his room to see how he was.

JAMIE [eagerly]   Yes, that's right, she did stop to listen outside his room. [hes-
itantly again] It was her being in the spare room that scared me. I couldn't
help remembering that when she starts sleeping alone in there, it has always
been a sign—

TYRONE   It isn't this time! It's easily explained. Where else could she go last
night to get away from my snoring? [He gives way to a burst of resentful
anger.] By God, how you can live with a mind that sees nothing but the
worst motives behind everything is beyond me!

JAMIE [stung]   Don't pull that! I've just said I was all wrong. Don't you suppose I'm as glad of that as you are!

TYRONE [mollifyingly]   I'm sure you are, Jamie. [A pause. His expression
becomes somber. He speaks slowly with a superstitious dread.] It would be
like a curse she can't escape if worry over Edmund—It was her long sickness
after bringing him into the world that she first—

JAMIE   She didn't have anything to do with it!

TYRONE   I'm not blaming her.

JAMIE [bitingly]   Then who are you blaming? Edmund, for being born?

TYRONE   You damned fool! No one was to blame.

JAMIE   The bastard of a doctor was! From what Mama's said, he was another
cheap quack like Hardy! You wouldn't pay for a first-rate—

TYRONE   That's a lie! [furiously] So I'm to blame! That's what you're driving
at, is it? You evil-minded loafer!

JAMIE [warningly as he hears his mother in the dining room]   Ssh!

[TYRONE gets hastily to his feet and goes to look out the windows at
right. JAMIE speaks with a complete change of tone.]

Well, if we're going to cut the front hedge today, we'd better go to work. [MARY *comes in from the back parlor. She gives a quick, suspicious glance from one to the other, her manner nervously self-conscious.*]

TYRONE [*turns from the window—with an actor's heartiness*]   Yes, it's too fine a morning to waste indoors arguing. Take a look out the window, Mary. There's no fog in the harbor. I'm sure the spell of it we've had is over now.

MARY [*going to him*]   I hope so, dear. [*to* JAMIE, *forcing a smile*] Did I actually hear you suggesting work on the front hedge, Jamie? Wonders will never cease! You must want pocket money badly.

JAMIE [*kiddingly*]   When don't I? [*He winks at her, with a derisive glance at his father.*] I expect a salary of at least one large iron man[9] at the end of the week—to carouse on!

MARY [*does not respond to his humor—her hands fluttering over the front of her dress*]   What were you two arguing about?

JAMIE [*shrugs his shoulders*]   The same old stuff.

MARY   I heard you say something about a doctor, and your father accusing you of being evil-minded.

JAMIE [*quickly*]   Oh, that. I was saying again Doc Hardy isn't my idea of the world's greatest physician.

MARY [*knows he is lying—vaguely*]   Oh. No, I wouldn't say he was either. [*changing the subject—forcing a smile*] That Bridget! I thought I'd never get away. She told me about her second cousin on the police force in St. Louis. [*then with nervous irritation*] Well, if you're going to work on the hedge why don't you go? [*hastily*] I mean, take advantage of the sunshine before the fog comes back. [*strangely, as if talking aloud to herself*] Because I know it will. [*Suddenly she is self-consciously aware that they are both staring fixedly at her—flurriedly, raising her hands*] Or I should say, the rheumatism in my hands knows. It's a better weather prophet than you are, James. [*She stares at her hands with fascinated repulsion.*] Ugh! How ugly they are! Who'd ever believe they were once beautiful?

[*They stare at her with a growing dread.*]

TYRONE [*takes her hands and gently pushes them down*]   Now, now, Mary. None of that foolishness. They're the sweetest hands in the world.

[*She smiles, her face lighting up, and kisses him gratefully. He turns to his son.*]

Come on Jamie. Your mother's right to scold us. The way to start work is to start work. The hot sun will sweat some of that booze fat off your middle.

[*He opens the screen door and goes out on the porch and disappears down a flight of steps leading to the ground.* JAMIE *rises from his chair and, taking off his coat, goes to the door. At the door he turns back but avoids looking at her, and she does not look at him.*]

JAMIE [*with an awkward, uneasy tenderness*]   We're all so proud of you, Mama, so darned happy.

[*She stiffens and stares at him with a frightened defiance. He flounders on.*]

But you've still got to be careful. You mustn't worry so much about Edmund. He'll be all right.

MARY [*with a stubborn, bitterly resentful look*]   Of course, he'll be all right. And I don't know what you mean, warning me to be careful.

---

9. Slang for "dollar."

JAMIE [*rebuffed and hurt, shrugs his shoulders*]   All right, Mama. I'm sorry
I spoke.
  [*He goes out on the porch. She waits rigidly until he disappears down
  the steps. Then she sinks down in the chair he had occupied, her face
  betraying a frightened, furtive desperation, her hands roving over the
  table top, aimlessly moving objects around. She hears* EDMUND
  *descending the stairs in the front hall. As he nears the bottom he has a
  fit of coughing. She springs to her feet, as if she wanted to run away
  from the sound, and goes quickly to the windows at right. She is looking
  out, apparently calm, as he enters from the front parlor, a book in one
  hand. She turns to him, her lips set in a welcoming, motherly smile.*]
MARY   Here you are. I was just going upstairs to look for you.
EDMUND   I waited until they went out. I don't want to mix up in any arguments. I feel too rotten.
MARY [*almost resentfully*]   Oh, I'm sure you don't feel half as badly as you
make out. You're such a baby. You like to get us worried so we'll make a
fuss over you. [*hastily*] I'm only teasing, dear. I know how miserably
uncomfortable you must be. But you feel better today, don't you? [*worriedly,
taking his arm*] All the same, you've grown much too thin. You need to rest
all you can. Sit down and I'll make you comfortable.
  [*He sits down in the rocking chair and she puts a pillow behind his
  back.*]
There, How's that?
EDMUND   Grand. Thanks, Mama.
MARY [*kisses him—tenderly*]   All you need is your mother to nurse you. Big
as you are, you're still the baby of the family to me, you know.
EDMUND [*takes her hand—with deep seriousness*]   Never mind me. You take
care of yourself. That's all that counts.
MARY [*evading his eyes*]   But I am, dear. [ *forcing a laugh*] Heavens, don't
you see how fat I've grown! I'll have to have all my dresses let out. [*She
turns away and goes to the windows at right. She attempts a light, amused
tone.*] They've started clipping the hedge. Poor Jamie! How he hates working in front where everyone passing can see him. There go the Chatfields
in their new Mercedes. It's a beautiful car, isn't it? Not like our secondhand
Packard. Poor Jamie! He bent almost under the hedge so they wouldn't
notice him. They bowed to your father and he bowed back as if he were
taking a curtain call. In that filthy old suit I've tried to make him throw
away. [*Her voice has grown bitter.*] Really, he ought to have more pride than
to make such a show of himself.
EDMUND   He's right not to give a damn what anyone thinks. Jamie's a fool to
care about the Chatfields. For Pete's sake, who ever heard of them outside
this hick burg?
MARY [*with satisfaction*]   No one. You're quite right, Edmund. Big frogs in a
small puddle. It is stupid of Jamie. [*She pauses, looking out the window—
then with an undercurrent of lonely yearning*] Still, the Chatfields and people like them stand for something. I mean they have decent, presentable
homes they don't have to be ashamed of. They have friends who entertain
them and whom they entertain. They're not cut off from everyone. [*She
turns back from the window.*] Not that I want anything to do with them. I've
always hated this town and everyone in it. You know that. I never wanted
to live here in the first place, but your father liked it and insisted on building
this house, and I've had to come here every summer.

EDMUND    Well, it's better than spending the summer in a New York hotel, isn't it? And this town's not so bad. I like it well enough. I suppose because it's the only home we've had.

MARY    I've never felt it was my home. It was wrong from the start. Everything was done in the cheapest way. Your father would never spend the money to make it right. It's just as well we haven't any friends here. I'd be ashamed to have them step in the door. But he's never wanted family friends. He hates calling on people, or receiving them. All he likes is to hobnob with men at the Club or in a barroom. Jamie and you are the same way, but you're not to blame. You've never had a chance to meet decent people here. I know you both would have been so different if you'd been able to associate with nice girls instead of—You'd never have disgraced yourselves as you have, so that now no respectable parents will let their daughters be seen with you.

EDMUND    [irritably]    Oh, Mama, forget it! Who cares? Jamie and I would be bored stiff. And about the Old Man, what's the use of talking? You can't change him.

MARY    [mechanically rebuking]    Don't call your father the Old Man. You should have more respect. [then dully] I know it's useless to talk. But sometimes I feel so lonely. [Her lips quiver and she keeps her head turned away.]

EDMUND    Anyway, you've got to be fair, Mama. It may have been all his fault in the beginning, but you know that later on, even if he'd wanted to, we couldn't have had people here—[He flounders guiltily.] I mean, you wouldn't have wanted them.

MARY    [wincing—her lips quivering pitifully]    Don't. I can't bear having you remind me.

EDMUND    Don't take it that way! Please, Mama! I'm trying to help. Because it's bad for you to forget. The right way is to remember. So you'll always be on your guard. You know what's happened before. [miserably] God, Mama, you know I hate to remind you. I'm doing it because it's been so wonderful having you home the way you've been, and it would be terrible—

MARY    [strickenly]    Please, dear. I know you mean it for the best, but—[A defensive uneasiness comes into her voice again.] I don't understand why you should suddenly say such things. What put it in your mind this morning?

EDMUND    [evasively]    Nothing. Just because I feel rotten and blue, I suppose.

MARY    Tell me the truth. Why are you so suspicious all of a sudden?

EDMUND    I'm not!

MARY    Oh, yes you are. I can feel it. Your father and Jamie, too—particularly Jamie.

EDMUND    Now don't start imagining things, Mama.

MARY    [her hands fluttering]    It makes it so much harder, living in this atmosphere of constant suspicion, knowing everyone is spying on me, and none of you believe in me, or trust me.

EDMUND    That's crazy, Mama. We do trust you.

MARY    If there was only some place I could go to get away for a day, or even an afternoon, some woman friend I could talk to—not about anything serious, simply laugh and gossip and forget for a while—someone besides the servants—that stupid Cathleen!

EDMUND    [gets up worriedly and puts his arm around her]    Stop it, Mama. You're getting yourself worked up over nothing.

MARY    Your father goes out. He meets his friends in barrooms or at the Club. You and Jamie have the boys you know. You go out. But I am alone. I've always been alone.

EDMUND    [soothingly]    Come now! You know that's a fib. One of us always

stays around to keep you company, or goes with you in the automobile
when you take a drive.
MARY [*bitterly*]   Because you're afraid to trust me alone! [*She turns on him—
sharply.*] I insist you tell me why you act so differently this morning—why
you felt you had to remind me—
EDMUND [*hesitates—then blurts out guiltily*]   It's stupid. It's just that I wasn't
asleep when you came in my room last night. You didn't go back to your
and Papa's room. You went in the spare room for the rest of the night.
MARY   Because your father's snoring was driving me crazy! For heaven's sake,
haven't I often used the spare room as my bedroom? [*bitterly*] But I see what
you thought. That was when—
EDMUND [*too vehemently*]   I didn't think anything!
MARY   So you pretended to be asleep in order to spy on me!
EDMUND   No! I did it because I knew if you found out I was feverish and
couldn't sleep, it would upset you.
MARY   Jamie was pretending to be asleep, too, I'm sure, and I suppose your
father—
EDMUND   Stop it, Mama!
MARY   Oh, I can't bear it, Edmund, when even you—! [*Her hands flutter up
to pat her hair in their aimless, distracted way. Suddenly a strange under-
current of revengefulness comes into her voice.*] It would serve all of you right
if it was true!
EDMUND   Mama! Don't say that! That's the way you talk when—
MARY   Stop suspecting me! Please, dear! You hurt me! I couldn't sleep
because I was thinking about you. That's the real reason! I've been so worried ever since you've been sick. [*She puts her arms around him and hugs
him with a frightened, protective tenderness.*]
EDMUND [*soothingly*]   That's foolishness. You know it's only a bad cold.
MARY   Yes, of course, I know that!
EDMUND   But listen, Mama. I want you to promise me that even if it should
turn out to be something worse, you'll know I'll soon be all right again,
anyway, and you won't worry yourself sick, and you'll keep on taking care
of yourself—
MARY [*frightenedly*]   I won't listen when you're so silly! There's absolutely no
reason to talk as if you expected something dreadful! Of course, I promise
you. I give you my sacred word of honor! [*then with a sad bitterness*] But I
suppose you're remembering I've promised before on my word of honor.
EDMUND   No!
MARY [*her bitterness receding into a resigned helplessness*]   I'm not blaming
you, dear. How can you help it? How can any one of us forget? [*strangely*]
That's what makes it so hard—for all of us. We can't forget.
EDMUND [*grabs her shoulder*]   Mama! Stop it!
MARY [*forcing a smile*]   All right, dear. I didn't mean to be so gloomy. Don't
mind me. Here. Let me feel your head. Why, it's nice and cool. You cer-
tainly haven't any fever now.
EDMUND   Forget! It's you—
MARY   But I'm quite all right, dear. [*with a quick, strange, calculating, almost
sly glance at him*] Except I naturally feel tired and nervous this morning,
after such a bad night. I really ought to go upstairs and lie down until lunch
time and take a nap.
      [*He gives her an instinctive look of suspicion—then, ashamed of him-
      self, looks quickly away. She hurries on nervously.*]
What are you going to do? Read here? It would be much better for you to

go out in the fresh air and sunshine. But don't get overheated, remember.
Be sure and wear a hat.
[*She stops, looking straight at him now. He avoids her eyes. There is a
tense pause. Then she speaks jeeringly.*]
Or are you afraid to trust me alone?
EDMUND [*tormentedly*]  No! Can't you stop talking like that! I think you ought
to take a nap. [*He goes to the screen door—forcing a joking tone*] I'll go down
and help Jamie bear up. I love to lie in the shade and watch him work.
[*He forces a laugh in which she makes herself join. Then he goes out on
the porch and disappears down the steps. Her first reaction is one of
relief. She appears to relax. She sinks down in one of the wicker armchairs at rear of table and leans her head back, closing her eyes. But
suddenly she grows terribly tense again. Her eyes open and she strains
forward, seized by a fit of nervous panic. She begins a desperate battle
with herself. Her long fingers, warped and knotted by rheumatism,
drum on the arms of the chair, driven by an insistent life of their own,
without her consent.*]

CURTAIN

Act Two

SCENE ONE

SCENE—*The same. It is around quarter to one. No sunlight comes into the room
now through the windows at right. Outside the day is still fine but increasingly
sultry, with a faint haziness in the air which softens the glare of the sun.*

EDMUND *sits in the armchair at left of table, reading a book. Or rather he is
trying to concentrate on it but cannot. He seems to be listening for some sound
from upstairs. His manner is nervously apprehensive and he looks more sickly
than in the previous act.*

*The second girl,* CATHLEEN, *enters from the back parlor. She carries a tray on
which is a bottle of bonded Bourbon, several whiskey glasses and a pitcher of ice
water. She is a buxom Irish peasant, in her early twenties, with a red-cheeked
comely face, black hair and blue eyes—amiable, ignorant, clumsy, and possessed by a dense, well-meaning stupidity. She puts the tray on the table.*
EDMUND *pretends to be so absorbed in his book he does not notice her, but she
ignores this.*

CATHLEEN [*with garrulous familiarity*]  Here's the whiskey. It'll be lunch time
soon. Will I call your father and Mister Jamie, or will you?
EDMUND [*without looking up from his book*]  You do it.
CATHLEEN  It's a wonder your father wouldn't look at his watch once in a
while. He's a divil for making the meals late, and then Bridget curses me as
if I was to blame. But he's a grand handsome man, if he is old. You'll never
see the day you're as good looking—nor Mister Jamie, either. [*She chuckles.*]
I'll wager Mister Jamie wouldn't miss the time to stop work and have his
drop of whiskey if he had a watch to his name!
EDMUND [*gives up trying to ignore her and grins*]  You win that one.
CATHLEEN  And here's another I'd win, that you're making me call them so
you can sneak a drink before they come.
EDMUND  Well, I hadn't thought of that—
CATHLEEN  Oh no, not you! Butter wouldn't melt in your mouth, I suppose.

EDMUND    But now you suggest it—

CATHLEEN  [*suddenly primly virtuous*]  I'd never suggest a man or a woman touch drink, Mister Edmund. Sure, didn't it kill an uncle of mine in the old country. [*relenting*] Still, a drop now and then is no harm when you're in low spirits, or have a bad cold.

EDMUND    Thanks for handing me a good excuse. [*then with forced casualness*] You'd better call my mother, too.

CATHLEEN  What for? She's always on time without any calling. God bless her, she has some consideration for the help.

EDMUND    She's been taking a nap.

CATHLEEN  She wasn't asleep when I finished my work upstairs a while back. She was lying down in the spare room with her eyes wide open. She'd a terrible headache, she said.

EDMUND [*his casualness more forced*]    Oh well then, just call my father.

CATHLEEN  [*goes to the screen door, grumbling good-naturedly*]  No wonder my feet kill me each night. I won't walk out in this heat and get sunstroke. I'll call from the porch.

[*She goes out on the side porch, letting the screen door slam behind her, and disappears on her way to the front porch. A moment later she is heard shouting.*]

Mister Tyrone! Mister Jamie! It's time!

[EDMUND, *who has been staring frightenedly before him, forgetting his book, springs to his feet nervously.*]

EDMUND    God, what a wench!

[*He grabs the bottle and pours a drink, adds ice water and drinks. As he does so, he hears someone coming in the front door. He puts the glass hastily on the tray and sits down again, opening his book.* JAMIE *comes in from the front parlor, his coat over his arm. He has taken off collar and tie and carries them in his hand. He is wiping sweat from his forehead with a handkerchief.* EDMUND *looks up as if his reading was interrupted.* JAMIE *takes one look at the bottle and glasses and smiles cynically.*]

JAMIE    Sneaking one, eh? Cut out the bluff, Kid. You're a rottener actor than I am.

EDMUND [*grins*]    Yes, I grabbed one while the going was good.

JAMIE [*puts a hand affectionately on his shoulder*]    That's better. Why kid me? We're pals, aren't we?

EDMUND    I wasn't sure it was you coming.

JAMIE    I made the Old Man look at his watch. I was halfway up the walk when Cathleen burst into song. Our wild Irish lark! She ought to be a train announcer.

EDMUND    That's what drove me to drink. Why don't you sneak one while you've got a chance?

JAMIE    I was thinking of that little thing. [*He goes quickly to the window at right.*] The Old Man was talking to old Captain Turner. Yes, he's still at it. [*He comes back and takes a drink.*] And now to cover up from his eagle eye. [*He measures two drinks of water and pours them in the whiskey bottle and shakes it up.*] There. That fixes it. [*He pours water in the glass and sets it on the table by* EDMUND.] And here's the water you've been drinking.

EDMUND    Fine! You don't think it will fool him, do you?

JAMIE    Maybe not, but he can't prove it. [*Putting on his collar and tie.*] I hope he doesn't forget lunch listening to himself talk. I'm hungry. [*He sits *across the table from* EDMUND—*irritably*] That's what I hate about working down in front. He puts on an act for every damned fool that comes along.

EDMUND [*gloomily*]    You're in luck to be hungry. The way I feel I don't care if I ever eat again.

JAMIE [*gives him a glance of concern*]    Listen, Kid. You know me. I've never lectured you, but Doctor Hardy was right when he told you to cut out the redeye.

EDMUND    Oh, I'm going to after he hands me the bad news this afternoon. A few before then won't make any difference.

JAMIE [*hesitates—then slowly*]    I'm glad you've got your mind prepared for bad news. It won't be such a jolt. [*He catches* EDMUND *staring at him.*] I mean, it's a cinch you're really sick, and it would be wrong dope to kid yourself.

EDMUND [*disturbed*]    I'm not. I know how rotten I feel, and the fever and chills I get at night are no joke. I think Doctor Hardy's last guess was right. It must be the damned malaria come back on me.

JAMIE    Maybe, but don't be too sure.

EDMUND    Why? What do you think it is?

JAMIE    Hell, how would I know? I'm no Doc. [*abruptly*] Where's Mama?

EDMUND    Upstairs.

JAMIE [*looks at him sharply*]    When did she go up?

EDMUND    Oh, about the time I came down to the hedge, I guess. She said she was going to take a nap.

JAMIE    You didn't tell me—

EDMUND [*defensively*]    Why should I? What about it? She was tired out. She didn't get much sleep last night.

JAMIE    I know she didn't.

     [*A pause. The brothers avoid looking at each other.*]

EDMUND    That damned foghorn kept me awake, too.

     [*Another pause.*]

JAMIE    She's been upstairs alone all morning, eh? You haven't seen her?

EDMUND    No. I've been reading here. I wanted to give her a chance to sleep.

JAMIE    Is she coming down to lunch?

EDMUND    Of course.

JAMIE [*dryly*]    No of course about it. She might not want any lunch. Or she might start having most of her meals alone upstairs. That's happened, hasn't it?

EDMUND [*with frightened resentment*]    Cut it out, Jamie! Can't you think anything but—? [*persuasively*] You're all wrong to suspect anything. Cathleen saw her not long ago. Mama didn't tell her she wouldn't be down to lunch.

JAMIE    Then she wasn't taking a nap?

EDMUND    Not right then, but she was lying down, Cathleen said.

JAMIE    In the spare room?

EDMUND    Yes. For Pete's sake, what of it?

JAMIE [*bursts out*]    You damned fool! Why did you leave her alone so long? Why didn't you stick around?

EDMUND    Because she accused me—and you and Papa—of spying on her all the time and not trusting her. She made me feel ashamed. I know how rotten it must be for her. And she promised on her sacred word of honor—

JAMIE [*with a bitter weariness*]    You ought to know that doesn't mean anything.

EDMUND    It does this time!

JAMIE   That's what we thought the other times. [*He leans over the table to give his brother's arm an affectionate grasp.*] Listen, Kid, I know you think I'm a cynical bastard, but remember I've seen a lot more of this game than you have. You never knew what was really wrong until you were in prep-school. Papa and I kept it from you. But I was wise ten years or more before we had to tell you. I know the game backwards and I've been thinking all morning of the way she acted last night when she thought we were asleep. I haven't been able to think of anything else. And now you tell me she got you to leave her alone upstairs all morning.

EDMUND   She didn't! You're crazy!

JAMIE [*placatingly*]   All right, Kid. Don't start a battle with me. I hope as much as you do I'm crazy. I've been as happy as hell because I'd really begun to believe that this time—[*He stops—looking through the front parlor toward the hall—lowering his voice, hurriedly*] She's coming downstairs. You win on that. I guess I'm a damned suspicious louse.

[*They grow tense with a hopeful, fearful expectancy.* JAMIE *mutters*] Damn! I wish I'd grabbed another drink.

EDMUND   Me, too.

[*He coughs nervously and this brings on a real fit of coughing.* JAMIE *glances at him with worried pity.* MARY *enters from the front parlor. At first one notices no change except that she appears to be less nervous, to be more as she was when we first saw her after breakfast, but then one becomes aware that her eyes are brighter, and there is a peculiar detachment in her voice and manner, as if she were a little withdrawn from her words and actions.*]

MARY [*goes worriedly to* EDMUND *and puts her arm around him*]   You mustn't cough like that. It's bad for your throat. You don't want to get a sore throat on top of your cold.

[*She kisses him. He stops coughing and gives her a quick apprehensive glance, but if his suspicions are aroused her tenderness makes him renounce them and he believes what he wants to believe for the moment. On the other hand,* JAMIE *knows after one probing look at her that his suspicions are justified. His eyes fall to stare at the floor, his face sets in an expression of embittered, defensive cynicism.* MARY *goes on, half sitting on the arm of* EDMUND's *chair, her arm around him, so her face is above and behind his and he cannot look into her eyes.*]

But I seem to be always picking on you, telling you don't do this and don't do that. Forgive me, dear. It's just that I want to take care of you.

EDMUND   I know, Mama. How about you? Do you feel rested?

MARY   Yes, ever so much better. I've been lying down ever since you went out. It's what I needed after such a restless night. I don't feel nervous now.

EDMUND   That's fine.

[*He pats her hand on his shoulder.* JAMIE *gives him a strange, almost contemptuous glance, wondering if his brother can really mean this.* EDMUND *does not notice but his mother does.*]

MARY [*in a forced teasing tone*]   Good heavens, how down in the mouth you look, Jamie. What's the matter now?

JAMIE [*without looking at her*]   Nothing.

MARY   Oh, I'd forgotten you've been working on the front hedge. That accounts for your sinking into the dumps, doesn't it?

JAMIE   If you want to think so, Mama.

MARY [*keeping her tone*]   Well, that's the effect it always has, isn't it? What a big baby you are! Isn't he, Edmund?

EDMUND    He's certainly a fool to care what anyone thinks.

MARY [*strangely*]   Yes, the only way is to make yourself not care.

[*She catches* JAMIE *giving her a bitter glance and changes the subject.*] Where is your father? I heard Cathleen call him.

EDMUND    Gabbing with old Captain Turner, Jamie says. He'll be late, as usual.

[ JAMIE *gets up and goes to the windows at right, glad of an excuse to turn his back.*]

MARY    I've told Cathleen time and again she must go wherever he is and tell him. The idea of screaming as if this were a cheap boardinghouse!

JAMIE [*looking out the window*]   She's down there now. [*sneeringly*] Interrupting the famous Beautiful Voice! She should have more respect.

MARY [*sharply—letting her resentment toward him come out*]   It's you who should have more respect. Stop sneering at your father! I won't have it! You ought to be proud you're his son! He may have his faults. Who hasn't? But he's worked hard all his life. He made his way up from ignorance and poverty to the top of his profession! Everyone else admires him and you should be the last one to sneer—you, who, thanks to him, have never had to work hard in your life!

[*Stung,* JAMIE *has turned to stare at her with accusing antagonism. Her eyes waver guiltily and she adds in a tone which begins to placate*] Remember your father is getting old, Jamie. You really ought to show more consideration.

JAMIE    *I* ought to?

EDMUND [*uneasily*]   Oh, dry up, Jamie!

[ JAMIE *looks out the window again.*]

And, for Pete's sake, Mama, why jump on Jamie all of a sudden?

MARY [*bitterly*]   Because he's always sneering at someone else, always looking for the worst weakness in everyone. [*then with a strange, abrupt change to a detached, impersonal tone*] But I suppose life has made him like that, and he can't help it. None of us can help the things life has done to us. They're done before you realize it, and once they're done they make you do other things until at last everything comes between you and what you'd like to be, and you've lost your true self forever.

[EDMUND *is made apprehensive by her strangeness. He tries to look up in her eyes but she keeps them averted.* JAMIE *turns to her—then looks quickly out of the window again.*]

JAMIE [*dully*]   I'm hungry. I wish the Old Man would get a move on. It's a rotten trick the way he keeps meals waiting, and then beefs because they're spoiled.

MARY [*with a resentment that has a quality of being automatic and on the surface while inwardly she is indifferent*]   Yes, it's very trying, Jamie. You don't know how trying. You don't have to keep house with summer servants who don't care because they know it isn't a permanent position. The really good servants are all with people who have homes and not merely summer places. And your father won't even pay the wages the best summer help ask. So every year I have stupid, lazy greenhorns to deal with. But you've heard me say this a thousand times. So has he, but it goes in one ear and out the other. He thinks money spent on a home is money wasted. He's lived too much in hotels. Never the best hotels, of course. Second-rate hotels. He doesn't understand a home. He doesn't feel at home in it. And yet, he wants a home. He's even proud of having this shabby place. He loves it here. [*She laughs—a hopeless and yet amused laugh.*] It's really funny, when you come to think of it. He's a peculiar man.

EDMUND [*again attempting uneasily to look up in her eyes*]   What makes you ramble on like that, Mama?

MARY [*quickly casual—patting his cheek*]   Why, nothing in particular, dear. It *is* foolish.

[*As she speaks,* CATHLEEN *enters from the back parlor.*]

CATHLEEN [*volubly*]   Lunch is ready, Ma'am, I went down to Mister Tyrone, like you ordered, and he said he'd come right away, but he kept on talking to that man, telling him of the time when—

MARY [*indifferently*]   All right, Cathleen. Tell Bridget I'm sorry but she'll have to wait a few minutes until Mister Tyrone is here.

[CATHLEEN *mutters,* "Yes, Ma'am," *and goes off through the back parlor, grumbling to herself.*]

JAMIE   Damn it! Why don't you go ahead without him? He told us to.

MARY [*with a remote, amused smile*]   He doesn't mean it. Don't you know your father yet? He'd be so terribly hurt.

EDMUND [ *jumps up—as if he was glad of an excuse to leave*]   I'll make him get a move on.

[*He goes out on the side porch. A moment later he is heard calling from the porch exasperatedly.*]

Hey! Papa! Come on! We can't wait all day!

[MARY *has risen from the arm of the chair. Her hands play restlessly over the table top. She does not look at* JAMIE *but she feels the cynically appraising glance he gives her face and hands.*]

MARY [*tensely*]   Why do you stare like that?

JAMIE   You know. [*He turns back to the window.*]

MARY   I don't know.

JAMIE   Oh, for God's sake, do you think you can fool me, Mama? I'm not blind.

MARY [*looks directly at him now, her face set again in an expression of blank, stubborn denial*]   I don't know what you're talking about.

JAMIE   No? Take a look at your eyes in the mirror!

EDMUND [*coming in from the porch*]   I got Papa moving. He'll be here in a minute. [*with a glance from one to the other, which his mother avoids— uneasily*] What happened? What's the matter, Mama?

MARY [*disturbed by his coming, gives way to a flurry of guilty, nervous excitement*]   Your brother ought to be ashamed of himself. He's been insinuating I don't know what.

EDMUND [*turns on* JAMIE]   God damn you!

[*He takes a threatening step toward him.* JAMIE *turns his back with a shrug and looks out the window.*]

MARY [*more upset, grabs* EDMUND's *arm—excitedly*]   Stop this at once, do you hear me? How dare you use such language before me! [*Abruptly her tone and manner change to the strange detachment she has shown before.*] It's wrong to blame your brother. He can't help being what the past has made him. Any more then your father can. Or you. Or I.

EDMUND [ *frightenedly—with a desperate hoping against hope*]   He's a liar! It's a lie, isn't it, Mama?

MARY [*keeping her eyes averted*]   What is a lie? Now you're talking in riddles like Jamie. [*Then her eyes meet his stricken, accusing look. She stammers*]

Edmund! Don't! [*She looks away and her manner instantly regains the quality of strange detachment—calmly*] There's your father coming up the steps now. I must tell Bridget.

[*She goes through the back parlor.* EDMUND *moves slowly to his chair. He looks sick and hopeless.*]

JAMIE [*from the window, without looking around*] Well?

EDMUND [*refusing to admit anything to his brother yet—weakly defiant*] Well, what? You're a liar.

[JAMIE *again shrugs his shoulders. The screen door on the front porch is heard closing.* EDMUND *says dully*] Here's Papa. I hope he loosens up with the old bottle.

[TYRONE *comes in through the front parlor. He is putting on his coat.*]

TYRONE Sorry I'm late. Captain Turner stopped to talk and once he starts gabbing you can't get away from him.

JAMIE [*without turning—dryly*] You mean once he starts listening.

[*His father regards him with dislike. He comes to the table with a quick measuring look at the bottle of whiskey. Without turning,* JAMIE *senses this.*]

It's all right. The level in the bottle hasn't changed.

TYRONE I wasn't noticing that. [*He adds caustically*] As if it proved anything with you around. I'm on to your tricks.

EDMUND [*dully*] Did I hear you say, let's all have a drink?

TYRONE [*frowns at him*] Jamie is welcome after his hard morning's work, but I won't invite you. Doctor Hardy—

EDMUND To hell with Doctor Hardy! One isn't going to kill me. I feel—all in, Papa.

TYRONE [*with a worried look at him—putting on a fake heartiness*] Come along, then. It's before a meal and I've always found that good whiskey, taken in moderation as an appetizer, is the best of tonics.

[EDMUND *gets up as his father passes the bottle to him. He pours a big drink.* TYRONE *frowns admonishingly.*]

I said, in moderation.

[*He pours his own drink and passes the bottle to* JAMIE, *grumbling.*]

It'd be a waste of breath mentioning moderation to you.

[*Ignoring the hint,* JAMIE *pours a big drink. His father scowls—then, giving it up, resumes his hearty air, raising his glass.*]

Well, here's health and happiness!

[EDMUND *gives a bitter laugh.*]

EDMUND That's a joke!

TYRONE What is?

EDMUND Nothing. Here's how. [*They drink.*]

TYRONE [*becoming aware of the atmosphere*] What's the matter here? There's gloom in the air you could cut with a knife. [*turns on* JAMIE *resentfully*] You got the drink you were after, didn't you? Why are you wearing that gloomy look on your mug?

JAMIE [*shrugging his shoulders*] You won't be singing a song yourself soon.

EDMUND Shut up, Jamie.

TYRONE [*uneasy now—changing the subject*] I thought lunch was ready. I'm hungry as a hunter. Where is your mother?

MARY [*returning through the back parlor, calls*] Here I am.

[*She comes in. She is excited and self-conscious. As she talks, she glances everywhere except at any of their faces.*]

I've had to calm down Bridget. She's in a tantrum over your being late again, and I don't blame her. If your lunch is dried up from waiting in the oven, she said it served you right, you could like it or leave it for all she cared. [*with increasing excitement*] Oh, I'm so sick and tired of pretending this is a home! You won't help me! You won't put yourself out the least bit! You don't know how to act in a home! You don't really want one! You never have wanted one—never since the day we were married! You should have remained a bachelor and lived in second-rate hotels and entertained your friends in barrooms! [*She adds strangely, as if she were now talking aloud to herself rather than to* TYRONE] Then nothing would ever have happened.

> [*They stare at her.* TYRONE *knows now. He suddenly looks a tired, bitterly sad old man.* EDMUND *glances at his father and sees that he knows, but he still cannot help trying to warn his mother.*]

EDMUND    Mama! Stop talking. Why don't we go in to lunch.

MARY [*Starts and at once the quality of unnatural detachment settles on her face again. She even smiles with an ironical amusement to herself.*] Yes, it is inconsiderate of me to dig up the past, when I know your father and Jamie must be hungry. [*putting her arm around* EDMUND's *shoulder—with a fond solicitude which is at the same time remote*] I do hope you have an appetite, dear. You really must eat more [*Her eyes become fixed on the whiskey glass on the table beside him—sharply*] Why is that glass there? Did you take a drink? Oh, how can you be such a fool? Don't you know it's the worst thing? [*She turns on* TYRONE.] You're to blame, James. How could you let him? Do you want to kill him? Don't you remember my father? He wouldn't stop after he was stricken. He said doctors were fools! He thought, like you, that whiskey is a good tonic! [*A look of terror comes into her eyes and she stammers*] But, of course, there's no comparison at all. I don't know why I— Forgive me for scolding you, James. One small drink won't hurt Edmund. It might be good for him, if it gives him an appetite.

> [*She pats* EDMUND's *cheek playfully, the strange detachment again in her manner. He jerks his head away. She seems not to notice, but she moves instinctively away.*]

JAMIE [*roughly, to hide his tense nerves*]    For God's sake, let's eat. I've been working in the damned dirt under the hedge all morning. I've earned my grub.

> [*He comes around in back of his father, not looking at his mother, and grabs* EDMUND's *shoulder.*]

Come on, Kid. Let's put on the feed bag.

> [EDMUND *gets up, keeping his eyes averted from his mother. They pass her, heading for the back parlor.*]

TYRONE [*dully*]    Yes, you go in with your mother, lads. I'll join you in a second.

> [*But they keep on without waiting for her. She looks at their backs with a helpless hurt and, as they enter the back parlor, starts to follow them.* TYRONE's *eyes are on her, sad and condemning. She feels them and turns sharply without meeting his stare.*]

MARY    Why do you look at me like that? [*Her hands flutter up to pat her hair.*] Is it my hair coming down? I was so worn out from last night, I thought I'd better lie down this morning. I drowsed off and had a nice refreshing nap. But I'm sure I fixed my hair again when I woke up. [*forcing a laugh*] Although, as usual, I couldn't find my glasses. [*sharply*] Please stop staring! One would think you were accusing me—[*then pleadingly*] James! You don't understand!

TYRONE [*with dull anger*]   I understand that I've been a God-damned fool to believe in you!

[*He walks away from her to pour himself a big drink.*]

MARY [*her face again sets in stubborn defiance*]   I don't know what you mean by "believing in me." All I've felt was distrust and spying and suspicion. [*then accusingly*] Why are you having another drink? You never have more than one before lunch. [*bitterly*] I know what to expect. You will be drunk tonight. Well, it won't be the first time, will it—or the thousandth? [*again she bursts out pleadingly*] Oh, James, please! You don't understand! I'm worried about Edmund! I'm so afraid he—

TYRONE   I don't want to listen to excuses, Mary.

MARY [*strickenly*]   Excuses? You mean—? Oh, you can't believe that of me! You mustn't believe that, James! [*then slipping away into her strange detachment—quite casually*] Shall we not go into lunch dear? I don't want anything but I know you're hungry.

[*He walks slowly to where she stands in the doorway. He walks like an old man. As he reaches her she bursts out piteously.*]

James! I tried so hard! I tried so hard! Please believe—!

TYRONE [*moved in spite of himself—helplessly*]   I suppose you did, Mary. [*then grief-strickenly*] For the love of God, why couldn't you have the strength to keep on?

MARY [*her face setting into that stubborn denial again*]   I don't know what you're talking about. Have the strength to keep on what?

TYRONE [*hopelessly*]   Never mind. It's no use now.

[*He moves on and she keeps beside him as they disappear in the back parlor.*]

CURTAIN

## Act Two

### SCENE TWO

SCENE—*The same, about a half hour later. The tray with the bottle of whiskey has been removed from the table. The family are returning from lunch as the curtain rises.* MARY *is the first to enter from the back parlor. Her husband follows. He is not with her as he was in the similar entrance after breakfast at the opening of Act One. He avoids touching her or looking at her. There is condemnation in his face, mingled now with the beginning of an old weary, helpless resignation.* JAMIE *and* EDMUND *follow their father.* JAMIE's *face is hard with defensive cynicism.* EDMUND *tries to copy this defense but without success. He plainly shows he is heartsick as well as physically ill.*

MARY *is terribly nervous again, as if the strain of sitting through lunch with them had been too much for her. Yet at the same time, in contrast to this, her expression shows more of that strange aloofness which seems to stand apart from her nerves and the anxieties which harry them.*

*She is talking as she enters—a stream of words that issues casually, in a routine of family conversation, from her mouth. She appears indifferent to the fact that their thoughts are not on what she is saying any more than her own are. As she talks, she comes to the left of the table and stands, facing front, one hand fumbling with the bosom of her dress, the other playing over the table top.*

TYRONE *lights a cigar and goes to the screen door, staring out.* JAMIE *fills a pipe from a jar on top of the bookcase at rear. He lights it as he goes to look out the window at right.* EDMUND *sits in a chair by the table, turned half away from his mother so he does not have to watch her.*

MARY It's no use finding fault with Bridget. She doesn't listen. I can't threaten her, or she'd threaten she'd leave. And she does do her best at times. It's too bad they seem to be just the times you're sure to be late, James. Well, there's this consolation: it's difficult to tell from her cooking whether she's doing her best or her worst. [*She gives a little laugh of detached amusement—indifferently*] Never mind. The summer will soon be over, thank goodness. Your season will open again and we can go back to second-rate hotels and trains. I hate them, too, but at least I don't expect them to be like a home, and there's no housekeeping to worry about. It's unreasonable to expect Bridget or Cathleen to act as if this was a home. They know it isn't as well as we know it. It never has been and it never will be.

TYRONE [*bitterly without turning around*] No, it never can be now. But it was once, before you—

MARY [*her face instantly set in blank denial*] Before I what? [*There is dead silence. She goes on with a return of her detached air.*] No, no. Whatever you mean, it isn't true, dear. It was never a home. You've always preferred the Club or barroom. And for me it's always been as lonely as a dirty room in a one-night stand hotel. In a real home one is never lonely. You forget I know from experience what a home is like. I gave up one to marry you— my father's home. [*At once, through an association of ideas she turns to* EDMUND. *Her manner becomes tenderly solicitous, but there is the strange quality of detachment in it.*] I'm worried about you, Edmund. You hardly touched a thing at lunch. That's no way to take care of yourself. It's all right for me not to have an appetite. I've been growing too fat. But you must eat. [*coaxingly maternal*] Promise me you will, dear, for my sake.

EDMUND [*dully*] Yes, Mama.

MARY [*pats his cheek as he tries not to shrink away*] That's a good boy.
[*There is another pause of dead silence. Then the telephone in the front hall rings and all of them stiffen startledly.*]

TYRONE [*hastily*] I'll answer. McGuire said he'd call me. [*He goes out through the front parlor.*]

MARY [*indifferently*] McGuire. He must have another piece of property on his list that no one would think of buying except your father. It doesn't matter any more, but it's always seemed to me your father could afford to keep on buying property but never to give me a home.
[*She stops to listen as* TYRONE'S *voice is heard from the hall.*]

TYRONE Hello. [*with forced heartiness*] Oh, how are you, Doctor?
[ JAMIE *turns from the window.* MARY'S *fingers play more rapidly on the table top.* TYRONE'S *voice, trying to conceal, reveals that he is hearing bad news.*]
I see—[*hurriedly*] Well, you'll explain all about it when you see him this afternoon. Yes, he'll be in without fail. Four o'clock. I'll drop in myself and have a talk with you before that. I have to go uptown on business, anyway. Goodbye, Doctor.

EDMUND [*dully*] That didn't sound like glad tidings.
[ JAMIE *gives him a pitying glance—then looks out the window again.* MARY'S *face is terrified and her hands flutter distractedly.* TYRONE

*comes in. The strain is obvious in his casualness as he addresses* EDMUND.]

TYRONE    It was Doctor Hardy. He wants you to be sure and see him at four.

EDMUND [*dully*]    What did he say? Not that I give a damn now.

MARY [*bursts out excitedly*]    I wouldn't believe him if he swore on a stack of Bibles. You mustn't pay attention to a word he says, Edmund.

TYRONE [*sharply*]    Mary!

MARY [*more excitedly*]    Oh, we all realize why you like him, James! Because he's cheap! But please don't try to tell me! I know all about Doctor Hardy. Heaven knows I ought to after all these years. He's an ignorant fool! There should be a law to keep men like him from practicing. He hasn't the slightest idea— When you're in agony and half insane, he sits and holds your hand and delivers sermons on will power! [*Her face is drawn in an expression of intense suffering by the memory. For the moment, she loses all caution. With bitter hatred*] He deliberately humiliates you! He makes you beg and plead! He treats you like a criminal! He understands nothing! And yet it was exactly the same type of cheap quack who first gave you the medicine—and you never knew what it was until too late! [*passionately*] I hate doctors! They'll sell their souls! What's worse, they'll sell yours, and you never know it till one day you find yourself in hell!

EDMUND    Mama! For God's sake, stop talking.

TYRONE [*shakily*]    Yes, Mary, it's no time—

MARY [*suddenly is overcome by guilty confusion—stammers*]    I—Forgive me, dear. You're right. It's useless to be angry now. [*There is again a pause of dead silence. When she speaks again, her face has cleared and is calm, and the quality of uncanny detachment is in her voice and manner.*] I'm going upstairs for a moment, if you'll excuse me. I have to fix my hair. [*she adds smilingly*] That is if I can find my glasses. I'll be right down.

TYRONE [*as she starts through the doorway—pleading and rebuking*]    Mary!

MARY [*turns to stare at him calmly*]    Yes, dear? What is it?

TYRONE [*helplessly*]    Nothing.

MARY [*with a strange derisive smile*]    You're welcome to come up and watch me if you're so suspicious.

TYRONE    As if that could do any good! You'd only postpone it. And I'm not your jailor. This isn't a prison.

MARY    No. I know you can't help thinking it's a home. [*She adds quickly with a detached contrition*] I'm sorry, dear. I don't mean to be bitter. It's not your fault.

[*She turns and disappears through the back parlor. The three in the room remain silent. It is as if they were waiting until she got upstairs before speaking.*]

JAMIE [*cynically brutal*]    Another shot in the arm!

EDMUND [*angrily*]    Cut out that kind of talk!

TYRONE    Yes! Hold your foul tongue and your rotten Broadway loafer's lingo! Have you no pity or decency? [*losing his temper*] You ought to be kicked out in the gutter! But if I did it, you know damned well who'd weep and plead for you, and excuse you and complain till I let you come back.

JAMIE [*a spasm of pain crosses his face*]    Christ, don't I know that? No pity? I have all the pity in the world for her. I understand what a hard game to beat she's up against—which is more than you ever have! My lingo didn't mean I had no feeling. I was merely putting bluntly what we all know, and have to live with now, again. [*bitterly*] The cures are no damned good except for a while. The truth is there is no cure and we've been saps to hope—[*cynically*] They never come back!

EDMUND [*scornfully parodying his brother's cynicism*]   They never come back! Everything is in the bag! It's all a frame-up! We're all fall guys and suckers and we can't beat the game! [*disdainfully*] Christ, if I felt the way you do—!

JAMIE [*stung for a moment—then shrugging his shoulders, dryly*]   I thought you did. Your poetry isn't very cheery. Nor the stuff you read and claim to admire. [*He indicates the small bookcase at rear.*] Your pet with the unpronounceable name, for example.

EDMUND   Nietzsche. You don't know what you're talking about. You haven't read him.

JAMIE   Enough to know it's a lot of bunk!

TYRONE   Shut up, both of you! There's little choice between the philosophy you learned from Broadway loafers, and the one Edmund got from his books. They're both rotten to the core. You've both flouted the faith you were born and brought up in—the one true faith of the Catholic Church— and your denial has brought nothing but self-destruction!

[*His two sons stare at him contemptuously. They forget their quarrel and are as one against him on this issue.*]

EDMUND   That's the bunk, Papa!

JAMIE   We don't pretend, at any rate. [*caustically*] I don't notice you've worn any holes in the knees of your pants going to Mass.

TYRONE   It's true I'm a bad Catholic in the observance, God forgive me. But I believe! [*angrily*] And you're a liar! I may not go to church but every night and morning of my life I get on my knees and pray!

EDMUND [*bitingly*]   Did you pray for Mama?

TYRONE   I did. I've prayed to God these many years for her.

EDMUND   Then Nietzsche must be right. [*He quotes from* Thus Spake Zarathustra.] "God is dead: of His pity for man hath God died."

TYRONE [*ignores this*]   If your mother had prayed, too— She hasn't denied her faith, but she's forgotten it, until now there's no strength of the spirit left in her to fight against her curse. [*then dully resigned*] But what's the good of talk? We've lived with this before and now we must again. There's no help for it. [*bitterly*] Only I wish she hadn't led me to hope this time. By God, I never will again.!

EDMUND   That's a rotten thing to say, Papa! [*defiantly*] Well, I'll hope! She's just started. It can't have got a hold on her yet. She can still stop. I'm going to talk to her.

JAMIE [*shrugs his shoulders*]   You can't talk to her now. She'll listen but she won't listen. She'll be here but she won't be here. You know the way she gets.

TYRONE   Yes, that's the way the poison acts on her always. Every day from now on, there'll be the same drifting away from us until by the end of each night—

EDMUND [*miserably*]   Cut it out, Papa! [*He jumps up from his chair.*] I'm going to get dressed. [*bitterly, as he goes*] I'll make so much noise she can't suspect I've come to spy on her.

[*He disappears through the front parlor and can be heard stamping noisily upstairs.*]

JAMIE [*after a pause*]   What did Doc Hardy say about the Kid?

TYRONE [*dully*]   It's what you thought. He's got consumption.

JAMIE   God damn it!

TYRONE    There is no possible doubt, he said.

JAMIE   He'll have to go to a sanatorium.

TYRONE    Yes, and the sooner the better, Hardy said, for him and everyone around him. He claims that in six months to a year Edmund will be cured, if he obeys orders. [He sighs—gloomily and resentfully] I never thought a child of mine— It doesn't come from my side of the family. There wasn't one of us that didn't have lungs as strong as an ox.

JAMIE    Who gives a damn about that part of it! Where does Hardy want to send him?

TYRONE    That's what I'm to see him about.

JAMIE    Well, for God's sake, pick out a good place and not some cheap dump!

TYRONE [stung]    I'll send him wherever Hardy thinks best!

JAMIE    Well, don't give Hardy your old over-the-hills-to-the-poorhouse song about taxes and mortgages.

TYRONE    I'm no millionaire who can throw money away! Why shouldn't I tell Hardy the truth?

JAMIE    Because he'll think you want him to pick a cheap dump, and because he'll know it isn't the truth—especially if he hears afterwards you've seen McGuire and let that flannel-mouth, gold-brick merchant sting you with another piece of bum property!

TYRONE    Keep your nose out of my business!

JAMIE    This is Edmund's business. What I'm afraid of is, with your Irish bog trotter idea that consumption is fatal, you'll figure it would be a waste of money to spend any more than you can help.

TYRONE    You liar!

JAMIE    All right. Prove I'm a liar. That's what I want. That's why I brought it up.

TYRONE [his rage still smouldering]    I have every hope Edmund will be cured. And keep your dirty tongue off Ireland! You're a fine one to sneer, with the map of it on your face!

JAMIE    Not after I wash my face. [Then before his father can react to this insult to the Old Sod he adds dryly, shrugging his shoulders] Well, I've said all I have to say. It's up to you. [abruptly] What do you want me to do this afternoon, now you're going uptown? I've done all I can do on the hedge until you cut more of it. You don't want me to go ahead with your clipping, I know that.

TYRONE    No. You'd get it crooked, as you get everything else.

JAMIE    Then I'd better go uptown with Edmund. The bad news coming on top of what's happened to Mama may hit him hard.

TYRONE [forgetting his quarrel]    Yes, go with him, Jamie. Keep up his spirits, if you can. [He adds caustically] If you can without making it an excuse to get drunk!

JAMIE    What would I use for money? The last I heard they were still selling booze, not giving it away. [He starts for the front-parlor doorway.] I'll get dressed.

[He stops in the doorway as he sees his mother approaching from the hall, and moves aside to let her come in. Her eyes look brighter, and her manner is more detached. This change becomes more marked as the scene goes on.]

MARY [vaguely]    You haven't seen my glasses anywhere, have you, Jamie? [She doesn't look at him. He glances away, ignoring her question but she doesn't seem to expect an answer. She comes forward, addressing her husband without looking at him.]

You haven't seen them, have you, James?

[*Behind her* JAMIE *disappears through the front parlor.*]

TYRONE [*turns to look out the screen door*]  No, Mary.

MARY  What's the matter with Jamie? Have you been nagging at him again? You shouldn't treat him with such contempt all the time. He's not to blame. If he'd been brought up in a real home, I'm sure he would have been different. [*She comes to the windows at right—lightly*] You're not much of a weather prophet, dear. See how hazy it's getting. I can hardly see the other shore.

TYRONE [*trying to speak naturally*]  Yes, I spoke too soon. We're in for another night of fog, I'm afraid.

MARY  Oh, well, I won't mind it tonight.

TYRONE  No, I don't imagine you will, Mary.

MARY [*flashes a glance at him—after a pause*]  I don't see Jamie going down to the hedge. Where did he go?

TYRONE  He's going with Edmund to the Doctor's. He went up to change his clothes. [*then, glad of an excuse to leave her*] I'd better do the same or I'll be late for my appointment at the Club.

[*He makes a move toward the front-parlor doorway, but with a swift impulsive movement she reaches out and clasps his arm.*]

MARY [*a note of pleading in her voice*]  Don't go yet, dear. I don't want to be alone. [*hastily*] I mean, you have plenty of time. You know you boast you can dress in one-tenth the time it takes the boys. [*vaguely*] There is something I wanted to say. What is it? I've forgotten. I'm glad Jamie is going uptown. You didn't give him any money, I hope.

TYRONE  I did not.

MARY  He'd only spend it on drink and you know what a vile, poisonous tongue he has when he's drunk. Not that I would mind anything he said tonight, but he always manages to drive you into a rage, especially if you're drunk, too, as you will be.

TYRONE [*resentfully*]  I won't. I never get drunk.

MARY [*teasing indifferently*]  Oh, I'm sure you'll hold it well. You always have. It's hard for a stranger to tell, but after thirty-five years of marriage—

TYRONE  I've never missed a performance in my life. That's the proof! [*then bitterly*] If I did get drunk it is not you who should blame me. No man has ever had a better reason.

MARY  Reason? What reason? You always drink too much when you go to the Club, don't you? Particularly when you meet McGuire. He sees to that. Don't think I'm finding fault, dear. You must do as you please. I won't mind.

TYRONE  I know you won't. [*He turns toward the front parlor, anxious to escape.*] I've got to get dressed.

MARY [*again she reaches out and grasps his arm—pleadingly*]  No, please wait a little while, dear. At least, until one of the boys comes down. You will all be leaving me so soon.

TYRONE [*with bitter sadness*]  It's you who are leaving us, Mary.

MARY  I? That's a silly thing to say, James. How could I leave? There is nowhere I could go. Who would I go to see? I have no friends.

TYRONE  It's your own fault—[*He stops and sighs helplessly—persuasively*] There's surely one thing you can do this afternoon that will be good for you, Mary. Take a drive in the automobile. Get away from the house. Get a little sun and fresh air. [*injuredly*] I bought the automobile for you. You know I don't like the damned things. I'd rather walk any day, or take a trolley. [*with growing resentment*] I had it here waiting for you when you came back from the sanatorium. I hoped it would give you pleasure and distract your mind. You used to ride in it every day, but you've hardly used it at all lately. I paid a lot of money I couldn't afford, and there's the chauffeur I have to board and lodge and pay high wages whether he drives you or not. [*bitterly*] Waste! The same old waste that will land me in the poorhouse in my old age! What good did it do you? I might as well have thrown the money out the window.

MARY [*with detached calm*]   Yes, it was a waste of money, James. You shouldn't have bought a secondhand automobile. You were swindled again as you always are, because you insist on secondhand bargains in everything.

TYRONE   It's one of the best makes! Everyone says it's better than any of the new ones!

MARY [*ignoring this*]   It was another waste to hire Smythe, who was only a helper in a garage and had never been a chauffeur. Oh, I realize his wages are less than a real chauffeur's, but he more than makes up for that, I'm sure, by the graft he gets from the garage on repair bills. Something is always wrong. Smythe sees to that, I'm afraid.

TYRONE   I don't believe it! He may not be a fancy millionaire's flunky but he's honest! You're as bad as Jamie, suspecting everyone!

MARY   You mustn't be offended, dear. I wasn't offended when you gave me the automobile. I knew you didn't mean to humiliate me. I knew that was the way you had to do everything. I was grateful and touched. I knew buying the car was a hard thing for you to do, and it proved how much you loved me, in your way, especially when you couldn't really believe it would do me any good.

TYRONE   Mary! [*He suddenly hugs her to him—brokenly*] Dear Mary! For the love of God, for my sake and the boys' sake and your own, won't you stop now?

MARY [*stammers in guilty confusion for a second*]   I—James! Please! [*Her strange, stubborn defense comes back instantly.*] Stop what? What are you talking about?

[*He lets his arm fall to his side brokenly. She impulsively puts her arm around him.*]

James! We've loved each other! We always will! Let's remember only that, and not try to understand what we cannot understand, or help things that cannot be helped—the things life has done to us we cannot excuse or explain.

TYRONE [*as if he hadn't heard—bitterly*]   You won't even try?

MARY [*her arms drop hopelessly and she turns away—with detachment*]   Try to go for a drive this afternoon, you mean? Why, yes, if you wish me to, although it makes me feel lonelier than if I stayed here. There is no one I can invite to drive with me, and I never know where to tell Smythe to go. If there was a friend's house where I could drop in and laugh and gossip awhile. But, of course, there isn't. There never has been. [*her manner becoming more and more remote*] At the Convent I had so many friends. Girls whose families lived in lovely homes. I used to visit them and they'd visit me in my father's home. But, naturally, after I married an actor—you know how actors were considered in those days—a lot of them gave me the cold shoulder. And then, right after we were married, there was the scandal of that woman who had been your mistress, suing you. From then on, all my old friends either pitied me or cut me dead. I hated the ones who cut me much less than the pitiers.

TYRONE [*with guilty resentment*]   For God's sake, don't dig up what's long forgotten. If you're that far gone in the past already, when it's only the beginning of the afternoon, what will you be tonight?

MARY [*stares at him defiantly now*]   Come to think of it, I do have to drive uptown. There's something I must get at the drugstore.

TYRONE [*bitterly scornful*]   Leave it to you to have some of the stuff hidden, and prescriptions for more! I hope you'll lay in a good stock ahead so we'll never have another night like the one when you screamed for it, and ran out of the house in your nightdress half crazy, to try and throw yourself off the dock!

MARY [*tries to ignore this*]   I have to get tooth powder and toilet soap and cold cream—[*She breaks down pitiably.*] James! You mustn't remember! You mustn't humiliate me so!

TYRONE [*ashamed*]   I'm sorry. Forgive me, Mary!

MARY [*defensively detached again*]   It doesn't matter. Nothing like that ever happened. You must have dreamed it.

> [*He stares at her hopelessly. Her voice seems to drift farther and farther away.*]

I was so healthy before Edmund was born. You remember, James. There wasn't a nerve in my body. Even traveling with you season after season, with week after week of one-night stands, in trains without Pullmans, in dirty rooms of filthy hotels, eating bad food, bearing children in hotel rooms, I still kept healthy. But bearing Edmund was the last straw. I was so sick afterwards, and that ignorant quack of a cheap hotel doctor—All he knew was I was in pain. It was easy for him to stop the pain.

TYRONE   Mary! For God's sake, forget the past!

MARY [*with strange objective calm*]   Why? How can I? The past is the present, isn't it? It's the future, too. We all try to lie out of that but life won't let us. [*going on*] I blame only myself. I swore after Eugene died I would never have another baby. I was to blame for his death. If I hadn't left him with my mother to join you on the road, because you wrote telling me you missed me and were so lonely, Jamie would never have been allowed, when he still had measles, to go in the baby's room. [*her face hardening*] I've always believed Jamie did it on purpose. He was jealous of the baby. He hated him. [*as TYRONE starts to protest*] Oh, I know Jamie was only seven, but he was never stupid. He'd been warned it might kill the baby. He knew. I've never been able to forgive him for that.

TYRONE [*with bitter sadness*]   Are you back with Eugene now? Can't you let our dead baby rest in peace?

MARY [*as if she hadn't heard him*]   It was my fault. I should have insisted on staying with Eugene and not have let you persuade me to join you, just because I loved you. Above all, I shouldn't have let you insist I have another baby to take Eugene's place, because you thought that would make me forget his death. I knew from experience by then that children should have homes to be born in, if they are to be good children, and women need homes, if they are to be good mothers. I was afraid all the time I carried Edmund. I knew something terrible would happen. I knew I'd proved by the way I'd left Eugene that I wasn't worthy to have another baby, and that God would punish me if I did. I never should have borne Edmund.

TYRONE [*with an uneasy glance through the front parlor*]   Mary! Be careful with your talk. If he heard you he might think you never wanted him. He's feeling bad enough already without—

MARY [*violently*]   It's a lie! I did want him! More than anything in the world!
You don't understand! I meant, for his sake. He has never been happy. He
never will be. Nor healthy. He was born nervous and too sensitive, and
that's my fault. And now, ever since he's been so sick I've kept remembering
Eugene and my father and I've been so frightened and guilty—[*then, catching herself, with an instant change to stubborn denial*] Oh, I know it's foolish to imagine dreadful things when there's no reason for it. After all,
everyone has colds and gets over them.

    [TYRONE *stares at her and sighs helplessly. He turns away toward the
    front parlor and sees* EDMUND *coming down the stairs in the hall.*]

TYRONE [*sharply, in a low voice*]   Here's Edmund. For God's sake try and be
yourself—at least until he goes! You can do that much for him!

    [*He waits, forcing his face into a pleasantly paternal expression. She
    waits frightenedly, seized again by a nervous panic, her hands flutter-
    ing over the bosom of her dress, up to her throat and hair, with a
    distracted aimlessness. Then, as* EDMUND *approaches the doorway, she
    cannot face him. She goes swiftly away to the windows at left and
    stares out with her back to the front parlor.* EDMUND *enters. He has
    changed to a ready-made blue serge suit, high stiff collar and tie, black
    shoes. With an actor's heartiness*]
Well! You look spic and span. I'm on my way up to change, too. [*He starts
to pass him.*]

EDMUND [*dryly*]   Wait a minute, Papa. I hate to bring up disagreeable topics,
but there's the matter of carfare. I'm broke.

TYRONE [*starts automatically on a customary lecture*]   You'll always be broke
until you learn the value—[*checks himself guiltily, looking at his son's sick
face with worried pity*] But you've been learning, lad. You worked hard
before you took ill. You've done splendidly. I'm proud of you.

    [*He pulls out a small roll of bills from his pants pocket and carefully
    selects one.* EDMUND *takes it. He glances at it and his face expresses
    astonishment. His father again reacts customarily—sarcastically*]
Thank you. [*He quotes*] "How sharper than a serpent's tooth it is—"

EDMUND   "To have a thankless child."[1] I know. Give me a chance, Papa. I'm
knocked speechless. This isn't a dollar. It's a ten spot.

TYRONE [*embarrassed by his generosity*]   Put it in your pocket. You'll probably
meet some of your friends uptown and you can't hold your end up and be
sociable with nothing in your jeans.

EDMUND   You meant it? Gosh, thank you, Papa. [*He is genuinely pleased
and grateful for a moment—then he stares at his father's face with uneasy
suspicion.*] But why all of a sudden—? [*cynically*] Did Doc Hardy tell you I
was going to die? [*Then he sees his father is bitterly hurt.*] No! That's a
rotten crack. I was only kidding, Papa. [*He puts an arm around his father
impulsively and gives him an affectionate hug.*] I'm very grateful. Honest,
Papa.

TYRONE [*touched, returns his hug*]   You're welcome, lad.

MARY [*suddenly turns to them in a confused panic of frightened anger*]   I won't
have it! [*She stamps her foot.*] Do you hear, Edmund! Such morbid nonsense! Saying you're going to die! It's the books you read! Nothing but sadness and death! Your father shouldn't allow you to have them. And some of
the poems you've written yourself are even worse! You'd think you didn't

----

1. Shakespeare, *King Lear* 1.4.312.

want to live! A boy of your age with everything before him! It's just a pose you get out of books! You're not really sick at all!

TYRONE   Mary! Hold your tongue!

MARY   [*instantly changing to a detached tone*]   But, James, it's absurd of Edmund to be so gloomy and make such a great to-do about nothing. [*turning to* EDMUND *but avoiding his eyes—teasingly affectionate*] Never mind, dear. I'm on to you. [*She comes to him.*] You want to be petted and spoiled and made a fuss over, isn't that it? You're still such a baby. [*She puts her arm around him and hugs him. He remains rigid and unyielding. Her voice begins to tremble.*] But please don't carry it too far, dear. Don't say horrible things. I know it's foolish to take them seriously but I can't help it. You've got me—so frightened.

> [*She breaks and hides her face on his shoulder, sobbing.* EDMUND *is moved in spite of himself. He pats her shoulder with an awkward tenderness.*]

EDMUND   Don't, mother. [*His eyes meet his father's.*]

TYRONE   [*huskily—clutching at hopeless hope*]   Maybe if you asked your mother now what you said you were going to—[*He fumbles with his watch.*] By God, look at the time! I'll have to shake a leg.

> [*He hurries away through the front parlor.* MARY *lifts her head. Her manner is again one of detached motherly solicitude. She seems to have forgotten the tears which are still in her eyes.*]

MARY   How do you feel, dear? [*She feels his forehead.*] Your head is a little hot, but that's just from going out in the sun. You look ever so much better than you did this morning. [*taking his hand*] Come and sit down. You mustn't stand on your feet so much. You must learn to husband your strength.

> [*She gets him to sit and she sits sideways on the arm of his chair, an arm around his shoulder, so he cannot meet her eyes.*]

EDMUND   [*starts to blurt out the appeal he now feels is quite hopeless*]   Listen, Mama—

MARY   [*interrupting quickly*]   Now, now! Don't talk. Lean back and rest. [*persuasively*] You know, I think it would be much better for you if you stayed home this afternoon and let me take care of you. It's such a tiring trip uptown in the dirty old trolley on a hot day like this. I'm sure you'd be much better off here with me.

EDMUND   [*dully*]   You forget I have an appointment with Hardy. [*trying again to get his appeal started*] Listen, Mama—

MARY   [*quickly*]   You can telephone and say you don't feel well enough. [*excitedly*] It's simply a waste of time and money seeing him. He'll only tell you some lie. He'll pretend he's found something serious the matter because that's his bread and butter. [*She gives a hard sneering little laugh.*] The old idiot! All he knows about medicine is to look solemn and preach will power!

EDMUND   [*trying to catch her eyes*]   Mama! Please listen! I want to ask you something! You— You're only just started. You can still stop. You've got the will power! We'll all help you. I'll do anything! Won't you, Mama?

MARY   [*stammers pleadingly*]   Please don't—talk about things you don't understand!

EDMUND   [*dully*]   All right, I give up. I knew it was no use.

MARY   [*in blank denial now*]   Anyway, I don't know what you're referring to. But I do know you should be the last one— Right after I returned from the sanatorium, you began to be ill. The doctor there had warned me I must have peace at home with nothing to upset me, and all I've done is worry about you. [*then distractedly*] But that's no excuse! I'm only trying to explain. It's not an excuse! [*She hugs him to her—pleadingly*] Promise me, dear, you won't believe I made you an excuse.

EDMUND [*bitterly*] What else can I believe?

MARY [*slowly takes her arm away—her manner remote and objective again*] Yes, I suppose you can't help suspecting that.

EDMUND [*ashamed but still bitter*] What do you expect?

MARY Nothing, I don't blame you. How could you believe me—when I can't believe myself? I've become such a liar. I never lied about anything once upon a time. Now I have to lie, especially to myself. But how can you understand, when I don't myself. I've never understood anything about it, except that one day long ago I found I could no longer call my soul my own. [*She pauses—then lowering her voice to a strange tone of whispered confidence*] But some day, dear, I will find it again—some day when you're all well, and I see you healthy and happy and successful, and I don't have to feel guilty any more—some day when the Blessed Virgin Mary forgives me and gives me back the faith in Her love and pity I used to have in my convent days, and I can pray to Her again—when She sees no one in the world can believe in me even for a moment any more, then She will believe in me, and with Her help it will be so easy. I will hear myself scream with agony, and at the same time I will laugh because I will be so sure of myself. [*then as EDMUND remains hopelessly silent, she adds sadly*] Of course, you can't believe that, either. [*She rises from the arm of his chair and goes to stare out the windows at right with her back to him—casually*] Now I think of it, you might as well go uptown. I forgot I'm taking a drive. I have to go to the drugstore. You would hardly want to go there with me. You'd be so ashamed.

EDMUND [*brokenly*] Mama! Don't!

MARY I suppose you'll divide that ten dollars your father gave you with Jamie. You always divide with each other, don't you? Like good sports. Well, I know what he'll do with his share. Get drunk someplace where he can be with the only kind of woman he understands or likes. [*She turns to him, pleading frightenedly*] Edmund! Promise me you won't drink! It's so dangerous! You know Doctor Hardy told you—

EDMUND [*bitterly*] I thought he was an old idiot. Anyway, by tonight, what will you care?

MARY [*pitifully*] Edmund!

   [ JAMIE's *voice is heard from the front hall,* "Come on, Kid, let's beat it." MARY's *manner at once becomes detached again.*]

Go on, Edmund. Jamie's waiting. [*She goes to the front-parlor doorway.*] There comes your father downstairs, too.

   [TYRONE's *voice calls,* "Come on, Edmund."]

EDMUND [ *jumping up from his chair*] I'm coming.

   [*He stops beside her—without looking at her.*]

Goodbye, Mama.

MARY [*kisses him with detached affection*] Goodbye, dear. If you're coming home for dinner, try not to be late. And tell your father. You know what Bridget is.

   [*He turns and hurries away.* TYRONE *calls from the hall,* "Goodbye, Mary," *and then* JAMIE, "Goodbye, Mama." *She calls back*]

Goodbye. [*The front screen door is heard closing after them. She comes and*

*stands by the table, one hand drumming on it, the other fluttering up to pat
her hair. She stares about the room with frightened, forsaken eyes and whispers to herself.*] It's so lonely here. [*Then her face hardens into bitter self-
contempt.*] You're lying to yourself again. You wanted to get rid of them.
Their contempt and disgust aren't pleasant company. You're glad they're
gone. [*She gives a little despairing laugh.*] Then Mother of God, why do I
feel so lonely?

CURTAIN

## Act Three

SCENE—*The same. It is around half past six in the evening. Dusk is gathering
in the living room, an early dusk due to the fog which has rolled in from the
Sound and is like a white curtain drawn down outside the windows. From a
lighthouse beyond the harbor's mouth, a foghorn is heard at regular intervals,
moaning like a mournful whale in labor, and from the harbor itself, intermittently, comes the warning ringing of bells on yachts at anchor.*

*The tray with the bottle of whiskey, glasses, and pitcher of ice water is on the
table, as it was in the pre-luncheon scene of the previous act.*

MARY *and the second girl,* CATHLEEN, *are discovered. The latter is standing
at left of table. She holds an empty whiskey glass in her hand as if she'd forgotten she had it. She shows the effects of drink. Her stupid, good-humored face
wears a pleased and flattered simper.*

MARY *is paler than before and her eyes shine with unnatural brilliance. The
strange detachment in her manner has intensified. She has hidden deeper
within herself and found refuge and release in a dream where present reality is
but an appearance to be accepted and dismissed unfeelingly—even with a hard
cynicism—or entirely ignored. There is at times an uncanny gay, free youthfulness in her manner, as if in spirit she were released to become again, simply
and without self-consciousness, the naive, happy, chattering schoolgirl of her
convent days. She wears the dress into which she had changed for her drive to
town, a simple, fairly expensive affair, which would be extremely becoming if it
were not for the careless, almost slovenly way she wears it. Her hair is no longer
fastidiously in place. It has a slightly disheveled, lopsided look. She talks to*
CATHLEEN *with a confiding familiarity, as if the second girl were an old, intimate friend. As the curtain rises, she is standing by the screen door looking out.
A moan of the foghorn is heard.*

MARY [*amused—girlishly*]   That foghorn! Isn't it awful, Cathleen?
CATHLEEN [*talks more familiarly than usual but never with intentional imperti-
    nence because she sincerely likes her mistress*]   It is indeed, Ma'am. It's like
    a banshee.
MARY [*Goes on as if she hadn't heard. In nearly all the following dialogue there
    is the feeling that she has* CATHLEEN *with her merely as an excuse to keep
    talking.*]   I don't mind it tonight. Last night it drove me crazy. I lay awake
    worrying until I couldn't stand it any more.
CATHLEEN   Bad cess to it.[2] I was scared out of my wits riding back from town.
    I thought that ugly monkey, Smythe, would drive us in a ditch or against a
    tree. You couldn't see your hand in front of you. I'm glad you had me sit in
    back with you, Ma'am. If I'd been in front with that monkey— He can't keep

2. Bad luck to it (Irish).

his dirty hands to himself. Give him half a chance and he's pinching me on the leg or you-know-where—asking your pardon, Ma'am, but it's true.

MARY [*dreamily*]   It wasn't the fog I minded, Cathleen, I really love fog.

CATHLEEN   They say it's good for the complexion.

MARY   It hides you from the world and the world from you. You feel that everything has changed, and nothing is what it seemed to be. No one can find or touch you any more.

CATHLEEN   I wouldn't care so much if Smythe was a fine, handsome man like some chauffeurs I've seen—I mean, if it was all in fun, for I'm a decent girl. But for a shriveled runt like Smythe—! I've told him, you must think I'm hard up that I'd notice a monkey like you. I've warned him, one day I'll give a clout that'll knock him into next week. And so I will!

MARY   It's the foghorn I hate. It won't let you alone. It keeps reminding you, and warning you, and calling you back. [*She smiles strangely.*] But it can't tonight. It's just an ugly sound. It doesn't remind me of anything. [*She gives a teasing, girlish laugh.*] Except, perhaps, Mr. Tyrone's snores. I've always had such fun teasing him about it. He has snored ever since I can remember, especially when he's had too much to drink, and yet he's like a child, he hates to admit it. [*She laughs, coming to the table.*] Well, I suppose I snore at times, too, and I don't like to admit it. So I have no right to make fun of him, have I? [*She sits in the rocker at right of table.*]

CATHLEEN   Ah, sure, everybody healthy snores. It's a sign of sanity, they say. [*then, worriedly*] What time is it, Ma'am? I ought to go back in the kitchen. The damp is in Bridget's rheumatism and she's like a raging divil. She'll bite my head off.

[*She puts her glass on the table and makes a movement toward the back parlor.*]

MARY [*with a flash of apprehension*]   No, don't go, Cathleen. I don't want to be alone, yet.

CATHLEEN   You won't be for long. The Master and the boys will be home soon.

MARY   I doubt if they'll come back for dinner. They have too good an excuse to remain in the barrooms where they feel at home.

[CATHLEEN *stares at her, stupidly puzzled.* MARY *goes on smilingly*] Don't worry about Bridget. I'll tell her I kept you with me, and you can take a big drink of whiskey to her when you go. She won't mind then.

CATHLEEN [*grins—at her ease again*]   No, Ma'am. That's the one thing can make her cheerful. She loves her drop.

MARY   Have another drink yourself, if you wish, Cathleen.

CATHLEEN   I don't know if I'd better, Ma'am. I can feel what I've had already. [*reaching for the bottle*] Well, maybe one more won't harm. [*She pours a drink.*] Here's your good health, Ma'am. [*She drinks without bothering about a chaser.*]

MARY [*dreamily*]   I really did have good health once, Cathleen. But that was long ago.

CATHLEEN [*worried again*]   The Master's sure to notice what's gone from the bottle. He has the eye of a hawk for that.

MARY [*amusedly*]   Oh, we'll play Jamie's trick on him. Just measure a few drinks of water and pour them in.

CATHLEEN [*does this—with a silly giggle*]   God save me, it'll be half water. He'll know by the taste.

MARY [*indifferently*]   No, by the time he comes home he'll be too drunk to

tell the difference. He has such a good excuse, he believes, to drown his
sorrows.

CATHLEEN [*philosophically*]   Well, it's a good man's failing. I wouldn't give a
trauneen[3] for a teetotaler. They've no high spirits. [*then, stupidly puzzled*]
Good excuse? You mean Master Edmund, Ma'am? I can tell the Master is
worried about him.

MARY [*stiffens defensively—but in a strange way the reaction has a mechanical
quality, as if it did not penetrate to real emotion*]   Don't be silly, Cathleen.
Why should he be? A touch of grippe is nothing. And Mr. Tyrone never is
worried about anything, except money and property and the fear he'll end
his days in poverty. I mean, deeply worried. Because he cannot really
understand anything else. [*She gives a little laugh of detached, affectionate
amusement.*] My husband is a very peculiar man, Cathleen.

CATHLEEN [*vaguely resentful*]   Well, he's a fine, handsome, kind gentleman
just the same, Ma'am. Never mind his weakness.

MARY   Oh, I don't mind. I've loved him dearly for thirty-six years. That
proves I know he's lovable at heart and can't help being what he is, doesn't
it?

CATHLEEN [*hazily reassured*]   That's right. Ma'am. Love him dearly, for any
fool can see he worships the ground you walk on. [ *fighting the effect of her
last drink and trying to be soberly conversational*] Speaking of acting,
Ma'am, how is it you never went on the stage?

MARY [*resentfully*]   I? What put that absurd notion in your head? I was
brought up in a respectable home and educated in the best convent in the
Middle West. Before I met Mr. Tyrone I hardly knew there was such a
thing as a theater. I was a very pious girl. I even dreamed of becoming a
nun. I've never had the slightest desire to be an actress.

CATHLEEN [*bluntly*]   Well, I can't imagine you a holy nun, Ma'am. Sure,
you never darken the door of a church, God forgive you.

MARY [*ignores this*]   I've never felt at home in the theater. Even though Mr.
Tyrone has made me go with him on all his tours, I've had little to do with
the people in his company, or with anyone on the stage. Not that I have
anything against them. They have always been kind to me, and I to them.
But I've never felt at home with them. Their life is not my life. It has always
stood between me and—[*She gets up—abruptly*] But let's not talk of old
things that couldn't be helped. [*She goes to the porch door and stares out.*]
How thick the fog is. I can't see the road. All the people in the world could
pass by and I would never know. I wish it was always that way. It's getting
dark already. It will soon be night, thank goodness. [*She turns back—
vaguely*] It was kind of you to keep me company this afternoon, Cathleen. I
would have been lonely driving uptown alone.

CATHLEEN   Sure, wouldn't I rather ride in a fine automobile than stay here
and listen to Bridget's lies about her relations? It was like a vacation, Ma'am.
[*She pauses—then stupidly*] There was only one thing I didn't like.

MARY [*vaguely*]   What was that, Cathleen?

CATHLEEN   The way the man in the drugstore acted when I took in the prescription for you. [*indignantly*] The impidence[4] of him!

MARY [*with stubborn blankness*]   What are you talking about? What drugstore? What prescription? [*then hastily, as CATHLEEN stares in stupid amazement*] Oh, of course, I'd forgotten. The medicine for the rheumatism in my

---

3. Coin of very low value (Irish).          4. Impudence.

hands. What did the man say? [*then with indifference*] Not that it matters, as long as he filled the prescription.

CATHLEEN    It mattered to me, then! I'm not used to being treated like a thief. He gave me a long look and says insultingly, "Where did you get hold of this?" and I says, "It's none of your damned business, but if you must know, it's for the lady I work for, Mrs. Tyrone, who's sitting out in the automobile." That shut him up quick. He gave a look out at you and said, "Oh," and went to get the medicine.

MARY [*vaguely*]    Yes, he knows me. [*She sits in the armchair at right rear of table. She adds in a calm, detached voice*] It's a special kind of medicine. I have to take it because there is no other that can stop the pain—all the pain—I mean, in my hands. [*She raises her hands and regards them with melancholy sympathy. There is no tremor in them now.*] Poor hands! You'd never believe it, but they were once one of my good points, along with my hair and eyes, and I had a fine figure, too. [*Her tone has become more and more far-off and dreamy.*] They were a musician's hands. I used to love the piano. I worked so hard at my music in the Convent—if you can call it work when you do something you love. Mother Elizabeth and my music teacher both said I had more talent than any student they remembered. My father paid for special lessons. He spoiled me. He would do anything I asked. He would have sent me to Europe to study after I graduated from the Convent. I might have gone—if I hadn't fallen in love with Mr. Tyrone. Or I might have become a nun. I had two dreams. To be a nun, that was the more beautiful one. To become a concert pianist, that was the other. [*She pauses, regarding her hands fixedly.* CATHLEEN *blinks her eyes to fight off drowsiness and a tipsy feeling.*] I haven't touched a piano in so many years. I couldn't play with such crippled fingers, even if I wanted to. For a time after my marriage I tried to keep up my music. But it was hopeless. One-night stands, cheap hotels, dirty trains, leaving children, never having a home—[*She stares at her hands with fascinated disgust.*] See, Cathleen, how ugly they are! So maimed and crippled! You would think they'd been through some horrible accident! [*She gives a strange little laugh.*] So they have, come to think of it. [*She suddenly thrusts her hands behind her back.*] I won't look at them. They're worse than the foghorn for reminding me— [*then with defiant self-assurance*] But even they can't touch me now. [*She brings her hands from behind her back and deliberately stares at them— calmly*] They're far away. I see them, but the pain has gone.

CATHLEEN [*stupidly puzzled*]    You've taken some of the medicine? It made you act funny, Ma'am. If I didn't know better, I'd think you'd a drop taken.

MARY [*dreamily*]    It kills the pain. You go back until at last you are beyond its reach. Only the past when you were happy is real. [*She pauses—then as if her words had been an evocation which called back happiness she changes in her whole manner and facial expression. She looks younger. There is a quality of an innocent convent girl about her, and she smiles shyly.*] If you think Mr. Tyrone is handsome now, Cathleen, you should have seen him when I first met him. He had the reputation of being one of the best looking men in the country. The girls in the Convent who had seen him act, or seen his photographs, used to rave about him. He was a great matinee idol then, you know. Women used to wait at the stage door just to see him come out. You can imagine how excited I was when my father wrote me he and James Tyrone had become friends, and that I was to meet him when I came home for Easter vacation. I showed the letter to all the girls, and how envious they

were! My father took me to see him act first. It was a play about the French
Revolution and the leading part was a nobleman. I couldn't take my eyes
off him. I wept when he was thrown in prison—and then was so mad at
myself because I was afraid my eyes and nose would be red. My father had
said we'd go backstage to his dressing room right after the play, and so we
did. [She gives a little excited, shy laugh.] I was so bashful all I could do was
stammer and blush like a little fool. But he didn't seem to think I was a fool.
I know he liked me the first moment we were introduced. [coquettishly] I
guess my eyes and nose couldn't have been red, after all. I was really very
pretty then, Cathleen. And he was handsomer than my wildest dream, in
his make-up and his nobleman's costume that was so becoming to him. He
was different from all ordinary men, like someone from another world. At
the same time he was simple, and kind, and unassuming, not a bit stuck-up
or vain. I fell in love right then. So did he, he told me afterwards. I forgot
all about becoming a nun or a concert pianist. All I wanted was to be his
wife. [She pauses, staring before her with unnaturally bright, dreamy eyes,
and a rapt, tender, girlish smile.] Thirty-six years ago, but I can see it as
clearly as if it were tonight! We've loved each other ever since. And in all
those thirty-six years, there has never been a breath of scandal about him. I
mean, with any other woman. Never since he met me. That has made me
very happy, Cathleen. It has made me forgive so many other things.
CATHLEEN [ fighting tipsy drowsiness—sentimentally] He's a fine gentleman
and you're a lucky woman. [then, fidgeting] Can I take the drink to Bridget,
Ma'am? It must be near dinnertime and I ought to be in the kitchen helping
her. If she don't get something to quiet her temper, she'll be after me with
the cleaver.
MARY [with a vague exasperation at being brought back from her dream] Yes,
yes, go. I don't need you now.
CATHLEEN [with relief] Thank you, Ma'am. [She pours out a big drink and
starts for the back parlor with it.] You won't be alone long. The Master and
the boys—
MARY [impatiently] No, no, they won't come. Tell Bridget I won't wait. You
can serve dinner promptly at half past six. I'm not hungry but I'll sit at the
table and we'll get it over with.
CATHLEEN You ought to eat something, Ma'am. It's a queer medicine if it
takes away your appetite.
MARY [has begun to drift into dreams again—reacts mechanically] What
medicine? I don't know what you mean. [in dismissal] You better take the
drink to Bridget.
CATHLEEN Yes, Ma'am.
    [She disappears through the back parlor. MARY waits until she hears
    the pantry door close behind her. Then she settles back in relaxed
    dreaminess, staring fixedly at nothing. Her arms rest limply along the
    arms of the chair, her hands with long, warped, swollen-knuckled, sen-
    sitive fingers drooping in complete calm. It is growing dark in the room.
    There is a pause of dead quiet. Then from the world outside comes the
    melancholy moan of the foghorn, followed by a chorus of bells, muffled
    by the fog, from the anchored craft in the harbor. MARY's face gives no
    sign she has heard, but her hands jerk and the fingers automatically
    play for a moment on the air. She frowns and shakes her head mechan-
    ically as if a fly had walked across her mind. She suddenly loses all the
    girlish quality and is an aging, cynically sad, embittered woman.]

MARY [*bitterly*]  You're a sentimental fool. What is so wonderful about that first meeting between a silly romantic schoolgirl and a matinee idol? You were much happier before you knew he existed, in the Convent when you used to pray to the Blessed Virgin. [*longingly*] If I could only find the faith I lost, so I could pray again! [*She pauses—then begins to recite the Hail Mary in a flat, empty tone.*] "Hail, Mary, full of grace! The Lord is with Thee; blessed art Thou among women." [*sneeringly*] You expect the Blessed Virgin to be fooled by a lying dope fiend reciting words! You can't hide from her! [*She springs to her feet. Her hands fly up to pat her hair distractedly.*] I must go upstairs. I haven't taken enough. When you start again you never know exactly how much you need. [*She goes toward the front parlor—then stops in the doorway as she hears the sound of voices from the front path. She starts guiltily.*] That must be them—[*She hurries back to sit down. Her face sets in stubborn defensiveness—resentfully*] Why are they coming back? They don't want to. And I'd much rather be alone. [*Suddenly her whole manner changes. She becomes pathetically relieved and eager.*] Oh, I'm so glad they've come! I've been so horribly lonely!

[*The front door is heard closing and* TYRONE *calls uneasily from the hall.*]

TYRONE  Are you there, Mary?

[*The light in the hall is turned on and shines through the front parlor to fall on* MARY.]

MARY [*rises from her chair, her face lighting up lovingly—with excited eagerness*]  I'm here, dear. In the living room. I've been waiting for you.

[TYRONE *comes in through the front parlor.* EDMUND *is behind him.* TYRONE *has had a lot to drink but beyond a slightly glazed look in his eyes and a trace of blur in his speech, he does not show it.* EDMUND *has also had more than a few drinks without much apparent effect, except that his sunken cheeks are flushed and his eyes look bright and feverish. They stop in the doorway to stare appraisingly at her. What they see fulfills their worst expectations. But for the moment* MARY *is unconscious of their condemning eyes. She kisses her husband and then* EDMUND. *Her manner is unnaturally effusive. They submit shrinkingly. She talks excitedly.*]

I'm so happy you've come. I had given up hope. I was afraid you wouldn't come home. It's such a dismal, foggy evening. It must be much more cheerful in the barrooms uptown, where there are people you can talk and joke with. No, don't deny it. I know how you feel. I don't blame you a bit. I'm all the more grateful to you for coming home. I was sitting here so lonely and blue. Come and sit down.

[*She sits at left rear of table,* EDMUND *at left of table, and* TYRONE *in the rocker at right of it.*]

Dinner won't be ready for a minute. You're actually a little early. Will wonders never cease. Here's the whiskey, dear. Shall I pour a drink for you? [*Without waiting for a reply she does so.*] And you, Edmund? I don't want to encourage you, but one before dinner, as an appetizer, can't do any harm.

[*She pours a drink for him. They make no move to take the drinks. She talks on as if unaware of their silence.*]

Where's Jamie? But, of course, he'll never come home so long as he has the price of a drink left. [*She reaches out and clasps her husband's hand— sadly*] I'm afraid Jamie has been lost to us for a long time, dear. [*Her face hardens.*] But we mustn't allow him to drag Edmund down with him, as he'd like to do. He's jealous because Edmund has always been the baby—just as he used to be of Eugene. He'll never be content until he makes Edmund as hopeless a failure as he is.

EDMUND [*miserably*]   Stop talking, Mama.

TYRONE [*dully*]   Yes, Mary, the less you say now—[*then to Edmund, a bit tipsily*] All the same there's truth in your mother's warning. Beware of that brother of yours, or he'll poison life for you with his damned sneering serpent's tongue!

EDMUND [*as before*]   Oh, cut it out, Papa.

MARY [*goes on as if nothing had been said*]   It's hard to believe, seeing Jamie as he is now, that he was ever my baby. Do you remember what a healthy, happy baby he was, James? The one-night stands and filthy trains and cheap hotels and bad food never made him cross or sick. He was always smiling or laughing. He hardly ever cried. Eugene was the same, too, happy and healthy, during the two years he lived before I let him die through my neglect.

TYRONE   Oh, for the love of God! I'm a fool for coming home!

EDMUND   Papa! Shut up!

MARY [*smiles with detached tenderness at* EDMUND]   It was Edmund who was the crosspatch when he was little, always getting upset and frightened about nothing at all. [*She pats his hand—teasingly*] Everyone used to say, dear, you'd cry at the drop of a hat.

EDMUND [*cannot control his bitterness*]   Maybe I guessed there was a good reason not to laugh.

TYRONE [*reproving and pitying*]   Now, now, lad. You know better than to pay attention—

MARY [*as if she hadn't heard—sadly again*]   Who would have thought Jamie would grow up to disgrace us. You remember, James, for years after he went to boarding school, we received such glowing reports. Everyone liked him. All his teachers told us what a fine brain he had, and how easily he learned his lessons. Even after he began to drink and they had to expel him, they wrote us how sorry they were, because he was so likable and such a brilliant student. They predicted a wonderful future for him if he would only learn to take life seriously. [*She pauses—then adds with a strange, sad detachment*] It's such a pity. Poor Jamie! It's hard to understand—[*Abruptly a change comes over her. Her face hardens and she stares at her husband with accusing hostility.*] No, it isn't at all. You brought him up to be a boozer. Since he first opened his eyes, he's seen you drinking. Always a bottle on the bureau in the cheap hotel rooms! And if he had a nightmare when he was little, or a stomach-ache, your remedy was to give him a teaspoonful of whiskey to quiet him.

TYRONE [*stung*]   So I'm to blame because that lazy hulk has made a drunken loafer of himself? Is that what I came home to listen to? I might have known! When you have the poison in you, you want to blame everyone but yourself!

EDMUND   Papa! You told me not to pay attention. [*then, resentfully*] Anyway it's true. You did the same thing with me. I can remember that teaspoonful of booze every time I woke up with a nightmare.

MARY [*in a detached reminiscent tone*]   Yes, you were continually having nightmares as a child. You were born afraid. Because I was so afraid to bring you into the world. [*She pauses—then goes on with the same detachment*] Please don't think I blame your father, Edmund. He didn't know any better.

He never went to school after he was ten. His people were the most ignorant kind of poverty-stricken Irish. I'm sure they honestly believed whiskey is the healthiest medicine for a child who is sick or frightened.

[TYRONE *is about to burst out in angry defense of his family but* EDMUND *intervenes.*]

EDMUND [*sharply*] Papa! [*changing the subject*] Are we going to have this drink, or aren't we?

TYRONE [*controlling himself—dully*] You're right. I'm a fool to take notice. [*He picks up his glass listlessly.*] Drink hearty, lad.

[EDMUND *drinks but* TYRONE *remains staring at the glass in his hand.* EDMUND *at once realizes how much the whiskey has been watered. He frowns, glancing from the bottle to his mother—starts to say something but stops.*]

MARY [*in a changed tone—repentantly*] I'm sorry if I sounded bitter, James. I'm not. It's all so far away. But I did feel a little hurt when you wished you hadn't come home. I was so relieved and happy when you came, and grateful to you. It's very dreary and sad to be here alone in the fog with night falling.

TYRONE [*moved*] I'm glad I came, Mary, when you act like your real self.

MARY I was so lonesome I kept Cathleen with me just to have someone to talk to. [*Her manner and quality drift back to the shy convent girl again.*] Do you know what I was telling her, dear? About the night my father took me to your dressing room and I first fell in love with you. Do you remember?

TYRONE [*deeply moved—his voice husky*] Can you think I'd ever forget, Mary?

[EDMUND *looks away from them, sad and embarrassed.*]

MARY [*tenderly*] No. I know you still love me, James, in spite of everything.

TYRONE [*His face works and he blinks back tears—with quiet intensity*] Yes! As God is my judge! Always and forever, Mary!

MARY And I love you, dear, in spite of everything.

[*There is a pause in which* EDMUND *moves embarrassedly. The strange detachment comes over her manner again as if she were speaking impersonally of people seen from a distance.*]

But I must confess, James, although I couldn't help loving you, I would never have married you if I'd known you drank so much. I remember the first night your barroom friends had to help you up to the door of our hotel room, and knocked and then ran away before I came to the door. We were still on our honeymoon, do you remember?

TYRONE [*with guilty vehemence*] I don't remember! It wasn't on our honeymoon! And I never in my life had to be helped to bed, or missed a performance!

MARY [*as though he hadn't spoken*] I had waited in that ugly hotel room hour after hour. I kept making excuses for you. I told myself it must be some business connected with the theater. I knew so little about the theater. Then I became terrified. I imagined all sorts of horrible accidents. I got on my knees and prayed that nothing had happened to you—and then they brought you up and left you outside the door. [*She gives a little, sad sigh.*] I didn't know how often that was to happen in the years to come, how many times I was to wait in ugly hotel rooms. I became quite used to it.

EDMUND [*bursts out with a look of accusing hate at his father*] Christ! No wonder—! [*He controls himself—gruffly*] When is dinner, Mama? It must be time.

TYRONE [*overwhelmed by shame which he tries to hide, fumbles with his watch*]

Yes. It must be. Let's see. [*He stares at his watch without seeing it—pleadingly*] Mary! Can't you forget—?

MARY [*with detached pity*]   No, dear. But I forgive. I always forgive you. So don't look so guilty. I'm sorry I remembered out loud. I don't want to be sad, or to make you sad. I want to remember only the happy part of the past. [*Her manner drifts back to the shy, gay convent girl.*] Do you remember our wedding, dear? I'm sure you've completely forgotten what my wedding gown looked like. Men don't notice such things. They don't think they're important. But it was important to me, I can tell you! How I fussed and worried! I was so excited and happy! My father told me to buy anything I wanted and never mind what it cost. The best is none too good, he said. I'm afraid he spoiled me dreadfully. My mother didn't. She was very pious and strict. I think she was a little jealous. She didn't approve of my marrying—especially an actor. I think she hoped I would become a nun. She used to scold my father. She'd grumble, "You never tell me, never mind what it costs, when I buy anything! You've spoiled that girl so, I pity her husband if she ever marries. She'll expect him to give her the moon. She'll never make a good wife." [*She laughs affectionately.*] Poor mother! [*She smiles at* TYRONE *with a strange, incongruous coquetry.*] But she was mistaken, wasn't she, James? I haven't been such a bad wife, have I?

TYRONE [*huskily, trying to force a smile*]   I'm not complaining, Mary.

MARY [*a shadow of vague guilt crosses her face*]   At least, I've loved you dearly, and done the best I could—under the circumstances. [*The shadow vanishes and her shy, girlish expression returns.*] That wedding gown was nearly the death of me and the dressmaker, too! [*She laughs.*] I was so particular. It was never quite good enough. At last she said she refused to touch it any more or she might spoil it, and I made her leave so I could be alone to examine myself in the mirror. I was so pleased and vain. I thought to myself, "Even if your nose and mouth and ears are a trifle too large, your eyes and hair and figure, and your hands, make up for it. You're just as pretty as any actress he's ever met, and you don't have to use paint." [ *She pauses, wrinkling her brow in an effort of memory.*] Where is my wedding gown now, I wonder? I kept it wrapped up in tissue paper in my trunk. I used to hope I would have a daughter and when it came time for her to marry— She couldn't have bought a lovelier gown, and I knew, James, you'd never tell her, never mind the cost. You'd want her to pick up something at a bargain. It was made of soft, shimmering satin, trimmed with wonderful old duchesse lace, in tiny ruffles around the neck and sleeves, and worked in with the folds that were draped round in a bustle effect at the back. The basque[5] was boned and very tight. I remember I held my breath when it was fitted, so my waist would be as small as possible. My father even let me have duchesse lace on my white satin slippers, and lace with orange blossoms in my veil. Oh, how I loved that gown! It was so beautiful! Where is it now, I wonder? I used to take it out from time to time when I was lonely, but it always made me cry, so finally a long while ago—[*She wrinkles her forehead again.*] I wonder where I hid it? Probably in one of the old trunks in the attic. Some day I'll have to look.

> [*She stops, staring before her.* TYRONE *sighs, shaking his head hopelessly, and attempts to catch his son's eye, looking for sympathy, but* EDMUND *is staring at the floor.*]

TYRONE [ *forces a casual tone*]   Isn't it dinner time, dear? [*with a feeble at-*

---

5. Tight-fitting bodice.

*tempt at teasing*] You're forever scolding me for being late, but now I'm on time for once, it's dinner that's late.
   [*She doesn't appear to hear him. He adds, still pleasantly*]
Well, if I can't eat yet, I can drink. I'd forgotten I had this.
   [*He drinks his drink.* EDMUND *watches him.* TYRONE *scowls and looks at his wife with sharp suspicion—roughly*]
Who's been tampering with my whiskey? The damned stuff is half water! Jamie's been away and he wouldn't overdo his trick like this, anyway. Any fool could tell— Mary, answer me! [*with angry disgust*] I hope to God you haven't taken to drink on top of—

EDMUND    Shut up, Papa! [*to his mother, without looking at her*] You treated Cathleen and Bridget, isn't that it, Mama?

MARY [*with indifferent casualness*]   Yes, of course. They work hard for poor wages. And I'm the housekeeper, I have to keep them from leaving. Besides, I wanted to treat Cathleen because I had her drive uptown with me, and sent her to get my prescription filled.

EDMUND    For God's sake, Mama! You can't trust her! Do you want everyone on earth to know?

MARY [*her face hardening stubbornly*]   Know what? That I suffer from rheumatism in my hands and have to take medicine to kill the pain? Why should I be ashamed of that? [*turns on* EDMUND *with a hard, accusing antagonism—almost a revengeful enmity*] I never knew what rheumatism was before you were born! Ask your father!
   [EDMUND *looks away, shrinking into himself.*]

TYRONE    Don't mind her, lad. It doesn't mean anything. When she gets to the stage where she gives the old crazy excuse about her hands she's gone far away from us.

MARY [*turns on him—with a strangely triumphant, taunting smile*]   I'm glad you realize that, James! Now perhaps you'll give up trying to remind me, you and Edmund! [*abruptly, in a detached, matter-of-fact tone*] Why don't you light the light, James? It's getting dark. I know you hate to, but Edmund has proved to you that one bulb burning doesn't cost much. There's no sense letting your fear of the poorhouse make you too stingy.

TYRONE [*reacts mechanically*]   I never claimed one bulb cost much! It's having them on, one here and one there, that makes the Electric Light Company rich. [*He gets up and turns on the reading lamp—roughly*] But I'm a fool to talk reason to you. [*to* EDMUND] I'll get a fresh bottle of whiskey, lad, and we'll have a real drink. [*He goes through the back parlor.*]

MARY [*with detached amusement*]   He'll sneak around to the outside cellar door so the servants won't see him. He's really ashamed of keeping his whiskey padlocked in the cellar. Your father is a strange man, Edmund. It took many years before I understood him. You must try to understand and forgive him, too, and not feel contempt because he's close-fisted. His father deserted his mother and their six children a year or so after they came to America. He told them he had a premonition he would die soon, and he was homesick for Ireland, and wanted to go back there to die. So he went and he did die. He must have been a peculiar man, too. Your father had to go to work in a machine shop when he was only ten years old.

EDMUND [*protests dully*]   Oh, for Pete's sake, Mama. I've heard Papa tell that machine shop story ten thousand times.

MARY    Yes, dear, you've had to listen, but I don't think you've ever tried to understand.

EDMUND [*ignoring this—miserably*]   Listen, Mama! You're not so far gone yet you've forgotten everything. You haven't asked me what I found out this afternoon. Don't you care a damn?

MARY [*shakenly*]   Don't say that! You hurt me, dear!

EDMUND   What I've got is serious, Mama. Doc Hardy knows for sure now.

MARY [*stiffens into scornful, defensive stubbornness*]   That lying old quack! I warned you he'd invent—!

EDMUND [*miserably dogged*]   He called in a specialist to examine me, so he'd be absolutely sure.

MARY [*ignoring this*]   Don't tell me about Hardy! If you heard what the doctor at the sanatorium, who really knows something, said about how he'd treated me! He said he ought to be locked up! He said it was a wonder I hadn't gone mad! I told him I had once, that time I ran down in my nightdress to throw myself off the dock. You remember that, don't you? And yet you want me to pay attention to what Doctor Hardy says. Oh, no!

EDMUND [*bitterly*]   I remember, all right. It was right after that Papa and Jamie decided they couldn't hide it from me any more. Jamie told me. I called him a liar! I tried to punch him in the nose. But I knew he wasn't lying. [*His voice trembles, his eyes begin to fill with tears.*] God, it made everything in life seem rotten!

MARY [*pitiably*]   Oh, don't. My baby! You hurt me so dreadfully!

EDMUND [*dully*]   I'm sorry, Mama. It was you who brought it up. [*then with a bitter, stubborn persistence*] Listen, Mama. I'm going to tell you whether you want to hear or not. I've got to go to a sanatorium.

MARY [*dazedly, as if this was something that had never occurred to her*]   Go away? [*violently*] No! I won't have it! How dare Doctor Hardy advise such a thing without consulting me! How dare your father allow him! What right has he? You are my baby! Let him attend to Jamie! [*more and more excited and bitter*] I know why he wants you sent to a sanatorium. To take you from me! He's always tried to do that. He's been jealous of every one of my babies! He kept finding ways to make me leave them. That's what caused Eugene's death. He's been jealous of you most of all. He knew I loved you most because—

EDMUND [*miserably*]   Oh, stop talking crazy, can't you, Mama! Stop trying to blame him. And why are you so against my going away now? I've been away a lot, and I've never noticed it broke your heart!

MARY [*bitterly*]   I'm afraid you're not very sensitive, after all. [*sadly*] You might have guessed, dear, that after I knew you knew—about me—I had to be glad whenever you were where you couldn't see me.

EDMUND [*brokenly*]   Mama! Don't! [*He reaches out blindly and takes her hand—but he drops it immediately, overcome by bitterness again.*] All this talk about loving me—and you won't even listen when I try to tell you how sick—

MARY [*with an abrupt transformation into a detached bullying motherliness*]   Now, now. That's enough! I don't care to hear because I know it's nothing but Hardy's ignorant lies.

[*He shrinks back into himself. She keeps on in a forced, teasing tone but with an increasing undercurrent of resentment.*]

You're so like your father, dear. You love to make a scene out of nothing so you can be dramatic and tragic. [*with a belittling laugh*] If I gave you the slightest encouragement, you'd tell me next you were going to die—

EDMUND   People do die of it. Your own father—

MARY [*sharply*]   Why do you mention him? There's no comparison at all with you. He had consumption. [*angrily*] I hate you when you become gloomy and morbid! I forbid you to remind me of my father's death, do you hear me?

EDMUND [*his face hard—grimly*]   Yes, I hear you, Mama. I wish to God I didn't! [*He gets up from his chair and stands staring condemningly at her— bitterly*] It's pretty hard to take at times, having a dope fiend for a mother!

[*She winces—all life seeming to drain from her face, leaving it with the appearance of a plaster cast. Instantly* EDMUND *wishes he could take back what he has said. He stammers miserably.*]

Forgive me, Mama. I was angry. You hurt me.

[*There is a pause in which the foghorn and the ships' bells are heard.*]

MARY [*goes slowly to the windows at right like an automaton—looking out, a blank, far-off quality in her voice*]   Just listen to that awful foghorn. And the bells. Why is it fog makes everything sound so sad and lost, I wonder?

EDMUND [*brokenly*]   I—I can't stay here. I don't want any dinner.

[*He hurries away through the front parlor. She keeps staring out the window until she hears the front door close behind him. Then she comes back and sits in her chair, the same blank look on her face.*]

MARY [*vaguely*]   I must go upstairs. I haven't taken enough. [*She pauses— then longingly*] I hope, sometime, without meaning it, I will take an over-dose. I never could do it deliberately. The Blessed Virgin would never forgive me, then.

[*She hears* TYRONE *returning and turns as he comes in, through the back parlor, with a bottle of whiskey he has just uncorked. He is fuming.*]

TYRONE [*wrathfully*]   The padlock is all scratched. That drunken loafer has tried to pick the lock with a piece of wire, the way he's done before. [*with satisfaction, as if this was a perpetual battle of wits with his elder son*] But I've fooled him this time. It's a special padlock a professional burglar couldn't pick. [*He puts the bottle on the tray and suddenly is aware of* EDMUND's *absence.*] Where's Edmund?

MARY [*with a vague far-away air*]   He went out. Perhaps he's going uptown again to find Jamie. He still has some money left, I suppose, and it's burning a hole in his pocket. He said he didn't want any dinner. He doesn't seem to have any appetite these days. [*then stubbornly*] But it's just a summer cold.

[TYRONE *stares at her and shakes his head helplessly and pours himself a big drink and drinks it. Suddenly it is too much for her and she breaks out and sobs.*]

Oh, James, I'm so frightened! [*She gets up and throws her arms around him and hides her face on his shoulder—sobbingly*] I know he's going to die!

TYRONE   Don't say that! It's not true! They promised me in six months he'd be cured.

MARY   You don't believe that! I can tell when you're acting! And it will be my fault. I should never have borne him. It would have been better for his sake. I could never hurt him then. He wouldn't have had to know his mother was a dope fiend—and hate her!

TYRONE [*his voice quivering*]   Hush, Mary, for the love of God! He loves you. He knows it was a curse put on you without your knowing or willing it. He's proud you're his mother! [*abruptly as he hears the pantry door opening*] Hush, now! Here comes Cathleen. You don't want her to see you crying.

[*She turns quickly away from him to the windows at right, hastily wiping her eyes. A moment later* CATHLEEN *appears in the back-parlor doorway. She is uncertain in her walk and grinning woozily.*]

CATHLEEN [*starts guiltily when she sees* TYRONE—*with dignity*]   Dinner is served, Sir. [*raising her voice unnecessarily*] Dinner is served, Ma'am. [*She forgets her dignity and addresses* TYRONE *with good-natured familiarity*] So you're here, are you? Well, well. Won't Bridget be in a rage! I told her the Madame said you wouldn't be home. [*then reading accusation in his eye*] Don't be looking at me that way. If I've a drop taken, I didn't steal it. I was invited.

[*She turns with huffy dignity and disappears through the back parlor.*]

TYRONE [*sighs—then summoning his actor's heartiness*]   Come along, dear. Let's have our dinner. I'm hungry as a hunter.

MARY [*comes to him—her face is composed in plaster again and her tone is remote*]   I'm afraid you'll have to excuse me, James. I couldn't possibly eat anything. My hands pain me dreadfully. I think the best thing for me is to go to bed and rest. Good night dear.

[*She kisses him mechanically and turns toward the front parlor.*]

TYRONE [*harshly*]   Up to take more of that God-damned poison, is that it? You'll be like a mad ghost before the night's over!

MARY [*starts to walk away—blankly*]   I don't know what you're talking about, James. You say such mean, bitter things when you've drunk too much. You're as bad as Jamie or Edmund.

[*She moves off through the front parlor. He stands a second as if not knowing what to do. He is a sad, bewildered, broken old man. He walks wearily off through the back parlor toward the dining room.*

CURTAIN

## Act Four

SCENE—*The same. It is around midnight. The lamp in the front hall has been turned out, so that now no light shines through the front parlor. In the living room only the reading lamp on the table is lighted. Outside the windows the wall of fog appears denser than ever. As the curtain rises, the foghorn is heard, followed by the ships' bells from the harbor.*

*TYRONE is seated at the table. He wears his pince-nez[6] and is playing solitaire. He has taken off his coat and has on an old brown dressing gown. The whiskey bottle on the tray is three-quarters empty. There is a fresh full bottle on the table, which he has brought from the cellar so there will be an ample reserve on hand. He is drunk and shows it by the owlish, deliberate manner in which he peers at each card to make certain of its identity, and then plays it as if he wasn't certain of his aim. His eyes have a misted, oily look and his mouth is slack. But despite all the whiskey in him, he has not escaped, and he looks as he appeared at the close of the preceding act, a sad, defeated old man, possessed by hopeless resignation.*

*As the curtain rises, he finishes a game and sweeps the cards together. He shuffles them clumsily, dropping a couple on the floor. He retrieves them with difficulty, and starts to shuffle again, when he hears someone entering the front door. He peers over his pince-nez through the front parlor.*

6. Eyeglasses clipped to the nose.

TYRONE [*his voice thick*]   Who's that? Is it you, Edmund?
    [EDMUND's *voice answers curtly, "Yes." Then he evidently collides with
    something in the dark hall and can be heard cursing. A moment later
    the hall lamp is turned on.* TYRONE *frowns and calls.*]
    Turn that light out before you come in.
    [*But* EDMUND *doesn't. He comes in through the front parlor. He is
    drunk now, too, but like his father he carries it well, and gives little
    physical sign of it except in his eyes and a chip-on-the-shoulder aggres-
    siveness in his manner.* TYRONE *speaks, at first with a warm, relieved
    welcome.*]
    I'm glad you've come, lad. I've been damned lonely. [*then resentfully*]
    You're a fine one to run away and leave me to sit alone here all night when
    you know—[*with sharp irritation*] I told you to turn out that light! We're
    not giving a ball. There's no reason to have the house ablaze with electricity
    at this time of night, burning up money!

EDMUND [*angrily*]   Ablaze with electricity! One bulb! Hell, everyone keeps a
    light on in the front hall until they go to bed. [*He rubs his knee.*] I damned
    near busted my knee on the hat stand.

TYRONE   The light from here shows in the hall. You could see your way well
    enough if you were sober.

EDMUND   If *I* was sober? I like that!

TYRONE   I don't give a damn what other people do. If they want to be wasteful
    fools, for the sake of show, let them be!

EDMUND   One bulb! Christ, don't be such a cheap skate! I've proved by figures
    if you left the light bulb on all night it wouldn't be as much as one drink!

TYRONE   To hell with your figures! The proof is in the bills I have to pay!

EDMUND [*sits down opposite his father—contemptuously*]   Yes, facts don't
    mean a thing, do they? What you want to believe, that's the only truth!
    [*derisively*] Shakespeare was an Irish Catholic, for example.

TYRONE [*stubbornly*]   So he was. The proof is in his plays.

EDMUND   Well he wasn't, and there's no proof of it in his plays, except to you!
    [ *jeeringly*] The Duke of Wellington, there was another good Irish Catholic!

TYRONE   I never said he was a good one. He was a renegade but a Catholic
    just the same.

EDMUND   Well, he wasn't. You just want to believe no one but an Irish Cath-
    olic general could beat Napoleon.

TYRONE   I'm not going to argue with you. I asked you to turn out that light
    in the hall.

EDMUND   I heard you, and as far as I'm concerned it stays on.

TYRONE   None of your damned insolence! Are you going to obey me or not?

EDMUND   Not! If you want to be a crazy miser put it out yourself!

TYRONE [*with threatening anger*]   Listen to me! I've put up with a lot from
    you because from the mad things you've done at times I've thought you
    weren't quite right in your head. I've excused you and never lifted my hand
    to you. But there's a straw that breaks the camel's back. You'll obey me and
    put out that light or, big as you are, I'll give you a thrashing that'll teach
    you—! [*Suddenly he remembers* EDMUND's *illness and instantly becomes
    guilty and shamefaced.*] Forgive me, lad. I forgot— You shouldn't goad me
    into losing my temper.

EDMUND [*ashamed himself now*]   Forget it, Papa. I apologize, too. I had no
    right being nasty about nothing. I am a bit soused, I guess. I'll put out the
    damned light. [*He starts to get up.*]

TYRONE   No, stay where you are. Let it burn.
[*He stands up abruptly—and a bit drunkenly—and begins turning on the three bulbs in the chandelier, with a childish, bitterly dramatic self-pity.*]
We'll have them all on! Let them burn! To hell with them! The poorhouse is the end of the road, and it might as well be sooner as later! [*He finishes turning on the lights.*]

EDMUND   [*has watched this proceeding with an awakened sense of humor—now he grins, teasing affectionately*]   That's a grand curtain. [*He laughs.*] You're a wonder, Papa.

TYRONE   [*sits down sheepishly—grumbles pathetically*]   That's right, laugh at the old fool! The poor old ham! But the final curtain will be in the poorhouse just the same, and that's not comedy! [*Then as* EDMUND *is still grinning, he changes the subject.*] Well, well, let's not argue. You've got brains in that head of yours, though you do your best to deny them. You'll live to learn the value of a dollar. You're not like your damned tramp of a brother. I've given up hope he'll ever get sense. Where is he, by the way?

EDMUND   How would I know?

TYRONE   I thought you'd gone back uptown to meet him.

EDMUND   No. I walked out to the beach. I haven't seen him since this afternoon.

TYRONE   Well, if you split the money I gave you with him, like a fool—

EDMUND   Sure I did. He's always staked me when he had anything.

TYRONE   Then it doesn't take a soothsayer to tell he's probably in the whorehouse.

EDMUND   What of it if he is? Why not?

TYRONE   [*contemptuously*]   Why not, indeed. It's the fit place for him. If he's ever had a loftier dream than whores and whiskey, he's never shown it.

EDMUND   Oh, for Pete's sake, Papa! If you're going to start that stuff, I'll beat it. [*He starts to get up.*]

TYRONE   [*placatingly*]   All right, all right, I'll stop. God knows, I don't like the subject either. Will you join me in a drink?

EDMUND   Ah! Now you're talking!

TYRONE   [*passes the bottle to him—mechanically*]   I'm wrong to treat you. You've had enough already.

EDMUND   [*pouring a big drink—a bit drunkenly*]   Enough is *not* as good as a feast. [*He hands back the bottle.*]

TYRONE   It's too much in your condition.

EDMUND   Forget my condition! [*He raises his glass.*] Here's how.

TYRONE   Drink hearty. [*They drink.*] If you walked all the way to the beach you must be damp and chilled.

EDMUND   Oh, I dropped in at the Inn on the way out and back.

TYRONE   It's not a night I'd pick for a long walk.

EDMUND   I loved the fog. It was what I needed. [*He sounds more tipsy and looks it.*]

TYRONE   You should have more sense than to risk—

EDMUND   To hell with sense! We're all crazy. What do we want with sense?
[*He quotes from Dowson[7] sardonically.*]
   "They are not long, the weeping and the laughter,
   Love and desire and hate:

---

7. Ernest Dowson (1867–1900), English poet.

I think they have no portion in us after
We pass the gate.

They are not long, the days of wine and roses:
Out of a misty dream
Our path emerges for a while, then closes
Within a dream."

[*staring before him*] The fog was where I wanted to be. Halfway down the
path you can't see this house. You'd never know it was here. Or any of the
other places down the avenue. I couldn't see but a few feet ahead. I didn't
meet a soul. Everything looked and sounded unreal. Nothing was what it
is. That's what I wanted—to be alone with myself in another world where
truth is untrue and life can hide from itself. Out beyond the harbor, where
the road runs along the beach, I even lost the feeling of being on land. The
fog and the sea seemed part of each other. It was like walking on the bottom
of the sea. As if I had drowned long ago. As if I was a ghost belonging to the
fog, and the fog was the ghost of the sea. It felt damned peaceful to be
nothing more than a ghost within a ghost. [*He sees his father staring at him
with mingled worry and irritated disapproval. He grins mockingly.*] Don't
look at me as if I'd gone nutty. I'm talking sense. Who wants to see life as it
is, if they can help it? It's the three Gorgons[8] in one. You look in their faces
and turn to stone. Or it's Pan.[9] You see him and you die—that is, inside
you—and have to go on living as a ghost.

TYRONE [*impressed and at the same time revolted*]   You have a poet in you
but it's a damned morbid one! [ *forcing a smile*] Devil take your pessimism.
I feel low-spirited enough. [*He sighs.*] Why can't you remember your Shakespeare and forget the third-raters. You'll find what you're trying to say in
him—as you'll find everything else worth saying. [*He quotes, using his fine
voice*] "We are such stuff as dreams are made on, and our little life is
rounded with a sleep."[1]

EDMUND [*ironically*]   Fine! That's beautiful. But I wasn't trying to say that.
We are such stuff as manure is made on, so let's drink up and forget it.
That's more my idea.

TYRONE [*disgustedly*]   Ach! Keep such sentiments to yourself. I shouldn't have
given you that drink.

EDMUND   It did pack a wallop, all right. On you, too. [*He grins with affectionate teasing.*] Even if you've never missed a performance! [*aggressively*] Well,
what's wrong with being drunk? It's what we're after, isn't it? Let's not kid
each other, Papa. Not tonight. We know what we're trying to forget. [*hurriedly*] But let's not talk about it. It's no use now.

TYRONE [*dully*]   No. All we can do is try to be resigned—again.

EDMUND   Or be so drunk you can forget. [*He recites, and recites well, with
bitter, ironical passion, the Symons' translation of Baudelaire's[2] prose poem.*]
"Be always drunken. Nothing else matters: that is the only question. If you
would not feel the horrible burden of Time weighing on your shoulders and
crushing you to the earth, be drunken continually.

Drunken with what? With wine, with poetry, or with virtue, as you will.
But be drunken.

---

8. In Greek mythology, three monstrous sisters so ugly
that the sight of them turned one to stone.
9. Greek god of woods, fields, and flocks, half man
and half goat, associated with wildness.

1. Shakespeare, *The Tempest* 4.1.156–58.
2. Charles Baudelaire (1821–1867), French poet. Arthur Symons (1865–1945), English poet and literary
critic.

And if sometimes, on the stairs of a palace, or on the green side of a ditch, or in the dreary solitude of your own room, you should awaken and the drunkenness be half or wholly slipped away from you, ask of the wind, or of the wave, or of the star, or of the bird, or of the clock, of whatever flies, or sighs, or rocks, or sings, or speaks, ask what hour it is; and the wind, wave, star, bird, clock, will answer you: 'It is the hour to be drunken! Be drunken, if you would not be martyred slaves of Time; be drunken continually! With wine, with poetry, or with virtue, as you will.' " [*He grins at his father provocatively.*]

TYRONE [*thickly humorous*]  I wouldn't worry about the virtue part of it, if I were you. [*then disgustedly*] Pah! It's morbid nonsense! What little truth is in it you'll find nobly said in Shakespeare. [*then appreciatively*] But you recited it well, lad. Who wrote it?

EDMUND  Baudelaire.

TYRONE  Never heard of him.

EDMUND [*grins provocatively*]  He also wrote a poem about Jamie and the Great White Way.

TYRONE  That loafer! I hope to God he misses the last car and has to stay uptown!

EDMUND [*goes on, ignoring this*]  Although he was French and never saw Broadway and died before Jamie was born. He knew him and Little Old New York just the same. [*He recites the Symons' translation of Baudelaire's "Epilogue."*]

"With heart at rest I climbed the citadel's
Steep height, and saw the city as from a tower,
Hospital, brothel, prison, and such hells,

Where evil comes up softly like a flower.
Thou knowest, O Satan, patron of my pain,
Not for vain tears I went up at that hour;

But like an old sad faithful lecher, fain
To drink delight of that enormous trull
Whose hellish beauty makes me young again.

Whether thou sleep, with heavy vapours full,
Sodden with day, or, new apparelled, stand
In gold-laced veils of evening beautiful,

I love thee, infamous city! Harlots and
Hunted have pleasures of their own to give,
The vulgar herd can never understand."

TYRONE [*with irritable disgust*]  Morbid filth! Where the hell do you get your taste in literature? Filth and despair and pessimism! Another atheist, I suppose. When you deny God, you deny hope. That's the trouble with you. If you'd get down on your knees—

EDMUND [*as if he hadn't heard—sardonically*]  It's a good likeness of Jamie, don't you think, hunted by himself and whiskey, hiding in a Broadway hotel room with some fat tart—he likes them fat—reciting Dowson's Cynara to her. [*He recites derisively, but with deep feeling*]

"All night upon mine heart I felt her warm heart beat,
Night-long within mine arms in love and sleep she lay;

Surely the kisses of her bought red mouth were sweet;
But I was desolate and sick of an old passion,
When I awoke and found the dawn was gray:
I have been faithful to thee, Cynara! in my fashion."
[ *jeeringly*] And the poor fat burlesque queen doesn't get a word of it, but
suspects she's being insulted! And Jamie never loved any Cynara, and was
never faithful to a woman in his life, even in his fashion! But he lies there,
kidding himself he is superior and enjoys pleasures "the vulgar herd can
never understand"! [*He laughs.*] It's nuts—completely nuts!

TYRONE [*vaguely—his voice thick*]   It's madness, yes. If you'd get on your
knees and pray. When you deny God, you deny sanity.

EDMUND [*ignoring this*]   But who am I to feel superior? I've done the same
damned thing. And it's no more crazy than Dowson himself, inspired by an
absinthe hangover, writing it to a dumb barmaid, who thought he was a
poor crazy souse, and gave him the gate to marry a waiter! [*He laughs—then
soberly, with genuine sympathy*] Poor Dowson. Booze and consumption got
him. [*He starts and for a second looks miserable and frightened. Then with
defensive irony*] Perhaps it would be tactful of me to change the subject.

TYRONE [*thickly*]   Where you get your taste in authors— That damned library
of yours! [*He indicates the small bookcase at rear.*] Voltaire, Rousseau,
Schopenhauer, Nietzsche, Ibsen! Atheists, fools, and madmen! And your
poets! This Dowson, and this Baudelaire, and Swinburne and Oscar Wilde,
and Whitman and Poe! Whore-mongers and degenerates! Pah! When I've
three good sets of Shakespeare there [*he nods at the large bookcase*] you
could read.

EDMUND [*provocatively*]   They say he was a souse, too.

TYRONE   They lie! I don't doubt he liked his glass—it's a good man's failing—
but he knew how to drink so it didn't poison his brain with morbidness and
filth. Don't compare him with the pack you've got in there. [*He indicates
the small bookcase again.*] Your dirty Zola! And your Dante Gabriel Rossetti
who was a dope fiend! [*He starts and looks guilty.*]

EDMUND [*with defensive dryness*]   Perhaps it would be wise to change the subject. [*a pause*] You can't accuse me of not knowing Shakespeare. Didn't I
win five dollars from you once when you bet me I couldn't learn a leading
part of his in a week, as you used to do in stock in the old days. I learned
Macbeth and recited it letter perfect, with you giving me the cues.

TYRONE [*approvingly*]   That's true. So you did. [*He smiles teasingly and
sighs.*] It was a terrible ordeal, I remember, hearing you murder the lines. I
kept wishing I'd paid over the bet without making you prove it.

[*He chuckles and* EDMUND *grins. Then he starts as he hears a sound
from upstairs—with dread*]
Did you hear? She's moving around. I was hoping she'd gone to sleep.

EDMUND   Forget it! How about another drink?

[*He reaches out and gets the bottle, pours a drink and hands it back.
Then with a strained casualness, as his father pours a drink*]
When did Mama go to bed?

TYRONE   Right after you left. She wouldn't eat any dinner. What made you
run away?

EDMUND   Nothing. [*Abruptly raising his glass.*] Well, here's how.

TYRONE [*mechanically*]   Drink hearty, lad. [*They drink.* TYRONE *again listens
to sounds upstairs—with dread*] She's moving around a lot. I hope to God
she doesn't come down.

EDMUND [*dully*]   Yes. She'll be nothing but a ghost haunting the past by this
  time. [*He pauses—then miserably*] Back before I was born—
TYRONE   Doesn't she do the same with me? Back before she ever knew me.
  You'd think the only happy days she's ever known were in her father's home,
  or at the Convent, praying and playing the piano. [ *jealous resentment in his
  bitterness*] As I've told you before, you must take her memories with a grain
  of salt. Her wonderful home was ordinary enough. Her father wasn't the
  great, generous, noble Irish gentleman she makes out. He was a nice
  enough man, good company and a good talker. I liked him and he liked
  me. He was prosperous enough, too, in his wholesale grocery business, an
  able man. But he had his weakness. She condemns my drinking but she
  forgets his. It's true he never touched a drop till he was forty, but after that
  he made up for lost time. He became a steady champagne drinker, the worst
  kind. That was his grand pose, to drink only champagne. Well, it finished
  him quick—that and the consumption—[*He stops with a guilty glance at
  his son.*]
EDMUND [*sardonically*]   We don't seem able to avoid unpleasant topics, do
  we?
TYRONE [*sighs sadly*]   No. [*then with a pathetic attempt at heartiness*] What
  do you say to a game or two of Casino, lad?
EDMUND   All right.
TYRONE [*shuffling the cards clumsily*]   We can't lock up and go to bed till
  Jamie comes on the last trolley—which I hope he won't—and I don't want
  to go upstairs, anyway, till she's asleep.
EDMUND   Neither do I.
TYRONE [*keeps shuffling the cards fumblingly, forgetting to deal them*]   As I
  was saying, you must take her tales of the past with a grain of salt. The piano
  playing and her dream of becoming a concert pianist. That was put in her
  head by the nuns flattering her. She was their pet. They loved her for being
  so devout. They're innocent women, anyway, when it comes to the world.
  They don't know that not one in a million who shows promise ever rises to
  concert playing. Not that your mother didn't play well for a schoolgirl, but
  that's no reason to take it for granted she could have—
EDMUND [*sharply*]   Why don't you deal, if we're going to play.
TYRONE   Eh? I am. [*dealing with very uncertain judgment of distance*] And
  the idea she might have become a nun. That's the worst. Your mother was
  one of the most beautiful girls you could ever see. She knew it, too. She
  was a bit of a rogue and a coquette, God bless her, behind all her shyness
  and blushes. She was never made to renounce the world. She was bursting
  with health and high spirits and the love of loving.
EDMUND   For God's sake, Papa! Why don't you pick up your hand?
TYRONE [ *picks it up—dully*]   Yes, let's see what I have here.
    [*They both stare at their cards unseeingly. Then they both start.*
    TYRONE *whispers*]
  Listen!
EDMUND   She's coming downstairs.
TYRONE [*hurriedly*]   We'll play our game. Pretend not to notice and she'll
  soon go up again.
EDMUND [*staring through the front parlor—with relief*]   I don't see her. She
  must have started down and then turned back.
TYRONE   Thank God.
EDMUND   Yes. It's pretty horrible to see her the way she must be now. [*with

*bitter misery*] The hardest thing to take is the blank wall she builds around her. Or it's more like a bank of fog in which she hides and loses herself. Deliberately, that's the hell of it! You know something in her does it deliberately—to get beyond our reach, to be rid of us, to forget we're alive! It's as if, in spite of loving us, she hated us!

TYRONE [*remonstrates gently*]    Now, now, lad. It's not her. It's the damned poison.

EDMUND [*bitterly*]    She takes it to get that effect. At least, I know she did this time! [*abruptly*] My play, isn't it? Here. [*He plays a card.*]

TYRONE [*plays mechanically—gently reproachful*]    She's been terribly frightened about your illness, for all her pretending. Don't be too hard on her, lad. Remember she's not responsible. Once that cursed poison gets a hold on anyone—

EDMUND [*his face grows hard and he stares at his father with bitter accusation*]    It never should have gotten a hold on her! I know damned well she's not to blame! And I know who is! You are! Your damned stinginess! If you'd spent money for a decent doctor when she was so sick after I was born, she'd never have known morphine existed! Instead you put her in the hands of a hotel quack who wouldn't admit his ignorance and took the easiest way out, not giving a damn what happened to her afterwards! All because his fee was cheap! Another one of your bargains!

TYRONE [*stung—angrily*]    Be quiet! How dare you talk of something you know nothing about! [*trying to control his temper*] You must try to see my side of it, too, lad. How was I to know he was that kind of a doctor? He had a good reputation—

EDMUND    Among the souses in the hotel bar, I suppose!

TYRONE    That's a lie! I asked the hotel proprietor to recommend the best—

EDMUND    Yes! At the same time crying poorhouse and making it plain you wanted a cheap one! I know your system! By God, I ought to after this afternoon!

TYRONE [*guiltily defensive*]    What about this afternoon?

EDMUND    Never mind now. We're talking about Mama! I'm saying no matter how you excuse yourself you know damned well your stinginess is to blame—

TYRONE    And I say you're a liar! Shut your mouth right now, or—

EDMUND [*ignoring this*]    After you found out she'd been made a morphine addict, why didn't you send her to a cure then, at the start, while she still had a chance? No, that would have meant spending some money! I'll bet you told her all she had to do was use a little will power! That's what you still believe in your heart, in spite of what doctors, who really know something about it, have told you!

TYRONE    You lie again! I know better than that now! But how was I to know then? What did I know of morphine? It was years before I discovered what was wrong. I thought she'd never got over her sickness, that's all. Why didn't I send her to a cure, you say? [*bitterly*] Haven't I? I've spent thousands upon thousands in cures! A waste. What good have they done her? She always started again.

EDMUND    Because you've never given her anything that would help her want to stay off it! No home except this summer dump in a place she hates and you've refused even to spend money to make this look decent, while you keep buying more property, and playing sucker for every con man with a gold mine, or a silver mine, or any kind of get-rich-quick swindle! You've dragged her around on the road, season after season, on one-night stands, with no one she could talk to, waiting night after night in dirty hotel rooms for you to come back with a bun on after the bars closed! Christ, is it any wonder she didn't want to be cured. Jesus, when I think of it I hate your guts!

TYRONE [*strickenly*]   Edmund! [*then in a rage*] How dare you talk to your father like that, you insolent young cub! After all I've done for you.

EDMUND   We'll come to that, what you're doing for me!

TYRONE [*looking guilty again—ignores this*]   Will you stop repeating your mother's crazy accusations, which she never makes unless it's the poison talking? I never dragged her on the road against her will. Naturally, I wanted her with me. I loved her. And she came because she loved me and wanted to be with me. That's the truth, no matter what she says when she's not herself. And she needn't have been lonely. There was always the members of my company to talk to, if she'd wanted. She had her children, too, and I insisted, in spite of the expense, on having a nurse to travel with her.

EDMUND [*bitterly*]   Yes, your one generosity, and that because you were jealous of her paying too much attention to us, and wanted us out of your way! It was another mistake, too! If she'd had to take care of me all by herself, and had that to occupy her mind, maybe she'd have been able—

TYRONE [*goaded into vindictiveness*]   Or for that matter, if you insist in judging things by what she says when she's not in her right mind, if you hadn't been born she'd never—[*He stops ashamed.*]

EDMUND [*suddenly spent and miserable*]   Sure. I know that's what she feels, Papa.

TYRONE [*protests penitently*]   She doesn't! She loves you as dearly as ever mother loved a son! I only said that because you put me in such a God-damned rage, raking up the past, and saying you hate me—

EDMUND [*dully*]   I didn't mean it, Papa. [*He suddenly smiles—kidding a bit drunkenly*] I'm like Mama, I can't help liking you, in spite of everything.

TYRONE [*grins a bit drunkenly in return*]   I might say the same of you. You're no great shakes as a son. It's a case of "A poor thing but mine own."[3] [*They both chuckle with real, if alcoholic, affection. TYRONE changes the subject.*] What's happened to our game? Whose play is it?

EDMUND   Yours, I guess.

[TYRONE *plays a card which* EDMUND *takes and the game gets forgotten again.*]

TYRONE   You mustn't let yourself be too downhearted, lad, by the bad news you had today. Both the doctors promised me, if you obey orders at this place you're going, you'll be cured in six months, or a year at most.

EDMUND [*his face hard again*]   Don't kid me. You don't believe that.

TYRONE [*too vehemently*]   Of course I believe it! Why shouldn't I believe it when both Hardy and the specialist—?

EDMUND   You think I'm going to die.

TYRONE   That's a lie! You're crazy!

EDMUND [*more bitterly*]   So why waste money? That's why you're sending me to a state farm—

TYRONE [*in guilty confusion*]   What state farm? It's the Hilltown Sanatorium, that's all I know, and both doctors said it was the best place for you.

EDMUND [*scathingly*]   For the money! That is, for nothing, or practically

3. Shakespeare, *As You Like It* 5.4.60.

nothing. Don't lie, Papa! You know damned well Hilltown Sanatorium is a state institution! Jamie suspected you'd cry poorhouse to Hardy and he wormed the truth out of him.

TYRONE [ *furiously* ]   That drunken loafer! I'll kick him out in the gutter! He's poisoned your mind against me ever since you were old enough to listen!

EDMUND   You can't deny it's the truth about the state farm, can you?

TYRONE   It's not true the way you look at it! What if it is run by the state? That's nothing against it. The state has the money to make a better place than any private sanatorium. And why shouldn't I take advantage of it? It's my right—and yours. We're residents. I'm a property owner. I help to support it. I'm taxed to death—

EDMUND [ *with bitter irony* ]   Yes, on property valued at a quarter of a million.

TYRONE   Lies! It's all mortgaged!

EDMUND   Hardy and the specialist know what you're worth. I wonder what they thought of you when they heard you moaning poorhouse and showing you wanted to wish me on charity!

TYRONE   It's a lie! All I told them was I couldn't afford any millionaire's sanatorium because I was land poor. That's the truth!

EDMUND   And then you went to the Club to meet McGuire and let him stick you with another bum piece of property! [ *as* TYRONE *starts to deny* ] Don't lie about it! We met McGuire in the hotel bar after he left you. Jamie kidded him about hooking you, and he winked and laughed!

TYRONE [ *lying feebly* ]   He's a liar if he said—

EDMUND   Don't lie about it! [ *with gathering intensity* ] God, Papa, ever since I went to sea and was on my own, and found out what hard work for little pay was, and what it felt like to be broke, and starve, and camp on park benches because I had no place to sleep, I've tried to be fair to you because I knew what you'd been up against as a kid. I've tried to make allowances. Christ, you have to make allowances in this damned family or go nuts! I have tried to make allowances for myself when I remember all the rotten stuff I've pulled! I've tried to feel like Mama that you can't help being what you are where money is concerned. But God Almighty, this last stunt of yours is too much! It makes me want to puke! Not because of the rotten way you're treating me. To hell with that! I've treated you rottenly, in my way, more than once. But to think when it's a question of your son having consumption, you can show yourself up before the whole town as such a stinking old tightwad! Don't you know Hardy will talk and the whole damned town will know! Jesus, Papa, haven't you any pride or shame? [ *bursting with rage* ] And don't think I'll let you get away with it! I won't go to any damned state farm just to save you a few lousy dollars to buy more bum property with! You stinking old miser—! [ *He chokes huskily, his voice trembling with rage, and then is shaken by a fit of coughing.* ]

TYRONE [ *has shrunk back in his chair under this attack, his guilty contrition greater than his anger—he stammers* ]   Be quiet! Don't say that to me! You're drunk! I won't mind you. Stop coughing, lad. You've got yourself worked up over nothing. Who said you had to go to this Hilltown place? You can go anywhere you like. I don't give a damn what it costs. All I care about is to have you get well. Don't call me a stinking miser, just because I don't want doctors to think I'm a millionaire they can swindle.

[ EDMUND *has stopped coughing. He looks sick and weak. His father stares at him frightenedly.* ]

You look weak, lad. You'd better take a bracer.

EDMUND [*grabs the bottle and pours his glass brimfull—weakly*] Thanks. [*He gulps down the whiskey.*]

TYRONE [*pours himself a big drink, which empties the bottle, and drinks it; his head bows and he stares dully at the cards on the table—vaguely*] Whose play is it? [*He goes on dully, without resentment.*] A stinking old miser. Well, maybe you're right. Maybe I can't help being, although all my life since I had anything I've thrown money over the bar to buy drinks for everyone in the house, or loaned money to sponges I knew would never pay it back—[*with a loose-mouthed sneer of self-contempt*] But, of course, that was in barrooms, when I was full of whiskey. I can't feel that way about it when I'm sober in my home. It was at home I first learned the value of a dollar and the fear of the poorhouse. I've never been able to believe in my luck since. I've always feared it would change and everything I had would be taken away. But still, the more property you own, the safer you think you are. That may not be logical, but it's the way I have to feel. Banks fail, and your money's gone, but you think you can keep land beneath your feet. [*Abruptly his tone becomes scornfully superior.*] You said you realized what I'd been up against as a boy. The hell you do! How could you? You've had everything—nurses, schools, college, though you didn't stay there. You've had food, clothing. Oh, I know you had a fling of hard work with your back and hands, a bit of being homeless and penniless in a foreign land, and I respect you for it. But it was a game of romance and adventure to you. It was play.

EDMUND [*dully sarcastic*] Yes, particularly the time I tried to commit suicide at Jimmie the Priest's, and almost did.

TYRONE You weren't in your right mind. No son of mine would ever—You were drunk.

EDMUND I was stone cold sober. That was the trouble. I'd stopped to think too long.

TYRONE [*with drunken peevishness*] Don't start your damned atheist morbidness again! I don't care to listen. I was trying to make plain to you—[*scornfully*] What do you know of the value of a dollar? When I was ten my father deserted my mother and went back to Ireland to die. Which he did soon enough, and deserved to, and I hope he's roasting in hell. He mistook rat poison for flour, or sugar, or something. There was gossip it wasn't by mistake but that's a lie. No one in my family ever—

EDMUND My bet is, it wasn't by mistake.

TYRONE More morbidness! Your brother put that in your head. The worst he can suspect is the only truth for him. But never mind. My mother was left, a stranger in a strange land, with four small children, me and a sister a little older and two younger than me. My two older brothers had moved to other parts. They couldn't help. They were hard put to it to keep themselves alive. There was no damned romance in our poverty. Twice we were evicted from the miserable hovel we called home, with my mother's few sticks of furniture thrown out in the street, and my mother and sisters crying. I cried, too, though I tried hard not to, because I was the man of the family. At ten years old! There was no more school for me. I worked twelve hours a day in a machine shop, learning to make files. A dirty barn of a place where rain dripped through the roof, where you roasted in summer, and there was no stove in winter, and your hands got numb with cold, where the only light came through two small filthy windows, so on grey days I'd have to sit bent over with my eyes almost touching the files in order to see! You talk of work!

And what do you think I got for it? Fifty cents a week! It's the truth! Fifty
cents a week! And my poor mother washed and scrubbed for the Yanks by
the day, and my older sister sewed, and my two younger stayed at home to
keep the house. We never had clothes enough to wear, nor enough food to
eat. Well I remember one Thanksgiving, or maybe it was Christmas, when
some Yank in whose house mother had been scrubbing gave her a dollar
extra for a present, and on the way home she spent it all on food. I can
remember her hugging and kissing us and saying with tears of joy running
down her tired face: "Glory be to God, for once in our lives we'll have
enough for each of us!" [He wipes tears from his eyes.] A fine, brave, sweet
woman. There never was a braver or finer.
EDMUND [moved]   Yes, she must have been.
TYRONE   Her one fear was she'd get old and sick and have to die in the poorhouse. [He pauses—then adds with grim humor] It was in those days I
learned to be a miser. A dollar was worth so much then. And once you've
learned a lesson, it's hard to unlearn it. You have to look for bargains. If I
took this state farm sanatorium for a good bargain, you'll have to forgive
me. The doctors did tell me it's a good place. You must believe that,
Edmund. And I swear I never meant you to go there if you didn't want to.
[vehemently] You can choose any place you like! Never mind what it costs!
Any place I can afford. Any place you like—within reason.
   [At this qualification, a grin twitches EDMUND's lips. His resentment
   has gone. His father goes on with an elaborately offhand, casual air.]
There was another sanatorium the specialist recommended. He said it had
a record as good as any place in the country. It's endowed by a group of
millionaire factory owners, for the benefit of their workers principally, but
you're eligible to go there because you're a resident. There's such a pile of
money behind it, they don't have to charge much. It's only seven dollars a
week but you get ten times that value. [hastily] I don't want to persuade you
to anything, understand. I'm simply repeating what I was told.
EDMUND [concealing his smile—casually]   Oh, I know that. It sounds like a
good bargain to me. I'd like to go there. So that settles that. [Abruptly he is
miserably desperate again—dully] It doesn't matter a damn now, anyway.
Let's forget it! [changing the subject] How about our game? Whose play is it?
TYRONE [mechanically]   I don't know. Mine, I guess. No, it's yours.
   [EDMUND plays a card. His father takes it. Then about to play from his
   hand, he again forgets the game.]
Yes, maybe life overdid the lesson for me, and made a dollar worth too
much, and the time came when that mistake ruined my career as a fine
actor. [sadly] I've never admitted this to anyone before, lad, but tonight I'm
so heartsick I feel at the end of everything, and what's the use of fake pride
and pretense. That God-damned play I bought for a song and made such a
great success in—a great money success—it ruined me with its promise of
an easy fortune. I didn't want to do anything else, and by the time I woke
up to the fact I'd become a slave to the damned thing and did try other
plays, it was too late. They had identified me with that one part, and didn't
want me in anything else. They were right, too. I'd lost the great talent I
once had through years of easy repetition, never learning a new part, never
really working hard. Thirty-five to forty thousand dollars net profit a season
like snapping your fingers! It was too great a temptation. Yet before I bought
the damned thing I was considered one of the three or four young actors
with the greatest artistic promise in America. I'd worked like hell. I'd left a

good job as a machinist to take supers'[4] parts because I loved the theater. I
was wild with ambition. I read all the plays ever written. I studied Shakespeare as you'd study the Bible. I educated myself. I got rid of an Irish
brogue you could cut with a knife. I loved Shakespeare. I would have acted
in any of his plays for nothing, for the joy of being alive in his great poetry.
And I acted well in him. I felt inspired by him. I could have been a great
Shakespearean actor, if I'd kept on. I know that! In 1874 when Edwin
Booth[5] came to the theater in Chicago where I was leading man, I played
Cassius to his Brutus one night, Brutus to his Cassius the next, Othello to
his Iago, and so on. The first night I played Othello, he said to our manager.
"That young man is playing Othello better than I ever did!" [*proudly*] That
from Booth, the greatest actor of his day or any other! And it was true! And
I was only twenty-seven years old! As I look back on it now, that night was
the high spot in my career. I had life where I wanted it! And for a time after
that I kept on upward with ambition high. Married your mother. Ask her
what I was like in those days. Her love was an added incentive to ambition.
But a few years later my good bad luck made me find the big money-maker.
It wasn't that in my eyes at first. It was a great romantic part I knew I could
play better than anyone. But it was a great box office success from the start—
and then life had me where it wanted me—at from thirty-five to forty thousand net profit a season! A fortune in those days—or even in these. [*bitterly*]
What the hell was it I wanted to buy, I wonder, that was worth—Well, no
matter. It's a late day for regrets. [*He glances vaguely at his cards.*] My play,
isn't it?

EDMUND [*moved, stares at his father with understanding—slowly*]   I'm glad
you've told me this, Papa. I know you a lot better now.

TYRONE [*with a loose, twisted smile*]   Maybe I shouldn't have told you. Maybe
you'll only feel more contempt for me. And it's a poor way to convince you
of the value of a dollar. [*Then as if this phrase automatically aroused an
habitual association in his mind, he glances up at the chandelier disapprovingly.*] The glare from those extra lights hurts my eyes. You don't mind if I
turn them out, do you? We don't need them, and there's no use making the
Electric Company rich.

EDMUND [*controlling a wild impulse to laugh—agreeably*]   No, sure not. Turn
them out.

TYRONE [*gets heavily and a bit waveringly to his feet and gropes uncertainly for
the lights—his mind going back to its line of thought*]   No, I don't know
what the hell it was I wanted to buy. [*He clicks out one bulb.*] On my solemn
oath, Edmund, I'd gladly face not having an acre of land to call my own,
nor a penny in the bank—[*He clicks out another bulb.*] I'd be willing to have
no home but the poorhouse in my old age if I could look back now on
having been the fine artist I might have been.

   [*He turns out the third bulb, so only the reading lamp is on, and sits
   down again heavily.* EDMUND *suddenly cannot hold back a burst of
   strained, ironical laughter.* TYRONE *is hurt.*]
What the devil are you laughing at?

EDMUND   Not at you, Papa. At life. It's so damned crazy.

TYRONE [*growls*]   More of your morbidness! There's nothing wrong with life.
It's we who—[*He quotes*] "The fault, dear Brutus, is not in our stars, but in

4. Supernumeraries', extras'.
5. Edwin Booth (1833–1893), American actor and theatrical manager.

ourselves that we are underlings."[6] [*He pauses—then sadly*] The praise
Edwin Booth gave my Othello. I made the manager put down his exact
words in writing. I kept it in my wallet for years. I used to read it every once
in a while until finally it made me feel so bad I didn't want to face it any
more. Where is it now, I wonder? Somewhere in this house. I remember I
put it away carefully—

EDMUND [*with a wry ironical sadness*]  It might be in an old trunk in the attic,
along with Mama's wedding dress. [*Then as his father stares at him, he adds
quickly*] For Pete's sake, if we're going to play cards, let's play.

     [*He takes the card his father had played and leads. For a moment,
they play the game, like mechanical chess players. Then* TYRONE *stops,
listening to a sound upstairs.*]

TYRONE  She's still moving around. God knows when she'll go to sleep.

EDMUND [*pleads tensely*]  For Christ's sake, Papa, forget it!

     [*He reaches out and pours a drink.* TYRONE *starts to protest, then gives
it up.* EDMUND *drinks. He puts down the glass. His expression changes.
When he speaks it is as if he were deliberately giving way to drunkenness and seeking to hide behind a maudlin manner.*]
Yes, she moves above and beyond us, a ghost haunting the past, and here
we sit pretending to forget, but straining our ears listening for the slightest
sound, hearing the fog drip from the eaves like the uneven tick of a rundown, crazy clock—or like the dreary tears of a trollop spattering in a puddle
of stale beer on a honky-tonk table top! [*He laughs with maudlin appreciation.*] Not so bad, that last, eh? Original, not Baudelaire. Give me credit!
[*then with alcoholic talkativeness*] You've just told me some high spots in
your memories. Want to hear mine? They're all connected with the sea.
Here's one. When I was on the Squarehead square rigger, bound for Buenos
Aires. Full moon in the Trades. The old hooker driving fourteen knots. I
lay on the bowsprit, facing astern, with the water foaming into spume under
me, the masts with every sail white in the moonlight, towering high above
me. I became drunk with the beauty and singing rhythm of it, and for a
moment I lost myself—actually lost my life. I was set free! I dissolved in the
sea, became white sails and flying spray, became beauty and rhythm,
became moonlight and the ship and the high dim-starred sky! I belonged,
without past or future, within peace and unity and a wild joy, within something greater than my own life, or the life of Man, to Life itself! To God, if
you want to put it that way. Then another time, on the American Line,
when I was lookout on the crow's nest in the dawn watch. A calm sea, that
time. Only a lazy ground swell and a slow drowsy roll of the ship. The
passengers asleep and none of the crew in sight. No sound of man. Black
smoke pouring from the funnels behind and beneath me. Dreaming, not
keeping lookout, feeling alone, and above, and apart, watching the dawn
creep like a painted dream over the sky and sea which slept together. Then
the moment of ecstatic freedom came. The peace, the end of the quest, the
last harbor, the joy of belonging to a fulfillment beyond men's lousy, pitiful,
greedy fears and hopes and dreams! And several other times in my life, when
I was swimming far out, or lying alone on a beach, I have had the same
experience. Became the sun, the hot sand, green seaweed anchored to a
rock, swaying in the tide. Like a saint's vision of beatitude. Like the veil of
things as they seem drawn back by an unseen hand. For a second you see—

---

6. Shakespeare, *Julius Caesar* 1.2.134.

and seeing the secret, are the secret. For a second there is meaning! Then the hand lets the veil fall and you are alone, lost in the fog again, and you stumble on toward nowhere, for no good reason! [*He grins wryly.*] It was a great mistake, my being born a man, I would have been much more successful as a sea gull or a fish. As it is, I will always be a stranger who never feels at home, who does not really want and is not really wanted, who can never belong, who must always be a little in love with death!

TYRONE [*stares at him—impressed*]  Yes, there's the makings of a poet in you all right. [*then protesting uneasily*] But that's morbid craziness about not being wanted and loving death.

EDMUND [*sardonically*]  The *makings* of a poet. No, I'm afraid I'm like the guy who is always panhandling for a smoke. He hasn't even got the makings. He's got only the habit. I couldn't touch what I tried to tell you just now. I just stammered. That's the best I'll ever do. I mean, if I live. Well, it will be faithful realism, at least. Stammering is the native eloquence of us fog people.

[*A pause. Then they both jump startledly as there is a noise from outside the house, as if someone had stumbled and fallen on the front steps.* EDMUND *grins.*]

Well, that sounds like the absent brother. He must have a peach of a bun on.

TYRONE [*scowling*]  That loafer! He caught the last car, bad luck to it. [*He gets to his feet.*] Get him to bed, Edmund. I'll go out on the porch. He has a tongue like an adder when he's drunk. I'd only lose my temper.

[*He goes out the door to the side porch as the front door in the hall bangs shut behind* JAMIE. EDMUND *watches with amusement* JAMIE's *wavering progress through the front parlor.* JAMIE *comes in. He is very drunk and woozy on his legs. His eyes are glassy, his face bloated, his speech blurred, his mouth slack like his father's, a leer on his lips.*]

JAMIE [*swaying and blinking in the doorway—in a loud voice*]  What ho! What ho!

EDMUND [*sharply*]  Nix on the loud noise!

JAMIE [*blinks at him*]  Oh, hello, Kid. [*with great seriousness*] I'm as drunk as a fiddler's bitch.

EDMUND [*dryly*]  Thanks for telling me your great secret.

JAMIE [*grins foolishly*]  Yes. Unneshesary information Number One, eh? [*He bends and slaps at the knees of his trousers.*] Had serious accident. The front steps tried to trample on me. Took advantage of fog to waylay me. Ought to be a lighthouse out there. Dark in here, too. [*scowling*] What the hell is this, the morgue? Lesh have some light on subject. [*He sways forward to the table, reciting Kipling[7]*]

> "Ford, ford, ford o' Kabul river,
> Ford o' Kabul river in the dark!
> Keep the crossing-stakes beside you, an' they
>      will surely guide you
> 'Cross the ford o' Kabul river in the dark."

[*He fumbles at the chandelier and manages to turn on the three bulbs.*] Thash more like it. The hell with old Gaspard.[8] Where is the old tightwad?

EDMUND  Out on the porch.

---

7. Rudyard Kipling (1865–1936), English author.      from a character in the popular drama *The Bells*.
8. Jamie's contemptuous name for his father, drawn

JAMIE    Can't expect us to live in the Black Hole of Calcutta.[9] [*His eyes fix on the full bottle of whiskey.*] Say! Have I got the d.t.'s?[1] [*He reaches out fumblingly and grabs it.*] By God, it's real. What's matter with the Old Man tonight? Must be ossified to forget he left this out. Grab opportunity by the forelock. Key to my success. [*He slops a big drink into a glass.*]

EDMUND    You're stinking now. That will knock you stiff.

JAMIE    Wisdom from the mouth of babes. Can the wise stuff, Kid. You're still wet behind the ears. [*He lowers himself into a chair, holding the drink carefully aloft.*]

EDMUND    All right. Pass out if you want to.

JAMIE    Can't, that's trouble. Had enough to sink a ship, but can't sink. Well, here's hoping. [*He drinks.*]

EDMUND    Shove over the bottle. I'll have one, too.

JAMIE    [*with sudden, big-brotherly solicitude, grabbing the bottle*]    No, you don't. Not while I'm around. Remember doctor's orders. Maybe no one else gives a damn if you die, but I do. My kid brother. I love your guts, Kid. Everything else is gone. You're all I've got left. [*pulling bottle closer to him*] So no booze for you, if I can help it. [*Beneath his drunken sentimentality there is a genuine sincerity.*]

EDMUND    [*irritably*]    Oh, lay off it.

JAMIE    [*is hurt and his face hardens*]    You don't believe I care, eh? Just drunken bull. [*He shoves the bottle over.*] All right. Go ahead and kill yourself.

EDMUND    [*seeing he is hurt—affectionately*]    Sure I know you care, Jamie, and I'm going on the wagon. But tonight doesn't count. Too many damned things have happened today. [*He pours a drink.*] Here's how. [*He drinks.*]

JAMIE    [*sobers up momentarily and with a pitying look*]    I know, Kid. It's been a lousy day for you. [*then with sneering cynicism*] I'll bet old Gaspard hasn't tried to keep you off booze. Probably give you a case to take with you to the state farm for pauper patients. The sooner you kick the bucket, the less expense. [*with contemptuous hatred*] What a bastard to have for a father! Christ, if you put him in a book, no one would believe it!

EDMUND    [*defensively*]    Oh, Papa's all right, if you try to understand him—and keep your sense of humor.

JAMIE    [*cynically*]    He's been putting on the old sob act for you, eh? He can always kid you. But not me. Never again. [*then slowly*] Although, in a way, I do feel sorry for him about one thing. But he has even that coming to him. He's to blame. [*hurriedly*] But to hell with that. [*He grabs the bottle and pours another drink, appearing very drunk again.*] That lash drink's getting me. This one ought to put the lights out. Did you tell Gaspard I got it out of Doc Hardy this sanatorium is a charity dump?

EDMUND    [*reluctantly*]    Yes. I told him I wouldn't go there. It's all settled now. He said I can go anywhere I want. [*He adds, smiling without resentment*] Within reason, of course.

JAMIE    [*drunkenly imitating his father*]    Of course, lad. Anything within reason. [*sneering*] That means another cheap dump. Old Gaspard, the miser in "The Bells," that's a part he can play without make-up.

EDMUND    [*irritably*]    Oh, shut up, will you. I've heard that Gaspard stuff a million times.

---

9. Small dungeon in Calcutta, India, where, on June 20, 1756, a total of 123 of 146 British prisoners died of suffocation. Hence, name for any small, cramped space.
1. Delirium tremens.

JAMIE [*shrugs his shoulders—thickly*]   Aw right, if you're shatisfied—let him get away with it. It's your funeral—I mean, I hope it won't be.
EDMUND [*changing the subject*]   What did you do uptown tonight? Go to Mamie Burns?
JAMIE [*very drunk, his head nodding*]   Sure thing. Where else could I find suitable feminine companionship? And love. Don't forget love. What is a man without a good woman's love? A God-damned hollow shell.
EDMUND [*chuckles tipsily, letting himself go now and be drunk*]   You're a nut.
JAMIE [*quotes with gusto from Oscar Wilde's[2] "The Harlot's House"*]
   "Then, turning to my love, I said,
   'The dead are dancing with the dead,
   The dust is whirling with the dust.'

   But she—she heard the violin,
   And left my side and entered in:
   Love passed into the house of lust.

   Then suddenly the tune went false,
   The dancers wearied of the waltz . . ."
[*He breaks off, thickly*] Not strictly accurate. If my love was with me, I didn't notice it. She must have been a ghost. [*He pauses.*] Guess which one of Mamie's charmers I picked to bless me with her woman's love. It'll hand you a laugh, Kid. I picked Fat Violet.
EDMUND [*laughs drunkenly*]   No, honest? Some pick! God, she weighs a ton. What the hell for, a joke?
JAMIE   No joke. Very serious. By the time I hit Mamie's dump I felt very sad about myself and all the other poor bums in the world. Ready for a weep on any old womanly bosom. You know how you get when John Barleycorn turns on the soft music inside you. Then, soon as I got in the door, Mamie began telling me all her troubles. Beefed how rotten business was, and she was going to give Fat Violet the gate. Customers didn't fall for Vi. Only reason she'd kept her was she could play the piano. Lately Vi's gone on drunks and been too boiled to play, and was eating her out of house and home, and although Vi was a goodhearted dumbbell, and she felt sorry for her because she didn't know how the hell she'd make a living, still business was business, and she couldn't afford to run a house for fat tarts. Well, that made me feel sorry for Fat Violet, so I squandered two bucks of your dough to escort her upstairs. With no dishonorable intentions whatever. I like them fat, but not that fat. All I wanted was a little heart-to-heart talk concerning the infinite sorrow of life.
EDMUND [*chuckles drunkenly*]   Poor Vi! I'll bet you recited Kipling and Swinburne and Dowson and gave her "I have been faithful to thee, Cynara, in my fashion."
JAMIE [*grins loosely*]   Sure—with the Old Master, John Barleycorn, playing soft music. She stood it for a while. Then she got good and sore. Got the idea I took her upstairs for a joke. Gave me a grand bawling out. Said she was better than a drunken bum who recited poetry. Then she began to cry. So I had to say I loved her because she was fat, and she wanted to believe that, and I stayed with her to prove it, and that cheered her up, and she kissed me when I left, and said she'd fallen hard for me, and we both cried

2. English author (1854–1900).

a little more in the hallway, and everything was fine, except Mamie Burns
thought I'd gone bughouse.

EDMUND [quotes derisively]

> "Harlots and
> Hunted have pleasures of their own to give,
> The vulgar herd can never understand."

JAMIE [nods his head drunkenly]   Egzactly! Hell of a good time, at that. You
should have stuck around with me, Kid. Mamie Burns inquired after you.
Sorry to hear you were sick. She meant it, too. [He pauses—then with
maudlin humor, in a ham-actor tone] This night has opened my eyes to a
great career in store for me, my boy! I shall give the art of acting back to the
performing seals, which are its most perfect expression. By applying my
natural God-given talents in their proper sphere, I shall attain the pinnacle
of success! I'll be the lover of the fat woman in Barnum and Bailey's circus!
[EDMUND laughs. JAMIE's mood changes to arrogant disdain.] Pah! Imagine
me sunk to the fat girl in a hick town hooker shop! Me! Who have made
some of the best-lookers on Broadway sit up and beg! [He quotes from Kipling's "Sestina of the Tramp-Royal"]

> "Speakin' in general, I 've tried 'em all,
> The 'appy roads that take you o'er the world."

[with sodden melancholy] Not so apt. Happy roads is bunk. Weary roads is
right. Get you nowhere fast. That's where I've got—nowhere. Where everyone lands in the end, even if most of the suckers won't admit it.

EDMUND [derisively]   Can it! You'll be crying in a minute.

JAMIE [starts and stares at his brother for a second with bitter hostility—thickly]
Don't get—too damned fresh. [then abruptly] But you're right. To hell with
repining! Fat Violet's a good kid. Glad I stayed with her. Christian act.
Cured her blues. Hell of a good time. You should have stuck with me, Kid.
Taken your mind off your troubles. What's the use coming home to get the
blues over what can't be helped. All over—finished now—not a hope! [He
stops, his head nodding drunkenly, his eyes closing—then suddenly he looks
up, his face hard, and quotes jeeringly.]

> "If I were hanged on the highest hill,
> Mother o' mine, O mother o' mine!
> I know whose love would follow me still . . ."

EDMUND [violently]   Shut up!

JAMIE [in a cruel, sneering tone with hatred in it]   Where's the hophead?
Gone to sleep?

[EDMUND jerks as if he'd been struck. There is a tense silence. EDMUND's
face looks stricken and sick. Then in a burst of rage he springs from
his chair.]

EDMUND   You dirty bastard!

[He punches his brother in the face, a blow that glances off the cheekbone. For a second JAMIE reacts pugnaciously and half rises from his
chair to do battle, but suddenly he seems to sober up to a shocked
realization of what he has said and he sinks back limply.]

JAMIE [miserably]   Thanks, Kid. I certainly had that coming. Don't know
what made me—booze talking— You know me, Kid.

EDMUND [his anger ebbing]   I know you'd never say that unless—But God,
Jamie, no matter how drunk you are, it's no excuse! [He pauses—miserably]
I'm sorry I hit you. You and I never scrap—that bad. [He sinks back on
his chair.]

JAMIE [*huskily*]   It's all right. Glad you did. My dirty tongue. Like to cut it
out. [*He hides his face in his hands—dully*] I suppose it's because I feel so
damned sunk. Because this time Mama had me fooled. I really believed she
had it licked. She thinks I always believe the worst, but this time I believed
the best. [*His voice flutters.*] I suppose I can't forgive her—yet. It meant so
much. I'd begun to hope, if she'd beaten the game, I could, too. [*He begins
to sob, and the horrible part of his weeping is that it appears sober, not the
maudlin tears of drunkenness.*]

EDMUND [*blinking back tears himself*]   God, don't I know how you feel! Stop
it, Jamie!

JAMIE [*trying to control his sobs*]   I've known about Mama so much longer
than you. Never forget the first time I got wise. Caught her in the act with
a hypo. Christ, I'd never dreamed before that any women but whores took
dope! [*He pauses.*] And then this stuff of you getting consumption. It's got
me licked. We've been more than brothers. You're the only pal I've ever
had. I love your guts. I'd do anything for you.

EDMUND [*reaches out and pats his arm*]   I know that, Jamie.

JAMIE [*his crying over—drops his hands from his face—with a strange bitterness*]   Yet I'll bet you've heard Mama and old Gaspard spill so much bunk
about my hoping for the worst, you suspect right now I'm thinking to myself
that Papa is old and can't last much longer, and if you were to die, Mama
and I would get all he's got, and so I'm probably hoping—

EDMUND [*indignantly*]   Shut up, you damned fool! What the hell put that in
your nut? [*He stares at his brother accusingly.*] Yes, that's what I'd like to
know. What put that in your mind?

JAMIE [*confusedly—appearing drunk again*]   Don't be a dumbbell! What I
said! Always suspected of hoping for the worst. I've got so I can't help—
[*then drunkenly resentful*] What are you trying to do, accuse me? Don't play
the wise guy with me! I've learned more of life than you'll ever know! Just
because you've read a lot of highbrow junk, don't think you can fool me!
You're only an overgrown kid! Mama's baby and Papa's pet! The family
White Hope! You've been getting a swelled head lately. About nothing!
About a few poems in a hick town newspaper! Hell, I used to write better
stuff for the Lit magazine in college! You better wake up! You're setting no
rivers on fire! You let hick town boobs flatter you with bunk about your
future—

[*Abruptly his tone changes to disgusted contrition.* EDMUND *has looked
away from him, trying to ignore this tirade.*]

Hell, Kid, forget it. That goes for Sweeny. You know I don't mean it. No
one hopes more than I do you'll knock 'em all dead. No one is prouder
you've started to make good. [*drunkenly assertive*] Why shouldn't I be
proud? Hell, it's purely selfish. You reflect credit on me. I've had more to
do with bringing you up than anyone. I wised you up about women, so
you'd never be a fall guy, or make any mistakes you didn't want to make!
And who steered you on to reading poetry first? Swinburne,[3] for example? I
did! And because I once wanted to write, I planted it in your mind that
someday you'd write! Hell, you're more than my brother. I made you!
You're my Frankenstein![4]

---

3. Algernon Charles Swinburne (1837–1909), English poet and critic.
4. In the novel *Frankenstein* by the English author
Mary Shelley (1797–1851), the scientist Dr. Franken-

stein creates a monster. Jamie confuses the scientist
with his creation, although it is possible that the mistake is O'Neill's.

[*He has risen to a note of drunken arrogance.* EDMUND *is grinning with amusement now.*]

EDMUND    All right, I'm your Frankenstein. So let's have a drink. [*He laughs.*] You crazy nut!

JAMIE [*thickly*]    I'll have a drink. Not you. Got to take care of you. [*He reaches out with a foolish grin of doting affection and grabs his brother's hand.*] Don't be scared of this sanatorium business. Hell, you can beat that standing on your head. Six months and you'll be in the pink. Probably haven't got consumption at all. Doctors lot of fakers. Told me years ago to cut out booze or I'd soon be dead—and here I am. They're all con men. Anything to grab your dough. I'll bet this state farm stuff is political graft game. Doctors get a cut for every patient they send.

EDMUND [*disgustedly amused*]    You're the limit! At the Last Judgment, you'll be around telling everyone it's in the bag.

JAMIE    And I'll be right. Slip a piece of change to the Judge and be saved, but if you're broke you can go to hell!

[*He grins at this blasphemy and* EDMUND *has to laugh.* JAMIE *goes on.*] "Therefore put money in thy purse."[5] That's the only dope. [*mockingly*] The secret of my success! Look what it's got me!

[*He lets* EDMUND's *hand go to pour a big drink, and gulps it down. He stares at his brother with bleary affection—takes his hand again and begins to talk thickly but with a strange, convincing sincerity.*] Listen, Kid, you'll be going away. May not get another chance to talk. Or might not be drunk enough to tell you truth. So got to tell you now. Something I ought to have told you long ago—for your own good.

[*He pauses—struggling with himself.* EDMUND *stares, impressed and uneasy. Jamie blurts out*] Not drunken bull, but "in vino veritas"[6] stuff. You better take it seriously. Want to warn you—against me. Mama and Papa are right. I've been rotten bad influence. And worst of it is, I did it on purpose.

EDMUND [*uneasily*]    Shut up! I don't want to hear—

JAMIE    Nix, Kid! You listen! Did it on purpose to make a bum of you. Or part of me did. A big part. That part that's been dead so long. That hates life. My putting you wise so you'd learn from my mistakes. Believed that myself at times, but it's a fake. Made my mistakes look good. Made getting drunk romantic. Made whores fascinating vampires instead of poor, stupid, diseased slobs they really are. Made fun of work as sucker's game. Never wanted you succeed and make me look even worse by comparison. Wanted you to fail. Always jealous of you. Mama's baby, Papa's pet! [*He stares at* EDMUND *with increasing enmity.*] And it was your being born that started Mama on dope. I know that's not your fault, but all the same, God damn you, I can't help hating your guts—!

EDMUND [*almost frightenedly*]    Jamie! Cut it out! You're crazy!

JAMIE    But don't get wrong idea, Kid. I love you more than I hate you. My saying what I'm telling you now proves it. I run the risk you'll hate me— and you're all I've got left. But I didn't mean to tell you that last stuff—go that far back. Don't know what made me. What I wanted to say is, I'd like to see you become the greatest success in the world. But you'd better be on your guard. Because I'll do my damnedest to make you fail. Can't help it. I hate myself. Got to take revenge. On everyone else. Especially you. Oscar

---

5. Shakespeare, *Othello* 1.3.354.                6. In wine there is truth (Latin).

Wilde's "Reading Gaol" has the dope twisted. The man was dead and so he had to kill the thing he loved. That's what it ought to be. The dead part of me hopes you won't get well. Maybe he's even glad the game has got Mama again! He wants company, he doesn't want to be the only corpse around the house! [*He gives a hard, tortured laugh.*]

EDMUND    Jesus, Jamie! You really have gone crazy!

JAMIE    Think it over and you'll see I'm right. Think it over when you're away from me in the sanatorium. Make up your mind you've got to tie a can to me—get me out of your life——think of me as dead—tell people, "I had a brother, but he's dead." And when you come back, look out for me. I'll be waiting to welcome you with that "my old pal" stuff, and give you the glad hand, and at the first good chance I get stab you in the back.

EDMUND    Shut up! I'll be God-damned if I'll listen to you any more—

JAMIE    [*as if he hadn't heard*]    Only don't forget me. Remember I warned you—for your sake. Give me credit. Greater love hath no man than this, that he saveth his brother from himself. [*very drunkenly, his head bobbing*] That's all. Feel better now. Gone to confession. Know you absolve me, don't you, Kid? You understand. You're a damned fine kid. Ought to be. I made you. So go and get well. Don't die on me. You're all I've got left. God bless you, Kid. [*His eyes close. He mumbles*] That last drink—the old K. O.

[*He falls into a drunken doze, not completely asleep.* EDMUND *buries his face in his hands miserably.* TYRONE *comes in quietly through the screen door from the porch, his dressing gown wet with fog, the collar turned up around his throat. His face is stern and disgusted but at the same time pitying.* EDMUND *does not notice his entrance.*]

TYRONE    [*in a low voice*]    Thank God he's asleep.

[EDMUND *looks up with a start.*]

I thought he'd never stop talking. [*He turns down the collar of his dressing gown.*] We'd better let him stay where he is and sleep it off.

[EDMUND *remains silent.* TYRONE *regards him—then goes on*]

I heard the last part of his talk. It's what I've warned you. I hope you'll heed the warning, now it comes from his own mouth.

[EDMUND *gives no sign of having heard.* TYRONE *adds pityingly*]

But don't take it too much to heart, lad. He loves to exaggerate the worst of himself when he's drunk. He's devoted to you. It's the one good thing left in him. [*He looks down on* JAMIE *with a bitter sadness.*] A sweet spectacle for me! My first-born, who I hoped would bear my name in honor and dignity, who showed such brilliant promise!

EDMUND    [*miserably*]    Keep quiet, can't you, Papa?

TYRONE    [*pours a drink*]    A waste! A wreck, a drunken hulk, done with and finished!

[*He drinks.* JAMIE *has become restless, sensing his father's presence, struggling up from his stupor. Now he gets his eyes open to blink up at* TYRONE. *The latter moves back a step defensively, his face growing hard.*]

JAMIE    [*suddenly points a finger at him and recites with dramatic emphasis*]
       "Clarence is come, false, fleeting, perjured Clarence,
       That stabbed me in the field by Tewksbury.
       Seize on him, Furies, take him into torment."[7]

7. Shakespeare, *Richard III* 1.4.55–57.

[*then resentfully*] What the hell are you staring at? [*He recites sardonically from Rossetti*[8]]
"Look in my face. My name is Might-Have-Been;
I am also called No More, Too Late, Farewell."

TYRONE    I'm well aware of that, and God knows I don't want to look at it.

EDMUND    Papa! Quit it!

JAMIE [*derisively*]    Got a great idea for you, Papa. Put on revival of "The Bells" this season. Great part in it you can play without make-up. Old Gaspard, the miser!

[TYRONE *turns away, trying to control his temper.*]

EDMUND    Shut up, Jamie!

JAMIE [*jeeringly*]    I claim Edwin Booth never saw the day when he could give as good a performance as a trained seal. Seals are intelligent and honest. They don't put up any bluffs about the Art of Acting. They admit they're just hams earning their daily fish.

TYRONE [*stung, turns on him in a rage*]    You loafer!

EDMUND    Papa! Do you want to start a row that will bring Mama down? Jamie, go back to sleep! You've shot off your mouth too much already.

[TYRONE *turns away.*]

JAMIE [*thickly*]    All right, Kid. Not looking for argument. Too damned sleepy.

[*He closes his eyes, his head nodding.* TYRONE *comes to the table and sits down, turning his chair so he won't look at* JAMIE. *At once he becomes sleepy, too.*]

TYRONE [*heavily*]    I wish to God she'd go to bed so that I could, too. [*drowsily*] I'm dog tired. I can't stay up all night like I used to. Getting old—old and finished. [*with a bone-cracking yawn*] Can't keep my eyes open. I think I'll catch a few winks. Why don't you do the same, Edmund? It'll pass the time until she—

*His voice trails off. His eyes close, his chin sags, and he begins to breathe heavily through his mouth.* EDMUND *sits tensely. He hears something and jerks nervously forward in his chair, staring through the front parlor into the hall. He jumps up with a hunted, distracted expression. It seems for a second he is going to hide in the back parlor. Then he sits down again and waits, his eyes averted, his hands gripping the arms of his chair. Suddenly all five bulbs of the chandelier in the front parlor are turned on from a wall switch, and a moment later someone starts playing the piano in there—the opening of one of Chopin's*[9] *simpler waltzes, done with a forgetful, stiff-fingered groping, as if an awkward schoolgirl were practicing it for the first time.* TYRONE *starts to wide-awakeness and sober dread, and* JAMIE's *head jerks back and his eyes open. For a moment they listen frozenly. The playing stops as abruptly as it began, and* MARY *appears in the doorway. She wears a sky-blue dressing gown over her nightdress, dainty slippers and pompons on her bare feet. Her face is paler than ever. Her eyes look enormous. They glisten like polished black jewels. The uncanny thing is that her face now appears so youthful. Experience seems ironed out of it. It is a marble mask of girlish innocence, the mouth caught in a shy smile. Her white hair is braided in two pigtails which hang over her breast. Over one arm, carried neglectfully, trailing on the floor, as if she had forgotten she held it, is an old-fashioned white satin wedding gown, trimmed with duchesse lace. She hesitates in the doorway,*

---

8. Dante Gabriel Rossetti (1821–1882), English poet and painter.

9. Frederic Chopin (1810–1849), Polish composer famous for works for the piano.

*glancing round the room, her forehead puckered puzzledly, like some-*
*one who has come to a room to get something but has become absent-*
*minded on the way and forgotten what it was. They stare at her. She*
*seems aware of them merely as she is aware of other objects in the room,*
*the furniture, the windows, familiar things she accepts automatically*
*as naturally belonging there but which she is too preoccupied to notice.*
JAMIE [*breaks the cracking silence—bitterly, self-defensively sardonic*] The
Mad Scene. Enter Ophelia![1]
     [*His father and brother both turn on him fiercely.* EDMUND *is quicker.*
     *He slaps* JAMIE *across the mouth with the back of his hand.*]
TYRONE [*his voice trembling with suppressed fury*]  Good boy, Edmund. The
dirty blackguard! His own mother!
JAMIE [*mumbles guiltily, without resentment*]  All right, Kid. Had it coming.
But I told you how much I'd hoped—[*He puts his hands over his face and*
*begins to sob.*]
TYRONE  I'll kick you out in the gutter tomorrow, so help me God. [*But*
JAMIE's *sobbing breaks his anger, and he turns and shakes his shoulder, plead-*
*ing*] Jamie, for the love of God, stop it!
     [*Then* MARY *speaks, and they freeze into silence again, staring at her.*
     *She has paid no attention whatever to the incident. It is simply a part*
     *of the familiar atmosphere of the room, a background which does not*
     *touch her preoccupation; and she speaks aloud to herself, not to them.*]
MARY  I play so badly now. I'm all out of practice. Sister Theresa will give me
a dreadful scolding. She'll tell me it isn't fair to my father when he spends
so much money for extra lessons. She's quite right, it isn't fair, when he's
so good and generous, and so proud of me. I'll practice every day from now
on. But something horrible has happened to my hands. The fingers have
gotten so stiff—[*She lifts her hands to examine them with a frightened puz-*
*zlement.*] The knuckles are all swollen. They're so ugly. I'll have to go to
the Infirmary and show Sister Martha. [*with a sweet smile of affectionate*
*trust*] She's old and a little cranky, but I love her just the same, and she has
things in her medicine chest that'll cure anything. She'll give me something
to rub on my hands, and tell me to pray to the Blessed Virgin, and they'll
be well again in no time. [*She forgets her hands and comes into the room,*
*the wedding gown trailing on the floor. She glances around vaguely, her*
*forehead puckered again.*] Let me see. What did I come here to find? It's
terrible, how absent-minded I've become. I'm always dreaming and
forgetting.
TYRONE [*in a stifled voice*]  What's that she's carrying, Edmund?
EDMUND [*dully*]  Her wedding gown, I suppose.
TYRONE  Christ! [*He gets to his feet and stands directly in her path—in*
*anguish*] Mary! Isn't it bad enough—? [*controlling himself—gently persua-*
*sive*] Here, let me take it, dear. You'll only step on it and tear it and get it
dirty dragging it on the floor. Then you'd be sorry afterwards.
     [*She lets him take it, regarding him from somewhere far away within*
     *herself, without recognition, without either affection or animosity.*]
MARY [*with the shy politeness of a well-bred young girl toward an elderly gentle-*
*man who relieves her of a bundle*]  Thank you. You are very kind. [*She*
*regards the wedding gown with a puzzled interest.*] It's a wedding gown. It's
very lovely, isn't it? [*A shadow crosses her face and she looks vaguely uneasy.*]
I remember now. I found it in the attic hidden in a trunk. But I don't know

---

1. An allusion to Shakespeare, *Hamlet.*

what I wanted it for. I'm going to be a nun—that is, if I can only find—[*She looks around the room, her forehead puckered again.*] What is it I'm looking for? I know it's something I lost. [*She moves back from* TYRONE, *aware of him now only as some obstacle in her path.*]

TYRONE [*in hopeless appeal*] Mary!
> [*But it cannot penetrate her preoccupation. She doesn't seem to hear him. He gives up helplessly, shrinking into himself, even his defensive drunkenness taken from him, leaving him sick and sober. He sinks back on his chair, holding the wedding gown in his arms with an unconscious clumsy, protective gentleness.*]

JAMIE [*drops his hand from his face, his eyes on the table top. He has suddenly sobered up, too—dully*] It's no good, Papa. [*He recites from Swinburne's "A Leave-taking" and does it well, simply but with a bitter sadness.*]
> "Let us rise up and part; she will not know.
> Let us go seaward as the great winds go,
> Full of blown sand and foam; what help is here?
> There is no help, for all these things are so,
> And all the world is bitter as a tear.
> And how these things are, though ye strove to show,
> She would not know."

MARY [*looking around her*] Something I miss terribly. It can't be altogether lost. [*She starts to move around in back of* JAMIE's *chair.*]

JAMIE [*turns to look up into her face—and cannot help appealing pleadingly in his turn*] Mama!
> [*She does not seem to hear. He looks away hopelessly.*]

Hell! What's the use? It's no good. [*He recites from "A Leave-taking" again with increased bitterness.*]
> "Let us go hence, my songs; she will not hear.
> Let us go hence together without fear;
> Keep silence now, for singing-time is over,
> And over all old things and all things dear.
> She loves not you nor me as all we love her.
> Yea, though we sang as angels in her ear,
> She would not hear."

MARY [*looking around her*] Something I need terribly. I remember when I had it I was never lonely nor afraid. I can't have lost it forever, I would die if I thought that. Because then there would be no hope.
> [*She moves like a sleepwalker, around the back of* JAMIE's *chair, then forward toward left front, passing behind* EDMUND.]

EDMUND [*turns impulsively and grabs her arm. As he pleads he has the quality of a bewilderedly hurt little boy.*] Mama! It isn't a summer cold! I've got consumption!

MARY [*For a second he seems to have broken through to her. She trembles and her expression becomes terrified. She calls distractedly, as if giving a command to herself.*] No! [*And instantly she is far away again. She murmurs gently but impersonally*] You must not try to touch me. You must not try to hold me. It isn't right, when I am hoping to be a nun.
> [*He lets his hand drop from her arm. She moves left to the front end of the sofa beneath the windows and sits down, facing front, her hands folded in her lap, in a demure school-girlish pose.*]

JAMIE [*gives Edmund a strange look of mingled pity and jealous gloating*] You damned fool. It's no good. [*He recites again from the Swinburne poem.*]

"Let us go hence, go hence; she will not see.
Sing all once more together; surely she,
She too, remembering days and words that were,
Will turn a little toward us, sighing; but we,
We are hence, we are gone, as though we had not been there.
Nay, and though all men seeing had pity on me,
She would not see."

TYRONE [*trying to shake off his hopeless stupor*] Oh, we're fools to pay any attention. It's the damned poison. But I've never known her to drown herself in it as deep as this. [*gruffly*] Pass me that bottle, Jamie. And stop reciting that damned morbid poetry. I won't have it in my house!

[ JAMIE *pushes the bottle toward him. He pours a drink without disarranging the wedding gown he holds carefully over his other arm and on his lap, and shoves the bottle back.* JAMIE *pours his and passes the bottle to* EDMUND, *who, in turn, pours one.* TYRONE *lifts his glass and his sons follow suit mechanically, but before they can drink* MARY *speaks and they slowly lower their drinks to the table, forgetting them.*]

MARY [*staring dreamily before her. Her face looks extraordinarily youthful and innocent. The shyly eager, trusting smile is on her lips as she talks aloud to herself.*] I had a talk with Mother Elizabeth. She is so sweet and good. A saint on earth. I love her dearly. It may be sinful of me but I love her better than my own mother. Because she always understands, even before you say a word. Her kind blue eyes look right into your heart. You can't keep any secrets from her. You couldn't deceive her, even if you were mean enough to want to. [*She gives a little rebellious toss of her head—with girlish pique*] All the same, I don't think she was so understanding this time. I told her I wanted to be a nun. I explained how sure I was of my vocation, that I had prayed to the Blessed Virgin to make me sure, and to find me worthy. I told Mother I had had a true vision when I was praying in the shrine of Our Lady of Lourdes, on the little island in the lake. I said I knew, as surely as I knew I was kneeling there, that the Blessed Virgin had smiled and blessed me with her consent. But Mother Elizabeth told me I must be more sure than that, even, that I must prove it wasn't simply my imagination. She said, if I was so sure, then I wouldn't mind putting myself to a test by going home after I graduated, and living as other girls lived, going out to parties and dances and enjoying myself; and then if after a year or two I still felt sure, I could come back to see her and we would talk it over again. [*She tosses her head—indignantly*] I never dreamed Holy Mother would give me such advice! I was really shocked. I said, of course, I would do anything she suggested, but I knew it was simply a waste of time. After I left her, I felt all mixed up, so I went to the shrine and prayed to the Blessed Virgin and found peace again because I knew she heard my prayer and would always love me and see no harm ever came to me so long as I never lost my faith in her. [*She pauses and a look of growing uneasiness comes over her face. She passes a hand over her forehead as if brushing cobwebs from her brain— vaguely*] That was in the winter of senior year. Then in the spring something happened to me. Yes, I remember. I fell in love with James Tyrone and was so happy for a time. [*She stares before her in a sad dream.* TYRONE *stirs in his chair.* EDMUND *and* JAMIE *remain motionless.*]

CURTAIN

1940

# KATHERINE ANNE PORTER

## 1890–1980

Katherine Anne Porter's literary output was small: over a long writing life she produced only four books of stories and one novel, *Ship of Fools*, which did not appear until she was over seventy. But each story was a masterpiece of technical skill and emotional power, combining traditional narrative ability with new symbolic techniques and modern subject matter like dreams and sex. It was to other writers that the difficulty of her achievement—her ability to sustain stylistic clarity and elegance while treating the most intense human emotions—was especially evident.

Callie Porter—she changed the name to the more sophisticated Katherine Anne when she became a writer—was born in the small settlement of Indian Creek, Texas; her young mother died soon after giving birth to her fourth child when Porter was not quite two years old. Her father moved them all to his mother's tiny home in Kyle, Texas. There the maternal grandmother raised the family in extreme poverty, and the father gave up all attempts to support them either financially or emotionally. The security provided by the strong, loving, but puritanically pious and stern grandmother ended with her death when Porter was eleven. She married to leave home immediately after her sixteenth birthday, only to find that rooted domesticity was not for her. Long before her divorce in 1915 she had separated from her first husband and begun a life of travel, activity, and changes of jobs.

She started writing in 1917 as a reporter for a Fort Worth newspaper. In 1918 she moved to Denver, the next year to New York City's Greenwich Village. Between 1920 and 1923 she lived mainly in Mexico, free-lancing, meeting artists and intellectuals, and becoming involved in revolutionary politics. In Mexico she found the resources of journalism inadequate to her ambitions; using an anecdote she had heard from an archaeologist as a kernel, she wrote her first story, *Maria Conception*, which was published in the prestigious *Century* magazine in 1922. Like all her stories, it dealt with powerful emotions and had a strong sense of locale. Critics praised her as a major talent.

Although she considered herself a serious writer from this time on, Porter was distracted from fiction by many crosscurrents. A self-supporting woman with expensive tastes, she hesitated to give up lucrative free-lance offers. She enjoyed travel and gladly took on jobs that sent her abroad. She became involved in political causes, including the Sacco-Vanzetti case. She was married four times.

Porter planned each story meticulously—taking extensive notes, devising scenarios, roughing out dialogue, and revising many times, sometimes over a period of years. She found the process of writing fiction to be emotionally painful. She did not write confessional or simple autobiographical fiction, but each story originated in an important real experience of her life—*Old Mortality*, for example, in her early marriage—and drew on her deepest feelings. And while each story mirrored real experience, it also reformed that experience into something more personally acceptable to her; Miranda's aristocratic southern background, for example, denies and disguises Porter's poor-white poverty. Although not a feminist, Porter devoted much of her work to exploring the tensions in women's lives in the modern era.

The story that made Porter famous for life, with the result that everything she published thereafter was looked on as a literary event, was *Flowering Judas* (1929), set in Mexico and dealing with revolutionary politics, love affairs, and betrayal. It appeared in the little magazine *Hound and Horn*. The collections *Flowering Judas* and *Noon Wine* came out in 1930 and 1937. In 1930 Porter went back to Mexico and the following year to Europe on a Guggenheim fellowship; she lived in Berlin, Paris, and Basel before returning to the United States in 1936. Two more collections of stories and novellas appeared in 1939 (*Pale Horse, Pale Rider*) and 1944 (*The Leaning Tower*). In these later collections there are several stories about Miranda Gay, the heroine of *The Fig Tree*, who is clearly a refraction of Porter herself.

Soon after arriving in Europe in 1931 Porter began working on a novel, but it was not until 1962 that *Ship of Fools*, which runs to almost five hundred printed pages, appeared. Set on board an ocean liner crossing the Atlantic to Germany in August 1931, it explores the characters and developing relationships of a large number of passengers; the ship, as Porter wrote in a preface, stands for "this world on its voyage to eternity." *Ship of Fools* was made into an ambitious film with several Hollywood stars and brought Porter a great deal of money. Capitalizing on the publicity, her publishers brought out the *Collected Stories* in 1965, from which followed the National Book Award, the Pulitzer Prize, the Gold Medal for fiction of the National Institute of Arts and Letters, and election to the American Academy of Letters, all in the next two years. During the last years of her life, she endowed and establishing the Katherine Anne Porter Room at the University of Maryland, not far from her last home near Washington, D.C.

# The Fig Tree

Old Aunt Nannie had a habit of gripping with her knees to hold Miranda while she brushed her hair or buttoned her dress down the back. When Miranda wriggled, Aunt Nannie squeezed still harder, and Miranda wriggled more, but never enough to get away. Aunt Nannie gathered up Miranda's scalp lock firmly, snapped a rubber band around it, jammed a freshly starched white chambray bonnet over her ears and forehead, fastened the crown to the lock with a large safety pin, and said: "Got to hold you still someways. Here now, don't you take this off your head till the sun go down."

"I didn't want a bonnet, it's too hot, I wanted a hat," said Miranda.

"You not goin' to get a hat, you goin' to get just what you got," said Aunt Nannie in the bossy voice she used for washing and dressing time, "and mo'over some of these days I'm goin' to sew this bonnet to your topknot. Your daddy says if you get freckles he blame me. Now, you're all ready to set out."

"Where are we going, Aunty?" Miranda could never find out about anything until the last minute. She was always being surprised. Once she went to sleep in her bed with her kitten curled on the pillow purring, and woke up in a stuffy tight bed in a train, hugging a hot-water bottle; and there was Grandmother stretched out beside her in her McLeod tartan dressing-gown, her eyes wide open. Miranda thought something wonderful had happened. "My goodness, Grandmother, where are we going?" And it was only for another trip to El Paso to see Uncle Bill.

Now Tom and Dick were hitched to the carry-all standing outside the gate with boxes and baskets tied on everywhere. Grandmother was walking alone through the house very slowly, taking a last look at everything. Now and then she put something else in the big leather portmoney on her arm until it was pretty bulgy. She carried a long black mohair skirt on her other arm, the one she put on over her other skirt when she rode horseback. Her son Harry,

Miranda's father, followed her saying: "I can't see the sense in rushing off to Halifax on five minutes' notice."

Grandmother said, walking on: "It's five hours exactly." Halifax wasn't the name of Grandmother's farm at all, it was Cedar Grove, but Father always called it Halifax. "Hot as Halifax," he would say when he wanted to describe something very hot. Cedar Grove was very hot, but they went there every summer because Grandmother loved it. "I went to Cedar Grove for fifty summers before you were born," she told Miranda, who remembered last summer very well, and the summer before a little. Miranda liked it for watermelons and grasshoppers and the long rows of blooming chinaberry trees where the hounds flattened themselves out and slept. They whined and winked their eyelids and worked their feet and barked faintly in their sleep, and Uncle Jimbilly said it was because dogs always dreamed they were chasing something. In the middle of the day when Miranda looked down over the thick green fields towards the spring she could simply see it being hot: everything blue and sleepy and the mourning doves calling.

"Are we going to Halifax, Aunty?"

"Now just ask your dad if you wanta know so much."

"Are we going to Halifax, Dad?"

Her father twitched her bonnet straight and pulled her hair forward so it would show. "You mustn't get sunburned. No, let it alone. Show the pretty curls. You'll be wading in the Whirlypool before supper this evening."

Grandmother said, "Don't say Halifax, child, say Cedar Grove. Call things by their right names."

"Yes, ma'am," said Miranda. Grandmother said again, to her son, "It's five hours, exactly, and your Aunt Eliza has had plenty of time to pack up her telescope, and take my saddle horse. She's been there three hours by now. I imagine she's got the telescope already set up on the hen-house roof. I hope nothing happens."

"You worry too much, Mammy," said her son, trying to conceal his impatience.

"I am not worrying," said Grandmother, shifting her riding skirt to the arm carrying the portmoney. "It will scarcely be any good taking this," she said; "I might in fact as well throw it away for this summer."

"Never mind, Mammy, we'll send to the Black Farm for Pompey, he's a good easy saddler."

"You may ride him yourself," said Grandmother. "I'll never mount Pompey while Fiddler is alive. Fiddler is my horse, and I hate having his mouth spoiled by a careless rider. Eliza never could ride, and she never will. . . ."

Miranda gave a little skip and ran away. So they were going to Cedar Grove. Miranda never got over being surprised at the way grown-up people simply did not seem able to give anyone a straight answer to any question, unless the answer was "No." Then it popped out with no trouble at all. At a little distance, she heard her grandmother say, "Harry, have you seen my riding crop lately?" and her father answered, at least maybe he thought it was an answer, "Now, Mammy, for God's sake let's get this thing over with." That was it, exactly.

Another strange way her father had of talking was called Grandmother "Mammy." Aunt Jane was Mammy. Sometimes he called Grandmother

"Mama," but she wasn't Mama either, she was really Grandmother. Mama was dead. Dead meant gone away forever. Dying was something that happened all the time, to people and everything else. Somebody died, and there was a long string of carriages going at a slow walk over the rocky ridge of the hill towards the river while the bell tolled and tolled, and that person was never seen again by anybody. Kittens and chickens and specially little turkeys died much oftener, and sometimes calves, but hardly ever cows or horses. Lizards on rocks turned into shells, with no lizard inside at all. If caterpillars all curled up and furry didn't move when you poked them with a stick, that meant they were dead—it was a sure sign.

When Miranda found any creature that didn't move or make a noise, or looked somehow different from the live ones, she always buried it in a little grave with flowers on top and a smooth stone at the head. Even grasshoppers. Everything dead had to be treated this way. "This way and no other!" Grandmother always said when she was laying down the law about all kinds of things. "It must be done *this* way, and no other!"

Miranda went down the crooked flat-stone walk hopping zigzag between the grass tufts. First there were pomegranate and cape jessamine bushes mixed together; then it got very dark and shady and that was the fig grove. She went to her favorite fig tree where the deep branches bowed down level with her chin, and she could gather figs without having to climb and skin her knees. Grandmother hadn't remembered to take any figs to the country the last time, she said there were plenty of them at Cedar Grove. But the ones at Cedar Grove were big soft greenish white ones, and these at home were black and sugary. It was strange that Grandmother did not seem to notice the difference. The air was sweet among the fig trees, and chickens were always getting out of the run and rushing there to eat the figs off the ground. One mother hen was scurrying around scratching and clucking. She would scratch around a fig lying there in plain sight and cluck to her children as if it was a worm and she had dug it up for them.

"Old smarty," said Miranda, "you're just pretending."

When the little chickens all ran to their mother under Miranda's fig tree, one little chicken did not move. He was spread out on his side with his eyes shut and his mouth open. He was yellow fur in spots and pinfeathers in spots, and the rest of him was naked and sunburned. "Lazy," said Miranda, poking him with her toe. Then she saw that he was dead.

Oh, and in no time at all they'd be setting out for Halifax. Grandmother never went away, she always set out for somewhere. She'd have to hurry like anything to get him buried properly. Back into the house she went on tiptoe hoping not to be seen, for Grandmother always asked: "Where are you going, child? What are you doing? What is that you're carrying? Where did you get it? Who gave you permission?" and after Miranda had explained all that, even if there turned out not to be anything wrong in it, nothing ever seemed so nice any more. Besides it took forever to get away.

Miranda slid open her bureau drawer, third down, left-hand side where her new shoes were still wrapped in tissue paper in a nice white box the right size for a chicken with pinfeathers. She pushed the rustling white folded things and the lavender bags out of the way and trembled a little. Down in front the carry-all wheels screeched and crunched on the gravel, with Old Uncle Jim-billy yelling like a foghorn, "Hiyi, thar, back up, you steeds! Back up thar, you!" and of course, that meant he was turning Tom and Dick around so they would be pointing towards Halifax. They'd be after her, calling and hurrying her, and she wouldn't have time for anything and they wouldn't listen to a word.

It wasn't hard work digging a hole with her little spade in the loose dry soil. Miranda wrapped the slimpsy chicken in tissue paper, trying to make it look pretty, laid it in the box carefully, and covered it up with a nice mound, just like people's. She had hardly got it piled up grave shape, kneeling and leaning to smooth it over, when a strange sound came from somewhere, a very sad little crying sound. It said Weep, weep, weep, three times like that slowly, and it seemed to come from the mound of dirt. "My goodness," Miranda asked herself aloud, "what's that?" She pushed her bonnet off her ears and listened hard. "Weep, weep," said the tiny sad voice. And people began calling and urging her, their voices coming nearer. She began to clamor, too.

"Yes, Aunty, wait a minute, Aunty!"

"You come right on here this minute, we're goin'!"

"You *have* to wait, Aunty!"

Her father was coming along the edge of the fig trees. "Hurry up, Baby, you'll get left!"

Miranda felt she couldn't bear to be left. She ran all shaking with fright. Her father gave her the annoyed look he always gave her when he said something to upset her and then saw that she was upset. His words were kind but his voice scolded: "Stop getting so excited, Baby, you know we wouldn't leave you for anything." Miranda wanted to talk back: "Then why did you say so?" but she was still listening for that tiny sound: "Weep, weep." She lagged and pulled backward, looking over her shoulder, but her father hurried her towards the carry-all. But things didn't make sounds if they were dead. They couldn't. That was one of the signs. Oh, but she had heard it.

Her father sat in front and drove, and Old Uncle Jimbilly didn't do anything but get down and open gates. Grandmother and Aunt Nannie sat in the back seat, with Miranda between them. She loved setting out somewhere, with everybody smiling and settling down and looking up at the weather, with the horses bouncing and pulling on the reins, the springs jolting and swaying with a creaky noise that made you feel sure you were traveling. That evening she would go wading with Maria and Paul and Uncle Jimbilly, and that very night she would lie out on the grass in her nightgown to cool off, and they would all drink lemonade before going to bed. Sister Maria and Brother Paul would already be burned like muffins because they were sent on ahead the minute school was out. Sister Maria got freckled and Father was furious. "Keep your bonnet on," he said to Miranda, sternly. "Now remember. I'm not going to have that face ruined, too." But oh, what had made that funny sound? Miranda's ears buzzed and she had a dull round pain in her just under her front ribs. She had to go back and let him out. He'd never get out by himself, all tangled up in tissue paper and that shoebox. He'd never get out without her.

"Grandmother, I've got to go back. Oh, I've *got* to go back!"

Grandmother turned Miranda's face around by the chin and looked at her closely, the way grown folks did. Grandmother's eyes were always the same. They never looked kind or sad or angry or tired or anything. They just looked, blue and still. "What is the matter with you, Miranda, what happened?"

"Oh, I've got to go back—I forg-got something important."

"Stop that silly crying and tell me what you want."

Miranda couldn't stop. Her father looked very anxious. "Mammy, maybe the Baby's sick." He reached out his handkerchief to her face. "What's the matter with my honey? Did you eat something?"

Miranda had to stand up to cry as hard as she wanted to. The wheels went grinding round in the road, the carry-all wobbled so that Grandmother had to take her by one arm, and her father by the other. They stared at each other over Miranda's head with a moveless gaze that Miranda had seen often, and their eyes looked exactly alike. Miranda blinked up at them, waiting to see who would win. Then Grandmother's hand fell away, and Miranda was handed over to her father. He gave the reins to Uncle Jimbilly, and lifted her over the top of the seat. She sprawled against his chest and knees as if he were an armchair and stopped crying at once. "We can't go back just for notions," he told her in the reasoning tone he always talked in when Grandmother scolded, and held the muffly handkerchief for her. "Now, blow hard. What did you forget, honey? We'll find another. Was it your doll?"

Miranda hated dolls. She never played with them. She always pulled the wigs off and tied them on the kittens, like hats. The kittens pulled them off instantly. It was fun. She put the doll clothes on the kittens and it took any one of them just half a minute to get them all off again. Kittens had sense. Miranda wailed suddenly, "Oh, I want my doll!" and cried again, trying to drown out the strange little sound, "Weep, weep"—

"Well now, if that's all," said her father comfortably, "there's a raft of dolls at Cedar Grove, and about forty fresh kittens. How'd you like that?"

"Forty?" asked Miranda.

"About," said Father.

Old Aunt Nannie leaned and held out her hand. "Look, honey, I toted you some nice black figs."

Her face was wrinkled and black and it looked like a fig upside down with a white ruffled cap. Miranda clenched her eyes tight and shook her head.

"Is that a pretty way to behave when Aunt Nannie offers you something nice?" asked Grandmother in her gentle reminding tone of voice.

"No, ma'am," said Miranda meekly. "Thank you, Aunt Nannie." But she did not accept the figs.

Great-Aunt Eliza, half way up a stepladder pitched against the flat-roofed chicken house, was telling Hinry just how to set up her telescope. "For a fellow who never saw or heard of a telescope," great-Aunt Eliza said to Grandmother, who was really her sister Sophia Jane, "he doesn't do so badly so long as I tell him."

"I do wish you'd stop clambering up stepladders, Eliza," said Grandmother, "at your time of life."

"You're nothing but a nervous wreck, Sophia, I declare. When did you ever know me to get hurt?"

"Even so," said Grandmother tartly, "there is such a thing as appropriate behavior at your time of . . ."

Great-Aunt Eliza seized a fold of her heavy brown pleated skirt with one hand, with the other she grasped the ladder one rung higher and ascended another step. "Now Hinry," she called, "just swing it around facing west and leave it level. I'll fix it the way I want when I'm ready. You can come on down now." She came down then herself, and said to her sister: "So long as you can go bouncing off on that horse of yours, Sophia Jane, I s'pose I can climb ladders. I'm three years younger than you, and *at your time of life* that makes all the difference!"

Grandmother turned pink as the inside of a seashell, the one on her sewing table that had the sound of the sea in it; Miranda knew that she had always been the pretty one, and she was pretty still, but great-Aunt Eliza was not pretty now and never had been. Miranda, watching and listening—for everything in the world was strange to her and something she had to know about— saw two old women, who were proud of being grandmothers, who spoke to children always as if they knew best about everything and children knew nothing, and they told children all day long to come here, go there, do this, do not do that, and they were always right and children never were except when they did anything they were told right away without a word. And here they were bickering like two little girls at school, or even the way Miranda and her sister Maria bickered and nagged and picked on each other and said things on purpose to hurt each other's feelings. Miranda felt sad and strange and a little frightened. She began edging away.

"Where are you going, Miranda?" asked Grandmother in her everyday voice.

"Just to the house," said Miranda, her heart sinking.

"Wait and walk with us," said Grandmother. She was very thin and pale and had white hair. Beside her, great-Aunt Eliza loomed like a mountain with her grizzled iron-colored hair like a curly wig, her steel-rimmed spectacles over her snuff-colored eyes, and snuff-colored woollen skirts billowing about her, and her smell of snuff. When she came through the door she quite filled it up. When she sat down the chair disappeared under her, and she seemed to be sitting solidly on herself from her waistband to the floor.

Now with Grandmother sitting across the room rummaging in her work basket and pretending not to see anything, great-Aunt Eliza took a small brown bottle out of her pocket, opened it, took a pinch of snuff in each nostril, sneezed loudly, wiped her nose with a big white starchy-looking handkerchief, pushed her spectacles up on her forehead, took a little twig chewed into a brush at one end, dipped and twisted it around in the little bottle, and placed it firmly between her teeth. Miranda had heard of this shameful habit in women of the lower classes, but no lady had been known to "dip snuff," and surely not in the family. Yet here was great-Aunt Eliza, a lady even if not a very pretty one, dipping snuff. Miranda knew how her grandmother felt about it; she stared fascinated at great-Aunt Eliza until her eyes watered. Great-Aunt Eliza stared back in turn.

"Look here, young one, d'ye s'pose if I gave you a gumdrop you'd get out from underfoot?"

She reached in the other pocket and took out a roundish, rather crushed-looking pink gumdrop with the sugar coating pretty badly crackled. "Now take this, and don't let me lay eyes on you any more today."

Miranda hurried away, clenching the gumdrop in her palm. When she reached the kitchen it was oozing through her fingers. She went to the tap and held her hand under the water and tried to wash off the snuffy smell. After this crime she did not really dare go near great-Aunt Eliza again soon. "What did you do with that gumdrop so quickly, child?" she could almost hear her asking.

Yet Miranda almost forgot her usual interests, such as kittens and other little

animals on the place, pigs, chickens, rabbits, anything at all so it was a baby
and would let her pet and feed it, for great-Aunt Eliza's ways and habits kept
Miranda following her about, gazing, or sitting across the dining-table, gazing,
for when great-Aunt Eliza was not on the roof before her telescope, always just
before daylight or just after dark, she was walking about with a microscope and
a burning glass, peering closely at something she saw on a tree trunk, something she found in the grass; now and then she collected fragments that looked
like dried leaves or bits of bark, brought them in the house, spread them out
on a sheet of white paper, and sat there, poring, as still as if she were saying
her prayers. At table she would dissect a scrap of potato peeling or anything
else she might be eating, and sit there, bowed over, saying, "Hum," from time
to time. Grandmother, who did not allow the children to bring anything to
the table to play with and who forbade them to do anything but eat while they
were there, ignored her sister's manners as long as she could, then remarked
one day, when great-Aunt Eliza was humming like a bee to herself over what
her microscope had found in a raisin, "Eliza, if it is interesting save it for me
to look at after dinner. Or tell me what it is."

"You wouldn't know if I told you," said great-Aunt Eliza, coolly, putting
her microscope away and finishing off her pudding.

When at last, just before they were all going back to town again, great-Aunt
Eliza invited the children to climb the ladder with her and see the stars
through her telescope, they were so awed they looked at each other like strangers, and did not exchange a word. Miranda saw only a great pale flaring disk
of cold light, but she knew it was the moon and called out in pure rapture,
"Oh, it's like another world!"

"Why, of course, child," said great-Aunt Eliza, in her growling voice, but
kindly, "other worlds, a million other worlds."

"Like this one?" asked Miranda, timidly.

"Nobody knows, child. . . ."

"Nobody knows, nobody knows," Miranda sang to a tune in her head, and
when the others walked on, she was so dazzled with joy she fell back by herself,
walking a little distance behind great-Aunt Eliza's swinging lantern and her
wide-swinging skirts. They took the dewy path through the fig grove, much
like the one in town, with the early dew bringing out the sweet smell of the
milky leaves. They passed a fig tree with low hanging branches, and Miranda
reached up by habit and touched it with her fingers for luck. From the earth
beneath her feet came a terrible, faint troubled sound. "Weep weep, weep
weep . . ." murmured a little crying voice from the smothering earth, the
grave.

Miranda bounded like a startled pony against the back of great-Aunt Eliza's
knees, crying out, "Oh, oh, oh, wait . . ."

"What on earth's the matter, child?"

Miranda seized the warm snuffy hand held out to her and hung on hard.
"Oh, there's something saying 'weep weep' out of the ground!"

Great-Aunt Eliza stooped, put her arm around Miranda and listened carefully, for a moment. "Hear them?" she said. "They're not in the ground at all.
They are the first tree frogs, means it's going to rain," she said, "weep weep—
hear them?"

Miranda took a deep trembling breath and heard them. They were in the
trees. They walked on again, Miranda holding great-Aunt Eliza's hand.

"Just think," said great-Aunt Eliza, in her most scientific voice, "when tree frogs shed their skins, they pull them off over their heads like little shirts, and they eat them. Can you imagine? They have the prettiest little shapes you ever saw—I'll show you one some time under the microscope."

"Thank you, ma'am," Miranda remembered finally to say through her fog of bliss at hearing the tree frogs sing, "Weep weep . . ."

1939

# ZORA NEALE HURSTON
## 1891–1960

Zora Neale Hurston is considered to be the most important and influential African-American woman who wrote before World War II. She was born in Eatonville, Florida, in 1891 an all-black town. Her family life was not happy, for her father, a Baptist preacher of considerable eloquence, was not a family man and made life difficult for his wife and eight children. The tie between mother and daughter was strong; Lucy Hurston was a driving force and strong support for all her children. But her death when Zora Hurston was about eleven left the child with little home life. Hitherto, the town of Eatonville had been like an extended family to her, and her early childhood was protected from racism because she encountered no white people. With her mother's death, Hurston's wanderings and her initiation into a racist society began. The early security had given her the core of self-confidence she needed to survive. She moved from one relative's home to another until old enough to support herself, and with her earnings she began slowly to pursue an education. She was so highly motivated that although she had never finished grade school in Eatonville she was able to enter and complete college. At Howard University in Washington, D.C. (the nation's leading African-American university at that time), in the early 1920s, she studied with the great black educator Alain Locke, who was to make history with his anthology *The New Negro* in 1925. After a short story, *Drenched in Light*, appeared in the New York African-American magazine *Opportunity*, she decided to move to Harlem and pursue a literary career there.

As her biographer, Robert Hemenway, writes, "Zora Hurston was an extraordinarily witty woman, and she acquired an instant reputation in New York for her high spirits and side-splitting tales of Eatonville life. She could walk into a room of strangers . . . and almost immediately gather people, charm, amuse, and impress them." Generous, outspoken, high spirited, and always interesting to be with, she was hired as a personal secretary by the politically liberal novelist Fanny Hurst and entered Barnard College. Her career now took two simultaneous directions: at Barnard she studied with the famous anthropologist Franz Boas and developed an interest in black folk traditions, and in Harlem she became well known as a storyteller, an informal performing artist. Thus she was doubly committed to the oral narrative, and her work excels in its representation of people, including herself, talking.

When she graduated from Barnard in 1927 she received a fellowship to return to Florida and study the oral traditions of Eatonville. From then on, she strove to achieve a balance between focusing on the folk and her origins and focusing on herself as an individual. After the fellowship money ran out, Hurston was supported by Mrs. R. Osgood Mason, an elderly white patron of the arts. Mason had firm ideas about what she wanted her protégés to produce; she liked the "primitive." And she required them all to get her permission before publishing any of the work that she had supported. In this relationship, Hurston experienced a difficulty that all the black artists of the Harlem Renaissance had to face—the fact that well-off white people were the sponsors of, and chief audience for, their work.

Hurston's work was not entirely popular with the male intellectual leaders of the Harlem community. Resolutely nonpolitical, she refused to align her work with anybody's ideologies and resisted the idea that a black writer's chief concern should be how blacks were being portrayed to the white reader. She did not write to "uplift her race," either; because in her view it was already uplifted, she was not embarrassed to present her characters as mixtures of good and bad, strong and weak. Some of the other Harlem writers thought her either naive or egotistical in ignoring appearances and in insisting on going her own way. But Hurston felt that freedom could only mean freedom from all coercion, no matter what the source.

The Great Depression brought the Harlem Renaissance to an end because the money that had supported it was no longer there. With the active intellectual social life gone, and no support for her fieldwork, Hurston turned all her energies to writing. Her most important work appeared in the mid-1930s when there was little interest in it, or in African-American writing in general. But she remained active during the decade, publishing *Jonah's Gourd Vine* in 1934 (a novel whose main character is based on her father); *Mules and Men* in 1935 (based on material from her field trips in Florida—this was her best-selling book, but it earned a total of only $943.75); and her masterpiece, *Their Eyes Were Watching God*, in 1937. This is a novel about an African-American woman's quest for selfhood. The main character in the novel is Janie Starks, who narrates her story to her best friend, Pheoby Watson. The tale is quickly carried forward by the voice of the narrator, returned to Janie only at the conclusion. It tells of Janie's young girlhood as she is brought up by her grandmother, who is obsessed with Janie's finding a good husband; her first marriage to an old farmer, Logan Killicks; her second to an entrepreneur and politician, Joe Starks; and a third relationship with a young migrant worker, Tea Cake. Through these three men Janie experiments with roles for black women and relationships with black men. Killicks and Starks are solid, stable citizens but their narrow goals and their inability to see Janie as a separate person stifle her. The footloose and imaginative Tea Cake, however unsuitable he may seem to be as a life partner, is the one who sets her free. At the end, though Janie is alone, she is content, having "been tuh de horizon and back."

*Their Eyes Were Watching God* is, as well as a woman's story, a description and critique of African-American society, showing its divisions and diversity. Technically, it is a loosely organized, highly metaphorical novel, with passages of broad folk humor and of extreme artistic compression. Its signal achievement was not recognized at first, in part because it did not fit readily into any fictional category. Other books followed in 1938 and 1939, and she wrote an autobiography —*Dust Tracks on a Road*— which appeared in 1942, with its occasional expression of antiwhite sentiments removed by her editors. At this point, however, Hurston simply had no audience. For the last decade of her life she lived in Florida, working from time to time as a maid.

The text for *How It Feels to Be Colored Me* is that of *I Love Myself When I Am Laughing . . . and Then Again When I Am Looking Mean and Impressive* (1979), edited by Alice Walker. The text for *Their Eyes Were Watching God* is from the 1937 edition.

# How It Feels to Be Colored Me

I am colored but I offer nothing in the way of extenuating circumstances except the fact that I am the only Negro in the United States whose grandfather on the mother's side was *not* an Indian chief.

I remember the very day that I became colored. Up to my thirteenth year I lived in the little Negro town of Eatonville, Florida. It is exclusively a colored town. The only white people I knew passed through the town going to or coming from Orlando. The native whites rode dusty horses, the Northern tourists chugged down the sandy village road in automobiles. The town knew the Southerners and never stopped cane chewing when they passed. But the Northerners were something else again. They were peered at cautiously from behind the curtains by the timid. The more venturesome would come out on the porch to watch them go past and got just as much pleasure out of the tourists as the tourists got out of the village.

The front porch might seem a daring place for the rest of the town, but it was a gallery seat for me. My favorite place was atop the gate-post. Proscenium box[1] for a born first-nighter. Not only did I enjoy the show, but I didn't mind the actors knowing that I liked it. I usually spoke to them in passing. I'd wave at them and when they returned my salute, I would say something like this: "Howdy-do-well-I-thank-you-where-you-goin'?" Usually automobile or the horse paused at this, and after a queer exchange of compliments, I would probably "go a piece of the way" with them, as we say in farthest Florida. If one of my family happened to come to the front in time to see me, of course negotiations would be rudely broken off. But even so, it is clear that I was the first "welcome-to-our-state" Floridian, and I hope the Miami Chamber of Commerce will please take notice.

During this period, white people differed from colored to me only in that they rode through town and never lived there. They liked to hear me "speak pieces" and sing and wanted to see me dance the parse-me-la, and gave me generously of their small silver for doing these things, which seemed strange to me for I wanted to do them so much that I needed bribing to stop. Only they didn't know it. The colored people gave no dimes. They deplored any joyful tendencies in me, but I was their Zora nevertheless. I belonged to them, to the nearby hotels, to the county—everybody's Zora.

But changes came in the family when I was thirteen, and I was sent to school in Jacksonville. I left Eatonville, the town of the oleanders, as Zora. When I disembarked from the river-boat at Jacksonville, she was no more. It seemed that I had suffered a sea change. I was not Zora of Orange County any more, I was now a little colored girl. I found it out in certain ways. In my heart as well as in the mirror, I became a fast brown—warranted not to rub nor run.

But I am not tragically colored. There is no great sorrow dammed up in my soul, nor lurking behind my eyes. I do not mind at all. I do not belong to the sobbing school of Negrohood who hold that nature somehow has given them a lowdown dirty deal and whose feelings are all hurt about it. Even in the helter-skelter skirmish that is my life, I have seen that the world is to the strong regardless of a little pigmentation more or less. No, I do not weep at the world—I am too busy sharpening my oyster knife.

Someone is always at my elbow reminding me that I am the granddaughter of slaves. It fails to register depression with me. Slavery is sixty years in the past. The operation was successful and the patient is doing well, thank you. The terrible struggle that made me an American out of a potential slave said

---

1. Box at the very front of the auditorium, closest to the stage.

"On the line!" The Reconstruction said "Get set!"; and the generation before said "Go!" I am off to a flying start and I must not halt in the stretch to look behind and weep. Slavery is the price I paid for civilization, and the choice was not with me. It is a bully adventure and worth all that I have paid through my ancestors for it. No one on earth ever had a greater chance for glory. The world to be won and nothing to be lost. It is thrilling to think—to know that for any act of mine, I shall get twice as much praise or twice as much blame. It is quite exciting to hold the center of the national stage, with the spectators not knowing whether to laugh or to weep.

The position of my white neighbor is much more difficult. No brown specter pulls up a chair beside me when I sit down to eat. No dark ghost thrusts its leg against mine in bed. The game of keeping what one has is never so exciting as the game of getting.

I do not always feel colored. Even now I often achieve the unconscious Zora of Eatonville before the Hegira.[2] I feel most colored when I am thrown against a sharp white background.

For instance at Barnard. "Besides the waters of the Hudson" I feel my race. Among the thousand white persons, I am a dark rock surged upon, and over-swept, but through it all, I remain myself. When covered by the waters, I am; and the ebb but reveals me again.

Sometimes it is the other way around. A white person is set down in our midst, but the contrast is just as sharp for me. For instance, when I sit in the drafty basement that is The New World Cabaret[3] with a white person, my color comes. We enter chatting about any little nothing that we have in common and are seated by the jazz waiters. In the abrupt way that jazz orchestras have, this one plunges into a number. It loses no time in circumlocutions, but gets right down to business. It constricts the thorax and splits the heart with its tempo and narcotic harmonies. This orchestra grows rambunctious, rears on its hind legs and attacks the tonal veil with primitive fury, rending it, clawing it until it breaks through to the jungle beyond. I follow those hea-then—follow them exultingly. I dance wildly inside myself; I yell within, I whoop; I shake my assegai[4] above my head, I hurl it true to the mark *yeeeeooww!* I am in the jungle and living in the jungle way. My face is painted red and yellow and my body is painted blue. My pulse is throbbing like a war drum. I want to slaughter something—give pain, give death to what, I do not know. But the piece ends. The men of the orchestra wipe their lips and rest their fingers. I creep back slowly to the veneer we call civilization with the last tone and find the white friend sitting motionless in his seat smoking calmly.

"Good music they have here," he remarks, drumming the table with his fingertips.

Music. The great blobs of purple and red emotion have not touched him. He has only heard what I felt. He is far away and I see him but dimly across the ocean and the continent that have fallen between us. He is so pale with his whiteness then and I am *so* colored.

At certain times I have no race, I am *me*. When I set my hat at a certain angle and saunter down Seventh Avenue, Harlem City, feeling as snooty as

2. Forced march of Mohammed from Mecca to Medina in A.D. 622; hence any forced flight or journey for
safety.

3. Popular Harlem nightclub in the 1920s.
4. A slender spear used by some South African tribes.

the lions in front of the Forty-Second Street Library, for instance. So far as my feelings are concerned, Peggy Hopkins Joyce on the Boule Mich[5] with her gorgeous raiment, stately carriage, knees knocking together in a most aristocratic manner, has nothing on me. The cosmic Zora emerges. I belong to no race nor time. I am the eternal feminine with its string of beads.

I have no separate feeling about being an American citizen and colored. I am merely a fragment of the Great Soul that surges within the boundaries. My country, right or wrong.

Sometimes, I feel discriminated against, but it does not make me angry. It merely astonishes me. How *can* any deny themselves the pleasure of my company? It's beyond me.

But in the main, I feel like a brown bag of miscellany propped against a wall. Against a wall in company with other bags, white, red and yellow. Pour out the contents, and there is discovered a jumble of small things priceless and worthless. A first-water diamond, an empty spool, bits of broken glass, lengths of string, a key to a door long since crumbled away, a rusty knife-blade, old shoes saved for a road that never was and never will be, a nail bent under the weight of things too heavy for any nail, a dried flower or two still a little fragrant. In your hand is the brown bag. On the ground before you is the jumble it held—so much like the jumble in the bags, could they be emptied, that all might be dumped in a single heap and the bags refilled without altering the content of any greatly. A bit of colored glass more or less would not matter. Perhaps that is how the Great Stuffer of Bags filled them in the first place—who knows?

1928

## From Their Eyes Were Watching God

2

Janie saw her life like a great tree in leaf with the things suffered, things enjoyed, things done and undone. Dawn and doom was in the branches.

"Ah know exactly what Ah got to tell yuh, but it's hard to know where to start at."

"Ah ain't never seen mah papa. And Ah didn't know 'im if Ah did. Mah mama neither. She was gone from round dere long before Ah wuz big enough tuh know. Mah grandma raised me. Mah grandma and de white folks she worked wid. She had a house out in de back-yard and dat's where Ah wuz born. They was quality white folks up dere in West Florida. Named Washburn. She had four gran'chillun on de place and all of us played together and dat's how come Ah never called mah Grandma nothin' but Nanny, 'cause dat's what everybody on de place called her. Nanny used to ketch us in our devilment and lick every youngun on de place and Mis' Washburn did de same. Ah reckon dey never hit us ah lick amiss 'cause dem three boys and us two girls wuz pretty aggravatin', Ah speck.

---

5. Boulevard St. Michel, a street on the Left Bank of Paris running near the Sorbonne University and through the Latin Quarter. It has never been a particularly fashionable street, but it is filled with cafés that were—and still are—much frequented by Americans in Paris. "Joyce": a socialite and heiress, much photographed.

"Ah was wid dem white chillun so much till Ah didn't know Ah wuzn't white till Ah was round six years old. Wouldn't have found it out then, but a man come long takin' pictures and without askin' anybody, Shelby, dat was de oldest boy, he told him to take us. Round a week later de man brought de picture for Mis' Washburn to see and pay him which she did, then give us all a good lickin'.

"So when we looked at de picture and everybody got pointed out there wasn't nobody left except a real dark little girl with long hair standing by Eleanor. Dat's where Ah wuz s'posed to be, but Ah couldn't recognize dat dark chile as me. So Ah ast, 'where is me? Ah don't see me.'

"Everybody laughed, even Mr. Washburn. Miss Nellie, de Mama of de chillun who come back home after her husband dead, she pointed to de dark one and said, 'Dat's you, Alphabet, don't you know yo' ownself?'

"Dey all useter call me Alphabet 'cause so many people had done named me different names. Ah looked at de picture a long time and seen it was mah dress and mah hair so Ah said:

" 'Aw, aw! Ah'm colored!'

"Den dey all laughed real hard. But before Ah seen de picture Ah thought Ah wuz just like de rest.

"Us lived dere havin' fun till de chillun at school got to teasin' me 'bout livin' in de white folks back-yard. Dere wuz uh knotty head gal name Mayrella dat useter git mad every time she look at me. Mis' Washburn useter dress me up in all de clothes her gran'chillun didn't need no mo' which still wuz better'n whut de rest uh de colored chillun had. And then she useter put hair ribbon on mah head fuh me tuh wear. Dat useter rile Mayrella uh lot. So she would pick at me all de time and put some others up tuh do de same. They'd push me 'way from de ring plays and make out they couldn't play wid nobody dat lived on premises. Den they'd tell me not to be takin' on over mah looks 'cause they mama told 'em 'bout de hound dawgs huntin' mah papa all night long. 'Bout Mr. Washburn and de sheriff puttin' de bloodhounds on de trail tuh ketch mah papa for whut he done tuh mah mama. Dey didn't tell about how he wuz seen tryin' tuh git in touch wid mah mama later on so he could marry her. Naw, dey didn't talk dat part of it atall. Dey made it sound real bad so as tuh crumple mah feathers. None of 'em didn't even remember whut his name wuz, but dey all knowed de bloodhound part by heart. Nanny didn't love tuh see me wid mah head hung down, so she figgered it would be mo'better fuh me if us had uh house. She got de land and everything and then Mis' Washburn helped out uh whole heap wid things."

Pheoby's hungry listening helped Janie to tell her story. So she went on thinking back to her young years and explaining them to her friend in soft, easy phrases while all around the house, the night time put on flesh and blackness.

She thought awhile and decided that her conscious life had commenced at Nanny's gate. On a late afternoon Nanny had called her to come inside the house because she had spied Janie letting Johnny Taylor kiss her over the gatepost.

It was a spring afternoon in West Florida. Janie had spent most of the day under a blossoming pear tree in the back-yard. She had been spending every minute that she could steal from her chores under that tree for the last three days. That was to say, ever since the first tiny bloom had opened. It had called her to come and gaze on a mystery. From barren brown stems to glistening leaf-buds; from the leaf-buds to snowy virginity of bloom. It stirred her tremendously. How? Why? It was like a flute song forgotten in another existence and remembered again. What? How? Why? This singing she heard that had nothing to do with her ears. The rose of the world was breathing out smell. It followed her through all her waking moments and caressed her in her sleep. It connected itself with other vaguely felt matters that had struck her outside observation and buried themselves in her flesh. Now they emerged and quested about her consciousness.

She was stretched on her back beneath the pear tree soaking in the alto chant of the visiting bees, the gold of the sun and the panting breath of the breeze when the inaudible voice of it all came to her. She saw a dust-bearing bee sink into the sanctum of a bloom; the thousand sister-calyxes arch to meet the love embrace and the ecstatic shiver of the tree from root to tiniest branch creaming in every blossom and frothing with delight. So this was a marriage! She had been summoned to behold a revelation. Then Janie felt a pain remorseless sweet that left her limp and languid.

After a while she got up from where she was and went over the little garden field entire. She was seeking confirmation of the voice and vision, and everywhere she found and acknowledged answers. A personal answer for all other creations except herself. She felt an answer seeking her, but where? When? How? She found herself at the kitchen door and stumbled inside. In the air of the room were flies tumbling and singing, marrying and giving in marriage. When she reached the narrow hallway she was reminded that her grandmother was home with a sick headache. She was lying across the bed asleep so Janie tipped on out of the front door. Oh to be a pear tree—any tree in bloom! With kissing bees singing of the beginning of the world! She was sixteen. She had glossy leaves and bursting buds and she wanted to struggle with life but it seemed to elude her. Where were the singing bees for her? Nothing on the place nor in her grandma's house answered her. She searched as much of the world as she could from the top of the front steps and then went on down to the front gate and leaned over to gaze up and down the road. Looking, waiting, breathing short with impatience. Waiting for the world to be made.

Through pollinated air she saw a glorious being coming up the road. In her former blindness she had known him as shiftless Johnny Taylor, tall and lean. That was before the golden dust of pollen had beglamored his rags and her eyes.

In the last stages of Nanny's sleep, she dreamed of voices. Voices far-off but persistent, and gradually coming nearer. Janie's voice. Janie talking in whispery snatches with a male voice she couldn't quite place. That brought her wide awake. She bolted upright and peered out of the window and saw Johnny Taylor lacerating her Janie with a kiss.

"Janie!"

The old woman's voice was so lacking in command and reproof, so full of crumbling dissolution,—that Janie half believed that Nanny had not seen her. So she extended herself outside of her dream and went inside of the house. That was the end of her childhood.

Nanny's head and face looked like the standing roots of some old tree that had been torn away by storm. Foundation of ancient power that no longer mattered. The cooling palma christi leaves that Janie had bound about her grandma's head with a white rag had wilted down and become part and parcel of the woman. Her eyes didn't bore and pierce. They diffused and melted Janie, the room and the world into one comprehension.

"Janie, youse uh 'oman, now, so—"

"Naw, Nanny, naw Ah ain't no real 'oman yet."

The thought was too new and heavy for Janie. She fought it away.

Nanny closed her eyes and nodded a slow, weary affirmation many times before she gave it voice.

"Yeah, Janie, youse got yo' womanhood on yuh. So Ah mout ez well tell yuh whut Ah been savin' up for uh spell. Ah wants to see you married right away."

"Me, married? Naw, Nanny, no ma'am! What Ah know 'bout uh husband?"

"Whut Ah seen just now is plenty for me, honey, Ah don't want no trashy nigger, no breath-and-britches, lak Johnny Taylor usin' yo' body to wipe his foots on."

Nanny's words made Janie's kiss across the gatepost seem like a manure pile after a rain.

"Look at me, Janie. Don't set dere wid yo' head hung down. Look at yo' ole grandma!" Her voice began snagging on the prongs of her feelings. "Ah don't want to be talkin' to you lak dis. Fact is Ah done been on mah knees to mah Maker many's de time askin' *please*—for Him not to make de burden too heavy for me to bear."

"Nanny, Ah just—Ah didn't mean nothin' bad."

"Dat's what makes me skeered. You don't mean no harm. You don't even know where harm is at. Ah'm ole now. Ah can't be always guidin' yo' feet from harm and danger. Ah wants to see you married right away."

"Who Ah'm goin' tuh marry off-hand lak dat? Ah don't know nobody."

"De Lawd will provide. He know Ah done bore de burden in de heat uh de day. Somebody done spoke to me 'bout you long time ago. Ah ain't said nothin' 'cause dat wasn't de way Ah placed you. Ah wanted yuh to school out and pick from a higher bush and a sweeter berry. But dat ain't yo' idea, Ah see."

"Nanny, who—who dat been askin' you for me?"

"Brother Logan Killicks. He's a good man, too."

"Naw, Nanny, no ma'am! Is dat whut he been hangin' round here for? He look like some ole skullhead in de grave yard."

The older woman sat bolt upright and put her feet to the floor, and thrust back the leaves from her face.

"So you don't want to marry off decent like, do yuh? You just wants to hug and kiss and feel around with first one man and then another, huh? You wants to make me suck de same sorrow yo' mama did, eh? Mah old head ain't gray enough. Mah back ain't bowed enough to suit yuh!"

The vision of Logan Killicks was desecrating the pear tree, but Janie didn't know how to tell Nanny that. She merely hunched over and pouted at the floor.

"Janie."

"Yes, ma'am."

"You answer me when Ah speak. Don't you set dere poutin' wid me after all Ah done went through for you!"

She slapped the girl's face violently, and forced her head back so that their eyes met in struggle. With her hand uplifted for the second blow she saw the huge tear that welled up from Janie's heart and stood in each eye. She saw the terrible agony and the lips tightened down to hold back the cry and desisted. Instead she brushed back the heavy hair from Janie's face and stood there suffering and loving and weeping internally for both of them.

"Come to yo' Grandma, honey. Set in her lap lak yo' use tuh. Yo' Nanny wouldn't harm a hair uh yo' head. She don't want nobody else to do it neither if she kin help it. Honey, de white man is de ruler of everything as fur as Ah been able tuh find out. Maybe it's some place way off in de ocean where de black man is in power, but we don't know nothin' but what we see. So de white man throw down de load and tell de nigger man tuh pick it up. He pick it up because he have to, but he don't tote it. He hand it to his womenfolks. De nigger woman is de mule uh de world so fur as Ah can see. Ah been prayin' fuh it tuh be different wid you. Lawd, Lawd, Lawd!"

For a long time she sat rocking with the girl held tightly to her sunken breast. Janie's long legs dangled over one arm of the chair and the long braids of her hair swung low on the other side. Nanny half sung, half sobbed a running chant-prayer over the head of the weeping girl.

"Lawd have mercy! It was a long time on de way but Ah reckon it had to come. Oh Jesus! Do, Jesus! Ah done de best Ah could."

Finally, they both grew calm.

"Janie, how long you been 'lowin' Johnny Taylor to kiss you?"

"Only dis one time, Nanny. Ah don't love him at all. Whut made me do it is—oh, Ah don't know."

"Thank yuh, Massa Jesus."

"Ah ain't gointuh do it no mo', Nanny. Please don't make me marry Mr. Killicks."

" 'Tain't Logan Killicks Ah wants you to have, baby, it's protection. Ah ain't gittin' ole, honey. Ah'm *done* ole. One mornin' soon, now, de angel wid de sword is gointuh stop by here. De day and de hour is hid from me, but it won't be long. Ah ast de Lawd when you was uh infant in mah arms to let me stay here till you got grown. He done spared me to see de day. Mah daily prayer now is tuh let dese golden moments rolls on a few days longer till Ah see you safe in life."

"Lemme wait, Nanny, please, jus' a lil bit mo'."

"Don't think Ah don't feel wid you, Janie, 'cause Ah do. Ah couldn't love yuh no more if Ah had uh felt yo' birth pains mahself. Fact uh de matter, Ah loves yuh a while heap more'n Ah do yo' mama, de one Ah did birth. But you got to take in consideration you ain't no everyday chile like most of 'em. You ain't got no papa, you might jus' as well say no mama, for de good she do yuh. You ain't got nobody but me. And mah head is ole and tilted towards de grave. Neither can you stand alone by yo'self. De thought uh you bein' kicked around from pillar tuh post is uh hurtin' thing. Every tear you drop squeezes a cup uh blood outa mah heart. Ah got tuh try and do for you befo' mah head is cold."

A sobbing sigh burst out of Janie. The old woman answered her with little soothing pats of the hand.

"You know, honey, us colored folks is branches without roots and that makes things come round in queer ways. You in particular. Ah was born back due in slavery so it wasn't for me to fulfill my dreams of whut a woman oughta be and to do. Dat's one of de hold-backs of slavery. But nothin' can't stop you from wishin'. You can't beat nobody down so low till you can rob 'em of they will. Ah didn't want to be used for a work-ox and a brood-sow and Ah didn't want mah daughter used dat way neither. It sho wasn't mah will for things to happen lak they did. Ah even hated de way you was born. But, all the de same Ah said thank God, Ah got another chance. Ah wanted to preach a great sermon about colored women sittin' on high, but they wasn't no pulpit for me. Freedom found me wid a baby daughter in mah arms, so Ah said Ah'd take a broom and a cook-pot and throw up a highway through de wilderness for her. She would expound what Ah felt. But somehow she got lost offa de highway and next thing Ah knowed here you was in de world. So whilst Ah was tendin' you of nights Ah said Ah'd save de text for you. Ah been waitin' a long time, Janie, but nothin' Ah been through ain't too much if you just take a stand on high ground lak Ah dreamed."

Old Nanny sat there rocking Janie like an infant and thinking back and back. Mind-pictures brought feelings, and feelings dragged out dramas from the hollows of her heart.

"Dat mornin' on de big plantation close to Savannah, a rider come in a gallop tellin' 'bout Sherman takin' Atlanta. Marse Robert's son had done been kilt at Chickamauga. So he grabbed his gun and straddled his best horse and went off wid de rest of de gray-headed men and young boys to drive de Yankees back into Tennessee.

"They was all cheerin' and cryin' and shoutin' for de men dat was ridin' off. Ah couldn't see nothin' cause yo' mama wasn't but a week old, and Ah was flat uh mah back. But pretty soon he let on he forgot somethin' and run into mah cabin and made me let down mah hair for de last time. He sorta wropped his hand in it, pulled mah big toe, lak he always done, and was gone after de rest lak lightnin'. Ah heard 'em give one last whoop for him. Then de big house and de quarters got sober and silent.

"It was de cool of de evenin' when Mistis come walkin' in mah door. She throwed de door wide open and stood dere lookin' at me outa her eyes and her face. Look lak she been livin' through uh hundred years in January without one day of spring. She come stood over me in de bed.

" 'Nanny, Ah come to see that baby uh yourn.'

"Ah tried not to feel de breeze off her face, but it got so cold in dere dat Ah was freezin' to death under the kivvers. So Ah couldn't move right away lak Ah aimed to. But Ah knowed Ah had to make haste and do it.

" 'You better git dat kivver offa dat youngun and dat quick!' she clashed at me. 'Look lak you don't know who is Mistis on dis plantation, Madam. But Ah aims to show you.'

"By dat time I had done managed tuh unkivver mah baby enough for her to see de head and face.

" 'Nigger, whut's yo' baby doin' wid gray eyes and yaller hair?' She begin tuh slap mah jaws ever which a'way. Ah never felt the fust ones 'cause Ah wuz too busy gittin' de kivver back over mah chile. But dem last lick burnt me lak fire. Ah had too many feelin's tuh tell which one tuh follow so Ah didn't cry and Ah didn't do nothin' else. But then she kept on astin me how come mah baby look white. She asted me dat maybe twenty-five or thirty times, lak she got tuh sayin' dat and couldn't help herself. So Ah told her, 'Ah don't know nothin' but what Ah'm told tuh do, 'cause Ah ain't nothin' but uh nigger and uh slave.'

"Instead of pacifyin' her lak Ah thought, look lak she got madder. But Ah reckon she was tired and wore out 'cause she didn't hit me no more. She went to de foot of de bed and wiped her hands on her handksher. 'Ah wouldn't dirty mah hands on yuh. But first thing in de mornin' de overseer will take you to de whippin' post and tie you down on yo' knees and cut de hide offa yo' yaller back. One hundred lashes wid a raw-hide on yo' bare back. Ah'll have you whipped till de blood run down to yo' heels! Ah mean to count de licks mahself. And if it kills you Ah'll stand de loss. Anyhow, as soon as dat brat is a month old Ah'm going to sell it offa dis place.'

"She flounced on off and left her wintertime wid me. Ah knowed mah body wasn't healed, but Ah couldn't consider dat. In de black dark Ah wrapped mah baby de best Ah knowed how and made it to de swamp by de river. Ah knowed de place was full uh moccasins and other bitin' snakes, but Ah was more skeered uh whut was behind me. Ah hide in dere day and night and suckled de baby every time she start to cry, for fear somebody might hear her and Ah'd git found. Ah ain't sayin' uh friend or two didn't feel mah care. And den de Good Lawd seen to it dat Ah wasn't taken. Ah don't see how come mah milk didn't kill mah chile, wid me so skeered and worried all de time. De noise uh de owls skeered me; de limbs of dem cypress trees look to crawlin' and movin' round after dark, and two three times Ah heered panthers prowlin' round. But nothin' never hurt me 'cause de Lawd knowed how it was.

"Den, one night Ah heard de big guns boomin' lak thunder. It kept up all night long. And de next mornin' Ah could see uh big ship at a distance and a great stirrin' round. So Ah wrapped Leafy up in moss and fixed her good in a tree and picked mah way on down to de landin'. The men was all in blue, and Ah heard people say Sherman was comin' to meet de boats in Savannah, and all of us slaves was free. So Ah run got mah baby and got in quotation wid people and found a place Ah could stay.

"But it was a long time after dat befo' de Big Surrender at Richmond. Den de big bell ring in Atlanta and all de men in gray uniforms had to go to Moultrie, and bury their swords in de ground to show they was never to fight about slavery no mo'. So den we knowed we was free.

"Ah wouldn't marry nobody, though Ah could have uh heap uh times, cause Ah didn't want nobody mistreating mah baby. So Ah got with some good white people and come down here in West Florida to work and make de sun shine on both sides of de street for Leafy.

"Mah Madam help me wid her just lak she been doin' wid you. Ah put her in school when it got so it was a school to put her in. Ah was 'spectin' to make a school teacher outa her.

"But one day she didn't come home at de usual time and Ah waited and waited, but she never come all dat night. Ah took a lantern and went round askin' everybody but nobody ain't seen her. De next mornin' she come crawlin' in on her hands and knees. A sight to see. Dat school teacher had done hid her in de woods all night long, and he had done raped mah baby and run on off just before day.

"She was only seventeen, and somethin' lak dat to happen! Lawd a'mussy! Look lak Ah kin see it all over again. It was a long time before she was well, and by dat time we knowed you was on de way. And after you was born she took to drinkin' likker and stayin' out nights. Couldn't git her to stay here and nowhere else. Lawd knows where she is right now. She ain't dead, 'cause Ah'd know it by mah feelings, but sometimes Ah wish she was at rest.

"And, Janie, maybe it wasn't much, but Ah done de best Ah kin by you. Ah raked and scraped and bought dis lil piece uh land so you wouldn't have to stay in de white folks' yard and tuck yo' head befo' other chillun at school. Dat was all right when you was little. But when you got big enough to understand things, Ah wanted you to look upon yo'self. Ah don't want yo' feathers always crumpled by folks throwin' up things in yo' face. And Ah can't die easy thinkin' maybe de menfolks white or black is makin' a spit cup outa you: Have some sympathy fuh me. Put me down easy, Janie, Ah'm a cracked plate."

## 3

There are years that ask questions and years that answer. Janie had had no chance to know things, so she had to ask. Did marriage end the cosmic loneliness of the unmated? Did marriage compel love like the sun the day?

In the few days to live before she went to Logan Killicks and his often-mentioned sixty acres, Janie asked inside of herself and out. She was back and forth to the pear tree continuously wondering and thinking. Finally out of Nanny's talk and her own conjectures she made a sort of comfort for herself. Yes, she would love Logan after they were married. She could see no way for it to come about, but Nanny and the old folks had said it, so it must be so. Husbands and wives always loved each other, and that was what marriage meant. It was just so. Janie felt glad of the thought, for then it wouldn't seem so destructive and mouldy. She wouldn't be lonely anymore.

Janie and Logan got married in Nanny's parlor of a Saturday evening with three cakes and big platters of fried rabbit and chicken. Everything to eat in abundance. Nanny and Mrs. Washburn had seen to that. But nobody put anything on the seat of Logan's wagon to make it ride glorious on the way to his house. It was a lonesome place like a stump in the middle of the woods where nobody had ever been. The house was absent of flavor, too. But anyhow Janie went on inside to wait for love to begin. The new moon had been up and down three times before she got worried in mind. Then she went to see Nanny in Mrs. Washburn's kitchen on the day for beaten biscuits.

Nanny beamed all out with gladness and made her come up to the bread board so she could kiss her.

"Lawd a'mussy, honey, Ah sho is glad tuh see mah chile! G'wan inside and let Mis' Washburn know youse heah. Umph! Umph! Umph! How is dat husband uh yourn?"

Janie didn't go in where Mrs. Washburn was. She didn't say anything to match up with Nanny's gladness either. She just fell on a chair with her hips and sat there. Between the biscuits and her beaming pride Nanny didn't notice for a minute. But after a while she found the conversation getting lonesome so she looked up at Janie.

"Whut's de matter, sugar? You ain't none too spry dis mornin'."

"Oh, nothin' much, Ah reckon. Ah come to get a lil information from you."

The old woman looked amazed, then gave a big clatter of laughter. "Don't tell me you done got knocked up already, less see—dis Saturday it's two month and two weeks."

"No'm, Ah don't think so anyhow." Janie blushed a little.

"You ain't got nothin' to be shamed of, honey, youse uh married 'oman.

You got yo' lawful husband same as Mis' Washburn or anybody else!"

"Ah'm all right dat way. Ah *know* 'tain't nothin' dere."

"You and Logan been fussin'? Lawd, Ah know dat grass-gut, liver-lipted nigger ain't done took and beat mah baby already! Ah'll take a stick and salivate 'im!"

"No'm, he ain't even talked 'bout hittin' me. He says he never mean to lay de weight uh his hand on me in malice. He chops all de wood he think Ah wants and den he totes it inside de kitchin for me. Keeps both water buckets full."

"Humph! don't 'spect all dat tuh keep up. He ain't kissin' yo' mouf when he carry on over yuh lak dat. He's kissin' yo' foot and 'tain't in uh man tuh kiss foot long. Mouf kissin' is on uh equal and dat's natural but when dey got to bow down tuh love, dey soon straightens up."

"Yes'm."

"Well, if he do all dat whut you come in heah wid uh face long as mah arm for?"

" 'Cause you told me Ah mus gointer love him, and, and Ah don't. Maybe if somebody was to tell me how, Ah could do it."

"You come heah wid yo' mouf full uh foolishness on uh busy day. Heah you got uh prop tuh lean on all yo' bawn days, and big protection, and everybody got tuh tip dey hat tuh you and call you Mis' Killicks, and you come worryin' me 'bout love."

"But Nanny, Ah wants to want him sometimes. Ah don't want him to do all de wantin'."

"If you don't want him, you sho oughta. Heah you is wid de onliest organ in town, amongst colored folks, in yo' parlor. Got a house bought and paid for and sixty acres uh land on de big road and . . . Lawd have mussy! Dat's de very prong all us black women gits hung on. Dis love! Dat's just whut's got us uh pullin' and uh haulin' and sweatin' and doin' from can't see in de mornin' till can't see at night. Dat's how come de ole folks say dat bein' uh fool don't kill nobody. It jus' makes you sweat. Ah betcha you wants some dressed up dude dat got to look at de sole of his shoe everytime he cross de street tuh see whether he got enough leather dere tuh make it across. You can buy and sell such as dem wid what you got. In fact you can buy 'em and give 'em away."

"Ah ain't studyin' 'bout none of 'em. At de same time Ah ain't takin' dat ole land tuh heart neither. Ah could throw ten acres of it over de fence every day and never look back to see where it fell. Ah feel de same way 'bout Mr. Killicks too. Some folks never was meant to be loved and he's one of 'em."

"How come?"

" 'Cause Ah hates de way his head is so long one way and so flat on de sides and dat pone uh fat back uh his neck."

"He never made his own head. You talk so silly."

"Ah don't keer who made it, Ah don't like de job. His belly is too big too, now, and his toe-nails look lak mule foots. And 'tain't nothin' in de way of him washin' his feet every evenin' before he comes tuh bed. 'Tain't nothin' tuh hinder him 'cause Ah places de water for him. Ah'd ruther be shot wid tacks than tuh turn over in de bed and stir up de air whilst he is in dere. He don't even never mention nothin' pretty."

She began to cry.

"Ah wants things sweet wid mah marriage lak when you sit under a pear tree and think. Ah . . ."

" 'Tain't no use in you cryin', Janie. Grandma done been long uh few roads herself. But folks is meant to cry 'bout somethin' or other. Better leave things de way dey is. Youse young yet. No tellin' whut mout happen befo' you die. Wait awhile, baby. Yo' mind will change."

Nanny sent Janie along with a stern mien, but she dwindled all the rest of the day as she worked. And when she gained the privacy of her own little shack she stayed on her knees so long she forgot she was there herself. There is a basin in the mind where words float around on thought and thought on sound and sight. Then there is a depth of thought untouched by words, and deeper still a gulf of formless feelings untouched by thought. Nanny entered this infinity of conscious pain again on her old knees. Towards morning she muttered, "Lawd, you know mah heart. Ah done de best Ah could do. De rest is left to you." She scuffled up from her knees and fell heavily across the bed. A month later she was dead.

So Janie waited a bloom time, and a green time and an orange time. But when the pollen again gilded the sun and sifted down on the world she began to stand around the gate and expect things. What things? She didn't know exactly. Her breath was gusty and short. She knew things that nobody had ever told her. For instance, the words of the trees and the wind. She often spoke to falling seeds and said, "Ah hope you fall on soft ground," because she had heard seeds saying that to each other as they passed. She knew the world was a stallion rolling in the blue pasture of ether. She knew that God tore down the old world every evening and built a new one by sun-up. It was wonderful to see it take form with the sun and emerge from the gray dust of its making. The familiar people and things had failed her so she hung over the gate and looked up the road towards way off. She knew now that marriage did not make love. Janie's first dream was dead, so she became a woman.

1937

---

# EDNA ST. VINCENT MILLAY
## 1892–1950

Edna St. Vincent Millay was a versatile writer, with an output ranging from Elizabethan sonnets through plays and sketches to political speeches. In the 1920s she became a kind of national symbol of the modern woman—liberated from Victorian mores, independent, self-supporting, full of energy and talent.

She was raised in a small town on the coast of Maine by her divorced mother, who supported herself and three daughters through work as a practical nurse. The mother provided her children with books and music lessons and encouraged ambition and independence. Millay began to write poetry in high school and published her first book of poetry, *Renascence and Other Poems*, in 1917, when she was only twenty-five. She went to Vassar College from 1913 to 1917 through the generosity of a benefactor impressed by her writing. At Vassar she studied languages, wrote songs and verse plays, and became interested in acting. After graduation she went to New York City, settling in the Greenwich Village section of the city and becoming associated with the Bohemian life of the literary and political rebels who lived there. A member of the Provincetown Players group, she acted and also wrote two plays for them. *The Ballad of the Harp-Weaver* (1923, later retitled *The Harp-Weaver and Other Poems*) was awarded a Pulitzer Prize.

Millay lived in Europe from 1921 to 1923 and, upon her return, married and moved with her businessman husband Eugene Boissevain to a farm in upstate New York. She participated in the protests against the sentencing of Sacco and Vanzetti in 1927 and during the 1930s wrote anti-Fascist newspaper verse, radio plays, and speeches. She was an advocate of early U.S. entrance into World War II.

Although as a young woman Millay achieved a certain degree of notoriety for love poetry that described free, guiltless sexuality, her poetic range was varied. The tone of her earliest work was flippantly cynical; later work became more muted and lyrical. Her New England poems, about nature and the familiar, fit into a regional tradition. Working with closed stanza forms and regular metrical lines, she displayed a high degree of technical virtuosity within quite deliberately chosen limits. "I will put chaos into fourteen lines," she wrote in one sonnet, joining the traditionalists like Robert Frost in a devotion to poetry as permanence.

The text of the poems included here is that of *Collected Poems: Edna St. Vincent Millay* (1956).

# Recuerdo[1]

We were very tired, we were very merry—
We had gone back and forth all night on the ferry.
It was bare and bright, and smelled like a stable—
But we looked into a fire, we leaned across a table,
We lay on a hill-top underneath the moon;      5
And the whistles kept blowing, and the dawn came soon.

We were very tired, we were very merry—
We had gone back and forth all night on the ferry;
And you ate an apple, and I ate a pear,
From a dozen of each we had bought somewhere;      10
And the sky went wan, and the wind came cold,
And the sun rose dripping, a bucketful of gold.

We were very tired, we were very merry,
We had gone back and forth all night on the ferry.
We hailed, "Good morrow, mother!" to a shawl-covered head,      15
And bought a morning paper, which neither of us read;
And she wept, "God bless you!" for the apples and pears,
And we gave her all our money but our subway fares.

1922

# I Think I Should Have Loved You Presently

I think I should have loved you presently,
And given in earnest words I flung in jest;
And lifted honest eyes for you to see,
And caught your hand against my cheek and breast;
And all my pretty follies flung aside      5
That won you to me, and beneath your gaze,

---

1. Remembrance, souvenir.

Naked of reticence and shorn of pride,
Spread like a chart my little wicked ways.
I, that had been to you, had you remained,
But one more waking from a recurrent dream,          10
Cherish no less the certain stakes I gained,
And walk your memory's halls, austere, supreme,
A ghost in marble of a girl you knew
Who would have loved you in a day or two.

                                              1922

## Apostrophe to Man

*(On reflecting that the world is ready to go to war again)*

Detestable race, continue to expunge yourself, die out.
Breed faster, crowd, encroach, sing hymns, build bombing airplanes;
Make speeches, unveil statues, issue bonds, parade;
Convert again into explosives the bewildered ammonia and the distracted
          cellulose;
Convert again into putrescent matter drawing flies          5
The hopeful bodies of the young; exhort,
Pray, pull long faces, be earnest, be all but overcome, be photographed;
Confer, perfect your formulae, commercialize
Bacteria harmful to human tissue,
Put death on the market;          10
Breed, crowd, encroach, expand, expunge yourself, die out,
*Homo* called *sapiens*.

                                              1934

## In the Grave No Flower[1]

Here dock and tare.
But there
No flower.

Here beggar-ticks, 'tis true;
Here the rank-smelling          5
Thorn-apple,—and who
Would plant this by his dwelling?
Here every manner of weed
To mock the faithful harrow:
Thistles, that feed          10
None but the finches; yarrow,
Blue vervain, yellow charlock; here
Bindweed, that chokes the struggling year;
Broad plantain and narrow.

---

1. This poem is the second of a pair of elegies to Millay's mother. The flowers named in the poem are those of common weeds.

But there no flower.      15

The rye is vexed and thinned,
The wheat comes limping home,
By vetch and whiteweed harried, and the sandy bloom
Of the sour-grass; here
Dandelions,—and the wind      20
Will blow them everywhere.

Save there.
There
No flower.

1934

## I Too beneath Your Moon, Almighty Sex

I too beneath your moon, almighty Sex,
Go forth at nightfall crying like a cat,
Leaving the lofty tower I laboured at
For birds to foul and boys and girls to vex
With tittering chalk; and you, and the long necks      5
Of neighbours sitting where their mothers sat
Are well aware of shadowy this and that
In me, that's neither noble nor complex.
Such as I am, however, I have brought
To what it is, this tower; it is my own;      10
Though it was reared To Beauty, it was wrought
From what I had to build with: honest bone
Is there, and anguish; pride; and burning thought;
And lust is there, and nights not spent alone.

1939

## I Forgot for a Moment

### July 1940

I forgot for a moment France; I forgot England; I forgot my care:
I lived for a moment in a world where I was free to be
With the things and people that I love, and I was happy there.
I forgot for a moment Holland, I forgot my heavy care.

I lived for a moment in a world so lovely, so inept      5
At twisted words and crookèd deeds, it was as if I slept and dreamt.

It seemed that all was well with Holland—not a tank had crushed
The tulips there.
Mile after mile the level lowlands blossomed—yellow square, white square,

Scarlet strip and mauve strip bright beneath the brightly clouded sky, the
    round clouds and the gentle air.                                          10
Along the straight canals between striped fields of tulips in the morning sailed
Broad ships, their hulls by tulip-beds concealed, only the sails showing.

It seemed that all was well with England—the harsh foreign voice hysterically
    vowing,
Once more, to keep its word, at length was disbelieved, and hushed.

It seemed that all was well with France, with her straight roads              15
Lined with slender poplars, and the peasants on the skyline ploughing.

                                                                              1940

---

# E. E. CUMMINGS
## 1894–1962

Beginning in the 1920s and 1930s, Edward Estlin Cummings built a reputation as
author of a particularly agreeable kind of modernist poetry, distinguished by clever
formal innovation, a tender lyricism, and the thematic celebration of individuals
against mass society. These qualities were evident in his first literary success, a
zesty prose account of his experience in a French prison camp during World War
I, *The Enormous Room* (1922). He and a friend had joined the ambulance corps
in France the day after the United States entered the war; their disdain for the
bureaucracy, expressed in outspoken letters home, aroused antagonism among
French officials and they were imprisoned. It took intervention from Cummings's
father and a letter to President Woodrow Wilson to get them out. To be made a
prisoner of one's own side struck Cummings as outrageous and yet funny; from the
experience he produced an ironic, earthy celebration of the ordinary soldier and
an attack on bureaucracy. His poetry continued the attack on depersonalized, commercial, exploitative mass culture and celebrated loners, lovers, and nonconformists.

He was born in Cambridge, Massachusetts. His father was a Congregationalist
minister and teacher at Harvard; the family was cultured and Cummings, a much-
loved son. While a student at Harvard (he graduated in 1915 and took an M.A. in
1916) he began to write poetry based on the intricate stanza patterns of the Pre-
Raphaelite and Metaphysical writers he was reading in English literature classes.
When he began to innovate—as he did after discovering the poetry of Ezra
Pound—he was able to build (like Pound himself) from a firm apprenticeship in
traditional techniques.

After the war, Cummings established a life that included a studio in Greenwich
Village, travel and sojourns in France, and summers at the family home in New
Hampshire. He was a painter as well as a poet; simple living and careful management of a small allowance from his mother, along with prizes, royalties, and commissions, enabled him to work full time as an artist. He was not in the least
interested in wealth or celebrity. He published four volumes of well-received poetry
in the 1920s and a book of collected poems toward the end of the 1930s. In the
1950s he visited and read at many college campuses, where students enjoyed his
tricks of verse and vocabulary and appreciated his tender yet earthy poetry. He
received a special citation by the National Book Award committee in 1955 and the
Bollingen Prize in 1957.

Cummings was less ambitious in his attempts to reshape poetry than Stein, Eliot, Pound, Stevens, or Williams, partly because he acknowledged more continuity with the American past than they. Standing up for the individual against society was, after all, the main theme of such nineteenth-century writers as Emerson, Thoreau, and Whitman, all three of whom, like Cummings, strove for flexible immediacy of style.

The special signature of Cummings's verse was its use of common speech and elements of popular culture in the diction, and its attention to the visual form of the poem—that is, the poem as it appears on the page as distinguished from its sound when read aloud. Experiments with capitalization or lack of it, punctuation, line breaks, hyphenation, and verse shapes were all carried out for the reader's eyes rather than ears. Some critics took this as mere trickery, but Cummings can be credited with awareness that he lived in a culture in which poems were read rather than spoken. To express his sense that life was always in process, he wrote untitled poems without beginnings and endings, consisting of fragmentary lines. There is always humor in his poetry, along with a willingness, even eagerness, to admit and express such traditional emotions as love and sadness. His love poems celebrate the body without guilt, free of the distrust or even loathing of the physical that pervades the work of so many other modernists. If his poetry was simpler in thought and technique than the major modernists of his day, it compensated by a gusto and humor that they often lacked.

The text of the poems included here is that of *Poems, 1923–1954* (1954).

## in Just-

in Just-
spring     when the world is mud-
luscious the little
lame balloonman

whistles     far     and wee                                                    5

and eddieandbill come
running from marbles and
piracies and it's
spring

when the world is puddle-wonderful                                   10

the queer
old balloonman whistles
far     and     wee
and bettyandisbel come dancing

from hop-scotch and jump-rope and                                    15

it's
spring
and
    the

        goat-footed                                                          20

balloonMan      whistles
far
and
wee

1920, 1923


## O sweet spontaneous

O sweet spontaneous
earth how often have
the
doting

      fingers of                                                 5
prurient philosophers pinched
and
poked

thee
,has the naughty thumb                                            10
of science prodded
thy

   beauty      .how
often have religions taken
thee upon their scraggy knees                                     15
squeezing and

buffeting thee that thou mightest conceive
gods
    (but
true                                                              20

to the incomparable
couch of death thy
rhythmic
lover

    thou answerest                                           25

them only with

      spring)

1920, 1923

# Poem, or Beauty Hurts Mr. Vinal

take it from me kiddo
believe me
my country, 'tis of

you, land of the Cluett
Shirt Boston Garter and Spearmint       5
Girl With The Wrigley Eyes(of you
land of the Arrow Ide
and Earl &
Wilson
Collars) of you i       10
sing: land of Abraham Lincoln and Lydia E. Pinkham,[1]
land above all of Just Add Hot Water And Serve—
from every B.V.D.[2]

let freedom ring

amen.    i do however protest, anent the un       15
-spontaneous and otherwise scented merde[3] which
greets one(Everywhere Why) as divine poesy per
that and this radically defunct periodical. i would

suggest that certain ideas gestures
rhymes, like Gillette Razor Blades       20
having been used and reused
to the mystical moment of dullness emphatically are
Not To Be Resharpened.    (Case in point

if we are to believe these gently O sweetly
melancholy trillers amid the thrillers       25
these crepuscular violinists among my and your
skyscrapers—Helen & Cleopatra[4] were Just Too Lovely,
The Snail's On The Thorn enter Morn and God's
In His andsoforth[5]

do you get me?) according       30
to such supposedly indigenous
throstles[6] Art is O World O Life
a formula: example, Turn Your Shirttails Into
Drawers and If It Isn't An Eastman It Isn't A
Kodak therefore my friends let       35
us now sing each and all fortissimo A-

---

1. Lydia E. Pinkham (1819–1883), manufacturer of a widely advertised patent medicine.
2. Trade name of a brand of men's underwear. In this and other stanzas Cummings uses brand names and advertising slogans to define a commercialized popular culture.
3. I.e., excrement (French).
4. Cleopatra (69–30 B.C.), queen of Egypt, Caesar's mistress, and lover of the Roman general and triumvir

Mark Antony. Helen, wife of Menelaus; her abduction by Paris occasioned the Trojan War in Homer's *Iliad*.
5. Parody of a song from *Pippas Passes* (lines 223–28), a verse drama by the English poet Robert Browning (1812–1889): "Morning's at seven; / The hillside's dew-pearled; / The lark's on the wing; / The snail's on the thorn; / God's in his heaven— / All's right with the world!"
6. European thrushes.

mer
i

ca,I
love,                                                                          40
You.    And there're a
hun-dred-mil-lion-oth-ers,like
all of you successfully if
delicately gelded (or spaded)[7]
gentlemen (and ladies)—pretty                                                  45

littleliverpill-
hearted-Nujolneeding[8]-There's-A-Reason
americans (who tensetendoned and with
upward vacant eyes, painfully
perpetually crouched,quivering,upon the                                        50
sternly allotted sandpile
—how silently
emit a tiny violetflavoured nuisance:Odor?

ono.[9]
comes out like a ribbon lies flat on the brush                                 55

                                                      1922, 1926


## i sing of Olaf glad and big

i sing of Olaf glad and big
whose warmest heart recoiled at war:
a conscientious object-or

his wellbelovéd colonel(trig
westpointer[1] most succinctly bred)                                            5
took erring Olaf soon in hand;
but—though an host of overjoyed
noncoms(first knocking on the head
him)do through icy waters roll
that helplessness which others stroke                                          10
with brushes recently employed
anent this muddy toiletbowl,
while kindred intellects evoke
allegiance per blunt instruments—
Olaf(being to all intents                                                      15
a corpse and wanting any rag
upon what God unto him gave)
responds, without getting annoyed
"I will not kiss your f.ing flag"

---

7. Common pronunciation of *spayed*.
8. Two commercial laxatives, Carters' Little Liver
Pills and Nujol.

9. Pun on *Odorono*, trade name of a deodorant.
1. Graduate of the U.S. Military Academy at West
Point, New York.

straightway the silver bird looked grave                    20
(departing hurriedly to shave)

but—though all kinds of officers
(a yearning nation's blueeyed pride)
their passive prey did kick and curse
until for wear their clarion                                25
voices and boots were much the worse,
and egged the firstclassprivates on
his rectum wickedly to tease
by means of skilfully applied
bayonets roasted hot with heat—                             30
Olaf(upon what were once knees)
does almost ceaselessly repeat
"there is some s. I will not eat"

our president, being of which
assertions duly notified                                    35
threw the yellowsonofabitch
into a dungeon, where he died

Christ(of His mercy infinite)
i pray to see; and Olaf, too

preponderatingly because                                    40
unless statistics lie he was
more brave than me:more blond than you.

                                                            1931


## somewhere i have never travelled, gladly beyond

somewhere i have never travelled, gladly beyond
any experience, your eyes have their silence:
in your most frail gesture are things which enclose me,
or which i cannot touch because they are too near

your slightest look easily will unclose me                  5
though i have closed myself as fingers,
you open always petal by petal myself as Spring opens
(touching skilfully, mysteriously)her first rose

or if your wish be to close me, i and
my life will shut very beautifully, suddenly,              10
as when the heart of this flower imagines
the snow carefully everywhere descending;

nothing which we are to perceive in this world equals
the power of your intense fragility:whose texture
compels me with the colour of its countries,              15
rendering death and forever with each breathing

(i do not know what it is about you that closes
and opens; only something in me understands
the voice of your eyes is deeper than all roses)
nobody,not even the rain,has such small hands          20

1931

## anyone lived in a pretty how town

anyone lived in a pretty how town
(with up so floating many bells down)
spring summer autumn winter
he sang his didn't he danced his did.

Women and men(both little and small)          5
cared for anyone not at all
they sowed their isn't they reaped their same
sun moon stars rain

children guessed(but only a few
and down they forgot as up they grew          10
autumn winter spring summer)
that noone loved him more by more

when by now and tree by leaf
she laughed his joy she cried his grief
bird by snow and stir by still          15
anyone's any was all to her

someones married their everyones
laughed their cryings and did their dance
(sleep wake hope and then)they
said their nevers they slept their dream          20

stars rain sun moon
(and only the snow can begin to explain
how children are apt to forget to remember
with up so floating many bells down)

one day anyone died i guess          25
(and noone stooped to kiss his face)
busy folk buried them side by side
little by little and was by was

all by all and deep by deep
and more by more they dream their sleep          30
noone and anyone earth by april
wish by spirit and if by yes.

Women and men(both dong and ding)
summer autumn winter spring

reaped their sowing and went their came     35
sun moon stars rain

1940

# my father moved through dooms of love

my father moved through dooms of love
through sames of am through haves of give,
singing each morning out of each night
my father moved through depths of height

this motionless forgetful where      5
turned at his glance to shining here;
that if(so timid air is firm)
under his eyes would stir and squirm

newly as from unburied which
floats the first who, his april touch      10
drove sleeping selves to swarm their fates
woke dreamers to their ghostly roots

and should some why completely weep
my father's fingers brought her sleep:
vainly no smallest voice might cry      15
for he could feel the mountains grow.

Lifting the valleys of the sea
my father moved through griefs of joy;
praised a forehead called the moon
singing desire into begin      20

joy was his song and joy so pure
a heart of star by him could steer
and pure so now and now so yes
the wrists of twilight would rejoice

keen as midsummer's keen beyond      25
conceiving mind of sun will stand,
so strictly(over utmost him
so hugely) stood my father's dream

his flesh was flesh his blood was blood:
no hungry man but wished him food;      30
no cripple wouldn't creep one mile
uphill to only see him smile.

Scorning the pomp of must and shall
my father moved through dooms of feel;
his anger was as right as rain      35
his pity was as green as grain

septembering arms of year extend
less humbly wealth to foe and friend
than he to foolish and to wise
offered immeasurable is                                    40

proudly and(by octobering flame
beckoned)as earth will downward climb,
so naked for immortal work
his shoulders marched against the dark

his sorrow was as true as bread:                           45
no liar looked him in the head;
if every friend became his foe
he'd laugh and build a world with snow.

My father moved through theys of we,
singing each new leaf out of each tree                     50
(and every child was sure that spring
danced when she heard my father sing)

then let men kill which cannot share,
let blood and flesh be mud and mire,
scheming imagine,passion willed,                           55
freedom a drug that's bought and sold

giving to steal and cruel kind,
a heart to fear,to doubt a mind,
to differ a disease of same,
conform the pinnacle of am                                 60

though dull were all we taste as bright,
bitter all utterly things sweet,
maggoty minus and dumb death
all we inherit,all bequeath

and nothing quite so least as truth                        65
—i say though hate were why men breathe—
because my father lived his soul
love is the whole and more than all

                                              1940


# what if a much of a which of a wind

what if a much of a which of a wind
gives the truth to summer's lie;
bloodies with dizzying leaves the sun
and yanks immortal stars awry?
Blow king to beggar and queen to seem                      5
(blow friend to fiend:blow space to time)
—when skies are hanged and oceans drowned,
the single secret will still be man

what if a keen of a lean wind flays
screaming hills with sleet and snow:     10
strangles valleys by ropes of thing
and stifles forests in white ago?
Blow hope to terror; blow seeing to blind
(blow pity to envy and soul to mind)
—whose hearts are mountains, roots are trees,     15
it's they shall cry hello to the spring

what if a dawn of a doom of a dream
bites this universe in two,
peels forever out of his grave
and sprinkles nowhere with me and you?     20
Blow soon to never and never to twice
(blow life to isn't:blow death to was)
—all nothing's only our hugest home;
the most who die, the more we live

1944

---

# JEAN TOOMER
## 1894–1967

In 1915, the section of New York City called Harlem had a black population of about fifty thousand; by 1929 it had more than three times that number and constituted the largest black urban area in the nation. Among newcomers to this "city within a city" were many talented men and women who made Harlem an intellectual and artistic center. For Jean Toomer, this Harlem Renaissance spurred the writing of one excellent book, *Cane* (1923). The strength of *Cane* lies in the interplay between a presentation of the image of the simple, rural black and the urban black sensibility that analyzes the image.

Toomer was born in Washington, D.C., and grew up with his mother and his grandfather, who had been an important Louisiana politician during the Reconstruction era but had fallen on hard times. Toomer never knew his father. He graduated from high school and attended several colleges—including the University of Wisconsin, the Massachusetts College of Agriculture, the American College of Physical Training in Chicago, the University of Chicago, and City College of New York—without earning a degree. He also held, briefly, a variety of jobs in different parts of the country.

Toomer began writing when he was in his middle twenties. He published poems and stories in several avant-garde little magazines, among them *Broom*, the *Little Review*, and *Prairie*, as well as such African-American publications as the *Liberator*, *Crisis*, and *Opportunity*. In 1921 he worked for four months as superintendent of a small black school in Sparta, Georgia, and there—his only sustained encounter with rural black people—absorbed the material from which *Cane* was distilled.

*Cane* is a three-part work, which incorporates short stories, sketches, poems, and a play; it has a general thematic unity in its representation of an alienated, questing black man who tries to find himself through connection with the black folk heritage. Part I, set in rural Georgia, depicts the difficult yet noble life of the rural black population. Part II shows black urban life in Washington, D.C., and

Chicago, where it has been corrupted by white materialism. Part III, the most autobiographical, shows an African-American intellectual teaching in the South, trying to establish roots in a style of life that he has never known before but that is nevertheless supposed to be "his." Although the circumstances are specifically black, the theme of returning to one's roots, or trying to and failing or even inventing the roots one never had, is persistent in modern fiction; we meet it in Katherine Anne Porter, Thomas Wolfe, and Ernest Hemingway, among others. *Cane* is also distinguished by its poetic, imagistic, evocative prose, its linguistic innovativeness, and its method of assembling pieces of writing like a mosaic. Toomer was attuned to modern literary method and greatly concerned with being literary in a recognizable sense—in contrast to Countee Cullen, who used traditional forms, and to Zora Neale Hurston and Langston Hughes, who tried to create a specifically African-American poetics.

Toomer continued to write after the appearance of *Cane* but had increasing difficulty in getting his work published—it was ever more abstract and less centered on black issues; eventually, he wrote for himself alone. There are numerous finished but unpublished works—short stories, novels, plays, and an autobiography—among his papers. He spent much of the last forty years of his life looking for a spiritual community that would satisfy his quest for psychic wholeness. For a while he was an ardent disciple of the Russian mystic George I. Gurdjieff, and in the 1940s he became a committed Quaker. Apparently concluding that the idea of a black identity was a fiction, he moved to the theme of individual connection with a transcendent divinity.

## From Cane[1]

### Georgia Dusk

The sky, lazily disdaining to pursue
    The setting sun, too indolent to hold
    A lengthened tournament for flashing gold,
Passively darkens for night's barbecue,

A feast of moon and men and barking hounds,                5
    An orgy for some genius of the South
    With blood-hot eyes and cane-lipped scented mouth,
Surprised in making folk-songs from soul sounds.

The sawmill blows its whistle, buzz-saws stop,
    And silence breaks the bud of knoll and hill,         10
    Soft settling pollen where plowed lands fulfill
Their early promise of a bumper crop.

Smoke from the pyramidal sawdust pile
    Curls up, blue ghosts of trees, tarrying low
    Where only chips and stumps are left to show           15
    The solid proof of former domicile.

1. Of the book's three sections, the first and the last are Georgia scenes. *Fern* appears in the first section, preceded immediately by the poem *Georgia Dusk*. The poem *Portrait in Georgia* appears in the first section immediately preceding a story of the lynching of a black woman's black lover by her white lover and his white cohorts. *Seventh Street* is the first sketch in the center section devoted to Washington, D.C., and Chicago. The text is that of the 1st edition (1923), as corrected in 1975.

Meanwhile, the men, with vestiges of pomp,
Race memories of king and caravan,
High-priests, an ostrich, and a juju-man,[2]
Go singing through the footpaths of the swamp.                    20

Their voices rise . . the pine trees are guitars,
Strumming, pine-needles fall like sheets of rain . .
Their voices rise . . the chorus of the cane
Is caroling a vesper to the stars. .

O singers, resinous and soft your songs                          25
Above the sacred whisper of the pines,
Give virgin lips to cornfield concubines,
Bring dreams of Christ to dusky cane-lipped throngs.

## Fern

Face flowed into her eyes. Flowed in soft cream foam and plaintive ripples,
in such a way that wherever your glance may momentarily have rested, it
immediately thereafter wavered in the direction of her eyes. The soft suggestion of down slightly darkened, like the shadow of a bird's wing might, the
creamy brown color of her upper lip. Why, after noticing it, you sought her
eyes, I cannot tell you. Her nose was aquiline, Semitic. If you have heard a
Jewish cantor[3] sing, if he has touched you and made your own sorrow seem
trivial when compared with his, you will know my feeling when I follow the
curves of her profile, like mobile rivers, to their common delta. They were
strange eyes. In this, that they sought nothing—that is, nothing that was obvious and tangible and that one could see, and they gave the impression that
nothing was to be denied. When a woman seeks, you will have observed, her
eyes deny. Fern's eyes desired nothing that you could give her; there was no
reason why they should withhold. Men saw her eyes and fooled themselves.
Fern's eyes said to them that she was easy. When she was young, a few men
took her, but got no joy from it. And then, once done, they felt bound to her
(quite unlike their hit and run with other girls), felt as though it would take
them a lifetime to fulfill an obligation which they could find no name for.
They became attached to her, and hungered after finding the barest trace of
what she might desire. As she grew up, new men who came to town felt as
almost everyone did who ever saw her: that they would not be denied. Men
were everlastingly bringing her their bodies. Something inside of her got tired
of them, I guess, for I am certain that for the life of her she could not tell why
or how she began to turn them off. A man in fever is no trifling thing to send
away. They began to leave her, baffled and ashamed, yet vowing to themselves
that some day they would do some fine thing for her: send her candy every
week and not let her know whom it came from, watch out for her wedding-
day and give her a magnificent something with no name on it, buy a house
and deed it to her, rescue her from some unworthy fellow who had tricked her
into marrying him. As you know, men are apt to idolize or fear that which
they cannot understand, especially if it be a woman. She did not deny them,

---

2. West African tribesman who controls the magical     3. Male singer in religious services.
fetish or charm, or "juju."

yet the fact was that they were denied. A sort of superstition crept into their consciousness of her being somehow above them. Being above them meant that she was not to be approached by anyone. She became a virgin. Now a virgin in a small southern town is by no means the usual thing, if you will believe me. That the sexes were made to mate is the practice of the South. Particularly, black folks were made to mate. And it is black folks whom I have been talking about thus far. What white men thought of Fern I can arrive at only by analogy. They let her alone.

Anyone, of course, could see her, could see her eyes. If you walked up the Dixie Pike most any time of day, you'd be most like to see her resting listless-like on the railing of her porch, back propped against a post, head tilted a little forward because there was a nail in the porch post just where her head came which for some reason or other she never took the trouble to pull out. Her eyes, if it were sunset, rested idly where the sun, molten and glorious, was pouring down between the fringe of pines. Or maybe they gazed at the gray cabin on the knoll from which an evening folk-song was coming. Perhaps they followed a cow that had been turned loose to roam and feed on cotton-stalks and corn leaves. Like as not they'd settle on some vague spot above the horizon, though hardly a trace of wistfulness would come to them. If it were dusk, then they'd wait for the search-light of the evening train which you could see miles up the track before it flared across the Dixie Pike, close to her home. Wherever they looked, you'd follow them and then waver back. Like her face, the whole countryside seemed to flow into her eyes. Flowed into them with the soft listless cadence of Georgia's South. A young Negro, once, was looking at her, spellbound, from the road. A white man passing in a buggy had to flick him with his whip if he was to get by without running him over. I first saw her on her porch. I was passing with a fellow whose crusty numbness (I was from the North and suspected of being prejudiced and stuck-up) was melting as he found me warm. I asked him who she was. "That's Fern," was all that I could get from him. Some folks already thought that I was given to nosing around; I let it go at that, so far as questions were concerned. But at first sight of her I felt as if I heard a Jewish cantor sing. As if his singing rose above the unheard chorus of a folk-song. And I felt bound to her. I too had my dreams: something I would do for her. I have knocked about from town to town too much not to know the futility of mere change of place. Besides, picture if you can, this cream-colored solitary girl sitting at a tenement window looking down on the indifferent throngs of Harlem. Better that she listen to folk-songs at dusk in Georgia, you would say, and so would I. Or, suppose she came up North and married. Even a doctor or a lawyer, say, one who would be sure to get along— that is, make money. You and I know, who have had experience in such things, that love is not a thing like prejudice which can be bettered by changes of town. Could men in Washington, Chicago, or New York, more than the men of Georgia, bring her something left vacant by the bestowal of their bodies? You and I who know men in these cities will have to say, they could not. See her out and out a prostitute along State Street in Chicago. See her move into a southern town where white men are more aggressive. See her become a white man's concubine . . . Something I must do for her. There was myself. What could I do for her? Talk, of course. Push back the fringe of pines upon new horizons. To what purpose? and what for? Her? Myself? Men in her case seem to lose their selfishness. I lost mine before I touched her. I ask you, friend (it makes no difference if you sit in the Pullman or the Jim Crow[4] as the train crosses her road), what thoughts would come to you—that is, after you'd finished with the thoughts that leap into men's minds at the sight of a pretty woman who will not deny them; what thoughts would come to you, had you seen her in a quick flash, keen and intuitively, as she sat there on her porch when your train thundered by? Would you have got off at the next station and come back for her to take her where? Would you have completely forgotten her as soon as you reached Macon, Atlanta, Augusta, Pasadena, Madison, Chicago, Boston, or New Orleans? Would you tell your wife or sweetheart about a girl you saw? Your thoughts can help me, and I would like to know. Something I would do for her . . .

One evening I walked up the Pike on purpose, and stopped to say hello. Some of her family were about, but they moved away to make room for me. Damn if I knew how to begin. Would you? Mr. and Miss So-and-So, people, the weather, the crops, the new preacher, the frolic, the church benefit, rabbit and possum hunting, the new soft drink they had at old Pap's store, the schedule of the trains, what kind of town Macon was, Negro's migration north, bollweevils, syrup, the Bible—to all these things she gave a yassur or nassur, without further comment. I began to wonder if perhaps my own emotional sensibility had played one of its tricks on me. "Lets take a walk," I at last ventured. The suggestion, coming after so long an isolation, was novel enough, I guess, to surprise. But it wasnt that. Something told me that men before me had said just that as a prelude to the offering of their bodies. I tried to tell her with my eyes. I think she understood. The thing from her that made my throat catch, vanished. Its passing left her visible in a way I'd thought, but never seen. We walked down the Pike with people on all the porches gaping at us. "Doesnt it make you mad?" She meant the row of petty gossiping people. She meant the world. Through a canebrake that was ripe for cutting, the branch was reached. Under a sweet-gum tree, and where reddish leaves had dammed the creek a little, we sat down. Dusk, suggesting the almost imperceptible procession of giant trees, settled with a purple haze about the cane. I felt strange, as I always do in Georgia, particularly at dusk. I felt that things unseen to men were tangibly immediate. It would not have surprised me had I had vision. People have them in Georgia more often than you would suppose. A black woman once saw the mother of Christ and drew her in charcoal on the courthouse wall . . . When one is on the soil of one's ancestors, most anything can come to one . . . From force of habit, I suppose, I held Fern in my arms—that is, without at first noticing it. Then my mind came back to her. Her eyes, unusually weird and open, held me. Held God. He flowed in as I've seen the countryside flow in. Seen men. I must have done something— what, I don't know, in the confusion of my emotion. She sprang up. Rushed some distance from me. Fell to her knees, and began swaying, swaying. Her body was tortured with something it could not let out. Like boiling sap it flooded arms and fingers till she shook them as if they burned her. It found her throat, and spattered inarticulately in plaintive, convulsive sounds, min-

---

4. In the segregated South, black persons were required to sit in the "Jim Crow" section of railway cars and were not allowed as passengers in the first-class "Pullman" lounges, or sleeping cars.

gled with calls to Christ Jesus. And then she sang, brokenly. A Jewish cantor singing with a broken voice. A child's voice, uncertain, or an old man's. Dusk hid her; I could hear only her song. It seemed to me as though she were pounding her head in anguish upon the ground. I rushed at her. She fainted in my arms.

There was talk about her fainting with me in the canefield. And I got one or two ugly looks from town men who'd set themselves up to protect her. In fact, there was talk of making me leave town. But they never did. They kept a watch-out for me, though. Shortly after, I came back North. From the train window I saw her as I crossed her road. Saw her on her porch, head tilted a little forward where the nail was, eyes vaguely focused on the sunset. Saw her face flow into them, the countryside and something that I call God, flowing into them . . . Nothing ever really happened. Nothing ever came to Fern, not even I. Something I would do for her. Some fine unnamed thing . . . And, friend, you? She is still living, I have reason to know. Her name, against the chance that you might happen down that way, is Fernie May Rosen.

*  *  *

## Portrait in Georgia

Hair—braided chestnut,
    coiled like a lyncher's rope,
Eyes—fagots,
Lips—old scars, or the first red blisters,
Breath—the last sweet scent of cane,        5
And her slim body, white as the ash
    of black flesh after flame.

*  *  *

## Seventh Street

Money burns the pocket, pocket hurts,
Bootleggers in silken shirts,
Ballooned, zooming Cadillacs,
Whizzing, whizzing down the street-car tracks.

Seventh Street is a bastard of Prohibition and the War.[5] A crude-boned, soft-skinned wedge of nigger life breathing its loafer air, jazz songs and love, thrusting unconscious rhythms, black reddish blood into the white and whitewashed wood of Washington. Stale soggy wood of Washington. Wedges rust in soggy wood . . . Split it! In two! Again! Shred it! . . the sun. Wedges are brilliant in the sun; ribbons of wet wood dry and blow away. Black reddish blood. Pouring for crude-boned soft-skinned life, who set you flowing? Blood suckers of the War would spin in a frenzy of dizziness if they drank your blood. Prohibition would put a stop to it. Who set you flowing? White and whitewash disappear in blood. Who set you flowing? Flowing down the smooth asphalt of Seventh Street, in shanties, brick office buildings, theaters, drug stores, restaurants, and cabarets? Eddying on the corners? Swirling like a blood-red smoke up where the buzzards fly in heaven? God would not dare to suck black red blood.

5. World War I.

A Nigger God! He would duck his head in shame and call for the Judgment
Day. Who set you flowing?

Money burns the pocket, pocket hurts,
Bootleggers in silken shirts,
Ballooned, zooming Cadillacs,
Whizzing, whizzing down the street-car tracks.

1923

---

# F. SCOTT FITZGERALD
## 1896–1940

In the aftermath of the American Revolution, the concept of "America" referred
primarily to ideas of political freedom. After the Civil War, a different kind of
imaginary America took shape, one promising the satisfaction of every material
desire. In the 1920s F. Scott Fitzgerald spoke both from within and against this
vision of America as a materialist utopia. On the one hand he argued that the
vision was unattainable and inherently corrupt; on the other, he documented its
allure.

Fitzgerald was born and raised in a middle-class neighborhood in St. Paul, Minnesota, descended on his mother's side from southern colonial landowners and
legislators, on his father's from Irish immigrants. The family was not prosperous
and it took an aunt's support to send him to a Catholic boarding school in New
Jersey in 1911. Two years later he entered Princeton University. His writings show
how much he was affected by the differences between himself and his rich young
classmates.

At Princeton Fitzgerald participated in extracurricular literary and dramatic
activities, forming friendships with campus intellectuals like Edmund Wilson who
were to help him in later years. But he failed to make the football team and felt
the disappointment for years. After three years of college Fitzgerald quit to join the
army, but the war ended before he saw active service. Stationed in Montgomery,
Alabama, he met and courted Zelda Zayre, a local belle who rejected him. In
1919 he went to New York City, determined to make a fortune and win Zelda.
Amazingly, he succeeded. A novel he had begun in college, revised, and published
in 1920 as *This Side of Paradise* became an immediate best-seller, making its
author a celebrity at the age of twenty-four. As one of the earliest examples of a
novel about college life, *This Side of Paradise* was accepted as the voice of the
younger generation in a society increasingly oriented toward youth. He combined
the traditional narrative and rhetorical gifts of a good fiction writer, it appeared,
with a thoroughly modern sensibility. A week after the novel appeared, Scott and
Zelda were married.

This is the point where fairy tales conclude with "and they lived happily ever
after." The Fitzgeralds had to live the story out to a different ending. They drank
too much and spent too much. Although Fitzgerald quickly learned that a life of
constant partying was incompatible with a serious literary career, he could not give
up the fun, and even when the fun came to an end, he kept on partying. Living
extravagantly in New York City and St. Paul, and on Long Island, they more than
spent the money Fitzgerald made from two collections of short stories—*Flappers
and Philosophers* (1921) and *Tales of the Jazz Age* (1922)—and a second novel, *The
Beautiful and Damned* (1922). Their only child, a daughter, was born in 1921.

In 1924, the Fitzgeralds moved to Europe to live more cheaply. They made friends with the American expatriates—Hemingway, Stein, and Pound among others—but were no more successful in managing their lives. During this time Fitzgerald published his masterpiece, *The Great Gatsby* (1925), and another book of short stories, *All the Sad Young Men* (1926). *The Great Gatsby* tells the story of a self-made young man whose dream of success, personified in a rich and beautiful young woman named Daisy, turns out to be a fantasy in every sense: Daisy belongs to a corrupt society, Gatsby corrupts himself in the quest for her, and above all, the rich have no intention of sharing their privileges. The novel is narrated from the point of view of Nick Carraway, an onlooker who is both moved and repelled by the tale he tells and whose responses form a sort of subplot: this experiment in narrative point of view was widely imitated. The structure of *The Great Gatsby* is compact, the style dazzling, and its images of modern American life—automobiles, parties, garbage heaps—are unforgettable.

Fitzgerald wrote dozens of short stories during the twenties. Despite the pace at which he worked—in all he wrote 178 short stories—the Fitzgeralds could not get out of debt. Scott became an alcoholic, and Zelda became mentally unstable. In 1930 she broke down and was consigned for most of the rest of her life—she died in 1947—to mental institutions. In 1931 Fitzgerald reestablished himself permanently in the United States, living at first near Baltimore where his wife was hospitalized. A second novel, *Tender Is the Night*, appeared in 1934. The novel follows the decline of a young American psychiatrist whose personal energies are sapped, and his professional career corroded, by his marriage to a beautiful and wealthy patient. As in *The Great Gatsby*, the character begins as a disciple of the work ethic and turns into a pursuer of wealth, and the American dream accordingly turns into a nightmare. The novel, with its characteristic thematic indictment of American materialism, seemed somewhat irrelevant to a country deep in a depression and was taken as a sign that during Fitzgerald's long stay in Europe he had lost touch with his age.

By 1937 Fitzgerald was sick, alcoholic, unable to write, and no longer earning royalties. He turned to Hollywood screenwriting; the money he made enabled him to pay for his wife's medical care and for the education of his daughter (although he had long since surrendered her upbringing to others). Toward the end of the decade things were looking up for him and he planned to revive his career as a fiction writer. But he died of a heart attack in Hollywood at the age of forty-four, leaving an unfinished novel about a film mogul, *The Last Tycoon*, which was brought out by Edmund Wilson in 1941. Wilson also successfully promoted Fitzgerald's posthumous reputation by editing a collection of his writings, which he called *The Crack-Up*, in 1945.

# Winter Dreams[1]

Some of the caddies were poor as sin and lived in one-room houses with a neurasthenic cow in the front yard, but Dexter Green's father owned the second best grocery-store in Black Bear—the best one was "The Hub," patronized by the wealthy people from Sherry Island—and Dexter caddied only for pocket-money.

In the fall when the days became crisp and gray, and the long Minnesota winter shut down like the white lid of a box, Dexter's skis moved over the snow that hid the fairways of the golf course. At these times the country gave him a feeling of profound melancholy—it offended him that the links should lie in

---

1. The text is that of *Tales of the Jazz Age* (1922).

enforced fallowness, haunted by ragged sparrows for the long season. It was dreary, too, that on the tees where the gay colors fluttered in summer there were now only the desolate sand-boxes knee-deep in crusted ice. When he crossed the hills the wind blew cold as misery, and if the sun was out he tramped with his eyes squinted up against the hard dimensionless glare.

In April the winter ceased abruptly. The snow ran down into Black Bear Lake scarcely tarrying for the early golfers to brave the season with red and black balls. Without elation, without an interval of moist glory, the cold was gone.

Dexter knew that there was something dismal about this Northern spring, just as he knew there was something gorgeous about the fall. Fall made him clinch his hands and tremble and repeat idiotic sentences to himself, and make brisk abrupt gestures of command to imaginary audiences and armies. October filled him with hope which November raised to a sort of ecstatic triumph, and in this mood the fleeting brilliant impressions of the summer at Sherry Island were ready grist to his mill. He became a golf champion and defeated Mr. T. A. Hedrick in a marvellous match played a hundred times over the fairways of his imagination, a match each detail of which he changed about untiringly—sometimes he won with almost laughable ease, sometimes he came up magnificently from behind. Again, stepping from a Pierce-Arrow automobile, like Mr. Mortimer Jones, he strolled frigidly into the lounge of the Sherry Island Golf Club—or perhaps, surrounded by an admiring crowd, he gave an exhibition of fancy diving from the spring-board of the club raft. . . . Among those who watched him in open-mouthed wonder was Mr. Mortimer Jones.

And one day it came to pass that Mr. Jones—himself and not his ghost—came up to Dexter with tears in his eyes and said that Dexter was the —— best caddy in the club, and wouldn't he decide not to quit if Mr. Jones made it worth his while, because every other —— caddy in the club lost one ball a hole for him—regularly——

"No, sir," said Dexter decisively, "I don't want to caddy any more." Then, after a pause: "I'm too old."

"You're not more than fourteen. Why the devil did you decide just this morning that you wanted to quit? You promised that next week you'd go over to the State tournament with me."

"I decided I was too old."

Dexter handed in his "A Class" badge, collected what money was due him from the caddy master, and walked home to Black Bear Village.

"The best —— caddy I ever saw," shouted Mr. Mortimer Jones over a drink that afternoon. "Never lost a ball! Willing! Intelligent! Quiet! Honest! Grateful!"

The little girl who had done this was eleven—beautifully ugly as little girls are apt to be who are destined after a few years to be inexpressibly lovely and bring no end of misery to a great number of men. The spark, however, was perceptible. There was a general ungodliness in the way her lips twisted down at the corners when she smiled, and in the—Heaven help us!—in the almost passionate quality of her eyes. Vitality is born in such women. It was utterly in evidence now, shining through her thin frame in a sort of glow.

She had come eagerly out on to the course at nine o'clock with a white linen nurse and five small new golf-clubs in a white canvas bag which the nurse was carrying. When Dexter first saw her she was standing by the caddy houses, rather ill at ease and trying to conceal the fact by engaging her nurse in an obviously unnatural conversation graced by startling and irrelevant grimaces from herself.

"Well, it's certainly a nice day, Hilda," Dexter heard her say. She drew down the corners of her mouth, smiled, and glanced furtively around, her eyes in transit falling for an instant on Dexter.

Then to the nurse:

"Well, I guess there aren't very many people out here this morning, are there?"

The smile again—radiant, blatantly artificial—convincing.

"I don't know what we're supposed to do now," said the nurse, looking nowhere in particular.

"Oh, that's all right. I'll fix it up."

Dexter stood perfectly still, his mouth slightly ajar. He knew that if he moved forward a step his stare would be in her line of vision—if he moved backward he would lose his full view of her face. For a moment he had not realized how young she was. Now he remembered having seen her several times the year before—in bloomers.

Suddenly, involuntarily, he laughed, a short abrupt laugh—then, startled by himself, he turned and began to walk quickly away.

"Boy!"

Dexter stopped.

"Boy—"

Beyond question he was addressed. Not only that, but he was treated to that absurd smile, that preposterous smile—the memory of which at least a dozen men were to carry into middle age.

"Boy, do you know where the golf teacher is?"

"He's giving a lesson."

"Well, do you know where the caddy-master is?"

"He isn't here yet this morning."

"Oh." For a moment this baffled her. She stood alternately on her right and left foot.

"We'd like to get a caddy," said the nurse. "Mr. Mortimer Jones sent us out to play golf, and we don't know how without we get a caddy."

Here she was stopped by an ominous glance from Miss Jones, followed immediately by the smile.

"There aren't any caddies here except me," said Dexter to the nurse, "and I got to stay here in charge until the caddy-master gets here."

"Oh."

Miss Jones and her retinue now withdrew, and at a proper distance from Dexter became involved in a heated conversation, which was concluded by Miss Jones taking one of the clubs and hitting it on the ground with violence. For further emphasis she raised it again and was about to bring it down smartly upon the nurse's bosom, when the nurse seized the club and twisted it from her hands.

"You damn little mean old *thing!*" cried Miss Jones wildly.

Another argument ensued. Realizing that the elements of comedy were implied in the scene, Dexter several times began to laugh, but each time restrained the laugh before it reached audibility. He could not resist the monstrous conviction that the little girl was justified in beating the nurse.

The situation was resolved by the fortuitous appearance of the caddy-master, who was appealed to immediately by the nurse.

"Miss Jones is to have a little caddy, and this one says he can't go."

"Mr. McKenna said I was to wait here till you came," said Dexter quickly.

"Well, he's here now." Miss Jones smiled cheerfully at the caddy-master. Then she dropped her bag and set off at a haughty mince toward the first tee.

"Well?" The caddy-master turned to Dexter. "What you standing there like a dummy for? Go pick up the young lady's clubs."

"I don't think I'll go out to-day," said Dexter.

"You don't—"

"I think I'll quit."

The enormity of his decision frightened him. He was a favorite caddy, and the thirty dollars a month he earned through the summer were not to be made elsewhere around the lake. But he had received a strong emotional shock, and his perturbation required a violent and immediate outlet.

It was not so simple as that, either. As so frequently would be the case in the future, Dexter was unconsciously dictated to by his winter dreams.

## II

Now, of course, the quality and the seasonability of these winter dreams varied, but the stuff of them remained. They persuaded Dexter several years later to pass up a business course at the State university—his father, prospering now, would have paid his way—for the precarious advantage of attending an older and more famous university in the East, where he was bothered by his scanty funds. But do not get the impression, because his winter dreams happened to be concerned at first with musings on the rich, that there was anything merely snobbish in the boy. He wanted not association with glittering things and glittering people—he wanted the glittering things themselves. Often he reached out for the best without knowing why he wanted it—and sometimes he ran up against the mysterious denials and prohibitions in which life indulges. It is with one of those denials and not with his career as a whole that this story deals.

He made money. It was rather amazing. After college he went to the city from which Black Bear Lake draws its wealthy patrons. When he was only twenty-three and had been there not quite two years, there were already people who liked to say: "Now *there's* a boy—" All about him rich men's sons were peddling bonds precariously, or investing patrimonies precariously, or plodding through the two dozen volumes of the "George Washington Commercial Course," but Dexter borrowed a thousand dollars on his college degree and his confident mouth, and bought a partnership in a laundry.

It was a small laundry when he went into it, but Dexter made a specialty of learning how the English washed fine woolen golf-stockings without shrinking them, and within a year he was catering to the trade that wore knickerbockers. Men were insisting that their Shetland hose and sweaters go to his laundry, just as they had insisted on a caddy who could find golf-balls. A little later he was doing their wives' lingerie as well—and running five branches in different parts of the city. Before he was twenty-seven he owned the largest string of laundries in his section of the country. It was then that he sold out and went to New York. But the part of his story that concerns us goes back to the days when he was making his first big success.

When he was twenty-three Mr. Hart—one of the gray-haired men who liked to say "Now there's a boy"—gave him a guest card to the Sherry Island Golf Club for a week-end. So he signed his name one day on the register, and that afternoon played golf in a foursome with Mr. Hart and Mr. Sandwood and Mr. T. A. Hedrick. He did not consider it necessary to remark that he had once carried Mr. Hart's bag over this same links, and that he knew every trap and gully with his eyes shut—but he found himself glancing at the four caddies who trailed them, trying to catch a gleam or gesture that would remind him of himself, that would lesson the gap which lay between his present and his past.

It was a curious day, slashed abruptly with fleeting, familiar impressions. One minute he had the sense of being a trespasser—in the next he was impressed by the tremendous superiority he felt toward Mr. T. A. Hedrick, who was a bore and not even a good golfer any more.

Then, because of a ball Mr. Hart lost near the fifteenth green, an enormous thing happened. While they were searching the stiff grasses of the rough there was a clear call of "Fore!" from behind a hill in their rear. And as they all turned abruptly from their search a bright new ball sliced abruptly over the hill and caught Mr. T. A. Hedrick in the abdomen.

"By Gad!" cried Mr. T. A. Hedrick, "they ought to put some of these crazy women off the course. It's getting to be outrageous."

A head and a voice came up together over the hill:

"Do you mind if we go through?"

"You hit me in the stomach!" declared Mr. Hedrick wildly.

"Did I?" The girl approached the group of men. "I'm sorry. I yelled 'Fore!' "

Her glance fell casually on each of the men—then scanned the fairway for her ball.

"Did I bounce into the rough?"

It was impossible to determine whether this question was ingenuous or malicious. In a moment, however, she left no doubt, for as her partner came up over the hill she called cheerfully:

"Here I am! I'd have gone on the green except that I hit something."

As she took her stance for a short mashie shot, Dexter looked at her closely. She wore a blue gingham dress, rimmed at throat and shoulders with a white edging that accentuated her tan. The quality of exaggeration, of thinness, which had made her passionate eyes and down-turning mouth absurd at eleven, was gone now. She was arrestingly beautiful. The color in her cheeks was centered like the color in a picture—it was not a "high" color, but a sort of fluctuating and feverish warmth, so shaded that it seemed at any moment it would recede and disappear. This color and the mobility of her mouth gave a continual impression of flux, of intense life, of passionate vitality—balanced only partially by the sad luxury of her eyes.

She swung her mashie impatiently and without interest, pitching the ball into a sand-pit on the other side of the green. With a quick, insincere smile and a careless "Thank you!" she went on after it.

"That Judy Jones!" remarked Mr. Hedrick on the next tee, as they waited—some moments—for her to play on ahead. "All she needs is to be turned up and spanked for six months and then to be married off to an old-fashioned cavalry captain."

"My God, she's good-looking!" said Mr. Sandwood, who was just over thirty.

"Good-looking!" cried Mr. Hedrick contemptuously. "She always looks as if she wanted to be kissed! Turning those big cow-eyes on every calf in town!"

It was doubtful if Mr. Hedrick intended a reference to the maternal instinct.

"She'd play pretty good golf it she'd try," said Mr. Sandwood.

"She has no form," said Mr. Hedrick solemnly.

"She has a nice figure," said Mr. Sandwood.

"Better thank the Lord she doesn't drive a swifter ball," said Mr Hart, winking at Dexter.

Later in the afternoon the sun went down with a riotous swirl of gold and varying blues and scarlets, and left the dry, rustling night of Western summer. Dexter watched from the veranda of the Golf Club, watched the even overlap of the waters in the little wind, silver molasses under the harvest-moon. Then the moon held a finger to her lips and the lake became a clear pool, pale and quiet. Dexter put on his bathing-suit and swam out to the farthest raft, where he stretched dripping on the wet canvas of the springboard.

There was a fish jumping and a star shining and the lights around the lake were gleaming. Over on a dark peninsula a piano was playing the songs of last summer and of summers before that—songs from "Chin-Chin" and "The Count of Luxemburg" and "The Chocolate Soldier"—and because the sound of a piano over a stretch of water had always seemed beautiful to Dexter he lay perfectly quiet and listened.

The tune the piano was playing at that moment had been gay and new five years before when Dexter was a sophomore at college. They had played it at a prom once when he could not afford the luxury of proms, and he had stood outside the gymnasium and listened. The sound of the tune precipitated in him a sort of ecstasy and it was with that ecstasy he viewed what happened to him now. It was a mood of intense appreciation, a sense that, for once, he was magnificently attuned to life and that everything about him was radiating a brightness and a glamour he might never know again.

A low, pale oblong detached itself suddenly from the darkness of the Island, spitting forth the reverberated sound of a racing motor-boat. Two white streamers of cleft water rolled themselves out behind it and almost immediately the boat was beside him, drowning out the hot tinkle of the piano in the drone of its spray. Dexter raising himself on his arms was aware of a figure standing at the wheel, of two dark eyes regarding him over the lengthening space of water—then the boat had gone by and was sweeping in an immense and purposeless circle of spray round and round in the middle of the lake. With equal eccentricity one of the circles flattened out and headed back toward the raft.

"Who's that?" she called, shutting off her motor. She was so near now that Dexter could see her bathing-suit, which consisted apparently of pink rompers.

The nose of the boat bumped the raft, and as the latter tilted rakishly he was precipitated toward her. With different degrees of interest they recognized each other.

"Aren't you one of those men we played through this afternoon?" she demanded.

He was.

"Well, do you know how to drive a motor-boat? Because if you do I wish you'd drive this one so I can ride on the surf-board behind. My name is Judy Jones"—she favored him with an absurd smirk—rather, what tried to be a smirk, for, twist her mouth as she might, it was not grotesque, it was merely beautiful—"and I live in a house over there on the Island, and in that house there is a man waiting for me. When he drove up at the door I drove out of the dock because he says I'm his ideal."

There was a fish jumping and a star shining and the lights around the lake were gleaming. Dexter sat beside Judy Jones and she explained how her boat was driven. Then she was in the water, swimming to the floating surf-board with a sinuous crawl. Watching her was without effort to the eye, watching a branch waving or a sea-gull flying. Her arms, burned to butternut, moved sinuously among the dull platinum ripples, elbow appearing first, casting the forearm back with a cadence of falling water, then reaching out and down, stabbing a path ahead.

They moved out into the lake; turning, Dexter saw that she was kneeling on the low rear of the now uptilted surf-board.

"Go faster," she called, "fast as it'll go."

Obediently he jammed the lever forward and the white spray mounted at the bow. When he looked around again the girl was standing up on the rushing board, her arms spread wide, her eyes lifted toward the moon.

"It's awful cold," she shouted. "What's your name?"

He told her.

"Well, why don't you come to dinner to-morrow night?"

His heart turned over like the fly-wheel of the boat, and, for the second time, her casual whim gave a new direction to his life.

*III*

Next evening while he waited for her to come down-stairs, Dexter peopled the soft deep summer room and the sun-porch that opened from it with the men who had already loved Judy Jones. He knew the sort of men they were— the men who when he first went to college had entered from the great prep schools with graceful clothes and the deep tan of healthy summers. He had seen that, in one sense, he was better than these men. He was newer and stronger. Yet in acknowledging to himself that he wished his children to be like them he was admitting that he was but the rough, strong stuff from which they eternally sprang.

When the time had come for him to wear good clothes, he had known who were the best tailors in America, and the best tailors in America had made him the suit he wore this evening. He had acquired that particular reserve peculiar to his university, that set it off from other universities. He recognized the value to him of such a mannerism and he had adopted it; he knew that to be careless in dress and manner required more confidence than to be careful. But carelessness was for his children. His mother's name had been Krimplich. She was a Bohemian[2] of the peasant class and she had talked broken English to the end of her days. Her son must keep to the set patterns.

At a little after seven Judy Jones came down-stairs. She wore a blue silk afternoon dress, and he was disappointed at first that she had not put on some-thing more elaborate. This feeling was accentuated when, after a brief greeting, she went to the door of a butler's pantry and pushing it open called: "You can serve dinner, Martha." He had rather expected that a butler would

---

2. Native of Bohemia, in the Czech Republic.

announce dinner, that there would be a cocktail. Then he put these thoughts behind him as they sat down side by side on a lounge and looked at each other.

"Father and mother won't be here," she said thoughtfully.

He remembered the last time he had seen her father, and he was glad the parents were not to be here to-night—they might wonder who he was. He had been born in Keeble, a Minnesota village fifty miles farther north, and he always gave Keeble as his home instead of Black Bear Village. Country towns were well enough to come from if they weren't inconveniently in sight and used as footstools by fashionable lakes.

They talked of his university, which she had visited frequently during the past two years, and of the near-by city which supplied Sherry Island with its patrons, and whither Dexter would return next day to his prospering laundries.

During dinner she slipped into a moody depression which gave Dexter a feeling of uneasiness. Whatever petulance she uttered in her throaty voice worried him. Whatever she smiled at—at him, at a chicken liver, at nothing— it disturbed him that her smile could have no root in mirth, or even in amusement. When the scarlet corners of her lips curved down, it was less a smile than an invitation to a kiss.

Then, after dinner, she led him out on the dark sun-porch and deliberately changed the atmosphere.

"Do you mind if I weep a little?" she said.

"I'm afraid I'm boring you," he responded quickly.

"You're not. I like you. But I've just had a terrible afternoon. There was a man I cared about, and this afternoon he told me out of a clear sky that he was poor as a church-mouse. He'd never even hinted it before. Does this sound horribly mundane?"

"Perhaps he was afraid to tell you."

"Suppose he was," she answered. "He didn't start right. You see, if I'd thought of him as poor—well, I've been mad about loads of poor men, and fully intended to marry them all. But in this case, I hadn't thought of him that way, and my interest in him wasn't strong enough to survive the shock. As if a girl calmly informed her fiancé that she was a widow. He might not object to widows, but—

"Let's start right," she interrupted herself suddenly. "Who are you, anyhow?"

For a moment Dexter hesitated. Then:

"I'm nobody," he announced. "My career is largely a matter of futures."

"Are you poor?"

"No," he said frankly, "I'm probably making more money than any man my age in the Northwest. I know that's an obnoxious remark, but you advised me to start right."

There was a pause. Then she smiled and the corners of her mouth drooped and an almost imperceptible sway brought her closer to him, looking up into his eyes. A lump rose in Dexter's throat, and he waited breathless for the experiment, facing the unpredictable compound that would form mysteriously from the elements of their lips. Then he saw—she communicated her excitement to him, lavishly, deeply, with kisses that were not a promise but a fulfilment. They aroused in him not hunger demanding renewal but surfeit that would demand more surfeit . . . kisses that were like charity, creating want by holding back nothing at all.

It did not take him many hours to decide that he had wanted Judy Jones ever since he was a proud, desirous little boy.

## IV

It began like that—and continued, with varying shades of intensity, on such a note right up to the dénouement. Dexter surrendered a part of himself to the most direct and unprincipled personality with which he had ever come in contact. Whatever Judy wanted, she went after with the full pressure of her charm. There was no divergence of method, no jockeying for position or premeditation of effects—there was a very little mental side to any of her affairs. She simply made men conscious to the highest degree of her physical loveliness. Dexter had no desire to change her. Her deficiencies were knit up with a passionate energy that transcended and justified them.

When, as Judy's head lay against his shoulder that first night, she whispered, "I don't know what's the matter with me. Last night I thought I was in love with a man and to-night I think I'm in love with you———"—it seemed to him a beautiful and romantic thing to say. It was the exquisite excitability that for the moment he controlled and owned. But a week later he was compelled to view this same quality in a different light. She took him in her roadster to a picnic supper, and after supper she disappeared, likewise in her roadster, with another man. Dexter became enormously upset and was scarcely able to be decently civil to the other people present. When she assured him that she had not kissed the other man, he knew she was lying—yet he was glad that she had taken the trouble to lie to him.

He was, as he found before the summer ended, one of a varying dozen who circulated about her. Each of them had at one time been favored above all others—about half of them still basked in the solace of occasional sentimental revivals. Whenever one showed signs of dropping out through long neglect, she granted him a brief honeyed hour, which encouraged him to tag along for a year or so longer. Judy made these forays upon the helpless and defeated without malice, indeed half unconscious that there was anything mischievous in what she did.

When a new man came to town every one dropped out—dates were automatically cancelled.

The helpless part of trying to do anything about it was that she did it all herself. She was not a girl who could be "won" in the kinetic sense—she was proof against cleverness, she was proof against charm; if any of these assailed her too strongly she would immediately resolve the affair to a physical basis, and under the magic of her physical splendor the strong as well as the brilliant played her game and not their own. She was entertained only by the gratification of her desires and by the direct exercise of her own charm. Perhaps from so much youthful love, so many youthful lovers, she had come, in self-defense, to nourish herself wholly from within.

Succeeding Dexter's first exhilaration came restlessness and dissatisfaction. The helpless ecstasy of losing himself in her was opiate rather than tonic. It was fortunate for his work during the winter that those moments of ecstasy came infrequently. Early in their acquaintance it had seemed for a while that there was a deep and spontaneous mutual attraction—that first August, for example—three days of long evenings on her dusky veranda, of strange wan

kisses through the late afternoon, in shadowy alcoves or behind the protecting
trellises of the garden arbors, of mornings when she was fresh as a dream and
almost shy at meeting him in the clarity of the rising day. There was all the
ecstasy of an engagement about it, sharpened by his realization that there was
no engagement. It was during those three days that, for the first time, he had
asked her to marry him. She said "maybe some day," she said "kiss me," she
said "I'd like to marry you," she said "I love you"—she said—nothing.

The three days were interrupted by the arrival of a New York man who
visited at her house for half September. To Dexter's agony, rumor engaged
them. The man was the son of the president of a great trust company. But at
the end of a month it was reported that Judy was yawning. At a dance one
night she sat all evening in a motor-boat with a local beau, while the New
Yorker searched the club for her frantically. She told the local beau that she
was bored with her visitor, and two days later he left. She was seen with him
at the station, and it was reported that he looked very mournful indeed.

On this note the summer ended. Dexter was twenty-four, and he found
himself increasingly in a position to do as he wished. He joined two clubs in
the city and lived at one of them. Though he was by no means an integral part
of the stag-lines at these clubs, he managed to be on hand at dances where
Judy Jones was likely to appear. He could have gone out socially as much as
he liked—he was an eligible young man, now, and popular with down-town
fathers. He confessed devotion to Judy Jones had rather solidified his position.
But he had no social aspirations and rather despised the dancing men who
were always on tap for the Thursday or Saturday parties and who filled in at
dinners with the younger married set. Already he was playing with the idea of
going East to New York. He wanted to take Judy Jones with him. No disillusion as to the world in which she had grown up could cure his illusion as to
her desirability.

Remember that—for only in the light of it can what he did for her be understood.

Eighteen months after he first met Judy Jones he became engaged to another
girl. Her name was Irene Scheerer, and her father was one of the men who
had always believed in Dexter. Irene was light-haired and sweet and honorable, and a little stout, and she had two suitors whom she pleasantly relinquished when Dexter formally asked her to marry him.

Summer, fall, winter, spring, another summer, another fall—so much he
had given of his active life to the incorrigible lips of Judy Jones. She had
treated him with interest, with encouragement, with malice, with indifference, with contempt. She had inflicted on him the innumerable little slights
and indignities possible in such a case—as if in revenge for having ever cared
for him at all. She had beckoned him and yawned at him and beckoned him
again and he had responded often with bitterness and narrowed eyes. She had
brought him ecstatic happiness and intolerable agony of spirit. She had caused
him untold inconvenience and not a little trouble. She had insulted him, and
she had ridden over him, and she had played his interest in her against his
interest in his work—for fun. She had done everything to him except to criticise him—this she had not done—it seemed to him only because it might
have sullied the utter indifference she manifested and sincerely felt toward
him.

When autumn had come and gone again it occurred to him that he could not have Judy Jones. He had to beat this into his mind but he convinced himself at last. He lay awake at night for a while and argued it over. He told himself the trouble and the pain she had caused him, he enumerated her glaring deficiencies as a wife. Then he said to himself that he loved her, and after a while he fell asleep. For a week, lest he imagined her husky voice over the telephone or her eyes opposite him at lunch, he worked hard and late, and at night he went to his office and plotted out his years.

At the end of a week he went to a dance and cut in on her once. For almost the first time since they had met he did not ask her to sit out with him or tell her that she was lovely. It hurt him that she did not miss these things—that was all. He was not jealous when he saw that there was a new man to-night. He had been hardened against jealousy long before.

He stayed late at the dance. He sat for an hour with Irene Scheerer and talked about books and about music. He knew very little about either. But he was beginning to be master of his own time now, and he had a rather priggish notion that he—the young and already fabulously successful Dexter Green— should know more about such things.

That was in October, when he was twenty-five. In January, Dexter and Irene became engaged. It was to be announced in June, and they were to be married three months later.

The Minnesota winter prolonged itself interminably, and it was almost May when the winds came soft and the snow ran down into Black Bear Lake at last. For the first time in over a year Dexter was enjoying a certain tranquillity of spirit. Judy Jones had been in Florida, and afterward in Hot Springs, and somewhere she had been engaged, and somewhere she had broken it off. At first, when Dexter had definitely given her up, it had made him sad that people still linked them together and asked for news of her, but when he began to be placed at dinner next to Irene Scheerer people didn't ask him about her any more—they told him about her. He ceased to be an authority on her.

May at last. Dexter walked the streets at night when the darkness was damp as rain, wondering that so soon, with so little done, so much of ecstasy had gone from him. May one year back had been marked by Judy's poignant, unforgivable, yet forgiven turbulence—it had been one of those rare times when he fancied she had grown to care for him. That old penny's worth of happiness he had spent for this bushel of content. He knew that Irene would be no more than a curtain spread behind him, a hand moving among gleaming tea-cups, a voice calling to children . . . fire and loveliness were gone, the magic of nights and the wonder of the varying hours and seasons . . . slender lips, down-turning, dropping to his lips and bearing him up into a heaven of eyes. . . . The thing was deep in him. He was too strong and alive for it to die lightly.

In the middle of May when the weather balanced for a few days on the thin bridge that led to deep summer he turned in one night at Irene's house. Their engagement was to be announced in a week now—no one could be surprised at it. And to-night they would sit to-gether on the lounge at the University Club and look on for an hour at the dancers. It gave him a sense of solidity to go with her—she was so sturdily popular, so intensely "great."

He mounted the steps of the brownstone house and stepped inside.

"Irene," he called.

Mrs. Scheerer came out of the living-room to meet him.

"Dexter," she said, "Irene's gone up-stairs with a splitting head-ache. She wanted to go with you but I made her go to bed."

"Nothing serious, I—"

"Oh, no. She's going to play golf with you in the morning. You can spare her for just one night, can't you, Dexter?"

Her smile was kind. She and Dexter liked each other. In the living-room he talked for a moment before he said good-night.

Returning to the University Club, where he had rooms, he stood in the doorway for a moment and watched the dancers. He leaned against the door-post, nodded at a man or two—yawned.

"Hello, darling."

The familiar voice at his elbow startled him. Judy Jones had left a man and crossed the room to him—Judy Jones, a slender enamelled doll in cloth of gold: gold in a band at her head, gold in two slipper points at her dress's hem. The fragile glow of her face seemed to blossom as she smiled at him. A breeze of warmth and light blew through the room. His hands in the pockets of his dinner-jacket tightened spasmodically. He was filled with a sudden excitement.

"When did you get back?" he asked casually.

"Come here and I'll tell you about it."

She turned and he followed her. She had been away—he could have wept at the wonder of her return. She had passed through enchanted streets, doing things that were like provocative music. All mysterious happenings, all fresh and quickening hopes, had gone away with her, come back with her now.

She turned in the doorway.

"Have you a car here? If you haven't, I have."

"I have a coupé."

In then, with a rustle of golden cloth. He slammed the door. Into so many cars she had stepped—like this—like that—her back against the leather, so—her elbow resting on the door—waiting. She would have been soiled long since had there been anything to soil her—except herself—but this was her own self outpouring.

With an effort he forced himself to start the car and back into the street. This was nothing, he must remember. She had done this before, and he had put her behind him, as he would have crossed a bad account from his books.

He drove slowly down-town and, affecting abstraction, traversed the deserted streets of the business section, peopled here and there where a movie was giving out its crowd or where consumptive or pugilistic youth lounged in front of pool halls. The clink of glasses and the slap of hands on the bars issued from saloons, cloisters of glazed glass and dirty yellow light.

She was watching him closely and the silence was embarrassing, yet in this crisis he could find no casual word with which to profane the hour. At a convenient turning he began to zigzag back toward the University Club.

"Have you missed me?" she asked suddenly.

"Everybody missed you."

He wondered if she knew of Irene Scheerer. She had been back only a day—her absence had been almost contemporaneous with his engagement.

"What a remark!" Judy laughed sadly—without sadness. She looked at him searchingly. He became absorbed in the dashboard.

"You're handsomer than you used to be," she said thoughtfully. "Dexter, you have the most rememberable eyes."

He could have laughed at this, but he did not laugh. It was the sort of thing that was said to sophomores. Yet it stabbed at him.

"I'm awfully tired of everything, darling." She called every one darling, endowing the endearment with careless, individual camaraderie. "I wish you'd marry me."

The directness of this confused him. He should have told her now that he was going to marry another girl, but he could not tell her. He could as easily have sworn that he had never loved her.

"I think we'd get along," she continued, on the same note, "unless probably you've forgotten me and fallen in love with another girl."

Her confidence was obviously enormous. She had said, in effect, that she found such a thing impossible to believe, that if it were true he had merely committed a childish indiscretion—and probably to show off. She would forgive him, because it was not a matter of any moment but rather something to be brushed aside lightly.

"Of course you could never love anybody but me," she continued, "I like the way you love me. Oh, Dexter, have you forgotten last year?"

"No, I haven't forgotten."

"Neither have I!"

Was she sincerely moved—or was she carried along by the wave of her own acting?

"I wish we could be like that again," she said, and he forced himself to answer:

"I don't think we can."

"I suppose not. . . . I hear you're giving Irene Scheerer a violent rush."

There was not the faintest emphasis on the name, yet Dexter was suddenly ashamed.

"Oh, take me home," cried Judy suddenly; "I don't want to go back to that idiotic dance—with those children."

Then, as he turned up the street that led to the residence district, Judy began to cry quietly to herself. He had never seen her cry before.

The dark street lightened, the dwellings of the rich loomed up around them, he stopped his coupé in front of the great white bulk of the Mortimer Joneses' house, somnolent, gorgeous, drenched with the splendor of the damp moonlight. Its solidity startled him. The strong walls, the steel of the girders, the breadth and beam and pomp of it were there only to bring out the contrast with the young beauty beside him. It was sturdy to accentuate her slightness—as if to show what a breeze could be generated by a butterfly's wing.

He sat perfectly quiet, his nerves in wild clamor, afraid that if he moved he would find her irresistibly in his arms. Two tears had rolled down her wet face and trembled on her upper lip.

"I'm more beautiful than anybody else," she said brokenly, "why can't I be happy?" Her moist eyes tore at his stability—her mouth turned slowly downward with an exquisite sadness: "I'd like to marry you if you'll have me, Dexter. I suppose you think I'm not worth having, but I'll be so beautiful for you, Dexter."

A million phrases of anger, pride, passion, hatred, tenderness fought on his lips. Then a perfect wave of emotion washed over him, carrying off with it a sediment of wisdom, of convention, of doubt, of honor. This was his girl who was speaking, his own, his beautiful, his pride.

"Won't you come in?" He heard her draw in her breath sharply.

Waiting.

"All right," his voice was trembling, "I'll come in."

## V

It was strange that neither when it was over nor a long time afterward did he regret that night. Looking at it from the perspective of ten years, the fact that Judy's flare for him endured just one month seemed of little importance. Nor did it matter that by his yielding he subjected himself to a deeper agony in the end and gave serious hurt to Irene Scheerer and to Irene's parents, who had befriended him. There was nothing sufficiently pictorial about Irene's grief to stamp itself on his mind.

Dexter was at bottom hard-minded. The attitude of the city on his action was of no importance to him, not because he was going to leave the city, but because any outside attitude on the situation seemed superficial. He was completely indifferent to popular opinion. Nor, when he had seen that it was no use, that he did not possess in himself the power to move fundamentally or to hold Judy Jones, did he bear any malice toward her. He loved her, and he would love her until the day he was too old for loving—but he could not have her. So he tasted the deep pain that is reserved only for the strong, just as he had tasted for a little while the deep happiness.

Even the ultimate falsity of the grounds upon which Judy terminated the engagement that she did not want to "take him away" from Irene—Judy, who had wanted nothing else—did not revolt him. He was beyond any revulsion or any amusement.

He went East in February with the intention of selling out his laundries and settling in New York—but the war[3] came to America in March and changed his plans. He returned to the West, handed over the management of the business to his partner, and went into the first officers' training-camp in late April. He was one of those young thousands who greeted the war with a certain amount of relief, welcoming the liberation from webs of tangled emotion.

## VI

This story is not his biography, remember, although things creep into it which have nothing to do with those dreams he had when he was young. We are almost done with them and with him now. There is only one more incident to be related here, and it happens seven years farther on.

It took place in New York, where he had done well—so well that there were no barriers too high for him. He was thirty-two years old, and, except for one flying trip immediately after the war, he had not been West in seven years. A man named Devlin from Detroit came into his office to see him in a business way, and then and there this incident occurred, and closed out, so to speak, this particular side of his life.

"So you're from the Middle West," said the man Devlin with careless curiosity. "That's funny—I thought men like you were probably born and raised on Wall Street. You know——wife of one of my best friends in Detroit came from your city. I was an usher at the wedding."

3. I.e., World War I, which America entered in 1917.

Dexter waited with no apprehension of what was coming.

"Judy Simms," said Devlin with no particular interest; "Judy Jones she was once."

"Yes, I knew her." A dull impatience spread over him. He had heard, of course, that she was married—perhaps deliberately he had heard no more.

"Awfully nice girl," brooded Devlin meaninglessly, "I'm sort of sorry for her."

"Why?" Something in Dexter was alert, receptive, at once.

"Oh, Lud Simms has gone to pieces in a way. I don't mean he ill-uses her, but he drinks and runs around—"

"Doesn't she run around?"

"No. Stays at home with her kids."

"Oh."

"She's a little too old for him," said Devlin.

"Too old!" cried Dexter. "Why, man, she's only twenty-seven."

He was possessed with a wild notion of rushing out into the streets and taking a train to Detroit. He rose to his feet spasmodically.

"I guess you're busy," Devlin apologized quickly. "I didn't realize—"

"No, I'm not busy," said Dexter, steadying his voice. "I'm not busy at all. Not busy at all. Did you say she was—twenty-seven? No, I said she was twenty-seven."

"Yes, you did," agreed Devlin dryly.

"Go on, then, Go on."

"What do you mean?"

"About Judy Jones."

Devlin looked at him helplessly.

"Well, that's—I told you all there is to it. He treats her like the devil. Oh, they're not going to get divorced or anything. When he's particularly outrageous she forgives him. In fact, I'm inclined to think she loves him. She was a pretty girl when she first came to Detroit."

A pretty girl! The phrase struck Dexter as ludicrous.

"Isn't she—a pretty girl, any more?"

"Oh, she's all right."

"Look here," said Dexter, sitting down suddenly. "I don't understand. You say she was a 'pretty girl' and now you say she's 'all right.' I don't understand what you mean—Judy Jones wasn't a pretty girl, at all. She was a great beauty. Why, I knew her, I knew her. She was—"

Devlin laughed pleasantly.

"I'm not trying to start a row," he said. "I think Judy's a nice girl and I like her. I can't understand how a man like Lud Simms could fall madly in love with her, but he did." Then he added: "Most of the women like her."

Dexter looked closely at Devlin, thinking wildly that there must be a reason for this, some insensitivity in the man or some private malice.

"Lots of women fade just like *that*," Devlin snapped his fingers. "You must have seen it happen. Perhaps I've forgotten how pretty she was at her wedding. I've seen her so much since then, you see. She has nice eyes."

A sort of dullness settled down upon Dexter. For the first time in his life he felt like getting very drunk. He knew that he was laughing loudly at something Devlin had said, but he did not know what it was or why it was funny. When, in a few minutes, Devlin went he lay down on his lounge and looked out the window at the New York sky-line into which the sun was sinking in dull lovely shades of pink and gold.

He had thought that having nothing else to lose he was invulnerable at last—but he knew that he had just lost something more, as surely as if he had married Judy Jones and seen her fade away before his eyes.

The dream was gone. Something had been taken from him. In a sort of panic he pushed the palms of his hands into his eyes and tried to bring up a picture of the waters lapping on Sherry Island and the moonlit veranda, and gingham on the golf-links and the dry sun and the gold color of her neck's soft down. And her mouth damp to his kisses and her eyes plaintive with melancholy and her freshness like new fine linen in the morning. Why, these things were no longer in the world! They had existed and they existed no longer.

For the first time in years the tears were streaming down his face. But they were for himself now. He did not care about mouth and eyes and moving hands. He wanted to care, and he could not care. For he had gone away and he could never go back any more. The gates were closed, the sun was gone down, and there was no beauty but the gray beauty of steel that withstands all time. Even the grief he could have borne was left behind in the country of illusion, of youth, of the richness of life, where his winter dreams had flourished.

"Long ago," he said, "long ago, there was something in me, but now that thing is gone. Now that thing is gone, that thing is gone. I cannot cry. I cannot care. That thing will come back no more."

1922

---

# WILLIAM FAULKNER
## 1897–1962

In each of the novels William Faulkner published between 1929 and 1936 it seemed as though fiction were being reinvented. He wrote about childhood, families, sex, race, obsessions, time, the past, his native South, and the modern world. He invented voices for characters ranging from sages to children, criminals, the insane, even the dead—sometimes all within one book. He developed, beyond this ventrilo- quism, his own unmistakable narrative voice, urgent, intense, highly rhetorical. He experimented with narrative chronology and with techniques for representing mind and memory. He invented an entire southern county and wrote its history.

He was a native Mississippian, born near Oxford, where his parents moved when he was about five. His great-grandfather had been a local legend: a colonel in the Civil War, lawyer, railroad builder, financier, politician, writer, and public figure who was shot and killed by a business and political rival in 1889. Faulkner's grandfather carried on some of the family enterprises, and his father worked first for the railroad (the Gulf and Chicago) and later as business manager of the University of Mississippi. The father was a reclusive man who loved to hunt, drink, and swap stories with his hunting friends; the mother, ambitious, sensitive, and literary, was a more profound influence on Faulkner, her favorite of four sons. In Faulkner's childhood his mother's mother also lived with them; she was a high-spirited, independent, and imaginative old lady whose death in 1907 seems to have affected Faulkner deeply.

Faulkner dropped out of high school in 1915 and had no further formal education beyond a year (1919–20) as a special student at the University of Mississippi. Through family connections, various jobs were made for him, but he was unhappy in all of them. In 1918 Estelle Oldham, his high school love, married someone else; Faulkner briefly left Oxford. First he went to New Haven where his best friend and informal tutor, Phil Stone, was in the Yale law school; then he enlisted in the British Royal Flying Corps and was sent to Canada to train. World War I ended before he saw active service; nevertheless, when he returned to Oxford in 1919 he was limping from what he claimed was a war wound.

Back at home, Faulkner drifted from one job to another and wrote poetry that was a mélange of Shakespearean, pastoral, Victorian, and Edwardian modes, with an overlay of French symbolism and T. S. Eliot. He published a volume of poetry, *The Marble Faun*, in 1924. In 1925 he went to New Orleans where, for the first time, he met and mingled with literary people, including Sherwood Anderson, who encouraged Faulkner to develop his own style, to concentrate on prose, and to use his region for material.

Faulkner wrote his first novel, *Soldier's Pay*, in New Orleans, and Anderson recommended it to his own publisher, Liveright; it appeared in 1926. He also published in the New Orleans magazine *The Double Dealer* and the newspaper *The Times Picayune*. He learned about the experimental writing of James Joyce and of the ideas of Sigmund Freud. After a trip to Europe at the end of the same year, he returned to Oxford. In 1929 he married Estelle Oldham, who had been divorced and had returned to Oxford with her two children. They bought a ruined mansion, Rowan Oak, in 1930 and began to restore it to its antebellum appearance. A daughter born in 1931 died in infancy; a second daughter, Jill, was born in 1933.

Faulkner's second novel was a satire on New Orleans intellectuals called *Mosquitos* (1927). His more typical subject matter emerged with his rejected novel *Flags in the Dust*, and the shortened version of it that appeared in 1929 as *Sartoris*. In this work Faulkner focused on the interconnections between a prominent southern family and the local community: the Sartoris family as well as many other characters appeared in later works, and the region, renamed Yoknapatawpha County, was to become the locale of Faulkner's imaginative world. But the social and historical emphasis in *Sartoris* was not directly followed up in the works Faulkner wrote next. *The Sound and the Fury* (1929)—Faulkner's favorite novel—and *As I Lay Dying* (1930) were dramatically experimental attempts to articulate the inexpressible aspects of individual psychology.

Neither these books nor his early short stories were very popular. *Sanctuary*, a sensational work about sex, gangsters, official corruption, and urban violence, attracted considerable attention, however. It appeared in 1931, and took its place among a great deal of hard-boiled fiction that appeared in the decade, notably by such authors as Dashiell Hammett and Raymond Chandler. During four different intervals—1932–1937, 1942–1945, 1951, and 1954—Faulkner spent time in Hollywood or on contract as a scriptwriter. He worked well with the director Howard Hawks, and wrote the scripts for two famous movies, an adaptation of Ernest Hemingway's *To Have and Have Not* and an adaptation of Raymond Chandler's *The Big Sleep*, both starring Humphrey Bogart and Lauren Bacall.

He continued to produce brilliant and inventive novels during these years. *Light in August* (1932) counterpointed a comic pastoral about the pregnant earth-mother figure Lena Grove with a grim tragedy about the embittered outcast Joe Christmas; it interrelated individual psychology and cultural pathology. *Absalom, Absalom!*, which followed in 1936, is thought by many to be Faulkner's masterpiece. The story of Thomas Sutpen, the ruthless would-be founder of a southern dynasty after the Civil War, is related by four different speakers, each trying to find "the meaning" of the story. The reader, observing how the story changes in each telling, comes to see that making stories is the human way of making meaning. Like Faulkner's earlier novels, *Absalom* is thus simultaneously about an individual, about the South, and about itself as a work of fiction. But its emphasis shifts from the private psychology that dominated in earlier work to social psychology: to the collective mind of the South.

With World War II, Faulkner's work became more traditional and less difficult. He began to write about the rise, in Yoknapatawpha County, of the poor white family named Snopes—this family had appeared in earlier works (like *Barn Burning*)—and the simultaneous decline of the region's "aristocratic" families. *The Hamlet* (1940) was the first of three novels devoted to the Snopeses. Because all his works had been set in Yoknapatawpha County and were interconnected, the region and its people began to take on an existence independent of any one book in which they appeared.

Faulkner's national reputation received a significant boost from the publication in 1946 of an anthology of his writings, *The Portable Faulkner*, edited by the critic Malcolm Cowley. He already had a major reputation abroad, especially in France, where his work in translation was a powerful influence on the French so-called new novel and its practitioners such as Michel Butor and Alain Robbe-Grillet. His antiracist *Intruder in the Dust* (1948) occasioned the award of the Nobel Prize in 1950, his last and greatest honor. In the 1950s Faulkner visited many college campuses. His writing took on more of the air of an old-fashioned yarn; he dealt with more legendary and local color materials; he rounded out the Snopes saga with *The Town* (1957) and *The Mansion* (1959). At the age of sixty-five he died of a heart attack.

# That Evening Sun

## I

Monday is no different from any other weekday in Jefferson now. The streets are paved now, and the telephone and electric companies are cutting down more and more of the shade trees—the water oaks, the maples and locusts and elms—to make room for iron poles bearing clusters of bloated and ghostly and bloodless grapes, and we have a city laundry which makes the rounds on Monday morning, gathering the bundles of clothes into bright-colored, specially-made motor cars: the soiled wearing of a whole week now flees apparitionlike behind alert and irritable electric horns, with a long diminishing noise of rubber and asphalt like tearing silk, and even the Negro women who still take in white people's washing after the old custom, fetch and deliver it in automobiles.

But fifteen years ago, on Monday morning the quiet, dusty, shady streets would be full of Negro women with, balanced on their steady, turbaned heads, bundles of clothes tied up in sheets, almost as large as cotton bales, carried so without touch of hand between the kitchen door of the white house and the blackened washpot beside a cabin door in Negro Hollow.

Nancy would set her bundle on the top of her head, then upon the bundle in turn she would set the black straw sailor hat which she wore winter and summer. She was tall, with a high, sad face sunken a little where her teeth were missing. Sometimes we would go a part of the way down the lane and across the pasture with her, to watch the balanced bundle and the hat that never bobbed nor wavered, even when she walked down into the ditch and up the other side and stooped through the fence. She would go down on her hands and knees and crawl through the gap, her head rigid, uptilted, the bundle steady as a rock or a balloon, and rise to her feet again and go on.

Sometimes the husbands of the washing women would fetch and deliver the clothes, but Jesus never did that for Nancy, even before father told him to stay away from our house, even when Dilsey was sick and Nancy would come to cook for us.

And then about half the time we'd have to go down the lane to Nancy's cabin and tell her to come on and cook breakfast. We would stop at the ditch, because father told us to not have anything to do with Jesus—he was a short black man, with a razor scar down his face—and we would throw rocks at Nancy's house until she came to the door, leaning her head around it without any clothes on.

"What yawl mean, chunking my house?" Nancy said. "What you little devils mean?"

"Father says for you to come on and get breakfast," Caddy said. "Father says it's over a half an hour now, and you've got to come this minute."

"I ain't studying no breakfast," Nancy said. "I going to get my sleep out."

"I bet you're drunk," Jason said. "Father says you're drunk. Are you drunk, Nancy?"

"Who says I is?" Nancy said. "I got to get my sleep out. I aint studying no breakfast."

So after a while we quit chunking the cabin and went back home. When she finally came, it was too late for me to go to school. So we thought it was whisky until that day they arrested her again and they were taking her to jail and they passed Mr Stovall. He was the cashier in the bank and a deacon in the Baptist church, and Nancy began to say:

"When you going to pay me, white man? When you going to pay me, white man? It's been three times now since you paid me a cent—" Mr Stovall knocked her down, but she kept on saying, "When you going to pay me, white man? It's been three times now since—" until Mr Stovall kicked her in the mouth with his heel and the marshal caught Mr Stovall back, and Nancy lying in the street, laughing. She turned her head and spat out some blood and teeth and said, "It's been three times now since he paid me a cent."

That was how she lost her teeth, and all that day they told about Nancy and Mr Stovall, and all that night the ones that passed the jail could hear Nancy singing and yelling. They could see her hands holding to the window bars, and a lot of them stopped along the fence, listening to her and to the jailer trying to make her stop. She didn't shut up until almost daylight, when the jailer began to hear a bumping and scraping upstairs and he went up there and found Nancy hanging from the window bar. He said that it was cocaine and not whisky, because no nigger would try to commit suicide unless he was full of cocaine, because a nigger full of cocaine wasn't a nigger any longer.

The jailer cut her down and revived her; then he beat her, whipped her. She had hung herself with her dress. She had fixed it all right, but when they arrested her she didn't have on anything except a dress and so she didn't have anything to tie her hands with and she couldn't make her hands let go of the window ledge. So the jailer heard the noise and ran up there and found Nancy hanging from the window, stark naked, her belly already swelling out a little, like a little balloon.

When Dilsey was sick in her cabin and Nancy was cooking for us, we could see her apron swelling out; that was before father told Jesus to stay away from the house. Jesus was in the kitchen, sitting behind the stove, with his razor scar on his black face like a piece of dirty string. He said it was a watermelon that Nancy had under her dress.

"It never come off of your vine, though," Nancy said.

"Off of what vine?" Caddy said.

"I can cut down the vine it did come off of," Jesus said.

"What makes you want to talk like that before these chillen?" Nancy said. "Whyn't you go on to work? You done et. You want Mr Jason to catch you hanging around his kitchen, talking that way before these chillen?"

"Talking what way?" Caddy said. "What vine?"

"I cant hang around white man's kitchen," Jesus said. "But white man can hang around mine. White man can come in my house, but I cant stop him. When white man want to come in my house, I aint got no house. I cant stop him, but he cant kick me outen it. He cant do that."

Dilsey was still sick in her cabin. Father told Jesus to stay off our place. Dilsey was still sick. It was a long time. We were in the library after supper.

"Isn't Nancy through in the kitchen yet?" mother said. "It seems to me that she has had plenty of time to have finished the dishes."

"Let Quentin go and see," father said. "Go and see if Nancy is through, Quentin. Tell her she can go on home."

I went to the kitchen. Nancy was through. The dishes were put away and the fire was out. Nancy was sitting in a chair, close to the cold stove. She looked at me.

"Mother wants to know if you are through," I said.

"Yes," Nancy said. She looked at me. "I done finished." She looked at me.

"What is it?" I said. "What is it?"

"I aint nothing but a nigger," Nancy said. "It aint none of my fault."

She looked at me, sitting in the chair before the cold stove, the sailor hat on her head. I went back to the library. It was the cold stove and all, when you think of a kitchen being warm and busy and cheerful. And with a cold stove and the dishes all put away, and nobody wanting to eat at that hour.

"Is she through?" mother said.

"Yessum," I said.

"What is she doing?" mother said.

"She's not doing anything. She's through."

"I'll go and see," father said.

"Maybe she's waiting for Jesus to come and take her home," Caddy said.

"Jesus is gone," I said. Nancy told us how one morning she woke up and Jesus was gone.

"He quit me," Nancy said. "Done gone to Memphis, I reckon. Dodging them city po-lice for a while, I reckon."

"And a good riddance," father said. "I hope he stays there."

"Nancy's scaired of the dark," Jason said.

"So are you," Caddy said.

"I'm not," Jason said.

"Scairy cat," Caddy said.

"I'm not," Jason said.

"You, Candace!" mother said. Father came back.

"I am going to walk down the lane with Nancy," he said. "She says that Jesus is back."

"Has she seen him?" mother said.

"No. Some Negro sent her word that he was back in town. I wont be long."

"You'll leave me alone, to take Nancy home?" mother said. "Is her safety more precious to you than mine?"

"I wont be long," father said.

"You'll leave these children unprotected, with that Negro about?"

"I'm going too," Caddy said. "Let me go, Father."

"What would he do with them, if he were unfortunate enough to have them?" father said.

"I want to go, too," Jason said.

"Jason!" mother said. She was speaking to father. You could tell that by the way she said the name. Like she believed that all day father had been trying to think of doing the thing she wouldn't like the most, and that she knew all the time that after a while he would think of it. I stayed quiet, because father and I both knew that mother would want him to make me stay with her if she just thought of it in time. So father didn't look at me. I was the oldest. I was nine[1] and Caddy was seven and Jason was five.

"Nonsense," father said. "We wont be long."

Nancy had her hat on. We came to the lane. "Jesus always been good to me," Nancy said. "Whenever he had two dollars, one of them was mine." We walked in the lane. "If I can just get through the lane," Nancy said. "I be all right then."

The lane was always dark. "This is where Jason got scared on Hallowe'en," Caddy said.

"I didn't," Jason said.

"Cant Aunt Rachel do anything with him?" father said. Aunt Rachel was old. She lived in a cabin beyond Nancy's, by herself. She had white hair and she smoked a pipe in the door, all day long; she didn't work any more. They said she was Jesus' mother. Sometimes she said she was and sometimes she said she wasn't any kin to Jesus.

"Yes, you did," Caddy said. "You were scairder than Frony. You were scairder than T.P. even. Scairder than niggers."

"Cant nobody do nothing with him," Nancy said. "He say I done woke up the devil in him and aint but one thing going to lay it down again."

"Well, he's gone now," father said. "There's nothing for you to be afraid of now. And if you'd just let white men alone."

"Let what white men alone?" Caddy said. "How let them alone?"

"He aint gone nowhere," Nancy said. "I can feel him. I can feel him now, in this lane. He hearing us talk, every word, hid somewhere, waiting. I aint seen him, and I aint going to see him again but once more, with that razor in his mouth. That razor on that string down his back, inside his shirt. And

1. The members of the family in this story reappear as the main characters of *The Sound and the Fury*, a novel which Faulkner wrote soon after finishing *The Evening Sun*. Quentin, who tells this story at about age 24 (see the second paragraph under section I, "fif-teen years ago"), commits suicide at age 18 in *The Sound and the Fury*—an example of how Faulkner modified the Yoknapatawpha world in the process of adding to it.

then I aint going to be even surprised."

"I wasn't scaired," Jason said.

"If you'd behave yourself, you'd have kept out of this," father said. "But it's all right now. He's probably in St. Louis now. Probably got another wife by now and forgot all about you."

"If he has, I better not find out about it," Nancy said. "I'd stand there right over them, and every time he wropped her, I'd cut that arm off. I'd cut his head off and I'd slit her belly and I'd shove—"

"Hush," father said.

"Slit whose belly, Nancy?" Caddy said.

"I wasn't scaired," Jason said. "I'd walk right down this lane by myself."

"Yah," Caddy said. "You wouldn't dare to put your foot down in it if we were not here too."

## II

Dilsey was still stick, so we took Nancy home every night until mother said, "How much longer is this going on? I to be left alone in this big house while you take home a frightened Negro?"

We fixed a pallet in the kitchen for Nancy. One night we waked up, hearing the sound. It was not singing and it was not crying, coming up the dark stairs. There was a light in mother's room and we heard father going down the hall, down the back stairs, and Caddy and I went into the hall. The floor was cold. Our toes curled away from it while we listened to the sound. It was like singing and it wasn't like singing, like the sounds that Negroes make.

Then it stopped and we heard father going down the back stairs, and we went to the head of the stairs. Then the sound began again, in the stairway, not loud, and we could see Nancy's eyes halfway up the stairs, against the wall. They looked like cat's eyes do, like a big cat against the wall, watching us. When we came down the steps to where she was, she quit making the sound again, and we stood there until father came back up from the kitchen, with his pistol in his hand. He went back down with Nancy and they came back with Nancy's pallet.

We spread the pallet in our room. After the light in mother's room went off, we could see Nancy's eyes again. "Nancy," Caddy whispered, "are you asleep, Nancy?"

Nancy whispered something. It was oh or no, I dont know which. Like nobody had made it, like it came from nowhere and went nowhere, until it was like Nancy was not there at all; that I had looked so hard at her eyes on the stairs that they had got printed on my eyeballs, like the sun does when you have closed your eyes and there is no sun. "Jesus," Nancy whispered. "Jesus."

"Was it Jesus?" Caddy said. "Did he try to come into the kitchen?"

"Jesus." Nancy said. Like this: Jeeeeeeeeeeeeeeeesus, until the sound went out, like a match or a candle does.

"It's the other Jesus she means," I said.

"Can you see us, Nancy?" Caddy whispered. "Can you see our eyes too?"

"I aint nothing but a nigger," Nancy said. "God knows. God knows."

"What did you see down there in the kitchen?" Caddy whispered. "What tried to get in?"

"God knows," Nancy said. We could see her eyes. "God knows."

Dilsey got well. She cooked dinner. "You'd better stay in bed a day or two longer," father said.

"What for?" Dilsey said. "If I had been a day later, this place would be to rack and ruin. Get on out of here now, and let me get my kitchen straight again."

Dilsey cooked supper too. And that night, just before dark, Nancy came into the kitchen.

"How do you know he's back?" Dilsey said. "You aint seen him."

"Jesus is a nigger," Jason said.

"I can feel him," Nancy said. "I can feel him laying yonder in the ditch."

"Tonight?" Dilsey said. "Is he there tonight?"

"Dilsey's a nigger too," Jason said.

"You try to eat something," Dilsey said.

"I dont want nothing," Nancy said.

"I aint a nigger," Jason said.

"Drink some coffee," Dilsey said. She poured a cup of coffee for Nancy. "Do you know he's out there tonight? How come you know it's tonight?"

"I know," Nancy said. "He's there, waiting. I know. I done lived with him too long. I know what he is fixing to do fore he know it himself."

"Drink some coffee," Dilsey said. Nancy held the cup to her mouth and blew into the cup. Her mouth pursed out like a spreading adder's, like a rubber mouth, like she had blown all the color out of her lips with blowing the coffee.

"I aint a nigger," Jason said. "Are you a nigger, Nancy?"

"I hellborn, child," Nancy said. "I wont be nothing soon. I going back where I come from soon."

### III

She began to drink the coffee. While she was drinking, holding the cup in both hands, she began to make the sound again. She made the sound into the cup and the coffee sploshed out onto her hands and her dress. Her eyes looked at us and she sat there, her elbows on her knees, holding the cup in both hands, looking at us across the wet cup, making the sound. "Look at Nancy," Jason said. "Nancy cant cook for us now. Dilsey's got well now."

"You hush up," Dilsey said. Nancy held the cup in both hands, looking at us, making the sound, like there were two of them: one looking at us and the other making the sound. "Whyn't you let Mr Jason telefoam the marshal?" Dilsey said. Nancy stopped then, holding the cup in her long brown hands. She tried to drink some coffee again, but it sploshed out of the cup, onto her hands and her dress, and she put the cup down. Jason watched her.

"I cant swallow it," Nancy said. "I swallows but it wont go down me."

"You go down to the cabin," Dilsey said. "Frony will fix you a pallet and I'll be there soon."

"Wont no nigger stop him," Nancy said.

"I aint a nigger," Jason said. "Am I, Dilsey?"

"I reckon not," Dilsey said. She looked at Nancy. "I dont reckon so. What you going to do, then?"

Nancy looked at us. Her eyes went fast, like she was afraid there wasn't time to look, without hardly moving at all. She looked at us, at all three of us at one time. "You remember that night I stayed in yawls' room?" she said. She told about how we waked up early the next morning, and played. We had to play quiet, on her pallet, until father woke up and it was time to get breakfast.

"Go and ask your maw to let me stay here tonight," Nancy said. "I wont need no pallet. We can play some more."

Caddy asked mother. Jason went too. "I cant have Negroes sleeping in the bedrooms," mother said. Jason cried. He cried until mother said he couldn't have any dessert for three days if he didn't stop. Then Jason said he would stop if Dilsey would make a chocolate cake. Father was there.

"Why dont you do something about it?" mother said. "What do we have officers for?"

"Why is Nancy afraid of Jesus?" Caddy said. "Are you afraid of father, mother?"

"What could the officers do?" father said. "If Nancy hasn't seen him, how could the officers find him?"

"Then why is she afraid?" mother said.

"She says he is there. She says she knows he is there tonight."

"Yet we pay taxes," mother said. "I must wait here alone in this big house while you take a Negro woman home."

"You know that I am not lying outside with a razor," father said.

"I'll stop if Dilsey will make a chocolate cake," Jason said. Mother told us to go out and father said he didn't know if Jason would get a chocolate cake or not, but he knew what Jason was going to get in about a minute. We went back to the kitchen and told Nancy.

"Father said for you to go home and lock the door, and you'll be all right," Caddy said. "All right from what, Nancy? Is Jesus made at you?" Nancy was holding the coffee cup in her hands again, her elbows on her knees and her hands holding the cup between her knees. She was looking into the cup. "What have you done that made Jesus mad?" Caddy said. Nancy let the cup go. It didn't break on the floor, but the coffee spilled out, and Nancy sat there with her hands still making the shape of the cup. She began to make the sound again, not loud. Not singing and not unsinging. We watched her.

"Here," Dilsey said. "You quit that, now. You get aholt of yourself. You wait here. I going to get Versh to walk home with you." Dilsey went out.

We looked at Nancy. Her shoulders kept shaking, but she quit making the sound. We watched her. "What's Jesus going to do to you?" Caddy said. "He went away."

Nancy looked at us. "We had fun that night I stayed in yawls' room, didn't we?"

"I didn't," Jason said. "I didn't have any fun."

"You were asleep in mother's room," Caddy said. "You were not there."

"Let's go down to my house and have some more fun," Nancy said.

"Mother wont let us," I said. "It's too late now."

"Dont bother her," Nancy said. We can tell her in the morning. She wont mind."

"She wouldn't let us," I said.

"Don't ask her now," Nancy said. "Dont bother her now."

"She didn't say we couldn't go," Caddy said.

"We didn't ask," I said.

"If you go, I'll tell," Jason said.

"We'll have fun," Nancy said. "They won't mind, just to my house. I been working for yawl a long time. They won't mind."

"I'm not afraid to go," Caddy said. "Jason is the one that's afraid. He'll tell."

"I'm not," Jason said.

"Yes, you are," Caddy said. "You'll tell."

"I won't tell," Jason said. "I'm not afraid."

"Jason ain't afraid to go with me," Nancy said. "Is you, Jason?"

"Jason is going to tell," Caddy said. The lane was dark. We passed the pasture gate. "I bet if something was to jump out from behind that gate, Jason would holler."

"I wouldn't," Jason said. We walked down the lane. Nancy was talking loud.

"What are you talking so loud for, Nancy?" Caddy said.

"Who; me?" Nancy said. "Listen at Quentin and Caddy and Jason saying I'm talking loud."

"You talk like there was five of us here," Caddy said. "You talk like father was here too."

"Who; me talking loud, Mr Jason?" Nancy said.

"Nancy called Jason 'Mister,' " Caddy said.

"Listen how Caddy and Quentin and Jason talk," Nancy said.

"We're not talking loud," Caddy said. "You're the one that's talking like father—"

"Hush," Nancy said; "hush, Mr. Jason."

"Nancy called Jason 'Mister' aguh—"

"Hush," Nancy said. She was talking loud when we crossed the ditch and stooped through the fence where she used to stoop through with the clothes on her head. Then we came to her house. We were going fast then. She opened the door. The smell of the house was like the lamp and the smell of Nancy was like the wick, like they were waiting for one another to begin to smell. She lit the lamp and closed the door and put the bar up. Then she quit talking loud, looking at us.

"What're we going to do?" Caddy said.

"What do yawl want to do?" Nancy said.

"You said we would have some fun," Caddy said.

There was something about Nancy's house; something you could smell besides Nancy and the house. Jason smelled it, even. "I don't want to stay here," he said. "I want to go home."

"Go home, then," Caddy said.

"I don't want to go by myself," Jason said.

"We're going to have some fun," Nancy said.

"How?" Caddy said.

Nancy stood by the door. She was looking at us, only it was like she had emptied her eyes, like she had quit using them. "What do you want to do?" she said.

"Tell us a story," Caddy said. "Can you tell a story?"

"Yes," Nancy said.

"Tell it," Caddy said. We looked at Nancy. "You don't know any stories."

"Yes," Nancy said. "Yes I do."

She came and sat in a chair before the hearth. There was a little fire there. Nancy built it up, when it was already hot inside. She built a good blaze. She told a story. She talked like her eyes looked, like her eyes watching us and her voice talking to us did not belong to her. Like she was living somewhere else, waiting somewhere else. She was outside the cabin. Her voice was inside and the shape of her, the Nancy that could stoop under a barbed wire fence with a bundle of clothes balanced on her head as though without weight, like a balloon, was there. But that was all. "And so this here queen come walking up to the ditch, where that bad man was hiding. She was walking up to the ditch, and she say, 'If I can just get past this here ditch,' was what she say . . ."

"What ditch?" Caddy said. "A ditch like that one out there? Why did a queen want to go into a ditch?"

"To get to her house," Nancy said. She looked at us. "She had to cross the ditch to get into her house quick and bar the door."

"Why did she want to go home and bar the door?" Caddy said.

## IV

Nancy looked at us. She quit talking. She looked at us. Jason's legs stuck straight out of his pants where he sat on Nancy's lap. "I don't think that's a good story," he said. "I want to go home."

"Maybe we had better," Caddy said. She got up from the floor. "I bet they are looking for us right now." She went toward the door.

"No," Nancy said. "Don't open it." She got up quick and passed Caddy. She didn't touch the door, the wooden bar.

"Why not?" Caddy said.

"Come back to the lamp," Nancy said. "We'll have fun. You don't have to go."

"We ought to go," Caddy said. "Unless we have a lot of fun." She and Nancy came back to the fire, the lamp.

"I want to go home," Jason said. "I'm going to tell."

"I know another story," Nancy said. She stood close to the lamp. She looked at Caddy, like when your eyes look up at a stick balanced on your nose. She had to look down to see Caddy, but her eyes looked like that, like when you are balancing a stick.

"I won't listen to it," Jason said. "I'll bang on the floor."

"It's a good one," Nancy said. "It's better than the other one."

"What's it about?" Caddy said. Nancy was standing by the lamp. Her hand was on the lamp, against the light, long and brown.

"Your hand is on that hot globe," Caddy said. "Don't it feel hot to your hand?"

Nancy looked at her hand on the lamp chimney. She took her hand away, slow. She stood there, looking at Caddy, wringing her long hand as though it were tied to her wrist with a string.

"Let's do something else," Caddy said.

"I want to go home," Jason said.

"I got some popcorn," Nancy said. She looked at Caddy and then at Jason and then at me and then at Caddy again. "I got some popcorn."

"I don't like popcorn," Jason said. "I'd rather have candy."

Nancy looked at Jason. "You can hold the popper." She was till wringing her hand; it was long and limp and brown.

"All right," Jason said. "I'll stay a while if I can do that. Caddy can't hold it. I'll want to go home again if Caddy holds the popper."

Nancy built up the fire. "Look at Nancy putting her hands in the fire," Caddy said. "What's the matter with you, Nancy?"

"I got popcorn," Nancy said. "I got some." She took the popper from under the bed. It was broken. Jason began to cry.

"Now we can't have any popcorn," he said.

"We ought to go home, anyway," Caddy said. "Come on, Quentin."

"Wait," Nancy said; "wait. I can fix it. Don't you want to help me fix it?"

"I don't think I want any," Caddy said. "It's too late now."

"You help me, Jason," Nancy said. "Don't you want to help me?"

"No," Jason said. "I want to go home."

"Hush," Nancy said; "hush. Watch. Watch me. I can fix it so Jason can hold it and pop the corn." She got a piece of wire and fixed the popper.

"It won't hold good," Caddy said.

"Yes, it will," Nancy said. "Yawl watch. Yawl help me shell some corn."

The popcorn was under the bed too. We shelled it into the popper and Nancy helped Jason hold the popper over the fire.

"It's not popping," Jason said. "I want to go home."

"You wait," Nancy said. "It'll begin to pop. We'll have fun then." She was sitting close to the fire. The lamp was turned up so high it was beginning to smoke.

"Why don't you turn it down some?" I said.

"It's all right," Nancy said. "I'll clean it. Yawl wait. The popcorn will start in a minute."

"I don't believe it's going to start," Caddy said. "We ought to start home, anyway. They'll be worried."

"No," Nancy said. "It's going to pop. Dilsey will tell um yawl with me. I been working for yawl long time. They won't mind if yawl at my house. You wait, now. It'll start popping any minute now."

Then Jason got some smoke in his eyes and he began to cry. He dropped the popper into the fire. Nancy got a wet rag and wiped Jason's face, but he didn't stop crying.

"Hush," she said. "Hush." But he didn't hush. Caddy took the popper out of the fire.

"It's burned up," she said. "You'll have to get some more popcorn, Nancy."

"Did you put all of it in?" Nancy said.

"Yes," Caddy said. Nancy look at Caddy. Then she took the popper and opened it and poured the cinders into her apron and began to sort the grains, her hands long and brown, and we watching her.

"Haven't you got any more?" Caddy said.

"Yes," Nancy said; "yes. Look. This here ain't burnt. All we need to do is—"

"I want to go home," Jason said. "I'm going to tell."

"Hush," Caddy said. We all listened. Nancy's head was already turned toward the barred door, her eyes filled with red lamplight. "Somebody is coming," Caddy said.

Then Nancy began to make that sound again, not loud, sitting there above the fire, her long hands dangling between her knees; all of a sudden water began to come out on her face in big drops, running down her face, carrying in each one a little turning ball of firelight like a spark until it dropped off her chin. "She's not crying," I said.

"I ain't crying," Nancy said. Her eyes were closed. "I ain't crying. Who is it?"

"I don't know," Caddy said. She went to the door and looked out. "We've got to go now," she said. "Here comes father."

"I'm going to tell," Jason said. "Yawl made me come."

The water still ran down Nancy's face. She turned in her chair. "Listen.

Tell him. Tell him we going to have fun. Tell him I take good care of yawl until in the morning. Tell him to let me come home with yawl and sleep on the floor. Tell him I won't need no pallet. We'll have fun. You remember last time how we had so much fun?"

"I didn't have fun," Jason said. "You hurt me. You put smoke in my eyes. I'm going to tell."

V

Father came in. He looked at us. Nancy did not get up.

"Tell him," she said.

"Caddy made us come down here," Jason said. "I didn't want to."

Father came to the fire. Nancy looked up at him. "Can't you go to Aunt Rachel's and stay?" he said. Nancy looked up at father, her hands between her knees. "He's not here," father said. "I would have seen him. There's not a soul in sight."

"He in the ditch," Nancy said. "He waiting in the ditch yonder."

"Nonsense," father said. He looked at Nancy. "Do you know he's there?"

"I got the sign," Nancy said.

"What sign?"

"I got it. It was on the table when I come in. It was a hogbone, with blood meat still on it, laying by the lamp. He's out there. When yawl walk out that door, I gone."

"Gone where, Nancy?" Caddy said.

"I'm not a tattletale," Jason said.

"Nonsense," father said.

"He out there," Nancy said. "He looking through that window this minute, waiting for yawl to go. Then I gone."

"Nonsense," father said. "Lock up your house and we'll take you on to Aunt Rachel's."

" 'Twont do no good," Nancy said. She didn't look at father now, but he looked down at her, at her long, limp moving hands. "Putting it off wont do no good."

"Then what do you want to do?" father said.

"I don't know," Nancy said. "I can't do nothing. Just put if off. And that don't do no good. I reckon it belong to me. I reckon what I going to get ain't no more than mine."

"Get what?" Caddy said. "What's yours?"

"Nothing," father said. "You all must get to bed."

"Caddy made me come," Jason said.

"Go on to Aunt Rachel's," father said.

"It won't do no good," Nancy said. She sat before the fire, her elbows on her knees, her long hands between her knees. "When even your own kitchen wouldn't do no good. When even if I was sleeping on the floor in the room with your chillen, and the next morning there I am, and blood—"

"Hush," father said. "Lock the door and put out the lamp and go to bed."

"I scared of the dark," Nancy said. "I scared for it to happen in the dark."

"You mean you're going to sit right here with the lamp lighted?" father said. Then Nancy began to make the sound again, sitting before the fire, her long hands between her knees. "Ah, damnation," father said. "Come along, chillen. It's past bedtime."

"When yawl go home, I gone," Nancy said. She talked quieter now, and her face looked quiet, like her hands. "Anyway, I got my coffin money saved up with Mr. Lovelady." Mr. Lovelady was a short, dirty man who collected the Negro insurance, coming around to the cabins or the kitchens every Saturday morning, to collect fifteen cents. He and his wife lived at the hotel. One morning his wife committed suicide. They had a child, a little girl. He and the child went away. After a week or two he came back alone. We would see him going along the lanes and the back streets on Saturday mornings.

"Nonsense," father said. "You'll be the first thing I'll see in the kitchen tomorrow morning."

"You'll see what you'll see, I reckon," Nancy said. "But it will take the Lord to say what that will be."

## VI

We left her sitting before the fire.

"Come and put the bar up," father said. But she didn't move. She didn't look at us again, sitting quietly there between the lamp and the fire. From some distance down the lane we could look back and see her through the open door.

"What, Father?" Caddy said. "What's going to happen?"

"Nothing," father said. Jason was on father's back, so Jason was the tallest of all of us. We went down into the ditch. I looked at it, quiet. I couldn't see much where the moonlight and the shadows tangled.

"If Jesus is hid here, he can see us, cant he?" Caddy said.

"He's not there," father said. "He went away a long time ago."

"You made me come," Jason said, high; against the sky it looked like father had two heads, a little one and a big one. "I didn't want to."

We went up out of the ditch. We could still see Nancy's house and the open door, but we couldn't see Nancy now, sitting before the fire with the door open, because she was tired. "I just done got tired," she said. "I just a nigger. It ain't no fault of mine."

But we could hear her, because she began just after we came up out of the ditch, the sound that was not singing and not unsinging. "Who will do our washing now, Father?" I said.

"I'm not a nigger," Jason said, high and close above father's head.

"You're worse," Caddy said, "you are a tattletale. If something was to jump out, you'd be scairder than a nigger."

"I wouldn't," Jason said.

"You'd cry," Caddy said.

"Caddy," father said.

"I wouldn't!" Jason said.

"Scairy cat," Caddy said.

"Candace!" father said.

1931

# A Rose for Emily

## I

When Miss Emily Grierson died, our whole town went to her funeral: the men through a sort of respectful affection for a fallen monument, the women mostly out of curiosity to see the inside of her house, which no one save an old manservant—a combined gardener and cook—had seen in at least ten years.

It was a big, squarish frame house that had once been white, decorated with cupolas and spires and scrolled balconies in the heavily lightsome style of the seventies, set on what had once been our most select street. But garages and cotton gins had encroached and obliterated even the august names of that neighborhood; only Miss Emily's house was left, lifting its stubborn and coquettish decay above the cotton wagons and the gasoline pumps—an eyesore among eyesores. And now Miss Emily had gone to join the representatives of those august names where they lay in the cedar-bemused cemetery among the ranked and anonymous graves of Union and Confederate soldiers who fell at the battle of Jefferson.

Alive, Miss Emily had been a tradition, a duty, and a care; a sort of heredi-tary obligation upon the town, dating from that day in 1894 when Colonel Sartoris, the mayor—he who fathered the edict that no Negro woman should appear on the streets without an apron—remitted her taxes, the dispensation dating from the death of her father on into perpetuity. Not that Miss Emily would have accepted charity. Colonel Sartoris invented an involved tale to the effect that Miss Emily's father had loaned money to the town, which the town, as a matter of business, preferred this way of repaying. Only a man of Colonel Sartoris' generation and thought could have invented it, and only a woman could have believed it.

When the next generation, with its more modern ideas, became mayors and aldermen, this arrangement created some little dissatisfaction. On the first of the year they mailed her a tax notice. February came, and there was no reply. They wrote her a formal letter, asking her to call at the sheriff's office at her convenience. A week later the mayor wrote her himself, offering to call or to send his car for her, and received in reply a note on paper of an archaic shape, in a thin, flowing calligraphy in faded ink, to the effect that she no longer went out at all. The tax notice was also enclosed, without comment.

They called a special meeting of the Board of Aldermen. A deputation waited upon her, knocked at the door through which no visitor had passed since she ceased giving china-painting lessons eight or ten years earlier. They were admitted by the old Negro into a dim hall from which a stairway mounted into still more shadow. It smelled of dust and disuse—a close, dank smell. The Negro led them into the parlor. It was furnished in heavy, leather-covered furniture. When the Negro opened the blinds of one window, they could see that the leather was cracked; and when they sat down, a faint dust rose slug-gishly about their thighs, spinning with slow motes in the single sun-ray. On a tarnished gilt easel before the fireplace stood a crayon portrait of Miss Emily's father.

They rose when she entered—a small, fat woman in black, with a thin gold chain descending to her waist and vanishing into her belt, leaning on an ebony cane with a tarnished gold head. Her skeleton was small and spare; perhaps that was why what would have been merely plumpness in another was obesity in her. She looked bloated, like a body long submerged in motionless water, and of that pallid hue. Her eyes, lost in the fatty ridges of her face, looked like two small pieces of coal pressed into a lump of dough as they moved from one face to another while the visitors stated their errand.

She did not ask them to sit. She just stood in the door and listened quietly until the spokesman came to a stumbling halt. Then they could hear the invisible watch ticking at the end of the gold chain.

Her voice was dry and cold. "I have no taxes in Jefferson. Colonel Sartoris explained it to me. Perhaps one of you can gain access to the city records and satisfy yourselves."

"But we have. We are the city authorities, Miss Emily. Didn't you get a notice from the sheriff, signed by him?"

"I received a paper, yes," Miss Emily said. "Perhaps he considers himself the sheriff . . . . I have no taxes in Jefferson."

"But there is nothing on the books to show that, you see. We must go by the—"

"See Colonel Sartoris. I have no taxes in Jefferson."

"But, Miss Emily—"

"See Colonel Sartoris." (Colonel Sartoris had been dead almost ten years.) "I have no taxes in Jefferson. Tobe!" The Negro appeared. "Show these gentlemen out."

## II

So she vanquished them, horse and foot, just as she had vanquished their fathers thirty years before about the smell. That was two years after her father's death and a short time after her sweetheart—the one we believed would marry her—had deserted her. After her father's death she went out very little; after her sweetheart went away, people hardly saw her at all. A few of the ladies had the temerity to call, but were not received, and the only sign of life about the place was the Negro man—a young man then—going in and out with a market basket.

"Just as if a man—any man—could keep a kitchen properly," the ladies said; so they were not surprised when the smell developed. It was another link between the gross, teeming world and the high and mighty Griersons.

A neighbor, a woman, complained to the mayor, Judge Stevens, eighty years old.

"But what will you have me do about it, madam?" he said.

"Why, send her word to stop it," the woman said. "Isn't there a law?"

"I'm sure that won't be necessary," Judge Stevens said. "It's probably just a snake or a rat that nigger of hers killed in the yard. I'll speak to him about it."

The next day he received two more complaints, one from a man who came in diffident deprecation. "We really must do something about it, Judge. I'd be the last one in the world to bother Miss Emily, but we've got to do something." That night the Board of Aldermen met—three gray-beards and one younger man, a member of the rising generation.

"It's simple enough," he said. "Send her word to have her place cleaned up. Give her a certain time to do it in, and if she don't . . . ."

"Dammit, sir," Judge Stevens said, "will you accuse a lady to her face of smelling bad?"

So the next night, after midnight, four men crossed Miss Emily's lawn and slunk about the house like burglars, sniffing along the base of the brickwork and at the cellar openings while one of them performed a regular sowing motion with his hand out of a sack slung from his shoulder. They broke open the cellar door and sprinkled lime there, and in all the outbuildings. As they recrossed the lawn, a window that had been dark was lighted and Miss Emily sat in it, the light behind her, and her upright torso motionless as that of an idol. They crept quietly across the lawn and into the shadow of the locusts that lined the street. After a week or two the smell went away.

That was when people had begun to feel really sorry for her. People in our town, remembering how old lady Wyatt, her great-aunt, had gone completely crazy at last, believed that the Griersons held themselves a little too high for what they really were. None of the young men were quite good enough for Miss Emily and such. We had long thought of them as a tableau; Miss Emily a slender figure in white in the background, her father a spraddled silhouette in the foreground, his back to her and clutching a horsewhip, the two of them framed by the back-flung front door. So when she got to be thirty and was still single, we were not pleased exactly, but vindicated; even with insanity in the family she wouldn't have turned down all of her chances if they had really materialized.

When her father died, it got about that the house was all that was left to her; and in a way, people were glad. At last they could pity Miss Emily. Being left alone, and a pauper, she had become humanized. Now she too would know the old thrill and the old despair of a penny more or less.

The day after his death all the ladies prepared to call at the house and offer condolence and aid, as is our custom. Miss Emily met them at the door, dressed as usual and with no trace of grief on her face. She told them that her father was not dead. She did that for three days, with the ministers calling on her, and the doctors, trying to persuade her to let them dispose of the body. Just as they were about to resort to law and force, she broke down, and they buried her father quickly.

We did not say she was crazy then. We believed she had to do that. We remembered all the young men her father had driven away, and we knew that with nothing left, she would have to cling to that which had robbed her, as people will.

### III

She was sick for a long time. When we saw her again, her hair was cut short, making her look like a girl, with a vague resemblance to those angels in colored church windows—sort of tragic and serene.

The town had just let the contracts for paving the sidewalks, and in the summer after her father's death they began to work. The construction company came with niggers and mules and machinery, and a foreman named Homer Barron, a Yankee—a big, dark, ready man, with a big voice and eyes lighter than his face. The little boys would follow in groups to hear him cuss the niggers, and the niggers singing in time to the rise and fall of picks. Pretty soon he knew everybody in town. Whenever you heard a lot of laughing anywhere about the square, Homer Barron would be in the center of the group.

Presently we began to see him and Miss Emily on Sunday afternoons driving in the yellow-wheeled buggy and the matched team of bays from the livery stable.

At first we were glad that Miss Emily would have an interest, because the ladies all said, "Of course a Grierson would not think seriously of a Northerner, a day laborer." But there were still others, older people, who said that even grief could not cause a real lady to forget *noblesse oblige*—without calling it *noblesse oblige*. They just said, "Poor Emily. Her kinsfolk should come to her." She had some kin in Alabama; but years ago her father had fallen out with them over the estate of old lady Wyatt, the crazy woman, and there was no communication between the two families. They had not even been represented at the funeral.

And as soon as the old people said, "Poor Emily," the whispering began. "Do you suppose it's really so?" they said to one another. "Of course it is. What else could . . . " This behind their hands; rustling of craned silk and satin behind jalousies closed upon the sun of Sunday afternoon as the thin, swift clop-clop-clop of the matched team passed: "Poor Emily."

She carried her head high enough—even when we believed that she was fallen. It was as if she demanded more than ever the recognition of her dignity as the last Grierson; as if it had wanted that touch of earthiness to reaffirm her imperviousness. Like when she bought the rat poison, the arsenic. That was over a year after they had begun to say "Poor Emily," and while the two female cousins were visiting her.

"I want some poison," she said to the druggist. She was over thirty then, still a slight woman, though thinner than usual, with cold, haughty black eyes in a face the flesh of which was strained across the temples and about the eyesockets as you imagine a lighthouse-keeper's face ought to look. "I want some poison," she said.

"Yes, Miss Emily. What kind? For rats and such? I'd recom—"

"I want the best you have. I don't care what kind."

The druggist named several. "They'll kill anything up to an elephant. But what you want is—"

"Arsenic," Miss Emily said. "Is that a good one?"

"Is . . . arsenic? Yes ma'am. But what you want—"

"I want arsenic."

The druggist looked down at her. She looked back at him, erect, her face like a strained flag. "Why, of course," the druggist said. "If that's what you want. But the law requires you to tell what you are going to use it for."

Miss Emily just stared at him, her head tilted back in order to look him eye for eye, until he looked away and went and got the arsenic and wrapped it up. The Negro delivery boy brought her the package; the druggist didn't come back. When she opened the package at home there was written on the box, under the skull and bones: "For rats."

## IV

So the next day we all said, "She will kill herself"; and we said it would be the best thing. When she had first begun to be seen with Homer Barron, we had said, "She will marry him." Then we said, "She will persuade him yet," because Homer himself had remarked—he liked men, and it was known that he drank with the younger men in the Elks' Club—that he was not a marrying man. Later we said, "Poor Emily," behind the jalousies as they passed on Sunday afternoon in the glittering buggy, Miss Emily with her head high and Homer Barron with his hat cocked and a cigar in his teeth, reins and whip in a yellow glove.

Then some of the ladies began to say that it was a disgrace to the town and a bad example to the young people. The men did not want to interfere, but at last the ladies forced the Baptist minister—Miss Emily's people were Episcopal—to call upon her. He would never divulge what happened during that interview, but he refused to go back again. The next Sunday they again drove about the streets, and the following day the minister's wife wrote to Miss Emily's relations in Alabama.

So she had blood-kin under her roof again and we sat back to watch developments. At first nothing happened. Then we were sure that they were to be married. We learned that Miss Emily had been to the jeweler's and ordered a man's toilet set in silver, with the letters H. B. on each piece. Two days later we learned that she had bought a complete outfit of men's clothing, including a nightshirt, and we said, "They are married." We were really glad. We were glad because the two female cousins were even more Grierson than Miss Emily had ever been.

So we were not surprised when Homer Barron—the streets had been finished some time since—was gone. We were a little disappointed that there was not a public blowing-off, but we believed that he had gone on to prepare for Miss Emily's coming, or to give her a chance to get rid of the cousins. (By that time it was a cabal, and we were all Miss Emily's allies to help circumvent the cousins.) Sure enough, after another week they departed. And, as we had expected all along, within three days Homer Barron was back in town. A neighbor saw the Negro man admit him at the kitchen door at dusk one evening.

And that was the last we saw of Homer Barron. And of Miss Emily for some time. The Negro man went in and out with the market basket, but the front door remained closed. Now and then we would see her at a window for a moment, as the men did that night when they sprinkled the lime, but for almost six months she did not appear on the streets. Then we knew that this was to be expected too; as if that quality of her father which had thwarted her woman's life so many times had been too virulent and too furious to die.

When we next saw Miss Emily, she had grown fat and her hair was turning gray. During the next few years it grew grayer and grayer until it attained an even pepper-and-salt iron-gray, when it ceased turning. Up to the day of her death at seventy-four it was still that vigorous iron-gray, like the hair of an active man.

From that time on her front door remained closed, save for a period of six or seven years, when she was about forty, during which she gave lessons in china-painting. She fitted up a studio in one of the downstairs rooms, where the daughters and granddaughters of Colonel Sartoris' contemporaries were sent to her with the same regularity and in the same spirit that they were sent on Sundays with a twenty-five-cent piece for the collection plate. Meanwhile her taxes had been remitted.

Then the newer generation became the backbone and the spirit of the town, and the painting pupils grew up and fell away and did not send their children to her with boxes of color and tedious brushes and pictures cut from the ladies' magazines. The front door closed upon the last one and remained closed for good. When the town got free postal delivery Miss Emily alone refused to let them fasten the metal numbers above her door and attach a mailbox to it. She would not listen to them.

Daily, monthly, yearly we watched the Negro grow grayer and more stooped, going in and out with the market basket. Each December we sent her a tax notice, which would be returned by the post office a week later, unclaimed. Now and then we would see her in one of the downstairs windows—she had evidently shut up the top floor of the house—like the carven torso of an idol in a niche, looking or not looking at us, we could never tell which. Thus she passed from generation to generation—dear, inescapable, impervious, tranquil, and perverse.

And so she died. Fell ill in the house filled with dust and shadows, with only a doddering Negro man to wait on her. We did not even know she was sick; we had long since given up trying to get any information from the Negro. He talked to no one, probably not even to her, for his voice had grown harsh and rusty, as if from disuse.

She died in one of the downstairs rooms, in a heavy walnut bed with a curtain, her gray head propped on a pillow yellow and moldy with age and lack of sunlight.

## V

The Negro met the first of the ladies at the front door and let them in, with their hushed, sibilant voices and their quick, curious glances, and then he disappeared. He walked right through the house and out the back and was not seen again.

The two female cousins came at once. They held the funeral on the second day, with the town coming to look at Miss Emily beneath a mass of bought flowers, with the crayon face of her father musing profoundly above the bier and the ladies sibilant and macabre; and the very old men—some in their brushed Confederate uniforms—on the porch and the lawn, talking of Miss Emily as if she had been a contemporary of theirs, believing that they had danced with her and courted her perhaps, confusing time with its mathematical progression, as the old do, to whom all the past is not a diminishing road, but, instead, a huge meadow which no winter ever quite touches, divided from them now by the narrow bottle-neck of the most recent decade of years.

Already we knew that there was one room in that region above stairs which no one had seen in forty years, and which would have to be forced. They waited until Miss Emily was decently in the ground before they opened it.

The violence of breaking down the door seemed to fill this room with pervading dust. A thin, acrid pall as of the tomb seemed to lie everywhere upon this room decked and furnished as for a bridal: upon the valance curtains of faded rose color, upon the rose-shaded lights, upon the dressing table, upon the delicate array of crystal and the man's toilet things backed with tarnished silver, silver so tarnished that the monogram was obscured. Among them lay a collar and tie, as if they had just been removed, which, lifted, left upon the surface a pale crescent in the dust. Upon a chair hung the suit, carefully folded; beneath it the two mute shoes and the discarded socks.

The man himself lay in the bed.

For a long while we just stood there, looking down at the profound and fleshless grin. The body had apparently once lain in the attitude of an embrace, but now the long sleep that outlasts love, that conquers even the grimace of love, had cuckolded him. What was left of him, rotted beneath what was left of the nightshirt, had become inextricable from the bed in which he lay; and upon him and upon the pillow beside him lay that even coating of the patient and biding dust.

Then we noticed that in the second pillow was the indentation of a head. One of us lifted something from it, and leaning forward, that faint and invisible dust dry and acrid in the nostrils, we saw a long strand of iron-gray hair.

1931

# Barn Burning[1]

The store in which the Justice of the Peace's court was sitting smelled of cheese. The boy, crouched on his nail keg at the back of the crowded room, knew he smelled cheese, and more: from where he sat he could see the ranked shelves close-packed with the solid, squat, dynamic shapes of tin cans whose labels his stomach read, not from the lettering which meant nothing to his mind but from the scarlet devils and the silver curve of fish—this, the cheese which he knew he smelled and the hermetic meat which his intestines believed he smelled coming in intermittent gusts momentary and brief between the other constant one, the smell and sense just a little of fear because mostly of despair and grief, the old fierce pull of blood. He could not see the table where the Justice sat and before which his father and his father's enemy (*our enemy* he thought in that despair; *ourn! mine and hisn both! He's my father!*) stood, but he could hear them, the two of them that is, because his father had said no word yet:

"But what proof have you, Mr. Harris?"

"I told you. The hog got into my corn. I caught it up and sent it back to him. He had no fence that would hold it. I told him so, warned him. The next time I put the hog in my pen. When he came to get it I gave him enough wire to patch up his pen. The next time I put the hog up and kept it. I rode down to his house and saw the wire I gave him still rolled on to the spool in his yard. I told him he could have the hog when he paid me a dollar pound fee. That evening a nigger came with the dollar and got the hog. He was a strange nigger. He said, 'He say to tell you wood and hay kin burn.' I said, 'What?' 'That whut he say to tell you,' the nigger said. 'Wood and hay kin burn.' That night my barn burned. I got the stock out but I lost the barn."

"Where is the nigger? Have you got him?"

"He was a strange nigger, I tell you. I don't know what became of him."

"But that's not proof. Don't you see that's not proof?"

"Get that boy up here. He knows." For a moment the boy thought too that the man meant his older brother until Harris said, "Not him. The little one. The boy," and, crouching, small for his age, small and wiry like his father, in patched and faded jeans even too small for him, with straight, uncombed,

1. The text is that of *Collected Stories* (1951).

brown hair and eyes gray and wild as storm scud, he saw the men between himself and the table part and become a lane of grim faces, at the end of which he saw the Justice, a shabby, collarless, graying man in spectacles, beckoning him. He felt no floor under his bare feet; he seemed to walk beneath the palpable weight of the grim turning faces. His father, stiff in his black Sunday coat donned not for the trial but for the moving, did not even look at him. *He aims for me to lie*, he thought, again with that frantic grief and despair. *And I will have to do hit.*

"What's your name, boy?" the Justice said.

"Colonel Sartoris Snopes,"[2] the boy whispered.

"Hey?" the Justice said. "Talk louder. Colonel Sartoris? I reckon anybody named for Colonel Sartoris in this country can't help but tell the truth, can they?" The boy said nothing. *Enemy! Enemy!* he thought; for a moment he could not even see, could not see that the Justice's face was kindly nor discern that his voice was troubled when he spoke to the man named Harris: "Do you want me to question this boy?" But he could hear, and during those subsequent long seconds while there was absolutely no sound in the crowded little room save that of quiet and intent breathing it was as if he had swung outward at the end of a grape vine, over a ravine, and at the top of the swing had been caught in a prolonged instant of mesmerized gravity, weightless in time.

"No!" Harris said violently, explosively. "Damnation! Send him out of here!" Now time, the fluid world, rushed beneath him again, the voices coming to him again through the smell of cheese and sealed meat, the fear and despair and the old grief of blood:

"This case is closed. I can't find against you, Snopes, but I can give you advice. Leave this country and don't come back to it."

His father spoke for the first time, his voice cold and harsh, level, without emphasis: "I aim to. I don't figure to stay in a country among people who . . ." he said something unprintable and vile, addressed to no one.

"That'll do," the Justice said. "Take your wagon and get out of this country before dark. Case dismissed."

His father turned, and he followed the stiff black coat, the wiry figure walking a little stiffly from where a Confederate provost's man's musket ball had taken him in the heel on a stolen horse thirty years ago, followed the two backs now, since his older brother had appeared from somewhere in the crowd, no taller than the father but thicker, chewing tobacco steadily, between the two lines of grim-faced men and out of the store and across the worn gallery and down the sagging steps and among the dogs and half-grown boys in the mild May dust, where as he passed a voice hissed:

"Barn burner!"

Again he could not see, whirling; there was a face in a red haze, moonlike, bigger than the full moon, the owner of it half again his size, he leaping in the red haze toward the face, feeling no blow, feeling no shock when his head struck the earth, scrabbling up and leaping again, feeling no blow this time either and tasting no blood, scrabbling up to see the other boy in full flight and himself already leaping into pursuit as his father's hand jerked him back, the harsh, cold voice speaking above him: "Go get in the wagon."

---

2. The boy is named for Colonal Sartoris, a leading citizen of Jefferson (Faulkner's invented town based on his hometown of Oxford, Mississippi) and officer in the Confederate Army. The Snopeses are a poor white family from the same region. Both families reappear in other works by Faulkner.

It stood in a grove of locusts and mulberries across the road. His two hulking sisters in their Sunday dresses and his mother and her sister in calico and sunbonnets were already in it, sitting on and among the sorry residue of the dozen and more movings which even the boy could remember—the battered stove, the broken beds and chairs, the clock inlaid with mother-of-pearl, which would not run, stopped at some fourteen minutes past two o'clock of a dead and forgotten day and time, which had been his mother's dowry. She was crying, though when she saw him she drew her sleeve across her face and began to descend from the wagon. "Get back," the father said.

"He's hurt. I got to get some water and wash his . . . ."

"Get back in the wagon," his father said. He got in too, over the tail-gate. His father mounted to the seat where the older brother already sat and struck the gaunt mules two savage blows with the peeled willow, but without heat. It was not even sadistic; it was exactly that same quality which in later years would cause his descendants to over-run the engine before putting a motor car into motion, striking and reining back in the same movement. The wagon went on, the store with its quiet crowd of grimly watching men dropped behind; a curve in the road hid it. *Forever* he thought. *Maybe he's done satisfied now, now that he has* . . . stopping himself, not to say it aloud even to himself. His mother's hand touched his shoulder.

"Does hit hurt?" she said.

"Naw," he said. "Hit don't hurt. Lemme be."

"Can't you wipe some of the blood off before hit dries?"

"I'll wash to-night," he said. "Lemme be, I tell you."

The wagon went on. He did not know where they were going. None of them ever did or ever asked, because it was always somewhere, always a house of sorts waiting for them a day or two days or even three days away. Likely his father had already arranged to make a crop on another farm before he . . . . Again he had to stop himself. He (the father) always did. There was something about his wolflike independence and even courage when the advantage was at least neutral which impressed strangers, as if they got from his latent ravening ferocity not so much a sense of dependability as a feeling that his ferocious conviction in the rightness of his own actions would be of advantage to all whose interest lay with his.

That night they camped, in a grove of oaks and beeches where a spring ran. The nights were still cool and they had a fire against it, of a rail lifted from a nearby fence and cut into lengths—a small fire, neat, niggard almost, a shrewd fire; such fires were his father's habit and custom always, even in freezing weather. Older, the boy might have remarked this and wondered why not a big one; why should not a man who had not only seen the waste and extravagance of war, but who had in his blood an inherent voracious prodigality with material not his own, have burned everything in sight? Then he might have gone a step farther and thought that that was the reason: that niggard blaze was the living fruit of nights passed during those four years in the woods hiding from all men, blue or gray, with his strings of horses (captured horses, he called them). And older still, he might have divined the true reason: that the element of fire spoke to some deep mainspring of his father's being, as the element of steel or of powder spoke to other men, as the one weapon for the preservation of integrity, else breath were not worth the breathing, and hence to be regarded with respect and used with discretion.

But he did not think this now and he had seen those same niggard blazes all his life. He merely ate his supper beside it and was already half asleep over his iron plate when his father called him, and once more he followed the stiff back, the stiff and ruthless limp, up the slope and on to the starlit road where, turning, he could see his father against the stars but without face or depth—a shape black, flat, and bloodless as though cut from tin in the iron folds of the frockcoat which had not been made for him, the voice harsh like tin and without heat like tin:

"You were fixing to tell them. You would have told him." He didn't answer. His father struck him with the flat of his hand on the side of the head, hard but without heat, exactly as he had struck the two mules at the store, exactly as he would strike either of them with any stick in order to kill a horse fly, his voice still without heat or anger: "You're getting to be a man. You got to learn. You got to learn to stick to your own blood or you ain't going to have any blood to stick to you. Do you think either of them, any man there this morning, would? Don't you know all they wanted was a chance to get at me because they knew I had them beat? Eh?" Later, twenty years later, he was to tell himself, "If I had said they wanted only truth, justice, he would have hit me again." But now he said nothing. He was not crying. He just stood there. "Answer me," his father said.

"Yes," he whispered. His father turned.

"Get on to bed. We'll be there tomorrow."

To-morrow they were there. In the early afternoon the wagon stopped before a paintless two-room house identical almost with the dozen others it had stopped before even in the boy's ten years, and again, as on the other dozen occasions, his mother and aunt got down and began to unload the wagon, although his two sisters and his father and brother had not moved.

"Likely hit ain't fitten for hawgs," one of the sisters said.

"Nevertheless, fit it will and you'll hog it and like it," his father said. "Get out of them chairs and help your Ma unload."

The two sisters got down, big, bovine, in a flutter of cheap ribbons; one of them drew from the jumbled wagon bed a battered lantern, the other a worn broom. His father handed the reins to the older son and began to climb stiffly over the wheel. "When they get unloaded, take the team to the barn and feed them." Then he said, and at first the boy thought he was still speaking to his brother: "Come with me."

"Me?" he said.

"Yes," his father said. "You."

"Abner," his mother said. His father paused and looked back—the harsh level stare beneath the shaggy, graying, irascible brows.

"I reckon I'll have a word with the man that aims to begin to-morrow owning me body and soul for the next eight months."

They went back up the road. A week ago—or before last night, that is—he would have asked where they were going, but not now. His father had struck him before last night but never before had he paused afterward to explain why; it was as if the blow and the following calm, outrageous voice still rang, repercussed, divulging nothing to him save the terrible handicap of being young, the light weight of his few years, just heavy enough to prevent his soaring free of the world as it seemed to be ordered but not heavy enough to keep him footed solid in it, to resist it and try to change the course of its events.

Presently he could see the grove of oaks and cedars and the other flowering trees and shrubs where the house would be, though not the house yet. They walked beside a fence massed with honeysuckle and Cherokee roses and came to a gate swinging open between two brick pillars, and now, beyond a sweep of drive, he saw the house for the first time and at that instant he forgot his father and the terror and despair both, and even when he remembered his father again (who had not stopped) the terror and despair did not return. Because, for all the twelve movings, they had sojourned until now in a poor country, a land of small farms and fields and houses, and he had never seen a house like this before. *Hit's big as a courthouse* he thought quietly, with a surge of peace and joy whose reason he could not have thought into words, being too young for that: *They are safe from him. People whose lives are a part of this peace and dignity are beyond his touch, he no more to them than a buzzing wasp: capable of stinging for a little moment but that's all; the spell of this peace and dignity rendering even the barns and stable and cribs which belong to it impervious to the puny flames he might contrive . . .* this, the peace and joy, ebbing for an instant as he looked again at the stiff black back, the stiff and implacable limp of the figure which was not dwarfed by the house, for the reason that it had never looked big anywhere and which now, against the serene columned backdrop, had more than ever that impervious quality of something cut ruthlessly from tin, depthless, as though, sidewise to the sun, it would cast no shadow. Watching him, the boy remarked the absolutely unde-viating course which his father held and saw the stiff foot come squarely down in a pile of fresh droppings where a horse had stood in the drive and which his father could have avoided by a simple change of stride. But it ebbed only for a moment, though he could not have thought this into words either, walking on in the spell of the house, which he could even want but without envy, without sorrow, certainly never with that ravening and jealous rage which unknown to him walked in the ironlike black coat before him: *Maybe he will feel it too. Maybe it will even change him now from what maybe he couldn't help but be.*

They crossed the portico. Now he could hear his father's stiff foot as it came down on the boards with clocklike finality, a sound out of all proportion to the displacement of the body it bore and which was not dwarfed either by the white door before it, as though it had attained to a sort of vicious and ravening minimum not to be dwarfed by anything—the flat, wide, black hat, the formal coat of broadcloth which had once been black but which had now that friction-glazed greenish cast of the bodies of old house flies, the lifted sleeve which was too large, the lifted hand like a curled claw. The door opened so promptly that the boy knew the Negro must have been watching them all the time, an old man with neat grizzled hair, in a linen jacket, who stood barring the door with his body, saying, "Wipe yo foots, white man, fo you come in here. Major ain't home nohow."

"Get out of my way, nigger," his father said, without heat too, flinging the door back and the Negro also and entering, his hat still on his head. And now the boy saw the prints of the stiff foot on the doorjamb and saw them appear on the pale rug behind the machinelike deliberation of the foot which seemed to bear (or transmit) twice the weight which the body compassed. The Negro was shouting "Miss Lula! Miss Lula!" somewhere behind them, then the boy, deluged as though by a warm wave by a suave turn of carpeted stair and a pendant glitter of chandeliers and a mute gleam of gold frames, heard the swift feet and saw her too, a lady—perhaps he had never seen her like before either—in a gray, smooth gown with lace at the throat and an apron tied at the waist and the sleeves turned back, wiping cake or biscuit dough from her hands with a towel as she came up the hall, looking not at his father at all but at the tracks on the blond rug with an expression of incredulous amazement.

"I tried," the Negro cried. "I tole him to . . ."

"Will you please go away?" she said in a shaking voice. "Major de Spain is not at home. Will you please go away?"

His father had not spoken again. He did not speak again. He did not even look at her. He just stood stiff in the center of the rug, in his hat, the shaggy iron-gray brows twitching slightly above the pebble-colored eyes as he appeared to examine the house with brief deliberation. Then with the same deliberation he turned; the boy watched him pivot on the good leg and saw the stiff foot drag round the arc of the turning, leaving a final long and fading smear. His father never looked at it, he never once looked down at the rug. The Negro held the door. It closed behind them, upon the hysteric and indistinguishable woman-wail. His father stopped at the top of the steps and scraped his boot clean on the edge of it. At the gate he stopped again. He stood for a moment, planted stiffly on the stiff foot, looking back at the house. "Pretty and white, ain't it?" he said. "That's sweat. Nigger sweat. Maybe it ain't white enough yet to suit him. Maybe he wants to mix some white sweat with it."

Two hours later the boy was chopping wood behind the house within which his mother and aunt and the two sisters (the mother and aunt, not the two girls, he knew that; even at this distance and muffled by walls the flat loud voices of the two girls emanated an incorrigible idle inertia) were setting up the stove to prepare a meal, when he heard the hooves and saw the linen-clad man on a fine sorrel mare, whom he recognized even before he saw the rolled rug in front of the Negro youth following on a fat bay carriage horse—a suffused, angry face vanishing, still at full gallop, beyond the corner of the house where his father and brother were sitting in the two tilted chairs; and a moment later, almost before he could have put the axe down, he heard the hooves again and watched the sorrel mare go back out of the yard, already galloping again. Then his father began to shout one of the sisters' names, who presently emerged backward from the kitchen door dragging the rolled rug along the ground by one end while the other sister walked behind it.

"If you ain't going to tote, go on and set up the wash pot," the first said.

"You, Sarty!" the second shouted. "Set up the wash pot!" His father appeared at the door, framed against that shabbiness, as he had been against that other bland perfection, impervious to either, the mother's anxious face at his shoulder.

"Go on," the father said. "Pick it up." The two sisters stooped, broad, lethargic; stooping, they presented an incredible expanse of pale cloth and a flutter of tawdry ribbons.

"If I thought enough of a rug to have to git hit all the way from France I wouldn't keep hit where folks coming in would have to tromp on hit," the first said. They raised the rug.

"Abner," the mother said. "Let me do it."

"You go back and git dinner," his father said. "I'll tend to this."

From the woodpile through the rest of the afternoon the boy watched them, the rug spread flat in the dust beside the bubbling wash-pot, the two sisters stooping over it with that profound and lethargic reluctance, while the father stood over them in turn, implacable and grim, driving them though never raising his voice again. He could smell the harsh homemade lye they were using; he saw his mother come to the door once and look toward them with an expression not anxious now but very like despair; he saw his father turn, and he fell to with the axe and saw from the corner of his eye his father raise from the ground a flattish fragment of field stone and examine it and return to the pot, and this time his mother actually spoke: "Abner. Abner. Please don't. Please, Abner."

Then he was done too. It was dusk; the whippoorwills had already begun. He could smell coffee from the room where they would presently eat the cold food remaining from the mid-afternoon meal, though when he entered the house he realized they were having coffee again probably because there was a fire on the hearth, before which the rug now lay spread over the backs of the two chairs. The tracks of his father's foot were gone. Where they had been were now long, water-cloudy scoriations resembling the sporadic course of a lilliputian mowing machine.

It still hung there while they ate the cold food and then went to bed, scattered without order or claim up and down the two rooms, his mother in one bed, where his father would later lie, the older brother in the other, himself, the aunt, and the two sisters on pallets on the floor. But his father was not in bed yet. The last thing the boy remembered was the depthless, harsh silhouette of the hat and coat bending over the rug and it seemed to him that he had not even closed his eyes when the silhouette was standing over him, the fire almost dead behind it, the stiff foot prodding him awake. "Catch up the mule," his father said.

When he returned with the mule his father was standing in the black door, the rolled rug over his shoulder. "Ain't you going to ride?" he said.

"No. Give me your foot."

He bent his knee into his father's hand, the wiry, surprising power flowed smoothly, rising, he rising with it, on to the mule's bare back (they had owned a saddle once; the boy could remember it though not when or where) and with the same effortlessness his father swung the rug up in front of him. Now in the starlight they retraced the afternoon's path, up the dusty road rife with honeysuckle, through the gate and up the black tunnel of the drive to the lightless house, where he sat on the mule and felt the rough warp of the rug drag across his thighs and vanish.

"Don't you want me to help?" he whispered. His father did not answer and now he heard again that stiff foot striking the hollow portico with that wooden and clocklike deliberation, that outrageous overstatement of the weight it carried. The rug, hunched, not flung (the boy could tell that even in the darkness) from his father's shoulder, struck the angle of wall and floor with a sound unbelievably loud, thunderous, then the foot again, unhurried and enormous; a light came on in the house and the boy sat, tense, breathing steadily and quietly and just a little fast, though the foot itself did not increase its beat at all, descending the steps now; now the boy could see him.

"Don't you want to ride now?" he whispered. "We kin both ride now," the light within the house altering now, flaring up and sinking. *He's coming down the stairs now*, he thought. He had already ridden the mule up beside the horse block; presently his father was up behind him and he doubled the reins

over and slashed the mule across the neck, but before the animal could begin
to trot the hard, thin arm came round him, the hard, knotted hand jerking the
mule back to a walk.

In the first red rays of the sun they were in the lot, putting plow gear on the
mules. This time the sorrel mare was in the lot before he heard it at all, the
rider collarless and even bareheaded, trembling, speaking in a shaking voice
as the woman in the house had done, his father merely looking up once before
stooping again to the hame he was buckling, so that the man on the mare
spoke to his stooping back:

"You must realize you have ruined that rug. Wasn't there anybody here,
any of your women . . ." he ceased, shaking, the boy watching him, the older
brother leaning now in the stable door, chewing, blinking slowly and steadily
at nothing apparently. "It cost a hundred dollars. But you never had a hundred
dollars. You never will. So I'm going to charge you twenty bushels of corn
against your crop. I'll add it in your contract and when you come to the commissary you can sign it. That won't keep Mrs. de Spain quiet but maybe it will
teach you to wipe your feet off before you enter her house again."

Then he was gone. The boy looked at his father, who still had not spoken
or even looked up again, who was now adjusting the logger-head in the hame.

"Pap," he said. His father looked at him—the inscrutable face, the shaggy
brows beneath which the gray eyes glinted coldly. Suddenly the boy went
toward him, fast, stopping as suddenly. "You done the best you could!" he
cried. "If he wanted hit done different why didn't he wait and tell you how?
He won't git no twenty bushels! He won't git none! We'll gether hit and hide
hit! I kin watch . . ."

"Did you put the cutter back in that straight stock like I told you?"

"No, sir," he said.

"Then go do it."

That was Wednesday. During the rest of that week he worked steadily, at
what was within his scope and some which was beyond it, with an industry
that did not need to be driven nor even commanded twice; he had this from
his mother, with the difference that some at least of what he did he liked to
do, such as splitting wood with the half-size axe which his mother and aunt
had earned, or saved money somehow, to present him with at Christmas. In
company with the two older women (and on one afternoon, even one of the
sisters), he built pens for the shoat and the cow which were a part of his father's
contract with the landlord, and one afternoon, his father being absent, gone
somewhere on one of the mules, he went to the field.

They were running a middle buster now, his brother holding the plow
straight while he handled the reins, and walking beside the straining mule, the
rich black soil shearing cool and damp against his bare ankles, he thought
*Maybe this is the end of it. Maybe even that twenty bushels that seems hard to
have to pay for just a rug will be a cheap price for him to stop forever and
always from being what he used to be*; thinking, dreaming now, so that his
brother had to speak sharply to him to mind the mule: *Maybe he even won't
collect the twenty bushels. Maybe it will all add up and balance and vanish—
corn, rug, fire; the terror and grief, the being pulled two ways like between two
teams of horses—gone, done with for ever and ever.*

Then it was Saturday; he looked up from beneath the mule he was harnessing and saw his father in the black coat and hat. "Not that," his father said.

"The wagon gear." And then, two hours later, sitting in the wagon bed behind his father and brother on the seat, the wagon accomplished a final curve, and he saw the weathered paintless store with its tattered tobacco- and patent-medicine posters and the tethered wagons and saddle animals below the gallery. He mounted the gnawed steps behind his father and brother, and there again was the lane of quiet, watching faces for the three of them to walk through. He saw the man in spectacles sitting at the plank table and he did not need to be told this was a Justice of the Peace; he sent one glare of fierce, exultant, partisan defiance at the man in collar and cravat now, whom he had seen but twice before in his life, and that on a galloping horse, who now wore on his face an expression not of rage but of amazed unbelief which the boy could not have known was at the incredible circumstance of being sued by one of his own tenants, and came and stood against his father and cried at the Justice: "He ain't done it! He ain't burnt . . ."

"Go back to the wagon," his father said.

"Burnt?" the Justice said. "Do I understand this rug was burned too?"

"Does anybody here claim it was?" his father said. "Go back to the wagon."

But he did not, he merely retreated to the rear of the room, crowded as that other had been, but not to sit down this time, instead, to stand pressing among the motionless bodies, listening to the voices:

"And you claim twenty bushels of corn is too high for the damage you did to the rug?"

"He brought the rug to me and said he wanted the tracks washed out of it. I washed the tracks out and took the rug back to him."

"But you didn't carry the rug back to him in the same condition it was in before you made the tracks on it."

His father did not answer, and now for perhaps half a minute there was no sound at all save that of breathing, the faint, steady suspiration of complete and intent listening.

"You decline to answer that, Mr. Snopes?" Again his father did not answer. "I'm going to find against you, Mr. Snopes. I'm going to find that you were responsible for the injury to Major de Spain's rug and hold you liable for it. But twenty bushels of corn seems a little high for a man in your circumstances to have to pay. Major de Spain claims it cost a hundred dollars. October corn will be worth about fifty cents. I figure that if Major de Spain can stand a ninety-five-dollar loss on something he paid cash for, you can stand a five-dollar loss you haven't earned yet. I hold you in damages to Major de Spain to the amount of ten bushels of corn over and above your contract with him, to be paid to him out of your crop at gathering time. Court adjourned."

It had taken no time hardly, the morning was but half begun. He thought they would return home and perhaps back to the field, since they were late, far behind all other farmers. But instead his father passed on behind the wagon, merely indicating with his hand for the older brother to follow with it, and crossed the road toward the blacksmith shop opposite, pressing on after his father, overtaking him, speaking, whispering up at the harsh, calm face beneath the weathered hat: "He won't git no ten bushels neither. He won't git one. We'll . . ." until his father glanced for an instant down at him, the face absolutely calm, the grizzled eyebrows tangled above the cold eyes, the voice almost pleasant, almost gentle:

"You think so? Well, we'll wait till October anyway."

The matter of the wagon—the setting of a spoke or two and the tightening of the tires—did not take long either, the business of the tires accomplished by driving the wagon into the spring branch behind the shop and letting it stand there, the mules nuzzling into the water from time to time, and the boy on the seat with the idle reins, looking up the slope and through the sooty tunnel of the shed where the slow hammer rang and where his father sat on an upended cypress bolt, easily, either talking or listening, still sitting there when the boy brought the dripping wagon up out of the branch and halted it before the door.

"Take them on to the shade and hitch," his father said. He did so and returned. His father and the smith and a third man squatting on his heels inside the door were talking, about crops and animals; the boy, squatting too in the ammoniac dust and hoof-parings and scales of rust, heard his father tell a long and unhurried story out of the time before the birth of the older brother even when he had been a professional horsetrader. And then his father came up beside him where he stood before a tattered last year's circus poster on the other side of the store, gazing rapt and quiet at the scarlet horses, the incredible poisings and convolutions of tulle and tights and the painted leers of comedians, and said "It's time to eat."

But not at home. Squatting beside his brother against the front wall, he watched his father emerge from the store and produce from a paper sack a segment of cheese and divide it carefully and deliberately into three with his pocket knife and produce crackers from the same sack. They all three squatted on the gallery and ate, slowly, without talking; then in the store again, they drank from a tin dipper tepid water smelling of the cedar bucket and of living beech trees. And still they did not go home. It was a horse lot this time, a tall rail fence upon and along which men stood and sat and out of which by one horses were led, to be walked and trotted and then cantered back and forth along the road while the slow swapping and buying went on and the sun began to slant westward, they—the three of them—watching and listening, the older brother with his muddy eyes and his steady, inevitable tobacco, the father commenting now and then on certain of the animals, to no one in particular.

It was after sundown when they reached home. They ate supper by lamplight, then, sitting on the doorstep, the boy watched the night fully accomplish, listening to the whippoorwills and the frogs, when he heard his mother's voice: "Abner! No! No! Oh, God. Oh, God. Abner!" and he rose, whirled, and saw the altered light through the door where a candle stub now burned in a bottle neck on the table and his father, still in the hat and coat, at once formal and burlesque as though dressed carefully for some shabby and ceremonial violence, emptying the reservoir of the lamp back into the five-gallon kerosene can from which it had been filled, while the mother tugged at his arm until he shifted the lamp to the other hand and flung her back, not savagely or viciously, just hard, into the wall, her hands flung out against the wall for balance, her mouth open and in her face the same quality of hopeless despair as had been in her voice. Then his father saw him standing in the door.

"Go to the barn and get that can of oil we were oiling the wagon with," he said. The boy did not move. Then he could speak.

"What . . ." he cried. "What are you . . ."

"Go get that oil," his father said. "Go."

Then he was moving, running, outside the house, toward the stable: this is the old habit, the old blood which he had not been permitted to choose for himself, which had been bequeathed him willy nilly and which had run for so long (and who knew where, battening on what of outrage and savagery and lust) before it came to him. *I could keep on*, he thought. *I could run on and on and never look back, never need to see his face again. Only I can't. I can't,* the rusted can in his hand now, the liquid sploshing in it as he ran back to the house and into it, into the sound of his mother's weeping in the next room, and handed the can to his father.

"Ain't you going to even send a nigger?" he cried. "At least you sent a nigger before!"

This time his father didn't strike him. The hand came even faster than the blow had, the same hand which had set the can on the table with almost excruciating care flashing from the can toward him too quick for him to follow it, gripping him by the back of his shirt and on to tiptoe before he had seen it quit the can, the face stooping at him in breathless and frozen ferocity, the cold, dead voice speaking over him to the older brother who leaned against the table, chewing with that steady, curious, sidewise motion of cows:

"Empty the can into the big one and go on. I'll catch up with you."

"Better tie him up to the bedpost," the brother said.

"Do like I told you," the father said. Then the boy was moving, his bunched shirt and the hard, bony hand between his shoulder-blades, his toes just touching the floor, across the room and into the other one, past the sisters sitting with spread heavy thighs in the two chairs over the cold hearth, and to where his mother and aunt sat side by side on the bed, the aunt's arms about his mother's shoulders.

"Hold him," the father said. The aunt made a startled movement. "Not you," the father said. "Lennie. Take hold of him. I want to see you do it." His mother took him by the wrist. "You'll hold him better than that. If he gets loose don't you know what he is going to do? He will go up yonder." He jerked his head toward the road. "Maybe I'd better tie him."

"I'll hold him," his mother whispered.

"See you do then." Then his father was gone, the stiff foot heavy and measured upon the boards, ceasing at last.

Then he began to struggle. His mother caught him in both arms, he jerking and wrenching at them. He would be stronger in the end, he knew that. But he had no time to wait for it. "Lemme go!" he cried. "I don't want to have to hit you!"

"Let him go!" the aunt said. "If he don't go, before God, I am going there myself!"

"Don't you see I can't!" his mother cried. "Sarty! Sarty! No! No! Help me, Lizzie!"

Then he was free. His aunt grasped at him but it was too late. He whirled, running, his mother stumbled forward on to her knees behind him, crying to the nearer sister: "Catch him, Net! Catch him!" But that was too late too, the sister (the sisters were twins, born at the same time, yet either of them now gave the impression of being, encompassing as much living meat and volume and weight as any other two of the family) not yet having begun to rise from the chair, her head, face, alone merely turned, presenting to him in the flying instant an astonishing expanse of young female features untroubled by any surprise even, wearing only an expression of bovine interest. Then he was out of the room, out of the house, in the mild dust of the starlit road and the heavy rifeness of honeysuckle, the pale ribbon unspooling with terrific slowness under his running feet, reaching the gate at last and turning in, running, his heart and lungs drumming, on up the drive toward the lighted house, the lighted door. He did not knock, he burst in, sobbing for breath, incapable for the moment of speech; he saw the astonished face of the Negro in the linen jacket without knowing when the Negro had appeared.

"De Spain!" he cried, panted. "Where's . . ." then he saw the white man too emerging from a white door down the hall. "Barn!" he cried. "Barn!"

"What?" the white man said. "Barn?"

"Yes!" the boy cried. "Barn!"

"Catch him!" the white man shouted.

But it was too late this time too. The Negro grasped his shirt, but the entire sleeve, rotten with washing, carried away, and he was out that door too and in the drive again, and had actually never ceased to run even while he was screaming into the white man's face.

Behind him the white man was shouting, "My horse! Fetch my horse!" and he thought for an instant of cutting across the park and climbing the fence into the road, but he did not know the park nor how high the vine-massed fence might be and he dared not risk it. So he ran on down the drive, blood and breath roaring; presently he was in the road again though he could not see it. He could not hear either: the galloping mare was almost upon him before he heard her, and even then he held his course, as if the very urgency of his wild grief and need must in a moment more find him wings, waiting until the ultimate instant to hurl himself aside and into the weed-choked roadside ditch as the horse thundered past and on, for an instant in furious silhouette against the stars, the tranquil early summer night sky which, even before the shape of the horse and rider vanished, stained abruptly and violently upward: a long, swirling roar incredible and soundless, blotting the stars, and he springing up and into the road again, running again, knowing it was too late yet still running even after he heard the shot and, an instant later, two shots, pausing now without knowing he had ceased to run, crying "Pap! Pap!", running again before he knew he had begun to run, stumbling, tripping over something and scrabbling up again without ceasing to run, looking backward over his shoulder at the glare as he got up, running on among the invisible trees, panting, sobbing, "Father! Father!"

At midnight he was sitting on the crest of a hill. He did not know it was midnight and he did not know how far he had come. But there was no glare behind him now and he sat now, his back toward what he had called home for four days anyhow, his face toward the dark woods which he would enter when breath was strong again, small, shaking steadily in the chill darkness, hugging himself into the remainder of his thin, rotten shirt, the grief and despair now no longer terror and fear but just grief and despair. *Father. My father*, he thought. "He was brave!" he cried suddenly, aloud but not loud, no more than a whisper: "He was! He was in the war! He was in Colonel Sartoris' cav'ry!" not knowing that his father had gone to that war a private in the fine old European sense, wearing no uniform, admitting the authority of and giving fidelity to no man or army or flag, going to war as Malbrouck[3] himself did:

---

3. Figure in an 18th-century French ballad, "Malbrouck Has Gone to the War," popularly identified with John Churchill, first duke of Marlborough (1650–1722), who rose through the ranks from private to become one of the most famous military commanders in history. Despite his military genius, he was often accused of greed and disloyalty.

for booty—it meant nothing and less than nothing to him if it were enemy booty or his own.

The slow constellations wheeled on. It would be dawn and then sun-up after a while and he would be hungry. But that would be to-morrow and now he was only cold, and walking would cure that. His breathing was easier now and he decided to get up and go on, and then he found that he had been asleep because he knew it was almost dawn, the night almost over. He could tell that from the whippoorwills. They were everywhere now among the dark trees below him, constant and inflectioned and ceaseless, so that, as the instant for giving over to the day birds drew nearer and nearer, there was no interval at all between them. He got up. He was a little stiff, but walking would cure that too as it would the cold, and soon there would be the sun. He went on down the hill, toward the dark woods within which the liquid silver voices of the birds called unceasing—the rapid and urgent beating of the urgent and quiring heart of the late spring night. He did not look back.

1938

---

# ERNEST HEMINGWAY
## 1899–1961

The narrator in Ernest Hemingway's A Farewell to Arms, reflecting on his war experiences, observes at one point, "I was always embarrassed by the words sacred, glorious, and sacrifice and the expression in vain. . . . I had seen nothing sacred, and the things that were glorious had no glory and the sacrifices were like the stockyards at Chicago if nothing was done with the meat except to bury it. There were many words that you could not stand to hear." Hemingway had not always been embarrassed by these grand words; he brought more to his writing than disillusionment or cynicism—he brought an ever-vivid sense of betrayal. His aim and achievement as a novelist and short-story writer were to convey his concerns in a prose style built from what was left after eliminating all the words one "could not stand to hear." As flamboyant in his personal style as he was severe in his writing, Hemingway became an international celebrity after the publication in 1926 of his first novel, The Sun Also Rises. At the time of his death, he was probably the most famous writer in the world.

He was born and raised in Oak Park, Illinois, one of six children. His mother was a strong, active woman: a music teacher, director of the church choir, a lover of high culture who had contemplated a career as an opera singer. His father was a successful physician who enjoyed hunting, fishing, and cooking and who shared in household responsibilities more than most men of his era. The family spent summers at their cottage in northern Michigan, where many of Hemingway's stories are set. After high school, Hemingway took a job on the Kansas City Star. When the United States entered the war in 1917, Hemingway was eager to go. An eye problem barred him from the army, so he joined the ambulance corps. Within three weeks he was wounded by shrapnel. After six months in the hospital Hemingway went home as a decorated hero: when wounded, he had carried a comrade more badly hurt than he to safety. He found readjustment difficult and became increasingly estranged from his family, especially his mother. Years later, when his father became ill and committed suicide, Hemingway blamed his mother for that death.

In 1920 he married Hadley Richardson and went with her to live in Paris. Supported partly by her money and partly by his journalism, Hemingway worked at becoming a writer. He came to know Gertrude Stein, Sherwood Anderson, Ezra Pound, F. Scott Fitzgerald, and others in the large community of expatriate artistic and literary Americans. Besides reading his manuscripts and advising him, Fitzgerald and Anderson, better known than he, used their influence to get his book of short stories, *In Our Time*, published in the United States in 1925. In this book, stories about the adolescent Nick Adams as he grows up in northern Michigan alternate with very brief, powerful vignettes of war and crime. The effect is to portray the world of adulthood as an arena of danger and violence.

In 1926 his novel *The Sun Also Rises* appeared; it presents the stripped-down "Hemingway style" at its finest. "I always try to write on the principle of the iceberg," he told an interviewer. "There is seven-eighths of it under water for every part that shows." Narrated by its protagonist, Jake Barnes, whose World War I wounds have made him sexually impotent, *The Sun Also Rises* contrasts the empty search for sensation of a group of English and American expatriates in Paris with the rich tradition of peasant life in Spain, especially as epitomized in bullfighting and the bullfighter. Much as they may admire traditional mores, Hemingway's heroes cannot return to that simplicity. They are too knowledgeable, too self-aware. The best they can do is develop a code by which to live with dignity and grace, while playing an unwinnable game.

In 1927 Hemingway brought out his second collection of stories, *Men Without Women*. Adapting journalistic techniques in telegraphic prose that minimized narrator commentary and depended heavily on uncontextualized dialogue, these stories developed a modern, speeded-up, streamlined style that has been endlessly imitated. His second novel, *A Farewell to Arms*, appeared in 1929. It described a romance between an American army officer, Frederick Henry, and a British nurse, Catherine Barkley. The two run away from war, trying to make "a separate peace," but their idyll is shattered when Catherine dies in childbirth. Life itself is implicated in violence and death, and there is no peace.

Hemingway's work has been much criticized for its depictions of women. The wholly good Catherine lives for Frederick Henry alone, and Maria, in his Spanish Civil War novel (*For Whom the Bell Tolls*, 1940), is a fantasy figure of total submissiveness. Characters like Brett Ashley in *The Sun Also Rises* and Pilar in *For Whom the Bell Tolls*, however, are strong, complex figures. Overall, Hemingway identified the rapid change in women's status after World War I and the general blurring of sex roles that accompanied the new sexual freedom as aspects of modernity that men were simultaneously attracted to and found hard to deal with. In retrospect, it is possible to see his work as preoccupied with the cultural and psychological meanings of masculinity.

As Hemingway aged, his interest in exclusively masculine forms of self-assertion and self-definition became more pronounced. War, hunting, and similar pursuits that he had used at first to show men manifesting dignity in the face of certain defeat increasingly became depicted (in his life as well as his writing) as occasions for competitive masculine display and triumph. Soon after the publication of *The Sun Also Rises*, his first marriage broke up; in all he was married four times. In the 1930s and 1940s he adopted the style of life of a celebrity.

In the 1930s two new themes entered his work. One was the ever-present thirties theme of politics. A political loner distrustful of all ideological abstractions, Hemingway was nevertheless drawn into antifascist politics by the Spanish Civil War. In *To Have and Have Not* (1937), the earliest of his political novels, the good characters are working-class people and the antagonists are idle rich. *For Whom the Bell Tolls* draws on Hemingway's experiences in Spain as a war correspondent, celebrating both the peasant loyalists and the Americans who fought on their behalf. Hemingway's opposition to fascism did not, however, keep him from viewing the pro-Loyalist communists with considerable skepticism, as his one play, *The Fifth Column*—which was printed along with his collected stories in 1938, and staged in 1940—makes clear.

The second new theme was that of the successful writer trying to preserve his talent in an atmosphere of celebrity, luxury, and leisure. It is clearly expressed in his story *The Snows of Kilimanjaro* (1936). The allegorical fable *The Old Man and the Sea* (1952) also involves this topic; published in the mass-circulation weekly *Life*, it won a Pulitzer Prize in 1953 and was crucial in bringing him the Nobel Prize in 1954.

Hemingway was fiercely anti-Nazi during World War II. As well as working as a war correspondent, he used his fishing boat to keep watch for German submarines off the coast of Cuba, where he had a home. When the war ended, he resumed his peripatetic life. In Africa on safari in October 1953 he was badly hurt in the crash of a light plane. He never fully recovered his mental health, and his productivity declined dramatically. Subject increasingly to despair and an incapacitating paranoia—afflictions that seem to have run in his family—he was hospitalized several times before killing himself in 1961. Several books have been published posthumously based on the voluminous manuscript collections he left. These include a book of reminiscences about his life in 1920s Paris, *A Moveable Feast* (1964); a novel about literary fame and sexual ambiguity constructed from several unfinished drafts, *Islands in the Stream* (1970); and *The Nick Adams Stories* (1972), a collection that added eight previously unpublished stories to the group.

# The Snows of Kilimanjaro[1]

*Kilimanjaro is a snow covered mountain 19,710 feet high, and is said to be the highest mountain in Africa. Its western summit is called the Masai "Ngàje Ngài," the House of God. Close to the western summit there is the dried and frozen carcass of a leopard. No one has explained what the leopard was seeking at that altitude.*

"The marvellous thing is that it's painless," he said. "That's how you know when it starts."

"Is it really?"

"Absolutely. I'm awfully sorry about the odor though. That must bother you."

"Don't! Please don't."

"Look at them," he said. "Now is it sight or is it scent that brings them like that?"

The cot the man lay on was in the wide shade of a mimosa tree and as he looked out past the shade onto the glare of the plain there were three of the big birds squatted obscenely, while in the sky a dozen more sailed, making quick-moving shadows as they passed.

"They've been there since the day the truck broke down," he said. "Today's the first time any have lit on the ground. I watched the way they sailed very carefully at first in case I ever wanted to use them in a story. That's funny now."

"I wish you wouldn't," she said.

"I'm only talking," he said. "It's much easier if I talk. But I don't want to bother you."

---

1. Mount Kilimanjaro is in Tanzania, near the border with Kenya. The text is that of *The Fifth Column and the First Forty-nine Stories* (1938).

"You know it doesn't bother me," she said. "It's that I've gotten so very nervous not being able to do anything. I think we might make it as easy as we can until the plane comes."

"Or until the plane doesn't come."

"Please tell me what I can do. There must be something I can do."

"You can take the leg off and that might stop it, though I doubt it. Or you can shoot me. You're a good shot now. I taught you to shoot didn't I?"

"Please don't talk that way. Couldn't I read to you?"

"Read what?"

"Anything in the book bag that we haven't read."

"I can't listen to it," he said. "Talking is the easiest. We quarrel and that makes the time pass."

"I don't quarrel. I never want to quarrel. Let's not quarrel any more. No matter how nervous we get. Maybe they will be back with another truck today. Maybe the plane will come."

"I don't want to move," the man said. "There is no sense in moving now except to make it easier for you."

"That's cowardly."

"Can't you let a man die as comfortably as he can without calling him names? What's the use of slanging me?"

"You're not going to die."

"Don't be silly. I'm dying now. Ask those bastards." He looked over to where the huge, filthy birds sat, their naked heads sunk in the hunched feathers. A fourth planed down, to run quick-legged and then waddle slowly toward the others.

"They are around every camp. You never notice them. You can't die if you don't give up."

"Where did you read that? You're such a bloody fool."

"You might think about some one else."

"For Christ's sake," he said, "That's been my trade."

He lay then and was quiet for a while and looked across the heat shimmer of the plain to the edge of the bush. There were a few Tommies[2] that showed minute and white against the yellow and, far off, he saw a herd of zebra, white against the green of the bush. This was a pleasant camp under big trees against a hill, with good water, and close by, a nearly dry water hole where sand grouse flighted in the mornings.

"Wouldn't you like me to read?" she asked. She was sitting on a canvas chair beside his cot. "There's a breeze coming up."

"No thanks."

"Maybe the truck will come."

"I don't give a damn about the truck."

"I do."

"You give a damn about so many things that I don't."

"Not so many, Harry."

"What about a drink?"

"It's supposed to be bad for you. It said in Black's to avoid all alcohol. You shouldn't drink."

"Molo!" he shouted.

---

2. Familiar name for the Thomson's gazelle of East Africa, smallest of the gazelles.

"Yes Bwana."

"Bring whiskey-soda."

"Yes Bwana."

"You shouldn't," she said. "That's what I mean by giving up. It says it's bad for you. I know it's bad for you."

"No," he said. "It's good for me."

So now it was all over, he thought. So now he would never have a chance to finish it. So this was the way it ended in a bickering over a drink. Since the gangrene started in his right leg he had no pain and with the pain the horror had gone and all he felt now was a great tiredness and anger that this was the end of it. For this, that now was coming, he had very little curiosity. For years it had obsessed him; but now it meant nothing in itself. It was strange how easy being tired enough made it.

Now he would never write the things that he had saved to write until he knew enough to write them well. Well, he would not have to fail at trying to write them either. Maybe you could never write them, and that was why you put them off and delayed the starting. Well he would never know, now.

"I wish we'd never come," the woman said. She was looking at him holding the glass and biting her lip. "You never would have gotten anything like this in Paris. You always said you loved Paris. We could have stayed in Paris or gone anywhere. I'd have gone anywhere. I said I'd go anywhere you wanted. If you wanted to shoot we could have gone shooting in Hungary and been comfortable."

"Your bloody money," he said.

"That's not fair," she said. "It was always yours as much as mine. I left everything and I went wherever you wanted to go and I've done what you wanted to do. But I wish we'd never come here."

"You said you loved it."

"I did when you were all right. But now I hate it. I don't see why that had to happen to your leg. What have we done to have that happen to us?"

"I suppose what I did was to forget to put iodine on it when I first scratched it. Then I didn't pay any attention to it because I never infect. Then, later, when it got bad, it was probably using that weak carbolic solution when the other antiseptics ran out that paralyzed the minute blood vessels and started the gangrene." He looked at her, "What else?"

"I don't mean that."

"If we would have hired a good mechanic instead of a half baked kikuyu driver, he would have checked the oil and never burned out that bearing in the truck."

"I don't mean that."

"If you hadn't left your own people, your goddamned Old Westbury, Saratoga, Palm Beach people to take me on—"

"Why, I loved you. That's not fair. I love you now. I'll always love you. Don't you love me?"

"No," said the man. "I don't think so. I never have."

"Harry, what are you saying? You're out of your head."

"No. I haven't any head to go out of."

"Don't drink that," she said. "Darling, please don't drink that. We have to do everything we can."

"You do it," he said. "I'm tired."

*Now in his mind he saw a railway station at Karagatch and he was standing with his pack and that was the headlight of the Simplon-Orient[3] cutting the dark now and he was leaving Thrace[4] then after the retreat. That was one of the things he had saved to write, with, in the morning at breakfast, looking out the window and seeing snow on the mountains in Bulgaria and Nansen's Secretary asking the old man if it were snow and the old man looking at it and saying, No, that's not snow. It's too early for snow. And the Secretary repeating to the other girls, No, you see. It's not snow and them all saying, It's not snow we were mistaken. But it was the snow all right and he sent them on into it when he evolved exchange of populations. And it was snow they tramped along in until they died that winter.*

*It was snow too that fell all Christmas week that year up in the Gauertal, that year they lived in the woodcutter's house with the big square porcelain stove that filled half the room, and they slept on mattresses filled with beech leaves, the time the deserter came with his feet bloody in the snow. He said the police were right behind him and they gave him woolen socks and held the gendarmes talking until the tracks had drifted over.*

*In Schrunz,[5] on Christmas day, the snow was so bright it hurt your eyes when you looked out from the weinstube and saw every one coming home from church. That was where they walked up the sleigh-smoothed urine-yellowed road along the river with the steep pine hills, skis heavy on the shoulder, and where they ran that great run down the glacier above the Madlener-haus, the snow as smooth to see as cake frosting and as light as powder and he remembered the noiseless rush the speed made as you dropped down like a bird.*

*They were snow-bound a week in the Madlener-haus that time in the blizzard playing cards in the smoke by the lantern light and the stakes were higher all the time as Herr Lent lost more. Finally he lost it all. Everything, the skischule money and all the season's profit and then his capital. He could see him with his long nose, picking up the cards and then opening, "Sans Voir."[6] There was always gambling then. When there was no snow you gambled and when there was too much you gambled. He thought of all the time in his life he had spent gambling.*

*But he had never written a line of that, nor of that cold, bright Christmas day with the mountains showing across the plain that Barker had flown across the lines to bomb the Austrian officers' leave train, machine-gunning them as they scattered and ran. He remembered Barker afterwards coming into the mess and starting to tell about it. And how quiet it got and then somebody saying, "You bloody murderous bastard."*

*Those were the same Austrians they killed then that he skied with later. No not the same. Hans, that he skied with all that year, had been in the Kaiser-Jägers[7] and when they went hunting hares together up the little valley above the saw-mill they had talked of the fighting on Pasubio and of the attack on Perticara and Asalone and he had never written a word of that. Nor of Monte Corono, nor the Sette Commumi, nor of Arsiero.*

3. A fast train going from Paris to Constantinople, crossing the Alps into Italy over the Simplon Pass.
4. A region spanning parts of Greece and Turkey, scene of savage border wars in 1922, which Hemingway covered as a war correspondent while living in Paris. Throughout *The Snows of Kilimanjaro*, Hemingway uses real place names to bring authenticity to his fiction.

5. Alpine ski resort in the western part of Austria.
6. Without seeing (French); a blind opening bet in poker or other gambling games.
7. The Kaiser's Hunters (German); name of crack Austrian troops. In World War I, Germany and Austria fought against the United Kingdom, France, Italy, and the United States.

*How many winters had he lived in the Vorarlberg and the Arlberg? It was four and then he remembered the man who had the fox to sell when they had walked into Bludenz, that time to buy presents, and the cherry-pit taste of good kirsch, the fast-slipping rush of running powder-snow on crust, singing "Hi! Ho! said Rolly!" as you ran down the last stretch to the steep drop, taking it straight, then running the orchard in three turns and out across the ditch and onto the icy road behind the inn. Knocking your bindings loose, kicking the skis free and leaning them up against the wooden wall of the inn, the lamplight coming from the window, where inside, in the smoky, new-wine smelling warmth, they were playing the accordion.*

"Where did we stay in Paris?" he asked the woman who was sitting by him in a canvas chair, now, in Africa.

"At the Crillon.[8] You know that."

"Why do I know that?"

"That's where we always stayed."

"No. Not always."

"There and at the Pavillion Henri-Quatre in St. Germain. You said you loved it there."

"Love is a dunghill," said Harry. "And I'm the cock that gets on it to crow."

"If you have to go away," she said, "is it absolutely necessary to kill off everything you leave behind? I mean do you have to take away everything? Do you have to kill your horse, and your wife and burn your saddle and your armour?"

"Yes," he said. "Your damned money was my armour. My Swift and my Armour."

"Don't."

"All right. I'll stop that. I don't want to hurt you."

"It's a little bit late now."

"All right then. I'll go on hurting you. It's more amusing. The only thing I ever really liked to do with you I can't do now."

"No, that's not true. You liked to do many things and everything you wanted to do I did."

"Oh, for Christ sake stop bragging, will you?"

He looked at her and saw her crying.

"Listen," he said. "Do you think that it is fun to do this? I don't know why I'm doing it. It's trying to kill to keep yourself alive, I imagine. I was all right when we started talking. I didn't mean to start this, and now I'm crazy as a coot and being as cruel to you as I can be. Don't pay any attention, darling, to what I say. I love you, really. You know I love you. I've never loved any one else the way I love you."

He slipped into the familiar lie he made his bread and butter by.

"You're sweet to me."

"You bitch," he said. "You rich bitch. That's poetry. I'm full of poetry now. Rot and poetry. Rotten poetry."

"Stop it. Harry, why do you have to turn into a devil now?"

"I don't like to leave anything," the man said. "I don't like to leave things behind."

---

8. Luxury hotel in Paris, as is the Henri-Quatre (below).

• • •

It was evening now and he had been asleep. The sun was gone behind the hill and there was a shadow all across the plain and the small animals were feeding close to camp; quick dropping heads and switching tails, he watched them keeping well out away from the bush now. The birds no longer waited on the ground. They were all perched heavily in a tree. There were many more of them. His personal boy was sitting by the bed.

"Memsahib's gone to shoot," the boy said. "Does Bwana want?"

"Nothing."

She had gone to kill a piece of meat and, knowing how he liked to watch the game, she had gone well away so she would not disturb this little pocket of the plain that he could see. She was always thoughtful, he thought. On anything she knew about, or had read, or that she had ever heard.

It was not her fault that when he went to her he was already over. How could a woman know that you meant nothing that you said; that you spoke only from habit and to be comfortable? After he no longer meant what he said, his lies were more successful with women than when he had told them the truth.

It was not so much that he lied as that there was no truth to tell. He had had his life and it was over and then he went on living it again with different people and more money, with the best of the same places, and some new ones.

You kept from thinking and it was all marvellous. You were equipped with good insides so that you did not go to pieces that way, the way most of them had, and you made an attitude that you cared nothing for the work you used to do, now that you could no longer do it. But, in yourself, you said that you would write about these people; about the very rich; that you were really not of them but a spy in their country; that you would leave it and write of it and for once it would be written by some one who knew what he was writing of. But he would never do it, because each day of not writing, of comfort, of being that which he despised, dulled his ability and softened his will to work so that, finally, he did no work at all. The people he knew now were all much more comfortable when he did not work. Africa was where he had been happiest in the good time of his life, so he had come out here to start again. They had made this safari with the minimum of comfort. There was no hardship; but there was no luxury and he had thought that he could get back into training that way. That in some way he could work the fat off his soul the way a fighter went into the mountains to work and train in order to burn it out of his body.

She had liked it. She said she loved it. She loved anything that was exciting, that involved a change of scene, where there were new people and where things were pleasant. And he had felt the illusion of returning strength of will to work. Now if this was how it ended, and he knew it was, he must not turn like some snake biting itself because its back was broken. It wasn't this woman's fault. If it had not been she it would have been another. If he lived by a lie he should try to die by it. He heard a shot beyond the hill.

She shot very well this good, this rich bitch, this kindly caretaker and destroyer of his talent. Nonsense. He had destroyed his talent himself. Why should he blame this woman because she kept him well? He had destroyed his talent by not using it, by betrayals of himself and what he believed in, by drinking so much that he blunted the edge of his perceptions, by laziness, by sloth, and by snobbery, by pride and by prejudice, by hook and by crook.[9] What was this? A catalogue of old books? What was his talent anyway? It was a talent all right but instead of using it, he had traded on it. It was never what he had done, but always what he could do. And he had chosen to make his living with something else instead of a pen or a pencil. It was strange, too, wasn't it, that when he fell in love with another woman, that woman should always have more money than the last one? But when he no longer was in love, when he was only lying, as to this woman, now, who had the most money of all, who had all the money there was, who had had a husband and children, who had taken lovers and been dissatisfied with them, and who loved him dearly as a writer, as a man, as a companion and as a proud possession; it was strange that when he did not love her at all and was lying, that he should be able to give her more for her money than when he had really loved.

We must all be cut out for what we do, he thought. However you make your living is where your talent lies. He had sold vitality, in one form or another, all his life and when your affections are not too involved you give much better value for the money. He had found that out but he would never write that, now, either. No, he would not write that, although it was well worth writing.

Now she came in sight, walking across the open toward the camp. She was wearing jodhpurs and carrying her rifle. The two boys had a Tommie slung and they were coming along behind her. She was still a good-looking woman, he thought, and she had a pleasant body. She had a great talent and appreciation for the bed, she was not pretty, but he liked her face, she read enormously, liked to ride and shoot and, certainly, she drank too much. Her husband had died when she was still a comparatively young woman and for a while she had devoted herself to her two just-grown children, who did not need her and were embarrassed at having her about, to her stable of horses, to books, and to bottles. She liked to read in the evening before dinner and she drank Scotch and soda while she read. By dinner she was fairly drunk and after a bottle of wine at dinner she was usually drunk enough to sleep.

That was before the lovers. After she had the lovers she did not drink so much because she did not have to be drunk to sleep. But the lovers bored her. She had been married to a man who had never bored her and these people bored her very much.

Then one of her two children was killed in a plane crash and after that was over she did not want the lovers, and drink being no anæsthetic she had to make another life. Suddenly, she had been acutely frightened of being alone. But she wanted some one that she respected with her.

It had begun very simply. She liked what he wrote and she had always envied the life he led. She thought he did exactly what he wanted to. The steps by which she had acquired him and the way in which she had finally fallen in love with him were all part of a regular progression in which she had built herself a new life and he had traded away what remained of his old life.

He had traded it for security, for comfort too, there was no denying that, and for what else? He did not know. She would have bought him anything he

9. "By pride and by prejudice": reference to title of a novel by the English writer Jane Austen (1775–1817); also other references to popular proverbs.

wanted. He knew that. She was a damned nice woman too. He would as soon be in bed with her as any one; rather with her, because she was richer, because she was very pleasant and appreciative and because she never made scenes. And now this life that she had built again was coming to a term because he had not used iodine two weeks ago when a thorn had scratched his knee as they moved forward trying to photograph a herd of waterbuck standing, their heads up, peering while their nostrils searched the air, their ears spread wide to hear the first noise that would send them rushing into the bush. They had bolted, too, before he got the picture.

Here she came now.

He turned his head on the cot to look toward her. "Hello," he said.

"I shot a Tommy ram," she told him. "He'll make you good broth and I'll have them mash some potatoes with the Klim.[1] How do you feel?"

"Much better."

"Isn't that lovely? You know I thought perhaps you would. You were sleeping when I left."

"I had a good sleep. Did you walk far?"

"No. Just around behind the hill. I made quite a good shot on the Tommy."

"You shoot marvellously, you know."

"I love it. I've loved Africa. Really. If *you're* all right it's the most fun that I've ever had. You don't know the fun it's been to shoot with you. I've loved the country."

"I love it too."

"Darling, you don't know how marvellous it is to see you feeling better. I couldn't stand it when you felt that way. You won't talk to me like that again, will you? Promise me?"

"No," he said. "I don't remember what I said."

"You don't have to destroy me. Do you? I'm only a middle-aged woman who loves you and wants to do what you want to do. I've been destroyed two or three times already. You wouldn't want to destroy me again, would you?"

"I'd like to destroy you a few times in bed," he said.

"Yes. That's the good destruction. That's the way we're made to be destroyed. The plane will be here tomorrow."

"How do you know?"

"I'm sure. It's bound to come. The boys have the wood all ready and the grass to make the smudge.[2] I went down and looked at it again today. There's plenty of room to land and we have the smudges ready at both ends."

"What makes you think it will come tomorrow?"

"I'm sure it will. It's overdue now. Then, in town, they will fix up your leg and then we will have some good destruction. Not that dreadful talking kind."

"Should we have a drink? The sun is down."

"Do you think you should?"

"I'm having one."

"We'll have one together. *Molo, letti dui whiskey-soda!*" she called.

"You'd better put on your mosquito boots," he told her.

"I'll wait till I bathe . . ."

While it grew dark they drank and just before it was dark and there was no

---

1. Powdered milk or milk substitute.
2. Fire made to produce a dense smoke, to guide the plane to a landing place.

longer enough light to shoot, a hyena crossed the open on his way around the hill.

"That bastard crosses there every night," the man said. "Every night for two weeks."

"He's the one makes the noise at night. I don't mind it. They're a filthy animal though."

Drinking together, with no pain now except the discomfort of lying in the one position, the boys lighting a fire, its shadow jumping on the tents, he could feel the return of acquiescence in this life of pleasant surrender. She *was* very good to him. He had been cruel and unjust in the afternoon. She was a fine woman, marvellous really. And just then it occurred to him that he was going to die.

It came with a rush; not as a rush of water nor of wind; but of a sudden evil-smelling emptiness and the odd thing was that the hyena slipped lightly along the edge of it.

"What is it, Harry?" she asked him.

"Nothing," he said. "You had better move over to the other side. To windward."

"Did Molo change the dressing?"

"Yes. I'm just using the boric now."

"How do you feel?"

"A little wobbly."

"I'm going in to bathe," she said. "I'll be right out. I'll eat with you and then we'll put the cot in."

So, he said to himself, we did well to stop the quarrelling. He had never quarrelled much with this woman, while with the women that he loved he had quarrelled so much they had finally, always, with the corrosion of the quarrelling, killed what they had together. He had loved too much, demanded too much, and he wore it all out.

*He thought about alone in Constantinople*[3] *that time, having quarrelled in Paris before he had gone out. He had whored the whole time and then, when that was over, and he had failed to kill his loneliness, but only made it worse, he had written her, the first one, the one who left him, a letter telling her how he had never been able to kill it. . . . How when he thought he saw her outside the* Regence *one time it made him go all faint and sick inside, and that he would follow a woman who looked like her in some way, along the Boulevard, afraid to see it was not she, afraid to lose the feeling it gave him. How every one he had slept with had only made him miss her more. How what she had done could never matter since he knew he could not cure himself of loving her. He wrote this letter at the Club, cold sober, and mailed it to New York asking her to write him at the office in Paris. That seemed safe. And that night missing her so much it made him feel hollow sick inside, he wandered up past Taxim's, picked a girl up and took her out to supper. He had gone to a place to dance with her afterward, she danced badly, and left her for a hot Armenian slut, that swung her belly against him so it almost scalded. He took her away from a British gunner subaltern after a row. The gunner asked him outside and they*

---

3. Now Istanbul, capital of Turkey. In the rest of the paragraph there are references to streets and places in and around the city.

*fought in the street on the cobbles in the dark. He'd hit him twice, hard, on the side of the jaw and when he didn't go down he knew he was in for a fight. The gunner hit him in the body, then beside his eye. He swung with his left again and landed and the gunner fell on him and grabbed his coat and tore the sleeve off and he clubbed him twice behind the ear and then smashed him with his right as he pushed him away. When the gunner went down his head hit first and he ran with the girl because they heard the M. P.'s coming. They got into a taxi and drove out to Rimmily Hissa along the Bosphorus, and around, and back in the cool night and went to bed and she felt as over-ripe as she looked but smoother, rose-petal, syrupy, smooth-bellied, big-breasted and needed no pillow under her buttocks, and he left her before she was awake looking blousy enough in the first daylight and turned up at the Pera Palace with a black eye, carrying his coat because one sleeve was missing.*

*That same night he left for Anatolia and he remembered, later on that trip, riding all day through fields of the poppies that they raised for opium and how strange it made you feel, finally, and all the distances seemed wrong, to where they had made the attack with the newly arrived Constantine officers, that did not know a goddamned thing, and the artillery had fired into the troops and the British observer had cried like a child.*

*That was the day he'd first seen dead men wearing white ballet skirts and upturned shoes with pompons on them. The Turks had come steadily and lumpily and he had seen the skirted men running and the officers shooting into them and running then themselves and he and the British observer had run too until his lungs ached and his mouth was full of the taste of pennies and they stopped behind some rocks and there were the Turks coming as lumpily as ever. Later he had seen the things that he could never think of and later still he had seen much worse. So when he got back to Paris that time he could not talk about it or stand to have it mentioned. And there in the café as he passed was that American poet with a pile of saucers in front of him and a stupid look on his potato face talking about the Dada movement[4] with a Roumanian who said his name was Tristan Tzara, who always wore a monocle and had a headache, and, back at the apartment with his wife that now he loved again, the quarrel all over, the madness all over, glad to be home, the office sent his mail up to the flat. So then the letter in answer to the one he'd written came in on a platter one morning and when he saw the handwriting he went cold all over and tried to slip the letter underneath another. But his wife said, "Who is that letter from, dear?" and that was the end of the beginning of that.*

*He remembered the good times with them all, and the quarrels. They always picked the finest places to have the quarrels. And why had they always quarrelled when he was feeling best? He had never written any of that because, at first, he never wanted to hurt any one and then it seemed as though there was enough to write without it. But he had always thought that he would write it finally. There was so much to write. He had seen the world change; not just the events; although he had seen many of them and had watched the people, but he had seen the subtler change and he could remember how the people were at different times. He had been in it and he had watched it and it was his duty to write of it; but now he never would.*

---

4. An international movement in painting, sculpture, and literature that flourished between 1916 and 1922, stressing fantasy, surrealism, and nonsense. The term is a child's cry, chosen because it has no meaning. Tristan Tzara (below) was the leading propagandist for the movement.

"How do you feel?" she said. She had come out from the tent now after her bath.

"All right."

"Could you eat now?" He saw Molo behind her with the folding table and the other boy with the dishes.

"I want to write," he said.

"You ought to take some broth to keep your strength up."

"I'm going to die tonight," he said. "I don't need my strength up."

"Don't be melodramatic, Harry, please," she said.

"Why don't you use your nose? I'm rotted half way up my thigh now. What the hell should I fool with broth for? Molo bring whiskey-soda."

"Please take the broth," she said gently.

"All right."

The broth was too hot. He had to hold it in the cup until it cooled enough to take it and then he just got it down without gagging.

"You're a fine woman," he said. "Don't pay any attention to me."

She looked at him with her well-known, well-loved face from *Spur* and *Town and Country*,[5] only a little the worse for drink, only a little the worse for bed, but *Town and Country* never showed those good breasts and those useful thighs and those lightly small-of-back-caressing hands, and as he looked and saw her well known pleasant smile, he felt death come again. This time there was no rush. It was a puff, as of a wind that makes a candle flicker and the flame go tall.

"They can bring my net out later and hang it from the tree and build the fire up. I'm not going in the tent tonight. It's not worth moving. It's a clear night. There won't be any rain."

So this was how you died, in whispers that you did not hear. Well, there would be no more quarrelling. He could promise that. The one experience that he had never had he was not going to spoil now. He probably would. You spoiled everything. But perhaps he wouldn't.

"You can't take dictation, can you?"

"I never learned," she told him.

"That's all right."

There wasn't time, of course, although it seemed as though it telescoped so that you might put it all into one paragraph if you could get it right.

*There was a log house, chinked white with mortar, on a hill above the lake. There was a bell on a pole by the door to call the people in to meals. Behind the house were fields and behind the fields was the timber. A line of lombardy poplars ran from the house to the dock. Other poplars ran along the point. A road went up to the hills along the edge of the timber and along that road he picked blackberries. Then that log house was burned down and all the guns that had been on deer foot racks above the open fire place were burned and afterwards their barrels, with the lead melted in the magazines, and the stocks burned away, lay out on the heap of ashes that were used to make lye for the big iron soap kettles, and you asked Grandfather if you could have them to play with, and he said, no. You see they were his guns still and he never bought any others. Nor did he hunt any more. The house was rebuilt in the same place out*

5. Two magazines designed for a wealthy audience.

*of lumber now and painted white and from its porch you saw the poplars and the lake beyond; but there were never any more guns. The barrels of the guns that had hung on the deer feet on the wall of the log house lay out there on the heap of ashes and no one ever touched them.*

*In the Black Forest,*[6] *after the war, we rented a trout stream and there were two ways to walk to it. One was down the valley from Triberg and around the valley road in the shade of the trees that bordered the white road, and then up a side road that went up through the hills past many small farms, with the big Schwarzwald*[7] *houses, until that road crossed the stream. That was where our fishing began.*

*The other way was to climb steeply up to the edge of the woods and then go across the top of the hills through the pine woods, and then out to the edge of a meadow and down across this meadow to the bridge. There were birches along the stream and it was not big, but narrow, clear and fast, with pools where it had cut under the roots of the birches. At the Hotel in Triberg the proprietor had a fine season. It was very pleasant and we were all great friends. The next year came the inflation and the money he had made the year before was not enough to buy supplies to open the hotel and he hanged himself.*

*You could dictate that, but you could not dictate the Place Contrescarpe*[8] *where the flower sellers dyed their flowers in the street and the dye ran over the paving where the autobus started and the old men and the women, always drunk on wine and bad marc;*[9] *and the children with their noses running in the cold; the smell of dirty sweat and poverty and drunkenness at the Café des Amateurs and the whores at the Bal Musette*[1] *they lived above. The Concierge who entertained the trooper of the Garde Republicaine in her loge, horse-hair-plumed helmet on a chair. The locataire across the hall whose husband was a bicycle racer and her joy that morning at the Cremerie when she had opened L'Auto and seen where he placed third in Paris-Tours, his first big race. She had blushed and laughed and then gone upstairs crying with the yellow sporting paper in her hand. The husband of the woman who ran the Bal Musette drove a taxi and when he, Harry, had to take an early plane the husband knocked upon the door to wake him and they each drank a glass of white wine at the zinc of the bar before they started. He knew his neighbors in that quarter then because they all were poor.*

*Around that Place there were two kinds; the drunkards and the sportifs. The drunkards killed their poverty that way; the sportifs took it out in exercise. They were the descendants of the Communards*[2] *and it was no struggle for them to know their politics. They knew who had shot their fathers, their relatives, their brothers, and their friends when the Versailles troops came in and took the town after the Commune and executed any one they could catch with calloused hands, or who wore a cap, or carried any other sign he was a working man. And in that poverty, and in that quarter across the street from a Boucherie Chevaline*[3] *and a wine co-operative he had written the start of all he was to do. There never was another part of Paris that he loved like that, the sprawling*

6. Wooded, mountainous region in southern Germany.
7. Black Forest (German).
8. Square in a working-class neighborhood of Paris.
9. White brandy (French).
1. Dance hall (French).

2. Participants in the 1871 workers' uprising in Paris and the Commune, a local government established on March 18, 1871, but suppressed by the Versailles government two months later.
3. A butcher shop selling horsemeat, once common in poorer neighborhoods throughout Europe.

*trees, the old white plastered houses painted brown below, the long green of the autobus in that round square, the purple flower dye upon the paving, the sudden drop down the hill of the rue Cardinal Lemoine to the River, and the other way the narrow crowded world of the rue Mouffetard.* The street that ran up toward the Pantheon and the other that he always took with the bicycle, the only asphalted street in all that quarter, smooth under the tires, with the high narrow houses and the cheap tall hotel where Paul Verlaine[4] had died. There were only two rooms in the apartments where they lived and he had a room on the top floor of that hotel that cost him sixty francs a month where he did his writing, and from it he could see the roofs and chimney pots and all the hills of Paris.

From the apartment you could only see the wood and coal man's place. He sold wine too, bad wine. The golden horse's head outside the Boucherie Chevaline where the carcasses hung yellow gold and red in the open window, and the green painted co-operative where they bought their wine; good wine and cheap. The rest was plaster walls and the windows of the neighbors. The neighbors who, at night, when some one lay drunk in the street, moaning and groaning in that typical French ivresse[5] that you were propaganded to believe did not exist, would open their windows and then the murmur of talk.

"Where is the policeman? When you don't want him the bugger is always there. He's sleeping with some concierge. Get the Agent." Till some one threw a bucket of water from a window and the moaning stopped. "What's that? Water. Ah, that's intelligent." And the windows shutting. Marie, his femme de menage,[6] protesting against the eight-hour day saying, "If a husband works until six he gets only a little drunk on the way home and does not waste too much. If he works only until five he is drunk every night and one has no money. It is the wife of the working man who suffers from this shortening of hours."

"Wouldn't you like some more broth?" the woman asked him now.

"No, thank you very much. It is awfully good."

"Try just a little."

"I would like a whiskey-soda."

"It's not good for you."

"No. It's bad for me. Cole Porter[7] wrote the words and the music. This knowledge that you're going mad for me."

"You know I like you to drink."

"Oh yes. Only it's bad for me."

When she goes, he thought. I'll have all I want. Not all I want but all there is. Ayee he was tired. Too tired. He was going to sleep a little while. He lay still and death was not there. It must have gone around another street. It went in pairs, on bicycles, and moved absolutely silently on the pavements.

No, he had never written about Paris. Not the Paris that he cared about. But what about the rest that he had never written?

What about the ranch and the silvered gray of the sage brush, the quick,

4. French Symbolist poet (1844–1896). Hemingway rented and worked in a room in which Verlaine had lived.
5. Drunkenness (French). Because the French drank only wine and brandy rather than hard liquor, it was often claimed that there was no real drunkenness among them.
6. Charwoman (French).
7. Popular American song composer (1893–1964).

*clear water in the irrigation ditches, and the heavy green of the alfalfa. The*
*trail went up into the hills and the cattle in the summer were shy as deer. The*
*bawling and the steady noise and slow moving mass raising a dust as you*
*brought them down in the fall. And behind the mountains, the clear sharpness*
*of the peak in the evening light and, riding down along the trail in the moon-*
*light, bright across the valley. Now he remembered coming down through the*
*timber in the dark holding the horse's tail when you could not see and all the*
*stories that he meant to write.*

*About the half-wit chore boy who was left at the ranch that time and told*
*not to let any one get any hay, and that old bastard from the Forks who had*
*beaten the boy when he had worked for him stopping to get some feed. The boy*
*refusing and the old man saying he would beat him again. The boy got the rifle*
*from the kitchen and shot him when he tried to come into the barn and when*
*they came back to the ranch he'd been dead a week, frozen in the corral, and*
*the dogs had eaten part of him. But what was left you packed on a sled wrapped*
*in a blanket and roped on and you got the boy to help you haul it, and the two*
*of you took it out over the road on skis, and sixty miles down to town to turn*
*the boy over. He having no idea that he would be arrested. Thinking he had*
*done his duty and that you were his friend and he would be rewarded. He'd*
*helped to haul the old man in so everybody could know how bad the old man*
*had been and how he'd tried to steal some feed that didn't belong to him, and*
*when the sheriff put the handcuffs on the boy he couldn't believe it. Then he'd*
*started to cry. That was one story he had saved to write. He knew at least*
*twenty good stories from out there and he had never written one. Why?*

"You tell them why," he said.

"Why what, dear?"

"Why nothing."

She didn't drink so much, now, since she had him. But if he lived he would
never write about her, he knew that now. Nor about any of them. The rich
were dull and they drank too much, or they played too much backgammon.
They were dull and they were repetitious. He remembered poor Julian and his
romantic awe of them and how he had started a story once that began, "The
very rich are different from you and me."[8] And how some one had said to
Julian, Yes, they have more money. But that was not humorous to Julian. He
thought they were a special glamourous race and when he found they weren't
it wrecked him just as much as any other thing that wrecked him.

He had been contemptuous of those who wrecked. You did not have to like
it because you understood it. He could beat anything, he thought, because no
thing could hurt him if he did not care.

All right. Now he would not care for death. One thing he had always
dreaded was the pain. He could stand pain as well as any man, until it went
on too long, and wore him out, but here he had something that had hurt
frightfully and just when he had felt it breaking him, the pain had stopped.

*He remembered long ago when Williamson, the bombing officer, had been*
*hit by a stick bomb some one in a German patrol had thrown as he was coming*

---

8. These are the opening words of *The Rich Boy* by F. Scott Fitzgerald. Hemingway originally used Fitzgerald's
name instead of "Julian," but was persuaded to make the change by his editor, Maxwell Perkins.

*in through the wire that night and, screaming, had begged every one to kill
him. He was a fat man, very brave, and a good officer, although addicted to
fantastic shows. But that night he was caught in the wire, with a flare lighting
him up and his bowels spilled out into the wire, so when they brought him in,
alive, they had to cut him loose. Shoot me, Harry. For Christ sake shoot me.
They had had an argument one time about our Lord never sending you anything you could not bear and some one's theory had been that meant that at a
certain time the pain passed you out automatically. But he had always remembered Williamson, that night. Nothing passed out Williamson until he gave
him all his morphine tablets that he had always saved to use himself and then
they did not work right away.*

Still this now, that he had, was very easy; and if it was no worse as it went
on there was nothing to worry about. Except that he would rather be in better
company.

He thought a little about the company that he would like to have.

No, he thought, when everything you do, you do too long, and do too late,
you can't expect to find the people still there. The people all are gone. The
party's over and you are with your hostess now.

I'm getting as bored with dying as with everything else, he thought.

"It's a bore," he said out loud.

"What is, my dear?"

"Anything you do too bloody long."

He looked at her face between him and the fire. She was leaning back in
the chair and the firelight shone on her pleasantly lined face and he could see
that she was sleepy. He heard the hyena make a noise just outside the range of
the fire.

"I've been writing," he said. "But I got tired."

"Do you think you will be able to sleep?"

"Pretty sure. Why don't you turn in?"

"I like to sit here with you."

"Do you feel anything strange?" he asked her.

"No. Just a little sleepy."

"I do," he said.

He had just felt death come by again.

"You know the only thing I've never lost is curiosity," he said to her.

"You've never lost anything. You're the most complete man I've ever
known."

"Christ," he said. "How little a woman knows. What is that? Your intuition?"

Because, just then, death had come and rested its head on the foot of the
cot and he could smell its breath.

"Never believe any of that about a scythe and a skull,"[9] he told her. "It can
be two bicycle policemen as easily, or be a bird. Or it can have a wide snout
like a hyena."

It had moved up on him now, but it had no shape any more. It simply
occupied space.

"Tell it to go away."

9. In medieval imagery death is often represented as a skeleton draped in a long cape so that only the skull shows.
He carries a scythe, with which he mows humans down.

It did not go away but moved a little closer.

"You've got a hell of a breath," he told it. "You stinking bastard."

It moved up closer to him still and he could not speak to it, and when it saw he could not speak it came a little closer, and now he tried to send it away without speaking, but it moved in on him so its weight was all upon his chest, and while it crouched there and he could not move, or speak, he heard the woman say, "Bwana is asleep now. Take the cot up very gently and carry it into the tent."

He could not speak to tell her to make it go away and it crouched now, heavier, so he could not breathe. And then, while they lifted the cot, suddenly it was all right and the weight went from his chest.

It was morning and had been morning for some time and he heard the plane. It showed very tiny and then made a wide circle and the boys ran out and lit the fires, using kerosene, and piled on grass so there were two big smudges at each end of the level place and the morning breeze blew them toward the camp and the plane circled twice more, low this time, and then glided down and levelled off and landed smoothly and, coming walking toward him, was old Compton in slacks, a tweed jacket and a brown felt hat.

"What's the matter, old cock?" Compton said.

"Bad leg," he told him. "Will you have some breakfast?"

"Thanks. I'll just have some tea. It's the Puss Moth[1] you know. I won't be able to take the Memsahib. There's only room for one. Your lorry is on the way."

Helen had taken Compton aside and was speaking to him. Compton came back more cheery than ever.

"We'll get you right in," he said. "I'll be back for the Mem. Now I'm afraid I'll have to stop at Arusha to refuel. We'd better get going."

"What about the tea?"

"I don't really care about it you know."

The boys had picked up the cot and carried it around the green tents and down along the rock and out onto the plain and along past the smudges that were burning brightly now, and the grass all consumed, and the wind fanning the fire, to the little plane. It was difficult getting him in, but once in he lay back in the leather seat, and the leg was stuck straight out to one side of the seat where Compton sat. Compton started the motor and got in. He waved to Helen and to the boys and, as the clatter moved into the old familiar roar, they swung around with Compie watching for wart-hog holes and roared, bumping, along the stretch between the fires and with the last bump rose and he saw them all standing below, waving, and the camp beside the hill, flattening now, and the plain spreading, clumps of trees, and the bush flattening, while the game trails ran now smoothly to the dry waterholes, and there was a new water that he had never known of. The zebra, small rounded backs now, and the wildebeeste, big-headed dots seeming to climb as they moved in long fingers across the plain, now scattering as the shadow came toward them, they were tiny now, and the movement had no gallop, and the plain as far as you could see, gray-yellow now and ahead old Compie's tweed back and the brown felt hat. Then they were over the first hills and the wildebeeste were trailing

1. A small, light airplane seating two people.

up them, and then they were over mountains with sudden depths of green-rising forest and the solid bamboo slopes, and then the heavy forest again, sculptured into peaks and hollows until they crossed, and hills sloped down and then another plain, hot now, and purple brown, bumpy with heat and Compie looking back to see how he was riding. Then there were other mountains dark ahead.

And then instead of going on to Arusha they turned left, he evidently figured that they had the gas, and looking down he saw a pink sifting cloud, moving over the ground, and in the air, like the first snow in a blizzard, that comes from nowhere, and he knew the locusts were coming up from the South. Then they began to climb and they were going to the East it seemed, and then it darkened and they were in a storm, the rain so thick it seemed like flying through a waterfall, and then they were out and Compie turned his head and grinned and pointed and there, ahead, all he could see, as wide as all the world, great, high, and unbelievably white in the sun, was the square top of Kilimanjaro. And then he knew that there was where he was going.

Just then the hyena stopped whimpering in the night and started to make a strange, human, almost crying sound. The woman heard it and stirred uneasily. She did not wake. In her dream she was at the house on Long Island and it was the night before her daughter's début. Somehow her father was there and he had been very rude. Then the noise the hyena made was so loud she woke and for a moment she did not know where she was and she was very afraid. Then she took the flashlight and shone it on the other cot that they had carried in after Harry had gone to sleep. She could see his bulk under the mosquito bar but somehow he had gotten his leg out and it hung down alongside the cot. The dressings had all come down and she could not look at it.

"Molo," she called, "Molo! Molo!"

Then she said, "Harry, Harry!" Then her voice rising, "Harry! Please, Oh Harry!"

There was no answer and she could not hear him breathing.

Outside the tent the hyena made the same strange noise that had awakened her. But she did not hear him for the beating of her heart.

1936, 1938

---

# HART CRANE
## 1899–1932

The French phrase *poète maudit* ("cursed poet") expresses a concept of the poet consumed by his vision and doomed in life because of his total commitment. The tortured life of Hart Crane—his bitter relationships with his parents, uncontrollable drinking, homosexual promiscuity, and suicide at the age of thirty-three—together with his ambition to create the "Great American Poem" have long been seen as fitting this familiar pattern. But his difficulties also had a practical base: without independent wealth, lacking wide popularity or institutional subsidy, he simply had no way to support himself as a poet.

Born and raised in Ohio, Crane went to New York City in 1917, ostensibly to prepare for college but in fact to investigate the possibility of a literary career.

Returning to Cleveland for four years (1919–23), he tried unsuccessfully to enter business as a means of financing an after-hours literary life. During these years he read widely and developed a large circle of intellectual friends and correspondents. He also published some of the poems that made his early reputation: *My Grandmother's Love Letters* in 1920, *Chaplinesque* in 1921, and *For the Marriage of Faustus and Helen* in 1922. He also began work on the love sequence *Voyages*. By 1923, believing himself ready to succeed as a writer, he moved back to New York City.

Between 1923 and 1927 he wrote the most and best of his poetry. He completed *Voyages* in 1924, published his first collection, *White Buildings*, in 1926, and composed ten of the fifteen poems that were to comprise *The Bridge* in 1926. He held occasional jobs, but received most of his support from his parents, friends, and above all from the patronage of a banker, Otto Kahn. Crane believed that poets had access to a higher state of consciousness than others; he defined himself as a follower of Walt Whitman in the visionary, prophetic, affirmative American tradition. His aim was nothing less than to master the techniques of modernism but also to reverse its direction—to make it positive, celebratory, and deeply meshed with contemporary American life—without sacrificing technical complexity or richness. For him as for the somewhat older William Carlos Williams, Eliot's *The Waste Land* was both threat and model. That poem could become an "absolute impasse," he wrote, unless one could "go *through* it to a different goal," leaving its negations behind. This was the task he attempted in *The Bridge*.

Crane's practice centered on metaphor—the device that, in his view, represented the difference between poetry and expository discourse. He believed that metaphor had preceded logic in the development of human thought and that it still remained the primary mode in which human knowledge was acquired and through which experience was connected to mind. The center of *The Bridge*, for example, is the Brooklyn Bridge—a tangible object transformed metaphorically into the sign of connection, technology, America, history, and the future. The poem, published in 1930, was not particularly well received by the critics; this was, of course, a great disappointment to Crane, and even though *Poetry* magazine awarded it a prize and the Guggenheim Foundation gave him a fellowship in the same year, he was perplexed about his future. In Mexico he completed work for a third book, *Key West*, but on the return trip to New York City he jumped overboard and was drowned.

*The Bridge* is a visionary poem made up of fifteen individual sections of varying lengths. It encapsulates a heroic quest, at once personal and epic, to find and enunciate "America." Like Walt Whitman's *Song of the Open Road*, which also focused on a symbol of expansion and dynamism, *The Bridge* moves westward in imagination from Brooklyn to California. It also goes back into the American past, dwelling on historical or legendary figures like Columbus, Pocahontas, and Rip Van Winkle. It moves upward under the guidance of Whitman; down in *The Tunnel* it meets the wandering spirit of Edgar Allan Poe. The material bridge stands at the center of all this motion and stands, finally, for the poem and poetry itself. The separate lyrics making up *The Bridge* are arranged like music, with recurring, modulated themes rather than a narrative or an expository line. As in most modernist poems, the verse is open and varied, the syntax complicated and often ambiguous, the references often dependent on a personal, sometimes inaccessible train of thought. Like his model Whitman, Crane wrote from the paradoxical, conflicted position of the outsider claiming to speak from and for the very center of America. Some critics have proposed that this conflicted stance is to be explained by Crane's homosexuality; this may be so, but many modernist poets have expressed a similar sense of cultural estrangement. What is perhaps unique to Crane among modernists is his nationalist idealism, his will to believe in America.

The text of the poems included here is that of *Complete Poems of Hart Crane*, edited by Marc Simon (1986).

# Chaplinesque[1]

We make our meek adjustments,
Contented with such random consolations
As the wind deposits
In slithered and too ample pockets.

For we can still love the world, who find                     5
A famished kitten on the step, and know
Recesses for it from the fury of the street,
Or warm torn elbow coverts.

We will sidestep, and to the final smirk
Dally the doom of that inevitable thumb                      10
That slowly chafes its puckered index toward us,
Facing the dull squint with what innocence
And what surprise!

And yet these fine collapses are not lies
More than the pirouettes of any pliant cane;                 15
Our obsequies[2] are, in a way, no enterprise.
We can evade you, and all else but the heart:
What blame to us if the heart live on.

The game enforces smirks; but we have seen
The moon in lonely alleys make                               20
A grail of laughter of an empty ash can,
And through all sound of gaiety and quest
Have heard a kitten in the wilderness.

                                          1921, 1926

# At Melville's Tomb[1]

Often beneath the wave, wide from this ledge
The dice of drowned men's bones he saw bequeath

---

1. Crane wrote in letters of his excitement at seeing
Charlie Chaplin's film *The Kid* (1921) and said that he
aimed "to put in words some of the Chaplin pantomime, so beautiful, and so full of eloquence, and so
modern." The film "made me feel myself, as a poet, as
being 'in the same boat' with him," Crane wrote; "Poetry, the human feelings, 'the kitten,' is so crowded out
of the humdrum, rushing, mechanical scramble of to-
day that the man who would preserve them must duck
and camouflage for dear life to keep them or keep himself from annihilation. . . . I have tried to express these
'social sympathies' in words corresponding somewhat
to the antics of the actor" (*Letters*, p. 68).

2. In the double sense of "funeral rites" and "obsequiousness."
1. This poem was published in *Poetry* magazine only
after Crane provided the editor, Harriet Monroe, with
a detailed explanation of its images. His letter, and
Monroe's inquiries and comments, were published
with the poem. Crane's letter (*Complete Poems and
Selected Letters and Prose*, pp. 234–40) insisted that
poetry, like his and that written by Eliot and William
Blake, derives from an "emotional dynamics," a
"dynamics of metaphor," that is distinct from the
"rationalized definitions" used in science and everyday experience; that poetry, exploiting the "illogical

An embassy. Their numbers as he watched,
Beat on the dusty shore and were obscured.[2]

And wrecks passed without sound of bells,                              5
The calyx of death's bounty giving back
A scattered chapter, livid hieroglyph,
The portent wound in corridors of shells.[3]

Then in the circuit calm of one vast coil,
Its lashings charmed and malice reconciled,                          10
Frosted eyes there were that lifted altars;[4]
And silent answers crept across the stars.

Compass, quadrant and sextant contrive
No farther tides[5] . . . High in the azure steeps
Monody shall not wake the mariner.                                    15
This fabulous shadow only the sea keeps.

1926

## From Voyages

### I

Above the fresh ruffles of the surf
Bright striped urchins flay each other with sand.
They have contrived a conquest for shell shucks,
And their fingers crumble fragments of baked weed
Gaily digging and scattering.                                         5

And in answer to their treble interjections
The sun beats lightning on the waves,

---

impingements of the connotations of words on the consciousness," depends on "something like short-hand"
as a "connective agent" when the poet explores "fresh
concepts, more inclusive evaluations" than those already worked out by his predecessors. Crane's detailed
comments in the letter are incorporated in the notes
below. The poem is a tribute to one of Crane's most
admired American predecessors, Herman Melville,
and evokes Meville's treatment of the horrors and mystery of the sea in such works as *Moby-Dick* (1851).
2. "Dice bequeath an embassy, in the first place, by
being ground (in this connection only, of course) in
little cubes from the bones of drowned men by the action of the sea, and are finally thrown up on the sand,
having 'numbers' but no identification. These being
the bones of dead men who never completed their voyage, it seems legitimate to refer to them as the only
surviving evidence of certain messages undelivered,
mute evidence of certain things. . . . Dice as a symbol
of chance and circumstance is also implied" [Crane's
note].
3. "This calyx refers in a double ironic sense both to a
cornucopia and the vortex made by a sinking vessel. As
soon as the water has closed over a ship this whirlpool
sends up broken spars, wreckage, etc., which can be

alluded to as livid *hieroglyphs*, making a *scattered chapter* so far as any complete record of the recent ship and
crew is concerned. In fact, about as much definite
knowledge might come from all this as anyone might
gain from the roar of his own veins, which is easily
heard (haven't you ever done it?) by holding a shell
close to one's ear" [Crane's note]. A calyx is a whorl of
leaves forming the outer casing of the bud of a plant.
4. "Refers simply to a conviction that a man, not
knowing perhaps a definite god yet being endowed with
a reverence for deity—such a man naturally postulates
a deity somehow, and the altar of that deity by the very
action of the eyes *lifted* in searching" [Crane's note].
5. "Hasn't it often occurred that instruments originally
invented for record and computation have inadvertently so extended the concepts of the entity they were
invented to measure (concepts of space, etc.) in the
mind and imagination that employed them, that they
may metaphorically be said to have extended the original boundaries of the entity measured? This little bit of
'relativity' ought not to be discredited in poetry now
that scientists are proceeding to measure the universe
on principles of pure *ratio*, quote as metaphorical, so
far as previous standards of scientific methods extended, as some of the axioms in *Job*" [Crane's note].

The waves fold thunder on the sand;
And could they hear me I would tell them:

O brilliant kids, frisk with your dog,                                    10
Fondle your shells and sticks, bleached
By time and the elements; but there is a line
You must not cross nor ever trust beyond it
Spry cordage of your bodies to caresses
Too lichen-faithful from too wide a breast.                               15
The bottom of the sea is cruel.

1923, 1926

V

Meticulous, past midnight in clear rime,
Infrangible and lonely, smooth as though cast
Together in one merciless white blade—
The bay estuaries fleck the hard sky limits.

—As if too brittle or too clear to touch!                                 5
The cables of our sleep so swiftly filed,
Already hang, shred ends from remembered stars.
One frozen trackless smile . . . What words
Can strangle this deaf moonlight? For we

Are overtaken. Now no cry, no sword                                       10
Can fasten or deflect this tidal wedge,
Slow tyranny of moonlight, moonlight loved
And changed . . . "There's

Nothing like this in the world," you say,
Knowing I cannot touch your hand and look                                 15
Too, into that godless cleft of sky
Where nothing turns but dead sands flashing.

"—And never to quite understand!" No,
In all the argosy of your bright hair I dreamed
Nothing so flagless as this piracy.                                       20

But now
Draw in your head, alone and too tall here.
Your eyes already in the slant of drifting foam;
Your breath sealed by the ghosts I do not know:
Draw in your head and sleep the long way home.                           25

1926

# THE BRIDGE

*From going to and fro in the earth,*
*and from walking up and down in it.*
—The Book of Job[1]

## To
## Brooklyn Bridge

How many dawns, chill from his rippling rest
The seagull's wings shall dip and pivot him,
Shedding white rings of tumult, building high
Over the chained bay waters Liberty—

Then, with inviolate curve, forsake our eyes          5
As apparitional as sails that cross
Some page of figures to be filed away;
—Till elevators drop us from our day . . .

I think of cinemas, panoramic sleights
With multitudes bent toward some flashing scene          10
Never disclosed, but hastened to again,
Foretold to other eyes on the same screen;

And Thee, across the harbor, silver-paced
As though the sun took step of thee, yet left
Some motion ever unspent in thy stride,—          15
Implicitly thy freedom staying thee!

Out of some subway scuttle, cell or loft
A bedlamite[2] speeds to thy parapets,
Tilting there momently, shrill shirt ballooning,
A jest falls from the speechless caravan.          20

Down Wall, from girder into street noon leaks,
A rip-tooth of the sky's acetylene;
All afternoon the cloud-flown derricks turn . . .
Thy cables breathe the North Atlantic still.

And obscure as that heaven of the Jews,          25
Thy guerdon . . . Accolade thou dost bestow
Of anonymity time cannot raise:
Vibrant reprieve and pardon thou dost show.

O harp and altar, of the fury fused,
(How could mere toil align thy choiring strings!)          30
Terrific threshold of the prophet's pledge,
Prayer of pariah, and the lover's cry,—

---

1. The formal pattern of the poem is suggested by this
quotation from the Book of Job (1.7), which gives Sa-
tan's answer to Jehovah when asked where he has been.     2. Madman, inmate of a hospital for the insane.

Again the traffic lights that skim thy swift
Unfractioned idiom, immaculate sigh of stars,
Beading thy path—condense eternity:                                35
And we have seen night lifted in thine arms.

Under thy shadow by the piers I waited;
Only in darkness is thy shadow clear.
The City's fiery parcels all undone,
Already snow submerges an iron year . . .                          40

O Sleepless as the river under thee,
Vaulting the sea, the prairies' dreaming sod,
Unto us lowliest sometime sweep, descend
And of the curveship lend a myth to God.

                                                        1927, 1930

## II. Powhatan's Daughter[1]

"—Pocahuntus, a well-featured but wanton yong girle . . . of the age of eleven
or twelve years, get the boyes forth with her into the market place, and make
them wheele, falling on their hands, turning their heels upwards, whom she
would followe, and wheele so herself, naked as she was, all the fort over."

                              *    *    *

### The River[2]

Stick your patent name on a signboard
brother—all over—going west—young man
Tintex—Japalac—Certain-teed Overalls ads[3]
and lands sakes! under the new playbill ripped          . . . and past
5  in the guaranteed corner—see Bert Williams[4] what?    the din and
Minstrels when you steal a chicken just                  slogans of
save me the wing for if it isn't                         the year—
Erie it ain't for miles around a
Mazda—and the telegraphic night coming on Thomas

10  a Ediford[5]—and whistling down the tracks
a headlight rushing with the sound—can you
imagine—while an EXPRESS makes time like

1. Powhatan was the Native American chief with whom English settlers in Virginia (1607) had to deal. Pocahontas (1595–1617) was his daughter, whom Crane associated with the American "continent," a "nature symbol" comparable to the "traditional Hertha of ancient Teutonic mythology." The epigraph is from William Strachey, History of Travaile into Virginia Britannica (1615).
2. Crane wrote to Mrs. T. W. Simpson (Letters, p. 303): "I'm trying in this part of the poem to chart the pioneer experience of our forefathers—and to tell the story backwards . . . on the 'backs' of hoboes. These hoboes are simply 'psychological ponies' to carry the reader across the country and back to the Mississippi, which you will notice is described as a great River of Time. I also unlatch the door to the pure Indian world which opens out in 'The Dance' section, so the reader is gradually led back in time to the pure savage world, while existing at the same time in the present." In the opening lines the image of a subway is translated into an image of a luxury express train, the Twentieth Century Limited, traveling from New York City to Chicago.
3. Advertising slogans: trade names of a dye, a varnish, and a brand of overalls.
4. Egbert A. Williams (1876–1922), popular, talented black minstrel show entertainer.
5. A mocking reference to Thomas A. Edison (1847–1931), inventor of the electric light bulb (trade name "Mazda"), and Henry Ford (1863–1947), automobile manufacturer.

SCIENCE—COMMERCE and the HOLYGHOST
RADIO ROARS IN EVERY HOME WE HAVE THE NORTHPOLE
15  WALLSTREET AND VIRGINBIRTH WITHOUT STONES OR
WIRES OR EVEN RUNning brooks connecting ears
and no more sermons windows flashing roar
breathtaking—as you like it . . . eh?[6]

　　　　So the 20th Century—so
20  whizzed the Limited—roared by and left
three men, still hungry on the tracks, ploddingly
watching the tail lights wizen and converge, slipping gimleted and neatly out of sight.

　　·　　　·　　　·　　　·　　　·　　　·　　　·

The last bear, shot drinking in the Dakotas
25  Loped under wires that span the mountain stream.
Keen instruments,[7] strung to a vast precision
Bind town to town and dream to ticking dream.
But some men take their liquor slow—and count
—Though they'll confess no rosary nor clue—

30  The river's minute by the far brook's year.
Under a world of whistles, wires and steam
Caboose-like they go ruminating through
Ohio, Indiana—blind baggage—
To Cheyenne tagging . . . Maybe Kalamazoo.

35  Time's rendings, time's blendings they construe
As final reckonings of fire and snow;
Strange bird-wit, like the elemental gist
Of unwalled winds they offer, singing low
*My Old Kentucky Home* and *Casey Jones,*
40  *Some Sunny Day.* I heard a road-gang chanting so.
And afterwards, who had a colt's eyes—one said,
"Jesus! Oh I remember watermelon days!" And sped
High in a cloud of merriment, recalled
"—And when my Aunt Sally Simpson smiled," he
drawled—
45  "It was almost Louisiana, long ago."
"There's no place like Booneville though, Buddy,"
One said, excising a last burr from his vest,
"—For early trouting." Then peering in the can,
"—But I kept on the tracks." Possessed, resigned,
50  He trod the fire down pensively and grinned,
Spreading dry shingles of a beard. . . .

　　　　　　　　　　Behind
My father's cannery works I used to see
Rail-squatters ranged in nomad raillery,
55  The ancient men—wifeless or runaway
Hobo-trekkers that forever search

*to those*
*whose*
*addresses*
*are never near*

---

6. An echo of Shakespeare, *As You Like It* (2.1.16–
17): "Books in the running brooks / Sermons in stones."

7. The telephone and telegraph.

An empire wilderness of freight and rails.
Each seemed a child, like me, on a loose perch,
Holding to childhood like some termless play.
60 John, Jake or Charley, hopping the slow freight
—Memphis to Tallahassee—riding the rods,
Blind fists of nothing, humpty-dumpty clods.

Yet they touch something like a key perhaps.
From pole to pole across the hills, the states
65 —They know a body under the wide rain;                *but who have*
Youngsters with eyes like fjords, old reprobates         *touched her,*
With racetrack jargon,—dotting immensity                 *knowing her*
They lurk across her, knowing her yonder breast          *without name*
Snow-silvered, sumac-stained or smoky blue—
70 Is past the valley-sleepers, south or west.
—As I have trod the rumorous midnights, too,

And past the circuit of the lamp's thin flame
(O Nights that brought me to her body bare!)
Have dreamed beyond the print that bound her name.
75 Trains sounding the long blizzards out—I heard
Wail into distances I knew were hers.
Papooses crying on the wind's long mane
Screamed redskin dynasties that fled the brain,
—Dead echoes! But I knew her body there,
80 Time like a serpent down her shoulder, dark,
And space, an eaglet's wing, laid on her hair.[8]

Under the Ozarks, domed by Iron Mountain,
The old gods of the rain lie wrapped in pools
Where eyeless fish curvet a sunken fountain             *nor the*
85 And re-descend with corn from querulous crows.         *myths of her*
Such pilferings make up their timeless eatage,          *fathers . . .*
Propitiate them for their timber torn
By iron, iron—always the iron dealt cleavage!
They doze now, below axe and powder horn.
90 And Pullman breakfasters glide glistening steel
From tunnel into field—iron strides the dew—
Straddles the hill, a dance of wheel on wheel.
You have a half-hour's wait at Siskiyou,
Or stay the night and take the next train through.
95 Southward, near Cairo passing, you can see
The Ohio merging,—borne down Tennessee;
And if it's summer and the sun's in dusk
Maybe the breeze will lift the River's musk
—As though the waters breathed that you might know
100 Memphis Johnny, Steamboat Bill, Missouri Joe.
Oh, lean from the window, if the train slows down,
As though you touched hands with some ancient clown,
—A little while gaze absently below
And hum *Deep River* with them while they go.

---

8. Feathered headdresses and serpents are familiar tokens of Native American culture.

105  Yes, turn again and sniff once more—look see,
     O Sheriff, Brakeman and Authority—
     Hitch up your pants and crunch another quid,[9]
     For you, too, feed the River timelessly.
     And few evade full measure of their fate;
110  Always they smile out eerily what they seem.
     I could believe he joked at heaven's gate—
     Dan Midland—jolted from the cold brake-beam.[1]

     Down, down—born pioneers in time's despite,
     Grimed tributaries to an ancient flow—
115  They win no frontier by their wayward plight,
     But drift in stillness, as from Jordan's[2] brow.

     You will not hear it as the sea; even stone
     Is not more hushed by gravity . . . But slow,
     As loth to take more tribute—sliding prone
120  Like one whose eyes were buried long ago

     The River, spreading, flows—and spends your dream.
     What are you, lost within this tideless spell?
     You are your father's father, and the stream—
     A liquid theme that floating niggers swell.

125  Damp tonnage and alluvial march of days—
     Nights turbid, vascular with silted shale
     And roots surrendered down of moraine clays:
     The Mississippi drinks the farthest dale.

     O quarrying passion, undertowed sunlight!
130  The basalt surface drags a jungle grace
     Ochreous and lynx-barred in lengthening might;
     Patience! and you shall reach the biding place!

     Over De Soto's bones the freighted floors
     Throb past the City storied of three thrones.[3]
135  Down two more turns the Mississippi pours
     (Anon tall ironsides up from salt lagoons)

     And flows within itself, heaps itself free.
     All fades but one thin skyline 'round . . . Ahead
     No embrace opens but the stinging sea;
140  The River lifts itself from its long bed,

     Poised wholly on its dream, a mustard glow

---

9. Chunk of chewing tobacco.
1. Structure on a railroad car where hoboes ride; Dan
Midland was a legendary hobo who fell to his death
from a train.
2. River mentioned frequently in the Bible; Jesus was
baptized in it.
3. New Orleans, at various times under Spanish,
French, and English rule. The body of the Spanish

explorer Hernando de Soto (1500–1542) was secretly
committed to the Mississippi River so that hostile
American Indians would continue to believe in his divinity. In 1862 Admiral David G. Farragut (1801–
1870) led a Union fleet up the Mississippi from the
Gulf and captured New Orleans. "Ironsides" (below) is
a term for warships, whether or not ironclad.

Tortured with history, its one will—flow!
—The Passion spreads in wide tongues, choked and slow,
Meeting the Gulf, hosannas silently below.

1930

## The Dance[4]

The swift red flesh, a winter king—
Who squired the glacier woman down the sky?
She ran the neighing canyons all the spring;
She spouted arms; she rose with maize—to die.

5  And in the autumn drouth, whose burnished hands
With mineral wariness found out the stone
Where prayers, forgotten, streamed the mesa sands?
He holds the twilight's dim, perpetual throne.

Mythical brows we saw retiring—loth,
10  Disturbed and destined, into denser green.
Greeting they sped us, on the arrow's oath:
Now lie incorrigibly what years between . . .

There was a bed of leaves, and broken play;
There was a veil upon you, Pocahontas, bride—
15  O Princess whose brown lap was virgin May;
And bridal flanks and eyes hid tawny pride.

I left the village for dogwood. By the canoe
Tugging below the mill-race, I could see
Your hair's keen crescent running, and the blue
20  First moth of evening take wing stealthily.

What laughing chains the water wove and threw!
I learned to catch the trout's moon whisper; I
Drifted how many hours I never knew,
But, watching, saw that fleet young crescent die,—

25  And one star, swinging, take its place, alone,
Cupped in the larches of the mountain pass—
Until, immortally, it bled into the dawn.
I left my sleek boat nibbling margin grass . . .

I took the portage climb, then chose
30  A further valley-shed; I could not stop.
Feet nozzled wat'ry webs of upper flows;
One white veil gusted from the very top.

O Appalachian Spring! I gained the ledge;
Steep, inaccessible smile that eastward bends

*Then you shall
see her truly
—your blood
remembering
its first
invasion of
her secrecy,
its first
encounters
with her kin,
her chieftain
lover . . . his
shade that
haunts the
lakes and hills*

---

4. This section presents Crane's imaginary consummation of his adventure westward and quest into the past. Crane intended to become "identified with the Indian and his world before it is over. . . . Pocahontas (the continent) is the common basis of our meeting, she survives the extinction of the Indian, who finally, after being assumed into the elements of nature . . . persists only as a kind of 'eye' in the sky, or a star" (*Letters*, p. 307).

35 And northward reaches in that violet wedge
Of Adirondacks!—wisped of azure wands,

Over how many bluffs, tarns, streams I sped!
—And knew myself within some boding shade:—
Grey tepees tufting the blue knolls ahead,
40 Smoke swirling through the yellow chestnut glade . . .

A distant cloud, a thunder-bud—it grew,
That blanket of the skies: the padded foot
Within,—I heard it; 'til its rhythm drew,
—Siphoned the black pool from the heart's hot root!

45 A cyclone threshes in the turbine crest,
Swooping in eagle feathers down your back;
Know, Maquokeeta, greeting; know death's best;
—Fall, Sachem,[5] strictly as the tamarack!

A birch kneels. All her whistling fingers fly.
50 The oak grove circles in a crash of leaves;
The long moan of a dance is in the sky.
Dance, Maquokeeta: Pocahontas grieves . . .

And every tendon scurries toward the twangs
Of lightning deltaed down your saber hair.
55 Now snaps the flint in every tooth; red fangs
And splay tongues thinly busy the blue air . . .

Dance, Maquokeeta! snake that lives before,
That casts his pelt, and lives beyond! Sprout, horn!
Spark, tooth! Medicine-man, relent, restore—
60 Lie to us,—dance us back the tribal morn!

Spears and assemblies: black drums thrusting on—
O yelling battlements,—I, too, was liege
To rainbows currying each pulsant bone:
Surpassed the circumstance, danced out the siege!

65 And buzzard-circleted, screamed from the stake;
I could not pick the arrows from my side.
Wrapped in that fire, I saw more escorts wake—
Flickering, sprint up the hill groins like a tide.

I heard the hush of lava wrestling your arms,
70 And stag teeth foam about the raven throat;
Flame cataracts of heaven in seething swarms
Fed down your anklets to the sunset's moat.

O, like the lizard in the furious noon,
That drops his legs and colors in the sun,
75 —And laughs, pure serpent, Time itself, and moon
Of his own fate, I saw thy change begun!

5. Chief (Algonquin). "Maquokeeta": the name of an American Indian cab driver who told Crane it meant "Big River" and signified a god whose rains refreshed the plains.

And saw thee dive to kiss that destiny
Like one white meteor, sacrosanct and blent
At last with all that's consummate and free
80   There, where the first and last gods keep thy tent.

·          ·          ·          ·

Thewed of the levin,[6] thunder-shod and lean,
Lo, through what infinite seasons dost thou gaze—
Across what bivouacs of thine angered slain,
And see'st thy bride immortal in the maize!

85   Totem and fire-gall, slumbering pyramid[7]—
Though other calendars now stack the sky,
Thy freedom is her largesse, Prince, and hid
On paths thou knewest best to claim her by.

High unto Labrador the sun strikes free
90   Her speechless dream of snow, and stirred again,
She is the torrent and the singing tree;
And she is virgin to the last of men . . .

West, west and south! winds over Cumberland
And winds across the llano[8] grass resume
95   Her hair's warm sibilance. Her breasts are fanned
O stream by slope and vineyard—into bloom!

And when the caribou slant down for salt
Do arrows thirst and leap? Do antlers shine
Alert, star-triggered in the listening vault
100  Of dusk?—And are her perfect brows to thine?

We danced, O Brave, we danced beyond their farms,
In cobalt desert closures made our vows . . .
Now is the strong prayer folded in thine arms,
The serpent with the eagle in the boughs.

                                                    1927, 1930


# VII. The Tunnel[1]

*To Find the Western path*
*Right thro' the Gates of Wrath.*
                    —Blake[2]


Performances, assortments, résumés—
Up Times Square to Columbus Circle lights
Channel the congresses, nightly sessions,
Refractions of the thousand theatres, faces—

---

6. Lightning.
7. Suggests the smoldering volcano Popocatepetl near Mexico City and the huge pyramids of the Mayans, used for sacrificial ceremonies and the astronomical measurement of time. "Fire-gall": charred ashes, like the excrescence made by insects on a tree.
8. Treeless plain.
1. *The Tunnel*, representing the epic convention of a descent into hell, renders the poet's descent into a subway and the interior of his mind, followed by the resurgence of desperate hope when he emerges to see the bridge and the East River leading to the distant sea.
2. The opening lines of *Morning*, by the visionary English poet William Blake (1757–1827), which foresees the return of dawn and the triumph of love after facing the crisis that tests it.

Mysterious kitchens. . . . You shall search them all.                    5
Someday by heart you'll learn each famous sight
And watch the curtain lift in hell's despite;
You'll find the garden in the third act dead,
Finger your knees—and wish yourself in bed
With tabloid crime-sheets perched in easy sight.                    10

    Then let you reach your hat
    and go.
    As usual, let you—also
    walking down—exclaim
    to twelve upward leaving                    15
    a subscription praise
    for what time slays.

Or can't you quite make up your mind to ride;
A walk is better underneath the L[3] a brisk
Ten blocks or so before? But you find yourself                    20
Preparing penguin flexions of the arms,—
As usual you will meet the scuttle yawn:
The subway yawns the quickest promise home.

Be minimum, then, to swim the hiving swarms
Out of the Square, the Circle burning bright[4]—                    25
Avoid the glass doors gyring at your right,
Where boxed alone a second, eyes take fright
—Quite unprepared rush naked back to light:
And down beside the turnstile press the coin
Into the slot. The gongs already rattle.                    30

    And so
    of cities you bespeak
    subways, rivered under streets
    and rivers. . . . In the car
    the overtone of motion                    35
    underground, the monotone
    of motion is the sound
    of other faces, also underground—

"Let's have a pencil Jimmy—living now
at Floral Park                    40
Flatbush—on the fourth of July—
like a pigeon's muddy dream—potatoes
to dig in the field—travlin the town—too—
night after night—the Culver line—the
girls all shaping up—it used to be—"                    45

Our tongues recant like beaten weather vanes.
This answer lives like verdigris,[5] like hair

---

3. Elevated railway (abbreviation).
4. An echo of Blake's poem *The Tyger*: "Tyger! Tyger!
burning bright / In the forests of the night, / What immortal hand or eye / Could frame thy fearful sym-

metry?"; also the lighted sign indicating a subway
station.
5. Green coating or stain on copper.

Beyond extinction, surcease of the bone;
And repetition freezes—"What

"what do you want? getting weak on the links?                50
fandaddle daddy don't ask for change—IS THIS
FOURTEENTH? it's half past six she said—if
you don't like my gate why did you
swing on it, why *didja*
swing on it                                                  55
anyhow—"

        And somehow anyhow swing—

The phonographs of hades in the brain
Are tunnels that re-wind themselves, and love
A burnt match skating in a urinal—                          60
Somewhere above Fourteenth TAKE THE EXPRESS
To brush some new presentiment of pain—

"But I want service in this office SERVICE
I said—after
the show she cried a little afterwards but—"                65

Whose head is swinging from the swollen strap?[6]
Whose body smokes along the bitten rails,
Bursts from a smoldering bundle far behind
In back forks of the chasms of the brain,—
Puffs from a riven stump far out behind                     70
In interborough fissures of the mind . . . ?

And why do I often meet your visage here,
Your eyes like agate lanterns—on and on
Below the toothpaste and the dandruff ads?
—And did their riding eyes right through your side,         75
And did their eyes like unwashed platters ride?
And Death, aloft,—gigantically down
Probing through you—toward me, O evermore![7]
And when they dragged your retching flesh,
Your trembling hands that night through Baltimore—          80
That last night on the ballot rounds, did you,
Shaking, did you deny the ticket, Poe?

For Gravesend Manor change at Chambers Street.
The platform hurries along to a dead stop.

The intent escalator lifts a serenade                       85
Stilly

---

6. The images of disfigurement and violent death in
this section introduce the tortured figure and haunted
imagination of Edgar Allan Poe. He died in Baltimore
in 1849, reputedly of a beating, while drunk, by a political gang who wanted him to cast multiple ballots ille-
gally for their ticket.
7. Echoes of "the agate lamp within thy hand" from
*To Helen*, "Death looks gigantically down" from *The
City in the Sea*, and of the refrain "Nevermore" in *The
Raven*, all poems by Poe.

Of shoes, umbrellas, each eye attending its shoe, then
Bolting outright somewhere above where streets
Burst suddenly in rain. . . . The gongs recur:
Elbows and levers, guard and hissing door.                          90
Thunder is galvothermic[8] here below. . . . The car
Wheels off. The train rounds, bending to a scream,
Taking the final level for the dive
Under the river—
And somewhat emptier than before,                                   95
Demented, for a hitching second, humps; then
Lets go. . . . Toward corners of the floor
Newspapers wing, revolve and wing.
Blank windows gargle signals through the roar.

And does the Daemon take you home, also,                            100
Wop washerwoman, with the bandaged hair?
After the corridors are swept, the cuspidors—
The gaunt sky-barracks cleanly now, and bare,
O Genoese,[9] do you bring mother eyes and hands
Back home to children and to golden hair?                           105

Daemon, demurring and eventful yawn!
Whose hideous laughter is a bellows mirth
—Or the muffled slaughter of a day in birth—
O cruelly to inoculate the brinking dawn
With antennae toward worlds that glow and sink;—                    110
To spoon us out more liquid than the dim
Locution of the eldest star, and pack
The conscience navelled in the plunging wind,
Umbilical to call—and straightway die!

O caught like pennies beneath soot and steam,                       115
Kiss of our agony thou gatherest;
Condensed, thou takest all—shrill ganglia
Impassioned with some song we fail to keep.
And yet, like Lazarus,[1] to feel the slope,
The sod and billow breaking,—lifting ground,                        120
—A sound of waters bending astride the sky
Unceasing with some Word that will not die . . . !

.        .        .        .        .

A tugboat, wheezing wreaths of steam,
Lunged past, with one galvanic blare stove up the River.
I counted the echoes assembling, one after one,                     125
Searching, thumbing the midnight on the piers.
Lights, coasting, left the oily tympanum of waters;
The blackness somewhere gouged glass on a sky.
And this thy harbor, O my City, I have driven under,
Tossed from the coil of ticking towers. . . . Tomorrow,             130

8. I.e., galvanothermic, producing heat by electricity.       1. He was resurrected from the grave by Jesus in John
9. The Italian-American mother is called Genoese to          11.43–44.
recall Genoa, Italy, the birthplace of Columbus.

And to be. . . . Here by the River that is East—
Here at the waters' edge the hands drop memory;
Shadowless in that abyss they unaccounting lie.
How far away the star has pooled the sea—
Or shall the hands be drawn away, to die?                           135

Kiss of our agony Thou gatherest,
                    O Hand of Fire
                              gatherest—

                                                       1927, 1930


# VIII. Atlantis[1]

*Music is then the knowledge of that which relates to love in harmony and*
*system.*                                                        —Plato[2]


Through the bound cable strands, the arching path
Upward, veering with light, the flight of strings,—
Taut miles of shuttling moonlight syncopate
The whispered rush, telepathy of wires.
Up the index of night, granite and steel—                          5
Transparent meshes—fleckless the gleaming staves—
Sibylline[3] voices flicker, waveringly stream
As though a god were issue of the strings. . . .

And through that cordage, threading with its call
One arc synoptic of all tides below—                               10
Their labyrinthine mouths of history
Pouring reply as though all ships at sea
Complighted in one vibrant breath made cry,—
"Make thy love sure—to weave whose song we ply!"
—From black embankments, moveless soundings hailed,               15
So seven oceans answer from their dream.

And on, obliquely up bright carrier bars
New octaves trestle the twin monoliths
Beyond whose frosted capes the moon bequeaths
Two worlds of sleep (O arching strands of song!)—                  20
Onward and up the crystal-flooded aisle
White tempest nets file upward, upward ring
With silver terraces the humming spars,
The loft of vision, palladium helm of stars.

Sheerly the eyes, like seagulls stung with rime—                   25
Slit and propelled by glistening fins of light—

---

1. In this section, the first that Crane wrote, the poet
imagines the perfect unison of his song with the vision
incarnate in *The Bridge*, celebrates the fusion of the
sacred and the aesthetic that spans the seas and eras of
history, and envisions the yet incomplete fulfillment of
his quest.
2. From Plato's *Republic* (3.403).
3. Enigmatic, prophetic; issuing from ancient oracles, sibyls.

Pick biting way up towering looms that press
Sidelong with flight of blade on tendon blade
—Tomorrows into yesteryear—and link
What cipher-script of time no traveller reads    30
But who, through smoking pyres of love and death,
Searches the timeless laugh of mythic spears.

Like hails, farewells—up planet-sequined heights
Some trillion whispering hammers glimmer Tyre:[4]
Serenely, sharply up the long anvil cry          35
Of inchling aeons silence rivets Troy.
And you, aloft there—Jason![5] hesting Shout!
Still wrapping harness to the swarming air!
Silvery the rushing wake, surpassing call,
Beams yelling Aeolus![6] splintered in the straits!    40

From gulfs unfolding, terrible of drums,
Tall Vision-of-the-Voyage, tensely spare—
Bridge, lifting night to cycloramic crest
Of deepest day—O Choir, translating time
Into what multitudinous Verb the suns            45
And synergy of waters ever fuse, recast
In myriad syllables,—Psalm of Cathay!
O Love, thy white, pervasive Paradigm . . . !

We left the haven hanging in the night—
Sheened harbor lanterns backward fled the keel.    50
Pacific here at time's end, bearing corn,—
Eyes stammer through the pangs of dust and steel.
And still the circular, indubitable frieze
Of heaven's meditation, yoking wave
To kneeling wave, one song devoutly binds—        55
The vernal strophe chimes from deathless strings!

O Thou steeled Cognizance whose leap commits
The agile precincts of the lark's return;
Within whose lariat sweep encinctured sing
In single chrysalis the many twain,—              60
Of stars Thou art the stitch and stallion glow
And like an organ, Thou, with sound of doom—
Sight, sound and flesh Thou leadest from time's realm
As love strikes clear direction for the helm.

Swift peal of secular light, intrinsic Myth        65
Whose fell unshadow is death's utter wound,—
O River-throated—iridescently upborne
Through the bright drench and fabric of our veins;
With white escarpments swinging into light,
Sustained in tears the cities are endowed          70
And justified conclamant with ripe fields

---

4. Ancient Phoenician port.
5. Leader of the Greek Argonauts in the search for the    Golden Fleece.
6. Keeper of the winds in Homer's epics.

Revolving through their harvests in sweet torment.

Forever Deity's glittering Pledge, O Thou
Whose canticle fresh chemistry assigns
To wrapt inception and beatitude,—                                    75
Always through blinding cables, to our joy,
Of thy white seizure springs the prophecy:
Always through spiring cordage, pyramids
Of silver sequel, Deity's young name
Kinetic of white choiring wings . . . ascends.                        80

Migrations that must needs void memory,
Inventions that cobblestone the heart,—
Unspeakable Thou Bridge to Thee, O Love.
Thy pardon for this history, whitest Flower,
O Answerer of all,—Anemone,[7]—                                       85
Now while thy petals spend the suns about us, hold—
(O Thou whose radiance doth inherit me)
Atlantis,—hold thy floating singer late!

So to thine Everpresence, beyond time,
Like spears ensanguined of one tolling star                           90
That bleeds infinity—the orphic[8] strings,
Sidereal phalanxes, leap and converge:
—One Song, one Bridge of Fire! Is it Cathay,
Now pity steeps the grass and rainbows ring
The serpent with the eagle in the leaves . . . ?                      95
Whispers antiphonal in azure swing.

                                                                    1930

---

7. Flower. At the end of the strife-torn love affair of
the goddess Venus and the mortal Adonis in Greek mythology, the white anemone sprang from her tears, the
red from Adonis's blood.
8. Prophetic and enchanting, so named from the

mythological poet and musician Orpheus, whose lyre
or harp could charm the powers of hell. Even after his
brutal murder by the Maenads, his severed head kept
singing as it floated down the river.

---

# LANGSTON HUGHES
## 1902–1967

Among the many talented black writers connected with the Harlem Renaissance,
Langston Hughes was the most popular, the most versatile, and the most durable.
Among his important achievements are the incorporation of the rhythms of African-American music into his poetry and the creation of an authentic black folk
speaker in the persona of Jesse B. Semple. Along with Zora Neale Hurston, and in
contrast to Jean Toomer and Countee Cullen (who wanted to work with purely
literary patterns, whether traditional or experimental), he wanted to capture the
dominant oral and improvisatory traditions of black culture in written form.

  Hughes was born in Joplin, Missouri, and in childhood, since his parents were
separated, he lived mainly with his maternal grandmother. He did, however, reside

intermittently with his mother in Detroit and Cleveland, where he finished high school and first began to write poetry, and with his father, who, disgusted with American racism, had gone to Mexico. Like other poets in this era—T. S. Eliot, Hart Crane, Edgar Lee Masters, and Robert Frost—Hughes had a mother sympathetic to his poetic ambitions and a businesslike father with whom he was in deep, scarring conflict.

Hughes entered Columbia University in 1920 but left after a year to travel and drift for several more: he shipped out as a merchant seaman, worked at a nightclub in Paris (France) and as a busboy in Washington, D.C. All this time, however, he was writing and publishing poetry, chiefly in the two important African-American periodicals *Opportunity* and *The Crisis*. Eleven of Hughes's poems were published in Alain Locke's pioneering anthology, *The New Negro* (1925), and he was also well represented in Countee Cullen's 1927 anthology, *Caroling Dusk*. Carl Van Vechten, one of the white patrons of African-American writing, helped get *The Weary Blues*, Hughes's first volume of poems, published in 1926. It was in this year, too, that his important essay *The Negro Artist and the Racial Mountain* appeared in the *Nation*; in this essay Hughes described the immense difficulties in store for the serious black artist "who would produce a racial art" but insisted on the need for courageous artists to make the attempt. Other patrons appeared: Amy Spingarn financed his college education at Lincoln University (Pennsylvania) and Charlotte Mason subsidized him in New York City between 1928 and 1930. The publication of his novel *Not without Laughter* in 1930 solidified his reputation and sales, enabling him to support himself. By the 1930s he was being called "the bard of Harlem."

The Great Depression brought an abrupt end to much African-American literary activity, but Hughes was already a public figure. In the activist 1930s he was much absorbed in radical politics. Hughes and other blacks were drawn by the American Communist party that made racial justice an important plank in its platform, promoting an image of working-class solidarity that nullified racial boundaries. He visited the Soviet Union in 1932 and produced a significant amount of radical writing up to the eve of World War II. He covered the Spanish Civil War for the *Baltimore Afro-American* in 1937. By the end of the decade he had also been involved in drama and screenplay writing and had begun an autobiography, all the while publishing poetry. In 1943 he invented the folksy, street-wise character Jesse B. Semple, whose commonsense prose monologues on race were eventually collected in four volumes; in 1949 he created Alberta K. Johnson, Semple's female equivalent.

In the 1950s and 1960s Hughes published a variety of anthologies for children and adults, including *First Book of Negroes* (1952), *The First Book of Jazz* (1955), and *The Book of Negro Folklore* (1958). In 1953 he was called to testify before Senator Joseph McCarthy's committee on subversive activities (HUAC) in connection with his 1930s radicalism. The FBI listed him as a security risk until 1959, and during these years, when he could not travel outside the United States, Hughes worked to rehabilitate his reputation as a good American by producing more-patriotic poetry. From 1960 to the end of his life he was again on the international circuit.

Like all the Harlem Renaissance writers (many of whom were not Harlemites), Hughes faced many difficulties in writing a self-proclaimed "Negro" poetry. Could or should any individual speak for an entire "race"? If he or she tried to, wouldn't that speech tend to homogenize and stereotype a diverse people? Harlem poets, aware that the audience for their poetry was almost all white, had to consider whether a particular image of black people would help or harm the cause. To the extent that they felt compelled to idealize black folk, their work risked lapsing into racist primitivism. African-American writers questioned, too, whether their work should emphasize their similarities to or differences from whites. Hughes's response to these problems was to turn his focus away from the rural black population and to the city folk. The shift to the contemporary urban context freed Hughes from the concerns over primitivism; he could be a realist and modernist. He could use stanza forms deriving from blues music and adapt the vocabulary of everyday black speech to poetry without affirming stereotypes. And he could insist that whatever the differences between black and white Americans, all Americans were equally entitled to liberty, justice, and opportunity.

## The Negro Speaks of Rivers

I've known rivers:
I've known rivers ancient as the world and older than the
    flow of human blood in human veins.

My soul has grown deep like the rivers.

I bathed in the Euphrates when dawns were young.                    5
I built my hut near the Congo and it lulled me to sleep.
I looked upon the Nile[1] and raised the pyramids above it.
I heard the singing of the Mississippi when Abe Lincoln
    went down to New Orleans, and I've seen its muddy
    bosom turn all golden in the sunset                            10

I've known rivers:
Ancient, dusky rivers.

My soul has grown deep like the rivers.

                                            1921, 1926

## Mother to Son

Well, son, I'll tell you:
Life for me ain't been no crystal stair.
It's had tacks in it,
And splinters,
And boards torn up,                                                5
And places with no carpet on the floor—
Bare.
But all the time
I'se been a-climbin' on,
And reachin' landin's,                                            10
And turnin' corners,
And sometimes goin' in the dark
Where there ain't been no light.
So boy, don't you turn back.
Don't you set down on the steps                                   15

---

1. The Euphrates River, cradle of ancient Babylonian civilization, flows from Turkey through Syria and Iraq. The Congo flows from the Republic of the Congo in central Africa into the Atlantic Ocean. The Nile, site of ancient Egyptian civilization, empties into the Mediterranean Sea.

'Cause you finds it's kinder hard.
Don't you fall now—
For I'se still goin', honey,
I'se still climbin',
And life for me ain't been no crystal stair.                    20

1922, 1926

## I, Too

I, too, sing America.

I am the darker brother.
They send me to eat in the kitchen
When company comes,
But I laugh,                                                     5
And eat well,
And grow strong.

Tomorrow,
I'll sit at the table
When company comes.                                             10
Nobody'll dare
Say to me,
"Eat in the kitchen,"
Then.

Besides,                                                        15
They'll see how beautiful I am
And be ashamed—

I, too, am America.

1932

## Mulatto

*I am your son, white man!*

Georgia dusk
And the turpentine woods.
One of the pillars of the temple fell.

        *You are my son!*                                       5
        *Like hell!*

The moon over the turpentine woods.
The Southern night
Full of stars,
Great big yellow stars.                                         10

What's a body but a toy?
  Juicy bodies
  Of nigger wenches
  Blue black
  Against black fences.                                    15
  O, you little bastard boy,
  What's a body but a toy?
The scent of pine wood stings the soft night air.
  *What's the body of your mother?*
Silver moonlight everywhere.                                20

      *What's the body of your mother?*
Sharp pine scent in the evening air.
      A nigger night,
      A nigger joy,
      A little yellow                                      25
      Bastard boy.

      *Naw, you ain't my brother.*
      *Niggers ain't my brother.*
      *Not ever.*
      *Niggers ain't my brother.*                          30
The Southern night is full of stars,
Great big yellow stars.
      O, sweet as earth,
      Dusk dark bodies
      Give sweet birth                                     35
To little yellow bastard boys.

      *Git on back there in the night,*
      *You ain't white.*

The bright stars scatter everywhere.
Pine wood scent in the evening air.                         40
      A nigger night,
      A nigger joy.

      *I am your son, white man!*

      A little yellow
      Bastard boy.                                         45

                                            1927


## Song for a Dark Girl

Way Down South in Dixie[1]
(Break the heart of me)

---

1. This ironic refrain is the last line of *Dixie*, the popular minstrel song, probably composed by Daniel D. Emmett (1815–1904), which became the rallying cry of southern patriotism during and after the Civil War.

They hung my black young lover
   To a cross roads tree.

Way Down South in Dixie                                    5
   (Bruised body high in air)
I asked the white Lord Jesus
   What was the use of prayer.

Way Down South in Dixie
   (Break the heart of me)                      10
Love is a naked shadow
   On a gnarled and naked tree.

1927

## Silhouette

Southern gentle lady,
Do not swoon.
They've just hung a black man
In the dark of the moon.

They've hung a black man                                    5
To a roadside tree
In the dark of the moon
For the world to see
How Dixie protects
Its white womanhood.                                        10

Southern gentle lady,
   Be good!
   Be good!

1949

## Visitors to the Black Belt

You can talk about
*Across* the railroad tracks—
To me it's *here*
On this side of the tracks.

You can talk about                                          5
*Up* in Harlem—
To me it's *here*
In Harlem.

You can say
Jazz on the South Side—                                     10
To me it's hell
On the South Side:

Kitchenettes
With no heat
And garbage                                          15
In the halls.

Who're you, outsider?

Ask me who am I.

1949


## Note on Commercial Theatre

You've taken my blues and gone—
You sing 'em on Broadway
And you sing 'em in Hollywood Bowl,
And you mixed 'em up with symphonies
And you fixed 'em                                     5
So they don't sound like me.
Yep, you done taken my blues and gone.

You also took my spirituals and gone.
You put me in *Macbeth* and *Carmen Jones*
And all kinds of *Swing Mikados*                     10
And in everything but what's about me—
But someday somebody'll
Stand up and talk about me,
And write about me—
Black and beautiful—                                 15
And sing about me,
And put on plays about me!

I reckon it'll be
Me myself!

Yes, it'll be me.                                    20

1949


## Democracy

Democracy will not come
Today, this year
    Nor ever
Through compromise and fear.

I have as much right                                 5
As the other fellow has
    To stand
On my two feet
And own the land.

I tire so of hearing people say,                                    10
*Let things take their course.*
*Tomorrow is another day.*
I do not need my freedom when I'm dead.
I cannot live on tomorrow's bread.

Freedom                                                            15
Is a strong seed
Planted
In a great need.

I live here, too.
I want freedom                                                     20
Just as you.

                                                                  1949

---

# JOHN STEINBECK
## 1902–1968

Most of John Steinbeck's fiction concerns his native California and the Great Depression. Among influential novels from the period between the wars, his Pulitzer Prize–winning novel about "Okies" (Oklahoma sharecroppers who were forced off their land after the Dust Bowl storms of 1937), *The Grapes of Wrath* (1939), was one of the most important. It combined naturalist and symbolist techniques to depict his characters' plights and expressed compassion, outrage, and admiration in response to their sufferings.

He was born and raised not far from San Francisco in the Salinas Valley region of wine and artichokes. His father was county treasurer, his mother a former schoolteacher. In the family library he found and read such standard authors as Milton, Dostoevsky, Flaubert, George Eliot, and Thomas Hardy. In high school he was a good student, president of his graduating class, and active in athletics and on the school newspaper. He began college at Stanford University as an English major but left school in 1925 and spent the next five years traveling, reading, and writing.

In 1930 he married (the first of three times) and moved to Pacific Grove, California, where his father provided a house and small allowance to support him. He achieved success in 1935 with *Tortilla Flat*, his third novel. It was an episodic, warmly humorous treatment of the lives of Salinas Valley *paisanos*—ethnically mixed Mexican-Indian-Caucasians—whose earthy, uninhibited lives provided a colorful contrast (in Steinbeck's view) to the valley's "respectable society." The subject of his second successful novel, *In Dubious Battle* (1936), was a fruit pickers' strike. The decency of the exploited workers is played off, on one side, against the cynical landowners and their vigilantes and, on the other, against the equally cynical Communist organizers who try to use the workers' grievances for their own purposes. His sympathy for the underdog was shown again in *Of Mice and Men* (1937), about two itinerant ranch hands, and in *The Grapes of Wrath*, about the Joad family, who, after losing their land, migrated westward to California on U.S. Highway 66 looking for, but not finding, a better life.

After World War II Steinbeck's work became more sentimental and more heavily symbolic. Postwar prosperity led to suburbia, television, and the explosion of a highly commercialized mass culture, from which he turned in disgust. *The Leader of the People* expresses his sense that America's best times are past and locates value in the story's socially marginal characters—a child, an old man, and a farmhand. In a prewar automobile with his poodle, named Charlie, he toured America; the title of his account, *Travels with Charlie in Search of America* (1962), again reveals this conviction that "America" was now hard to find. He won the Novel Prize in 1963.

# The Leader of the People[1]

On Saturday afternoon Billy Buck, the ranch-hand, raked together the last of the old years' haystack and pitched small forkfuls over the wire fence to a few mildly interested cattle. High in the air small clouds like puffs of cannon smoke were driven eastward by the March wind. The wind could be heard whishing in the brush on the ridge crests, but no breath of it penetrated down into the ranch-cup.

The little boy, Jody, emerged from the house eating a thick piece of buttered bread. He saw Billy working on the last of the haystack. Jody tramped down scuffling his shoes in a way he had been told was destructive to good shoe-leather. A flock of white pigeons flew out of the black cypress tree as Jody passed, and circled the tree and landed again. A half-grown tortoise-shell cat leaped from the bunkhouse porch, galloped on stiff legs across the road, whirled and galloped back again. Jody picked up a stone to help the game along, but he was too late, for the cat was under the porch before the stone could be discharged. He threw the stone into the cypress tree and started the white pigeons on another whirling flight.

Arriving at the used-up haystack, the boy leaned against the barbed wire fence. "Will that be all of it, do you think?" he asked.

The middle-aged ranch-hand stopped his careful raking and stuck his fork into the ground. He took off his black hat and smoothed down his hair. "Nothing left of it that isn't soggy from ground moisture," he said. He replaced his hat and rubbed his dry leathery hands together.

"Ought to be plenty mice," Jody suggested.

"Lousy with them," said Billy. "Just crawling with mice."

"Well, maybe, when you get all through, I could call the dogs and hunt the mice."

"Sure, I guess you could," said Billy Buck. He lifted a forkful of the damp ground-hay and threw it into the air. Instantly three mice leaped out and burrowed frantically under the hay again.

Jody sighed with satisfaction. Those plump, sleek, arrogant mice were doomed. For eight months they had lived and multiplied in the haystack. They had been immune from cats, from traps, from poison and from Jody. They had grown smug in their security, overbearing and fat. Now the time of disaster had come; they would not survive another day.

Billy looked up at the top of the hills that surrounded the ranch. "Maybe you better ask your father before you do it," he suggested.

"Well, where is he? I'll ask him now."

---

1. This is the fourth story in *The Red Pony* (1945), the source of the text included here.

"He rode up to the ridge ranch after dinner. He'll be back pretty soon."

Jody slumped against the fence post. "I don't think he'd care."

As Billy went back to his work he said ominously, "You'd better ask him anyway. You know how he is."

Jody did know. His father, Carl Tiflin, insisted upon giving permission for anything that was done on the ranch, whether it was important or not. Jody sagged farther against the post until he was sitting on the ground. He looked up at the little puffs of wind-driven cloud. "Is it like to rain, Billy?"

"It might. The wind's good for it, but not strong enough."

"Well, I hope it don't rain until after I kill those damn mice." He looked over his shoulder to see whether Billy had noticed the mature profanity. Billy worked on without comment.

Jody turned back and looked at the side-hill where the road from the outside world came down. The hill was washed with lean March sunshine. Silver thistles, blue lupins and a few poppies bloomed among the sage bushes. Half-way up the hill Jody could see Doubletree Mutt, the black dog, digging in a squirrel hole. He paddled for a while and then paused to kick bursts of dirt out between his hind legs, and he dug with an earnestness which belied the knowledge he must have had that no dog had ever caught a squirrel by digging in a hole.

Suddenly, while Jody watched, the black dog stiffened, and backed out of the hole and looked up the hill toward the cleft in the ridge where the road came through. Jody looked up too. For a moment Carl Tiflin on horseback stood out against the pale sky and then he moved down the road toward the house. He carried something white in his hand.

The boy started to his feet. "He's got a letter," Jody cried. He trotted away toward the ranch house, for the letter would probably be read aloud and he wanted to be there. He reached the house before his father did, and ran in. He heard Carl dismount from his creaking saddle and slap the horse on the side to send it to the barn where Billy would unsaddle it and turn it out.

Jody ran into the kitchen. "We got a letter!" he cried.

His mother looked up from a pan of beans. "Who has?"

"Father has. I saw it in his hand."

Carl strode into the kitchen then, and Jody's mother asked, "Who's the letter from, Carl?"

He frowned quickly. "How did you know there was a letter?"

She nodded her head in the boy's direction. "Big-Britches Jody told me."

Jody was embarrassed.

His father looked down at him contemptuously. "He *is* getting to be a Big-Britches," Carl said. "He's minding everybody's business but his own. Got his big nose into everything."

Mrs. Tiflin relented a little. "Well, he hasn't enough to keep him busy. Who's the letter from?"

Carl still frowned on Jody. "I'll keep him busy if he isn't careful." He held out a sealed letter. "I guess it's from your father."

Mrs. Tiflin took a hairpin from her head and slit open the flap. Her lips pursed judiciously. Jody saw her eyes snap back and forth over the lines. "He says," she translated, "he says he's going to drive out Saturday to stay for a little while. Why, this is Saturday. The letter must have been delayed." She looked at the postmark. "This was mailed day before yesterday. It should have been here yesterday." She looked up questioningly at her husband, and then her face darkened angrily. "Now what have you got that look on you for? He doesn't come often."

Carl turned his eyes away from her anger. He could be stern with her most of the time, but when occasionally her temper arose, he could not combat it.

"What's the matter with you?" she demanded again.

In his explanation there was a tone of apology Jody himself might have used. "It's just that he talks," Carl said lamely. "Just talks."

"Well, what of it? You talk yourself."

"Sure I do. But your father only talks about one thing."

"Indians!" Jody broke in excitedly. "Indians and crossing the plains!"

Carl turned fiercely on him. "You get out, Mr. Big-Britches! Go on, now! Get out!"

Jody went miserably out the back door and closed the screen with elaborate quietness. Under the kitchen window his shamed, downcast eyes fell upon a curiously shaped stone, a stone of such fascination that he squatted down and picked it up and turned it over in his hands.

The voices came clearly to him through the open kitchen window. "Jody's damn well right," he heard his father say. "Just Indians and crossing the plains. I've heard that story about how the horses got driven off about a thousand times. He just goes on and on, and he never changes a word in the things he tells."

When Mrs. Tiflin answered her tone was so changed that Jody, outside the window, looked up from his study of the stone. Her voice had become soft and explanatory. Jody knew how her face would have changed to match the tone. She said quietly, "Look at it this way, Carl. That was the big thing in my father's life. He led a wagon train clear across the plains to the coast, and when it was finished, his life was done. It was a big thing to do, but it didn't last long enough. Look!" she continued, "it's as though he was born to do that, and after he finished it, there wasn't anything more for him to do but think about it and talk about it. If there'd been any farther west to go, he'd have gone. He's told me so himself. But at last there was the ocean. He lives right by the ocean where he had to stop."

She had caught Carl, caught him and entangled him in her soft tone.

"I've seen him," he agreed quietly. "He goes down and stares off west over the ocean." His voice sharpened a little. "And then he goes up to the Horse-shoe Club in Pacific Grove, and he tells people how the Indians drove off the horses."

She tried to catch him again. "Well, it's everything to him. You might be patient with him and pretend to listen."

Carl turned impatiently away. "Well, if it gets too bad, I can always go down to the bunkhouse and sit with Billy," he said irritably. He walked through the house and slammed the front door after him.

Jody ran to his chores. He dumped the grain to the chickens without chasing any of them. He gathered the eggs from the nests. He trotted into the house with the wood and interlaced it so carefully in the wood-box that two armloads seemed to fill it to overflowing.

His mother had finished the beans by now. She stirred up the fire and brushed off the stove-top with a turkey wing. Jody peered cautiously at her to see whether any rancor toward him remained. "Is he coming today?" Jody asked.

"That's what his letter said."

"Maybe I better walk up the road to meet him."

Mrs. Tiflin clanged the stove-lid shut. "That would be nice," she said. "He'd probably like to be met."

"I guess I'll just do it then."

Outside, Jody whistled shrilly to the dogs. "Come on up the hill," he commanded. The two dogs waved their tails and ran ahead. Along the roadside the sage had tender new tips. Jody tore off some pieces and rubbed them on his hands until the air was filled with the sharp wild smell. With a rush the dogs leaped from the road and yapped into the brush after a rabbit. That was the last Jody saw of them, for when they failed to catch the rabbit, they went back home.

Jody plodded on up the hill toward the ridge top. When he reached the little cleft where the road came through, the afternoon wind struck him and blew up his hair and ruffled his shirt. He looked down on the little hills and ridges below and then out at the huge green Salinas Valley. He could see the white town of Salinas far out in the flat and the flash of its windows under the waning sun. Directly below him, in an oak tree, a crow congress had convened. The tree was black with crows all cawing at once.

Then Jody's eyes followed the wagon road down from the ridge where he stood, and lost it behind a hill, and picked it up again on the other side. On that distant stretch he saw a cart slowly pulled by a bay horse. It disappeared behind the hill. Jody sat down on the ground and watched the place where the cart would reappear again. The wind sang on the hilltops and the puff-ball clouds hurried eastward.

Then the cart came into sight and stopped. A man dressed in black dismounted from the seat and walked to the horse's head. Although it was so far away, Jody knew he had unhooked the check-rein, for the horse's head dropped forward. The horse moved on, and the man walked slowly up the hill beside it. Jody gave a glad cry and ran down the road toward them. The squirrels bumped along off the road, and a road-runner flirted its tail and raced over the edge of the hill and sailed out like a glider.

Jody tried to leap into the middle of his shadow at every step. A stone rolled under his foot and he went down. Around a little bend he raced, and there, a short distance ahead, were his grandfather and the cart. The boy dropped from his unseemly running and approached at a dignified walk.

The horse plodded stumble-footedly up the hill and the old man walked beside it. In the lowering sun their giant shadows flickered darkly behind them. The grandfather was dressed in a black broadcloth suit and he wore kid congress gaiters[2] and a black tie on a short, hard collar. He carried his black slouch hat in his hand. His white beard was cropped close and his white eyebrows overhung his eyes like mustaches. The blue eyes were sternly merry. About the whole face and figure there was a granite dignity, so that every motion seemed an impossible thing. Once at rest, it seemed the old man would be stone, would never move again. His steps were slow and certain. Once made, no step could ever be retraced; once headed in a direction, the path would never bend nor the pace increase nor slow.

When Jody appeared around the bend, Grandfather waved his hat slowly in

---

2. A high-topped shoe, or spats. Grandfather is dressed quite formally, in keeping with his old-fashioned sense of dignity.

welcome, and he called, "Why, Jody! Come down to meet me, have you?"

Jody sidled near and turned and matched his step to the old man's step and stiffened his body and dragged his heels a little. "Yes, sir," he said. "We got your letter only today."

"Should have been here yesterday," said Grandfather. "It certainly should. How are all the folks?"

"They're fine, sir." He hesitated and then suggested shyly, "Would you like to come on a mouse hunt tomorrow, sir?"

"Mouse hunt, Jody?" Grandfather chuckled. "Have the people of this generation come down to hunting mice? They aren't very strong, the new people, but I hardly thought mice would be game for them."

"No, sir. It's just play. The haystack's gone. I'm going to drive out the mice to the dogs. And you can watch, or even beat the hay a little."

The stern, merry eyes turned down on him. "I see. You don't eat them, then. You haven't come to that yet."

Jody explained, "The dogs eat them, sir. It wouldn't be much like hunting Indians, I guess."

"No, not much—but then later, when the troops were hunting Indians and shooting children and burning teepees, it wasn't much different from your mouse hunt."

They topped the rise and started down into the ranch-cup, and they lost the sun from their shoulders. "You've grown," Grandfather said. "Nearly an inch, I should say."

"More" Jody boasted. "Where they mark me on the door, I'm up more than an inch since Thanksgiving even."

Grandfather's rich throaty voice said, "Maybe you're getting too much water and turning to pith and stalk. Wait until you head out, and then we'll see."

Jody looked quickly into the old man's face to see whether his feelings should be hurt, but there was no will to injure, no punishing nor putting-in-your-place light in the keen blue eyes. "We might kill a pig," Jody suggested.

"Oh, no! I couldn't let you do that. You're just humoring me. It isn't the time and you know it."

"You know Riley, the big boar, sir?"

"Yes, I remember Riley well."

"Well, Riley ate a hole into that same haystack, and it fell down on him and smothered him."

"Pigs do that when they can," said Grandfather.

"Riley was a nice pig, for a boar, sir. I rode him sometimes, and he didn't mind."

A door slammed at the house below them, and they saw Jody's mother standing on the porch waving her apron in welcome. And they saw Carl Tiflin walking up from the barn to be at the house for the arrival.

The sun had disappeared from the hills by now. The blue smoke from the house chimney hung in flat layers in the purpling ranch-cup. The puff-ball clouds, dropped by the falling wind, hung listlessly in the sky.

Billy Buck came out of the bunkhouse and flung a wash basin of soapy water on the ground. He had been shaving in mid-week, for Billy held Grandfather in reverence, and Grandfather said that Billy was one of the few men of the new generation who had not gone soft. Although Billy was in middle age, Grandfather considered him a boy. Now Billy was hurrying toward the house too.

When Jody and Grandfather arrived, the three were waiting for them in front of the yard gate.

Carl said, "Hello, sir. We've been looking for you."

Mrs. Tiflin kissed Grandfather on the side of his beard, and stood still while his big hand patted her shoulder. Billy shook hands solemnly, grinning under his straw mustache. "I'll put up your horse," said Billy, and he led the rig away.

Grandfather watched him go, and then, turning back to the group, he said as he had said a hundred times before, "There's a good boy. I knew his father, old Mule-tail Buck. I never knew why they called him Mule-tail except he packed mules."

Mrs. Tiflin turned and led the way into the house. "How long are you going to stay, Father? Your letter didn't say."

"Well, I don't know. I thought I'd stay about two weeks. But I never stay as long as I think I'm going to."

In a short while they were sitting at the white oilcloth table eating their supper. The lamp with the tin reflector hung over the table. Outside the dining-room windows the big moths battered softly against the glass.

Grandfather cut his steak into tiny pieces and chewed slowly. "I'm hungry," he said. "Driving out here got my appetite up. It's like when we were crossing. We all got so hungry every night we could hardly wait to let the meat get done. I could eat about five pounds of buffalo meat every night."

"It's moving around does it," said Billy. "My father was a government packer. I helped him when I was a kid. Just the two of us could about clean up a deer's ham."

"I knew your father, Billy," said Grandfather. "A fine man he was. They called him Mule-tail Buck. I don't know why except he packed mules."

"That was it," Bill agreed. "He packed mules."

Grandfather put down his knife and fork and looked around the table. "I remember one time we ran out of meat—" His voice dropped to a curious low sing-song, dropped into a tonal groove the story had worn for itself. "There was no buffalo, no antelope, not even rabbits. The hunters couldn't even shoot a coyote. That was the time for the leader to be on the watch. I was the leader, and I kept my eyes open. Know why? Well, just the minute the people began to get hungry they'd start slaughtering the team oxen. Do you believe that? I've heard of parties that just ate up their draft cattle. Started from the middle and worked toward the ends. Finally they'd eat the lead pair, and then the wheelers. The leader of a party had to keep them from doing that."

In some manner a big moth got into the room and circled the hanging kerosene lamp. Billy got up and tried to clap it between his hands. Carl struck with a cupped palm and caught the moth and broke it. He walked to the window and dropped it out.

"As I was saying," Grandfather began again, but Carl interrupted him. "You'd better eat some more meat. All the rest of us are ready for our pudding."

Jody saw a flash of anger in his mother's eyes. Grandfather picked up his knife and fork. "I'm pretty hungry, all right," he said. "I'll tell you about that later."

When supper was over, when the family and Billy Buck sat in front of the fireplace in the other room, Jody anxiously watched Grandfather. He saw the signs he knew. The bearded head leaned forward; the eyes lost their sternness and looked wonderingly into the fire; the big lean fingers laced themselves on the black knees. "I wonder," he began, "I just wonder whether I ever told you how those thieving Piutes drove off thirty-five of our horses."

"I think you did," Carl interrupted. "Wasn't it just before you went up into the Tahoe country?"

Grandfather turned quickly toward his son-in-law. "That's right. I guess I must have told you that story."

"Lots of times," Carl said cruelly, and he avoided his wife's eyes. But he felt the angry eyes on him, and he said, " 'Course I'd like to hear it again."

Grandfather looked back at the fire. His fingers unlaced and laced again. Jody knew how he felt, how his insides were collapsed and empty. Hadn't Jody been called a Big-Britches that very afternoon? He arose to heroism and opened himself to the term Big-Britches again. "Tell about Indians," he said softly.

Grandfather's eyes grew stern again. "Boys always want to hear about Indians. It was a job for men, but boys want to hear about it. Well, let's see. Did I ever tell you how I wanted each wagon to carry a long iron plate?"

Everyone but Jody remained silent. Jody said, "No. You didn't."

"Well, when the Indians attacked, we always put the wagons in a circle and fought from between the wheels. I thought that if every wagon carried a long plate with rifle holes, the men could stand the plates on the outside of the wheels when the wagons were in the circle and they would be protected. It would save lives and that would make up for the extra weight of the iron. But of course the party wouldn't do it. No party had done it before and they couldn't see why they should go to the expense. They lived to regret it, too."

Jody looked at his mother, and knew from her expression that she was not listening at all. Carl picked at a callus on his thumb and Billy Buck watched a spider crawling up the wall.

Grandfather's tone dropped into its narrative groove again. Jody knew in advance exactly what words would fall. The story droned on, speeded up for the attack, grew sad over the wounds, struck a dirge at the burials on the great plains. Jody sat quietly watching Grandfather. The stern blue eyes were detached. He looked as though he were not very interested in the story himself.

When it was finished, when the pause had been politely respected as the frontier of the story, Billy Buck stood up and stretched and hitched his trousers. "I guess I'll turn in," he said. Then he faced Grandfather. "I've got an old powder horn and a cap and ball pistol down to the bunkhouse. Did I ever show them to you?"

Grandfather nodded slowly. "Yes, I think you did, Billy. Reminds me of a pistol I had when I was leading the people across." Billy stood politely until the story was done, and then he said, "Good night," and went out of the house.

Carl Tiflin tried to turn the conversation then. "How's the country between here and Monterey?[3] I've heard it's pretty dry."

"It is dry," said Grandfather. "There's not a drop of water in the Laguna Seca.[4] But it's a long pull from '87. The whole country was powder then, and in '61 I believe all the coyotes starved to death. We had fifteen inches of rain this year."

"Yes, but it all came too early. We could do with some now." Carl's eye fell on Jody. "Hadn't you better be getting to bed?"

---

3. Peninsula jutting into the Pacific Ocean south of San Francisco—the western-most tip of the continent.    4. Dry Lagoon (Spanish).

Jody stood up obediently. "Can I kill the mice in the old haystack, sir?"
"Mice? Oh! Sure, kill them all off. Billy said there isn't any good hay left."
Jody exchanged a secret and satisfying look with Grandfather. "I'll kill every one tomorrow," he promised.

Jody lay in his bed and thought of the impossible world of Indians and buffaloes, a world that had ceased to be forever. He wished he could have been living in the heroic time, but he knew he was not of heroic timber. No one living now, save possibly Billy Buck, was worthy to do the things that had been done. A race of giants had lived then, fearless men, men of a staunchness unknown in this day. Jody thought of the wide plains and of the wagons moving across like centipedes. He thought of Grandfather on a huge white horse, marshaling the people. Across his mind marched the great phantoms, and they marched off the earth and they were gone.

He came back to the ranch for a moment, then. He heard the dull rushing sound that space and silence make. He heard one of the dogs, out in the doghouse, scratching a flea and bumping his elbow against the floor with every stroke. Then the wind arose again and the black cypress groaned and Jody went to sleep.

He was up half an hour before the triangle sounded for breakfast. His mother was rattling the stove to make the flames roar when Jody went through the kitchen. "You're up early," she said. "Where are you going?"

"Out to get a good stick. We're going to kill the mice today."

"Who is 'we'?"

"Why, Grandfather and I."

"So you've got him in it. You always like to have someone in with you in case there's blame to share."

"I'll be right back," said Jody. "I just want to have a good stick ready for after breakfast."

He closed the screen door after him and went out into the cool blue morning. The birds were noisy in the dawn and the ranch cats came down from the hill like blunt snakes. They had been hunting gophers in the dark, and although the four cats were full of gopher meat, they sat in a semi-circle at the back door and mewed piteously for milk. Doubletree Mutt and Smasher moved sniffing along the edge of the brush, performing the duty with rigid ceremony, but when Jody whistled, their heads jerked up and their tails waved. They plunged down to him, wriggling their skins and yawning. Jody patted their heads seriously, and moved on to the weathered scrap pile. He selected an old broom handle and a short piece of inch-square scrap wood. From his pocket he took a shoelace and tied the ends of the sticks loosely together to make a flail. He whistled his new weapon through the air and struck the ground experimentally, while the dogs leaped aside and whined with apprehension.

Jody turned and started down past the house toward the old haystack ground to look over the field of slaughter, but Billy Buck, sitting patiently on the back steps, called to him, "You better come back. It's only a couple of minutes till breakfast."

Jody changed his course and moved toward the house. He leaned his flail against the steps. "That's to drive the mice out," he said. "I'll bet they're fat. I'll bet they don't know what's going to happen to them today."

"No, nor you either," Billy remarked philosophically, "nor me, nor anyone."

Jody was staggered by this thought. He knew it was true. His imagination twitched away from the mouse hunt. Then his mother came out on the back porch and struck the triangle, and all thoughts fell in a heap.

Grandfather hadn't appeared at the table when they sat down. Billy nodded at his empty chair. "He's all right? He isn't sick?"

"He takes a long time to dress," said Mrs. Tiflin. "He combs his whiskers and rubs up his shoes and brushes his clothes."

Carl scattered sugar on his mush. "A man that's led a wagon train across the plains has got to be pretty careful how he dresses."

Mrs. Tiflin turned on him. "Don't do that, Carl! Please don't!" There was more of threat than of request in her tone. And the threat irritated Carl.

"Well, how many times do I have to listen to the story of the iron plates, and the thirty-five horses? That time's done. Why can't he forget it, now it's done?" He grew angrier while he talked, and his voice rose. "Why does he have to tell them over and over? He came across the plains. All right! Now it's finished. Nobody wants to hear about it over and over."

The door into the kitchen closed softly. The four at the table sat frozen. Carl laid his mush spoon on the table and touched his chin with his fingers.

Then the kitchen door opened and Grandfather walked in. His mouth smiled tightly and his eyes were squinted. "Good morning," he said, and he sat down and looked at his mush dish.

Carl could not leave it there. "Did—did you hear what I said?"

Grandfather jerked a little nod.

"I don't know what got into me, sir. I didn't mean it. I was just being funny."

Jody glanced in shame at his mother, and he saw that she was looking at Carl, and that she wasn't breathing. It was an awful thing that he was doing. He was tearing himself to pieces to talk like that. It was a terrible thing to him to retract a word, but to retract it in shame was infinitely worse.

Grandfather looked sidewise. "I'm trying to get right side up," he said gently. "I'm not being mad. I don't mind what you said, but it might be true, and I would mind that."

"It isn't true," said Carl. "I'm not feeling well this morning. I'm sorry I said it."

"Don't be sorry, Carl. An old man doesn't see things sometimes. Maybe you're right. The crossing is finished. Maybe it should be forgotten, now it's done."

Carl got up from the table. "I've had enough to eat. I'm going to work. Take your time, Billy!" He walked quickly out of the dining-room. Billy gulped the rest of his food and followed soon after. But Jody could not leave his chair.

"Won't you tell any more stories?" Jody asked.

"Why, sure I'll tell them, but only when—I'm sure people want to hear them."

"I like to hear them, sir."

"Oh! Of course you do, but you're a little boy. It was a job for men, but only little boys like to hear about it."

Jody got up from his place. "I'll wait outside for you, sir. I've got a good stick for those mice."

He waited by the gate until the old man came out on the porch. "Let's go down and kill the mice now," Jody called.

"I think I'll just sit in the sun, Jody. You go kill the mice."

"You can use my stick if you like."

"No, I'll just sit here a while."

Jody turned disconsolately away, and walked down toward the old haystack. He tried to whip up his enthusiasm with thoughts of the fat juicy mice. He beat the ground with his flail. The dogs coaxed and whined about him, but he could not go. Back at the house he could see Grandfather sitting on the porch, looking small and thin and black.

Jody gave up and went to sit on the steps at the old man's feet.

"Back already? Did you kill the mice?"

"No, sir. I'll kill them some other day."

The morning flies buzzed close to the ground and the ants dashed about in front of the steps. The heavy smell of sage slipped down the hill. The porch boards grew warm in the sunshine.

Jody hardly knew when Grandfather started to talk. "I shouldn't stay here, feeling the way I do." He examined his strong old hands. "I feel as though the crossing wasn't worth doing." His eyes moved up the side-hill and stopped on a motionless hawk perched on a dead limb. "I tell those old stories, but they're not what I want to tell. I only know how I want people to feel when I tell them.

"It wasn't Indians that were important, nor adventures, nor even getting out here. It was a whole bunch of people made into one big crawling beast. And I was the head. It was westering and westering. Every man wanted something for himself, but the big beast that was all of them wanted only westering. I was the leader, but if I hadn't been there, someone else would have been the head. The thing had to have a head.

"Under the little bushes the shadows were black at white noonday. When we saw the mountains at last, we cried—all of us. But it wasn't getting here that mattered, it was movement and westering.

"We carried life out here and set it down the way those ants carry eggs. And I was the leader. The westering was as big as God, and the slow steps that made the movement piled up and piled up until the continent was crossed.

"Then we came down to the sea, and it was done." He stopped and wiped his eyes until the rims were red. "That's what I should be telling instead of stories."

When Jody spoke, Grandfather started and looked down at him. "Maybe I could lead the people some day," Jody said.

The old man smiled. "There's no place to go. There's the ocean to stop you. There's a line of old men along the shore hating the ocean because it stopped them."

"In boats I might, sir."

"No place to go, Jody. Every place is taken. But that's not the worst—no, not the worst. Westering has died out of the people. Westering isn't a hunger any more. It's all done. Your father is right. It is finished." He laced his fingers on his knee and looked at them.

Jody felt very sad. "If you'd like a glass of lemonade I could make it for you."

Grandfather was about to refuse, and then he saw Jody's face. "That would be nice," he said. "Yes, it would be nice to drink a lemonade."

Jody ran into the kitchen where his mother was wiping the last of the breakfast dishes. "Can I have a lemon to make a lemonade for Grandfather?"

His mother mimicked—"And another lemon to make a lemonade for you."

"No, ma'am. I don't want one."

"Jody! You're sick!" Then she stopped suddenly. "Take a lemon out of the cooler," she said softly. "Here, I'll reach the squeezer down to you."

1945

---

# COUNTEE CULLEN
## 1903–1946

The African-American artists associated with the Harlem Renaissance faced difficult problems as they attempted to enunciate a collective identity for themselves and their people. Should they demonstrate excellence by working within traditional art forms, or should they develop new forms specifically derived from black experience? Should they write (or paint, or sing) only about their experiences as black people, or should they write like Americans, or about universal issues? If the answer was always to write as blacks, could it be maintained that there was just one black experience common to all African-Americans? Countee Cullen, a black middle-class New Yorker, experienced these issues in a particularly divisive fashion: he wanted to be a traditional poet but felt it his duty to articulate a black experience that was not entirely his own.

He was the adopted son of a Methodist minister and enjoyed a secure, comfortable childhood. He attended New York public schools, and traveled to Europe. He earned a Phi Beta Kappa key at New York University, where he received his B.A. in 1925; he took an M.A. at Harvard in 1926. He returned to New York as a public-school teacher. His first book of poems, *Color*, appeared in 1925, when he was only twenty-two. His youth, his technical proficiency, and the themes of the poems—truth, beauty, and goodness, in the world of time and circumstance—established him as the "black Keats," a prodigy.

Cullen's anthology of black poetry, *Caroling Dusk* (1927), was an important document for Harlem Renaissance poets. He prefaced his selection with the assertion that the forms of English poetry, not transcriptions of black dialects or militant manifestos, were the proper tools of the artist. In this idea he went counter to the practices of such other Harlem writers as Zora Neale Hurston and Langston Hughes; he wanted to be a poet as he understood poets to be. Nevertheless, the titles of his books—*Color* as well as *Copper Sun* in 1927 and *The Ballad of the Brown Girl* in 1928—showed that he felt a responsibility to write about being black even if he did so in modes alien to black folk traditions. And he acknowledged in the preface to *Caroling Dusk* that it was not easy to be both a black and an American.

Cullen won a Guggenheim Fellowship to complete *The Black Christ* in 1929 and published a novel, *One Way to Heaven*, in 1932. He succeeded in his aim of becoming a literary man recognized for his skill as a traditional artist, but it is an important part of his achievement that in an era when American society was far more racially segregated than it is now he worked to bring black themes to the awareness of white readers who admired him because he exploited poetic modes that they found familiar.

The text of *From the Dark Tower* is that of *Copper Sun* (1927); the text of the other poems included here is that of *Color* (1925).

# Yet Do I Marvel

I doubt not God is good, well-meaning, kind,
And did He stoop to quibble could tell why
The little buried mole continues blind,
Why flesh that mirrors Him must some day die,
Make plain the reason tortured Tantalus[1]     5
Is baited by the fickle fruit, declare
If merely brute caprice dooms Sisyphus
To struggle up a never-ending stair.
Inscrutable His ways are, and immune
To catechism by a mind too strewn     10
With petty cares to slightly understand
What awful brain compels His awful hand.
Yet do I marvel at this curious thing:
To make a poet black, and bid him sing!

1925

# Incident

Once riding in old Baltimore,
    Heart-filled, head-filled with glee,
I saw a Baltimorean
    Keep looking straight at me.

Now I was eight and very small,     5
    And he was no whit bigger,
And so I smiled, but he poked out
    His tongue, and called me, "Nigger."

I saw the whole of Baltimore
    From May until December;     10
Of all the things that happened there
    That's all that I remember.

1925

# Heritage

What is Africa to me:
Copper sun or scarlet sea,
Jungle star or jungle track,
Strong bronzed men, or regal black
Women from whose loins I sprang     5
When the birds of Eden sang?
*One three centuries removed*

---

1. Tantalus and Sisyphus (line 7) are figures in Greek mythology who were punished in Hades for crimes committed on earth. Tantalus's punishment was to be offered food and water that was then instantly snatched away. Sisyphus's torment was to roll a heavy stone to the top of a hill and, after it rolled back down, to repeat the ordeal perpetually.

*From the scenes his fathers loved,*
*Spicy grove, cinnamon tree,*
*What is Africa to me?*                                    10

So I lie, who all day long
Want no sound except the song
Sung by wild barbaric birds
Goading massive jungle herds,
Juggernauts[1] of flesh that pass                          15
Trampling tall defiant grass
Where young forest lovers lie,
Plighting troth beneath the sky.
So I lie, who always hear,
Though I cram against my ear                               20
Both my thumbs, and keep them there,
Great drums throbbing through the air.
So I lie, whose fount of pride,
Dear distress, and joy allied,
Is my somber flesh and skin,                              25
With the dark blood dammed within
Like great pulsing tides of wine
That, I fear, must burst the fine
Channels of the chafing net
Where they surge and foam and fret.                       30

Africa? A book one thumbs
Listlessly, till slumber comes.
Unremembered are her bats
Circling through the night, her cats
Crouching in the river reeds,                             35
Stalking gentle flesh that feeds
By the river brink; no more
Does the bugle-throated roar
Cry that monarch claws have leapt
From the scabbards where they slept.                      40
Silver snakes that once a year
Doff the lovely coats you wear,
Seek no covert in your fear
Lest a mortal eye should see;
What's your nakedness to me?                              45
Here no leprous flowers rear
Fierce corollas[2] in the air;
Here no bodies sleek and wet,
Dripping mingled rain and sweat,
Tread the savage measures of                              50
Jungle boys and girls in love.
What is last year's snow to me,[3]

---

1. The juggernaut is a sacred Hindu idol dragged on a huge car in the path of which devotees were believed to throw themselves. Hence any power demanding blind sacrifice, here spliced with the image of elephants.
2. The whorl of petals forming the inner envelope of a flower.
3. An echo of the lament "Where are the snows of yesteryear?" from the poem *Grand Testament* by the 15th-century French poet François Villon.

Last year's anything? The tree
Budding yearly must forget
How its past arose or set—                                    55
Bough and blossom, flower, fruit,
Even what shy bird with mute
Wonder at her travail there,
Meekly labored in its hair.
*One three centuries removed*                                 60
*From the scenes his fathers loved,*
*Spicy grove, cinnamon tree,*
*What is Africa to me?*

So I lie, who find no peace
Night or day, no slight release                              65
From the unremittant beat
Made by cruel padded feet
Walking through my body's street.
Up and down they go, and back,
Treading out a jungle track.                                 70
So I lie, who never quite
Safely sleep from rain at night—
I can never rest at all
When the rain begins to fall;
Like a soul gone mad with pain                               75
I must match its weird refrain;
Ever must I twist and squirm,
Writhing like a baited worm,
While its primal measures drip
Through my body, crying, "Strip!                             80
Doff this new exuberance.
Come and dance the Lover's Dance!"
In an old remembered way
Rain works on me night and day.

Quaint, outlandish heathen gods                              85
Black men fashion out of rods,
Clay, and brittle bits of stone,
In a likeness like their own,
My conversion came high-priced;
I belong to Jesus Christ,                                    90
Preacher of humility;
Heathen gods are naught to me.

Father, Son, and Holy Ghost,
So I make an idle boast;
Jesus of the twice-turned cheek[4]                           95
Lamb of God, although I speak
With my mouth thus, in my heart
Do I play a double part.

---

4. In his Sermon on the Mount (Matthew 5.39), Jesus declared that when struck on one cheek, one should turn the other cheek rather than strike back.

Ever at Thy glowing altar
Must my heart grow sick and falter,                          100
Wishing He I served were black,
Thinking then it would not lack
Precedent of pain to guide it,
Let who would or might deride it;
Surely then this flesh would know                            105
Yours had borne a kindred woe.
Lord, I fashion dark gods, too,
Daring even to give You
Dark despairing features where,
Crowned with dark rebellious hair,                           110
Patience wavers just so much as
Mortal grief compels, while touches
Quick and hot, of anger, rise
To smitten cheek and weary eyes.
Lord, forgive me if my need                                  115
Sometimes shapes a human creed.
*All day long and all night through,*
*One thing only must I do:*
*Quench my pride and cool my blood,*
*Lest I perish in the flood.*                                120
*Lest a hidden ember set*
*Timber that I thought was wet*
*Burning like the dryest flax,*
*Melting like the merest wax,*
*Lest the grave restore its dead.*                           125
*Not yet has my heart or head*
*In the least way realized*
*They and I are civilized.*

                                                    1925

---

# RICHARD WRIGHT
## 1908–1960

With the 1940 publication of *Native Son* Richard Wright became the first black American author of a best-seller. *Native Son* is an uncompromising study of an African-American underclass youth who is goaded to brutal violence by the oppression, hatred, and incomprehension of the white world. The sensational story disregarded conventional wisdom about how black authors should approach a white reading audience. Bigger Thomas, the main character, embodied everything that such an audience might fear and detest, but by situating the point of view within this character's consciousness Wright forced readers to see the world through Bigger's eyes and thus to understand him. The novel was structured like a hard-boiled detective story, contained layers of literary allusion and symbol, and combined Marxist social analysis with existential philosophy—in brief, it was at once a powerful social statement and a complex work of literary art.

Wright was born near Natchez, Mississippi. When he was five, his father abandoned the family—Wright, his younger brother, and his mother—and for the next ten years Wright was raised by a series of relatives in Mississippi. By 1925, when he went to Memphis on his own, he had moved twenty times. Extreme poverty, a constantly interrupted education that never went beyond junior high school, and the religious fundamentalism of his grandmother, along with the constant experiences of humiliation and hatred in a racially segregated South: all these contributed to Wright's growing sense that the hidden anger of black people was justified and that only by acknowledging and expressing it could they move beyond it. The title of Native Son made the point that the United States is as much the country of black as of white; the story showed that blacks had been deprived of their inheritance.

Two years after moving to Memphis, Wright went north to Chicago. Here he took a series of odd jobs and then joined the WPA Writers' Project (a government project of the Depression years to help support authors) as a writer of guidebooks and as a director of the Federal Negro Theater. He began to study Marxist theory, contributing poetry to leftist literary magazines and joining the Communist party in 1932. By 1935 he had become the center of a group of African-American Chicago writers and had started to write fiction. He was influenced by the naturalistic fiction of James T. Farrell, whose study of sociology at the University of Chicago had helped give structure to his popular Studs Lonigan trilogy about Irish working people.

Wright moved to New York in 1937 to write for the New York Writers' Project and as a reporter on the Communist Daily Worker. In 1938 he published Uncle Tom's Children, a collection of four short stories. (An earlier novel, Lawd Today, was not published until after his death.) Set in the rural South, the stories center on racial conflict and physical violence. Wright's theme of the devastating effect of relentless, institutionalized hatred and humiliation on the black male's psyche was paramount in all of them.

After Native Son, Wright turned to autobiographical writings that eventuated in Black Boy, published in 1945. Many consider this to be his best book, and such writers as Ralph Ellison and James Baldwin took it as a model for their own work in the 1950s and 1960s. A Communist activist in the early 1940s, Wright became increasingly disillusioned and broke completely with the party in 1944. Visiting France in 1946, he was warmly received by leading writers and philosophers. In 1947 he settled permanently in that country, where he was perceived from the first as one of the important experimental modernist prose writers and was ranked on a level with Hemingway, Fitzgerald, and Faulkner. An existential novel, The Outsider (1953), was followed by five more books: two novels and three collections of lectures, travel writings, and sociopolitical commentary. The collection Eight Men, from which the story printed here is taken, was the last literary project he worked on and appeared the year after his death.

Wright's immersion in Marxist doctrine gave him tools for representing society as divided into antagonistic classes and run for the benefit of the few. But in each of his works he portrays individuals who, no matter how they are deformed and brutalized by oppression and exploitation, retain a transcendent spark of selfhood. Ultimately, it is in this spark that Wright put his faith. His writing from first to last affirmed the dignity and humanity of society's outcasts without romanticizing them, and indicted those who had cast them out. As Ralph Ellison expressed it, Wright's example "converted the American Negro impulse toward self-annihilation and 'going underground' into a will to confront the world" and to "throw his findings unashamedly into the guilty conscience of America."

# The Man Who Was Almost a Man[1]

Dave struck out across the fields, looking homeward through paling light. Whut's the use talkin wid em niggers in the field? Anyhow, his mother was putting supper on the table. Them niggers can't understan nothing. One of these days he was going to get a gun and practice shooting, then they couldn't talk to him as though he were a little boy. He slowed, looking at the ground. Shucks, Ah ain scareda them even ef they are biggern me! Aw, Ah know whut Ahma do. Ahm going by ol Joe's sto n git that Sears Roebuck catlog n look at them guns. Mebbe Ma will lemme buy one when she gits mah pay from ol man Hawkins. Ahma beg her t gimme some money. Ahm ol ernough to hava gun. Ahm seventeen. Almost a man. He strode, feeling his long loose-jointed limbs. Shucks, a man oughta hava little gun aftah he done worked hard all day.

He came in sight of Joe's store. A yellow lantern glowed on the front porch. He mounted steps and went through the screen door, hearing it bang behind him. There was a strong smell of coal oil and mackerel fish. He felt very confident until he saw fat Joe walk in through the rear door, then his courage began to ooze.

"Howdy, Dave! Whutcha want?"

"How yuh. Mistah Joe? Aw, Ah don wanna buy nothing. Ah jus wanted t see ef yuhd lemme look at tha catlog erwhile."

"Sure! You wanna see it here?"

"Nawsuh. Ah wans t take it home wid me. Ah'll bring it back termorrow when Ah come in from the fiels."

"You plannin on buying something?"

"Yessuh."

"Your ma lettin you have your own money now?"

"Shucks. Mistah Joe, Ahm gittin t be a man like anybody else!"

Joe laughed and wiped his greasy white face with a red bandanna.

"Whut you plannin on buyin?"

Dave looked at the floor, scratched his head, scratched his thigh, and smiled. Then he looked up shyly.

"Ah'll tell yuh, Mistah Joe, ef yuh promise yuh won't tell."

"I promise."

"Waal, Ahma buy a gun."

"A gun? What you want with a gun?"

"Ah wanna keep it."

"You ain't nothing but a boy. You don't need a gun."

"Aw, lemme have the catlog, Mistah Joe. Ah'll bring it back."

Joe walked through the rear door. Dave was elated. He looked around at barrels of sugar and flour. He heard Joe coming back. He craned his neck to see if he were bringing the book. Yeah, he's got it. Gawddog, he's got it!

"Here, but be sure you bring it back. It's the only one I got."

"Sho, Mistah Joe."

"Say, if you wanna buy a gun, why don't you buy one from me? I gotta gun to sell."

---

1. This story was first published in *Harper's Bazaar* (1939) under the title *Almos' a Man*. Under its present title it appeared in *Eight Men* (1961), a posthumous collection of Wright's short fiction.

"Will it shoot?"

"Sure it'll shoot."

"Whut kind is it?"

"Oh, it's kinda old . . . a left-hand Wheeler. A pistol. A big one."

"Is it got bullets in it?"

"It's loaded."

"Kin Ah see it?"

"Where's your money?"

"What yuh wan fer it?"

"I'll let you have it for two dollars."

"Just two dollahs? Shucks, Ah could buy tha when Ah git mah pay."

"I'll have it here when you want it."

"Awright, suh. Ah be in fer it."

He went through the door, hearing it slam again behind him. Ahma git some money from Ma n buy me a gun! Only two dollahs! He tucked the thick catalogue under his arm and hurried.

"Where yuh been, boy?" His mother held a steaming dish of black-eyed peas.

"Aw, Ma, Ah just stopped down the road t talk wid the boys."

"Yuh know bettah t keep suppah waitin."

He sat down, resting the catalogue on the edge of the table.

"Yuh git up from there and git to the well n wash yosef! Ah ain feedin no hogs in mah house!"

She grabbed his shoulder and pushed him. He stumbled out of the room, then came back to get the catalogue.

"Whut this?"

"Aw, Ma, it's jusa catlog."

"Who yuh git it from?"

"From Joe, down at the sto."

"Waal, thas good. We kin use it in the outhouse."

"Naw, Ma." He grabbed for it. "Gimme ma catlog, Ma."

She held onto it and glared at him.

"Quit hollerin at me! Whut's wrong wid yuh? Yuh crazy?"

"But Ma, please. It ain mine! It's Joe's! He tol me t bring it back t im termorrow."

She gave up the book. He stumbled down the back steps, hugging the thick book under his arm. When he had splashed water on his face and hands, he groped back to the kitchen and fumbled in a corner for the towel. He bumped into a chair; it clattered to the floor. The catalogue sprawled at his feet. When he had dried his eyes he snatched up the book and held it again under his arm. His mother stood watching him.

"Now, ef yuh gonna act a fool over that ol book, Ah'll take it n burn it up."

"Naw, Ma, please."

"Waal, set down n be still!"

He sat down and drew the oil lamp close. He thumbed page after page, unaware of the food his mother set on the table. His father came in. Then his small brother.

"Whutcha got there, Dave?" his father asked.

"Jusa catlog," he answered, not looking up.

"Yeah, here they is!" His eyes glowed at blue-and-black revolvers. He glanced up, feeling sudden guilt. His father was watching him. He eased the book under the table and rested it on his knees. After the blessing was asked, he ate. He scooped up peas and swallowed fat meat without chewing. Buttermilk helped to wash it down. He did not want to mention money before his father. He would do much better by cornering his mother when she was alone. He looked at his father uneasily out of the edge of his eye.

"Boy, how come yuh don quit foolin wid tha book n eat yo suppah?"

"Yessuh."

"How you n ol man Hawkins gitten erlong?"

"Suh?"

"Can't yuh hear? Why don yuh lissen? Ah ast yu how wuz yuh n ol man Hawkins gittin erlong?"

"Oh, swell, Pa. Ah plows mo lan than anybody over there."

"Waal, yuh oughta keep yo mind on whut yuh doin."

"Yessuh."

He poured his plate full of molasses and sopped it up slowly with a chunk of cornbread. When his father and brother had left the kitchen, he still sat and looked again at the guns in the catalogue, longing to muster courage enough to present his case to his mother. Lawd, ef Ah only had tha pretty one! He could almost feel the slickness of the weapon with his fingers. If he had a gun like that he would polish it and keep it shining so it would never rust. N Ah'd keep it loaded, by Gawd!

"Ma?" His voice was hesitant.

"Hunh?"

"Ol man Hawkins give yuh mah money yit?"

"Yeah, but ain no usa yuh thinking bout throwin nona it erway. Ahm keepin tha money sos yuh kin have cloes t go to school this winter."

He rose and went to her side with the open catalogue in his palms. She was washing dishes, her head bent low over a pan. Shyly he raised the book. When he spoke, his voice was husky, faint.

"Ma, Gawd knows Ah wans one of these."

"One of whut?" she asked, not raising her eyes.

"One of these," he said again, not daring even to point. She glanced up at the page, then at him with wide eyes.

"Nigger, is yuh gone plumb crazy?"

"Aw, Ma—"

"Git outta here! Don yuh talk t me bout no gun! Yuh a fool!"

"Ma, Ah kin buy one fer two dollahs."

"Not ef Ah knows it, yuh ain!"

"But yuh promised me one—"

"Ah don care whut Ah promised! Yuh ain nothing but a boy yit!"

"Ma, ef yuh lemme buy one Ah'll *never* ast yuh fer nothing no mo."

"Ah tol yuh t git outta here! Yuh ain gonna toucha penny of tha money fer no gun! Thas how come Ah has Mistah Hawkins t pay yo wages t me, cause Ah knows yuh ain got no sense."

"But, Ma, we needa gun. Pa ain got no gun. We needa gun in the house. Yuh kin never tell whut might happen."

"Now don yuh try to maka fool outta me, boy! Ef we did hava gun, yuh wouldn't have it!"

He laid the catalogue down and slipped his arm around her waist.

"Aw, Ma, Ah done worked hard alla summer n ain ast yuh fer nothin, is Ah, now?"

"Thas whut yuh spose t do!"

"But Ma, Ah wans a gun. Yuh kin lemme have two dollahs outta mah money. Please, Ma. I kin give it to Pa . . . Please, Ma! Ah loves yuh, Ma."

When she spoke her voice came soft and low.

"What yuh wan wida gun, Dave? Yuh don need no gun. Yuh'll git in trouble. N ef yo pa jus thought Ah let yuh have money t buy a gun he'd hava fit."

"Ah'll hide it, Ma. It ain but two dollahs."

"Lawd, chil, whut's wrong wid yuh?"

"Ain nothing wrong, Ma. Ahm almos a man now. Ah wans a gun."

"Who gonna sell yuh a gun?"

"Ol Joe at the sto."

"N it don cos but two dollahs?"

"Thas all, Ma. Just two dollahs. Please, Ma."

She was stacking the plates away; her hands moved slowly, reflectively. Dave kept an anxious silence. Finally, she turned to him.

"Ah'll let yuh git tha gun ef yuh promise me one thing."

"Whut's tha, Ma?"

"Yuh bring it straight back t me, yuh hear? It be fer Pa."

"Yessum! Lemme go now, Ma."

She stooped, turned slightly to one side, raised the hem of her dress, rolled down the top of her stocking, and came up with a slender wad of bills.

"Here," she said. "Lawd knows yuh don need no gun. But yer pa does. Yuh bring it right back t me, yuh hear? Ahma put it up. Now ef yuh don, Ahma have yuh pa pick yuh so hard yuh won fergit it."

"Yessum."

He took the money, ran down the steps, and across the yard.

"Dave! Yuuuuuh Daaaaave!"

He heard, but he was not going to stop now. "Naw, Lawd!"

The first movement he made the following morning was to reach under his pillow for the gun. In the gray light of dawn he held it loosely, feeling a sense of power. Could kill a man with a gun like this. Kill anybody, black or white. And if he were holding his gun in his hand, nobody could run over him; they would have to respect him. It was a big gun, with a long barrel and a heavy handle. He raised and lowered it in his hand, marveling at its weight.

He had not come straight home with it as his mother had asked; instead he had stayed out in the fields, holding the weapon in his hand, aiming it now and then at some imaginary foe. But he had not fired it; he had been afraid that his father might hear. Also he was not sure he knew how to fire it.

To avoid surrendering the pistol he had not come into the house until he knew that they were all asleep. When his mother had tiptoed to his bedside late that night and demanded the gun, he had first played possum; then he had told her that the gun was hidden outdoors, that he would bring it to her in the morning. Now he lay turning it slowly in his hands. He broke it, took out the cartridges, felt them, and then put them back.

He slid out of bed, got a long strip of old flannel from a trunk, wrapped the gun in it, and tied it to his naked thigh while it was still loaded. He did not go

in to breakfast. Even though it was not yet daylight, he started for Jim Hawkins'
plantation. Just as the sun was rising he reached the barns where the mules
and plows were kept.

"Hey! That you, Dave?"

He turned. Jim Hawkins stood eying him suspiciously.

"What're yuh doing here so early?"

"Ah didn't know Ah wuz gittin up so early, Mistah Hawkins. Ah wuz fixin
t hitch up ol Jenny n take her t the fiels."

"Good. Since you're so early, how about plowing that stretch down by the
woods?"

"Suits me, Mistah Hawkins."

"'O.K. Go to it!'"

He hitched Jenny to a plow and started across the fields. Hot dog! This was
just what he wanted. If he could get down by the woods, he could shoot his
gun and nobody would hear. He walked behind the plow, hearing the traces
creaking, feeling the gun tied tight to his thigh.

When he reached the woods, he plowed two whole rows before he decided
to take out the gun. Finally, he stopped, looked in all directions, then untied
the gun and held it in his hand. He turned to the mule and smiled.

"Know whut this is, Jenny? Naw, yuh wouldn know! Yuhs jusa ol mule!
Anyhow, this is a gun, n it kin shoot, by Gawd!"

He held the gun at arm's length. Whut t hell, Ahma shoot this thing! He
looked at Jenny again.

"'Lissen here, Jenny! When Ah pull this ol trigger, Ah don wan yuh t run
n acka fool now!"

Jenny stood with head down, her short ears pricked straight. Dave walked
off about twenty feet, held the gun far out from him at arm's length, and
turned his head. Hell, he told himself, Ah ain afraid. The gun felt loose in his
fingers; he waved it wildly for a moment. Then he shut his eyes and tightened
his forefinger. Bloom! A report half deafened him and he thought his right
hand was torn from his arm. He heard Jenny whinnying and galloping over
the field, and he found himself on his knees, squeezing his fingers hard
between his legs. His hand was numb; he jammed it into his mouth, trying to
warm it, trying to stop the pain. The gun lay at his feet. He did not quite know
what had happened. He stood up and stared at the gun as though it were a
living thing. He gritted his teeth and kicked the gun. Yuh almos broke mah
arm! He turned to look for Jenny; she was far over the fields, tossing her head
and kicking wildly.

"Hol on there, ol mule!"

When he caught up with her she stood trembling, walling her big white
eyes at him. The plow was far away; the traces had broken. Then Dave stopped
short, looking, not believing. Jenny was bleeding. Her left side was red and
wet with blood. He went closer. Lawd, have mercy! Wondah did Ah shoot
this mule? He grabbed for Jenny's mane. She flinched, snorted, whirled, tossing her head.

"Hol on now! Hol on."

Then he saw the hole in Jenny's side, right between the ribs. It was round,
wet, red. A crimson stream streaked down the front leg, flowing fast. Good
Gawd! Ah wuzn't shootin at tha mule. He felt panic. He knew he had to stop
that blood, or Jenny would bleed to death. He had never seen so much blood

in all his life. He chased the mule for a half a mile, trying to catch her. Finally she stopped, breathing hard, stumpy tail half arched. He caught her mane and led her back to where the plow and gun lay. Then he stooped and grabbed handfuls of damp black earth and tried to plug the bullet hole. Jenny shuddered, whinnied, and broke from him.

"Hol on! Hol on now!"

He tried to plug it again, but blood came anyhow. His fingers were hot and sticky. He rubbed dirt into his palms, trying to dry them. Then again he attempted to plug the bullet hole, but Jenny shied away, kicking her heels high. He stood helpless. He had to do something. He ran at Jenny; she dodged him. He watched a red stream of blood flow down Jenny's leg and form a bright pool at her feet.

"Jenny . . . Jenny," he called weakly.

His lips trembled. She's bleeding t death! He looked in the direction of home, wanting to go back, wanting to get help. But he saw the pistol lying in the damp black clay. He had a queer feeling that if he only did something, this would not be; Jenny would not be there bleeding to death.

When he went to her this time, she did not move. She stood with sleepy, dreamy eyes; and when he touched her she gave a low-pitched whinny and knelt to the ground, her front knees slopping in blood.

"Jenny . . . Jenny . . ." he whispered.

For a long time she held her neck erect; then her head sank, slowly. Her ribs swelled with a mighty heave and she went over.

Dave's stomach felt empty, very empty. He picked up the gun and held it gingerly between his thumb and forefinger. He buried it at the foot of a tree. He took a stick and tried to cover the pool of blood with dirt—but what was the use? There was Jenny lying with her mouth open and her eyes walled and glassy. He could not tell Jim Hawkins he had shot his mule. But he had to tell something. Yeah, Ah'll tell em Jenny started gittin wil n fell on the joint of the plow. . . . But that would hardly happen to a mule. He walked across the field slowly, head down.

It was sunset. Two of Jim Hawkins' men were over near the edge of the woods digging a hole in which to bury Jenny. Dave was surrounded by a knot of people, all of whom were looking down at the dead mule.

"I don't see how in the world it happened," said Jim Hawkins for the tenth time.

The crowd parted and Dave's mother, father, and small brother pushed into the center.

"Where Dave?" his mother called.

"There he is," said Jim Hawkins.

His mother grabbed him.

"Whut happened, Dave? Whut yuh done?"

"Nothin."

"C mon, boy, talk," his father said.

Dave took a deep breath and told the story he knew nobody believed.

"Waal," he drawled. "Ah brung ol Jenny down here sos Ah could do mah plowin. Ah plowed bout two rows, just like yuh see." He stopped and pointed at the long rows of upturned earth. "Then somethin musta been wrong wid ol Jenny. She wouldn ack right a-tall. She started snortin n kickin her heels. Ah tried t hol her, but she pulled erway, rearin n goin in. Then when the point of the plow was stickin up in the air, she swung erroun n twisted herself back on it . . . She stuck herself n started t bleed. N fo Ah could do anything, she wuz dead."

"Did you ever hear of anything like that in all your life?" asked Jim Hawkins.

There were white and black standing in the crowd. They murmured. Dave's mother came close to him and looked hard into his face. "Tell the truth, Dave," she said.

"Looks like a bullet hole to me," said one man.

"Dave, whut yuh do wid the gun?" his mother asked.

The crowd surged in, looking at him. He jammed his hands into his pockets, shook his head slowly from left to right, and backed away. His eyes were wide and painful.

"Did he hava gun?" asked Jim Hawkins.

"By Gawd, Ah tol yuh tha wu a gun wound," said a man, slapping his thigh.

His father caught his shoulders and shook him till his teeth rattled.

"Tell whut happened, yuh rascal! Tell whut . . ."

Dave looked at Jenny's stiff legs and began to cry.

"Whut yuh do wid tha gun?" his mother asked.

"Whut wuz he doin wida gun?" his father asked.

"Come on and tell the truth," said Hawkins. "Ain't nobody going to hurt you . . ."

His mother crowded close to him.

"Did yuh shoot tha mule, Dave?"

Dave cried, seeing blurred white and black faces.

"Ahh ddinn gggo tt sshooot hher . . . Ah ssswear ffo Gawd Ahh ddin. . . . Ah wuz a-tryin t sssee ef the old gggun would sshoot—"

"Where yuh git the gun from?" his father asked.

"Ah got it from Joe, at the sto."

"Where yuh git the money?"

"Ma give it t me."

"He kept worryin me, Bob. Ah had t. Ah tol im t bring the gun right back to me . . . It was fer yuh, the gun."

"But how yuh happen to shoot that mule?" asked Jim Hawkins.

"Ah wuzn shootin at the mule, Mistah Hawkins. The gun jumped when Ah pulled the trigger . . . N fo Ah knowed anythin Jenny was there a-bleedin."

Somebody in the crowd laughed. Jim Hawkins walked close to Dave and looked into his face.

"Well, looks like you have bought you a mule, Dave."

"Ah swear fo Gawd, Ah didn go t kill the mule, Mistah Hawkins!"

"But you killed her!"

All the crowd was laughing now. They stood on tiptoe and poked heads over one another's shoulders.

"Well, boy, looks like yuh done bought a dead mule! Hahaha!"

"Ain tha ershame."

"Hohohohoho."

Dave stood, head down, twisting his feet in the dirt.

"Well, you needn't worry about it, Bob," said Jim Hawkins to Dave's father. "Just let the boy keep on working and pay me two dollars a month."

"Whut yuh wan fer yo mule, Mistah Hawkins?"

Jim Hawkins screwed up his eyes.

"Fifty dollars."
"Whut yuh do wid tha gun?" Dave's father demanded.
Dave said nothing.
"Yuh wan me t take a tree n beat yuh till yuh talk!"
"Nawsuh!"
"Whut yuh do wid it?"
"Ah throwed it erway."
"Where?"
"Ah . . . Ah throwed it in the creek."
"Waal, c mon home. N firs thing in the mawnin git to tha creek n fin tha gun."
"Yessuh."
"Whut yuh pay fer it?"
"Two dollahs."
"Take tha gun n git yo money back n carry it t Mistah Hawkins, yuh near? N don fergit Ahma lam you black bottom good fer this! Now march yosef on home, suh!"

Dave turned and walked slowly. He heard people laughing. Dave glared, his eyes welling with tears. Hot anger bubbled in him. Then he swallowed and stumbled on.

That night Dave did not sleep. He was glad that he had gotten out of killing the mule so easily, but he was hurt. Something hot seemed to turn over inside him each time he remembered how they had laughed. He tossed on his bed, feeling his hard pillow. *N Pa says he's gonna beat me . . .* He remembered other beatings, and his back quivered. *Naw, naw, Ah sho don wan im t beat me tha way no mo. Dam em all! Nobody ever gave him anything. All he did was work. They treat me like a mule, n then they beat me.* He gritted his teeth. *N Ma had t tell on me.*

Well, if he had to, he would take old man Hawkins that two dollars. But that meant selling the gun. And he wanted to keep that gun. Fifty dollars for a dead mule.

He turned over, thinking how he had fired the gun. He had an itch to fire it again. *Ef other men kin shoota gun, by Gawd, Ah kin!* He was still, listening. *Mebbe they all sleepin now.* The house was still. He heard the soft breathing of his brother. *Yes, now!* He would go down and get that gun and see if he could fire it! He eased out of bed and slipped into overalls.

The moon was bright. He ran almost all the way to the edge of the woods. He stumbled over the ground, looking for the spot where he had buried the gun. *Yeah, here it is.* Like a hungry dog scratching for a bone, he pawed it up. He puffed his black cheeks and blew dirt from the trigger and barrel. He broke it and found four cartridges unshot. He looked around; the fields were filled with silence and moonlight. He clutched the gun stiff and hard in his fingers. But, as soon as he wanted to pull the trigger, he shut his eyes and turned his head. *Naw, An can't shoot wid mah eyes closed n mah head turned.* With effort he held his eyes open; then he squeezed. *Bloooom!* He was stiff, not breathing. The gun was still in his hands. *Dammit, he'd done it!* He fired again. *Blooooom!* He smiled. *Blooooom! Blooooom! Click, click.* There! It was empty. If anybody could shoot a gun, he could. He put the gun into his hip pocket and started across the fields.

When he reached the top of a ridge he stood straight and proud in the moonlight, looking at Jim Hawkins' big white house, feeling the gun sagging in his pocket. Lawd, ef Ah had just one mo bullet Ah'd taka shot at tha house. Ah'd like t scare ol man Hawkins jusa little . . . Jusa enough t let im know Dave Saunders is a man.

To his left the road curved, running to the tracks of the Illinois Central. He jerked his head, listening. From far off came a faint *hooof-hoooof; hoooof-hoooof; hoooof-hoooof.* . . . He stood rigid. Two dollahs a mont. Les see now . . . Tha means it'll take bout two years. Shucks! Ah'll be dam!

He started down the road, toward the tracks. Yeah, here she comes! He stood beside the track and held himself stiffly. Here she comes, erroun the ben . . . C mon, yuh slow poke! C mon! He had his hand on his gun; something quivered in his stomach. Then the train thundered past, the gray and brown box cars rumbling and clinking. He gripped the gun tightly; then he jerked his hand out of his pocket. Ah betcha Bill wouldn't do it! Ah betcha. . . . The cars slid past, steel grinding upon steel. Ahm ridin yuh ternight, so hep me Gawd! He was hot all over. He hesitated just a moment; then he grabbed, pulled atop of a car, and lay flat. He felt his pocket; the gun was still there. Ahead the long rails were glinting in the moonlight, stretching away, away to somewhere, somewhere where he could be a man . . .

1939, 1961

---

# MURIEL RUKEYSER
## 1913–1980

Rukeyser was born in New York City, the child of comfortably wealthy Jewish parents who gave her a good education, sending her to the Fieldston School, Vassar College, and Columbia University. As though uncomfortable with privilege, she was attracted early on to radical causes, identifying herself throughout life with the disadvantaged and oppressed and associating with the Socialists, Communists, labor activists, and free-spirited artists who formed a lively heterogeneous subculture of their own in New York City during the 1920s and 1930s. Active on behalf of Sacco and Vanzetti, she was most outraged at the plight of labor, appalled at dangerous working conditions and low wages in factories. She perceived the idealism and solidarity of the labor movement as a liberating alternative to the emptiness and shallowness of affluent individualism, which she portrayed in surrealistic imagistic montages of destruction and despair.

While vigorously forwarding a program of social consciousness in poetry, however, Rukeyser was equally vigorously dedicated to the principle of artistic freedom and personally devoted to an aesthetic of poetic complexity; thus unlike many social poets of the 1930s she did not try to write in the supposed style of simple working people. She denied that there was any conflict between poetry written at a high level of technical and textual sophistication and poetry that was politically motivated and dedicated. For her poetry was a way of seeing the world, an instrument for writing about anything and everything. As an artist she devoted her life to demonstrating how the same supple and subtle verse could serve to write about nature, about private life, and about the most public concerns.

Rukeyser began to publish poetry while still a student at Vassar and published her first collection of poetry, *Theory of Flight*, in 1935. Next came *U.S. 1* in 1938 and *A Turning Wind* in 1939. With the outbreak of World War II, Rukeyser's main motif became the atrocities of war, a theme that is prominent in *Beast in*

*View* (1944). She was briefly married, and soon after World War II, while living
for a short while in California, she became a single parent. Returning to New York
with a child to rear and support, she divided her time between income-producing
work like teaching and work on her own poetry. She was less prolific in the 1950s
than she had been earlier and concentrated more on autobiographical than social
poetry during that decade. When, after the "silent fifties," social issues again came
to the fore in American thinking during the 1960s, Rukeyser returned to social
themes and produced some fine feminist poetry in the 1970s. Like many poets, she
began writing elaborately decorated, intricate verse and evolved toward increasing
simplicity and terseness of diction; at each point in her career, the poetry continued
to display the same concern for technical skill.

## Effort at Speech Between Two People

:  Speak to me.   Take my hand.   What are you now?
   I will tell you all.   I will conceal nothing.
   When I was three, a little child read a story about a rabbit
   who died, in the story, and I crawled under a chair   :
   a pink rabbit   :   it was my birthday, and a candle                    5
   burnt a sore spot on my finger, and I was told to be happy.

:  Oh, grow to know me.   I am not happy.   I will be open:
   Now I am thinking of white sails against a sky like music,
   like glad horns blowing, and birds tilting, and an arm about me.
   There was one I loved, who wanted to live, sailing.                    10

:  Speak to me.   Take my hand.   What are you now?
   When I was nine, I was fruitily sentimental,
   fluid   :   and my widowed aunt played Chopin,[1]
   and I bent my head on the painted woodwork, and wept.
   I want now to be close to you.   I would                               15
   link the minutes of my days close, somehow, to your days.

:  I am not happy.   I will be open.
   I have liked lamps in evening corners, and quiet poems.
   There has been fear in my life.   Sometimes I speculate
   On what a tragedy his life was, really.                                20

:  Take my hand.   Fist my mind in your hand.   What are you now?
   When I was fourteen, I had dreams of suicide,
   and I stood at a steep window, at sunset, hoping toward death   :
   if the light had not melted clouds and plains to beauty,
   if light had not transformed that day, I would have leapt.             25
   I am unhappy.   I am lonely.   Speak to me.

:  I will be open.   I think he never loved me:
   he loved the bright beaches, the little lips of foam
   that ride small waves, he loved the veer of gulls:
   he said with a gay mouth: I love you.   Grow to know me.               30

1. Frédéric François Chopin (1810–1849), Polish composer who settled in Paris in 1831 and is known for his
Romantic works for the piano.

What are you now?   If we could touch one another,
if these our separate entities could come to grips,
clenched like a Chinese puzzle . . . yesterday
I stood in a crowded street that was live with people,
and no one spoke a word, and the morning shone.                    35
Everyone silent, moving. . . . Take my hand.   Speak to me.

1935

## For Fun

It was long before the national performance,
preparing for heroes,
carnival-time, time of
political decorations and the tearing of treaties.
Long before the prophecies came true.                               5
For cities also play their brilliant lives.
They have their nightmares.   They have their nights of peace.
Senility, wisecracks, tomb, tomb.

Bunting, plaster of Paris whores, electrified unicorns.
Pyramids of mirrors and the winking sphinx,                         10
flower mosaics on the floors of stores,
ballets of massacres.   Cut-glass sewers,
red velvet hangings stained the walls of jails,
white lacquer chairs in the abortionists',
boxers, mummies for policemen, wigs                                 15
on the meat at the butchers', murderers
eating their last meal under the Arch of Peace.

The unemployed brought all the orange trees,
cypress trees, tubbed rubber-plants, and limes,
conifers, loblolly and the tamaracks,                               20
incongruous flowers to a grove wherein
they sat, making oranges.   For in that cold season
fruit was golden could not be guaranteed.

It was long before the riderless horse came streaming
hot to the Square.   I walked at noon and saw                       25
that face run screaming through the crowd saying Help
but its mouth would not open and they could not hear.

It was long before the troops entered the city
that I looked up and saw the Floating Man.
Explain yourself I cried at the last.   I am                        30
the angel waste, your need which is your guilt,
answered, affliction and a fascist death.

It was long before the city was bombed I saw
fireworks, mirrors, gilt, consumed in flame,
we show this you said the flames, speak it speak it                 35
but I was employed then making straw oranges.

Everything spoke : flames, city, glass, but I
had heavy mystery thrown against the heart.

It was long before the fall of the city.
Ten days before the appearance of the skull.                    40
Five days until the skull showed clean,
and now the entry is prepared.
Carnival's ready.
Let's dance a little before we go home to hell.

1939

## "Long Enough"

"Long enough. Long enough,"
I heard a woman say—
I am that woman who too long
Under the web lay.
Long enough in the empire                    5
Of his darkened eyes
Bewildered in the greying silver
Light of his fantasies.

I have been lying here too long,
From shadow-begin to shadow-began                    10
Where stretches over me the subtle
Rule of the Floating Man.
A young man and an old-young woman
My dive in the river between
And rise, the children of another country;                    15
That riverbank, that green.

But too long, too long, too long
Is the journey through the ice
And too secret are the entrances
To my stretched hidingplace.                    20
Walk out of the pudorweb[1]
And into a lifetime
Said the woman; and I sleeper began to wake
And to say my own name.

1958

## The Poem as Mask

### Orpheus[1]

When I wrote of the women in their dances and wildness, it was a mask,
on their mountain, gold-hunting, singing, in orgy,

---

1. The confining meshes of female shame.                    by the Bacchante, his female admirers.
1. Greek god of music and song who was torn to pieces

it was a mask; when I wrote of the god,
fragmented, exiled from himself, his life, the love gone down with song,
it was myself, split open, unable to speak, in exile from myself.　　　5

There is no mountain, there is no god, there is memory
of my torn life, myself split open in sleep, the rescued child
beside me among the doctors, and a word
of rescue from the great eyes.

No more masks! No more mythologies!　　　10

Now, for the first time, the god lifts his hand,
the fragments join in me with their own music.

　　　　　　　　　　　　　　　　　　　　　　　1968

## Myth

Long afterward, Oedipus, old and blinded, walked the
roads.　　　He smelled a familiar smell.　　　It was
the Sphinx.　　　Oedipus said, "I want to ask one question.
Why didn't I recognize my mother?"　　　"You gave the
wrong answer," said the Sphinx.　　　"But that was what　　　5
made everything possible," said Oedipus.　　　"No," she said.
"When I asked, What walks on four legs in the morning,
two at noon, and three in the evening, you answered,
Man.　　　You didn't say anything about woman."
"When you say Man," said Oedipus, "you include women　　　10
too. Everyone knows that."　　　She said, "That's what
you think."

　　　　　　　　　　　　　　　　　　　　　　　1973

## Painters

In the cave with a long-ago flare
a woman stands, her arm up. Red twig, black twig, brown twig.
A wall of leaping darkness over her.
The men are out hunting in the early light
But here in this flicker, one or two men, painting　　　5
and a woman among them.
Great living animals grow on the stone walls,
their pelts, their eyes, their sex, their hearts,
and the cave-painters touch them with life, red, brown, black,
a woman among them, painting.　　　10

　　　　　　　　　　　　　　　　　　　　　　　1973

# American Prose
# since 1945

When in 1942 a young critic named Alfred Kazin published his first book, *On Native Grounds*, a survey of American writing from late-nineteenth-century realism up through the literature of the 1930s, he judged "the greatest single fact about our modern American writing" to be "our writers' absorption in every last detail of their American world together with their deep and subtle alienation from it." Three years later, on August 6, 1945, the explosion of an atomic bomb over Hiroshima in Japan brought about a hasty conclusion to World War II and also introduced into human life a new reality so unimaginable as to make terms like *crisis* and *alienation* seem understatements, scarcely adequate to the nature of the postwar era. What was one to feel, what were American writers to feel, about such an event, and what difference would it make to the kind of work they were hoping to do?

Fifty years later we can look back on a number of cataclysmic upheavals that followed the ones at Hiroshima and Nagasaki. A short list might include the Cold War, with its attendant fears of nuclear annihilation, culminating in the Cuban missile crisis of 1962; the civil rights movement of the 1960s, with its stark message that there were races in this country who lived neither on equal nor on amicable terms; the assassination of John F. Kennedy in November 1963, and the assassinations five years later of his brother and of Martin Luther King, Jr., chief spokesman for civil rights and a leader of black Americans; the extended, seemingly endless war of attrition and folly in Vietnam; violence in the urban ghettos; the killing of four students by the National Guard at Kent State University in 1970, bringing violence in the universities to a head; the resignation in 1974, after Watergate, of President Richard Nixon; turbulence and war in the Middle East; and the AIDS epidemic. These and lesser crises may persuade us, as the media work to persuade us, that each day brings a new and intolerable threat to our lives.

But literature is not life, even though certain episodes from our recent history wear the aspects of both tragedy and farce, and no list of crucial public events should be seized on as responsible for the literature that is contemporaneous with or that succeeded them. Even though a novel-fantasy like Robert Coover's *The Public Burning* (1977) could not have been written without the public events that the novelist uses as his imaginative materials—in this case, the execution of the Rosenbergs in 1953 for treason and the career of Richard Nixon—the directness of relation between literature and contemporary events depends on the books or writers one selects. (In fact Philip Roth's *Our Gang*, published two years before the Watergate fiasco, was unable in its attempt at far-out satiric display to equal the real thing when it occurred.) In the best of postwar American novels and stories the relation has seldom been that direct. To name just three examples from serious writers in the 1950s: the work of Saul Bellow, Flannery O'Connor, and Ralph Ellison surely manifested, in Kazin's terms, "absorption in every last detail of their American world" as well as their "deep and subtle alienation from it." Yet no public event can account for why *The Adventures of Augie March* or *A Good Man*

*Is Hard to Find* or *Invisible Man* should have occurred when they did, or indeed should have occurred at all.

Certain novels did, however, get written as a direct result of World War II, most notably Norman Mailer's *The Naked and the Dead* (1948) and James Jones's *From Here to Eternity* (1951). Mailer had been planning his novel ever since the war began; with hindsight, we can see that he got it out of his system—writing a best-seller in the process—then went on to produce many different although not unrelated books. Jones, on the other hand, never found another subject; the final volume of his trilogy about the war was not published until after his death in 1978. World War II novels were long, usually swollen chronicles that looked backward to the naturalism of 1930s writers and were unambitious in their form and style. Perhaps the war novelists were intimidated by Hemingway's *A Farewell to Arms* and were persuaded that there was nothing new or profound to say about their subject. Perhaps the novels sank under their conventional story lines or perhaps it was just too soon to expect highly imaginative writing about the event. At any rate the most compellingly original treatments of that war are to be found in Joseph Heller's *Catch-22* (1961) and Thomas Pynchon's *Gravity's Rainbow* (1973), both written many years after it had ended.

## SOUTHERN WRITERS

Taking the years 1945–60 as a unit, we can identify two main groupings of literary energies and principles in the postwar period. The "southern" writers are much less to be thought of as a group than as a number of individually talented novelists and short-story writers, many of them women, and all of them touched by the large shadow of William Faulkner. (Faulkner remained busily at work completing the Snopes trilogy he had begun with *The Hamlet* in 1940, while visiting universities and producing other work until his death in 1962.) The older writers of this group, Katherine Anne Porter and Eudora Welty, remained active—the former occupied with the writing of a lengthy novel, *Ship of Fools* (1962), the latter providing a host of distinguished short fiction and novels of which *The Golden Apples* (1949) is perhaps the finest. Other highly acclaimed writers were Carson McCullers—whose first novel *The Heart Is a Lonely Hunter* (1940) was a critical success and whose short novel *The Member of the Wedding* (1946) is her best work—and Truman Capote, whose *Other Voices, Other Rooms* was published to much fanfare in 1948 when he was twenty-four (Carson McCullers was twenty-three when her first novel appeared).

The absorption of these younger writers in the grotesque, their fascination with extreme and perverse incongruities of character and scene, and their cultivation of verbal effects can be understood as a commitment to "art"—to a use of the creative imagination and language unchecked by any presumed realities of life as it was lived in America in 1948 or 1960. On the other hand, such features of their writing may be defended as the only true and adequate response the artist can make to that bizarre life. Or so Flannery O'Connor, perhaps the most talented, certainly the most humorous of the younger southern writers, implied when she remarked wryly, "Of course I have found that any fiction that comes out of the South is going to be called grotesque by the Northern reader—unless it is grotesque, in which case it's going to be called realistic." In any case these artists (to whom one should add the gifted storyteller Peter Taylor and the novelist Walker Percy) absorbed—often brilliantly created—American speech, manners, habits of eating or praying or loving, while holding back in the main from any topical engagement with the public and social happenings around them.

## NEW YORK WRITERS

With proper consciousness of the umbrellalike nature of the label, we can distinguish another principal group of writers and the critics who wrote about and publicized them. Here the milieu is urban Jewish, the concerns recognizably more public and political—although less overtly so in the novelists than in the essayist-intellectuals who criticized them. The major periodical for these writers was *Partisan Review* (for a time *Commentary* shared some of the same interests and personnel), a magazine published monthly, bimonthly, or quarterly throughout the 1940s and 1950s and still extant, although a shadow of its former self. *Partisan* was remarkable for the way it managed, despite its inception in highly political circumstances and controversies in the 1930s, to maintain an extremely wide range of interests in poetry, fiction, drama, and fine arts and in Continental literature, politics, and sociological thought. Its favorite fiction writers during the postwar years were Bellow (parts of *The Adventures of Augie March* and all of *Seize the Day* appeared there), Bernard Malamud, Mailer (occasionally), and Delmore Schwartz. But *Partisan* also looked beyond urban-Jewish writing, publishing stories by Flannery O'Connor and James Baldwin and the prologue to Ellison's *Invisible Man*. Among the distinguished critics who contributed steadily to the magazine over these years on a variety of literary and political subjects, one should mention Lionel Trilling—whose *The Liberal Imagination* (1948) was perhaps the most widely read and influential of New York critical works—as well as Philip Rahv, Irving Howe, Elizabeth Hardwick, and Diana Trilling. Mary McCarthy reviewed plays and published some of her fiction there, and Hannah Arendt's political writing and Clement Greenberg's art criticism were regular features of the journal.

By 1960 regional and ethnic senses of identity became diluted as the various parts of America began more and more to resemble each other. This cultural dilution can be observed at work in some of the "assimilated" Jews depicted in Philip Roth's *Goodbye, Columbus* (1959) or in the southerners who inhabit Walker Percy's novels generally. To be a southern novelist in 1960 was no more exotic than to be a Jewish novelist. At about that time *Partisan Review* began to lose its distinctiveness, especially after 1963, when during a New York City newspaper strike a new magazine was formed, the *New York Review of Books*. This organ, while making use of many of the *Partisan* writers, appeared biweekly rather than quarterly and was able to give essayists and reviewers as much room as they desired. Its striking success has continued to the present day.

### THE "TRANQUILLIZED FIFTIES"

The heading for this section is taken from *Memories of West Street and Lepke*, a poem Robert Lowell published in 1958 during the years of Eisenhower's presidency (1953–61) when

> . . . even the man
> scavenging filth in the back alley trash cans,
> has two children, a beach wagon, a helpmate,
> and is a "young Republican."

They were years when attention to serious public matters probably meant attention to the Cold War and what should be done about the real or mythical Communists whom Senator Joseph McCarthy was crusading against, or whether a ban on nuclear testing could be accomplished before the United States and the former Soviet Union contrived to blow up the world. At home, although there was a famously named "recession" (a Republican word brought into play so as not to recall the Great Depression of 1929 and beyond), the majority of Americans were employed, paid better than they had ever been paid, and exposed to an ever-increasing number of household "labor-saving devices" and automotive finery like the beach wagon of Lowell's poem. Citizens were generally encouraged to think well of their country, while poor people largely remained, in a phrase coined by the Socialist critic Michael Harrington, "our invisible poor." And although there was a flurry of confrontations over the Supreme Court's decision in 1954 that public schools could not be maintained on a segregated, "separate but equal" basis, the dramatic beginning to the civil rights struggles that were to mark the 1960s took place largely in the South and was mainly unremarked by novelists preoccupied with other matters.

For all the abuse the 1950s have received as a success-oriented, socially and ecologically irresponsible, fearfully smug decade, they look in retrospect (though they were surely not felt as such at the time) to have been a good time for serious American writers, and not the less so for the individual writer's assurance that he or she could not possibly be appreciated or understood by a philistine and materialistic nation run by businessmen, generals, and golfers. So the "deep and subtle alienation" Kazin spoke of was also seen as a necessary, sometimes even an attractive, condition, that furnished a rich vein for fictional exploration. Bellow expressed the mood most masterfully in his short novel *Seize the Day* (1956) through his portrayal of a disastrous day in the life of Tommy Wilhelm, a young man who cannot succeed in, eventually cannot even breathe in, a world of optimists, boosters, yea-sayers to family, commerce, and life. Or there is the hero of Ellison's *Invisible Man* (1952), who tells us in the novel's prologue that he lives underground in New York City, the city of light, serviced by a company he calls "Monopolated Light and Power" and who chooses for his hero the jazz cornetist Louis Armstrong, who has "made poetry out of being invisible." And in *The Man Who Studied Yoga* (1952), Mailer inspects his unheroic hero Sam Svoboda to observe the sadness and anxieties lying not far below the surface of middle-class "ordinary" American married couples. Each of these three works lives through its detailed absorption in the urban scene from which its hero is alienated, whether as observed in Harlem, in Brooklyn, or on Manhattan's Upper West Side.

### OTHER CRITICISMS OF AMERICA

The most stunning fictional success of the 1950s was J. D. Salinger's *The Catcher in the Rye*, a book with a young hero who is out of step with the educational, commercial, and sexual customs of adult society and who is able to see through and expose its falsities and "phoniness." For a time in the late 1950s and early 1960s, one could assume that all college students had read this book, as attested by their "identification" with Holden Caulfield, who summed up and rendered both poignant and funny their own presumed predicaments, enabling them to feel better about being unhappy, even to cherish the illusion that it was virtuous to be so. By 1975 this slippery and astonishing book, although never on the best-seller lists for any one year, had sold nearly six million copies.

Readers of Salinger in the 1950s were probably also reading sociological studies like David Riesman's *The Lonely Crowd* (1950), which classified American behavior as mainly "other-directed," a condition for which the accepted standards and criteria for behavior came from outside the self rather than from within. Or they were learning about the "gray-flannel suit" ethos by reading Vance Packard's popular reporting or Sloan Wilson's forgotten best-seller, *The Man in the Gray Flannel Suit* (1955). At a more polemical and radical level, a smaller, predominantly university audience read the social criticism of C. Wright Mills in *White Collar* (1951) and *The Power Elite* (1956). There was also much general interest in the popularized psychological, religious, and philosophical movements that surfaced after World War II. The meaning of existentialism, as imported from France and abstracted from the novels of Albert Camus and Jean-Paul Sartre or from Mailer's novels and essays, was solemnly discussed by those in search of a post-Christian, philosophically respectable attitude toward life. There was much interest in the psychological theories of Erich Fromm and Erik Erikson or, at a lower level, in the self-help best-sellers like Norman Vincent Peale's *The Power of Positive Thinking* (1952), which sold five million copies. One could even decide that all of Western thinking was at fault and so turn to the East and learn about Zen Buddhism through books by Alan Watts or D. T. Suzuki. The stories of Salinger increasingly featured young people unable to talk to their parents or accept "the American way of life," who became prey to extreme versions of experience, sometimes mystical and sometimes suicidal.

As the 1950s drew to a close, these criticisms of American institutional and social styles over the decade grew more extreme and more specific in the hands of radical critics. Mailer's pamphlet *The White Negro* (1957) defined the American world as essentially "square": stultifying, sickly, infected with pieties and timidities, obedient to authoritarian voices. As a cure for this sickness he proposed a "new breed of adventurer" named "the hipster" who would live according to what Mailer termed the black man's code of "ever-threatening danger" and who would dramatically confront and reject the square world. At a no less passionate level, although less violent in its emphasis, was Paul Goodman's *Growing Up Absurd* (1959), the most forceful of many books he wrote in opposition to the technological America he saw around him. Goodman pushed for a return to decentralized, Jeffersonian principles of social organization, to smaller cars, and to meaningful work; his plea especially focused on the kids (as he liked to call them) who needed jobs more worthwhile than making tail fins for America's enormous late-fifties automobiles if they were to respect either their country or themselves.

But the most publicized literary expression of disaffection with official American life was made by the Beat writers, of whom Jack Kerouac was the prose laureate. Advertised as the "Beat generation" and known also, more accurately, as the San Francisco school, the group included most notably the poets Allen Ginsberg and Gregory Corso. Its influence radiated from the City Lights Bookstore run by Lawrence Ferlinghetti, who was himself a poet. Beat poets sometimes read their works to a jazz accompaniment; among their objects of veneration were Whitman, the Buddha and Eastern religions generally, and (in Kerouac's case at least) large quantities of Western beer. Their experiments with drugs anticipated the more drastic and often disastrous use of them in the 1960s. The Beats were in favor of spontaneity and against constricting forms, poetic or political; indeed, Kerouac proved it was possible to let oneself go and write a novel (*The Subterraneans*, 1958) in three nights. Briefly, the Beat writers constituted a challenge to the many carefully worked-over lyrics or ingeniously worked-out novels that had been characteristic products of the 1950s. They were also good at clowning, and the comic touches that dot their work probably will prove most enduring.

### LETTING GO IN THE 1960s

The first years of the sixties decade seemed truly a time when new possibilities and opportunities presented themselves on both public and private levels. The election of John F. Kennedy to the presidency brought to Washington a glamorous and humorous leader who was thought to be committed both to social justice and to culture—perhaps even bringing in the "new Augustan age of poetry and power" Robert Frost wrote about in his inaugural poem. The agreement with the former Soviet Union to cease nuclear testing in the atmosphere; the increasing concern for changes in the relationship between whites and blacks; the loosening of sexual codes and of official censorship, coincident with the marketing of an effective new oral contraceptive—these and other events seemed in the minds of some to promise a more life-affirming, less restrictive era than the preceding one. With particular regard to the matter of censorship, it may be noted that for many years Americans who wished to read Henry Miller's novels had to smuggle in from Paris their copies of *Tropic of Cancer* and *Tropic of Capricorn*, while in the mid-1950s Vladimir Nabokov's *Lolita* had to be obtained in a similar way. When in 1956, however, *Lolita* was first published in this country, there was no legal prosecution, and in 1959 the successful publication by Grove Press of D. H. Lawrence's *Lady Chat-*

*terley's Lover* cleared the way for novels of more explicit sexual reference. When Mailer published *The Naked and the Dead* in 1948, a well-known four-letter word had to be spelled "fug," evidently to spare the delicate sensibilities of its readers. By 1959, when he published his comic tour de force *The Time of Her Time*, about a sexual warrior's candidly explicit adventures with women in his Greenwich Village loft, hardly anyone raised an eyebrow.

The novelists also seemed, as in the title of Philip Roth's first novel in 1962, to be "letting go" by indulging to the fullest their verbal, storytelling propensities. Between 1961 and 1963 four novels were published (three of them first efforts) by writers whose interest was in the active, exuberant exploration of fantasies, of extremities of experience, and of comic modes that would later on come to be known as "black humor." These books, like many that followed them, turned their backs on ordinary experience, on the mundane continuities of existence in small town or big city, which American writers had so devotedly investigated over the first fifty-odd years of the twentieth century. John Barth's *The Sot-Weed Factor* (1961), Joseph Heller's *Catch-22* (1961), Ken Kesey's *One Flew over the Cuckoo's Nest* (1962), and most bizarre Thomas Pynchon's *V* (1963), all attested to the fact that no verbal resource, no gimmick or extravagance of style need be rejected in the pursuit of putting on a brilliantly entertaining performance. These novels (Kesey's perhaps excluded) were highly self-conscious, parodied other literary styles, and built those parodies into their individually odd designs at the same time as they were ironic and playful about their own fictional assumptions.

The 1960s were also to see a corresponding "liberation" from official standards of correctness in the realm of the journalistic essay, or—as everyone who wrote in that mode called it—a "piece." Norman Podhoretz noted that everyone he knew was engaged in writing lively essays instead of laboring over novels and poems, and there were many collections of such pieces on subjects ranging from the Beat generation phenomenon to the trial of Adolf Eichmann. Mailer's *Advertisements for Myself* (1959), the father of the mode, had shown how unconventional and various a book of essays—which also included stories, newspaper columns, interviews—might be, and he produced two more such books in the first half of the new decade. In the hands of Tom Wolfe, style became something to cultivate and exaggerate; the subject of his "New Journalism" might be the doings of a racing-car star or a New York disco celebrity, but in fact, didn't matter all that much, because it was there mainly for the style to perform upon. A young critic, Susan Sontag, titled a group of her essays *Against Interpretation* (1966) and made the case for more playful, aesthetically oriented responses to both life and art. That the title essay was originally published in *Partisan Review*, a serious high-culture periodical, suggested that the winds were changing, as did the fact that literary critics like Richard Poirier and Benjamin DeMott were to be observed writing full-dress pieces on listening to the Beatles and on the morals of *Playboy* magazine.

## SATIRIC PERFORMANCES

The relation of such expansive and experimental writing to the major public disaster of this time—the assassination of John Kennedy in November 1963—we are not in a position to determine, nor can we determine the effect on literary modes of such events as the following: the increasingly desperate adventure in Vietnam; the riots in the black ghettos of our decaying cities; the turmoil in the universities consequent on the war; the murders of Robert Kennedy and Martin Luther King, Jr.; the omnipresence of drugs, hard and soft; the rise of pornography as a feature of the sexual "revolution"; the decline of the family and the exacerbations in the relations between men and women pointed out at the decade's end by the women's movement and documented in the divorce statistics; the Stonewall rebellion of 1969 and its importance to the gay rights movement. Taken together or singly, these severe dislocations proved to be unavailable for writers to deal with in the representational and realistic modes of portrayal handed down to them by novelists such as Howells, Dreiser, and Dos Passos.

Although satire has been a traditional way of dealing with disasters or upheavals, what sort of "satire" could possibly be adequate to events that seemed beyond the reach of even a gifted writer's words? The middle and late 1960s saw the term *black humor* employed as a tent to cover any literary creation that played fast and loose with ordinary values and standards, frequently employing elements of cruelty and shock to make us see the awful, the ugly, the "sick" in a new way, for what it was. The great humorist in this line—he was a moralist as well—may turn out to have been not a novelist at all but a stand-up comedian, Lenny Bruce, whose violent and obscene rehearsals of clichés in language and in American life gave novelists something to live up to. His was an art of solo performance, dependent (as Frost once said all poetic performance must be) on Bruce's prowess and feats of association.

Similar displays by the writer as satiric performer may be viewed in the works of major novelists and prose entertainers from the later 1960s and early 1970s: in Mailer's speech to Lyndon Johnson (in 1965) urging him, with as much obscenity and crude familiarity as the lecturer could display, to get us out of Vietnam immediately; in the eloquent pleadings and threatening lashing of James Baldwin's attempts to make whites see and accept blacks; in the daffy brilliance of Pynchon's language throughout *The Crying of Lot 49* (1966); and in the forceful charm with which Roth as comedian came up with one amusing routine after another in *Portnoy's Complaint* (1969). The major performer of them all was undoubtedly Vladimir Nabokov, who in a series of startling novels projected his comic fantasies in a style by turns antic, icy, and weird. When at the end of the decade two of our best, but more conservative, novelists tried to render critically, in vivid detail but in a more traditional narrative, their reservations about American life in the late 1960s, they offended some readers by acting as if such a rendering by an individual imagination could still be made. Bellow's *Mr. Sammler's Planet* (1970) and John Updike's *Rabbit Redux* (1971) remain interestingly combative and tendentious views of the liberations of a just-ended decade.

### SUMMARY: OLD AND NEW WRITERS IN THE 1970s, 1980s, AND 1990s

It may be folly—given the fact that our appreciation of a particular writer has so much to do with the gender, class, age, or taste of the appreciator—to name the major American novelists of the post–World War II decades. Nevertheless, in the eyes of this anthologist they appear to be Bellow, Updike, and Roth. Mailer's distinction as a writer, certainly over the past quarter-century, has lain in nonfiction and fictional reportage (there is no good name for it) like *The Armies of the Night* (with its two sections, "History as a Novel," "The Novel as History") and *The Executioner's Song*, rather than in bona fide fiction. And Thomas Pynchon, whose recent *Vineland* (1990) was his first novel since *Gravity's Rainbow* (1973), remains in a category by himself. But Bellow, Updike, and Roth, all three of them, have produced steadily and amply, while keeping their eyes directed at the novel's truest subject: matters of love and death, race and sex, culture and anarchy—especially as such matters have played themselves out in late-twentieth-century America.

Yet even applying exclusive standards, we can easily name fifty or so American novelists and storywriters who are artists of real distinction, who have produced and are producing work that can be read with pleasure and that bring us news about where we are, as we near the end of a century. So the making of a short list of major novelists may be less to the point than noting that the oft-repeated complaint, heard earlier in the twentieth century, about how the novel was in decline, or was dead, is now rarely uttered. We are more likely to hear praise of its richness and diversity, not least in that part of the period that began in the mid-1970s.

There is no doubt that the women's movement, which became a powerful cultural force at the end of the 1960s, has made us all as readers attend more closely to women's voices in novels and stories, as well as in the prose of memoir, essay, and polemic. Perhaps the most influential polemic, although it is also a work of cultural and sociological analysis, was Kate Millett's Sexual Politics (1970), the most memorable sections of which consist of hard-swinging criticisms of three male novelists—D. H. Lawrence, Henry Miller, and Norman Mailer—whose fiction Millett found full of antifemale actions and attitudes. The book provoked Mailer into a fighting reply (in The Prisoner of Sex, 1971). In a less directly combative but no less critical way, essayists like Mary McCarthy and Susan Sontag continued to produce work of varied focuses and impressive range. McCarthy wrote about Vietnam and Watergate (in The Seventeenth Degree, 1974) and the novel (The Writing on the Wall, 1970); while Sontag, in her book-length essays On Photography (1976) and Illness as Metaphor (1979), cast a usefully cold eye on certain received ideas about the moral virtue of photography and about promiscuous uses of the "disease" metaphor. Her Aids and Its Metaphors (1989) continued in this analytic tradition.

Joan Didion's miniature but ambitious cultural reports on New York and Los Angeles, first glimpsed in Slouching toward Bethlehem (1968), was seen later in books about El Salvador and Miami. Elizabeth Hardwick and Cynthia Ozick, both certified novelists, also turned out critical work that was consistently repaying. Hardwick's essays in the New York Review of Books (collected in Bartleby in Manhattan, 1983) unfailingly turned up fresh perspectives, as did Ozick's, whose revaluations of T. S. Eliot and Henry James (in The New Yorker and The New Criterion, respectively) brought provocative rethinking to the cases of important reputations.

The most prolific American woman novelist in recent decades has been Joyce Carol Oates, although her very productivity has probably counted against any single book of hers receiving sustained and admiring attention. In addition to writers anthologized here, like Ann Beattie and Bobbie Ann Mason (whose special affinity is with the short story), a number of expert novelists have built solid reputations on the basis of continuing work. One should mention Gail Godwin, Anne Tyler, and Maureen Howard, all of them writers about suburbs and small-town America. Father Melancholy's Daughter (1991), Godwin's portrait of a young daughter of a minister growing up in Romolus, Virginia, is etched with affectionate noticings that do not exclude deeper tones. Tyler's explorations of ordinary-extraordinary people living in the Baltimore area manage to blend comedy with pathos in wholly original ways, especially in Dinner at the Homesick Restaurant (1982) and Saint Maybe (1991). Most recently, Howard's Natural History (1992), a highly ambitious work that goes about memorializing the people, places, and ambiance of a once-alive Bridgeport, Connecticut, does so through language of dazzling virtuosity and with narrative juxtapositions of singular boldness.

Two of the most widely admired novels of the last decade (both of them won Pulitzers) were written by women at the height of their creative powers. Toni Morrison's Beloved (1987) is a densely textured, passionate evocation of a woman haunted by the spirit of her dead child. Beloved is both a historical novel (it takes place in rural Ohio after the Civil War) and a contemporary meditation on relations between blacks and whites. The shadow of Faulkner looms large at times, but Morrison's stylistic modes are various—sometimes traditional, at other times daringly experimental. Coming as it did after a number of strong earlier successes (The Bluest Eye, 1970; Song of Solomon, 1977), Beloved confirmed her reputation as in the front rank of American novelists; indeed, Morrison was awarded the Nobel Prize for literature in 1993. And although the work of Jane Smiley has not yet quite attained such a reputation—her significant fiction having been published only beginning in 1987—her novel A Thousand Acres will be read for a long time. Centering on a large farm in Iowa in 1959, it dramatizes the struggles of three sisters with their father, their husbands, and with each other but also with the land itself in its ever present, unforgiving circumstances. Ingeniously manipulating the plot of Shakespeare's *King Lear*, *A Thousand Acres* creates new perspectives through a wealth of farm lore and keen observation generally. It is the peak, thus far, of an achievement that also includes a fine novella, *The Age of Grief* (1987), as well as two other novellas, *Ordinary Love & Good Will* (1989). And having singled out these works by Morrison and Smiley, and indeed of the other women glanced at above, we should remind ourselves that they cannot be penned into such a category as, for purposes of convenience and classification, we have penned them.

In general, contemporary novelists spend less time than they did forty years ago taking part in symposia about the "Future of the Novel" and more time in getting on with their writing lives. It may be a related fact that much contemporary fiction is less severe or "modernist" in its comportment, more relaxed about its status as "art," less certain that—in the English critic Cyril Connolly's dictum—the writer's only task is to produce a masterpiece (with Faulkner and Joyce as role models). One notes also that substantially fewer novels present themselves as examples of language and feeling run wild. It is not enough to title something *Superworm* or *The Bushwacked Piano* (two forgotten novels from twenty years ago) and hope it will survive. This is not to say that fantasy has been downplayed in favor of a muted or timid realism. William Gaddis's relentless parodies, in *JB* (1975) and *Carpenter's Gothic* (1985), and Robert Coover's zany extravagances, in *Gerald's Party* (1986) and *Pinocchio in Venice* (1991), have recently been on display. On a more humanly conceived scale, we have seen elaborate blends of fantasy and realism in works like John Gardner's *The Sunlight Dialogues* (1972) and *October Light* (1976), in Paul Theroux's *The Family Arsenal* (1976) and *Chicago Loop* (1991), and in Frederick Buechner's tetralogy, *The Book of Bebb* (1980). Perhaps the single most powerful influence on writers of short fiction has been the spare and fastidious procedures of Raymond Carver, whose stories in *Where I'm Calling From* (1988) depict unglamorous scenes from unheroic American lives. Meanwhile, novelists such as Thomas Berger, Stanley Elkin, and Don DeLillo have produced impressive bodies of work: Berger's *The Houseguest* (1986), Elkin's *The Maguffin* (1991), and DeLillo's *White Noise* (1985) are but three examples of such work. Other distinctive achievements include Gore Vidal's series of novels about American history and George V. Higgins's artful renderings of petty criminal life along the eastern seaboard.

One of the strongest arguments for the continuing liveliness of American prose in the final decade of the twentieth century is the emergence largely over the past twenty years of Native American, Asian-American, and Latino writers. Critical and historical treatment of their books and the traditions in which those books figure has been an accompanying aspect of this emergence. In addition to writers represented in this section, one might single out novels, stories, and essays by Maxine Hong Kingston, Amy Tan, James Welch, Bharati Mukherjee, and Sandra Cisneros. Kingston's *The Woman Warrior* (1976) is probably the most widely read book by an Asian-American writer, and its imaginative, poetic treatment of her Chinese-American heritage as it has influenced her growing up in America (she was born in California) is written with metaphorical vividness and shrewd analysis. A more recent success, Tan's *The Joy Luck Club* (1989), gives witty and affectionate treatment to the stories of four Chinese-American women and their families, showing—as Alice Walker puts it—"the mystery of the mother-daughter bond in ways that we have not experienced before." Welch, who along with Louise Erdrich is the Native American writer whose standing is most assured, has occupied himself with the lives of American Indian men in all their complex fates. In *Winter in the Blood* (1974) and *The Death of Jim Loney* (1979) especially, Welch has constructed narratives of action and adventure, in the tradition of his predecessors, Faulkner and Hemingway. Inevitably the atmosphere is somber and the protagonist's trajectory a violent and unhappy one. Mukherjee, author of a lively book of stories, *The Middleman* (1988), has written arrestingly, in her novel *Jasmine* (1989), of the transformations in an Indian village girl who becomes an inhabitant of New York's Upper West Side and of a small town in Iowa. Mukherjee's unusual angle of vision is made memorable by her sharply comic sense of incongruities, expressed through crisply turned sentences.

But any broadly sweeping overview, like the one that has been attempted here, becomes embarrassed at itself for what it leaves out and how it simplifies—for purposes of classification—what really matters: gifted writers pursuing their craft with vigorous anxiety, acknowledging their membership in a literary community while measuring themselves against each other, sometimes with beady eye. In recognizing their contributions to what this anthology calls, with open-ended unfinality, "American Prose Since 1945," it is appropriate to end with a list of writers, thus far unmentioned, who have enriched that prose by giving us memorable examples of it. Some of these writers are unjustly neglected, some will eventually have their day; some are dead, others are just beginning to realize themselves. In no particular order, then, alphabetic or chronologic: James Gould Cozzens, Wright Morris, J. F. Powers, Evan S. Connell, Thomas Savage, Cynthia Seton, Richard Yates, Louis Auchincloss, John Irving, John Hersey, Jean Stafford, Alan Lelchuk, Susan Kenney, Theodore Weesner, William Styron, Russell Banks, Andre Dubus, Sue Miller, Rand Richards Cooper. America is a large country.

---

# EUDORA WELTY
## b. 1909

In her essay titled *Place in Fiction*, Eudora Welty spoke of her work as filled with the spirit of place: "Location is the ground conductor of all the currents of emotion and belief and moral conviction that charge out from the story in its course." Both her outwardly uneventful life and her writing are most intimately connected to the topography and atmosphere, the season and the soil of the native Mississippi that has been her lifelong home.

Born in Jackson in 1909, to parents who came from the North, and raised in comfortable circumstances (her father headed an insurance company), she attended Mississippi State College for Women, then graduated from the University of Wisconsin in 1929. After a course in advertising at the Columbia University School of Business, she returned to Mississippi, first working as a radio writer and newspaper society editor, then for the Works Progress Administration, taking photographs of and interviewing local residents. Those travels would be reflected in her fiction and also in a book of her photographs, *One Time and Place*, published in 1971.

She began writing fiction after her return to Mississippi in 1931, and five years later published her first story, *Death of a Traveling Salesman*, in a small magazine. Over the next two years, six of her stories were published in the *Southern Review*, a serious literary magazine one of whose editors was the poet and novelist Robert Penn Warren. She also received strong support from Katherine Anne Porter, who contributed an introduction to Welty's first book of stories, *A Curtain of Green* (1941). That introduction hailed the arrival of another gifted southern fiction writer, and in fact the volume contained some of the best stories she was ever to write, such as *Petrified Man* (printed here). Her profusion of metaphor and the difficult surface of her narrative—often oblique and indirect in its effect—were in part a mark of her admiration for modern writers like Virginia Woolf and (as with any young southern writer) William Faulkner. Although Welty's stories were as shapely as her mentor's, Porter, they were more richly idiomatic and comic in their inclination. A second collection, *The Wide Net*, appeared two years later; and her first novel, *The Robber Bridegroom*, was published in 1942.

In that year and the next she was awarded the O. Henry Memorial Prize for the best piece of short fiction, and from then on she received a steady stream of awards and prizes, including the Pulitzer Prize for her novel *The Optimist's Daughter* (1972). Her most ambitious and longest piece of fiction is *Losing Battles* (1970), in which she aimed to compose a narrative made up almost wholly out of her characters' voices in mainly humorous interplay. Like Robert Frost, Welty loves gossip in all its actuality and intimacy, and if that love failed in the novels to produce compelling, extended sequences, it did result in many lively and entertaining pages. Perhaps her finest single book after *A Curtain of Green* was *The Golden Apples* (1949), a sequence of tales about a fabulous, invented, small Mississippi community named Morgana. Her characters appear and reappear in these related stories and come together most memorably in the brilliant *June Recital*, perhaps her masterpiece.

As an entertainer, her wonderfully sharp sense of humor is strongly evident. Although the characters and themes that fill the pages of her fiction consist, in part, of involuted southern families, physically handicapped, mentally retarded, or generally unstable kinfolk—and although this fiction is shot through with undercurrents of death, violence, and degradation—everything Welty touches is transformed by the incorrigibly humorous twist of her narrative idiom. No matter how desperate a situation may be, she makes us listen to the way a character talks about it; it is style rather than information we find ourselves paying attention to. And although her attitude toward human folly is satiric, it is satire devoid of the wish to undermine and make mockery of her characters. Instead, they are given irresistible life and a memorable expressiveness in the vivid realizations of her prose. Her narrative unfolds on the principle of varied repetitions or reiterations that have (she has claimed) the function of a deliberate double exposure in photography. She once remarked in an essay that "fine story writers seem to be in a sense obstructionists." By making us pay attention to who is speaking and what the implications are of that speech, by asking us to imagine the way in which a silent character is responding to that speech, and by making us read behind the deceptively simple response she gives to that character, we are made active readers, playfully engaged in the complicated scene of a typical Welty story. *Why I Live at the P.O.*, *Keela, the Outcast Indian Maiden*, the unforgettable *Powerhouse* with its Fats Waller–like hero, *Petrified Man*, *June Recital*, and many others are solid proof of both the strength and the joy of her art. And although she has been called a "regional" writer, she herself has noted the condescending nature of that term, which she says is an "outsider's term; it has no meaning for the insider who is doing the writing, because as far as he knows he is simply writing about life" (*On Writing*). So it is with Eudora Welty's fiction.

# Petrified Man[1]

"Reach in my purse and git me a cigarette without no powder in it if you kin, Mrs. Fletcher, honey," said Leota to her ten o'clock shampoo-and-set customer. "I don't like no perfumed cigarettes."

Mrs. Fletcher gladly reached over to the lavender shelf under the lavender-framed mirror, shook a hair net loose from the clasp of the patent-leather bag,

1. Published in *A Curtain of Green* (1941).

and slapped her hand down quickly on a powder puff which burst out when the purse was opened.

"Why, look at the peanuts, Leota!" said Mrs. Fletcher in her marvelling voice.

"Honey, them goobers has been in my purse a week if they's been in it a day. Mrs. Pike bought them peanuts."

"Who's Mrs. Pike?" asked Mrs. Fletcher, settling back. Hidden in this den of curling fluid and henna[2] packs, separated by a lavender swing-door from the other customers, who were being gratified in other booths, she could give her curiosity its freedom. She looked expectantly at the black part in Leota's yellow curls as she bent to light the cigarette.

"Mrs. Pike is this lady from New Orleans," said Leota, puffing, and pressing into Mrs. Fletcher's scalp with strong red-nailed fingers. "A friend, not a customer. You see, like maybe I told you last time, me and Fred and Sal and Joe all had us a fuss, so Sal and Joe up and moved out, so we didn't do a thing but rent out their room. So we rented it to Mrs. Pike. And Mr. Pike." She flicked an ash into the basket of dirty towels. "Mrs. Pike is a very decided blonde. *She* bought me the peanuts."

"She must be cute," said Mrs. Fletcher.

"Honey, 'cute' ain't the word for what she is. I'm tellin' you, Mrs. Pike is attractive. She has her a good time. She's got a sharp eye out, Mrs. Pike has."

She dashed the comb through the air, and paused dramatically as a cloud of Mrs. Fletcher's hennaed hair floated out of the lavender teeth like a small storm-cloud.

"Hair fallin'."

"Aw, Leota."

"Uh-huh, commencin' to fall out," said Leota, combing again, and letting fall another cloud.

"Is it any dandruff in it?" Mrs. Fletcher was frowning, her hair-line eyebrows diving down toward her nose, and her wrinkled, beady-lashed eyelids batting with concentration.

"Nope." She combed again. "Just fallin' out."

"Bet it was that last perm'nent you gave me that did it," Mrs. Fletcher said cruelly. "Remember you cooked me fourteen minutes."

"You had fourteen minutes comin' to you," said Leota with finality.

"Bound to be somethin'," persisted Mrs. Fletcher. "Dandruff, dandruff. I couldn't of caught a thing like that from Mr. Fletcher, could I?"

"Well," Leota answered at last, "you know what I heard in here yestiddy, one of Thelma's ladies was settin' over yonder in Thelma's booth gittin' a machineless, and I don't mean to insist or insinuate or anything, Mrs. Fletcher, but Thelma's lady just happ'med to throw out—I forgotten what she was talkin' about at the time—that you was p-r-e-g., and lots of times that'll make your hair do awful funny, fall out and God knows what all. It just ain't our fault, is the way I look at it."

There was a pause. The women stared at each other in the mirror.

"Who was it?" demanded Mrs. Fletcher.

"Honey, I really couldn't say," said Leota. "Not that you look it."

"Where's Thelma? I'll get it out of her," said Mrs. Fletcher.

2. Reddish brown dye for tinting hair.

"Now, honey, I wouldn't go and git mad over a little thing like that," Leota said, combing hastily, as though to hold Mrs. Fletcher down by the hair. "I'm sure it was somebody didn't mean no harm in the world. How far gone are you?"

"Just wait," said Mrs. Fletcher, and shrieked for Thelma, who came in and took a drag from Leota's cigarette.

"Thelma, honey, throw your mind back to yestiddy if you kin," said Leota, drenching Mrs. Fletcher's hair with a thick fluid and catching the overflow in a cold wet towel at her neck.

"Well, I got my lady half wound for a spiral," said Thelma doubtfully.

"This won't take but a minute," said Leota. "Who is it you got in there, old Horse Face? Just cast your mind back and try to remember who your lady was yestiddy who happ'm to mention that my customer was pregnant, that's all. She's dead to know."

Thelma drooped her blood-red lips and looked over Mrs. Fletcher's head into the mirror. "Why, honey, I ain't got the faintest," she breathed. "I really don't recollect the faintest. But I'm sure she meant no harm. I declare, I forgot my hair finally got combed and thought it was a stranger behind me."

"Was it that Mrs. Hutchinson?" Mrs. Fletcher was tensely polite.

"Mrs. Hutchinson? Oh, Mrs. Hutchinson." Thelma batted her eyes. "Naw, precious, she come on Thursday and didn't ev'm mention your name. I doubt if she ev'm knows you're on the way."

"Thelma!" cried Leota staunchly.

"All I know is, whoever it is 'll be sorry some day. Why, I just barely knew it myself!" cried Mrs. Fletcher. "Just let her wait!"

"Why? What're you gonna do to her?"

It was a child's voice, and the women looked down. A little boy was making tents with aluminum wave pinchers[3] on the floor under the sink.

"Billy Boy, hon, mustn't bother nice ladies," Leota smiled. She slapped him brightly and behind her back waved Thelma out of the booth. "Ain't Billy Boy a sight? Only three years old and already just nuts about the beauty-parlor business."

"I never saw him here before," said Mrs. Fletcher, still unmollified.

"He ain't been here before, that's how come," said Leota. "He belongs to Mrs. Pike. She got her a job but it was Fay's Millinery. He oughtn't to try on those ladies' hats, they come down over his eyes like I don't know what. They just git to look ridiculous, that's what, an' of course he's gonna put 'em on: hats. They tole Mrs. Pike they didn't appreciate him hangin' around there. Here, he couldn't hurt a thing."

"Well! I don't like children that much," said Mrs. Fletcher.

"Well!" said Leota moodily.

"Well! I'm almost tempted not to have this one," said Mrs. Fletcher. "That Mrs. Hutchinson! Just looks straight through you when she sees you on the street and then spits at you behind your back."

"Mr. Fletcher would beat you on the head if you didn't have it now," said Leota reasonably. "After going this far."

Mrs. Fletcher sat up straight. "Mr. Fletcher can't do a thing with me."

"He can't!" Leota winked at herself in the mirror.

3. Clip used to form and hold (or set) hair curl or wave.

"No, siree, he can't. If he so much as raises his voice against me, he knows good and well I'll have one of my sick headaches, and then I'm just not fit to live with. And if I really look that pregnant already—"

"Well, now, honey, I just want you to know—I habm't told any of my ladies and I ain't goin' to tell 'em—even that you're losin' your hair. You just get you one of those Stork-a-Lure dresses and stop worryin'. What people don't know don't hurt nobody, as Mrs. Pike says."

"Did you tell Mrs. Pike?" asked Mrs. Fletcher sulkily.

"Well, Mrs. Fletcher, look, you ain't ever goin' to lay eyes on Mrs. Pike or her lay eyes on you, so what diffunce does it make in the long run?"

"I knew it!" Mrs. Fletcher deliberately nodded her head so as to destroy a ringlet Leota was working on behind her ear. "Mrs. Pike!"

Leota sighed. "I reckon I might as well tell you. It wasn't any more Thelma's lady tole me you was pregnant than a bat."

"Not Mrs. Hutchinson?"

"Naw, Lord! It was Mrs. Pike."

"Mrs. Pike!" Mrs. Fletcher could only sputter and let curling fluid roll into her ear. "How could Mrs. Pike possibly know I was pregnant or otherwise, when she doesn't even know me? The nerve of some people!"

"Well, here's how it was. Remember Sunday?"

"Yes," said Mrs. Fletcher.

"Sunday, Mrs. Pike an' me was all by ourself. Mr. Pike and Fred had gone over to Eagle Lake, sayin' they was goin' to catch 'em some fish, but they didn't a course. So we was gettin' in Mrs. Pike's car, it's a 1939 Dodge—"

"1939, eh," said Mrs. Fletcher.

"—An' we was gettin' us a Jax beer apiece—that's the beer that Mrs. Pike says is made right in N.O., so she won't drink no other kind. So I seen you drive up to the drugstore an' run in for just a secont, leavin' I reckon Mr. Fletcher in the car, an' come runnin' out with looked like a perscription. So I says to Mrs. Pike, just to be makin' talk, 'Right yonder's Mrs. Fletcher, and I reckon that's Mr. Fletcher—she's one of my regular customers,' I says."

"I had on a figured print," said Mrs. Fletcher tentatively.

"You sure did," agreed Leota. "So Mrs. Pike, she give you a good look— she's very observant, a good judge of character, cute as a minute, you know— and she says, 'I bet you another Jax that lady's three months on the way.'"

"What gall!" said Mrs. Fletcher. "Mrs. Pike!"

"Mrs. Pike ain't goin' to bite you," said Leota. "Mrs. Pike is a lovely girl, you'd be crazy about her, Mrs. Fletcher. But she can't sit still a minute. We went to the travellin' freak show yestiddy after work. I got through early—nine o'clock. In the vacant store next door. What, you ain't been?"

"No, I despise freaks," declared Mrs. Fletcher.

"Aw. Well, honey, talkin' about bein' pregnant an' all, you ought to see those twins in a bottle, you really owe it to yourself."

"What twins?" asked Mrs. Fletcher out of the side of her mouth.

"Well, honey, they got these two twins in a bottle, see? Born joined plumb together—dead a course." Leota dropped her voice into a soft lyrical hum. "They was about this long—pardon—must of been full time, all right, wouldn't you say?—an' they had these two heads an' two faces an' four arms an' four legs, all kind of joined *here*. See, this face looked this-a-way, and the other face looked that-a-way, over their shoulder, see. Kinda pathetic."

"Glah!" said Mrs. Fletcher disapprovingly.

"Well, ugly? Honey, I mean to tell you—their parents was first cousins and all like that. Billy Boy, git me a fresh towel from off Teeny's stack—this 'n's wringin' wet—an' quit ticklin' my ankles with that curler. I declare! He don't miss nothin'."

"Me and Mr. Fletcher aren't one speck of kin, or he could never of had me," said Mrs. Fletcher placidly.

"Of course not!" protested Leota. "Neither is me an' Fred, not that we know of. Well, honey, what Mrs. Pike liked was the pygmies. They've got these pygmies down there, too, an' Mrs. Pike was just wild about 'em. You know, the teeniniest men in the universe? Well, honey, they can just rest back on their little bohunkus an' roll around an' you can't hardly tell if they're sittin' or standin'. That'll give you some idea. They're about forty-two years old. Just suppose it was your husband!"

"Well, Mr. Fletcher is five foot nine and one half," said Mrs. Fletcher quickly.

"Fred's five foot ten," said Leota, "but I tell him he's still a shrimp, account of I'm so tall." She made a deep wave over Mrs. Fletcher's other temple with the comb. "Well, these pygmies are a kind of a dark brown, Mrs. Fletcher. Not bad lookin' for what they are, you know."

"I wouldn't care for them," said Mrs. Fletcher. "What does that Mrs. Pike see in them?"

"Aw, I don't know," said Leota. "She's just cute, that's all. But they got this man, this petrified man, that ever'thing ever since he was nine years old, when it goes through his digestion, see, somehow Mrs. Pike says it goes to his joints and has been turning to stone."

"How awful!" said Mrs. Fletcher.

"He's forty-two too. That looks like a bad age."

"Who said so, that Mrs. Pike? I bet she's forty-two," said Mrs. Fletcher.

"Naw," said Leota, "Mrs. Pike's thirty-three, born in January, an Aquarian. He could move his head—like this. A course his head and mind ain't a joint, so to speak, and I guess his stomach ain't, either—not yet, anyways. But see— his food, he eats it, and it goes down, see, and then he digests it"—Leota rose on her toes for an instant—"and it goes out to his joints and before you can say 'Jack Robinson,' it's stone—pure stone. He's turning to stone. How'd you liked to be married to a guy like that? All he can do, he can move his head just a quarter of an inch. A course he *looks* just *terrible*."

"I should think he would," said Mrs. Fletcher frostily. "Mr. Fletcher takes bending exercises every night of the world. I make him."

"All Fred does is lay around the house like a rug. I wouldn't be surprised if he woke up some day and couldn't move. The petrified man just sat there moving his quarter of an inch though," said Leota reminiscently.

"Did Mrs. Pike like the petrified man?" asked Mrs. Fletcher.

"Not as much as she did the others," said Leota deprecatingly. "And then she likes a man to be a good dresser, and all that."

"Is Mr. Pike a good dresser?" asked Mrs. Fletcher sceptically.

"Oh, well, yeah," said Leota, "but he's twelve or fourteen years older'n her. She ast Lady Evangeline about him."

"Who's Lady Evangeline?" asked Mrs. Fletcher.

"Well, it's this mind reader they got in the freak show," said Leota. "Was real good. Lady Evangeline is her name, and if I had another dollar I wouldn't do a thing but have my other palm read. She had what Mrs. Pike said was the 'sixth mind' but she had the worst manicure I ever saw on a living person."

"What did she tell Mrs. Pike?" asked Mrs. Fletcher.

"She told her Mr. Pike was as true to her as he could be and besides, would come into some money."

"Humph!" said Mrs. Fletcher. "What does he do?"

"I can't tell," said Leota, "because he don't work. Lady Evangeline didn't tell me enough about my nature or anything. And I would like to go back and find out some more about this boy. Used to go with this boy until he got married to this girl. Oh, shoot, that was about three and a half years ago, when you was still goin' to the Robert E. Lee Beauty Shop in Jackson. He married her for her money. Another fortune-teller tole me that at the time. So I'm not in love with him any more, anyway, besides being married to Fred, but Mrs. Pike thought, just for the hell of it, see, to ask Lady Evangeline was he happy."

"Does Mrs. Pike know everything about you already?" asked Mrs. Fletcher unbelievingly. "Mercy!"

"Oh, yeah, I tole her ever'thing about ever'thing, from now on back to I don't know when—to when I first started goin' out," said Leota. "So I ast Lady Evangeline for one of my questions, was he happily married, and she says, just like she was glad I ask her, 'Honey,' she says, 'naw, he idn't. You write down this day, March 8, 1941,' she says, 'and mock it down: three years from today him and her won't be occupyin' the same bed.' There it is, up on the wall with them other dates—see, Mrs. Fletcher? And she says, 'Child, you ought to be glad you didn't git him, because he's so mercenary.' So I'm glad I married Fred. He sure ain't mercenary, money don't mean a thing to him. But I sure would like to go back and have my other palm read."

"Did Mrs. Pike believe in what the fortune-teller said?" asked Mrs. Fletcher in a superior tone of voice.

"Lord, yes, she's from New Orleans. Ever'body in New Orleans believes ever'thing spooky. One of 'em in New Orleans before it was raided says to Mrs. Pike one summer she was goin' to go from State to State and meet some grey-headed men, and, sure enough, she says she went on a beautician convention up to Chicago. . . ."

"Oh!" said Mrs. Fletcher. "Oh, is Mrs. Pike a beautician too?"

"Sure she is," protested Leota. "She's a beautician. I'm goin' to git her in here if I can. Before she married. But it don't leave you. She says sure enough, there was three men who was a very large part of making her trip what it was, and they all three had grey in their hair and they went in six States. Got Christmas cards from 'em. Billy Boy, go see if Thelma's got any dry cotton. Look how Mrs. Fletcher's a-drippin'."

"Where did Mrs. Pike meet Mr. Pike?" asked Mrs. Fletcher primly.

"On another train," said Leota.

"I met Mr. Fletcher, or rather he met me, in a rental library," said Mrs. Fletcher with dignity, as she watched the net come down over her head.

"Honey, me an' Fred, we met in a rumble seat[4] eight months ago and we was practically on what you might call the way to the altar inside of half an hour," said Leota in a guttural voice, and bit a bobby pin open. "Course it don't last. Mrs. Pike says nothin' like that ever lasts."

---

4. Folding seat at the rear of an automobile.

"Mr. Fletcher and myself are as much in love as the day we married," said Mrs. Fletcher belligerently as Leota stuffed cotton into her ears.

"Mrs. Pike says it don't last," repeated Leota in a louder voice. "Now go git under the dryer. You can turn yourself on, can't you? I'll be back to comb you out. Durin' lunch I promised to give Mrs. Pike a facial. You know—free. Her bein' in the business, so to speak."

"I bet she needs one," said Mrs. Fletcher, letting the swing-door fly back against Leota. "Oh, pardon me."

A week later, on time for her appointment, Mrs. Fletcher sank heavily into Leota's chair after first removing a drug-store rental book, called *Life Is Like That*, from the seat. She stared in a discouraged way into the mirror.

"You can tell it when I'm sitting down, all right," she said.

Leota seemed preoccupied and stood shaking out a lavender cloth. She began to pin it around Mrs. Fletcher's neck in silence.

"I said you sure can tell it when I'm sitting straight on and coming at you this way," Mrs. Fletcher said.

"Why, honey, naw you can't," said Leota gloomily. "Why, I'd never know. If somebody was to come up to me on the street and say, 'Mrs. Fletcher is pregnant!' I'd say, 'Heck, she don't look it to me.' "

"If a certain party hadn't found it out and spread it around, it wouldn't be too late even now," said Mrs. Fletcher frostily, but Leota was almost choking her with the cloth, pinning it so tight, and she couldn't speak clearly. She paddled her hands in the air until Leota wearily loosened her.

"Listen, honey, you're just a virgin compared to Mrs. Montjoy," Leota was going on, still absent-minded. She bent Mrs. Fletcher back in the chair and, sighing, tossed liquid from a teacup on to her head and dug both hands into her scalp. "You know Mrs. Montjoy—her husband's that premature-grey-headed fella?"

"She's in the Trojan Garden Club, is all I know," said Mrs. Fletcher.

"Well, honey," said Leota, but in a weary voice, "she come in here not the week before and not the day before she had her baby—she come in here the very selfsame day, I mean to tell you. Child, we was all plumb scared to death. There she was! Come for her shampoo an' set. Why, Mrs. Fletcher, in an hour an' twenty minutes she was layin' up there in the Babtist Hospital with a seb'm-pound son. It was that close a shave. I declare, if I hadn't been so tired I would of drank up a bottle of gin that night."

"What gall," said Mrs. Fletcher. "I never knew her at all well."

"See, her husband was waitin' outside in the car, and her bags was all packed an' in the back seat, an' she was all ready, 'cept she wanted her shampoo an' set. An' havin' one pain right after another. Her husband kep' comin' in here, scared-like, but couldn't do nothin' with her a course. She yelled bloody murder, too, but she always yelled her head off when I give her a perm'nent."

"She must of been crazy," said Mrs. Fletcher. "How did she look?"

"Shoot!" said Leota.

"Well, I can guess," asid Mrs. Fletcher. "Awful."

"Just wanted to look pretty while she was havin' her baby, is all," said Leota airily. "Course, we was glad to give the lady what she was after—that's our motto—but I bet a hour later she wasn't payin' no mind to them little end curls. I bet she wasn't thinkin' about she ought to have on a net. It wouldn't of done her no good if she had."

"No, I don't suppose it would," said Mrs. Fletcher.

"Yeah man! She was a-yellin'. Just like when I give her perm'nent."

"Her husband ought to make her behave. Don't it seem that way to you?" asked Mrs. Fletcher. "He ought to put his foot down."

"Ha," said Leota. "A lot he could do. Maybe some women is soft."

"Oh, you mistake me, I don't mean for her to get soft—far from it! Women have to stand up for themselves, or there's just no telling. But now you take me—I ask Mr. Fletcher's advice now and then, and he appreciates it, especially on something important, like is it time for a permanent—not that I've told him about the baby. He says, 'Why, dear, go ahead!' Just ask their *advice*."

"Huh! If I ever ast Fred's advice we'd be floatin' down the Yazoo River on a houseboat or somethin' by this time," said Leota. "I'm sick of Fred. I told him to go over to Vicksburg."

"Is he going?" demanded Mrs. Fletcher.

"Sure. See, the fortune-teller—I went back and had my other palm read, since we've got to rent the room agin—said my lover was goin' to work in Vicksburg, so I don't know who she could mean, unless she meant Fred. And Fred ain't workin' here—that much is so."

"Is he going to work in Vicksburg?" asked Mrs. Fletcher. "And—"

"Sure. Lady Evangeline said so. Said the future is going to be brighter than the present. He don't want to go, but I ain't gonna put up with nothin' like that. Lays around the house an' bulls—did bull—with that good-for-nothin' Mr. Pike. He says if he goes who'll cook, but I says I never get to eat anyway—not meals. Billy Boy, take Mrs. Grover that *Screen Secrets* and leg it."

Mrs. Fletcher heard stamping feet go out the door.

"Is that that Mrs. Pike's little boy here again?" she asked, sitting up gingerly.

"Yeah, that's still him." Leota stuck out her tongue.

Mrs. Fletcher could hardly believe her eyes. "Well! How's Mrs. Pike, your attractive new friend with the sharp eyes who spreads it around town that perfect strangers are pregnant?" she asked in a sweetened tone.

"Oh, Mizziz Pike." Leota combed Mrs. Fletcher's hair with heavy strokes.

"You act like you're tired," said Mrs. Fletcher.

"Tired? Feel like it's four o'clock in the afternoon already," said Leota. "I ain't told you the awful luck we had, me and Fred? It's the worst thing you ever heard of. Maybe *you* think Mrs. Pike's got sharp eyes. Shoot, there's a limit! Well, you know, we rented out our room to this Mr. and Mrs. Pike from New Orleans when Sal an' Joe Fentress got mad at us 'cause they drank up some home-brew we had in the closet—Sal an' Joe did. So, a week ago Sat'day Mr. and Mrs. Pike moved in. Well, I kinda fixed up the room, you know—put a sofa pillow on the couch and picked some ragged robbins and put in a vase, but they never did say they appreciated it. Anyway, then I put some old magazines on the table."

"I think that was lovely," said Mrs. Fletcher.

"Wait. So, come night 'fore last, Fred and this Mr. Pike, who Fred just took up with, was back from they said they was fishin', bein' as neither one of 'em has got a job to his name, and we was all settin' around their room. So Mrs. Pike was settin' there, readin' a old *Startling G-Man Tales* that was mine, mind you, I'd bought it myself, and all of a sudden she jumps!—into the air—you'd 'a' thought she'd set on a spider—an' says, 'Canfield'—ain't that silly, that's Mr. Pike—'Canfield, my God A'mighty,' she says, 'honey,' she says, 'we're rich, and you won't have to work.' Not that he turned one hand anyway."

Well, me and Fred rushes over to her, and Mr. Pike, too, and there she sets, pointin' her finger at a photo in my copy of *Startling G-Man*. 'See that man?' yells Mrs. Pike. 'Remember him, Canfield?' 'Never forget a face,' says Mr. Pike. 'It's Mr. Petrie, that we stayed with him in the apartment next to ours in Toulouse Street in N.O. for six weeks. Mr. Petrie.' 'Well,' says Mrs. Pike, like she can't hold out one secont longer, 'Mr. Petrie is wanted for five hundred dollars cash, for rapin' four women in California, and I know where he is.' "

"Mercy!" said Mrs. Fletcher. "Where was he?"

At some time Leota had washed her hair and now she yanked her up by the back locks and sat her up.

"Know where he was?"

"I certainly don't," Mrs. Fletcher said. Her scalp hurt all over.

Leota flung a towel around the top of her customer's head. "Nowhere else but in that freak show! I saw him just as plain as Mrs. Pike. *He* was the petrified man!"

"Who would ever have thought that!" cried Mrs. Fletcher sympathetically.

"So Mr. Pike says, 'Well whatta you know about that', an' he looks real hard at the photo and whistles. And she starts dancin' and singin' about their good luck. She meant our bad luck! I made a point of tellin' that fortune-teller the next time I saw her. I said, 'Listen, that magazine was layin' around the house for a month, and there was the freak show runnin' night an' day, not two steps away from my own beauty parlor, with Mr. Petrie just settin' there waitin'. An' it had to be Mr. and Mrs. Pike, almost perfect strangers.' "

"What gall," said Mrs. Fletcher. She was only sitting there, wrapped in a turban, but she did not mind.

"Fortune-tellers don't care. And Mrs. Pike, she goes around actin' like she thinks she was Mrs. God," said Leota. "So they're goin' to leave tomorrow, Mr. and Mrs. Pike. And in the meantime I got to keep that mean, bad little ole kid here, gettin' under my feet ever' minute of the day an' talkin' back too."

"Have they gotten the five hundred dollars' reward already?" asked Mrs. Fletcher.

"Well," said Leota, "at first Mr. Pike didn't want to do anything about it. Can you feature that? Said he kinda liked that ole bird and said he was real nice to 'em, lent 'em money or somethin'. But Mrs. Pike simply tole him he could just go to hell, and I can see her point. She says, 'You ain't worked a lick in six months, and here I make five hundred dollars in two seconds, and what thanks do I get for it? You go to hell, Canfield,' she says. So," Leota went on in a despondent voice, "they called up the cops and they caught the ole bird, all right, right there in the freak show where I saw him with my own eyes, thinkin' he was petrified. He's the one. Did it under his real name—Mr. Petrie. Four women in California, all in the month of August. So Mrs. Pike gits five hundred dollars. And my magazine, and right next door to my beauty parlor. I cried all night, but Fred said it wasn't a bit of use and to go to sleep, because the whole thing was just a sort of coincidence—you know: can't do nothin' about it. He says it put him clean out of the notion of goin' to Vicksburg for a few days till we rent out the room agin—no tellin' who we'll git this time."

"But can you imagine anybody knowing this old man, that's raped four women?" persisted Mrs. Fletcher, and she shuddered audibly. "Did Mrs. Pike *speak* to him when she met him in the freak show?"

Leota had begun to comb Mrs. Fletcher's hair. "I says to her, I says, 'I didn't notice you fallin' on his neck when he was the petrified man—don't tell me you didn't recognize your fine friend?' And she says, 'I didn't recognize him with that white powder all over his face. He just looked familiar,' Mrs. Pike says, 'and lots of people look familiar.' But she says that ole petrified man did put her in mind of somebody. She wondered who it was! Kep' her awake, which man she'd ever knew it reminded her of. So when she seen the photo, it all come to her. Like a flash. Mr. Petrie. The way he'd turn his head and look at her when she took him in his breakfast."

"Took him in his breakfast!" shrieked Mrs. Fletcher. "Listen—don't tell me. I'd 'a' felt something."

"Four women. I guess those women didn't have the faintest notion at the time they'd be worth a hundred an' twenty-five bucks apiece some day to Mrs. Pike. We ast her how old the fella was then, an's she says he musta had one foot in the grave, at least. Can you beat it?"

"Not really petrified at all, of course," said Mrs. Fletcher meditatively. She drew herself up. "I'd 'a' felt something," she said proudly.

"Shoot! I did feel somethin'," said Leota. "I tole Fred when I got home I felt so funny. I said, 'Fred, that ole petrified man sure did leave me with a funny feelin'.' He says, 'Funny-haha or funny-peculiar?' and I says, 'Funny-peculiar.' " She pointed her comb into the air emphatically.

"I'll bet you did," said Mrs. Fletcher.

They both heard a crackling noise.

Leota screamed, "Billy Boy! What you doin' in my purse?"

"Aw, I'm just eatin' these ole stale peanuts up," said Billy Boy.

"You come here to me!" screamed Leota, recklessly flinging down the comb, which scattered a whole ashtray full of bobby pins and knocked down a row of Coca-Cola bottles. "This is the last straw!"

"I caught him! I caught him!" giggled Mrs. Fletcher. "I'll hold him on my lap. You bad, bad boy, you! I guess I better learn how to spank little old bad boys," she said.

Leota's eleven o'clock customer pushed open the swing-door upon Leota's paddling him heartily with the brush, while he gave angry but belittling screams which penetrated beyond the booth and filled the whole curious beauty parlor. From everywhere ladies began to gather round to watch the paddling. Billy Boy kicked both Leota and Mrs. Fletcher as hard as he could, Mrs. Fletcher with her new fixed smile.

Billy Boy stomped through the group of wild-haired ladies and went out the door, but flung back the words, "If you're so smart, why ain't you rich?"

1941

---

# TENNESSEE WILLIAMS

## 1911–1983

Speaking of Blanche DuBois, the heroine of A *Streetcar Named Desire*, Tennessee Williams once said, "She was a demonic creature; the size of her feeling was too great for her to contain." In Williams's plays—he wrote and rewrote more than twenty full-length dramas as well as films and shorter works—his characters are driven by the size of their feelings, much as Williams himself felt driven to write about them.

He was born Thomas Lanier Williams in Columbus, Mississippi, on March 26, 1911. His mother, "Miss Edwina," the daughter of an Episcopalian minister, was repressed and genteel, very much the southern belle in her youth. His father, Cornelius, was a traveling salesman, often away from his family and often violent and drunk when at home. As a child, Williams was sickly and overly protected by his mother; he was closely attached to his sister, Rose, repelled by the roughhouse world of boys, and alienated from his father. The family's move from Mississippi to St. Louis, where Cornelius became a sales manager of the shoe company he had traveled for, was a shock to Mrs. Williams and her young children, used to living in small southern towns where a minister's daughter was an important person. Yet Mrs. Williams was a woman who could take care of herself, a "survivor."

Williams went to the University of Missouri, but left after two years; his father then found him a job in the shoe-factory warehouse. He worked there for ten months, writing feverishly at night. His closest friend at the time was a burly co-worker, easygoing and attractive to women, named Stanley Kowalski. Williams found the life so difficult, however, that he succumbed to a nervous breakdown. After recovering at the home of his beloved grandparents, he went on to further studies, finally graduating at the age of twenty-seven. Meanwhile Rose had been suffering increasing mental imbalance; the final trauma was apparently brought on by one of Cornelius's alcoholic rages, in which he beat Edwina and, trying to calm Rose, made a gesture that she took to be a sexual one. Shortly thereafter, Edwina signed the papers allowing Rose to be "tragically becalmed" by a prefrontal lobotomy. She spent most of her life in sanatoriums, except when Williams brought her out for visits.

The next year Williams left for New Orleans, the first of many temporary homes; it would provide the setting for A Streetcar Named Desire. In New Orleans, he changed his name to "Tennessee," later giving—as often when discussing his life—various romantic reasons for doing so. There also he actively entered the homosexual world.

Williams had had plays produced at local theaters, and in 1939 he won a prize for a collection of one-act plays, American Blues. The next year, Battle of Angels failed (it would later be rewritten as Orpheus Descending, 1957). His first success was The Glass Menagerie (1945). Williams called it a "memory play," seen through the recollections of the writer Tom, who talks to the audience about himself and about the scenes depicting his mother Amanda, poverty-stricken but genteelly living on memories of her southern youth and her "gentlemen callers"; his crippled sister, Laura, who finds refuge in her "menagerie" of little glass animals; and the traumatic effect of a modern "gentleman caller" on them. While there are similarities between Edwina, Rose, and Tennessee, on the one hand, and Amanda, Laura, and Tom on the other, there are also differences: the play is not literally autobiographical.

The financial success of Menagerie was at first exhilarating, then debilitating. Williams fled to Mexico, to work full-time on an earlier play, The Poker Night. It had begun as The Moth; its first image, as Williams's biographer, Donald Spoto, tells us, was "simply that of a woman, sitting with folded hands near a window, while moonlight streamed in and she awaited in vain the arrival of her boy friend": named Blanche, she was at first intended as a young Amanda. During rehearsals of Menagerie, Williams had asked members of the stage crew to teach him to play poker, and he began to visualize the play as a series of confrontations between working-class poker players and two refined southern women.

As the focus of his attention changed from Stanley to Blanche, The Poker Night gradually turned into A Streetcar Named Desire. When it opened in 1947, it was an even greater success than *Glass Menagerie*, and it won the Pulitzer Prize. Williams was able to travel and to buy a home in Key West, Florida, where he did much of his ensuing work. At about this time his "transitory heart" found "a home at last" in a young man named Frank Merlo.

For more than a decade thereafter, a new Williams play appeared almost every two years. Among the most successful were *The Rose Tattoo* (1950), in which the tempestuous heroine Serafina, worshiping the memory of her dead husband, finds love again; the Pulitzer Prize–winning *Cat on a Hot Tin Roof* (1955), which portrays the conflict of the dying Big Daddy and his impotent son, Brick, watched and controlled by Brick's wife, "Maggie the Cat"; and *The Night of the Iguana* (1961), which brings a varied group of tormented people together at a rundown hotel on the Mexican coast. His plays were produced widely abroad and also became equally successful films. Yet some of the ones now regarded as the best of this period were commercial failures: *Summer and Smoke* (1948), for example, and the surrealistic and visionary *Camino Real* (1953).

For years, Williams had depended on a wide variety of drugs, especially to help him sleep and to keep him awake in the early mornings when he invariably worked. In the 1960s, these began to take a real toll. Other factors contributed to the decline of his later years: the death of Frank Merlo, the emergence of younger playwrights of whom he felt blindly jealous, and the violent nature of the 1960s themselves, which seemed both to mirror his own inner chaos and to leave him behind.

Yet, despite Broadway failures, critical disparagements, and a breakdown for which he was hospitalized, he kept valiantly working. His biographer notes that in his late work, Rose was "the source and inspiration of everything he wrote, either directly—with a surrogate character representing her—or indirectly, in the situation of romanticized mental illness or unvarnished verisimilitude." This observation is certainly true of his last Broadway play, the failed *Clothes for a Summer Hotel* (1980), ostensibly about the ghosts of Scott and Zelda Fitzgerald, and of the play he obsessively wrote and rewrote, *The Two Character Play*, which chronicles the descent into madness and death of a brother and sister who are also lovers.

Despite Williams's self-destructiveness, both in his writing and in his social life, the work of his great years was now being seriously studied and often revived by regional and community theaters. Critics began to see that he was one of America's best and most dedicated playwrights. And he kept on working. He was collaborating on a film of two stories about Rose when he died on February 23, 1983, apparently having choked to death on the lid of a pill bottle.

Williams, who was always reluctant to talk about his work (likening it to a "bird that will be startled away, as by a hawk's shadow"), did not see himself in a tradition in American dramaturgy. He acknowledged the influence of Anton Chekhov, the nineteenth-century Russian writer of dramas with lonely, searching characters; of D. H. Lawrence, the British novelist who emphasized the theme of a sexual life force; and above all of the American Hart Crane, homosexual *poète maudit*, who, he said, "touched fire that burned [himself] alive," adding that "perhaps it is only through self-immolation of such a nature that we living beings can offer to you the entire truth of ourselves." Such a statement indicates the deeply confessional quality of Williams's writing, even in plays not directly autobiographical.

Although he never acknowledged any debt to Eugene O'Neill, Williams shared with that playwright an impatience over realistic theater conventions. *The Glass Menagerie*, for example, uses screened projections, lighting effects, and music to emphasize that it takes place in Tom's memory. *A Streetcar Named Desire* moves in and out of the house on Elysian Fields, while music and lighting reinforce all the major themes. Williams also relies on the effects of language, especially of a vivid and colloquial southern speech that may be compared with that of William Faulkner, Eudora Welty, or Flannery O'Connor. Rhythms of language become almost a musical indication of character, distinguishing Blanche from other characters. Reading or seeing his plays, we become aware of how symbolic repetitions—in Blanche's and Stanley's turns of phrase, the naked light bulb and the paper lantern, the Mexican woman selling flowers for the dead, the "Varsouviana" waltz and the reverberating voices—produce a heightening of reality: what Williams called "poetic realism."

Forty or more years later, does the destruction of Blanche, the "lady," still have the power to move us? Elia Kazan, in his director's notes, thought of her as "an outdated creature, approaching extinction . . . like a dinosaur." But Blythe Danner, who played Blanche in a 1988 revival, acutely observes that Williams "was attached to the things that were going to destroy him" and that Blanche, similarly, is both attracted and repelled by Stanley: "It's Tennessee fighting, fighting, fighting what he doesn't want to get into, what is very prevalent in his mind. That incredible contradiction in so many people is what he captures better than any other playwright."

From our present perspective, moreover, we are less concerned over contemporary criticisms of Williams's plays for their violence and their obsession with sexuality, which in some of the later work was regarded by some critics as an almost morbid preoccupation with "perversion"—murder, rape, drugs, incest, nymphomania. We now know that the shriller voices making such accusations were attacking Williams for his homosexuality, which, we must remember, could not be publicly spoken of in this country until comparatively recently. These topics, however, also figure as instances of his deeper subject, the themes of desire and loneliness. As he said in an interview, "Desire is rooted in a longing for companionship, a release from the loneliness that haunts every individual." Loneliness and desire propel his characters into extreme behavior, no doubt, but such behavior literally dramatizes the plight that Williams saw as universal.

# A Streetcar Named Desire[1]

*And so it was I entered the broken world*
*To trace the visionary company of love, its voice*
*An instant in the wind (I know not whither hurled)*
*But not for long to hold each desperate choice.*
*—"The Broken Tower" by Hart Crane[2]*

## THE CHARACTERS

| | |
|---|---|
| BLANCHE | PABLO |
| STELLA | A NEGRO WOMAN |
| STANLEY | A DOCTOR |
| MITCH | A NURSE |
| EUNICE | A YOUNG COLLECTOR |
| STEVE | A MEXICAN WOMAN |

## Scene One

*The exterior of a two-story corner building on a street in New Orleans which is named Elysian Fields and runs between the L & N tracks and the river.[3] The section is poor but, unlike corresponding sections in other American cities, it*

1. The text is taken from *The Theatre of Tennessee Williams*, Vol. 1 (1971).
2. American poet (1899–1932).
3. Elysian Fields is in fact a New Orleans street at the northern tip of the French Quarter, between the Louisville & Nashville railroad tracks and the Mississippi River. In Greek mythology, the Elysian Fields are the abode of the blessed in the afterlife.

*has a raffish charm. The houses are mostly white frame, weathered grey, with rickety outside stairs and galleries and quaintly ornamented gables. This building contains two flats, upstairs and down. Faded white stairs ascend to the entrances of both.*

*It is first dark of an evening early in May. The sky that shows around the dim white building is a peculiarly tender blue, almost a turquoise, which invests the scene with a kind of lyricism and gracefully attenuates the atmosphere of decay. You can almost feel the warm breath of the brown river beyond the river warehouses with their faint redolences of bananas and coffee. A corresponding air is evoked by the music of Negro entertainers at a barroom around the corner. In this part of New Orleans you are practically always just around the corner, or a few doors down the street, from a tinny piano being played with the infatuated fluency of brown fingers. This "Blue Piano" expresses the spirit of the life which goes on here.*

*Two women, one white and one colored, are taking the air on the steps of the building. The white woman is* EUNICE, *who occupies the upstairs flat; the colored woman a neighbor, for New Orleans is a cosmopolitan city where there is a relatively warm and easy intermingling of races in the old part of town.*

*Above the music of the "Blue Piano" the voices of people on the street can be heard overlapping.*

[*Two men come around the corner,* STANLEY KOWALSKI *and* MITCH. *They are about twenty-eight or thirty years old, roughly dressed in blue denim work clothes.* STANLEY *carries his bowling jacket and a red-stained package from a butcher's. They stop at the foot of the steps.*]

STANLEY [*bellowing*]   Hey there! Stella, baby!

[STELLA *comes out on the first floor landing, a gentle young woman, about twenty-five, and of a background obviously quite different from her husband's.*]

STELLA [*mildly*]   Don't holler at me like that. Hi, Mitch.

STANLEY   Catch!

STELLA   What?

STANLEY   Meat!

[*He heaves the package at her. She cries out in protest but manages to catch it: then she laughs breathlessly. Her husband and his companion have already started back around the corner.*]

STELLA [*calling after him*]   Stanley! Where are you going?

STANLEY   Bowling!

STELLA   Can I come watch?

STANLEY   Come on. [*He goes out.*]

STELLA   Be over soon. [*to the white woman*] Hello, Eunice. How are you?

EUNICE   I'm all right. Tell Steve to get him a poor boy's sandwich 'cause nothing's left here.

[*They all laugh; the colored woman does not stop.* STELLA *goes out.*]

COLORED WOMAN   What was that package he th'ew at 'er? [*She rises from steps, laughing louder.*]

EUNICE   You hush, now!

NEGRO WOMAN   Catch *what!*

[*She continues to laugh.* BLANCHE *comes around the corner, carrying a valise. She looks at a slip of paper, then at the building, then again at the slip and again at the building. Her expression is one of shocked disbelief. Her appearance is incongruous to this setting. She is daintily dressed in a white suit with a fluffy bodice, necklace and earrings of pearl, white gloves and hat, looking as if she were arriving at a summer tea or cocktail party in the garden district. She is about five years older than* STELLA. *Her delicate beauty must avoid a strong light. There is something about her uncertain manner, as well as her white clothes, that suggests a moth.*]

EUNICE [*finally*]   What's the matter, honey? Are you lost?

BLANCHE [*with faintly hysterical humor*]   They told me to take a street-car named Desire, and then transfer to one called Cemeteries[4] and ride six blocks and get off at—Elysian Fields!

EUNICE   That's where you are now.

BLANCHE   At Elysian Fields?

EUNICE   This here is Elysian Fields.

BLANCHE   They mustn't have—understood—what number I wanted . . .

EUNICE   What number you lookin' for?

[BLANCHE *wearily refers to the slip of paper.*]

BLANCHE   Six thirty-two.

EUNICE   You don't have to look no further.

BLANCHE [*uncomprehendingly*]   I'm looking for my sister, Stella DuBois, I mean—Mrs. Stanley Kowalski.

EUNICE   That's the party.—You just did miss her, though.

BLANCHE   This—can this be—her home?

EUNICE   She's got the downstairs here and I got the up.

BLANCHE   Oh. She's—out?

EUNICE   You noticed that bowling alley around the corner?

BLANCHE   I'm—not sure I did.

EUNICE   Well, that's where she's at, watchin' her husband bowl. [*There is a pause.*] You want to leave your suitcase here an' go find her?

BLANCHE   No.

NEGRO WOMAN   I'll go tell her you come.

BLANCHE   Thanks.

NEGRO WOMAN   You welcome. [*She goes out.*]

EUNICE   She wasn't expecting you?

BLANCHE   No. No, not tonight.

EUNICE   Well, why don't you just go in and make yourself at home till they get back.

BLANCHE   How could I—do that?

EUNICE   We own this place so I can let you in.

[*She gets up and opens the downstairs door. A light goes on behind the blind, turning it light blue.* BLANCHE *slowly follows her into the downstairs flat. The surrounding areas dim out as the interior is lighted. Two rooms can be seen, not too clearly defined. The one first entered is primarily a kitchen but contains a folding bed to be used by* BLANCHE. *The room beyond this is a bedroom. Off this room is a narrow door to a bathroom.*]

EUNICE [*defensively, noticing* BLANCHE'S *look*]   It's sort of messed up right now but when it's clean it's real sweet.

BLANCHE   Is it?

EUNICE   Uh-huh, I think so. So you're Stella's sister?

BLANCHE   Yes. [*wanting to get rid of her*] Thanks for letting me in.

---

4. Desire is a street in New Orleans; Cemeteries, the end of a streetcar line that stopped at a cemetery.

EUNICE     *Por nada,*[5] as the Mexicans say, *por nada!* Stella spoke of you.
BLANCHE     Yes?
EUNICE     I think she said you taught school.
BLANCHE     Yes.
EUNICE     And you're from Mississippi, huh?
BLANCHE     Yes.
EUNICE     She showed me a picture of your home-place, the plantation.
BLANCHE     Belle Reve?[6]
EUNICE     A great big place with white columns.
BLANCHE     Yes . . .
EUNICE     A place like that must be awful hard to keep up.
BLANCHE     If you will excuse me, I'm just about to drop.
EUNICE     Sure, honey. Why don't you set down?
BLANCHE     What I meant was I'd like to be left alone.
EUNICE [*offended*]     Aw. I'll make myself scarce, in that case.
BLANCHE     I didn't meant to be rude, but—
EUNICE     I'll drop by the bowling alley an' hustle her up. [*She goes out the door.*]

> [BLANCHE *sits in a chair very stiffly with her shoulders slightly hunched and her legs pressed close together and her hands tightly clutching her purse as if she were quite cold. After a while the blind look goes out of her eyes and she begins to look slowly around. A cat screeches. She catches her breath with a startled gesture. Suddenly she notices something in a half opened closet. She springs up and crosses to it, and removes a whiskey bottle. She pours a half tumbler of whiskey and tosses it down. She carefully replaces the bottle and washes out the tumbler at the sink. Then she resumes her seat in front of the table.*]

BLANCHE [*faintly to herself*]     I've got to keep hold of myself! [STELLA *comes quickly around the corner of the building and runs to the door of the downstairs flat.*]
STELLA [*calling out joyfully*]     Blanche!

> [*For a moment they stare at each other. Then* BLANCHE *springs up and runs to her with a wild cry.*]

BLANCHE     Stella, oh, Stella, Stella! Stella for Star!

> [*She begins to speak with feverish vivacity as if she feared for either of them to stop and think. They catch each other in a spasmodic embrace.*]

BLANCHE     Now, then, let me look at you. But don't you look at me, Stella, no, no, no, not till later, not till I've bathed and rested! And turn that overlight off! Turn that off! I won't be looked at in this merciless glare! [STELLA *laughs and complies.*] Come back here now! Oh, my baby! Stella! Stella for Star! [*She embraces her again.*] I thought you would never come back to this horrible place! What am I saying? I didn't mean to say that. I meant to be nice about it and say—Oh, what a convenient location and such—Ha-a-ha! Precious lamb! You haven't said a *word* to me.
STELLA     You haven't given me a chance to, honey! [*She laughs, but her glance at* BLANCHE *is a little anxious.*]
BLANCHE     Well, now you talk. Open your pretty mouth and talk while I look around for some liquor! I know you must have some liquor on the place! Where could it be, I wonder? Oh, I spy, I spy!

---

5. It's nothing.                    6. Beautiful Dream.

[*She rushes to the closet and removes the bottle; she is shaking all over and panting for breath as she tries to laugh. The bottle nearly slips from her grasp.*]

STELLA [*noticing*]   Blanche, you sit down and let me pour the drinks. I don't know what we've got to mix with. Maybe a coke's in the icebox. Look'n see, honey, while I'm—

BLANCHE   No coke, honey, not with my nerves tonight! Where—where—where is—?

STELLA   Stanley? Bowling! He loves it. They're having a—found some soda!—tournament . . .

BLANCHE   Just water, baby, to chase it! Now don't get worried, your sister hasn't turned into a drunkard, she's just all shaken up and hot and tired and dirty! You sit down, now, and explain this place to me! What are you doing in a place like this?

STELLA   Now, Blanche—

BLANCHE   Oh, I'm not going to be hypocritical, I'm going to be honestly critical about it! Never, never, never in my worst dreams could I picture— Only Poe! Only Mr. Edgar Allan Poe!—could do it justice! Out there I suppose is the ghoul-haunted woodland of Weir![7] [*She laughs.*]

STELLA   No, honey, those are the L & N tracks.

BLANCHE   No, now seriously, putting joking aside. Why didn't you tell me, why didn't you write me, honey, why didn't you let me know?

STELLA [*carefully, pouring herself a drink*]   Tell you what, Blanche?

BLANCHE   Why, that you had to live in these conditions!

STELLA   Aren't you being a little intense about it? It's not that bad at all! New Orleans isn't like other cities.

BLANCHE   This has got nothing to do with New Orleans. You might as well say—forgive me, blessed baby! [*She suddenly stops short.*] The subject is closed!

STELLA [*a little drily*]   Thanks.

[*During the pause,* BLANCHE *stares at her. She smiles at* BLANCHE.]

BLANCHE [*looking down at her glass, which shakes in her hand*]   You're all I've got in the world, and you're not glad to see me!

STELLA [*sincerely*]   Why, Blanche, you know that's not true.

BLANCHE   No?—I'd forgotten how quiet you were.

STELLA   You never did give me a chance to say much, Blanche. So I just got in the habit of being quiet around you.

BLANCHE [*vaguely*]   A good habit to get into . . . [*then, abruptly*] You haven't asked me how I happened to get away from the school before the spring term ended.

STELLA   Well, I thought you'd volunteer that information—if you wanted to tell me.

BLANCHE   You thought I'd been fired?

STELLA   No, I—thought you might have—resigned . . .

BLANCHE   I was so exhausted by all I'd been through my—nerves broke. [*nervously tamping cigarette*] I was on the verge of—lunacy, almost! So Mr. Graves—Mr. Graves is the high school superintendent—he suggested I take a leave of absence. I couldn't put all of those details into the wire . . . [*She drinks quickly.*] Oh, this buzzes right through me and feels so *good*!

STELLA   Won't you have another?

---

7. From the refrain of Poe's gothic ballad *Ulalume* (1847).

BLANCHE    No, one's my limit.

STELLA    Sure?

BLANCHE    You haven't said a word about my appearance.

STELLA    You look just fine.

BLANCHE    God love you for a liar! Daylight never exposed so total a ruin! But you—you've put on some weight, yes, you're just as plump as a little partridge! And it's so becoming to you!

STELLA    Now, Blanche—

BLANCHE    Yes, it is, it is or I wouldn't say it! You just have to watch around the hips a little. Stand up.

STELLA    Not now.

BLANCHE    You hear me? I said stand up! [STELLA *complies reluctantly.*] You messy child, you, you've spilt something on that pretty white lace collar! About your hair—you ought to have it cut in a feather bob with your dainty features. Stella, you have a maid, don't you?

STELLA    No. With only two rooms it's—

BLANCHE    What? *Two* rooms, did you say?

STELLA    This one and—[*She is embarrassed.*]

BLANCHE    The other one? [*She laughs sharply. There is an embarrassed silence.*]

BLANCHE    I am going to take just one little tiny nip more, sort of to put the stopper on, so to speak. . . . Then put the bottle away so I won't be tempted. [*She rises.*] I want you to look at *my* figure! [*She turns around.*] You know I haven't put on one ounce in ten years, Stella? I weigh what I weighed the summer you left Belle Reve. The summer Dad died and you left us . . .

STELLA    [*a little wearily*] It's just incredible, Blanche, how well you're looking.

BLANCHE    [*They both laugh uncomfortably.*] But, Stella, there's only two rooms, I don't see where you're going to put me!

STELLA    We're going to put you in here.

BLANCHE    What kind of bed's this—one of those collapsible things? [*She sits on it.*]

STELLA    Does it feel all right?

BLANCHE    [*dubiously*] Wonderful, honey. I don't like a bed that gives much. But there's no door between the two rooms, and Stanley—will it be decent?

STELLA    Stanley is Polish, you know.

BLANCHE    Oh, yes. They're something like Irish, aren't they?

STELLA    Well—

BLANCHE    Only not so—highbrow? [*They both laugh again in the same way.*] I brought some nice clothes to meet all your lovely friends in.

STELLA    I'm afraid you won't think they are lovely.

BLANCHE    What are they like?

STELLA    They're Stanley's friends.

BLANCHE    Polacks?

STELLA    They're a mixed lot, Blanche.

BLANCHE    Heterogeneous—types?

STELLA    Oh, yes. Yes, types is right!

BLANCHE    Well—anyhow—I brought nice clothes and I'll wear them. I guess you're hoping I'll say I'll put up at a hotel, but I'm not going to put up at a hotel. I want to be *near* you, got to be *with* somebody, I *can't* be *alone*! Because—as you must have noticed—I'm—*not* very *well*. . . . [*Her voice drops and her look is frightened.*]

STELLA   You seem a little bit nervous or overwrought or something.
BLANCHE   Will Stanley like me, or will I be just a visiting in-law, Stella? I couldn't stand that.
STELLA   You'll get along fine together, if you'll just try not to—well—compare him with men that we went out with at home.
BLANCHE   Is he so—different?
STELLA   Yes. A different species.
BLANCHE   In what way; what's he like?
STELLA   Oh, you can't describe someone you're in love with! Here's a picture of him! [*She hands a photograph to* BLANCHE.]
BLANCHE   An officer?
STELLA   A Master Sergeant in the Engineers' Corps. Those are decorations!
BLANCHE   He had those on when you met him?
STELLA   I assure you I wasn't just blinded by all the brass.
BLANCHE   That's not what I—
STELLA   But of course there were things to adjust myself to later on.
BLANCHE   Such as his civilian background! [STELLA *laughs uncertainly.*] How did he take it when you said I was coming?
STELLA   Oh, Stanley doesn't know yet.
BLANCHE [*frightened*]   You—haven't told him?
STELLA   He's on the road a good deal.
BLANCHE   Oh. Travels?
STELLA   Yes.
BLANCHE   Good. I mean—isn't it?
STELLA [*half to herself*]   I can hardly stand it when he is away for a night . . .
BLANCHE   Why, Stella!
STELLA   When he's away for a week I nearly go wild!
BLANCHE   Gracious!
STELLA   And when he comes back I cry on his lap like a baby . . . [*She smiles to herself.*]
BLANCHE   I guess that is what is meant by being in love . . . [STELLA *looks up with a radiant smile.*] Stella—
STELLA   What?
BLANCHE [*in an uneasy rush*]   I haven't asked you the things you probably thought I was going to ask. And so I'll expect you to be understanding about what I have to tell you.
STELLA   What, Blanche? [*Her face turns anxious.*]
BLANCHE   Well, Stella—you're going to reproach me, I know that you're bound to reproach me—but before you do—take into consideration—you left! I stayed and struggled! You came to New Orleans and looked out for yourself! I stayed at *Belle Reve* and tried to hold it together! I'm not meaning this in any reproachful way, but *all* the burden descended on *my* shoulders.
STELLA   The best I could do was make my own living, Blanche.
    [BLANCHE *begins to shake again with intensity.*]
BLANCHE   I know, I know. But you are the one that abandoned Belle Reve, not I! I stayed and fought for it, bled for it, almost died for it!
STELLA   Stop this hysterical outburst and tell me what's happened? What do you mean fought and bled? What kind of—
BLANCHE   I knew you would, Stella. I knew you would take this attitude about it!
STELLA   About—what?—please!
BLANCHE [*slowly*]   The loss—the loss . . .

STELLA   Belle Reve? Lost, is it? No!

BLANCHE   Yes, Stella.

   [*They stare at each other across the yellow-checked linoleum of the table.* BLANCHE *slowly nods her head and* STELLA *looks slowly down at her hands folded on the table. The music of the "Blue Piano" grows louder.* BLANCHE *touches her handkerchief to her forehead.*]

STELLA   But how did it go? What happened?

BLANCHE   [*springing up*]   You're a fine one to ask me how it went!

STELLA   Blanche!

BLANCHE   You're a fine one to sit there *accusing me* of it!

STELLA   *Blanche!*

BLANCHE   I, I, *I* took the blows in my face and my body! All of those deaths! The long parade to the graveyard! Father, mother! Margaret, that dreadful way! So big with it, it couldn't be put in a coffin! But had to be burned like rubbish! You just came home in time for the funerals, Stella. And funerals are pretty compared to deaths. Funerals are quiet, but deaths—not always. Sometimes their breathing is hoarse, and sometimes it rattles, and sometimes they even cry out to you, "Don't let me go!" Even the old, sometimes, say, "Don't let me go." As if you were able to stop them! But funerals are quiet, with pretty flowers. And, oh, what gorgeous boxes they pack them away in! Unless you were there at the bed when they cried out, "Hold me!" you'd never suspect there was the struggle for breath and bleeding. You didn't dream, but I saw! *Saw! Saw!* And now you sit there telling me with your eyes that I let the place go! How in hell do you think all that sickness and dying was paid for? Death is expensive, Miss Stella! And old Cousin Jessie's right after Margaret's, hers! Why, the Grim Reaper had put up his tent on our doorstep! . . . Stella. Belle Reve was his headquarters! Honey— that's how it slipped through my fingers! Which of them left us a fortune? Which of them left a cent of insurance even? Only poor Jessie—one hundred to pay for her coffin. That was all, Stella! And I with my pitiful salary at the school. Yes, accuse me! Sit there and stare at me, thinking I let the place go! *I* let the place go? Where were *you!* In bed with your—Polack!

STELLA   [*springing*]   Blanche! You be still! That's enough! [*She starts out.*]

BLANCHE   Where are you going?

STELLA   I'm going into the bathroom to wash my face.

BLANCHE   Oh, Stella, Stella, you're crying!

STELLA   Does that surprise you?

BLANCHE   Forgive me—I didn't mean to—

   [*The sound of men's voices is heard.* STELLA *goes into the bathroom, closing the door behind her. When the men appear, and* BLANCHE *realizes it must be* STANLEY *returning, she moves uncertainly from the bathroom door to the dressing table, looking apprehensively toward the front door.* STANLEY *enters, followed by* STEVE *and* MITCH. STANLEY *pauses near his door,* STEVE *by the foot of the spiral stair, and* MITCH *is slightly above and to the right of them, about to go out. As the men enter, we hear some of the following dialogue.*]

STANLEY   Is that how he got it?

STEVE   Sure that's how he got it. He hit the old weather-bird for 300 bucks on a six-number-ticket.

MITCH   Don't tell him those things; he'll believe it.

   [*Mitch starts out.*]

STANLEY   [*restraining Mitch*]   Hey, Mitch—come back here.

[BLANCHE, *at the sound of voices, retires in the bedroom. She picks up* STANLEY's *photo from dressing table, looks at it, puts it down. When* STANLEY *enters the apartment, she darts and hides behind the screen at the head of bed.*]

STEVE [*to* STANLEY *and* MITCH]   Hey, are we playin' poker tomorrow?

STANLEY   Sure—at Mitch's.

MITCH [*hearing this, returns quickly to the stair rail*]   No—not at my place. My mother's still sick!

STANLEY   Okay, at my place . . .   [MITCH *starts out again.*]   But you bring the beer!

   [MITCH *pretends not to hear—calls out "Good night, all," and goes out, singing.* EUNICE's *voice is heard, above.*]
Break it up down there! I made the spaghetti dish and ate it myself.

STEVE [*going upstairs*]   I told you and phoned you we was playing. [*to the men*] Jax[8] beer!

EUNICE   You never phoned me once.

STEVE   I told you at breakfast—and phoned you at lunch . . .

EUNICE   Well, never mind about that. You just get yourself home here once in a while.

STEVE   You want it in the papers?

   [*More laughter and shouts of parting come from the men.* STANLEY *throws the screen door of the kitchen open and comes in. He is of medium height, about five feet eight or nine, and strongly, compactly built. Animal joy in his being is implicit in all his movements and attitudes. Since earliest manhood the center of his life has been pleasure with women, the giving and taking of it, not with weak indulgence, dependently, but with the power and pride of a richly feathered male bird among hens. Branching out from this complete and satisfying center are all the auxiliary channels of his life, such as his heartiness with men, his appreciation of rough humor, his love of good drink and food and games, his car, his radio, everything that is his, that bears his emblem of the gaudy seed-bearer. He sizes women up at a glance, with sexual classifications, crude images flashing into his mind and determining the way he smiles at them.*]

BLANCHE [*drawing involuntarily back from his stare*]   You must be Stanley. I'm Blanche.

STANLEY   Stella's sister?

BLANCHE   Yes.

STANLEY   H'lo. Where's the little woman?

BLANCHE   In the bathroom.

STANLEY   Oh. Didn't know you were coming in town.

BLANCHE   I—uh—

STANLEY   Where you from, Blanche?

BLANCHE   Why, I—live in Laurel.

   [*He has crossed to the closet and removed the whiskey bottle.*]

STANLEY   In Laurel, huh? Oh, yeah. Yeah, in Laurel, that's right. Not in my territory. Liquor goes fast in hot weather. [*He holds the bottle to the light to observe its depletion.*] Have a shot?

BLANCHE   No, I—rarely touch it.

STANLEY   Some people rarely touch it, but it touches them often.

8. A local brand of beer.

BLANCHE [*faintly*]   Ha-ha.

STANLEY   My clothes're stickin' to me. Do you mind if I make myself comfortable? [*He starts to remove his shirt.*]

BLANCHE   Please, please do.

STANLEY   Be comfortable is my motto.

BLANCHE   It's mine, too. It's hard to stay looking fresh. I haven't washed or even powdered my face and—here you are!

STANLEY   You know you can catch cold sitting around in damp things, especially when you been exercising hard like bowling is. You're a teacher, aren't you?

BLANCHE   Yes.

STANLEY   What do you teach, Blanche?

BLANCHE   English.

STANLEY   I never was a very good English student. How long you here for, Blanche?

BLANCHE   I—don't know yet.

STANLEY   You going to shack up here?

BLANCHE   I thought I would if it's not inconvenient for you all.

STANLEY   Good.

BLANCHE   Traveling wears me out.

STANLEY   Well, take it easy.

[*A cat screeches near the window.* BLANCHE *springs up.*]

BLANCHE   What's that?

STANLEY   Cats . . . Hey, Stella!

STELLA [*faintly, from the bathroom*]   Yes, Stanley.

STANLEY   Haven't fallen in, have you? [*He grins at* BLANCHE. *She tries unsuccessfully to smile back. There is a silence.*] I'm afraid I'll strike you as being the unrefined type. Stella's spoke of you a good deal. You were married once, weren't you?

[*The music of the polka rises up, faint in the distance.*]

BLANCHE   Yes. When I was quite young.

STANLEY   What happened?

BLANCHE   The boy—the boy died. [*She sinks back down.*] I'm afraid I'm—going to be sick! [*Her head falls on her arms.*]

## Scene Two

*It is six o'clock the following evening.* BLANCHE *is bathing.* STELLA *is completing her toilette.* BLANCHE's *dress, a flowered print, is laid out on* STELLA's *bed.*

STANLEY *enters the kitchen from outside, leaving the door open on the perpetual "Blue Piano" around the corner.*

STANLEY   What's all this monkey doings?

STELLA   Oh, Stan! [*She jumps up and kisses him, which he accepts with lordly composure.*] I'm taking Blanche to Galatoire's for supper and then to a show, because it's your poker night.

STANLEY   How about my supper, huh? I'm not going to no Galatoire's for supper!

STELLA   I put you a cold plate on ice.

STANLEY   Well, isn't that just dandy!

STELLA   I'm going to try to keep Blanche out till the party breaks up because I don't know how she would take it. So we'll go to one of the little places in the Quarter afterward and you'd better give me some money.

STANLEY    Where is she?

STELLA    She's soaking in a hot tub to quiet her nerves. She's terribly upset.

STANLEY    Over what?

STELLA    She's been through such an ordeal.

STANLEY    Yeah?

STELLA    Stan, we've—lost Belle Reve!

STANLEY    The place in the country?

STELLA    Yes.

STANLEY    How?

STELLA [*vaguely*]    Oh, it had to be—sacrificed or something. [*There is a pause while* STANLEY *considers.* STELLA *is changing into her dress.*] When she comes in be sure to say something nice about her appearance. And, oh! Don't mention the baby. I haven't said anything yet, I'm waiting until she gets in a quieter condition.

STANLEY [*ominously*]    So?

STELLA    And try to understand her and be nice to her, Stan.

BLANCHE [*singing in the bathroom*]    "From the land of the sky blue water, They brought a captive maid!"

STELLA    She wasn't expecting to find us in such a small place. You see I'd tried to gloss things over a little in my letters.

STANLEY    So?

STELLA    And admire her dress and tell her she's looking wonderful. That's important with Blanche. Her little weakness!

STANLEY    Yeah. I get the idea. Now let's skip back a little to where you said the country place was disposed of.

STELLA    Oh!—yes . . .

STANLEY    How about that? Let's have a few more details on that subjeck.

STELLA    It's best not to talk much about it until she's calmed down.

STANLEY    So that's the deal, huh? Sister Blanche cannot be annoyed with business details right now!

STELLA    You saw how she was last night.

STANLEY    Uh-hum, I saw how she was. Now let's have a gander at the bill of sale.

STELLA    I haven't seen any.

STANLEY    She didn't show you no papers, no deed of sale or nothing like that, huh?

STELLA    It seems like it wasn't sold.

STANLEY    Well, what in hell was it then, give away? To charity?

STELLA    Shhh! She'll hear you.

STANLEY    I don't care if she hears me. Let's see the papers!

STELLA    There weren't any papers, she didn't show any papers, I don't care about papers.

STANLEY    Have you ever heard of the Napoleonic code?[9]

STELLA    No, Stanley, I haven't heard of the Napoleonic code and if I have, I don't see what it—

STANLEY    Let me enlighten you on a point or two, baby.

STELLA    Yes?

STANLEY    In the state of Louisiana we have the Napoleonic code according to which what belongs to the wife belongs to the husband and vice versa. For instance if I had a piece of property, or you had a piece of property—

STELLA    My head is swimming!

---

9. This codification of French law (1802), made by Napoleon as emperor, is the basis for Louisiana's civil law.

STANLEY   All right. I'll wait till she gets through soaking in a hot tub and then I'll inquire if *she* is acquainted with the Napoleonic code. It looks to me like you have been swindled, baby, and when you're swindled under the Napoleonic code I'm swindled *too*. And I don't like to be *swindled*.

STELLA   There's plenty of time to ask her questions later but if you do now she'll go to pieces again. I don't understand what happened to Belle Reve but you don't know how ridiculous you are being when you suggest that my sister or I or anyone of our family could have perpetrated a swindle on anyone else.

STANLEY   Then where's the money if the place was sold?

STELLA   Not sold—*lost, lost!*
[*He stalks into bedroom, and she follows him.*]
Stanley!
[*He pulls open the wardrobe trunk standing in middle of room and jerks out an armful of dresses.*]

STANLEY   Open your eyes to this stuff! You think she got them out of a teacher's pay?

STELLA   Hush!

STANLEY   Look at these feathers and furs that she come here to preen herself in! What's this here? A solid-gold dress, I believe! And this one! What is these here? Fox-pieces! [*He blows on them.*] Genuine fox fur-pieces, a half a mile long! Where are your fox-pieces, Stella? Bushy snow-white ones, no less! Where are your white fox-pieces?

STELLA   Those are inexpensive summer furs that Blanche has had a long time.

STANLEY   I got an acquaintance who deals in this sort of merchandise. I'll have him in here to appraise it. I'm willing to bet you there's thousands of dollars invested in this stuff here!

STELLA   Don't be such an idiot, Stanley!
[*He hurls the furs to the day bed. Then he jerks open a small drawer in the trunk and pulls up a fistful of costume jewelry.*]

STANLEY   And what have we here? The treasure chest of a pirate!

STELLA   Oh, Stanley!

STANLEY   Pearls! Ropes of them! What is this sister of yours, a deep-sea diver? Bracelets of solid gold, too! Where are your pearls and gold bracelets?

STELLA   Shhh! Be still, Stanley!

STANLEY   And diamonds! A crown for an empress!

STELLA   A rhinestone tiara she wore to a costume ball.

STANLEY   What's rhinestone?

STELLA   Next door to glass.

STANLEY   Are you kidding? I have an acquaintance that works in a jewelry store. I'll have him in here to make an appraisal of this. Here's your plantation, or what was left of it, here!

STELLA   You have no idea how stupid and horrid you're being! Now close that trunk before she comes out of the bathroom!
[*He kicks the trunk partly closed and sits on the kitchen table.*]

STANLEY   The Kowalskis and the DuBoises have different notions.

STELLA [*angrily*]   Indeed they have, thank heavens!—*I'm* going outside. [*She snatches up her white hat and gloves and crosses to the outside door.*] You come out with me while Blanche is getting dressed.

STANLEY   Since when do you give me orders?

STELLA   Are you going to stay here and insult her?

STANLEY   You're damn tootin' I'm going to stay here.

[STELLA *goes out to the porch.* BLANCHE *comes out of the bathroom in a red satin robe.*]

BLANCHE [*airily*]   Hello, Stanley! Here I am, all freshly bathed and scented, and feeling like a brand new human being!
[*He lights a cigarette.*]

STANLEY   That's good.

BLANCHE [*drawing the curtains at the windows*]   Excuse me while I slip on my pretty new dress!

STANLEY   Go right ahead, Blanche.
[*She closes the drapes between the rooms.*]

BLANCHE   I understand there's to be a little card party to which we ladies are cordially *not* invited!

STANLEY [*ominously*]   Yeah?
[BLANCHE *throws off her robe and slips into a flowered print dress.*]

BLANCHE   Where's Stella?

STANLEY   Out on the porch.

BLANCHE   I'm going to ask a favor of you in a moment.

STANLEY   What could that be, I wonder?

BLANCHE   Some buttons in back! You may enter!
[*He crosses through drapes with a smoldering look.*]
How do I look?

STANLEY   You look all right.

BLANCHE   Many thanks! Now the buttons!

STANLEY   I can't do nothing with them.

BLANCHE   You men with your big clumsy fingers. May I have a drag on your cig?

STANLEY   Have one for yourself.

BLANCHE   Why, thanks! . . . It looks like my trunk has exploded.

STANLEY   Me an' Stella were helping you unpack.

BLANCHE   Well, you certainly did a fast and thorough job of it!

STANLEY   It looks like you raided some stylish shops in Paris.

BLANCHE   Ha-ha! Yes—clothes are my passion!

STANLEY   What does it cost for a string of fur-pieces like that?

BLANCHE   Why, those were a tribute from an admirer of mine!

STANLEY   He must have had a lot of—admiration!

BLANCHE   Oh, in my youth I excited some admiration. But look at me now!
[*She smiles at him radiantly.*] Would you think it possible that I was once considered to be—attractive?

STANLEY   Your looks are okay.

BLANCHE   I was fishing for a compliment, Stanley.

STANLEY   I don't go in for that stuff.

BLANCHE   What—stuff?

STANLEY   Compliments to women about their looks. I never met a woman that didn't know if she was good-looking or not without being told, and some of them give themselves credit for more than they've got. I once went out with a doll who said to me, "I am the glamorous type, I am the glamorous type!" I said, "So what?"

BLANCHE   And what did she say then?

STANLEY   She didn't say nothing. That shut her up like a clam.

BLANCHE   Did it end the romance?

STANLEY   It ended the conversation—that was all. Some men are took in by this Hollywood glamor stuff and some men are not.

BLANCHE   I'm sure you belong in the second category.

STANLEY   That's right.

BLANCHE   I cannot imagine any witch of a woman casting a spell over you.

STANLEY   That's—right.

BLANCHE   You're simple, straightforward and honest, a little bit on the primitive side I should think. To interest you a woman would have to—[*She pauses with an indefinite gesture.*]

STANLEY [*slowly*]   Lay . . . her cards on the table.

BLANCHE [*smiling*]   Well, I never cared for wishy-washy people. That was why, when you walked in here last night, I said to myself—"My sister has married a man!"—Of course that was all that I could tell about you.

STANLEY [*booming*]   Now let's cut the re-bop![1]

BLANCHE [*pressing hands to her ears*]   Ouuuuu!

STELLA [*calling from the steps*]   Stanley! You come out here and let Blanche finish dressing!

BLANCHE   I'm through dressing, honey.

STELLA   Well, you come out, then.

STANLEY   Your sister and I are having a little talk.

BLANCHE [*lightly*]   Honey, do me a favor. Run to the drugstore and get me a lemon Coke with plenty of chipped ice in it!—Will you do that for me, sweetie?

STELLA [*uncertainly*]   Yes. [*She goes around the corner of the building.*]

BLANCHE   The poor little thing was out there listening to us, and I have an idea she doesn't understand you as well as I do. . . . All right; now, Mr. Kowalski, let us proceed without any more double-talk. I'm ready to answer all questions. I've nothing to hide. What is it?

STANLEY   There is such a thing in this state of Louisiana as the Napoleonic code, according to which whatever belongs to my wife is also mine—and vice versa.

BLANCHE   My, but you have an impressive judicial air!

[*She sprays herself with her atomizer; then playfully sprays him with it. He seizes the atomizer and slams it down on the dresser. She throws back her head and laughs.*]

STANLEY   If I didn't know that you was my wife's sister I'd get ideas about you!

BLANCHE   Such as what!

STANLEY   Don't play so dumb. You know what!

BLANCHE [*she puts the atomizer on the table*]   All right. Cards on the table. That suits me. [*She turns to* STANLEY.] I know I fib a good deal. After all, a woman's charm is fifty per cent illusion, but when a thing is important I tell the truth, and this is the truth: I haven't cheated my sister or you or anyone else as long as I have lived.

STANLEY   Where's the papers? In the trunk?

BLANCHE   Everything that I own is in that trunk.

[STANLEY *crosses to the trunk, shoves it roughly open and begins to open compartments.*]

BLANCHE   What in the name of heaven are you thinking of! What's in the back of that little boy's mind of yours? That I am absconding with something, attempting some kind of treachery on my sister?—Let me do that! It will be faster and simpler . . . [*She crosses to the trunk and takes out a box.*] I keep my papers mostly in this tin box. [*She opens it.*]

STANLEY   What's them underneath? [*He indicates another sheaf of paper.*]

---

1. Nonsense syllables (from "bop," a form of jazz).

BLANCHE These are love-letters, yellowing with antiquity, all from one boy. [*He snatches them up. She speaks fiercely.*] Give those back to me!

STANLEY I'll have a look at them first!

BLANCHE The touch of your hands insults them!

STANLEY Don't pull that stuff!

[*He rips off the ribbon and starts to examine them.* BLANCHE *snatches them from him, and they cascade to the floor.*]

BLANCHE Now that you've touched them I'll burn them!

STANLEY [*staring, baffled*] What in hell are they?

BLANCHE [*on the floor gathering them up*] Poems a dead boy wrote. I hurt him the way that you would like to hurt me, but you can't! I'm not young and vulnerable any more. But my young husband was and I—never mind about that! Just give them back to me!

STANLEY What do you mean by saying you'll have to burn them?

BLANCHE I'm sorry, I must have lost my head for a moment. Everyone has something he won't let others touch because of their—intimate nature . . .

[*She now seems faint with exhaustion and she sits down with the strong box and puts on a pair of glasses and goes methodically through a large stack of papers.*]

Ambler & Ambler. Hmmmm . . . . Crabtree. . . . More Ambler & Ambler.

STANLEY What is Ambler & Ambler?

BLANCHE A firm that made loans on the place.

STANLEY Then it was lost on a mortgage.

BLANCHE [*touching her forehead*] That must've been what happened.

STANLEY I don't want no ifs, ands or buts! What's all the rest of them papers?

[*She hands him the entire box. He carries it to the table and starts to examine the paper.*]

BLANCHE [*picking up a large envelope containing more papers*] There are thousands of papers, stretching back over hundreds of years, affecting Belle Reve as, piece by piece, our improvident grandfathers and father and uncles and brothers exchanged the land for their epic fornications—to put it plainly! [*She removes her glasses with an exhausted laugh.*] The four-letter word deprived us of our plantation, till finally all that was left—and Stella can verify that!—was the house itself and about twenty acres of ground, including a graveyard, to which now all but Stella and I have retreated. [*She pours the contents of the envelope on the table.*] Here all of them are, all papers! I hereby endow you with them! Take them, peruse them—commit them to memory, even! think it's wonderfully fitting that Belle Reve should finally be this bunch of old papers in your big, capable hands! . . . I wonder if Stella's come back with my lemon Coke . . . [*She leans back and closes her eyes.*]

STANLEY I have a lawyer acquaintance who will study these out.

BLANCHE Present them to him with a box of aspirin tablets.

STANLEY [*becoming somewhat sheepish*] You see, under the Napoleonic code—a man has to take an interest in his wife's affairs—especially now that she's going to have a baby.

[BLANCHE *opens her eyes. The* "Blue Piano" *sounds louder.*]

BLANCHE Stella? Stella going to have a baby? [*dreamily*] I didn't know she was going to have a baby!

[*She gets up and crosses to the outside door.* STELLA *appears around the corner with a carton from the drugstore.* STANLEY *goes into the bedroom with the envelope and the box. The inner rooms fade to darkness and the outside wall of the house is visible.* BLANCHE *meets* STELLA *at the foot of the steps to the sidewalk.*]

BLANCHE   Stella, Stella for star! How lovely to have a baby! It's all right. Everything's all right.

STELLA   I'm sorry he did that to you.

BLANCHE   Oh, I guess he's just not the type that goes for jasmine perfume, but maybe he's what we need to mix with our blood now that we've lost Belle Reve. We thrashed it out. I feel a bit shaky, but I think I handled it nicely, I laughed and treated it all as a joke. [STEVE *and* PABLO *appear, carrying a case of beer.*] I called him a little boy and laughed and flirted. Yes, I was flirting with your husband! [*as the men approach*] The guests are gathering for the poker party. [*The two men pass between them, and enter the house.*] Which way do we go now, Stella—this way?

STELLA   No, this way. [*She leads* BLANCHE *away.*]

BLANCHE [*laughing*]   The blind are leading the blind!

[*A tamale* VENDOR *is heard calling.*]

VENDOR'S VOICE   Red-hot!

## Scene Three

### THE POKER NIGHT

*There is a picture of Van Gogh's[2] of a billiard-parlor at night. The kitchen now suggests that sort of lurid nocturnal brilliance, the raw colors of childhood's spectrum. Over the yellow linoleum of the kitchen table hang an electric bulb with a vivid green glass shade. The poker players—*STANLEY, STEVE, MITCH *and* PABLO*—wear colored shirts, solid blues, a purple, a red-and-white check, a light green, and they are men at the peak of their physical manhood, as coarse and direct and powerful as the primary colors. There are vivid slices of watermelon on the table, whiskey bottles and glasses. The bedroom is relatively dim with only the light that spills between the portieres and through the wide window on the street.*

*For a moment, there is absorbed silence as a hand is dealt.*

STEVE   Anything wild this deal?

PABLO   One-eyed jacks are wild.

STEVE   Give me two cards.

PABLO   You, Mitch?

MITCH   I'm out.

PABLO   One.

MITCH   Anyone want a shot?

STANLEY   Yeah. Me.

PABLO   Why don't somebody go to the Chinaman's and bring back a load of chop suey?

STANLEY   When I'm losing you want to eat! Ante up! Openers? Openers! Get your ass off the table, Mitch. Nothing belongs on a poker table but cards, chips and whiskey.

[*He lurches up and tosses some watermelon rinds to the floor.*]

MITCH   Kind of on your high horse, ain't you?

---

2. *The Night Café*, by Vincent Van Gogh (1853–1890), Dutch postimpressionist painter. *The Poker Night* was Williams's first title for *A Streetcar Named Desire*.

STANLEY    How many?

STEVE    Give me three.

STANLEY    One.

MITCH    I'm out again. I oughta go home pretty soon.

STANLEY    Shut up.

MITCH    I gotta sick mother. She don't go to sleep until I come in at night.

STANLEY    Then why don't you stay home with her?

MITCH    She says to go out, so I go, but I don't enjoy it. All the while I keep wondering how she is.

STANLEY    Aw, for the sake of Jesus, go home, then!

PABLO    What've you got?

STEVE    Spade flush.

MITCH    You all are married. But I'll be alone when she goes.—I'm going to the bathroom.

STANLEY    Hurry back and we'll fix you a sugar-tit.

MITCH    Aw, go rut. [*He crosses through the bedroom into the bathroom.*]

STEVE [*dealing a hand*]    Seven card stud.[3] [*telling his joke as he deals*] This ole farmer is out in back of his house sittin' down th'owing corn to the chickens when all at once he hears a loud cackle and this young hen comes lickety split around the side of the house with the rooster right behind her and gaining on her fast.

STANLEY [*impatient with the story*]    Deal!

STEVE    But when the rooster catches sight of the farmer th'owing the corn he puts on the brakes and lets the hen get away and starts pecking corn. And the old farmer says, "Lord God, I hopes I never gits *that* hungry!"

[STEVE *and* PABLO *laugh. The sisters appear around the corner of the building.*]

STELLA    The game is still going on.

BLANCHE    How do I look?

STELLA    Lovely, Blanche.

BLANCHE    I feel so hot and frazzled. Wait till I powder before you open the door. Do I look done in?

STELLA    Why no. You are as fresh as a daisy.

BLANCHE    One that's been picked a few days.

[STELLA *opens the door and they enter.*]

STELLA    Well, well, well. I see you boys are still at it?

STANLEY    Where you been?

STELLA    Blanche and I took in a show. Blanche, this is Mr. Gonzales and Mr. Hubbell.

BLANCHE    Please don't get up.

STANLEY    Nobody's going to get up, so don't be worried.

STELLA    How much longer is this game going to continue?

STANLEY    Till we get ready to quit.

BLANCHE    Poker is so fascinating. Could I kibitz?

STANLEY    You could not. Why don't you women go up and sit with Eunice?

STELLA    Because it is nearly two-thirty. [BLANCHE *crosses into the bedroom and partially closes the portieres.*] Couldn't you call it quits after one more hand?

[*A chair scrapes.* STANLEY *gives a loud whack of his hand on her thigh.*]

STELLA [*sharply*]    That's not fun, Stanley.

[*The men laugh.* STELLA *goes into the bedroom.*]

3. An adventurous and risky variant of poker.

STELLA   It makes me so mad when he does that in front of people.
BLANCHE   I think I will bathe.
STELLA   Again?
BLANCHE   My nerves are in knots. Is the bathroom occupied?
STELLA   I don't know.
    [BLANCHE *knocks.* MITCH *opens the door and comes out, still wiping his*
    *hands on a towel.*]
BLANCHE   Oh!—good evening.
MITCH   Hello. [*He stares at her.*]
STELLA   Blanche, this is Harold Mitchell. My sister, Blanche DuBois.
MITCH [*with awkward courtesy*]   How do you do, Miss DuBois.
STELLA   How is your mother now, Mitch?
MITCH   About the same, thanks. She appreciated your sending over that cus-
    tard.—Excuse me, please.
    [*He crosses slowly back into the kitchen, glancing back at* BLANCHE *and*
    *coughing a little shyly. He realizes he still has the towel in his hands*
    *and with an embarrassed laugh hands it to* STELLA. BLANCHE *looks*
    *after him with a certain interest.*]
BLANCHE   That one seems—superior to the others.
STELLA   Yes, he is.
BLANCHE   I thought he had a sort of sensitive look.
STELLA   His mother is sick.
BLANCHE   Is he married?
STELLA   No.
BLANCHE   Is he a wolf?
STELLA   Why, Blanche! [BLANCHE *laughs.*] I don't think he would be.
BLANCHE   What does—what does he do? [*She is unbuttoning her blouse.*]
STELLA   He's on the precision bench in the spare parts department. At the
    plant Stanley travels for.
BLANCHE   Is that something much?
STELLA   No. Stanley's the only one of his crowd that's likely to get anywhere.
BLANCHE   What makes you think Stanley will?
STELLA   Look at him.
BLANCHE   I've looked at him.
STELLA   Then you should know.
BLANCHE   I'm sorry, but I haven't noticed the stamp of genius even on Stan-
    ley's forehead.
    [*She takes off the blouse and stands in her pink silk brassiere and white*
    *skirt in the light through the portieres. The game has continued in*
    *undertones.*]
STELLA   It isn't on his forehead and it isn't genius.
BLANCHE   Oh. Well, what is it, and where? I would like to know.
STELLA   It's a drive that he has. You're standing in the light, Blanche!
BLANCHE   Oh, am I!
    [*She moves out of the yellow streak of light.* STELLA *has removed her*
    *dress and put on a light blue satin kimona.*]
STELLA [*with girlish laughter*]   You ought to see their wives.
BLANCHE [*laughingly*]   I can imagine. Big, beefy things, I suppose.
STELLA   You know that one upstairs? [*more laughter*] One time [*laughing*] the
    plaster—[*laughing*] cracked—
STANLEY   You hens cut out that conversation in there!
STELLA   You can't hear us.

STANLEY   Well, you can hear me and I said to hush up!

STELLA   This is my house and I'll talk as much as I want to!

BLANCHE   Stella, don't start a row.

STELLA   He's half drunk!—I'll be out in a minute.

[*She goes into the bathroom.* BLANCHE *rises and crosses leisurely to a small white radio and turns it on.*]

STANLEY   Awright, Mitch, you in?

MITCH   What? Oh!—No, I'm out!

[BLANCHE *moves back into the streak of light. She raises her arms and stretches, as she moves indolently back to the chair. Rhumba music comes over the radio.* MITCH *rises at the table.*]

STANLEY   Who turned that on in there?

BLANCHE   I did. Do you mind?

STANLEY   Turn it off!

STEVE   Aw, let the girls have their music.

PABLO   Sure, that's good, leave it on!

STEVE   Sounds like Xavier Cugat!⁴

[STANLEY *jumps up and, crossing to the radio, turns it off. He stops short at the sight of* BLANCHE *in the chair. She returns his look without flinching. Then he sits again at the poker table. Two of the men have started arguing hotly.*]

STEVE   I didn't hear you name it.

PABLO   Didn't I name it, Mitch?

MITCH   I wasn't listenin'.

PABLO   What were you doing, then?

STANLEY   He was looking through them drapes. [*He jumps up and jerks roughly at curtains to close them.*] Now deal the hand over again and let's play cards or quit. Some people get ants when they win.

[MITCH *rises as* STANLEY *returns to his seat.*]

STANLEY [*yelling*]   Sit down!

MITCH   I'm going to the "head." Deal me out.

PABLO   Sure he's got ants now. Seven five-dollar bills in his pants pocket folded up tight as spitballs.

STEVE   Tomorrow you'll see him at the cashier's window getting them changed into quarters.

STANLEY   And when he goes home he'll deposit them one by one in a piggy bank his mother give him for Christmas. [*dealing*] This game is Spit in the Ocean.⁵

[MITCH *laughs uncomfortably and continues through the portieres. He stops just inside.*]

BLANCHE [*softly*]   Hello! The Little Boys' Room is busy right now.

MITCH   We've—been drinking beer.

BLANCHE   I hate beer.

MITCH   It's—a hot weather drink.

BLANCHE   Oh, I don't think so; it always makes me warmer. Have you got any cigs? [*She has slipped on the dark red satin wrapper.*]

MITCH   Sure.

BLANCHE   What kind are they?

MITCH   Luckies.

---

4. Cuban band leader, well known for composing and playing rhumbas.   5. Another variant of poker.

BLANCHE   Oh, good. What a pretty case. Silver?

MITCH   Yes. Yes; read the inscription.

BLANCHE   Oh, is there an inscription? I can't make it out. [*He strikes a match and moves closer.*] Oh! [*reading with feigned difficulty*] "And if God choose, /I shall but love thee better—after—death!" Why, that's from my favorite sonnet by Mrs. Browning![6]

MITCH   You know it?

STELLA   Certainly I do!

MITCH   There's a story connected with that inscription.

BLANCHE   It sounds like a romance.

MITCH   A pretty sad one.

BLANCHE   Oh?

MITCH   The girl's dead now.

BLANCHE [*in a tone of deep sympathy*]   Oh!

MITCH   She knew she was dying when she give me this. A very strange girl, very sweet—very!

BLANCHE   She must have been fond of you. Sick people have such deep, sincere attachments.

MITCH   That's right, they certainly do.

BLANCHE   Sorrow makes for sincerity, I think.

MITCH   It sure brings it out in people.

BLANCHE   The little there is belongs to people who have experienced some sorrow.

MITCH   I believe you are right about that.

BLANCHE   I'm positive that I am. Show me a person who hasn't known any sorrow and I'll show you a shuperficial—Listen to me! My tongue is a lit-tle—thick! You boys are responsible for it. The show let out at eleven and we couldn't come home on account of the poker game so we had to go somewhere and drink. I'm not accustomed to having more than one drink. Two is the limit—and *three*! [*She laughs.*] Tonight I had three.

STANLEY   Mitch!

MITCH   Deal me out. I'm talking to Miss—

BLANCHE   DuBois.

MITCH   Miss DuBois?

BLANCHE   It's a French name. it means woods and Blanche means white, so the two together mean white woods. Like an orchard in spring! You can remember it by that.

MITCH   You're French?

BLANCHE   We are French by extraction. Our first American ancestors were French Huguenots.

MITCH   You are Stella's sister, are you not?

BLANCHE   Yes, Stella is my precious little sister. I call her little in spite of the fact she's somewhat older than I. Just slightly. Less than a year. Will you do something for me?

MITCH   Sure. What?

BLANCHE   I bought this adorable little colored paper lantern at a Chinese shop on Bourbon. Put it over the light bulb! Will you, please?

MITCH   Be glad to.

BLANCHE   I can't stand a naked light bulb, any more than I can a rude remark or a vulgar action.

---

6. Elizabeth Barrett Browning, 19th-century British poet, was most famous for her sequence of love poems, *Sonnets from the Portuguese.*

MITCH [*adjusting the lantern*]   I guess we strike you as being a pretty rough bunch.

BLANCHE   I'm very adaptable—to circumstances.

MITCH   Well, that's a good thing to be. You are visiting Stanley and Stella?

BLANCHE   Stella hasn't been so well lately, and I came down to help her for a while. She's very run down.

MITCH   You're not—?

BLANCHE   Married? No, no. I'm an old maid schoolteacher!

MITCH   You may teach school but you're certainly not an old maid.

BLANCHE   Thank you, sir! I appreciate your gallantry!

MITCH   So you are in the teaching profession?

BLANCHE   Yes. Ah, yes . . .

MITCH   Grade school or high school or—

STANLEY [*bellowing*]   Mitch!

MITCH   Coming!

BLANCHE   Gracious, what lung-power! . . . I teach high school. In Laurel.

MITCH   What do you teach? What subject?

BLANCHE   Guess!

MITCH   I bet you teach art or music? [BLANCHE *laughs delicately*.] Of course I could be wrong. You might teach arithmetic.

BLANCHE   Never arithmetic, sir; never arithmetic! [*with a laugh*] I don't even know my multiplication tables! No, I have the misfortune of being an English instructor. I attempt to instill a bunch of bobby-soxers and drugstore Romeos with reverence for Hawthorne and Whitman and Poe!

MITCH   I guess that some of them are more interested in other things.

BLANCHE   How very right you are! Their literary heritage is not what most of them treasure above all else! But they're sweet things! And in the spring, it's touching to notice them making their first discovery of love! As if nobody had ever known it before!

[*The bathroom door opens and* STELLA *comes out.* BLANCHE *continues talking to* MITCH.]

Oh! Have you finished? Wait—I'll turn on the radio.

[*She turns the knobs on the radio and it begins to play* "Wien, Wien, nur du allein."[7] BLANCHE *waltzes to the music with romantic gestures.* MITCH *is delighted and moves in awkward imitation like a dancing bear.* STANLEY *stalks fiercely through the portieres into the bedroom. He crosses to the small white radio and snatches it off the table. With a shouted oath, he tosses the instrument out the window.*]

STELLA   Drunk—drunk—animal thing, you! [*She rushes through to the poker table.*] All of you—please go home! If any of you have one spark of decency in you—

BLANCHE [*wildly*]   Stella, watch out, he's—

[STANLEY *charges after* STELLA.]

MEN [*feebly*]   Take it easy, Stanley. Easy, fellow.—Let's all—

STELLA   You lay your hands on me and I'll—

[*She backs out of sight. He advances and disappears. There is the sound of a blow.* STELLA *cries out.* BLANCHE *screams and runs into the kitchen. The men rush forward and there is grappling and cursing. Something is overturned with a crash.*]

BLANCHE [*shrilly*]   My sister is going to have a baby!

7. Vienna, Vienna, you are my only (German); a waltz from an operetta by Franz Lehar.

MITCH    This is terrible.

BLANCHE    Lunacy, absolute lunacy!

MITCH    Get him in here, men.

[STANLEY *is forced, pinioned by the two men, into the bedroom. He nearly throws them off. Then all at once he subsides and is limp in their grasp. They speak quietly and lovingly to him and he leans his face on one of their shoulders.*]

STELLA [*in a high, unnatural voice, out of sight*]    I want to go away, I want to go away!

MITCH    Poker shouldn't be played in a house with women.

[BLANCHE *rushes into the bedroom.*]

BLANCHE    I want my sister's clothes! We'll go to that woman's upstairs!

MITCH    Where is the clothes?

BLANCHE [*opening the closet*]    I've got them! [*She rushes through to* STELLA.] Stella, Stella, precious! Dear, dear little sister, don't be afraid!

[*With her arm around* STELLA, BLANCHE *guides her to the outside door and upstairs.*]

STANLEY [*dully*]    What's the matter; what's happened?

MITCH    You just blew your top, Stan.

PABLO    He's okay, now.

STEVE    Sure, my boy's okay!

MITCH    Put him on the bed and get a wet towel.

PABLO    I think coffee would do him a world of good, now.

STANLEY [*thickly*]    I want water.

MITCH    Put him under the shower!

[*The men talk quietly as they lead him to the bathroom.*]

STANLEY    Let the rut go of me, you sons of bitches!

[*Sounds of blows are heard. The water goes on full tilt.*]

STEVE    Let's get quick out of here!

[*They rush to the poker table and sweep up their winnings on their way out.*]

MITCH [*sadly but firmly*]    Poker should not be played in a house with women.

[*The door closes on them and the place is still. The Negro entertainers in the bar around the corner play "Paper Doll"[8] slow and blue. After a moment* STANLEY *comes out of the bathroom dripping water and still in his clinging wet polka dot drawers.*]

STANLEY    Stella! [*There is a pause.*] My baby doll's left me!

[*He breaks into sobs. Then he goes to the phone and dials, still shuddering with sobs.*]

Eunice? I want my baby! [*He waits a moment; then he hangs up and dials again.*] Eunice! I'll keep on ringin' until I talk with my baby!

[*An indistinguishable shrill voice is heard. He hurls phone to floor. Dissonant brass and piano sounds as the rooms dim out to darkness and the outer walls appear in the night light. The "Blue Piano" plays for a brief interval. Finally,* STANLEY *stumbles half-dressed out to the porch and down the wooden steps to the pavement before the building. There he throws back his head like a baying hound and bellows his wife's name: "Stella! Stella, sweetheart! Stella!"*]

STANLEY    Stell-*lahhhhh!*

---

8. Popular song of the early 1940s by Johnny Black.

EUNICE [*calling down from the door of her upper apartment*]   Quit that howl-
ing out there an' go back to bed!
STANLEY   I want my baby down here. Stella, Stella!
EUNICE   She ain't comin' down so you quit! Or you'll git th' law on you!
STANLEY   Stella!
EUNICE   You can't beat on a woman an' then call 'er back! She won't come!
And her goin' t' have a baby! . . . You stinker! You whelp of a Polack, you!
I hope they do haul you in and turn the fire hose on you, same as the
last time!
STANLEY [*humbly*]   Eunice, I want my girl to come down with me!
EUNICE   Hah! [*She slams her door.*]
STANLEY [*with heaven-splitting violence*]   STELL-LAHHHHH!
[*The low-tone clarinet moans. The door upstairs opens again.* STELLA
*slips down the rickety stairs in her robe. Her eyes are glistening with
tears and her hair loose about her throat and shoulders. They stare at
each other. Then they come together with low, animal moans. He falls
to his knees on the steps and presses his face to her belly, curving a
little with maternity. Her eyes go blind with tenderness as she catches
his head and raises him level with her. He snatches the screen door
open and lifts her off her feet and bears her into the dark flat.* BLANCHE
*comes out the upper landing in her robe and slips fearfully down the
steps.*]
BLANCHE   Where is my little sister? Stella? Stella?
[*She stops before the dark entrance of her sister's flat. Then catches her
breath as if struck. She rushes down to the walk before the house. She
looks right and left as if for a sanctuary. The music fades away.* MITCH
*appears from around the corner.*]
MITCH   Miss DuBois?
BLANCHE   Oh!
MITCH   All quiet on the Potomac now?
BLANCHE   She ran downstairs and went back in there with him.
MITCH   Sure she did.
BLANCHE   I'm terrified!
MITCH   Ho-ho! There's nothing to be scared of. They're crazy about each
other.
BLANCHE   I'm not used to such—
MITCH   Naw, it's a shame this had to happen when you just got here. But
don't take it serious.
BLANCHE   Violence! Is so—
MITCH   Set down on the steps and have a cigarette with me.
BLANCHE   I'm not properly dressed.
MITCH   That don't make no difference in the Quarter.
BLANCHE   Such a pretty silver case.
MITCH   I showed you the inscription, didn't I?
BLANCHE   Yes. [*During the pause, she looks up at the sky.*] There's so much—
so much confusion in the world . . . [*He coughs diffidently.*] Thank you for
being so kind! I need kindness now.

## Scene Four

*It is early the following morning. There is a confusion of street cries like a
choral chant.*

STELLA *is lying down in the bedroom. Her face is serene in the early morning sunlight. One hand rests on her belly, rounding slightly with new maternity. From the other dangles a book of colored comics. Her eyes and lips have that almost narcotized tranquility that is in the faces of Eastern idols.*

*The table is sloppy with remains of breakfast and the debris of the preceding night, and* STANLEY's *gaudy pyjamas lie across the threshold of the bathroom. The outside door is slightly ajar on a sky of summer brilliance.*

BLANCHE *appears at this door. She has spent a sleepless night and her appearance entirely contrasts with* STELLA's. *She presses her knuckles nervously to her lips as she looks through the door, before entering.*

BLANCHE    Stella?
STELLA [*stirring lazily*]    Hmmh?
            [BLANCHE *utters a moaning cry and runs into the bedroom, throwing*
            *herself down beside* STELLA *in a rush of hysterical tenderness.*]
BLANCHE    Baby, my baby sister!
STELLA [*drawing away from her*]    Blanche, what is the matter with you?
            [BLANCHE *straightens up slowly and stands beside the bed looking down*
            *at her sister with knuckles pressed to her lips.*]
BLANCHE    He's left?
STELLA    Stan? Yes.
BLANCHE    Will he be back?
STELLA    He's gone to get the car greased. Why?
BLANCHE    Why! I've been half crazy, Stella! When I found out you'd been
    insane enough to come back in here after what happened—I started to rush
    in after you!
STELLA    I'm glad you didn't.
BLANCHE    What were you thinking of? [STELLA *makes an indefinite gesture.*]
    Answer me! What? What?
STELLA    Please, Blanche! Sit down and stop yelling.
BLANCHE    All right, Stella. I will repeat the question quietly now. How could
    you come back in this place last night? Why, you must have slept with him!
            [STELLA *gets up in a calm and leisurely way.*]
STELLA    Blanche, I'd forgotten how excitable you are. You're making much
    too much fuss about this.
BLANCHE    Am I?
STELLA    Yes, you are, Blanche. I know how it must have seemed to you and
    I'm awful sorry it had to happen, but it wasn't anything as serious as you
    seem to take it. In the first place, when men are drinking and playing poker
    anything can happen. It's always a powder-keg. He didn't know what he was
    doing. . . . He was as good as a lamb when I came back and he's really
    very, very ashamed of himself.
BLANCHE    And that—that makes it all right?
STELLA    No, it isn't all right for anybody to make such a terrible row, but—
    people do sometimes. Stanley's always smashed things. Why, on our wed-
    ding night—soon as we came in here—he snatched off one of my slippers
    and rushed about the place smashing light bulbs with it.
BLANCHE    He did—*what?*
STELLA    He smashed all the light bulbs with the heel of my slipper! [*She
    laughs.*]
BLANCHE    And you—you *let* him? Didn't *run*, didn't *scream?*
STELLA    I was—sort of—thrilled by it. [*She waits for a moment.*] Eunice and
    you had breakfast?

BLANCHE   Do you suppose I wanted any breakfast?
STELLA   There's some coffee left on the stove.
BLANCHE   You're so—matter of fact about it, Stella.
STELLA   What other can I be? He's taken the radio to get it fixed. It didn't
land on the pavement so only one tube was smashed.
BLANCHE   And you are standing there smiling!
STELLA   What do you want me to do?
BLANCHE   Pull yourself together and face the facts.
STELLA   What are they, in your opinion?
BLANCHE   In my opinion?. You're married to a madman!
STELLA   No!
BLANCHE   Yes, you are, your fix is worse than mine is! Only you're not being
sensible about it. I'm going to *do* something. Get hold of myself and make
myself a new life!
STELLA   Yes?
BLANCHE   But you've given in. And that isn't right, you're not old! You can
get out.
STELLA   [*slowly and emphatically*]   I'm not in anything I want to get out of.
BLANCHE   [*incredulously*]   What—Stella?
STELLA   I said I am not in anything that I have a desire to get out of. Look at
the mess in this room! And those empty bottles! They went through two
cases last night! He promised this morning that he was going to quit having
these poker parties, but you know how long such a promise is going to keep.
Oh, well, it's his pleasure, like mine is movies and bridge. People have got
to tolerate each other's habits, I guess.
BLANCHE   I don't understand you. [STELLA *turns toward her.*] I don't under-
stand your indifference. Is this a Chinese philosophy you've—cultivated?
STELLA   Is what—what?
BLANCHE   This—shuffling about and mumbling—'One tube smashed—beer
bottles—mess in the kitchen!'—as if nothing out of the ordinary has hap-
pened! [STELLA *laughs uncertainly and picking up the broom, twirls it in
her hands.*]
BLANCHE   Are you deliberately shaking that thing in my face?
STELLA   No.
BLANCHE   Stop it. Let go of that broom. I won't have you cleaning up for him!
STELLA   Then who's going to do it? Are you?
BLANCHE   I? I!
STELLA   No, I didn't think so.
BLANCHE   Oh, let me think, if only my mind would function! We've got to
get hold of some money, that's the way out!
STELLA   I guess that money is always nice to get hold of.
BLANCHE   Listen to me. I have an idea of some kind. [*Shakily she twists a
cigarette into her holder.*] Do you remember Shep Huntleigh? [STELLA
*shakes her head.*] Of course you remember Shep Huntleigh. I went out with
him at college and wore his pin for a while. Well—
STELLA   Well?
BLANCHE   I ran into him last winter. You know I went to Miami during the
Christmas holidays?
STELLA   No.
BLANCHE   Well, I did. I took the trip as an investment, thinking I'd meet
someone with a million dollars.
STELLA   Did you?
BLANCHE   Yes. I ran into Shep Huntleigh—I ran into him on Biscayne Boule-

vard, on Christmas Eve, about dusk . . . getting into his car—Cadillac convertible; must have been a block long!

STELLA    I should think it would have been—inconvenient in traffic!

BLANCHE    You've heard of oil wells?

STELLA    Yes—remotely.

BLANCHE    He has them, all over Texas. Texas is literally spouting gold in his pockets.

STELLA    My, my.

BLANCHE    Y'know how indifferent I am to money. I think of money in terms of what it does for you. But he could do it, he could certainly do it!

STELLA    Do what, Blanche?

BLANCHE    Why—set us up in a—shop!

STELLA    What kind of a shop?

BLANCHE    Oh, a—shop of some kind! He could do it with half what his wife throws away at the races.

STELLA    He's married?

BLANCHE    Honey, would I be here if the man weren't married?

> [STELLA *laughs a little.* BLANCHE *suddenly springs up and crosses to phone. She speaks shrilly.*] How do I get Western Union?—Operator! Western Union!

STELLA    That's a dial phone, honey.

BLANCHE    I can't dial, I'm too—

STELLA    Just dial O.

BLANCHE    O?

STELLA    Yes, "O" for Operator! [BLANCHE *considers a moment; then she puts the phone down.*]

BLANCHE    Give me a pencil. Where is a slip of paper? I've got to write it down first—the message, I mean . . . [*She goes to the dressing table, and grabs up a sheet of Kleenex and an eyebrow pencil for writing equipment.*] Let me see now . . . [*She bites the pencil.*] 'Darling Shep. Sister and I in desperate situation.'

STELLA    I beg your pardon!

BLANCHE    'Sister and I in desperate situation. Will explain details later. Would you be interested in—?' [*She bites the pencil again.*] 'Would you be—interested—in . . .' [*She smashes the pencil on the table and springs up.*] You never get anywhere with direct appeals!

STELLA  [*with a laugh*]   Don't be so ridiculous, darling!

BLANCHE    But I'll think of something, I've *got* to think of—*some*thing! Don't laugh at me, Stella! Please, please don't—I—I want you to look at the contents of my purse! Here's what's in it! [*She snatches her purse open.*] Sixty-five measly cents in coin of the realm!

STELLA  [*crossing to bureau*]   Stanley doesn't give me a regular allowance, he likes to pay bills himself, but—this morning he gave me ten dollars to smooth things over. You take five of it, Blanche, and I'll keep the rest.

BLANCHE    Oh, no. No, Stella.

STELLA  [*insisting*]   I know how it helps your morale just having a little pocket-money on you.

BLANCHE    No, thank you—I'll take to the streets!

STELLA    Talk sense! How did you happen to get so low on funds?

BLANCHE    Money just goes—it goes places. [*She rubs her forehead.*] Sometime today I've got to get hold of a Bromo![9]

---

9. Short for Bromo-seltzer, a headache remedy.

STELLA    I'll fix you one now.

BLANCHE    Not yet—I've got to keep thinking!

STELLA    I wish you'd just let things go, at least for a—while. . .

BLANCHE    Stella, I can't live with him! You can, he's your husband. But how could I stay here with him, after last night, with just those curtains between us?

STELLA    Blanche, you saw him at his worst last night.

BLANCHE    On the contrary, I saw him at his best! What such a man has to offer is animal force and he gave a wonderful exhibition of that! But the only way to live with such a man is to—go to bed with him! And that's your job—not mine!

STELLA    After you've rested a little, you'll see it's going to work out. You don't have to worry about anything while you're here. I mean—expenses . . .

BLANCHE    I have to plan for us both, to get us both—out!

STELLA    You take it for granted that I am in something that I want to get out of.

BLANCHE    I take it for granted that you still have sufficient memory of Belle Reve to find this place and these poker players impossible to live with.

STELLA    Well, you're taking entirely too much for granted.

BLANCHE    I can't believe you're in earnest.

STELLA    No?

BLANCHE    I understand how it happened—a little. You saw him in uniform, an officer, not here but—

STELLA    I'm not sure it would have made any difference where I saw him.

BLANCHE    Now don't say it was one of those mysterious electric things between people! If you do I'll laugh in your face.

STELLA    I am not going to say anything more at all about it!

BLANCHE    All right, then, don't!

STELLA    But there are things that happen between a man and a woman in the dark—that sort of make everything else seem—unimportant. [*Pause.*]

BLANCHE    What you are talking about is brutal desire—just—Desire!—the name of that rattle-trap streetcar that bangs through the Quarter, up one old narrow street and down another . . .

STELLA    Haven't you ever ridden on that streetcar?

BLANCHE    It brought me here.—Where I'm not wanted and where I'm ashamed to be . . .

STELLA    Then don't you think your superior attitude is a bit out of place?

BLANCHE    I am not being or feeling at all superior, Stella. Believe me I'm not! It's just this. This is how I look at it. A man like that is someone to go out with—once—twice—three times when the devil is in you. But live with? Have a child by?

STELLA    I have told you I love him.

BLANCHE    Then I *tremble* for you! I just—*tremble* for you. . . .

STELLA    I can't help your trembling if you insist on trembling!
          [*There is a pause.*]

BLANCHE    May I—speak—*plainly?*

STELLA    Yes, do. Go ahead. As plainly as you want to.
          [*Outside, a train approaches. They are silent till the noise subsides. They are both in the bedroom. Under cover of the train's noise STANLEY enters from outside. He stands unseen by the women, holding some packages in his arms, and overhears their following conversation. He wears an undershirt and grease-stained seersucker pants.*]

BLANCHE    Well—if you'll forgive me—he's *common!*

STELLA   Why, yes, I suppose he is.

BLANCHE   Suppose! You can't have forgotten that much of our bringing up, Stella, that you just *suppose* that any part of a gentleman's in his nature! *Not one particle, no!* Oh, if he was just—*ordinary!* Just *plain*—but good and wholesome, but—*no.* There's something downright—*bestial*—about him! You're hating me saying this, aren't you?

STELLA [*coldly*]   Go on and say it all, Blanche.

BLANCHE   He acts like an animal, has an animal's habits! Eats like one, moves like one, talks like one! There's even something—sub-human—something not quite to the stage of humanity yet! Yes, something—ape-like about him, like one of those pictures I've seen in—anthropological studies! Thousands and thousands of years have passed him right by, and there he is—Stanley Kowalski—survivor of the Stone Age! Bearing the raw meat home from the kill in the jungle! And you—*you* here—*waiting* for him! Maybe he'll strike you or maybe grunt and kiss you! That is, if kisses have been discovered yet! Night falls and the other apes gather! There in the front of the cave, all grunting like him, and swilling and gnawing and hulking! His poker night! you call it—this party of apes! Somebody growls—some creature snatches at something—the fight is on! *God!* Maybe we are a long way from being made in God's image, but Stella—my sister—there has been *some* progress since then! Such things as art—as poetry and music—such kinds of new light have come into the world since then! In some kinds of people some tenderer feelings have had some little beginning! That we have got to make *grow!* And *cling* to, and hold as our flag! In this dark march toward whatever it is we're approaching. . . . *Don't*—*don't hang back with the brutes!*

[*Another train passes outside.* STANLEY *hesitates, licking his lips. Then suddenly he turns stealthily about and withdraws through front door. The women are still unaware of his presence. When the train has passed he calls through the closed front door.*]

STANLEY   Hey! Hey, Stella!

STELLA [*who has listened gravely to* BLANCHE]   Stanley!

BLANCHE   Stell, I—

[*But* STELLA *has gone to the front door.* STANLEY *enters casually with his packages.*]

STANLEY   Hiyuh, Stella. Blanche back?

STELLA   Yes, she's back.

STANLEY   Hiyuh, Blanche. [*He grins at her.*]

STELLA   You must've got under the car.

STANLEY   Them darn mechanics at Fritz's don't know their ass fr'm—Hey!

[STELLA *has embraced him with both arms, fiercely, and full in the view of* BLANCHE. *He laughs and clasps her head to him. Over her head he grins through the curtains at* BLANCHE. *As the lights fade away, with a lingering brightness on their embrace, the music of the "Blue Piano" and trumpet and drums is heard.*]

### Scene Five

BLANCHE *is seated in the bedroom fanning herself with a palm leaf as she reads over a just-completed letter. Suddenly she bursts into a peal of laughter.* STELLA *is dressing in the bedroom.*

STELLA   What are you laughing at, honey?

BLANCHE   Myself, myself, for being such a liar! I'm writing a letter to Shep.

[*She picks up the letter.*] "Darling Shep. I am spending the summer on the wing, making flying visits here and there. And who knows, perhaps I shall take a sudden notion to *swoop* down on *Dallas!* How would you feel about that? Ha-ha! [*She laughs nervously and brightly, touching her throat as if actually talking to* SHEP.] Forewarned is forearmed, as they say!"—How does that sound?

STELLA    Uh-huh . . .

BLANCHE [*going on nervously*]    "Most of my sister's friends go north in the summer but some have homes on the Gulf and there has been a continued round of entertainments, teas, cocktails, and luncheons—"
    [*A disturbance is heard upstairs at the Hubbells' apartment.*]

STELLA    Eunice seems to be having some trouble with Steve.
    [EUNICE'*s voice shouts in terrible wrath.*]

EUNICE    I heard about you and that blonde!

STEVE    That's a damn lie!

EUNICE    You ain't pulling the wool over my eyes! I wouldn't mind if you'd stay down at the Four Deuces, but you always going up.

STEVE    Who ever seen me up?

EUNICE    I seen you chasing her 'round the balcony—I'm gonna call the vice squad!

STEVE    Don't you throw that at me!

EUNICE [*shrieking*]    You hit me! I'm gonna call the police!
    [*A clatter of aluminum striking a wall is heard, followed by a man's angry roar, shouts and overturned furniture. There is a crash; then a relative hush.*]

BLANCHE [*brightly*]    Did he *kill* her?
    [EUNICE *appears on the steps in daemonic disorder.*]

STELLA    No! She's coming downstairs.

EUNICE    Call the police, I'm going to call the police! [*She rushes around the corner.*]
    [*They laugh lightly.* STANLEY *comes around the corner in his green and scarlet silk bowling shirt. He trots up the steps and bangs into the kitchen.* BLANCHE *registers his entrance with nervous gestures.*]

STANLEY    What's a matter with Eun-uss?

STELLA    She and Steve had a row. Has she got the police?

STANLEY    Naw. She's gettin' a drink.

STELLA    That's much more practical!
    [STEVE *comes down nursing a bruise on his forehead and looks in the door.*]

STEVE    She here?

STANLEY    Naw, naw. At the Four Deuces.

STEVE    That rutting hunk! [*He looks around the corner a bit timidly, then turns with affected boldness and runs after her.*]

BLANCHE    I must jot that down in my notebook. Ha-ha! I'm compiling a notebook of quaint little words and phrases I've picked up here.

STANLEY    You won't pick up nothing here you ain't heard before.

BLANCHE    Can I count on that?

STANLEY    You can count on it up to five hundred.

BLANCHE    That's a mighty high number. [*He jerks open the bureau drawer, slams it shut and throws shoes in a corner. At each noise* BLANCHE *winces slightly. Finally she speaks.*] What sign were you born under?

STANLEY [*while he is dressing*]    Sign?

BLANCHE    Astrological sign. I bet you were born under Aries. Aries people are forceful and dynamic. They dote on noise! They love to bang things around! You must have had lots of banging around in the army and now that you're out, you make up for it by treating inanimate objects with such a fury!

[STELLA *has been going in and out of closet during this scene. Now she pops her head out of the closet.*]

STELLA   Stanley was born just five minutes after Christmas.

BLANCHE   Capricorn—the Goat!

STANLEY   What sign were *you* born under?

BLANCHE   Oh, my birthday's next month, the fifteenth of September; that's under Virgo.

STANLEY   What's Virgo?

BLANCHE   Virgo is the Virgin.

STANLEY   [*contemptuously*]   Hah! [*He advances a little as he knots his tie.*] Say, do you happen to know somebody named Shaw?

[*Her face expresses a faint shock. She reaches for the cologne bottle and dampens her handkerchief as she answers carefully.*]

BLANCHE   Why, everybody knows somebody named Shaw!

STANLEY   Well, this somebody named Shaw is under the impression he met you in Laurel, but I figure he must have got you mixed up with some other party because this other party is someone he met at a hotel called the Flamingo.

[BLANCHE *laughs breathlessly as she touches the cologne-dampened handkerchief to her temples.*]

BLANCHE   I'm afraid he does have me mixed up with this "other party." The Hotel Flamingo is not the sort of establishment I would dare to be seen in!

STANLEY   You know of it?

BLANCHE   Yes, I've seen it and smelled it.

STANLEY   You must've got pretty close if you could smell it.

BLANCHE   The odor of cheap perfume is penetrating.

STANLEY   That stuff you use is expensive?

BLANCHE   Twenty-five dollars an ounce! I'm nearly out. That's just a hint if you want to remember my birthday! [*She speaks lightly but her voice has a note of fear.*]

STANLEY   Shaw must've got you mixed up. He goes in and out of Laurel all the time so he can check on it and clear up any mistake.

[*He turns away and crosses to the portieres.* BLANCHE *closes her eyes as if faint. Her hand trembles as she lifts the handkerchief again to her forehead.* STEVE *and* EUNICE *come around corner.* STEVE's *arm is around* EUNICE's *shoulder and she is sobbing luxuriously and he is cooing love-words. There is a murmur of thunder as they go slowly upstairs in a tight embrace.*]

STANLEY   [*to* STELLA]   I'll wait for you at the Four Deuces!

STELLA   Hey! Don't I rate one kiss?

STANLEY   Not in front of your sister.

[*He goes out.* BLANCHE *rises from her chair. She seems faint; looks about her with an expression of almost panic.*]

BLANCHE   Stella! What have you heard about me?

STELLA   Huh?

BLANCHE   What have people been telling you about me?

STELLA   Telling?

BLANCHE   You haven't heard any—unkind—gossip about me?

STELLA   Why, no, Blanche, of course not!

BLANCHE Honey, there was—a good deal of talk in Laurel.

STELLA About *you*, Blanche?

BLANCHE I wasn't so good the last two years or so, after Belle Reve had started to slip through my fingers.

STELLA All of us do things we—

BLANCHE I never was hard or self-sufficient enough. When people are soft— soft people have got to shimmer and glow—they've got to put on soft colors, the colors of butterfly wings, and put a—paper lantern over the light. . . . It isn't enough to be soft. You've got to be soft *and attractive*. And I—I'm fading now! I don't know how much longer I can turn the trick.

[*The afternoon has faded to dusk.* STELLA *goes into the bedroom and turns on the light under the paper lantern. She holds a bottled soft drink in her hand.*]

BLANCHE Have you been listening to me?

STELLA I don't listen to you when you are being morbid! [*She advances with the bottled Coke.*]

BLANCHE [*with abrupt change to gaiety*] Is that Coke for me?

STELLA Not for anyone else!

BLANCHE Why, you precious thing, you! Is it just Coke?

STELLA [*turning*] You mean you want a shot in it!

BLANCHE Well, honey, a shot never does a Coke any harm! Let me! You mustn't wait on me!

STELLA I like to wait on you, Blanche. It makes it seem more like home.

[*She goes into the kitchen, finds a glass and pours a shot of whiskey into it.*]

BLANCHE I have to admit I love to be waited on . . .

[*She rushes into the bedroom.* STELLA *goes to her with the glass.* BLANCHE *suddenly clutches* STELLA's *free hand with a moaning sound and presses the hand to her lips.* STELLA *is embarrassed by her show of emotion.* BLANCHE *speaks in a choked voice.*]

You're—you're—so *good* to me! And I—

STELLA Blanche.

BLANCHE I know, I won't! You hate me to talk sentimental! But honey, *believe* I feel things more than I *tell* you! I *won't* stay long! I won't, I *promise* I—

STELLA Blanche!

BLANCHE [*hysterically*] I won't, I promise, *I'll* go! Go *soon*! I will *really*! I *won't* hang around until he—throws me out . . .

STELLA Now will you stop talking foolish?

BLANCHE Yes, honey. Watch how you pour—that fizzy stuff foams over!

[BLANCHE *laughs shrilly and grabs the glass, but her hand shakes so it almost slips from her grasp.* STELLA *pours the Coke into the glass. It foams over and spills.* BLANCHE *gives a piercing cry.*]

STELLA [*shocked by the cry*] Heavens!

BLANCHE Right on my pretty white skirt!

STELLA Oh . . . Use my hanky. Blot gently.

BLANCHE [*slowly recovering*] I know—gently—gently . . .

STELLA Did it stain?

BLANCHE Not a bit. Ha-ha! Isn't that lucky? [*She sits down shakily, taking a grateful drink. She holds the glass in both hands and continues to laugh a little.*]

STELLA Why did you scream like that?

BLANCHE I don't know why I screamed! [*continuing nervously*] Mitch— Mitch is coming at seven. I guess I am just feeling nervous about our relations. [*She begins to talk rapidly and breathlessly.*] He hasn't gotten a thing but a good-night kiss, that's all I have given him, Stella. I want his respect. And men don't want anything they get too easy. But on the other hand men lose interest quickly. Especially when the girl is over—thirty. They think a girl over thirty ought to—the vulgar term is—"put out." . . . And I—I'm not "putting out." Of course he—he doesn't know—I mean I haven't informed him—of my real age!

STELLA   Why are you sensitive about your age?

BLANCHE   Because of hard knocks my vanity's been given. What I mean is— he thinks I'm sort of—prim and proper, you know! [*She laughs out sharply.*] I want to *deceive* him enough to make him—want me . . .

STELLA   Blanche, do you want *him?*

BLANCHE   I want to *rest!* I want to breathe quietly again! Yes—I *want* Mitch . . . *very badly!* Just think! If it happens! I can leave here and not be any-one's problem . . .

   [STANLEY *comes around the corner with a drink under his belt.*]

STANLEY [*bawling*]   Hey, Steve! Hey, Eunice! Hey, Stella!

   [*There are joyous calls from above. Trumpet and drums are heard from around the corner.*]

STELLA [*kissing* BLANCHE *impulsively*]   It *will* happen!

BLANCHE [*doubtfully*]   It will?

STELLA   It *will!* [*She goes across into the kitchen, looking back at* BLANCHE.] It will, honey, *it will.* . . . But don't take another drink! [*Her voice catches as she goes out the door to meet her husband.*]

   [BLANCHE *sinks faintly back in her chair with her drink.* EUNICE *shrieks with laughter and runs down the steps.* STEVE *bounds after her with goat-like screeches and chases her around corner.* STANLEY *and* STELLA *twine arms as they follow, laughing. Dusk settles deeper. The music from the Four Deuces is slow and blue.*]

BLANCHE   Ah, me, ah, me, ah, me . . .

   [*Her eyes fall shut and the palm leaf fan drops from her fingers. She slaps her hand on the chair arm a couple of times. There is a little glimmer of lightning about the building. A* YOUNG MAN *comes along the street and rings the bell.*]

BLANCHE   Come in.

   [*The* YOUNG MAN *appears through the portieres. She regards him with interest.*]

BLANCHE   Well, well! What can I do for *you?*

YOUNG MAN   I'm collecting for *The Evening Star.*

BLANCHE   I didn't know that stars took up collections.

YOUNG MAN   It's the paper.

BLANCHE   I know, I was joking—feebly! Will you—have a drink?

YOUNG MAN   No, ma'am. No, thank you. I can't drink on the job.

BLANCHE   Oh, well, now, let's see. . . . No, I don't have a dime! I'm not the lady of the house. I'm her sister from Mississippi. I'm one of those poor relations you've heard about.

YOUNG MAN   That's all right. I'll drop by later. [*He starts to go out. She approaches a little.*]

BLANCHE   Hey! [*He turns back shyly. She puts a cigarette in a long holder.*] Could you give me a light? [*She crosses toward him. They meet at the door between the two rooms.*]

YOUNG MAN   Sure. [*He takes out a lighter.*] This doesn't always work.

BLANCHE   It's temperamental? [*It flares.*] Ah!—thank you. [*He starts away again.*] Hey! [*He turns again, still more uncertainly. She goes close to him.*] Uh—what time is it?

YOUNG MAN   Fifteen of seven, ma'am.

BLANCHE   So late? Don't you just love these long rainy afternoons in New Orleans when an hour isn't just an hour—but a little piece of eternity dropped into your hands—and who knows what to do with it? [*She touches his shoulders.*] You—uh—didn't get wet in the rain?

YOUNG MAN   No, ma'am. I stepped inside.

BLANCHE   In a drugstore? And had a soda?

YOUNG MAN   Uh-huh.

BLANCHE   Chocolate?

YOUNG MAN   No, ma'am. Cherry.

BLANCHE [*laughing*]   Cherry!

YOUNG MAN   A cherry soda.

BLANCHE   You make my mouth water. [*She touches his cheek lightly, and smiles. Then she goes to the trunk.*]

YOUNG MAN   Well, I'd better be going—

BLANCHE [*stopping him*]   Young man!

> [*He turns. She takes a large, gossamer scarf from the trunk and drapes it about her shoulders. In the ensuing pause, the "Blue Piano" is heard. It continues through the rest of this scene and the opening of the next. The young man clears his throat and looks yearningly at the door.*]

Young man! Young, young, young man! Has anyone ever told you that you look like a young Prince out of the Arabian Nights?

> [*The* YOUNG MAN *laughs uncomfortably and stands like a bashful kid.* BLANCHE *speaks softly to him.*]

Well, you do, honey lamb! Come here. I want to kiss you, just once, softly and sweetly on your mouth!

> [*Without waiting for him to accept, she crosses quickly to him and presses her lips to his.*]

Now run along, now, quickly! It would be nice to keep you, but I've got to be good—and keep my hands off children.

> [*He stares at her a moment. She opens the door for him and blows a kiss at him as he goes down the steps with a dazed look. She stands there a little dreamily after he has disappeared. Then* MITCH *appears around the corner with a bunch of roses.*]

BLANCHE [*gaily*]   Look who's coming! My Rosenkavalier! Bow to me first . . . now present them! Ahhhh—Merciiii![1]

> [*She looks at him over them, coquettishly pressing them to her lips. He beams at her self-consciously.*]

## Scene Six

*It is about two A.M. on the same evening. The outer wall of the building is visible.* BLANCHE *and* MITCH *come in. The utter exhaustion which only a neurasthenic personality can know is evident in* BLANCHE'*s voice and manner.* MITCH *is stolid but depressed. They have probably been out to the amusement park on Lake Pontchartrain, for* MITCH *is bearing, upside down, a plaster statu-*

---

1. "Merci": thank you (French). "My Rosenkavalier": Knight of the Rose (German); title of a romantic opera (1911) by Richard Strauss.

*ette of Mae West, the sort of prize won at shooting galleries and carnival games of chance.*

BLANCHE [*stopping lifelessly at the steps*]  Well— [MITCH *laughs uneasily.*] Well . . .

MITCH  I guess it must be pretty late—and you're tired.

BLANCHE  Even the hot tamale man has deserted the street, and he hangs on till the end. [MITCH *laughs uneasily again.*] How will you get home?

MITCH  I'll walk over to Bourbon and catch an owl-car.

BLANCHE [*laughing grimly*]  Is that streetcar named Desire still grinding along the tracks at this hour?

MITCH [*heavily*]  I'm afraid you haven't gotten much fun out of this evening, Blanche.

BLANCHE  I spoiled it for *you.*

MITCH  No, you didn't, but I felt all the time that I wasn't giving you much—entertainment.

BLANCHE  I simply couldn't rise to the occasion. That was all. I don't think I've ever tried so hard to be gay and made such a dismal mess of it. I get ten points for trying!—I *did* try.

MITCH  Why did you try if you didn't feel like it, Blanche?

BLANCHE  I was just obeying the law of nature.

MITCH  Which law is that?

BLANCHE  The one that says the lady must entertain the gentleman—or no dice! See if you can locate my door key in this purse. When I'm so tired my fingers are all thumbs!

MITCH [*rooting in her purse*]  This it?

BLANCHE  No, honey, that's the key to my trunk which I must soon be packing.

MITCH  You mean you are leaving here soon?

BLANCHE  I've outstayed my welcome.

MITCH  This it?

          [*The music fades away.*]

BLANCHE  Eureka! Honey, you open the door while I take a last look at the sky. [*She leans on the porch rail. He opens the door and stands awkwardly behind her.*] I'm looking for the Pleiades, the Seven Sisters, but these girls are not out tonight. Oh, yes they are, there they are! God bless them! All in a bunch going home from their little bridge party. . . . Y' get the door open? Good boy! I guess you—want to go now . . .

          [*He shuffles and coughs a little.*]

MITCH  Can I—uh—kiss you—good night?

BLANCHE  Why do you always ask me if you may?

MITCH  I don't know whether you want me to or not.

BLANCHE  Why should you be so doubtful?

MITCH  That night when we parked by the lake and I kissed you, you—

BLANCHE  Honey, it wasn't the kiss I objected to. I liked the kiss very much. It was the other little—familiarity—that I—felt obliged to—discourage. . . . I didn't resent it! Not a bit in the world! In fact, I was somewhat flattered that you—desired me! But, honey, you know as well as I do that a single girl, a girl alone in the world, has got to keep a firm hold on her emotions or she'll be lost!

MITCH [*solemnly*]  Lost?

BLANCHE  I guess you are used to girls that like to be lost. The kind that get lost immediately, on the first date!

MITCH  I like you to be exactly the way that you are, because in all my—
experience—I have never known anyone like you.
  [BLANCHE *looks at him gravely; then she bursts into laughter and then
  claps a hand to her mouth.*]
MITCH  Are you laughing at me?
BLANCHE  No, honey. The lord and lady of the house have not yet returned,
  so come in. We'll have a nightcap. Let's leave the lights off. Shall we?
MITCH  You just—do what you want to.
  [BLANCHE *precedes him into the kitchen. The outer wall of the building
  disappears and the interiors of the two rooms can be dimly seen.*]
BLANCHE [*remaining in the first room*]  The other room's more comfortable—
  go on in. This crashing around in the dark is my search for some liquor.
MITCH  You want a drink?
BLANCHE  I want *you* to have a drink! You have been so anxious and solemn
  all evening, and so have I; we have both been anxious and solemn and now
  for these few last remaining moments of our lives together—I want to create—*joie de vivre!* I'm lighting a candle.
MITCH  That's good.
BLANCHE  We are going to be very Bohemian. We are going to pretend that
  we are sitting in a little artists' cafe on the Left Bank in Paris! [*She lights a
  candle stub and puts it in a bottle.*] *Je suis la Dame aux Camellias! Vous
  êtes—Armand!*[2] Understand French?
MITCH [*heavily*]  Naw. Naw, I—
BLANCHE  *Voulez-vous couchez avec moi ce soir? Vous ne comprenez pas? Ah,
  quelle dommage!*[3]—I mean it's a damned good thing. . . . I've found some
  liquor! Just enough for two shots without any dividends, honey . . .
MITCH [*heavily*]  That's—good.
  [*She enters the bedroom with the drinks and the candle.*]
BLANCHE  Sit down! Why don't you take off your coat and loosen your collar?
MITCH  I better leave it on.
BLANCHE  No. I want you to be comfortable.
MITCH  I am ashamed of the way I perspire. My shirt is sticking to me.
BLANCHE  Perspiration is healthy. If people didn't perspire they would die in
  five minutes. [*She takes his coat from him.*] This is a nice coat. What kind
  of material is it?
MITCH  They call that stuff alpaca.
BLANCHE  Oh. Alpaca.
MITCH  It's very light-weight alpaca.
BLANCHE  Oh. Light-weight alpaca.
MITCH  I don't like to wear a wash-coat even in summer because I sweat
  through it.
BLANCHE  Oh.
MITCH  And it don't look neat on me. A man with a heavy build has got to be
  careful of what he puts on him so he don't look too clumsy.
BLANCHE  You are not too heavy.
MITCH  You don't think I am?
BLANCHE  You are not the delicate type. You have a massive bone-structure
  and a very imposing physique.

---

2. I am the Lady of the Camellias! You are—Armand!
(French). Both are characters in the popular romantic
play *La Dame aux Camélias* (1852) by the French author Alexandre Dumas (*fils*); she is a courtesan who
gives up her true love, Armand.
3. Would you like to sleep with me this evening? You
don't understand? Ah, what a pity! (French).

MITCH  Thank you. Last Christmas I was given a membership to the New Orleans Athletic Club.

BLANCHE  Oh, good.

MITCH  It was the finest present I ever was given. I work out there with the weights and I swim and I keep myself fit. When I started there, I was getting soft in the belly but now my belly is hard. It is so hard now that a man can punch me in the belly and it don't hurt me. Punch me! Go on! See? [*She pokes lightly at him.*]

BLANCHE  Gracious. [*Her hand touches her chest.*]

MITCH  Guess how much I weigh, Blanche?

BLANCHE  Oh, I'd say in the vicinity of—one hundred and eighty?

MITCH  Guess again.

BLANCHE  Not that much?

MITCH  No. More.

BLANCHE  Well, you're a tall man and you can carry a good deal of weight without looking awkward.

MITCH  I weigh two hundred and seven pounds and I'm six feet one and one half inches tall in my bare feet—without shoes on. And that is what I weigh stripped.

BLANCHE  Oh, my goodness, me! It's awe-inspiring.

MITCH [*embarrassed*]  My weight is not a very interesting subject to talk about. [*He hesitates for a moment.*] What's yours?

BLANCHE  My weight?

MITCH  Yes.

BLANCHE  Guess!

MITCH  Let me lift you.

BLANCHE  Samson![4] Go on, lift me. [*He comes behind her and puts his hands on her waist and raises her lightly off the ground.*] Well?

MITCH  You are light as a feather.

BLANCHE  Ha-ha! [*He lowers her but keeps his hands on her waist.* BLANCHE *speaks with an affectation of demureness.*] You may release me now.

MITCH  Huh?

BLANCHE [*gaily*]  I said unhand me, sir. [*He fumblingly embraces her. Her voice sounds gently reproving.*] Now, Mitch. Just because Stanley and Stella aren't at home is no reason why you shouldn't behave like a gentleman.

MITCH  Just give me a slap whenever I step out of bounds.

BLANCHE  That won't be necessary. You're a natural gentleman, one of the very few that are left in the world. I don't want you to think that I am severe and old maid school-teacherish or anything like that. It's just—well—

MITCH  Huh?

BLANCHE  I guess it is just that I have—old-fashioned ideals! [*She rolls her eyes, knowing he cannot see her face.* MITCH *goes to the front door. There is a considerable silence between them.* BLANCHE *sighs and* MITCH *coughs self-consciously.*]

MITCH [*finally*]  Where's Stanley and Stella tonight?

BLANCHE  They have gone out. With Mr. and Mrs. Hubbell upstairs.

MITCH  Where did they go?

BLANCHE  I think they were planning to go to a midnight prevue at Loew's State.

MITCH  We should all go out together some night.

---

4. Legendary strong man, in the Old Testament.

BLANCHE   No. That wouldn't be a good plan.

MITCH   Why not?

BLANCHE   You are an old friend of Stanley's?

MITCH   We was together in the Two-forty-first. [5]

BLANCHE   I guess he talks to you frankly?

MITCH   Sure.

BLANCHE   Has he talked to you about me?

BLANCHE   Oh—not very much.

BLANCHE   The way you say that, I suspect that he has.

MITCH   No, he hasn't said much.

BLANCHE   But what he *has* said. What would you say his attitude toward me was?

MITCH   Why do you want to ask that?

BLANCHE   Well—

MITCH   Don't you get along with him?

BLANCHE   What do you think?

MITCH   I don't think he understands you.

BLANCHE   That is putting it mildly. If it weren't for Stella about to have a baby, I wouldn't be able to endure things here.

MITCH   He isn't—nice to you?

BLANCHE   He is insufferably rude. Goes out of his way to offend me.

MITCH   In what way, Blanche?

BLANCHE   Why, in every conceivable way.

MITCH   I'm surprised to hear that.

BLANCHE   Are you?

MITCH   Well, I—don't see how anybody could be rude to you.

BLANCHE   It's really a pretty frightful situation. You see, there's no privacy here. There's just these portieres between the two rooms at night. He stalks through the rooms in his underwear at night. And I have to ask him to close the bathroom door. That sort of commonness isn't necessary. You probably wonder why I don't move out. Well, I'll tell you frankly. A teacher's salary is barely sufficient for her living expenses. I didn't save a penny last year and so I had to come here for the summer. That's why I have to put up with my sister's husband. And he has to put up with me, apparently so much against his wishes. . . . Surely he must have told you how much he hates me!

MITCH   I don't think he hates you.

BLANCHE   He hates me. Or why would he insult me? The first time I laid eyes on him I thought to myself, that man is my executioner! That man will destroy me, unless——

MITCH   Blanche—

BLANCHE   Yes, honey?

MITCH   Can I ask you a question?

BLANCHE   Yes. What?

MITCH   How old are you?

[*She makes a nervous gesture.*]

BLANCHE   Why do you want to know?

MITCH   I talked to my mother about you and she said, "How old is Blanche?" And I wasn't able to tell her. [*There is another pause.*]

BLANCHE   You talked to your mother about me?

MITCH   Yes.

---

5. Battalion of engineers, in World War II.

BLANCHE   Why?

MITCH   I told my mother how nice you were, and I liked you.

BLANCHE   Were you sincere about that?

MITCH   You know I was.

BLANCHE   Why did your mother want to know my age?

MITCH   Mother is sick.

BLANCHE   I'm sorry to hear it. Badly?

MITCH   She won't live long. Maybe just a few months.

BLANCHE   Oh.

MITCH   She worries because I'm not settled.

BLANCHE   Oh.

MITCH   She wants me to be settled down before she—[*His voice is hoarse and he clears his throat twice, shuffling nervously around with his hands in and out of his pockets.*]

BLANCHE   You love her very much, don't you?

MITCH   Yes.

BLANCHE   I think you have a great capacity for devotion. You will be lonely when she passes on, won't you? [MITCH *clears his throat and nods.*] I understand what that is.

MITCH   To be lonely?

BLANCHE   I loved someone, too, and the person I loved I lost.

MITCH   Dead? [*She crosses to the window and sits on the sill, looking out. She pours herself another drink.*] A man?

BLANCHE   He was a boy, just a boy, when I was a very young girl. When I was sixteen, I made the discovery—love. All at once and much, much too completely. It was like you suddenly turned a blinding light on something that had always been half in shadow, that's how it struck the world for me. But I was unlucky. Deluded. There was something different about the boy, a nervousness, a softness and tenderness which wasn't like a man's, although he wasn't the least bit effeminate looking—still—that thing was there. . . . He came to me for help. I didn't know that. I didn't find out anything till after our marriage when we'd run away and come back and all I knew was I'd failed him in some mysterious way and wasn't able to give the help he needed but couldn't speak of! He was in the quicksands and clutching at me—but I wasn't holding him out, I was slipping in with him! I didn't know that. I didn't know anything except I loved him unendurably but without being able to help him or help myself. Then I found out. In the worst of all possible ways. By coming suddenly into a room that I thought was empty— which wasn't empty, but had two people in it . . . the boy I had married and an older man who had been his friend for years . . .

[*A locomotive is heard approaching outside. She claps her hands to her ears and crouches over. The headlight of the locomotive glares into the room as it thunders past. As the noise recedes she straightens slowly and continues speaking.*]

Afterward we pretended that nothing had been discovered. Yes, the three of us drove out to Moon Lake Casino, very drunk and laughing all the way.

[*Polka music sounds, in a minor key faint with distance.*]

We danced the Varsouviana![6] Suddenly in the middle of the dance the boy I had married broke away from me and ran out of the casino. A few moments later—a shot!

---

6. Fast Polish dance, similar to the polka.

[*The polka stops abruptly.* BLANCHE *rises stiffly. Then, the polka resumes in a major key.*]

I ran out—all did!—all ran and gathered about the terrible thing at the edge of the lake! I couldn't get near for the crowding. Then somebody caught my arm. "Don't go any closer! Come back! You don't want to see!" See? See what! Then I heard voices say—Allan! Allan! The Grey boy! He'd stuck the revolver into his mouth, and fired—so that the back of his head had been— blown away!

[*She sways and covers her face.*]

It was because—on the dance floor—unable to stop myself—I'd suddenly said—"I saw! I know! You disgust me . . ." And then the searchlight which had been turned on the world was turned off again and never for one moment since has there been any light that's stronger than this—kitchen— candle . . .

[MITCH *gets up awkwardly and moves toward her a little. The polka music increases.* MITCH *stands beside her.*]

MITCH [*drawing her slowly into his arms*]  You need somebody. And I need somebody, too. Could it be—you and me, Blanche?

[*She stares at him vacantly for a moment. Then with a soft cry huddles in his embrace. She makes a sobbing effort to speak but the words won't come. He kisses her forehead and her eyes and finally her lips. The Polka tune fades out. Her breath is drawn and released in long, grateful sobs.*]

BLANCHE  Sometimes—there's God—so quickly!

## Scene Seven

*It is late afternoon in mid-September.*
*The portieres are open and a table is set for a birthday supper, with cake and flowers.*
STELLA *is completing the decorations as* STANLEY *comes in.*

STANLEY  What's all this stuff for?
STELLA  Honey, it's Blanche's birthday.
STANLEY  She here?
STELLA  In the bathroom.
STANLEY [*mimicking*]  "Washing out some things"?
STELLA  I reckon so.
STANLEY  How long she been in there?
STELLA  All afternoon.
STANLEY [*mimicking*]  "Soaking in a hot tub"?
STELLA  Yes.
STANLEY  Temperature 100 on the nose, and she soaks herself in a hot tub.
STELLA  She says it cools her off for the evening.
STANLEY  And you run out an' get her cokes, I suppose? And serve 'em to Her Majesty in the tub? [STELLA *shrugs.*] Set down here a minute.
STELLA  Stanley, I've got things to do.
STANLEY  Set down! I've got th' dope on your big sister, Stella.
STELLA  Stanley, stop picking on Blanche.
STANLEY  That girl calls *me* common!
STELLA  Lately you been doing all you can think of to rub her the wrong way, Stanley, and Blanche is sensitive and you've got to realize that Blanche and

I grew up under very different circumstances than you did.

STANLEY   So I been told. And told and told and told! You know she's been feeding us a pack of lies here?

STELLA   No, I don't, and—

STANLEY   Well, she has, however. But now the cat's out of the bag! I found out some things!

STELLA   What—things?

STANLEY   Things I already suspected. But now I got proof from the most reliable sources—which I have checked on!

[BLANCHE *is singing in the bathroom a saccharine popular ballad which is used contrapuntally with* STANLEY's *speech.*]

STELLA [*to* STANLEY]   Lower your voice!

STANLEY   Some canary bird, huh!

STELLA   Now please tell me quietly what you think you've found out about my sister.

STANLEY   Lie Number One: All this squeamishness she puts on! You should just know the line she's been feeding to Mitch. He thought she had never been more than kissed by a fellow! But Sister Blanche is no lily! Ha-ha! Some lily she is!

STELLA   What have you heard and who from?

STANLEY   Our supply-man down at the plant has been going through Laurel for years and he knows all about her and everybody else in the town of Laurel knows all about her. She is as famous in Laurel as if she was the President of the United States, only she is not respected by any party! This supply-man stops at a hotel called the Flamingo.

BLANCHE [*singing blithely*]   "Say, it's only a paper moon, Sailing over a cardboard sea—But it wouldn't be make-believe If you believed in me!"[7]

STELLA   What about the—Flamingo?

STANLEY   She stayed there, too.

STELLA   My sister lived at Belle Reve.

STANLEY   This is after the home-place had slipped through her lily-white fingers! She moved to the Flamingo! A second-class hotel which has the advantage of not interfering in the private social life of the personalities there! The Flamingo is used to all kinds of goings-on. But even the management of the Flamingo was impressed by Dame Blanche! In fact they was so impressed by Dame Blanche that they requested her to turn in her room key—for permanently! This happened a couple of weeks before she showed here.

BLANCHE [*singing*]   "It's a Barnum and Bailey world, Just as phony as it can be—But it wouldn't be make-believe If you believed in me!"

STELLA   What—contemptible—lies!

STANLEY   Sure, I can see how you would be upset by this. She pulled the wool over your eyes as much as Mitch's!

STELLA   It's pure invention! There's not a word of truth in it and if I were a man and this creature had dared to invent such things in my presence—

BLANCHE [*singing*]   "Without your love, It's a honky-tonk parade! Without your love, It's a melody played In a penny arcade . . ."

STANLEY   Honey, I told you I thoroughly checked on these stories! Now wait till I finished. The trouble with Dame Blanche was that she couldn't put on her act any more in Laurel! They got wised up after two or three dates with her and then they quit, and she goes on to another, the same old line, same

7. From "It's Only a Paper Moon" (1933), a popular song by Harold Arlen.

old act, same old hooey! But the town was too small for this to go on forever! And as time went by she became a town character. Regarded as not just different but downright loco—nuts. [STELLA *draws back*.] And for the last year or two she has been washed up like poison. That's why she's here this summer, visiting royalty, putting on all this act—because she's practically told by the mayor to get out of town! Yes, did you know there was an army camp near Laurel and your sister's was one of the places called "Out-of-Bounds"?

BLANCHE  "It's only a paper moon, Just as phony as it can be—But it wouldn't be make-believe If you believed in me!"

STANLEY  Well, so much for her being such a refined and particular type of girl. Which brings us to Lie Number Two.

BLANCHE  I don't want to hear any more!

STANLEY  She's not going back to teach school! In fact I am willing to bet you that she never had no idea of returning to Laurel! She didn't resign temporarily from the high school because of her nerves! No, siree, Bob! She didn't. They kicked her out of that high school before the spring term ended—and I hate to tell you the reason that step was taken! A seventeen-year-old boy—she'd gotten mixed up with!

BLANCHE  "It's a Barnum and Bailey world, Just as phony as it can be—"
[*In the bathroom the water goes on loud; little breathless cries and peals of laughter are heard as if a child were frolicking in the tub.*]

STELLA  This is making me—sick!

STANLEY  The boy's dad learned about it and got in touch with the high school superintendent. Boy, oh, boy, I'd like to have been in that office when Dame Blanche was called on the carpet! I'd like to have seen her trying to squirm out of that one! But they had her on the hook good and proper that time and she knew that the jig was all up! They told her she better move on to some fresh territory. Yep, it was practickly a town ordinance passed against her!
[*The bathroom door is opened and* BLANCHE *thrusts her head out, holding a towel about her hair.*]

BLANCHE  Stella!

STELLA [*faintly*]  Yes, Blanche?

BLANCHE  Give me another bath-towel to dry my hair with. I've just washed it.

STELLA  Yes, Blanche. [*She crosses in a dazed way from the kitchen to the bathroom door with a towel.*]

BLANCHE  What's the matter, honey?

STELLA  Matter? Why?

BLANCHE  You have such a strange expression on your face!

STELLA  Oh—[*she tries to laugh*] I guess I'm a little tired!

BLANCHE  Why don't you bathe, too, soon as I get out?

STANLEY [*calling from the kitchen*]  How soon is that going to be?

BLANCHE  Not so terribly long! Possess your soul in patience!

STANLEY  It's not my soul, it's my kidneys I'm worried about!
[BLANCHE *slams the door.* STANLEY *laughs harshly.* STELLA *comes slowly back into the kitchen.*]

STANLEY  Well, what do you think of it?

STELLA  I don't believe all of those stories and I think your supply-man was mean and rotten to tell them. It's possible that some of the things he said are partly true. There are things about my sister I don't approve of—things that caused sorrow at home. She was always—flighty!

STANLEY  Flighty!

STELLA  But when she was young, very young, she married a boy who wrote poetry. . . . He was extremely good-looking. I think Blanche didn't just love him but worshipped the ground he walked on! Adored him and thought him almost too fine to be human! But then she found out—

STANLEY  What?

STELLA  This beautiful and talented young man was a degenerate. Didn't your supply-man give you that information?

STANLEY  All we discussed was recent history. That must have been a pretty long time ago.

STELLA  Yes, it was—a pretty long time ago . . .

[STANLEY *comes up and takes her by the shoulders rather gently. She gently withdraws from him. Automatically she starts sticking little pink candles in the birthday cake.*]

STANLEY  How many candles you putting in that cake?

STELLA  I'll stop at twenty-five.

STANLEY  Is company expected?

STELLA  We asked Mitch to come over for cake and ice-cream.

[STANLEY *looks a little uncomfortable. He lights a cigarette from the one he has just finished.*]

STANLEY  I wouldn't be expecting Mitch over tonight.

[STELLA *pauses in her occupation with candles and looks slowly around at* STANLEY.]

STELLA  Why?

STANLEY  Mitch is a buddy of mine. We were in the same outfit together— Two-forty-first Engineers. We work in the same plant and now on the same bowling team. You think I could face him if—

STELLA  Stanley Kowalski, did you—did you repeat what that—?

STANLEY  You're goddam right I told him! I'd have that on my conscience the rest of my life if I knew all that stuff and let my best friend get caught!

STELLA  Is Mitch through with her?

STANLEY  Wouldn't you be if—?

STELLA  I said, *Is Mitch through with her?*

[BLANCHE'*s voice is lifted again, serenely as a bell. She sings* "But it wouldn't be make-believe If you believed in me."]

STANLEY  No, I don't think he's necessarily through with her—just wised up!

STELLA  Stanley, she thought Mitch was—going to—going to marry her. I was hoping so, too.

STANLEY  Well, he's not going to marry her. Maybe he *was*, but he's not going to jump in a tank with a school of sharks—now! [*He rises.*] Blanche! Oh, Blanche! Can I please get in my bathroom? [*There is a pause.*]

BLANCHE  Yes, indeed, sir! Can you wait one second while I dry?

STANLEY  Having waited one hour I guess one second ought to pass in a hurry.

STELLA  And she hasn't got her job? Well, what will she do!

STANLEY  She's not stayin' here after Tuesday. You know that, don't you? Just to make sure I bought her ticket myself. A bus ticket.

STELLA  In the first place, Blanche wouldn't go on a bus.

STANLEY  She'll go on a bus and like it.

STELLA  No, she won't, no, she won't, Stanley!

STANLEY  *She'll go!* Period. P.S. She'll go *Tuesday!*

STELLA [*slowly*]  What'll—she—do? What on earth will she—*do!*

STANLEY  Her future is mapped out for her.

STELLA  What do you mean?

    [BLANCHE *sings.*]

STANLEY  Hey, canary bird! Toots! Get OUT of the BATHROOM!

    [*The bathroom door flies open and* BLANCHE *emerges with a gay peal of laughter, but as* STANLEY *crosses past her, a frightened look appears in her face, almost a look of panic. He doesn't look at her but slams the bathroom door shut as he goes in.*]

BLANCHE  [*snatching up a hairbrush*]  Oh, I feel so good after my long, hot bath, I feel so good and cool and—rested!

STELLA  [*sadly and doubtfully from the kitchen*]  Do you, Blanche?

BLANCHE  [*snatching up a hairbrush*]  Yes, I do, so refreshed! [*She tinkles her highball glass.*] A hot bath and a long, cold drink always give me a brand new outlook on life! [*She looks through the portieres at* STELLA, *standing between them, and slowly stops brushing.*] Something has happened!— What is it?

STELLA  [*turning away quickly*]  Why, nothing has happened, Blanche.

BLANCHE  You're lying! Something has!

    [*She stares fearfully at* STELLA, *who pretends to be busy at the table. The distant piano goes into a hectic breakdown.*]

## Scene Eight

*Three quarters of an hour later.*

*The view through the big windows is fading gradually into a still-golden dusk. A torch of sunlight blazes on the side of a big water-tank or oil-drum across the empty lot toward the business district which is now pierced by pin-points of lighted windows or windows reflecting the sunset.*

*The three people are completing a dismal birthday supper.* STANLEY *looks sullen.* STELLA *is embarrassed and sad.*

BLANCHE *has a tight, artificial smile on her drawn face. There is a fourth place at the table which is left vacant.*

BLANCHE  [*suddenly*]  Stanley, tell us a joke, tell us a funny story to make us all laugh. I don't know what's the matter, we're all so solemn. Is it because I've been stood up by my beau?

    [STELLA *laughs feebly.*]

It's the first time in my entire experience with men, and I've had a good deal of all sorts, that I've actually been stood up by anybody! Ha-ha! I don't know how to take it. . . . Tell us a funny little story, Stanley! Something to help us out.

STANLEY  I didn't think you liked my stories, Blanche.

BLANCHE  I like them when they're amusing but not indecent.

STANLEY  I don't know any refined enough for your taste.

BLANCHE  Then let me tell one.

STELLA  Yes, you tell one, Blanche. You used to know lots of good stories.

    [*The music fades.*]

BLANCHE  Let me see, now. . . . I must run through my repertoire! Oh, yes— I love parrot stories! Do you all like parrot stories? Well, this one's about the old maid and the parrot. This old maid, she had a parrot that cursed a blue streak and knew more vulgar expressions than Mr. Kowalski!

STANLEY  Huh.

BLANCHE  And the only way to hush the parrot up was to put the cover back on its cage so it would think it was night and go back to sleep. Well, one morning the old maid had just uncovered the parrot for the day—when who should she see coming up the front walk but the preacher! Well, she rushed back to the parrot and slipped the cover back on the cage and then she let in the preacher. And the parrot was perfectly still, just as quiet as a mouse, but just as she was asking the preacher how much sugar he wanted in his coffee—the parrot broke the silence with a loud—[*She whistles.*]—and said—"God *damn*, but that was a short day!"

> [*She throws back her head and laughs.* STELLA *also makes an ineffectual effort to seem amused.* STANLEY *pays no attention to the story but reaches way over the table to spear his fork into the remaining chop which he eats with his fingers.*]

BLANCHE   Apparently Mr. Kowalski was not amused.

STELLA   Mr. Kowalski is too busy making a pig of himself to think of anything else!

STANLEY   That's right, baby.

STELLA   Your face and your fingers are disgustingly greasy. Go and wash up and then help me clear the table.

> [*He hurls a plate to the floor.*]

STANLEY   That's how I'll clear the table! [*He seizes her arm.*] Don't ever talk that way to me! "Pig—Polack—disgusting—vulgar—greasy!"—them kind of words have been on your tongue and your sister's too much around here! What do you two think you are? A pair of queens? Remember what Huey Long[8] said—"Every Man is a King!" And I am the king around here, so don't forget it! [*He hurls a cup and saucer to the floor.*] My place is cleared! You want me to clear your places?

> [STELLA *begins to cry weakly.* STANLEY *stalks out on the porch and lights a cigarette. The Negro entertainers around the corner are heard.*]

BLANCHE   What happened while I was bathing? What did he tell you, Stella?

STELLA   Nothing, nothing, nothing!

BLANCHE   I think he told you something about Mitch and me! You know why Mitch didn't come but you won't tell me! [STELLA *shakes her head helplessly.*] I'm going to call him!

STELLA   I wouldn't call him, Blanche.

BLANCHE   I am, I'm going to call him on the phone.

STELLA [*miserably*]   I wish you wouldn't.

BLANCHE   I intend to be given some explanation from someone!

> [*She rushes to the phone in the bedroom.* STELLA *goes out on the porch and stares reproachfully at her husband. He grunts and turns away from her.*]

STELLA   I hope you're pleased with your doings. I never had so much trouble swallowing food in my life, looking at that girl's face and the empty chair! [*She cries quietly.*]

BLANCHE [*at the phone*]   Hello. Mr. Mitchell, please. . . . Oh. . . . I would like to leave a number if I may. Magnolia 9047. And say it's important to call. . . . Yes, very important. . . . Thank you.

> [*She remains by the phone with a lost, frightened look.*]
> [STANLEY *turns slowly back toward his wife and takes her clumsily in his arms.*]

STANLEY   Stell, it's gonna be all right after she goes and after you've had the

---

8. Demagogic Louisiana political leader, governor, and senator (1893–1935).

baby. It's gonna be all right again between you and me the way that it was. You remember the way that it was? Them nights we had together? God, honey, it's gonna be sweet when we can make noise in the night the way that we used to and get the colored lights going with nobody's sister behind the curtains to hear us!

[*Their upstairs neighbors are heard in bellowing laughter at something.* STANLEY *chuckles.*] Steve an' Eunice . . .

STELLA    Come on back in. [*She returns to the kitchen and starts lighting the candles on the white cake.*] Blanche?

BLANCHE    Yes. [*She returns from the bedroom to the table in the kitchen.*] Oh, those pretty, pretty little candles! Oh, don't burn them, Stella.

STELLA    I certainly will.

[STANLEY *comes back in.*]

BLANCHE    You ought to save them for baby's birthdays. Oh, I hope candles are going to glow in his life and I hope that his eyes are going to be like candles, like two blue candles lighted in a white cake!

STANLEY [*sitting down*]    What poetry!

BLANCHE [*she pauses reflectively for a moment*]    I shouldn't have called him.

STELLA    There's lots of things could have happened.

BLANCHE    There's no excuse for it, Stella. I don't have to put up with insults. I won't be taken for granted.

STANLEY    Goddamn, it's hot in here with the steam from the bathroom.

BLANCHE    I've said I was sorry three times. [*The piano fades out.*] I take hot baths for my nerves. Hydrotherapy, they call it. You healthy Polack, without a nerve in your body, of course you don't know what anxiety feels like!

STANLEY    I am not a Polack. People from Poland are Poles, not Polacks. But what I am is a one-hundred-per-cent American, born and raised in the greatest country on earth and proud as hell of it, so don't ever call me a Polack.

[*The phone rings.* BLANCHE *rises expectantly.*]

BLANCHE    Oh, that's for me, I'm sure.

STANLEY    I'm not sure. Keep your seat. [*He crosses leisurely to phone.*] H'lo. Aw, yeh, hello, Mac.

[*He leans against wall, staring insultingly in at* BLANCHE. *She sinks back in her chair with a frightened look.* STELLA *leans over and touches her shoulder.*]

BLANCHE    Oh, keep your hands off me, Stella. What is the matter with you? Why do you look at me with that pitying look?

STANLEY [*bawling*]    QUIET IN THERE!—We've got a noisy woman on the place.—Go on, Mac. At Riley's? No, I don't wanta bowl at Riley's. I had a little trouble with Riley last week. I'm the team captain, ain't I? All right, then, we're not gonna bowl at Riley's, we're gonna bowl at the West Side or the Gala! All right, Mac. See you!

[*He hangs up and returns to the table.* BLANCHE *fiercely controls herself, drinking quickly from her tumbler of water. He doesn't look at her but reaches in a pocket. Then he speaks slowly and with false amiability.*]

Sister Blanche, I've got a little birthday remembrance for you.

BLANCHE    Oh, have you, Stanley? I wasn't expecting any, I—I don't know why Stella wants to observe my birthday! I'd much rather forget it—when you—reach twenty-seven! Well—age is a subject that you'd prefer to—ignore!

STANLEY   Twenty-seven?
BLANCHE [*quickly*]   What is it? Is it for *me?*
       [*He is holding a little envelope toward her.*]
STANLEY   Yes, I hope you like it!
BLANCHE   Why, why—Why, it's a—
STANLEY   Ticket! Back to Laurel! On the Greyhound! Tuesday!
       [*The Varsouviana music steals in softly and continues playing.* STELLA
       *rises abruptly and turns her back.* BLANCHE *tries to smile. Then she
       tries to laugh. Then she gives both up and springs from the table and
       runs into the next room. She clutches her throat and then runs into the
       bathroom. Coughing, gagging sounds are heard.*]
   Well!
STELLA   You didn't need to do that.
STANLEY   Don't forget all that I took off her.
STELLA   You needn't have been so cruel to someone alone as she is.
STANLEY   Delicate piece she is.
STELLA   She is. She was. You didn't know Blanche as a girl. Nobody,
   nobody, was tender and trusting as she was. But people like you abused her,
   and forced her to change.
       [*He crosses into the bedroom, ripping off his shirt, and changes into a
       brilliant silk bowling shirt. She follows him.*]
   Do you think you're going bowling now?
STANLEY   Sure.
STELLA   You're not going bowling. [*She catches hold of his shirt.*] Why did
   you do this to her?
STANLEY   I done nothing to no one. Let go of my shirt. You've torn it.
STELLA   I want to know why. Tell me why.
STANLEY   When we first met, me and you, you thought I was common. How
   right you was, baby. I was common as dirt. You showed me the snapshot of
   the place with the columns. I pulled you down off them columns and how
   you loved it, having them colored lights going! And wasn't we happy
   together, wasn't it all okay till she showed here?
       [STELLA *makes a slight movement. Her look goes suddenly inward as if
       some interior voice had called her name. She begins a slow, shuffling
       progress from the bedroom to the kitchen, leaning and resting on the
       back of the chair and then on the edge of a table with a blind look and
       listening expression.* STANLEY, *finishing with his shirt, is unaware of
       her reaction.*]
   And wasn't we happy together? Wasn't it all okay? Till she showed here.
   Hoity-Toity, describing me as an ape. [*He suddenly notices the change in*
   STELLA.] Hey, what is it, Stel? [*He crosses to her.*]
STELLA [*quietly*]   Take me to the hospital.
       [*He is with her now, supporting her with his arm, murmuring indistin-
       guishably as they go outside.*]

### Scene Nine

*A while later that evening.* BLANCHE *is seated in a tense hunched position in a
bedroom chair that she has recovered with diagonal green and white stripes. She
has on her scarlet satin robe. On the table beside chair is a bottle of liquor and
a glass. The rapid, feverish polka tune, the "Varsouviana," is heard. The music*

*is in her mind; she is drinking to escape it and the sense of disaster closing in on her, and she seems to whisper the words of the song. An electric fan is turning back and forth across her.*

MITCH *comes around the corner in work clothes: blue denim shirt and pants. He is unshaven. He climbs the steps to the door and rings.* BLANCHE *is startled.*

BLANCHE  Who is it, please?

MITCH [*hoarsely*]  Me. Mitch.

> [*The polka tune stops.*]

BLANCHE  Mitch!—Just a minute.

> [*She rushes about frantically, hiding the bottle in a closet, crouching at the mirror and dabbing her face with cologne and powder. She is so excited that her breath is audible as she dashes about. At last she rushes to the door in the kitchen and lets him in.*]

Mitch!—Y'know, I really shouldn't let you in after the treatment I have received from you this evening! So utterly uncavalier! But hello, beautiful!

> [*She offers him her lips. He ignores it and pushes past her into the flat. She looks fearfully after him as he stalks into the bedroom.*]

My, my, what a cold shoulder! And such uncouth apparel! Why, you haven't even shaved! The unforgivable insult to a lady! But I forgive you. I forgive you because it's such a relief to see you. You've stopped that polka tune that I had caught in my head. Have you ever had anything caught in your head? No, of course you haven't, you dumb angel-puss, you'd never get anything awful caught in your head!

> [*He stares at her while she follows him while she talks. It is obvious that he has had a few drinks on the way over.*]

MITCH  Do we have to have that fan on?

BLANCHE  No!

MITCH  I don't like fans.

BLANCHE  Then let's turn it off, honey. I'm not partial to them!

> [*She presses the switch and the fan nods slowly off. She clears her throat uneasily as* MITCH *plumps himself down on the bed in the bedroom and lights a cigarette.*]

I don't know what there is to drink. I—haven't investigated.

MITCH  I don't want Stan's liquor.

BLANCHE  It isn't Stan's. Everything here isn't Stan's. Some things on the premises are actually mine! How is your mother? Isn't your mother well?

MITCH  Why?

BLANCHE  Something's the matter tonight, but never mind. I won't cross-examine the witness. I'll just— [*She touches her forehead vaguely. The polka tune starts up again.*] —pretend I don't notice anything different about you! That—music again . . .

MITCH  What music?

BLANCHE  The "Varsourviana"! The polka tune they were playing when Allan— Wait!

> [*A distant revolver shot is heard.* BLANCHE *seems relieved.*]

There now, the shot! It always stops after that.

> [*The polka music dies out again.*]

Yes, now it's stopped.

MITCH  Are you boxed out of your mind?

BLANCHE  I'll go and see what I can find in the way of— [*She crosses into the closet, pretending to search for the bottle.*] Oh, by the way, excuse me for

not being dressed. But I'd practically given you up! Had you forgotten your
invitation to supper?

MITCH    I wasn't going to see you any more.

BLANCHE    Wait a minute. I can't hear what you're saying and you talk so little
that when you do say something, I don't want to miss a single syllable of it.
. . . What am I looking around here for? Oh, yes—liquor! We've had so
much excitement around here this evening that I *am* boxed out of my mind!
[*She pretends suddenly to find the bottle. He draws his foot up on the bed
and stares at her contemptuously.*] Here's something. Southern Comfort!
What is that, I wonder?

MITCH  · If you don't know, it must belong to Stan.

BLANCHE    Take your foot off the bed. It has a light cover on it. Of course you
boys don't notice things like that. I've done so much with this place since
I've been here.

MITCH    I bet you have.

BLANCHE    You saw it before I came. Well, look at it now! This room is
almost—dainty! I want to keep it that way. I wonder if this stuff ought to be
mixed with something? Ummm, it's sweet, so sweet! It's terribly, terribly
sweet! Why, it's a *liqueur*, I believe! Yes, that's what it *is*, a liqueur! [MITCH
*grunts.*] I'm afraid you won't like it, but try it, and maybe you will.

MITCH    I told you already I don't want none of his liquor and I mean it. You
ought to lay off his liquor. He says you been lapping it up all summer like a
wild cat!

BLANCHE    What a fantastic statement! Fantastic of him to say it, fantastic of
you to repeat it! I won't descend to the level of such cheap accusations to
answer them, even!

MITCH    Huh.

BLANCHE    What's in your mind? I see something in your eyes!

MITCH [*getting up*]    It's dark in here.

BLANCHE    I like it dark. The dark is comforting to me.

MITCH    I don't think I ever seen you in the light. [BLANCHE *laughs breathlessly.*] That's a fact!

BLANCHE    Is it?

MITCH    I've never seen you in the afternoon.

BLANCHE    Whose fault is that?

MITCH    You never want to go out in the afternoon.

BLANCHE    Why, Mitch, you're at the plant in the afternoon!

MITCH    Not Sunday afternoon. I've asked you to go out with me sometimes
on Sundays but you always make an excuse. You never want to go out till
after six and then it's always some place that's not lighted much.

BLANCHE    There is some obscure meaning in this but I fail to catch it.

MITCH    What it means is I've never had a real good look at you, Blanche.
Let's turn the light on here.

BLANCHE [*fearfully*]    Light? Which light? What for?

MITCH    This one with the paper thing on it. [*He tears the paper lantern off
the light bulb. She utters a frightened gasp.*]

BLANCHE    What did you do that for?

MITCH    So I can take a look at you good and plain!

BLANCHE    Of course you don't really mean to be insulting!

MITCH    No, just realistic.

BLANCHE    I don't want realism. I want magic! [MITCH *laughs.*] Yes, yes,
magic! I try to give that to people. I misrepresent things to them. I don't tell

truth, I tell what *ought* to be truth. And if that is sinful, then let me be damned for it!—*Don't turn the light on!*
[MITCH *crosses to the switch. He turns the light on and stares at her. She cries out and covers her face. He turns the lights off again.*]
MITCH [*slowly and bitterly*]   I don't mind you being older than what I thought. But all the rest of it—Christ! That pitch about your ideals being so old-fashioned and all the malarkey that you've dished out all summer. Oh, I knew you weren't sixteen any more. But I was a fool enough to believe you was straight.
BLANCHE   Who told you I wasn't—"straight"? My loving brother-in-law. And you believed him.
MITCH   I called him a liar at first. And then I checked on the story. First I asked our supply-man who travels through Laurel. And then I talked directly over long-distance to this merchant.
BLANCHE   Who is this merchant?
MITCH   Kiefaber.
BLANCHE   The merchant Kiefaber of Laurel! I know the man. He whistled at me. I put him in his place. So now for revenge he makes up stories about me.
MITCH   Three people, Kiefaber, Stanley and Shaw, swore to them!
BLANCHE   Rub-a-dub-dub, three men in a tub! And such a filthy tub!
MITCH   Didn't you stay at a hotel called The Flamingo?
BLANCHE   Flamingo? No! Tarantula was the name of it! I stayed at a hotel called The Tarantula Arms!
MITCH [*stupidly*]   Tarantula?
BLANCHE   Yes, a big spider! That's where I brought my victims. [*She pours herself another drink.*] Yes, I had many intimacies with strangers. After the death of Allan—intimacies with strangers was all I seemed able to fill my empty heart with. . . . I think it was panic, just panic, that drove me from one to another, hunting for some protection—here and there, in the most—unlikely places—even, at last, in a seventeen-year-old boy but—somebody wrote the superintendent about it—"This woman is morally unfit for her position!"
[*She throws back her head with convulsive, sobbing laughter. Then she repeats the statement, gasps, and drinks.*]
True? Yes, I suppose—unfit somehow—anyway. . . . So I came here. There was nowhere else I could go. I was played out. You know what played out is? My youth was suddenly gone up the water-spout, and—I met you. You said you needed somebody. Well, I needed somebody, too. I thanked God for you, because you seemed to be gentle—a cleft in the rock of the world that I could hide in! But I guess I was asking, hoping—too much! Kiefaber, Stanley and Shaw have tied an old tin can to the tail of the kite.
[*There is a pause.* MITCH *stares at her dumbly.*]
MITCH   You lied to me, Blanche.
BLANCHE   Don't say I lied to you.
MITCH   Lies, lies, inside and out, all lies.
BLANCHE   Never inside, I didn't lie in my heart . . .
[A VENDOR *comes around the corner. She is a blind* MEXICAN WOMAN *in a dark shawl, carrying bunches of those gaudy tin flowers that lower-class Mexicans display at funerals and other festive occasions. She is calling barely audibly. Her figure is only faintly visible outside the building.*]

MEXICAN WOMAN    Flores. Flores, Flores para los muertos.[9] Flores. Flores.

BLANCHE    What? Oh! Somebody outside . . . [*She goes to the door, opens it and stares at the* MEXICAN WOMAN.]

MEXICAN WOMAN [*she is at the door and offers* BLANCHE *some of her flowers*]    Flores? Flores para los muertos?

BLANCHE [*frightened*]    No, no! Not now! Not now!

     [*She darts back into the apartment, slamming the door.*]

MEXICAN WOMAN [*she turns away and starts to move down the street*]    Flores para los muertos.

     [*The polka tune fades in.*]

BLANCHE [*as if to herself*]    Crumble and fade and—regrets—recriminations . . . . "If you'd done this, it wouldn't've cost me that!"

MEXICAN WOMAN    Corones[1] para los muertos. Corones . . .

BLANCHE    Legacies! Huh. . . . And other things such as bloodstained pillow-slips—"Her linen needs changing"—"Yes, Mother. But couldn't we get a colored girl to do it?" No, we couldn't of course. Everything gone but the—

MEXICAN WOMAN    Flores.

BLANCHE    Death—I used to sit here and she used to sit over there and death was as close as you are. . . . We didn't dare even admit we had ever heard of it!

MEXICAN WOMAN    Flores para los muertos, flores—flores . . .

BLANCHE    The opposite is desire. So do you wonder? How could you possibly wonder! Not far from Belle Reve, before we had lost Belle Reve, was a camp where they trained young soldiers. On Sunday nights they would go in town to get drunk—

MEXICAN WOMAN [*softly*]    Corones . . .

BLANCHE    —and on the way back they would stagger onto my lawn and call—"Blanche! Blanche!"—the deaf old lady remaining suspected nothing. But sometimes I slipped outside to answer their calls. . . . Later the paddy-wagon would gather them up like daisies . . . the long way home . . .

     [*The* MEXICAN WOMAN *turns slowly and drifts back off with her soft mournful cries.* BLANCHE *goes to the dresser and leans forward on it. After a moment,* MITCH *rises and follows her purposefully. The polka music fades away. He places his hands on her waist and tries to turn her about.*]

BLANCHE    What do you want?

MITCH [*fumbling to embrace her* ]    What I been missing all summer.

BLANCHE    Then marry me, Mitch!

MITCH    I don't think I want to marry you any more.

BLANCHE    No?

MITCH [*dropping his hands from her waist*]    You're not clean enough to bring in the house with my mother.

BLANCHE    Go away, then. [*He stares at her.*] Get out of here quick before I start screaming fire! [*Her throat is tightening with hysteria.*] Get out of here quick before I start screaming fire.

     [*He still remains staring. She suddenly rushes to the big window with its pale blue square of the soft summer light and cries wildly.*]

Fire! Fire! Fire!

     [*With a startled gasp,* MITCH *turns and goes out the outer door, clatters awkwardly down the steps and around the corner of the building.*

---

9. Flowers for the dead (Spanish).              1. Wreaths (Spanish).

BLANCHE *staggers back from the window and falls to her knees. The distant piano is slow and blue.*]

## Scene Ten

*It is a few hours later that night.*
BLANCHE *has been drinking fairly steadily since* MITCH *left. She has dragged her wardrobe trunk into the center of the bedroom. It hangs open with flowery dresses thrown across it. As the drinking and packing went on, a mood of hysterical exhilaration came into her and she has decked herself out in a somewhat soiled and crumpled white satin evening gown and a pair of scuffed silver slippers with brilliants set in their heels.*

*Now she is placing the rhinestone tiara on her head before the mirror of the dressing-table and murmuring excitedly as if to a group of spectral admirers.*

BLANCHE   How about taking a swim, a moonlight swim at the old rock-quarry? If anyone's sober enough to drive a car! Ha-ha! Best way in the world to stop your head buzzing! Only you've got to be careful to dive where the deep pool is—if you hit a rock you don't come up till tomorrow . . .
[*Tremblingly she lifts the hand mirror for a closer inspection. She catches her breath and slams the mirror face down with such violence that the glass cracks. She moans a little and attempts to rise.*
STANLEY *appears around the corner of the building. He still has on the vivid green silk bowling shirt. As he rounds the corner the honky-tonk music is heard. It continues softly throughout the scene. He enters the kitchen, slamming the door. As he peers in at* BLANCHE, *he gives a low whistle. He has had a few drinks on the way and has brought some quart beer bottles home with him.*]
BLANCHE   How is my sister?
STANLEY   She is doing okay.
BLANCHE   And how is the baby?
STANLEY [*grinning amiably*]   The baby won't come before morning so they told me to go home and get a little shut-eye.
BLANCHE   Does that mean we are to be alone in here?
STANLEY   Yep. Just me and you, Blanche. Unless you got somebody hid under the bed. What've you got on those fine feathers for?
BLANCHE   Oh, that's right. You left before my wire came.
STANLEY   You got a wire?
BLANCHE   I received a telegram from an old admirer of mine.
STANLEY   Anything good?
BLANCHE   I think so. An invitation.
STANLEY   What to? A fireman's ball?
BLANCHE [*throwing back her head*]   A cruise of the Caribbean on a yacht!
STANLEY   Well, well. What do you know?
BLANCHE   I have never been so surprised in my life.
STANLEY   I guess not.
BLANCHE   It came like a bolt from the blue!
STANLEY   Who did you say it was from?
BLANCHE   An old beau of mine.
STANLEY   The one that give you the white fox-pieces?
BLANCHE   Mr. Shep Huntleigh. I wore his ATO pin my last year at college. I hadn't seen him again until last Christmas. I ran in to him on Biscayne

Boulevard. Then—just now—this wire—inviting me on a cruise of the Caribbean! The problem is clothes. I tore into my trunk to see what I have that's suitable for the tropics!

STANLEY And come up with that—gorgeous—diamond—tiara?

BLANCHE This old relic? Ha-ha! It's only rhinestones.

STANLEY Gosh. I thought it was Tiffany diamonds. [*He unbuttons his shirt.*]

BLANCHE Well, anyhow, I shall be entertained in style.

STANLEY Uh-huh. It goes to show, you never know what is coming.

BLANCHE Just when I thought my luck had begun to fail me—

STANLEY Into the picture pops this Miami millionaire.

BLANCHE This man is not from Miami. This man is from Dallas.

STANLEY This man is from Dallas?

BLANCHE Yes, this man is from Dallas where gold spouts out of the ground!

STANLEY Well, just so he's from somewhere! [*He starts removing his shirt.*]

BLANCHE Close the curtains before you undress any further.

STANLEY [*amiably*] This is all I'm going to undress right now. [*He rips the sack off a quart beer bottle*] Seen a bottle-opener?

[*She moves slowly toward the dresser, where she stands with her hands knotted together.*]

I used to have a cousin who could open a beer bottle with his teeth. [*pounding the bottle cap on the corner of table*] That was his only accomplishment, all he could do—he was just a human bottle-opener. And then one time, at a wedding party, he broke his front teeth off! After that he was so ashamed of himself he used t' sneak out of the house when company came . . .

[*The bottle cap pops off and a geyser of foam shoots up. Stanley laughs happily, holding up the bottle over his head.*]

Ha-ha! Rain from heaven! [*He extends the bottle toward her*] Shall we bury the hatchet and make it a loving-cup? Huh?

BLANCHE No, thank you.

STANLEY Well, it's a red-letter night for us both. You having an oil millionaire and me having a baby.

[*He goes to the bureau in the bedroom and crouches to remove something from the bottom drawer.*]

BLANCHE [*drawing back*] What are you doing in here?

STANLEY Here's something I always break out on special occasions like this. The silk pyjamas I wore on my wedding night!

BLANCHE Oh.

STANLEY When the telephone rings and they say, "You've got a son!" I'll tear this off and wave it like a flag! [*He shakes out a brilliant pyjama coat.*] I guess we are both entitled to put on the dog. [*He goes back to the kitchen with the coat over his arm.*]

BLANCHE When I think of how divine it is going to be to have such a thing as privacy once more—I could weep with joy!

STANLEY This millionaire from Dallas is not going to interfere with your privacy any?

BLANCHE It won't be the sort of thing you have in mind. This man is a gentleman and he respects me. [*improvising feverishly*] What he wants is my companionship. Having great wealth sometimes makes people lonely! A cultivated woman, a woman of intelligence and breeding, can enrich a man's life—immeasurably! I have those things to offer, and this doesn't take them away. Physical beauty is passing. A transitory possession. But beauty of the mind and richness of the spirit and tenderness of the heart—and I have all of those things—aren't taken away, but grow! Increase with the years! How strange that I should be called a destitute woman! When I have all of these treasures locked in my heart. [*A choked sob comes from her.*] I think of myself as a very, very rich woman! But I have been foolish—casting my pearls before swine!

STANLEY Swine, huh?

BLANCHE Yes, swine! Swine! And I'm thinking not only of you but of your friend, Mr. Mitchell. He came to see me tonight. He dared to come here in his work clothes! And to repeat slander to me, vicious stories that he had gotten from you! I gave him his walking papers . . .

STANLEY You did, huh?

BLANCHE But then he came back. He returned with a box of roses to beg my forgiveness! He implored my forgiveness. But some things are not forgivable. Deliberate cruelty is not forgivable. It is the one unforgivable thing in my opinion and it is the one thing of which I have never, never been guilty. And so I told him, I said to him, "Thank you," but it was foolish of me to think that we could ever adapt ourselves to each other. Our ways of life are too different. Our attitudes and our backgrounds are incompatible. We have to be realistic about such things. So farewell, my friend! And let there be no hard feelings . . .

STANLEY Was this before or after the telegram came from the Texas oil millionaire?

BLANCHE What telegram? No! No, after! As a matter of fact, the wire came just as—

STANLEY As a matter of fact there wasn't no wire at all!

BLANCHE Oh, oh!

STANLEY There isn't no millionaire! And Mitch didn't come back with roses 'cause I know where he is—

BLANCHE Oh!

STANLEY There isn't a goddam thing but imagination!

BLANCHE Oh!

STANLEY And lies and conceit and tricks!

BLANCHE Oh!

STANLEY And look at yourself! Take a look at yourself in that worn-out Mardi Gras outfit, rented for fifty cents from some rag-picker! And with the crazy crown on! What queen do you think you are?

BLANCHE Oh—God . . .

STANLEY I've been on to you from the start! Not once did you pull any wool over this boy's eyes! You come in here and sprinkle the place with powder and spray perfume and cover the light-bulb with a paper lantern, and lo and behold the place has turned into Egypt and you are the Queen of the Nile! Sitting on your throne and swilling down my liquor! I say—Ha!—Ha! Do you hear me? Ha—ha—ha! [*He walks into the bedroom.*]

BLANCHE Don't come in here!

[*Lurid reflections appear on the walls around* BLANCHE. *The shadows are of a grotesque and menacing form. She catches her breath, crosses to the phone and jiggles the hook.* STANLEY *goes into the bathroom and closes the door.*]

Operator, operator! Give me long-distance, please. . . . I want to get in touch with Mr. Shep Huntleigh of Dallas. He's so well known he doesn't require any address. Just ask anybody who—Wait!!—No, I couldn't find it right now. . . . Please understand, I—No! No, wait! . . . One moment!

Someone is—Nothing! Hold on, please!

[*She sets the phone down and crosses warily into the kitchen. The night is filled with inhuman voices like cries in a jungle. The shadows and lurid reflections move sinuously as flames along the wall spaces. Through the back wall of the rooms, which have become transparent, can be seen the sidewalk. A prostitute has rolled a drunkard. He pursues her along the walk, overtakes her and there is a struggle. A policeman's whistle breaks it up. The figures disappear. Some moments later the Negro Woman appears around the corner with a sequined bag which the prostitute had dropped on the walk. She is rooting excitedly through it.* BLANCHE *presses her knuckles to her lips and returns slowly to the phone. She speaks in a hoarse whisper.*]

BLANCHE  Operator! Operator! Never mind long-distance. Get Western Union. There isn't time to be—Western—Western Union!

[*She waits anxiously.*]

Western Union? Yes! I—want to—Take down this message! "In desperate, desperate circumstances! Help me! Caught in a trap. Caught in—" Oh!

[*The bathroom door is thrown open and* STANLEY *comes out in the brilliant silk pyjamas. He grins at her as he knots the tasseled sash about his waist. She gasps and backs away from the phone. He stares at her for a count of ten. Then a clicking becomes audible from the telephone, steady and rasping.*]

STANLEY  You left th' phone off th' hook.

[*He crosses to it deliberately and sets it back on the hook. After he has replaced it, he stares at her again, his mouth slowly curving into a grin, as he weaves between* BLANCHE *and the outer door. The barely audible "Blue Piano" begins to drum up louder. The sound of it turns into the roar of an approaching locomotive.* BLANCHE *crouches, pressing her fists to her ears until it has gone by.*]

BLANCHE  [*finally straightening*]  Let me—let me get by you!

STANLEY  Get by me? Sure. Go ahead. [*He moves back a pace in the doorway.*]

BLANCHE  You—you stand over there! [*She indicates a further position.*]

STANLEY  [*grinning*]  You got plenty of room to walk by me now.

BLANCHE  Not with you there! But I've got to get out somehow!

STANLEY  You think I'll interfere with you? Ha-ha!

[*The "Blue Piano" goes softly. She turns confusedly and makes a faint gesture. The inhuman jungle voices rise up. He takes a step toward her, biting his tongue which protrudes between his lips.*]

STANLEY  [*softly*]  Come to think of it—maybe you wouldn't be bad to—interfere with . . .

[BLANCHE *moves backward through the door into the bedroom.*]

BLANCHE  Stay back! Don't you come toward me another step or I'll—

STANLEY  What?

BLANCHE  Some awful thing will happen! It will!

STANLEY  What are you putting on now?

[*They are now both inside the bedroom.*]

BLANCHE  I warn you, don't, I'm in danger!

[*He takes another step. She smashes a bottle on the table and faces him, clutching the broken top.*]

STANLEY  What did you do that for?

BLANCHE  So I could twist the broken end in your face!

STANLEY  I bet you would do that!

BLANCHE  I would! I will if you—

STANLEY  Oh! So you want some roughhouse! All right, let's have some roughhouse!

[*He springs toward her, overturning the table. She cries out and strikes at him with the bottle top but he catches her wrist.*]

Tiger—tiger! Drop the bottle-top! Drop it! We've had this date with each other from the beginning!

[*She moans. The bottle-top falls. She sinks to her knees: He picks up her inert figure and carries her to the bed. The hot trumpet and drums from the Four Deuces sound loudly.*]

### Scene Eleven

*It is some weeks later.* STELLA *is packing* BLANCHE's *things. Sounds of water can be heard running in the bathroom.*

*The portieres are partly open on the poker players*—STANLEY, STEVE, MITCH *and* PABLO—*who sit around the table in the kitchen. The atmosphere of the kitchen is now the same raw, lurid one of the disastrous poker night.*

*The building is framed by the sky of turquoise.* STELLA *has been crying as she arranges the flowery dresses in the open trunk.*

EUNICE *comes down the steps from her flat above and enters the kitchen. There is an outburst from the poker table.*

STANLEY  Drew to an inside straight and made it, by God.

PABLO  *Maldita sea tu suerto!*

STANLEY  Put it in English, greaseball.

PABLO  I am cursing your rutting luck.

STANLEY  [*prodigiously elated*]  You know what luck is? Luck is believing you're lucky. Take at Salerno.[2] I believed I was lucky. I figured that 4 out of 5 would not come through but I would . . . and I did. I put that down as a rule. To hold front position in this rat-race you've got to believe you are lucky.

MITCH  You . . . you . . . you . . . Brag . . . brag . . . bull . . . bull.

[STELLA *goes into the bedroom and starts folding a dress.*]

STANLEY  What's the matter with him?

EUNICE  [*walking past the table*]  I always did say that men are callous things with no feelings, but this does beat anything. Making pigs of yourselves.

[*She comes through the portieres into the bedroom.*]

STANLEY  What's the matter with her?

STELLA  How is my baby?

EUNICE  Sleeping like a little angel. Brought you some grapes. [*She puts them on a stool and lowers her voice.*] Blanche?

STELLA  Bathing.

EUNICE  How is she?

STELLA  She wouldn't eat anything but asked for a drink.

EUNICE  What did you tell her?

STELLA  I—just told her that—we'd made arrangements for her to rest in the country. She's got it mixed in her mind with Shep Huntleigh.

[BLANCHE *opens the bathroom door slightly.*]

BLANCHE  Stella.

---

2. Important beachhead in the Allied invasion of Italy in World War II.

STELLA   Yes, Blanche.

BLANCHE   If anyone calls while I'm bathing take the number and tell them
I'll call right back.

STELLA   Yes.

BLANCHE   That cool yellow silk—the bouclé. See if it's crushed. If it's not too
crushed I'll wear it and on the lapel that silver and turquoise pin in the
shape of a seahorse. You will find them in the heart-shaped box I keep my
accessories in. And Stella . . . Try and locate a bunch of artificial violets in
that box, too, to pin with the seahorse on the lapel of the jacket.

[*She closes the door.* STELLA *turns to* EUNICE.]

STELLA   I don't know if I did the right thing.

EUNICE   What else could you do?

STELLA   I couldn't believe her story and go on living with Stanley.

EUNICE   Don't ever believe it. Life has got to go on. No matter what happens,
you've got to keep on going.

[*The bathroom door opens a little.*]

BLANCHE [*looking out*]   Is the coast clear?

STELLA   Yes, Blanche. [*to* EUNICE] Tell her how well she's looking.

BLANCHE   Please close the curtains before I come out.

STELLA   They're closed.

STANLEY   —How many for you?

PABLO   Two.

STEVE   Three.

[BLANCHE *appears in the amber light of the door. She has a tragic
radiance in her red satin robe following the sculptural lines of her body.
The "Varsouviana" rises audibly as* BLANCHE *enters the bedroom.*]

BLANCHE [*with faintly hysterical vivacity*]   I have just washed my hair.

STELLA   Did you?

BLANCHE   I'm not sure I got the soap out.

EUNICE   Such fine hair!

BLANCHE [*accepting the compliment*]   It's a problem. Didn't I get a call?

STELLA   Who from, Blanche?

BLANCHE   Shep Huntleigh . . .

STELLA   Why, not yet, honey!

BLANCHE   How strange! I—

[*At the sound of* BLANCHE'*s voice* MITCH'*s arm supporting his cards
has sagged and his gaze is dissolved into space.* STANLEY *slaps him on
the shoulder.*]

STANLEY   Hey, Mitch, come to!

[*The sound of this new voice shocks* BLANCHE. *She makes a shocked
gesture, forming his name with her lips.* STELLA *nods and looks quickly
away.* BLANCHE *stands quite still for some moments—the silver-backed
mirror in her hand and a look of sorrowful perplexity as though all
human experience shows on her face.* BLANCHE *finally speaks but with
sudden hysteria.*]

BLANCHE   What's going on here?

[*She turns from* STELLA *to* EUNICE *and back to* STELLA. *Her rising voice
penetrates the concentration of the game.* MITCH *ducks his head lower
but* STANLEY *shoves back his chair as if about to rise.* STEVE *places a
restraining hand on his arm.*]

BLANCHE [*continuing*]   What's happened here? I want an explanation of
what's happened here.

STELLA [*agonizingly*]   Hush! Hush!

EUNICE   Hush! Hush! Honey.

STELLA   Please, Blanche.

BLANCHE   Why are you looking at me like that? Is something wrong with me?

EUNICE   You look wonderful, Blanche. Don't she look wonderful?

STELLA   Yes.

EUNICE   I understand you are going on a trip.

STELLA   Yes, Blanche *is*. She's going on a vacation.

EUNICE   I'm green with envy.

BLANCHE   Help me, help me get dressed!

STELLA [*handing her dress*]   Is this what you—

BLANCHE   Yes, it will do! I'm anxious to get out of here—this place is a trap!

EUNICE   What a pretty blue jacket.

STELLA   It's lilac colored.

BLANCHE   You're both mistaken. It's Della Robbia blue.[3] The blue of the robe in the old Madonna pictures. Are these grapes washed?

[*She fingers the bunch of grapes which* EUNICE *had brought in.*]

EUNICE   Huh?

BLANCHE   Washed, I said. Are they washed?

EUNICE   They're from the French Market.

BLANCHE   That doesn't mean they've been washed. [*The cathedral bells chime.*] Those cathedral bells—they're the only clean thing in the Quarter. Well, I'm going now. I'm ready to go.

EUNICE [*whispering*]   She's going to walk out before they get here.

STELLA   Wait, Blanche.

BLANCHE   I don't want to pass in front of those men.

EUNICE   Then wait'll the game breaks up.

STELLA   Sit down and . . .

[BLANCHE *turns weakly, hesitantly about. She lets them push her into a chair.*]

BLANCHE   I can smell the sea air. The rest of my time I'm going to spend on the sea. And when I die, I'm going to die on the sea. You know what I shall die of? [*She plucks a grape.*] I shall die of eating an unwashed grape one day out on the ocean. I will die—with my hand in the hand of some nice-looking ship's doctor, a very young one with a small blond mustache and a big silver watch. "Poor lady," they'll say, "the quinine did her no good. That unwashed grape has transported her soul to heaven." [*The cathedral chimes are heard.*] And I'll be buried at sea sewn up in a clean white sack and dropped overboard—at noon— in the blaze of summer—and into an ocean as blue as [*chimes again*] my first lover's eyes!

[*A* DOCTOR *and a* MATRON *have appeared around the corner of the building and climbed the steps to the porch. The gravity of their profession is exaggerated—the unmistakable aura of the state institution with its cynical detachment. The* DOCTOR *rings the doorbell. The murmur of the game is interrupted.*]

EUNICE [*whispering to* STELLA]   That must be them.

[STELLA *presses her fists to her lips.*]

BLANCHE [*rising slowly*]   What is it?

EUNICE [*affectedly casual*]   Excuse me while I see who's at the door.

STELLA   Yes.

---

3. A shade of light blue seen in terra cottas made by the Della Robbia family in the Italian Renaissance.

[EUNICE *goes into the kitchen.*]
BLANCHE [*tensely*]   I wonder if it's for me.
[*A whispered colloquy takes place at the door.*]
EUNICE [*returning, brightly*]   Someone is calling for Blanche.
BLANCHE   It *is* for me, then! [*She looks fearfully from one to the other and then to the portieres. The "Varsouviana" faintly plays.*] Is it the gentleman I was expecting from Dallas?
EUNICE   I think it is, Blanche.
BLANCHE   I'm not quite ready.
STELLA   Ask him to wait outside.
BLANCHE   I . . .
[EUNICE *goes back to the portieres. Drums sound very softly.*]
STELLA   Everything packed?
BLANCHE   My silver toilet articles are still out.
STELLA   Ah!
EUNICE [*returning*]   They're waiting in front of the house.
BLANCHE   They! Who's "they"?
EUNICE   There's a lady with him.
BLANCHE   I cannot imagine who this "lady" could be! How is she dressed?
EUNICE   Just—just a sort of a—plain-tailored outfit.
BLANCHE   Possibly she's— [*Her voice dies out nervously.*]
STELLA   Shall we go, Blanche?
BLANCHE   Must we go through that room?
STELLA   I will go with you.
BLANCHE   How do I look?
STELLA   Lovely.
EUNICE [*echoing*]   Lovely.
[BLANCHE *moves fearfully to the portieres.* EUNICE *draws them open for her.* BLANCHE *goes into the kitchen.*]
BLANCHE [*to the men*]   Please don't get up. I'm only passing through.
[*She crosses quickly to outside door.* STELLA *and* EUNICE *follow. The poker players stand awkwardly at the table—all except* MITCH, *who remains seated, looking down at the table.* BLANCHE *steps out on a small porch at the side of the door. She stops short and catches her breath.*]
DOCTOR   How do you do?
BLANCHE   You are not the gentleman I was expecting. [*She suddenly gasps and starts back up the steps. She stops by* STELLA, *who stands just outside the door, and speaks in a frightening whisper.*] That man isn't Shep Hunt- leigh.
[*The "Varsouviana" is playing distantly.* STELLA *stares back at* BLANCHE. EUNICE *is holding* STELLA's *arm. There is a moment of silence—no sound but that of* STANLEY *steadily shuffling the cards.* BLANCHE *catches her breath again and slips back into the flat. She enters the flat with a peculiar smile, her eyes wide and brilliant. As soon as her sister goes past her,* STELLA *closes her eyes and clenches her hands.* EUNICE *throws her arms comfortingly about her. Then she starts up to her flat.* BLANCHE *stops just inside the door.* MITCH *keeps staring down at his hands on the table, but the other men look at her curiously. At last she starts around the table toward the bedroom. As she does,* STANLEY *suddenly pushes back his chair and rises as if to block her way. The* MATRON *follows her into the flat.*]
STANLEY   Did you forget something?

BLANCHE [*shrilly*]   Yes! Yes, I forgot something!

[*She rushes past him into the bedroom. Lurid reflections appear on the walls in odd, sinuous shapes. The "Varsouviana" is filtered into a weird distortion, accompanied by the cries and noises of the jungle.* BLANCHE *seizes the back of a chair as if to defend herself.*]

STANLEY [*sotto voce*][4]   Doc, you better go in.

DOCTOR [*sotto voce, motioning to the* MATRON]   Nurse, bring her out.

[*The* MATRON *advances on one side,* STANLEY *on the other. Divested of all the softer properties of womanhood, the* MATRON *is a peculiarly sinister figure in her severe dress. Her voice is bold and toneless as a firebell.*]

MATRON   Hello, Blanche.

[*The greeting is echoed and re-echoed by other mysterious voices behind the walls, as if reverberated through a canyon of rock.*]

STANLEY   She says that she forgot something.

[*The echo sounds in threatening whispers.*]

MATRON   That's all right.

STANLEY   What did you forget, Blanche?

BLANCHE   I—I—

MATRON   It don't matter. We can pick it up later.

STANLEY   Sure. We can send it along with the trunk.

BLANCHE [*retreating in panic*]   I don't know you—I don't know you. I want to be—left alone—please!

MATRON   Now, Blanche!

ECHOES [*rising and falling*]   Now, Blanche—now, Blanche—now, Blanche!

STANLEY   You left nothing here but spilt talcum and old empty perfume bottles—unless it's the paper lantern you want to take with you. You want the lantern?

[*He crosses to dressing table and seizes the paper lantern, tearing it off the light bulb, and extends it toward her. She cries out as if the lantern was herself. The* MATRON *steps boldly toward her. She screams and tries to break past the* MATRON. *All the men spring to their feet.* STELLA *runs out to the porch, with* EUNICE *following to comfort her, simultaneously with the confused voices of the men in the kitchen.* STELLA *rushes into* EUNICE's *embrace on the porch.*]

STELLA   Oh, my God, Eunice help me! Don't let them do that to her, don't let them hurt her! Oh, God, oh, please God, don't hurt her! What are they doing to her? What are they doing? [*She tries to break from* EUNICE's *arms.*]

EUNICE   No, honey, no, no, honey. Stay here. Don't go back in there. Stay with me and don't look.

STELLA   What have I done to my sister? Oh, God, what have I done to my sister?

EUNICE   You done the right thing, the only thing you could do. She couldn't stay here; there wasn't no other place for her to go.

[*While* STELLA *and* EUNICE *are speaking on the porch the voices of the men in the kitchen overlap them.* MITCH *has started toward the bedroom.* STANLEY *crosses to block him.* STANLEY *pushes him aside.* MITCH *lunges and strikes at* STANLEY. STANLEY *pushes* MITCH *back.* MITCH *collapses at the table, sobbing. During the preceding scenes, the* MATRON *catches hold of* BLANCHE's *arm and prevents her flight.*]

---

4. In an undertone.

BLANCHE *turns wildly and scratches at the* MATRON. *The heavy woman pinions her arms.* BLANCHE *cries out hoarsely and slips to her knees.*]

MATRON    These fingernails have to be trimmed. [*The* DOCTOR *comes into the room and she looks at him.*] Jacket, Doctor?

DOCTOR    Not unless necessary.

[*He takes off his hat and now he becomes personalized. The unhuman quality goes. His voice is gentle and reassuring as he crosses to* BLANCHE *and crouches in front of her. As he speaks her name, her terror subsides a little. The lurid reflections fade from the walls, the inhuman cries and noises die out and her own hoarse crying is calmed.*]

DOCTOR    Miss DuBois.

[*She turns her face to him and stares at him with desperate pleading. He smiles; then he speaks to the* MATRON.]

It won't be necessary.

BLANCHE [*faintly*]    Ask her to let go of me.

DOCTOR [*to the* MATRON]    Let go.

[*The* MATRON *releases her.* BLANCHE *extends her hands toward the* DOCTOR. *He draws her up gently and supports her with his arm and leads her through the portieres.*]

BLANCHE [*holding tight to his arm*]    Whoever you are—I have always depended on the kindness of strangers.

[*The poker players stand back as* BLANCHE *and the* DOCTOR *cross the kitchen to the front door. She allows him to lead her as if she were blind. As they go out on the porch,* STELLA *cries out her sister's name from where she is crouched a few steps up on the stairs.*]

STELLA    Blanche! Blanche, Blanche!

[BLANCHE *walks on without turning, followed by the* DOCTOR *and the* MATRON. *They go around the corner of the building.* EUNICE *descends to* STELLA *and places the child in her arms. It is wrapped in a pale blue blanket.* STELLA *accepts the child, sobbingly.* EUNICE *continues downstairs and enters the kitchen where the men, except for* STANLEY, *are returning silently to their places about the table.* STANLEY *has gone out on the porch and stands at the foot of the steps looking at* STELLA.]

STANLEY [*a bit uncertainly*]    Stella?

[*She sobs with inhuman abandon. There is something luxurious in her complete surrender to crying now that her sister is gone.*]

STANLEY [*voluptuously, soothingly*]    Now, honey. Now, love. Now, now, love. [*He kneels beside her and his fingers find the opening of her blouse.*] Now, now, love, Now, love. . . .

[*The luxurious sobbing, the sensual murmur fade away under the swelling music of the "Blue Piano" and the muted trumpet.*]

STEVE    This game is seven-card stud.

CURTAIN

1947

# RALPH ELLISON

## 1914–1994

"If the Negro, or any other writer, is going to do what's expected of him, he's lost the battle before he takes the field." This remark of Ralph Ellison's, taken from his *Paris Review* interview of 1953, serves in more than one sense as an appropriate motto for his own career. He did not do what his critics, literary or political ones, suggested that he ought to but insisted on being a writer rather than a spokesman for a cause or a representative figure. His importance to American letters is partly due to this independence. It is also true, however, that he did the unexpected in not following his fine first novel with the others that were predicted. Except for the twelve stories he published since the novel appeared, *Invisible Man*—more than three decades after its appearance—still remains the sole indicator of Ellison's artistic significance.

Ellison was born in Oklahoma, grew up in Oklahoma City, won a state scholarship, and attended Tuskegee Institute, where he was a music major, his instrument the trumpet. His musical life was wide enough to embrace both "serious music" and the world of Southwest–Kansas City jazz just reaching its heyday when Ellison was a young man. He became friends with Jimmy Rushing, the blues singer, and was acquainted with other members of what would be the great Count Basie band of the 1930s; this "deep, rowdy stream of jazz" figured for him as an image of the power and control that constituted art. Although he was a serious student of music and composition, his literary inclinations eventually dominated his musical ones; but testimony to his abiding knowledge and love of music may be found in some of the essays from *Shadow and Act* (1964), a collection of his prose.

When Ellison left Tuskegee he went north to make his way in New York City. There, in 1936, he met Richard Wright, who encouraged him as a writer, and Ellison began to publish reviews and short stories. *Invisible Man*, begun in 1945, was published seven years later and won the National Book Award. Ellison subsequently received a number of awards and lectureships, taught at the Salzburg Seminar, at Bard College, and at the University of Chicago, and in 1970 was named Albert Schweitzer Professor of the Humanities at New York University, where he taught until his retirement. Yet he admitted to being troubled by the terms in which *Invisible Man*'s success—and perhaps his own career as well—were defined. In the *Paris Review* interview he deprecatingly referred to his novel as largely a failure, wished that rather than a "statement" about the American Negro it could be read "simply as a novel," and hoped that in twenty years it would be so read, casually adding, "if it's around that long."

That twenty-year period is now well passed and *Invisible Man* is very much around, though the attempt to view it "simply as a novel" is a complex activity. Near the beginning of the book the young hero dreams that the following message is engraved on a document presented to him at his high school graduation: "To Whom It May Concern: Keep This Nigger-Boy Running." Ellison keeps him running throughout the novel, from his term at Southern College to his flight north into the dizzying sequence of adventures and the various brands of political and racial rhetoric he encounters in Harlem. The novel presents a gallery of extraordinary characters and circumstances, expressed through different narrative styles, against which the ordinary hero defines—or fails to define—himself. And we are to remember that the whole book is conceived and understood to be narrated from a "hole" into which the Invisible Man has retired and where he thinks about the great black jazz trumpet player, Louis Armstrong: "Perhaps I like Louis Armstrong because he's made poetry out of being invisible."

In the late 1960s some black intellectuals and writers found Ellison's work irrelevant to their more activist designs. And earlier in the decade the white critic Irving Howe published an essay praising Richard Wright for writing "protest" works like *Native Son* while (Howe claimed) Ellison and James Baldwin were evading their tragic responsibilities as black victims by being too sanguine about the possibilities of human freedom. Ellison's answer to Howe's charge is printed in an important essay called *The World and the Jug* (in *Shadow and Act*) and in essence runs like this: "I am a human being, not just the black successor to Richard Wright, and there are ways of celebrating my experience more complex than terms like 'protest' can suggest." In Ellison's own words, "To deny in the interest of revolutionary posture that . . . such possibilities of human richness exist for others" is to impoverish both life and art.

Ellison surely felt the sting and seriousness of these charges by black and white critics, but one of the things he shared with his invisible-man protagonist was that, as with Armstrong or any good jazz improviser, he never quite stayed on the beat, especially when the beat was laid down by somebody else. It is not yet clear if or when the uncompleted manuscript of the long-awaited successor to *Invisible Man* will be published. If it is, we can predict that it will provide further confirmation of the genius of an original writer.

# *From* Invisible Man[1]

## Chapter I

### [BATTLE ROYAL]

It goes a long way back, some twenty years. All my life I had been looking for something, and everywhere I turned someone tried to tell me what it was. I accepted their answers too, though they were often in contradiction and even self-contradictory. I was naïve. I was looking for myself and asking everyone except myself questions which I, and only I, could answer. It took me a long time and much painful boomeranging of my expectations to achieve a realization everyone else appears to have been born with: That I am nobody but myself. But first I had to discover that I am an invisible man!

And yet I am no freak of nature, nor of history. I was in the cards, other things having been equal (or unequal) eighty-five years ago. I am not ashamed of my grandparents for having been slaves. I am only ashamed of myself for having at one time been ashamed. About eighty-five years ago they were told that they were free, united with others of our country in everything pertaining to the common good, and, in everything social, separate like the fingers of the hand. And they believed it. They exulted in it. They stayed in their place, worked hard, and brought up my father to do the same. But my grandfather is the one. He was an odd old guy, my grandfather, and I am told I take after him. It was he who caused the trouble. On his death-bed he called my father to him and said, "Son, after I'm gone I want you to keep up the good fight. I never told you, but our life is a war and I have been a traitor all my born days, a spy in the enemy's country ever since I give up my gun back in the Reconstruction. Live with your head in the lion's mouth. I want you to over-

1. This selection from *Invisible Man* (1952) consists of the novel's Prologue and Chapter 1. Ras the Destroyer, Rinehart, and Brother Jack, mentioned in the Prologue, are characters who will appear later.

come 'em with yeses, undermine 'em with grins, agree 'em to death and destruction, let 'em swoller you till they vomit or bust wide open." They thought the old man had gone out of his mind. He had been the meekest of men. The younger children were rushed from the room, the shades drawn and the flame of the lamp turned so low that it sputtered on the wick like the old man's breathing. "Learn it to the younguns," he whispered fiercely; then he died.

But my folks were more alarmed over his last words than over his dying. It was as though he had not died at all, his words caused so much anxiety. I was warned emphatically to forget what he had said and, indeed, this is the first time it has been mentioned outside the family circle. It had a tremendous effect upon me, however. I could never be sure of what he meant. Grandfather had been a quiet old man who never made any trouble, yet on his deathbed he had called himself a traitor and a spy, and he had spoken of his meekness as a dangerous activity. It became a constant puzzle which lay unanswered in the back of my mind. And whenever things went well for me I remembered my grandfather and felt guilty and uncomfortable. It was as though I was carrying out his advice in spite of myself. And to make it worse, everyone loved me for it. I was praised by the most lily-white men of the town. I was considered an example of desirable conduct—just as my grandfather had been. And what puzzled me was that the old man had defined it as *treachery*. When I was praised for my conduct I felt a guilt that in some way I was doing something that was really against the wishes of the white folks, that if they had understood they would have desired me to act just the opposite, that I should have been sulky and mean, and that that really would have been what they wanted, even though they were fooled and thought they wanted me to act as I did. It made me afraid that some day they would look upon me as a traitor and I would be lost. Still I was more afraid to act any other way because they didn't like that at all. The old man's words were like a curse. On my graduation day I delivered an oration in which I showed that humility was the secret, indeed, the very essence of progress. (Not that I believed this—how could I, remembering my grandfather?—I only believed that it worked.) It was a great success. Everyone praised me and I was invited to give the speech at a gathering of the town's leading white citizens. It was a triumph for our whole community.

It was in the main ballroom of the leading hotel. When I got there I discovered that it was on the occasion of a smoker, and I was told that since I was to be there anyway I might as well take part in the battle royal to be fought by some of my schoolmates as part of the entertainment. The battle royal came first.

All of the town's big shots were there in their tuxedoes, wolfing down the buffet foods, drinking beer and whiskey and smoking black cigars. It was a large room with a high ceiling. Chairs were arranged in neat rows around three sides of a portable boxing ring. The fourth side was clear, revealing a gleaming space of polished floor. I had some misgivings over the battle royal, by the way. Not from a distaste for fighting, but because I didn't care too much for the other fellows who were to take part. They were tough guys who seemed to have no grandfather's curse worrying their minds. No one could mistake their toughness. And besides, I suspected that fighting a battle royal might detract from the dignity of my speech. In those pre-invisible days I visualized myself as a potential Booker T. Washington. But the other fellows didn't care too much for me either, and there were nine of them. I felt superior to them in my way, and I didn't like the manner in which we were all crowded together into the servants' elevator. Nor did they like my being there. In fact, as the warmly lighted floors flashed past the elevator we had words over the fact that I, by taking part in the fight, had knocked one of their friends out of a night's work.

We were led out of the elevator through a rococo hall into an anteroom and told to get into our fighting togs. Each of us was issued a pair of boxing gloves and ushered out into the big mirrored hall, which we entered looking cautiously about us and whispering, lest we might accidentally be heard above the noise of the room. It was foggy with cigar smoke. And already the whiskey was taking effect. I was shocked to see some of the most important men of the town quite tipsy. They were all there—bankers, lawyers, judges, doctors, fire chiefs, teachers, merchants. Even one of the more fashionable pastors. Something we could not see was going on up front. A clarinet was vibrating sensuously and the men were standing up and moving eagerly forward. We were a small tight group, clustered together, our bare upper bodies touching and shining with anticipatory sweat; while up front the big shots were becoming increasingly excited over something we still could not see. Suddenly I heard the school superintendent, who had told me to come, yell, "Bring up the shines, gentlemen! Bring up the little shines!"

We were rushed up to the front of the ballroom, where it smelled even more strongly of tobacco and whiskey. Then we were pushed into place. I almost wet my pants. A sea of faces, some hostile, some amused, ringed around us, and in the center, facing us, stood a magnificent blonde—stark naked. There was dead silence. I felt a blast of cold air chill me. I tried to back away, but they were behind me and around me. Some of the boys stood with lowered heads, trembling. I felt a wave of irrational guilt and fear. My teeth chattered, my skin turned to goose flesh, my knees knocked. Yet I was strongly attracted and looked in spite of myself. Had the price of looking been blindness, I would have looked. The hair was yellow like that of a circus kewpie doll, the face heavily powdered and rouged, as though to form an abstract mask, the eyes hollow and smeared a cool blue, the color of a baboon's butt. I felt a desire to spit upon her as my eyes brushed slowly over her body. Her breasts were firm and round as the domes of East Indian temples, and I stood so close as to see the fine skin texture and beads of pearly perspiration glistening like dew around the pink and erected buds of her nipples. I wanted at one and the same time to run from the room, to sink through the floor, or go to her and cover her from my eyes and the eyes of the others with my body; to feel the soft thighs, to caress her and destroy her, to love her and murder her, to hide from her, and yet to stroke where below the small American flag tattooed upon her belly her thighs formed a capital V. I had a notion that of all in the room she saw only me with her impersonal eyes.

And then she began to dance, a slow sensuous movement; the smoke of a hundred cigars clinging to her like the thinnest of veils. She seemed like a fair bird-girl girdled in veils calling to me from the angry surface of some gray and threatening sea. I was transported. Then I became aware of the clarinet playing and the big shots yelling at us. Some threatened us if we looked and others if we did not. On my right I saw one boy faint. And now a man grabbed a silver pitcher from a table and stepped close as he dashed ice water upon him and stood him up and forced two of us to support him as his head hung and moans issued from his thick bluish lips. Another boy began to plead to go home. He was the largest of the group, wearing dark red fighting trunks much too small to conceal the erection which projected from him as though in answer to the insinuating low-registered moaning of the clarinet. He tried to hide himself with his boxing gloves.

And all the while the blonde continued dancing, smiling faintly at the big shots who watched her with fascination, and faintly smiling at our fear. I noticed a certain merchant who followed her hungrily, his lips loose and drooling. He was a large man who wore diamond studs in a shirtfront which swelled with the ample paunch underneath, and each time the blonde swayed her undulating hips he ran his hand through the thin hair of his bald head and, with his arms upheld, his posture clumsy like that of an intoxicated panda, wound his belly in a slow and obscene grind. This creature was completely hypnotized. The music had quickened. As the dancer flung herself about with a detached expression on her face, the men began reaching out to touch her. I could see their beefy fingers sink into the soft flesh. Some of the others tried to stop them and she began to move around the floor in graceful circles, as they gave chase, slipping and sliding over the polished floor. It was mad. Chairs went crashing, drinks were spilt, as they ran laughing and howling after her. They caught her just as she reached a door, raised her from the floor, and tossed her as college boys are tossed at a hazing, and above her red, fixed-smiling lips I saw the terror and disgust in her eyes, almost like my own terror and that which I saw in some of the other boys. As I watched, they tossed her twice and her soft breasts seem to flatten against the air and her legs flung wildly as she spun. Some of the more sober ones helped her to escape. And I started off the floor, heading for the anteroom with the rest of the boys.

Some were still crying and in hysteria. But as we tried to leave we were stopped and ordered to get into the ring. There was nothing to do but what we were told. All ten of us climbed under the ropes and allowed ourselves to be blindfolded with broad bands of white cloth. One of the men seemed to feel a bit sympathetic and tried to cheer us up as we stood with our backs against the ropes. Some of us tried to grin. "See that boy over there?" one of the men said. "I want you to run across at the bell and give it to him right in the belly. If you don't get him, I'm going to get you. I don't like his looks." Each of us was told the same. The blindfolds were put on. Yet even then I had been going over my speech. In my mind each word was as bright as flame. I felt the cloth pressed into place, and frowned so that it would be loosened when I relaxed.

But now I felt a sudden fit of blind terror. I was unused to darkness. It was as though I had suddenly found myself in a dark room filled with poisonous cottonmouths. I could hear the bleary voices yelling insistently for the battle royal to begin.

"Get going in there!"

"Let me at that big nigger!"

I strained to pick up the school superintendent's voice, as though to squeeze some security out of that slightly more familiar sound.

"Let me at those black sonsabitches!" someone yelled.

"No, Jackson, no!" another voice yelled. "Here, somebody, help me hold Jack."

"I want to get at that ginger-colored nigger. Tear him limb from limb," the first voice yelled.

I stood against the ropes trembling. For in those days I was what they called ginger-colored, and he sounded as though he might crunch me between his teeth like a crisp ginger cookie.

Quite a struggle was going on. Chairs were being kicked about and I could hear voices grunting as with a terrific effort. I wanted to see, to see more desperately than ever before. But the blindfold was tight as a thick skin-puckering scab and when I raised my gloved hands to push the layers of white aside a voice yelled, "Oh, no you don't, black bastard! Leave that alone!"

"Ring the bell before Jackson kills him a coon!" someone boomed in the sudden silence. And I heard the bell clang and the sound of the feet scuffling forward.

A glove smacked against my head. I pivoted, striking out stiffly as someone went past, and felt the jar ripple along the length of my arm to my shoulder. Then it seemed as though all nine of the boys had turned upon me at once. Blows pounded me from all sides while I struck out as best I could. So many blow landed upon me that I wondered if I were not the only blindfolded fighter in the ring, or if the man called Jackson hadn't succeeded in getting me after all.

Blindfolded, I could no longer control my motions. I had no dignity. I stumbled about like a baby or a drunken man. The smoke had become thicker and with each new blow it seemed to sear and further restrict my lungs. My saliva became like hot bitter glue. A glove connected with my head, filling my mouth with warm blood. It was everywhere. I could not tell if the moisture I felt upon my body was sweat or blood. A blow landed hard against the nape of my neck. I felt myself going over, my head hitting the floor. Streaks of blue light filled the black world behind the blindfold. I lay prone, pretending that I was knocked out, but felt myself seized by hands and yanked to my feet. "Get going, black boy! Mix it up!" My arms were like lead, my head smarting from blows. I managed to feel my way to the ropes and held on, trying to catch my breath. A glove landed in my mid-section and I went over again, feeling as though the smoke had become a knife jabbed into my guts. Pushed this way and that by the legs milling around me, I finally pulled erect and discovered that I could see the black, sweat-washed forms weaving in the smoky-blue atmosphere like drunken dancers weaving to the rapid drum-like thuds of blows.

Everyone fought hysterically. It was complete anarchy. Everybody fought everybody else. No group fought together for long. Two, three, four, fought one, then turned to fight each other, were themselves attacked. Blows landed below the belt and in the kidney, with the gloves open as well as closed, and with my eye partly opened now there was not so much terror. I moved carefully, avoiding blows, although not too many to attract attention, fighting from group to group. The boys groped about like blind, cautious crabs crouching to protect their mid-sections, their heads pulled in short against their shoulders, their arms stretched nervously before them, with their fists testing the smoke-filled air like the knobbed feelers of hypersensitive snails. In one corner I glimpsed a boy violently punching the air and heard him scream in pain as he smashed his hand against a ring post. For a second I saw him bent over holding his hand, then going down as a blow caught his unprotected head. I played one group against the other, slipping in and throwing a punch then stepping out of range while pushing the others into the melee to take the blows blindly aimed at me. The smoke was agonizing and there were no rounds, no bells at three minute intervals to relieve our exhaustion. The room spun around me, a swirl of lights, smoke, sweating bodies surrounded by tense white faces. I bled from both nose and mouth, the blood spattering upon my chest.

The men kept yelling, "Slug him, black boy! Knock his guts out!"

"Uppercut him! Kill him! Kill that big boy!"

Taking a fake fall, I saw a boy going down heavily beside me as though we were felled by a single blow, saw a sneaker-clad foot shoot into his groin as the two who had knocked him down stumbled upon him. I rolled out of range, feeling a twinge of nausea.

The harder we fought the more threatening the men became. And yet, I had begun to worry about my speech again. How would it go? Would they recognize my ability? What would they give me?

I was fighting automatically when suddenly I noticed that one after another of the boys was leaving the ring. I was surprised, filled with panic, as though I had been left alone with an unknown danger. Then I understood. The boys had arranged it among themselves. It was the custom for the two men left in the ring to slug it out for the winner's prize. I discovered this too late. When the bell sounded two men in tuxedoes leaped into the ring and removed the blindfold. I found myself facing Tatlock, the biggest of the gang. I felt sick at my stomach. Hardly had the bell stopped ringing in my ears than it clanged again and I saw him moving swiftly toward me. Thinking of nothing else to do I hit him smash on the nose. He kept coming, bringing the rank sharp violence of stale sweat. His face was a black blank of a face, only his eyes alive—with hate of me and aglow with a feverish terror from what had happened to us all. I became anxious. I wanted to deliver my speech and he came at me as though he meant to beat it out of me. I smashed him again and again, taking his blows as they came. Then on a sudden impulse I struck him lightly and as we clinched, I whispered, "Fake like I knocked you out, you can have the prize."

"I'll break your behind," he whispered hoarsely.

"For *them*?"

"For *me*, sonofabitch!"

They were yelling for us to break it up and Tatlock spun me half around with a blow, and as a joggled camera sweeps in a reeling scene, I saw the howling red faces crouching tense beneath the cloud of blue-gray smoke. For a moment the world wavered, unraveled, flowed, then my head cleared and Tatlock bounced before me. That fluttering shadow before my eyes was his jabbing left hand. Then falling forward, my head against his damp shoulder, I whispered,

"I'll make it five dollars more."

"Go to hell!"

But his muscles relaxed a trifle beneath my pressure and I breathed, "Seven?"

"Give it to your ma," he said, ripping me beneath the heart.

And while I still held him I butted him and moved away. I felt myself bombarded with punches. I fought back with hopeless desperation. I wanted to deliver my speech more than anything else in the world, because I felt that only these men could judge truly my ability, and now this stupid clown was ruining my chances. I began fighting carefully now, moving in to punch him and out again with my greater speed. A lucky blow to his chin and I had him going too—until I heard a loud voice yell, "I got my money on the big boy."

Hearing this, I almost dropped my guard. I was confused: Should I try to win against the voice out there? Would not this go against my speech, and was not this a moment for humility, for nonresistance? A blow to my head as I danced about sent my right eye popping like a jack-in-the-box and settled my dilemma. The room went red as I fell. It was a dream fall, my body languid and fastidious as to where to land, until the floor became impatient and smashed up to meet me. A moment later I came to. An hypnotic voice said FIVE emphatically. And I lay there, hazily watching a dark red spot of my own blood shaping itself into a butterfly, glistening and soaking into the soiled gray world of the canvas.

When the voice drawled TEN I was lifted up and dragged to a chair. I sat dazed. My eye pained and swelled with each throb of my pounding heart and I wondered if now I would be allowed to speak. I was wringing wet, my mouth still bleeding. We were grouped along the wall now. The other boys ignored me as they congratulated Tatlock and speculated as to how much they would be paid. One boy whimpered over his smashed hand. Looking up front, I saw attendants in white jackets rolling the portable ring away and placing a small square rug in the vacant space surrounded by chairs. Perhaps, I thought, I will stand on the rug to deliver my speech.

Then the M.C. called to us, "Come on up here boys and get your money."

We ran forward to where the men laughed and talked in their chairs, waiting. Everyone seemed friendly now.

"There it is on the rug," the man said. I saw the rug covered with coins of all dimensions and a few crumpled bills. But what excited me, scattered here and there, were the gold pieces.

"Boys, it's all yours," the man said. "You get all you grab."

"That's right, Sambo," a blond man said, winking at me confidentially.

I trembled with excitement, forgetting my pain. I would get the gold and the bills, I thought. I would use both hands. I would throw my body against the boys nearest me to block them from the gold.

"Get down around the rug now," the man commanded, "and don't anyone touch it until I give the signal."

"This ought to be good," I heard.

As told, we got around the square rug on our knees. Slowly the man raised his freckled hand as we followed it upward with our eyes.

I heard, "These niggers look like they're about to pray!"

Then, "Ready," the man said. "Go!"

I lunged for a yellow coin lying on the blue design of the carpet, touching it and sending a surprised shriek to join those rising around me. I tried frantically to remove my hand but could not let go. A hot, violent force tore through my body, shaking me like a wet rat. The rug was electrified. The hair bristled up on my head as I shook myself free. My muscles jumped, my nerves jangled, writhed. But I saw that this was not stopping the other boys. Laughing in fear and embarrassment, some were holding back and scooping up the coins knocked off by the painful contortions of the others. The men roared above us as we struggled.

"Pick it up, goddamnit, pick it up!" someone called like a bass-voiced parrot. "Go on, get it!"

I crawled rapidly around the floor, picking up the coins, trying to avoid the coppers and to get greenbacks and the gold. Ignoring the shock by laughing,

as I brushed the coins off quickly, I discovered that I could contain the electricity—a contradiction, but it works. Then the men began to push us onto the
rug. Laughing embarrassedly, we struggled out of their hands and kept after
the coins. We were all wet and slippery and hard to hold. Suddenly I saw a
boy lifted into the air, glistening with sweat like a circus seal, and dropped, his
wet back landing flush upon the charged rug, heard him yell and saw him
literally dance upon his back, his elbows beating a frenzied tattoo upon the
floor, his muscles twitching like the flesh of a horse stung by many flies. When
he finally rolled off, his face was gray and no one stopped him when he ran
from the floor amid booming laughter.

"Get the money," the M.C. called. "That's good hard American cash!"

And we snatched and grabbed, snatched and grabbed. I was careful not to
come too close to the rug now, and when I felt the hot whiskey breath descend
upon me like a cloud of foul air I reached out and grabbed the leg of a chair.
It was occupied and I held on desperately.

"Leggo, nigger! Leggo!"

The huge face wavered down to mine as he tried to push me free. But my
body was slippery and he was too drunk. It was Mr. Colcord, who owned a
chain of movie houses and "entertainment palaces." Each time he grabbed me
I slipped out of his hands. It became a real struggle. I feared the rug more than
I did the drunk, so I held on, surprising myself for a moment by trying to
topple *him* upon the rug. It was such an enormous idea that I found myself
actually carrying it out. I tried not to be obvious, yet when I grabbed his leg,
trying to tumble him out of the chair, he raised up roaring with laughter, and,
looking at me with soberness dead in the eye, kicked me viciously in the chest.
The chair leg flew out of my hand and I felt myself going and rolled. It was as
though I had rolled through a bed of hot coals. It seemed a whole century
would pass before I would roll free, a century in which I was seared through
the deepest levels of my body to the fearful breath within me and the breath
seared and heated to the point of explosion. It'll all be over in a flash, I thought
as I rolled clear. It'll all be over in a flash.

But not yet, the men on the other side were waiting, red faces swollen as
though from apoplexy as they bent forward in their chairs. Seeing their fingers
coming toward me I rolled away as a fumbled football rolls off the receiver's
fingertips, back into the coals. That time I luckily sent the rug sliding out of
place and heard the coins ringing against the floor and the boys scuffling to
pick them up and the M.C. calling, "All right, boys, that's all. Go get dressed
and get your money."

I was limp as a dish rag. My back felt as though it had been beaten with
wires.

When we had dressed the M.C. came in and gave us each five dollars,
except Tatlock, who got ten for being last in the ring. Then he told us to leave.
I was not to get a chance to deliver my speech, I thought. I was going out into
the dim alley in despair when I was stopped and told to go back. I returned to
the ballroom, where the men were pushing back their chairs and gathering in
groups to talk.

The M.C. knocked on a table for quiet. "Gentlemen," he said, "we almost
forgot an important part of the program. A most serious part, gentlemen. This
boy was brought here to deliver a speech which he made at his graduation
yesterday . . ."

"Bravo!"

"I'm told that he is the smartest boy we've got out there in Greenwood. I'm told that he knows more big words than a pocket-sized dictionary."

Much applause and laughter.

"So now, gentlemen, I want you to give him your attention."

There was still laughter as I faced them, my mouth dry, my eye throbbing. I began slowly, but evidently my throat was tense, because they began shouting, "Louder! Louder!"

"We of the younger generation extol the wisdom of that great leader and educator," I shouted, "who first spoke these flaming words of wisdom: 'A ship lost at sea for many days suddenly sighted a friendly vessel. From the mast of the unfortunate vessel was seen a signal: "Water, water; we die of thirst!" The answer from the friendly vessel came back: "Cast down your bucket where you are." The captain of the distressed vessel, at last heeding the injunction, cast down his bucket, and it came up full of fresh sparkling water from the mouth of the Amazon River.' And like him I say, and in his words, 'To those of my race who depend upon bettering their condition in a foreign land, or who underestimate the importance of cultivating friendly relations with the Southern white man, who is his next-door neighbor, I would say: "Cast down your bucket where you are"—cast it down in making friends in every manly way of the people of all races by whom we are surrounded . . .' "

I spoke automatically and with such fervor that I did not realize that the men were still talking and laughing until my dry mouth, filling up with blood from the cut, almost strangled me. I coughed, wanting to stop and go to one of the tall brass, sand-filled spittoons to relieve myself, but a few of the men, especially the superintendent, were listening and I was afraid. So I gulped it down, blood, saliva and all, and continued. (What powers of endurance I had during those days! What enthusiasm! What a belief in the rightness of things!) I spoke even louder in spite of the pain. But still they talked and still they laughed, as though deaf with cotton in dirty ears. So I spoke with greater emotional emphasis. I closed my ears and swallowed blood until I was nauseated. The speech seemed a hundred times as long as before, but I could not leave out a single word. All had to be said, each memorized nuance considered, rendered. Nor was that all. Whenever I uttered a word of three or more syllables a group of voices would yell for me to repeat it. I used the phrase "social responsibility," and they yelled:

"What's that word you say, boy?"

"Social responsibility," I said.

"What?"

"Social . . ."

"Louder."

". . . responsibility."

"More!"

"Respon—"

"Repeat!"

"—sibility."

The room filled with the uproar of laughter until, no doubt, distracted by having to gulp down my blood, I made a mistake and yelled a phrase I had often seen denounced in newspaper editorials, heard debated in private.

"Social . . ."

"What?" they yelled.

". . . equality—"

The laughter hung smokelike in the sudden stillness. I opened my eyes, puzzled. Sounds of displeasure filled the room. The M.C. rushed forward. They shouted hostile phrases at me. But I did not understand.

A small dry mustached man in the front row blared out, "Say that slowly, son!"

"What, sir?"

"What you just said!"

"Social responsibility, sir," I said.

"You weren't being smart, were you, boy?" he said, not unkindly.

"No, sir!"

"You sure that about 'equality' was a mistake?"

"Oh, yes, sir," I said. "I was swallowing blood."

"Well, you had better speak more slowly so we can understand. We mean to do right by you, but you've got to know your place at all times. All right, now, go on with your speech."

I was afraid. I wanted to leave but I wanted also to speak and I was afraid they'd snatch me down.

"Thank you, sir," I said, beginning where I had left off, and having them ignore me as before.

Yet when I finished there was a thunderous applause. I was surprised to see the superintendent come forth with a package wrapped in white tissue paper, and, gesturing for quiet, address the men.

"Gentlemen, you see that I did not overpraise the boy. He makes a good speech and some day he'll lead his people in the proper paths. And I don't have to tell you that that is important in these days and times. This is a good, smart boy, and so to encourage him in the right direction, in the name of the Board of Education I wish to present him a prize in the form of this . . ."

He paused, removing the tissue paper and revealing a gleaming calfskin brief case.

". . . in the form of this first-class article from Shad Whitmore's shop."

"Boy," he said, addressing me, "take this prize and keep it well. Consider it a badge of office. Prize it. Keep developing as you are and some day it will be filled with important papers that will help shape the destiny of your people."

I was so moved that I could hardly express my thanks. A rope of bloody saliva forming a shape like an undiscovered continent drooled upon the leather and I wiped it quickly away. I felt an importance that I had never dreamed.

"Open it and see what's inside," I was told.

My fingers a-tremble, I complied, smelling the fresh leather and finding an official-looking document inside. It was a scholarship to the state college for Negroes. My eyes filled with tears and I ran awkwardly off the floor.

I was overjoyed; I did not even mind when I discovered that the gold pieces I had scrambled for were brass pocket tokens advertising a certain make of automobile.

When I reached home everyone was excited. Next day the neighbors came to congratulate me. I even felt safe from grandfather, whose deathbed curse usually spoiled my triumphs. I stood beneath his photograph with my brief case in hand and smiled triumphantly into his stolid black peasant's face. It was a face that fascinated me. The eyes seemed to follow everywhere I went.

That night I dreamed I was at a circus with him and that he refused to laugh at the clowns no matter what they did. Then later he told me to open my brief case and read what was inside and I did, finding an official envelope stamped with the state seal; and inside the envelope I found another and another, endlessly, and I thought I would fall of weariness. "Them's years," he said. "Now open that one." And I did and in it I found an engraved document containing a short message in letters of gold. "Read it," my grandfather said. "Out loud!"

"To Whom It May Concern," I intoned. "Keep This Nigger-Boy Running."

I awoke with the old man's laughter ringing in my ears.

(It was a dream I was to remember and dream again for many years after. But at that time I had no insight into its meaning. First I had to attend college.)

1952

# SAUL BELLOW
## b. 1915

When Saul Bellow was awarded the Nobel Prize for literature in 1976 his citation read: "For the human understanding and subtle analysis of contemporary culture that are combined in his work." Except for the poet Robert Lowell, no American writer of the post–World War II period has a better claim to these virtues than Bellow, who has devoted himself almost exclusively and passionately to the novel and its attempt to imagine life in the United States, particularly in the great cities of Chicago and New York.

He was born in Lachine, Quebec, grew up in the Jewish ghetto of Montreal, and moved to Chicago when he was nine. He attended the University of Chicago, then transferred to Northwestern, where he took a degree in anthropology and sociology, the effects of which study are everywhere evident in the novels he was to write. He taught English for a time, served in the merchant marine during World War II, then after the war spent some fifteen years away from Chicago, teaching at New York University and Princeton and living in Paris. In 1962 he returned to Chicago and since then has been a lecturer at the University of Chicago. He has married five times.

Bellow's first novel, *Dangling Man*, was not published until he was nearly thirty and is a short series of elegantly morose meditations, told through the journal of a young man waiting to be inducted into the army and with the "freedom" of having nothing to do but wait. Eventually he is drafted: "Long live regimentation," he sardonically exults. His second novel, *The Victim* (1947), continues the investigation of ways people strive to be relieved of self-determination. This book concerns a week in the life of Asa Leventhal, alone in New York City while his wife visits a relative, who is suddenly confronted by a figure from the past (Kirby Allbee, a Gentile) who succeeds in implicating Leventhal with the past and its present manifestations. *The Victim* is Bellow's most somberly naturalistic depiction of a man brought up against forces larger than himself, yet from the opening sentence ("On some nights New York is as hot as Bangkok") a poetic dimension makes itself felt and helps create the sense of mystery and disturbance felt by both the main character and the reader.

*Dangling Man* and *The Victim* are highly wrought, mainly humorless books; in two long novels published in the 1950s Bellow opened up into new ranges of aspiration and situational zaniness, which brought him respectful admiration from many critics. *The Adventures of Augie March* (1953) and *Henderson the Rain King*

(1959) are each narrated by an "I" who, like his predecessor Huck Finn, is good at lighting out for the territory ahead of whoever means to tie him down. The hero's adventures, whether occurring in Chicago, Mexico, or Africa, are exuberantly delivered in an always stimulating and sometimes overactive prose. *Augie* is filled with sights and sounds, colors and surfaces; its tone is self-involved, affectionate, and affirmative in its ring; *Henderson*, Bellow's most extravagant narrative, has the even more fabulous air of a quest-romance in which the hero returns home from Africa at peace with the world he had been warring against.

The ironic motto for Bellow's novels of the 1950s may well be "Seize the Day," as in the title of perhaps his finest piece of fiction. This short novel is both painful and exhilarating because it so fully exposes its hero (Tommy Wilhelm, an aging out-of-work ex-actor) to the insults of other people who don't understand him, to a city (New York's Upper West Side) impervious to his needs, and to a narrative prose that mixes ridicule and affection so thoroughly as to make them scarcely distinguishable. *Seize the Day* combines, within Tommy's monologues, a wildness and pathos of bitter comedy that was a powerful new element in Bellow's work.

In *Where Do We Go from Here: The Future of Fiction*, an essay published in 1965, Bellow pointed out that nineteenth-century American literature—Emerson, Thoreau, Whitman, Melville—was highly didactic in its efforts to "instruct a young and raw nation." Bellow sees himself in this instructive tradition and in the international company of "didactic" novelists like Dostoyevsky, D. H. Lawrence, and Joseph Conrad; he believes also that "the imagination is looking for new ways to express virtue . . . we have barely begun to comprehend what a human being is." These concerns animate the novels Bellow has written in the years since *Henderson*. In *Herzog* (1964) the hero is another down-and-outer, a professor-intellectual, a student of Romanticism and of the glorification of Self, which Herzog believes both modern life and modernist literature have been working to undercut. At the same time he is a comic and pathetic victim of marital disorder; like all Bellow's heroes, Herzog has a terrible time with women, yet cannot live without them. In *Mr. Sammler's Planet* (1970), written out of the disorders of the late 1960s, the atmosphere is grimmer. Sammler, an aging Jew living (again) on New York's West Side, analyzes and judges but cannot understand the young or blacks, or the mass of people gathered at Broadway and Ninety-sixth Street. He sees about him everywhere "poverty of soul" but admits that he too has "a touch of the same disease—the disease of the single self explaining what was what and who was who."

These novels, as well as *Humboldt's Gift* (1975), have been accused of parading too single-handedly attitudes toward which their author is sympathetic, whereas *The Dean's December* (1982) was criticized by John Updike, in a review, for being too much "*about* Saul Bellow," even though indirectly. Most recently, a collection of shorter fiction, *Him With His Foot in His Mouth* (1984); a novel, *More Die of Heartbreak* (1987); and a novella, *The Bellarosa Connection* (1989), exhibit various talky, informal protagonists and narrators with a lot on their minds. Matters of form and plot in these works seem less important than the ideas and active energy struck off by human beings in turmoil—usually comic turmoil. What Bellow finds moving in Theodore Dreiser's work, "his balkiness and sullenness, and then his allegiance to life," is still found in his own: complaint and weariness, fault-finding, accusation of self and others—these gestures directed at "life" also make up the stuff of life and the "allegiance" out of which Bellow's heroes are made. We read him for this range of interest, for flexibility and diversity of style and idiom, and for the eloquences of nostalgia, invective, and lamentation that make up his intensely imagined world.

# Looking for Mr. Green[1]

*Whatsoever thy hand findeth to do, do it with thy might. . . .*

Hard work? No, it wasn't really so hard. He wasn't used to walking and stair-climbing, but the physical difficulty of his new job was not what George Grebe felt most. He was delivering relief checks in the Negro district, and although he was a native Chicagoan this was not a part of the city he knew much about—it needed a depression to introduce him to it. No, it wasn't literally hard work, not as reckoned in foot-pounds, but yet he was beginning to feel the strain of it, to grow aware of its peculiar difficulty. He could find the streets and numbers, but the clients were not where they were supposed to be, and he felt like a hunter inexperienced in the camouflage of his game. It was an unfavorable day, too—fall, and cold, dark weather, windy. But, anyway, instead of shells in his deep trenchcoat pocket he had the cardboard of checks, punctured for the spindles of the file, the holes reminding him of the holes in player-piano paper. And he didn't look much like a hunter, either; his was a city figure entirely, belted up in this Irish conspirator's coat.[2] He was slender without being tall, stiff in the back, his legs looking shabby in a pair of old tweed pants gone through and fringy at the cuffs. With this stiffness, he kept his head forward, so that his face was red from the sharpness of the weather; and it was an indoors sort of face with gray eyes that persisted in some kind of thought and yet seemed to avoid definiteness of conclusion. He wore sideburns that surprised you somewhat by the tough curl of the blond hair and the effect of assertion in their length. He was not so mild as he looked, nor so youthful; and nevertheless there was no effort on his part to seem what he was not. He was an educated man; he was a bachelor; he was in some ways simple; without lushing, he liked a drink; his luck had not been good. Nothing was deliberately hidden.

He felt that his luck was better than usual today. When he had reported for work that morning he had expected to be shut up in the relief office at a clerk's job, for he had been hired downtown as a clerk, and he was glad to have, instead, the freedom of the streets and welcomed, at least at first, the vigor of the cold and even the blowing of the hard wind. But on the other hand he was not getting on with the distribution of the checks. It was true that it was a city job; nobody expected you to push too hard at a city job. His supervisor, that young Mr. Raynor, had practically told him that. Still, he wanted to do well at it. For one thing, when he knew how quickly he could deliver a batch of checks, he would know also how much time he could expect to clip for himself. And then, too, the clients would be waiting for their money. That was not the most important consideration, though it certainly mattered to him. No, but he wanted to do well, simply for doing-well's sake, to acquit himself decently of a job because he so rarely had a job to do that required just this sort of energy. Of this peculiar energy he now had a superabundance; once it had started to flow, it flowed all too heavily. And, for the time being anyway, he was balked. He could not find Mr. Green.

---

1. From *Mosby's Memoirs and Other Stories* (1968). The epigraph comes from Ecclesiastes 9.10; the verse continues, "for there is no work, nor device, nor knowledge, nor wisdom, in the grave, whither thou goest."

2. Like those worn by members of the anti-British underground in Ireland.

So he stood in his big-skirted trenchcoat with a large envelope in his hand and papers showing from his pocket, wondering why people should be so hard to locate who were too feeble or sick to come to the station to collect their own checks. But Raynor had told him that tracking them down was not easy at first and had offered him some advice on how to proceed. "If you can see the postman, he's your first man to ask, and your best bet. If you can't connect with him, try the stores and tradespeople around. Then the janitor and the neighbors. But you'll find the closer you come to your man the less people will tell you. They don't want to tell you anything."

"Because I'm a stranger."

"Because you're white. We ought to have a Negro doing this, but we don't at the moment, and of course you've got to eat, too, and this is public employment. Jobs have to be made. Oh, that holds for me too. Mind you, I'm not letting myself out. I've got three years of seniority on you, that's all. And a law degree. Otherwise, you might be back of the desk and I might be going out into the field this cold day. The same dough pays us both and for the same, exact, identical reason. What's my law degree got to do with it? But you have to pass out these checks, Mr. Grebe, and it'll help if you're stubborn, so I hope you are."

"Yes, I'm fairly stubborn."

Raynor sketched hard with an eraser in the old dirt of his desk, left-handed, and said, "Sure, what else can you answer to such a question. Anyhow, the trouble you're going to have is that they don't like to give information about anybody. They think you're a plain-clothes dick or an installment collector, or summons-server or something like that. Till you've been seen around the neighborhood for a few months and people know you're only from the relief."

It was dark, ground-freezing, pre-Thanksgiving weather; the wind played hob with the smoke, rushing it down, and Grebe missed his gloves, which he had left in Raynor's office. And no one would admit knowing Green. It was past three o'clock and the postman had made his last delivery. The nearest grocer, himself a Negro, had never heard the name Tulliver Green, or said he hadn't. Grebe was inclined to think that it was true, that he had in the end convinced the man that he wanted only to deliver a check. But he wasn't sure. He needed experience in interpreting looks and signs and, even more, the will not to be put off or denied and even the force to bully if need be. If the grocer did know, he had got rid of him easily. But since most of his trade was with reliefers, why should he prevent the delivery of a check? Maybe Green, or Mrs. Green, if there was a Mrs. Green, patronized another grocer. And was there a Mrs. Green? It was one of Grebe's great handicaps that he hadn't looked at any of the case records. Raynor should have let him read files for a few hours. But he apparently saw no need for that, probably considering the job unimportant. Why prepare systematically to deliver a few checks?

But now it was time to look for the janitor. Grebe took in the building in the wind and gloom of the late November day—trampled, frost-hardened lots on one side; on the other, an automobile junk yard and then the infinite work of Elevated frames, weak-looking, gaping with rubbish fires; two sets of leaning brick porches three stories high and a flight of cement stairs to the cellar. Descending, he entered the underground passage, where he tried the doors until one opened and he found himself in the furnace room. There someone rose toward him and approached, scraping on the coal grit and bending under the canvas-jacketed pipes.

"Are you the janitor?"

"What do you want?"

"I'm looking for a man who's supposed to be living here. Green."

"What Green?"

"Oh, you maybe have more than one Green?" said Grebe with new, pleasant hope. "This is Tulliver Green."

"I don't think I c'n help you, mister. I don't know any."

"A crippled man."

The janitor stood bent before him. Could it be that he was crippled? Oh, God! what if he was. Grebe's gray eyes sought with excited difficulty to see. But no, he was only very short and stooped. A head awakened from meditation, a strong-haired beard, low, wide shoulders. A staleness of sweat and coal rose from his black shirt and the burlap sack he wore as an apron.

"Crippled how?"

Grebe thought and then answered with the light voice of unmixed candor, "I don't know. I've never seen him." This was damaging, but his only other choice was to make a lying guess, and he was not up to it. "I'm delivering checks for the relief to shut-in cases. If he weren't crippled he'd come to collect himself. That's why I said crippled. Bedridden, chair-ridden—is there anybody like that?"

This sort of frankness was one of Grebe's oldest talents, going back to childhood. But it gained him nothing here.

"No suh. I've got four buildin's same as this that I take care of. I don' know all the tenants, leave alone the tenants' tenants. The rooms turn over so fast, people movin' in and out every day. I can't tell you."

The janitor opened his grimy lips but Grebe did not hear him in the piping of the valves and the consuming pull of air to flame in the body of the furnace. He knew, however, what he had said.

"Well, all the same, thanks. Sorry I bothered you. I'll prowl around upstairs again and see if I can turn up someone who knows him."

Once more in the cold air and early darkness he made the short circle from the cellarway to the entrance crowded between the brickwork pillars and began to climb to the third floor. Pieces of plaster ground under his feet; strips of brass tape from which the carpeting had been torn away marked old boundaries at the sides. In the passage, the cold reached him worse than in the street; it touched him to the bone. The hall toilets ran like springs. He thought grimly as he heard the wind burning around the building with a sound like that of the furnace, that this was a great piece of constructed shelter. Then he struck a match in the gloom and searched for names and numbers among the writings and scribbles on the walls. He saw WHOODY-DOODY GO TO JESUS, and zigzags, caricatures, sexual scrawls, and curses. So the sealed rooms of pyramids were also decorated, and the caves of human dawn.

The information on his card was, TULLIVER GREEN—APT 3D. There were no names, however, and no numbers. His shoulders drawn up, tears of cold in his eyes, breathing vapor, he went the length of the corridor and told himself that if he had been lucky enough to have the temperament for it he would bang on one of the doors and bawl out "Tulliver Green!" until he got results. But it wasn't in him to make an uproar and he continued to burn matches, passing the light over the walls. At the rear, in a corner off the hall, he discovered a door he had not seen before and he thought it best to investigate. It sounded empty when he knocked, but a young Negress answered, hardly more than a girl. She opened only a bit, to guard the warmth of the room.

"Yes suh?"

"I'm from the district relief station on Prairie Avenue. I'm looking for a man named Tulliver Green to give him his check. Do you know him?"

No, she didn't; but he thought she had not understood anything of what he had said. She had a dream-bound, dream-blind face, very soft and black, shut off. She wore a man's jacket and pulled the ends together at her throat. Her hair was parted in three directions, at the sides and transversely, standing up at the front in a dull puff.

"Is there somebody around here who might know?"

"I jus' taken this room las' week."

He observed that she shivered, but even her shiver was somnambulistic and there was no sharp consciousness of cold in the big smooth eyes of her handsome face.

"All right, miss, thank you. Thanks," he said, and went to try another place.

Here he was admitted. He was grateful, for the room was warm. It was full of people, and they were silent as he entered—ten people, or a dozen, perhaps more, sitting on benches like a parliament. There was no light, properly speaking, but a tempered darkness that the window gave, and everyone seemed to him enormous, the men padded out in heavy work clothes and winter coats, and the women huge, too, in their sweaters, hats, and old furs. And, besides, bed and bedding, a black cooking range, a piano piled towering to the ceiling with papers, a dining-room table of the old style of prosperous Chicago. Among these people Grebe, with his cold-heightened fresh color and his smaller stature, entered like a schoolboy. Even though he was met with smiles and good will, he knew, before a single word was spoken, that all the currents ran against him and that he would make no headway. Nevertheless he began. "Does anybody here know how I can deliver a check to Mr. Tulliver Green?"

"Green?" It was the man that had let him in who answered. He was in short sleeves, in a checkered shirt, and had a queer, high head, profusely overgrown and long as a shako;[3] the veins entered it strongly, from his forehead. "I never heard mention of him. Is this where he live?"

"This is the address they gave me at the station. He's a sick man, and he'll need his check. Can't anybody tell me where to find him?"

He stood his ground and waited for a reply, his crimson wool scarf wound about his neck and drooping outside his trenchcoat, pockets weighted with the block of checks and official forms. They must have realized that he was not a college boy employed afternoons by a bill collector, trying foxily to pass for a relief clerk, recognized that he was an older man who knew himself what need was, who had had more than an average seasoning in hardship. It was evident enough if you looked at the marks under his eyes and at the sides of his mouth.

"Anybody know this sick man?"

"No suh." On all sides he saw heads shaken and smiles of denial. No one knew. And maybe it was true, he considered, standing silent in the earthen, musky human gloom of the place as the rumble continued. But he could never really be sure.

"What's the matter with this man?" said shako-head.

_____

3. Stiff military headdress with a high crown and a plume.

"I've never seen him. All I can tell you is that he can't come in person for his money. It's my first day in this district."

"Maybe they given you the wrong number?"

"I don't believe so. But where else can I ask about him?" He felt that this persistence amused them deeply, and in a way he shared their amusement that he should stand up so tenaciously to them. Though smaller, though slight, he was his own man, he retracted nothing about himself, and he looked back at them, gray-eyed, with amusement and also with a sort of courage. On the bench some man spoke in his throat, the words impossible to catch, and a woman answered with a wild, shrieking laugh, which was quickly cut off.

"Well, so nobody will tell me?"

"Ain't nobody who knows."

"At least, if he lives here, he pays rent to someone. Who manages the building?"

"Greatham Company. That's on Thirty-ninth Street."

Grebe wrote it in his pad. But, in the street again, a sheet of wind-driven paper clinging to his leg while he deliberated what direction to take next, it seemed a feeble lead to follow. probably this Green didn't rent a flat, but a room. Sometimes there were as many as twenty people in an apartment; the real-estate agent would know only the lessee. And not even the agent could tell you who the renters were. In some places the beds were even used in shifts, watchmen or jitney drivers or short-order cooks in night joints turning out after a day's sleep and surrendering their beds to a sister, a nephew, or perhaps a stranger, just off the bus. There were large numbers of newcomers in this terrific, blight-bitten portion of the city between Cottage Grove and Ashland, wandering from house to house and room to room. When you saw them, how could you know them? They didn't carry bundles on their backs or look picturesque. You only saw a man, a Negro, walking in the street or riding in the car, like everyone else, with his thumb closed on a transfer. And therefore how were you supposed to tell? Grebe thought the Greatham agent would only laugh at his question.

But how much it would have simplified the job to be able to say that Green was old, or blind, or consumptive. An hour in the files, taking a few notes, and he needn't have been at such a disadvantage. When Raynor gave him the block of checks he asked, "How much should I know about these people?" Then Raynor had looked as though he were preparing to accuse him of trying to make the job more important than it was. He smiled, because by then they were on fine terms, but nevertheless he had been getting ready to say something like that when the confusion began in the station over Staika and her children.

Grebe had waited a long time for this job. It came to him through the pull of an old schoolmate in the Corporation Counsel's office, never a close friend, but suddenly sympathetic and interested—pleased to show, moreover, how well he had done, how strongly he was coming on even in these miserable times. Well, he was coming through strongly, along with the Democratic administration itself. Grebe had gone to see him in City Hall, and they had had a counter lunch or beers at least once a month for a year, and finally it had been possible to swing the job. He didn't mind being assigned the lowest clerical grade, nor even being a messenger, though Raynor thought he did. This Raynor was an original sort of guy and Grebe had taken to him immediately. As was proper on the first day, Grebe had come early, but he waited long, for Raynor was late. At last he darted into his cubicle of an office as though he had just jumped from one of those hurtling huge red Indian Avenue cars. His thin, rough face was wind-stung and he was grinning and saying something breathlessly to himself. In his hat, a small fedora, and his coat, the velvet collar a neat fit about his neck, and his silk muffler that set off the nervous twist of his chin, he swayed and turned himself in his swivel chair, feet leaving the ground; so that he pranced a little as he sat. Meanwhile he took Grebe's measure out of his eyes, eyes of an unusual vertical length and slightly sardonic. So the two men sat for a while, saying nothing, while the supervisor raised his hat from his miscombed hair and put it in his lap. His cold-darkened hands were not clean. A steel beam passed through the little makeshift room, from which machine belts once had hung. The building was an old factory.

"I'm younger than you; I hope you won't find it hard taking orders from me," said Raynor. "But I don't make them up, either. You're how old, about?"

"Thirty-five."

"And you thought you'd be inside doing paper work. But it so happens I have to send you out."

"I don't mind."

"And it's mostly a Negro load we have in this district."

"So I thought it would be."

"Fine. You'll get along. *C'est un bon boulot.*[4] Do you know French?"

"Some."

"I thought you'd be a university man."

"Have you been in France?" said Grebe.

"No, that's the French of the Berlitz School. I've been at it for more than a year, just as I'm sure people have been, all over the world, office boys in China and braves in Tanganyika. In fact, I damn well know it. Such is the attractive power of civilization. It's overrated, but what do you want? *Que voulez-vous?*[5] I get *Le Rire* and all the spicy papers, just like in Tanganyika. It must be mystifying, out there. But my reason is that I'm aiming at the diplomatic service. I have a cousin who's a courier, and the way he describes it is awfully attractive. He rides in the *wagon-lits*[6] and reads books. While we—What did you do before?"

"I sold."

"Where?"

"Canned meat at Stop and Shop. In the basement."

"And before that?"

"Window shades, at Goldblatt's."

"Steady work?"

"No, Thursdays and Saturdays. I also sold shoes."

"You've been a shoe-dog too. Well. And prior to that? Here it is in your folder." He opened the record. "Saint Olaf's College, instructor in classical languages. Fellow, University of Chicago, 1926–27. I've had Latin, too. Let's trade quotations—'*Dum spiro spero.*' "

" '*Da dextram misero.*' "

---

4. "It's a good meal" (French slang).
5. "What do you want?"
6. European railroad sleeping-cars.

" '*Alea jacta est.*' "
" '*Excelsior.*' "[7]

Raynor shouted with laughter, and other workers came to look at him over the partition. Grebe also laughed, feeling pleased and easy. The luxury of fun on a nervous morning.

When they were done and no one was watching or listening, Raynor said rather seriously, "What made you study Latin in the first place? Was it for the priesthood?"

"No."

"Just for the hell of it? For the culture? Oh, the things people think they can pull!" He made his cry hilarious and tragic. "I ran my pants off so I could study for the bar, and I've passed the bar, so I get twelve dollars a week more than you as a bonus for having seen life straight and whole. I'll tell you, as a man of culture, that even though nothing looks to be real, and everything stands for something else, and that thing for another thing, and that thing for a still further one—there ain't any comparison between twenty-five and thirty-seven dollars a week, regardless of the last reality. Don't you think that was clear to your Greeks? They were a thoughtful people, but they didn't part with their slaves."

This was a great deal more than Grebe had looked for in his first interview with his supervisor. He was too shy to show all the astonishment he felt. He laughed a little, aroused, and brushed at the sunbeam that covered his head with its dust. "Do you think my mistake was so terrible?"

"Damn right it was terrible, and you know it now that you've had the whip of hard times laid on your back. You should have been preparing yourself for trouble. Your people must have been well off to send you to the university. Stop me, if I'm stepping on your toes. Did your mother pamper you? Did your father give in to you? Were you brought up tenderly, with permission to go and find out what were the last things that everything else stands for while everybody else labored in the fallen world of appearances?"

"Well, no, it wasn't exactly like that." Grebe smiled. *The fallen world of appearances!* no less. But now it was his turn to deliver a surprise. "We weren't rich. My father was the last genuine English butler in Chicago—"

"Are you kidding?"

"Why should I be?"

"In a livery?"

"In livery. Up on the Gold Coast."

"And we wanted you to be educated like a gentleman?"

"He did not. He sent me to the Armor Institute to study chemical engineering. But when he died I changed schools."

He stopped himself, and considered how quickly Raynor had reached him. In no time he had your valise on the table and all your stuff unpacked. And afterward, in the streets, he was still reviewing how far he might have gone, and how much he might have been led to tell if they had not been interrupted by Mrs. Stakia's great noise.

But just then a young woman, one of Raynor's workers, ran into the cubicle exclaiming, "Haven't you heard all the fuss?"

---

7. "Where there's life there's hope" (literally, "while I breathe I hope"); "give the right hand to the wretched"; "the die is cast"; "higher!"

"We haven't heard anything."

"It's Staika, giving out with all her might. The reporters are coming. She said she phoned the papers, and you know she did."

"But what is she up to?" said Raynor.

"She brought her wash and she's ironing it here, with our current, because the relief won't pay her electric bill. She has her ironing board set up by the admitting desk, and her kids are with her, all six. They never are in school more than once a week. She's always dragging them around with her because of her reputation."

"I don't want to miss any of this," said Raynor, jumping up. Grebe, as he followed with the secretary, said, "Who is this Staika?"

"They call her the 'Blood Mother of Federal Street.' She's a professional donor at the hospitals. I think they pay ten dollars a pint. Of course it's no joke, but she makes a very big thing out of it and she and the kids are in the papers all the time."

A small crowd, staff and clients divided by a plywood barrier, stood in the narrow space of the entrance, and Staika was shouting in a gruff, mannish voice, plunging the iron on the board and slamming it on the metal rest.

"My father and mother came in a steerage, and I was born in our house, Robey by Huron. I'm no dirty immigrant. I'm a U.S. citizen. My husband is a gassed veteran from France with lungs weaker'n paper, that hardly can he go to the toilet by himself. These six children of mine, I have to buy the shoes for their feet with my own blood. Even a lousy little white Communion necktie, that's a couple drops of blood; a little piece of mosquito veil for my Vadja so she won't be ashamed in church for the other girls, they take my blood for it by Goldblatt. That's how I keep goin'. A fine thing if I had to depend on the relief. And there's plenty of people on the rolls—fakes! There's nothin' *they* can't get, that can go and wrap bacon at Swift and Armour any time. They're lookin' for them by the Yards. They never have to be out of work. Only they rather lay in their lousy beds and eat the public's money." She was not afraid, in a predominantly Negro station, to shout this way about Negroes.

Grebe and Raynor worked themselves forward to get a closer view of the woman. She was flaming with anger and with pleasure at herself, broad and huge, a golden-headed woman who wore a cotton cap laced with pink ribbon. She was barelegged and had on black gym shoes, her Hoover apron[8] was open and her great breasts, not much restrained by a man's undershirt, hampered her arms as she worked at the kid's dress on the iron board. And the children, silent and white, with a kind of locked obstinacy, in sheepskins and lumberjackets, stood behind her. She had captured the station, and the pleasure this gave her was enormous. Yet her grievances were true grievances. She was telling the truth. But she behaved like a liar. The look of her small eyes was hidden, and while she raged she also seemed to be spinning and planning.

"They send me out college case workers in silk pants to talk me out of what I got comin'. Are they better'n me? Who told them? Fire them. Let 'em go and get married, and then you won't have to cut electric from people's budget."

The chief supervisor, Mr. Ewing, couldn't silence her and he stood with folded arms at the head of his staff, bald, bald-headed, saying to his subordinates like the ex-school principal he was, "Pretty soon she'll be tired and go."

---

8. Woman's coverall, popular during World War I.

"No she won't," said Raynor to Grebe. "She'll get what she wants. She knows more about the relief even then Ewing. She's been on the rolls for years, and she always gets what she wants because she puts on a noisy show. Ewing knows it. He'll give in soon. He's only saving face. If he gets bad publicity, the Commissioner'll have him on the carpet, downtown. She's got him submerged; she'll submerge everybody in time, and that includes nations and governments."

Grebe replied with his characteristic smile, disagreeing completely. Who would take Staika's orders, and what changes could her yelling ever bring about?

No, what Grebe saw in her, the power that made people listen, was that her cry expressed the war of flesh and blood, perhaps turned a little crazy and certainly ugly, on this place and this condition. And at first, when he went out, the spirit of Staika somehow presided over the whole district for him, and it took color from her; he saw her color, in the spotty curb fires, and the fires under the El, the straight alley of flamy gloom. Later, too, when he went into a tavern for a shot of rye, the sweat of beer, association with West Side Polish streets, made him think of her again.

He wiped the corners of his mouth with his muffler, his handkerchief being inconvenient to reach for, and went out again to get on with the delivery of his checks. The air bit cold and hard and a few flakes of snow formed near him. A train struck by and left a quiver in the frames and a bristling icy hiss over the rails.

Crossing the street, he descended a flight of broad steps into a basement grocery, setting off a little bell. It was a dark, long store and it caught you with its stinks of smoked meat, soap, dried peaches, and fish. There was a fire wrinkling and flapping in the little stove, and the proprietor was waiting, an Italian with a long, hollow face and stubborn bristles. He kept his hands warm under his apron.

No, he didn't know Green. You knew people but not names. The same man might not have the same name twice. The police didn't know, either, and mostly didn't care. When somebody was shot or knifed they took the body away and didn't look for the murderer. In the first place, nobody would tell them anything. So they made up a name for the coroner and called it quits. And in the second place, they didn't give a goddamn anyhow. But they couldn't get to the bottom of a thing even if they wanted to. Nobody would get to know even a tenth of what went on among these people. They stabbed and stole, they did every crime and abomination you ever heard of, men and men, women and women, parents and children, worse than the animals. They carried on their own way, and the horrors passed off like a smoke. There was never anything like it in the history of the whole world.

It was a long speech, deepening with every word in its fantasy and passion and becoming increasingly senseless and terrible: a swarm amassed by suggestion and invention, a huge, hugging, despairing knot, a human wheel of heads, legs, bellies, arms, rolling through his shop.

Grebe felt that he must interrupt him. He said sharply, "What are you talking about! All I asked was whether you knew this man."

"That isn't even the half of it. I been here six years. You probably don't want to believe this. But suppose it's true?"

"All the same," said Grebe, "there must be a way to find a person."

The Italian's close-spaced eyes had been queerly concentrated, as were his muscles, while he leaned across the counter trying to convince Grebe. Now he gave up the effort and sat down on his stool. "Oh—I suppose. Once in a while. But I been telling you, even the cops don't get anywhere."

"They're always after somebody. It's not the same thing."

"Well, keep trying if you want. I can't help you."

But he didn't keep trying. He had no more time to spend on Green. He slipped Green's check to the back of the block. The next name on the list was FIELD, WINSTON.

He found the back-yard bungalow without the least trouble; it shared a lot with another house, a few feet of yard between. Grebe knew these two-shack arrangements. They had been built in vast numbers in the days before the swamps were filled and the streets raised, and they were all the same—a board-walk along the fence, well under street level, three or four ball-headed posts for clotheslines, greening wood, dead shingles, and a long, long flight of stairs to the rear door.

A twelve-year-old boy let him into the kitchen, and there the old man was, sitting by the table in a wheel chair.

"Oh, it's d' Government man," he said to the boy when Grebe drew out his checks. "Go bring me my box of papers." He cleared a space on the table.

"Oh, you don't have to go to all that trouble," said Grebe. But Field laid out his papers: Social Security card, relief certification, letters from the state hospital in Manteno, and a naval discharged dated San Diego, 1920.

"That's plenty," Grebe said. "Just sign."

"You got to know who I am," the old man said. "You're from the Government. It's not your check, it's a Government check and you got no business to hand it over till everything is proved."

He loved the ceremony of it, and Grebe made no more objections. Field emptied his box and finished out the circle of cards and letters.

"There's everything I done and been. Just the death certificate and they can close book on me." He said this with a certain happy pride and magnificence. Still he did not sign; he merely held the little pen upright on the golden-green corduroy of his thigh. Grebe did not hurry him. He felt the old man's hunger for conversation.

"I got to get better coal," he said. I send my little gran'son to the yard with my order and they fill his wagon with screening. The stove ain't made for it. It fall through the grate. The order says Franklin County egg-size coal."

"I'll report it and see what can be done."

"Nothing can be done, I expect. You know and I know. There ain't no little ways to make things better, and the only big thing is money. That's the only sunbeams, money. Nothing is black where it shines, and the only place you see black is where it ain't shining. What we colored have to have is our own rich. There ain't no other way.

Grebe sat, his reddened forehead bridged levelly by his close-cut hair and his cheeks lowered in the wings of his collar—the caked fire shone hard within the isinglass-and-iron frames but the room was not comfortable—sat and listened while the old man unfolded his scheme. This was to create one Negro millionaire a month by subscription. One clever, good-hearted young fellow elected every month would sign a contract to use the money to start a business employing Negroes. This would be advertised by chain letters and word of mouth, and every Negro wage earner would contribute a dollar a month. Within five years there would be sixty millionaires.

"That'll fetch respect," he said with a throat-stopped sound that came out like a foreign syllable. "You got to take and organize all the money that gets thrown away on the policy wheel and horse race. As long as they can take it away from you, they got no respect for you. Money, that's d' sun of human kind!" Field was a Negro of mixed blood, perhaps Cherokee, or Natchez; his skin was reddish. And he sounded, speaking about a golden sun in this dark room, and looked, shaggy and slab-headed, with the mingled blood of his face and broad lips, the little pen still upright in his hand, like one of the underground kings of mythology, old judge Minos himself.

And now he accepted the check and signed. Not to soil the slip, he held it down with his knuckles. The table budged and creaked, the center of the gloomy, heathen midden of the kitchen covered with bread, meat, and cans, and the scramble of papers.

"Don't you think my scheme'd work?"

"It's worth thinking about. Something ought to be done, I agree."

"It'll work if people will do it. That's all. That's the only thing, any time. When they understand it in the same way, all of them."

"That's true," said Grebe, rising. His glance met the old man's.

"I know you got to go," he said. "Well, God bless you, boy, you ain't been sly with me. I can tell in a minute."

He went back through the buried yard. Someone nursed a candle in a shed, where a man unloaded kindling wood from a sprawl-wheeled baby buggy and two voices carried on a high conversation. As he came up the sheltered passage he heard the hard boost of the wind in the branches and against the house fronts, and then, reaching the sidewalk, he saw the needle-eye red of cable towers in the open icy height hundreds of feet above the river and the factories—those keen points. From here, his view was obstructed all the way to the South Branch and its timber banks, and the cranes beside the water. Rebuilt after the Great Fire,[9] this part of the city was, not fifty years later, in ruins again, factories boarded up, buildings deserted or fallen, gaps of prairie between. But it wasn't desolation that this made you feel, but rather a faltering of organization that set free a huge energy, an escaped, unattached, unregulated power from the giant raw place. Not only must people feel it but, it seemed to Grebe, they were compelled to match it. In their very bodies. He no less than others, he realized. Say that his parents had been servants in their time, whereas he was not supposed to be one. He thought that they had never done any service like this, which no one visible asked for, and probably flesh and blood could not even perform. Nor could anyone show why it should be performed; or see where the performance would lead. That did not mean that he wanted to be released from it, he realized with a grimly pensive face. On the contrary. He had something to do. To be compelled to feel this energy and yet have no task to do—that was horrible; that was suffering; he knew what that was. It was now quitting time. Six o'clock. He could go home if he liked, to his room, that is, to wash in hot water, to pour a drink, lie down on his quilt, read the paper, eat some liver paste on crackers before going out to dinner. But to think of this actually made him feel a little sick as though he

9. The Chicago Fire of 1871.

had swallowed hard air. Her had six checks left, and he was determined to deliver at least one of these: Mr. Green's check.

So he started again. He had four or five dark blocks to go, past open lots, condemned houses, old foundations, closed schools, black churches, mounds, and he reflected that there must be many people alive who had once seen the neighborhood rebuilt and new. Now there was a second layer of ruins; centuries of history accomplished through human massing. Numbers had given the place forced growth; enormous numbers had also broken it down. Objects once so new, so concrete that it could have occurred to anyone they stood for other things, had crumbled. Therefore, reflected Grebe, the secret of them was out. It was that they stood for themselves by agreement, and were natural and not unnatural by agreement, and when the things themselves collapsed the agreement became visible. What was it, otherwise, that kept cities from looking peculiar? Rome, that was almost permanent, did not give rise to thoughts like these. And was it abidingly real? But in Chicago, where the cycles were so fast and the familiar died out, and again rose changed, and died again in thirty years, you saw the common agreement or convenant, and you were forced to think about appearances and realities. (He remembered Raynor and he smiled. Raynor was a clever boy.) Once you had grasped this, a great many things became intelligible. For instance, why Mr. Field should conceive such a scheme. Of course, if people were to agree to create a millionaire, a real millionaire would come into existence. And if you wanted to know how Mr. Field was inspired to think of this, why, he had within sight of his kitchen window the chart, the very bones of a successful scheme—the El with its blue and green confetti of signals. People consented to pay dimes and ride the crash-box cars, and so it was a success. Yet how absurd it looked; how little reality there was to start with. And yet Yerkes,[1] the great financier who built it, had known that he could get people to agree to do it. Viewed as itself, what a scheme of a scheme if seemed, how close to an appearance. Then why wonder at Mr. Field's idea? He had grasped the principle. And then Grebe remembered, too, that Mr. Yerkes had established the Yerkes Observatory and endowed it with millions. Now how did the notion come to him in his New York museum of a palace or his Aegean-bound yacht to give money to astronomers? Was he awed by the success of his bizarre enterprise and therefore ready to spend money to find out where in the universe being and seeming were identical? Yes, he wanted to know what abides; and whether flesh is Bible grass; and he offered money to be burned in the fire of suns. Okay, then, Grebe thought further, these things exist because people consent to exist with them—we have got so far—and also there is a reality which doesn't depend on consent but within which consent is a game. But what about need, the need that keeps so many vast thousands in position? You tell me that, you *private little gentleman* and *decent* soul—he used these words against himself scornfully. Why is the consent given to misery? And why so painfully ugly? Because there is *something* that is dismal and permanently ugly? Here he sighed and gave it up, and thought it was enough for the present moment that he had a real check in his pocket for a Mr. Green who must be real beyond question. If only his neighbors didn't think they had to conceal him.

This time he stopped at the second floor. He struck a match and found a

1. Charles Tyson Yerkes (1837–1905), American financier.

door. Presently a man answered his knock and Grebe had the check ready and showed it even before he began. "Does Tulliver Green live here? I'm from the relief."

The man narrowed the opening and spoke to someone at his back.

"Does he live here?"

"Uh-uh. No."

"Or anywhere in this building? He's a sick man and he can't come for his dough." He exhibited the check in the light, which was smoky—the air smelled of charred lard—and the man held off the brim of his cap to study it.

"Uh-uh. Never seen the name."

"There's nobody around here that uses crutches?"

He seemed to think, but it was Grebe's impression that he was simply waiting for a decent interval to pass.

"No, suh. Nobody I ever see."

"I've been looking for this man all afternoon"—Grebe spoke out with sudden force—"and I'm going to have to carry this check back to the station. It seems strange not to be able to find a person to *give* him something when you're looking for him for a good reason. I suppose if I had bad news for him I'd find him quick enough."

There was a responsive motion in the other man's face. "That's right, I reckon."

"It almost doesn't do any good to have a name if you can't be found by it. It doesn't stand for anything. He might as well not have any," he went on, smiling. It was as much of a concession as he could make to his desire to laugh.

"Well, now, there's a little old knot-back man I see once in a while. He might be the one you lookin' for. Downstairs."

"Where? Right side or left? Which door?"

"I don't know which. Thin-face little knot-back with a stick."

But no one answered at any of the doors on the first floor. He went to the end of the corridor, searching by matchlight, and found only a stairless exit to the yard, a drop of about six feet. But there was a bungalow near the alley, an old house like Mr. Field's. To jump was unsafe. He ran from the front door, through the underground passage and into the yard. The place was occupied. There was a light through the curtains, upstairs. The name on the ticket under the broken, scoop-shaped mailbox was Green! He exultantly rang the bell and pressed against the locked door. Then the lock clicked faintly and a long staircase opened before him. Someone was slowly coming down—a woman. He had the impression in the weak light that she was shaping her hair as she came, making herself presentable, for he saw her arms raised. But it was for support that they were raised; she was feeling her way downward, down the wall, stumbling. Next he wondered about the pressure of her feet on the treads; she did not seem to be wearing shoes. And it was a freezing stairway. His ring had got her out of bed, perhaps, and she had forgotten to put them on. And then he saw that she was not only shoeless but naked; she was entirely naked, climbing down while she talked to herself, a heavy woman, naked and drunk. She blundered into him. The contact of her breasts, though they touched only his coat, made him go back against the door with a blind shock. See what he had tracked down, in his hunting game!

The woman was saying to herself, furious with insult. "So I cain't ——k, huh? I'll show that son-of-a-bitch kin I, cain't I."

What should he do now? Grebe asked himself. Why, he should go. He should turn away and go. He couldn't talk to this woman. He couldn't keep her standing naked in the cold. But when he tried he found himself unable to turn away.

He said, "Is this where Mr. Green lives?"

But she was still talking to herself and did not hear him.

"Is this Mr. Green's house?"

At last she turned her furious drunken glance on him. "What do you want?"

Again her eyes wandered from him; there was a dot of blood in their enraged brilliance. He wondered why she didn't feel the cold.

"I'm from the relief."

"Awright, what?"

"I've got a check for Tulliver Green."

This time she heard him and put out her hand.

"No, no, for Mr. Green. He's got to sign," he said. How was he going to get Green's signature tonight!

"I'll take it. He cain't."

He desperately shook his head, thinking of Mr. Field's precautions about identification. "I can't let you have it. It's for him. Are you Mrs. Green?"

"Maybe I is, and maybe I ain't. Who want to know?"

"Is he upstairs?"

"Awright. Take it up yourself, you goddamn fool."

Sure, he was a goddamn fool. Of course he could not go up because Green would probably be drunk and naked, too. And perhaps he would appear on the landing soon. He looked eagerly upward. Under the light was a high narrow brown wall. Empty! It remained empty!

"Hell with you, then!" he heard her cry. To deliver a check for coal and clothes, he was keeping her in the cold. She did not feel it, but his face was burning with frost and self-ridicule. He backed away from her.

"I'll come tomorrow, tell him."

"Ah, hell with you. Don' never come. What you doin' here in the night-time? Don' come back." She yelled so that he saw the breadth of her tongue. She stood astride in the long cold box of the hall and held on to the banister and the wall. The bungalow itself was shaped something like a box, a clumsy, high box pointing into the freezing air with its sharp, wintry lights.

"If you are Mrs. Green, I'll give you the check," he said, changing his mind.

"Give here, then." She took it, took the pen offered with it in her left hand, and tried to sign the receipt on the wall. He looked around, almost as though to see whether his madness was being observed, and came near believing that someone was standing on a mountain of used tires in the auto-junking shop next door.

"But are you Mrs. Green?" he now thought to ask. But she was already climbing the stairs with the check, and it was too late, if he had made an error, if he was now in trouble, to undo the thing. But he wasn't going to worry about it. Though she might not be Mrs. Green, he was convinced that Mr. Green was upstairs. Whoever she was, the woman stood for Green, whom he was not to see this time. Well, you silly bastard, he said to himself, so you think you found him. So what? Maybe you really did find him—what of it? But it was important that there was a real Mr. Green whom they could not keep him from reaching because he seemed to come as an emissary from hostile appearances. And though the self-ridicule was slow to diminish, and his face still blazed with it, he had, nevertheless, a feeling of elation, too. "For after all," he said, "he *could* be found!"

1951, 1968

---

# NORMAN MAILER
## b. 1923

"The sour truth is that I am imprisoned with a perception which will settle for nothing less than making a revolution in the consciousness of our time. Whether rightly or wrongly, it is then obvious that I should go so far as to think it is my present and future work which will have the deepest influence of any work being done by an American novelist in these years." Taken from the introductory "advertisement" in Norman Mailer's first collection of his occasional journalism, reviews, and stories, these two sentences lay out the terms in which the writer insists his work be considered and judged. As Richard Poirier has put it, Mailer "has exhibited a literary ambition that can best be called imperialistic. He has wanted to translate his life into a literary career and then to translate that literary career into history." Like all imperialists, he has offended many people by his ambitious exhibitions, but they are also the very stuff of his achievement.

He was born in New Jersey, grew up in Brooklyn, went to Harvard College, where by the end of his first semester (and just before turning seventeen) he "formed the desire to be a major writer." Mailer took a number of writing courses at Harvard (as well as ones in engineering), won various literary prizes, then upon graduation entered the army with the intention of writing a "great war novel" about either the European or the Pacific conflict, whichever was to be his personal fate. He served in the Pacific and came home to write, over the course of fifteen months, *The Naked and the Dead.* If not obviously a "great war novel," it is a good one, strong when it evokes place and action, lively as a drama of debate, of ideas in conflict. It was also a best-seller and got Mailer off to a success that would take some work to live up to.

His uncertain and turbulent career in the ten years after the war is described in *Advertisements for Myself* (1959): marriages and divorces, disillusionment with leftist politics (Mailer supported former vice-president Henry Wallace's ill-fated campaign for the presidency in 1948), and experiments with drugs and with new fictional styles. The novels from these years, *Barbary Shore* (1951) and *The Deer Park* (1955), were largely treated as fallings-off from his first book. But in *Barbary Shore* Mailer ambitiously attempted and at least partially succeeded in weaving an eerie Cold War fantasy about sex, power, and totalitarianism, all played out within a Brooklyn rooming house. And *The Deer Park* moved across country to Hollywood, continuing to explore relationships among sex, politics, and money as well as demonstrating Mailer's stylistic debt to F. Scott Fitzgerald.

After *The Deer Park* appeared in 1955, Mailer began to write a column for the *Village Voice*, a Greenwich Village weekly he had helped found. Concurrently, he became fascinated with a phenomenon he called "hip" and with its embodiment in the "hipster," a heroic, cool, but potentially violent figure whose essential being contradicted everything Mailer saw as the dull pieties of social adjustment fashionable in the years of Eisenhower's presidency. "The shits are killing us," was Mailer's war cry, as he set out to confound the "square" mentality by finding suitable antagonists for it, such as the "existential hero" he saw in John F. Kennedy or the comic warrior Sergius O'Shaugnessy who appears in Mailer's fiction or (most luridly and pompously) in the notion of himself as an investigator of "psychic mysteries" like rape, suicide, and orgasm. The fullest development of these theories is found in his essay *The White Negro* (1959), while his culminating fictional portrayal of the hero-as-hipster is Stephen Rojack, the narrator of *An American Dream* (1964) who murders his wife in the novel's second chapter. Adverse critics of the book saw Rojack as no more than a crude projection of his author's destructive fantasies. But Mailer is larger than his character, and the novel an ingenious if not altogether convincing attempt to create a more human and a healthier consciousness.

As his work became increasingly subversive of traditional distinctions among fiction, essay, poetry, and sociology, Mailer's style grew bolder in metaphor, more daring in its improvisations. And as the country plunged ever deeper into the Vietnam tragedy, his imagination was stung to the composition of a brilliantly obscene improvisation (officially a novel) *Why Are We in Vietnam?* (1967), then to perhaps his finest book, *The Armies of the Night* (1968). Here, for once, the power of the man and of the moment came together in an extended piece of writing that is at once history, fiction, and prophecy. Springing from Mailer's involvement in the 1967 march on the Pentagon in protest of the war, it plays off private, even ignoble concerns against the public significances borne by the event. The "Mailer" who moves through its pages is a less-than-heroic figure, often available for comic and satiric treatment by the author, although not exclusively so, and in that quality *Armies* resembles no book in American letters so much as *The Education of Henry Adams*. Thick with often humorously observed particularity, its tone and feeling are eventually deeper and more humanly compelling than anything he had written before or has written since.

That last assertion might be challenged by admirers of *The Executioner's Song* (1979), which is distinct from Mailer's other writings in that it adopts a toneless, documentary style to tell the story of Gary Gilmore, a convicted murderer. Thus far, fewer readers have declared themselves with respect to *Ancient Evenings* (1983), his immense "historical" novel set in an Egypt that one reviewer, George Stade, compared to the "repressed unconscious." The reviewer claimed that the book contained the fullest working out "not only of Mailer's psychosomatics but also of his poetics," while others have praised its complicated wordplay. These claims may be true, but do not mean that reading *Ancient Evenings* is necessarily a pleasure. *Tough Guys Don't Dance* (1984), an existential thriller set in Provincetown, Massachusetts, is easier going than *Ancient Evenings* and has some good comic moments, but it is hard to take seriously. Most recently, *Harlot's Ghost* (1991), his long-meditated (and at 1328 pages very long indeed) novel about the CIA, makes its claim to be the most imperialistic of all Mailer's projects.

In the years since *Armies of the Night* was published, Mailer has done such colorful things as run for mayor of New York City, marry and divorce more women (he now lives with his sixth wife), father many children, and make various films. His books have been ambitiously varied in subject: *A Fire on the Moon* (1970) is one of the best things written about the astronauts and their space flights, while *The Prisoner of Sex* (1971) is a fevered polemic against certain aspects of the women's movement. He has also written a biography of Marilyn Monroe and a blow-by-blow account of the heavyweight championship fight between George Foreman and Muhammed Ali in Zaire. His fascinating coverages of the Republican and Democratic political conventions, from 1952 through 1972, are to be found in *Some Honorable Men* (1975). Throughout these books, as well as in his personal appearances on late-night talk shows, his comic sense has shown to good advantage the ability in uncertain or unpleasant situations to interpolate, mimic, turn a phrase against the world or himself, sometimes against both at the same time. Whether Mailer's literary production has as yet or will ever live up to the immense promise he made for himself—to make "a revolution in the consciousness of our time"—there is fertility and variety in his performances as an entertainer, diagnostician, and prophet committed to nothing less than what Emerson, in *The American Scholar*, called the "conversion of the world."

# *From* The Armies of the Night[1]

## *Part I*

### 5. TOWARD A THEATER OF IDEAS

The guests were beginning to leave the party for the Ambassador, which was two blocks away. Mailer did not know this yet, but the audience there had been waiting almost an hour. They were being entertained by an electronic folk rock guitar group, so presumably the young were more or less happy, and the middle-aged dim. Mailer was feeling the high sense of clarity which accompanies the light show of the aurora borealis when it is projected upon the inner universe of the chest, the lungs, and the heart. He was happy. On leaving, he had appropriated a coffee mug and filled it with bourbon. The fresh air illumined the bourbon, gave it a cerebrative edge; words entered his brain with the agreeable authority of fresh minted coins. Like all good professionals, he was stimulated by the chance to try a new if related line of work. Just as professional football players love sex because it is so close to football, so he was fond of speaking in public because it was thus near to writing. An extravagant analogy? Consider that a good half of writing consists of being sufficiently sensitive to the moment to reach for the next promise which is usually hidden in some word or phrase just a shift to the side of one's conscious intent. (Consciousness, that blunt tool, bucks in the general direction of the truth; instinct plucks the feather. Cheers!) Where public speaking is an exercise from prepared texts to demonstrate how successfully a low order of consciousness can beat upon the back of a collective flesh, public speaking being, therefore, a sullen expression of human possibility metaphorically equal to a bugger on his victim, speaking-in-public (as Mailer liked to describe any speech which was more or less improvised, impromptu, or dangerously written) was an activity like writing; one had to trick or seize or submit to the grace of each moment, which, except for those unexpected and sometimes well-deserved moments when consciousness and grace came together (and one felt on the consequence, heroic) were usually occasions of some mystery. The pleasure of speaking in public was the sensitivity it offered: with every phrase one was better or worse, close or less close to the existential promise of truth, *it feels true*, which hovers on good occasions like a presence between speaker and audience. Sometimes one was better, and worse, at the same moment; so strategic choices on the continuation of the attack would soon have to be decided, a moment to know the blood of the gambler in oneself.

Intimations of this approaching experience, obviously one of Mailer's preferred pleasures in life, at least when he did it well, were now connected to

---

1. The following selection consists of chapter 5 (Part I) from *The Armies of the Night* (1968). The occasion is the anti-Vietnam War march on the Pentagon in October 1967. Mailer, despite some reservations, has agreed to participate in this march and also in a premarch evening rally at a Washington theater. In this chapter, which describes that evening, the principal actors are Mailer; the poet Robert Lowell; Dwight Macdonald, a leading American critic and journalist of politics and literature; Paul Goodman, poet and cultural critic, author of *Growing Up Absurd* (1959); and Ed de Grazia, one of the organizers of the march.

the professional sense of intrigue at the new task: tonight he would be both speaker and master of ceremonies. The two would conflict, but interestingly. Already he was looking in his mind for kind even celebrative remarks about Paul Goodman which would not violate every reservation he had about Goodman's dank glory. But he had it. It would be possible with no violation of truth to begin by saying that the first speaker looked very much like Nelson Algren,[2] because in fact the first speaker was Paul Goodman, and both Nelson Algren and Paul Goodman looked like old cons. Ladies and Gentlemen, without further ado let me introduce one of young America's favorite old cons, Paul Goodman! (It would not be necessary to add that where Nelson Algren looked like the sort of skinny old con who was in on every make in the joint, and would sign away Grandma's farm to stay in the game, Goodman looked like the sort of old con who had first gotten into trouble in the YMCA, and hadn't spoken to anyone since.)

All this while, Mailer had in clutch *Why Are We in Vietnam?*[3] He had neglected to bring his own copy to Washington and so had borrowed the book from his hostess on the promise he would inscribe it. (Later he was actually to lose it—working apparently on the principle that if you cannot make a hostess happy, the next best charity is to be so evil that the hostess may dine out on tales of your misconduct.) But the copy of the book is now noted because Mailer, holding it in one hand and the mug of whisky in the other, was obliged to notice on entering the Ambassador Theater that he had an overwhelming urge to micturate. The impulse to pass urine, being for some reason more difficult to restrain when both hands are occupied, there was no thought in the Master of Ceremonies' mind about the alternatives—he would have to find The Room before he went on stage.

That was not so immediately simple as one would have thought. The twenty guests from the party, looking a fair piece subdued under the fluorescent lights, had therefore the not unhaggard look of people who have arrived an hour late at the theater. No matter that the theater was by every evidence sleazy (for neighborhood movie houses built on the dream of the owner that some day Garbo or Harlow or Lombard would give a look in, aged immediately they were not used for movies anymore) no matter, the guests had the uneasiness of very late arrivals. Apologetic, they were therefore in haste for the speakers to begin.

Mailer did not know this. He was off already in search of The Room, which, it developed was up on the balcony floor. Imbued with the importance of his first gig as Master of Ceremonies, he felt such incandescence of purpose that he could not quite conceive it necessary to notify de Grazia he would be gone for a minute. Incandescence is the *satori*[4] of the Romantic spirit which spirit would insist—this is the essence of the Romantic—on accelerating time. The greater the power of any subjective state, the more total is a Romantic's assumption that everyone understands exactly what he is about to do, therefore waste not a moment by stopping to tell them.

Flush with his incandescence, happy in all the anticipations of liberty which this Götterdämmerung[5] of a urination was soon to provide, Mailer did not

---

2. Chicago-based contemporary American novelist, author of *The Man with the Golden Arm* (1949) and other works.
3. Mailer's novel (1967)

4. Zen Buddhist term for spiritual enlightenment.
5. Twilight of the Gods (German); i.e., on a grand scale.

know, but he had already and unwitting to himself metamorphosed into the Beast. Wait and see!

He was met on the stairs by a young man from *Time* magazine, a stringer presumably, for the young man lacked that I-am-damned look in the eye and rep tie of those whose work for *Time* has become a life addiction. The young man had a somewhat ill-dressed look, a map showed on his skin of an old adolescent acne, and he gave off the unhappy furtive presence of a fraternity member on probation for the wrong thing, some grievous mis-deposit of vomit, some hanky panky with frat-house tickets.

But the Beast was in a great good mood. He was soon to speak; that was food for all. So the Beast greeted the *Time* man with the geniality of a surrogate Hemingway unbending for the Luce-ites (Loo-sights was the pun)[6] made some genial cryptic remark or two about finding Herr John, said cheerfully in answer to why he was in Washington that he had come to protest the war in Vietnam, and taking a sip of bourbon from the mug he kept to keep all fires idling right, stepped off into the darkness of the top balcony floor, went through a door into a pitch-black men's room, and was alone with his need. No chance to find the light switch for he had no matches, he did not smoke. It was therefore a matter of locating what's what with the probing of his toes. He found something finally which seemed appropriate, and pleased with the precision of these generally unused senses in his feet, took aim between them at a point twelve inches ahead, and heard in the darkness the sound of his water striking the floor. Some damn mistake had been made, an assault from the side doubtless instead of the front, the bowl was relocated now, and Master of Ceremonies breathed deep of the great reveries of this utterly non-Sisyphian[7] release—at last!!—and thoroughly enjoyed the next forty-five seconds, being left on the aftermath not a note depressed by the condition of the premises. No, he was off on the Romantic's great military dream, which is: seize defeat, convert it to triumph. Of course, pissing on the floor was bad; very bad; the attendant would probably gossip to the police (if the *Time* man did not sniff it out first) and The Uniformed in turn would report it to The Press who were sure to write about the scandalous condition in which this meeting had left the toilets. And all of this contretemps merely because the management, bitter with their lost dream of Garbo and Harlow and Lombard, were now so pocked and stingy they doused the lights. (Out of such stuff is a novelist's brain.)

Well, he could convert this deficiency to an asset. From gap to gain is very American. He would confess straight out to all aloud that he was the one who wet the floor in the men's room, he alone! While the audience was recovering from the existential anxiety of encountering an orator who confessed to such a crime, he would be able—their attention now riveted—to bring them up to a contemplation of deeper problems, of, indeed, the deepest problems, the most chilling alternatives, and would from there seek to bring them back to a restorative view of man. Man might be a fool who peed in the wrong pot, man was also a scrupulous servant of the self-damaging admission; man was therefore a philosopher who possessed the magic stone; he could turn loss to philosophical gain, and so illumine the deeps, find the poles, and eventually learn to cultivate his most special fool's garden: *satori*, incandescence, and the hard gem-

6. Employees of the publishing empire owned by Henry Luce (*Time, Life*, etc.). Lucite is a durable synthetic or plastic, but Mailer also plays on "loo" (British for toilet) "sights" (sites).

7. Sisyphus was condemned to push a huge boulder up a hill with, unlike Mailer, no prospect of relief.

like flame[8] of bourbon burning in the furnaces of metabolism.

Thus composed, illumined by these first stages of Emersonian transcendence, Mailer left the men's room, descended the stairs, entered the back of the orchestra, all opening remarks held close file in his mind like troops ranked in order before the parade, and then suddenly, most suddenly saw, with a cancerous swoop of albatross wings, that de Grazia was on the stage, was acting as M.C., was—no calling it back—launched into the conclusion of a gentle stammering stumbling—small orator, de Grazia!—introduction of Paul Goodman. All lost! The magnificent opening remarks about the forces gathered here to assemble on Saturday before the Pentagon, this historic occasion, let us hold it in our mind and focus on a puddle of passed water on the floor above and see if we assembled here can as leftists and proud dissenters contain within our minds the grandeur of the two—all lost!—no chance to do more than pick up later—later! after de Grazia and Goodman had finished dead-assing the crowd. Traitor de Grazia! Sicilian de Grazia!

As Mailer picked his way between people sitting on the stone floor (orchestra seats had been removed—the movie house was a dance hall now with a stage) he made a considerable stir in the orchestra. Mailer had been entering theaters for years, mounting stages—now that he had put on weight, it would probably have been fair to say that he came to the rostrum like a poor man's version of Orson Welles,[9] some minor note of the same contemplative presence. A titter and rise of expectation followed him. He could not resist its appeal. As he passed de Grazia, he scowled, threw a look from Lower Shakespearian "Et tu Bruté," and proceeded to slap the back of his hand against de Grazia's solar plexus. It was not a heavy blow, but then de Grazia was not a heavy man; he wilted some hint of an inch. And the audience pinched off a howl, squeaked on their squeal. It was not certain to them what had taken place.

Picture the scene two minutes later from the orchestra floor. Paul Goodman, now up at the microphone with no podium or rostrum, is reading the following lines:

. . . these days my contempt for the misrulers of my country is icy and my indignation raucous.

It is impossible to tell what he is reading. Off at the wing of the stage where the others are collected—stout Macdonald, noble Lowell, beleaguered de Grazia, and Mailer, Prince of Bourbon, the acoustics are atrocious. One cannot hear a word the speaker is saying. Nor are there enough seats. If de Grazia and Macdonald are sitting in folding chairs, Mailer is squatting on his haunches, or kneeling on one knee like a player about to go back into the ball game. Lowell has the expression on his face of a dues payer who is just about keeping up with the interest on some enormous debt. As he sits on the floor with his long arms clasped mournfully about his long Yankee legs, "I am here," says his expression, "but I do not have to pretend I like what I see." The hollows in his cheeks give a hint of the hanging judge. Lowell is of a good weight, not too heavy, not too light, but the hollows speak of the great Puritan gloom in which the country was founded—man was simply not good enough for God.

---

8. The English critic Walter Pater (1839–1894) advocated in *Studies in the History of the Renaissance* that one should cultivate such an intense response to art.
9. Actor and film director (1915–1985) of large bulk.

At this moment, it is hard not to agree with Lowell. The cavern of the theater seems to resonate behind the glare of the footlights, but this is no resonance of a fine bass voice—it is rather electronics on the march. The public address system hisses, then rings in a random chorus of electronic music, sounds of cerebral mastication from some horror machine of Outer Space (where all that electricity doubtless comes from, child!) then a hum like the squeak in the hinges of the gates of Hell—we are in the penumbra of psychedelic netherworlds, ghost-odysseys from the dead brain cells of adolescent trysts with LSD, some ultrapurple spotlight from the balcony (not ultraviolet—ultrapurple, deepest purple one could conceive) there out in the dark like some neon eye of the night, the media is the message,[1] and the message is purple, speaks of the monarchies of Heaven, madnesses of God, and clamvaults of people on a stone floor. Mailer's senses are now tuned to absolute pitch or sheer error—he marks a ballot for absolute pitch—he is certain there is a profound pall in the audience. Yes, they sit there, stricken, inert, in terror of what Saturday will bring, and so are unable to rise to a word the speaker is offering them. It will take dynamite to bring life. The shroud of burned-out psychedelic dreams is in this audience, Cancer Gulch with open maw—and Mailer thinks of the vigor and the light (from marijuana?) in the eyes of those American soldiers in Vietnam who have been picked by the newsreel cameras to say their piece, and the happy healthy never unintelligent faces of all those professional football players he studies so assiduously on television come Sunday (he has neglected to put his bets in this week) and wonders how they would poll out on sentiment for the war.

HAWKS 95     DOVES 6

NFL Footballers Approve Vietnam War

Doubtless. All the healthy Marines, state troopers, professional athletes, movie stars, rednecks, sensuous life-loving Mafia, cops, mill workers, city officials, nice healthy-looking easy-grafting politicians full of the light (from marijuana?) in their eye of a life they enjoy—yes, they would be for the war in Vietnam. Arrayed against them as hard-core troops: an elite! the Freud-ridden members of Marxism, good old American anxiety strata—the urban middle-class with their proliferated monumental adenoidal resentments, their secret slavish love for the oncoming hegemony of the computer and the suburb, yes, they and their children, by the sheer ironies, the sheer ineptitude, the *kinks* of history, were now being compressed into more and more militant stands, their resistance to the war some hopeless melange, somehow firmed, of Pacifism and closet Communism. And their children—on a freak-out from the suburbs to a love-in on the Pentagon wall.

It was the children in whom Mailer had some hope, a gloomy hope. These mad middle-class children with their lobotomies from sin, their nihilistic embezzlement of all middle-class moral funds, their innocence, their lust for apocalypse, their unbelievable indifference to waste: twenty generations of buried hopes perhaps engraved in their chromosomes, and now conceivably burning like faggots in the secret inquisitional fires of LSD. It was a devil's drug—

---

1. Herbert Marshall McLuhan (b. 1911), a Canadian critic and communications theorist, coined this slogan in *Understanding Media* (1964) to say that each me-dium of communication (television, print, etc.) determines its appropriate mode of response, whatever the "subject" of its address.

designed by the Devil to consume the love of the best, and leave them liver-wasted, weeds of the big city. If there had been a player piano, Mailer might have put in a quarter to hear "In the Heart of the City Which Has No Heart."

Yes, these were the troops; middle-class cancer-pushers and drug-gutted flower children. And Paul Goodman to lead them. Was he now reading this?

> Once American faces were beautiful to me but now they look cruel and
> as if they had narrow thoughts.

Not much poetry, but well put prose. And yet there was always Goodman's damnable tolerance for all the varieties of sex. Did he know nothing of evil or entropy? Sex was the superhighway to your own soul's entropy if it was used without a constant sharpening of the taste. And orgies? What did Goodman know of orgies, real ones, not lib-lab college orgies to carry out the higher program of the Great Society, but real ones with murder in the air, and witches on the shoulder. The collected Tory[2] in Mailer came roaring to the surface like a cocked hat in a royal coach.

"When Goodman finishes, I'm going to take over as M.C.," he whispered to de Grazia. (The revery we have just attended took no more in fact than a second. Mailer's melancholy assessment of the forces now mounting in America took place between two consecutive lines of Goodman's poem—not because Mailer cerebrated that instantly, but because he had had the revery many a time before—he had to do no more than sense the audience, whisper Cancer Gulch to himself and the revery went by with a mental ch-ch-ch Click! reviewed again.) In truth, Mailer was now in a state. He had been prepared to open the evening with apocalyptic salvos to announce the real gravity of the situation, and the intensely peculiar American aspect of it—which is that the urban and suburban middle class were to be offered on Saturday an opportunity for glory—what other nation could boast of such option for its middle class? Instead—lost. The benignity and good humor of his planned opening remarks now subjugated to the electronic hawking and squabbling and *hum* of the P.A., the maniacal necessity to *wait* was on this hiatus transformed into a violent concentration of purpose, all intentions reversed. He glared at de Grazia. "How could you do this?" he whispered to his ear.

De Grazia looked somewhat confused at the intensity. Meetings to de Grazia were obviously just meetings, assemblages of people who coughed up for large admissions or kicked in for the pitch; at best, some meetings were less boring than others. De Grazia was much too wise and guilty-spirited to brood on apocalypse. "I couldn't find you," he whispered back.

"You didn't trust me long enough to wait one minute?"

"We were over an hour late," de Grazia whispered again. "We had to begin."

Mailer was all for having the conversation right then on stage: to hell with reciprocal rights and polite incline of the ear to the speaker. The Beast was ready to grapple with the world. "Did you think I wouldn't show up?" he asked de Grazia.

"Well, I was wondering."

In what sort of mumbo-jumbo of promise and betrayal did de Grazia live?

---

2. Member of the Conservative party in the United Kingdom, generally in support of established authority.

How could de Grazia ever suppose he would not show up? He had spent his life showing up at the most boring and onerous places. He gave a blast of his eyes to de Grazia. But Macdonald gave a look at Mailer, as if to say, "You're creating disturbance."

Now Goodman was done.

Mailer walked to the stage. He did not have any idea any longer of what he would say, his mind was empty, but in a fine calm, taking for these five instants a total rest. While there was no danger of Mailer ever becoming a demagogue since if the first idea he offered could appeal to a mob, the second in compensation would be sure to enrage them, he might nonetheless have made a fair country orator, for he loved to speak, he loved in fact to holler, and liked to hear a crowd holler back. (Of how many New York intellectuals may that be said?)

"I'm here as your original M.C., temporarily displaced owing to a contre-temps"—which was pronounced purposefully as contretempse—"in the men's room," he said into the microphone for opening, but the gentle high-strung beast of a device pushed into a panic by the electric presence of a real Beast, let loose a squeal which shook the welds in the old foundation of the Ambassa-dor. Mailer immediately decided he had had enough of public address systems, electronic fields of phase, impedance, and spooks in the circuitry. A hex on collaborating with Cancer Gulch. He pushed the microphone away, squared off before the audience. "Can you hear me?" he bellowed.

"Yes."

"Can you hear me in the balcony?"

"Yes."

"Then let's do away with electronics," he called out.

Cries of laughter came back. A very small pattern of applause. (Not too many on his side for electrocuting the public address system, or so his orators ear recorded the vote.)

"Now I missed the beginning of this occasion, or I would have been here to introduce Paul Goodman, for which we're all sorry, right?"

Confused titters. Small reaction.

"What are you, dead-heads?" he bellowed at the audience. "Or are you all"—here he put on his false Irish accent—"in the nature of becoming dead ahsses?" Small laughs. A whistle or two. "No," he said, replying to the whis-tles, "I invoke these dead asses as part of the gravity of the occasion. The middle class plus one hippie surrealistic symbolic absolutely insane March on the Pentagon, bless us all," beginning of a big applause which offended Mailer for it came on "bless" and that was too cheap a way to win votes, "bless us all—shit!" he shouted, "I'm trying to say the middle class plus shit, I mean plus revolution, is equal to one big collective dead ass." Some yells of approval, but much shocked curious rather stricken silence. He had broken the shank of his oratorical charge. Now he would have to sweep the audience together again. (Perhaps he felt like a surgeon delivering a difficult breech—nothing to do but plunge to the elbows again.)

"To resume our exposition," a good warm titter, then a ripple of laughter, not unsympathetic to his ear; the humor had been unwitting, but what was the life of an orator without some bonus? "To resume this orderly marshalling of concepts"—a conscious attempt at humor which worked less well; he was beginning to recognize for the first time that bellowing without a mike

demanded a more forthright style—"I shall now *engage* in confession." More
Irish accent. (He blessed Brendan Behan[3] for what he had learned from him.)
"A public speaker may offer you two opportunities. Instruction or confession."
Laughter now. "Well, you're all college heads, so my instruction would be as
pearls before—I dare not say it." Laughs. Boos. A voice from the balcony:
"Come on, Norman, say something!"

"Is there a black man in the house?" asked Mailer. He strode up and down
the stage pretending to peer at the audience. But in fact they were illumined
just well enough to emphasize one sad discovery—if black faces there were
they were certainly not in plenty. "Well ah'll just have to be the *impromptu*
Black Power for tonight. Woo-eeeee! Woo-eeeee! HMmmmmmmm." He
grunted with some partial success, showing hints of Cassius Clay.[4] "Get your
white butts moving."

"The confession. The confession!" screamed some adolescents from up
front.

He came to a stop, shifted his voice. Now he spoke in a relaxed tone. "The
confession, yeah!" Well, at least the audience was awake. He felt as if he had
driven away some sepulchral phantoms of a variety which inhabited the profound middle-class schist. Now to charge the center of vested spookery.

"Say," he called out into the semidarkness with the ultrapurple light coming
off the psychedelic lamp on the rail of the balcony, and the spotlights blaring
against his eyes, "say," all happiness again, "I think of Saturday, and that
March and do you know, fellow carriers of the holy unendurable grail, for the
first time in my life I don't know whether I have the piss or the shit scared out
of me most." It was an interesting concept, thought Mailer, for there was a
difference between the two kinds of fear—pursue the thought, he would, in
quieter times—"we are up, face this, all of you, against an existential situation—we do not know how it is going to turn out, and what is even more
inspiring of dread is that the government doesn't know either."

Beginning of a real hand, a couple of rebel yells. "We're going to try to
stick it up the government's ass," he shouted, "right into the sphincter of the
Pentagon." Wild yells and chills of silence from different reaches of the crowd.
Yeah, he was cooking now. "Will reporters please get every word accurately,"
he called out dryly to warm the chill.

But humor may have been too late. *The New Yorker* did not have strictures
against the use of sh*t for nothing; nor did Dwight Macdonald love *The New
Yorker* for nothing, he also had strictures against sh*t's metaphorical associations. Mailer looked to his right to see Macdonald approaching, a book in his
hands, arms at his side, a sorrowing look of concern in his face. "Norman,"
said Macdonald quietly, "I can't possibly follow you after all this. Please introduce me, and get it over with."

Mailer was near to stricken. On the one hand interrupted on a flight; on the
other, he had fulfilled no duty whatsoever as M.C. He threw a look at Macdonald which said; give me this. I'll owe you one.

But de Grazia was there as well. "Norman, let me be M.C. now," he said.

They were being monstrous unfair, thought Mailer. They didn't understand
what he had been doing, how good he had been, what he would do next. Fatal

---

3. Large, loud Irish playwright and performer (1925–1964).
4. Muhammad Ali (b. 1942), boxer and world heavyweight champion.

to walk off now—the verdict would claim he was unbalanced. Still, he could not hold the stage by force. That was unthinkably worse.

For the virtuous, however, deliverance (like buttercups) pops up everywhere. Mailer now took the microphone and turned to the audience. He was careful to speak in a relaxed voice. "We are having a disagreement about the value of the proceedings. Some think de Grazia should resume his post as Master of Ceremonies. I would like to keep the position. It is an existential moment. We do not know how it will turn out. So let us vote on it." Happy laughter from the audience at these comic effects. Actually Mailer did not believe it was an existential situation any longer. He reckoned the vote would be well in his favor. "Will those," he asked, "who are in favor of Mr. de Grazia succeeding me as Master of Ceremonies please say aye."

A good sound number said aye.

Now for the ovation. "Will those opposed to this, please say no." The no's to Mailer's lack of pleasure were no greater in volume. "It seems the ayes and no's are about equal," said Mailer. (He was thinking to himself that he had posed the issue all wrong—the ayes should have been reserved for those who would keep him in office.) "Under the circumstances," he announced, "I will keep the chair." Laughter at this easy cheek. He stepped into the middle of such laughter. "You have all just learned an invaluable political lesson." He waved the microphone at the audience. "In the absence of a definitive vote, the man who holds the power, keeps it."

"Hey, de Grazia," someone yelled from the audience, "why do you let him have it?"

Mailer extended the microphone to de Grazia who smiled sweetly into it. "Because if I don't," he said in a gentle voice, "he'll beat the shit out of me." The dread word had been used again.

"Please, Norman," said Macdonald retreating.

So Mailer gave his introduction to Macdonald. It was less than he would have attempted if the flight had not been grounded, but it was certainly respectable. Under the military circumstances, it was a decent cleanup operation. For about a minute he proceeded to introduce Macdonald as a man with whom one might seldom agree, but could never disrespect because he always told the truth as he saw the truth, a man therefore of the most incorruptible integrity. "Pray heaven, I am right," said Mailer to himself, and walked past Macdonald who was on his way to the mike. Both men nodded coolly to each other.

In the wing, visible to the audience, Paul Goodman sat on a chair clearly avoiding any contaminatory encounter with The Existentialist. De Grazia gave his "It's tough all over" smile. Lowell sat in a mournful hunch on the floor, his eyes peering over his glasses to scrutinize the metaphysical substance of his boot, now hide? now machine? now, where the joining and to what? foot to boot, boot to earth—cease all speculations as to what was in Lowell's head. "The one mind a novelist cannot enter is the mind of a novelist superior to himself," said once to Mailer by Jean Malaquais.[5] So, by corollary, the one mind a minor poet may not enter . . . .

Lowell looked most unhappy. Mailer, minor poet, had often observed that Lowell had the most disconcerting mixture of strength and weakness in his

---

5. French novelist (b. 1908) whose *Reflections on Hip* Mailer admired.

presence, a blending so dramatic in its visible sign of conflict that one had to assume he would be sensationally attractive to women. He had something untouchable, all insane in its force; one felt immediately there were any number of causes for which the man would be ready to die, and for some he would fight, with an axe in his hand and a Cromwellian[6] light in his eye. It was even possible that physically he was very strong—one couldn't tell at all—he might be fragile, he might have the sort of farm mechanic's strength which could manhandle the rear axle and differential off a car and into the back of a pickup. But physical strength or no, his nerves were all too apparently delicate. Obviously spoiled by everyone for years, he seemed nonetheless to need the spoiling. These nerves—the nerves of a consummate poet—were not tuned to any battering. The squalls of the mike, now riding up a storm on the erratic piping breath of Macdonald's voice, seemed to tear along Lowell's back like a gale. He detested tumult—obviously. And therefore saw everything which was hopeless in a rife situation: the dank middle-class depths of the audience, the strident squalor of the mike, the absurdity of talent gathered to raise money— for what, dear God? who could finally know what this March might convey, or worse, purvey, and worst of all—to be associated now with Mailer's butcher boy attack. Lowell's eyes looked up from the shoe, and passed one withering glance by the novelist, saying much, saying, "Every single bad thing I have ever heard about you is not exaggerated."

Mailer, looking back, thought bitter words he would not say: "You, Lowell, beloved poet of many, what do you know of the dirt and the dark deliveries of the necessary? What do you know of dignity hard-achieved, and dignity lost through innocence, and dignity lost by sacrifice for a cause one cannot name. What do you know about getting fat against your will, and turning into a clown of an arriviste baron when you would rather be an eagle or a count, or rarest of all, some natural aristocrat from these damned democratic states. No, the only subject we share, you and I, is that species of perception which shows that if we are not very loyal to our unendurable and most exigent inner light, then some day we may burn. How dare you condemn me! You know the diseases which inhabit the audience in this accursed psychedelic house. How dare you scorn the explosive I employ?"

And Lowell with a look of the greatest sorrow as if all this *mess* were finally too shapeless for the hard Protestant smith of his own brain, which would indeed burst if it could not forge his experience into the iron edge of the very best words and the most unsinkable relation of words, now threw up his eyes like an epileptic as if turned out of orbit by a turn of the vision—and fell backward, his head striking the floor with no last instant hesitation to cushion the blow, but like a baby, downright sudden, savagely to himself, as if from the height of a foot he had taken a pumpkin and dropped it splat on the floor. "There, much-regarded, much-protected brain, you have finally taken a blow," Lowell might have said to himself, for he proceeded to lie there, resting quietly, while Macdonald went on reading from "The White Man's Burden," Lowell seeming as content as if he had just tested the back of his cranium against a policeman's club. What a royal head they had all to lose!

---

6. Oliver Cromwell (1599–1658) led the Puritan revolt against Charles I.

# JAMES BALDWIN
## 1924–1987

James Baldwin was born in Harlem, the first of nine children. From his novel *Go Tell It on the Mountain* (1953) and his story *The Rockpile*, we learn how extremely painful was the relationship between the father and his eldest son. David Baldwin, son of a slave, was a lay preacher rigidly committed to a vengeful God who would eventually judge white people as they deserved; in the meantime, much of the vengeance was taken out on James. His father's "unlimited capacity for introspection and rancor," as the son later put it, must have had a profound effect on the sermonizing style Baldwin was to develop. Just as important was his conversion and resulting service as a preacher in his father's church, as we can see from both the rhythm and message of his prose—which is very much a *spoken* prose.

Baldwin did well in school and, having received a hardship deferment from military service (his father was dying), began to attach himself to Greenwich Village, where he concentrated on the business of becoming a writer. In 1944 he met Richard Wright, at that time "the greatest black writer in the world for me," in whose early books Baldwin "found expressed, for the first time in my life, the sorrow, the rage, and the murderous bitterness which was eating up my life and the lives of those about me." Wright helped him win a Eugene Saxton fellowship, and in 1948, when Baldwin went to live in Paris, he was following Wright's footsteps (Wright had become an expatriate to the same city a year earlier). It is perhaps for this reason that in his early essays written for *Partisan Review* and published in 1955 as *Notes of a Native Son* (with the title's explicit reference to Wright's novel) Baldwin dissociated himself from the image of American life found in Wright's "protest work" and, as Ralph Ellison was also doing, went about protesting in his own way.

As far as his novels are concerned, Baldwin's way involved a preoccupation with the intertwining of sexual with racial concerns, particularly in America. His interest in what it means to be black and homosexual in relation to white society is most fully and interestingly expressed in his long and somewhat ragged third novel, *Another Country* (1962). (He had previously written *Go Tell It on the Mountain*, and a second novel, *Giovanni's Room*, 1955, about a white expatriate in Paris and his male lover.) *Another Country* contains scenes full of lively detail and intelligent reflection, although it lacks—as do all his novels—a compelling design that draws the book together. In his novels Baldwin made slight use of the talents for irony and sly teasing he is master of in his essays; nor, unlike Ellison or Mailer, did he show much interest in stylistic experimentation.

Baldwin's imagination is intensely social and reveals itself most passionately and variously in his collections of essays, of which *Notes of a Native Son* is probably the best, and in what many would judge his finest piece of writing, *Letter from a Region of My Mind* (in *The Fire Next Time*, 1963). This essay, the first half of which is printed here, was first published in *The New Yorker* and probably had a greater effect on white liberals than on the blacks who read it. In its firm rejection of separatism between the races as preached by the Black Muslims and their leader, Elijah Muhammad, it spoke out for love as the difficult and necessary way out of slavery and race hatred. Today, with all that has happened since its appearance, it is still a fresh and moving utterance, directed as the best of Baldwin's essays are by a beautifully controlled speaking voice, alternately impressing on us its accents of polite directness, sardonic irony, or barely controlled fury.

His later novels, *Tell Me How Long the Train's Been Gone* (1968) and *Just Above My Head* (1979), were overlong and tended toward the shapeless. Like Mailer,

Baldwin risked advertising himself too strenuously and sometimes fell into stridency and sentimentality. Like Ellison he experienced many pressures to be something more than just a writer, but he nevertheless produced a respectable series of novels and stories, even if no single fiction of his is comparable in breadth and daring to *Invisible Man*. There has surely been no black writer better able to imagine white experience, to speak in various tones of different kinds and behaviors of people or places other than his own. In its sensitivity to shades of discrimination and moral shape, and in its commitment—despite everything—to America, his voice was comparable in importance to that of any person of letters from recent decades, and tributes paid to him at his death were agreed on that fact.

# *From* The Fire Next Time[1]

## [Part I]

I underwent, during the summer that I became fourteen, a prolonged religious crisis. I use the word "religious" in the common, and arbitrary, sense, meaning that I then discovered God, His saints and angels, and His blazing Hell. And since I had been born in a Christian nation, I accepted this Deity as the only one. I supposed Him to exist only within the walls of a church— in fact, of *our* church—and I also supposed that God and safety were synonymous. The word "safety" brings us to the real meaning of the word "religious" as we use it. Therefore, to state it in another, more accurate way, I became, during my fourteenth year, for the first time in my life, afraid—afraid of the evil within me and afraid of the evil without. What I saw around me that summer in Harlem was what I had always seen; nothing had changed. But now, without any warning, the whores and pimps and racketeers on the Avenue[2] had become a personal menace. It had not before occurred to me that I could become one of them, but now I realized that we had been produced by the same circumstances. Many of my comrades were clearly headed for the Avenue, and my father said that I was headed that way, too. My friends began to drink and smoke, and embarked—at first avid, then groaning—on their sexual careers. Girls, only slightly older than I was, who sang in the choir or taught Sunday school, the children of holy parents, underwent, before my eyes, their incredible metamorphosis, of which the most bewildering aspect was not their budding breasts or their rounding behinds but something deeper and more subtle, in their eyes, their heat, their odor, and the inflection of their voices. Like the strangers on the Avenue, they became, in the twinkling of an eye, unutterably different and fantastically *present*. Owing to the way I had been raised, the abrupt discomfort that all this aroused in me and the fact that I had no idea what my voice or my mind or my body was likely to do next caused me to consider myself one of the most depraved people on earth. Matters were not helped by the fact that these holy girls seemed rather to enjoy my

1. *Letter from a Region of My Mind*, of which the first half is printed here, was originally published in *The New Yorker* in 1962, then combined with a shorter essay to make up *The Fire Next Time* (1963). In the second half of the *Letter*, Baldwin describes in detail his impressions of the Black Muslims and their leader, Elijah Muhammad. The book's epigraph—"God gave Noah the rainbow sign, / No more water, the fire next

time!"—alludes to what Baldwin terms at the book's conclusion "the fulfillment of that prophecy, recreated from the Bible in song by a slave," which we will suffer if we do not "end the racial nightmare, and achieve our country."
2. Lenox Avenue, the main street running through Harlem.

terrified lapses, our grim, guilty, tormented experiments, which were at once as chill and joyless as the Russian steppes and hotter, by far, than all the fires of Hell.

Yet there was something deeper than these changes, and less definable, that frightened me. It was real in both the boys and the girls, but it was, somehow, more vivid in the boys. In the case of the girls, one watched them turning into matrons before they had become women. They began to manifest a curious and really rather terrifying single-mindedness. It is hard to say exactly how this was conveyed: something implacable in the set of the lips, something farseeing (seeing what?) in the eyes, some new and crushing determination in the walk, something peremptory in the voice. They did not tease us, the boys, any more; they reprimanded us sharply, saying, "You better be thinking about your soul!" For the girls also saw the evidence on the Avenue, knew what the price would be, for them, of one misstep, knew that they had to be protected and that we were the only protection there was. They understood that they must act as God's decoys, saving the souls of the boys for Jesus and binding the bodies of the boys in marriage. For this was the beginning of our burning time, and "It is better," said St. Paul—who elsewhere, with a most unusual and stunning exactness, described himself as a "wretched man"—"to marry than to burn."[3] And I began to feel in the boys a curious, wary, bewildered despair, as though they were now settling in for the long, hard winter of life. I did not know then what it was that I was reacting to; I put it to myself that they were letting themselves go. In the same way that the girls were destined to gain as much weight as their mothers, the boys, it was clear, would rise no higher than their fathers. School began to reveal itself, therefore, as a child's game that one could not win, and boys dropped out of school and went to work. My father wanted me to do the same. I refused, even though I no longer had any illusions about what an education could do for me; I had already encountered too many college-graduate handymen. My friends were now "downtown," busy, as they put it, "fighting the man." They began to care less about the way they looked, the way they dressed, the things they did; presently, one found them in twos and threes and fours, in a hallway, sharing a jug of wine or a bottle of whiskey, talking, cursing, fighting, sometimes weeping: lost, and unable to say what it was that oppressed them, except that they knew it was "the man"—the white man. And there seemed to be no way whatever to remove this cloud that stood between them and the sun, between them and love and life and power, between them and whatever it was that they wanted. One did not have to be very bright to realize how little one could do to change one's situation; one did not have to be abnormally sensitive to be worn down to a cutting edge by the incessant and gratuitous humiliation and danger one encountered every working day, all day long. The humiliation did not apply merely to working days, or workers; I was thirteen and was crossing Fifth Avenue on my way to the Forty-second Street library, and the cop in the middle of the street muttered as I passed him, "Why don't you niggers stay uptown where you belong?" When I was ten, and didn't look, certainly, any older, two policemen amused themselves with me by frisking me, making comic (and terrifying) speculations concerning my ancestry and probable sexual prowess, and for good measure, leaving me flat on my back in one of Harlem's empty lots. Just before and then

---

3. 1 Corinthians 7.9

during the Second World War, many of my friends fled into the service, all to be changed there, and rarely for the better, many to be ruined, and many to die. Others fled to other states and cities—that is, to other ghettos. Some went on wine or whiskey or the needle, and are still on it. And others, like me, fled into the church.

For the wages of sin were visible everywhere, in every wine-stained and urine-splashed hallway, in every clanging ambulance bell, in every scar on the faces of the pimps and their whores, in every helpless, newborn baby being brought into this danger, in every knife and pistol fight on the Avenue, and in every disastrous bulletin: a cousin, mother of six, suddenly gone mad, the children parcelled out here and there; an indestructible aunt rewarded for years of hard labor by a slow, agonizing death in a terrible small room; someone's bright son blown into eternity by his own hand; another turned robber and carried off to jail. It was a summer of dreadful speculations and discoveries, of which these were not the worst. Crime became real, for example—for the first time—not as *a* possibility but as *the* possibility. One would never defeat one's circumstances by working and saving one's pennies; one would never, by working, acquire that many pennies, and, besides, the social treatment accorded even the most successful Negroes proved that one needed, in order to be free, something more than a bank account. One needed a handle, a lever, a means of inspiring fear. It was absolutely clear that the police would whip you and take you in as long as they could get away with it, and that everyone else— housewives, taxi-drivers, elevator boys, dishwashers, bartenders, lawyers, judges, doctors, and grocers—would never, by the operation of any generous human feeling, cease to use you as an outlet for his frustrations and hostilities. Neither civilized reason nor Christian love would cause any of those people to treat you as they presumably wanted to be treated; only the fear of your power to retaliate would cause them to do that, or to seem to do it, which was (and is) good enough. There appears to be a vast amount of confusion on this point, but I do not know many Negroes who are eager to be "accepted" by white people, still less to be loved by them; they, the blacks, simply don't wish to be beaten over the head by the whites every instant of our brief passage on this planet. White people in this country will have quite enough to do in learning how to accept and love themselves and each other, and when they have achieved this—which will not be tomorrow and may very well be never—the Negro problem will no longer exist, for it will no longer be needed.

People more advantageously placed than we in Harlem were, and are, will no doubt find the psychology and the view of human nature sketched above dismal and shocking in the extreme. But the Negro's experience of the white world cannot possibly create in him any respect for the standards by which the white world claims to live. His own condition is overwhelming proof that white people do not live by these standards. Negro servants have been smuggling odds and ends out of white homes for generations, and white people have been delighted to have them do it, because it has assuaged a dim guilt and testified to the intrinsic superiority of white people. Even the most doltish and servile Negro could scarcely fail to be impressed by the disparity between his situation and that of the people for whom he worked; Negroes who were neither doltish nor servile did not feel that they were doing anything wrong when they robbed white people. In spite of the Puritan-Yankee equation of virtue with well-being, Negroes had excellent reasons for doubting that money was made or kept by any very striking adherence to the Christian virtues; it certainly did not work that way for black Christians. In any case, white people, who had robbed black people of their liberty and who profited by this theft every hour that they lived, had no moral ground on which to stand. They had the judges, the juries, the shotguns, the law—in a word, power. But it was a criminal power, to be feared but not respected, and to be outwitted in any way whatever. And those virtues preached but not practiced by the white world were merely another means of holding Negroes in subjection.

It turned out, then, that summer, that the moral barriers that I had supposed to exist between me and the dangers of a criminal career were so tenuous as to be nearly nonexistent. I certainly could not discover any principled reason for not becoming a criminal, and it is not my poor, God-fearing parents who are to be indicted for the lack but this society. I was icily determined—more determined, really, than I then knew—never to make my peace with the ghetto but to die and go to Hell before I would let any white man spit on me, before I would accept my "place" in this republic. I did not intend to allow the white people of this country to tell me who I was, and limit me that way, and polish me off that way. And yet, of course, at the same time, I *was* being spat on and defined and described and limited, and could have been polished off with no effort whatever. Every Negro boy—in my situation during those years, at least—who reaches this point realizes, at once, profoundly, because he wants to live, that he stands in great peril and must find, with speed, a "thing," a gimmick, to lift him out, to start him on his way. *And it does not matter what the gimmick is.* It was this last realization that terrified me and—since it revealed that the door opened on so many dangers—helped to hurl me into the church. And, by an unforeseeable paradox, it was my career in the church that turned out, precisely, to be my gimmick.

For when I tried to assess my capabilities, I realized that I had almost none. In order to achieve the life I wanted, I had been dealt, it seemed to me, the worst possible hand. I could not become a prizefighter—many of us tried but very few succeeded. I could not sing. I could not dance. I had been well conditioned by the world in which I grew up, so I did not yet dare take the idea of becoming a writer seriously. The only other possibility seemed to involve my becoming one of the sordid people on the Avenue, who were not really as sordid as I then imagined but who frightened me terribly, both because I did not want to live that life and because of what they made me feel. Everything inflamed me, and that was bad enough, but I myself had also become a source of fire and temptation. I had been far too well raised, alas, to suppose that any of the extremely explicit overtures made to me that summer, sometimes by boys and girls but also, more alarmingly, by older men and women, had anything to do with my attractiveness. On the contrary, since the Harlem idea of seduction is, to put it mildly, blunt, whatever these people saw in me merely confirmed my sense of my depravity.

It is certainly sad that the awakening of one's senses should lead to such a merciless judgment of oneself—to say nothing of the time and anguish one spends in the effort to arrive at any other—but it is also inevitable that a literal attempt to mortify the flesh should be made among black people like those with whom I grew up. Negroes in this country—and Negroes do not, strictly or legally speaking, exist in any other—are taught really to despise themselves from the moment their eyes open on the world. This world is white and they are black. White people hold the power, which means that they are superior to blacks (intrinsically, that is: God decreed it so), and the world has innumerable ways of making this difference known and felt and feared. Long before the Negro child perceives this difference, and even longer before he understands it, he has begun to react to it, he has begun to be controlled by it. Every effort made by the child's elders to prepare him for a fate from which they cannot protect him causes him secretly, in terror, to begin to await, without knowing that he is doing so, his mysterious and inexorable punishment. He must be "good" not only in order to please his parents and not only to avoid being punished by them; behind their authority stands another, nameless and impersonal, infinitely harder to please, and bottomlessly cruel. And this filters into the child's consciousness through his parents' tone of voice as he is being exhorted, punished, or loved; in the sudden, uncontrollable note of fear heard in his mother's or his father's voice when he has strayed beyond some particular boundary. He does not know what the boundary is, and he can get no explanation of it, which is frightening enough, but the fear he hears in the voices of his elders is more frightening still. The fear that I heard in my father's voice, for example, when he realized that I really *believed* I could do anything a white boy could do, and had every intention of proving it, was not at all like the fear I heard when one of us was ill or had fallen down the stairs or strayed too far from the house. It was another fear, a fear that the child, in challenging the white world's assumptions, was putting himself in the path of destruction. A child cannot, thank Heaven, know how vast and how merciless is the nature of power, with what unbelievable cruelty people treat each other. He reacts to the fear in his parents' voices because his parents hold up the world for him and he has no protection without them. I defended myself, as I imagined, against the fear my father made me feel by remembering that he was very old-fashioned. Also, I prided myself on the fact that I already knew how to outwit him. To defend oneself against a fear is simply to insure that one will, one day, be conquered by it; fears must be faced. As for one's wits, it is just not true that one can live by them—not, that is, if one wishes really to live. That summer, in any case, all the fears with which I had grown up, and which were now a part of me and controlled my vision of the world, rose up like a wall between the world and me, and drove me into the church.

As I look back, everything I did seems curiously deliberate, though it certainly did not seem deliberate then. For example, I did not join the church of which my father was a member and in which he preached. My best friend in school, who attended a different church, had already "surrendered his life to the Lord," and he was very anxious about my soul's salvation. (I wasn't, but any human attention was better than none.) One Saturday afternoon, he took me to his church. There were no services that day, and the church was empty, except for some women cleaning and some other women praying. My friend took me into the back room to meet his pastor—a woman. There she sat, in her robes, smiling, an extremely proud and handsome woman, with Africa, Europe, and the America of the American Indian blended in her face. She was perhaps forty-five or fifty at this time, and in our world she was a very celebrated woman. My friend was about to introduce me when she looked at me and smiled and said, "Whose little boy are you?" Now this, unbelievably, was precisely the phrase used by pimps and racketeers on the Avenue when they suggested, both humorously and intensely, that I "hang out" with them.

Perhaps part of the terror they had caused me to feel came from the fact that I unquestionably wanted to be *somebody's* little boy. I was so frightened, and at the mercy of so many conundrums, that inevitably, that summer, *someone* would have taken me over; one doesn't, in Harlem, long remain standing on any auction block. It was my good luck—perhaps—that I found myself in the church racket instead of some other, and surrendered to a spiritual seduction long before I came to any carnal knowledge. For when the pastor asked me, with that marvellous smile, "Whose little boy are you?" my heart replied at once, "Why, yours."

The summer wore on, and things got worse. I became more guilty and more frightened, and kept all this bottled up inside me, and naturally, inescapably, one night, when this woman had finished preaching, everything came roaring, screaming, crying out, and I fell to the ground before the altar. It was the strangest sensation I have ever had in my life—up to that time, or since. I had not known that it was going to happen, or that it could happen. One moment I was on my feet, singing and clapping and, at the same time, working out in my head the plot of a play I was working on then; the next moment, with no transition, no sensation of falling, I was on my back, with the lights beating down into my face and all the vertical saints above me. I did not know what I was doing down so low, or how I had got there. And the anguish that filled me cannot be described. It moved in me like one of those floods that devastate counties, tearing everything down, tearing children from their parents and lovers from each other, and making everything an unrecognizable waste. All I really remember is the pain, the unspeakable pain; it was as though I were yelling up to Heaven and Heaven would not hear me. And if Heaven would not hear me, if love could not descend from Heaven—to wash me, to make me clean—then utter disaster was my portion. Yes, it does indeed mean something—something unspeakable—to be born, in a white country, an Anglo-Teutonic, antisexual country, black. You very soon, without knowing it, give up all hope of communion. Black people, mainly, look down or look up but do not look at each other, not at you, and white people, mainly, look away. And the universe is simply a sounding drum; there is no way, no way whatever, so it seemed then and has sometimes seemed since, to get through a life, to love your wife and children, or your friends, or your mother and father, or to be loved. The universe, which is not merely the stars and the moon and the planets, flowers, grass, and trees, but *other people*, has evolved no terms for your existence, has made no room for you, and if love will not swing wide the gates, no other power will or can. And if one despairs—as who has not?—of human love, God's love alone is left. But God—and I felt this even then, so long ago, on that tremendous floor, unwillingly—is white. And if His love was so great, and if He loved all His children, why were we, the blacks, cast down so far? Why? In spite of all I said thereafter, I found no answer on the floor—not *that* answer, anyway—and I was on the floor all night. Over me, to bring me "through," the saints sang and rejoiced and prayed. And in the morning, when they raised me, they told me that I was "saved."

Well, indeed I was, in a way, for I was utterly drained and exhausted, and released, for the first time, from all my guilty torment. I was aware then only of my relief. For many years, I could not ask myself why human relief had to be achieved in a fashion at once so pagan and so desperate—in a fashion at once so unspeakably old and so unutterably new. And by the time I was able to ask myself this question, I was also able to see that the principles governing the rites and customs of the churches in which I grew up did not differ from the principles governing the rites and customs of other churches, white. The principles were Blindness, Loneliness, and Terror, the first principle necessarily and actively cultivated in order to deny the two others. I would love to believe that the principles were Faith, Hope, and Charity, but this is clearly not so for most Christians, or for what we call the Christian world.

I was saved. But at the same time, out of a deep, adolescent cunning I do not pretend to understand, I realized immediately that I could not remain in the church merely as another worshipper. I would have to give myself something to do, in order not to be too bored and find myself among all the wretched unsaved of the Avenue. And I don't doubt that I also intended to best my father on his own ground. Anyway, very shortly after I joined the church, I became a preacher—a Young Minister—and I remained in the pulpit for more than three years. My youth quickly made me a much bigger drawing card than my father. I pushed this advantage ruthlessly, for it was the most effective means I had found of breaking his hold over me. That was the most frightening time of my life, and quite the most dishonest, and the resulting hysteria lent great passion to my sermons—for a while. I relished the attention and the relative immunity from punishment that my new status gave me, and I relished, above all, the sudden right to privacy. It had to be recognized, after all, that I was still a schoolboy, with my schoolwork to do, and I was also expected to prepare at least one sermon a week. During what we may call my heyday, I preached much more often than that. This meant that there were hours and even whole days when I could not be interrupted—not even by my father. I had immobilized him. It took rather more time for me to realize that I had also immobilized myself, and had escaped from nothing whatever.

The church was very exciting. It took a long time for me to disengage myself from this excitement, and on the blindest, most visceral level, I never really have, and never will. There is no music like that music, no drama like the drama of the saints rejoicing, the sinners moaning, the tambourines racing, and all those voices coming together and crying holy unto the Lord. There is still, for me, no pathos quite like the pathos of those multicolored, worn, somehow triumphant and transfigured faces, speaking from the depths of a visible, tangible, continuing despair of the goodness of the Lord. I have never seen anything to equal the fire and excitement that sometimes, without warning, fill a church, causing the church, as Leadbelly[4] and so many others have testified, to "rock." Nothing that has happened to me since equals the power and the glory that I sometimes felt when, in the middle of a sermon, I knew that I was somehow, by some miracle, really carrying, as they said, "the Word"—when the church and I were one. Their pain and their joy were mine, and mine were theirs—they surrendered their pain and joy to me, I surrendered mine to them—and their cries of "Amen!" and "Hallelujah!" and "Yes, Lord!" and "Praise His name!" and "Preach it, brother!" sustained and whipped on my solos until we all became equal, wringing wet, singing and dancing, in anguish and rejoicing, at the foot of the altar. It was, for a

---

4. Huddie Ledbetter (1888–1949), or Leadbelly, folk and blues singer who had enormous influence on other singers.

long time, in spite of—or, not inconceivably, because of—the shabbiness of my motives, my only sustenance, my meat and drink. I rushed home from school, to the church, to the altar, to be alone there, to commune with Jesus, my dearest Friend, who would never fail me, who knew all the secrets of my heart. Perhaps He did, but I didn't, and the bargain we struck, actually, down there at the foot of the cross, was that He would never let me find out.

He failed His bargain. He was a much better Man than I took Him for. It happened, as things do, imperceptibly, in many ways at once. I date it—the slow crumbling of my faith, the pulverization of my fortress—from the time, about a year after I had begun to preach, when I began to read again. I justified this desire by the fact that I was still in school, and I began, fatally, with Dostoevski. By this time, I was in a high school that was predominantly Jewish. This meant that I was surrounded by people who were, by definition, beyond any hope of salvation, who laughed at the tracts and leaflets I brought to school, and who pointed out that the Gospels had been written long after the death of Christ. This might not have been so distressing if it had not forced me to read the tracts and leaflets myself, for they were indeed, unless one believed their message already, impossible to believe. I remember feeling dimly that there was a kind of blackmail in it. People, I felt, ought to love the Lord *because* they loved Him, and not because they were afraid of going to Hell. I was forced, reluctantly, to realize that the Bible itself had been written by men, and translated by men out of languages I could not read, and I was already, without quite admitting it to myself, terribly involved with the effort of putting words on paper. Of course, I had the rebuttal ready: These men had all been operating under divine inspiration. *Had* they? *All* of them? And I also knew by now, alas, far more about divine inspiration than I dared admit, for I knew how I worked myself up into my own visions, and how frequently—indeed, incessantly—the visions God granted to me differed from the visions He granted to my father. I did not understand the dreams I had at night, but I knew that they were not holy. For that matter, I knew that my waking hours were far from holy. I spent most of my time in a state of repentance for things I had vividly desired to do but had not done. The fact that I was dealing with Jews brought the whole question of color, which I had been desperately avoiding, into the terrified center of my mind. I realized that the Bible had been written by white men. I knew that, according to many Christians, I was a descendant of Ham,[5] who had been cursed, and that I was therefore predestined to be a slave. This had nothing to do with anything I was, or contained, or could become; my fate had been sealed forever, from the beginning of time. And it seemed, indeed, when one looked out over Christendom, that this was what Christendom effectively believed. It was certainly the way it behaved. I remembered the Italian priests and bishops blessing Italian boys who were on their way to Ethiopia.

Again, the Jewish boys in high school were troubling because I could find no point of connection between them and the Jewish pawnbrokers and landlords and grocery-store owners in Harlem. I knew that these people were Jews—God knows I was told it often enough—but I thought of them only as white. Jews, as such, until I got to high school, were all incarcerated in the

---

5. One of the sons of Noah, Ham was cursed with slavery for seeing his drunken father's nakedness (Genesis 9.18–27). He was also regarded as the progenitor of the African peoples.

Old Testament, and their names were Abraham, Moses, Daniel, Ezekiel, and Job, and Shadrach, Meshach, and Abednego. It was bewildering to find them so many miles and centuries out of Egypt, and so far from the fiery furnace.[6] My best friend in high school was a Jew. He came to our house once, and afterward my father asked, as he asked about everyone, "Is he a Christian?"— by which he meant "Is he saved?" I really do not know whether my answer came out of innocence or venom, but I said coldly, "No. He's Jewish." My father slammed me across the face with his great palm, and in that moment everything flooded back—all the hatred and all the fear, and the depth of a merciless resolve to kill my father rather than allow my father to kill me—and I knew that all those sermons and tears and all that repentance and rejoicing had changed nothing. I wondered if I was expected to be glad that a friend of mine, or anyone, was to be tormented forever in Hell, and I also thought, suddenly, of the Jews in another Christian nation, Germany. They were not so far from the fiery furnace after all, and my best friend might have been one of them. I told my father, "He's a better Christian than you are," and walked out of the house. The battle between us was in the open, but that was all right; it was almost a relief. A more deadly struggle had begun.

Being in the pulpit was like being in the theatre; I was behind the scenes and knew how the illusion was worked. I knew the other ministers and knew the quality of their lives. And I don't mean to suggest by this the "Elmer Gantry"[7] sort of hypocrisy concerning sensuality; it was a deeper, deadlier, and more subtle hypocrisy than that, and a little honest sensuality, or a lot, would have been like water in an extremely bitter desert. I knew how to work on a congregation until the last dime was surrendered—it was not very hard to do— and I knew where the money for "the Lord's work" went. I knew, though I did not wish to know it, that I had no respect for the people with whom I worked. I could not have said it then, but I also knew that if I continued I would soon have no respect for myself. And the fact that I was "the young Brother Baldwin" increased my value with those same pimps and racketeers who had helped to stampede me into the church in the first place. They still saw the little boy they intended to take over. They were waiting for me to come to my senses and realize that I was in a very lucrative business. They knew that I did not yet realize this, and also that I had not yet begun to suspect where my own needs, *coming up* (they were very patient), could drive me. They themselves did know the score, and they knew that the odds were in their favor. And, really, I knew it, too. I was even lonelier and more vulnerable than I had been before. And the blood of the Lamb had not cleansed me in any way whatever. I was just as black as I had been the day that I was born. Therefore, when I faced a congregation, it began to take all the strength I had not to stammer, not to curse, not to tell them to throw away their Bibles and get off their knees and go home and organize, for example, a rent strike. When I watched all the children, their copper, brown, and beige faces staring up at me as I taught Sunday school, I felt that I was committing a crime in talking about the gentle Jesus, in telling them to reconcile themselves to their misery on earth in order to gain the crown of eternal life. Were only Negroes to gain this crown? Was Heaven, then, to be merely another ghetto? Perhaps I might have been able

6. Shadrach, Meshach, and Abednego appear in the Old Testament (Daniel 3.19–24), where they are cast into the fiery furnace for refusing to worship the divinities of Babylon and disobeying King Nebuchadnezzar.
7. Hero of Sinclair Lewis's novel of that title whose preaching is at odds with his lechery.

to reconcile myself even to this if I had been able to believe that there was any loving-kindness to be found in the haven I represented. But I had been in the pulpit too long and I had seen too many monstrous things. I don't refer merely to the glaring fact that the minister eventually acquires houses and Cadillacs while the faithful continue to scrub floors and drop their dimes and quarters and dollars into the plate. I really mean that there was no love in the church. It was a mask for hatred and self-hatred and despair. The transfiguring power of the Holy Ghost ended when the service ended, and salvation stopped at the church door. When we were told to love everybody, I had thought that that meant *everybody*. But no. It applied only to those who believed as we did, and it did not apply to white people at all. I was told by a minister, for example, that I should never, on any public conveyance, under any circumstances, rise and give my seat to a white woman. White men never rose for Negro women. Well, that was true enough, in the main—I saw his point. But what was the point, the purpose, of *my* salvation if it did not permit me to behave with love toward others, no matter how they behaved toward me? What others did was their responsibility, for which they would answer when the judgment trumpet sounded. But what *I* did was *my* responsibility, and I would have to answer, too—unless, of course, there was also in Heaven a special dispensation for the benighted black, who was not to be judged in the same way as other human beings, or angels. It probably occurred to me around this time that the vision people hold of the world to come is but a reflection, with predictable wishful distortions, of the world in which they live. And this did not apply only to Negroes, who were no more "simple" or "spontaneous" or "Christian" than anybody else—who were merely more oppressed. In the same way that we, for white people, were the descendants of Ham, and were cursed forever, white people were, for us, the descendants of Cain. And the passion with which we loved the Lord was a measure of how deeply we feared and distrusted and, in the end, hated almost all strangers, always, and avoided and despised ourselves.

But I cannot leave it at that; there is more to it than that. In spite of everything, there was in the life I fled a zest and a joy and a capacity for facing and surviving disaster that are very moving and very rare. Perhaps we were, all of us—pimps, whores, racketeers, church members, and children—bound together by the nature of our oppression, the specific and peculiar complex of risks we had to run; if so, within these limits we sometimes achieved with each other a freedom that was close to love. I remember, anyway, church suppers and outings, and, later, after I left the church, rent and waistline parties[8] where rage and sorrow sat in the darkness and did not stir, and we ate and drank and talked and laughed and danced and forgot all about "the man." We had the liquor, the chicken, the music, and each other, and had no need to pretend to be what we were not. This is the freedom that one hears in some gospel songs, for example, and in jazz. In all jazz, and especially in the blues, there is something tart and ironic, authoritative and double-edged. White Americans seem to feel that happy songs are *happy* and sad songs are *sad*, and that, God help us, is exactly the way most white Americans sing them—sounding, in both cases, so helplessly, defenselessly fatuous that one dare not speculate on the temperature of the deep freeze from which issue their brave

---

8. Gatherings held in houses or apartments to raise money to pay the rent.

and sexless little voices. Only people who have been "down the line," as the song puts it, know what this music is about. I think it was Big Bill Broonzy[9] who used to sing "I Feel So Good," a really joyful song about a man who is on his way to the railroad station to meet his girl. She's coming home. It is the singer's incredibly moving exuberance that makes one realize how leaden the time must have been while she was gone. There is no guarantee that she will stay this time, either, as the singer clearly knows, and, in fact, she has not yet actually arrived. Tonight, or tomorrow, or within the next five minutes, he may very well be singing "Lonesome in My Bedroom," or insisting, "Ain't we, ain't we, going to make it all right? Well, if we don't today, we will tomorrow night." White Americans do not understand the depths out of which such an ironic tenacity comes, but they suspect that the force is sensual, and they are terrified of sensuality and do not any longer understand it. The word "sensual" is not intended to bring to mind quivering dusky maidens or priapic black studs. I am referring to something much simpler and much less fanciful. To be sensual, I think, is to respect and rejoice in the force of life, of life itself, and to be *present* in all that one does, from the effort of loving to the breaking of bread. It will be a great day for America, incidentally, when we begin to eat bread again, instead of the blasphemous and tasteless foam rubber that we have substituted for it. And I am not being frivolous now, either. Something very sinister happens to the people of a country when they begin to distrust their own reactions as deeply as they do here, and become as joyless as they have become. It is this individual uncertainty on the part of white American men and women, this inability to renew themselves at the fountain of their own lives, that makes the discussion, let alone elucidation, of any conundrum—that is, any reality—so supremely difficult. The person who distrusts himself has no touchstone for reality—for this touchstone can be only oneself. Such a person interposes between himself and reality nothing less than a labyrinth of attitudes. And these attitudes, furthermore, though the person is usually unaware of it (is unaware of so much!), are historical and public attitudes. They do not relate to the present any more than they relate to the person. Therefore, whatever white people do not know about Negroes reveals, precisely and inexorably, what they do not know about themselves.

White Christians have also forgotten several elementary historical details. They have forgotten that the religion that is now identified with their virtue and their power—"God is on our side," says Dr. Verwoerd[1]—came out of a rocky piece of ground in what is now known as the Middle East before color was invented, and that in order for the Christian church to be established, Christ had to be put to death, by Rome, and that the real architect of the Christian church was not the disreputable, sun-baked Hebrew who gave it his name but the mercilessly fanatically and self-righteous St. Paul. The energy that was buried with the rise of the Christian nations must come back into the world; nothing can prevent it. Many of us, I think, both long to see this happen and are terrified of it, for though this transformation contains the hope of liberation, it also imposes a necessity for great change. But in order to deal with the untapped and dormant force of the previously subjugated, in order to survive as a human, moving, moral weight in the world, America and all the

---

9. Blues singer and guitarist (1893–1958).
1. Dr. Henrik Verwoerd was a dedicated proponent of

*apartheid* (separation of the races) and prime minister of South Africa in the late 1950s.

Western nations will be forced to reexamine themselves and release themselves from many things that are now taken to be sacred, and to discard nearly all the assumptions that have been used to justify their lives and their anguish and their crimes so long.

"The white man's Heaven," sings a Black Muslim minister, "is the black man's Hell." One may object—possibly—that this puts the matter somewhat too simply, but the song is true, and it has been true for as long as white men have ruled the world. The Africans put it another way: When the white man came to Africa, the white man had the Bible and the African had the land, but now it is the white man who is being, reluctantly and bloodily, separated from the land, and the African who is still attempting to digest or to vomit up the Bible. The struggle, therefore, that now begins in the world is extremely complex, involving the historical role of Christianity in the realm of power— that is, politics—and in the realm of morals. In the realm of power, Christianity has operated with an unmitigated arrogance and cruelty—necessarily, since a religion ordinarily imposes on those who have discovered the true faith the spiritual duty of liberating the infidels. This particular true faith, moreover, is more deeply concerned about the soul than it is about the body, to which fact the flesh (and the corpses) of countless infidels bears witness. It goes without saying, then, that whoever questions the authority of the true faith also contests the right of the nations that hold this faith to rule over him—contests, in short, their title to his land. The spreading of the Gospel, regardless of the motives or the integrity or the heroism of some of the missionaries, was an absolutely indispensable justification for the planting of the flag. Priests and nuns and school-teachers helped to protect and sanctify the power that was so ruthlessly being used by people who were indeed seeking a city, but not one in the heavens, and one to be made, very definitely, by captive hands. The Christian church itself—again, as distinguished from some of its ministers—sanctified and rejoiced in the conquests of the flag, and encouraged, if it did not formulate, the belief that conquest, with the resulting relative well-being of the Western populations, was proof of the favor of God. God had come a long way from the desert—but then so had Allah, though in a very different direction. God, going north, and rising on the wings of power, had become white, and Allah, out of power, and on the dark side of Heaven, had become—for all practical purposes, anyway—black. Thus, in the realm of morals the role of Christianity has been, at best, ambivalent. Even leaving out of account the remarkable arrogance that assumed that the ways and morals of others were inferior to those of Christians, and that they therefore had every right, and could use any means, to change them, the collision between cultures—and the schizophrenia in the mind of Christendom—had rendered the domain of morals as chartless as the sea once was, and as treacherous as the sea still is. It is not too much to say that whoever wishes to become a truly moral human being (and let us not ask whether or not this is possible; I think we must *believe* that it is possible) must first divorce himself from all the prohibitions, crimes, and hypocrisies of the Christian church. If the concept of God has any validity or any use, it can only be to make us larger, freer, and more loving. If God cannot do this, then it is time we got rid of Him.

1962, 1963

# FLANNERY O'CONNOR
## 1925–1964

Flannery O'Connor, one of this century's finest writers of short stories, was born in Savannah; lived with her mother in Milledgeville, Georgia, for much of her life; and died before her fortieth birthday—victim like her father of disseminated lupus, a rare and incurable disease. She was stricken with the disease in 1950 while at work on her first novel, but injections of a cortisone derivative managed to arrest it, though the cortisone weakened her bones to the extent that from 1955 on she could only get around on crutches. She was able to write, travel, and lecture until 1964 when the lupus reactivated itself and killed her. A Roman Catholic throughout her life, she is quoted as having remarked, apropos of a trip to Lourdes, "I had the best-looking crutches in Europe." This remark suggests the kind of hair-raising jokes that centrally inform her writing as well as a refusal to indulge in self-pity over her fate.

She published two novels, *Wise Blood* (1952) and *The Violent Bear It Away* (1960), both weighty with symbolic and religious concerns and ingeniously contrived in the black-humored manner of Nathanael West, her American predecessor in this mode. But her really memorable creations of characters and actions take place in the stories, which are extremely funny, sometimes unbearably so, and finally we may wonder just what it is we are laughing at. Upon consideration the jokes are seen to be dreadful ones, as with Manley Pointer's treatment of Joy Hopewell's artificial leg in *Good Country People*.

Another American "regionalist," the poet Robert Frost, whose own work contains its share of dreadful jokes, once confessed to being more interested in people's speech than in the people themselves. A typical Flannery O'Connor story consists at its most vital level in people talking, clucking their endless reiterations of clichés about life, death, and the universe. These clichés are captured with beautiful accuracy by an artist who had spent her life listening to them, lovingly and maliciously keeping track until she could put them to use. Early in her life she hoped to be a cartoonist, and there is cartoonlike mastery in her vivid renderings of character through speech and other gesture. Critics have called her a maker of grotesques, a label that like other ones—regionalist, southern lady, or Roman Catholic novelist—might have annoyed if it didn't obviously amuse her too. She once remarked tartly that "anything that comes out of the South is going to be called grotesque by the Northern reader, unless it is grotesque, in which case it is going to be called realistic."

Of course, this capacity for mockery, along with a facility in portraying perverse behavior, may work against other demands we make of the fiction writer, and it is true that O'Connor seldom suggests that her characters have inner lives that are imaginable, let alone worth respect. Instead, the emphasis is on the sharp eye and the ability to tell a tale and keep it moving inevitably toward completion. These completions are usually violent, occurring when the character—in many cases a woman—must confront an experience that she cannot handle by the old trustworthy language and habit-hardened responses. O'Connor's art lies partly in making it impossible for us merely to scorn the banalities of expression and behavior by which these people get through their lives. However dark the comedy, it keeps in touch with the things of this world, even when some force from another world threatens to annihilate the embattled protagonist. And although the stories are filled with religious allusions and parodies, they do not try to inculcate a doctrine. One of her best ones is titled *Revelation*, but a reader often finishes a story with no simple, unambiguous sense of what has been revealed. Instead, we must trust the internal fun and richness of each tale to reveal what it has to reveal. We can agree also, in sadness, with the critic Irving Howe's conclusion to his review of her posthumous collection of stories that it is intolerable for such a writer to have died at the age of thirty-nine.

# Good Country People[1]

Besides the neutral expression that she wore when she was alone, Mrs. Freeman had two others, forward and reverse, that she used for all her human dealings. Her forward expression was steady and driving like the advance of a heavy truck. Her eyes never swerved to left or right but turned as the story turned as if they followed a yellow line down the center of it. She seldom used the other expression because it was not often necessary for her to retract a statement, but when she did, her face came to a complete stop, there was an almost imperceptible movement of her black eyes, during which they seemed to be receding, and then the observer would see that Mrs. Freeman, though she might stand there as real as several grain sacks thrown on top of each other, was no longer there in spirit. As for getting anything across to her when this was the case, Mrs. Hopewell had given it up. She might talk her head off. Mrs. Freeman could never be brought to admit herself wrong on any point. She would stand there and if she could be brought to say anything, it was something like, "Well, I wouldn't of said it was and I wouldn't of said it wasn't," or letting her gaze range over the top kitchen shelf where there was an assortment of dusty bottles, she might remark, "I see you ain't ate many of them figs you put up last summer."

They carried on their important business in the kitchen at breakfast. Every morning Mrs. Hopewell got up at seven o'clock and lit her gas heater and Joy's. Joy was her daughter, a large blonde girl who had an artificial leg. Mrs. Hopewell thought of her as a child though she was thirty-two years old and highly educated. Joy would get up while her mother was eating and lumber into the bathroom and slam the door, and before long, Mrs. Freeman would arrive at the back door. Joy would hear her mother call, "Come on in," and then they would talk for a while in low voices that were indistinguishable in the bathroom. By the time Joy came in, they had usually finished the weather report and were on one or the other of Mrs. Freeman's daughters, Glynese or Carramae. Joy called them Glycerin and Caramel. Glynese, a redhead, was eighteen and had many admirers; Carramae, a blonde, was only fifteen but already married and pregnant. She could not keep anything on her stomach. Every morning Mrs. Freeman told Mrs. Hopewell how many times she had vomited since the last report.

Mrs. Hopewell liked to tell people that Glynese and Carramae were two of the finest girls she knew and that Mrs. Freeman was a *lady* and that she was never ashamed to take her anywhere or introduce her to anybody they might meet. Then she would tell how she had happened to hire the Freemans in the first place and how they were a godsend to her and how she had had them four years. The reason for her keeping them so long was that they were not trash. They were good country people. She had telephoned the man whose name

1. From *A Good Man Is Hard to Find* (1955).

they had given as a reference and he had told her that Mr. Freeman was a good farmer but that his wife was the nosiest woman ever to walk the earth. "She's got to be into everything," the man said. "If she don't get there before the dust settles, you can bet she's dead, that's all. She'll want to know all your business. I can stand him real good," he had said, "but me nor my wife neither could have stood that woman one more minute on this place." That had put Mrs. Hopewell off for a few days.

She had hired them in the end because there were no other applicants but she had made up her mind beforehand exactly how she would handle the woman. Since she was the type who had to be into everything, then, Mrs. Hopewell had decided, she would not only let her be into everything, she would *see to it* that she was into everything—she would give her the responsibility of everything, she would put her in charge. Mrs. Hopewell had no bad qualities of her own but she was able to use other people's in such a constructive way that she never felt the lack. She had hired the Freemans and she had kept them four years.

Nothing is perfect. This was one of Mrs. Hopewell's favorite sayings. Another was: that is life! And still another, the most important, was: well, other people have their opinions too. She would make these statements, usually at the table, in a tone of gentle insistence as if no one held them but her, and the large hulking Joy, whose constant outrage had obliterated every expression from her face, would stare just a little to the side of her, her eyes icy blue, with the look of someone who has achieved blindness by an act of will and means to keep it.

When Mrs. Hopewell said to Mrs. Freeman that life was like that, Mrs. Freeman would say, "I always said so myself." Nothing had been arrived at by anyone that had not first been arrived at by her. She was quicker than Mr. Freeman. When Mrs. Hopewell said to her after they had been on the place a while, "You know, you're the wheel behind the wheel," and winked, Mrs. Freeman had said, "I know it. I've always been quick. It's some that are quicker than others."

"Everybody is different," Mrs. Hopewell said.

"Yes, most people is," Mrs. Freeman said.

"It takes all kinds to make the world."

"I always said it did myself."

The girl was used to this kind of dialogue for breakfast and more of it for dinner; sometimes they had it for supper too. When they had no guest they ate in the kitchen because that was easier. Mrs. Freeman always managed to arrive at some point during the meal and to watch them finish it. She would stand in the doorway if it were summer but in the winter she would stand with one elbow on top of the refrigerator and look down on them, or she would stand by the gas heater, lifting the back of her skirt slightly. Occasionally she would stand against the wall and roll her head from side to side. At no time was she in any hurry to leave. All this was very trying on Mrs. Hopewell but she was a woman of great patience. She realized that nothing is perfect and that in the Freemans she had good country people and that if, in this day and age, you get good country people, you had better hang onto them.

She had had plenty of experience with trash. Before the Freemans she had averaged one tenant family a year. The wives of these farmers were not the kind you would want to be around you for very long. Mrs. Hopewell, who had divorced her husband long ago, needed someone to walk over the fields with her; and when Joy had to be impressed for these services, her remarks were usually so ugly and her face so glum that Mrs. Hopewell would say, "If you can't come pleasantly, I don't want you at all," to which the girl, standing square and rigid-shouldered with her neck thrust slightly forward, would reply, "If you want me, here I am—LIKE I AM."

Mrs. Hopewell excused this attitude because of the leg (which had been shot off in a hunting accident when Joy was ten). It was hard for Mrs. Hopewell to realize that her child was thirty-two now and that for more than twenty years she had had only one leg. She thought of her still as a child because it tore her heart to think instead of the poor stout girl in her thirties who had never danced a step or had any *normal* good times. Her name was really Joy but as soon as she was twenty-one and away from home, she had had it legally changed. Mrs. Hopewell was certain that she had thought and thought until she had hit upon the ugliest name in any language. Then she had gone and had the beautiful name, Joy, changed without telling her mother until after she had done it. Her legal name was Hulga.

When Mrs. Hopewell thought the name, Hulga, she thought of the broad blank hull of a battleship. She would not use it. She continued to call her Joy to which the girl responded but in a purely mechanical way.

Hulga had learned to tolerate Mrs. Freeman who saved her from taking walks with her mother. Even Glynese and Carramae were useful when they occupied attention that might otherwise have been directed at her. At first she had thought she could not stand Mrs. Freeman for she had found that it was not possible to be rude to her. Mrs. Freeman would take on strange resentments and for days together she would be sullen but the source of her displeasure was always obscure; a direct attack, a positive leer, blatant ugliness to her face—these never touched her. And without warning one day, she began calling her Hulga.

She did not call her that in front of Mrs. Hopewell who would have been incensed but when she and the girl happened to be out of the house together, she would say something and add the name Hulga to the end of it, and the big spectacled Joy-Hulga would scowl and redden as if her privacy had been intruded upon. She considered the name her personal affair. She had arrived at it first purely on the basis of its ugly sound and then the full genius of its fitness had struck her. She had a vision of the name working like the ugly sweating Vulcan who stayed in the furnace and to whom, presumably, the goddess had to come when called.[2] She saw it as the name of her highest creative act. One of her major triumphs was that her mother had not been able to turn her dust into Joy, but the greater one was that she had been able to turn it herself into Hulga. However, Mrs. Freeman's relish for using the name only irritated her. It was as if Mrs. Freeman's beady steel-pointed eyes had penetrated far enough behind her face to reach some secret fact. Something about her seemed to fascinate Mrs. Freeman and then one day Hulga realized that it was the artificial leg. Mrs. Freeman had a special fondness for the details of secret infections, hidden deformities, assaults upon children. Of diseases, she preferred the lingering or incurable. Hulga had heard Mrs. Hopewell give her the details of the hunting accident, how the leg had been literally

---

2. Vulcan was the Greek god of fire whom Venus, goddess of love, "presumably" obeyed as her consort.

blasted off, how she had never lost consciousness. Mrs. Freeman could listen to it any time as if it had happened an hour ago.

When Hulga stumped into the kitchen in the morning (she could walk without making the awful noise but she made it—Mrs. Hopewell was certain—because it was ugly-sounding), she glanced at them and did not speak. Mrs. Hopewell would be in her red kimono with her hair tied around her head in rags. She would be sitting at the table, finishing her breakfast and Mrs. Freeman would be hanging by her elbow outward from the refrigerator, looking down at the table. Hulga always put her eggs on the stove to boil and then stood over them with her arms folded, and Mrs. Hopewell would look at her— a kind of indirect gaze divided between her and Mrs. Freeman—and would think that if she would only keep herself up a little, she wouldn't be so bad looking. There was nothing wrong with her face that a pleasant expression wouldn't help. Mrs. Hopewell said that people who looked on the bright side of things would be beautiful even if they were not.

Whenever she looked at Joy this way, she could not help but feel that it would have been better if the child had not taken the Ph.D. It had certainly not brought her out any and now that she had it, there was no more excuse for her to go to school again. Mrs. Hopewell thought it was nice for girls to go to school to have a good time but Joy had "gone through." Anyhow, she would not have been strong enough to go again. The doctors had told Mrs. Hopewell that with the best of care, Joy might see forty-five. She had a weak heart. Joy had made it plain that if it had not been for this condition, she would be far from these red hills and good country people. She would be in a university lecturing to people who knew what she was talking about. And Mrs. Hopewell could very well picture her there, looking like a scarecrow and lecturing to more of the same. Here she went about all day in a six-year-old skirt and a yellow sweat shirt with a faded cowboy on a horse embossed on it. She thought this was funny; Mrs. Hopewell thought it was idiotic and showed simply that she was still a child. She was brilliant but she didn't have a grain of sense. It seemed to Mrs. Hopewell that every year she grew less like other people and more like herself—bloated, rude, and squint-eyed. And she said such strange things! To her own mother she had said—without warning, without excuse, standing up in the middle of a meal with her face purple and her mouth half full—"Woman! do you ever look inside? Do you ever look inside and see what you are *not*? God!" she had cried sinking down again and staring at her plate, "Malebranche[3] was right: we are not our own light. We are not our own light!" Mrs. Hopewell had no idea to this day what brought that on. She had only made the remark, hoping Joy would take it in, that a smile never hurt anyone.

The girl had taken the Ph.D. in philosophy and this left Mrs. Hopewell at a complete loss. You could say, "My daughter is a nurse," or "My daughter is a school teacher," or even, "My daughter is a chemical engineer." You could not say, "My daughter is a philosopher." That was something that had ended with the Greeks and Romans. All day Joy sat on her neck in a deep chair, reading. Sometimes she went for walks but she didn't like dogs or cats or birds or flowers or nature or nice young men. She looked at nice young men as if she could smell their stupidity.

One day Mrs. Hopewell had picked up one of the books the girl had just

3. Nicolas Malebranche, French philosopher (1638–1715).

put down and opening it at random, she read, "Science, on the other hand, has to assert its soberness and seriousness afresh and declare that it is concerned solely with what-is. Nothing—how can it be for science anything but a horror and a phantasm? If science is right, then one thing stands firm: science wishes to know nothing of nothing. Such is after all the strictly scientific approach to Nothing. We know it by wishing to know nothing of Nothing." These words had been underlined with a blue pencil and they worked on Mrs. Hopewell like some evil incantation in gibberish. She shut the book quickly and went out of the room as if she were having a chill.

This morning when the girl came in, Mrs. Freeman was on Carramae. "She thrown up four times after supper," she said, "and was up twict in the night after three o'clock. Yesterday she didn't do nothing but ramble in the bureau drawer. All she did. Stand up there and see what she could run up on."

"She's got to eat," Mrs. Hopewell muttered, sipping her coffee, while she watched Joy's back at the stove. She was wondering what the child had said to the Bible salesman. She could not imagine what kind of a conversation she could possibly have had with him.

He was a tall gaunt hatless youth who had called yesterday to sell them a Bible. He had appeared at the door, carrying a large black suitcase that weighted him so heavily on one side that he had to brace himself against the door facing. He seemed on the point of collapse but he said in a cheerful voice, "Good morning, Mrs. Cedars!" and set the suitcase down on the mat. He was not a bad-looking young man though he had on a bright blue suit and yellow socks that were not pulled up far enough. He had prominent face bones and a streak of sticky-looking brown hair falling across his forehead.

"I'm Mrs. Hopewell," she said.

"Oh!" he said, pretending to look puzzled but with his eyes sparkling, "I saw it said 'The Cedars' on the mailbox so I thought you was Mrs. Cedars!" and he burst out in a pleasant laugh. He picked up the satchel and under cover of a pant, he fell forward into her hall. It was rather as if the suitcase had moved first, jerking him after it. "Mrs. Hopewell!" he said and grabbed her hand. "I hope you are well!" and he laughed again and then all at once his face sobered completely. He paused and gave her a straight earnest look and said, "Lady, I've come to speak of serious things."

"Well, come in," she muttered, none too pleased because her dinner was almost ready. He came into the parlor and sat down on the edge of a straight chair and put the suitcase between his feet and glanced around the room as if he were sizing her up by it. Her silver gleamed on the two sideboards; she decided he had never been in a room as elegant as this.

"Mrs. Hopewell," he began, using her name in a way that sounded almost intimate, "I know you believe in Chrustian service."

"Well yes," she murmured.

"I know," he said and paused, looking very wise with his head cocked on one side, "that you're a good woman. Friends have told me."

Mrs. Hopewell never liked to be taken for a fool. "What are you selling?" she asked.

"Bibles," the young man said and his eye raced around the room before he added, "I see you have no family Bible in your parlor, I see that is the one lack you got!"

Mrs. Hopewell could not say, "My daughter is an atheist and won't let me keep the Bible in the parlor." She said, stiffening slightly, "I keep my Bible by my bedside." This was not the truth. It was in the attic somewhere.

"Lady," he said, "the word of God ought to be in the parlor."

"Well, I think that's a matter of taste," she began. "I think . . ."

"Lady," he said, "for a Chrustian, the word of God ought to be in every room in the house besides in his heart. I know you're a Chrustian because I can see it in every line of your face."

She stood up and said, "Well, young man, I don't want to buy a Bible and I smell my dinner burning."

He didn't get up. He began to twist his hands and looking down at them, he said softly, "Well lady, I'll tell you the truth—not many people want to buy one nowadays and besides, I know I'm real simple. I don't know how to say a thing but to say it. I'm just a country boy." He glanced up into her unfriendly face. "People like you don't like to fool with country people like me!"

"Why!" she cried, "good country people are the salt of the earth! Besides, we all have different ways of doing, it takes all kinds to make the world go 'round. That's life!"

"You said a mouthful," he said.

"Why, I think there aren't enough good country people in the world!" she said, stirred. "I think that's what's wrong with it!"

His face had brightened. "I didn't inraduce myself," he said. "I'm Manley Pointer from out in the country around Willohobie, not even from a place, just from near a place."

"You wait a minute," she said. "I have to see about my dinner." She went out to the kitchen and found Joy standing near the door where she had been listening.

"Get rid of the salt of the earth," she said, "and let's eat."

Mrs. Hopewell gave her a pained look and turned the heat down under the vegetables. "I can't be rude to anybody," she murmured and went back into the parlor.

He had opened the suitcase and was sitting with a Bible on each knee.

"You might as well put those up," she told him. "I don't want one."

"I appreciate your honesty," he said. "You don't see any more real honest people unless you go way out in the country."

"I know," she said, "real genuine folks!" Through the crack in the door she heard a groan.

"I guess a lot of boys come telling you they're working their way through college," he said, "but I'm not going to tell you that. Somehow," he said, "I don't want to go to college. I want to devote my life to Chrustian service. See," he said, lowering his voice, "I got this heart condition. I may not live long. When you know it's something wrong with you and you may not live long, well then, lady . . ." He paused, with his mouth open, and stared at her.

He and Joy had the same condition! She knew that her eyes were filling with tears but she collected herself quickly and murmured, "Won't you stay for dinner? We'd love to have you!" and was sorry the instant she heard herself say it.

"Yes mam," he said in an abashed voice, "I would sher love to do that!"

Joy had given him one look on being introduced to him and then throughout the meal had not glanced at him again. He had addressed several remarks to her, which she had pretended not to hear. Mrs. Hopewell could not understand deliberate rudeness, although she lived with it, and she felt she had always to overflow with hospitality to make up for Joy's lack of courtesy. She urged him to talk about himself and he did. He said he was the seventh child of twelve and that his father had been crushed under a tree when he himself was eight years old. He had been crushed very badly, in fact, almost cut in two and was practically not recognizable. His mother had got along the best she could by hard working and she had always seen that her children went to Sunday School and that they read the Bible every evening. He was now nineteen years old and he had been selling Bibles for four months. In that time he had sold seventy-seven Bibles and had the promise of two more sales. He wanted to become a missionary because he thought that was the way you could do most for people. "He who losest his life shall find it," he said simply and he was so sincere, so genuine and earnest that Mrs. Hopewell would not for the world have smiled. He prevented his peas from sliding onto the table by blocking them with a piece of bread which he later cleaned his plate with. She could see Joy observing sidewise how he handled his knife and fork and she saw too that every few minutes, the boy would dart a keen appraising glance at the girl as if he were trying to attract her attention.

After dinner Joy cleared the dishes off the table and disappeared and Mrs. Hopewell was left to talk with him. He told her again about his childhood and his father's accident and about various things that had happened to him. Every five minutes or so she would stifle a yawn. He sat for two hours until finally she told him she must go because she had an appointment in town. He packed his Bibles and thanked her and prepared to leave, but in the doorway he stopped and wrung her hand and said that not on any of his trips had he met a lady as nice as her and he asked if he could come again. She had said she would always be happy to see him.

Joy had been standing in the road, apparently looking at something in the distance, when he came down the steps toward her, bent to the side with his heavy valise. He stopped where she was standing and confronted her directly. Mrs. Hopewell could not hear what he said but she trembled to think what Joy would say to him. She could see that after a minute Joy said something and that then the boy began to speak again, making an excited gesture with his free hand. After a minute Joy said something else at which the boy began to speak once more. Then to her amazement, Mrs. Hopewell saw the two of them walk off together, toward the gate. Joy had walked all the way to the gate with him and Mrs. Hopewell could not imagine what they had said to each other, and she had not yet dared to ask.

Mrs. Freeman was insisting upon her attention. She had moved from the refrigerator to the heater so that Mrs. Hopewell had to turn and face her in order to seem to be listening. "Glynese gone out with Harvey Hill again last night," she said. "She had this sty."

"Hill," Mrs. Hopewell said absently, "is that the one who works in the garage?"

"Nome, he's the one that goes to chiropracter school," Mrs. Freeman said. "She had this sty. Been had it two days. So she says when he brought her in the other night he says, 'Lemme get rid of that sty for you,' and she says, 'How?' and he says, 'You just lay yourself down acrost the seat of that car and I'll show you.' So she done it and he popped her neck. Kept on a-popping it several times until she made him quit. This morning," Mrs. Freeman said, "she ain't got no sty. She ain't got no traces of a sty."

"I never heard of that before," Mrs. Hopewell said.

"He ast her to marry him before the Ordinary,"[4] Mrs. Freeman went on, "and she told him she wasn't going to be married in no *office*."

"Well, Glynese is a fine girl," Mrs. Hopewell said. "Glynese and Carramae are both fine girls."

"Carramae said when her and Lyman was married Lyman said it sure felt sacred to him. She said he said he wouldn't take five hundred dollars for being married by a preacher."

"How much would he take?" the girl asked from the stove.

"He said he wouldn't take five hundred dollars," Mrs. Freeman repeated.

"Well we all have work to do," Mrs. Hopewell said.

"Lyman said it just felt more sacred to him," Mrs. Freeman said. "The doctor wants Carramae to eat prunes. Says instead of medicine. Says them cramps is coming from pressure. You know where I think it is?"

"She'll be better in a few weeks," Mrs. Hopewell said.

"In the tube," Mrs. Freeman said. "Else she wouldn't be as sick as she is."

Hulga had cracked her two eggs into a saucer and was bringing them to the table along with a cup of coffee that she had filled too full. She sat down carefully and began to eat, meaning to keep Mrs. Freeman there by questions if for any reason she showed an inclination to leave. She could perceive her mother's eye on her. The first round-about question would be about the Bible salesman and she did not wish to bring it on. "How did he pop her neck?" she asked.

Mrs. Freeman went into a description of how he had popped her neck. She said he owned a '55 Mercury but that Glynese said she would rather marry a man with only a '36 Plymouth who would be married by a preacher. The girl asked what if he had a '32 Plymouth and Mrs. Freeman said what Glynese had said was a '36 Plymouth.

Mrs. Hopewell said there were not many girls with Glynese's common sense. She said what she admired in those girls was their common sense. She said that reminded her that they had had a nice visitor yesterday, a young man selling Bibles. "Lord," she said, "he bored me to death but he was so sincere and genuine I couldn't be rude to him. He was just good country people, you know," she said, "—just the salt of the earth."

"I seen him walk up," Mrs. Freeman said, "and then later—I seen him walk off," and Hulga could feel the slight shift in her voice, the slight insinuation, that he had not walked off alone, had he? Her face remained expressionless but the color rose into her neck and she seemed to swallow it down with the next spoonful of egg. Mrs. Freeman was looking at her as if they had a secret together.

"Well, it takes all kinds of people to make the world go 'round," Mrs. Hopewell said. "It's very good we aren't all alike."

"Some people are more alike than others," Mrs. Freeman said.

Hulga got up and stumped, with about twice the noise that was necessary, into her room and locked the door. She was to meet the Bible salesman at ten o'clock at the gate. She had thought about it half the night. She had started thinking of it as a great joke and then she had begun to see profound implications in it. She had lain in bed imagining dialogues for them that were insane on the surface but that reached below to depths that no Bible salesman would

4. Justice of the peace who performs the marriage ceremony in chambers rather than in public.

be aware of. Their conversation yesterday had been of this kind.

He had stopped in front of her and had simply stood there. His face was bony and sweaty and bright, with a little pointed nose in the center of it, and his look was different from what it had been at the dinner table. He was gazing at her with open curiosity, with fascination, like a child watching a new fantastic animal at the zoo, and he was breathing as if he had run a great distance to reach her. His gaze seemed somehow familiar but she could not think where she had been regarded with it before. For almost a minute he didn't say anything. Then on what seemed an insuck of breath, he whispered, "You ever ate a chicken that was two days old?"

The girl looked at him stonily. He might have just put this question up for consideration at the meeting of a philosophical association. "Yes," she presently replied as if she had considered it from all angles.

"It must have been mighty small!" he said triumphantly and shook all over with little nervous giggles, getting very red in the face, and subsiding finally into his gaze of complete admiration, while the girl's expression remained exactly the same.

"How old are you?" he asked softly.

She waited some time before she answered. Then in a flat voice she said, "Seventeen."

His smiles came in succession like waves breaking on the surface of a little lake. "I see you got a wooden leg," he said. "I think you're brave. I think you're real sweet."

The girl stood blank and solid and silent.

"Walk to the gate with me," he said. "You're a brave sweet little thing and I liked you the minute I seen you walk in the door."

Hulga began to move forward.

"What's your name?" he asked, smiling down on the top of her head.

"Hulga," she said.

"Hulga," he murmured, "Hulga. Hulga. I never heard of anybody name Hulga before. You're shy, aren't you, Hulga?" he asked.

She nodded, watching his large red hand on the handle of the giant valise.

"I like girls that wear glasses," he said. "I think a lot. I'm not like these people that a serious thought don't ever enter their heads. It's because I may die."

"I may die too," she said suddenly and looked up at him. His eyes were very small and brown, glittering feverishly.

"Listen," he said, "don't you think some people was meant to meet on account of what all they got in common and all? Like they both think serious thoughts and all?" He shifted the valise to his other hand so that the hand nearest her was free. He caught hold of her elbow and shook it a little. "I don't work on Saturday," he said. "I like to walk in the woods and see what Mother Nature is wearing. O'er the hills and far away. Pic-nics and things. Couldn't we go on a pic-nic tomorrow? Say yes, Hulga," he said and gave her a dying look as if he felt his insides about to drop out of him. He had even seemed to sway slightly toward her.

During the night she had imagined that she seduced him. She imagined that the two of them walked on the place until they came to the storage barn beyond the two back fields and there, she imagined, that things came to such a pass that she very easily seduced him and that then, of course, she had to reckon with his remorse. True genius can get an idea across even to an inferior mind. She imagined that she took his remorse in hand and changed it into a deeper understanding of life. She took all his shame away and turned it into something useful.

She set off for the gate at exactly ten o'clock, escaping without drawing Mrs. Hopewell's attention. She didn't take anything to eat, forgetting that food is usually taken on a picnic. She wore a pair of slacks and a dirty white shirt, and as an afterthought, she had put some Vapex on the collar of it since she did not own any perfume. When she reached the gate no one was there.

She looked up and down the empty highway and had the furious feeling that she had been tricked, that he had only meant to make her walk to the gate after the idea of him. Then suddenly he stood up, very tall, from behind a bush on the opposite embankment. Smiling, he lifted his hat which was new and wide-brimmed. He had not worn it yesterday and she wondered if he had bought it for the occasion. It was toast-colored with a red and white band around it and was slightly too large for him. He stepped from behind the bush still carrying the black valise. He had on the same suit and the same yellow socks sucked down in his shoes from walking. He crossed the highway and said, "I knew you'd come!"

The girl wondered acidly how he had known this. She pointed to the valise and asked, "Why did you bring your Bibles?"

He took her elbow, smiling down on her as if he could not stop. "You can never tell when you'll need the word of God, Hulga," he said. She had a moment in which she doubted that this was actually happening and then they began to climb the embankment. They went down into the pasture toward the woods. The boy walked lightly by her side, bouncing on his toes. The valise did not seem to be heavy today; he even swung it. They crossed half the pasture without saying anything and then, putting his hand easily on the small of her back, he asked softly, "Where does your wooden leg join on?"

She turned an ugly red and glared at him and for an instant the boy looked abashed. "I didn't mean you no harm," he said. "I only meant you're so brave and all. I guess God takes care of you."

"No," she said, looking forward and walking fast, "I don't even believe in God."

At this he stopped and whistled. "No!" he exclaimed as if he were too astonished to say anything else.

She walked on and in a second he was bouncing at her side, fanning with his hat. "That's very unusual for a girl," he remarked, watching her out of the corner of his eye. When they reached the edge of the wood, he put his hand on her back again and drew her against him without a word and kissed her heavily.

The kiss, which had more pressure than feeling behind it, produced that extra surge of adrenalin in the girl that enables one to carry a packed trunk out of a burning house, but in her, the power went at once to the brain. Even before he released her, her mind, clear and detached and ironic anyway, was regarding him from a great distance, with amusement but with pity. She had never been kissed before and she was pleased to discover that it was an unexceptional experience and all a matter of the mind's control. Some people might enjoy drain water if they were told it was vodka. When the boy, looking expectant but uncertain, pushed her gently away, she turned and walked on, saying nothing as if such business, for her, were common enough.

He came along panting at her side, trying to help her when he saw a root that she might trip over. He caught and held back the long swaying blades of thorn vine until she had passed beyond them. She led the way and he came breathing heavily behind her. Then they came out on a sunlit hillside, sloping softly into another one a little smaller. Beyond, they could see the rusted top of the old barn where the extra hay was stored.

The hill was sprinkled with small pink weeds. "Then you ain't saved?" he asked suddenly, stopping.

The girl smiled. It was the first time she had smiled at him at all. "In my economy," she said, "I'm saved and you are damned but I told you I didn't believe in God."

Nothing seemed to destroy the boy's look of admiration. He gazed at her now as if the fantastic animal at the zoo had put its paw through the bars and given him a loving poke. She thought he looked as if he wanted to kiss her again and she walked on before he had the chance.

"Ain't there somewheres we can sit down sometime?" he murmured, his voice softening toward the end of the sentence.

"In that barn," she said.

They made for it rapidly as if it might slide away like a train. It was a large two-story barn, cool and dark inside. The boy pointed up the ladder that led into the loft and said, "It's too bad we can't go up there."

"Why can't we?" she asked.

"Yer leg," he said reverently.

The girl gave him a contemptuous look and putting both hands on the ladder, she climbed it while he stood below, apparently awestruck. She pulled herself expertly through the opening and then looked down at him and said, "Well, come on if you're coming," and he began to climb the ladder, awkwardly bringing the suitcase with him.

"We won't need the Bible," she observed.

"You never can tell," he said, panting. After he had got into the loft, he was a few seconds catching his breath. She had sat down in a pile of straw. A wide sheath of sunlight, filled with dust particles, slanted over her. She lay back against a bale, her face turned away, looking out the front opening of the barn where hay was thrown from a wagon into the loft. The two pink-speckled hillsides lay back against a dark ridge of woods. The sky was cloudless and cold blue. The boy dropped down by her side and put one arm under her and the other over her and began methodically kissing her face, making little noises like a fish. He did not remove his hat but it was pushed far enough back not to interfere. When her glasses got in his way, he took them off of her and slipped them into his pocket.

The girl at first did not return any of the kisses but presently she began to and after she had put several on his cheek, she reached his lips and remained there, kissing him again and again as if she were trying to draw all the breath out of him. His breath was clear and sweet like a child's and the kisses were sticky like a child's. He mumbled about loving her and about knowing when he first seen her that he loved her, but the mumbling was like the sleepy fretting of a child being put to sleep by his mother. Her mind, throughout this, never stopped or lost itself for a second to her feelings. "You ain't said you loved me none," he whispered finally, pulling back from her. "You got to say that."

She looked away from him off into the hollow sky and then down at a black ridge and then down farther into what appeared to be two green swelling lakes. She didn't realize he had taken her glasses but this landscape could not seem exceptional to her for she seldom paid any close attention to her surroundings.

"You got to say it," he repeated. "You got to say you love me."

She was always careful how she committed herself. "In a sense," she began, "if you use the word loosely, you might say that. But it's not a word I use. I don't have illusions. I'm one of those people who see *through* to nothing."

The boy was frowning. "You got to say it. I said it and you got to say it," he said.

The girl looked at him almost tenderly. "You poor baby," she murmured. "It's just as well you don't understand," and she pulled him by the neck, face-down against her. "We are all damned," she said, "but some of us have taken off our blindfolds and see that there's nothing to see. It's a kind of salvation."

The boy's astonished eyes looked blankly through the ends of her hair. "Okay," he almost whined, "but do you love me or don'tcher?"

"Yes," she said and added, "in a sense. But I must tell you something. There mustn't be anything dishonest between us." She lifted his head and looked him in the eye. "I am thirty years old," she said. "I have a number of degrees."

The boy's look was irritated but dogged. "I don't care," he said. "I don't care a thing about what all you done. I just want to know if you love me or don'tcher?" and he caught her to him and wildly planted her face with kisses until she said, "Yes, yes."

"Okay then," he said, letting her go. "Prove it."

She smiled, looking dreamily out on the shifty landscape. She had seduced him without even making up her mind to try. "How?" she asked, feeling that he should be delayed a little.

He leaned over and put his lips to her ear. "Show me where your wooden leg joins on," he whispered.

The girl uttered a sharp little cry and her face instantly drained of color. The obscenity of the suggestion was not what shocked her. As a child she had sometimes been subject to feelings of shame but education had removed the last traces of that as a good surgeon scrapes for cancer; she would no more have felt it over what he was asking than she would have believed in his Bible. But she was as sensitive about the artificial leg as a peacock about his tail. No one ever touched it but her. She took care of it as someone else would his soul, in private and almost with her own eyes turned away. "No," she said.

"I known it," he muttered, sitting up. "You're just playing me for a sucker."

"Oh no no!" she cried. "It joins on at the knee. Only at the knee. Why do you want to see it?"

The boy gave her a long penetrating look. "Because," he said, "it's what makes you different. You ain't like anybody else."

She sat staring at him. There was nothing about her face or her round freezing-blue eyes to indicate that this had moved her; but she felt as if her heart had stopped and left her mind to pump her blood. She decided that for the first time in her life she was face to face with real innocence. This boy, with an instinct that came from beyond wisdom, had touched the truth about her. When after a minute, she said in a hoarse high voice, "All right," it was like surrendering to him completely. It was like losing her own life and finding it again, miraculously, in his.

Very gently he began to roll the slack leg up. The artificial limb, in a white sock and brown flat shoe, was bound in a heavy material like canvas and ended in an ugly jointure where it was attached to the stump. The boy's face and his voice were entirely reverent as he uncovered it and said, "Now show me how to take it off and on."

She took it off for him and put it back on again and then he took it off himself, handling it as tenderly as if it were a real one. "See!" he said with a delighted child's face. "Now I can do it myself!"

"Put it back on," she said. She was thinking that she would run away with him and that every night he would take the leg off and every morning put it back on again. "Put it back on," she said.

"Not yet," he murmured, setting it on its foot out of her reach. "Leave it off for a while. You got me instead."

She gave a cry of alarm but he pushed her down and began to kiss her again. Without the leg she felt entirely dependent on him. Her brain seemed to have stopped thinking altogether and to be about some other function that it was not very good at. Different expressions raced back and forth over her face. Every now and then the boy, his eyes like two steel spikes, would glance behind him where the leg stood. Finally she pushed him off and said, "Put it back on me now."

"Wait," he said. He leaned the other way and pulled the valise toward him and opened it. It had a pale blue spotted lining and there were only two Bibles in it. He took one of these out and opened the cover of it. It was hollow and contained a pocket flask of whiskey, a pack of cards, and a small blue box with printing on it. He laid these out in front of her one at a time in an evenly-spaced row, like one presenting offerings at the shrine of a goddess. He put the blue box in her hand. THIS PRODUCT TO BE USED ONLY FOR THE PREVENTION OF DISEASE, she read, and dropped it. The boy was unscrewing the top of the flask. He stopped and pointed, with a smile, to the deck of cards. It was not an ordinary deck but one with an obscene picture on the back of each card. "Take a swig," he said, offering her the bottle first. He held it in front of her, but like one mesmerized, she did not move.

Her voice when she spoke had an almost pleading sound. "Aren't you," she murmured, "aren't you just good country people?"

The boy cocked his head. He looked as if he were just beginning to understand that she might be trying to insult him. "Yeah," he said, curling his lip slightly, "but it ain't held me back none. I'm as good as you any day in the week."

"Give me my leg," she said.

He pushed it farther away with his foot. "Come on now, let's begin to have us a good time," he said coaxingly. "We ain't got to know one another good yet."

"Give me my leg!" she screamed and tried to lunge for it but he pushed her down easily.

"What's the matter with you all of a sudden?" he asked, frowning as he screwed the top on the flask and put it quickly back inside the Bible. "You just a while ago said you didn't believe in nothing. I thought you was some girl!"

Her face was almost purple. "You're a Christian!" she hissed. "You're a fine Christian! You're just like them all—say one thing and do another. You're a perfect Christian, you're . . ."

The boy's mouth was set angrily. "I hope you don't think," he said in a lofty indignant tone, "that I believe in that crap! I may sell Bibles but I know which end is up and I wasn't born yesterday and I know where I'm going!"

"Give me my leg!" she screeched. He jumped up so quickly that she barely saw him sweep the cards and the blue box into the Bible and throw the Bible into the valise. She saw him grab the leg and then she saw it for an instant slanted forlornly across the inside of the suitcase with a Bible at either side of its opposite ends. He slammed the lid shut and snatched up the valise and swung it down the hole and then stepped through himself.

When all of him had passed but his head, he turned and regarded her with a look that no longer had any admiration in it. "I've gotten a lot of interesting things," he said. "One time I got a woman's glass eye this way. And you needn't to think you'll catch me because Pointer ain't really my name. I use a different name at every house I call at and don't stay nowhere long. And I'll tell you another thing, Hulga," he said, using the name as if he didn't think much of it, "you ain't so smart. I been believing in nothing ever since I was born!" and then the toast-colored hat disappeared down the hole and the girl was left, sitting on the straw in the dusty sunlight. When she turned her churning face toward the opening, she saw his blue figure struggling successfully over the green speckled lake.

Mrs. Hopewell and Mrs. Freeman, who were in the back pasture, digging up onions, saw him emerge a little later from the woods and head across the meadow toward the highway. "Why, that looks like that nice dull young man that tried to sell me a Bible yesterday," Mrs. Hopewell said, squinting. "He must have been selling them to the Negroes back in there. He was so simple," she said, "but I guess the world would be better off if we were all that simple."

Mrs. Freeman's gaze drove forward and just touched him before he disappeared under the hill. Then she returned her attention to the evil-smelling onion shoot she was lifting from the ground. "Some can't be that simple," she said. "I know I never could."

1955

# JOHN BARTH
## b. 1930

During a prolonged student strike at the State University of New York in Buffalo, John Barth, teaching there at the time, when asked his opinion of the strike answered that it was important but boring. To judge from his fiction, this response also characterizes Barth's attitude toward everyday human affairs. Although gifted with strong representational powers, as demonstrated in his first two novels, he is uninterested in providing carefully rendered imitations of life but does care passionately about the activity of storytelling, of narrative itself—to the extent that a reviewer of one of his most elaborate pieces of fiction (*Chimera*, 1972) called him a "narrative chauvinist pig."

He was born in Cambridge, Maryland, and after a brief time spent at the Juilliard School of Music entered Johns Hopkins University in Baltimore, from which he graduated and where he currently teaches writing. In the first three and the last three months of 1955, Barth accomplished the noteworthy feat of writing his first two novels, books preoccupied with "ultimate" philosophical and moral questions a gifted young man might have asked at Johns Hopkins. The hero of *The Floating Opera* (1956) is such a young man, named Todd Andrews, who plans to kill himself on the day on which the novel is set, and who describes the title thus: "It's a floating opera, friend, chock-full of curiosities, melodrama, spectacle, instruction and entertainment, but it floats willy-nilly on the tide of my vagrant prose." No better description has been made of Barth's work as a whole.

The *Floating Opera* was nominated for the National Book Award and remains compelling for its playful, colloquial speech and for Barth's ability to spin marvelously funny yarns fringed with metaphysical speculation. It is also notable for its intimate feeling for the Maryland coastal region, at moments reminding us of Melville's similarly genial treatment of New England in *Moby-Dick*, our literature's grandest floating opera. Barth's second novel, *The End of the Road* (1958), was to be his last "realistic" one, although it is also filled with narrative games. In the manic monologues and dialectical skirmishes with others, engaged in by its hero Jacob Horner, Barth practices an inventive and amusing questioning of moral and philosophical values. This extremely funny book turns suddenly grim at its conclusion, when Horner is left with nothing but words (he is an evasive teacher of grammar) to deal with the horror of an event beyond them and for which he is in part responsible.

After the rapid composition of these books, Barth ceased to be interested in writing books that were tied even minimally to conventional realistic fiction. In the immensely long and sometimes labored productions that followed—*The Sot-Weed Factor* (1960) and *Giles Goat-Boy* (1966)—he constructed gigantic parody-histories filled with gags, sexual bawdy, and lore of all sorts to dislocate and entertain the reader. Barth is saying in these books, among other things, that fiction is stranger than "fiction," that the reader must understand he is not reading about Life—events that really take place in a world out there—but is instead reading words. So *Giles* is as much "about" itself as a book can be: its comically pedantic and self-footnoting procedure and its strategy of pretending that the Universe is really the University are only two of the devices by which Barth attempts to dazzle and ensnare us.

The selection printed here is taken from a volume (*Lost in the Funhouse*, 1968) subtitled *Fiction for Print, Tape, Live Voice*, and at one point a voice addresses us as follows: "The reader! You, dogged, uninsultable, print-oriented bastard, it's you I'm addressing, who else, from inside this monstrous fiction." *Life-Story* is one of Barth's most extreme attempts to confuse the realms of art and life, imagination and reality—but Barth did not stop there. With *Chimera* he exercised his disruptively playful imagination on three ancient myths, of which the Scheherazade story is most memorable. He then spent seven years writing probably his most complicated and (excepting *The Sot-Weed Factor*) his longest book. *Letters* (1979) is an epistolary novel, or parody of an epistolary novel, consisting of exchanges of letters between a number of characters, some of whom appeared in earlier novels of Barth. The self-reflexive tendency in his work is carried to ingenious lengths in his most recent novels, *Sabbatical* (1982), *The Tidewater Tales* (1987), and *The Last Voyage of Somebody the Sailor* (1991), all of them firmly located in the waters of coastal Maryland but reaching out to realms of legend and myth. Like his earlier books, they are animated by the spirit of good-humored, restless experimentation that has characterized and will continue to characterize his art.

# Life-Story[1]

## 1

Without discarding what he'd already written he began his story afresh in a somewhat different manner. Whereas his earlier version had opened in a straight-forward documentary fashion and then degenerated or at least modulated intentionally into irrealism and dissonance he decided this time to tell his tale from start to finish in a conservative, "realistic," unself-conscious way. He being by vocation an author of novels and stories it was perhaps inevitable that one afternoon the possibility would occur to the writer of these lines that his own life might be a fiction, in which he was the leading or an accessory char- acter. He happened at the time[2] to be in his study attempting to draft the opening pages of a new short story; its general idea had preoccupied him for some months along with other general ideas, but certain elements of the conceit, without which he could scarcely proceed, remained unclear. More specifically: narrative plots may be imagined as consisting of a "ground-situation" (Scheherazade desires not to die) focused and dramatized by a "vehicle-situation" (Scheherazade beguiles the King with endless stories), the several incidents of which have their final value in terms of their bearing upon the "ground-situation." In our author's case it was the "vehicle" that had vouch-safed itself, first as a germinal proposition in his commonplace book—D comes to suspect that the world is a novel, himself a fictional personage—subsequently as an articulated conceit explored over several pages of the workbook in which he elaborated more systematically his casual inspirations: since D is writing a fictional account of this conviction he has indisputably a fictional existence in his account, replicating what he suspects to be his own situation. Moreover E, hero of D's account, is said to be writing a similar account, and so the replication is in both ontological directions, et cetera. But the "ground-situation"—some state of affairs on D's part which would give dramatic resonance to his attempts to prove himself factual, assuming he made such attempts obstinately withheld itself from his imagination. As is commonly the case the question reduced to one of stakes: what were to be the consequences of D's—and finally E's—disproving or verifying his suspicion, and why should a reader be interested?

What a dreary way to begin a story he said to himself upon reviewing his long introduction. Not only is there no "ground-situation," but the prose style is heavy and somewhat old-fashioned, like an English translation of Thomas Mann,[3] and the so-called "vehicle" itself is at least questionable: self-conscious, vertiginously arch, fashionably solipsistic, unoriginal—in fact a convention of twentieth-century literature. Another story about a writer writing a story! Another regressus in infinitum! Who doesn't prefer art that at least overtly imitates something other than its own processes? That doesn't continually proclaim "Don't forget I'm an artifice!"? That takes for granted its mimetic nature instead of asserting it in order (not so slyly after all) to deny it, or vice-versa? Though his critics sympathetic and otherwise described his own work as avant-garde, in his heart of hearts he disliked literature of an experimental,

---

1. From Lost in the Funhouse: Fiction for Print, Tape, Live Voice (1968).
2. "9:00 A.M., Monday, June 20, 1966" [Barth's note].

3. German novelist (1875–1955), author of The Magic Mountain and others.

self-despising, or overtly metaphysical character, like Samuel Beckett's, Marian Cutler's, Jorge Borges's.[4] The logical fantasies of Lewis Carroll pleased
him less than straight-forward tales of adventure, subtly sentimental romances,
even densely circumstantial realisms like Tolstoy's. His favorite contemporary
authors were John Updike, Georges Simenon, Nicole Riboud.[5] He had no
use for the theater of absurdity, for "black humor," for allegory in any form,
for apocalyptic preachments meretriciously tricked out in dramatic garb.

Neither had his wife and adolescent daughters, who for that matter preferred
life to literature and read fiction when at all for entertainment. Their kind of
story (his too, finally) would begin if not once upon a time at least with
arresting circumstance, bold character, trenchant action. C flung away the
whining manuscript and pushed impatiently through the french doors leading
to the terrace from his oak-wainscoted study. Pausing at the stone balustrade
to light his briar he remarked through a lavender cascade of wisteria that lithe-
limbed Gloria, Gloria of timorous eye and militant breast, had once again
chosen his boat-wharf as her basking-place.

By Jove he exclaimed to himself. It's particularly disquieting to suspect not
only that one is a fictional charcter but that the fiction one's in—the fiction
one is—is quite the sort one least prefers. His wife entered the study with
coffee and an apple-pastry, set them at his elbow on his work table, returned
to the living room. Ed' pelut' kondo nedode; nyoing nyang.[6] One manifestation of schizophrenia as everyone knows is the movement from reality toward
fantasy, a progress which not infrequently takes the form of distorted and fragmented representation, abstract formalism, an increasing preoccupation, even
obsession, with pattern and design for their own sakes—especially patterns of
a baroque, enormously detailed character—to the (virtual) exclusion of representative "content." There are other manifestations. Ironically, in the case of
graphic and plastic artists for example the work produced in the advanced
stages of their affliction may be more powerful and interesting than the realistic
productions of their earlier "sanity." Whether the artists themselves are gratified by this possibility is not reported.

B called upon a literary acquaintance, B_____, summering with Mrs. B and
children on the Eastern Shore of Maryland. "You say you lack a ground-
situation. Has it occurred to you that that circumstance may be your ground-
situation? What occurs to me is that if it is it isn't. And conversely. The case
being thus, what's really wanting after all is a well-articulated vehicle, a foreground or upstage situation to dramatize the narrator's or author's grundlage.
His what. To write merely C comes to suspect that the world is a novel, himself a fictional personage is but to introduce the vehicle; the next step must be
to initiate its uphill motion by establishing and complicating some conflict. I
would advise in addition the eschewal of overt and self-conscious discussion of
the narrative process. The via negativa and its positive counterpart are it is to
be remembered poles after all of the same cell. Returning to his study.

If I'm going to be a fictional character G declared to himself I want to be in
a rousing good yarn as they say, not some piece of avant-garde preciousness. I
want passion and bravura action in my plot, heroes I can admire, heroines I
can love, memorable speeches, colorful accessory characters, poetical lan-

4. Samuel Beckett (1906–1989), Irish writer, dramatist, poet. Marian Cutler, one of Barth's invented authors. Jorge Luis Borges (1899–1986), Argentinian
short-story writer.

5. Georges Simenon (1903–1989), Belgian-Swiss
writer of detective novels. Nicole Riboud, another of
Barth's invented authors.
6. Nonsense words.

guage. It doesn't matter to me how naively linear the anecdote is; never mind modernity! How reactionary J appears to be. How will such nonsense sound thirty-six years from now?[7] As if. If he can only get K through his story I reflected grimly; if he can only retain his self-possession to the end of this sentence; not go mad; not destroy himself and/or others. Then what I wondered grimly. Another sentence fast, another story. Scheherazade my only love! All those nights you kept your secret from the King my rival, that after your defloration he was unnecessary, you'd have killed yourself in any case when your invention failed.

Why could he not begin his story afresh X wondered, for example with the words why could he not begin his story afresh et cetera? Y's wife came into the study as he was about to throw out the baby with the bathwater. "Not for an instant to throw out the baby while every instant discarding the bathwater is perhaps a chief task of civilized people at this hour of the world.[8] I used to tell B____ that without success. What makes you so sure it's not a film he's in or a theater-piece?

Because U responded while he certainly felt rather often that he was merely acting his own role or roles he had no idea who the actor was, whereas even the most Stanislavsky-methodist would presumably if questioned closely recollect his offstage identity even onstage in mid-act. Moreover a great part of T's "drama," most of his life in fact, was non-visual, consisting entirely in introspection, which the visual dramatic media couldn't manage easily. He had for example mentioned to no one his growing conviction that he was a fictional character, and since he was not given to audible soliloquizing a "spectator" would take him for a cheerful, conventional fellow, little suspecting that et cetera. It was of course imaginable that much goes on in the mind of King Oedipus in addition to his spoken sentiments; any number of interior dramas might be being played out in the actors' or characters' minds, dramas of which the audience is as unaware as are V's wife and friends of his growing conviction that he's a fictional character. But everything suggested that the medium of his life was prose fiction—moreover a fiction narrated from either the first-person or the third-person-omniscient point of view.

Why is it L wondered with mild disgust that both K and M for example choose to write such stuff when life is so sweet and painful and full of such a variety of people, places, situations, and activities other than self-conscious and after all rather blank introspection? Why is it N wondered et cetera that both M and O et cetera when the world is in such parlous explosive case? Why et cetera et cetera et cetera when the word, which was in the beginning, is now evidently nearing the end of its road? Am I being strung out in this ad libitum fashion I wondered merely to keep my author from the pistol? What sort of story is it whose drama lies always in the next frame out? If Sinbad sinks it's Scheherazade who drowns; whose neck one wonders is on her line?

2

Discarding what he'd already written as he could wish to discard the mumbling pages of his life he began his story afresh, resolved this time to eschew overt and self-conscous discussion of his narrative process and to recount

7. "10:00 A.M., Monday, June 20, 1966" [Barth's note].    8. "11:00 A.M., Monday, June 20, 1966" [Barth's note].

instead in the straight-forwardest manner possible the several complications of his character's conviction that he was a character in a work of fiction, arranging them into dramatically ascending stages if he could for his readers' sake and leading them (the stages) to an exciting climax and dénouement if he could.

He rather suspected that the medium and genre in which he worked—the only ones for which he felt any vocation—were moribund if not already dead. The idea pleased him. One of the successfullest men he knew was a blacksmith of the old school who et cetera. He meditated upon the grandest sailing-vessel ever built, the *France II*, constructed in Bordeaux in 1911 not only when but because the age of sail had passed. Other phenomena that consoled and inspired him were the great flying-boat *Hercules*, the zeppelin *Hindenburg*, the *Tsar Psuhka* cannon, the then-record Dow-Jones industrial average of 381.17 attained on September 3, 1929.

He rather suspected that the society in which he persisted—the only one with which he felt any degree of identification—was moribund if not et cetera. He knew beyond any doubt that the body which he inhabited—the only one et cetera—was et cetera. The idea et cetera. He had for thirty-six years lacking a few hours been one of our dustmote's three billion tenants give or take five hundred million, and happening to be as well a white male citizen of the United States of America he had thirty-six years plus a few hours more to cope with one way or another unless the actuarial tables were mistaken, not bloody likely, or his term was unexpectedly reduced.

Had he written for his readers' sake? The phrase implied a thitherto-unappreciated metaphysical dimension. Suspense. If his life was a fictional narrative it consisted of three terms—teller, tale, told—each dependent on the other two but not in the same ways. His author could as well tell some other character's tale or some other tale of the same character as the one being told as he himself could in his own character as author; his "reader" could as easily read some other story, would be well advised to; but his own "life" depended absolutely on a particular author's original persistence, thereafter upon some reader's. From this consideration any number of things followed, some less tiresome than others. No use appealing to his author, of whom he'd come to dislike even to think. The idea of his playing with his characters' and his own self-consciousness! He himself tended in that direction and despised the tendency. The idea of his or her smiling smugly to himself as the "words" flowed from his "pen" in which his the protagonist's unhappy inner life was exposed! Ah he had mistaken the nature of his narrative; he had thought it very long, longer than Proust's, longer than any German's, longer than *The Thousand Nights and a Night* in ten quarto volumes. Moreover he'd thought it the most prolix and pedestrian *tranche-de-vie* realism, unredeemed by even the limited virtues of colorful squalor, solid specification, an engaging variety of scenes and characters—in a word a bore, of the sort he himself not only would not write but would not read either. Now he understood that his author might as probably resemble himself and the protagonist of his own story-in-progress. Like himself, like his character aforementioned, his author not impossibly deplored the obsolescence of humanism, the passing of *savoir-vivre*, et cetera; admired the outmoded values of fidelity, courage, tact, restraint, amiability, self-discipline, et cetera; preferred fictions in which were to be found stirring actions, characters to love as well as ditto to despise, speeches and deeds to affect us strongly, et cetera. He too might wish to make some final effort to put by his fictional character and achieve factuality or at least to figure in if not be hero of a more attractive fiction, but be caught like the writer of these lines in some more or less desperate tour de force. For him to attempt to come to an understanding with such an author were as futile as for one of his own creations to et cetera.

But the reader! Even if his author were his only reader as was he himself of his work-in-progress as of the sentence-in-progress and his protagonist of his, et cetera, his character as reader was not the same as his character as author, a fact which might be turned to account. What suspense.

As he prepared to explore this possibility one of his mistresses whereof he had none entered his brown study unannounced. "The passion of love," she announced, "which I regard as no less essential to a satisfying life than those values itemized above and which I infer from my presence here that you too esteem highly, does not in fact play in your life a role of sufficient importance to sustain my presence here. It plays in fact little role at all outside your imaginative and/or ary life. I tell you this not in a criticizing spirit, for I judge you to be as capable of the sentiment aforementioned as any other imagin[ative], deep-feeling man in good physical health more or less precisely in the middle of the road of our life. What hampers, even cripples you in this regard is your final preference, which I refrain from analyzing, for the sedater, more responsible pleasures of monogamous fidelity and the serener affections of domesticity, notwithstanding the fact that your enjoyment of these is correspondingly inhibited though not altogether spoiled by an essentially romantical, unstable, irresponsible, death-wishing fancy. V. S. Pritchett,[9] English critic and author, will put the matter succinctly in a soon-to-be-written essay on Flaubert, whose work he'll say depicts the course of ardent longings and violent desires that rise from the horrible, the sensual, and the sadistic. They turn into the virginal and mystical, only to become numb by satiety. At this point pathological boredom leads to a final desire for death and nothingness—the Romantic syndrome. If, not to be unfair, we qualify somewhat the terms horrible and sadistic and understand satiety to include a large measure of vicariousness, this description undeniably applies to one aspect of yourself and your work; and while your ditto has other, even contrary aspects, the net fact is that you have elected familial responsibilities and rewards—indeed, straight-laced middle-classness in general—over the higher expenses of spirit and wastes of shame attendant upon a less regular, more glamorous style of life. So to elect is surely admirable for the layman, even essential if the social fabric, without which there can be no culture, is to be preserved. For the artist, however, and in particular the writer, whose traditional material has been the passions of men and women, the choice is fatal. You have made it I bid you goodnight probably forever."

Even as she left he reached for the sleeping pills cached conveniently in his writing desk and was restrained from their administration only by his being in the process of completing a sentence, which he cravenly strung out at some sacrifice of rhetorical effect upon realizing that he was et cetera. Moreover he added hastily he had not described the intruder for his readers' vicarious satiety: a lovely woman she was, whom he did not after all describe for his readers' et cetera inasmuch as her appearance and character were inconstant. Her inter-

---

9. English literary critic and autobiographer (b. 1900).

ruption of his work inspired a few sentences about the extent to which his fiction inevitably made public his private life, though the trespasses in this particular were as nothing beside those of most of his profession. That is to say, while he did not draw his characters and situations directly from life nor permit his author-protagonist to do so, any moderately attentive reader of his oeuvre, his what, could infer for example that its author feared for example schizophrenia, impotence creative and sexual, suicide—in short living and dying. His fictions were preoccupied with these fears among their other, more serious preoccupations. Hot dog. As of the sentence-in-progress he was not in fact unmanageably schizophrenic, impotent in either respect, or dead by his own hand, but there was always the next sentence to worry about. But there was always the next sentence to worry about. In sum he concluded hastily such limited self-exposure did not constitute a misdemeanor, representing or mis as it did so small an aspect of his total self, negligible a portion of his total life—even which totalities were they made public would be found remarkable only for their being so unremarkable. Well shall he continue.

Bearing in mind that he had not developed what he'd mentioned earlier about turning to advantage his situation vis-à-vis his "reader" (in fact he deliberately now postponed his return to that subject, sensing that it might well constitute the climax of his story) he elaborated one or two ancillary questions, perfectly aware that he was trying, even exhausting, whatever patience might remain to whatever readers might remain to whoever elaborated yet another ancillary question. Was the novel of his life for example a *roman à clef?*[1] Of that genre he was as contemptuous as of the others aforementioned; but while in the introductory adverbial clause it seemed obvious to him that he didn't "stand for" anyone else, any more than he was an actor playing the role of himself, by the time he reached the main clause he had to admit that the question was unanswerable, since the "real"man to whom he'd correspond in a *roman à clef* would not be also in the *roman à clef* and the characters in such works were not themselves aware of their irritating correspondences.

Similarly unanswerable were such questions as when "his" story (so he regarded it for convenience and consolement though for all he knew he might be not the central character; it might be his wife's story, one of his daughters's, his imaginary mistress's, the man-who-once-cleaned-his-chimney's) began. Not impossibly at his birth or even generations earlier: a *Bildungsroman*, an *Erziehungsroman*, a *roman fleuve!*[2] More likely at the moment he became convinced of his fictional nature: that's where he'd have begun it, as he'd begun the piece currently under his pen. If so it followed that the years of his childhood and younger manhood weren't "real," he'd suspected as much, in the first-order sense, but a mere "background" consisting of a few well-placed expositiory insinuations, perhaps misleading, or inferences, perhaps unwarranted, from strategic hints in his present reflections. God so to speak spare his readers from heavy-footed forced expositions of the sort that begin in the countryside near _____ in May of the year _____ it occurred to the novelist _____ that his own life might be a _____, in which he was the leading or an accessory character. He happened at the time to be in the oak-wainscoted study of the old family summer residence; through a lavender cascade of hyste-

---

1. Novel about "real" persons and "actual" events.
2. *Bildungsroman*: novel about education and development of its hero. *Erziehungsroman*: novel with a thesis. *Roman fleuve*: extended chronicle novel about related people.

ria he observed that his wife had once again chosen to be the subject of this clause, itself the direct object of his observation. A lovely woman she was, whom he did not describe in keeping with his policy against drawing characters from life as who should draw a condemnee to the gallows. Begging his pardon. Flinging his tiresome tale away he pushed impatiently through the french windows leading from his study to a sheer drop from the then-record high into a nearly fatal depression.

He clung onto his narrative depressed by the disproportion of its ratiocination to its dramatization, reflection to action. One had heard *Hamlet* criticized as a collection of soliloquies for which the implausible plot was a mere excuse; witnessed Italian operas whose dramatic portions were no more than interstitial relief and arbitrary continuity between the arias. If it was true that he didn't take his "real" life seriously enough even when it had him by the throat, the fact didn't lead him to consider whether the fact was a cause or a consequence of his tale's tedium or both.

Concluding these reflections he concluded these reflections: that there was at this advancèd page still apparently no ground-situation suggested that his story was dramatically meaningless. If one regarded the absence of a ground-situation, more accurately the protagonist's anguish at that absence and his vain endeavors to supply the defect, as itself a sort of ground-situation, did his life-story thereby take on a kind of meaning? A "dramatic" sort he supposed, though of so sophistical a character as more likely to annoy than to engage.

3

The reader! You, dogged, uninsultable, print-oriented bastard, it's you I'm addressing, who else, from inside this monstrous fiction. You've read me this far, then? Even this far? For what discreditable motive? How is it you don't go to a movie, watch TV, stare at the wall, play tennis with a friend, make amorous advances to the person who comes to your mind when I speak of amorous advances? Can nothing surfeit, saturate you, turn you off? Where's your shame?

Having let go this barrage of rhetorical or at least unanswered questions and observing himself nevertheless in midst of yet another sentence he concluded and caused the "hero" of his story to conclude that one or more of three things must be true: 1) his author was his sole and indefatigable reader; 2) he was in a sense his own author, telling his story to himself, in which case in which case; and/or 3) his reader was not only tireless and shameless but sadistic, masochistic if he was himself.

For why do you suppose—you! you!—he's gone on so, so relentlessly refusing to entertain you as he might have at a less desperate than this hour of the world[3] with felicitous language, exciting situation, unforgettable character and image? Why has he as it were ruthlessly set about not to win you over but to turn you away? Because your own author bless and damn you his life is in your hands! He writes and reads himself; don't you think he knows who gives his creatures their lives and deaths? Do they exist except as he or others read their words? Age except we turn their pages? And can he die until you have no more of him? Time was obviously when his author could have turned the

---

3. "11:00 P.M., Monday, June 20, 1966" [Barth's note].

trick; his pen had once to left-to-right it through these words as does your kindless eye and might have ceased at any one. This. This. And did not as you see but went on like an Oriental torturemaster to the end.

But you needn't! He exclaimed to you. In vain. Had he petitioned you instead to read slowly in the happy parts, what happy parts, swiftly in the painful no doubt you'd have done the contrary or cut him off entirely. But as he longs to die and can't without your help you force him on, force him on. Will you deny you've read this sentence? This? To get away with murder doesn't appeal to you, is that it? As if your hands weren't inky with other dyings! As if he'd know you'd killed him! Come on. He dares you.

In vain. You haven't: the burden of his knowledge. That he continues means that he continues, a fortiori you too. Suicide's impossible: he can't kill himself without your help. Those petitions aforementioned, even his silly plea for death—don't you think he understands their sophistry, having authored their like for the wretches he's authored? Read him fast or slow, intermittently, continuously, repeatedly, backward, not at all, he won't know it; he only guesses someone's reading or composing his sentences, such as this one, because he's reading or composing sentences such as this one; the net effect is that there's a net effect, of continuity aad an apparently consistent flow of time, though his pages do seem to pass more swiftly as they near his end.

To what conclusion will he come? He'd been about to append to his own tale inasmuch as the old analogy between Author and God, novel and world, can no longer be employed unless deliberately as a false analogy, certain things follow: 1) fiction must acknowledge its fictiousness and metaphoric invalidity or 2) choose to ignore the question or deny its relevance or 3) establish some other, acceptable relation between itself, its author, its reader. Just as he finished doing so however his real wife and imaginary mistresses entered his study; "It's a little past midnight" she announced with a smile; "do you know what that means?"

Though she'd come into his story unannounced at a critical moment he did not describe her, for even as he recollected that he'd seen his first light just thirty-six years before the night incumbent he saw his last: that he could not after all be a character in a work of fiction inasmuch as such a fiction would be of an entirely different character from what he thought of as fiction. Fiction consisted of such monuments of the imagination as Cutler's *Morganfield*, Riboud's *Tales Within Tales*, his own creations; fact of such as for example read those fictions. More, he could demonstrate by syllogism that the story of his life was a work of fact: though assaults upon the boundary between life and art, reality and dream, were undeniably a staple of his own and his century's literature as they'd been of Shakespeare's and Cervantes's, yet it was a fact that in the corpus of fiction as far as he knew no fictional character had become convinced as had he that he was a character in a work of fiction. This being the case and he having in fact become thus convinced it followed that his conviction was false. "Happy birthday," and his wife et cetera, kissing him et cetera to obstruct his view of the end of the sentence he was nearing the end of, playfully refusing to be nay-said so that in fact he did at last as did his fictional character end his ending story endless by interruption, cap his pen.

1968

# JOHN UPDIKE

## b. 1932

"To transcribe middleness with all its grits, bumps and anonymities, in its fullness of satisfaction and mystery: is it possible . . . or worth doing?" John Updike's novels and stories give a positive answer to the question he asks in his early memoir, *The Dogwood Tree: A Boyhood*; for he is arguably the most significant transcriber, or creator rather, of "middleness" in American writing since William Dean Howells (about whom he has written appreciatively). Falling in love in high school, meeting a college roommate, going to the eye-doctor or dentist, eating supper on Sunday night, visiting your mother with your wife and son—these activities are made to yield up their possibilities to a writer as responsively curious in imagination and delicately precise in his literary expression as Updike has shown himself to be.

Born in Reading, Pennsylvania, an only child, he grew up in the neighboring small town of Shillington. He was gifted at drawing and caricature, and after graduating summa cum laude from Harvard in 1954, he spent a year studying art in England, then returned to America and went to work for *The New Yorker*, where his first stories appeared and to which he is still a regular contributor. When later in the 1950s he left the magazine, he also left New York City and with his wife and children settled in Ipswich, Massachusetts. There he pursued "his solitary trade as methodically as the dentist practiced his," resisting the temptations of university teaching as successfully as the blandishments of media talk shows. Like Howells, his ample production has been achieved through dedicated, steady work; his books are the fruit of patience, leisure, and craft.

Since 1958 when his first novel, *The Poorhouse Fair*, appeared, Updike has published not only many novels and stories but also six books of poetry, a play, and a vast store of book reviews and other prose writings. He is most admired by some readers as the author of the "Olinger" stories, about life in an imaginary Pennsylvania town that takes on its colors from the real Shillington of his youth. The heroes of these stories are adolescents straining to break out of their fast-perishing environments, as they grow up and as their small town turns into something else. Updike treats them with a blend of affection and ironic humor that is wonderfully assured in its touch, although his sense of place, of growing up during the Depression and the years of World War II, is always vividly present. Like Howells (whose fine memoir of his youthful days in Ohio, *A Boy's Town*, is an ancestor of Updike's *The Dogwood Tree*) he shows how one's spirit takes on its coloration from the material circumstances—houses, clothes, landscape, food, parents—one is bounded by.

This sense of place, which is also a sense of life, is found in the stories and in the novels too, although Updike has found it harder to invent convincing forms in which to tell longer tales. His most ambitious novel is probably *The Centaur* (1964), memorable for its portrayal of three days of confusion and error in the life of an American high school teacher seen through his son's eyes, but the book is also burdened with an elaborate set of mythical trappings that seem less than inevitable. *Couples* (1968), a novel that gained him a good deal of notoriety as a chronicler of sexual relationships, marital and adulterous, is jammed with much interesting early-1960s lore about suburban life but seems uncertain whether it is an exercise in realism or a creative fantasy, as does *Marry Me* (1976).

It is in the four "Rabbit" novels that Updike found his most congenial and engaging subject for longer fiction. In each book he has managed to render the sense of an era—the 1950s in *Rabbit, Run*; the late 1960s in *Rabbit Redux*; the great gasoline crisis of 1979 in *Rabbit Is Rich*; the end of the Reagan era (and the end of

Rabbit) in *Rabbit at Rest* (1990)—through the eyes of a hero who both is and is
not like his creator. Harry "Rabbit" Angstrom, ex–high school basketball star, a
prey to nostalgia and in love with his own past, perpetually lives in a present he
can't abide. *Rabbit, Run* shows him trying to escape from his town, his job, his
wife and child, by a series of disastrously sentimental and humanly irresponsible
actions; yet Updike makes us feel Rabbit's yearnings even as we judge the painful
consequences of yielding to them. Ten years later the fading basketball star has
become a fortyish, dispirited printer with a wayward wife and a country that is both
landing on the moon and falling to pieces. *Rabbit Redux* is masterly in presenting
a small town rotting away from its past certainties; it also attempts to deal with the
Vietnam War and the black revolution. *Rabbit Is Rich* is a more gentle, sadder
chronicling of the hero's settling into grandfatherhood as he draws ever closer to
death; while *Rabbit at Rest*, the longest and richest of the four novels, brings him
to a moving conclusion. In *Roger's Version* (1986) and *S* (1988) Updike has
adopted—or permitted his protagonists to adopt—a more broadly, sometimes a
harsher, satiric view of contemporary religion, computer technology, feminism,
and other forms of "liberation." Still, for all his virtuosity as a novelist, his best
work may be found in the stories and in his short novel *Of the Farm* (1965). In
*Separating* (printed here) the boy from *The Happiest I've Been*, one of the Olinger
stories, has grown up, married, and fathered children and is now about to leave
them as he moves into divorce. It is a beautiful example of Updike's careful, poised
sense of how things work, a sense that can also be observed in the poem *Dog's
Death* and in his memoir *Self-Consciousness* (1989).

Near the end of *The Dogwood Tree* he summarized his boyish dream of becoming an artist:

> He saw art—between drawing and writing he ignorantly made no distinc-
> tion—as a method of riding a thin pencil out of Shillington, out of time
> altogether, into an infinity of unseen and even unborn hearts. He pictured
> this infinity as radiant. How innocent!

Most writers would name that innocence only to deplore it. Updike maintains
instead that, as with the Christian faith he still professes, succeeding years have
given him no better assumptions with which to replace it. In any case, his fine
sense of fact has protected him from fashionable extravagances in black humor and
experimental narratives, while enabling him to be both a satirist and a celebrator
of our social and domestic conditions.

# Separating[1]

The day was fair. Brilliant. All that June the weather had mocked the
Maples' internal misery with solid sunlight—golden shafts and cascades of
green in which their conversations had wormed unseeing, their sad murmuring selves the only stain in Nature. Usually by this time of the year they had
acquired tans; but when they met their elder daughter's plane on her return
from a year in England they were almost as pale as she, though Judith was too
dazzled by the sunny opulent jumble of her native land to notice. They did
not spoil her homecoming by telling her immediately. Wait a few days, let her
recover from jet lag, had been one of their formulations, in that string of gray
dialogues—over coffee, over cocktails, over Cointreau—that had shaped the

---

1. From *The New Yorker*, June 23, 1975.

strategy of their dissolution, while the earth performed its annual stunt of renewal unnoticed beyond their closed windows. Richard had thought to leave at Easter; Joan had insisted they wait until the four children were at last assembled, with all exams passed and ceremonies attended, and the bauble of summer to console them. So he had drudged away, in love, in dread, repairing screens, getting the mowers sharpened, rolling and patching their new tennis court. The court, clay, had come through its first winter pitted and windswept bare of redcoat. Years ago the Maples had observed how often, among their friends, divorce followed a dramatic home improvement, as if the marriage were making one last twitchy effort to live; their own worst crisis had come amid the plaster dust and exposed plumbing of a kitchen renovation. Yet, a summer ago, as canary-yellow bulldozers gaily churned a grassy, daisy-dotted knoll into a muddy plateau, and a crew of pigtailed young men raked and tamped clay into a plane, this transformation did not strike them as ominous, but festive in its impudence; their marriage could rend the earth for fun. The next spring, waking each day at dawn to a sliding sensation as if the bed were being tipped, Richard found the barren tennis court, its net and tapes still rolled in the barn, an environment congruous with his mood of purposeful desolation, and the crumbling of handfuls of clay into cracks and holes (dogs had frolicked on the court in a thaw; rivulets had evolved trenches) an activity suitably elemental and interminable. In his sealed heart he hoped the day would never come.

Now it was here. A Friday. Judith was reacclimated; all four children were assembled, before jobs and camps and visits again scattered them. Joan thought they should be told one by one. Richard was for making an announcement at the table. She said, "I think just making an announcement is a cop-out. They'll start quarrelling and playing to each other instead of focussing. They're each individuals, you know, not just some corporate obstacle to your freedom."

"O.K., O.K. I agree." Joan's plan was exact. That evening, they were giving Judith a belated welcome-home dinner, of lobster and champagne. Then, the party over, they, the two of them, who nineteen years before would push her in a baby carriage along Tenth Street to Washington Square,[2] were to walk her out of the house, to the bridge across the salt creek, and tell her, swearing her to secrecy. Then Richard Jr., who was going directly from work to a rock concert in Boston, would be told, either late when he returned on the train or early Saturday morning before he went off to his job; he was seventeen and employed as one of a golf-course maintenance crew. Then the two younger children, John and Margaret, could, as the morning wore on, be informed.

"Mopped up, as it were," Richard said.

"Do you have any better plan? That leaves you the rest of Saturday to answer any questions, pack, and make your wonderful departure."

"No," he said, meaning he had no better plan, and agreed to hers, though it had an edge of false order, a plea for control in the semblance of its achievement, like Joan's long chore lists and financial accountings and, in the days when he first knew her, her too copious lecture notes. Her plan turned one hurdle for him into four—four knife-sharp walls, each with a sheer blind drop on the other side.

---

2. In Greenwich Village, an area in lower Manhattan, New York City.

All spring he had been morbidly conscious of insides and outsides, of barriers and partitions. He and Joan stood as a thin barrier between the children and the truth. Each moment was a partition, with the past on one side and the future on the other, a future containing this unthinkable *now*. Beyond four knifelike walls a new life for him waited vaguely. His skull cupped a secret, a white face, a face both frightened and soothing, both strange and known, that he wanted to shield from tears, which he felt all about him, solid as the sunlight. So haunted, he had become obsessed with battening down the house against his absence, replacing screens and sash cords, hinges and latches—a Houdini[3] making things snug before his escape.

The lock. He had still to replace a lock on one of the doors of the screened porch. The task, like most such, proved more difficult than he had imagined. The old lock, aluminum frozen by corrosion, had been deliberately rendered obsolete by manufacturers. Three hardware stores had nothing that even approximately matched the mortised hole its removal (surprisingly easy) left. Another hole had to be gouged, with bits too small and saws too big, and the old hole fitted with a block of wood—the chisels dull, the saw rusty, his fingers thick with lack of sleep. The sun poured down, beyond the porch, on a world of neglect. The bushes already needed pruning, the windward side of the house was shedding flakes of paint, rain would get in when he was gone, insects, rot, death. His family, all those he would lose, filtered through the edges of his awareness as he struggled with screw holes, splinters, opaque instructions, minutiae of metal.

Judith sat on the porch, a princess returned from exile. She regaled them with stories of fuel shortages, of bomb scares in the Underground, of Pakistani workmen loudly lusting after her as she walked past on her way to dance school. Joan came and went, in and out of the house, calmer than she should have been, praising his struggles with the lock as if this were one more and not the last of their chain of shared chores. The younger of his sons, John, now at fifteen suddenly, unwittingly handsome, for a few minutes held the rickety screen door while his father clumsily hammered and chiselled, each blow a kind of sob in Richard's ears. His younger daughter, having been at a slumber party, slept on the porch hammock through all the noise—heavy and pink, trusting and forsaken. Time, like the sunlight, continued relentlessly; the sunlight slowly slanted. Today was one of the longest days. The lock clicked, worked. He was through. He had a drink; he drank it on the porch, listening to his daughter. "It was so sweet," she was saying, "during the worst of it, how all the butcher's and bakery shops kept open by candlelight. They're all so plucky and cute. From the papers, things sounded so much worse here—people shooting people in gas lines, and everybody freezing."

Richard asked her, "Do you still want to live in England forever?" *Forever:* the concept, now a reality upon him, pressed and scratched at the back of his throat.

"No," Judith confessed, turning her oval face to him, its eyes still childishly far apart, but the lips set as over something succulent and satisfactory. "I was anxious to come home. I'm an American." She was a woman. They had raised her; he and Joan had endured together to raise her, alone of the four. The

3. Harry Houdini (1874–1926), American magician and escape artist.

others had still some raising left in them. Yet it was the thought of telling Judith—the image of her, their first baby, walking between them arm in arm to the bridge—that broke him. The partition between himself and the tears broke. Richard sat down to the celebratory meal with the back of his throat aching; the champagne, the lobster seemed phases of sunshine; he saw them and tasted them through tears. He blinked, swallowed, croakily joked about hay fever. The tears would not stop leaking through; they came not through a hole that could be plugged but through a permeable spot in a membrane, steadily, purely, endlessly, fruitfully. They became, his tears, a shield for himself against these others—their faces, the fact of their assembly, a last time as innocents, at a table where he sat the last time as head. Tears dropped from his nose as he broke the lobster's back; salt flavored his champagne as he sipped it; the raw clench at the back of his throat was delicious. He could not help himself.

His children tried to ignore his tears. Judith on his right, lit a cigarette, gazed upward in the direction of her too energetic, too sophisticated exhalation; on her other side, John earnestly bent his face to the extraction of the last morsels—legs, tail segments—from the scarlet corpse. Joan, at the opposite end of the table, glanced at him surprised, her reproach displaced by a quick grimace, of forgiveness, or of salute to his superior gift of strategy. Between them, Margaret, no longer called Bean, thirteen and large for her age, gazed from the other side of his pane of tears as if into a shopwindow at something she coveted—at her father, a crystalline heap of splinters and memories. It was not she, however, but John who, in the kitchen, as they cleared the plates and carapaces away, asked Joan the question: "Why is Daddy crying?"

Richard heard the question but not the murmured answer. Then he heard Bean cry, "Oh, no-oh!"—the faintly dramatized exclamation of one who had long expected it.

John returned to the table carrying a bowl of salad. He nodded tersely at his father and his lips shaped the conspiratorial words "She told."

"Told what?" Richard asked aloud, insanely.

The boy sat down as if to rebuke his father's distraction with the example of his own good manners and said quietly, "The separation."

Joan and Margaret returned; the child, in Richard's twisted vision, seemed diminished in size, and relieved, relieved to have had the boogeyman at last proved real. He called out to her—the distances at the table had grown immense—"You knew, you always knew," but the clenching at the back of his throat prevented him from making sense of it. From afar he heard Joan talking, levelly, sensibly, reciting what they had prepared: it was a separation for the summer, an experiment. She and Daddy both agreed it would be good for them; they needed space and time to think; they liked each other but did not make each other happy enough, somehow.

Judith, imitating her mother's factual tone, but in her youth off-key, too cool, said, "I think it's silly. You should either live together or get divorced."

Richard's crying, like a wave that has crested and crashed, had become tumultuous; but it was overtopped by another tumult, for John, who had been so reserved, now grew larger and larger at the table. Perhaps his younger sister's being credited with knowing set him off. "Why didn't you *tell* us?" he asked, in a large round voice quite unlike his own. "You should have *told* us you weren't getting along."

Richard was startled into attempting to force words through his tears. "We *do* get along, that's the trouble, so it doesn't show even to us—" "That we do not love each other" was the rest of the sentence; he couldn't finish it.

Joan finished for him, in her style. "And we've always, *especially*, loved our children."

John was not mollified. "What do you care about *us?*" he boomed. "We're just little things you *had.*" His sisters' laughing forced a laugh from him, which he turned hard and parodistic: "Ha ha *ha.*" Richard and Joan realized simultaneously that the child was drunk, on Judith's homecoming champagne. Feeling bound to keep the center of the stage, John took a cigarette from Judith's pack, poked it into his mouth, let it hang from his lower lip, and squinted like a gangster.

"You're not little things we had," Richard called to him. "You're the whole point. But you're grown. Or almost."

The boy was lighting matches. Instead of holding them to his cigarette (for they had never seen him smoke; being "good" had been his way of setting himself apart), he held them to his mother's face, closer and closer, for her to blow out. Then he lit the whole folder—a hiss and then a torch, held against his mother's face. Prismed by tears, the flame filled Richard's vision; he didn't know how it was extinguished. He heard Margaret say, "Oh stop showing off," and saw John, in response, break the cigarette in two and put the halves entirely into his mouth and chew, sticking out his tongue to display the shreds to his sister.

Joan talked to him, reasoning—a fountain of reason, unintelligible. "Talked about it for years . . . our children must help us . . . Daddy and I both want . . . ." As the boy listened, he carefully wadded a paper napkin into the leaves of his salad, fashioned a ball of paper and lettuce, and popped it into his mouth, looking around the table for the expected laughter. None came. Judith said, "Be mature," and dismissed a plume of smoke.

Richard got up from this stifling table and led the boy outside. Though the house was in twilight, the outdoors still brimmed with light, the long waste light of high summer. Both laughing, he supervised John's spitting out the lettuce and paper and tobacco into the pachysandra.[4] He took him by the hand—a square gritty hand, but for its softness a man's. Yet, it held on. They ran together up into the field, past the tennis court. The raw banking left by the bulldozers was dotted with daisies. Past the court and a flat stretch where they used to play family baseball stood a soft green rise glorious in the sun, each weed and species of grass distinct as illumination on parchment. "I'm sorry, so sorry," Richard cried. "You were the only one who ever tried to help me with all the goddam jobs around this place."

Sobbing, safe within his tears and the champagne, John explained, "It's not just the separation, it's the whole crummy year, I *hate* that school, you can't make any friends, the history teacher's a scud."[5]

They sat on the crest of the rise, shaking and warm from their tears but easier in their voices, and Richard tried to focus on the child's sad year—the weekdays long with homework, the weekends spent in his room with model airplanes, while his parents murmured down below, nursing their separation. How selfish, how blind, Richard thought; his eyes felt scoured. He told his

---

4. Green, leafy plant, frequently used as groundcover.     5. Disagreeable, objectionable person.

son, "We'll think about getting you transferred. Life's too short to be miserable."

They had said what they could, but did not want the moment to heal, and talked on, about the school, about the tennis court, whether it would ever again be as good as it had been that first summer. They walked to inspect it and pressed a few more tapes more firmly down. A little stiltedly, perhaps trying to make too much of the moment, to prolong it, Richard led the boy to the spot in the field where the view was best, of the metallic blue river, the emerald marsh, the scattered islands velvet with shadow in the low light, the white bits of beach far away. "See," he said. "It goes on being beautiful. It'll be here tomorrow."

"I know," John answered, impatiently. The moment had closed.

Back in the house, the others had opened some white wine, the champagne being drunk, and still sat at the table, the three females, gossiping. Where Joan sat had become the head. She turned, showing him a tearless face, and asked, "All right?"

"We're fine," he said, resenting it, though relieved, that the party went on without him.

In bed she explained, "I couldn't cry I guess because I cried so much all spring. It really wasn't fair. It's your idea, and you made it look as though I was kicking you out."

"I'm sorry," he said. "I couldn't stop. I wanted to but couldn't."

"You *didn't* want to. You loved it. You were having your way, making a general announcement."

"I love having it over," he admitted. "God, those kids were great. So brave and funny." John, returned to the house, had settled to a model airplane in his room, and kept shouting down to them, "I'm O.K. No sweat." "And the way," Richard went on, cozy in his relief, "they never questioned the reasons we gave. No thought of a third person. Not even Judith."

"That *was* touching," Joan said.

He gave her a hug. "You were great too. Thank you." Guiltily, he realized he did not feel separated.

"You still have Dickie to do," she told him. These words set before him a black mountain in the darkness; its cold breath, its near weight affected his chest. Of the four children Dickie was most nearly his conscience. Joan did not need to add, "That's one piece of your dirty work I won't do for you."

"I know. I'll do it. You go to sleep."

Within minutes, her breathing slowed, became oblivious and deep. It was quarter to midnight. Dickie's train from the concert would come in at one-fourteen. Richard set the alarm for one. He had slept atrociously for weeks. But whenever he closed his lids some glimpse of the last hours scorched them—Judith exhaling toward the ceiling in a kind of aversion, Bean's mute staring, the sunstruck growth of the field where he and John had rested. The mountain before him moved closer, moved within him; he was huge, momentous. The ache at the back of his throat felt stale. His wife slept as if slain beside him. When, exasperated by his hot lids, his crowded heart, he rose from bed and dressed, she awoke enough to turn over. He told her then, "If I could undo it all, I would."

"Where would you begin?" she asked. There was no place. Giving him courage, she was always giving him courage. He put on shoes without socks in the dark. The children were breathing in their rooms, the downstairs was hollow. In their confusion they had left lights burning. He turned off all but one, the kitchen overhead. The car started. He had hoped it wouldn't. He met only moonlight on the road; it seemed a diaphanous companion, flickering in the leaves along the roadside, haunting his rearview mirror like a pursuer, melting under his headlights. The center of town, not quite deserted, was eerie at this hour. A young cop in uniform kept company with a gang of T-shirted kids on the steps of the bank. Across from the railroad station, several bars kept open. Customers, mostly young, passed in and out of the warm night, savoring summer's novelty. Voices shouted from cars as they passed; an immense conversation seemed in progress. Richard parked and in his weariness put his head on the passenger seat, out of the commotion and wheeling lights. It was as when, in the movies, an assassin grimly carries his mission through the jostle of a carnival—except the movies cannot show the precipitous, palpable slope you cling to within. You cannot climb back down; you can only fall. The synthetic fabric of the car seat, warmed by his cheek, confided to him an ancient, distant scent of vanilla.

A train whistle caused him to lift his head. It was on time; he had hoped it would be late. The slender drawgates descended. The bell of approach tingled happily. The great metal body, horizontally fluted, rocked to a stop, and sleepy teen-agers disembarked, his son among them. Dickie did not show surprise that his father was meeting him at this terrible hour. He sauntered to the car with two friends, both taller than he. He said "Hi" to his father and took the passenger's seat with an exhausted promptness that expressed gratitude. The friends got into the back, and Richard was grateful; a few more minutes' postponement would be won by driving them home.

He asked, "How was the concert?"

"Groovy," one boy said from the back seat.

"It bit," the other said.

"It was O.K.," Dickie said, moderate by nature, so reasonable that in his childhood the unreason of the world had given him headaches, stomach aches, nausea. When the second friend had been dropped off at his dark house, the boy blurted, "Dad, my eyes are killing me with hay fever! I'm out there cutting that mothering grass all day!"

"Do we still have those drops?"

"They didn't do any good last summer."

"They might this." Richard swung a U-turn on the empty street. The drive home took a few minutes. The mountain was here, in his throat. "Richard," he said, and felt the boy, slumped and rubbing his eyes, go tense at his tone, "I didn't come to meet you just to make your life easier. I came because your mother and I have some news for you, and you're a hard man to get ahold of these days. It's sad news."

"That's O.K." The reassurance came out soft, but quick, as if released from the tip of a spring.

Richard had feared that his tears would return and choke him, but the boy's manliness set an example, and his voice issued forth steady and dry. "It's sad news, but it needn't be tragic news, at least for you. It should have no practical effect on your life, though it's bound to have an emotional effect. You'll work at your job, and go back to school in September. Your mother and I are really proud of what you're making of your life; we don't want that to change at all."

"Yeah," the boy said lightly, on the intake of his breath, holding himself up. They turned the corner; the church they went to loomed like a gutted fort. The home of the woman Richard hoped to marry stood across the green. Her bedroom light burned.

"Your mother and I," he said, "have decided to separate. For the summer. Nothing legal, no divorce yet. We want to see how it feels. For some years now, we haven't been doing enough for each other, making each other as happy as we should be. Have you sensed that?"

"No," the boy said. It was an honest, unemotional answer: true or false in a quiz.

Glad for the factual basis, Richard pursued, even garrulously, the details. His apartment across town, his utter accessibility, the split vacation arrangements, the advantages to the children, the added mobility and variety of the summer. Dickie listened, absorbing. "Do the others know?"

Richard described how they had been told.

"How did they take it?"

"The girls pretty calmly. John flipped out; he shouted and ate a cigarette and made a salad out of his napkin and told us how much he hated school."

His brother chuckled. "He did?"

"Yeah. The school issue was more upsetting for him than Mom and me. He seemed to feel better for having exploded."

"He did?" The repetition was the first sign that he was stunned.

"Yes. Dickie, I want to tell you something. This last hour, waiting for your train to get in, has been about the worst of my life. I hate this. *Hate* it. My father would have died before doing it to me." He felt immensely lighter, saying this. He had dumped the mountain on the boy. They were home. Moving swiftly as a shadow, Dickie was out of the car, through the bright kitchen. Richard called after him, "Want a glass of milk or anything?"

"No thanks."

"Want us to call the course tomorrow and say you're too sick to work?"

"No, that's all right." The answer was faint, delivered at the door to his room; Richard listened for the slam of a tantrum. The door closed normally. The sound was sickening.

Joan had sunk into that first deep trough of sleep and was slow to awake. Richard had to repeat, "I told him."

"What did he say?"

"Nothing much. Could you go say good night to him? Please."

She left their room, without putting on a bathrobe. He sluggishly changed back into his pajamas and walked down the hall. Dickie was already in bed, Joan was sitting beside him, and the boy's bedside clock radio was murmuring music. When she stood, an inexplicable light—the moon?—outlined her body through the nightie. Richard sat on the warm place she had indented on the child's narrow mattress. He asked him, "Do you want the radio on like that?"

"It always is."

"Doesn't it keep you awake? It would me."

"No."

"Are you sleepy?"

"Yeah."

"Good. Sure you want to get up and go to work? You've had a big night."

"I want to."

Away at school this winter he had learned for the first time that you can go short of sleep and live. As an infant he had slept with an immobile, sweating intensity that had alarmed his babysitters. As the children aged, he became the first to go to bed, earlier for a time than his younger brother and sister. Even now, he would go slack in the middle of a television show, his sprawled legs hairy and brown. "O.K. Good boy. Dickie, listen. I love you so much, I never knew how much until now. No matter how this works out, I'll always be with you. Really."

Richard bent to kiss an averted face but his son, sinewy, turned and with wet cheeks embraced him and gave him a kiss, on the lips, passionate as a woman's. In his father's ear he moaned one word, the crucial, intelligent word: "Why?"

Why. It was a whistle of wind in a crack, a knife thrust, a window thrown open on emptiness. The white face was gone, the darkness was featureless. Richard had forgotten why.

1975

---

# PHILIP ROTH

## b. 1933

From the moment Philip Roth's collection of stories *Goodbye, Columbus* won the Houghton Mifflin Literary Fellowship for 1959, his career has received the ambiguous reward of much anxious concern, directed at it by critics and centered on whether he would develop the promise displayed in this first book. Ten years later, with *Portnoy's Complaint*, Roth became overnight the famous author of a "dirty" best-seller, yet his success only made his critics more uneasy. Was this gifted portrayer of Jewish middle-class life really more interested in scoring points off caricatures than in creating and exploring characters? Did his very facility with words inhibit the exercise of deeper sympathies and more humanly generous purposes?

Roth grew up in Newark, New Jersey, attended the branch of Rutgers University there, graduated from Bucknell University, took an M.A. in English literature at the University of Chicago, then served in the army. Over the years he has taught at a number of universities while receiving many awards and fellowships. Like John Barth, another "university" writer, Roth is an ironic humorist, although the impulse behind his early stories is darker and less playful. *Goodbye, Columbus* is about Jews on the verge of being or already having been assimilated into the larger American culture, and the stories confidently take the measure of their embattled heroes, as in *The Conversion of the Jews* or *Epstein* or the long title story. *Defender of the Faith* (printed here), arguably the best piece in the collection, is distinguished for the way Roth explores rather than exploits the conflict between personal feelings and religious loyalties as they are felt by Nathan Marx, a U.S. Army sergeant in a Missouri training company near the end of World War II. Throughout *Goodbye, Columbus* the narrator's voice is centrally important: in some stories it is indistinguishable from that of a campus wiseguy; in others it reaches out to a calmer and graver sense of disparities between promises and performance.

Roth's first two novels, *Letting Go* (1962) and *When She Was Good* (1967), markedly extended the territory charted in *Goodbye, Columbus* and showed him eager and equipped to write about people other than Jews. *Letting Go* is conventional in technique and in its subjects—love, marriage, university life—but Roth's easy mastery of the look and feel of places and things is everywhere evident. F. Scott Fitzgerald is the American writer whose presence in these early novels is most strongly felt; in particular, the section from *Letting Go* told in the first person by a graduate student in English betrays its indebtedness to Fitzgerald's Nick Carraway, the narrator of *The Great Gatsby*. This Fitzgeraldian atmosphere, with its nostalgic presentation of adolescence and early romantic visions, is even more evident in *When She Was Good*, which is strong in its rendering of middle-American living rooms and kitchens, the flushed atmosphere of late-night 1950s sex in parked cars, or the lyrics of popular songs—bits of remembered trivia that Roth, like his predecessor, has a genius for bringing to life.

The less-than-overwhelming reception of his second novel probably helped Roth move away from relatively sober realism; certainly *Portnoy's Complaint* (1969) is a louder and more virtuoso performance than the earlier books. Alexander Portnoy's recollections of early childhood miseries are really a pretext for Roth to perform a succession of clever numbers in the inventive mode of a stand-up comic. Memories of growing up in New Jersey, listening to radio programs, playing softball, ogling girls at the ice-skating rink, or (most sensationally) masturbating in outlandish ways add up to an entertaining narrative that is sometimes crude but more often delicate and precise.

After *Portnoy* Roth moved toward fantasy and further showmanly operations: *Our Gang* (1970) attempted to do for Richard Nixon and his associates what actual events were to do one better; *The Breast* (1971) is a rather unamusing fable about a man's metamorphosis into that object; *The Great American Novel* (1973) threatened to sink under its weight of baseball lore dressed up in tall tales and sick jokes. But in *My Life As a Man* (1974) and *The Professor of Desire* (1977) he returned to matters that have traditionally preoccupied the social novelist and that inform his own best work: marriage, divorce, the family, being a Jew, and being psychoanalyzed—the pressures of civilization and the resultant individual discontents.

His finest work is to be found in the Zuckerman trilogy (*Zuckerman Bound*, 1985) and its successor, *The Counterlife* (1987). In these novels Roth created a hero-as-novelist whose experience parallels in important ways his creator's. A scandalous novel, "Carnovsky," refers to *Portnoy's Complaint*; a critic named Milton Appel is a stand-in for the real critic Irving Howe, who once subjected Roth's work to hostile criticism. Yet for all the dangers of self-pity or self-absorption such autobiographical reference involves, the novels add up to something much deeper, more comic and touching, than self-advertisement and complaint. Scenes like the death of Zuckerman's father in a Florida hospital and the subsequent return of the son to the vanished Newark where he grew up are moving expressions of the generous purposes and human sympathies we find in Roth's work at its best. And those purposes and sympathies are also evident in his autobiographical writing: in *The Facts* (1988) and especially in *Patrimony* (1991), a most attractive and poignant memoir of his father.

Most recently, with *Operation Shylock* (1993), Roth develops his art of impersonation into its most excessive and audacious form. Subtitled "A Confession" (he has insisted that it is not fiction, but truth), it recounts an adventure in which the novelist (Roth 1) encounters an imposter (Roth 2) who claims to be the novelist, right down to his name and physical appearance. The struggle between them, enacted mainly in Jerusalem and environs, involves much verbal argument and soliloquy about the Jews, past, present, and future. Whether novel or confession, it is full of controversial and extremely funny talk, and it shows Roth at the height of his powers as a virtuoso.

# Defender of the Faith[1]

In May of 1945, only a few weeks after the fighting had ended in Europe, I was rotated back to the States, where I spent the remainder of the war with a training company at Camp Crowder, Missouri. We had been racing across Germany so swiftly during the late winter and spring that when I boarded the plane that drizzly morning in Berlin, I couldn't believe our destination lay to the west. My mind might inform me otherwise, but there was an inertia of the spirit that told me we were flying to a new front where we would disembark and continue our push eastward—eastward until we'd circled the globe, marching through villages along whose twisting, cobbled streets crowds of the enemy would watch us take possession of what up till then they'd considered their own. I had changed enough in two years not to mind the trembling of the old people, the crying of the very young, the uncertain fear in the eyes of the once-arrogant. After two years I had been fortunate enough to develop an infantryman's heart which, like his feet, at first aches and swells, but finally grows horny enough for him to travel the weirdest paths without feeling a thing.

Captain Paul Barrett was to be my C. O. at Camp Crowder. The day I reported for duty he came out of his office to shake my hand. He was short, gruff, and fiery, and indoors or out he wore his polished helmet liner[2] down on his little eyes. In Europe he had received a battlefield commission and a serious chest wound, and had been returned to the States only a few months before. He spoke easily to me, but was, I thought, unnecessarily abusive towards the troops. At the evening formation, he introduced me.

"Gentlemen," he called. "Sergeant Thurston, as you know, is no longer with this Company. Your new First Sergeant is Sergeant Nathan Marx here. He is a veteran of the European theater and consequently will take no shit."

I sat up late in the orderly room that evening, trying halfheartedly to solve the riddle of duty rosters, personnel forms, and morning reports. The CQ[3] slept with his mouth open on a mattress on the floor. A trainee stood reading the next day's duty roster, which was posted on the bulletin board directly inside the screen door. It was a warm evening and I could hear the men's radios playing dance music over in the barracks.

The trainee, who I knew had been staring at me whenever I looked groggily into the forms, finally took a step in my direction.

"Hey, Sarge—we having a G.I. party tomorrow night?" A G.I. party is a barracks-cleaning.

"You usually have them on Friday nights?"

"Yes," and then he added mysteriously, "that's the whole thing."

"Then you'll have a G.I. party."

He turned away and I heard him mumbling. His shoulders were moving and I wondered if he was crying.

"What's your name, soldier?" I asked.

He turned, not crying at all. Instead his green-speckled eyes, long and narrow, flashed like fish in the sun. He walked over to me and sat on the edge of my desk.

---

1. From *Goodbye, Columbus* (1959).
2. Plastic liner worn under a helmet to prevent chafing or bruising.
3. Noncommissioned officer in charge of quarters at night or on weekends.

He reached out a hand. "Sheldon," he said.

"Stand on your own two feet, Sheldon."

Climbing off the desk, he said, "Sheldon Grossbart." He smiled wider at the intimacy into which he'd led me.

"You against cleaning the barracks Friday night, Grossbart? Maybe we shouldn't have G.I. parties—maybe we should get a maid." My tone startled me: I felt like a Charlie McCarthy, with every top sergeant I had ever known as my Edgar Bergen.[4]

"No, Sergeant." He grew serious, but with a seriousness that seemed only to be the stifling of a smile. "It's just G.I. parties on Friday night, of all nights . . ."

He slipped up to the corner of the desk again—not quite sitting, but not quite standing either. He looked at me with those speckled eyes flashing and then made a gesture with his hand. It was very slight, no more than a rotation back and forth of the wrist, and yet it managed to exclude from our affairs everything else in the orderly room, to make the two of us the center of the world. It seemed, in fact, to exclude everything about the two of us except our hearts. "Sergeant Thurston was one thing," he whispered, an eye flashing to the sleeping CQ, "but we thought with you here, things might be a little different."

"We?"

"The Jewish personnel."

"Why?" I said, harshly.

He hesitated a moment, and then, uncontrollably, his hand went up to his mouth. "I mean . . ." he said.

"What's on your mind?" Whether I was still angry at the "Sheldon" business or something else, I hadn't a chance to tell—but clearly I was angry.

". . . we thought you . . . Marx, you know, like Karl Marx. The Marx brothers. Those guys are all . . . M-A-R-X, isn't that how you spell it, Sergeant?"

"M-A-R-X."

"Fishbein said—" He stopped. "What I mean to say, Sergeant—" His face and neck were red, and his mouth moved but no words came out. In a moment, he raised himself to attention, gazing down at me. It was as though he had suddenly decided he could expect no more sympathy from me than from Thurston, the reason being that I was of Thurston's faith and not his. The young man had managed to confuse himself as to what my faith really was, but I felt no desire to straighten him out. Very simply, I didn't like him.

When I did nothing but return his gaze, he spoke, in an altered tone. "You see, Sergeant," he explained to me, "Friday nights, Jews are supposed to go to services."

"Did Sergeant Thurston tell you you couldn't go to them when there was a G.I. party?"

"No."

"Did he say you had to stay and scrub the floors?"

"No, Sergeant."

"Did the Captain say you had to stay and scrub the floors?"

"That isn't it, Sergeant. It's the other guys in the barracks." He leaned

---

4. Bergen, a ventriloquist, and Charlie McCarthy, his dummy, were a popular radio comedy team.

toward me. "They think we're goofing off. But we're not. That's when Jews go
to services, Friday night. We have to."

"Then go."

"But the other guys make accusations. They have no right."

"That's not the Army's problem, Grossbart. It's a personal problem you'll
have to work out yourself."

"But it's un*fair*."

I got up to leave. "There's nothing I can do about it," I said.

Grossbart stiffened in front of me. "But this is a matter of *religion*, sir."

"Sergeant."

"I mean 'Sergeant,' " he said, almost snarling.

"Look, go see the chaplain. The I.G.[5] You want to see Captain Barrett, I'll
arrange an appointment."

"No, no. I don't want to make trouble, Sergeant. That's the first thing they
throw up to you. I just want my rights!"

"Damn it, Grossbart, stop whining. You have your rights. You can stay and
scrub floors or you can go to *shul*[6]—"

The smile swam in again. Spittle gleamed at the corners of his mouth. "You
mean church, Sergeant."

"I mean *shul*, Grossbart!" I walked past him and outside. Near me I heard
the scrunching of a guard's boots on gravel. In the lighted windows of the
barracks the young men in T-shirts and fatigue pants were sitting on their
bunks, polishing their rifles. Suddenly there was a light rustling behind me. I
turned and saw Grossbart's dark frame fleeing back to the barracks, racing to
tell his Jewish friends that they were right—that like Karl and Harpo, I was
one of them.

The next morning, while chatting with the Captain, I recounted the incident of the previous evening, as if to unburden myself of it. Somehow in the
telling it seemed to the Captain that I was not so much explaining Grossbart's
position as defending it.

"Marx, I'd fight side by side with a nigger if the fellow proved to me he was
a man. I pride myself," the Captain said looking out the window, "that I've
got an open mind. Consequently, Sergeant, nobody gets special treatment
here, for the good or the bad. All a man's got to do is prove himself. A man
fires well on the range, I give him a weekend pass. He scores high in PT, he
gets a weekend pass. He *earns* it." He turned from the window and pointed a
finger at me. "You're a Jewish fellow, am I right, Marx?"

"Yes, sir."

"And I admire you. I admire you because of the ribbons on your chest, not
because you had a hem stitched on your dick before you were old enough to
even know you had one. I judge a man by what he shows me on the field of
battle, Sergeant. It's what he's got *here*," he said, and then, though I expected
he would point to his heart, he jerked a thumb towards the buttons straining
to hold his blouse across his belly. "Guts," he said.

"Okay, sir, I only wanted to pass on to you how the men felt."

"Mr. Marx, you're going to be old before your time if you worry about how

5. Inspector-general, who, apart from the chaplain,        registered.
provided the only route by which complaints could be     6. Synagogue.

the men feel. Leave that stuff to the Chaplain—pussy, the clap, church picnics with the little girls from Joplin, that's all his business, not yours. Let's us train these fellas to shoot straight. If the Jewish personnel feels the other men are accusing them of goldbricking . . . well, I just don't know. Seems awful funny how suddenly the Lord is calling so loud in Private Grossman's ear he's just got to run to church."

"Synagogue," I said.

"Synagogue is right, Sergeant. I'll write that down for handy reference. Thank you for stopping by."

That evening, a few minutes before the company gathered outside the orderly room for the chow formation, I called the CQ, Corporal Robert LaHill, in to see me. LaHill was a dark burly fellow whose hair curled out of his clothes wherever it could. He carried a glaze in his eyes that made one think of caves and dinosaurs. "LaHill," I said, "when you take the formation, remind the men that they're free to attend church services *whenever* they are held, provided they report to the orderly room before they leave the area."

LaHill didn't flicker; he scratched his wrist, but gave no indication that he'd heard or understood.

"LaHill," I said, "*church*. You remember? Church, priest, Mass, confession . . ."

He curled one lip into a ghastly smile; I took it for a signal that for a second he had flickered back up into the human race.

"Jewish personnel who want to attend services this evening are to fall out in front of the orderly room at 1900." And then I added, "By order of Captain Barrett."

A little while later, as a twilight softer than any I had seen that year dropped over Camp Crowder, I heard LaHill's thick, inflectionless voice outside my window: "Give me your ears, troopers. Toppie says for me to tell you that at 1900 hours all Jewish personnel is to fall out in front here if they wants to attend the Jewish Mass."

At seven o'clock, I looked out of the orderly-room window and saw three soldiers in starched khakis standing alone on the dusty quadrangle. They looked at their watches, and fidgeted while they whispered back and forth. It was getting darker, and alone on the deserted field they looked tiny. When I walked to the door I heard the noises of the G.I. party coming from the surrounding barracks—bunks being pushed to the wall, faucets pounding water into buckets, brooms whisking at the wooden floors. In the windows big puffs of cloth moved round and round, cleaning the dirt away for Saturday's inspection. I walked outside and the moment my foot hit the ground I thought I heard Grossbart, who was now in the center, call to the other two, "Ten-*hut!*" Or maybe when they all three jumped to attention, I imagined I heard the command.

At my approach, Grossbart stepped forward. "Thank you, sir," he said.

"Sergeant, Grossbart," I reminded him. "You call officers 'Sir.' I'm not an officer. You've been in the Army three weeks—you know that."

He turned his palms out at his sides to indicate that, in truth, he and I lived beyond convention. "Thank you, anyway," he said.

"Yes," the tall boy behind him said. "Thanks a lot."

And the third whispered, "Thank you," but his mouth barely fluttered so that he did not alter by more than a lip's movement, the posture of attention.

"For what?" I said.

Grossbart snorted, happily. "For the announcement before. The Corporal's announcement. It helped. It made it . . ."

"Fancier." It was the tall boy finishing Grossbart's sentence.

Grossbart smiled. "He means formal, sir. Public," he said to me. "Now it won't seem as though we're just taking off, goldbricking, because the work has begun."

"It was by order of Captain Barrett," I said.

"Ahh, but you pull a little weight . . ." Grossbart said. "So we thank you." Then he turned to his companions. "Sergeant Marx, I want you to meet Larry Fishbein."

The tall boy stepped forward and extended his hand. I shook it. "You from New York?" he asked.

"Yes."

"Me too." He had a cadaverous face that collapsed inward from his cheekbone to his jaw, and when he smiled—as he did at the news of our communal attachment—revealed a mouthful of bad teeth. He blinked his eyes a good deal, as though he were fighting back tears. "What borough?" he asked.

I turned to Grossbart. "It's five after seven. What time are services?"

"*Shul*," he smiled, "is in ten minutes. I want you to meet Mickey Halpern. This is Nathan Marx, our Sergeant."

The third boy hopped forward. "Private Michael Halpern." He saluted.

"Salute officers, Halpern." The boy dropped his hand, and in his nervousness checked to see if his shirt pockets were buttoned on the way down.

"Shall I march them over, sir?" Grossbart asked, "or are you coming along?"

From behind Grossbart, Fishbein piped up. "Afterwards they're having refreshments. A Ladies' Auxiliary from St. Louis, the rabbi told us last week."

"The chaplain," whispered Halpern.

"You're welcome to come along," Grossbart said.

To avoid his plea, I looked away, and saw, in the windows of the barracks, a cloud of faces staring out at the four of us.

"Look, hurry out of here, Grossbart."

"Okay, then," he said. He turned to the others. "Double time, *march!*" and they started off, but ten feet away Grossbart spun about, and running backwards he called to me, "Good *shabus*,[7] sir." And then the three were swallowed into the Missouri dusk.

Even after they'd disappeared over the parade grounds, whose green was now a deep twilight blue, I could hear Grossbart singing the double-time cadence, and as it grew dimmer and dimmer it suddenly touched some deep memory—as did the slant of light—and I was remembering the shrill sounds of a Bronx playground, where years ago, beside the Grand Concourse,[8] I had played on long spring evenings such as this. Those thin fading sounds . . . It was a pleasant memory for a young man so far from peace and home, and it brought so very many recollections with it that I began to grow exceedingly tender about myself. In fact, I indulged myself to a reverie so strong that I felt within as though a hand had opened and was reaching down inside. It had to

---

7. Sabbath.                    8. Bronx, New York, expressway.

reach so very far to touch me. It had to reach past those days in the forests of Belgium and the dying I'd refused to weep over; past the nights in those German farmhouses whose books we'd burned to warm us, and which I couldn't bother to mourn; past those endless stretches when I'd shut off all softness I might feel for my fellows, and managed even to deny myself the posture of a conqueror—the swagger that I, as a Jew, might well have worn as my boots whacked against the rubble of Münster, Braunschweig, and finally Berlin.

But now one night noise, one rumor of home and time past, and memory plunged down through all I had anesthetized and came to what I suddenly remembered to be myself. So it was not altogether curious that in search of more of me I found myself following Grossbart's tracks to Chapel No. 3 where the Jewish services were being held.

I took a seat in the last row, which was empty. Two rows in front sat Grossbart, Fishbein, and Halpern, each holding a little white dixie cup. Fishbein was pouring the contents of his cup into Grossbart's, and Grossbart looked mirthful as the liquid drew a purple arc between his hand and Fishbein's. In the glary yellow light, I saw the chaplain on the pulpit chanting the first line of the responsive reading. Grossbart's prayerbook remained closed on his lap; he swished the cup around. Only Halpern responded in prayer. The fingers of his right hand were spread wide across the cover of the book, and his cap was pulled down low onto his brow so that it was round like a *yarmulke*[9] rather than long and pointed. From time to time, Grossbart wet his lips at the cup's edge; Fishbein, his long yellow face, a dying light bulb, looked from here to there, leaning forward at the neck to catch sight of the faces down the row, in front—then behind. He saw me and his eyelids beat a tattoo. His elbow slid into Grossbart's side, his neck inclined towards his friend, and then, when the congregation responded, Grossbart's voice was among them. Fishbein looked into his book now too; his lips, however, didn't move.

Finally it was time to drink the wine. The chaplain smiled down at them as Grossbart swigged in one long gulp, Halpern sipped, meditating, and Fishbein faked devotion with an empty cup.

At last the chaplain spoke: "As I look down amongst the congregation—" he grinned at the word, "this night, I see many new faces, and I want to welcome you to Friday night services here at Camp Crowder. I am Major Leo Ben Ezra, your chaplain . . ." Though an American, the chaplain spoke English very deliberately, syllabically almost, as though to communicate, above all, to the lip-readers in the audience. "I have only a few words to say before we adjourn to the refreshment room where the kind ladies of the Temple Sinai, St. Louis, Missouri, have a nice setting for you."

Applause and whistling broke out. After a momentary grin, the chaplain raised his palms to the congregation, his eyes flicking upward a moment, as if to remind the troops where they were and Who Else might be in attendance. In the sudden silence that followed, I thought I heard Grossbart's cackle—"Let the goyim[1] clean the floors!" Were those the words? I wasn't sure, but Fishbein, grinning, nudged Halpern. Halpern looked dumbly at him, then went back to his prayerbook, which had been occupying him all through the rabbi's talk. One hand tugged at the black kinky hair that stuck out under his cap. His lips moved.

9. Skullcap.     1. Gentiles.

The rabbi continued. "It is about the food that I want to speak to you for a moment. I know, I know, I know," he intoned, wearily, "how in the mouths of most of you the *trafe*[2] food tastes like ashes. I know how you gag, some of you, and how your parents suffer to think of their children eating foods unclean and offensive to the palate. What can I tell you? I can only say close your eyes and swallow as best you can. Eat what you must to live and throw away the rest. I wish I could help more. For those of you who find this impossible, may I ask that you try and try, but then come to see me in private where, if your revulsion is such, we will have to seek aid from those higher up."

A round of chatter rose and subsided; then everyone sang "Ain Kelohanoh," after all those years I discovered I still knew the words.

Suddenly, the service over, Grossbart was upon me. "Higher up? He means the General?"

"Hey, Shelly," Fishbein interrupted, "he means God." He smacked his face and looked at Halpern. "How high can you go!"

"Shhh!" Grossbart said. "What do you think, Sergeant?"

"I don't know. You better ask the chaplain."

"I'm going to. I'm making an appointment to see him in private. So is Mickey."

Halpern shook his head. "No, no, Sheldon . . ."

"You have rights, Mickey. They can't push us around."

"It's okay. It bothers my mother, not me . . ."

Grossbart looked at me. "Yesterday he threw up. From the hash. It was all ham and God knows what else."

"I have a cold—that was why," Halpern said. He pushed his *yamalkah* back into a cap.

"What about you, Fishbein?" I asked. "You kosher too?"

He flushed, which made the yellow more gray than pink. "A little. But I'll let it ride. I have a very strong stomach. And I don't eat a lot anyway . . ." I continued to look at him, and he held up his wrist to re-enforce what he'd just said. His watch was tightened to the last hole and he pointed that out to me. "So I don't mind."

"But services are important to you?" I asked him.

He looked at Grossbart. "Sure, sir."

"Sergeant."

"Not so much at home," said Grossbart, coming between us, "but away from home it gives one a sense of his Jewishness."

"We have to stick together," Fishbein said.

I started to walk towards the door; Halpern stepped back to make way for me.

"That's what happened in Germany," Grossbart was saying, loud enough for me to hear. "They didn't stick together. They let themselves get pushed around."

I turned. "Look, Grossbart, this is the Army, not summer camp."

He smiled. "So?" Halpern tried to sneak off, but Grossbart held his arm. "So?" he said again.

"Grossbart," I asked, "how old are you?"

"Nineteen."

"And you?" I said to Fishbein.

2. Unkosher—unfit to eat.

"The same. The same month even."

"And what about him?" I pointed to Halpern, who'd finally made it safely to the door.

"Eighteen," Grossbart whispered. "But he's like he can't tie his shoes or brush his teeth himself. I feel sorry for him."

"I feel sorry for all of us, Grossbart, but just act like a man. Just don't overdo it."

"Overdo what, sir?"

"The sir business. Don't overdo that," I said, and I left him standing there. I passed by Halpern but he did not look up. Then I was outside, black surrounded me—but behind I heard Grossbart call, "Hey, Mickey, *liebschen*,[3] come on back. Refreshments!"

*Liebschen!* My grandmother's word for me!

One morning, a week later, while I was working at my desk, Captain Barrett shouted for me to come into his office. When I entered, he had his helmet liner squashed down so that I couldn't even see his eyes. He was on the phone, and when he spoke to me, he cupped one hand over the mouthpiece.

"Who the fuck is Grossbart?"

"Third platoon, Captain," I said. "A trainee."

"What's all this stink about food? His mother called a goddam congressman about the food . . ." He uncovered the mouthpiece and slid his helmet up so I could see the curl of his bottom eyelash. "Yes, sir," he said into the phone. "Yes, sir. I'm still here, sir. I'm asking Marx here right now . . ."

He covered the mouthpiece again and looked back to me. "Lightfoot Harry's on the phone," he said, between his teeth. "This congressman calls General Lyman who calls Colonel Sousa who calls the Major who calls me. They're just dying to stick this thing on me. What's a matter," he shook the phone at me, "I don't feed the troops? What the hell is this?"

"Sir, Grossbart is strange . . ." Barrett greeted that with a mockingly indulgent smile. I altered my approach. "Captain, he's a very orthodox Jew and so he's only allowed to eat certain foods."

"He throws up, the congressman said. Every time he eats something his mother says he throws up!"

"He's accustomed to observing the dietary laws, Captain."

"So why's his old lady have to call the White House!"

"Jewish parents, sir, they're apt to be more protective than you expect. I mean Jews have a very close family life. A boy goes away from home, sometimes the mother is liable to get very upset. Probably the boy *mentioned* something in a letter and his mother misinterpreted."

"I'd like to punch him one right in the mouth. There's a goddam war on and he wants a silver platter!"

"I don't think the boy's to blame, sir. I'm sure we can straighten it out by just asking him. Jewish parents worry—"

"*All* parents worry, for Christ sake. But they don't get on their high horse and start pulling strings—"

I interrupted, my voice higher, tighter than before. "The home life, Captain, is so very important . . . but you're right, it may sometimes get out of

3. Darling.

hand. It's a very wonderful thing, Captain, but because it's so close, this kind of thing—"

He didn't listen any longer to my attempt to present both myself and Lightfoot Harry with an explanation for the letter. He turned back to the phone. "Sir?" he said. "Sir, Marx here tells me Jews have a tendency to be pushy. He says he thinks he can settle it right here in the Company . . . Yes, sir . . . I *will* call back, sir, soon as I can . . ." He hung up. "Where are the men, Sergeant?"

"On the range."

With a whack on the top, he crushed his helmet over his eyes, and charged out of his chair. "We're going for a ride."

The Captain drove and I sat beside him. It was a hot spring day and under my newly starched fatigues it felt as though my armpits were melting down onto my sides and chest. The roads were dry and by the time we reached the firing range, my teeth felt gritty with dust though my mouth had been shut the whole trip. The Captain slammed the brakes on and told me to get the hell out and find Grossbart.

I found him on his belly, firing wildly at the 500 feet target. Waiting their turns behind him were Halpern and Fishbein. Fishbein, wearing a pair of rimless G.I. glasses I hadn't seen on him before, gave the appearance of an old peddler who would gladly have sold you the rifle and cartridges that were slung all over him. I stood back by the ammo boxes, waiting for Grossbart to finish spraying the distant targets. Fishbein straggled back to stand near me.

"Hello, Sergeant Marx."

"How are you?" I mumbled.

"Fine, thank you. Sheldon's really a good shot."

"I didn't notice."

"I'm not so good, but I think I'm getting the hang of it now . . . Sergeant, I don't mean to, you know, ask what I shouldn't . . ." The boy stopped. He was trying to speak intimately but the noise of the shooting necessitated that he shout at me.

"What is it?" I asked. Down the range I saw Captain Barrett standing up in the jeep, scanning the line for me and Grossbart.

"My parents keep asking and asking where we're going. Everybody says the Pacific. I don't care, but my parents . . . If I could relieve their minds I think I could concentrate more on my shooting."

"I don't know where, Fishbein. Try to concentrate anyway."

"Sheldon says you might be able to find out—"

"I don't know a thing, Fishbein. You just take it easy, and don't let Sheldon—"

"*I'm* taking it easy, Sergeant. It's at home—"

Grossbart had just finished on the line and was dusting his fatigues with one hand. I left Fishbein's sentence in the middle.

"Grossbart, the Captain wants to see you."

He came toward us. His eyes blazed and twinkled. "Hi!"

"Don't point that goddam rifle!"

"I wouldn't shoot you, Sarge." He gave me a smile wide as a pumpkin as he turned the barrel aside.

"Damn you, Grossbart—this is no joke! Follow me."

I walked ahead of him and had the awful suspicion that behind me Grossbart was *marching*, his rifle on his shoulder, as though he were a one-man detachment.

At the jeep he gave the Captain a rifle salute. "Private Sheldon Grossbart, sir."

"At ease, Grossman." The Captain slid over to the empty front seat, and crooking a finger, invited Grossbart closer.

"Bart, sir. Sheldon Gross*bart*. It's a common error." Grossbart nodded to me—*I* understand, he indicated. I looked away, just as the mess truck pulled up to the range, disgorging a half dozen K.P.'s with rolled-up sleeves. The mess sergeant screamed at them while they set up the chow line equipment.

"Grossbart, your mama wrote some congressman that we don't feed you right. Do you know that?" the Captain said.

"It was my father, sir. He wrote to Representative Franconi that my religion forbids me to eat certain foods."

"What religion is that, Grossbart?"

"Jewish."

"Jewish, *sir*," I said to Grossbart.

"Excuse me, sir. 'Jewish, sir.' "

"What have you been living on?" the Captain asked. "You've been in the Army a month already. You don't look to me like you're falling to pieces."

"I eat because I have to, sir. But Sergeant Marx will testify to the fact that I don't eat one mouthful more than I need to in order to survive."

"Marx," Barrett asked, "is that so?"

"I've never seen Grossbart eat, sir," I said.

"But you heard the rabbi," Grossbart said. "He told us what to do, and I listened."

The Captain looked at me. "Well, Marx?"

"I still don't know what he eats and doesn't eat, sir."

Grossbart raised his rifle, as though to offer it to me. "But, Sergeant—"

"Look, Grossbart, just answer the Captain's questions!" I said sharply.

Barrett smiled at me and I resented it. "All right, Grossbart," he said, "What is it you want? The little piece of paper? You want out?"

"No, sir. Only to be allowed to live as a Jew. And for the others, too."

"What others?"

"Fishbein, sir, and Halpern."

"They don't like the way we serve either?"

"Halpern throws up, sir. I've seen it."

"I thought *you* threw up."

"Just once, sir. I didn't know the sausage was sausage."

"We'll give menus, Grossbart. We'll show training films about the food, so you can identify when we're trying to poison you."

Grossbart did not answer. Out before me, the men had been organized into two long chow lines. At the tail end of one I spotted Fishbein—or rather, his glasses spotted me. They winked sunlight back at me like a friend. Halpern stood next to him, patting inside his collar with a khaki handkerchief. They moved with the line as it began to edge up towards the food. The mess sergeant was still screaming at the K.P.'s, who stood ready to ladle out the food, bewildered. For a moment I was actually terrorized by the thought that somehow the mess sergeant was going to get involved in Grossbart's problem.

"Come over here, Marx," the Captain said to me. "Marx, you're a Jewish fella, am I right?"

I played straight man. "Yes, sir."

"How long you been in the Army? Tell this boy."

"Three years and two months."

"A year in combat, Grossbart. Twelve goddam months in combat all through Europe. I admire this man," the Captain said, snapping a wrist against my chest. But do you hear him peeping about the food? Do you? I want an answer, Grossbart. Yes or no."

"No, sir."

"And why not? He's a Jewish fella."

"Some things are more important to some Jews than other things to other Jews."

Barrett blew up. "Look, Grossbart, Marx here is a good man, a goddam *hero*. When you were sitting on your sweet ass in high school, Sergeant Marx was killing Germans. Who does more for the Jews, you by throwing up over a lousy piece of sausage, a piece of firstcut meat—or Marx by killing those Nazi bastards? If I was a Jew, Grossbart, I'd kiss this man's feet. He's a goddam hero, you know that? And *he* eats what we give him. Why do you have to cause trouble is what I want to know! What is it you're buckin' for, a discharge?"

"No, sir."

"I'm talking to a *wall*! Sergeant, get him out of my way." Barrett pounced over to the driver's seat. "I'm going to see the chaplain!" The engine roared, the jeep spun around, and then, raising a whirl of dust, the Captain was headed back to camp.

For a moment, Grossbart and I stood side by side, watching the jeep. Then he looked at me and said, "I don't want to start trouble. That's the first thing they toss up to us."

When he spoke I saw that his teeth were white and straight, and the sight of them suddenly made me understand that Grossbart actually did have parents: that once upon a time someone had taken little Sheldon to the dentist. He was someone's son. Despite all the talk about his parents, it was hard to believe in Grossbart as a child, an heir—as related by blood to anyone, mother, father, or, above all, to me. This realization led me to another.

"What does your father do, Grossbart?" I asked, as we started to walk back towards the chow line.

"He's a tailor."

"An American?"

"Now, yes. A son in the Army," he said, jokingly.

"And your mother?" I asked.

He winked. "A *ballabusta*[4]—she practically sleeps with a dustcloth in her hand."

"She's also an immigrant?"

"All she talks is Yiddish, still."

"And your father too?"

"A little English. 'Clean,' 'Press,' 'Take the pants in . . .' That's the extent of it. But they're good to me . . ."

"Then, Grossbart—" I reached out and stopped him. He turned towards me

---

4. Good housekeeper.

and when our eyes met his seemed to jump back, shiver in their sockets. He looked afraid. "Grossbart, then you were the one who wrote that letter, weren't you?"

It took only a second or two for his eyes to flash happy again. "Yes." He walked on, and I kept pace. "It's what my father *would* have written if he had known how. It was his name, though. *He* signed it. He even mailed it. I sent it home. For the New York postmark."

I was astonished, and he saw it. With complete seriousness, he thrust his right arm in front of me. "Blood is blood, Sergeant," he said, pinching the blue vein in his wrist.

"What the hell *are* you trying to do, Grossbart? I've seen you eat. Do you know that? I told the Captain I don't know what you eat, but I've seen you eat like a hound at chow."

"We work hard, Sergeant. We're in training. For a furnace to work, you've got to feed it coal."

"If you wrote the letter, Grossbart, then why did you say you threw up all the time?"

"I was really talking about Mickey there. But he would never write, Sergeant, though I pleaded with him. He'll waste away to nothing if I don't help. Sergeant, I used my name, my father's name, but it's Mickey and Fishbein too I'm watching out for."

"You're a regular Messiah,[5] aren't you?"

We were at the chow line now.

"That's a good one, Sergeant." He smiled. "But who knows? Who can tell? Maybe you're the Messiah . . . a little bit. What Mickey says is the Messiah is a collective idea. He went to Yeshivah,[6] Mickey, for a while. He says *together* we're the Messiah. Me a little bit, you a little bit . . . You should hear that kid talk, Sergeant, when he gets going."

"Me a little bit, you a little bit. You'd like to believe that, wouldn't you, Grossbart? That makes everything so clean for you."

"It doesn't seem too bad a thing to believe, Sergeant. It only means we should all give a little, is all . . ."

I walked off to eat my rations with the other noncoms.

Two days later a letter addressed to Captain Barrett passed over my desk. It had come through the chain of command—from the office of Congressman Franconi, where it had been received, to General Lyman, to Colonel Sousa, to Major Lamont, to Captain Barrett. I read it over twice while the Captain was at the officers' mess. It was dated May 14th, the day Barrett had spoken with Grossbart on the rifle range.

Dear Congressman:

First let me thank you for your interest in behalf of my son, Private Sheldon Grossbart. Fortunately, I was able to speak with Sheldon on the phone the other night, and I think I've been able to solve our problem. He is, as I mentioned in my last letter, a very religious boy, and it was only with the greatest difficulty that I could persuade him that the religious thing to do—what God Himself would want Sheldon to do—would be to suffer the pangs of religious

5. The deliverer who will rule over the people of Israel    6. Jewish institution of learning.
at the end of time.

remorse for the good of his country and all mankind. It took some doing, Congressman, but finally he saw the light. In fact, what he said (and I wrote down the words on a scratch pad so as never to forget), what he said was, "I guess you're right, Dad. So many millions of my fellow Jews gave up their lives to the enemy, the least I can do is live for a while minus a bit of my heritage so as to help end this struggle and regain for all the children of God dignity and humanity." That, Congressman, would make any father proud.

By the way, Sheldon wanted me to know—and to pass on to you—the name of a soldier who helped him reach this decision: SERGEANT NATHAN MARX. Sergeant Marx is a combat veteran who is Sheldon's First Sergeant. This man has helped Sheldon over some of the first hurdles he's had to face in the Army, and is in part responsible for Sheldon's changing his mind about the dietary laws. I know Sheldon would appreciate any recognition Marx could receive.

Thank you and good luck. I look forward to seeing your name on the next election ballot.

Respectfully,<br>Samuel E. Grossbart

Attached to the Grossbart communiqué was a communiqué addressed to General Marshall Lyman, the post commander, and signed by Representative Charles E. Franconi of the House of Representatives. The communiqué informed General Lyman that Sergeant Nathan Marx was a credit to the U.S. Army and the Jewish people.

What was Grossbart's motive in recanting? Did he feel he'd gone too far? Was the letter a strategic retreat—a crafty attempt to strengthen what he considered our alliance? Or had he actually changed his mind, via an imaginary dialogue between Grossbart *père* and *fils*? I was puzzled, but only for a few days—that is, only until I realized that whatever his reasons, he had actually decided to disappear from my life: he was going to allow himself to become just another trainee. I saw him at inspection but he never winked; at chow formations but he never flashed me a sign; on Sundays, with the other trainees, he would sit around watching the noncoms' softball team, for whom I pitched, but not once did he speak an unnecessary or unusual word to me. Fishbein and Halpern retreated from sight too, at Grossbart's command I was sure. Apparently he'd seen that wisdom lay in turning back before he plunged us over into the ugliness of privilege undeserved. Our separation allowed me to forgive him our past encounters, and, finally, to admire him for his good sense.

Meanwhile, free of Grossbart, I grew used to my job and my administrative tasks. I stepped on a scale one day and discovered I had truly become a noncombatant: I had gained seven pounds. I found patience to get past the first three pages of a book. I thought about the future more and more, and wrote letters to girls I'd known before the war—I even got a few answers. I sent away to Columbia for a Law School catalogue. I continued to follow the war in the Pacific, but it was not my war and I read of bombings and battles like a civilian. I thought I could see the end in sight and sometimes at night I dreamed that I was walking on the streets of Manhattan—Broadway, Third Avenue, and 116th Street, where I had lived those three years I'd attended Columbia College. I curled myself around these dreams and I began to be happy.

And then one Saturday when everyone was away and I was alone in the orderly room reading a month-old copy of *The Sporting News*, Grossbart reappeared.

"You a baseball fan, Sergeant?"

I looked up. "How are you?"

"Fine," Grossbart said. "They're making a soldier out of me."

"How are Fishbein and Halpern?"

"Coming along," he said. "We've got no training this afternoon. They're at the movies."

"How come you're not with them?"

"I wanted to come over and say hello."

He smiled—a shy, regular-guy smile, as though he and I well knew that our friendship drew its sustenance from unexpected visits, remembered birthdays, and borrowed lawnmowers. At first it offended me, and then the feeling was swallowed by the general uneasiness I felt at the thought that everyone on the post was locked away in a dark movie theater and I was here alone with Grossbart. I folded my paper.

"Sergeant," he said, "I'd like to ask a favor. It is a favor and I'm making no bones about it."

He stopped, allowing me to refuse him a hearing—which, of course, forced me into a courtesy I did not intend. "Go ahead."

"Well, actually it's two favors."

I said nothing.

"The first one's about these rumors. Everybody says we're going to the Pacific."

"As I told your friend Fishbein, I don't know. You'll just have to wait to find out. Like everybody else."

"You think there's a chance of any of us going East?"

"Germany," I said, "maybe."

"I meant New York."

"I don't think so, Grossbart. Offhand."

"Thanks for the information, Sergeant," he said.

"It's not information, Grossbart. Just what I surmise."

"It certainly would be good to be near home. My parents . . . you know."

He took a step towards the door and then turned back. "Oh the other thing. May I ask the other?"

"What is it?"

"The other thing is—I've got relatives in St. Louis and they say they'll give me a whole Passover dinner if I can get down there. God, Sergeant, that'd mean an awful lot to me."

I stood up. "No passes during basic, Grossbart."

"But we're off from now till Monday morning, Sergeant. I could leave the post and no one would even know."

"I'd know. You'd know."

"But that's all. Just the two of us. Last night I called my aunt and you should have heard her. 'Come, come,' she said. 'I got gefilte fish, *chrain*,[7] the works!' Just a day, Sergeant, I'd take the blame if anything happened."

"The captain isn't here to sign a pass."

"You could sign."

_____

7. Horseradish.

"Look, Grossbart—"

"Sergeant, for two months practically I've been eating *trafe* till I want to die."

"I thought you'd made up your mind to live with it. To be minus a little bit of heritage."

He pointed a finger at me. "You!" he said. "That wasn't for you to read!"

"I read it. So what."

"That letter was addressed to a congressman."

"Grossbart, don't feed me any crap. You *wanted* me to read it."

"Why are you persecuting me, Sergeant?"

"Are you kidding!"

"I've run into this before," he said, "but never from my own!"

"Get out of here, Grossbart! Get the hell out of my sight!"

He did not move. "Ashamed, that's what you are. So you take it out on the rest of us. They say Hitler himself was half a Jew. Seeing this, I wouldn't doubt it!"

"What are you trying to do with me, Grossbart? What are you after? You want me to give you special privileges, to change the food, to find out about your orders, to give you weekend passes."

"You even talk like a goy!" Grossbart shook his fist. "Is this a weekend pass I'm asking for? Is a Seder[8] sacred or not?"

Seder! It suddenly occurred to me that Passover had been celebrated weeks before. I confronted Grossbart with the fact.

"That's right," he said. "Who says no? A month ago, and *I* was in the field eating hash! And now all I ask is a simple favor—a Jewish boy I thought would understand. My aunt's willing to go out of her way—to make a Seder a month later—" He turned to go, mumbling.

"Come back here!" I called. He stopped and looked at me. "Grossbart, why can't you be like the rest? Why do you have to stick out like a sore thumb? Why do you beg for special treatment?"

"Because I'm a Jew, Sergeant. I *am* different. Better, maybe not. But different."

"This is a war, Grossbart. For the time being *be* the same."

"I refuse."

"What?"

"I refuse. I can't stop being me, that's all there is to it." Tears came to his eyes. "It's a hard thing to be a Jew. But now I see what Mickey says—it's a harder thing to stay one." He raised a hand sadly toward me. "Look at you."

"Stop crying!"

"Stop this, stop that, stop the other thing! You stop, Sergeant. Stop closing your heart to your own!" And wiping his face with his sleeve, he ran out the door. "The least we can do for one another . . . the least . . ."

An hour later I saw Grossbart headed across the field. He wore a pair of starched khakis and carried only a little leather ditty bag. I went to the door and from the outside felt the heat of the day. It was quiet—not a soul in sight except over by the mess hall four K.P.'s sitting round a pan, sloped forward from the waists, gabbing and peeling potatoes in the sun.

"Grossbart!" I called.

---

8. Ceremonial dinner on the first evening of Passover.

He looked toward me and continued walking.

"Grossbart, get over here!"

He turned and stepped into his long shadow. Finally he stood before me.

"Where are you going?" I said.

"St. Louis. I don't care."

"You'll get caught without a pass."

"So I'll get caught without a pass."

"You'll go to the stockade."

"I'm in the stockade." He made an about-face and headed off.

I let him go only a step: "Come back here," I said, and he followed me into the office, where I typed out a pass and signed the Captain's name and my own initials after it.

He took the pass from me and then, a moment later, he reached out and grabbed my hand. "Sergeant, you don't know how much this means to me."

"Okay. Don't get in any trouble."

"I wish I could show you how much this means to me."

"Don't do me any favors. Don't write any more congressmen for citations."

Amazingly, he smiled. "You're right. I won't. But let me do something."

"Bring me a piece of that gefilte fish. Just get out of here."

"I will! With a slice of carrot and a little horseradish. I won't forget."

"All right. Just show your pass at the gate. And don't tell *anybody*."

"I won't. It's a month late, but a good Yom Tov to you."

"Good Yom Tov,[9] Grossbart," I said.

"You're a good Jew, Sergeant. You like to think you have a hard heart, but underneath you're a fine decent man. I mean that."

Those last three words touched me more than any words from Grossbart's mouth had the right to. "All right, Grossbart. Now call me 'sir' and get the hell out of here."

He ran out the door and was gone. I felt very pleased with myself—it was a great relief to stop fighting Grossbart. And it had cost me nothing. Barrett would never find out, and if he did, I could manage to invent some excuse. For a while I sat at my desk, comfortable in my decision. Then the screen door flew back and Grossbart burst in again. "Sergeant!" he said. Behind him I saw Fishbein and Halpern, both in starched khakis, both carrying ditty bags exactly like Grossbart's.

"Sergeant, I caught Mickey and Larry coming out of the movies. I almost missed them."

"Grossbart, did I say tell no one?"

"But my aunt said I could bring friends. That I should, in fact."

"I'm the Sergeant, Grossbart—not your aunt!"

Grossbart looked at me in disbelief; he pulled Halpern up by his sleeve. "Mickey, tell the Sergeant what this would mean to you."

"Grossbart, for God's sake, spare us—"

"Tell him what you told me, Mickey. How much it would mean."

Halpern looked at me and, shrugging his shoulders, made his admission. "A lot."

Fishbein stepped forward without prompting. "This would mean a great deal to me and my parents, Sergeant Marx."

9. Praise the day.

"No!" I shouted.

Grossbart was shaking his head. "Sergeant, I could see you denying me, but how you can deny Mickey, a Yeshivah boy, that's beyond me."

"I'm not denying Mickey anything. You just pushed a little too hard, Grossbart. *You* denied him."

"I'll give him my pass, then," Grossbart said. "I'll give him my aunt's address and a little note. At least let him go."

In a second he had crammed the pass into Halpern's pants' pocket. Halpern looked at me, Fishbein too. Grossbart was at the door, pushing it open. "Mickey, bring me a piece of gefilte fish at least." And then he was outside again.

The three of us looked at one another and then I said, "Halpern, hand that pass over."

He took it from his pocket and gave it to me. Fishbein had now moved to the doorway, where he lingered. He stood there with his mouth slightly open and then pointed to himself. "And me?" he asked.

His utter ridiculousness exhausted me. I slumped down in my seat and I felt pulses knocking at the back of my eyes. "Fishbein," I said, "you understand I'm not trying to deny you anything, don't you? If it was my Army I'd serve gefilte fish in the mess hall. I'd sell kugel[1] in the PX, honest to God."

Halpern smiled.

"You understand, don't you, Halpern?"

"Yes, Sergeant."

"And you, Fishbein? I don't want enemies. I'm just like you—I want to serve my time and go home. I miss the same things you miss."

"Then, Sergeant," Fishbein interrupted, "Why don't you come too?"

"Where?"

"To St. Louis. To Shelley's aunt. We'll have a regular Seder. Play hide-the-matzah." He gave a broad, black-toothed smile.

I saw Grossbart in the doorway again, on the other side of the screen.

"Pssst!" He waved a piece of paper. "Mickey, here's the address. Tell her I couldn't get away."

Halpern did not move. He looked at me and I saw the shrug moving up his arms into his shoulders again. I took the cover off my typewriter and made out passes for him and Fishbein. "Go," I said, "the three of you."

I thought Halpern was going to kiss my hand.

That afternoon, in a bar in Joplin, I drank beer and listened with half an ear to the Cardinal game. I tried to look squarely at what I'd become involved in, and began to wonder if perhaps the struggle with Grossbart wasn't as much my fault as his. What was I that I had to *muster* generous feelings? Who was I to have been feeling so grudging, so tight-hearted? After all, I wasn't being asked to move the world. Had I a right, then, or a reason, to clamp down on Grossbart, when that meant clamping down on Halpern, too? And Fishbein, that ugly agreeable soul, wouldn't he suffer in the bargain also? Out of the many recollections that had tumbled over me these past few days, I heard from some childhood moment my grandmother's voice: "What are you making a *tsimas*?"[2] It was what she would ask my mother when, say, I had cut myself

1. Baked pudding of noodles or potatoes.
2. Fuss (Yiddish), here a side dish made of mixed cooked vegetables and fruit.

with a knife and her daughter was busy bawling me out. I would need a hug and a kiss and my mother would moralize! But my grandmother knew—mercy overrides justice. I should have known it, too. Who was Nathan Marx to be such a pennypincher with kindness? Surely, I thought, the Messiah himself— if he should ever come—won't niggle over nickels and dimes. God willing, he'll hug and kiss.

The next day, while we were playing softball over on the Parade Grounds, I decided to ask Bob Wright, who was noncom in charge over at Classification and Assignment, where he thought our trainees would be sent when their cycle ended in two weeks. I asked casually, between innings, and he said, "They're pushing them all into the Pacific. Shulman cut the orders on your boys the other day."

The news shocked me, as though I were father to Halpern, Fishbein, and Grossbart.

That night I was just sliding into sleep when someone tapped on the door. "What is it?"

"Sheldon."

He opened the door and came in. For a moment I felt his presence without being able to see him. "How was it?" I asked, as though to the darkness.

He popped into sight before me. "Great, Sergeant." I felt my springs sag; Grossbart was sitting on the edge of the bed. I sat up.

"How about you?" he asked. "Have a nice weekend?"

"Yes."

He took a deep paternal breath. "The others went to sleep . . ." We sat silently for a while, as a homey feeling invaded my ugly little cubicle: the door was locked, the cat out, the children safely in bed.

"Sergeant, can I tell you something? Personal?"

I did not answer and he seemed to know why. "Not about me. About Mickey. Sergeant, I never felt for anybody like I feel for him. Last night I heard Mickey in the bed next to me. He was crying so, it could have broken your heart. Real sobs."

"I'm sorry to hear that."

"I had to talk to him to stop him. He held my hand, Sergeant—he wouldn't let it go. He was almost hysterical. He kept saying if he only knew where we were going. Even if he knew it *was* the Pacific, that would be better than nothing. Just to know."

Long ago, someone had taught Grossbart the sad law that only lies can get the truth. Not that I couldn't believe in Halpern's crying—his eyes *always* seemed red-rimmed. But, fact or not, it became a lie when Grossbart uttered it. He was entirely strategic. But then—it came with the force of indictment— so was I! There are strategies of aggression, but there are strategies of retreat, as well. And so, recognizing that I myself, had been without craft and guile, I told him what I knew. "It is the Pacific."

He let out a small gasp, which was not a lie. "I'll tell him. I wish it was otherwise."

"So do I."

He jumped on my words. "You mean you think you could do something? A change maybe?"

"No, I couldn't do a thing."

"Don't you know anybody over at C & A?"

"Grossbart, there's nothing I can do. If your orders are for the Pacific then it's the Pacific."

"But Mickey."

"Mickey, you, me—everybody, Grossbart. There's nothing to be done. Maybe the war'll end before you go. Pray for a miracle."

"But—"

"Good night, Grossbart." I settled back, and was relieved to feel the springs upbend again as Grossbart rose to leave. I could see him clearly now; his jaw had dropped and he looked like a dazed prizefighter. I noticed for the first time a little paper bag in his hand.

"Grossbart"—I smiled—"my gift?"

"Oh, yes, Sergeant. Here, from all of us." He handed me the bag. "It's egg roll."

"Egg roll?" I accepted the bag and felt a damp grease spot on the bottom. I opened it, sure that Grossbart was joking.

"We thought you'd probably like it. You know, Chinese egg roll. We thought you'd probably have a taste for—"

"Your aunt served egg roll?"

"She wasn't home."

"Grossbart, she invited you. You told me she invited you and your friends."

"I know. I just reread the letter. Next week."

I got out of bed and walked to the window. It was black as far off as I could see. "Grossbart," I said. But I was not calling him.

"What?"

"What are you, Grossbart? Honest to God, what are you?"

I think it was the first time I'd asked him a question for which he didn't have an immediate answer.

"How can you do this to people?" I asked.

"Sergeant, the day away did us all a world of good. Fishbein, you should see him, he *loves* Chinese food."

"But the Seder," I said.

"We took second best, Sergeant."

Rage came charging at me. I didn't sidestep—I grabbed it, pulled it in, hugged it to my chest.

"Grossbart, you're a liar! You're a schemer and a crook! You've got no respect for anything! Nothing at all! Not for me, for the truth, not even for poor Halpern! You use us all—"

"Sergeant, Sergeant, I feel for Mickey, honest to God, I do. I *love* Mickey. I try—"

"You try! You feel!" I lurched towards him and grabbed his shirt front. I shook him furiously. "Grossbart, get out. Get out and stay the hell away from me! Because if I see you, I'll make your life miserable. *You understand that?*"

"Yes."

I let him free, and when he walked from the room I wanted to spit on the floor where he had stood. I couldn't stop the fury from rising in my heart. It engulfed me, owned me, till it seemed I could only rid myself of it with tears or an act of violence. I snatched from the bed the bag Grossbart had given me and with all my strength threw it out the window. And the next morning, as the men policed the area around the barracks, I heard a great cry go up from one of the trainees who'd been anticipating only this morning handful of cigarette butts and candy wrappers. "Egg roll!" he shouted. "Holy Christ, Chinese goddam egg roll!"

A week later when I read the orders that had come down from C & A I couldn't believe my eyes. Every single trainee was to be shipped to Camp Stoneham, California, and from there to the Pacific. Every trainee but one: Private Sheldon Grossbart was to be sent to Fort Monmouth, New Jersey. I read the mimeographed sheet several times. Dee, Farrell, Fishbein, Fuselli, Fylypowycz, Glinicki, Gromke, Gucwa, Halpern, Hardy, Helebrandt . . . right down to Anton Zygadlo, all were to be headed West before the month was out. All except Grossbart. He had pulled a string and I wasn't it.

I lifted the phone and called C & A.

The voice on the other end said smartly, "Corporal Shulman, sir."

"Let me speak to Sergeant Wright."

"Who is this calling, sir?"

"Sergeant Marx."

And to my surprise, the voice said, "Oh." Then: "Just a minute, Sergeant." Shulman's *oh* stayed with me while I waited for Wright to come to the phone. Why *oh*? Who was Shulman? And then, so simply, I knew I'd discovered the string Grossbart had pulled. In fact, I could hear Grossbart the day he'd discovered Shulman, in the PX, or the bowling alley, or maybe even at services. "Glad to meet you. Where you from? Bronx? Me too. Do you know so-and-so? And so-and-so? Me too! You work at C & A? Really? Hey, how's chances of getting East? Could you do something? Change something? Swindle, cheat, lie? We gotta help each other, you know . . . if the Jews in Germany . . ."

At the other end Bob Wright answered. "How are you, Nate? How's the pitching arm?"

"Good. Bob, I wonder if you could do me a favor." I heard clearly my own words and they so reminded me of Grossbart that I dropped more easily than I could have imagined into what I had planned. "This may sound crazy, Bob, but I got a kid here on orders to Monmouth who wants them changed. He had a brother killed in Europe and he's hot to go to the Pacific. Says he'd feel like a coward if he wound up stateside. I don't know, Bob, can anything be done? Put somebody else in the Monmouth slot?"

"Who?" he asked cagily.

"Anybody. First guy on the alphabet. I don't care. The kid just asked if something could be done."

"What's his name?"

"Grossbart, Sheldon."

Wright didn't answer.

"Yeah," I said, "he's a Jewish kid, so he thought I could help him out. You know."

"I guess I can do something," he finally said. "The Major hasn't been around here for weeks—TDY[3] to the golf course. I'll try, Nate that's all I can say."

"I'd appreciate it, Bob. See you Sunday," and I hung up, perspiring.

---

3. Temporary Duty, an army orders term used ironically here.

And the following day the corrected orders appeared: Fishbein, Fuselli, Fylypowycz, Glinicki, Grossbart, Gucwa, Halpern, Hardy . . . Lucky Private Harley Alton was to go to Fort Monmouth, New Jersey, where for some reason or other, they wanted an enlisted man with infantry training.

After chow that night I stopped back at the orderly room to straighten out the guard duty roster. Grossbart was waiting for me. He spoke first.

"You son of a bitch!"

I sat down at my desk and while he glared down at me I began to make the necessary alterations in the duty roster.

"What do you have against me?" he cried. "Against my family? Would it kill you for me to be near my father, God knows how many months he has left to him."

"Why?"

"His heart," Grossbart said. "He hasn't had enough troubles in a lifetime, you've got to add to them. I curse the day I ever met you, Marx! Shulman told me what happened over there. There's no limit to your anti-Semitism, is there! The damage you've done here isn't enough. You have to make a special phone call! You really want me dead!"

I made the last few notations in the duty roster and got up to leave. "Good night, Grossbart."

"You owe me an explanation!" He stood in my path.

"Sheldon, you're the one who owes explanations."

He scowled. "To *you*?"

"To me, I think so, yes. Mostly to Fishbein and Halpern."

"That's right, twist things around. I owe nobody nothing, I've done all I could do for them. Now I think I've got the right to watch out for myself."

"For each other we have to learn to watch out, Sheldon. You told me yourself."

"You call this watching out for me, what you did?"

"No. For all of us."

I pushed him aside and started for the door. I heard his furious breathing behind me, and it sounded like steam rushing from the engine of his terrible strength.

"You'll be all right," I said from the door. And, I thought, so would Fishbein and Halpern be all right, even in the Pacific, if only Grossbart could continue to see in the obsequiousness of the one, the soft spirituality of the other, some profit for himself.

I stood outside the orderly room, and I heard Grossbart weeping behind me. Over in the barracks, in the lighted windows, I could see the boys in their T-shirts sitting on their bunks talking about their orders, as they'd been doing for the past two days. With a kind of quiet nervousness, they polished shoes, shined belt buckles, squared away underwear, trying as best they could to accept their fate. Behind me, Grossbart swallowed hard, accepting his. And then, resisting with all my will an impulse to turn and seek pardon for my vindictiveness, I accepted my own.

1959

# N. SCOTT MOMADAY
## b. 1934

"In a certain sense," writes N. Scott Momaday in *Man Made of Words*, "we are all made of words; . . . our most essential being consists in language. It is the element in which we think and dream and act, in which we live our daily lives." Since the publication of his Pulitzer Prize–winning novel *House Made of Dawn* (1968), Momaday's writing has crossed boundaries of language, form, and genre, thereby creating for Momaday himself, through will and imagination, an American Indian identity in words.

Navarre Scott Momaday was born at the Kiowa and Comanche Indian Hospital in Lawton, Oklahoma, the only child of Al Momaday, a Kiowa, and Natachee Scott, who was part Cherokee. He spent most of his early years in New Mexico and Arizona, moving in 1946 to Jemez Pueblo in New Mexico's Rio Grande Valley. There his parents, both artists and teachers, took jobs at a small day school. Growing up on reservations, including those of the Navajo and the Apache, and then in Jemez Pueblo, Momaday experienced the rhythms of traditional tribal life, but saw, too, the changes wrought by postwar material culture, and their human costs—the alcoholism, underemployment, and personal disintegration that mark the life of Abel, the returning veteran in *House Made of Dawn*. Early on, Momaday's mother instilled in him the value of a bicultural education that would open the future without closing off his native heritage. Momaday attended reservation, public, and mission schools, then graduated from military high school in Virginia and the University of New Mexico. He received his Ph.D. in 1963 from Stanford University, where his mentor in his studies of American and English literature was the poet and critic Yvor Winters. Since then his teaching career has taken him to Santa Barbara, Berkeley, the University of Moscow, Stanford, and the University of Arizona.

What some scholars call the "Native American Renaissance" is usually said to have begun with the publication of *House Made of Dawn* in 1968 and its reception of the Pulitzer Prize the following year. And, indeed, from 1968 to the present, Native American writers have published a substantial body of fine poetry, fiction, and autobiography, gaining considerable notice both in the United States and abroad.

Over the decades since the publication of *House Made of Dawn*, Momaday has published a second novel, *The Ancient Child* (1989); three volumes of poems, *Angle of Geese and Other Poems* (1974), *The Gourd Dancer* (1976), and *In the Presence of the Sun* (1992); and three works of autobiography, *The Journey to Tai-me* (1967, privately published), *The Way to Rainy Mountain* (1969), and *The Names: A Memoir* (1976) as well as scholarly works. His deliberate engagement with a variety of forms—oral and written poetry, prose fiction and nonfiction, autobiography, legend, history, photography, painting—all "forms of discovery," in Winters's words, has helped him to lay claim to his Kiowa past.

Momaday's idea of the past as a journey is consciously expressed in *The Journey of Tai-me*. This work relates the story of the Sun Dance—a ceremony for spiritual guidance and power performed by many Plains Indian groups that his grandmother Aho saw outlawed in the late 1800s—to his revelatory memory on journeying to Oklahoma to see the sacred Tai-me bundle: "I became more keenly aware of myself as someone who had walked through time and in whose blood there is something inestimably old and undying. It was as if I had remembered something that happened two hundred years ago. I meant then to seek after the source of my memory and myself." In *The Way to Rainy Mountain* (1969), Momaday undertakes this search, collecting, with his father as translator, Kiowa tales and myths and clustering them with brief, loose historical commentaries and personal family stories. What seem to be fragments come together in a complex structure—twenty-four "quintessential novels," divided into three sections, framed by poems and prose pieces—that follow the Kiowa from emergence through maturity to decline as a Plains Indian culture. Central to *Rainy Mountain*, and to all of Momaday's writing, is the land, the focal point of memory, the defining place for Kiowa culture. The same rootedness that defines Momaday's ancestors gives his work its conjuring power, a power that comes from distilling in words and pictures, as Momaday writes, "the glare of noon and all the colors of the dawn and dusk."

## *From* The Way to Rainy Mountain

### *Headwaters*

Noon in the intermountain plain:
There is scant telling of the marsh—
A log, hollow and weather-stained,
An insect at the mouth, and moss—
Yet waters rise against the roots,                                    5
Stand brimming to the stalks. What moves?
What moves on this archaic force
Was wild and welling at the source.

### *Introduction*

A single knoll rises out of the plain in Oklahoma, north and west of the Wichita Range. For my people, the Kiowas,[1] it is an old landmark, and they gave it the name Rainy Mountain. The hardest weather in the world is there. Winter brings blizzards, hot tornadic winds arise in the spring, and in summer the prairie is an anvil's edge. The grass turns brittle and brown, and it cracks beneath your feet. There are green belts along the rivers and creeks, linear groves of hickory and pecan, willow and witch hazel. At a distance in July or August the steaming foliage seems almost to writhe in fire. Great green and yellow grasshoppers are everywhere in the tall grass, popping up like corn to sting the flesh, and tortoises crawl about on the red earth, going nowhere in the plenty of time. Loneliness is an aspect of the land. All things in the plain are isolate; there is no confusion of objects in the eye, but *one* hill or *one* tree or *one* man. To look upon that landscape in the early morning, with the sun at your back, is to lose the sense of proportion. Your imagination comes to life, and this, you think, is where Creation was begun.

I returned to Rainy Mountain in July. My grandmother had died in the spring, and I wanted to be at her grave. She had lived to be very old and at last infirm. Her only living daughter was with her when she died, and I was told that in death her face was that of a child.

I like to think of her as a child. When she was born, the Kiowas were living the last great moment of their history. For more than a hundred years they

---

1. The Kiowa were a mobile hunting and gathering people of the Southern Plains.

had controlled the open range from the Smoky Hill River to the Red, from the headwaters of the Canadian to the fork of the Arkansas and Cimarron. In alliance with the Comanches, they had ruled the whole of the southern Plains. War was their sacred business, and they were among the finest horsemen the world has ever known. But warfare for the Kiowas was preeminently a matter of disposition rather than of survival, and they never understood the grim, unrelenting advance of the U.S. Cavalry. When at last, divided and ill-provisioned, they were driven onto the Staked Plains in the cold rains of autumn, they fell into panic. In Palo Duro Canyon[2] they abandoned their crucial stores to pillage and had nothing then but their lives. In order to save themselves, they surrendered to the soldiers at Fort Sill[3] and were imprisoned in the old stone corral that now stands as a military museum. My grandmother was spared the humiliation of those high gray walls by eight or ten years, but she must have known from birth the affliction of defeat, the dark brooding of old warriors.

Her name was Aho, and she belonged to the last culture to evolve in North America. Her forebears came down from the high country in western Montana nearly three centuries ago. They were a mountain people, a mysterious tribe of hunters whose language has never been positively classified in any major group. In the late seventeenth century they began a long migration to the south and east. It was a journey toward the dawn, and it led to a golden age. Along the way the Kiowas were befriended by the Crows, who gave them the culture and religion of the Plains. They acquired horses, and their ancient nomadic spirit was suddenly free of the ground. They acquired Tai-me,[4] the sacred Sun Dance doll, from that moment the object and symbol of their worship, and so shared in the divinity of the sun. Not least, they acquired the sense of destiny, therefore courage and pride. When they entered upon the southern Plains they had been transformed. No longer were they slaves to the simple necessity of survival; they were a lordly and dangerous society of fighters and thieves, hunters and priests of the sun. According to their origin myth, they entered the world through a hollow log. From one point of view, their migration was the fruit of an old prophecy, for indeed they emerged from a sunless world.

Although my grandmother lived out her long life in the shadow of Rainy Mountain, the immense landscape of the continental interior lay like memory in her blood. She could tell of the Crows, whom she had never seen, and of the Black Hills, where she had never been. I wanted to see in reality what she had seen more perfectly in the mind's eye, and traveled fifteen hundred miles to begin my pilgrimage.

Yellowstone, it seemed to me, was the top of the world, a region of deep lakes and dark timber, canyons and waterfalls. But, beautiful as it is, one might have the sense of confinement there. The skyline in all directions is close at hand, the high wall of the woods and deep cleavages of shade. There is a perfect freedom in the mountains, but it belongs to the eagle and the elk, the badger and the bear. The Kiowas reckoned their stature by the distance they could see, and they were bent and blind in the wilderness.

2. Palo Duro Canyon is on the Staked Plains, or the Texas Panhandle, that part of the state jutting north between New Mexico and Oklahoma.
3. U.S. cavalry fort in Oklahoma and site of the Ki-

owa-Comanche Agency.
4. The sacred being who aids the Kiowa in times of trouble; this being is embodied in the holy doll central to Kiowa ritual.

Descending eastward, the highland meadows are a stairway to the plain. In July the inland slope of the Rockies is luxuriant with flax and buckwheat, stonecrop and larkspur. The earth unfolds and the limit of the land recedes. Clusters of trees, and animals grazing far in the distance, cause the vision to reach away and wonder to build upon the mind. The sun follows a longer course in the day, and the sky is immense beyond all comparison. The great billowing clouds that sail upon it are shadows that move upon the grain like water, dividing light. Farther down, in the land of the Crows and Blackfeet, the plain is yellow. Sweet clover takes hold of the hills and bends upon itself to cover and seal the soil. There the Kiowas paused on their way; they had come to the place where they must change their lives. The sun is at home on the plains. Precisely there does it have the certain character of a god. When the Kiowas came to the land of the Crows, they could see the dark lees of the hills at dawn across the Bighorn River, the profusion of light on the grain shelves, the oldest deity ranging after the solstices. Not yet would they veer southward to the caldron of the land that lay below; they must wean their blood from the northern winter and hold the mountains a while longer in their view. They bore Tai-me in procession to the east.

A dark mist lay over the Black Hills, and the land was like iron. At the top of a ridge I caught sight of Devil's Tower upthrust against the gray sky as if in the birth of time the core of the earth had broken through its crust and the motion of the world was begun. There are things in nature that engender an awful quiet in the heart of man; Devil's Tower is one of them. Two centuries ago, because they could not do otherwise, the Kiowas made a legend at the base of the rock. My grandmother said:

> Eight children were there at play, seven sisters and their brother. Suddenly the boy was struck dumb; he trembled and began to run upon his hands and feet. His fingers became claws, and his body was covered with fur. Directly there was a bear where the boy had been. The sisters were terrified; they ran, and the bear after them. They came to the stump of a great tree, and the tree spoke to them. It bade them climb upon it, and as they did so it began to rise into the air. The bear came to kill them, but they were just beyond its reach. It reared against the tree and scored the bark all around with its claws. The seven sisters were borne into the sky, and they became the stars of the Big Dipper.

From that moment, and so long as the legend lives, the Kiowas have kinsmen in the night sky. Whatever they were in the mountains, they could be no more. However tenuous their well-being, however much they had suffered and would suffer again, they had found a way out of the wilderness.

My grandmother had a reverence for the sun, a holy regard that now is all but gone out of mankind. There was a wariness in her, and an ancient awe. She was a Christian in her later years, but she had come a long way about, and she never forgot her birthright. As a child she had been to the Sun Dances; she had taken part in those annual rites, and by them she had learned the restoration of her people in the presence of Tai-me. She was about seven when the last Kiowa Sun Dance was held in 1887 on the Washita River above Rainy Mountain Creek. The buffalo were gone. In order to consummate the ancient sacrifice—to impale the head of a buffalo bull upon the medicine tree—a delegation of old men journeyed into Texas, there to beg and barter for an animal from the Goodnight herd. She was ten when the Kiowas came together for the last time as a living Sun Dance culture. They could find no buffalo; they had to hang an old hide from the sacred tree. Before the dance could begin, a company of soldiers rode out from Fort Sill under orders to disperse the tribe. Forbidden without cause the essential act of their faith,[5] having seen the wild herds slaughtered and left to rot upon the ground, the Kiowas backed away forever from the medicine tree. That was July 20, 1890, at the great bend of the Washita. My grandmother was there. Without bitterness, and for as long as she lived, she bore a vision of deicide.

Now that I can have her only in memory, I see my grandmother in the several postures that were peculiar to her: standing at the wood stove on a winter morning and turning meat in a great iron skillet; sitting at the south window, bent above her beadwork, and afterwards, when her vision failed, looking down for a long time into the fold of her hands; going out upon a cane, very slowly as she did when the weight of age came upon her; praying. I remember her most often at prayer. She made long, rambling prayers out of suffering and hope, having seen many things. I was never sure that I had the right to hear, so exclusive were they of all mere custom and company. The last time I saw her she prayed standing by the side of her bed at night, naked to the waist, the light of a kerosene lamp moving upon her dark skin. Her long, black hair, always drawn and braided in the day, lay upon her shoulders and against her breasts like a shawl. I do not speak Kiowa, and I never understood her prayers, but there was something inherently sad in the sound, some merest hesitation upon the syllables of sorrow. She began in a high and descending pitch, exhausting her breath to silence; then again and again—and always the same intensity of effort, of something that is, and is not, like urgency in the human voice. Transported so in the dancing light among the shadows of her room, she seemed beyond the reach of time. But that was illusion; I think I knew then that I should not see her again.

Houses are like sentinels in the plain, old keepers of the weather watch. There, in a very little while, wood takes on the appearance of great age. All colors wear soon away in the wind and rain, and then the wood is burned gray and the grain appears and the nails turn red with rust. The windowpanes are black and opaque; you imagine there is nothing within, and indeed there are many ghosts, bones given up to the land. They stand here and there against the sky, and you approach them for a longer time than you expect. They belong in the distance; it is their domain.

Once there was a lot of sound in my grandmother's house, a lot of coming and going, feasting and talk. The summers there were full of excitement and reunion. The Kiowas are a summer people; they abide the cold and keep to themselves, but when the season turns and the land becomes warm and vital they cannot hold still; an old love of going returns upon them. The aged visitors who came to my grandmother's house when I was a child were made of lean and leather, and they bore themselves upright. They wore great black hats and bright ample shirts that shook in the wind. They rubbed fat upon their hair and wound their braids with strips of colored cloth. Some of them

---

5. From the 1880s on, the U.S. government sought to ban all "heathenish" practices among the Native American peoples in a continuing effort to Christianize and "civilize" them.

painted their faces and carried the scars of old and cherished enmities. They were an old council of warlords, come to remind and be reminded of who they were. Their wives and daughters served them well. The women might indulge themselves; gossip was at once the mark and compensation of their servitude. They made loud and elaborate talk among themselves, full of jest and gesture, fright and false alarm. They went abroad in fringed and flowered shawls, bright beadwork and German silver. They were at home in the kitchen, and they prepared meals that were banquets.

There were frequent prayer meetings, and great nocturnal feasts. When I was a child I played with my cousins outside, where the lamplight fell upon the ground and the singing of the old people rose up around us and carried away into the darkness. There were a lot of good things to eat, a lot of laughter and surprise. And afterwards, when the quiet returned, I lay down with my grandmother and could hear the frogs away by the river and feel the motion of the air.

Now there is a funeral silence in the rooms, the endless wake of some final word. The walls have closed in upon my grandmother's house. When I returned to it in mourning, I saw for the first time in my life how small it was. It was late at night, and there was a white moon, nearly full. I sat for a long time on the stone steps by the kitchen door. From there I could see out across the land; I could see the long row of trees by the creek, the low light upon the rolling plains, and the stars of the Big Dipper. Once I looked at the moon and caught sight of a strange thing. A cricket had perched upon the handrail, only a few inches away from me. My line of vision was such that the creature filled the moon like a fossil. It had gone there, I thought, to live and die, for there, of all places, was its small definition made whole and eternal. A warm wind rose up and purled like the longing within me.

The next morning I awoke at dawn and went out on the dirt road to Rainy Mountain. It was already hot, and the grasshoppers began to fill the air. Still, it was early in the morning, and the birds sang out of the shadows. The long yellow grass on the mountain shone in the bright light, and a scissortail hied above the land. There, where it ought to be, at the end of a long and legendary way, was my grandmother's grave. Here and there on the dark stones were ancestral names. Looking back once, I saw the mountain and came away.

## IV

They lived at first in the mountains. They did not yet know of Tai-me, but this is what they knew: There was a man and his wife. They had a beautiful child, a little girl whom they would not allow to go out of their sight. But one day a friend of the family came and asked if she might take the child outside to play. The mother guessed that would be all right, but she told the friend to leave the child in its cradle and to place the cradle in a tree. While the child was in the tree, a redbird came among the branches. It was not like any bird that you have seen; it was very beautiful, and it did not fly away. It kept still upon a limb, close to the child. After a while the child got out of its cradle and began to climb after the redbird. And at the same time the tree began to grow taller, and the child was borne up into the sky. She was then a woman, and she found herself in a strange place. Instead of a redbird, there was a young man standing before her. The man spoke to her and said: "I have been watching you for a long time, and I knew that I would find a way to bring you here. I have brought you here to be my wife." The woman looked all around; she saw that he was the only living man there. She saw that he was the sun.

*There the land itself ascends into the sky. These mountains lie at the top of the continent, and they cast a long rain shadow on the sea of grasses to the east. They arise out of the last North American wilderness, and they have wilderness names: Wasatch, Bitterroot, Bighorn, Wind River.*

*I have walked in a mountain meadow bright with Indian paintbrush, lupine, and wild buckwheat, and I have seen high in the branches of a lodgepole pine the male pine grosbeak, round and rose-colored, its dark, striped wings nearly invisible in the soft, mottled light. And the uppermost branches of the tree seemed very slowly to ride across the blue sky.*

## XIII

If an arrow is well made, it will have tooth marks upon it. That is how you know. The Kiowas made fine arrows and straightened them in their teeth. Then they drew them to the bow to see if they were straight. Once there was a man and his wife. They were alone at night in their tipi. By the light of the fire the man was making arrows. After a while he caught sight of something. There was a small opening in the tipi where two hides were sewn together. Someone was there on the outside, looking in. The man went on with his work, but he said to his wife: "Someone is standing outside. Do not be afraid. Let us talk easily, as of ordinary things." He took up an arrow and straightened it in his teeth; then, as it was right for him to do, he drew it to the bow and took aim, first in this direction and then in that. And all the while he was talking, as if to his wife. But this is how he spoke: "I know that you are there on the outside, for I can feel your eyes upon me. If you are a Kiowa, you will understand what I am saying, and you will speak your name." But there was no answer, and the man went on in the same way, pointing the arrow all around. At last his aim fell upon the place where his enemy stood, and he let go of the string. The arrow went straight to the enemy's heart.

*The old men were the best arrowmakers, for they could bring time and patience to their craft. The young men—the fighters and hunters—were willing to pay a high price for arrows that were well made.*

When my father was a boy, an old man used to come to Mammedaty's[6] house and pay his respects. He was a lean old man in braids and was impressive in his age and bearing. His name was Cheney, and he was an arrowmaker. Every morning, my father tells me, Cheney would paint his wrinkled face, go out, and pray aloud to the rising sun. In my mind I can see that man as if he were there now. I like to watch him as he makes his prayer. I know where he stands and where his voice goes on the rolling grasses and where the sun comes up on the land. There, at dawn, you can feel the silence. It is cold and clear and deep like water. It takes hold of you and will not let you go.

---

6. Momaday's paternal grandfather.

## XVII

Bad women are thrown away. Once there was a handsome young man. He was wild and reckless, and the chief talked to the wind about him. After that, the man went hunting. A great whirlwind passed by, and he was blind. The Kiowas have no need of a blind man; they left him alone with his wife and child. The winter was coming on and food was scarce. In four days the man's wife grew tired of caring for him. A herd of buffalo came near, and the man knew the sound. He asked his wife to hand him a bow and an arrow. "You must tell me," he said, "when the buffalo are directly in front of me." And in that way he killed a bull, but his wife said that he had missed. He asked for another arrow and killed another bull, but again his wife said that he had missed. Now the man was a hunter, and he knew the sound an arrow makes when it strikes home, but he said nothing. Then his wife helped herself to the meat and ran away with her child. The man was blind; he ate grass and kept himself alive. In seven days a band of Kiowas found him and took him to their camp. There in the firelight a woman was telling a story. She told of how her husband had been killed by enemy warriors. The blind man listened, and he knew her voice. That was a bad woman. At sunrise they threw her away.

*In the Kiowa calendars[7] there is graphic proof that the lives of women were hard, whether they were "bad women" or not. Only the captives, who were slaves, held lower status. During the Sun Dance of 1843, a man stabbed his wife in the breast because she accepted Chief Dohasan's invitation to ride with him in the ceremonial procession. And in the winter of 1851–52, Big Bow stole the wife of a man who was away on a raiding expedition. He brought her to his father's camp and made her wait outside in the bitter cold while he went in to collect his things. But his father knew what was going on, and he held Big Bow and would not let him go. The woman was made to wait in the snow until her feet were frozen.*

*Mammedaty's grandmother, Kau-au-ointy,[8] was a Mexican captive, taken from her homeland when she was a child of eight or ten years. I never knew her, but I have been to her grave at Rainy Mountain.*

KAU-AU-OINTY
BORN 1834
DIED 1929
AT REST

*She raised a lot of eyebrows, they say, for she would not play the part of a Kiowa woman. From slavery she rose up to become a figure in the tribe. She owned a great herd of cattle, and she could ride as well as any man. She had blue eyes.*

7. The Kiowa recorded their history in pictures that functioned as calendars.
8. Momaday's great-great grandmother.

## XXIV

East of my grandmother's house, south of the pecan grove, there is buried a woman in a beautiful dress. Mammedaty used to know where she is buried, but now no one knows. If you stand on the front porch of the house and look eastward towards Carnegie, you know that the woman is buried somewhere within the range of your vision. But her grave is unmarked. She was buried in a cabinet, and she wore a beautiful dress. How beautiful it was! It was one of those fine buckskin dresses, and it was decorated with elk's teeth and beadwork. That dress is still there, under the ground.

*Aho's high moccasins are made of softest, cream-colored skins. On each instep there is a bright disc of beadwork—an eight-pointed star, red and pale blue on a white field—and there are bands of beadwork at the soles and ankles. The flaps of the leggings are wide and richly ornamented with blue and red and green and white and lavender beads.*

*East of my grandmother's house the sun rises out of the plain. Once in his life a man ought to concentrate his mind upon the remembered earth, I believe. He ought to give himself up to a particular landscape in his experience, to look at it from as many angles as he can, to wonder about it, to dwell upon it. He ought to imagine that he touches it with his hands at every season and listens to the sounds that are made upon it. He ought to imagine the creatures there and all the faintest motions of the wind. He ought to recollect the glare of noon and all the colors of the dawn and dusk.*

## Epilogue

During the first hours after midnight on the morning of November 13, 1833, it seemed that the world was coming to an end. Suddenly the stillness of the night was broken; there were brilliant flashes of light in the sky, light of such intensity that people were awakened by it. With the speed and density of a driving rain, stars were falling in the universe. Some were brighter than Venus; one was said to be as large as the moon.

That most brilliant shower of Leonid meteors has a special place in the memory of the Kiowa people. It is among the earliest entries in the Kiowa calendars, and it marks the beginning as it were of the historical period in the tribal mind. In the preceding year Tai-me had been stolen by a band of Osages, and although it was later returned, the loss was an almost unimaginable tragedy; and in 1837 the Kiowas made the first of their treaties[9] with the United States. The falling stars seemed to image the sudden and violent disintegration of an old order.

But indeed the golden age of the Kiowas had been short-lived, ninety or a hundred years, say, from about 1740. The culture would persist for a while in decline, until about 1875, but then it would be gone, and there would be very little material evidence that it had ever been. Yet it is within the reach of memory still, though tenuously now, and moreover it is even defined in a remarkably rich and living verbal tradition which demands to be preserved for its own sake. The living memory and the verbal tradition which transcends it were brought together for me once and for all in the person of Ko-sahn.

A hundred-year-old woman came to my grandmother's house one afternoon in July. Aho was dead; Mammedaty had died before I was born. There were very few Kiowas left who could remember the Sun Dances; Ko-sahn was one of them; she was a grown woman when my grandparents came into the world. Her body was twisted and her face deeply lined with age. Her thin white hair was held in place by a cap of black netting, though she wore braids as well, and she had but one eye. She was dressed in the manner of a Kiowa matron, a dark, full-cut dress that reached nearly to the ankles, full, flowing sleeves, and a wide, apron-like sash. She sat on a bench in the arbor so concentrated in her great age that she seemed extraordinarily small. She was quiet for a time—she might almost have been asleep—and then she began to speak and to sing. She spoke of many things, and once she spoke of the Sun Dance:

> My sisters and I were very young; that was a long time ago. Early one morning they came to wake us up. They had brought a great buffalo in from the plain. Everyone went out to see and to pray. We heard a great many voices. One man said that the lodge was almost ready. We were told to go there, and someone gave me a piece of cloth. It was very beautiful. Then I asked what I ought to do with it, and they said that I must tie it to the Tai-me tree. There were other pieces of cloth on the tree, and so I put mine there as well.
> When the lodge frame was finished, a woman—sometimes a man— began to sing. It was like this:

9. This treaty provided for the passage of settlers through Kiowa and Comanche lands.

*Everything is ready.*
*Now the four societies must go out.*
*They must go out and get the leaves,*
    *the branches for the lodge.*

And when the branches were tied in place, again there was singing:

*Let the boys go out.*
*Come on, boys, now we must get the earth.*

The boys began to shout. Now they were not just ordinary boys, not all
of them; they were those for whom prayers had been made, and they
were dressed in different ways. There was an old, old woman. She had
something on her back. The boys went out to see. The old woman had a
bag full of earth on her back. It was a certain kind of sandy earth. That is
what they must have in the lodge. The dancers must dance upon the
sandy earth. The old woman held a digging tool in her hand. She turned
towards the south and pointed with her lips. It was like a kiss, and she
began to sing:

*We have brought the earth.*
*Now it is time to play;*
*As old as I am, I still have the feeling of play.*

That was the beginning of the Sun Dance. The dancers treated themselves with buffalo medicine, and slowly they began to take their steps.
. . . And all the people were around, and they wore splendid things—
beautiful buckskin and beads. The chiefs wore necklaces, and their pen-
dants shone like the sun. There were many people, and oh, it was beautiful! That was the beginning of the Sun Dance. It was all for Tai-me, you
know, and it was a long time ago.

It was—all of this and more—a quest, a going forth upon the way to Rainy
Mountain. Probably Ko-sahn too is dead now. At times, in the quiet of evening, I think she must have wondered, dreaming, who she was. Was she
become in her sleep that old purveyor of the sacred earth, perhaps, that ancient
one who, old as she was, still had the feeling of play? And in her mind, at
times, did she see the falling stars?

### Rainy Mountain Cemetery

Most is your name the name of this dark stone.
Deranged in death, the mind to be inheres
Forever in the nominal unknown,
The wake of nothing audible he hears
Who listens here and now to hear your name.          5

The early sun, red as a hunter's moon,
Runs in the plain. The mountain burns and shines;
And silence is the long approach of noon
Upon the shadow that your name defines—
And death this cold, black density of stone.          10

1969

# THOMAS PYNCHON
## b. 1937

Thomas Pynchon has managed to remain the most private of contemporary American writers, without so much as a photograph of him in circulation. A few facts are known: born on Long Island, graduated from Cornell University (where he was a student in Vladimir Nabokov's course) in the late 1950s, served a term in the navy, and now lives—it is said—in southern, or is it northern, California. Beyond that, silence, which has been broken only by four strange and distinctive novels, plus a few short stories.

The first of these, V (1963), cannot be understood by reference to convenient fictional signposts. Although it showed an indebtedness to Faulkner and Joyce (an indebtedness shared by most ambitious American novelists), Pynchon's style was already wholly his own. In writing that was by turns labyrinthine, eloquent, and colloquial, he showed a particular fondness for imitating other styles and writing. But these imitations and parodies instead of disparaging or minimizing their subjects radiated a generous spirit of exuberance that extended to the many characters who inhabit V and whose individual paranoias—Pynchon's word to characterize the human attempt to make connections between events—propel them into unbelievably complicated and absurd plots. The interest of V was largely in the remarkably unending inventiveness with which Pynchon developed those plots, which might involve anything from diplomatic spy stories in nineteenth-century Africa to the bombing of Malta during World War II, to surgical reconstruction of a young woman's nose, or a hunt for alligators in the sewers of New York City.

The comic talent shown in various New York episodes from V was also evident in *The Crying of Lot 49* (1966), of which the first chapter is printed here. This short, perfectly controlled novel teases us and itself with questions about the meaning of our American heritage, as embodied in the form of the mysterious legacy left to its heroine, Oedipa Maas. (The jokey yet portentous name exemplifies Pynchon's teasing way of playing at "significance.") What is the connection between this legacy and the mysterious alternative to the U.S. Postal System on which Oedipa believes she has stumbled? Is there a secret network of alienated citizens carrying on their lives outside the ordinary systems and institutions of American life? Or is it all Oedipa's delusion, her private paranoia? These questions are considered through a style that continually surprises and unsettles us, though it is less discontinuous than V's. In Pynchon's world everything serious has its silly aspects (the Marx Brothers, among countless other comic acts, are in the background), while bits of trivia and foolery are suddenly elevated, through the style, into objects of sublime contemplation—as the novel's end when Oedipa thinks of "squatters" who

> . . . slept in junkyards in the stripped shells of wrecked Plymouths, or even, daring, spent the night up some pole in a lineman's tent like caterpillars, swung among a web of telephone wires, living in the very copper rigging and secular miracle of communication, untroubled by the dumb voltages flickering their miles, the night long, in the thousand of unheard messages.

Here his sentences enact the daring freedom he admires, in contrast to the institutions of a technological society.

Pynchon's longest and most daring and exhaustive effort came with the publication, in 1973, of *Gravity's Rainbow*. This encyclopedic fantasy operates through brilliant improvisations, tall tales, obscene parables, and burlesque stage routines, all of which work together into a story of supersonic capabilities and annihilative retributions. A huge cast of characters, each with a crazy name and a plot to unravel, is located all over the map, but mainly in World War II London and in postwar Germany. As the four main and the countless subsidiary plots take shape, characters—and the reader as well—attempt to "read" the messages flickering, the dumb intent to communicate, in the most casual as well as the most portentous sign. Pynchon's knowingness and fascination with popular culture is overwhelmingly evident in *Gravity's Rainbow* as is his preoccupation with the lore of theoretical science, of obscure historical tales, and of contemporary comic books. No one denies the formidably encyclopedic nature of this astonishing effort; the question is, as Warner Berthoff has asked it, whether that effort may not also be "encyclopedically monotonous and static." More readers begin *Gravity's Rainbow* than finish it.

After 1973, except for the publication in 1984 of some of his early stories (in *Slow Learner*), all was silent on the Pynchon front until *Vineland* appeared in 1990. *Vineland* is wonderful on the California terrain and has much free-wheeling and funny inventiveness; at other times Pynchon seems to be flogging his material and repeating himself. But although there is still no consensus on his stature as an enduring American writer, there is general recognition of the quirky, uncanny exactitude of his imagination. Pynchon's theatrical spellbindings as a man of metaphor, his feats of association (in Robert Frost's phrase), are employed on subjects— like the rocket in *Gravity's Rainbow*—that were thought to be beyond words. For daring, wit, and exuberance, there is no contemporary writer who excels him.

## *From* The Crying of Lot 49[1]

### 1

One summer afternoon Mrs Oedipa Maas came home from a Tupperware party whose hostess had put perhaps too much kirsch in the fondue to find that she, Oedipa, had been named executor, or she supposed executrix, of the estate of one Pierce Inverarity, a California real estate mogul who had once lost two million dollars in his spare time but still had assets numerous and tangled enough to make the job of sorting it all out more than honorary. Oedipa stood in the living room, stared at by the greenish dead eye of the TV tube, spoke the name of God, tried to feel as drunk as possible. But this did not work. She thought of a hotel room in Mazatlán whose door had just been slammed, it seemed forever, waking up two hundred birds down in the lobby; a sunrise over the library slope at Cornell University that nobody out on it had seen because the slope faced west; a dry, disconsolate tune from the fourth movement of the Bartók Concerto for Orchestra; a whitewashed bust of Jay Gould that Pierce kept over the bed on a shelf so narrow for it she'd always had the hovering fear it would someday topple on them. Was that how he'd died, she wondered, among dreams, crushed by the only ikon in the house? That only made her laugh, out loud and helpless: You're so sick, Oedipa, she told herself, or the room, which knew.

The letter was from the law firm of Warpe, Wistfull, Kubitschek and McMingus, of Los Angeles, and signed by somebody named Metzger. It said Pierce had died back in the spring, and they'd only just now found the will. Metzger was to act as co-executor and special counsel in the event of any

---

1. Chapter 1 is printed here.

involved litigation. Oedipa had been named also to execute the will in a codicil dated a year ago. She tried to think back to whether anything unusual had
happened around then. Through the rest of the afternoon, through her trip to
the market in downtown Kinneret-Among-the-Pines to buy ricotta and listen
to the Muzak (today she came through the bead-curtained entrance around
bar 4 of the Fort Wayne Settecento Ensemble's variorum recording of the
Vivaldi Kazoo Concerto, Boyd Beaver, soloist); then through the sunned gathering of her marjoram and sweet basil from the herb garden, reading of book
reviews in the latest *Scientific American*, into the layering of a lasagna, gar-
licking of a bread, tearing up of romaine leaves, eventually, oven on, into the
mixing of the twilight's whiskey sours against the arrival of her husband, Wendell ("Mucho") Maas from work, she wondered, wondered, shuffling back
through a fat deckful of days which seemed (wouldn't she be first to admit it?)
more or less identical, or all pointing the same way subtly like a conjurer's
deck, any odd one readily clear to a trained eye. It took her till the middle of
Huntley and Brinkley to remember that last year at three or so one morning
there had come this long-distance call, from where she would never know
(unless now he'd left a diary) by a voice beginning in heavy Slavic tones as
second secretary at the Transylvanian Consulate, looking for an escaped bat;
modulated to comic-Negro, then on into hostile Pachuco dialect, full of chin-
gas and maricones; then a Gestapo officer asking her in shrieks did she have
relatives in Germany and finally his Lamont Cranston voice, the one he'd
talked in all the way down to Mazatlán. "Pierce, please," she'd managed to get
in, "I thought we had—"

"But Margo," earnestly, "I've just come from Commissioner Weston, and
that old man in the fun house was murdered by the same blowgun that killed
Professor Quackenbush," or something.

"For God's sake," she said. Mucho had rolled over and was looking at her.

"Why don't you hang up on him," Mucho suggested, sensibly.

"I heard that," Pierce said. "I think it's time Wendell Maas had a little visit
from The Shadow." Silence, positive and thorough, fell. So it was the last of
his voices she ever heard. Lamont Cranston. That phone line could have
pointed any direction, been any length. Its quiet ambiguity shifted over, in the
months after the call, to what had been revived: memories of his face, body,
things he'd given her, things she had now and then pretended not to've heard
him say. It took him over, and to the verge of being forgotten. The shadow
waited a year before visiting. But now there was Metzger's letter. Had Pierce
called last year then to tell her about this codicil? Or had he decided on it
later, somehow because of her annoyance and Mucho's indifference? She felt
exposed, finessed, put down. She had never executed a will in her life, didn't
know where to begin, didn't know how to tell the law firm in L.A. that she
didn't know where to begin.

"Mucho, baby," she cried, in an access of helplessness.

Mucho Maas, home, bounded through the screen door. "Today was
another defeat," he began.

"Let me tell you," she also began. But let Mucho go first.

He was a disk jockey who worked further along the Peninsula and suffered
regular crises of conscience about his profession. "I don't believe in any of it,
Oed," he could usually get out. "I try, I truly can't," way down there, further
down perhaps than she could reach, so that such times often brought her near

panic. It might have been the sight of her so about to lose control that seemed to bring him back up.

"You're too sensitive." Yeah, there was so much else she ought to be saying also, but this was what came out. It was true, anyway. For a couple years he'd been a used car salesman and so hyperaware of what *that* profession had come to mean that working hours were exquisite torture to him. Mucho shaved his upper lip every morning three times with, three times against the grain to remove any remotest breath of a moustache, new blades he drew blood invariably but kept at it; bought all natural-shoulder suits, then went to a tailor to have the lapels made yet more abnormally narrow, on his hair used only water, combing it like Jack Lemmon to throw them further off. The sight of sawdust, even pencil shavings, made him wince, his own kind being known to use it for hushing sick transmissions, and though he dieted he could still not as Oedipa did use honey to sweeten his coffee for like all things viscous it distressed him, recalling too poignantly what is often mixed with motor oil to ooze dishonest into gaps between piston and cylinder wall. He walked out of a party one night because somebody used the word "creampuff," it seemed maliciously, in his hearing. The man was a refugee Hungarian pastry cook talking shop, but there was your Mucho: thin-skinned.

Yet at least he had believed in the cars. Maybe to excess: how could he not, seeing people poorer than him come in, Negro, Mexican, cracker, a parade seven days a week, bringing the most godawful of trade-ins: motorized, metal extensions of themselves, of their families and what their whole lives must be like, out there so naked for anybody, a stranger like himself, to look at, frame cockeyed, rusty underneath, fender repainted in a shade just off enough to depress the value, if not Mucho himself, inside smelling hopelessly of children, supermarket booze, two, sometimes three generations of cigarette smokers, or only of dust—and when the cars were swept out you had to look at the actual residue of these lives, and there was no way of telling what things had been truly refused (when so little he supposed came by that out of fear most of it had to be taken and kept) and what had simply (perhaps tragically) been lost: clipped coupons promising savings of 5 or 10¢, trading stamps, pink flyers advertising specials at the markets, butts, tooth-shy combs, help-wanted ads, Yellow Pages torn from the phone book, rags of old underwear or dresses that already were period costumes, for wiping your own breath off the inside of a windshield with so you could see whatever it was, a movie, a woman or car you coveted, a cop who might pull you over just for drill, all the bits and pieces coated uniformly, like a salad of despair, in a gray dressing of ash, condensed exhaust, dust, body wastes—it made him sick to look, but he had to look. If it had been an outright junkyard, probably he could have stuck things out, made a career: the violence that had caused each wreck being infrequent enough, far enough away from him, to be miraculous, as each death, up till the moment of our own, is miraculous. But the endless rituals of trade-in, week after week, never got as far as violence or blood, and so were too plausible for the impressionable Mucho to take for long. Even if enough exposure to the unvarying gray sickness had somehow managed to immunize him, he could still never accept the way each owner, each shadow, filed in only to exchange a dented, malfunctioning version of himself for another, just as futureless, automotive projection of somebody else's life. As if it were the most natural thing. To Mucho it was horrible. Endless, convoluted incest.

Oedipa couldn't understand how he could still get so upset even now. By the time he married her he'd already been two years at the station, KCUF, and the lot on the pallid, roaring arterial was far behind him, like the Second World or Korean Wars were for older husbands. Maybe, God help her, he should have been in a war, Japs in trees, Krauts in Tiger tanks, gooks with trumpets in the night he might have forgotten sooner than whatever it was about the lot that had stayed so alarmingly with him for going on five years. Five years. You comfort them when they wake pouring sweat or crying out in the language of bad dreams, yes, you hold them, they calm down, one day they lose it: she knew that. But when was Mucho going to forget? She suspected the disk jockey spot (which he'd got through his good buddy the KCUF advertising manager, who'd visited the lot once a week, the lot being a sponsor) was a way of letting the Top 200, and even the news copy that came jabbering out of the machine—all the fraudulent dream of teenage appetites—be a buffer between him and that lot.

He had believed too much in the lot, he believed not at all in the station. Yet to look at him now, in the twilit living room, gliding like a large bird in an updraft toward the sweating shakerful of booze, smiling out of his fat vortex ring's centre, you'd think all was flat calm, gold, serene.

Until he opened his mouth. "Today Funch," he told her, pouring, "had me in, wanted to talk about my image, which he doesn't like." Funch being the program director, and Mucho's great foe. "I'm too horny, now. What I should be is a young father, a big brother. These little chicks call in with requests, naked lust, to Funch's ear, throbs in every word I say. So now I'm supposed to tape all the phone talk. Funch personally will edit out anything he considers offensive, meaning all of my end of the conversation. Censorship, I told him, 'fink,' I muttered, and fled." He and Funch went through some such routine maybe once a week.

She showed him the letter from Metzger. Mucho knew all about her and Pierce: it had ended a year before Mucho married her. He read the letter and withdrew along a shy string of eyeblinks.

"What am I going to do?" she said.

"Oh, no," said Mucho, "you got the wrong fella. Not me. I can't even make out our income tax right. Execute a will, there's nothing I can tell you, see Roseman." Their lawyer.

"Mucho. Wendell. It was *over*. *Before* he put my name on it."

"Yeah, yeah. I meant only that, Oed. I'm not capable."

So next morning that's what she did, went and saw Roseman. After a half hour in front of her vanity mirror drawing and having to redraw dark lines along her eyelids that each time went ragged or wavered violently before she could take the brush away. She'd been up most of the night, after another three-in-the-morning phone call, its announcing bell clear cardiac terror, so out of nothing did it come, the instrument one second inert, the next screaming. It brought both of them instantly awake and they lay, joints unlocking, not even wanting to look at each other for the first few rings. She finally, having nothing she knew of to lose, had taken it. It was Dr Hilarius, her shrink or psychotherapist. But he sounded like Pierce doing a Gestapo officer.

"I didn't wake you up, did it," he began, dry. "You sound so frightened. How are the pills, not working?"

"I'm not taking them," she said.

"You feel threatened by them?"

"I don't know what's inside them."

"You don't believe that they're only tranquilizers."

"Do I trust you?" She didn't, and what he said next explained why not.

"We still need a hundred-and-fourth for the bridge." Chuckled aridly. The bridge, die Brücke, being his pet name for the experiment he was helping the community hospital run on effects of LSD-25, mescaline, psilocybin, and related drugs on a large sample of suburban housewives. The bridge inward.

"When can you let us fit you into our schedule."

"No," she said, "you have half a million others to choose from. It's three in the morning."

"We want you." Hanging in the air over her bed she now beheld the well-known portrait of Uncle that appears in front of all our post offices, his eyes gleaming unhealthily, his sunken yellow cheeks most violently rouged, his finger pointing between her eyes. I want you. She had never asked Dr Hilarius why, being afraid of all he might answer.

"I am having a hallucination now. I don't need drugs for that."

"Don't describe it," he said quickly. "Well. Was there anything else you wanted to talk about."

"Did I call you?"

"I thought so," he said, "I had this feeling. Not telepathy. But rapport with a patient is a curious thing sometimes."

"Not this time." She hung up. And then couldn't get to sleep. But would be damned if she'd take the capsules he'd given her. Literally damned. She didn't want to get hooked in any way, she'd told him that.

"So," he shrugged, "on me you are not hooked? Leave then. You're cured."

She didn't leave. Not that the shrink held any dark power over her. But it was easier to stay. Who'd know the day she was cured? Not him, he'd admitted that himself. "Pills are different," she pleaded. Hilarius only made a face at her, one he'd made before. He was full of these delightful lapses from orthodoxy. His theory being that a face is symmetrical like a Rorschach blot, tells a story like a TAT picture, excites a response like a suggested word, so why not. He claimed to have once cured a case of hysterical blindness with his number 37, the "Fu-Manchu" (many of the faces having like German symphonies, both a number and nickname), which involved slanting the eyes up with the index fingers, enlarging the nostrils with the middle fingers, pulling the mouth wide with the pinkies and protruding the tongue. On Hilarius it was truly alarming. And in fact, as Oedipa's Uncle Sam hallucination faded, it was this Fu-Manchu face that came dissolving in to replace it and stay with her for what was left of the hours before dawn. It put her in hardly any shape to see Roseman.

But Roseman had also spent a sleepless night, brooding over the Perry Mason television program the evening before, which his wife was fond of but toward which Roseman cherished a fierce ambivalence, wanting at once to be a successful trial lawyer like Perry Mason and, since this was impossible, to destroy Perry Mason by undermining him. Oedipa walked in more or less by surprise to catch her trusted family lawyer stuffing with guilty haste a wad of different-sized and colored papers into a desk drawer. She knew it was the rough draft of *The Profession v. Perry Mason, A Not-so-hypothetical Indictment,* and had been in progress for as long as the TV show had been on the air.

"You didn't use to look guilty, as I remember," Oedipa said. They often went to the same group therapy sessions, in a car pool with a photographer from Palo Alto who thought he was a volleyball. "That's a good sign, isn't it?"

"You might have been one of Perry Mason's spies," said Roseman. After thinking a moment he added, "Ha, ha."

"Ha, ha," said Oedipa. They looked at each other. "I have to execute a will," she said.

"Oh, go ahead then," said Roseman, "don't let me keep you."

"No," said Oedipa, and told him all.

"Why would he do a thing like that," Roseman puzzled, after reading the letter.

"You mean die?"

"No," said Roseman, "name you to help execute it."

"He was unpredictable." They went to lunch. Roseman tried to play footsie with her under the table. She was wearing boots, and couldn't feel much of anything. So, insulated, she decided not to make any fuss.

"Run away with me," said Roseman when the coffee came.

"Where?" she asked. That shut him up.

Back in the office, he outlined what she was in for: learn intimately the books and the business, go through probate, collect all debts, inventory the assets, get an appraisal of the estate, decide what to liquidate and what to hold on to, pay off claims, square away taxes, distribute legacies . . .

"Hey," said Oedipa, "can't I get somebody to do it for me?"

"Me," said Roseman, "some of it, sure. But aren't you even interested?"

"In what?"

"In what you might find out."

As things developed, she was to have all manner of revelations. Hardly about Pierce Inverarity, or herself; but about what remained yet had somehow, before this, stayed away. There had hung the sense of buffering, insulation, she had noticed the absence of an intensity, as if watching a movie, just perceptibly out of focus, that the projectionist refused to fix. And had also gently conned herself into the curious, Rapunzel-like[2] role of a pensive girl somehow, magically, prisoner among the pines and salt fogs of Kinneret, looking for somebody to say hey, let down your hair. When it turned out to be Pierce she'd happily pulled out the pins and curlers and down it tumbled in its whispering, dainty avalanche, only when Pierce had got maybe halfway up, her lovely hair turned, through some sinister sorcery, into a great unanchored wig, and down he fell, on his ass. But dauntless, perhaps using one of his many credit cards for a shim, he'd slipped the lock on her tower door and come up the conchlike stairs, which, had true guile come more naturally to him, he'd have done to begin with. But all that had then gone on between them had really never escaped the confinement of that tower. In Mexico City they somehow wandered into an exhibition of paintings by the beautiful Spanish exile Remedios Varo: in the central painting of a triptych, titled "Bordando el Manto Terrestre," were a number of frail girls with heart-shaped faces, huge eyes, spun-gold hair, prisoners in the top room of a circular tower, embroidering a kind of tapestry which spilled out the slit windows and into a void,

---

2. Rapunzel, a maiden from a Grimm's fairy tale, was imprisoned in a tower, but let down her hair to her lover, who climbed to her by means of it.

seeking hopelessly to fill the void: for all the other buildings and creatures, all the waves, ships and forests of the earth were contained in this tapestry, and the tapestry was the world. Oedipa, perverse, had stood in front of the painting and cried. No one had noticed; she wore dark green bubble shades. For a moment she'd wondered if the seal around her sockets were tight enough to allow the tears simply to go on and fill up the entire lens space and never dry. She could carry the sadness of the moment with her that way forever, see the world refracted through those tears, those specific tears, as if indices as yet unfound varied in important ways from cry to cry. She had looked down at her feet and known, then, because of a painting, that what she stood on had only been woven together a couple thousand miles away in her own tower, was only by accident known as Mexico, and so Pierce had taken her away from nothing, there'd been no escape. What did she so desire to escape from? Such a captive maiden, having plenty of time to think, soon realizes that her tower, its height and architecture, are like her ego only incidental: that what really keeps her where she is is magic, anonymous and malignant, visited on her from outside and for no reason at all. Having no apparatus except gut fear and female cunning to examine this formless magic, to understand how it works, how to measure its field strength, count its lines of force, she may fall back on superstition, or take up a useful hobby like embroidery, or go mad, or marry a disk jockey. If the tower is everywhere and the knight of deliverance no proof against its magic, what else?

---

# JOYCE CAROL OATES
## b. 1938

When in 1987 Mikhail Gorbachev and his wife, Raisa, visited this country, a number of entertainers and artists were invited to a party in their honor. Among the invited was the novelist and storywriter Joyce Carol Oates, whom both the Gorbachevs assured of their admiration for her work. If the admiration was real, it may have had something to do with the astonishing and continuous productivity this writer has enjoyed since her first collection of stories, *By the North Gate*, was published in 1963. In the intervening years she has brought out more than a score of novels—often with only a year's gap separating one from the next—as well as volumes of stories, many poems, and essays. Under the pseudonym of Rosamond Smith she has written a number of thrillers. Even for a prolific "serious" writer, this output is cause for wonder—if not alarm. Can anyone who writes this much be trusted as to the quality of her product? How many of her books had the Gorbachevs actually read?

Oates's origins were Catholic, working class, and rural. She grew up on her maternal grandparents' farm in Erie County, outside Lockport, New York, went to a high school near Buffalo, then entered Syracuse University where she performed spectacularly. A Phi Beta Kappa class valedictorian, she was characterized by her creative-writing teacher, Donald A. Dike, as the most brilliant student he had ever seen at Syracuse. One of her stories won the *Mademoiselle* College Fiction contest, her first in a series of awards and prizes. After graduating from college she took an M.A. at Wisconsin, married Raymond Joseph Smith (himself a teacher of English), and went on to study and teach literature at Rice, the University of

Detroit, and the University of Windsor in Ontario, Canada. More recently she has moved to Princeton where she teaches at the university and, with her husband, edits a magazine, the *Ontario Review*.

Critics have often remarked on Oates's fascination with violence, and it is probably true that there is a higher density of murder, rape, and general physical distress in her books than in those of any American writer since Faulkner (whose work was a powerful influence on hers). She has put the issue this way in answer to the question of whether she is "personally haunted by the fear of violence," or simply reflects "everyone else's feelings about it": "I sense it around me, both the fear and the desire, and perhaps I simply have appropriated it from other people." The answer does not of course explain the pervasive and joyless obsessiveness with which terrible things happen to the people in Oates's novels and stories. *them*, her novel of 1969, which won the National Book Award, is perhaps the most powerful embodiment of such happenings, in the lives of two generations of a slum family in Detroit. Maureen Wendall, the novel's heroine, becomes a prostitute at age sixteen and is so seriously beaten by her stepfather that she goes into a catatonic state, emerging from it to take a writing course with a character named Joyce Carol Oates. Maureen's brother Jules, after a string of adventures (in one of which he is shot in the chest by a woman), kills a policeman in the Detroit race riots. Oates writes in the novel's preface that nothing has been exaggerated to dramatize "the various sordid and shocking events of slum life." But as an early critic of her work, Elizabeth Dalton, pointed out, "The dosage of violence is so high and so regular . . . that the reader becomes immune to it, and none of it seems to matter much." This charge, made frequently by critics of Oates's work, is one that individual readers must prove or disprove on their own pulses.

But there is no doubt that the torrent of words delivered to us by this writer over the last two decades has made it extremely difficult to keep up with her, and temptingly easy to neglect her. Such "Gothic" imitations as the novels she published early in the 1980s—*Bellefleur* (1980), *A Bloodsmoor Romance* (1982), and *The Mysteries of Winterthurn* (1984)—tested the staying power of some of Oates's strongest admirers. Although on occasion she has essayed satiric looks at academic folk—in the novel *Unholy Loves* (1979) and in such a marvelous story as *In the Autumn of the Year* (from *A Sentimental Education*, 1980)—her truest place of focus has been the upstate New York territory she early along staked out and returned to in the novel *You Must Remember This* (1987). In it,

> numbing familiar sights passed blurred with rain dreamlike in succession— the Ajax car wash with its big yellow sign, the White Tower restaurant at the corner of Clinton and Lock, the Esso service station . . . then Carrier Furnaces, then the Clinton Street Bank of Port Oriskany, then blocks of brick rowhouses mean and cramped and then slightly larger houses, duplexes like the Stevicks' covered in shingle-board in gunmetal gray or dark brown or green, with wide porches and steep slanting roofs and small plots of grass or no grass at all, just scrubby soil, weeds.

The relentless style is appropriate to the sense of place and life conveyed, as the unforgiving small city, Port Oriskany, with the canal running through it, rises before our eyes. *You Must Remember This* is in part a history of America in the 1950s and also contains some of the most vivid writing about boxing ever encountered in a book (to the point of making one of its admirers, John Updike, declare that on the basis of her description of the death of a young fighter in the ring, the sport should be outlawed).

*Golden Gloves*, the story printed here, has some of that vividness in its writing about life in the ring (Oates has published a pictorial study of boxing), but it also dramatizes, once again, the deterministic victimization painfully, if vaguely, felt by her characters as they sink under life's current. It is still too early to make clear distinctions among the many parts of Oates's work, but she is on her way to creating an oeuvre that makes a strong claim to the accolade bestowed on her by Updike when he said, "If the phrase 'woman of letters' existed, she would be, foremost in this country, entitled to it."

# Golden Gloves[1]

He was a premature baby, seven months old, born with deformed feet: the tiny arches twisted, the toes turned inward like fleshy claws. He didn't learn to walk until the age of three; then he tottered and lurched from side to side, his small face contorted with an adult rage, a rim of white showing above the irises of his eyes. His parents watched him in pity and despair—his father with a kind of embarrassment as well. Even at that age he hated to be helped to walk. Sometimes he hated to be touched.

Until the age of eight, when both his feet were finally operated on, he was always stumbling, falling, hurting himself, but he was accustomed to pain, he rarely cried. He wasn't like other children! At school, on the playground, out on the street, the cruelest children mocked him, called him names—Cripple, Freak—sometimes they even tripped him—but as he got older and stronger they learned to keep their distance. If he could grab them he'd hurt them with his hard pummeling fists, he'd make them cry. And even with his handicap he was quick: quick and clever and sinewy as a snake.

After the operation on his feet his father began to take him to boxing matches downtown in the old sports arena. He will remember all his life the excitement of his first Golden Gloves tournament, some of the boxers as young as fifteen, ribs showing, backs raw with acne, hard tight muscles, tiny glinting gold crosses on chains around their necks. He remembers the brick-red leather gloves that looked as if they must be soft to the touch, the bodies hotly gleaming with sweat, white boys, black boys, their amazing agility, the quickness of their feet and hands, high-laced shoes and ribbed socks halfway to their knees. They wore trunks like swimming trunks, they wore robes like bathrobes, and all with such nonchalance, in public. He remembers the dazzling lights focused upon the elevated ring, the shouts of the crowd that came in waves, the warm rippling applause when one boy of a pair was declared the winner of his match, his arm held aloft by the referee. What must it be, to be that boy!—to stand in his place!

*He* was seated in a child's wheelchair in the aisle, close beside his father's seat. Both legs encased in plaster from hip to toe: and him trapped inside. He was a quiet child, a friendly child, uncomplaining and perhaps even shy, showing none of the emotion that welled up in him—hurt, anger, shame—when people stared. They were curious, mainly—didn't mean to be insulting. Just ignore them, honey, his mother always said. But when he was alone with his father and people looked at him a little too long his father bristled with irritation. If anyone dared ask what had happened to him his father would say, Who wants to know? in a certain voice. And the subject was quickly dropped.

To him his father said, Let the sons of bitches mind their own business and we'll mind ours. Right?

1. From *Raven's Wing* (1987).

The operation had lasted nine hours but he remembered little of it afterward except the needle going into his arm, into a vein, the careening lights, then waking alone and frightened in a room so cold his teeth began to chatter. Such cold, and such silence: he thought he must have died. Then the pain began and he knew he was alive, he cried in short breathless incredulous sobs until the first shock was past. A nurse stood over him telling him he'd be all right. He'd been a brave, brave little boy, she said.

The promise all along had been: he'd be able to walk now like any other boy. As soon as the casts were removed.

And: he'd be able to run. (Until now he'd crawled on his hands and knees faster than he'd been able to walk, like something scuttling along a beach.)

In his wheelchair at the Golden Gloves tournament he told himself he would be a boxer: he told himself at the conclusion of the first three-round match when a panting grinning boy was declared the winner of his match, on points, his arm held high, the gleaming brick-red glove raised for all to see. And the applause!—immediate, familial, rising and swelling like a heartbeat gone wild. The boy's father was in the ring with him, other boys who might have been his brothers or cousins—they were hugging one another in their happiness at the victory. Then the ring was emptied except for the referee, and the next young boxers and their seconds appeared.

He knew: he would be up there in the ring one day in the lights, rows of people watching. He would be there in the lighted ring, not in a wheelchair. Not in the audience at all.

After the casts were removed he had to learn to walk again.

They stood him carefully against a wall like a small child and encouraged him, Don't be afraid, take a step, take another step, come to them as best he could. They told him it wouldn't hurt and though it did hurt he didn't care, he plunged out lurching, swaying, falling panicked into his mother's arms. Yes, said the mother. Like that. Come *on*, said his father. Try again.

It was a year before he could walk inside the house without limping or turning his left foot helplessly inward. It was another year before he could run in the yard or in the school playground. By then his father had bought him a pair of child's boxing gloves, soft simulated dark brown leather. The gloves were the size of melons and so beautiful his eyes filled with tears when he first saw them. He would remember their sharp pungent smell through his life.

His father laced on the gloves, crouched to spar with him, taught him a few basic principles—how to hold his guard, how to stand at an angle with his chin tucked against his shoulder (Joe Louis style), how to jab, how to keep moving—later arranged for him to take boxing lessons at the YMCA. His father had wanted to be a boxer himself when he was a boy, he'd fought in a few three-round matches at a local club but had won only the first match; his reflexes, he said, were just slightly off: when his opponent's jab got to him he forgot everything he knew and wanted to slug it out. He'd known enough to quit before he got hurt. Either you have the talent or you don't, his father said. It can't be faked.

He began to train at the Y, he worked out every day after school and on Saturday mornings; by the age of sixteen he'd brought his weight up to 130 pounds standing five foot six, he could run ten, twelve, as many as fifteen miles without tiring. He was quick, light, shrewd, he was good at boxing and he knew he was good, everyone acknowledged it, everyone watched him with interest. When he wasn't at the gym—when he had to be in school, or in church, or at home, even in bed—he was thinking about the gym, the ring, himself in his boxing trunks and leather gloves, Vaseline smeared on his face and his headgear on his head, he was in his crouch but getting ready to move, his knees bent, his hands closed into fists. He was ready! He couldn't be taken unawares! He couldn't be stopped! He became obsessed with some of the boys and young men he knew at the gym, their weights, their heights, the reach of their arms, could they knock him out if he fought them, could he knock them out? What did they think about *him*? There were weeks when he was infatuated with one or another boy who might be a year or two older than he, a better boxer, until it was revealed that he wasn't a better boxer after all: he had his weaknesses, his bad habits, his limitations. He concentrated a good deal on the feel of his own body, building up his muscles, strengthening his stomach, his neck, learning not to wince at pain—not to show pain at all. He loved the sinewy springiness of his legs and feet, the tension in his shoulders; he loved the way his body came to life, moving, it seemed, of its own will, knowing by instinct how to strike his opponent how to get through his opponent's guard how to hurt him and hurt him again and make it last. His clenched fists inside the shining gloves. His teeth in the mouthpiece. Eyes narrowed and shifting behind the hot lids as if they weren't his own eyes merely but those belonging to someone he didn't yet know, an adult man, a man for whom all things were possible.

Sometimes on Saturday afternoons the boys were shown film clips and documentaries of the great fighters. Jack Dempsey—Gene Tunney—Benny Leonard—Joe Louis—Billy Conn—Archie Moore—Sandy Saddler—Carmen Basilio—Sugar Ray Robinson—Jersey Joe Walcott—Rocky Marciano. He watched entranced, staring at the flickering images on the screen; some of the films were aged and poorly preserved, the blinds at the windows fitted loosely so that the room wasn't completely darkened, and the boxers took on an odd ghostly insubstantial look as they crouched and darted and lunged at one another. Feinting, clinching, backing off, then the flurry of gloves so swift the eye couldn't follow, one man suddenly down and the other in a neutral corner, the announcer's voice rising in excitement as if it were all happening now right now and not decades ago. More astonishing than the powerful blows dealt were the blows taken, the punishment absorbed as if really finally one could not be hurt by an opponent, only stopped by one's own failure of nerve or judgment. If you're hurt you deserve to be hurt! If you're hurt badly you deserve to be hurt badly! Turning to the referee to protest a low blow, his guard momentarily lowered—there was Jack Sharkey, knocked out by Jack Dempsey with a fast left hook. Like that! And the fight was over. And there was aging Archie Moore knocked down repeatedly, savagely, by young Yvon Durrelle, staggering on his feet part-conscious but indomitable—how had he come back to win? how had he done it?—boasting he wasn't tired afterward, he could fight the fight all over again. Young Joe Louis baffled and outboxed by stylish Billy Conn for twelve rounds, then suddenly as Conn swarmed all over him trying to knock him out Louis came alive, turned into a machine for hitting, combinations so rapid the eye couldn't follow, left hooks, right crosses, uppercuts, a dozen punches within seconds and Conn was finished—that was the great Joe Louis in his prime. And here, Jersey Joe Walcott outboxing Rocky Marciano until suddenly Marciano connected with his right, that terrible incalculably powerful right, Let's see the knockout in slow motion, the announcer said, and you could see this time how it happened, Walcott hit so hard his face so stunned so distorted it was no longer a human face, no longer recognizable. And Rocky Marciano and Ezzard Charles fighting for Marciano's heavyweight title in 1954—after fifteen rounds both men covered in blood from cuts and gashes in their faces but embracing each other like brothers, smiling, laughing it seemed, in mutual respect and admiration and it didn't—almost—seem to matter that one man had to lose and the other had to win: they'd fought one of the great fights of the century and everyone knew it.

And *he* knew he was of their company. If only he might be allowed to show it.

He was sixteen years old, he was seventeen years old, boxing in local matches, working his way steadily up into state competitions, finally into the Golden Gloves Tri-State tournament. He had a good trainer, his father had seen to that. He had trophies, plaques, photographs taken at ringside, part of the liv- ing room was given over to his boxing as to a shrine. What do your friends think about your boxing? his relatives asked. Isn't it a dangerous sport? But he hadn't any friends that mattered and if his classmates had any opinion about him he couldn't have guessed what it might be, or cared. And, no, it wasn't a dangerous sport. It was only dangerous if you made mistakes.

It was said frequently at the gym that he was "coming along." The sportswriter for the local newspaper did a brief piece on him and a few other "promising" amateurs. He was quick and clever and intuitive, he knew to let a blow slide by his shoulder then to get his own in then to retreat, never to panic, never to shut his eyes, never to breathe through his mouth, it was all a matter of breath you might say, a matter of the most exquisite timing, momentum, a dancer's intelligence in his legs, the instinct to hit, to hit hard, and to hit again. He was a young Sandy Saddler they said—but he didn't fight dirty! No, he was a young Sugar Ray. Styled a bit on that brilliant new heavyweight Cassius Clay, who'd surprised the boxing world by knocking out Sonny Liston. He hadn't a really hard punch but he was working on it, working constantly, in any case he was winning all his matches or fighting to a draw, there's nothing wrong in fighting to a draw his father told him, though he could see his father was disappointed sometimes, there were fights he should have won but just didn't—couldn't. The best times were when he won a match by a knockout, his opponent suddenly falling, and down, not knocked out really, just sitting there on the canvas dazed and frightened, blinking, looking as if he were about to cry but no one ever cried, that never happened.

You have real talent, he was told. Told repeatedly.

You have a future!

The promise was—he seemed to know—that he couldn't lose. He'd understood that years before, watching one or another of the films, young Dempsey fierce as a tiger against the giant Jess Willard, twenty-year-old Joe Louis in action, Sugar Ray Robinson who'd once killed an opponent in the ring with the force of his blows: he was of their company and he knew it and he knew he couldn't lose, he couldn't even be seriously hurt, that seemed to be part of the promise. But sometimes he woke in the night in his bed not knowing at first where he was, was he in the gym, in the ring, staring panicked across the wide lighted canvas to his opponent shadowy in the opposite corner, he lay shivering, his heart racing, the bedclothes damp with sweat. He liked to sweat most of the time, he liked the rank smell of his own body, but this was not one of those times. His fists when he woke would be clenched so hard his fingernails would be cutting into his palms, his toes curled in tight and cramped as if still deformed, secretly deformed. Cripple! Freak! The blow you can't see coming is the blow that knocks you out—the blow out of nowhere. How can you protect yourself against a blow out of nowhere? How can you stop it from happening again? He'd been surprised like that only a few times, sparring, not in real fights. But the surprise had stayed with him.

Yet there was a promise. Going back to when he was very small, before the operation.

And his father adored him, his father was so happy for him, placing bets on him, not telling him until afterward—after he'd won. Just small bets. Just for fun. His father said, I don't want you to feel any pressure, it's just for fun.

Then of course he was stopped and his "career" ended abruptly and unromantically. As he should have foreseen. Just a few weeks before his eighteenth birthday.

It happened midway in the first round of a Golden Gloves semifinal lightweight match in Buffalo, New York, when a stocky black boy from Trenton, New Jersey, came bounding at him like a killer, pushing and crowding and bulling him back into the ropes, forcing him backward as he'd never been forced; the boy brushed aside his jabs and ignored his feints, popped him with a hard left then landed a blow to his exposed mouth that drove his upper front teeth back through his slack lower lip but somehow at the same time smashed the teeth upward into his palate. He'd lost his mouthpiece in the confusion, he'd never seen the punch coming, he was told afterward it had been a hard straight right like no amateur punch anyone could recall.

He fell dazed into the ropes, he fell to the canvas, he hid his bleeding face with his gloves, gravity pulled him down and his instinct was to submit to curl up into a tight ball to lie very still maybe he wouldn't be hit again maybe it was all over.

And so it happened.

That was his career as an amateur boxer. Twenty or so serious matches: that was it.

Never again, he told himself. That *was* it.

(The black boy from New Jersey—Roland Bush Jr.—was eighteen years old at the time of the fight but had the face of a mature man, heavy-lidded eyes, broad flat nose, scars in his forehead and fanning his eyes. An inch shorter than his white opponent but his shoulder and leg muscles rippled with highstrung nervous strength, he'd thickened his neck muscles to withstand all blows, he was ready, he was hot, he couldn't be stopped. His skin was very dark and the whites of his eyes were an eerie bluish-white, luminous, threaded almost invisibly with blood. He weighed no more than his opponent but he had a skull and a body built to absorb punishment, he was solid, hard, relentless, taking no joy in his performance just doing it, doing it superbly, getting it done, he went on to win the Golden Gloves title in his division with another spectacular knockout and a few months later turned professional and was advanced swiftly through the lightweight ranks then into the junior welterweights where he was ranked number fourteen by *Ring* magazine at the time of his death—he died aged twenty of a cerebral hemorrhage following a ten-round fight in Houston, Texas, which he'd lost in the ninth round by a technical knockout.[2])

. . . . .

The fight was stopped, the career of "promise" was stopped, now he is thirty-four years old and it seems to him his life is passing swiftly. But at a distance. It doesn't seem in fact to belong to him, it might be anybody's life.

In his professional career, in his social life, he is successful, no doubt enviable, but he finds himself dreaming frequently these days of the boy with the crippled feet. Suppose he'd never had the operation: what then! He sees the creature on its hands and knees crawling crablike along the ground, there is a jeering circle of boys, now the terrible blinding lights of the operating room snuff him out and he's gone. And now seated in his aluminum wheelchair staring down helplessly at the white plaster casts: his punishment. Hips to toes, toes to hips. His punishment.

The adults of the world conspire in lies leaning over him smiling into his face. He will be able to walk he will be able to run he won't feel any pain he won't be hurt again doesn't he want to believe?—and of course he does. He does.

His wife's name is Annemarie, a name melodic and lovely he sometimes shapes with his lips, in silence: an incantation.

He had fallen in love with Annemarie seeing her for the first time amid a large noisy gathering of relatives and friends. When they were introduced and he was told her name he thought extravagantly, Annemarie, yes—she's the one!

From the first she inspired him to such extravagant fancies, such violations of his own self. Which is why he loves her desperately.

Annemarie is twenty-nine years old but has the lithe small-boned features of a girl. Her hair is light brown, wavy, silvery in sunshine, her eyes wide-set and intelligent, watchful. Most of the time she appears to be wonderfully assured, her center of gravity well inside her, yet in the early weeks of the pregnancy she cried often and asked him half angrily, Do you love me? And he told her, Yes, of course. Of course I love you. But shortly afterward she asked him again, as if she hadn't believed him, Do you love me—*really*? More than before, or less? and he laughed as if she were joking, as if it were one of her jokes, closing his arms around her to comfort her. This was Annemarie's second pregnancy after all: the first had ended in a miscarriage.

Don't be absurd, Annemarie, he tells her.

Most of the time, of course, she is good-natured, sunny, uncomplaining; she loves being pregnant and she is eager to have the baby. She chooses her maternity outfits with care and humor: flowing waistless dresses in colorful

2. I.e., on points scored; not a knockout.

fabrics, blouses with foppish ties, shawls, Indian beads, cloth flowers in her hair. Some of the outfits are from secondhand shops in the city, costumes from the forties and fifties, long skirts, culottes, silk pants suits, a straw boater with clusters of artificial berries on the rim: to divert the eye from her prominent belly, she says. But the childlike pleasure Annemarie takes in dressing is genuine and her husband is charmed by it, he adores her for all that is herself, yes, he'd fight to the death to protect her he'd die in her place if required.

Odd how, from the start, she has had the power to inspire him to such melodramatic extravagant claims.

The miscarriage took place in the fifth month of the first pregnancy. One night Annemarie woke with mock-labor pains and began to bleed, she bled until nothing remained in her womb of what was to have been their son. And they were helpless, helpless to stop it.

They'd known for weeks that the fetus was impaired, the pregnancy might not go to term; still, the premature labor and the premature death were blows from which each was slow to recover. Annemarie wept in his arms and, he thought, in his place: her angry childish mourning helped purge his soul. And Annemarie was the first to recover from the loss for after all—as her doctor insisted—it wasn't anything personal, *it's just physical.* The second pregnancy has nothing at all to do with the first.

So we'll try again, Annemarie said reasonably.

And he hesitated saying, Not now. Saying, Isn't it too soon? You aren't recovered.

And she said, Of course I'm recovered.

And he said, But I think we should wait.

And she said, chiding, *Now.* When if not *now?*

(Twenty-nine years old isn't young, in fact it is "elderly" in medical terms for a woman pregnant with her first child. And they want more than one child, after all. They want a family.)

So they made love. And they made love. And he gave himself up to her in love, in love, in a drowning despairing hope, it's just physical after all it doesn't mean anything. Such failures of the physical life don't mean anything. You take the blow then get on with living isn't that the history of the world? Of course it is.

He's an adult man now, not a boy any longer. He knows.

He cradles his wife's belly in his hands. Stroking her gently. Kissing her. Fiercely attentive to the baby's secret life, that mysterious interior throb, that ghostly just-perceptible kick. Through the doctor's stethoscope each listened to the baby's heartbeat, a rapid feverish-sounding beat, *I am, I am, I am.* This pregnancy, unlike the first, has been diagnosed as "normal." This fetus unlike the first has been promised as "normal."

Approximately fifteen days yet to go: the baby has begun its descent head first into the pelvic cavity and Annemarie has begun, oddly, to feel more comfortable than she has felt in months. She assures him she is excited—not frightened—and he remembers the excitement of boxing, the excitement of climbing through the ropes knowing he couldn't turn back. Elation or panic? euphoria or terror?—that heartbeat beating everywhere in his body.

For months they have attended natural childbirth classes together and he oversees, genially but scrupulously, her exercises at home: he will be in the delivery room with her, he'll be there all the while.

This time, like last time, the fetus is male, and again they have drawn up a list of names. But the names are entirely different from the first list, Patrick, William, Alan, Seth, Sean, Raymond; sometimes Annemarie favors one and sometimes another but she doesn't want to choose a name until the baby is born. Safely born.

Why hasn't he ever told Annemarie about his amateur boxing, his "career" in the Golden Gloves?—he has told her virtually everything else about his life. But it is a matter of deep shame to him, recalling not only the evening of his public defeat but his hope, his near-lunatic hope that he would be a hero, a star! a great champion! He has told her he'd been a premature baby, born with a "slight deformity" of one foot which was corrected by surgery immediately after his birth: this is as near to the truth as he can manage.

Which foot was it? Annemarie asks sympathetically.

He tells her he doesn't remember which foot, it isn't important.

But one night he asks her to caress his feet. They are in bed, he is feeling melancholy, worried, not wholly himself. He has begun to profoundly dislike his work in proportion to his success at it and this is a secret he can't share with Annemarie; there are other secrets too he can't share, won't share, he fears her ready sympathy, the generosity of her spirit. At such times he feels himself vulnerable to memory, in danger of reliving that last fight, experiencing moments he hadn't in a sense experienced at the time—it had all happened too swiftly. Roland Bush Jr. pressing through his defense, jabbing him with precise machinelike blows, that gleaming black face those narrowed eyes seeking him out. White boy! White boy who are *you!* Bush was the true fighter stalking his prey. Bush was the one.

He hadn't been a fighter at all, merely a victim.

He asks Annemarie to caress his feet. Would she hold them? Warm them? Would she . . . ? It would mean so much, he can't explain.

Perhaps he is jealous of their son so cozy and tight upside down beneath his wife's heart but this is a thought he doesn't quite think.

Of course Annemarie is delighted to massage his feet, it's the sort of impulsive whimsical thing she loves to do, no need for logic, no need for explanations, she has wanted all along to nourish the playful side of his personality. So she takes his feet between her small dry warm hands and gently massages them. She brings to the intimate task a frowning concentration that flatters him, fills him with love. What is she thinking? he wonders. Then suddenly he is apprehensive: What does she know of me? What can she guess? Annemarie says, smiling, Your feet are so terribly cold! But I'll make them warm.

The incident is brief, silly, loving, quickly forgotten. One of those moments between a husband and a wife not meant to be analyzed, or even remembered. It never occurs a second time, never again does Annemarie offer to caress his feet and out of pride and shame he certainly isn't going to ask.

The days pass, the baby is due in less than a week, he keeps thinking, dreaming, of that blow to his mouth: the terrible power of the punch out of nowhere. His skull shook with a fierce reverberation that ran through his entire body and he'd known then that no one had ever hit him before.

It was his own death that had crashed into him—yet no more than he deserved. He was hit as one is hit only once in a lifetime. He was hit and time stopped. He was hit in the second minute of the first round of a long-forgotten amateur boxing match in Buffalo, New York; he was hit and he died and they carried him along a corridor of blinding lights, strapped to a stretcher, drooling blood and saliva, eyes turned up in his head. Something opened, lifted, a space of some kind clearing for him to enter, his own death but he hadn't had the courage to step forward.

Someone whose face he couldn't see was sinking a needle deep into his forearm, into the fleshy part of his forearm, afterward they spoke calmly and reassuringly saying it isn't really serious, a mild concussion not a serious fracture, his nose wasn't broken, only his mouth and teeth injured, that could be fixed. He flinched remembering the blow flying at him out of nowhere. He flinched, remembering. It happened once in a lifetime after that you're dead white boy but you pick yourself up and keep going.

There followed then the long period—months, years—when his father shrank from looking him fully in the face. Sometimes, however, his father examined his mouth, wasn't entirely pleased with the plastic surgeon's work. It had cost so damned much after all. But the false teeth were lifelike, wonderfully convincing, some consolation at least. Expensive too but everyone in the family was impressed with the white perfect teeth affixed to their lightweight aluminum plate.

All that the old tales of pregnancy promise of a female beauty luminous and dewy, lit from within, was true: here is Annemarie with eyes moist and bright as he'd rarely seen them, a skin with a faint rosy bloom, feverish to the touch. Here is the joy of the body as he had known it long ago and had forgotten.

There were days, weeks, when she felt slightly unwell yet the bloom of pregnancy had held and deepened month following month. A woman fully absorbed in herself, suffused with light, heat, radiance, entranced by the plunge into darkness she is to take. Pain—the promised pain of childbirth— frightens yet fascinates her: she means to be equal to it. She doesn't shrink from hearing the most alarming stories, labors of many hours without anesthetic, cesarean deliveries where natural childbirth had been expected, sudden losses of blood. She means to triumph.

Within the family they joke—it's the father-to-be, not Annemarie, who is having difficulty sleeping these past few weeks. But that too is natural, isn't it?

One night very late in her term Annemarie stares down at herself as if she'd never seen herself before—the enormous swollen belly, the blue-veined stretched skin with its uncanny luminous pallor—and because she has been feeling melancholy for days, because she is fatigued, suddenly doubting, not altogether herself, she exclaims with a harsh little laugh, God look at me, at this, how can you love anything like—*this!*

His nerves are torn like silk. He knows she isn't serious, he knows it is the lateness of the hour and the strain of waiting, it can't be Annemarie herself speaking. Quickly he says, Don't be absurd.

But that night as he falls slowly asleep he hears himself explaining to Annemarie in a calm measured voice that she will be risking something few men can risk, she should know herself exalted, privileged, in a way invulnerable to hurt even if she is very badly hurt, she'll be risking something he himself cannot risk again in his life. And maybe he never risked it at all.

You'll be going to a place I can't reach, he says.

He would touch her, in wonder, in dread, he would caress her, but his body is heavy with sleep, growing distant from him. He says softly, I'm not sure I'll be here when you come back.

But by now Annemarie's breathing is so deep and rhythmic she must be asleep. In any case she gives no sign of having heard.

1987

---

# BOBBIE ANN MASON
## b. 1940

In Bobbie Ann Mason's story *Drawing Names* (printed here), the following exchange occurs between a mother and her daughter: " 'Hattie Smoot brought these over,' said Mom. 'I made a pants suit for her last week,' she said to Carolyn. 'The one that had stomach bypass?' " It was of course Hattie (who had brought over some chocolate creams) and not her pants suit that had the stomach bypass. The amusing collocation of disparate items is typical of those we encounter in Mason's fiction. Her characters play hearts or rook or canasta, drink a lot of Pepsi-Cola with their tacos, watch "Charlie's Angels" and "M.A.S.H" and countless other programs on television. Vaguely disturbed or confused about life in their once-rural Kentucky that is approaching the standard condition of tacky American urban, they contemplate matters with more surprise than resentment. In *Shiloh*, the title story of Mason's first collection of stories, a truck driver named Leroy, recuperating from an injury, notes "how much the town has changed. Subdivisions are spreading across western Kentucky like an oil slick. . . . The farmers who used to gather around the courthouse square on Saturday afternoons to play checkers and spit tobacco juice have gone." They have disappeared without Leroy's noticing, and against this backdrop of quietly disappearing landmarks Mason's characters enact their less-than-tragic affairs.

Raised on a farm near Mayfield, Kentucky, Mason graduated from the University of Kentucky, then went north to New York City, after which she took graduate degrees in English from S.U.N.Y. Binghamton and the University of Connecticut. For a number of years she taught English and journalism at Mansfield State College in Pennsylvania and in the 1970s published two critical books: a "feminist" guide to young women's fiction (titled *The Girl Sleuth*) and a guide to Nabokov's *Ada*. Meanwhile she worked for years on an unpublished novel, while sending story after story to *The New Yorker*, each of them rejected until its editors accepted her twentieth try. Her career launched, she published *Shiloh* in 1982 and three years later followed it with a novel, *In Country*. Speaking of those years before breaking into print, she noted that it took time for her to discover her true calling, "which was to write about my roots and the kinds of people I'd known, but from a contemporary perspective." Coming from a "sheltered and isolated background," she experienced her years of living in the north as culture shock, and she added that it wasn't until she was in her thirties that she could command "enough detachment and objectivity to see that many of those people back home were going through culture shock too."

The temptation Mason may have felt, but that she successfully resisted, was to use "those people back home" in a satiric way, by presenting them as caricatures to be ridiculed or pitied by a presumably more sensitive author and reader. More than one young writer from the provinces had made a career out of doing just that. But

Mason's relationship to her roots is deeper and more benign than is suggested by
the term *satire*, because she is truly fascinated by the way her people talk, the
things they buy and do and eat. And she is more interested in registering such
events on the surface of her prose than in analyzing or citing them as evidence of
late-century American vulgarity, ineptitude, or other misdemeanors. Although she
is sometimes compared—in her subject matter and approach—with her contemporary Raymond Carver, she seems less depressed than he by the life her characters
live, more willing to see what can be said for it, what can be seen in it.

In *Country* is about a young woman, Sam Hughes, whose father died in Vietnam and who lives with her uncle Emmett, a Vietnam survivor. Full of Mason's
familiar people and territory, it moves—by exploring Sam's attempt to understand
what Vietnam was like, what it meant and now means to her—into a realm beyond
satire in which personal and public realities are movingly portrayed, especially
Sam's relationship with her uncle. In the novel's concluding sequence, the characters visit the Vietnam Veterans Memorial in Washington, D.C., and Mason's
comic and touching rendering of this event is one of the best things she has done.
But it is her noticing care for things, passing on even as they are named—from dirt
bikes to Agent Orange to "Cyndi Lauper and her fat face"—that makes for the
affectionate solidity of her fictional world.

# Drawing Names[1]

On Christmas Day, Carolyn Sisson went early to her parents' house to help
her mother with the dinner. Carolyn had been divorced two years before, and
last Christmas, coming alone, she felt uncomfortable. This year she had
invited her lover, Kent Ballard, to join the family gathering. She had even
brought him a present to put under the tree, so he wouldn't feel left out. Kent
was planning to drive over from Kentucky Lake by noon. He had gone there
to inspect his boat because of an ice storm earlier in the week. He felt compelled to visit his boat on the holiday, Carolyn thought, as if it were a sad old
relative in a retirement home.

"We're having baked ham instead of turkey," Mom said. "Your daddy never
did like ham baked, but whoever heard of fried ham on Christmas? We have
that all year round and I'm burnt out on it."

"I love baked ham," said Carolyn.

"Does Kent like it baked?"

"I'm sure he does." Carolyn placed her gifts under the tree. The number of
packages seemed unusually small.

"It don't seem like Christmas with drawed names," said Mom.

"Your star's about to fall off." Carolyn straightened the silver ornament at
the tip of the tree.

"I didn't decorate as much as I wanted to. I'm slowing down. Getting old, I
guess." Mom had not combed her hair and she was wearing a workshirt and
tennis shoes.

"You always try to do too much on Christmas, Mom."

Carolyn knew the agreement to draw names had bothered her mother. But
the four daughters were grown, and two had children. Sixteen people were
expected today. Carolyn herself could not afford to buy fifteen presents on her

1. From *Shiloh and Other Stories* (1982).

salary as a clerk at J. C. Penney's, and her parents' small farm had not been profitable in years.

Carolyn's father appeared in the kitchen and he hugged her so tightly she squealed in protest.

"That's all I can afford this year," he said, laughing.

As he took a piece of candy from a dish on the counter, Carolyn teased him. "You'd better watch your calories today."

"Oh, not on Christmas!"

It made Carolyn sad to see her handsome father getting older. He was a shy man, awkward with his daughters, and Carolyn knew he had been deeply disappointed over her failed marriage, although he had never said so. Now he asked, "Who bought these 'toes'?"

He would no longer say "nigger toes," the old name for the chocolate-covered creams.

"Hattie Smoot brought those over," said Mom. "I made a pants suit for her last week," she said to Carolyn. "The one that had stomach bypass?"

"When PeeWee McClain had that, it didn't work and they had to fix him back like he was," said Dad. He offered Carolyn a piece of candy, but she shook her head no.

Mom said, "I made Hattie a dress back last spring for her boy's graduation, and she couldn't even find a pattern big enough. I had to 'low a foot. But after that bypass, she's down to a size twenty."

"I think we'll all need a stomach bypass after we eat this feast you're fixing," said Carolyn.

"Where's Kent?" Dad asked abruptly.

"He went to see about his boat. He said he'd be here."

Carolyn looked at the clock. She felt uneasy about inviting Kent. Everyone would be scrutinizing him, as if he were some new character on a soap opera. Kent, who drove a truck for the Kentucky Loose-Leaf Floor, was a part-time student at Murray State. He was majoring in accounting. When Carolyn started going with him early in the summer, they went sailing on his boat, which had "Joyce" painted on it. Later he painted over the name, insisting he didn't love Joyce anymore—she was a dietician who was always criticizing what he ate—but he had never said he loved Carolyn. She did not know if she loved him. Each seemed to be waiting for the other to say it first.

While Carolyn helped her mother in the kitchen, Dad went to get her grandfather, her mother's father. Pappy, who had been disabled by a stroke, was cared for by a live-in housekeeper who had gone home to her own family for the day. Carolyn diced apples and pears for fruit salad while her mother shaped sweet potato balls with marshmallow centers and rolled them in crushed cornflakes. On TV in the living room, *Days of Our Lives* was beginning, but the Christmas tree blocked their view of the television set.

"Whose name did you draw, Mom?" Carolyn asked, as she began seeding the grapes.

"Jim's."

"You put Jim's name in the hat?"

Mom nodded. Jim Walsh was the man Carolyn's youngest sister, Laura Jean, was living with in St. Louis. Laura Jean was going to an interior decorating school, and Jim was a textiles salesman she had met in a class. "I made him a shirt," Mom said.

"I'm surprised at you."

"Well, what was I to do?"

"I'm just surprised." Carolyn ate a grape and spit out the seeds. "Emily Post says the couple should be offered the same room when they visit."

"You know we'd never stand for that. I don't think your dad's ever got over her stacking up with that guy."

"You mean shacking up."

"Same thing." Mom dropped the potato masher, and the metal rattled on the floor. "Oh, I'm in such a tizzy," she said.

As the family began to arrive, the noise of the TV played against the greetings, the slam of the storm door, the outside wind rushing in. Carolyn's older sisters, Peggy and Iris, with their husbands and children, were arriving all at once, and suddenly the house seemed small. Peggy's children Stevie and Cheryl, without even removing their jackets, became involved in a basketball game on TV. In his lap, Stevie had a Merlin electronic toy, which beeped randomly. Iris and Ray's children, Deedee and Jonathan, went outside to look for cats.

In the living room, Peggy jiggled her baby, Lisa, on her hip and said, "You need you one of these, Carolyn."

"Where can I get one?" said Carolyn, rather sharply.

Peggy grinned. "At the gittin' place, I reckon."

Peggy's critical tone was familiar. She was the only sister who had had a real wedding. Her husband, Cecil, had a Gulf franchise, and they owned a motor cruiser, a pickup truck, a camper, a station wagon, and a new brick colonial home. Whenever Carolyn went to visit Peggy, she felt apologetic for not having a man who would buy her all these things, but she never seemed to be attracted to anyone steady or ambitious. She had been wondering how Kent would get along with the men of the family. Cecil and Ray were standing in a corner talking about gas mileage. Cecil, who was shorter than Peggy and was going bald, always worked on Dad's truck for free, and Ray usually agreed with Dad on politics to avoid an argument. Ray had an impressive government job in Frankfort. He had coordinated a ribbon-cutting ceremony when the toll road opened. What would Kent have to say to them? She could imagine him insisting that everyone go outside later to watch the sunset. Her father would think that was ridiculous. No one ever did that on a farm, but it was the sort of thing Kent would think of. Yet she knew that spontaneity was what she liked in him.

Deedee and Jonathan, who were ten and six, came inside then and immediately began shaking the presents under the tree. All the children were wearing new jeans and cowboy shirts, Carolyn noticed.

"Why are y'all so quiet?" she asked. "I thought kids whooped and hollered on Christmas."

"They've been up since *four*," said Iris. She took a cigarette from her purse and accepted a light from Cecil. Exhaling smoke, she said to Carolyn, "We heard Kent was coming." Before Carolyn could reply, Iris scolded the children for shaking the packages. She seemed nervous.

"He's supposed to be here by noon," said Carolyn.

"There's somebody now. I hear a car."

"It might be Dad, with Pappy."

It was Laura Jean, showing off Jim Walsh as though he were a splendid Christmas gift she had just received.

"Let me kiss everybody!" she cried, as the women rushed toward her. Laura Jean had not been home in four months.

"Merry Christmas!" Jim said in a booming official-sounding voice, something like a TV announcer, Carolyn thought. He embraced all the women and then, with a theatrical gesture, he handed Mom a bottle of Rebel Yell bourbon and a carton of boiled custard which he took from a shopping bag. The bourbon was in a decorative Christmas box.

Mom threw up her hands. "Oh, no, I'm afraid I'll be a alky-holic."

"Oh, that's ridiculous, Mom," said Laura Jean, taking Jim's coat. "A couple of drinks a day are good for your heart."

Jim insisted on getting coffee cups from a kitchen cabinet and mixing some boiled custard and bourbon. When he handed a cup to Mom, she puckered up her face.

"Law, don't let the preacher in," she said, taking a sip. "Boy, that sends my blood pressure up."

Carolyn waved away the drink Jim offered her. "I don't start this early in the day," she said, feeling confused.

Jim was a large, dark-haired man with a neat little beard, like a bird's nest cupped on his chin. He had a Northern accent. When he hugged her, Carolyn caught a whiff of cologne, something sweet, like chocolate syrup. Last summer, when Laura Jean brought him home for the first time, she had made a point of kissing and hugging him in front of everyone. Dad had virtually ignored him. Now Carolyn saw that Jim was telling Cecil that he always bought Gulf gas. Red-faced, Ray accepted a cup of boiled custard. Carolyn fled to the kitchen and began grating cheese for potatoes au gratin. She dreaded Kent's arrival.

When Dad arrived with Pappy, Cecil and Jim helped set up the wheelchair in a corner. Afterward, Dad and Jim shook hands, and Dad refused Jim's offer of bourbon. From the kitchen, Carolyn could see Dad hugging Laura Jean, not letting go. She went into the living room to greet her grandfather.

"They roll me in this buggy too fast," he said when she kissed his forehead.

Carolyn hoped he wouldn't notice the bottle of bourbon, but she knew he never missed anything. He was so deaf people had given up talking to him. Now the children tiptoed around him, looking at him with awe. Somehow, Carolyn expected the children to notice that she was alone, like Pappy.

At ten minutes of one, the telephone rang. Peggy answered and handed the receiver to Carolyn. "It's Kent," she said.

Kent had not left the lake yet. "I just got here an hour ago," he told Carolyn. "I had to take my sister over to my mother's."

"Is the boat O.K.?"

"Yeah. Just a little scraped paint. I'll be ready to go in a little while." He hesitated, as though waiting for assurance that the invitation was real.

"This whole gang's ready to eat," Carolyn said. "Can't you hurry?" She should have remembered the way he tended to get sidetracked. Once it took them three hours to get to Paducah, because he kept stopping at antique shops.

After she hung up the telephone, her mother asked, "Should I put the rolls in to brown yet?"

"Wait just a little. He's just now leaving the lake."

"When's this Kent feller coming?" asked Dad impatiently, as he peered into the kitchen. "It's time to eat."

"He's on his way," said Carolyn.

"Did you tell him we don't wait for stragglers?"

"No."

"When the plate rattles, we eat."

"I know."

"Did you tell him that?"

"No, I didn't!" cried Carolyn, irritated.

When they were alone in the kitchen, Carolyn's mother said to her, "Your dad's not his self today. He's fit to be tied about Laura Jean bringing that guy down here again. And him bringing that whiskey."

"That was uncalled for," Carolyn agreed. She had noticed that Mom had set her cup of boiled custard in the refrigerator.

"Besides, he's not too happy about that Kent Ballard you're running around with."

"What's it to him?"

"You know how he always was. He don't think anybody's good enough for one of his little girls, and he's afraid you'll get mistreated again. He don't think Kent's very dependable."

"I guess Kent's proving Dad's point."

Carolyn's sister Iris had dark brown eyes, unique in the family. When Carolyn was small, she tried to say "Iris's eyes" once and called them "Irish eyes," confusing them with a song their mother sometimes sang, "When Irish Eyes Are Smiling." Thereafter, they always teased Iris about her smiling Irish eyes. Today Iris was not smiling. Carolyn found her in a bedroom smoking, holding an ashtray in her hand.

"I drew your name," Carolyn told her. "I got you something I wanted myself."

"Well, if I don't want it, I guess I'll have to give it to you."

"What's wrong with you today?"

"Ray and me's getting a separation," said Iris.

"Really?" Carolyn was startled by the note of glee in her response. Actually, she told herself later, it was because she was glad her sister, whom she saw infrequently, had confided in her.

"The thing of it is, I had to beg him to come today, for Mom and Dad's sake. It'll kill them. Don't let on, will you?"

"I won't. What are you going to do?"

"I don't know. He's already moved out."

"Are you going to stay in Frankfort?"

"I don't know. I have to work things out."

Mom stuck her head in the door. "Well, is Kent coming or not?"

"He *said* he'd be here," said Carolyn.

"Your dad's about to have a duck with a rubber tail. He can't stand to wait on a meal."

"Well, let's go ahead, then. Kent can eat when he gets here."

When Mom left, Iris said, "Aren't you and Kent getting along?"

"I don't know. He said he'd come today, but I have a feeling he doesn't really want to."

"To hell with men." Iris laughed and stubbed out her cigarette. "Just look at us—didn't we turn out awful? First your divorce. Now me. And Laura Jean bringing that guy down. Daddy can't stand him. Did you see the look he gave him?"

"Laura Jean's got a lot more nerve than I've got," said Carolyn, nodding. "I could wring Kent's neck for being late. Well, none of us can do anything right—except Peggy."

"Daddy's precious little angel," said Iris mockingly. "Come on, we'd better get in there and help."

While Mom went to change her blouse and put on lipstick, the sisters brought the food into the dining room. Two tables had been put together. Peggy cut the ham with an electric knife, and Carolyn filled the iced tea glasses.

"Pappy gets buttermilk and Stevie gets Coke," Peggy directed her.

"I know," said Carolyn, almost snapping.

As the family sat down, Carolyn realized that no one ever asked Pappy to "turn thanks"[2] anymore at holiday dinners. He was sitting there expectantly, as if waiting to be asked. Mom cut up his ham into small bits. Carolyn waited for a car to drive up, the phone to ring. The TV was still on.

"Y'all dig in," said Mom. "Jim? Make sure you try some of these dressed eggs like I fix."

"I thought your new boyfriend was coming," said Cecil to Carolyn.

"So did I!" said Laura Jean. "That's what you wrote me."

Everyone looked at Carolyn as she explained. She looked away.

"You're looking at that pitiful tree," Mom said to her. "I just know it don't show up good from the road."

"No, it looks fine." No one really noticed the tree. Carolyn seemed to be seeing it for the first time in years—broken red plastic reindeer, Styrofoam snowmen with crumbling top hats, silver walnuts which she remembered painting when she was about twelve.

Dad began telling a joke about some monks who had taken a vow of silence. At each Christmas dinner, he said, one monk was allowed to speak.

"Looks like your vocal cords would rust out," said Cheryl.

"Shut up, Cheryl. Granddaddy's trying to tell something," said Cecil.

"So the first year it was the first monk's turn to talk, and you know what he said? He said, 'These taters is lumpy.' "

When several people laughed, Stevie asked, "Is that the joke?"

Carolyn was baffled. Her father had never told a joke at the table in his life. He sat at the head of the table, looking out past the family at the cornfield through the picture window.

"Pay attention now," he said. "The second year Christmas rolled around again and it was the second monk's turn to say something. He said, 'You know, I think you're right. The taters *is* lumpy.' "

Laura Jean and Jim laughed loudly.

"Reach me some light-bread," said Pappy. Mom passed the dish around the table to him.

"And so the third year," Dad continued, "the third monk got to say something. What he said"—Dad was suddenly overcome with mirth—"what he

2. Say grace.

said was, 'If y'all don't shut up arguing about them taters, I'm going to leave this place!' "

After the laughter died, Mom said, "Can you imagine anybody not a-talking all year long?"

"That's the way monks are, Mom," said Laura Jean. "Monks are economical with everything. They're not wasteful, not even with words."

"The Trappist Monks are really an outstanding group," said Jim. "And they make excellent bread. No preservatives."

Cecil and Peggy stared at Jim.

"You're not eating, Dad," said Carolyn. She was sitting between him and the place set for Kent. The effort at telling the joke seemed to have taken her father's appetite.

"He ruined his dinner on nigger toes," said Mom.

"Dottie Barlow got a Barbie doll for Christmas and it's black," Cheryl said.

"Dottie Barlow ain't black, is she?" asked Cecil.

"No."

"That's funny," said Peggy. "Why would they give her a black Barbie doll?"

"She just wanted it."

Abruptly, Dad left the table, pushing back his place. He sat down in the recliner chair in front of the TV. The Blue-Gray game was beginning, and Cecil and Ray were hurriedly finishing in order to join him. Carolyn took out second helpings of ham and jello salad, feeling as though she were eating for Kent in his absence. Jim was taking seconds of everything, complimenting Mom. Mom apologized for not having fancy napkins. Then Laura Jean described a photography course she had taken. She had been photographing close-ups of car parts—fenders, headlights, mud flaps.

"That sounds goofy," said one of the children, Deedee.

Suddenly Pappy spoke. "Use to, the menfolks would eat first, and the children separate. The womenfolks would eat last, in the kitchen."

"You know what I could do with you all, don't you?" said Mom, shaking her fist at him. "I could set up a plank out in the field for y'all to eat on." She laughed.

"Times are different now, Pappy," said Iris loudly. "We're just as good as the men."

"She gets that from television," said Ray, with an apologetic laugh.

Carolyn noticed Ray's glance at Iris. Just then Iris matter-of-factly plucked an eyelash from Ray's cheek. It was as though she had momentarily forgotten about the separation.

Later, after the gifts were opened, Jim helped clear the tables. Kent still had not come. The baby slept, and Laura Jean, Jim, Peggy, and Mom played a Star Trek board game at the dining room table, while Carolyn and Iris played Battlestar Galactica with Cheryl and Deedee. The other men were quietly engrossed in the football game, a blur of sounds. No one had mentioned Kent's absence, but after the children had distributed the gifts, Carolyn refused to tell them what was in the lone package left under the tree. It was the most extravagantly wrapped of all the presents, with an immense ribbon, not a stick-on bow. An icicle had dropped on it, and it reminded Carolyn of an abandoned float, like something from a parade.

At a quarter to three, Kent telephoned. He was still at the lake. "The gas stations are all closed," he said. "I couldn't get any gas."

"We already ate and opened the presents," said Carolyn.

"Here I am, stranded. Not a thing I can do about it."

Kent's voice was shaky and muffled, and Carolyn suspected he had been drinking. She did not know what to say, in front of the family. She chattered idly, while she played with a ribbon from a package. The baby was awake, turning dials and knobs on a Busy Box. On TV, the Blues picked up six yards on an end sweep. Carolyn fixed her eyes on the tilted star at the top of the tree. Kent was saying something about Santa Claus.

"They wanted me to play Santy at Mama's house for the littluns. I said—you know what I said? 'Bah, humbug!' Did I ever tell you what I've got against Christmas?"

"Maybe not." Carolyn's back stiffened against the wall.

"When I was little bitty, Santa Claus came to town. I was about five. I was all fired up to go see Santy, and Mama took me, but we were late, and he was about to leave. I had to run across the courthouse square to get to him. He was giving away suckers, so I ran as hard as I could. He was climbing up on the fire engine—are you listening?"

"Unh-huh." Carolyn was watching her mother, who was folding Christmas paper to save for next year.

Kent said, "I reached up and pulled at his old red pants leg, and he looked down at me, and you know what he said?"

"No—what?"

"He said, 'Piss off, kid.' "

"Really?"

"Would I lie to you?"

"I don't know."

"Do you want to hear the rest of my hard-luck story?"

"Not now."

"Oh, I forgot this was long distance. I'll call you tomorrow. Maybe I'll go paint the boat. That's what I'll do! I'll go paint it right this minute."

After Carolyn hung up the telephone, her mother said, "I think my Oriental casserole was a failure. I used the wrong kind of mushroom soup. It called for cream of mushroom and I used golden mushroom."

"Won't you *ever* learn, Mom?" cried Carolyn. "You always cook too much. You make *such* a big deal—"

Mom said, "What happened with Kent this time?"

"He couldn't get gas. He forgot the gas stations were closed."

"Jim and Laura Jean didn't have any trouble getting gas," said Peggy, looking up from the game.

"We tanked up yesterday," said Laura Jean.

"Of course you did," said Carolyn distractedly. "You always think ahead."

"It's your time," Cheryl said, handing Carolyn the Battlestar Galactica toy. "I did lousy."

"Not as lousy as I did," said Iris.

Carolyn tried to concentrate on shooting enemy missiles, raining through space. Her sisters seemed far away, like the spaceships. She was aware of the men watching football, their hands in action as they followed an exciting play. Even though Pappy had fallen asleep, with his blanket in his lap he looked like a king on a throne. Carolyn thought of the quiet accommodation her father had made to his father-in-law, just as Cecil and Ray had done with Dad, and her ex-husband had tried to do once. But Cecil had bought his way in, and now Ray was getting out. Kent had stayed away. Jim, the newcomer, was with the women, playing Star Trek as if his life depended upon it. Carolyn was glad now that Kent had not come. The story he told made her angry, and his pity for his childhood made her think of something Pappy had often said: "Christmas is for children." Earlier, she had listened in amazement while Cheryl listed on her fingers the gifts she had received that morning: a watch, a stereo, a nightgown, hot curls, perfume, candles, a sweater, a calculator, a jewelry box, a ring. Now Carolyn saw Kent's boat as his toy, more important than the family obligations of the holiday.

Mom was saying, "I wanted to make a Christmas tablecloth out of red checks with green fringe. You wouldn't think knit would do for a tablecloth, but Hattie Smoot has the prettiest one."

"You can do incredible things with knit," said Jim with sudden enthusiasm. The shirt Mom had made him was bonded knit.

"Who's Hattie Smoot?" asked Laura Jean. She was caressing the back of Jim's neck, as though soothing his nerves.

Carolyn laughed when her mother began telling Jim and Laura Jean about Hattie Smoot's operation. Jim listened attentively, leaning forward with his elbows on the table, and asked eager questions, his eyes as alert as Pappy's.

"Is she telling a joke?" Cheryl asked Carolyn.

"No. I'm not laughing at you, Mom," Carolyn said, touching her mother's hand. She felt relieved that the anticipation of Christmas had ended. Still laughing, she said, "Pour me some of that Rebel Yell, Jim. It's about time."

"I'm with you," Jim said, jumping up.

In the kitchen, Carolyn located a clean spoon while Jim washed some cups. Carolyn couldn't find the cup Mom had left in the refrigerator. As she took out the carton of boiled custard, Jim said, "It must be a very difficult day for you."

Carolyn was startled. His tone was unexpectedly kind, genuine. She was struck suddenly by what he must know about her, because of his intimacy with her sister. She knew nothing about him. When he smiled, she saw a gold cap on a molar, shining like a Christmas ornament. She managed to say, "It can't be any picnic for you either. Kent didn't want to put up with us."

"Too bad he couldn't get gas."

"I don't think he wanted to get gas."

"Then you're better off without him." When Jim looked at her, Carolyn felt that he must be examining her resemblances to Laura Jean. He said, "I think your family's great."

Carolyn laughed nervously. "We're hard on you. God, you're brave to come down here like this."

"Well, Laura Jean's worth it."

They took the boiled custard and cups into the dining room. As Carolyn sat down, her nephew Jonathan begged her to tell what was in the gift left under the tree.

"I can't tell," she said.

"Why not?"

"I'm saving it till next year, in case I draw some man's name."

"I hope it's mine," said Jonathan.

Jim stirred bourbon into three cups of boiled custard, then gave one to Carolyn and one to Laura Jean. The others had declined. Then he leaned back in his chair—more relaxed now—and squeezed Laura Jean's hand. Carolyn wondered what they said to each other when they were alone in St. Louis. She knew with certainty that they would not be economical with words, like the monks in the story. She longed to be with them, to hear what they would say. She noticed her mother picking at a hangnail, quietly ignoring the bourbon. Looking at the bottle's gift box, which showed an old-fashioned scene, children on sleds in the snow, Carolyn thought of Kent's boat again. She felt she was in that snowy scene now with Laura Jean and Jim, sailing in Kent's boat into the winter breeze, into falling snow. She thought of how silent it was out on the lake, as though the whiteness of the snow were the absence of sound. "Cheers!" she said to Jim, lifting her cup.

1981

---

# MAXINE HONG KINGSTON
## b. 1940

Maxine Hong Kingston was born in Stockton, California, to parents who had emigrated from China. Before they emigrated, Kingston's father was a schoolteacher and a poet; her mother was a rural doctor in a profession consisting almost entirely of men. In America they took on quite different identities: her father, at times unemployed, worked in a gambling house and a laundry; her mother raised six children, of whom Kingston was the eldest.

Kingston graduated from the University of California, Berkeley, studying there in the turbulent middle sixties. Her debut as a writer was auspicious: in 1976, an unknown, she published her first and most widely read book, *The Woman Warrior*, and was catapulted to literary fame. Subtitled "Memoirs of a Girlhood among Ghosts," it draws upon autobiographical fact and combines it with legends, especially Asian ones, to make a distinct imaginative creation. Reviews of the book, almost universally laudatory, emphasized its poetic and lyric beauty. *The Woman Warrior* is about the cultural conflicts Americans of Chinese descent must confront. Still, what remains in the mind is its quality of vivid particularity, as for example at the beginning of *Shaman*, the book's third section:

> Once in a long while, four times so far for me, my mother brings out the metal tube that holds her medical diploma. On the tube are gold circles crossed with seven red lines each—"joy" ideographs in abstract. There are also little flowers that look like gears for a gold machine. . . . When I open it the smell of China flies out, a thousand-year-old bat flying heavy-handed out of the Chinese caverns where bats are as white as dust, a smell that comes from long ago, far back in my brain.

Although *The Woman Warrior* received the National Book Critics' Circle award for general nonfiction, there is nothing "general" in the sensuous density of its reference.

The importance of storytelling to Kingston's enterprise in *The Woman Warrior* and its successor, *China Men* (1980), cannot be overemphasized. The Chinese phrase for storytelling is "talking story," and in *No Name Woman* (anthologized here), the first section from *Warrior*, the narrator's mother "talks" her a story—

which she is instructed to keep silent about—of the suicide in China of her father's sister. This woman, the narrator's aunt, became pregnant out of wedlock (she may have been raped); and in response to this violation of a taboo, the village treats her with a vengeful hostility that leads to her own and her infant's death. The narrator (Kingston in no disguise) is fascinated and appalled by this family secret; how can she, as a writer, presume to publish it to the world? In an interview with Bill Moyers on public television, Kingston says that her attempt was to push the account toward "form" by giving it a "redemptive" meaning, making it a "beautiful" story rather than a sordid one. As is the case typically with her practice as a writer, her effort is to mediate between present and past: "I think that my stories have a constant breaking in and out of the present and past. So the reader might be walking along very well in the present, but the past breaks through and changes and enlightens the present and vice versa."

Kingston had originally conceived of *The Woman Warrior* and *China Men* as one long book, but decided to preserve an overall division by gender: *Warrior* is about her female antecedents; while *China Men*, which won the 1980 National Book Award for nonfiction, deals with her relation to her father and complements that relation by providing epiclike biographies of earlier male forebears, especially those Chinese who came to America and worked on building the railroads. In a final section, she writes about her brother who served in the U.S. Navy during the Vietnam war. Interestingly enough, as she said in the interview with Moyers, her father annotated both of these memoir-meditations, thus carrying further the conversation between the generations.

Her first and as yet only novel, *Tripmaster Monkey* (1989), is an exercise as excessive as the young fifth-generation American hero, Wittman Ah Sing, who is portrayed there. Subtitled "His Fake Book," the novel is an extended, picaresque account of Wittman's adventures as an aspiring playwright who imagines himself to be an incarnation of the legendary Monkey King—a trickster hero said to have brought the Buddha's teaching to China. Combining magic, realism, and black humor, *Tripmaster Monkey* is about a young male's search for a community in America. Although Kingston's myth-laden narratives have been called "exotic," she dislikes the word, since she has dedicated her art to exploring what it means to be a human being in American society. In fact, she thinks of her books as more American than Chinese, sees William Carlos Williams's *In the American Grain* as a true prose predecessor, and probably would not be unhappy to think of the hero of *Tripmaster Monkey* as a later, different version of Huck Finn or Augie March.

# No Name Woman

"You must not tell anyone," my mother said, "what I am about to tell you. In China your father had a sister who killed herself. She jumped into the family well. We say that your father has all brothers because it is as if she had never been born.

"In 1924 just a few days after our village celebrated seventeen hurry-up weddings—to make sure that every young man who went 'out on the road' would responsibly come home—your father and his brothers and your grandfather and his brothers and your aunt's new husband sailed for America, the Gold Mountain. It was your grandfather's last trip. Those lucky enough to get contracts waved good-bye from the decks. They fed and guarded the stowaways and helped them off in Cuba, New York, Bali, Hawaii. 'We'll meet in California next year,' they said. All of them sent money home.

"I remember looking at your aunt one day when she and I were dressing; I had not noticed before that she had such a protruding melon of a stomach. But I did not think, 'She's pregnant,' until she began to look like other pregnant women, her shirt pulling and the white tops of her black pants showing. She could not have been pregnant, you see, because her husband had been gone for years. No one said anything. We did not discuss it. In early summer she was ready to have the child, long after the time when it could have been possible.

"The village had also been counting. On the night the baby was to be born the villagers raided our house. Some were crying. Like a great saw, teeth strung with lights, files of people walked zigzag across our land, tearing the rice. Their lanterns doubled in the disturbed black water, which drained away through the broken bunds.[1] As the villagers closed in, we could see that some of them, probably men and women we knew well, wore white masks. The people with long hair hung it over their faces. Women with short hair made it stand up on end. Some had tied white bands around their foreheads, arms, and legs.

"At first they threw mud and rocks at the house. Then they threw eggs and began slaughtering our stock. We could hear the animals scream their deaths—the roosters, the pigs, a last great roar from the ox. Familiar wild heads flared in our night windows; the villagers encircled us. Some of the faces stopped to peer at us, their eyes rushing like searchlights. The hands flattened against the panes, framed heads, and left red prints.

"The villagers broke in the front and the back doors at the same time, even though we had not locked the doors against them. Their knives dripped with the blood of our animals. They smeared blood on the doors and walls. One woman swung a chicken, whose throat she had slit, splattering blood in red arcs about her. We stood together in the middle of our house, in the family hall with the pictures and tables of the ancestors around us, and looked straight ahead.

"At that time the house had only two wings. When the men came back, we would build two more to enclose our courtyard and a third one to begin a second courtyard. The villagers pushed through both wings, even your grandparents' rooms, to find your aunt's, which was also mine until the men returned. From this room a new wing for one of the younger families would grow. They ripped up her clothes and shoes and broke her combs, grinding them underfoot. They tore her work from the loom. They scattered the cooking fire and rolled the new weaving in it. We could hear them in the kitchen breaking our bowls and banging the pots. They overturned the great waist-high earthenware jugs; duck eggs, pickled fruits, vegetables burst out and mixed in acrid torrents. The old woman from the next field swept a broom through the air and loosed the spirits-of-the-broom over our heads. 'Pig,' 'Ghost,' 'Pig,' they sobbed and scolded while they ruined our house.

"When they left, they took sugar and oranges to bless themselves. They cut pieces from the dead animals. Some of them took bowls that were not broken and clothes that were not torn. Afterward we swept up the rice and sewed it

---

1. Embankments built to control the flow of water, here probably irrigation water.

back up into sacks. But the smells from the spilled preserves lasted. Your aunt gave birth in the pigsty that night. The next morning when I went for the water, I found her and the baby plugging up the family well.

"Don't let your father know that I told you. He denies her. Now that you have started to menstruate, what happened to her could happen to you. Don't humiliate us. You wouldn't like to be forgotten as if you had never been born. The villagers are watchful."

Whenever she had to warn us about life, my mother told stories that ran like this one, a story to grow up on. She tested our strength to establish realities. Those in the emigrant generations who could not reassert brute survival died young and far from home. Those of us in the first American generations have had to figure out how the invisible world the emigrants built around our childhoods fits in solid America.

The immigrants confused the gods by diverting their curses, misleading them with crooked streets and false names. They must try to confuse their offspring as well, who, I suppose, threaten them in similar ways—always trying to get things straight, always trying to name the unspeakable. The Chinese I know hide their names; sojourners take new names when their lives change and guard their real names with silence.

Chinese-Americans, when you try to understand what things in you are Chinese, how do you separate what is peculiar to childhood, to poverty, insanities, one family, your mother who marked your growing with stories, from what is Chinese? What is Chinese tradition and what is the movies?

If I want to learn what clothes my aunt wore, whether flashy or ordinary, I would have to begin, "Remember Father's drowned-in-the-well sister?" I cannot ask that. My mother has told me once and for all the useful parts. She will add nothing unless powered by Necessity, a riverbank that guides her life. She plants vegetable gardens rather than lawns; she carries the odd-shaped tomatoes home from the fields and eats food left for the gods.

Whenever we did frivolous things, we used up energy; we flew high kites. We children came up off the ground over the melting cones our parents brought home from work and the American movie on New Year's Day—*Oh, You Beautiful Doll* with Betty Grable one year, and *She Wore a Yellow Ribbon* with John Wayne another year. After the one carnival ride each, we paid in guilt; our tired father counted his change on the dark walk home.

Adultery is extravagance. Could people who hatch their own chicks and eat the embryos and the heads for delicacies and boil the feet in vinegar for party food, leaving only the gravel, eating even the gizzard lining—could such people engender a prodigal aunt? To be a woman, to have a daughter in starvation time was a waste enough. My aunt could not have been the lone romantic who gave up everything for sex. Women in the old China did not choose. Some man had commanded her to lie with him and be his secret evil. I wonder whether he masked himself when he joined the raid on her family.

Perhaps she had encountered him in the fields or on the mountain where the daughters-in-law collected fuel. Or perhaps he first noticed her in the marketplace. He was not a stranger because the village housed no strangers. She had to have dealings with him other than sex. Perhaps he worked an adjoining field, or he sold her the cloth for the dress she sewed and wore. His demand must have surprised, then terrified her. She obeyed him; she always did as she was told.

When the family found a young man in the next village to be her husband, she had stood tractably beside the best rooster, his proxy,[2] and promised before they met that she would be his forever. She was lucky that he was her age and she would be the first wife, an advantage secure now. The night she first saw him, he had sex with her. Then he left for America. She had almost forgotten what he looked like. When she tried to envision him, she only saw the black and white face in the group photograph the men had had taken before leaving.

The other man was not, after all, much different from her husband. They both gave orders: she followed. "If you tell your family, I'll beat you. I'll kill you. Be here again next week." No one talked sex, ever. And she might have separated the rapes from the rest of living if only she did not have to buy her oil from him or gather wood in the same forest. I want her fear to have lasted just as long as rape lasted so that the fear could have been contained. No drawnout fear. But women at sex hazarded birth and hence lifetimes. The fear did not stop but permeated everywhere. She told the man, "I think I'm pregnant." he organized the raid against her.

On nights when my mother and father talked about their life back home, sometimes they mentioned an "outcast table" whose business they still seemed to be settling, their voices tight. In a commensal tradition,[3] where food is precious, the powerful older people made wrongdoers eat alone. Instead of letting them start separate new lives like the Japanese, who could become samurais and geishas,[4] the Chinese family, faces averted but eyes glowering sideways, hung on to the offenders and fed them leftovers. My aunt must have lived in the same house as my parents and eaten at an outcast table. My mother spoke about the raid as if she had seen it, when she and my aunt, a daughter-in-law to a different household, should not have been living together at all. Daughters-in-law lived with their husbands' parents, not their own; a synonym for marriage in Chinese is "taking a daughter-in-law." Her husband's parents could have sold her, mortgaged her, stoned her. But they had sent her back to her own mother and father, a mysterious act hinting at disgraces not told me. Perhaps they had thrown her out to deflect the avengers.

She was the only daughter; her four brothers went with her father, husband, and uncles "out on the road" and for some years became western men. when the goods were divided among the family, three of the brothers took land, and the youngest, my father, chose an education. After my grandparents gave their daughter away to her husband's family, they had dispensed all the adventure and all the property. They expected her alone to keep the traditional ways, which her brothers, now among the barbarians, could fumble without detection. The heavy, deep-rooted women were to maintain the past against the flood, safe for returning. But the rare urge west had fixed upon our family, and so my aunt crossed boundaries not delineated in space.

The work of preservation demands that the feelings playing about in one's guts not be turned into action. Just watch their passing like cherry blossoms. But perhaps my aunt, my forerunner, caught in a slow life, let dreams grow and fade and after some months or years went toward what persisted. Fear at the enormities of the forbidden kept her desires delicate, wire and bone. She looked at a man because she liked the way the hair was tucked behind his ears,

---

2. Someone or something that has the power to substitute or act for another.
3. A tradition in which people eat together at the

same table.
4. In Japanese society women trained to entertain men. *Samurai:* the Japanese warrior elite.

or she liked the question-mark line of a long torso curving at the shoulder and straight at the hip. For warm eyes or a soft voice or a slow walk—that's all—a few hairs, a line, a brightness, a sound, a pace, she gave up family. She offered us up for a charm that vanished with tiredness, a pigtail that didn't toss when the wind died. Why, the wrong lighting could erase the dearest thing about him.

It could very well have been, however, that my aunt did not take subtle enjoyment of her friend, but, a wild woman, kept rollicking company. Imagining her free with sex doesn't fit, through. I don't know any women like that, or men either. Unless I see her life branching into mine, she gives me no ancestral help.

To sustain her being in love, she often worked at herself in the mirror, guessing at the colors and shapes that would interest him, changing them frequently in order to hit on the right combination. She wanted him to look back.

On a farm near the sea, a woman who tended her appearance reaped a reputation for eccentricity. All the married women blunt-cut their hair in flaps about their ears or pulled it back in tight buns. No nonsense. Neither style blew easily into heart-catching tangles. And at their weddings they displayed themselves in their long hair for the last time. "It brushed the backs of my knees," my mother tells me. "It was braided, and even so, it brushed the backs of my knees."

At the mirror my aunt combed individuality into her bob. A bun could have been contrived to escape into black streamers blowing in the wind or in quiet wisps about her face, but only the older women in our picture album wear buns. She brushed her hair back from her forehead, tucking the flaps behind her ears. She looped a piece of thread, knotted into a circle between her index fingers and thumbs, and ran the double strand across her forehead. When she closed her fingers as if she were making a pair of shadow geese bite, the string twisted together catching the little hairs. Then she pulled the thread away from her skin, ripping the hair out neatly, her eyes watering from the needles of pain. Opening her fingers, she cleaned the thread, then rolled it along her hairline and the tops of her eyebrows. My mother did the same to me and my sisters and herself. I used to believe that the expression "caught by the short hairs" meant a captive held with a depilatory string. It especially hurt at the temples, but my mother said we were lucky we didn't have to have our feet bound when we were seven. Sisters used to sit on their beds and cry together, she said, as their mothers or their slave removed the bandages for a few minutes each night and let the blood gush back into their veins. I hope that the man my aunt loved appreciated a smooth brow, that he wasn't just a tits-and-ass man.

Once my aunt found a freckle on her chin, at a spot that the almanac said predestined her for unhappiness. She dug it out with a hot needle and washed the wound with peroxide.

More attention to her looks than these pullings of hairs and pickings at spots would have caused gossip among the villagers. They owned work clothes and good clothes, and they wore good clothes for feasting the new seasons. But since a woman combing her hair hexes beginnings, my aunt rarely found an occasion to look her best. Women looked like great sea snails—the corded wood, babies, and laundry they carried were the whorls on their backs. The

Chinese did not admire a bent back; goddesses and warriors stood straight. Still there must have been a marvelous freeing of beauty when a worker laid down her burden and stretched and arched.

Such commonplace loveliness, however, was not enough for my aunt. She dreamed of a lover for the fifteen days of New Year's, the time for families to exchange visits, money, and food. She plied her secret comb. And sure enough she cursed the year, the family, the village, and herself.

Even as her hair lured her imminent lover, many other men looked at her. Uncles, cousins, nephews, brothers would have looked, too, had they been home between journeys. Perhaps they had already been restraining their curiosity, and they left, fearful that their glances, like a field of nesting birds, might be startled and caught. Poverty hurt, and that was their first reason for leaving. But another, final reason for leaving the crowded house was the never-said.

She may have been unusually beloved, the precious only daughter, spoiled and mirror gazing because of the affection the family lavished on her. When her husband left, they welcomed the chance to take her back from the in-laws; she could live like the little daughter for just a while longer. There are stories that my grandfather was different from other people, "crazy ever since the little Jap bayoneted him in the head." He used to put his naked penis on the dinner table, laughing. And one day he brought home a baby girl, wrapped up inside his brown western-style greatcoat.[5] He had traded one of his sons, probably my father, the youngest, for her. My grandmother made him trade back. When he finally got a daughter of his own, he doted on her. They must have all loved her, except perhaps my father, the only brother who never went back to China, having once been traded for a girl.

Brothers and sisters, newly men and women, had to efface their sexual color and present plain miens. Disturbing hair and eyes, a smile like no other, threatened the ideal of five generations living under one roof. To focus blurs, people shouted face to face and yelled from room to room. The immigrants I know have loud voices, unmodulated to American tones even after years away from the village where they called their friendships out across the fields. I have not been able to stop my mother's screams in public libraries or over telephones. Walking erect (knees straight, toes pointed forward, not pigeon-toed, which is Chinese-feminine) and speaking in an inaudible voice, I have tried to turn myself American-feminine. Chinese communication was loud, public. Only sick people had to whisper. But at the dinner table, where the family members came nearest one another, no one could talk, not the outcasts nor any eaters. Every word that falls from the mouth is a coin lost. Silently they gave and accepted food with both hands. A preoccupied child who took his bowl with one hand got a sideways glare. A complete moment of total attention is due everyone alike. Children and lovers have no singularity here, but my aunt used a secret voice, a separate attentiveness.

She kept the man's name to herself throughout her labor and dying; she did not accuse him that he be punished with her. To save her inseminator's name she gave silent birth.

He may have been somebody in her own household, but intercourse with a man outside the family would have been no less abhorrent. All the village were kinsmen, and the titles shouted in loud country voices never let kinship

5. A heavy overcoat.

be forgotten. Any man within visiting distance would have been neutralized as a lover—"brother," "younger brother," "older brother"—one hundred and fifteen relationship titles. Parents researched birth charts probably not so much to assure good fortune as to circumvent incest in a population that has but one hundred surnames. Everybody has eight million relatives. How useless then sexual mannerisms, how dangerous.

As if it came from an atavism[6] deeper than fear, I used to add "brother" silently to boys' names. It hexed the boys, who would or would not ask me to dance, and made them less scary and as familiar and deserving of benevolence as girls.

But, of course, I hexed myself also—no dates. I should have stood up, both arms waving, and shouted out across libraries, "Hey, you! Love me back." I had no idea, though, now to make attraction selective, how to control its direction and magnitude. If I made myself American-pretty so that the five or six Chinese boys in the class fell in love with me, everyone else—the Caucasian, Negro, and Japanese boys—would too. Sisterliness, dignified and honorable, made much more sense.

Attraction eludes control so stubbornly that whole societies designed to organize relationships among people cannot keep order, not even when they bind people to one another from childhood and raise them together. Among the very poor and the wealthy, brothers married their adopted sisters, like doves. Our family allowed some romance, paying adult brides' prices and providing dowries so that their sons and daughters could marry strangers. Marriage promises to turn strangers into friendly relatives—a nation of siblings.

In the village structure, spirits shimmered among the live creatures, balanced and held in equilibrium by time and land. But one human being flaring up into violence could open up a black hole, a maelstrom[7] that pulled in the sky. The frightened villagers, who depended on one another to maintain the real, went to my aunt to show her a personal, physical representation of the break she had made in the "roundness." Misallying couples snapped off the future, which was to be embodied in true offspring. The villagers garnished her for acting as if she could have a private life, secret and apart from them.

If my aunt had betrayed the family at a time of large grain yields and peace, when many boys were born, and wings were being built on many houses, perhaps she might have escaped such severe punishment. But the men—hungry, greedy, tired of planting in dry soil—had been forced to leave the village in order to send food-money home. There were ghost plagues, bandit plagues, wars with the Japanese, floods. My Chinese brother and sister had died of an unknown sickness. Adultery, perhaps only a mistake during good times, became a crime when the village needed food.

The round moon cakes and round doorways, the round tables of graduated size that fit one roundness inside another, round windows and rice bowls—these talismans had lost their power to warn this family of the law: a family must be whole, faithfully keeping the descent line by having sons to feed the old and the dead, who in turn look after the family. The villagers came to show my aunt and her lover-in-hiding a broken house. The villagers were speeding up the circling of events because she was too shortsighted to see that her infidelity had already harmed the village, that waves of consequences

---

6. A trait with origins farther back than the preceding     7. A powerful, violent whirlpool.
generation—a throwback.

would return unpredictably, sometimes in disguise, as now, to hurt her. This roundness had to be made coin-sized so that she would see its circumference: punish her at the birth of her baby. Awaken her to the inexorable. People who refused fatalism because they could invent small resources insisted on culpability. Deny accidents and wrest fault from the stars.

After the villagers left, their lanterns now scattering in various directions toward home, the family broke their silence and cursed her. "Aiaa, we're going to die. Death is coming. Death is coming. Look what you've done. You've killed us. Ghost! Dead ghost! Ghost! You've never been born." She ran out into the fields, far enough from the house so that she could no longer hear their voices, and pressed herself against the earth, her own land no more. When she felt the birth coming, she thought that she had been hurt. Her body seized together. "They're hurt me too much," she thought. "This is gall, and it will kill me." With forehead and knees against the earth, her body convulsed and then relaxed. She turned on her back, lay on the ground. The black well of sky and stars went out and out and out forever; her body and her complexity seemed to disappear. She was one of the stars, a bright dot in blackness, without home, without a companion, in eternal cold and silence. An agoraphobia[8] rose in her, speeding higher and higher, bigger and bigger; she would not be able to contain it; there would be no end to fear.

Flayed, unprotected against space, she felt pain return, focusing her body. This pain chilled her—a cold, steady kind of surface pain. Inside, spasmodically, the other pain, the pain of the child, heated her. For hours she lay on the ground, alternately body and space. Sometimes a vision of normal comfort obliterated reality: she saw the family in the evening gambling at the dinner table, the young people massaging their elder's backs. She saw them congratulating one another, high joy on the mornings the rice shoots came up. When these pictures burst, the stars drew yet further apart. Black space opened.

She got to her feet to fight better and remembered that old-fashioned women gave birth in their pigsties to fool the jealous, pain-dealing gods, who do not snatch piglets. Before the next spasms could stop her, she ran to the pigsty, each step a rushing out into emptiness. She climbed over the fence and knelt in the dirt. It was good to have a fence enclosing her, a tribal person alone.

Laboring, this women who had carried her child as a foreign growth that sickened her every day, expelled it at last. She reached down to touch the hot, wet, moving mass, surely smaller than anything human, and could feel that it was human after all—fingers, toes, nails, nose. She pulled it up on to her belly, and it lay curled there, but in the air, feet precisely tucked one under the other. She opened her loose shirt and buttoned the child inside. After resting, it squirmed and thrashed and she pushed it up to her breast. It turned its head this way and that until it found her nipple. There, it made little snuffling noises. She clenched her teeth at its preciousness, lovely as a young calf, a piglet, a little go.

She may have gone to the pigsty as a last act of responsibility: she would protect this child as she had protected its father. It would look after her soul, leaving supplies on her grave. But how would this tiny child without family find her grave when there would be no marker for her anywhere, neither in the earth nor the family hall? No one would give her a family hall name. She had taken the child with her into the wastes. At its birth the two of them had

8. An abnormal fear of open space.

felt the same raw pain of separation, a wound that only the family pressing tight could close. A child with no descent line would not soften her life but only trail after her, ghostlike, begging her to give it purpose. At dawn the villagers on their way to the fields would stand around the fence and look.

Full of milk, the little ghost slept. When it awoke, she hardened her breasts against the milk that crying loosens. Toward morning she picked up the baby and walked to the well.

Carrying the baby to the well shows loving. Otherwise abandon it. Turn its face into the mud. Mothers who love their children take them along. It was probably a girl; there is some hope of forgiveness for boys.

"Don't tell anyone you had an aunt. Your father does not want to hear her name. She has never been born." I have believed that sex was unspeakable and words so strong and fathers so frail that "aunt" would do my father mysterious harm. I have thought that my family, having settled among immigrants who had also been their neighbors in the ancestral land, needed to clean their name, and a wrong word would incite the kinspeople even here. But there is more to this silence: they want me to participate in her punishment. And I have.

In the twenty years since I heard this story I have not asked for details nor said my aunt's name; I do not know it. People who can comfort the dead can also chase after them to hurt them further—a reverse ancestor worship. The real punishment was not the raid swiftly inflicted by the villagers, but the family's deliberately forgetting her. Her betrayal so maddened them, they saw to it that she would suffer forever, even after death. Always hungry, always needing, she would have to beg food from other ghosts, snatch and steal it from those whose living descendants give them gifts. She would have to fight the ghosts massed at crossroads for the buns a few thoughtful citizens leave to decoy her away from village and home so that the ancestral spirits could feast unharassed. At peace, they could act like gods, not ghosts, their descent lines providing them with paper suits and dresses, spirit money, paper houses, paper automobiles, chicken, meat, and rice[9] into eternity—essences delivered up in smoke and flames, steam and incense rising from each rice bowl. In an attempt to make the Chinese care for people outside the family, Chairman Mao[1] encourages us now to give our paper replicas to the spirits of outstanding soldiers and workers, no matter whose ancestors they may be. My aunt remains forever hungry. Goods are not distributed evenly among the dead.

My aunt haunts me—her ghost drawn to me because now, after fifty years of neglect, I alone devote pages of paper to her, though not origamied into houses and clothes. I do not think she always means me well. I am telling on her, and she was a spite suicide, drowning herself in the drinking water. The Chinese are always very frightened of the drowned one, whose weeping ghost, wet hair hanging and skin bloated, waits silently by the water to pull down a substitute.

1976

9. Traditionally, offerings left at the graves of ancestors.
1. Mao Tse-Tung (1893–1976), head of the Chinese Communist Party and leader of China from 1949 to 1959 and 1969 to 1976.

# ALICE WALKER
## b. 1944

In her essay *Beyond the Peacock*, Alice Walker, born to sharecropper parents in Eatonton, Georgia, describes the moment when she visited the country house of Flannery O'Connor—by then deceased—outside nearby Milledgeville. As she prepared to knock at the door of the empty but still cared-for house, with peacocks strutting about in the sun, Walker thought of the shack in which she herself was born, minutes away from and on the same road as O'Connor's "Andalusia":

> What I feel at the moment of knocking is fury that someone is paid to take care of her house, though no one lives in it, and that her house still, in fact, stands, while mine—which of course we never owned anyway—is slowly rotting into dust. Her house becomes—in an instant—the symbol of my own disinheritance, and for that instant I hate her guts.

She goes on to reflect that "it all comes back to houses," and that the difference between rich and poor—as, on that economic basis, between white and black—is a fact and a wrong that will not be changed by what she terms the currently fashionable "literary separatism"—black and white writers staying apart, minding their own business and writing only for readers of the same color.

That O'Connor's house provoked such a response in Walker is a measure of how seriously and with what admiration she read O'Connor's work, which first convinced her that a separatist, segregated literature was an inadequate literature. Just as she could read O'Connor with instructive pleasure, so her own work would speak not merely to African-American readers. As a college student in the 1960s, first at Spelman College and then at Sarah Lawrence, she read O'Connor—as she later noted—"scarcely conscious of the difference between her racial and economic background and my own." At Sarah Lawrence she wrote her first novel (it would be published in 1970 as *The Third Life of Grange Copeland*). But the crucial moment of her college experience seems to have been when, as she relates it in *From an Interview*, pregnant and suicidal, she had an abortion and in its aftermath wrote the poems that were to make up her first book, *Once*. She gave those poems to her teacher, Muriel Rukeyser, who admired them and sent them to an agent. Published in 1968, the poems are notable not so much for their formal skill as for their sensitive renderings of the Africa which she had visited and her native Georgia (particularly in the poem *Once*) as it was embroiled in the struggle for civil rights. Upon graduating from Sarah Lawrence she received a writing fellowship and planned to spend it in Senegal, West Africa. But instead, after working as a caseworker in the New York City welfare department, she volunteered in the summer of 1966 to work at the voter registration drive in Mississippi. This decision came, as she was to put it later, out of "the realization that I could never live happily in Africa—or anywhere else—until I could live freely in Mississippi."

Her career as a writer began to flower, as she taught at Jackson State, at Tougaloo, and at Wellesley College and was a fellow at the Radcliffe Institute from 1971 to 1973. In that last year she published her first collection of stories, *In Love & Trouble*. With its subtitle, *Stories of Black Women*, such ones as *Her Sweet Jerome*, *To Hell with Dying*, and *Everyday Use* (printed here) register with delicate precision and some humor lives that tell themselves in an idiom as colorful as the following:

> Last night while Ruel snored on his side of the bed I washed the prints of his hands off my body. Then I plugged in one of his chain saws and tried to slice

off his head. This failed because of the noise. Ruel woke up in the nick of time. (*Really, Doesn't Crime Pay?*)

Walker married Mel Leventhal, a white activist civil rights lawyer, and together they had a daughter (they have since separated). A second collection of her poems, *Revolutionary Petunias*, was published in 1973 and nominated for the National Book Award. In 1976 she published *Meridian*, a novel whose heroine is involved in the civil rights movement. More conventional in its writing than either her poems or her stories, it is mainly interesting as a register of social history. In later years have appeared a second collection of stories, *You Can't Keep a Good Woman Down* (1979), and her much-admired novel *The Color Purple* (1982), an American Book Award winner, notable for its imaginative use of epistolary convention to create a richly vernacular speech.

In her collection of "womanist" prose writings, *In Search of Our Mothers' Gardens* (1983), and as an ironic parallel to the visit to O'Connor's house, Walker describes (in *Looking for Zora*) her discovery of Zora Neale Hurston's grave in a decaying Florida cemetery. (Walker edited a collection of Hurston's work, *I Love Myself When I Am Laughing . . .* , 1979.) She admires her black forebear's insistence on the richness of African-American folk culture and admires too her anger, her rejection of "the sobbing school of Negrohood" in favor of livelier, more energetic creativeness. Concluding her essay, Walker remarks that

> there are times—and finding Zora Hurston's grave was one of them—when normal responses of grief, horror, and so on do not make sense because they bear no real relation to the depth of the emotion one feels.

Unable to cry, and remembering that Hurston was not a "teary sort of person herself," she feels the absurdity of grief: "And at this point, laughter gushes up to retrieve sanity." Something like that mixture of feelings and attitudes is what we encounter in the varied kinds of awareness expressed in Walker's own work.

# Everyday Use[1]

## *For Your Grandmama*

I will wait for her in the yard that Maggie and I made so clean and wavy yesterday afternoon. A yard like this is more comfortable than most people know. It is not just a yard. It is like an extended living room. When the hard clay is swept clean as a floor and the fine sand around the edges lined with tiny, irregular grooves, anyone can come and sit and look up into the elm tree and wait for the breezes that never come inside the house.

Maggie will be nervous until after her sister goes: she will stand hopelessly in corners, homely and ashamed of the burn scars down her arms and legs, eyeing her sister with a mixture of envy and awe. She thinks her sister has held life always in the palm of one hand, that "no" is a word the world never learned to say to her.

You've no doubt seen those TV shows where the child who has "made it" is confronted, as a surprise, by her own mother and father, tottering in weakly from backstage. (A pleasant surprise, of course: What would they do if parent

---

1. From *In Love & Trouble* (1973).

and child came on the show only to curse out and insult each other?) On TV mother and child embrace and smile into each other's faces. Sometimes the mother and father weep, the child wraps them in her arms and leans across the table to tell how she would not have made it without their help. I have seen these programs.

Sometimes I dream a dream in which Dee and I are suddenly brought together on a TV program of this sort. Out of a dark and soft-seated limousine I am ushered into a bright room filled with many people. There I meet a smiling, gray, sporty man like Johnny Carson who shakes my hand and tells me what a fine girl I have. Then we are on the stage and Dee is embracing me with tears in her eyes. She pins on my dress a large orchid, even though she has told me once that she thinks orchids are tacky flowers.

In real life I am a large, big-boned woman with rough, man-working hands. In the winter I wear flannel nightgowns to bed and overalls during the day. I can kill and clean a hog as mercilessly as a man. My fat keeps me hot in zero weather. I can work outside all day, breaking ice to get water for washing; I can eat pork liver cooked over the open fire minutes after it comes steaming from the hog. One winter I knocked a bull calf straight in the brain between the eyes with a sledge hammer and had the meat hung up to chill before nightfall. But of course all this does not show on television. I am the way my daughter would want me to be: a hundred pounds lighter, my skin like an uncooked barley pancake. My hair glistens in the hot bright lights. Johnny Carson has much to do to keep up with my quick and witty tongue.

But that is a mistake. I know even before I wake up. Who ever knew a Johnson with a quick tongue? Who can even imagine me looking a strange white man in the eye? It seems to me I have talked to them always with one foot raised in flight, with my head turned in whichever way is farthest from them. Dee, though. She would always look anyone in the eye. Hesitation was no part of her nature.

"How do I look, Mama?" Maggie says, showing just enough of her thin body enveloped in pink skirt and red blouse for me to know she's there, almost hidden by the door.

"Come out into the yard," I say.

Have you ever seen a lame animal, perhaps a dog run over by some careless person rich enough to own a car, sidle up to someone who is ignorant enough to be kind to them? That is the way my Maggie walks. She has been like this, chin on chest, eyes on ground, feet in shuffle, ever since the fire that burned the other house to the ground.

Dee is lighter than Maggie, with nicer hair and a fuller figure. She's a woman now, though sometimes I forget. How long ago was it that the other house burned? Ten, twelve years? Sometimes I can still hear the flames and feel Maggie's arms sticking to me, her hair smoking and her dress falling off her in little black papery flakes. Her eyes seemed stretched open, blazed open by the flames reflected in them. And Dee. I see her standing off under the sweet gum tree she used to dig gum out of; a look of concentration on her face as she watched the last dingy gray board of the house fall in toward the red-hot brick chimney. Why don't you do a dance around the ashes? I'd wanted to ask her. She had hated the house that much.

I used to think she hated Maggie, too. But that was before we raised the money, the church and me, to send her to Augusta to school. She used to read to us without pity; forcing words, lies, other folks' habits, whole lives upon us two, sitting trapped and ignorant underneath her voice. She washed us in a river of make-believe, burned us with a lot of knowledge we didn't necessarily need to know. Pressed us to her with the serious way she read, to shove us away at just the moment, like dimwits, we seemed about to understand.

Dee wanted nice things. A yellow organdy dress to wear to her graduation from high school; black pumps to match a green suit she'd made from an old suit somebody gave me. She was determined to stare down any disaster in her efforts. Her eyelids would not flicker for minutes at a time. Often I fought off the temptation to shake her. At sixteen she had a style of her own: and knew what style was.

I never had an education myself. After second grade the school was closed down. Don't ask me why: in 1927 colored asked fewer questions than they do now. Sometimes Maggie reads to me. She stumbles along good-naturedly but can't see well. She knows she is not bright. Like good looks and money, quickness passed her by. She will marry John Thomas (who has mossy teeth in an earnest face) and then I'll be free to sit here and I guess just sing church songs to myself. Although I never was a good singer. Never could carry a tune. I was always better at a man's job. I used to love to milk till I was hooked in the side in '49. Cows are soothing and slow and don't bother you, unless you try to milk them the wrong way.

I have deliberately turned my back on the house. It is three rooms, just like the one that burned, except the roof is tin; they don't make shingle roofs any more. There are no real windows, just some holes cut in the sides, like the portholes in a ship, but not round and not square, with rawhide holding the shutters up on the outside. This house is in a pasture, too, like the other one. No doubt when Dee sees it she will want to tear it down. She wrote me once that no matter where we "choose" to live, she will manage to come see us. But she will never bring her friends. Maggie and I thought about this and Maggie asked me, "Mama, when did Dee ever *have* any friends?"

She had a few. Furtive boys in pink shirts hanging about on washday after school. Nervous girls who never laughed. Impressed with her they worshiped the well-turned phrase, the cute shape, the scalding humor that erupted like bubbles in lye. She read to them.

When she was courting Jimmy T she didn't have much time to pay to us, but turned all her faultfinding power on him. He *flew* to marry a cheap city girl from a family of ignorant flashy people. She hardly had time to recompose herself.

When she comes I will meet—but there they are!

Maggie attempts to make a dash for the house, in her shuffling way, but I stay her with my hand. "Come back here," I say. And she stops and tries to dig a well in the sand with her toe.

It is hard to see them clearly through the strong sun. But even the first glimpse of leg out of the car tells me it is Dee. Her feet were always neat-looking, as if God himself had shaped them with a certain style. From the other side of the car comes a short, stocky man. Hair is all over his head a foot long and hanging from his chin like a kinky mule tail. I hear Maggie suck in her breath. "Uhnnnh," is what it sounds like. Like when you see the wriggling end of a snake just in front of your foot on the road. "Uhnnnh."

Dee next. A dress down to the ground, in this hot weather. A dress so loud it hurts my eyes. There are yellows and oranges enough to throw back the light of the sun. I feel my whole face warming from the heat waves it throws out. Earrings gold, too, and hanging down to her shoulders. Bracelets dangling and making noises when she moves her arm up to shake the folds of the dress out of her armpits. The dress is loose and flows, and as she walks closer, I like it. I hear Maggie go "Uhnnnh" again. It is her sister's hair. It stands straight up like the wool on a sheep. It is black as night and around the edges are two long pigtails that rope about like small lizards disappearing behind her ears.

"Wa-su-zo-Tean-o!" she says, coming on in that gliding way the dress makes her move. The short stocky fellow with the hair to his navel is all grinning and he follows up with "Asalamalakim, my mother and sister!" He moves to hug Maggie but she falls back, right up against the back of my chair. I feel her trembling there and when I look up I see the perspiration falling off her chin.

"Don't get up," says Dee. Since I am stout it takes something of a push. You can see me trying to move a second or two before I make it. She turns, showing white heels through her sandals, and goes back to the car. Out she peeks next with a Polaroid. She stoops down quickly and lines up picture after picture of me sitting there in front of the house with Maggie cowering behind me. She never takes a shot without making sure the house is included. When a cow comes nibbling around the edge of the yard she snaps it and me and Maggie *and* the house. Then she puts the Polaroid in the back seat of the car, and comes up and kisses me on the forehead.

Meanwhile Asalamalakim is going through motions with Maggie's hand. Maggie's hand is as limp as a fish, and probably as cold, despite the sweat, and she keeps trying to pull it back. It looks like Asalamalakim wants to shake hands but wants to do it fancy. Or maybe he don't know how people shake hands. Anyhow, he soon gives up on Maggie.

"Well," I say. "Dee."

"No, Mama," she says. "Not 'Dee,' Wangero Leewanika Kemanjo!"

"What happened to 'Dee'?" I wanted to know.

"She's dead," Wangero said. "I couldn't bear it any longer, being named after the people who oppress me."

"You know as well as me you was named after your aunt Dicie," I said. Dicie is my sister. She named Dee. We called her "Big Dee" after Dee was born.

"But who was *she* named after?" asked Wangero.

"I guess after Grandma Dee," I said.

"And who was she named after?" asked Wangero.

"Her mother," I said, and saw Wangero was getting tired. "That's about as far back as I can trace it," I said. Though, in fact, I probably could have carried it back beyond the Civil War through the branches.

"Well," said Asalamalakim, "there you are."

"Uhnnnh," I heard Maggie say.

"There I was not," I said, "before 'Dicie' cropped up in our family, so why should I try to trace it that far back?"

He just stood there grinning, looking down on me like somebody inspecting

a Model A car. Every once in a while he and Wangero sent eye signals over
my head.

"How do you pronounce this name?" I asked.

"You don't have to call me by it if you don't want to," said Wangero.

"Why shouldn't I?" I asked. "If that's what you want us to call you, we'll
call you."

"I know it might sound awkward at first," said Wangero.

"I'll get used to it," I said. "Ream it out again."

Well, soon we got the name out of the way. Asalamalakim had a name
twice as long and three times as hard. After I tripped over it two or three times
he told me to just call him Hakim-a-barber. I wanted to ask him was he a
barber, but I didn't really think he was, so I didn't ask.

"You must belong to those beef-cattle peoples down the road," I said. They
said "Asalamalakim" when they met you, too, but they didn't shake hands.
Always too busy: feeding the cattle, fixing the fences, putting up salt-lick shelters, throwing down hay. When the white folks poisoned some of the herd the
men stayed up all night with rifles in their hands. I walked a mile and a half
just to see the sight.

Hakim-a-barber said, "I accept some of their doctrines, but farming and
raising cattle is not my style." (They didn't tell me, and I didn't ask, whether
Wangero (Dee) had really gone and married him.)

We sat down to eat and right away he said he didn't eat collards and pork
was unclean. Wangero, though, went on through the chitlins and corn bread,
the greens and everything else. She talked a blue streak over the sweet potatoes.
Everything delighted her. Even the fact that we still used the benches her
daddy made for the table when we couldn't afford to buy chairs.

"Oh, Mama!" she cried. Then turned to Hakim-a-barber. "I never knew
how lovely these benches are. You can feel the rump prints," she said, running
her hands underneath her and along the bench. Then she gave a sigh and her
hand closed over Grandma Dee's butter dish. "That's it!" she said. "I knew
there was something I wanted to ask you if I could have." She jumped up from
the table and went over in the corner where the churn stood, the milk in it
clabber by now. She looked at the churn and looked at it.

"This churn top is what I need," she said. "Didn't Uncle Buddy whittle it
out of a tree you all used to have?"

"Yes," I said.

"Uh huh," she said happily. "And I want the dasher, too."

"Uncle Buddy whittle that, too?" asked the barber.

Dee (Wangero) looked up at me.

"Aunt Dee's first husband whittled the dash," said Maggie so low you almost
couldn't hear her. "His name was Henry, but they called him Stash."

"Maggie's brain is like an elephant's," Wangero said, laughing. "I can use
the churn top as a centerpiece for the alcove table," she said, sliding a plate
over the churn, "and I'll think of something artistic to do with the dasher."

When she finished wrapping the dasher the handle stuck out. I took it for a
moment in my hands. You didn't even have to look close to see where hands
pushing the dasher up and down to make butter had left a kind of sink in the
wood. In fact, there were a lot of small sinks; you could see where thumbs and
fingers had sunk into the wood. It was beautiful light yellow wood, from a tree
that grew in the yard where Big Dee and Stash had lived.

After dinner Dee (Wangero) went to the trunk at the foot of my bed and started rifling through it. Maggie hung back in the kitchen over the dishpan. Out came Wangero with two quilts. They had been pieced by Grandma Dee and then Big Dee and me had hung them on the quilt frames on the front porch and quilted them. One was in the Lone Star pattern. The other was Walk Around the Mountain. In both of them were scraps of dresses Grandma Dee had worn fifty and more years ago. Bits and pieces of Grandpa Jarrell's Paisley shirts. And one teeny faded blue piece, about the size of a penny matchbox, that was from Great Grandpa Ezra's uniform that he wore in the Civil War.

"Mama," Wangero said sweet as a bird. "Can I have these old quilts?"

I heard something fall in the kitchen, and a minute later the kitchen door slammed.

"Why don't you take one or two of the others?" I asked. "These old things was just done by me and Big Dee from some tops your grandma pieced before she died."

"No," said Wangero. "I don't want those. They are stitched around the borders by machine."

"That'll make them last better," I said.

"That's not the point," said Wangero. "These are all pieces of dresses Grandma used to wear. She did all this stitching by hand. Imagine!" She held the quilts securely in her arms, stroking them.

"Some of the pieces, like those lavender ones, come from old clothes her mother handed down to her," I said, moving up to touch the quilts. Dee (Wangero) moved back just enough so that I couldn't reach the quilts. They already belonged to her.

"Imagine!" she breathed again, clutching them closely to her bosom.

"The truth is," I said, "I promised to give them quilts to Maggie, for when she marries John Thomas."

She gasped like a bee had stung her.

"Maggie can't appreciate these quilts!" she said. "She'd probably be backward enough to put them to everyday use."

"I reckon she would," I said. "God knows I been saving 'em for long enough with nobody using 'em. I hope she will!" I didn't want to bring up how I had offered Dee (Wangero) a quilt when she went away to college. Then she had told me they were old-fashioned, out of style.

"But they're *priceless!*" she was saying now, furiously; for she has a temper. "Maggie would put them on the bed and in five years they'd be in rags. Less than that!"

"She can always make some more," I said. "Maggie knows how to quilt."

Dee (Wangero) looked at me with hatred. "You just will not understand. The point is these quilts, *these* quilts!"

"Well," I said, stumped. "What would *you* do with them?"

"Hang them," she said. As if that was the only thing you *could* do with quilts.

Maggie by now was standing in the door. I could almost hear the sound her feet made as they scraped over each other.

"She can have them, Mama," she said, like somebody used to never winning anything, or having anything reserved for her. "I can 'member Grandma Dee without the quilts."

I looked at her hard. She had filled her bottom lip with checkerberry snuff and it gave her a face a kind of dopey, hangdog look. It was Grandma Dee and Big Dee who taught her how to quilt herself. She stood there with her scarred hands hidden in the folds of her skirt. She looked at her sister with something like fear but she wasn't mad at her. This was Maggie's portion. This was the way she knew God to work.

When I looked at her like that something hit me in the top of my head and ran down to the soles of my feet. Just like when I'm in church and the spirit of God touches me and I get happy and shout. I did something I never had done before: hugged Maggie to me, then dragged her on into the room, snatched the quilts out of Miss Wangero's hands and dumped them into Maggie's lap. Maggie just sat there on my bed with her mouth open.

"Take one or two of the others," I said to Dee.

But she turned without a word and went out to Hakim-a-barber.

"You just don't understand," she said, as Maggie and I came out to the car.

"What don't I understand?" I wanted to know.

"Your heritage," she said. And then she turned to Maggie, kissed her, and said, "You ought to try to make something of yourself, too, Maggie. It's really a new day for us. But from the way you and Mama still live you'd never know it."

She put on some sunglasses that hid everything above the tip of her nose and her chin.

Maggie smiled; maybe at the sunglasses. But a real smile, not scared. After we watched the car dust settle I asked Maggie to bring me a dip of snuff. And then the two of us sat there just enjoying, until it was time to go in the house and go to bed.

1973

---

# ANN BEATTIE
## b. 1947

The American 1960s, a highly publicized decade, was bound to produce a writer who would be held responsible for chronicling the fortunes of its young people, as they grew up, got married and divorced, worked at different jobs and went to the same parties. There is some truth in the claim that Ann Beattie, who graduated from high school in 1965, is that writer; indeed she has picked up some of the mythical reputation that adheres to the film *The Big Chill* as somehow "representative" in its representation of late-sixties idealism and conviction gone flat or sour. Yet to stress Beattie's importance as portraitist of a generation may be to do her a disservice, since she is above all else a writer, and one with an unrepresentative, even idiosyncratic, style. Her stories and novels should not be taken merely as vehicles for displaying social attitudes and manners, but as mannerist compositions that need to be not only looked at but listened to. Her style is too pronounced, too carefully contrived, to be treated as a transparent medium through which "reality" is given us directly.

On its surface her life has been relatively uneventful, from growing up in a middle-class suburb of Washington, D.C. ("an artsy little thing . . . you know, painting pictures, writing," as she put it), taking her undergraduate degree at American University, then going on to graduate study for a time at the University of Connecticut. She soon began to send stories to *The New Yorker* (one of her collections is dedicated to Roger Angell, of that magazine) and after the usual spate of rejections had one accepted, then others. By the time she was in her mid-twenties she had become a publishing writer in the most sought-after place, and in 1976 on the verge of her thirtieth birthday she brought out simultaneously a collection of her stories, *Distortions*, and her first novel, *Chilly Scenes of Winter*.

The stories—some of them more experimental in style than her more recent work—are about transient, usually unsatisfactory relationships between people, married and single, male and female. Their work provides them with little pleasure or fulfillment; almost anything threatens to become "just a job." What they do best, and incessantly, is talk to each other about themselves, how they feel about their lives. In fact such talk is the essential ingredient in her fiction. As one of her more severe critics, Joseph Epstein, has pointed out, what she strives for in her writing is not "development of character, accounts of motivation or moral resolution" but rather "states of feeling." In stories from her second collection, *Secrets and Surprises* (1978), such as *A Reasonable Man*, *Lawn Party*, and *Weekend*, feelings are talked around, hinted at, never quite said, but are the only "thing" that happens in the story. In *Weekend* (printed here) the happening has a force that is cumulative and disturbing.

Like many fiction writers, Beattie acknowledges the influence of Hemingway ("I sound like someone talking in *The Sun Also Rises*," says a character in *The Lawn Party*), but her kinship with him is especially strong in that each uses language, exchanges between characters, to suggest—by all that is left unsaid in the spare, often dull sentences, the platitudinous conversations—that something interesting lies behind the words, that conversation. Hemingway manages in his best stories to make us feel the presence of something powerful behind the conventional words. Beattie's characters, decades later, yearn for there to be something real or interesting behind their banal words, but the poignancy of her comedy—she is frequently a comic writer—lies in the hint that, as the characters themselves half guess, there may be nothing much behind them. Something important got lost, back there in the sixties.

Of her four novels, the longest and most ambitious is *Falling in Place* (1980), which spreads the usual urban and suburban anomie over the usual Beattie cast of dispirited seekers after a better day. But the book comes to life—a rather chilling, comic life—when it focuses on a fifteen-year-old girl named Mary (whose favorite characterizing response to things is "Suck-O") and her younger brother John Joel, a compulsive eater who loves violent comics but little else in the world. This twosome, who could give the most obnoxious of Flannery O'Connor's fictional children a run for their money, is observed with satiric verve, and although as a whole the book doesn't add up very satisfactorily, it contains a number of brilliant parts. Beattie is essentially a writer of scenes rather than a contriver of extended sequences, just as the people she writes about can only deal with life—and that just barely—a moment at a time.

Like her contemporary the short-fiction writer Raymond Carver, Beattie has many imitators, "minimalists" who try to prove that less is more and most often make the attempt with less than maximum talents. In fact, like all distinctive stylists, she cannot be imitated, only travestied. Her sharp, idiomatic humor, often operating so quietly the reader almost misses it, is an insurance against airlessness in her fiction. Now that she has fully developed her distinctive style, the question is whether she can avoid further bureaucratizing of it—continuing efficiently to turn out the same product—and move instead in directions new and surprising to her readers.

# Weekend[1]

On Saturday morning Lenore is up before the others. She carries her baby into the living room and puts him in George's favorite chair, which tilts because its back legs are missing, and covers him with a blanket. Then she lights a fire in the fireplace, putting fresh logs on a few embers that are still glowing from the night before. She sits down on the floor beside the chair and checks the baby, who has already gone back to sleep—a good thing, because there are guests in the house. George, the man she lives with, is very hospitable and impetuous; he extends invitations whenever old friends call, urging them to come spend the weekend. Most of the callers are his former students— he used to be an English professor—and when they come it seems to make things much worse. It makes *him* much worse, because he falls into smoking too much and drinking and not eating, and then his ulcer bothers him. When the guests leave, when the weekend is over, she has to cook bland food: apple-sauce, oatmeal, puddings. And his drinking does not taper off easily anymore; in the past he would stop cold when the guests left, but lately he only tapers down from Scotch to wine, and drinks wine well into the week—a lot of wine, perhaps a whole bottle with his meal—until his stomach is much worse. He is hard to live with. Once when a former student, a woman named Ruth, visited them—a lover, she suspected—she overheard George talking to her in his study, where he had taken her to see a photograph of their house before he began repairing it. George had told Ruth that she, Lenore, stayed with him because she was simple. It hurt her badly, made her actually dizzy with sur-prise and shame, and since then, no matter who the guests are, she never feels quite at ease on the weekends. In the past she enjoyed some of the things she and George did with their guests, but since overhearing what he said to Ruth she feels that all their visitors have been secretly told the same thing about her. To her, though, George is usually kind. But she is sure that is the reason he has not married her, and when he recently remarked on their daughter's intelligence (she is five years old, a girl named Maria) she found that she could no longer respond with simple pride; now she feels spite as well, feels that Maria exists as proof of her own good genes. She has begun to expect perfec-tion of the child. She knows this is wrong, and she has tried hard not to com-municate her anxiety to Maria, who is already, as her kindergarten teacher says, "untypical."

At first Lenore loved George because he was untypical, although after she had moved in with him and lived with him for a while she began to see that he was not exceptional but a variation on a type. She is proud of observing that, and she harbors the discovery—her silent response to his low opinion of her. She does not know why he found her attractive—in the beginning he did—because she does not resemble the pretty, articulate young women he likes to invite, with their lovers or girl friends, to their house for the weekend. None of these young women have husbands; when they bring a man with them at all they bring a lover, and they seem happy not to be married. Lenore, too, is happy to be single—not out of conviction that marriage is wrong but because she knows that it would be wrong to be married to George if he thinks she is simple. She thought at first to confront him with what she had over-

1. From *Secrets and Surprises* (1978).

heard, to demand an explanation. But he can weasel out of any corner. At best, she can mildly fluster him, and later he will only blame it on Scotch. Of course she might ask why he has all these women come to visit, why he devotes so little time to her or the children. To that he would say that it was the quality of the time they spent together that mattered, not the quantity. He has already said that, in fact, without being asked. He says things over and over so that she will accept them as truths. And eventually she does. She does not like to think long and hard, and when there is an answer—even his answer—it is usually easier to accept it and go on with things. She goes on with what she has always done: tending the house and the children and George, when he needs her. She likes to bake and she collects art postcards. She is proud of their house, which was bought cheaply and improved by George when he was still interested in that kind of work, and she is happy to have visitors come there, even if she does not admire them or even like them.

Except for teaching a night course in photography at a junior college once a week, George has not worked since he left the university two years ago, after he was denied tenure. She cannot really tell if he is unhappy working so little, because he keeps busy in other ways. He listens to classical music in the morning, slowly sipping herbal teas, and on fair afternoons he lies outdoors in the sun, no matter how cold the day. He takes photographs, and walks alone in the woods. He does errands for her if they need to be done. Sometimes at night he goes to the library or goes to visit friends; he tells her that these people often ask her to come too, but he says she would not like them. This is true— she would not like them. Recently he has done some late-night cooking. He has always kept a journal, and he is a great letter writer. An aunt left him most of her estate, ten thousand dollars, and said in her will that he was the only one who really cared, who took the time, again and again, to write. He had not seen his aunt for five years before she died, but he wrote regularly. Sometimes Lenore finds notes that he has left for her. Once, on the refrigerator, there was a long note suggesting clever Christmas presents for her family that he had thought of while she was out. Last week he scotch-taped a slip of paper to a casserole dish that contained leftover veal stew, saying "This was delicious." He does not compliment her verbally, but he likes to let her know that he is pleased.

A few nights ago—the same night they got a call from Julie and Sarah, saying they were coming for a visit—she told him that she wished he would talk more, that he would confide in her.

"Confide what?" he said.

"You always take that attitude," she said. "You pretend that you have no thoughts. Why does there have to be so much silence?"

"I'm not a professor anymore," he said. "I don't have to spend every minute *thinking*."

But he loves to talk to the young women. He will talk to them on the phone for as much as an hour; he walks with them through the woods for most of the day when they visit. The lovers the young women bring with them always seem to fall behind; they give up and return to the house to sit and talk to her, or to help with the preparation of the meal, or to play with the children. The young woman and George come back refreshed, ready for another round of conversation at dinner.

A few weeks ago one of the young men said to her, "Why do you let it go on?" They had been talking lightly before that—about the weather, the children—and then, in the kitchen, where he was sitting shelling peas, he put his head on the table and said, barely audibly, "Why do you let it go on?" He did not raise his head, and she stared at him, thinking that she must have imagined his speaking. She was surprised—surprised to have heard it, and surprised that he had said nothing after that, which made her doubt that he had spoken.

"Why do I let what go on?" she said.

There was a long silence. "Whatever this sick game is, I don't want to get involved in it," he said at last. "It was none of my business to ask. I understand that you don't want to talk about it."

"But it's really cold out there," she said. "What could happen when it's freezing out?"

He shook his head, the way George did, to indicate that she was beyond understanding. But she wasn't stupid, and she knew what might be going on. She had said the right thing, had been on the right track, but she had to say what she felt, which was that nothing very serious could be happening at that moment because they were walking in the woods. There wasn't even a barn on the property. She knew perfectly well that they were talking.

When George and the young woman had come back, he fixed hot apple juice, into which he trickled rum. Lenore was pleasant, because she was sure of what had not happened; the young man was not, because he did not think as she did. Still at the kitchen table, he ran his thumb across a pea pod as though it were a knife.

This weekend Sarah and Julie are visiting. They came on Friday evening. Sarah was one of George's students—the one who led the fight to have him rehired. She does not look like a troublemaker; she is pale and pretty, with freckles on her cheeks. She talks too much about the past, and this upsets him, disrupts the peace he has made with himself. She tells him that they fired him because he was "in touch" with everything, that they were afraid of him because he was so in touch. The more she tells him the more he remembers, and then it is necessary for Sarah to say the same things again and again; once she reminds him, he seems to need reassurance—needs to have her voice, to hear her bitterness against the members of the tenure committee. By evening they will both be drunk. Sarah will seem both agitating and consoling, Lenore and Julie and the children will be upstairs, in bed. Lenore suspects that she will not be the only one awake listening to them. She thinks that in spite of Julie's glazed look she is really very attentive. The night before, when they were all sitting around the fireplace talking, Sarah made a gesture and almost upset her wineglass, but Julie reached for it and stopped it from toppling over. George and Sarah were talking so energetically that they did not notice. Lenore's eyes met Julie's as Julie's hand shot out. Lenore feels that she is like Julie: Julie's face doesn't betray emotion, even when she is interested, even when she cares deeply. Being the same kind of person, Lenore can recognize this.

Before Sarah and Julie arrived Friday evening, Lenore asked George if Sarah was his lover.

"Don't be ridiculous," he said. "You think every student is my lover? Is Julie my lover?"

She said, "That wasn't what I said."

"Well, if you're going to be preposterous, go ahead and say that," he said. "If you think about it long enough, it would make a lot of sense, wouldn't it?" He would not answer her question about Sarah. He kept throwing Julie's name into it. Some other woman might then think that he was protesting too strongly—that Julie really was his lover. She thought no such thing. She also stopped suspecting Sarah, because he wanted that, and it was her habit to oblige him.

He is twenty-one years older than Lenore. On his last birthday he was fifty-five. His daughter from his first marriage (his *only* marriage; she keeps reminding herself that they are not married, because it often seems that they might as well be) sent him an Irish country hat. The present made him irritable. He kept putting it on and pulling it down hard on his head. "She wants to make me a laughable old man," he said. "She wants me to put this on and go around like a fool." He wore the hat all morning, complaining about it, frightening the children. Eventually, to calm him, she said, "She intended *nothing.*" She said it with finality, her tone so insistent that he listened to her. But having lost his reason for bitterness, he said, "Just because you don't think doesn't mean others don't think." Is he getting old? She does not want to think of him getting old. In spite of his ulcer, his body is hard. He is tall and handsome, with a thick mustache and a thin black goatee, and there is very little gray in his kinky black hair. He dresses in tight-fitting blue jeans and black turtleneck sweaters in the winter, and old white shirts with the sleeves rolled up in the summer. He pretends not to care about his looks, but he does. He shaves carefully, scraping slowly down each side of his goatee. He orders his soft leather shoes from a store in California. After taking one of his long walks—even if he does it twice a day—he invariably takes a shower. He always looks refreshed, and very rarely admits any insecurity. A few times, at night in bed, he has asked, "Am I still the man of your dreams?" And when she says yes he always laughs, turning it into a joke, as if he didn't care. She knows he does. He pretends to have no feeling for clothing, but actually he cares so strongly about his turtlenecks and shirts (a few are Italian silk) and shoes that he will have no others. She has noticed that the young women who visit are always vain. When Sarah arrived, she was wearing a beautiful silk scarf, pale as conch shells.

Sitting on the floor on Saturday morning, Lenore watches the fire she has just lit. The baby, tucked in George's chair, smiles in his sleep, and Lenore thinks what a good companion he would be if only he were an adult. She gets up and goes into the kitchen and tears open a package of yeast and dissolves it, with sugar and salt, in hot water, slushing her fingers through it and shivering because it is so cold in the kitchen. She will bake bread for dinner—there is always a big meal in the early evening when they have guests. But what will she do for the rest of the day? George told the girls the night before that on Saturday they would walk in the woods, but she does not really enjoy hiking, and George will be irritated because of the discussion the night before, and she does not want to aggravate him. "You are unwilling to challenge anyone," her brother wrote her in a letter that came a few days ago. He has written her for years—all the years she has been with George—asking when she is going to end the relationship. She rarely writes back because she knows that her answers sound too simple. She has a comfortable house. She cooks. She keeps busy and she loves her two children. "It seems unkind to say *but*," her brother writes, "but . . ." It is true; she likes simple things. Her brother, who is a lawyer in Cambridge, cannot understand that.

Lenore rubs her hand down the side of her face and says good morning to Julie and Sarah, who have come downstairs. Sarah does not want orange juice; she already looks refreshed and ready for the day. Lenore pours a glass for Julie. George calls from the hallway, "Ready to roll?" Lenore is surprised that he wants to leave so early. She goes into the living room. George is wearing a denim jacket, his hands in the pockets.

"Morning," he says to Lenore. "You're not up for a hike, are you?"

Lenore looks at him, but does not answer. As she stands there, Sarah walks around her and joins George in the hallway and he holds the door open for her. "Let's walk to the store and get Hershey bars to give us energy for a long hike," George says to Sarah. They are gone. Lenore finds Julie still in the kitchen, waiting for the water to boil. Julie says that she had a bad night and she is happy not to be going with George and Sarah. Lenore fixes tea for them. Maria sits next to her on the sofa, sipping orange juice. The baby likes company, but Maria is a very private child; she would rather that she and her mother were always alone. She has given up being possessive about her father. Now she gets out a cardboard box and takes out her mother's collection of postcards, which she arranges on the floor in careful groups. Whenever she looks up, Julie smiles nervously at her; Maria does not smile, and Lenore doesn't prod her. Lenore goes into the kitchen to punch down the bread, and Maria follows. Maria has recently gotten over chicken pox, and there is a small new scar in the center of her forehead. Instead of looking at Maria's blue eyes, Lenore lately has found herself focusing on the imperfection.

As Lenore is stretching the loaves onto the cornmeal-covered baking sheet, she hears the rain start. It hits hard on the garage roof.

After a few minutes Julie comes into the kitchen. "They're caught in this downpour," Julie says. "If Sarah had left the car keys, I could go get them."

"Take my car and pick them up," Lenore says, pointing with her elbow to the keys hanging on a nail near the door.

"But I don't know where the store is."

"You must have passed it driving to our house last night. Just go out of the driveway and turn right. It's along the main road."

Julie gets her purple sweater and takes the car keys. "I'll be right back," she says.

Lenore can sense that she is glad to escape from the house, that she is happy the rain began.

In the living room Lenore turns the pages of a magazine, and Maria mutters a refrain of "Blue, blue, dark blue, green blue," noticing the color every time it appears. Lenore sips her tea. She puts a Michael Hurley record on George's stereo. Michael Hurley is good rainy-day music. George has hundreds of records. His students used to love to paw through them. Cleverly, he has never made any attempt to keep up with what is currently popular. Everything is jazz or eclectic: Michael Hurley, Keith Jarrett, Ry Cooder.[2]

Julie comes back. "I couldn't find them," she says. She looks as if she expects to be punished.

---

2. Musical performers who combine elements of folk, jazz, and rock.

Lenore is surprised. She is about to say something like "You certainly didn't look very hard, did you?" but she catches Julie's eye. She looks young and afraid, and perhaps even a little crazy.

"Well, we tried," Lenore says.

Julie stands in front of the fire, with her back to Lenore. Lenore knows she is thinking that she is dense—that she does not recognize the implications.

"They might have walked through the woods instead of along the road," Lenore says. "That's possible."

"But they would have gone out to the road to thumb when the rain began, wouldn't they?"

Perhaps she misunderstood what Julie was thinking. Perhaps it has never occurred to Julie until now what might be going on.

"Maybe they got lost," Julie says. "Maybe something happened to them."

"Nothing happened to them," Lenore says. Julie turns around and Lenore catches that small point of light in her eye again. "Maybe they took shelter under a tree," she says. "Maybe they're screwing. How should I know?"

It is not a word Lenore often uses. She usually tries not to think about that at all, but she can sense that Julie is very upset.

"Really?" Julie says. "Don't you care, Mrs. Anderson?"

Lenore is amused. There's a switch. All the students call her husband George and her Lenore; now one of them wants to think there's a real adult here to explain all this to her.

"What am I going to do?" Lenore says. She shrugs.

Julie does not answer.

"Would you like me to pour you tea?" Lenore asks.

"Yes," Julie says. "Please."

George and Sarah return in the middle of the afternoon. George says that they decided to go on a spree to the big city—it is really a small town he is talking about, but calling it the big city gives him an opportunity to speak ironically. They sat in a restaurant bar, waiting for the rain to stop, George says, and then they thumbed a ride home. "But I'm completely sober," George says, turning for the first time to Sarah. "What about you?" He is all smiles. Sarah lets him down. She looks embarrassed. Her eyes meet Lenore's quickly, and jump to Julie. The two girls stare at each other, and Lenore, left with only George to look at, looks at the fire and then gets up to pile on another log.

Gradually it becomes clear that they are trapped together by the rain. Maria undresses her paper doll and deliberately rips a feather off its hat. Then she takes the pieces to Lenore, almost in tears. The baby cries, and Lenore takes him off the sofa, where he has been sleeping under his yellow blanket, and props him in the space between her legs as she leans back on her elbows to watch the fire. It's her fire, and she has the excuse of presiding over it.

"How's my boy?" George says. The baby looks, and looks away.

It gets dark early, because of the rain. At four-thirty George uncorks a bottle of Beaujolais and brings it into the living room, with four glasses pressed against his chest with his free arm. Julie rises nervously to extract the glasses, thanking him too profusely for the wine. She gives a glass to Sarah without looking at her.

They sit in a semicircle in front of the fire and drink the wine. Julie leafs through magazines—*New Times*, *National Geographic*—and Sarah holds a small white dish painted with gray-green leaves that she has taken from the coffee table; the dish contains a few shells and some acorn caps, a polished stone or two, and Sarah lets these objects run through her fingers. There are several such dishes in the house, assembled by George. He and Lenore gathered the shells long ago, the first time they went away together, at a beach in North Carolina. But the acorn caps, the shiny turquoise and amethyst stones—those are there, she knows, because George likes the effect they have on visitors; it is an expected unconventionality, really. He has also acquired a few small framed pictures, which he points out to guests who are more important than worshipful students—tiny oil paintings of fruit, prints with small details from the unicorn tapestries. He pretends to like small, elegant things. Actually, when they visit museums in New York he goes first to El Grecos and big Mark Rothko canvases. She could never get him to admit that what he said or did was sometimes false. Once, long ago, when he asked if he was still the man of her dreams, she said, "We don't get along well anymore." "Don't talk about it," he said—no denial, no protest. At best, she could say things and get away with them; she could never get him to continue such a conversation.

At the dinner table, lit with white candles burning in empty wine bottles, they eat off his grandmother's small flowery plates. Lenore looks out a window and sees, very faintly in the dark, their huge oak tree. The rain has stopped. A few stars have come out, and there are glints on the wet branches. The oak tree grows very close to the window. George loved it when her brother once suggested that some of the bushes and trees should be pruned away from the house so it would not always be so dark inside; it gave him a chance to rave about the beauty of nature, to say that he would never tamper with it. "It's like a tomb in here all day," her brother had said. Since moving here, George has learned the names of almost all the things growing on the land: he can point out abelia bushes, spirea, laurels. He subscribes to *National Geographic* (although she rarely sees him looking at it). He is at last in touch, he says, being in the country puts him in touch. He is saying it now to Sarah, who has put down her ivory-handled fork to listen to him. He gets up to change the record. Side two of the Telemann[3] record begins softly.

Sarah is still very much on guard with Lenore; she makes polite conversation with her quickly when George is out of the room. "You people are so wonderful," she says. "I wish my parents could be like you."

"George would be pleased to hear that," Lenore says, lifting a small piece of pasta to her lips.

When George is seated again, Sarah, anxious to please, tells him, "If only my father could be like you."

"Your father," George says. "I won't have that analogy." He says it pleasantly, but barely disguises his dismay at the comparison.

"I mean, he cares about nothing but business," the girl stumbles on.

The music, in contrast, grows lovelier.

Lenore goes into the kitchen to get the salad and hears George say, "I simply won't let you girls leave. Nobody leaves on a Saturday."

There are polite protests, there are compliments to Lenore on the meal—

---

3. German composer of the 18th century.

there is too much talk. Lenore has trouble caring about what's going on. The food is warm and delicious. She pours more wine and lets them talk.

"Godard, yes, I know . . . panning that row of honking cars so slowly, that long line of cars stretching on and on."[4]

She has picked up the end of George's conversation. His arm slowly waves out over the table, indicating the line of motionless cars in the movie.

"That's a lovely plant," Julie says to Lenore.

"It's Peruvian ivy," Lenore says. She smiles. She is supposed to smile. She will not offer to hack shoots off her plant for these girls.

Sarah asks for a Dylan record when the Telemann finishes playing. White wax drips onto the wood table. George waits for it to solidify slightly, then scrapes up the little circles and with thumb and index finger flicks them gently toward Sarah. He explains (although she asked for no particular Dylan record) that he has only Dylan before he went electric. And "Planet Waves"—"because it's so romantic. That's silly of me, but true." Sarah smiles at him. Julie smiles at Lenore. Julie is being polite, taking her cues from Sarah, really not understanding what's going on. Lenore does not smile back. She has done enough to put them at ease. She is tired now, brought down by the music, a full stomach, and again the sounds of rain outside. For dessert there is homemade vanilla ice cream, made by George, with small black vanilla-bean flecks in it. He is still drinking wine, though; another bottle has been opened. He sips wine and then taps his spoon on his ice cream, looking at Sarah. Sarah smiles, letting them all see the smile, then sucks the ice cream off her spoon. Julie is missing more and more of what's going on. Lenore watches as Julie strokes her hand absently on her napkin. She is wearing a thin silver choker and—Lenore notices for the first time—a thin silver ring on the third finger of her hand.

"It's just terrible about Anna," George says, finishing his wine, his ice cream melting, looking at no one in particular, although Sarah was the one who brought up Anna the night before, when they had been in the house only a short time—Anna dead, hit by a car, hardly an accident at all. Anna was also a student of his. The driver of the car was drunk, but for some reason charges were not pressed. (Sarah and George have talked about this before, but Lenore blocks it out. What can she do about it? She met Anna once: a beautiful girl, with tiny, childlike hands, her hair thin and curly—wary, as beautiful people are wary.) Now the driver has been flipping out, Julie says, and calling Anna's parents, wanting to talk to them to find out why it has happened.

The baby begins to cry. Lenore goes upstairs, pulls up more covers, talks to him for a minute. He settles for this. She goes downstairs. The wine must have affected her more than she realizes; otherwise, why is she counting the number of steps?

In the candlelit dining room, Julie sits alone at the table. The girl has been left alone again; George and Sarah took the umbrellas, decided to go for a walk in the rain.

It is eight o'clock. Since helping Lenore load the dishes into the dishwasher, when she said what a beautiful house Lenore had, Julie has said very little. Lenore is tired, and does not want to make conversation. They sit in the living room and drink wine.

4. A famous scene from Jean Luc Godard's film *Weekend* (1969).

"Sarah is my best friend," Julie says. She seems apologetic about it. "I was so out of it when I came back to college. I was in Italy, with my husband, and suddenly I was back in the States. I couldn't make friends. But Sarah wasn't like the other people. She cared enough to be nice to me."

"How long have you been friends?"

"For two years. She's really the best friend I've ever had. We understand things—we don't always have to talk about them."

"Like her relationship with George," Lenore says.

Too direct. Too unexpected. Julie has no answer.

"You act as if you're to blame," Lenore says.

"I feel strange because you're such a nice lady."

A nice lady! What an odd way to speak. Has she been reading Henry James? Lenore has never known what to think of herself, but she certainly thinks of herself as being more complicated than a "lady."

"Why do you look that way?" Julie asks. "You *are* nice. I think you've been very nice to us. You've given up your whole weekend."

"I always give up my weekends. Weekends are the only time we socialize, really. In a way, it's good to have something to do."

"But to have it turn out like this . . ." Julie says. "I think I feel so strange because when my own marriage broke up I didn't even suspect. I mean, I couldn't act the way you do, anyway, but I—"

"For all I know, nothing's going on," Lenore says. "For all I know, your friend is flattering herself, and George is trying to make me jealous." She puts two more logs on the fire. When these are gone, she will either have to walk to the woodshed or give up and go to bed. "Is there something . . . *major* going on?" she asks.

Julie is sitting on the rug, by the fire, twirling her hair with her finger. "I didn't know it when I came out here," she says. "Sarah's put me in a very awkward position."

"But do you know how far it has gone?" Lenore asks, genuinely curious now.

"No," Julie says.

No way to know if she's telling the truth. Would Julie speak the truth to a lady? Probably not.

"Anyway," Lenore says with a shrug, "I don't want to think about it all the time."

"I'd never have the courage to live with a man and not marry," Julie says. "I mean, I wish I had, that we hadn't gotten married, but I just don't have that kind of . . . I'm not secure enough."

"You have to live somewhere," Lenore says.

Julie is looking at her as if she does not believe that she is sincere. Am I? Lenore wonders. She has lived with George for six years, and sometimes she thinks she has caught his way of playing games, along with his colds, his bad moods.

"I'll show you something," Lenore says. She gets up, and Julie follows. Lenore puts on the light in George's study, and they walk through it to a bathroom he has converted to a darkroom. Under a table, in a box behind another box, there is a stack of pictures. Lenore takes them out and hands them to Julie. They are pictures that Lenore found in his darkroom last summer; they were left out by mistake, no doubt, and she found them when she went in with some contact prints he had left in their bedroom. They are high-contrast photographs of George's face. In all of them he looks very serious and very sad; in some of them his eyes seem to be narrowed in pain. In one, his mouth is open. It is an excellent photograph of a man in agony, a man about to scream.

"What are they?" Julie whispers.

"Pictures he took of himself," Lenore says. She shrugs. "So I stay," she says. Julie nods. Lenore nods, taking the pictures back. Lenore has not thought until this minute that this may be why she stays. In fact, it is not the only reason. It is just a very demonstrable, impressive reason. When she first saw the pictures, her own face had become as distorted as George's. She had simply not known what to do. She had been frightened and ashamed. Finally she put them in an empty box, and put the box behind another box. She did not even want him to see the horrible pictures again. She does not know if he has ever found them, pushed back against the wall in that other box. As George says, there can be too much communication between people.

Later, Sarah and George come back to the house. It is still raining. It turns out that they took a bottle of brandy with them, and they are both drenched and drunk. He holds Sarah's finger with one of his. Sarah, seeing Lenore, lets his finger go. But then he turns—they have not even said hello yet—and grabs her up, spins her around, stumbling into the living room, and says, "I am in love."

Julie and Lenore watch them in silence.

"See no evil," George says, gesturing with the empty brandy bottle to Julie. "Hear no evil," George says, pointing to Lenore. He hugs Sarah closer. "I speak no evil. I speak the truth. I am in love!"

Sarah squirms away from him, runs from the room and up the stairs in the dark.

George looks blankly after her, then sinks to the floor and smiles. He is going to pass it off as a joke. Julie looks at him in horror, and from upstairs Sarah can be heard sobbing. Her crying awakens the baby.

"Excuse me," Lenore says. She climbs the stairs and goes into her son's room, and picks him up. She talks gently to him, soothing him with lies. He is too sleepy to be alarmed for long. In a few minutes he is asleep again, and she puts him back in his crib. In the next room Sarah is crying more quietly now. Her crying is so awful that Lenore almost joins in, but instead she pats her son. She stands in the dark by the crib and then at last goes out and down the hallway to her bedroom. She takes off her clothes and gets into the cold bed. She concentrates on breathing normally. With the door closed and Sarah's door closed, she can hardly hear her. Someone taps lightly on her door.

"Mrs. Anderson," Julie whispers. "Is this your room?"

"Yes," Lenore says. She does not ask her in.

"We're going to leave. I'm going to get Sarah and leave. I didn't want to just walk out without saying anything."

Lenore just cannot think how to respond. It was really very kind of Julie to say something. She is very close to tears, so she says nothing.

"Okay," Julie says, to reassure herself. "Good night. We're going."

There is no more crying. Footsteps. Miraculously, the baby does not wake up again, and Maria has slept through all of it. She has always slept well.

Lenore herself sleeps worse and worse, and she knows that George walks much of the night, most nights. She hasn't said anything about it. If he thinks she's simple, what good would her simple wisdom do him?

The oak tree scrapes against the window in the wind and rain. Here on the second floor, under the roof, the tinny tapping is very loud. If Sarah and Julie say anything to George before they leave, she doesn't hear them. She hears the car start, then die out. It starts again—she is praying for the car to go—and after conking out once more it rolls slowly away, crunching gravel. The bed is no warmer; she shivers. She tries hard to fall asleep. The effort keeps her awake. She squints her eyes in concentration instead of closing them. The only sound in the house is the electric clock, humming by her bed. It is not even midnight.

She gets up, and without turning on the light, walks downstairs. George is still in the living room. The fire is nothing but ashes and glowing bits of wood. It is as cold there as it was in the bed.

"That damn bitch," George says. "I should have known she was a stupid little girl."

"You went too far," Lenore says. "I'm the only one you can go too far with."

"Damn it," he says and pokes the fire. A few sparks shoot up. "Damn it," he repeats under his breath.

His sweater is still wet. His shoes are muddy and ruined. Sitting on the floor by the fire, his hair matted down on his head, he looks ugly, older, unfamiliar.

She thinks of another time, when it was warm. They were walking on the beach together, shortly after they met, gathering shells. Little waves were rolling in. The sun went behind the clouds and there was a momentary illusion that the clouds were still and the sun was racing ahead of them. "Catch me," he said, breaking away from her. They had been talking quietly, gathering shells. She was so surprised at him for breaking away that she ran with all her energy and did catch him, putting her hand out and taking hold of the band of his swimming trunks as he veered into the water. If she hadn't stopped him, would he really have run far out into the water, until she couldn't follow anymore? He turned on her, just as abruptly as he had run away, and grabbed her and hugged her hard, lifted her high. She had clung to him, held him close. He had tried the same thing when he came back from the walk with Sarah, and it hadn't worked.

"I wouldn't care if their car went off the road," he says bitterly.

"Don't say that," she says.

They sit in silence, listening to the rain. She slides over closer to him, puts her hand on his shoulder and leans her head there, as if he could protect her from the awful things he has wished into being.

1978

# DENISE CHÁVEZ
## b. 1948

In recent Latino literature, a number of women have emerged as distinct talents, of whom one of the most impressive is Denise Chávez, author of *The Last of the Menu Girls*, a book of seven related stories—they add up to a sort of novel—about the experience of a teenage New Mexican girl named Rocío Esquibel. Speaking of her view of this literature, Chávez calls it optimistic and affirmative, because "our literature and our art are just coming into their own. Now is a marvelous time for creativity and imagination." Chávez's voice has some of the vitality and hopefulness of the young heroine in her work, who—in the title story (printed here)—spends a summer working as a "menu girl," distributing them to patients in a hospital. "You're the Florence Nightingale of Altavista Memorial Hospital, that's it!" says one of her friends at the end of her tenure. Rocío Esquibel is full of dreams of fame and beauty, eventually of becoming an artist, but these fantasies are played out against the tragi-comic situation of hospital life, in its banality and its sadness. Chávez writes with sensitivity and some poignancy about her hospital characters, resisting sentimentality, in presenting them, through the frequent use of sharp, idiomatic language.

She has been hailed—among others, by the Mexican-American novelist Rudolfo Anaya—as an important figure in "the ranks of writers who are rounding out the parameters of Chicano literature." But as one reviewer of her stories has pointed out, that praise may unfairly limit her appeal, since it could be argued that the more universal quality of her voice and her situation as a woman is at least as strong as any regional or ethnic appeal. Chávez's language gives pleasure for the way it brings to comic grotesque life Rocío Esquibel's employer at the hospital, a Mr. Smith who is hunchbacked (and who, at the interview, offers Rocío iced tea at nine in the morning):

> Was I to work for this gnome? I wanted to rescue souls, not play attendant to this crippled, dried up specimen, this cartilaginous insect with his misshapen head and eyes that peered out to me like the marbled eyes of statues one sees in museums.

And she proceeds to imagine the unenobling consequences of herself as a "menu girl": "I faced Dietary Awards, Degrees in Food Management, menus for Low Salt and Fluids; the word Jello leaped out at every turn." There is mischief and irrepressible verbal energy in the way one phrase or sentence calls up the next.

Chávez was born in Las Cruces, New Mexico, took degrees in drama and in creative writing (she has written many plays and worked with bilingual theater companies), and edited a poetry anthology put together from inmates at the Radium Springs Center for Women. She is very much a community-oriented artist, who gives frequent, highly theatrical readings from her work, while running a number of workshops in poetry, fiction, and drama. Like the young heroine of *The Last of the Menu Girls*, she possessed an active imagination, gave herself to fantasies of becoming a writer, and transposed her own experiences into literature. "I read a lot. To write you must first read. At first I copied stories and poems I liked. In reading you sense that events have meaning." From what she describes as an unimpressive eighth grader in a Catholic school—"a dud, skinny, with an inferiority complex"—Chávez developed into someone convinced she had a special gift: "I managed to get a sense of myself. What I was trying to do was stand out in the landscape of the Southwest." Thus the regional commitment is acknowledged directly, yet as with her identity as a Latina writer, it is wise not to hang the labels too heavily around her neck. At times she shows a propensity to be too lyrically solemn, as when she writes about Rocío making "that awesome leap into myself that steamy summer of illness and dread." But such momentary solemnity invariably has the starch taken out of it by her playful knowledge that as Rocío Esquibel is *not* Florence Nightingale so Chávez's own literary identity is at least as individual as it is representative of any group or region.

## The Last of the Menu Girls[1]

NAME: Rocío Esquibel
AGE: Seventeen
PREVIOUS EXPERIENCE WITH THE SICK AND DYING: My Great
  Aunt Eutilia
PRESENT EMPLOYMENT: Work-study aide at Altavista[2] Memorial

I never wanted to be a nurse. My mother's aunt died in our house, seventy-seven years old and crying in her metal crib: "Put a pillow on the floor. I can jump," she cried. "Go on, let me jump. I want to get away from here, far away."

Eutilia's mattress was covered with chipped clothlike sheaves of yellowed plastic. She wet herself, was a small child, undependable, helpless. She was an old lady with a broken hip, dying without having gotten down from that rented bed. Her blankets were sewn by my mother: corduroy patches, bright yellows, blues and greens, and still she wanted to jump!

"Turn her over, turn her over, turn her, wait a minute, wait—turn . . ."
Eutilia faced the wall. It was plastered white. The foamed, concrete turnings of some workman's trowel revealed daydreams: people's faces, white clouds, phantom pianos slowly playing half lost melodies, "Las Mañanitas," "Cielito Lindo,"[3] songs formulated in expectation, dissolved into confusion. Eutilia's blurred faces, far off tunes faded into the white walls, into jagged, broken waves.

I never wanted to be a nurse, ever. All that gore and blood and grief. I was not as squeamish as my sister Mercy, who could not stand to put her hands into a sinkful of dirty dishes filled with floating food—wet bread, stringy vegetables and bits of softened meat. Still, I didn't like the touch, the smells. How could I? When I touched my mother's feet, I looked away, held my nose with one hand, the other with finger laced along her toes, pulling and popping them into place. "It really helps my arthritis, baby—you don't know. Pull my toes, I'll give you a dollar, find my girdle, and I'll give you two. Ouch. Ouch. Not so hard. There, that's good. Look at my feet. You see the veins? Look at them. Aren't they ugly? And up here, look where I had the operations . . . ugly, they stripped them and still they hurt me."

She rubbed her battered flesh wistfully, placed a delicate and lovely hand on her right thigh. Mother said proudly, truthfully, "I still have lovely thighs."

---

1. Title story of *The Last of the Menu Girls* (1986).
2. High View (Spanish, literal trans.).
3. Both are songs. The first, "Little Morning," is traditionally sung as a morning serenade to a girl turning

fifteen. The second, "Beautiful Little Sky," has become almost a national folk song: in it a boy praises his girl's eyes, which possess, for him, the lovely, light-giving qualities of the sky.

PREVIOUS EXPERIENCE WITH THE SICK AND DYING: Let me
think . . .

Great Aunt Eutilia came to live with us one summer and seven months
later she died in my father's old study, the walls lined with books, whatever
answers were there—unread.

Great Aunt Eutilia smelled like the mercilessly sick. At first, a vague, softened aroma of tiredness and spilled food. And later, the full-blown emptyings
of the dying: gas, putrefaction and fetid lucidity. Her body poured out long,
held-back odors. She wet her diapers and sheets and knocked over medicines
and glasses of tepid water, leaving in the air an unpleasant smell.

I danced around her bed in my dreams, naked, smiling, jubilant. It was an
exultant adolescent dance for my dying aunt. It was necessary, compulsive. It
was a primitive dance, a full moon offering that led me slithering into her
room with breasts naked and oily at thirteen . . .

No one home but me.

Led me to her room, my father's refuge, those halcyon days now that he
was gone—and all that remained were dusty books, cast iron bookends,
reminders of the spaces he filled. Down the steps I leaped into Eutilia's faded
and foggy consciousness where I whirled and danced and sang: I am your
flesh and my mother's flesh and you are . . . are . . . Eutilia stared at me. I
turned away.

I danced around Eutilia's bed. I hugged the screen door, my breasts
indented in the meshed wire. In the darkness Eutilia moaned, my body wet,
her body dry. Steamy we were, and full of prayers.

Could I have absolved your dying by my life? Could I have lessened your
agony with my spirit-filled dance in the deep darkness? The blue fan stirred,
then whipped nonstop the solid air; little razors sliced through consciousness
and prodded the sick and dying woman, whose whitened eyes screeched: Ay!
Ay! Let me jump, put a pillow, I want to go away . . . let me . . . let me . . .

One day while playing "Cielito Lindo" on the piano in the living room,
Eutilia got up and fell to the side of the piano stool. Her foot caught on the
rug, "¡Ay! ¡Ay! ¡Ay! ¡Ay! Canta y no llores⁴ . . ."

All requests were silenced. Eutilia rested in her tattered hospital gown, having shredded it to pieces. She was surrounded by little white strips of raveled
cloth. Uncle Toño, her babysitter, after watching the evening news, found her
naked and in a bed of cloth. She stared at the ceiling, having played the piano
far into the night. She listened to sounds coming from around the back of her
head. Just listened. Just looked. Just shredded. Shredded the rented gown,
shredded it. When the lady of the house returned and asked how was she,
meaning, does she breathe, Toño answered, "Fine."

Christ on his crucifix! He'd never gone into the room to check on her.
Later, when they found her, Toño cried, his cousin laughed. They hugged
each other, then cried, then laughed, then cried. Eutilia's fingers never rested.
They played beautiful tunes. She was a little girl in tatters in her metal bed
with sideboards that went up and down, up and down . . .

The young girls danced they played they danced they filled out forms.

---

4. Sing and don't cry (Spanish).

PREVIOUS EMPLOYMENT: None.

There was always a first job, as there was the first summer of the very first boyfriend. That was the summer of our first swamp cooler. The heat bore down and congealed sweat. It made rivulets trace the body's meridian and, before it stopped, was wiped away, never quite dismissed.

On the tops of the neighbors' houses old swamp coolers, with their jerky grating and droning moans, strained to ease the southern implacabilities. Whrr whrr cough whrr.

Regino Suárez climbed up and down the roof, first forgetting his hammer and then the cooler filter. His boy, Eliterio, stood at the bottom of the steps that led to the sun deck and squinted dumbly at the blazing sun. For several days Regino tramped over my dark purple bedroom. I had shut the curtains to both father and son and rested in violet contemplation of my first boyfriend.

Regino stomped his way to the other side of the house where Eutilia lay in her metal crib, trying to sleep, her weary eyes uncomprehending. The noise was upsetting, she could not play. The small blue fan wheezed freshness. Regino hammered and paced then climbed down. When lunchtime came, a carload of fat daughters drove Regino and the handsome son away.

If Eutilia could have read a book, it would have been the *Bible*, or maybe her novena to the Santo Niño de Atocha,[5] he was her boy . . .

PREVIOUS EXPERIENCE WITH THE SICK AND DYING:

This question reminds me of a story my mother told me about a very old woman, Doña Mercedes, who was dying of cancer. Doña Mercedes lived with her daughter, Corina, who was my mother's friend. The old woman lay in bed, day after day, moaning and crying softly, not actually crying out, but whimpering in a sad, hopeless way. "Don't move me," she begged when her daughter tried to change the sheets or bathe her. Every day this ordeal of maintenance became worse. It was a painful thing and full of dread for the old woman, the once fastidious and upright Doña Mercedes. She had been a lady, straight and imposing, and with a headful of rich dark hair. Her ancestors were from Spain. "You mustn't move me, Corina," Doña Mercedes pleaded, "never, please. Leave me alone, mi'jita,"[6] and so the daughter acquiesced. Cleaning around her tortured flesh and delicately wiping where they could, the two women attended to Doña Mercedes. She died in the daytime, as she had wanted.

When the young women went to lift the old lady from her death bed, they struggled to pull her from the sheets; and, when finally they turned her on her side, they saw huge gaping holes in her back where the cancer had eaten through the flesh. The sheets were stained, the bedsores lost in a red wash of bloody pus. Doña Mercedes' cancer had eaten its way through her back and onto those sheets. "Don't move me, please don't move me," she had cried.

The two young women stuffed piles of shredded disinfected rags soaked in Lysol into Doña Mercedes' chest cavity, filling it, and horrified, with cloths over their mouths, said the prayers for the dead. Everyone remembered her as tall and straight and very Spanish.

---

5. Holy Child of Atocha (Spanish), very likely a local saint. "Novena": Roman Catholic devotion or prayer.　　6. My little daughter (Spanish).

PRESENT EMPLOYMENT: Work-study aide at Altavista Memorial Hospital

I never wanted to be a nurse. Never. The smells. The pain. What was I to do then, working in a hospital, in that place of white women, whiter men with square faces? I had no skills. Once in the seventh grade I'd gotten a penmanship award. Swirling R's in boredom, the ABC's ad infinitum. Instead of dipping chocolate cones at the Dairy Queen next door to the hospital, I found myself a frightened girl in a black skirt and white blouse standing near the stairwell to the cafeteria.

I stared up at a painting of a dark-haired woman in a stiff nurse's cap and grey tunic, tending to men in old fashioned service uniforms. There was a beauty in that woman's face whoever she was. I saw myself in her, helping all of mankind, forgetting and absolving all my own sick, my own dying, especially relatives, all of them so far away, removed. I never wanted to be like Great Aunt Eutilia, or Doña Mercedes with the holes in her back, or my mother, her scarred legs, her whitened thighs.

## MR. SMITH

Mr. Smith sat at his desk surrounded by requisition forms. He looked up to me with glassy eyes like filmy paperweights.

MOTHER OF GOD, MR. SMITH WAS A WALLEYED HUNCHBACK!

"Mr. Smith, I'm Rocío Esquibel, the work-study student from the university and I was sent down here to talk to you about my job."

"Down here, down here," he laughed, as if it were a private joke. "Oh, yes, you must be the new girl. Menus," he mumbled. "Now just have a seat and we'll see what we can do. Would you like some iced tea?"

It was nine o'clock in the morning, too early for tea. "No, well, yes, that would be nice."

"It's good tea, everyone likes it. Here, I'll get you some." Mr. Smith got up, more hunchbacked than I'd imagined. He tiptoed out of the room whispering, "Tea, got to get this girl some tea."

There was a bit of the gruesome Golom[7] in him, a bit of the twisted spider in the dark. Was I to work for this gnome? I wanted to rescue souls, not play attendant to this crippled, dried up specimen, this cartilaginous insect with his misshapen head and eyes that peered out to me like the marbled eyes of statues one sees in museums. History preserves its freaks. God, was my job to do the same? No, never!

I faced Dietary Awards, Degrees in Food Management, menus for Low Salt and Fluids; the word Jello leaped out at every turn. I touched the walls. They were moist, never having seen the light.

In my dreams, Mr. Smith was encased in green Jello; his formaldehyde breath reminded me of other smells—decaying, saddened dead things; my great aunt, biology class in high school, my friend Dolores Casaus. Each of us held a tray with a dead frog pinned in place, served to us by a tall stoop-shouldered Viking turned farmer, our biology teacher Mr. Franke, pink-eyed, half blind. Dolores and I cut into the chest cavity and explored that small

---

7. Or *golem*, an automaton in Hebrew folklore not unlike Frankenstein's monster.

universe of dead cold fibers. Dolores stopped at the frog's stomach, then squeezed out its last meal, a green mash, spinach-colored, a viscous fluid— that was all that remained in that miniaturized, unresponding organ, all that was left of potential life.

Before Eutilia died she ate a little, mostly drank juice through bent and dripping hospital straws. The straws littered the floor where she'd knocked them over in her wild frenzy to escape. "Diooooooooos," she cried in that shrill voice. "Dios mío, Diosito, por favor. Ay, I won't tell your mamá, just help me get away . . . Diosito de mi vida . . . Diosito de mi corazón . . . agua, agua . . . por favor, por favor[8] . . ."

Mr. Smith returned with my iced tea.
"Sugar?"
Sugar, yes, sugar. Lots of it. Was I to spend all summer in this smelly cage? What was I to do? What? And for whom? I had no business here. It was summertime and my life stretched out magically in front of me: there was my boyfriend, my freedom. Senior year had been the happiest of my life; was it to change?
"Anytime you want to come down and get a glass of tea, you go right ahead. We always have it on hand. Everyone likes my tea," he said with pride.
"About the job?" I asked.
Mr. Smith handed me a pile of green forms. They were menus.
In the center of the menu was listed the day of the week, and to the left and coming down in a neat order were the three meals, breakfast, lunch and dinner. Each menu had various choices for each meal.

LUNCH:

| | |
|---|---|
| ☐ Salisbury Steak | ☐ Mashed potatoes and gravy |
| ☐ Fish sticks | ☐ Macaroni and cheese |
| ☐ Enchiladas | ☐ Broccoli and onions |
| ☐ Rice almondine | |
| *Drinks* | *Dessert* |
| ☐ Coffee | ☐ Jello |
| ☐ Tea | ☐ Carrot cake |
| ☐ 7-Up | ☐ Ice Cream, vanilla |
| ☐ Other | |

"Here you see a menu for Friday, listing the three meals. Let's take lunch. You have a choice of Salisbury steak, enchiladas, they're really good, Trini makes them, she's been working for me for twenty years. Her son George Jr. works for me, too, probably his kids one day." At this possibility, Mr. Smith laughed at himself. "Oh, and fish sticks. You a . . . ?"
"Our Lady of the Holy Scapular."
"Sometimes I'll get a menu back with a thank you written on the side, 'Thanks for the liver, it was real good', or 'I haven't had rice pudding since I was a boy.' Makes me feel good to know we've made our patients happy."
Mr. Smith paused, reflecting on the positive aspects of his job.

8. My God, oh, my dear God, please. . . . Dear God of my life . . . dear God of my heart . . . water, water . . . please, please (Spanish).

"Mind you, these menus are only for people on regular diets, not everybody, but a lot of people. I take care of the other special diets, that doesn't concern you. I have a girl working for me now, Arlene Rutschman. You know . . ."

My mind raced forward, backward. Arlene Rutschman, the Arlene from Holy Scapular, Arlene of the soft voice, the limp mannerisms, the plain, too goodly face, Arlene, president of Our Lady's Sodality, in her white and navy blue beanie, her bobby socks and horn-rimmed glasses, the Arlene of the school dances with her perpetual escort, Bennie Lara, the toothy better-than-no-date date, the Arlene of the high grades, the muscular, yet turned-in legs, the curly unattractive hair, *that* Arlene, the dud?

"Yes, I know her."

"Good!"

"We went to school together."

"Wonderful!"

"She works here?"

"Oh, she's a nice girl. She'll help you, show you what to do, how to distribute the menus."

"Distribute the menus?"

"Now you just sit there, drink your tea and tell me about yourself."

This was the first of many conversations with Mr. Smith, the hunchbacked dietician, a man who was never anything but kind to me.

"Hey," he said proudly, "these are my kids. Norma and Bardwell. Norma's in Junior High, majoring in boys, and Bardwell is graduating from the Military Institute."

"Bardwell. That's an unusual name," I said as I stared at a series of 5 x 7's on Mr. Smith's desk.

"Bardwell, well, that was my father's name. Bardwell B. Smith. The Bard, they called him!" At this he chuckled to himself, myopically recalling his father, tracing with his strange eyes patterns of living flesh and bone.

"He used to recite."

The children looked fairly normal. Norma was slight, with a broad toothy smile. Bardwell, or Bobby, as he was called, was not unhandsome in his uniform, if it weren't for one ragged, splayed ear that slightly cupped forward, as if listening to something.

Mr. Smith's image was nowhere in sight. "Camera shy," he said. To the right of Mr. Smith's desk hung a plastic gold framed prayer beginning with the words: "Oh Lord of Pots and Pans." To the left, near a dried out water-cooler was a sign, "Bless This Mess."

Over the weeks I began to know something of Mr. Smith's convoluted life, its anchorings. His wife and children came to life, and Mr. Smith acquired a name: Marion, and a vague disconcerting sexuality. It was upsetting for me to imagine him fathering Norma and Bardwell. I stared into the framed glossies full of disbelief. Who was Mrs. Smith? What was she like?

Eutilia never had any children. She'd been married to José Esparza, a good man, a handsome man. They ran a store in Agua Tibia. They prospered, until one day, early in the morning, about three a.m., several men from El Otro Lado[9] called out to them in the house. "Don José, wake up! We need to buy

---

9. The other side (Spanish), i.e., of the tracks.

supplies." Eutilia was afraid, said, "No, José, don't let them in." He told her, "Woman, what are we here for?" And she said, "But at this hour, José? At this hour?" Don José let them into the store. The two men came in carrying two sacks, one that was empty, and another that they said was full of money. They went through the store, picking out hats, clothing, tins of corned beef, and stuffing them into the empty sack. "So many things, José," Eutilia whispered, "*too* many things!" "Oh no," one man replied, "we have the money, don't you trust us, José?" "Cómo no, compadre,"[1] he replied easily. "We need the goods, don't be afraid, compadre." "Too many things, too many things," Eutilia sighed, huddled in the darkness in her robe. She was a small woman, with the body of a little girl. Eutilia looked at José, and it was then that they both knew. When the two men had loaded up, they turned to Don José, took out a gun, which was hidden in a sack, and said, "So sorry, compadre, but you know . . . stay there, don't follow us." Eutilia hugged the darkness, saying nothing for the longest time. José was a handsome man, but dumb.

The village children made fun of José Esparza, laughed at him and pinned notes and pieces of paper to his pants. "Tonto, tonto"[2] and "I am a fool." He never saw these notes, wondered why they laughed.

"I've brought you a gift, a bag of rocks"; all fathers have said that to their children. Except Don José Esparza. He had no children, despite his looks. "At times a monkey can do better than a prince," la comadre[3] Lucaya used to say to anyone who would listen.

The bodies of patients twisted and moaned and cried out, and cursed, but for the two of us in that basement world, all was quiet save for the occasional clinking of an iced tea glass and the sporadic sound of Mr. Smith clearing his throat.

"There's no hurry," Mr. Smith always said. "Now you just take your time. Always in a hurry. A young person like you."

## ARLENE RUTSCHMAN

"You're so lucky that you can speak Spanish," Arlene intoned. She stood tiptoes, held her breath, then knocked gently on the patient's door. No sound. A swifter knock. "I could never remember what a turnip was," she said.

"Whatjawant?" a voice bellowed.

"I'm the menu girl; can I take your order?"

Arlene's high tremulous little girl's voice trailed off, "Good morning, Mr. Samaniego! What'll it be? No, it's not today you leave, tomorrow, after lunch. Your wife is coming to get you. So, what'll it be for your third-to-the-last meal? Now we got poached or fried eggs. Poached. P-o-a-c-h-e-d. That's like a little hard in the middle, but a little soft on the outside. Firm. No, not like scrambled. Different. Okay, you want scrambled. Juice? We got grape or orange. You like grape? Two grape. And some coffee, black."

A tall Anglo man, gaunt and yellowed like an old newspaper, his eyes rubbed black like an old raccoon's, ranged the hallway. The man talked quietly to himself and smoked numbers of cigarettes as he weaved between attendants

---

1. Of course, pal (Spanish).
2. Stupid (Spanish).
3. The godmother of one's daughter (Spanish). Both mother and godmother are considered, and consider themselves as, co-mothers.

with half-filled urinals and lugubrious I.V.'s. He reminded me of my father's friends, angular Anglos in their late fifties, men with names like Bud or Earl, men who owned garages or steak houses, men with firm hairy arms, clear blue eyes and tattoos from the war.

"That's Mr. Ellis, 206." Arlene whispered, "jaundice."

"Oh," I said, curiously contemptuous and nervous at the same time, unhappy and reeling from the phrase, "I'm the menu girl!" How'd I ever manage to get such a dumb job? At least the Candy Stripers wore a cute uniform, and they got to do fun things like deliver flowers and candy.

"Here comes Mrs. Samaniego. The wife."

"Mr. Ellis's wife?" I said, with concern.

"No, Mr. Samaniego's wife, Donelda." Arlene pointed to a wizened and giggly old woman who was sneaking by the information desk, past the silver-haired volunteer, several squirmy grandchildren in tow. Visiting hours began at two p.m., but Donelda Samaniego had come early to beat the rush. From the hallway, Arlene and I heard loud smacks, much kidding and general merriment. The room smelled of tamales.

"Old Mr. Phillips in 304, that's the Medical Floor, he gets his cath[4] at eleven, so don't go ask him about his menu then. It upsets his stomach."

Mrs. Daniels in 210 told Arlene weakly, "Honey, yes, you, honey, who's the other girl? Who is she? You'll just have to come back later, I don't feel good. I'm a dying woman, can't you see that?" When we came back an hour later, Mrs. Daniels was asleep, snoring loudly.

Mrs. Gustafson, a sad wet-eyed, well-dressed woman in her late sixties, dismissed us from the shade of drawn curtains as her husband, G.P. "Gus" Gustafson, the judge, took long and fitful naps only to wake up again, then go back to sleep, beginning once more his inexorable round of disappearances.

"Yesterday I weighed myself in the hall and I'm getting fat. Oh, and you're so thin."

"The hips," I said, "the hips."

"You know, you remind me of that painting," Arlene said, thoughtfully.

"Which?"

"Not which, who. The one in the stairwell. Florence Nightingale, she looks like you."

"That's who that is!"

"The eyes."

"She does?"

"The eyes."

"The eyes?"

"And the hair."

"The eyes and the hair? Maybe the hair, but not the eyes."

"Yes."

"I don't think so."

"Oh yes! Every time I look at it."

"Me?"

Arlene and I sat talking at our table in the cafeteria, that later was to become *my* table. It faced the dining room. From that vantage point I could see everything and not be seen.

---

4. Catheter, a medical device inserted into a body aperture for extraction or injection of fluids.

We talked, two friends almost, if only she weren't so, so, little girlish with ribbons. Arlene was still dating Bennie and was majoring in either home ec or biology. They seemed the same in my mind: babies, menus and frogs. Loathsome, unpleasant things.

It was there, in the coolness of the cafeteria, in that respite from the green forms, at our special table, drinking tea, laughing with Arlene, that I, still shy, still judgmental, still wondering and still afraid, under the influence of caffeine, decided to stick it out. I would not quit the job.

"How's Mr. Prieto in 200?"

"He left yesterday, but he'll be coming back. He's dying."

"Did you see old Mr. Carter? They strapped him to the wheelchair finally."

"It was about time. He kept falling over."

"Mrs. Domínguez went to bland."[5]

"She was doing so well."

"You think so? She couldn't hardly chew. She kept choking."

"And that grouch, what's her name, the head nurse, Stevens in 214 . . ."

"She's the head nurse? I didn't know that—god, I filled out her menu for her . . . she was sleeping and I . . . no wonder she was mad . . . how did I know she was the head nurse?"

"It's okay. She's going home or coming back, I can't remember which. Esperanza González is gonna be in charge."

"She was real mad."

"Forget it, it's okay."

"The woman will never forgive me, I'll lose my job," I sighed.

I walked home past the Diary Queen. It took five minutes at the most. I stopped midway at the ditch's edge, where the earth rose and where there was a concrete embankment on which to sit. To some this was the quiet place, where neighborhood lovers met on summer nights to kiss, and where older couples paused between their evening walks to rest. It was also the talking place, where all the neighbor kids discussed life while eating hot fudge sundae with nuts. The bench was large; four could sit on it comfortably. It faced an open field in the middle of which stood a huge apricot tree. Lastly, the bench was a stopping place, the "throne," we called it. We took off hot shoes and dipped our cramped feet into the cool ditch water, as we sat facing the southern sun at the quiet talking place, at our thrones, not thinking anything, eyes closed, but sun. The great red velvet sun.

One night I dreamt of food, wading through hallways of food, inside some dark evil stomach. My boyfriend waved to me from the ditch's bank. I sat on the throne, ran alongside his car, a blue Ford, in which he sat, on clear plastic seat covers, with that hungry Church-of-Christ smile of his. He drove away, and when he returned, the car was small and I was too big to get inside.

Eutilia stirred. She was tired. She did not recognize anyone. I danced around the bed, crossed myself, en el nombre del padre, del hijo y del espíritu santo,[6] crossed forehead, chin and breast, begged for forgiveness even as I danced.

And on waking, I remembered. *Nabos. Turnips.* But of course.

---

5. I.e., was put on a bland diet.
6. In the name of the Father, of the Son, and of the Holy Ghost (Spanish).

It seemed right to me to be working in a hospital, to be helping people, and yet: why was I only a menu girl? Once a menu was completed, another would take its place and the next day another. It was a never ending round of food and more food. I thought of Judge Gustafson.

When Arlene took a short vacation to the Luray Caverns, I became the official menu girl. That week was the happiest of my entire summer.

That week I fell in love.

## ELIZABETH RAINEY

Elizabeth Rainey, Room 240, was in for a D and C.[7] I didn't know what a D and C was, but I knew it was mysterious and to me, of course, this meant it had to do with sex. Elizabeth Rainey was propped up in bed with many pillows, a soft blue, homemade quilt at the foot of her bed. Her cheeks were flushed, her red lips quivering. She looked fragile, and yet her face betrayed a harsh indelicate bitterness. She wore a creme-colored gown on which her loose hair fell about her like a cape. She was a beautiful woman, full-bodied, with the translucent beauty certain women have in the midst of sorrow—clear and unadorned, her eyes bright with inexplicable and self-contained suffering.

She cried out to me rudely, as if I personally had offended her. "What do you want? Can't you see I want to be alone. Now close the door and go away! Go away!"

"I'm here to get your menu." I could not bring myself to say, I'm the menu girl.

"Go away, go away, I don't want anything. I don't want to eat. Close the door!"

Elizabeth Rainey pulled her face away from me and turned to the wall, and, with deep and self-punishing exasperation, grit her teeth, and from the depths of her self-loathing a small inarticulate cry escaped—"Oooooh."

I ran out, frightened by her pain, yet excited somehow. She was so beautiful and so alone. I wanted in my little girl's way to hold her, hold her tight and in my woman's way never to feel her pain, ever, whatever it was.

"Go away, go away," she said, her trembling mouth rimmed with pain, "go away!"

She didn't want to eat, told me to go away. How many people yelled to me to go away that summer, have yelled since then, countless people, of all ages, sick people, really sick people, dying people, people who were well and still rudely tied into their needs for privacy and space, affronted by these constant impositions from, of all people, the menu girl!

"Move over and move out, would you? Go away! Leave me alone!"

And yet, of everyone who told me to go away, it was this woman in her solitary anguish who touched me the most deeply. How could I, age seventeen, not knowing love, how could I presume to reach out to this young woman in her sorrow, touch her and say, "I know, I understand."

Instead, I shrank back into myself and trembled behind the door. I never went back into her room. How could I? It was too terrible a vision, for in her I saw myself, all life, all suffering. What I saw both chilled and burned me. I stood long in that darkened doorway, confused in the presence of human pain.

---

7. Dilation and curettage; expanding and cleaning the uterus by scraping.

I wanted to reach out . . . I wanted to . . . I wanted to . . . But *how?*

As long as I live I will carry Elizabeth Rainey's image with me: in a creme-colored gown she is propped up, her hair fanning pillows in a room full of deep sweet acrid and overspent flowers. Oh, I may have been that summer girl, but yes, I knew, I understood. I would have danced for her, Eutilia, had I but dared.

## DOLORES CASAUS

Dolores of the frog entrails episode, who'd played my sister Ismene in the world literature class play,[8] was now a nurse's aide on the surgical floor, changing sheets, giving enemas and taking rectal temperatures.

It was she who taught me how to take blood pressure, wrapping the cuff around the arm, counting the seconds and then multiplying beats. As a friend, she was rude, impudent, delightful; as an aide, most dedicated. One day for an experiment, with me as a guinea pig, she took the blood pressure of my right leg. That day I hobbled around the hospital, the leg cramped and weak. In high school Dolores had been my double, my confidante and the best Ouija board partner I ever had. When we set our fingers to the board, the dial raced and spun, flinging out letters—notes from the long dead, the crying out. Together we contacted la Llorona[9] and would have unraveled *that* mystery if Sister Esperidiana hadn't caught us in the religion room during lunchtime communing with that distressed spirit who had so much to tell!

Dolores was engaged. She had a hope chest. She wasn't going to college because she had to work, and her two sisters-in-law, the Nurses González and González—Esperanza, male, and Bertha, female, were her supervisors.

As a favor to Dolores, González the Elder, Esperanza would often give her a left-over tray of "regular" food, the patient having checked out or on to other resting grounds. Usually I'd have gone home after the ritualistic glass of tea but one day, out of boredom perhaps, most likely out of curiosity, I hung around the surgical floor talking to Dolores, my only friend in all the hospital. I clung to her sense of wonder, her sense of the ludicrous, to her humor in the face of order, for even in that environment of restriction, I felt her still probing the whys and wherefores of science, looking for vestiges of irregularity with immense childlike curiosity.

The day of the left-over meal found Dolores and me in the laundry room, sandwiched between bins of feces and urine stained sheets to be laundered. There were also dripping urinals waiting to be washed. Hunched over a tray of fried chicken, mashed potatoes and gravy, lima beans and vanilla ice cream, we devoured crusty morsels of Mr. Smith's fried chicken breasts. The food was good. We fought over the ice cream. I resolved to try a few more meals before the summer ended, perhaps in a more pleasant atmosphere.

That day, I lingered at the hospital longer than usual. I helped Dolores with Francisca Pacheco, turning the old woman on her side as we fitted the sheet on the mattress. "Cuidado, no me toquen,"[1] she cried. When Dolores took her temperature rectally, I left the room, but returned just as quickly, ashamed

---

8. The Greek tragedy *Antigone*, by Sophocles. Dolores had played the weaker sister, Ismene, to Rocío's strong-willed Antigone.

9. The Weeper-Ghost (Spanish) of a dead woman, in folklore.

1. Careful, don't touch me (Spanish).

of my timidity. I was always the passing menu girl, too afraid to linger, too unwilling to see, too busy with summer illusions. Every day I raced to finish the daily menus, punching in my time card, greeting the beginning of what I considered to be my *real* day outside those long and smelly corridors where food and illness intermingled, leaving a sweet thick air of exasperation in my lungs. The "ooooh" of Elizabeth Rainey's anxious flesh.

The "ay ay ay" of Great Aunt Eutilia's phantom cries awaited me in my father's room. On the wall the portrait of his hero Napoleon hung, shielded by white sheets. The sun was too bright that summer for delicate fading eyes, the heat too oppressive. The blue fan raced to bring freshness to that acrid tomb full of ghosts.

I walked home slowly, not stopping at the quiet place. Compadre Regino Suárez was on the roof. The cooler leaked. Impatient with Regino and his hearty wave, his habit of never doing any job thoroughly, I remembered that I'd forgotten my daily iced tea. The sun was hot. All I wanted was to rest in the cool darkness of my purple room.

The inside of the house smelled of burnt food and lemons. My mother had left something on the stove again. To counteract the burnt smell she'd placed lemons all over the house. Lemons filled ashtrays and bowls, they lay solidly on tables and rested in hot corners. I looked in the direction of Eutilia's room. Quiet. She was sleeping. She'd been dead five years but, still, the room was hers. She was sleeping peacefully. I smelled the cleansing bitterness of lemons.

## MRS. DANIELS

When I entered rooms and saw sick, dying women in their forties, I always remembered room 210, Mrs. Daniels, the mother of my cousin's future wife.

Mrs. Daniels usually lay in bed, whimpering like a little dog, moaning to her husband, who always stood nearby, holding her hand, saying softly, "Now, Martha, Martha. The little girl only wants to get your order."

"Send her away, goddammit!"

On those days that Mr. Daniels was absent, Mrs. Daniels whined for me to go away. "Leave me alone, can't you see I'm dying" she said and looked toward the wall. She looked so pale, sick, near death to me, but somehow I knew, not really having imagined death without the dying, not having felt the outrage and loathing, I knew and saw her outbursts for what they really were: deep hurts, deep distresses. I saw her need to release them, to fling them at others, dribbling pain / anguish / abuse, trickling away those vast torrential feelings of sorrow and hate and fear, letting them fall wherever they would, on whomever they might. I was her white wall. I was her whipping girl upon whom she spilled her darkened ashes. She cried out obscenely to me, sending me reeling from her room, that room of loathing and dread. That room anxious with worms.

Who of us has not heard the angry choked words of crying people, listened, not wanting to hear, then shut our ears, said enough, I don't want to. Who has not seen the fearful tear-streamed faces, known the blank eyes and felt the holding back, and, like smiling thoughtless children, said: "I was in the next room, I couldn't help hearing, I heard, I saw, you didn't know, did you? I know."

We rolled up the pain, assigned it a shelf, placed it in the hardened place, along with a certain self-congratulatory sense of wonder at the world's unfortunates like Mrs. Daniels. We were embarrassed to be alive.

## JUAN MARIA / THE NOSE

"Cómo se dice[2] when was the last time you had a bowel movement?" Nurse Luciano asked. She was from Yonkers, a bright newlywed. Erminia, the ward secretary, a tall thin horsey woman with a postured Juárez hairdo of exaggerated sausage ringlets, replied through chapped lips, "Oh, who cares, he's sleeping."

"He's from México, huh?" Luciano said with interest.

"An illegal alien," Rosario retorted. She was Erminia's sister, the superintendent's secretary, with the look of a badly scarred bulldog. She'd stopped by to invite Erminia to join her for lunch.

"So where'd it happen?" Luciano asked.

"At the Guadalajara Bar on Main Street," Erminia answered, moistening her purple lips nervously. It was a habit of hers.

"Hey, I remember when we used to walk home from school. You remember, Rocío?" Dolores asked, "We'd try to throw each other through the swinging doors. It was real noisy in there."

"Father O'Kelley said drink was the defilement of men, the undoing of staunch, god-fearing women," I said.

"Our father has one now and then," Rosario replied, "that doesn't mean anything. It's because he was one of those aliens."

"Those kind of problems are bad around here I heard," Luciano said, "people sneaking across the border and all."

"Hell, you don't know the half of it," Nurse González said as she came up to the desk where we all stood facing the hallway. "It's an epidemic."

"I don't know, my mother always had maids, and they were all real nice except the one who stole her wedding rings. We had to track her all the way to Piedras Negras and even then she wouldn't give them up," Erminia interjected.

"Still, it doesn't seem human the way they're treated at times."

"Some of them, they ain't human."

"Still, he was drunk, he wasn't full aware."

"Full aware, my ass," retorted Esperanza angrily, "he had enough money to buy booze. If that's not aware, I don't know what aware is. Ain't my goddam fault the bastard got into a fight and someone bit his nose off. Ain't *my* fault he's here and *we* gotta take care of him. Christ! If *that* isn't aware, I don't know what aware is!"

Esperanza González, head surgical floor nurse, the short but highly respected Esperanza of no esperanzas,[3] the Esperanza of the short-bobbed hair, the husky deferential voice, the commands, the no-nonsense orders and briskness, Esperanza the future sister-in-law of Dolores, my only friend, Esperanza the dyke, who was later killed in a car accident on the way to somewhere, said: "Now get back to work all of you, we're just here to clean up the mess."

Later when Esperanza was killed my aunt said, "How nice. In the paper they called her lover her sister. How nice!"

---

2. How do you say (Spanish).   3. Hope of no hopes (Spanish).

"Hey, Erminia, lunch?" asked Rosario, almost sheepishly. "You hungry?"

"Coming, Rosario," yelled Erminia from the back office where she was getting her purse. "Coming!"

"God, I'm starving," Rosario said, "can you hear my stomach?"

"Go check Mr. Carter's cath, Dolores, will you?" said Esperanza in a softer tone.

"Well, I don't know, I just don't know," Luciano pondered. "It doesn't seem human, does it? I mean how in the world could anyone in their right mind bite off another person's nose? How? You know it, González, you're a tough rooster. If I didn't know you so well already, you'd scare the hell out of me. How long you been a nurse?"

"Too long, Luciano. Look, I ain't a new bride, that's liable to make a person soft. Me, I just clean up the mess."

"Luciano, what you know about people could be put on the head of a pin. You just leave these alien problems to those of us who were brought up around here and know what's going on. Me, I don't feel one bit sorry for that bastard," Esperanza said firmly. "Christ, Luciano, what do you expect, he don't speak no Engleesh!"

"His name is Juan María Mejía," I ventured.

Luciano laughed. Esperanza laughed. Dolores went off to Mr. Carter's room, and Rosario chatted noisily with Erminia as they walked toward the cafeteria.

"Hey, Rosario," Luciano called out, "what happened to the rings?"

It was enchilada day. Trini was very busy.

Juan María the Nose was sleeping in the hallway; all the other beds were filled. His hospital gown was awry, the grey sheet folded through sleep-deadened limbs. His hands were tightly clenched. The hospital screen barely concealed his twisted private sleep of legs akimbo, moist armpits and groin. It was a sleep of sleeping off, of hard drunken wanderings, with dreams of a bar, dreams of a fight. He slept the way little boys sleep, carelessly half exposed. I stared at him.

Esperanza complained and muttered under her breath, railing at the Anglo sons of bitches and at all the lousy wetbacks, at everyone, male and female, goddamn them and their messes. Esperanza was dark and squat, pura india[4] tortured by her very face. Briskly, she ordered Dolores and now me about. I had graduated overnight, as if in a hazy dream, to assistant, but unofficial, ward secretary.

I stared across the hallway to Juan María the Nose. He faced the wall, a dangling I.V. at the foot of the bed. Esperanza González, R.N., looked at me.

"Well, and *who* are you?"

"I'm the menu, I mean, I *was* the menu . . ." I stammered. "I'm helping Erminia."

"So get me some cigarettes. Camels. I'll pay you tomorrow when I get paid."

Yes, it was really González, male, who ran the hospital.

Arlene returned from the Luray Caverns with a stalactite charm bracelet for me. She announced to Mr. Smith and me that she'd gotten a job with an insurance company.

"I'll miss you, Rocío."

4. Pure Indian.

"Me, too, Arlene." God knows it was the truth. I'd come to depend on her, our talks over tea. No one ever complimented me like she did.

"You never get angry, do you?" she said admiringly.

"Rarely," I said. But inside, I was always angry.

"What do you want to do?"

"Want to do?"

"Yeah."

I want to be someone else, somewhere else, someone important and responsible and sexy. I want to be sexy.

"I don't know. I'm going to major in drama."

"You're sweet," she said. "Everyone likes you. It's in your nature. You're the Florence Nightingale of Altavista Memorial, that's it!"

"Oh God, Arlene, I don't want to be a nurse, *ever!* I can't take the smells. No one in our family can stand smells."

"You look like that painting. I always did think it looked like you . . . ."

"You did?"

"Yeah."

"Come on, you're making me sick, Arlene."

"Everyone likes you."

"Well . . ."

"So keep in touch. I'll see you at the University."

"Home Ec?"

"Biology."

We hugged.

The weeks progressed. My hours at the hospital grew. I was allowed to check in patients, to take their blood pressures and temperatures. I flipped through the patients' charts, memorizing names, room numbers, types of diet. I fingered the doctors' reports with reverence. Perhaps someday I would begin to write in them as Erminia did: "2:15 p.m., Mrs. Daniels, pulse normal, temp normal, Dr. Blasse checked patient, treatment on schedule, medication given to quiet patient."

One day I received a call at the ward desk. It was Mr. Smith.

"Ms. Esquibel? Rocío? This is Mr. Smith, you know, down in the cafeteria."

"Yes, Mr. Smith! How are you? Is there anything I can do? Are you getting the menus okay? I'm leaving them on top of your desk."

"I've been talking to Nurse González, surgical; she says they need you there full time to fill in and could I do without you?"

"Oh, I can do both jobs; it doesn't take that long, Mr. Smith."

"No, we're going by a new system. Rather, it's the old system. The aides will take the menu orders like they used to before Arlene came. So, you come down and see me, Rocío, have a glass of iced tea. I never see you any more since you moved up in the world. Yeah, I guess you're the last of the menu girls."

The summer passed. June, July, August, my birth month. There were serious days, hurried admissions, feverish errands, quick notes jotted in the doctor's charts. I began to work Saturdays. In my eagerness to "advance," I unwittingly had created more work for myself, work I really wasn't skilled to do.

My heart reached out to every person, dragged itself through the hallways with the patients, cried when they did, laughed when they did. I had no business in the job. I was too emotional.

Now when I walked into a room I knew the patient's history, the cause of illness. I began to study individual cases with great attention, turning to a copy of *The Family Physician*, which had its place among my father's old books in his abandoned study.

Gone were the idle hours of sitting in the cafeteria, leisurely drinking iced tea, gone were the removed reflections of the outsider.

My walks home were measured, pensive. I hid in my room those long hot nights, nights full of wrestling, injured dreams. Nothing seemed enough.

Before I knew it, it was the end of August, close to that autumnal time of setting out. My new life was about to begin. I had made that awesome leap into myself that steamy summer of illness and dread—confronting at every turn, the flesh, its lingering cries.

"Ay, Ay, Ay, Ay, Canta y no llores! Porque cantando se alegran, Cielito Lindo, los corazones[5] . . ." The little thin voice of an old woman sang from one of the back rooms. She pumped the gold pedals with fast furious and fervent feet, she smiled to the wall, its faces, she danced on the ceiling.

Let me jump.

"Goodbye, Dolores, it was fun."

"I'll miss you, Rocío! But you know, gotta save some money. I'll get back to school someday, maybe."

"What's wrong, Erminia? You mad?" I asked.

"I thought you were gonna stay and help me out here on the floor."

"Goddamn right!" complained Esperanza. "Someone told me this was your last day, so why didn't you tell me? Why'd I train you for, so you could leave us? To go to school? What for? So you can get those damned food stamps? It's a disgrace all those wetbacks and healthy college students getting our hard earned tax money. Makes me sick. Christ!" Esperanza shook her head with disgust.

"Hey, Erminia, you tell Rosario goodbye for me and Mrs. Luciano, too," I said sadly.

"Yeah, okay. They'll be here tomorrow," she answered tonelessly. I wanted to believe she was sad.

"I gotta say goodbye to Mr. Smith," I said, as I moved away.

"Make him come up and get some sun," González snickered. "Hell no, better not, he might get sunstroke and who'd fix my fried chicken?"

I climbed down the steps to the basement, past the cafeteria, past my special table, and into Mr. Smith's office, where he sat, adding numbers.

"Miss Esquibel, Rocío!"

"This is my last day, Mr. Smith. I wanted to come down and thank you. I'm sorry about . . ."

"Oh no, it worked out all right. It's nothing."

5. Sing and don't cry! Because when they sing, Beautiful Little Sky, hearts rejoice (Spanish).

Did I see, from the corner of my eye, a set of Friday's menus he himself was tabulating—salisbury steak, macaroni and cheese . . .

"We'll miss you, Rocío. You were an excellent menu girl."

"It's been a wonderful summer."

"Do you want some tea?"

"No, I really don't have the time."

"I'll get . . ."

"No, thank you, Mr. Smith, I *really* have to go, but thanks. It's really good tea."

I extended my hand, and for the first time, we touched. Mr. Smith's eyes seemed fogged, distracted. He stood up and hobbled closer to my side. I took his grave cold hand, shook it softly, and turned to the moist walls. When I closed the door, I saw him in front of me, framed in paper, the darkness of that quiet room. Bless this mess.

Eutilia's voice echoed in the small room. Goodbye. Goodbye. And let me jump.

I turned away from the faces, the voices, now gone: Father O'Kelley, Elizabeth Rainey, Mrs. Luciano, Arlene Rutschman, Mrs. Daniels, Juan María the Nose, Mr. Samaniego and Donelda, his wife, their grandchildren, Mr. Carter, Earl Ellis, Dolores Casaus, Erminia and her sister, the bulldog. Esperanza González, Francisca Pacheco, Elweena Twinbaum, the silver-haired volunteer whose name I'd learned the week before I left Altavista Memorial. I'd made a list on a menu of all the people I'd worked with. To remember. It seemed right.

From the distance I heard Marion Smith's high voice: "Now you come back and see us!"

Above the stairs the painting of Florence Nightingale stared solidly into weary soldiers' eyes. Her look encompassed all the great unspeakable sufferings of every war. I thought of Arlene typing insurance premiums.

Farther away, from behind and around my head, I heard the irregular but joyful strains of "Cielito Lindo" played on a phantom piano by a disembodied but now peaceful voice that sang with great quivering emotion: De la sierra morena. Cielito Lindo . . . viene bajando[6] . . .

Regino fixed the cooler. I started school. Later that year I was in a car accident. I crashed into a brick wall at the cemetery. I walked to Dolores' house, holding my bleeding face in my hands. Dolores and her father argued all the way to the hospital. I sat quietly in the back seat. It was a lovely morning. So clear. When I woke up I was on the surgical floor. Everyone knew me. I had so many flowers in the room I could hardly breathe. My older sister, Ronelia, thought I'd lost part of my nose in the accident and she returned to the cemetery to look for it. It wasn't there.

Mr. Smith came to see me once. I started to cry.

"Oh no, no, no, now don't you do that, Rocío. You want some tea?"

No one took my menu order. I guess that system had finally died out. I ate the food, whatever it was, walked the hallways in my grey hospital gown slit in the back, railed at the well-being of others, cursed myself for being so stupid.

---

6. From the dark mountains. Beautiful Little Sky . . . you are descending (Spanish); the boy is contrasting her light with his own inner darkness.

I only wanted to be taken home, down the street, past the quiet-talking place, a block away, near the Dairy Queen, to the darkness of my purple room. It was time.

PREVIOUS EMPLOYMENT: Altavista Memorial Hospital
SUPERVISORS: Mr. Marion Smith, Dietician, and Miss Esperanza González, R.N., Surgical Floor.
DATES: June 1966 to August 1966
IN A FEW SENTENCES GIVE A BRIEF DESCRIPTION OF YOUR JOB: As Ward Secretary, I was responsible for . . . let me think . . .

1986

---

# LOUISE ERDRICH
## b. 1954

Louise Erdrich grew up in the small town of Wahpeton, North Dakota, just on the Minnesota border. Her mother was French-Chippewa, her maternal grandmother was tribal chairman on the Turtle Mountain Reservation, and both her mother and father worked in the Bureau of Indian Affairs boarding school in Wahpeton. Although she wrote stories as a child, encouraged by her father who paid her a nickel for each one, Erdrich's growing up was marked by no special awareness of her Chippewa background. She has said that she never thought about "what was Native American and what wasn't. . . . There wasn't a political climate at the time about Indian rights." The eldest of seven children, she "grew up just taking it all in as something that was part of me."

In 1972 she entered Dartmouth College, participating in a Native American Studies program run by Michael Dorris—himself part American Indian and a writer—whom eventually she would marry and who she admits is her most serious and supportive critic. In her undergraduate years she won prizes for poetry and fiction and worked at a variety of jobs, such as teaching poetry in prisons, editing a Boston Indian Council newspaper, and flag-signaling on a construction site. Deciding on a career as a writer, she took an M.A. degree at Johns Hopkins, for which degree she submitted a number of poems—later to appear in her collection, *Jacklight*—as well as part of a novel. There followed the usual sending out of poems and stories, the rejection slips, eventually the acceptances.

Her first novel, *Love Medicine*, which won the National Book Critics Circle award for 1984, began as a short story. Working closely with her husband, she not only expanded the story into a novel but planned that novel as the first of a tetralogy, ranging over different periods of time and focusing on the lives of two Chippewa families. Her interest in the interactions between characters and their families and friends lies at the center of her fiction. As Erdrich has explained, she and her husband "continuously plot and continuously talk about who the characters are, what they eat, what clothes they wear, what their favorite colors are and what's going to happen to them. In that way, I think it's a true kind of collaboration."

Successive chapters of *Love Medicine* jump from 1981 to 1934 to 1948, each chapter told through a particular character's point of view (sometimes we see the same event from succeeding points of view). But the individual chapter is more a discrete whole than is the case with a traditional novel.

Erdrich's style is easy, offhand, quietly unostentatious, but always with a kick in the language, as in the first paragraph of *The Red Convertible*, whose protagonist, Lyman Lamartine, tells us:

> I was the first one to drive a convertible on my reservation. And of course, it was red, a red Olds. I owned that car along with my brother Henry Junior. We owned it together until his boots filled with water on a windy night and he bought out my share. Now Henry owns the whole car, and his younger brother (that's myself) Lyman walks everywhere he goes.

Such clarity and directness is only part of the story, however, since her style also calls upon lyric resources, notable in the following sentence from her second novel, *The Beet Queen*:

> After the miraculous sheets of black ice came the floods, stranding boards and snaky knots of debris high in the branches, leaving brown leeches to dry like raisins on the sidewalks when the water receded, and leaving the smell of river mud, a rotten sweetness, in the backyards and gutters.

*The Beet Queen* moves outside the reservation, where the two families in *Love Medicine* lived, to a small town near it called Argus, made up of whites and a few Chippewas. The novel focuses on a sister and brother, abandoned by their mother in 1932, and takes them up through forty years to a time when the family gathers at a town beet festival. Different members of the extended family pick up and lay down the narrative, while an omniscient voice intersperses itself between those of the characters. If anything, *The Beet Queen* is a more poised and finished piece of writing than the earlier novel, auguring well for the books to come. Erdrich writes without sentimentality, yet with a real feeling for place and people, for individual lives as they extend themselves over time and space. She is a strongly regional and ethnic writer, yet in reading her one feels those qualities not as limitations but as rooted solidities out of which ranging, even universal, values and situations may be experienced.

# Lulu's Boys[1]

On the last day that Lulu Lamartine spent as Henry's widow, her boys were outside drinking beers and shooting plastic jugs. Her deceased husband's brother, Beverly, was sitting across from her at the kitchen table. Having a name some people thought of as feminine had turned Beverly Lamartine to building up his muscles in his youth, and they still bulged, hard as ingots in some places, now lost in others. His plush belly strained open the bottom buttons of his black shirt, and Lulu saw his warm skin peeking through. She also saw how the tattoos he and Henry had acquired on their arms, and which Lulu had always admired, were now deep black and so fuzzy around the edges that she could hardly tell what they were.

Beverly saw her looking at the old tattoos and pushed his sleeves up over his biceps. "Get an eyeful," he grinned. As of old, he stretched his arms across the table, and she gazed at the figures commemorating the two brothers' drunken travels outside her life.

There was a doll, a skull with a knife stuck in it, an eagle, a swallow, and Beverly's name, rank, and serial number. Looking at the arm made Lulu

---

1. From *Love Medicine* (1984).

remember her husband's tattoos. Henry's arms had been imprinted with a banner bearing some other woman's name, a rose with a bleeding thorn, two lizards, and like his brother's, with his name, rank, and serial number.

Sometimes Lulu could not help it. She thought of everything so hard that her mind felt warped and sodden as a door that swells up in spring. It would not close properly to keep the troublesome thoughts out.

Right now she thought of those two lizards on either one of Henry's arms. She imagined them clenching together when he put his arms around her. Then she thought of them coupling the same way she and Henry did. She thought of this while looking at Beverly's lone swallow, a bird with outstretched wings deep as ink and bleeding into his flesh. She remembered Beverly's trick: the wings were carefully tattooed on certain muscles, so that when he flexed his arm the bird almost seemed to hover in a dive or swoop.

Lulu hadn't seen her husband's brother since the funeral in 1950, with the casket closed because of how badly Henry had suffered in the car wreck. Drunk, he had started driving the old Northern Pacific tracks and either fallen asleep or passed out, his car straddling the rails. As he'd left the bar that night everyone who had been there remembered his words.

"She comes barreling through, you'll never see me again."

At first they had thought he was talking about Lulu. But even at the time they knew she didn't lose her temper over drinking. It was the train Henry had been talking about. They realized that later when the news came and his casket was sealed.

Beverly Lamartine had shown up from the Twin Cities[2] one hour before his brother's service was held. He had brought along the trophy flag—a black swastika on torn red cloth—that he had captured to revenge the oldest Lamartine, a quiet boy, hardly spoken of now, who was killed early on while still in boot camp.

When the men from the veteran's post had lowered Henry's casket into the grave on ropes, there was a U.S. flag draped across it already. Beverly had shaken out the trophy flag. He'd let it go in the air, and the wind seemed to suck it down, the black arms of the insignia whirling like a spider.

Watching it, Lulu had gone faint. The sudden spokes of the black wheel flashed before her eyes and she'd toppled dizzily, then stumbled over the edge of the grave.

The men were still lowering Henry on ropes. Lulu plunged heavily down with the trophy flag, and the ropes burned out of the pallbearers' hands. The box hit bottom. People screamed and there was a great deal of commotion, during which Beverly jumped down to revive Lulu. All together, the pallbearers tugged and hoisted her out. The black garments seemed to make her even denser than she was. Her round face and chubby hands were a pale dough color, cold and wet with shock. For hours afterward she trembled, uttered senseless vowels, jumped at sounds and touches. Some people, assuming that she had jumped in the grave to be buried along with Henry, thought much better of her for a while.

But most of her life Lulu had been known as a flirt. And that was putting it mildly. Tongues less kind had more indicting things to say.

2. Minneapolis and St. Paul, Minnesota.

For instance, besides the fact of Lulu Lamartine's first husband, why did each of the boys currently shooting milk jugs out front of Henry's house look so different? There were eight of them. Some of them even had her maiden name. The three oldest were Nanapushes. The next oldest were Morrisseys who took the name Lamartine, and then there were more assorted younger Lamartines who didn't look like one another, either. Red hair and blond abounded; there was some brown. The black hair on the seven-year-old at least matched his mother's. This boy was named Henry Junior, and he had been born approximately nine months after Henry Senior's death.

Give or take a week, Beverly thought, looking from Henry Junior out the window back to the woman across the table. Beverly was quite certain that he, and not his brother, was the father of that boy. In fact, Beverly had come back to the reservation with a hidden purpose.

Beverly Lamartine wanted to claim Henry Junior and take him home.

In the Twin Cities there were great relocation opportunities for Indians with a certain amount of natural stick-to-it-iveness and pride. That's how Beverly saw it. He was darker than most, but his parents had always called themselves French or Black Irish and considered those who thought of themselves as Indians quite backward. They had put the need to get ahead in Beverly. He worked devilishly hard.

Door to door, he'd sold children's after-school home workbooks for the past eighteen years. The wonder of it was that he had sold any workbook sets at all, for he was not an educated man and if the customers had, as they might naturally do, considered him an example of his product's efficiency they might not have entrusted their own children to those pages of sums and reading exercises. But they did buy the workbook sets regularly, for Bev's ploy was to use his humble appearance and faulty grammar to ease into conversation with his hardworking get-ahead customers. They looked forward to seeing the higher qualities, which they could not afford, inculcated in their own children. Beverly's territory was a small-town world of earnest dreamers. Part of Bev's pitch, and the one that usually sold the books, was to show the wife or husband a wallet-sized school photo of his son.

That was Henry Junior. The back of the photo was inscribed "To Uncle Bev," but the customer never saw that, because the precious relic was encased in a cardboard-backed sheet of clear plastic. This covering preserved it from thousands of mill-toughened thumbs in the working-class sections of Minneapolis and small towns within its one-hundred-mile radius. Every year or so Beverly wrote to Lulu, requesting another picture. It was sent to him in perfect goodwill. With every picture Beverly grew more familiar with his son and more inspired in the invention of tales he embroidered, day after day, on front porches that were to him the innocent stages for his routine.

His son played baseball in a sparkling-white uniform stained across the knees with grass. He pitched no-hitters every few weeks. Teachers loved the boy for getting so far ahead of the other students on his own initiative. They sent him on to various higher grades, and he was invited to the parties of children in the wealthy suburb of Edina. Henry Junior cleared the hurdles of class and intellect with an ease astonishing to Beverly, who noted to his wistful customers how swiftly the young surpass the older generation.

"Give them wings!" he would urge, flipping softly through the cheap pulp-flecked pages. The sound of the ruffled paper was like the panic of fledglings before they learn how to glide. People usually bought, and only later, when they found themselves rolling up a work-skills book to slaughter a fly or scribbling phone numbers down on the back of *Math Enrichment*, would they realize that their children had absolutely no interest in taking the world by storm through self-enlightenment.

Some days, after many hours of stories, the son became so real in Bev's mind that when he came home to the apartment, he half expected the boy to pounce on him before he put his key in the door. But when the lock turned his son vanished, for Elsa would be there, and she was not particularly interested in children, real or not. She was a typist who changed jobs incessantly. Groomed with exquisite tawdriness, she'd fashioned for Bev the image of a modern woman living the ideal career life. Her salary only fluctuated by pennies from firm to firm, but her importance and value as a knower-of-ropes swelled. She believed herself indispensable, but she heartlessly left employers hanging in their times of worst need to go on to something better.

Beverly adored her.

She was a natural blond with birdlike legs and, true, no chin, but great blue snapping eyes. She smoked exotically, rolling smoke off her tongue, and often told Bev that two weeks from now he might not be seeing her again. Then she would soften toward him. The possibilities she gave up to be with him impressed Bev so much, every time, that it ceased to bother him that Elsa only showed him off to her family in Saint Cloud at the height of summer, when they admired his perfect tan.

The boy, though, who was everywhere in his life and yet nowhere, fit less easily into Bev's fantasy of how he lived. The boy made him ache in hidden, surprising places sometimes at night when he lay next to Elsa, his knuckles resting lightly against her emphatic spine. That was the limit of touching she would tolerate in slumber. She even took her sleeping breath with a certain rigid meanness, holding it stubbornly and releasing it with small explosive sighs. Bev hardly noticed, though, for beside her his mind raced through the ceilings and walls.

One night he saw himself traveling. He was driving his sober green car westward, past the boundaries of his salesman's territory, then over the state line and on across to the casual and lonely fields, the rich, dry violet hills of the reservation. Then he was home where his son really lived. Lulu came to the door. He habitually blotted away her face and body, so that in his thoughts she was a doll of flour sacking with a curly black mop on her head. She was simply glad that he had come at last to take the son she had such trouble providing for off her hands. She was glad Henry Junior would be wafted into a new and better metropolitan existence.

This scenario became so real through the quite hours he lay beside Elsa that Bev even convinced himself that his wife would take to Henry Junior, in spite of the way she shuddered at children in the streets and whispered "Monkeys!" And then, by the time the next workday was half over, he'd arranged for a vacation and made an appointment to have a once-over done on his car.

Of course, Lulu was not made of flour sacking and yarn. Beverly had realized that in the immediacy of her arms. She grabbed him for a hug when he got out of his car, and, tired by the long trip, his head whirled for a moment in a haze of yellow spots. When she released him, the boys sauntered up, poker-faced and mildly suspicious, to stand in a group around him and await their introductions. There seemed to be so many that at first he was speechless. Each of them was Henry Junior in a different daydream, at a different age, and so alike were their flat expressions he couldn't even pick out the one whose picture sold the record number of home workbooks in the Upper Midwestern Regional Division.

Henry Junior, of course, was perfectly recognizable after Lulu introduced him. After all, he did look exactly like the picture in Bev's wallet. He put his hand out and shook manfully like his older brothers, which pleased Bev, although he had trouble containing a moment of confusion at the utter indifference in the boy's eyes. He had to remember the boy was meeting him for the first time. In a child's world strange grown-ups are indistinguishable as trees in a forest. Even the writing on the back of those photographs was probably, now that he thought of it, Lulu's.

They went away, started shooting their guns, and then Bev was left with the unexpected problem of the mother of his son, the woman he would just as soon forget. During a moment of adjustment, however, he decided to go through whatever set of manipulations were necessary. He wanted to handle the situation in the ideal, firm, but diplomatic manner. And then, after he'd recovered from the strength of her hug, he had absolutely no doubt that things would go on according to his plan.

"My my my," he said to Lulu now. She was buttering a piece of bread soft as the plump undersides of her arms. "Lot of water under the dam."

She agreed, taking alert nips of her perfectly covered slice. She had sprinkled a teaspoon of sugar over it, carefully distributing the grains. That was how she was. Even with eight boys her house was neat as a pin. The candy bowl on the table sat precisely on its doily. All her furniture was brushed and straightened. Her coffee table held a neat stack of *Fate* and *True Adventure* magazines. On her walls she'd hung matching framed portraits of poodles, kittens, and an elaborate embroidered portrait of Chief Joseph.[3] Her windowsills were decorated with pincushions in the shapes of plump little hats and shoes.

"I make these." She cupped a tiny blue sequined pump in her hand. "You have a girl friend? I'll give it to you. Here."

She pushed the little shoe across the table. It skittered over the edge, fell into his lap, and Beverly retrieved it quickly, for he saw that her hand was following. He set the blue slipper between them without addressing her implicit question on his status—girl friend, married, or just looking around. He was intent on bringing up the subject of Henry Junior.

"Remember that time . . ." he started. Then he didn't know what he was going to say. What did come out surprised him. "You and me and Henry were playing cards before you got married and the boys were sleeping?"

He could have kicked himself for having blurted that out. Even after all these years he couldn't touch on the memory without running a hand across his face or whistling tunelessly to drive it from his mind. It didn't seem to have bothered her all these years though. She picked up the story smoothly and went on.

"Oh, you men," she laughed chidingly. Her face was so little like Beverly's

---

3. Eminent Nez Percé tribal chief and military leader against the whites (c. 1840–1904).

flour sacking doll he wondered how he had stood imagining her that way all these years. Her mouth was small, mobile, like a puckering flower, and her teeth were unusually tiny and white. He remembered having the urge to lick their smoothness once. But now she was talking.

"I suppose you thought you could take advantage of a poor young woman. I don't know who it was, you or Henry, that suggested after several too many beers that we change our pennyante poker game to strip. Well I still have to laugh. I had you men right down to your boxer shorts in no time flat, and I was sitting there, warm and cozy as you please. I was still in my dress with my shoes on my feet."

"You had them beads on, clip earrings, bangle bracelets, silk stockings," Beverly pouted.

"Garters and other numerous foundation garments. Of course I did. I am a woman of detachable parts. You should know by now. You simply weren't playing in your league with strip poker."

She had the grace to put a hand to her lips as they uncurved, hiding the little gap-toothed smile he'd doted over at the time of that game.

"Want to know something I never told before?" she said. "It was after I won your shorts with my pair of deuces and Henry's with my eights, and you were naked, that I decided which one to marry."

Beverly was shocked at this statement, bold even for Lulu. His wind felt knocked out of him for a moment, because her words called up the old times so clearly, the way he felt when she decided to marry his brother. He'd buried the feelings eventually in the knowledge that she wasn't right for him, man of the world that he was becoming. He congratulated himself for years after on getting free of her slack, ambitionless, but mindlessly powerful female clutches. Right now his reasoning had ripped wide open, however, and jealousy kicked him in the stomach.

Lulu cooed. Her voice was like a wind chime rattling. Cheap, sweet, maddening. "Some men react in that situation and some don't," she told him. "It was reaction I looked for, if you know what I mean."

Beverly was silent.

Lulu winked at him with her bold, gleaming blackberry eyes. She had smooth tight skin, wrinkled only where she laughed, always fragrantly powdered. At the time her hair was still dark and thickly curled. Later she would burn it off when her house caught fire, and it would never grow back. Because her face was soft and yet alert, vigilant as some small cat's, plump and tame but with a wildness in its breast, Beverly had always felt exposed, preyed on, undressed around her, even before the game in which she'd stripped him naked and now, as he found, appraised him in his shame.

You got your reaction when you needed it, he wanted to say.

Yet, even in his mounting exasperation, he did not lose control and stoop to discussing what had happened after Henry's wake, when they both went outside to get some air. He rolled his sleeves down and fished a soft pack of Marlboros from her side of the table. She watched his hand as he struck the match, and her eyes narrowed. They were so black the iris sometimes showed within like blue flames. He thought her heartless, suddenly, and wondered if she even remembered the two of them in the shed after Henry's wake. But there was no good way he could think of to ask without getting back down to her level.

Henry Junior came to the window, hungry, and Lulu made a sandwich for him with baloney and hot-dog relish. The boy was seven years old, sturdy, with Lulu's delicate skin and the almost Asian-looking eyes of all the Lamartines. Beverly watched the boy with electrified attention. He couldn't really say if anything about the child reminded him of himself, unless it was the gaze. Beverly had tried to train his gaze like a hawk to use in barroom staredowns during his tour of duty. It came in handy, as well, when he made a sale, although civilian life had long ago taken the edge off his intensity, as it had his muscles, his hero's stubborn, sagging flesh that he could still muster in a crisis. There was a crisis now. The boy seemed to have acquired the staredown technique naturally. Beverly was the first to look away.

"Uncle Bev," Henry Junior said. "I always heard about the bird on your arm. Could you make it fly?"

So Beverly rolled up shirt sleeve once more and forced his blood up. He flexed powerfully, over and over, until the boy was bored, satisfied, and fled back to his brothers. Beverly let his arm down carefully. It was numb. The sound of the .22 reports came thick and fast for a while, then all the boys paused to reload and set the jugs in a line against the fence and argue over whose shot went where.

"They're teaching him to shoot," explained Lulu. "We had two bucks brought down last fall. And pheasants? Those boys will always put meat on my table."

She rambled on about them all, and Bev listened with relief, gathering his strength to pull the conversation back his way again.

One of the oldest boys was going down to Haskell Junior College, while another, Gerry, was testing the limits of the mission school system,[4] at twelve. Lulu pointed Gerry out among the others. Bev could see Lulu most clearly in this boy. He laughed at everything, or seemed barely to be keeping amusement in. His eyes were black, sly, snapping with sparks. He led the rest in play without a hint of effort, just like Lulu, whose gestures worked as subtle magnets. He was a big boy, a born leader, light on his feet and powerful. His mind seemed quick. It would not surprise Bev to hear, after many years passed on, that this Gerry grew up to be both a natural criminal and a hero whose face appeared on the six-o'clock news.

Lulu managed to make the younger boys obey perfectly. Bev noticed, while the older ones adored her to the point that they did not tolerate anything less from anyone else. As her voice swirled on, Bev thought of some Tarzan book he had read. In that book there was a queen protected by bloodthirsty warriors who smoothly dispatched all of her enemies. Lulu's boys had grown into a kind of pack. They always hung together. When a shot went true, their gangling legs, encased alike in faded denim, shifted as if a ripple went through them collectively. They moved in dance steps too intricate for the noninitiated eye to imitate or understand. Clearly they were of one soul. Handsome, rangy, wildly various, they were bound in total loyalty, not by oath but by the simple, unquestioning belongingness of part of one organism.

Lulu had gone silent, suddenly, to fetch something from her icebox. In that quiet moment something about the boys outside struck Beverly as almost dangerous.

---

4. Schools taught by white missionaries for American Indian children.

He watched them close around Henry Junior in an impenetrable mass of black-and-white sneakers, sweatshirts, baseball hats, and butts of Marlin rifles. Through the chinks between their bodies Beverly saw Gerry, dark and electric as his mother, kneel behind Henry Junior and arm-over-arm instruct him how to cradle, aim, and squeeze-fire the .22. When Henry Junior stumbled, kicked backward by the recoil, missing the jug, the boys dusted him clean and set him back behind the rifle again. Slowly, as he watched, Beverly's uneasy sense of menace gave way to some sweet apprehension of their kinship. He was remembering the way he and Henry and Slick, the oldest of his brothers, used to put themselves on the line for each other in high school. People used to say you couldn't drive a knife edge between the Lamartines. Nothing ever came between them. Nothing ever did or would.

Even while he was thinking that, Beverly knew it wasn't true.

What had come between them was a who, and she was standing across from him now at the kitchen counter. Lulu licked some unseen sweetness from her fingers, having finished her sugared bread. Her tongue was small, flat, and pale as a little cat's. Her eyes had shut in mystery. He wondered if she knew his thoughts.

She padded easily toward him, and he stood up in an odd panic as she approached. He felt his heart knock urgently as a stranger in trouble, and then she touched him through his pants. He was helpless. His mouth fell on hers and kept traveling, through the walls and ceilings, down the levels, through the broad, warm reaches of the years.

The boys came back very late in the afternoon. By then, Beverly had drastically revised his plans for Henry Junior to the point where he had no plans at all. In a dazed, immediate, unhappy bewilderment he sat on the doily-bedecked couch opening and closing his hands in his lap. Lulu was bustling about the kitchen in a calm, automatic frenzy. She seemed to fill pots with food by pointing at them and take things from the oven that she'd never put in. The table jumped to set itself. The pop foamed into glasses, and the milk sighed to the lip. The youngest boy, Lyman, crushed in a high chair, watched eagerly while things placed themselves around him. Everyone sat down. Then the boys began to stuff themselves with a savage and astonishing efficiency. Before Bev had cleaned his plate once, they'd had thirds, and by the time he looked up from dessert, they had melted through the walls. The youngest had levitated from his high chair and was sleeping out of sight. The room was empty except for Lulu and himself.

He looked at her. She turned to the sinkful of dishes and disappeared in a cloud of steam. Only the round rear of her blue flowered housedress was visible, so he watched that. It was too late now. He had fallen. He could not help but remember their one night together.

They had gone into the shed while the earth was still damp and the cut flowers in their foam balls still exuded scent over Henry's grave. Beverly had kissed the small cries back onto Lulu's lips. He remembered. Then passion overtook them. She hung on to him like they were riding the tossing ground, her teeth grinding in his ear. He wasn't man or woman. None of that mattered. Yet he was more of a man than he'd ever been. The grief of loss for the beloved made their tiny flames of life so sad and precious it hardly mattered who was what. The flesh was only given so that the flame could touch in a

union however less than perfect. Afterward they lay together, breathing the
dark in and out. He had wept the one other time in his life besides post combat, and after a while he came into her again, tasting his own miraculous continuance.

Lulu left him sitting on the couch and went back into the sacred domain of
her femininity. That was the bedroom with the locking door that she left open
just a crack. She pulled down the blue-and-white-checked bedspread, put the
pillows aside, and lay down carefully with her hands folded on her stomach.
She closed her eyes and breathed deep. She went into herself, sinking through
her body as if on a raft of darkness, until she reached the very bottom of her
soul where there was nothing to do but wait.

Things had gotten by Beverly. Night came down. His sad dazzlement abated
and he tried to avoid thinking of Elsa. But she was there filing her orange nails
whichever way he ducked. And then there was the way he was proud of living
his life. He wanted to go back and sell word-enrichment books. No one on the
reservation would buy them, he knew, and the thought panicked him. He
realized that the depth and danger of his situation was great if he had forgotten
that basic fact. The moon went black. The bushes seemed to close around
the house.
   Retrench, he told himself, as the boys turned heavily and mumbled in their
invisible cots and all along the floors around him. Retreat if you have to and
forget about Henry Junior. He finally faced surrender and knew it was the only
thing he could possibly have the strength for.
   He planned to get into his car while it was still dark, before dawn, and drive
back to Minneapolis without Henry Junior. He would simply have to bolt
without saying good-bye to Lulu. But when he rose from the couch, he walked
down the hall to her bedroom door. He didn't pause but walked right through.
It was like routine he'd built up over time in marriage. The close dark was
scented with bath lilac. Glowing green spears told the hour in her side-table
clock. The bedclothes rustled. He stood holding the lathed wooden post. And
then his veins were full of warm ash and his tongue swelled in his throat.
   He lay down in her arms.
   Whirling blackness swept through him, and there was nothing else to do.
   The wings didn't beat as hard as they used to, but the bird still flew.

1984

# American Poetry
# since 1945

More than a decade after the end of World War II, two important and transforming shocks were administered to American poetry: Allen Ginsberg's *Howl* (1956) and Robert Lowell's *Life Studies* (1959). Ginsberg first delivered his poem aloud, during a reading at the Six Gallery in San Francisco in the fall of 1955; the following year it was published by Lawrence Ferlinghetti's City Lights Bookshop. In a single stroke, with the energy of a reborn Whitman, Ginsberg made poetry one of the rallying points for underground protest and prophetic denunciation of the prosperous, complacent, gray-spirited Eisenhower years. The setting in which the poem appeared is also significant, for *Howl*, like other work associated with what came to be known as the San Francisco Renaissance, challenged the conventions of a literary tradition dominated by the East Coast. With its open, experimental form and strong oral emphasis, *Howl* sounded a departure from the well-shaped lyric. Lowell, a more "difficult," less popular poet, was rooted in the literary culture of Boston. But with *Life Studies* he too challenged the literary status quo, bringing a new directness and autobiographical intensity into American poetry as he exposed the psychological turbulence suffered by an inbred New Englander. Lowell's movement into a more open, less heavily symbolic style was inspired, in part, by hearing the work of Ginsberg and others while on a reading tour of the West Coast.

The connection between these two volumes and the times in which they were written is direct and apparent. Their poems anticipated and explored strains in American social relationships that were to issue in the open conflicts of the 1960s and 1980s: public unrest about the uses of government and industrial power; the institutions of marriage and the family; the rights and powers of racial minorities, women, and homosexuals; the use of drugs; alternative states of consciousness. Taken together the books also suggested that the invigorating energies of postwar American poetry would arise from diverse regions of the country, their common aim restoring poetry to a more vital relation with contemporary life.

### THE 1940s: OLDER POETS AND YOUNGER

Social pressures alone do not fully explain why American poets such as Lowell and Ginsberg felt ready to claim new authority and new areas of experience in their writing. However radical the changes in the style and content of American poetry in the 1950s and 1960s, its assurance was rooted in subtle, far-reaching developments of the decade before. American poetry had flourished in the late 1940s because of a new confidence in native literary traditions, derived in part from the achievements of the early modernists in the first half of the century. The two most prominent figures, T. S. Eliot and Ezra Pound, both were expatriates whose work continued to dominate the literary scene into the 1940s. Eliot's *Four Quartets*, written in England, was arguably the best "American" poem of the 1940s, and another candidate for that honor, Pound's *Pisan Cantos*, which forms one of the finest sections in his lifelong epic, was written during the poet's incarceration for treason in Italy and published in 1948. Although the reputations of these two poets overshadowed for some time those of their contemporaries (with the possible exception of Robert Frost, who won the Pulitzer Prize in 1931), the postwar period saw the emergence of other important models. For example, the work of William Carlos Williams only became influential for younger poets after the war, with the appearance of the first two books of his *Paterson* in 1946 and 1948 and his important collection *The Desert Music* in 1954. For postwar poets like Allen Ginsberg, Denise Levertov, and Robert Creeley, Williams's work offered a poetic alternative to Eliot's version of modernism. Wallace Stevens also emerged as an influence in the 1940s and 1950s, publishing *Transport to Summer* in 1947, *The Auroras of Autumn* in 1950, and his *Collected Poems* in 1954. Stevens's meditative style and "gaiety of language" became important to many poets, including Theodore Roethke, James Merrill, and John Ashbery. In addition, the impact of two major women modernists, H. D. and Gertrude Stein (both of whom lived in Europe for most of their careers), was not fully felt until after the war. H. D. completed her book-length sequence, *Trilogy*, in 1946 and her meditative epic, *Helen in Egypt*, appeared in 1961. Her work provided for Robert Duncan, Denise Levertov, and others a model elsewhere unavailable for the union of visionary power with energy of language. Although Gertrude Stein died in 1946, a number of her radical experiments in poetic language were first published only in the late 1950s. Indeed, the importance of her work for contemporary experimental poets in the 1980s recalls the composer Virgil Thompson's epithet for Stein: "The Mother of Us All."

As the accomplishments of an older generation emerged, confirming for postwar poets the strength of American poetry, they also cast a daunting shadow against which a subsequent generation measured itself. Following the revolutionary experiments and ambitious designs of their predecessors, it was possible for postwar poets to feel there was little left to do. Nonetheless, during and immediately after 1945, younger poets who were to prove themselves among the strongest and most important of their generation began publishing notable books: Gwendolyn Brooks's *A Street in Bronzeville* (1945); Elizabeth Bishop's first volume, *North & South* (1946); Robert Lowell's *Lord Weary's Castle* (1946); Denise Levertov's first book, published in England, *The Double Image* (1946); Richard Wilbur's *The Beautiful Changes* (1947); Robert Duncan's *Heavenly City, Earthly City* (1947); John Berryman's *The Dispossessed* (1948); and the important second volume by Theodore Roethke, *The Lost Son* (1948). In addition, postwar poets soon began to claim their independence in poetic manifestos. One of the most provocative of these was Charles Olson's *Projective Verse* (1950), which called for a unit of poetic expression based not on a predetermined metrical foot but on the poet's "breath" and the rhythms of the body.

By the end of the 1940s, with the death of the great Irish poet W. B. Yeats in 1939 and the immigration to the United States of his most notable English successor, W. H. Auden, it was clear that the center of poetic activity in the English language had shifted from Britain to America. Indeed, Denise Levertov would later describe her own move from England to the United States in 1947 as a discovery of the vitality of life and speech in American poetry.

### A NEW CLIMATE FOR POETS AND POETRY

In the 1950s and 1960s poets acquired a new visibility in American life. Earlier poets had been relatively isolated from the public: Pound, Eliot, and H. D. lived in Europe; Wallace Stevens was a businessman in Hartford; William Carlos Williams was a small-town doctor in New Jersey. Poetry readings had been relatively rare performances by the few famous poets of the familiar poems the audience already knew but wanted to hear from the illustrious presence of the author. After the war, writers' conferences and workshops, recordings, and published and broadcast interviews became more common. A network of poets traveling to give readings and of poets-in-residence at universities began to form. In the 1960s and 1970s, readings became less formal, more numerous and accessible, held not only in auditoriums but in coffeehouses, bars, and lofts. The purpose of these more casual readings was often to introduce new poets or, perhaps, new poems by an already recognized writer. The poet coming of age after the war was, as one of them, Richard Wilbur, put it, more a "poet-citizen" than an alienated artist. Poets often made a living by putting together a combination of teaching positions, readings, and foundation grants.

A poet's education in the 1950s differed from that of poets in an earlier generation. Written poetry in the postwar years became firmly linked to the English literature curriculum in ways that it had not been in the past. Many of the young poets were taught to read verse and sometimes to write it by influential literary critics who were often poets themselves: John Crowe Ransom, Yvor Winters, Robert Penn Warren, R. P. Blackmur, and Allen Tate. There was, for better or worse, the college major in English literature, as there had not been in so narrow and disciplined a sense for the poetic giants of a generation earlier. Eliot, for example, had done graduate work in philosophy, Pound in Romance philology, Williams had gone to medical school, and each had forged his own literary criticism. A younger poet, on the other hand, *studied* Eliot's essays, or learned critical approaches to literature in English courses such as the ones Allen Ginsberg took from Mark Van Doren and Lionel Trilling at Columbia or James Merrill from Reuben Brower at Amherst. A popular critical text, *Understanding Poetry* (1938) by Cleanth Brooks and Robert Penn Warren, taught students to be close readers of English Metaphysical poems of the seventeenth century, such as those by John Donne and Andrew Marvell. As the poet W. D. Snodgrass testifies, "In school we had been taught to write a very difficult and very intellectual poem. We tried to achieve the obscure and dense texture of the French Symbolists (very intuitive and often deranged poets), but by using methods similar to those of the very intellectual and conscious poets of the English Renaissance, especially the Metaphysical poets."

A young writer, thus trained to read intricate traditional lyrics, did not expect to encounter much, if any, contemporary verse in the classroom. The student had to seek out modern poems in the literary quarterlies or come on them through the chance recommendations of informed friends and teachers. And whether a beginning poet fell, in this private, accidental way, under the influence of Eliot's ironic elegies or Stevens's high rhapsodies or William Carlos Williams's homemade documentaries or H. D.'s visionary powers, he or she was prepared to think of a poem as something separate from the poet's self: objective, free from the quirks of the personal.

### THE 1950s AND THE 1960s: LYRIC MEDITATIONS AND THE "CHILDREN OF MIDAS"

In the 1950s, although there was no dominant prescription for a poem, the short lyric meditation was held in high regard. Avoiding the first person, poets would find an object, a landscape, or an observed encounter that epitomized and clarified their feelings. A poem was the product of retrospection, a gesture of composure following the initial shock or stimulus that provided the occasion for writing. Often composed in intricate stanzas and skillfully rhymed, such a poem deployed its mastery of verse form as one sign of the civilized mind's power to explore, tame, and distill raw experience. Richard Wilbur's verse was especially valued for its speculative neatness, a poise that was often associated with the awareness of the historical values of European culture. It was a time of renewed travel in Europe; there were Fulbright fellowships for American students to study abroad, prizes for writers who wanted to travel and write in Europe. Wilbur and others wrote poems about European art and artifacts and landscapes as a way of testing American experience against the alternative ways of life; for example, they contrasted American Puritanism and its notions of virtue with such complicated pleasures as those embodied in the seventeenth-century sculpted fountain described in Wilbur's *A Baroque Wall-Fountain in the Villa Sciarra*. Unlike the pessimistic Eliot of *The Waste Land*, such poets found the treasures of the past—its art and literature—nourishing in poems whose chief pleasure was that of evaluation and balancing, of weighing such alternatives as spirituality and worldliness.

That was one side of the picture. The other side, equally important, was the way many of these same young poets reacted to (*to*, rather than *against*) their training. Richard Howard, in a happy phrase, calls this postwar generation of poets "the children of Midas." He is thinking of the last phases of the classical myth, when King Midas, having discovered that everything he touches inconveniently turns to gold, prays to lose the gift of the golden touch. "What seems to me especially proper to these poets," Howard says, ". . . is the last development, the longing to *lose* the gift of order, despoiling the self of all that had been, merely, *propriety*." In the 1950s and 1960s there were some very extreme examples of poets transforming themselves: Allen Ginsberg, who began by writing formal quatrains, became the free and rambunctious poet of *Howl*; Sylvia Plath, who began as a well-mannered imitator of Eliot and Dylan Thomas, turned into the intense protagonist of *Ariel* (1966). It is a special mark of this period that a poet as bookish, as literary, as academic as John Berryman, who started out writing like Auden and Yeats, should also have written the wildest and most disquieting lyrics of his time, the *Dream Songs* (1964, 1968).

The new confidence and technical sophistication of American poetry in the 1940s fostered the more exploratory styles of the 1950s and 1960s. Some changes were more noticeable and notorious than others. For one thing, poetry extended its subject matter to more explicit and extreme areas of autobiography: insanity, sex, divorce, and alcoholism. The convenient but not very precise label *confessional* came to be attached to certain books: Robert Lowell's *Life Studies*, which explored the disorders of several generations of his New England family; Anne Sexton's *To Bedlam and Part Way Back* (1960) and *All My Pretty Ones* (1962), which dealt openly with abortion, women's sexuality, the poet's own life in mental hospitals; W. D. Snodgrass's *Heart's Needle* (1969), whose central lyric sequence chronicled the stages of divorce from the point of view of a husband separated from his wife and child; and John Berryman's *Dream Songs*, which exposed his alcoholism and struggle with insanity. Allen Ginsberg's *Howl* celebrated his homosexuality. Sylvia Plath's *Ariel* explored the heightened energies of a woman on the edge.

Some of the poetry of this period was avowedly political, tending in the 1950s to general protest and in the 1960s to more specifically focused critiques. The Beats of the 1950s—with *Howl* as their manifesto—had no one particular object of protest. Their work envisioned freer life-styles and explored underground alternatives to life in a standardized or mechanized society. The pun on the word *beat* linked them on the one side to a downtrodden drifting underground community—drugs, homosexuality, political radicalism—and, on the other, to a new "beatitude," made available by Eastern religious cults, that many members of this generation espoused. Gary Snyder, who in the 1950s was with the Beats in San Francisco, is one example of how their protests were extended and focused in the next decades. In his books of the 1960s and 1970s such as *Earth House Hold* and *Turtle Island*, he dramatizes a very specific alternative to American suburban and urban sprawl: he describes and advocates a life of almost Thoreauvian simplicity in a commune in the Sierras.

Many poets in the 1960s identified themselves with specific reform and protest movements. Denise Levertov, Adrienne Rich, and Robert Lowell, among others, directed poems against American participation in the Vietnam War and our government's support of the corrupt South Vietnam regime. Robert Lowell publicly refused President Johnson's invitation to a White House dinner and was a participant in the 1967 march against the Pentagon, which Norman Mailer describes in *Armies of the Night*. Robert Bly and others used the occasion of receiving poetry prizes to make antiwar statements. The important freedom movements of the 1960s—advocating black power, women's liberation, and gay rights—had supporters among committed poets. Black poets such as Gwendolyn Brooks and LeRoi Jones (later Imamu Amiri Baraka) who had already had considerable success with white audiences, turned to address exclusively black constituencies. Small presses, notably the Broadside Press, were founded for the publication of African-American poets, and others devoted themselves to feminist writing. Some poetry of the late 1960s had the insistence, urgency, and single-mindedness of political tracts. But the more enduring effect of political protest on poetry was to make a broader, more insistent range of voices available to verse; poems dramatized individual predicaments, stressing the underlying angers and desires that also issue in political action. African-American poets experimented in bringing out the distinctive speech rhythms of black English; they stressed the oral values of verse—its openness to song, to angry chant, and to the cadenced complaint of the "blues." With this emphasis on the power of voice, and with their recovery of non-European traditions, especially those of Africa, black poets in the 1960s and 1970s exerted powerful influences on contemporary American poetry. Their work helped to define the increasing importance of oral traditions in poetry of the 1970s and 1980s, and spurred the opening up of American poetry to other, non-European traditions, including those of Native American societies and the Caribbean, Mexico, and Latin America. At the same time the feminist movement made many poets aware of the need for a poetic language to explore the experiences of women hitherto silenced or unrepresented in literature. Among these was Adrienne Rich, whose significantly titled collections *Diving into the Wreck* and *The Dream of a Common Language* suggest the necessity to probe what lies beneath the surface and to forge a language of shared experience.

In an indirect but vital sense the heightened energies of almost all poetry in the 1960s and 1970s had political implications. With the increasing standardization of speech, a documented decline in reading skills in the schools, and the dominance of nationwide television, poems provided a special resource for individual expression, a resistance to the leveling force of official language, and access to profoundly individual areas of consciousness. In that context poets as superficially apolitical as James Wright, W. S. Merwin, Elizabeth Bishop, James Merrill, and John Ashbery were by their very cultivation of private vision making distinctly political choices.

## THE 1950S AND THE 1960S: POETIC FORMS

In response to the pressures, inner and outer, of the 1950s and 1960s, new kinds of poems took their place alongside the favored "objective" poems of the late 1940s. As some poets aimed more at exposing than at composing the self, they demanded more open forms to suggest vagaries, twists, and confusions of mind or else its potential directness and spontaneity. Their poems depended on less rhyme, sparer use of regular stanzas and metrics, even new ways of spacing a poem on the page. Critics talked of "organic" form, using free verse, which took its length of line or its visual form on the page from the poet's provisional or intense feelings at the moment of composition. The most insistent formulations of this attitude are to be found in the manifestos of the so-called Black Mountain school, a group of poets gathered at Black Mountain College in North Carolina and very much influenced by its rector, Charles Olson. Ordinary lineation, straight left-hand margins, and regular meters and verse forms were to be discarded in favor of a placement of lines and phrases that corresponded to the mental and physical energy enlisted to get the words on the page. Olson's purpose was to put the poem in touch—as in certain forms of meditation or yoga—with the body, with an individual poet's natural rhythms, often buried by acquired verbal skills. The poet was not to revise poems to any great extent; he or she might make considerable mental preparation or store up intense feeling before writing, but the poem itself was to represent feeling at the moment of composition. Another corollary of Olson's theories was the notion that a poem was provisional. In contrast to the 1940s model of a poem as a completed and permanent object, a number of poets saw their work as transitory, incomplete, an instrument of passage. Olson himself, of course, saw his *Maximus Poems* as a continually open, lifelong work, whereas other poets, Adrienne Rich and Allen Ginsberg among them, carefully date each of their poems as if to suggest that the feelings involved are peculiarly subject to revision by later experience.

A parallel development—only very loosely related to the San Francisco Beat explosion and Black Mountain manifestos—took place among a group of poets involved with and inspired by the work of nonrepresentational or abstract expressionist painters in New York. The so-called New York school included John Ashbery, Kenneth Koch, James Schuyler, and the figure whose friendship and enthusiasm held them all together, Frank O'Hara. It was O'Hara with his breezy diary poems, almost throwaways, who most typified their belief in the poem as a chronicle of its occasion and of the act of composing it. As O'Hara said in his offhand parody of sober poetic credos, *Personism: A Manifesto* (1959): "The poem is at last between two persons instead of two pages. . . . In all modesty, I confess that it may be the death of literature as we know it."

### THE 1970s AND THE 1980s: CONSOLIDATION, EXPERIMENTATION, AND MULTIPLE TRADITIONS

The 1960s had changed the face of American poetry. For many poets in the 1970s the task seemed not so much to innovate as to consolidate and perhaps reinterpret the achievement of the previous three decades. But a fresh impetus of experimentation and poetic commitment came from poets of minority traditions who gained access to presses and publication in the 1970s and 1980s. A flourishing Latino literature was first disseminated by the publishing house Quinto Sol in the early 1970s, and in the 1980s the Arte Publico Press of Houston published a number of fine writers. We now have available the work of such poets as Denise Chávez, Lucha Corpi, Pat Mora, Alberto Ríos, Ricardo Sanchez, Bernice Zamora, and Lorna Dee Cervantes. In 1983 Joseph Bruhac edited and published an important collection of contemporary Native American poetry, *Songs from This Earth on Turtle's Back*, and several notable volumes of poetry by Native Americans appeared in the late 1970s and 1980s, among them works by Paula Gunn Allen, Joy Harjo, Linda Hogan, and Simon Ortiz. More recently several arresting books have appeared from poets whose backgrounds are Asian-American, including Mei-mei Berssenbrugge, Marilyn Chin, Garret Kaoru Hongo, and Cathy Song. In addition, the resurgence of African-American traditions that fired the 1960s and early 1970s has found diverse and gifted heirs. The legacy of Robert Hayden's historical imagination and formal skill and the dynamic example of Gwendolyn Brooks's continuing evolution as well as Audre Lorde's recovery of the power of African myth are among the resources available to poets like Michael Harper, Rita Dove, and Nathaniel Mackey.

What best characterizes the world of contemporary American poetry is its pluralism and the power of its best poets to absorb a variety of influences. Despite a distressing tendency on the part of some poets and critics to define "schools" of poetry as if they were mutually exclusive, no vital tradition in American poetry is self-enclosed. The finest contemporary poems testify to an enlivening interaction between traditions, affirming the imagination's freedom to draw from many sources. The work of Richard Hugo has been important to both James Welch and

Simon Ortiz, Hawaiian oral traditions find their way into the poetry of W. S. Merwin, Adrienne Rich has taken inspiration from the work of Chicana poets, Gary Snyder draws on Hopi sources, and the presence of Elizabeth Bishop makes itself felt in some of Cathy Song's work. In addition, a significant number of American poets have understood their translations of poetry from other languages, among them Spanish and Russian, as an important aspect of their own work. As the earlier modernists reached out to traditions beyond the Western—Pound to the Chinese ideograph, H. D. to Egyptian and Phoenician myths, and later Charles Olson to Mayan Indian culture—American poets of the past thirty years have been redefining what constitutes *America*.

### THE 1970s AND 1980s: POETIC FORMS

Just as recent poets have turned to alternative traditions for other ways of thinking about the world, they have also explored alternative poetic forms. Traditional verse and metrics have not been left behind but have taken their place among a number of resources, rather than serving as the obligatory models of poetic decorum. The reach of the early modernists in their epic constructions had suggested extensions of poetic possibility, but in the past thirty years poets have sought their own ways to combine an ambition for inclusive structures with their feeling for life's fluidity. The model of the poetic diary or journal has provided one way. Robert Creeley's *Pieces* and *A Day Book* both emphasize the activity of writing rather than the finished work. In a related effort, Robert Lowell said of his *Notebook*, "If I saw something one day, I wrote it that day, or the next, or the next. Things I felt or saw or read were drift to the whirlpool, the squeeze of the sonnet and the loose ravel of blank verse." Adrienne Rich's sequence *Contradictions* also shares this quality of form grounded in an occasion and open to experience.

Sequences of poems provide another way of countering neat closure and emphasizing the complexity of consciousness and fluidity of external life. John Berryman's *Dream Songs*, however strict its stanzaic form and use of rhyme, has enormous flexibility of voice and rich varied exposures of the self, and Robert Hayden's *Elegies for Paradise Valley*, from his final book, *American Journal*, creates through a related series of instants the whole sweep of a particular time and place and reveals his deepest origins. Other poets have conceived of part of their work as ongoing sequences to which they continue to add over the years. This is how Robert Duncan understood his *The Structure of Rime* and *Passages* and how Gary Snyder understands his *Mountains and Rivers Without End*, begun in the 1960s.

Long poems provide still another alternative to the lyric. James Merrill's series of three book-length *Divine Comedies*, and the coda that followed, were a sign that poetic ambition was taking a new direction. Before his death in February 1988, Duncan completed the collection of later poems, which had been gestating for twenty years: *Ground Work: Before the War* and *Ground Work II: In the Dark*. Both, he wrote in a poem, "underwrite the grand design." In a younger generation, Rita Dove's book-length sequence *Thomas and Beulah* shows a poet finding her own way to render the larger scope of time, place, and social movements through a series of particular instants. Many American poets do not want to think of their work as the fragments of modern literature. They perhaps remember that Whitman desired to put the whole of America into *Leaves of Grass*, or that Wallace Stevens, whose first published volume was *Harmonium*, wanted to call his collected poems *The Whole of Harmonium*. As poetry has moved away from the single lyrics of the immediate postwar period, shorter poetic efforts open into larger constructions, and the rigid boundary between poetry and prose often dissolves. Oral traditions, with an emphasis on storytelling and on repetition and variation, often refute generic categories, whereas the work of John Ashbery; the interconnected essays and poems of "Language" poets like Charles Bernstein, Michael Palmer, and

Susan Howe; or the "talk poems" of performance artists like David Antin challenge definitions of poetry restricted to the enclosed lyric. The contemporary interest in longer poems or related series of poems lies not in an effort to create an "objective correlative" for a small, poetic truth. Rather, these poets seek an extended power that presents particular and diverse models of the mind's continuing struggle for insight and of the rich and mysterious interaction between language and the world.

### CONTEMPORARY POETRY: ABSENCES AND PRESENCES

The distinctive work of individual writers who constitute a literary period makes all generalizations provisional. Remarkable poems often come from poets who simply pursue their own course. The example of Elizabeth Bishop comes to mind—her work includes no extended sequences, no epic structures, simply a body of dazzling poems. In addition, the living world of contemporary poetry changes: new poets emerge, and existing poets, previously inaccessible or neglected, make themselves heard. The work of younger poets teaches us not only to reread and reevaluate the great modernists but also to return to the work of poets like Louis Zukofsky, Charles Reznikoff, George Oppen, and Lorine Niedecker and others who were read only by small audiences in the 1950s and 1960s and who have been largely ignored in classrooms since.

The landscape of American poetry in the 1990s is marked by absences—there were no new poems from Robert Lowell or Elizabeth Bishop, both of whom died between 1975 and 1980. James Wright and Richard Hugo, two of the strongest heirs of Theodore Roethke's "western" romanticism, both died in the early 1980s as did one of the most influential members of the San Francisco Renaissance, Robert Duncan, and one of our finest African-American poets, Robert Hayden. The late 1980s also saw the death of Robert Penn Warren, who wrote poems of blazing vitality into his own eighth decade, reminding us (as he once wrote) that "in the heart's last kingdom only the old are young." Yet essential poets whose careers span the period from the 1950s to the present continue to do innovative work, at times reminding us of how the shape of a career can change before our eyes. Denise Levertov continues to demonstrate her distinctive ability to write poems of both sensual and visionary power in *Breathing the Water* and *A Door in the Hive*; A. R. Ammons continues to discover provisional forms true to the motion that, for him, characterizes life. James Merrill, already known for his shorter lyrics of "love and loss," gathered these and other strengths into a trilogy of epics and new cosmologies, *The Changing Light at Sandover*, and John Ashbery's work retains its fresh and surprising investigation of language and of an inner life. Robert Creeley's most recent work shows him exploring the ways memory invades the present, while W. S. Merwin and Gary Snyder in their strong recent books bring to bear not only personal memory but a larger ecological consciousness of the earth's losses. Many of our best poets have found ways both to witness pressing contemporary issues and to open up new possibilities of language. Until her death in 1992, Audre Lorde's work offered one model of such explorations; the work of Gwendolyn Brooks, Adrienne Rich, and Philip Levine continues to offer others. Indeed, the work of many of these poets in the late 1980s and early 1990s seems only to grow in power, as Rich's *Time's Power* and *An Atlas of the Difficult World*, Ashbery's *Flow Chart*, or Levine's *A Walk with Thomas Jefferson* and *What Work Is* amply demonstrate. The connections between poetry and cultural criticism are also deepened by many of the poets of a younger generation represented in this book, including Simon Ortiz, Rita Dove, and Lorna Dee Cervantes. And an important and lively group of writers, most often grouped together under the rubric Language poets, is producing experimental work that both exposes and unsettles some of the ways language shapes our selves and our world.

There are, of course, other important poets who deserve our attention after years of distinguished writing. One thinks of Charles Bernstein, Olga Broumas, Hayden

Carruth, Mona Van Duyn, Michael Harper, Donald Justice, Galway Kinnell, Jerome Rothenberg, and Diane Wakoski, to name only a few. A younger generation also promises poets whose work will sustain us in years to come: Rita Dove, Jorie Graham, Joy Harjo, Robert Hass, Susan Howe, Li-Young Lee, Nathaniel Mackey, Sandra McPherson, Sharon Olds, Simon Ortiz, Alberto Ríos, Michael Palmer, Charles Simic, Dave Smith, Cathy Song, Gary Soto, C. K. Williams, and Sherley Williams provide only a partial list. No group of selections definitively represents a contemporary period still in the process of shaping itself. As much as we can delight in the work of the poets represented here, whose poems witness the strength and variety of American poetry since 1945, we need to keep listening for other voices: those we have not yet understood or have neglected, and those that are just emerging. Meanwhile, the poets whose work appears in the following pages are diverse. They represent three generations, come from various backgrounds and regions of the country, and often work in very different styles. But they each have as a touchstone a vital, imaginative use of language, and in reading them our sense of poetry's rich possibilities quickens.

# ROBERT PENN WARREN
## 1905–1989

In 1969, with a long, distinguished career as a man of letters already behind him, Robert Penn Warren published his long poem *Audubon: A Vision*, the book that announced that here was a major poet. Although Warren wrote poetry throughout his life, until the 1960s he was best known for his fiction. In the six books of poetry that followed *Audubon*, Warren laid claim to a powerful, distinctive, American voice. The distinguishing mark of Warren's poetry is passion, a passion directed toward the physical world and toward a knowledge of truth. He is a poet full of yearning for more, more than what life usually discloses, yet an intense love for the world accompanies this yearning.

Warren was born in 1905 in Guthrie in southern Kentucky, and much of his writing reflects his engagement with the lessons of history as they can be read in the experience of the American South. He took this sense of history most immediately from his father, who read history and poetry aloud to the family, and from his maternal grandfather, Gabriel Telemachus Penn. Warren spent his boyhood summers on this grandfather's isolated tobacco farm. There the old man, who fought on the Confederate side in the Civil War, told Warren tales of war while the two mapped out battles together, or the boy listened while his grandfather recited poetry "by the yard," especially Sir Walter Scott and Robert Burns. The memory of an idyllic boyhood spent dreaming amid the natural world informs many of Warren's poems, among them *American Portrait: Old Style* where he returns, in his seventies, to visit both the place of that boyhood and his childhood friend, K.

The decisive literary moment in Warren's life came when, at the age of sixteen, he enrolled at Vanderbilt University in Nashville. He had wanted to be a naval officer but an eye injury prevented him from taking up his commission at Annapolis. Vanderbilt was enjoying a feverish interest in poetry at the time. (Even football players, Warren reported, seemed to be writing verse, and Warren remembers that people lined up for the latest issues of the *Dial* and other literary periodicals in which they might find new work by Yeats or Eliot or Hart Crane.) Part of the excitement was due to the presence of the poet John Crowe Ransom, who taught

Warren's freshman composition class and soon involved him, even as an undergraduate, with the Fugitives, a group of faculty members and "bookish, intelligent young businessmen" who met to discuss literature and philosophy. By the time Warren joined, it was largely a poetry club at which Ransom and others read and criticized one another's work. It was here that Warren met Allen Tate, the gifted poet and critic, who found the redheaded undergraduate, five years his junior, "the most gifted person I have ever known." For years to come they constituted a kind of southern axis in American letters and in 1930 joined several other southern writers in a political manifesto, *I'll Take My Stand.* The collection of twelve essays envisioned an agrarian South with strong local cultures as the only humane alternative to an increasingly self-destructive industrialism centered in the North.

Warren attended graduate school at the University of California, at Yale, and then as a Rhodes Scholar at Oxford University in England. From 1935 to 1942 he was on the English faculty at Louisiana State University. Along with Cleanth Brooks and Charles W. Pipkin, he was the founder there of the *Southern Review,* which for the seven years of their involvement was the most influential literary quarterly in the country. It was the principal forum for pioneering interpretative essays by "New Critics" such as Ransom, Kenneth Burke, and R. P. Blackmur. (Brooks and Warren were also the editors of *Understanding Poetry,* the important school anthology and text that introduced students to "close reading" on New Critical principles.) In addition, *Southern Review* published the best fiction by emerging southern writers such as Katherine Anne Porter and Eudora Welty.

Warren's own fiction brought him wide critical attention in the 1940s. *All the King's Men* (1946), which was conceived as a verse play before it became a novel, won the Pulitzer Prize and later became a film. It portrayed the rise and fall of a southern demagogue who closely resembled Huey Long, the Louisiana governor and senator who was assassinated in the rotunda of the Louisiana statehouse in 1935. Warren's interest was in showing the tangled motives of his protagonist Willie Stark, a depression governor, who led a regime both corrupt and yet progressive in its social programs. In choosing violent subjects with historical and psychological resonance, Warren's fiction anticipates the focus of his sequence *Audubon.* Other novels like *World Enough and Time* (1950), set in the Kentucky of the 1820s, are based on documents and grow out of his ongoing study of and response to the history of the South.

For ten years, from 1944 to 1954, Warren was intensely active in fiction, and published almost no poems. In 1952 he married the writer Eleanor Clark, his second wife, and prompted by the landscapes where they lived in Europe and by the birth of a son and daughter in the mid-1950s, he returned to poetry with a new intimacy and autobiographical intensity. His earlier work had been strongly influenced by the formal control and the elegant, well-mannered rationality of John Crowe Ransom's verse. But beginning with the volume *Promises* (1957), and revealed fully in *Audubon,* Warren's poetic line loosened up, moved with vigor and rawenergy. Although the tone of his poems sometimes grows too insistent or rhetorical, his muscular syntax and rhythm forged a "voice-instrument calibrated to experience," in the words of Dave Smith, a poet of a younger generation, indebted to Warren's work.

In *Democracy and Poetry* (1975), his Jefferson Lecture in the Humanities, Warren said, "What poetry most significantly celebrates is the capacity of man to face the deep, dark inwardness of his nature and fate." In his book-length poem *Audubon: A Vision,* Warren's version of the historical John James Audubon must enter what Yeats once called "the abyss of the self" to create an heroic selfhood at the center of the poetry. Ornithologist and painter of *Birds of America,* Audubon (1785–1851) was artist and scientist, solitary searcher and classifier, consumed by his tasks. Basing part of his poem on Audubon's autobiographical account, Warren imagines a man launched into his true vision after an encounter with a violence at the heart of experience: he narrowly escapes being robbed and murdered in the wilderness by a crone and her sons. In this incident Audubon must also confront the violent desire of his own "lust of the eye" and thereby reconcile in himself the need for both passion and reverence toward existence. Passion directs Warren's hero to slay the birds in order to paint them, to put them "In our imagination" (*Audubon* VI, "Love and Knowledge"). But reverence demands the heart's total response to the beauty of existence itself. This is why Warren commands his hero and himself: "Continue to walk in the world. Yes, love it!" While the most representative figure in Warren's poems is solitary—the individual, like Audubon, confronting versions of the American sublime—Warren has also written a number of fine poems in other registers, among them some moving love poems, such as *After the Dinner Party* and *The Birth of Love*. The sense of history that animates so much of his fiction has become, in his poems, the persistent struggle of memory to overcome the passage of time, to make *then* into *now*, as reflected in the title of his volume *Now and Then: Poems 1976–1978* (1978). The struggle with time is one aspect of the heroic engagement with existence, which is the dramatic center of Warren's work. Until his death in 1989, he continued to write poems of passion and vigor.

## From Audubon[1]

### I. Was Not the Lost Dauphin

[A]

Was not the lost dauphin, though handsome was only
Base-born and not even able
To make a decent living, was only
Himself, Jean Jacques, and his passion—what
Is man but his passion?                                                                 5

                  Saw,
Eastward and over the cypress swamp, the dawn,
Redder than meat, break;
And the large bird,
Long neck outthrust, wings crooked to scull air, moved             10
In a slow calligraphy, crank, flat, and black against
The color of God's blood spilt, as though
Pulled by a string.

              Saw
It proceed across the inflamed distance.                                      15

Moccasins set in hoar frost, eyes fixed on the bird,
Thought: "On that sky it is black."
Thought: "In my mind it is white."
Thinking: "*Ardea occidentalis*, heron, the great one."

---

1. Jean-Jacques Audubon (1785–1851), natural son of French parents, but later an American citizen. Painter, ornithologist, Kentucky settler, he dedicated his life to the pursuit, classification, and depiction of the *Birds of* *America* (first published in England, 1827). Among the stories told about his birth was one (false) that he was the Dauphin, the son of the dethroned Louis XVI and Marie Antoinette of France.

Dawn: his heart shook in the tension of the world.                    20

Dawn: and what is your passion?

[B]

October: and the bear,
Daft in the honey-light, yawns.

The bear's tongue, pink as a baby's, out-crisps to the curled tip,
It bleeds the black blood of the blueberry.                    25

The teeth are more importantly white
Than has ever been imagined.

The bear feels his own fat
Sweeten, like a drowse, deep to the bone.

Bemused, above the fume of ruined blueberries,                    30
The last bee hums.

The wings, like mica, glint
In the sunlight.

He leans on his gun. Thinks
How thin is the membrane between himself and the world.                    35

### VI. *Love and Knowledge*

Their footless dance
Is of the beautiful liability of their nature.
Their eyes are round, boldly convex, bright as a jewel,
And merciless. They do not know
Compassion, and if they did,                    5
We should not be worthy of it. They fly
In air that glitters like fluent crystal
And is hard as perfectly transparent iron, they cleave it
With no effort. They cry
In a tongue multitudinous, often like music.                    10

He slew them, at surprising distances, with his gun.
Over a body held in his hand, his head was bowed low,
But not in grief.

He put them where they are, and there we see them:
In our imagination.                    15

What is love?

Our name for it is knowledge.

## VII. *Tell Me a Story*

### [A]

Long ago, in Kentucky, I, a boy, stood
By a dirt road, in first dark, and heard
The great geese hoot northward.

I could not see them, there being no moon
And the stars sparse. I heard them.                          5

I did not know what was happening in my heart.

It was the season before the elderberry blooms,
Therefore they were going north.

The sound was passing northward.

### [B]

Tell me a story.                                             10

In this century, and moment, of mania,
Tell me a story.

Make it a story of great distances, and starlight.

The name of the story will be Time,
But you must not pronounce its name.                         15

Tell me a story of deep delight.

1969

# Acquaintance with Time in Early Autumn

Never—yes, never—before these months just passed
Had I known the nature of Time, and felt its strong heart,
Stroke by stroke, against my own, like love,
But love without face, or shape, or history—
Pure Being that, by being, our being denies.                 5

Summer fulfills the field, the heart, the womb,
While summerlong, infinitesimally,
Leaf stem, at bough-juncture, dries,
Even as our tireless bodies plunge,
With delicious muscular flexion and heart's hilarity,        10
White to the black ammoniac purity of
A mountain pool. But black
Is blue as it stares up at summer's depthless azure,
And azure was what we saw beneath

At the timeless instant hanging                                    15
At arc-height.

Voices of joy how distant seem!
I float, pubic hair awash, and gaze
At one lone leaf, flame-red—the first—alone
Above summer's bulge of green,                                     20
High-hung against the sky.

Yes, sky was blue, but water, I suddenly felt,
Was black, and striped with cold, and one cold claw
Reached ghostly up
To find my flesh, to pierce                                        25
The heart, as though
Releasing, in that dark inwardness,
A single drop. Oh, leaf,

Cling on! For I have felt knee creak on stair,
And sometimes, dancing, notice how rarely                          30
A girl's inner thigh will brush my own,
Like a dream. Whose dream?

The sun
Pours down on the leaf its lacquer of Chinese red.

Then, in the lucent emptiness,                                     35
While cries of joy of companions fade,
I feel that I see, even in
The golden paradox of air unmoving
Each tendon of that stem, by its own will,
Release                                                            40
Its tiny claw-hooks, and trust
A shining destiny. The leaf—it is
Too moorless not to fall. But
Does not. Minutely,
It slides—calm, calm—along the air sidewise,                      45
Sustained by the kiss of under-air.

While ages pass, I watch the red-gold leaf,
Sunlit, descend to water I know is black.
It touches. Breath
Comes back, and I hate God                                         50
As much as gravity or the great globe's tilt.

How shall we know the astrolabe[1] of joy?
Shall gratitude run forward as well as back?
Who once would have thought that the heart,
Still ravening on the world's provocation and beauty, might,       55
After time long lost

---

1. Old instrument for observing and calculating the position of heavenly bodies.

In the tangled briars of youth,
Have picked today as payday, the payment

In life's dime-thin, thumb-worn, two-sided, two-faced coin?

1980

# Mortal Limit

I saw the hawk ride updraft in the sunset over Wyoming.
It rose from coniferous darkness, past gray jags
Of mercilessness, past whiteness, into the gloaming
Of dream-spectral light above the last purity of snow-snags.

There—west—were the Tetons.[1] Snow-peaks would soon be          5
In dark profile to break constellations. Beyond what height
Hangs now the black speck? Beyond what range will gold eyes see
New ranges rise to mark a last scrawl of light?

Or, having tasted that atmosphere's thinness, does it
Hang motionless in dying vision before                            10
It knows it will accept the mortal limit,
And swing into the great circular downwardness that will restore

The breath of earth? Of rock? Of rot? Of other such
Items, and the darkness of whatever dream we clutch?

1985

# Little Girl Wakes Early

Remember when you were the first one awake, the first
To stir in the dawn-curdled house, with little bare feet
Cold on boards, every door shut and accurst,
And behind shut doors no breath perhaps drew, no heart beat.

You held your breath and thought how all over town          5
Houses had doors shut, and no whisper of breath sleeping,
And that meant no swinging, nobody to pump up and down,
No hide-and-go-seek, no serious play at housekeeping.

So you ran outdoors, bare feet from the dew wet,
And climbed the fence to the house of your dearest friend,     10
And opened your lips and twisted your tongue, all set
To call her name—but the sound wouldn't come in the end,

For you thought how awful, if there was no breath there
For answer. Tears start, you run home, where now mother,

---

1. High mountain range in northwest Wyoming.

Over the stove, is humming some favorite air.                                    15
You seize her around the legs, but tears aren't over,

And won't get over, not even when she shakes you—
And shakes you hard—and more when you can't explain.
Your mother's long dead. And you've learned that when loneliness takes
     you
There's nobody ever to explain to—though you try again and again.        20

                                                                         1985

## After the Dinner Party

You two sit at the table late, each, now and then,
Twirling a near-empty wine glass to watch the last red
Liquid climb up the crystalline spin to the last moment when
Centrifugality fails: with nothing now said.

What is left to say when the last logs sag and wink?                      5
The dark outside is streaked with the casual snowflake
Of winter's demise, all guests long gone home, and you think
Of others who never again can come to partake

Of food, wine, laughter, and philosophy—
Though tonight one guest has quoted a killing phrase we owe               10
To a lost one whose grin, in eternal atrophy,
Now in dark celebrates some last unworded jest none can know.

Now a chair scrapes, sudden, on tiles, and one of you
Moves soundless, as in hypnotic certainty,
The length of table. Stands there a moment or two,                        15
Then sits, reaches out a hand, open and empty.

How long it seems till a hand finds that hand there laid,
While ash, still glowing, crumbles, and silence is such
That the crumbling of ash is audible. Now naught's left unsaid
Of the old heart-concerns, the last, tonight, which                       20

Had been of the absent children, whose bright gaze
Over-arches the future's horizon, in the mist of your prayers.
The last log is black, while ash beneath displays
No last glow. You snuff candles. Soon the old stairs

Will creak with your grave and synchronized tread as each mounts         25
To a briefness of light, then true weight of darkness, and then
That heart-dimness in which neither joy nor sorrow counts.
Even so, one hand gropes out for another, again.

                                                                         1985

# THEODORE ROETHKE
## 1908–1963

Theodore Roethke had the kind of childhood a poet might have invented. He was born in Saginaw, Michigan, where both his German grandfather and his father kept greenhouses for a living. The greenhouse world, he later said, represented for him "both heaven and hell, a kind of tropics created in the savage climate of Michigan, where austere German-Americans turned their love of order and their terrifying efficiency into something truly beautiful." Throughout his life he was haunted both by the ordered, protected world of the greenhouse—the constant activity of growth, the cultivated flowers—and by the desolate landscape of his part of Michigan. "The marsh, the mire, the Void, is always there, immediate and terrifying. It is a splendid place for schooling the spirit. It is America."

Roethke's poetry often reenacted this "schooling" of the spirit by revisiting the landscapes of his childhood: the nature poems that make up the largest part of his early work try to bridge the distance between a child's consciousness and the adult mysteries presided over by his father. Roethke arranged and rearranged these poems to give the sense of a spiritual autobiography, especially in preparing the volumes *The Lost Son* (1948), *Praise to the End!* (1951), and *The Waking* (1953). The greenhouse world emerged as a "reality harsher than reality," the cultivator's activity pulsating and threatening. Its overseers, like "Frau Bauman, Frau Schmidt, and Frau Schwartze," emerge as gods, fates, muses, and witches all in one. It was by focusing on the minute processes of botanical growth—the rooting, the budding—that the poet found a way of participating in the mysteries of this once alien world, "alive in a slippery grave."

In his books *The Lost Son and Other Poems* and *Praise to the End!* Roethke explored the regenerative possibilities of prerational speech (like children's riddles) in which language as sound recaptures nonlogical states of being. In these poems, his most dazzling and original work, Roethke opened up the possibilities of language. One of the sections of the long poem *The Lost Son* is called "The Gibber," a pun, because the word means both a meaningless utterance and the pouch at the base of the calyx of a flower. The pun identifies principles of growth with the possibilities of speech freed from logical meanings, and the sequence as a whole suggests the power of both nature and language to revive the spirit of an adult life: "A lively understandable spirit / Once entertained you. / It will come again. / Be still. / Wait."

If the nature poems of Roethke's first four books explore the anxieties with him since childhood, his later love poems show him in periods of release and momentary pleasure:

> And I dance round and round,
> A fond and foolish man,
> And see and suffer myself
> In another being at last.

The love poems, many of them included in *Words for the Wind* (1958) and *The Far Field* (1964), are among the most appealing in modern American verse. They stand in sharp relief to the suffering Roethke experienced in other areas of his personal life—several mental breakdowns and periods of alcoholism—which led to a premature death. *The Far Field*, a posthumous volume, includes fierce, strongly rhymed lyrics in which Roethke tried "bare, even terrible statement," pressing toward the threshold of spiritual insight:

> A man goes far to find out what he is—
> Death of the self in a long, tearless night,
> All natural shapes blazing unnatural light.

The nature poems of this last volume, gathered as "The North American Sequence" (from which the title poem of the book, *The Far Field*, is taken) use extended landscape to find natural analogies for the human passage toward the dark unknown, hoping "in their rhythms to catch the very movement of mind itself."

Roethke is remembered as one of the great teachers of poetry, especially by those young poets and critics who studied with him at the University of Washington from 1948 until the time of his death in 1963. James Wright, David Wagoner, and Richard Hugo, among others, attended his classes. He was noted for his mastery of sound and metrics. Although his own poetry was intensely personal, his starting advice to students always deemphasized undisciplined self-expression. "Write like someone else," was his instruction to beginners. In Roethke's own career, however, this advice had its costs. His apprenticeship to Yeats, in particular, endangered his own poetic voice; in some late poems the echo of this great predecessor makes Roethke all but inaudible.

Roethke was much honored later in his career: a Pulitzer Prize for *The Waking* (1953); a National Book Award and Bollingen Prize for the collected poems, *Words for the Wind* (1958); and a posthumous National Book Award for *The Far Field* (1964).

## Cuttings

> Sticks-in-a-drowse droop over sugary loam,
> Their intricate stem-fur dries;
> But still the delicate slips keep coaxing up water;
> The small cells bulge;
>
> One nub of growth        5
> Nudges a sand-crumb loose,
> Pokes through a musty sheath
> Its pale tendrilous horn.

1948

## Cuttings

### *(later)*

> This urge, wrestle, resurrection of dry sticks,
> Cut stems struggling to put down feet,
> What saint strained so much,
> Rose on such lopped limbs to a new life?
>
> I can hear, underground, that sucking and sobbing,       5
> In my veins, in my bones I feel it,—
> The small waters seeping upward,
> The tight grains parting at last.

When sprouts break out,
Slippery as fish                                                    10
I quail, lean to beginnings, sheath-wet.

1948


# Frau Bauman, Frau Schmidt, and Frau Schwartze[1]

Gone the three ancient ladies
Who creaked on the greenhouse ladders,
Reaching up white strings
To wind, to wind
The sweet-pea tendrils, the smilax,                                 5
Nasturtiums, the climbing
Roses, to straighten
Carnations, red
Chrysanthemums; the stiff
Stems, jointed like corn,                                           10
They tied and tucked,—
These nurses of nobody else.
Quicker than birds, they dipped
Up and sifted the dirt;
They sprinkled and shook;                                           15
They stood astride pipes,
Their skirts billowing out wide into tents,
Their hands twinkling with wet;
Like witches they flew along rows
Keeping creation at ease;                                           20
With a tendril for needle
They sewed up the air with a stem;
They teased out the seed that the cold kept asleep,—
All the coils, loops, and whorls.
They trellised the sun; they plotted for more than themselves.      25

I remember how they picked me up, a spindly kid,
Pinching and poking my thin ribs
Till I lay in their laps, laughing,
Weak as a whiffet;[2]
Now, when I'm alone and cold in my bed,                             30
They still hover over me,
These ancient leathery crones,
With their bandannas stiffened with sweat,
And their thorn-bitten wrists,
And their snuff-laden breath blowing lightly over me in my first sleep.   35

1948

---

1. Women who worked in the greenhouse owned by    2. A small, young, or unimportant person (probably
Roethke's father.                                   from *whippet*, a small dog).

# My Papa's Waltz

The whiskey on your breath
Could make a small boy dizzy;
But I hung on like death:
Such waltzing was not easy.

We romped until the pans                    5
Slid from the kitchen shelf;
My mother's countenance
Could not unfrown itself.

The hand that held my wrist
Was battered on one knuckle;                 10
At every step you missed
My right ear scraped a buckle.

You beat time on my head
With a palm caked hard by dirt,
Then waltzed me off to bed                   15
Still clinging to your shirt.

1948

# Night Crow

When I saw that clumsy crow
Flap from a wasted tree,
A shape in the mind rose up:
Over the gulfs of dream
Flew a tremendous bird                       5
Further and further away
Into a moonless black,
Deep in the brain, far back.

1948

# I Knew a Woman

I knew a woman, lovely in her bones,
When small birds sighed, she would sigh back at them;
Ah, when she moved, she moved more ways than one:
The shapes a bright container can contain!
Of her choice virtues only gods should speak,          5
Or English poets who grew up on Greek
(I'd have them sing in chorus, cheek to cheek).

How well her wishes went! She stroked my chin,
She taught me Turn, and Counter-turn, and Stand;[1]

1. Parts of a Pindaric ode.

She taught me Touch, that undulant white skin;                    10
I nibbled meekly from her proffered hand;
She was the sickle; I, poor I, the rake,
Coming behind her for her pretty sake
(But what prodigious mowing we did make).

Love likes a gander, and adores a goose:                          15
Her full lips pursed, the errant note to seize;
She played it quick, she played it light and loose;
My eyes, they dazzled at her flowing knees;
Her several parts could keep a pure repose,
Or one hip quiver with a mobile nose                              20
(She moved in circles, and those circles moved).

Let seed be grass, and grass turn into hay:
I'm martyr to a motion not my own;
What's freedom for? To know eternity.
I swear she cast a shadow white as stone.                         25
But who would count eternity in days?
These old bones live to learn her wanton ways:
(I measure time by how a body sways).

                                                              1958


# The Far Field[1]

## 1

I dream of journeys repeatedly:
Of flying like a bat deep into a narrowing tunnel,
Of driving alone, without luggage, out a long peninsula,
The road lined with snow-laden second growth,
A fine dry snow ticking the windshield,                            5
Alternate snow and sleet, no on-coming traffic,
And no lights behind, in the blurred side-mirror,
The road changing from glazed tarface to a rubble of stone,
Ending at last in a hopeless sand-rut,
Where the car stalls,                                             10
Churning in a snowdrift
Until the headlights darken.

## 2

At the field's end, in the corner missed by the mower,
Where the turf drops off into a grass-hidden culvert,
Haunt of the cat-bird, nesting-place of the field-mouse,          15
Not too far away from the ever-changing flower-dump,
Among the tin cans, tires, rusted pipes, broken machinery,—
One learned of the eternal;

---

1. The penultimate of six poems in Roethke's "North American Sequence" from the book *The Far Field*.

And in the shrunken face of a dead rat, eaten by rain and ground-beetles
(I found it lying among the rubble of an old coal bin)                          20
And the tom-cat, caught near the pheasant-run,
Its entrails strewn over the half-grown flowers,
Blasted to death by the night watchman.

I suffered for birds, for young rabbits caught in the mower,
My grief was not excessive.                                                     25
For to come upon warblers in early May
Was to forget time and death:
How they filled the oriole's elm, a twittering restless cloud, all one morning,
And I watched and watched till my eyes blurred from the bird shapes,—
Cape May, Blackburnian, Cerulean,[2]—                                          30
Moving, elusive as fish, fearless,
Hanging, bunched like young fruit, bending the end branches,
Still for a moment,
Then pitching away in half-flight,
Lighter than finches,                                                          35
While the wrens bickered and sang in the half-green hedgerows,
And the flicker[3] drummed from his dead tree in the chicken-yard.

—Or to lie naked in sand,
In the silted shallows of a slow river,
Fingering a shell,
Thinking:                                                                      40
Once I was something like this, mindless,
Or perhaps with another mind, less peculiar;
Or to sink down to the hips in a mossy quagmire;
Or, with skinny knees, to sit astride a wet log,                               45
Believing:
I'll return again,
As a snake or a raucous bird,
Or, with luck, as a lion.

I learned not to fear infinity,                                                50
The far field, the windy cliffs of forever,
The dying of time in the white light of tomorrow,
The wheel turning away from itself,
The sprawl of the wave,
The on-coming water.                                                          55

3

The river turns on itself,
The tree retreats into its own shadow.
I feel a weightless change, a moving forward
As of water quickening before a narrowing channel
When banks converge, and the wide river whitens;                               60
Or when two rivers combine, the blue glacial torrent
And the yellowish-green from the mountainy upland,—

2. Types of warblers.                    3. A kind of woodpecker.

At first a swift rippling between rocks,
Then a long running over flat stones
Before descending to the alluvial plain,                            65
To the clay banks, and the wild grapes hanging from the elmtrees.
The slightly trembling water
Dropping a fine yellow silt where the sun stays;
And the crabs bask near the edge,
The weedy edge, alive with small snakes and bloodsuckers,—          70

I have come to a still, but not a deep center,
A point outside the glittering current;
My eyes stare at the bottom of a river,
At the irregular stones, iridescent sandgrains,
My mind moves in more than one place,                              75
In a country half-land, half-water.

I am renewed by death, thought of my death,
The dry scent of a dying garden in September,
The wind fanning the ash of a low fire.
What I love is near at hand,                                       80
Always, in earth and air.


                              4

The lost self changes,
Turning toward the sea,
A sea-shape turning around,—
An old man with his feet before the fire,                         85
In robes of green, in garments of adieu.

A man faced with his own immensity
Wakes all the waves, all their loose wandering fire.
The murmur of the absolute, the why
Of being born falls on his naked ears.                            90
His spirit moves like monumental wind
That gentles on a sunny blue plateau.
He is the end of things, the final man.

All finite things reveal infinitude:
The mountain with its singular bright shade                       95
Like the blue shine on freshly frozen snow,
The after-light upon ice-burdened pines;
Odor of basswood on a mountain-slope,
A scent beloved of bees;
Silence of water above a sunken tree:                            100
The pure serene of memory in one man,—
A ripple widening from a single stone
Winding around the waters of the world.

                                              1964

## Wish for a Young Wife

My lizard, my lively writher,
May your limbs never wither,
May the eyes in your face
Survive the green ice
Of envy's mean gaze;                                    5
May you live out your life
Without hate, without grief,
And your hair ever blaze,
In the sun, in the sun,
When I am undone,                                       10
When I am no one.

1964

## In a Dark Time

In a dark time, the eye begins to see,
I meet my shadow in the deepening shade;
I hear my echo in the echoing wood—
A lord of nature weeping to a tree.
I live between the heron and the wren,                  5
Beasts of the hill and serpents of the den.

What's madness but nobility of soul
At odds with circumstance? The day's on fire!
I know the purity of pure despair,
My shadow pinned against a sweating wall.               10
That place among the rocks—is it a cave,
Or winding path? The edge is what I have.

A steady storm of correspondences!
A night flowing with birds, a ragged moon,
And in broad day the midnight come again!               15
A man goes far to find out what he is—
Death of the self in a long, tearless night,
All natural shapes blazing unnatural light.

Dark, dark my light, and darker my desire.
My soul, like some heat-maddened summer fly,            20
Keeps buzzing at the sill. Which I is I?
A fallen man, I climb out of my fear.
The mind enters itself, and God the mind,
And one is One, free in the tearing wind.

1964

# CHARLES OLSON

## 1910–1970

Writing of the sense of place in Charles Olson's poems, Robert Creeley says, "In short, the world is not separable, and we *are* in it." Being in the world, for Olson, meant experiencing it as present; for him, what happens in a poem happens now. Art, he said, "does not seek to describe but to enact." In an influential essay, *Projective Verse*, he rejected the partitioning of reality that separates the human from the natural world. His aim, he wrote, was to get "rid of the lyrical interference of the individual as ego, of the 'subject' and his soul, that peculiar presumption by which western man has interposed himself between what he is as a creature of nature . . . and those other creations of nature." To read Olson is to enter a critical and theoretical force field made up of his essays, lectures, and poems. His ultimate concern was reimagining the world, returning language (as Creeley writes) "to its place *in* experience." Although this ambition is inconsistently realized in Olson's poems, it directed his lifelong effort. And in this effort he was an extraordinarily influential figure for a group of poets whose work was beginning to be known in the 1950s, among them Creeley, Denise Levertov, and Robert Duncan.

Olson's influence grew out of his years at Black Mountain, an experimental college in North Carolina where he had served as an instructor and then as head or rector, succeeding the artist Josef Albers. In its flourishing years under the direction of Olson, the college included among its teachers and students key figures of the avant-garde: John Cage in music, Merce Cunningham in dance, Franz Kline and Robert Rauschenberg in painting. Just before going to Black Mountain, Olson published a critical study of Herman Melville and *Moby-Dick*, *Call Me Ishmael* (1947), which declared his new independence of the formal academic systems. (He had been, as he put it, "uneducated" at Wesleyan, Yale, and Harvard, had taught at Clark University in Worcester, Massachusetts, and had taken an advanced degree in American Civilization at Harvard.) *Call Me Ishmael*, unlike most literary studies, was fiercely personal and unorthodox—almost a prose poem proclaiming new bearings in American literature, especially the symbolic importance of the Pacific, the "unwarped primal world" that, according to the poet, was the true center of the American experience.

Olson claimed that "the substances of history now useful lie outside, under, right here, anywhere but in the direct continuum of society as we have had it." Therefore his own work, as he makes clear in *The Kingfishers*, sharply cultivates the primitive sources of energy almost buried by civilized responses and instruments. As a sometime archaeologist, Olson "hunted among stones." He studied earlier North American cultures and worked among the Mayan ruins in the Yucatán, trying to recover the living elements of an archaic way of life. For Olson, the imagination of ancient cultures exists in the present as much as does a walk down the street in one's native town.

In his lifetime poetic project, the Maximus poems, Olson sought to do for his own life what the anthropologist does for a lost civilization; he aimed at recapturing or reinstating lost links to the unconscious sources of his being. Ezra Pound's *Cantos*, with their mosaic of disjoined and recurrent images, provided a formal model, but in Olson's eyes, Pound was too devoted to reviving the values of European culture. The Maximus poems were designed to capture the mythical spirit of place—the fishing town of Gloucester, Massachusetts, where Olson grew up in a neighborhood called Dogtown. Maximus is an enlarged version of its author. The facts of Olson's own life in Gloucester (including perhaps even a joking allusion in the name Maximus to the fact that Olson was six foot eight) are used as a point of departure for an ambitious effort to project the entire historical, geological, and social presence of the town. Through the heightened awareness of Maximus, Olson tries to find the hidden energies that shape consciousness, "the primal features of those founders who lie buried in us." These features include the backgrounds and racial inheritance of his own Swedish father and the Irish-American mother. They also include the communal dependence on and subjection to the sea around the town.

So, for example, the opening Maximus poem, *I, Maximus of Gloucester, to You*, renders the emergence of the central character out of the sea ("hot from boiling water"), identifying him with that element, and recalling Homer's identification of Odysseus as seafarer. Beginning from a perspective offshore, the poem moves from sea to land, taking us into the harbor section of Gloucester and connecting the activity and skill of the poet to that of the fishermen, responsive to the natural world. Yet Olson knows that, even in Gloucester, the "mu-sick, mu-sick, mu-sick" of mass culture threatens this way of life. Later in the sequence he confronts his own difficulties in establishing the right relation to the world embodied in the fishermen; in *Maximus, to Himself*, he writes, "The sea was not, finally, my trade / But even my trade, at it, I stood estranged / from that which was most familiar." The Maximus poems enact a quest to overcome such estrangement and to attain a wholeness celebrated in *Celestial Evening, October 1967*, where the poet feels the "full volume of all which ever was" and the separation between inner and outer worlds dissolves.

In Olson's proposed "open form," ordinary lineation, straight left-hand margin, regular meters, and verse forms are to be discarded in favor of a free placement of lines and phrases over the page. This "composition by field" would allow, through typographical adjustments, for something like a musical score in which the length of pauses, the degree of emphasis, even changes of speed could be indicated. The unit of poetic expression was not a predetermined metrical foot, but the length of breath of the particular poet. The arrangement of words on the page would convey rhythms of thinking, breathing, and gesturing. Olson hoped to get closer to the individuality of a poet by making the poem a graph of the process through which it was produced. "A poem is energy transferred from where the poet got it . . . by way of the poem itself to, all the way over to, the reader." The energetic movement of the opening Maximus poem is a fine example of Olson's theory become practice.

Like certain techniques of meditation and yoga, Olson's theory seems an effort to bring mental activity (here, writing) in touch with its instinctive physical origins. Although Olson extended many of Pound's notions of poetic immediacy, he transferred the authority for perceiving mythic truth from the mind dependent on European culture to the mind striving to get in touch with the instinctive roots of its own behavior. Throughout his life he sought the origins of things, and in the end, the most memorable and accurate description of Olson is his own: "an archeologist of morning."

# FROM THE MAXIMUS POEMS

## Maximus, to Himself

I have had to learn the simplest things
last. Which made for difficulties.
Even at sea I was slow, to get the hand out, or to cross
a wet deck.
          The sea was not, finally, my trade.

5

But even my trade, at it, I stood estranged
from that which was most familiar.[1] Was delayed,
and not content with the man's argument
that such postponement
is now the nature of                                          10
obedience,

             that we are all late
             in a slow time,
             that we grow up many
             And the single                                15
             is not easily
             known

It could be, though the sharpness (the *achiote*[2])
I note in others,
makes more sense                                              20
than my own distances. The agilities

             they show daily
             who do the world's
             businesses
             And who do nature's                           25
             as I have no sense
             I have done either

I have made dialogues,
have discussed ancient texts,
have thrown what light I could, offered            30
what pleasures
doceat[3] allows

             But the known?
This, I have had to be given,
a life, love, and from one man                     35
the world.

             Tokens.
             But sitting here
             I look out as a wind
             and water man, testing            40
             And missing
             some proof

I know the quarters
of the weather, where it comes from,
where it goes. But the stem of me,                45
this I took from their welcome,
or their rejection, of me

---

1. An echo of the Greek philosopher Heraclitus: "We are estranged from that with which we are most familiar."
2. The seed of the annatto tree, which yields a reddish dye, resembling red (sharp) pepper.
3. "That he teach." One of the three functions of a poet, according to medieval theorists. Pound modernized the concept in his essay *Make It New*.

And my arrogance
was neither diminished
nor increased,                                          50
by the communication

2

It is undone business
I speak of, this morning,
with the sea
stretching out                                          55
from my feet

1953

## Celestial Evening, October 1967

Advanced out toward the external from
the time I did actually lose space control,
here on the Fort [1] and kept turning left
like my star-nosed mole batted
on the head, not being able to                          5
get home 50 yards as I was
from it. There is a vast

internal life, a sea or organism
full of sounds & memoried
objects swimming or sunk                                10
in the great fall of it as,
when one further
ring of the 9 bounding
Earth & Heaven runs
into the daughter of God's                              15
particular place, cave, palace—a tail

of Ocean whose waters then
are test if even a god
lies will tell & he or she spend
9 following years out of the company                    20
of their own. The sounds

and objects of the great
10th within us are
what we hear see are motived by
dream belief care for discriminate                      25
our loves & choices cares & failures unless
in this forbidding Earth & Heaven by

enclosure 9 times round plus
all that stream collecting as,
into her hands it comes: the                             30

---

1. A district in Gloucester, Massachusetts, where Olson settled after leaving Black Mountain in 1957.

full volume of all which ever was which we
as such have that which is our part of it,
all history existence places splits of moon
& slightest oncoming smallest stars at
sunset, fears & horrors, grandparents'                          35
lives as much as we have also features
and their forms, whatever grace or ugliness our legs
etc possess, it all

comes in as also outward leads
us after itself as though then                                  40
the horn of the nearest moon was
truth. I bend my ear, as,
if I were Amoghasiddi[2] and,
here on this plain where
like my mole I have                                             45
been knocked flat, attend,
to turn & turn within
the steady stream & collect which
within me ends as in her hall and I

hear all, the new moon new in all                               50
the ancient sky

1967                                                          1975

2. In Tibetan Buddhism, one of the five Dhyana-Buddhas, or Buddhas of contemplation.

---

# ELIZABETH BISHOP

## 1911–1979

"The enormous power of reticence," the poet Octavio Paz said in a tribute, "—
that is the great lesson of Elizabeth Bishop." Bishop's reticence originates in a
temperament indistinguishable from her style; her remarkable formal gifts allowed
her to create ordered and lucid structures that hold strong feelings in place. Chief
among these feelings was a powerful sense of loss. The crucial events of Bishop's
life occurred within her first eight years. Born in Worcester, Massachusetts, in
1911, she was eight months old when her father died. Her mother suffered a series
of breakdowns and was permanently institutionalized when her daughter was five.
"I've never concealed this," Bishop once wrote, "although I don't like to make too
much of it. But of course it is an important fact, to me. I didn't see her again."
The understatement in this remark is characteristic. When Bishop wrote about her
early life—as she first did in several poems and stories in the 1950s and last did in
her extraordinary final book, *Geography III* (1976)—she resisted sentimentality and
self-pity. It was as if she could look at the events of her own life with the same
unflinching gaze she turned on the landscapes that so consistently compelled her.
The deep feeling in her poems rises up out of direct and particular description,
but Bishop does more than simply observe. Whether writing about her childhood
landscape of Nova Scotia or her adopted Brazil, she often opens a poem with long

perspectives on time, with landscapes that dwarf the merely human, emphasizing the dignified frailty of a human observer and the pervasive mysteries that surround her.

Examining her own case, she traces the observer's instinct to early childhood. *In the Waiting Room*, a poem written in the early 1970s, probes the sources and motives behind her interest in detail. Using an incident from 1918 when she was seven—a little girl waits for her aunt in the dentist's anteroom—Bishop shows how in the course of the episode she became aware, as if wounded, of the utter strangeness and engulfing power of the world. The spectator in that poem hangs on to details as a kind of lifejacket; she observes because she has to.

After her father's death, Bishop and her mother went to live with Bishop's maternal grandparents in Great Village, Nova Scotia. She remained there for several years after her mother was institutionalized, until she was removed ("kidnapped," she describes herself feeling in one of her stories) by her paternal grandparents and taken to live in Worcester, Massachusetts. This experience was followed by a series of illnesses (eczema, bronchitis, and asthma), which plagued her for many years. Bishop later lived with an aunt and attended Walnut Hill School, a private high school. She graduated from Vassar College in 1934, where while a student she had been introduced to Marianne Moore. Moore's meticulous taste for fact was to influence Bishop's poetry, but more immediately, Moore's independent life as a poet made that life seem an alternative to Bishop's vaguer intentions to attend medical school. Bishop lived in New York City and in Key West, Florida; a traveling fellowship took her to Brazil, which so appealed to her that she stayed there for more than sixteen years.

Exile and travel were at the heart of Bishop's poems from the very start. The title of her very first book, *North & South* (1946), looks forward to the tropical worlds she was to choose so long as home and backward to the northern seas of Nova Scotia. Her poems are set among these landscapes, where she can stress the sweep and violence of encircling and eroding geological powers or, in the case of Brazil, a bewildering botanical plenty. *Questions of Travel* (1965), her third volume, constitutes a sequence of poems initiating her, with her botanist-geologist-anthropologist's curiosity, into the life of Brazil and the mysteries of what questions a traveler-exile should ask. In this series with its increasing penetration of a new country, a process is at work similar to one Bishop identifies in the great English naturalist Charles Darwin, of whom Bishop once said: "One admires the beautiful solid case being built up out of his endless, heroic observations, almost unconscious or automatic—and then comes a sudden relaxation, a forgetful phrase, and one feels the strangeness of his undertaking, sees the lonely young man, his eyes fixed on facts and minute details, sinking or sliding giddily off into the unknown."

In 1969 Bishop's *Complete Poems* appeared, an ironic title in light of the fact that she continued to write and publish new poetry. *Geography III* contains some of her very best work, poems that, from the settled perspective of her return to the United States, look back and evaluate the appetite for exploration apparent in her earlier verse. Having left Brazil, Bishop lived in Boston from 1970 and taught at Harvard University until 1977. She received the Pulitzer Prize for the combined volume *North & South and A Cold Spring* (1955), the National Book Award for *The Complete Poems*, and in 1976 was the first woman and the first American to receive the Books Abroad Neustadt International for Literature Prize. Since Bishop's death in 1979, most of her published work has been gathered in two volumes: *The Complete Poems 1929–1979* and *The Collected Prose*.

# The Unbeliever

*He sleeps on the top of a mast.*—Bunyan [1]

He sleeps on the top of a mast
with his eyes fast closed.
The sails fall away below him
like the sheets of his bed,
leaving out in the air of the night the sleeper's head.          5

Asleep he was transported there,
asleep he curled
in a gilded ball on the mast's top,
or climbed inside
a gilded bird, or blindly seated himself astride.               10

"I am founded on marble pillars,"
said a cloud. "I never move.
See the pillars there in the sea?"
Secure in introspection
he peers at the watery pillars of his reflection.               15

A gull had wings under his
and remarked that the air
was "like marble." He said: "Up here
I tower through the sky
for the marble wings on my tower-top fly."                      20

But he sleeps on the top of his mast
with his eyes closed tight.
The gull inquired into his dream,
which was, "I must not fall.
The spangled sea below wants me to fall.                        25
It is hard as diamonds; it wants to destroy us all."

1946

# The Fish

I caught a tremendous fish
and held him beside the boat
half out of water, with my hook
fast in a corner of his mouth.
He didn't fight.                                                5
He hadn't fought at all.
He hung a grunting weight,
battered and venerable
and homely. Here and there
his brown skin hung in strips                                   10
like ancient wallpaper,

---

1. John Bunyan (1628–1688), English author of *Pilgrim's Progress*, an allegory of Christian's progress to salvation.

and its pattern of darker brown
was like wallpaper:
shapes like full-blown roses
stained and lost through age.                                15
He was speckled with barnacles,
fine rosettes of lime,
and infested
with tiny white sea-lice,
and underneath two or three                                 20
rags of green weed hung down.
While his gills were breathing in
the terrible oxygen
—the frightening gills,
fresh and crisp with blood,                                 25
that can cut so badly—
I thought of the coarse white flesh
packed in like feathers,
the big bones and the little bones,
the dramatic reds and blacks                                30
of his shiny entrails,
and the pink swim-bladder
like a big peony.
I looked into his eyes
which were far larger than mine                             35
but shallower, and yellowed,
the irises backed and packed
with tarnished tinfoil
seen through the lenses
of old scratched isinglass. [1]                             40
They shifted a little, but not
to return my stare.
—It was more like the tipping
of an object toward the light.
I admired his sullen face,                                  45
the mechanism of his jaw,
and then I saw
that from his lower lip
—if you could call it a lip—
grim, wet, and weaponlike,                                  50
hung five old pieces of fish-line,
or four and a wire leader
with the swivel still attached,
with all their five big hooks
grown firmly in his mouth.                                  55
A green line, frayed at the end
where he broke it, two heavier lines,
and a fine black thread
still crimped from the strain and snap
when it broke and he got away.                              60

---

1. A whitish, semitransparent substance, originally obtained from the swim bladders of some freshwater fish and occasionally used for windows.

Like medals with their ribbons
frayed and wavering,
a five-haired beard of wisdom
trailing from his aching jaw.
I stared and stared                                    65
and victory filled up
the little rented boat,
from the pool of bilge
where oil had spread a rainbow
around the rusted engine                               70
to the bailer rusted orange,
the sun-cracked thwarts,
the oarlocks on their strings,
the gunnels—until everything
was rainbow, rainbow, rainbow!                         75
And I let the fish go.

                                          1946

## At the Fishhouses

Although it is a cold evening,
down by one of the fishhouses
an old man sits netting,
his net, in the gloaming almost invisible
a dark purple-brown,                                    5
and his shuttle worn and polished.
The air smells so strong of codfish
it makes one's nose run and one's eyes water.
The five fishhouses have steeply peaked roofs
and narrow, cleated gangplanks slant up               10
to storerooms in the gables
for the wheelbarrows to be pushed up and down on.
All is silver: the heavy surface of the sea,
swelling slowly as if considering spilling over,
is opaque, but the silver of the benches,             15
the lobster pots, and masts, scattered
among the wild jagged rocks,
is of an apparent translucence
like the small old buildings with an emerald moss
growing on their shoreward walls.                      20
The big fish tubs are completely lined
with layers of beautiful herring scales
and the wheelbarrows are similarly plastered
with creamy iridescent coats of mail,
with small iridescent flies crawling on them.         25
Up on the little slope behind the houses,
set in the sparse bright sprinkle of grass,
is an ancient wooden capstan,[1]

---

1. Cylindrical drum around which rope is wound, used for hauling.

cracked, with two long bleached handles
and some melancholy stains, like dried blood,                    30
where the ironwork has rusted.
The old man accepts a Lucky Strike.[2]
He was a friend of my grandfather.
We talk of the decline in the population
and of codfish and herring                                       35
while he waits for a herring boat to come in.
There are sequins on his vest and on his thumb.
He has scraped the scales, the principal beauty,
from unnumbered fish with that black old knife,
the blade of which is almost worn away.                          40

Down at the water's edge, at the place
where they haul up the boats, up the long ramp
descending into the water, thin silver
tree trunks are laid horizontally
across the gray stones, down and down                            45
at intervals of four or five feet.

Cold dark deep and absolutely clear,
element bearable to no mortal,
to fish and to seals . . . One seal particularly
I have seen here evening after evening.                          50
He was curious about me. He was interested in music;
like me a believer in total immersion,[3]
so I used to sing him Baptist hymns.
I also sang "A Mighty Fortress Is Our God."
He stood up in the water and regarded me                         55
steadily, moving his head a little.
Then he would disappear, then suddenly emerge
almost in the same spot, with a sort of shrug
as if it were against his better judgment.
Cold dark deep and absolutely clear,                             60
the clear gray icy water . . . Back, behind us,
the dignified tall firs begin.
Bluish, associating with their shadows,
a million Christmas trees stand
waiting for Christmas. The water seems suspended                 65
above the rounded gray and blue-gray stones.
I have seen it over and over, the same sea, the same,
slightly, indifferently swinging above the stones,
icily free above the stones,
above the stones and then the world.                             70
If you should dip your hand in,
your wrist would ache immediately,
your bones would begin to ache and your hand would burn
as if the water were a transmutation of fire
that feeds on stones and burns with a dark gray flame.           75
If you tasted it, it would first taste bitter,

---

2. Brand of cigarettes.                    3. Form of baptism used by Baptists.

then briny, then surely burn your tongue.
It is like what we imagine knowledge to be:
dark, salt, clear, moving, utterly free,
drawn from the cold hard mouth                                          80
of the world, derived from the rocky breasts
forever, flowing and drawn, and since
our knowledge is historical, flowing, and flown.

                                                              1955

# The Armadillo

*for Robert Lowell*

This is the time of year
when almost every night
the frail, illegal fire balloons appear.
Climbing the mountain height,

rising toward a saint                                                    5
still honored in these parts,
the paper chambers flush and fill with light
that comes and goes, like hearts.

Once up against the sky it's hard
to tell them from the stars—                                            10
planets, that is—the tinted ones:
Venus going down, or Mars,

or the pale green one. With a wind,
they flare and falter, wobble and toss;
but if it's still they steer between                                     15
the kite sticks of the Southern Cross,

receding, dwindling, solemnly
and steadily forsaking us,
or, in the downdraft from a peak,
suddenly turning dangerous.                                             20

Last night another big one fell.
It splattered like an egg of fire
against the cliff behind the house.
The flame ran down. We saw the pair

of owls who nest there flying up                                        25
and up, their whirling black-and-white
stained bright pink underneath, until
they shrieked up out of sight.

The ancient owls' nest must have burned.
Hastily, all alone,                                                     30

a glistening armadillo left the scene,
rose-flecked, head down, tail down,

and then a baby rabbit jumped out,
*short*-eared, to our surprise.
So soft!—a handful of intangible ash                    35
with fixed, ignited eyes.

*Too pretty, dreamlike mimicry!*
*O falling fire and piercing cry*
*and panic, and a weak mailed fist*[2]
*clenched ignorant against the sky!*                    40

1965

## Sestina[1]

September rain falls on the house.
In the failing light, the old grandmother
sits in the kitchen with the child
beside the Little Marvel Stove,
reading the jokes from the almanac,                    5
laughing and talking to hide her tears.

She thinks that her equinoctial tears
and the rain that beats on the roof of the house
were both foretold by the almanac,
but only known to a grandmother.                    10
The iron kettle sings on the stove.
She cuts some bread and says to the child,

*It's time for tea now;* but the child
is watching the teakettle's small hard tears
dance like mad on the hot black stove,                    15
the way the rain must dance on the house.
Tidying up, the old grandmother
hangs up the clever almanac

on its string. Birdlike, the almanac
hovers half open above the child,                    20
hovers above the old grandmother
and her teacup full of dark brown tears.
She shivers and says she thinks the house
feels chilly, and puts more wood in the stove.

*It was to be,* says the Marvel Stove.                    25
*I know what I know,* says the almanac.
With crayons the child draws a rigid house

2. The armadillo, curled tight. It is protected against
everything but fire.
1. A fixed verse form in which the end words of the

first six-line stanza must be used at the ends of the lines
in the next stanza in a rotating order; the final three
lines must contain all six words.

and a winding pathway. Then the child
puts in a man with buttons like tears
and shows it proudly to the grandmother.                    30

But secretly, while the grandmother
busies herself about the stove,
the little moons fall down like tears
from between the pages of the almanac
into the flower bed the child                    35
has carefully placed in the front of the house.

*Time to plant tears*, says the almanac.
The grandmother sings to the marvellous stove
and the child draws another inscrutable house.

                                                   1965

## In the Waiting Room

In Worcester, Massachusetts,
I went with Aunt Consuelo
to keep her dentist's appointment
and sat and waited for her
in the dentist's waiting room.                    5
It was winter. It got dark
early. The waiting room
was full of grown-up people,
arctics and overcoats,
lamps and magazines.                    10
My aunt was inside
what seemed like a long time
and while I waited I read
the *National Geographic*
(I could read) and carefully                    15
studied the photographs:
the inside of a volcano,
black, and full of ashes;
then it was spilling over
in rivulets of fire.                    20
Osa and Martin Johnson[1]
dressed in riding breeches,
laced boots, and pith helmets.
A dead man slung on a pole
—"Long Pig,"[2] the caption said.                    25
Babies with pointed heads
wound round and round with string;
black, naked women with necks
wound round and round with wire
like the necks of light bulbs.                    30

---

1. Famous explorers and travel writers.          2. Polynesian cannibals' name for the human carcass.

Their breasts were horrifying.
I read it right straight through.
I was too shy to stop.
And then I looked at the cover:
the yellow margins, the date.                                    35

Suddenly, from inside,
came an *oh!* of pain
—Aunt Consuelo's voice—
not very loud or long.
I wasn't at all surprised;                                       40
even then I knew she was
a foolish, timid woman.
I might have been embarrassed,
but wasn't. What took me
completely by surprise                                           45
was that it was *me:*
my voice, in my mouth.
Without thinking at all
I was my foolish aunt,
I—we—were falling, falling,                                      50
our eyes glued to the cover
of the *National Geographic,*
February, 1918.

I said to myself: three days
and you'll be seven years old.                                   55
I was saying it to stop
the sensation of falling off
the round, turning world
into cold, blue-black space.
But I felt: you are an *I,*                                       60
you are an *Elizabeth,*
you are one of *them.*
*Why* should you be one, too?
I scarcely dared to look.
to see what it was I was.                                         65
I gave a sidelong glance
—I couldn't look any higher—
at shadowy gray knees,
trousers and skirts and boots
and different pairs of hands                                      70
lying under the lamps.
I knew that nothing stranger
had ever happened, that nothing
stranger could ever happen.
Why should I be my aunt,                                          75
or me, or anyone?
What similarities—
boots, hands, the family voice
I felt in my throat, or even
the *National Geographic*                                         80

and those awful hanging breasts—
held us all together
or made us all just one?
How—I didn't know any
word for it—how "unlikely" . . .                    85
How had I come to be here,
like them, and overhear
a cry of pain that could have
got loud and worse but hadn't?

The waiting room was bright                          90
and too hot. It was sliding
beneath a big black wave,
another, and another.

Then I was back in it.
The War was on. Outside,                             95
in Worcester, Massachusetts,
were night and slush and cold,
and it was still the fifth
of February, 1918.

                                                     1976


## The Moose

### for Grace Bulmer Bowers

From narrow provinces
of fish and bread and tea,
home of the long tides
where the bay leaves the sea
twice a day and takes                                 5
the herrings long rides,

where if the river
enters or retreats
in a wall of brown foam
depends on if it meets                               10
the bay coming in,
the bay not at home;

where, silted red,
sometimes the sun sets
facing a red sea,                                    15
and others, veins the flats'
lavender, rich mud
in burning rivulets;

on red, gravelly roads,
down rows of sugar maples,                           20

past clapboard farmhouses
and neat, clapboard churches,
bleached, ridged as clamshells,
past twin silver birches,

through late afternoon                                    25
a bus journeys west,
the windshield flashing pink,
pink glancing off of metal,
brushing the dented flank
of blue, beat-up enamel;                                  30

down hollows, up rises,
and waits, patient, while
a lone traveller gives
kisses and embraces
to seven relatives                                        35
and a collie supervises.

Goodbye to the elms,
to the farm, to the dog.
The bus starts. The light
grows richer; the fog,                                    40
shifting, salty, thin,
comes closing in.

Its cold, round crystals
form and slide and settle
in the white hens' feathers,                              45
in gray glazed cabbages,
on the cabbage roses
and lupins like apostles;

the sweet peas cling
to their wet white string                                 50
on the whitewashed fences;
bumblebees creep
inside the foxgloves,
and evening commences.

One stop at Bass River.                                   55
Then the Economies—
Lower, Middle, Upper;
Five Islands, Five Houses, [1]
where a woman shakes a tablecloth
out after supper.                                         60

A pale flickering. Gone.
The Tantramar marshes
and the smell of salt hay.

---

1. These are small towns and villages in Nova Scotia, near Halifax.

An iron bridge trembles
and a loose plank rattles                              65
but doesn't give way.

On the left, a red light
swims through the dark:
a ship's port lantern.
Two rubber boots show,                                70
illuminated, solemn.
A dog gives one bark.

A woman climbs in
with two market bags,
brisk, freckled, elderly.                             75
"A grand night. Yes, sir,
all the way to Boston."
She regards us amicably.

Moonlight as we enter
the New Brunswick woods,                              80
hairy, scratchy, splintery;
moonlight and mist
caught in them like lamb's wool
on bushes in a pasture.

The passengers lie back.                              85
Snores. Some long sighs.
A dreamy divagation
begins in the night,
a gentle, auditory,
slow hallucination. . . .                             90

In the creakings and noises,
an old conversation
—not concerning us,
but recognizable, somewhere,
back in the bus:                                      95
Grandparents' voices

uninterruptedly
talking, in Eternity:
names being mentioned,
things cleared up finally;                           100
what he said, what she said,
who got pensioned;

deaths, deaths and sicknesses;
the year he remarried;
the year (something) happened.                       105
She died in childbirth.
That was the son lost
when the schooner foundered.

He took to drink. Yes.
She went to the bad.                                        110
When Amos began to pray
even in the store and
finally the family had
to put him away.

"Yes . . ." that peculiar                                   115
affirmative. "Yes . . ."
A sharp, indrawn breath,
half groan, half acceptance,
that means "Life's like that.
We know *it* (also death)."                                 120

Talking the way they talked
in the old featherbed,
peacefully, on and on,
dim lamplight in the hall,
down in the kitchen, the dog                                125
tucked in her shawl.

Now, it's all right now
even to fall asleep
just as on all those nights.
—Suddenly the bus driver                                    130
stops with a jolt,
turns off his lights.

A moose has come out of
the impenetrable wood
and stands there, looms, rather,                            135
in the middle of the road.
It approaches; it sniffs at
the bus's hot hood.

Towering, antlerless,
high as a church,                                           140
homely as a house
(or, safe as houses).
A man's voice assures us
"Perfectly harmless. . . ."

Some of the passengers                                      145
exclaim in whispers,
childishly, softly,
"Sure are big creatures."
"It's awful plain."
"Look! It's a she!"                                         150

Taking her time,
she looks the bus over,
grand, otherworldly.

Why, why do we feel
(we all feel) this sweet                                               155
sensation of joy?

"Curious creatures,"
says our quiet driver,
rolling his r's.
"Look at that, would you."                                            160
Then he shifts gears.
For a moment longer,

by craning backward,
the moose can be seen
on the moonlit macadam;                                               165
then there's a dim
smell of moose, an acrid
smell of gasoline.

1976

## One Art

The art of losing isn't hard to master;
so many things seem filled with the intent
to be lost that their loss is no disaster.

Lose something every day. Accept the fluster
of lost door keys, the hour badly spent.                              5
The art of losing isn't hard to master.

Then practice losing farther, losing faster:
places, and names, and where it was you meant
to travel. None of these will bring disaster.

I lost my mother's watch. And look! my last, or                       10
next-to-last, of three loved houses went.
The art of losing isn't hard to master.

I lost two cities, lovely ones. And, vaster,
some realms I owned, two rivers, a continent.
I miss them, but it wasn't a disaster.                                15

—Even losing you (the joking voice, a gesture
I love) I shan't have lied. It's evident
the art of losing's not too hard to master
though it may look like (*Write* it!) like disaster.

1976

# ROBERT HAYDEN
## 1913–1980

"Hayden is by far the best chronicler and rememberer of the African-American heritage in these Americas that I know of," the poet Michael Harper, whose own sense of history is indebted to Robert Hayden's work, has said. Hayden's poems save what has vanished, what has been lost to standard histories: a depression prize-fighter from the Midwest (*Free Fantasia: Tiger Flowers*), a miner trapped in Cystal Cave (*Beginnings, V*), a storefront gypsy who conducts seances (*Elegies for Paradise Valley*). He records the loss of what others never noticed as missing, and in their recovery he discovers a significance in the passing moment, the passed-over figure, the inarticulate gesture, which lasts through time. Always, in his words, "opposed to the chauvinistic and the doctrinaire" in art, he cherished the freedom of the poet to write about whatever seized the imagination. But his imagination was in its nature elegiac and historical. As he remembers and recreates the African-American heritage, he speaks to the struggles of the individual spirit for freedom and to pain-ful self-divisions people of many times and places know. But if the circumstances he confronts in his poems are often harsh, his work captures the energy and joy-fulness that make survival possible.

Born in Detroit, Michigan, Hayden grew up in a poor neighborhood called by its inhabitants, with affectionate irony, "Paradise Valley." His powerful sequence *Elegies for Paradise Valley* (1978) resurrects the neighborhood in its racial and ethnic mix and, through the power of imagination and memory, brings alive again the vanished occupants. Memory for Hayden is an act of love that leads to self-awareness; writing about his own past, he confronts its pain and preserves its sus-taining moments of happiness. Although the sequence originates in autobiography, the poet's consciousness works inclusively to join the memory of a single life to other lives, past and present, remembered and forgotten. As he recreates his own experience of growing up—the experience of the outsider—he discovers in his neighborhood a community of outsiders. His parents warn him against the Gypsies ("pornographers of gaudy otherness"), but he realizes that, in their very otherness, they are "like us like us" (*Elegies for Paradise Valley, VII*).

Hayden had a deep understanding of conflicts that divide the self. His family history gave him an early acquaintance with such self-division: his parents' mar-riage ended when he was young, and his mother left him in the care of foster parents (whose surname he adopted) when she left Detroit to look for work. He remained with the Haydens although his mother returned to Detroit when he was a teen-ager and lived for a period with his foster family until conflict arose between her and his foster mother. "I lived in the midst of so much turmoil all the time I didn't know if I loved or hated," he once said. As an African-American and as a poet Hayden also lived between worlds. He courageously maintained his sense of vocation through years of critical neglect and amid the demands of full-time teach-ing at Fisk University from 1946 to 1968. He published his first book, *Heart-Shape in the Dust*, in 1940, but his mature work did not appear in quantity until his volume *Ballad of Remembrance* (1962). At the same time, his belief that the poet should not be restricted by any set of themes, racial or otherwise, and the highly formal quality of his work led to criticism on the part of some young African-American writers in the 1960s. But Hayden never abandoned his belief in the power of art to speak universally. In an interview conducted in 1974, he told Den-nis Gendron of rereading Yeats's poem *Easter 1916* in the wake of the riots in Detroit—"that is the kind of poetry I want to write," he said, in admiration of the ways Yeats conceived a particular historical and political moment so that it speaks across time and place.

In fact, Hayden wrote that kind of poetry. His most famous poem, *Middle Passage*, demonstrates his transfiguring imagination and the knowledge of historical documents, which began early in his career. In 1936, leaving college because of increasingly difficult economic conditions, Hayden joined the Federal Writers Project of the Works Progress Administration and for two years researched the history of abolition movements and the Underground Railroad in Michigan. *Middle Passage* is a collage of accounts of the slave ships that transported men and women from Africa into slavery in the New World. Through the multiple voices in the poem, Hayden lets the accounts of those who participated in (and profited from) the slave trade reveal the evidence of their own damnation. The blindness that attacks one of the ships becomes a symbol of the devastating suffering of those transported into slavery and of the moral blindness everywhere evident in the traders' accounts. The technique of collage allows Hayden to suggest the fragmentation of the story; the silences in the poem evoke the missing voices of those who suffered and died on the voyages or in the intolerable conditions of slavery. At the heart of the poem is the account of a rebellion led by one of the slaves (Cinquez) on the ship *The Amistad*. Cinquez is one of several figures in Hayden's poems who dramatize "The deep immortal human wish / the timeless will" (*Middle Passage*) which for Hayden is the indomitable struggle for freedom. This "timeless will" and struggle also appear in his poems about Harriet Tubman (*Runagate Runagate*), Nat Turner, Frederick Douglass, Phillis Wheatley, and the later figures of Paul Robeson and Bessie Smith.

Hayden's experiment with collage technique in *Middle Passage* connects him to modernist poets like T. S. Eliot and William Carlos Williams and to an African-American tradition acutely aware of the power of voice. He continued to experiment with poetic form and with the creation of different voices throughout his life, and although some of these poems are not successful, he was always engaged with testing the possibilities of craft, with forging a language to express what he knew and felt. His sequences *Beginnings* and *Elegies for Paradise Valley* demonstrate his formal originality, as does his late poem *American Journal*, with its long lines and its approximation to prose. Hayden loved language and was unafraid to be lushly descriptive, even exotic, as well as to be precisely imagistic. His work summons us to notice the world as we had not before and offers us candor, clearsightedness, and a transforming gaiety.

From 1968 until his death, Hayden was professor of English at the University of Michigan at Ann Arbor. In 1976 he became the first African-American to be appointed poetry consultant to the Library of Congress.

# Middle Passage[1]

## *I*

*Jesús, Estrella, Esperanza, Mercy*[2]

Sails flashing to the wind like weapons,
sharks following the moans the fever and the dying;
horror the corposant and compass rose.[3]

---

1. Main route for the slave trade in the South Atlantic between Africa and the West Indies.
2. Names of slave ships. *"Esperanza"*: hope (Spanish).

3. Circle printed on a map showing compass directions. "Corposant": a fiery luminousness that can appear on the decks of ships during electrical storms.

Middle Passage:                                                    5
    voyage through death
            to life upon these shores.

"10 April 1800—
Blacks rebellious. Crew uneasy. Our linguist says
their moaning is a prayer for death,                               10
ours and their own. Some try to starve themselves.
Lost three this morning leaped with crazy laughter
to the waiting sharks, sang as they went under."

Desire, Adventure, Tartar, Ann:


    Standing to America, bringing home                             15
    black gold, black ivory, black seed.


    *Deep in the festering hold thy father lies,*
    *of his bones New England pews are made,*
    *those are altar lights that were his eyes.*[4]

Jesus   Saviour   Pilot   Me                                       20
Over   Life's   Tempestuous   Sea[5]

We pray that Thou wilt grant, O Lord,
safe passage to our vessels bringing
heathen souls unto Thy chastening.

Jesus   Saviour                                                    25

    "8 bells. I cannot sleep, for I am sick
    with fear, but writing eases fear a little
    since still my eyes can see these words take shape
    upon the page & so I write, as one
    would turn to exorcism. 4 days scudding,                       30
    but now the sea is calm again. Misfortune
    follows in our wake like sharks (our grinning
    tutelary gods). Which one of us
    has killed an albatross?[6] A plague among
    our blacks—Ophthalmia: blindness—& we                         35
    have jettisoned the blind to no avail.
    It spreads, the terrifying sickness spreads.
    Its claws have scratched sight from the Capt.'s eyes
    & there is blindness in the fo'c'sle[7]
    & we must sail 3 weeks before we come                          40
    to port."

        *What port awaits us, Davy Jones'*
        *or home? I've heard of slavers drifting, drifting,*

---

4. "Full fathom five thy father lies; / Of his bones are
coral made; / Those are pearls that were his eyes"
(Shakespeare's *Tempest* 1.2.399–401). The sprite Ariel
is singing about the supposed death by water of the king
of Naples.
5. A Protestant hymn.

6. A bird of good omen; to kill one is an unlucky and
impious act (as in Samuel Taylor Coleridge's *Rime of
the Ancient Mariner*).
7. Short for forecastle, the place in a ship where sailors
are quartered.

*playthings of wind and storm and chance, their crews*
*gone blind, the jungle hatred*                                     45
*crawling up on deck.*

Thou   Who   Walked   On   Galilee

"Deponent further sayeth *The Bella J*
left the Guinea Coast
with cargo of five hundred blacks and odd                          50
for the barracoons[8] of Florida:

"That there was hardly room 'tween-decks for half
the sweltering cattle stowed spoon-fashion there;
that some went mad of thirst and tore their flesh
and sucked the blood:                                              55

"That Crew and Captain lusted with the comeliest
of the savage girls kept naked in the cabins;
that there was one they called The Guinea Rose
and they cast lots and fought to lie with her:

"That when the Bo's'n piped all hands,[9] the flames               60
spreading from starboard already were beyond
control, the negroes howling and their chains
entangled with the flames:

"That the burning blacks could not be reached,
that the Crew abandoned ship,                                      65
leaving their shrieking negresses behind,
that the Captain perished drunken with the wenches:

"Further Deponent sayeth not."

Pilot   Oh   Pilot   Me

## II

Aye, lad, and I have seen those factories,                         70
Gambia, Rio Pongo, Calabar;[1]
have watched the artful mongos[2] baiting traps
of war wherein the victor and the vanquished

Were caught as prizes for our barracoons.
Have seen the nigger kings whose vanity                            75
and greed turned wild black hides of Fellatah,
Mandingo, Ibo, Kru[3] to gold for us.

And there was one—King Anthracite we named him—
fetish face beneath French parasols

---

8. Barracks or enclosures for slaves.
9. I.e., when the boatswain (petty officer aboard a
ship) signaled to all the crew on deck.
1. "Gambia": a river and nation in west Africa. "Rio

Pongo": a watercourse, dry for most of the year, in east
Africa. "Calabar": a city in southeast Nigeria.
2. I.e., Africans.
3. African tribes.

of brass and orange velvet, impudent mouth                          80
whose cups were carven skulls of enemies:

He'd honor us with drum and feast and conjo[4]
and palm-oil-glistening wenches deft in love,
and for tin crowns that shone with paste,
red calico and German-silver trinkets                               85

Would have the drums talk war and send
his warriors to burn the sleeping villages
and kill the sick and old and lead the young
in coffles[5] to our factories.

Twenty years a trader, twenty years,                                90
for there was wealth aplenty to be harvested
from those black fields, and I'd be trading still
but for the fevers melting down my bones.

### III

Shuttles in the rocking loom of history,
the dark ships move, the dark ships move,                           95
their bright ironical names
like jests of kindness on a murderer's mouth;
plough through thrashing glister toward
fata morgana's lucent melting shore,
weave toward New World littorals[6] that are                        100
mirage and myth and actual shore.

Voyage through death,
                    voyage whose chartings are unlove.

A charnel stench, effluvium of living death
spreads outward from the hold,                                      105
where the living and the dead, the horribly dying,
lie interlocked, lie foul with blood and excrement.

> Deep in the festering hold thy father lies,
> the corpse of mercy rots with him,
> rats eat love's rotten gelid eyes.                                110

> But, oh, the living look at you
> with human eyes whose suffering accuses you,
> whose hatred reaches through the swill of dark
> to strike you like a leper's claw.

> You cannot stare that hatred down                                 115
> or chain the fear that stalks the watches
> and breathes on you its fetid scorching breath;

---

4. Dance.
5. Train of slaves fastened together.

6. Coastal regions. "Fata morgana": mirage.

*cannot kill the deep immortal human wish,*
*the timeless will.*

"But for the storm that flung up barriers                    120
of wind and wave, *The Amistad*,[7] señores,
would have reached the port of Príncipe in two,
three days at most; but for the storm we should
have been prepared for what befell.
Swift as the puma's leap it came. There was        125
that interval of moonless calm filled only
with the water's and the rigging's usual sounds,
then sudden movement, blows and snarling cries
and they had fallen on us with machete
and marlinspike. It was as though the very          130
air, the night itself were striking us.
Exhausted by the rigors of the storm,
we were no match for them. Our men went down
before the murderous Africans. Our loyal
Celestino ran from below with gun                     135
and lantern and I saw, before the cane-
knife's wounding flash, Cinquez,
that surly brute who calls himself a prince,
directing, urging on the ghastly work.[8]
He hacked the poor mulatto down, and then     140
he turned on me. The decks were slippery
when daylight finally came. It sickens me
to think of what I saw, of how these apes
threw overboard the butchered bodies of
our men, true Christians all, like so much jetsam.  145
Enough, enough. The rest is quickly told:
Cinquez was forced to spare the two of us
you see to steer the ship to Africa,
and we like phantoms doomed to rove the sea
voyaged east by day and west by night,               150
deceiving them, hoping for rescue,
prisoners on our own vessel, till
at length we drifted to the shores of this
your land, America, where we were freed
from our unspeakable misery. Now we                   155
demand, good sirs, the extradition of
Cinquez and his accomplices to La
Havana.[9] And it distresses us to know
there are so many here who seem inclined
to justify the mutiny of these blacks.               160
We find it paradoxical indeed
that you whose wealth, whose tree of liberty
are rooted in the labor of your slaves

---

7. "Friendship"; a Spanish ship carrying fifty-three il-
legally obtained slaves out of Havana, Cuba, in July
1839.
8. During the mutiny the Africans, led by a man
called Cinqué, or Cinquez, killed the captain, his slave
Celestino, and the mate, but spared the two slave

owners.
9. *The Amistad* reached Long Island Sound after two
months, where it was detained by the American ship
*Washington*, the slaves were imprisoned, and the owners were freed. The owners began litigation to force the
slaves' return to Havana to be tried for murder.

should suffer the august John Quincy Adams
to speak with so much passion of the right                    165
of chattel slaves to kill their lawful masters
and with his Roman rhetoric weave a hero's
garland for Cinquez.[1] I tell you that
we are determined to return to Cuba
with our slaves and there see justice done. Cinquez—    170
or let us say 'the Prince'—Cinquez shall die."

The deep immortal human wish,
the timeless will:

Cinquez its deathless primaveral image,
life that transfigures many lives.                            175

Voyage through death
            to life upon these shores.

                                                        1962


## Homage to the Empress of the Blues[1]

Because there was a man somewhere in a candystripe silk shirt,
gracile and dangerous as a jaguar and because a woman moaned
for him in sixty-watt gloom and mourned him Faithless Love
Twotiming Love Oh Love Oh Careless Aggravating Love,

    She came out on the stage in yards of pearls, emerging like        5
    a favorite scenic view, flashed her golden smile and sang.

Because grey laths began somewhere to show from underneath
torn hurdygurdy[2] lithographs of dollfaced heaven;
and because there were those who feared alarming fists of snow
on the door and those who feared the riot-squad of statistics,        10

    She came out on the stage in ostrich feathers, beaded satin,
    and shone that smile on us and sang.

                                                        1962


## Those Winter Sundays

Sundays too my father got up early
and put his clothes on in the blueblack cold,
then with cracked hands that ached

---

1. The case reached the Supreme Court in 1841; the
Africans were defended by former president John
Quincy Adams, and the court released the thirty-seven
survivors to return to Africa.
1. Bessie Smith (1895–1937), one of the greatest

American blues singers. Her flamboyant style, which
grew out of the black vaudeville tradition, made her
popular in the 1920s.
2. A disreputable kind of dance hall. "Laths": the strips
of wood that form a backing for plaster.

from labor in the weekday weather made
banked fires blaze. No one ever thanked him.                    5

I'd wake and hear the cold splintering, breaking.
When the rooms were warm, he'd call,
and slowly I would rise and dress,
fearing the chronic angers of that house,

Speaking indifferently to him,                    10
who had driven out the cold
and polished my good shoes as well.
What did I know, what did I know
of love's austere and lonely offices?

1962


## Free Fantasia: Tiger Flowers[1]

*for Michael*

The sporting people
along St. Antoine—
that scufflers'
paradise of ironies—
            bet salty money                    5
on his righteous
            hook and jab.

I was a boy then, running
(unbeknownst to Pa)
errands for Miss Jackie                    10
and Stack-o'-Diamonds' Eula Mae.
. . . Their perfumes,
rouged Egyptian faces.
            Their pianolas jazzing.

O Creole babies,                    15
Dixie odalisques,[2]
speeding through cutglass
dark to see the macho angel
            trick you'd never
turn, his bluesteel prowess                    20
            in the ring.

Hardshell believers
amen'd the wreck
as God A'mighty's
will. I'd thought                    25
            such gaiety could not

---

1. A midwestern boxer during the Depression years.   champion.
He was the first African-American middleweight   2. Female slaves or concubines in a harem.

die. Nor could our
    elegant avenger.

*The Virgin Forest*
by Rousseau[3]—                         30
its psychedelic flowers
towering, its deathless
        dark dream figure
death the leopard
        claws—I choose it                35
now as elegy
        for Tiger Flowers.

                              1975

# Elegies for Paradise Valley[1]

## I

My shared bedroom's window
opened on alley stench.
A junkie died in maggots there.
I saw his body shoved into a van.
I saw the hatred for our kind            5
glistening like tears
in the policemen's eyes.

## II

No place for Pestalozzi's
fiorelli.[2] No time of starched
and ironed innocence. Godfearing       10
elders, even Godless grifters, tried
as best they could to shelter
us. Rats fighting in their walls.

## III

Waxwork Uncle Henry
(murdered Uncle Crip)            15
lay among floral pieces
in the front room where
the Christmas tree had stood.

Mister Hong of the
Chinese Lantern (there           20
Auntie as waitress queened it
nights) brought freesias, wept
beside the coffin.

---

3. Henri Rousseau (1844–1910), French painter known for jungle scenes and exotic colors.
1. The name of the Detroit neighborhood where Hayden grew up.

2. Small flowers. Johann Pestalozzi developed a system of education based on a child's individual development.

Beautiful, our neighbors
murmured; he would be proud.                                        25
Is it mahogany?
Mahogany—I'd heard
the victrola voice of

dead Bert Williams[3]
talk-sing that word as macabre                                      30
music played, chilling
me. Uncle Crip
had laughed and laughed.

### IV

Whom now do you guide, Madam Artelia?
Who nowadays can summon you to speak                                35
from the spirit place your ghostly home
of the oh-riental wonders there—
of the fate, luck, surprises, gifts

awaiting us out here? Oh, Madam,
part Seminole and confidante                                        40
("Born with a veil over my face")
of all our dead, how clearly you
materialize before the eye

of memory—your AfroIndian features,
Gypsy dress, your silver crucifix                                   45
and manycolored beads. I see
again your waitingroom, with its wax
bouquets, its plaster Jesus of the Sacred Heart.

I watch blue smoke of incense curl
from a Buddha's lap as I wait with Ma                               50
and Auntie among your nervous clients.
You greet us, smiling, lay your hand
in blessing on my head, then lead

the others into a candlelit room
I may not enter. She went into a trance,                            55
Auntie said afterward, and spirits
talked, changing her voice to suit
their own. And Crip came.

Happy yes I am happy here,
he told us; dying's not death. Do not grieve.                       60
Remembering, Auntie began to cry
and poured herself a glass of gin.
Didn't sound a bit like Crip, Ma snapped.

3. Comedian and songwriter (1876?–1922).

## V

And Belle the classy dresser, where is she,
who changed her frocks three times a day?                        65
　　Where's Nora, with her laugh, her comic flair.
　　stagestruck Nora waiting for her chance?
Where's fast Iola, who so loved to dance
she left her sickbed one last time to whirl
in silver at The Palace till she fell?                           70
　　Where's mad Miss Alice, who ate from garbage cans?
　　Where's snuffdipping Lucy, who played us 'chunes'
on her guitar? Where's Hattie? Where's Melissabelle?
Let vanished rooms, let dead streets tell.

Where's Jim, Watusi prince and Good Old Boy,                     75
who with a joke went off to fight in France?
　　Where's Tump the defeated artist, for meals or booze
　　daubing with quarrelsome reds, disconsolate blues?
Where's Les the huntsman? Tough Kid Chocolate, where
is he? Where's dapper Jess? Where's Stomp the shell-             80
shocked, clowning for us in parodies of war?
　　Where's taunted Christopher, sad queen of night?
　　And Ray, who cursing crossed the color line?
Where's gentle Brother Davis? Where's dopefiend Mel?
Let vanished rooms, let dead streets tell.                       85

## VI

Of death. Of loving too:
Oh sweet sweet jellyroll:[4]
so the sinful hymned it while
the churchfolk loured.

I scrounged for crumbs:                                          90
I yearned to touch the choirlady's hair,
I wanted Uncle Crip

to kiss me, but he danced
with me instead;
we Balled-the-Jack                                              95
to Jellyroll

Morton's[5] brimstone
piano on the phonograph,
laughing, shaking the gasolier[6]
a later stillness dimmed.                                        100

---

4. All-purpose slang word for sexual activity, sexual
organs, or sexual parts.
5. Jelly Roll Morton (1890–1941), jazz innovator
whose style grew out of Dixieland and ragtime. Balling

the Jack is an energetic dance accompanied by hand
clapping.
6. Chandelier equipped with gas lights.

## VII

Our parents warned us: Gypsies
kidnap you. And we must never play
with Gypsy children: Gypsies
all got lice in their hair.

Their queen was dark as Cleopatra                    105
in the Negro History Book. Their king's
sinister arrogance flashed fire
like the diamonds on his dirty hands.

Quite suddenly he was dead,
his tribe clamoring in grief.                    110
They take on bad as Colored Folks,
Uncle Crip allowed. Die like us too.

Zingaros: Tzigeune: Gitanos:[7] Gypsies:
pornographers of gaudy otherness:
aliens among the alien: thieves,                    115
carriers of sickness: like us like us.

## VIII

Of death, of loving,
of sin and hellfire too.
Unsaved, old Christians
gossiped; pitched                    120

from the gamblingtable—
Lord have mercy on
his wicked soul—
face foremost into hell.

We'd dance there, Uncle                    125
Crip and I,
for though I spoke
my pieces well in Sunday School,

I knew myself (precocious
in the ways of guilt                    130
and secret pain)
the devil's own rag babydoll.

1978

---

7. Italian, Hungarian, and Spanish names for Gypsies—a reflection of the neighborhood's mixed ethnic population.

# RANDALL JARRELL
## 1914–1965

"Monstrously knowing and monstrously innocent. . . . A Wordsworth with the obsession of a Lewis Carroll"—so Robert Lowell once described his friend and fellow poet Randall Jarrell. Jarrell was teacher and critic as well as poet, and for many writers of his generation—Lowell, Delmore Schwartz, and John Berryman among them—Jarrell was the critic whose taste was most unerring, who seemed to know instantly what was genuine and what was not. An extraordinary teacher, he loved the activity, both in and out of the classroom; "the gods who had taken away the poet's audience had given him students," he once said. The novelist Peter Taylor recalls that when he came to Vanderbilt University as a freshman in the mid-1930s, Jarrell, then a graduate student, had already turned the literary students into disciples; he held court discussing Chekhov on the sidelines of touch football games. For all his brilliance Jarrell was, at heart, democratic. Believing that poetry belongs to every life, his teaching, his literary criticism, and his poetry aimed to recapture and reeducate a general audience lost to poetry in an age of specialization. Jarrell's interests were democratic as well; his lifelong fascination with popular culture may have originated in a childhood spent in Long Beach, California, and a year spent with grandparents in Hollywood. Witty and incisive, Jarrell could be intimidating; at the same time he remained deeply in touch with childhood's mystery and enchantment. It was as if, Hannah Arendt once said, he "had emerged from the enchanted forests." He loved fairy tales, translated a number of them, and wrote several books for children, among them *The Bat-Poet*. The childlike quality of the person informs Jarrell's poems as well; he is unembarrassed by the adult heart still in thrall to childhood's wishes.

Jarrell was born in Nashville, Tennessee, but spent much of his childhood in California. When his parents divorced, the child, then eleven, remained for a year with his grandparents, then returned to live with his mother in Nashville. He majored in psychology at Vanderbilt and stayed on there to do graduate work in English. In 1937 he left Nashville to teach at Kenyon College (Gambier, Ohio) on the invitation of his old Vanderbilt professor John Crowe Ransom, the New Critic and Fugitive poet. From that time on, Jarrell almost always had some connection with a university: after Kenyon, the University of Texas, Sarah Lawrence College, and from 1947 until his death, the Women's College of the University of North Carolina at Greensboro. But, as his novel *Pictures from an Institution* (1954) with its mixed satiric and tender views of academic life suggests, he was never satisfied with a cloistered education. As poetry editor of the *Nation* (1946), and then in a series of essays and reviews collected as *Poetry and the Age* (1953), he introduced readers to the work of his contemporaries—Elizabeth Bishop, Robert Lowell, John Berryman, the William Carlos Williams of *Paterson*—and influentially reassessed the reputations of Whitman and Robert Frost.

Among the poets who emerged after World War II, Jarrell stands out for his colloquial plainness. While others—Richard Wilbur and the early Robert Lowell, for example—were writing highly structured poems with complicated imagery, Jarrell's work feels and sounds close to what he calls in one poem the "dailiness of life" (*Well Water*). He is master of the heartbreak of everyday and identifies with ordinary forms of loneliness. Jarrell's gift of imaginative sympathy appears in the treatment of soldiers in his war poems, the strongest to come out of World War II. He had been trained as an army air force pilot and after that as a control operator, and he had a sense of the war's special casualties. With their understanding of soldiers as both destructive and innocent at the same time, these poems make his volumes *Little Friend, Little Friend* (1945) and *Losses* (1948) powerful and moving. Jarrell also empathized with the dreams, loneliness, and disappointments of women, whose perspective he often adopted, as in the title poem of his collection *The Woman at the Washington Zoo* (1960) and his poem *Next Day.*

Against the blasted or unrealized possibilities of adult life, Jarrell often poised the rich mysteries of childhood. Many of the poems reinterpret fairy tales; in *The Märchen* Jarrell mixes and transmutes these tales to give his poem the power and complexity of a dream. The title poem of his last book, *The Lost World* (1965), looks back to his Los Angeles playtime, the movie sets and plaster dinosaurs and pterodactyls against whose eternal gay presence he measures his own aging. The poem has Jarrell's characteristic sense of loss but also his capacity for a mysterious happiness, which animates the poem even as he holds "nothing" in his hands.

Jarrell suffered a nervous breakdown in February 1965 but returned to teaching that fall. In October he was struck down by a car and died. His *Complete Poems* were published posthumously (1969), as were a translation of Goethe's *Faust*, Part I, in preparation at his death, and two books of essays, *The Third Book of Criticism* (1969) and *Kipling, Auden & Co.* (1980).

## The Death of the Ball Turret Gunner[1]

From my mother's sleep I fell into the State,
And I hunched in its belly till my wet fur froze.
Six miles from earth, loosed from its dream of life,
I woke to black flak[2] and the nightmare fighters.
When I died they washed me out of the turret with a hose.     5

1945

## Second Air Force

Far off, above the plain the summer dries,
The great loops of the hangars sway like hills.
Buses and weariness and loss, the nodding soldiers
Are wire, the bare frame building, and a pass
To what was hers; her head hides his square patch     5
And she thinks heavily: My son is grown.
She sees a world: sand roads, tar-paper barracks,
The bubbling asphalt of the runways, sage,
The dunes rising to the interminable ranges,
The dim flights moving over clouds like clouds.     10
The armorers in their patched faded green,
Sweat-stiffened, banded with brass cartridges,
Walk to the line; their Fortresses,[1] all tail,
Stand wrong and flimsy on their skinny legs,
And the crews climb to them clumsily as bears.     15

1. "A ball turret was a plexiglass sphere set into the belly of a B-17 or B-24 [oomber], and inhabited by two .50 caliber machine-guns and one man, a short, small man. When this gunner tracked with his machine-guns a fighter attacking his bomber from below, he revolved with the turret; hunched upside-down in his little sphere, he looked like the foetus in the womb. The fighters which attacked him were armed with cannon firing explosive shells. The hose was a steam hose" [Jarrell's note].
2. Antiaircraft fire.
1. Flying Fortresses, a type of bomber in World War II.

The head withdraws into its hatch (a boy's),
The engines rise to their blind laboring roar,
And the green, made beasts run home to air.
Now in each aspect death is pure.
(At twilight they wink over men like stars                                    20
And hour by hour, through the night, some see
The great lights floating in—from Mars, from Mars.)
How emptily the watchers see them gone.

They go, there is silence; the woman and her son
Stand in the forest of the shadows, and the light                             25
Washes them like water. In the long-sunken city
Of evening, the sunlight stills like sleep
The faint wonder of the drowned; in the evening,
In the last dreaming light, so fresh, so old,
The soldiers pass like beasts, unquestioning,                                 30
And the watcher for an instant understands
What there is then no need to understand;
But she wakes from her knowledge, and her stare,
A shadow now, moves emptily among
The shadows learning in their shadowy fields                                  35
The empty missions.
                    Remembering,
She hears the bomber calling, *Little Friend!*[2]
To the fighter hanging in the hostile sky,
And sees the ragged flame eat, rib by rib,                                    40
Along the metal of the wing into her heart:
The lives stream out, blossom, and float steadily
To the flames of the earth, the flames
That burn like stars above the lands of men.

She saves from the twilight that takes everything                            45
A squadron shipping, in its last parade—
Its dogs run by it, barking at the band—
A gunner walking to his barracks, half-asleep,
Starting at something, stumbling (above, invisible,
The crews in the steady winter of the sky                                     50
Tremble in their wired fur); and feels for them
The love of life for life. The hopeful cells
Heavy with someone else's death, cold carriers
Of someone else's victory, grope past their lives
Into her own bewilderment: The years meant *this?*                           55

But for them the bombers answer everything.

                                                          1945

---

2. "In 'Second Air Force' the woman visiting her son remembers what she has read on the front page of her newspaper the week before, a conversation between a bomber, in flames over Germany, and one of the fighters protecting it: 'Then I heard the bomber call me in: "Little Friend, Little Friend, I got two engines on fire. Can you see me, Little Friend?" I said, "I'm crossing right over you. Let's go home" ' " [Jarrell's note].

# Next Day

Moving from Cheer to Joy, from Joy to All,
I take a box
And add it to my wild rice, my Cornish game hens.
The slacked or shorted, basketed, identical
Food-gathering flocks                                                    5
Are selves I overlook. Wisdom, said William James,[1]

Is learning what to overlook. And I am wise
If that is wisdom.
Yet somehow, as I buy All from these shelves
And the boy takes it to my station wagon,                                10
What I've become
Troubles me even if I shut my eyes.

When I was young and miserable and pretty
And poor, I'd wish
What all girls wish: to have a husband,                                  15
A house and children. Now that I'm old, my wish
Is womanish:
That the boy putting groceries in my car

See me. It bewilders me he doesn't see me.
For so many years                                                        20
I was good enough to eat: the world looked at me
And its mouth watered. How often they have undressed me,
The eyes of strangers!
And, holding their flesh within my flesh, their vile

Imaginings within my imagining,                                          25
I too have taken
The chance of life. Now the boy pats my dog
And we start home. Now I am good.
The last mistaken,
Ecstatic, accidental bliss, the blind                                    30

Happiness that, bursting, leaves upon the palm
Some soap and water—
It was so long ago, back in some Gay
Twenties, Nineties, I don't know . . . Today I miss
My lovely daughter                                                       35
Away at school, my sons away at school,

My husband away at work—I wish for them.
The dog, the maid,
And I go through the sure unvarying days
At home in them. As I look at my life,                                   40
I am afraid
Only that it will change, as I am changing:

---

1. From *Principles of Psychology*, by the American philosopher William James (1842–1910).

I am afraid, this morning, of my face.
It looks at me
From the rear-view mirror, with the eyes I hate,                    45
The smile I hate. Its plain, lined look
Of gray discovery
Repeats to me: "You're old." That's all, I'm old.

And yet I'm afraid, as I was at the funeral
I went to yesterday.                                              50
My friend's cold made-up face, granite among its flowers,
Her undressed, operated-on, dressed body
Were my face and body.
As I think of her I hear her telling me

How young I seem; I *am* exceptional;                             55
I think of all I have.
But really no one is exceptional,
No one has anything, I'm anybody,
I stand beside my grave
Confused with my life, that is commonplace and solitary.          60

                                                        1965


# Well Water

What a girl called "the dailiness of life"
(Adding an errand to your errand. Saying,
"Since you're up . . ." Making you a means to
A means to a means to) is well water
Pumped from an old well at the bottom of the world.               5
The pump you pump the water from is rusty
And hard to move and absurd, a squirrel-wheel
A sick squirrel turns slowly, through the sunny
Inexorable hours. And yet sometimes
The wheel turns of its own weight, the rusty                      10
Pump pumps over your sweating face the clear
Water, cold, so cold! you cup your hands
And gulp from them the dailiness of life.

                                                        1965


# Thinking of the Lost World

This spoonful of chocolate tapioca
Tastes like—like peanut butter, like the vanilla
Extract Mama told me not to drink.
Swallowing the spoonful, I have already traveled
Through time to my childhood. It puzzles me                       5
That age is like it.
            Come back to that calm country

Through which the stream of my life first meandered,
My wife, our cat, and I sit here and see
Squirrels quarreling in the feeder, a mockingbird
Copying our chipmunk, as our end copies                          10
Its beginning.
           Back in Los Angeles, we missed
Los Angeles. The sunshine of the Land
Of Sunshine is a gray mist now, the atmosphere
Of some factory planet: when you stand and look
You see a block or two, and your eyes water.                     15
The orange groves are all cut down . . . My bow
Is lost, all my arrows are lost or broken,
My knife is sunk in the eucalyptus tree
Too far for even Pop to get it out,
And the tree's sawed down. It and the stair-sticks               20
And the planks of the tree house are all firewood
Burned long ago; its gray smoke smells of Vicks.[1]

Twenty Years After, thirty-five years after,
Is as good as ever—better than ever,
Now that D'Artagnan[2] is no longer old—                          25
Except that it is unbelievable.
I say to my old self: "I believe. Help thou
Mine unbelief."
           I believe the dinosaur
Or pterodactyl's married the pink sphinx
And lives with those Indians in the undiscovered                 30
Country between California and Arizona
That the mad girl told me she was princess of—
Looking at me with the eyes of a lion,
Big, golden, without human understanding,
As she threw paper-wads from the back seat                       35
Of the car in which I drove her with her mother
From the jail in Waycross to the hospital
In Daytona. If I took my eyes from the road
And looked back into her eyes, the car would—I'd be—

Or if only I could find a crystal set[3]                          40
Sometimes, surely, I could still hear their chief
Reading to them from Dumas or Amazing Stories;
If I could find in some Museum of Cars
Mama's dark blue Buick, Lucky's electric,
Couldn't I be driven there? Hold out to them,                    45
The paraffin half picked out, Tawny's dewclaw—
And have walk to me from among their wigwams
My tall brown aunt, to whisper to me: "Dead?
They told you I was dead?"
           As if you could die!
If I never saw you, never again                                  50

---

1. A remedy for colds.
2. Hero of *The Three Musketeers* (1844) by Alexandre

Dumas *père*; its sequel was *Twenty Years After* (1845).
3. Old-fashioned radio receiver.

Wrote to you, even, after a few years,
How often you've visited me, having put on,
As a mermaid puts on her sealskin, another face
And voice, that don't fool me for a minute—
That are yours for good . . . All of them are gone                    55
Except for me; and for me nothing is gone—
The chicken's body is still going round
And round in widening circles, a satellite
From which, as the sun sets, the scientist bends
A look of evil on the unsuspecting earth.                    60
Mama and Pop and Dandeen are still there
In the Gay Twenties.
                    The Gay Twenties! You say
The Gay Nineties . . . But it's all right: they *were* gay,
O so gay! A certain number of years after,
Any time is Gay, to the new ones who ask:                    65
"Was that the first World War or the second?"
Moving between the first world and the second,
I hear a boy call, now that my beard's gray:
"Santa Claus! Hi, Santa Claus!" It *is* miraculous
To have the children call you Santa Claus.                    70
I wave back. When my hand drops to the wheel,
It is brown and spotted, and its nails are ridged
Like Mama's. Where's my own hand? My smooth
White bitten-fingernailed one? I seem to see
A shape in tennis shoes and khaki riding-pants                    75
Standing there empty-handed; I reach out to it
Empty-handed, my hand comes back empty,
And yet my emptiness is traded for its emptiness,
I have found that Lost World in the Lost and Found
Columns whose gray illegible advertisements                    80
My soul has memorized world after world:
LOST—NOTHING. STRAYED FROM NOWHERE. NO REWARD.
I hold in my own hands, in happiness,
Nothing: the nothing for which there's no reward.

                                                        1965

---

# JOHN BERRYMAN

## 1914–1972

From a generation whose ideal poem was short, self-contained, and ironic, John Berryman emerged as the author of two extended and passionate works: *Homage to Mistress Bradstreet* and the lyric sequence called *The Dream Songs*. It was as if Berryman needed more space than the single lyric provided—a larger theater to play out an unrelenting psychic drama. He had written shorter poems—songs and sonnets—but it was his discovery of large-scale dramatic situations and strange new voices that astonished his contemporaries.

Berryman seemed fated to intense suffering and self-preoccuption. His father, a banker, shot himself outside his son's window when the boy was twelve. The suicide haunted Berryman to the end of his own life, which also came by suicide.

Berryman, who was born John Smith, took a new name from his stepfather, also a banker. His childhood was a series of displacements: ten years near McAlester, Oklahoma, then Tampa, Florida, and after his father's suicide, Gloucester, Massachusetts, and New York City. His mother's second marriage ended in divorce, but his stepfather sent him to private school in Connecticut. Berryman graduated from Columbia College in 1936 and won a fellowship to Clare College, Cambridge, England.

He was later to say of himself, "I masquerade as a writer. Actually I am a scholar." However misleading this may be about his poetry, it reminds us that all his life Berryman drew nourishment from teaching—at Wayne State, at Harvard (1940–43), then off and on at Princeton, and from 1955 until his death, at the University of Minnesota. He chose to teach, not creative writing, but literature and the "history of civilization" and claimed that such teaching forced him into areas in which he wouldn't otherwise have done detailed work. A mixture of bookishness and wildness characterizes all his writing: five years of research lay behind the intensities of *Homage to Mistress Bradstreet*, while an important constituent of "huffy Henry's" personality in *The Dream Songs* is his professorial awkwardness and exhibitionism.

Berryman seemed drawn to borrowing identities in his poetry. In his first important volume, *The Dispossessed* (1948), he had experimented with various dramatic voices in short *Nervous Songs: The Song of the Demented Priest, A Professor's Song, The Song of the Tortured Girl, The Song of the Man Forsaken and Obsessed*. The *dispossession* of the book's title had two opposite and urgent meanings for him: "the miserable, *put out of one's own*, and the relieved, saved, undevilled, de-spelled." Taking on such roles was for Berryman both a revelation of his cast-out, fatherless state and an exorcism of it. It was perhaps in that spirit that he entered into an imaginary dialogue with what he felt as the kindred nature of the Puritan poet Anne Bradstreet. "Both of our worlds unhanded us." What started out to be a poem of fifty lines emerged as the fifty-seven stanzas of *Homage to Mistress Bradstreet* (1956), a work so absorbing that after completing it Berryman claimed to be "a ruin for two years." It was not Bradstreet's poetry that engaged him. Quite the contrary: he was fascinated by the contrast between her "bald abstract rime" and her life of passionate suffering. The poem explores the kinship between Bradstreet and Berryman as figures of turbulence and rebellion.

Berryman took literary encouragement from another American poet of the past, Stephen Crane, about whom he wrote a book-length critical study in 1950. Crane's poems, he said, have "the character of a 'dream,' something seen naively in a new relation." Berryman's attraction to a poetry that accommodated the nightmare antics of the dream world became apparent in his own long work, *The Dream Songs*. It was modeled, he claimed, on "the greatest American poem," Whitman's *Song of Myself*, in which the speaker assumes a fluid, ever-changing persona. *77 Dream Songs* was published in 1964. Additional poems, to a total of 385, appeared in *His Toy, His Dream, His Rest* (1968). (Some uncollected "Dream Songs" were published posthumously in *Henry's Fate*, 1977, and drafts of others remained in manuscript.) There are obvious links between Berryman and other so-called confessional writers such as Robert Lowell, Sylvia Plath, and Anne Sexton. But the special autobiographical flavor of *The Dream Songs* is that of a psychic vaudeville; as in dreams, the poet represents himself through a fluid series of *alter egos*, whose voices often flow into one another in single poems. One of these voices is that of a blackface minstrel, and Berryman's appropriation of this dialect prompted Michael Harper's poem *Tongue-Tied in Black and White*. Despite the suffering that these poems enact, Berryman seemed to find a secret strength through the staginess, variety, resourcefulness, and renewals of these poems.

The *Dream Songs* brought Berryman a success that was not entirely beneficial.
The collection *Love and Fame* (1970) shows him beguiled by his own celebrity
and wrestling with some of its temptations. In an unfinished, posthumously published novel, *Recovery*, he portrays himself as increasingly prey to alcoholism. Berryman had been married twice before, and his hospitalization for drinking and for
periods of insanity had put a strain on his third marriage. He came to distrust his
poetry as a form of exhibitionism and was clearly, in his use of the discipline of
prose and in the prayers that crowd his last two volumes of poetry (*Delusions, Etc.*
appeared posthumously), in search of some new and humbling style. Having been
raised a strict Catholic and fallen away from the church, he tried to return to it in
his last years, speaking of his need for a "God of rescue." On January 7, 1972,
Berryman committed suicide by leaping from a Minneapolis bridge.

## FROM DREAM SONGS[1]

### 29

There sat down, once, a thing on Henry's heart
so heavy, if he had a hundred years
& more, & weeping, sleepless, in all them time
Henry could not make good.
Starts again always in Henry's ears                                    5
the little cough somewhere, an odour, a chime.

And there is another thing he has in mind
like a grave Sienese face[2] a thousand years
would fail to blur the still profiled reproach of. Ghastly,
with open eyes, he attends, blind.                                     10
All the bells say: too late. This is not for tears;
thinking.

But never did Henry, as he thought he did,
end anyone and hacks her body up
and hide the pieces, where they may be found.                          15
He knows: he went over everyone, & nobody's missing.
Often he reckons, in the dawn, them up.
Nobody is ever missing.

### 45

He stared at ruin. Ruin stared straight back.
He thought they was old friends. He felt on the stair

---

1. These poems were written over a period of thirteen
years. (*77 Dream Songs* was published in 1964, and the
remaining poems appeared in *His Toy, His Dream, His
Rest* in 1968. Some uncollected Dream Songs were included in the volume *Henry's Fate*, which appeared
five years after Berryman committed suicide in 1972.)
Berryman placed an introductory note at the head of
*His Toy, His Dream, His Rest*: "The poem then, whatever its wide cast of characters, is essentially about an
imaginary character (not the poet, not me) named

Henry, a white American in early middle age sometimes in blackface, who has suffered an irreversible loss
and talks about himself sometimes in the first person,
sometimes in the third, sometimes even in the second;
he has a friend, never named, who addresses him as
Mr. Bones and variants thereof. Requiescant in pace."
2. Alluding to the somber, austere mosaiclike religious
portraits by the Italian painters who worked in Siena
during the 13th and 14th centuries.

where her papa found them bare
they became familiar. When the papers were lost
rich with pals' secrets, he thought he had the knack          5
of ruin. Their paths crossed

and once they crossed in jail; they crossed in bed;
and over an unsigned letter their eyes met,
and in an Asian city
directionless & lurchy at two & three,                       10
or trembling to a telephone's fresh threat,
and when some wired his head

to reach a wrong opinion, 'Epileptic'.
But he noted now that: they were not old friends.
He did not know this one.                                    15
This one was a stranger, come to make amends
for all the imposters, and to make it stick.
Henry nodded, un-.

## 385

My daughter's heavier. Light leaves are flying.
Everywhere in enormous numbers turkeys will be dying
and other birds, all their wings.
They never greatly flew. Did they wish to?
I should know. Off away somewhere once I knew               5
such things.

Or good Ralph Hodgson[1] back then did, or does.
The man is dead whom Eliot[2] praised. My praise
follows and flows too late.
Fall is grievy, brisk. Tears behind the eyes                10
almost fall. Fall comes to us as a prize
to rouse us toward our fate.

My house is made of wood and it's made well,
unlike us. My house is older than Henry;
that's fairly old.                                          15
If there were a middle   ground between things and the
        soul
or if the sky resembled more the sea,
I wouldn't have to scold

                              my heavy daughter.

                                            1968

---

1. An English poet (1871–1962) who wrote balladlike       birds for commercial uses.
lyrics. Berryman may be alluding to Hodgson's *Hymn*      2. T. S. Eliot (1888–1965), American poet and critic.
*to Moloch*, in which the poet protests the slaughter of

# ROBERT LOWELL

## 1917–1977

In *North Haven*, her poem in memory of Robert Lowell, Elizabeth Bishop translates the song of the birds as Lowell seemed to hear it: "repeat, repeat, repeat, revise, revise, revise." Repeatedly, even obsessively, Lowell returned to certain subjects in his poems. Each return confirmed an existing pattern even as it opened the possibility for revision. In fact, Lowell's life was full of revision. Descended from Protestant New Englanders, he converted to Catholicism, then fell away from it; he married three times; and he changed his poetic style more than once. In the later part of his career, Lowell revised even his published poems and did so repeatedly. "Revision is inspiration," he once said, "no reading of the finished work as exciting as writing the last changes." Revision allowed for Lowell's love of stray events, his attraction to the fluidity of life (in this, he resembles Wallace Stevens). But Lowell also wanted to organize life into formal patterns, to locate the random moment in the design of an epic history (his Catholicism can be seen, in part, as an expression of this desire). History offered plot and repetition: just as patterns of his childhood recurred in adult life, the sins of his New England ancestors were reenacted by contemporary America. Lowell's vision of history leaned toward apocalypse, toward the revelation of a prior meaning the poet agonized to determine, and yet he cherished the freedom of "human chances," with all their indeterminacy. His poems had to accommodate these opposing impulses. Concerning the sequence of poems in *Notebook 1967–1968*, begun as a poetic diary, he said: "Accident threw up the subject and the plot swallowed them—famished for human chances." If Lowell often swallowed up the casual, the random, the ordinary, and the domestic into the forms of his poems, his best plots have a spontaneity whose meanings cannot be fixed.

The burden of family history was substantial for Lowell, whose ancestors included members of Boston's patrician families. His grandfather was a well-known Episcopal minister and head of the fashionable St. Mark's School, which the poet was later to attend. His great-granduncle James Russell Lowell had been a poet and ambassador to England. The family's light note was provided by the poet Amy Lowell, "big and a scandal, as if Mae West were a cousin." In the context of this history, Lowell's father, who fared badly in business after his retirement from service as a naval officer, appeared as a diminished figure.

Lowell's first act of revising family history was to leave the East after two years at Harvard (1935–37) to study at Kenyon College with John Crowe Ransom, the poet and critic. The move brought him in closer touch with the New Criticism and its predilections for "formal difficult poems," the wit and irony of English Metaphysical writers such as John Donne. He also, through Ransom and the poet Allen Tate, came into contact with (although never formally joined) the Fugitive movement, whose members were southern agrarians opposed to what they regarded as the corrupting values of northern industrialism.

Two of the acts that most decisively separated Lowell from family history were his conversion to Roman Catholicism (1940) and his resistance to American policies in World War II. Although he did try to enlist in the navy, he refused to be drafted into the army. He opposed the saturation bombing of Hamburg and the Allied policy of unconditional surrender and was as a result sentenced to a year's confinement in New York's West Street jail. The presiding judge at his hearing admonished him for "marring" his family traditions. In his first book, *Lord Weary's Castle* (1946), his Catholicism provided a set of symbols and a distanced platform from which to express his violent antagonism to Protestant mercantile Boston. The stunning, apocalyptic conclusions of these early poems ("the Lord survives the rainbow of his will" or "The blue kingfisher dives on you in fire") render the devastating judgment of the eternal on the fallen history of the individual and the nation.

Alongside those poems drawing on Old Testament anger, there were those poems in *Lord Weary's Castle* such as *Mr. Edwards and the Spider* that explored from within the nervous intensity which underlay Puritan revivalism. Later dramatic narratives with modern settings such as *The Mills of the Kavanaghs* and *Falling Asleep over the Aeneid* reveal his psychological interest in and obsession with ruined New England families.

In *Life Studies* (1959), Lowell changed his style dramatically. His subjects became explicitly autobiographical, and his language more open and direct. In 1957 he gave readings in California, where Allen Ginsberg and the other Beats had just made their strongest impact in San Francisco. By contrast to their candid, breezy writing, Lowell felt his own seemed "distant, symbol-ridden, and willfully difficult. . . . I felt my old poems hid what they were really about, and many times offered a stiff, humorless and even impenetrable surface." Although more controlled and severe than Beat writers, he was stimulated by Ginsberg's self-revelations to write more openly than he had about his parents and grandparents, about the mental breakdowns he suffered in the 1950s, and about the difficulties of marriage. (Lowell divorced his first wife, the novelist Jean Stafford, and married the critic Elizabeth Hardwick in 1949).

*Life Studies*, by and large, records his ambivalence toward the New England where he resettled after the war, on Boston's "hardly passionate Marlborough Street." Revising his stance toward New England and family history, he no longer denounces the city of his fathers as if he were a privileged outsider. In complicated psychological portraits of his childhood, his relation to his parents and his wives, he assumes a portion of the weakness and vulnerability for himself.

In 1960 Lowell left Boston to live in New York City. *For the Union Dead* (1964), the book that followed, continued the autobiographical vein of *Life Studies*. Lowell called it a book about "witheredness . . . lemony, soured and dry, the drouth I had touched with my own hands." These poems seem more carefully controlled than his earlier *Life Studies*. Often they organize key images from the past into a pattern that illuminates the present. The book includes a number of poems that fuse private and public themes, such as *Fall 1961* and the volume's title poem.

In 1969 Lowell published *Notebook 1967–1968*, and then revised these poems for a second, augmented edition, called simply *Notebook* (1970). In 1973, in a characteristic act, he once more revised, rearranged, and expanded *Notebook's* poems, and published them in two separate books. The more personal poems, recording the breakup of his second marriage and his separation from his wife and daughter, were published as *For Lizzie and Harriet*. Those dealing more with public subjects, past and present, were published under the title *History*. Taken together, these two books show Lowell once again engaged with the relations between the random event, or the moment out of a personal life, and an epic design. In these unrhymed, loosely blank verse revisions of the sonnet Lowell responded to the books he was reading, to the events of his personal life, and to the national issue of the Vietnam War, of which he was an outspoken critic. "Things I felt or saw, or read were drift in the whirlpool."

At the same time, a new collection of sonnets, *The Dolphin* (1973), appeared, recording his marriage to Lady Caroline Blackwood. He divided his time between her home in England and periods of teaching writing and literature at Harvard—a familiar pattern for him in which the old tensions between New England and "elsewhere" were being constantly explored and renewed. His last book, *Day by Day* (1977), records those stresses as well as new marital difficulties. It also contains some of his most powerful poems about his childhood.

For those who cherish the work of the early Lowell, with its manic, rhythmic energy and its enjambed lines building to fierce power or those who admire the passionate engagement of *Life Studies* or *For the Union Dead*, the poems of his last four books can be disappointing. At times flat and dispirited, they can seem worked up rather than fully imagined. Yet in poems like *Returning Turtle* or the two titled *No Hearing*, the later Lowell demonstrates his substantial gifts in a quieter mode. The excitement in these poems lies in the way his language quickens with changing feelings and reveals the heart surprised by an ordinary moment or event.

Lowell's career included an interest in the theater, for which he wrote a version of *Prometheus Bound*, a translation of Racine's *Phaedra*, and adaptations of Melville and Hawthorne stories gathered as *The Old Glory*. He also translated from modern European poetry and the classics, often freely as "imitations," which brought important poetic voices into English currency. His *Selected Poems* (his own choices) appeared in 1976. When he died suddenly at the age of sixty, he was the dominant and most honored poet of his generation—not only for his ten volumes of verse but for his broad activity as a man of letters. He took the role of poet as public figure, sometimes at great personal cost. He was with the group of writers who led Vietnam War protesters against the Pentagon in 1967, where Norman Mailer, a fellow protester, observed that "Lowell gave off at times the unwilling haunted saintliness of a man who was repaying the moral debts of ten generations of ancestors."

# The Quaker Graveyard in Nantucket

## [*For Warren Winslow,*[1] *Dead at Sea*]

*Let man have dominion over the fishes of the sea and the fowls of the air and the beasts of the whole earth, and every creeping creature that moveth upon the earth.*[2]

### I

A brackish reach of shoal off Madaket[3]—
The sea was still breaking violently and night
Had steamed into our North Atlantic Fleet,
When the drowned sailor clutched the drag-net. Light
Flashed from his matted head and marble feet,                5
He grappled at the net
With the coiled, hurdling muscles of his thighs:
The corpse was bloodless, a botch of reds and whites,
Its open, staring eyes
Were lustreless dead-lights[4]                                10
Or cabin-windows on a stranded hulk
Heavy with sand. We weight the body, close
Its eyes and heave it seaward whence it came,
Where the heel-headed dogfish barks its nose
On Ahab's[5] void and forehead; and the name            15
Is blocked in yellow chalk.

---

1. A cousin of Lowell's who died in the sinking of a naval vessel during World War II.
2. From Genesis 1.26, the account of the creation of man.
3. On Nantucket Island.
4. Shutters over portholes to keep out water in a storm. The images in lines 4–11 come from "The Shipwreck,"

the opening chapter of *Cape Cod* by Henry David Thoreau (1817–1862).
5. Protagonist of Herman Melville's *Moby-Dick* who drowns as a result of his obsessive hunt for the white whale. Melville uses Ahab's domineering forehead as an emblem of his monomaniac passion.

Sailors, who pitch this portent at the sea
Where dreadnaughts shall confess
Its hell-bent deity,
When you are powerless                                         20
To sand-bag this Atlantic bulwark, faced
By the earth-shaker, green, unwearied, chaste
In his steel scales: ask for no Orphean lute
To pluck life back.[6] The guns of the steeled fleet
Recoil and then repeat                                        25
The hoarse salute.

### II

Whenever winds are moving and their breath
Heaves at the roped-in bulwarks of this pier,
The terns and sea-gulls tremble at your death
In these home waters. Sailor, can you hear                   30
The Pequod's[7] sea wings, beating landward, fall
Headlong and break on our Atlantic wall
Off 'Sconset, where the yawing S-boats splash
The bellbuoy, with ballooning spinnakers,
As the entangled, screeching mainsheet clears               35
The blocks: off Madaket, where lubbers[8] lash
The heavy surf and throw their long lead squids
For blue-fish? Sea-gulls blink their heavy lids
Seaward. The winds' wings beat upon the stones,
Cousin, and scream for you and the claws rush               40
At the sea's throat and wring it in the slush
Of this old Quaker graveyard where the bones
Cry out in the long night for the hurt beast
Bobbing by Ahab's whaleboats in the East.

### III

All you recovered from Poseidon died                        45
With you, my cousin, and the harrowed brine
Is fruitless on the blue beard of the god,
Stretching beyond us to the castles in Spain,
Nantucket's westward haven. To Cape Cod
Guns, cradled on the tide,                                    50
Blast the eelgrass about a waterclock
Of bilge and backwash, roil the salt and sand
Lashing earth's scaffold, rock
Our warships in the hand
Of the great God, where time's contrition blues            55
Whatever it was these Quaker[9] sailors lost
In the mad scramble of their lives. They died

---

6. In Greek mythology, Orpheus through his music
tried to win the freedom of his bride Eurydice from the
Underworld. "Earth-shaker": an epithet for Poseidon,
the Greek god of the oceans.
7. Ahab's ship, destroyed by Moby-Dick.

8. Sailor's term for an awkward crew member. "Yawing": steering wildly in heavy seas. "S-boats": type of
large racing sailboats.
9. The whaling population of Nantucket included
many Quakers.

When time was open-eyed,
Wooden and childish; only bones abide
There, in the nowhere, where their boats were tossed                    60
Sky-high, where mariners had fabled news
Of IS,[1] the whited monster. What it cost
Them is their secret. In the sperm-whale's slick
I see the Quakers drown and hear their cry:
"If God himself had not been on our side,                               65
If God himself had not been on our side,
When the Atlantic rose against us, why,
Then it had swallowed us up quick."


                              IV

This is the end of the whaleroad[2] and the whale
Who spewed Nantucket bones on the thrashed swell                       70
And stirred the troubled waters to whirlpools
To send the Pequod packing off to hell:
This is the end of them, three-quarters fools,
Snatching at straws to sail
Seaward and seaward on the turntail whale,                             75
Spouting out blood and water as it rolls,
Sick as a dog to these Atlantic shoals:
Clamavimus,[3] O depths. Let the sea-gulls wail

For water, for the deep where the high tide
Mutters to its hurt self, mutters and ebbs.                            80
Waves wallow in their wash, go out and out,
Leave only the death-rattle of the crabs,
The beach increasing, its enormous snout
Sucking the ocean's side.
This is the end of running on the waves;                               85
We are poured out like water. Who will dance
The mast-lashed master of Leviathans
Up from this field of Quakers in their unstoned graves?


                              V

When the whale's viscera go and the roll
Of its corruption overruns this world                                 90
Beyond tree-swept Nantucket and Woods Hole[4]
And Martha's Vineyard, Sailor, will your sword
Whistle and fall and sink into the fat?
In the great ash-pit of Jehoshaphat[5]
The bones cry for the blood of the white whale,                       95
The fat flukes arch and whack about its ears,

1. The white whale is here imagined as a force like the God of Exodus 3.14, who, when asked his name by Moses, replies, "I AM THAT I AM." Also an abbreviation of Jesus Salvator.
2. An Anglo-Saxon epithet for the sea.
3. We have called (Latin). Adapting the opening of Psalm 130: "Out of the depths have I cried unto thee,

O Lord."
4. On the coast of Massachusetts near the island of Martha's Vineyard.
5. "The day of judgment. The world, according to some prophets, will end in fire" [Lowell's note]. In Joel 3, the Last Judgment takes place in the valley of Jehoshaphat.

The death-lance churns into the sanctuary, tears
The gun-blue swingle,[6] heaving like a flail,
And hacks the coiling life out: it works and drags
And rips the sperm-whale's midriff into rags,                          100
Gobbets of blubber spill to wind and weather,
Sailor, and gulls go round the stoven timbers
Where the morning stars sing out together
And thunder shakes the white surf and dismembers
The red flag hammered in the mast-head.[7] Hide,                      105
Our steel, Jonas Messias, in Thy side.[8]


### VI.  OUR LADY OF WALSINGHAM[9]

There once the penitents took off their shoes
And then walked barefoot the remaining mile;
And the small trees, a stream and hedgerows file
Slowly along the munching English lane,                                110
Like cows to the old shrine, until you lose
Track of your dragging pain.
The stream flows down under the druid tree,
Shiloah's[1] whirlpools gurgle and make glad
The castle of God. Sailor, you were glad                              115
And whistled Sion by that stream. But see:

Our Lady, too small for her canopy,
Sits near the altar. There's no comeliness
At all or charm in that expressionless
Face with its heavy eyelids. As before,                               120
This face, for centuries a memory,
*Non est species, neque decor,*[2]
Expressionless, expresses God: it goes
Past castled Sion. She knows what God knows,
Not Calvary's Cross nor crib at Bethlehem                             125
Now, and the world shall come to Walsingham.


### VII

The empty winds are creaking and the oak
Splatters and splatters on the cenotaph,
The boughs are trembling and a gaff
Bobs on the untimely stroke                                           130
Of the greased wash exploding on a shoal-bell
In the old mouth of the Atlantic. It's well;
Atlantic, you are fouled with the blue sailors,
Sea-monsters, upward angel, downward fish:

---

6. Knifelike wooden instrument for beating flax.
7. At the end of *Moby-Dick*, the arm of the American Indian Tashtego appears from the waves and nails Ahab's flag to the sinking mast.
8. Because he emerged alive from the belly of a whale, the prophet Jonah is often linked with the messiah as a figure of salvation. Lowell imagines that a harpoon strikes Jonah inside the whale as the Roman soldier's spear struck Jesus on the cross.
9. Lowell took these details from E. I. Watkin's *Catholic Art and Culture*, which includes a description of the medieval shrine of the Virgin at Walsingham.
1. The stream that flows past God's Temple on Mount Sion (Isaiah 8.6). In Isaiah 51.11, the redeemed come "singing into Zion."
2. There is no ostentation or elegance (Latin).

Unmarried and corroding, spare of flesh                              135
Mart once of supercilious, wing'd clippers,
Atlantic, where your bell-trap guts its spoil
You could cut the brackish winds with a knife
Here in Nantucket, and cast up the time
When the Lord God formed man from the sea's slime                    140
And breathed into his face the breath of life,
And blue-lung'd combers lumbered to the kill.
The Lord survives the rainbow[3] of His will.

                                                                     1946


# Mr. Edwards and the Spider[1]

I saw the spiders marching through the air,
Swimming from tree to tree that mildewed day
    In latter August when the hay
    Came creaking to the barn. But where
        The wind is westerly,                                        5
Where gnarled November makes the spiders fly
    Into the apparitions of the sky,
    They purpose nothing but their ease and die
Urgently beating east to sunrise and the sea;

What are we in the hands of the great God?[2]                       10
It was in vain you set up thorn and briar
    In battle array against the fire
    And treason crackling in your blood;
        For the wild thorns grow tame
And will do nothing to oppose the flame;                            15
    Your lacerations tell the losing game
    You play against a sickness past your cure.
How will the hands be strong? How will the heart endure?

A very little thing, a little worm,
Or hourglass-blazoned spider,[3] it is said,                        20
    Can kill a tiger. Will the dead
    Hold up his mirror and affirm
        To the four winds the smell
And flash of his authority? It's well
    If God who holds you to the pit of hell,                        25
    Much as one holds a spider, will destroy,
Baffle and dissipate your soul. As a small boy

3. Alluding to God's covenant with Noah after the
Flood. The rainbow symbolized the fact that humanity
would never again be destroyed by flood (Genesis
9.11).
1. Jonathan Edwards (1703–1758), Puritan preacher
and theologian. Lowell quotes his writings throughout.
The details of the first stanza come from his youthful
essay *Of Insects* ("The Habits of Spiders").

2. This stanza draws on Edwards's sermon "Sinners in
the Hands of an Angry God," whose point of departure
is Ezekiel 22.14: "Can thine heart endure or can thine
hands be strong in the days that I shall deal with thee"
(cf. line 18).
3. The poisonous black widow spider has, on the underside of its abdomen, a red marking that resembles
an hourglass.

On Windsor Marsh,[4] I saw the spider die
When thrown into the bowels of fierce fire:
    There's no long struggle, no desire        30
    To get up on its feet and fly—
        It stretches out its feet
And dies. This is the sinner's last retreat;
Yes, and no strength exerted on the heat
Then sinews the abolished will, when sick        35
And full of burning, it will whistle on a brick.

But who can plumb the sinking of that soul?
Josiah Hawley,[5] picture yourself cast
    Into a brick-kiln where the blast
    Fans your quick vitals to a coal—        40
        If measured by a glass,
How long would it seem burning! Let there pass
A minute, ten, ten trillion; but the blaze
Is infinite, eternal: this is death,
To die and know it. This is the Black Widow, death.    45

    1946

# Memories of West Street and Lepke[1]

Only teaching on Tuesdays, book-worming
in pajamas fresh from the washer each morning,
I hog a whole house on Boston's
"hardly passionate Marlborough Street,"[2]
where even the man        5
scavenging filth in the back alley trash cans,
has two children, a beach wagon, a helpmate,
and is a "young Republican."
I have a nine months' daughter,
young enough to be my granddaughter.        10
Like the sun she rises in her flame-flamingo infants' wear.

These are the tranquillized *Fifties,*
and I am forty. Ought I to regret my seedtime?
I was a fire-breathing Catholic C.O.,[3]
and made my manic statement,        15
telling off the state and president, and then
sat waiting sentence in the bull pen
beside a Negro boy with curlicues
of marijuana in his hair.

Given a year.        20
I walked on the roof of the West Street Jail, a short

---

4. East Windsor, Connecticut, Edwards's childhood home.
5. Edwards's uncle, Joseph Hawley.
1. In 1943 Lowell was sentenced to a year in New York's West Street jail for his refusal to serve in the armed forces. Among the prisoners was Lepke Bu-

chalter, head of Murder Incorporated, an organized crime syndicate, who had been convicted of murder.
2. William James's phrase for a street in the elegant Back Bay section of Boston, where Lowell lived in the 1950s.
3. Conscientious objector (to war).

enclosure like my school soccer court,
and saw the Hudson River once a day
through sooty clothesline entanglements
and bleaching khaki tenements.                                    25
Strolling, I yammered metaphysics with Abramowitz,
a jaundice-yellow ("it's really tan")
and fly-weight pacifist,
so vegetarian,
he wore rope shoes and preferred fallen fruit.                   30
He tried to convert Bioff and Brown,
the Hollywood pimps, to his diet.
Hairy, muscular, suburban,
wearing chocolate double-breasted suits,
they blew their tops and beat him black and blue.                35

I was so out of things, I'd never heard
of the Jehovah's Witnesses.[4]
"Are you a C.O.?" I asked a fellow jailbird.
"No," he answered, "I'm a J.W."
He taught me the "hospital tuck,"[5]                             40
and pointed out the T-shirted back
of *Murder Incorporated's* Czar Lepke,
there piling towels on a rack,
or dawdling off to his little segregated cell full
of things forbidden the common man:                             45
a portable radio, a dresser, two toy American
flags tied together with a ribbon of Easter palm.
Flabby, bald, lobotomized,
he drifted in a sheepish calm,
where no agonizing reappraisal                                   50
jarred his concentration on the electric chair—
hanging like an oasis in his air
of lost connections. . . .

                                                               1959


# Skunk Hour

## for Elizabeth Bishop[1]

Nautilus Island's[2] hermit
heiress still lives through winter in her Spartan cottage;
her sheep still graze above the sea.
Her son's a bishop. Her farmer
is first selectman in our village;                               5
she's in her dotage.

---

4. A Christian revivalist sect strongly opposed to war
and denying the power of the state in matters of conscience.
5. The authorized, efficient way of making beds in a
hospital.

1. Lowell's poem is a response to Elizabeth Bishop's
*The Armadillo.*
2. The poem is set in Castine, Maine, where Lowell
had a summer house.

Thirsting for
the hierarchic privacy
of Queen Victoria's century,
she buys up all                                                                    10
the eyesores facing her shore,
and lets them fall.

The season's ill—
we've lost our summer millionaire,
who seemed to leap from an L. L. Bean                                              15
catalogue.[3] His nine-knot yawl
was auctioned off to lobstermen.
A red fox stain covers Blue Hill.

And now our fairy
decorator brightens his shop for fall;                                             20
his fishnet's filled with orange cork,
orange, his cobbler's bench and awl;
there is no money in his work,
he'd rather marry.

One dark night,                                                                    25
my Tudor Ford climbed the hill's skull;
I watched for love-cars. Lights turned down,
they lay together, hull to hull,
where the graveyard shelves on the town. . . .
My mind's not right.                                                               30

A car radio bleats,
"Love, O careless Love. . . ." I hear
my ill-spirit sob in each blood cell,
as if my hand were at its throat. . . .
I myself am hell;[4]                                                               35
nobody's here—

only skunks, that search
in the moonlight for a bite to eat.
They march on their soles up Main Street:
white stripes, moonstruck eyes' red fire                                           40
under the chalk-dry and spar spire
of the Trinitarian Church.

I stand on top
of our back steps and breathe the rich air—
a mother skunk with her column of kittens swills the garbage pail.                 45
She jabs her wedge-head in a cup
of sour cream, drops her ostrich tail,
and will not scare.

1959

---

3. A mail-order house in Maine, which deals primarily with sporting and camping goods.

4. "Which way I fly is Hell, myself am Hell" (Satan in Milton's *Paradise Lost* 4.75).

# Soft Wood

*for Harriet Winslow*

Sometimes I have supposed seals
must live as long as the Scholar Gypsy.[1]
Even in their barred pond at the zoo they are happy,
and no sunflower turns
more delicately to the sun                                                    5
without a wincing of the will.

Here too in Maine things bend to the wind forever.
After two years away, one must get used
to the painted soft wood staying bright and clean,
to the air blasting an all-white wall whiter,                                 10
as it blows through curtain and screen
touched with salt and evergreen.

The green juniper berry spills crystal-clear gin,
and even the hot water in the bathtub
is more than water,                                                           15
and rich with the scouring effervescence
of something healing,
the illimitable salt.

Things last, but sometimes for days here
only children seem fit to handle children,                                    20
and there is no utility or inspiration
in the wind smashing without direction.
The fresh paint
on the captains' houses hides softer wood.

Their square-riggers[2] used to whiten                                         25
the four corners of the globe,
but it's no consolation to know
the possessors seldom outlast the possessions,
once warped and mothered by their touch.
Shed skin will never fit another wearer.                                       30

Yet the seal pack will bark past my window
summer after summer.
This is the season
when our friends may and will die daily.
Surely the lives of the old                                                    35
are briefer than the young.

Harriet Winslow, who owned this house,
was more to me than my mother.
I think of you far off in Washington,

---

1. Hero of a poem (1853) by Matthew Arnold, derived
from the old legend of a poor Oxford scholar who
joined the Gypsies roaming the countryside and who
still haunts Oxford.
2. Sailing ships of the later 19th century.

breathing in the heat wave                                                    40
and air-conditioning, knowing
each drug that numbs alerts another nerve to pain.

1965

# For the Union Dead[1]

*"Relinquunt Omnia Servare Rem Publicam."*[2]

The old South Boston Aquarium stands
in a Sahara of snow now. Its broken windows are boarded.
The bronze weathervane cod has lost half its scales.
The airy tanks are dry.

Once my nose crawled like a snail on the glass;                               5
my hand tingled
to burst the bubbles
drifting from the noses of the cowed, compliant fish.

My hand draws back. I often sigh still
for the dark downward and vegetating kingdom                                  10
of the fish and reptile. One morning last March,
I pressed against the new barbed and galvanized

fence on the Boston Common. Behind their cage,
yellow dinosaur steamshovels were grunting
as they cropped up tons of mush and grass                                     15
to gouge their underworld garage.

Parking spaces luxuriate like civic
sandpiles in the heart of Boston.
A girdle of orange, Puritan-pumpkin colored girders
braces the tingling Statehouse,                                               20

shaking over the excavations, as it faces Colonel Shaw
and his bell-cheeked Negro infantry
on St. Gaudens' shaking Civil War relief,
propped by a plank splint against the garage's earthquake.

Two months after marching through Boston,                                     25
half the regiment was dead;

---

1. First published under the title *Colonel Shaw and the Massachusetts' 54th* in a paperback edition of *Life Studies* (1960). With a change of title, it became the title poem of *For the Union Dead* (1964).
2. Robert Gould Shaw (1837–1863) led the first all-African-American regiment in the North during the Civil War. He was killed in the attack against Fort Wagner, South Carolina. A bronze relief by the sculptor Augustus Saint-Gaudens (1848–1897), dedicated in 1897, standing opposite the Massachusetts State House on Boston Common, commemorates the deaths. A Latin inscription on the monument reads *Omnia Reliquit Servare Rem Publicam* ("He leaves all behind to serve the Republic"). Lowell's epigraph alters the inscription slightly, changing the third-person singular (*he*) to the third-person plural: "*They* give up everything to serve the Republic."

at the dedication
William James[3] could almost hear the bronze Negroes breathe.

Their monument sticks like a fishbone
in the city's throat.                                                    30
Its Colonel is as lean
as a compass-needle.

He has an angry wrenlike vigilance,
a greyhound's gentle tautness;
he seems to wince at pleasure,                                           35
and suffocate for privacy.

He is out of bounds now. He rejoices in man's lovely,
peculiar power to choose life and die—
when he leads his black soldiers to death,
he cannot bend his back.                                                 40

On a thousand small town New England greens,
the old white churches hold their air
of sparse, sincere rebellion; frayed flags
quilt the graveyards of the Grand Army of the Republic.

The stone statues of the abstract Union Soldier                         45
grow slimmer and younger each year—
wasp-waisted, they doze over muskets
and muse through their sideburns . . .

Shaw's father wanted no monument
except the ditch,                                                       50
where his son's body was thrown[4]
and lost with his "niggers."

The ditch is nearer.
There are no statues for the last war[5] here;
on Boylston Street,[6] a commercial photograph                          55
shows Hiroshima boiling

over a Mosler Safe, the "Rock of Ages"
that survived the blast. Space is nearer.
When I crouch to my television set,
the drained faces of Negro school-children rise like balloons.[7]       60

Colonel Shaw
is riding on his bubble,
he waits
for the blessed break.

---

3. Philosopher and psychologist (1842–1910) who
taught at Harvard.
4. By the Confederate soldiers at Fort Wagner.
5. World War II.

6. In Boston, where the poem is set.
7. Probably news photographs connected with contemporary civil rights demonstrations to secure deseg-
regation of schools in the South.

The Aquarium is gone. Everywhere,                              65
giant finned cars nose forward like fish;
a savage servility
slides by on grease.

                                                    1960, 1964


## Epilogue[1]

Those blessèd structures, plot and rhyme—
why are they no help to me now
I want to make
something imagined, not recalled?
I hear the noise of my own voice:                              5
*The painter's vision is not a lens,*
*it trembles to caress the light.*
But sometimes everything I write
with the threadbare art of my eye
seems a snapshot,                                              10
lurid, rapid, garish, grouped,
heightened from life,
yet paralyzed by fact.
All's misalliance.
Yet why not say what happened?                                 15
Pray for the grace of accuracy
Vermeer[2] gave to the sun's illumination
stealing like the tide across a map
to his girl solid with yearning.
We are poor passing facts,                                     20
warned by that to give
each figure in the photograph
his living name.

                                                            1977

---

1. The poem is printed as the last piece (excluding a      2. Jan Vermeer (1632–1675), Dutch painter noted for
few translations) in Lowell's last book, *Day by Day*      his subtle handling of the effects of light.
(1977).

---

# GWENDOLYN  BROOKS
## b.  1917

"If there was ever a born poet," Alice Walker once said in an interview, "I think it
is Brooks." A passionate sense of language and an often daring use of formal structures are hallmarks of Gwendolyn Brooks's poetry. She has used these gifts in a
career characterized by dramatic evolution, a career that links two very different
generations of African-American poets. "Until 1967," Brooks has said, "my own
Blackness did not confront me with a shrill spelling of itself." Since that time she
has grouped herself with militant black writers and defined her work as belonging

primarily to the African-American community. In her earlier work, however, Brooks had followed the example of the older writers of the Harlem Renaissance, Langston Hughes and Countee Cullen among them, who honored the ideal of an integrated society. In that period her work had received support largely from white audiences. But Brooks's changing sense of her commitments should not obscure her persistent, underlying concerns. She has never been a poet without political awareness, and in remarkably versatile poems, both early and late, she has written powerfully about black experience and black rage, with a particular awareness of the complex lives of black women.

Brooks was born in Topeka, Kansas; she grew up in Chicago and is closely identified with the energies and problems of its black community. She went to Chicago's Englewood High School and graduated from Wilson Junior College. Brooks remembers writing poetry from the time she was seven and keeping poetry notebooks from the time she was eleven. She got her education in the moderns— Pound and Eliot—under the guidance of a rich Chicago socialite, Inez Cunningham Stark, who was a reader for *Poetry* magazine and taught a poetry class at the Southside Community Art Center. Her first book, A *Street in Bronzeville* (1945), took its title from the name journalists gave to the Chicago black ghetto. Her poems portrayed the waste and loss that are the inevitable result of what Langston Hughes called the blacks' "dream deferred." With her second book of poems, *Annie Allen* (1949), Brooks became the first African-American to receive the Pulitzer Prize for poetry.

In *Annie Allen* and in her Bronzeville poems (*Bronzeville Boys and Girls*, 1956, continued the work begun in A *Street in Bronzeville*), Brooks concentrated on portraits of what Langston Hughes called "the ordinary aspects of black life." In character sketches she stressed the vitality and the often subversive morality of ghetto figures; good girls who want to be bad, the boredom of the children of hardworking pious mothers, the laments of black mothers and women abandoned by their men. Brooks's diction was a combination of the florid biblical speech of black Protestant preachers, street talk, and the main speech patterns of English and American verse. She wrote vigorous, strongly accented, and strongly rhymed lines with a great deal of alliteration. She also cultivated traditional lyric forms; for example, she was one of the few modern poets to write extensively in the sonnet form.

A great change in Brooks's life came with the Second Black Writers' Conference at Fisk University in 1967, in whose charged activist atmosphere she encountered many of the new young black poets. After this, Brooks became interested in writing poetry exclusively for black audiences. She drew closer to militant political groups as a result of conducting poetry workshops for some members of the Blackstone Rangers, a teenage gang in Chicago. In autobiographical writings such as her prose *Report from Part One*, Brooks became more self-conscious about her own potential role as a leader of black feminists. She left her New York publisher to have her work printed by African-American publishers, especially the Broadside Press. Brooks's poetry, too, has changed, in both its focus and its technique. Her subjects tend to be more explicitly political and to deal with questions of revolutionary violence and issues of African-American identity. In style, too, her work has evolved out of the concentrated imagery and narratives of her earlier writing, with its often formal diction, and has moved toward an increased use of the energetic, improvisatory rhythms of jazz, the combinations of African chants, and an emphatically spoken language. The result is a poetry constantly revising itself and the world, open to change but evocative of history. Reading Brooks, as Alice Walker also remarked in her interview, "your whole spiritual past begins to float around in your throat."

FROM A STREET IN BRONZEVILLE

*to David and Keziah Brooks*

## kitchenette building

We are things of dry hours and the involuntary plan,
Grayed in, and gray. "Dream" makes a giddy sound, not strong
Like "rent," "feeding a wife," "satisfying a man."

But could a dream send up through onion fumes
Its white and violet, fight with fried potatoes                    5
And yesterday's garbage ripening in the hall,
Flutter, or sing an aria down these rooms

Even if we were willing to let it in,
Had time to warm it, keep it very clean,
Anticipate a message, let it begin?                                10

We wonder. But not well! not for a minute!
Since Number Five is out of the bathroom now,
We think of lukewarm water, hope to get in it.

1945

## the mother

Abortions will not let you forget.
You remember the children you got that you did not get,
The damp small pulps with a little or with no hair,
The singers and workers that never handled the air.
You will never neglect or beat                                     5
Them, or silence or buy with a sweet.
You will never wind up the sucking-thumb
Or scuttle off ghosts that come.
You will never leave them, controlling your luscious sigh,
Return for a snack of them, with gobbling mother-eye.              10

I have heard in the voices of the wind the voices of my dim
        killed children.
I have contracted. I have eased
My dim dears at the breasts they could never suck.
I have said, Sweets, if I sinned, if I seized
Your luck                                                          15
And your lives from your unfinished reach,
If I stole your births and your names,
Your straight baby tears and your games,
Your stilted or lovely loves, your tumults, your marriages, aches,
        and your deaths,
If I poisoned the beginnings of your breaths,                     20
Believe that even in my deliberateness I was not deliberate.
Though why should I whine,

Whine that the crime was other than mine?—
Since anyhow you are dead.
Or rather, or instead,                                           25
You were never made.

But that too, I am afraid,
Is faulty: oh, what shall I say, how is the truth to be said?
You were born, you had body, you died.
It is just that you never giggled or planned or cried.          30

Believe me, I loved you all.
Believe me, I knew you, though faintly, and I loved, I loved you
All.

                                                                1945


## the vacant lot

Mrs. Coley's three-flat brick
Isn't here any more.
All done with seeing her fat little form
Burst out of the basement door;
And with seeing her African son-in-law                          5
(Rightful heir to the throne)
With his great white strong cold squares of teeth
And his little eyes of stone;
And seeing the squat fat daughter
Letting in the men                                              10
When majesty has gone for the day—
And letting them out again.

                                                                1945


## The White Troops Had Their Orders But the Negroes Looked Like Men

They had supposed their formula was fixed.
They had obeyed instructions to devise
A type of cold, a type of hooded gaze.
But when the Negroes came they were perplexed.
These Negroes looked like men. Besides, it taxed               5
Time and the temper to remember those
Congenital iniquities that cause
Disfavor of the darkness. Such as boxed
Their feelings properly, complete to tags—
A box for dark men and a box for Other—                        10
Would often find the contents had been scrambled.
Or even switched. Who really gave two figs?
Neither the earth nor heaven ever trembled.
And there was nothing startling in the weather.

                                                                1945

## The Bean Eaters

They eat beans mostly, this old yellow pair.
Dinner is a casual affair.
Plain chipware on a plain and creaking wood,
Tin flatware.

Two who are Mostly Good.                                                    5
Two who have lived their day,
But keep on putting on their clothes
And putting things away.

And remembering . . .
Remembering, with twinklings and twinges,                                  10
As they lean over the beans in their rented back room that is full of beads and
    receipts and dolls and cloths, tobacco crumbs, vases and fringes.

1960


## The Last Quatrain of the Ballad of Emmett Till[1]

after the murder,
after the burial

Emmett's mother is a pretty-faced thing;
        the tint of pulled taffy.
She sits in a red room,                                                    5
        drinking black coffee.
She kisses her killed boy.
        And she is sorry.
Chaos in windy grays
        through a red prairie.                                             10

1960


## To the Diaspora[2]

*you did not know you were Afrika*

When you set out for Afrika
you did not know you were going.
Because
you did not know you were Afrika.
You did not know the Black continent                                       5
that had to be reached
was you.

---

1. A fourteen-year-old African-American boy lynched
in Mississippi in 1955 for allegedly "leering" at a
white woman.

2. People settled far from their ancestral homelands.

I could not have told you then that some sun
would come,
somewhere over the road,                                        10
would come evoking the diamonds
of you, the Black continent—
somewhere over the road.
You would not have believed my mouth.

When I told you, meeting you somewhere close            15
to the heat and youth of the road,
liking my loyalty, liking belief,
you smiled and you thanked me but very little believed me.

Here is some sun. Some.
Now off into the places rough to reach.                         20
Though dry, though drowsy, all unwillingly a-wobble,
into the dissonant and dangerous crescendo.
Your work, that was done, to be done to be done to be done.

                                                                1981

## The Coora Flower

Today I learned the *coora* flower
grows high in the mountains of Itty-go-luba Bésa.
Province Meechee.
Pop. 39.

Now I am coming home.                                            5
This, at least, is Real, and what I know.

It was restful, learning nothing necessary.
School is tiny vacation. At least you can sleep.
At least you can think of love or feeling your boy friend against you
(which is not free from grief).                                  10

But now it's Real Business.
I am Coming Home.

My mother will be screaming in an almost dirty dress.
The crack is gone. So a Man will be in the house.

I must watch myself.                                             15
I must not dare to sleep.

                                                                1991

# ROBERT DUNCAN
## 1919–1988

In *The Truth & Life of Myth: An Essay in Essential Autobiography* (1968), Robert Duncan writes: "In the very beginning, in the awakening of childhood back of this later awakening of the man I was to be, there had been my mother's voice reading the fairy tales and myths that were to remain the charged ground of my poetic reality." Myth remained for Duncan the ground of poetic reality throughout his life, expressing for him the relation between the individual life and the life of the universe. Duncan believes in the enduring truth of myth as a story of soul making, which for him, as for Keats, is the poet's primary activity. A poet learned and widely read, Duncan makes use of myths from many traditions (in this, he reminds us of Ezra Pound), including those of Christianity, Jewish mysticism, and classical and Egyptian mythology.

Duncan's deepest concerns as a poet are expressed in the myth of Eros and Psyche, which he retells in *A Poem Beginning with a Line by Pindar.* He once wrote, "Psyche must doubt and seek to know; reading must become life and writing; and all go wrong. There is no way then but Psyche's search, the creative work of a union in knowledge and experience." This description of Psyche's work might serve to describe his own: in *A Poem Beginning with a Line by Pindar* Duncan carries out the work of poets before him (Pound, William Carlos Williams, and especially, Walt Whitman): the creative work of understanding experience (both the individual's and the nation's) and of recovering lost possibility. As Psyche's task is the recovery of Eros, Duncan is a love poet in the fullest sense. Love, for him, necessarily involves loss and recovery, death and life. The recurring image of Atlantis in his work reinforces this sense of a paradise lost through catastrophe, to be recovered by the poet, as by Psyche, through trial and through the effort of imagination.

Duncan's life began with loss: born in Oakland, California, his mother died at his birth, and he himself has connected this birth memory to his fascination with "the mother-country that has been lost in legend." He was adopted at six months by Edwin and Minnehaha Symmes, both of whom engaged in Hermetic and Rosicrucian studies. From them he took his continuing interest in the magical and the occult. Duncan grew to his early manhood and to his vocation as a poet during World War II, and his understanding of his own personal strife has always been linked for him to a sense of national strife, as in *A Poem Beginning with a Line by Pindar.* In 1936 he entered the University of California at Berkeley and found there the first of several artistic and social communities that would always be an important part of his life. In 1938 he moved east, and during the early 1940s lived in New York City, where he was part of a group of writers that included Anaïs Nin, Henry Miller, Kenneth Patchen, and George Barker. (The poems of his book *Caesar's Gate*, published in 1955, describe what he has called the "adolescent dismay" of this period.) In New York he also came in contact with the abstract expressionist painters, and when he returned to Berkeley in 1946, he brought with him the excitement of what he had seen. There, under the mentorship of Kenneth Rexroth, Duncan along with the poets Jack Spicer and Robin Blaser began a "renaissance," which he has described as "a reinterpretation of the work of Stein, Joyce, Pound, H. D., Williams, D.H. Lawrence, not as 'we moderns' but as links in a spiritual tradition."

*Heavenly City Earthly City*, Duncan's first book, appeared in 1947. In the 1950s he encountered the poetics of Charles Olson, whose understanding of the poem as "a field of action" confirmed and invigorated Duncan's own thinking about poetic forms. In 1956 he taught for several months at Black Mountain College in North

Carolina, where Olson was rector. Also in the 1950s he began a domestic life with the painter Jess Collins, which was to inform his work for the rest of his life. The household they created together existed, for Duncan, in vital relation to his sense of place in the universe as a whole ("The imagination of this cosmos is as immediate to me as the imagination of my household or myself," he wrote in his essay *Toward an Open Universe*). Both hearth and cosmos are governed by love, the creator for Duncan of growth and harmony but also the source of fury and suffering. Since his essay *The Homosexual in Society* (1944), Duncan had declared his homoeroticism, and his work gives powerful expression to the struggles of the passional self.

The publication of *The Opening of the Field* (1960) marked, Duncan has said, the beginning of his mature work as a poet and the poems of this book remain some of his finest. Close to this time he also began his important prose work, *The H.D. Book*, a work-in-progress of which more than ten chapters appeared in little magazines during his life. Duncan first read H. D.'s *Trilogy* in the 1940s and her poems were relatively unknown when he began his study of her. In what may be one of the most important works of criticism by an American poet in the twentieth century, he explores not only the connections between his own work and H. D.'s but his vision of the generative power of imagination and the life-restoring nature of poetry. His commentaries on modernism in various chapters of this book are often brilliant and provocative. Duncan's work on H. D. issues from his effort as a poet to renew traditions and knowledge lost to modern life and to open up the possibilities of language when "all the nets of words are gone" (as he writes in his moving poem for H. D., *Doves*). Duncan writes to reclaim the poetic ground from which mythology arises, a place (like the meadow in *Often I am Permitted to Return to a Meadow*) that permits return to the "first feeling" of childhood and recovery of a tradition of spiritual testimony. To paraphrase the title of one of William Carlos Williams's essays, the basis of Duncan's faith in art is his belief in the regenerative possibilities of language, its capacity to renew and reorder. For him (as for William Blake, whom he began to study in the 1950s), the domain of imagination encompasses the entire universe.

Duncan used *traditional* as an adjective of praise and understood his work as recovering the past in present meanings. His models included not only H. D. and Blake but also the major figures of Whitman and Dante. He was drawn toward Whitman and Dante, he wrote, as each "projected a poem central to his civilization and his vision of ultimate reality—*Leaves of Grass*, like *The Divina Commedia*, being not an epic narrative but the spiritual testament of self-realization." In the work of H. D., Whitman, and Dante, Duncan found the wholeness for which his Psyche searched.

Given that, for Duncan, everything in the universe is related, it is not surprising that his personal sense of apocalypse extended into explicitly political poems. In his introduction to *Bending the Bow* (1971) he wrote, "We enter again and again the last days of our own history, for everywhere living productive forms in the evolution of forms fail, weaken or grow monstrous, destroying the terms of their existence." Duncan felt history grow monstrous especially during the events of the Vietnam War, and he struggled in his work to confront the meanings of that experience. One sign of the seriousness and difficulty of that struggle was his decision, in the 1970s, not to publish another book for at least ten years. The work gestating during that time emerged in two volumes: *Ground Work: Before the War* (1983) and *Ground Work II: In the Dark* (1987). Together the collections represent the culmination of Duncan's years of effort as a poet. Among the poems in these volumes are several sequences, including a group inspired by Dante and a sequence inspired by (and improvising on) the work of the Metaphysical poets, *Seventeenth Century Suite* (previously printed privately in 1973). In a poem from this sequence, he powerfully revises Robert Southwell's *The Burning Babe* to accommodate his own torment as he sees the photographs of children burned by napalm. What sets Duncan apart from many other poets who addressed the Vietnam War is that he does not separate himself from "the nation's store of crimes long / unacknowledged, unrepented" (*From Robert Southwell's "The Burning Babe"*). In this and other poems Duncan confronts his own implication in the evils of war, in the nation's crimes, and understands the task of self-restoration as both a personal and political act.

Duncan's spiritual vision, which he distinguished from any religious orthodoxy, and his serious interest in mysticism set him apart from the mainstreams of contemporary American poetry. This, combined with fifteen years in which he chose to publish relatively little until his last books appeared, led to a neglect of his astonishing achievement as a poet. For Duncan, poetry has a generative function that is at the heart of life, and this makes his poems ambitious. If his work does not always achieve the wholeness to which it aspires, this may be, in part, because he aspires to so much. He believed that no single poem is ever complete in its meaning; each poem awakens the possibility of a new beginning. Although his range of reference can sometimes leave the reader behind, Duncan's best work reaches beyond itself, stirring the reader into just such an awakened sense of life.

# A Poem Beginning with a Line by Pindar[1]

## I

The light foot hears you and the brightness begins[2]
god-step at the margins of thought,
        quick adulterous tread at the heart.
Who is it that goes there?
        Where I see your quick face                                    5
notes of an old music pace the air,
torse-reverberations of a Grecian lyre.

In Goya's canvas Cupid and Psyche[3]
have a hurt voluptuous grace
bruised by redemption. The copper light                               10
falling upon the brown boy's slight body

---

1. Greek lyric poet (c. 522–c. 438 B.C.), author of celebratory odes. "When in the inception of a 'Poem Beginning with a Line by Pindar,' reading late at night the third line of the first Pythian Ode in the translation by Wade-Gery and Bowra, my mind lost hold of Pindar's sense and was faced with certain puns in that the words *light, foot, hears, you, brightness, begins* moved in a world beyond my reading; these were no longer words alone but powers in a theogony, having resonances in Hesiodic and Orphic cosmogonies where the foot that moves in the dance of the poem appears as the pulse of measures in first things. Immediately, sight of Goya's great canvas, once seen in the Marquis deCambo's collection in Barcelona, came to me like a wave carrying the vision—out of the evocation of the fragment from Pindar and out of Goya's pictorial evocation, to add to the masterly powers of my own—the living vision, Cupid and Psyche were there; then the power of a third master, not a master of poetry or of picture but of storytelling, the power of Lucius Apuleius was there too . . . the living genius of these three stood as my masters, and I stood in the very presence

of the story of Cupid and Psyche" (Duncan, *The Truth and Life of Myth*). A *theogony* is an account of the origin and descent of the gods; a *cosmogony*, an account of the origin of the world or universe. Hesiod was a Greek poet (fl. 800 B.C.), among whose works was a *Theogony*. *Orphic* has to do with the legendary Greek poet-musician Orpheus or the rites ascribed to him. For Goya, Cupid and Psyche, and Apuleius, see n. 3, below.
2. The third line of Pindar's Pythian Ode.
3. Francisco José de Goya (1746–1828), Spanish artist, painted a canvas called *Cupid and Psyche*. The story of Cupid and Psyche is told by the Latin writer Lucius Apuleius (fl. c. A.D. 155) in *The Golden Ass*. Psyche (the Greek personification of the soul) marries Cupid, or Eros (the god of love). As a condition of their union Cupid forbids her to look at him and comes to her only in darkness, leaving before dawn. Prompted by her sisters, Psyche disobeys, and Cupid flees. Through a series of trials, however, she becomes immortal and is reunited with Cupid forever.

is carnal fate that sends the soul wailing
up from blind innocence, ensnared
     by dimness
into the deprivations of desiring sight.                                          15

But the eyes in Goya's painting are soft,
diffuse with rapture absorb the flame.
Their bodies yield out of strength.
     Waves of visual pleasure
wrap them in a sorrow previous to their impatience.                               20

A bronze of yearning, a rose that burns
     the tips of their bodies, lips,
ends of fingers, nipples. He is not wingd.
His thighs are flesh, are clouds
     lit by the sun in its going down,                                            25
Hot luminescence at the loins of the visible.

          But they are not in a landscape.
          They exist in an obscurity.

The wind spreading the sail serves them.
The two jealous sisters eager for her ruin                                         30
     serve them.
That she is ignorant, ignorant of what Love will be,
     serves them.
The dark serves them.
The oil scalding his shoulder serves them,[4]                                      35
serves their story. Fate, spinning,
     knots the threads for Love.

Jealousy, ignorance, the hurt . . . serve them.

                              *II*

This is magic. It is passionate dispersion.
What if they grow old? The gods                                                    40
     would not allow it.
     Psyche is preserved.

In time we see a tragedy, a loss of beauty
     the glittering youth
of the god retains—but from this threshold                                        45
     it is age
that is beautiful. It is toward the old poets
     we go, to their faltering,
     their unaltering wrongness that has style,
          their variable truth,                                                   50
          the old faces,

---

4. In the story, Psyche holds an oil lamp above the sleeping Cupid to see him, but a drop of oil spills onto his shoulder. He wakes and flees.

words shed like tears from
a plenitude of powers time stores.

A stroke. These little strokes. A chill.
The old man, feeble, does not recoil[5]        55
Recall. A phase so minute,
    only a part of the word in- jerrd.

    *The Thundermakers descend,*

damerging a nuv. A nerb.
    The present dented of the U        60
nighted stayd. States. The heavy clod?
    Cloud. Invades the brain. What
    if lilacs last in *this* dooryard bloomd?[6]

Hoover, Roosevelt, Truman, Eisenhower[7]—
where among these did the power reside        65
that moves the heart? What flower of the nation
bride-sweet broke to the whole rapture?
Hoover, Coolidge, Harding, Wilson[8]
hear the factories of human misery turning out commodities.
For whom are the holy matins of the heart ringing?        70
Noble men in the quiet of morning hear
Indians singing the continent's violent requiem.
Harding, Wilson, Taft,[9] Roosevelt,
idiots fumbling at the bride's door,
hear the cries of men in meaningless debt and war.        75
Where among these did the spirit reside
that restores the land to productive order?
McKinley, Cleveland, Harrison, Arthur,
Garfield, Hayes, Grant, Johnson,[1]
dwell in the roots of the heart's rancor.        80
How sad "amid lanes and through old woods"[2]
    echoes Whitman's love for Lincoln!

There is no continuity then. Only a few
    posts of the good remain. I too
that am a nation sustain the damage        85
    where smokes of continual ravage
obscure the flame.
            It is across great scars of wrong
    I reach toward the song of kindred men

5. A reference to the poet William Carlos Williams (1883–1963), who suffered a series of strokes that injured his capacity for speech. Duncan phonetically presents this damage.
6. *When Lilacs Last in the Dooryard Bloom'd*, Walt Whitman's elegy for Abraham Lincoln, published in 1866.
7. U.S. presidents (terms of office follow): Herbert Hoover (1929–33), Franklin Roosevelt (1933–45), Harry Truman (1945–52), and Dwight Eisenhower (1953–61).
8. U.S. presidents: Calvin Coolidge (1923–29), War-

ren Harding (1921–23), and Woodrow Wilson (1913–21).
9. William Taft, U.S. president 1909–13.
1. U.S. presidents: William McKinley (1897–1901), Grover Cleveland (1885–89; 1893–97), Benjamin Harrison (1889–93), Chester Arthur (1881–85), James Garfield (March–September 1881; assassinated), Rutherford Hayes (1869–77), and Andrew Johnson (1865–69).
2. From Whitman's *When Lilacs Last in the Dooryard Bloom'd.*

and strike again the naked string                                            90
old Whitman sang from. Glorious mistake!
    that cried:

    "The theme is creative and has vista."
    "He is the president of regulation."[3]

I see always the under side turning,                                         95
fumes that injure the tender landscape.
    From which up break
lilac blossoms of courage in daily act
    striving to meet a natural measure.


            III      *(for Charles Olson)*[4]

                        Psyche's tasks—the sorting of seeds      100
wheat      barley      oats      poppy      coriander
anise      beans       lentils   peas       —every grain
                    in its right place
                            before nightfall;


gathering the gold wool from the cannibal sheep                  105
(for the soul must weep
        and come near upon death);

harrowing Hell for a casket Proserpina keeps
                            that must not
        be opend . . . containing beauty?                        110

no!   Melancholy coild like a serpent
                        that is deadly sleep
        we are not permitted
                to succumb to.
        These are the old tasks.[5]                              115
        You've heard them before.


    They must be impossible. Psyche
must despair, be brought to her
                        insect instructor;
must obey the counsels of the green reed;                        120
saved from suicide by a tower speaking,
        must follow to the letter
        freakish instructions.[6]

---

3. From Whitman's *Preface* to the 1855 edition of *Leaves of Grass* in which he declares the great, creative theme of the American republic and the role of the poet in the United States: "Their Presidents shall not be their common referee so much as their poets shall."
4. Charles Olson, American poet and friend of Duncan's. His essay *Projective Verse* encouraged Duncan's sense of the poem as a "field."
5. To be reunited with Cupid, Psyche must accomplish a series of tasks set by Venus (Cupid's mother):

she must separate and sort a storehouse of seeds, she must bring Venus some of the gold fleece from a flock of cannibal sheep, and she must descend to Hell to bring back to Venus a measure of the beauty of Proserpina, queen of the Underworld.
6. In these tasks Psyche is aided by ants, who help sort the grain; by the river god, who instructs her in how to gather fleece; and by a voice from a tower, which instructs her in how to reach Hell safely and what she must do on return.

In the story the ants help. The old man at Pisa[7]
    mixd in whose mind                                          125
(to draw the sorts) are all seeds
       *as a lone ant from a broken ant-hill*[8]
had part restored by an insect, was
    upheld by a lizard

            (to draw the sorts)                    130
*the wind is part of the process*[9]
        defines a nation of the wind—

    father of many notions,
              Who?
let the light into the dark?   began                          135
the many movements of the passion?
               West
from east   men push.
           The islands are blessd
(cursed)   that swim below the sun,                         140

    *man upon whom the sun has gone down!*[1]

There is the hero who struggles east
widdershins[2] to free the dawn   and must
            woo Night's daughter,
sorcery, black passionate rage, covetous queens,                 145
so that the fleecy sun go   back from Troy,
    Colchis,[3] India . . . all the blazing armies
spent, he must struggle alone toward the pyres of Day.

           The light that is Love
rushes on toward passion. It verges upon dark.                   150
    Roses and blood flood the clouds.
    Solitary first riders advance into legend.

    This land, where I stand, was all legend
in my grandfathers' time: cattle raiders,
    animal tribes, priests, gold.                              155
It was the West.[4] Its vistas painters saw
    in diffuse light, in melancholy,
in abysses left by glaciers as if they had been the sun
    primordial carving empty enormities
            out of the rock.                          160

7. Ezra Pound, American poet, from whose *Pisan Cantos* (part of his long poem *The Cantos*) Duncan quotes. Pound wrote these cantos while imprisoned for treason by American forces in Italy.
8. Pound, *Canto LXXVI*. "Draw the sorts": draw lots, cast fortunes.
9. Pound, *Canto LXXIV*.
1. A reference to Odysseus, hero of *The Odyssey*. Duncan here quotes Pound's epithet for the hero, whose movement is toward home, in his *Canto LXXIV*. In this section of the poem Duncan is fusing several mythic questors, among them Psyche, Odysseus, and Jason.
2. In a contrary direction; here, opposite to the usual course of the sun.
3. An ancient country on the eastern shore of the Black Sea, the land where Jason and the Argonauts sought a golden fleece. "Fleecy sun": i.e., the golden fleece Psyche must bring to Venus. The ancient city of Troy was the site of the Trojan War, after which Odysseus began his journey home.
4. The American West.

                             Snakes lurkd
          guarding secrets.    Those first ones
                             survived solitude.

                Scientia
          holding the lamp, driven by doubt;[5]                              165
          Eros naked in foreknowledge
          smiling in his sleep;   and the light
          spilld, burning his shoulder—the outrage
                that conquers legend—
          passion, dismay, longing, search                                   170
                flooding up where
          the Beloved is lost.   Psyche travels
          life after life, my life, station
                after station,
          to be tried                                                        175

                without break, without
          news, knowing only—but what did she know?
                The oracle at Miletus had spoken
          truth surely: that he was Serpent-Desire
                that flies thru the air,                                      180
          a monster-husband.[6] But she saw him fair

          whom Apollo's mouthpiece said spread
                pain
          beyond cure    to those
                wounded by his arrows.                                       185

          Rilke torn by a rose thorn[7]
          blackend toward Eros.    Cupidinous Death!
                that will not take no for an answer.

                             *IV*

                Oh yes!    Bless the footfall where
          step by step    the boundary walker                                190
          (in Maverick Road    the snow
          thud by thud    from the roof
          circling the house—another tread)

                that foot    informd
          by the weight of all things                                        195
                that can be elusive
          no more than a nearness to the mind
                of a single image

---

5. The desire to know what Cupid looks like drives
Psyche to her mistake. "Scientia": knowledge.
6. In Apuleius's story, Psyche's parents consult the oracle (shrine from which a god reveals the future) of
Apollo at Miletus before her marriage to Eros. The oracle responds that Psyche is destined for no mortal lover

and that her husband will be a monster "whom neither
gods nor men can resist."
7. Rainer Maria Rilke, German lyric poet whose work
expresses the interconnections of life, death, and love;
he died from a rose thorn scratch.

       Oh yes!  this
most dear
    the catalyst force that renders clear
the days of a life from the surrounding medium!        200

       Yes, beautiful rare wilderness!
wildness that verifies strength of my tame mind,
    clearing held against indians,        205
health that prepared to meet death,
    the stubborn hymns going up
into the ramifications of the hostile air

    that, deceptive, gives way.

Who is there?  O, light the light!        210
    The Indians give way,   the clearing falls.
Great Death gives way   and unprepares us.
    Lust gives way.   The Moon gives way.
Night gives way.   Minutely,   the Day gains.

She saw the body of her beloved        215
    dismemberd in waking . . . or was it
in sight?  *Finders Keepers* we sang
    when we were children   or were taught to sing
before our histories began   and we began
    who were beloved   our animal life       220
toward the Beloved,   sworn to be Keepers.

       On the hill before the wind came
the grass moved toward the one sea,
    blade after blade dancing in waves.

There the children turn the ring to the left.        225
There the children turn the ring to the right.
    Dancing . . . Dancing . . .

And the lonely psyche goes up thru the boy to the king
    that in the caves of history dreams.
Round and round the children turn.        230
    London Bridge that is a kingdom falls.[8]

We have come so far that all the old stories
  whisper once more.
    Mount Segur, Mount Victoire, Mount Tamalpais[9] . . .
    *rise to adore the mystery of Love!*       235

(An ode? Pindar's art, the editors tell us, was not a statue but a mosaic, an accumulation of metaphor. But if he was archaic, not classic, a survival of obsolete mode, there may have been old voices in the survival that

---

8. The children's song "London Bridge Is Falling Down."

9. Duncan's list of mountains moves from east to west:

to Mount Tamalpais, in western California, across the Golden Gate from San Francisco, where Duncan lived.

directed the heart. So, a line from a hymn came in a novel I was reading
to help me. Psyche, poised to leap—and Pindar too, the editors write,     240
goes too far, topples over—listend to a tower that said, *Listen to me!* The
oracle[1] had said, *Despair! The Gods themselves abhor his power.* And then
the virgin flower of the dark falls back flesh of our flesh from which everywhere . . .

> the information flows                                      245
>     that is yearning. A line of Pindar
> moves from the area of my lamp
>     toward morning.

> In the dawn that is nowhere
>     I have seen the willful children                       250

> clockwise and counter-clockwise turning.

1960

## *From* Seventeenth Century Suite

### 4

*Robert Southwell,     The Burning Babe[1]*

*As I in hoarie Winters night stoode shivering in the snow,*
*Surpris'd I was with sodaine heate, which made my hart to glow;*
*And lifting up a fearefull eye, to view what fire was neare,*
*A pretty Babe all burning bright did in the ayre appeare;*
*Who scorched with excessive heate, such floods of teares did shed,*
*As though his floods should quench his flames, which with his teares were bred;*
*Alas (quoth he) but newly borne, in fierie heates I frie,*
*Yet none approach to warme their harts or feele my fire, but I;*
*My faultlesse breast the furnace is, the fuell wounding thornes:*
*Love is the fire, and sighs the smoake, the ashes, shames and scornes;*
*The mettall in this furnace wrought, are mens defiled soules:*
*For which, as now on fire I am to worke them to their good,*
*So will I melt into a bath, to wash them in my blood.*
*With this he vanisht out of sight, and swiftly shrunk away,*
*And straight I called unto minde, that it was Christmasse day.*

[St Peter's Complaint with other Poems, April 1595—following his martyrdom in the Roman Catholic cause by edict of Queen Elizabeth on February
21st, 1595, at Tyburn, after three years imprisonment with rack and torture]

### *From Robert Southwell's* The Burning Babe

> The vision of a burning babe    I see
> doubled in my sight.      The one

---

1. I.e., the tower that spoke to Psyche on her quest
and the oracle of Apollo that warned Psyche's parents.
1. Southwell (1561–1595) was an English Jesuit poet
venerated as a martyr by Roman Catholics. Duncan

reproduces the text of Southwell's poem as the source
and inspiration for his variations that follow, along the
line of a musical theme and variations.

alight in that fire of passion that tries the soul
is such a Child as Southwell saw his Christ to be:

This is not a baby on fire but a babe of fire,                              5
flesh burning with its own flame,   not toward death
    but alive with flame,   suffering its *self*
the heat of the heart the rose was hearth of;

    so there *was* a rose,   there was a flame,
    consubstantial with the heart,                         10

long burning me through and through,
    long time ago I knew   and came
to a knowledge of the bitter core of me,
the clinker[2] soul, the stubborn residue
that needed the fire and refused to burn.                                   15

Envy of the living was its name,   black jealousy
    of what I loved it was,   and
the pain was not living,   it was ashes of the wood;
the burning was not living,   it was
    without Truth's heat,                                  20
a cold of utter Winter that refused the Sun,
an adversary in the body against its youth.

In this I am self possesst of such a hoarie Winter's night
    as Southwell stood in shivering—
a shivering runs me through and through.                                    25

O Infant Joy that in Desire burns bright!
Bright Promise that I might in Him burn free!
His faultless breast the furnace,
my inner refusal the thorny fuel!

All the doors of Life's wounds I have long closed in me               30
break open from His body and pour forth
therefrom fire that is His blood
    relentlessly

"Who scorcht with excessive heat, such
    floods of tears did shed"                              35

—it is no more than an image in Poetry—as though

"his floods should quench his flames,
    which with his tears were bred"   until

tears breeding flames, flames breeding tears,
I am undone from what I am,   and in Imagination's alchemy            40
    the watery Moon and fiery Sun   are wed.

---

2. Brick burned too much in a kiln.

The burning Babe, the Rose,
the Wedding of the Moon and Sun,
wherever in the World I read
such Mysteries come to haunt the Mind,                          45
the Language of What Is        and I
              are one.


                              5

"A *pretty Babe*"—that burning Babe
            the poet Southwell saw—
a scorching, a crying, that made his cold heart glow,
            a fuel of passion in which
the thought of wounds delites the soul.                         5
            He's Art's epiphany[3] of Art new born,
a Christ of Poetry, the burning spirit's show;
He leaves no shadow, where he dances in the air,
            of misery below.


Another Christ, if he be, as we are,                            10
Man, cries out in utter misery;
and every Holy Martyr must have cried
            forsaken in some moment
that from Christ's "Why hast Thou forsaken me?"
            has entered our Eternity                            15
or else is not true to itself.        But now


            I am looking upon burnd faces
that have known catastrophe incommensurate
            with meaning,   beyond hate or loss or
Christian martyrdom, unredeemd.        My heart                 20
            caves into a space it seems
to have long feard.


I cannot imagine, gazing upon photographs
            of these young girls,   the mind
transcending what's been done to them.                          25


            From the broild flesh of these heretics,
by napalm monstrously   baptised
            in a new name,   every delicate and
sensitive curve of lip and eyelid
            blasted away,   surviving . . .                     30
            eyes?     Can this horror be calld their
*fate?* Our fate grows a mirroring face
in the accusation beyond accusation
            of such eyes,
a kind of hurt that drives into the root                        35
of understanding,   their very lives
            burnd into us   we live by.


3. Appearance or manifestation of perception or of the divine.

Victor and victim know not what they do
     —the deed exceeding what we would *know*;
the knowledge in the sight of those eyes                    40
     goes deep into the heart's fatalities.
And in our nation's store of crimes    long
     unacknowledged, unrepented,
the sum of abject suffering, of dumb incalculable
     injury increases                    45
the sore of conscience we long avoid.

What can I feel of it?    All hurt
rushes in to illustrate that glare
and fails.    What can I feel of what was done?
All hatred cringes from the sight of it                    50
and would contract into self-loathing
to ease the knowledge of what no man
can compensate.    I think I could bear it.

I cannot think I could bear it.

                                              1977


## Interrupted Forms

Long slumbering, often coming forward,
haunting the house I am the house I live in
resembles so, does he recall me or I
recall him?    Seeing you the other day
long I lookt to see your face his, longing                    5
without reason.    I meant to tell
or spell your name, to dwell in the charm
I almost felt in the stone,    the impassive
weight of old feeling, the cold awakening
I meant to tell you of, as if telling could reach you,                    10
at last come into your embrace again, my arms
hold you, mounting, coming into your life
my life and interruption of all long lasting
         inertia in feeling,
arousal.                    15

         In dreams
insubstantially you have come before my eyes'
expectations, and, even in waking,
taking over the field of sight    fleetingly
stronger than what my eyes see,                    20
the thought of you thought has eyes to see
has eyes to meet your answering eyes
thought raises.    I am speaking of a ghost
the heart is glad to have return,    of a room
I have often been lonely in,    of a desertion                    25
that remains even where I am most cherisht

and surrounded by Love's company,    of a form,
wholly fulfilling the course of my life, interrupted,
of a cold in the full warmth of the sunlight
that seeks to come in close to your heart                        30
            for warmth.

                                                        1984

---

# RICHARD WILBUR
## b. 1921

Richard Wilbur was born in New York City and grew up in the country in New
Jersey. His father was a painter, and his mother came from a family prominent in
journalism. He was educated at Amherst College, where Robert Frost was a frequent guest and teacher, and Wilbur's remarkable gifts as a prosodist often remind
us of the older poet. Of the effects of his college years, Wilbur says: "Most American poets of my generation were taught to admire the English metaphysical poets
of the seventeenth century and such contemporary masters of irony as John Crowe
Ransom. We were led by our teachers and by the critics whom we read to feel
that the most adequate and convincing poetry is that which accommodates mixed
feelings, clashing ideas, and incongruous images." Wilbur was to remain true to
this preference for the ironic meditative lyric, the single perfect poem, rather than
longer narratives or dramatic sequences.

After graduation and service in the infantry in Italy and France (1943–45), Wilbur returned to study for an M.A. at Harvard, with a firm notion of what he
expected to get out of poetry. "My first poems were written in answer to the inner
and outer disorders of the second World War and they helped me . . . to take ahold
of raw events and convert them, provisionally, into experience." He reasserted the
balance of mind against instinct and violence: "The praiseful, graceful soldier /
Shouldn't be fired by his gun." The poised lyrics in *The Beautiful Changes* (1947)
and *Ceremony* (1950) also reclaimed a sense of Europe obscured by the war: the
value of pleasure, defined as an interplay of intelligence with sensuous enjoyment.
Whether looking at a real French landscape, as in *Grasse: The Olive Trees*, or a
French landscape painting, as in *Ceremony*, the point was to show the witty shaping power of the mind in nature.

Wilbur prefers strict stanzaic forms and meters; "limitation makes for power: the
strength of the genie comes of his being confined in a bottle." In individual lines
and the structure of an entire poem, his emphasis is on a civilized balancing of
perceptions. A *World without Objects Is a Sensible Emptiness* begins with the "tall
camels of the spirit" but qualifies our views of lonely spiritual impulses. The poem
summons us back to find visionary truth grasped through sensual experience. "All
shining things need to be shaped and borne." Wilbur favors "a spirituality which is
not abstracted, not dissociated and world-renouncing. A good part of my work
could, I suppose, be understood as a public quarrel with the aesthetics of Edgar
Allan Poe"—presumably with Poe's notion that poetry provided *indefinite* sensations and aspired to the abstract condition of music.

Wilbur was among the first of the younger postwar poets to adopt a style of living
and working different from the masters of an earlier generation—from Eliot, ironic
priestlike modernist who lived as a publisher-poet in England, or William Carlos
Williams, a doctor in Paterson, or Wallace Stevens, a remote insurance executive
in Hartford. Wilbur was a teacher-poet and gave frequent readings. Instead of
thinking of himself as an alienated artist, he came to characterize himself as a

"poet-citizen," part of what he judged a widening community of poets addressing themselves to an audience increasingly responsive to poetry. Wilbur's taste for civilized wit and his metrical skill made him an ideal translator of the seventeenth-century satirical comedies of Molière, *Tartuffe* (1963) and *The Misanthrope* (1955). They are frequently played, as is the musical version of Voltaire's *Candide* for which Wilbur was one of the collaborating lyricists. Wilbur has taught most recently at Smith. He received the Pulitzer Prize for his volume *Things of This World* (1956) and served as the second poet laureate consultant in poetry in 1987–88.

# The Death of a Toad

A toad the power mower caught,
Chewed and clipped of a leg, with a hobbling hop has got
 To the garden verge, and sanctuaried him
 Under the cineraria leaves, in the shade
 Of the ashen heartshaped leaves, in a dim,                5
 Low, and a final glade.

The rare original heartsblood goes,
Spends on the earthen hide, in the folds and wizenings, flows
 In the gutters of the banked and staring eyes. He lies
 As still as if he would return to stone,                 10
 And soundlessly attending, dies
 Toward some deep monotone,

Toward misted and ebullient seas
And cooling shores, toward lost Amphibia's emperies.[1]
 Day dwindles, drowning, and at length is gone             15
 In the wide and antique eyes, which still appear
 To watch, across the castrate lawn,
 The haggard daylight steer.

                                                         1950

# Ceremony

A striped blouse in a clearing by Bazille[1]
Is, you may say, a patroness of boughs
Too queenly kind[2] toward nature to be kin.
But ceremony never did conceal,
Save to the silly[3] eye, which all allows,                5
How much we are the woods we wander in.

Let her be some Sabrina[4] fresh from stream,
Lucent as shallows slowed by wading sun,
Bedded on fern, the flowers' cynosure:[5]

1. Empires (archaic). Amphibia is imagined to be the spiritual ruler of the toad's universe.
1. Jean Frédéric Bazille (1841–1871), French painter noted for painting figures in forest landscapes; he was associated with the impressionists.
2. An original meaning of *nature* was "kind."
3. Innocent, homely.
4. A nymph, the presiding deity of the river Severn in Milton's masque *Comus* (1634).
5. Center of attraction; also from the constellation Ursa Minor, whose center is the Pole Star.

Then nymph and wood must nod and strive to dream          10
That she is airy earth, the trees, undone,
Must ape her languor natural and pure.

Ho-hum. I am for wit and wakefulness,
And love this feigning lady by Bazille.
What's lightly hid is deepest understood,          15
And when with social smile and formal dress
She teaches leaves to curtsey and quadrille,[6]
I think there are most tigers in the wood.

1950

## "A World without Objects Is a Sensible Emptiness"[1]

The tall camels of the spirit
Steer for their deserts, passing the last groves loud
With the sawmill shrill of the locust, to the whole honey
           of the arid
Sun. They are slow, proud,

And move with a stilted stride          5
To the land of sheer horizon, hunting Traherne's
Sensible emptiness, there where the brain's lantern-slide
Revels in vast returns.

O connoisseurs of thirst,
Beasts of my soul who long to learn to drink          10
Of pure mirage, those prosperous islands are accurst
That shimmer on the brink

Of absence; auras, lustres,
And all shinings need to be shaped and borne.
Think of those painted saints, capped by the early masters          15
With bright, jauntily-worn

Aureate plates, or even
Merry-go-round rings. Turn, O turn
From the fine sleights of the sand, from the long empty oven
Where flames in flamings burn          20

Back to the trees arrayed
In bursts of glare, to the halo-dialing run
Of the country creeks, and the hills' bracken tiaras made
Gold in the sunken sun,

Wisely watch for the sight          25
Of the supernova[2] burgeoning over the barn,

6. A square dance, of French origin, performed by four couples.
1. From Meditation 65, by the English Metaphysical poet Thomas Traherne (c. 1638–1674): "Life without objects is sensible emptiness, and that is a greater mis- ery than death or nothing." Sensible is used to mean "palpable to the senses."
2. A scientific term for an exploding star, here associated with the Star of Bethlehem.

Lampshine blurred in the stream of beasts, the spirit's right
    Oasis, light incarnate.

                                                      1950


# The Mind-Reader

### Lui parla.[1]

#### FOR CHARLES AND EULA

Some things are truly lost. Think of a sun-hat
Laid for the moment on a parapet
While three young women—one, perhaps, in mourning—
Talk in the crenellate shade.[2] A slight wind plucks
And budges it; it scuffs to the edge and cartwheels                5
Into a giant view of some description:
Haggard escarpments,[3] if you like, plunge down
Through mica shimmer to a moss of pines
Amidst which, here or there, a half-seen river
Lobs up a blink of light. The sun-hat falls,                     10
With what free flirts and stoops you can imagine,
Down through that reeling vista or another,
Unseen by any, even by you or me.
It is as when a pipe-wrench, catapulted
From the jounced back of a pick-up truck, dives headlong         15
Into a bushy culvert;[4] or a book
Whose reader is asleep, garbling the story,
Glides from beneath a steamer chair and yields
Its flurried pages to the printless sea.

It is one thing to escape from consciousness                     20
As such things do, another to be pent
In the dream-cache or stony oubliette[5]
Of someone's head.

                    They found, when I was little,
That I could tell the place of missing objects.                  25
I stood by the bed of a girl, or the frayed knee
Of an old man whose face was lost in shadow.
When did you miss it?, people would be saying,
Where did you see it last? And then those voices,
Querying or replying, came to sound                              30
Like cries of birds when the leaves race and whiten
And a black overcast is shelving over.
The mind is not a landscape, but if it were
There would in such case be a tilted moon
Wheeling beyond the wood through which you groped,               35
Its fine spokes breaking in the tangled thickets.
There would be obfuscations, paths which turned

---

1. He [the mind-reader, an Italian] speaks.
2. That is, the shade provided by battlements.
3. Worn cliffs.

4. Drain under a road. "Pipe-wrench": wrench for
gripping and turning metal pipe.
5. Dungeon pit (French oublier, "to forget").

To dried-up stream-beds, hemlocks which invited
Through shiny clearings to a groundless shade;
And yet in a sure stupor you would come                      40
At once upon dilapidated cairns,
Abraded moss, and half-healed blazes[6] leading
To where, around the turning of a fear,
The lost thing shone.

                Imagine a railway platform—          45
The long cars come to a cloudy halt beside it,
And the fogged windows offering a view
Neither to those within nor those without,
Now, in the crowd—forgive my predilection—
Is a young woman standing amidst her luggage,               50
Expecting to be met by you, a stranger.
See how she turns her head, the eyes engaging
And disengaging, pausing and shying away.
It is like that with things put out of mind,
As the queer saying goes: a lost key hangs                  55
Trammeled by threads in what you come to see
As the webbed darkness of a sewing-basket,
Flashing a little; or a photograph,
Misplaced in an old ledger, turns its bled
Oblivious profile to rebuff your vision,                    60
Yet glistens with the fixative of thought.
What can be wiped from memory? Not the least
Meanness, obscenity, humiliation,
Terror which made you clench your eyes, or pulse
Of happiness which quickened your despair.                  65
Nothing can be forgotten, as I am not
Permitted to forget.

                It was not far
From that to this—this corner café table
Where, with my lank grey hair and vatic[7] gaze,           70
I sit and drink at the receipt of custom.
They come here, day and night, so many people:
Sad women of the quarter, dressed in black,
As to a black confession; blinking clerks
Who half-suppose that Taurus ruminates                     75
Upon their destinies;[8] men of affairs
Down from Milan to clear it with the magus[9]
Before they buy or sell some stock or other;
My fellow-drunkards; fashionable folk,
Mocking and ravenously credulous,                          80
And skeptics bent on proving me a fraud
For fear that some small wonder, unexplained,
Should leave a fissure in the world, and all
Saint Michael's host[1] come flapping back.

6. Cuts on trees to mark a path in a forest. "Cairns" (of which Taurus, the bull, is one).
(piles of stones) and rubbed-away moss would serve the   9. Expert in the occult.
same purpose.                         1. St. Michael the archangel and his host of angels,
7. I.e., staring like a prophet.           whose war in heaven is predicted in Revelation 12.7–9.
8. I.e., that they are influenced by astrological signs

                                    I give them                    85
Paper and pencil, turn away and light
A cigarette, as you have seen me do;
They write their questions; fold them up; I lay
My hand on theirs and go into my frenzy,
Raising my eyes to heaven, snorting smoke,                          90
Lolling my head as in the fumes of Delphi,[2]
And then, with shaken, spirit-guided fingers,
Set down the oracle. All that, of course,
Is trumpery,[3] since nine times out of ten
What words float up within another's thought                       95
Surface as soon as mine, unfolding there
Like paper flowers in a water-glass.
In the tenth case, I sometimes cheat a little.
That shocks you? But consider: what I do
Cannot, so most conceive, be done at all,                          100
And when I fail, I am a charlatan
Even to such as I have once astounded—
Whereas a tailor can mis-cut my coat
And be a tailor still. I tell you this
Because you know that I have the gift, the burden.                 105
Whether or not I put my mind to it,
The world usurps me ceaselessly; my sixth
And never-resting sense is a cheap room
Black with the anger of insomnia,
Whose wall-boards vibrate with the mutters, plaints,              110
And flushings of the race.[4]

                    What should I tell them?
I have no answers. *Set your fears at rest,*
I scribble when I must. *Your paramour*
*Is faithful, and your spouse is unsuspecting.*                    115
*You were not seen, that day, beneath the fig-tree.*
*Still, be more cautious. When the time is ripe,*
*Expect promotion. I foresee a message*
*From a far person who is rich and dying.*
*You are admired in secret. If, in your judgment,*                 120
*Profit is in it, you should take the gamble.*
*As for these fits of weeping, they will pass.*

It makes no difference that my lies are bald
And my evasions casual. It contents them
Not to have spoken, yet to have been heard.                        125
What more do they deserve, if I could give it,
Mute breathers as they are of selfish hopes
And small anxieties? Faith, justice, valor,
All those reputed rarities of soul
Confirmed in marble by our public statues—                        130
You may be sure that they are rare indeed
Where the soul mopes in private, and I listen.

---

2. Site of the most famous Greek oracle, at which, for     3. Worthless nonsense.
a fee, seekers could have their questions answered by a    4. That is, the human race. "Plaints, / And flushings":
priestess drugged by the "fumes."                          complaints and sudden rushes of emotion.

Sometimes I wonder if the blame is mine,
If through a sullen fault of the mind's ear
I miss a resonance in all their fretting.　　　　　　　　　135
Is there some huge attention, do you think,
Which suffers us and is inviolate,
To which all hearts are open, which remarks
The sparrow's weighty fall,[5] and overhears
In the worst rancor a deflected sweetness?　　　　　　　140
I should be glad to know it.

　　　　　　　　　　　　　Meanwhile, saved
By the shrewd habit of concupiscence,
which, like a visor, narrows my regard,
And drinking studiously until my thought　　　　　　　145
Is a blind lowered almost to the sill,
I hanker for that place beyond the sparrow
Where the wrench beds in mud, the sun-hat hangs
In densest branches, and the book is drowned.[6]
Ah, you have read my mind. One more, perhaps . . .　　　150
A mezzo-litro. Grazie, professore.[7]

1976

5. Hamlet, just before his death, speaks of the "special providence in the fall of a sparrow" (5.2.220).
6. At the end of Shakespeare's *The Tempest*, the magician Prospero renounces his island and his magic, saying, "Deeper than ever did plummet sound / I'll drown my book" (5.1.56–57).
7. The speaker thanks the listening "professore" for the offer of another half-liter of wine.

---

# DENISE LEVERTOV
## b. 1923

Denise Levertov once wrote of her predecessor, the poet H. D.: "She showed a way to penetrate mystery; which means, not to flood darkness with light so that darkness is destroyed, but to *enter into* darkness, mystery, so that it is experienced." Along with Robert Duncan, Levertov has carried out in her own distinctive way H. D.'s tradition of visionary poetry. More grounded than her predecessor in observing the natural world and in appreciating daily life, Levertov's own work connects the concrete to the invisible, as suggested by the image of *The Jacob's Ladder* (1961), the title of her fifth book. She desires that a poem be "hard as a floor, sound as a bench" but also that it be "mysterious" (*Illustrious Ancestors*), and in her poems ordinary events open into the unknown. The origins of Levertov's magical sense of the world are not difficult to trace. She was born in England and has written of her parents: "My mother was descended from the Welsh Tailor and mystic Angel Jones of Mold, my father from the noted Hasid, Schneour Zaiman (d. 1831), the 'Rav of Northern White Russia.' " In *Illustrious Ancestors*, Levertov claims a connection to her forefathers, both mystical and Hasidic: "some line still taut between me and them." Hasidim, a sect of Judaism that emphasizes the soul's communion with God rather than formal religious observance and encourages what Levertov has called "a wonder at creation," was an important influence on her father, Paul Philip Levertoff. He had converted to Christianity as a student and later became an Anglican priest, but he retained his interest in Judaism and told

Hasidic legends to Levertov and her older sister, Olga, throughout their child-hoods. From her mother, Beatrice Spooner-Jones, Levertov learned to look closely at the world around her, and we might say of her work what she says of her mother: "with how much gazing / her life had paid tribute to the world's body" (*The 90th Year*).

In 1947, Levertov married an American, Mitchell Goodman (they have since divorced), and moved to the United States. She describes this move as crucial to her development as a poet; it "necessitated the finding of new rhythms in which to write, in accordance with new rhythms of life and speech." In this discovery of a new idiom, the stylistic influence of William Carlos Williams was especially important to her; without it, she has said, "I could not have developed from a British Romantic with an almost Victorian background to an American poet of any vitality." Levertov embraced Williams's interest in an organic poetic form, growing out of the poet's relation to her subject, and like Duncan and Robert Creeley, she has actively explored the relations between the line and the unit of breath, as they control rhythm, melody, and stress. But if Levertov became the poet she is by becoming an American poet, her European heritage also enriches her sense of influence. Although her poem *September 1961* acknowledges her link to "the old great ones" (Ezra Pound, Williams, and H. D.), she is as at home with German lyric poet Rilke as with Emerson. And in the United States she discovered the work of Martin Buber, the Jewish theologian and philosopher, which renewed her interest "in the Hasidic ideas with which I was dimly acquainted as a child." Her eclecticism lets her move easily between plain and richly descriptive language, between a vivid perception of the "thing itself" and the often radiant mystery that, for Levertov, arises from such seeing.

From 1956 to 1959 Levertov lived with her husband and son in Mexico. They were joined there by her mother, who, after her daughter's departure, remained in Mexico for the final eighteen years of her life (she died in 1977). Several moving poems in Levertov's collection *Life in the Forest* (1978) address her mother's last years, among them *The 90th Year* and *Death in Mexico*. In the late 1960s, the political crisis prompted by the Vietnam War turned Levertov's work more directly to public woes, as reflected in her following four books. Not all of the poems in these books explicitly concern political issues (*The Sorrow Dance*, for example, contains her sequence in memory of her sister, Olga, one of her finest, most powerful poems); nonetheless, many poems originate in a need for public testimony. Her overtly political poems are not often among her best, however; their very explicitness restricts her distinctive strengths as a poet, which include a feeling for the inexplicable, a language lyrical enough to express wish and desire, and a capacity for playfulness. But it is a mistake to separate too rigidly the political concerns in her work from a larger engagement with the world. As she has written, "If a degree of intimacy is a condition of lyric expression, surely—at times when events make feelings run high—that intimacy between writer and political belief does exist, and is as intense as other emotions."

The power of Levertov's poems depends on her capacity to balance, however precariously, her two-sided vision, to keep alive both terms of what one critic calls her "magical realism." At its best, her work seems to spring from experience deep within her, stirred into being by a source beyond herself (as *Caedmon* is suddenly "affrighted" by an angel or the poet at sixteen dreams deeply, "sunk in the well"). Her finest poems render the inexplicable nature of our ordinary lives and their capacity for unexpected beauty. But Levertov's capacity for pleasure in the world never strays too far from the knowledge that the very landscapes that delight us contain places "that can pull you / down" (*Zeroing In*), as our inner landscapes also contain places " 'that are bruised forever, that time / never assuages, never.' "

Levertov has published two collections of prose, *The Poet in the World* (1973) and *Light Up the Cave* (1981). In 1987 she published her fifteenth book of poems,

*Breathing the Water.* This book contains a long sequence, *The Showings: Lady Julian of Norwich, 1342–1416,* which continues the link between Levertov's work and a visionary tradition. A *Door in the Hive* appeared in 1989. She has taught widely and since 1982 has been professor of English at Stanford University, where she is an important teacher for a younger generation of writers.

# To the Snake

Green Snake, when I hung you round my neck
and stroked your cold, pulsing throat
    as you hissed to me, glinting
arrowy gold scales, and I felt
    the weight of you on my shoulders,     5
and the whispering silver of your dryness
    sounded close at my ears—

Green Snake—I swore to my companions that certainly
    you were harmless! But truly
I had no certainty, and no hope, only desiring    10
    to hold you, for that joy,
                which left
a long wake of pleasure, as the leaves moved
and you faded into the pattern
of grass and shadows, and I returned    15
smiling and haunted, to a dark morning.

                                  1960

# The Jacob's Ladder[1]

The stairway is not
a thing of gleaming strands
a radiant evanescence
for angels' feet that only glance in their tread, and need not
touch the stone.    5

It is of stone.
A rosy stone that takes
a glowing tone of softness
only because behind it the sky is a doubtful, a doubting
night gray.    10

A stairway of sharp
angles, solidly built.
One sees that the angels must spring
down from one step to the next, giving a little
lift of the wings:    15

---

1. Jacob dreamed of "a ladder set up on the earth, and the top of it reached to heaven: and behold the angels of God ascending and descending on it" (Genesis 28.12).

and a man climbing
must scrape his knees, and bring
the grip of his hands into play. The cut stone
consoles his groping feet. Wings brush past him.
The poem ascends.                                                    20

1961

## Illustrious Ancestors[1]

The Rav
of Northern White Russia declined,
in his youth, to learn the
language of birds, because
the extraneous did not interest him; nevertheless          5
when he grew old it was found
he understood them anyway, having
listened well, and as it is said, 'prayed
            with the bench and the floor.' He used
what was at hand—as did                                           10
Angel Jones of Mold,[2] whose meditations
were sewn into coats and britches.
            Well, I would like to make,
thinking some line still taut between me and them,
poems direct as what the birds said,                              15
hard as a floor, sound as a bench,
mysterious as the silence when the tailor
would pause with his needle in the air.

1961

## In Mind

There's in my mind a woman
of innocence, unadorned but

fair-featured, and smelling of
apples or grass. She wears

a utopian smock or shift, her hair                               5
is light brown and smooth, and she

is kind and very clean without
ostentation—
            but she has
no  imagination.                                                 10
            And there's a
      turbulent moon-ridden girl

---

1. Rabbi (or Rav) Schneour Zaimon and Angel Jones     of Levertov's father and mother, respectively.
were mystics who were also the "illustrious ancestors"     2. A town in Wales.

or old woman, or both,
dressed in opals and rags, feathers

and torn taffeta,                                          15
who knows strange songs—

but she is not kind.

1964

# Death in Mexico[1]

Even two weeks after her fall,
three weeks before she died, the garden
began to vanish. The rickety fence gave way
as it had threatened, and the children threw
broken plastic toys—vicious yellow,                        5
unresonant red, onto the path, into the lemontree;
or trotted in through the gap, trampling small plants.
For two weeks no one watered it, except
I did, twice, but then I left. She was still conscious then
and thanked me. I begged the others to water it—          10
but the rains began; when I got back there were violent,
sudden, battering downpours each afternoon.
                            Weeds flourished,
dry topsoil was washed away swiftly
into the drains. Oh, there was green, still,               15
but the garden was disappearing—each day
less sign of the ordered,
thought-out oasis, a squared circle her mind
constructed for rose and lily, begonia
and rosemary-for-remembrance.                              20
Twenty years in the making—
less than a month to undo itself;
and those who had seen it grow,
living around it those decades,
did nothing to hold it. Oh, Alberto did,                   25
one day, patch up the fence a bit,
when I told him a future tenant would value
having a garden. But no one believed
the garden-maker would live (I least of all),
so her pain if she were to see the ruin                    30
remained abstract, an incomprehensible concept,
impelling no action. When they carried her past
                            on a stretcher,
on her way to the *sanatorio*, failing sight
transformed itself into a mercy: certainly                 35
she could have seen no more than a greenish blur.
But to me the weeds, the flowerless rosebushes, broken

---

1. One of a sequence of poems on the death of Levertov's mother.

stems of the canna lilies and amaryllis, all
a lusterless jungle green, presented—
even before her dying was over—                                    40
an obdurate, blind, all-seeing gaze:
I had seen it before, in the museums,
in stone masks of the gods and victims.
A gaze that admits no tenderness; if it smiles, it
only smiles with sublime bitterness—no,                          45
not even bitter: it admits
no regret, nostalgia has no part in its cosmos,
bitterness is irrelevant.
If it holds a flower—and it does,
a delicate brilliant silky flower that blooms only              50
a single day—it holds it clenched
between sharp teeth.
Vines may crawl, and scorpions, over its face,
but though the centuries blunt
eyelid and flared nostril, the stone gaze                        55
is utterly still, fixed, absolute,
smirk of denial facing eternity.
Gardens vanish. She was an alien here,
as I am. Her death
was not Mexico's business. The garden though                     60
was a hostage. Old gods
took back their own.

1978

## Caedmon[1]

All others talked as if
talk were a dance.
Clodhopper I, with clumsy feet
would break the gliding ring.
Early I learned to                                                5
hunch myself
close by the door:
then when the talk began
I'd wipe my
mouth and wend                                                   10
unnoticed back to the barn
to be with the warm beasts,
dumb among body sounds
of the simple ones.
I'd see by a twist                                               15
of lit rush[2] the motes
of gold moving

1. "The story comes, of course, from the Venerable
Bede's *History of the English Church and People*, but I
first read it as a child in John Richard Green's *History
of the English People*, 1855" [Levertov's note]. Caedmon (fl. 658–680) was, according to the story, an illiterate cowherd employed by a monastery; one night he
received a divine call to sing verses in praise of God.
He is the earliest known Christian poet in English.
2. The piths of rush plants were used for candlewicks.

from shadow to shadow
slow in the wake
of deep untroubled sighs.                                                    20
The cows
munched or stirred or were still. I
was at home and lonely,
both in good measure. Until
the sudden angel affrighted me—light effacing                                25
my feeble beam,
a forest of torches, feathers of flame, sparks upflying:
but the cows as before
were calm, and nothing was burning,
        nothing but I, as that hand of fire                                        30
touched my lips and scorched my tongue
and pulled my voice
           into the ring of the dance.

1987

---

# A. R. AMMONS
## b. 1926

A. R. Ammons writes that he "was born big and jaundiced (and ugly) on February 18, 1926, in a farmhouse 4 miles southwest of Whiteville, North Carolina, and 2 miles northwest of New Hope Elementary School and New Hope Baptist Church." It is characteristic of Ammons to be laconic, self-deprecating, unfailingly local, and unfailingly exact. He belongs to the homemade strain of American writers rather than the Europeanized or cosmopolitan breed. His poems are filled with the landscapes in which he has lived: North Carolina, the south Jersey coast, and the surroundings of Ithaca, New York, where he now lives and teaches in the English department of Cornell University.

Ammons's career did not start out with a traditional literary education. At Wake Forest College in North Carolina he studied mostly scientific subjects, especially biology and chemistry, and that scientific training has strongly colored his poems. Only later (1951–52) did he study English literature for three semesters at the University of California in Berkeley. He had worked briefly as a high-school principal in North Carolina. When he returned from Berkeley he spent twelve years as an executive for a firm that made biological glass in southern New Jersey.

In 1955, his thirtieth year, Ammons published his first book of poems, *Ommateum*. The title refers to the compound structure of an insect's eye and foreshadows a twofold impulse in Ammons's work. On one hand he is involved in the minute observation of natural phenomena; on the other hand he is frustrated by the physical limitations analogous to those of the insects' vision. We see the world, as insects do, in small portions and in impulses that take in but do not totally resolve the many images we receive. "Overall is beyond me," says Ammons in *Corsons Inlet*, an important poem in which the shifting details of shoreline and dunes represent a severe challenge to the poet-observer. There are no straight lines. The contours differ every day, every hour, and they teach the poet the endless adjustments he must make to nature's fluidity.

"A poem is a walk," Ammons has said, and his work is characterized by the motion he finds everywhere in nature, a motion answered by the activity of his own mind. Both near- and farsighted, he looks closely at vegetation, small animals, the minute shifts of wind and weather and light, yet over and over again seems drawn to Emerson's visionary aspirations for poetry. "Poetry," Emerson remarked, "was all written before time was, and whenever we are so finely organized that we can penetrate into that region where the air is music, we hear those primal warnings and attempt to write them down." Much of Ammons's poetry tests this farsighted, transcendental promise to see if it yields a glimpse of supernatural order.

The self in Ammons's poems is a far more modest presence than in the work of many other American writers. Sometimes he is a "surrendered self among unwelcoming forms" (as he writes in the conclusion of *Gravelly Run*); in many other poems he is at home in a universe, both human and natural, whose variety delights him. He is that rare thing, a contemporary poet of praise, one who says "I can find nothing lowly / in the universe" (*Still*) and convinces us he speaks the truth.

Ammons began his career writing short lyrics, almost journal entries in an unending career of observation. But the laconic notations—of a landslide, a shift in the shoreline from one day to the next—often bore abstract titles—*Clarity, Saliences*—as if to suggest the connections he feels between concrete experience and speculative thought. Ammons has often conducted experiments with poetic form in his effort to make his verse responsive to the engaging but evasive particularity of natural process. This formal inventiveness is part of the appeal of his work. "Stop on any word and language gives way: / the blades of reason, unlightened by motion, sink in," he remarks in his *Essay on Poetics*. Preparing *Tape for the Turn of the Year* (1965) he typed a book-length day-to-day verse diary along an adding machine tape. The poem ended when the tape did. This was his first and most flamboyant attempt to turn his verse into something beyond mere gatherings. Since then he has discovered that the long poem is the form best adapted to his continuing, indeed endless, dialogue between the specific and the general.

The poems tend to make use of the colon—what one critic calls "the most democratic punctuation," suggesting as it does equivalence on both sides. Used in place of the period, it keeps the poem from coming to a halt or stopping the flow in which the mind feverishly suggests analogies among its minutely perceived experiences. Many notable examples of Ammons's extended forms are gathered in *The Selected Longer Poems* (1980), although that book does not include his remarkable *Sphere: The Form of a Motion* (1974). A single, book-length poem, with no full stops, 155 sections of four tercets each, it aspires to be what Wallace Stevens called "the poem of the act of the mind." The only unity in *Sphere* is the mind's power to make analogies between the world's constant "diversifications." As he demonstrates in this poem and in *Garbage* (1993), which won the National Book Award for poetry, Ammons is committed to the provisional, the self-revising, and this commitment has kept his poetry fresh over a long career. Writing of his sense of the world in *The Dwelling*, from *Sumerian Vistas* (1987), Ammons says, "here the plainnest / majesty gave us what it could." The same might be said of his wonderfully generous and witty poems.

# So I Said I Am Ezra

So I said I am Ezra
and the wind whipped my throat
gaming for the sounds of my voice
    I listened to the wind
go over my head and up into the night        5
Turning to the sea I said

                    I am Ezra
but there were no echoes from the waves
The words were swallowed up
          in the voice of the surf                              10
or leaping over the swells
lost themselves oceanward
          Over the bleached and broken fields
I moved my feet and turning from the wind
          that ripped sheets of sand                            15
          from the beach and threw them
          like seamists across the dunes
swayed as if the wind were taking me away
and said
                    I am Ezra                                   20
As a word too much repeated
falls out of being
so I Ezra went out into the night
like a drift of sand
and splashed among the windy oats                              25
that clutch the dunes
of unremembered seas

                                                            1955

## Corsons Inlet

I went for a walk over the dunes again this morning
to the sea,
then turned right along
          the surf
                    rounded a naked headland                    5
                    and returned

          along the inlet shore:

it was muggy sunny, the wind from the sea steady and high,
crisp in the running sand,
          some breakthroughs of sun                            10
          but after a bit

continuous overcast:

the walk liberating, I was released from forms,
from the perpendiculars,
          straight lines, blocks, boxes, binds                 15
of thought
into the hues, shadings, rises, flowing bends and blends
          of sight:

                    I allow myself eddies of meaning:
yield to a direction of significance                           20
running

like a stream through the geography of my work:
    you can find
in my sayings
            swerves of action                                    25
            like the inlet's cutting edge:
        there are dunes of motion,
organizations of grass, white sandy paths of remembrance
in the overall wandering of mirroring mind:

but Overall is beyond me: is the sum of these events                30
I cannot draw, the ledger I cannot keep, the accounting
beyond the account:

in nature there are few sharp lines: there are areas of
primrose
        more or less dispersed;                                35
disorderly orders of bayberry; between the rows
of dunes,
irregular swamps of reeds,
though not reeds alone, but grass, bayberry, yarrow, all . . .
predominantly reeds:                                               40

I have reached no conclusions, have erected no boundaries,
shutting out and shutting in, separating inside
        from outside: I have
        drawn no lines:
        as                                                      45

manifold events of sand
change the dune's shape that will not be the same shape
tomorrow,

so I am willing to go along, to accept
the becoming                                                       50
thought, to stake off no beginnings or ends, establish
      no walls:

by transitions the land falls from grassy dunes to creek
to undercreek: but there are no lines, though
      change in that transition is clear                        55
      as any sharpness: but "sharpness" spread out,
allowed to occur over a wider range
than mental lines can keep:

the moon was full last night: today, low tide was low:
black shoals of mussels exposed to the risk                         60
of air
and, earlier, of sun,
waved in and out with the waterline, waterline inexact,
caught always in the event of change:
      a young mottled gull stood free on the shoals               65
      and ate
to vomiting: another gull, squawking possession, cracked a crab,

picked out the entrails, swallowed the soft-shelled legs, a ruddy
turnstone[1] running in to snatch leftover bits:

risk is full: every living thing in                                          70
siege: the demand is life, to keep life: the small
white blacklegged egret, how beautiful, quietly stalks and spears
      the shallows, darts to shore
          to stab—what? I couldn't
      see against the black mudflats—a frightened          75
      fiddler crab?

      the news to my left over the dunes and
reeds and bayberry clumps was
      fall: thousands of tree swallows
      gathering for flight:                                       80
      an order held
      in constant change: a congregation
rich with entropy: nevertheless, separable, noticeable
      as one event,
          not chaos: preparations for                      85
flight from winter,
cheet, cheet, cheet, cheet, wings rifling the green clumps,
beaks
at the bayberries
      a perception full of wind, flight, curve,                  90
      sound:
      the possibility of rule as the sum of rulelessness:
the "field" of action
with moving, incalculable center:

in the smaller view, order tight with shape:                                 95
blue tiny flowers on a leafless weed: carapace of crab:
snail shell:
      pulsations of order
      in the bellies of minnows: orders swallowed,
broken down, transferred through membranes                                   100
to strengthen larger orders: but in the large view, no
lines or changeless shapes: the working in and out, together
      and against, of millions of events: this,
          so that I make
          no form of                                       105
          formlessness:

orders as summaries, as outcomes of actions override
or in some way result, not predictably (seeing me gain
the top of a dune,
the swallows                                                                 110
could take flight—some other fields of bayberry
      could enter fall
      berryless) and there is serenity:

---

1. A ploverlike migratory bird.

no arranged terror: no forcing of image, plan,
or thought:                                                                          115
no propaganda, no humbling of reality to precept:

terror pervades but is not arranged, all possibilities
of escape open: no route shut, except in
   the sudden loss of all routes:

      I see narrow orders, limited tightness, but will            120
not run to that easy victory:
    still around the looser, wider forces work:
    I will try
      to fasten into order enlarging grasps of disorder, widening
scope, but enjoying the freedom that                                                 125
Scope eludes my grasp, that there is no finality of vision,
that I have perceived nothing completely,
    that tomorrow a new walk is a new walk.

                             1965

## The City Limits

When you consider the radiance, that it does not withhold
itself but pours its abundance without selection into every
nook and cranny not overhung or hidden; when you consider

that birds' bones make no awful noise against the light but
lie low in the light as in a high testimony; when you consider      5
the radiance, that it will look into the guiltiest

swervings of the weaving heart and bear itself upon them,
not flinching into disguise or darkening; when you consider
the abundance of such resource as illuminates the glow-blue

bodies and gold-skeined wings of flies swarming the dumped          10
guts of a natural slaughter or the coil of shit and in no
way winces from its storms of generosity; when you consider

that air or vacuum, snow or shale, squid or wolf, rose or lichen,
each is accepted into as much light as it will take, then
the heart moves roomier, the man stands and looks about, the        15

leaf does not increase itself above the grass, and the dark
work of the deepest cells is of a tune with May bushes
and fear lit by the breadth of such calmly turns to praise.

                             1971

# Easter Morning

I have a life that did not become,
that turned aside and stopped,
astonished:
I hold it in me like a pregnancy or
as on my lap a child                                                  5
not to grow or grow old but dwell on

it is to his grave I most
frequently return and return
to ask what is wrong, what was
wrong, to see it all by                                              10
the light of a different necessity
but the grave will not heal
and the child,
stirring, must share my grave
with me, an old man having                                           15
gotten by on what was left

when I go back to my home country in these
fresh far-away days, it's convenient to visit
everybody, aunts and uncles, those who used to say,
look how he's shooting up, and the                                   20
trinket aunts who always had a little
something in their pocketbooks, cinnamon bark
or a penny or nickel, and uncles who
were the rumored fathers of cousins
who whispered of them as of great, if                                25
troubled, presences, and school
teachers, just about everybody older
(and some younger) collected in one place
waiting, particularly, but not for
me, mother and father there, too, and others                         30
close, close as burrowing
under skin, all in the graveyard
assembled, done for, the world they
used to wield, have trouble and joy
in, gone                                                             35

the child in me that could not become
was not ready for others to go,
to go on into change, blessings and
horrors, but stands there by the road
where the mishap occurred, crying out for                            40
help, come and fix this or we
can't get by, but the great ones who
were to return, they could not or did
not hear and went on in a flurry and
now, I say in the graveyard, here                                    45
lies the flurry, now it can't come
back with help or helpful asides, now

we all buy the bitter
incompletions, pick up the knots of
horror, silently raving, and go on                              50
crashing into empty ends not
completions, not rondures the fullness
has come into and spent itself from
I stand on the stump
of a child, whether myself                                      55
or my little brother who died, and
yell as far as I can, I cannot leave this place, for
for me it is the dearest and the worst,
it is life nearest to life which is
life lost: it is my place where                                 60
I must stand and fail,
calling attention with tears
to the branches not lofting
boughs into space, to the barren
air that holds the world that was my world              65

though the incompletions
(& completions) burn out
standing in the flash high-burn
momentary structure of ash, still it
is a picture-book, letter-perfect                               70
Easter morning: I have been for a
walk: the wind is tranquil: the brook
works without flashing in an abundant
tranquility: the birds are lively with
voice: I saw something I had                                    75
never seen before: two great birds,
maybe eagles, blackwinged, whitenecked
and -headed, came from the south oaring
the great wings steadily; they went
directly over me, high up, and kept on               80
due north: but then one bird,
the one behind, veered a little to the
left and the other bird kept on seeming
not to notice for a minute: the first
began to circle as if looking for                               85
something, coasting, resting its wings
on the down side of some of the circles:
the other bird came back and they both
circled, looking perhaps for a draft;
they turned a few more times, possibly             90
rising—at least, clearly resting—
then flew on falling into distance till
they broke across the local bush and
trees: it was a sight of bountiful
majesty and integrity: the having                               95
patterns and routes, breaking
from them to explore other patterns or
better way to routes, and then the

return: a dance sacred as the sap in
the trees, permanent in its descriptions                          100
as the ripples round the brook's
ripplestone: fresh as this particular
flood of burn breaking across us now
from the sun.

1981

## Autonomy

I am living without you because
    of terror, a farfetched
notion that I
can't live without you

which I must narrow down & quell,                                 5
    for how can I live
worthy of you, in the
freedom of your limber engagements,

in the casual uptakes of your
    sweetest compliances                                         10
if stricken in your presence
by what your absence stills:

to have you, I school myself
    to let you go; how terrible
to buy that absence                                              15
before the fragrance of any presence comes:

but though I am living without
    you, surely
I can't live
without you: the thought of                                     20

you hauls my heavy
    body up,
floats me around,
gives my motions point, just the thought.

1987

# JAMES MERRILL
## 1926–1995

When James Merrill's *First Poems* were published in 1950, he was immediately recognized as one of the most gifted and polished poets of his generation. But it was not until *Water Street* (1962), his third volume of poems, that Merrill began to enlist his brilliant technique and sophisticated tone in developing a poetic autobiography. The book takes its title from the street where he lived in the seaside village of Stonington, Connecticut. The opening poem, *An Urban Convalescence*, explores his decision to leave New York, which he sees as a distracting city that destroys its past. He portrays his move as a rededication to his personal past and an attempt through poetry "to make some kind of house / Out of the life lived, out of the love spent."

The metaphor of *home* is an emotional center to which Merrill's writing often returns, as in *Lost in Translation*, where the narrator recalls a childhood summer in a home mysteriously without parents. *The Broken Home* similarly recalls elements of Merrill's own experience as the son of parents who divorced when he was young. He had been born to the second marriage of Charles E. Merrill, financier and founder of the best-known brokerage firm in America. *The Broken Home* and *Lost in Translation* show how memory and the act of writing have the power to reshape boyhood pain and conflict so as to achieve "the unstiflement of the entire story." Such an attitude distinguishes Merrill from his contemporaries (Robert Lowell, Anne Sexton, and Sylvia Plath), whose autobiographical impulse expresses itself primarily in the present tense and the use of poems as an urgent journal true to the moment.

As an undergraduate at Amherst College, Merrill had written an honors thesis on the French novelist Marcel Proust (1871–1922). His poetry was clearly affected by Proust's notion that the literary exercise of memory slowly discloses the patterns of childhood experience that we are destined to relive. Proust showed in his *Remembrance of Things Past* how such power over chaotic material of the past is often triggered involuntarily by an object or an episode in the present whose associations reach back into formative childhood encounters. The questions he asked were asked by Freud as well: What animates certain scenes—and not others—for us? It is to answer such questions that some of Merrill's poems are told from the viewpoint of an observant child. In other poems the poet is explicitly present, at his desk, trying to incorporate into his adult understanding of the contours of his life the pain and freshness of childhood memories. The poems are narrative (one of his early books was called *Short Stories*) as often as lyric, in the hope that dramatic *action* will reveal the meanings with which certain objects have become charged. As Merrill saw it, "You hardly ever need to *state* your feelings. The point is to feel and keep the eyes open. Then what you feel is expressed, is mimed back at you by the scene. A room, a landscape. I'd go a step further. We don't *know* what we feel until we see it distanced by this kind of translation."

Merrill traveled extensively and presented landscapes from his travels as ways of exploring alternative or buried states of his own mind, the "translations" of which he spoke. Poems such as *Days of 1964* and *After the Fire* reflect his experiences in Greece, where he used to spend a portion of each year. They respectively anticipate and comment on *The Fire Screen* (1969), a sequence of poems describing the rising and falling curve of a love affair partly in terms of an initiation into Greece with its power to strip away urban sophistication. The books that followed served as initiations into other psychic territories. Problems of family relationships and the erotic entanglements of homosexual love previously seen on an intimate scale were in *Braving the Elements* (1972) acted out against a wider backdrop: the long land-scapes, primitive geological perspectives, and erosions of the American Far West. Here human experience, examined in his earlier work in close-up, is seen as part of a longer process of evolution comprehensible in terms of enduring nonhuman patterns.

In *Divine Comedies* (which received the Pulitzer Prize in 1977) Merrill began his most ambitious work: two-thirds of it is devoted to *The Book of Ephraim*, a long narrative. It is not only a recapitulation of his career but also an attempt to locate individual psychic energies as part of a larger series of nourishing influences: friends living and dead, literary predecessors, scientific theories of the growth of the universe and the mind, the life of other periods and even other universes—all conducted through a set of encounters with the "other world" in seances at the Ouija board. It is a witty and original and assured attempt to take the intimate material of the short lyric that has characterized his earlier work and cast it onto an epic scale. The second and third volumes of the trilogy, *Mirabell: Books of Number* and *Scripts for the Pageant*, appeared in 1978 and 1980, respectively; the entire work, with an epilogue titled *Coda: The Higher Keys* was collected in 1982 under the title *The Changing Light at Sandover*. His final collections of shorter poems are *Late Settings* (1985) and *The Inner Room* (1988).

## An Urban Convalescence

Out for a walk, after a week in bed,
I find them tearing up part of my block
And, chilled through, dazed and lonely, join the dozen
In meek attitudes, watching a huge crane
Fumble luxuriously in the filth of years.                                     5
Her jaws dribble rubble. An old man
Laughs and curses in her brain,
Bringing to mind the close of *The White Goddess*.[1]

As usual in New York, everything is torn down
Before you have had time to care for it.                                      10
Head bowed, at the shrine of noise, let me try to recall
What building stood here. Was there a building at all?
I have lived on this same street for a decade.

Wait. Yes. Vaguely a presence rises
Some five floors high, of shabby stone                                        15
—Or am I confusing it with another one
In another part of town, or of the world?—
And over its lintel into focus vaguely
Misted with blood (my eyes are shut)
A single garland sways, stone fruit, stone leaves,                            20
Which years of grit had etched until it thrust
Roots down, even into the poor soil of my seeing.
When did the garland become part of me?

---

1. The book (1948) in which English poet Robert Graves sets forth the impassioned theory that authentic poetry is inspired by a primitive goddess who is both creative and destructive. The crane is her sacred bird, which through a pun the poet here associates with the mechanical crane. Its operator seems like a crazed parody poet, committed only to demolition.

I ask myself, amused almost,
Then shiver once from head to toe,                                    25

Transfixed by a particular cheap engraving of garlands
Bought for a few francs long ago,
All calligraphic tendril and cross-hatched rondure,
Ten years ago, and crumpled up to stanch
Boughs dripping, whose white gestures filled a cab,                   30
And thought of neither then nor since.
Also, to clasp them, the small, red-nailed hand
Of no one I can place. Wait. No. Her name, her features
Lie toppled underneath that year's fashions.
The words she must have spoken, setting her face                      35
To fluttering like a veil, I cannot hear now,
Let alone understand.

So that I am already on the stair,
As it were, of where I lived,
When the whole structure shudders at my tread                        40
And soundlessly collapses, filling
The air with motes of stone.
Onto the still erect building next door
Are pressed levels and hues—
Pocked rose, streaked greens, brown whites.                          45
Who drained the pousse-café?[2]
Wires and pipes, snapped off at the roots, quiver.

Well, that is what life does. I stare
A moment longer, so. And presently
The massive volume of the world                                      50
Closes again.

Upon that book I swear
To abide by what it teaches:
Gospels of ugliness and waste,
Of towering voids, of soiled gusts,                                  55
Of a shrieking to be faced
Full into, eyes astream with cold—

With cold?
All right then. With self-knowledge.

Indoors at last, the pages of *Time* are apt                         60
To open, and the illustrated mayor of New York,
Given a glimpse of how and where I work,
To note yet one more house that can be scrapped.

Unwillingly I picture
My walls weathering in the general view.                             65
It is not even as though the new
Buildings did very much for architecture.

2. An after-dinner drink made up of layers of different-colored cordials.

Suppose they did. The sickness of our time requires
That these as well be blasted in their prime.
You would think the simple fact of having lasted                70
Threatened our cities like mysterious fires.

There are certain phrases which to use in a poem
Is like rubbing silver with quicksilver. Bright
But facile, the glamour deadens overnight.
For instance, how "the sickness of our time"                     75

Enhances, then debases, what I feel.
At my desk I swallow in a glass of water
No longer cordial, scarcely wet, a pill
They had told me not to take until much later.

With the result that back into my imagination                    80
The city glides, like cities seen from the air,
Mere smoke and sparkle to the passenger
Having in mind another destination

Which now is not that honey-slow descent
Of the Champs-Elysées,[3] her hand in his,                       85
But the dull need to make some kind of house
Out of the life lived, out of the love spent.

                                                          1962


# The Broken Home

Crossing the street,
I saw the parents and the child
At their window, gleaming like fruit
With evening's mild gold leaf.

In a room on the floor below,                                    5
Sunless, cooler—a brimming
Saucer of wax, marbly and dim—
I have lit what's left of my life.

I have thrown out yesterday's milk
And opened a book of maxims.                                     10
The flame quickens. The word stirs.

Tell me, tongue of fire,
That you and I are as real
At least as the people upstairs.
                                        •
My father, who had flown in World War I,                         15
Might have continued to invest his life
In cloud banks well above Wall Street and wife.

---

3. A stylish boulevard in Paris.

But the race was run below, and the point was to win.

Too late now, I make out in his blue gaze
(Through the smoked glass of being thirty-six)                    20
The soul eclipsed by twin black pupils, sex
And business; time was money in those days.

Each thirteenth year he married. When he died
There were already several chilled wives
In sable orbit—rings, cars, permanent waves.                    25
We'd felt him warming up for a green bride.

He could afford it. He was "in his prime"
At three score ten. But money was not time.

                                        •

When my parents were younger this was a popular act:
A veiled woman would leap from an electric, wine-dark car       30
To the steps of no matter what—the Senate or the Ritz Bar—
And bodily, at newsreel speed, attack

No matter whom—Al Smith or José Maria Sert
Or Clemenceau[1]—veins standing out on her throat
As she yelled *War mongerer! Pig! Give us the vote!*,          35
And would have to be hauled away in her hobble skirt.

What had the man done? Oh, made history.
Her business (he had implied) was giving birth,
Tending the house, mending the socks.

Always that same old story—                                    40
Father Time and Mother Earth,[2]
A marriage on the rocks.

                                        •

One afternoon, red, satyr-thighed
Michael, the Irish setter, head
Passionately lowered, led                                      45
The child I was to a shut door. Inside,

Blinds beat sun from the bed.
The green-gold room throbbed like a bruise.
Under a sheet, clad in taboos
Lay whom we sought, her hair undone, outspread,               50

And of a blackness found, if ever now, in old
Engravings where the acid bit.
I must have needed to touch it
Or the whiteness—was she dead?

1. Georges Clemenceau (1841–1929), premier of
France during World War I, visited the United States
in 1922. Alfred E. Smith (1873–1944), a governor of
New York and in 1928 candidate for the presidency.
Sert (1876–1945), a Spanish painter who decorated the
lobby of the Waldorf Astoria Hotel in New York

(1930).
2. In one sense a reference to Cronus (Greek for
"Time"), ruler of the ancient Titans, and to his wife,
Rhea, an earth deity known as Mother of the Gods.
Because Cronus ate their children as soon as they were
born, Rhea plotted his overthrow.

Her eyes flew open, startled strange and cold.                    55
The dog slumped to the floor. She reached for me. I fled.
                              •

Tonight they have stepped out onto the gravel.
The party is over. It's the fall
Of 1931. They love each other still.

She: Charlie, I can't stand the pace.                             60
He: Come on, honey—why, you'll bury us all!

A lead soldier guards my windowsill:
Khaki rifle, uniform, and face.
Something in me grows heavy, silvery, pliable.

How intensely people used to feel!                                65
Like metal poured at the close of a proletarian novel,[3]
Refined and glowing from the crucible,
I see those two hearts, I'm afraid,
Still. Cool here in the graveyard of good and evil,
They are even so to be honored and obeyed.                        70
                              •

. . . Obeyed, at least, inversely. Thus
I rarely buy a newspaper, or vote.
To do so, I have learned, is to invite
The tread of a stone guest[4] within my house.

Shooting this rusted bolt, though, against him,                  75
I trust I am no less time's child than some
Who on the heath impersonate Poor Tom[5]
Or on the barricades risk life and limb.

Nor do I try to keep a garden, only
An avocado in a glass of water—                                   80
Roots pallid, gemmed with air. And later,

When the small gilt leaves have grown
Fleshy and green, I let them die, yes, yes,
And start another. I am earth's no less.
                              •

A child, a red dog roam the corridors,                            85
Still, of the broken home. No sound. The brilliant
Rag runners halt before wide-open doors.
My old room! Its wallpaper—cream, medallioned
With pink and brown—brings back the first nightmares,
Long summer colds, and Emma, sepia-faced,                         90
Perspiring over broth carried upstairs
Aswim with golden fats I could not taste.

The real house became a boarding-school.
Under the ballroom ceiling's allegory

---

3. Socialist novel that romanticized laborers.
4. The *commendatore* in Mozart's *Don Giovanni* (1787) returns as a statue to get his revenge.

5. Edgar, in Shakespeare's *King Lear*, disowned by his father, wanders the heath disguised as a madman.

Someone at last may actually be allowed                        95
To learn something; or, from my window, cool
With the unstiflement of the entire story,
Watch a red setter stretch and sink in cloud.

1966

# FROM THE CHANGING LIGHT AT SANDOVER[1]

## From The Book of Ephraim

Maya[2] in the city has a dream:
People in evening dress move through a blaze
Of chandeliers, white orchids, silver trays
Dense with bubbling glassfuls. Suavities
Of early talking pictures, although no                         5
Word is spoken. One she seems to know
Has joined her, radiant with his wish to please.
She is a girl again, his fire-clear eyes
Turning her beautiful, limber, wise,
Except that she alone wears mourning weeds                     10
That weigh unbearably until he leads
Her to a spring, or source, oh wonder! in
Whose shining depths her gown turns white, her jet
To diamonds, and black veil to bridal snow.
Her features are unchanged, yet her pale skin                 15
Is black, with glowing nostrils—a not yet
Printed self . . . Then it is time to go.
Long trials, his eyes convey, must intervene
Before they meet again. A first, last kiss
And fadeout. Dream? She wakes from it in bliss.               20

So what does that turn out to mean?
Well, Maya has lately moved to the top floor

---

1. James Merrill's trilogy provides a series of overlapping fictions to explain the poet's sense of participation in "other worlds." Three successive "worlds" are revealed to him through "dictation" on a Ouija board:

> Heavy cardboard sheet
> Over which the letters A to Z
> Spread in an arc, our covenant
> With whom it would concern; also
> The Arabic numerals, and YES and NO.

(Messages are spelled out by the pointer, the handle of a cup on which the poet JM and his friend DJ [David Jackson] each rest a hand.) In *The Book of Ephraim* they feel the presence of now dead friends, figures who have been in one way or another exemplary for the poet. They are imagined as part of a vast system of reincarnation and eventual purification in a series of stages that free them from earthly ties. In *Mirabell's Books of Number* human perspective is augmented, even replaced, by a scientific fiction: the presence of nonhuman, batlike figures who are said to speak from within the atom. *The Book of Ephraim* is divided into twenty-six sections, each identified by a letter of the alphabet; our selection is from M (identified by the large initial letter). *Mirabell* is divided into numerical sections from 1 through 9; our selection is the first part of section 9.

2. "Deren, Elanora ('Maya'), 1917–61, doyenne of our American experimental film. Mistress moreover of a life style not For twenty years to seem conventional. Fills her Village flat with sacred objects: Dolls, drums, baubles that twirl and shimmer, Stills from work in progress, underfoot The latest in a lineage of big, black, Strangely accident-prone Haitian cats. Dresses her high-waisted, maiden-breasted Person—russet afro, agate eyes— In thriftshop finery" [from section D].

Of a brownstone whence, a hundred and six years
Ago, a lady more or less her age
Passed respectably to the First Stage.                                    25
Now (explains Ephraim) in a case like this
At least a century goes by before
One night comes when the soul, revisiting
Its deathplace here below, locates and enters
On the spot a sleeping form its own                                        30
Age and sex (easier said than done
In rural or depopulated areas:
E treats us here to the hilarious
Upshot of a Sioux brave's having chosen
By mistake a hibernating bear).                                            35
Masked in that sleeping person, then, the soul
For a few outwardly uneventful hours—
Position shifting, pillowcrease, a night
Of faint sounds, gleams, moonset, mosquito bite—
Severs what LAST THREADS bind it to the world.                            40
Meanwhile (here comes the interesting bit)
The sleeper's soul, dislodged, replaces it
In Heaven. Ephraim now, remembering
Her from that distant weekend, pulls a string
THIS TIME AT LEAST NO GRIZZLY ON RAMPAGE                                  45
Transferring Maya's dream to his own Stage.
And who was her admirer? CANT U GUESS
But is that how you generally dress,
You dead, in 1930's evening clothes?
WE ARE CORRECT IN STYLES THE DREAMER KNOWS                               50

This dream, he blandly adds, is a low-budget
Remake—imagine—of the *Paradiso*.[3]
Not otherwise its poet toured the spheres
While Someone very highly placed up there,
Donning his bonnet, in and out through that                               55
Now famous nose haled the cool Tuscan night.
The resulting masterpiece takes years to write;
More, since the dogma of its day
Calls for a Purgatory, for a Hell,
Both of which Dante thereupon, from footage                               60
Too dim or private to expose, invents.
His Heaven, though, as one cannot but sense,
Tercet by tercet, is pure Show and Tell.

1976, 1982

---

3. The trilogy is loosely based on the three-part structure of *The Divine Comedy* of the Italian Dante Alighieri (1265–1321). Dante (whose prominent nose was
familiar from contemporary portraits) organized his
dream vision as an ascent from Inferno, or Hell,
through Purgatory to Paradise. The poem was written
in *terza rima*, an intricately rhymed series of "tercets"
(three-line stanzas).

# *From* Mirabell's Books of Number

### 9.1

And maddening—it's all by someone else![1]
In your voice, Wystan, or in Mirabell's.
I want it mine, but cannot spare those twenty
Years in a cool dark place that *Ephraim* took
In order to be palatable wine.                    5
This book by contrast, immature, supine,
Still kicks against its archetypal cradle
LESS I SHD THINK BY CONTRAST THAN DESIGN?
A MUSE IN HER RECURRENT INFANCY
PRESIDES AS U MY DEAR WERE FIRST TO SEE:          10
URANIA[2] BABBLING ON THE THRESHOLD OF
OUR NEW ATOMIC AGE     THE LITTLE LOVE
AT PLAY WITH WORDS WHOSE SENSE SHE CANNOT YET
FACE LEARNING     Very pretty, but I'd set
My whole heart, after *Ephraim*, on returning      15
To private life, to my own words. Instead,
Here I go again, a vehicle
In this cosmic carpool. Mirabell once said
He taps my word banks. I'd be happier
If *I* were tapping them. Or thought I were.        20

YR SCRUPLES DEAR BOY ARE INCONSEQUENT
IF I MAY SAY SO     CAN U STILL BE BENT,
AFTER OUR COURSE IN HOW TO SEE PAST LONE
AUTONOMY TO POWERS BEHIND THE THRONE,
ON DOING YR OWN THING: EACH TEENY BIT              25
(PARDON MME[3]) MADE PERSONAL AS SHIT?
GRANTED THAT IN 1ST CHILDHOOD WE WERE NOT
PRAISED ENOUGH FOR GETTING OFF THE POT
IT'S TIME TO DO SO NOW     THINK WHAT A MINOR
PART THE SELF PLAYS IN A WORK OF ART               30
COMPARED TO THOSE GREAT GIVENS     THE ROSEBRICK MANOR
ALL TOPIARY[4] FORMS & METRICAL
MOAT ARIPPLE! FROM ANTHOLOGIZED
PERENNIALS TO HERB GARDEN OF CLICHES
FROM LATIN-LABELED HYBRIDS TO THE FAWN             35
4 LETTER FUNGI THAT ENRICH THE LAWN,
IS NOT ARCADIA TO DWELL AMONG
GREENWOOD PERSPECTIVES OF THE MOTHER TONGUE
ROOTSYSTEMS UNDERFOOT WHILE OVERHEAD
THE SUN GOD SANG & SHADES OF MEANING SPREAD        40

1. By contrast with *The Book of Ephraim*, which looks back over twenty years of experience at the Ouija board and is told largely in Merrill's own voice, *Mirabell* occurs in an almost continuous present. The poet W. H. Auden (1907–1973), the other character in this dialogue, is one of the poet JM's tutelary spirits in this trilogy; he speaks from the "other world" in five-foot iambic capitalized lines. "Wystan" is Auden's first name.

2. Traditionally, the classical muse of astronomy, but here, in a larger sense, of scientific, especially atomic, knowledge.

3. (Madame) Maria Mitsotaki, a Greek woman who, along with Auden, "educates" JM and DJ from the world of the dead.

4. Elaborately trimmed and shaped shrubbery and vegetation. "Rosebrick Manor": poetic tradition imagined as a manor house.

& FAR SNOWCAPPED ABSTRACTIONS GLITTERED NEAR
OR FAIRLY MELTED INTO ATMOSPHERE?
AS FOR THE FAMILY ITSELF MY DEAR
JUST GAPE UP AT THAT CORONETED FRIEZE:[5]
SWEET WILLIAMS & FATE-FLAVORED EMILIES                                45
THE DOUBTING THOMAS & THE DULCET ONE
(HARDY MY BOY WHO ELSE? & CAMPION)
MILTON & DRYDEN OUR LONG JOHNS   IN SHORT
IN BED AT PRAYERS AT MUSIC FLUSHED WITH PORT
THE DULL THE PRODIGAL THE MEAN THE MAD                                50
IT WAS THE GREATEST PRIVILEGE TO HAVE HAD
A BARE LOWCEILINGED MAID'S ROOM AT THE TOP
Stop! you've convinced me. Better yet, don't stop.

I SHALL ONCE I HAVE TAKEN UP YR CHIEF
& EARLIEST ANXIETY: BELIEF                                            55
FACTS JM WERE ALL U KNEW TO WANT.
WRETCHED RICKETY RECALCITRANT
URCHINS,   THE FEW WHO LIVE GROW UP TO BE
IMPS OF THE ANTIMASQUE[6]—RUDE SCENERY
& GUTTURAL STOMPINGS, WHEN THE SOVEREIGN NODS,                        60
SOUNDLESSLY DIVIDE & HERE A TABLE
IS SET & LAMPS LIT FOR THE FEASTING GODS
OBERON'S COURT (OR MY FRIEND'S CAVE) APPEARS.
THE ELDER FACTS IN LIVERY OF FABLE
HAVE JOINED THE DANCE   FOR FACT IS IS IS FABLE:                      65
THIS IS OUR GIFT FROM MIRABELL MY DEARS.

                                                        1978, 1982

5. Among the aristocratic coats of arms are flowers and vines identified by punning names with figures in literary history—first generally with the famous Williams and Emilies, then specifically with the novelist Thomas Hardy (1840–1928), the poet Thomas Campion (1567–1620), and the poets John Milton (1608–1674) and John Dryden (1631–1700).
6. An integral part of masques—dramas performed before royal personages especially in the 17th century—was the antimasque in which the forces of disorder temporarily cavort and prevail. They are brought to order by a figure representing the sovereign (here, Oberon, king of the fairies, or Plato in his cave). Merrill imagines unassimilated facts as "imps of the antimasque."

---

# ROBERT CREELEY
## b. 1926

"I was shy of the word 'poet,' " Robert Creeley once said, "and all its associations in a world I was then intimate with. It was not, in short, a fit attention for a young man raised in the New England manner, compact of Puritanically deprived senses of speech and sensuality. Life was real and life was earnest, and one had best get on with it." Despite the "constant, restless moving" that Creeley himself has called a pattern in his life, his work retains its connections to his New England background (he was born in Massachusetts), with its economy of speech and natural resources, and with the lingering heritage of its Puritanism. His chosen vocabulary is spare (someone once noted that 80 percent of his volume *Words*, 1967, is made up of monosyllables), but his work is, in part, a reaction against the strictures of his background, as seen most clearly in his explicit treatment of the erotic and sensual. Like William Carlos Williams, he sees the poet's role as overthrowing repression and creating the possibility for contact. But Creeley's poems are especially interesting for the ways they conduct a struggle between the self-conscious mind and the instincts of the body, for their exposure of the mind's relentless self-regard. The effort of the poet is to break through the mind's enclosures and to enter fully into the world. Such a breakthrough is evident in a poem like *The Birds*, which captures the poet's desire to give himself over to the world in the way the birds "ride the air," and its rhythms and language enact a realization of this desire. Other poems, however, are grounded in the difficulty of release from a painful self-consciousness. Whether joyful or agonized, Creeley's work as a whole is characterized by an awareness of his own act of thinking about what he feels. He may be the most self-conscious passionate poet we have.

After the death of his father, a doctor, when Creeley was four, he was brought up in a family of five women. He began his life of restless motion in 1944, when he dropped out of Harvard after a year and joined the American Field Service in India and Burma. He returned to Harvard a year later but left again in 1947 without receiving a degree. In 1946 he married for the first time, and he and his wife lived for a period on Cape Cod (commuting by boat to his classes at Harvard), then on a farm in New Hampshire. Early in 1950, with his friend Jacob Leed, Creeley attempted to publish an alternative literary magazine, and wrote to every writer he knew, and some he did not, soliciting contributions. One of his correspondents sent him several of Charles Olson's poems. Although the magazine was never founded, a correspondence between Creeley and Olson began in 1950 that would run to thousands of letters (the correspondence at one point, according to Creeley, took up eight hours of each day). After a period in Aix-en-Provence and then in Mallorca, where he founded the Divers Press, he accepted Olson's invitation to join the faculty at Black Mountain College, where he founded and edited the *Black Mountain Review* (Olson solved the problem of Creeley's never having graduated from Harvard by having Black Mountain grant him a degree). Olson, Creeley said, "taught me to how to write. Not how to write poems that he wrote, but how to write poems that I write. This is a very curious and specific difference." The richly reciprocal nature of the friendship between the two poets led Olson to quote Creeley's now famous statement on organic form, "Form is never more than an extension of content," in bold print in his essay on "Projective Verse," and to dedicate *The Maximus Poems* to him.

In the company of poets to whom Creeley feels most indebted—Whitman, Hart Crane, Olson, and Williams—Williams remains the one with whom his work shares most (epigraphs from Williams's poems open several of Creeley's books). In the work of Creeley, as in the work of Williams, women are a recurrent presence: wife, mother, daughter, queen, or muse, the figure of the woman is composite. Her presence in his poems expresses Creeley's need for contact with what he has called "the most persistent *other* of our existence, eschewing male order, allowing us to live at last." For Creeley, this contact can be invigorating, erotic, difficult, and confusing, and his frequent poems about marriage, such as *For Love*, dedicated to his second wife, Bobbie Louise Hall, render "tedium / despair, a painful / sense of isolation" even as they celebrate "the company of love." "He continues the art of the troubadours with its themes of love and trial," Robert Duncan once wrote of him. While Creeley has written often of love's trials (he has been married three times) he remains a poet in its service. Visited by the muse in *Kore* (as happens also in *The Door* and *The Finger*), the poet can only ask "O love, / where are you / leading / me now?"

The question Creeley asks in *Kore* suggests that for him the poem is a discovery of what might be said, an activity or a form of wandering ("life tracking itself," as he has called it) in which the destination or subject is not known beforehand. His poems often enact a walk, where the poet's particular form of walking is presented as stumbling (as in *The Door*, where he writes, "The Lady has always moved to the next town / and you stumble on after Her"). The stumbling walk is, of course, open to error, and the form of Creeley's poems presents a wandering that at times missteps in search of its true form or subject. His presentation of himself as a stumbler also suggests his humorous self-awareness. The playfulness of some of his poems, like *The Messengers*, or like the moment in *An Illness* when, remembering "pastures / of my childhood," he says, "I will not / bore you with their / boulders and cows," contrasts with their sometimes agonized uncertainty. "I am *given* to write poems," Creeley has said, "I cannot anticipate their occasion. I have used all the intelligence I can muster to follow the possibilities that the poem . . . is declaring, but I cannot anticipate the necessary conclusion in the activity." As this comment suggests, Creeley emphasizes process and discovery, to the pursuit of "the particular instance." Such an emphasis necessarily makes his work uneven—some poems wander without discovery, others capture an instant that may not be worth capturing. But in his best poems, Creeley measures both thinking and feeling, measures out the uncertain pursuit of an instant's possibility. His poetic form is shaped by an acute awareness of himself, the moment, and the line as a rhythmic unit, and the pleasures of his poems lie in this awareness and in their openness to discovery. If he is a wanderer in the poems as he has been in his life, his wandering repeatedly takes him home: to domesticity, to love, to the work of memory, and, most characteristically, to a fresh sense of the present, as when he sees "the light then / of the sun coming / for another morning / in the world" (*The World*).

# Kore[1]

As I was walking
   I came upon
chance walking
   the same road upon.

As I sat down                                                      5
   by chance to move
later
   if and as I might,

light the wood was,
   light and green,                                   10
and what I saw
   before I had not seen.

It was a lady
   accompanied
by goat men[2]
   leading her.                                           15

---

1. Kore, literally "maiden," is an epithet for the Greek earth goddess Persephone. While picking flowers with some companions, she was kidnapped by Hades (who had been struck by one of Eros's arrows) and taken to the Underworld. There she spends part of the year as queen of the dead; part of the time she lives above-ground with her mother, Demeter. Her annual reemergence is linked with the reemergence of earth's fertility in spring and summer.
2. Or satyrs, creatures of Greek mythology with the upper bodies of men and the legs of goats.

Her hair held earth.
    Her eyes were dark.
A double flute[3]
    made her move.                                     20

"O love,
    where are you
leading
    me now?"

                          1959


# The Door

### for Robert Duncan

It is hard going to the door
cut so small in the wall where
the vision which echoes loneliness
brings a scent of wild flowers in a wood.

What I understood, I understand.                     5
My mind is sometime torment,
sometimes good and filled with livelihood,
and feels the ground.

But I see the door,
and knew the wall, and wanted the wood,              10
and would get there if I could
with my feet and hands and mind.

Lady, do not banish me
for digressions. My nature
is a quagmire of unresolved                          15
confessions. Lady, I follow.

I walked away from myself,
I left the room, I found the garden,
I knew the woman
in it, together we lay down.                         20

Dead night remembers. In December
we change, not multiplied but dispersed,
sneaked out of childhood,
the ritual of dismemberment.

Mighty magic is a mother,                            25
in her there is another issue
of fixture, repeated form, the race renewal,
the charge of the command.

3. Ancient Greek musical instrument.

The garden echoes across the room.
It is fixed in the wall like a mirror                                    30
that faces a window behind you
and reflects the shadows.

May I go now?
Am I allowed to bow myself down
in the ridiculous posture of renewal,                                   35
of the insistence of which I am the virtue?

Nothing for You is untoward.
Inside You would also be tall,
more tall, more beautiful.
Come toward me from the wall, I want to be with You.                     40

So I screamed to You,
who hears as the wind, and changes
multiply, invariably,
changes in the mind.

Running to the door, I ran down                                         45
as a clock runs down. Walked backwards,
stumbled, sat down
hard on the floor near the wall.

Where were You.
How absurd, how vicious.                                                50
There is nothing to do but get up.
My knees were iron, I rusted in worship, of You.

For that one sings, one
writes the spring poem, one goes on walking.
The Lady has always moved to the next town                              55
and you stumble on after Her.

The door in the wall leads to the garden
where in the sunlight sit
the Graces[1] in long Victorian dresses,
of which my grandmother had spoken.                                     60

History sings in their faces.
They are young, they are obtainable,
and you follow after them also
in the service of God and Truth.

But the Lady is indefinable,                                            65
she will be the door in the wall
to the garden in sunlight.
I will go on talking forever.

---

1. In Greek mythology, the personification of beauty and grace.

I will never get there.
Oh Lady, remember me                                          70
who in Your service grows older
not wiser, no more than before.

How can I die alone.
Where will I be then who am now alone,
what groans so pathetically                                   75
in this room where I am alone?

I will go to the garden.
I will be a romantic. I will sell
myself in hell,
in heaven also I will be.                                     80

In my mind I see the door,
I see the sunlight before me across the floor
beckon to me, as the Lady's skirt
moves small beyond it.

                                                      1959


# The Messengers

### for Allen Ginsberg

The huge dog, Broderick, and
the smile of the quick eyes
of Allen light a kind world.

Their feelings, under some distance
of remote skin, must touch,                                    5
wondering at what impatience does

block them. So little love
to share among so many, so much
yellow-orange hair, on the one,

and on the other, such a darkness                             10
of long hanging hair now, such
slightness of body, and a voice that

rises on the sounds of feeling.
Aie! It raises the world, lifts,
falls, like a sudden sunlight, like                           15

that edge of the black night sweeps
the low lying fields, of soft grasses,
bodies, fills them with quiet longing.

                                                      1967

# The Birds

### *for Jane and Stan Brakhage*

I'll miss the small birds that come
for the sugar you put out
and the bread crumbs. They've

made the edge of the sea domestic
and, as I am, I welcome that.                              5
Nights my head seemed twisted

with dreams and the sea wash,
I let it all come quiet, waking,
counting familiar thoughts and objects.

Here to rest, like they say, I best                        10
liked walking along the beach
past the town till one reached

the other one, around the corner
of rock and small trees. It was
clear, and often empty, and                                15

peaceful. Those lovely ungainly
pelicans fished there, dropping
like rocks, with grace, from the air,

headfirst, then sat on the water,
letting the pouch of their beaks                           20
grow thin again, then swallowing

whatever they'd caught. The birds,
no matter they're not of our kind,
seem most like us here. I want

to go where they go, in a way, if                          25
a small and common one. I want
to ride that air which makes the sea

seem down there, not the element
in which one thrashes to come up.
I love water, I *love* water—                              30

but I also love air, and fire.

1972

# Fathers

Scattered, aslant
faded faces a column

a rise of the packed
peculiar place to a
modest height makes                5
a view of common lots
in winter then, a ground
of battered snow crusted
at the edges under
it all, there under                10
my fathers their
faded women, friends,
the family all echoed,
names trees more tangible
physical place more tangible         15
the air of this place the road
going past to Watertown[1]
or down to my mother's
grave, my father's grave, not
now this resonance of           20
each other one was his, his
survival only, his curious
reticence, his dead state,
his emptiness, his acerbic
edge cuts the hands to          25
hold him, hold on, wants
the ground, *wants* this frozen ground.

1986

1. Town in Massachusetts, just west of Boston.

---

# ALLEN GINSBERG
## b. 1926

"Hold back the edges of your gowns, Ladies, we are going through hell." William Carlos Williams's introduction to Allen Ginsberg's *Howl* (1956) was probably the most auspicious public welcome from one poet to another since Emerson had hailed the unknown Whitman in a letter that Whitman prefaced to the second edition of *Leaves of Grass* one hundred years before. *Howl* combined apocalyptic criticism of the dull, prosperous Eisenhower years with exuberant celebration of an emerging counterculture. It was the best known and most widely circulated book of poems of its time, and with its appearance Ginsberg became part of the history of publicity as well as the history of poetry. *Howl* and Jack Kerouac's novel *On the Road* were the pocket Bibles of the generation whose name Kerouac had coined—"Beat," with its punning overtones of "beaten down" and "beatified."

Allen Ginsberg was born in 1926, son of Louis Ginsberg, a schoolteacher in New Jersey, himself a poet, and of Naomi Ginsberg, a Russian émigrée, whose madness and eventual death her son memorialized in *Kaddish* (1959). His official education took place at Columbia University, but for him as for Jack Kerouac the presence of William Burroughs in New York was equally influential. Burroughs (b. 1914), later the author of *Naked Lunch*, one of the most inventive experiments in American prose, was at that time a drug addict about to embark on an expatriate life in Mexico and Tangier. He helped Ginsberg discover modern writers: Kafka, Yeats, Céline, Rimbaud. Ginsberg responded to Burroughs's liberated kind of life, to his comic-apocalyptic view of American society, and to his bold literary use of autobiography, as when writing about his own experience with addicts and addiction in *Junkie*, whose chapters Ginsberg was reading in manuscript form in 1950.

Ginsberg's New York career has passed into mythology for a generation of poets and readers. In 1945, his sophomore year, he was expelled from Columbia: he had sketched some obscene drawings and phrases in the dust of his dormitory window to draw the attention of a neglectful cleaning woman to the grimy state of his room. Then, living periodically with Burroughs and Kerouac, he shipped out for short trips as a messman on merchant tankers and worked in addition as a welder, a night porter, and a dishwasher.

One summer, in a Harlem apartment, Ginsberg underwent what he was always to represent as the central conversion experience of his life. He had an "auditory vision" of the English poet William Blake reciting his poems: first *Ah! Sunflower*, and then a few minutes later the same oracular voice intoning *The Sick Rose*. It was "like hearing the doom of the whole universe, and at the same time the inevitable beauty of that doom." Ginsberg was convinced that the presence of "this big god over all . . . and that the whole purpose of being born was to wake up to Him."

Ginsberg eventually finished Columbia in 1948 with high grades but under a legal cloud. Herbert Huncke, a colorful but irresponsible addict friend, had been using Ginsberg's apartment as a storage depot for the goods he stole to support his drug habit. To avoid prosecution as an accomplice, Ginsberg had to plead insanity and spent eight months in the Columbia Psychiatric Institute.

After more odd jobs and a considerable success as a market researcher in San Francisco, Ginsberg left the straight, nine-to-five world for good. He was drawn to San Francisco, he said, by its "long honorable . . . tradition of Bohemian— Buddhist—Wobbly [the I.W.W., an early radical labor movement]—mystical— anarchist social involvement." In the years after 1954 he met San Francisco poets such as Robert Duncan, Kenneth Rexroth, Gary Snyder (who was studying Chinese and Japanese at Berkeley), and Lawrence Ferlinghetti, whose City Lights Bookshop became the publisher of *Howl*. The night Ginsberg read the new poem aloud at the Six Gallery has been called "the birth trauma of the Beat Generation."

*Howl*'s spontaneity of surface conceals but grows out of Ginsberg's care and self-consciousness about rhythm and meter. Under the influence of William Carlos Williams, who had befriended him in Paterson after he left the mental hospital, Ginsberg had started carrying around a notebook to record the rhythms of voices around him. Kerouac's *On the Road* gave him further examples of "frank talk" and, in addition, of an "oceanic" prose "sometimes as sublime as epic line." Under Kerouac's influence Ginsberg began the long tumbling lines that were to become his trademark. He carefully explained that all of *Howl and Other Poems* was an experiment in what could be done with the long line, the longer unit of breath that seemed natural for him. "My feeling is for a big long clanky statement," one that accommodates "not the way you would *say* it, a thought, but the way you would think it—i.e., we think rapidly, in visual images as well as words, and if each successive thought were transcribed in its confusion . . . you get a slightly different prosody than if you were talking slowly."

The long line is something Ginsberg learned as well from biblical rhetoric, from the eighteenth-century English poet Christopher Smart, and above all, from Whitman and Blake. His first book pays tribute to both these latter poets. *A Supermarket in California*, with its movement from exclamations to sad questioning, is Ginsberg's melancholy reminder of what has become, after a century, of Whitman's vision of American plenty. In *Sunflower Sutra* he celebrates the battered nobility beneath our industrial "skin of grime." Ginsberg at his best gives a sense of both doom and beauty, whether in the denunciatory impatient prophecies of *Howl* or in the catalog of suffering in *Kaddish*. His disconnected phrases can accumulate as narrative shrieks or, at other moments, can build as a litany of praise.

By the end of the 1960s Ginsberg was widely known and widely traveled. For him it was a decade in which he conducted publicly his own pursuit of inner peace during a long stay with Buddhist instructors in India and at home served as a kind of guru himself for many young people disoriented by the Vietnam War. Ginsberg read his poetry and held "office hours" in universities all over America, a presence at everything from "be-ins"—mass outdoor festivals of chanting, costumes, and music—to antiwar protests. He was a gentle and persuasive presence at hearings for many kinds of reform: revision of severe drug laws and laws against homosexuality. Ginsberg himself had lived for years with the poet Peter Orlovsky and wrote frankly about their relationship. His poems record his drug experiences as well, and *The Change*, written in Japan in 1963, marks his decision to keep away from what he considered the nonhuman domination of drugs and to lay new stress on "living in and inhabiting the human form."

In *The Fall of America* (1972) Ginsberg turned to "epic," a poem including history and registering the ups and downs of his travels across the United States. These "transit" poems sometimes seem like tape-recorded random lists of sights, sounds, and names, but at their best they give a sense of how far America has fallen, by measuring the provisional and changing world of nuclear America against the traces of nature still visible in our landscape and place names. Ginsberg now lives on a farm near Woodstock, New York, and has added ecology to the causes for which he is a patient and attractive spokesman.

## From Howl

### for Carl Solomon[1]

#### I

I saw the best minds of my generation destroyed by madness, starving
    hysterical naked,
dragging themselves through the negro streets at dawn looking for an angry fix,
angelheaded hipsters burning for the ancient heavenly connection[2] to the
    starry dynamo in the machinery of night,
who poverty and tatters and hollow-eyed and high sat up smoking in the
    supernatural darkness of cold-water flats floating across the tops of cities
    contemplating jazz,
who bared their brains to Heaven under the El[3] and saw Mohammedan angels
    staggering on tenement roofs illuminated,               5
who passed through universities with radiant cool eyes hallucinating Arkansas
    and Blake-light[4] tragedy among the scholars of war,
who were expelled from the academies for crazy & publishing obscene odes
    on the windows of the skull,
who cowered in unshaven rooms in underwear, burning their money in
    wastebaskets and listening to the Terror through the wall,

1. Ginsberg met Carl Solomon (b. 1928) while both were patients in the Columbia Psychiatric Institute in 1949 and called him "an intuitive Bronx Dadaist and prose-poet." Many details in *Howl* come from the "apocryphal history" that Solomon told Ginsberg in 1949. In *More Mishaps* (1968), Solomon admits that these adventures were "compounded partly of truth, but for the most [of] raving self-justification, crypto-bohemian boasting . . . effeminate prancing and esoteric aphorisms."
2. In one sense, a person who can supply drugs.
3. The elevated railway in New York City; also, a Hebrew word for God.
4. Refers to Ginsberg's apocalyptic vision of the English poet William Blake (1757–1827).

who got busted in their pubic beards returning through Laredo with a belt of
　　marijuana for New York,
who ate fire in paint hotels or drank turpentine in Paradise Alley,[5] death, or
　　purgatoried their torsos night after night　　　　　　　　　　　　　　10
with dreams, with drugs, with waking nightmares, alcohol and cock and end-
　　less balls,
incomparable blind streets of shuddering cloud and lightning in the mind
　　leaping toward poles of Canada & Paterson,[6] illuminating all the
　　motionless world of Time between,
Peyote solidities of halls, backyard green tree cemetery dawns, wine drunken-
　　ness over the rooftops, storefront boroughs of teahead joyride neon blink-
　　ing traffic light, sun and moon and tree vibrations in the roaring winter
　　dusks of Brooklyn, ashcan rantings and kind king light of mind,
who chained themselves to subways for the endless ride from Battery to holy
　　Bronx[7] on benzedrine until the noise of wheels and children brought
　　them down shuddering mouth-wracked and battered bleak of brain all
　　drained of brilliance in the drear light of Zoo,
who sank all night in submarine light of Bickford's floated out and sat through
　　the stale beer afternoon in desolate Fugazzi's, listening to the crack of
　　doom on the hydrogen jukebox,　　　　　　　　　　　　　　　　　15
who talked continuously seventy hours from park to pad to bar to Bellevue[8] to
　　museum to the Brooklyn Bridge,
a lost battalion of platonic conversationalists jumping down the stoops off fire
　　escapes off windowsills off Empire State out of the moon,
yacketayakking screaming vomiting whispering facts and memories and anec-
　　dotes and eyeball kicks and shocks of hospitals and jails and wars,
whole intellects disgorged in total recall for seven days and nights with brilliant
　　eyes, meat for the Synagogue cast on the pavement,
who vanished into nowhere Zen New Jersey leaving a trail of ambiguous pic-
　　ture postcards of Atlantic City Hall,　　　　　　　　　　　　　　　20
suffering Eastern sweats and Tangerian bone-grindings and migraines of
　　China[9] under junk-withdrawal in Newark's bleak furnished room,
who wandered around and around at midnight in the railroad yard wondering
　　where to go, and went, leaving no broken hearts,
who lit cigarettes in boxcars boxcars boxcars racketing through snow toward
　　lonesome farms in grandfather night,
who studied Plotinus Poe St. John of the Cross[1] telepathy and bop kaballah[2]
　　because the cosmos instinctively vibrated at their feet in Kansas,
who loned it through the streets of Idaho seeking visionary indian angels who
　　were visionary indian angels,　　　　　　　　　　　　　　　　　25
who thought they were only mad when Baltimore gleamed in supernatural
　　ecstasy,
who jumped in limousines with the Chinaman of Oklahoma on the impulse
　　of winter midnight streetlight smalltown rain,
who lounged hungry and lonesome through Houston seeking jazz or sex or

---

5. A tenement courtyard in New York's East Village;
setting of Kerouac's *The Subterraneans* (1958).
6. Ginsberg's hometown, also the town celebrated by
William Carlos Williams in his long poem *Paterson*.
7. Opposite ends of a New York subway line; the
Bronx Zoo was the northern terminus.
8. New York public hospital to which mental patients
are generally committed.

9. African and Asian sources of drugs.
1. Spanish visionary and poet (1542–1591), author of
*The Dark Night of the Soul.* Plotinus (205–270), visionary philosopher. Edgar Allan Poe (1809–1849),
American poet and author of supernatural tales.
2. Bop was the jazz style of the 1940s. The "kaballah"
is a mystical tradition of interpretation of Hebrew
scripture.

· soup, and followed the brilliant Spaniard to converse about America and
Eternity, a hopeless task, and so took ship to Africa,

who disappeared into the volcanoes of Mexico leaving behind nothing but the
shadow of dungarees and the lava and ash of poetry scattered in fireplace
Chicago,

who reappeared on the West Coast investigating the FBI in beards and shorts
with big pacifist eyes sexy in their dark skin passing out incomprehensible leaflets,                                                          30

who burned cigarette holes in their arms protesting the narcotic tobacco haze
of Capitalism,

who distributed Supercommunist pamphlets in Union Square weeping and
undressing while the sirens of Los Alamos[3] wailed them down, and
wailed down Wall,[4] and the Staten Island ferry also wailed,

who broke down crying in white gymnasiums naked and trembling before the
machinery of other skeletons,

who bit detectives in the neck and shrieked with delight in policecars for
committing no crime but their own wild cooking pederasty and intoxication,

who howled on their knees in the subway and were dragged off the roof waving
genitals and manuscripts,                                              35

who let themselves be fucked in the ass by saintly motorcyclists, and screamed
with joy,

who blew and were blown by those human seraphim, the sailors, caresses of
Atlantic and Caribbean love,

who balled in the morning in the evenings in rosegardens and the grass of
public parks and cemeteries scattering their semen freely to whomever
come who may,

who hiccupped endlessly trying to giggle but wound up with a sob behind a
partition in a Turkish Bath when the blonde & naked angel came to
pierce them with a sword,[5]

who lost their loveboys to the three old shrews of fate the one eyed shrew of
the heterosexual dollar the one eyed shrew that winks out of the womb
and the one eyed shrew that does nothing but sit on her ass and snip the
intellectual golden threads of the craftsman's loom,                  40

who copulated ecstatic and insatiate with a bottle of beer a sweetheart a package of cigarettes a candle and fell off the bed, and continued along the
floor and down the hall and ended fainting on the wall with a vision of
ultimate cunt and come eluding the last gyzym of consciousness,

who sweetened the snatches of a million girls trembling in the sunset, and
were red eyed in the morning but prepared to sweeten the snatch of the
sunrise, flashing buttocks under barns and naked in the lake,

who went out whoring through Colorado in myriad stolen nightcars, N.C.,[6]
secret hero of these poems, cocksman and Adonis of Denver—joy to the
memory of his innumerable lays of girls in empty lots & diner backyards,
moviehouses' rickety rows, on mountaintops in caves or with gaunt wait-

---

3. In New Mexico, a center for the development of
the atomic bomb. "Union Square": a gathering place
for radical speakers in New York in the 1930s.
4. Wall Street, but also alludes to the Wailing Wall, a
place of public lamentation in Jerusalem.
5. An allusion to *The Ecstasy of St. Teresa*, a sculpture
by Lorenzo Bernini (1598–1680) based on St. Teresa's
(1515–1582) distinctly erotic description of a religious

vision. The three fates (line 40) in Greek mythology
were goddesses who determine a mortal's life by spinning out a length of thread and cutting it at the time
of death.
6. Neal Cassady, hip companion of Jack Kerouac and
the original Dean Moriarty, one of the leading figures
in *On the Road*.

resses in familiar roadside lonely petticoat upliftings & especially secret
    gas-station solipsisms of johns, & hometown alleys too,
who faded out in vast sordid movies, were shifted in dreams, woke on a sudden
    Manhattan, and picked themselves up out of basements hungover with
    heartless Tokay[7] and horrors of Third Avenue iron dreams & stumbled to
    unemployment offices,
who walked all night with their shoes full of blood on the snowbank docks
    waiting for a door in the East River to open to a room full of steamheat
    and opium,                                                                    45
who created great suicidal dramas on the apartment cliff-banks of the Hudson
    under the wartime blue floodlight of the moon & their heads shall be
    crowned with laurel in oblivion,
who ate the lamb stew of the imagination or digested the crab at the muddy
    bottom of the rivers of Bowery,[8]
who wept at the romance of the streets with their pushcarts full of onions and
    bad music,
who sat in boxes breathing in the darkness under the bridge, and rose up to
    build harpsichords in their lofts,
who coughed on the sixth floor of Harlem crowned with flame under the
    tubercular sky surrounded by orange crates of theology,                      50
who scribbled all night rocking and rolling over lofty incantations which in
    the yellow morning were stanzas of gibberish,
who cooked rotten animals lung heart feet tail borsht & tortillas dreaming of
    the pure vegetable kingdom,
who plunged themselves under meat trucks looking for an egg,
who threw their watches off the roof to cast their ballot for Eternity outside of
    Time, & alarm clocks fell on their heads every day for the next decade,
who cut their wrists three times successively unsuccessfully, gave up and were
    forced to open antique stores where they thought they were growing old
    and cried,                                                                    55
who were burned alive in their innocent flannel suits on Madison Avenue[9]
    amid blasts of leaden verse & the tanked-up clatter of the iron regiments
    of fashion & the nitroglycerine shrieks of the fairies of advertising & the
    mustard gas of sinister intelligent editors, or were run down by the
    drunken taxicabs of Absolute Reality,
who jumped off the Brooklyn Bridge this actually happened and walked away
    unknown and forgotten into the ghostly daze of Chinatown soup alley-
    ways & firetrucks, not even one free beer,
who sang out of their windows in despair, fell out of the subway window,
    jumped in the filthy Passaic,[1] leaped on negroes, cried all over the street,
    danced on broken wineglasses barefoot smashed phonograph records of
    nostalgic European 1930's German jazz finished the whiskey and threw
    up groaning into the bloody toilet, moans in their ears and the blast of
    colossal steamwhistles,
who barreled down the highways of the past journeying to each other's hotrod-
    Golgotha[2] jail-solitude watch or Birmingham jazz incarnation,
who drove crosscountry seventytwo hours to find out if I had a vision or you
    had a vision or he had a vision to find out Eternity,                        60
who journeyed to Denver, who died in Denver, who came back to Denver &

---

7. An aromatic wine made in Hungary.
8. Southern extension of Third Avenue in New York
City; traditional haunt of derelicts and alcoholics.

9. Center of New York advertising agencies.
1. River flowing past Paterson, New Jersey.
2. Site of Christ's crucifixion.

waited in vain, who watched over Denver & brooded & loned in Denver
    and finally went away to find out the Time, & now Denver is lonesome
    for her heroes,
who fell on their knees in hopeless cathedrals praying for each other's salvation
    and light and breasts, until the soul illuminated its hair for a second,
who crashed through their minds in jail waiting for impossible criminals with
    golden heads and the charm of reality in their hearts who sang sweet blues
    to Alcatraz,
who retired to Mexico to cultivate a habit, or Rocky Mount to tender Buddha
    or Tangiers to boys or Southern Pacific to the black locomotive or Har-
    vard to Narcissus to Woodlawn[3] to the daisychain or grave,
who demanded sanity trials accusing the radio of hypnotism & were left with
    their insanity & their hands & a hung jury,                                     65
who threw potato salad at CCNY lecturers on Dadaism[4] and subsequently
    presented themselves on the granite steps of the madhouse with shaven
    heads and harlequin speech of suicide, demanding instantaneous
    lobotomy,
and who were given instead the concrete void of insulin metrasol electricity
    hydrotherapy psychotherapy occupational therapy pingpong & amnesia,
who in humorless protest overturned only one symbolic pingpong table, rest-
    ing briefly in catatonia,
returning years later truly bald except for a wig of blood, and tears and fingers,
    to the visible madman doom of the wards of the madtowns of the East,
Pilgrim State's Rockland's and Greystone's[5] foetid halls, bickering with the
    echoes of the soul, rocking and rolling in the midnight solitude-bench
    dolmen-realms of love, dream of life a nightmare, bodies turned to stone
    as heavy as the moon,                                                          70
with mother finally * * * * * * *, and the last fantastic book flung out of the
    tenement window, and the last door closed at 4 AM and the last telephone
    slammed at the wall in reply and the last furnished room emptied down
    to the last piece of mental furniture, a yellow paper rose twisted on a wire
    hanger in the closet, and even that imaginary, nothing but a hopeful little
    bit of hallucination—
ah, Carl,[6] while you are not safe I am not safe, and now you're really in the
    total animal soup of time—
and who therefore ran through the icy streets obsessed with a sudden flash of
    the alchemy of the use of the ellipse the catalog the meter & the vibrat-
    ing plane,
who dreamt and made incarnate gaps in Time & Space through images juxta-
    posed, and trapped the archangel of the soul between 2 visual images and
    joined the elemental verbs and set the noun and dash of consciousness
    together jumping with sensation of Pater Omnipotens Aeterna Deus[7]

3. A cemetery in the Bronx. "Southern Pacific" is a railroad company. The references in this line are to the lives of Kerouac, Cassidy, and William Burroughs (an author and fellow Beat).
4. This and the following incidents probably derived from the "apocryphal history of my adventures" related by Solomon to Ginsberg. "Dadaism": artistic cult of absurdity (c. 1916–1920). "CCNY": City College of New York.
5. Three mental hospitals near New York. Solomon was institutionalized at Pilgrim State and Rockland; Ginsberg's mother, Naomi, was permanently institu-
tionalized at Greystone after years of suffering hallucinations and paranoid attacks. She died there in 1956, the year after *Howl* was written.
6. Solomon.
7. All Powerful Father, Eternal God (Latin). An allusion to a phrase used by the French painter Paul Cézanne (1839–1906), in a letter describing the effects of nature (1904). Ginsberg, in an interview, compared his own method of sharply juxtaposed images with Cézanne's foreshortening of perspective in landscape painting.

to recreate the syntax and measure of poor human prose and stand before you
  speechless and intelligent and shaking with shame, rejected yet confessing
  out the soul to conform to the rhythm of thought in his naked and endless head,                                                                    75
the madman bum and angel beat in Time, unknown, yet putting down here
  what might be left to say in time come after death,
and rose reincarnate in the ghostly clothes of jazz in the goldhorn shadow of
  the band and blew the suffering of America's naked mind for love into an
  eli eli lamma lamma sabacthani[8] saxophone cry that shivered the cities
  down to the last radio
with the absolute heart of the poem of life butchered out of their own bodies
  good to eat a thousand years.

                                                                        1956


## A Supermarket in California

What thoughts I have of you tonight, Walt Whitman,[1] for I walked down
the sidestreets under the trees with a headache self-conscious looking at the
full moon.

In my hungry fatigue, and shopping for images, I went into the neon fruit
supermarket, dreaming of your enumerations!

What peaches and what penumbras![2] Whole families shopping at night!
Aisles full of husbands! Wives in the avocados, babies in the tomatoes!—and
you, Garcia Lorca,[3] what were you doing down by the watermelons?

I saw you, Walt Whitman, childless, lonely old grubber, poking among the
meats in the refrigerator and eyeing the grocery boys.

I heard you asking questions of each: Who killed the pork chops? What
price bananas? Are you my Angel?                                               5

I wandered in and out of the brilliant stacks of cans following you, and
followed in my imagination by the store detective.

We strode down the open corridors together in our solitary fancy tasting
artichokes, possessing every frozen delicacy, and never passing the cashier.

Where are we going, Walt Whitman? The doors close in an hour. Which
way does your beard point tonight?

(I touch your book and dream of our odyssey in the supermarket and feel
absurd.)

Will we walk all night through solitary streets? The trees add shade to shade,
lights out in the houses, we'll both be lonely.                               10

Will we stroll dreaming of the lost America of love past blue automobiles in
driveways, home to our silent cottage?

Ah, dear father, graybeard, lonely old courage-teacher, what America did

---

8. Christ's last words on the Cross: My God, my God,
why have you forsaken me? (Aramaic).
1. American poet (1819–1892), author of *Leaves of
Grass*, against whose homosexuality and vision of
American plenty Ginsberg measures himself.

2. Partial shadows.
3. Spanish poet and dramatist (1899–1936), author of
*A Poet in New York*, whose work is characterized by
surrealist and homoerotic inspiration.

you have when Charon quit poling his ferry and you got out on a smoking
bank and stood watching the boat disappear on the black waters of Lethe?[4]

Berkeley 1955                                                    1956

# To Aunt Rose

Aunt Rose—now—might I see you
  with your thin face and buck tooth smile and pain
    of rheumatism—and a long black heavy shoe
      for your bony left leg
limping down the long hall in Newark on the running carpet     5
    past the black grand piano
      in the day room
        where the parties were
  and I sang Spanish loyalist[1] songs
    in a high squeaky voice                10
      (hysterical) the committee listening
    while you limped around the room
      collected the money—
Aunt Honey, Uncle Sam, a stranger with a cloth arm
    in his pocket                   15
      and huge young bald head
        of Abraham Lincoln Brigade[2]

—your long sad face
    your tears of sexual frustration
      (what smothered sobs and bony hips      20
        under the pillows of Osborne Terrace)
—the time I stood on the toilet seat naked
    and you powdered my thighs with Calomine
      against the poison ivy—my tender
        and shamed first black curled hairs     25
what were you thinking in secret heart then
    knowing me a man already—
and I an ignorant girl of family silence on the thin pedestal
    of my legs in the bathroom—Museum of Newark.
           Aunt Rose               30
Hitler is dead, Hitler is in Eternity; Hitler is with
    Tamburlane and Emily Brontë[3]

Though I see you walking still, a ghost on Osborne Terrace
    down the long dark hall to the front door
      limping a little with a pinched smile     35
        in what must have been a silken

4. Forgetfulness. In Greek mythology, one of the rivers of Hades. Charon was the boatman who ferried the
dead to hell.
1. During the Spanish Civil War (1936–39), many
left-wing Americans—among them Ginsberg's relatives in Newark—sympathized with the Spanish loyalists who were resisting Francisco Franco's (1892–1975)
efforts to become dictator of Spain.
2. American volunteers who fought against the Fas-
cists in the Spanish Civil War.
3. English poet and novelist (1818–1848), author of
*Wuthering Heights*. Tamburlane was the Mideastern
"scourge" and conqueror (hero of Christopher Marlowe's *Tamburlane*, 1588).

flower dress
welcoming my father, the Poet, on his visit to Newark
—see you arriving in the living room
dancing on your crippled leg                          40
and clapping hands his book
had been accepted by Liveright[4]

Hitler is dead and Liveright's gone out of business
*The Attic of the Past* and *Everlasting Minute* are out of print
Uncle Harry sold his last silk stocking                45
Claire quit interpretive dancing school
Buba sits a wrinkled monument in Old
Ladies Home blinking at new babies

last time I saw you was the hospital
pale skull protruding under ashen skin                 50
blue veined unconscious girl
in an oxygen tent
the war in Spain has ended long ago
Aunt Rose

Paris 1958                                              1961


# Ego Confession

I want to be known as the most brilliant man in America
Introduced to Gyalwa Karmapa heir of the Whispered Transmission Crazy
   Wisdom Practice Lineage
as the secret young wise man who visited him and winked anonymously
   decade ago in Gangtok
Prepared the way for Dharma[1] in America without mentioning Dharma—
   scribbled laughter
Who saw Blake[2] and abandoned God                                     5
To whom the Messianic Fink sent messages darkest hour sleeping on steel
   sheets "somewhere in the Federal Prison system" Weathermen[3] got no
   Moscow Gold
who went backstage to Cecil Taylor serious chat chord structure & Time in
   a nightclub
who fucked a rose-lipped rock star in a tiny bedroom slum watched by a statue
   of Vajrasattva—
and overthrew the CIA with a silent thought—
Old Bohemians many years hence in Viennese beergardens'll recall         10
his many young lovers with astonishing faces and iron breasts
gnostic apparatus and magical observation of rainbow-lit spiderwebs
extraordinary cooking, lung stew & Spaghetti a la Vongole and recipe for salad
   dressing 3 parts oil one part vinegar much garlic and honey a spoonful

4. Leading American publisher of the 1920s and
1930s (now a subsidiary of W. W. Norton); published
*The Everlasting Minute* (1937), poems by Allen Ginsberg's father, Louis, whose first book was *The Attic of
the Past* (1920).

1. In Buddhism, divine law.
2. William Blake (1757–1827), English poet and mystic, whom Ginsberg had seen in a hallucinatory vision.
3. Revolutionary terrorist student group during the
1960s.

his extraordinary ego, at service of Dharma and completely empty
unafraid of its own self's spectre                                                                    15
parroting gossip of gurus and geniuses famous for their reticence—
Who sang a blues made rock stars weep and moved an old black guitarist to
    laughter in Memphis—
I want to be the spectacle of Poesy triumphant over trickery of the world
Omniscient breathing its own breath thru War tear gas spy hallucination
whose common sense astonished gaga Gurus and rich Artistes—                        20
who called the Justice department & threaten'd to Blow the Whistle
Stopt Wars, turned back petrochemical Industries' Captains to grieve & groan
    in bed
Chopped wood, built forest houses & established farms
distributed monies to poor poets & nourished imaginative genius of the land
Sat silent in jazz roar writing poetry with an ink pen—                                        25
wasn't afraid of God or Death after his 48th year—
let his brains turn to water under Laughing Gas his gold molar pulled by
    futuristic dentists
Seaman knew ocean's surface a year
carpenter late learned bevel and mattock
son, conversed with elder Pound[4] & treated his father gently                          30
—All empty all for show, all for the sake of Poesy
to set surpassing example of sanity as measure for late generations
Exemplify Muse Power to the young avert future suicide
accepting his own lie & the gaps between lies with equal good humor
Solitary in worlds full of insects & singing birds all solitary                                 35
—who had no subject but himself in many disguises
some outside his own body including empty air-filled space forests & cities—
Even climbed mountains to create his mountain, with ice ax & crampons &
    ropes, over Glaciers—

San Francisco, October 1974                                                                        1977

4. Ezra Pound (1885–1972), poet and critic who was a leader of the modernist movement in America.

---

# GALWAY KINNELL
## b. 1927

In an interview in 1971, Galway Kinnell praised Whitman's *Song of Myself*: "The final action of the poem where Whitman dissolves into the air and into the ground, is for me one of the great moments of self-transcendence in poetry. In one way or another, consciously or not, all poems try to pass beyond the self." This capacity for self-transcendence is dramatized in Kinnell's own work, where he enters the lives of animals (*The Porcupine* and *The Bear*) and experiences himself as part of the natural world, like the flower he speaks for in *Flower Herding on Mount Monadnock*. "Part of poetry's usefulness in the world," he has said, "is that it pays some of our huge unpaid tribute to the things and creatures that share the earth with us." Many of his poems pay such tribute by discovering the way "everything flowers, from within, of self-blessing" (*Saint Francis and the Sow*). His work moves between a vivid sense of the world's physical actuality and an equally vivid sense of its dissolution, for mortality is Kinnell's great theme. It appears in his work both as

extinction and as "the flowing away into the universe which we desire." This theme
is worked out at length in his sequence *The Book of Nightmares* (1978). Speaking
to his infant daughter in a poem from that book, *Little Sleep's-Head Sprouting
Hair in the Moonlight*, he instructs her on the perishability of all living things.
This poem, like many others of Kinnell's, reveals the way the unconditional fact
of mortality gives radiance to life. Like Wallace Stevens, whose poem *Sunday
Morning* declares that "Death is the mother of beauty," Kinnell finds a music for
poetry in "The still undanced cadence of vanishing" (*Little Sleep's-Head*).

Kinnell grew up in Providence, Rhode Island, and attended Princeton University, where he and a classmate, W. S. Merwin, sometimes read each other their
poems. He has written continuously since that time, combining his life of poetry
with political commitments. Among his various activities Kinnell has been director
of an adult education program in Chicago, a journalist in Iran, and a field-worker
for the Congress of Racial Equality in Louisiana. More recently, he has taught at
a large number of colleges and universities.

Kinnell's experiences working for voter registration in the South in the 1960s
make their way into his long poem *The Last River* from his volume *Body Rags*
(1969). Over the years, Kinnell has frequently written poems that unite personal
life with the events of the nation. His work includes powerful war poems such as
*Vapor Trail Reflected in the Frog Pond* and *The Dead Shall Be Raised Incorruptible*, and in *The Past* (1985) he meditates on, and imagines his way into, the
consequences of the dropping of the atom bomb on Hiroshima and Nagasaki (*The
Fundamental Project of Technology*). Elsewhere he has suggested that poetry is an
alternative to a technological world in which domination of nature represses the
knowledge of death.

Kinnell's earliest work, as seen in *What a Kingdom It Was* (1960) and *First
Poems 1946–1954* (1970), is formally intricate. The course of his career has been
a movement to a looser line, a more uncluttered diction. His sense of form arises
from what he calls the "inner shape" of the poem: "saying in its own music what
matters most." Over the years he has come to write poems that maintain musicality
and a richness of language while never departing too far from the speaking voice.
Kinnell's attraction to the nonhuman world, which may remind us of Theodore
Roethke and Gary Snyder, gives his work a vivid sense of life's diversity. But he
has sometimes elevated the instinctual at the expense of a shaping, conscious
awareness and has written as if the very need for poetic form were, in and of itself,
repressive. The finest of Kinnell's poems combine self-transcendence with self-
awareness in rhythms that convey a powerful physical energy and an empathetic
imagination. His description of Whitman can serve as a description of Kinnell's
own work at its best: "All his feelings for existence, for himself, for his own place,
come out in what he says about them. . . . He rescues these things from death
and lets them live in his poems and, in turn, they save him from incoherence
and silence."

# The Porcupine

1

Fatted
on herbs, swollen on crabapples,
puffed up on bast and phloem,[1] ballooned
on willow flowers, poplar catkins, first

---

1. I.e., plant tissues.

leafs of aspen and larch,
the porcupine
drags and bounces his last meal through ice,
mud, roses and goldenrod, into the stubbly high fields. 5


2


In character
he resembles us in seven ways: 10
he puts his mark on outhouses,
he alchemizes by moonlight,
he shits on the run,
he uses his tail for climbing,
he chuckles softly to himself when scared, 15
he's overcrowded if there's more than one of him per five acres,
his eyes have their own inner redness.


3


Digger of
goings across floors, of hesitations
at thresholds, of 20
handprints of dread
at doorpost or window jamb, he would
gouge the world
empty of us, hack and crater
it 25
until it is nothing, if that
could rinse it of all our sweat and pathos.

Adorer of ax
handles aflow with grain, of arms
of Morris chairs,[2] of hand 30
crafted objects
steeped in the juice of fingertips,
of surfaces wetted down
with fist grease and elbow oil,
of clothespins that have 35
grabbed our body-rags by underarm and crotch . . .

Unimpressed—bored—
by the whirl of the stars, by *these*
he's astonished, ultra-
Rilkean[3] angel! 40

for whom the true
portion of the sweetness of earth
is one of those bottom-heavy, glittering, saccadic

---

2. Easy chairs.
3. Rainer Maria Rilke (1875–1926), German poet. He wrote in the letter that "the 'angel' of the [Duino] Elegies has nothing to do with the angel of the Christian heaven. . . . The angel of the Elegies is that being which stands for the idea of recognizing a higher order of reality in invisibility."

bits
of salt water that splash down                                    45
the haunted ravines of a human face.

4

A farmer shot a porcupine three times
as it dozed on a tree limb. On
the way down it tore open its belly
on a broken                                                       50
branch, hooked its gut,
and went on falling. On the ground
it sprang to its feet, and
paying out gut heaved
and spartled through a hundred feet of goldenrod            55
before
the abrupt emptiness.

5

The Avesta[4]
puts porcupine killers
into hell for nine generations, sentencing them            60
to gnaw out
each other's hearts for the
salts of desire.

I roll
this way and that in the great bed, under                   65
the quilt
that mimics this country of broken farms and woods,
the fatty sheath of the man
melting off,
the self-stabbing coil                                      70
of bristles reversing, blossoming outward—
a red-eyed, hard-toothed, arrow-stuck urchin
tossing up mattress feathers,
pricking the
woman beside me until she cries.                            75

6

In my time I have
crouched, quills erected,
Saint
Sebastian[5] of the
scared heart, and been                                      80
beat dead with a locust club

---

4. Book of the sacred writings of Zoroastrianism, a
Persian religion.
5. St. Sebastian (d. 288), an early Christian saint and

martyr. He was shot full of arrows by an execution
squad and miraculously survived, only to be beaten to
death later.

on the bare snout.
And fallen from high places
I have fled, have
jogged 85
over fields of goldenrod,
terrified, seeking home,
and among flowers
I have come to myself empty, the rope
strung out behind me 90
in the fall sun
suddenly glorified with all my blood.

7

And tonight I think I prowl broken
skulled or vacant as a
sucked egg in the wintry meadow, softly chuckling, blank 95
template of myself, dragging
a starved belly through the lichflowered acres,
where
burdock looses the ark of its seed
and thistle holds up its lost blooms 100
and rosebushes in the wind scrape their dead limbs
for the forced-fire
of roses.

1969

## Saint Francis[1] and the Sow

The bud
stands for all things,
even for those things that don't flower,
for everything flowers, from within, of self-blessing;
though sometimes it is necessary 5
to reteach a thing its loveliness,
to put a hand on its brow
of the flower
and retell it in words and in touch
it is lovely
until it flowers again from within, of self-blessing; 10
as Saint Francis
put his hand on the creased forehead
of the sow, and told her in words and in touch
blessings of earth on the sow, and the sow 15
began remembering all down her thick length,
from the earthen snout all the way
through the fodder and slops to the spiritual curl of the tail,
from the hard spininess spiked out from the spine

1. St. Francis of Assisi (c. 1181–1226), who preached poverty and humility.

down through the great broken heart                                        20
to the sheer blue milken dreaminess spurting and shuddering
from the fourteen teats into the fourteen mouths sucking and blowing
    beneath them:
the long, perfect loveliness of sow.

                                                                1980

## The Fundamental Project of Technology

> "A flash! A white flash sparkled!"
> —Tatsuichiro Akizuki,[1] *Concentric Circles of Death*

Under glass: glass dishes which changed
in color; pieces of transformed beer bottles;
a household iron; bundles of wire become solid
lumps of iron; a pair of pliers; a ring of skull-
bone fused to the inside of a helmet; a pair of eyeglasses          5
taken off the eyes of an eyewitness, without glass,
which vanished, when a white flash sparkled.

An old man, possibly a soldier back then,
now reduced down to one who soon will die,
sucks at the cigarette dangling from his lip, peers               10
at the uniform, scorched, of some tiniest schoolboy,
sighs out bluish mists of his own ashes over
a pressed tin lunch box well crushed back then when
the word *future* first learned, in a white flash, to jerk tears.

On the bridge outside, in navy black, a group                    15
of schoolchildren line up, hold it, grin at a flash-pop,
scatter like pigeons across grass, see a stranger, cry
*hello! hello! hello!* and soon *goodbye! goodbye!*
having pecked up the greetings that fell half unspoken
and the going-sayings that those who went the day            20
it happened a white flash sparkled did not get to say.

If all a city's faces were to shrink back all at once
from their skulls, would a new sound come into existence,
audible above moans eaves extract from wind that smoothes
the grass on graves, or raspings heart's-blood greases still,      25
or wails infants trill born already skillful at the grandpa's rattle,
or infra-screams bitter-knowledge's speechlessness
memorized, at that white flash, inside closed-forever mouths?

To de-animalize human mentality, to purge it of obsolete
evolutionary characteristics, in particular of death,            30
which foreknowledge terrorizes the contents of skulls with,
is the fundamental project of technology; however,

---

1. Author of writings about the destruction of Nagasaki by the atomic bomb in 1945.

*pseudologica fantastica's*[2] mechanisms require:
to establish deathlessness it is necessary to eliminate
those who die; a task attempted, when a white flash sparkled.                    35

Unlike the trees of home, which continually evaporate
along the skyline, the trees here have been enticed down
toward world-eternity. No one knows which gods they enshrine.
Does it matter? Awareness of ignorance is as devout
as knowledge of knowledge. Or more so. Even though not knowing,        40
sometimes we weep, from surplus of gratitude, even though knowing,
twice already on earth sparkled a flash, a white flash.

The children go away. By nature they do. And by memory,
in scorched uniforms, holding tiny crushed lunch tins.
All the ecstasy-groans of each night call them back, satori[3]                    45
their ghostliness back into the ashes, in the momentary shrines,
the thankfulness of arms, from which they will go
again and again, until the day flashes and no one lives
to look back and say, a flash, a white flash sparkled.

                                                                    1985

2. I.e., fantastic lying.                3. In Zen Buddhism, intuitive enlightenment.

---

# JOHN ASHBERY
## b. 1927

John Ashbery has described his writing this way: "I think that any one of my poems might be considered to be a snapshot of whatever is going on in my mind at the time—first of all the desire to write a poem, after that wondering if I've left the oven on or thinking about where I must be in the next hour." Ashbery has developed a style hospitable to quicksilver changes in tone and attention. His work often moves freely between different modes of discourse, between a language of popular culture and commonplace experience and a heightened rhetoric often associated with poetic vision. His poems show an awareness of the various linguistic codes (including clichés and conventional public speech) in which we live and through which we define ourselves. This awareness includes an interest in what he has called "prose voices," and he has often written in a way that challenges arbitrary boundaries between poetry and prose.

Ashbery's poetry was not always so open to contradictory notions and impulses. His early books rejected the mere surfaces of realism and the momentary to get at "remoter areas of consciousness." The protagonist of *Illustration* (from his first book, *Some Trees*) is a cheerful nun about to leave behind the irrelevancies of the world by leaping from a skyscraper. Her act implies "Much that is beautiful must be discarded / So that we may resemble a taller / impression of ourselves." To reach the "remoter areas of consciousness," Ashbery tried various technical experiments. He used highly patterned forms such as the sestina in *Some Trees* and *The Tennis Court Oath* (1962) not with any show of mechanical brilliance but to explore: "I once told somebody that writing a sestina was rather like riding downhill on a bicycle and having the pedals push your feet. I wanted my feet to be pushed into places they wouldn't normally have taken."

Ashbery was born in Rochester, New York, in 1927. He attended Deerfield Academy and Harvard, graduating in 1949. He received an M.A. in English from Columbia in 1951. In France first as a Fulbright scholar, he returned in 1958 for eight years and was art critic for the European edition of the *New York Herald Tribune* and reported the European shows and exhibitions for *Art News* and *Arts International.* He returned to New York in 1965 to be executive editor of *Art News,* a position he held until 1972. Since then he has been professor of English in the creative writing program of Brooklyn College and art critic for *Newsweek* magazine.

Ashbery's interest in art played a formative role in his poetry. He is often associated with Frank O'Hara, James Schuyler, and Kenneth Koch as part of the "New York school" of poets. The name refers to their common interest in the New York school of abstract painters of the 1940s and 1950s, some of whose techniques they wished to adapt in poetry. These painters avoided realism to stress the work of art as a representation of the creative act that produced it—as in the action paintings of Jackson Pollock. Ashbery's long poem *Self-Portrait in a Convex Mirror* gives as much attention to the rapidly changing feelings of the poet in the act of writing his poem as it does to the Renaissance painting that inspired him. The poem moves back and forth between the distracted energies that feed a work of art and the completed composition, which the artist feels as both a triumph and a falsification of complex feelings. Ashbery shares with O'Hara a sense of the colloquial brilliance of daily life in New York and sets this in tension with the concentration and stasis of art.

*Self-Portrait in a Convex Mirror* (1975) was followed by *Houseboat Days* (1977), *As We Know* (1979), *Shadow Train* (1981), and *A Wave* (1984). His important recent book, *Flow Chart,* appeared in 1991. Ashbery's work, especially his earlier, more highly experimental poems, has become particularly influential for a younger generation identified as Language poets, such as Charles Bernstein, Lyn Hejinian, Michael Palmer, and Susan Howe. They have been attracted to the linguistic playfulness of Ashbery's poetry and to its resistance to being read as a single, personal voice. Exposing and sometimes breaking through the dominant uses of language in our world, Ashbery's poems open new possibilities of meaning: "We are all talkers / It is true, but underneath the talk lies / The moving and not wanting to be moved, the loose / Meaning, untidy and simple like the threshing floor" (*Soonest Mended*).

# Illustration

## I

A novice[1] was sitting on a cornice
High over the city. Angels

Combined their prayers with those
Of the police, begging her to come off it.

One lady promised to be her friend.                                    5
"I do not want a friend," she said.

A mother offered her some nylons
Stripped from her very legs. Others brought

---

1. Student in the first stage of instruction to be a nun.

ILLUSTRATION          2575

Little offerings of fruit and candy,
The blind man all his flowers. If any          10

Could be called successful, these were,
For that the scene should be a ceremony

Was what she wanted. "I desire
Monuments," she said. "I want to move

Figuratively, as waves caress          15
The thoughtless shore. You people I know

Will offer me every good thing
I do not want. But please remember

I died accepting them." With that, the wind
Unpinned her bulky robes, and naked          20

As a roc's[2] egg, she drifted softly downward
Out of the angels' tenderness and the minds of men.

### II

Much that is beautiful must be discarded
So that we may resemble a taller

Impression of ourselves. Moths climb in the flame,          25
Alas, that wish only to be the flame:

They do not lessen our stature.
We twinkle under the weight

Of indiscretions. But how could we tell
That of the truth we know, she was          30

The somber vestment? For that night, rockets sighed
Elegantly over the city, and there was feasting:

There is so much in that moment!
So many attitudes toward that flame,

We might have soared from earth, watching her
glide          35
Aloft, in her peplum[3] of bright leaves.

But she, of course, was only an effigy
Of indifference, a miracle

Not meant for us, as the leaves are not
Winter's because it is the end.          40

1956

2. Legendary bird of prey.
3. In ancient Greece, a drapery about the upper part of the body.

# Soonest Mended

Barely tolerated, living on the margin
In our technological society, we were always having to be rescued
On the brink of destruction, like heroines in *Orlando Furioso*[1]
Before it was time to start all over again.
There would be thunder in the bushes, a rustling of coils,     5
And Angelica, in the Ingres painting,[2] was considering
The colorful but small monster near her toe, as though wondering whether forgetting
The whole thing might not, in the end, be the only solution.
And then there always came a time when
Happy Hooligan[3] in his rusted green automobile     10
Came plowing down the course, just to make sure everything was O.K.,
Only by that time we were in another chapter and confused
About how to receive this latest piece of information.
*Was* it information? Weren't we rather acting this out
For someone else's benefit, thoughts in a mind     15
With room enough and to spare for our little problems (so they began to seem),
Our daily quandary about food and the rent and bills to be paid?
To reduce all this to a small variant,
To step free at last, minuscule on the gigantic plateau—
This was our ambition: to be small and clear and free.     20
Alas, the summer's energy wanes quickly,
A moment and it is gone. And no longer
May we make the necessary arrangements, simple as they are.
Our star was brighter perhaps when it had water in it.
Now there is no question even of that, but only     25
Of holding on to the hard earth so as not to get thrown off,
With an occasional dream, a vision: a robin flies across
The upper corner of the window, you brush your hair away
And cannot quite see, or a wound will flash
Against the sweet faces of the others, something like:     30
This is what you wanted to hear, so why
Did you think of listening to something else? We are all talkers
It is true, but underneath the talk lies
The moving and not wanting to be moved, the loose
Meaning, untidy and simple like a threshing floor.[4]     35

These then were some hazards of the course,
Yet though we knew the course *was* hazards and nothing else
It was still a shock when, almost a quarter of a century later,
The clarity of the rules dawned on you for the first time.
*They* were the players, and we who had struggled at the game     40
Were merely spectators, though subject to its vicissitudes
And moving with it out of the tearful stadium, borne on shoulders, at last.

---

1. Fantastic epic poem by Ludovico Ariosto (1474–1533), whose romantic heroine Angelica is constantly being rescued from imminent perils such as monsters and ogres.
2. *Roger Delivering Angelica* (1819), a painting based on a scene from Ariosto, by the French artist Jean Au-
guste Dominique Ingres (1780–1867).
3. The good-natured, simple title character of a popular comic strip of the 1920s and 1930s.
4. Used at harvest time to separate the wheat from the chaff, which is to be discarded.

Night after night this message returns, repeated
In the flickering bulbs of the sky, raised past us, taken away from us,
Yet ours over and over until the end that is past truth,                    45
The being of our sentences, in the climate that fostered them,
Not ours to own, like a book, but to be with, and sometimes
To be without, alone and desperate.
But the fantasy makes it ours, a kind of fence-sitting
Raised to the level of an esthetic ideal. These were moments, years,        50
Solid with reality, faces, namable events, kisses, heroic acts,
But like the friendly beginning of a geometrical progression
Not too reassuring, as though meaning could be cast aside some day
When it had been outgrown. Better, you said, to stay cowering
Like this in the early lessons, since the promise of learning               55
Is a delusion, and I agreed, adding that
Tomorrow would alter the sense of what had already been learned,
That the learning process is extended in this way, so that from this standpoint
None of us ever graduates from college,
For time is an emulsion,[5] and probably thinking not to grow up            60
Is the brightest kind of maturity for us, right now at any rate.
And you see, both of us were right, though nothing
Has somehow come to nothing; the avatars[6]
Of our conforming to the rules and living
Around the home have made—well, in a sense, "good citizens" of us,          65
Brushing the teeth and all that, and learning to accept
The charity of the hard moments as they are doled out,
For this is action, this not being sure, this careless
Preparing, sowing the seeds crooked in the furrow,
Making ready to forget, and always coming back                             70
To the mooring of starting out, that day so long ago.

                                                              1970


# Syringa[1]

Orpheus liked the glad personal quality
Of the things beneath the sky. Of course, Eurydice was a part
of this.[2] Then one day, everything changed. He rends
Rocks into fissures with lament. Gullies, hummocks
Can't withstand it. The sky shudders from one horizon                       5
To the other, almost ready to give up wholeness.
Then Apollo[3] quietly told him: "Leave it all on earth.
Your lute, what point? Why pick at a dull pavan[4] few care to
Follow, except a few birds of dusty feather,
Not vivid performances of the past." But why not?                          10
All other things must change too.

5. A chemical solution in which the particles of one liquid are suspended in another.
6. Incarnations.
1. The genus name for lilac, it is derived from a word meaning "pipe" and has been applied to mock orange because sheperd's pipes were once made from the pithy stems.
2. Orpheus was a legendary musician and poet; his wife, Eurydice, died of a snake bite.
3. God of music and song.
4. Stately court dance. "Lute": stringed instrument, forerunner of the guitar.

The seasons are no longer what they once were,
But it is the nature of things to be seen only once,
As they happen along, bumping into other things, getting along
Somehow. That's where Orpheus made his mistake.                              15
Of course Eurydice vanished into the shade;
She would have even if he hadn't turned around.[5]
No use standing there like a gray stone toga[6] as the whole wheel
Of recorded history flashes past, struck dumb, unable to utter an intelligent
Comment on the most thought-provoking element in its train.                  20
Only love stays on the brain, and something these people,
These other ones, call life. Singing accurately
So that the notes mount straight up out of the well of
Dim noon and rival the tiny, sparkling yellow flowers
Growing around the brink of the quarry, encapsulizes                         25
The different weights of the things.
                                But it isn't enough
To just go on singing. Orpheus realized this
And didn't mind so much about his reward being in heaven
After the Bacchantes had torn him apart,[7] driven                           30
Half out of their minds by his music, what it was doing to them.
Some say it was for his treatment of Eurydice.
But probably the music had more to do with it, and
The way music passes, emblematic
Of life and how you cannot isolate a note of it                             35
And say it is good or bad. You must
Wait till it's over. "The end crowns all,"
Meaning also that the "tableau"[8]
Is wrong. For although memories, of a season, for example,
Melt into a single snapshot, one cannot guard, treasure                     40
That stalled moment. It too is flowing, fleeting;
It is a picture of flowing, scenery, though living, mortal,
Over which an abstract action is laid out in blunt,
Harsh strokes. And to ask more than this
Is to become the tossing reeds of that slow,                                45
Powerful stream, the trailing grasses
Playfully tugged at, but to participate in the action
No more than this. Then in the lowering gentian[9] sky
Electric twitches are faintly apparent first, then burst forth
Into a shower of fixed, cream-colored flares. The horses                    50
Have each seen a share of the truth, though each thinks,
"I'm a maverick. Nothing of this is happening to me,
Though I can understand the language of birds, and
The itinerary of the lights caught in the storm is fully apparent to me.
Their jousting ends in music much                                           55
As trees move more easily in the wind after a summer storm
And is happening in lacy shadows of shore-trees, now, day after day."

But how late to be regretting all this, even
Bearing in mind that regrets are always late, too late!

---

5. Orpheus descended to Hades to retrieve Eurydice; Pluto allowed her to depart, on the condition that Orpheus not look back at her as they returned to the surface of the earth. He failed the test, and she vanished.
6. Roman robe, as on a statue.

7. The Bacchantes, or Maenads, were female votaries of Dionysus, god of wine and inspiration. In one of their intoxicated frenzies, they tore Orpheus to pieces.
8. Image, picture.
9. I.e., gentian blue, a purplish blue.

To which Orpheus, a bluish cloud with white contours,               60
Replies that these are of course not regrets at all,
Merely a careful, scholarly setting down of
Unquestioned facts, a record of pebbles along the way.
And no matter how all this disappeared,
Or got where it was going, it is no longer                          65
Material for a poem. Its subject
Matters too much, and not enough, standing there helplessly
While the poem streaked by, its tail afire, a bad
Comet screaming hate and disaster, but so turned inward
That the meaning, good or other, can never                          70
Become known. The singer thinks
Constructively, builds up his chant in progressive stages
Like a skyscraper, but at the last minute turns away.
The song is engulfed in an instant in blackness
Which must in turn flood the whole continent                        75
With blackness, for it cannot see. The singer
Must then pass out of sight, not even relieved
Of the evil burthen of the words. Stellification[1]
Is for the few, and comes about much later
When all record of these people and their lives                     80
Has disappeared into libraries, onto microfilm.
A few are still interested in them. "But what about
So-and-so?" is still asked on occasion. But they lie
Frozen and out of touch until an arbitrary chorus
Speaks of a totally different incident with a similar name          85
In whose tale are hidden syllables
Of what happened so long before that
In some small town, one indifferent summer.

                                                          1977

# The Lonedale Operator

The first movie I ever saw was the Walt Disney cartoon *The Three Little
Pigs*. My grandmother took me to it. It was back in the days when you
went "downtown." There was a second feature, with live actors, called
*Bring 'Em Back Alive*, a documentary about the explorer Frank Buck. In
this film you saw a python swallow a live pig. This wasn't scary. In fact,     5
it seemed quite normal, the sort of thing you *would* see in a movie—
"reality."

A little later we went downtown again to see a movie of *Alice in Wonderland*, also with live actors. This wasn't very surprising either. I think I
knew something about the story; maybe it had been read to me. That       10
wasn't why it wasn't surprising, though. The reason was that these famous
movie actors, like W. C. Fields and Gary Cooper, were playing different
roles, and even though I didn't know who they were, they were obviously
important for doing other kinds of acting, and so it didn't seem strange
that they should be acting in a special way like this, pretending to be       15
characters that people already knew about from a book. In other words, I

---

1. Being made into a star or placed among stars.

imagined specialties for them just from having seen this one example.
And I was right, too, though not about the film, which I liked. Years later
I saw it when I was grown up and thought it was awful. How could I have
been wrong the first time? I knew it wasn't inexperience, because some-         20
how I was experienced the first time I saw a movie. It was as though my
taste had changed, though I had not, and I still can't help feeling that
I was right the first time, when I was still relatively unencumbered by
my experience.

I forget what were the next movies I saw and will skip ahead to one I         25
saw when I was grown up, *The Lonedale Operator*, a silent short by D.
W. Griffith,[1] made in 1911 and starring Blanche Sweet. Although I was
in my twenties when I saw it at the Museum of Modern Art, it seems as
remote from me in time as my first viewing of *Alice in Wonderland*. I can
remember almost none of it, and the little I can remember may have been         30
in another Griffith short, *The Lonely Villa*, which may have been on the
same program. It seems that Blanche Sweet was a heroic telegraph operator who managed to get through to the police and foil some gangsters who
were trying to rob a railroad depot, though I also see this living room—
small, though it was supposed to be in a large house—with Mary Pickford[2]         35
running around, and this may have been a scene in *The Lonely Villa*. At
that moment the memories stop, and terror, or tedium, sets in. It's hard
to tell which is which in this memory, because the boredom of living in
a lonely place or having a lonely job, and even of being so far in the past
and having to wear those funny uncomfortable clothes and hairstyles is         40
terrifying, more so than the intentional scariness of the plot, the criminals,
whoever they were.

Imagine that innocence (Lilian Harvey) encounters romance (Willy
Fritsch) in the home of experience (Albert Basserman). From there it is
only a step to terror, under the dripping boughs outside. Anything can         45
change as fast as it wants to, and in doing so may pass through a more or
less terrible phase, but the true terror is in the swiftness of changing, forward or backward, slipping always just beyond our control. The actors are
like people on drugs, though they aren't doing anything unusual—as a
matter of fact, they are performing brilliantly.         50

1984

1. Pioneer American director of silent films (1875–
1948).
2. American movie star (1893–1979), known as

"America's sweetheart" for roles in, especially, Griffith's films.

---

# JAMES WRIGHT
## 1927–1980

"My name is James A. Wright, and I was born / Twenty-five miles from this infected
grave, / In Martins Ferry, Ohio, where one slave / To Hazel-Atlas Glass became
my father"; so James Wright introduced himself in an early poem, *At the Executed
Murderer's Grave*. The angry assertiveness in these lines suggests his embattled
relations with an America he both loves and hates. This America is symbolized for
him by the landscape of Ohio, in particular by Martins Ferry, just across the Ohio

River from Wheeling, West Virginia, the home of Wheeling Steel and of the glass factory where his father worked for fifty years. In Wright's work this landscape is harsh evidence of the way the social world has contaminated a natural world infinitely more beautiful and self-restoring. The same social world that destroys the landscape also turns its back on those whose lives meet failure or defeat, and Wright's deep knowledge of defeat and his anger at this exclusion lead him to the murderer's grave. It is not simply that Wright sympathizes with social outcasts, but rather, as Robert Hass acutely pointed out, "the suffering of other people, particularly the lost and the derelict, is actually a part of his own emotional life. It is what he writes from, not what he writes about." As a poet who writes out of loss, Wright is elegiac, memorializing a vanished beauty, and lost hopes. So deep is his sense of loss that he will sometimes identify with anyone and anything that is scarred or wounded ("I am not a happy man by talent," he once said. "Sometimes I have been very happy, but characteristically I'm a miserable son of a bitch"). Any serious reading of his work has to contend with sorting out those poems in which this identification is unthinking and sentimental, poems where Wright suggests that all forms of suffering and defeat are equal and alike. What remains in some of his best work is a curiously tough-minded tenderness at work in his exploration of despair. He admires, for example, the sumac flourishing in the Ohio landscape, its bark so tough it "will turn aside hatchets and knife blades" (*The Sumac in Ohio*).

When Wright finished high school, he joined the army. In 1948 he left the military to attend Kenyon College in Ohio on the GI Bill ("I applied to several schools in Ohio," he once said, "and they all said no except Kenyon College. So I went there"). He was lucky in his teachers; at Kenyon he studied with John Crowe Ransom and, after a Fulbright scholarship to the University of Vienna, he went to the University of Washington, where he studied with the poet Theodore Roethke and also became a close friend of Richard Hugo's. At Washington he wrote a Ph.D. dissertation on Charles Dickens and received the degree in 1959. Thereafter he became a teacher himself, first at the University of Minnesota, Minneapolis (1957–64), and later at Hunter College, New York (1966–80).

From both Ransom and Roethke, Wright learned poetic form. From Ransom in particular he took what he called "the Horatian ideal" of the carefully made, unified poem. Wright would later say that were he to choose a master, he would choose the Latin poet Horace, "who was able to write humorously and kindly in flawless verse." The Horatian impulse in Wright—restrained, formal, sometimes satirical—helps hold in check a deep-seated romanticism that idealizes nature and the unconscious. His first two books, *The Green Wall* (1957), chosen to appear in the Yale Younger Poets series, and *Saint Judas* (1959), are formal and literary in style although much of their subject matter (the murderer, the lunatic, a deaf child) might be called romantic. Wright seems in these books closest to Thomas Hardy, Robert Frost, and Edwin Arlington Robinson. But in the 1960s, like a great many other American poets, he moved away from traditional forms, loosened his poetic organization, and began to depend heavily on what his fellow poet Robert Bly called "the deep image." Wright had been translating the work of Spanish poets often associated with surrealism—Pablo Neruda, Cesar Vallejo, and Juan Ramon Jimenez—as well as the German Georg Trakl (whom he translated in collaboration with Robert Bly), and he took from them, in part, a reliance on the power of a poetic image to evoke association deep within the unconscious. He followed his volume *The Branch Will Not Break* (1963) with two books, *Shall We Gather at the River* (1968) and *Two Citizens* (1974), in which he began to overwork certain images ("stone," "dark"), as if repetition were a substitute for clarity. Some of the poems in these books succeed in carrying us into areas of experience that resist the discursive, but the effect of a number of poems is to exclude conscious intelligence, to celebrate "whatever is not mind," as Robert Hass has pointed out. It is as if Wright responded to the scarred landscape outside (and inside) him by fleeing to an inwardness so deep it could not partake of thought or expression.

But Wright's love of clarity and form and his ability to see through pretensions (including his own) resurface in *Moments of the Italian Summer* (1976), *To a Blossoming Pear Tree* (1977), and in his last, posthumous collection, *This Journey* (1982). Restored to a unity of thinking and feeling, many of the poems in these books convey the flawed beauty of the world with a loving and witty tenderness. He often writes with particular feeling about the creatures of the world—finches, lizards, hermit crabs—whose liveliness and fragility touch him. In *A Finch Sitting Out a Windstorm*, his final portrait of the finch suggests admiration of its stubbornness in the face of loss: "But his face is as battered / As Carmen Basillio's. / He never listens / To me."

Though the poems of his final book do not abandon the anger he feels thinking of the ruined landscapes of Ohio, the European setting of many of the poems extends his sense of ruin into a knowledge of how time chips away at all human creation, with or without the help of men and women. For a man who claimed to be constitutionally unhappy, the poems of *This Journey* suggest that before his death from cancer a deep happiness took him by surprise. We turn to Wright's work for its fierce understanding of defeat, for its blend of American speech rhythms with the formal music of poetry, and for the loveliness he finds in the imperfect and neglected. Accustomed to expect the worst, he had an enduring capacity to be astonished by this loveliness, as in this childhood memory of a trip to the icehouse with his father: "We stood and breathed the rising steam of that amazing winter, and carried away in our wagon the immense fifty-pound diamond, while the old man chipped us each a jagged little chunk and then walked behind us, his hands so calm they were trembling for us, trembling with exquisite care" (*The Ice House*).

## Autumn Begins in Martins Ferry, Ohio

In the Shreve High football stadium,
I think of Polacks nursing long beers in Tiltonsville,
And gray faces of Negroes in the blast furnace at Benwood,[1]
And the ruptured night watchman of Wheeling Steel,
Dreaming of heroes.                                                                 5

All the proud fathers are ashamed to go home.
Their women cluck like starved pullets,[2]
Dying for love.

Therefore,
Their sons grow suicidally beautiful                                              10
At the beginning of October,
And gallop terribly against each other's bodies.

1963

## To the Evening Star: Central Minnesota

Under the water tower at the edge of town
A huge Airedale ponders a long ripple

---

1. A town south of Martins Ferry, where the Wheeling Steel Works are located. Tiltonsville is a town in far east Ohio, north of Martins Ferry.
2. Young hens.

In the grass fields beyond.
Miles off, a whole grove silently
Flies up into the darkness.                                              5
One light comes on in the sky,
One lamp on the prairie.

Beautiful daylight of the body, your hands carry seashells.
West of this wide plain,
Animals wilder than ours                                               10
Come down from the green mountains in the darkness.
Now they can see you, they know
The open meadows are safe.

                                                                    1963

# A Blessing

Just off the highway to Rochester, Minnesota,
Twilight bounds softly forth on the grass.
And the eyes of those two Indian ponies
Darken with kindness.
They have come gladly out of the willows                              5
To welcome my friend and me.
We step over the barbed wire into the pasture
Where they have been grazing all day, alone.
They ripple tensely, they can hardly contain their happiness
That we have come.                                                    10
They bow shyly as wet swans. They love each other.
There is no loneliness like theirs.
At home once more,
They begin munching the young tufts of spring in the darkness.
I would like to hold the slenderer one in my arms,                    15
For she has walked over to me
And nuzzled my left hand.
She is black and white,
Her mane falls wild on her forehead,
And the light breeze moves me to caress her long ear                  20
That is delicate as the skin over a girl's wrist.
Suddenly I realize
That if I stepped out of my body I would break
Into blossom.

                                                                    1963

# A Finch Sitting out a Windstorm

Solemnly irritated by the turn
The cold air steals,
He puffs out his most fragile feathers,
His breast down,

And refuses to move.                                                    5
If I were he,
I would not clamp my claws so stubbornly around
The skinny branch.
I would not keep my tiny glitter
Fixed over my beak, or return                                          10
The glare of the wind.
Too many Maytime snowfalls have taught me
The wisdom of hopelessness.

But the damned fool
Squats there as if he owned                                            15
The earth, bought and paid for.
Oh, I could advise him plenty
About his wings. Give up, drift,
Get out.

But his face is as battered                                            20
As Carmen Basilio's.[1]
He never listens
To me.

                                                                    1982

## The Journey

Anghiari[2] is medieval, a sleeve sloping down
A steep hill, suddenly sweeping out
To the edge of a cliff, and dwindling.
But far up the mountain, behind the town,
We too were swept out, out by the wind,                                 5
Alone with the Tuscan grass.

Wind had been blowing across the hills
For days, and everything now was graying gold
With dust, everything we saw, even
Some small children scampering along a road,                           10
Twittering Italian to a small caged bird.
We sat beside them to rest in some brushwood,
And I leaned down to rinse the dust from my face.

I found the spider web there, whose hinges
Reeled heavily and crazily with the dust,                              15
Whole mounds and cemeteries of it, sagging
And scattering shadows among shells and wings.
And then she stepped into the center of air
Slender and fastidious, the golden hair
Of daylight along her shoulders, she poised there,                     20

1. A famous boxer.
2. Village in Tuscany, a province in western Italy.

While ruins crumbled on every side of her.
Free of the dust, as though a moment before
She had stepped inside the earth, to bathe herself.

I gazed, close to her, till at last she stepped
Away in her own good time.                                    25

Many men
Have searched all over Tuscany and never found
What I found there, the heart of the light
Itself shelled and leaved, balancing
On filaments themselves falling. The secret                   30
Of this journey is to let the wind
Blow its dust all over your body,
To let it go on blowing, to step lightly, lightly
All the way through your ruins, and not to lose
Any sleep over the dead, who surely                           35
Will bury their own, don't worry.

                                                        1982

---

# ADRIENNE RICH

## b. 1929

A childhood of reading and hearing poems taught Adrienne Rich to love the sound of words; her adult life taught her that poetry must "consciously situate itself amid political conditions." Over the years she has conducted a passionate struggle to honor these parts of herself, in her best poems brilliantly mixing what she calls "the poetry of the actual world with the poetry of sound." Extending the dialogue between art and politics she first discovered in W. B. Yeats, whose poems she read as an undergraduate at Radcliffe, her work addresses with particular power the experiences of women, experiences often omitted from history and misrepresented in literature. Our culture, she believes, is "split at the root" (to adapt the title of one of her essays); art is separated from politics and the poet's identity as a woman is separated from her art. Rich's work seeks a language that will expose and integrate these divisions in the self and in the world. To do this she has written "directly and overtly as a woman, out of a woman's body and experience," for "to take women's existence seriously as theme and source for art, was something I had been hungering to do, needing to do, all my writing life."

Rich's first book was published in the Yale series of Younger Poets, a prize particularly important for poets of her generation (others in the series have included James Wright, John Ashbery, and W. S. Merwin). W. H. Auden, the judge for the series in the 1950s, said of Rich's volume *A Change of World* (1951) that her poems "were neatly and modestly dressed . . . respect their elders, but are not cowed by them and do not tell fibs." Rich, looking back at that period from the vantage point of 1972, renders a more complicated sense of things. In an influential essay, *When We Dead Awaken*, she recalls this period as one in which the chief models for poetry were men; it was from those models that she first learned her craft. Even in looking at the poetry of older women writers she found herself "looking . . . for the same things I found in the poetry of men . . . , to be equal was still confused with sounding the same." Twenty years and five volumes after *A Change of World* she published *The Will to Change*, taking its title from the opening line of Charles Olson's *The Kingfishers:* "What does not change / is the will to change." The shift of emphasis in Rich's titles signals an important turn in her work—from acceptance of change as a way of the world to an active sense of change as willed or desired.

In 1953 Rich married the economist Alfred Conrad and in her twenties gave birth to three children within four years, "a radicalizing experience," she said, and a vital transforming event in both her personal and writing lives. Trying to be the ideal faculty wife and hostess, undergoing difficult pregnancies, and taking care of three small sons, she had little time or energy for writing. In 1955 her second book, *The Diamond Cutters*, appeared, but eight years were to pass before she published another. It was during this time that Rich experienced most severely that gap between what she calls the "energy of creation" and the "energy of relation. . . . In those early years I always felt the conflict as a failure of love in myself." In her later work Rich came to identify the source of that conflict not as individual but social and, in 1976, published a book of prose, *Of Woman Born: Motherhood as Experience and Institution*. Part autobiography and part history and anthropology, it contrasts the actual experience of bearing and raising children with the myths fostered by our medical, social, and political institutions.

With her third and fourth books, *Snapshots of a Daughter-in-Law* (1963) and *Necessities of Life* (1966), Rich began explicitly to treat problems that have engaged her ever since. The title poem of *Snapshots* exposes the gap between literary versions of women's experience and the day-to-day truths of their lives. Fragments of familiar poems praising and glamorizing women are juxtaposed with scenes from ordinary home life—in a way that adapts the technique of Eliot's *The Waste Land* to more overtly social protest.

Rich's poems aim at self-definition, at establishing boundaries of the self, but they also fight off the notion that insights remain solitary and unshared. Many of her poems proceed by means of intimate argument, sometimes with externalized parts of herself, as if to dramatize the way identity forms from the self's movement beyond fixed boundaries. In some of her most powerful later poems, she pushes her imagination to recognize the multiple aspects of the self ("My selves," she calls them in her poem *Integrity*); in *Transcendental Etude*, she writes:

> *I am the lover and the loved,*
> *home and wanderer, she who splits*
> *firewood and she who knocks, a stranger*
> *in the storm.*

In other important later poems she has carried out a dialogue with lives similar to and different from her own (*To Ethel Rosenberg* and *Frame*). As she writes in *Blood, Bread and Poetry*, in her development as a poet she came to feel "more and more urgently the dynamic between poetry as language and poetry as a kind of action, probing, burning, stripping, placing itself in dialogue with others."

When Rich and her husband moved to New York City in 1966 they became increasingly involved in radical politics, especially in the opposition to the Vietnam War. These new concerns are reflected in the poems of *Leaflets* (1969) and *The Will to Change* (1971). Along with new subject matter came equally important changes in style. Rich's poems throughout the 1960s moved away from formal verse patterns to more jagged utterance. Sentence fragments, lines of varying length, irregular spacing to mark off phrases—all these devices emphasized a voice of greater urgency. Ever since *Snapshots of a Daughter-in-Law*, Rich had been dating each poem, as if to mark them as provisional, true to the moment but instruments of passage, like entries in a journal in which feelings are subject to continual revision.

In the 1970s Rich dedicated herself increasingly to feminism. As poet, as prose writer, and as public speaker her work took on a new unity and intensity. The continuing task was to see herself—as she put it in 1984—neither as "unique nor universal, but a person in history, a woman and not a man, a white and also Jewish inheritor of a particular Western consciousness, from the making of which most women have been excluded." Poetry becomes a means for discovering inner worlds of women, just as the telescope was for exploring the heavens. As she says in *Planetarium,*

> I am an instrument in the shape
> of a woman trying to translate pulsations
> into images for the relief of the body
> and the reconstruction of the mind.

Rich's collections of prose—*Of Woman Born; On Lies, Secrets, and Silence: Selected Prose 1966–1978;* and *Blood, Bread, and Poetry: Selected Prose 1979–1985*—provide an important context for her poems. In these works she addresses issues of women's education and their literary traditions, Jewish identity, and what she has called "the erasure of lesbian existence from so much of scholarly feminist literature." As a young woman Rich had been stirred by James Baldwin's comment that "any real change implies the breakup of the world as one has always known it, the loss of all that gave one an identity, the end of safety." In many ways her essays, like her poems, track the forces that resist such change and the human conditions that require it. Her essay *Compulsory Heterosexuality and Lesbian Existence* is an important example of such an examination. There she writes that "woman identification is a source of energy, a potential spring-head of female power, curtailed and contained under the institution of heterosexuality."

In the long poem *Sources* (1982) she began to disentangle two complicated relationships: that with her Jewish husband, who died (a suicide) in 1970, and his connection to her powerful father—Jewish, intellectual, a doctor, who practically raised her as a "son." She continues to explore the differences and connections that constitute the community of women, an exploration in which her honesty is often courageous. Although Rich's individual poems do not consistently succeed in expressing a political vision without sacrificing "intensity of language," her work is best read as a continuous process. The books have an air of ongoing, pained investigation, almost scientific in intention but with an ardor suggested by their titles: *The Dream of a Common Language* (1977), *A Wild Patience Has Taken Me Thus Far* (1981), *The Fact of a Doorframe* (1984), and *Your Native Land, Your Life* (1986). Rich's most recent books, *Time's Power* (1989) and *An Atlas of the Difficult World* (1991), demonstrate an ongoing power of language and deepening poetic vision. Reading through her poems we may sometimes wish for more relaxation and playfulness, for a liberating comic sense of self almost never present in her work. What we find, however, is invaluable—a poet whose imagination confronts and resists the harsh necessities of our times and keeps alive a vision of what is possible: "a whole new poetry beginning here" (*Transcendental Etude*).

# Storm Warnings

The glass[1] has been falling all the afternoon,
And knowing better than the instrument

---

1. Barometer.

What winds are walking overhead, what zone
Of gray unrest is moving across the land,
I leave the book upon a pillowed chair                              5
And walk from window to closed window, watching
Boughs strain against the sky

And think again, as often when the air
Moves inward toward a silent core of waiting,
How with a single purpose time has traveled                        10
By secret currents of the undiscerned
Into this polar realm. Weather abroad
And weather in the heart alike come on
Regardless of prediction.

Between foreseeing and averting change                             15
Lies all the mastery of elements
Which clocks and weatherglasses cannot alter.
Time in the hand is not control of time,
Nor shattered fragments of an instrument
A proof against the wind; the wind will rise,                      20
We can only close the shutters.

I draw the curtains as the sky goes black
And set a match to candles sheathed in glass
Against the keyhole draught, the insistent whine
Of weather through the unsealed aperture.                          25
This is our sole defense against the season;
These are the things that we have learned to do
Who live in troubled regions.

                                                          1951

## Snapshots of a Daughter-in-Law

### 1

You, once a belle in Shreveport,
with henna-colored hair, skin like a peachbud,
still have your dresses copied from that time,
and play a Chopin prelude
called by Cortot: "*Delicious recollections*                      5
*float like perfume through the memory.*"[1]

Your mind now, moldering like wedding-cake,
heavy with useless experience, rich
with suspicion, rumor, fantasy,
crumbling to pieces under the knife-edge                           10
of mere fact. In the prime of your life.

---

1. A remark made by Alfred Cortot (1877–1962), a well-known French pianist, in his *Chopin: 24 Preludes* (1930);
he is referring specifically to Chopin's Prelude No. 7, Andantino, A Major.

Nervy, glowering, your daughter
wipes the teaspoons, grows another way.


2

Banging the coffee-pot into the sink
she hears the angels chiding, and looks out                    15
past the raked gardens to the sloppy sky.
Only a week since They said: *Have no patience.*

The next time it was: *Be insatiable.*
Then: *Save yourself; others you cannot save.*
Sometimes she's let the tapstream scald her arm,              20
a match burn to her thumbnail,

or held her hand above the kettle's snout
right in the woolly steam. They are probably angels,
since nothing hurts her anymore, except
each morning's grit blowing into her eyes.                     25


3

A thinking woman sleeps with monsters.[2]
The beak that grips her, she becomes. And Nature,
that sprung-lidded, still commodious
steamer-trunk of *tempora* and *mores*[3]
gets stuffed with it all:   the mildewed orange-flowers,       30
the female pills, the terrible breasts
of Boadicea[4] beneath flat foxes' heads and orchids.

Two handsome women, gripped in argument,
each proud, acute, subtle, I hear scream
across the cut glass and majolica                              35
like Furies[5] cornered from their prey:
The argument *ad feminam*,[6] all the old knives
that have rusted in my back, I drive in yours,
*ma semblable, ma soeur!*[7]


4

Knowing themselves too well in one another:                    40
their gifts no pure fruition, but a thorn,

2. A reference to W. B. Yeats's *Leda and the Swan*, a poem about the rape of a maiden by Zeus in the form of a giant bird. The poem ends: "Did she put on his knowledge with his power / Before the indifferent beak could let her drop?"
3. Times and customs (Latin, literal trans.). This alludes perhaps to the Roman orator Cicero's famous phrase, "O Tempora! O Mores!" ("Alas for the degeneracy of our times and the low standard of our morals!")
4. British queen in the time of the Emperor Nero; she led her people in a large, although ultimately unsuccessful, revolt against Roman rule. "Female pills":

remedies for menstrual pain.
5. Greek goddesses of vengeance. "Majolica": a kind of earthenware with a richly colored glaze.
6. Feminine version of the Latin phrase *ad hominem* (literally, "to the man"), referring to an argument directed not to reason but to personal prejudices and emotions.
7. The last line of Charles Baudelaire's French poem *Au Lecteur* addresses "*Hypocrite lecteur!—mon semblable—mon frère!*" ("Hypocrite reader, like me, my brother!"); Rich here instead addresses "*ma soeur*" ("my sister"). See also T. S. Eliot, *The Waste Land* 76.

the prick filed sharp against a hint of scorn . . .
Reading while waiting
for the iron to heat,
writing, *My Life had stood—a Loaded Gun*[8]—                              45
in that Amherst pantry while the jellies boil and scum,
or, more often,
iron-eyed and beaked and purposed as a bird,
dusting everything on the whatnot every day of life.

### 5

*Dulce ridens, dulce loquens,*[9]                                          50
she shaves her legs until they gleam
like petrified mammoth-tusk.

### 6

When to her lute Corinna sings[1]
neither words nor music are her own;
only the long hair dipping                                                 55
over her cheek, only the song
of silk against her knees
and these
adjusted in reflections of an eye.

Poised, trembling and unsatisfied, before                                  60
an unlocked door, that cage of cages,
tell us, you bird, you tragical machine—
is this *fertilisante douleur?*[2] Pinned down
by love, for you the only natural action,
are you edged more keen                                                    65
to prise the secrets of the vault? has Nature shown
her household books to you, daughter-in-law,
that her sons never saw?

### 7

*"To have in this uncertain world some stay*
*which cannot be undermined, is*                                           70
*of the utmost consequence."*[3]
                              Thus wrote
a woman, partly brave and partly good,
who fought with what she partly understood.
Few men about her would or could do more,                                  75
hence she was labeled harpy, shrew and whore.

---

8. *"Emily Dickinson, Complete Poems,* ed. T. H.
Johnson, 1960, p. 369" [Rich's note]; this is the poem
numbered 754 in the Johnson edition. Amherst is the
town where Dickinson lived her entire life (1830–
1886).
9. Sweetly laughing, sweetly speaking (Latin, from
Horace, *Odes,* 22.23–24).
1. First line of a lyric poem of Thomas Campion

(1567–1620) about the extent to which a courtier is
moved by Corinna's beautiful music.
2. Fertilizing (or life-giving) sorrow (French).
3. "From Mary Wollstonecraft, *Thoughts on the Edu-*
*cation of Daughters,* London, 1787" [Rich's note].
Wollstonecraft (1759–1797), one of the first feminist
thinkers, is best known for her *Vindication of the*
*Rights of Woman.*

8

"You all die at fifteen," said Diderot,[4]
and turn part legend, part convention.
Still, eyes inaccurately dream
behind closed windows blankening with steam.                    80
Deliciously, all that we might have been,
all that we were—fire, tears,
wit, taste, martyred ambition—
stirs like the memory of refused adultery
the drained and flagging bosom of our middle years.                    85

9

*Not that it is done well, but*
*that it is done at all?*[5] Yes, think
of the odds! or shrug them off forever.
This luxury of the precocious child,
Time's precious chronic invalid,—                    90
would we, darlings, resign it if we could?
Our blight has been our sinecure:
mere talent was enough for us—
glitter in fragments and rough drafts.

Sigh no more, ladies.                    95
                    Time is male
and in his cups drinks to the fair.
Bemused by gallantry, we hear
our mediocrities over-praised,
indolence read as abnegation,                    100
slattern thought styled intuition,
every lapse forgiven, our crime
only to cast too bold a shadow
or smash the mold straight off.

For that, solitary confinement,                    105
tear gas, attrition shelling.
Few applicants for that honor.

10

                                        Well,
she's long about her coming, who must be
more merciless to herself than history.                    110
Her mind full to the wind, I see her plunge
breasted and glancing through the currents,
taking the light upon her

4. Denis Diderot (1713–1784): French philosopher,
encyclopedist, playwright, and critic. " 'You all die at
fifteen': '*Vous mourez toutes à quinze ans,*' from the
*Lettres à Sophie Volland,* quoted by Simone de Beauvoir in *Le Deuxième Sexe,* Vol. II, pp. 123–24"

[Rich's note].
5. An allusion to Samuel Johnson's remark to James
Boswell: "Sir, a woman's preaching is like a dog's walking on his hinder legs. It is not done well; but you are
surprised to find it done at all" (July 31, 1763).

at least as beautiful as any boy
or helicopter,[6]                                        115
        poised, still coming,
her fine blades making the air wince

but her cargo
no promise then:
delivered                                              120
palpable
ours.

1958–60                                               1963


## "I Am in Danger—Sir—"[1]

"Half-cracked" to Higginson,[2] living,
afterward famous in garbled versions,
your hoard of dazzling scraps a battlefield,
now your old snood

mothballed at Harvard                                    5
and you in your variorum monument[3]
equivocal to the end—
who are you?

Gardening the day-lily,
wiping the wine-glass stems,                             10
your thought pulsed on behind
a forehead battered paper-thin,

you, woman, masculine
in single-mindedness,
for whom the word was more                              15
than a symptom—

a condition of being.
Till the air buzzing with spoiled language
sang in your ears
of Perjury                                             20

---

6. "She comes down from the remoteness of ages, from Thebes, from Crete, from Chichén-Itzá; and she is also the totem set deep in the African jungle; she is a helicopter and she is a bird; and there is this, the greatest wonder of all: under her tinted hair the forest murmur becomes a thought, and words issue from her breasts" (Simone de Beauvoir, *The Second Sex*, trans. H. M. Parshlev [New York, 1953], 729). (A translation of the passage from *Le Deuxième Sexe*, Vol. II, 574, cited in French by Rich.)
1. A sentence in a letter from Emily Dickinson to Thomas Wentworth Higginson (1823–1911), a critic and editor with whom she opened correspondence in

1862 and to whom she sent some of her poems. She writes: "You think my gait 'spasmodic'—I am in danger—Sir—You think me 'uncontrolled'—I have no Tribunal."
2. Higginson in a letter described Emily Dickinson as "my partially cracked Poetess at Amherst."
3. *The Poems of Emily Dickinson*, ed. Thomas H. Johnson, 3 vols. (Cambridge, Mass., 1955) is a "variorum" in that it contains all the variant readings in her manuscripts. "Mothballed at Harvard": the Houghton Rare Books Library at Harvard University has a collection of Emily Dickinson manuscripts and memorabilia.

and in your half-cracked way you chose
silence for entertainment,
chose to have it out at last
on your own premises.

1964                                                          1966

# Orion[1]

Far back when I went zig-zagging
through tamarack pastures
you were my genius, you
my cast-iron Viking, my helmed
lion-heart king[2] in prison.                                    5
Years later now you're young

my fierce half-brother, staring
down from that simplified west
your breast open, your belt dragged down
by an oldfashioned thing, a sword                               10
the last bravado you won't give over
though it weighs you down as you stride

and the stars in it are dim
and maybe have stopped burning.
But you burn, and I know it;                                    15
as I throw back my head to take you in
an old transfusion happens again:
divine astronomy is nothing to it.

Indoors I bruise and blunder,
break faith, leave ill enough                                   20
alone, a dead child born in the dark.
Night cracks up over the chimney,
pieces of time, frozen geodes[3]
come showering down in the grate.

A man reaches behind my eyes                                    25
and finds them empty
a woman's head turns away
from my head in the mirror
children are dying my death
and eating crumbs of my life.                                   30

Pity is not your forte.
Calmly you ache up there
pinned aloft in your crow's nest,[4]

---

1. A constellation of the winter sky, popularly known
as the Hunter, which appears as a giant with a belt
and sword.
2. Allusion to King Richard the Lion-Heart of England (1157–1199), imprisoned in Austria on his return
from the Crusades. "Genius": a guardian spirit.
3. Small, spheroid stones, with a cavity usually lined
with crystals.
4. Lookout post on the mast of old ships.

my speechless pirate!
You take it all for granted                                    35
and when I look you back

it's with a starlike eye
shooting its cold and egotistical[5] spear
where it can do least damage.
Breathe deep! No hurt, no pardon                               40
out here in the cold with you
you with your back to the wall.

1965                                                          1969

## A Valediction Forbidding Mourning[1]

My swirling wants. Your frozen lips.
The grammar turned and attacked me.
Themes, written under duress.
Emptiness of the notations.

They gave me a drug that slowed the healing of wounds.          5

I want you to see this before I leave:
the experience of repetition as death
the failure of criticism to locate the pain
the poster in the bus that said:
*my bleeding is under control.*                                10

A red plant in a cemetery of plastic wreaths.

A last attempt: the language is a dialect called metaphor.
These images go unglossed: hair, glacier, flashlight.
When I think of a landscape I am thinking of a time.
When I talk of taking a trip I mean forever.                   15
I could say: those mountains have a meaning
but further than that I could not say.

To do something very common, in my own way.

1970                                                          1971

## Diving into the Wreck

First having read the book of myths,
and loaded the camera,
and checked the edge of the knife-blade,

---

5. "One of two phrases suggested by Gottfried Benn's essay, *Artists and Old Age* in *Primal Vision*, edited by E. B. Ashton, New Directions" [Rich's note]. Benn's advice to the modern artist is: "Don't lose sight of the cold and egotistical element in your mission. . . . With your back to the wall, care-worn and weary, in the gray light of the void, read Job and Jeremiah and keep going" (pp. 206–7).
1. Title of a famous poem by John Donne (1572–1631), in which the English poet forbids his wife to lament his departure for a trip to the Continent.

I put on
the body-armor of black rubber                                    5
the absurd flippers
the grave and awkward mask.
I am having to do this
not like Cousteau[2] with his
assiduous team                                                   10
aboard the sun-flooded schooner
but here alone.

There is a ladder.
The ladder is always there
hanging innocently                                               15
close to the side of the schooner.
We know what it is for,
we who have used it.
Otherwise
it's a piece of maritime floss                                   20
some sundry equipment.

I go down.
Rung after rung and still
the oxygen immerses me
the blue light                                                   25
the clear atoms
of our human air.
I go down.
My flippers cripple me,
I crawl like an insect down the ladder                           30
and there is no one
to tell me when the ocean
will begin.

First the air is blue and then
it is bluer and then green and then                              35
black I am blacking out and yet
my mask is powerful
it pumps my blood with power
the sea is another story
the sea is not a question of power                               40
I have to learn alone
to turn my body without force
in the deep element.

And now: it is easy to forget
what I came for                                                  45
among so many who have always
lived here
swaying their crenellated fans
between the reefs

2. Jacques-Yves Cousteau (b. 1910), a French underwater explorer and author.

and besides                                                     50
you breathe differently down here.

I came to explore the wreck.
The words are purposes.
The words are maps.
I came to see the damage that was done                         55
and the treasures that prevail.
I stroke the beam of my lamp
slowly along the flank
of something more permanent
than fish or weed                                              60

the thing I came for:
the wreck and not the story of the wreck
the thing itself and not the myth
the drowned face[3] always staring
toward the sun                                                 65
the evidence of damage
worn by salt and sway into this threadbare beauty
the ribs of the disaster
curving their assertion
among the tentative haunters.                                  70

This is the place.
And I am here, the mermaid whose dark hair
streams black, the merman in his armored body
We circle silently
about the wreck                                                75
we dive into the hold.
I am she: I am he

whose drowned face sleeps with open eyes
whose breasts still bear the stress
whose silver, copper, vermeil cargo lies                       80
obscurely inside barrels
half-wedged and left to rot
we are the half-destroyed instruments
that once held to a course
the water-eaten log                                            85
the fouled compass

We are, I am, you are
by cowardice or courage
the one who find our way
back to this scene                                             90
carrying a knife, a camera
a book of myths
in which
our names do not appear.

1972                                                     1973

3. Referring to the ornamental female figurehead that formed the prow of many old sailing ships.

## From Twenty-One Love Poems

### I

Wherever in this city, screens flicker
with pornography, with science-fiction vampires,
victimized hirelings bending to the lash,
we also have to walk . . . if simply as we walk
through the rainsoaked garbage, the tabloid cruelties          5
of our own neighborhoods.
We need to grasp our lives inseparable
from those rancid dreams, that blurt of metal, those disgraces,
and the red begonia perilously flashing
from a tenement sill six stories high,          10
or the long-legged young girls playing ball
in the junior highschool playground.
No one has imagined us. We want to live like trees,
sycamores blazing through the sulfuric air,
dappled with scars, still exuberantly budding,          15
our animal passion rooted in the city.


### (The Floating Poem. Unnumbered)

Whatever happens with us, your body
will haunt mine—tender, delicate
your lovemaking, like the half-curled frond
of the fiddlehead fern in forests
just washed by sun. Your traveled, generous thighs          5
between which my whole face has come and come—
the innocence and wisdom of the place my tongue has found there—
the live, insatiate dance of your nipples in my mouth—
your touch on me, firm, protective, searching
me out, your strong tongue and slender fingers          10
reaching where I had been waiting years for you
in my rose-wet cave—whatever happens, this is.

1974–1976                                                                      1978


## Transcendental Etude[1]

### for Michelle Cliff

This August evening I've been driving
over backroads fringed with queen anne's lace
my car startling young deer in meadows—one
gave a hoarse intake of her breath and all
four fawns sprang after her          5
into the dark maples.
Three months from today they'll be fair game

---

1. A piece of music played for the practice of a point of technique or a composition built on technique but played for its artistic value.

for the hit-and-run hunters, glorying
in a weekend's destructive power,
triggers fingered by drunken gunmen, sometimes          10
so inept as to leave the shattered animal
stunned in her blood. But this evening deep in summer
the deer are still alive and free,
nibbling apples from early-laden boughs
so weighted, so englobed                                  15
with already yellowing fruit
they seem eternal, Hesperidean[2]
in the clear-tuned, cricket-throbbing air.

Later I stood in the dooryard,
my nerves singing the immense                             20
fragility of all this sweetness,
this green world already sentimentalized, photographed,
advertised to death. Yet, it persists
stubbornly beyond the fake Vermont
of antique barnboards glazed into discothèques,          25
artificial snow, the sick Vermont of children
conceived in apathy, grown to winters
of rotgut violence,
poverty gnashing its teeth like a blind cat at their lives.
Still, it persists. Turning off onto a dirt road         30
from the raw cuts bulldozed through a quiet village
for the tourist run to Canada,
I've sat on a stone fence above a great, soft, sloping field
of musing heifers, a farmstead
slanting its planes calmly in the calm light,            35
a dead elm raising bleached arms
above a green so dense with life,
minute, momentary life—slugs, moles, pheasants, gnats,
spiders, moths, hummingbirds, groundhogs, butterflies—
a lifetime is too narrow                                  40
to understand it all, beginning with the huge
rockshelves that underlie all that life.

No one ever told us we had to study our lives,
make of our lives a study, as if learning natural history
or music, that we should begin                           45
with the simple exercises first
and slowly go on trying
the hard ones, practicing till strength
and accuracy became one with the daring
to leap into transcendence, take the chance              50
of breaking down in the wild arpeggio
or faulting the full sentence of the fugue.[3]
—And in fact we can't live like that: we take on
everything at once before we've even begun

---

2. I.e., like the golden apples of the tree guarded by
the Hesperides, daughters of Atlas, in Greek mythology.

3. Musical piece characterized by the interweaving of
several voices. "Arpeggio": production of tones of a
chord in succession.

to read or mark time, we're forced to begin                55
in the midst of the hardest movement,
the one already sounding as we are born.
At most we're allowed a few months
of simply listening to the simple line
of a woman's voice singing a child                         60
against her heart. Everything else is too soon,
too sudden, the wrenching-apart, that woman's heartbeat
heard ever after from a distance,
the loss of that ground-note echoing
whenever we are happy, or in despair.                      65

Everything else seems beyond us,
we aren't ready for it, nothing that was said
is true for us, caught naked in the argument,
the counterpoint, trying to sightread
what our fingers can't keep up with, learn by heart        70
what we can't even read. And yet
it *is* this we were born to. We aren't virtuosi
or child prodigies, there are no prodigies
in this realm, only a half-blind, stubborn
cleaving to the timbre, the tones of what we are           75
——even when all the texts describe it differently.

And we're not performers, like Liszt,[4] competing
against the world for speed and brilliance
(the 79-year-old pianist said, when I asked her
*What makes a virtuoso?—Competitiveness.*)                 80
The longer I live the more I mistrust
theatricality, the false glamour cast
by performance, the more I know its poverty beside
the truths we are salvaging from
the splitting-open of our lives.                           85
The woman who sits watching, listening,
eyes moving in the darkness
in rehearsing in her body, hearing-out in her blood
a score touched off in her perhaps
by some words, a few chords, from the stage:               90
a tale only she can tell.

But there come times—perhaps this is one of them—
when we have to take ourselves more seriously or die;
when we have to pull back from the incantations,
rhythms we've moved to thoughtlessly,                      95
and disenthrall ourselves, bestow
ourselves to silence, or a severer listening, cleansed
of oratory, formulas, choruses, laments, static
crowding the wires. We cut the wires,
find ourselves in free-fall, as if                         100
our true home were the undimensional

---

4. Franz Liszt, 19th-century Hungarian composer and pianist, noted for his virtuoso performances.

solitudes, the rift
in the Great Nebula.[5]
No one who survives to speak
new language, has avoided this:                                    105
the cutting-away of an old force that held her
rooted to an old ground
the pitch of utter loneliness
where she herself and all creation
seem equally dispersed, weightless, her being a cry               110
to which no echo comes or can ever come.

But in fact we were always like this,
rootless, dismembered: knowing it makes the difference.
Birth stripped our birthright from us,
tore us from a woman, from women, from ourselves                  115
so early on
and the whole chorus throbbing at our ears
like midges, told us nothing, nothing
of origins, nothing we needed
to know, nothing that could re-member us.                         120

Only: that it is unnatural,
the homesickness for a woman, for ourselves,
for that acute joy at the shadow her head and arms
cast on a wall, her heavy or slender
thighs on which we lay, flesh against flesh,                      125
eyes steady on the face of love; smell of her milk, her sweat,
terror of her disappearance, all fused in this hunger
for the element they have called most dangerous, to be
lifted breathtaken on her breast, to rock within her
—even if beaten back, stranded against, to apprehend             130
in a sudden brine-clear thought
trembling like the tiny, orbed, endangered
egg-sac of a new world:
*This is what she was to me, and this*
*is how I can love myself—*                                       135
*as only a woman can love me.*

*Homesick for myself, for her*—as, after the heatwave
breaks, the clear tones of the world
manifest: cloud, bough, wall, insect, the very soul of light:
*homesick* as the fluted vault of desire                          140
articulates itself: *I am the lover and the loved,*
*home and wanderer, she who splits*
*firewood and she who knocks, a stranger*
*in the storm,* two women, eye to eye
measuring each other's spirit, each other's                      145
limitless desire,
              a whole new poetry beginning here.

---

5. A nebula is an immense body of rarefied gas or dust
in interstellar space. Rich may be referring to the Great
Nebula in the Orion constellation or to a body of dark
nebulae, usually called the "Great Rift," which in photographs appears to divide the Milky Way.

Vision begins to happen in such a life
as if a woman quietly walked away
from the argument and jargon in a room                                    150
and sitting down in the kitchen, began turning in her lap
bits of yarn, calico and velvet scraps,
laying them out absently on the scrubbed boards
in the lamplight, with small rainbow-colored shells
sent in cotton-wool from somewhere far away,                             155
and skeins of milkweed from the nearest meadow—
original domestic silk, the finest findings—
and the darkblue petal of the petunia,
and the dry darkbrown lace of seaweed;
not forgotten either, the shed silver                                   160
whisker of the cat,
the spiral of paper-wasp-nest curling
beside the finch's yellow feather.
Such a composition has nothing to do with eternity,
the striving for greatness, brilliance—                                 165
only with the musing of a mind
one with her body, experienced fingers quietly pushing
dark against bright, silk against roughness,
pulling the tenets of a life together
with no mere will to mastery,                                           170
only care for the many-lived, unending
forms in which she finds herself,
becoming now the sherd of broken glass
slicing light in a corner, dangerous
to flesh, now the plentiful, soft leaf                                  175
that wrapped round the throbbing finger, soothes the wound;
and now the stone foundation, rockshelf further
forming underneath everything that grows.

1977                                                                    1978

# For a Friend in Travail

Waking from violence:   the surgeon's probe left in the foot
paralyzing the body from the waist down.
Dark before dawn:   wrapped in a shawl, to walk the house
the Drinking-Gourd slung in the northwest,
half-slice of moon to the south                                         5
through dark panes.   A time to speak to you.

*What are you going through?* she said, is the great question.[1]
Philosopher of oppression, theorist
of the victories of force.

---

1. "The love of our neighbor in all its fullness simply
means being able to say to him: 'What are you going
through?' Simone Weil, *Waiting for God* (New York:
Putnam, 1951), p. 115" [Rich's note]. Weil (1909–
1943) was a French philosopher and mystic whose writings include meditations on the nature of violence
and suffering.

We write from the marrow of our bones.    What she did not          10
ask, or tell:    how victims save their own lives.

That crawl along the ledge, then the ravelling span of fibre strung
from one side to the other, I've dreamed that too.
Waking, not sure we made it.    Relief, appallment, of waking.
Consciousness.    O, no.    To sleep again.                         15
O to sleep without dreaming.

How day breaks, when it breaks, how clear and light the moon
melting into moon-colored air
moist and sweet, here on the western edge.
Love for the world, and we are part of it.                         20
How the poppies break from their sealed envelopes
she did not tell.

What are you going through, there on the other edge?

1990                                                              1991

---

# GARY  SNYDER
## b.  1930

"I try to hold both history and wildness in my mind, that my poems may approach
the true measure of things and stand against the unbalance and ignorance of our
time," Gary Snyder has said. Throughout his life Snyder has sought alternatives to
this imbalance. His quest has led him to the natural world, to the study of mythology and the discipline of Eastern religions, and to living oral traditions including
those of Native American societies. Snyder understands the work of poetry as recovery and healing. Like the shaman-poet of primitive cultures whose power to "heal
disease and resist death" is "acquired from dreams" (as he writes in *Poetry and the
Primitive*), he seeks to restore contact with a vital universe in which all things are
interdependent. The journey of Snyder's life and work has taken him back to what
he calls "the most archaic values on earth." His poems are acts of cultural criticism,
challenges to the dominant values of the contemporary world.

The American West Coast is Snyder's native landscape; its forests and mountains
have always attracted him and they inspire many of his poems. He was born in
San Francisco, grew up in the state of Washington, and later moved with his
family to Portland, Oregon. In 1947, he entered Reed College, where he studied
anthropology and developed a special interest in Native American cultures (Northwest Coast Indian myths and tales inform his second book, *Myths and Tests*, 1960).
After doing graduate work in linguistics at Indiana University, he returned to the
West, where he became associated with Kenneth Rexroth and Philip Whalen and
with Jack Kerouac and Allen Ginsberg, all of whom participated in what came to
be called the San Francisco Renaissance. In this period, Snyder also studied classical Chinese at the University of California at Berkeley and translated some of the
*Cold Mountain Poems* of the Zen poet Han-shan. In the mid 1950s Snyder went
to Japan, where he resided, except intermittently, until 1968; in Japan he took
formal instruction in Buddhism under Zen masters. The various traditions Snyder
has studied come together in his poetic vision quest *The Blue Sky*, a magical celebration of the overarching heavens.

Snyder's poems, like his life, combine reading and formal study with physical activity; he has worked as a timber scaler, a forest fire lookout (one of his lookouts inspired *August at Sourdough*), a logger, and a hand on a tanker in the South Pacific. "My poems follow the rhythms of the physical work I'm doing and the life I'm leading at any given time," he has remarked. The title of his first book, *Riprap* (1959), is a forester's term; a riprap, he explains, is "a cobble of stone laid on steep slick rock to make a trail for horses in the mountains." Snyder's poems often follow a trail of ascent or descent, as in *Straight-Creek—Great Burn* from his Pulitzer Prize–winning volume, *Turtle Island* (1975). Hiking with friends, he experiences the world as dynamic and flowing (running water and "changing clouds"), but the journey brings the walkers to a still point; they lie "resting on dry fern and / watching." From such a stillness the central image of a Snyder poem often rises, like the birds who "arch and loop," then "settle down." The achievement of stillness in a universe of change is, for Snyder, pivotal. The mind empties itself, the individual ego is erased, and the local place reveals the universal.

If Snyder's poems contain a Zen-like stillness, they also exhibit an appealing energy, one source of which is his love of wildness. Like the Thoreau of *Walden* explicitly evoked in sections of *Myths and Texts*, Snyder finds a tonic wildness in the natural world, but unlike Thoreau, he is an unabashed celebrant of erotic experience (his earlier poems make it clear that he also knows the destructive possibilities in such experience). He renders some of the various faces of Eros in *Beneath My Hand and Eye the Distant Hills. Your Body* (from *The Back Country*, 1968) and in *Song of the Taste* (from *Regarding Wave*, 1970).

Some of Snyder's numerous essays on politics and ecology are included in his influential *Earth House Hold* (1969) and *The Practice of the Wild* (1990). His collections, *Axe Handles* (1983) and *Left Out in the Rain* (1986), confirm that his poems are bound up in the same concerns. Although his didactic impulse sometimes leads him to oversimplification, Snyder's political vision remains one of the strengths of his poetry. The potential in this vision for self-importance and overseriousness is tempered by his sense of humor and the conviction, palpable in his best poems, that his experiences are common and shared. Snyder's poems suggest diverse contexts: his belief in the writer as cultural critic links him to Thoreau and Robert Duncan, his rhythms and strong images recall Ezra Pound, his meticulous attention to the natural world reminds us of Robert Frost and A. R. Ammons. Eclectic yet respectful of ancient traditions, Snyder is an American original who sees his own work as part of a "continual creation," one manifestation of the energy which sustains all life.

# Riprap[1]

Lay down these words
Before your mind like rocks.
        placed solid, by hands
In choice of place, set
Before the body of the mind                        5
        in space and time:
Solidity of bark, leaf, or wall
        riprap of things:
Cobble of milky way,
        straying planets,                       10
These poems, people,
        lost ponies with

---

1. "A cobble of stone laid on steep slick rock to make a trail for horses in the mountains" [Snyder's note].

Dragging saddles—
        and rocky sure-foot trails.
The worlds like an endless            15
        four-dimensional
Game of Go. [2]
        ants and pebbles
In the thin loam, each rock a word
        a creek-washed stone      20
Granite: ingrained
        with torment of fire and weight
Crystal and sediment linked hot
        all change, in thoughts,
As well as things.      25

          1959

## August on Sourdough, [1] A Visit from Dick Brewer

You hitched a thousand miles
        north from San Francisco
Hiked up the mountainside  a mile in the air
The little cabin—one room—
        walled in glass      5
Meadows and snowfields,  hundreds of peaks.
We lay in our sleeping bags
        talking half the night;
Wind in the guy-cables  this summer mountain rain.
Next morning I went with you      10
        as far as the cliffs,
Loaned you my poncho—  the rain across the shale—
You down the snowfield
        flapping in the wind
Waving a last goodbye  half hidden in the clouds  15
To go on hitching
        clear to New York;
Me back to my mountain  and far, far, west.

          1968

## Beneath My Hand and Eye the Distant Hills. Your Body

What my hand follows on your body
Is the line. A stream of love
    of heat, of light,    what my
    eye        lascivious

---

2. An ancient Japanese game played with black and white stones, placed one after the other on a checkered board.

1. Mountain in Alaska where Snyder was stationed as a fire watcher.

licks                                                          5
over, watching
far snow-dappled Uintah mountains[1]
Is that stream.
Of power.        what my
   hand curves over, following the line.              10
   "hip" and "groin"

Where "I"
   follow by hand and eye
   the swimming limit of your body.
As when vision idly dallies on the hills             15
Loving what it feeds on.
   soft cinder cones and craters;
   —Drum Hadley in the Pinacate[2]
   took ten minutes more to look again—
A leap of power unfurling:                           20
   left,     right—right—
My heart beat faster looking
   at the snowy Uintah mountains.

As my hand feeds on you
   runs down your side and curls beneath your hip.   25
oil pool; stratum; water—

What "is" within    not known
   but feel it
   sinking with a breath
   pusht ruthless, surely, down.                     30

Beneath this long caress of hand and eye
   "we" learn the flower burning,
      outward, from "below".

                                                1968

## Song of the Taste

Eating the living germs of grasses
Eating the ova[1] of large birds

   the fleshy sweetness packed
   around the sperm of swaying trees

The muscles of the flanks and thighs of             5
      soft-voiced cows
   the bounce in the lamb's leap
   the swish in the ox's tail

1. Mountain range in northeastern Utah.              1. Eggs.
2. Town in California.

Eating roots grown swoll
　　inside the soil                                                    10

Drawing on life of living
　　clustered points of light spun
　　　　out of space
hidden in the grape.

Eating each other's seed                                              15
　　　　eating
ah, each other.

Kissing the lover in the mouth of bread:
　　lip to lip.

1970

---

# SYLVIA PLATH

## 1932–1963

In an introduction to Sylvia Plath's *Ariel* (1965), published two years after her
suicide in London, Robert Lowell wrote: "In these poems . . . Sylvia Plath
becomes herself, becomes something imaginary, newly, wildly, and subtly created— . . . one of those super-real, hypnotic great classical heroines." Lowell had
first met Plath in 1958, during her regular visits to his poetry seminar at Boston
University, where he remembered her "air of maddening docility." Later, writing
his introduction, he recognized her astonishing creation of a poetic self. The
poems of *Ariel* were written at white heat, two or three a day, in the last months of
Plath's life, but there is nothing hurried in their language or structure. Taken
together, with the poems posthumously published in *Crossing the Water* (1971)
and *Winter Trees* (1972), a coherent persona emerges: larger than life, operatic in
feeling. Although this focus on the self often excludes attention to the larger world,
it generates the dynamic energy of her work. Plath appropriates a centrally American tradition: the heroic ego confronting the sublime, but she brilliantly revises
this tradition by turning Emerson's "great and crescive self" into a heroine instead
of a hero. Seizing a mythic power, the Plath of the poems transmutes the domestic
and the ordinary into the hallucinatory, the utterly strange. Her revision of the
romantic ego dramatizes its tendency toward disproportion and excess, and she is
fully capable of both using and mocking this heightened sense of self, as she does
in her poem *Lady Lazarus*.

Plath's well-known autobiographical novel, *The Bell Jar*, has nothing of the brilliance of her poems, but it effectively dramatizes the stereotyping of women's roles
in the 1950s and the turmoil of a young woman only partly aware that her gifts
and ambitions greatly exceed the options available to her. In the novel, Plath makes
use of her experience as a guest editor of a young women's magazine (in real life,
*Mademoiselle*), and then, in an abrupt shift, presents her heroine's attempted suicide and hospitalization. Plath herself had suffered a serious breakdown and
attempted suicide between her junior and senior years in college. The popularity
of *The Bell Jar* may be one reason why attention to Plath's life has sometimes
obscured the accomplishments of her art. While her poems often begin in autobiography, their success depends on Plath's imaginative transformations of experi-

ence into myth, as in a number of her poems (such as *Daddy*) where the figure of
her Prussian father is transformed into an emblem for masculine authority. Otto
Plath was an entomologist and the author of a treatise on bumblebees. His death
in 1940 from gangrene (the consequence of a diabetic condition he refused to
treat), when Plath was eight, was the crucial event of her childhood. After his
death, her mother, Aurelia, while struggling to support two small children,
encouraged her daughter's literary ambitions.

In many ways Plath embodied the bright, young, middle-class woman of the
1950s. She went to Smith College on a scholarship and graduated summa cum
laude. On a Fulbright grant she studied in England at Cambridge University,
where she met and married the poet Ted Hughes. On the face of it, her marriage
must have seemed the perfect fate for such a young woman; it combined romance,
two poets beginning careers together (Plath's first book, *The Colossus*, appeared in
1960) and, later, two children (Frieda, born in 1960, and Nicholas, born in 1962),
with a country house in Devon, England. In her poems, however, we find the
strains of such a life; the work is galvanized by suffering, by a terrible constriction
against which she unlooses "The lioness, / The shriek in the bath, / The cloak of
holes" (*Purdah*). In articulating a dark vision of domestic life, Plath was adopting
the license of Robert Lowell and Anne Sexton, a fellow student in Lowell's poetry
seminar, to write about "private and taboo subjects."

The marriage broke up in the summer of 1962 and Plath found herself with two
small children, living in a London flat in one of the coldest winters in recent
British history. There she began the poems of *Ariel*, writing furiously until February 1963, when she took her life. Fueled by an anger toward her husband and
father, she speaks in these poems as one whose feelings are more than her own; it
is as if she were the character in George Eliot's *Daniel Deronda* who appears suddenly before the novel's heroine and says, "I am a woman's life." These powerful,
angry poems, mining a limited range of deep feeling, are Plath's best-known work.
Other poems, however, demonstrate her ability to render a wider variety of emotion; they include poems about her children (such as *Morning Song, Child,* and
*Parliament Hill Fields*) and a number of arresting poems about the natural world.
In the vastness of natural processes, the romantic ego finds something as large as
itself, and Plath's response to nature is intense, often uncanny. Her poems offer an
eccentricity of vision where (as in *Blackberrying*) the appearance of the natural
world is never separable from the consciousness of the one who sees it.

For all her courting of excess, Plath is a remarkably controlled writer; her lucid
stanzas, her clear diction, her dazzling alterations of sound are evidence of that
control. The imaginative intensity of her poems is her own, triumphant creation
out of the difficult circumstances of her life. She once remarked, "I cannot sympathize with those cries from the heart that are informed by nothing except a needle
or a knife. . . . I believe that one should be able to control and manipulate experiences, even the most terrifying . . . with an informed and intelligent mind." The
influence of her style, and of the persona she created, continues to be felt in the
work of a wide variety of contemporary poets.

# Morning Song

Love set you going like a fat gold watch.
The midwife slapped your footsoles, and your bald cry
Took its place among the elements.

Our voices echo, magnifying your arrival. New statue.
In a drafty museum, your nakedness                                            5
Shadows our safety. We stand round blankly as walls.

I'm no more your mother
Than the cloud that distills a mirror to reflect its own slow
Effacement at the wind's hand.

All night your moth-breath                                        10
Flickers among the flat pink roses. I wake to listen:
A far sea moves in my ear.

One cry, and I stumble from bed, cow-heavy and floral
In my Victorian nightgown.
Your mouth opens clean as a cat's. The window square          15

Whitens and swallows its dull stars. And now you try
Your handful of notes;
The clear vowels rise like balloons.

1961                                                           1966

## Lady Lazarus[1]

I have done it again.
One year in every ten
I manage it——

A sort of walking miracle, my skin
Bright as a Nazi lampshade,[2]                                  5
My right foot

A paperweight,
My face a featureless, fine
Jew linen.

Peel off the napkin                                            10
O my enemy.
Do I terrify?——

The nose, the eye pits, the full set of teeth?
The sour breath
Will vanish in a day.                                          15

Soon, soon the flesh
The grave cave ate will be
At home on me

And I a smiling woman.
I am only thirty.                                              20
And like the cat I have nine times to die.

---

1. Lazarus was raised from the dead by Jesus (John 11.1–45).      2. In the Nazi death camps, the skins of victims were sometimes used to make lampshades.

This is Number Three.
What a trash
To annihilate each decade.

What a million filaments.                                    25
The peanut-crunching crowd
Shoves in to see

Them unwrap me hand and foot——
The big strip tease.
Gentlemen, ladies                                            30

These are my hands
My knees.
I may be skin and bone,

Nevertheless, I am the same, identical woman.
The first time it happened I was ten.                        35
It was an accident.

The second time I meant
To last it out and not come back at all.
I rocked shut

As a seashell.                                               40
They had to call and call
And pick the worms off me like sticky pearls.

Dying
Is an art, like everything else.
I do it exceptionally well.                                  45

I do it so it feels like hell.
I do it so it feels real.
I guess you could say I've a call.

It's easy enough to do it in a cell.
It's easy enough to do it and stay put.                      50
It's the theatrical

Comeback in broad day
To the same place, the same face, the same brute
Amused shout:

'A miracle!'                                                 55
That knocks me out.
There is a charge

For the eyeing of my scars, there is a charge
For the hearing of my heart——
It really goes.                                              60

And there is a charge, a very large charge
For a word or a touch
Or a bit of blood

Or a piece of my hair or my clothes.
So, so, Herr[3] Doktor.                                          65
So, Herr Enemy.

I am your opus,
I am your valuable,
The pure gold baby

That melts to a shriek.                                          70
I turn and burn.
Do not think I underestimate your great concern.

Ash, ash—
You poke and stir.
Flesh, bone, there is nothing there——                            75

A cake of soap,
A wedding ring,
A gold filling.[4]

Herr God, Herr Lucifer
Beware
Beware.                                                          80

Out of the ash[5]
I rise with my red hair
And I eat men like air.

1962                                                           1966


# Daddy

You do not do, you do not do
Any more, black shoe
In which I have lived like a foot
For thirty years, poor and white,
Barely daring to breathe or Achoo.                               5

Daddy, I have had to kill you.
You died before I had time——
Marble-heavy, a bag full of God,
Ghastly statue with one grey toe[1]
Big as a Frisco seal                                             10

---

3. Mr.
4. The Nazis used human remains in the making of
soap and scavenged corpses for jewelry and gold teeth.
5. An allusion to the phoenix, a mythical bird that dies

by fire and is reborn out of its own ashes.
1. Plath's father's toe turned black from gangrene, a
complication of diabetes.

And a head in the freakish Atlantic
Where it pours bean green over blue
In the waters of beautiful Nauset.[2]
I used to pray to recover you.
Ach, du.[3]                                              15

In the German tongue, in the Polish town[4]
Scraped flat by the roller
Of wars, wars, wars.
But the name of the town is common.
My Polack friend                                        20

Says there are a dozen or two.
So I never could tell where you
Put your foot, your root,
I never could talk to you.
The tongue stuck in my jaw.                              25

It stuck in a barb wire snare.
Ich, ich, ich, ich,[5]
I could hardly speak.
I thought every German was you.
And the language obscene                                 30

An engine, an engine
Chuffing me off like a Jew.
A Jew to Dachau, Auschwitz, Belsen.[6]
I began to talk like a Jew.
I think I may well be a Jew.                             35

The snows of the Tyrol,[7] the clear beer of Vienna
Are not very pure or true.
With my gypsy ancestress and my weird luck
And my Taroc[8] pack and my Taroc pack
I may be a bit of a Jew.                                 40

I have always been scared of *you*,
With your Luftwaffe,[9] your gobbledygoo.
And your neat mustache
And your Aryan eye, bright blue.
Panzer[1]-man, panzer-man, O You——                      45

Not God but a swastika
So black no sky could squeak through.

2. Beach south of Boston.
3. Ah, you: the first of a series of references to her father's German origins.
4. The poet's father, although of German descent, was born in Grabow, Poland.
5. I.
6. German concentration camps, where millions of Jews were murdered during World War II.
7. Austrian Alpine region.

8. Variation of Tarot, ancient fortune-telling cards. Gypsies, like Jews, were objects of Nazi genocidal ambition; many died in the concentration camps.
9. The German air force.
1. Armor (German); refers to the Nazi tank corps in World War II. Hitler preached the superiority of the Aryans—people of German stock with blond hair and blue eyes.

Every woman adores a Fascist,
The boot in the face, the brute
Brute heart of a brute like you.                                    50

You stand at the blackboard, daddy,
In the picture I have of you,
A cleft in your chin instead of your foot
But no less a devil for that, no not
And less the black man who                                         55

Bit my pretty red heart in two.
I was ten when they buried you.
At twenty I tried to die
And get back, back, back to you.
I thought even the bones would do.                                 60

But they pulled me out of the sack,
And they stuck me together with glue.[2]
And then I knew what to do.
I made a model of you,
A man in black with a Meinkampf[3] look                            65

And a love of the rack and the screw.
And I said I do, I do.
So daddy, I'm finally through.
The black telephone's off at the root,
The voices just can't worm through.                                70

If I've killed one man, I've killed two——
The vampire who said he was you
And drank my blood for a year,
Seven years, if you want to know.
Daddy, you can lie back now.                                       75

There's a stake in your fat black heart
And the villagers never liked you.
They are dancing and stamping on you.
They always *knew* it was you.
Daddy, daddy, you bastard, I'm through.                            80

1962                                                               1966

# Parliament Hill Fields[1]

On this bald hill the new year hones its edge.
Faceless and pale as china
The round sky goes on minding its business.

---

2. An allusion to Plath's first suicide attempt.
3. A reference to Hitler's political autobiography, *Mein Kampf* (My struggle), written and published be- fore his rise to power, in which the future dictator out-

lined his plans for world conquest.
1. Large tract of open land near Highgate, north of London.

Your absence is inconspicuous;
Nobody can tell what I lack.                                    5

Gulls have threaded the river's mud bed back
To this crest of grass. Inland, they argue,
Settling and stirring like blown paper
Or the hands of an invalid. The wan
Sun manages to strike such tin glints                          10

From the linked ponds that my eyes wince
And brim; the city melts like sugar.
A crocodile of small girls[2]
Knotting and stopping, ill-assorted, in blue uniforms,
Opens to swallow me. I'm a stone, a stick,                     15

One child drops a barrette of pink plastic;
None of them seem to notice.
Their shrill, gravelly gossip's funnelled off.
Now silence after silence offers itself.
The wind stops my breath like a bandage.                       20

Southward, over Kentish Town, an ashen smudge
Swaddles roof and tree.
It could be a snowfield or a cloudbank.
I suppose it's pointless to think of you at all.
Already your doll grip lets go.                                25

The tumulus,[3] even at noon, guards its black shadow:
You know me less constant,
Ghost of a leaf, ghost of a bird.
I circle the writhen[4] trees. I am too happy.
These faithful dark-boughed cypresses[5]                       30

Brood, rooted in their heaped losses.
Your cry fades like the cry of a gnat.
I lose sight of you on your blind journey,
While the heath grass glitters and the spindling rivulets
Unspool and spend themselves. My mind runs with them,          35

Pooling in heel-prints, fumbling pebble and stem.
The day empties its images
Like a cup or a room. The moon's crook whitens,
Thin as the skin seaming a scar.
Now, on the nursery wall,                                      40

The blue night plants, the little pale blue hill
In your sister's birthday picture start to glow.
The orange pompons, the Egyptian papyrus
Light up. Each rabbit-eared
Blue shrub behind the glass                                    45

---

2. I.e., a line of girls.                    4. Intertwined, twisted.
3. Artificial mound (as over a grave).       5. Trees symbolic of mourning.

Exhales an indigo nimbus,[6]
A sort of cellophane balloon.
The old dregs, the old difficulties take me to wife.
Gulls stiffen to their chill vigil in the draughty half-light;
I enter the lit house.                                              50

1961                                                               1971


# Blackberrying

Nobody in the lane, and nothing, nothing but blackberries,
Blackberries on either side, though on the right mainly,
A blackberry alley, going down in hooks, and a sea
Somewhere at the end of it, heaving. Blackberries
Big as the ball of my thumb, and dumb as eyes                       5
Ebon in the hedges, fat
With blue-red juices. These they squander on my fingers.
I had not asked for such a blood sisterhood; they must love me.
They accommodate themselves to my milkbottle, flattening their sides.

Overhead go the choughs[1] in black, cacophonous flocks—            10
Bits of burnt paper wheeling in a blown sky.
Theirs is the only voice, protesting, protesting.
I do not think the sea will appear at all.
The high, green meadows are glowing, as if lit from within.
I come to one bush of berries so ripe it is a bush of flies,        15
Hanging their bluegreen bellies and their wing panes in a Chinese screen.
The honey-feast of the berries has stunned them; they believe in heaven.
One more hook, and the berries and bushes end.

The only thing to come now is the sea.
From between two hills a sudden wind funnels at me,                  20
Slapping its phantom laundry in my face.
These hills are too green and sweet to have tasted salt.
I follow the sheep path between them. A last hook brings me
To the hills' northern face, and the face is orange rock
That looks out on nothing, nothing but a great space                25
Of white and pewter lights, and a din like silversmiths
Beating and beating at an intractable metal.

1961                                                               1971


# Child

Your clear eye is the one absolutely beautiful thing.
I want to fill it with color and ducks,
The zoo of the new

---

6. I.e., a blue luminous cloud.                    1. Small, chattering birds of the crow family.

Whose names you meditate—
April snowdrop, Indian pipe,                                    5
Little

Stalk without wrinkle,
Pool in which images
Should be grand and classical

Not this troublous                                            10
Wringing of hands, this dark
Ceiling without a star.

1963                                                        1972

---

# AUDRE LORDE

## 1934–1992

Audre Lorde's poetry wages what she called "a war against the tyrannies of silence";
it articulates what has been passed over out of fear or discomfort, what has been
kept hidden and secret. Reading her we feel the violence inherent in breaking a
silence, perhaps most often as she probes the experience of anger—the anger of
black toward white or white toward black, a woman's anger at men and other
women, and men's anger toward women (the subject of her powerful poem *Need:
A Choral of Black Women's Voices*). "My Black woman's anger," she wrote in her
collection of essays, *Sister Outsider*, "is a molten pond at the core of me, my
most fiercely guarded secret." Having admitted this secret into her poems, Lorde
transforms our expectations of what is fit subject for the lyric. Her work is often
deliberately disturbing, the powerful voice of the poem cutting through denial,
politeness, and fear. In the development of this voice, Lorde drew on African
resources, especially the matriarchal mythology and history of West Africa. Her
seventh book, *The Black Unicorn* (1978), reflects the time she spent in Africa studying, in particular, Yoruba mythology and reclaiming her connection to the rich
African cultures. The African presence is evident in one of her last books, *Our
Dead Behind Us* (1986), as well. From the start, Lorde's work suggests that she
always connected poetry to the speaking voice, but her study of African materials
deepened her connection to oral traditions (like the chant or the call) and taught
her the power of voice to cut across time and place. From African writers, she said,
she learned that "we live in accordance with, in a kind of correspondence with,
the rest of the world as a whole." A powerful voice informed by personal and
cultural history creates the possibility, for Lorde, of bridging the differences her
work does not seek to erase. "It is not difference that immobilizes us," she wrote,
"but silence."

Her work both celebrates difference and confounds it. In Adrienne Rich's words,
Lorde wrote "as a Black woman, a mother, a daughter, a Lesbian, a feminist, a
visionary." Her poem *Coal* affirms an *I* that is "the total black, being spoken / from
the earth's inside." This total blackness was, for her, also associated with Eros and
with creativity; she celebrated this source as what she called "woman's place of
power within each of us," which is "neither white nor surface; it is dark, it is
ancient; and it is deep." Her best work calls on the deepest places of her own life—
on the pain she experienced, on her rage (her second book was titled *Cables to*

*Rage*, 1972), on her longing and desire. One of the silences her poems broke concerns love between women, and she wrote a number of poems that are erotic, precise, and true to both the power and delicacy of feeling. Unafraid of anger, she was also capable of tenderness; this is perhaps most clear not only in her love poems but in poems that address a younger generation. Her poem *Chain* is a moving response to a news item in which two young girls who, having borne children by their natural father, were sent to foster homes but petitioned the court to be returned to their parents.

Lorde was born in New York City and lived in New York almost all her life. Her parents were West Indian, and her mother was light skinned. "I grew up in a genuine confusion / between grass and weeds and flowers / and what colored meant," Lorde wrote in her poem *Outside*. Part of that confusion was the conflict represented by her father's blackness and her mother's desire for whiteness (in *Black Mother Woman* Lorde speaks of the mother as "split with deceitful longings"). Lorde's understanding of identity forged out of conflict began, then, for her in her own family history with its legacy of "conflicting rebellions" (*Black Mother Woman*). In 1961 she received a B.A. from Hunter College and later a Master's of Library Science from Columbia University. The following year she married (she divorced in 1970), and the marriage produced a daughter and a son. In 1968 she became poet-in-residence for a year at Tougaloo College in Mississippi, her first experience in the American South. Thereafter she knew her work to be that of a writer and teacher; she taught at John Jay College of Criminal Justice in New York City and, from 1981, was professor of English at Hunter College. In the last years of her life Lorde traveled extensively, not only to Africa but to Australia (where she met with aborigine women) and Germany. During her last years she lived much of the time in St. Croix.

"I have come to believe over and over again," Lorde said, "that what is most important to me must be spoken, made verbal and shared, even at the risk of having it bruised or misunderstood." This drive toward expression made Lorde a prolific writer and led her to several prose works in which she shared experiences often restricted to privacy: *The Cancer Journals* (1980), an account of her struggle with breast cancer, and *Zami: A New Spelling of My Name* (1982), a "biomythography" of her growing up and her emergent lesbian identity. The urgency Lorde felt to make experience "verbal and shared," however, sometimes overrode the distinction between poetry and rhetoric, which she knew was crucial to her art. She preserved this distinction in her best work by listening and responding to other voices in herself and in the world around her. With their combination of pain, anger, and tenderness, her finest poems are poetry as illumination, poetry in which, as she said, "we give name to those ideas which are—until the poem— nameless, formless, about to be birthed, but already felt."

# Coal

### I

is the total black, being spoken
from the earth's inside.
There are many kinds of open
how a diamond comes into a knot of flame          5
how sound comes into a word, coloured
by who pays what for speaking.

Some words are open like a diamond
on glass windows

singing out within the passing crash of sun                    10
Then there are words like stapled wagers
in a perforated book,—buy and sign and tear apart—
and come whatever wills all chances
the stub remains
and ill-pulled tooth with a ragged edge.                    15
Some words live in my throat
breeding like adders. Others know sun
seeking like gypsies over my tongue
to explode through my lips
like young sparrows bursting from shell.                    20
Some words
bedevil me.

Love is a word, another kind of open.
As the diamond comes into a knot of flame
I am Black because I come from the earth's inside                    25
now take my word for jewel in the open light.

                                                    1968


## The Woman Thing

The hunters are back from beating the winter's face
in search of a challenge or task
in search of food
making fresh tracks for their children's hunger
they do not watch the sun                    5
they cannot wear its heat for a sign
of triumph or freedom;
The hunters are treading heavily homeward
through snow that is marked
with their own bloody footprints.                    10
emptyhanded, the hunters return
snow-maddened, sustained by their rages.

In the night after food they may seek
young girls for their amusement. But now
the hunters are coming                    15
and the unbaked girls flee from their angers.
All this day I have craved
food for my child's hunger
Emptyhanded the hunters come shouting
injustices drip from their mouths                    20
like stale snow melted in sunlight.

Meanwhile
the woman thing my mother taught me
bakes off its covering of snow
like a rising blackening sun.                    25

                                                    1968

# From the House of Yemanjá[1]

My mother had two faces and a frying pot
where she cooked up her daughters
into girls
before she fixed our dinner.
My mother had two faces                                         5
and a broken pot
where she hid out a perfect daughter
who was not me
I am the sun and moon and forever hungry
for her eyes.                                                   10

I bear two women upon my back
one dark and rich and hidden
in the ivory hungers of the other
mother
pale as a witch                                                15
yet steady and familiar
brings me bread and terror
in my sleep
her breasts as huge exciting anchors
in the midnight storm.                                         20

All this has been
before
in my mother's bed
time has no sense
I have no brothers                                             25
and my sisters are cruel.

Mother I need
mother I need
mother I need your blackness now
as the august earth needs rain.                               30

I am
the sun and moon and forever hungry
the sharpened edge
where day and night shall meet
and not be                                                     35
one.

1978

1. "Mother of the other *Orisha* [gods and goddesses of
the Yoruba peoples, western Nigeria], Yemanjá is also
the goddess of oceans. Rivers are said to flow from her
breasts. One legend has it that a son tried to rape her.
She fled until she collapsed, and from her breasts, the
rivers flowed. Another legend says that a husband insulted Yemanjá's long breasts, and when she fled with
her pots he knocked her down. From her breasts flowed
the rivers, and from her body then sprang forth all the
other *Orisha*. River-smooth stones are Yemanjá's symbol, and the sea is sacred to her followers. Those who
please her are blessed with many children" [Lorde's
note].

## Harriet

Harriet there was always somebody calling us crazy
or mean or stuck-up or evil or black
or black
and we were
nappy girls quick as cuttlefish[1]                                        5
scurrying for cover
trying to speak trying to speak
trying to speak
the pain in each others mouths
until we learned                                                         10
on the edge of a lash
or a tongue
on the edge of the other's betrayal
that respect
meant keeping our distance                                               15
in silence
averting our eyes
from each other's face in the street
from the beautiful dark mouth
and cautious familiar eyes                                               20
passing alone.

I remember you Harriet
before we were broken apart
we dreamed the crossed swords
of warrior queens                                                        25
while we avoided each other's eyes
and we learned to know lonely
as the earth learns to know dead
Harriet Harriet
what name shall we call our selves now                                   30
our mother is gone?

1978

## Chain

News item: Two girls, fifteen and sixteen, were sent to foster homes, because
they had borne children by their natural father. Later, they petitioned the New
York courts to be returned to their parents, who, the girls said, loved them.
And the courts did so.

*I*

Faces surround me that have no smell or color no time
only strange laughing testaments
vomiting promise like love
but look at the skeleton children

1. Ten-armed shellfish. "Nappy": with closely twisted or curled hair.

advancing against us                                          5
beneath their faces there is no sunlight
no darkness
no heart remains
no legends
to bring them back as women                                 10
into their bodies at dawn.

Look at the skeleton children
advancing against us
we will find womanhood
in their eyes                                               15
as they cry
which of you bore me
will love me
will claim my blindness as yours
and which of you marches to battle                          20
from between my legs?

## II

On the porch outside my door
girls are lying
like felled maples in the path of my feet
I cannot step past them nor over them                       25
their slim bodies roll like smooth tree trunks
repeating themselves over and over
until my porch is covered with the bodies
of young girls.
Some have a child in their arms.                            30
To what death shall I look for comfort?
Which mirror to break or mourn?

Two girls repeat themselves in my doorway
their eyes are not stone.
Their flesh is not wood nor steel                           35
but I can not touch them.
Shall I warn them of night
or offer them bread
or a song?
They are sisters. Their father has known[1]                 40
them over and over. The twins they carry
are his. Whose death shall we mourn
in the forest
unburied?
Winter has come and the children are dying.                 45

One begs me to hold her between my breasts
Oh write me a poem mother
here, over my flesh

---

1. Probably also in the old sense, "has had sexual intercourse with."

get your words upon me
as he got this child upon me                                    50
our father lover
thief in the night
do not be so angry with us. We told him
your bed was wider
but he said if we did it then                                   55
we would be his
good children if we did it
then he would love us
oh make us a poem mother
that will tell us his name                                      60
in your language
is he father or lover

we will leave your word
for our children
engraved on a whip or a golden scissors                        65
to tell them the lies
of their birth.

Another says mother
I am holding your place.
Do you know me better than I knew him                           70
or myself?
Am I his daughter or girlfriend
am I your child or your rival
you wish to be gone from his bed?
Here is your granddaughter mother                               75
give us your blessing before I sleep
what other secrets
do you have to tell me
how do I learn to love her
as you have loved me?                                           80

                                                      1978

# AMIRI BARAKA (LeRoi Jones)

## b. 1934

The poet who in 1966 returned to the slums of Newark, New Jersey, as a black activist named Imamu Amiri Baraka had been born in that city thirty-two years before as LeRoi Jones. Baraka came to say that "the Black Artist's role in America is to aid in the destruction of America as he knows it." But he arrived at that attitude after almost fifteen years of attempting to make a go of the idea of an integrated society, or at least of a multiracial literary world.

Baraka was a precocious child who graduated from high school two years early. He attended Howard University, spent two and a half years as an aerial climatogra-

pher in the air force, then studied at Columbia, taking an M.A. in German literature. He associated himself with Beat poets such as Allen Ginsberg and with poets
of the New York school such as Frank O'Hara. "For me, Lorca, Williams, Pound,
and Charles Olson have had the greatest influence," Baraka said in 1959. At that
time his desire was to find a poetic style that would fully and freely express "whatever I think I am." In more particular terms, this meant new metrics and ways of
notation on the page so that he could stress the way he *sounds*, his individual
cadence. It was natural that he should turn for tonal models on the one side to the
"projective verse" of Olson, and on the other to the rhythms he knew from African-
American music like the blues.

Baraka's early poems tried to describe or convey a personal anguish for which
the poet projected no political solution. "I am inside someone / who hates me, I
look / out from his eyes." He returns over and over to the predicament of a divided
self, part of whose pain stems from being a black intellectual in a white world. For
the most part, the speakers in these poems, as in *I Substitute for the Dead Lecturer*,
are paralyzed by their guilt and fears:

> And I am frightened
> that the flame of my sickness
> will burn off my face. And leave
> the bones, my stewed black skull,
> an empty cage of failure.

Baraka's first two volumes of poetry (written as Jones) were *Preface to a Twenty
Volume Suicide Note* (1961) and *The Dead Lecturer* (1964). Later in his career, he
was to look back at those earlier poems as symptomatic not of personal disorders
but of a sick society. "You notice the preoccupation with death, with suicide. . . .
Always my own, caught up in the deathurge of the twisted society. The work a
cloud of abstraction and disjointedness, that was just whiteness. . . . There is a
spirituality always trying to get through, to triumph, to walk across those dead
bodies like stuntin for disciples, walking the water of dead bodies europeans call
their minds."

Looking back at his university and army experience, Baraka was to say: "The
Howard thing let me understand the Negro sickness. They teach you how to pretend to be white. But the Air Force made me understand the white sickness."

Feeling these pressures, Baraka became increasingly outspoken and separate
from the white literary circles of which he was an important part. In 1958 with his
first wife, who was white, he had started *Yugen* magazine and then the Totem
Press, printing work by poets such as Charles Olson, Robert Duncan, Gary Snyder,
and Frank O'Hara. But in a series of influential plays in the mid-1960s, Baraka
turned to explore the violent bases of relationships between blacks and whites. In
*Dutchman* (1964), an encounter involving a young black and a white woman in a
subway ends in the gratuitous murder of the black.

In his book reviews, Baraka became strongly critical of what he called "The
Myth of a Negro Literature." He claimed that most African-American literature
was mediocre because "most of the Negroes who've found themselves in a position
to become writers were middle-class Negroes who thought of literature as a way of
proving they were not 'inferior' (and quite a few who wanted to prove they were)."

The answer was to move out of the range of white literary institutions. He first
went to Harlem and began the Black Arts Repertory Theater. Then the focus of
his activities became avowedly social and political. In 1966 he set up Spirit House
in Newark. Baraka was involved in the Newark riots in the summer of 1967 and,
after appealing a stiff sentence, acquitted of carrying a concealed weapon. His book
of poems *Black Magic* (1969) marked a real point of departure in his writings. The
titles of its three sections tell a great deal about its concerns: Sabotage, Target

Study, and Black Art. "We want a black poem. And a / Black World. / Let all the world be a Black Poem," he says at the conclusion of *Black Art*, "And Let All Black People Speak This Poem / Silently / or LOUD." The capital letters suggest how strongly the poems have moved toward chant, oral presentation, and political rallying. Having taken a Muslim name, Imamu Amiri Baraka (he would later drop the religious title Imamu), Baraka helped found in 1968 the Black Community Development and Defense Organization, an enclave in Newark that has remained strongly separatist and politically and economically radical.

## An Agony. As Now.

I am inside someone
who hates me. I look
out from his eyes. Smell
what fouled tunes come in
to his breath. Love his            5
wretched women.

Slits in the metal, for sun. Where
my eyes sit turning, at the cool air
the glance of light, or hard flesh
rubbed against me, a woman, a man,      10
without shadow, or voice, or meaning.

This is the enclosure (flesh,
where innocence is a weapon. An
abstraction. Touch. (Not mine,
Or yours, if you are the soul I had      15
and abandoned when I was blind and had
my enemies carry me as a dead man
(if he is beautiful, or pitied.

It can be pain. (As now, as all his
flesh hurts me.) It can be that. Or      20
pain. As when she ran from me into
that forest.
          Or pain, the mind
silver spiraled whirled against the
sun, higher than even old men thought      25
God would be. Or pain. And the other. The
*yes*. (Inside his books, his fingers. They
are withered yellow flowers and were never
beautiful.) The yes. You will, lost soul, say
'beauty.' Beauty, practiced, as the tree. The      30
slow river. A white sun in its wet sentences.

Or, the cold men in their gale. Ecstasy. Flesh
or soul. The yes. (Their robes blown. Their bowls
empty. They chant at my heels, not at yours.) Flesh
or soul, as corrupt. Where the answer moves too quickly.      35
Where the God is a self, after all.)

Cold air blown through narrow blind eyes. Flesh,
white hot metal. Glows as the day with its sun.
It is a human love, I live inside. A bony skeleton
you recognize as words or simple feeling.                    40

But it has no feeling. As the metal, is hot, it is not,
given to love.

It burns the thing
inside it. And that thing
screams.                                                     45

1964


# A Poem for Willie Best[1]

### I

The face sings, alone
at the top
          of the body. All
flesh, all song, aligned. For hell
is silent, at those cracked lips                             5
flakes of skin and mind
twist and whistle softly
as they fall.
                    It was your own death
you saw. Your own face, stiff                               10
and raw. This
without sound, or
movement. Sweet afton, the
dead beggar bleeds
yet. His blood, for a time                                  15
alive, and huddled in a door
way, struggling to sing. Rain
washes it into cracks. Pits
whose bottoms are famous. Whose sides
are innocent broadcasts                                     20
of another life.


### II

At this point, neither
front nor back. A point, the
dimensionless line. The top
of a head, seen from Christ's                               25
heaven, stripped of history
or desire.
          Fixed, perpendicular
to shadow. (Even speech, vertical,

---

1. "Willie Best was a negro character actor whose Hollywood name was Sleep'n'eat" [Baraka's note].

leaves no trace. Born in to death                                      30
held fast to it, where
the lover spreads his arms, the line
he makes to threaten Gods with history.
The fingers stretch to emptiness. At
each point, after flesh, even light                                    35
is speculation. But an end, his end,
failing a beginning.


2

A cross. The gesture, symbol, line
arms held stiff, nailed stiff, with
no sign, of what gave them strength.                                   40
The point, become a line, a cross, or
the man, and his material, driven in
the ground. If the head rolls back
and the mouth opens, screamed into
existence, there will be perhaps                                       45
only the slightest hint of movement—
a smear; no help will come. No one
will turn to that station again.


III

At a cross roads, sits the
player. No drum, no umbrella, even                                     50
though it's raining. Again, and we
are somehow less miserable because
here is a hero, used to being wet.
One road is where you are standing now
(reading this, the other, crosses then                                55
rushes into a wood.
                      5 lbs neckbones.
                      5 lbs hog innards.
                      10 bottles cheap wine.
                                        (the contents               60
of a paper bag, also shoes, with holes
for the big toe, and several rusted
knives. This is a literature, of
symbols. And it is his gift, as the
bag is.                                                                65
          (The contents
again, holy saviours,
                  300 men on horseback
                  75 bibles
                  the quietness                                        70
of a field. A rich
man, though wet through
by the rain.
          I said,

47 howitzers                                    75
7 polished horse jaws
a few trees being waved
softly back under
the black night
            All This should be              80
invested.


## IV

Where
ever,
      he has gone. Who ever
mourns                                          85
or sits silent
to remember

There is nothing of pity
here. Nothing
of sympathy.                                    90

## V

This is the dance of the raised
leg. Of the hand on the knee
quickly.
            As a dance it punishes
speech. 'The house burned. The         95
old man killed.'
            As a dance it
is obscure.

## VI

This is the song
of the highest C.                               100
            The falsetto. An elegance
that punishes silence. This is the song
of the toes pointed inward, the arms swung, the
hips, moved, for fucking, slow, from side
to side. He is quote                            105
saying, "My father was
never a jockey,
            but
                  he did teach me
                    how to ride."              110

## VII

The balance.
            (Rushed in, swarmed of dark, cloaks,
and only red lights pushed a message

to the street. Rub.
            This is the lady,               115
I saw you with.
This is your mother.
This is the lady I wanted
some how to sleep with.
                As a dance, or            120
our elegant song. Sun red and grown
from trees, fences, mud roads in dried out
river beds. This is for me, with no God
but what is given. Give me
                  Something more      125
than what is here. I must tell you
my body hurts.

The balance.
            Can you hear? Here
I am again. Your boy, dynamite. Can       130
you hear? My soul is moved. The soul
you gave me. I say, my soul, and it
is moved. That soul
you gave me.
            Yes, I'm sure        135
this is the lady. You
slept with her. Witness, your boy,
here, dynamite. Hear?
                I mean
can you?                        140

The balance.
            He was tired of losing. (And
his walking buddies tired
of walking.
            Bent slightly,        145
at the waist. Left hand low, to flick
quick showy jabs ala Sugar.[2] The right
cocked, to complete,
                any combination.
                      He was        150
tired of losing, but he was fighting
a big dumb "farmer."
                Such a blue bright
afternoon, and only a few hundred yards
from the beach. He said, I'm tired     155
of losing.
         "I *got* ta cut'cha."

## VIII

A renegade
behind the mask. And even

2. Sugar Ray Robinson, a boxer.

the mask, a renegade                                      160
disguise. Black skin
and hanging lip.
        Lazy
        Frightened
        Thieving                                 165
        Very potent sexually
        Scars
        Generally inferior
                (but natural
rhythms.                                                  170

His head is
at the window. The only
part
    that sings.

(The word he used                                         175
        (we are passing St. Mark's place
        and those crazy jews who fuck)
                to provoke
in neon, still useful
in the rain,                                              180
        to provoke
some meaning, where before
there was only hell. I said
silence, at his huddled blood.
        It is an obscene invention.            185
        A white sticky discharge.
        "Jism," in white chalk
        on the back of Angel's garage.
        Red jackets with the head of
           Hobbes[3] staring into space. "Jasm"   190
        the name the leader took, had it
        stenciled on his chest.
                And he sits
wet at the crossroads, remembering distinctly
each weightless face that eases by. (Sun at               195
the back door, and that hideous mindless grin.
              (Hear?

                          1964

---

3. Thomas Hobbes (1588–1679), English philosopher who believed a "social contract" was necessary between rulers and the ruled. Here he represents the Western, white, materialist tradition.

# MICHAEL S. HARPER

## b. 1938

"I've been listening to music all my life," Michael S. Harper has said, and his first book of poems, *Dear John, Dear Coltrane* (1970), took its title from his poem to the great American jazz saxophonist. Recalling Coltrane's life in his prose piece *Don't They Speak Jazz*, Harper tells this story: "Trane was searching for a particular tone on his horn; he had what we thought was a perfect embouchure, but his teeth hurt constantly, so he searched for the soft reed which would ease the pain. After searching for a year, each session killing his chops, he gave it up completely; there was no easy way to get that sound: play through the pain to *a love supreme.*" Playing through the pain is a part of what Harper brings to his poetry. Like the great blues singers and jazz musicians, his work celebrates life as song, especially as tragic song, full of losses and griefs, but song nevertheless. Sometimes the pain Harper sings through is personal, like the death of one of his sons in *Deathwatch* (he and his wife lost two of their infant sons shortly after birth), sometimes the pain belongs to family history (as in *Grandfather*). Sometimes it is the pain of history more generally, its violence and oppression.

History is Harper's second love as a poet, following right behind music. His poem for Coltrane, while dependent on the techniques of jazz and the blues, also reflects Harper's concern with an imaginative recovery of history, especially black history, in an America where (as he once put it) the "amnesia level" is high. "I think the important thing about Americans is that they're not very good historians," Harper has said. "And Americans are really bad historians when it comes to moral ideas because they can't keep them in their heads very long." For Harper, to be a poet is to be a good historian; history identifies and inscribes moral issues that continue to engage us in the present. In college, Harper has recalled, he read William Carlos Williams's *In the American Grain* (1925), in which Williams announces that "History for us begins with murder and enslavement, not with discovery." Like Williams, Harper wants to bring his personal imagination in contact with an American history (black and white) essentially tragic, tragic because, he says, "so many possibilities exist and there's been so much waste." This tragic sense informs Harper's work perhaps most clearly in his volume *Nightmare Begins Responsibility* (1975)—the title is a variation on one of Yeats's epigraphs—where a personal sense of loss is never separable from the sufferings of black history or of human history more generally. His collections *Images of Kin* (1977) and *Healing Song for the Inner Ear* (1985) followed.

Born in Brooklyn, New York, Harper remembers a childhood in which "my parents weren't rich, but they had a good record collection." He grew up hearing the blues and jazz, but also reading the work of Langston Hughes, and later James Baldwin and Ralph Ellison, and his poetic technique owes something to his literary as well as to his musical sensibility. An additional resource was a family tradition of oral storytelling ("My people were good storytellers," he has said), out of which some of his poems have grown. In fact, the jazz techniques of variation on a theme, of improvisation around an existing form, recall traditions of oral storytelling, and both jazz and oral traditions influenced the formal experiments of an Ellison or a Baldwin. After high school, Harper took a B.A. and M.A. at what is now California State University, then went to the University of Iowa for an M.F.A. His travels abroad, first to Mexico and Europe, and later (1977) to South Africa, intensified his historical sense both of his own family roots and of their connection with racial history (a connection he probes in his poem *The Militance of a Photograph in the Passbook of a Bantu under Detention*). Since 1970 he has been at

Brown University, where he is professor of English and director of the writing program.

"Most great art is finally testamental," Harper has written; "its technical brilliance never shadows the content of the song." Harper writes poems to remember and to witness, but at times the urgency of the content overpowers his form and his language cannot sustain the urgency the poem asserts. This may be the cost for a poet whose engagement with moral issues, whose deep historical sense, and whose rhythmic inventiveness make him capable of creating powerful and moving poems. His finest work is possessed of what he admires in Coltrane: "the energy and passion with which he approached his instrument and music," resembling the energy it takes "to break oppressive conditions, oppressive musical structures and oppressive societal structures." Harper's inclusive sense of history lets him write (in *Blue Ruth: America*) that "*history is your own heartbeat*" but also lets him hear his own heart beat in time with those who lived in other times, other places. Responsible to memory, Harper also shares the affirmative impulse he finds in the blues: "the blues say 'Yes' to life no matter what it is. That doesn't mean you're going to survive it. But it means you're going to say yes to it."

# Dear John, Dear Coltrane[1]

> *a love supreme, a love supreme*
> *a love supreme, a love supreme*

Sex fingers toes
in the marketplace
near your father's church
in Hamlet, North Carolina[2]—
witness to this love                                         5
in this calm fallow
of these minds,
there is no substitute for pain:
genitals gone or going,
seed burned out,                                            10
you tuck the roots in the earth,
turn back, and move
by river through the swamps,
singing: *a love supreme, a love supreme;*
what does it all mean?                                      15
Loss, so great each black
woman expects your failure
in mute change, the seed gone.
You plod up into the electric city—
your song now crystal and                                   20
the blues. You pick up the horn
with some will and blow
into the freezing night:
*a love supreme, a love supreme—*

Dawn comes and you cook                                     25
up the thick sin 'tween
impotence and death, fuel

---

1. John Coltrane (1926–1967), avant-garde jazz musi-    2. Coltrane's birthplace.
cian. The epigraph is the title of one of his songs.

the tenor sax cannibal
heart, genitals and sweat
that makes you clean—                                                30
*a love supreme, a love supreme—*

*Why you so black?*
*cause I am*
*why you so funky?*
*cause I am*                                                        35
*why you so black?*
*cause I am*
*why you so sweet?*
*cause I am*
*why you so black?*                                                 40
*cause I am*
*a love supreme, a love supreme:*

So sick
you couldn't play *Naima,*[3]
so flat we ached                                                   45
for song you'd concealed
with your own blood,
your diseased liver gave
out its purity,
the inflated heart                                                 50
pumps out, the tenor[4] kiss,
tenor love:
*a love supreme, a love supreme—*
*a love supreme, a love supreme—*

1970

# American History

## *for John Callahan*

Those four black girls blown up
in that Alabama church[1]
remind me of five hundred
middle passage blacks,[2]
in a net, under water                                               5
in Charleston harbor
so    *redcoats*[3]   wouldn't   find
them.
Can't find what you can't see
can you?

1970

3. Another song that Coltrane made famous.
4. Perhaps an allusion to the tenor saxophone, Coltrane's instrument.
1. By white racists as a reprisal against civil rights demonstrations.

2. Captured, and en route from Africa (along the "Middle Passage," the usual route for slave ships) to be sold as slaves.
3. I.e., British soldiers.

# Deathwatch

Twitching in the cactus
hospital gown, a loon
on hairpin wings,
she tells me how
her episiotomy[1]                                                     5
is perfectly sewn
and doesn't hurt
while she sits in a pile
of blood
which once cleaned                                                   10
the placenta
my third son should be in.
She tells me how early
he is, and how strong,
like his father,                                                     15
and long, like a black-
stemmed Easter rose
in a white hand.

Just under five pounds
you lie there, a collapsed                                           20
balloon doll, burst in your
fifteenth hour, with the face
of your black father,
his fingers, his toes,
and eight voodoo                                                     25
adrenalin holes in
your pinwheeled hair-lined
chest; you witness
your parents sign the autopsy
and disposal papers                                                  30
shrunken to duplicate
in black ink
on white paper
like the country
you were born in,                                                    35
unreal, asleep,
silent, almost alive.

This is a dedication
to our memory
of three sons—                                                       40
two dead, one alive—
a reminder of a letter
to DuBois[2]
from a student
at Cornell—on behalf                                                 45

---

1. Surgical enlargement of the vulval opening at
childbirth.

2. W. E. B. Du Bois (1868–1963), African-American
leader.

of his whole history class.
The class is confronted
with a question,
and no one—
not even the professor— 50
is sure of the answer:
"Will you please tell us
whether or not it is true
that negroes
are not able to cry?" 55

America needs a killing.
America needs a killing.
*Survivors will be human.*

1970

## Martin's[1] Blues

He came apart in the open,
the slow motion cameras
falling quickly
neither alive nor kicking;
stone blind dead 5
on the balcony
that old melody
etched his black lips
in a pruned echo:
*We shall overcome*[2]
*some day*— 10

Yes we did!
Yes we did!

1971

## Nightmare Begins Responsibility[1]

I place these numbed wrists to the pane
watching white uniforms whisk over
him in the tube-kept
prison
fear what they will do in experiment 5
watch my gloved stickshifting gasolined hands
breathe *boxcar-information-please* infirmary tubes
distrusting white-pink mending paperthin

---

1. Martin Luther King, Jr., American civil rights
leader, was assassinated in 1968 on a motel balcony.
2. Hymn made famous by King's followers.
1. Cf. the title of a book by the American poet Delmore Schwartz, *In Dreams Begin Responsibilities*
(1938); Schwartz took the title from a line in the Irish
poet William Butler Yeats's *Responsibilities* (1913).

silkened end hairs, distrusting tubes
shrunk in his *trunk-skincapped*           10
shaven head, in thighs
*distrusting-white-hands-picking-baboon-light*
on this son who will not make his second night
of this wardstrewn intensive airpocket
where his father's asthmatic           15
hymns of *night-train*, train done gone
his mother can only know that he has flown
up into essential calm unseen corridor
going boxscarred home, *mamaborn, sweetsonchild*
*gonedowntown* into *researchtestingwarehousebatteryacid*     20
*mama-son-done-gone* / me telling her 'nother
train tonight, no music, no breathstroked
heartbeat in my infinite distrust of them:

and of my distrusting self
*white-doctor-who-breathed-for-him-all-night*       25
say it for two sons gone,
say nightmare, say it loud
panebreaking heartmadness:
nightmare begins responsibility.

1975

---

# SIMON J. ORTIZ
## b. 1941

In his poem *A Designated National Park*, Simon Ortiz tells of visiting Montezuma Castle in Verde Valley, Arizona, where he experiences as present in himself the life of the people there: "Hear / in my cave, sacred song. / Morning feeling, sacred song. / We shall plant today." His connection to that landscape, however, is complicated by the fact that it is now a "DESIGNATED FEDERAL RECRE- ATION FEE AREA": "This morning / I have to buy a permit to get back home." Ortiz's treatment of Verde Valley is characteristic of the way he inhabits a con- flicted landscape. He was born and raised in the Acoma Pueblo Community in Albuquerque, New Mexico. One meaning for the name *Acoma* is "the place that always was," and in this sense, it transcends the poet's personal place of origin and represents for him the Native American way of life. Ortiz continually returns to this abiding sense of origin after traveling great distances away from it. Often his poems enact a journey, and as Joseph Bruhac reminds us, in American Indian cultures the theme of traveling implicitly recalls the "tragic epic movements of Native American nations." Many of his poems dramatize Ortiz's disorientation as he moves within an America where Indian names are reduced to billboard signs, where rivers burn from industrial wastes and construction fills up the spaces of the earth. His sense of contemporary life, especially its absurdities, is acute.

But the America he travels conceals within it an older landscape, one animated by spirit, where the earth is alive with "wind visions" and "The Mountains dream / about pine brothers and friends" (*Vision Shadows*); to travel it is to seek "the center of the center" (*Between Albuquerque and Santa Fe*), the place where the spirits enter the world. Asked in an interview, "Why do you write?" Ortiz once responded, "Because Indians always tell a story. . . . The only way to continue is to tell a story and there is no other way. Your children will not survive unless you tell something about them—how they were born, how they came to this certain place, how they continued." Tellingly, Ortiz chose to reprint these comments at the beginning of his collection A *Good Journey* (1977). The stories his poems narrate are evidence that the Native American way of life is continuous, despite all the forces that attempt to eradicate it. But his work also tells of the painful costs involved in survival.

Schooled within the Bureau of Indian Affairs on the Acoma Reservation, Ortiz later attended the University of New Mexico, and the University of Iowa, where he received an M.F.A. He has since taught at San Diego State University and the University of New Mexico. "I never decided to become a poet," Ortiz has said, suggesting that his relatives transmitted to him the power of words. "An old-man relative with a humpback used to come to our home when I was a child, and he would carry me on his back. He told me stories. . . . That contact must have contributed the language of myself." His father, a stonemason, carpenter, and woodcarver, would talk and sing as he worked. In A *Story of How a Wall Stands*, he remembers his father saying "Underneath / what looks like loose stone, / there is stone woven together." This sense of underlying connection is true of Ortiz's poetry as well, often at its finest when revealing how a moment or event fits into the ongoing cycles celebrated by ritual. His best poems are carefully made, sometimes surprising in the way the apparently loose details suddenly blaze into an arrangement. Characteristically, this happens through powerful repetitions culminating in the last movements of a poem, making Ortiz a writer whose work depends on rereading. His collection *Going for Rain* appeared in 1976; its poems sometimes show a writer whose strong feelings have not yet found a distinctive language or rhythm. His next book, *The Good Journey*, is more assured and its range, significantly broader. Since then he has published *From Sand Creek*, which won the 1982 Pushcart Prize, A *Poem Is a Journey* (1981), and an edition that collects earlier volumes together with new work, *Woven Stone* (1992). He has also published several works of fiction. Ortiz is a poet with a mission—continuance and preservation—and sometimes a didactic impulse shapes his work too rigidly. But his finest poems have a richness of experience and a vital, imaginative sense of the earth that refuses any single conceptual or moral frame.

A recurring image in several Ortiz poems is the "Wisconsin horse" he once saw standing "within a fence / / silent in the hot afternoon" while one mile away new construction was going on: "I tell the horse, / 'That's America building something' " (*The Wisconsin Horse*). The spirit of the horse, restrained by the chainlink fence and threatened by the approaching construction, suggests Ortiz's sense of constriction in the VA hospitals (his experience in one of these prompted his sequence *Poems from the Veterans Hospital*), as well as in small-town bars, in the Salvation Army store, or in the boundaries of the designated National Parks. Something threatens to break loose in these poems; feelings precariously held in check shake the formal structures. Other poems, like *Earth and Rain, the Plants & Sun*, have the freedom and buoyancy of the hawk's flight; the words move in a space that seems immense. Instead of explosive anger or despair, the tone of the poem is close to song or prayer. What is so moving in Simon Ortiz's work is that these voices are both his; together they suggest the fracture of identity and the possibility of reintegration.

# Earth and Rain, the Plants & Sun

Once near San Ysidro
on the way to Colorado,
I stopped and looked.

The sound of a meadowlark
through smell of fresh cut alfalfa.          5

Raho would say,
"Look, Dad." A hawk

sweeping
            its wings

clear through                                10
       the blue
of whole and pure
            the wind
                  the sky.

It is writhing                               15
overhead.
Hear. The Bringer.
            The Thunderer.

Sunlight falls
through cloud curtains,                      20
a straight bright shaft.

It falls,
       it falls,
       down
       to earth,                             25
a green plant.

Today, the Katzina[1] come.
The dancing prayers.
Many times, the Katzina.
The dancing prayers.                         30
It shall not end,
son, it will not end,
this love.

Again and again,
the earth is new again.                      35
They come, listen, listen.
Hold on to your mother's hand.
They come

---

1. Or "kachina," elaborately masked dancers at Southwest Indian ceremonies who impersonate deified ancestral
spirits.

O great joy, they come.
The plants with bells.                                    40
The stones with voices.
Listen, son, hold my hand.

                                                          1977


# Vision Shadows

Wind visions are honest.
Eagles clearly soar
into the craggy peaks
of the mind.
The mind is full                                          5
of sunprayer
and childlaughter.

The Mountains dream
about pine brothers and friends,
the mystic realm of boulders                              10
which shelter
rabbits, squirrels, wrens.
They believe in the power.
They also believe
in quick eagle death.                                     15

The eagle loops
into the wind power.
He can see a million miles
and more because of it.

All believe things                                        20
of origin and solitude.

          *But what has happened*
(I hear strange news from Wyoming
of thallium sulphate.[1] Ranchers
bearing arms in helicopters.)                             25
*to these visions?*
I hear foreign tremors.
Breath comes thin and shredded.
I hear the scabs of strange deaths
falling off.                                              30

Snake hurries through the grass.
Coyote is befuddled by his own tricks.
And Bear whimpers pain into the wind.

Poisonous fumes cross our sacred paths.
The wind is still.                                        35

---

1. A chemical used by farmers as a rat poison.

O Blue Sky, O Mountain, O Spirit, O
what has stopped?

Eagles tumble dumbly into shadows
that swallow them with dull thuds.
The sage can't breathe.                                          40
Jackrabbit is lonely and alone
with eagle gone.

It is painful, aiiee, without visions
to soothe dry whimpers
or repair the flight of eagle, our own brother.                  45

1977


## *From* Poems from the Veterans Hospital

### 8:50 AM Ft. Lyons VAH

The Wisconsin Horse[1] hears the geese.

They wheel from the west.
First the unfamiliar sounds,
and then the memory recalls
ancient songs.                                                    5

Sky is gray and thick.
Sometimes it is the horizon
and the sky weighs less.

The Wisconsin Horse cranes
his neck.                                                         10
The geese veer
out of sight
past the edge of a building.

The building is not old,
built in 1937.                                                    15
Contains men broken
from three American wars.

Less and less, the sound,
and it becomes
the immense sky.                                                  20

1977

---

1. See headnote "Simon J. Ortiz" (p. 2635).

## *From* From Sand Creek

At the Salvation Army
a clerk
caught me
wandering
among old spoons                                        5
        and knives,
        sweaters and shoes.

I couldn't have stolen anything;
my life was stolen already.

In protest though,                                      10
I should have stolen.
My life. My life.

She caught me;
Carson[1] caught Indians,
secured them with his lies.                              15
Bound them with his belief.

After winter,
our own lives fled.

I reassured her
what she believed.                                      20
Bought a sweater.

And fled.

I should have stolen.
My life. My life.

                                                1981

---

1. Christopher ("Kit") Carson (1809–1868), Indian agent who killed many Native Americans.

---

# RITA DOVE
## b. 1952

What she has called the "friction" between the beauty of a poetic form and a difficult or painful subject appeals to Rita Dove. Her own formal control and discipline create a beautiful design and a haunting music in *Parsley*, a poem based on a murderous event: in 1957 the dictator of the Dominican Republic, Rafael Trujillo, ordered twenty thousand black Haitians killed because they could not pronounce the letter "r" in the Spanish word for parsley. What compels Dove in this poem is the way a "single, beautiful word" has the power of life and death. More astonishing is that she writes from the perspective of both the Haitians in the cane fields and General Trujillo in his palace. When asked in an interview about her capacity to imagine Trujillo, Dove responded, "I frankly don't believe anyone who says they've never felt any evil, that they cannot understand that process of evil. It was important to me to try to understand that arbitrary quality of his cruelty. . . . Making us get into his head may shock us all into seeing what the human being is capable of, because if we can go that far into his head, we're halfway there ourselves." An ability to enter into different points of view in a single poem is characteristic of Dove's disinterested imagination. Her method is to avoid commentary, to let the imagined person or object, the suggestive detail, speak for itself. Often her work suggests what Keats called "negative capability," the gift of the poet to become what he or she is not.

Born in Akron, Dove attended Miami University of Ohio and, after her graduation, studied modern European literature as a Fulbright/Hays fellow at the University of Tübingen in Germany. When she returned from Europe she took an M.F.A. at the University of Iowa (in 1977). Later she taught creative writing at Arizona State University before joining the University of Virginia, where she is now Commonwealth Professor of English. Over the past two decades since her Fulbright year she has also returned to live abroad frequently, in Ireland, Israel, France, and especially Germany. Her travel in Europe and elsewhere suggests part of the imperative she feels as a poet: to range widely through fields of experience, to cross boundaries of space as well as time. Her first book, *The Yellow House on the Corner* (1980), is notable for its intense poems about adolescence; her second book, *Museum* (1983), dramatically extends the range of her work. "When I started *Museum*," she has said, "I was in Europe, and I had a way of looking back on America and distancing myself from my experience." As well as several fine poems about her father (a subject that may also have needed distance), the book is remarkable for the way distance allowed Dove to move out of her immediate experience, freed her to imagine widely different lives.

As if to show that it is also possible to travel widely while staying at home, Dove's *Thomas and Beulah* (1986) is an extended sequence based on her grandparents' lives. Her continuing fascination with imagining different perspectives on the same event is evident in this sequence. Dove herself has described the origins of the book this way:

> My grandmother had told me a story that had happened to my grandfather when he was young, coming up on a riverboat to Akron, Ohio, my hometown. But that was all I had basically. And the story so fascinated me that I tried to write about it. I started off writing stories about my grandfather and soon, because I ran out of real fact, in order to keep going, I made up facts for this character, Thomas. . . . then this poem "Dusting" appeared, really out of nowhere. I didn't realize this was Thomas's wife saying, "I want to talk. And you can't do his side without my side . . ."

This is the story, in part, of a marriage and of a black couple's life in the industrial Midwest in the period from 1900 to 1960. Thomas's point of view controls the poems of the book's first section, while the second part imagines his wife's. The larger framework of the sequence links family history to social history. Thomas's journey from the rural South to the industrial city of Akron (where he finds employment in the Goodyear Zeppelin factory until the Depression puts him out of work) is part of the larger social movement of southern African-Americans into northern industrial cities in the first part of this century. The individual lyrics of Dove's sequence create and sustain the story through distinct and often ordinary moments in which each life is vividly portrayed. It is part of Dove's gift that she can render the apparently unimportant moments that inform a life and set them against a background of larger historical forces, as do Robert Hayden in *Elegies for Paradise Valley* and Robert Lowell in *Notebook*.

Many of the figures in Dove's poems are displaced, on the border between different worlds: for example, Thomas and Beulah and Benjamin Banneker (*Banneker*). The experience of displacement, of what she has called living in "two different worlds, seeing things with double vision," consistently compels this poet's imagination. It takes both detachment and control to maintain (and to live with) such doubleness. This may be why Dove's rich sense of language and her love of sound are joined to a disciplined formal sense. The form of her poems often holds in place difficult or ambiguous feelings, and keeps the expression of feeling understated. While restraint is one of the strengths of Dove's poems, her work can sometimes seem austere. She is perhaps too careful not to risk excess. Such careful control recalls Elizabeth Bishop's early work, also highly controlled and even, at times, guarded. As Bishop grew to relax her restraints, to open into an extraordinary expressiveness, so Dove, now only in her early forties, has gifts to suggest a similar growth, and her most recent collection, *Grace Notes* (1989), suggests just such a relaxing of the poet's guard. The evidence so far is that with each book she asks something more from herself, and there is every reason to believe she will become one of our indispensable poets. Dove was named U.S. poet laureate in 1993.

# Banneker[1]

What did he do except lie
under a pear tree, wrapped in
a great cloak, and meditate
on the heavenly bodies?
*Venerable*, the good people of Baltimore          5
whispered, shocked and more than
a little afraid. After all it was said
he took to strong drink.
Why else would he stay out
under the stars all night          10
and why hadn't he married?

But who would want him! Neither
Ethiopian nor English, neither
lucky nor crazy, a capacious bird
humming as he penned in his mind          15
another enflamed letter
to President Jefferson[2]—he imagined
the reply, polite and rhetorical.
Those who had been to Philadelphia
reported the statue          20
of Benjamin Franklin
before the library

his very size and likeness.
A wife? No, thank you.

---

1. "Benjamin Banneker (1731–1806), first black man to devise an almanac and predict a solar eclipse accurately, was also appointed to the commission that surveyed and laid out what is now Washington, D.C." [Dove's note].

2. After hearing that Jefferson doubted the mental capacity of black people, Banneker wrote him a letter that invoked ideals of human equality and asked for Jefferson's help in the abolition of slavery.

At dawn he milked                               25
the cows, then went inside
and put on a pot to stew
while he slept. The clock
he whittled as a boy
still ran.[3] Neighbors                          30
woke him up
with warm bread and quilts.
At nightfall he took out

his rifle—a white-maned
figure stalking the darkened                     35
breast of the Union—and
shot at the stars, and by chance
one went out. Had he killed?
*I assure thee, my dear Sir!*
Lowering his eyes to fields                      40
sweet with the rot of spring, he could see
a government's domed city
rising from the morass and spreading
in a spiral of lights. . . .

1983

# Parsley[1]

## 1. The Cane[2] Fields

There is a parrot imitating spring
in the palace, its feathers parsley green.
Out of the swamp the cane appears

to haunt us, and we cut it down. El General
searches for a word; he is all the world          5
there is. Like a parrot imitating spring,

we lie down screaming as rain punches through
and we come up green. We cannot speak an R—
out of the swamp, the cane appears

and then the mountain we call in whispers *Katalina*.[3]    10
The children gnaw their teeth to arrowheads.
There is a parrot imitating spring.

El General has found his word: *perejil*.
Who says it, lives. He laughs, teeth shining
out of the swamp. The cane appears                15

---

3. The first all-wood clock ever made in America, which Banneker carved as an experiment after studying only a common pocketwatch.
1. "On October 2, 1937, Rafael Trujillo (1891–1961), dictator of the Dominican Republic, ordered 20,000 blacks killed because they could not pronounce the letter 'r' in *perejil*, the Spanish word for parsley" [Dove's note].
2. I.e., sugar cane.
3. Katarina (because "we cannot speak an R").

in our dreams, lashed by wind and streaming.
And we lie down. For every drop of blood
there is a parrot imitating spring.
Out of the swamp the cane appears.

2. *The Palace*

The word the general's chosen is parsley.                                    20
It is fall, when thoughts turn
to love and death; the general thinks
of his mother, how she died in the fall
and he planted her walking cane at the grave
and it flowered, each spring stolidly forming                                25
four-star blossoms. The general

pulls on his boots, he stomps to
her room in the palace, the one without
curtains, the one with a parrot
in a brass ring. As he paces he wonders                                      30
Who can I kill today. And for a moment
the little knot of screams
is still. The parrot, who has traveled

all the way from Australia in an ivory
cage, is, coy as a widow, practising                                         35
spring. Ever since the morning
his mother collapsed in the kitchen
while baking skull-shaped candies
for the Day of the Dead,[4] the general
has hated sweets. He orders pastries                                         40
brought up for the bird; they arrive

dusted with sugar on a bed of lace.
The knot in his throat starts to twitch;
he sees his boots the first day in battle
splashed with mud and urine                                                  45
as a soldier falls at his feet amazed—
how stupid he looked!—at the sound
of artillery. *I never thought it would sing*
the soldier said, and died. Now

the general sees the fields of sugar                                         50
cane, lashed by rain and streaming.
He sees his mother's smile, the teeth
gnawed to arrowheads. He hears
the Haitians sing without R's
as they swing the great machetes:                                           55
*Katalina*, they sing, *Katalina*,

*mi madle, mi amol en muelte.*[5] God knows
his mother was no stupid woman; she

4. Corpus Christi ("Body of Christ"), a Roman Catho-        5. I.e., *mi madre, mi amor en muerte*, "my mother,
lic festival.                                               my love in death."

could roll an R like a queen. Even
a parrot can roll an R! In the bare room                              60
the bright feathers arch in a parody
of greenery, as the last pale crumbs
disappear under the blackened tongue. Someone

calls out his name in a voice
so like his mother's, a startled tear                              65
splashes the tip of his right boot.
*My mother, my love in death.*
The general remembers the tiny green sprigs
men of his village wore in their capes
to honor the birth of a son. He will                              70
order many, this time, to be killed

for a single, beautiful word.

1983

## FROM THOMAS AND BEULAH[1]

### The Event

Ever since they'd left the Tennessee ridge
with nothing to boast of
but good looks and a mandolin,

the two Negroes leaning
on the rail of a riverboat                              5
were inseparable: Lem plucked

to Thomas' silver falsetto.
But the night was hot and they were drunk.
They spat where the wheel

churned mud and moonlight,                              10
they called to the tarantulas
down among the bananas

to come out and dance.
*You're so fine and mighty; let's see
what you can do,* said Thomas, pointing                              15

to a tree-capped island.
Lem stripped, spoke easy: *Them's chestnuts,
I believe.* Dove

---

1. The story in this sequence of poems begins with
Thomas as he makes his way north to Akron, Ohio.
He loses his best friend, who, on a drunken dare from
Thomas, drowns, leaving his mandolin behind.
Thomas carries the mandolin with him and eventually
hangs it on his parlor wall. He and Beulah marry when
he is twenty-four and she is twenty; they have four
daughters. Thomas works at the Goodyear Zeppelin
factory (a zeppelin is a cylindrical airship kept aloft by
gas). The Depression puts him out of work, so he
sweeps offices for a living until Goodyear rehires him
at the advent of World War II. Beulah works in a dress
shop and later makes hats. Thomas dies at sixty-three
from his second heart attack; Beulah dies six years later.

quick as a gasp. Thomas, dry
on deck, saw the green crown shake                    20
as the island slipped

under, dissolved
in the thickening stream.
At his feet

a stinking circle of rags,                            25
the half-shell mandolin.
Where the wheel turned the water

gently shirred.[2]

                                                      1986

## Straw Hat

In the city, under the saw-toothed leaves of an oak
overlooking the tracks, he sits out
the last minutes before dawn, lucky
to sleep third shift. Years before
he was anything, he lay on                            5
so many kinds of grass, under stars,
the moon's bald eye opposing.

He used to sleep like a glass of water
held up in the hand of a very young girl.
Then he learned he wasn't perfect, that             10
no one was perfect. So he made his way
North under the bland roof of a tent
too small for even his lean body.

The mattress ticking he shares in the work barracks
is brown and smells                                  15
from the sweat of two other men.
One of them chews snuff:
he's never met either.
To him, work is a narrow grief
and the music afterwards                             20
is like a woman
reaching into his chest
to spread it around. When he sings

he closes his eyes.
He never knows when she'll be coming               25
but when she leaves, he always
tips his hat.

                                                      1986

2. Drew together.

## Dusting

Every day a wilderness—no
shade in sight. Beulah[1]
patient among knicknacks,
the solarium a rage
of light, a grainstorm      5
as her gray cloth brings
dark wood to life.

Under her hand scrolls
and crests gleam
darker still. What      10
was his name, that
silly boy at the fair with
the rifle booth? And his kiss and
the clear bowl with one bright
fish, rippling      15
wound!

Not Michael—
something finer. Each dust
stroke a deep breath and
the canary in bloom.      20
Wavery memory: home
from a dance, the front door
blown open and the parlor
in snow, she rushed
the bowl to the stove, watched      25
as the locket of ice
dissolved and he
swam free.

That was years before
Father gave her up      30
with her name, years before
her name grew to mean
Promise, then
Desert-in-Peace.
Long before the shadow and      35
sun's accomplice, the tree.

Maurice.

1986

## Poem in Which I Refuse Contemplation

A letter from my mother was waiting:
read in standing, one a.m.,
just arrived at my German mother-in-law

---

1. Hebrew for "married one" or "possessed." In the Bible it is used to refer to the Promised Land.

six hours from Paris by car.
Our daughter hops on Oma's bed,                                    5
happy to be back in a language

she knows. *Hello, all! Your postcard*
*came on the nineth*—familiar misspelled
words, exclamations. I wish my body

wouldn't cramp and leak; I want to—                                    10
as my daughter says, pretending to be
"Papa"—pull on boots and go for a long walk

alone. *Your cousin Ronnie in D.C.—*
*remember him?—he was the one*
*a few months younger than you—*                                    15

*was strangulated at some chili joint,*
*your Aunt May is beside herself!*
Mom skips to the garden which is

*producing—onions, swiss chard,*
*lettuce, lettuce, lettuce, turnip greens and more lettuce*                                    20
*so far! The roses are flurishing.*

Haven't I always hated gardening? And German,
with its patient, grunting building blocks,
and for that matter, English, too,

Americanese's chewy twang? *Raccoons*                                    25
*have taken up residence*
we were ten *in the crawl space*

but I can't feel his hand *who knows*
anymore *how we'll get them out?*
I'm still standing. Bags to unpack.                                    30

*That's all for now. Take care.*

                                                                1989

---

# ALBERTO RÍOS
## b. 1952

The poet Rita Dove once recalled in an interview W. E. B. Du Bois's remark on the "second sight that comes from having to live in two different cultures." As a Latino whose heritage includes Spanish and English, Alberto Ríos often writes poems possessed of literal second sight. His work gives us magical and poetic ways of understanding the world, like his grandmother's account of the nature of scorpions in *Advice to a First Cousin*, where a knowledge inaccessible in books is transmitted. "The way the world works is like this," the poem begins. In Ríos's best poems we feel both that anything can happen and that everything has happened before; we hear a particular voice whose rhythms recall stories passed from generation to generation.

Ríos has said of his background, "My father, born in southern Mexico, and my mother, born in England, gave me a language-rich, story-fat upbringing." He was born in Nogales, Arizona (on the border of Mexico), and earned an M.F.A. at the University of Arizona. He has worked on the Arizona Commission on the Arts and presently is on the faculty of Arizona State University in Tempe. His first book, *Whispering to Fool the Wind* (1982), won the Walt Whitman Award. He has since published *Five Indiscretions* (1985), *The Lime Orchard Women* (1989), and *Teodora Luna's Two Kisses* (1990). Not surprising for a poet with his gifts, he has also published a volume of fiction, *The Iguana Killer: Twelve Stories of the Heart* (1984). Ríos is a talented teller of stories, whose poems often suggest oral traditions, including Spanish ballads. For him, stories are forms of remembering and means of understanding; they honor the claims of dream and fact, past and present. Whether he is writing with humorous self-awareness about a childhood visit to a fortune-teller (*Madre Sofía*) or rendering the unbearable reality behind the newspaper accounts of those among the "disappeared" (in *Taking Away the Name of a Nephew*), the details of his poems accumulate to reveal a startling sense of the world. At times, however, the story the poem tells must overcome too predictable uses of the line. If Ríos's magical sense of the world sometimes yields too easily to the surreal, the pleasures of his poems often lie in their fluid movement between layers of reality, their deft integration of the factual and fantastic. Given Ríos's sense of the possibilities in language, the epigraph for his first book, taken from the Chilean poet Pablo Neruda, is especially fitting: "You see there are in our countries rivers which have no names, trees which nobody knows, and birds which nobody has described. . . . Our duty, then, as we understand it, is to express what is unheard of." Flavored with the music of Spanish and English, Ríos's poems create a new landscape: a contemporary America beneath which lives an older way of life, and the country of the imagination we discover in genuine poems.

# Madre Sofía[1]

My mother took me because she couldn't
wait the second ten years to know.
This was the lady rumored to have been
responsible for the box-wrapped baby
among the presents at that wedding,   5
but we went in, anyway, through the curtains.
Loose jar-top, half turned
and not caught properly in the threads
her head sat mimicking its original intention
like the smile of a child hitting himself.   10
Central in that head grew unfamiliar poppies
from a face mahogany, eyes half yellow
half gray at the same time, goat and fog,
slit eyes of the devil, his tweed suit, red
lips, and she smelled of smoke, cigarettes,   15
but a diamond smoke, somehow; I inhaled
sparkles, I could feel them, throat, stomach.
She did not speak, and as a child

---

1. Mother Sofia (Spanish). *Sofia* derives from the Greek word meaning "wisdom."

I could only answer, so that together
we were silent, cold and wet, dry and hard:
from behind my mother pushed me forward.
The lady put her hand on the face
of a thin animal wrap, tossing that head
behind her to be pressured incredibly
as she sat back in the huge chair and leaned.
And then I saw the breasts as large as her
head, folded together, coming out of her dress
as if it didn't fit, not like my mother's.
I could see them, how she kept them
penned up, leisurely, in maroon feed bags,
horse nuzzles of her wide body,
but exquisitely penned up
circled by pearl reins and red scarves.
She lifted her arm, but only with the tips
of her fingers motioned me to sit opposite.
She looked at me but spoke to my mother
words dark, smoky like the small room,
words coming like red ants stepping occasionally
from a hole on a summer day in the valley,
red ants from her mouth, her nose, her ears,
tears from the corners of her cinched eyes.
And suddenly she put her hand full on my head
pinching tight again with those finger tips
like a television healer, young Oral Roberts
half standing, quickly, half leaning
those breasts swinging toward me
so that I reach with both my hands to my lap
protecting instinctively whatever it is
that needs protection when a baseball is thrown
and you're not looking but someone yells,
the hand, then those breasts coming toward me
like the quarter-arms of the amputee Joaquín
who came back from the war to sit
in the park, reaching always for children
until one day he had to be held back.
I sat there, no breath, and could see only
hair around her left nipple, like a man.
Her clothes were old.
Accented, in a language whose spine had been
snapped, she whispered the words of a city
witch, and made me happy, alive like a man:
*The future will make you tall.*

1982

# Wet Camp

We have been here before, but we are lost.
The earth is black and the trees are bent
and broken and piled as if the game

of pick-up-sticks were ready and the children
hiding, waiting their useless turns.                                    5
The west bank of the river is burned
and the Santa Cruz[1] has poured onto it.
The grit brown ponds
sit like dirty lilies in the black.
The afternoon is gone grazing                                          10
over the thin mountains.
The night is colder here without leaves.
Nothing holds up the sky.

                                                                      1982


## Advice to a First Cousin

The way the world works is like this:
for the bite of scorpions, she says,
my grandmother to my first cousin,
because I might die and someone must know,
go to the animal jar                                                   5
the one with the soup of green herbs
mixed with the scorpions I have been putting in
still alive. Take one out
put it on the bite. It has had time to think
there with the others—put the lid back tight—                        10
and knows that a biting is not the way to win
a finger or a young girl's foot.
It will take back into itself the hurting
the redness and the itching and its marks.

But the world works like this, too:                                    15
look out for the next scorpion you see,
she says, and makes a big face to scare me
thereby instructing my cousin, look out!
for one of the scorpion's many
illegitimate and unhappy sons.                                         20
It will be smarter, more of the devil.
It will have lived longer than these dead ones.
It will know from them something more
about the world, in the way mothers know
when something happens to a child, or how                              25
I knew from your sadness you had been bitten.
It will learn something stronger than biting.
Look out most for that scorpion, she says,
making a big face to scare me again and it works
I go—crying—she lets me go—they laugh,                                30
the way you must look out for men
who have not yet bruised you.

                                                                      1985

1. River in southern Arizona.

# Seniors

William cut a hole in his Levi's pocket
so he could flop himself out in class
behind the girls so the other guys
could see and shit what guts we all said.
All Konga wanted to do over and over          5
was the rubber band trick, but he showed
everyone how, so nobody wanted to see
anymore and one day he cried, just cried
until his parents took him away forever.
Maya had a Hotpoint refrigerator standing          10
in his living room, just for his family to show
anybody who came that they could afford it.

Me, I got a French kiss, finally, in the catholic
darkness, my tongue's farthest half vacationing
loudly in another mouth like a man in Bermudas,          15
and my body jumped against a flagstone wall,
I could feel it through her thin, almost
nonexistent body: I had, at that moment, that moment,
a hot girl on a summer night, the best of all
the things we tried to do. Well, she          20
let me kiss her, anyway, all over.

Or it was just a flagstone wall
with a flaw in the stone, an understanding cavity
for burning young men with smooth dreams—
the true circumstance is gone, the true          25
circumstances about us all then
are gone. But when I kissed her, all water,
she would close her eyes, and they into somewhere
would disappear. Whether she was there
or not, I remember her, clearly, and she moves          30
around the room, sometimes, until I sleep.

I have lain on the desert in watch
low in the back of a pick-up truck
for nothing in particular, for stars, for
the things behind stars, and nothing comes          35
more than the moment: always now, here in a truck,
the moment again to dream of making love and sweat,
this time to a woman, or even to all of them
in some allowable way, to those boys, then,
who couldn't cry, to the girls before they were          40
women, to friends, me on my back, the sky over me
pressing its simple weight into her body
on me, into the bodies of them all, on me.

1985

# CATHY SONG
## b. 1955

In many of Cathy Song's poems, a particular moment or event becomes a window through which we enter a field of vision. "What frames the view," she has written, "is the mind in the diamond pinpoint light of concentration tunneling into memory, released by the imagination." As the title of her second book, *Frameless Windows, Squares of Light*, suggests, Song's poems capture the way a warm afternoon, a childhood Easter, a picnic in the park, are openings for memory and reflection. The visual quality of her poems can suggest a photograph or painting, and she herself feels a connection between her work and that of the Japanese printmaker Kitagawa Utamaro and the American painter Georgia O'Keeffe. Her first book, *Picture Bride* (1983), contains a number of poems inspired by the work of these artists. Writing, in *Beauty and Sadness*, of the way Utamaro's prints rendered "Teahouse waitresses, actresses, / geishas, courtesans and maids" in "their fleeting loveliness," Song suggests that the artist and poet capture the moment, knowing that it is always dissolving.

Song's first book was chosen by Richard Hugo for the Yale series of Younger Poets. In the title poem, *Picture Bride*, she comes as close as imagination allows to the experience of her grandmother, who, the poem implies, was chosen as a bride from a photograph, and summoned from Korea to Hawaii. But Song is also aware of the limits of imaginative identification and the difficulty of knowing the full truth of the past. She respects the mystery of another's identity. The grandmother in *Picture Bride*, the woman in *Lost Sister*, the mother in *Humble Jar*, and the geishas painted by Utamaro possess a privacy that the poet discloses but cannot fully enter. Song's tactful sense of both the power and the limits of imagination is one of her distinctive marks as a poet.

She was born in Honolulu, Hawaii, and grew up in Wahiawa, a small town on the island of Oahu. The setting of sugar cane fields, of island life where "the sound of the ocean / could be heard through the ironwoods" (*Waialaua*), and of the rain that comes "even when the sun was shining" (*A Pale Arrangement of Hands*), is central to her work. That landscape belongs to her present but also evokes her childhood and the memory of another, more distant landscape—the Asia of her ancestors. Many of Song's poems render the mysteries of what she has called "familial and personal ties; lives overlapping," and her sense of these ties extends backward to ancestors as well as forward to her own children. She began her college education at the University of Hawaii and then attended Wellesley College. After her graduation from Wellesley, she received an M.A. in creative writing from Boston University and has since taught creative writing at a number of colleges and universities.

Song's ability to write about her own or another's experience as an acute observer may have to do with her multicultural background, which often places her on the boundary of what she sees. Her capacity to let the power of observation give rise to feeling recalls at times the work of Elizabeth Bishop and also suggests Song's resemblance to the Utamaro of her poem *Beauty and Sadness*, whose "invisible presence / one feels in these prints." At other times Song writes about herself more directly. She has, for example, deftly rendered the erotic nature of her own experience: "But there is this slow arousal. / The small buttons / of my cotton blouse / are pulling away from my body" (*The White Porch*). The careful composition of her poems, with their vivid detail, blend the accidental and spontaneous quality of life with the design of art, like the Japanese floral arrangement she describes in her poem *Ikebana*. Although her work can sometimes seem too composed, too

removed from the sharp impact of experience, her strongest poems balance a sense
of tradition with a feel for contemporary life and catch in the patterns of art the
transient instant: "the flicker of a dragonfly's delicate wing."

## The White Porch

I wrap the blue towel
after washing,
around the damp
weight of hair, bulky
as a sleeping cat,                                                    5
and sit out on the porch.
Still dripping water,
it'll be dry by supper,
by the time the dust
settles off your shoes,                                              10
though it's only five
past noon. Think
of the luxury: how to use
the afternoon like the stretch
of lawn spread before me.                                           15
There's the laundry,
sun-warm clothes at twilight,
and the mountain of beans
in my lap. Each one,
I'll break and snap                                                 20
thoughtfully in half.

But there is this slow arousal.
The small buttons
of my cotton blouse
are pulling away from my body.                                      25
I feel the strain of threads,
the swollen magnolias
heavy as a flock of birds
in the tree. Already,
the orange sponge cake                                              30
is rising in the oven.
I know you'll say it makes
your mouth dry
and I'll watch you
drench your slice of it                                             35
in canned peaches
and lick the plate clean.

So much hair, my mother
used to say, grabbing
the thick braided rope                                              40
in her hands while we washed
the breakfast dishes, discussing
dresses and pastries.

My mind often elsewhere
as we did the morning chores together.                                    45
Sometimes, a few strands
would catch in her gold ring.
I worked hard then,
anticipating the hour
when I would let the rope down                                            50
at night, strips of sheets,
knotted and tied,
while she slept in tight blankets.
My hair, freshly washed
like a measure of wealth,                                                 55
like a bridal veil.
Crouching in the grass,
you would wait for the signal,
for the movement of curtains
before releasing yourself                                                 60
from the shadow of moths.
Cloth, hair and hands,
smuggling you in.

                                                                    1983


# Beauty and Sadness

### for Kitagawa Utamaro[1]

He drew hundreds of women
in studies unfolding
like flowers from a fan.
Teahouse waitresses, actresses,
geishas,[2] courtesans and maids.                                        5
They arranged themselves
before this quick, nimble man
whose invisible presence
one feels in these prints
is as delicate                                                           10
as the skinlike paper
he used to transfer
and retain their fleeting loveliness.

Crouching like cats,
they purred amid the layers of kimono[3]                                 15
swirling around them
as though they were bathing
in a mountain pool with irises
growing in the silken sunlit water.
Or poised like porcelain vases,                                          20

---

1. Japanese artist (1753–1806), who specialized in studies of sensuous and beautiful women.
2. Women trained to provide entertaining, light-hearted company for men.
3. Traditional Japanese robe with long sleeves.

slender, erect and tall; their heavy
brocaded hair was piled high
with sandalwood combs and blossom sprigs
poking out like antennae.
They resembled beautiful iridescent insects,                    25
creatures from a floating world.[4]

Utamaro absorbed these women of Edo[5]
in their moments of melancholy
as well as of beauty.
He captured the wisp of shadows,                                30
the half-draped body
emerging from a bath; whatever
skin was exposed
was powdered white as snow.
A private space disclosed.                                      35
Portraying another girl
catching a glimpse of her own vulnerable
face in the mirror, he transposed
the trembling plum lips
like a drop of blood                                            40
soaking up the white expanse of paper.

At times, indifferent to his inconsolable
eye, the women drifted
through the soft gray feathered light,
maintaining stillness, the moments in between.                  45
Like the dusty ash-winged moths
that cling to the screens in summer
and that the Japanese venerate
as ancestors reincarnated;
Utamaro graced these women with immortality                     50
in the thousand sheaves of prints
fluttering into the reverent hands of keepers:
the dwarfed and bespectacled painter
holding up to a square of sunlight
what he had carried home beneath his coat                       55
one afternoon in winter.

                                                        1983

## Lost Sister

### 1

In China,
even the peasants
named their first daughters
Jade—

---

4. The pictures "were called 'pictures of the floating
world' because of their preoccupation with the pleasures of the moment" [Song's note].
5. "Present-day Tokyo" [Song's note].

the stone that in the far fields                                            5
could moisten the dry season,
could make men move mountains
for the healing green of the inner hills
glistening like slices of winter melon.

And the daughters were grateful:                                          10
they never left home.
To move freely was a luxury
stolen from them at birth.
Instead, they gathered patience,
learning to walk in shoes                                                  15
the size of teacups,
without breaking—
the arc of their movements
as dormant as the rooted willow,
as redundant as the farmyard hens.                                        20
But they traveled far
in surviving,
learning to stretch the family rice,
to quiet the demons,
the noisy stomachs.                                                        25

2

There is a sister
across the ocean,
who relinquished her name,
diluting jade green
with the blue of the Pacific.                                             30
Rising with a tide of locusts,
she swarmed with others
to inundate another shore.
In America,
there are many roads                                                      35
and women can stride along with men.

But in another wilderness,
the possibilities,
the loneliness,
can strangulate like jungle vines.                                        40
The meager provisions and sentiments
of once belonging—
fermented roots, Mah-Jongg[1] tiles and firecrackers—
set but a flimsy household
in a forest of nightless cities.                                          45
A giant snake rattles above,
spewing black clouds into your kitchen.
Dough-faced landlords
slip in and out of your keyholes,

1. A game of Chinese origins.

making claims you don't understand,                                    50
tapping into your communication systems
of laundry lines and restaurant chains.

You find you need China:
your one fragile identification,
a jade link                                                            55
handcuffed to your wrist.
You remember your mother
who walked for centuries,
footless—
and like her,                                                          60
you have left no footprints,
but only because
there is an ocean in between,
the unremitting space of your rebellion.

                                                                    1983

# Heaven

He thinks when we die we'll go to China.
Think of it—a Chinese heaven
where, except for his blond hair,
the part that belongs to his father,
everyone will look like him.                                           5
China, that blue flower on the map,
bluer than the sea
his hand must span like a bridge
to reach it.
An octave away.                                                        10

I've never seen it.
It's as if I can't sing that far.
But look—
on the map, this black dot.
Here is where we live,                                                 15
on the pancake plains
just east of the Rockies,
on the other side of the clouds.
A mile above the sea,
the air is so thin, you can starve on it.                              20
No bamboo trees
but the alpine equivalent,
reedy aspen with light, fluttering leaves.
Did a boy in Guangzhou[1] dream of this
as his last stop?                                                      25

I've heard the trains at night
whistling past our yards,

1. Or Canton, seaport city in southeastern China.

what we've come to own,
the broken fences, the whiny dog, the rattletrap cars.
It's still the wild west,                                        30
mean and grubby,
the shootouts and fistfights in the back alley.
With my son the dreamer
and my daughter, who is too young to walk,
I've sat in this spot                                           35
and wondered why here?
Why in this short life,
this town, this creek they call a river?

He had never planned to stay,
the boy who helped to build                                     40
the railroads for a dollar a day.[2]
He had always meant to go back.
When did he finally know
that each mile of track led him further away,
that he would die in his sleep,                                 45
dispossessed,
having seen Gold Mountain,
the icy wind tunneling through it,
these landlocked, makeshift ghost towns?

It must be in the blood,                                        50
this notion of returning.
It skipped two generations, lay fallow,
the garden an unmarked grave.
On a spring sweater day
it's as if we remember him.                                     55
I call to the children.
We can see the mountains
shimmering blue above the air.
If you look really hard
says my son the dreamer,                                        60
leaning out from the laundry's rigging,
the work shirts fluttering like sails,
you can see all the way to heaven.

1988

2. The Chinese provided much of the cheap labor that laid the tracks of the transcontinental railroads in the
19th century.

---

# LI-YOUNG LEE
## b. 1957

In his poem *Persimmons* Li-Young Lee remembers his father saying, "Some things never leave a person." Many of the poems in Lee's two books, *Rose* (1986) and *The City in Which I Love You* (1990), testify to a sense of the past, especially his father's past, which never leaves Lee. The figure of the father in Lee's poems is both personal and mythic; it is he who instructs the poet-son in "the art of memory." Lee's father, born in China, served as a personal physician to Mao Tse-tung. He later was jailed for nineteen months, a political prisoner of the Indonesian dictator Sukarno. Lee was born in Jakarta, Indonesia. In 1959 the family fled Indonesia and traveled in the Far East (Hong Kong, Macao, and Japan), finally arriving in America, where Lee's father became a Presbyterian minister in a small town in western Pennsylvania. Many of Lee's poems seek to remember and understand his father's life and to come to terms with Lee's own differences from that powerful figure.

Lee's work reminds us of the ancient connections between the arts of memory and poetry. In his work, memory is often sweet; it draws the poet to the past even when, as in *Eating Alone*, that sweetness is as dizzying as the juice of a rotten pear in which a hornet spins. But memory can also be a burden, and its pull is countered in Lee's work by a sensuous apprehension of the present. As in his poem *This Room and Everything in It*, the erotic immediacy of the moment can disrupt any effort to fix that moment in the orders of memory. Everywhere in Lee's work is the evidence of all the senses: hearing, taste, smell, and touch as much as sight. If the poet's bodily presence in the world recalls Walt Whitman, Lee's fluid motion between the physical world and the domain of memory, dream, or vision also carries out Whitman's visionary strain and links Lee to the work of Theodore Roethke, James Wright, and Denise Levertov, among others. The intensity of Lee's poems, however, is often leavened by a subtle and winning humor and playfulness; such qualities are especially valuable in a poet at times too easily seduced by beauty.

Lee studied at the University of Pittsburgh (where one of his teachers was the poet Gerald Stern), the University of Arizona, and the State University of New York, College at Brockport. He has since taught at various universities. The links Lee makes between an individual life and a powerful past and his ability to work within registers ranging from plain speech to a lushness evocative of biblical language enrich contemporary American poetry.

# Persimmons

In sixth grade Mrs. Walker
slapped the back of my head
and made me stand in the corner
for not knowing the difference
between *persimmon* and *precision*.     5
How to choose

persimmons. This is precision.
Ripe ones are soft and brown-spotted.
Sniff the bottoms. The sweet one
will be fragrant. How to eat:     10
put the knife away, lay down newspaper.
Peel the skin tenderly, not to tear the meat.
Chew the skin, suck it,
and swallow. Now, eat
the meat of the fruit,     15
so sweet,
all of it, to the heart.

Donna undresses, her stomach is white.
In the yard, dewy and shivering
with crickets, we lie naked,                                    20
face-up, face-down.
I teach her Chinese.
Crickets:    *chiu chiu.* Dew:    I've forgotten.
Naked:    I've forgotten.
*Ni, wo:*    you and me.                                        25
I part her legs,
remember to tell her
she is beautiful as the moon.

Other words
that got me into trouble were                                   30
*fight* and *fright, wren* and *yarn.*
Fight was what I did when I was frightened,
fright was what I felt when I was fighting.
Wrens are small, plain birds,
yarn is what one knits with.                                    35
Wrens are soft as yarn.
My mother made birds out of yarn.
I loved to watch her tie the stuff;
a bird, a rabbit, a wee man.

Mrs. Walker brought a persimmon to class                        40
and cut it up
so everyone could taste
a *Chinese apple.* Knowing
it wasn't ripe or sweet, I didn't eat
but I watched the other faces.                                  45

My mother said every persimmon has a sun
inside, something golden, glowing,
warm as my face.

Once, in the cellar, I found two wrapped in newspaper,
forgotten and not yet ripe.                                     50
I took them and set both on my bedroom windowsill,
where each morning a cardinal
sang, *The sun, the sun.*

Finally understanding
he was going blind,                                             55
my father sat up all one night
waiting for a song, a ghost.
I gave him the persimmons,
swelled, heavy as sadness,
and sweet as love.                                              60

This year, in the muddy lighting
of my parents' cellar, I rummage, looking
for something I lost.

My father sits on the tired, wooden stairs,
black cane between his knees, 65
hand over hand, gripping the handle.

He's so happy that I've come home.
I ask how his eyes are, a stupid question.
*All gone,* he answers.

Under some blankets, I find a box. 70
Inside the box I find three scrolls.
I sit beside him and untie
three paintings by my father:
Hibiscus leaf and a white flower.
Two cats preening. 75
Two persimmons, so full they want to drop from the cloth.

He raises both hands to touch the cloth,
asks, *Which is this?*

*This is persimmons, Father.*

*Oh, the feel of the wolftail on the silk,* 80
*the strength, the tense*
*precision in the wrist.*
*I painted them hundreds of times*
*eyes closed. These I painted blind.*
*Some things never leave a person:* 85
*scent of the hair of one you love,*
*the texture of persimmons,*
*in your palm, the ripe weight.*

1986

## Eating Alone

I've pulled the last of the year's young onions.
The garden is bare now. The ground is cold,
brown and old. What is left of the day flames
in the maples at the corner of my
eye. I turn, a cardinal vanishes. 5
By the cellar door, I wash the onions,
then drink from the icy metal spigot.

Once, years back, I walked beside my father
among the windfall pears. I can't recall
our words. We may have strolled in silence. But 10
I still see him bend that way—left hand braced
on knee, creaky—to lift and hold to my
eye a rotten pear. In it, a hornet
spun crazily, glazed in slow, glistening juice.

It was my father I saw this morning                    15
waving to me from the trees. I almost
called to him, until I came close enough
to see the shovel, leaning where I had
left it, in the flickering, deep green shade.

White rice steaming, almost done. Sweet green peas      20
fried in onions. Shrimp braised in sesame
oil and garlic. And my own loneliness.
What more could I, a young man, want.

                                                    1986

## Eating Together

In the steamer is the trout
seasoned with slivers of ginger,
two sprigs of green onion, and sesame oil.
We shall eat it with rice for lunch,
brothers, sister, my mother who will                   5
taste the sweetest meat of the head,
holding it between her fingers
deftly, the way my father did
weeks ago. Then he lay down
to sleep like a snow-covered road                      10
winding through pines older than him,
without any travelers, and lonely for no one.

                                                    1986

## This Room and Everything in It

Lie still now
while I prepare for my future,
certain hard days ahead,
when I'll need what I know so clearly this moment.

I am making use                                        5
of the one thing I learned
of all the things my father tried to teach me:
the art of memory.

I am letting this room
and everything in it                                   10
stand for my ideas about love
and its difficulties.

I'll let your love-cries,
those spacious notes
of a moment ago,                                       15
stand for distance.

Your scent,
that scent
of spice and a wound,
I'll let stand for mystery.                                    20

Your sunken belly
is the daily cup
of milk I drank
as a boy before morning prayer.

The sun on the face                                           25
of the wall
is God, the face
I can't see, my soul,

and so on, each thing
standing for a separate idea,                                 30
and those ideas forming the constellation
of my greater idea.
And one day, when I need
to tell myself something intelligent
about love,                                                   35

I'll close my eyes
and recall this room and everything in it:
My body is estrangement.
This desire, perfection.
Your closed eyes my extinction.                               40
Now I've forgotten my
idea. The book
on the windowsill, riffled by wind . . .
the even-numbered pages are
the past, the odd-                                            45
numbered pages, the future.
The sun is
God, your body is milk . . .

useless, useless . . .
your cries are song, my body's not me . . .                   50
no good . . . my idea
has evaporated . . . your hair is time, your thighs are song . . .
it had something to do
with death . . . it had something
to do with love.                                              55

1990

# Selected Bibliographies

## LITERATURE TO 1620

Few major studies address the great body of writings produced in various European languages, or codified in Native American ones, in the period up to 1620; those that do concern themselves more with matters of context than with patterns of language. For the basic outline of European expansion westward, Samuel Eliot Morison's *The European Discovery of America*, 2 vols. (1971–74) is useful. For North America, David Beers Quinn's thorough *North America from Earliest Discovery to First Settlements* (1977) and his *England and the Discovery of America, 1481–1620* (1973) give detailed narrative and analysis, as does Gary Nash's *Red, White, and Black: The People of Early America* (1974). Edmundo O'Gorman's insightful *The Invention of America* (1961) shifts the discussion away from the geographical discoveries of Renaissance Europe and toward the cultural responses that those discoveries called forth, a theme followed out as well in J. H. Elliot's brief *The Old World and the New, 1492–1650* (1970) and in Stephen Greenblatt's *Marvelous Possessions: The Wonder of the New World* (1991). Roy Harvey Pearce's *Savagism and Civilization: A Study of the Indian and the American Mind* (1953; 1988) goes from 1609 to the mid-nineteenth century and serves as an indispensable starting point for the literary impact of the Native American on "the American mind." In a related vein, Alfred W. Crosby traces the biological exchanges between the hemispheres in his influential *The Columbian Exchange: Biological and Cultural Consequences of 1492* (1972), while Carl O. Sauer takes up the question of how the Caribbean was altered after 1492 in *The Early Spanish Main* (1966). A similar project is carried out for New England in William Cronon's excellent *Changes in the Land: Indians, Colonists, and the Ecology of New England* (1983); for the South, see Timothy Silver, *A New Face on the Countryside: Indians, Colonists, and Slaves in the South Atlantic Forests, 1500–1800* (1990).

Among books that deal with the verbal shape of the early documents, William Carlos Williams's *In the American Grain* (1925) gives brief but evocative guidance. Howard Mumford Jones places early American culture in the context of Renaissance Europe in *O Strange New World: American Culture, the Formative Years* (1964). In *The Machine in the Garden: Technology and the Pastoral Ideal in America* (1964), Leo Marx offers insightful readings of some Renaissance texts (such as Shakespeare's *The Tempest*) that reflect on the new lands suddenly opened to the Old World; responses to the New World (and a reading, again, of *The Tempest*) are considered in Eric Cheyfitz's *The Poetics of Imperialism: Translation and Colonization from "The Tempest" to "Tarzan"* (1991). A feminist perspective guides Annette Kolodny's *The Lay of the Land; Metaphor as Experience and History in American Life and Letters* (1975), and the opening chapters of Richard Drinnon's *Facing West: The Metaphysics of Indian-Hating and Empire-Building* (1980) offer a psychohistorical perspective. William C. Spengemann argues for the centrality of early American texts in the transformation of Western writing generally in *The Adventurous Muse: The Poetics of American Fiction, 1789–1900* (1977), John Seelye offers ingenious readings of many early texts in *Prophetic Waters: The River in Early American Life and Literature* (1977), and Wayne Franklin gives attention to sixteenth-century works in *Discoverers, Explorers, Settlers: The Diligent Writers of Early America* (1979). No generally inclusive bibliography of the literary texts of the period is available, although Joseph Sabin's massive *Biblioteca Americana: A Dictionary of Books Relating to America, from its Discovery to the Present Time*, 29 vols. (1868–1936) is invaluable. Among anthologies, the most useful are David Beers Quinn's *New American World: A Documentary History of North America to 1612*, 5 vols. (1979) and the modern editions of Richard Hakluyt's collection of 1598–1600, *The Principall Navigations, Voyages, Traffiques, & Discoveries of the English Nation*, 12 vols. (1903–1905) and Samuel Purchas's 1625 sequel to it, *Hakluytus Posthumus, or Purchas His Pilgrimes*, 20 vols. (1905–1907). The Hakluyt volumes also were reprinted in the Everyman's Library, 8 vols. (1907). A companion series to Quinn's is John H. Parry and Robert G. Keith, *New Iberian World: A Documentary History of the Discovery and Settlement of Latin America to the Early 17th Century*, 5 vols. (1984).

### Samuel de Champlain

The standard (bilingual) edition is *The Works of Samuel de Champlain*, 6 vols. (1922–36), edited by H. P. Biggar and others. A useful 1-vol. English version, edited by W. L. Grant in the *Original Narratives of Early American History* series, is *Voyages of Samuel de Champlain, 1604–1618* (1907). Samuel Eliot Morison's recent biography, *Samuel de Champlain: Father of New France* (1972) is useful.

## Christopher Columbus

Cecil Jane's *Select Documents Illustrating the Four Voyages of Columbus* (1930–33; 1988) is the best bilingual edition of various writings. It does not include the "journal" of the first voyage, which survives only in summaries and unreliable transcriptions by others. The best text of that problematic work is Oliver Dunn and James E. Kelley's bilingual *The Diario of Christopher Columbus's First Voyage to America, 1492–93* (1989); on the problems associated with this text (and others), see David Heninge's *In Search of Columbus: The Sources for the First Voyage* (1991). Biographies include Samuel Eliot Morison's now somewhat dated *Admiral of the Ocean Sea* (1942) and Kirkpatrick Sale's contentious *The Conquest of Paradise: Christopher Columbus and the Columbian Legacy* (1990). James Axtell's *After Columbus* (1988) and *Beyond 1492* (1992) offer excellent and broad coverage of key topics.

## Thomas Harriot

Muriel Rukeyser's *The Traces of Thomas Harriot* (1971) is an innovative biography. John W. Shirley's edited volume *Thomas Harriot, Renaissance Scientist* (1974) collects a number of modern studies. David Beers Quinn includes Harriot among his topics in *England and the Discovery of America, 1481–1620* (1974) and gives the best text of Harriot's *A Brief and True Report of the New Found Land of Virginia* in *The Roanoke Voyages, 1584–1590*, 2 vols. (1955; 1991). The collaborative edition of that work illustrated with engravings based on John White's drawings and watercolors has been reprinted (1972).

## Iroquois Creation Stories

First published in 1851, Lewis Henry Morgan's *League of the Iroquois* remains a fine overview and introduction (1972, with an introduction by William Fenton) to all things Iroquoian. Daniel K. Richter's *The Ordeal of the Longhouse: The Peoples of the Iroquois League in the Era of European Colonization* (1992) is a brilliant recent volume that covers the basic elements of Iroquois language, culture, and history and begins with a fine overview of Iroquois cosmogonic myths. It refers to and builds on the work of the leading specialist in Iroquois culture, William Fenton, whose "This Island, the World on the Turtle's Back," *Journal of American Folklore*, 75 (1962), 283–300, is probably still the richest analysis of Iroquois mythology available. For the most detailed versions of the stories themselves, the reader must consult J. N. B.

Hewitt's "Iroquoian Cosmology," part I, Bureau of American Ethnology, *Annual Report, 1899–1900* (1903) and "Iroquoian Cosmology," part II, Bureau of American Ethnology, *Annual Report, 1925–6* (1928). Also worth consulting is the Seneca ethnologist Arthur C. Parker's *Seneca Myths and Folk Tales*, Buffalo Historical Society Publications No. 27 (1923). In addition to these scholarly accounts, Edmund Wilson's meditation on the Iroquois, *Apologies to the Iroquois* (1960) remains fascinating. Also worth consulting is the work of the contemporary Abenaki poet and storyteller Joseph Bruchac, in particular his *Iroquois Stories: Heroes and Heroines, Monsters and Magic* (1985) and his edited volume, *New Voices from the Longhouse: An Anthology of Contemporary Iroquois Writing* (1989).

## Native American Oral Literature

A. Lavonne Brown Ruoff's *American Indian Literatures: An Introduction, Bibliographic Review, and Selected Bibliography* (1990) is a good sourcebook on oral literature, as is William M. Clements and Frances M. Malpezzi's *Native American Folklore, 1879–1979* (1984), which presents a useful bibliography for the study of many sorts of oral literature. Ruoff's "The Survival of Tradition: American Indian Oral and Written Narratives," *Massachusetts Review* (1986) begins by surveying Native American oral story and storytelling traditions. John Miles Foley, in *Oral Tradition in Literature: Interpretation in Context* (1986), offers six essays that deal with the aesthetics of oral and orally derived works. Although focused on the European oral tradition, the essays raise issues of concern for the study of American Indian oral literatures. Paula Gunn Allen has edited *Studies in Native American Literature: Critical Essays and Course Designs* (1983), which begins with a section on oral literature. The first two chapters of Andrew Wiget's *Native American Literature* (1985) also are valuable introductions to oral narrative and oratory and oral poetry. Karl Kroeber has edited *Traditional Literatures of the American Indian: Texts and Interpretations* (1981), which presents, as the title indicates, both texts and interpretations, the best of which are Dennis Tedlock's "The Spoken Word and the Work of Interpretation in American Indian Religion" and Barre Toelken and Tacheeni Scott's "Poetic Retranslation and the 'Pretty Languages' of Yellowman." Toelken transcribes another tale by the Navajo storyteller Yellowman in "Life and Death in the Navajo Coyote Tales," in *Recovering the Word: Essays on Native American Literatures*, edited by Brian Swann and Arnold Krupat (1987), the introduction to which is also useful. Swann's edited volume *On the Translation of Native American Literatures* (1992) contains several fine essays. Krupat has edited *New Voices in Native American Literary Criticism* (1993), which contains some of the most recent work on oral narrative both in

English and in native languages (see especially the essays by Geoffrey Kimball, Ridie Wilson Ghezzi, and Kathleen Danker).

**Álvar Núñez Cabeza de Vaca**
An excellent colloquial translation of *La Relacion* is Cyclone Covey's *Cabeza de Vaca's Adventures in the Unknown Interior of America* (1961; 1983). This relies on studies of Cabeza de Vaca's itinerary by Cleve Hallenbeck, *Álvar Núñez Cabeza de Vaca: The Journey and Route of the First European to Cross the Continent of North America, 1534–1536* (1940; 1971) and Carl O. Sauer, *Sixteenth-Century North America* (1971). Morris Bishop's *The Odyssey of Cabeza de Vaca* (1933) treats the whole of the life, including the later South American episodes. Cabeza de Vaca's Río de la Plata narrative, *Comentarios* (1555), was translated by Luis L. Dominguez in *The Conquest of the River Plate* (1891). A fictional account of Estevánico, the Moorish slave who was one of the four survivors of the Cabeza de Vaca party, is offered in Daniel Panger, *Black Ulysses* (1982). Interesting later notes on Cabeza de Vaca and Estevánico are to be found in the various narratives of the Coronado expedition collected in George Parker Winship and Frederick Webb Hodge, *The Journey of Francisco Vázquez de Coronado, 1540–1542* (1933; 1990).

**Pima Creation Stories**
Ruth M. Underhill's studies in the 1930s and 1940s of the Pima (and their close relatives the Tohono O'odham [Papago] are still useful for the student who would like to learn more about the history and culture of these Southwestern desert peoples. Her *Singing for Power: The Song Magic of the Papago Indians of Southern Arizona* (1938, 1973, 1993) is still valuable, as is her *Rainhouse and Ocean: Speeches for the Papago Year* (1979). Dean Saxton and Lucille Saxton's *Legends and Lore of the Papago and Pima Indians* (1973)

offers some creation stories in both English translation and the original language. Somewhat more specialized, but of great importance, is Donald M. Bahr's *Pima and Papago Ritual Oratory: A Study of Three Texts* (1975, 1988). Bahr's *Oriole Songs* (1994) is a collection, with extended commentaries, of one variety of Pima "dream songs" still being sung today. For an intimate and personal view of these people, see Underhill's *Maria Chona: The Autobiography of a Papago Woman*, which was reprinted as *Papago Woman* (1979). A specifically Pima autobiography is that of Anna Moore Shaw, *A Pima Past* (1974), which details the customs of the Pimas.

**John Smith**
A recent, definitive edition of Smith's many writings is *The Complete Works of Captain John Smith*, edited by Philip Barbour in 3 vols. (1986). The best single book on John Smith is Everett H. Emerson's *Captain John Smith* (1971), but for a more expansive treatment of Smith's life the student can turn to Bradford Smith's *Captain John Smith, His Life and Legend* (1953) and Philip L. Barbour's *The Three Worlds of Captain John Smith* (1964). A useful descriptive bibliography can be found in *American Prose in 1820*, edited by Donald Yanella and John H. Roche (1979).

**John White**
David Beers Quinn surveys what is known of White's life in *Set Fair for Roanoke: Voyages and Colonies, 1584–1606* (1985) and gives a good text of White's various writings in *The Roanoke Voyages, 1584–1590*, 2 vols. (1955; 1991). The graphic works are described in the latter book, and reproduced in Quinn and Paul Hulton, *The American Drawings of John White* (1964). Hulton has also published *America 1585: The Complete Drawings of John White* (1984).

## EARLY AMERICAN LITERATURE 1620–1820

The classic study of the Puritans remains Perry Miller's *The New England Mind: The Seventeenth Century* (1939) and *The New England Mind: From Colony to Province* (1953). Useful essays by Miller are included in *Errand into the Wilderness* ("The Marrow of Puritan Divinity" and "From Edwards to Emerson" are especially important) (1956). Miller and Thomas H. Johnson edited an anthology of *The Puritans: A Sourcebook of Their Writings* in 1938 (rev. ed., 1963), which contains useful introductions. A valuable collection, *Seventeenth-Century American Poetry* (1968), was compiled by Harrison T. Meserole. Peter White edited *Puritan Poets and Poetics* in 1985. Patricia Caldwell discusses Puritan "relations" (accounts of conversions or spiritual autobiographies) in *The Puritan Conversion Narrative* (1983). Other books

of general interest are Edmund S. Morgan's *Visible Saints: The History of a Puritan Idea* (1963) and Kenneth B. Murdock's *Literature and Theology in Colonial New England* (1949). On Puritan historians, see Peter Gay's *Loss of Mastery* (1966) and David Levin's *In Defense of Historical Literature* (1967). Sacvan Bercovich has edited a useful collection of essays on the Puritans in *The American Puritan Imagination: Essays in Revaluation* (1974); it contains a good selected bibliography. Another useful revaluation of Puritans which brings together some hard-to-come-by essays is Michael McGiffert's *Puritanism and the American Experience* (1969). Some of the best accounts of the intellectual and cultural life of the 17th century are to be found in the biographies of writers included in this anthology. One important study of a writer not included is Edmund Morgan's life of Ezra Stiles, *The Gentle Puritan* (1962).

Although the bicentennial year produced a number of useful studies of American culture in the 18th century, nothing has replaced Moses Coit Tyler's monumental *A History of American Literature during the Colonial Period, 1607–1765*, 2 vols. (1878; rev. ed., 1897; 1-vol. reprint, 1949) and *The Literary History of the American Revolution, 1763–1783*, 2 vols. (1897; 1-vol. reprint, 1941). Readers should be warned, however, to check biographical details with more recent studies. Russel B. Nye's *The Cultural Life of the New Nation* (1960), Kenneth Silverman's *A Cultural History of the American Revolution* (1976), and Michael Kammer's *A Season of Youth* (1978) are useful surveys of the arts of this period. On the American Revolution, see Edmund S. Morgan's *The American Revolution: Two Centuries of Interpretation* (1965). *Fifteen American Authors before 1900: Bibliograhic Essays on Research and Criticism*, ed. Robert A. Rees and Earl N. Harbert (1971), contains discursive chapters on the scholarship and criticism that had appeared up to that date on three authors in this period: Edwards, Franklin, and Taylor. *American Prose to 1820: A Guide to Information Sources*, ed. Donald Yannella and John H. Roch (1979), provides a helpful description of primary works and secondary sources. Writers like Anne Bradstreet and Edward Taylor are included because they wrote prose as well as poetry. Mason Lowance discusses metaphor and symbol from the Puritans to the Transcendentalists in *The Language of Canaan* (1980).

**Elizabeth Ashbridge**
The best discussion of Mrs. Ashbridge's *Account* will be found in Daniel B. Shea, Jr.'s *Spiritual Autobiography in Early America* (1968). All editions other than that published in Nantwich, England, in 1774 and reprinted here should be treated skeptically.

**William Bradford**
Samuel Eliot Morison's edition of *Of Plymouth Plantation* (1952) is the standard edition of Bradford's history, and his life of Bradford in *The Dictionary of American Biography* (1933) is useful. For a discussion of Puritan historians, see Kenneth B. Murdock's *Literature and Theology in Colonial New England* (1949) and David Levin's "William Bradford: The Value of Puritan Historiography," in E. H. Emerson's *Major Writers of Early American Literature* (1972), pp. 11–31.

**Anne Bradstreet**
The standard edition is now Jeannine Hensley's *The Works of Anne Bradstreet* (1967), with an introduction by Adrienne Rich. Useful critical discussions may be found in Josephine K. Piercy's *Anne Bradstreet* (1965), Elizabeth W. White's *Anne Bradstreet: The Tenth Muse* (1971), and Ann

Stanford's *Anne Bradstreet: The Worldly Puritan* (1974).

**J. Hector St. John de Crèvecoeur**
*Sketches of Eighteenth Century America, More Letters of St. John de Crèvecoeur* (1925) was edited by H. L. Bourdin *et al. Eighteenth Century Travels in Pennsylvania and New York* (1962) was edited by P. G. Adams. The best biographies are by Thomas Philbrick (1970) and Gay Wilson Allen and Roger Asselineau (1987).

**Jonathan Edwards**
Yale University Press is in the process of publishing a complete edition of the works of Jonathan Edwards. A selection from Edwards's writings edited by Clarence H. Faust and Thomas H. Johnson (1935) contains a useful introduction and bibliography. David Levin's *Jonathan Edwards: A Profile* (1969) includes Samuel Hopkins's *Life and Character of the Late Rev. Mr. Jonathan Edwards* (1765). Perry Miller's *Jonathan Edwards* (1949) and essays included in *Errand into the Wilderness* (1956) are indispensable. Daniel B. Shea, Jr., includes a discussion of the *Personal Narrative* in his *Spiritual Autobiography in Early America* (1968). Richard Bushman writes of "Jonathan Edwards as a Great Man" in *Soundings*, Vol. 52 (1969), pp. 15–46, and Patricia J. Tracy considers the implications of his career in *Jonathan Edwards, Pastor* (1980).

**Olaudah Equiano**
*The Interesting Narrative* has been edited by Paul Edwards (1969) using the edition of 1789, and Henry Louis Gates (in his *Classic Slave Narratives* (1987)) using the edition of 1814. Both contain useful introductions. Sidney Kaplan in his study of *The Black Presence in the Era of the American Revolution 1770–1800* (1973) discusses the American publication of Equiano's *Narrative*.

**Benjamin Franklin**
*The Papers of Benjamin Franklin* are being published by Yale University Press under the general editorship of Leonard W. Labaree. A good selection of Franklin's writings may be found in *Benjamin Franklin: Representative Selections* (1936), ed. F. L. Mott and C. L. Jorgenson. The standard biography is by Carl Van Doren (1938). Useful critical studies include Bruce I. Granger's *Benjamin Franklin, an American Man of Letters* (1964) and Alfred O. Aldridge's *Benjamin Franklin and Nature's God* (1967). See also David Levin, "The Autobiography of Benjamin Franklin: The Puritan Experimenter in Life and Art," *Yale Review*, Vol. 53 (1964), pp. 258–75. A famous unfavorable response to Franklin can be found in D. H. Lawrence's *Studies in Classic American Literature* (1923). Franklin's early years are discussed in A. B. Tourtellot's *Benjamin Franklin: The Boston Years* (1977).

## Philip Freneau

The standard edition of *The Poems of Philip Freneau* is that of F. L. Pattee, 3 vols. (1902–1907). Lewis Leary, who edited *The Last Poems of Philip Freneau* (1945), wrote the best biography, *That Rascal Freneau: A Study in Literary Failure* (1941). A very useful introduction to Freneau can be found in Harry H. Clark's edition of *Philip Freneau: Representative Selections* (1929). Richard C. Vitzhum offers a study of Freneau's lyrics in *Land and Sea* (1978).

## Thomas Jefferson

Princeton University Press, under the general editorship of Julian P. Boyd, is currently engaged in publishing the *Papers of Thomas Jefferson.* The best biography is Dumas Malone's six-volume *Jefferson and His Time* (1948–1981). Mr. Malone's article on Jefferson in *The Dictionary of American Biography* is very helpful. Recent critical studies include those of M. D. Peterson, *Thomas Jefferson and the New Nation* (1970) and Garry Wills, *Inventing America: Jefferson's Declaration of Independence* (1978). Fawn Brodie published a controversial biograpy in 1974. Jefferson's Monticello is the subject of a distinguished study by William Howard Adams (1983).

## Thomas Paine

Moncure D. Conway, who edited *The Writings of Thomas Paine*, 4 vols. (1894–1896), wrote the best life of Paine (1892). H. H. Clark's *Thomas Paine: Representative Selections* (1944) contains a very helpful introduction. Cecil Kenyon's "Where Paine Went Wrong," *American Political Science Review*, Vol. 45 (1951), pp. 1086–89, is a challenging critical assessment. A more recent biography is that by David F. Hawke (1974).

## Mary Rowlandson

Richard Slotkin's *Regeneration through Violence* (1973) contains a useful discussion of Mrs. Rowlandson's captivity. See also R. H. Pearce's "The Significance of the Captivity Narrative," *American Literature*, Vol. 19 (1947), pp. 1–20.

## Samuel Sewall

*The Diary of Samuel Sewall, 1674–1729*, ed. M. Halsey Thomas (1973), is now the standard edition and preferred over that published by the Massachusetts Historical Society from 1878 to 1882. Thomas's edition includes "The Selling of Joseph," but the introduction and commentary in Sidney Kaplan's edition (1969) is valuable for what it tells us about slavery in New England. Ola E. Winslow has written a succinct biography (1964).

## Edward Taylor

The standard edition of *The Poems of Edward Taylor* is by Donald E. Stanford (1960). Taylor's *Diary* was edited by Francis Murphy (1964) and his *Christographia* sermons (1962) and *Treatise Concerning the Lord's Supper* (1966) by Norman S. Grabo, who has also written the best critical biography (1961). Thomas M. and Virginia L. Davis are presently editing the "unpublished" writings of Edward Taylor: *Church Records and Related Sermons; Edward Taylor vs. Solomon Stoddard;* and *The Minor Poetry* appeared in 1981. All three volumes contain significant introductory material.

## Phillis Wheatley

The best edition of the poems is that edited by Julian D. Mason (1966). Shirley Graham's *The Story of Phillis Wheatley* (1969) and William G. Allen's *Wheatley, Banneker and Horton* (1970) are useful critical biographies.

## John Winthrop

The standard edition of Winthrop's work is *The Winthrop Papers*, ed. A. Forbes, 5 vols. (1929–1945). For critical biographies see D. B. Rutman's *Winthrop's Boston* (1965) and Edmund Morgan's *The Puritan Dilemma: The Story of John Winthrop* (1965). For a history of the Journal see Richard S. Dunn's "John Winthrop Writes his Journal," *William and Mary Quarterly*, Vol. 41 (1984), pp. 185–212. A more sympathetic treatment of Mrs. Hutchinson can be found in Philip F. Gura's *A Glimpse of Sion's Glory* (1984).

## AMERICAN LITERATURE 1820–1865

*Eight American Authors: A Review of Research and Criticism* (rev. ed.), edited by James Woodress (1971), contains chapters on the scholarship and criticism that had appeared on Poe, Emerson, Hawthorne, Thoreau, Whitman, and Melville up to 1969 (the other two of the eight authors are Clemens and James). *Fifteen American Authors before 1900: Bibliographic Essays on Research and Criticism*, edited by Robert A. Rees and Earl N. Harbert (1971, 1984), contains chapters on Bryant, Cooper, Dickinson, Holmes, Irving, Longfellow, Lowell, and Whittier as well as a section on the Southern humorists. The essays in these two volumes may be supplemented (especially for recent scholarship and criticism) by the various volumes of *American Literary Scholarship: An Annual*, published each year since 1965. Separate chapters in *American Literary Scholarship* are devoted to Hawthorne, Poe, and Melville, while one chapter is devoted to "Emerson, Thoreau, and Transcendentalism" and another to "Whitman and Dickinson." Work on other writers of this period is covered in the chapter on "19th-century Litera-ture." (The volumes appear two years after the works they discuss.)

Documentary discoveries in the last three decades have rendered all histories of American literature badly out of date, although the chapters on this period in the most ambitious such work, the mammoth *Literary History of the United States*, edited by Robert E. Spiller et al. (1948, 1974), are still useful; the second volume of the 1974 edition is an updated biography of studies on American writers. *The Columbia Literary History of the United States* (1988), edited by Emory Elliott, is a product of the "New Historicism." According to the general introduction, traditional sources of knowledge about episodes of literary his-tory ("old records, diaries, letters, newspapers, official firsthand documents") are eschewed by the writers of the chapters, who are described not as truthtellers but as storytellers who aim to convince their readers "not by facts but by persuasive rhetoric and narrative skill." The most influential critical study of this period remains F. O. Matthiessen's *American Renaissance: Art and Expression in the Age of Emerson and Whitman* (1941, 1968), although it is outdated, especially in its reliance on now-superseded biographies. Walter Harding has called Lawrence Buell's *Literary Transcendental-ism* (1973) "perhaps the most significant volume in the field since Matthiessen's." Still more important is Buell's *New England Literary Cul-ture: From Revolution through Renaissance* (1986). Essential are *Critical Essays on American Tran-scendentalism*, edited by Philip F. Gura and Joel Myerson (1982), and *The Transcendentalists: A Review of Research and Criticism*, edited by Joel Myerson (1984). For study of the poetry of the period Roy Harvey Pearce's *The Continuity of American Poetry* (1961) is now supplemented by Hyatt H. Waggoner's *American Poets from the Puritans to the Present* (1968) and Philip K. Jason's *Nineteenth Century Poetry: An Annotated Bibliog-raphy* (1989). A useful discussion of literature pop-ular at the time of *The Scarlet Letter* and *Moby-Dick* is David Reynolds's *Beneath the American Renaissance* (1988). Gale is printing a multivol-ume *Dictionary of Literary Biography* (DAB), arranged by regions and unevenly edited. Two especially good volumes, both edited by Joel Myer-son, are *The American Renaissance in New England* (1978) and *Antebellum Writers in New York and the South* (1979). Stanley Trachtenberg edited *American Humorists 1800–1950* (1982). Important specialized works are *The History of Southern Literature*, by Louis D. Rubin, Jr., et al. (1985, 1990) and Blyden Jackson's *A History of Afro-American Literature: The Long Beginnings, 1746–1895* (1989). Major new studies in literary history, biography, and criticism are appearing as scholars and critics assimilate information about the period, notably that being published in vol-umes sponsored by the Center for Editions of American Authors and, subsequently, by the Cen-ter for Scholarly Editions.

### William Apess

As early as 1928, Ernest Sutherland Bates wrote about Apess for the *Dictionary of American Biogra-phy*, and in 1983 James D. Hart also noticed Apess in *The Oxford Companion to American Literature*. Kim McQuaid's "William Apes, A Pequot: An Indian Reformer in the Jackson Era," *New England Quarterly* (1977), 605–25, is probably the first study fully to recognize the potential signifi-cance of Apess's work. Arnold Krupat, in *The Voice in the Margin: Native American Literature and the Canon* (1989) and *Ethnocriticism: Ethnography, History, Literature* (1992), has offered readings of Apess's major works. A. Lavonne Brown Ruoff's essay "Three Nineteenth-Century American-Indian Autobiographers," in Ruoff and Jerry Ward, Jr.'s edited *Redefining American Literary History* (1990), also comments on Apess. David Murray's *Forked Tongues: Speech, Writing, and Representa-tion in North American Indian Texts* (1991) has some informative and sophisticated discussions of Apess. The complete works of Apess have been superbly edited by Barry O'Connell, in a volume called *On Our Own Ground: The Complete Writ-ings of William Apess, A Pequot* (1992). O'Con-nell's lengthy introduction and notes provide the indispensable starting point for any further study of Apess.

### William Cullen Bryant

Bryant's poetry has not been reedited according to modern standards, and his newspaper writing is mostly buried in the files of the *New York Evening Post*. William Cullen Bryant II and Thomas G. Voss edited in six volumes *The Letters of William Cullen Bryant* (1975–92). Earlier biographies are superseded by Charles H. Brown's *William Cullen Bryant* (1971). Judith Turner Phair has compiled *A Bibliography of William Cullen Bryant and His Critics, 1808–1972* (1975). The best guide to work on Bryant is the chapter by James E. Rocks in *Fif-teen American Authors before 1900*, edited by Rob-ert A. Rees and Earl N. Harbert (1971, 1984), supplemented by the annual *American Literary Scholarship* (1963– ).

### James Fenimore Cooper

The late James Franklin Beard was editor-in-chief of a long-planned and, after 1979, fast-appearing collected edition of Cooper's *Writings*, well edited and enhanced by contemporary illustrations, including many of scenes from Cooper's novels. Beard edited the six-volume *Letters and Journals of James Fenimore Cooper* (1960–1968), the most important work of Cooper scholarship.

Reputation studies include Marcel Clavel's *Fen-imore Cooper and His Critics: American, British and French Criticisms of the Novelist's Early Work*

(1938) and George Dekker and John P. McWilliams's *Fenimore Cooper: The Critical Heritage* (1973). The early collection *James Fenimore Cooper: A Re-Appraisal*, edited by Mary E. Cunningham (1954), lived up to its title, consolidating gains in the understanding of Cooper and pointing toward needed work. The best guide to work on Cooper is the chapter by James Franklin Beard in *Fifteen American Authors before 1900*, edited by Robert A. Rees and Earl N. Harbert (1971, 1984), supplemented by the annual *American Literary Scholarship* (1963–    ).

### Rebecca Harding Davis

Until recently Davis has been best known in the writings about her son Richard Harding Davis, especially her son Charles Belmont Davis's *The Adventures and Letters of Richard Harding Davis* (1917) and Gerald Langford's *The Richard Harding Davis Years* (1961). Davis published some reminiscences in *Bits of Gossip* (1904). The fullest recent account is Tillie Olsen's very personal "Biographical Interpretation" in the Feminist Press reprint of *Life in the Iron-Mills* (1972).

### Emily Dickinson

Three volumes of *The Poems of Emily Dickinson* (1955) were edited by Thomas H. Johnson, and he and Theodora Ward edited three companion volumes of *The Letters of Emily Dickinson* (1958). Of great importance to Dickinson scholars is R. W. Franklin's brilliantly edited and magnificently reproduced *The Manuscript Books of Emily Dickinson* (1981), which provides, in two volumes, facsimiles of the handsewn fascicles of poems Dickinson left behind at her death. Jay Leyda's *The Years and Hours of Emily Dickinson* (1960) provides two volumes of documents crucial to the understanding of her life and time. Richard B. Sewall's *The Life of Emily Dickinson* (1974) is the most ambitious and detailed life, but Thomas H. Johnson's *Emily Dickinson: An Interpretive Biography* (1955) remains a valuable treatment. Also important is Ralph W. Franklin's *The Editing of Emily Dickinson: A Reconsideration* (1967). The sensational story of the love affair between Austin Dickinson and Mabel Loomis Todd is at last told in Polly Longsworth's *Austin and Mabel: The Amherst Affair* (1984). Two valuable resources are Vivian Pollak, *A Poet's Parents: The Courtship Letters of Emily Norcross and Edward Dickinson* (1988) and Polly Longsworth's *The World of Emily Dickinson* (1990).

Since the rediscovery of Dickinson in the 1930s and 1940s, the quality of critical studies has been immense.

Two works have been particularly influential in the move in recent years to consider Dickinson from a feminist perspective: Sandra M. Gilbert and Susan Gubar's *The Madwoman in the Attic: The Woman Writer and the Nineteenth-Century Literary Imagination* (1979) and Margaret Homans's *Women Writers and Poetic Identity* (1980). Books that pursue this line of inquiry include Barbara Antonina Clarke Mossberg's *Emily Dickinson: When a Writer Is a Daughter* (1982), Susan Juhasz's *The Undiscovered Continent: Emily Dickinson and the Space of the Mind* (1983), and the same author's collection of essays, *Feminist Critics Read Emily Dickinson* (1983). Tendentious but thorough is Cynthia Griffin Wolff, *Emily Dickinson* (1986). The masterpiece of this feminist scholarship and criticism is Judith Farr's *The Passion of Emily Dickinson* (1992).

Valuable research tools are Joseph Duchac's *The Poems of Emily Dickinson: An Annotated Guide to Commentary Published in English, 1890–1977* (1979), Karen Dandurand, *Dickinson Scholarship: An Annotated Bibliography 1969–1985* (1988), and the treasure-trove compiled by Willis J. Buckingham, *Emily Dickinson's Reception in the 1890s* (1989). S. P. Rosenbaum has compiled *A Concordance to the Poems of Emily Dickinson* (1964).

### Frederick Douglass

No uniform edition of Douglass's writings is available, but one is under way at Yale University under the editorship of John Blassingame. Four volumes have appeared since 1979. Houston A. Baker, Jr., has edited and supplied a useful introduction to a reprint of the 1st edition of Douglass's *Narrative of the Life of Frederick Douglass, an American Slave* (1982). Philip S. Foner edited *The Life and Writings of Frederick Douglass* in five volumes (195075). Foner's biography, *Frederick Douglass: A Biography* (1964), has been replaced as the standard work by William S. McFeely's superb *Frederick Douglass* (1991), which also contains an extensive bibliography. Other biographies of interest include Charles W. Chesnutt's *Frederick Douglass* (1899), Benjamin Quarles's excellent *Frederick Douglass* (1948), Arna W. Bontemps's *Free at Last: The Life of Frederick Douglass* (1971), and Nathan Irvin Huggins's *Slave and Citizen: The Life of Frederick Douglass* (1980). Brilliant historical detective work is contained in Dickson J. Preston's *Young Frederick Douglass* (1980); Waldo E. Martin, Jr.'s *The Mind of Frederick Douglass* (1984), as its title suggests, offers a full-scale intellectual biography. Important pioneering essays dealing with the *Narrative* are to be found in the collection edited by Robert B. Stepto and Dexter Fisher, *Afro-American Literature: The Reconstruction of Instruction* (1978), and an unusually rich group of original essays in Eric J. Sundquist's *Frederick Douglass: New Literary and Historical Essays* (1990); William L. Andrews's *Critical Essays on Frederick Douglass* (1991) contains both early reviews and current views. Vol. 1 of Blyden Jackson's *A History of Afro-American Literature: The Long Beginning, 1746–1895* (1989) puts Douglass in one of his contexts. These volumes will in turn introduce the reader to the rapidly growing scholarship on Douglass, slave narratives, and traditions of writing by black men and women that have begun to be recovered and interpreted.

## Ralph Waldo Emerson

The outstanding achievement in Emerson scholarship is the *Journals and Miscellaneous Notebooks*, edited by George P. Clark, Merrell R. Davis, Alfred R. Ferguson, Harrison Hayford, and Merton M. Sealts, Jr., later joined by Linda Allardt, Ralph H. Orth, J. E. Parsons, A. W. Plumstead, and Susan Sutton Smith under editor-in-chief William H. Gilman (1960–1977), and completed under Orth's direction. Robert E. Spiller and Alfred R. Ferguson edited the 1849 *Nature, Addresses, and Lectures* (1971). Stephen E. Whicher, Robert E. Spiller, and Wallace E. Williams edited *Early Lectures*, 3 vols. (1959–1972). Ralph H. Orth is editor-in-chief of *The Topical Notebooks of Ralph Waldo Emerson*; Susan Sutton Smith edited the first volume (1990). *The Complete Sermons of Ralph Waldo Emerson* are available in four volumes (1989), under the chief editorship of Albert J. von Frank. Merton M. Sealts, Jr., and Alfred R. Ferguson edited *Emerson's "Nature": Origin, Growth, Meaning* (1969), of which Sealts has prepared a revision (1979). Ralph L. Rusk's six-volume *Letters* (1939) must be supplemented by *The Correspondence of Emerson and Carlyle*, edited by Joseph Slater (1964), and other compilations. Eric W. Carlson has edited *Emerson's Literary Criticism* (1979).

The most detailed biography is Ralph L. Rusk's *The Life of Ralph Waldo Emerson* (1949), now supplemented by Joel Porte's *Representative Man: Ralph Waldo Emerson in His Time* (1979) and Gay Wilson Allen's *Waldo Emerson* (1981). Emerson's life is partly told in *The Life of Lidiian Jackson Emerson by Ellen Tucker Emerson*, edited by Delores Bird Carpenter (1980), and *The Letters of Ellen Tucker Emerson*, edited by Edith E. W. Gregg, 2 vols. (1982).

Kenneth W. Cameron prepared *Emerson's Workshop: An Analysis of His Reading in Periodicals through 1836* (1964), which should be used along with Walter Harding's *Emerson's Library* (1967). Cameron's *Emerson among His Contemporaries* (1967) includes reviews of Emerson's books and reminiscences from those who knew him. William J. Sowder edited *Emerson's Reviewers and Commentators: A Biographical and Bibliographical Analysis of Nineteenth-Century Periodical Criticism* (1968) and Joel Myerson edited *Emerson and Thoreau: The Contemporary Reviews* (1992). Milton R. Konvitz and Stephen E. Whicher edited *Emerson: A Collection of Critical Essays* (1962) and Jackson R. Bryer and Robert A. Rees compiled *A Checklist of Emerson Criticism, 1951–1961* (1964).

Important collections of work on Emerson are *Emerson Centenary Essays*, edited by Joel Myerson (1982) and *Critical Essays on Ralph Waldo Emerson*, edited by Robert E. Burkholder and Joel Myerson (1983). Joel Myerson has published the much-praised *Ralph Waldo Emerson: A Descriptive Bibliography* (1982).

Because Frederic Ives Carpenter's *Emerson Handbook* (1953) is out of print and out of date, the best guide to scholarship and criticism on Emerson is Floyd Stovall's chapter in *Eight American Authors*, edited by James Woodress (1971), supplemented by the annual chapter on the Transcendentalists in *American Literary Scholarship* (1963–   ).

## Margaret Fuller

The guarded, sanitized *Memoirs of Margaret Fuller Ossoli* (1852) was prepared by W. H. Channing, James Freeman Clarke, and Ralph Waldo Emerson, friends who casually vandalized the manuscripts they worked with. There are substantial recent collections: Bell Gale Chevigny's *The Woman and the Myth: Margaret Fuller's Life and Writings* (1976), a selection of Fuller's writings interspersed with contemporary comments on her; Joel Myerson's *Margaret Fuller: Essays on American Life and Letters* (1978); *"These Sad but Glorious Days": Dispatches from Europe, 1846–1850*, edited by Larry J. Reynolds and Susan Belasco Smith (1991); and *The Essential Margaret Fuller*, edited by Jeffrey Steele (1992). Robert N. Hudspeth's excellent edition of Fuller's *Letters* is complete in five volumes (1983–1988). Three good biographies are Madeleine B. Stern's *The Life of Margaret Fuller* (1942), Joseph J. Deiss's *The Roman Years of Margaret Fuller* (1969), and Laurie James's *Men, Women, and Margaret Fuller* (1990). The most valuable work on Fuller is *Margaret Fuller: An American Romantic Life / The Private Years* (1992), Vol. 1 of Charles Capper's projected two-volume biography.

## Nathaniel Hawthorne

The texts of the Ohio State University Centenary volumes of short stories and romances, all edited by Fredson Bowers, have proved unreliable, but in all these volumes there is much information about the history of composition and publication, including quotations from previously unpublished letters. Some volumes of the Centenary Edition are distinguished: Claude M. Simpson's edition of *The American Notebooks* (1972) and the editions of the romances Hawthorne left unfinished at his death, *The American Claimant Manuscripts* (1977) and *The Elixir of Life Manuscripts* (1977), both edited by Edward H. Davidson, Claude M. Simpson, and L. Neal Smith. Randall Stewart edited *The English Notebooks* (1941), and L. Neal Smith and Thomas Woodson have edited *The French and Italian Notebooks* (1979), always known in the incomplete *Passages* published in 1872. For generations the darkest shame of Hawthorne scholarship was the lack of a collected edition of the letters; continuing the work begun by Norman Holmes Pearson, Smith and Woodson have lifted that shame with four volumes of *Letters* (1984–1987) in the Centenary Edition. For the same edition Bill Ellis edited *The Consular Letters of Nathaniel Hawthorne*, 2 vols. (1988). Very useful is Rita Gollin, *Portraits of Nathaniel Hawthorne* (1983).

Lacking access to many important letters, scholars had been unable to produce a solid, comprehensive biography. Students of Hawthorne must still rely on documents cited in works such as Julian Hawthorne's two-volume *Hawthorne and His Wife* (1884, 1968); Lawrence S. Hall, *Hawthorne: Critic of Society* (1944); Robert Cantwell's *Nathaniel Hawthorne: The American Years* (1948); Louise H. Tharp, *The Peabody Sisters of Salem* (1950); and Vernon Loggins, *The Hawthornes: The Story of Seven Generations* (1951). Randall Stewart's *Nathaniel Hawthorne: A Biography* (1948) is often cited as standard, but it lacks richness of detail and sophistication of critical judgment. Arlin Turner's *Nathaniel Hawthorne: A Biography* (1980) is, like Stewart's, disappointingly thin; more readable is James Mellow's *Nathaniel Hawthorne in His Times* (1980). The latest biography is Edwin Haviland Miller's *Salem is my Dwelling Place: A Life of Nathaniel Hawthorne* (1991). Raymona Hull's *Nathaniel Hawthorne: The English Experience* (1980) is well researched.

These books survey Hawthorne's reputation: Kenneth W. Cameron's *Hawthorne among His Contemporaries* (1968); B. Barnard Cohen's *The Recognition of Nathaniel Hawthorne* (1969); and J. Donald Crowley's *Hawthorne: The Critical Heritage* (1970). Other useful collections are *Hawthorne Centenary Essays*, edited by Roy Harvey Pearce (1964); *Hawthorne: A Collection of Critical Essays*, edited by A. N. Kaul (1966); and *Nathaniel Hawthorne: A Collection of Criticism*, edited by J. Donald Crowley (1975).

The best overview of scholarship and criticism on Hawthorne is Walter Blair's chapter in *Eight American Authors*, edited by James Woodress (1971), but it must be supplemented by Buford Jones's *A Checklist of Hawthorne Criticism: 1951– 1966* (1967) and Jones's "Hawthorne Studies: The Seventies," *Studies in the Novel*, Vol. 2 (Winter, 1970). A superb resource is Gary Scharnhorst's *Nathaniel Hawthorne: An Annotated Bibliography of Comment and Criticism Before 1900* (1988). Also essential is the annual Hawthorne chapter in *American Literary Scholarship* (1963–     ) as well as the new trash-and-treasures annual *Nathaniel Hawthorne Journal* (1971–     ). C. E. Frazer Clark, Jr.'s *Nathaniel Hawthorne: A Descriptive Bibliography* (1978) has been praised as the best bibliography of a 19th-century American writer. Valuable is Robert L. Gale's *A Nathaniel Hawthorne Encyclopedia* (1991).

## Washington Irving

The *Complete Works of Washington Irving*, organized under the chief editorship of Henry A. Pochmann, was continued by Herbert L. Kleinfield then by Richard Dilworth Rust. It includes the *Journals and Notebooks*, edited in three volumes by Nathalia Wright and Walter A. Reichart (1969–1970); it includes a comprehensive collection of his letters in four volumes, completed in 1982. In the various introductory essays to this edition the history of Irving's career is being written in greater detail than ever before. The standard biography is Stanley T. Williams's two-volume *Life of Washington Irving* (1935), a brilliant and learned study marred only by Williams's unremitting disparagement of Irving. William L. Hedges's *Washington Irving: An American Study, 1802–1832* (1965) reacts too strongly against Williams in exalting Irving's "relevance." Important documentary studies are Walter A. Reichart's *Washington Irving in Germany* (1957) and Ben Harris McClary's *Washington Irving and the House of Murray* (1969). The best discursive guide to work on Irving is Pochmann's chapter in *Fifteen American Authors before 1900*, edited by Robert A. Rees and Earl N. Harbert (1971, 1984), supplemented by the annual review of current work in *American Literary Scholarship* (1963–     ). Two valuable recent works are Haskell Springer's comprehensive *Washington Irving: A Reference Guide* (1976) and Andrew B. Myers's *A Century of Commentary on the Works of Washington Irving* (1976). Edwin T. Bowden prepared a descriptive bibliography, *Washington Irving: Bibliography* (1989).

## Harriet Jacobs

Jean Fagin Yellin's edition of *Incidents in the Life of a Slave Girl* (1987) is extensively annotated and provides the fullest account of Jacobs's life available along with an excellent interpretive discussion. There are as yet no book-length studies of Jacobs, and there is relatively little scholarly discussion thus far. Good commentary may be found in Valerie Smith's *Self-Discovery and Authority in Afro-American Narrative* (1987) and *Within the Plantation Household: Black and White Women in the Old South*, by Elizabeth Fox-Genovese (1989). Consult the journal *Black American Literature Forum* for scholarly essays. For general discussion of pre–Civil War slave narratives, see Robert Stepto, *From Behind the Veil: A Study of Afro-American Narrative* (1979) and Frances Smith Foster, *Witnessing Slavery: The Development of Ante-bellum Slave Narratives* (1979).

## Abraham Lincoln

The most comprehensive collection is *The Collected Works of Abraham Lincoln*, edited by Roy P. Basler et al., 9 vols. (1953). Basler also edited in one volume *Abraham Lincoln: His Speeches and Writings* (1946); his introduction is useful both for the critical reflections on Lincoln as a man and as a writer and for information on the history of the texts. Writings on Lincoln constitute a library in themselves. For beginners, Carl Sandburg's detailed, passionate, and adulatory two-volume biography, *Abraham Lincoln: The Prairie Years* (1926) and his four-volume *Abraham Lincoln: The War Years* (1939) were abridged in one volume in 1954. More recent, more dispassionate accounts may be found in Benjamin Thomas's *Abraham Lincoln* (1952), one of the best short accounts; David Donald's *Lincoln Reconsidered* (1956); Steven B. Oates's *With Malice Towards None: The Life of Abraham Lincoln* (1977), and Roger Bruns's *Abraham Lincoln* (1986). A good specialized examination of *Lincoln the Writer: The Development of His Style* was published by Herbert Joseph Edwards and John Erskine Hankins in 1962.

### Henry Wadsworth Longfellow

Lawrence Buell edited *Selected Poems* (1988). The outstanding modern work on Longfellow is Andrew Hilen's *The Letters of Henry Wadsworth Longfellow* (1966–    ). The fullest biography is still Samuel Longfellow's two-volume *Life of Henry Wadsworth Longfellow* (1886–1887) and his *Final Memorials of Henry Wadsworth Longfellow* (1887), but Hilen's edition of the letters reveals much that Samuel Longfellow—the poet's brother—suppressed. Recent well-documented biographies are Lawrance R. Thompson's *Young Longfellow (1807–1843)* (1938, 1969) and Edward Wagenknecht's *Longfellow: A Full-Length Portrait* (1955). Useful are Andrew Hilen's edition of *Clara Crowninshield's Diary: A European Tour with Longfellow, 1835–1836* (1956) and Wagenknecht's edition of *Mrs. Longfellow: Selected Letters and Journals of Fanny Appleton Longfellow (1817–1861)* (1956). There are important discussions of Longfellow's earnings in William Charvat's *The Profession of Authorship in America, 1800–1870* (1968). The best guide to work on Longfellow is Richard Dilworth Rust's chapter in *Fifteen American Authors before 1900*, edited by Robert A. Rees and Earl N. Harbert (1971), supplemented by the annual *American Literary Scholarship* (1963–    ).

### Herman Melville

The Northwestern-Newberry Edition of *The Writings of Herman Melville*, edited by Harrison Hayford, Hershel Parker, and G. Thomas Tanselle (1968–    ) is standard. Textual discoveries reported in the Norton Critical Edition of *Moby-Dick*, edited by Harrison Hayford and Hershel Parker (1967) went into the chief volume in this edition, *Moby-Dick* (1988), in which the "Historical Note" was the first study to make full use of the massive trove of new documents acquired by the New York Public Library in 1983. Until Robert C. Ryan's volume appears in the Northwestern-Newberry Edition, there will be no satisfactory texts of Melville's poems, but otherwise scholarly editions

or facsimiles of most of Melville's works are now available.

The 19th-century biographical accounts are reprinted and analyzed in Merton M. Sealts, Jr.'s *The Early Lives of Melville* (1974). The first full-length biography, Raymond Weaver's *Herman Melville: Mariner and Mystic* (1921), has been superseded by Leon Howard's *Herman Melville: A Biography* (1951) and by Jay Leyda's monumental compilation of documents, *The Melville Log* (1951; reprinted with supplement, 1969). The 3rd edition, *The New Melville Log*, by Jay Leyda and Hershel Parker, is forthcoming in three or four volumes, with items from the 1969 supplement and any new items interspersed chronologically among the items of the 1951 edition. Hershel Parker's two-volume biography of Melville is due out in 1995.

Merton M. Sealts, Jr.'s *Melville's Reading* (1988) is a compilation of books Melville owned or used. Melville's annotations in his surviving books are recorded in W. Walker Cowen's Harvard dissertation, *Melville's Marginalia* (1965). For contemporary reviews see Kevin Hayes and Hershel Parker, *A Checklist of Melville Reviews* (1991). Some reviews and later essays are reprinted in *The Recognition of Herman Melville*, edited by Hershel Parker (1967). "*Moby-Dick*" *as Doubloon*, edited by Parker and Hayford (1970), includes all the then-known reviews of *Moby-Dick* and much later criticism. Watson G. Branch's *Melville: The Critical Heritage* (1974) prints a lavish sampling of reviews. Of the compilations of modern criticism on Melville's masterpiece, the fullest are in *Doubloon* and the Brian Higgins and Hershel Parker *Critical Essays on Herman Melville's "Moby-Dick"* (1992). The best bibliography of Melville criticism is Brian Higgins's *Herman Melville: An Annotated Bibliography, 1846–1930* (1979) along with his *Herman Melville: A Reference Guide, 1931–1960* (1987). Merton M. Sealts's *Pursuing Melville: 1940–1980* (1982) reprints now-classic early essays in addition to new material such as Sealts's correspondence with Charles Olson and some remarkable recent essays, notably one on Melville and Emerson and one on the chronology of Melville's magazine pieces of 1853–56. A *Companion to Melville Studies* (1986), edited by John Bryant, is a 906-page guide by some two dozen Melvillians, old and young.

The best guide to work on Melville is Nathalia Wright's chapter in *Eight American Authors*, edited by James Woodress (1971), supplemented by the annual chapter in *American Literary Scholarship* (1963–    ) as well as news in *Melville Society Extracts*.

### Edgar Allan Poe

There is no modern scholarly edition of Poe, although there are a number of facsimile reprints of early editions as well as modern editions of the poems by Floyd Stovall (1965) and by Thomas O. Mabbott (1969). Burton R. Pollin is continuing Mabbott's long-projected edition of the *Collected Writings*; the first volume appeared in 1981. Of recent popular editions, *The Short Fiction of Edgar Allan Poe*, edited by Stuart Levine and Susan Levine (1976), is especially well annotated. John W. Ostrom edited *The Letters of Edgar Allan Poe* (1948: reprinted with additional letters, 1966). Partly because of forgeries and calumnies by Poe's literary executor Rufus Griswold, Poe biography became and has remained enmeshed in legends. John Carl Miller's *Building Poe Biography* (1977) lucidly traces the gradual emergence of documents concerning Poe. Although weak in its literary judgments and given to excessive argument in favor of certain dubious biographical points, Arthur Hobson Quinn's *Edgar Allan Poe: A Critical Biography* (1941) remains valuable. The best recent biography is Kenneth Silverman's *Edgar A. Poe* (1991). Robert D. Jacobs's *Poe: Journalist and Critic* (1969) is highly detailed and discriminating.

Poe's early reputation is traced in Eric Carlson's *The Recognition of Edgar Allan Poe* (1966) and in Jean Alexander's *Affidavits of Genius: Edgar Allan Poe and the French Critics, 1847–1924* (1971). Modern criticism is sampled in *Poe: A Collection of Critical Essays*, edited by Robert Regan (1967); *Twentieth Century Interpretations of Poe's Tales*, edited by William L. Howarth (1971); and *Papers on Poe*, edited by Richard P. Veler (1972). Benjamin Franklin Fisher IV's *Poe and His Times* (1990) is a collection of essays by various critics on Poe in his contemporary contexts. A comprehensive listing of works on Poe is Esther F. Hyneman's *Edgar Allan Poe: An Annotated Bibliography of Books and Articles in English, 1827–1973* (1974). The best guide to work on Poe is Jay B. Hubbell's chapter in *Eight American Authors*, edited by James Woodress (1971), supplemented, as in mentions of newly published letters, by the annual discussion in *American Literary Scholarship* (1963–    ), where Poe has been given a chapter to himself since 1973, and by *Poe Studies* (1968–    ). G. R. Thompson's selection in the Library of America series, *Edgar Allan Poe: Essays and Revisions* makes many elusive documents readily available. The most important recent work of Poe scholarship, and the most useful single reference book on Poe, is *The Poe Log: A Documentary Life of Edgar Allan Poe, 1809–1849*, edited by Dwight Thomas and David K. Jackson (1987).

**Harriet Beecher Stowe**

Though not complete, *The Writings of Harriet Beecher Stowe* (1896), in sixteen volumes, is still the most substantial collection. John M. Moran, Jr., edited *Collected Poems* (1967), and Elizabeth Ammons has edited a Norton Critical Edition of *Uncle Tom's Cabin*.

Several "official" biographies were written dur-ing Stowe's lifetime or soon after she died, but Joan D. Hedrick's *Harriet Beecher Stowe: A Life* (1993) is complete and dependable. Other biographies include Robert Forrest Wilson's *Crusader in Crinoline: The Life of Harriet Beecher Stowe* (1941); Johanna Johnston's *Runaway to Heaven: The Story of Harriet Beecher Stowe* (1963); Edward Wagenknecht's "psychographic" study, *Harriet Beecher Stowe: The Known and the Unknown* (1965); and Noel B. Gerson's *Harriet Beecher Stowe: A Biography* (1976).

The best critical studies include Charles H. Foster's *The Rungless Ladder: Harriet Beecher Stowe and New England Puritanism* (1954); John R. Adams's *Harriet Beecher Stowe* (1963); Alice C. Crozier's *The Novels of Harriet Beecher Stowe* (1969); Edwin Bruce Kirkham's *The Building of Uncle Tom's Cabin* (1977); Ellen Moers's monograph, *Harriet Beecher Stowe and American Literature* (1978); and Gayle Kimball's *The Religious Ideas of Harriet Beecher Stowe* (1982).

Josephine Donovan's *New England Local Color Literature: A Women's Tradition* (1983) locates Stowe in the larger tradition she helped to initiate. Two volumes will be of particular interest to researchers: Jean Ashton's *Harriet Beecher Stowe: A Reference Guide* (1977) and Elizabeth Ammons's *Critical Essays on Harriet Beecher Stowe* (1980). Eric Sundquist's edition of *New Essays on "Uncle Tom's Cabin"* (1986) reflects the recovery of Stowe as a major writer and recent perspectives on her most famous novel. Theodore Hovet's *The Master Narrative: Harriet Beecher Stowe's Subversive Story of Master and Slave in "Uncle Tom's Cabin" and "Dred"* (1989) may be recommended. Jane Tompkins's chapter on *"Uncle Tom's Cabin* and the Politics of Literary History" in her *Sensational Designs: The Cultural Work of American Fiction, 1790–1860* (1985) stimulated fresh interest in Stowe.

**Henry David Thoreau**

The Princeton Edition (1971–    ) will be standard. Of the volumes published so far, *Walden*, edited by J. Lyndon Shanley, must be supplemented by Shanley's own *The Making of "Walden"* (1957; reprinted 1966) and by further study of the next-to-final form of the manuscript. The Princeton Edition includes the journals (1981–    ), previously available in an imperfectly transcribed edition (1906; reprinted 1962) as well as Walter Harding's re-edited *Correspondence*. For now, Thoreau's letters are mostly available in Carl Bode and Walter Harding's *Correspondence of Henry David Thoreau* (1958), supplemented by Kenneth W. Cameron's *Companion to Thoreau's Correspondence* (1964). *Collected Poems*, edited by Carl Bode (1964) is being reedited for Princeton by Elizabeth Wetherell. Among the separate editions of *Walden* the miscalled "Variorum" edited by Harding is very valuable for its lavish annotations, as is Philip Van Doren Stern's *Annotated Walden* (1970).

The most reliable biography is Walter Harding's *The Days of Henry Thoreau: A Biography* (1965). Also valuable is Harding's *Thoreau: Man of Concord* (1960), recollections by dozens of people who knew Thoreau, and Harding's *Thoreau's Library* (1957). William L. Howarth edited Robert F. Stowell's *A Thoreau Gazeteer* (1970), which includes many maps and photographs of places Thoreau knew. Essential is Robert Sattelmeyer, *Thoreau's Reading: A Study in Intellectual History with Bibliographical Catalogue* (1988). Thoreau's reputation is surveyed in *Thoreau: A Century of Criticism*, edited by Walter Harding (1954); Wendell Glick's *The Recognition of Henry David Thoreau* (1969); and in Joel Myerson's *Emerson and Thoreau: The Contemporary Reviews* (1992). Among the more frequently cited recent books about Thoreau are Sherman Paul's *The Shores of America: Thoreau's Inward Exploration* (1958); Joel Porte's *Emerson and Thoreau: Transcendentalists in Conflict* (1966); Michael Meyer's *Several More Lives to Live: Thoreau's Political Reputation in America* (1977); and Robert F. Sayre's *Thoreau and the American Indians* (1977). Sherman Paul edited *Thoreau: A Collection of Critical Essays* (1962). Walter Harding's *Thoreau Handbook* (1959), long out of print, has been revised by Harding and Meyer (1980). Lewis Leary's chapter in *Eight American Authors*, edited by James Woodress (1971), must be supplemented by the annual chapter on the Transcendentalists in *American Literary Scholarship* (1963– ), issues of the *Thoreau Society Bulletin* (1941– ), and Raymond R. Borst's *Henry David Thoreau: A Reference Guide: 1835–1899* (1987). Raymond R. Borst has published *Henry David Thoreau: A Descriptive Bibliography* (1982).

**Walt Whitman**

The *Collected Writings of Walt Whitman* is in progress under the general editorship of Gay Wilson Allen; part of this edition is the five-volume *Walt Whitman: The Correspondence*, edited by Edwin H. Miller (1961–1969). The growth of *Leaves of Grass* may be studied conveniently in the *Comprehensive Reader's Edition*, edited by Harold W. Blodgett and Sculley Bradley (1965; reprinted 1968); the same two edited the Norton Critical Edition of *Leaves of Grass* (1973). There are a variety of useful facsimiles of early editions, especially of the 1855 *Leaves of Grass*, and Arthur Golden edited *Walt Whitman's Blue Book* (1968), a facsimile of Whitman's marked-up copy of the 1860 edition. Essential, in three volumes, is *"Leaves of Grass": A Textual Variorum of the Printed Poems* (1980), edited by Bradley, Blodgett, Golden, and William White.

The standard biography, essential for its week-by-week story of Whitman's life, is Gay Wilson

Allen's *The Solitary Singer* (1967). More popular in nature is Justin Kaplan's *Walt Whitman: A Life* (1980). Allen also wrote *A Reader's Guide to Walt Whitman* (1970) and the extremely valuable *New Walt Whitman Handbook* (1975). Some other recent work based on study of documentary evidence are Thomas L. Brasher's *Whitman as Editor of the Brooklyn Daily Eagle* (1970); Joseph Jay Rubin's *The Historic Whitman* (1973); Floyd Stovall's *The Foreground of "Leaves of Grass"* (1974); and Jerome M. Loving's *Civil War Letters of George Washington Whitman* (1975), the writer of the letters being Whitman's brother. New documents are in *Dear Brother Walt: The Letters of Thomas Jefferson Whitman*, edited by Dennis Berthold and Kenneth Price (1984). Of recent collections of writing on Whitman, these are especially useful: *The Presence of Walt Whitman*, edited by R. W. B. Lewis (1962); *Whitman: A Collection of Critical Essays*, edited by Roy Harvey Pearce (1962); *The Poet and the President: Whitman's Lincoln Poems*, edited by William Coyle (1962); *Whitman the Poet*, edited by John C. Broderick (1962); *Whitman's "Song of Myself": Origin, Growth, Meaning*, edited by James E. Miller, Jr. (1964); *A Century of Whitman Criticism*, edited by Edwin H. Miller (1969); *Walt Whitman*, edited by Francis Murphy (1969); and *Whitman: The Critical Heritage*, edited by Milton Hindus (1971). A notable recent critical book is Edwin H. Miller's *Walt Whitman's Poetry: A Psychological Journey* (1968). An important new study is Paul Zweig, *Walt Whitman: The Making of the Poet* (1984). Important documents are in *Notebooks and Unpublished Prose Manuscripts*, edited by Edward P. Grier, 6 vols. (1984).

Indispensable are Scott Giantvalley's *Walt Whitman, 1838–1939: A Reference Guide* (1981) and Donald D. Kummings's *Walt Whitman, 1940–1975: A Reference Guide* (1982). These two books may be supplemented by Roger Asselineau's chapter in *Eight American Authors*, edited by James Woodress (1971), supplemented by the discussions in *American Literary Scholarship* (1963– ) and by the *Walt Whitman Review* (1955– ).

**John Greenleaf Whittier**

Whittier's poetry has been steadily available, but much of his prose, especially his newspaper writings, has never been collected or else was collected but is out of print. Samuel T. Pickard's *Life and Letters of John Greenleaf Whittier* (1894), long standard, is being superseded by recent works such as John A. Pollard's *John Greenleaf Whittier: Friend of Man* (1949), John B. Pickard's *John Greenleaf Whittier: An Introduction and Interpretation* (1961), and John B. Pickard's three-volume *Letters of John Greenleaf Whittier* (1975). John B. Pickard also edited an important collection of criticism, *Memorabilia of John Greenleaf Whittier*

(1968), and Donald C. Freeman, John B. Pickard, and Roland H. Woodwell assembled the illustration-filled *Whittier and Whittierland: Portrait of a Poet and His World* (1976). Woodwell also published *John Greenleaf Whittier: A Biography*

(1985). The best guide to work on Whittier is Karl Keller's chapter in *Fifteen American Authors before 1900*, edited by Robert A. Rees and Earl N. Harbert (1971, 1984), supplemented by the annual *American Literary Scholarship* (1963– ).

## AMERICAN LITERATURE 1865–1914

The titles of the following highly selective list of general historical and critical studies typically suggest their coverage within this period: Daniel Aaron, *The Unwritten War: American Writers and the Civil War* (1973); Lars Åhnebrink, *The Beginnings of Naturalism in American Fiction* (1950); Elizabeth Ammons, *Conflicting Stories: American Women Writers at the Turn of the Century* (1991); Louis Auchincloss, *Pioneers and Caretakers: A Study of Nine American Women Novelists* (1965); Barbara Bardes and Suzanne Gossett, *Declarations of Independence: Women and Political Power in Nineteenth Century American Fiction* (1990); Bernard W. Bell, *The Afro-American Novel and Its Tradition* (1987); Sacvan Bercovitch, ed., *Reconstructing American Literary History* (1986); Warner Berthoff, *The Ferment of Realism: American Literature, 1884–1919* (1965); William Boelhower, *Through a Glass Darkly: Ethnic Semiosis in American Literature* (1987); Richard Bridgman, *The Colloquial Style in America* (1966); Edwin H. Cady, *The Light of Common Day* (1971); Richard Chase, *The American Novel and Its Tradition* (1957); Henry Steele Commager, *The American Mind: An Interpretation of American Thought and Character Since the 1880's* (1950); John Conder, *Naturalism in American Fiction: The Classic Phase* (1984); Thomas Cooley, *Educated Lives: The Rise of Modern Autobiography in America* (1977); Marcus Cunliffe, *The Literature of the United States* (1961); Cathy N. Davidson, *Revolution and the Word: The Rise of the Novel in America* (1986); Josephine Donovan, *New England Local Color Literature: A Women's Tradition* (1983); Ann Douglas, *The Feminization of American Culture* (1977); Paul John Eakin, *American Autobiography: Restrospect and Prospect* (1991); Emory Elliott, ed., *Columbia Literary History of the United States* (1988) and *Columbia History of the American Novel* (1991); Robert Falk, *The Victorian Mode in American Fiction, 1865–1885* (1965); Robert A. Ferguson, *Law and Letters in American Culture* (1984); Leslie A. Fiedler, *Love and Death in the American Novel* (1960); Philip Fisher, *Hard Facts: Setting and Form in the American Novel* (1985); Henry Louis Gates, Jr., *Figures in Black: Words, Signs, and the "Racial" Self* (1987); Seymour L. Gross and John Edward Hardy, eds., *Images of the Negro in American Literature* (1966); Huck Gutman, ed., *As Others Read Us: International Perspectives on American Literature* (1991); Alfred

Habegger, *Gender, Fantasy, and Realism in American Literature* (1982); Susan K. Harris, *Nineteenth-Century American Women's Novels* (1990); Daniel Hoffman, *Form and Fable in American Fiction* (1961); Richard Hofstadter, *Social Darwinism in American Thought* (1944); June Howard, *Form and History in American Literary Naturalism* (1985); Leon Howard, *Literature and the American Tradition* (1960); Howard Mumford Jones, *The Age of Energy: Varieties of American Experience, 1865–1915* (1971); Amy Kaplan, *The Social Construction of American Realism* (1988); Alfred Kazin, *On Native Grounds: An Interpretation of Modern American Prose Literature* (1942) and *American Procession* (1984); Marcus Klein, *Foreigners: The Making of American Literature, 1900–1940* (1981); Harold Kolb, *The Illusion of Life: American Realism as a Literary Form* (1969); Annette Kolodny, *The Lay of the Land: Metaphor as Experience and History* (1975); T. J. Jackson Lears, *No Place of Grace: Antimodernism and the Transformation of American Culture, 1880–1920* (1981); Brian Lee, *American Fiction 1865–1940* (1987); Glen A. Love, *New Americans: The Westerner and the Modern Experience in the American Novel* (1982); Richard M. Ludwig and Clifford A. Nault, Jr., eds., *Annals of American Literature, 1602–1983* (1985); Jay Martin, *Harvests of Change: American Literature, 1865–1914* (1967); Ronald E. Martin, *American Literature and the Universe of Force* (1981); Leo Marx, *The Machine in the Garden: Technology and the Pastoral Ideal in America* (1964); Janet Holmgrin McKay, *Narration and Discourse in American Realistic Fiction* (1982); Walter B. Michaels, *The Gold Standard and the Logic of Naturalism: American Literature at the Turn of the Century* (1987); Ruth Miller, *Backgrounds to Black American Literature* (1971); Lee Clark Mitchell, *Determined Fictions: American Literary Naturalism* (1989); Vernon L. Parrington, *Main Currents in American Thought: An Interpretation of American Literature from the Beginnings to 1920*, 3 vols. (1927–1930); Roy Harvey Pearce, *The Continuity of American Poetry* (1961); Richard Poirier, *A World Elsewhere: The Place of Style in American Literature* (1966); David Perkins, *A History of American Poetry: From the 1890s to the High Modernist Mode* (1976); Carolyn Porter, *Seeing and Being: The Plight of the Participant Observer in Emerson, James, Adams and Faulkner* (1981); Russell Reising, *The Unusable*

Part: Theory and the Study of American Literature (1986); Constance Rourke, American Humor: A Study of the National Character (1931); John Carlos Rowe, Through the Custom-House: Nineteenth Century American Fiction and Modern Theory (1982); A. La Vonne Brown Ruoff, American Indian Literatures: An Introduction, Bibliographic Review, and Selected Bibliography (1990); A. LaVonne Brown Ruoff and Jerry Ward, eds., Redefining American Literary History (1990); Alan Shucard, Fred Moramarco, and William Sullivan, Modern American Poetry, 1865–1950 (1989); Robert Shulman, Social Criticism and Nineteenth Century American Fictions (1987); Richard Slotkin, The Fatal Environment: The Myth of the Frontier in the Age of Industrialization, 1800–1890 (1985); Henry Nash Smith, Virgin Land: The American West as Symbol and Myth (1950) and Democracy and the Novel: Popular Resistance to Classic American Writers (1978); Valerie Smith, Self-Discovery and Authority in Afro-American Narrative (1987); Carroll Smith-Rosenberg, Disorderly Conduct: Visions of Gender in Victorian America (1986); Werner Sollers, Beyond Ethnicity: Consent and Descent in American Culture (1986); Michael Spindler, American Literature and Social Change: William Dean Howells to Arthur Miller (1983); Eric J. Sundquist, ed., American Realism: New Essays (1982); Tony Tanner, The Reign of Wonder: Naivety and Reality in American Literature (1965); Gordon O. Taylor, Chapters of Experience: Studies in Twentieth Century American Autobiography (1983); Alan Trachtenberg, The Incorporation of America: Culture and Society in the Gilded Age (1982); Hyatt H. Waggoner, American Poets from the Puritans to the Present (1968); Charles C. Walcutt, American Literary Naturalism: A Divided Stream (1956); Robert Wiebe, Search for Order, 1877–1920 (1967); Edmund Wilson, Patriotic Gore: Studies in the Literature of the American Civil War (1962); Larzer Ziff, The American 1890s: Life and Times of a Lost Generation (1966).

Eight American Authors: A Review of Research and Criticism, ed. James Woodress (1977), contains discursive chapters on the secondary literature that had appeared, up to 1969, on two authors in this period—Clemens and James; Fifteen American Authors before 1900: Bibliographic Essays on Research and Criticism, ed. Robert A. Rees and Earl N. Harbert (1984), contains chapters on Adams, Crane, Howells, and Norris; Sixteen Modern Authors, ed. Jackson R. Bryer (1973), contains essays on Crane and Dreiser. For guidance to more recent general books on American literature in this period, see the first section of "Key to Abbreviations" list, and the "Themes, Topics, Criticism" and "Nineteenth-Century Literature" chapters in annual volumes of American Literary Scholarship. Annual volumes of the Modern Language Association Bibliography should also be consulted. Up-to-

date bibliographies and reviews may be found in such standard journals as American Literature and American Literary Realism, 1870–1910 as well as in the publications of societies devoted to individual authors in this period.

## Henry Adams

No uniform, authoritatively edited collection of Adams's writings exists. Ernest Samuels's annotated edition of The Education sets a high standard for those who would undertake such a project in the future. In 1920, 1930, and 1938, Worthington C. Ford edited three volumes of Adams's excellent letters. More recently, J. C. Levenson et al. have edited six generous volumes of The Letters of Henry Adams (1982–88). The standard biography is a trilogy by Ernest Samuels: The Young Henry Adams (1948); Henry Adams, The Middle Years (1958); and Henry Adams, the Major Phase (1964). A sound one-volume life is Elizabeth Stevenson's Henry Adams, a Biography (1956).

Earl N. Harbert's The Force So Much Closer Home: Henry Adams and the Adams Family (1977) situates Adams within his family tradition. George Hochfield's Henry Adams: An Introduction and Interpretation (1962) delivers well what its title promises. Different aspects of Adams are dealt with in Max I. Baym's The French Education of Henry Adams (1951); John J. Conder's A Formula of His Own: Henry Adams' Literary Experiment (1970); William H. Jordy's Henry Adams: Scientific Historian (1952); Harold Kaplan's Power and Order: Henry Adams and the Naturalist Tradition in American Fiction (1981); J. C. Levenson's The Mind and Art of Henry Adams (1957), a difficult and distinguished work; John Carlos Rowe's Henry Adams and Henry James: The Emergence of a Modern Consciousness (1976); Ernest Scheyer's The Circle of Henry Adams: Art and Artists (1970); and Vern Wagner's The Suspension of Henry Adams: A Study of Manner and Matter (1969), which effectively treats Adams's humor. R. P. Blackmur's Henry Adams (1980), Joseph F. Byrnes's The Virgin of Chartres: An Intellectual and Psychological History of Henry Adams (1981), Edward Chalfant's Both Sides of the Ocean: A Biography of Henry Adams: His First Life, 1838–1862 (1982), and William Wasserstrom's The Ironies of Progress (1984) are stimulating studies. William Merrill Decker's The Literary Vocation of Henry Adams (1990) skillfully analyzes the rhetoric of Adams's major works.

## Ambrose Bierce

The fullest edition of Bierce's writings, Collected Works of Ambrose Bierce (1909–1912), was edited by Walter Neale. Ernest Jerome Hopkins's The Complete Short Stories of Ambrose Bierce (1970, 1984) contains his commentary and a foreword by Cathy N. Davidson. The largest collection of Bierce's letters is available in Bertha C. Pope's edition of The Letters of Ambrose Bierce (1921).

Vincent Starrett's pioneer appreciative biography

*Ambrose Bierce* (1920) should be supplemented by Walter Neale's *Life of Ambrose Bierce* (1929); by Carey McWilliams's *Ambrose Bierce: A Biography* (1929); by the standard critical biography, Paul Fatout's *Ambrose Bierce, the Devil's Lexicographer* (1951); and by Mary Elizabeth Grenander's *Ambrose Bierce* (1971). Stuart C. Woodruff's *The Short Stories of Ambrose Bierce: A Study in Polarity* (1964) is a useful survey of the short fiction and Robert A. Wiggins's *Ambrose Bierce* (1964) is a serviceable introductory overview. By far the best critical study of Bierce's work is Cathy W. Davidson's *The Experimental Fictions of Ambrose Bierce: Structuring the Ineffable* (1984). Davidson also edited *Critical Essays on Ambrose Bierce* (1982).

### Gertrude Simmons Bonnin
See Zitkala Ša.

### Kate Chopin
*The Complete Works of Kate Chopin* (1969) was edited in two volumes by Per Seyersted, who also wrote the excellent *Kate Chopin: A Critical Biography* (1969). Per Seyersted and Emily Toth have edited *A Kate Chopin Miscellany* (1980), a collection of unpublished short fiction, poems, letters, etc.; their *Kate Chopin's Private Papers* is forthcoming. An early critical biography is Daniel Rankin's *Kate Chopin and Her Creole Stories* (1932); Peggy Skaggs's *Kate Chopin* is a good introduction to the life and work, as is Barbara C. Ewell's *Kate Chopin* (1986). Emily Toth's monumental critical biography *Kate Chopin* (1990) has established her as perhaps the leading Chopin scholar. Bernard J. Koloski has edited a varied and useful collection, *Approaches to Teaching Kate Chopin's "The Awakening"* (1988). Lynda S. Boren and Sara deSaussure Davis have edited a fresh collection of essays, *Kate Chopin Reconsidered: Beyond the Bayou* (1992).

### Samuel Clemens
The present standard edition of *The Writings of Mark Twain*, 37 vols., ed. Albert Bigelow Paine (1922–1925), is being superseded by the ongoing editions of *The Mark Twain Papers* (1969– ), under the supervision of Robert Hirst, and *The Works of Mark Twain* (1972– ), under the supervision of John Gerber. Three volumes of letters have appeared so far in the *Papers*, and other Clemens letters are available in several scattered volumes, the most interesting of which is *The Correspondence of Samuel L. Clemens and William Dean Howells, 1872–1910*, ed. Henry Nash Smith and William M. Gibson (1960).

Albert Bigelow Paine's *Mark Twain, a Biography* (1912) is vivid, unreliable, and still indispensable. Justin Kaplan's *Mr. Clemens and Mark Twain, a Biography* (1966) is a lively, popular account. Van Wyck Brooks's polemical and controversial *The Ordeal of Mark Twain* (1920) should be read together with Bernard De Voto's corrective

*Mark Twain's America* (1932). De Lancey Ferguson's *Mark Twain: Man and Legend* (1943) is still the best full-length critical biography, though Everett Emerson's *The Authentic Mark Twain: A Literary Biography of Samuel L. Clemens* (1985) is the best critical study we have within its announced limits.

The criticism of Clemens is enormous in quantity, variety, and quality. Two excellent general studies are Henry Nash Smith's *Mark Twain: The Development of a Writer* (1962) and William M. Gibson's *The Art of Mark Twain* (1976). James M. Cox's perceptive *Mark Twain: The Fate of Humor* (1966), Gladys Bellamy's *Mark Twain as a Literary Artist* (1950), Edgar M. Branch's *The Literary Apprenticeship of Mark Twain* (1950), and Albert E. Stone's *The Innocent Eye: Childhood in Mark Twain's Imagination* (1961) are all distinguished contributions to Clemens scholarship. More specialized studies of distinction include Henry Seidel Canby's *Turn West, Turn East* (1951), which concentrates on Clemens and Henry James; Louis J. Budd's *Mark Twain: Social Philosopher* (1962); Bernard De Voto's *Mark Twain at Work* (1942); Paul Fatout's *Mark Twain on the Lecture Circuit* (1960); Sydney J. Krause's *Mark Twain as Critic* (1967); Howard Baetzhold's *Mark Twain and John Bull* (1970); and Walter Blair's *Mark Twain and Huckleberry Finn* (1960). More recent studies of permanent interest include Louis J. Budd's *Our Mark Twain: The Making of His Public Personality* (1983), Hamlin Hill's *Mark Twain: God's Fool* (1973), James L. Johnson's *Mark Twain and the Limits of Power: Emerson's God in Ruins* (1982), Sherwood Cummings's excellent *Mark Twain and Science: Adventures of a Mind* (1989), Susan Gillman's *Dark Twins: Imposture and Identity in Mark Twain's America* (1991), Maria Ornella Marotti's *The Duplicating Imagination: Twain and the Twain Papers* (1991), and David E. Sloane's *Mark Twain as a Literary Comedian* (1979). Among the many collections of criticism, Robert Sattlemeyer and J. Donald Crowley's *One Hundred Years of "Huckleberry Finn": The Boy, His Book, and American Culture* (1985) merits special notice. Victor Doyno's masterful study, *Writing "Huck Finn": Mark Twain's Creative Process* (1991), will soon be revised to incorporate the discovery of additional *Huckleberry Finn* manuscript materials.

### Stephen Crane
Fredson Bowers is the textual editor of *The Works of Stephen Crane* (1969–1976), a complete edition that has come in for some criticism despite its endorsement by the Center for Editions of American Authors. *Stephen Crane: Letters* (1960) was edited by R. W. Stallman and Lillian Gilkes; Joseph Katz edited both *The Portable Stephen Crane* (1969) and *The Poems of Stephen Crane: A Critical Edition* (1966).

Thomas Beer's early biography *Stephen Crane:*

A *Study in American Letters* (1923) is still important, although it lacks documentation. The poet John Berryman prepared a stimulating and more factually reliable biography in 1950, and R. W. Stallman's massive, polemical *Stephen Crane: A Critical Biography* (1968) incorporates the substantial new material discovered in the interim.

Edwin H. Cady's *Stephen Crane* (1980) is an excellent critical introduction to Crane's life and work. Eric Solomon's *Stephen Crane: From Parody to Realism* (1966), Donald B. Gibson's *The Fiction of Stephen Crane* (1968), Daniel G. Hoffman's *The Poetry of Stephen Crane* (1957), Marston La France's *A Reading of Stephen Crane* (1971), Frank Bergon's *Stephen Crane's Artistry* (1975), James Nagel's *Stephen Crane and Literary Impressionism* (1980), Chester L. Wolford's *The Anger of Stephen Crane: Fiction and the Epic Tradition* (1983), James B. Colvert's *Stephen Crane* (1984), Bettina L. Knapp's *Stephen Crane* (1987), and David Halliburton's *The Color of the Sky: A Study of Stephen Crane* (1991) are among the best of the surprisingly few significant book-length studies.

**Theodore Dreiser**

Most of Dreiser's novels and short stories are in print, but his poetry, plays, and other writings generally are not, and a well-edited uniform edition of Dreiser's writings is badly needed. The University of Pennsylvania has begun to satisfy this need; so far James L. W. West III, textual editor, and Neda Westlake, general editor, have overseen the publication of *American Diaries: 1902–1926* (edited and with an introduction by Thomas P. Riggio) and *Sister Carrie* (John C. Berkey and Alice M. Winters, historical editors). Donald Pizer has made an important contribution with *Theodore Dreiser: A Selection of Uncollected Prose* (1977). Robert H. Elias has edited three volumes of *Letters of Theodore Dreiser* (1959).

W. A. Swanberg's lively *Dreiser* (1965) and Robert H. Elias's *Theodore Dreiser: Apostle of Nature* (1949) are still valuable, but Richard Lingeman's two-volume biography is now standard: *Theodore Dreiser: At the Gates of the City, 1891–1907* (1986) and *Theodore Dreiser: An American Journey, 1908–1945* (1990); Marguerite Tjader's *Theodore Dreiser: A New Dimension* (1965) sheds light on his later life especially. Ellen Moers's *Two Dreisers* (1969) examines the biographical circumstances surrounding (and the compositional histories of) *Sister Carrie* and *An American Tragedy*.

Good introductions to Dreiser's life and work may be found in Philip L. Gerber's *Theodore Dreiser* (1964) and John J. McAleer's *Theodore Dreiser: An Introduction and Interpretation* (1968). F. O. Matthiessen's *Theodore Dreiser* (1951) is still illuminating, but subsequent critical studies by Charles Shapiro, *Theodore Dreiser: Our Bitter Patriot* (1962); Richard Lehan, *Theodore Dreiser:*

*His World and His Novels* (1974); R. N. Mookerjee, *Theodore Dreiser: His Thought and Social Criticism* (1974); Donald Pizer, *The Novels of Theodore Dreiser* (1976); Voshinobu Habutani, *Young Dreiser: A Critical Study* (1979); Lawrence E. Hussman, Jr., *Dreiser and His Fiction: A Twentieth-Century Quest* (1983); and Joseph Griffin's *The Small Canvas: An Introduction to Dreiser's Short Stories* (1985) have advanced our appreciation and understanding considerably.

**W. E. B. Du Bois**

There is no collected edition of Du Bois's prolific output. Several interesting collections of Du Bois's writings are available: Philip S. Foner's *W. E. B. DuBois Speaks: Speeches and Addresses* (1970), Meyer Weinberg's *W. E. B. Du Bois: A Reader* (1970), Andrew G. Paschol, *A W. E. B. DuBois Reader* (1971), Herbert Lee Moon's *The Emerging Thought of W. E. B. DuBois: Essays and Editorials from the "Crisis"* (1972), and Dan S. Green and Edwin D. Driver's *W. E. B. DuBois on Sociology in the Black Community* (1978), which includes sixteen articles by Du Bois. Herbert Aptheker has edited three volumes of *The Correspondence of W. E. B. DuBois* (1973–1978) and *Selections from "Phylon"* (1980).

Significant background to Du Bois's place in American intellectual thought may be found in August Meier's *Negro Thought in America, 1880–1915* (1963) and John Hope Franklin's *From Slavery to Freedom: A History of American Negroes* (1967). Over the past decades several biographies of Du Bois have appeared: Leslie A. Lacey's *Cheer the Lonesome Traveler: The Life of W. E. B. DuBois* (1970), Shirley Graham's *His Day Is Marching On: A Memoir of W. E. B. Du Bois* (1971), and Arnold Rampersad's excellent critical study *The Art and Imagination of W. E. B. DuBois* (1976). Francis Broderick's *W. E. B. DuBois, Negro Leader in a Time of Crisis* (1959), Elliot M. Rudwick's *W. E. B. DuBois: Voice of the Black Protest Movement* (1960), and Jack B. Moore's *W. E. B. DuBois* (1981) provide a brief critical biography and introductory survey of his writings, while Joseph P. De Marco's *The Social Thought of W. E. B. DuBois* (1983) is thorough and helpful on this complex topic. William L. Andrews's *Critical Essays on W. E. B. DuBois* (1985) is the best such collection.

**Mary E. Wilkins Freeman**

The only collection of Freeman's work, *The Best Stories of Mary E. Wilkins* (1927), was edited by Henry W. Lanier. It has been superseded by *Selected Stories of Mary E. Wilkins Freeman* (1983), ed. Marjorie Pryse. Perry D. Westbrook's full-length study, *Mary Wilkins Freeman* (1988), is a good introduction to Freeman's life and work. Abigail Ann Hamblen's *The New England Art of Mary E. Wilkins Freeman* (1966) delivers what its title promises. The introduction to Judith Fetterley and Marjorie Pryse's anthology *American Women Regionalists: 1850–1910* (1992) contextualizes Freeman's fiction.

## Charlotte Perkins Gilman

No collected edition of Gilman's writings exists, but the intense interest in her work has resulted in several reprints of such key titles as *The Living of Charlotte Perkins Gilman: An Autobiography* (1975); *Women and Economics* (1966), ed. Carl Degler; *Herland* (1979), ed. Ann J. Lane; *The Charlotte Perkins Gilman Reader* (1980), ed. Ann J. Lane; *Herland and Selected Stories by Charlotte Perkins Gilman* (1992), ed. Barbara Solomon. Lane's full-scale critical biography, *To Herland and Beyond: The Life and Work of Charlotte Perkins Gilman* (1990), is now standard. Mary A. Hill's *Charlotte Perkins Gilman: The Making of a Radical Feminist* (1980) and her edition, *Endure: The Diaries of Charles Walter Stetson* (1985) illuminate Gilman's early years. Three other books are also worthy of note: Gary Scharnhorst's *Charlotte Perkins Gilman* (1985), Polly Wynn Allen's *Building Domestic Liberty: Charlotte Perkins Gilman's Architectural Feminism* (1988), and Sheryl L. Meyering's *Charlotte Perkins Gilman: The Woman and Her Work* (1989). Catherine Golden has edited *The Captive Imagination: A Casebook on "The Yellow Wallpaper"* (1991).

## W. D. Howells

*A Selected Edition of W. D. Howells* (1968– ) will provide the first authoritatively edited collection (in thirty or more volumes) of Howells's massive literary production. In the meantime, individual reprints must be sought out and may be supplemented by such collections of his letters as the two volumes edited by Henry Nash Smith and William M. Gibson, *The Correspondence of Samuel L. Clemens and William Dean Howells, 1872–1910* (1960), his daughter Mildred Howells's edition in two volumes of *Life in Letters of William Dean Howells* (1928), George Monteir and Brenda Murphy's *John Hay-Howells Letters* (1980), and Walter J. Meserve's *The Complete Plays of W. D. Howells* (1960). Thomas Wortham edited *The Early Prose Writings of William Dean Howells* (1990). Three volumes of *Selected Criticism* appeared in 1993.

The standard critical biography is Edwin H. Cady's two-volume work, *The Road to Realism: The Early Years, 1837–1885* (1956) and *The Realist at War: The Mature Years, 1885–1920* (1958). Van Wyck Brooks's *Howells: His Life and Work* (1959) reveals Howells in relation to his contemporaries. A more recent biography is Kenneth S. Lynn's *William Dean Howells: An American Life* (1971).

In the last four decades critical studies of Howells have appeared regularly. The introduction to Clara M. Kirk and Rudolph Kirk's *William Dean Howells: Representative Selections* (1950) contains much useful information. An excellent brief introduction is William M. Gibson's *William Dean Howells* (1967). Kenneth Eugene Eble's *William Dean Howells* (1982) is a more comprehensive introductory study. Everett Carter's *Howells and the Age of Realism* (1954) was one of the first to argue Howells's centrality to his age and its chief literary development. Other general studies of interest are George N. Bennett's *William Dean Howells: The Development of a Novelist* (1959), the same author's *The Realism of William Dean Howells, 1889–1920* (1973), George C. Carrington's *The Immense Complex Drama* (1966), William McMurray's *The Literary Realism of William Dean Howells* (1967), and Robert L. Hough's *The Quiet Rebel: William Dean Howells as a Social Commentator* (1959). Kermit Vanderbilt's fresh and illuminating *The Achievement of William Dean Howells: A Reinterpretation* (1968) concentrates on five of Howells's novels. Other important, more specialized studies are James Woodress's *Howells and Italy* (1952), Olov W. Fryckstedt's *In Quest of America: A Study of Howells' Early Development as a Novelist* (1958), James L. Dean's *Travels toward Art* (1970), Elizabeth Stevens Prioleau's *The Circle of Eros: Sexuality in the Work of William Dean Howells* (1983), John William Crowley's *The Black Heart's Truth: The Early Career of W. D. Howells* (1985) and *The Mask of Fiction: Essays on W. D. Howells* (1989); and Elsa Nettels's *Language, Race, and Social Class in Howells's America* (1988).

## Henry James

*The Novels and Tales of Henry James* (The New York Edition) in twenty-six volumes, originally published in 1907–1917, was reissued 1962–1965. Other collections of James's diverse writings are available in Leon Edel's edition of *The Complete Plays of Henry James* (1949), R. P. Blackmur's *The Art of the Novel* (1935), Morris Shapiro's edition of *Selected Literary Criticism* (1963), Morton D. Zabel's edition of James's travel writings, *The Art of Travel* (1958), F. O. Matthiessen and Kenneth B. Murdoch's *The Notebooks of Henry James* (1947), F. W. Dupee's edition of the three volumes of *Henry James: Autobiography* (1956), and in various collections of essays and letters edited by Leon Edel.

Edel is also author of the definitive biography of James in five volumes, published between 1953 and 1972. F. O. Matthiessen's *The James Family* (1947) reveals Henry's relationship to this extraordinary American family, which included his brother, William, the celebrated psychologist and philosopher, and sister, Alice, whose diary has attracted considerable attention since its publication in 1964.

F. W. Dupee's *Henry James* (1951) and Bruce McElderry's *Henry James* (1965) are among the best of the introductory books that survey the life and career. Since the 1940s, critical studies of James have abounded. Among the best of these, in chronological order, are J. W. Beach's pioneering *The Method of Henry James* (1918), Morris Roberts's *Henry James's Criticism* (1929), F. O. Matthiessen's *Henry James: The Major Phase* (1944), Quentin Anderson's *The American Henry James* (1957), Richard Poirier's *The Comic Sense of Henry James* (1960), Oscar Cargill's thorough *The Novels of Henry James* (1961), Dorothea Krook's *The Ordeal of Consciousness in Henry James* (1962), Laurence B. Holland's *The Expense of Vision* (1964), J. A. Ward's *Search for Form: Studies in the Structure of James's Fiction* (1967), Sallie Sears's *The Negative Imagination: Form and Perspective in the Novels of Henry James* (1968), Viola Hopkins Winner's *Henry James and the Visual Arts* (1969), James Kraft's *The Early Tales of Henry James* (1970), Martha Banta's *Henry James and the Occult* (1972), Ruth Bernard Yeazell's *Language and Knowledge in the Late Novels of Henry James* (1976), Charles Robert Anderson's *Person, Place, and Thing in Henry James's Novels* (1977), Strother Purdy's *The Hole in the Fabric: Science, Contemporary Literature, and Henry James* (1977), Shlomith Rummon's *The Concept of Ambiguity: The Example of James* (1977), Sergio Perosa's *Henry James and the Experimental Novel* (1978), Daniel J. Schneider's *The Crystal Cage: Adventures of the Imagination in the Fiction of Henry James* (1978), Mary Doyle Springer's *A Rhetoric of Literary Character: Some Women of Henry James* (1978), Edward Wagenknecht's *Eve and Henry James: Portraits of Women and Girls in His Fiction* (1978), Nicola Bradbury's *Henry James: The Later Novels* (1979), Susanne Kappeler's *Writing and Reading in Henry James* (1980), Philip Sicker's *Love and the Quest for Identity in the Fiction of Henry James* (1980), Alwyn Buland's *Culture and Conduct in the Novels of Henry James* (1981), Sarah B. Daugherty's *The Literary Criticism of Henry James* (1981), Daniel Mark Fogel's *Henry James and the Structure of the Romantic Imagination* (1981), William W. Stowe's *Balzac, James, and the Realistic Novel* (1983), John Carlos Rowe's *The Theoretical Dimensions of Henry James* (1984), Roger Sale's *Literary Inheritance* (1984), and Edward Wagenknecht's *The Novels of Henry James* (1983) and *The Tales of Henry James* (1984); Sharon Cameron, *Thinking in Henry James* (1989); Alfred Habegger, *Henry James and the "Woman Business"* (1989); Sarah S. Chapman, *Henry James's Portrait of the Writer as Hero* (1989); Philip Horne, *Henry James and Revision* (1990); Edwin S. Fussell, *The French Side of Henry James* (1990); Richard A. Hocks, *Henry James: A Study of the Short Fiction* (1990).

**Sarah Orne Jewett**

There is no collected edition of Jewett's writings. Jewett's *Stories and Tales* were published in seven volumes in 1910, but a more readily available collection, *The Best Stories of Sarah Orne Jewett* (1925), was edited in two volumes with a foreword by Willa Cather. Richard Cary edited *The Uncollected Short Stories of Sarah Orne Jewett* (1971). Cary also edited *Sarah Orne Jewett Letters* (1967).

The earliest critical biography is F. O. Matthiessen's *Sarah Orne Jewett* (1929). A more complete critical survey of her life and work is Richard Cary's *Sarah Orne Jewett* (1961). Margaret Thorp's brief *Sarah Orne Jewett* (1966) is a good introductory study, as is Josephine Donovan's *Sarah Orne Jewett* (1980). More recently, Perry D. Westbrook's *Acres of Flint: Sarah Orne Jewett and Her Contemporaries* (1981), Louis A. Renza's *"A White Heron" and The Question of Minor Literature*, and Sarah Way Sherman's *Sarah Orne Jewett: An American Persephone* (1989) have both clarified and complicated our understanding of Jewett. Gwen L. Nagel's *Critical Essays on Sarah Orne Jewett* (1984) offers a rich selection, and her introduction is useful.

**Jack London**

No standard edition in English of London's voluminous writings is available; the rare (and incomplete) Sonoma edition (1928) printed twenty-eight titles in twenty-one volumes; the British Fitzroy *Works* reprinted twenty titles in the 1960s. The best collection of London's letters is King Hendricks and Irving Shepard's *Letters from Jack London* (1965). This volume has been replaced by the scholarly *The Letters of Jack London*, 3 vols., ed. Earl Labor, Robert C. Leitz III, and I. Milo Shepard (1988).

The most substantial early biography of London was written by his daughter Joan: *Jack London and His Times: An Unconventional Biography* (1939). Andrew Sinclair's *Jack: A Biography of Jack London* (1977) is sound. Earl Labor's *Jack London* (1974) effectively combines biography and criticism and is the best introduction to London. Three other biographies are worthy of note: Andrew Sinclair's *Jack: A Biography of Jack London* (1977), John Perry's *Jack London: An American Myth* (1981), and Clarice Stasz's *American Dreamers: Charmian and Jack London* (1988).

Specialized studies of special merit are Philip S. Foner's *Jack London, American Rebel* (1947), Franklin Walker's *Jack London and the Klondike* (1966), James I. McClintock's *White Logic: Jack London's Short Stories* (1975), Joan D. Hedrick's *Solitary Comrade: Jack London and His Work* (1982), Charles N. Watson, Jr.'s careful and penetrating *The Novels of Jack London: A Reappraisal* (1983), and James Lundquist's *Jack London: Adventures, Ideas and Fiction* (1987). Joan R. Sherman's *Jack London: A Reference Guide* (1977) is an especially useful review of the secondary literature. Jacquelin Tavernier-Courtin's *Critical Essays on Jack London* (1983) supplies both older and more recent views of London's writings.

## Native American Chants and Songs

John Miles Foley's *Oral Tradition in Literature: Interpretation in Context* (1986) is a collection of six essays that deal with the problem of establishing an aesthetics for oral and orally derived works in our text-oriented culture. Although focused mainly on the European oral tradition, the discussions bear on issues important to the study of American Indian oral literatures. William M. Clements and Frances M. Malpezzi edited *Native American Folklore, 1879–1979* (1984), a useful bibliography that, under the heading of "folklore," includes a whole range of American Indian performances. Although Natalie Curtis Burlin's *The Indians' Book* (1907, 1968) is marked by a desire to see the literature of indigenous people as a priceless relic of the past, it does gather an extensive selection of songs, which are scored as well as translated. In *The Sky Clears: Poetry of the American Indians* (1951) A. Grove Day also emphasizes the "literary" over the "literal," but the more than two hundred songs from forty native American peoples make this an important anthology. Margot Astrov's *American Indian Prose and Poetry* (1962, originally published as *The Winged Serpent: An Anthology of American Indian Poetry*, 1946), remains the most wide-ranging collection of traditional chants and songs, also including "prayers," and some brief narratives. Several of John Bierhorst's sensitive compilations are well worth consulting, in particular *In the Trail of the Wind: American Indian Poems and Ritual Orations* (1971), *Four Masterworks of American Indian Literature: Quetzalcoatl/The Ritual of Condolence/Cuceb/The Night Chant* (1974), and *Cry from the Earth: Music of the North American Indians* (1979). Larry Evers and Felipe Molina's *Yaqui Deer Songs, Maso Bwi- kam* (1987) explains Yaqui culture and the song's place in it. Among recent works from the domain of ethnograpy is Judith Vander's *Songprints: The Musical Experience of Five Shoshone Women* (1988), which shows how music was a part of five women's lives and how song is a living, changing art form in Native American life. Gerald Vizenor's *Summer in the Spring: Anishinaabe Lyric Poems and Stories* (1965, 1993) contains song lyrics and tales, with a glossary of Anishinaabemowin—Chippewa—words. Frances Densmore's *Bureau of American Ethnography Bulletins* were reprinted by the Da Capo Press as part of its music reprint series in 1972, and these include *Chippewa Music*, 2 vols. (1910, 1913); *Papago Music* (1929); and *Teton Sioux Music* (1918). Finally, there is Charlotte Heth's, *Traditional Music of North American Indians* (1980), a collection of essays on American Indian song.

## Native American Oratory

Euro-Americans even in the seventeenth century were interested in the speeches of American Indians, as shown in the missionary John Eliot's collection, *The Dying Speeches of Several Indians* (1685).

A good, recent account of the issues involved in any consideration of Indian oratory exists in David Murray, *Forked Tongues: Speech, Writing, and Representation in North American Indian Texts* (1991). A history of Indian speeches to Euro-Americans may be found in Louis Thomas Jones's *Aboriginal American Oratory: The Tradition of Eloquence among the Indians of the United States* (1965), which provides historical information for the speeches considered but does not pay attention to issues of transcription and translation. Virginia Armstrong's *I Have Spoken: American History through the Voices of Indians* (1971) is a chronologically arranged collection of Native American speeches, beginning in 1609 and ending in 1971, although the majority of the speeches are from the nineteenth century. W. C. Vanderwerth's *Indian Oratory: Famous Speeches by Noted Indian Chieftains* (1971) covers the period from the late eighteenth century to the early twentieth century and provides biographical information on each speaker. Peter Nabokov, in *Native American Testimony: A Chronicle of Indian-White Relations from Prophecy to Present, 1492–1992* (1991), has chronologically and thematically grouped both written and oral native accounts. For accounts of oratorical practices in their traditional and contemporary form, one must turn to the anthropologists and linguists, in particular to such studies as Donald Bahr's *Pima and Papago Ritual Oratory: A Study of Three Texts* (1975), and Michael Foster's *From the Earth to Beyond the Sky: An Ethnographic Approach to Four Longhouse Iroquois Speech Events* (1974).

## Booker T. Washington

Louis R. Harlan has edited *The Booker T. Washington Papers* in thirteen volumes (1972–84). August Meier's *Negro Thought in America, 1880–1915* (1963) and John Hope Franklin's *From Slavery to Freedom: A History of American Negroes* (1967) are two useful background books. E. L. Thornborough's biographical study *Booker T. Washington* (1969) should be supplemented by the fine critical biography by Louis R. Harlan, *Booker T. Washington: The Making of a Black Leader, 1865–1901* (1972) and *Booker T. Washington The Wizard of Tuskegee, 1901–1915* (1983). Specialized studies of interest are Basil Matthews's *Booker T. Washington: Educator and Interracial Interpreter* (1948) and G. R. Spencer's *Booker T. Washington and the Negro's Place in American Life* (1955). James M. Cox's chapter "Autobiography and Washington" in his *Recovering Literature's Lost Ground: Essays in American Autobiography* (1989) is especially perceptive.

## Edith Wharton

There is no uniform edition of Wharton's writings. Louis Auchincloss edited *The Edith Wharton Reader* (1965) and R. W. B. Lewis edited in two volumes *The Collected Short Stories of Edith*

Wharton (1968) and (with Nancy Lewis) The Letters of Edith Wharton (1988).

Lewis, using the extensive Wharton Papers at Yale, prepared the definitive Edith Wharton: A Biography (1975). Millicent Bell's Edith Wharton and Henry James: The Story of Their Friendship (1965) is still useful.

Two excellent introductory studies are Louis Auchincloss's brief Edith Wharton (1961) and Margaret B. McDowell's Edith Wharton (1976). Book-length studies of importance include Blake Nevius's Edith Wharton: A Study of Her Fiction (1953), Marilyn J. Lyde's Edith Wharton: Convention and Morality in the Work of a Novelist (1959), Gary H. Lindberg's Edith Wharton and the Novel of Manners (1975), Cynthia Griffin Wolff's A Feast of Words: The Triumph of Edith Wharton (1977), Richard H. Lawson's Edith Wharton (1977), Elizabeth Ammons's Edith Wharton's Argument with America (1980), Geoffrey Walton's Edith Wharton, a Critical Interpretation (1982), Wendy Gimbel's Edith Wharton: Orphancy and Survival (1984), Carol Wershoven's The Female Intruder in the Novels of Edith Wharton (1983),

Catherine M. Rae's Edith Wharton's New York Quartet (1984), Susan Goodman's Edith Wharton's Women (1990), Janet Goodwyn's Edith Wharton: Traveller in the Land of Letters (1990), and Penelope Vita-Finzi's Edith Wharton and the Art of Fiction (1990).

### Zitkala Ša [Gertrude Bonnin]

Dexter Fisher's 1986 edition of Zitkala Ša's American Indian Stories (1921) includes an expert and insightful introduction to this collection of autobiography, fiction, and nonfiction prose. The best recent discursive bibliography of Native American literature is A. LaVonne Brown Ruoff's American Indian Literatures: An Introduction, Bibliographic Review, and Selected Bibliography (1990), a comprehensive and judicious survey of the field. Two other titles may be recommended to anyone interested in Native American autobiography: A. David Brumble III's American Indian Autobiography (1988) and Arnold Krupat's essay "Native American Autobiography and the Synechdochic Self" in Paul John Eakin's American Autobiography: Retrospect and Prospect (1991).

## AMERICAN LITERATURE BETWEEN THE WARS, 1914–1945

General thematic or chronological approaches to the literature in this period include John Aldridge, After the Lost Generation: A Critical Study of the Writers of Two Wars (1951); Modernism and the Harlem Renaissance, ed. Houston Baker, Jr. (1987); Shari Benstock, Women of the Left Bank: Paris 1900–1940 (1986); Richard Bridgman, The Colloquial Style in America (1966); three books by Malcolm Cowley: Exile's Return (rev. 1951), After the Genteel Tradition: American Writers, 1910–1930 (rev. 1964), and A Second Flowering: Works and Days of the Lost Generation (1973); Noel Riley Fitch, Sylvia Beach and the Lost Generation: A Literary History of Paris in the Twenties and Thirties (1983); Gillian Hanscombe and Virginia L. Sayers, Writing for Their Lives: The Modernist Women 1910–1940 (1987); Frederick J. Hoffman, The Twenties: American Writing in the Postwar Decade (1955); Nathan I. Huggins, Harlem Renaissance (1971); Bruce Kellner, ed., The Harlem Renaissance: A Historical Dictionary for the Era (1984); Marcus Klein, Foreigners: The Making of American Literature, 1900–1940 (1981); Dale Kramer, Chicago Renaissance: The Literary Life in the Midwest, 1910–1930 (1966); David Levering Lewis, When Harlem Was in Vogue (1981); Edward Margolies, Native Sons: A Critical Study of Twentieth-Century Negro American Authors (1968); Louis D. Rubin, Writers of the Modern South (1963); A. LaVonne Brown Ruoff, American Indian Literatures (1990); Lawrence H. Schwartz, Creating Faulkner's Reputation: The Politics of

Modern Literary Criticism (1988); Daniel J. Singal, The War Within: From Victorian to Modernist Thought in the South 1919–1945 (1982); Benjamin T. Spencer, Patterns of Nationality: Twentieth-Century Literary Versions of America (1981); Cecilia Tichi, Shifting Gears: Technology, Literature, Culture in Modernist America (1987); and Edmund Wilson, The Shores of Light: A Literary Chronicle of the Twenties and Thirties (1952).

Among major studies of American drama of the era are Brooks Atkinson, Broadway: Nineteen Hundred to Nineteen Seventy (1970); C. W. E. Bigsby, A Critical Introduction to Twentieth-Century American Drama, Vol. 1: 1900–1940 (1985); Harold Clurman, The Fervent Years: The Story of the Group Theatre and the Thirties (repr. 1957); Alan S. Downer, Fifty Years of American Drama, 1900–1950 (1951); Glenn Hughes, A History of the American Theater, 1700–1950 (1951); Joseph Wood Krutch, The American Drama Since 1918 (rev. 1957); Ethan Mordden, The American Theatre (1981); Brenda Murphy, American Realism and American Drama, 1880–1940 (1987); Arthur Hobson Quinn, A History of the American Drama from the Civil War to the Present Day (rev. 1936); and Howard Taubmann, The Making of the American Theater (1965).

Important general studies of American poetry since World War I include Louise Bogan, Achievement in American Poetry, 1900–1950 (1951); L. S. Dembo, Conceptions of Reality in Modern American Poetry (1966); William Drake, The First Wave:

*Women Poets in America, 1914–1945* (1987); Edwin Fussell, *Lucifer in Harness* (1973); Albert Gelpi, *The Tenth Muse: The Psyche of the American Poet* (1975) and *A Coherent Splendor: The American Poetic Renaissance, 1910–1950* (1987); Maureen Honey, ed., *Shadowed Dreams: Women's Poetry of the Harlem Renaissance* (1989); Graham Hough, *Image and Experience: Studies in a Literary Revolution* (1960); Hugh Kenner, *The Pound Era* (1971) and *A Homemade World: The American Modernist Writers* (1975); J. Hillis Miller, *Poets of Reality* (1965); Cary Nelson, *Repression and Recovery: Modern American Poetry and the Politics of Cultural Memory, 1910–1945* (1989); Roy Harvey Pearce, *The Continuity of American Poetry* (1961); David Perkins, *A History of Modern Poetry* (1976); M. L. Rosenthal and Sally M. Gall, *The Modern Poetic Sequence: The Genius of Modern Poetry* (1984); Donald E. Stanford, *Revolution and Convention in Modern Poetry* (1983); and Lisa M. Steinman, *Made in America: Science, Technology, and American Modernist Poets* (1987).

Studies of fiction include Daniel Aaron, *Writers on the Left* (1961); Joseph Warren Beach, *American Fiction: 1920–1940* (1941); Joseph Blotner, *The Modern American Political Novel* (1966); Hazel V. Carby, *Reconstructing Womanhood: The Emergence of the Afro-American Woman Novelist* (1987); Leon Edel, *The Psychological Novel, 1900–1950* (1955); Warren French, *The Social Novel at the End of an Era* (1966); W. M. Frohock, *The Novel of Violence in America* (rev. 1957); Maxwell Geismar, *Writers in Crisis: The American Novel between Two Wars* (1942); Alfred Kazin, *On Native Grounds: An Interpretation of Modern American Prose Literature* (1942); Michael Milgate, *American Social Fiction* (1967); Walter Rideout, *The Radical Novel in the United States, 1900–1954* (1956); and Linda Wagner-Martin, *The Modern American Novel 1914–1945* (1990).

For bibliographies of authors consult *Sixteen Modern American Authors* (1963) and *Sixteen Modern American Authors, Vol. 2: A Survey of Research and Criticism Since 1972* (1990), ed. Jackson R. Bryer, and the series *American Literary Scholarship: An Annual*, ed. James Woodress and J. Albert Robbins (1965–).

### Sherwood Anderson

There is no collected edition of Anderson's writing. In addition to works mentioned in the author's introduction, Anderson published *The Modern Writer* (1925); *Sherwood Anderson's Notebook* (1925); *Alice and the Lost Novel* (1929); *Nearer the Grass Roots* (1929); *The American Country Fair* (1930); and *Home Town* (1940). *The Letters of Sherwood Anderson* (1953) were edited by Howard Mumford Jones and Walter Rideout. See also *Sherwood Anderson: Selected Letters*, ed. Charles E. Modlin (1984) and *Letters to Bab: Sherwood*

*Anderson to Marietta D. Finley, 1916–1933* (1985). Eugene P. Seehy and Kenneth A. Lohf compiled *Sherwood Anderson: A Bibliography* (1960); Kim Townsend has written *Sherwood Anderson: A Biography* (1987); for critical commentary see David D. Anderson, *Sherwood Anderson: An Introduction and Interpretation* (1967); *Critical Essays on Sherwood Anderson*, ed. David D. Anderson (1981); *Homage to Sherwood Anderson*, ed. Paul F. Appel (1970); Rex Burbank, *Sherwood Anderson* (1964); Irving Howe, *Sherwood Anderson* (1951); *Sherwood Anderson: A Collection of Critical Essays*, ed. Walter Rideout (1974); James Schevill, *Sherwood Anderson* (1951); Brom Weber, *Sherwood Anderson* (1964); and *The Achievement of Sherwood Anderson: Essays in Criticism*, ed. R. L. White (1966).

### Black Elk

*Black Elk Speaks* was published in 1932 and reissued in 1961. The best account of Black Elk's life is found in Raymond J. DeMallie's *The Sixth Grandfather: Black Elk's Teachings Given to John G. Neihardt* (1984). DeMallie also gives the complete texts of Black Elk's interviews with John Neihardt, analyzes Black Elk's vision from an anthropological perspective, and discusses Neihardt's role in producing the book. See also Julian Rice, *Black Elk's Story: Distinguishing Its Lakota Purpose* (1991). Neihardt's contribution is also considered in Lucile F. Aly's *John G. Neihardt: A Critical Biography* (1977).

The first literary study of *Black Elk Speaks* was Robert F. Sayre's "Vision and Experience in *Black Elk Speaks*," *College English*, 32 (1971): 509–35. Also see Sally McCluskey, "*Black Elk Speaks*: And So Does John Neihardt," *Western American Literature* 6 (1972): 231–42; Albert Stone, *Autobiographical Occasions and Original Acts* (1982); Janet Varner Gunn's *Autobiography: Toward a Poetics of Experience* (1982).

Works considering *Black Elk Speaks* both in its own right and in relation to more recent native American authors are Michael Castro, *Interpreting the Indian: Twentieth Century Poets and the Native American* (1983); Kenneth Lincoln, "Native American Literatures: 'old like hills, like stars' " in *Three American Literatures*, ed. Houston A. Baker, Jr. (1982); Jarold Ramsey, *Reading the Fire: Essays in the Traditional Indian Literatures of the Far West* (1983); A. LaVonne Brown Ruoff, *American IndianLiteratures* (1990); Andrew Wiget, *Native American Literature* (1985); Arnold Krupat, *For Those Who Come After: A Study of Native American Autobiography* (1985); and *Recovering the Word: Essays on Native American Literature*, ed. Brian Swann and Arnold Krupat (1987).

### Willa Cather

Cather's volume of verse, *April Twilights* (1903; rev. 1923), and her collection of essays, *Not under*

*Forty* (1936), supplement the standard edition of her fiction, *The Novels and Stories of Willa Cather* (1937–1941). Her tales and novels have been published in two volumes by the Library of America with notes by Sharon O'Brien (1987, 1990). Other sources include *Willa Cather on Writing* (1949); *Writings from Willa Cather's Campus Years*, ed. James Shively (1950); and *The Kingdom of Art: Willa Cather's First Principles and Critical Statements*, ed. Bernice Slote (1967). William M. Curtin has collected her articles and reviews in the two-volume *The World and the Parish* (1970). *Willa: The Life of Willa Cather*, by Phyllis C. Robinson (1982), is a full-length biography, as is *Willa Cather: A Literary Life* by James Woodress (1987). Sharon O'Brien's *Willa Cather: The Emerging Voice* (1987) concentrates on Cather's early years. Critical studies of Cather are David Daiches's *Willa Cather* (1951); Dorothy Van Ghent's *Willa Cather* (1964); David Stouck's *Willa Cather's Imagination* (1975); Philip Gerber's *Willa Cather* (1975); Marilyn Arnold's *Willa Cather's Short Fiction* (1984); and Susan J. Rosowski, *The Voyage Perilous: Willa Cather's Romanticism* (1986). Personal memoirs include Edith Lewis's *Willa Cather Living* (1953) and Elizabeth Sergeant's *Willa Cather: A Memoir* (1953). Commentaries on Cather are gathered in *Willa Cather and Her Critics*, ed. James Schroeter (1967).

### Hart Crane

Marc Simon edited *Complete Poems of Hart Crane* (1993), the best current text. Also of use is Brom Weber, *The Complete Poems and Selected Letters and Prose of Hart Crane* (1966). Crane's *Collected Poems*, edited by his friend Waldo Frank, appeared in 1933. Other sources of primary and bibliographical material are *The Letters of Hart Crane*, ed. Brom Weber (1965); *The Letters of Hart Crane and His Family*, ed. Thomas S. W. Lewis (1974); *Hart Crane: An Annotated Critical Bibliography*, ed. Joseph Schwartz (1970); and *Hart Crane: A Descriptive Bibliography*, ed. Joseph Schwartz and Robert C. Schweik (1972). Gary Lane compiled *A Concordance to the Poems of Hart Crane* (1972).

Biographies of Crane are Philip Horton, *Hart Crane: The Life of an American Poet* (1937; repr. 1957), Brom Weber, *Hart Crane: A Biographical and Critical Study* (1948) and John Unterecker, *Voyager: A Life of Hart Crane* (1969).

Three poet-critics contributed important early essays on Crane: Richard P. Blackmur in *The Double Agent* (1935); Allen Tate in *Reactionary Essays on Poetry and Ideas* (1936); and Yvor Winters in *In Defense of Reason* (1947). Full-length critical studies are L. S. Dembo's *Hart Crane's Sanscrit Charge: A Study of "The Bridge"* (1960); R. W. B. Lewis's *The Poetry of Hart Crane* (1967); Vincent Quinn's *Hart Crane* (1963); Samuel Hazo's *Hart Crane: An Introduction and Interpretation* (1963); Monroe K. Spears's *Hart Crane* (1965); R. W. But-

terfield's *The Broken Arc: A Study of Hart Crane* (1969); Hunce Voelcker's *The Hart Crane Voyages* (1967); Richard P. Sugg's *Hart Crane's "The Bridge"* (1976); Samuel Hazo's *Smithereened Apart: A Critique of Hart Crane* (1977); Helge Norman Nilsen's *Hart Crane's Divided Vision: An Analysis of "The Bridge"* (1980); Edward Brunner's *Hart Crane and the Making of "The Bridge"* (1984); and Thomas E. Yingling, *Hart Crane and the Homosexual Text* (1990).

### Countee Cullen

For extended studies of Cullen see Stephen H. Bronz, *Roots of Negro Racial Consciousness—The 1920's: Three Harlem Renaissance Authors* (1954); Helen J. Dinger, *A Study of Countee Cullen* (1953); Margaret Perry, *A Bio-Bibliography of Countee P. Cullen* (1969); and Blanche E. Ferguson, *Countee Cullen and the Negro Renaissance* (1966).

### E. E. Cummings

*Complete Poems 1904–62*, edited by George J. Firmage, was published in 1991. George J. Firmage also edited *Three Plays and a Ballet* (1967). Cummings's prose fiction includes *The Enormous Room* (1922) and *EIMI* (1933). *E. E. Cummings: A Miscellany Revised*, ed. George J. Firmage (1965), contains previously uncollected short prose pieces. *Six Nonlectures* (1953) consists of the talks that Cummings delivered at Harvard in the same year. *Selected Letters of E. E. Cummings* (1969) was edited by F. W. Dupee and George Stade. George J. Firmage edited *E. E. Cummings: A Bibliography* (1960).

Several of Cummings's earlier individual works have been reedited by George J. Firmage in the Cummings Typescript Editions. These include *Tulips & Chimneys* (1976); *No Thanks* (1978); *The Enormous Room*, including illustrations by Cummings (1978); *ViVa* (1979); *XAIPE* (1979); and *Etcetera*, the unpublished poems (1983).

*The Magic Maker*, a biography by Cummings's friend Charles Norman, was published in 1958 and reissued after the poet's death. A biography is *Dreams in the Mirror*, by Richard S. Kennedy (1979). Norman Friedman's *E. E. Cummings: The Art of His Poetry* (1960) focuses on Cummings's language and the techniques of his poetry. Friedman's second book, *E. E. Cummings: The Growth of a Writer* (1964), discusses Cummings's texts in roughly chronological order. Barry A. Marks's *E. E. Cummings* (1964) analyzes individual poems and considers the relation between Cummings's graphic art and the principles of his poetry. Robert E. Wegner's *The Poetry and Prose of E. E. Cummings* (1965), Bethany K. Dumas's *E. E. Cummings: A Remembrance of Miracles* (1974), and *E. E. Cummings, An Introduction to the Poetry* by Rushworth Kidder (1979) provide introductions to Cummings's work. See also *I Am, A Study of E. E. Cummings' Poems* by Cary Lane (1976).

*E. E. Cummings and the Critics* is edited by S. V. Baum (1962). Norman Friedman edited *E. E. Cummings: A Collection of Critical Essays* (1972).

**Hilda Doolittle (H. D.)**
The poetry through 1944 has been collected and edited by Louis L. Martz in *Collected Poems 1912–1944* (1983). *Collected Poems of H. D.* was published in 1925. Subsequent volumes of poetry include *Red Rose for Bronze* (1931); the trilogy of war poems *The Walls Do Not Fall* (1944), *Tribute to the Angels* (1945), and *The Flowering of the Rod* (1946); the dramatic monologue *Helen in Egypt* (1961); the major collection of her late poems, *Hermetic Definition* (1972); and the long poem *Vale Ave* (1992). H. D.'s other book-length verse dramas are *Hippolytus Temporizes* (1927) and the translation of Euripides' *Ion* (1937). *Palimpsest* (1926), *Hadylus* (1928), *Bid Me to Live* (1961), and *HERmione* (1981) comprise her major prose fiction. *By Avon River* (1949) celebrates Shakespeare in prose and verse. *Tribute to Freud* (1956) is her account of her psychoanalysis by Freud. Also important are two autobiographical works: *End to Torment* (1979) and *The Gift* (1982).

*Herself Defined: The Poet H. D. and Her World*, by Barbara Guest (1984), is a biography, while *H. D.: The Career of That Struggle*, by Rachel Blau DuPlessie (1986), *Psyche Reborn: The Emergence of H. D.* by Susan S. Friedman (1981), and *H. D.: The Life and Work of an American Poet* by Janice S. Robinson (1982) combine biography and literary analysis. Two earlier full-length studies are Thomas Burnett Swann's *The Classical World of H. D.* (1962) and Vincent Quinn's *Hilda Doolittle* (1967); more recent are Gary Barnett, *H. D.: Between Image and Epic, The Mysteries of Her Poetics* (1990) and Susan Stanford Friedman, *Penelope's Web: Gender, Modernity, and H. D.'s Fiction* (1990).

**T. S. Eliot**
Eliot's poetic works have been collected in *Collected Poems, 1909–1962* (1963) and *The Complete Poems and Plays of T. S. Eliot* (1969). The indispensable manuscript to *The Waste Land* is in *The Waste Land: A Facsimile and Transcript of the Original Drafts Including the Annotations of Ezra Pound*, ed. Valerie Eliot (1971). Important critical writings include *The Use of Poetry and the Use of Criticism* (1933); *Poetry and Drama* (1951); *The Three Voices of Poetry* (1953); *On Poetry and Poets* (1957); and *To Criticize the Critic and Other Writings* (1965). Three volumes of social commentary are *After Strange Gods* (1934); *The Idea of a Christian Society* (1939); and *Notes toward the Definition of Culture* (1948). Valerie Eliot has edited *The Letters of T. S. Eliot, Vol. 1: 1898–1922* (1988).

The most complete biographical study is *T. S. Eliot: A Life*, by Peter Ackroyd (1984). Even more detailed are Lyndall Gordon's *Eliot's Early Years* (1977) and *Eliot's New Life* (1988).

Influential earlier studies of Eliot include F. O. Matthiessen's *The Achievement of T. S. Eliot* (rev. 1947); Helen Gardner's *The Art of T. S. Eliot* (1950); Hugh Kenner's *The Invisible Poet* (1959); Northrop Frye's *T. S. Eliot* (1963); and Stephen Spender's *T. S. Eliot* (1976). Useful introductions include Elizabeth Drew's *T. S. Eliot: The Design of His Poetry* (1949); George Williamson's *A Reader's Guide to T. S. Eliot* (1953); and Grover Smith's *T. S. Eliot's Poetry and Plays* (1956) and his *The Waste Land, by T. S. Eliot* (1983). Among virtually countless critical studies are David E. Jones, *The Plays of T. S. Eliot* (1960); Carol Smith, *T. S. Eliot's Poetry and Plays* (1963); John Margolies, *T. S. Eliot's Intellectual Development, 1922–1939* (1972); Helen Gardener, *The Composition of Four Quartets* (1978); Derek Traversi, *T. S. Eliot: The Longer Poems* (1976); Ronald Bush, *T. S. Eliot: A Study in Character and Style* (1984); Louis Menand, *Discovering Modernism: T. S. Eliot and His Context* (1987); Eric Svary, "The Men of 1914": *T. S. Eliot and Early Modernism* (1988); Eric Sigg, *The American T. S. Eliot: A Study of the Early Writings* (1989); and Jewel Spears Brooker and Joseph Bentley, *Reading "The Waste Land": Modernism and the Limits of Interpretation* (1990). For collections of critical essays about Eliot, see *Twentieth Century Interpretations of The Waste Land*, ed. Jay Martin (1968); *T. S. Eliot: A Collection of Criticism*, ed. Linda W. Wagner (1974); and *T. S. Eliot: The Modernist in History*, ed. Ronald Bush (1991).

Donald C. Gallup compiled the standard bibliography, *T. S. Eliot: A Bibliography* (rev. 1969).

**William Faulkner**
There is no collected edition of Faulkner's works. In addition to volumes mentioned in the author's headnote are *Early Prose and Poetry*, ed. Carvel Collins (1962); *Dr. Martino and Other Stories* (1934); *Pylon* (1935); *The Unvanquished* (1938); *Intruder in the Dust* (1948); *Knight's Gambit* (1949); *Collected Stories of William Faulkner* (1950); *Requiem for a Nun* (1951); *Notes on a Horsethief* (1951); *Big Woods* (1955); and *Essays, Speeches, and Public Letters*, ed. James B. Meriwether (1965). Transcripts of discussion sessions and interviews with Faulkner include *Faulkner at Nagano*, ed. Robert A. Jelliffe (1956); *Faulkner in the University*, ed. Frederick L. Gwynn and Joseph L. Blotner (1959); *Faulkner at West Point*, ed. Joseph L. Fant and Robert Ashley (1964); and *The Lion in the Garden*, ed. James B. Meriwether and Michael Millgate (1968). Letters are collected in *The Faulkner–Cowley File*, ed. Malcolm Cowley (1961), and *Selected Letters of William Faulkner*, ed. Joseph L. Blotner (1977). Noel Polk has produced editions of several Faulkner novels based on study of the manuscripts.

The full-length *Faulkner: A Biography*, 2 vols. (1974), by Joseph L. Blotner has been condensed and updated in *Faulkner* (1984). Two shorter biographies based on Blotner's work are *William Faulkner: His Life and Work* by David Minter (1980) and *Faulkner: The Transfiguration of Biography* by Judith Wittenberg (1979).

A comprehensive guide is *Faulkner's World: A Directory of His People and Synopsis of Actions in His Published Works*, by Thomas E. Connolly (1988). David Dowling's *William Faulkner* (1989) is a general introduction. Full-length early studies include Michael Millgate's *The Achievement of William Faulkner* (1966); Cleanth Brooks's *William Faulkner: The Yoknapatawpha Country* (1963); Irving Howe's *William Faulkner* (1952; rev. 1962); and Hyatt H. Waggoner's *William Faulkner: From Jefferson to the World* (1959). More recent studies include John Hunt's *William Faulkner: Art in Theological Tension* (1965); Melvin Backman's *Faulkner: The Major Years* (1966); H. Richardson's *William Faulkner, the Journey to Self-Discovery* (1969); John T. Irwin's *Doubling and Incest, Repetition and Revenge: A Speculative Reading of Faulkner* (1975); Thadious M. Davis's *Faulkner's "Negro": Art and the Southern Context* (1983); Eric J. Sundquist's *Faulkner: The House Divided* (1983); Robert Dale Parker, *Faulkner and the Novelistic Imagination* (1985); Warwick Wadlington's *Reading Faulknerian Tragedy* (1987); Stephen M. Ross, *Fiction Inexhaustible Voice: Speech and Writing in Faulkner* (1989); and Minrose C. Gwin, *The Feminine and Faulkner: Reading (Beyond) Sexual Difference* (1990).

Edited collections of critical essays include Frederick J. Hoffman and Olga Vickery, *William Faulkner: Three Decades of Criticism* (1960); Linda Wagner, *William Faulkner: Four Decades of Criticism* (1973); Dean M. Schmitter, ed., *William Faulkner: A Collection of Criticism* (1973); Doreen Fowler and Ann J. Abadie, *Faulkner and Race* (1987); and Louis J. Budd and Edwin Cady, *On Faulkner* (1989).

### F. Scott Fitzgerald

Fitzgerald's novels are *This Side of Paradise* (1920); *The Beautiful and Damned* (1922); *The Great Gatsby* (1925); *Tender Is the Night* (1934; rev. 1939; repr. 1953); and the unfinished *The Last Tycoon* (1941). His collections of stories are *Flappers and Philosophers* (1921); *Tales of the Jazz Age* (1922); *All the Sad Young Men* (1926); and *Taps at Reveille* (1935). A satirical play, *The Vegetable, or From Presidents to Postman*, was published in 1923. Among collections of Fitzgerald's writings are *The Apprentice Fiction of F. Scott Fitzgerald*, ed. John Kuehl (1965); *F. Scott Fitzgerald in His Own Time: A Miscellany*, ed. Jackson R. Bryer and Matthew J. Bruccoli (1971); and *Afternoon of an Author*, ed. Arthur Mizener (1957). *The Crack-Up*, ed. Edmund Wilson (1945), collects essays, notebook entries, and letters from the 1930s.

The fullest collection of letters is *Correspondence of F. Scott Fitzgerald*, ed. Matthew J. Bruccoli and

Margaret M. Duggan (1980). Other volumes of letters are *Dear Scott / Dear Max: The Fitzgerald–Perkins Correspondence*, ed. John Kuehl and Jackson R. Bryer (1971) and *As Ever, Scott Fitz*, ed. Matthew J. Bruccoli and Jennifer McCabe Atkinson (1972) (letters between Fitzgerald and his literary agent, Harold Ober). Fitzgerald's biographers are Arthur Mizener, *The Far Side of Paradise* (1951; rev. 1965); Andrew Turnbull, *Scott Fitzgerald* (1962); Matthew J. Bruccoli, *Some Sort of Epic Grandeur: The Life of F. Scott Fitzgerald* (1981); Andre le Vot, *F. Scott Fitzgerald: A Biography* (1983); Scott Donaldson, *Fool for Love: F. Scott Fitzgerald, A Biographical Portrait* (1983); and James Mellow, *Invented Lives* (1984).

Critical introductions to Fitzgerald's work include Kenneth Eble's *F. Scott Fitzgerald* (1963); Henry Dan Piper's *F. Scott Fitzgerald: A Critical Portrait* (1965); and Richard D. Lehan's *F. Scott Fitzgerald and the Craft of Fiction* (1966). Among earlier general and specialized studies are James E. Miller's *The Fictional Technique of F. Scott Fitzgerald* (1957); William Goldhurst's *F. Scott Fitzgerald and His Contemporaries* (1963); Matthew J. Bruccoli's *The Composition of Tender Is the Night* (1963); Robert Sklar's *F. Scott Fitzgerald: The Last Laocoön* (1967); Milton R. Stern's *The Golden Moment: The Novels of F. Scott Fitzgerald* (1970); and John F. Callahan's *The Illusions of a Nation: Myth and History in the Novels of F. Scott Fitzgerald* (1972). More recent are *The Achieving of "The Great Gatsby": F. Scott Fitzgerald, 1920–1925*, by Robert Emmet Long (1979) and *F. Scott Fitzgerald and the Art of Social Fiction*, by Brian Way (1980). Recent collections of critical essays are *The Short Stories of F. Scott Fitzgerald: New Approaches in Criticism*, ed. Jackson R. Bryer (1983) and *New Essays on "The Great Gatsby,"* ed. Matthew J. Bruccoli (1985). Jackson R. Bryer has edited *The Critical Reputation of F. Scott Fitzgerald: A Bibliographical Study* (1967).

### Robert Frost

*The Poetry of Robert Frost* (1969) incorporated *Complete Poems* (1949) and Frost's last volume, *In the Clearing* (1962). Eleven early essays on farming, edited by Edward C. Lathem and Lawrance Thompson, appear in *Robert Frost: Farm Poultryman* (1963). Important collections of letters appear in *Selected Letters of Robert Frost*, ed. Lawrance Thompson (1964); *The Letters of Robert Frost to Louis Untermeyer* (1963); and Margaret Anderson, *Robert Frost and John Bartlett: The Record of a Friendship* (1963). His critical essays have been collected in *Selected Prose*, ed. Hyde Cox and Edward C. Lathem (1966). Collections of conversations and interviews with Frost include Edward C. Lathem's *Interviews with Robert Frost* (1966); Reginald L. Cook's *The Dimensions of Robert Frost* (1964); Daniel Smythe's *Robert Frost Speaks* (1954); and Louis Mertin's *Robert Frost: Life and Talks–Walking* (1965).

Lawrance Thompson finished two volumes of the authorized biography before his death: *Robert Frost: The Early Years, 1874–1915* (1966) and *Robert Frost: The Years of Triumph, 1915–1938* (1970). The third volume, *Robert Frost, the Later Years*, was completed by Richard Winnick (1976), and Edward C. Lathem produced a shorter version of the biography in *Robert Frost: A Biography* (1981). William H. Pritchard in *Frost: A Literary Life Reconsidered* (1984) provides a biography more interested in the poet's art than his personal life. The early *Robert Frost: A Bibliography*, ed. W. B. Shubrick Clymer and Charles Green (1937), may be supplemented by W. B. S. Clymer, *Robert Frost: A Bibliography* (1972). James L. Potter's *Robert Frost Handbook* (1980) is a useful guide.

Two brief critical introductions to Frost's poetry are Lawrance Thompson's *Robert Frost* (1964) and Philip L. Gerber's *Robert Frost* (1966). Longer critical studies are John F. Lynen's *The Pastoral Art of Robert Frost* (1964); Reginald L. Cook's *The Dimensions of Robert Frost* (1958); Radcliffe Squires's *The Major Themes of Robert Frost* (1963); Richard Poirier, *Robert Frost, The Work of Knowing* (1977); and John C. Kemp, *Robert Frost and New England: The Poet as Regionalist* (1979). Collections of critical essays include *Robert Frost: A Collection of Critical Essays*, ed. James M. Cox (1962); *Recognition of Robert Frost*, ed. Richard Thornton (1970); and *Robert Frost: Studies of the Poetry*, ed. Kathryn Gibbs Harris (1979).

### Angelina Weld Grimké

It has been diffiult to undertake criticism of Grimké with little of her work in print. This situation is being corrected. *The Selected Works of Angelina Weld Grimké*, ed. Carolivia Herron (1991), prints about one-third of the poetry and half the stories, along with the play *Rachel*; it also has an excellent biographical and critical introduction. Grimké is one of three writers discussed in Gloria T. Hull's, *Color, Sex, and Poetry* (1987). The journal *Sage: A Scholarly Journal on Black Women* has published a few essays on Grimké over the years.

### Ernest Hemingway

There is no collected edition of Hemingway's writings. In addition to works mentioned in the author's headnote, his fiction includes *Today Is Friday* (1926) and *God Rest You Merry Gentlemen* (1933). His tribute to Spain, *The Spanish Earth*, and his play *The Fifth Column* appeared in 1938, the latter in a collection *The Fifth Column and the First Forty-nine Stories*. His journalism has been collected in *The Wild Years*, ed. Gene Z. Hanrahan (1962), and *By-Line: Ernest Hemingway, Selected Articles and Dispatches of Four Decades*, ed. William White (1967). Audre Hanneman's *Ernest Hemingway: A Comprehensive Bibliography* (1967) is thorough. Scribners has published *The Complete Short Stories of Ernest Hemingway* (1987).

The authorized biography is Carlos Baker's

*Ernest Hemingway: A Life Story* (1969). Jeffrey Meyers's *Hemingway: A Biography* (1985) and Kenneth S. Lynn's *Hemingway* (1987) are also important, while Michael Reynolds's *The Young Hemingway* (1986) is the fullest and most accurate treatment of Hemingway's early years as is his *Hemingway: The Paris Years* (1989) for Hemingway's life in Paris. A succinct overview is Scott Donaldson's *By Force of Will: The Life and Art of Ernest Hemingway* (1977). *The Hemingway Women*, by Bernice Kertner (1983), tells about Hemingway's mother, wives, and lovers; *Fame Became of Him: Hemingway as Public Writer*, by John Raeburn (1984), compares the life with the public image.

*A Reader's Guide to Ernest Hemingway* by Arthur Waldhorn (1972) and *A Reader's Guide to the Short Stories of Ernest Hemingway* by Paul Smith (1989) are useful handbooks. Full-length critical works include Carlos Baker's *Ernest Hemingway: The Writer as Artist* (1952; rev. 1956 and 1963) and Philip Young's *Ernest Hemingway* (1952; rev. 1966). For collections of critical essays on Hemingway, see *Ernest Hemingway: The Man and His Work*, ed. John K. M. McCaffrey (1950); *Hemingway and His Critics*, ed. Carlos Baker (1961); *Hemingway: A Collection of Critical Essays*, ed. Robert P. Weeks (1962); *Ernest Hemingway: Six Decades of Criticism*, ed. Linda Wagner-Martin (1987); and *New Critical Approaches to the Short Stories of Ernest Hemingway*, ed. Jackson J. Benson (1991). Specialized studies include Charles A. Fenton's *The Apprenticeship of Ernest Hemingway: The Early Years* (1954); Robert W. Lewis's *Hemingway on Love* (1965); Robert O. Stephen's *Hemingway's Nonfiction: The Public Voice* (1968); Bernard Oldsey's *Hemingway's Hidden Craft: The Writing of "A Farewell to Arms"* (1979); Wirt Williams's *The Tragic Art of Ernest Hemingway* (1982); and Mark Spilka's, *Hemingway's Quarrel with Androgyny* (1990).

### Langston Hughes

*The Selected Poems of Langston Hughes* (1959 and 1965) draws on his earlier volumes, the most important of which were *The Weary Blues* (1926); *Fine Clothes to the Jew* (1927); *The Dream Keeper and Other Poems* (1932); *Scottsboro Limited: Four Poems and a Play in Verse* (1932); and *Montage of a Dream Deferred* (1951). More recent is *The Panther and the Lash: Poems of our Times* (1967). Faith Berry has edited *Good Morning Revolution: Uncollected Social Protest Writings* by Langston Hughes (1973). Hughes's autobiographical volumes include *The Big Sea* (1940) and *I Wonder as I Wander* (1956). Charles H. Nichols has edited *Arna Bontemps–Langston Hughes, Letters 1925–1967* (1980).

Early biographies of Hughes include Milton Meltzer's *Langston Hughes: A Biography* (1968); Charlemae Rollins's *Black Troubador: Langston*

Hughes (1970); and James S. Haskins's *Always Movin' On: The Life of Langston Hughes* (1976). Faith Berry's *Langston Hughes: Before and Beyond Harlem* (1983) contained much new research about Hughes's life to 1940. Arnold Rampersad's two-volume *Life of Langston Hughes*—Vol. I, 1902–1941: *I, Too, Sing America* (1986) and Vol. II, 1941–1967: *I Dream a World* (1988)—is definitive.

James A. Emmanuel's *Langston Hughes* (1967) is an excellent introduction to Hughes's writing. Full-length critical studies are Onwuchekwa Jemie's *Langston Hughes: An Introduction to the Poetry* (1976); Richard K. Barksdale's *Langston Hughes: The Poet and His Critics* (1977); Steven C. Tracy, *Langston Hughes and the Blues* (1988); and R. Baxter Miller, *The Art and Imagination of Langston Hughes* (1989). Therman B. O'Daniel has edited *Langston Hughes, Black Genius: A Critical Evaluation* (1972). Useful reference works include Donald C. Dickinson's *A Bio-Bibliography of Langston Hughes, 1902–1967* (1967) and the compilation by Peter Mandelik and Stanley Schatt, *A Concordance to the Poetry of Langston Hughes* (1975).

**Zora Neale Hurston**

An excellent biography is by Robert Hemenway, *Zora Neale Hurston, a Literary Biography* (1977); book-length studies are Lillie P. Howard, *Zora Neale Hurston* (1980) and *The Character of the Word: The Texts of Zora Zeale Hurston* by Karla F. C. Holloway (1987). *Modern Critical Studies: Zora Neale Hurston*, ed. Harold Bloom (1986), collects previously published essays.

**Robinson Jeffers**

Stanford University Press has begun to publish Jeffers's complete poetry, edited by Tim Hunt. Vol. I, 1920–1928 appeared in 1988 and Vol. II, 1928–1938 in 1989. L. C. Powell, *Robinson Jeffers, The Man and His Work* (1934, rev. 1940); M. C. Monjian, *Robinson Jeffers* (1958); and Melba Bennett, *The Stone Mason of Tor House: The Life and Work of Robinson Jeffers* (1966) are biographical and analytical studies. Ann N. Ridgway has edited *The Selected Letters of Robinson Jeffers, 1897–1962* (1968). Among books of critical analysis are Brother Antoninus, *Robinson Jeffers: Fragments of an Older Fury* (1968); Arthur B. Coffin, *Robinson Jeffers, Poet of Inhumanism* (1970); Robert Brophy, *Robinson Jeffers, Myth, Ritual, and Symbol in His Narrative Poems* (1973); Marlan Beilke, *Shining Clarity: God and Man in the Works of Robinson Jeffers* (1977); and *The Cliffs of Solitude: A Reading of Robinson Jeffers*, by Robert Zaller (1983). *Critical Essays on Robinson Jeffers*, ed. James Karmen, appeared in 1990.

**Amy Lowell**

Lowell's complete poems were published in 1955. Ferris Greenslet, who was her editor at Houghton Mifflin, has written an excellent family chronicle from the first settler to Amy Lowell, *The Lowells and Their Seven Worlds* (1945). Additional biographical material may be found in S. Foster Damon, *Amy Lowell: A Chronicle, with Extracts from Her Correspondence* (1935) and *Florence Ayscough and Amy Lowell: Correspondence of a Friendship*, ed. Harley Farnsworth MacNair (1945). Critical estimates of Lowell include Horace Gregory, *Amy Lowell: Portrait of the Poet in Her Time* (1958); S. Foster Damon, *Amy Lowell* (1966); Jean Gould, *Amy: The World of Amy Lowell and the Imagist Movement* (1975); Glenn Richard Ruihley, *The Thorn of a Rose: Amy Lowell Reconsidered* (1975); and Richard Benvenuto, *Amy Lowell* (1985).

**Edna St. Vincent Millay**

Millay's *Collected Sonnets* (1941) and *Collected Lyrics* (1943) were followed by *Collected Poems: Edna St. Vincent Millay*, ed. Norma Millay (1956). Her prose sketches, *Distressing Dialogues*, published under the pseudonym Nancy Boyd, appeared in 1924. Her three verse plays (*Aria da Capo*, 1920; *The Lamp and the Bell*, 1921; and *Two Slatterns and a King*, 1921) were collected in *Three Plays* (1926).

Karl Yost compiled *A Bibliography of the Works of Edna St. Vincent Millay* in 1937. Allan Ross Macdougall edited *Letters of Edna St. Vincent Millay* in 1952. Millay is one of the subjects in Joan Dash's *A Life of One's Own: Three Gifted Women and the Men They Married* (1973). Fuller treatments are Jean Gould's *The Poet and Her Book* (1969) and Miriam Gurko's *Restless Spirit* (1957). Useful introductions are James Gray's *Edna St. Vincent Millay* (1967), Norman A. Brittin's rev. *Edna St. Vincent Millay* (1982), and Judith Nierman's *Edna St. Vincent Millay: A Reference Guide* (1977). William B. Thessig has edited *Critical Essays on Edna St. Vincent Millay* (1993).

**Marianne Moore**

No collection of Moore's verse is authoritative because each excluded some earlier poems while subjecting others to extensive revisions and changes in format. Her separate volumes include *Poems* (1921); *Observations* (1924); *The Pangolin and Other Verse* (1936); *What Are Years?* (1941); *Nevertheless* (1944); *Like a Bulwark* (1956); *O to Be a Dragon* (1959); and *Tell Me, Tell Me* (1966). Collections include *Selected Poems* (1935); *Collected Poems* (1951); and *The Complete Poems of Marianne Moore* (1967, repr. 1981, 1987), which included selections from her translation of *The Fables of La Fontaine* (1954). Patricia C. Willis has brought together Moore's published prose in *The Complete Prose of Marianne Moore* (1986). The first biography to appear is *Marianne Moore: A Literary Life*, by Charles Molesworth (1990). Earlier book-length studies include Bernard F. Engel's *Marianne Moore* (1963, rev. 1989); Jean Garrigue's *Marianne Moore* (1965); George W.

Nitchie's *Marianne Moore: An Introduction to the Poetry* (1969); Pamela W. Hadas's *Marianne Moore, Poet of Affection* (1977); and Donald Hall's *Marianne Moore: The Cage and the Animal* (1970). More recent are Laurence Stapleton's *Marianne Moore: The Poet's Advance* (1978); *Marianne Moore; Imaginary Possessions*, by Bonnie Costello (1982); John M. Slatin's *The Savage's Romance: The Poetry of Marianne Moore* (1986); Grace Schulman's *Marianne Moore: The Poetry of Engagement* (1987); and Margaret Holley's *The Poetry of Marianne Moore: A Study in Voice and Value* (1987). M. J. Tambimuttu edited *Festschrift for Marianne Moore's Seventy-fifth Birthday—by Various Hands* in 1964, and Charles Tomlinson edited *Marianne Moore: A Collection of Critical Essays* in 1969. Eugene P. Sheehy and Kenneth A. Lohf compiled *The Achievement of Marianne Moore: A Bibliography, 1907–1957* in 1958, and Craig S. Abbott compiled *Marianne Moore: A Descriptive Bibliography* in 1977. Gary Lane's *A Concordance to the Poems of Marianne Moore* appeared in 1972.

### Eugene O'Neill

The standard biography of O'Neill is by Arthur and Barbara Gelb, *O'Neill* (1962, rev. 1973). Other biographical treatments are Frederic I. Carpenter, *Eugene O'Neill* (1964, rev. 1979) and L. Schaeffer, *O'Neill, Son and Playwright* (1968). *The Theatre We Worked For: The Letters of Eugene O'Neill to Kenneth Macgowan*, ed. Jackson R. Bryer (1982), documents O'Neill's attitudes to the theater of his day. Bryer, along with Travers Bogard, have edited *Selected Letters of Eugene O'Neill* (1988). O'Neill's reputation is studied in *O'Neill and His Plays: Four Decades of Criticism*, ed. Oscar Cargill (1961), and James Miller, *Eugene O'Neill and the American Critic* (1962). *The Eugene O'Neill Companion*, by Margaret Loftus Ranald (1984), is informative. Literary analysis of O'Neill's plays can be found in Edwin A. Engel, *The Haunted Heroes of Eugene O'Neill* (1953); Doris V. Falk, *Eugene O'Neill and the Tragic Tension* (1958); Doris Alexander, *The Tempering of Eugene O'Neill* (1962); J. Raleigh, *The Plays of Eugene O'Neill* (1965); Travis Bogard, *Contour in Time: The Plays of Eugene O'Neill* (1972, rev. 1987); L. Chabrower, *Ritual and Pathos, The Theater of O'Neill* (1976); *Eugene O'Neill: A Collection of Criticism*, ed. E. Griffin (1976); *Eugene O'Neill's New Language of Kinship*, by Michael Manheim (1982); Judith E. Barlow, *Final Acts: The Creation of Three Late O'Neill Plays* (1985); and Virginia Floyd, *The Plays of Eugene O'Neill: A New Assessment* (1985).

### Katherine Anne Porter

There is no standard collection of Porter's works. *Katherine Anne Porter, A Life*, by Joan Givner (1983, rev. 1991), is the first full-scale biography. The bibliographies are Edward Schwartz's *Katherine Anne Porter, a Critical Bibliography: Bulletin of the New York Public Library* (1957) and *A Bibliography of the Works of Katherine Anne Porter*, ed. Louise Waldrip and Shirley Ann Bauer (1969). For surveys of her career and writings, see Ray West's *Katherine Anne Porter* (1963); George Hendrick's *Katherine Anne Porter* (1965, rev., with Willene Hendrick, 1988); M. M. Liberman's *Katherine Anne Porter's Fiction* (1971); Harry J. Mooney's *The Fiction and Criticism of Katherine Anne Porter* (1962); William L. Nance's *Katherine Anne Porter and the Art of Rejection* (1964); W. S. Emmons's *Katherine Anne Porter: The Regional Stories* (1967); Paul R. Baumgarter's *Katherine Anne Porter* (1969); John L. Hardy's *Katherine Anne Porter* (1973); Jane Krause DeMouy's *Katherine Anne Porter's Women: The Eye of Her Fiction* (1983); and two books by Darlene Harbour Unrue, *Truth and Vision in Katherine Anne Porter's Fiction* (1985) and *Understanding Katherine Anne Porter* (1988).

### Ezra Pound

Pound's early poetry, from *A Lume Spento* (1908) through *Ripostes* (1912), has been collected in the authoritative *Collected Early Poems of Ezra Pound*, ed. Michael King (1976). The same volumes, along with later volumes *Hugh Selwyn Mauberley* and *Homage to Sextus Propertius*, are collected in *Personae: The Collected Shorter Poems* (rev. ed. 1949; 2nd rev. ed. 1990). Earlier editions of *The Cantos* have been superseded by *The Cantos* (1986). The most important of Pound's critical writings are *The Spirit of Romance* (rev. 1952); *Gaudier-Brzeska: A Memoir* (1916); *Instigations* (1920); *Make It New* (1934); *The ABC of Reading* (1934); *Guide to Kulchur* (1938); and *Patria Mia* (1950). Also important are *Translations* (1963) and the additional volumes of Confucian translations *Confucius* (1969) and *The Confucian Odes: The Classic Anthology Defined by Confucius* (1954). His criticism has been collected in *Literary Essays of Ezra Pound*, ed. T. S. Eliot (1954), and *Selected Prose, 1909–1965*, ed. William Cookson (1973). *Ezra Pound Speaking: Radio Speeches of World War II*, ed. Leonard W. Doob (1978), is a collection of wartime radio addresses. D. D. Paige edited *The Letters of Ezra Pound, 1907–1941* (1950). Other important correspondence is collected in *Ezra Pound and Dorothy Shakespear: Their Letters, 1909–1914*, ed. Omar Pound and A. Walton Litz (1984), and *Pound / Lewis: The Letters of Ezra Pound and Wyndham Lewis*, ed. Timothy Materer (1985). A revised edition of *Selected Poems of Ezra Pound* (1949) and *Ezra Pound: Selected Cantos* appeared in 1957 and 1967 respectively.

There is biographical material in Pound's autobiographical pamphlet *Indiscretions* (1923); Noel Stock's *Ezra Pound's Pennsylvania* (1976); Michael Reck's *Ezra Pound: A Close-Up* (1967); Harry M. Meachman's *The Caged Panther: Ezra Pound at St. Elizabeth's* (1968); *The Trial of Ezra Pound* (1966) by Pound's lawyer, Julien Cornell; *The*

*Roots of Treason: Ezra Pound and the Secrets of St. Elizabeth's* by E. Fuller Torrey (1984); and the memoir by Pound's daughter, Mary de Rachewiltz, *Discretions* (1972). Major biographies are Charles Norman's *Ezra Pound* (1960); Noel Stock's *The Life of Ezra Pound* (1970, expanded 1982); C. David Haymann's *Ezra Pound, the Last Rower: A Political Profile* (1976); James J. Wilhelm's *The American Roots of Ezra Pound* (1985); and Humphrey Carpenter, *A Serious Character: The Life of Ezra Pound* (1988).

Influential books on Pound are Hugh Kenner's *The Pound Era* (1972); Donald Davie's brief *Pound* (1975); and the latter's *Ezra Pound: Poet as Sculptor* (1964). M. L. Rosenthal's *A Primer of Ezra Pound* (1960) is a good introduction, as are Christine Brooke-Rose's *A ZBC of Ezra Pound* (1971) and James Knapp's *Ezra Pound* (1972). On Pound's early verse see N. Christophe de Nagy's *The Poetry of Ezra Pound: The Pre-Imagist Stage* (rev. 1968); Thomas H. Jackson's *The Early Poetry of Ezra Pound* (1968); Hugh Witemeyer's *The Poetry of Ezra Pound: Forms and Renewal, 1908–1920* (1969); and K. K. Ruthven's *A Guide to Ezra Pound's Personae* (1969).

On *The Cantos* see the *Annotated Index to the Cantos of Ezra Pound* (through Canto LXXXIV), ed. John H. Edwards and William W. Vasse (1957); George Dekker's *The Cantos of Ezra Pound* (1963); Noel Stock's *Reading the Cantos* (1967); Ronald Bush's *The Genesis of Pound's Cantos* (1976); John Wilhelm's *The Later Cantos of Ezra Pound* (1977); Carrol F. Terrill's *A Companion to the Cantos of Ezra Pound* (1980); George Kearn's *Guide to Ezra Pound's Selected Cantos* (1980); and Anthony Woodward's *Ezra Pound and "The Pisan Cantos"* (1980). *Ezra Pound and Italian Fascism* by Tim Redman (1991) addresses the poet's politics.

Donald C. Gallup's *A Bibliography of Ezra Pound* appeared in 1963, and Gary Lane issued *A Con- cordance to Personae: The Shorter Poems of Ezra Pound* in 1974.

### Edwin Arlington Robinson

*Collected Poems of Edwin Arlington Robinson* (1921) was enlarged periodically through 1937. In addition to a considerable body of shorter verse, Robinson wrote a number of long narrative poems. *Merlin* (1917), *Lancelot* (1920), and *Tristram* (1927) evoke an Arthurian world embroiled in "modern" moral and political crises. Robinson's other explorations of human character in modern life include *Roman Bartholomew* (1923); *The Man Who Died Twice* (1924); *Cavender's House* (1929); *The Glory of the Nightingales* (1930); *Matthias at the Door* (1931); *Talifer* (1933); *Amaranth* (1934); and *King Jasper* (1935). Ridgely Torrence compiled *Selected Letters* (1940). Denham Sutcliffe edited *Untriangulated Stars: Letters of Edwin Arlington Robinson to Harry de Forest Smith,*

*1890–1905* (1947). Richard Cary edited *Edwin Arlington Robinson's Letters to Edith Brower* (1968). *A Bibliography of Edwin Arlington Robinson,* ed. Charles Bescher Hogan, appeared in 1936. William White compiled *Edwin Arlington Robinson: A Supplementary Bibliography* (1971).

Two biographies, both entitled *Edwin Arlington Robinson,* are by Hermann Hagedorn (1938) and Emery Neff (1948). Richard Cary documented *The Early Reception of Edwin Arlington Robinson* (1974). Ellsworth Barnard's *Edwin Arlington Robinson: A Critical Study* (1952) is the best introduction to Robinson's work. Others include Wallace L. Anderson's *Edwin Arlington Robinson: A Critical Introduction* (1967); Hoyt C. Franchere's *Edwin Arlington Robinson* (1968); and Louis O. Coxe's *Edwin Arlington Robinson: The Life of Poetry* (1969). Edwin S. Fussell examines the cultural and intellectual influences on Robinson in *Edwin Arlington Robinson: The Literary Background of a Traditional Poet* (1954). Ellsworth Barnard edited *Edwin Arlington Robinson: Centenary Essays* (1969). Other collections are *Appreciation of Edwin Arlington Robinson: Twenty-eight Interpretive Essays,* ed. Richard Cary (1969), and *Edwin Arlington Robinson: A Collection of Critical Essays,* ed. Francis Murphy (1970).

### Muriel Rukeyser

Rukeyser's poems were collected in 1978. She also published several translations and biographies as well as children's books. A full-length study is *The Poetic Vision of Muriel Rukeyser* by Louise Kertesz (1980).

While most of Rukeyser's work is out of print, renewed interest in her has led to two recent publications: *Out of Silence: Selected Poems* (1992), edited by Kate Daniels; and *A Muriel Rukeyser Reader* (1994), edited by Jan Heller Levi, with an introduction by Adrienne Rich, which includes selections of poetry and prose.

### Carl Sandburg

*The Complete Poems of Carl Sandburg* (1950) was revised and expanded in 1969. In addition to seven full-length volumes of poetry, Sandburg wrote a Pulitzer Prize–winning study of Abraham Lincoln (*Abraham Lincoln: The Prairie Years,* 2 vols., 1926, and *Abraham Lincoln: The War Years,* 4 vols., 1939), two collections of journalism and social commentary, a novel, and several books for children. *The Letters of Carl Sandburg* (1968) was edited by Herbert Mitgang. Mark Van Doren published *Carl Sandburg: With a Bibliography of Sandburg Materials in the Collections of the Library of Congress* (1969).

*Always the Young Strangers* (1952) and *Ever the Winds of Chance,* ed. Margaret Sandburg and George Hendrick (1983), are segments of Sandburg's autobiography. A full-scale biography is Penelope Niven's *Carl Sandburg: A Biography* (1991). Critical studies include Richard Crowder's

*Carl Sandburg* (1964); Hazel Durnell's *The America of Carl Sandburg* (1965); and Gay Wilson Allen's *Carl Sandburg* (1972).

**John Steinbeck**
There is no collected edition of Steinbeck's writings. *The True Adventures of John Steinbeck, Writer*, by Jackson J. Benson (1984), is a full-scale biography. Critical studies of Steinbeck include Peter Liska's *The Wide World of John Steinbeck* (1958); Warren French's *John Steinbeck* (1961); Joseph Fontenrose's *John Steinbeck: An Introduction and Interpretation* (1963); Howard Levant, *The Novels of John Steinbeck* (1974); Peter Lisca, *John Steinbeck, Nature and Myth* (1978); Paul McCarthy, *John Steinbeck* (1980); and R. S. Hughes, *Beyond the Red Pony: A Reader's Guide to Steinbeck's Complete Short Stories* (1987). R. David edited *John Steinbeck: A Collection of Critical Essays* (1972); more recent collections are *Rediscovering Steinbeck*, ed. Cliff Lewis and Carroll Britch (1989); *Critical Essays on Steinbeck's Grapes of Wrath*, ed. John Ditsky; and *Short Novels of John Steinbeck*, ed. Jackson J. Benson (1990).

**Wallace Stevens**
*The Collected Poems of Wallace Stevens* was published in 1954. *Opus Posthumous* (1957, rev. ed. 1989) by Milton J. Bates includes previously uncollected poems, plays, and essays primarily found among Stevens's numerous contributions to magazines and anthologies. Another edition, by Holly Stevens, is *The Palm at the End of the Mind* (1971). *The Necessary Angel: Essays on Reality and the Imagination* (1951) is Stevens's prose statement on poetry. Other sources are *Letters of Wallace Stevens*, ed. Holly Stevens (1966); *Concordance to the Poetry of Wallace Stevens*, ed. Thomas Walsh (1963); and *Wallace Stevens: A Descriptive Bibliography*, compiled by J. M. Edelstein (1973).

Samuel French Morse's *Wallace Stevens: Poetry as Life* (1970) is a critical biography. *Wallace Stevens: The Early Years, 1879–1923* by Joan Richardson is a thorough biography of the poet's youth (1986) and her *Wallace Stevens: The Later Years, 1923–1955* (1988) completes the story. Two early studies, William Van O'Connor's *The Shaping Spirit* (1950) and Robert Pack's *Wallace Stevens* (1958), provide introductions to Stevens's work. Robert Buttel's *Wallace Stevens: The Making of Harmonium* (1967) and Walton A. Litz's *Introspective Voyager: The Poetic Development of Wallace Stevens* (1972) trace Stevens's thought and style through his early and middle years. Frank Doggett's *Stevens' Poetry of Thought* (1966), Michel Benamou's *Wallace Stevens and the Symbolist Imagination* (1972), and Harold Bloom's *Wallace Stevens: The Poems of Our Climate* (1977) consider some intellectual influences on Stevens. Joseph N. Riddle's *The Clairvoyant Eye: The Poetry and Poetics of Wallace Stevens* (1965), Ronald Sukenick's *Wallace Stevens: Musing the Obscure* (1967), and

Merle E. Brown's *Wallace Stevens: The Poem as Act* (1971) offer readings of many individual poems. Other useful full-length studies include Daniel Fuchs's *The Comic Spirit of Wallace Stevens* (1963); Eugene Paul Nassar's *Wallace Stevens: An Anatomy of Figuration* (1965); James Baird's *The Dome and the Rock: Structure in the Poetry of Wallace Stevens* (1968); Helen H. Vendler's *On Extended Wings: Wallace Stevens' Longer Poems* (1969); Frank Doggett's *Wallace Stevens: The Making of the Poem* (1980); Rajeev S. Patke, *The Long Poems of Wallace Stevens: An Interpretive Study* (1985); Eleanor Cook's *Poetry, Word-Play, and Word-War in Wallace Stevens* (1988); and Robert Rehder's *The Poetry of Wallace Stevens* (1988). Frank Doggett and Robert Buttel edited *Wallace Stevens: A Celebration* (1980); Albert Gelpi collects essays on the poet in *Wallace Stevens: The Poetics of Modernism* (1985).

**Jean Toomer**
Toomer's published works include *Cane* (1923, repr. 1975, pub. also in a Norton Critical Edition, 1988); *Essentials* (1931); *Portage Potential* (1932); and an address, "The Flavor of Man" (1949). His *Collected Poems*, edited by Robert B. Jones and Margery Toomer Latimer, were published in 1988. On Toomer, see Arna Bontemps's "Jean Toomer and the Harlem Writers of the 1920's," in *Anger and Beyond: The Negro Writer in the United States*, ed. Herbert Hill (1966); Edward Margolies's *Native Sons* (1968); Hugh M. Gloster's *Negro Voices in American Fiction* (1948); and Robert A. Bone's *The Negro Novel in America* (rev. 1965). *Jean Toomer*, by Brian Joseph Benson and Mabel Mayle Dillard (1980); *Jean Toomer, Artist: A Study of His Literary Life and Work, 1894–1936*, by Nellie Y. McKay (1984); and *The Lives of Jean Toomer: A Hunger for Wholeness*, by Cynthia Earl Kerman and Richard Eldridge (1987) are biographies. Frank Durham edited *Studies in Cane* (1971); a more general collection of essays is *Jean Toomer: A Critical Evaluation*, ed. Therman B. O'Daniel (1988).

**William Carlos Williams**
Williams's poems were first collected in three volumes: *Collected Earlier Poems of William Carlos Williams* (1951); *Collected Later Poems of William Carlos Williams* (1950); and *Pictures from Brueghel* (1962). More recent are *The Collected Poems of William Carlos Williams, Volume 1, 1909–1939*, edited by A. Walton Litz and Christopher MacGowan (1986) and *Volume 2, 1939–1962*, edited by Christopher MacGowan (1988). These volumes exclude *Paterson*, whose five books, published individually between 1946 and 1958, were issued in one volume in 1963 and then reedited by Christopher MacGowan (1992). *Kora in Hell*, Williams's important volume of prose poetry, is contained in the collection *Imaginations*, ed. Webster Schott (1970), which also contains essays,

fiction, and creative prose. Williams's short stories are collected in *Make Light of It* (1950) and again, with several additions, in *The Farmers' Daughters* (1961). His novels are *A Voyage to Pagany* (1928); *White Mule* (1937); *In the Money* (1940); and *The Build Up* (1946). His dramatic pieces were published together in *Many Loves and Other Plays* (1961). His most important essays are contained in *In the American Grain* (1925; reissued 1940); *Selected Essays of William Carlos Williams* (1954); and *Imaginations*, ed. Webster Schott (1970). Williams's prose also includes *The Autobiography of William Carlos Williams* (1951); a book of recollections dictated to Edith Heal, *I Wanted to Write a Poem* (1958); and *Yes, Mrs. Williams* (1959), a portrait of the poet's mother. J. C. Thirlwall edited *The Selected Letters of William Carlos Williams* (1957) and Emily Mitchell Wallace compiled *A Bibliography of William Carlos Williams* (1968). Reed Whittemore's *William Carlos Williams: Poet from Jersey* (1975) is a critical biography, as is Paul Mariani's more detailed *William Carlos Williams: A New World Naked* (1981).

James E. Breslin's *William Carlos Williams: An American Artist* (1970) is a good overview of Williams's work. Other general introductions are Linda Wagner's *The Poems of William Carlos Williams* (1964); Alan Ostrom's *The Poetic World of William Carlos Williams* (1966); Thomas Whitaker's *William Carlos Williams* (1968); James Guimond's *The Art of William Carlos Williams: A Discovery and Possession of America* (1968); Sherman Paul's *The Music of Survival: A Biography of a Poem by William Carlos Williams* (1968); and Thomas R. Whitaker's *William Carlos Williams* (1989). Bram Dijkstra's *The Hieroglyphics of a New Speech: Cubism, Stieglitz, and the Early Poetry of William Carlos Williams* (1969); Mike Weaver's *William Carlos Williams: The American Background* (1971); Jerome Mazzaro's *William Carlos Williams: The Later Poems* (1973); Joseph N. Riddel's *The Inverted Bell: Modernism and the Counter-Poetics of William Carlos Williams* (1974); Charles Doyle's *William Carlos Williams*

*and the American Poem* (1982); Henry M. Sayre's *The Visual Text of William Carlos Williams* (1983); Kerry Driscoll's, *William Carlos Williams and the Maternal Muse* (1987); and Ann W. Fisher-Wirth's, *William Carlos Williams and Autobiography: The Woods of His Own Nature* (1989) are more specialized.

Linda Wagner, *The Prose of William Carlos Williams* (1970) and Robert Coles, *William Carlos Williams: The Knack of Survival in America* (1975) discuss Williams's prose. For *Paterson*, see W. S. Peterson's *An Approach to Paterson* (1967); Joel Conarroe's *William Carlos Williams' Paterson: Language and Landscape* (1970); and Benjamin Sankey's *A Companion to William Carlos Williams's Paterson* (1971). Paul Mariani, *William Carlos Williams: The Poet and His Critics* (1975), considers Williams's critical reception, as does *William Carlos Williams, The Critical Heritage*, ed. Charles Doyle (1980).

### Richard Wright

Wright's fiction includes *Uncle Tom's Children* (1938), *Native Son* (1940), *The Outsider* (1953), and *Eight Men* (1961). *Black Boy* (1945) is his autobiography; *White Man, Listen!* (1957) is an important work of nonfiction. For a complete bibliography of his writings, see *Richard Wright: A Primary Bibliography*, compiled by Charles T. Davis and Michel Fabre (1982). A good example of re- views can be found in *Richard Wright: The Crit- ical Reception*, edited by John M. Reilly (1978); a massive bibliography of Wright criticism around the world has been assembled by Keneth Kinna- mon (1988). The best critical biography is Michel Fabre's *The Unfinished Quest of Richard Wright* (1973); three basic studies are Edward Margolies, *The Art of Richard Wright* (1969); Russell C. Brignano, *Richard Wright: An Introduction to the Man and His Works* (1970); and Keneth Kinna- mon, *The Emergence of Richard Wright* (1972). Collections of criticism are Yoshinobu Haku- tani's *Critical Essays on Richard Wright* (1982) and Keneth Kinnamon's *New Essays on Native Son* (1990).

## AMERICAN PROSE SINCE 1945

Many of the writers anthologized here have books devoted to them in the Twayne American Authors Series. The *Critical Essays on American Literature* series, published by G. K. Hall, and the *Modern Critical Views* series, edited by Harold Bloom and published by Chelsea House, also include a number of these writers as does the Prentice-Hall Twentieth Century Views series. The University Press of Mississippi has put out "Conversations" with Welty, O'Connor, Cheever, Taylor, and more to follow. There are relevant sections of *The Columbia Literary History of the United States* (1988) and *The Harvard Guide to Contemporary Writing*

(1979). In *American Fictions 1940–1980* (1983), Frederick R. Karl has written a history and critical evaluation of this large subject. *Three American Literatures*, ed. Houston A. Baker, Jr. (1982) is a collection of essays on Hispanic, Native American, and Asian-American literature. *Native American Renaissance*, by Kenneth Lincoln (1983), consists of essays about American Indian literatures and contains photographs and a good selected bibliography. But there are no indispensable surveys or histories of the period, and the most useful discussions of books and writers are found in collections of essays by several critics. Warner Berthoff's *Fic-

*tions and Events* (1971) has a good study of Edmund Wilson as well as an essay on books by Mailer and Malcolm X. A *Literature Without Qualities: American Writing Since 1945* (1979), also by Warner Berthoff, is a brilliantly succinct consideration of, among other things, postwar novelists. Richard Poirier's *The Performing Self* (1971) has interesting material on Barth, Pynchon, and others of recent reputation. In *Bright Book of Life* (1973), Alfred Kazin discusses American novelists and storytellers from Hemingway to Mailer. Tony Tanner's *City of Words: American Fiction 1935– 1970* (1971) provides a full treatment of many figures from this period, while Frank MacConnell's *Four Postwar American Novelists* (1977) contains analyses of the literary careers of Bellow, Mailer, Barth, and Pynchon. Irving Howe's essay on Ralph Ellison and on "The New York Intellectuals" may be found in his *Collected Essays* (1990). Leslie Fiedler's *Collected Essays* (1971) and Norman Podhoretz's *Doings and Undoings* (1964) include essays and reviews of most of the writers anthologized here. Arthur Mizener's *The Sense of Life in the Modern Novel* (1964) is useful on Salinger and Updike. Roger Sale's *On Not Being Good Enough* (1979) has lively writing about many recent novelists, some of them not very well known. *Black Fiction* (1974), by Roger Rosenblatt, is thoughtful and incisive. Morris Dickstein's *Gates of Eden: American Culture in the Sixties* (1977) is a wide-ranging, personal view of the period. *Plausible Prejudices*, by Joseph Epstein (1985), contains lively, often adverse, accounts of some recent novelists, as does Bruce Bawer's *Diminishing Fictions* (1988). The *Afro-American Novel and Its Traditions*, by Bernard Bell (1987), is thorough in its range and treatment. Finally, the twenty-six issues of *The New American Review*, edited by Theodore Solotaroff, are excellent places to encounter much interesting fiction and other prose published between 1968 and 1978.

### James Baldwin

Baldwin's six novels are *Go Tell It on the Mountain* (1953), *Giovanni's Room* (1956), *Another Country* (1962), *Tell Me How Long the Train's Been Gone* (1968), *If Beale Street Could Talk* (1974), and *Just above My Head* (1979). A collection of short stories, *Going to Meet the Man*, was published in 1965.

*The Price of the Ticket* (1985) collects Baldwin's essays and other nonfiction. He wrote two plays: *Blues for Mr. Charlie* (1964) and *The Amen Corner* (1968).

*Talking at the Gates: A Life of James Baldwin*, by James Campbell (1991) is a biographical study. Recent critical books are *Stealing the Fire: The Art and Protest of James Baldwin*, by Horace Porter (1989), and *James Baldwin: Artist on Fire*, by William J. Weatherby (1989). Kenneth Kinnamon has edited the Prentice-Hall collection of critical essays on Baldwin (1974).

### John Barth

Barth is the author of eight novels, the first three of which were altered when republished: *The Floating Opera* (1956, 1967); *The End of the Road* (1958, 1967); *The Sot-Weed Factor* (1960, 1967); *Giles Goat-Boy*, or, *The Revised New Syllabus* (1966); *LETTERS* (1979); *Sabbatical* (1982); *The Tidewater Tales* (1987); and *The Last Voyage of Somebody the Sailor* (1991). *Lost in the Funhouse: Fiction for Print, Tape, Live Voice* (1968) is a collection of stories. *Chimera* (1972) consists of three novellas. *The Friday Book* (1984) is a collection of his essays and other nonfiction.

*John Barth* by Gerhard Joseph (1970) is a biographical and critical pamphlet in the University of Minnesota series. *John Barth: An Introduction* by David Morell (1976) is an intelligent survey of Barth's work, containing much lively information and manuscript material plus an excellent bibliography. *Passionate Virtuosity: The Fiction of John Barth*, by Charles B. Harris (1983), is a more recent study.

### Ann Beattie

Beattie's novels are *Chilly Scenes of Winter* (1976), *Falling in Place* (1981), *Love Always* (1985), and *Picturing Will* (1989). Her collections of short stories are *Distortions* (1976), *Secrets and Surprises* (1978), *The Burning House* (1982), *Where You'll Find Me* (1986), and *What Was Mine* (1991). Christina Murphy has written a book about Beattie in the Twayne Authors series (1986).

### Saul Bellow

Among Bellow's works are the following novels: *Dangling Man* (1944), *The Victim* (1947), *The Adventures of Augie March* (1953), *Seize the Day* (1956), *Henderson the Rain King* (1959), *Herzog* (1964), *Mr. Sammler's Planet* (1970), *Humboldt's Gift* (1975), *The Dean's December* (1981), and *More Die of Heartbreak* (1987). His two collections of shorter fiction are *Mosby's Memoirs* (1968) and *Him with His Foot in His Mouth* (1984). Two recent novellas are *The Theft* (1989) and *The Bellarosa Connection* (1989). His play, *The Last Analysis*, produced in New York in 1964, was published in 1965. *To Jerusalem and Back* (1976) is an account of a visit to Israel. Also of interest is a lecture, "Some Notes on Recent American Fiction," *Encounter* (November 1963).

A useful collection of critical essays on Bellow's work that also includes his essay "Where Do We Go from Here: The Future of Fiction" is *Saul Bellow and the Critics*, ed. Irving Malin (1967). Books about him include *Saul Bellow: In Defense of Man*, by John Clayton (1979); *Saul Bellow*, by Robert R. Dutton (1982); *Saul Bellow: Vision and Revision*, by Daniel Fuchs (1983); and *Saul Bellow: Against the Grain*, by Ellen Pifer (1990).

### Denise Chávez

Chávez's collection of short stories, *The Last of the Menu Girls*, was published in 1986.

## Ralph Ellison

Ellison published three books: his novel, *Invisible Man* (1952), and two collections of essays, *Shadow and Act* (1964) and *Going to the Territory* (1986). There are also a number of uncollected short stories as well as excerpts from the novel that he left unpublished when he died. (See Bernard Benoit and Michel Fabre, "A Bibliography of Ralph Ellison's Published Writings," in *Studies in Black Literature*, 1971.)

The Prentice-Hall collection of critical essays (1974), edited by John Hersey, has a number of useful items, including interviews with Ellison by Hersey and James McPherson and a further selected bibliography, *Studies in Invisible Man*, ed. Ronald Gottesman (1971), is a shorter collection. Irving Howe's essay contrasting Ellison with Richard Wright appears in *A World More Attractive* (1963). A recent study is *The Craft of Ralph Ellison*, by Robert G. O'Mealley (1980), who has also edited *New Essays on Invisible Man* (1988).

## Louise Erdrich

Erdrich's novels are *Love Medicine* (1984), *The Beet Queen* (1986), and *Tracks* (1988). Her two collections of poems are *Jacklight* (1984) and *Baptism of Desire* (1989). She is coauthor (with Michael Dorris) of a novel, *The Crown of Columbus* (1991).

## Maxine Hong Kingston

Kingston's two memoirs are *The Woman Warrior* (1976) and *China Men* (1980). Her novel, *Tipmaster Monkey*, was published in 1989.

Critical essays on Kingston include Patricia Lin Blinde, "Icicle in the Desert: Perspective and Form in the Works of Two Chinese American Women Writers," *MELUS* 6 (1979), 51–71; Leslie Rabin, "No Lost Paradise: Social Gender and Symbolic Gender in the Writings of Maxine Hong Kingston," *Signs* 12 (1987), 471–92; Sau-ling Wong, "Necessity and Extravagance in Maxine Hong Kingston's *The Woman Warrior*: Art and the Ethnic Experience," *MELUS* 15 (1988), 4–26; and King-kok Cheung, " 'Don't Tell': Imposed Silences in *The Color Purple* and *The Woman Warrior*," *PMLA* 103 (1988), 162–74. John Paul Eakin, *Fictions in Autobiography: Studies in the Art of Self-Invention* (1985), includes some discussion of *The Woman Warrior* and *China Men*. Published in 1991 was Shirley Lim, ed., *Teaching Approaches to Maxine Hong Kingston's* The Woman Warrior.

## Norman Mailer

Mailer's novels are *The Naked and the Dead* (1948), *Barbary Shore* (1951), *The Deer Park* (1955), *An American Dream* (1965), *Why Are We in Vietnam?* (1967), *Ancient Evenings* (1983), *Tough Guys Don't Dance* (1984), and *Harlot's Ghost* (1991). Among collections of essays and miscellaneous materials are *Advertisements for Myself* (1959), *The Presidential Papers* (1963), *Cannibals and Christians* (1966), *Existential Essays* (1972), and *Pieces and Pontifications* (1982). *The Armies of the Night: History as a Novel, the Novel as History*, was published in 1968. His writings about political conventions are collected in *Some Honorable Men* (1975). Some further titles are *Of a Fire on the Moon* (1971), *The Prisoner of Sex* (1972), *Marilyn* (1973), and *The Executioner's Song* (1979). His films include *Maidstone* (1968) and *Tough Guys Don't Dance* (1987).

*Mailer: A Biography*, by Hilary Mills, appeared in 1982. *Lives of Norman Mailer*, by Carl Rollyson (1991) is a recent biographical study. The best critical treatment is Richard Poirier's *Norman Mailer* in the Modern Masters series (1973). Also good is *Down Mailer's Way* (1974), by Robert Solotaroff, and *Radical Fictions and the Novels of Norman Mailer*, by Nigel Leigh (1990). *Squaring Off* (1976), by W. J. Weatherby, has some interesting personal glimpses. *Mailer: His Life and Times* (1985), by Peter Manso, is an enormous oral biography that provides more than anyone will want to hear about the writer.

## Bobbie Ann Mason

Mason has published two collections of stories, *Shiloh* (1983) and *Love Life* (1990). Her novels are *In Country* (1985), *Spence & Lila* (1988), and *Feather Crowns* (1993).

## N. Scott Momaday

A complete listing of Momaday's works would include *The Journey of Tai-me* (1967), *House Made of Dawn* (1968), *Colorado: Summer, Fall, Winter, Spring* (with photographer David Muench, 1973), *Angle of Geese and Other Poems* (1974), *The Colors of Night* (1976), *The Gourd Dancer: Poems* (1976), *The Ancient Child* (a novel, 1989), *The Names: A Memoir* (1976), and *In the Presence of the Sun: Stories and Poems 1961–1991* (1992). Many of these publications overlap and reprint some of the same materials.

A book-length study of Momaday is *N. Scott Momaday: The Cultural and Literary Background* (1985) by Matthias Schubnell. The poet Linda Hogan, in "Who Puts Together," in *Studies in American Literature: Critical Essays and Course Designs*, edited by Paula Gunn Allen (1983), has traced the relationship between *House Made of Dawn* and the Navajo Night Chant. Of the many interviews with Momaday, early and noteworthy is Joseph Bruchac's "The Magic of Words: An Interview with N. Scott Momaday," in *Survival This Way: Interviews with American Indian Poets*, edited by Bruchac (1987). Charles L. Woodward's *Ancestral Voices: Conversations with N. Scott Momaday* (1989) prints the edited texts of interviews with Momaday that took place in 1986–87. Louis Owens's "N. Scott Momaday," in *This Is about Vision: Interviews with Southwestern Writers*, edited by William Balassi, John F. Crawford, and Annie O. Eysturoy (1990), also offers quite a good interview. Kenneth M. Roemer edited *Approaches to Teaching Momaday's "The Way to Rainy Mountain"* (1988), which is useful. Arnold

Krupat's *The Voice in the Margin: Native American Literature and the Canon* (1989) has a chapter comparing the autobiographical writing of Momaday and Leslie Marmon Silko. Susan Scarberry-Garcia's *Landmarks of Healing: A Study of "House Made of Dawn"* (1990) fills in some of the multitribal mythic context necessary for understanding that novel. Gerald Vizenor edited *Narrative Chance: Postmodern Discourse on Native American Indian Literatures* (1989), which contains three articles on Momaday. A fine recent account, focusing predominantly on *House Made of Dawn*, is in Louis Owens's *Other Destinies: Understanding the American Indian Novel* (1992).

**Joyce Carol Oates**

Among Oates's many novels are *With Shuddering Fall* (1964), *Expensive People* (1968), *them* (1969), *Wonderland* (1971), *Unholy Loves* (1979), *Angel of Light* (1981), *Solstice* (1985), *Marya: A Life* (1986), *You Must Remember This* (1987), *American Appetites* (1990), *Because It Is Bitter, and Because It Is My Heart* (1990), *Black Water* (1992), and *Foxfire: The Story of a Girl Gang* (1993). Under the pseudonym of Rosamond Smith, Oates has published three thrillers, of which *Snake Eyes* (1992) is the most recent. Two of her collections of stories are *Marriages and Infidelities* (1972) and *Last Days* (1983). She has written a number of books of poems and criticism and a book about boxing (*On Boxing*, 1987).

*Joyce Carol Oates, Artist in Residence* (1987), by Eileen Teper Bender, is one study of the writer.

**Flannery O'Connor**

O'Connor's novels and stories (ed. Sally Fitzgerald), form a recent volume in the *Library of America* series (1988). Her novels are *Wise Blood* (1952) and *The Violent Bear It Away* (1960). Two collections of stories, *A Good Man Is Hard to Find* (1955) and *Everything That Rises Must Converge* (1965), are included—plus some earlier previously uncollected stories—in *Complete Stories* (1971). Her letters are collected in *The Habit of Being: The Letters of Flannery O'Connor* (1979). *The Presence of Grace, and Other Book Reviews* (1983) collects some of her critical prose.

A collection of her essays and other occasional prose is *Mystery and Manners*, ed. Sally Fitzgerald and Robert Fitzgerald (1969). There are a number of books about her fiction, the most interesting of which is probably *The Added Dimension: The Art and Mind of Flannery O'Connor*, ed. M. J. Freedman and L. A. Lawson (1966). Robert Fitzgerald's memoir, prefaced to *Everything That Rises Must Converge*, is an excellent portrait. Stanley Edgar Hyman's pamphlet in the University of Minnesota series (1966) is a good short introduction.

**Thomas Pynchon**

Pynchon's novels are *V* (1961), *The Crying of Lot 49* (1966), *Gravity's Rainbow* (1973), and *Vineland* (1990). A collection of his early stories, *Slow*

*Learner* (1984), has been published. Two useful books of critical essays about him are the Prentice-Hall Twentieth Century Views volume, edited by Edward Mendelson (1978), and *Mindful Pleasures: Essays on Thomas Pynchon*, edited by George Levine (1976).

**Philip Roth**

Roth's fiction consists of *Goodbye, Columbus* (1959), a novella and five short stories, and the following novels: *Letting Go* (1962), *When She Was Good* (1967), *Portnoy's Complaint* (1969), *Our Gang* (1971), *The Breast* (1972), *The Great American Novel* (1973), *My Life as a Man* (1974), *The Professor of Desire* (1977), *The Ghost Writer* (1979), *Zuckerman Unbound* (1981), and *The Anatomy Lesson* (1983). (The last three have been published together, with an epilogue, as *Zuckerman Bound*, 1985.) *The Counterlife* (1987), *Deception* (1990), and *Operation Shylock* (1993) are more recent titles. *Reading Myself and Others* (1975) is a collection of essays and interviews. *The Facts: A Novelist's Autobiography* (1988) is Roth's memoir. A memoir of his father, *Patrimony*, was published in 1991.

*Philip Roth*, by Hermione Lee (1982), is an excellent short introduction. Interesting essays about Roth are Theodore Solotaroff's "The Journey of Philip Roth," in *The Red Hot Vacuum* (1970), and Irving Howe's adversely critical "Philip Roth Reconsidered," in *The Critical Point* (1973).

**John Updike**

Updike's novels are *The Poorhouse Fair* (1958); *Rabbit, Run* (1961); *The Centaur* (1963); *Of the Farm* (1965); *Couples* (1968); *Rabbit Redux* (1971); *A Month of Sundays* (1975); *Marry Me* (1976); *The Coup* (1978); *Rabbit Is Rich* (1981); *The Witches of Eastwick* (1984); *Roger's Version* (1986); *S.* (1988); *Rabbit at Rest* (1990), and *Memories of the Ford Administration* (1992). Collections of short fiction are *The Same Door* (1959), *Pigeon Feathers* (1962), *The Music School* (1966), *Bech: A Book* (1970), *Museums and Women* (1973), *Problems* (1979), *Bech Is Back* (1982), and *Trust Me* (1987). *Self-Consciousness* (1989) is a memoir; *Just Looking* (1989), a collection of essays about paintings and artists. His poems and light verse are in *Collected Poems* (1993). His occasional articles, interviews, and reviews are found in *Assorted Prose* (1965), *Picked-Up Pieces* (1975), *Hugging the Shore* (1983), and *Odd Jobs* (1991). Charles Thomas Samuels's pamphlet in the University of Minnesota series (1969) is usefully critical, if outdated. Donald J. Grenier's *The Other John Updike* (1979) and *John Updike's Novels* (1984) are of critical and bibliographical interest.

**Alice Walker**

Walker's novels are *The Third Life of Grange Copeland* (1970), *Meridian* (1976), *The Color Purple* (1982), *The Temple of My Familiar* (1989), and

*Possessing the Secret of Joy* (1992). Her two volumes of short fiction are *In Love and Trouble* (1973) and *You Can't Keep a Good Woman Down* (1979). Her poems are collected in *Her Blue Body Everything We Know: Earthling Poems, 1965–1990* (1991). In *Search of Our Mothers' Gardens* (1983) and *Living by the Word* (1988) are collections of essays, including autobiographical material.

### Eudora Welty

Eudora Welty's short fiction may be found in *Collected Stories* (1980). Among her novels are *Losing Battles* (1970) and *The Optimist's Daughter* (1972). A selection from her prose is *The Eye of the Story: Selected Essays and Reviews* (1978), and she has published a memoir, *One Writer's Beginnings* (1984). Full-length studies of her include *Eudora Welty* by Ruth M. Vande Kieft (1962, rev. ed. 1987) and *Eudora Welty* by J. A. Bryant, Jr. (1968). A collection of essays is *Eudora Welty: Critical Essays*, ed. Peggy Whitman Prenshaw (1979). *Eudora Welty, a Bibliography*, by Richard David Ramsey, appeared in 1971.

### Tennessee Williams

Most of Williams's plays are collected in the seven-volume *The Theatre of Tennessee Williams* (1971–1981). Some later dramas are available in separate editions; a few others are still to be published. Other writings include a novel, *The Roman Spring of Mrs. Stone* (1950); short stories printed in several volumes and finally brought together in *Collected Stories* (1986), by Gore Vidal; a volume of screenplays, *Stopped Rocking and Other Screenplays* (1984); and poems collected in *In the Winter of Cities* (1956, 1964) and *Androgyne, Mon Amour* (1977). *Where I Live: Selected Essays*, edited by Christine R. Day and Bob Woods, appeared in 1978.

Williams's *Memoirs* (1975) is interestingly revelatory but is not a reliable biographical guide; neither is Dotson Rader, *Tennessee: Cry of the Heart* (1985). Donald Spoto's *A Kindness of Strangers: The Life of Tennessee Williams* (1985) is workmanlike. Harold Bloom (1986) and Jac L. Tharpe (1980) have edited collections of critical essays, and Drewey W. Gunn has compiled *Tennessee Williams: A Bibliography*.

## AMERICAN POETRY SINCE 1945

The diversity of postwar American poetry requires diverse works of criticism. Some of the most valuable commentary has occurred when one poet writes about another or meditates on the work of poetry itself. Such essays are available in collections like Charles Bernstein's *A Poetics* (1992), Robert Creeley's *A Quick Graph* (1970), Randall Jarrell's *Poetry and the Age* (1953), Denise Levertov's *The Poet in the World* (1973) and *Light Up the Cave* (1981), and Robert Lowell's *Collected Prose* (1987). Among the many critical books that provide valuable studies of the period and of particular poets are Harold Bloom's *The Ringers in the Tower* (1971) and *Figures of Capable Imagination* (1976), James E. B. Breslin's *From Modern to Contemporary* (1984), Richard Howard's *Alone with America* (1969), David Kalstone's *Five Temperaments* (1977), J. D. McClatchey's *White Paper* (1990), Sherman Paul's *The Lost America of Love* (1981), Marjorie Perloff's *The Poetics of Indeterminacy* (1981) and *The Dance of the Intellect* (1985), Robert Pinsky's *The Situation of Poetry* (1976), Helen Vendler's *Part of Nature, Part of Us* (1980) and *The Music of What Happens* (1988), and Alan Williamson's *Introspection and Contemporary Poetry* (1984). Donald Allen's *Poetics of the New American Poetry* (1973) collects a number of theoretical pieces from important contemporary poets. Ours is an age of the interview, and interviews with a variety of poets may be found in the several volumes of *Writers at Work: The Paris Review Interviews* and in current editions of the *Paris Review*

itself. Many other journals and reviews frequently feature interviews with contemporary poets.

Collections of individual poets' interviews and prose have also been published in the *Poets on Poetry* series (University of Michigan). Also valuable are John O'Brien's *Interviews with Black Writers* (1973), *Black Women Writers at Work*, edited by Claudia Tate (1988), and *Survival This Way: Interviews with American Indian Poets*, edited by Joseph Bruhac (1987).

### A. R. Ammons

Collections of A. R. Ammons's poetry include *Really Short Poems of A. R. Ammons* (1991), *Selected Longer Poems* (1980), *The Selected Poems: Expanded Edition* (1986), and *Collected Poems: 1951–1971*. His individual volumes include *Sphere: The Form of a Motion* (1974), *Diversifications* (1975), *Snow Poems* (1977), *A Coast of Trees* (1981), *Lake Effect Country* (1983), *Sumerian Vistas* (1987) and *Garbage* (1993). There are useful critical essays on his work in Richard Howard, *Alone with America* (1969); in Harold Bloom, *The Ringers in the Tower*; and in Helen Vendler, *The Music of What Happens* (1988). An interview with Ammons appeared in a special issue of *Diacritics* 3, no. 5 (Winter 1973), devoted to studies of his work.

### John Ashbery

John Ashbery's volumes of poetry include *Some Trees* (1956), *The Tennis Court Oath* (1962), *Rivers and Mountains* (1966), *The Double Dream of Spring* (1970), *Three Poems* (1972), *Self-Portrait in a Convex Mirror* (1975), *Houseboat Days* (1977), *As We Know* (1979), *Shadow Train* (1981), *A Wave* (1984), *Selected Poems* (1985), *April Galleons* (1988), and *Flow Chart* (1991). With James Schuyler he is co-author of the comic novel *A Nest of Ninnies* (1969). Among useful critical essays are the chapters on Ashbery in Richard Howard's *Alone with America* (1969) and David Kalstone's *Five Temperaments* (1977), and a study by Harold Bloom in *Contemporary Poetry in America: Essays and Introductions*, edited by Robert Boyers (1973). David K. Kermani's *John Ashbery: A Comprehensive Bibliography* (1975) is indispensable and amusing. See also *Beyond Amazement: New Essays on John Ashbery*, edited by David Lehman (1980). An interview with Ashbery appears in *Code of Signals*, edited by Michael Palmer (1983).

### Amiri Baraka (LeRoi Jones)

Amiri Baraka's *Selected Poetry* appeared in 1979. His other volumes include *Preface to a Twenty Volume Suicide Note* (1962), *The Dead Lecturer* (1965), *Black Art* (1966), *Black Magic: Poetry 1961–1967* (1969), *Spirit Reach* (1972), *Afrikan Revolution* (1973), *Hard Facts* (1976), and *Reggae or Not!* (1982). He is the author of several important plays, among them *Dutchman and Slave* (1964), *The Baptism* and *The Toilet* (1967), and *Four Black Revolutionary Plays* (1969). His prose writings include *Home: Social Essays* (1966); *Raise Race Rays Raze* (1972); *Daggers and Javelins: Essays, 1974–1979* (1984); *The Autobiography of Leroi Jones / Amiri Baraka* (1984); and *The Music: Reflections on Jazz and Blues* (1987). William J. Harris, *The Poetry and Poetics of Amiri Baraka: The Jazz Aesthetic* (1985) is a book-length critical study of Baraka's work, and *Iamamu Amiri Baraka*, edited by Kimberly W. Benston (1979), is a collection of critical essays.

### John Berryman

John Berryman's *Collected Poems: 1937–1971* appeared in 1991; *Homage to Mistress Bradstreet* (1956) and a selection of his *Short Poems* (1948) were issued together in paperback format in 1968. His other volumes of poetry include *77 Dream Songs* (1964); *Berryman's Sonnets* (1967); *His Toy, His Dream, His Rest* (1968); *Love and Fame* (1970; rev. 1972); *Delusions, Etc.* (1972); and a posthumous volume, *Henry's Fate* (1977). Berryman's critical biography, *Stephen Crane*, appeared in 1950, and a collection of his short fiction and literary essays was issued under the title *The Freedom of the Poet* (1976). Berryman's unfinished novel about his alcoholism, *Recovery*, appeared in 1973. A valuable critical introduction to Berryman's poetry is to be found in Martin Dodsworth's essay on him in *The Survival of Poetry*, edited by Martin Dodsworth (1970). John Haffenden's *The Life of John Berryman* (1982) and Eileen Simpson's *Poets in Their Youth* (1982) are useful biographical studies.

### Elizabeth Bishop

Elizabeth Bishop's poems are now available in *The Complete Poems 1927–1979*. *The Collected Prose* (1984) includes a number of memoirs and stories, especially *In the Village*, invaluable for a reading of her poems. She has also translated from the Portuguese *The Diary of "Helena Morley"* (1957, 1977, 1991), an enchanting memoir of provincial life in Brazil. Anne Stevenson's biographical and critical study, *Elizabeth Bishop*, appeared in 1966. Useful critical essays on Bishop appear in the issue of *World Literature Today* (1976) dedicated to her, in Lorrie Glodensohn, *Elizabeth Bishop: The Biography of a Poetry* (1992); in David Kalstone, *Becoming a Poet* (1989); in Helen Vendler, *Part of Nature, Part of Us* (1980); and in *Elizabeth Bishop and Her Art*, edited by Lloyd Schwartz and Sybil P. Estess (1983), which includes two interviews as well. A provocative essay on Bishop also appears in Adrienne Rich, *Blood, Bread and Poetry* (1986). Candace MacMahon's *Elizabeth Bishop: A Bibliography* (1980) is indispensable.

### Gwendolyn Brooks

Gwendolyn Brooks's volumes of poetry include *A Street in Bronzeville* (1945); *Annie Allen* (1949); *Selected Poems* (1963); *In the Time of Detachment, In the Time of Cold* (1965); *In the Mecca* (1968); *Riot* (1969); *Family Pictures* (1970); *Aloneness* (1972); *Aurora* (1972); *Beckonings* (1975); *To Disembark* (1981); *Winnie* (1989); and *Children Coming Home* (1991). Many of her poems are collected in the volume *Blacks* (1991). She has also written a prose autobiography, *Report from Part One* (1972). Other useful biographical material appears in *A Life Distilled*, edited by M. K. Mootry and others. Valuable discussions of Brooks's poetry appear in *Black Women Writers (1950–1980)*, edited by Mari Evans (1984). D. H. Melhem's critical study, *Gwendolyn Brooks: Poetry and the Heroic Voice*, appeared in 1987.

### Robert Creeley

*The Collected Poems of Robert Creeley 1945–1975* appeared in 1982 and a *Selected Poems*, in 1991. *The Collected Prose* appeared in 1988, and *The Collected Essays* in 1989. Creeley's many volumes of poetry include *The Whip* (1957), *A Form of Women* (1959), *For Love* (1962), *A Day Book* (1970, 1972), *Away* (1976), *Selected Poems* (1976), *Later* (1978), *Echoes* (1982), *Memories* (1984), *Memory Gardens* (1986), and *The Company* (1988). Creeley has also written fiction, including *The Gold Diggers* (1954) and *The Island* (1963). *Contexts of Poetry: Interviews 1961–1971*, edited by Donald Allen (1973), is engaging and valuable. Many of the essays in Creeley's *Collected Essays* illuminate Creeley's work; the collection also includes important commentary on the work of other poets. Nine volumes of *Charles Olson and Robert Creeley: The Complete Correspondence* have been edited and published by George Butterick

(1950–1952) and they constitute a remarkable glimpse into the history of contemporary poetry.

An important critical discussion of Creeley's poetry appears in Sherman Paul, *The Lost America of Love* (1971). Robert von Hallberg, *American Poetry and Culture, 1945–1980* (1985), also includes a discussion of Creeley.

## Rita Dove

Rita Dove has published five volumes of poetry: *The Yellow House on the Corner* (1980), *Museum* (1983), *Thomas and Beulah* (1986), *Grace Notes* (1989), and *Selected Poems* (1993). She has also published *Fifth Sunday*, a collection of fiction, and a novel, *Through the Ivory Gate* (1992). Useful interviews with Dove have appeared in a number of journals, among them *Black American Literature Forum* (Vol. 20, Fall 1986), *Gargoyle* (no. 27, 1985), *Iowa Review* (1989), *Christian Science Monitor* (1993), *AWP Newsletter* (1993), and *Poets & Writers* (1994).

## Robert Duncan

Robert Duncan's poems have not been collected in a single volume, but a number of his books gather together poems from his many fugitive pamphlet publications. Volumes of selected work include *The Years as Catches, First Poems 1939–1941* (1966); *Selected Poems 1942–1950* (1959); *The First Decade: Selected Poems, Vol. 1* (1968); and *Derivations: Selected Poems, 1950–1956*. Duncan's two final volumes of poetry, *Ground Work: Before the War* (1984) and *Ground Work II: In the Dark* (1987) contain many major poems written over a fifteen-year period. Other important books of his poetry are *The Opening of the Field* (1960), *Roots and Branches* (1964), and *Bending the Bow* (1968). Duncan's prose collection, *Fictive Certainties* (1979), is invaluable to a reader of his poems.

*Robert Duncan: Scales of the Marvelous* (1979) collects essays on Duncan's work from a range of poets and critics. Also important is the discussion of Duncan in Sherman Paul, *The Lost America of Love* (1981). Robert J. Bertholf, *Robert Duncan: A Descriptive Bibliography* (1986) is a necessary guide to Duncan's many uncollected writings.

## Allen Ginsberg

Allen Ginsberg's *Collected Poems, 1947–1980* appeared in 1984 and *White Shroud: Poems, 1980–1985* in 1986. His individual volumes, with the exception of *Empty Mirror* (early poems collected in 1961), have been issued in the now unmistakable City Lights paperbacks. They include *Howl* (1956); *Kaddish and Other Poems, 1958–1960* (1961); *Reality Sandwiches* (1963); *Planet News, 1961–1967* (1968); *The Fall of America, Poems of These States, 1965–1971* (1973); and *Mind Breaths, Poems 1972–1977* (1977). Ginsberg has published a great number of pages from his journals, dealing with his travels, such as the *Indian Journals* (1970). *Allen Verbatim* (1974) includes

transcripts of some of his "lectures on poetry." In 1977 he published *Letters: Early Fifties Early Sixties* (1977) and in 1980 *Composed on the Tongue; Literary Conversations 1967–1977*, edited by Donald Allen. Among the many interviews, the *Paris Review* dialogue conducted by Tom Clarkin, *Writers at Work: Third Series* (1967), is extremely valuable. Jane Kramer's *Allen Ginsberg in America* (1969) is a brilliant documentary piece on Ginsberg in the 1960s. *On the Poetry of Allen Ginsberg*, edited by Lewis Hyde (1980), is a collection of essays by different hands.

## Michael S. Harper

Michael Harper's poems appear in *Dear John, Dear Coltrane* (1970); *History Is Your Own Heartbeat* (1971); *Photographs: Negatives: History as Apple Tree* (1972); *Song: I Want a Witness* (1972); *Nightmare Begins Responsibility* (1974); *Images of Kin: New and Selected Poems* (1977); and *Healing Song for the Inner Ear* (1984). His book-length poem *Debridement* appeared in 1973. Harper has also edited (with Robert Stepto) a collection of African-American literature, art, and scholarship, *Chants of Saints* (1976).

## Robert Hayden

Robert Hayden's *Collected Poems* appeared in 1985; his *Collected Prose* appeared the previous year. Both were edited by Frederick Glaysher. Fred M. Fetrow's *Robert Hayden* (1984) is a critical study of Hayden's work.

## Randall Jarrell

Randall Jarrell's *Complete Poems* were published in 1969 and a *Selected Poems* appeared in 1991. His novel satirizing American academic life, *Pictures from an Institution*, appeared in 1954. Jarrell's critical essays have been collected in *Poetry and the Age* (1953), *A Sad Heart at the Supermarket* (1962), and *The Third Book of Criticism* (1969). Some of the most valuable commentary on Jarrell's life and work is to be found in a memorial volume of essays edited by Robert Lowell, Peter Taylor, and Robert Penn Warren, *Randall Jarrell, 1914–1965* (1967). Suzanne Ferguson's *The Poetry of Randall Jarrell* is a useful book-length study, and William Pritchard's fine *Randall Jarrell: A Literary Life* (1990) illumines both Jarrell's life and his work.

## Galway Kinnell

Galway Kinnell's *Selected Poems* appeared in 1982. Earlier collected volumes of his work were *First Poems 1946–1954* (1970) and *The Avenue Bearing the Initial of Christ into the New World: Poems 1946–1964* (1974). Important individual volumes of Kinnell's poetry are *What a Kingdom It Was* (1960), *The Book of Nightmares* (1971), *Mortal Acts, Mortal Words* (1980), *The Past* (1985), and *When One Has Lived a Long Time Alone* (1990). He has also published a collection of criticism, *The Poetics of the Physical World* (1969) and selected interviews, *Walking Down the Stairs*, edited by Donald Hall (1978). A critical discussion of Kinnell's work appears in Ralph J. Mills, Jr., *Cry of the Human: Essays on Contemporary American Poetry* (1975).

**Li-Young Lee**
Li-Young Lee's two volumes of poetry are *Rose* (1986) and *The City in Which I Love You* (1990). Gerald Stern's foreword to *Rose* provides useful biographical material about Lee's family. Available on videotape, as part of the series *The Power of the Word*, is "Voices of Memory," in which Bill Moyers conducts a valuable interview with Lee and Lee reads from and talks about his poetry.

**Denise Levertov**
Some of Denise Levertov's poems have been collected in *Collected Earlier Poems 1940–1960* (1979) and *Poems 1960–1967* (1983). Her individual volumes include *The Double Image* (1946), *Here and Now* (1957), *Overland to the Islands* (1958), *With Eyes at the Back of Our Heads* (1960), *The Jacob's Ladder* (1962), *O Taste and See* (1964), *The Sorrow Dance* (1967), *Relearning the Alphabet* (1970), *To Stay Alive* (1971), *Footprints* (1972), *The Freedom of the Dust* (1973), *Life in the Forest* (1978), *Candles in Babylon* (1982), *Oblique Prayers* (1984), *Breathing the Water* (1987), and *A Door in the Hive* (1989). *The Poet in the World* (1973) and *Light Up the Cave* (1981) include essays on her own work, memoirs, reviews of other poets, and some theoretical essays. Linda Wagner, *Denise Levertov* (1967) is a critical introduction to Levertov's work through the mid-1960s. James E. Breslin's *From Modern to Contemporary: American Poetry 1945–1965* (1984) contains a useful discussion of Levertov and Linda Wagner-Martin has edited *Critical Essays on Denise Levertov* (1990).

**Audre Lorde**
*Chosen Poems, Old and New* (1982) provides a selection of Audre Lorde's poetry from several books, including *Cables to Rage* (1970) and *New York Head Shop and Museum* (1975). Her poems also appear in *The Black Unicorn* (1978) and *Our Dead Behind Us* (1986). A collection of essays and speeches, *Sister Outsider* (1984), provides a powerful context for reading her work. Her autobiographical writing includes *The Cancer Journals* (1980) and *Zami: A New Spelling of My Name* (1982). *Black Women Writers at Work*, edited by Claudia Tate (1988), includes an interview with Lorde. Essays on Lorde's work appear in *Black Women Writers*, edited by Mari Evans (1984).

**Robert Lowell**
In 1976, the year before his death, Robert Lowell prepared his *Selected Poems*, which drew on all his volumes of poetry except *Day by Day*, which appeared in 1977. The interested reader will still have to look back to individual volumes, because Lowell frequently revised his poems and could only

print a small proportion of his work in *Selected Poems*. His earlier books of verse include *Lord Weary's Castle* (1946), *The Mills of the Kavenaughs* (1951), *Life Studies* (1959), *Imitations* (1961), *For the Union Dead* (1964), *Near the Ocean* (1967), *Notebook* (1969; rev. and exp. 1970), *The Dolphin* (1973), *For Lizzie and Harriet* (1973), and *History* (1973). For the stage Lowell prepared adaptations of Racine's *Phaedra* (1961) and Aeschylus's *Prometheus Bound* (1969) as well as versions of Hawthorne and Melville stories grouped under the title *The Old Glory* (1965). His *Collected Prose*, which appeared in 1987, is an indispensable companion to Lowell's poetry and contains valuable essays on the work of other writers. Among the many useful critical works on Lowell are Philip Cooper's *The Autobiographical Myth of Robert Lowell* (1970); Jerome Mazzaro's *The Poetic Themes of Robert Lowell* (1965); Hugh B. Staple's *Robert Lowell, the First Twenty Years* (1962); Stephen Yenser's *Circle to Circle* (1975); Steven Axelrod's *Robert Lowell: Life and Art* (1978); and Vereen Bell's *Robert Lowell, Nihilist as Hero* (1983). *Robert Lowell: A Collection of Critical Essays*, edited by Thomas Parkinson (1968), includes an important interview with the poet. A partial bibliography of Lowell's work can be found in Jerome Mazzaro, *The Achievement of Robert Lowell, 1939–1959* (1960). Ian Hamilton's biography, *Robert Lowell*, appeared in 1982.

**James Merrill**
James Merrill's shorter poems are collected in *From the First Nine, Poems 1946–1976* (1982). His three book-length poems along with an epilogue are published as *The Changing Light at Sandover* (1982). The trilogy is concluded by *Scripts for the Pageant* (1980), which also includes the "Coda." Merrill also published *Marbled Paper* (1982) and *Late Settings* (1985). A collection of his prose, *Recitative*, appeared in 1986. He also wrote two novels, *The Seraglio* (1957) and *The (Diblos) Notebook* (1965). Among useful critical essays are the chapters on Merrill in Richard Howard's *Alone with America* (1969), David Kalstone's *Five Temperaments* (1977), and Robert von Hallberg's *American Poetry and Culture* (1985), as well as those in *James Merrill: Essays in Criticism*, edited by Lehman and Berger (1983).

**Charles Olson**
The best single introduction to Charles Olson is Robert Creeley's *Selected Writings of Charles Olson* (1967). A complete edition of *The Maximus Poems*, edited by George F. Butterick, appeared in 1983. *The Collected Poems*, edited by George Butterick, appeared in 1987. Among Olson's many works of prose are his study of Melville, *Call Me Ishmael* (1947); *Mayan Letters* (1953); and a two-volume collection of his lectures and interviews, *Mathologos*, edited by George F. Butterick (1976–79).

The seven volumes of *Charles Olson and Robert Creeley: The Complete Correspondence*, edited by George F. Butterick (1980–1986), provide as extensive a discussion of life and poetry as we are ever likely to see. Among the critical studies of Olson's poetry, some of the most useful are Ed Dorn, *What I See in the Maximus Poems* (1960); Sherman Paul, *Olson's Push* (1978); and Robert von Hallberg, *Charles Olson: The Scholar's Art* (1978). For any reader of *The Maximus Poems*, George Butterick's *A Guide to the Maximus Poems* is indispensable. Various "Charles Olson Issues" appeared in the journal *Boundary 2*, 1973–74.

**Simon Ortiz**

Simon Ortiz has published *Naked in the Wind* (1970); *Going for Rain* (1976); *A Good Journey* (1977); *Song, Poetry, Language* (1978); *From Sand Creek: Rising in This Heart Which Is Our America* (1981); and *A Poem Is a Journey* (1981). His work has been gathered together in the volume *Woven Stone* (1992). Two collections of his short stories have also appeared: *Howbah Indians* (1978) and *Fightin': New and Collected Stories* (1983). He has also edited a collection, *These Hearts, These Poems* (1984). A discussion of Ortiz's poetry appears in Kenneth Lincoln's *Native American Renaissance* (1983), which also provides a valuable context for Native American literature more generally.

**Sylvia Plath**

Sylvia Plath's books of poetry include *The Colossus and Other Poems* (1962), *Ariel* (1966), *Crossing the Water* (1971), and *Winter Trees* (1972). Her novel *The Bell Jar* was first published in England in 1963. Plath's mother, Aurelia Schober Plath, selected and edited the useful *Letters Home: Correspondence 1950–63* (1975), and Ted Hughes and Frances McCullough have edited *The Journals of Sylvia Plath* (1983). There are a number of biographical and critical studies of Plath's work. Among them are Judith Kroll, *Chapters in a Mythology* (1976); Anne Stevenson, *Bitter Frame: The Undiscovered Life of Sylvia Plath* (1988); and Linda Wagner-Martin, *Sylvia Plath: A Biography*. A number of informative essays also appear in *The Art of Sylvia Plath*, edited by Charles Newman (1970), and *Critical Essays on Sylvia Plath*, edited by Linda Wagner (1984).

**Adrienne Rich**

A convenient starting point is *The Fact of a Doorframe: Poems Selected and New 1950–1984* (1984), which draws poems from Adrienne Rich's earlier books: *A Change of World* (1951), *The Diamond Cutters* (1955), *Snapshots of a Daughter-in-Law* (1963), *Necessities of Life* (1966), *Leaflets* (1969), *The Will to Change* (1971), *Diving Into the Wreck* (1973), *The Dream of a Common Language* (1978), and *A Wild Patience Has Taken Me This Far* (1981). Since the publication of this selection, Rich has published *Your Native Land, Your Life*

(1986); *Time's Power: Poems 1985–1988* (1989); and *An Atlas of the Difficult World: Poems 1988–1991* (1991). Two valuable collections gather together Rich's essays, lectures, and speeches: *On Lies, Secrets, and Silence* (1979) and *Blood, Bread, and Poetry* (1986). Rich is also the author of an important study, *Of Woman Born: Motherhood as Experience and Institution* (1976).

Valuable critical essays and an interview appear in *Adrienne Rich's Poetry* (1975), edited by Barbara Charlesworth Gelpi and Albert Gelpi. Other studies are *Reading Adrienne Rich* (1984), edited by Jane Roberta Cooper; Wendy Martin, *An American Triptych: Anna Bradstreet, Emily Dickinson and Adrienne Rich* (1984); Paula Bennett, *My Life, a Loaded Gun: Female Creativity and Feminist Poetics* (1986); and Terence Des Pres, *Praises and Dispraises: Poetry, Politics, the Twentieth Century* (1988).

**Alberto Ríos**

Alberto Ríos has published several collections of poetry, *Whispering to Fool the Wind* (1982), *Five Indiscretions* (1985), *The Dime Orchard Woman* (1988), and *Teodora Luna's Two Kisses* (1992). He has also published a collection of short stories, *The Iguana Killer* (1984). A discussion of Ríos's work and the larger contexts of Latino poetry appears in Cordelia Candelaria, *Chicano Poetry: A Critical Introduction* (1986).

**Theodore Roethke**

*The Collected Poems of Theodore Roethke* was published in 1966. Useful comments on poetic tradition and his own poetic practice are to be found in several collections of Roethke's prose: *On the Poet and His Craft: Selected Prose of Theodore Roethke*, edited by Ralph J. Mills, Jr. (1965); *Straw for the Fire: From the Notebooks of Theodore Roethke, 1948–63*, edited by David Wagoner (1972); and *The Selected Letters of Theodore Roethke*, edited by Ralph J. Mills, Jr. (1970). Among the useful studies of Roethke's work are *Theodore Roethke: An Introduction to the Poetry* by Karl Malkoff (1966); Rosemary Sullivan's *Theodore Roethke: The Garden Master* (1975); and *Theodore Roethke: Essays on the Poetry*, edited by Arnold Stein (1965). Allan Seager's *The Glass House* (1968) contains useful biographical material.

**Gary Snyder**

Gary Snyder's poems have been published by several different presses, often with duplication of poems. *Riprap*, originally published in 1959, is most easily obtained in *Riprap and Cold Mountain Poems* (1965, 1991). *Myths and Texts* first appeared in 1960. *The Blue Sky* first appeared in 1969 and reappeared in *Six Sections of Mountains and Rivers without End plus One* (1970). Other volumes include *The Back Country* (1968), *Regarding Wave* (1970), *Six Sections of Mountains and Rivers without End plus One* (1970), *Turtle*

*Island* (1974), *Axe Handles*, (1983), and *Left Out in the Rain: New Poems 1947–1985* (1986). He has also published an important prose collection dealing with ecology, *Earth House Hold* (1969). Helpful critical discussion of Synder's work can be found in Bob Steuding, *Gary Snyder* (1976); Charles Altieri, *Self and Sensibility in Contemporary American Poetry* (1984); and Sherman Paul, *In Search of the Primitive* (1986).

**Cathy Song**

Cathy Song has published *Picture Bride* (1983) and *Frameless Windows, Squares of Light* (1988).

**Robert Penn Warren**

Robert Penn Warren's last retrospective collection of his verse appeared as *New and Selected Poems 1925–1985* (1985). It includes his book-length poem, "Audubon: A Vision," first published in 1969. Because Warren often reselected his work, many poems are only to be found in his individual volumes, including *Incarnations* (1968); *Or Else: Poem / Poems 1968–1974*; *Now and Then* (1978); *Being Here* (1980); *Rumor Verified* (1981); and *Chief Joseph of the Nez Perce* (1983). His best-known novels are *All the King's Men* (1946) and *World Enough and Time* (1950). His Thomas Jefferson lectures, *Democracy and Poetry*, appeared in 1975. Also available is a collection of interviews, *Robert Penn Warren Talking*, edited by Floyd Watkins and John Tiers (1980). The best critical study of Warren's poetry is Calvin Bedient's *In the Heart's Last Kingdom* (1986). Also valuable are the essays collected in *Robert Penn Warren*, edited by Harold Bloom (1986), and in *Critical Essays on Robert Penn Warren*, edited by William Bedford Clark (1982).

**Richard Wilbur**

Richard Wilbur's *New and Collected Poems* appeared in 1989 and draws from *The Beautiful Changes* (1947); *Ceremony and Other Poems* (1950); *Things of This World* (1956); *Advice to a Prophet* (1961); *Walking to Sleep* (1969); and *The Mind-Reader* (1976). His translations from Molière include *The Misanthrope* (1955); *Tartuffe* (1963); and *Molière: Four Comedies* (1982). He has also published *Responses* (1976), a collection of prose pieces. Critical discussion of his work can be found in *Richard Wilbur's Creation*, edited by Wendy Salinger (1983), and various journals, among them *Parnassus* (Spring–Summer 1977).

**James Wright**

A collection of James Wright's complete poems, *Above the River*, appeared in 1990 and includes the work of his individual volumes: *The Green Wall* (1956), *Saint Judas* (1963), *Shall We Gather at the River* (1968), the lovely *Moments of the Italian Summer* (1976), *To a Blossoming Pear Tree* (1977), and *This Journey* (1982). An edition of his *Collected Prose*, edited by Anne Wright, appeared in 1983. Some of Wright's translations from the Spanish and Geman are available in *Twenty Poems of Georg Trakl* (1963), *Twenty Poems of Cesar Vallejo* (1964), and *Twenty Poems of Pablo Neruda* (with Robert Bly, 1968). The best critical discussion of Wright's work appears in the essays collected in *The Pure Clear Word: Essays on the Poetry of James Wright* (1982), edited by Dave Smith.

**Henry Adams:** Excerpts from THE EDUCATION OF HENRY ADAMS copyright © 1918 by the Massachusetts Historical Society. Copyright, 1946 by Charles F. Adams. Houghton Mifflin Company.

**A. R. Ammons:** "So I Said I Am Ezra," "Corsons Inlet," "The City Limits," and "Easter Morning" are reprinted from THE SELECTED POEMS OF A. R. AMMONS, Expanded Edition, with the permission of W. W. Norton & Company, Inc. Copyright © 1986, 1977, 1975, 1974, 1972, 1971, 1970, 1966, 1965, 1964, 1955 by A. R. Ammons. "Autonomy" reprinted from SUMERIAN VISTAS, Poems by A. R. Ammons, with the permission of W. W. Norton & Company, Inc. Copyright © 1987 by A. R. Ammons.

**Sherwood Anderson:** "Mother" from WINESBURG, OHIO by Sherwood Anderson, Introduction, Malcolm Cowley. Copyright 1919 by B. W. Huebsch. Copyright 1947 by Eleanor Copenhaver Anderson. Used by permission of Viking Penguin, a division of Penguin Books USA Inc. "The Egg" from THE TRIUMPH OF THE EGG by Sherwood Anderson. Reprinted by permission of Harold Ober Associates Incorporated. Copyright 1921 by B. W. Huebsch, Inc. Copyright renewed 1948 by Eleanor C. Anderson.

**John Ashbery:** "Syringa" from HOUSEBOAT DAYS by John Ashbery (New York: Viking, 1977). Reprinted by permission of Georges Borchardt, Inc. for the author. "The Lonedale Operator" from A WAVE by John Ashbery (New York: Viking, 1984). Reprinted by permission of Georges Borchardt, Inc. for the author. Copyright © 1981, 1982, 1983, 1984 by John Ashbery. "Illustration" and "Soonest Mended" by John Ashbery from THE DOUBLE DREAM OF SPRING (New York: The Ecco Press, 1975). Reprinted by permission of Georges Borchardt, Inc. for the author. Copyright © 1970, 1969, 1968, 1967, 1966 by John Ashbery.

**James Baldwin:** Part 1 from THE FIRE NEXT TIME by James Baldwin (Vintage, 1993). Copyright © James Baldwin, 1963. Reprinted by permission of the James Baldwin Estate.

**Amiri Baraka:** "An Agony. As Now" and "A Poem for Willie Best" from THE DEAD LECTURER by Amiri Baraka. Copyright © 1964, 1969 by Amiri Baraka. Reprinted by permission of Sterling Lord Literistic, Inc.

**John Barth:** "Life-Story" copyright © 1968 by John Barth from LOST IN THE FUNHOUSE by John Barth. Used by permission of Doubleday, a division of Bantam Doubleday Dell Publishing Group, Inc.

**Ann Beattie:** "Weekend" from SECRETS AND SURPRISES by Ann Beattie. Copyright © 1976, 1977, 1978 by Ann Beattie. Reprinted by permission of Random House, Inc.

**Saul Bellow:** "Looking for Mr. Green," copyright 1951, 1979 by Saul Bellow, from MOSBY'S MEMOIRS & OTHER STORIES by Saul Bellow. Used by permission of Viking Penguin, a division of Penguin Books USA Inc.

**John Berryman:** "Dream Songs" 29, 45, and 385 from THE DREAM SONGS by John Berryman. Copyright © 1969 by John Berryman. Reprinted by permission of Farrar, Straus & Giroux, Inc.

**John Bierhorst:** Excerpts from FOUR MASTERWORKS OF AMERICAN INDIAN LITERATURE: QUETZALCOATL, THE RITUAL OF CONDOLENCE, CUCEV, THE NIGHT CHANT, edited by John Bierhorst. (1974, 1984) University of Arizona Press. Reprinted by permission of John Bierhorst.

**Elizabeth Bishop:** "The Unbeliever," "The Fish," "At the Fishhouses," "The Armadillo," "Sestina," "In the Waiting Room," "The Moose," "One Art" from THE COMPLETE POEMS 1927–1979 by Elizabeth Bishop. Copyright © 1979, 1983 by Alice Helen Methfessel. Reprinted by permission of Farrar, Straus & Giroux, Inc.

**Black Elk:** Excerpts from BLACK ELK SPEAKS by John G. Neihardt, by permission of the University of Nebraska Press. Copyright 1932, 1959, 1972 by John G. Neihardt. Copyright © 1961 by the John G. Neihardt Trust.

**William Bradford:** Excerpts from OF PLYMOUTH PLANTATION by William Bradford, edited by Samuel Eliot Morison. Copyright © 1952 by Samuel Eliot Morison and renewed 1980 by Emily M. Beck. Reprinted by permission of Alfred A. Knopf, Inc.

**Anne Bradstreet:** Excerpts from THE WORKS OF ANNE BRADSTREET, edited by Jeannine Hensley, Cambridge, Mass.: Harvard University Press, Copyright © 1967 by the President and Fellows of Harvard College. Reprinted by permission of Harvard University Press.

**Gwendolyn Brooks:** "kitchenette building," "the mother," "the vacant lot," "The White

Outright," "Directive" from THE POETRY OF ROBERT FROST, edited by Edward Connery Lathem. Copyright 1936, 1942, 1944, 1951, 1956, © 1958, 1962 by Robert Frost. Copyright © 1964, 1967, 1970, 1975, by Leslie Frost Ballantine. Copyright 1916, 1923, 1928, 1930, 1934, 1939, 1947, © 1967, 1969 by Henry Holt and Company, Inc. Reprinted by permission of Henry Holt and Company, Inc.

**Allen Ginsberg:** "Howl, Part I," "A Supermarket in California," copyright © 1955 by Allen Ginsberg. "To Aunt Rose" copyright © 1958 by Allen Ginsberg. "Ego Confession" copyright © 1974 by Allen Ginsberg. All from COLLECTED POEMS 1947–1980 by Allen Ginsberg. Reprinted by permission of HarperCollins Publishers.

**Angelina Weld Grimké:** "To Clarissa Scott Delaney" (33–10, folder 164), "At April" (33–10, folder 162), "Trees" (33–10, folder 164), "The Eyes of My Regret" (38–10, folder 163), and "Tenebris" (38–10, folder 156) reprinted by permission of the Angelina Grimké Papers, Moorland-Spingarn Research Center, Howard University. "El Beso" from NEGRO POETS AND THEIR POEMS, edited by Robert T. Kerlin (1923). Reprinted by permission of the Associated Publishers, Inc., 1407 14th Street, N.W., Washington, D.C. 20005-3704.

**Michael S. Harper:** "Martin's Blues" from HISTORY IS YOUR OWN HEART BEAT, copyright © 1971 by Michael S. Harper. "Nightmare Begins Responsibility" from NIGHTMARE BEGINS RESPONSIBILITY copyright © 1975 by Michael S. Harper. Reprinted by permission of the University of Illinois Press. "Dear John, Dear Coltrane," "American History," and "Deathwatch" from DEAR JOHN, DEAR COLTRANE by Michael S. Harper. Copyright © 1970, 1985 by Michael S. Harper. Reprinted by permission of the author.

**Robert Hayden:** "Middle Passage," "Homage to the Empress of the Blues," "Those Winter Sundays," "Free Fantasia: Tiger Flowers," "Elegies for Paradise Valley" from COLLECTED POEMS OF ROBERT HAYDEN, edited by Frederich Glaysher. Copyright © 1985 by Erma Hayden. Reprinted by permission of Liveright Publishing Corporation.

**Ernest Hemingway:** "The Snows of Kilimanjaro." Reprinted with permission of Scribners, an imprint of Simon & Schuster, from THE COMPLETE SHORT STORIES OF ERNEST HEMINGWAY. Copyright © 1936 by Ernest Hemingway; renewal copyright © 1964 by Mary Hemingway.

**Langston Hughes:** "The Negro Speaks of Rivers," "Mother to Son," "I, Too," copyright 1926 by Alfred A. Knopf, Inc. and renewed 1954 by Langston Hughes; "Mulatto," "Song for a Dark Girl" copyright 1927 by Alfred A. Knopf, Inc. and renewed 1955 by Langston Hughes; "Silhouette," "Note on Commercial Theatre," "Democracy" copyright 1948 by Alfred A. Knopf, Inc. From SELECTED POEMS by Langston Hughes. Reprinted by permission of Alfred A. Knopf, Inc. "Visitors to the Black Belt" from ONE WAY TICKET by Langston Hughes. Copyright 1948 by Alfred A. Knopf, Inc. Copyright renewed 1976 by George Houston Bass. Reprinted by permission of Harold Ober Associates Incorporated.

**Zora Neale Hurston:** Parts 2 and 3 from THEIR EYES WERE WATCHING GOD by Zora Neale Hurston. Copyright 1937 by Harper & Row Publishers, Inc. Copyright renewed 1965 by John C. Hurston and Joel Hurston. Reprinted by permission of HarperCollins Publishers, Inc. "How It Feels to Be Colored Me" from I LOVE MYSELF WHEN I AM LAUGHING . . . AND THEN AGAIN WHEN I AM LOOKING MEAN AND IMPRESSIVE by Zora Neale Hurston, reprinted by permission of Lucy Hurston.

**Henry James:** "The Real Thing," "The Beast in the Jungle," "The Art of Fiction," from THE TALES OF HENRY JAMES, the New York Edition, and "Daisy Miller: A Study." Reprinted by permission of Alexander R. James, Literary Executor.

**Randall Jarrell:** "The Death of the Ball Turret Gunner" and "Second Air Force" from THE COMPLETE POEMS by Randall Jarrell. Copyright © 1969 by Mrs. Randall Jarrell. Reprinted by permission of Farrar, Straus & Giroux, Inc. "Next Day," "Well Water," and "Thinking of the Lost World," copyright © 1965 by Randall Jarrell from THE LOST WORLD in RANDALL JARRELL: THE COMPLETE POEMS, published by Farrar, Straus & Giroux, Inc. Reprinted by permission of the Rhoda Weyr Agency.

**Robinson Jeffers:** "To the Stone-Cutters," "Shine, Perishing Republic" copyright 1925 and renewed 1953 by Robinson Jeffers, from SELECTED POETRY OF ROBINSON JEFFERS by Robinson Jeffers. "Carmel Point" copyright © 1954 by Robinson Jeffers, "Birds & Fishes" copyright © 1963 by Steuben Glass from SELECTED POEMS by Robinson Jeffers. Reprinted by permission of Random House, Inc.

**Thomas Jefferson:** Excerpts from NOTES ON THE STATE OF VIRGINIA, by Thomas Jefferson. Edited by William Peden. Published for the Institute of Early American History

Grave No Flower" copyright © 1934, 1962 by Edna St. Vincent Millay and Norma Millay Ellis. "I, Too, Beneath Your Moon, Almighty Sex" copyright © 1939, 1967 by Edna St. Vincent Millay and Norma Millay Ellis. "I Forgot for a Moment" copyright © 1940, 1968 by Edna St. Vincent Millay and Norma Millay Ellis. All of the above from COLLECTED POEMS, HarperCollins. Reprinted by permission of Elizabeth Barnett, literary executor.

**N. Scott Momaday:** Introduction reprinted from THE WAY TO RAINY MOUNTAIN, N. Scott Momaday, © 1969, The University of New Mexico Press. "Headwaters," IV, XIII, XVII, XXIV, Epilogue, "Rainy Mountain Cemetery" reprinted from THE WAY TO RAINY MOUNTAIN, © 1969, The University of New Mexico Press.

**Marianne Moore:** "To a Snail," and "Poetry," reprinted with the permission of Simon & Schuster from COLLECTED POEMS OF MARIANNE MOORE. Copyright 1935 by Marianne Moore, and renewed 1963 by Marianne Moore and T. S. Eliot. "The Mind Is an Enchanting Thing," reprinted with permission of Simon & Schuster from COLLECTED POEMS OF MARIANNE MOORE. Copyright 1944, and renewed 1972 by Marianne Moore. "Keeping Their World Large" reprinted with permission of Simon & Schuster from COLLECTED POEMS OF MARIANNE MOORE. Copyright 1951 by Marianne Moore, renewed 1978 by Lawrence E. Brinn and Louise Crane. "O to Be a Dragon" copyright © 1957 by Marianne Moore, renewed 1985 by Lawrence E. Brinn and Louise Crane, Executors of the Estate of Marianne Moore, from THE COMPLETE POEMS OF MARIANNE MOORE by Marianne Moore. Used by permission of Viking Penguin, a divison of Penguin Books USA Inc.

**James Mooney:** Ghost Dance Songs, "Songs of the Arapaho," Songs of the Sioux, Wovoka: The Messiah Letter (version by James Mooney) and The Messiah Letter (Cheyenne version) from THE GHOST-DANCE RELIGION AND THE SIOUX OUTBREAK OF 1890 by James Mooney, abridged by A. F. C. Wallace. 1965. Reprinted by permission of the University of Chicago Press.

**Flannery O'Connor:** "Good Country People" copyright © 1955 by Flannery O'Connor and renewed 1983 by Regina O'Connor, from A GOOD MAN IS HARD TO FIND AND OTHER STORIES by Flannery O'Connor. Reprinted by permission of Harcourt Brace & Company.

**Eugene O'Neill:** *Long Day's Journey into Night*, copyright © 1955 by Carlotta Monterey O'Neill. Copyright © renewed 1983 by Oona O'Neill Chaplin and Yale University. Reprinted by permission.

**Joyce Carol Oates:** "Golden Gloves" from RAVEN'S WING by Joyce Carol Oates. Copyright © 1986 by *The Ontario Review*. Used by permission of Dutton Signet, a division of Penguin Books USA Inc.

**Charles Olson:** "Maximus, to Himself," and "Celestial Evening, October 1967" from Charles Olson: MAXIMUS POEMS, translated and edited by George Butterick. Copyright © 1983 The Regents of the University of California. Reprinted by permission.

**Simon J. Ortiz:** "Earth and Rain," the Plants & Sun," "Vision Shadows," "8:50 AM Ft. Lyons VAH" from A GOOD JOURNEY. Reprinted by permission of Simon J. Ortiz. "At the Salvation Army" from FROM SAND CREEK by Simon J. Ortiz. Copyright © 1981 by Simon J. Ortiz. Used by permission of the publisher, Thunder's Mouth Press.

**Sylvia Plath:** "Morning Song" copyright © 1961 by Ted Hughes. Copyright renewed. "Lady Lazarus" copyright © 1963 by Ted Hughes. Copyright renewed. "Daddy" copyright © 1963 by Ted Hughes. Copyright renewed. All from ARIEL by Sylvia Plath. "Parliament Hill Fields" copyright © 1961 by Ted Hughes. Copyright renewed. Reprinted from CROSSING THE WATER by Sylvia Plath. "Blackberrying" copyright © 1962 by Ted Hughes. Copyright renewed. This poem originally appeared in UNCOLLECTED POEMS, Turret Books, London, and in the *Hudson Review*. "Child" copyright © 1963 by Ted Hughes. Copyright renewed. Reprinted from WINTER TREES by Sylvia Plath. Reprinted by permission of HarperCollins Publishers Inc.

**Katherine Anne Porter:** THE FIG TREE reprinted by permission of Barbara Thompson Davis for the Literary Estate of Katherine Anne Porter.

**Ezra Pound:** "Portrait d'une Femme," "A Virginal," "A Pact," "The Rest," "In a Station of the Metro," "The River Merchant's Wife: A Letter," "Hugh Selwyn Mauberley: Life and Contacts." Ezra Pound: PERSONAE, copyright 1926 by Ezra Pound. "Canto I," "Canto XLV." Ezra Pound: THE CANTOS OF EZRA POUND, copyright 1934, 1937, 1948 by Ezra Pound. Reprinted by permission of New Directions Publishing Corporation.

**Thomas Pynchon:** Chapter 1 from THE CRYING OF LOT 49 by Thomas Pynchon. Copyright © 1965, 1966 by Thomas Pynchon. Copyright renewed 1993, 1994 by Thomas

**Pynchon.** Reprinted by permission of HarperCollins Publishers, Inc.

**Adrienne Rich:** "Storm Warnings," "Snapshots of a Daughter-in-Law," "I Am in Danger—Sir—," "Orion," "A Valediction Forbidding Mourning," "Diving into the Wreck," "Twenty-One Love Poems: I, (The Floating Poem, Unnumbered)," "Transcendental Etude" from THE FACT OF A DOORFRAME: POEMS SELECTED AND NEW, 1950–1984 by permission of W. W. Norton & Company, Inc. Copyright © 1984 by Adrienne Rich. Copyright © 1975, 1978 by W. W. Norton & Company, Inc. Copyright © 1981 by Adrienne Rich. "For a Friend in Travail" from AN ATLAS OF THE DIFFICULT WORLD, Poems 1988–1991, by Adrienne Rich, by permission of W. W. Norton & Company, Inc. Copyright © 1991 by Adrienne Rich.

**Alberto Ríos:** "Madre Sofia" and "Wet Camp" from WHISPERING TO FOOL THE WIND, copyright © 1982 by Alberto Ríos. "Advice to a First Cousin," and "Seniors" from FIVE INDISCRETIONS, copyright © 1985 by Alberto Ríos. Reprinted by permission of Alberto Ríos.

**Edwin Arlington Robinson:** "The Mill" copyright 1920 by Edwin Arlington Robinson, renewed 1948 by Ruth Nivison. "Mr. Flood's Party" copyright 1921 by Edwin Arlington Robinson, renewed 1949 by Ruth Nivison. Reprinted with permission of Simon & Schuster from COLLECTED POEMS OF EDWIN ARLINGTON ROBINSON.

**Theodore Roethke:** "Cuttings" copyright 1948 by Theodore Roethke, "Cuttings (Later)" copyright 1948 by Theodore Roethke. "I Knew a Woman" copyright 1954 by Theodore Roethke. "In a Dark Time" copyright © 1960 by Beatrice Roethke, Administratrix of the Estate of Theodore Roethke. "The Far Field" copyright © 1962 by Beatrice Roethke, Administratrix of the Estate of Theodore Roethke. "Wish for a Young Wife" copyright © 1963 by Beatrice Roethke, Administratrix of the Estate of Theodore Roethke. "My Papa's Waltz" copyright 1942 by Hearst Magazines, Inc. "Night Crow" copyright 1944 by Saturday Review Association, Inc. "Frau Bauman, Frau Schmidt and Frau Schwartze" copyright 1952 by Theodore Roethke. All from THE COLLECTED POEMS OF THEODORE ROETHKE by Theodore Roethke. Reprinted by permission of Doubleday, a division of Bantam Doubleday Dell Publishing Group, Inc.

**Philip Roth:** "Defender of the Faith" from GOODBYE, COLUMBUS by Philip Roth. Copyright © 1959, renewed 1987 by Philip Roth. Reprinted by permission of Houghton Mifflin Company. All rights reserved.

**Muriel Rukeyser:** "Effort at Speech Between Two People," " 'Long Enough,' " "The Poem as Mask," "Poem" and "Myth" by Muriel Rukeyser from OUT OF SILENCE, copyright © William L. Rukeyser, 1992, TriQuarterly Books, Evanston, IL. "For Fun" and "Painters" from COLLECTED POEMS copyright © Muriel Rukeyser, 1978, McGraw-Hill, NY, by permission of William L. Rukeyser.

**Carl Sandburg:** "Chicago" and "Fog" from CHICAGO POEMS by Carl Sandburg, copyright 1916 by Holt Rinehart and Winston, Inc. and renewed 1944 by Carl Sandburg. "Grass" from CORNHUSKERS by Carl Sandburg, copyright © 1918 by Holt, Rinehart and Winston, Inc. and renewed 1946 by Carl Sandburg. Reprinted by permission of Harcourt Brace and Company.

**Samuel Sewall:** Excerpts from THE DIARY OF SAMUEL SEWALL, 1674–1729, edited by M. Halsey Thomas. Copyright © 1973 by Farrar, Straus & Giroux, Inc.

**John Smith:** Excerpts from THE COMPLETE WORKS OF CAPTAIN JOHN SMITH, 1580–1631, edited by Philip L. Barbour. Published for the Institute of Early American History and Culture, Williamsburg, Virginia. Copyright © 1986 by the University of North Carolina Press.

**Gary Snyder:** "Riprap" from RIPRAP AND COLD MOUNTAIN POEMS by Gary Snyder. Copyright © 1958, 1959, 1965 by Gary Snyder. Reprinted by permission of North Point Press, a division of Farrar, Straus & Giroux, Inc. "August on Sourdough" and "Beneath My Hand and Eye" from THE BACK COUNTRY by Gary Snyder. Copyright © 1974 by Gary Snyder. "Song of the Taste" from REGARDING WAVE. Copyright © 1968 by Gary Snyder. First printed in POETRY. Reprinted by permission of New Directions Publishing Corporation.

**Cathy Song:** "The White Porch," "Beauty and Sadness," and "Lost Sister" from PICTURE BRIDE (1983) by Cathy Song. Reprinted by permission of Yale University Press. "Heaven" is reprinted from FRAMELESS WINDOWS, SQUARES OF LIGHT, Poems by Cathy Song. Copyright © 1988 by Cathy Song. Reprinted by permission of W. W. Norton & Company, Inc.

**John Steinbeck:** "The Leader of the People" from THE LONG VALLEY by John Steinbeck.

# Index